KEY TO PRONUNCIATION

A shortened form of this key appears at the bottom of every right-hand page of the dictionary. A fuller explanation of the symbols will be found in the section on "How to Use Your Dictionary."

Symbol	Key Words	Symbol	Key Words	Symbol	Key Words
a	ask, fat, parrot	ə	a in ago	r	red, port, dear
ā	ape, date, play		e in agent	s	sell, castle, pass
ä	ah, car, father		i in sanity	t	top, cattle, hat
e	elf, ten, berry		o in comply	v	vat, hovel, have
ē	even, meet, money		u in focus	w	will, always, swear
i	is, hit, mirror	ər	perhaps, murder	y	yet, onion, yard
ī	ice, bite, high	b	bed, fable, dub	z	zebra, dazzle, haze
ō	open, tone, go	d	dip, beadle, had	ch	chin, catcher, arch
ô	all, horn, law	f	fall, after, off	sh	she, cushion, dash
o͞o	ooze, tool, crew	g	get, haggle, dog	th	thin, nothing, truth
o͝o	look, pull, moor	h	he, ahead, hotel	*th*	then, father, lathe
yo͞o	use, cute, few	j	joy, agile, badge	zh	azure, leisure
yo͝o	united, cure, globule	k	kill, tackle, bake	ŋ	ring, anger, drink
oi	oil, point, toy	l	let, yellow, ball	'	able (ā'b'l)
ou	out, crowd, plow	m	met, camel, trim		
u	up, cut, color	n	not, flannel, ton	(see also *Foreign Sounds*
ʉr	urn, fur, deter	p	put, apple, tap	below)

FOREIGN SOUNDS

à This symbol stands for the sound of *a* in the French word *bal* (bàl), which can best be described as halfway between (a) and (ä).

ë This symbol stands for the sound of the three vowels in the French word *coeur* (kër), which can be made by rounding the lips as for (ô) and pronouncing (e).

ö This symbol stands for the sound of *eu* in the French word *feu* (fö) or of *ö* (or *oe*) in the German name *Göthe* (or *Goethe*) (gö'tə); the sound can be made by rounding the lips as for (ō) and pronouncing (ā).

ô This symbol stands for sounds ranging from (ō) to (ô), such as those heard in French *coq* (kôk), German *doch* (dôкh), Italian *poco* (pô'kô), Spanish *torero* (tô re'rô), etc.

ü This symbol stands for the sound of *u* in the French word *duc* (dük) or in the German word *grün* (grün), which can be made by rounding the lips as for (o͞o) and pronouncing (ē).

kh This symbol stands for the sound heard in the German word *doch* (dôкh). It can be made by bringing the back of the tongue up to the roof of the mouth, as in pronouncing (k), but allowing the breath to escape in a stream, as in pronouncing (h).

H This symbol stands for a sound similar to the one just above, except that it is formed closer to the front of the roof of the mouth, as in German *ich* (iH). Speakers of English sometimes hear the sound as (sh) and pronounce it that way.

n This symbol tells you that the vowel just in front of it should be sounded with the nasal passage left open so that the breath passes through both the mouth and nose. This nasalized sound is heard in such words as French *mon* (mō*n*).

r This symbol stands for sounds used in languages other than English for the consonant *r*. It may stand for the flap or trill of the *r* in French *reste* (rest) or *sur* (sür), German *Reuter* (roi'tər), Italian *ricotta* (rē kôt'tä), etc.

' The apostrophe is used as a symbol after a final *l* or *r* sound in certain French words to show that the *l* or *r* is pronounced with little or no voice, as in *lettre* (let'r').

Webster's New World Dictionary

Student Edition

Webster's
New World
Dictionary

Student Edition

DAVID B. GURALNIK, **Editor in Chief**

Simon and Schuster   New York, N.Y.

Prentice-Hall, Inc.   Englewood Cliffs, N.J.

A Simon & Schuster Division of Gulf & Western Corporation
Simon and Schuster Building
Rockefeller Center
1230 Avenue of the Americas
New York, New York 10020

SIMON AND SCHUSTER, TREE OF KNOWLEDGE, WEBSTER'S NEW WORLD, and colophons are trademarks of Simon and Schuster.

10   9

ISBN 0-13-947747-0

CONTENTS

EDITORIAL STAFF

FOREWORD

Two conflicting forces are constantly at work in a living language. One is the effort to keep the language stable and unchanging so that each generation may continue to understand the one before. The other is the continual change that takes place so that the language may deal with the altered conditions and attitudes and the new technologies that time always brings. The record that we keep of the words of the constant language and of the changing language is called a dictionary.

This dictionary, the newest addition to the well-known family of *Webster's New World Dictionaries,* was specially prepared for students. It contains more than 108,000 vocabulary entries, chosen as the ones students are most likely to come across in reading the classics, textbooks, and other classroom assignments, but also the daily newspapers and current magazines and novels. These entries were chosen from among the hundreds of thousands that have been collected by our readers (called *citators*) who regularly read through current publications in order to keep a record of the old and new terms as they are used in writing. Present-day slang and other informal words and expressions that are much used, especially by younger people, have also been entered if they have been around for some time and show signs of remaining active in the language for at least a while longer. For example, you will find here the current slang uses of *heavy, dude, up-tight,* and *cop-out.*

The editors of this dictionary have tried to anticipate the kinds of questions students might put to a dictionary and to give the answers in the most direct form possible, so that no time will be lost in checking through a number of long supplements or in following up one cross-reference to another to still another. For that reason, all entries, including the names of persons and places, abbreviations, and the like, are entered in one alphabetical listing, so that you need look in only one place to find **nat.** (abbreviation for *national* or *native*), **natal** (of one's birth), **Natal** (province of South Africa), **Natalie** (a girl's name), and **Gamal Abdel Nasser** (former president of Egypt), instead of searching in five different sections, as in some dictionaries.

To help make sure that the information supplied is that which students will be looking for, and that it is presented in a form that will make it readily understandable, the editorial staff asked a number of teachers and educators to serve as an Advisory Council. This group,

whose names will be found on page **vi**, helped in the planning of the dictionary and offered valuable suggestions during the time that it was being compiled, and we take this opportunity to thank them for their expert assistance.

The section on the following pages was prepared in some detail to help you get the most from your dictionary. It tells you the kinds of information that it contains, how it is arranged, and how you can put it to its most effective use. We urge you to read through the section and to refer to it from time to time until you are so familiar with the dictionary that you know all the ways in which it can help you in writing, speaking, and understanding our American language.

Because this is an American dictionary, special attention has been paid to Americanisms, those usages that first appeared in English in this country. For more information on Americanisms, see the section beginning on page **xi**. Also, for the first time in any school dictionary, the origins of the names of American cities, States, rivers, and the like are given. This is also the first students' dictionary to give complete little histories of the origins (called *etymologies*) of words, tracing them back to their Indo-European roots and showing the relationships among the words. For more information on the etymologies, see the section beginning on page **xvi**.

Words that are registered trademarks but that are commonly used in a general way are entered, always with a note indicating the fact that they are trademarks.

In order to help the user of this dictionary understand more clearly the meanings of the words, thousands of examples of terms used in typical phrases and sentences are shown. And, in addition, more than 1500 clear pictures have been included to help you understand even more quickly what has been described in words. Among the illustrations are a number of little maps showing the exact locations of geographical and historical places and areas. The printing type faces of this dictionary, which was set on a computer, have been specially chosen because they are large, clear, and easily read.

Words are the most important tools you will ever use. The more you know about them and the better you understand how to use them, the more satisfying your life will be. We hope this dictionary will help you gain greater mastery of them.

David B. Guralnik

HOW TO USE YOUR DICTIONARY

This Student Edition of *Webster's New World Dictionary* is a reference book about words. It is a book you will refer to again and again for information and help on words—words you meet with in your studies, your reading, your listening to radio and television, and your conversation. You will find that your dictionary is day to day the most important reference book you use.

It is a complicated book with many things in it on the tens of thousands of words you may have questions about. In it you can learn how words are spelled, how they are pronounced, what meanings they have, what their histories are, how they are used in sentences. It gathers together all this information and more about the English language as it is spoken in America.

MAIN ENTRIES

You will find as main entries in boldface type single words and compound words, names of people and places, abbreviations, prefixes, and suffixes. All are arranged in alphabetical order, as in the following list. Notice that only the family name of a biographical entry counts in alphabetizing main entries.

acme	*a noun*
Addams, Jane	*a proper name (person)*
adolescent	*an adjective and noun*
Ba	*a chemical symbol*
B.A.	*an abbreviation*
Bangladesh	*a proper name (place)*
brown rice	*a two-word compound*
cloak-and-dagger	*an adjective formed with hyphens*
com-	*a prefix*
escalate	*a verb*
King, Martin Luther, Jr.	*a proper name (person)*
kingly	*an adjective and adverb*
-ness	*a suffix*
zap	*a verb, noun, and interjection*

Now look at these two entries that are next to each other in your dictionary.

Jack·son . . . capital of Miss., . . .

Jack·son . . . 1. Andrew, . . . 2. Thomas Jonathan, . . .

The first entry deals with a place, the second with persons. Both have the name *Jackson* in common. Notice that the geographical entry is kept separate from the biographical entry. Notice also that persons with the same last name are dealt with in a single block and placed in alphabetical order by first names. This pattern is followed in all such cases.

Just remember that all main entries are in strict alphabetical order. Thus, although the "Saint" in **Saint Bernard** and the "St." in **St. Louis** are pronounced the same way, the two entries will be found many pages apart, **Saint Bernard** with the *sa-* words, **St. Louis** with the *st-* words.

Canonized persons as such are entered by their given names. Thus Saint Patrick will be found in the P's but Saint Patrick's Day will be found in the S's.

GUIDE WORDS

The word in boldface type at the top of the left-hand side of the page is the same as the first main-entry word on the page. The word on the right-hand side is the same as the last main-entry word on the page. If you are looking for the entry word **dialysis**, you will find on page 265 the guide words **dialectic** and **diatribe**. You know that **dialysis** belongs on this page because it comes after **dialectic** and before **diatribe** in alphabetical order.

THE PROBLEM OF SPELLING

Very often someone will say, "But how can I find a word in the dictionary if I don't know how to spell it?" That is a common problem with English spellings, which often no longer agree with the pronunciations that may have changed over the years while the spellings remained the same. You may hear someone mention a kind of rock that sounds as though it might be spelled "nice," but there is no such definition at that spelling. By studying the WORD FINDER TABLE below, you will learn the various combinations of letters that may be used in spelling the common sounds of English. You will find, for example, that the first sound of "nice" may be spelled *gn,* that the middle vowel sound may be spelled *ei,* and the final sound may be *ss.* By trying out the various combinations, you will soon find the word **gneiss** listed and defined in your dictionary.

In your day-to-day reading you do get to know most of the patterns of spelling by seeing them in very common words, and you will put this knowledge to use when looking up a word whose spelling you are not sure of. Most often you will find the word without using the WORD FINDER TABLE at all. But when you do need it, it is a helpful tool.

WORD FINDER TABLE

If the sound is like the . . .	try also the spelling . . .	as in the words . . .
a in fat	ai, au	pl*ai*d, dr*au*ght
a in lane	ai, ao, au, ay, ea, ei, eigh, et, ey	r*ai*n, g*ao*l, g*au*ge, r*ay*, br*ea*k, r*ei*n, w*ei*gh, sach*et*, th*ey*
a in care	ai, ay, e, ea, ei	*ai*r, pr*ay*er, th*e*re, w*ea*r, th*ei*r
a in father	au, e, ea	g*au*nt, s*e*rgeant, h*ea*rth
a in ago	e, i, o, u, *and combinations, as* ou	*a*gent, san*i*ty, c*o*mply, foc*u*s, vici*ou*s
b in big	bb	ru*bb*er
ch in chin	tch, ti, tu	ca*tch*, ques*ti*on, na*tu*re
d in do	dd, ed	pu*dd*le, call*ed*
e in get	a, ae, ai, ay, ea, ei, eo, ie, u	*a*ny, *ae*sthete, s*ai*d, s*ay*s, br*ea*d, h*ei*fer, l*eo*pard, fr*ie*nd, b*u*ry
e in equal	ae, ay, ea, ee, ei, eo, ey, i, ie, oe	alumn*ae*, qu*ay*, l*ea*n, fr*ee*, dec*ei*t, p*eo*ple, k*ey*, mach*i*ne, ch*ie*f, ph*oe*be
e in here	ea, ee, ei, ie	*ea*r, ch*ee*r, w*ei*rd, b*ie*r
er in over	ar, ir, or, our, re, ur, ure, yr	li*ar*, elix*ir*, auth*or*, glam*our*, ac*re*, aug*ur*, meas*ure*, zeph*yr*
f in fine	ff, gh, lf, ph	cli*ff*, lau*gh*, ca*lf*, *ph*rase
g in go	gg, gh, gu, gue	e*gg*, *gh*oul, *gu*ard, prolo*gue*
h in hat	wh	*wh*o
i in it	a, e, ee, ia, ie, o, u, ui, y	us*a*ge, *E*nglish, b*ee*n, carr*ia*ge, s*ie*ve, w*o*men, b*u*sy, b*ui*lt, h*y*mn
i in kite	ai, ay, ei, ey, ie, igh, uy, y, ye	*ai*sle, *ay*e, sl*ei*ght, *ey*e, t*ie*, n*igh*, b*uy*, fl*y*, r*ye*
j in jam	d, dg, di, dj, g, gg	gra*d*uate, ju*dg*e, sol*di*er, a*dj*ective, ma*g*ic, exa*gg*erate
k in keep	c, cc, ch, ck, cqu, cu, lk, q, qu, que	*c*an, a*cc*ount, *ch*orus, ta*ck*, la*cqu*er, bis*cu*it, wa*lk*, *q*uick, li*qu*or, baro*que*
l in let	ll, sl	ca*ll*, i*sl*e
m in me	chm, gm, lm, mb, mm, mn	dra*chm*, paradi*gm*, ca*lm*, li*mb*, dru*mm*er, hy*mn*
n in no	gn, kn, mn, nn, pn	*gn*u, *kn*eel, *mn*emonic, di*nn*er, *pn*eumatic

Continued

Continued

If the sound is like the . . .	try also the spelling . . .	as in the words . . .
ng in ring	n, ngue	pink, tongue
o in go	au, eau, eo, ew, oa, oe, oh, oo, ou, ough, ow	mauve, beau, yeoman, sew, boat, toe, oh, brooch, soul, dough, row
o in long	a, ah, au, aw, oa, ou	all, Utah, fraud, thaw, broad, ought
oo in tool	eu, ew, o, oe, ou, ough, u, ue, ui	maneuver, drew, move, shoe, group, through, rule, blue, fruit
oo in look	o, ou, u	wolf, would, pull
oi in oil	oy	toy
ou in out	ough, ow	bough, crowd
p in put	pp	clipper
r in red	rh, rr, wr	rhyme, berry, wrong
s in sew	c, ce, ps, sc, sch, ss	cent, rice, psychology, scene, schism, miss
sh in ship	ce, ch, ci, s, sch, sci, se, si, ss, ssi, ti	ocean, machine, facial, sure, schwa, conscience, nauseous, tension, issue, fission, nation
t in top	ed, ght, pt, th, tt	walked, bought, ptomaine, thyme, better
u in cuff	o, oe, oo, ou	son, does, flood, double
u in use	eau, eu, eue, ew, ieu, iew, ue, ui, you, yu	beauty, feud, queue, few, adieu, view, cue, suit, youth, yule
ur in fur	ear, er, eur, ir, or, our, yr	learn, germ, hauteur, bird, word, scourge, myrtle
v in vat	f, lv, ph	of, salve, Stephen
w in will	o, u, wh	choir, quaint, wheat
y in you	i, j	onion, hallelujah
z in zero	s, sc, ss, x, zz	busy, discern, scissors, xylophone, buzzer
z in azure	ge, s, si, zi	garage, leisure, fusion, glazier

Sometimes, certain letter combinations (rather than single sounds) cause problems when you are trying to find a word. Here are some common ones:

If you've tried . . .	then try . . .	If you've tried . . .	then try . . .	If you've tried . . .	then try . . .
pre	per, pro, pri, pra, pru	cks, gz us	x ous	fiz ture	phys teur
per	pre, pir, pur, par, por	tion	sion, cion, cean, cian	tious air	seous are
is	us, ace, ice	le	tle, el, al	ance	ence

Continued

Continued

If you've tried . . .	then try . . .	If you've tried . . .	then try . . .	If you've tried . . .	then try . . .
ere	eir, ear, ier	kw	qu	ant	ent
wi	whi	cer	cre	able	ible
we	whe	ei	ie	sin	syn, cin,
zi	xy	si	psy, ci		cyn

VARIANTS

If a word may be spelled in more than one way, and if the spellings are different enough so that the forms appear some distance apart in the dictionary, the definition is given under the spelling most frequently used and other spellings of the word are cross-referred to it. Throughout this dictionary words printed in small capital letters are cross-references, words that you must turn to in order to find the definition or other information you are looking for.

ae·on . . . *n. same as* EON

kerb . . . *n. Brit. sp. of* CURB (*n.* 4)

If the spellings are almost the same, and both spellings are very common, they are placed together at the head of the entry.

the·a·ter, the·a·tre . . . *n.* . . . .

Neither spelling is considered "more correct," but the one listed first is usually the one used more often today.

Some variant spellings are listed at the end of an entry block.

judg·ment . . . *n.* . . . . Also sp. **judge′ment**

Putting the *judge-* spelling at the end of the entry in this way tells you that it is used less often. When no special pronunciation is shown for a variant, it is pronounced like the word of which it is a variant.

In addition to spellings, there are other variant forms that may be cross-referred to another main entry. Here are some of the different cross-references that you will find.

aer·o·plane . . . *n. Brit. var. of* AIRPLANE

Indian corn *same as* CORN¹ (sense 2)

cop·ter . . . *n. shortened form of* HELICOPTER

lib . . . *n. clipped form of* LIBERATION (sense 2)

pick·er·el . . . *n.* . . . . **2.** *a local name for* WALLEYED PIKE

re·ceipt . . . *n.* **1.** *old-fashioned var. of* RECIPE **2.** . . . .

HOMOGRAPHS

Words that are spelled alike but have different meanings and origins are called *homographs*. In this dictionary, homographs are marked with small numerals just after the boldface spellings. If one or another needs to be referred to in other parts of the dictionary, it will always be shown with its numeral.

ball¹ . . . *n.* **1.** any round object; sphere; globe . . .

ball² . . . *n.* **1.** a formal social dance . . .

bal·let . . . [< Fr. < It. *balletto* . . . see BALL²]

AMERICANISMS

An open star before a word or meaning marks it as an Americanism—as a usage that first appeared in the English language in our country. This dictionary is the only school dictionary that tells you which words and meanings were born in America.

Noah Webster added the verb *demoralize* to our vocabulary. Before him Benjamin Franklin had coined the word *electrician* and Thomas Jefferson the word *belittle.* All three words are still very much alive today.

Back in colonial days, the American settlers started making new words by putting together old words, as in *backwoods,* or by adding endings to old words, as in *lengthy.* They also added new meanings to existing English words: *creek* (which had earlier meant "a narrow bay") came to mean "a small stream" in America; *lumber* (which had meant "discarded articles") developed a new meaning here, "timber sawed into boards, beams, etc."; and *store* (which had meant simply "supplies") took on an additional meaning, "a retail shop."

From the Indians, who were the first Americans, the American language borrowed such words as *rac-*

coon, moccasin, and *succotash*. From the French settlers came such words as *prairie*, *picayune*, and *chowder*. From the Dutch colonists we got such words as *boss*, *coleslaw*, and *cookie*. The Spanish-speaking people in the Southwest gave us such words as *bonanza*, *canyon*, and *ranch* as well as *avocado*, *chili*, and *coyote* from Nahuatl, the language of the Aztecs. The African natives, brought here as slaves, gave us, among other words, *banjo*, *goober*, and *jumbo*.

Later immigrants all contributed generously to the American language. From the Chinese came *gung-ho*, *tycoon*, and *chop suey;* from the Swedish, *smorgasbord* and *lingonberry;* from the Germans, *delicatessen*, *hoodlum*, *pretzel*, and the suffix *-fest* (used in *gabfest*, *slugfest*, etc.); from the Yiddish-speaking Americans, *kibitzer*, *schlemiel*, and *shtick;* from the Italians, *gondola* (applied to types of river barge, freight car, and aerial car) and *pizza;* and the list could go on and on. Among recent Americanisms are such words as *hard hat*, *backpack*, *cloning*, *quadraphonic*, *Ms.*, *oceanaut*, *groove* (in the slang senses), *moonquake*, *dune buggy*, and *environmentalist*. The Americanisms in your *Webster's New World Dictionary* number in the thousands, and you will keep on being surprised, as you learn from the stars marking them, which words and meanings were born in our country.

When you see the star in front of the main entry word, it means that every meaning and every form of the word given in the block is an Americanism.

☆ **las·so** . . . *n., pl.* **-sos, -soes** . . . a long rope with a sliding noose at one end, used to catch cattle or horses —*vt.* **-soed, -so·ing** to catch with a lasso — **las′so·er** *n.*

If a star is placed before a particular part of speech, all senses of that part of speech are Americanisms. If the star is placed before a single definition or part of a definition, only that definition or part is an Americanism.

ap·pre·ci·ate . . . *vt.* **-at′ed, -at′ing** . . . ☆ **5.** to raise the price of . . . —☆ *vi.* to rise in value . . .

FOREIGN WORDS AND PHRASES

Foreign words and phrases are marked in a special way, too. The symbol ‡, called a double dagger, is placed in front of an entry word or phrase that is not yet felt to be a part of the English vocabulary although it is heard and seen fairly often in English speech and writing.

‡ma·chis·mo . . . *n.* [Sp.] . . .

‡au na·tu·rel . . . [Fr.] . . .

This mark, ‡, is a signal telling you that such a word or phrase is usually printed in italic type or underlined in writing. The pronunciation shown for an entry marked ‡ is the one it has in its own language. If the word now also has an English pronunciation that differs somewhat from the foreign one, it is added.

PREFIXES, SUFFIXES, AND COMBINING FORMS

Some main entries end or begin with a hyphen. Those are the entries for prefixes, suffixes, and combining forms, and the hyphen indicates that they are not really words but parts of words. You will find them joined to regular words or to other such forms.

Prefixes or combining forms used at the beginning of words have a hyphen placed at the end of the entry form.

re- . . . *a prefix meaning:* **1.** back *[repay]* **2.** again, anew *[reappear]* . . .

bio- . . . *a combining form meaning* life, of living things, biological *[biography, biochemistry]*

Suffixes or combining forms used at the end of words have the hyphen at the beginning of the entry form.

-hood . . . *a suffix meaning:* **1.** state, quality, condition *[childhood]* **2.** the whole group of (a specified class, profession, etc.) *[priesthood]*

Many such forms are entered and make it possible for you to figure out the meaning of words that are made with these forms but are not themselves entered. You will, of course, find a great many words made with these forms in the dictionary, some as main entries with definitions, others as run-in entries listed at the end of a main entry. You will find a fuller explanation of these run-in entries under the heading "Derived Words" on Guide page xvi.

DIVISION OF WORDS INTO SYLLABLES

The large, centered dots in a main entry or run-in form show you at what points a word may be broken at the end of a line of written or printed matter when the whole word does not fit on the line.

neigh·bor·hood

ste·nog·ra·pher

You may break the word *neighborhood* at *neigh-* or at *neighbor-*. You may break *stenographer* at *ste-*, *stenog-*, or *stenogra-*.

Try not to divide short words or leave a syllable of one or two letters on a line by itself. To leave the *a-* of a·ban·don at the end of a line or put the *y* of might·y at the beginning of the next line makes it hard to read the next lines, even though these single letters are indeed syllables.

Never divide words of one syllable, such as scrounged or through, no matter how long they are.

Compound entries such as cabin cruiser, cost of living, and security blanket do not have center dots for syllable division. That is because each word of the compound is syllabified at its own entry.

If the stress given to the syllables of a word shifts when that word is used as another part of speech, the syllable division is shown only for the first part of speech given. In the case of a word such as progress, you may want to change the syllable division from prog·ress, when the noun is meant, to pro·gress when the verb is meant. The pronunciation shown for the verb serves as a guide for this change.

PRONUNCIATIONS

We all speak American English, but people in different parts of our country pronounce many words differently. These differences are not important, and the speech of educated people of one region is no "better" or "more correct" than that of another region.

In order to go into these slight dialectal differences, we must first look at the symbols that are used to show how a word is pronounced. The pronunciation of the word is printed with these symbols and comes after the heavy boldface entry word, enclosed in parentheses. These symbols tell you how the word sounds.

co·coa (kō′kō)

de·nun·ci·a·tion (di nun′sē ā′shən)

Try sounding these words aloud by looking at the sound symbols and stress marks. Check yourself by using the full pronunciation key below. The special marks above the letters are called diacritical marks. The key gives a list of all the symbols used in the pronunciations. Each symbol is followed by sample words that show the sound of the symbol. The sound of the symbol (a) is that of *a* in the key word *ask*, and so on.

THE PRONUNCIATION KEY

Symbol	Key Words	Symbol	Key Words
a	ask, fat, parrot	b	bed, fable, dub
ā	ape, date, play	d	dip, beadle, had
ä	ah, car, hot	f	fall, after, off
		g	get, haggle, dog
e	elf, ten, care	h	he, ahead, hotel
ē	even, meet, city	j	joy, agile, badge
		k	kill, tackle, bake

i	is, hit, mirror	l	let, yellow, ball
ī	ice, bite, high	m	met, camel, trim
		n	not, flannel, ton
ō	open, tone, go	p	put, apple, tap
ô	all, horn, law	r	red, port, dear
ᴏᴏ	ooze, tool, crew	s	sell, castle, pass
oo	look, pull, moor	t	top, cattle, hat
yᴏᴏ	use, cute, few	v	vat, hovel, have
yoo	united, cure, globule	w	will, always, swear
oi	oil, point, toy	y	yet, onion, yard
ou	out, crowd, plow	z	zebra, dazzle, haze
u	up, cut, color	ch	chin, catcher, arch
ʉr	urn, fur, deter	sh	she, cushion, dash
ə	a in ago	th	thin, nothing, truth
	e in agent	*th*	then, father, lathe
	i in sanity	zh	azure, leisure
	o in comply	ŋ	ring, anger, drink
	u in focus	′	[see the explanation
ər	perhaps, murder		below and also *Foreign sounds* below]

A heavy stress mark ′ is placed after a syllable that gets a strong accent, as in de·vel·op (di vel′əp).

A light stress mark ′ is placed after a syllable that also gets a stress, but of a weaker kind, as after the third syllable of dic·tion·ar·y (dik′shə ner′ē).

A shortened form of this key is given at the bottom of every right-hand page of the dictionary. Thus, when the book is spread open at any page and you want to check on a symbol, you can glance down and find it.

With the key words given for each speech sound, a speaker of American English in any part of the U.S. will automatically read the pronunciation of his own region into any symbol shown here. Let us examine the differences in the sounds heard for the various symbols.

a The New Englander who sees ask as one of the key words for the symbol **a** naturally sounds the **a** in this word, and certain other words, more like the **a** in *father* than like the **a** in *fat,* which is heard in most other regions.

ä Some words shown with the symbol **ä,** such as *alms* (ämz), *hot* (hät), *rod* (räd), etc. are heard in the speech of some regions with the vowel sound ô (ômz), (hôt), (rôd).

e The symbol **e** stands for the vowel in the word *ten,* but it is also used, followed by **r,** for the vowel sound of *care* (ker). For this sound, vowels ranging from ā (kār *or* kā′ər) to a (kar) are sometimes heard.

ē The symbol **ē** stands for the vowel of *meet* and is also used for the vowel in the unstressed last syllable of such words as *lucky* (luk′ē) or *pretty* (prit′ē). In such words, the vowel sometimes seem closer to **i** (luk′i), (prit′i), etc., but the sound generally heard is not quite as long as **ē** in *meet* or as short as **i** in *hit.*

i The symbol **i** stands for the vowel of *hit,* but is also used for the unstressed syllables of such words as *gar-bage* (gär′bij), *goodness* (good′nis), *preface* (pref′is), *deny* (di nī′), etc. In such unstressed syllables, the schwa (ə) is also often heard (gär′bəj, də nī′), etc. The symbol **i** is used, followed by **r,** for the vowel sound of *dear* (dir). For this sound, a vowel closer to ē (dēr *or* dē′ər) is sometimes heard.

ô The symbol **ô** stands for the vowel of *all.* When followed by **r,** as in *more* (môr), a vowel more like ō (mōr *or* mō′ər) is sometimes heard. In words like *cough* (kôf), *lawn* (lôn), etc., a vowel closer to ä (käf), (län) is sometimes heard.

ur and **ər,** and other vowels with **r** The two symbols **ur** and **ər** stand for the stressed and unstressed sounds heard in the two syllables of *murder* (mur′dər). Where these symbols are shown, some speakers, especially in the South and along the eastern seaboard, automatically "drop their r's" in pronouncing them. These speakers do not sound the r's following certain other vowels, as in words like *car, dear,* etc.

oo and **ōō** The symbol **oo** stands for the vowel of *look* and the symbol **ōō** for the vowel of *tool.* With **y** they form the symbols for the sounds heard in *pure* (pyoor) and *use* (yōōz). After some consonants **yoo** and **yōō** are sometimes heard instead of **oo** and **ōō,** as in *during* (door′iŋ, dyoor′in), *news* (nōōz, nyōōz), and *tube* (tōōb, tyōōb). The second pronunciations may be heard, for example, along the eastern seaboard. This dictionary does not give the **yoo** and **yōō** sounds after *l* and *s* because they are not often heard in American speech. If you wonder why, try using them in *lute* and *sue.*

ə The symbol **ə,** called the schwa, stands for the vowel heard in the unstressed syllables of *ago, agent, focus,* etc. In many words, such as *neuritis,* this vowel is sometimes heard as **i** (noo rīt′is).

ŋ The symbol **ŋ** stands for the nasal sound of the **ng** in *sing* and of the **n** before the consonants **k** and **g** in words such as *drink* (driŋk) and *finger* (fiŋ′gər).

' The apostrophe used as a symbol before **l, m,** and **n** shows that these consonants form syllables in the word by themselves with practically no vowel sound coming before, as in *battle* (bat′l), *happen* (hap′'n). In the speech of some persons, a fuller sound (hap′ən) is heard. You will find other uses of the apostrophe as a symbol in the next section, *Foreign Sounds.*

The pronunciation of "wh" in a word such as *where* is given as (hwer, wer). The first pronunciation begins with a forcing out of the breath as in sounding *h,* unlike the second in which the *w* is pronounced exactly as it is in the word *wear.* Both pronunciations are given for such "wh" words since both are heard so commonly in American speech.

FOREIGN SOUNDS

Most of the symbols in the key above have been used in the pronunciations of words in foreign languages. Along with these, the following added symbols (and the apostrophe again) are needed to show sounds that cannot be dealt with using the general key.

ȧ This sound is halfway between (a) and (ä). It is heard in words such as French *bal* (bȧl).

ë For this sound you round the lips as you would for (ô) and pronounce (e). It is heard in words such as French *coeur* (kër).

ö For this sound you round your lips as you would for (ō) and pronounce (ā). It is heard in French *feu* (fö), German *Göthe* or *Goethe* (gö′tə), etc.

ô̂ This symbol stands for any of a range of sounds between (ō) and (ô), such as those heard in French *coq* (kôk), German *doch* (dôkh), Italian *poco* (pô′kô), Spanish *torero* (tô re′rô), etc.

ü For this sound you round the lips as you would for (ōō) and pronounce (ē). It is heard in French *duc* (dük), German *grün* (grün), etc.

kh For this sound you bring the back of the tongue up to the roof of the mouth almost as you would for (k) and let your breath pass through in a stream, as in pronouncing (h). This sound is heard in words such as German *doch* (dôkh).

H This sound is similar to the one just above, except that it is formed closer to the front of the roof of the mouth. It is heard in such German words as *ich* (iH) and is sometimes mistaken by speakers of English for the sound (sh).

n This symbol tells you that the vowel just in front of it should be sounded so that much of the breath passes through the nose as well as through the mouth. This nasalized sound is heard in such words as French *mon* (mōn).

r This symbol stands for any of various trilled sounds made by vibrating the tip of the tongue against the fleshy ridge along the inside of the upper front teeth, or by vibrating the hanging flap of flesh at the back of the mouth against the back of the tongue. Such sounds are heard for the r in French, German, Italian, and Russian words.

' The apostrophe is used as a symbol after a final *l* or *r* sound in certain French words and names to show that the *l* or *r* is pronounced with little or no voice, as in French *lettre* (let′r') or *table* (tȧ′ bl').

HOW PRONUNCIATIONS ARE SHORTENED

Shortened pronunciations are given for main entries when you can quickly and easily form the full pronunciation by glancing at a preceding entry that is very close.

gear (gir)

gear·ing (gir′iŋ)

gear·shift (-shift′)

gear·wheel (-hwēl′, -wēl′)

The first, strongly stressed syllable (gir′), given in the pronunciation of *gearing* for *gear-*, applies also to the pronunciations of *gearshift* and *gearwheel*, each of which has a hyphen in front to show that the first part needs to be filled in by you.

Variant pronunciations for the same word are also cut short wherever possible, with only that syllable or those syllables shown in which change takes place. A hyphen at the end of a shortened pronunciation tells you that the last part does not change, and a hyphen at the beginning, that the first part does not change. Hyphens before and after a variant tell you the change is in the middle of the word.

ac·cept (ək sept′, ak-)

rec·ti·tude (rek′tə tōōd′, -tyōōd′)

fu·tu·ri·ty (fyōō tōōr′ə tē, -tyōōr′-, -choor′-)

Shortened forms of this kind are also used inside the parentheses when there is a change for different parts of speech or for a certain sense under a part-of-speech label.

des·ig·nate (dez′ig nāt′; *for adj., also* -nit) *adj.* . . . —
vt. . . .

en·sign (en′sīn; *also, and for 4 always,* -s′n) *n.* **1.** . . . .
2. . . . . **3.** . . . . **4.** . . . .

Such shortened forms are also often used for showing pronunciation of words in boldface inside an entry, such as plural forms, derived forms, etc.

cha·peau (sha pō′) *n., pl.* **-peaus′, -peaux′** (-pōz′)

fore·close (fôr klōz′) *vt.* . . . . —**fore·clo′sure**
(-klō′zhər) *n.*

PART-OF-SPEECH LABELS

Almost all definitions in your dictionary are given under part-of-speech labels. These are abbreviated *n.* for noun, *vt.* for transitive verb, *vi.* for intransitive verb, *adj.* for adjective, *adv.* for adverb, *prep.* for preposition, *conj.* for conjunction, *pron.* for pronoun, and *interj.* for interjection. If you have any trouble with the names and what they stand for, refer to the entries for them in your dictionary for explanations and examples. Remember that words can on occasion be used as almost any part of speech and some such uses get to be part of the language, as can be seen in the adjective-to-noun change of *married* in "the young marrieds" and the adjective-to-verb change of *tough* in "to tough it out." Almost all

nouns can be used as adjectives, as in *coffee* flavor, *picnic* basket, and *energy* crisis.

PLURALS OF NOUNS

Plurals formed by simply adding *-s* or *-es* to the singular form are not normally shown. Plurals are shown when the *y* ending of the singular form is changed to *i* before adding *-es*. Plural forms are shortened, as below, when there is no change in spelling and stress in the first syllable or syllables.

sky (skī) *n., pl.* **skies** . . .

can·dy (kan′dē) *n., pl.* **-dies** . . .

cer·e·mo·ny (ser′ə mō′nē) *n., pl.* **-nies** . . .

Plurals of nouns ending in *o* are shown so that you will know whether they are formed with *-s* or *-es* or, as in the case of some nouns, with either ending.

dom·i·no (däm′ə nō′) *n., pl.* **-noes′, -nos′** . . .

he·ro (hir′ō, hē′rō) *n., pl.* **-roes** . . .

ra·di·o (rā′dē ō′) *n., pl.* **-os′** . . .

Many nouns have plurals that are not formed simply by adding *-s* or *-es,* and such plural forms are always shown. For a full explanation of the different ways plurals are formed, see the entry **plural** in your dictionary. You will find that some noun entries have plural forms with notes referring the user to specific parts of the entry for **plural.**

COMPARATIVE AND SUPERLATIVE FORMS

Many common adjectives and adverbs of one or two syllables have a comparative form (abbreviated *compar.*) showing a degree of being "more," and a superlative form (abbreviated *superl.*) showing a degree of being "most." Thus *fast* has the forms *faster* and *fastest.* Where these forms are made, as with *fast,* by simply adding *-er* or *-est,* they are not shown in the dictionary.

Comparatives and superlatives are shown with the main entry if the spelling is changed when *-er* and *-est* are added, as in **rare, happy,** and **big** below, or if there is a complete change in form. The comparative *worse* and superlative *worst* for the adjective **bad,** for example, come from a different Old English word than the word **bad** itself.

rare (rer) *adj.* **rar′er, rar′est** . . .

hap·py (hap′ē) *adj.* **-pi·er, -pi·est** . . .

big (big) *adj.* **big′ger, big′gest** . . .

good (good) *adj.* **bet′ter, best** . . .

bad (bad) *adj.* **worse, worst** . . .

Notice the shortened forms given with **happy.**

PRINCIPAL PARTS OF VERBS

Every verb has basic forms called **principal parts**, used in building other forms of the verb. The infinitive is the first principal part. The second is the past tense and the third is the past participle. Another important form, the present participle, is sometimes regarded as a principal part. Look at these forms for the verbs *walk* and *march*.

Infinitive	Past Tense	Past Participle	Present Participle
walk	walked	walked	walking
march	marched	marched	marching

The principal parts of most verbs are formed in a regular way, as shown above, by adding *-ed* to form the past tense and the past participle and adding *-ing* to form the present participle. For the third person singular in the present tense, you add *-s (walks)* or *-es (marches)*. You will find **walk** and **march** listed as main entries. You will not find other forms shown for these verbs because they are regular. When principal parts are not shown with a verb, you can assume that the regular rules are followed in forming them.

Principal parts are shown even when the irregularity consists only of dropping the letter *e* (as with *taste*, shown below) before adding *-ed* or *-ing*.

Where two inflected forms are given for a verb, the first is the form for the past tense and the past participle, and the second is the form for the present participle.

taste (tāst) *vt.* **tast′ed, tast′ing** . . .

snap (snap) *vi.* **snapped, snap′ping** . . .

Where three forms are given, separated from one another by commas, the first is the form for the past tense, the second the form for the past participle, and the third the form for the present participle.

do (dо̄о̄) *vt.* **did, done, do′ing** . . .

go (gо̄) *vi.* **went, gone, go′ing** . . .

Where there are alternative forms for any of the principal parts, these are shown as follows:

dive (dīv) *vi.* **dived** or **dove, dived, div′ing** . . .

fo·cus (fо̄′kəs) . . . —*vt.* **-cused** or **-cussed, -cus·ing** or **-cus·sing** . . .

Note that the principal parts of **focus** are cut short since there is no change in the spelling or stress of the first part.

DERIVED WORDS

Among the words formed from main-entry words and placed in the same blocks with them are the run-in derived words. These are formed by adding suffixes to the entry words. Thus greatness, liveliness, and new-ness, each formed with the suffix -ness, are run in at the end of the entries for great, lively, and new. The meanings of these derived words can be clearly understood from the base word and the suffix -ness, which is a separate entry in the dictionary and means "state, quality, or instance of being." So greatness means "the state, quality, or an instance of being great."

Many words that are formed with common suffixes such as -able, -er, -less, -like, -ly, and -tion are listed as run-in entries with the word from which they are derived. Let us look at several examples from your dictionary.

def·i·nite (def′ə nit) *adj.* . . . . —**def′i·nite·ly** *adv.* —**def′i·nite·ness** *n.*

dis·sect (di sekt′) *vt.* . . . —**dis·sec′tion** *n.* —**dis·sec′tor** *n.*

for·give (fər giv′, fôr-) *vt.* . . . —**for·giv′a·ble** *adj.* —**for·giv′er** *n.*

home (hōm) *n.* . . . . —**home′less** *adj.* —**home′like** *adj.*

Notice that the run-in entries are all syllabified and that accents are placed where the stress occurs. When necessary, pronunciation is shown, in full or in part.

ETYMOLOGIES: THE HISTORIES OF WORDS

Short etymologies, or little histories of words, have been included in your dictionary. The etymology will be found immediately before the definition, set off in heavy brackets. The symbols and abbreviations used in the etymologies (such as < meaning "derived from" and the abbreviations of language labels) are explained in the list of Abbreviations and Symbols that you will find at the end of this Guide.

Etymologies will help you to have a clearer understanding of today's meanings of the words. You see how a word may gradually change in form and meaning in its journey from language to language until finally the word in Modern English is quite different in form or meaning from the original word. Some words have been borrowed unchanged from foreign languages. The words in our language have come to us not only from Old English and other Germanic languages but also from Greek and Latin and the Romance languages (especially French) that developed from Latin. These have been the main sources, but there have been others as well, as the languages of the American Indians, Africans, and Asians.

Students of language, starting several hundred years ago, began to notice similarities among words of the same meaning in various European languages and the languages of India and Persia. For example, the English word *father* is matched by Old Norse *fathir*, German *vater* (pronounced fä′tər), Latin *pater*, Greek *patēr,* and Sanskrit *pitár.* As linguists kept comparing words in this way, it became clear to them that certain languages belonged to the same family, a family descended from a language that existed before recorded history.

The linguists were able to put together an outline of this primitive language from bases, or roots, that are common to many of the words in the member languages living and dead. No record of this language exists, but it has been given a name. It is called Indo-European (abbreviated IE.), because the languages descended from it are spoken throughout almost all of Europe and in an area southeastward into India.

One of the main branches of the Indo-European family is the Germanic branch, which includes German, Dutch, the Scandinavian languages, and our own English. The Italic branch includes along with Latin the Romance languages, French, Italian, Spanish, etc., that sprang from Latin. Another important branch of the Indo-European family is the Slavic, to which Russian, Polish, Czech, Serbo-Croatian, etc. belong.

Two other main branches are the Greek and the Celtic. The only branch that developed outside of Europe and still survives today is the Indo-Iranian, which includes most of the languages of India, Pakistan, Afganistan, and Iran. Inside Europe only a very few languages—Basque and a group that includes Finnish, Estonian, and Hungarian—do not belong to the Indo-European family.

People familiar with two or more of the Indo-European languages may be aware that they are related in some way. Linguists studying the languages noticed that they underwent certain fixed changes of consonants and of vowels from group to group and from branch to branch. For example, look at the etymology of **bear**[1], meaning "to carry."

> **bear**[1] (ber) *vt.* . . . [OE. *beran* < IE. base *bher-*, to carry, bring, from which also come L. *ferre* & Gr. *pherein,* both meaning "to bear"]

Note that the (bh) sound that you see in the Indo-European base *bher-* became an (f) sound in Greek and Latin words. In English and other Germanic languages it turned into the (b) sound we use when we pronounce the word *bear.*

By making use of the information contained in the etymology for *bear* (to carry), you will find that words you might never have imagined have any connection with each other are indeed related. In words like **bier**, **birth**, and **burden** you can see the different ways you are told to look back at the entry **bear**[1] for the Indo-European base which relates these words to one another. The word *bear* appears in small capitals as a cross reference in each etymology.

The following words with widely different meanings are all related to the English word *bear* because they all come from the Latin verb *ferre,* which in turn comes from the IE. base *bher-:* **confer, conifer, differ, prefer,** and **transfer.** Then we have words that come from the Greek verb *pherein,* which also derives from the IE. base *bher-.* Here are some of them: **euphoria, metaphor, periphery,** and **semaphore.**

Other etymologies tell interesting stories. For example, at the entry **bacitracin,** meaning "an antibiotic gotten from a strain of bacteria and used in treating bacterial infections, esp. of the skin," you will find the following etymology: [<BACI(LLUS) + (Margaret) *Trac(y),* Am. girl (1963 -   ) from whose wounds the strain was isolated + –IN[1]] . . . You discover that *Tracy,* the family name of the American girl from whom the bacillus was isolated, is memorialized in the word **bacitracin,** whose other parts are made up of *baci-* from *bacillus* and the suffix *-in.*

There are surprises of many kinds in the etymologies. Would you have guessed that the word **scold**, meaning "to find fault (with) harshly or angrily," comes from the Old Norse word for the Viking poets—*skald?* The skaids wrote sharply satirical poems and won themselves a special place in the English language for it.

The etymology for *salver,* a word applied simply to a kind of tray, suggests a curious history. The word comes to us through the French from the Spanish noun *salva,* which also referred to a tray—one used to hold food that was to be tasted before being served to kings and nobles. The noun in turn goes back to the Latin verb *salvare,* meaning "to save." The tasting of food was in fact the testing of food—to make sure it was not poisoned.

You will find that no etymology is shown where one is not needed because the parts that make up the word can be checked for their etymologies, as in the word **precondition.** And, of course, for some words the definition itself clearly explains the etymology. See **bluebottle** for an example of this. Where no etymology is known for certain, the following appears: [< ?]. If we are fairly sure, but not certain, about an etymology, it will be shown with "?" before it.

Remember that all cross-references are printed in small capitals. For some words etymologies are simply shown by cross-references to the parts of which they are formed and which are entered separately.

> **en·dog·a·my** . . . *n.* [ENDO- + -GAMY]
>
> **ra·don** . . . *n.* [RAD(IUM) + -ON]

IDIOMATIC PHRASES

An idiom is a phrase or expression that has a meaning different from that which the words suggest in their usual meaning in the language. If someone says,

"Mary is a real friend—she stood by me when I was sick," we know that Mary isn't being complimented for having stood beside a sickbed twenty-four hours a day. Or again, if we overhear one ham radio operator say to another, "Stand by, I'll get back to you in a minute," we don't think he is asking the other person to get up out of his chair and stand, while waiting for the message to continue. The expression "stand by" is a fairly common one, and many of us never stop to think that the words as used in these examples make little sense if taken literally.

This idiomatic phrase, along with thousands of others in American English, is entered and defined in your *Webster's New World Dictionary*. Some of the phrases are as familiar to you as the one above. Many others you will need to look up because they seem to have a meaning other than the literal meaning. Such phrases are run in to the entry for the key word of each phrase, or the word that needs explaining.

SYNONYMIES

At the end of certain main entries for words you will find a block of words in slightly smaller type that begins with *SYN*. These blocks of words are called "synonymies" and will help you see the differences in meaning between "synonyms," words that are closely related in meaning, such as *follow, ensue,* and *result.* When there are slight differences in meaning, these are pointed out, so that you see that something that *follows* something else in time comes after it but is not always caused by it, and that something that *ensues* or *results* not only comes after something else but is also caused by it. Usually there are also short phrases and sentences to show the words in use: [sunshine *followed* by rain], [dark clouds appeared and rain *ensued*], [superstition *results* from ignorance].

To make it easy for you to find a particular synonymy, a cross-reference to the word where the synonymy appears has been put into the entry for each of the other words discussed in the synonymy. For example, in the entries for *ensue* and *result,* there is a cross-reference to *follow,* that reads "see *SYN.* at FOLLOW." At the end of some synonymies you may find a cross-reference to another synonymy. For example, at the end of the synonymy for *kind* as an adjective, you will find a cross-reference to *type,* where there is a synonymy that treats *kind* as a noun. Also at the end of some synonymies you may find antonyms, or words that have opposite meanings to the words in the synonymies. For example, at the end of the synonymy at *care,* you will find "*ANT.* unconcern, indifference."

USAGE LABELS AND USAGE NOTES

Usage—the way people use their language—varies from one time or period to another, from one place or region to another, and from one person or group to another. Because of these variations people speak and write in various dialects, according to the period they live in, the place where they live, and the groups they belong to. These differences show up in the spellings, pronunciations, and meanings of words, and in other ways. People cannot make full use of their language or of a dictionary unless they understand these differences in usage. Usage is concerned with what is suitable or appropriate in speech or writing for a particular person to use at a certain time and place and in a specific situation or for a specific audience. Good usage in English is a matter of taste and education and depends on the time, the place, and the occasion. Good usage does not demand that a user of the language should always follow conventional or standard usage, but it does demand that one know the difference between standard and nonstandard usage. *Standard English* is the dialect that has developed to meet the need for a single dialect, especially in written or printed form, that can be used as a standard and understood by people anywhere in the United States. A dictionary intended for use in the schools is mainly a record of Standard English and standard usages, but many common nonstandard usages are also included. Your dictionary calls attention to differences in usage in various ways: by putting labels inside brackets or in italics and by the use of notes or comments. Here are the most important usage labels, with the meanings they have in this dictionary.

Obsolete: The word or sense is no longer used but may be found in writing of an earlier period. Abbreviated as Obs.

Archaic: The word or sense is no longer much used at the present time except in certain situations, as in church services, but may be found in writing of an earlier period.

Rare: The word or sense is rarely used.

Poetic: The word or sense is used chiefly in poetry, especially in poetry of an earlier period. Abbreviated as Poet.

Dialect: The word or sense is used regularly only in some geographical areas or in a certain specified area (*South, Southwest, West,* etc.) of the United States. Abbreviated as Dial.

British (or *Canadian, Scottish,* etc.): The word or sense is used in British English (or Canadian English, Scottish English, etc.) but not in American English. When *chiefly* is put before the label, it indicates that the word or sense is also used in the United States, but less frequently. *British dialect* indicates that the word or sense is used regularly only in certain geographical areas of Great Britain, usually in northern England. Abbreviated as Brit., Canad., Scot., etc.

Colloquial: The word or sense is used in the informal, or everyday, speech and writing of educated people.

Colloquial English is Standard English on an informal level; it is not to be regarded as substandard or illiterate. Abbreviated as Colloq.

Slang: The word or sense is not generally regarded as conventional or standard usage but is used, even by the best speakers, in very informal situations. Slang includes words that are made up, like *pizazz,* as well as old, well-known words, like *cool,* when they are given new, slang meanings. Slang words are usually very popular for a time and then disappear from use or become part of the standard vocabulary.

These usage labels are usually placed in brackets. If the label comes right after a part-of-speech label or after a boldface entry term, it applies to all the senses given for that part of speech or that term. If the label comes after a numeral or letter, it applies only to the sense having that numeral or letter.

When a usage that is not standard is entered in the dictionary, you will find at the entry a usage label, such as [Slang] or [Dial.] or a usage note, such as "not a polite use" (for *guts)* or ["he *don't,"* "she *don't,"* and "it *don't"* are not now considered to be standard].

The eleventh sense of *leave* as a transitive verb, "to let or allow," is not only labeled [Dial.] but also has a note, "in this sense not a standard usage." The label and the note together tell you that a usage may belong to a *regional dialect,* spoken in a certain area of the country, as well as to a *social dialect,* spoken by those who belong to a certain social group, based mainly on education. Whether one says "leave us go" or "let us go" depends on what social group one is in and where that group is located. A character in one of T. S. Eliot's poems says, "Let us go then, you and I." A character in John Steinbeck's *The Grapes of Wrath* says, "Leave me salt the meat." The usage of one character is standard; the usage of the other is not standard. But what is more important is that the usage of each is appropriate to his situation.

Standard English has developed from the various regional and social dialects of our American language. A dialect that is understood well only in a certain region or only in a certain social group serves the people in that region or group very well and deserves respect as part of a rich cultural heritage, but a regional dialect or a social dialect cannot serve all groups in the way that Standard English can.

There are three main regional dialects in the United States: Northern, Midland, and Southern. The Northern dialect area includes New England, New York, and those States and parts of States that border on the Great Lakes. The Midland dialect area begins in parts of New Jersey, Pennsylvania, Delaware, etc. and broadens in the Middle West, spreading north and south from it to include most of the area to the west. The Southern dialect area includes most of Delaware, Maryland, and Virginia and the Southern and Gulf States and part of Texas.

You may have been born in New England and learned to say *idea* with an "r" sound at the end, when it comes before a vowel, and *dear* without any "r" sound. Then you moved to the South and discovered that words like *idea* do not have any "r" sound added but that words like *dear* sound almost the same as in New England. Or you moved to the Midwest and discovered that words like *dear* are usually spoken with the "r" sounded at all times and that an "r" sound is never added to words like *idea.* You may have grown up in the North and learned to pronounce *greasy* with an "s" sound. Then you moved to the South and found people pronouncing *greasy* with a "z" sound.

There are dialect differences in vocabulary as well as in pronunciation. The usage labels in your dictionary for words such as *goober, grits,* and the third meaning of *frappé* make you aware of these differences.

FIELD LABELS

A field label may be placed right before a certain sense so as to indicate that the word is used in that sense by people engaged in a special field of knowledge or activity. Sometimes these labels are abbreviated. In long entries where there are many general and specialized senses, these labels are arranged after the general senses in alphabetical order, in order to help the user find a special sense quickly.

form . . . *n.* . . . **15.** *Gram.* . . . **17.** *Printing* . . .

dou·ble . . . *n.* . . . . **8.** *Baseball* . . . **9.** *Bridge* . . .

A Final Word

A dictionary cannot teach you how to write and speak, but it can tell you many things about how words and phrases are used. And few things are more important than words. You use them to pass on information and to express your feelings. You need them if you are to understand others. You use them at work and at play. They are tools of communication and sources of pleasure. You find them on the labels of cans and in the lyrics of rock songs. You shout them at football games and whisper them to the one you love. You tell jokes and make puns with them. Politicians use them to get your vote. Poets use them to sway your emotions. Without them you would be unable even to think. They are as much a part of your life as the air you breathe and the food you eat.

abbrev. abbreviated; abbreviation
abl. ablative
acc. accusative
adj. adjective; adjectival
adv. adverb; adverbial
Aeron. Aeronautics
Afr. African
Afrik. Afrikaans
alt. alternative
Am. American
AmFr. American French
AmInd. American Indian
AmSp. American Spanish
Anat. Anatomy
Anglo-Fr. Anglo-French
Anglo-Ind. Anglo-Indian
Anglo-Ir. Anglo-Irish
Anglo-L. Anglo-Latin
Anglo-N. Anglo-Norse
Anglo-Norm. Anglo-Norman
ANT. antonym
Ar. Arabic
Aram. Aramaic
Archaeol. Archaeology
Archit. Architecture
Arith. Arithmetic
Arm. Armenian
art. article
assoc. associated
Assyr. Assyrian
Astrol. Astrology
Astron. Astronomy
at. no. atomic number
at. wt. atomic weight
Bab. Babylonian
Beng. Bengali
Biochem. Biochemistry
Biol. Biology
Bohem. Bohemian
Bot. Botany
Braz. Brazilian
Bret. Breton
Brit. British
Bulg. Bulgarian
C Celsius; Central
c. century (in etym.); circa
Canad. Canadian
CanadFr. Canadian French
cap. capital
Celt. Celtic

cent. century; centuries
cf. compare
Ch. Chaldean; Church
Chem. Chemistry
Chin. Chinese
Colloq. colloquial
comp. compound
compar. comparative
conj. conjunction
contr. contracted; contraction
Cop. Coptic
Corn. Cornish
cu. cubic
Cym. Cymric
Dan. Danish
dat. dative
deriv. derivative
Dial.; dial. dialectal
dim. diminutive
Du. Dutch
E eastern
E. East; English (in etym. & pronun.)
Early ModDu. Early Modern Dutch
Early ModE. Early Modern English
Early ModG. Early Modern German
EC east central
Eccles. Ecclesiastical
Ecol. Ecology
Econ. Economics
Educ. Education
e.g. for example
Egypt. Egyptian
Elec. Electricity
Eng. English
equiv. equivalent
Esk. Eskimo
esp. especially
est. estimated
Eth. Ethiopic
etym. etymology
Ex. example
F Fahrenheit
fem. feminine
ff. following (entry, sense, etc.)
fig. figurative; figuratively
Finn. Finnish

Fl. Flemish
fl. flourished
Fr. French
Frank. Frankish
Fris. Frisian
ft. feet
fut. future
G. German (in etym. & pronun.)
Gael. Gaelic
gal. gallon; gallons
Gaul. Gaulish
gen. genitive
Geog. Geography
Geol. Geology
Geom. Geometry
Ger. German
ger. gerund
Gmc. Germanic
Goth. Gothic
Gr. Greek
Gram. Grammar
Haw. Hawaiian
Heb. Hebrew
Hort. Horticulture
Hung. Hungarian
Ice. Icelandic
IE. Indo-European
i.e. that is
imper. imperative
imperf. imperfect
in. inch; inches
incl. including
Ind. Indian
indic. indicative
inf. infinitive
infl. influenced
intens. intensive
interj. interjection
Ir. Irish
Iran. Iranian
IrGael. Irish Gaelic
irreg. irregular
It. Italian
Jap. Japanese
Jpn. Japanese
KJV King James Version
L Late
L. Latin
lb. pound; pounds
LGr. Late Greek

Linguis. Linguistics
lit. literally
Lith. Lithuanian
LL. Late Latin
LME. Late Middle English
LowG. Low German
M Middle; Medieval
Math. Mathematics
MDu. Middle Dutch
ME. Middle English
Mech. Mechanics
Med. Medicine; Medieval
met. metropolitan
Meteorol. Meteorology
Mex. Mexican
MexSp. Mexican Spanish
MFr. Middle French
MGr. Medieval Greek
MHG. Middle High German
mi. mile; miles
Mil. Military
ML. Medieval Latin
MLowG. Middle Low German
Mod, Mod. Modern
ModGr. Modern Greek
ModHeb. Modern Hebrew
ModL. Modern Latin
Mongol. Mongolic
Myth. Mythology
N northern
N. North
n. noun
Naut., naut. nautical usage
NC north central
NE northeastern
neut. neuter
n.fem. feminine form of noun
n.masc. masculine form of noun
nom. nominative
Norm, Norm. Norman
Norw. Norwegian
n.pl. plural form of noun
n.sing. singular form of noun
N.T. New Testament
NW northwestern
O Old
Obs., obs. obsolete
occas. occasionally
OE. Old English
OFr. Old French
OHG. Old High German
OIce. Old Icelandic
OIr. Old Irish
OIt. Old Italian
OL. Old Latin

ON. Old Norse
ONormFr. Old Norman French
orig. origin; originally
OS. Old Saxon
OSp. Old Spanish
O.T. Old Testament
oz. ounce; ounces
P Primitive
p. page
part. participle
pass. passive
Per. Persian
perf. perfect
pers. person
Peruv. Peruvian
Philos. Philosophy
Phoen. Phoenician
Phonet. Phonetics
Photog. Photography
phr. phrase
Phys. Ed. Physical Education
Physiol. Physiology
PidE. Pidgin English
pl. plural
Poet. poetic
Pol. Polish
pop. popular; population
Port. Portuguese
poss. possessive
pp. pages; past participle
Pr. Provençal
prec. preceding
prep. preposition
pres. present
prin. pts. principal parts
prob. probably
pron. pronoun; pronunciation
pronun. pronunciation
prp. present participle
pseud. pseudonym
Psychol. Psychology
pt. past tense
qt. quart; quarts
R.C.Ch. Roman Catholic Church
refl. reflexive
Rom. Roman
R.S.F.S.R. Russian Soviet
  Federated Socialist Republic
RSV Revised Standard Version
Russ. Russian
S southern
S. South
Sans. Sanskrit
SC south central
Scand. Scandinavian

Scot, Scot. Scottish
ScotGael. Scottish Gaelic
SE southeastern
Sem. Semitic
Serb. Serbian
sing. singular
Sinh. Sinhalese
Slav. Slavic
Sp. Spanish
sp. spelled; spelling
specif. specifically
sq. square
S.S.R. Soviet Socialist Republic
subj. subjunctive
superl. superlative
SW southwestern
Sw. Swedish (in etym. & pronun.)
Swed. Swedish
SYN. synonymy
Syr. Syriac
Tag. Tagalog
Theol. Theology
transl. translation
Turk. Turkish
TV television
ult. ultimately
UN United Nations
U.S. United States
U.S.S.R. Union of Soviet
  Socialist Republics
v. verb
var. variant; variety
v.aux. auxiliary verb
Vet. Veterinary Medicine
vi. intransitive verb
VL. Vulgar Latin
vt. transitive verb
Vulg. Vulgate
W western
W. Welsh; West
WAfr. West African
WC west central
WGmc. West Germanic
WInd. West Indian
yd. yard; yards
Yid. Yiddish
Zool. Zoology

‡ foreign word or phrase
☆ Americanism
+ plus
< derived from
? uncertain; possibly; perhaps
& and

A

A, a (ā) *n., pl.* **A's, a's** **1.** the first letter of the English alphabet **2.** a sound of *A* or *a* **3.** *a symbol for* the first in a sequence or group

A (ā) *n.* ☆**1.** *Educ.* a grade indicating excellence **2.** *Music a)* the sixth tone in the ascending scale of C major *b)* the scale having A as the keynote —*adj.* shaped like *A*

a (ə; *stressed* ā) *adj., indefinite article* [form of AN¹] **1.** one; one sort of **2.** each; any one [*a spider has eight legs*] **3.** [orig. a prep. < OE. *an*, in, on, at] to each; in each; per [*once a day*] Before words beginning with a consonant sound or a sounded *h*, *a* is used [*a child, a home, a uniform*]; before words beginning with a vowel sound or a silent *h*, *an* is used [*an eye, an* ultimatum, *an* honor]

a-¹ [weakened form of OE. *an, on,* in, on, at] *a prefix meaning:* **1.** in, into, on, at, to [*abed, ashore*] **2.** in the act or state of [*asleep*]

a-² *a prefix of various origins and meanings:* **1.** [OE. *a-*, out of, up] up, out: now generally used to add emphasis [*awake, arise*] **2.** [OE. *of-, af-*] off, of [*akin*] **3.** [Gr. *a-, an-*, not] not, without [*atypical*]: before vowels *an-* is used [*anastigmatic*]

A. **1.** *Physics* Absolute **2.** angstrom

a. **1.** about **2.** acre(s) **3.** adjective **4.** alto **5.** ampere **6.** anode **7.** anonymous **8.** answer

A.A. Associate in (or of) Arts

AAA, A.A.A. American Automobile Association

Aa·chen (ä′kən; *G.* ä′khən) city in W West Germany, on the Belgian border: pop. 177,000

A & R Artists and Repertoire (or Repertory)

aard·vark (ärd′värk′) *n.* [obs. Afrik., earth pig] a burrowing African mammal that feeds on ants and termites: it has a long snout

aard·wolf (-woolf′) *n., pl.* **-wolves′** (-woolvz′) [Afrik., earth wolf] a mammal of southern and eastern Africa resembling the hyena but feeding chiefly on termites and insect larvae

Aar·on (er′ən) [LL. < Gr. < Heb. *aharōn,* lit., the exalted one] **1.** a masculine name **2.** *Bible* the older brother of Moses and first high priest of the Hebrews

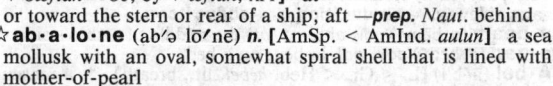

AARDVARK
(c. 2 ft. high at shoulder)

Ab (äb; *Heb.* äv) *n.* [Heb.] *see* JEWISH CALENDAR

ab- [L.] *a prefix meaning* away, from, from off, down [*abdicate*]: shortened to *a-* before *m, p,* and *v;* often *abs-* before *c* or *t* [*abstract*]

A.B. [ML. *Artium Baccalaureus*] Bachelor of Arts

a·ba (ä′bə) *n.* [Ar.] **1.** a fabric of wool or hair fiber with a finish like felt **2.** a loose, sleeveless robe worn by Arabs

a·ba·cá (ab′ə kə) *n.* [Tag.] **1.** *same as* MANILA HEMP (sense 1) **2.** the Philippine plant yielding Manila hemp

a·back (ə bak′) *adv.* **1.** [Archaic] backward; back **2.** backward against the mast, as sails in a wind from straight ahead —**taken aback** startled and confused; surprised

ab·a·cus (ab′ə kəs, ə bak′əs) *n., pl.* **ab′a·cus·es, ab′a·ci′** (-sī′) [L. < Gr. *abax*] **1.** a frame with beads or balls sliding back and forth on wires or in slots, for doing arithmetic **2.** *Archit.* a slab forming the uppermost part of the capital of a column

A·ba·dán (ä′bä dän′) city in W Iran, on an island in the Shatt-al-Arab: pop. 302,000

a·baft (ə baft′) *adv.* [< OE. *on,* on + *bæftan* < *be,* by + *æftan,* AFT] at or toward the stern or rear of a ship; aft —*prep. Naut.* behind

☆**ab·a·lo·ne** (ab′ə lō′nē) *n.* [AmSp. < AmInd. *aulun*] a sea mollusk with an oval, somewhat spiral shell that is lined with mother-of-pearl

a·ban·don (ə ban′dən) *vt.* [< OFr. < *mettre a bandon,* to put under (someone else's) ban] **1.** to give up (something) completely [*to abandon* all hope] **2.** to leave; desert [*the crew abandoned* ship] **3.** to yield (oneself) completely, as to a feeling —*n.* unrestrained freedom of action or emotion —**a·ban′don·ment** *n.*

SYN.—**abandon** implies leaving a person or thing either because of necessity [*to abandon* a sinking ship] or from a lack of responsibility [she *abandoned* her child]; **desert** emphasizes leaving because one is deliberately violating one's obligation, duty, etc. [the soldier *deserted* his post]; **forsake** emphasizes a rejecting of a person or thing that was once dear to one [*to forsake* a cause]—see also **SYN.** at RELINQUISH —**ANT.** reclaim

a·ban·doned (-dənd) *adj.* **1.** given up; forsaken; deserted **2.** shamefully wicked **3.** unrestrained

a·base (ə bās′) *vt.* **a·based′, a·bas′ing** [< OFr. < ML. *abassare,* to lower < L. *ad-,* to + LL. *bassus,* low] to humble or humiliate—see **SYN.** at DEGRADE —**a·base′ment** *n.*

a·bash (ə bash′) *vt.* [OFr. *esbahir,* to astonish < L. *ex* + *ba,* interj. of surprise] to make ashamed and ill at ease—see **SYN.** at EMBARRASS —**a·bashed′** *adj.*

a·bate (ə bāt′) *vt.* **a·bat′ed, a·bat′ing** [< OFr. *abattre,* to beat down: see AD- & BATTER¹] **1.** to make less in amount, degree, etc. **2.** to deduct **3.** *Law* to put a stop to; end —*vi.* to become less; subside —see **SYN.** at WANE —**a·bate′ment** *n.*

ab·a·tis, ab·at·tis (ab′ə tis) *n., pl.* **-a·tis, -at·tis** [Fr.: see prec.] a barricade of cut-down trees laid so that the branches face the enemy

ab·at·toir (ab′ə twär′, ab′ə twär′) *n.* [Fr.: see ABATE] a slaughterhouse

ab·ba·cy (ab′ə sē) *n., pl.* **-cies** an abbot's position, jurisdiction, or term of office

ab·bé (a′bā; *Fr.* à bā′) *n.* [Fr. < LL.: see ABBOT] a French title of respect for a priest, minister, etc.

ab·bess (ab′əs) *n.* [< LL.: see ABBOT] a woman who is head of an abbey of nuns

ab·bey (ab′ē) *n.* **1.** a monastery headed by an abbot or a convent of nuns headed by an abbess **2.** a church or building belonging to an abbey

---

fat, āpe, cär; ten, ēven; is, bīte; gō, hôrn, to͞ol, lo͝ok; oil, out; up, fur; get; joy; yet; chin; she; thin, then; zh, leisure; ŋ, ring; ə for *a* in *ago, e* in *agent, i* in *sanity, o* in *comply, u* in *focus;* ′ as in *able* (ā′b'l); Fr. bâl; ë, Fr. coeur; ö, Fr. feu; Fr. mon; ô, Fr. coq; ü, Fr. duc; r, Fr. cri; H, G. ich; kh, G. doch; ‡foreign; ☆ Americanism; < derived from. See inside front cover.

ab·bot (ab′ət) *n.* [< OE. < LL. < Gr. < Aram. *abbā*, father] a man who heads an abbey of monks

abbr., abbrev. 1. abbreviated **2.** abbreviation

ab·bre·vi·ate (ə brē′vē āt′) *vt.* **-at′ed, -at′ing** [< LL. pp. of *abbreviare* < L. < *ad-*, to + *brevis*, BRIEF] **1.** to make shorter **2.** to shorten (a word or phrase) by leaving out or substituting letters —**ab·bre′vi·a′tor** *n.*

ab·bre·vi·a·tion (ə brē′vē ā′shən) *n.* **1.** a making shorter **2.** the state or fact of being made shorter **3.** a shortened form of a word or phrase, as *N.Y.* for *New York*, *Mr.* for *Mister*, *lb.* for *pound*

A B C (ā′ bē′ sē′) *n., pl.* **A B C's 1.** [*usually pl.*] the alphabet **2.** the basic elements (*of* a subject); rudiments

ABC American Broadcasting Company

ABC soil a vertical section of soil in three distinct layers: the top layer (*A-horizon*) is mostly humus, the middle layer (*B-horizon*) is of clay and other oxidized material, and the bottom layer (*C-horizon*) consists of loose rock and other mineral materials

ab·di·cate (ab′də kāt′) *vt., vi.* **-cat′ed, -cat′ing** [< L. pp. of *abdicare* < *ab-*, off + *dicare*, to proclaim] **1.** to give up formally (a high office, etc.) **2.** to surrender (a right, responsibility, etc.) —**ab′di·ca′tion** *n.* —**ab′di·ca′tor** *n.*

ab·do·men (ab′də mən, ab dō′-) *n.* [L.] **1.** the part of the body between the diaphragm and the pelvis, containing the stomach, intestines, etc.; belly **2.** in insects and crustaceans, the hind part of the body, beyond the thorax

ABDOMEN OF
HONEY BEE

ab·dom·i·nal (ab däm′ə n'l) *adj.* of, in, on, or for the abdomen

ab·duct (ab dukt′) *vt.* [< L. pp. of *abducere* < *ab-*, away + *ducere*, to lead: for IE. base see DUKE] **1.** to kidnap (a person) **2.** to move (a part of the body) away from the median axis of the body, as in lifting an arm sideways —**ab·duc′tion** *n.* —**abduc′tor** *n.*

a·beam (ə bēm′) *adv.* abreast (*of*) the middle of a ship's side

a·bed (ə bed′) *adv., adj.* in bed; on a bed

A·bel (ā′b'l) [L. < Gr. < Heb. *hebel*, lit., breath] **1.** a masculine name **2.** *Bible* the second son of Adam and Eve, killed by his brother Cain: Gen. 4

Ab·é·lard (à bā làr′), **Pierre** (pyer) 1079–1142; Fr. philosopher & teacher: Eng. name **Peter Ab·e·lard** (ab′ə lärd′): see also HÉLOÏSE

Ab·er·deen (ab′ər dēn′) seaport in E Scotland, on the North Sea: pop. 182,000 —**Ab′er·do′ni·an** (-dō′nē ən) *adj., n.*

Aberdeen Angus any of a breed of black, hornless cattle, originally from Scotland, raised for beef

ab·er·rant (a ber′ənt) *adj.* [< L. prp. of *aberrare* < *ab-*, from + *errare*, to wander] turning aside from what is true, normal, or typical —**ab·er′rance, ab·er′ran·cy** *n.*

ab·er·ra·tion (ab′ər ā′shən) *n.* **1.** a turning aside from what is right, true, normal, or typical **2.** mental disorder or lapse **3.** *Optics a)* the failure of light rays from one point to converge to a single focus *b)* an error in a lens or mirror causing such failure

a·bet (ə bet′) *vt.* **a·bet′ted, a·bet′ting** [< OFr. *abeter*, to incite < *a-*, to + *beter*, to BAIT] to urge on or help, esp. in wrongdoing —**a·bet′ment** *n.* —**a·bet′tor, a·bet′ter** *n.*

a·bey·ance (ə bā′əns) *n.* [< Anglo-Fr. < OFr. *abeance*, expectation < *a-*, at + *bayer*, to gape] temporary suspension, as of an activity or function

ab·hor (ab hôr′, əb-) *vt.* **-horred′, -hor′ring** [< L. *abhorrere* < *ab-*, away, from + *horrere*, to shudder: see HORRID] to shrink from in disgust or hatred; detest

ab·hor·rence (-hôr′əns) *n.* an abhorring or something abhorred —see SYN. at AVERSION

ab·hor·rent (-ənt) *adj.* **1.** causing disgust, hatred, etc.; detestable **2.** opposed (*to*) [*abhorrent* to his principles] —**ab·hor′rent·ly** *adv.*

a·bide (ə bīd′) *vi.* **a·bode′** or **a·bid′ed, a·bid′ing** [OE. *abidan* < *a-*, thoroughly + *bidan*, to remain] **1.** to stand fast; remain **2.** [Archaic] to stay; reside (*in* or *at*) —*vt.* **1.** to await **2.** to submit to; put up with [some people cannot *abide* loud noises] —see SYN. at CONTINUE —**abide by 1.** to live up to (a promise, etc.) **2.** to submit to and carry out (a rule, decision, etc.) —**a·bid′ance** *n.*

a·bid·ing (ə bīd′iŋ) *adj.* continuing without change; lasting —**a·bid′ing·ly** *adv.*

Ab·i·djan (äb′i jän′) seaport and capital of the Ivory Coast: pop. 282,000

Ab·i·gail (ab′ə gāl′) [Heb. *abīgayil*, lit., father is rejoicing] a feminine name: dim. *Abby, Gail*

Ab·i·lene (ab′ə lēn′) [< a Biblical name: see Luke 3:1] city in C Tex.: pop. 90,000

a·bil·i·ty (ə bil′ə tē) *n., pl.* **-ties** [see ABLE] **1.** a being able; power to do (something physical or mental) **2.** skill or talent [musical *ability*]

-a·bil·i·ty (ə bil′ə tē) *pl.* **-ties** [L. *-abilitas*: see -ABLE & -ITY] a suffix used to form nouns from adjectives ending in -ABLE [*durability*]

ab·ject (ab′jekt, ab jekt′) *adj.* [< L. pp. of *abjicere* < *ab-*, away, from + *jacere*, to throw: see JET[1]] **1.** of the lowest degree; miserable [*abject* poverty] **2.** lacking self-respect; degraded [an *abject* coward] —see SYN. at BASE[2] —**ab′ject·ly** *adv.* —**ab′ject·ness, ab·jec′tion** *n.*

ab·jure (əb joor′, ab-) *vt.* **-jured′, -jur′ing** [< L. *abjurare* < *ab-*, away, from + *jurare*, to swear: see JURY[1]] **1.** to swear to give up (rights, allegiance, etc.); renounce **2.** to give up (opinions) publicly; recant —**ab·ju·ra·tion** (ab′jə rā′shən) *n.* —**ab·jur′er** *n.*

ab·late (ab lāt′) *vt.* **-lat′ed, -lat′ing** [back-formation < *ablation* < LL. < L. *ablatus*: see ABLATIVE] **1.** to remove, as by surgery **2.** *Astrophysics* to melt, vaporize, etc. (surface material) during high-speed movement through the atmosphere —*vi.* to become ablated —**ab·la′tion** *n.*

ab·la·tive (ab′lə tiv; *for adj. 2* ab lāt′iv) *n.* [< L. < *ablatus*, pp. of *auferre* < *ab-*, away + *ferre*, to BEAR[1]] **1.** the grammatical case in Latin and some other languages used to express "away from," "out of," "derived from," etc. **2.** a word in this case —*adj.* **1.** of or in the ablative **2.** *Astrophysics* that ablates

ab·laut (ab′lout, ab′-; *G.* äp′lout) *n.* [G. < *ab-*, off, from + *laut*, sound] the change of base vowels in related words to show changes in tense, meaning, etc. (Ex.: dr*i*nk, dr*a*nk, dr*u*nk) —*adj.* of or characterized by ablaut

a·blaze (ə blāz′) *adj.* **1.** flaming; gleaming **2.** greatly excited; eager

a·ble (ā′b'l) *adj.* **a′bler** (-blər), **a′blest** (-blist) [< OFr. < L. *habilis*, handy < *habere*, to have, hold: see HABIT] **1.** having enough power, skill, etc. (*to* do something) **2.** having the necessary skill or talent; skilled [an *able* teacher] —**a′bly** *adv.*

SYN.—**able** implies power or ability to do something [*able* to make payments] but sometimes suggests special power or skill [an *able* speaker]; **capable** usually implies that only ordinary requirements are met [a *capable* machinist]; **competent** and **qualified** both imply that the necessary qualifications for something are met, but **qualified** emphasizes that certain specified requirements are complied with [a *competent* critic of modern art; a *qualified* voter] —ANT. inept

-a·ble (ə b'l) [< OFr. < L. *-abilis*] a suffix meaning: **1.** able to [*durable*] **2.** capable of being [*drinkable*] **3.** worthy of being [*lovable*] **4.** having qualities of [*comfortable*] **5.** tending or inclined to [*peaceable*]

a·ble-bod·ied (ā′b'l bäd′ēd) *adj.* healthy and strong

able-bodied seaman a trained, highly skilled sailor: also **able seaman**

a·bloom (ə blōōm′) *adj.* in bloom; in flower

ab·lu·tion (ab lōō′shən, əb-) *n.* [< L. *ablutio* < *abluere* < *ab-*, off + *luere*, to LAVE] a washing of the body, esp. as a religious ceremony

-a·bly (ə blē) a suffix used to form adverbs from adjectives ending in -ABLE [*peaceably*]

ABM anti-ballistic missile

ab·ne·gate (ab′nə gāt′) *vt.* **-gat′ed, -gat′ing** [< L. pp. of *abnegare* < *ab-*, away, from + *negare*, to deny] to give up (rights, claims, etc.); renounce —**ab′ne·ga′tor** *n.*

ab·ne·ga·tion (ab′nə gā′shən) *n.* a giving up of rights, claims, etc.; self-denial [a hermit lives a life of *abnegation*]

Ab·ner (ab′nər) [L. < Heb. *'abnēr*, lit., the father is a light] a masculine name

ab·nor·mal (ab nôr′m'l) *adj.* [earlier *anormal* < Fr. < LL. < Gr. *anōmalos* (see ANOMALOUS) infl. by L. *abnormis* < *ab-*, from + *norma*, NORM] not normal; not average; not typical; irregular, esp. to a considerable degree —see SYN. at IRREGULAR —**ab·nor′mal·ly** *adv.*

ab·nor·mal·i·ty (ab′nôr mal′ə tē) *n.* **1.** the condition of being abnormal **2.** *pl.* **-ties** an abnormal thing

abnormal psychology the study of the behavior of abnormal people, esp. of neurotic, psychotic, or mentally retarded people

a·board (ə bôrd′) *adv.* on board; on, in, or into a ship, airplane, etc. —*prep.* on board of; on; in —☆**all aboard!** get on! get in!: a warning to passengers that the train, car, etc. will start soon

a·bode[1] (ə bōd′) *n.* [see ABIDE] a place where one lives or stays; home; residence

a·bode[2] (ə bōd′) *alt. pt. and pp. of* ABIDE

a·bol·ish (ə bäl′ish) *vt.* [< OFr. < L. *abolescere*, to decay < L. *abolere*, to destroy] to do away with completely; put an end to; esp., to make (a law, etc.) null and void —**a·bol′ish·ment** *n.*
SYN.—**abolish** means to completely do away with something, as an institution, custom, condition, etc. [*to abolish* slavery, ignorance, etc.]; **annul** emphasizes a canceling by law [the marriage was *annulled* by the court]; **rescind, revoke,** and **repeal** all agree in describing the setting aside of laws, orders, permits, etc. [*to rescind* in order; *revoke* a charter; *repeal* an Amendment] —**ANT. establish**

ab·o·li·tion (ab′ə lish′ən) *n.* 1. an abolishing or being abolished; annulment 2. [*occas.* A-] the abolishing of slavery in the U.S. —**ab′o·li′tion·ar′y** *adj.*

ab·o·li·tion·ist (-ist) *n.* one in favor of abolishing some law, custom, etc.; specif. [*occas.* A-], one who favored the abolition of slavery in the U.S.

ab·o·ma·sum (ab′ə mā′səm) *n., pl.* **-ma·sa** (-sə) [ModL. < L. *ab-*, from + *omasum*, paunch] the fourth, or digesting, chamber of the stomach of a cud-chewing animal, as the cow

☆**A-bomb** (ā′bäm′) *n. same as* ATOMIC BOMB —*vt.* to attack or destroy with an atomic bomb

a·bom·i·na·ble (ə bäm′ə nə b'l) *adj.* [see ABOMINATE] 1. disgusting; vile; loathsome [an *abominable* crime] 2. very bad or unpleasant [*abominable* taste in art] —**a·bom′i·na·bly** *adv.*

Abominable Snowman a large, hairy, manlike animal reputed to live in the Himalayas

a·bom·i·nate (ə bäm′ə nāt′) *vt.* **-nat′ed, -nat′ing** [< L. pp. of *abominari*, to regard as an ill omen] 1. to feel hatred and disgust for; loathe 2. to dislike very much —**a·bom′i·na′tor** *n.*

a·bom·i·na·tion (ə bäm′ə nā′shən) *n.* 1. hatred and disgust 2. anything hateful and disgusting

ab·o·rig·i·nal (ab′ə rij′ə n'l) *adj.* 1. existing from earliest days; first; indigenous 2. of aborigines —see **SYN.** at NATIVE — **ab′o·rig′i·nal·ly** *adv.*

ab·o·rig·i·ne (ab′ə rij′ə nē′) *n., pl.* **-nes** [L. < *ab-*, from + *origine*, the beginning] 1. any of the earliest known inhabitants of a region; native 2. [*pl.*] the native animals or plants of a region

a·born·ing (ə bôr′niŋ) *adv.* while being born or created [the plan died *aborning*]

a·bort (ə bôrt′) *vi.* [< L. pp. of *aboriri*, to miscarry] 1. to have a miscarriage 2. to fail to be completed —*vt.* 1. to cause to have an abortion 2. to check (a disease) before fully developed ☆3. to cut short (an operation of an aircraft, missile, etc.) as because of an equipment failure

a·bor·tion (ə bôr′shən) *n.* 1. expulsion of a fetus from the womb before it is developed enough to survive; miscarriage 2. an aborted fetus 3. anything immature and incomplete, as a badly developed plan

☆**a·bor·tion·ist** (-ist) *n.* a person who causes abortions, esp. unlawfully

a·bor·tive (ə bôr′tiv) *adj.* 1. coming to nothing; unsuccessful 2. *Biol.* rudimentary 3. *Med.* causing abortion —**a·bor′tive·ly** *adv.*

ABO system the system of classifying human blood types in accordance with their compatibility for transfusion: there are four major types (A, B, AB, and O), determined by the antigens inherited

a·bound (ə bound′) *vi.* [< OFr. < L. *abundare*, to overflow < *ab-*, away + *undare*, to rise in waves < *unda*, a wave] 1. to be plentiful; exist in large numbers [tropical plants *abound* in the jungle] 2. to have plenty; be rich (*in*) or teem (*with*) [woods *abounding* with game]

a·bout (ə bout′) *adv.* [< OE. *onbutan*, around, on the outside (of)] 1. all around [look *about*] 2. here and there [travel *about*] 3. near [it is somewhere *about*] 4. in the opposite direction [turn it *about*] 5. in succession or rotation [play fair— turn and turn *about*] 6. nearly [*about* four years old] 7. [Colloq.] almost [just *about* ready] —*adj.* [*used only in the predicate*] 1. active [he is up and *about* again] 2. in the vicinity [typhoid is *about*] —*prep.* 1. around; on all sides of 2. here and there in; everywhere in 3. near to 4. with; on (one's person) [have your wits *about* you] 5. attending to [go *about* your business] 6. intending; on the point of [he is *about* to speak] 7. having

to do with; concerning [a book *about* ships] —**how** (or **what**) **about** [Colloq.] what is your wish or opinion concerning? —**how about that!** [Colloq.] isn't that interesting!

☆**a·bout-face** (ə bout′fās′; *for v.* ə bout′fās′) *n.* 1. a sharp turn to the opposite direction, esp. in response to a military command 2. a sharp change, as in opinion —*vi.* **-faced′, -fac′ing** to turn or face in the opposite direction

a·bove (ə buv′) *adv.* [OE. *abufan*] 1. in, at, or to a higher place; overhead; up 2. in or to heaven 3. at a previous place (in a piece of writing) 4. higher in power, status, etc. —*prep.* 1. higher than; over 2. beyond; past [the road *above* the town] 3. at a point upstream of 4. better than [*above* the average] 5. more than [*above* fifty dollars] —*adj.* placed, found, written, mentioned, etc. above or earlier —*n.* something that is above —**above all** most of all; mainly

a·bove·board (-bôrd′) *adv., adj.* without dishonesty or concealment; straightforward

ab·ra·ca·dab·ra (ab′rə kə dab′rə) *n.* [LL.] 1. a word supposed to have magic powers, used in incantations, etc. 2. foolish or meaningless talk

ab·rade (ə brād′) *vt., vi.* **-rad′ed, -rad′ing** [< L. *abradere* < *ab-*, away + *radere*, to scrape] to rub off; wear away by scraping —**ab·rad′er** *n.*

A·bra·ham (ā′brə ham′) [Heb., lit., father of many] 1. a masculine name: dim. *Abe;* var. *Abram* 2. *Bible* the first patriarch and ancestor of the Hebrews —**in Abraham's bosom** 1. at rest with one's dead ancestors 2. in a state of heavenly bliss, peace, etc.

Abraham, Plains of plateau in the city of Quebec, on the St. Lawrence: site of a battle (1759) in which the British defeated the French, giving Britain control of Canada

a·bran·chi·ate (ā braŋ′kē it, -āt) *adj.* [< Gr. *a-*, not + *branchia*, gills + -ATE[1]] without gills —*n.* an animal without gills Also **a·bran′chi·al** (-əl)

ab·ra·sion (ə brā′zhən) *n.* 1. a scraping or rubbing off, as of skin 2. a wearing away by rubbing or scraping, as of rock by wind, water, etc. 3. an abraded spot or area

ab·ra·sive (ə brā′siv) *adj.* causing abrasion —*n.* a substance used for grinding, polishing, etc.

a·breast (ə brest′) *adv., adj.* [A-[1] + BREAST] 1. side by side [walking four *abreast*] 2. informed (*of*) or familiar (*with*) recent developments

a·bridge (ə brij′) *vt.* **a·bridged′, a·bridg′ing** [< OFr. < LL. *abbreviare:* see ABBREVIATE] 1. to reduce in size, etc.; shorten 2. to shorten by using fewer words but keeping the main contents 3. to lessen (rights, authority, etc.) —see **SYN.** at SHORTEN —**a·bridg′a·ble, a·bridge′a·ble** *adj.* —**a·bridg′er** *n.*

a·bridg·ment, a·bridge·ment (ə brij′mənt) *n.* 1. an abridging or being abridged 2. an abridged or condensed version of a book, etc.
SYN.—**abridgment** describes a work that is shortened from a larger work, but that keeps the main contents more or less unchanged; an **abstract** is a short statement of the main contents as of a court record or a technical writing; a **summary** usually restates the main points of the matter that has gone before; a **synopsis** is a condensed, orderly treatment, as of the plot of a novel; a **digest** is a concise, systematic treatment, generally broader in scope than a synopsis —**ANT. expansion**

a·broad (ə brôd′) *adv.* 1. broadly; far and wide 2. circulating [a report is *abroad* that he is ill] 3. outdoors [to stroll *abroad*] 4. to or in foreign countries —**from abroad** from a foreign land

ab·ro·gate (ab′rə gāt′) *vt.* **-gat′ed, -gat′ing** [< L. pp. of *abrogare*, to repeal < *ab-*, away + *rogare*, to propose] to cancel or repeal (a law, treaty, etc.) by authority; annul —**ab′ro·ga·ble** (-gə b'l) *adj.* —**ab′ro·ga′tion** *n.* —**ab′ro·ga′tor** *n.*

a·brupt (ə brupt′) *adj.* [< L. pp. of *abrumpere* < *ab-*, off + *rumpere*, to break] 1. happening suddenly or unexpectedly 2. curt or brusque in speech or manner 3. very steep 4. jumping from topic to topic without connection; disconnected —see **SYN.** at STEEP[1] —**a·brupt′ly** *adv.* —**a·brupt′ness** *n.*

Ab·sa·lom (ab′sə ləm) *Bible* David's favorite son, who rebelled against his father: II Sam. 18

ab·scess (ab′ses) *n.* [< L. < *abscidere* < *ab(s)-*, from + *cedere*, to go: from the old notion that humors go into the swelling] a swollen, inflamed area in body tissues, in which pus gathers —*vi.* to form an abscess —**ab′scessed** *adj.*

---

fat, āpe, cär; ten, ēven; is, bīte; gō, hôrn, tōōl, lŏŏk; oil, out; up, fur; get; joy; yet; chin; she; thin, then; zh, leisure; ŋ, ring; ə for *a* in *ago, e* in *agent, i* in *sanity, o* in *comply, u* in *focus;* ′ as in *able* (ā′b'l); Fr. bäl; ë, Fr. coeur; ö, Fr. feu; Fr. mon; ô, Fr. coq; ü, Fr. duc; r, Fr. cri; H, G. ich; ᴋh, G. doch; ‡foreign; ☆ Americanism; < derived from. See inside front cover.

ab·scis·sa (ab sis′ə) *n., pl.* **-sas, -sae** (-ē) [L. *abscissa* (*linea*), (a line) cut off < pp. of *abscindere* < *ab-*, from, off + *scindere*, to cut] *Math.* in a system of coordinates, the distance of a point from the vertical axis as measured along a line parallel to the horizontal axis: cf. ORDINATE

ab·scis·sion (ab sizh′ən) *n.* [L. *abscissio:* see prec.] **1.** a cutting off, as by surgery **2.** the process by which fruit, leaves, etc. normally separate from plants

ab·scond (əb skänd′, ab-) *vi.* [< L. *abscondere* < *ab(s)-*, from, away + *condere*, to hide] to run away and hide, esp. in order to escape the law

ABSCISSA
(x, the abscissa of P;
y, the ordinate of P)

ab·sence (ab′s'ns) *n.* **1.** the state of being absent, or away **2.** the time of being away **3.** the fact of being without; lack [in the *absence* of proof]

ab·sent (ab′s'nt; *for v.* ab sent′) *adj.* [< OFr. < L. prp. of *abesse* < *ab-*, away + *esse*, to be] **1.** not present; away **2.** not existing; lacking [vitamin C was *absent* from his diet] **3.** not attentive; absorbed in thought —*vt.* to keep (oneself) away [he *absents* himself from classes]

ab·sen·tee (ab′s'n tē′) *n.* a person who is absent, as from work —*adj.* designating or of a landlord who lives away from the property he owns

☆**absentee ballot** a ballot to be marked by a person (**absentee voter**) before an election during which he will be absent from his voting district

ab·sen·tee·ism (-iz'm) *n.* absence from work, school, etc., esp. when deliberate or habitual

ab·sent·ly (ab′s'nt lē) *adv.* in an absent manner; not paying attention

ab·sent-minded (ab′s'nt mīn′did) *adj.* **1.** so lost in thought as not to pay attention to what is going on around one **2.** habitually forgetful —**ab′sent-mind′ed·ly** *adv.* —**ab′sent-mind′ed·ness** *n.*

SYN.—**absent-minded** suggests a wandering, often habitual, of the mind away from the situation at hand; **abstracted** suggests withdrawal of the mind from the situation around one because of a serious concern with some other matter; **preoccupied** suggests that one's attention cannot be easily turned to something new because of concern with a present matter; **distraught** suggests an inability to concentrate, esp. because of worry, grief, etc.; **inattentive** suggests a failure to pay attention, esp. because of lack of discipline

ab·sinthe, ab·sinth (ab′sinth) *n.* [< OFr. < L. < Gr. *apsinthion* < OPer.] **1.** wormwood **2.** a green liqueur with the flavor of wormwood and anise

ab·so·lute (ab′sə lōōt′, ab′sə lōōt′) *adj.* [< L. pp. of *absolvere:* see ABSOLVE] **1.** perfect; complete [*absolute* silence] **2.** not mixed; pure [*absolute* alcohol] **3.** not limited; unrestricted [an *absolute* ruler] **4.** positive; definite [an *absolute* certainty] **5.** actual; real [an *absolute* truth] **6.** without reference to anything else; not relative **7.** *Gram.* a) forming part of a sentence, but not in the usual relations of syntax [in the sentence "The weather being good, they went," *the weather being good* is an *absolute* construction] b) with no expressed object: said of a verb usually transitive c) used alone, with the noun understood: said of a pronoun or an adjective, such as *ours* and *brave* in the sentence "Ours are the brave." **8.** *Physics* of the absolute-temperature scale —*n.* something that is absolute —**ab′so·lute′ly** *adv.* —**ab′so·lute′ness** *n.*

absolute music music that does not seek to suggest a story, scene, etc. but is concerned only with tone, structure, etc.

absolute pitch the ability to identify the pitch of any tone, or to sing a given tone, without having a known pitch sounded beforehand

absolute temperature temperature measured from absolute zero

absolute value 1. the value of a number, regardless of a prefixed plus or minus sign [the *absolute value* of −4 is 4] **2.** the positive square root of the sum of the squares of the real and imaginary parts of a complex number

absolute zero a point of temperature theoretically equal to −273.15°C or −459.67°F: the hypothetical point at which a substance would have no movement of its molecules and hence no heat

ab·so·lu·tion (ab′sə lōō′shən) *n.* [< OFr. < L. *absolutio* < *absolvere:* see ABSOLVE] **1.** a formal freeing (*from* guilt); for-giveness **2.** a forgiving (*of* sin) or a releasing from its penalty; specif., in some churches, such a release formally given by a priest in the sacrament of penance

ab·so·lut·ism (ab′sə lōō′tiz'm) *n.* government in which the ruler has unlimited powers; despotism —**ab′so·lut′ist** *n., adj.*

ab·solve (əb zälv′, ab-; -sälv′) *vt.* **-solved′, -solv′ing** [< L. *absolvere* < *ab-*, from + *solvere*, to loose] **1.** to pronounce free from guilt or blame; acquit **2.** *a)* to give religious absolution to *b)* to forgive (a sin) **3.** to free (someone *from* an obligation) —**ab·solv′ent** *adj., n.* —**ab·solv′er** *n.*

SYN.—**absolve** suggests a setting free from responsibilities, duties, etc. [*absolved* from her promise] or from the penalties for violating them; **acquit** means to declare not guilty, usually for lack of evidence; to **exonerate** is to relieve of the blame for a wrongdoing; to **pardon** is to release from punishment for an offense [the prisoner was *pardoned* by the governor]; **forgive** suggests the giving up of vengeful feelings and the desire to punish [to *forgive* one's enemies]; to **vindicate** is to clear (a person or thing under attack) through evidence of the unfairness of the charge —**ANT. blame**

ab·sorb (əb zôrb′, ab-; -sôrb′) *vt.* [< L. *absorbere* < *ab-*, from + *sorbere*, to drink in] **1.** to suck up [sponges *absorb* water] **2.** to take up fully the attention of; engross **3.** to take in and incorporate; assimilate [the city *absorbed* the neighboring town] **4.** to take in (a shock, jolt, etc.) with little or no recoil or reaction **5.** to take in and not reflect (light, sound, etc.) —**ab·sorbed′** *adj.*

ab·sorb·ent (əb zôr′b'nt, ab-; -sôr′-) *adj.* capable of absorbing moisture, light, etc. —*n.* a thing that absorbs moisture, etc. —**ab·sorb′en·cy** *n.*

ab·sorb·ing (əb zôr′biŋ, ab-; -sôr′-) *adj.* very interesting; engrossing [an *absorbing* tale]

ab·sorp·tion (əb zôrp′shən, ab-; -sôrp′-) *n.* **1.** an absorbing or being absorbed **2.** great interest; engrossment **3.** *Biol.* the passing of digested food material into the blood or lymph —**ab·sorp′tive** *adj.* —**ab′sorp·tiv′i·ty** *n.*

ab·stain (əb stān′, ab-) *vi.* [< OFr. < L. *abstinere* < *ab(s)-*, from + *tenere*, to hold: see TENANT] to do without voluntarily; refrain (*from*) [to *abstain* from eating meat] —see SYN. at RE-FRAIN¹] —**ab·stain′er** *n.*

ab·ste·mi·ous (əb stē′mē əs, ab-) *adj.* [< L. < *ab(s)-*, from + root of *temetum*, strong drink] moderate, esp. in eating and drinking; temperate —**ab·ste′mi·ous·ly** *adv.* —**ab·ste′mi·ous·ness** *n.*

ab·sten·tion (əb sten′shən, ab-) *n.* an abstaining; specif., a refraining from voting on some issue

ab·sti·nence (ab′stə nəns) *n.* **1.** an abstaining from some or all food, drink, or other pleasures **2.** an abstaining from alcoholic liquors — **ab′sti·nent** *adj.* —**ab′sti·nent·ly** *adv.*

ab·stract (ab strakt′; *also, and for n. 1 & v. 4 always,* ab′strakt) *adj.* [< L. pp. of *abstrahere* < *ab(s)-*, from + *trahere*, to DRAW] **1.** thought of apart from any particular instances or material objects [an *abstract* idea of justice] **2.** expressing a quality so thought of ["beauty" is an *abstract* word] **3.** not easy to understand; abstruse **4.** theoretical; not practical or applied **5.** designating or of art that does not depict objects realistically but in patterns or forms of lines, masses, or colors —*n.* **1.** a brief statement of the essential thoughts of a book, article, etc.; summary **2.** an abstract thing, condition, etc. —*vt.* **1.** to take away **2.** to steal **3.** to think of (a quality) apart from any particular instance or from any object that has it **4.** to summarize; make an abstract of —see SYN. at ABRIDGMENT —**in the abstract** in theory as apart from practice —**ab·stract′er** *n.* —**ab·stract′ly** *adv.* —**ab·stract′ness** *n.*

ABSTRACT ART

ab·stract·ed (ab strak′tid) *adj.* **1.** removed or separated (*from* something) **2.** withdrawn in mind; preoccupied —see SYN. at ABSENT-MINDED —**ab·stract′ed·ly** *adv.*

ab·strac·tion (ab strak′shən) *n.* **1.** an abstracting or being abstracted **2.** formation of an idea, as of the qualities of a thing, by separating it mentally from any particular instances or material objects **3.** an idea so formed, or a word for it ["honesty" is an *abstraction*] **4.** an unrealistic notion **5.** a being lost in thought; absent-mindedness **6.** a picture, sculpture, etc. that is wholly or partly abstract

ab·struse (ab strōōs′) *adj.* [< L. pp. of *abstrudere* < *ab(s)-*, away + *trudere*, to THRUST] hard to understand; deep —**ab·struse′ly** *adv.* —**ab·struse′ness** *n.*

ab·surd (ab surd′, ab-; -zurd′) *adj.* [< Fr. < L. *absurdus*, not to be heard of < *ab-*, intens. + *surdus*, dull, deaf] so clearly untrue or unreasonable as to be laughable or ridiculous —**ab·surd′ly** *adv.* —**ab·surd′ness** *n.*
SYN.—*absurd* means so inconsistent with what is judged as reasonable or true as to be laughable [*an absurd* hypothesis]; *ludicrous* is applied to what is so incongruous or exaggerated as to be laughable [a *ludicrous* facial expression]; *preposterous* is used to describe anything extremely absurd or ludicrous; *foolish* describes that which shows lack of good judgment or of common sense [I don't take *foolish* chances]; *ridiculous* applies to whatever causes amusement or contempt because of its extreme foolishness —**ANT.** sensible, logical

ab·surd·i·ty (ab surd′ə tē, ab-; -zurd′-) *n.* **1.** the quality or state of being absurd; foolishness **2.** *pl.* **-ties** an absurd idea or thing

a·bun·dance (ə bun′dəns) *n.* [< OFr. < L. prp. of *abundare:* see ABOUND] **1.** a great supply; an amount more than enough **2.** wealth

a·bun·dant (-dənt) *adj.* **1.** very plentiful; more than enough **2.** well-supplied; rich [a lake *abundant* in fish]—see SYN. at PLENTIFUL —**a·bun′dant·ly** *adv.*

a·buse (ə byo͞oz′; *for n.* ə byo͞os′) *vt.* **a·bused′, a·bus′ing** [< OFr. < L. pp. of *abuti*, to misuse < *ab-*, away, from + *uti*, to use] **1.** to use wrongly; misuse [to *abuse* a privilege] **2.** to hurt by treating badly; mistreat **3.** to use insulting language about or to; revile **4.** [Obs.] to deceive —*n.* **1.** wrong or excessive use **2.** mistreatment; injury **3.** a bad or corrupt custom or practice **4.** insulting language —**a·bus′er** *n.*

a·bu·sive (ə byo͞os′iv) *adj.* **1.** abusing; mistreating **2.** insulting in language; scurrilous —**a·bu′sive·ly** *adv.* —**a·bu′sive·ness** *n.*

a·but (ə but′) *vi.* **a·but′ted, a·but′ting** [< OFr. < *a-*, to + *bout*, end] to end (*on*) or lean (*upon*) at one end; border (*on*) —*vt.* to border upon

a·but·ment (-mənt) *n.* **1.** an abutting **2.** that part of a support which carries the weight of an arch **3.** the supporting structure at either end of a bridge

a·buzz (ə buz′) *adj.* **1.** filled with buzzing **2.** full of activity, talk, etc.

a·bys·mal (ə biz′m'l) *adj.* **1.** of or like an abyss; bottomless **2.** bad or wretched beyond measure [*abysmal* poverty] —**a·bys′mal·ly** *adv.*

ABUTMENT

a·byss (ə bis′) *n.* [< L. < Gr. < *a-*, without + *byssos*, bottom] **1.** a deep crack in the earth; bottomless gulf; chasm **2.** anything too deep for measurement [an *abyss* of shame] **3.** the ocean depths **4.** *Theol.* the chaos that existed before the Creation —**a·bys·sal** (ə bis′'l) *adj.*

Ab·ys·sin·i·a (ab′ə sin′ē ə) *same as* ETHIOPIA —**Ab′ys·sin′i·an** *adj., n.*

-ac (ak, ək) [Fr. *-aque* < L. *-acus* < Gr. *-akos* (or directly < any of these)] *a suffix meaning:* **1.** characteristic of [*elegiac*] **2.** of; relating to [*cardiac*] **3.** affected by or having [*maniac*]

Ac *Chem.* actinium

AC, A.C., a.c. alternating current

A/C, a/c *Bookkeeping* **1.** account **2.** account current

a·ca·cia (ə kā′shə) *n.* [< OFr. < L. < Gr. *akakia*, thorny tree; prob. < *akē*, a point] **1.** a tree or shrub of the legume family, with clusters of yellow or white flowers: some yield gum arabic or dyes ☆**2.** the flower ☆**3.** *same as* LOCUST (sense 3)

ac·a·dem·ic (ak′ə dem′ik) *adj.* [see ACADEMY] **1.** of colleges, universities, etc.; scholastic **2.** having to do with the liberal arts rather than technical or vocational education **3.** following fixed rules; formalistic **4.** having no practical application; merely theoretical [an *academic* question] Also **ac′a·dem′i·cal** —*n.* a teacher or student at a college or university —**ac′a·dem′i·cal·ly** *adv.*

ACACIA

☆**academic freedom** freedom of a teacher or student to hold and express views without fear of arbitrary interference by officials

a·cad·e·mi·cian (ə kad′ə mish′ən, ak′ə də-) *n.* a member of an academy (sense 3)

a·cad·e·my (ə kad′ə mē) *n., pl.* **-mies** [< Fr. < L. < Gr. *akadēmeia*, the grove of *Akadēmos* (legendary figure), where Plato taught] **1.** a private secondary or high school **2.** a school offering training in a special field [a music *academy*] **3.** an association of scholars, writers, artists, etc., for advancing literature, art, or science

A·ca·di·a (ə kā′dē ə) French colony (1604–1713) that later became Nova Scotia and New Brunswick —**A·ca′di·an** *adj., n.*

Acadia National Park national park mostly on an island (*Mount Desert Island*) off the S coast of Maine

a·can·thus (ə kan′thəs) *n., pl.* **-thus·es, -thi** (-thī) [L. < Gr. *akantha*, thorn < *akē*, a point] **1.** a thistlelike Mediterranean plant with lobed, often spiny leaves **2.** *Archit.* a conventional representation of its leaf, esp. on the capitals of Corinthian columns —**a·can·thine** (-thin) *adj.*

a cap·pel·la (ä′ kə pel′ə) [It., in chapel style < L. *ad*, to + ML. *capella*, CHAPEL] without instrumental accompaniment: said of choral singing

acc. **1.** accompanied **2.** account **3.** accusative

ac·cede (ak sēd′) *vi.* **-ced′ed, -ced′ing** [< L. *accedere* < *ad-*, to + *cedere*, to yield] **1.** to enter upon the duties (of an office); attain (*to*) **2.** to give assent; give in; agree (*to*) —see SYN. at CONSENT —**ac·ced′ence** *n.* —**ac·ced′er** *n.*

ac·cel·er·an·do (ak sel′ə ran′dō; *It.* ät che′le rän′dô) *adv., adj.* [It.] *Music* with gradually quickening tempo

ac·cel·er·ate (ək sel′ə rāt′, ak-) *vt.* **-at′ed, -at′ing** [< L. pp. of *accelerare* < *ad-*, to + *celerare*, to hasten < *celer*, swift < IE. base *kel-*, to drive] **1.** to increase the speed of **2.** to hasten or bring about sooner [new industries *accelerated* the city's growth] **3.** *Physics* to cause a change in the rate of velocity of (a moving body) —*vi.* to go or progress faster —**ac·cel·er·a′tive** *adj.*

ac·cel·er·a·tion (ək sel′ə rā′shən, ak-) *n.* **1.** an accelerating or being accelerated **2.** change in the velocity of a moving body, or the rate of such change

ac·cel·er·a·tor (ək sel′ə rāt′ər, ak-) *n.* **1.** one that accelerates **2.** a device, as the foot throttle of an automobile, for speeding up something **3.** *Chem.* a substance that speeds up a reaction **4.** *Nuclear Physics* a device that accelerates charged particles to high energies

ac·cent (ak′sent; *for v. also* ak sent′) *n.* [Fr. < L. < *ad-*, to + *cantus*, pp. of *canere*, to sing] **1.** the emphasis given to a particular syllable or word in speaking it **2.** a mark used to show this emphasis, as primary (′) and secondary (′) accents **3.** a mark used to distinguish between various sounds of the same letter [in French there are acute (´), grave (`), and circumflex (ˆ) *accents*] **4.** a distinguishing regional or national way of pronouncing **5.** [*pl.*] [Poet.] speech; words [in *accents* mild] **6.** something that lends emphasis, as by contrast with its surroundings **7.** special emphasis [to put the *accent* on safety] **8.** *Music* emphasis or stress on a note or chord **9.** *Prosody* rhythmic stress or beat —*vt.* **1.** to pronounce with special stress **2.** to mark with an accent **3.** to emphasize

ac·cen·tu·al (ak sen′choo wəl) *adj.* **1.** of or having to do with accent **2.** having rhythm based on stress, as some poetry —**ac·cen′tu·al·ly** *adv.*

ac·cen·tu·ate (ak sen′choo wāt′) *vt.* **-at′ed, -at′ing** **1.** to pronounce or mark with an accent or stress **2.** to emphasize [the short hairdo *accentuated* her long neck] —**ac·cen′tu·a′tion** *n.*

ac·cept (ək sept′, ak-) *vt.* [< OFr. < L. *acceptare* < *accipere* < *ad-*, to + *capere*, to take] **1.** to take (what is offered or given); receive willingly **2.** to receive favorably; approve [to *accept* a current style] **3.** to agree or consent to [he will not *accept* defeat] **4.** to believe in [to *accept* the proposition that all men are created equal] **5.** to reply "yes" to [to *accept* an invitation] **6.** *Business* to agree to pay —*vi.* to accept something offered —**ac·cept′er** *n.*

ac·cept·a·ble (ək sep′tə b'l, ak-) *adj.* worth accepting; satisfactory or, sometimes, merely adequate —**ac·cept′a·bil′i·ty** *n.* —**ac·cept′a·bly** *adv.*

ac·cept·ance (ək sep′təns, ak-) *n.* **1.** an accepting or being accepted **2.** approving reception; approval **3.** belief in; assent **4.** a written order to pay a certain sum at a set future time

ac·cep·ta·tion (ak′sep tā′shən) *n.* the generally accepted meaning (of a word or expression)

ac·cept·ed (ək sep′tid, ak-) *adj.* generally regarded as true, proper, etc.; conventional; approved

ac·cess (ak′ses) *n.* [< OFr. < L. pp. of *accedere*, ACCEDE] 1. a coming toward; approach 2. a means of approaching, using, etc. [the *access* to the farm is by this road] 3. a being able or allowed to enter, approach, or use [he has *access* to the information] 4. increase or growth 5. an outburst [an *access* of anger]

ac·ces·sa·ry (ək ses′ər ē, ak-) *adj., n., pl.* **-ries** same as ACCESSORY

ac·ces·si·ble (ak ses′ə b'l) *adj.* [see ACCESS] 1. that can be approached or entered 2. easy to approach or enter 3. obtainable 4. open to the influence of (with *to*) [not *accessible* to pity] —**ac·ces′si·bil′i·ty** *n.* —**ac·ces′si·bly** *adv.*

ac·ces·sion (ak sesh′ən) *n.* [see ACCESS] 1. the act of attaining (a throne, power, etc.) 2. an assenting, or agreeing 3. *a*) increase by addition *b*) an item added, as to a library —**ac·ces′sion·al** *adj.*

ac·ces·so·ry (ək ses′ər ē, ak-) *adj.* [< ML. < L. pp. of *accedere*, ACCEDE] 1. helping in a secondary way; extra; additional 2. *Law* helping in an unlawful act —*n., pl.* **-ries** 1. something extra added to help in a secondary way; specif., *a*) an article to complete one's costume, as a purse, gloves, etc. *b*) a piece of optional equipment, as on an automobile, for convenience, comfort, etc. 2. *Law* a person who, though absent, helps another to break or escape the law —**accessory before (or after) the fact** one who, though absent at the committing of a crime, helps the accused before (or after) its commission —**ac·ces·so·ri·al** (ak′sə sôr′ē əl) *adj.*

☆**access time** in computers, the time between the moment when information is requested from (or presented for) storage and the moment of its delivery (or storage)

ac·ci·dence (ak′sə dəns) *n.* [see ACCIDENT] the part of grammar dealing with inflection of words

ac·ci·dent (ak′sə dənt) *n.* [< OFr. < L. prp. of *accidere*, happen < *ad-*, to + *cadere*, to fall] 1. a happening that is not expected, foreseen, or intended 2. an unintended happening that results in injury, loss, etc. 3. chance [to meet by *accident*] 4. an attribute that is not essential

ac·ci·den·tal (ak′sə den′t'l) *adj.* 1. happening by chance 2. belonging but not essential; incidental —*n. Music* 1. a sign, as a sharp or flat, placed before a note to show a change of pitch from that indicated by the key signature 2. the tone of such a note —**ac′ci·den′tal·ly** *adv.*

SYN. **accidental** describes that which occurs by chance [an *accidental* encounter]; **fortuitous** suggests a complete lack of cause, and now usually refers to chance events of a fortunate nature; **casual** describes something unplanned or informal [a *casual* visit, remark, dress, etc.]; **incidental** emphasizes the secondary importance of something not essential [an *incidental* consideration]

ac·ci·dent-prone (ak′sə dənt prōn′) *adj.* tending to become involved in accidents

ac·claim (ə klām′) *vt.* [< L. *acclamare* < *ad-*, to + *clamare*, to cry out: see CLAMOR] 1. to greet with loud applause or approval 2. to announce with much applause or praise; hail [they *acclaimed* him president] —*n.* loud applause or strong approval

ac·cla·ma·tion (ak′lə mā′shən) *n.* 1. an acclaiming or being acclaimed 2. loud applause or strong approval 3. an enthusiastic approving vote by voice without an actual count —**ac·clam·a·to·ry** (ə klam′ə tôr′ē) *adj.*

ac·cli·mate (ak′lə māt′, ə klī′mət) *vt., vi.* **-mat·ed, -mat·ing** [< Fr.: see AD- & CLIMATE] to accustom or become accustomed to a different climate, situation, etc. —**ac′cli·ma′tion** *n.*

ac·cli·ma·tize (ə klī′mə tīz′) *vt., vi.* **-tized′, -tiz′ing** same as ACCLIMATE —**ac·cli′ma·ti·za′tion** *n.*

ac·cliv·i·ty (ə kliv′ə tē) *n., pl.* **-ties** [< L. < *ad-*, up + *clivus*, hill] an upward slope of ground

ac·co·lade (ak′ə lād′) *n.* [Fr. < Pr. < It. pp. of *accollare*, to embrace < L. *ad*, to + *collum*, neck] 1. formerly, an embrace (now, a touch with a sword) used in conferring knighthood 2. anything done or given as a sign of great respect, appreciation, etc.

ac·com·mo·date (ə käm′ə dāt′) *vt.* **-dat·ed, -dat·ing** [< L. pp. of *accommodare* < *ad-*, to + *com-*, with + *modus*, a measure] 1. to make fit; adjust; adapt [to *accommodate* oneself to changes] 2. to adjust and settle (differences) 3. to help by supplying (*with* something) 4. to do a favor for 5. to have room for —*vi.* to become adjusted, as the lens of the eye in focusing —see SYN. at ADAPT and at CONTAIN

ac·com·mo·dat·ing (-dāt′iŋ) *adj.* ready to help; obliging —**ac·com′mo·dat′ing·ly** *adv.*

ac·com·mo·da·tion (ə käm′ə dā′shən) *n.* 1. adaptation (*to* a purpose); adjustment 2. settlement of differences 3. willingness to do favors 4. a help or convenience 5. [*pl.*] lodgings or space, as in a hotel, on a ship, etc. 6. the self-adjustment of the lens of the eye in focusing

ac·com·pa·ni·ment (ə kump′ni mənt, ə kum′pə nē mənt) *n.* 1. anything that accompanies something else 2. *Music* a part, usually for an instrument, performed along with and in support of a main part [the piano *accompaniment* to a song]

ac·com·pa·nist (ə kum′pə nist) *n.* a person who plays an accompaniment

ac·com·pa·ny (ə kum′pə nē) *vt.* **-nied, -ny·ing** [< MFr. < *ac-*, to + OFr. *compagnon*: see COMPANION[1]] 1. to go or be together with 2. to send (*with*); add to; supplement [to *accompany* words with acts] 3. to play an accompaniment for or to

ac·com·plice (ə käm′plis) *n.* [< A-[1] + OFr. *complice* < LL. *complex*, accomplice: see COMPLEX] a person who knowingly helps another in an unlawful act

ac·com·plish (ə käm′plish) *vt.* [< OFr. < L. *ad-*, AD- + *complere*: see COMPLETE] to do; succeed in doing; complete —see SYN. at PERFORM —**ac·com′plish·a·ble** *adj.*

ac·com·plished (-plisht) *adj.* 1. done; completed 2. skilled; proficient [an *accomplished* pianist] 3. trained in the social arts or skills

ac·com·plish·ment (-plish mənt) *n.* 1. an accomplishing or being accomplished; completion 2. something accomplished or done successfully; achievement 3. a social art or skill: *usually used in pl.*

ac·cord (ə kôrd′) *vt.* [< OFr. < L. *ad-*, to + *cor* (gen. *cordis*), HEART] 1. to make agree or harmonize 2. to give, grant, or award [he was *accorded* many honors] —*vi.* to agree or harmonize (*with*) —*n.* 1. mutual agreement; harmony 2. an informal agreement, as between nations 3. harmony of sound, color, etc. —see SYN. at AGREE —**of one's own accord** willingly, without being asked —**with one accord** all agreeing

ac·cord·ance (-'ns) *n.* agreement; harmony; conformity [in *accordance* with the plans] —**ac·cord′ant** *adj.* —**ac·cord′ant·ly** *adv.*

ac·cord·ing (-iŋ) *adj.* agreeing; in harmony —**according to** 1. in agreement with [we left *according to* schedule] 2. in the order of [seated *according to* age] 3. as stated by

ac·cord·ing·ly (-iŋ lē) *adv.* 1. in a way that is fitting and proper 2. therefore

ac·cor·di·on (ə kôr′dē ən) *n.* [< G., prob. < It. *accordare*, be in tune] a musical instrument with a bellows which is pulled out and pressed together to produce tones by forcing air through metal reeds opened by fingering keys —*adj.* having folds, or folding, like an accordion's bellows —**ac·cor′di·on·ist** *n.*

ACCORDION

ac·cost (ə kôst′, -käst′) *vt.* [< Fr. < It. < L. < *ad-*, to + *costa*, rib, side] to approach and speak to, esp. in a bold or forward manner

ac·count (ə kount′) *vt.* [< OFr. < *a-*, to + *conter*, to tell < L. *computare*: see COMPUTE] to consider or judge to be; deem [his idea was *accounted* of little value] —*vi.* 1. to furnish a reckoning of money received and paid out 2. to make satisfactory amends (*for*) [made to *account* for his crime] 3. to give satisfactory reasons or an explanation (*for*) 4. to be the cause or source of (with *for*) [what *accounts* for his anger?] 5. to do away with as by killing (with *for*) —*n.* 1. *a*) a record of the financial transactions of a person, business, etc. *b*) same as CHARGE ACCOUNT *c*) a business that is a customer or client, esp. on a credit basis 2. *same as* BANK ACCOUNT 3. worth; importance [a thing of small *account*] 4. an explanation [no satisfactory *account* of their failure has been given] 5. a report; description [he gave an *account* of his travels] —**call to account** 1. to demand an explanation of 2. to reprimand —**give a good account of oneself** to conduct oneself well —**on account** as partial payment —**on account of** because of —**on no account** under no circumstances —**on (someone's) account** for (someone's) sake —**take account of** 1. to allow for 2. to take notice of —**take into account** to take into consideration —**turn to account** to get use from

ac·count·a·ble (-ə b'l) *adj.* 1. obliged to account for one's acts; responsible [held *accountable* for the losses] 2. that can be accounted for; explainable —see **SYN.** at **RESPONSIBLE** —**ac·count′a·bil′i·ty** n. —**ac·count′a·bly** adv.

ac·count·an·cy (ə kount′'n se) n. the keeping or inspecting of financial accounts; work of an accountant

ac·count·ant (ə kount′'nt) n. a person whose work is to inspect or keep financial accounts: see **CERTIFIED PUBLIC ACCOUNTANT**

account executive an executive in an advertising agency or similar business who is in charge of certain accounts of the business, keeping direct contact with established customers and trying to get new ones

ac·count·ing (ə koun′tiŋ) n. **1.** the principles or practice of setting up and auditing financial accounts **2.** a settling or balancing of accounts

ac·cou·ter (ə koot′ər) vt. [Fr., prob. < L. con-, together + suere, to sew] to equip or attire: also **ac·cou′tre** -**tred,** -**tring**

ac·cou·ter·ments, ac·cou·tre·ments (ə koot′ər mənts, -koo′trə-) n.pl. **1.** clothes; dress **2.** equipment; furnishings; trappings

Ac·cra (ə krä′) capital of Ghana, on the Atlantic: pop. 533,000

ac·cred·it (ə kred′it) vt. [< Fr.: see **CREDIT**] **1.** to bring into credit or favor; believe in **2.** to give credentials to [an accredited representative] **3.** to certify as meeting certain standards [an accredited college] **4.** to attribute; credit —**ac·cred′it·a′tion** (-ə tā′shən) n.

ac·cre·tion (ə krē′shən) n. [< L. accretio < accrescere < ad-, to + crescere, to grow] **1.** growth in size, esp. by addition or accumulation **2.** a growing together of separate parts **3.** accumulated matter **4.** a part added separately; addition —**ac·cre′tive** adj.

ac·crue (ə kroo′) vi. -**crued′,** -**cru′ing** [< OFr. < L.: see **ACCRETION**] **1.** to come as a natural growth, advantage, or right (to) [the rights that accrue to all citizens] **2.** to be added periodically as an increase [interest accrues to a savings account] —**ac·cru′al** n.

acct. account

☆**ac·cul·tu·rate** (ə kul′chə rāt′) vi., vt. -**rat′ed,** -**rat′ing** to undergo, or alter by, acculturation

☆**ac·cul·tu·ra·tion** (ə kul′chə rā′shən) n. [**AC-** (see **AD-**) + **CULTUR(E)** + -**ATION**] **1.** the conditioning of a child to the patterns of a culture **2.** a becoming adapted to a different culture **3.** the mutual influence of different cultures in close contact

ac·cu·mu·late (ə kyoom′yə lāt′) vt., vi. -**lat′ed,** -**lat′ing** [< L. pp. of accumulare < ad-, to + cumulare, to heap] to pile up or collect, esp. over a period of time —**ac·cu′mu·la·ble** (-lə b'l) adj.

ac·cu·mu·la·tion (ə kyoom′yə lā′shən) n. **1.** an accumulating; collection **2.** accumulated or collected material

ac·cu·mu·la·tive (ə kyoom′yə lāt′iv) adj. **1.** resulting from accumulation **2.** tending to accumulate —**ac·cu′mu·la·tive·ly** adv. —**ac·cu′mu·la′tive·ness** n.

ac·cu·mu·la·tor (-lāt′ər) n. **1.** one that accumulates **2.** [Brit.] a storage battery **3.** a device, as in a computer, that stores a quantity and that will add to that quantity others, storing the sum

ac·cu·ra·cy (ak′yər ə sē) n. the quality or state of being accurate; precision; exactness

ac·cu·rate (ak′yər it) adj. [< L. pp. of accurare, to take care < ad-, to + cura, care] **1.** careful and exact **2.** free from errors; precise **3.** adhering closely to a standard [an accurate thermometer] —see **SYN.** at **CORRECT** —**ac′cu·rate·ly** adv. —**ac′cu·rate·ness** n.

ac·curs·ed (ə kur′sid, ə kurst′) adj. **1.** under a curse; sure to end badly **2.** deserving to be cursed; damnable Also **ac·curst′** (ə kurst′) —**ac·curs′ed·ly** adv. —**ac·curs′ed·ness** n.

ac·cu·sa·tion (ak′yə zā′shən) n. **1.** an accusing or being accused **2.** the wrong that one is accused of

ac·cu·sa·tive (ə kyoo′zə tiv) adj. [< L. < pp. of accusare: see **ACCUSE**] **1.** designating or in the grammatical case, as in Latin, used for the direct object of a verb and after certain prepositions **2.** same as **ACCUSATORY** —n. **1.** the accusative case **2.** a word in this case —**ac·cu′sa·tive·ly** adv.

ac·cu·sa·to·ry (-tôr′ē) adj. making or containing an accusation; accusing

ac·cuse (ə kyooz′) vt. -**cused′,** -**cus′ing** [< OFr. < L. accusare < ad-, to + causa, a cause or lawsuit] **1.** to find at fault;

blame **2.** to bring formal charges against (of breaking the law, etc.) —**the accused** Law the person formally charged with committing a crime —**ac·cus′er** n. —**ac·cus′ing·ly** adv.

ac·cus·tom (ə kus′təm) vt. to make used (to something) as by custom or regular use; habituate

ac·cus·tomed (-təmd) adj. **1.** customary; usual; characteristic [he spoke with his accustomed ease] **2.** used (to); in the habit of [accustomed to obeying orders] —see **SYN.** at **USUAL**

ace (ās) n. [< L. as, unit] **1.** a playing card, domino, etc. marked with one spot **2.** a) a serve, as in tennis, that one's opponent is unable to return b) the point thus made **3.** Golf a hole in one: see entry **HOLE 4.** a combat pilot who has destroyed many enemy planes **5.** an expert —adj. [Colloq.] first-rate; expert [an ace salesman] —vt. **aced** (āst), **ac′ing** to score an ace against (an opponent) in tennis, or on (a hole) in golf

-**a·ce·a** (ā′shə, ā′shē ə) [L., neut. pl. of -aceus] a plural suffix used in forming zoological names of classes or orders: see -**ACEOUS**

-**a·ce·ae** (ā′si ē′) [L., fem. pl. of -aceus] a plural suffix used in forming botanical names of families: see -**ACEOUS**

☆**ace in the hole 1.** Stud Poker an ace dealt and kept face down until the deal is over **2.** [Slang] any advantage held in reserve until needed

-**a·ceous** (ā′shəs) [L. -aceus] a suffix meaning of the nature of, like, belonging to, producing, etc. [herbaceous]: often used to form adjectives corresponding to nouns ending in -**ACEA,** -**ACEAE**

a·cerb (ə surb′) adj. [< Fr. < L. acerbus, bitter] **1.** sour in taste **2.** bitter or harsh in temper, language, etc.

ac·er·bate (as′ər bāt′) vt. -**bat′ed,** -**bat′ing** [< L. pp. of acerbare] **1.** to make sour or bitter **2.** to irritate; vex

a·cer·bi·ty (ə sur′bə tē) n., pl. -**ties** [< Fr. < L. < acerbus, bitter] **1.** a sour, astringent quality **2.** sharpness or harshness of temper, words, etc.

ac·e·tab·u·lum (as′ə tab′yoo ləm) n., pl. -**la** (-lə), -**lums** [L., orig., vinegar cup < acetum: see **ACETO-**] Anat. the cup-shaped socket of the hipbone

ac·et·an·i·lide (as′ə tan′ə līd′, -′l id) n. [**ACET(O)-** + **ANIL(INE)** + -**IDE**] a white, crystalline organic substance, C_8H_9NO, used to lessen pain and fever

ac·e·tate (as′ə tāt′) n. [**ACET(O)-** + -**ATE²**] **1.** a salt or ester of acetic acid **2.** same as **CELLULOSE ACETATE 3.** an article or material made with cellulose acetate —**ac′e·tat′ed** adj.

a·ce·tic (ə sēt′ik, -set′-) adj. [< L. acetum: see **ACETO-**] of, like, containing, or producing acetic acid or vinegar

acetic acid a sour, colorless liquid, $C_2H_4O_2$, having a sharp odor: it is found in vinegar

a·cet·i·fy (ə set′ə fī′, -sēt′-) vt., vi. -**fied′,** -**fy′ing** to change into vinegar or acetic acid —**a·cet′i·fi·ca′tion** n.

ac·e·to- [< L. acetum, vinegar] a combining form meaning of or from acetic acid: also, before a vowel, **acet-**

ac·e·tone (as′ə tōn′) n. [**ACET(O)-** + -**ONE**] a colorless, flammable, volatile liquid, C_3H_6O, used as a paint remover and as a solvent for certain oils, etc.

ac·e·to·phe·net·i·din (ə sēt′ō fə net′ə din) n. [**ACETO-** + **PHEN-** + **ET(HYL)** + -**ID(E)** + -**IN¹**] a white, crystalline powder, $C_{10}H_{13}O_2N$, used to reduce fever and to relieve headaches and muscular pains; phenacetin

a·cet·y·lene (ə set′'l ēn′) n. [**ACET(O)-** + -**YL** + -**ENE**] a colorless, poisonous, highly flammable gaseous hydrocarbon, C_2H_2, used for lighting, and as a fuel with oxygen to produce a hot flame, as in a blowtorch

ac·e·tyl·sal·i·cyl·ic acid (ə sēt′'l sal′ə sil′ik, as′ə t'l-) same as **ASPIRIN**

A·chae·an (ə kē′ən) n. **1.** a native or inhabitant of Achaea, an ancient province in the Peloponnesus **2.** loosely, a Greek

A·cha·tes (ə kāt′ēz) in Virgil's Aeneid, a loyal friend of Aeneas —n. a loyal friend

ache (āk) vi. **ached, ach′ing** [OE. acan] **1.** to have or give dull, steady pain **2.** to feel pity, etc. (for) **3.** [Colloq.] to yearn or long: with for or an infinitive [she ached to go home again] —n. a dull, continuous pain

a·chene (ā kēn′) n. [< ModL. < Gr. a-, not + chainein, to gape] any small, dry fruit with one seed, whose thin outer cov-

---

fat, āpe, cär; ten, ēven; is, bīte; gō, hôrn, tool, look; oil, out; up, fur; get; joy; yet; chin; she; thin, then; zh, leisure; ŋ, ring; ə for a in ago, e in agent, i in sanity, o in comply, u in focus; ' as in able (ā′b'l); Fr. bāl; ë, Fr. coeur; ö, Fr. feu; Fr. mon; ô, Fr. coq; ü, Fr. duc; r, Fr. cri; H, G. ich; kh, G. doch; ‡foreign; ☆ Americanism; < derived from. See inside front cover.

ering (*pericarp*) does not burst when ripe —**a·che′ni·al** (-kē′-nē əl) *adj.*

Ach·er·on (ak′ə rän′) [L. < Gr.] *Gr. & Rom. Myth.* the river in Hades across which Charon ferried the dead

a·chieve (ə chēv′) *vt.* **a·chieved′, a·chiev′ing** [< OFr. < *a-*, to + *chief:* see CHIEF] **1.** to succeed in doing; accomplish; do **2.** to get by trying hard; gain —*vi.* to do things successfully —see SYN. at PERFORM and at REACH —**a·chiev′a·ble** *adj.* —**a·chiev′er** *n.*

a·chieve·ment (-mənt) *n.* **1.** an achieving **2.** a thing achieved, esp. by skill, work, etc.; feat

A·chil·les (ə kil′ēz) *Gr. Myth.* Greek hero in the Trojan War, who killed Hector and was killed by Paris with an arrow that struck his vulnerable heel: he is the hero of Homer's *Iliad*

Achilles' heel (one's) vulnerable spot

Achilles' tendon the tendon connecting the back of the heel to the muscles of the calf of the leg

ach·ro·mat·ic (ak′rə mat′ik) *adj.* [< Gr. < *a-*, without + *chrōma*, color + *-IC*] **1.** colorless **2.** refracting white light without breaking it up into its component colors **3.** forming visual images whose outline is free from prismatic colors [an *achromatic* lens] **4.** *Music same as* DIATONIC —**ach′ro·mat′i·cal·ly** *adv.*

a·chro·mic (ā krō′mik) *adj.* [< Gr. < *a-*, without + *chrōma*, color + *-IC*] without color: also **a·chro′mous** (-məs)

ach·y (ā′kē) *adj.* **ach′i·er, ach′i·est** having an ache, or dull, steady pain

ac·id (as′id) *adj.* [L. *acidus*, sour < IE. base *ak-*, sharp, from which also comes EAR²] **1.** sharp and biting to the taste; sour **2.** sharp or sarcastic in speech, etc. **3.** that is or has the properties of an acid **4.** having too much acid —*n.* **1.** a sour substance **2.** [Slang] *same as* LSD **3.** *Chem.* any compound that reacts with a base to form a salt, produces hydrogen ions in water solution, and turns blue litmus paper red —see SYN. at SOUR —**ac′id·ly** *adv.* —**ac′id·ness** *n.*

a·cid·ic (ə sid′ik) *adj.* **1.** forming acid **2.** acid

a·cid·i·fy (ə sid′ə fī′) *vt., vi.* **-fied′, -fy′ing 1.** to make or become sour or acid **2.** to change into an acid —**a·cid′i·fi′a·ble** *adj.* —**a·cid′i·fi·ca′tion** *n.* —**a·cid′i·fi′er** *n.*

a·cid·i·ty (ə sid′ə tē) *n., pl.* **-ties 1.** *a)* acid quality or condition; sourness *b)* the degree of this **2.** *same as* HYPERACIDITY

ac·i·do·sis (as′ə dō′sis) *n. Med.* a condition in which the body's alkali reserve is below normal —**ac′i·dot′ic** (-dät′ik) *adj.*

acid test [orig., a *test* of gold by *acid*] a crucial, final test of value or quality

a·cid·u·lous (ə sij′oo ləs) *adj.* [< L. dim. of *acidus*, sour] **1.** somewhat acid or sour **2.** somewhat sarcastic

-a·cious (ā′shəs) [< L. *-ax* (gen. *-acis*) + *-OUS*] a suffix meaning characterized by, inclined to, full of [*tenacious*]

-ac·i·ty (as′ə tē) a suffix used to form nouns corresponding to adjectives ending in -ACIOUS [*tenacity*]

ac·knowl·edge (ək näl′ij, ak-) *vt.* **-edged, -edg·ing** [< ME. *knowleche* (see KNOWLEDGE): infl. by ME. *aknowen* < OE. *oncnawan*, to understand] **1.** to admit to be true; confess **2.** to recognize the authority or claims of **3.** to recognize and answer (a greeting, introduction, etc.) **4.** to express thanks for **5.** to state that one has received (a letter, gift, etc.) **6.** *Law* to certify in legal form [to *acknowledge* a deed] —**ac·knowl′edge·a·ble** *adj.*

SYN.—**acknowledge** implies the reluctant disclosure of something one might have kept secret [he *acknowledged* having written the letter]; to **admit** is to concede (something), but only after persuasion, and often after a denial [I'll *admit* you're right]; **avow** suggests affirming or emphasizing a statement [he *avowed* that he had been mistaken]; **confess** implies a formal acknowledgment of a crime or sin, and also is used, as is **admit**, in making a simple declaration [I *confess* I don't like her] —**ANT. deny**

ac·knowl·edged (-ijd) *adj.* commonly recognized or accepted [the *acknowledged* writer of the speech]

ac·knowl·edg·ment, ac·knowl·edge·ment (-ij mənt) *n.* **1.** an acknowledging; admission **2.** something done or given in acknowledging, as thanks **3.** recognition, as of authority or claims

ACLU, A.C.L.U. American Civil Liberties Union

ac·me (ak′mē) *n.* [Gr. *akmē*, a point, top] the highest point; peak [playing Hamlet was the *acme* of his career] —see SYN. at SUMMIT

ac·ne (ak′nē) *n.* [ModL., ? orig. error for Gr. *akmē*: see prec.] a common skin disease, esp. among young people, in which the oil-secreting glands in the skin become inflamed and cause pimples on the face, back, and chest

ac·o·lyte (ak′ə līt′) *n.* [< ML. < Gr. *akolouthos*, follower] **1.** *R.C.Ch.* a member of the highest of the four minor orders, who serves at Mass **2.** *same as* ALTAR BOY **3.** an attendant

A·con·ca·gua (ä′kôn kä′gwä) mountain of the Andes in W Argentina: 22,835 ft.

ac·o·nite (ak′ə nīt′) *n.* [< L. < Gr. *akoniton*] **1.** any of a genus of plants of the buttercup family, with blue, purple, or yellow, hoodlike flowers: most species are poisonous **2.** a drug made from the dried roots of one species, formerly used in medicine

ACOLYTE

a·corn (ā′kôrn′) *n.* [< OE. *æcern*, nut] the fruit of the oak tree; oak nut

☆**acorn squash** a kind of winter squash, acorn-shaped with a dark-green, ridged skin

a·cous·tic (ə koos′tik) *adj.* [< Fr. < Gr. < *akouein*, to hear] **1.** having to do with hearing or with sound as it is heard **2.** of acoustics

a·cous·ti·cal (ə koos′ti k'l) *adj.* acoustic; specif., having to do with the control of sound [*acoustical* tile absorbs sounds]

a·cous·ti·cal·ly (-tik lē, -tik 'l ē) *adv.* with reference to, or from the standpoint of, acoustics

a·cous·tics (ə koos′tiks) *n.pl.* **1.** the qualities of a room, etc. that have to do with how clearly sounds can be heard or transmitted in it **2.** [with sing. v.] the branch of physics dealing with sound, esp. with its transmission

ac·quaint (ə kwānt′) *vt.* [< OFr. < ML. < L. *ad*, to + *cognitus*, pp. of *cognoscere*, to know thoroughly: see KNOW] **1.** to give knowledge to; inform [to *acquaint* oneself with the facts] **2.** to cause to know personally; make familiar (*with*) [are you *acquainted* with my brother?] —see SYN. at NOTIFY

ac·quaint·ance (-'ns) *n.* **1.** knowledge (of something) got from personal experience or study **2.** the state of being acquainted (*with* someone) **3.** a person whom one knows only slightly —**make (someone's) acquaintance** to become an acquaintance of (someone) —**ac·quaint′ance·ship′** *n.*

ac·qui·esce (ak′wē es′) *vi.* **-esced′, -esc′ing** [< Fr. < L. *acquiescere* < *ad-*, to + *quiescere:* see QUIET] to consent quietly without protest, but without enthusiasm (often with *in*) [to *acquiesce* in a decision] —see SYN. at CONSENT

ac·qui·es·cence (-es′'ns) *n.* an acquiescing; agreement or consent without protest —**ac′qui·es′cent** *adj.* —**ac′qui·es′cent·ly** *adv.*

ac·quire (ə kwīr′) *vt.* **-quired′, -quir′ing** [L. *acquirere* < *ad-*, to + *quaerere*, to seek] **1.** to get by one's own efforts [to *acquire* an education] **2.** to come to have as one's own [to *acquire* certain traits] —see SYN. at GET —**ac·quir′a·ble** *adj.*

acquired character *Biol.* a change of structure or function caused by factors in the environment: it is now generally believed that such a change is not inheritable: also **acquired characteristic**

ac·quire·ment (ə kwīr′mənt) *n.* **1.** an acquiring **2.** something acquired, as a skill, etc.

ac·qui·si·tion (ak′wə zish′ən) *n.* **1.** an acquiring or being acquired **2.** something acquired

ac·quis·i·tive (ə kwiz′ə tiv) *adj.* eager to acquire; good at getting and holding wealth, ideas, etc. —see SYN. at GREEDY —**ac·quis′i·tive·ly** *adv.* —**ac·quis′i·tive·ness** *n.*

ac·quit (ə kwit′) *vt.* **-quit′ted, -quit′ting** [< OFr. < ML. *acquitare*, to settle a claim < L. *ad*, to + *quietare*, to quiet] **1.** to release from a duty, obligation, etc. **2.** to declare not guilty of a charge; exonerate **3.** to conduct (oneself); behave [the novice *acquitted* himself like a veteran] —see SYN. at ABSOLVE —**ac·quit′ter** *n.*

ac·quit·tal (ə kwit′'l) *n.* **1.** an acquitting **2.** *Law* a setting free or being set free by a court

ac·quit·tance (-'ns) *n.* a written release as from debt or liability

a·cre (ā′kər) *n.* [OE. *æcer*, field < IE. base *agros-*, field, from which also comes L. *ager*] **1.** a measure of land, 43,560 sq. ft. **2.** [pl.] specific land holdings

a·cre·age (ā′kər ij, ā′krij) *n.* acres collectively

ac·rid (ak′rid) *adj.* [< L. *acris*, sharp: for IE. base see ACID] **1.** sharp, bitter, or irritating to the taste or smell **2.** bitter or sarcastic in speech, etc. —**a·crid·i·ty** (a krid′ə tē, ə-), **ac′rid·ness** *n.* —**ac′rid·ly** *adv.*

ac·ri·mo·ni·ous (ak′rə mō′nē əs) *adj.* [see ACRIMONY] bitter or harsh in temper, manner, or speech —**ac′ri·mo′ni·ous·ly** *adv.* —**ac′ri·mo′ni·ous·ness** *n.*

ac·ri·mo·ny (ak′rə mō′nē) *n.* [< L. < *acer*, sharp: for IE. base see ACID] bitterness or harshness of manner or speech; asperity

ac·ro- [< Gr. *akros*, at the end or top] *a combining form meaning* highest, at the extremities [*acrogen*]

ac·ro·bat (ak′rə bat′) *n.* [< Fr. < Gr. *akrobatos*, walking on tiptoe < *akros* (see prec.) + *bainein*, to go] an expert performer of tricks in tumbling or on the trapeze, tightrope, etc.; skilled gymnast —**ac′ro·bat′ic** *adj.* —**ac′ro·bat′i·cal·ly** *adv.*

ac·ro·bat·ics (ak′rə bat′iks) *n.pl.* [*also with sing. v.*] **1.** the skill or tricks of an acrobat **2.** tricks requiring great skill [*mental acrobatics*]

ac·ro·gen (ak′rə jən) *n.* [ACRO- + -GEN] a plant, such as a fern or moss, having a perennial stem with the growing point at the tip

ac·ro·meg·a·ly (ak′rō meg′ə lē) *n.* [< Fr.: see ACRO- & MEGALO-] abnormal enlargement of the bones of the head, hands, and feet, resulting from overproduction of growth hormone by the pituitary gland —**ac′ro·me·gal′ic** (-mə gal′ik) *adj.*

☆**ac·ro·nym** (ak′rə nim) *n.* [ACRO- + Gr. *onyma*, NAME] a word formed from the first (or first few) letters of a series of words, as *radar*, from *radio detecting and ranging* —**ac′ro·nym′ic** *adj.*

ac·ro·pho·bi·a (ak′rə fō′bē ə) *n.* [ACRO- + PHOBIA] an abnormal fear of being in high places

a·crop·o·lis (ə kräp′′l is) *n.* [< Gr. < *akros* (see ACRO-) + *polis*, city] the fortified upper part of an ancient Greek city, esp. [A-] that of Athens, on which the Parthenon was built

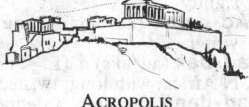

ACROPOLIS

a·cross (ə krôs′) *adv.* **1.** crossed; crosswise **2.** from one side to the other **3.** on or to the other side —*prep.* **1.** from one side to the other of; so as to cross [*go across the street*] **2.** on or to the other side of; over [*he lives across the river*] **3.** into contact with by chance [*he came across an old friend*]

☆**across-the-board** (ə krôs′*th*ə bôrd′) *adj.* **1.** *Horse Racing* combining win, place, and show, as a bet **2.** including or affecting all classes or groups

a·cros·tic (ə krôs′tik) *n.* [< Gr. < *akros* (see ACRO-) + *stichos*, line of verse] a verse or arrangement of words in which certain letters in each line, as the first or last, when taken in order spell out a word, motto, etc. —*adj.* of or like an acrostic —**a·cros′ti·cal·ly** *adv.*

a·cryl·ic fiber (ə kril′ik) [ult. < ACR(ID) + -YL + -IC] any of a group of synthetic fibers derived from a compound of hydrogen cyanide and acetylene, and made into fabrics

acrylic resin any of a group of transparent thermoplastic resins, as Lucite

act (akt) *n.* [< Fr. < L. *actus*, a doing, *actum*, thing done, pp. of *agere*, to do < IE. base *ag-*, to drive] **1.** a thing done; deed [*an act of bravery*] **2.** an action; doing [*caught in the act of stealing*] **3.** a decision (of a court, legislature, etc.) **4.** a document formally stating what has been done, etc. **5.** one of the main divisions of a drama or opera **6.** any of the separate performances on a variety program **7.** insincere behavior, put on just for effect —*vt.* **1.** to play the part of. **2.** to perform in (a play) **3.** to behave like [*don't act the child*] —*vi.* **1.** to perform on the stage; play a role **2.** to behave as though playing a role **3.** to behave; comport oneself [*act like a lady*] **4.** to do something [*act quickly in an emergency*] **5.** to serve or function [*the fence acts as a barrier*] **6.** to serve as spokesman (*for*) **7.** to have an effect [*acids act on metal*] **8.** to appear to be [*he acted very angry*] —**act up** [Colloq.] **1.** to be playful **2.** to misbehave **3.** to become inflamed, painful, etc.

act·a·ble (ak′tə b′l) *adj.* that can be acted: said of a play, a role, etc. —**act′a·bil′i·ty** *n.*

☆**ACTH** [<*a(dreno)c(ortico)t(rophic) h(ormone)*] a hormone secreted by the pituitary gland, that stimulates the production of hormones by the adrenal cortex

act·ing (ak′tiŋ) *adj.* **1.** adapted for performance [*an acting version of a play*] **2.** that acts; functioning **3.** temporarily taking over the duties of a position [*the acting chairman*] —*n.* the art or occupation of performing in plays

ac·tin·ic (ak tin′ik) *adj.* having to do with actinism —**ac·tin′i·cal·ly** *adv.*

actinic rays light rays occurring in the violet and ultraviolet parts of the spectrum, that produce chemical changes, as in photography

ac·ti·nide series (ak′tə nīd′) a group of radioactive chemical elements from element 90 (thorium) through element 103 (lawrencium)

ac·tin·ism (ak′tən iz′m) *n.* [< Gr. *aktis* (gen. *aktinos*), ray & -ISM] that property of ultraviolet light, X-rays, etc. by which chemical changes are produced

ac·tin·i·um (ak tin′ē əm) *n.* [ModL. < Gr. *aktis* (gen. *aktinos*), ray] a radioactive chemical element found in pitchblende and other minerals: symbol, Ac; at. wt., 227(?); at. no., 89

ac·ti·no·my·cin (ak′ti nō mī′s′n) *n.* [< ModL. *Actinomyces*, a genus of bacteria] any of various antibiotic substances derived from soil bacteria

ac·tion (ak′shən) *n.* [< OFr. < L. *actio* < pp. of *agere*: see ACT] **1.** the doing of something; a being in motion **2.** an act or thing done **3.** [*pl.*] behavior; habitual conduct **4.** bold and energetic activity [*a man of action*] **5.** an effect [*the action of a drug*] **6.** the way of moving, working, etc., as of a machine **7.** the moving parts or mechanism, as of a gun, piano, etc. **8.** the sequence of happenings in a story or play **9.** a legal proceeding; lawsuit **10.** combat in war; battle [*wounded in action*] **11.** [Slang] activity or excitement —**bring action** to start a lawsuit —**see action** to take part in military combat —**take action 1.** to become active **2.** to start a lawsuit

ac·tion·a·ble (-ə b′l) *adj. Law* that gives cause for an action, or lawsuit

ac·ti·vate (ak′tə vāt′) *vt.* **-vat′ed, -vat′ing 1.** to make active **2.** to put (an inactive military unit) on an active status **3.** to make radioactive **4.** to make capable of reacting or of accelerating a chemical reaction **5.** to treat (sewage) with air so that aerobes will purify it —**ac′ti·va′tion** *n.* —**ac′ti·va′tor** *n.*

activated carbon a highly porous carbon that can adsorb gases, vapors, and colloidal particles: also called **activated charcoal**

ac·tive (ak′tiv) *adj.* [< OFr. < L. *activus* < base *act-* as in *actus*: see ACT] **1.** acting, functioning, working, moving, etc. **2.** capable of acting, functioning, etc. **3.** causing motion or change **4.** full of action; lively, busy, quick, etc. [*an active mind, an active boy*] **5.** involving action [*an active role*] **6.** necessitating action or work [*active sports*] **7.** in current operation, effect, etc. [*an active law*] **8.** *Gram.* denoting the voice or form of a verb whose subject is shown as performing the action of the verb —*n. Gram.* the active voice —**ac′tive·ly** *adv.* —**ac′tive·ness** *n.*

☆**active duty** (or **service**) full-time service, esp. in the armed forces

active immunity immunity (to a disease) resulting from the production of antibodies by the body

ac·tiv·ism (ak′tə viz′m) *n.* the doctrine or policy of taking positive, direct action, esp. for political or social ends —**ac′tiv·ist** *adj., n.*

ac·tiv·i·ty (ak tiv′ə tē) *n., pl.* **-ties 1.** the state of being active; action **2.** energetic action; liveliness **3.** a normal function of the body or mind **4.** an active force **5.** any specific action or pursuit [*recreational activities*]

ac·tiv·ize (ak′tə vīz′) *vt.* **-ized′, -iz′ing** same as ACTIVATE

act of God *Law* an occurrence, esp. a disaster, that is due to the forces of nature and could not reasonably have been prevented

ac·tor (ak′tər) *n.* **1.** a person who does something **2.** a person who acts in plays, movies, etc.

ac·tress (ak′tris) *n.* a woman or girl who acts in plays, movies, etc.

Acts (akts) a book of the New Testament: full title, **The Acts of the Apostles**

ac·tu·al (ak′chōō wəl) *adj.* [< LL. < L. *actus*: see ACT] **1.** existing in reality or fact; not merely possible, but real [*the actual cost was lower than the estimate*] **2.** existing at present or at the time —see SYN. at TRUE

ac·tu·al·i·ty (ak′chōō wal′ə tē) *n.* **1.** the state of being actual; reality **2.** *pl.* **-ties** an actual thing or condition; fact

ac·tu·al·ize (ak′chōō wə līz′) *vt.* **-ized′, -iz′ing** to make actual or real —**ac′tu·al·i·za′tion** *n.*

ac·tu·al·ly (ak′chōō wəl ē, ak′chə lē) *adv.* as a matter of actual fact; really

ac·tu·ar·y (ak′chōō wer′ē) *n., pl.* **-ar′ies** [L. *actuarius*, clerk < *actus*: see ACT] a person who calculates risks, premiums, etc. for insurance —**ac′tu·ar′i·al** *adj.* —**ac′tu·ar′i·al·ly** *adv.*

ac·tu·ate (ak′chōō wāt′) *vt.* **-at′ed, -at′ing 1.** to put into action or motion [the starter is *actuated* by turning the key] **2.** to cause to take action [what motives *actuated* him?] —**ac′tu·a′tion** *n.* —**ac′tu·a′tor** *n.*

a·cu·i·ty (ə kyōō′ə tē) *n.* [< Fr. < L. *acus*, a needle] keenness, as of thought or vision; acuteness

a·cu·men (ə kyōō′mən, ak′yoo-) *n.* [L., a point < *acuere*, to sharpen: for IE. base see ACID] keenness and quickness of mind; shrewdness [political *acumen*]

a·cu·mi·nate (ə kyōō′mə nit; *for v.* -nāt′) *adj.* [< L. pp. of *acuminare* < *acumen*: see prec.] pointed; tapering to a point —*vt.* **-nat′ed, -nat′ing** to make sharp or pointed —**a·cu′mi·na′tion** *n.*

ac·u·punc·ture (ak′yoo puŋk′chər) *n.* [< L. *acus*, needle + PUNCTURE] the ancient practice, esp. as carried on by the Chinese, of piercing parts of the body with needles in seeking to treat disease or relieve pain

a·cute (ə kyōōt′) *adj.* [< L. pp. of *acuere*: see ACUMEN] **1.** having a sharp point. **2.** keen or quick of mind; shrewd **3.** sensitive [*acute* hearing] **4.** severe and sharp [*acute* pain or jealousy] **5.** severe but of short duration, as some diseases; not chronic **6.** very serious; critical [an *acute* shortage] **7.** of less than 90° [an *acute* angle] —**a·cute′ly** *adv.* —**a·cute′ness** *n.*

ACUTE ANGLE

SYN.—acute, in this comparison, suggests a situation that is growing more serious and will soon reach a turning point [an *acute* shortage of skilled workers]; **critical** is applied to a turning point that will determine a final outcome [the patient is in *critical* condition]; **crucial** is used in referring to a trial or decision that will determine a future line of action [a *crucial* debate on foreign policy] —see also SYN. at SHARP

acute accent a mark (′) used to show: **1.** the quality or length of a vowel, as in French *idée* **2.** primary stress, as in *typewriter*

-a·cy (ə sē) [variously < Fr. < L. < Gr. *-ateia*] *a suffix meaning* quality, condition, position, etc. [celibacy, curacy]

ad¹ (ad) *n.* [Colloq.] an advertisement

ad² (ad) *n. Tennis* advantage: said of the first point scored after deuce

ad- [L., to, at, toward; akin to AT¹] *a prefix meaning variously* motion toward, addition to, nearness to [admit, adjoin, adrenal]: changed in words of Latin origin to **ac-** before *c* or *q*, **af-** before *f*, **ag-** before *g*, **al-** before *l*, **an-** before *n*, **ap-** before *p*, **ar-** before *r*, **as-** before *s*, **at-** before *t*, and **a-** before *sc, sp,* and *st*

A.D. [L. *Anno Domini*, in the year of the Lord] of the Christian era: used with dates

A·da, A·dah (ā′də) [Heb. *'ādhā*, beauty] a feminine name

ad·age (ad′ij) *n.* [Fr. < L. < *ad-*, to + *aio*, I say] an old saying that has been popularly accepted as a truth —see SYN. at SAYING

a·da·gio (ə dä′jō, -jē ō) *adv.* [It. *ad agio*, lit., at ease] *Music* slowly and leisurely —*adj.* slow —*n., pl.* **-gios 1.** a slow movement in music **2.** a slow ballet dance, esp. by a mixed couple

Ad·am (ad′əm) [Heb. *ādām*, lit., a human being] **1.** a masculine name **2.** *Bible* the first man: Gen. 1–5 —**not know (a person) from Adam** not know (a person) at all

ad·a·mant (ad′ə mənt, -mant′) *n.* [OFr. < L. < Gr. *adamas* (gen. *adamantos*) < *a-*, not + *daman*, to subdue] in ancient times, a substance that was supposedly unbreakable —*adj.* **1.** too hard to be broken **2.** not giving in; unyielding —**ad·a·man·tine** (ad′ə man′tēn, -tīn, -tin) *adj.* —**ad′a·mant·ly** *adv.*

Ad·ams (ad′əmz) **1. Henry (Brooks)**, 1838–1918; U.S. historian & writer **2. John**, 1735–1826; 2d president of the U.S. (1797–1801) **3. John Quin·cy** (kwin′sē), 1767–1848; 6th president of the U.S. (1825–29): son of *prec.* **4. Samuel**, 1722–1803; Am. statesman & Revolutionary leader

Adam's apple the bulge formed in the front of the throat by the thyroid cartilage, esp. in men

A·da·na (ä′dä nä′) city in S Turkey: pop. 290,000

a·dapt (ə dapt′) *vt.* [< Fr. < L. *adaptare* < *ad-*, to + *aptare*, to fit] **1.** to make fit or suitable by changing or adjusting **2.** to adjust (oneself) to new or changed circumstances —*vi.* to adjust oneself

SYN.—adapt implies a changing to suit new conditions and suggests flexibility [to *adapt* oneself to a new environment]; **adjust** suggests the bringing of things into a proper relationship by using skill and judgment [to

adjust brakes; to *adjust* differences]; **accommodate** suggests an adjusting to meet the needs of another, as by the use of concession or compromise [he *accommodated* his walk to the slow steps of his friend]; **conform** means to bring or act in harmony with some standard pattern, principle, etc. [to *conform* to specifications]

a·dapt·a·ble (ə dap′tə b'l) *adj.* **1.** that can be adapted or made suitable **2.** able to adjust oneself to changes —**a·dapt′a·bil′i·ty** *n.*

ad·ap·ta·tion (ad′əp tā′shən) *n.* **1.** an adapting or being adapted **2.** a thing resulting from adapting [a movie *adaptation* of a novel] **2.** *Biol.* a change in structure, function, etc. of a plant or animal that produces better adjustment to the environment Also **a·dap·tion** (ə dap′shən) —**ad′ap·ta′tion·al** *adj.*

a·dapt·er, a·dap·tor (ə dap′tər) *n.* **1.** a device for adapting apparatus to new uses **2.** a connecting device for parts that would not otherwise fit together

a·dap·tive (ə dap′tiv) *adj.* **1.** showing adaptation **2.** able to adapt —**a·dap′tive·ly** *adv.*

A·dar (ä där′) *n.* [Heb.] see JEWISH CALENDAR

A.D.C., ADC aide-de-camp

add (ad) *vt.* [< L. *addere* < *ad-*, to + *dare*, to give] **1.** to join or unite (*to*) so as to increase the quantity, number, etc. **2.** to state further **3.** to combine (numbers) into a sum or total —*vi.* **1.** to cause an increase (*to*) [it will *add* to your pleasure] **2.** to figure a total —**add up** to seem reasonable [his excuse just doesn't *add up*] —**add up to 1.** to reach a total of **2.** to mean; signify

Ad·ams (ad′əmz), **Jane** 1860–1935; U.S. social worker & writer

ad·dax (ad′aks) *n.* [L. < native Afr. word] a large antelope of N Africa, with long, twisted horns

ad·dend (ad′end, ə dend′) *n.* [< ADDENDUM] a number or quantity to be added to another

ad·den·dum (ə den′dəm) *n., pl.* **-da** (-də) [L., gerundive of *addere*: see ADD] a thing added; esp., an appendix or supplement

ad·der (ad′ər) *n.* [ME. < *a nadder* (by faulty separation of *a nadder*) < OE. *nædre*] **1.** a small poisonous snake of Europe; common viper **2.** any of various other snakes, as the puff adder of Africa, the milk snake of North America, etc.

ad·der's-tongue (ad′ərz tuŋ′) *n.* ☆**1.** *same as* DOGTOOTH VIOLET **2.** a fern with a narrow spike

ad·dict (ə dikt′; *for n.* ad′ikt) *vt.* [< L. pp. of *addicere*, to give assent < *ad-*, to + *dicere*, to say: see DICTION] **1.** to give (oneself) up (*to* some strong habit): usually in the passive **2.** to make an addict of —*n.* one addicted to a habit, esp. to the use of a narcotic drug —**ad·dic′tion** *n.* —**ad·dic′tive** *adj.*

☆**adding machine** a machine that automatically performs addition (and often subtraction, division, etc.) when certain keys are pressed

Ad·dis A·ba·ba (ä′dis ä′bə bə) capital of Ethiopia: pop. 644,000

Ad·di·son (ad′ə s'n), **Joseph** 1672–1719; Eng. essayist & poet —**Ad′di·so′ni·an** (-sō′nē ən) *adj.*

ad·di·tion (ə dish′ən) *n.* **1.** an adding of numbers to get a number called the sum **2.** a joining of a thing to another thing **3.** a thing or part added; specif., a room or rooms added to a building —**in addition (to)** besides; as well (as)

ad·di·tion·al (-əl) *adj.* more; extra; added —**ad·di·tion·al·ly** *adv.*

ad·di·tive (ad′ə tiv) *adj.* **1.** showing or relating to addition **2.** to be added —*n.* a substance added to another in small quantities for a desired effect, as a preservative added to food, an antiknock added to gasoline, etc.

ad·dle (ad′'l) *adj.* [< OE. *adela*, mire, mud] **1.** rotten: said of an egg **2.** muddled; confused —*vt., vi.* **-dled, -dling 1.** to make or become rotten **2.** to make or become muddled or confused

ad·dle·brained (-brānd′) *adj.* having an addle brain; muddled: also **ad′dle·head′ed, ad′dle·pat′ed** (-pāt′id)

ad·dress (ə dres′; *for n., esp. 2, 3, & 4, also* ad′res) *vt.* [< OFr. < *a-*, to + *dresser*, to direct < L. *dirigere*: see DIRECT] **1.** to direct (spoken or written words *to*) **2.** to speak to or write to [to *address* an audience] **3.** to write the destination on (a letter or parcel) **4.** to use a proper form in speaking to [how does one *address* the mayor?] **5.** to apply (oneself) or direct (one's energies) [*address* yourselves to the problem] **6.** to take a stance, as in aiming the club at (a golf ball), facing (a target), etc. —*n.* **1.** a speech, esp. a formal one **2.** the place to which mail can be sent to one; place where one lives or works **3.** the writing on mail showing its destination. **4.** the location in a computer's storage compartment of an item of information **5.** social skill and tact **6.** conversational manner —see *SYN.* at SPEECH —**ad·dress′er, ad·dres′sor** *n.*

☆**ad·dress·ee** (ad′res ē′) *n.* the person to whom mail, etc. is addressed

ad·duce (ə dōōs′, -dyōōs′) *vt.* **-duced′, -duc′ing** [< L. *adducere* < *ad-*, to + *ducere:* see DUCT] to give as a reason or proof; cite —**ad·duc′er** *n.* —**ad·duc′i·ble, ad·duce′a·ble** *adj.*

ad·duct (a dukt′, ə-) *vt.* [< L. pp. of *adducere:* see prec.] to pull (a part of the body) toward the median axis: said of a muscle —**ad·duc′tive** (-duk′tiv) *adj.* —**ad·duc′tor** *n.*

ad·duc·tion (a duk′shən, ə-) *n.* **1.** an adducing or citing **2.** an adducting

-ade (ād) [ult. < L. *-ata*] *a suffix meaning:* **1.** the act of [*blockade*] **2.** the result or product of [*pomade*] **3.** participant(s) in an action [*brigade*] **4.** [after LEMONADE] drink made from [*limeade*]

Ad·e·laide (ad′'l ād′) [< Fr. < G. < OHG. *Adalheit*, lit., nobility] **1.** a feminine name: dim. *Addie;* var. *Adeline, Adelina, Adele* **2.** city in S Australia: pop. 727,000

A·den (äd′'n, ād′-) **1.** former Brit. colony in SW Arabia: now part of YEMEN (sense 2) **2.** seaport in this region, the capital of YEMEN (sense 2): pop. 250,000 **3. Gulf of,** arm of the Arabian Sea, between S Arabia and E Africa

ad·e·nine (ad′'n ēn′) *n.* [ADEN(O)- + -INE⁴] a white, crystalline purine base, $C_5H_5N_5$, found in nucleic acid in the spleen, pancreas, etc.

ad·e·no- [< Gr. *adēn*, gland] *a combining form meaning* of a gland or glands: also, before a vowel, **aden-**

ad·e·noi·dal (ad′'n oid′'l) *adj.* **1.** *a)* glandular *b)* of or like lymphoid tissue: also **ad′e·noid′ 2.** having adenoids **3.** having the characteristic difficult breathing or nasal tone due to enlarged adenoids

ad·e·noids (ad′'n oidz′) *n.pl.* [< ADEN(O)- + -OID] lymphoid growths in the throat behind the nose: they can swell up and obstruct breathing

ad·e·no·ma (ad′'n ō′mə) *n.* [ADEN(O)- + -OMA] a benign tumor of glandular origin or glandlike cell structure

a·den·o·sine (ə den′ə s'n, -sēn′) *n.* [arbitrary blend < ADENINE + RIBOSE] a white, crystalline powder, $C_{10}H_{13}N_5O_4$, obtained from the hydrolysis of yeast nucleic acid: see also ADP, ATP

ad·ept (ə dept′; *for n.* ad′ept) *adj.* [< L. pp. of *adipisci* < *ad-*, to + *apisci*, to pursue, attain] highly skilled; expert —*n.* an expert —**ad·ept′ly** *adv.* —**ad·ept′ness** *n.*

ad·e·qua·cy (ad′ə kwə sē) *n.* the quality or state of being adequate

ad·e·quate (ad′ə kwət) *adj.* [< L. pp. of *adaequare* < *ad-*, to + *aequare*, to make equal] **1.** enough or good enough; sufficient; suitable **2.** barely satisfactory —**ad′e·quate·ly** *adv.*

ad·here (əd hir′, ad-) *vi.* **-hered′, -her′ing** [< L. *adhaerere* < *ad-*, to + *haerere*, to stick] **1.** to stick fast; stay attached **2.** to stay firm in supporting or approving [he *adhered* to the original plan] —**ad·her′er** *n.*

ad·her·ence (əd hir′əns, ad-) *n.* an adhering; attachment or devotion (*to* a person, cause, etc.)

ad·her·ent (-ənt) *adj.* **1.** sticking fast; attached **2.** *Bot.* grown together —*n.* a supporter or follower (*of* a person, cause, etc.) —see *SYN.* at FOLLOWER

ad·he·sion (əd hē′zhən, ad-) *n.* [Fr. < L. *adhaesio* < *adhaerere:* see ADHERE] **1.** a sticking or being stuck together **2.** devoted attachment; adherence **3.** *Med. a)* the joining together, by fibrous tissue, of bodily parts normally separate *b)* such fibrous tissue **4.** *Physics* the force that holds together the molecules of unlike substances whose surfaces are in contact: distinguished from COHESION

ad·he·sive (əd hē′siv, ad-; -ziv) *adj.* **1.** sticking and not coming loose; clinging **2.** gummed; sticky —*n.* an adhesive substance, as glue —**ad·he′sive·ly** *adv.* —**ad·he′sive·ness** *n.*

adhesive tape tape with a sticky substance on one side, used for holding bandages in place, etc.

ad hoc (ad′ häk′) [L., to this] for a special case or purpose only [an *ad hoc* committee]

ad·i·a·bat·ic (ad′ē ə bat′ik) *adj.* [< Gr. < *a-*, not + *dia*, through + *bainein*, to go] *Physics* involving expansion or compression without loss or gain of heat —**ad′i·a·bat′i·cal·ly** *adv.*

a·dieu (ə dyōō′, -dōō′; *Fr.* à dyö′) *interj., n., pl.* **a·dieus′;** *Fr.* **a·dieux′** (-dyö′) [Fr. < OFr. < L. *ad*, to + *Deus*, God] goodbye

ad in·fi·ni·tum (ad in′fə nīt′əm) [L., to infinity] endlessly; forever; without limit

ad in·ter·im (ad in′tər im) [L.] **1.** in the meantime **2.** temporary [an *ad interim* appointment]

☆**a·di·os** (ä′dē ōs′, ä′-; *Sp.* ä dyôs′) *interj.* [Sp. *adiós* < L. *ad*, to + *Deus*, God] goodbye

ad·i·pose (ad′ə pōs′) *adj.* [< ModL. < L. *adeps* (gen. *adipis*), fat] of, like, or containing animal fat; fatty —*n.* animal fat in the connective tissue —**ad′i·pos′i·ty** (-päs′ə tē) *n.*

Ad·i·ron·dack Mountains (ad′ə rän′dak) mountain range of the Appalachians, in NE N.Y.: also **Ad′i·ron′dacks**

adj. 1. adjective **2.** adjourned **3.** adjutant

ad·ja·cent (ə jā′s'nt) *adj.* [< L. prp. of *adjacere* < *ad-*, to + *jacere*, to lie] near or close (*to* something); adjoining —**ad·ja′cen·cy** *n.* —**ad·ja′cent·ly** *adv.*

SYN.—**adjacent** things may or may not be in actual contact with each other but they are not separated by things of the same kind [*adjacent* angles; *adjacent* buildings]; that which is **adjoining** something else touches it at some point or along some line [*adjoining* rooms]; things are **contiguous** when they touch along the whole or most of one side [*contiguous* lots]; **tangent** implies contact at a single point on a curved line or surface [a line *tangent* to a circle]

adjacent angles two angles having the same vertex and a side in common

ad·jec·tive (aj′ik tiv) *n.* [< L. < pp. of *adjicere*, to add to < *ad-*, to + *jacere*, to throw] **1.** any of a class of words used to limit or qualify a noun or other substantive [*good, every,* and *Aegean* are *adjectives*] **2.** any phrase or clause similarly used —*adj.* of, or having the nature or function of, an adjective —**ad′jec·ti·val** (-tī′v'l) *adj.* —**ad′jec·ti·val·ly** *adv.*

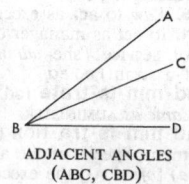

ADJACENT ANGLES
(ABC, CBD)

ad·join (ə join′) *vt.* [< OFr. < L. *adjungere* < *ad-*, to + *jungere:* see JOIN] to be next to [a playground *adjoins* the school] —*vi.* to be next to each other; be in contact —see *SYN.* at ADJACENT —**ad·join′ing** *adj.*

ad·journ (ə jurn′) *vt.* [< OFr. < *a*, at + *jorn*, day < L. *diurnum*, daily < *dies*, day] to put off or suspend until a future day —*vi.* **1.** to close a session or meeting for a time **2.** [Colloq.] to go (*to* another place) [let's *adjourn* to the patio] —**ad·journ′ment** *n.*

ad·judge (ə juj′) *vt.* **-judged′, -judg′ing** [< OFr. < L. *adjudicare* < *ad-*, to + *judicare*, to judge < *judex*, JUDGE] **1.** to judge or decide by law [he was *adjudged* innocent] **2.** to declare or order by law **3.** to award (costs, etc.) by law **4.** [Rare] to regard; deem

ad·ju·di·cate (ə jōō′də kāt′) *vt.* **-cat′ed, -cat′ing** [< L. pp. of *adjudicare:* see prec.] *Law* to hear and decide (a case); adjudge —*vi.* to serve as a judge (*in* or *on* a matter) —**ad·ju′di·ca′tion** *n.* —**ad·ju′di·ca′tive** *adj.* —**ad·ju′di·ca′tor** *n.* —**ad·ju′di·ca·to′ry** (-kə tôr′ē) *adj.*

ad·junct (aj′uŋkt) *n.* [< L. pp. of *adjungere:* see ADJOIN] **1.** a thing added to something else, but secondary [the orchard was an *adjunct* to his farm] **2.** a subordinate associate **3.** *Gram.* a modifier —*adj.* connected in a subordinate way —**ad·junc·tive** (ə juŋk′tiv) *adj.* —**ad·junc′tive·ly** *adv.* —**ad·junct′ly** *adv.*

ad·jure (ə jōōr′) *vt.* **-jured′, -jur′ing** [< L. *adjurare* < *ad-*, to + *jurare:* see JURY¹] **1.** to charge solemnly, often under oath or penalty [the judge *adjured* him to tell all he knew] **2.** to entreat earnestly —**ad·ju·ra·tion** (aj′oo rā′shən) *n.* —**ad·jur′a·to′ry** (-ə tôr′ē) *adj.* —**ad·jur′er, ad·ju′ror** *n.*

ad·just (ə just′) *vt.* [< OFr. < *a-*, to + *j(o)uster* (see JOUST); infl. by OFr. *juste* < L. *justus*, JUST¹] **1.** to change so as to fit, conform, make suitable, etc. **2.** to regulate [to *adjust* a watch] **3.** to settle or arrange rightly [to *adjust* accounts] **4.** to resolve or bring into accord **5.** to decide how much is to be paid on (an insurance claim) —*vi.* to adapt oneself, as to one's surroundings —see *SYN.* at ADAPT —**ad·just′a·ble** *adj.* —**ad·just′er, ad·jus′tor** *n.*

---

ad·just·ment (-mənt) *n.* **1.** an adjusting or being adjusted **2.** a means by which parts are adjusted to one another **3.** the settlement of a claim

ad·ju·tant (aj′ə tənt) *n.* [< L. prp. of *adjutare* < *adjuvare* < *ad-*, to + *juvare*, to help] **1.** an assistant **2.** *Mil.* a staff officer who is an administrative assistant to the commanding officer **3.** a large stork of India and Africa

adjutant general *pl.* **adjutants general 1.** an army officer who is the chief administrative assistant of a commanding general **2.** [A- G-] *U.S. Army* the general in charge of the department that handles records, correspondence, etc.

ad-lib (ad′lib′) ☆ *vt., vi.* **-libbed′, -lib′bing** [< AD LIBITUM] [Colloq.] to improvise (words, etc. not in the script); extemporize —☆ *n.* [Colloq.] an ad-libbed remark: also **ad lib** —*adj.* spoken or done without preparation —*adv.* [Colloq.] freely; as one pleases; without restraint: also **ad lib**

ADJU-TANT STORK (to 60 in. high)

ad lib·i·tum (ad′ lib′i təm) [ML. < L. *ad*, at + *libitum* < *libet*, it pleases] at pleasure; as one pleases: used esp. as a musical direction that a section may be altered to suit the performer

Adm. 1. Admiral **2.** Admiralty

☆ **ad·man** (ad′man′) *n., pl.* **-men′** (-men′) a man whose work or business is advertising: also **ad man**

ad·min·is·ter (əd min′ə stər, ad-) *vt.* [< OFr. < L. *administrare* < *ad-*, to + *ministrare*, to serve] **1.** to manage or direct **2.** to give out or dispense (punishment, etc.) **3.** to give or apply (medicine, etc.) **4.** to direct the taking of (an oath, pledge, etc.) **5.** *Law* to act as executor or administrator of (an estate) —*vi.* **1.** to act as manager or administrator **2.** to furnish help or be of service [she *administered* to the sick] —**ad·min′is·trant** (-ə strənt) *n., adj.*

ad·min·is·trate (əd min′ə strāt′, ad-) *vt.* **-trat′ed, -trat′ing** same as ADMINISTER

ad·min·is·tra·tion (əd min′ə strā′shən, ad-) *n.* **1.** management, specif. of the affairs of a government, business, etc. **2.** *a)* [often A-] the executive officials of a government, business, etc., and their policies *b)* their term of office **3.** the administering (of medicine, an oath, etc.) **4.** *Law* the management and settling (of an estate) —**ad·min′is·tra′tive** *adj.* —**ad·min′is·tra′tive·ly** *adv.*

ad·min·is·tra·tor (əd min′ə strāt′ər, ad-) *n.* **1.** one who administers, or manages affairs **2.** *Law* a person appointed by a court to settle the estate of someone who has died: cf. EXECUTOR

ad·mi·ra·ble (ad′mər ə b′l) *adj.* inspiring or deserving admiration or praise; splendid —**ad′mi·ra·bil′i·ty** *n.* —**ad′mi·ra·bly** *adv.*

ad·mi·ral (ad′mər əl) *n.* [< OFr. < Ar. *amîr alʿāli*, high leader; spelling influenced by ADMIRABLE] **1.** the commanding officer of a navy or fleet **2.** a naval officer of the highest rank **3.** [orig. ADMIRABLE] any of certain colorful butterflies

ad·mi·ral·ty (-tē) *n., pl.* **-ties 1.** the rank, position, or authority of an admiral **2.** *a)* [often A-] the governmental department for naval affairs, as in England *b)* maritime law or court

ad·mi·ra·tion (ad′mə rā′shən) *n.* **1.** an admiring **2.** wonder, delight, and pleased approval at anything fine, skillful, beautiful, etc. **3.** a thing or person inspiring such feelings

ad·mire (əd mīr′, ad-) *vt.* **-mired′, -mir′ing** [< OFr. < L. *admirari* < *ad-*, at + *mirari*, to wonder] **1.** to regard with wonder, delight, and approval **2.** to have high regard for **3.** [Dial.] to like or wish (*to* do something) —see SYN. at REGARD —**ad·mir′er** *n.* —**ad·mir′ing·ly** *adv.*

ad·mis·si·ble (əd mis′ə b′l, ad-) *adj.* [Fr. < L. pp. of *admittere*, ADMIT] **1.** that can be properly accepted or allowed [*admissible* evidence] **2.** that ought to be admitted —**ad·mis′si·bil′i·ty** *n.* —**ad·mis′si·bly** *adv.*

ad·mis·sion (əd mish′ən, ad-) *n.* **1.** an admitting or being admitted **2.** the right to enter **3.** an entrance fee **4.** a conceding, or granting of the truth, of something **5.** a confessing to some crime, fault, etc. —**ad·mis′sive** *adj.*

ad·mit (əd mit′, ad-) *vt.* **-mit′ted, -mit′ting** [< L. *admittere* < *ad-*, to + *mittere*, to send: see MISSION] **1.** to permit to enter or use **2.** to entitle to enter [this ticket *admits* two] **3.** to allow, or leave room for **4.** to have room for; hold [the hall *admits* 500 people] **5.** to concede or grant **6.** to acknowledge or confess **7.** to permit to practice [*admitted* to the bar] —*vi.* **1.** to give entrance (*to* a place) **2.** to allow or warrant (with *of*) —see SYN. at ACKNOWLEDGE

ad·mit·tance (-′ns) *n.* **1.** an admitting or being admitted

2. permission or right to enter **3.** *Elec.* the ratio of effective current to effective voltage in an AC circuit; the reciprocal of impedance

ad·mit·ted·ly (əd mit′id lē) *adv.* by admission or agreement; confessedly [*admittedly* afraid]

ad·mix (ad miks′) *vt., vi.* [< ADMIXTURE] to mix (a thing) in; mix with something

ad·mix·ture (-miks′chər) *n.* [< L. pp. of *admiscere* < *ad-*, to + *miscere*, to MIX + -URE] **1.** a mixture **2.** a thing or ingredient added in mixing

ad·mon·ish (əd män′ish, ad-) *vt.* [< OFr. < L. *admonere* < *ad-*, to + *monere*, to warn] **1.** to caution against specific faults; warn [the judge *admonished* him to drive more slowly] **2.** to criticize mildly [she was *admonished* for coming home late] **3.** to urge or exhort **4.** to inform or remind, by way of a warning —**ad·mon′ish·ing·ly** *adv.* —**ad·mon′ish·ment** *n.*

ad·mo·ni·tion (ad′mə nish′ən) *n.* **1.** an admonishing, or warning to correct some fault **2.** a mild criticism; reprimand

ad·mon·i·tor (əd män′ə tər, ad-) *n.* a person who admonishes —**ad·mon′i·to′ry** (-tôr′ē) *adj.*

ad nau·se·am (ad′ nô′zē əm, -shē-, -sē-) [L., to nausea] to the point of disgust

a·do (ə dōō′) *n.* [ME. < dial. inf. *at do*, to do] fuss; trouble; excitement

☆ **a·do·be** (ə dō′bē) *n.* [Sp. < Ar. < Coptic *tōbe*, brick] **1.** unburnt, sun-dried brick **2.** the clay of which such brick is made **3.** a building made of adobe, esp. in the Southwest

ADOBE

ad·o·les·cence (ad′'l es′'ns) *n.* **1.** the state or quality of being adolescent **2.** the time of life between puberty and maturity

ad·o·les·cent (-'nt) *adj.* [Fr. < L. prp. of *adolescere*, to mature < *ad-*, to + *alescere*, to increase, grow up < *alere*, to feed] **1.** developing from childhood to maturity; growing up **2.** of or characteristic of adolescence; youthful, exuberant, immature, etc. —*n.* a boy or girl from puberty to adulthood; person in his teens —see SYN. at YOUNG

Ad·olph (ad′älf, ā′dôlf) [< L. < OHG. < *adal*, nobility + *wolf*, wolf] a masculine name

A·don·is (ə dän′is, -dō′nis) *Gr. Myth.* a young man loved by Aphrodite —*n.* any very handsome young man

a·dopt (ə däpt′) *vt.* [< L. *adoptare* < *ad-*, to + *optare*, to choose: see OPTION] **1.** to choose and bring into a certain relationship; specif., to take into one's own family by legal process and raise as one's own child **2.** to take up and use (an idea, etc.) as one's own **3.** to choose and follow (a course) **4.** to vote to accept (a motion, etc.) **5.** to select as a required textbook —**a·dopt′a·ble** *adj.* —**a·dopt′er** *n.* —**a·dop′tion** *n.*

a·dop·tive (ə däp′tiv) *adj.* **1.** of adoption **2.** having become so by adopting [*adoptive* parents]

a·dor·a·ble (ə dôr′ə b′l) *adj.* **1.** [Now Rare] worthy of adoration **2.** [Colloq.] delightful; charming —**a·dor′a·bil′i·ty** *n.* —**a·dor′a·bly** *adv.*

ad·o·ra·tion (ad′ə rā′shən) *n.* **1.** a worshiping or paying homage **2.** great love or devotion

a·dore (ə dôr′) *vt.* **a·dored′, a·dor′ing** [< OFr. < L. *adorare* < *ad-*, to + *orare*, to speak: see ORATION] **1.** to worship as divine **2.** to love or honor greatly; idolize **3.** [Colloq.] to like very much —**a·dor′er** *n.* —**a·dor′ing·ly** *adv.*

a·dorn (ə dôrn′) *vt.* [< OFr. < L. *adornare* < *ad-*, to + *ornare*, to deck out] **1.** to be an ornament to; add beauty or distinction to **2.** to put decorations on; ornament

SYN.—**adorn** is used of that which adds beauty to something because it itself is beautiful [roses *adorned* her hair]; **decorate** implies that something added makes attractive that which would otherwise be plain [to *decorate* a wall with pictures]; **ornament** refers to accessories which improve the appearance [a crown *ornamented* with jewels]; **embellish** suggests the adding of showy details for effect [a musical phrase *embellished* with trills]; **bedeck** emphasizes the addition of many showy things [*bedecked* with ornate jewelry]

a·dorn·ment (-mənt) *n.* **1.** an adorning or being adorned **2.** a decoration or ornament

ADP [A(DENOSINE) *d(i)p(hosphate)*] an important substance, $C_{10}H_{15}N_5O_{10}P_2$, of all living cells, that is essential to the energy processes of life

‡ **ad rem** (ad′ rem′) [L., to (the) thing] to the point at issue; to the matter at hand

ad·re·nal (ə drē′n′l) *adj.* [AD- + RENAL] **1.** near the kidneys **2.** of or from the adrenal glands —*n.* same as ADRENAL GLAND

adrenal gland either of a pair of endocrine organs lying immediately above the kidney and producing a variety of hormones

☆**Ad·ren·al·in** (ə dren′′l in) [AD-RENAL + -IN¹] *a trademark for* EPINEPHRINE —*n.* [a-] epinephrine: also **ad·ren′al·ine** (-in)

ad·re·no- *a combining form meaning:* 1. adrenal glands 2. epinephrine Also, before a vowel, **adren-**

A·dri·at·ic (Sea) (ā′drē at′ik) arm of the Mediterranean between Italy and Yugoslavia

a·drift (ə drift′) *adv., adj.* 1. floating freely without being steered; drifting 2. without any particular aim or purpose [unemployed youth, *adrift* in society]

a·droit (ə droit′) *adj.* [Fr. *à*, to + *droit*, right < L. pp. of *dirigere*, DIRECT] skillful and clever [his *adroit* handling of an awkward situation] —see SYN. at DEXTEROUS —**a·droit′ly** *adv.* —**a·droit′ness** *n.*

ad·sorb (ad sôrb′, -zôrb′) *vt.* [< AD- + L. *sorbere* (see ABSORB)] to collect (a gas, liquid, or dissolved substance) in condensed form on a surface —**ad·sorb′a·ble** *adj.* —**ad·sor′bent** *adj., n.*

ad·sorp·tion (ad sôrp′shən, -zôrp′-) *n.* adhesion of the molecules of a gas, liquid, or dissolved substance to a surface —**ad·sorp′tive** *adj.*

ad·u·late (aj′ə lāt′) *vt.* -lat′ed, -lat′ing [< L. pp. of *adulari*, to fawn upon] to praise or flatter too greatly —**ad′u·la′tion** *n.* —**ad′u·la′tor** *n.* —**ad′u·la·to′ry** (-lə tôr′ē) *adj.*

a·dult (ə dult′, ad′ult) *adj.* [< L. pp. of *adolescere*: see ADOLESCENT] 1. grown up; fully developed in size, strength, mind, etc. 2. of or for adult persons [an *adult* novel] —*n.* 1. a mature person 2. a mature animal or plant 3. a person who has reached the age at which he has full legal rights and responsibilities —**a·dult′hood** *n.* —**a·dult′ness** *n.*

a·dul·ter·ant (ə dul′tər ənt) *n.* a substance used to adulterate something —*adj.* adulterating

a·dul·ter·ate (ə dul′tə rāt′) *vt.* -at′ed, -at′ing [< L. pp. of *adulterare*, to falsify < *ad-*, to + *alter*, other] to make inferior, impure, etc. by adding a harmful, inferior, or unnecessary substance —**a·dul′ter·a′tion** *n.* —**a·dul′ter·a′tor** *n.*

a·dul·ter·er (ə dul′tər ər) *n.* a person (esp. a man) who commits adultery —**a·dul′ter·ess** *n.fem.*

a·dul·ter·ous (-əs) *adj.* relating to or guilty of adultery —**a·dul′ter·ous·ly** *adv.*

a·dul·ter·y (ə dul′tər ē) *n., pl.* -ter·ies [L. *adulterium* < *adulter*: see ADULTERATE] voluntary sexual intercourse between a married person and someone other than his wife or her husband

ad·um·brate (ad um′brāt, ad′əm brāt′) *vt.* -brat·ed, -brat·ing [< L. pp. of *adumbrari* < *ad-*, to + *umbra*, shade] 1. to outline vaguely; sketch 2. to foreshadow vaguely 3. to obscure; overshadow —**ad′um·bra′tion** *n.* —**ad·um′bra·tive** (-brə tiv) *adj.*

adv. 1. adverb 2. adverbial 3. advertisement 4. advisory

ad va·lo·rem (ad′ və lôr′əm) [L.] in proportion to the value: said of duties levied on imports according to their invoiced value: abbrev. **ad val.**

ad·vance (əd vans′) *vt.* -vanced′, -vanc′ing [< OFr. *avancer*, to forward < L. *ab-*, from + *ante*, before] 1. to bring or move forward 2. to raise in rank, importance, etc. 3. to help; further [to *advance* a building project] 4. to put forward; propose [to *advance* a scheme] 5. to cause to happen earlier 6. to raise the rate of; increase [to *advance* prices] 7. to pay (money) before due 8. to lend —*vi.* 1. to go forward 2. to improve; progress; develop 3. to rise in rank, importance, price, etc. —*n.* 1. a moving forward 2. an improvement; progress 3. a rise in value or cost 4. [*pl.*] approaches to gain favor, become acquainted, etc. 5. a payment made before due, as of wages 6. a loan —*adj.* 1. in front [*advance* guard] 2. beforehand [*advance* information] —**in advance** 1. in front 2. ahead of time

ad·vanced (əd vanst′) *adj.* 1. in advance; in front 2. far on in life; old 3. ahead or beyond in progress, more complex, etc. [*advanced* studies] 4. higher than usual [*advanced* prices]

advance guard a detachment of troops sent ahead to reconnoiter and protect the line of march

ad·vance·ment (əd vans′mənt) *n.* 1. an advancing or being advanced 2. promotion, as to a higher rank 3. progress or improvement; furtherance

ad·van·tage (əd van′tij) *n.* [< OFr. *avant*, before < L. *ab ante*, from before] 1. a more favorable position; superiority or a better chance 2. a favorable circumstance, event, etc. 3. gain or benefit 4. *Tennis* the first point scored after deuce —**take advantage of** 1. to use for one's own benefit 2. to impose upon —**to advantage** so as to result in a good effect [I can use that money *to advantage*]

ad·van·ta·geous (ad′vən tā′jəs) *adj.* favorable; profitable —**ad′van·ta′geous·ly** *adv.*

Ad·vent (ad′vent) *n.* [< L. pp. of *advenire* < *ad-*, to + *venire*, to come] 1. the period including the four Sundays just before Christmas 2. *Theol. a)* Christ's birth *b) same as* SECOND COMING 3. [a-] a coming or arrival

☆**Ad·vent·ist** (ad′vən tist) *n.* a member of a Christian sect based on the belief that Christ's second coming will soon occur —**Ad′vent·ism** *n.*

ad·ven·ti·tious (ad′vən tish′əs) *adj.* [< L., *adventicius*, coming from abroad: see ADVENT] 1. added from outside; accidental 2. *Biol.* occurring in unusual or abnormal places [*adventitious* leaves on a plant] —see SYN. at ACCIDENTAL —**ad′ven·ti′tious·ly** *adv.* —**ad′ven·ti′tious·ness** *n.*

ad·ven·tive (ad ven′tiv) *adj. Bot.* not native to the environment

ad·ven·ture (əd ven′chər) *n.* [< OFr. < L. *advenire*: see ADVENT] 1. the encountering of, or a liking for, danger 2. an exciting and dangerous undertaking 3. an unusual, stirring experience, often of a romantic nature 4. a business venture or speculation —*vt.* -tured, -tur·ing to risk or venture —*vi.* 1. to engage in adventure 2. to take a risk

ad·ven·tur·er (-ər) *n.* 1. a person who has or likes to have adventures 2. *same as* SOLDIER OF FORTUNE 3. a person who speculates in business ventures 4. a person who seeks to become rich, powerful, etc. by tricky schemes —**ad·ven′tur·ess** *n.fem.*

ad·ven·ture·some (-səm) *adj.* willing to take risks; adventurous

ad·ven·tur·ism (-iz′m) *n.* actions, esp. in international relations, regarded as reckless and risky —**ad·ven′tur·ist** *n., adj.*

ad·ven·tur·ous (-əs) *adj.* 1. fond of adventure; daring 2. full of danger; risky —**ad·ven′tur·ous·ly** *adv.* —**ad·ven′tur·ous·ness** *n.*

ad·verb (ad′vurb) *n.* [< L. *adverbium* < *ad-*, to + *verbum*, a WORD] 1. any of a class of words used to modify a verb, an adjective, another adverb, a phrase, or a clause, as by showing time, place, manner, degree, cause, etc. 2. any phrase or clause similarly used —**ad·ver′bi·al** *adj., n.* —**ad·ver′bi·al·ly** *adv.*

ad·ver·sar·y (ad′vər ser′ē) *n., pl.* -sar′ies [< OFr. < L. < *adversus*, ADVERSE] a person who opposes or fights against another; opponent; enemy —see SYN. at OPPONENT

ad·ver·sa·tive (ad vur′sə tiv, əd-) *adj.* [< LL. < L. pp. of *adversari*, to be opposed to] expressing opposition or a contrast of thoughts —*n.* an adversative word, such as *but, yet, however*

ad·verse (ad vurs′, əd-; ad′vərs) *adj.* [< OFr. < L. *adversus*, turned opposite to, pp. of *advertere*: see ADVERT] 1. opposite in position or direction [*adverse* currents in the river] 2. unfavorable; harmful [*adverse* weather conditions] —**ad·verse′ly** *adv.*

ad·ver·si·ty (ad vur′sə tē, əd-) *n.* 1. a state of wretchedness; poverty and trouble 2. *pl.* -ties an instance of misfortune; calamity

ad·vert (ad vurt′, əd-) *vi.* [< OFr. < L. *advertere* < *ad-*, to + *vertere*, to turn: see VERSE] to call attention (*to*); refer or allude

ad·vert·ent (-'nt) *adj.* attentive; heedful —**ad·vert′ence, ad·vert′en·cy** *n.* —**ad·vert′ent·ly** *adv.*

ad·ver·tise (ad′vər tīz′) *vt.* -tised′, -tis′ing [< OFr. *advertir*, to call attention to < L. *advertere*: see ADVERT] 1. to tell about or praise (a product, service, etc.), as through newspapers, radio, or the like, so as to promote sales 2. to make known —*vi.* 1. to call the public's attention to things for sale, for rent, etc., as by printed notices 2. to ask (*for*) publicly by printed notice, etc. [*advertise* for a maid] —**ad·ver′tis′er** *n.*

ad·ver·tise·ment (ad′vər tīz′mənt, əd vur′tiz mənt) *n.*

1. the act of advertising **2.** a public announcement, usually paid for, as of things for sale, needs, etc.

ad·ver·tis·ing (ad′vər tī′ziŋ) *n.* **1.** printed or spoken matter that advertises **2.** the business or work of preparing and issuing advertisements

ad·ver·tize (ad′vər tīz′) *vt., vi.* **-tized′, -tiz′ing** *same as* ADVERTISE **—ad′ver·tize′ment** *n.*

ad·vice (əd vīs′) *n.* [< OFr. < ML. *advisum* < pp. of *advidere* < L. < *ad-*, at + *videre*, to look: see VISION] **1.** opinion given as to what to do or how to deal with something; counsel **2.** [*usually pl.*] information or report [diplomatic *advices*]

ad·vis·a·ble (əd vī′zə b'l) *adj.* being good advice; wise; sensible [it is *advisable* to leave early] **—ad·vis′a·bil′i·ty** *n.* **—ad·vis′a·bly** *adv.*

ad·vise (əd vīz′) *vt.* **-vised′, -vis′ing** [< OFr. < ML. *advisum:* see ADVICE] **1.** to give advice to; counsel [the doctor *advised* him to relax] **2.** to offer as advice; recommend [I *advise* a long vacation] **3.** to notify; inform [we *advised* him of the facts] **—vi. 1.** to discuss or consult (*with*) **2.** to give advice **—ad·vis′er, ad·vi′sor** *n.*

ad·vised (əd vīzd′) *adj.* showing or resulting from thought or advice: now chiefly in WELL-ADVISED, ILL-ADVISED

ad·vis·ed·ly (əd vī′zid lē) *adv.* with due consideration; deliberately

ad·vise·ment (əd vīz′mənt) *n.* careful consideration **—take under advisement** to consider carefully

ad·vi·so·ry (əd vī′zər ē) *adj.* **1.** advising or empowered to advise [the president's *advisory* board] **2.** relating to, or containing, advice [an *advisory* message] **—n., pl. -ries** a warning, esp. one from the National Weather Service about weather conditions

ad·vo·ca·cy (ad′və kə sē) *n.* an advocating; a speaking or writing in support (*of* something)

ad·vo·cate (ad′və kit, -kāt′; *for v.* -kāt′) *n.* [< OFr. < L. *advocatus*, a counselor < *ad-*, to + *vocare*, to call] **1.** a person who pleads another's cause; specif., a lawyer **2.** a person who speaks or writes in support of something [an *advocate* of lower taxes] **—vt. -cat′ed, -cat′ing** to speak or write in support of; be in favor of **—see** SYN. at SUPPORT **—ad′vo·ca′tor** *n.*

advt. *pl.* **advts.** advertisement

adz, adze (adz) *n.* [OE. *adesa*] an axlike tool for trimming and smoothing wood, etc., with a curved blade at right angles to the handle

A.E.C., AEC Atomic Energy Commission

a·ë·des (ā ē′dēz) *n., pl.* **a·ë′des** [ModL. < Gr. *aēdēs* < *a-*, not + *hēdys*, sweet] the mosquito that carries the virus of yellow fever

ae·dile (ē′dīl) *n.* [< L. < *aedes*, building] in ancient Rome, an official in charge of buildings, roads, public games, etc.

ADZ

Ae·ge·an (Sea) (ē jē′ən) sea between Greece and Turkey: an arm of the Mediterranean

ae·gis (ē′jis) *n.* [L. < Gr. *aigis*, goatskin] **1.** *Gr. Myth.* a shield borne by Zeus and, later, by Athena **2.** a protection **3.** sponsorship or support [he spoke under the *aegis* of the university]

Ae·ne·as (i nē′əs) *Gr. & Rom. Myth.* a Trojan warrior who escaped from ruined Troy and wandered for years before coming to Latium

Ae·ne·id (i nē′əd) a Latin epic poem by Virgil, about Aeneas and his adventures

Ae·o·li·an (ē ō′lē ən) *adj.* **1.** of Aeolus **2.** [*often* a-] of the wind

aeolian harp a boxlike stringed instrument that makes musical sounds when air blows on it

Ae·o·lus (ē′ə ləs) *Gr. Myth.* the god of the winds

ae·on (ē′ən, ē′än) *n.* *same as* EON

ae·o·ni·an (ē ō′nē ən) *adj.* lasting for eons; eternal

aer·ate (er′āt′, ā′ər-) *vt.* **-at′ed, -at′ing** [AER(O)- + -ATE¹] **1.** to expose to air, or cause air to circulate through **2.** to supply oxygen to (the blood) by respiration **3.** to charge (liquid) with gas, as in making soda water **—aer·a′tion** *n.* **—aer′a·tor** *n.*

aer·i- *same as* AERO-

aer·i·al (er′ē əl; *occas. for adj.* ā ir′ē əl) *adj.* [< L. *aerius* < *aer* (see AIR) + -AL] **1.** of, in, or

AEOLIAN HARP

by the air **2.** like air; light as air **3.** not substantial; unreal; imaginary **4.** high up; lofty **5.** of, for, or by means of aircraft or flying [an *aerial* photograph] **6.** growing in the air instead of in soil or water **—n.** an antenna (sense 2) **—aer′i·al·ly** *adv.*

aer·i·al·ist (er′ē əl ist) *n.* an acrobat who performs on a trapeze, high wire, etc.

aer·ie (er′ē, ir′ē) *n.* [< OFr. < ML. *aeria*, area; sp. & meaning infl. by L. *aer*, air & ME. *ei*, egg] **1.** the nest of an eagle or other bird of prey that builds in a high place **2.** a house or stronghold on a high place

aer·o (er′ō, ā′ə rō′) *adj.* of or for aeronautics or aircraft

aer·o- [< Gr. *aēr*, air] *a combining form meaning:* **1.** air; of the air [*aerolite*] **2.** of aircraft or flying [*aerobatics*] **3.** of gases [*aerodynamics*]

aer·o·bat·ics (er′ə bat′iks) *n.pl.* [prec. + (ACRO)BATICS] **1.** spectacular feats done with an airplane, as loops, rolls, etc. **2.** [*with sing. v.*] the art of performing such feats

aer·obe (er′ōb) *n.* [< AERO- + Gr. *bios*, life] a microorganism that can live and grow only where free oxygen is present **—aer·o′bic** *adj.*

aer·o·drome (er′ə drōm′) *n. Brit. var. of* AIRDROME

aer·o·dy·nam·ics (er′ō dī nam′iks) *n.pl.* [*with sing. v.*] the branch of aeromechanics dealing with the forces exerted by air or other gases in motion **—aer′o·dy·nam′ic** *adj.* **—aer′o·dy·nam′i·cal·ly** *adv.*

aer·o·em·bo·lism (er′ō em′bə liz'm) *n.* **1.** *same as* DECOMPRESSION SICKNESS **2.** nitrogen bubbles formed in the blood during decompression sickness

aer·o·lite (er′ə līt′) *n.* [AERO- + -LITE] a stony meteorite **—aer′o·lit′ic** (-lit′ik) *adj.*

aer·ol·o·gy (er äl′ə jē) *n.* [AERO- + -LOGY] the branch of meteorology concerned with the study of air, esp. in the upper atmosphere **—aer·ol′o·gist** *n.*

aer·o·me·chan·ics (er′ō mə kan′iks) *n.pl.* [*with sing. v.*] the branch of mechanics dealing with air or other gases in motion or equilibrium: it includes aerodynamics and aerostatics **—aer′o·me·chan′ic** *adj.*

aer·o·med·i·cine (-med′ə s'n) *n.* the branch of medicine dealing with the diseases and disorders associated with airplane flights: see SPACE MEDICINE

aer·o·naut (er′ə nôt′) *n.* [< Fr. < Gr. *aēr*, air + *nautēs*, sailor] the pilot of a balloon or dirigible: now chiefly a historical term

aer·o·nau·tics (er′ə nôt′iks) *n.pl.* [*with sing. v.*] [see prec. & -ICS] the science, art, or work of designing, making, and operating aircraft **—aer′o·nau′ti·cal, aer′o·nau′tic** *adj.* **—aer′o·nau′ti·cal·ly** *adv.*

aer·o·pause (er′ō pôz′) *n.* a region at the upper level of the earth's atmosphere, regarded as the boundary between the atmosphere and outer space

aer·o·plane (er′ə plān′) *n. Brit. var. of* AIRPLANE

aer·o·pulse (-puls′) *n.* [AERO- + PULSE¹] *same as* PULSEJET (ENGINE)

☆**aer·o·space** (er′ō spās′) *n.* [altered < AIR + SPACE] the earth's atmosphere together with the space outside it **—adj.** of aerospace, or of spacecraft or missiles designed to fly in it

aer·o·stat (-stat′) *n.* [< Fr.: see AERO- & -STAT] a dirigible, balloon, or other airship that is lifted by a container filled with a gas that is lighter than air

aer·o·stat·ics (er′ō stat′iks) *n.pl.* [*with sing. v.*] the branch of aeromechanics dealing with the equilibrium of air or other gases, and with the equilibrium of solid bodies, such as aerostats, floating in air or other gases **—aer′o·stat′ic** *adj.*

aer·y (er′ē, ir′ē) *n. same as* AERIE

Aes·chy·lus (es′kə ləs) 525?-456 B.C.; Gr. writer of tragedies **—Aes·chy·le·an** (es′kə lē′ən) *adj.*

Aes·cu·la·pi·us (es′kyoo lā′pē əs) *Rom. Myth.* the god of medicine and of healing: identified with the Greek god Asclepius **—Aes′cu·la′pi·an** *adj.*

Ae·sir (ā′sir, ē′-) *n.pl.* [ON., pl. of *ass*, a god] the principal gods of Norse mythology

Ae·sop (ē′säp, -səp) real or legendary Gr. author of fables: supposed to have lived 6th cent. B.C.

Ae·so·pi·an (ē sō′pē ən) *adj.* **1.** of Aesop or like his fables **2.** having an additional, secret meaning for members of an ingroup [*Aesopian* language]

aes·thete (es′thēt′) *n.* [Gr. *aisthētēs*, one who perceives] **1.** a person highly sensitive to art and beauty **2.** a person who makes a great show of his sensitivity to art and beauty —**aes·thet·i·cism** (es thet′ə siz′m) *n.*

aes·thet·ic (es thet′ik) *adj.* **1.** of aesthetics **2.** of beauty **3.** keenly aware of and loving what is beautiful; artistic Also **aes·thet′i·cal** —**aes·thet′i·cal·ly** *adv.*

aes·thet·ics (-iks) *n.pl.* [*with sing. v.*] the study or theory of beauty and of the psychological responses to it; specif., the branch of philosophy dealing with art and its forms, effects, etc.

aes·ti·vate (es′tə vāt′) *vi.* **-vat′ed, -vat′ing** *same as* ESTIVATE —**aes′ti·va′tion** *n.*

aet., aetat. [L. *aetatis*] at the age of

ae·ther (ē′thər) *n. earlier var. of* ETHER

Aet·na (et′nə) *same as* ETNA

a.f., A.F. audio-frequency

a·far (ə fär′) *adv.* [Poet. or Archaic] at or to a distance —**from afar** from a distance

A·fars and Is·sas (ə färz′ ənd ē zäs′) French territory in E Africa, on the Gulf of Aden: 8,500 sq. mi.; pop. 81,000; cap. Djibouti

AFB Air Force Base

A.F.C., AFC automatic frequency control

a·feard, a·feared (ə fird′) *adj.* [< OE. < *a-* (see A-[2]) + *færan*, to frighten] [Dial. or Archaic] frightened; afraid

af·fa·ble (af′ə b'l) *adj.* [< L. *affabilis* < *fari*, to speak: see FAME] **1.** easy to approach and talk to; friendly **2.** gentle and kindly [an *affable* smile] —see SYN. at AMIABLE —**af′fa·bil′i·ty** *n.* —**af′fa·bly** *adv.*

af·fair (ə fer′) *n.* [< OFr. < *a faire*, to do < L. *ad-*, to + *facere*, to do: see FACT] **1.** a thing to be done; business **2.** [*pl.*] matters of business or concern **3.** any matter, occurrence, or thing **4.** an event arousing public controversy **5.** a social gathering **6.** a sexual relationship outside of marriage

af·fect[1] (ə fekt′; *for n.* af′ekt) *vt.* [< L. *affectare*, to strive after < pp. of *afficere*, to influence < *ad-*, to + *facere*, to do: see FACT] **1.** to have an effect on; influence [bright light *affects* the eyes] **2.** to make feel sad or sympathetic [his death *affected* us deeply] —*n. Psychol.* emotion or emotional response

af·fect[2] (ə fekt′) *vt.* [< OFr. < L. *affectare*, AFFECT[1]] **1.** to like to have, use, wear, etc. [she *affects* plaid coats] **2.** to pretend to have, feel, like, etc.; feign [to *affect* indifference]

af·fec·ta·tion (af′ek tā′shən) *n.* **1.** an affecting or pretending to like, have, etc.; show or pretense **2.** artificial behavior meant to impress others

af·fect·ed[1] (ə fek′tid) *adj.* **1.** diseased or injured [he bathed the *affected* eye] **2.** influenced; acted upon **3.** emotionally moved; feeling sympathy

af·fect·ed[2] (ə fek′tid) *adj.* **1.** assumed for effect; artificial [affected gaiety] **2.** behaving in an artificial way to impress people —**af·fect′ed·ly** *adv.*

af·fect·ing (ə fek′tiŋ) *adj.* emotionally touching; causing one to feel pity, sympathy, etc. —see SYN. at MOVING

af·fec·tion (ə fek′shən) *n.* **1.** a tendency **2.** fond or tender feeling; warm liking **3.** a disease [an *affection* of the liver] **4.** an affecting or being affected —see SYN. at LOVE

af·fec·tion·ate (-it) *adj.* full of affection; tender and loving —**af·fec′tion·ate·ly** *adv.*

af·fec·tive (ə fek′tiv) *adj.* of affects, or feelings; emotional —**af·fec′tive·ly** *adv.*

af·fer·ent (af′ər ənt) *adj.* [< L. prp. of *afferre* < *ad-*, to + *ferre*, to BEAR[1]] *Physiol.* bringing inward to a central part; specif., designating nerves that transmit impulses toward a nerve center: opposed to EFFERENT

af·fi·ance (ə fi′əns) *vt.* **-anced, -anc·ing** [< OFr. *afier* < ML. < *ad-*, to + *fidare*, to trust] to pledge, esp. in marriage; betroth

☆**af·fi·ant** (ə fi′ənt) *n.* [< prp. of OFr. *afier*: see prec.] a person who makes an affidavit

af·fi·da·vit (af′ə dā′vit) *n.* [ML., he has made oath] a written statement sworn to be true, as before a notary public

af·fil·i·ate (ə fil′ē āt′; *for n.* -it) *vt.* **-at′ed, -at′ing** [< ML. pp. of *affiliare*, to adopt as a son < L. *ad-*, to + *filius*, son] **1.** to take in as a member or branch **2.** to connect or associate (oneself *with*) —*vi.* to associate closely; join —*n.* an affiliated person or organization —**af·fil′i·a′tion** *n.*

af·fin·i·ty (ə fin′ə tē) *n., pl.* **-ties** [< OFr. < L. *affinis*, adjacent < *ad-*, to + *finis*, end: see FINISH] **1.** relationship by marriage **2.** close relationship; connection **3.** a similarity of structure, as of biological species, that implies origin from the same source **4.** a natural liking; esp., a mutual attraction **5.** a person of the opposite sex who especially attracts one **6.** the force that causes the atoms of certain elements to combine and stay combined —**af·fin′i·tive** *adj.*

af·firm (ə furm′) *vt.* [< OFr. < L. *affirmare* < *ad-*, to + *firmare*, to make firm] **1.** to declare positively; assert to be true **2.** to confirm; ratify (a law, decision, or judgment) —*vi. Law* to declare solemnly, but not under oath —**af·firm′a·ble** *adj.* —**af·firm′er,** *law* **af·firm′ant** *n.*

af·fir·ma·tion (af′ər mā′shən) *n.* **1.** an affirming **2.** a positive declaration; assertion **3.** *Law* a solemn declaration instead of an oath, made by a person whose conscience will not allow him to take oaths

af·firm·a·tive (ə fur′mə tiv) *adj.* **1.** answering "yes" [an *affirmative* reply] **2.** bold or confident, as in asserting [take *affirmative* action] —*n.* **1.** a word or expression indicating agreement **2.** an affirmative statement —**the affirmative** the side that is in favor of the proposition being debated —**af·firm′a·tive·ly** *adv.*

☆**affirmative action** a positive plan that is meant to make up for earlier discrimination in the hiring or education of members of certain minority groups, women, etc.

af·fix (ə fiks′; *for n.* af′iks) *vt.* [< L. pp. of *affigere* < *ad-*, to + *figere*, FIX] **1.** to fasten; attach [affix a label to the jar] **2.** to add at the end [affix your signature to the petition] —*n.* **1.** a thing affixed **2.** a prefix or suffix

af·fla·tus (ə flāt′əs) *n.* [< L. pp. of *afflare* < *ad-*, to + *flare*, to blow] inspiration, as of an artist

af·flict (ə flikt′) *vt.* [< L. *afflictare* < pp. of *affligere* < *ad-*, to + *fligere*, to strike] to cause suffering to; distress very much

af·flic·tion (ə flik′shən) *n.* **1.** an afflicted condition; pain; suffering **2.** anything causing pain or distress; calamity

af·flic·tive (-tiv) *adj.* causing pain or misery

af·flu·ence (af′loo wəns; *now sometimes* ə flōō′-) *n.* [< L. < *affluere* < *ad-*, to + *fluere*, to flow: see FLUCTUATE] **1.** great plenty; abundance **2.** much riches; wealth; opulence

af·flu·ent (-wənt) *adj.* **1.** plentiful; abundant **2.** wealthy; prosperous; rich [the *affluent* society] —*n.* a stream flowing into a river; tributary —see SYN. at RICH —**af′flu·ent·ly** *adv.*

af·ford (ə fôrd′) *vt.* [OE. *geforthian*, to advance < *forthian*, to further] **1.** to have enough or the means for; bear the cost of without serious inconvenience: usually with *can* or *be able* **2.** to be able (*to* do something) with little risk [you can *afford* to speak frankly] **3.** to give; yield; furnish [music *affords* her much pleasure]

af·fray (ə frā′) *n.* [< OFr. < *esfraer*, to frighten < L. *ex*, out of + Gmc. base *frith-*, peace] a noisy brawl or quarrel; riot

af·fri·cate (af′rə kit) *n.* [< L. pp. of *affricare* < *ad-*, to + *fricare*, to rub] *Phonet.* a sound produced when a slowly released stop is followed immediately by a fricative, as (t) followed by (sh) to produce (ch)

af·fright (ə frit′) *vt.* [Archaic] to frighten; terrify —*n.* [Archaic] great fright or terror

af·front (ə frunt′) *vt.* [< OFr. *afronter*, to encounter < ML. < *ad-*, to + *frons*, forehead] **1.** to insult openly or on purpose **2.** to confront defiantly —*n.* an open or intentional insult —see SYN. at OFFEND

Af·ghan (af′gan, -gən) *n.* **1.** a native of Afghanistan **2.** any of a breed of hunting dog with silky hair and a long, narrow head **3.** [a-] a soft blanket or shawl, crocheted or knitted, esp. in a geometrical design —*adj.* of Afghanistan, its people, etc.

af·ghan·i (af gan′ē) *n., pl.* **-is** *see* MONETARY UNITS, table (Afghanistan)

Af·ghan·i·stan (af gan′ə stan′) country in SW Asia, between Iran and Pakistan: 250,000 sq. mi.; pop. 16,516,000; cap. Kabul

a·fi·cio·na·do (ə fish′ə nä′dō, -fis′ē ə-) *n., pl.* **-dos** [Sp., pp. of *aficionar*, to be devoted to < L.

AFGHAN
(to 28 in. high
at shoulder)

---

fat, āpe, cär, ten, ēven, is, bīte; gō, hôrn, tōol, look; oil, out; up, fur; get; joy; yet; chin; she; thin, then; zh, leisure; ŋ, ring; ə for *a* in *ago*, *e* in *agent*, *i* in *sanity*, *o* in *comply*, *u* in *focus*; ′ as in *able* (ā′b'l); Fr. bal; ë, Fr. coeur; ö, Fr. feu; Fr. mon; ô, Fr. coq; ü, Fr. duc; r, Fr. cri; H, G. ich; kh, G. doch; ‡foreign; ☆ Americanism; < derived from. See inside front cover.

affectio, warm liking] a devoted follower of some sport, art, etc.; fan

a·field (ə fēld′) *adv.* 1. in, on, or to the field 2. away (from home) 3. off the right path; astray

a·fire (ə fīr′) *adv., adj.* 1. on fire 2. greatly excited

a·flame (ə flām′) *adv., adj.* 1. in flames 2. glowing [trees *aflame* with fall colors] 3. greatly excited

AFL-CIO American Federation of Labor and Congress of Industrial Organizations

a·float (ə flōt′) *adv.* 1. floating freely 2. on board ship; at sea 3. flooded [the deck is *afloat*] 4. drifting about 5. in circulation [rumors are *afloat*] 6. free of trouble, debt, etc. [he kept the business *afloat*]

a·flut·ter (ə flut′ər) *adv., adj.* in a flutter

a·foot (ə foot′) *adv.* 1. on foot; walking 2. in motion or operation; in progress; astir [there is trouble *afoot*]

a·fore (ə fôr′) *adv., prep., conj.* [Archaic or Dial. except in compounds and nautical use] before

a·fore·men·tioned (ə fôr′men′shənd) *adj.* mentioned before or previously

a·fore·said (-sed′) *adj.* spoken of before; mentioned previously

a·fore·thought (-thôt′) *adj.* thought out beforehand; premeditated

a for·ti·o·ri (ā fôr′tē ôr′ē, -shē ôr′ī) [L., for a stronger (reason)] all the more: said of a conclusion that follows with even more logical force another already accepted

☆**a·foul** (ə foul′) *adv., adj.* in a collision or a tangle —**run** (or **fall**) **afoul of** to get into trouble with [he ran *afoul of* the law]

Afr. 1. Africa 2. African

a·fraid (ə frād′) *adj.* [< ME. pp. of *affraien*, to frighten: see AFFRAY] feeling fear; frightened [with *of, that,* or an infinitive): often used colloquially to indicate regret [I'm *afraid* that I can't go]

SYN.—afraid is broadly applied to a general feeling of fear [*afraid* of the dark; *afraid* to die]; **frightened** and **scared** imply a sudden, usually brief, feeling of fear, often fear of bodily harm [when the dog growled, the *frightened* child cowered; he ran like a *scared* rabbit]; **fearful** implies a tendency to worry, often without an immediate reason [*fearful* of the future]; **terrified** suggests a feeling of intense, overwhelming fear [he stood *terrified* as the tiger charged] —**ANT.** brave, bold, self-controlled

☆**A-frame** (ā′frām′) *n.* a structural framework, as of a house, with steeply angled sides meeting at the top like the sides of the letter A

a·fresh (ə fresh′) *adv.* again; anew

Af·ri·ca (af′ri kə) second largest continent, situated in the Eastern Hemisphere, south of Europe: c. 11,500,000 sq. mi.; pop. c. 345,000,000

Af·ri·can (-kən) *adj.* of Africa, its peoples (esp. Negro peoples), their cultures, etc. —*n.* 1. a member of a native ethnic group of Africa, esp. a Negro 2. any native or inhabitant of Africa

African violet any of several tropical African plants with violet, white, or pinkish flowers and hairy, dark-green leaves, often grown as house plants

AFRICAN VIOLET

Af·ri·kaans (af′ri känz′, -käns′, -kanz′) *n.* [Afrik. < *Afrika*, Africa] an official language of South Africa, a development from 17th-cent. Dutch

Af·ri·ka·ner (af′ri kän′ər) *n.* [Du.] a South African of European, esp. Dutch, ancestry; Boer

☆**Af·ro** (af′rō) *adj.* [< AFRO-] designating or of a full, bouffant hair style, as worn by some blacks

Af·ro- *a combining form meaning:* 1. Africa 2. African Also, before a vowel, **Afr-**

☆**Af·ro-A·mer·i·can** (af′rō ə mer′ə kən) *adj.* of black Americans, their culture; etc. —*n.* a black American

Af·ro-A·sian (-ā′zhən) *adj.* of Africa and Asia jointly [an Afro-Asian conference]

aft (aft) *adv.* [< OE. < *afta*, behind] at, near, or toward the stern of a ship or rear of an aircraft

af·ter (af′tər) *adv.* [OE. *æfter* < *of*, off + -*ter*, old compar. suffix] behind in place or time; later or next —*prep.* 1. behind in place 2. later in time; next 3. in search of [what are you *after*?] 4. as a result of [after what has happened, he

AFRO

won't go] 5. in spite of [after all his bad luck, he is still cheerful] 6. following next to in rank or importance 7. in the manner of [a novel *after* Dickens' style] 8. for; in honor of [named *after* Lincoln] 9. concerning [she asked *after* you] — *conj.* following the time when [they left the party *after* we did] —*adj.* 1. next; later [in the *after* period of his career] 2. nearer the rear (esp. of a ship or aircraft)

af·ter·birth (-burth′) *n.* the placenta and fetal membranes expelled from the womb after childbirth

af·ter·burn·er (-bur′nər) *n.* 1. a device attached to the tailpipe of some jet engines for obtaining additional thrust by using the hot exhaust gases to burn extra fuel 2. a device, as on an incinerator, for burning undesirable exhaust gases

af·ter·damp (-damp′) *n.* an asphyxiating gas left in a mine after an explosion of firedamp

af·ter·ef·fect (-ə fekt′) *n.* an effect coming later, or as a secondary result [a drug with no *aftereffects*]

af·ter·glow (-glō′) *n.* 1. the glow remaining after a light has gone, as after sunset 2. a pleasant feeling after an enjoyable experience

af·ter·im·age (-im′ij) *n.* a visual image that continues after the stimulus causing it is withdrawn

af·ter·life (-līf′) *n.* 1. a life after death 2. one's later years

af·ter·math (-math′) *n.* [AFTER + dial. *math* < OE. *mæth*, cutting of grass] a result or consequence, esp. an unpleasant one

af·ter·most (-mōst′) *adj.* 1. hindmost; last 2. nearest to the stern

af·ter·noon (af′tər nōōn′, af′tər nōōn′) *n.* the time of day from noon to evening —*adj.* of, in, or for the afternoon

af·ter·noons (-nōōnz′) *adv.* during every afternoon or most afternoons [afternoons he studies]

af·ter·taste (af′tər tāst′) *n.* 1. a taste lingering on in the mouth, as after eating 2. the feeling remaining after an experience

af·ter·thought (-thôt′) *n.* 1. an idea, explanation, etc. coming or added later 2. a thought coming too late to be apt, useful, etc.

af·ter·ward (-wərd) *adv.* at a later time; subsequently: also **af′ter·wards**

Ag [L. *argentum*] *Chem.* silver

AG Adjutant General

Ag. August

A.G. Attorney General

a·gain (ə gen′; chiefly Brit. -gān′) *adv.* [OE. *ongegn* < *on-*, toward + *gegn*, direct] 1. back into a former position or condition [home *again*, well *again*] 2. once more; a second time [read it *again*] 3. besides; further [*again*, we should note] 4. on the other hand [he may, and then *again* he may not] — **again and again** often; repeatedly —**as much again** twice as much

a·gainst (ə genst′; chiefly Brit. -gānst′) *prep.* [see AGAIN] 1. in opposition to [*against* my will] 2. toward so as to strike [throw the ball *against* the wall] 3. opposite to the direction of [drive *against* the traffic] 4. in contrast with [green *against* the gold] 5. next to; adjoining 6. in preparation for [we provided *against* a poor crop] 7. as a charge on [a bill was entered *against* his account] —**over against** 1. opposite to 2. as compared with

Ag·a·mem·non (ag′ə mem′nän, -nən) *Gr. Myth.* king of Mycenae and commander in chief of the Greek army in the Trojan War

A·ga·ña (ä gän′yə) capital of Guam: pop. 2,000

a·gape[1] (ə gāp′) *adv., adj.* [A-[1] + GAPE] 1. with the mouth wide open, as in wonder 2. wide open

ag·a·pe[2] (ä′gä pā′, ag′ə pē) *n.* [< LL. < Gr. *agapē*, love] *Christian Theol.* 1. God's love for man 2. spontaneous, altruistic love

a·gar-a·gar (ä′gär ä′gär, ag′ər ag′ər) *n.* [Malay] a gelatinous extract of seaweed, used for bacterial cultures, as a laxative, etc.: also **a′gar**

ag·ar·ic (ə ger′ik, ag′ər ik) *n.* [< L. < Gr. < *Agaria*, ancient European town] any gill fungus, as the common edible mushroom, etc.

Ag·as·siz (ag′ə sē), (**Jean**) **Louis** (**Rodolphe**) 1807–73; U.S. zoologist & geologist, born in Switzerland

ag·ate (ag′ət) *n.* [OFr. < L. < Gr. *achatēs* < ?] 1. a hard, semiprecious stone, a variety of chalcedony, with striped or clouded coloring 2. a little ball made of this stone or of glass, used in playing marbles 3. a small size of type, 5½ point

Ag·a·tha (ag′ə thə) [L. < Gr. *Agathē*, lit., good, fem. of *agathos*, good] a feminine name

a·ga·ve (ə gä′vē) *n.* [ModL. < Gr. *Agauē*, a proper name, lit., illustrious] any of several American desert plants, as the century plant, having tall flower stalks and fleshy leaves

a·gaze (ə gāz′) *adv., adj.* gazing

agcy. agency

age (āj) *n.* [< OFr. < L. *aetas* < IE. base *aiw-*, vitality] **1.** the time that a person or thing has existed since birth or beginning **2.** the lifetime **3.** a stage of life [the awkward *age*] **4.** the condition of being old [bent with *age*] **5.** a generation [future *ages* will honor him] **6.** *a)* any interval of geologic time *b)* any prehistoric or historic cultural period [the Stone *Age*, the Space *Age*] **7.** [often *pl.*] [Colloq.] a long time [I haven't seen her for *ages*] —*vi.* **aged, ag′ing** or **age′ing** to grow old or become mature —*vt.* to make old or cause to become mature —**of age** having reached the age of full legal rights

-age (ij, əj) [OFr. < LL. *-aticum*, belonging to] *a suffix meaning:* **1.** the act, condition, or result of [*marriage*] **2.** amount or number of [*acreage*] **3.** cost of [*postage*] **4.** place of [*steerage*] **5.** collection of [*peerage*] **6.** home of [*hermitage*]

a·ged (ā′jid *for 1 & 2;* ājd *for 3 & 4) adj.* **1.** grown old [her *aged* aunt] **2.** of old age **3.** brought to a desired state of aging **4.** of the age of [a boy *aged* ten] —**the aged** (ā′jid) old people

age·ism (āj′iz′m) *n.* [AGE + (RAC)ISM] discrimination against people, specif. older people, because of age

age·less (āj′lis) *adj.* **1.** seemingly not growing older **2.** eternal —**age′less·ly** *adv.*

age·long (-lôŋ′) *adj.* lasting a very long time

a·gen·cy (ā′jən sē) *n., pl.* **-cies** [see AGENT] **1.** that by which something is done; means [electricity is the *agency* by which our homes are lighted] **2.** the work or place of work of any person, firm, etc. authorized to act for another [an insurance *agency;* social work *agency*] **3.** an administrative division of government [U.S. Information *Agency*]

a·gen·da (ə jen′də) *n., pl.* **-das** [L., pl. of *agendum* < *agere,* ACT] program of things to be done; specif., a list of things to be dealt with at a meeting: also **a·gen′dum** (-dəm), *pl.* **-da** (-də), **-dums**

a·gent (ā′jənt) *n.* [< L. *agens* (gen. *agentis*), prp. of *agere,* ACT] **1.** a person or thing that brings about a certain result [education is a powerful *agent* in human understanding] **2.** a force or substance that produces an effect [chemical *agent*] **3.** a person, firm, etc. authorized to act for another [a theatrical *agent*] ☆**4.** a representative of a government agency

‡**a·gent pro·vo·ca·teur** (à zhän′ prô vô kà ter′) *pl.* **a·gents pro·vo·ca·teurs** (à zhän′ prô vô kà ter′) [Fr.] a secret agent hired to join some group in order to incite its members to commit unlawful acts

age-old (āj′ōld′) *adj.* ages old; ancient

ag·er·a·tum (aj′ə rāt′əm) *n.* [ModL. < Gr. < *agēratos,* not growing old < *a-,* not + *gēras,* old age] a plant of the composite family, with small, thick heads of usually bluish flowers

ag·glom·er·ate (ə gläm′ə rāt′; *for adj. & n.* -ər it) *vt., vi.* **-at′ed, -at′ing** [< L. pp. of *agglomerare* < *ad-,* to + *glomerare,* to form into a ball] to gather into a mass or ball —*adj.* gathered into a mass or ball —*n.* a jumbled heap, mass, etc. —**ag·glom′er·a′tion** *n.* —**ag·glom′er·a′tive** *adj.*

ag·glu·ti·nant (ə glōōt′′n ənt) *adj.* [see AGGLUTINATE] sticking together —*n.* a sticky substance

ag·glu·ti·nate (ə glōōt′′n it; *for v.* -āt′) *adj.* [< L. pp. of *agglutinare* < *ad-,* to + *gluten,* glue] **1.** stuck together, as with glue **2.** *Linguis.* forming words by agglutination —*vt., vi.* **-nat′ed, -nat′ing 1.** to stick together, as with glue **2.** *Linguis.* to form (words) by agglutination **3.** *Med. & Bacteriology* to clump, as blood cells, microorganisms, etc. suspended in fluid —**ag·glu′ti·na′tive** *adj.*

ag·glu·ti·na·tion (ə glōōt′′n ā′shən) *n.* **1.** an agglutinating or being agglutinated **2.** a mass of agglutinated parts **3.** *Linguis.* the combining of words into compounds without marked change of form or loss of meaning

ag·glu·ti·nin (ə glōōt′′n in) *n.* a substance that causes agglutination of bacteria, blood cells, etc.

ag·gran·dize (ə gran′dīz′, ag′rən-) *vt.* **-dized′, -diz′ing** [< Fr. < *a-,* to + *grandir,* to increase < L. *grandire* < *grandis,* great] **1.** to make (esp. oneself) greater, more powerful, richer, etc. **2.** to make seem greater —**ag·gran′dize·ment** (-diz mənt) *n.* —**ag·gran′diz′er** *n.*

ag·gra·vate (ag′rə vāt′) *vt.* **-vat′ed, -vat′ing** [< L. pp. of *aggravare* < *ad-,* to + *gravis,* heavy] **1.** to make worse, more troublesome, etc. [to *aggravate* a sprained ankle by walking] **2.** [Colloq.] to exasperate; annoy —**ag′gra·va′tion** *n.*

ag·gre·gate (ag′rə gət; *for v.* -gāt′) *adj.* [< L. pp. of *aggregare* < *ad-,* to + *gregare,* to herd < *gregis,* genitive of *grex,* a herd] **1.** gathered into, or considered as, a whole; total [the *aggregate* number of unemployed] **2.** *Geol.* made up of a mixture of mineral fragments, crystals, etc. [*aggregate* rock] —*n.* **1.** a group or mass of distinct things gathered into, or considered as, a whole; total **2.** the sand or pebbles added to cement in making concrete or mortar —*vt.* **-gat′ed, -gat′ing 1.** to gather into a whole or mass **2.** to amount to; total —**in the aggregate** taken all together; on the whole —**ag′gre·ga′tion** *n.* —**ag′gre·ga′tive** *adj.*

ag·gress (ə gres′) *vi.* [< L. pp. of *aggredi,* to attack < *ad-,* to + *gradi,* to step] to start a quarrel or be the first to attack

ag·gres·sion (ə gresh′ən) *n.* **1.** an unprovoked attack or warlike act **2.** the practice or habit of being aggressive, or quarrelsome **3.** *Psychiatry* forceful or hostile behavior

ag·gres·sive (ə gres′iv) *adj.* **1.** starting, or ready to start, fights or quarrels **2.** ready to engage in direct action **3.** full of energy and ideas; bold and active —**ag·gres′sive·ly** *adv.* —**ag·gres′sive·ness** *n.*
SYN. —**aggressive** implies boldness and forcefulness in seeking to reach one's goals, either in an unfavorable sense connoting ruthlessness or quarrelsomeness, or in a more favorable sense connoting energy, a daring to take risks, etc.; **assertive** suggests self-confidence and strong persistence in expressing oneself or one's views; **militant** implies vigorous, unwavering support of a cause, movement, etc., usually with no notion of personal gain; **pushy** is used in a critical way to imply a boldness in making one's way that is shown by rudeness, domineering, etc.

ag·gres·sor (-ər) *n.* a person, nation, etc. that is guilty of aggression, or makes an unprovoked attack

ag·grieve (ə grēv′) *vt.* **-grieved′, -griev′ing** [< OFr. < L. *aggravare,* AGGRAVATE] **1.** to cause grief or injury to; offend **2.** to do a wrong to in some legal matter

a·ghast (ə gast′) *adj.* [< ME. < *a-* (see A-[2]) + *gastan* < OE. *gæstan,* to terrify < *gast,* GHOST] feeling great horror or dismay; horrified

ag·ile (aj′′l; *chiefly Brit.* -īl) *adj.* [Fr. < L. < *agere,* ACT] **1.** quick and easy of movement; nimble **2.** keen and lively [an *agile* wit] —**ag′ile·ly** *adv.* —**a·gil·i·ty** (ə jil′ə tē) *n.*
SYN. —**agile** and **nimble** both imply quickness and lightness of movement, but **agile** stresses general skill and ease in the use of the limbs, while **nimble** suggests quick sureness in carrying out a particular act [*nimble* fingers at the keyboard]; **quick** implies speed or promptness with no indication of the degree of skill; **spry** suggests nimbleness, esp. as displayed by a vigorous, elderly person; **sprightly** suggests liveliness, gaiety, etc. —**ANT.** torpid, sluggish, lethargic

ag·ism (āj′iz′m) *n. same as* AGEISM

ag·i·tate (aj′ə tāt′) *vt.* **-tat′ed, -tat′ing** [< L. pp. of *agitare* to put in motion < *agere,* ACT] **1.** to move violently; stir up or shake up **2.** to excite or disturb the feelings of —*vi.* to stir up support through speeches and writing so as to produce changes [to *agitate* for reform] —**ag′i·tat′ed·ly** *adv.*

ag·i·ta·tion (aj′ə tā′shən) *n.* **1.** an agitating or being agitated; violent motion or stirring **2.** emotional disturbance **3.** discussion meant to stir up people and produce changes

‡**a·gi·ta·to** (ä′jē tä′tô) *adj., adv.* [It.: see AGITATE] *Music* fast and with excitement

ag·i·ta·tor (aj′ə tāt′ər) *n.* **1.** a person who tries to stir up people in support of a social or political cause: often used in disapproval **2.** an apparatus for shaking or stirring, as in a washing machine

ag·it·prop (aj′it präp′) *adj.* [< Russ. *agit(atsiya) prop(aganda),* agitation propaganda] of or for agitating and propagandizing

a·gleam (ə glēm′) *adv., adj.* gleaming

a·gley (ə glē′, -glī′, -glā′) *adv.* [Scot.] awry

a·glit·ter (ə glit′ər) *adv., adj.* glittering

a·glow (ə glō′) *adj.* in a glow (of color or emotion) [her face was *aglow* with joy]

Ag·nes (ag′nis) [< Fr. < L. < Gr. *hagnē,* fem. of *hagnos,* chaste] a feminine name: dim. **Aggie**

ag·nos·tic (ag näs′tik) *n.* [< Gr. < *a-,* not + base of *gignōskein,* to KNOW] a person who believes that one cannot know whether there is a God or an ultimate cause —*adj.* of or characteristic of an agnostic —see **SYN.** at ATHEIST —**ag·nos′ti·cal·ly** *adv.* —**ag·nos′ti·cism** *n.*

Ag·nus De·i (ag′nŏŏs dā′ē; ag′nəs dē′ī) [L., Lamb of God] **1.** a representation of Christ as a lamb, often holding a cross or flag **2.** *R.C.Ch.* a prayer in the Mass, beginning *Agnus Dei*, or music for it

a·go (ə gō′) *adj.* [< OE. *agan* < *a-*, + *gan*, go] gone by; past [*years ago*, a month *ago*] —*adv.* in the past [long *ago*]

a·gog (ə gäg′) *adv., adj.* [OFr. < *a-*, to + *gogue*, joyfulness] with eager interest or excitement

-a·gogue, -a·gog (ə gäg′, -gôg) [< Gr. prp. of *agein*, to lead] *a combining form meaning* leading, directing, inciting [*demagogue*]

ag·o·nize (ag′ə nīz′) *vi.* **-nized′, -niz′ing** **1.** to make desperate efforts; struggle **2.** to be in agony —*vt.* to torture —**ag′o·niz′ing·ly** *adv.*

ag·o·ny (ag′ə nē) *n., pl.* **-nies** [< L. < Gr. *agōnia*, a contest < *agōn*, an assembly (as for athletic contests)] **1.** great mental or physical pain **2.** death pangs **3.** a desperate struggle **4.** a sudden outburst (*of* emotion) —see **SYN.** at DISTRESS

a·go·ra[1] (ag′ə rə) *n., pl.* **-rae′** (-rē′), **-ras** [Gr. < *ageirein*, to assemble] in ancient Greece, an assembly or a place of assembly, esp. a marketplace

a·go·ra[2] (ä′gō rä′) *n., pl.* **-rot′** (-rōt′) [ModHeb. *'agōrāh*] *see* MONETARY UNITS, table (Israel)

ag·o·ra·pho·bi·a (ag′ər ə fō′bē ə) *n.* [AGORA[1] + -PHOBIA] an abnormal fear of being in open spaces

a·gou·ti, a·gou·ty (ə gōō′tē) *n., pl.* **-tis, -ties:** see PLURAL, II, D, 1 [Fr. < Sp. < Guarani] a rodent related to the guinea pig, found in tropical America

A·gra (ä′grə) city in N India: site of the Taj Mahal: pop. 509,000

AGOUTI
(17–25 in. long)

a·grar·i·an (ə grer′ē ən) *adj.* [< L. *ager*, a field: see ACRE] **1.** relating to land or to the ownership or division of land **2.** of agriculture —*n.* a person who favors a more even division of land among those who work it —**a·grar′i·an·ism** *n.*

a·gree (ə grē′) *vi.* **-greed′, -gree′ing** [< OFr. < *a gre*, favorably < L. *ad*, to + *gratus*, pleasing] **1.** to consent or accede (*to*); say "yes" **2.** to be in harmony or accord [our tastes in art *agree*] **3.** to be of the same opinion; concur (*with*) **4.** to arrive at a satisfactory understanding (*about* prices, terms, etc.) **5.** to be suitable, healthful, etc. (followed by *with*) [the climate *agrees* with him] **6.** *Gram.* to correspond in number, person, case, or gender [the verb should *agree* with its subject] —*vt.* to grant or acknowledge [we *agreed* that it was true] **SYN.—agree** is the general term used to express a fitting or going together without conflict; **conform** emphasizes agreement in form or basic character [specifications must *conform* to the building code]; **accord** emphasizes fitness for each other of the things being considered together [his story does not *accord* with the facts]; **harmonize** implies a combining of different things in an orderly or pleasing arrangement [*harmonizing* colors]; **correspond** is applied to that which matches, complements, or is comparable to something else [their Foreign Office *corresponds* to our State Department]; **coincide** stresses that the things being considered are identical [their interests *coincide*] —see also **SYN.** at CONSENT —**ANT.** differ

a·gree·a·ble (-ə b'l) *adj.* [see prec.] **1.** pleasing or pleasant [an *agreeable* odor] **2.** willing or ready to consent [she was *agreeable* to our plan] **3.** in harmony or accord —see **SYN.** at PLEASANT —**a·gree′a·bil′i·ty, a·gree′a·ble·ness** *n.* —**a·gree′a·bly** *adv.*

a·greed (ə grēd′) *adj.* settled by mutual consent [pay the *agreed* price]

a·gree·ment (ə grē′mənt) *n.* **1.** an agreeing, or being in harmony **2.** an understanding between two or more people, countries, etc. **3.** a contract

ag·ri·cul·ture (ag′ri kul′chər) *n.* [Fr. < L. < *ager*, a field (see ACRE) + *cultura*, cultivation] the science and art of farming; work of cultivating the soil, producing crops, and raising livestock —**ag′ri·cul′tur·al** *adj.* —**ag′ri·cul′tur·al·ly** *adv.*

ag·ri·cul·tur·ist (ag′ri kul′chər ist) *n.* **1.** an expert in agriculture **2.** a farmer Also **ag′ri·cul′tur·al·ist**

ag·ri·mo·ny (ag′rə mō′nē) *n., pl.* **-nies** [< OE. & OFr. < L. < Gr. *argemōnē*] a plant of the rose family, having little yellow flowers on spiky stalks and bearing burlike fruits

ag·ro·bi·ol·o·gy (ag′rō bī äl′ə jē) *n.* the science of plant growth and nutrition as applied to improvement of crops and control of soil

a·gron·o·my (ə grän′ə mē) *n.* [< Fr. < Gr. < *agros*, field + *nemein*, to manage] the science and economics of crop production; management of farm land —**ag·ro·nom·ic** (ag′rə-näm′ik), **ag′ro·nom′i·cal** *adj.* —**a·gron′o·mist** *n.*

a·ground (ə ground′) *adv., adj.* on or onto the shore, a reef, etc. [the ship ran *aground*]

agt. agent

a·gue (ā′gyōō) *n.* [< OFr. < ML. (*febris*) *acuta*, violent (fever)] **1.** a fever, usually that of malaria, marked by regularly recurring chills **2.** a chill; fit of shivering —**a′gu·ish** *adj.*

ah (ä, ô) *interj.* an exclamation expressing pain, delight, regret, disgust, surprise, etc.

a·ha (ä hä′) *interj.* an exclamation expressing satisfaction, pleasure, triumph, etc., often mixed with irony or mockery

A·hab (ā′hab) *Bible* a wicked king of Israel, husband of Jezebel: I Kings 16:29

a·head (ə hed′) *adv., adj.* **1.** in or to the front **2.** forward; onward **3.** in advance **4.** winning or leading **5.** having something as a profit or advantage [he ended up $10 *ahead*] —**ahead of** in advance of; before —**get ahead** to advance socially, financially, etc. —**get ahead of** to outdo or excel

a·hem (ə hem′) *interj.* a cough or similar sound made to get attention, fill a pause, etc.

a·him·sa (ə him′sə) *n.* [< Sans. < *a-*, not + *himsā*, injury] the Buddhist and Hindu principle of not harming any living creature

Ah·med·a·bad, Ah·mad·a·bad (ä′məd ə bäd′) city in W India: pop. 1,206,000

A·ho·ri·zon (ā′hə rī′z'n) *n. see* ABC SOIL

a·hoy (ə hoi′) *interj. Naut.* a call used in hailing [ship *ahoy!*]

A·hu·ra Maz·da (ä′hŏŏ rə maz′də) *same as* ORMAZD

a·i (ä′ē) *n., pl.* **a′is** (-ēz) [Tupi *ai hai* < the animal's cry] a S. American sloth with three toes

AID Agency for International Development

aid (ād) *vt., vi.* [< OFr. < L. *adjutare*: see ADJUTANT] to give help (to); assist —*n.* **1.** help; assistance **2.** a helper; assistant [a nurse's *aid*] **3.** a helpful device [a hearing *aid*] **4.** same as AIDE-DE-CAMP —see **SYN.** at HELP

aide (ād) *n.* [Fr.: see AID] **1.** an assistant **2.** same as AIDE-DE-CAMP

aide-de-camp (ād′də kamp′) *n., pl.* **aides-de-camp** [Fr., lit., camp assistant] an officer in the army, navy, etc. serving as assistant and confidential secretary to a superior

aid·man (ād′man′) *n., pl.* **-men′** (-men′) an enlisted man in a medical corps in a combat area

☆ **aid station** *Mil.* a medical station in a combat area, where emergency treatment is given

ai·grette, ai·gret (ā′gret, ā gret′) *n.* [see EGRET] **1.** the long, white plumes of the egret, once worn for ornament by women **2.** any ornament like this

Ai·ken (āk′n), **Conrad (Potter)** 1889–1973; U.S. poet & fiction writer

ail (āl) *vt.* [< OE. *eglian*, to afflict with dread, trouble < *egle*, harmful] to be the cause of pain to; trouble —*vi.* to be in poor health; be ill

ai·lan·thus (ā lan′thəs) *n., pl.* **-thus·es** [ModL. < native name in Malacca] a tree with pointed leaflets, fine-grained wood, and clusters of small, greenish flowers with an unpleasant odor; tree of heaven

Ai·leen (ī lēn′, ā-) *var. of* EILEEN

ai·le·ron (ā′lə rän′) *n.* [Fr. < OFr. < *aile* < L. *ala*, wing] a movable hinged section at the trailing edge of an airplane wing for controlling rolling movements

ail·ing (āl′iŋ) *adj.* in poor health; sickly —see **SYN.** at SICK[1]

ail·ment (āl′mənt) *n.* an illness, esp. a mild one

aim (ām) *vi., vt.* [< OFr. *aesmer* < L. < *ad-*, to + *aestimare*, to ESTIMATE] **1.** to point (a weapon) or direct (a blow, remark, etc.) **2.** to direct (one's efforts) [we *aimed* at complete victory] **3.** to try or intend (*to* do or be) [aim to please] —*n.* **1.** the act of aiming **2.** the direction of a missile, blow, etc. **3.** intention or purpose —**take aim** to point a weapon, as by viewing along a sight

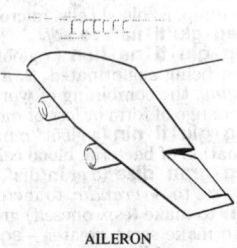
AILERON

aim·less (ām′ləs) *adj.* having no aim or purpose —**aim′less·ly** *adv.* —**aim′less·ness** *n.*

ain't (ānt) [early assimilation of *amn't*, contr. of *am not;* later confused with *a'nt* (are not), *i'nt* (is not), *ha'nt* (has not, have not)] [Colloq.] am not: also a dialectal or substandard contraction for *is not, are not, has not,* and *have not: ain't* was formerly standard for *am not* and is still sometimes defended as a useful contraction for *am not* in questions [I'm going too, *ain't* I?]

Ai·nu (ī'nōō) *n.* [Ainu, lit., man] **1.** *pl.* **-nus, -nu** a member of a native, light-skinned people of Japan **2.** their language, unrelated to any other

air (er) *n.* [< OFr. < L. *aer* < Gr. *aēr,* air, mist] **1.** the elastic, invisible mixture of gases (chiefly nitrogen and oxygen, as well as hydrogen, carbon dioxide, etc.) that surrounds the earth; atmosphere **2.** space above the earth; sky **3.** a movement of air; breeze; wind **4.** *same as* COMPRESSED AIR **5.** an outward appearance [an *air* of luxury] **6.** a person's manner or bearing **7.** [*pl.*] affected, superior manners **8.** public expression [give *air* to your opinions] **9.** transportation by aircraft **10.** the medium through which radio signals are transmitted: a figurative use **11.** a song or melody —*adj.* of aircraft, air forces, etc. [*air* power] —*vt.* **1.** to let air into or through **2.** to publicize —*vi.* to become aired, dried, etc. —see SYN. at MELODY —☆**give** (or **get**) **the air** [Slang] to reject (or be rejected) —**in the air 1.** prevalent **2.** not decided —**on** (or **off**) **the air** *Radio & TV* that is (or is not) broadcasting or being broadcast —**take the air** to go outdoors, as for fresh air —**up in the air** not settled or decided —**walk on air** to feel very happy or exalted

☆**air bag** a bag of nylon, plastic, etc. that inflates automatically within an automobile at the instant a collision occurs, to protect riders from being thrown forward

air base a base of operations for military aircraft

air bladder a sac with air or gas in it, found in most fishes and in some other animals and some plants

air·borne (er'bôrn') *adj.* **1.** carried by or through the air **2.** aloft or flying

☆**air brake** a brake operated by the action of compressed air on a piston

☆**air·brush** (er'brush') *n.* a kind of atomizer operated by compressed air and used for spraying on paint or other liquid: also **air brush** —*vt.* to spray with such an atomizer

air chamber a cavity or compartment full of air, esp. one used in hydraulics

air coach an airliner with lower passenger rates and less luxurious accommodations than first class

☆**air command** *U.S. Air Force* the largest organizational unit

☆**air conditioning** a method of filtering air and regulating its humidity and temperature in buildings, cars, planes, etc. —**air'-con·di'tion** *vt.* —**air conditioner**

air-cooled (er'kōōld') *adj.* cooled by having air passed over, into, or through it —**air'-cool'** *vt.*

air·craft (er'kraft') *n., pl.* **-craft'** any machine designed for flying, whether heavier or lighter than air; airplane, balloon, helicopter, etc.

aircraft carrier a warship that carries aircraft, with a large, flat deck for taking off and landing

air curtain (or **door**) a downward draft of air at an open entrance for keeping even temperatures within

☆**air·drome** (er'drōm') *n.* [AIR + -DROME] the physical facilities of an air base

air·drop (-dräp') *n.* the delivery of supplies or troops by parachute from an aircraft —*vt.* **-dropped', -drop'ping** to deliver by airdrop

Aire·dale (er'dāl') *n.* [after *Airedale* in Yorkshire, England] a large terrier having a hard, wiry, tan coat with black markings

☆**air express** a system for transporting packages rapidly by airlines

air·field (er'fēld') *n.* a field where aircraft can take off and land

☆**air·foil** (-foil') *n.* a part with a flat or curved surface, as a wing, rudder, etc., used to keep an aircraft up or control its movements

air force 1. the branch of the armed forces made up of the airplanes, men, etc. needed for air warfare **2.** *U.S. Air Force* a unit lower than an air command

AIREDALE
(23 in. high
at shoulder)

air gun 1. a gun operated by compressed air **2.** a gunlike device used to spray paint, insecticide, etc. by means of compressed air

air hole 1. a hole that permits passage of air **2.** an unfrozen or open place in the ice covering a body of water

air·i·ly (er'ə lē) *adv.* in an airy or gay, light manner; jauntily; breezily

air·i·ness (-ē nis) *n.* **1.** a being airy, or full of fresh air **2.** gay lightness; jauntiness

air·ing (-iŋ) *n.* **1.** exposure to the air, as for drying **2.** exposure to public knowledge [to give a scandal an *airing*] **3.** a walk or ride outdoors

air lane a prescribed route for travel by air; airway

air·less (-lis) *adj.* **1.** without air; esp., without fresh air [a musty, *airless* attic] **2.** without wind or breeze

air·lift (-lift') *n.* a system of transporting troops, supplies, etc. by aircraft, as when ground routes are blocked —*vt.* to transport by airlift

☆**air·line** (-līn') *n.* **1.** a direct line; beeline: also **air line 2.** a system or company for moving freight and passengers by aircraft **3.** a route for travel by air —*adj.* of or on an airline [*airline* personnel]

air·lin·er (-lī'nər) *n.* a large aircraft operated by an airline for carrying passengers

air lock an airtight compartment, with adjustable air pressure, between places that do not have the same air pressure

air·mail (-māl') *n.* **1.** the system of transporting mail by aircraft **2.** mail so transported —*vt.* to send by airmail

air·man (-mən) *n., pl.* **-men 1.** an aviator **2.** an enlisted man or woman in the U.S. Air Force, specif. one in any of the four lowest grades

air mass *Meteorol.* a large body of air having virtually uniform conditions of temperature and moisture in a horizontal cross section

air-mind·ed (er'mīn'dəd) *adj.* interested in or promoting aviation, aircraft, air power, etc.

air·plane (er'plān') *n.* an aircraft, heavier than air, that is kept aloft by the aerodynamic forces of air upon its wings and is driven forward by a screw propeller, by jet propulsion, etc.

air pocket an atmospheric condition that causes an aircraft to make sudden, short drops

air·port (-pôrt') *n.* a place where aircraft can land and take off, usually with facilities for repair, accommodations for passengers, etc.

air power total capacity of a nation for air war

air pressure the pressure of the atmosphere or of compressed air

air·proof (-prōōf') *adj.* that cannot be penetrated by air —*vt.* to make airproof

air pump a machine for removing or compressing air or for forcing it through something

air raid an attack by aircraft, esp. bombers

☆**air rifle** a rifle in which the force of compressed air is used to shoot BB's, etc.

air sac any of the air-filled cavities in a bird's body, having connections to the lungs

air shaft 1. a passage through which fresh air can enter a tunnel, mine, etc. **2.** *same as* AIR WELL

air·ship (-ship') *n.* any self-propelled aircraft that is lighter than air and can be steered

air·sick (-sik') *adj.* sick or nauseated from traveling in an aircraft —**air'sick'ness** *n.*

air·space (-spās') *n.* **1.** space for maneuvering an aircraft **2.** the space extending upward above a particular land area

air·speed (-spēd') *n.* the speed of an aircraft relative to the air rather than to the ground

air·strip (-strip') *n.* a hard-surfaced area used as a temporary airplane runway

☆**air taxi** a small or medium-sized airplane operated by an airline for carrying passengers, and often mail, to places not regularly served by scheduled airlines

air·tight (er'tīt') *adj.* **1.** too tight for air or gas to enter or escape **2.** giving no opening for attack; without weak points [an *airtight* alibi]

air-to-air (er'tə er') *adj.* fired from an aircraft at a target in the air [an *air-to-air* missile]

air-to-ground (-ground′) *adj.* fired from an aircraft at a target on land [an *air-to-ground* missile]

air·waves (-wāvz′) *n.pl.* the medium through which radio signals are transmitted

air·way (-wā′) *n.* 1. *same as:* a) AIR SHAFT (sense 1) b) AIR LANE c) [*pl.*] AIRWAVES 2. a passage for air, as to the lungs

☆**air well** an open shaft passing through the floors of a building, for ventilation

air·wor·thy (-wur′thē) *adj.* fit and safe to fly: said of aircraft —**air′wor′thi·ness** *n.*

air·y (er′ē) *adj.* **air′i·er**, **air′i·est** 1. of or in the air [the *airy* heights of the Alps] 2. open to the air; breezy [an *airy* room] 3. unsubstantial as air; not practical [*airy* schemes] 4. light as air; delicate; graceful [*airy* music] 5. lighthearted; gay [*airy* merriment] 6. flippant

aisle (īl) *n.* [< OFr. *aile:* see AILERON: the *-s-* is through confusion with ISLE] 1. a part of a church set off by a row of columns or piers 2. a passageway, as between rows of seats

Aisne (ān) river in N France: 175 mi.

Aix-la-Cha·pelle (eks lä shä pel′) *Fr. name for* AACHEN

A·jac·cio (ä yät′chō) chief city of Corsica: birthplace of Napoleon: pop. 41,000

a·jar[1] (ə jär′) *adv., adj.* [ME. *on char* < OE. *cier,* a turn: see CHORE] slightly open [the door stood *ajar*]

a·jar[2] *adv., adj.* [A-[1], on + JAR, *v.*] not in harmony

A·jax (ā′jaks) *Gr. Myth.* a Greek hero in the Trojan War

AK Alaska

a k a, a.k.a. also known as: used before an alias [George Decatur *a k a* George Destry]

a·kim·bo (ə kim′bō) *adv., adj.* [ME. *in kenebowe,* lit., in keen bow; a folk etym. < ON. < *keng,* bent + *bogi,* a bow] with hands on hips and elbows bent outward [with arms *akimbo*]

a·kin (ə kin′) *adj.* 1. of one kin, or family; related 2. having similar qualities; similar

Ak·ron (ak′rən) [< Gr. *akron,* highest point] city in N Ohio: pop. 275,000 (met. area 679,000)

-al (əl, 'l) [< Fr. < L. *-alis*] 1. *a suffix meaning* of, like, or suitable for [*comical, hysterical*] 2. *a suffix meaning* the act or process of [*avowal*] 3. [AL(DEHYDE)] *Chem. a suffix denoting:* a) an aldehyde [*chloral*] b) a barbiturate [*phenobarbital*]

Al *Chem.* aluminum

A.L. American League

a·la (ā′lə) *n., pl.* **a′lae** (-lē) [L., a wing] 1. *Zool.* a wing 2. a winglike structure, as the ear lobe

à la, a la (ä′lə, -lä; al′ə) [Fr.] in the manner or style of

Al·a·bam·a (al′ə bam′ə) [< Fr. < AmInd. tribal name] Southern State of SE U.S.: 51,609 sq. mi.; pop. 3,444,000; cap. Montgomery: abbrev. **Ala., AL** —**Al′a·bam′i·an** (-ē ən) *adj., n.*

al·a·bas·ter (al′ə bas′tər) *n.* [< OFr. < L. < Gr. < Egypt. name for "vessel of (the goddess) Bast"] 1. a translucent, whitish, fine-grained variety of gypsum 2. a streaked or mottled variety of calcite —**al′a·bas′trine** (-trin) *adj.*

a la carte (ä′lə kärt′, al′ə-) [Fr., by the bill of fare] with a separate price for each item on the menu: opposed to TABLE D'HÔTE

a·lack (ə lak′) *interj.* [A(H) + LACK] [Archaic] an exclamation of regret, surprise, dismay, etc.

a·lac·ri·ty (ə lak′rə tē) *n.* [< OFr. < L. < *alacer,* lively] eager willingness or readiness, often shown by quick, lively action [she ran to the door with *alacrity*] —**a·lac′ri·tous** *adj.*

A·lad·din (ə lad′'n) a boy in *The Arabian Nights* who found a magic lamp and a magic ring, with which he could call up a jinni to do his bidding

à la king (ä′lə kiŋ′) [lit., in kingly style] diced and served in a sauce containing mushrooms, pimentos, and green peppers

Al·a·me·da (al′ə mē′də, -mā′-) [Sp. < *álamo,* poplar tree] city on an island in San Francisco Bay, Calif.: pop. 71,000

Al·a·mo (al′ə mō′) [see prec.] Franciscan mission at San Antonio, Tex.: scene of a siege and massacre of Texans by Mexican troops (1836)

a la mode (al′ə mōd′, ä′lə) [Fr. *à la mode*] 1. in the fashion; stylish 2. made or served in a certain style, as (pie) with ice cream, or (beef) braised with vegetables in sauce Also **à la mode, alamode**

Al·an (al′ən) [ML. *Alanus,* of Breton origin] a masculine name

a·lar (ā′lər) *adj.* [< L. < *ala,* a wing] 1. of or like a wing 2. having wings

Al·a·ric (al′ə rik) 370–410 A.D.; king of the Visigoths (395?–410): captured Rome (410)

a·larm (ə lärm′) *n.* [< OFr. < It. *all'arme,* to arms] 1. [Archaic] a sudden call to arms 2. a signal, sound, etc. to warn of danger [a bugle was blown to sound the *alarm*] 3. a mechanism designed to warn of danger or trespassing [a burglar *alarm*] 4. the bell, buzzer, etc. of an alarm clock 5. fear caused by the sudden realization of danger —*vt.* 1. to warn of approaching danger 2. to make suddenly afraid or anxious

alarm clock a clock that can be set to ring, buzz, or flash a light at any particular time, as to awaken a person from sleep

a·larm·ing (-iŋ) *adj.* that alarms, or makes suddenly afraid; frightening [an *alarming* symptom] —**a·larm′ing·ly** *adv.*

a·larm·ist (-ist) *n.* 1. one who habitually spreads alarming rumors, etc. 2. one who usually expects the worst to happen — *adj.* of or like an alarmist

a·las (ə las′) *interj.* [< OFr. < *a,* ah + *las,* wretched < L. *lassus,* weary] an exclamation of sorrow, pity, regret, etc.

A·las·ka (ə las′kə) [< Esk. *Alákshak*] 1. State of the U.S. in northwestern N. America: 586,400 sq. mi.; pop. 302,000; cap. Juneau: abbrev. **Alas., AK** 2. **Gulf of,** inlet of the Pacific in the S coast of Alaska —**A·las′kan** *adj., n.*

Alaska Highway highway between E British Columbia, Canada, and Fairbanks, Alas.: 1,523 mi.

☆**Alaskan malamute** a large, strong dog, orig. of Alaska, with a thick coat and a bushy tail

Alaska Range mountain range in SC Alaska: highest peak, Mount McKINLEY

☆**Alaska Standard Time** *see* STANDARD TIME

a·late (ā′lāt) *adj.* [< L. < *ala,* a wing] having wings or winglike attachments: also **a′lat·ed**

alb (alb) *n.* [< OE. *albe,* ult. < L. *albus,* white] a long, white linen robe with sleeves tapering to the wrist, worn by a priest at Mass

al·ba·core (al′bə kôr′) *n., pl.* **-cores′, -core′:** see PLURAL, II, D, 1 [Port. < Ar. *al,* the + *bakūrah,* albacore] 1. *a*) a warm-water tuna with unusually long pectoral fins *b*) *same as* TUNA[1] 2. any of several related saltwater fishes, as the bonito

Al·ba·ni·a (al bā′nē ə, -bān′yə) country in the W Balkan Peninsula, on the Adriatic: 11,099 sq. mi.; pop. 2,019,000; cap. Tirana —**Al·ba′ni·an** *adj., n.*

Al·ba·ny (ôl′bə nē) [after the Duke of York and *Albany,* later JAMES II] 1. capital of N.Y., on the Hudson: pop. 115,000 2. city in SW Ga.: pop. 73,000

al·ba·tross (al′bə trôs′, -träs′) *n., pl.* **-tross′es, -tross′:** see PLURAL, II, D, 1 [< Sp. < Port. < Ar. *al qādūs,* water container < Gr. *kados,* cask; prob. < Heb. *kad,* water jug] 1. any of several large, web-footed sea birds related to the petrel 2. [from the bird used as a guilt symbol in a poem by S. T. COLERIDGE] a source of worry or trouble, esp. when it keeps one from doing things effectively: often in the phrase **an albatross around one's neck**

al·be·do (al bē′dō) *n.* [LL., whiteness < L. *albus,* white] 1. *Astron.* the reflecting power of a planet or satellite 2. *Physics* the degree to which a surface reflects cosmic rays or neutron currents that strike it

al·be·it (ôl bē′it, al-) *conj.* [ME. *al be it,* al(though) it be] although; even though

Al·be·marle Sound (al′bə märl′) [after G. Monk (1608–70), Duke of *Albemarle*] arm of the Atlantic extending into northeastern N.C.: see map at DISMAL SWAMP

Al·bé·niz (äl bā′nith, -nis), **Isaac** (**Manuel Francisco**) 1860–1909; Sp. composer & pianist

Al·bert (al′bərt) [Fr. < OHG. *Adalbrecht,* lit., bright through nobility] 1. a masculine name: dim. *Al, Bert;* var. *Adelbert, Elbert* 2. Prince (*Albert of Saxe-Coburg Gotha*) 1819–61; husband of Queen Victoria of England

Al·ber·ta (al bur′tə) [fem. of ALBERT] 1. a feminine name: var. *Albertina, Albertine* 2. [after Princess Louise *Alberta,* 4th daughter of Queen Victoria] province of SW Canada: 255,285 sq. mi.; pop. 1,838,000; cap. Edmonton: abbrev. **Alta.**

ARMS AKIMBO

ALB

ALBATROSS
(wingspread
to 7 ft.)

Al·bi·gen·ses (al'bə jen'sēz) *n.pl.* a religious sect in France c.1020–1250 A.D.: it was suppressed for heresy —**Al'bi·gen'si·an** (-sē ən) *adj., n.*

al·bi·no (al bi'nō) *n., pl.* **-nos** [< Port. < L. *albus*, white] **1.** a person whose skin, hair, and eyes lack normal coloring: albinos have a white skin, whitish hair, and pink eyes **2.** any animal or plant abnormally lacking in color —**al·bin'ic** (-bin'ik) *adj.* —**al·bi·nism** (al'bə niz'm) *n.*

Al·bi·on (al'bē ən) *poet.* name for ENGLAND

al·bum (al'bəm) *n.* [L., neut. of *albus*, white] **1.** a book with blank pages for mounting pictures, clippings, stamps, etc., or for collecting autographs **2.** *a*) a booklike holder for phonograph records *b*) a set of records in such a holder *c*) a single long-playing record, not part of a set **3.** an anthology, picture book, or the like

al·bu·men (al byōō'mən) *n.* [L. < *albus*, white] **1.** the white of an egg; nutritive substance surrounding the yolk **2.** *same as* ALBUMIN

al·bu·min (al byōō'mən) *n.* [ALBUM(EN) + -IN¹] any of a class of water-soluble proteins found in milk, egg, muscle, blood, and in many plants

al·bu·mi·nous (-mə nəs) *adj.* of, like, or containing albumin or albumen

Al·bu·quer·que (al'bə kur'kē) [after the Duke of *Albuquerque*, Mex. Viceroy (1702–11)] city in central N.Mex.: pop. 244,000

al·bur·num (al bur'nəm) *n.* [< L. < *albus*, white] *same as* SAPWOOD

Al·ca·traz (al'kə traz') [< Sp. *Isla de Alcatraces*, Island of Pelicans] small island in San Francisco Bay: site of a Federal prison (1934–63)

al·caz·ar (al'kə zär, al kaz'ər; *Sp.* äl kä'thär) *n.* [Sp. < Ar. *al-qasr*, the castle] a palace or fortress of the Moors in Spain; specif. [A-], such a palace in Seville, later used by the Spanish kings

al·che·mist (al'kə mist) *n.* one who practiced alchemy —**al'che·mis'tic, al'che·mis'ti·cal** *adj.*

al·che·my (al'kə mē) *n.* [< OFr. < ML. < Ar. *al-kīmiyā* < ? Gr. *cheein*, to pour] **1.** an early form of chemistry studied in the Middle Ages: its chief aims were to change the baser metals, as iron or lead, into gold and to find a substance that would keep people young forever **2.** a means of changing one thing into another; esp., the seemingly miraculous change of a thing into something better —**al·chem·ic** (al kem'ik), **al·chem'i·cal** *adj.* —**al·chem'i·cal·ly** *adv.*

Alc·me·ne (alk mē'nē) *see* AMPHITRYON

al·co·hol (al'kə hôl', -häl') *n.* [ML. < Ar. *al kuhl*, powder of antimony] **1.** a colorless, strong-smelling liquid, C_2H_5OH, that evaporates readily and burns with a hot flame: it is used in industry and medicine, and is the element in whiskey, wine, beer, etc. that causes intoxication: also called *ethyl alcohol* **2.** any intoxicating liquor with this liquid in it **3.** any of a series of similarly constructed organic compounds with a hydroxyl group, as methyl (or wood) alcohol

al·co·hol·ic (al'kə hôl'ik, -häl'-) *adj.* **1.** of, containing, or caused by alcohol **2.** suffering from alcoholism —*n.* one who has chronic alcoholism

al·co·hol·ism (al'kə hôl'iz'm, -häl'-) *n.* the habitual drinking of alcoholic liquor to excess, or a diseased condition caused by this

al·co·hol·ize (al'kə hôl īz', -häl-) *vt.* **-ized', -iz'ing** **1.** to saturate or treat with alcohol **2.** to convert into alcohol

Al·cott (ôl'kət), **Louisa May** 1832–88; U.S. novelist

al·cove (al'kōv) *n.* [Fr. < Sp. < Ar. < *al*, the + *qubba*, an arch, vault] **1.** a section of a room that is set back from the main part, as a breakfast nook **2.** a secluded bower in a garden

Ald., Aldm. Alderman

Al·deb·a·ran (al deb'ər ən) a brilliant red star in the constellation Taurus

al·de·hyde (al'də hīd') *n.* [< AL(COHOL) + L. *de*, without + HYD(ROGEN)] **1.** a colorless, volatile fluid, CH_3CHO, with a strong, unpleasant odor, obtained from alcohol by oxidation **2.** any of a class of organic compounds containing the CHO group, as formaldehyde —**al'de·hy'dic** (-hī'dik) *adj.*

Al·den (ôl'd'n), **John** 1599?–1687; Pilgrim settler in Plymouth Colony

al·der (ôl'dər) *n.* [< OE. *alor*] any of a group of trees and shrubs of the birch family, having durable wood and growing in cool, moist regions

al·der·man (ôl'dər mən) *n., pl.* **-men** [< OE. < *eald*, old + *man*, man] **1.** in some U.S. cities, a member of the municipal council, usually representing a certain district or ward **2.** in England and Ireland, a senior member of a county or borough council —**al'der·man·cy** (-sē) *n.* —**al'·der·man'ic** (-man'ik) *adj.*

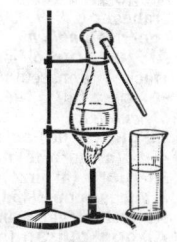

ALDER
(leaves & catkins)

Al·der·ney (ôl'dər nē) *n., pl.* **-neys** any of a breed of small dairy cattle originally from Alderney, one of the Channel Islands

al·do·ste·rone (al däs'tə rōn', al'dōs-) *n.* [< ALD(EHYDE) + STER(OL) + -ONE] a steroid hormone secreted by the adrenal cortex, that regulates the metabolism of sodium and potassium in the body

☆**al·drin** (al'drin) *n.* [G., after K. *Alder*, 20th-c. G. chemist] an insecticide especially effective against insects that are resistant to DDT

ale (āl) *n.* [< OE. *ealu*] a fermented drink made from malt and hops, like beer, but produced by rapid fermentation at a relatively high temperature

a·le·a·to·ry (ā'lē ə tôr'ē) *adj.* [< L. < *alea*, chance] depending on chance or luck: also **a'le·a·to'ric**

a·lee (ə lē') *adv., adj. Naut.* on or toward the side of a ship away from the wind; leeward

ale·house (āl'hous') *n.* a place where ale is sold and served; saloon; tavern

Aleichem, Sholom *see* SHOLOM ALEICHEM

Alembert, Jean le Rond d' *see* D'ALEMBERT

a·lem·bic (ə lem'bik) *n.* [< OFr. < ML. < Ar. < *al*, the + *anbīq*, a still < Gr. *ambix*, a cup] **1.** an apparatus of glass or metal, formerly used for distilling **2.** anything that refines or purifies

a·leph (ä'lif) *n.* [Heb., lit., ox, leader] the first letter of the Hebrew alphabet

A·lep·po (ə lep'ō) city in NW Syria: pop. 563,000

a·lert (ə lurt') *adj.* [< Fr. < It. *all' erta*, on the watch < L. *erigere*, to ERECT] **1.** watchful and ready, as in facing danger **2.** quick and active; nimble —*n.* **1.** a warning signal, as of an expected air raid **2.** the period when such a warning is in effect —*vt.* to warn to be ready or watchful [the troops were *alerted*] —see SYN. at INTELLIGENT and at WATCHFUL —**on the alert** watchful; vigilant —**a·lert'ly** *adv.* —**a·lert'ness** *n.*

ALEMBIC

A·leut (ə lōōt', al'ōōt) *n.* [< Russ. < ? native name] **1.** *pl.* **A·leuts', A·leut'** any of a native people of the Aleutian Islands and parts of mainland Alaska **2.** either of the two languages of these people

A·leu·tian (ə lōō'shən) *adj.* **1.** of the Aleutian Islands **2.** of the Aleuts, their culture, etc. —*n. same as* ALEUT

Aleutian Islands chain of islands of Alaska, extending c. 1,200 miles from the SW coast: see map at BERING SEA

ale·wife (āl'wīf') *n., pl.* **-wives'** (-wīvz') [< ?] ☆an edible N. American fish resembling the herring

Al·ex·an·der (al'ig zan'dər) [< L. < Gr. *alexein*, to defend + *andros*, gen. of *anēr*, man] a masculine name: dim. *Alex* **2. Alexander II** 1818–81; czar of Russia (1855–81): son of NICHOLAS I

Alexander Nev·ski (nef'skē) 1220?–63; Russ. military hero, statesman, & saint

Alexander the Great 356–323 B.C.; king of Macedonia (336–323); military conqueror

Al·ex·an·dri·a (al'ig zan'drē ə) **1.** seaport in Egypt, on the Mediterranean: pop. 1,513,000 **2.** [< prec., but with allusion to the *Alexander* family, owners of the town site] city in NE Va., near Washington, D.C.: pop. 111,000

Al·ex·an·dri·an (-ən) *adj.* **1.** of Alexander the Great **2.** of Alexandria, Egypt **3.** *same as* ALEXANDRINE

al·ex·an·drine (al'ig zan'drin) *n.* [*occas.* **A-**] an iambic line of poetry having six feet; iambic hexameter —*adj.* of an alexandrine or alexandrines

a·lex·i·a (ə lek'sē ə) *n.* [ModL. < Gr. *a-*, without + *lexis*, speech < *legein*, to speak] a loss of the ability to read, caused by brain injury

al·fal·fa (al fal'fə) *n.* [Sp. < Ar. *al-faṣfaṣah*, the best fodder] a deep-rooted plant of the legume family, grown throughout the U.S. for fodder, pasture, and as a cover crop

‡al fi·ne (äl fē'ne) [It.] *Music* to the end (of a repeated section)

Al·fred (al'frid) [OE. *Ælfred*, lit., wise counselor] a masculine name: dim. *Al, Alf*

Alfred the Great 849–900? A.D.; king of Wessex (871–900?); promoted English culture

al·fres·co (al fres'kō) *adv.* [It. < *al* (for *a il*), in the + *fresco*, fresh, cool] in the open air; outdoors —*adj.* outdoor Also **al fresco**

Alg. 1. Algeria 2. Algerian

alg. algebra

al·gae (al'jē) *n.pl., sing.* **al'ga** (-gə) [pl. of L. *alga*, seaweed] a group of plants, either one-celled or many-celled, often growing in colonies: algae contain chlorophyll and other pigments, but have no true root, stem, or leaf: they are found in water or damp places and include seaweed, pond scum, etc. —**al'gal** (-gəl) *adj.*

☆**al·gae·cide** (al'jə sīd') *n.* [ALGAE + -CIDE] a substance used to prevent or get rid of algae

al·ge·bra (al'jə brə) *n.* [ML. < Ar. < *al*, the + *jabr*, reunion of broken parts] a form of mathematics used to carry out certain arithmetical operations by permitting letters or other symbols to stand for numbers: it is used esp. in the solution of polynomial equations: see also BOOLEAN ALGEBRA —**al'ge·bra'ist** *n.*

al·ge·bra·ic (al'jə brā'ik) *adj.* of, like, or used in algebra —**al'ge·bra'i·cal·ly** *adv.*

Al·ger (al'jər), **Horatio** 1832–99; U.S. writer of boys' stories

Al·ge·ri·a (al jir'ē ə) country in N Africa, on the Mediterranean: c. 919,000 sq. mi.; pop. 13,547,000; cap. Algiers —**Al·ge'ri·an** *adj., n.*

Al·ger·non (al'jər nən) [prob. < OFr. *al grenon*, with a mustache] a masculine name: dim. *Algie, Algy*

-al·gi·a (al'jə, -jē ə) [< Gr. *algos*, pain] a suffix meaning pain [*neuralgia*]

al·gid (al'jid) *adj.* [< Fr. < L. *algidus*] cold; chilly —**al·gid·i·ty** (al jid'ə tē) *n.*

Al·giers (al jirz') capital of Algeria; seaport on the Mediterranean: pop. 943,000

Al·gol (al'gäl) a bright variable star in the constellation Perseus

Al·gon·qui·an (al gän'kē ən, -kwē-) *adj.* designating or of a widespread family of languages used by a number of N. American Indian tribes, including the Arapaho, Cheyenne, Blackfoot, etc. —*n.* 1. this family of languages 2. a member of any tribe using one of these languages

Al·gon·quin (al gän'kwin, -kin) *n.* [< AmInd.] 1. a member of a tribe of Algonquian Indians who live in the area of the Ottawa River, Canada 2. their Algonquian language

al·go·rism (al'gər iz'm) *n.* [< ME. & OFr. < ML. *algorismus* < name of 9th-c. Ar. mathematician] a system of counting; esp., the decimal system

al·go·rithm (al'gər ith'm) *n.* [altered (after ARITHMETIC) < prec.] *Math.* any special method of solving a certain kind of problem; specif., the repetitive calculations used in finding the greatest common divisor of two numbers

Al·ham·bra (al ham'brə) [Sp. < Ar. *al ḥamrā*, lit., the red (house)] 1. early palace of the Moorish kings near Granada, Spain 2. city in SW Calif.: pop. 62,000 —**Al·ham·bresque'** (-bresk') *adj.*

a·li·as (ā'lē əs, āl'yəs) *n., pl.* **a'li·as·es** [< L. *alius*, other] a name assumed by a person to hide who he really is —*adv.* having the alias of [John Bell *alias* Joe Brown]

A·li Ba·ba (ä'lē bä'bə, al'ē bab'ə) in *The Arabian Nights*, a poor woodcutter who finds the treasure of forty thieves in a cave

al·i·bi (al'ə bī') *n., pl.* **-bis'** [L., contr. < *alius ibi*, elsewhere] 1. *Law* the plea or fact that an accused person was elsewhere than at the scene of the crime ☆2. [Colloq.] an excuse —*vi.* **-bied'**, **-bi'ing** [Colloq.] to offer an excuse

Al·ice (al'is) [< OFr. < OHG. *Adalheit*: see ADELAIDE] a feminine name: dim. *Elsie*; var. *Alicia*

al·ien (āl'yən, -ē ən) *adj.* [< OFr. < L. *alienus* < *alius*, other] 1. belonging to another country or people; foreign 2. not natural; strange [*foods* alien to their diet] 3. opposed or repugnant [*cruelty* was alien to his nature] 4. of aliens —*n.*

1. a foreigner 2. a resident in a country who is not a citizen of it 3. an outsider —see SYN. at EXTRINSIC

al·ien·a·ble (-ə b'l) *adj.* capable of being transferred to a new owner —**al'ien·a·bil'i·ty** *n.*

al·ien·ate (-āt') *vt.* **-at'ed**, **-at'ing** 1. to transfer the ownership of (property) to another 2. to make unfriendly; estrange [behavior that *alienated* his friends] 3. to cause to be withdrawn or detached, as from society 4. to cause (one's affection) to be transferred to another —**al'ien·a'tion** *n.* —**al'ien·a'tor** *n.*

al·ien·ee (āl'yə nē', āl'ē ə-) *n.* a person to whom property is transferred or conveyed

al·ien·ist (āl'yən ist, āl'ē ən-) *n.* a psychiatrist, esp. one who testifies in a law court

al·ien·or (-ôr', -ər) *n.* a person from whom property is transferred or conveyed

al·i·form (al'ə fôrm', ā'lə-) *adj.* [< L. *ala*, a wing + -FORM] shaped like a wing

a·light¹ (ə līt') *vi.* **a·light'ed** or **a·lit'**, **a·light'ing** [< ME. < *a-*, out, off + *lihtan*, to dismount] 1. to get down or off; dismount [she *alighted* from her horse] 2. to come down after flight; settle [the bird *alighted* on the ground]

a·light² (ə līt') *adj.* lighted up; glowing [a face *alight* with joy]

a·lign (ə līn') *vt.* [< Fr. < *a*, to + *ligner* < *ligne*, LINE¹] 1. to bring into a straight line 2. to bring (parts, as the wheels of a car) into proper coordination 3. to bring into agreement, close cooperation, etc. [he *aligned* himself with the liberals] —*vi.* to come into line; line up

a·lign·ment (-mənt) *n.* 1. an aligning or being aligned; esp., *a*) arrangement in a straight line *b*) a condition of close cooperation [a new *alignment* of European nations] 2. a line or lines formed by aligning

a·like (ə līk') *adj.* [< OE. *gelic, onlike*: see A-¹ & LIKE¹] like one another; similar: usually in the predicate [they look *alike*] —*adv.* 1. in the same manner; similarly [they dress *alike*] 2. to the same degree; equally [they are treated *alike*] —**a·like'ness** *n.*

al·i·ment (al'ə mənt) *n.* [L. *alimentum* < *alere*, to nourish] 1. anything that nourishes; food 2. means of support —**al'i·men'tal** (-men't'l) *adj.*

al·i·men·ta·ry (al'ə men'tər ē) *adj.* [see prec.] 1. connected with food or nutrition 2. nourishing

alimentary canal (or **tract**) the passage in the body through which food passes to be digested: it extends from the mouth to the anus

al·i·men·ta·tion (al'ə men tā'shən) *n.* 1. nourishment; nutrition 2. support; sustenance

al·i·mo·ny (al'ə mō'nē) *n.* [< L. < *alere*, to nourish] an allowance paid, esp. to a woman, by the spouse or former spouse after a legal separation or divorce

a·line (ə līn') *vt., vi.* **a·lined'**, **a·lin'ing** *same as* ALIGN —**a·line'ment** *n.*

al·i·quant (al'ə kwənt) *adj.* [< L. *alius*, other + *quantus*, how much] *Math.* that does not divide a number evenly but leaves a remainder [8 is an *aliquant* part of 25]: see ALIQUOT

al·i·quot (al'ə kwət) *adj.* [L. < *alius*, other + *quot*, how many] *Math.* that divides a number evenly and leaves no remainder [8 is an *aliquot* part of 24]: see ALIQUANT

Al·i·son (al'ə s'n) [< OFr.: see ALICE] a feminine name

a·lit (ə lit') *alt. pt. & pp. of* ALIGHT¹

a·live (ə līv') *adj.* [< OE. *on*, in + *life*, life] [usually used in the predicate] 1. having life; living 2. in existence, operation, etc. [to keep his memory *alive*] 3. lively; alert [*Alive* is used as an interjection in such phrases as man *alive!* sakes *alive!* etc. —see SYN. at LIVING —**alive to** fully aware of; perceiving —**alive with** teeming with; full of [streets *alive* with bicyclists]

a·liz·a·rin (ə liz'ər in) *n.* [G., ult. < Ar. *al aṣārah*, the juice < *aṣara*, to press] a reddish-yellow crystalline compound, $C_{14}H_8O_4$, used in dyes: also **a·liz'a·rine** (-in, -ēn')

ALIMENTARY CANAL (A, gallbladder; B, liver; C, appendix; D, esophagus; E, stomach; F, spleen; G, pancreas; H, colon; I, rectum; J, anus; K, small intestine)

al·ka·li (al′kə lī′) *n., pl.* **-lies′, -lis′** [< Ar. *al*, the + *qili*, ashes (of saltwort)] **1.** any base or hydroxide, as soda, potash, etc., that gives a high concentration of hydroxyl ions in solution **2.** any soluble mineral salt or mixture of salts found in desert soils and capable of neutralizing acids

alkali metals the group of metallic chemical elements consisting of lithium, sodium, potassium, rubidium, cesium, and francium

al·ka·line (al′kə lin, -līn′) *adj.* of, like, or containing an alkali; basic —**al′ka·lin′i·ty** (-lin′ə tē) *n.*

al·ka·line-earth metals (al′kə lin ʉrth′, -līn′-) a group of metallic chemical elements, including calcium, strontium, barium, and sometimes beryllium, magnesium, and radium: the oxides of these metals are called **alkaline earths**

al·ka·lin·ize (al′kə lə nīz′) *vt.* **-ized′, -iz′ing** *same as* ALKALIZE

al·ka·lize (al′kə līz′) *vt.* **-lized′, -liz′ing** to make alkaline —**al′ka·li·za′tion** *n.*

al·ka·loid (-loid′) *n.* [ALKAL(I) + -OID] any of a number of colorless, bitter, basic organic substances, as caffeine, morphine, quinine, etc., found in certain plants —**al′ka·loid′al** *adj.*

al·kane (al′kān) *n.* [ALK(YL) + (METH)ANE] any hydrocarbon of the methane series

Al·ko·ran (al′kō ran′, -rän′) *n.* the Koran

al·kyd (al′kid) *n.* [ult. < ALKALI + ACID] any of several synthetic resins used as coatings, and in paints, varnishes, etc.: also **alkyd resin**

all (ôl) *adj.* [OE. *eall*] **1.** the whole quantity, extent, or number of [*all* the gold, *all* day] **2.** every one of [*all* men must eat] **3.** the greatest possible [said in *all* sincerity] **4.** any; any whatever [true beyond *all* question] **5.** every [*all* manner of men] **6.** alone; only [life is not *all* pleasure] **7.** seeming to be nothing but [he was *all* arms and legs] —*pron.* **1.** [*with pl. v.*] everyone [*all* are present] **2.** [*with pl. v.*] every one [*all* of us are going] **3.** everything [*all* is over between them] **4.** every part or bit [*all* of it is eaten] —*n.* everything one has [give your *all*] —*adv.* **1.** wholly; entirely [*all* worn out] **2.** apiece [a score of thirty *all*] —**after all** nevertheless; in spite of everything —**all but 1.** all except **2.** nearly; almost —☆**all in** [Colloq.] very tired —**all in all 1.** considering everything **2.** as a whole —**all over 1.** ended **2.** everywhere **3.** [Colloq.] typically [that's Mary *all over*] —**all the (better, worse,** etc.) so much the (better, worse, etc.) —**all the (farther, closer,** etc.) [Colloq. or Dial.] as (far, close, etc.) as —**all the same 1.** nevertheless **2.** of no importance —**at all 1.** in the least; to the slightest degree **2.** in any way **3.** under any conditions —**for all** in spite of —**in all** altogether

all- *a combining form meaning:* **1.** wholly; entirely; exclusively [*all*-American] **2.** for every [*all*-purpose] **3.** of every part [*all*-inclusive]

Al·lah (al′ə, ä′lə, ä lä′) [Ar. *Allāh* < *al*, the + *ilāh*, god] *the Moslem name for* GOD

Al·la·ha·bad (al′ə hä bäd′) city in N India, on the Ganges: pop. 431,000

☆**all-A·mer·i·can** (ôl′ə mer′ə kən) *adj.* **1.** made up wholly of Americans or of American elements **2.** representative of the U.S. as a whole, or chosen as best in the U.S. **3.** of all the Americas —*n.* **1.** a hypothetical football (or other) team of college players voted the best of the year in the U.S. **2.** a player chosen for such a team

Al·lan (al′ən) *var. of* ALAN

☆**all-a·round** (ôl′ə round′) *adj.* having many abilities, talents, or uses; versatile

al·lay (ə lā′) *vt.* **-layed′, -lay′ing** [< OE. < *a-*, down + *lecgan*, to lay] **1.** to put (fears, etc.) to rest; calm **2.** to lessen or relieve (pain, etc.) —see SYN. at RELIEVE

all-clear (ôl′klir′) *n.* a siren or other signal that an air raid or practice alert is over

al·le·ga·tion (al′ə gā′shən) *n.* **1.** an alleging **2.** something alleged; assertion **3.** a statement made without proof **4.** *Law* a statement made by a person who proposes to support it with evidence

al·lege (ə lej′) *vt.* **-leged′, -leg′ing** [ME. *aleggen*, to produce as evidence < OFr., ult. < L. *ex-*, out of + *litigare*: see LITIGATE] **1.** to state positively, or declare, esp. without proof **2.** to give as a plea, excuse, etc. [in his defense, he *alleged* that he was merely following orders] —**al·lege′a·ble** *adj.* —**al·leg′er** *n.*

al·leged (ə lejd′, ə lej′id) *adj.* **1.** so declared, but without proof [the *alleged* assassin] **2.** so-called [his *alleged* friends] —**al·leg′ed·ly** *adv.*

Al·le·ghe·ny (al′ə gā′nē) [< AmInd. < ?] river in W Pa., joining the Monongahela to form the Ohio: 325 mi.

Allegheny Mountains mountain range of the Appalachians, in C Pa., Md., Va., and W.Va.: also **Al′le·ghe′nies**

al·le·giance (ə lē′jəns) *n.* [< OFr. *a-*, to + *ligeance* < *liege*: see LIEGE] **1.** the obligation to support and be loyal to one's ruler or country **2.** loyalty or devotion, as to a cause, person, etc. —**al·le′giant** (-jənt) *adj., n.*

SYN.—*allegiance* refers to a citizen's duty to his government or a similar obligation to support a cause, leader, etc.; *fidelity* suggests strong faithfulness to an obligation, trust, etc.; *loyalty* suggests a firm and unquestioning devotion that one may feel for one's family, friends, or country; *fealty*, now chiefly a literary word, suggests faithfulness that one has sworn to uphold, as that of a vassal to his lord —**ANT.** faithlessness, disaffection

al·le·gor·i·cal (al′ə gôr′i k'l, -gär′-) *adj.* **1.** of or characteristic of allegory **2.** that is or contains an allegory Also **al′le·gor′ic** —**al′le·gor′i·cal·ly** *adv.*

al·le·go·rist (al′ə gôr′ist, -gər ist) *n.* one who writes allegories

al·le·go·rize (al′ə gə rīz′) *vt.* **-rized′, -riz′ing 1.** to make into or treat as an allegory **2.** to interpret in an allegorical sense —*vi.* to make or use allegories —**al′le·go·ri·za′tion** *n.* —**al′le·go·riz′er** *n.*

al·le·go·ry (al′ə gôr′ē) *n., pl.* **-ries** [< L. < Gr. < *allos*, other + *agoreuein*, to speak < *agora*, AGORA¹] **1.** a story in which people, things, and events have a hidden or symbolic meaning besides the one that is readily seen: allegories are used for teaching or explaining ideas, moral principles, etc. **2.** the presenting of ideas by such stories

al·le·gret·to (al′ə gret′ō) *adj., adv.* [It., dim. of ALLEGRO] *Music* moderately fast; somewhat slower than *allegro* —*n., pl.* **-tos** an allegretto movement or passage

al·le·gro (ə leg′rō, -lā′grō) *adj., adv.* [It. < L. *alacer*, brisk] *Music* fast, but not so fast as *presto* —*n., pl.* **-gros** a fast movement or passage

al·lele (ə lēl′) *n.* [G. *allel* < Gr. *allēlōn*, of one another] either of a pair of genes in the same position on both members of a pair of chromosomes and bearing characters inherited alternatively according to Mendelian law: also **al·le·lo·morph** (ə lel′ə môrf′, ə lē′lə-) —**al·le·lic** (ə lel′ik, ə lē′lik) *adj.*

al·le·lu·ia (al′ə lōō′yə) *interj., n. same as* HALLELUJAH

Al·len (al′ən) *var. of* ALAN

Al·len·town (al′ən toun′) [after Wm. *Allen*, the founder] city in E Pa.: pop. 110,000

☆**al·ler·gen** (al′ər jən) *n.* [G. < *allergie*, ALLERGY + -*gen*, -GEN] a substance causing an allergic state or reaction —**al′ler·gen′ic** (-jen′ik) *adj.*

☆**al·ler·gic** (ə lʉr′jik) *adj.* **1.** of or caused by allergy **2.** having an allergy **3.** unwilling or not inclined (*to*): a humorous usage [*allergic* to study]

☆**al·ler·gist** (al′ər jist) *n.* a doctor who specializes in treating allergies

☆**al·ler·gy** (al′ər jē) *n., pl.* **-gies** [< G. < Gr. *allos*, other + -*ergeia*, as in *energeia* (see ENERGY)] **1.** abnormal sensitivity to a specific substance (such as a food, pollen, dust, etc.) or condition (as heat or cold) that is not harmful to most people **2.** a strong dislike

al·le·vi·ate (ə lē′vē āt′) *vt.* **-at′ed, -at′ing** [< LL. pp. of *alleviare* < L. < *ad-*, to + *levis*, LIGHT²] **1.** to make less hard to bear; relieve (pain, etc.) **2.** to reduce or decrease [to *alleviate* poverty] —see SYN. at RELIEVE —**al·le′vi·a′tion** *n.* —**al·le′vi·a′tive** *adj.* —**al·le′vi·a′tor** *n.*

al·ley (al′ē) *n., pl.* **-leys** [< OFr. *alee*, a going < *aler* (Fr. *aller*), to go < ML. < L. *ambulare*, to walk] **1.** a lane in a garden or park **2.** a narrow street or walk; specif., a lane behind a row of buildings **3.** *Bowling* **a)** the long, narrow lane along which the balls are rolled: now usually LANE **b)** [*occas. pl.*] a bowling establishment —☆**up** (or **down**) **one's alley** [Slang] suited to one's tastes or abilities

☆**al·ley·way** (al′ē wā′) *n.* **1.** an alley between buildings **2.** any narrow passageway

All Fools' Day *same as* APRIL FOOLS' DAY

All·hal·lows (ôl′hal′ōz) *n.* [< OE. *ealle halgan*: see ALL & HALLOW] [Archaic] *same as* ALL SAINTS' DAY

---

fat, āpe, cär; ten, ēven; is, bīte; gō, hôrn, tōōl, lōōk; oil, out; up, fʉr; get; joy; yet; chin; she; thin, then; zh, leisure; ŋ, ring; ə for *a* in *ago*, *e* in *agent*, *i* in *sanity*, *o* in *comply*, *u* in *focus*; ' as in *able* (ā′b'l); Fr. bàl; ë, Fr. coeur; ö, Fr. feu; Fr. mon; ô, Fr. coq; ü, Fr. duc; r, Fr. cri; H, G. ich; kh, G. doch; ‡foreign; ☆ Americanism; < derived from. See inside front cover.

al·li·ance (ə lī′əns) *n.* [< OFr. < *alier:* see ALLY] **1.** an allying or being allied; specif., a union, as of families by marriage **2.** *a)* a close association for a common goal, as of nations, parties, etc. *b)* the agreement for such an association *c)* the countries, groups, etc. in such association **3.** a joining by some relationship in characteristics

SYN.—**alliance** refers to any association entered into for mutual benefit; **league** stresses a formal organization and a definite purpose; a **coalition** is a temporary alliance of parties usually opposed to one another; **confederacy** and **confederation** refer to an association of independent states under a central government that has only certain functions, as defense or customs; a **federation** is a league of states or organizations that give up part of their independence to a central authority; **union** implies a close, permanent alliance in a single political entity

al·lied (ə līd′; *also, esp. for 3,* al′īd) *adj.* **1.** united by kinship, treaty, etc. **2.** closely related [*allied* sciences] **3.** [A-] of the Allies

Al·lies (al′īz, ə līz′) *n.pl.* **1.** in World War I, the nations allied by treaty against Germany and the other Central Powers; orig., Great Britain, France, and Russia, later joined by the U.S., Italy, Japan, etc. **2.** in World War II, the nations associated against the Axis; esp., Great Britain, the Soviet Union, and the U.S.: see UNITED NATIONS

al·li·ga·tor (al′ə gāt′ər) *n.* [< Sp. *el,* the + *lagarto* < L. *lacerta,* LIZARD] **1.** a large reptile of the crocodile group, found in tropical rivers and marshes of the U.S. and in China **2.** a scaly leather made from its hide

alligator pear *same as* AVOCADO

all-im·por·tant (ôl′im pôr′t'nt) *adj.* essential

al·lit·er·ate (ə lit′ə rāt′) *vi., vt.* -at′ed, -at′ing to show or cause to show alliteration

ALLIGATOR
(8–12 ft. long)

al·lit·er·a·tion (ə lit′ə rā′shən) *n.* [< ML. < L. *ad-,* to + *littera,* letter] repetition of a beginning sound, usually of a consonant, in two or more words of a phrase, line of poetry, etc. (Ex.: "Full *f*athom *f*ive thy *f*ather lies")

al·lit·er·a·tive (ə lit′ə rāt′iv, -ər ə tiv) *adj.* of, showing, or using alliteration —**al·lit′er·a′tive·ly** *adv.*

al·lo- [< Gr. *allos,* other] *a combining form meaning* different, variant [*allotropy*]

al·lo·cate (al′ə kāt′) *vt.* -cat′ed, -cat′ing [< ML. pp. of *allocare* < L. *ad-,* to + *locus,* a place] **1.** to set apart for a specific purpose [to *allocate* funds for housing] **2.** to distribute in shares; allot [*allocate* the cost among the departments] —see SYN. at ALLOT —**al′lo·ca′tion** *n.*

al·lom·er·ism (ə läm′ər iz′m) *n.* [< ALLO- + Gr. *meros,* part + -ISM] variation in chemical makeup without change in crystalline form —**al·lom′er·ous** *adj.*

al·lo·morph (al′ə môrf′) *n.* [ALLO- + -MORPH] any of the variant forms of a morpheme [the *-es* of *boxes* and the *-s* of *cats* are *allomorphs* of the plural ending]

al·lo·path (al′ə path′) *n.* a person who practices or advocates allopathy: also **al·lop·a·thist** (ə läp′ə thist)

al·lop·a·thy (ə läp′ə thē) *n.* [< G.: see ALLO- & -PATHY] treatment of disease by remedies that produce effects different from those produced by the disease: opposed to HOMEOPATHY —**al·lo·path·ic** (al′ə path′ik) *adj.* —**al′lo·path′i·cal·ly** *adv.*

al·lo·phone (al′ə fōn′) *n.* [ALLO- + PHONE¹] any of the variant forms of a phoneme [the sounds of *d* in *dog* and *lid* are *allophones* of (d)]

al·lot (ə lät′) *vt.* -lot′ted, -lot′ting [OFr. *aloter* < *a-,* to + *lot,* lot] **1.** to distribute by lot or in shares; apportion [the land was *allotted* equally to all] **2.** to give or assign as one's share [each speaker is *allotted* five minutes]

SYN.—**allot** and **assign** both imply the giving of a share or portion with no indication of even division; **assign** also suggesting greater authority [I was *assigned* the task of *allotting* seats]; **apportion** suggests the fair, often even, distribution of a fixed number of portions [state legislatures must be *apportioned* on the basis of population]; **allocate** usually suggests the allotment of a fixed amount for a specific purpose [Congress *allocated* funds for pollution control]

al·lot·ment (-mənt) *n.* **1.** an allotting or being allotted **2.** a thing allotted; portion

al·lo·trope (al′ə trōp′) *n.* an allotropic form

al·lo·trop·ic (al′ə träp′ik) *adj.* of or having allotropy: also **al′lo·trop′i·cal** —**al′lo·trop′i·cal·ly** *adv.*

al·lot·ro·py (ə lät′rə pē) *n.* [< Gr. < ALLO- + *tropos,* way, manner] the property that certain chemical elements have of existing in two or more different forms, as carbon in the form of charcoal, diamond, etc.: also **al·lot′ro·pism**

al·lot·tee (ə lät′ē′) *n.* a person to whom something is allotted

all-out (ôl′out′) *adj.* complete or wholehearted [an *all-out* effort]

al·low (ə lou′) *vt.* [< OFr. *alouer* < ML. < L. < *ad-,* to + *locus,* a place: associated with OFr. *alouer* < L. *ad-,* to + *laudare,* to praise] **1.** to let do, happen, etc.; permit [*allow* me to thank you] **2.** to let have [they *allowed* him no vacation] **3.** to let enter [dogs not *allowed*] **4.** to admit (a claim or the like); acknowledge as true **5.** to provide or allot (an amount, period, etc.) for a purpose [*allow* an inch for shrinkage] **6.** [Dial.] to think; give as one's opinion —see SYN. at LET¹ —**allow for** to keep in mind [*allow for* the difference in time] —**allow of** to be subject to; admit of

al·low·a·ble (-ə b'l) *adj.* that can be allowed; permissible —**al·low′a·bly** *adv.*

al·low·ance (-əns) *n.* **1.** an allowing, permitting, etc. **2.** something allowed; specif., an amount of money given regularly, as to a child, or for a specific purpose, as to a soldier [travel *allowance*] **3.** a reduction in price in return for a large order, a trade-in, etc. —*vt.* -anced, -anc·ing to put on an allowance —**make allowance** (or **allowances**) to take circumstances into consideration —**make allowance** (or **allowances**) **for 1.** to keep in mind things that will help explain or excuse (something) **2.** to leave room, time, etc. for

al·low·ed·ly (ə lou′id lē) *adv.* admittedly

al·loy (al′oi; *also, and for v. usually,* ə loi′) *n.* [< Anglo-Fr. < OFr. < L. *alligare:* see ALLY] **1.** a substance that is a mixture of two or more metals, or of a metal and something else **2.** *a)* formerly, a less valuable metal mixed with a more valuable one, often to give hardness *b)* something that lowers the value of another thing when mixed with it —*vt.* **1.** to make (a metal) less pure by mixing with a less valuable metal **2.** to mix (metals) to form an alloy **3.** to make less valuable by mixing with something inferior

all-pur·pose (ôl′pur′pəs) *adj.* useful in many ways

all right 1. satisfactory; adequate [your work is *all right*] **2.** unhurt; safe **3.** correct **4.** yes; very well [*all right*, I'll do it] **5.** [Colloq.] certainly [he's the one, *all right*]

all-round (ôl′round′) *adj. same as* ALL-AROUND

All Saints' Day an annual church festival (November 1) in honor of all the saints

All Souls' Day in some Christian churches, a day (usually November 2) of prayer for the dead

all·spice (ôl′spīs′) *n.* **1.** the berry of a West Indian tree of the myrtle family **2.** the spice made from this berry: its flavor seems to combine the tastes of several spices **3.** the tree itself

☆**all-star** (-stär′) *adj.* made up entirely of outstanding or star performers

all-time (-tīm′) *adj.* not exceeded or surpassed up to the present time [an *all-time* record]

al·lude (ə lood′) *vi.* -lud′ed, -lud′ing [L. *alludere,* to jest < *ad-,* to + *ludere,* to play: for IE. base see LUDICROUS] to refer in a casual or indirect way (*to*) —see SYN. at REFER

al·lure (ə loor′) *vt., vi.* -lured′, -lur′ing [< OFr. < *a-,* to + *lurer,* to LURE] to tempt with something desirable; attract; entice —*n.* the power of alluring; fascination —see SYN. at ATTRACT

al·lure·ment (-mənt) *n.* **1.** an alluring or tempting **2.** fascination; charm **3.** something that allures

al·lur·ing (ə loor′iŋ) *adj.* tempting strongly; highly attractive; charming —**al·lur′ing·ly** *adv.*

al·lu·sion (ə loo′zhən) *n.* **1.** an alluding **2.** an indirect reference; casual mention

al·lu·sive (ə loos′iv) *adj.* **1.** containing an allusion **2.** using allusion; full of allusions —**al·lu′sive·ly** *adv.* —**al·lu′sive·ness** *n.*

al·lu·vi·al (ə loo′vē əl) *adj.* of, composed of, or found in alluvium —*n. same as* ALLUVIUM

al·lu·vi·um (ə loo′vē əm) *n.* -vi·ums, -vi·a (-vē ə) [< L. < *alluere* < *ad-,* to + *luere,* to LAVE] sand, clay, etc. gradually deposited by moving water, as along a river bed

al·ly (ə lī′; *also, and for n. usually,* al′ī) *vt.* -lied′, -ly′ing [< OFr. *alier* < L. *alligare* < *ad-,* to + *ligare,* to bind] **1.** to unite (families) by marriage, (nations) by treaty, etc. **2.** to relate by similarity of structure, qualities, etc.: usually in the passive [the onion is *allied* to the lily] —*vi.* to become allied —*n., pl.* -lies **1.** a country or person joined with another for a common purpose: see also ALLIES **2.** a plant, animal, or thing closely related in structure, etc. to another **3.** an associate; helper —see SYN. at ASSOCIATE

Al·ma (al′mə) [L. fem. of *almus*, nourishing] a feminine name

al·ma ma·ter (al′mə mät′ər, mät′ər) [L., fostering mother] **1.** the college or school that one attended **2.** its anthem, or hymn

al·ma·nac (ôl′mə nak′, al′-) *n.* [< ML. < LGr. *almenichiaka*, calendar] **1.** a calendar with astronomical data, weather forecasts, etc. **2.** a book published annually, containing information, usually statistical, on many subjects

al·might·y (ôl mīt′ē) *adj.* [< OE. < *eal*, all + *mihtig*, mighty] **1.** having unlimited power; all-powerful **2.** [Slang] great; extreme —*adv.* [Slang] extremely —**the Almighty** God —**al·might′i·ly** *adv.* —**al·might′i·ness** *n.*

al·mond (ä′mənd, am′ənd, al′mənd) *n.* [< OFr. < L. < Gr. *amygdalē*] **1.** the edible, nutlike kernel of a small, dry, peachlike fruit **2.** the tree bearing this fruit **3.** anything shaped like an almond, oval and pointed at one or both ends —**al′mond·like′** *adj.*

al·mon·er (al′mən ər, ä′mən-) *n.* one who distributes alms, as for a church, etc.

al·most (ôl′mōst, ôl′mōst′) *adv.* [OE. *eallmæst:* see ALL & MOST] very nearly but not completely

alms (ämz) *n., pl.* **alms** [< OE. < LL. < Gr. *eleēmosynē*, alms < *eleos*, pity] money, food, etc. given to poor people —**alms′giv′er** *n.*

alms·house (-hous′) *n.* formerly, a home for people too poor to support themselves; poorhouse

al·oe (al′ō) *n., pl.* **-oes** [< L. < Gr. *aloē* < ? Heb.] **1.** a South African plant of the lily family, with fleshy, spiny leaves **2.** [*pl.*, *with sing. v.*] a laxative drug made from the juice of certain aloe leaves

a·loft (ə lôft′) *adv.* [ME. *o, on*, on + *loft* < ON. *lopt:* see LOFT] **1.** far above the ground [he swung *aloft* into the upper tree branches] **2.** in the air; flying **3.** high above a ship's deck

☆**a·lo·ha** (ə lō′ə, ä lō′hä) *n., interj.* [Haw., lit., love] a word used as a greeting or farewell

a·lone (ə lōn′) *adj., adv.* [ME. < *al*, ALL + *one*, ONE] **1.** apart from anything or anyone else [the hut stood *alone* in the woods] **2.** without any other person [to walk *alone*] **3.** with nothing more; only [the box *alone* weighs two pounds] **4.** without equal or peer —**let alone 1.** to refrain from bothering **2.** not to mention [we hadn't a dime, *let alone* a dollar] —**let well enough alone** to be content with things as they are —**a·lone′-ness** *n.*

SYN.—**alone** denotes the simple fact of being by oneself or itself; **solitary** suggests more strongly the lack of companionship or association [a *solitary* tree in the meadow], and may also suggest a being alone by choice; **lonely**, and the more poetic **lone**, carry a greater sense of solitude and gloom [the *lonely* sentinel walks his post]; **lonesome** suggests a longing for companionship, often for a particular person —**ANT.** accompanied

a·long (ə lôn′) *prep.* [< OE. *andlang*, along < *and-*, over against + *-lang*, long] **1.** on or beside the length of [*along* the wall is a hedge] **2.** in conformity with [to think *along* certain lines] —*adv.* **1.** in a line; lengthwise [they stood *along* by the road] **2.** progressively onward [he walked *along* by himself] **3.** as a companion [come *along* with us] **4.** with one [she took her book *along*] ☆**5.** advanced [well *along* in years] ☆**6.** [Colloq.] approaching [*along* toward evening] —**all along** from the very beginning —**along with 1.** together with **2.** in addition to —☆**be along** [Colloq.] to come or arrive [I'll *be along* soon] —**get along 1.** to go forward **2.** to manage [he gets *along* on $50 a week] **3.** to succeed **4.** to be on friendly terms; agree [we can't *get along*] **5.** [Colloq.] to go away

a·long·shore (ə lôn′shôr′) *adv.* along the shore; near or beside the shore

a·long·side (-sīd′) *adv.* at or by the side; side by side —*prep.* at the side of; side by side with —**alongside of** at the side of; beside

a·loof (ə lōōf′) *adv.* [*a-*, on + *loof* < Du. *loef*, LUFF, to windward] at a distance but in view; apart [he stood *aloof* from the others] —*adj.* distant in sympathy, interest, etc. [an *aloof* manner] —**a·loof′ly** *adv.* —**a·loof′ness** *n.*

a·loud (ə loud′) *adv.* **1.** loudly [to cry *aloud*] **2.** with the normal voice [read the letter *aloud*]

Al·o·ys·i·us (al′ə wish′əs) [< ML.; prob. < OFr. *Loeis:* see LOUIS] a masculine name

alp (alp) *n.* [< L. *Alpes*, the Alps] a high mountain, esp. in Switzerland: see ALPS

al·pac·a (al pak′ə) *n., pl.* **-pac′as, -pac′a:** see PLURAL, II, D, 1 [Sp. < SAmInd. *allpaca*] **1.** a domesticated S. American mammal related to the llama, with brown or black fleecy wool **2.** this wool **3.** a cloth woven from this wool, often mixed with other fibers **4.** a glossy cloth of cotton and wool, used for linings, suits, etc.

al·pen·horn (al′pən hôrn′) *n.* [G., Alpine horn] a curved, wooden, powerful-sounding horn, from five to twelve feet long, used by Swiss Alpine herdsmen for signaling: also **alp′horn′**

ALPENHORN

al·pen·stock (-stäk′) *n.* [G., Alpine staff] an iron-pointed staff used by mountain climbers

al·pha (al′fə) *n.* [Gr. < Phoen. name whence Heb. *āleph:* see ALEPH] **1.** the first letter of the Greek alphabet (A, α) **2.** the beginning of anything **3.** the brightest star in a constellation

al·pha·bet (al′fə bet′) *n.* [< LL. < LGr. < Gr.: see ALPHA & BETA] **1.** the letters of a language, arranged in a traditional order **2.** a system of signs or symbols used to indicate letters or speech sounds **3.** the first elements, as of a subject

al·pha·bet·i·cal (al′fə bet′i k'l) *adj.* **1.** of or using an alphabet **2.** in the usual order of the alphabet Also **al′pha·bet′ic** —**al′pha·bet′i·cal·ly** *adv.*

al·pha·bet·ize (al′fə bə tīz′) *vt.* **-ized′, -iz′ing 1.** to arrange in alphabetical order **2.** to express by or provide with an alphabet —**al′pha·bet′i·za′tion** (-bet′i zā′shən) *n.*

al·pha·nu·mer·ic (al′fə nōō mer′ik, -nyōō-) *adj.* [ALPHA-(BET) + NUMERIC(AL)] having or using both alphabetical and numerical symbols

alpha particle a positively charged particle given off by certain radioactive substances: it consists of two protons and two neutrons

alpha ray 1. *same as* ALPHA PARTICLE **2.** a stream of alpha particles, less penetrating than a beta ray

Al·pine (al′pīn) *adj.* **1.** of the Alps or their inhabitants **2.** [a-] *a)* of or like high mountains *b)* growing on high slopes above the timberline

Alps (alps) mountain system of SC Europe: highest peak, Mont Blanc

al·read·y (ôl red′ē) *adv.* **1.** by or before the given or implied time [when we arrived, dinner had *already* begun] **2.** even now or even then [he is *already* an hour late]

al·right (ôl rīt′) *adv. var. of* ALL RIGHT: a spelling objected to by some, but in common use

Al·sace (al sās′, al′sas; *Fr.* àl zàs′) former province of NE France —**Al·sa′tian** (-sā′shən) *adj., n.*

Al·sace-Lor·raine (-lô rān′; *Fr.* -lô ren′) region in NE France consisting of the former provinces of Alsace and Lorraine

al·so (ôl′sō) *adv.* [< OE. < *eal*, all + *swa*, so] in addition; too: sometimes used in place of *and*

☆**al·so-ran** (-ran′) *n.* [Colloq.] a loser, esp. one trailing badly, in a competition, election, etc.

alt. 1. alternate **2.** altitude **3.** alto

Alta. Alberta (Canada)

Al·ta·ic (al tā′ik) *adj.* **1.** of the Altai Mountains or the people living there **2.** designating or of a family of languages including Turkic and Mongolic

Al·tai Mountains (al′tī, al tī′) mountain system in SC U.S.S.R., NW China, and W Mongolia

Al·ta·ir (al tä′ir) [Ar. *al tā′ir*, the bird] the brightest star in the constellation Aquila

al·tar (ôl′tər) *n.* [< OE. & OFr.; both ult. < L. < *altus*, high] **1.** a raised platform where sacrifices are made to a god, etc. **2.** a table, stand, etc. used for sacred purposes in a place of worship, as the Communion table in Christian churches —**lead to the altar** to marry

altar boy a boy or man who helps a priest, vicar, etc. at religious services, esp. at Mass

al·tar·piece (-pēs′) *n.* an ornamental carving, painting, etc. above and behind an altar

al·ter (ôl′tər) *vt.* [< ML. *alterare* < L. *alter*, other] **1.** to make different in details; modify **2.** to resew parts of (a garment) for a better fit ☆**3.** to castrate or spay —*vi.* to become different; change —see SYN. at CHANGE —**al'ter·a·ble** *adj.*

al·ter·a·tion (ôl'tə rā'shən) *n.* **1.** an altering or being altered **2.** the result of this; change

al·ter·a·tive (ôl'tə rāt'iv, -tər ə tiv) *adj.* **1.** causing alteration **2.** *Med.* gradually restoring to health —*n.* an alterative medicine or treatment

al·ter·cate (ôl'tər kāt') *vi.* -cat'ed, -cat'ing [< L. pp. of *altercari*, to dispute < *alter*, other] to argue angrily; quarrel

al·ter·ca·tion (ôl'tər kā'shən) *n.* an angry or heated argument —see SYN. at QUARREL[2]

al·ter e·go (ôl'tər ē'gō, eg'ō) [L., lit., other I] **1.** another aspect of oneself **2.** a very close friend or constant companion

al·ter·nate (ôl'tər nit, al'-; *for v.* -nāt') *adj.* [< L. pp. of *alternare*, to do by turns < *alternus*, one after the other < *alter*, other] **1.** succeeding each other; first one and then the other [*alternate* stripes of blue and yellow] **2.** every other [*alternate* Fridays] **3.** being one of two or more choices; alternative [an *alternate* route] **4.** *Bot.* growing along the stem singly at intervals —*n.* a person chosen to take the place of another if necessary; substitute —*vt.* -nat'ed, -nat'ing to do, use, or make happen by turns —*vi.* **1.** to act, happen, etc. by turns [good times *alternate* with bad] **2.** to take turns **3.** to exchange places, etc. regularly **4.** *Elec.* to reverse direction at regular intervals: said of a current —**al'ter·nate·ly** *adv.* —**al'ter·na'tion** *n.*

alternate angles two angles at opposite ends and on opposite sides of a line crossing two others

alternating current an electric current that reverses its direction at regular intervals

alternation of generations *Biol.* the occurrence of generations in alternate order, esp. of one that reproduces sexually (*gametophyte*) with one that reproduces asexually (*sporophyte*)

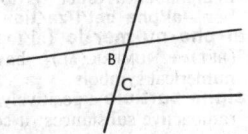

ALTERNATE ANGLES (B,C)

al·ter·na·tive (ôl tur'nə tiv, al-) *adj.* providing or being a choice between two (or, less strictly, among more than two) things —*n.* **1.** a choice between two or more things **2.** any of the things to be chosen **3.** something remaining to be chosen [is there an *alternative* to going?] —see SYN. at CHOICE —**al·ter'na·tive·ly** *adv.*

al·ter·na·tor (ôl'tər nāt'ər, al'-) *n.* an electric generator or dynamo producing alternating current

al·the·a, al·thae·a (al thē'ə) *n.* [< L. < Gr. *althaia*, wild mallows] **1.** any of a genus of plants in the mallow family, as the hollyhock **2.** *same as* ROSE OF SHARON (sense 1)

alt·horn (alt'hôrn') *n.* a brass-wind instrument, the alto saxhorn: also **alto horn**

al·though (ôl thō') *conj.* [ME. < *all, al*, even (emphatic) + *though*] in spite of the fact that; though: now sometimes sp. **altho**

al·tim·e·ter (al tim'ə tər; *chiefly Brit.* al'tə mēt'ər) *n.* [< L. *altus*, high + -METER] an instrument for measuring altitude; esp., in aircraft, an aneroid barometer that tells how high the craft is flying —**al·tim'e·try** *n.*

al·ti·tude (al'tə tōod', -tyōod') *n.* [< L. < *altus*, high] **1.** height; esp., the height of a thing above the earth's surface or above sea level **2.** a high place or region: *usually in pl.* **3.** a high level, rank, etc. **4.** *Astron.* the angular height of a planet, star, etc. above the horizon **5.** *Geom.* the perpendicular distance from the base of a figure to its highest point —**al'ti·tu'di·nal** (-'n əl) *adj.*

al·to (al'tō) *n., pl.* -tos [It. < L. *altus*, high] **1.** the range of the lowest female voice or, esp. formerly, the highest male voice **2.** a voice or singer with such range **3.** an instrument with the second highest range within a family of instruments, as the alto saxophone **4.** a part for such a voice or instrument —*adj.* of, in, for, or having this range

alto clef *see* C CLEF

al·to·geth·er (ôl'tə geth'ər, ôl'tə geth'ər) *adv.* [see ALL & TOGETHER] **1.** wholly; completely [*altogether* right] **2.** in all [he wrote six books *altogether*] **3.** on the whole [*altogether* a success] —**in the altogether** [Colloq.] nude

Al·too·na (al tōo'nə) [< *Altona*, former Ger. seaport] city in C Pa.: pop. 63,000

al·tru·ism (al'trōo iz'm) *n.* [< Fr. < It. *altrui*, of or to others < L. *alter*, another] unselfish concern for the welfare of others —**al'tru·ist** *n.*

al·tru·is·tic (al'trōo is'tik) *adj.* of, or acting because of, altruism —**al'tru·is'ti·cal·ly** *adv.*

al·um[1] (al'əm) *n.* [< OFr. < L. *alumen*] **1.** a hydrated double sulfate of a trivalent metal and a univalent metal; esp., a double sulfate of potassium and aluminum, used in medicine and in making dyes, paper, etc. **2.** aluminum sulfate: erroneous use

☆**a·lum**[2] (ə lum') *n.* [Colloq.] an alumnus or alumna

a·lu·mi·na (ə lōo'mi nə) *n.* an oxide of aluminum, Al_2O_3, present in bauxite and clay and found as different forms of corundum, including emery, sapphires, rubies, etc.

a·lu·min·i·um (al'yoo min'yəm, -ē əm) *n. Brit. var. of* ALUMINUM

a·lu·mi·nize (ə lōo'mə nīz') *vt.* -nized', -niz'ing to cover, or treat, with aluminum

a·lu·mi·nous (-nəs) *adj.* of or containing alum, alumina, or aluminum

a·lu·mi·num (ə lōo'mə nəm) *n.* [ModL. < L. *alumen*, alum] a silvery, lightweight, metallic chemical element that is easily worked, resists corrosion, and is found abundantly, but only in combination: symbol, Al; at. wt., 26.9815; at. no., 13 —*adj.* of, containing, or made of aluminum

aluminum oxide *same as* ALUMINA

☆**a·lum·na** (ə lum'nə) *n., pl.* -nae (-nē) [L., fem. of ALUMNUS] a girl or woman alumnus

a·lum·nus (-nəs) *n., pl.* -ni (-nī) [L., foster son < *alere*, to nourish] ☆a person, esp. a boy or man, who has attended or is a graduate of a particular school, college, etc.

al·ve·o·lar (al vē'ə lər) *adj.* **1.** of or like an alveolus; socket-like **2.** *Anat. a)* of the part of the jaws containing the sockets of the teeth *b)* designating the ridge of the gums behind the upper front teeth *c)* of the air cells in the lungs **3.** pronounced by bringing the tip of the tongue to or near to the alveolar ridge [*t, d,* and *s* are *alveolar* consonants] —*n.* an alveolar sound

al·ve·o·late (-lit) *adj.* full of small cavities: also **al·ve'o·lat'ed** (-lāt'id) —**al·ve'o·la'tion** *n.*

al·ve·o·lus (al vē'ə ləs) *n., pl.* -li' (-lī') [L., dim. of *alveus*, a cavity < *alvus*, the belly] **1.** *Anat., Zool.* a small cavity or hollow, as an air cell of a lung, a tooth socket, etc. **2.** [*usually pl.*] the alveolar ridge

Al·vin (al'v'n) [< G. < OHG. *adal*, nobility + *wini*, friend] a masculine name

al·way (ôl'wā) *adv.* [Archaic] always

al·ways (ôl'wiz, -wāz) *adv.* [see ALL & WAY] **1.** in every instance; invariably [he's *always* late] **2.** all the time; forever [*always* present in the atmosphere] **3.** at any time [you can *always* leave]

a·lys·sum (ə lis'əm) *n.* [ModL. < Gr. < *alyssos*, curing madness < *a-*, without + *lyssa*, rage] **1.** any of a genus of plants of the mustard family, with white or yellow flowers **2.** *same as* SWEET ALYSSUM

am (am; *unstressed* əm) [OE. *eom*: see BE] *the first person singular in the present tense of* BE

Am *Chem.* americium

AM amplitude modulation

Am. **1.** America **2.** American

A.M., AM [L. *Artium Magister*] master of arts

A.M., a.m., AM [L. *ante meridiem*] before noon: used to designate the time from midnight to noon

AMA, A.M.A. American Medical Association

a·mah (ä'mə) *n.* [Anglo-Ind. < Port. *ama*] in the Orient, a woman servant, esp. one who serves as a baby's nurse

a·main (ə mān') *adv.* [A-[1], on + MAIN] [Archaic or Poet.] **1.** forcefully; vigorously **2.** at or with great speed **3.** hastily; suddenly **4.** greatly

a·mal·gam (ə mal'gəm) *n.* [< ML., prob. < Ar. < Gr. *malagma*, an emollient < *malassein*, to soften] **1.** any alloy of mercury with another metal or metals [silver *amalgam* is used as a dental filling] **2.** any mixture or blend

a·mal·ga·mate (-gə māt') *vt., vi.* -mat'ed, -mat'ing **1.** to combine in an amalgam **2.** to join together into one; unite — **a·mal'gam·a·ble** (-gəm ə b'l) *adj.* —**a·mal'ga·ma'tion** *n.* — **a·mal'ga·ma'tive** *adj.* —**a·mal'ga·ma'tor** *n.*

A·man·da (ə man'də) [L., lit., worthy to be loved < *amare*, to love] a feminine name: dim. **Mandy**

a·man·u·en·sis (ə man'yoo wen'sis) *n., pl.* -ses (-sēz) [L. < *a-* (ab), from + *manus*, a hand + *-ensis*, relating to] an assistant who takes dictation or copies something already written; secretary: now mainly a humorous usage

am·a·ranth (am'ə ranth') *n.* [< L. < Gr. *amarantos*, unfading < *a-*, not + *marainein*, to die away] **1.** any of a genus of plants, usually with colorful leaves, including love-lies-bleeding, etc. **2.** [Poet.] an imaginary flower that never fades or dies **3.** a dark purplish red —**am′a·ran′thine** (-ran′thin) *adj.*

Am·a·ril·lo (am′ə ril′ō) [Sp., yellow] city in NW Texas: pop. 127,000

am·a·ryl·lis (am′ə ril′əs) *n.* [< L. & Gr.; conventional name for a shepherdess] **1.** a bulb plant bearing several white, purple, pink, or red lilylike flowers on a single stem **2.** any of several plants closely related to this

a·mass (ə mas′) *vt.* [< Fr. < ML. < *a*-, to + VL. *massare*, to pile up < L. *massa*, a MASS] **1.** to pile up; collect together **2.** to accumulate (esp. wealth) —**a·mass′er** *n.* —**a·mass′ment** *n.*

am·a·teur (am′ə chər, -toor, -tyoor) *n.* [Fr. < L. *amator*, a lover < *amare*, to love] **1.** a person who engages in some art, science, sport, etc. for pleasure rather than as a profession; specif., an athlete who is forbidden by rule to profit from his athletic activity **2.** a person who does something without professional skill —*adj.* **1.** of or done by or as by an amateur or amateurs **2.** being an amateur or made up of amateurs

SYN.—**amateur** refers to someone who does something for pleasure rather than for pay, and often implies a relative lack of skill; **novice** and **neophyte** both refer to one who is just a beginner in some activity and is therefore inexperienced, **neophyte** suggesting youthful enthusiasm as well; **tyro** refers to an inexperienced beginner and suggests a clumsy lack of skill and, often, unjustified self-confidence —**ANT. professional, expert**

am·a·teur·ish (am′ə choor′ish, -toor′-, -tyoor′-) *adj.* like an amateur; unskillful; not expert —**am′a·teur′ish·ly** *adv.* —**am′a·teur′ish·ness** *n.*

am·a·teur·ism (am′ə chər iz′m, -toor-, -tyoor-) *n.* **1.** an amateurish method or quality **2.** the nonprofessional status of an amateur

am·a·to·ry (am′ə tôr′ē) *adj.* [< L. pp. of *amare*, to love] of or showing love, esp. sexual love

a·maze (ə māz′) *vt.* **a·mazed′, a·maz′ing** [< OE. *amasian*: see MAZE] to fill with great surprise or sudden wonder; astonish —*n.* [Poet.] amazement —see SYN. at SURPRISE —**a·maz′ed·ly** (-id lē) *adv.* —**a·maz′ing·ly** *adv.*

a·maze·ment (-mənt) *n.* an amazed condition; great surprise or wonder; astonishment

Am·a·zon (am′ə zän′, -zən) river in S. America, flowing from the Andes in Peru across N Brazil into the Atlantic: c. 3,300 mi. —*n.* [L. < Gr. < ?, but derived by folk etym. < *a*-, without + *mazos*, breast, hence the story that the Amazons cut off one breast to facilitate archery] **1.** *Gr. Myth.* any of a race of female warriors supposed to have lived in Scythia **2.** [a-] a large, strong, masculine woman —**Am′a·zo′ni·an** (-zō′nē ən) *adj.*

am·bas·sa·dor (am bas′ə dər) *n.* [< MFr. < OIt. < Pr. < *ambaissa*, task, mission] **1.** the highest-ranking diplomatic representative appointed by a government to represent it in another country: an ☆**ambassador-at-large** is one accredited to no particular country; an **ambassador extraordinary** is one on a special diplomatic mission; an **ambassador plenipotentiary** has the power to make treaties **2.** an official messenger with a special mission —**am·bas′sa·do′ri·al** (-dôr′ē əl) *adj.* —**am·bas′sa·dor·ship′** *n.*

am·ber (am′bər) *n.* [< OFr. < Ar. ′*anbar*, ambergris] **1.** a yellow or brownish-yellow translucent fossil resin used in jewelry, pipestems, etc. **2.** the color of amber —*adj.* **1.** made of or like amber **2.** having the color of amber

am·ber·gris (-grēs′, -gris′) *n.* [< OFr. < *ambre gris*, gray AMBER] a grayish, waxy substance from the intestines of sperm whales, found floating in tropical seas and used in some perfumes

☆**am·ber·jack** (-jak′) *n.* [AMBER + JACK (fish): from its color] any of several food and game fishes found in warm seas

am·bi- [L. < *ambo*, both] *a combining form meaning* both [*ambidextrous*]

am·bi·ance (am′bē əns) *n.* [Fr.: see AMBIENT] an environment or its distinct atmosphere; milieu: also **am′bi·ence**

am·bi·dex·trous (am′bə dek′strəs) *adj.* [< L. AMBI- + *dexter*, right hand + -OUS] **1.** able to use both hands with equal ease, as in writing or throwing **2.** very skillful or versatile **3.** deceitful —**am′bi·dex·ter′i·ty** (-dek ster′ə tē) *n.* —**am′bi·dex′trous·ly** *adv.*

am·bi·ent (am′bē ənt) *adj.* [< L. prp. of *ambire* < *ambi-*,

around + *ire*, to go] surrounding; on all sides [warm, *ambient* waters]

am·bi·gu·i·ty (am′bə gyōō′ə tē) *n.* **1.** the quality or state of being ambiguous; unclearness or uncertainty of meaning **2.** *pl.* **-ties** an ambiguous word, statement, etc.

am·big·u·ous (am big′yoo wəs) *adj.* [< L. < *ambigere*, to wander < *ambi-*, around + *agere*, to ACT] **1.** having two or more possible meanings **2.** not clear; indefinite; vague —see SYN. at OBSCURE —**am·big′u·ous·ly** *adv.* —**am·big′u·ousness** *n.*

am·bi·tion (am bish′ən) *n.* [< OFr. < L. *ambitio*, a going around (to solicit votes) < pp. of *ambire*: see AMBIENT] **1.** a strong desire for success, fame, power, wealth, etc. **2.** the thing strongly desired [his *ambition* is to be an engineer]

am·bi·tious (-əs) *adj.* **1.** full of or showing ambition **2.** greatly desirous (*of* something) **3.** needing great effort, skill, enterprise, etc. [an *ambitious* project] —**am·bi′tious·ly** *adv.* —**am·bi′tious·ness** *n.*

SYN.—**ambitious** implies a striving for success, wealth, power, etc. and is used in either a favorable or unfavorable sense; **aspiring** means a striving to reach a goal considered beyond one's normal reach [an *aspiring* young poet]; **enterprising** implies eagerness to undertake new or risky projects in order to succeed

am·biv·a·lence (am biv′ə ləns) *n.* [AMBI- + VALENCE] strong mixed feelings toward a person or thing, as love and hate felt at the same time —**am·biv′a·lent** *adj.* —**am·biv′a·lent·ly** *adv.*

am·ble (am′b'l) *vi.* **-bled, -bling** [< OFr. < L. *ambulare*, to walk] **1.** to move at a smooth, easy gait by raising first both legs on one side, then both on the other: said of a horse, etc. **2.** to walk in a leisurely manner —*n.* **1.** a horse's ambling gait **2.** a leisurely walking pace —**am′bler** *n.*

Am·brose (am′brōz) [< L. < Gr. < *ambrotos*: see AMBROSIA] a masculine name

am·bro·sia (am brō′zhə) *n.* [L. < Gr. < *ambrotos* < *a*-, not + *brotos*, mortal: for IE. base see MORBID] **1.** *Gr. & Rom. Myth.* the food of the gods and immortals **2.** anything that tastes or smells delicious —**am·bro′sial, am·bro′sian** *adj.*

am·bu·lance (am′byə ləns) *n.* [< Fr. (*hôpital*) *ambulant*, mobile (hospital) < L. prp. of *ambulare*, to walk] a specially equipped vehicle for carrying the sick or wounded

am·bu·lant (am′byə lənt) *adj.* moving; walking

am·bu·late (am′byə lāt′) *vi.* **-lat′ed, -lat′ing** [< L. pp. of *ambulare*, to walk] to move about; walk —**am′bu·la′tion** *n.*

am·bu·la·to·ry (-lə tôr′ē) *adj.* **1.** of or for walking **2.** able to walk and not confined to bed [an *ambulatory* patient] **3.** moving from one place to another; movable **4.** *Law* that can be changed or revoked [an *ambulatory* will] —*n., pl.* **-ries** any sheltered place for walking, as in a cloister

am·bus·cade (am′bəs kād′; *also for n.* am′bəs kād′) *n., vt., vi.* **-cad′ed, -cad′ing** [< Fr. < OFr. *embuschier*: see AMBUSH] *same as* AMBUSH

am·bush (am′boosh) *n.* [< OFr. *embuschier* < ML. *imboscare*, to set an ambush < *in-*, in + *boscus*, woods] **1.** an arrangement of persons in hiding to make a surprise attack **2.** *a*) the persons in hiding *b*) their place of hiding **3.** the act of so lying in wait to attack —*vt., vi.* **1.** to hide in ambush **2.** to attack from ambush —**am′bush·ment** *n.*

a·me·ba (ə mē′bə) *n., pl.* **-bas, -bae** (-bē) *same as* AMOEBA — **a·me′bic** *adj.* —**a·me′boid** *adj.*

amebic dysentery a form of dysentery caused by an amoeba

a·meer (ə mir′) *n. same as* AMIR

A·me·lia (ə mēl′yə, -ē ə) [of Gmc. origin; lit., ? diligent < base of *amal*, work] a feminine name

a·mel·io·rant (ə mēl′yər ənt) *n.* a thing that ameliorates

a·mel·io·rate (ə mēl′yə rāt′) *vt., vi.* **-rat′ed, -rat′ing** [< Fr. < OFr. *ameillorer* < *a-*, to + *meillor* < L. *melior*, better] to make or become better; improve [to *ameliorate* working conditions] —see SYN. at IMPROVE —**a·mel′io·ra·ble** (-yər ə b'l) *adj.* —**a·mel′io·ra′tion** *n.* —**a·mel′io·ra′tive** *adj.* —**a·mel′io·ra′tor** *n.*

A·men (ä′mən) *same as* AMON

a·men (ä′men′, ā′-) *interj.* [< L. < Gr. < Heb. *āmēn*, truly, certainly] may it be so! so it is!: used after a prayer or to express approval —*n.* a speaking or writing of "amen"

a·me·na·ble (ə mē′nə b'l, -men′ə-) *adj.* [Anglo-Fr. < OFr. < *a-*, to + *mener*, to lead < L. *minare*, to drive (animals)] **1.**

responsible or answerable **2.** able to be controlled or influenced; responsive [*amenable* to suggestion; an illness *amenable* to treatment] **3.** that can be tested by (with *to*) [*amenable* to the laws of physics] —see SYN. at OBEDIENT —**a·me′na·bil′i·ty** *n.* —**a·me′na·bly** *adv.*

amen corner ☆in some rural Protestant churches, the seats to the minister's right, once occupied by those leading the responsive amens

a·mend (ə mend′) *vt.* [< OFr. < L. *emendare*, to correct: see EMEND] **1.** to make better; improve [to *amend* one's manners] **2.** to remove the faults of; correct **3.** to change or revise (a legislative bill, a law, etc.) —*vi.* to improve one's conduct — **a·mend′a·ble** *adj.* —☆**a·mend′a·to·ry** *adj.*

a·mend·ment (ə mend′mənt) *n.* **1.** a change for the better; improvement **2.** a correction of errors, faults, etc. **3.** a revision or addition proposed or made in a law, constitution, etc.

a·mends (ə mendz′) *n.pl.* [< OFr., pl. of *amende*, a fine: see AMEND] [*sometimes with sing. v.*] something given or done to make up for injury, loss, etc. that one has caused [he made *amends* for his rudeness by apologizing]

a·men·i·ty (ə men′ə tē, -mē′nə-) *n., pl.* **-ties** [< OFr. < L. *amoenitas* < *amoenus*, pleasant] **1.** pleasant quality; attractiveness **2.** *a)* an attractive or desirable feature, as of a place, climate, etc. *b)* anything that adds to one's comfort; convenience **3.** [*pl.*] the courtesies of polite social behavior

am·ent (am′ənt, ā′mənt) *n.* [< L. *amentum*, thong] *same as* CATKIN —**am·en·ta·ceous** (am′ən tā′shəs) *adj.*

a·men·tia (ā men′shə) *n.* [L., madness < *amens* < *a-* (*ab*), away + *mens*, mind] a severe mental deficiency that is present from birth

a·merce (ə murs′) *vt.* **a·merced′, a·merc′ing** [< Anglo-Fr. < OFr. *a merci*, at the mercy of] **1.** to punish by imposing an arbitrary fine **2.** to punish generally —**a·merce′ment** *n.*

A·mer·i·ca (ə mer′ə kə) [name traditionally associated with *Amerigo* VESPUCCI, but < ? Sp. *Amerrique* (< AmInd. *Americ*), name of a Nicaraguan mountain range] **1.** North America and South America considered together **2.** either North America or South America ☆**3.** the United States —**the Americas** America (sense 1)

A·mer·i·can (ə mer′ə kən) *adj.* **1.** of or in America [the *American* Indians] ☆**2.** of, in, or characteristic of the U.S., its people, etc. [the *American* language] —*n.* **1.** a native or inhabitant of America; specif., *a)* an American Indian ☆*b)* a citizen of the U.S. ☆**2.** the English language spoken in the U.S.

☆**A·mer·i·ca·na** (ə mer′ə kan′ə, -kä′nə) *n.pl.* [see -ANA] books, papers, objects, etc. having to do with America, its people, and its history

☆**American cheese** a kind of fairly hard, mild Cheddar cheese, popular in the U.S.

American Indian *same as* INDIAN (*n.* 2)

☆**A·mer·i·can·ism** (ə mer′ə kən iz'm) *n.* **1.** a custom, characteristic, or belief of or originating in the U.S. **2.** a word, phrase, or usage originating in or peculiar to American English **3.** devotion or loyalty to the U.S., or to its traditions, etc.

☆**A·mer·i·can·ize** (-īz′) *vt., vi.* **-ized′, -iz′ing** to make or become American in character, manners, methods, ideals, etc.; assimilate to U.S. customs, speech, etc. —**A·mer′i·can·i·za′tion** *n.*

☆**American plan** a system of hotel operation in which the charge to guests covers room, service, and meals: distinguished from EUROPEAN PLAN

American Revolution 1. a sequence of actions (1763–83) by American colonists against British domination, culminating in the Revolutionary War **2.** the Revolutionary War (1775–83), fought by the American colonies to gain independence from England

American Samoa *see* SAMOA

American Standard Version a revision of the King James Version of the Bible, published in the U.S. in 1901

☆**am·er·ic·i·um** (am′ə rish′ē əm, -ris′-) *n.* [ModL. < AMERICA] a chemical element, one of the transuranic elements produced from plutonium: symbol, Am; at. wt., 243.13; at. no., 95

☆**Am·er·ind** (am′ə rind′) *n.* [AMER(ICAN) + IND(IAN)] an American Indian or Eskimo —**Am′er·in′di·an** *adj., n.* —**Am′er·in′dic** *adj.*

am·e·thyst (am′ə thist) *n.* [< OFr. < L. < Gr. < *a-*, not + *methystos*, drunken (it was believed to prevent intoxication)] **1.** a purple or violet variety of quartz, used in jewelry **2.** popularly, a purple corundum, used in jewelry: also called *Oriental amethyst* **3.** purple or violet

Am·har·ic (am har′ik, äm här′-) *n.* the Semitic language used officially in Ethiopia

a·mi·a·ble (ā′mē ə b'l) *adj.* [< OFr. < LL. *amicabilis*, friendly < L. *amicus*, friend] having a pleasant, friendly disposition; good-natured —**a′mi·a·bil′i·ty** *n.* —**a′mi·a·bly** *adv.*

SYN.—**amiable** and **affable** both suggest friendliness and an easygoing temperament that make one likable, **affable** also implying a readiness to talk and be sociable; a **good-natured** person is one who tends to like others as well as to be liked by them, and is sometimes easily imposed on; **obliging** implies a ready, often cheerful, desire to be helpful [the *obliging* clerk answered my questions]; **genial** suggests cheerful sociability [our *genial* host]; **cordial** suggests sincerity and warmth [a *cordial* welcome] —**ANT.** surly, ill-natured

am·i·ca·ble (am′i kə b'l) *adj.* [< LL. *amicabilis:* see AMIABLE] friendly in feeling; showing good will; peaceable [an *amicable* discussion] —**am′i·ca·bil′i·ty** *n.* —**am′i·ca·bly** *adv.*

am·ice (am′is) *n.* [< OFr. < L. *amictus*, a cloak] an oblong cloth of white linen worn about the neck and shoulders by a priest at Mass

a·mi·cus cu·ri·ae (ə mī′kəs kyoor′i ē′) [L., friend of the court] *Law* a person who is called in to advise a court on some legal matter

a·mid (ə mid′) *prep.* [ME. < *on*, at + *middan*, middle] in the middle of; among

am·ide (am′īd, -id) *n.* [AM(MONIA) + -IDE] **1.** any of a group of organic compounds containing the $CO \cdot NH_2$ radical or an acid radical in place of one hydrogen atom of an ammonia molecule **2.** any of the ammonia bases in which one hydrogen atom of the ammonia molecule is replaced by a metal —**a·mid·ic** (ə mid′ik) *adj.*

am·i·dol (am′ə dōl′, -dôl′) *n.* [< AMID(E) + (PHEN)OL] a colorless, crystalline compound used as a developer in photography

a·mid·ships (ə mid′ships′) *adv., adj.* in or toward the middle of a ship: also **a·mid′ship′**

a·midst (ə midst′) *prep. same as* AMID

☆**a·mi·go** (ə mē′gō) *n., pl.* **-gos** [Sp.] a friend

a·mine (ə mēn′; am′ēn, -in) *n.* [AM(MONIA) + -INE⁴] *Chem.* a derivative of ammonia in which hydrogen atoms have been replaced by radicals containing hydrogen and carbon atoms

a·mi·no (ə mē′nō) *adj.* [< prec.] of or containing the NH_2 radical in combination with certain organic radicals

amino acids a group of organic compounds that contain the amino radical and serve as units of structure of the proteins

a·mir (ə mir′) *n.* [Ar.] in some Moslem countries, a ruler, prince, or commander: see also EMIR

☆**Am·ish** (ä′mish, am′ish) *n.pl.* [after Jacob *Ammann* (or *Amen*), the founder] Mennonites of a sect founded in the 17th cent. —*adj.* of this sect

a·miss (ə mis′) *adv.* [ME.: see A-¹ & MISS¹] in a wrong way; astray, wrongly, faultily, etc. [don't take his remarks *amiss*] — *adj.* wrong, faulty, improper, etc.: used predicatively

a·mi·to·sis (ā′mī tō′sis, am′ə-) *n.* [A-² (sense 3) + MITOSIS] *Biol.* cell division in which the nucleus and cytoplasm divide by simple constriction and without halving of chromosomes; direct cell division: opposed to MITOSIS —**a′mi·tot′ic** (-tät′ik) *adj.*

am·i·ty (am′ə tē) *n., pl.* **-ties** [< OFr. *amistie* < L. *amicus*, friend] friendly, peaceful relations, as between nations; friendship

Am·man (äm′än) capital of Jordan: pop. 330,000

am·me·ter (am′mēt′ər) *n.* [AM(PERE) + -METER] an instrument for measuring the strength of an electric current in terms of amperes

am·mo (am′ō) *n.* [Slang] ammunition

Am·mon (am′ən) Amon, the ancient Egyptian god: identified by the Greeks with Zeus and by the Romans with Jupiter

am·mo·nia (ə mōn′yə) *n.* [< (SAL) AMMONIAC] **1.** a colorless, pungent gas, NH_3: its compounds are used in fertilizers, cleaning fluids, etc. **2.** a water solution of this gas: in full, **ammonia water**

am·mo·ni·ac (ə mō′nē ak′) *n.* [< L. < Gr. *ammōniakon*, gum resin said to come from near the temple of Jupiter AMMON in Libya] an Asian gum resin used in perfumes, porcelain cements, etc.

am·mo·ni·ate (ə mō′nē āt′; *for n.* -it) *vt.* **-at′ed, -at′ing** to mix or combine with ammonia —*n.* any of several compounds containing ammonia —**am·mo′ni·a′tion** *n.*

☆**am·mo·ni·fi·ca·tion** (ə mō′nə fi kā′shən, -män′ə-) *n.* **1.** an ammoniating **2.** the forming of ammonia by bacterial action in the decay of nitrogenous organic matter —**am·mo′ni·fy′** *vt., vi.* **-fied′, -fy′ing**

am·mo·nite (am′ə nīt′) *n.* [< L. (*cornu*) *Ammonis*, (horn) of

Ammon] any of the flat, usually coiled fossil shells of a mollusk of the Mesozoic era

am·mo·ni·um (ə mō′nē əm) *n.* the radical NH₄, present in salts produced by the reaction of ammonia with an acid: its compounds are like those of the alkali metals

ammonium chloride a white, crystalline compound, NH₄Cl, produced by the reaction of ammonia with hydrochloric acid: it is used in medicine, and also in dry cells, dyes, etc.: also called **sal ammoniac**

ammonium hydroxide an alkali, NH₄OH, formed by dissolving ammonia in water

ammonium sulfate an ammonium salt, (NH₄)₂SO₄, used in making fertilizers, in treating water, etc.

am·mu·ni·tion (am′yə nish′ən) *n.* [< Fr., by faulty reading of *la munition* as *l'amunition:* see MUNITIONS] **1.** anything hurled by a weapon or exploded as a weapon, as bullets, shells, bombs, grenades, etc. **2.** any means of attack or defense [the books provided him with *ammunition* for his argument]

am·ne·sia (am nē′zhə, -zhē ə) *n.* [ModL. < Gr. *a-*, not + *mnasthai*, to remember: for IE. base see MIND] a loss of memory, partial or total, caused by brain injury, or by shock, repression, etc. —**am·ne′si·ac′** (-zē ak′), **am·ne′sic** (-sik, -zik) *adj., n.*

am·nes·ty (am′nəs tē) *n., pl.* **-ties** [< Fr. < L. < Gr. *amnēstia*, a forgetting: see prec.] a general pardon, esp. for political offenses against a government —*vt.* **-tied, -ty·ing** to grant amnesty to; pardon

am·ni·on (am′nē ən, -än′) *n., pl.* **-ni·ons, -ni·a** (-ə) [Gr., dim. of *amnos*, lamb] the innermost membrane of the sac enclosing the embryo of a mammal, reptile, or bird: it is filled with a watery fluid (**amniotic fluid**) —**am′ni·ot′ic** (-ät′ik) *adj.*

a·moe·ba (ə mē′bə) *n., pl.* **-bas, -bae** (-bē) [ModL. < Gr. *amoibē* < *ameibein*, to change] **1.** a microscopic, one-celled animal found commonly in fresh and salt water: it moves by making continual changes in its shape, feeds by engulfing bits of food, and multiplies by fission **2.** a similar animal that is a parasite in higher animals and man Also sp. **a·me′ba**

NUCLEUS
VACUOLE
PSEUDOPODIUM
AMOEBA

a·moe·bic (-bik) *adj.* **1.** of or like an amoeba or amoebas **2.** caused by amoebas Also sp. **a·me′bic**

a·mok (ə muk′) *adj., adv.* [Malay *amoq*] in a frenzy to kill; in a violent rage —**run** (or **go**) **amok 1.** to rush about in a frenzy to kill **2.** to lose control of oneself

A·mon (ä′mən) an ancient Egyptian deity, later identified with the sun god: see AMON-RE, AMMON

a·mong (ə muŋ′) *prep.* [OE. *on gemang*, in the company (of) < *on*, in + *gemang*, a crowd < *gemengan*, to MINGLE] **1.** in the company of; surrounded by [*among* friends] **2.** from place to place in [pass *among* the crowd] **3.** in the group or class of [fairest *among* women] **4.** by or with many of [rebellion *among* the youth] **5.** as compared with [one *among* thousands] **6.** with a share for each of [divided *among* us] **7.** with one another [talking *among* ourselves] **8.** by the joint action of [we have, *among* us, finished the work]

a·mongst (ə muŋst′) *prep. same as* AMONG

A·mon-Re (ä′mən rā′) the ancient Egyptian sun god: also **A′mon-Ra′** (-rä′)

a·mon·til·la·do (ə män′tə lä′dō) *n.* [Sp. < *Montilla*, a town in Spain] a pale, rather dry sherry

a·mor·al (ā môr′əl, -mär′-) *adj.* **1.** not to be judged by moral values; neither moral nor immoral **2.** not capable of distinguishing between right and wrong —**a·mor·al·i·ty** (ā′mə ral′ə tē) *n.* —**a·mor′al·ly** *adv.*

am·o·rous (am′ər əs) *adj.* [< OFr. < LL. *amorosus* < L. *amor*, love < *amare*, to love] **1.** fond of making love **2.** in love; enamored or fond (*of*) **3.** full of or showing love or sexual desire [*amorous* words] **4.** of sexual love or lovemaking —**am′o·rous·ly** *adv.* —**am′o·rous·ness** *n.*

a·mor·phous (ə môr′fəs) *adj.* [< ModL. < Gr. *a-*, without + *morphē*, form] **1.** without definite form; shapeless **2.** of no definite type [an *amorphous* style of architecture] **3.** indefinite, unorganized, vague, etc. [an *amorphous* plan] **4.** *Biol.* without

specialized structure, as some lower forms of life **5.** *Chem., Mineralogy* not crystalline [a lump of *amorphous* charcoal] —**a·mor′phism** *n.* —**a·mor′phous·ly** *adv.*

am·or·tize (am′ər tīz′, ə môr′-) *vt.* **-tized′, -tiz′ing** [< OFr. *amortir*, to extinguish < ML. < L. *ad*, to + *mors*, death: see MORTAL] **1.** to put money aside at intervals, as in a sinking fund, for gradual payment of (a debt, etc.) **2.** *Accounting* to write off (expenditures) by prorating over a fixed period Chiefly Brit. sp. **am′or·tise′, -tised′, -tis′ing** —**am′or·tiz′a·ble** *adj.* —**am′or·ti·za′tion** *n.*

A·mos (ā′məs) [Heb. *'āmōs*, lit., borne (by God?)] **1.** a masculine name **2.** *Bible a)* a Hebrew prophet of the 8th cent. B.C. *b)* the book containing prophecies attributed to him

a·mount (ə mount′) *vi.* [< OFr. *amonter* < *amont*, upward < *a-* (L. *ad*), to + *mont* < L. *mons*, mountain: see MOUNT¹] **1.** to add up; total [the bill *amounts* to $4.50] **2.** to be equal in meaning, value, or effect [her reply *amounts* to a refusal] —*n.* **1.** the sum of two or more quantities; total **2.** a principal sum plus its interest **3.** a quantity [a small *amount* of rain]

a·mour (ə moor′) *n.* [Fr. < Pr. < L. *amor*, love] a love affair, esp. a secret one

amp. 1. amperage **2.** ampere(s)

am·per·age (am′pər ij, am pir′-) *n.* the strength of an electric current, measured in amperes

am·pere (am′pir) *n.* [after A. M. *Ampère* (1775-1836), Fr. physicist] the standard unit for measuring the strength of an electric current; rate of flow of charge of one coulomb per second

am·per·sand (am′pər sand′) *n.* [< *and per se and*, lit., (the sign) & by itself (is) *and*] a sign (& or ▮), meaning *and:* it represents the Latin word *et* (and)

☆ **am·phet·a·mine** (am fet′ə mēn′, -min) *n.* [*alpha*-methyl-*beta*-*phenyl*-*ethyl*-*amine*] a compound, C₉H₁₃N, used as a drug to overcome depression, fatigue, etc. and to lessen the appetite

am·phi- [< Gr.] *a prefix meaning:* **1.** on both sides or ends **2.** of both kinds **3.** around; about

am·phib·i·an (am fib′ē ən) *n.* [see AMPHIBIOUS] **1.** any of a class of vertebrates, including frogs, toads, salamanders, etc., that usually begin life in the water as tadpoles with gills, and later develop lungs: they are cold-blooded and scaleless **2.** any amphibious animal or plant **3.** an aircraft that can take off from and come down on either land or water **4.** a vehicle that can travel on either land or water —*adj.* **1.** of the amphibians **2.** *same as* AMPHIBIOUS

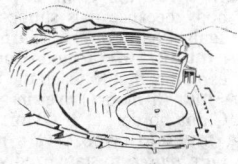

AMPHIBIAN (sense 4)

am·phib·i·ous (am fib′ē əs) *adj.* [< Gr. < *amphi-*, AMPHI- + *bios*, life] **1.** that can live both on land and in water **2.** that can operate on both land and water **3.** of or for a military operation involving the landing of troops from seaborne transports —**am·phib′i·ous·ly** *adv.*

am·phi·bole (am′fə bōl′) *n.* [Fr. < LL. *amphibolus*, ambiguous < Gr. *amphiballein*, to be uncertain < *amphi-*, AMPHI- + *ballein*, to throw] any of a group of rock-forming minerals, as hornblende or asbestos, composed largely of silica, calcium, iron, and magnesium —**am′phi·bol′ic** (-bäl′ik) *adj.*

am·phi·ox·us (am′fē äk′səs) *n.* [< AMPHI- + Gr. *oxys*, sharp] *same as* LANCELET

am·phi·the·a·ter, am·phi·the·a·tre (am′fə thē′ə tər) *n.* [< L. < Gr.: see AMPHI- & THEATER] **1.** a round or oval building with an open space (arena) surrounded by rising rows of seats **2.** any place where a contest is held **3.** a level place surrounded by rising ground

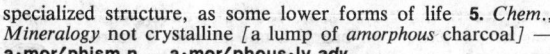

AMPHITHEATER

Am·phi·tri·te (am′fi trīt′ē) *Gr. Myth.* goddess of the sea and wife of Poseidon

Am·phi·try·on (am fit′rē ən) *Gr. Myth.* a king of Thebes: his wife, Alcmene, became the mother of Hercules by Zeus

fat, āpe, cär; ten, ēven; is, bīte; gō, hôrn, tōol, look; oil, out; up, fur; get; joy; yet; chin; she; thin, then; zh, leisure; ŋ, ring; ə for a in ago, e in agent, i in sanity, o in comply, u in focus; ' as in able (ā′b'l); Fr. bâl; ë, Fr. coeur; ö, Fr. feu; Fr. mon; ô, Fr. coq; ü, Fr. duc; r, Fr. cri; H, G. ich; kh, G. doch; ‡ foreign; ☆ Americanism; < derived from. See inside front cover.

am·pho·ra (am'fər ə) *n., pl.* **-rae** (-ē̄), **-ras** [L. < Gr. < *amphi-*, AMPHI- + *pherein*, to bear] a tall jar with a narrow neck and base and two handles, used by the ancient Greeks and Romans

am·pho·ter·ic (am'fə ter'ik) *adj.* [< Gr. < *amphō*, var. of AMPHI-] *Chem.* that can react as either an acid or a base

AM-
PHORA

am·ple (am'p'l) *adj.* **-pler, -plest** [OFr. < L. *amplus* < IE. base *am-*, to contain] **1.** large in size, extent, etc.; spacious; roomy [ten can be seated in the *ample* kitchen] **2.** more than enough; abundant [he contributed generously from his *ample* funds] **3.** enough; adequate [the food supply is *ample* for the winter] —see SYN. at PLENTIFUL —**am'ple·ness** *n.*

am·plex·i·caul (am plek'sə kôl') *adj.* [< L. pp. of *amplectari*, to twine around + *caulis*, stem] *Bot.* growing directly from the main stem and encircling it, as corn leaves

am·pli·fi·ca·tion (am'plə fi kā'shən) *n.* **1.** an amplifying or being amplified **2.** additional details **3.** a statement, etc. with something added

am·pli·fi·er (am'plə fī'ər) *n.* **1.** a person or thing that amplifies **2.** *Electronics* a device, esp. one with electron tubes or semiconductors, used to increase electrical signal strength

am·pli·fy (am'plə fī') *vt.* **-fied', -fy'ing** [< OFr. < L. *amplificare* < *amplus*, AMPLE + *facere*, to make] **1.** to make stronger; increase (power, authority, etc.) **2.** to develop more fully, as with details, examples, etc. [to *amplify* a point in a debate] **3.** *Electronics* to strengthen (an electrical signal) by means of an amplifier —*vi.* to speak or write at length; expatiate

am·pli·tude (am'plə tōōd', -tyōōd') *n.* [< L. < *amplus*, AMPLE] **1.** extent; largeness **2.** abundance; fullness **3.** scope or breadth, as of mind **4.** the extreme range of a fluctuating quantity, as the swing of a pendulum, measured from the average or mean to the extreme

amplitude modulation **1.** the changing of the amplitude of the transmitting radio wave in accordance with the signal being broadcast **2.** a broadcasting system that uses this Distinguished from FREQUENCY MODULATION

am·ply (am'plē) *adv.* to an ample degree; liberally; fully [he will be *amply* rewarded]

am·pul (am'pool, -pul) *n.* [Fr. < L. *ampulla*, AMPULLA] a small, sealed glass container for one dose of a medicine to be injected hypodermically: also **am'pule** (-pyool), **am'poule** (-pōōl)

am·pul·la (am pul'ə, -pool'ə) *n., pl.* **-pul'lae** (-ē) [< OE. < L. *ampulla*, dim. of AMPHORA] **1.** a nearly round bottle with two handles, used by the ancient Greeks and Romans **2.** a container used in churches for holy oil, consecrated wine, etc.

am·pu·tate (am'pyə tāt') *vt.* **-tat'ed, -tat'ing** [< L. pp. of *amputare* < *am-*, for AMBI- + *putare*, to cut: see PAVE] to cut off (an arm, leg, etc.), esp. by surgery —**am'pu·ta'tion** *n.* —**am'pu·ta'tor** *n.*

AMPUL

am·pu·tee (am'pyə tē') *n.* [see -EE] a person who has had a limb or limbs amputated

Am·rit·sar (əm rit'sər) city in Punjab, N India: pop. 398,000

Am·ster·dam (am'stər dam') constitutional capital of the Netherlands: pop. 868,000: see also The HAGUE

amt. amount

amu, AMU atomic mass unit

a·muck (ə muk') *adj., adv. same as* AMOK

am·u·let (am'yə lit) *n.* [< Fr. < L.] something worn on the body because it is supposed to have magic power to protect against harm or evil; charm

A·mund·sen (ä'moon sən), **Ro·ald** (rō'äl) 1872–1928; Norw. explorer; first to reach the South Pole (1911)

A·mur (ä moor') river in NE Asia, flowing along the U.S.S.R.-China border: c. 2,700 mi.

a·muse (ə myōoz') *vt.* **a·mused', a·mus'ing** [< Fr. < *à*, at + OFr. *muser*, to stare fixedly] **1.** to keep pleasantly interested or entertained **2.** to make laugh, smile, etc. by being comical or humorous —**a·mus'a·ble** *adj.* —**a·mus'er** *n.*

SYN.—**amuse** suggests keeping the mind occupied in a pleasant way, often, esp., by something that appeals to the sense of humor [the monkey's antics *amused* him]; to **divert** is to take the mind from worry, daily concerns, etc. to something gay or light [the crossword puzzles helped to *divert* her]; **entertain** implies planned amusement or diversion [another guest *entertained* us with folk songs] —ANT. bore

a·muse·ment (-mənt) *n.* **1.** the condition of being amused **2.** something that amuses or entertains

☆**amusement park** an outdoor place with devices for entertainment, as a merry-go-round

a·mus·ing (ə myōo'ziŋ) *adj.* **1.** entertaining; diverting **2.** causing laughter —see SYN. at FUNNY —**a·mus'ing·ly** *adv.*

A·my (ā'mē) [< OFr. *Amee*, lit., beloved < pp. of *aimer*, to love < L. *amare*] a feminine name

am·yl (am'il) *n.* [AM(YLUM) + -YL] any of various isomeric forms of the monovalent radical C_5H_{11}

amyl alcohol a colorless, sharp-smelling alcohol, $C_5H_{11}OH$, found in fusel oil

am·yl·ase (am'ə lās') *n.* an enzyme that helps change starch into sugar: it is found in saliva, pancreatic juice, etc.: see also DIASTASE

am·y·loid (am'ə loid') *n.* a starchy substance

am·y·lop·sin (am'ə läp'sin) *n.* [< AMYLUM + TRYPSIN] the enzyme (amylase) of pancreatic juice: it splits starch into glucose

am·y·lum (am'ə ləm) *n.* [< L. < Gr.] *Chem. a technical name for* STARCH

an[1] (ən; *stressed* an) *adj., indefinite article* [weakened variant of ONE < OE. *an*, the numeral one] **1.** one; one sort of [an apple pie] **2.** each; any one [pick *an* apple] **3.** to each; in each; for each; per [two *an* hour] *An* is used (instead of *a*) before all words beginning with a vowel sound or silent *h* [an orange, an honor]; *an* is sometimes used, esp. in older usage, before *h* in an unstressed initial syllable [an hotel] and, in British usage, before the sound (yōō) or (yoo) [an union] See also A, *adj.*

an[2], **an'** (ən) *conj.* [< *and*] **1.** [Dial.] and **2.** [Archaic] if

an- *same as* A-[2] (not, without): used before vowels

-an (ən, 'n) [< L. *-anus*] *a suffix meaning:* **1.** (one) belonging to or having some relation to [*diocesan*] **2.** (one) born in or living in [*American*] **3.** (one) believing in or following [*Mohammedan*]

an. **1.** [L. *anno*] in the year **2.** anonymous

an·a- [L. < Gr. *ana*, up, on, again] *a prefix meaning:* **1.** up [*anadromous*] **2.** back, backward [*anagram*] **3.** again [*Anabaptist*] **4.** throughout [*analysis*] **5.** according to, similar to [*analogy*]

-a·na (an'ə, ä'nə, ā'nə) [neut. pl. of L. *-anus*] *a suffix meaning* sayings, writings, anecdotes, or facts of [*Americana*]

An·a·bap·tist (an'ə bap'tist) *n.* [< LL. < Gr. < *ana-*, again + *baptizein*, to baptize] a member of a 16th-cent. Protestant sect, that held that only baptism of adults was valid and rejected infant baptism —*adj.* of this sect —**An'a·bap'tism** *n.*

an·a·bat·ic (an'ə bat'ik) *adj.* [Gr. *anabatikos* < *anabainein*, to go up] moving upward: said of air currents

a·nab·o·lism (ə nab'ə liz'm) *n.* [< Gr. *anabolē*, a rising up + -ISM] the process in a plant or animal by which food is changed into living tissue; constructive metabolism: opposed to CATABOLISM —**an·a·bol·ic** (an'ə bäl'ik) *adj.*

a·nach·ro·nism (ə nak'rə niz'm) *n.* [< MGr. *anachronizein*, to refer to a wrong time < *ana-*, against + *chronos*, time] **1.** the representation of something as existing or occurring at other than its proper historical time [the striking of the clock in Shakespeare's *Julius Caesar* is an *anachronism*] **2.** anything out of its proper time in history [a belief in magic today is an *anachronism*] —**a·nach'ro·nis'tic, a·nach'ro·nous** (-nəs) *adj.* —**a·nach'ro·nis'ti·cal·ly** *adv.*

an·a·co·lu·thon (an'ə kə lōō'thän) *n., pl.* **-tha** (-thə), **-thons** [Gr. < *anakolouthos*, inconsequent < *an-*, not + *akolouthos*, following] a change from one grammatical construction to another in the middle of a sentence, sometimes for rhetorical effect (Ex.: "If you refuse—but, let's not talk about it.")

an·a·con·da (an'ə kän'də) *n.* [< ? Sinhalese *henakandaya*, whip snake] **1.** a long, heavy S. American snake of the boa family **2.** any similar large snake that crushes its victim in its coils

an·a·cru·sis (an'ə krōōs'is) *n.* [ModL. < Gr. < *ana-*, back + *krouein*, to strike] one or more unaccented syllables at the beginning of a line of verse before the meter proper begins

a·nad·ro·mous (ə nad'rə məs) *adj.* [< Gr. < *ana-*, upward + *dramein*, to run] going up rivers to spawn: said of salmon, shad, etc.

a·nae·mi·a (ə nē'mē ə, -myə) *n. same as* ANEMIA —**a·nae'mic** *adj.*

ANACONDA
(to 30 ft. long)

an·aer·obe (an er'ōb, an'ə rōb') *n.* [< ANAEROBIUM] an anaerobic microorganism

an·aer·o·bic (an′er ō′bik, -ə rō′-) *adj.* **1.** able to live and grow where there is no air or free oxygen, as certain bacteria **2.** of or produced by anaerobes

an·aer·o·bi·um (an′er ō′bē əm, -ə rō′-) *n., pl.* **-bi·a** (-bē ə) [ModL. < Gr. *an-*, AN- + *aero-*, AERO- + *bios*, life] *same as* ANAEROBE

an·aes·the·sia (an′əs thē′zhə) *n. same as* ANESTHESIA — **an·aes·thet·ic** (-thet′ik) *adj., n.* —**an·aes·the·tist** (ə nes′thə tist) *n.* —**an·aes·the·tize** *vt.* **-tized′, -tiz′ing**

an·a·gram (an′ə gram′) *n.* [< ModL. < Gr. *anagrammatizein*, to transpose letters < *ana-*, back + *gramma*, letter < *graphein*, to write: see GRAPHIC] **1.** a word or phrase made from another by rearranging its letters [*dare* is an anagram of *read*] **2.** [*pl., with sing. v.*] a game in which players seek to form words by arranging letters drawn at random —**an′a·gram·mat′ic** (-grə mat′ik), **an′a·gram·mat′i·cal** *adj.*

An·a·heim (an′ə hīm′) [< Santa *Ana* (St. Anne, reputed mother of the Virgin Mary) + G. *heim*, home] city in SW Calif.: pop. 167,000

a·nal (ā′n′l) *adj.* of or near the anus —**a′nal·ly** *adv.*

an·a·lects (an′ə lekts′) *n.pl.* [< L. < Gr. *analegein*, to collect < *ana-*, up + *legein*, to gather] collected literary excerpts: also **an′a·lec′ta** (-lek′tə) —**the Analects** a collection of Confucius' teachings

an·al·ge·si·a (an′′l jē′zē ə, -sē ə) *n.* [ModL. < Gr. *an-*, without + *algēsia*, pain] a state of not feeling pain although fully conscious

an·al·ge·sic (-zik, -sik) *adj.* stopping or easing pain without causing unconsciousness; producing analgesia —*n.* a drug that produces analgesia

analog computer an electronic computer that uses voltages to represent the numerical data of physical quantities (as lengths): see also DIGITAL COMPUTER

an·a·log·i·cal (an′ə läj′i k′l) *adj.* of, expressing, or based upon analogy —**an′a·log′i·cal·ly** *adv.*

a·nal·o·gize (ə nal′ə jīz′) *vi.* **-gized′, -giz′ing** to use, or reason by, analogy —*vt.* to explain or liken by analogy —**a·nal′o·gist** (-jist) *n.*

a·nal·o·gous (-gəs) *adj.* [see ANALOGY] **1.** similar or alike in some ways [the grammars of all languages are *analogous*] **2.** *Biol.* similar in function but not in origin and structure — **a·nal′o·gous·ly** *adv.*

an·a·logue, an·a·log (an′ə lôg′, -läg′) *n.* a thing or part that is analogous —*adj.* of or by means of an analog computer: usually **analog**

a·nal·o·gy (ə nal′ə jē) *n., pl.* **-gies** [< ME. & OFr. < L. < Gr. *analogia*, proportion < *ana-*, according to + *logos*, ratio: see LOGIC] **1.** similarity in some ways between things otherwise unlike; resemblance in part [the *analogy* between a computer and the human brain] **2.** a comparing of something point by point with something similar **3.** *Biol.* similarity in function but not in origin and structure **4.** *Linguis.* the process by which new words, etc. conform to the pattern of older ones [*energize* is formed from *energy* by analogy with *apologize* from *apology*] **5.** *Logic* the inference that if there are certain admitted resemblances between things, they will probably be similar in other ways

a·nal·y·sand (ə nal′ə sand′) *n.* a person who is undergoing psychoanalysis

an·a·lyse (an′ə līz′) *vt.* **-lysed′, -lys′ing** *chiefly Brit. sp. of* ANALYZE

a·nal·y·sis (ə nal′ə sis) *n., pl.* **-ses′** (-sēz′) [ML. < Gr., a dissolving < *ana-*, up, throughout + *lysis*, a loosing < *lyein*, to loose] **1.** *a)* a breaking up of any whole into its parts so as to find out their nature, function, etc. *b)* a statement of these findings **2.** *same as* PSYCHOANALYSIS **3.** *Chem.* the separation of compounds and mixtures into their constituent substances to determine the nature (*qualitative analysis*) or the proportion (*quantitative analysis*) of the constituents **4.** *Linguis.* the use of word order and function words rather than inflection to express relationships of syntax

an·a·lyst (an′ə list) *n.* **1.** a person who analyzes [a news *analyst*] **2.** *same as* PSYCHOANALYST

an·a·lyt·ic (an′ə lit′ik) *adj.* **1.** designating or of a language that is characterized by analysis rather than inflection **2.** *same as* ANALYTICAL

an·a·lyt·i·cal (-i k′l) *adj.* **1.** of analysis or analytics **2.** skilled in or using analysis **3.** *same as* ANALYTIC (sense 1) — **an′a·lyt′i·cal·ly** *adv.*

analytic geometry the use of algebra in dealing with geometry by employing a system of coordinates for locating points on a plane

an·a·lyt·ics (-iks) *n.pl.* [*with sing. v.*] the part of logic having to do with analyzing

an·a·lyze (an′ə līz′) *vt.* **-lyzed′, -lyz′ing** [< Fr. < *analyse*, ANALYSIS] **1.** to separate (a thing, idea, etc.) into its parts so as to find out their nature, function, etc. [to *analyze* a chemical] **2.** to examine in detail so as to determine the nature or tendencies of [to *analyze* the causes of war] **3.** to psychoanalyze — **an′a·lyz′a·ble** *adj.* —**an′a·lyz′er** *n.*

an·a·pest, an·a·paest (an′ə pest′) *n.* [< L. < Gr. < *ana-*, back + *paiein*, to strike] a metrical foot consisting of two unaccented syllables followed by an accented one, as in English verse (Ex.: "And thĕ shéen/ŏf thĕir spéars/wăs lĭke stárs/ŏn thĕ séa") —**an′a·pes′tic, an′a·paes′tic** *adj.*

an·a·phor·a (ə naf′ər ə) *n.* [L. < Gr. < *ana-*, up, back + *pherein*, to BEAR¹] the repetition of a word or phrase at the beginning of successive clauses or sentences as a rhetorical device

an·aph·ro·dis·i·ac (an af′rə diz′ē ak) *adj.* that lessens sexual desire —*n.* a drug, etc. that lessens sexual desire

an·a·phy·lax·is (an′ə fə lak′sis) *n.* [ModL. < Gr. *ana-*, ANA- + *phylaxis*, a guarding] abnormal sensitivity to a substance that one was exposed to earlier, resulting in shock —**an′a·phy·lac′tic** (-lak′tik) *adj.*

an·ar·chic (an är′kik) *adj.* **1.** of, like, or promoting anarchy **2.** without controls; lawless Also **an·ar′chi·cal** —**an·ar′chi·cal·ly** *adv.*

an·ar·chism (an′ər kiz′m) *n.* [ANARCH(Y) + -ISM] **1.** the theory that all forms of government interfere unjustly with individual liberty and should be replaced by a system of voluntary cooperation **2.** resistance, sometimes by terrorism, to government

an·ar·chist (-kist) *n.* **1.** a person who believes in or advocates anarchism **2.** a person who promotes anarchy —**an′ar·chis′tic** *adj.*

an·ar·chy (-kē) *n., pl.* **-chies** [< Gr. < *an-*, without + *archos*, leader] **1.** the complete absence of government **2.** political disorder and violence **3.** disorder or confusion in any kind of activity

an·as·tig·mat·ic (an as′tig mat′ik, an′ə stig-) *adj.* free from, or corrected for, astigmatism

a·nas·to·mose (ə nas′tə mōz′) *vt., vi.* **-mosed′, -mos′ing** to join by anastomosis

a·nas·to·mo·sis (ə nas′tə mō′sis) *n., pl.* **-ses** (-sēz) [ModL. < Gr. *anastomōsis*, opening < *ana-*, again + *stoma*, mouth] **1.** interconnection as between blood vessels or veins of a leaf **2.** the surgical operation of joining tubular parts or organs

a·nas·tro·phe (ə nas′trə fē) *n.* [Gr. < *ana-*, back + *strephein*, to turn] reversal of the usual word order of a sentence (Ex.: "Came the dawn")

anat. **1.** anatomical **2.** anatomist **3.** anatomy

a·nath·e·ma (ə nath′ə mə) *n., pl.* **-mas** [LL. < Gr., thing devoted to evil < *anatithenai*, to dedicate < *ana-*, up + *tithenai*, to set] **1.** a thing or person accursed or hated **2.** a formal curse, as in excommunicating a person from a church **3.** any strong curse

a·nath·e·ma·tize (ə nath′ə mə tīz′) *vt., vi.* **-tized′, -tiz′ing** to utter an anathema (against); curse —**a·nath′e·ma·ti·za′tion** *n.*

An·a·to·li·a (an′ə tō′lē ə) **1.** formerly, Asia Minor **2.** the part of modern Turkey that is in Asia —**An′a·to′li·an** *adj., n.*

an·a·tom·i·cal (an′ə täm′i k′l) *adj.* **1.** of or connected with anatomy **2.** structural Also **an′a·tom′ic** —**an′a·tom′i·cal·ly** *adv.*

a·nat·o·mist (ə nat′ə mist) *n.* **1.** a person skilled in anatomy **2.** a person who anatomizes

a·nat·o·mize (-mīz′) *vt., vi.* **-mized′, -miz′ing** [see ANATOMY] **1.** to dissect (an animal or plant) in order to examine the structure **2.** to analyze in great detail —**a·nat′o·mi·za′tion** *n.*

a·nat·o·my (ə nat′ə mē) *n., pl.* **-mies** [< ME. & OFr. < LL. < Gr. < *ana-*, up + *temnein*, to cut] **1.** the dissecting of an animal or plant in order to study its structure **2.** the science of the structure of animals or plants **3.** the structure of a particular animal or plant [the *anatomy* of a frog] **4.** a detailed analysis

An·ax·ag·o·ras (an′ak sag′ər əs) 500?–428? B.C.; Gr. philosopher

-ance (əns, ′ns) [< Fr. < L. *-antia, -entia,* or directly < L.] *a suffix meaning:* **1.** the act of [*assistance*] **2.** the quality or state of being [*vigilance*] **3.** a thing that [*conveyance*] **4.** a thing that is [*dissonance, inheritance*]

an·ces·tor (an′ses′tər) *n.* [< ME. & OFr. < L. *antecessor,* one who goes before < *ante-,* before + *cedere,* to go] **1.** any person from whom one is descended; forebear **2.** an early type of animal from which later kinds have evolved **3.** a precursor or predecessor [the clavichord is an *ancestor* of the piano] **4.** *Law* the person from whom an estate has been inherited —**an′ces′tress** (-trəs) *n.fem.*

an·ces·tral (an ses′trəl) *adj.* of or inherited from ancestors

an·ces·try (an′ses′trē) *n., pl.* **-tries 1.** family descent or lineage [a man of Czech *ancestry*] **2.** ancestors collectively

an·chor (aŋ′kər) *n.* [< OE. < L. < Gr. *ankyra,* a hook: for IE. base see ANKLE] **1.** a heavy object, usually a shaped iron weight with flukes, lowered to the bottom of a body of water by cable or chain to keep a ship from drifting **2.** anything that keeps something or someone stable or secure [in time of trouble, her home was her *anchor*] **3.** *same as* ANCHORMAN —*vt.* **1.** to hold firm and steady by or as by an anchor **2.** to act as an anchorman on —*vi.* **1.** to lower the anchor overboard **2.** to be or become fixed —**at anchor** anchored —**drop** (or **cast**) **anchor 1.** to lower the anchor overboard **2.** to settle (*in* a place) — **weigh anchor 1.** to raise the anchor **2.** to leave; go away

ANCHOR

an·chor·age (aŋ′kər ij) *n.* **1.** money charged for the right to anchor **2.** an anchoring or being anchored **3.** a place to anchor **4.** something that can be firmly held on to or relied on

an·cho·rite (aŋ′kə rīt′) *n.* [< OFr. < LL. < Gr. *anachōrētēs* < *ana-,* back + *chōrein,* to retire] a person who lives alone for religious meditation; hermit —**an′cho·rit′ic** (-rit′ik) *adj.*

an·chor·man (aŋ′kər man′) *n., pl.* **-men** (-men′) **1.** the final contestant, as on a relay team **2.** *Radio & TV* that member of a team of newscasters who coordinates various reports —**an′chor·wom′an** *n.fem., pl.* **-wom′en**

an·chor·per·son (-pur′s′n) *n. same as* ANCHORMAN: preferred by some who use this term not suggesting a man

an·cho·vy (an′chō′vē, -chə-; an′chō′vē) *n., pl.* **-vies, -vy:** see PLURAL, II, D, 1 [< Port. *anchova,* prob. ult. < Gr. *aphyē,* small fry] a very small, herringlike fish: anchovies are usually canned in oil or made into a salty paste

an·chy·lose (aŋ′kə lōs′) *vt., vi.* **-losed′, -los′ing** *same as* ANKYLOSE —**an′chy·lo′sis** (-lō′sis) *n.*

‡**an·cien ré·gime** (äṅ syaṅ rā zhēm′) [Fr., old order] the former social and political system, esp. that in France before the Revolution of 1789

an·cient (än′shənt) *adj.* [< OFr., ult. < L. *ante,* before] **1.** of times long past; esp., of the time before the end of the Western Roman Empire in 476 A.D. **2.** very old **3.** old-fashioned —*n.* **1.** a person who lived in ancient times **2.** an aged person —**the ancients** the people who lived in ancient times; esp., the classical writers and artists of Greco-Roman times

an·cient·ly (-lē) *adv.* in ancient times

an·cil·lar·y (an′sə ler′ē) *adj.* [< L. < *ancilla,* maidservant] **1.** subordinate (*to*) **2.** auxiliary

an·con (aŋ′kän) *n., pl.* **an·co·nes** (aŋ kō′nēz) [L. < Gr. < *ankos,* a bend] a bracketlike projection supporting a cornice

-an·cy (ən sē, ′n sē) *same as* -ANCE

and (ənd, ən, ′n; *stressed* and) *conj.* [OE.] **1.** also; in addition; as well as: used to join words of the same grammatical class [apples *and* pears, to beg *and* borrow] **2.** plus [6 *and* 2 equals 8] **3.** as a result [he told her *and* she wept] **4.** [Colloq.] to [try *and* get it] **5.** [Archaic] then [*and* it came to pass] **6.** [Obs.] if

An·da·lu·sia (an·də lōō′zhə, -shə) region of S Spain

an·dan·te (än dän′tā, an dan′tē) *adj., adv.* [It., prp. of *andare,* to walk] *Music* moderate, not fast, in tempo —*n.* an andante movement or passage

an·dan·ti·no (än′dän tē′nō, an′dan-) *adj., adv.* [It., dim. of *andante*] *music* slightly faster than andante —*n., pl.* **-nos** an andantino movement or section of music

An·der·sen (an′dər s′n), **Hans Christian** 1805–75; Dan. novelist & writer of fairy tales

An·der·son (an′dər s′n) [after a Delaware Indian, Chief *Anderson*] city in EC Ind.: pop. 71,000

An·der·son (an′dər s′n), **Sher·wood** (shur′wood) 1876–1941; U.S. novelist & short-story writer

An·des (Mountains) (an′dēz) mountain system along the length of western S. America: highest peak, ACONCAGUA —**An·de·an** (an dē′ən, an′dē-) *adj.*

and·i·ron (an′dī′ərn) *n.* [< OFr. *andier* (with ending altered after IRON)] either of a pair of metal supports with front uprights, used to hold the wood in a fireplace

and/or either *and* or *or,* according to what is meant; either or both [money *and/or* real estate]

An·dor·ra (an dôr′ə, -där′ə) republic in the E Pyrenees, between Spain and France: 180 sq. mi.; pop. 19,000 —**An·dor′ran** *adj., n.*

Andrea del Sarto *see* SARTO

An·drew (an′drōō) [< OFr. < L. < Gr. *Andreas,* lit., manly < *andros,* genitive of *anēr,* man] **1.** a masculine name: dim. *Andy* **2.** *Bible* one of the twelve apostles

an·dro- [< Gr. *andros,* genitive of *anēr,* man] *a combining form meaning:* **1.** man, male, masculine [*androgynous*] **2.** anther, stamen

An·dro·cles (an′drə klēz′) *Rom. Legend* a slave spared in the arena by a lion that recognized him as the man who had once pulled a thorn from its paw

an·droe·ci·um (an drē′shē əm, -sē-) *n., pl.* **-ci·a** (-ə) [ModL. < ANDRO- + Gr. *oikos,* house] *Bot.* the stamens and the parts belonging to them, as a group

an·dro·gen (an′drə jən) *n.* [ANDRO- + -GEN] a male sex hormone that can give rise to masculine characteristics —**an′dro·gen′ic** (-jen′ik) *adj.*

an·drog·y·nous (an dräj′ə nəs) *adj.* [< L. < Gr. < *anēr* (gen. *andros*), man + *gynē,* woman] **1.** both male and female in one; hermaphroditic **2.** *Bot.* bearing flowers with stamens and flowers with pistils in the same cluster —**an·drog′y·ny** (-ə nē) *n.*

an·droid (an′droid) *n.* [ANDR(O)- + -OID] in science fiction, an automaton that looks human

An·drom·a·che (an dräm′ə kē) *Gr. Myth.* the wife of Hector

An·drom·e·da (an dräm′ə də) **1.** *Gr. Myth.* an Ethiopian princess whom Perseus rescued from a sea monster and then married **2.** *Astron.* a N constellation just south of Cassiopeia

an·dros·ter·one (an dräs′tə rōn′) *n.* [ANDRO- + STER(OL) + -ONE] a steroid that is a male sex hormone

-an·drous (an′drəs) [< Gr. *anēr:* see ANDRO-] *a suffix meaning* having stamens

-ane (ān) [arbitrary formation] *a suffix denoting* a hydrocarbon of the paraffin series [*methane*]

an·ec·dote (an′ik dōt′) *n.* [Fr. < ML. < Gr. *anekdotos,* unpublished < *an-,* not + *ek-,* out + *didonai,* to give] a short, entertaining story of some happening, usually personal or biographical —see SYN. at STORY[1] —**an′ec·dot′al** (-dōt′′l) *adj.* —**an′ec·dot′ist** (-dōt′ist) *n.*

an·e·cho·ic (an′e kō′ik) *adj.* [AN- + ECHOIC] free from echoes [an *anechoic* recording chamber]

a·ne·mi·a (ə nē′mē ə, -myə) *n.* [ModL. < Gr. < *a-, an-,* without + *haima,* blood] **1.** a condition in which there is a lack of red blood corpuscles or of hemoglobin in the bloodstream **2.** lack of vigor; lifelessness —**a·ne′mic** (-mik) *adj.*

a·nem·o·graph (ə nem′ə graf′) *n.* [< Gr. *anemos,* the wind + -GRAPH] an instrument for recording the speed and direction of the wind

an·e·mom·e·ter (an′ə mäm′ə tər) *n.* [< Gr. *anemos,* the wind + -METER] a gauge for determining the force or speed of the wind, and sometimes its direction —**an′e·mo·met′ric** (-mō met′rik) *adj.* —**an′e·mom′e·try** *n.*

a·nem·o·ne (ə nem′ə nē′) *n.* [L. < Gr., infl. by *anemos,* wind] **1.** any of various plants with cup-shaped flowers, usually white, purple, or red **2.** *same as* SEA ANEMONE

a·nent (ə nent′) *prep.* [< OE. *on efen,* lit., on even (with), level (with)] concerning; as regards

an·er·oid (an′ər oid) *adj.* [< Gr. *a-,* without + *nēros,* liquid + -OID] not using liquid —*n. same as* ANEROID BAROMETER

aneroid barometer a barometer consisting of a box in which a partial vacuum is maintained: changes in atmospheric pressure cause its elastic top to bend in or out, thus moving a pointer

an·es·the·sia (an′əs thē′zhə, -zhē ə) *n.* [< Gr. *a-,* without + *aisthēsis,* feeling] **1.** a partial or total loss of the sense of pain, temperature, touch, etc. produced by disease ☆**2.** a loss of sensation caused by an anesthetic and affecting a specific area (**local anesthesia**) or producing unconsciousness (**general anesthesia**)

☆**an·es·the·si·ol·o·gist** (an'əs thē'zē äl'ə jist) *n.* a doctor who specializes in anesthesiology

☆**an·es·the·si·ol·o·gy** (-jē) *n.* the science of anesthesia and anesthetics

☆**an·es·thet·ic** (an'əs thet'ik) *adj.* **1.** of or with anesthesia **2.** producing anesthesia —*n.* a drug, gas, etc. used to produce anesthesia, as before surgery —**anesthetic to** incapable of feeling or responding to —**an'es·thet'i·cal·ly** *adv.*

an·es·the·tist (ə nes'thə tist) *n.* a nurse or other person trained to give anesthetics

an·es·the·tize (-tīz') *vt.* **-tized', -tiz'ing** to cause anesthesia in as by giving an anesthetic —**an'es·the·ti·za'tion** *n.*

an·eu·rysm, an·eu·rism (an'yər iz'm) *n.* [ModL. < Gr. < *ana-*, up + *eurys*, broad] a sac formed when the wall of an artery, weakened by disease or injury, becomes enlarged —**an'eu·rys'mal, an'eu·ris'mal** (-yə riz'm'l) *adj.*

a·new (ə nō͞o', -nyō͞o') *adv.* **1.** once more; again **2.** in a new manner or form

an·gel (ān'j'l) *n.* [< OFr. or OE. < L. *angelus* < Gr. *angelos*, messenger < Iran.] **1.** *Theol.* a) a messenger of God b) a supernatural being, either good or bad, with more power, intelligence, etc. than human beings **2.** a guiding spirit [one's good *angel*] **3.** an image of a figure in human form with wings and a halo, representing an angel **4.** a person regarded as beautiful, good, innocent, etc. ☆**5.** [Colloq.] a supporter who provides money, as for producing a play —☆*vt.* [Slang] to support with money

An·ge·la (an'jə lə) [< ML. < L. *angelicus*, angelic] a feminine name: var. *Angelica, Angelina*

☆**An·gel·e·no** (an'jə lē'nō) *n., pl.* **-nos** [AmSp.] a native or inhabitant of Los Angeles

an·gel·fish (ān'j'l fish') *n., pl.* **-fish', -fish'es:** see FISH **1.** a shark with winglike pectoral fins **2.** any of a number of bright-colored tropical fishes with spiny fins

☆**angel food cake** a light, spongy, white cake made with egg whites and no shortening: also **angel cake**

an·gel·ic (an jel'ik) *adj.* **1.** of an angel or the angels **2.** like an angel in beauty, goodness, etc. Also **an·gel'i·cal** —**an·gel'i·cal·ly** *adv.*

an·gel·i·ca (an jel'i kə) *n.* [ML. (*herba*) *angelica*, lit., the angelic (herb)] a plant of the parsley family, with roots and fruit used in flavoring, medicine, etc.

ANGELFISH
(4–24 in. long)

An·gel·i·co (an jel'ə kō'), **Fra** (frä) (*Giovanni da Fiesole*) 1387–1455; It. painter

An·ge·lus (an'jə ləs) *n.* [L.: see ANGEL] [*also* a-] *R.C.Ch.* **1.** a prayer said at morning, noon, and evening in commemoration of the Incarnation **2.** a bell rung to announce the time for this

an·ger (aŋ'gər) *n.* [ON. *angr*, distress, sorrow] a feeling of displeasure and hostility that one has because of being injured, mistreated, opposed, etc. —*vt.* to make angry —*vi.* to become angry
SYN.—**anger** is the general word for the feeling of strong displeasure mixed with resentment or a desire for revenge; **rage** suggests a violent outburst of anger in which self-control is lost [*their insults drove him into a rage*]; **fury** suggests a rage so violent that it is almost madness [*the fury of a rejected lover*]; **indignation** implies anger caused by action that seems unjust, immoral, or insulting [*he viewed racial discrimination with indignation*]; **wrath** suggests strong indignation with a desire to punish or get revenge [*the wrath of the gods*] —**ANT.** pleasure, forbearance

An·ge·vin, An·ge·vine (an'jə vin) *adj.* [Fr.] of Anjou or the Plantagenets —*n.* **1.** a native of Anjou **2.** any of the Plantagenets

an·gi·na (an jī'nə, an'jə-) *n.* [L., quinsy < Gr. < *anchein*, to squeeze] **1.** any inflammatory disease of the throat, esp. one characterized by fits of suffocation **2.** any sudden spasm of pain **3.** *same as* ANGINA PECTORIS —**an·gi'nal, an·gi·nose** (an'jə nōs'), **an·gi'nous** (-nəs) *adj.*

angina pec·to·ris (pek'tər is) [L., angina of the breast] a condition marked by sharp pain recurring from time to time in the chest and left arm, caused by a sudden decrease of blood supply to the heart

an·gi·o·ma (an'jē ō'mə) *n., pl.* **-ma·ta** (-mə tə), **-mas** [< Gr.

angeion, vessel + -OMA] a tumor made up mainly of blood vessels and lymph vessels

an·gi·o·sperm (an'jē ə spurm') *n.* [< Gr. *angeion*, capsule + -SPERM] any flowering plant having the seeds enclosed in an ovary

Angl. 1. Anglican **2.** Anglicized

an·gle¹ (aŋ'g'l) *n.* [ME. & OFr. < L. *angulus*, a corner < Gr. *ankylos*, bent: for IE. base see ANKLE] **1.** a) the shape made by two straight lines meeting in a point, or by two plane surfaces meeting along a line b) the space between such lines or surfaces c) the amount of difference in direction between them, measured in degrees **2.** a sharp corner **3.** the way one looks at something; point of view [consider this from all *angles*] **4.** [Colloq.] a selfish motive or tricky plan —*vt., vi.* **-gled, -gling** **1.** to move or bend at an angle **2.** [Colloq.] to give a specific point of view to (a story, report, etc.)

an·gle² (aŋ'g'l) *vi.* **-gled, -gling** [OE. *angul*, fishhook: for IE. base see ANKLE] **1.** to fish with a hook and line **2.** to use tricks to get something [he *angled* for her attention by looking moody]

angle iron a piece of iron or steel in the form of an angle, used for joining or reinforcing two beams, girders, etc.

angle of incidence the angle that a light ray or electromagnetic wave striking a surface makes with a line perpendicular to the surface

an·gler (aŋ'glər) *n.* [< ANGLE²] **1.** a fisherman **2.** one who uses tricks to get something **3.** a saltwater fish that feeds on other fish attracted by a filament on its head

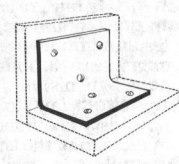

ANGLE IRON

An·gles (aŋ'g'lz) *n.pl.* a Germanic people that settled in eastern England in the 5th cent. A.D. —**An'gli·an** (-glē ən) *adj., n.*

☆**an·gle·worm** (aŋ'g'l wurm') *n.* an earthworm: so called because used as fishing bait

An·gli·can (aŋ'gli kən) *adj.* [< ML. < *Anglicus*, of England, of the Angles] **1.** of England; English **2.** of the Church of England or any related church with the same faith and forms —*n.* a member of an Anglican church —**An'gli·can·ism** *n.*

An·gli·cism (aŋ'glə siz'm) *n.* **1.** a word or idiom peculiar to English, esp. British English; Briticism **2.** a typically English trait, custom, etc. **3.** the quality of being English

An·gli·cize (aŋ'glə sīz') *vt., vi.* **-cized', -ciz'ing** [*also* a-] to change to English form, pronunciation, customs, etc. [*lariat* is a Spanish word that has been *Anglicized*] —**An'gli·ci·za'tion** *n.*

☆**An·gli·fy** (-fī') *vt.* **-fied', -fy'ing** *same as* ANGLICIZE

an·gling (aŋ'gliŋ) *n.* [< ANGLE²] the act or skill of fishing with hook and line

An·glo (aŋ'glō) *n., pl.* **-glos** [< ANGLO-AMERICAN] [Southwest] a white person of non-Mexican descent

An·glo- [< L. *Anglus*, sing. of *Angli*, ANGLES] *a combining form meaning* English [*Anglophile*]

☆**An·glo-A·mer·i·can** (aŋ'glō ə mer'ə kən) *adj.* English and American; of or between England and the U.S. —*n.* an American of English birth or ancestry

An·glo-French (-french') *adj.* English and French; of or between England and France —*n.* the French spoken in England from the Norman Conquest through the Middle Ages: see NORMAN FRENCH

An·glo-In·di·an (-in'dē ən) *adj.* **1.** of England and India **2.** of Anglo-Indians or their English speech —*n.* **1.** a person of English and Indian ancestry **2.** words borrowed into English from the languages of India

☆**An·glo·ma·ni·a** (-mā'nē ə) *n.* an exaggerated liking for and imitation of English customs, manners, institutions, etc. —**An'·glo·ma'ni·ac'** (-ak') *n.*

An·glo-Nor·man (-nôr'mən) *adj.* English and Norman —*n.* **1.** a Norman settler in England after the Norman Conquest **2.** the Anglo-French dialect spoken by such settlers

An·glo·phile (aŋ'glə fīl') *n.* [*often* a-] a person characterized by Anglophilia

An·glo·phil·i·a (aŋ'glə fil'ē ə) *n.* [*often* a-] extreme admiration for England, its people, customs, etc.

An·glo·phobe (aŋ'glə fōb') *n.* [*often* a-] a person characterized by Anglophobia

☆**An·glo·pho·bi·a** (aŋ′glə fō′bē ə) *n.* [*often* a-] hatred or fear of England, its people, customs, etc. —**An′glo·pho′bic** (-fō′bik) *adj.*

An·glo-Sax·on (aŋ′glō sak′s'n) *n.* [< ML.: see ANGLES & SAXON] **1.** a member of the Germanic peoples (Angles, Saxons, and Jutes) living in England at the time of the Norman Conquest **2.** *same as* OLD ENGLISH **3.** plain, blunt language of Old English origin **4.** a person of English nationality or descent — *adj.* **1.** of the Anglo-Saxons or their language **2.** of their descendants; english

An·go·la (aŋ gō′lə, an-) country on the W coast of Africa: 481,351 sq. mi.; pop. 6,761,000; cap. Luanda

An·go·ra (aŋ gôr′ə, an-) *n.* [former name of ANKARA] **1.** a kind of cat with long, silky fur **2.** *a*) a kind of goat raised for its long, silky hair *b*) a cloth made from this hair; mohair **3.** *a*) a long-eared rabbit, raised for its long, silky hair *b*) a soft yarn made from this hair and woven into sweaters, etc. Also **angora** for senses 2*b*, 3*b*

an·gos·tu·ra (bark) (an′gəs toor′ə, -tyoor′-) [after *Angostura*, former name of Ciudad Bolívar, city in Venezuela] a bitter bark used as a medicinal tonic and as a flavoring in bitters

an·gri·ly (aŋ′grə lē) *adv.* in an angry way

an·gry (aŋ′grē) *adj.* -gri·er, -gri·est **1.** feeling, showing, or resulting from anger [an *angry* reply] **2.** wild and stormy [an *angry* sea] **3.** inflamed and sore [an *angry* wound] —**an′gri·ness** (-grē nis) *n.*

ang·strom (aŋ′strəm) *n.* [after A. J. *Angström*, 19th-c. Swed. physicist] one hundred-millionth of a centimeter, a unit used in measuring the length of light waves: also **angstrom unit**

An·guil·la (aŋ gwil′ə) island in the Leeward group in the West Indies; a Brit. colony: 35 sq. mi.; pop. 6,000

an·guish (aŋ′gwish) *n.* [< OFr. < L. *angustia*, tightness < *angustus*, narrow] great suffering, as from worry, grief, or pain; agony [his disappearance caused her much *anguish*] —*vi., vt.* to feel or make feel anguish —see SYN. at DISTRESS —**an′guished** (-gwisht) *adj.*

an·gu·lar (aŋ′gyə lər) *adj.* **1.** having or forming an angle or angles; having sharp corners **2.** measured by an angle [*angular* distance] **3.** with bones that jut out; gaunt [an *angular* face] **4.** without ease or grace; awkward [an *angular* stride] —**an′gu·lar·ly** *adv.*

an·gu·lar·i·ty (aŋ′gyə lar′ə tē) *n., pl.* -ties **1.** the quality or condition of being angular **2.** [*pl.*] angular forms; sharp corners; angles

An·gus (aŋ′gəs) [< Gael. & Ir. < *aon*, one] **1.** a masculine name **2.** the Celtic god of love

an·hy·dride (an hī′drīd) *n.* [< Gr. *anhydros* (see ANHYDROUS) + -IDE] **1.** an oxide that reacts with water to form an acid or a base **2.** any compound formed by the removal of water, usually from an acid

an·hy·drous (-drəs) *adj.* [Gr. *anhydros* < *an-*, without + *hydōr*, water] **1.** without water **2.** *Chem.* having no water of crystallization

an·il (an′il) *n.* [Fr. < Port. < Ar. *al*, the + *nīl*, blue] **1.** a West Indian shrub from which indigo is made **2.** *same as* INDIGO

an·ile (an′īl, ā′nīl) *adj.* [< L. < *anus*, old woman] like a weak or infirm old woman

an·i·line (an′'l in, -ēn′, -īn′) *n.* [ANIL + -INE⁴] a colorless, poisonous, oily liquid, $C_6H_5NH_2$, gotten from benzene and used in making dyes, synthetic resins, rocket fuel, etc.

aniline dye 1. any dye made from aniline **2.** commonly, any synthetic dye made from coal tar

an·i·ma (an′ə mə) *n.* [L.] life principle; soul

an·i·mad·ver·sion (an′ə mad vur′zhən, -shən) *n.* [see ANIMADVERT] **1.** a critical, esp. unfavorable, comment (*on* or *upon* something) **2.** the act of criticizing unfavorably

an·i·mad·vert (-vurt′) *vi.* [< L. < *animus*, mind + *advertere*, to turn: see ANIMUS & ADVERT] to comment (*on* or *upon*), esp. with disapproval; criticize unfavorably

an·i·mal (an′ə m'l) *n.* [L. < *anima, animus*, breath, life principle, soul] **1.** any living organism except a plant or bacterium: most animals can move about voluntarily and are unable to make their own food by photosynthesis, as plants do **2.** any such organism other than a human being, esp. a mammal or, sometimes, any four-footed creature **3.** a person who is like a beast or brute —*adj.* **1.** of, like, or from an animal **2.** gross, coarse, bestial, sensual, etc. [he lives an *animal* existence] —**an′i·mal·ly** *adv.*

animal cracker a small, sweet cracker shaped like any of various animals

an·i·mal·cule (an′ə mal′kyool) *n.* [< ModL., dim.: see

ANIMAL] a tiny or microscopic animal: also **an′i·mal′cu·lum** (-kyə ləm) *n., pl.* -la (-lə) —**an′i·mal′cu·lar** (-kyə lər) *adj.*

animal husbandry the raising of farm animals, as cattle, sheep, horses, etc.

an·i·mal·ism (an′ə m'l iz'm) *n.* **1.** the activity, appetites, nature, etc. of animals **2.** the doctrine that man is a mere animal with no soul —**an′i·mal·ist** *n.* —**an′i·mal·is′tic** *adj.*

an·i·mal·i·ty (an′ə mal′ə tē) *n.* **1.** animal characteristics or nature **2.** the animal instincts or nature in man

animal magnetism 1. *old term for* HYPNOTISM **2.** the power to attract others in a sensual way

animal spirits healthy, lively vigor

an·i·mate (an′ə māt′; *for adj.* -mit) *vt.* -mat′ed, -mat′ing [< L. pp. of *animare*, to make alive < *anima*: see ANIMAL] **1.** to give life to; bring to life **2.** to make lively or spirited **3.** to cause to act; inspire [she is *animated* by a desire to help others] **4.** to give motion to [a breeze *animating* the leaves] **5.** to make move so as to seem lifelike [to *animate* puppets] ☆**6.** to produce as an animated cartoon [to *animate* a fairy tale] —*adj.* **1.** living; having life, esp. animal life **2.** lively; spirited —see SYN. at LIVING —**an′i·ma′tor, an′i·mat′er** *n.*

an·i·mat·ed (-māt′id) *adj.* **1.** alive or seeming alive; living **2.** lively; spirited [an *animated* conversation] —see SYN. at LIVING —**an′i·mat′ed·ly** *adv.*

☆**animated cartoon** a motion picture made by filming a series of drawings, each slightly changed from the one before, so that the figures in them seem to move when the film is projected

an·i·ma·tion (an′ə mā′shən) *n.* **1.** an animating or being animated **2.** life **3.** liveliness; spirit [they spoke with *animation*] ☆**4.** the making of animated cartoons ☆**5.** *same as* ANIMATED CARTOON

‡**a·ni·ma·to** (ä′nē mä′tô) *adj., adv.* [It.] *Music* with animation; lively

an·i·mism (an′ə miz'm) *n.* [< Fr. & G. < L. *anima*: see ANIMAL & -ISM] **1.** the doctrine that all life is produced by a spiritual force **2.** the belief that all natural objects and phenomena have souls **3.** a belief in the existence of spirits, demons, etc. —**an′i·mist** *n.* —**an′i·mis′tic** *adj.*

an·i·mos·i·ty (an′ə mäs′ə tē) *n., pl.* -ties [< L. *animositas*, spirit < *animus*: see ANIMUS] a feeling of strong dislike or hatred; enmity; ill will — see SYN. at ENMITY

an·i·mus (an′ə məs) *n.* [L., soul, mind, passion: see ANIMAL] **1.** an animating force; intention **2.** a feeling of ill will or enmity; animosity

an·i·on (an′ī′ən) *n.* [< Gr. neut. prp. of *anienai*, to go up < *ana-*, up + *ienai*, to go] a negatively charged ion: in electrolysis, anions move toward the anode —**an·i·on·ic** (an′ī än′ik) *adj.*

an·ise (an′is) *n.* [< ME. & OFr. < L. < Gr. *anēson*] **1.** a plant of the parsley family, with fragrant seeds used for flavoring **2.** *same as* ANISEED

an·i·seed (an′ə sēd′) *n.* the seed of anise

A·ni·ta (ə nēt′ə) [Sp. dim. of *Ana*, equiv. of ANNA] a feminine name

An·jou (an′joō; *Fr.* än zhoō′) former province of W France

An·ka·ra (aŋ′kə rə, äŋ′-) capital of Turkey: pop. 906,000

ankh (aŋk) *n.* [Egypt., life, soul] a cross with a loop at the top, an ancient Egyptian symbol of life

an·kle (aŋ′k'l) *n.* [OE. *ancleow* < IE. base *ang-*, limb, var. of *ank-*, to bend] **1.** the joint that connects the foot and the leg **2.** the part of the leg between the foot and calf

an·kle·bone (-bōn′) *n.* the bone of the ankle; talus

an·klet (aŋ′klit) *n.* **1.** anything worn around the ankle as an ornament or fetter **2.** a short sock

an·ky·lose (aŋ′kə lōs′) *vt., vi.* -losed′, -los′ing to stiffen or join by ankylosis

an·ky·lo·sis (aŋ′kə lō′sis) *n.* [Gr. < *ankyloun*, to stiffen < *ankylos*, bent: for IE. base see ANKLE] *Med.* an abnormal growing together and stiffening of a joint —**an′ky·lot′ic** (-lät′ik) *adj.*

ann. 1. annual **2.** annuity

An·na (an′ə) [< Fr. < L. < Gr. < Heb. *hannāh*, lit., grace] a feminine name: var. *Ann, Anne, Hannah*

ANIMATED FILM

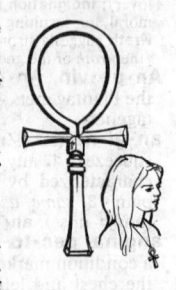

ANKH

an·na (an′ə, ä′nə) *n.* [Hindi *ānā*] a former coin of India, Pakistan, and Burma, equal to 1/16 of a rupee

An·na·bel, An·na·belle (an′ə bel′) [? altered < *Amabel* < L. *amabilis*, lovable < *amare*, to love] a feminine name

an·nal·ist (an′'l ist) *n.* a writer of annals —**an′nal·is′tic** *adj.*

an·nals (an′'lz) *n.pl.* [< L. < *annus*, year] **1.** a written account of events year by year in chronological order **2.** historical records; history [he held a unique place in the *annals* of our country] **3.** any journal containing reports of a society, etc.

An·nam (an am′, an′am) region in EC Indochina, divided between North Vietnam and South Vietnam —**An′na·mese′** (-ə mēz′) *adj., n., pl.* -**mese′**

An·nap·o·lis (ə nap′ə lis) [< ANNA + Gr. *polis*, city] capital of Md., on Chesapeake Bay: pop. 30,000

An·na·pur·na (än′ə poor′nə, an′ə pur′-) mountain mass of the Himalayas, C Nepal: highest peak, 26,500 ft.

Ann Ar·bor (an är′bər) [prob. after *Ann* Allen, early settler] city in SE Mich.: pop. 100,000

Anne (an) **1.** a feminine name: see ANNA **2.** 1665–1714; queen of Great Britain & Ireland (1702–14)

an·neal (ə nēl′) *vt.* [OE. *anælan*, to burn < *an-*, on + *ælan*, to burn < *æl*, fire] **1.** to heat (glass, metals, etc.) and then cool slowly to prevent brittleness **2.** to strengthen or toughen (the mind, will, etc.) —**an·neal′er** *n.*

an·ne·lid (an′'l id) *n.* [< Fr. < L. *annellus*, dim. of *anulus*, a ring: see ANNULAR] a worm with a body made of joined segments· or rings, as the earthworm, leech, etc. —*adj.* of such worms

An·nette (an et′, ə net′) [Fr. dim. of *Anne:* see ANNA] a feminine name

an·nex (ə neks′; *for n.* an′eks) *vt.* [< OFr. < L. pp. of *annectere* < *ad-*, to + *nectere*, to tie, bind] **1.** to add on or attach, esp. to something larger **2.** to add as a condition, consequence, etc. [power is often *annexed* to wealth] **3.** to incorporate into a state, etc. the territory of (another state, etc.) **4.** to take, esp. without asking —*n.* something added on; esp., an addition built on or near a building —**an·nex′a·ble** *adj.* —**an·nex·a·tion** (an′ek sā′shən) *n.* —**an′nex·a′tion·ist** *n.*

an·ni·hi·late (ə nī′ə lāt′) *vt.* -**lat′ed,** -**lat′ing** [< L. pp. of *annihilare*, to bring to nothing < *ad-*, to + *nihil*, nothing] **1.** to destroy completely; demolish [an atomic bomb can *annihilate* a city] **2.** to kill **3.** to conquer decisively; crush —see SYN. at DESTROY —**an·ni′hi·la·ble** (-lə b'l) *adj.* —**an·ni′hi·la′tion** *n.* — **an·ni′hi·la′tive** *adj.* —**an·ni′hi·la′tor** *n.*

an·ni·ver·sa·ry (an′ə vur′sər ē) *n., pl.* -**ries** [< L. < *annus*, year + pp. of *vertere*, to turn: see VERSE] **1.** the date on which some event occurred in an earlier year **2.** the celebration of such an event on that date in following years —*adj.* of, being, or connected with an anniversary

‡**an·no Do·mi·ni** (än′ō dō′mə nē, an′ō däm′ə nī) [L., lit., in the year of the Lord] in the (given) year since the beginning of the Christian Era

an·no·tate (an′ə tāt′, -ō-) *vt., vi.* -**tat′ed,** -**tat′ing** [< L. pp. of *annotare* < *ad-*, to + *nota*, to mark: see NOTE] to add notes that explain or offer opinions about (a literary work, etc.) —**an′no·ta′tive** *adj.* —**an′no·ta′tor** *n.*

an·no·ta·tion (an′ə tā′shən, -ō-) *n.* **1.** an annotating or being annotated **2.** a note or notes added to explain something or offer opinions

an·nounce (ə nouns′) *vt.* -**nounced′,** -**nounc′ing** [< OFr. < L. *annuntiare* < *ad-*, to + *nuntiare*, to report < *nuntius*, messenger] **1.** to give notice of publicly; proclaim [to *announce* the opening of a new store] **2.** to say or tell [he *announced* that he was pleased] **3.** to make known the arrival, etc. of [the butler *announced* the guests] **4.** *Radio & TV* to act as an announcer for [who will *announce* the World Series?] —*vi.* **1.** to serve as an announcer ☆**2.** to declare one's candidacy or endorsement (with *for*)

an·nounce·ment (-mənt) *n.* **1.** an announcing or being announced **2.** something announced **3.** a written or printed notice [an engraved wedding *announcement*]

an·nounc·er (-ər) *n.* a person who announces; specif., one who introduces radio or television programs, identifies the station, reads the news, etc.

an·noy (ə noi′) *vt.* [< OFr. < VL. < *in odio habere*, to have in hate: see ODIUM] **1.** to irritate, bother, or make somewhat an-

gry **2.** to harm by repeated attacks; harass —*vi.* to be annoying —**an·noy′er** *n.* —**an·noy′ing** *adj.* —**an·noy′ing·ly** *adv.*

SYN.—**annoy** implies temporary disturbance of the mind caused by something that displeases one or makes one impatient [I was *annoyed* by his mumbling]; **vex** suggests a greater disturbance and, often, worry [his failure to write home *vexed* her]; **irk** emphasizes a wearing down of one's patience by continuing annoyance [the many detours *irked* the driver]; **bother** implies minor disturbance of one's peace of mind and may suggest mild confusion or anxiety [don't *bother* him with mere details]; **plague** suggests mental pain that can be compared to physical suffering [financial worries continually *plagued* them] —**ANT.** comfort, soothe

an·noy·ance (-əns) *n.* **1.** an annoying or being annoyed **2.** a thing or person that annoys

an·nu·al (an′yoo wəl) *adj.* [< ME. & OFr. < L. < *annus*, year] **1.** of or measured by a year [its *annual* growth] **2.** happening once a year; yearly [their *annual* picnic] **3.** for a year's time, work, etc. [an *annual* wage] **4.** living for only one year or season [an *annual* plant] —*n.* **1.** a yearly publication; specif., a yearbook of a school senior class **2.** a plant that lives only one year or season —**an′nu·al·ly** *adv.*

an·nu·i·tant (ə nōō′ə tənt, -nyōō′-) *n.* a person receiving an annuity

an·nu·i·ty (ə nōō′ə tē, -nyōō′-) *n., pl.* -**ties** [< ME. & OFr. < ML. < L. *annus*, year] **1.** a payment of a fixed sum of money at regular intervals, esp. yearly **2.** an investment yielding such payments

an·nul (ə nul′) *vt.* -**nulled′,** -**nul′ling** [< OFr. < LL. *annullare*, to bring to nothing < *ad-*, to + *nullum*, nothing: see NULL] **1.** to do away with **2.** to make no longer binding under the law; cancel [the marriage was *annulled*] —see SYN. at ABOLISH

an·nu·lar (an′yoo lər) *adj.* [< L. < *anulus*, a ring] of, like, or forming a ring —**an′nu·lar′i·ty** (-lar′ə tē) *n.* —**an′nu·lar·ly** *adv.*

annular eclipse an eclipse in which a ring of sunlight can be seen around the disk of the moon

annular ligament the ligament surrounding the ankle joint or wrist joint

an·nu·late (an′yoo lit, -lāt′) *adj.* [see ANNULAR] marked with, or made up of, rings: also **an′nu·lat′ed** —**an′nu·la′tion** *n.*

an·nu·let (an′yoo lət) *n.* [< L. *anulus*, a ring + -ET] **1.** a small ring **2.** *Archit.* a ringlike molding near the top of a column

an·nul·ment (ə nul′mənt) *n.* **1.** an annulling or being annulled **2.** a formal statement by a court that a marriage is no longer legally binding

an·nu·lus (an′yoo ləs) *n., pl.* -**li′** (-lī′), -**lus·es** [L. *anulus*] any ringlike part or mark

an·nun·ci·ate (ə nun′sē āt′, -shē-) *vt.* -**at′ed,** -**at′ing** [< L. pp. of *annuntiare*] to announce —**an·nun′ci·a′tor** *n.*

an·nun·ci·a·tion (ə nun′sē ā′shən, -shē-) *n.* **1.** an announcing or being announced **2.** [A-] *a*) the angel Gabriel's announcement to Mary that she was to give birth to Jesus: Luke 1:26–38 *b*) the church festival (March 25) commemorating this

an·ode (an′ōd) *n.* [< Gr. < *ana-*, up + *hodos*, way] **1.** a positively charged electrode, as in an electrolytic cell, electron tube, etc. **2.** the negative electrode in a battery supplying current

an·o·dize (an′ə dīz′) *vt.* -**dized′,** -**diz′ing** to put a protective oxide film on (a light metal) by an electrolytic process in which the metal serves as the anode

an·o·dyne (an′ə dīn′) *adj.* [< L. < Gr. < *an-*, without + *odyne,* pain] relieving or lessening pain —*n.* anything that relieves pain or soothes —**an′o·dyn′ic** (-din′ik) *adj.*

a·noint (ə noint′) *vt.* [< OFr. < L. *inungere* < *in-*, on + *ungere*, to smear] **1.** to rub oil or ointment on **2.** to put oil on in a ceremony of making holy or placing in a high office —**a·noint′er** *n.* —**a·noint′ment** *n.*

Anointing of the Sick *R.C.Ch.* the sacrament in which a priest prays for and anoints a person dying or critically ill

a·nom·a·lis·tic (ə näm′ə lis′tik) *adj.* **1.** tending to be anomalous **2.** of an anomaly

a·nom·a·lous (ə näm′ə ləs) *adj.* [< L. < Gr. < *an-*, not + *homalos* < *homos*, the SAME] **1.** not following the general rule; abnormal **2.** being, or seeming to be, inconsistent or a contradiction [a soldier's *anomalous* role in peacetime] —see SYN. at IRREGULAR —**a·nom′a·lous·ly** *adv.*

a·nom·a·ly (-lē) *n., pl.* -**lies** [< L. < Gr. *anōmalia*, inequality:

see prec.] **1.** departure from what is regular or usual; abnormality **2.** anything anomalous *[a four-leaf clover is an anomaly]*

an·o·mie, an·o·my (an′ə mē) *n.* [< Fr. < Gr. < *a-*, without + *nomos*, law] lack of purpose, identity, or ethical values in a person or in a society; rootlessness **—a·nom·ic** (ə näm′ik) *adj.*

a·non (ə nän′) *adv.* [OE. *on an*, in one, straightway] **1.** soon; shortly; also, at another time: now nearly archaic **2.** [Archaic] at once **—ever and anon** now and then

anon. anonymous

an·o·nym·i·ty (an′ə nim′ə tē) *n.* the condition or fact of being anonymous

a·non·y·mous (ə nän′ə məs) *adj.* [< Gr. < *an-*, without + *onyma*, name] **1.** with no name known *[an anonymous writer]* **2.** given, written, etc. by a person whose name is withheld or unknown *[an anonymous gift]* **3.** lacking in distinctive features *[an anonymous face]* **—a·non′y·mous·ly** *adv.*

a·noph·e·les (ə näf′ə lēz′) *n.* [ModL. < Gr. *anōphelēs*, harmful < *an-*, without + *ophelēs*, use] the mosquito that can carry the malaria parasite and transmit the disease

an·o·rex·i·a (an′ə rek′sē ə) *n.* [ModL. < Gr. < *an-*, without + *orexis*, a desire for] lack of appetite for food; specif., **anorexia ner·vo·sa** (nər vō′sə) an emotional problem, chiefly in young women, in which they find food unpleasant, starve themselves to keep losing weight, etc.

an·oth·er (ə nuth′ər) *adj.* [ME. *an other*] **1.** one more; an additional *[have another cup of tea]* **2.** a different *[at another time]* **3.** one of the same kind as *[another Caesar]* **—pron.** **1.** one additional **2.** a different one **3.** one of the same kind

an·ox·i·a (an äk′sē ə) *n.* [AN- + OX(YGEN) + -IA] the condition of not having enough oxygen in the body tissues

ans. answer

an·ser·ine (an′sər īn′, -in) *adj.* [< L. < *anser*, goose] **1.** of or like a goose **2.** stupid; foolish

an·swer (an′sər) *n.* [< OE. < *and-*, against + *swerian*, to SWEAR] **1.** something said or written in return to a question, letter, etc. **2.** any act in response or retaliation **3.** a solution to a problem, as in arithmetic **4.** *Law* a defense **—vi.** **1.** to reply in words, by an action, etc. **2.** to react or respond *(to)* *[the horse answered to its rider's touch]* **3.** to be sufficient **4.** to be responsible *(to* a person *for* an action, etc.) **5.** to correspond *(to)* *[she answers to the description]* **—vt.** **1.** to reply to in some way **2.** to respond to the signal of (a telephone, doorbell, etc.) **3.** to be sufficient for; serve *[to answer a purpose]* **4.** to defend oneself against (an accusation, criticism, etc.); refute **5.** to agree with; suit *[she answers the description]* **—answer back** [Colloq.] to reply forcefully, rudely, or impertinently

SYN. answer implies a saying, writing, or acting in return, as required by the situation *[to answer a letter]*; **respond** implies something said or done in reacting to a stimulus *[to respond to an appeal]*; **reply** in its most exact sense refers to an answer that satisfies the question asked *[he replied at length to the reporter's inquiries]*; **retort** suggests a sharp or witty reply, as to a criticism; **rejoin** suggests an answer, originally to a reply, now often to an objection **—ANT. question, ask, inquire**

an·swer·a·ble (-ə b'l) *adj.* **1.** responsible; accountable *[answerable* for one's actions*]* **2.** that can be answered or shown to be wrong *[an answerable* argument*]* **—see SYN.** at RESPONSIBLE

ant (ant) *n.* [OE. *æmete*] any of a family of insects, generally wingless, that live in colonies with a complex division of labor

-ant (ənt, 'nt) [Fr. < L. *-antem* or *-entem*, acc. prp. ending] *a suffix meaning:* **1.** that has, shows, or does *[defiant, radiant]* **2.** a person or thing that *[occupant, accountant]*

WORKER ANT

ant. **1.** antenna **2.** antonym

ant·ac·id (ant′as′id) *adj.* that neutralizes acids **—n.** an antacid substance

an·tag·o·nism (an tag′ə niz'm) *n.* [see ANTAGONIZE] **1.** the state of being opposed or hostile; opposition or hostility **2.** an opposing force, principle, etc. **—see SYN.** at ENMITY

an·tag·o·nist (-nist) *n.* **1.** a person who opposes or fights with another **2.** a muscle, drug, etc. that acts in opposition to or counteracts another **—see SYN.** at OPPONENT

an·tag·o·nis·tic (an tag′ə nis′tik) *adj.* showing antagonism; acting in opposition **—an·tag′o·nis′ti·cal·ly** *adv.*

an·tag·o·nize (an tag′ə nīz′) *vt.* **-nized**, **-niz′ing** [< Gr. < *anti-*, against + *agōn*, a contest: see AGONY] **1.** to oppose or counteract **2.** to incur the dislike of; make an enemy of

ant·al·ka·li (ant al′kə lī′) *n., pl.* **-lies′, -lis′** a substance that neutralizes an alkali

An·ta·na·na·ri·vo (än′tä nä nä rē′vōō) capital of Madagascar, in the central part: pop. 322,000

ant·arc·tic (ant ärk′tik, -är′-) *adj.* [< OFr. < L. < Gr. < *anti*, opposite + *arktikos*, ARCTIC] of or near the South Pole or the region around it **—the antarctic** same as ANTARCTICA

Ant·arc·ti·ca (-ti kə) land area about the South Pole, covered by ice: sometimes called a continent: c. 5,000,000 sq. mi.

Antarctic Circle [also **a- c-**] an imaginary circle parallel to the equator, 66°33′ south of it

Antarctic Ocean the parts of the Atlantic, Pacific, and Indian oceans surrounding Antarctica

An·tar·es (an ter′ēz) the brightest star in the constellation Scorpio

ant bear a large anteater of tropical S. America

☆**an·te** (an′tē) *n.* [L., before] **1.** *Poker* the stake that each player must put into the pot before receiving cards **2.** [Colloq.] the amount one must pay as one's share **—vt., vi. -ted** or **-teed, -te·ing** **1.** *Poker* to put in (one's stake) **2.** [Colloq.] to pay (one's share) **—ante up** to ante one's stake or share

an·te- [< L. *ante*, before] *a prefix meaning:* **1.** before; prior (to) *[antecedent]* **2.** before; in front (of) *[anteroom]*

ant·eat·er (ant′ēt′ər) *n.* any of several mammals that feed mainly on ants: anteaters have a long, sticky tongue and a long snout

☆**an·te·bel·lum** (an′ti bel′əm) *adj.* [L.] before the war; specif., before the American Civil War

an·te·cede (an′tə sēd′) *vt., vi.* **-ced′ed, -ced′ing** [< L. *antecedere* < *ante*, before + *cedere*, to go] to go before in place, time, etc.

an·te·ced·ence (-sēd′'ns) *n.* [see prec.] a going before; precedence: also **an′te·ced′en·cy** (-'n sē)

an·te·ced·ent (-sēd′'nt) *adj.* [see ANTECEDE] coming or happening before; prior; previous **—n.** **1.** any thing prior to another **2.** anything logically preceding **3.** [*pl.*] one's ancestry, past life, etc. **4.** *Gram.* the word, phrase, or clause to which a pronoun refers *[*"girl" is the *antecedent* of "who" in "the girl who spoke"*]* **5.** *Math.* the first term of a ratio **—see SYN.** at CAUSE and at PREVIOUS

GIANT ANTEATER
(5–7 ft. long,
including tail)

an·te·cham·ber (an′ti chām′bər) *n.* [< Fr.: see ANTE- & CHAMBER] a smaller room leading into a larger or main room

an·te·date (-dāt) *vt.* **-dat′ed, -dat′ing** **1.** to put a date on that is earlier than the actual date *[to antedate* a check*]* **2.** to happen earlier than; come before **3.** to set an earlier date for

an·te·di·lu·vi·an (an′ti də lōō′vē ən) *adj.* [< ANTE- + L. *diluvium*, a flood + -AN] **1.** of the time before the Biblical Flood **2.** very old or old-fashioned

an·te·lope (an′tə lōp′) *n., pl.* **-lopes′, -lope′:** see PLURAL, II, D, 1 [< ME. & OFr. < ML. < MGr. *antholops*, deer] **1.** *a)* any of a group of swift, cud-chewing, hollow-horned animals that are like deer but are related to oxen, sheep, and goats ☆*b)* same as PRONGHORN **2.** leather made from an antelope's hide

an·te me·ri·di·em (an′tē mə rid′ē əm) [L.] before noon: abbrev. **A.M., a.m., AM**

an·ten·na (an ten′ə) *n.* [< L. < *antemna*, sail yard] **1.** *pl.* **-nae** (-ē), **-nas** either of a pair of movable sense organs on the head of an insect, crab, etc.; feeler **2.** *pl.* **-nas** *Radio & TV* an arrangement of wires, metal rods, etc. used in sending and receiving electromagnetic waves; aerial

ANTELOPE
(to 70 in. high
at shoulder)

an·te·pe·nult (an′ti pē′nəlt) *n.* [see ANTE- & PENULT] the third last syllable in a word, as *-lu-* in *an·te·di·lu·vi·an*

an·te·pe·nul·ti·mate (-pi nul′tə mit) *adj.* third from the end **—n.** **1.** anything third from the end **2.** an antepenult

an·te·ri·or (an tir′ē ər) *adj.* [L., compar. of *ante*, before] **1.** at or toward the front; forward: opposed to POSTERIOR **2.** coming before in time, order, etc.; earlier; previous

an·te·room (an′ti rōōm′, -room′) *n.* a room leading to a larger or more important one; waiting room

an·them (an′thəm) *n.* [< OE. *antefn* < ML. < Gr. *antiphōnos*, sounding back < *anti-*, over against + *phōnē*, voice: see PHONO-] **1.** a religious choral song usually based on words from the Bible **2.** a song of praise or devotion, as to a nation

an·ther (an'thər) *n.* [< Fr. < ModL. < Gr. *anthēros*, blooming < *anthos*, a flower] the part of a stamen that contains the pollen

an·ther·id·i·um (an'thə rid'ē əm) *n., pl.* **-id'i·a** (-ə) [ModL. < prec. + Gr. dim. suffix *-idion*] in flowerless and seedless plants, the organ in which the male sex cells are developed —**an'ther·id'i·al** *adj.*

ant·hill (ant'hil') *n.* the soil carried away by ants in digging their underground nest, heaped in a mound around its entrance

an·thol·o·gize (an thäl'ə jīz') *vi.* **-gized'**, **-giz'ing** to make anthologies —*vt.* to make an anthology of or include in an anthology — **an·thol'o·gist** *n.*

an·thol·o·gy (an thäl'ə jē) *n., pl.* **-gies** [< Gr. *anthologia*, a garland < *anthos*, flower + *legein*, to gather] a collection of poems, stories, etc. —**an·tho·log·i·cal** (an'thə läj'i k'l) *adj.*

An·tho·ny (an'thə nē; *also, for 1 & 2*, -tə-) [< L. *Antonius*, name of a Roman gens] **1.** a masculine name: dim. *Tony*; var. *Antony* **2.** **Mark**, *see* ANTONY **3.** **Susan B**(rownell), 1820-1906; U.S. leader in the women's suffrage movement

an·tho·zo·an (an'thə zō'ən) *n.* [< ModL. < Gr. *anthos*, flower + *zōion*, animal + -AN] any of a class of saltwater coelenterates, comprising corals, sea anemones, etc. —*adj.* of the anthozoans

an·thra·cene (an'thrə sēn') *n.* [< Gr. *anthrax*, coal + -ENE] a crystalline hydrocarbon, $C_{14}H_{10}$, a product of coal-tar distillation used in making dyes and as a radiation detector

an·thra·cite (an'thrə sīt') *n.* [< Gr. < *anthrax*, coal] hard coal, which burns with much heat but little flame and smoke

an·thrax (an'thraks) *n.* [< Gr., (burning) coal, hence carbuncle] an infectious disease of wild and domesticated animals, esp. cattle and sheep, which is caused by a bacillus and can be transmitted to man: it is characterized by black pustules

an·thro·po- [< Gr. *anthrōpos*, man] *a combining form meaning* man, human [*anthropology*]: also, before a vowel, **anthrop-**

an·thro·po·cen·tric (an'thrə pə sen'trik) *adj.* [prec. + CENTRIC] regarding man as the central fact of the universe and viewing everything in terms of human values

an·thro·poid (an'thrə poid') *adj.* [ANTHROP(O)- + -OID] **1.** resembling man; manlike; esp., designating or of any of the most highly developed apes, including the chimpanzee, gorilla, orangutan, and gibbon **2.** apelike [*anthropoid* features] —*n.* any anthropoid ape —**an'thro·poi'dal** *adj.*

an·thro·pol·o·gist (an'thrə päl'ə jist) *n.* a student of or specialist in anthropology

an·thro·pol·o·gy (an'thrə päl'ə jē) *n.* [ANTHROPO- + -LOGY] the study of man, esp. of the variety, distribution, characteristics, cultures, etc. of mankind —**an'thro·po·log'i·cal** (-pə läj'i k'l), **an'thro·po·log'ic** *adj.* —**an'thro·po·log'i·cal·ly** *adv.*

an·thro·pom·e·try (-päm'ə trē) *n.* [ANTHROPO- + -METRY] the science dealing with measurement of the human body in comparing individual and group differences —**an'thro·po·met'ric** (-pə met'rik), **an'thro·po·met'ri·cal** *adj.*

an·thro·po·mor·phic (an'thrə pə môr'fik) *adj.* of, characterized by, or resulting from anthropomorphism —**an'thro·po·mor'phi·cal·ly** *adv.*

an·thro·po·mor·phism (-môr'fiz'm) *n.* [ANTHROPOMORPH(OUS) + -ISM] the practice of thinking of gods, animals, or certain inanimate things as having human form or characteristics

an·thro·po·mor·phize (-môr'fīz) *vt., vi.* **-phized**, **-phiz·ing** to think of (a god, animal, etc.) as having human form or characteristics

an·thro·po·mor·phous (-môr'fəs) *adj.* [< Gr. < *anthrōpos*, a man + *morphē*, form, shape] having human form and characteristics

an·thro·poph·a·gi (an'thrə päf'ə jī') *n.pl., sing.* **-a·gus** (-ə gəs) [L. < Gr. < *anthropos*, man + *phagein*, to eat] cannibals

an·thro·poph·a·gy (-päf'ə jē) *n.* [see prec.] cannibalism — **an'thro·poph'a·gous** (-gəs), *adj.*

an·thu·ri·um (an thoor'ē əm) *n.* [ModL. < Gr. *anthos*, flower + *oura*, tail] a tropical American plant having a long spike with a flaring, heart-shaped spathe around its base

ANTHER

an·ti (an'tī, -tē) *n., pl.* **-tis** [< ANTI-] [Colloq.] a person opposed to some policy, proposal, etc. —*prep.* [Colloq.] opposed to; against

an·ti- (an'ti; *also variously* -tē, -tī, -tə) [< Gr. < *anti*, against] *a prefix meaning:* **1.** against; hostile to [*antilabor*] **2.** that operates against [*antiaircraft*] **3.** that prevents, cures, or neutralizes [*antitoxin*] **4.** opposite; reverse [*antimatter*] **5.** rivaling [*antipope*]

an·ti·air·craft (an'tē er'kraft, -tī-) *adj.* used for defense against enemy aircraft [*antiaircraft* gun]

an·ti·bac·te·ri·al (-bak tir'ē əl) *adj.* that checks the growth or effect of bacteria

an·ti·bal·lis·tic missile (-bə lis'tik) a ballistic missile intended to intercept and destroy another ballistic missile in flight

an·ti·bi·o·sis (-bī ō'sis) *n.* [ModL. < ANTI- + Gr. *biōsis*, way of life < *bios*, life] *Biol.* an association between organisms which is harmful to one of them

☆**an·ti·bi·ot·ic** (-bī ät'ik, -bē-) *adj.* **1.** of antibiosis **2.** destroying, or stopping the growth of, bacteria and other microorganisms —*n.* an antibiotic substance produced by various microorganisms, as by bacteria or fungi: antibiotics, such as penicillin, streptomycin, etc., are used to treat various infectious diseases

☆**an·ti·bod·y** (an'ti bäd'ē) *n., pl.* **-bod'ies** a protein produced in the body as a reaction to an antigen: it neutralizes the antigen, and in this way creates immunity

an·tic (an'tik) *adj.* [< It. < L. *antiquus*: see ANTIQUE] **1.** [Archaic] fantastic and queer **2.** odd and funny —*n.* **1.** a playful or silly act, trick, etc.; caper **2.** [Archaic] a clown or buffoon —*vi.* **-ticked**, **-tick·ing** to perform antics; caper

an·ti·christ (an'ti krīst', -tī-) *n.* an opponent of Christ —[A-] *Bible* the great antagonist of Christ: I John 2:18

an·tic·i·pant (an tis'ə pənt) *adj.* expecting; anticipating (with *of*) —*n.* a person who anticipates

an·tic·i·pate (an tis'ə pāt') *vt.* **-pat'ed**, **-pat'ing** [< L. pp. of *anticipare* < *ante-*, before + *capere*, to take] **1.** to look forward to; expect [to *anticipate* a good time] **2.** to prevent by action in advance; forestall [to *anticipate* an opponent's blows] **3.** to foresee and take care of in advance [to *anticipate* a request] **4.** to use or enjoy in advance [to *anticipate* a legacy] **5.** to be ahead of in doing or achieving something [did the vikings *anticipate* Columbus in visiting America?] —**an·tic'i·pa'tor** *n.* —*see* **SYN.** at EXPECT

an·tic·i·pa·tion (an tis'ə pā'shən) *n.* **1.** an anticipating or being anticipated **2.** something anticipated or expected **3.** foreknowledge; presentiment

an·tic·i·pa·tive (an tis'ə pāt'iv) *adj.* of or full of anticipation —**an·tic'i·pa'tive·ly** *adv.*

an·tic·i·pa·to·ry (an tis'ə pə tôr'ē) *adj.* of or expressing anticipation —**an·tic'i·pa·to'ri·ly** *adv.*

an·ti·cler·i·cal (an'ti kler'ə k'l, -tī-) *adj.* opposed to the influence of the clergy or church in public affairs —**an'ti·cler'i·cal·ism** *n.*

an·ti·cli·max (-klī'maks) *n.* **1.** a sudden drop from the dignified or important to the commonplace or trivial **2.** a final event which is in disappointing contrast to those coming before —**an'ti·cli·mac'tic** (-mak'tik) *adj.*

an·ti·cline (an'ti klīn') *n.* [< ANTI- + Gr. *klinein*, to incline] *Geol.* a fold of stratified rock in which the strata slope downward in opposite directions from the central axis: opposed to SYNCLINE —**an'ti·cli'nal** *adj.*

an·ti·co·ag·u·lant (an'ti kō ag'yə lənt, -tī-) *n.* a drug or substance that delays or prevents the clotting of blood

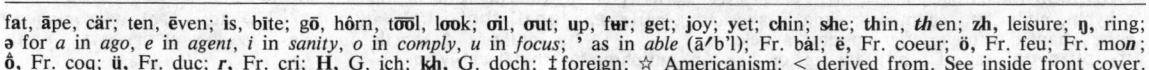

ANTICLINE

an·ti·cy·clone (-sī'klōn) *n.* a condition of high barometric pressure over a wide area, with the winds at the edge blowing outward —**an'ti·cy·clon'ic** (-klän'ik) *adj.*

an·ti·de·pres·sant (-di pres'ənt) *adj.* designating or of any drug used to treat emotional depression —*n.* an antidepressant drug

an·ti·dote (an'tə dōt') *n.* [ME. & OFr. < L. < Gr. < *anti-*, against + *dotos*, given < *didonai*, to give] **1.** a remedy to counteract a poison [milk and olive oil are common *antidotes*] **2.** anything that works against an evil or unwanted condition [education is a good *antidote* for prejudice] —**an'ti·dot'al** *adj.*

---

fat, āpe, cär; ten, ēven; is, bīte; gō, hôrn, to͞ol, lo͝ok; oil, out; up, fur; get; joy; yet; chin; she; thin, *th*en; zh, leisure; ŋ, ring; ə for *a* in *ago*, *e* in *agent*, *i* in *sanity*, *o* in *comply*, *u* in *focus*; ' as in *able* (ā'b'l); Fr. bal; ë, Fr. coeur; ö, Fr. feu; Fr. mon; ô, Fr. coq; ü, Fr. duc; r, Fr. cri; H, G. ich; kh, G. doch; ‡foreign; ☆ Americanism; < derived from. See inside front cover.

An·tie·tam (an tēt′əm) [AmInd. < ?] creek in W Md.: site of a Civil War battle (1862)

☆**an·ti·fed·er·al·ist** (an′ti fed′ər ə list, -tī-; -fed′rə-) *n.* **1.** one opposed to federalism **2.** [A-] one who opposed the Federalists and the adoption of the U.S. Constitution

☆**an·ti·freeze** (an′ti frēz′, -tī-) *n.* a substance of low freezing point added esp. to the water in automobile radiators to prevent freezing

an·ti·fric·tion (an′ti frik′shən, -tī-) *adj.* reducing friction —*n.* any lubricant, etc. for reducing friction

☆**an·ti·gen** (an′tə jən) *n.* [ANTI- + -GEN] an enzyme, toxin, etc. to which the body reacts by producing antibodies —**an′ti·gen′ic** (-jen′ik) *adj.*

An·tig·o·ne (an tig′ə nē′) *Gr. Myth.* daughter of Oedipus: she defied her uncle by performing funeral rites for her brother

An·ti·gua (an tē′gə, -gwə) self-governing island under Brit. protection, in the Leeward group of the West Indies: 108 sq. mi.; pop. 57,000

an·ti·he·ro (an′ti hir′ō, -tī-) *n.* the main character of a novel, play, etc. who lacks the virtues of a traditional hero

an·ti·his·ta·mine (an′ti his′tə mēn′, an′tī-; -mən) *n.* any drug used to lessen the action of histamine and relieve the symptoms in allergies such as hay fever and hives —**an′ti·his′ta·min′ic** (-min′ik) *adj.*

☆**an·ti·knock** (an′ti näk′, -tī-) *n.* a substance added to the fuel of internal-combustion engines to do away with noise caused by too rapid combustion

an·ti·la·bor (an′ti lā′bər, -tī-) *adj.* opposed to labor unions or to the interests of workers

An·til·les (an til′ez) main island group of the West Indies: see GREATER ANTILLES, LESSER ANTILLES —**An·til′le·an** (-ē ən, an′-tə lē′ən) *adj.*

an·ti·log·a·rithm (an′ti lôg′ə rith′m, -tī-; -läg′-) *n.* the number corresponding to a given logarithm [the *antilogarithm* of 1 is 10]

an·ti·ma·cas·sar (an′ti mə kas′ər) *n.* [ANTI- + *macassar* (oil), a former hair oil] a small cover to protect the back or arms of a chair, etc. from soiling

an·ti·mag·net·ic (an′ti.mag net′ik, -tī-) *adj.* made of metals that resist magnetism [an *antimagnetic* watch]

an·ti·ma·lar·i·al (-mə ler′ē əl) *adj.* preventing or relieving malaria —*n.* an antimalarial drug

an·ti·mat·ter (an′ti mat′ər, -tī-) *n.* a form of matter in which the electrical charge or other property of each constituent particle is the reverse of that in the usual matter of our universe

ANTIMACASSARS

an·ti·mis·sile (-mis′'l) *adj.* designed as a defense against ballistic missiles

an·ti·mo·ny (an′tə mō′nē) *n.* [< OFr. < ML. *antimonium*] a silvery-white, brittle, metallic chemical element, found only in combination: used to harden alloys, etc.: symbol, Sb; at. wt., 121.75; at. no., 51

An·ti·och (an′tē äk′) capital of ancient Syria: now, a city in S Turkey: pop. 46,000

an·ti·ox·i·dant (an′ti äk′sə dənt, -tī-) *n.* a substance that slows down the oxidation of oils, fats, etc. and so is used as a preservative

an·ti·par·ti·cle (an′ti pär′tə k'l, an′tī-) *n.* any of the constituent particles of antimatter

an·ti·pas·to (an′ti pas′tō, -päs′-) *n.* [It. < *anti-* (L. *ante*), before + *pasto* < L. *pastus*, food] a dish of salted fish, meat, olives, etc. served as an appetizer

an·ti·pa·thet·ic (an′ti pə thet′ik) *adj.* **1.** having antipathy **2.** opposite or contrary in character, tendency, etc. Also **an′ti·pa·thet′i·cal** —**an′ti·pa·thet′i·cal·ly** *adv.*

an·tip·a·thy (an tip′ə thē) *n., pl.* -thies [< L. < Gr. < *anti-*, against + *patheia* < *pathein*, to feel] **1.** a strong dislike **2.** the object of such dislike —see SYN. at AVERSION

an·ti·per·son·nel (an′ti pur′sə nel′, -tī-) *adj.* directed against, or intended to destroy, people rather than material objects [*antipersonnel* mines]

an·ti·per·spir·ant (-pur′spər ənt) *n.* an astringent applied to the skin to reduce perspiration

an·ti·phon (an′tə fän′) *n.* [< ML. < Gr.: see ANTHEM] **1.** a hymn, psalm, etc. chanted or sung in alternating parts **2.** verses chanted before or after a psalm, canticle, etc.

an·tiph·o·nal (an tif′ə n'l) *adj.* of or like an antiphon;

chanted or sung in alternating parts —*n. same as* ANTIPHONARY

an·tiph·o·nar·y (an tif′ə ner′ē) *n., pl.* -nar′ies a book of antiphons

an·ti·pode (an′tə pōd′) *n.* [back-formation of ANTIPODES] an exact opposite

an·tip·o·des (an tip′ə dēz′) *n.pl.* [ML. < L. < Gr., pl. of *anti-pous* < *anti-*, opposite + *pous*, FOOT] **1.** any two places directly opposite each other on the earth **2.** [*with pl. or sing. v.*] a place on the opposite side of the earth: in British usage, New Zealand and Australia are usually meant **3.** two opposite or contrary things —**an·tip′o·dal** *adj.* —**an·tip′o·de′an** (-dē′ən) *adj., n.*

an·ti·pope (an′ti pōp′, -tī-) *n.* a pope set up against the one chosen by church laws, as in a schism

an·ti·py·ret·ic (an′ti pī ret′ik, -tī-) *adj.* reducing fever —*n.* anything that reduces fever

an·ti·quar·i·an (an′tə kwer′ē ən) *adj.* **1.** of antiques or antiquities **2.** of antiquaries **3.** of, or dealing in, rare old books —*n.* an antiquary

an·ti·quar·y (an′tə kwer′ē) *n., pl.* -quar′ies one who collects or studies relics and ancient art

an·ti·quate (an′tə kwāt′) *vt.* -quat′ed, -quat′ing [< L. pp. of *antiquare* < *antiquus*: see ANTIQUE] to make obsolete or old-fashioned —**an′ti·qua′tion** *n.*

an·ti·quat·ed (-kwāt′id) *adj.* old-fashioned, out-of-date, etc.

an·tique (an tēk′) *adj.* [Fr. < L. *antiquus*, ancient < *ante*, before] **1.** of ancient times; ancient **2.** old-fashioned; out-of-date **3.** in the style of classical antiquity **4.** of, or in the style of, a former period **5.** dealing in antiques [an *antique* store] —*n.* **1.** an ancient relic **2.** the ancient style, esp. of Greek or Roman sculpture, etc. **3.** a piece of furniture, silverware, etc. made in a former period, generally more than 100 years ago **4.** *Printing* a variety of boldface type —*vt.* -tiqued′, -tiqu′ing to make look antique —**an·tique′ly** *adv.* —**an·tique′ness** *n.*

an·tiq·ui·ty (an tik′wə tē) *n., pl.* -ties [see prec.] **1.** the early period of history, esp. before the Middle Ages **2.** great age; oldness [a statue of great *antiquity*] **3.** the people of ancient times **4.** [*pl.*] *a*) relics, monuments, etc. of the distant past *b*) ancient manners, customs, etc.

an·ti·scor·bu·tic (an′ti skôr byoo′tik, -tī-) *adj.* that cures or prevents scurvy

an·ti·Se·mit·ic (-sə mit′ik) *adj.* **1.** having or showing prejudice against Jews **2.** discriminating against or persecuting Jews —**an′ti·Sem′ite** (-sem′īt) *n.* —**an′ti·Sem′i·tism** (-sem′ə tiz′m) *n.*

an·ti·sep·sis (an′tə sep′sis) *n.* [ANTI- + SEPSIS] **1.** the technique of preventing infection, the growth of microorganisms, etc. **2.** the condition of being antiseptic **3.** the use of antiseptics

an·ti·sep·tic (-sep′tik) *adj.* **1.** preventing infection, decay, etc. by stopping the action of microorganisms [an *antiseptic* solution] **2.** using antiseptics **3.** free from infection; sterile [an *antiseptic* room] **4.** untouched by life, its problems, etc. [an *antiseptic* mind] —*n.* any antiseptic substance, as alcohol or iodine —**an′ti·sep′ti·cal·ly** *adv.*

an·ti·sep·ti·cize (-sep′tə sīz′) *vt.* -cized′, -ciz′ing to make antiseptic; apply antiseptics to

an·ti·se·rum (an′ti sir′əm) *n.* a serum with antibodies in it

☆**an·ti·slav·er·y** (an′ti slā′vər ē, -tī-) *adj.* against slavery

an·ti·so·cial (-sō′shəl) *adj.* **1.** not liking to be with other people; unsociable **2.** harmful to the welfare of the people generally —see SYN. at UNSOCIAL

an·ti·spas·mod·ic (-spaz mäd′ik) *adj.* relieving or preventing spasms —*n.* an antispasmodic drug

an·ti·stat·ic (-stat′ik) *adj.* reducing static electric charges, as on textiles, polishes, etc., by keeping enough moisture to provide electrical conduction

an·tis·tro·phe (an tis′trə fē) *n.* [L. < Gr. < *anti-*, opposite + *strephein*, to turn] **1.** *a*) the return movement, left to right, made by the chorus of an ancient Greek play in answering a strophe *b*) the part of a choric song performed during this **2.** a stanza following a strophe, often in the same form —**an·ti·stroph·ic** (an′tə sträf′ik) *adj.*

an·ti·tank (an′ti taŋk′, -tī-) *adj.* for use against tanks in war

an·tith·e·sis (an tith′ə sis) *n., pl.* -ses′ (-sēz′) [L. < Gr. < *anti-*, against + *tithenai*, to place] **1.** a contrast of thoughts, usually in two phrases, clauses, etc. (Ex.: "Man proposes, but God disposes") **2.** a contrast or opposition **3.** the exact opposite [joy is the *antithesis* of sorrow]

an·ti·thet·i·cal (an′tə thet′i k'l) *adj.* **1.** of or containing antithesis **2.** exactly opposite —see SYN. at OPPOSITE —**an′ti·thet′i·cal·ly** *adv.*

an·ti·tox·in (an′ti täk′sin, -tī-) *n.* **1.** an antibody formed by the body to act against a specific toxin **2.** a serum containing an antitoxin: taken from the blood of an immunized animal, such a serum is injected into a person to prevent a specific disease, such as diphtheria or tetanus —**an′ti·tox′ic** *adj.*

an·ti·trades (an′ti trādz′) *n.pl.* westerly winds that blow above and opposite to the trade winds

☆**an·ti·trust** (an′ti trust′, -tī-) *adj.* opposed to or regulating trusts, or business monopolies

an·ti·ven·in (-ven′ən) *n.* [ANTI- + VEN(OM) + -IN¹] **1.** an antitoxin for venom, as of snakes, produced by gradually increased injections of the specific venom **2.** a serum containing this antitoxin

an·ti·viv·i·sec·tion (-viv′ə sek′shən) *n.* opposition to medical research on living animals —**an′ti·viv′i·sec′tion·ist** *n., adj.*

ant·ler (ant′lər) *n.* [< OFr. < L. < *ante-*, before + *ocularis*, of the eyes] **1.** the branched horn of any animal of the deer family, that is grown and shed annually **2.** any branch of such a horn —**ant′lered** *adj.*

ant lion **1.** the large-jawed larva of certain winged insects that digs a pit for trapping ants, etc. on which it feeds **2.** the adult insect

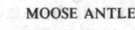

MOOSE ANTLERS

An·toi·nette (an′twə net′, -tə-) **1.** a feminine name: dim. *Nettie, Netty* **2. Marie,** see MARIE ANTOINETTE

An·to·ny (an′tə nē) **1.** *var. of* ANTHONY **2. Mark** or **Marc,** (L. name *Marcus Antonius*) 83?–30 B.C.; Rom. general & statesman

an·to·nym (an′tə nim′) *n.* [< Gr. < *anti-*, opposite + *onyma*, name] a word that is opposite in meaning to another word ["sad" is an *antonym* of "happy"] —**an·ton·y·mous** (an tän′ə məs) *adj.*

an·trum (an′trəm) *n., pl.* **-tra** (-trə), **-trums** [L. < Gr. *antron*, cave] *Anat.* a cavity; esp., either of a pair of sinuses in the upper jaw

Ant·werp (an′twərp) seaport in N Belgium, on the Scheldt River: pop. 240,000

A·nu·bis (ə nyo͞o′bis, -no͞o′-) an Egyptian god, depicted with the head of a jackal, who led the dead to judgment

an·u·re·sis (an′yoo rē′sis) *n.* [ModL. < AN- + Gr. *ouresis*, urination] the condition of being unable to pass one's urine

a·nus (ā′nəs) *n., pl.* **a′nus·es, a′ni** (-nī) [L., a ring] the opening at the lower end of the alimentary canal

an·vil (an′vəl) *n.* [< OE. *anfilt* < *an-*, on + hyp. *filtan*, to beat] **1.** an iron or steel block on which metal objects are hammered into shape **2.** the incus, one of the three bones of the middle ear: see illustration at EAR

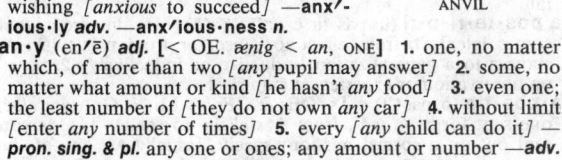

ANVIL

anx·i·e·ty (aŋ zī′ə tē) *n., pl.* **-ties** [see ANXIOUS] **1.** a state of being uneasy or worried about what may happen **2.** an eager but often uneasy desire [*anxiety* to do well] —see SYN. at CARE

anx·ious (aŋk′shəs, aŋ′-) *adj.* [L. *anxius < angere*, to choke] **1.** uneasy in mind; worried **2.** causing or full of anxiety [an *anxious* hour] **3.** eagerly wishing [*anxious* to succeed] —**anx′·ious·ly** *adv.* —**anx′ious·ness** *n.*

an·y (en′ē) *adj.* [< OE. *ænig < an*, ONE] **1.** one, no matter which, of more than two [*any* pupil may answer] **2.** some, no matter what amount or kind [he hasn't *any* food] **3.** even one; the least number of [they do not own *any* car] **4.** without limit [enter *any* number of times] **5.** every [*any* child can do it] —*pron. sing. & pl.* any one or ones; any amount or number —*adv.* to any degree or extent; at all [is he *any* better?]

an·y·bod·y (-bud′ē, -bäd′ē) *pron.* **1.** any person; anyone **2.** a person of fame, importance, etc. [everybody who was *anybody* came to the party]

an·y·how (-hou′) *adv.* **1.** no matter in what way [it's fine *anyhow* you look at it] **2.** in any case [I didn't want to go *anyhow*] **3.** carelessly [don't do it just *anyhow*]

an·y·more (-môr′) *adv.* now; nowadays: usually used only in a negative clause [he doesn't live here *anymore*]: also **any more**

an·y·one (en′ē wun′) *pron.* any person; anybody

any one any single (person or thing)

☆**an·y·place** (en′ē plās′) *adv.* [Colloq.] in, at, or to any place; anywhere —**get anyplace** [Colloq.] to succeed

an·y·thing (-thiŋ′) *pron.* any object, event, fact, etc. —*n.* a thing, no matter of what kind —*adv.* in any way; at all [is it *anything* like yours?] —**anything but** not at all [I'm *anything but* sad]

an·y·way (-wā′) *adv.* **1.** in any manner or way **2.** in any case; anyhow **3.** haphazardly; carelessly

an·y·where (-hwer′, -wer′) *adv.* **1.** in, at, or to any place **2.** [Colloq.] at all; to any extent —☆**anywhere from** [Colloq.] any amount, time, etc. between (stated limits) [*anywhere from* $5 to $10] —**get anywhere** [Colloq.] to have any success

an·y·wise (-wīz′) *adv.* in any manner; at all

A/O, a/o account of

☆**A-OK** (ā′ō kā′) *adj.* [A(LL) OK] [Colloq.] excellent, fine, in working order, etc.: also **A′-O·kay′**

A one (ā′ wun′) [Colloq.] first-class; first-rate; superior: also **A 1, A number 1**

a·or·ta (ā ôr′tə) *n., pl.* **-tas, -tae** (-tē) [ModL. < Gr. < *aeirein*, to raise] the main artery of the body, carrying blood from the left ventricle of the heart to arteries in all organs and parts: see illustration at HEART —**a·or′tic, a·or′tal** *adj.*

a·ou·dad (ä′oo dad′) *n.* [Fr. < Moorish *audad*] a wild North African sheep with large, curved horns and a heavy growth of hair on the chest

a·pace (ə pās′) *adv.* at a fast pace; swiftly

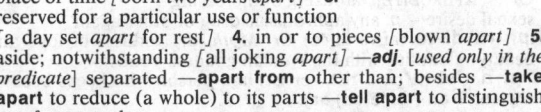

A·pach·e (ə pach′ē) *n.* [AmSp., prob. < Zuñi *ápachu*, enemy] **1.** *pl.* **A·pach′es, A·pach′e** any member of a group of tribes of Indians of northern Mexico and the southwestern U.S. **2.** any of their Athapascan languages

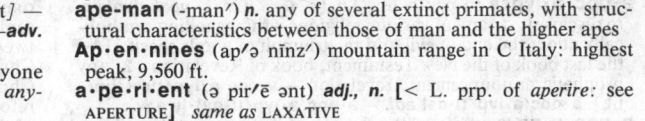

AOUDAD
(to 39 in. high
at shoulder)

a·part (ə pärt′) *adv.* [< OFr. < L. *ad*, to, at + *partem*, acc. of *pars*, a part, side] **1.** to one side; aside **2.** away in place or time [born two years *apart*] **3.** reserved for a particular use or function [a day set *apart* for rest] **4.** in or to pieces [blown *apart*] **5.** aside; notwithstanding [all joking *apart*] —*adj.* [used only in the predicate] separated —**apart from** other than; besides —**take apart** to reduce (a whole) to its parts —**tell apart** to distinguish one from another

a·part·heid (ə pärt′hāt, -hīt) *n.* [Afrik., apartness] in South Africa, the policy of strict racial segregation and discrimination imposed on blacks and other non-Caucasoids

a·part·ment (ə pärt′mənt) *n.* [< Fr. < It. < *appartare*, to separate < *parte*, PART] **1.** a room or suite of rooms to live in ☆**2.** *same as* APARTMENT HOUSE

☆**apartment house** a building divided into a number of apartments: also **apartment building**

ap·a·thet·ic (ap′ə thet′ik) *adj.* [< APATHY, after PATHETIC] **1.** feeling no emotion; unmoved **2.** not interested; indifferent —see SYN. at IMPASSIVE —**ap′a·thet′i·cal·ly** *adv.*

ap·a·thy (ap′ə thē) *n., pl.* **-thies** [< Fr. < L. < Gr. < *a-*, without + *pathos*, emotion] **1.** lack of emotion **2.** lack of interest; indifference

APC tablet a tablet containing aspirin, phenacetin, and caffeine, for relieving headaches, etc.

ape (āp) *n.* [OE. *apa*] **1.** any of a family of large, tailless monkeys; specif., a chimpanzee, gorilla, orangutan, or gibbon **2.** any monkey **3.** a person who imitates; mimic **4.** an uncouth person —*vt.* aped, ap′ing to imitate or mimic —**ape′like′** *adj.*

ape-man (-man′) *n.* any of several extinct primates, with structural characteristics between those of man and the higher apes

Ap·en·nines (ap′ə ninz′) mountain range in C Italy: highest peak, 9,560 ft.

a·pe·ri·ent (ə pir′ē ənt) *adj., n.* [< L. prp. of *aperire*: see APERTURE] *same as* LAXATIVE

a·pe·ri·od·ic (ā′pir ē äd′ik) *adj.* **1.** occurring irregularly **2.** *Physics* without periodic vibrations

a·pe·ri·tif (ä′pā rə tēf′) *n.* [< Fr. < L. *apertus*: see ff.] an alcoholic drink, esp. a wine, taken before meals to stimulate the appetite

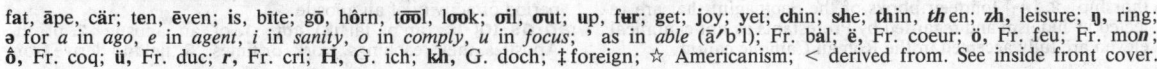

ap·er·ture (ap′ər chər) ***n.*** [< L. < *apertus*, pp. of *aperire*, to open] **1.** an opening; hole; gap **2.** the diameter of the opening in a camera, etc., through which light passes into the lens

a·pet·a·lous (ā pet′'l əs) ***adj.*** *Bot.* without petals

a·pex (ā′peks) ***n.***, *pl.* **a′pex·es, ap′i·ces** (ap′ə sēz′, ā′pə-) [L., a point] **1.** the highest point; peak; vertex **2.** the pointed end; tip **3.** the highest point of interest, excitement, etc.; climax —see ***SYN.*** at SUMMIT

a·pha·si·a (ə fā′zhə, -zhē ə) ***n.*** [ModL. < Gr. < *a-*, not + *phanai*, to speak] a total or partial loss of the power to use or understand words, usually caused by brain disease or injury —**a·pha′sic** (-zik), **a·pha′si·ac′** (-zē ak′) ***adj., n.***

a·phe·li·on (ə fē′lē ən) ***n.***, *pl.* **-li·ons, -li·a** (-ə) [ModL. < Gr. *apo*, from + *hēlios*, sun] the point farthest from the sun in the orbit around it of a planet, comet, or man-made satellite: opposed to PERIHELION

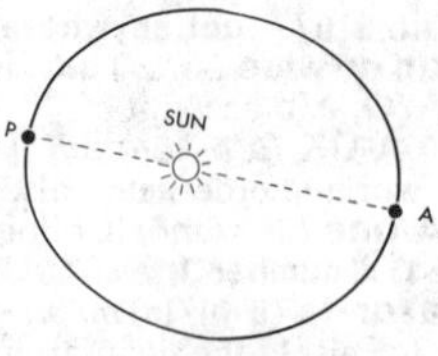

APHELION
(planet at aphelion A and at perihelion P)

a·pher·e·sis, a·phaer·e·sis (ə fer′ə sis) ***n.*** [< L. < Gr. < *apo-*, away + *hairein*, to take] the dropping of a sound or sounds at the beginning of a word (Ex.: *'cause* for *because*)

a·phid (ā′fid, af′id) ***n.*** [ModL. *aphis* (pl. *aphides*) < Gr. *apheidēs*, lavish] any of a group of small insects that suck the juice from plants; plant louse: also **a·phis** (ā′fis, af′is), *pl.* **a·ph·i·des** (af′ə dēz′) —**a·phid·i·an** (ə fid′ē ən) ***adj., n.***

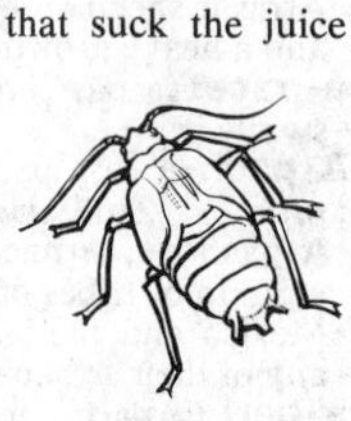

APHID
(to 1/4 in. long)

aph·o·rism (af′ə riz'm) ***n.*** [< Fr. < Gr. < *aphorizein*, to divide < *apo-*, from + *horizein*, to bound: see HORIZON] **1.** a short, concise statement of a principle **2.** a short sentence expressing a wise observation or a general truth —see ***SYN.*** at SAYING —**aph′o·ris′tic** ***adj.*** —**aph′o·ris′ti·cal·ly** ***adv.***

aph·ro·dis·i·ac (af′rə diz′ē ak′) ***adj.*** [< Gr. < APHRODITE] arousing or increasing sexual desire —***n.*** any aphrodisiac drug or other agent

Aph·ro·di·te (af′rə dīt′ē) *Gr. Myth.* the goddess of love and beauty: identified with the Roman goddess Venus

a·pi·a·rist (ā′pē ə rist, -er′ist) ***n.*** a person who keeps bees —**a′pi·ar′i·an** (-er′ē ən) ***adj.***

a·pi·ar·y (ā′pē er′ē) ***n.***, *pl.* **-ar′ies** [< L. < *apis*, bee] a place where bees are kept for their honey, generally consisting of a number of hives

ap·i·cal (ap′i k'l, ā′pi-) ***adj.*** of, at, or constituting the apex

ap·i·ces (ap′ə sēz′, ā′pə-) ***n.*** *alt. pl. of* APEX

a·pi·cul·ture (ā′pə kul′chər) ***n.*** [< L. *apis*, bee + CULTURE] the raising and care of bees; beekeeping —**a′pi·cul′tur·al** ***adj.*** —**a′pi·cul′tur·ist** ***n.ce***

a·piece (ə pēs′) ***adv.*** [see A & PIECE] for each one; each *[*candy bars ten cents *apiece]*

ap·ish (āp′ish) ***adj.*** **1.** like an ape **2.** foolishly imitative **3.** silly, affected, mischievous, etc. —**ap′ish·ly** ***adv.*** —**ap′ish·ness** ***n.***

a·plen·ty (ə plen′tē) ***adj., adv.*** [Colloq.] in abundance *[*there's room *aplenty]*

a·plomb (ə pläm′, -plum′) ***n.*** [Fr., lit., perpendicularity < *à*, to + *plomb*, a PLUMB] self-possession; poise

ap·o- [< Gr. *apo*, off] *a prefix meaning* off, from, or away from *[apogee]*

APO Army Post Office

Apoc. **1.** Apocalypse **2.** Apocrypha

a·poc·a·lypse (ə päk′ə lips′) ***n.*** [< L. < Gr. < *apokalyptein*, to disclose] **1.** any of various religious writings telling symbolically about the end of evil and the triumph of good; specif., [**A-**] the last book of the New Testament; book of Revelation **2.** any prophetic announcement; revelation —**a·poc′a·lyp′tic** (-lip′tik), **a·poc′a·lyp′ti·cal** ***adj.*** —**a·poc′a·lyp′ti·cal·ly** ***adv.***

a·poc·o·pe (ə päk′ə pē′) ***n.*** [< Gr. < *apo-*, from + *koptein*, to cut off] the dropping of a sound or sounds at the end of a word (Ex.: *mos'* for *most*)

a·poc·ry·pha (ə päk′rə fə) ***n.pl.*** [< LL. < Gr. *apokryphos*, hidden, obscure < *apo-*, away + *kryptein*, to hide: see CRYPT] **1.** any writings, anecdotes, etc. of doubtful authenticity or authorship **2.** [**A-**] fourteen books of the Septuagint that are rejected in Judaism and regarded by Protestants as not canonical: eleven are fully accepted in the Roman Catholic canon

a·poc·ry·phal (-f'l) ***adj.*** **1.** of doubtful authorship or authenticity **2.** not genuine; false; counterfeit **3.** [**A-**] of or like the Apocrypha

ap·o·gee (ap′ə jē′) ***n.*** [< Fr. < L. < Gr. < *apo-*, from + *gē*, earth] **1.** the point farthest from the earth, the moon, or another planet, in the orbit of a satellite or spacecraft around it **2.** the highest or farthest point —**ap′o·ge′an** (-jē′ən), **ap′o·ge′al** ***adj.***

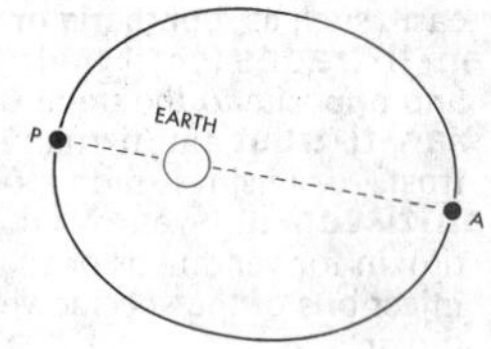

APOGEE
(moon at apogee A and at perigee P)

a·po·lit·i·cal (ā′pə lit′ə k'l) ***adj.*** not concerned with political matters —**a′po·lit′i·cal·ly** ***adv.***

A·pol·lo (ə päl′ō) **1.** *Gr. & Rom. Myth.* the god of music, poetry, prophecy, and medicine: later identified with HELIOS **2.** any of a series of U.S. spaceships; specif., **Apollo 11**, that first landed men on the moon (July 20, 1969) —***n.***, *pl.* **-los** any handsome young man

A·pol·lyon (ə päl′yən) Satan: name used in Rev. 9:11

a·pol·o·get·ic (ə päl′ə jet′ik) ***adj.*** making apology; esp., showing that one is aware of and regrets a fault, wrong, etc.: also **a·pol′o·get′i·cal** —***n.*** a formal defense of belief, cause, etc. —**a·pol′o·get′i·cal·ly** ***adv.***

a·pol·o·get·ics (-iks) ***n.pl.*** [*with sing. v.*] [see APOLOGY] the branch of theology that seeks to prove and defend the authority of Christianity

ap·o·lo·gi·a (ap′ə lō′jē ə) ***n.*** an apology, esp. a formal defense of an idea, religion, etc.

a·pol·o·gist (ə päl′ə jist) ***n.*** a person who writes or speaks in defense or justification of a doctrine, faith, action, etc.

a·pol·o·gize (ə päl′ə jīz′) ***vi.*** **-gized′, -giz′ing** to make an apology; esp., to state that one is aware of and regrets a fault, wrong, etc.

ap·o·logue (ap′ə lôg′, -läg′) ***n.*** [Fr. < L. < Gr.] a short allegorical story with a moral; fable

a·pol·o·gy (ə päl′ə jē) ***n.***, *pl.* **-gies** [< LL. < Gr. *apologia*, a speaking in defense < *apo-*, from + *logos*, word] **1.** a formal spoken or written defense of some idea, doctrine, etc. **2.** a statement that one is aware of having committed a fault or wrong, regrets it, and asks for pardon **3.** an inferior substitute *[*he is a poor *apology* for an actor*]*

ap·o·phthegm (ap′ə them′) ***n.*** *same as* APOTHEGM

ap·o·plec·tic (ap′ə plek′tik) ***adj.*** **1.** of, like, or causing apoplexy **2.** having apoplexy **3.** seemingly about to have apoplexy *[apoplectic* with rage*]* Also **ap′o·plec′ti·cal** —***n.*** a person having or likely to have apoplexy —**ap′o·plec′ti·cal·ly** ***adv.***

ap·o·plex·y (ap′ə plek′sē) ***n.*** [< ME. & OFr. < L. < Gr. < *apo-*, down + *plēssein*, to strike] sudden paralysis with some loss of consciousness and feeling, caused when a blood vessel in the brain breaks or becomes clogged; stroke

a·port (ə pôrt′) ***adv.*** *Naut.* on or to the left, or port, side

a·pos·ta·sy (ə päs′tə sē) ***n.***, *pl.* **-sies** [< LL. < Gr. < *apo-*, away + *stasis*, a standing] an abandoning of something that one once believed in, as a faith, cause, etc.

a·pos·tate (ə päs′tāt′, -tit) ***n.*** a person guilty of apostasy —***adj.*** guilty of apostasy

a·pos·ta·tize (-tə tīz′) ***vi.*** **-tized′, -tiz′ing** to become an apostate

a pos·te·ri·o·ri (ā′ päs tir′ē ôr′ī, -ôr′ē) [ML., lit., from what comes later] **1.** from effect to cause, or from particular instances to a generalization; inductive or inductively **2.** based on observation or experience; empirical

a·pos·tle (ə päs′'l) ***n.*** [< OE. & OFr. < LL. < Gr. *apostolos*, one sent forth < *apo-*, from + *stellein*, to send] **1.** a person sent out on a special mission; specif., [*usually* **A-**] any of the twelve disciples sent out by Jesus to teach the gospel **2.** the first Christian missionary in a place **3.** any of a group of early Christian missionaries **4.** an early advocate or leader, as of a reform movement **5.** any of the twelve administrative officials of the Mormon Church —**a·pos′tle·ship′** ***n.***

Apostles' Creed a statement of belief in the basic Christian doctrines, coming from an early period and formerly thought to have been composed by the twelve Apostles: it begins, "I believe in God, the Father Almighty . . ."

a·pos·to·late (ə päs′t'l it, -tə lāt′) ***n.*** the office, duties, or period of activity of an apostle

ap·os·tol·ic (ap′əs täl′ik) ***adj.*** **1.** of an apostle **2.** of the Apostles, their teachings, work, or times **3.** held to derive from the Apostles in a direct line of succession 4. [*often* A-] of the Pope; papal Also **ap′os·tol′i·cal**

apostolic delegate a church official who represents the Pope in a country that does not have diplomatic relations with the Vatican

Apostolic See *R.C.Ch.* the Pope's see at Rome

a·pos·tro·phe[1] (ə päs′trə fē) *n.* [L. < Gr. *apostrophē*, a turning away to address one person < *apo-*, from + *strephein*, to turn] words addressed to a person or thing, whether absent or present, generally in the form of an exclamation —**ap·os·troph·ic** (ap′ə sträf′ik) *adj.*

a·pos·tro·phe[2] (ə päs′trə fē) *n.* [Fr. < LL. < Gr. *apostrophos* (*prosōdia*), averted (accent): see prec.] the mark (′) used: **1.** to show the omission of a letter or letters from a word (Ex.: *it's* for *it is*) **2.** to indicate the possessive case (Ex.: *Mary's* dress, the *girls'* club) **3.** in forming some plurals, as of figures and letters (Ex.: five *6's*, dot the *i's*)

a·pos·tro·phize (-fīz′) *vt., vi.* **-phized′, -phiz′ing** to speak or write an apostrophe (to)

apothecaries' measure a system of units used in measuring liquids in pharmacy: see TABLES OF WEIGHTS AND MEASURES in the Supplements

apothecaries' weight a system of weights used in pharmacy: see TABLES OF WEIGHTS AND MEASURES in the Supplements

a·poth·e·car·y (ə päth′ə ker′ē) *n., pl.* **-car′ies** [< OFr. < ML. < L. < Gr. *apothēkē*, storehouse < *apo-*, away + *tithenai*, to put] a pharmacist, or druggist: apothecaries formerly also prescribed drugs

ap·o·thegm (ap′ə them′) *n.* [< Gr. < *apo-*, from + *phthengesthai*, to utter] a short, pithy saying (Ex.: "Brevity is the soul of wit") —**ap′o·theg·mat′ic** (-theg mat′ik), **ap′o·theg·mat′i·cal** *adj.*

a·poth·e·o·sis (ə päth′ē ō′sis, ap′ə thē′ə sis) *n., pl.* **-ses′** (-sēz′) [L. < Gr. *apotheoun*, to deify < *apo-*, from + *theos*, a god] **1.** the act of raising a person to the status of a god; deification **2.** the glorification of a person or thing **3.** an ideal or exact type [she is the *apotheosis* of beauty]

a·poth·e·o·size (ə päth′ē ə sīz′, ap′ə thē′ə sīz′) *vt.* **-sized′, -siz′ing** [APOTHEOS(IS) + -IZE] **1.** to make a god of; deify **2.** to glorify; idealize

app. **1.** appendix **2.** appointed **3.** approved **4.** approximate

ap·pal (ə pôl′) *vt.* **-palled′, -pal′ling** same as APPALL

Ap·pa·la·chi·a (ap′ə lā′chə, -chē ə; -lach′ə) the highland region of the E U.S., including the central and southern Appalachians: characterized generally by economic depression and poverty

Ap·pa·la·chi·an Mountains (-lā′chən, -chē ən; -lach′ən) [< ? *Apalachee* Indians < ?] mountain system in E N. America, extending from S Quebec to N Ala.: highest peak, 6,684 ft.: also **Appalachians** —**Ap′pa·la′chi·an** *adj.*

ap·pall (ə pôl′) *vt.* [< OFr. *apalir* < *a-*, to + *palir*, to grow pale < L. *pallidus*, pale] to fill with horror or dismay; shock —see SYN. at DISMAY

ap·pall·ing (-iŋ) *adj.* causing horror, shock, or dismay —**ap·pal′ling·ly** *adv.*

☆**ap·pa·loo·sa** (ap′ə lōō′sə) *n.* [altered < *a palouse*, after the *Palouse* Indians of the NW U.S.] any of a sturdy breed of Western saddle horses with spotted markings on the rump and loins

ap·pa·nage (ap′ə nij) *n.* [< Fr. < ML. < L. *ad*, to + *panis*, bread] **1.** money, land, etc. granted by a monarch for the support of his younger children **2.** a person's rightful privilege; perquisite **3.** something that naturally accompanies; adjunct [the *appanages* of high office]

APPALOOSA

ap·pa·ra·tus (ap′ə rat′əs, ap′ə rāt′-) *n., pl.* **-ra′tus, -ra′tus·es** [L., a making ready < *apparare* < *ad-*, to + *parare*, to prepare] **1.** the instruments, equipment, etc. for a specific use **2.** any complex device or system [the *apparatus* of government] **3.** *Physiol.* a set of organs having a specific function [the digestive *apparatus*]

ap·par·el (ə per′əl, -par′-) *n.* [< OFr., ult. < L. *apparare*: see prec.] clothing; attire —*vt.* **-eled** or **-elled, -el·ing** or **-el·ling** **1.** to clothe; dress **2.** to adorn; bedeck

ap·par·ent (ə per′ənt, -par′-) *adj.* [< OFr. < L. prp. of *parere*, APPEAR] **1.** readily seen; visible **2.** readily understood; obvious [it's *apparent* that he's angry] **3.** appearing to be real or true; seeming See also HEIR APPARENT —see SYN. at EVIDENT —**ap·par′ent·ly** *adv.*

ap·pa·ri·tion (ap′ə rish′ən) *n.* [< OFr. < ML. < L. *apparere*: see APPEAR] **1.** anything that appears unexpectedly or in a strange way; esp., a ghost **2.** the act of appearing or becoming visible —**ap′pa·ri′tion·al** *adj.*

▸**ap·peal** (ə pēl′) *vt.* [< OFr. < L. *appellare*, to accost, appeal < *ad-*, to + *pellere*: see COMPEL] to make a request to a higher court for the rehearing of (a case) —*vi.* **1.** to appeal a law case to a higher court **2.** to make an urgent request (*to* a person *for* help, sympathy, etc.) **3.** to resort (*to*) for decision, justification, etc. [to *appeal* to logic] **4.** to be attractive, interesting, etc. —*n.* **1.** a call upon some authority for a decision, etc. **2.** an urgent request for help, etc. **3.** a quality that arouses interest, sympathy, etc.; attraction **4.** *Law* *a*) a request that a case be transferred to a higher court for rehearing or review *b*) the right to request this —**ap·peal′a·ble** *adj.* —**ap·peal′ing** *adj.* —**ap·peal′ing·ly** *adv.*

SYN.—**appeal** implies an earnest request, often one based on moral values [*appeal* to his sense of fair play] and, in legal usage, connotes resort to a higher court; **plead** suggests urgency and an attempt to persuade by argument [he *pleaded* for tolerance]; **petition** implies a formal request, usually in writing and in accordance with established rights; **pray** and **supplicate** suggest humility and imply that the request is addressed to God or to a superior authority; **sue** is highly formal and suggests respectful seeking of relief, a favor, etc.

ap·pear (ə pir′) *vi.* [< OFr. < L. *apparere* < *ad-*, to + *parere*, to come forth] **1.** to come into sight [a ship *appeared* over the horizon] **2.** to come into being [freckles *appear* on his face every summer] **3.** to become understood [it *appears* he left] **4.** to seem; look [he *appears* to be healthy] **5.** to present oneself formally, as in court **6.** to come before the public [he *appeared* in Hamlet] **7.** to be published [her book *appeared* in May]

ap·pear·ance (-əns) *n.* **1.** an appearing **2.** the outward look of anything **3.** an outward show; pretense [to give the *appearance* of being busy] **4.** [*pl.*] the way things seem to be [from all *appearances*, he's innocent] —**keep up appearances** to try to give the impression of being proper, well-off, etc. —**put in an appearance** to be present for a short time, as at a party

SYN.—**appearance** and **look** refer generally to the outward impression of a thing, but the former may imply mere show [an *appearance* of innocence] while the latter refers to physical details [the *look* of an abandoned house]; **aspect** also refers to features which appear to the eye, esp. as at a given time and place [the colorful trees in their autumn *aspect*]; **semblance** refers to the outward impression as contrasted with inner reality, but without any intent to deceive [a *semblance* of order]; **guise** is usually used of a deliberately misleading appearance [under the *guise* of patriotism]

ap·pease (ə pēz′) *vt.* **-peased′, -peas′ing** [< OFr. < *a-*, to + *pais* < L. *pax*, PEACE] **1.** to make peaceful or quiet, esp. by giving in to the demands of **2.** to satisfy or relieve [water *appeases* thirst] —see SYN. at PACIFY —**ap·peas′a·ble** *adj.* —**ap·peas′er** *n.*

ap·pease·ment (-mənt) *n.* **1.** an appeasing or being appeased **2.** the policy of giving in to demands of a hostile power in an attempt to keep peace

ap·pel·lant (ə pel′ənt) *adj. Law* relating to appeals; appealing —*n.* a person who appeals, esp. to a higher court

ap·pel·late (ə pel′it) *adj.* [< L. pp. of *appellare*, APPEAL] *Law* relating to, or having the right to review, appeals [an *appellate* court]

ap·pel·la·tion (ap′ə lā′shən) *n.* [< L. < pp. of *appellare*, APPEAL] **1.** the act of calling by a name **2.** a name or title that describes or identifies [Czar Ivan IV's *appellation* was "the Terrible"]

ap·pel·la·tive (ə pel′ə tiv) *adj.* of appellation; naming —*n.* a name or title

ap·pend (ə pend′) *vt.* [< OFr. < L. *appendere* < *ad-*, to + *pendere*, to suspend] to attach or affix; add as a supplement or appendix

ap·pend·age (ə pen′dij) *n.* **1.** anything appended; adjunct

2. *Biol.* any secondary, external organ or part, as a tree branch or a dog's tail

ap·pend·ant, ap·pend·ent (-dənt) *adj.* [Fr.: see APPEND] 1. attached or added 2. associated with as a consequence —*n.* an appendage

☆**ap·pen·dec·to·my** (ap'ən dek'tə mē) *n., pl.* **-mies** [APPEND(IX) + -ECTOMY] the surgical operation of removing the vermiform appendix

☆**ap·pen·di·ci·tis** (ə pen'də sīt'əs) *n.* [< APPENDIX + -ITIS] inflammation of the vermiform appendix

ap·pen·dix (ə pen'diks) *n., pl.* **-dix·es, -di·ces'** (-də sēz') [L.: see APPEND] 1. additional material at the end of a book 2. *Anat.* an outgrowth of an organ; esp., a small sac (**vermiform appendix**) extending from the cecum of the large intestine: it serves no known purpose: see illustration at ALIMENTARY CANAL

ap·per·ceive (ap'ər sēv') *vt.* **-ceived', -ceiv'ing** [< OFr. < L. *ad-*, to + *percipere*, PERCEIVE] *Psychol.* to assimilate and interpret (a new perception) by the help of past experience

ap·per·cep·tion (ap'ər sep'shən) *n.* [< Fr. < *apercevoir*, APPERCEIVE] 1. an apperceiving 2. the state of the mind in being conscious of its own consciousness —**ap'per·cep'tive** *adj.*

ap·per·tain (ap'ər tān') *vi.* [< OFr. < L. *appertinere* < *ad-*, to + *pertinere*: see PERTAIN] to belong properly as a function, part, etc.; pertain [the house and all fixtures *appertaining* to it]

ap·pe·ten·cy (ap'ə tən sē) *n., pl.* **-cies** [< L. prp. of *appetere*: see APPETITE] 1. a strong desire 2. an instinctive tendency; propensity 3. a natural attraction, as between some chemical elements; affinity Also **ap'pe·tence** (-təns)

ap·pe·tite (ap'ə tīt') *n.* [< ME. & OFr. < L. *appetitus*, pp. of *appetere* < *ad-*, to + *petere*, to seek] 1. a desire for food or for a specific food 2. any strong desire or craving [an *appetite* for learning]

ap·pe·tiz·er (ap'ə tī'zər) *n.* a small portion of a tasty food or a drink to stimulate the appetite at the beginning of a meal

ap·pe·tiz·ing (-tī'ziŋ) *adj.* 1. stimulating the appetite 2. savory; tasty —**ap'pe·tiz'ing·ly** *adv.*

ap·plaud (ə plôd') *vt., vi.* [L. *applaudere* < *ad-*, to + *plaudere*, to clap hands] 1. to show approval (of) by clapping the hands, cheering, etc. 2. to praise; approve —**ap·plaud'er** *n.*

ap·plause (ə plôz') *n.* approval or praise, esp. as shown by clapping hands, cheering, etc.

ap·ple (ap''l) *n.* [OE. *æppel*] 1. *a)* a round, firm, fleshy, edible fruit with a red, yellow, or green skin and a seed core, growing on any of a genus of trees in temperate regions *b)* any of these trees 2. any of various plants bearing applelike fruits, as the May apple

☆**apple butter** a kind of jam made from apples stewed with spices

ap·ple·jack (-jak') *n.* ☆a brandy distilled from apple cider

apple of one's eye 1. the pupil of one's eye 2. any person or thing that one cherishes

ap·ple-pie order (ap''l pī') [Colloq.] neat order

ap·ple·sauce (-sôs') *n.* 1. apples cooked to a pulp in water ☆2. [Slang] nonsense; hokum

Ap·ple·seed (ap''l sēd'), **Johnny** (nickname of *John Chapman*) 1775-1845; U.S. frontiersman who planted apple trees throughout the Midwest

Ap·ple·ton (ap''l tən) [after S. *Appleton*, 19th-c. Boston philanthropist] city in E Wis.: pop. 57,000

ap·pli·ance (ə plī'əns) *n.* a device or machine for a specific task, esp. one worked mechanically or by electricity [stoves, irons, etc. are household *appliances*]

ap·pli·ca·ble (ap'li kə b'l) *adj.* that can be applied; appropriate; suitable [that rule is not *applicable* in his case] —**ap'pli·ca·bil'i·ty** *n.*

ap·pli·cant (ap'li kənt) *n.* a person who applies, as for employment, help, etc.

ap·pli·ca·tion (ap'lə kā'shən) *n.* 1. the act or a way of applying or being applied [the *application* of force to a door that is stuck] 2. anything applied, esp. a remedy [an *application* containing zinc oxide] 3. a request, or the form filled out in making a request [an *application* for employment] 4. continued effort; close attention [to succeed by *application* to one's studies] 5. relevance or practicality [this idea has no *application* to the case]

ap·pli·ca·tor (ap'lə kāt'ər) *n.* any device for applying medicine or paint, polish, etc.

ap·pli·ca·to·ry (-kə tôr'ē) *adj.* that can be applied or used; practical: also **ap'pli·ca'tive** (-kāt'iv)

ap·plied (ə plīd') *adj.* used in actual practice or to work out practical problems [applied science]

ap·pli·qué (ap'lə kā') *n.* [Fr. < L. *applicare*: see APPLY] a decoration made of one material attached by sewing, etc. to another —*adj.* applied as such a decoration —*vt.* **-quéd', -qué'ing** 1. to decorate with appliqué 2. to put on as appliqué

APPLIQUÉ

ap·ply (ə plī') *vt.* **-plied', -ply'ing** [< OFr. < L. *applicare*, to attach to < *ad-*, to + *plicare*, to fold] 1. to put on [to *apply* salve] 2. to use practically [to *apply* one's knowledge] 3. to refer to a person or thing with (an epithet or suitable term) [she *applies* the word "fantastic" indiscriminately] 4. to concentrate (one's faculties); employ (oneself) diligently —*vi.* 1. to make a formal request [to *apply* for a job] 2. to be suitable or relevant [this rule *applies* to everyone] —**ap·pli'er** *n.*

ap·pog·gia·tu·ra (ə päj'ə toor'ə) *n.* [It. < *appoggiare*, to lean. < L. *ad-*, to + *podium*, PODIUM] *Music* an auxiliary note like a grace note but rhythmically more prominent than the melodic note that it precedes

ap·point (ə point') *vt.* [< OFr. *apointer*, to make ready, ult. < L. *ad-*, to + *punctum*, a POINT] 1. to set (a date, place, etc.); decree 2. to name for an office, etc. [to *appoint* a chairman] 3. to furnish and arrange: now usually in *well-appointed*, etc.

ap·point·ee (ə poin'tē') *n.* a person appointed to some position

ap·point·ive (ə poin'tiv) *adj.* to which one is appointed, not elected [an *appointive* office]

ap·point·ment (ə point'mənt) *n.* 1. an appointing or being appointed; specif., a naming for an office, etc. 2. a person so named 3. an office held in this way 4. an arrangement to meet a person; engagement 5. [*pl.*] furnishings

Ap·po·mat·tox (Court House) (ap'ə mat'əks) [< Algonquian tribal name] former village in C Va., where Lee surrendered to Grant (April 9, 1865), ending the Civil War

ap·por·tion (ə pôr'shən) *vt.* [< OFr.: see AD- & PORTION] to divide and distribute in shares according to a plan [the drinking water was *apportioned* according to age] —see SYN. at ALLOT

ap·por·tion·ment (-mənt) *n.* 1. an apportioning 2. proportional distribution, as of U.S. Representatives among the States

ap·pos·a·ble (ə pōz'ə b'l) *adj.* that can be apposed; specif., that can move so as to touch each of the four fingers [the human thumb is *apposable*]

ap·pose (ə pōz') *vt.* **-posed', -pos'ing** [< Fr. < L. *appositus*, pp. of *apponere* < *ad-*, near + *ponere*, to put] to put side by side, next, or near

ap·po·site (ap'ə zit) *adj.* [see prec.] appropriate; apt —see SYN. at RELEVANT —**ap'po·site·ly** *adv.* —**ap'po·site·ness** *n.*

ap·po·si·tion (ap'ə zish'ən) *n.* 1. an apposing or being apposed 2. the position resulting from this 3. *Gram. a)* the placing of a word or expression beside another so that the second explains and has the same grammatical construction as the first *b)* the relationship between such terms ["my cousin" is in *apposition* with "Mary" in "Mary, my cousin, is here"] —**ap'po·si'tion·al** *adj.*

ap·pos·i·tive (ə päz'ə tiv) *adj.* of or in apposition —*n.* a word, phrase, or clause in apposition —**ap·pos'i·tive·ly** *adv.*

ap·prais·al (ə prā'z'l) *n.* 1. an appraising 2. an appraised value; esp., an expert valuation as for taxation or sale Also **ap·praise'ment**

ap·praise (ə prāz') *vt.* **-praised', -prais'ing** [< OFr. < LL. *appretiare* < L. *ad*, to + *pretium*, PRICE; Eng. sp. infl. by PRAISE] 1. to set a price for; decide the value of, esp. officially 2. to estimate the quantity or quality of —see SYN. at ESTIMATE —**ap·prais'er** *n.* —**ap·prais'ing·ly** *adv.*

ap·pre·ci·a·ble (ə prē'shə b'l, -shē ə-) *adj.* enough to be perceived; noticeable; measurable [an *appreciable* difference] —see SYN. at PERCEPTIBLE —**ap·pre'ci·a·bly** *adv.*

ap·pre·ci·ate (ə prē'shē āt') *vt.* **-at'ed, -at'ing** [< LL. pp. of *appretiare*, APPRAISE] 1. to think well of; understand and enjoy [he *appreciates* the music of Bach] 2. to recognize and be grateful for [I *appreciate* your help] 3. to estimate the quality or worth of 4. to be fully or sensitively aware of [I *appreciate* your problem] ☆ 5. to raise the price of: opposed to DEPRECIATE —☆*vi.* to rise in value —**ap·pre'ci·a'tor** *n.* —**ap·pre'ci·a·to'ry** (-shə tôr'ē, -shē ə-) *adj.*

SYN.—**appreciate** implies enough understanding and judgment to see the value or enjoy [he *appreciates* good music]; to **value** is to rate highly because of worth [I *value* your friendship]; to **prize** is to think highly of or take great satisfaction in [he *prizes* his art collection]; to **treasure** is to regard as precious and implies special care and protection; to **esteem** is to hold in high regard or respect *[an esteemed* statesman*]*; to **cherish** is to prize or treasure, but connotes greater affection for the thing cherished *[he cherished his family] —see also* **SYN.** at UNDERSTAND *—ANT.* despise, disdain

ap·pre·ci·a·tion (ə prē´shē ā´shən) *n.* **1.** an appreciating; specif., *a)* proper estimation *b)* grateful recognition, as of a favor *c)* sensitive awareness or enjoyment, as of art *d)* an evaluation or judgment ☆**2.** a rise in value or price

ap·pre·ci·a·tive (ə prē´shə tiv, -shē ə-; -shē āt´iv) *adj.* feeling or showing appreciation —**ap·pre´ci·a·tive·ly** *adv.* —**ap·pre´ci·a·tive·ness** *n.*

ap·pre·hend (ap´rə hend´) *vt.* **[** < L. *apprehendere,* to take hold of < *ad-,* to + *prehendere,* to seize**] 1.** to capture or arrest *[to apprehend* a criminal*]* **2.** to grasp mentally; understand *[to apprehend* a problem*]* **3.** to expect anxiously; dread *[to apprehend* disaster*]*

ap·pre·hen·sion (-hen´shən) *n.* **1.** capture or arrest **2.** mental grasp or understanding **3.** an anxious feeling or dread

ap·pre·hen·sive (-hen´siv) *adj.* **1.** able or quick to understand **2.** uneasy or fearful about the future —**ap´pre·hen´sive·ly** *adv.* —**ap´pre·hen´sive·ness** *n.*

ap·pren·tice (ə pren´tis) *n.* **[** < OFr. < *aprendre,* to teach < L. *apprehendere,* APPREHEND**] 1.** a person under legal agreement to work a specified length of time for a master craftsman in a craft or trade in return for instruction and, formerly, support **2.** a person, usually a member of a labor union, learning a trade, etc. under specified conditions **3.** any learner or beginner —*vt.* **-ticed, -tic·ing** to place or accept as an apprentice

ap·pren·tice·ship (-ship´) *n.* the condition or period of being an apprentice

ap·prise¹, ap·prize¹ (ə prīz´) *vt.* **-prised´** or **-prized´, -pris´ing** or **-priz´ing [** < Fr. pp. of *apprendre,* to teach, inform < L. *apprehendere,* APPREHEND**]** to inform or notify —see **SYN.** at NOTIFY

ap·prize², ap·prise² (ə prīz´) *vt.* **-prized´** or **-prised´, -priz´ing** or **-pris´ing** *same as* APPRAISE

ap·proach (ə prōch´) *vi.* **[** < OFr. < LL. *appropiare* < L. *ad,* to + *propius,* compar. of *prope,* near**]** to come closer or draw nearer *[vacation time approaches]* —*vt.* **1.** to come near or nearer to *[we're approaching* home*]* **2.** to be similar to; approximate *[that color approaches* what we want*]* **3.** to make advances, a proposal, or a request to *[he approached* me for a loan*]* **4.** to begin dealing with *[to approach* a task*]* —*n.* **1.** a coming closer *[the approach* of spring*]* **2.** an approximation or similarity **3.** an advance or overture *(to* someone): *often used in pl.* **4.** a way of getting to a person, place, or thing; path; road; access *[a new approach* to the subject; there are several *approaches* to the city*]* **5.** *Golf* a shot to drive the ball from the fairway onto the putting green —**ap·proach´a·bil´i·ty** *n.* —**ap·proach´a·ble** *adj.*

ap·pro·ba·tion (ap´rə bā´shən) *n.* **[** < L. < *approbare,* APPROVE**]** official approval, permission, or praise —**ap´pro·ba´tive, ap·pro·ba·to·ry** (ə prō´bə tôr´ē) *adj.*

ap·pro·pri·ate (ə prō´prē āt´; *for adj.* -it) *vt.* **-at´ed, -at´ing [** < LL. pp. of *appropriare* < L. < *ad-,* to + *proprius,* one's own**] 1.** to take for one's own use **2.** to take improperly, as without permission **3.** to set aside for a specific use *[to appropriate* funds for schools*]* —*adj.* right for the purpose; suitable —see **SYN.** at FIT¹ —**ap·pro´pri·ate·ly** (-it lē) *adv.* —**ap·pro´pri·ate·ness** *n.* —**ap·pro´pri·a´tor** *n.*

ap·pro·pri·a·tion (ə prō´prē ā´shən) *n.* **1.** an appropriating or being appropriated **2.** a thing appropriated; esp., money set aside for a specific use

ap·prov·al (ə pro͞o´v'l) *n.* **1.** an approving **2.** favorable attitude or opinion **3.** formal consent or permission —**on approval** for the customer to examine and decide whether to buy or return

ap·prove (ə pro͞ov´) *vt.* **-proved´, -prov´ing [** < OFr. < L. *approbare* < *ad-,* to + *probare,* to try, test < *probus,* good**] 1.** to give one's consent to; sanction *[the mayor must approve* the plan*]* **2.** to judge to be good, satisfactory, etc. —*vi.* to have a favorable opinion *(of)* *[does she approve* of your friends?*]* —**ap·prov´ing·ly** *adv.*

SYN.—approve, the most general of these terms, means simply to regard as good or satisfactory; **endorse,** in addition, suggests active support *[to en-*

dorse a candidate for office*]*; **sanction** suggests official approval *[a practice sanctioned* by the courts*]*; **certify** implies official approval given because requirements or standards have been satisfied *[a certified* public accountant*]* *—ANT.* disapprove, reject

approx. 1. approximate **2.** approximately

ap·prox·i·mate (ə präk´sə mit; *for v.* -māt´) *adj.* **[** < LL. pp. of *approximare* < L. *ad,* to + *proximus,* superl. of *prope,* near**] 1.** near in position **2.** much like; resembling **3.** not exact, but almost so *[the approximate* price is $10*]* —*vt.* **-mat´ed, -mat´ing 1.** to come near to; be almost the same as *[a painting that approximates* reality*]* **2.** to bring near *(to* something) —*vi.* to come near; be almost the same —**ap·prox´i·mate·ly** *adv.*

ap·prox·i·ma·tion (ə präk´sə mā´shən) *n.* **1.** an approximating **2.** a fairly close estimate or guess *[give us your approximation* of the costs*]*

ap·pur·te·nance (ə pur´t'n əns) *n.* **[** < Anglo-Fr. < OFr. < L. prp. of *appertinere,* APPERTAIN**] 1.** something added to a more important thing; adjunct **2.** *[pl.]* accessories **3.** *Law* an additional, subordinate right or privilege —**ap·pur´te·nant** *adj., n.*

a·prax·i·a (ə prak´sē ə) *n.* **[**ModL. < Gr. *apraxia,* nonaction**]** loss of memory of how to perform complex muscular movements, resulting from brain damage —**a·prax´ic** (-prak´sik), **a·prac´tic** (-prak´tik) *adj.*

a·près (a´prā´; *Fr.* à pre´) *prep.* **[**Fr.**]** after: often in hyphenated compounds *[an après-ski party]*

a·pri·cot (ap´rə kät´, ā´prə-) *n.* **[** < Fr. < Port. < Ar. < MGr. < L. *praecoquus,* early matured, pp. of *precoquere:* see PRECOCIOUS**] 1.** a small, yellowish-orange fruit related to the peach **2.** the tree it grows on **3.** yellowish orange

A·pril (ā´prəl) *n.* **[** < OFr. < L. < *apero-,* second (in the ancient Rom. calendar, the year began with March)**]** the fourth month of the year, having 30 days: abbrev. **Apr.**

April fool a victim of jokes on April Fools' Day

April Fools' Day April 1, All Fools' Day, when practical jokes are traditionally played

APRICOTS

a pri·o·ri (ā´prē ôr´ē, ā´prī ôr´ī) **[**L., from something prior**] 1.** from cause to effect or from a generalization to particular instances; deductive or deductively **2.** based on theory instead of on experience or experiment

a·pron (ā´prən, -pərn) *n.* **[**by faulty separation < ME. *a napron* < OFr. *naperon* < *nape,* a cloth < L. *mappa,* a napkin**] 1.** a garment worn over the front part of the body, usually to protect one's clothes **2.** anything like an apron; specif., *a)* a protective covering for or edging on a structure, machine, etc. *b)* the hard-surfaced area in front of a hangar *c)* a broadened part of a driveway *d)* the part of a stage in front of the curtain —*vt.* to put an apron on or provide an apron for

apron string a string for tying an apron on —**tied to one's mother's** (or **wife's,** etc.) **apron strings** dominated by one's mother (or wife, etc.)

ap·ro·pos (ap´rə pō´) *adv.* **[**Fr. *à propos,* to the purpose**]** at the right time; opportunely —*adj.* fitting; apt —see **SYN.** at RELEVANT —**apropos of** in connection with; with regard to

apse (aps) *n.* **[** < L. < Gr. *hapsis,* an arch, fastening < *haptein,* to fasten**]** a part of a building that is set back, esp. at the east end of a church, and generally is shaped like a half circle with a domed roof —**ap´si·dal** (ap´sid 'l) *adj.*

apt (apt) *adj.* **[** < ME. & OFr. < L. *aptus,* pp. of *apere,* to fasten**] 1.** appropriate; fitting *[an apt* remark*]* **2.** tending or inclined; likely *[apt* to rain*]* **3.** quick to learn or understand *[an apt* student*]* —see **SYN.** at FIT¹ and at LIKELY —**apt´ly** *adv.* —**apt´ness** *n.*

apt. *pl.* **apts.** apartment

ap·ter·ous (ap´tər əs) *adj.* **[** < Gr. < *a-,* without + *pteron,* a wing**]** *Biol.* having no wings; wingless

APSE

ap·ter·yx (ap′tər iks) *n.* [< Gr. *a-*, without + *pteryx*, wing] *same as* KIWI

ap·ti·tude (ap′tə tōōd′, -tyōōd′) *n.* [< ML. < L. *aptus*: see APT] **1.** a natural tendency, inclination, or ability [an *aptitude* for sports] **2.** quickness to learn or understand —see SYN. at TALENT

☆**aptitude test** a test for finding out how successful a person is likely to be in some activity in which he is not yet trained

aq·ua (ak′wə, äk′-) *n., pl.* **aq′uas, aq′uae** (-wē) [L.] water; esp., *Pharm.* a solution of a substance in water —*adj.* [< AQUAMARINE] bluish-green

aq·ua·cul·ture (ak′wə kul′chər, äk′-) *n.* [prec. + CULTURE] cultivation of water plants and animals for human use

aqua for·tis (fôr′təs) [L., strong water] *same as* NITRIC ACID

Aq·ua-lung (ak′wə luŋ′, äk′-) [AQUA + LUNG] *a trademark for* a kind of self-contained underwater breathing apparatus: see SCUBA —*n.* an apparatus of this kind: usually **a′qua·lung′**

aq·ua·ma·rine (ak′wə mə rēn′, äk′-) *n.* [L. *aqua marina*, sea water] **1.** a transparent, pale bluish-green mineral: a variety of beryl, used in jewelry **2.** its color —*adj.* bluish-green

☆**aq·ua·naut** (ak′wə nôt′, äk′-) *n.* [AQUA + (ASTRO)NAUT] **1.** any of a group of persons using a watertight underwater chamber as a base for experiments in the oceans **2.** *same as* SKIN DIVER

☆**aq·ua·plane** (ak′wə plān′, äk′-) *n.* [AQUA + PLANE⁴] a board on which one rides standing up as it is pulled over water by a motorboat —*vi.* **-planed′, -plan′ing** to ride on such a board as a sport

aqua re·gi·a (rē′jē ə) [L., lit., kingly water: it dissolves the "noble metals," gold and platinum] a mixture of nitric and hydrochloric acids

☆**a·quar·ist** (ə kwer′ist) *n.* the keeper of an aquarium

a·quar·i·um (ə kwer′ē əm) *n., pl.* **-i·ums, -i·a** (-ē ə) [L., neut. of *aquarius*, of water < *aqua*, water] **1.** a tank, usually with glass sides, or a pool, bowl, etc., for keeping live water animals and water plants **2.** a building where such collections are exhibited

A·quar·i·us (ə kwer′ē əs) [L., the water carrier] **1.** a large S constellation **2.** the eleventh sign of the zodiac: see ZODIAC

a·quat·ic (ə kwät′ik, -kwat′-) *adj.* [< L. < *aqua*, water] **1.** growing or living in or upon water **2.** done in or upon the water [*aquatic* sports] —*n.* [*pl.*, *often with sing. v.*] aquatic sports or performances —**a·quat′i·cal·ly** *adv.*

aq·ua·tint (ak′wə tint′, äk′-) *n.* [< Fr. < It. *acqua tinta*, dyed in water] **1.** a process by which spaces rather than lines are etched with acid to produce an etching that looks like a watercolor **2.** such an etching —*vt.* to etch in this way

aqua vi·tae (vīt′ē) [L., water of life] **1.** *Alchemy* alcohol **2.** brandy or other strong liquor

aq·ue·duct (ak′wə dukt′) *n.* [< L. < *aqua*, water + pp. of *ducere*, to lead] **1.** a large pipe or conduit for bringing water from a distant source **2.** a bridgelike structure for carrying a water conduit or canal across a river or valley

a·que·ous (ā′kwē əs, ak′wē-) *adj.* [see AQUA & -OUS] **1.** of, like, or containing water; watery **2.** *Geol.* formed by the action of water

aqueous humor a watery fluid in the space between the cornea and the lens of the eye

aq·ui·cul·ture (ak′wi kul′chər, äk′-) *n. same as* AQUACULTURE

☆**aq·ui·fer** (ak′wə fər, äk′-) *n.* [ModL.: see AQUA & -FER] an underground layer of rock, sand, etc. containing water, into which wells can be sunk

Aq·ui·la (ak′wi lə) [L., eagle] a N constellation in the Milky Way

aq·ui·line (ak′wə līn′, -lən) *adj.* [< L. < *aquila*, eagle] **1.** of or like an eagle **2.** curved or hooked like an eagle's beak [an *aquiline* nose]

A·qui·nas (ə kwī′nəs), Saint **Thomas** 1225?-74; It. theologian & philosopher

Aq·ui·taine (ak′wə tān′) region of SW France

-ar (ər) [< ME. < OFr. < L. *-aris* or *-arius;* or directly < L.] **1.** *a suffix meaning* of, relating to, like, of the nature of [*singular, polar*] **2.** *a suffix denoting* agency [*bursar, vicar*]

Ar *Chem.* argon

AR 1. Airman Recruit **2.** Arkansas **3.** Army Regulation

Ar. 1. Arabic **2.** Aramaic

ar. 1. arrival **2.** arrives

A.R. Autonomous Republic

AQUILINE NOSE

Ar·ab (ar′əb) *n.* **1.** a native or inhabitant of Arabia **2.** any of a Semitic people originating in Arabia; commonly, a Bedouin **3.** any of a breed of swift, graceful horses native to Arabia —*adj. same as* ARABIAN

ar·a·besque (ar′ə besk′) *n.* [Fr. < It. < *Arabo*, Arab < Ar. *'arab:* with reference to Moorish designs] **1.** an elaborate design of intertwined flowers, foliage, geometrical patterns, etc. **2.** *Ballet* a position in which one leg is extended back and the arms are extended, usually one back and one forward —*adj.* of or done in arabesque; fantastic and elaborate

ARABESQUE

A·ra·bi·a (ə rā′bē ə) peninsula, largely a desert, in SW Asia: also **Arabian Peninsula**

A·ra·bi·an (-ən) *adj.* of Arabia or the Arabs —*n. same as* ARAB (senses 1 & 3)

Arabian Nights, The a collection of ancient tales from Arabia, India, Persia, etc.

Arabian Sea part of the Indian Ocean, between India and Arabia

Ar·a·bic (ar′ə bik) *adj.* **1.** of Arabia **2.** of the Arabs, their language, culture, etc. —*n.* the Semitic language of the Arabs, spoken in Arabia, Syria, Jordan, Iraq, northern Africa, etc.

Arabic numerals the figures 1, 2, 3, 4, 5, 6, 7, 8, 9, and the 0 (zero), orig. used in India and often called **Hindu-Arabic numerals**

ar·a·ble (ar′ə b'l) *adj.* [Fr. < L. < *arare*, to plow] suitable for plowing and producing crops —*n.* arable land —**ar′a·bil′i·ty** *n.*

Arab League a confederation of a number of Arabic-speaking nations

Ar·a·by (ar′ə bē) [Archaic or Poet.] Arabia

a·rach·nid (ə rak′nid) *n.* [ModL. < Gr. *arachnē*, spider] any of a large group of arthropods, including spiders, scorpions, and mites, with four pairs of legs and with breathing tubes or lung-like sacs —**a·rach′ni·dan** (-ni dən) *adj., n.*

Ar·a·gon (ar′ə gän′) region & former kingdom in NE Spain: see map at CASTILE —**Ar′a·go·nese′** (-gə nēz′) *adj., n., pl.* **-nese′**

Ar·al Sea (ar′əl) inland body of salt water in SW Asiatic U.S.S.R., east of the Caspian Sea: also **Lake Aral**

Ar·am (ar′əm) [Heb.] *Biblical name for* ancient Syria —**Ar·a·mae·an, Ar·a·me·an** (ar′ə mē′ən) *adj., n.*

Aram. Aramaic

Ar·a·ma·ic (ar′ə mā′ik) *n.* a group of northwestern Semitic languages of Biblical times, including that of Palestine

A·rap·a·ho (ə rap′ə hō′) *n.* [< ? Crow, lit., enemy] **1.** *pl.* **-hos′, -ho′** any member of a tribe of Indians orig. from the area between the upper Platte and Arkansas rivers **2.** their Algonquian language

Ar·a·rat (ar′ə rat′) mountain in E Turkey: supposed landing place of Noah's Ark (Gen. 8:4)

ar·ba·lest, ar·ba·list (är′bə list) *n.* [< OFr. < L. < *arcus*, a bow + *ballista*, BALLISTA] a medieval crossbow with a steel bow

ar·bi·ter (är′bə tər) *n.* [L., orig., one who goes to a place, a witness < *ad-*, to + *baetere*, to go] **1.** a person selected to judge a dispute; umpire; arbitrator **2.** a person given full power to judge or decide —**ar′bi·tral** (-trəl) *adj.* —**ar′bi·tress** *n.fem.*

ARBALEST

ar·bi·tra·ble (är′bə trə b'l) *adj.* that can be decided by arbitration

ar·bit·ra·ment (är bit′rə mənt) *n.* **1.** arbitration **2.** an arbitrator's decision

ar·bi·trar·y (är′bə trer′ē) *adj.* [< L. < *arbiter*, ARBITER] **1.** not fixed by rules but left to one's own choice [*arbitrary* judgment] **2.** based on one's whim or notion; capricious [*arbitrary* rules] **3.** absolute; despotic —see SYN. at DICTATORIAL —**ar′bi·trar′i·ly** *adv.* —**ar′bi·trar′i·ness** *n.*

ar·bi·trate (är′bə trāt′) *vt.* **-trat′ed, -trat′ing** [< L. pp. of *arbitrari*, to give a decision < *arbiter*, ARBITER] **1.** to give to an arbitrator to decide [get them to *arbitrate* their dispute] **2.** to decide (a dispute) as an arbitrator —*vi.* **1.** to act as an arbitrator (*in* a dispute, *between* persons) **2.** to submit a dispute to arbitration

ar·bi·tra·tion (är′bə trā′shən) *n.* settlement of a dispute by someone chosen to hear both sides and come to a decision —**ar′bi·tra′tion·al** *adj.*

ar·bi·tra·tor (är′bə trāt′ər) *n.* a person chosen to arbitrate a dispute

ar·bor[1] (är′bər) *n.* [< OFr. < LL. *herbarium,* HERBARIUM] a place shaded by trees or shrubs, or, esp., by vines on latticework: Brit. sp. **ar′bour** —**ar′bored** *adj.*

ar·bor[2] (är′bər) *n., pl.* **ar′bo·res** (-bə rēz′) [L.] *Bot.* a tree

ar·bor[3] (är′bər) *n.* [< Fr. *arbre* < L. *arbor,* tree, beam] *Mech.* **1.** a shaft; beam **2.** a spindle; axle **3.** a bar that holds cutting tools

Arbor Day a tree-planting day observed in most States of the U.S., usually in April

ar·bo·re·al (är bôr′ē əl) *adj.* **1.** of or like a tree **2.** living in trees [*arboreal* toads]

ar·bo·res·cent (är′bə res′′nt) *adj.* treelike in form or growth; branching —**ar′bo·res′cence** *n.*

ar·bo·re·tum (är′bə rēt′əm) *n., pl.* **-tums, -ta** (-ə) [L.] a place where many kinds of trees and shrubs are grown for exhibition or study

ar·bor·vi·tae (är′bər vīt′ē) *n.* [L., tree of life] any of several evergreen trees related to the cypress, with flattened sprays of scalelike leaves

ar·bu·tus (är byōōt′əs) *n.* [L., wild strawberry tree] **1.** a tree or shrub of the heath family, with dark-green leaves and berries like strawberries **2.** a related trailing plant with clusters of white or pink flowers

arc (ärk) *n.* [OFr. < L. *arcus,* a bow, arch] **1.** a bowlike curved line or object **2.** *Elec.* the band of sparks or incandescent light formed when an electric current passes from one electrode or conducting surface to another **3.** *Geom. a)* any part of a curve, esp. of a circle *b)* the angular measurement of this —*vi.* **arced** or **arcked, arc′ing** or **arck′ing** **1.** to move in a curved course **2.** *Elec.* to form an arc

Arc, Jeanne d' (zhän därk′) *see* JOAN OF ARC

ar·cade (är kād′) *n.* [Fr. < Pr. < ML. < L. *arcus,* arch] **1.** a covered passageway, as through a building, often with an arched roof; esp., such a passage with shops along the sides **2.** a line of arches and their supporting columns —*vt.* **-cad′ed, -cad′ing** to make into or provide with an arcade

Ar·ca·di·a (är kā′dē ə) a pastoral district of ancient Greece: see map at GREECE —*n.* any place of rural peace and simplicity Also [Poet.] **Ar·ca·dy** (är′kə dē) —**Ar·ca·di·an** (är kā′dē ən) *adj., n.*

ar·cane (är kān′) *adj.* [see ARCANUM] that is understood by only a few; esoteric [an *arcane* theory]

ar·ca·num (-kā′nəm) *n., pl.* **-na** (-nə), **-nums** [L., hidden < *arcere,* to shut up] a secret; mystery

arch[1] (ärch) *n.* [< OFr. < ML. < L. *arcus,* a bow, arch] a curved structure, as of masonry, that supports the weight of material over an open space, as in a bridge, doorway, etc. **2.** the form of an arch **3.** anything shaped like an arch [the *arch* of the foot] —*vt.* **1.** to provide with an arch or arches **2.** to curve into an arch [the cat *arched* its back] —*vi.* **1.** to form an arch **2.** to form an arch over; span

arch[2] (ärch) *adj.* [< ARCH-] **1.** main; chief [the *arch* villain] **2.** gaily mischievous; pert [an *arch* smile] —**arch′ly** *adv.* —**arch′ness** *n.*

arch- [< OE. < L. < Gr. *archos,* ruler] a prefix meaning main, chief [*archbishop, archduke*]

-arch (ärk; *occas.* ərk) [< Gr. *archos,* ruler] a suffix meaning ruler [*matriarch*]

arch. **1.** archaic **2.** archaism **3.** archipelago **4.** architect **5.** architectural **6.** architecture

ar·chae·ol·o·gy (är′kē äl′ə jē) *n.* [< Gr. *archaios,* ancient < *arche,* the beginning + -LOGY] the scientific study of the life and culture of ancient peoples, as by digging up the remains of ancient cities, etc. —**ar′chae·o·log′i·cal** (-ə läj′i k′l) *adj.* —**ar′chae·o·log′i·cal·ly** *adv.* —**ar′chae·ol′o·gist** *n.*

ar·chae·op·ter·yx (är′kē äp′tər iks) *n.* [< Gr. *archaios* (see prec.) + *pteryx,* wing] an extinct bird of the Jurassic Period that had teeth and some other features of reptiles

ARCHES
(A, semicircular;
B, horseshoe;
C, pointed)

ar·cha·ic (är kā′ik) *adj.* [< Gr. < *archaios,* ancient] **1.** belonging to an earlier time; ancient or old-fashioned **2.** that is now seldom used except in poetry, church ritual, etc., as the word *thou* —**ar·cha′i·cal·ly** *adv.*

ar·cha·ism (är′kē iz′m, -kā-) *n.* **1.** the use or imitation of archaic words, technique, etc. **2.** an archaic word, usage, etc. —**ar′cha·ist** *n.* —**ar′cha·is′tic** *adj.* —**ar′cha·is′ti·cal·ly** *adv.*

arch·an·gel (ärk′ān′j′l) *n.* a chief angel

Arch·an·gel (ärk′ān′j′l) seaport in NW R.S.F.S.R., on the White Sea: pop. 313,000

arch·bish·op (ärch′bish′əp) *n.* a chief bishop, who presides over an archbishopric or archdiocese

arch·bish·op·ric (-bish′ə prik′) *n.* the office, rank, term, or church district of an archbishop

arch·dea·con (ärch′dē′k′n) *n.* [see ARCH- & DEACON] a church official ranking just below a bishop, as in the Anglican Church —**arch′dea′con·ry** *n., pl.* **-ries**

arch·di·o·cese (-dī′ə sis, -sēs) *n.* the diocese of an archbishop —**arch′di·oc′e·san** (-dī äs′ə sən) *adj.*

arch·du·cal (-dōōk′′l, -dyōōk′′l) *adj.* of an archduke or archduchy

arch·duch·ess (-duch′is) *n.* **1.** the wife or widow of an archduke **2.** a princess of the former Austrian royal family

arch·duch·y (-duch′ē) *n., pl.* **-ies** the territory of an archduke or of an archduchess

arch·duke (-dōōk′, -dyōōk′) *n.* a chief duke, esp. a prince of the former Austrian royal family

ar·che·go·ni·um (är′kə gō′nē əm) *n., pl.* **-ni·a** (-nē ə) [ModL. < Gr. < *archos,* first + *gonos,* offspring] the flask-shaped female reproductive organ in mosses, ferns, etc.

arch·en·e·my (ärch′en′ə mē) *n., pl.* **-mies** a chief enemy —**the archenemy** Satan

ar·che·ol·o·gy (är′kē äl′ə jē) *n. same as* ARCHAEOLOGY —**ar′che·o·log′i·cal** *adj.* —**ar′che·ol′o·gist** *n.*

arch·er (är′chər) *n.* [< ME. & OFr. < VL. < L. < *arcus,* a bow] a person who shoots with bow and arrow; bowman —**[A-]** the constellation Sagittarius

arch·er·y (är′chər ē) *n.* **1.** the practice, art, or sport of shooting with bow and arrow **2.** an archer's equipment **3.** archers as a group

ar·che·type (är′kə tīp′) *n.* [< L. < Gr. < *archos,* first + *typos:* see TYPE, *n.*] **1.** the original pattern or model of something; prototype **2.** a perfect example of a type or group —**ar′che·typ′al** (-tīp′əl), **ar′che·typ′i·cal** (-tip′i k′l) *adj.*

arch·fiend (ärch′fēnd′) *n.* a chief fiend —**the archfiend** Satan

Ar·chi·bald (är′chə bôld′) [of Gmc. origin, prob. nobly bold] a masculine name

ar·chi·di·ac·o·nal (är′kə dī ak′ə n′l) *adj.* of an archdeacon or archdeaconry —**ar′chi·di·ac′o·nate** (-nit) *n.*

ar·chi·e·pis·co·pal (är′kē ə pis′kə p′l) *adj.* of an archbishop or archbishopric —**ar′chi·e·pis′co·pate** (-pət, -pāt′) *n.*

Ar·chi·me·des (är′kə mē′dēz) 287?-212 B.C.; Gr. mathematician & inventor —**Ar′chi·me′de·an** (-mē′dē ən, -mi·dē′ən) *adj.*

ar·chi·pel·a·go (är′kə pel′ə gō′) *n., pl.* **-goes, -gos′** [< It. < MGr. < Gr. *archi-,* chief + *pelagos,* sea] **1.** a sea with many islands **2.** such a group of islands —**ar′chi·pe·lag′ic** (-pə laj′ik) *adj.*

ar·chi·tect (är′kə tekt′) *n.* [< L. < Gr. < *archi-,* chief + *tektōn,* carpenter: for IE. base see TECHNIC] **1.** a person whose profession is designing plans for buildings, bridges, etc. and generally administering construction **2.** any planner or creator

ar·chi·tec·ton·ic (är′kə tek tän′ik) *adj.* [see prec.] **1.** of architecture or architectural methods, etc. **2.** having structure or design like that of architecture —*n. same as* ARCHITECTONICS

ar·chi·tec·ton·ics (-tän′iks) *n.pl.* [with *sing. v.*] **1.** the science of architecture **2.** structural design, as of a symphony

ar·chi·tec·ture (är′kə tek′chər) *n.* [Fr. < L. *architectura:* see ARCHITECT] **1.** the science, art, or profession of designing and constructing buildings, bridges, etc. **2.** a building, or buildings collectively **3.** a style of construction [modern *architecture*] **4.** design and construction [the *architecture* of a beehive] **5.** any framework, system, etc. —**ar′chi·tec′tur·al** *adj.* —**ar′chi·tec′tur·al·ly** *adv.*

ar·chi·trave (är′kə trāv′) *n.* [Fr. < It. < L. *archi-,* first + *trabs,* a beam] *Archit.* **1.** the lowest part of an entablature, a beam resting directly on the tops of the columns **2.** the molding around a doorway, window, etc. See illustration at ENTABLATURE

ar·chives (är′kīvz) *n.pl.* [Fr. < L. < Gr. *archeion*, town hall < *archē*, the beginning] **1.** a place where public records, documents, etc. are kept **2.** the public records, documents, etc. kept there —**ar·chi·val** (är′kī′v′l, är kī′v′l) *adj.*

ar·chi·vist (är′kə vist, är′kī′vist) *n.* a person having charge of archives

ar·chon (är′kän) *n.* [< Gr. < *archein*, to be first, rule] **1.** one of the nine chief magistrates of ancient Athens **2.** a ruler

arch·way (ärch′wā) *n.* a passage under an arch

-ar·chy (är kē, ər kē) [< Gr. < *archein*, to rule] *a suffix meaning* a ruling, or that which is ruled [*matriarchy, monarchy*]

arc lamp a lamp in which the light is produced by an arc between electrodes: also **arc light**

arc·tic (ärk′tik, är′-) *adj.* [< OFr. < L. < Gr. *arktikos*, lit., of the (constellation) of the Bear (Gr. *arktos*), northern] **1.** of, characteristic of, or near the North Pole or the region around it **2.** very cold —**the Arctic** the region around the North Pole

Arctic Circle [*also* **a- c-**] an imaginary circle parallel to the equator, 66°33′ north of it

Arctic Ocean ocean surrounding the North Pole, north of the Arctic Circle

☆**arc·tics** (är′tiks, ärk′-) *n.pl.* [< ARCTIC] high, warm, water-proof overshoes, usually with buckles

Arc·tu·rus (ärk toor′əs, -tyoor′-) [L. < Gr. *Arktouros* < *arktos*, a bear + *ouros*, a guard] a giant red star of the first magnitude, the brightest in the constellation Boötes

arc welding the welding of metal parts using the extreme heat of an electric arc

-ard (ərd) [OFr. < MHG. *hart*, bold] *a suffix denoting* one who carries an action too far or has too much of some quality [*sluggard, drunkard*]

Ar·den (är′d′n) wooded area in C England

ar·dent (är′d′nt) *adj.* [< L. prp. of *ardere*, to burn] **1.** warm or intense in feeling; passionate [*ardent* love] **2.** very enthusiastic or devoted; zealous [an *ardent* follower] **3.** glowing or burning —see SYN. at PASSIONATE —**ar′den·cy** (-d′n sē) *n.* —**ar′dent·ly** *adv.*

ar·dor (är′dər) *n.* [< OFr. < L. < *ardere*, to burn] **1.** very warm feeling; passion [an orator who spoke with *ardor*] **2.** enthusiasm; zeal [he lost his *ardor* for adventure] **3.** intense heat; fire —see SYN. at PASSION

ar·dour (är′dər) *n.* Brit. *sp.* of ARDOR

ar·du·ous (är′joo wəs) *adj.* [L. *arduus*, steep] **1.** difficult to do; laborious [*arduous* work] **2.** using much energy; strenuous [*arduous* efforts] **3.** hard to climb —see SYN. at HARD —**ar′du·ous·ly** *adv.* —**ar′du·ous·ness** *n.*

are[1] (är; *unstressed* ər) [OE. (Northumbrian) *aron*] *the plural & second person singular in the present tense of* BE

are[2] (er, är) *n.* [Fr. < L. *area*: see AREA] a unit of measure in the metric system, equal to 100 square meters (119.6 sq. yd.)

ar·e·a (er′ē ə) *n.* [L., vacant place, courtyard] **1.** orig., a level surface **2.** a part of the earth's surface; region [tropical *areas*] **3.** the measure, in square units, of a closed figure on a plane or of the surface of a solid **4.** a particular part of a house, city, etc. [dining *area*, slum *area*] **5.** a part of any surface **6.** range or extent, as of an operation —**ar′e·al** *adj.*

☆**area code** any of the groups of three numerals assigned as a telephone code to each of the more than 120 areas into which the U.S. and Canada are divided

☆**ar·e·a·way** (-wā′) *n.* **1.** a sunken yard leading into a cellar **2.** a passage between buildings

a·re·na (ə rē′nə) *n.* [L., sand, sandy place, arena] **1.** the central part of an ancient Roman amphitheater, for gladiatorial contests **2.** any place of struggle or conflict [a boxing *arena*; the political *arena*]

☆**arena theater** a theater having a central stage without a proscenium, surrounded by seats

aren't (ärnt) are not: also, occas., a substitute for a contraction of *am not* in questions: see also AIN'T

a·re·o·la (ə rē′ə lə) *n., pl.* **-lae** (-lē′) **-las** [L., dim. of *area*: see AREA] **1.** a small space, as between the veins of a leaf **2.** Anat. a small, surrounding area, as the dark ring around a nipple Also **ar·e·ole** (ar′ē ōl′) —**a·re·o·lar** (-lər) *adj.*

Ar·e·op·a·gus (ar′ē äp′ə gəs)

ARENA THEATER

[L. < Gr. < *Areios*, of Ares + *pagos*, hill] a rocky hill northwest of the Acropolis in Athens —*n.* the high court of justice that met there

Ar·es (er′ēz) *Gr. Myth.* the god of war: identified with the Roman god Mars

ar·ga·li (är′gə lē) *n., pl.* **-lis, -li:** see PLURAL, II, D, 1 [Mongol.] a wild sheep of Asia, with large, curved horns

ar·gent (är′jənt) *n.* [Fr. < L. *argentum*, silver] [Archaic or Poet.] silver —*adj.* [Poet.] of silver: also **ar·gen′tal** (-jen′t′l)

ar·gen·tif·er·ous (är′jən tif′ər əs) *adj.* [see prec. & -FEROUS] containing silver, as ore

Ar·gen·ti·na (är′jən tē′nə) country in southern S. America: 1,084,120 sq. mi.; pop. 23,983,000; cap. Buenos Aires —**Ar′gen·tine′** (-tēn′, -tīn′), **Ar′gen·tin′e·an** (-tin′ē ən) *adj., n.*

ar·gen·tine (är′jən tin, -tīn′, -tēn′) *adj.* of or like silver —*n.* silver or a silvery substance

ar·gil·la·ceous (är′jə lā′shəs) *adj.* [< L. *argilla*, clay < Gr. < *argos*, white] like or containing clay

Ar·go (är′gō) *Gr. Myth.* the ship on which Jason sailed to find the Golden Fleece

ar·gon (är′gän) *n.* [Gr., inert < *a-*, without + *ergon*, work] one of the chemical elements, an inert, odorless, colorless gas forming nearly one percent of the atmosphere: it is used in radio tubes, welding, etc.: symbol, Ar; at. wt., 39.948; at. no., 18

Ar·go·naut (är′gə nôt′) *n.* [< L. < Gr. < ARGO + *nautēs*, sailor] *Gr. Myth.* **1.** any of the men who sailed with Jason to search for the Golden Fleece ☆**2.** [*also* **a-**] any of the persons who went to California to search for gold in the gold rush of 1848–1849

Ar·gonne (är′gän; *Fr.* àr gôn′) wooded region in NE France, near the Belgian border

ar·go·sy (är′gə sē) *n., pl.* **-sies** [earlier *ragusy* < It. (*nave*) *Ragusea*, (vessel of) Ragusa, ancient Dalmatian port; sp. influenced by ARGO] [Poet.] **1.** a large ship **2.** a fleet of such ships

ar·got (är′gō, -gət) *n.* [Fr., orig. (in thieves' jargon), the company of beggars < *argoter*, to beg, prob. < *ergot*, claw] the specialized vocabulary and idioms of a particular group, as the secret slang of criminals —see SYN. at DIALECT

ar·gu·a·ble (är′gyoo wə b′l) *adj.* that can be argued about; not certain either way —**ar′gu·a·bly** *adv.*

ar·gue (är′gyoo) *vi.* **-gued, -gu·ing** [< OFr. < L. *argutare*, to prattle < *arguere*, to prove] **1.** to give reasons (*for* or *against* a proposal, etc.) **2.** to have a disagreement; quarrel —*vt.* **1.** to give reasons for and against; debate [to *argue* a point of law] **2.** to try to prove by giving reasons; contend [to *argue* that something is true] **3.** to give evidence of; indicate [his manners *argue* a good upbringing] **4.** to persuade (*into* or *out of* an opinion, etc.) by giving reasons —see SYN. at DISCUSS —**ar′gu·er** *n.*

ar·gu·fy (är′gyə fī′) *vt., vi.* **-fied′, -fy′ing** [< ARGU(E) + -FY] [Colloq. or Dial.] to argue, esp. merely for the sake of arguing

ar·gu·ment (är′gyə mənt) *n.* [Fr. < L. *argumentum*: see ARGUE] **1.** a reason or reasons offered for or against something **2.** the offering of such reasons; reasoning **3.** discussion in which there is disagreement; dispute; debate **4.** a short statement of subject matter; summary

SYN.—**argument** refers to a discussion in which there is disagreement and suggests the use of reasoning and the bringing forth of facts to support or disprove a point; **dispute** basically refers to a disagreement involving debate in which there is strong feeling or anger [an international boundary *dispute*]; **controversy** suggests a disagreement that lasts a long time and has to do with a matter of some importance [the continuing *controversy* over some of Freud's theories]

ar·gu·men·ta·tion (är′gyə men tā′shən) *n.* **1.** the process of arriving at reasons and conclusions; arguing **2.** debate; discussion

ar·gu·men·ta·tive (-men′tə tiv) *adj.* **1.** containing argument; controversial **2.** apt to argue Also **ar′gu·men′tive** —**ar′gu·men′ta·tive·ly** *adv.* —**ar′gu·men′ta·tive·ness** *n.*

Ar·gus (är′gəs) [L. < Gr. < *argos*, bright] *Gr. Myth.* a giant with a hundred eyes, killed by Hermes —*n.* an alert watchman

Ar·gus-eyed (-īd′) *adj.* keenly observant; vigilant

ar·gyle (är′gīl) *adj.* [orig. a clan tartan of *Argyll*, county of Scotland] knitted or woven in a pattern of diamond-shaped figures of different colors —*n.* [*pl.*] argyle socks

a·ri·a (är′ē ə, er′-) *n.* [It. < L. *aer*, AIR] an air or melody in an opera, cantata, or oratorio, esp. for solo voice with instrumental accompaniment

-a·ri·a (er′ē ə, ā′rē ə) [ModL. < L. *-arius*] *Biol.* a plural suffix used in names of taxonomic groups

Ar·i·ad·ne (ar/ē ad/nē) *Gr. Myth.* King Minos' daughter, who gave Theseus the thread by which he found his way out of the Labyrinth

Ar·i·an[1] (er/ē ən, ar/-) *n., adj. same as* ARYAN

Ar·i·an[2] (er/ē ən, ar/-) *adj.* of Arius or Arianism —*n.* a believer in Arianism

-ar·i·an (er/ē ən, ar/-) [L. *-arius* + *-anus*] *a suffix denoting:* **1.** age [*octogenarian*] **2.** sect [*Unitarian*] **3.** social belief [*utilitarian*] **4.** occupation [*antiquarian*]

Ar·i·an·ism (er/ē ə niz/m, ar/-) *n.* the doctrines of Arius, who taught that Jesus was not of the same substance as God

ar·id (ar/id, er/-) *adj.* [< L. < *arere*, to be dry: for IE. base see ASH[1]] **1.** dry and barren [a desert is an *arid* region] **2.** not interesting; dull —**a·rid·i·ty** (ə rid/ə tē), **ar/id·ness** *n.* —**ar/id·ly** *adv.*

Ar·i·el (er/ē əl, ar/-) in Shakespeare's *The Tempest*, an airy spirit who is Prospero's servant

Ar·i·es (er/ēz, ar/-; -i ēz/) [L., the Ram] **1.** a N constellation **2.** the first sign of the zodiac: see ZODIAC

a·right (ə rīt/) *adv.* in a right way; correctly

ar·il (ar/il, er/-) *n.* [ModL. *arillus* < ML., dried grape] an additional covering that forms on certain seeds after fertilization — **ar/il·late** (-ə lāt/) *adj.*

a·ri·o·so (är/ē ō/sō) *adj., adv.* [It. < *aria*, ARIA] like an aria —*n.* an arioso composition

a·rise (ə rīz/) *vi.* **a·rose** (-rōz/), **a·ris·en** (-riz/'n), **a·ris·ing** [OE. < *a-*, out + *risan*, to rise] **1.** to get up, as from sleeping or sitting; rise **2.** to move upward; ascend [swarms of flies *arose* from the field] **3.** to come into being; originate [no questions have *arisen* as yet] **4.** to result or spring (*from* something) [hate *arises* from fear] —see SYN. at RISE

Ar·is·ti·des (ar/ə stī/dēz) 530?–468? B.C.; Athenian general & statesman: called *the Just*

ar·is·toc·ra·cy (ar/ə stäk/rə sē) *n., pl.* **-cies** [< L. < Gr. < *aristos*, best + *kratein*, to rule] **1.** orig., government by the best citizens **2.** government by a small upper class, whose wealth and social position are usually inherited **3.** a country with such government **4.** a privileged ruling class; nobility **5.** those considered the best in some way [an *aristocracy* of scientists]

a·ris·to·crat (ə ris/tə krat/, ar/is-) *n.* **1.** a member of the aristocracy; nobleman **2.** a person with the manners, beliefs, etc. of the upper class **3.** one who believes in aristocracy as a form of government

a·ris·to·crat·ic (ə ris/tə krat/ik, ar/is-) *adj.* **1.** of or favoring aristocracy as a form of government **2.** of an aristocracy or upper class **3.** like an aristocrat: used with either a favorable meaning (proud, noble, etc.) or an unfavorable one (snobbish, haughty, etc.) —**a·ris/to·crat/i·cal·ly** *adv.*

Ar·is·toph·a·nes (ar/ə stäf/ə nēz/) 448?–380? B.C.; Gr. writer of satirical comedies

Ar·is·to·te·li·an (ar/is tə tēl/yən, -tē/lē ən) *adj.* of Aristotle or his philosophy —*n.* **1.** a follower of Aristotle **2.** a person who is empirical or practical in his thinking —**Ar/is·to·te/li·an·ism** *n.*

Ar·is·tot·le (ar/ə stät/'l) 384–322 B.C.; Gr. philosopher, pupil of Plato

a·rith·me·tic (ə rith/mə tik; *for adj.* ar/ith met/ik) *n.* [OFr. < L. < Gr. < *arithmein*, to count < *arithmos*, number] **1.** the science of computing by positive, real numbers, specif. by adding, subtracting, multiplying, and dividing **2.** skill in this science —*adj.* of or using arithmetic: also **ar/ith·met/i·cal** — **ar/ith·met/i·cal·ly** *adv.*

a·rith·me·ti·cian (ar/ith mə tish/ən, ə rith/mə-) *n.* a person skilled in arithmetic

ar·ith·met·ic mean (ar/ith met/ik) the average obtained by dividing a sum by the number of quantities that have been added to make up the sum

arithmetic progression a sequence of terms each of which, after the first, is derived by adding the same quantity to the term before it (Ex.: 5, 9, 13, 17)

A·ri·us (ə rī/əs, er/ē əs) 256?–336 A.D.; Christian theologian of Alexandria: see ARIANISM

Ar·i·zo·na (ar/ə zō/nə) [AmSp. < AmInd. *Arizonac*, "little springs"] State of the SW U.S., on the border with Mexico: 113,909 sq. mi.; pop. 1,772,000; cap. Phoenix: abbrev. **Ariz., AZ** —**Ar/i·zo/nan, Ar/i·zo/ni·an** (-nē ən) *adj., n.*

ark (ärk) *n.* [< OE. *earc* < L. *arca* < *arcere*, to enclose] **1.** *Bible* the huge boat in which Noah, his family, and two of every kind of creature survived the Flood: Gen. 6–9 ☆**2.** formerly, a large, flat-bottomed river boat **3.** *a)* same as ARK OF THE COVENANT *b)* the place in a synagogue or temple where the scrolls of the Torah are kept

ARK (in a synagogue)

Ar·kan·sas (är/k'n sô/; *for 2, also* är kan/zəs) [< Fr. < Siouan tribal name] **1.** State of the SC U.S.: 53,104 sq. mi.; pop. 1,923,000; cap. Little Rock: abbrev. **Ark., AR 2.** river flowing from Colorado southeast into the Mississippi: 1,450 mi. —**Ar·kan/san** (-kan/z'n) *adj., n.*

ark of the covenant *Bible* the chest in which the stone tablets inscribed with the Ten Commandments were kept: Ex. 25:10

Ark·wright (ärk/rīt/), Sir **Richard** 1732–92; Eng. inventor of a cotton-spinning machine

Ar·ling·ton (är/liŋ tən) [orig. after a place name in England] **1.** urban county in Va., near Washington, D.C.: pop. 174,000: site of a national cemetery (**Arlington National Cemetery**) **2.** city in NE Tex.: suburb of Fort Worth: pop. 91,000

arm[1] (ärm) *n.* [OE. *earm*: for IE. base see ART[1]] **1.** the part of the human body between the shoulder and the hand; upper limb **2.** anything like this in form or use [an *arm* of the sea]; esp., *a)* the forelimb of a vertebrate animal *b)* any limb of an octopus, starfish, etc. *c)* a branch of a tree *d)* a sleeve *e)* a support for the arm, as on a chair **3.** power to seize, control, etc. [the *arm* of the law] ☆**4.** *Sports* ability to pitch or throw a ball —**arm in arm** with arms joined, as two people walking together —**at arm's length** at a distance; aloof —**with open arms** in a warm and friendly way —**arm/less** *adj.* —**arm/like** *adj.*

arm[2] (ärm) *n.* [< OFr. *armes*, pl. < L. *arma*, implements, weapons] **1.** any weapon: *usually used in pl.*: see also SMALL ARMS **2.** [*pl.*] warfare; fighting **3.** [*pl.*] insignia used in heraldry: see COAT OF ARMS **4.** any combatant branch of the military forces, as the infantry or artillery —*vt.* **1.** to provide with weapons, tools, etc. **2.** to provide with something that protects **3.** to prepare for or against attack [reporters *armed* with questions] **4.** to equip with needed parts [to *arm* a missile with a warhead] —*vi.* to equip oneself with weapons, etc., esp. for war —**bear arms** to serve in the armed forces —**take up arms 1.** to go to war **2.** to enter a dispute —**to arms!** get ready to fight! —**under arms** equipped with weapons —**up in arms** angry and prepared to fight

ar·ma·da (är mä/də, -mā/-) *n.* [Sp. < L. *armata*, fem. pp. of *armare*, to arm < *arma*: see ARM[2]] **1.** *a)* a fleet of warships *b)* [A-] such a fleet sent against England by Spain in 1588 but destroyed: also **Spanish Armada 2.** a fleet of military aircraft

ar·ma·dil·lo (är/mə dil/ō) *n., pl.* **-los** [Sp., dim. of *armado*: see prec.] any of a family of burrowing mammals of Texas and Central and South America, that have an armorlike covering of bony plates and are active mostly at night

Ar·ma·ged·don (är/mə ged/'n) *Bible* the place described as the scene of the last, deciding battle between good and evil: Rev. 16:16

ar·ma·ment (är/mə mənt) *n.* [< L. < *armare*: see ARMADA] **1.** [*often pl.*] all the military forces and equipment of a nation **2.** a combat force **3.** all the military equipment of a warship, fortification, etc. **4.** an arming or being armed for war **5.** anything serving to protect or defend

ARMADILLO
(head & body to 40 in. long; tail to 20 in. long)

ar·ma·ture (är/mə chər) *n.* [< L. *armatura*, arms, equipment < pp. of *armare*: see ARMADA] **1.** any protective covering; armor **2.** any part of an animal useful for offense or defense **3.** a soft iron bar placed across the poles of a magnet **4.** *a)* the laminated iron core wound around with wire, usually a revolving part, in a generator or motor *b)* the vibrating part in an electric relay, bell, etc. **5.** *Sculpture* a framework for supporting the clay, etc. in modeling

arm·chair (ärm′cher′) *n.* a chair with supports at the sides for one's arms or elbows —*adj.* offering opinions or advice but not actually taking part [an *armchair* general]

armed (ärmd) *adj.* **1.** provided with arms (weapons), armor, etc. **2.** having arms (limbs) of a specified kind [long-*armed*]

armed forces all the military, naval, and air forces of a country or group of countries

Ar·me·ni·a (är mē′nē ə, -mēn′yə) **1.** former kingdom of SW Asia, south of the Caucasus Mts. **2.** republic of the U.S.S.R., including most of this region: 11,500 sq. mi.; pop. 2,300,000; cap. Yerevan: in full, **Armenian Soviet Socialist Republic** — **Ar·me′ni·an** *adj., n.*

arm·ful (ärm′fool) *n., pl.* **-fuls** as much as the arms or one arm can hold

arm·hole (-hōl′) *n.* an opening for the arm in a garment

Ar·min·i·us (är min′ē əs), **Ja·co·bus** (jə kō′bəs) 1560–1609; Dutch theologian —**Ar·min′i·an** *adj., n.*

ar·mi·stice (är′mə stis) *n.* [Fr. < L. *arma*, arms + *sistere*, to cause to stand] a temporary stopping of warfare by agreement on both sides; truce

Armistice Day November 11, the anniversary of the armistice of World War I in 1918: see VETERANS DAY

arm·let (ärm′lit) *n.* **1.** a band worn for ornament around the upper arm **2.** a small inlet of the sea

arm·lock (-läk′) *n. Wrestling* a hold in which one contestant's arm is locked by the other's arm

ar·mor (är′mər) *n.* [< OFr. < L. *armatura*: see ARMATURE] **1.** covering worn to protect the body against weapons **2.** any defensive or protective covering, as the shell of a turtle or the metal plating on warships **3.** armored forces, as tanks —*vt., vi.* to put armor on

ar·mor·bear·er (-ber′ər) *n.* a person who carried the armor or weapons of a warrior

ar·mored (är′mərd) *adj.* **1.** covered with armor [an *armored* car] **2.** equipped with tanks and other armored vehicles

ar·mor·er (är′mər ər) *n.* **1.** formerly, one who made or repaired armor **2.** a maker of firearms **3.** *Mil.* an enlisted man in charge of small arms

ar·mo·ri·al (är môr′ē əl) *adj.* of coats of arms; heraldic

HELMET
BEAVER
GORGET
PAULDRON
BREASTPLATE
TASSE
GAUNTLET
CUISSE
KNEEPIECE
GREAVE
SOLLERET

ARMOR

armor plate a protective covering of steel plates, as on a tank —**ar′mor-plat′ed** *adj.*

ar·mor·y (är′mər ē) *n., pl.* **-mor·ies** [< OFr. < *arme*: see ARM²] **1.** a storehouse for weapons; arsenal ☆**2.** a building housing the drill hall and offices of a National Guard unit ☆**3.** a place where firearms are made

ar·mour (är′mər) *n., vi., vt.* Brit. sp. of ARMOR

arm·pit (ärm′pit′) *n.* the hollow under the arm where it joins the shoulder; axilla

arm·rest (-rest′) *n.* a support for one's arm

ar·my (är′mē) *n., pl.* **-mies** [< OFr. < L. *armata*: see ARMADA] **1.** a large, organized body of soldiers for waging war, esp. on land **2.** a military unit of two or more corps **3.** [often **A-**] a large organization of persons for a specific cause [the Salvation *Army*] **4.** any large number of persons, animals, etc. [the *army* of the unemployed]

army ant any of certain ants that travel in large groups and devour insects and animals

☆**army worm** any of the larvae of certain moths that travel in large groups, ruining crops

Arn·hem (ärn′hem) city on the Rhine, in E Netherlands: pop. 135,000

ar·ni·ca (är′ni kə) *n.* [ModL.] **1.** any of a number of plants bearing yellow flowers **2.** a preparation made from certain of these plants, formerly used for treating sprains, bruises, etc.

Ar·nold (är′nəld) [< G. < Gmc. bases *aran*, eagle + *wald*, power] **1.** a masculine name **2. Benedict,** 1741–1801; Am. Revolutionary general who became a traitor **3. Matthew,** 1822–88; Eng. poet, essayist, & critic

a·roint (ə roint′) *vt.* [< ?] [Obs.] begone!: used in the imperative, usually followed by *thee*

a·ro·ma (ə rō′mə) *n.* [LL. < Gr. *arōma*, sweet spice] **1.** a pleasant, often spicy odor; fragrance, as of a plant, cooking, etc.

2. a characteristic quality or atmosphere [the *aroma* of a large city]

ar·o·mat·ic (ar′ə mat′ik) *adj.* **1.** of or having an aroma **2.** *Chem.* containing one or more benzene rings in the molecule —*n.* an aromatic plant, substance, or chemical —**ar′o·mat′i·cal·ly** *adv.*

a·rose (ə rōz′) *pt. of* ARISE

a·round (ə round′) *adv.* [ME. < *a-*, on + *round*] **1.** in a circle; along a circular course [the wheel turned *around*] **2.** in or through a course or circuit, as from one place to another **3.** in every direction [there are mountains all *around*] **4.** in circumference [the ball measures six inches *around*] **5.** in or to the opposite direction, belief, etc. [he turned *around*] **6.** in various places [they went in and looked *around*] **7.** in sequence [his turn came *around*] **8.** throughout [the year *around*] **9.** for everyone [not enough to go *around*] **10.** [Colloq.] nearby [stay *around*] ☆**11.** [Colloq.] to a (specified) place [come *around* to see us] —*prep.* **1.** so as to encircle, surround, or envelop [trees grew *around* the lake] **2.** on the border of [there is a fence *around* the property] **3.** on all sides of [the suburbs around the city] **4.** in various places in or on [books scattered *around* the room] **5.** so as to rotate about (a center) ☆**6.** close to; about [*around* 1890] —*adj.* [*used only in the predicate*] **1.** on the move; about [he's up and *around* now] **2.** existing [when dinosaurs were *around*] See ROUND —☆**have been around** [Colloq.] to have had wide experience; be sophisticated See also phrases under BRING, COME, GET, etc.

a·rouse (ə rouz′) *vt.* **a·roused′**, **a·rous′ing** [A-² (sense 1) + ROUSE] **1.** to awaken, as from sleep **2.** to stir, as to action **3.** to bring forth or work up (some action or feeling); excite —*vi.* to become aroused —see SYN. at INCITE and at STIR¹ —**a·rous′al** *n.*

ar·peg·gio (är pej′ō, -pej′ē ō) *n., pl.* **-gios** [It. < *arpeggiare*, to play on a harp < *arpa*, a harp] **1.** the playing of the notes of a chord quickly one after another instead of all together **2.** a chord so played

ar·que·bus (är′kwə bəs) *n. same as* HARQUEBUS

arr. 1. arranged **2.** arrival

ar·rack (ar′ək) *n.* [< Fr. < Ar. *'araq*, sweat, liquor] in the Orient, strong alcoholic drink, esp. that made from rice, molasses, or coconut milk

ar·raign (ə rān′) *vt.* [< OFr. < ML. < L. *ad*, to + *ratio*, reason] to bring before a law court to hear and answer charges —**ar·raign′er** *n.* —**ar·raign′ment** *n.*

ar·range (ə rānj′) *vt.* **-ranged′**, **-rang′ing** [< OFr. < *a-*, to + *renc*, rank: see RANGE] **1.** to put in the correct or suitable order **2.** to prepare or plan [to *arrange* a concert appearance] **3.** to settle or adjust (matters) **4.** *Music* to adapt (a composition) to other instruments or voices than those for which it was written, or to the style of a certain band or orchestra —*vi.* **1.** to come to an agreement (*with* a person, *about* a thing) **2.** to make plans [*arrange* to be here later] **3.** *Music* to write arrangements —**ar·range′a·ble** *adj.* —**ar·rang′er** *n.*

ar·range·ment (-mənt) *n.* **1.** an arranging or being arranged **2.** the way in which something is arranged [a new *arrangement* of furniture in the room] **3.** something made by arranging parts in a particular way **4.** [*usually pl.*] a plan or preparation [*arrangements* for the party] **5.** a settlement or adjustment, as of a dispute **6.** *Music a)* an adaptation of a composition for other instruments, voices, etc. *b)* the composition as thus adapted

ar·rant (ar′ənt) *adj.* [var. of ERRANT] that is plainly such; out-and-out [an *arrant* fool] —**ar′rant·ly** *adv.*

ar·ras (ar′əs) *n.* [after *Arras*, city in France, where it was made] **1.** an elaborate kind of tapestry **2.** a wall hanging, esp. of tapestry

ar·ray (ə rā′) *vt.* [< OFr. < ML. *arredare*, to put in order < *ad-*, to + Gmc. base *raid-*, order] **1.** to put in the proper order; marshal (troops, etc.) **2.** to dress in fine clothes —*n.* **1.** an orderly grouping, esp. of troops **2.** a military force so grouped **3.** an impressive display of persons or things [an *array* of fine china] **4.** fine clothes —**ar·ray′al** *n.* —**ar·ray′er** *n.*

ar·rear·age (ə rir′ij) *n.* arrears or the state of being in arrears

ar·rears (ə rirz′) *n.pl.* [< OFr. *ariere*, backward < VL. < L. *ad*, to + *retro*, behind] **1.** overdue debts **2.** unfinished work, etc. —**in arrears** (or **arrear**) behind in paying a debt, in one's work, etc.

ar·rest (ə rest′) *vt.* [< OFr. < L. *ad-*, to + *restare*, to stop] **1.** to stop or check [a coat of paint will *arrest* the rust] **2.** to seize or take into custody by authority of the law **3.** to catch and keep (one's attention, etc.) —*n.* an arresting or being arrested —**under arrest** in legal custody, as of the police —**ar·rest′·er, ar·res′tor** *n.*

ar·rest·ing (-iŋ) *adj.* attracting attention; interesting; striking —**ar·rest′ing·ly** *adv.*

Ar·rhe·ni·us (ä rā′nē oos), **Svan·te Au·gust** (svän′te ou′goost) 1859–1927; Swed. chemist

ar·ris (ar′əs) *n.* [< OFr. < L. *arista*, awn of grain] the edge made by two surfaces coming together at an angle, as in a molding

ar·riv·al (ə rī′v'l) *n.* **1.** the act of arriving **2.** a person or thing that arrives or has arrived

ar·rive (ə rīv′) *vi.* **-rived′, -riv′ing** [< OFr. < L. *ad-*, to + *ripa*, shore] **1.** to reach one's destination; come to a place **2.** to come [the time has *arrived*] **3.** to attain fame, etc. [he has *arrived* as a musician] —**arrive at 1.** to reach by traveling **2.** to reach by thinking, etc. [to *arrive* at a decision]

‡**ar·ri·ve·der·ci** (ä rē′ve der′chē) *interj.* [It.] until we meet again; goodbye

‡**ar·ri·viste** (á rē vēst′) *n.* [Fr. < *arriver* (see ARRIVE) + *-iste*, -IST] *same as* PARVENU

ar·ro·gance (ar′ə gəns) *n.* [see ARROGANT] a feeling of too great pride or self-importance, that makes one act haughty

ar·ro·gant (-gənt) *adj.* [OFr. < L. prp. of *arrogare*, ARROGATE] full of or due to arrogance; overbearing; haughty —see SYN. at PROUD —**ar′ro·gant·ly** *adv.*

ar·ro·gate (-gāt′) *vt.* **-gat′ed, -gat′ing** [< L. pp. of *arrogare* < *ad-*, for + *rogare*, to ask] **1.** to claim or seize without right [they had *arrogated* to themselves all political power] **2.** to ascribe or attribute without reason [she *arrogated* to herself a certain importance] —**ar′ro·ga′tion** *n.*

‡**ar·ron·disse·ment** (á rōn dēs män′) *n., pl.* **-ments′** (-män′) [Fr. < *arrondir*, to make round] in France, **1.** the largest subdivision of a department **2.** a municipal subdivision, as of Paris

ar·row (ar′ō) *n.* [OE. *earh, arwe*] **1.** a slender shaft, usually pointed at one end and feathered at the other, for shooting from a bow **2.** anything like an arrow in form, etc. **3.** a sign (←) used to indicate direction —**ar′row·y** *adj.*

ar·row·head (-hed′) *n.* **1.** the pointed tip of an arrow **2.** anything shaped like an arrowhead, as an indicating mark **3.** a marsh plant with arrow-shaped leaves and small, white flowers

ar·row·root (-rōōt′, -root′) *n.* [from its use as an antidote for poisoned arrows] **1.** a tropical American plant with starchy roots **2.** the edible starch made from its roots

☆**ar·roy·o** (ə roi′ō) *n., pl.* **-os** [Sp. < L. *arrugia*, mine shaft] [Southwest] **1.** a dry gully **2.** a rivulet or stream

ar·se·nal (är′s'n əl, -snəl) *n.* [It. *arsenale*, a dock < Ar. *dār* (eṣ) ṣināʼ, wharf, workshop] **1.** a place for making or storing weapons and other munitions **2.** a store or collection [an *arsenal* of facts used in a debate]

ar·se·nate (är′s'n āt′, -it) *n.* [ARSEN(IC) + -ATE²] a salt or ester of arsenic acid

ar·se·nic (är′s'n ik, -snik; *for adj.* är sen′ik) *n.* [OFr. < L. < Gr. *arsenikon*, a yellow sulfide of arsenic; ult. < Per. *zar*, gold] **1.** a silvery-white, brittle, very poisonous chemical element, compounds of which are used in making insecticides, medicines, etc.: symbol, As; at. wt., 74.9216; at. no., 33 **2.** loosely, arsenic trioxide, a poisonous, tasteless, white powder, used to exterminate insects and rodents —*adj.* of or containing arsenic, esp. with a valence of five

arsenic acid a white, poisonous, crystalline compound, H_3AsO_4, used in insecticides, etc.

ar·sen·i·cal (är sen′ə k'l) *adj.* of or containing arsenic —*n.* an arsenical drug, insecticide, etc.

ar·se·ni·ous (är sē′nē əs) *adj.* of or containing arsenic, esp. with a valence of three: also **ar·se·nous** (är′s'n əs)

‡**ars gra·ti·a ar·tis** (ärz′ grā′shē ə är′tis; grä′tē ə) [L.] art for art's sake

ar·son (är′s'n) *n.* [OFr. < L. pp. of *ardere*, to burn] the crime of purposely setting fire to a building or property —**ar′son·ist** *n.*

art¹ (ärt) *n.* [< OFr. < L. *ars* (gen. *artis*), art < IE. base *ar-*, to join, fit together] **1.** human ability to make or do things; creativity **2.** skill [to use *art* in one's cooking] **3.** any specific skill or its application [the *art* of making friends] **4.** any craft or profession, or its principles [the cobbler's *art*] **5.** a making or doing of things that have form and beauty; creative work: see

also FINE ART **6.** any branch of creative work, esp. painting, drawing, sculpture, etc. **7.** products of creative work; paintings, statues, etc. **8.** a branch of learning; specif., [pl.] the liberal arts as distinguished from the sciences **9.** trick; wile: *usually used in pl.* —*adj.* of or for works of art or artists [an *art* gallery]

art² (ärt) *archaic 2d person singular, present indicative,* of BE: *used with* thou

-art (ərt) *same as* -ARD

art. 1. article **2.** artificial

ar·te·fact (är′tə fakt′) *n. var. sp.* of ARTIFACT

Ar·te·mis (är′tə mis) *Gr. Myth.* the goddess of the moon and hunting, Apollo's twin sister: identified with the Roman goddess Diana

ar·te·ri·al (är tir′ē əl) *adj.* **1.** of or like an artery or arteries **2.** designating or of the bright-red, oxygenated blood in the arteries **3.** of or being a main road with many branches —**ar·te′ri·al·ly** *adv.*

ar·te·ri·al·ize (-īz′) *vt.* **-ized′, -iz′ing** to change (venous blood) into arterial blood by oxygenation —**ar·te′ri·al·i·za′tion** *n.*

ar·te·ri·ole (är tir′ē ōl′) *n.* a small artery

ar·te·ri·o·scle·ro·sis (är tir′ē ō sklə rō′sis) *n.* [see ARTERY & SCLEROSIS] a thickening and hardening of the walls of the arteries, as in old age —**ar·te′ri·o·scle·rot′ic** (-rät′ik) *adj.*

ar·ter·y (är′tər ē) *n., pl.* **-ter·ies** [< L. < Gr.; prob. < *aeirein*, to raise] **1.** any of the system of tubes carrying blood from the heart to all parts of the body: cf. VEIN **2.** a main road or channel [the traffic *arteries* that lead from downtown]

ar·te·sian well (är tē′zhən) [Fr. *artésien*, lit., of Artois, former Fr. province] a well in which ground water is forced up by the pressure of the water itself which has drained down from higher ground above the well

art·ful (ärt′fəl) *adj.* **1.** skillful or clever, esp. in achieving a purpose [*artful* reasoning] **2.** sly or cunning [an *artful* swindle] **3.** using or showing considerable art or skill **4.** artificial; imitative —**art′ful·ly** *adv.* —**art′ful·ness** *n.*

ARTESIAN WELL

ar·thral·gia (är thral′jə) *n.* [see ARTHRITIS & -ALGIA] neuralgic pain in a joint or joints

ar·thri·tis (är thrīt′əs) *n.* [Gr. < *arthron*, a joint + -ITIS] inflammation of a joint or joints: see also RHEUMATOID ARTHRITIS —**ar·thrit′ic** (-thrit′ik) *adj.* —**ar·thrit′i·cal·ly** *adv.*

ar·thro·pod (är′thrə päd′) *n.* [< Gr. *arthron*, a joint + -POD] any member of a large group of invertebrate animals with jointed legs and a segmented body, as insects, crustaceans, arachnids, etc. —**ar·throp·o·dal** (är thräp′ə d'l), **ar·throp′o·dous** (-dəs) *adj.*

Ar·thur (är′thər) [ML. *Arthurus*] **1.** a masculine name: dim. *Art* **2.** a legendary king of Britain in the 6th century, who led the knights of the Round Table **3. Chester Alan,** 1830–86; 21st president of the U.S. (1881–85)

Ar·thu·ri·an (är thoor′ē ən) *adj.* of King Arthur and his knights

ar·ti·choke (är′tə chōk′) *n.* [< It. < Sp. < Ar. *al-ḫaršūf*] **1.** a thistlelike plant **2.** its flower head, cooked as a vegetable **3.** *short for* JERUSALEM ARTICHOKE

ar·ti·cle (är′ti k'l) *n.* [OFr. < L. *articulus*, dim. of *artus*, a joint: for IE. base see ART¹] **1.** any of the sections of a written document, as of a treaty **2.** a complete piece of writing that is part of a newspaper, magazine, or book **3.** a separate item [an *article* of luggage] **4.** a thing for sale; commodity **5.** *Gram.* any one of the words *a, an,* or *the* (and their equivalents in other languages), used as adjectives —*vt.* **-cled, -cling** to bind by the articles of an agreement or contract [an *articled* apprentice]

ARTICHOKE
(head in cross section)

Articles of Confederation the first

constitution of the thirteen original States, in effect from 1781 to 1789

ar·tic·u·lar (är tik′yə lər) *adj.* [< L. < *articulus:* see prec.] of a joint or joints [an *articular* inflammation]

ar·tic·u·late (är tik′yə lit; *for v.* -lāt′) *adj.* [< L. pp. of *articulare,* to disjoint < *articulus:* see ARTICLE] **1.** having parts [*articulate* limbs]: usually **ar·tic′u·lat·ed 2.** made up of distinct syllables or words that have meaning, as human speech **3.** able to speak **4.** expressing oneself easily and clearly [an *articulate* spokesman] **5.** clearly presented [an *articulate* argument] —*vt.* **-lat′ed, -lat′ing 1.** to put together by joints **2.** to fit together; correlate [to *articulate* a science program for all grades] **3.** to pronounce carefully; enunciate **4.** to express clearly **5.** *Phonet.* to produce (a speech sound) by moving an articulator —*vi.* **1.** to speak distinctly **2.** to be jointed [the arm *articulates* with the body at the shoulder] —**ar·tic′u·late·ly** *adv.* —**ar·tic′u·late·ness** *n.* —**ar·tic′u·la·tive** *adj.*

ar·tic·u·la·tion (är tik′yə lā′shən) *n.* **1.** a jointing or being jointed **2.** the way in which parts are joined together **3.** way of talking or pronouncing **4.** a spoken sound **5.** a joint, as between bones **6.** *Bot.* a node, or a space between two nodes

ar·tic·u·la·tor (är tik′yə lāt′ər) *n.* **1.** a person or thing that articulates **2.** *Phonet.* any organ in the mouth or throat used in making speech sounds —**ar·tic′u·la·to·ry** (-lə tôr′ē) *adj.*

ar·ti·fact (är′tə fakt′) *n.* [< L. *ars* (gen. *artis*), ART[1] + *factum,* thing made (see FACT)] any object made by human work; esp., a primitive tool, etc.

ar·ti·fice (är′tə fis) *n.* [Fr. < L. < *ars,* ART[1] + *facere,* to make] **1.** skill or ingenuity **2.** trickery or craft **3.** a sly or artful trick —see SYN. at TRICK

ar·tif·i·cer (är tif′ə sər) *n.* [see prec. & -ER] **1.** a skilled craftsman **2.** an inventor **3.** a military mechanic

ar·ti·fi·cial (är′tə fish′əl) *adj.* [< OFr. < L.: see ARTIFICE] **1.** made by human work or art; not natural [*artificial* ice] **2.** made in imitation of something natural; simulated [*artificial* teeth] **3.** unnatural in an affected way [an *artificial* smile] —**ar′ti·fi·ci·al′i·ty** (-fish′ē al′ə tē) *n., pl.* **-ties** —**ar′ti·fi′cial·ly** *adv.* —**ar′ti·fi′cial·ness** *n.*

artificial insemination the impregnation of a female by introducing semen taken from a male without sexual intercourse

artificial respiration the act of trying to start or keep a person breathing by artificial means, as by forcing breath into the mouth

ar·til·ler·y (är til′ər ē) *n.* [< OFr. < Pr. *artilla,* fortifications; ult. < L. *ars,* ART[1]] **1.** heavy mounted guns, as cannon or missile launchers **2.** the science of guns; gunnery —**the artillery** the military branch specializing in the use of artillery —**ar·til′·ler·ist, ar·til′ler·y·man** (-mən) *n., pl.* **-men**

ar·ti·san (är′tə z'n, -s'n) *n.* [Fr. < It.; ult. < L. *ars,* ART[1]] a skilled workman; craftsman

art·ist (är′tist) *n.* [ML. *artista,* craftsman < L. *ars,* ART[1]] **1.** a person who is skilled in any of the fine arts, esp. in painting, sculpture, etc. **2.** a person who does anything very well, with a feeling for form, etc. **3.** *same as* ARTISTE

ar·tiste (är tēst′) *n.* [Fr.] **1.** a professional in any of the performing arts **2.** a person very skilled in his work: often used in a joking way

ar·tis·tic (är tis′tik) *adj.* **1.** of art or artists **2.** done skillfully and tastefully **3.** having a sensitive appreciation of art and beauty —**ar·tis′ti·cal·ly** *adv.*

art·ist·ry (är′tis trē) *n.* artistic work or skill

art·less (ärt′lis) *adj.* **1.** lacking skill or art **2.** uncultured; ignorant **3.** simple; natural [an *artless* style of singing] **4.** without guile or deceit [*artless* affection] —see SYN. at NAIVE —**art′less·ly** *adv.* —**art′less·ness** *n.*

‡art nou·veau (är′ noo vō′) [Fr., lit., new art] an art movement of the late 19th and early 20th cent., emphasizing curved, flowing lines and designs of plants

art·y (är′tē) *adj.* **art′i·er, art′i·est** [Colloq.] pretending or striving to be artistic —**art′i·ness** *n.*

ar·um (er′əm, ar′-) *n.* [L. < Gr. *aron,* the wake-robin] any of a family of plants bearing small flowers on a fleshy spike enclosed by a hoodlike leaf, as the jack-in-the-pulpit

A.R.V. American (Standard) Revised Version (of the Bible), printed in 1901

-ar·y (er′ē; *chiefly Brit.* ər i) [L. *-arius, -aria, -arium*] **1.** a *suffix meaning: a)* related to; connected with [*auxiliary*] *b)*

ART NOUVEAU

a person or thing connected with [*missionary*] *c)* a place for [*granary*] **2.** [L. *-aris*] *a suffix meaning* like; of the same kind [*military*]

Ar·y·an (er′ē ən, ar′-) *adj.* [< Sans. *ārya,* noble, lord (used as a tribal name)] **1.** *earlier term for* INDO-EUROPEAN **2.** *same as* INDO-IRANIAN **3.** of the Aryans —*n.* **1.** formerly, the hypothetical language from which all Indo-European languages are supposed to be descended **2.** a person belonging to, or supposed to be a descendant of, the prehistoric peoples who spoke this language **3.** loosely, as in Nazi usage, a non-Jewish Caucasoid, a Nordic, etc.

as[1] (az; *unstressed* əz) *adv.* [weakened form of ALSO < OE. *ealswa,* quite so, just as: see ALSO] **1.** to the same amount or degree; equally [he's just *as* happy at home] **2.** for instance; thus [a card game, *as* bridge] —*conj.* **1.** to the same amount or degree that [it flew straight *as* an arrow] **2.** in the same manner that [do *as* he does] **3.** at the same time that; while [she wept *as* she spoke] **4.** because [*as* you object, we won't go] **5.** that the result is or was [a question so obvious *as* to need no reply] **6.** though [full *as* he was, he kept eating] **7.** [Colloq.] that [I don't know *as* I should] —*pron.* **1.** a fact that [he is tired, *as* anyone can see] **2.** that (preceded by *such* or *the same*) [the same color *as* yours (is)] —*prep.* **1.** in the role, function, capacity, or sense of [he poses *as* a friend] **2.** like [the same *as* mine] —**as ... as** a construction used to indicate the equality or sameness of two things [*as* large *as*, *as* many *as*, etc.] —**as for** with reference to; concerning —**as if** (or **though**) **1.** as it (or one) would if **2.** that [it seems *as if* she's never home] —☆**as is** [Colloq.] just as it is; without any changes: said of damaged goods for sale —**as it were** as if it were so; so to speak —☆**as of** up to, on, or from (a specified time) —**as to 1.** concerning **2.** as if to

as[2] (as) *n., pl.* **as′ses** (-əz, -ēz) [L.] **1.** an ancient Roman unit of weight equal to about twelve ounces **2.** an ancient Roman coin of copper alloy

As *Chem.* arsenic

AS., A.S., A.-S. Anglo-Saxon

as·a·fet·i·da, as·a·foet·i·da (as′ə fet′ə də) *n.* [ML. *asa* < Per. *āzā,* gum + L. *f(o)etida,* FETID] a bad-smelling gum resin obtained from various Asiatic plants of the parsley family, formerly used in folk medicine to repel disease

as·bes·tos, as·bes·tus (as bes′təs, az-) *n.* [< L. < Gr. *asbestos,* inextinguishable < *a-,* not + *sbennynai,* to extinguish] a grayish mineral, esp. an amphibole, that separates into long, threadlike fibers: some varieties resist heat and chemicals and are used in fireproof curtains, roofing, etc. —*adj.* woven of or containing asbestos

as·ca·rid (as′kə rid) *n.* [< Gr. *askaris*] a roundworm that is a parasite in mammals

as·cend (ə send′) *vi.* [< OFr. < L. < *ad-,* to + *scandere,* to climb] **1.** to go up; move upward; rise [the elevator *ascended* quietly] **2.** to slope or lead upward [the path *ascended* near the cliffs —*vt.* **1.** to move upward along; climb [he *ascended* the stairs] **2.** to succeed to (a throne) —**as·cend′a·ble, as·cend′i·ble** *adj.* —**as·cend′er** *n.*

as·cend·an·cy, as·cend·en·cy (ə send′ən sē) *n.* a position of control or power; supremacy; domination: also **as·cend′ance, as·cend′ence**

as·cend·ant, as·cend·ent (-ənt) *adj.* **1.** rising; ascending **2.** in control; dominant; superior —*n.* **1.** a dominating position; ascendancy **2.** *Astrol.* the sign of the zodiac just above the eastern horizon at any given moment —**in the ascendant** at or approaching the height of power, fame, etc.

as·cen·sion (ə sen′shən) *n.* **1.** an ascending; ascent **2.** [A-] *same as* ASCENSION DAY —**the Ascension** *Bible* the bodily ascent of Jesus into heaven on the fortieth day after the Resurrection: Acts 1:9 —**as·cen′sion·al** *adj.*

Ascension Day the fortieth day after Easter, celebrating the Ascension

as·cent (ə sent′) *n.* **1.** an ascending or rising [an *ascent* in a balloon] **2.** an advancement, as in rank, fame, etc. [a rapid *ascent* to leadership] **3.** *a)* an upward slope [the *ascent* of the mountain] *b)* the degree of such slope

as·cer·tain (as′ər tān′) *vt.* [< OFr. < *a-,* to + *certain,* CERTAIN] to find out in such a way as to be certain —see SYN. at LEARN —**as′cer·tain′a·ble** *adj.* —**as′cer·tain′ment** *n.*

as·cet·ic (ə set′ik) *adj.* [< Gr. < *askein,* to train the body] of or like ascetics or their way of life; self-denying; austere: also **as·cet′i·cal** —*n.* a person who leads a life of contemplation, without the usual pleasures and comforts of people, esp. for some religious purpose —**as·cet′i·cal·ly** *adv.*

as·cet·i·cism (ə set′ə siz′m) *n.* **1.** the way of life of an ascetic **2.** the religious doctrine that one can reach a higher spiritual state by denying oneself comforts

as·cid·i·an (ə sid′ē ən) *n.* [< Gr. *askidion:* see ASCIDIUM] any of a class of sea animals that are sac-shaped and have a tough outer covering

as·cid·i·um (-əm) *n., pl.* **-i·a** (-ə) [ModL. < Gr. dim. of *askos,* a bag, bladder] *Bot.* a pitcherlike leaf or structure, as of the pitcher plant

As·cle·pi·us (as klē′pē əs) *Gr. Myth.* the god of healing and medicine: identified with the Roman god Aesculapius

as·co·my·cete (as′kə mī sēt′) *n.* [< Gr. *askos,* bladder + *mykēs,* fungus] any of a class of fungi, including the mildews, yeasts, etc., that develop spores in a saclike structure —**as′co·my′ce′tous** *adj.*

a·scor·bic acid (ə skôr′bik) [A-² (sense 3) + SCORB(UTIC) + -IC] a water-soluble vitamin, $C_6H_8O_6$, occurring in citrus fruits, tomatoes, etc.: it prevents and cures scurvy; vitamin C

as·cot (as′kət, -kät′) *n.* **1.** [A-] an annual horse-racing meet at Ascot Heath, Berkshire, England **2.** a necktie or scarf with very broad ends hanging from the knot, one upon the other: supposedly first worn at the Ascot

as·cribe (ə skrīb′) *vt.* **-cribed′, -crib′ing** [< OFr. < L. < *ad-,* to + *scribere,* to write] **1.** to put down (*to* a supposed cause); attribute [*he ascribed* his success to hard work] **2.** to regard as belonging (*to*) or coming from someone [poems *ascribed* to Homer] —**as·crib′a·ble** *adj.*

ASCOT

as·crip·tion (ə skrip′shən) *n.* **1.** the act of ascribing **2.** a statement that ascribes

-ase (ās, āz) [< (DIAST)ASE] *a suffix denoting* an enzyme, esp. one of vegetable origin [*amylase*]

a·sep·sis (ā sep′sis, ə-) *n.* **1.** the condition of being aseptic **2.** any method of keeping a thing or place aseptic

a·sep·tic (-tik) *adj.* not septic; free from microorganisms that cause disease —**a·sep′ti·cal·ly** *adv.*

a·sex·u·al (ā sek′shoo wəl) *adj.* **1.** having no sex or sexual organs; sexless **2.** of reproduction without the joining of male and female germ cells —**a·sex′u·al′i·ty** (-wal′ə tē) *n.* —**a·sex′u·al·ly** *adv.*

As·gard (as′gärd, az′-) *Norse Myth.* the home of the gods and slain heroes: also **As′garth** (-gärth)

ash¹ (ash) *n.* [OE. *æsce* < IE. base *as-,* to burn] **1.** the white or grayish powder left after something has been thoroughly burned **2.** fine, volcanic lava **3.** the silvery-gray color of wood ash See also ASHES

ash² (ash) *n.* [OE. *æsc*] **1.** a timber and shade tree of the olive family, having tough, elastic, straight-grained wood **2.** the wood

a·shamed (ə shāmd′) *adj.* **1.** feeling shame or embarrassment [he was *ashamed* of having lost his temper] **2.** unwilling because afraid that one will feel shame [she was *ashamed* to ask for help] —**a·sham·ed·ly** (ə shā′mid lē) *adv.*

A·shan·ti (ə shän′tē, -shan′-) region in C Ghana, orig. a native kingdom —*n.* **1.** *pl.* **-ti, -tis** any member of the W African people of Ashanti **2.** their language

☆**ash·can** (ash′kan′) *n.* a can for ashes and trash

ash·en¹ (ash′ən) *adj.* **1.** of ashes **2.** like ashes, esp. in color; pale; pallid —see SYN. at PALE¹

ash·en² (ash′ən) *adj.* [Archaic] of the ash tree or its wood

ash·es (ash′iz) *n.pl.* **1.** the unburned particles and grayish powder left after a thing has been burned **2.** human remains, esp. after cremation **3.** the ruins or remains of something destroyed

Ashe·ville (ash′vil) [after S. Ashe (1725–1813), governor of N.C.] city in western N.C.: pop. 58,000

Ash·ke·naz·im (ash′kə naz′im, äsh′kə näz′im) *n.pl., sing.* **-naz′, -naz′i** (-ē) [Heb.: see Jer. 51:27] the Jews who settled in C and N Europe after the Diaspora, or their descendants: see SEPHARDIM —**Ash′ke·naz′ic** *adj.*

ash·lar, ash·ler (ash′lər) *n.* [< OFr. < L. *assis,* board] **1.** a square stone used in building **2.** masonry made of ashlar

a·shore (ə shôr′) *adv., adj.* **1.** to or on the shore [row the boat *ashore*] **2.** to or on land

ash·ram (ash′rəm) *n.* [< Sans. < *ā,* toward + *srama,* fatigue,

penance] a secluded place for a community of Hindus leading a life of religious meditation

Ash·to·reth (ash′tə reth′) the ancient Phoenician and Syrian goddess of love and fertility: identified with ASTARTE

ash·tray (ash′trā′) *n.* a container for smokers' tobacco ashes: also **ash tray**

A·shur (ä′shoor) the chief god of the ancient Assyrians

Ash Wednesday the first day of Lent: from the putting of ashes on the forehead in penitence

ash·y (ash′ē) *adj.* **ash′i·er, ash′i·est** **1.** of, like, or covered with ashes **2.** of ash color; pale

A·sia (ā′zhə, -shə) largest continent, situated in the Eastern Hemisphere and separated from N Europe by the Ural Mountains: 16,900,000 sq. mi.; pop. 2,035,000,000 —**A′sian, A·si·at·ic** (ā′zhē at′ik) *adj., n.*

Asia Minor large peninsula in W Asia, between the Black Sea and the Mediterranean, including most of Asiatic Turkey

Asian influenza a widespread influenza caused by a strain of virus first isolated in Singapore in 1957: also **Asian flu**

Asiatic cholera an acute, infectious disease characterized by severe diarrhea, sharp cramps, and loss of water from the body

a·side (ə sīd′) *adv.* **1.** on or to one side [pull the curtains *aside*] **2.** away; in reserve [put this *aside* for me] **3.** out of the way; out of one's mind [let's lay the proposal *aside*] ☆**4.** apart; notwithstanding [joking *aside,* I mean it] —*n.* an actor's words spoken as to the audience and supposedly not heard by the other actors —☆**aside from 1.** except for [he reads little *aside from* magazines] **2.** besides [*aside from* much knowledge, he also has good sense]

as·i·nine (as′ə nīn′) *adj.* [< L. < *asinus,* ass] like an ass; esp., having qualities thought of as asslike; stupid, silly, obstinate, etc. —see SYN. at SILLY —**as′i·nine′ly** *adv.* —**as′i·nin′i·ty** (-nin′ə tē) *n., pl.* **-ties**

ask (ask) *vt.* [OE. *ascian*] **1.** to use words in seeking the answer to (a question); inquire about **2.** to put a question to (a person); inquire of **3.** to request; solicit; beg [*ask* no favors of anyone] **4.** to demand or expect as a price [he's *asking* ten dollars for the lamp] **5.** to invite [they *asked* us to the party] —*vi.* **1.** to make a request (*for*) **2.** to inquire (*about, after,* or *for*) **3.** to behave so as to appear to be looking (*for* trouble, etc.) —**ask′er** *n.* —**ask′ing** *n.*

SYN.—**ask** and the more formal **inquire** and **query** usually suggest no more than the seeking of an answer or information, but **query** also often implies doubt as to the correctness of something [the printer *queried* the spelling of several words]; **question** and **interrogate** imply the asking of a series of questions [to *question* a witness], and **interrogate** further suggests a systematic questioning [to *interrogate* a prisoner of war] —**ANT.** answer, tell

a·skance (ə skans′) *adv.* [< ME. *askoin* < *a-,* on + *skwyn* < Du. *schuin,* sidewise] **1.** with a sidewise glance; obliquely **2.** with suspicion, disapproval, etc. [they looked *askance* at the plan for moving] Also [Archaic or Poet.] **a·skant′**

a·skew (ə skyoo′) *adv.* to one side; awry; crookedly —*adj.* on one side; awry

asking price the price asked by a seller, esp. when he will accept less after bargaining

a·slant (ə slant′) *adv.* on a slant; slantingly —*prep.* on a slant across —*adj.* slanting

a·sleep (ə slēp′) *adj.* **1.** in a condition of sleep; sleeping **2.** inactive; dull; sluggish **3.** numb except for a prickly feeling [my arm is *asleep*] **4.** dead —*adv.* into a sleeping or inactive condition [to fall *asleep*]

a·slope (ə slōp′) *adv., adj.* at a slant

As·ma·ra (äs mä′rä) capital of Eritrea, in N Ethiopia: pop. 146,000

a·so·cial (ā sō′shəl) *adj.* **1.** not social; withdrawing from others **2.** selfish —see SYN. at UNSOCIAL

LAMPSHADE
ASKEW

asp (asp) *n.* [< OFr. < L. < Gr. *aspis*] any of several small, poisonous snakes of Africa and Europe, as the horned viper

as·par·a·gus (ə spar′ə gəs) *n.* [L. < Gr. *asparagos,* a sprout] **1.** a plant of the lily family, with small, scalelike leaves and many needlelike branches **2.** the tender shoots of this plant, eaten as a cooked vegetable

a·spar·kle (ə spär′k'l) *adj.* sparkling

---

fat, āpe, cär; ten, ēven; is, bīte; gō, hôrn, tōol, look; oil, out; up, fur; get; joy; yet; chin; she; thin, then; zh, leisure; ŋ, ring; ə for *a* in *ago, e* in *agent, i* in *sanity, o* in *comply, u* in *focus;* ′ as in *able* (ā′b'l); Fr. bal; ë, Fr. coeur; ö, Fr. feu; Fr. mon; ô, Fr. coq; ü, Fr. duc; r, Fr. cri; H, G. ich; kh, G. doch; ‡foreign; ☆ Americanism; < derived from. See inside front cover.

A.S.P.C.A. American Society for the Prevention of Cruelty to Animals

as·pect (as′pekt) *n.* [< L. pp. of *aspicere* < *ad-*, to, at + *specere*, to look] **1.** look or appearance [his face had a gloomy *aspect*] **2.** any of the possible ways in which an idea, problem, etc. may be regarded [that's an *aspect* of the matter that I overlooked] **3.** a side facing in a given direction [the eastern *aspect* of the house] **4.** *Astrol.* the position of stars in relation to each other or to the observer, as it supposedly influences human affairs —see **SYN.** at APPEARANCE

as·pen (as′pən) *n.* [OE. æspe] a kind of poplar tree with leaves that flutter in the least breeze —*adj.* of or like an aspen; esp., fluttering; trembling

as·per·i·ty (as per′ə tē) *n., pl.* **-ties** [ME. & OFr. < L. < *asper*, rough] **1.** roughness or harshness, as of surface, sound, etc. **2.** sharpness of temper

as·perse (ə spurs′) *vt.* **-persed′, -pers′ing** [< L. pp. of *aspergere* < *ad-*, to + *spargere*, to sprinkle] to spread false or damaging rumors about; slander —**as·pers′er** *n.*

as·per·sion (ə spur′zhən, -shən) *n.* **1.** an act of slander or libel **2.** a damaging or false remark; slander

as·phalt (as′fôlt) *n.* [< ML. < Gr.; prob. < *a-*, not + *sphallein*, to cause to fall] **1.** a brown or black tarlike substance, a variety of bitumen, found in a natural state or obtained by evaporating petroleum **2.** a mixture of this with sand or gravel, for paving, roofing, etc. —*vt.* to pave, roof, etc. with asphalt —**as·phal′tic** *adj.*

as·phal·tum (as fôl′təm) *n. same as* ASPHALT

as·pho·del (as′fə del′) *n.* [< L. < Gr. *asphodelos*] a plant of the lily family, having fleshy roots, narrow leaves, and white or yellow flowers

as·phyx·i·a (as fik′sē ə) *n.* [ModL. < Gr., a stopping of the pulse < *a-*, not + *sphyzein*, to throb] loss of consciousness as a result of too little oxygen and too much carbon dioxide in the blood: suffocation causes asphyxia —**as·phyx′i·ant** *adj., n.*

as·phyx·i·ate (-āt′) *vt.* **-at′ed, -at′ing 1.** to cause asphyxia in **2.** to suffocate —*vi.* to undergo asphyxia —**as·phyx′i·a′tion** *n.* —**as·phyx′i·a′tor** *n.*

as·pic (as′pik) *n.* [Fr. < OFr. *aspe*, ASP] **1.** [Archaic] an asp **2.** [Fr., from its asplike colorfulness] a jelly of meat juice, tomato juice, etc., molded, often with meat, seafood, etc., and eaten as a relish

as·pi·dis·tra (as′pə dis′trə) *n.* [ModL. < Gr. *aspis*, a shield + *astron*, a star] a plant of the lily family, with stiff, glossy evergreen leaves

as·pir·ant (as′pər ənt, ə spīr′ənt) *adj.* aspiring —*n.* a person who aspires; esp., one who seeks to get honors, a high position, etc.

as·pi·rate (as′pə rāt′; *for n. & adj.* -pər it) *vt.* **-rat′ed, -rat′ing** [< L. pp. of *aspirare:* see ASPIRE] **1.** to begin (a word or syllable) with the sound of English *h* in *home* **2.** to follow (a consonant) with a puff of suddenly released breath [the "p" in "puff" is *aspirated*] **3.** to draw in, as by inhaling [*aspirating* dust into the lungs] **4.** *Med.* to remove (fluid or gas), as from a body cavity —*n.* **1.** the speech sound represented by English *h* **2.** a breath puff such as follows *p, t,* or *k* when it begins a syllable —*adj.* preceded or followed by an aspirate: also **as′pi·rat′ed**

as·pi·ra·tion (as′pə rā′shən) *n.* **1.** *a)* strong desire or ambition *b)* the thing so desired **2.** an aspirating **3.** an aspirate

as·pi·ra·tor (as′pə rāt′ər) *n.* a suction apparatus for removing air, fluids, etc. as from a body cavity

as·pir·a·to·ry (ə spīr′ə tôr′ē) *adj.* of or suited for breathing or suction

as·pire (ə spīr′) *vi.* **-pired′, -pir′ing** [< L. *aspirare* < *ad-*, to + *spirare*, to breathe] **1.** to be ambitious (*to* get or do something grand); yearn or seek (*after*) [Jim *aspired* to play in the major leagues; Jane *aspired* after fame as a writer] **2.** [Archaic] to rise high; tower —see **SYN.** at AMBITIOUS —**as·pir′ing·ly** *adv.*

as·pi·rin (as′pər in, as′prin) *n.* [G. < *a(cetyl)* + *spir(säure)*, salicylic acid + *-IN*[1]] a white, crystalline powder, acetylsalicylic acid, $C_9H_8O_4$, used for reducing fever, relieving headaches, etc.

a·squint (ə skwint′) *adv., adj.* [ME. *of skwyn* (see ASKANCE): infl. by SQUINT] with a squint; out of the corner of the eye

ass (as) *n.* [OE. *assa* < L. *asinus*] **1.** an animal related to the horse but having longer ears and a shorter mane: donkeys and burros are domesticated asses **2.** a stupid or silly person; fool

as·sa·fet·i·da, as·sa·foet·i·da (as′ə fet′ə də) *n. same as* ASAFETIDA

as·sa·gai (as′ə gī′) *n.* [< Port. < Ar. *al,* the + *zaghāyah,* spear] a slender spear with an iron tip, used in southern Africa

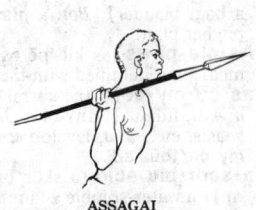

ASSAGAI

‡as·sa·i (äs sä′ē) *adv.* [It.] *Music* very: used in indicating tempo [adagio *assai*]

as·sail (ə sāl′) *vt.* [< OFr. < L. *assilire* < *ad,* to + *salire,* to leap] **1.** to attack with force and violence **2.** to attack with arguments, questions, etc. **3.** to begin working on (a task, etc.) with energy **4.** to have a forceful effect on [noise *assailed* my ears] —**as·sail′a·ble** *adj.*

as·sail·ant (-ənt) *n.* a person who assails; attacker

As·sam (a sam′, as′am) border state of NE India —**As·sa·mese** (as′ə mēz′, -mēs′) *adj., n., pl.* **-mese′**

as·sas·sin (ə sas′′n) *n.* [Fr. < Ar. *hash-shāshīn,* hashish users < *hashīsh,* hemp] **1.** [A-] a member of a secret cult of Moslems who killed Crusaders, supposedly while under the influence of hashish **2.** a murderer who strikes suddenly; esp., the killer of a politically important person

as·sas·si·nate (-āt′) *vt.* **-nat′ed, -nat′ing 1.** to murder (esp. a politically important person) **2.** to harm or ruin (a reputation, etc.), as by slander —**as·sas′si·na′tion** *n.*

as·sault (ə sôlt′) *n.* [< OFr. < L. *ad,* to + *saltare,* to leap] **1.** a violent attack, either physical or with words **2.** *Law* an unlawful threat or unsuccessful attempt to physically harm another —*vt., vi.* to make an assault (upon) —**as·sault′ive** *adj.*

assault and battery *Law* the carrying out of threatened physical harm or violence

as·say (as′ā, a sā′; *for v.* a sā′, ə-) *n.* [OFr. *essai,* trial, test < L. *exagium,* a weighing < *ex-,* out + *agere,* to ACT] **1.** an examination or testing **2.** the analysis of an ore, etc. to find out the nature and proportion of the ingredients **3.** a substance to be analyzed in this way **4.** the result or report of such analysis —*vt.* **1.** to make an assay of; test; analyze **2.** to try; attempt —☆*vi.* to be shown by analysis to contain a certain proportion of some substance [this ore *assays* high in gold] —**as·say′er** *n.*

as·sem·blage (ə sem′blij) *n.* **1.** an assembling or being assembled **2.** a group of persons or things gathered together; assembly **3.** a form of art in which a number of unrelated objects are arranged together to form a kind of sculptural collage

as·sem·ble (ə sem′b'l) *vt.* **-bled, -bling** [< OFr. < L. < *ad-*, to + *simul,* together] **1.** to gather into a group; collect ☆**2.** to fit or put together the parts of (a machine, etc.) —see **SYN.** at GATHER —**as·sem′bler** *n.*

as·sem·bly (ə sem′blē) *n., pl.* **-blies 1.** an assembling or being assembled **2.** a group of persons gathered together, as for a meeting **3.** [A-] in some States, the lower house of the legislature **4.** *a)* a fitting together of parts to form a complete unit, as in making automobiles *b)* the parts so fitted together [an airplane's tail *assembly*] **5.** a call, as by bugle or drum, for soldiers to assemble in ranks

☆**assembly line** in many factories, an arrangement by which each worker does a single operation in assembling the work as it is passed along, often on a slowly moving belt or track

as·sem·bly·man (ə sem′blē mən) *n., pl.* **-men** (-mən, -men′) a member of a legislative assembly; specif., [A-] in some States, a member of the lower house of the legislature —**as·sem′bly·wom′an** *n.fem., pl.* **-wom′en**

as·sent (ə sent′) *vi.* [< OFr. < L. < *assentire* < *ad-*, to + *sentire,* to feel] to say that one will accept an opinion, proposal, etc.; agree (*to*) —*n.* consent or agreement —see **SYN.** at CONSENT

as·sert (ə surt′) *vt.* [< L. pp. of *asserere* < *ad-*, to + *serere,* to join] **1.** to state positively; declare **2.** to insist on or defend (one's rights, a claim, etc.) —**assert oneself** to insist on one's rights, or on being recognized —**as·sert′er, as·ser′tor** *n.*

as·ser·tion (ə sur′shən) *n.* **1.** an asserting **2.** a positive statement; declaration

as·ser·tive (-tiv) *adj.* stubbornly positive or confident —see **SYN.** at AGGRESSIVE —**as·ser′tive·ly** *adv.* —**as·ser′tive·ness** *n.*

as·sess (ə ses′) *vt.* [< OFr. < ML. *assessare,* to set a rate < L. pp. of *assidere,* sit beside, assist < *ad-*, to + *sedere,* sit]

1. to set an estimated value on (property, etc.) for taxation **2.** to set the amount of (damages, a fine, etc.) **3.** to impose a fine, tax, etc. on (a person or property) **4.** to impose (an amount) as a fine, tax, etc. **5.** to estimate or determine the importance or value of

as·sess·ment (-mənt) *n.* **1.** an assessing **2.** an amount assessed

as·ses·sor (-ər) *n.* a person who assesses property, etc. for taxation —**as·ses·so·ri·al** (as′ə sôr′ē əl) *adj.* —**as·ses′sor·ship′** *n.*

as·set (as′et) *n.* [< Anglo-Fr. *assetz*, enough < OFr.; ult. < L. *ad*, to + *satis*, enough] **1.** anything owned that has exchange value **2.** a valuable or desirable thing [charm is her chief *asset*] **3.** [*pl.*] the entries on a balance sheet showing all the resources of a person or business, as land, buildings, machinery, cash, money due, etc.

as·sev·er·ate (ə sev′ə rāt′) *vt.* -**at**′**ed,** -**at**′**ing** [< L. pp. of *asseverare* < *ad-*, to + *severus*, earnest] to state seriously or positively; assert —**as·sev′er·a′tion** *n.*

as·si·du·i·ty (as′ə dyōō′ə tē, -dōō′-) *n., pl.* -**ties 1.** the quality or condition of being assiduous; diligence **2.** [*pl.*] constant personal attention

as·sid·u·ous (ə sij′ōō wəs) *adj.* [< L. < *assidere:* see ASSESS] working with constant and careful attention; diligent; persevering [an *assiduous* student] —see SYN. at BUSY —**as·sid′u·ous·ly** *adv.* —**as·sid′u·ous·ness** *n.*

as·sign (ə sīn′) *vt.* [< OFr. < L. *assignare*, to allot < *ad-*, to + *signare*, SIGN] **1.** to set apart or mark for a specific purpose; designate [*assign* a day for the meeting] **2.** to place at some task or duty [I was *assigned* to watch the road] **3.** to give out as a task; allot [the teacher *assigned* a new lesson] **4.** to ascribe (a motive, reason, etc.) **5.** *Law* to transfer (a claim, property, etc.) to another —*vi. Law* to transfer property, etc. to another —*n.* [*usually pl.*] an assignee —see SYN. at ALLOT —**as·sign′a·bil′i·ty** *n.* —**as·sign′a·ble** *adj.* —**as·sign′er, *Law* as·sign′or** (-ər, -ôr′) *n.*

as·sig·na·tion (as′ig nā′shən) *n.* **1.** an assigning **2.** anything assigned **3.** an appointment to meet, esp. one made secretly by lovers; rendezvous

as·sign·ee (ə sī′nē′) *n. Law* a person to whom a claim, property, etc. is transferred

as·sign·ment (ə sīn′mənt) *n.* **1.** an assigning or being assigned **2.** anything assigned, as a lesson, task, etc. **3.** *Law a)* a transfer of a claim, property, etc. *b)* a deed, etc. authorizing this

as·sim·i·late (ə sim′ə lāt′) *vt.* -**lat**′**ed,** -**lat**′**ing** [< L. pp. of *assimilare* < *ad-*, to + *similare*, make similar to < *similis*, like] **1.** to change (food) into a form that can be taken up by, and made part of, the body **2.** to take in and make part of one's thinking [to *assimilate* what one reads] **3.** to absorb (groups of different cultures) into the main culture **4.** to make like or alike (with *to*) [he *assimilated* his attitudes to those of his son] —*vi.* to become assimilated —**as·sim′i·la·ble** *adj.* —**as·sim′i·la′tor** *n.*

as·sim·i·la·tion (ə sim′ə lā′shən) *n.* an assimilating or being assimilated; specif., *a)* the absorption of a minority group into the main culture *b) Phonet.* the process by which a sound tends to become like a neighboring sound [the *p* in *cupboard* has been lost by assimilation to *b*] *c) Physiol.* the change of digested food into the protoplasm of an animal; also, the absorption of food elements by plants

as·sim·i·la·tive (ə sim′ə lāt′iv) *adj.* of or causing assimilation; assimilating

as·sist (ə sist′) *vt.* [< OFr. < L. *assistere* < *ad-*, to + *sistere*, to make stand < *stare*, to stand] **1.** to give help to; aid **2.** to work as an assistant to —*vi.* to give help; aid —*n.* **1.** an instance or act of helping **2.** *Baseball* a defensive play by a fielder that helps a teammate to make a putout **3.** *Hockey* the passing of the puck in such a way as to help a teammate to score a goal —see SYN. at HELP —**assist at** to be present at; attend

as·sist·ance (ə sis′təns) *n.* the act of assisting or the help given; aid

as·sist·ant (-tənt) *adj.* assisting; helping —*n.* **1.** a person who assists another or serves in a lower position; helper **2.** a thing that aids

as·size (ə sīz′) *n.* [< OFr. < L. *assidere:* see ASSESS] **1.** orig., a legislative assembly or any of its decrees **2.** [*pl.*] *a)* court sessions held at regular times in each county of England *b)* the time or place of these

assn. association

assoc. 1. associate **2.** associated **3.** association

as·so·ci·ate (ə sō′shē āt′, -sē-; *for n. & adj., usually* -it) *vt.* -**at**′**ed,** -**at**′**ing** [< L. pp. of *associare* < *ad-*, to + *sociare*, to join < *socius*, companion] **1.** to join together; connect; combine **2.** to bring (a person) into relationship as companion, partner, friend, etc. **3.** to connect in the mind [to *associate* rain with grief] —*vi.* **1.** to join (*with* another or others) as a companion, partner, friend, etc. **2.** to join together; unite —*n.* **1.** a friend, partner, fellow worker, etc. **2.** a member of less than full status, as of a society **3.** anything joined with another thing or things ☆**4.** a degree granted by a junior college to those completing the regular two-year course [an *Associate* in (or of) Arts] —*adj.* **1.** joined with others, as in some work [an *associate* justice] **2.** of less than full status [an *associate* membership] **SYN.**—**associate** refers to a person who is frequently in one's company, usually because of working together [business *associates*]; **companion** refers to a person who actually accompanies one and usually implies friendship [the *companions* of his youth]; **comrade** refers to a close associate who shares in one's activities, etc. [*comrades* in arms]; **colleague** denotes a fellow worker, esp. in one of the professions, and may or may not imply personal friendship [his *colleagues* at the university]; **ally** now usually refers to one who is joined with others in a common cause [they were *allies* in the fight against pollution]; a **confederate** is one who joins with others for some common purpose, esp. to commit a crime

as·so·ci·a·tion (ə sō′sē ā′shən, -shē-) *n.* **1.** the act of associating **2.** companionship; fellowship; partnership **3.** an organization of persons having the same interests, purposes, etc.; society **4.** a connection in the mind between ideas, feelings, etc. [the *association* of the color blue with coolness] **5.** a group of plants of several species living together in the same environment —**as·so′ci·a′tion·al** *adj.*

association football *British name for* SOCCER

as·so·ci·a·tive (ə sō′shē āt′iv, -sē-) *adj.* **1.** of, characterized by, or causing association **2.** *Math.* describing an operation, as the multiplication of three numbers, in which the result is the same regardless of the way the elements are grouped [Ex.: $2(3 \times 4) = (2 \times 3)4$]

as·so·nance (as′ə nəns) *n.* [Fr. < L. prp. of *assonare* < *ad-*, to + *sonare*, to SOUND[1]] **1.** likeness of sound, esp. of vowels, as in a series of words or syllables **2.** a partial rhyme in which the stressed vowel sounds are alike but the consonant sounds are not, as in *late* and *make* —**as′so·nant** *adj., n.*

as·sort (ə sôrt′) *vt.* [< OFr. < *a-* (L. *ad*), to + *sorte*, SORT] to sort or classify —**as·sort′er** *n.*

as·sort·ed (-id) *adj.* **1.** of different sorts; miscellaneous [a box of *assorted* candies] **2.** sorted into groups according to kind [it comes in *assorted* sizes] **3.** matched [a poorly *assorted* pair]

as·sort·ment (-mənt) *n.* **1.** an assorting or being assorted; classification **2.** an assorted, or miscellaneous, group or collection; variety

ASSR, A.S.S.R. Autonomous Soviet Socialist Republic

asst. assistant

as·suage (ə swāj′) *vt.* -**suaged**′, -**suag**′**ing** [< OFr. < L. *ad*, to + *suavis*, SWEET] **1.** to lessen (pain, distress, etc.); allay **2.** to calm (passion, anger, etc.); pacify **3.** to satisfy or slake (thirst, appetite, etc.) —see SYN. at RELIEVE —**as·suage′ment** *n.* —**as·suag′er** *n.*

as·sume (ə sōōm′, -syōōm′) *vt.* -**sumed**′, -**sum**′**ing** [< L. *assumere*, to claim < *ad-*, to + *sumere*, to take] **1.** to take on or put on (the appearance, form, role, etc. *of*) **2.** to take over; seize [to *assume* control] **3.** to take upon oneself; undertake [to *assume* an obligation] **4.** to take for granted; suppose [we *assumed* that he was loyal] **5.** to pretend to have; feign [to *assume* an air of innocence] —see SYN. at PRESUME —**as·sum′a·ble** *adj.* —**as·sum′er** *n.*

as·sumed (ə sōōmd′, -syōōmd′) *adj.* **1.** not real; pretended [an *assumed* name] **2.** taken for granted

as·sum·ing (ə sōō′miŋ, -syōō′-) *adj.* taking too much for granted; presumptuous

as·sump·tion (ə sump′shən) *n.* **1.** the act of assuming [an *assumption* of power] **2.** anything taken for granted; supposition [our *assumption* of his innocence proved correct] **3.** [A-]

R.C.Ch. a) the taking up of the body and soul of the Virgin Mary into heaven after her death *b)* a church festival on August 15 celebrating this —**as·sump′tive** *adj.*

as·sur·ance (ə shoor′əns) *n.* 1. the act of assuring 2. a being assured; sureness; confidence [I have no *assurance* that we will win] 3. something that inspires confidence, as a promise, positive statement, etc.; guarantee [she had received *assurances* of financial aid] 4. self-confidence [the new salesman lacks *assurance*] 5. bold forwardness; presumption 6. [Chiefly Brit.] insurance —see SYN. at CERTAINTY

as·sure (ə shoor′) *vt.* **-sured′, -sur′ing** [< OFr. < ML. *assecurare* < L. *ad*, to + *securus*, SECURE] 1. to make (a person) sure of something; convince [we *assured* him of our friendship] 2. to give confidence to [the news *assured* us] 3. to declare to or promise confidently [I *assure* you I'll be there] 4. to make (a doubtful thing) certain; guarantee [his help *assured* our success] 5. [Brit.] to insure against loss —**as·sur′er** *n.*

as·sured (ə shoord′) *adj.* 1. made sure; certain [an *assured* income] 2. confident [an *assured* manner] 3. insured —*n.* 1. the person to whom an insurance policy is payable 2. the person whose life or property is insured —**as·sur·ed·ly** (ə shoor′id lē) *adv.* —**as·sur′ed·ness** *n.*

As·syr·i·a (ə sir′ē ə) ancient empire in SW Asia in the region of the upper Tigris River

As·syr·i·an (-ən) *adj.* of Assyria, its people, language, etc. —*n.* 1. a native or inhabitant of Assyria 2. the Semitic language of the Assyrians

As·tar·te (as tär′tē) a Phoenician goddess of love and fertility

☆**as·ta·tine** (as′tə tēn′) *n.* [< Gr. *astatos*, unstable + -INE⁴] a radioactive chemical element formed from bismuth when it is bombarded by alpha particles: symbol, At; at. wt., 210(?); at. no., 85

as·ter (as′tər) *n.* [L. < Gr. *astēr*, STAR] 1. a plant of the composite family, with purplish, blue, pink, or white daisylike flowers 2. *Zool.* a star-shaped structure formed around a centrosome during mitosis

-as·ter (as′tər) [L. dim. suffix] *a suffix meaning* inferior or worthless [*poetaster*]

as·ter·isk (as′tər isk) *n.* [< LL. < Gr. dim. of *astēr*, STAR] a starlike sign (*) used in printing to call attention to a footnote or the like, or to show that something has been left out

as·ter·ism (as′tər iz'm) *n.* [< Gr. < *astēr*, STAR] 1. a starlike figure formed by light in some crystals 2. *Astron.* a group or cluster of stars

a·stern (ə sturn′) *adv.* 1. behind a ship or aircraft 2. at or toward the back of a ship or aircraft 3. backward; in a reverse direction

NEW ENGLAND ASTER

as·ter·oid (as′tə roid′) *adj.* [< Gr. < *astēr*, STAR + -OID] like a star or starfish —*n.* 1. any of the many small planets with orbits between those of Mars and Jupiter; planetoid 2. a starfish

as·the·ni·a (as thē′nē ə) *n.* [ML. < Gr. < *a-*, without + *sthenos*, strength] bodily weakness —**as·then′ic** (-then′ik) *adj.*

asth·ma (az′mə) *n.* [Gr.] a chronic disorder in which there are attacks of wheezing, coughing, difficulty in breathing, and a suffocating feeling, usually caused by an allergy

asth·mat·ic (az mat′ik) *adj.* of or having asthma: also **asth·mat′i·cal** —*n.* a person who has asthma —**asth·mat′i·cal·ly** *adv.*

as·tig·mat·ic (as′tig mat′ik) *adj.* 1. of or having astigmatism 2. correcting astigmatism [an *astigmatic* lens] 3. having a distorted view or judgment —**as·tig·mat′i·cal·ly** *adv.*

a·stig·ma·tism (ə stig′mə tiz'm) *n.* [< Gr. *a-*, without + *stigma*, a mark + -ISM] 1. an irregularity in the curvature of a lens, esp. of the eye, so that light rays do not meet in a single focal point and images are distorted 2. a distorted view or judgment, as because of prejudice

a·stir (ə stur′) *adv., adj.* 1. in motion; in excited activity 2. out of bed

as·ton·ish (ə stän′ish) *vt.* [< OFr. < L. < *ex-*, emphatic + *tonare*, to thunder] to fill with sudden wonder or great surprise; amaze —see SYN. at SURPRISE —**as·ton′ish·ing** *adj.* —**as·ton′ish·ing·ly** *adv.*

as·ton·ish·ment (-mənt) *n.* 1. a being astonished; great amazement 2. anything that astonishes

As·tor (as′tər), **John Jacob** 1763-1848; U.S. fur merchant & financier, born in Germany

as·tound (ə stound′) *vt.* [< ME. pp. of *astonien*, ASTONISH] to bewilder with sudden surprise; astonish greatly; amaze —see SYN. at SURPRISE —**as·tound′ing** *adj.* —**as·tound′ing·ly** *adv.*

a·strad·dle (ə strad′'l) *adv.* in a straddling position

As·tra·khan (as′trə kan′; *Russ.* äs′trə khän′y′) seaport in S European R.S.F.S.R.: pop. 376,000

as·tra·khan (as′trə kən) *n.* 1. a loosely curled fur from the pelt of very young lambs orig. bred near Astrakhan 2. a wool fabric made to look like this Also sp. **as′tra·chan**

as·tral (as′trəl) *adj.* [< L. < Gr. *astron*, star < *astēr*, STAR] of, from, or like the stars

a·stray (ə strā′) *adv.* 1. off the right path 2. so as to be in error [led *astray* by false evidence]

a·stride (ə strīd′) *adv.* 1. with a leg on either side; astraddle 2. with legs far apart —*prep.* 1. with a leg on either side of (a horse, etc.) 2. extending over or across [a bridge *astride* the river]

as·trin·gent (ə strin′jənt) *adj.* [< L. prp. of *astringere*, to contract < *ad-*, to + *stringere*, to draw] 1. that contracts or tightens body tissues and stops bleeding from capillaries 2. having a harsh, biting quality [an *astringent* wit] —*n.* an astringent substance, such as alum —**as·trin′gen·cy** *n.* —**as·trin′gent·ly** *adv.*

as·tro- [< Gr. *astron:* see ASTRAL] *a combining form meaning* of a star or stars [*astrophysics*]

as·tro·dome (as′trə dōm′) *n.* a transparent dome on top of an aircraft fuselage for the navigator

astrol. 1. astrologer 2. astrology

as·tro·labe (as′trə lāb′) *n.* [< OFr. < ML. < Gr. < *astron*, a star + *lambanein*, to take] an instrument formerly used to find the altitude of a star, etc.: it was replaced by the sextant

as·trol·o·gy (ə sträl′ə jē) *n.* [< L. & Gr. < *astron*, star + -*logia*, -LOGY] 1. orig., primitive astronomy 2. a pseudoscience based on the notion that the positions of the moon, sun, and stars affect human affairs and that one can foretell the future by studying the stars, etc. —**as·trol′o·ger** *n.* —**as·tro·log·i·cal** (as′trə läj′i k'l) *adj.* —**as′tro·log′i·cal·ly** *adv.*

astron. 1. astronomer 2. astronomy

as·tro·naut (as′trə nôt′) *n.* [< Fr.: see ASTRONAUTICS] a person trained to make rocket flights in outer space

as·tro·nau·tics (as′trə nôt′iks) *n.pl.* [with sing. v.] [< Fr.: see ASTRO- & AERONAUTICS] the science that deals with spacecraft and with travel in outer space —**as′tro·nau′ti·cal** *adj.*

as·tron·o·mer (ə strän′ə mər) *n.* an expert in astronomy

as·tro·nom·i·cal (as′trə näm′i k'l) *adj.* 1. of or having to do with astronomy 2. extremely large, as the numbers or quantities used in astronomy Also **as′tro·nom′ic** —**as′tro·nom′i·cal·ly** *adv.*

astronomical unit a unit of length equal to the mean radius of the earth's orbit (c. 93 million mi.) used in measuring distances in astronomy

as·tron·o·my (ə strän′ə mē) *n.* [< ME. & OFr. < L. < Gr. < *astron*, star + *nomos*, system of laws < *nemein*, to arrange] the science of the stars, planets, and all other heavenly bodies, dealing with their composition, motion, relative position, size, etc.

as·tro·phys·ics (as′trō fiz′iks) *n.pl.* [with sing. v.] the science dealing with the physical properties and chemical makeup of the stars, planets, etc. —**as′tro·phys′i·cal** *adj.* —**as′tro·phys′i·cist** (-ə sist) *n.*

as·tute (ə stoot′, -styoot′) *adj.* [< L. < *astus*, craft, cunning] having or showing a clever or shrewd mind; keen [an *astute* politician] —see SYN. at SHREWD —**as·tute′ly** *adv.* —**as·tute′ness** *n.*

A·sun·ción (ä soon syôn′) capital of Paraguay, on the Paraguay River: pop. 305,000

a·sun·der (ə sun′dər) *adv.* [see SUNDER] 1. into parts or pieces [the cart fell *asunder*] 2. apart [they moved *asunder*]

As·wan (äs wän′, as-; as′wän′) city on the Nile, in SE Egypt: pop. 48,000: a dam (**Aswan High Dam**) has been built just south of this city

a·sy·lum (ə sī′ləm) *n.* [L. < Gr. *asylon*, asylum < *a-*, without + *sylē*, right of seizure] 1. formerly, a sanctuary, as a temple, where criminals, etc. were safe from arrest 2. any refuge 3. the protection given by one country to refugees from another 4. *an old term for* a place for the care of the mentally ill, or of the aged, poor, etc.: this term has been replaced by such terms as *psychiatric hospital, nursing home,* etc.

a·sym·me·try (ā sim′ə trē) *n.* lack of symmetry —**a·sym·met·ri·cal** (ā′sə met′ri k'l), **a′sym·met′ric** *adj.* —**a′sym·met′ri·cal·ly** *adv.*

as·ymp·tote (as′im tōt′) *n.* [ModL. < Gr. < *a-*, not + *syn-*, together + *piptein*, to fall] a straight line always approaching but never meeting a curve —**as′ymp·tot′ic** (-tät′ik), **as′ymp·tot′i·cal** *adj.*

ASYMPTOTE
(A, asymptote of curve C)

at[1] (at; *unstressed* ət) *prep.* [OE. *æt*] **1.** on; in; near; by [*at* the office] **2.** to or toward [look *at* her] **3.** through [enter *at* the gate] **4.** from [get the facts *at* their source] **5.** attending [*at* the party] **6.** occupied in; busy with [*at* work] **7.** in a state of [*at* war] **8.** in the manner of [*at* a trot] **9.** because of [terrified *at* the sight] **10.** according to [*at* his discretion] **11.** with reference to [good *at* tennis] **12.** in the amount, degree, price, etc. of [*at* five cents each] **13.** from an interval of [*at* half a mile] **14.** on or close to the time or age of [*at* five o'clock] **15.** during the period of [to happen *at* night]

at[2] (ät, at) *n., pl.* **at** *see* MONETARY UNITS, table (Laos)

At *Chem.* astatine

at. **1.** airtight **2.** atmosphere **3.** atomic

☆**At·a·brine** (at′ə brin, -brēn′) [G. *atebrin*] *a trademark for* a synthetic drug used in treating malaria and other diseases —*n.* [a-] this drug

At·a·lan·ta (at′'l an′tə) *Gr. Myth.* a beautiful, swift-footed maiden who offered to marry any man able to defeat her in a race

at·a·rac·tic (at′ə rak′tik) *n.* [< Gr. *ataraxia*, calmness < *a-*, not + *tarassein*, to disturb] a tranquilizing drug —*adj.* of or having to do with tranquilizing drugs or their effects Also **at′a·rax′ic** (-rak′sik)

at·a·vism (at′ə viz′m) *n.* [< Fr. < L. *atavus*, ancestor < *at-*, beyond + *avus*, grandfather: for IE. base see UNCLE] **1.** the appearance in an individual of a characteristic found in an early ancestor but not in more recent ones **2.** *a)* such a characteristic *b)* an individual with such a characteristic: also **at′a·vist** —**at′a·vis′tic** *adj.* —**at′a·vis′ti·cal·ly** *adv.*

a·tax·i·a (ə tak′sē ə) *n.* [Gr., disorder < *a-*, not + *tassein*, to arrange] inability to coordinate movements of parts of the body —**a·tax′ic** *adj., n.*

A·te (ā′tē) *Gr. Myth.* the goddess personifying criminal folly or reckless ambition

ate (āt; *Brit.*, or *U.S. dial.*, et) *pt.* of EAT

-ate[1] (āt *for 1*; it, āt *for 2*) [< L. *-atus*, pp. ending] **1.** *a suffix meaning:* *a)* to become [maturate] *b)* to cause to become [invalidate] *c)* to produce [salivate] *d)* to provide or treat with [vaccinate] *e)* to put in the form of [triangulate] *f)* to arrange for [orchestrate] *g)* to combine or treat with [oxygenate] **2.** *a suffix meaning:* *a)* of or characteristic of [collegiate] *b)* having or filled with [passionate] *c)* *Biol.* having or characterized by [chordate]

-ate[2] (āt, it) [L. *-atus*, a noun ending] *a suffix denoting:* **1.** a function, agent, or official [directorate, potentate] **2.** [L. *-atum*, neut. of *-atus*] *Chem.* a salt made from (an acid with a name ending in *-ic*) [acetate, nitrate]

at·el·ier (at′'l yā′) *n.* [Fr., ult. < L. *assula*, dim. of *assis*, board] a studio or workshop

a tem·po (ä tem′pō) [It.] *Music* in time: a direction to return to the original tempo

Ath·a·na·sius (ath′ə nā′shəs), Saint 296?–373 A.D.; Alexandrian bishop, who opposed Arianism —**Ath′a·na′sian** (-zhən) *adj., n.*

Ath·a·pas·can, Ath·a·pas·kan (ath′ə pas′kən) *adj.* [< Cree *athap-askaw*, lit., grass here and there] designating or of the most widely scattered language family of N. American Indians, including the Navahos and Apaches —*n.* an Athapascan Indian or language Also **Ath′a·bas′can, Ath′a·bas′kan** (-bas′-)

a·the·ism (ā′thē iz′m) *n.* [< Fr. < Gr. < *a-*, without + *theos*, god] the belief that there is no God —**a′the·is′tic, a′the·is′ti·cal** *adj.*

a·the·ist (-ist) *n.* a person who believes that there is no God

SYN.—an **atheist** rejects all religious belief and denies that a God or gods exist; an **agnostic** questions whether God exists and is unwilling to accept supernatural revelation; a **freethinker** rejects the beliefs of formal religion as being opposed to reason; **infidel** is a term sometimes used of a person who does not believe in a particular religion —ANT. theist

A·the·na (ə thē′nə) *Gr. Myth.* the goddess of wisdom, skills, and warfare, identified with the Roman goddess Minerva: also **A·the′ne** (-nē)

Ath·e·nae·um, Ath·e·ne·um (ath′ə nē′əm) the temple of Athena at Athens, where writers and scholars met —*n.* [a-] ☆**1.** a literary or scientific club **2.** a library or reading room

Ath·ens (ath′′nz) capital of Greece: pop. (of the metropolitan area) 2,530,000: the ancient center of Greek culture and capital of ancient Attica —**A·the·ni·an** (ə thē′nē ən) *adj., n.*

ath·er·o·scle·ro·sis (ath′ər ō sklə rō′sis) *n.* [ModL. < Gr. *athērōma*, tumor filled with grainy matter + SCLEROSIS] a thickening and hardening of the walls of arteries, with the deposit of fatty lumps on the inner walls —**ath′er·o·scle·rot′ic** (-rät′ik) *adj.*

a·thirst (ə thurst′) *adj.* **1.** [Archaic] thirsty **2.** eager; longing [athirst for knowledge]

ath·lete (ath′lēt′) *n.* [< L. < Gr. < *athlein*, to contest for a prize < *athlon*, a prize] a person trained in exercises, games, or contests requiring physical strength, skill, speed, etc.

athlete's foot a common fungous infection of the skin of the feet; ringworm of the feet

ath·let·ic (ath let′ik) *adj.* **1.** of, like, or proper to athletes or athletics **2.** physically strong, skillful, muscular, etc. —**ath·let′i·cal·ly** *adv.*

ath·let·ics (-iks) *n.pl.* [*sometimes with sing. v.*] sports, games, etc. requiring physical strength, skill, stamina, speed, etc.

at-home (ət hōm′) *n.* an informal reception at one's home, usually in the afternoon

a·thwart (ə thwôrt′) *prep.* **1.** from one side to the other of; across **2.** in opposition to; against **3.** *Naut.* across the course or length of —*adv.* **1.** crosswise **2.** so as to block or thwart

-at·ic (at′ik) [< Fr. or L. < Gr. *-atikos*] *a suffix meaning* of, of the kind of [lymphatic, chromatic]

a·tilt (ə tilt′) *adj., adv.* tilted

a·tin·gle (ə tiŋ′g'l) *adj.* tingling; excited

-a·tion (ā′shən) [< Fr. or L.] *a suffix meaning:* **1.** the act of [alteration] **2.** the condition of being [gratification] **3.** the result of [compilation]

-a·tive (ə tiv, āt′iv) [< Fr. or L.] *a suffix meaning* of or relating to, serving to, tending to [demonstrative, informative, talkative]

At·lan·ta (ət lan′tə, at-) [< Western & *Atlantic* Railroad] capital of Ga., in the NC part: pop. 497,000 (met. area 1,390,000)

At·lan·tic (ət lan′tik, at-) [< L. *Atlanticum* (*mare*), Atlantic (ocean) < *Atlanticus*, of the Atlas Mts.] ocean touching the American continents to the west and Europe and Africa to the east —*adj.* of, in, on, or near this ocean

Atlantic City city & ocean resort in N.J., on the Atlantic: pop. 48,000

Atlantic Standard Time *see* STANDARD TIME

At·lan·tis (ət lan′tis, at-) legendary island or continent west of Gibraltar, supposed to have sunk in the Atlantic —**At·lan·te·an** (at′lan tē′ən) *adj.*

At·las (at′ləs) [L. < Gr.; ult. < *tlan*, bearing] *Gr. Myth.* a Titan forced to hold the heavens on his shoulders —*n.* [a-] **1.** a book of maps: such books used to have a picture of Atlas holding the earth **2.** a book of tables, charts, etc. on a specific subject

Atlas Mountains mountain system in NW Africa, extending across Morocco, Algeria, and Tunisia

atm. **1.** atmosphere **2.** atmospheric

at·man (ät′mən) *n.* [Sans., breath, soul] *Hinduism* **1.** the individual soul **2.** [A-] the universal soul, that is the source of all individual souls

at·mos·phere (at′məs fir′) *n.* [< ModL. < Gr. *atmos*, vapor + *sphaira*, sphere] **1.** all the air surrounding the earth, consisting of oxygen, nitrogen, and other gases **2.** the gaseous mass surrounding any star, etc. **3.** the air in any given place **4.** the general feeling or spirit of a place; mood [a city with the *atmosphere* of a small town] **5.** [Colloq.] an interesting effect produced by decoration, etc. [a restaurant with *atmosphere*] **6.** *Physics* a unit of pressure equal to 14.69 lb. per sq. in.

ATLAS

at·mos·pher·ic (at′məs fer′ik, -fir′-) *adj.* **1.** of or in the atmosphere [*atmospheric* lightning] **2.** caused or produced by the atmosphere [*atmospheric* pressure] **3.** creating an atmosphere, or mood Also **at′mos·pher′i·cal** —**at′mos·pher′i·cal·ly** *adv.*

at·mos·pher·ics (-iks) *n.pl. same as* STATIC (*n.* 1)

at. no. atomic number

at·oll (a′tôl, ā′-; -täl) *n.* [< Maldive Is. term] a ring-shaped coral island nearly or completely surrounding a lagoon

at·om (at′əm) *n.* [< OFr. < L. < Gr. *atomos*, uncut < *a-*, not + *temnein*, to cut] **1.** orig., any of the tiny particles that ancient philosophers imagined as the basic component of all matter **2.** a tiny particle; jot **3.** *Chem. & Physics* any of the smallest particles of an element that combine with similar particles of other elements to produce compounds: atoms consist of electrons revolving about a positively charged nucleus —**the atom** *same as* ATOMIC ENERGY

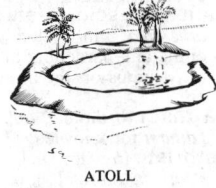

ATOLL

at·om-bomb (at′əm bäm′) *vt.* to destroy with an atomic bomb

atom bomb *same as* ATOMIC BOMB

a·tom·ic (ə täm′ik) *adj.* **1.** of an atom or atoms **2.** of or using atomic energy or atomic bombs **3.** having its atoms in an uncombined form **4.** very small; minute —**a·tom′i·cal·ly** *adv.*

☆**Atomic Age** the period since the creation of the first self-sustaining nuclear chain reaction on December 2, 1942

☆**atomic bomb** an extremely destructive type of bomb, the power of which comes from the very great quantity of energy that is suddenly released when a chain reaction of nuclear fission is set off: first used in warfare in 1945 by the United States

atomic clock a highly accurate clock regulated by the constant frequency at which atoms or molecules of certain substances, as of cesium, absorb or give forth electromagnetic radiation

☆**atomic cocktail** a dose of medicine to be swallowed, containing a radioactive element and used as in diagnosing or treating cancer

atomic energy the energy released from an atom in nuclear fission or nuclear fusion, or by radioactive decay

at·o·mic·i·ty (at′ə mis′ə tē) *n.* **1.** the state of being made up of atoms **2.** *Chem. a)* the number of atoms in a molecule *b) same as* VALENCE

atomic mass unit a unit of mass, exactly one twelfth of the mass of an atom of the most common isotope of carbon

atomic number *Chem.* a number representing the relative position of an element in the periodic table; number representing the number of protons in the nucleus of the atom of an element

☆**atomic pile** *early name for* NUCLEAR REACTOR

atomic theory the theory that all material objects and substances are composed of atoms

atomic weight *Chem.* a number representing the weight of one atom of an element as compared with an arbitrary number representing the weight of one atom of another element taken as the standard (now usually carbon at 12)

at·om·ize (at′ə mīz′) *vt.* **-ized′, -iz′ing 1.** to separate into atoms **2.** to reduce (a liquid) to a fine spray **3.** to destroy by atomic weapons **4.** to disintegrate —**at′om·i·za′tion** *n.*

at·om·iz·er (-mī′zər) *n.* a device used to shoot out a fine spray, as of medicine or perfume

☆**atom smasher** *same as* ACCELERATOR (sense 4)

a·ton·al (ā tōn′′l) *adj.* having atonality —**a·ton′al·ism** *n.* —**a·ton′al·ist** *n.* —**a·ton′al·is′tic** *adj.* —**a·ton′al·ly** *adv.*

a·to·nal·i·ty (ā′tō nal′ə tē) *n. Music* **1.** lack of tonality **2.** a style of writing music by using chromatic tones that have no relation to a central keynote

a·tone (ə tōn′) *vi.* **a·toned′, a·ton′ing** [ME. *at-onen*, become reconciled < *at one*, in accord] to make amends (*for* wrongdoing, etc.) —**a·ton′er** *n.*

ATOMIZER

a·tone·ment (-mənt) *n.* **1.** an atoning **2.** something done to make up for wrongdoing, etc.; amends **3.** [A-] *Theol.* the reconciliation of God to man by means of Jesus' sufferings and death

a·top (ə täp′) *adv.* on the top; at the top —*prep.* on the top of

-a·to·ry (ə tôr′ē, ə tō′rē) [< L. *-atorius*] *a suffix meaning* of, characterized by, produced by [*accusatory*]

ATP [A(DENOSINE) *t(ri)p(hosphate)*] a vital substance, $C_{10}H_{16}P_3O_{13}N_5$, found in all living cells: it is the immediate source of muscular energy

a·trem·ble (ə trem′b′l) *adv.* [Poet.] trembling

a·tri·um (ā′trē əm) *n., pl.* **a′tri·a** (-ə), **a′tri·ums** [L.] **1.** the main room of an ancient Roman house **2.** a hall or entrance court **3.** *Anat.* a chamber or cavity, esp. either of the upper chambers of the heart: see illustration at HEART —**a′tri·al** (-əl) *adj.*

a·tro·cious (ə trō′shəs) *adj.* [< L. *atrox* (gen. *atrocis*), fierce < *ater*, black + *-ous*] **1.** very cruel, evil, etc. **2.** appalling or dismaying **3.** [Colloq.] very bad, offensive, inferior, etc. [an *atrocious* joke] —see SYN. at OUTRAGEOUS —**a·tro′cious·ly** *adv.* —**a·tro′cious·ness** *n.*

a·troc·i·ty (ə träs′ə tē) *n., pl.* **-ties 1.** atrocious behavior; brutality, etc. **2.** an atrocious act **3.** [Colloq.] a very offensive thing

at·ro·phy (at′rə fē) *n.* [< Fr. < L. < Gr. < *a-*, not + *trephein*, to nourish] a wasting away, or the failure to grow, of an organ, etc., because of insufficient nutrition —*vi.* **-phied, -phy·ing** to waste away or fail to develop —*vt.* to cause atrophy in —**a·troph·ic** (ə träf′ik) *adj.*

at·ro·pine (at′rə pēn′, -pin) *n.* [< ModL. < Gr. *Atropos* (see ATROPOS) + *-INE*[4]] a poisonous, crystalline alkaloid obtained from belladonna and similar plants, used to relieve spasms or to dilate the pupil of the eye: also **at′ro·pin** (-pin)

At·ro·pos (at′rə päs′) *Gr. & Rom. Myth.* that one of the three Fates who cuts the thread of life

att. 1. attention **2.** attorney

at·tach (ə tach′) *vt.* [< OFr. < *estachier* < *estache*, a post] **1.** to fasten by tying, etc. **2.** to cause (oneself or another) to join [he *attached* himself to us] **3.** to bring close together by feelings of love or affection **4.** to affix (a signature, etc.) **5.** to ascribe [I *attach* much meaning to his remark] **6.** *Law* to take (property or a person) into custody by a court order **7.** *Mil.* to join (troops, etc.) temporarily to another unit —*vi.* to be joined; belong [certain duties *attach* to the position] —see SYN. at TIE —**at·tach′a·ble** *adj.*

at·ta·ché (at′ə shā′; *chiefly Brit.* ə tash′ā; *Fr.* à tà shā′) *n.* [Fr., pp. of *attacher*, ATTACH] a person with special duties on the staff of an ambassador or minister

attaché case a flat, rectangular case for carrying documents, papers, etc.

at·tach·ment (ə tach′mənt) *n.* **1.** the act of attaching something **2.** anything that attaches; fastening **3.** devotion **4.** anything attached **5.** an accessory for an electrical appliance, etc. [a power drill with all the *attachments*] **6.** *Law* a taking of a person, property, etc. into custody, or a writ for this —see SYN. at LOVE

ATTACHÉ CASE

at·tack (ə tak′) *vt.* [< Fr. < It. < OFr.: see ATTACH] **1.** to use force against in order to harm **2.** to speak or write against **3.** to begin working on energetically [to *attack* a problem] **4.** to begin acting upon harmfully [the disease *attacked* him suddenly] —*vi.* to make an assault —*n.* **1.** an attacking; onslaught **2.** an onset or return of a disease **3.** a beginning of a task, undertaking, etc. —**at·tack′er** *n.*

at·tain (ə tān′) *vt.* [< OFr. < L. *attingere* < *ad-*, to + *tangere*, to touch] **1.** to gain through effort; achieve [to *attain* fame] **2.** to reach or come to; arrive at [to *attain* a ripe old age] —*vi.* to succeed in reaching or coming (*to* a goal) —see SYN. at REACH —**at·tain′a·bil′i·ty, at·tain′a·ble·ness** *n.* —**at·tain′a·ble** *adj.*

at·tain·der (ə tān′dər) *n.* [OFr. *ataindre*, to attain] the loss of a person's civil rights and property because he has been sentenced to death or outlawed: see BILL OF ATTAINDER

at·tain·ment (ə tān′mənt) *n.* **1.** an attaining or being attained **2.** anything attained; esp., a skill that one has developed; accomplishment

at·taint (ə tānt′) *vt.* **1.** to punish by attainder **2.** [Archaic] to disgrace or dishonor —*n.* an attainder

at·tar (at′ər) *n.* [< Per. < Ar. *'itr*, perfume] a perfume made from the petals of flowers, esp. of damask roses (**attar of roses**)

at·tempt (ə tempt′) *vt.* [< OFr. < L. *attemptare* < *ad-*, to + *temptare*, to try] to try to do, get, etc.; endeavor [to *attempt* a 20-mile hike; we *attempted* to cheer her up] —*n.* **1.** a try; endeavor **2.** an attack, as on a person's life —see SYN. at TRY — **attempt the life of** to try to kill —**at·tempt′a·ble** *adj.*

at·tend (ə tend′) *vt.* [< OFr. < L. *attendere*, to give heed to < *ad-*, to + *tendere*, to stretch: for IE. base see TEND²] **1.** [Now Rare] to take care or charge of **2.** *a)* to wait on; serve *b)* to serve as doctor to during an illness **3.** to go with [*the governor was* attended *by his staff*] **4.** to accompany as a result [*success* attended *his efforts*] **5.** to be present at [*we* attend *school five days a week*] —*vi.* **1.** to pay attention **2.** to wait (*on* or *upon*) **3.** to devote oneself (*to*) **4.** to give the required care or attention (*to*)

at·tend·ance (ə ten′dəns) *n.* **1.** an attending **2.** the number of persons present [*attendance* at the game was more than 30,000] **3.** the degree of regularity in attending [*he has a record of poor* attendance]

at·tend·ant (-dənt) *adj.* **1.** attending or serving [an *attendant* nurse] **2.** being present **3.** accompanying [*attendant* difficulties] —*n.* **1.** one who attends or serves [an *attendant* at the zoo] **2.** a person present **3.** an accompanying thing

at·ten·tion (ə ten′shən) *n.* **1.** *a)* the act of keeping one's mind closely on something; concentration *b)* readiness for concentration **2.** notice or observation [*her smile caught my* attention] **3.** care or consideration **4.** *a)* thoughtful consideration for others *b)* an act of consideration, courtesy, etc.: *usually used in pl.* **5.** *a)* a position of soldiers in which they stand straight and still, as in waiting for a command *b)* a command to take this position

at·ten·tive (ə ten′tiv) *adj.* **1.** paying attention [an *attentive* audience] **2.** courteous, devoted, etc. [an *attentive* husband] —see SYN. at THOUGHTFUL —**at·ten′tive·ly** *adv.* —**at·ten′tive·ness** *n.*

at·ten·u·ate (ə ten′yoo wāt′) *vt.* **-at′ed, -at′ing** [< L. pp. of *attenuare* < *ad-*, to + *tenuare* < *tenuis*, thin] **1.** to make slender or thin **2.** to dilute; rarefy **3.** to lessen or weaken **4.** to reduce the strength of (an electrical impulse) —*vi.* to become thin, weak, etc. —**at·ten′u·a·ble** *adj.* —**at·ten′u·a′tion** *n.* —**at·ten′u·a′tor** *n.*

at·test (ə test′) *vt.* [< Fr. < L. *attestari* < *ad-*, to + *testari*, to bear witness < *testis*, a witness] **1.** to declare to be true or genuine [*the value of the gem was* attested *by a jeweler*] **2.** to certify, as by oath **3.** to serve as proof of —*vi.* to bear witness; testify (*to*) —**at·tes·ta·tion** (at′es tā′shən) *n.* —**at·test′er, at·tes′tor** *n.*

At·tic (at′ik) *adj.* **1.** of Attica **2.** Athenian **3.** classical in a simple, restrained way [an *Attic* style] —*n.* **1.** the Greek dialect of Attica, the literary language of ancient Greece **2.** an Athenian

at·tic (at′ik) *n.* [< Fr. < prec.] **1.** a low wall or story above the cornice of a classical façade **2.** the room or space just below the roof of a house; garret

At·ti·ca (at′i kə) province of SE Greece: in ancient times, a region dominated by Athens: see map at GREECE

At·ti·la (at′l ə, ə til′ə) 406?–453 A.D.; king of the Huns (433?–453)

at·tire (ə tīr′) *vt.* **-tired′, -tir′ing** [< OFr. *atirier*, put in order < *a* (L. *ad*), to + *tire*, row, order] to dress, esp. in fine garments; clothe; array —*n.* clothes, esp. very fine clothes

at·ti·tude (at′ə tood′, -tyood′) *n.* [Fr. < It. < LL. *aptitudo* < L. *aptus*, APT] **1.** the posture of the body in connection with an action, mood, etc. [we knelt in an *attitude* of prayer] **2.** a way of acting, feeling, or thinking; one's disposition, mental set, etc. [a friendly *attitude*] **3.** the position of an aircraft or spacecraft in relation to a given line or plane, as the horizon —**strike an attitude** to act in an affected or theatrical way —**at′ti·tu′di·nal** *adj.*

at·ti·tu·di·nize (at′ə tood′'n īz′, -tyood′-) *vi.* **-nized′, -niz′-ing** to strike an attitude; pose

at·to- [< Dan. *atten*, eighteen] *a combining form meaning* one quintillionth, the factor 10⁻¹⁸ [*attosecond*]

at·tor·ney (ə tur′nē) *n., pl.* **-neys** [< OFr. < *a-* (L. *ad*), to + *torner*: see TURN] any person having the legal power to act for another; esp. (also **attorney at law**), a lawyer —see SYN. at LAWYER

attorney general *pl.* **attorneys general, attorney generals 1.** the chief law officer of a national or State government **2.** [A-G-] the head of the U.S. Department of Justice: he is a member of the President's Cabinet

at·tract (ə trakt′) *vt.* [< L. pp. of *attrahere* < *ad-*, to + *trahere*, to DRAW] **1.** to draw to itself or oneself [a magnet *attracts* iron] **2.** to get the admiration, attention, etc. of; allure —*vi.* to be attractive —**at·tract′a·ble** *adj.* —**at·tract′er, at·trac′tor** *n.* SYN.—**attract** implies the existence of a force such as magnetism to draw a person or thing and suggests that the person or thing is susceptible to the force; **allure** implies attraction by something that offers pleasure, delight, reward, etc.; **charm** suggests such pleasing qualities in a person or thing that they seem to cast a spell; **fascinate** and **enchant** both also suggest a power that seems magical, **fascinate** stressing that the subject is irresistible; **captivate** implies a capturing of the attention or affection, but suggests that it may be only for a brief time —ANT. repel

at·trac·tion (ə trak′shən) *n.* **1.** an attracting or the power of attracting; esp., charm or fascination **2.** anything that attracts **3.** *Physics* the mutual action by which bodies or particles of matter tend to draw together or cohere: opposed to REPULSION

at·trac·tive (-tiv) *adj.* that attracts or has the power to attract; esp., charming, pretty, etc. —**at·trac′tive·ly** *adv.* —**at·trac′-tive·ness** *n.*

attrib. 1. attribute **2.** attributive

at·trib·ute (ə trib′yoot; *for n.* a′trə byoot′) *vt.* **-ut·ed, -ut·ing** [< L. pp. of *attribuere* < *ad-*, to + *tribuere*, to assign < *tribus*: see TRIBE] **1.** to think of as belonging to or coming from a particular person or thing; assign or ascribe (*to*) [a play that is *attributed* to Shakespeare] **2.** to regard as a characteristic or quality [she *attributed* an envious nature to him] —*n.* **1.** a characteristic or quality of a person or thing **2.** an object used in the arts as a symbol for a person, office, etc. [winged feet are the *attribute* of Mercury] **3.** a word or phrase used as an adjective —see SYN. at QUALITY —**at·trib′ut·a·ble** *adj.* —**at′tri·bu′tion** *n.*

at·trib·u·tive (ə trib′yoo tiv) *adj.* **1.** attributing **2.** of or like an attribute **3.** *Gram.* joined directly to the substantive it modifies, esp., in English, coming just before it: said of an adjective —*n.* an attributive adjective, as *black* in *black cat* —**at·trib′u·tive·ly** *adv.*

at·tri·tion (ə trish′ən) *n.* [< L. < pp. of *atterere*, to wear < *ad-*, to + *terere*, to rub] **1.** a wearing away by friction **2.** any gradual wearing, or weakening [a siege is a battle of *attrition*] **3.** loss of personnel in the normal course of events, as because of death, retirement, etc.

at·tune (ə toon′, -tyoon′) *vt.* **-tuned′, -tun′ing 1.** to tune **2.** to bring into harmony or agreement [his methods are not *attuned* to the times]

atty. attorney

a·twit·ter (ə twit′ər) *adv., adj.* twittering

at. wt. atomic weight

a·typ·i·cal (ā tip′i k'l) *adj.* not typical; not characteristic: also **a·typ′ic** —**a·typ′i·cal·ly** *adv.*

Au [L. *aurum*] *Chem.* gold

au·burn (ô′bərn) *adj., n.* [< OFr. < L. *alburnus* < *albus*, white; meaning infl. by ME. *brun*, brown] reddish brown

Auck·land (ôk′lənd) seaport on North Island, New Zealand: pop. 152,000 (met. area 577,000)

‡au cou·rant (ō koo rän′) [Fr., lit., with the current] fully informed; up-to-date

auc·tion (ôk′shən) *n.* [< L. < pp. of *augere*, to increase: see AUGMENT] **1.** a public sale at which each item is sold to the person bidding the highest price **2.** *same as* AUCTION BRIDGE —*vt.* to sell at auction

auction bridge a variety of the game of bridge in which the players bid for the right to say what suit shall be trump or to declare no-trump

auc·tion·eer (ôk′shə nir′) *n.* one whose work is selling things at auction —*vt.* to auction

auc·to·ri·al (ôk tôr′ē əl) *adj.* [< L. *auctor*, author] of or by an author

aud. 1. audit **2.** auditor

au·da·cious (ô dā′shəs) *adj.* [< L. < *audax*, bold < *audere*, to dare] **1.** bold or daring; fearless **2.** rudely bold; brazen; insolent —see SYN. at BRAVE —**au·da′cious·ly** *adv.* —**au·da′cious·ness** *n.*

au·dac·i·ty (ô das′ə tē) *n.* **1.** bold courage; daring **2.** brazen boldness; insolence **3.** *pl.* **-ties** an audacious act or remark —see SYN. at TEMERITY

Au·den (ôd′'n), **W(ystan) H(ugh)** 1907–73; U.S. poet, born in England

au·di·ble (ô′də b'l) *adj.* [< ML. < L. *audire*, to hear] loud enough to be heard [an *audible* sigh] —**au′di·bil′i·ty** *n.* —**au′di·bly** *adv.*

au·di·ence (ô′dē əns) *n.* [ME. & OFr. < L. *audientia*, a hearing < prp. of *audire*, to hear < IE. base *awis-*, to perceive, grasp] **1.** a group assembled to see and hear a play, concert, etc. **2.** those who are tuned in to a certain radio or TV program or who read a certain book ☆**3.** those who pay attention to what one writes or says **4.** a chance to be heard; hearing **5.** a formal interview with a person of high rank

au·di·o (ô′dē ō) *adj.* [< L. *audire*, hear] **1.** of frequencies corresponding to sound waves that can normally be heard by the human ear ☆**2.** of or relating to sound reproduction, esp. to the sound phase of TV

au·di·o-fre·quen·cy (ô′dē ō frē′kwən sē) *adj.* of the band of audible sound frequencies or corresponding electric current frequencies, from about 20 to 20,000 hertz

au·di·ol·o·gy (ô′dē äl′ə jē) *n.* the science of hearing, esp. as it relates to the rehabilitation of persons who have hearing defects —**au′di·o·log′i·cal** (-ə läj′i k'l) *adj.* —**au′di·ol′o·gist** *n.*

au·di·om·e·ter (ô′dē äm′ə tər) *n.* an instrument for measuring hearing

au·di·o·phile (ô′dē ə fīl′) *n.* a devotee of high-fidelity sound reproduction

au·di·o-vis·u·al (ô′dē ō vizh′oo wəl) *adj.* **1.** involving both hearing and sight **2.** designating or of such teaching aids as filmstrips, radio, etc.

au·dit (ô′dit) *n.* [< L. pp. of *audire*, to hear] **1.** a formal, often periodic examination and checking of accounts or financial records **2.** a settlement or adjustment of accounts **3.** an account thus examined and adjusted, or a statement of this —*vt., vi.* **1.** to examine and check (accounts, claims, etc.) ☆**2.** to attend (a college course) as a listener receiving no credits

au·di·tion (ô dish′ən) *n.* **1.** the act or sense of hearing **2.** a hearing to test the ability or fitness of an actor, musician, etc. —☆*vt.* to give an audition to [they *auditioned* several sopranos] —☆*vi.* to perform in an audition [three men *auditioned* for the role]

au·di·tor (ô′də tər) *n.* **1.** a hearer or listener **2.** a person who is authorized to audit accounts ☆**3.** a person who audits a college course

au·di·to·ri·um (ô′də tôr′ē əm) *n.* **1.** a room for an audience, as in a school, library, etc. ☆**2.** a building or hall for speeches, concerts, etc.

au·di·to·ry (ô′də tôr′ē) *adj.* of hearing or the sense of hearing —**au′di·to′ri·ly** *adv.*

Au·drey (ô′drē) [< OE. *æthelthryth*, lit., noble might < *æthel*, noble + *thryth*, might] a feminine name

Au·du·bon (ô′də bän′), **John James** 1785–1851; U.S. naturalist, famous for his paintings of birds

‡**auf Wie·der·se·hen** (ouf vē′dər zā′ən) [G.] till we see each other again; goodbye

Aug. August

Au·ge·an (ô jē′ən) *adj.* **1.** *Gr. Legend* of King Augeas or his large, filthy stable, which Hercules cleaned in one day **2.** very filthy

au·ger (ô′gər) *n.* [by faulty separation of ME. *a nauger* < OE. *nafu*, nave (of a wheel) + *gar*, a spear] **1.** a tool with a spiral cutting edge for boring holes in wood **2.** a similar but larger tool, as for boring in the earth

aught (ôt) *n.* [OE. *awiht* < *a*, one + *wiht*, a creature, WIGHT] **1.** anything whatever [for *aught* I know] **2.** [< *a naught* (see NAUGHT), wrongly divided *an aught*] a zero —*adv.* (Archaic) in any degree

TYPES OF AUGER

aug·ment (ôg ment′) *vt., vi.* [< OFr. < L. *augmentare* < *augere*, to increase < IE. base *aug-*, to multiply] to make or become greater; increase —see SYN. at INCREASE —**aug·ment′a·ble** *adj.* —**aug·ment′er** *n.*

aug·men·ta·tion (ôg′men tā′shən) *n.* **1.** an augmenting or being augmented **2.** an addition; increase

aug·men·ta·tive (ôg men′tə tiv) *adj.* augmenting —*n.* a word or affix that increases the force of meaning of a word, as *up* in "eat up" or *in-* in "inflammable"

au gra·tin (ō grät′'n, ô-; grat′-) [Fr., lit., with scrapings] made with a lightly browned crust of bread crumbs and grated cheese [potatoes *au gratin*]

Augs·burg (ôgz′bərg; *G.* ouks′boork) city in Bavaria, S West Germany: pop. 211,000

au·gur (ô′gər) *n.* [L., orig., a priest at rituals of fertility; prob. < *augere* (see AUGMENT)] **1.** in ancient Rome, any of a group of officials who interpreted omens as favorable or unfavorable for an undertaking **2.** a fortuneteller; soothsayer —*vt., vi.* **1.** to foretell or prophesy **2.** to be an omen (of) [cloudy skies *augur* rain] —**augur ill** (or **well**) to be a bad (or good) omen

au·gu·ry (ô′gyər ē) *n., pl.* **-ries** **1.** the rite conducted by an augur **2.** an omen or sign

Au·gust (ô′gəst) [L. < AUGUSTUS (Caesar)] a masculine name —*n.* the eighth month of the year, having 31 days: abbrev. **Aug., Ag.**

au·gust (ô gust′) *adj.* [L. *augustus*, orig., prob. "consecrated by the augurs"] **1.** inspiring awe and reverence; imposing **2.** worthy of respect; venerable —**au·gust′ly** *adv.* —**au·gust′ness** *n.*

Au·gus·ta (ô gus′tə) [L., fem. of AUGUSTUS] **1.** a feminine name **2.** city in E Ga.: pop. 60,000 **3.** capital of Me.: pop. 22,000

Au·gus·tan (ô gus′tən) *adj.* **1.** of or characteristic of Augustus Caesar, his reign (27 B.C.–14 A.D.), or his times **2.** of or like any similar age, as the early 18th cent. in England; classical; elegant —*n.* a writer living in an Augustan age

Au·gus·tine (ô′gəs tēn′, ô gus′t'n) [< L. dim. of AUGUSTUS] **1.** a masculine name: var. *Austin, Augustin* **2.** Saint *a*) 354–430 A.D.; Christian church father & bishop in North Africa *b*) ?–604? A.D.; Roman monk sent to convert the English to Christianity —**Au′gus·tin′i·an** (-tin′ē ən) *adj., n.*

Au·gus·tus (ô gus′təs) [L. < *augustus*, AUGUST] **1.** a masculine name: dim. *Gus* **2.** (*Gaius Julius Caesar Octavianus*) 63 B.C.–14 A.D.; 1st Roman emperor (27 B.C.–14 A.D.): grandnephew of Julius Caesar: also called *Octavian*

au jus (ō zhōō′, ō jōōs′; *Fr.* ō zhü′) [Fr., with the juice] served in its natural gravy: said of meat

auk (ôk) *n.* [dial. *alk* < ON. *alka*] any of a number of related diving birds of the northern seas, with webbed feet and short wings used as paddles

‡**au lait** (ō le′) [Fr.] with milk

auld (ôld) *adj.* [Dial. & Scot.] old

auld lang syne (ôld′ laŋ′ zīn′, sīn′) [Scot., lit., old long since] old times; the good old days

‡**au na·tu·rel** (ō nà tü rel′) [Fr.] **1.** in the natural state **2.** naked **3.** cooked or served simply

aunt (ant, änt) *n.* [< ME. & OFr. < L. *amita*, paternal aunt] **1.** a sister of one's mother or father **2.** the wife of one's uncle

aunt·ie, aunt·y (an′tē, än′-) *n.* aunt: a familiar or affectionate form

GREAT AUK
(to 30 in. high)

au·ra (ôr′ə) *n., pl.* **-ras, -rae** (-ē) [L. < Gr., akin to *aēr*, air] **1.** an invisible flow or vapor that comes forth from something, as the smell of flowers **2.** a particular atmosphere or quality that seems to arise from and surround a person or thing [an *aura* of gentleness about the old doctor]

au·ral (ôr′əl) *adj.* [< L. *auris*, ear + -AL] of or received through the ear or the sense of hearing —**au′ral·ly** *adv.*

au·re·ate (ôr′ē it) *adj.* [< LL. < L. *aureus* < *aurum*, gold] **1.** golden; gilded **2.** splendid or brilliant, often in a way that is affected

Au·re·li·us (ô rē′lē əs, -rēl′yəs), **Marcus** (*Marcus Aurelius Antoninus*) 121–180 A.D.; Roman emperor (161–180) & Stoic philosopher

au·re·ole (ôr′ē ōl′) *n.* [< L. *aureola* (*corona*), golden (crown) < L. *aureus*: see AUREATE] **1.** a halo **2.** a fringe of light around the sun, as when it is viewed in a mist Also **au·re·o·la** (ô rē′ə lə)

☆**Au·re·o·my·cin** (ôr′ē ō mīs′'n) [< L. *aureus*, golden + Gr. *mykēs*, fungus + -IN′] *a trademark for* CHLORTETRACYCLINE

au re·voir (ō′rə vwär′) [Fr. < *au*, to the + *revoir*, a seeing again < L. < *re-*, again + *videre*, to see] until we meet again; goodbye

au·ri·cle (ôr′ə k'l) *n.* [< L. *auricula*, dim. of *auris*, EAR¹] **1.** *Anat. a*) the external part of the ear; pinna *b*) an atrium of the heart **2.** *Biol.* an earlike part or organ

au·ric·u·lar (ô rik′yoo lər) *adj.* **1.** of or near the ear, or having to do with the sense of hearing **2.** spoken directly into the ear **3.** ear-shaped **4.** *Anat.* of an auricle —**au·ric′u·lar·ly** *adv.*

au·rif·er·ous (ô rif′ər əs) *adj.* [< L. < *aurum*, gold + *ferre*, to BEAR¹ + -OUS] bearing or yielding gold

au·ri·form (ôr′ə fôrm′) *adj.* ear-shaped

au·rochs (ô′räks) *n., pl.* **au′rochs** [G. *auerochs* < OHG. *urohso* < *uro*, aurochs + *ohso*, ox] **1.** the wild ox of Europe, now extinct; urus **2.** the nearly extinct European bison; wisent

Au·ro·ra (ô rôr′ə, ə-) [L., lit., dawn] **1.** *Rom. Myth.* the goddess of dawn **2.** [directly or ultimately after the goddess] *a)* city in NE Ill., near Chicago: pop. 74,000 *b)* city in NC Colo., near Denver: pop. 75,000 —*n.* [a-] *pl.* **-ras, -rae** (-ē) **1.** the dawn **2.** *same as* AURORA AUSTRALIS or AURORA BOREALIS —**au·ro′ral, au·ro′re·an** (-ē ən) *adj.*

aurora aus·tra·lis (ô strā′lis) [L.: see prec. & AUSTRAL] luminous bands of light like the aurora borealis, but in the Southern Hemisphere

aurora bo·re·a·lis (bôr′ē al′is) [L.: see AURORA & BOREAS] luminous bands or streamers of light sometimes appearing in the night sky of the Northern Hemisphere, believed to be electrical discharges in the ionized air; northern lights

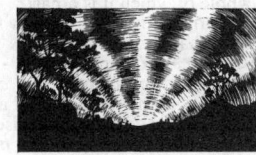
AURORA BOREALIS

Au·schwitz (ou′shvits) city in SW Poland: site of a Nazi concentration camp where millions of victims were killed: Pol. name, OŚWIĘCIM

aus·cul·ta·tion (ôs′kəl tā′shən) *n.* [< pp. of L. *auscultare*, to listen] **1.** a listening **2.** a listening, often with a stethoscope, to sounds in the chest, abdomen, etc., as in a medical examination —**aus′cul·tate′** *vt., vi.* **-tat′ed, -tat′ing** —**aus′cul·ta′tor** *n.*

aus·pice (ôs′pis) *n., pl.* **-pic·es** (-pə sēz′) [Fr. < L. *auspicium*, omen] **1.** an omen, esp. a favorable one **2.** [*pl.*] guiding sponsorship; patronage [a plan under government *auspices*]

aus·pi·cious (ôs pish′əs) *adj.* **1.** of good omen; favorable [his first victory was an *auspicious* beginning to the match] **2.** favored by fortune; successful [on this *auspicious* occasion]—**aus·pi′cious·ly** *adv.* —**aus·pi′cious·ness** *n.*

Aus·ten (ôs′tən), **Jane** 1775–1817; Eng. novelist

aus·tere (ô stir′) *adj.* [< OFr. < L. < Gr. *austēros* < *auos*, dry] **1.** having a stern manner; forbidding **2.** showing strict self-discipline; ascetic **3.** very plain; without luxury [a room with *austere* furnishings]—see SYN. at SEVERE —**aus·tere′ly** *adv.* —**aus·tere′ness** *n.*

aus·ter·i·ty (ô ster′ə tē) *n., pl.* **-ties 1.** an austere quality, state, act, or practice; sternness, strictness, etc. **2.** an economy in which there are shortages, as of consumers' goods

Aus·tin (ôs′tən) **1.** a masculine name: see AUGUSTINE **2.** [after S. F. *Austin*, Am. pioneer in Tex.] capital of Tex., on the Colorado River: pop. 252,000

aus·tral (ôs′trəl) *adj.* [< L. < *auster*, the south] **1.** southern; southerly **2.** [A-] Australian

Aus·tral·a·sia (ôs′trə lā′zhə, -shə) the islands of the SW Pacific; specif., *a)* Australia, New Zealand, and adjacent islands *b)* Australia, New Zealand, the Malay Archipelago, and Oceania —**Aus′tral·a′sian** *adj., n.*

Aus·tral·ia (ô strāl′yə) [< L. (*terra*) *australis*, southern (land)] **1.** island continent between the S Pacific and Indian oceans **2.** country comprising this continent and Tasmania: a member of the Commonwealth; 2,971,081 sq. mi.; pop. 12,446,000; cap. Canberra —**Aus·tral′ian** *adj., n.*

☆**Australian ballot** an official ballot listing candidates for election to public office, marked by the voter in secrecy

Aus·tra·loid (ôs′trə loid′) *adj.* [AUSTRAL(IA) + -OID] designating or of an ethnic group of mankind that includes the Australian aborigines, the Ainu, etc. —*n.* any member of this group

Aus·tri·a (ôs′trē ə) country in C Europe: 32,375 sq. mi.; pop. 7,371,000; cap. Vienna: Ger. name, ÖSTERREICH —**Aus′tri·an** *adj., n.*

Aus·tri·a-Hun·ga·ry (-huŋ′gər ē) former monarchy in C Europe (1867–1918) —**Aus·tro-Hun·gar·i·an** (ôs′trō huŋ ger′-ē ən) *adj.*

Aus·tro-[1] *a combining form meaning* Austria

Aus·tro-[2] [< L. *auster*, south] *a combining form meaning* South, Southern

Aus·tro-A·si·at·ic (ôs′trō ā′zhē at′ik) *adj.* of a family of languages widely scattered throughout SE Asia, including Vietnamese

Aus·tro·ne·sia (ôs′trō nē′zhə, -shə) islands of the Pacific, extending from Madagascar east to Hawaii and Easter Island

Aus·tro·ne·sian (-zhən, -shən) *adj.* **1.** of Austronesia, its people, etc. **2.** *same as* MALAYO-POLYNESIAN

au·tar·chy (ô′tär kē) *n., pl.* **-chies** [< Gr. < *autarchos*, absolute ruler < *autos*, self + *archos*, first, ruler] **1.** absolute rule; autocracy **2.** a country under such rule **3.** *same as* AUTARKY —**au·tar′chic, au·tar′chi·cal** *adj.*

au·tar·ky (ô′tär kē) *n.* [Gr. *autarkeia* < *autos*, self + *arkein*, to suffice] the policy of keeping a nation economically self-sufficient, so that it does not need to import goods —**au·tar′-kic, au·tar′ki·cal** *adj.*

auth. 1. author **2.** authority **3.** authorized

au·then·tic (ô then′tik) *adj.* [< OFr. < LL. < Gr. *authentikos* < *authentēs*, one who does things himself] **1.** that can be believed; reliable [an *authentic* report] **2.** genuine; real [an *authentic* antique] **3.** legally executed, as a deed —**au·then′-ti·cal·ly** *adv.*

au·then·ti·cate (-tə kāt′) *vt.* **-cat′ed, -cat′ing** to establish as authentic, or true, valid, genuine, etc. —see SYN. at CONFIRM —**au·then′ti·ca′tion** *n.* —**au·then′ti·ca′tor** *n.*

au·then·tic·i·ty (ô′thən tis′ə tē) *n.* the condition of being authentic; genuineness

au·thor (ô′thər) *n.* [< OFr. < L. *auctor* < *augere*, to increase: for IE. base see AUGMENT] **1.** one who makes or originates something; creator ["*author* of liberty"] **2.** the writer (of a book, article, etc.) **3.** an author's writings [to translate French *authors* into English] —*vt.* to be the author of —**au′thor·ess** [Now Rare] *n.fem.* —**au·tho·ri·al** (ô thôr′ē əl) *adj.*

au·thor·i·tar·i·an (ə thôr′ə ter′ē ən, -thär′-) *adj.* believing in or characterized by unquestioning obedience to authority rather than individual freedom —*n.* a person who believes in or enforces such obedience —**au·thor′i·tar′i·an·ism** *n.*

au·thor·i·ta·tive (ə thôr′ə tāt′iv, -thär′-) *adj.* **1.** having authority; official **2.** reliable because coming from an authority or expert [an *authoritative* reference book] **3.** asserting authority; dictatorial [he spoke in an *authoritative* manner] —**au·thor′i-ta′tive·ly** *adv.* —**au·thor′i·ta′tive·ness** *n.*

au·thor·i·ty (ə thôr′ə tē, -thär′-) *n., pl.* **-ties** [< OFr. < L. *auctoritas* < *auctor*: see AUTHOR] **1.** *a)* the power or right to give commands, enforce obedience, take action, or make final decisions; jurisdiction *b)* the position of one having such power [the man in *authority*] *c)* such power as delegated; authorization [she has my *authority* to make the choice] **2.** power or influence resulting from knowledge, prestige, etc. **3.** a writing, decision, etc. cited in support of an opinion, action, etc. **4.** *a)* [*pl.*] persons, esp. in government, having the power to enforce orders, laws, etc. *b)* a government agency that administers a project **5.** an expert whose opinion is considered reliable [an *authority* on drugs] **6.** self-assurance that comes with being an expert [he plays the piano with *authority*] —see SYN. at POWER

au·thor·i·za·tion (ô′thər i zā′shən) *n.* **1.** the act of authorizing **2.** legal power or right [do you have *authorization* to hire someone?]

au·thor·ize (ô′thə rīz′) *vt.* **-ized′, -iz′ing 1.** to give official approval to or permission for [who *authorized* that expense?] **2.** to give power or authority to; empower; commission [the mayor *authorized* her to write the report] **3.** to give justification for; warrant [a spelling *authorized* by usage] —**au′thor·iz′-er** *n.*

Authorized Version the revised English translation of the Bible published in England in 1611 with the authorization of King James I: also called *King James Version*

au·thor·ship (ô′thər ship′) *n.* **1.** the profession of a writer **2.** the origin (of a book, idea, etc.) with reference to its author or originator [a story of unknown *authorship*]

☆**au·tis·tic** (ô tis′tik) *adj.* [AUT(O)- + -ISTIC] of or in a state of emotional disorder in which there is extreme mental withdrawal from the people and things around one [an *autistic* child] —**au′tism** *n.*

☆**au·to** (ôt′ō) *n., pl.* **-tos** an automobile —*vi.* **-toed, -to·ing** to go by automobile: an earlier usage

au·to- [Gr. *autos*, self] *a combining form meaning:* **1.** of or for oneself; self [*autobiography*] **2.** by oneself or itself [*automobile*] Also, before a vowel, **aut-**

‡**Au·to·bahn** (ou′tō bän′; E. ôt′ə bän′) *n., pl.* **-bahn′en** (-bä′nən); E. **-bahns′** [G.] in Germany, an automobile expressway

au·to·bi·og·ra·phy (ôt′ə bī äg′rə fē, -bē-) *n., pl.* **-phies** the story of one's own life written or dictated by oneself —**au′to·bi·og′ra·pher** *n.* —**au′to·bi′o·graph′i·cal** (-bī′ə graf′i k'l), **au′to·bi′o·graph′ic** *adj.* —**au′to·bi′o·graph′i·cal·ly** *adv.*

au·to·clave (ôt′ə klāv′) *n.* [Fr. < *auto-*, AUTO- + L. *clavis*, a key] a container for sterilizing, cooking, etc. by superheated steam under pressure —*vt.* **-claved′, -clav′ing** to sterilize, etc. in this

au·toc·ra·cy (ô täk′rə sē) *n., pl.* **-cies** [< Gr. < *autokratēs:* see AUTOCRAT] **1.** a government in which one person has supreme power; dictatorship **2.** unlimited power or authority over others

au·to·crat (ôt′ə krat′) *n.* [< Fr. < Gr. *autokratēs*, absolute ruler < *autos*, self + *kratos*, power] **1.** a ruler with absolute power; dictator; despot **2.** anyone having unlimited power over others **3.** any domineering, self-willed person —**au′to·crat′ic**, **au′to·crat′i·cal** *adj.* —**au′to·crat′i·cal·ly** *adv.*

au·to·da·fé (ôt′ō də fā′, out′-) *n., pl.* **au′tos-da-fé′** [Port., lit., act of the faith] **1.** the public ceremony in which the Inquisition judged and sentenced those tried as heretics **2.** the carrying out of the sentence; esp., the public burning of a person judged to be a heretic

au·tog·a·my (ô täg′ə mē) *n.* [AUTO- + -GAMY] the process of self-fertilization, as in a flower receiving pollen from its own stamens —**au·tog′a·mous** *adj.*

au·to·gi·ro, au·to·gy·ro (ôt′ə jī′rō) *n., pl.* **-ros** [orig. a trademark < AUTO- + Gr. *gyros*, a circle] an earlier kind of aircraft having both a propeller and a large horizontal rotor

au·to·graph (ôt′ə graf′) *n.* [< L. < Gr. *autographos* < *autos*, self + *graphein*, to write] **1.** something written in a person's own handwriting; esp., a signature **2.** a thing written in one's own handwriting; holograph —*vt.* **1.** to write (something) with one's own hand **2.** to write one's signature on or in —**au′to·graph′ic**, **au′to·graph′i·cal** *adj.* —**au′to·graph′i·cal·ly** *adv.*

☆**au·to·harp** (ôt′ō härp′) *n.* [AUTO- + HARP] a type of zither for accompanying a singer, on which chords can be played by means of a series of dampers worked by keys

au·to·hyp·no·sis (ôt′ō hip nō′sis) *n.* a hypnotizing of oneself or the state of being so hypnotized

au·to·in·tox·i·ca·tion (-in täk′sə kā′shən) *n.* poisoning by substances formed within the body

au·to·mat (ôt′ə mat′) *n.* [see AUTOMATIC] a restaurant in which patrons get food from small compartments opened by putting coins into slots

AUTOHARP

☆**au·to·mate** (ôt′ə māt′) *vt.* **-mat′ed, -mat′ing** [back-formation < AUTOMATION] **1.** to convert (a factory, process, etc.) to automation **2.** to use the techniques of automation in [*automated* teaching]

au·to·mat·ic (ôt′ə mat′ik) *adj.* [Gr. *automatos*, self-moving] **1.** done without conscious thought, as if mechanically, or from force of habit [his *automatic* refusal] **2.** involuntary or reflex, as some muscle action **3.** *a)* moving, operating, etc. by itself [*automatic* machinery] *b)* done with automatic equipment [*automatic* navigation] **4.** *Firearms* using the force of the explosion of a shell to eject, reload, and fire again, so that shots continue in rapid succession with one trigger pull: cf. SEMI-AUTOMATIC —*n.* **1.** an automatic pistol, rifle, etc. **2.** any automatic machine —see SYN. at SPONTANEOUS —**au′to·mat′i·cal·ly** *adv.*

☆**au·to·ma·tion** (ôt′ə mā′shən) *n.* [AUTOMA(TIC) + -TION] **1.** in manufacturing, a system or method in which many or all of the processes are automatically performed or controlled by machinery, electronic devices, etc. **2.** any system using equipment to replace people **3.** the state of being automated

au·tom·a·tism (ô täm′ə tiz′m) *n.* **1.** the quality or condition of being automatic **2.** automatic action **3.** *Physiol.* action that takes place without outside stimulus or conscious control

au·tom·a·tize (-tīz′) *vt.* **-tized′, -tiz′ing 1.** to make automatic **2.** *same as* AUTOMATE —**au·tom′a·ti·za′tion** *n.*

au·tom·a·ton (ô täm′ə tän′, -tən) *n., pl.* **-tons′, -ta** (-tə) [Gr., neut. of *automatos:* see AUTOMATIC] **1.** anything that can move or act of itself **2.** an apparatus that works or moves by responding to preset controls or computerized instructions **3.** a person acting in a mechanical way

☆**au·to·mo·bile** (ôt′ə mə bēl′, -mō-; ôt′ə mə bēl′; ôt′ə mō′bēl) *n.* [Fr.: see AUTO- & MOBILE] a passenger car propelled

by an engine, esp. an internal-combustion engine, and used for traveling on streets or roads; motorcar

au·to·mo·tive (ôt′ə mōt′iv) *adj.* [AUTO- + -MOTIVE] **1.** moving by its own power; self-moving **2.** of or having to do with motor vehicles

au·to·nom·ic (ôt′ə näm′ik) *adj.* **1.** of or controlled by the autonomic nervous system **2.** *Biol.* resulting from internal causes, as through a mutation —**au′to·nom′i·cal·ly** *adv.*

autonomic nervous system the divisions of the nervous system that control the motor functions of the heart, lungs, intestines, smooth muscles, glands, etc.

au·ton·o·mous (ô tän′ə məs) *adj.* [< Gr. < *autos*, self + *nomos*, law] **1.** of an autonomy **2.** *a)* having self-government *b)* existing, functioning, or developing independently of the whole of which it is a part

au·ton·o·my (-mē) *n.* **1.** self-government **2.** *pl.* **-mies** any state that governs itself

au·top·sy (ô′täp′sē) *n., pl.* **-sies** [< ML. & Gr. *autopsia*, a seeing with one's own eyes < *autos*, self + *opsis*, a sight] an examination and dissection of a dead body to discover the cause of death, damage done by a disease, etc.; post-mortem

au·to·some (ôt′ə sōm′) *n.* [AUTO- + (CHROMO)SOME] any chromosome that is not a sex chromosome

au·to·sug·ges·tion (ôt′ō səg jes′chən) *n.* suggestion to oneself arising within one's own mind and having effects on one's thinking and bodily function

au·tumn (ôt′əm) *n.* [< OFr. < L. *autumnus;* prob. of Etruscan origin] **1.** the season that comes between summer and winter; fall **2.** any period of maturity or of beginning decline [the *autumn* of the actor's career] —*adj.* of, in, characteristic of, or like autumn [*autumn* leaves] —**au·tum·nal** (ô tum′n'l) *adj.* —**au·tum′nal·ly** *adv.*

aux. auxiliary

aux·il·ia·ry (ôg zil′yər ē, -zil′ər-) *adj.* [< L. < *auxilium*, aid < pp. of *augere*, AUGMENT] **1.** giving help or aid; assisting **2.** acting in a lesser but helpful way; additional; supplementary; reserve [a sailboat with an *auxiliary* engine] —*n., pl.* **-ries 1.** an auxiliary person or thing **2.** [*pl.*] foreign troops aiding a country at war **3.** a supplementary group or organization [a women's *auxiliary*]

auxiliary verb a verb that helps form tenses, moods, or voices of other verbs, as *have, be, may, can, must, do, shall, will* [In the sentence "You must come," "must" is an *auxiliary* verb]

Av., av. avenue

av. 1. average **2.** avoirdupois

A.V. Authorized Version (of the Bible)

a·vail (ə vāl′) *vi., vt.* [< OFr. *a* (L. *ad*), to + *valoir*, to be worth < L. *valere*, to be strong: see VALUE] to be of use, help, worth, or advantage (to), as in accomplishing an end [force alone will not *avail* us] —*n.* effective use or help; advantage [of no *avail*] —**avail oneself of** to take advantage of (an opportunity, etc.); utilize

a·vail·a·ble (ə vā′lə b'l) *adj.* **1.** that can be used [use any *available* excuse] **2.** that can be got, had, or reached; accessible [he is *available* at his office Fridays] ☆**3.** qualified and willing to run for public office —**a·vail′a·bil′i·ty** *n.* —**a·vail′a·bly** *adv.*

av·a·lanche (av′ə lanch′) *n.* [Fr. (altered after *avaler*, to descend) < *lavanche* < LL. < L. < *labi*, to slip, glide down] **1.** a large mass of loosened snow, earth, rocks, etc. suddenly and swiftly sliding down a mountain **2.** anything that comes suddenly in overwhelming number [an *avalanche* of mail] —*vi., vt.* **-lanched′, -lanch′ing** to come down (on) like an avalanche

Av·a·lon (av′ə län′) [Fr. < ML. < W. (*ynys yr*) *Afallon*, (island of) apples] in Celtic legend, an island paradise in the west where King Arthur and other heroes were taken after death

a·vant-garde (ä vänt′gärd′; Fr. à vän gàrd′) *n.* [Fr., lit., advance guard] the leaders in new or unconventional movements, esp. in the arts; vanguard —*adj.* of such movements, ideas, etc. —**a·vant′-gard′ism** *n.* —**a·vant′-gard′ist** *n.*

av·a·rice (av′ər is) *n.* [< OFr. < L. < *avarus*, greedy < *avere*, to desire] too great a desire to have wealth; greed for riches; cupidity

av·a·ri·cious (av′ə rish′əs) *adj.* full of avarice; greedy for riches —see SYN. at GREEDY —**av′a·ri′cious·ly** *adv.* —**av′a·ri′cious·ness** *n.*

a·vast (ə vast′) *interj.* [< Du. *houd vast*, hold fast] *Naut.* stop! cease! halt!

av·a·tar (av′ə tär′) *n.* [Sans. *avatāra*, descent] **1.** *Hinduism* a god's coming down in bodily form to the earth; incarnation **2.** any embodiment, as of a quality in a person [he is the very *avatar* of democracy]

a·vaunt (ə vônt′, -vänt′) *interj.* [< OFr. < L. *ab*, from + *ante*, before] [Archaic] begone! go away!

avdp. avoirdupois

a·ve (ä′vā, ä′vē) *interj.* [L., imperative of *avere*, to be well] **1.** hail! **2.** farewell! —*n.* **1.** the salutation *ave* **2.** [A-] the prayer AVE MARIA

Ave., ave. avenue

A·ve Ma·ri·a (ä′vā mə rē′ə, -vē) [L. (Luke 1:28)] **1.** "Hail, Mary," the first words of a prayer to the Virgin Mary used in the Roman Catholic Church **2.** this prayer **3.** a musical setting of this

a·venge (ə venj′) *vt.*, *vi.* **a·venged′**, **a·veng′ing** [< OFr. < *a-* (L. *ad*), to + *vengier* < L. *vindicare*, to claim: see VINDICATE] **1.** to get revenge for (an injury, wrong, etc.) **2.** to take vengeance on behalf of, as for a wrong [Hamlet *avenged* his murdered father] —**a·veng′er** *n.*
SYN.—**avenge** and **revenge** both refer to the inflicting of punishment for a wrong done, but **avenge** suggests that the motive is a wish to see justice done, whereas **revenge** implies that one wishes to get even, usually for an injury against oneself, and suggests bitter feelings of hatred and resentment

av·e·nue (av′ə noo̅′, -nyoo̅′) *n.* [Fr. < L. *advenire*: see AD-VENT] **1.** a road, path, or drive, often one bordered with trees **2.** a way of approach to something [books are *avenues* to knowledge] ☆**3.** a street, esp. a wide, principal one

a·ver (ə vur′) *vt.* **a·verred′**, **a·ver′ring** [< OFr. *averrer* < L. *ad*, to + *verus*, true] **1.** to declare to be true; affirm **2.** *Law* to state or declare formally; assert; allege —**a·ver′ment** *n.*

av·er·age (av′rij, av′ər ij) *n.* [< Fr. *avarie*, damage to a ship < It. < Ar. *'awār*, damaged goods; sense development from *n.* 4] **1.** the number obtained by dividing the sum of two or more quantities by the number of quantities; an arithmetic mean [the *average* of 7, 9, and 17 is 33÷3, or 11] **2.** any similar value [a grade *average* of C] **3.** the usual or normal kind, amount, quality, etc. [her intelligence is above the *average*] **4.** *Marine Law a)* a loss caused by damage to a ship or its cargo *b)* the even division of such a loss among the interested parties —*adj.* **1.** being a numerical average **2.** usual; normal; ordinary [the *average* weather] —*vi.* **-aged, -ag·ing 1.** to be or amount to on the average **2.** to buy or sell more shares, goods, etc. at intervals so as to get a better average price —*vt.* **1.** to calculate the average or mean of **2.** to do, take, etc. on the average [to *average* eight hours of sleep a night] **3.** to divide proportionately among more than two —**average out** to arrive at an average eventually —**on the** (or **an**) **average** as an average quantity, rate, etc. [he works 40 hours a week *on the average*]

A·ver·nus (ə vur′nəs) **1.** a small lake in an extinct volcano near Naples, Italy: the ancient Romans imagined the entrance to Hades to be near this lake **2.** *same as* HADES

a·verse (ə vurs′) *adj.* [< L. pp. of *avertere*, AVERT] not willing; opposed (*to*) [he is *averse* to quarreling] —see SYN. at RELUCTANT —**a·verse′ly** *adv.* —**a·verse′ness** *n.*

a·ver·sion (ə vur′zhən, -shən) *n.* **1.** a strong or definite dislike; antipathy; repugnance **2.** the object arousing such dislike
SYN.—**aversion** and **antipathy** both imply an instinctive dislike of something unpleasant or offensive, **aversion** suggesting that one seeks to avoid it and **antipathy** suggesting actual hostility; **repugnance** implies a feeling of deep distaste for something which does not agree with one's tastes, ideas, etc.; **abhorrence** indicates a feeling of disgust, often in reacting to something that is felt to be highly immoral; **loathing** and **revulsion** indicate extreme disgust, with **revulsion** suggesting an actual drawing back or a feeling of nausea —**ANT.** attraction, affinity

a·vert (ə vurt′) *vt.* [< L. *avertere* < *a-* (*ab-*), from + *vertere*, to turn: see VERSE] **1.** to turn away [to *avert* one's eyes] **2.** to keep from happening; avoid; prevent [better apologize to *avert* a catastrophe] —see SYN. at PREVENT —**a·vert′i·ble** *adj.*

A·ves·ta (ə ves′tə) *n.* [< Per.] the sacred writings of Zoroastrianism, in an ancient Iranian language —**A·ves′tan** *adj.*, *n.*

avg. average

☆**av·gas** (av′gas′) *n.* [AV(IATION) GAS(OLINE)] gasoline for aircraft

a·vi·an (ā′vē ən) *adj.* [< L. *avis*, bird + -AN] of or having to do with birds

a·vi·ar·y (ā′vē er′ē) *n.*, *pl.* **-ar·ies** [< L. < *avis*, bird] a large cage or building for keeping many birds

a·vi·a·tion (ā′vē ā′shən) *n.* [Fr. < L. *avis*, bird] **1.** the art or science of flying airplanes **2.** the development and operation of heavier-than-air craft **3.** military aircraft, collectively

a·vi·a·tor (ā′vē āt′ər) *n.* an airplane pilot; flier —**a′vi·a·trix** (-ā′triks) *n.fem.*

a·vi·cul·ture (ā′və kul′chər, av′ə-) *n.* [< L. *avis*, bird + *cultura*, culture] the raising and care of birds —**a′vi·cul′tur·ist** *n.*

av·id (av′id) *adj.* [L. *avidus* < *avere*, to desire] **1.** having an intense desire or craving; greedy [*avid* for power] **2.** eager and enthusiastic [an *avid* reader] —**a·vid·i·ty** (ə vid′ə tē) *n.* —**av′id·ly** *adv.*

A·vi·gnon (à vē nyôn′) city in SE France: seat of the popes (1309–77): pop. 73,000

a·vi·on·ics (ā′vē än′iks) *n.pl.* [AVI(ATION) + (ELECTR)ONICS] [*with sing. v.*] the branch of electronics dealing with the use of electronic equipment in aviation and astronautics —**a′vi·on′ic** *adj.*

☆**av·o·ca·do** (av′ə kä′dō, äv′-) *n.*, *pl.* **-dos** [Sp. < MexSp. *aguacate* < Nahuatl *ahuacatl*] **1.** a thick-skinned, pear-shaped tropical fruit, yellowish green to purplish black, with a single large seed and yellow, buttery flesh, used in salads; alligator pear **2.** the tree that it grows on

av·o·ca·tion (av′ə kā′shən) *n.* [< L. pp. of *avocare* < *ab-*, away + *vocare*, to call] something one does in addition to his regular work, and usually for pleasure; hobby [Dr. Miller makes pottery as an *avocation*] —**av′o·ca′tion·al** *adj.*

av·o·cet (av′ə set′) *n.* [< Fr. < It.] a long-legged wading bird with webbed feet and a slender bill that curves upward

AVOCADO

A·vo·ga·dro's law (äv′ə gä′drōz) the theory that equal volumes of all gases under identical conditions of temperature and pressure contain equal numbers of molecules: formulated by Amedeo Avogadro (1776–1856), It. chemist & physicist

a·void (ə void′) *vt.* [< Anglo-Fr. < OFr. *esvuidier*, to empty < *es-* (< L. *ex*), out + *vuidier*: see VOID] **1.** to make void; annul, invalidate, or quash (a plea, etc. in law) **2.** to keep away from; shun [to *avoid* crowds] **3.** to keep from happening [remove your boots to *avoid* dirtying the floor] —see SYN. at ESCAPE —**a·void′a·ble** *adj.* —**a·void′a·bly** *adv.* —**a·void′ance** *n.*

AVOCET
(to 18 in. high)

av·oir·du·pois (av′ər də poiz′, av′ər də poiz′) *n.* [< OFr. *aveir de peis*, goods having weight] **1.** *same as* AVOIRDUPOIS WEIGHT ☆**2.** [Colloq.] heaviness or weight, esp. of a person

avoirdupois weight an English and American system of weights based on a pound of 16 ounces: see TABLES OF WEIGHTS AND MEASURES in Supplements

A·von (ā′vən, -vän; av′ən) any of three rivers in England: Stratford, Shakespeare's birthplace, is on the Avon in the SW part of England

a·vouch (ə vouch′) *vt.* [< OFr. *avochier* < L. *advocare*: see AD-VOCATE] **1.** to vouch for; guarantee **2.** to declare the truth of; affirm **3.** to acknowledge openly; avow —**a·vouch′ment** *n.*

a·vow (ə vou′) *vt.* [< OFr. *avouer* < L. *advocare*: see ADVOCATE] **1.** to declare openly or admit frankly [she *avowed* that she had not read the book] **2.** to acknowledge or claim (oneself) to be [he *avowed* himself a patriot] —see SYN. at ACKNOWLEDGE

a·vow·al (ə vou′əl) *n.* an open declaration or admission

a·vowed (ə voud′) *adj.* openly declared or frankly admitted [his *avowed* goal] —**a·vow·ed·ly** (ə vou′id lē) *adv.*

a·vun·cu·lar (ə vuŋ′kyə lər) *adj.* [< L. *avunculus*, maternal uncle, dim. of *avus*, ancestor: for IE. base see UNCLE] of, like, or in the relationship of, an uncle

aw (ô, ä) *interj.* an exclamation of protest, dislike, disgust, sympathy, etc.

a·wait (ə wāt′) *vt.* [< ONormFr. < *a-* (L. *ad*), to + *waitier*, WAIT] **1.** to wait for; expect [I *await* your call] **2.** to be in store for; be ready for [a thrill *awaits* you] —*vi.* to wait —see SYN. at EXPECT

a·wake (ə wāk′) **vt. a·woke′** or **a.waked′, a.waked′,
a.wak′ing**; occas. Brit. pp. **a·woke′** or **a·wok′en** [< OE. *awa-
can* (on- + *wacan*, to arise, awake) & OE. *awacian* (on- + *wacian*, to be awake, watch)] **1.** to rouse from sleep; wake **2.** to
rouse from inactivity; stir up **3.** to call forth (memories, etc.) —
vi. 1. to come out of sleep; wake **2.** to become active **3.** to
become aware (with *to*) —**adj. 1.** not asleep **2.** active or alert
a·wak·en (ə wāk′'n) **vt., vi.** to awake; wake up; rouse —see
SYN. at STIR¹ —**a·wak′en·er** n.
a·wak·en·ing (-iŋ) **n., adj. 1.** (a) waking up **2.** (an) arousing,
as of impulses, interest, etc.
a·ward (ə wôrd′) **vt.** [< Anglo-Fr. < ONormFr. < *es-* (< L. *ex*)
+ Gmc. *wardon*: see GUARD, n.] **1.** to give by the decision of a
law court or arbitrator [to *award* damages] **2.** to give as the result of judging, as in a contest [to *award* prizes] —**n. 1.** a
decision, as by a judge **2.** something awarded; prize
a·ware (ə wer′) **adj.** [< OE. *gewær* < *wær*, cautious] **1.** orig.,
on one's guard **2.** knowing or realizing; conscious; informed
[I'm not *aware* of any difference] —**a·ware′ness** n.
SYN. —**aware** implies having knowledge of something as a result of paying close attention to what occurs around one [*aware* of muffled footsteps outside]; **conscious** suggests a less precise recognition of some sensation, feeling, fact, etc. [*conscious* of a draft in the room]; **cognizant** implies knowledge gotten by deliberate mental effort [*cognizant* of the
terms of the will]; **sensible** suggests awareness of something not openly
expressed [*sensible* of her unspoken gratitude]
a·wash (ə wôsh′, -wäsh′) **adv., adj. 1.** just above the surface
of the water so that waves, tide, etc. flow over **2.** floating on
the water **3.** flooded with water
a·way (ə wā′) **adv.** [< OE. *aweg* < *on*, on + *weg*, way] **1.** from
any given place; off [to run *away*] **2.** in another place, esp. the
proper place [put tools *away*] **3.** in another direction [look
away] **4.** far [*away* behind] **5.** off; aside [to clear snow *away*]
6. from one's possession [give it *away*] **7.** out of existence [to
fade *away*] **8.** at once [fire *away*] **9.** without stopping [to work
away all night] **10.** into action [*away* we go!] —**adj. 1.** absent;
gone [she is *away*] **2.** at a distance [a mile *away*] **☆3.** not
played on the home team's field [an *away* game] **☆4.** *Baseball*
out [one *away* in this inning] —**interj. 1.** begone! **2.** let's go! —
away with 1. take away [*away with* the knave!] **2.** go or come
away [*away with* you!] —**do away with 1.** to get rid of **2.** to kill
awe (ô) **n.** [ON. *agi* < IE. base *agh-*, to be afraid] deep respect
mixed with fear and wonder —**vt. awed, aw′ing** to inspire awe
in; fill with awe [we were *awed* by the force of the hurricane] —
stand (or **be**) **in awe of** to respect and fear
SYN. —**awe** indicates a feeling of deep respect mixed with fear felt for
that which is so majestic, powerful, etc. that it overwhelms one; **reverence** refers to a feeling of deep respect and love for something considered to be sacred or of the highest worth and suggests that this feeling is
shown in acts of courtesy and honor; **veneration** implies the deepest
kind of reverence felt for a person or thing and often suggests acts of religious devotion
a·weigh (ə wā′) **adj.** *Naut.* just clear of the bottom: said of an
anchor that is being weighed
awe·some (ô′səm) **adj. 1.** inspiring awe **2.** showing awe —
awe′some·ly adv. —**awe′some·ness** n.
awe-struck (ô′struk′) **adj.** filled with awe or wonder: also
awe′-strick′en (-strik′'n)
aw·ful (ô′fəl) **adj.** [see AWE & -FUL] **1.** inspiring awe [his *awful*
majesty] **2.** causing fear; terrifying [an *awful* massacre] **3.**
[colloq.] *a)* very bad, unpleasant, etc. [an *awful* joke] *b)* great
[an *awful* bore] —**☆adv.** [Colloq.] very; extremely [*awful*
happy] —**aw′ful·ness** n.
aw·ful·ly (ô′fə lē, ô′flē) **adv. 1.** in a way to inspire awe **☆2.**
[Colloq.] badly or offensively [to behave *awfully*] **3.** [Colloq.]
very; extremely [I'm *awfully* glad you came]
a·while (ə wīl′, -hwīl′) **adv.** for a while; for a short time [stop
and rest *awhile*]
awk·ward (ôk′wərd) **adj.** [< ON. *ofugr*,
turned backward + OE. *-weard*, -WARD]
1. not having grace or skill; clumsy;
bungling [that was an *awkward* catch]
2. hard to handle and use; unwieldy [an
awkward tool] **3.** inconvenient; uncomfortable [an *awkward* position] **4.** embarrassed or embarrassing [an *awkward*
remark] **5.** not easy to deal with; delicate [an *awkward* situation] —**awk′-
ward·ly** adv. —**awk′ward·ness** n.
awl (ôl) **n.** [< OE. *æl, awel* < IE. base
ela] a small, pointed tool for making
holes in wood, leather, etc.

AWL

awn (ôn) **n.** [ON. *ǫgn*, chaff: for IE. base see ACID] any of the
bristly fibers on a head of barley, oats, etc., or,
usually, such fibers collectively; beard —**awned**
adj. —**awn′less** adj.
awn·ing (ô′niŋ) **n.** [< ? MFr. *auvans*, pl. of *au-
vent*, window shade] a structure of canvas, metal,
etc. extended before a window or door or over a
patio, deck, etc. as a protection from sun or rain
a·woke (ə wōk′) *alt. pt. & occas. Brit. pp.* of
AWAKE
a·wok·en (ə wōk′'n) *occas. Brit. pp.* of AWAKE
☆A·WOL, a·wol (ā′wôl′) **adj.** [*a(bsent)
w(ith)o(ut) l(eave)] *Mil.* absent without leave, but
with no intention of deserting —**n.** one who is
AWOL

AWN

a·wry (ə rī′) **adv., adj.** [see A-¹ (sense 1) & WRY]
1. with a twist to a side; askew **2.** wrong; amiss [our plans
went *awry*]
ax, axe (aks) **n., pl. ax′es** [OE. *eax, æx* < IE. base *agw(e)si*] **1.**
a tool with a long handle and a metal head with a blade, for
chopping trees and splitting wood **2.** any similar tool or
weapon, as a battle-ax —**vt. axed, ax′ing 1.** to trim, split, etc.
with an ax **2.** to get rid of —**☆get the ax** [Colloq.] **1.** to be beheaded **2.** to be discharged from one's job —**☆have an ax to
grind** [Colloq.] to have a special reason of one's own for being
involved in something
ax·es (ak′siz) **n.** pl. of AX
ax·es² (ak′sēz) **n.** pl. of AXIS
ax·i·al (ak′sē əl) **adj. 1.** of, like, or forming an axis **2.** around
or along an axis —**ax′i·al·ly** adv.
ax·il (ak′sil) **n.** [< L. *axilla*: see AXILLA] the upper angle between a leaf, twig, etc. and the stem from which it grows
ax·il·la (ak sil′ə) **n., pl. -lae** (-ē), -**las** [L., armpit] **1.** the armpit **2.** *Bot.* an axil
ax·il·lar (ak′sə lər) **adj.** *same as* AXILLARY —**n.** any one of the
stiff feathers on the underside of a bird's wing
ax·il·la·ry (ak′sə ler′ē) **adj. 1.** *Anat.* of or near the axilla **2.**
Bot. of, in, or growing from an axil —**n., pl. -ries** *same as* AXIL-
LAR
ax·i·om (ak′sē əm) **n.** [< Fr. < L. < Gr. *axiōma*, authority <
axios, worthy] **1.** a statement widely accepted as true; truism
2. an established principle or law of a science, art, etc. **3.** *Logic,
Math.* a statement that needs no proof because its truth is obvious, or one accepted as true without proof [it is an *axiom* that
things equal to the same thing are equal to each other]
ax·i·o·mat·ic (ak′sē ə mat′ik) **adj. 1.** of or like an axiom; obvious **2.** full of axioms —**ax′i·o·mat′i·cal·ly** adv.
ax·is (ak′sis) **n., pl. ax′es** (-sēz) [L. < IE. base *aks-*] **1.** a real
or imaginary straight line on which an object rotates or is regarded as rotating [the earth's *axis*] **2.** a real or imaginary
straight line around which the parts of a thing, system, etc. are
arranged in a balanced way **3.** a straight line for reference or
measurement, as in a graph [x-*axis*, y-*axis*] **4.** *Bot., Zool.* any
of various axial or central parts, as the main stem of a plant —
the Axis the countries that were joined against the United Nations in World War II, chiefly Germany and Italy, and later
Japan
ax·le (ak′s'l) **n.** [< AXLETREE] **1.** a rod on which a wheel turns,
or one connected to a wheel so that they turn together **2.** a bar
connecting opposite wheels, as of an automobile
ax·le·tree (-trē′) **n.** [< ON. < *oxull*, axle (for IE. base see AXIS)
+ *tre*, tree, beam] a bar connecting two opposite wheels of a
carriage, wagon, etc.
Ax·min·ster (aks′min stər) **n.** [< *Axminster*, town in
England] a type of patterned carpet with a cut pile
ax·o·lotl (ak′sə lät′'l) **n.** [< Nahuatl, lit., water toy] a salamander of Mexico and the western U.S. that matures sexually
while remaining in the larval stage
ax·on (ak′sän) **n.** [ModL. < Gr. *axōn*, AXIS] that part of a
nerve cell that has no branches and through which impulses
travel away from the cell body
ay·ah (ä′yə) **n.** [< Hindi < Port. *aia*, governess] a native nurse-
maid or lady's maid in India
ay·a·tol·lah (ī′ə tō′lə) **n.** [Ar., lit., sign of God] a leader of one
of the sects of the Moslem religion, serving as teacher, judge,
and administrator
aye¹ (ā) **adv.** [ON. *ei*: for IE. base see AGE] [Poet.] always;
ever: also sp. **ay**
aye² (ī) **adv.** [< ? prec.] yes; yea —**n.** a vote of "yes" or a person
so voting Also sp. **ay** —**aye, aye** I understand and will obey:
used by sailors in response to a command

aye-aye (ī′ī′) *n.* [Fr. < Malagasy: echoic of its cry] a lemur of Madagascar, with shaggy fur, large ears, fingerlike claws, and a long, bushy tail

Ayr·shire (er′shir) *n.* [orig. bred in the county of *Ayr*, in Scotland] any of a breed of reddish-brown and white dairy cattle

AZ Arizona

a·zal·ea (ə zāl′yə) *n.* [ModL. < Gr. fem. of *azaleos*, dry: because it thrives in dry soil] 1. any of several rhododendrons, having flowers of various colors and leaves that are usually shed in the fall 2. the flower of any of these plants

Az·er·bai·jan (äz′ər bī jän′, az′-) 1. region of NW Iran 2. republic of the U.S.S.R., on the Caspian Sea: 33,436 sq. mi.; pop. 4,900,000; cap. Baku: in full, **Azerbaijan Soviet Socialist Republic** Also sp. **Azerbaidzhan, Azerbaydzhan**

Az·er·bai·ja·ni (-jä′nē) *n., pl.* **-nis, -ni** 1. a native or inhabitant of Azerbaijan 2. the Turkic dialect spoken there

az·i·muth (az′ə məth) *n.* [< OFr. < Ar. *as-sumūt* < *al*, the + *sumūt*, pl. of *samt*, way, path] *Astron., Surveying,* etc. distance in angular degrees in a clockwise direction from the north point

AYE-AYE
(34–41 in. long, including tail)

or, in the Southern Hemisphere, south point —**az·i·muth·al** (az′ə muth′əl) *adj.*

az·o (az′ō, ā′zō) *adj.* [< *azote*, obs. name for nitrogen] containing the nitrogen radical -N:N- *[azo dyes]:* used also as a prefix, **az·o-**

A·zores (ā′zôrz, ə zôrz′) group of Portuguese islands in the N Atlantic, west of Portugal

A·zov (ā′zôf; *Russ.* ä′zôf), **Sea of** northern arm of the Black Sea, in S European U.S.S.R.

Az·tec (az′tek) *n.* [< Nahuatl *Aztatlán*, name of their legendary place of origin] 1. *pl.* **-tecs, -tec** a member of a people who lived in Mexico and had an advanced civilization before the conquest of Mexico by Cortés in 1519 2. their Uto-Aztecan language, usually called Nahuatl —*adj.* of the Aztecs, their language, culture, etc.: also **Az′tec·an**

az·ure (azh′ər) *adj.* [OFr. *azur* < Ar. < Per. *lāzhuward*, lapis lazuli] of or like the color of a clear sky; sky-blue —*n.* 1. sky blue or any similar blue 2. [Poet.] the blue sky

az·u·rite (azh′ə rīt′) *n.* [AZUR(E) + -ITE] 1. a brilliantly blue mineral, $2CuCO_3 \cdot Cu(OH)_2$, an ore of copper 2. a semiprecious gem cut from it

az·y·gous (az′i gəs) *adj.* [Gr. *azygos*, unmatched < *a-*, not + *zygon*, yoke] not one of a pair; unpaired; odd *[an azygous muscle]*

B

B, b (bē) *n., pl.* **B's, b's** **1.** the second letter of the English alphabet **2.** the sound of *B* or *b* **3.** *a symbol for* the second in a sequence or group

B¹ (bē) *n.* **1.** *Chem.* boron **2.** *Educ.* a grade indicating above-average work **3.** *Music a)* the seventh tone in the ascending scale of C major *b)* the scale having B as the keynote

B² *Chess* bishop

B- bomber

B. 1. Bible **2.** British **3.** Brotherhood

B., b. 1. bachelor **2.** bacillus **3.** *Baseball a)* base *b)* baseman **4.** *Music* bass **5.** bay **6.** book **7.** born **8.** brother

Ba *Chem.* barium

B.A. [L. *Baccalaureus Artium*] Bachelor of Arts

baa (bä) *n.* [echoic] the cry of a sheep or goat —*vi.* to make this cry; bleat

Ba·al (bā′əl, bāl) *n., pl.* **Ba′al·im** (-im), **Ba′als 1.** among some ancient Semitic peoples, any of several fertility gods; later, a chief god **2.** a false god; idol —**Ba′al·ism** *n.*

☆**bab·bitt¹** (bab′it) *n. same as* BABBITT METAL

☆**bab·bitt²**, **Bab·bitt** (bab′it) *n.* [after the title character of a novel by Sinclair Lewis (1922)] a smugly conventional person who is interested chiefly in business and social success and who ignores or scorns art, learning, etc. —**bab′bitt·ry, Bab′bitt·ry** *n.*

☆**Babbitt metal** [after Isaac *Babbitt* (1799–1862), U.S. inventor] a soft alloy of tin, copper, and antimony, used to reduce friction in bearings, etc.

bab·ble (bab′'l) *vi.* **-bled, -bling** [of echoic origin] **1.** to make meaningless sounds, as a baby does; prattle **2.** to talk foolishly or too much **3.** to make a low, bubbling sound *[a babbling brook]* —*vt.* **1.** to say indistinctly or in a confused way **2.** to say foolishly; blab —*n.* **1.** confused, indistinct vocal sounds **2.** foolish or meaningless talk **3.** a low, bubbling sound —**bab′bler** *n.*

babe (bāb) *n.* [ME., prob. formed in imitation of baby sounds] **1.** a baby **2.** a naive, gullible, or helpless person: also **babe in the woods** ☆**3.** [Slang] a girl or young woman

Ba·bel (bā′b'l, bab′'l) *Bible* a city where people tried to build a tower to the sky and were stopped by God, who caused them suddenly to speak in different languages: Gen. 11:1–9 —*n.* [*also* b-] **1.** a confusion of voices, languages, or sounds; tumult **2.** a place of such confusion

ba·biche (bä bēsh′) *n.* [< CanadFr. < Algonquian] [Chiefly Canad.] thongs or lacings of rawhide, used for tying or weaving, esp. in snowshoes

ba·bies' breath (bā′bēz) *same as* BABY'S BREATH

bab·i·ru·sa, bab·i·rous·sa, bab·i·rus·sa (bab′ə rōōs′ə, bä′bä-) *n.* [Malay *babi*, hog + *rūsa*, deer] a wild hog of the East Indies, with large, curving tusks: the upper pair grow through the skin of the snout and curve backwards

Bab·ism (bäb′iz'm) *n.* a Persian religion founded c. 1844: see BAHAISM —**Bab′ist, Bab′ite** *n., adj.*

ba·boon (ba bōōn′) *n.* [< OFr. *babuin*, ape, fool < *baboue*, lip (of animals) < *bab*, echoic] any of various large and fierce, short-tailed monkeys of Africa and Arabia, having a doglike snout, cheek pouches, and bare calluses on the rump —**ba·boon′er·y** *n.* —**ba·boon′ish** *adj.*

BABOON
(35–58 in. long,
including tail)

ba·bu, ba·boo (bäb′ōō) *n.* [Hindi *bābu*] **1.** a Hindu title equivalent to *Mr.* or *Sir* **2.** a native clerk in India who can write English

ba·bush·ka (bə bōōsh′kə) *n.* [Russ., grandmother] a scarf worn on the head by a woman or girl and tied under the chin

ba·by (bā′bē) *n., pl.* **-bies** [ME. *babi*, dim. of BABE] **1.** a very young child; infant **2.** a person who behaves like an infant; esp., a timid person **3.** a very young animal **4.** the youngest or smallest in a group ☆**5.** [Slang] *a)* a girl or young woman *b)* any person or thing —*adj.* **1.** of or for an infant *[baby* food] **2.** very young or small *[baby* lima beans] **3.** infantile or childish *[baby* talk] —*vt.* **-bied, -by·ing 1.** to treat like a baby; pamper; coddle **2.** [Colloq.] to handle with great care *[to baby* a new car] —see SYN. at INDULGE —**ba′by·hood′** *n.* —**ba′by·ish** *adj.* —**ba′by·ish·ly** *adv.* —**ba′by·like** *adj.*

☆**baby beef** meat from a heifer or steer fattened for butchering when one to two years old

☆**baby carriage** a light carriage for wheeling a baby about: also **baby buggy**

baby grand a small grand piano

Bab·y·lon (bab′ə lən, -län′) ancient capital of Babylonia, famous for wealth, luxury, and wickedness —*n.* any city of great wealth, luxury, and vice

Bab·y·lo·ni·a (bab′ə lō′nē ə) ancient empire in SW Asia, in the lower valley of the Tigris & Euphrates rivers: flourished c. 2100–538 B.C. —**Bab′y·lo′ni·an** *adj., n.*

ba·by's breath (bā′bēz breth′) **1.** any of several plants of the pink family, having small, delicate, white or pink flowers **2.** any of several other plants with small, sweet-smelling flowers

☆**ba·by-sit** (bā′bē sit′) *vi., vt.* **-sat′, -sit′ting** to act as a baby sitter (to)

☆**baby sitter** a person hired to take care of a child or children, as when parents are away for an evening

ASSYRIA

Tigris

Euphrates

Babylon

BABYLONIA

ARABIA

PERSIAN
GULF

BABYLONIA (c. 2100 B.C.)

bac·ca·lau·re·ate (bak′ə lôr′ē it) *n.* [< ML. < *baccalaris*, vassal farmer, bachelor < ? L. *baculum*, staff] **1.** the degree of Bachelor of Arts (or Science, etc.) ☆**2.** a speech or sermon to a graduating class at commencement: also **baccalaureate address** (or **sermon**)

bac·ca·rat, bac·ca·ra (bak′ə rä′, bäk′-) *n.* [Fr. < ?] a gambling game played with cards

bac·cate (bak′āt) *adj.* [L. < *bacca*, berry] **1.** like a berry, as in form **2.** bearing berries

Bac·chae (bak′ē) *n.pl.* priestesses and other women who attended Bacchus or took part in the Bacchanalia

bac·cha·nal (bak′ə nəl, -nal′; bak′ə nal′) *n.* [L., place devoted to Bacchus] **1.** a worshiper of Bacchus **2.** a drunken carouser **3.** [*pl.*] the Bacchanalia **4.** a dance or song in honor of Bacchus **5.** a drunken party; orgy —*adj.* **1.** of Bacchus or his worship **2.** carousing

Bac·cha·na·li·a (bak′ə nāl′yə, -nā′lē ə) *n.pl.* **1.** an ancient Roman festival honoring Bacchus **2.** [b-] a drunken party; orgy —**bac′cha·na′li·an** *adj., n.*

bac·chant (bak′ənt, bə kant′) *n., pl.* **bac′chants, bac·chan′tes** (-kan′tēz) **1.** a priest or worshiper of Bacchus **2.** a drunken carouser —**bac·chan·te** (bə kan′tē, -kant′) *n.fem.* —**bac·chan′tic** *adj.*

Bac·chus (bak′əs) an ancient Greek and Roman god of wine and wild merrymaking: earlier called *Dionysus* by the Greeks — **Bac′chic, bac′chic** *adj.*

☆**bach** (bach) *vi.* [< BACHELOR] [Slang] to live alone or keep house for oneself, as a bachelor: usually in the phrase **bach it** —*n.* [Slang] a bachelor

Bach (bäkh; *E. also* bäk) **1. Jo·hann Christian** (yō′hän), 1735–82; Ger. organist & composer: son of *Johann Sebastian* **2. Johann Sebastian**, 1685–1750; Ger. organist & composer **3. Karl Philipp Emanuel**, 1714–88; Ger. composer: son of *prec.*

bach·e·lor (bach′l ər, bach′lər) *n.* [< OFr. < ML. *baccalaris:* see BACCALAUREATE] **1.** orig., a young knight who served under another's banner **2.** a man who has not married **3.** a person who is a BACHELOR OF ARTS (or SCIENCE, etc.) —*adj.* of or for a bachelor —**bach′e·lor·hood′** *n.*

Bachelor of Arts (or **Science**, etc.) **1.** a degree given by a college or university to one who has completed a four-year course in the humanities (or in science, etc.) **2.** one who has this degree

bachelor's button any of several plants of the composite family, as the cornflower, having flowers shaped somewhat like buttons

bac·il·lar·y (bas′ə ler′ē, bə sil′ər ē) *adj.* [ModL. *bacillarius:* see BACILLUS] **1.** rod-shaped: also **ba·cil·li·form** (bə sil′ə fôrm′) **2.** consisting of rodlike structures **3.** of, like, characterized by, or caused by bacilli Also **ba·cil·lar** (bə sil′ər)

ba·cil·lus (bə sil′əs) *n., pl.* **ba·cil′li** (-ī) [ModL. < LL. < L. dim. of *baculus*, a stick < IE. base *bak-*, staff, from which also come Gr. *baktron* & PEG] **1.** any of the rod-shaped bacteria: see illustration at BACTERIA **2.** [*usually pl.*] loosely, any of the bacteria, esp. those causing disease

☆**bac·i·tra·cin** (bas′ə trās′n) *n.* [< BACI(LLUS) + (Margaret) *Trac(y)*, Am. girl (1936–   ) from whose wounds the strain was isolated + -IN¹] an antibiotic gotten from a strain of bacteria and used in treating bacterial infections, esp. of the skin

back (bak) *n.* [< OE. *bæc*] **1.** the part of the body opposite to the front; in man and other animals, the part from the nape of the neck to the end of the spine **2.** the backbone **3.** the part of a chair that supports one's back **4.** the part of a garment that fits on the back **5.** the rear part of anything [the *back* of the bus; the *back* of his head] **6.** the part or side that is less often used, seen, etc. [the *back* of a rug] **7.** the part of a book where the sections are fastened together **8.** *Sports* a player or position behind the front line —*adj.* **1.** at the rear; behind [a *back* wheel] **2.** distant or remote [*back* country] **3.** of or for a time in the past [*back* pay] **4.** backward; reversed [a *back* step] **5.** *Phonet.* pronounced with the tongue toward the back of the mouth [(o͞o) is a *back* vowel] —*adv.* **1.** at, to, or toward the rear [please move *back*] **2.** to or toward a former position [throw the ball *back*] **3.** into or toward a previous condition [she nursed him *back* to health] **4.** to or toward an earlier time [think *back* to last year] **5.** in concealment [to hold *back* information] **6.** in return [to pay one *back*] —*vt.* **1.** to cause to move backward (often with *up*) [*back* the car up] **2.** to stand behind **3.** to support or help [to *back* a project] **4.** to bet on **5.** to get on the back of; mount **6.** to provide with a back or backing **7.** to form the back of —*vi.* **1.** to go backward **2.** to move (*into* a better position) only because an opponent has performed badly [they lost and we *backed* into first place] **3.** to have the back facing [the house *backs* on a lake] —see SYN. at SUPPORT —**back and fill 1.** to handle sails so that they fill with wind and spill wind in turn **2.** to have trouble making up one's mind —**back and forth** to and fro —☆**back down** to withdraw from a position, etc. —**back out (of) 1.** to withdraw from an enterprise **2.** to break a promise or engagement —**back up 1.** to support **2.** to go backward: also **back away, back out,** etc. **3.** to accumulate as the result of a stoppage [traffic *backed up*] —**back water 1.** to use oars, a propeller, etc. to move backward or to stay in place ☆**2.** to withdraw from a position, etc. —**be (flat) on one's back** to be ill, bedridden, etc. —**behind one's back** without one's knowledge or consent —☆**get off one's back** [Slang] to stop nagging or harassing one —**get** (or put) one's back up to make or become angry or obstinate —☆**go back on 1.** to betray **2.** to fail to keep (a promise, etc.) —☆**(in) back of** behind —**turn one's back on** to desert; fail —**with one's back to the wall** in a desperate position

back·ache (bak′āk′) *n.* an ache or pain in the back

back·bench·er (-ben′chər) *n.* a legislator, esp. in the British House of Commons, who is not a leader in his party

back·bite (-bīt′) *vt., vi.* **-bit′, -bit′ten** or **-bit′, -bit′ing** to slander (an absent person) —**back′bit′er** *n.*

back·board (-bôrd′) *n.* a board that forms the back of something; specif., ☆a flat surface just behind the basket in basketball

back·bone (-bōn′) *n.* **1.** the column of bones (vertebrae) along the center of the back; spine **2.** main support or most important part [steel, the *backbone* of our economy] **3.** a main ridge of mountains **4.** willpower, courage, etc.

back·break·ing (-brāk′iŋ) *adj.* very tiring

back court *n.* **1.** *Basketball* a team's defensive half of the court **2.** *Tennis* the area from the service line to the base line on either side of the net

back·drop (-dräp′) *n.* a curtain hung at the back of a stage, often painted to represent a scene

backed (bakt) *adj.* having a (specified kind of) back [canvas-*backed*]

back·er (bak′ər) *n.* **1.** a patron; supporter **2.** a person who bets on a contestant

☆**back·field** (-fēld′) *n. Football* the players stationed behind the line of scrimmage; esp., the offensive unit

back·fill (-fil′) *vt.* to refill (an excavation), as with earth previously removed

back·fire (-fīr′) *n.* ☆**1.** a fire started to stop a prairie fire or forest fire by creating a burned area in its path **2.** a premature explosion in a cylinder of an internal-combustion engine **3.** an explosive force toward the breech of a firearm —*vi.* **-fired′, -fir′ing** ☆**1.** to use or set a backfire **2.** to explode as a backfire **3.** to have an unwanted result; go awry; boomerang [his plan *backfired*]

back-for·ma·tion (-fôr mā′shən) *n.* **1.** a word formed from, but looking as if it were the base of, another word [the verb *peddle* is a *back-formation* from *peddler*] **2.** the forming of such a word

back·gam·mon (-gam′ən) *n.* [BACK + GAMMON²] a game played on a special board by two people, with pieces moved according to the throw of dice

back·ground (-ground′) *n.* **1.** the part of a scene or picture toward the back **2.** surroundings behind something, providing harmony or contrast [white stars on a blue *background*] **3.** a position that is unimportant or attracts no attention [try to stay in the *background*] **4.** the whole of one's study, training, and experience [he has a good *background* for politics] **5.** the events that lead up to something and help to explain it [the *background* of the Civil War] **6.** music (in full, **background music**) or sound effects accompanying action, as in movies

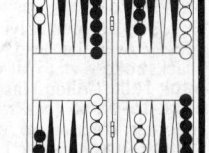

BACKGAMMON BOARD

back·hand (-hand′) *n.* **1.** handwriting that slants backward, up to the left **2.** a stroke, as in tennis, with the back of the hand turned forward —*adj.* **1.** done with the back of the hand **2.** done or performed with a backhand —*adv.* with a backhand —*vt.* ☆to catch (a ball) with the back of the hand turned inward and the arm across the body

back·hand·ed (-han′did) *adj.* **1.** *same as* BACKHAND **2.** indirect or sarcastic; not sincere [a *backhanded* compliment] **3.** performed by backhanding the ball —*adv.* with a backhand

back·ing (-iŋ) *n.* **1.** something forming a back for support or strength **2.** support given to a person or cause **3.** those giving such support **4.** [Slang] a musical accompaniment

BACKHAND STROKE

back·lash (-lash′) *n.* **1.** a quick, sharp recoil **2.** a sudden, strong reaction, as to a political or social movement or development **3.** a snarl in a reeled fishing line caused by an imperfect cast

☆**back·log** (-lôg′, -läg′) *n.* **1.** a large log at the back of a fireplace **2.** a reserve of something stored, served, etc. **3.** an accumulation of unfilled orders, unfinished work, etc. —*vi.*, *vt.* **-logged′, -log′ging** to accumulate as a backlog

back order an order not yet filled

☆**back·pack** (bak′pak′) *n.* **1.** a pack or kit worn on the back; specif., a kind of knapsack **2.** a piece of equipment, as a radio transmitter, used while being carried on the back —*vt.*, *vi.* to carry (supplies, etc.) on the back or in a backpack, as when hiking —**back′pack′er** *n.*

back·ped·al (-ped′'l) *vi.* **-ped′aled** or **-ped′alled, -ped′al·ing** or **-ped′al·ling 1.** to press backward on bicycle pedals, as in braking ☆**2.** to move backward quickly, as in boxing to avoid a blow ☆**3.** to retract an earlier opinion

☆**back road** a road that is away from the main road; country road, esp. an unpaved one

back seat a less important or less obvious position

☆**back-seat driver** (-sēt′) an automobile passenger who offers unwanted advice about driving

back·sheesh, back·shish (bak′shēsh′, bäk′-) *n. same as* BAKSHEESH

back·side (bak′sīd′) *n.* **1.** the back or hind part **2.** the rump; buttocks

☆**back·slap·per** (-slap′ər) *n.* [Colloq.] a person who is friendly in a way that is excessive or too hearty

back·slide (-slīd′) *vi.* **-slid′, -slid′** or **-slid′den, -slid′ing** to slide back into former wrong ways of acting or believing; often, to lose religious faith —**back′slid′er** *n.*

back·space (-spās′) *vi.* **-spaced′, -spac′ing** to move a typewriter carriage back a space at a time by pressing a certain key **(backspacer)**

back·spin (-spin′) *n.* a backward spin given to a propelled ball, wheel, etc. that causes it, upon hitting the ground, etc., to bound backward

back·stage (-stāj′) *adv.* in the wings or dressing rooms of a theater —*adj.* **1.** situated backstage **2.** of the life of people in show business

back·stay (-stā′) *n.* a stay or rope extending aft from a masthead to the side or stern of the ship

back·stop (-stäp′) *n.* ☆a screen, etc., as behind a baseball catcher, to stop balls from going too far; also, the catcher

☆**back·stretch** (-strech′) *n.* the part of a race track farthest from the grandstand

back·stroke (-strōk′) *n.* **1.** a backhand stroke **2.** a stroke made by a swimmer lying face upward, stretching the arms alternately over the head —*vi.* **-stroked′, -strok′ing** to perform a backstroke —*vt.* to hit with a backstroke

back talk [Colloq.] insolent or disrespectful answers

back-to-back (bak′tə bak′) *adj.* ☆[Colloq.] one right after another; consecutive [*back-to-back* home runs]

☆**back·track** (-trak′) *vi.* **1.** to return by the same path **2.** to withdraw from a position, etc.

back·up, back-up (-up′) *adj.* **1.** alternate or auxiliary [a *backup* pilot] **2.** supporting [a *backup* effort] —*n.* **1.** an accumulation because of a stoppage [a *backup* of water in a sink] **2.** a support or help

back·ward (-wərd) *adv.* **1.** toward the back; behind [to look *backward*] **2.** with the back or rear foremost [to walk *backward*] **3.** in reverse [to count from 10 *backward*] **4.** into the past [think *backward* to last week] **5.** from a better to a worse state Also **back′wards** —*adj.* **1.** turned or directed toward the rear or in the opposite way [with a *backward* look] **2.** hesitant or shy, as in meeting people **3.** late in developing; retarded — **bend** (or **lean**) **over backward 1.** to try earnestly (to please, pacify, etc.) **2.** to offset a tendency, bias, etc. by an effort in the opposite direction —**back′ward·ly** *adv.* —**back′ward·ness** *n.*

back·wash (-wôsh′, -wäsh′) *n.* **1.** water moved backward, as by a ship, an oar, etc. **2.** a backward current, as of air from an airplane propeller

back·wa·ter (-wôt′ər, -wät′-) *n.* **1.** water moved backward or held back by a dam, etc. **2.** stagnant water in a stream **3.** a place or condition where there is no progress or growth —*adj.* stagnant; backward

☆**back·woods** (-woodz′) *n.pl.* [occas. with sing. v.] **1.** heavily wooded areas far from centers of population **2.** any remote place with few inhabitants —*adj.* in, from, or like the backwoods: also **back′wood′** —**back′woods′man** *n.*, *pl.* **-men**

ba·con (bāk′'n) *n.* [OFr. < OS. *baco*, side of bacon] salted and smoked meat from the back or sides of a hog —**bring home the bacon** [Colloq.] **1.** to earn a living **2.** to succeed; win

Ba·con (bāk′'n) **1. Francis,** 1561–1626; Eng. philosopher, es-

sayist, & statesman **2. Roger,** 1214?–94; Eng. philosopher & scientist

bac·te·ri·a (bak tir′ē ə) *n.pl., sing.* **-ri·um** (-əm) [ModL. < Gr. dim. of *baktron*, a staff: for IE. base see BACILLUS] microorganisms that usually have only one cell, contain no chlorophyll, multiply by simple division, and occur in three main forms, spherical (*cocci*), rod-shaped (*bacilli*), and spiral (*spirilla*): some bacteria cause diseases, but others are necessary for fermentation, nitrogen fixation, etc. —**bac·te′ri·al** *adj.* —**bac·te′ri·al·ly** *adv.*

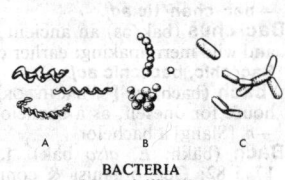

BACTERIA
(A, spirilla; B, cocci; C, bacilli)

bac·te·ri·cide (bak tir′ə sīd′) *n.* [BACTERI(O)- + -CIDE] a substance that destroys bacteria —**bac·te′ri·ci′dal** *adj.*

bac·te·ri·o- *a combining form meaning* of bacteria

bac·te·ri·ol·o·gy (bak tir′ē äl′ə jē) *n.* the study of bacteria, as in medicine, or for food processing, agriculture, etc. —**bac·te′ri·o·log′ic** (-ē ə läj′ik), **bac·te′ri·o·log′i·cal** *adj.* —**bac·te′ri·o·log′i·cal·ly** *adv.* —**bac·te′ri·ol′o·gist** *n.*

bac·te·ri·o·phage (bak tir′ē ə fāj′) *n.* [BACTERIO- + -PHAGE] any virus that destroys bacteria

bac·te·ri·um (bak tir′ē əm) *n. sing. of* BACTERIA

Bac·tri·an camel (bak′trē ən) [< *Bactria*, ancient country in W Asia] a camel with two humps, native to C Asia, shorter and hairier than the dromedary

bad[1] (bad) *adj.* **worse, worst** [ME.] **1.** not good; not as it should be [*bad* workmanship] **2.** defective in quality [*bad* plumbing] **3.** unfit; not skilled; poor [a *bad* poet] **4.** not pleasant; unfavorable [*bad* news] **5.** rotten; spoiled [a *bad* egg] **6.** incorrect; faulty [*bad* spelling] **7.** *a)* wicked; immoral *b)* mischievous **8.** causing injury; harmful [*bad* for one's health] **9.** severe [a *bad* storm] **10.** ill; in poor health **11.** sorry; distressed [he feels *bad* about it]: see BADLY **12.** *Law* not valid [a *bad* title] —*adv.* [Colloq.] badly —*n.* **1.** anything bad; bad quality or state [to go from *bad* to worse] **2.** wickedness —☆**in bad** [Colloq.] in trouble or disfavor —**not bad** [Colloq.] good; fairly good; not unsatisfactory: also **not half bad, not so bad** —**the bad** those who are wicked —**bad′ness** *n.*

BACTRIAN CAMEL
(to 6 ft. high
at shoulder)

bad[2] (bad) *archaic pt. of* BID

bad blood a feeling of being enemies; hostility

☆**bad·die, bad·dy** (bad′ē) *n., pl.* **-dies** [Slang] a bad or wicked person, esp. such a character in a play, movie, etc.

bade (bad; *occas.* bād) *alt. pt. of* BID

☆**bad egg** [Slang] a mean or dishonest person: also **bad actor, bad apple, bad hat, bad lot,** etc.

Ba·den (bäd′'n) **1.** region in SW West Germany **2.** city & health resort there: in full, **Baden-Baden**

badge (baj) *n.* [ME. *bage*] **1.** a token, emblem, or sign worn to show rank, membership, etc. **2.** any distinguishing mark or sign

badg·er (baj′ər) *n., pl.* **-ers, -er:** see PLURAL, II, D, 1 [< ? obs. *badger*, grain dealer] **1.** a meat-eating, burrowing mammal with a broad back and thick, short legs **2.** its fur —*vt.* to nag at; pester [the crowd began to *badger* the speaker] —see SYN. at BAIT

BADGER
(body 16–18 in. long)

bad·i·nage (bad′ə näzh′, bad′'n ij) *n.* [Fr. < *badiner*, to jest < Pr. < ML. *badare*, to gape] playful, teasing talk; banter

☆**bad·lands** (bad′landz′) *n.pl.* **1.** any section of barren land where deep erosion has cut the dry soil or soft rocks into strange shapes **2.** [B-] any section like this in the western U.S., esp. in southwestern S.Dak.: also **Bad Lands**

bad·ly (bad′lē) *adv.* **worse, worst 1.** in a bad manner; harmfully, unpleasantly, incorrectly, etc. **2.** [Colloq.] very much; greatly [he's *badly* mistaken] Also used informally as an adjective meaning "sorry" although *bad* is preferred in formal use [she feels *bad* (or *badly*) about the loss]

☆**bad·man** (bad′man′) *n., pl.* **-men** (-men′) a cattle thief, desperado, or hired gunman of the old West

bad·min·ton (bad′min t'n) *n.* [after *Badminton*, estate of the Duke of Beaufort] a game in which a feathered cork (*shuttlecock*) is batted back and forth with light rackets across a net

☆**bad-mouth** (bad′mouth′) *vt.* [Slang] to find fault with or criticize harshly

bad-tem·pered (bad′tem′pərd) *adj.* having a bad temper or cranky disposition; irritable

Bae·de·ker (bā′də kər) *n.* **1.** any of a series of guidebooks to foreign countries first published in Germany by Karl Baedeker (1801–59) **2.** loosely, any guidebook

Baf·fin Bay (baf′in) arm of the N Atlantic, between Greenland & Baffin Island

Baffin Island [after William *Baffin* (1584–1622), Eng. explorer] large island off the NE coast of Canada, in the Northwest Territories: c.200,000 sq. mi.

baf·fle (baf′'l) *vt.* **-fled, -fling** [16th-c. Scot.; prob. respelling of obs. Scot. *bauchle*] **1.** to confuse so as to keep from understanding or solving; puzzle; confound [a crime that has *baffled* the police] **2.** to hinder; impede **3.** to check the interference of (sound waves) by a baffle —*n.* **1.** a baffling or being baffled **2.** a wall or screen to deflect the flow of liquids, gases, etc.: also **baf′fle-plate′ 3.** a mounting that checks the transmission of sound waves between the front and rear of a loudspeaker of a radio, phonograph, etc. —**baf′fle·ment** *n.* —**baf′fler** *n.* —**baf′fling** *adj.*

bag (bag) *n.* [ON. *baggi*] **1.** a container made of fabric, paper, leather, etc., with an opening at the top that can be closed; sack **2.** the amount a bag holds **3.** a piece of hand luggage; as a suitcase **4.** a woman's handbag; purse **5.** *a)* a container for game *b)* the amount of game caught or killed **6.** anything shaped or bulging like a bag [*bags* under the eyes] **7.** an udder or sac ☆**8.** [Slang] one's special interest, talent, obsession, etc. [music is not her *bag*] **9.** [Slang] an unattractive woman **10.** *Baseball* a base —*vt.* **bagged, bag′ging 1.** to make bulge **2.** to enclose within a bag **3.** to capture **4.** to kill in hunting **5.** [Slang] to get —*vi.* **1.** to bulge **2.** to hang loosely —**bag and baggage** [Colloq.] **1.** with all one's possessions **2.** entirely —**be left holding the bag** [Colloq.] to be left to suffer the bad consequences or the blame —☆**in the bag** [Slang] having its success assured

ba·gasse (bə gas′) *n.* [Fr. < Pr. *bagasso*, refuse from processing grapes, etc. < L. *baca*, berry] the part of sugar cane left after the juice has been extracted, or the residue of certain other processed plants: used for making fiberboard, etc.

bag·a·telle (bag′ə tel′) *n.* [Fr. < It. *bagatella*, dim. < L. *baca*, berry] **1.** something of little value; trifle **2.** a game, somewhat like billiards, played with nine balls on a table

Bag·dad (bag′dad, bäg′ däd′) *same as* BAGHDAD

ba·gel (bā′g'l) *n.* [< Yid., ult. < G. *beugen*, to bend: for IE. base see BOW¹] a hard, doughnut-shaped bread roll that is simmered in water before being baked

bag·ful (bag′fool′) *n., pl.* **-fuls′ 1.** the amount that a bag will hold **2.** a large amount

bag·gage (bag′ij) *n.* [< OFr. < *bagues*, baggage < ML. *baga*, chest] **1.** the bags and other equipment of a traveler **2.** the supplies and gear of an army **3.** a saucy or lively girl **4.** unnecessary or outdated ideas, practices, etc.

bag·gy (bag′ē) *adj.* **-gi·er, -gi·est 1.** puffed in a baglike way **2.** hanging loosely [*baggy* trousers] —**bag′gi·ly** *adv.* —**bag′gi·ness** *n.*

Bagh·dad (bag′dad, bäg däd′) capital of Iraq, on the Tigris River: pop. c. 1,000,000

bag·man (bag′mən) *n., pl.* **-men 1.** [Brit.] a traveling salesman ☆**2.** [Slang] a go-between in offering bribes, collecting ransom money, etc.

bagn·io (ban′yō, bän′-) *n., pl.* **-ios** [< It. < L. < Gr. *balaneion*, bath] a house of prostitution; brothel

bag·pipe (bag′pīp′) *n.* [*often pl.*] a shrill-toned musical instrument with several pipes, sounded by air forced from a leather bag, which the player keeps filled by blowing air into it: now played chiefly in Scotland —**bag′pip′er** *n.*

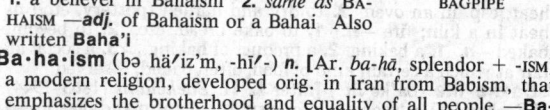
BAGPIPE

ba·guette, ba·guet (ba get′) *n.* [< Fr. < It. < L. *baculum*, a staff (see BACILLUS)] **1.** a gem, etc. cut in the shape of a narrow oblong **2.** this shape

bah (bä, ba) *interj.* an exclamation expressing contempt, scorn, or disgust

Ba·hai (bə hī′, bə hä′ē) *n., pl.* **Ba·hais′ 1.** a believer in Bahaism **2.** *same as* BAHAISM —*adj.* of Bahaism or a Bahai Also written **Baha'i**

Ba·ha·ism (bə hä′iz'm, -hī′-) *n.* [Ar. *ba-hā*, splendor + -ISM] a modern religion, developed orig. in Iran from Babism, that emphasizes the brotherhood and equality of all people —**Ba·ha′ist** *n., adj.*

Ba·ha·mas (bə hä′məz, -hä′-) island country in the West Indies, southeast of Fla.: a member of the Commonwealth: 4,404 sq. mi.; pop. 180,000; cap. Nassau —**Ba·ha′mi·an** *adj., n.*

Bah·rain, Bah·rein (bä rän′) independent Arab sheikdom consisting of a group of islands in the Persian Gulf: a member of the Commonwealth: 231 sq. mi.; pop. 200,000

baht (bät) *n., pl.* **bahts, baht** [Thai *bāt*] *see* MONETARY UNITS, table (Thailand)

Bai·kal (bī käl′), **Lake** large lake in SE Siberia: deepest lake in the world (c.5,700 ft.): 12,000 sq. mi.

bail¹ (bāl) *n.* [OFr., power, control < *baillir*, keep in custody < L. *bajulare*, bear a burden < *bajulus*, porter] **1.** money or credit deposited with the court as a guarantee that an arrested person who has been released will appear for trial **2.** the release thus brought about **3.** the person giving bail —*vt.* **1.** to set (an arrested person) free on bail or have (an arrested person) set free by giving bail (often with *out*) **2.** to help out of financial or other difficulty (often with *out*) —**go bail for** to furnish bail for —**bail′a·ble** *adj.*

bail² (bāl) *n.* [< OFr. < VL. *bajula*, vessel < *bajulare*: see prec.] a bucket, etc. for dipping up water from a boat —*vi., vt.* **1.** to remove water from (a boat) as with a bail **2.** to dip out (water, etc.) as with a bail —**bail out** to make a parachute jump from an aircraft —**bail′er** *n.*

bail³ (bāl) *n.* [< ON. *beygla* < *beygja*, to bend: for IE. base see BOW¹] **1.** a hoop-shaped support, as for a canopy **2.** a hoop-shaped handle for a bucket, etc. **3.** a bar on a typewriter to hold the paper against the platen

bail⁴ (bāl) *n.* [< OFr., ult. < L. *bajulus*, porter] *Cricket* either of two pieces of wood laid across the three stumps to form a wicket

bai·lie (bā′lē) *n.* [Scot. < OFr. < *bailif:* see BAILIFF] in Scotland, a municipal official corresponding to an alderman in England

bai·liff (bā′lif) *n.* [OFr. *bailif* < *baillir:* see BAIL¹] **1.** a deputy sheriff who serves processes, etc. **2.** a court officer who guards jurors, keeps order in the courtroom, etc. **3.** in England, an administrative official of a district **4.** [Chiefly Brit.] an overseer or steward of an estate

bai·li·wick (bā′lə wik) *n.* [ME. < *bailif*, BAILIFF + *wik* < OE. *wic*, village] **1.** a bailiff's district **2.** one's particular area of activity, authority, etc.

bails·man (bālz′mən) *n., pl.* **-men** a person who gives bail to get someone released until his trial

bairn (bern) *n.* [< OE. *bearn* < *beran*, to BEAR¹] [Scot.] a son or daughter; child

bait (bāt) *vt.* [ON. *beita*, to make bite < *bīta*, to BITE] **1.** to set attacking dogs against for sport [to *bait* bears] **2.** to torment or harass with unprovoked, repeated attacks **3.** to tease or goad **4.** to put food, etc. on (a hook or trap) so as to lure animals or fish **5.** to lure; tempt; entice —*n.* **1.** food, etc. put on a hook or trap to lure fish or animals **2.** any lure; enticement —**bait′er** *n.*

SYN.—to **bait** is to torment or provoke esp. because the persecutor gets cruel pleasure from the act; to **badger** is to pester so persistently as to make frantic and confused; to **hound** is to keep after stubbornly in a way that wears the victim down; to **heckle** is to annoy or taunt (a public speaker or performer) with critical or jeering remarks; to **hector** suggests a continual bullying in order to frighten or weaken; to **torment**, in this comparison, is to keep attacking, annoying, etc. in a way that causes great suffering; **ride** is colloquial and implies a persistent teasing as by ridiculing

☆**bait-and-switch** (bāt''n swich') *adj.* of or using a dishonest sales method in which a seller attracts customers by advertising a bargain item which may not exist and then tries to switch their attention to more expensive items

baize (bāz) *n.* [< OFr. *baies,* pl. of *baie* < L. *badius,* chestnut-brown] a feltlike, thick woolen cloth, often green, used to cover billiard tables, etc.

Ba·ja Ca·li·for·nia (bä'hä kä'lē fôr'nyä) peninsula in Mexico, between the Pacific & the Gulf of California: 55,634 sq. mi.

bake (bāk) *vt.* **baked, bak'ing** [OE. *bacan* < IE. base *bhe-,* to warm, from which also comes BATH] **1.** to cook (food) by dry heat, esp. in an oven **2.** to dry and harden (pottery, etc.) by heat in a kiln; fire —*vi.* **1.** to bake bread, etc. **2.** to become baked —*n.* **1.** a baking **2.** a product of baking ☆**3.** a social affair at which a certain kind of food, often baked, is served

☆**Ba·ke·lite** (bā'kə līt') [after L. H. *Baekeland* (1863–1944), U.S. chemist] *a trademark for* a synthetic resin and plastic —*n.* [b-] this resin

bak·er (bāk'ər) *n.* **1.** one whose work or business is baking bread, etc. ☆**2.** a small, portable oven

baker's dozen thirteen

Bak·ers·field (bāk'ərz fēld') [after Col. *Baker,* early landowner] city in SC Calif.: pop. 70,000

☆**bak·er·y** (bāk'ər ē) *n.* **1.** *pl.* **-er·ies** a place where bread, pastries, etc. are baked or sold **2.** baked goods; bread, etc.

bake·shop (bāk'shäp') *n.* a bakery

☆**baking powder** a substance used to make dough rise in baking biscuits, cake, etc.: it contains baking soda and an acid substance, such as cream of tartar, which together produce carbon dioxide in the presence of water

baking soda sodium bicarbonate, NaHCO³, used to neutralize acids and to make dough rise in baking

bak·sheesh, bak·shish (bak'shēsh) *n.* [via Turk. or Ar. < Per. < *bakhshidan,* to give] in Turkey, Egypt, India, etc., a tip, gratuity, or alms

Ba·ku (bä koo') capital of the Azerbaijan S.S.R., on the Caspian Sea: pop. 1,224,000

Ba·ku·nin (bä koo'nyin; *E.* bə kyoo'nin), **Mi·kha·il** (**Aleksandrovich**) (mē khä ēl') 1814–76; Russ. anarchist

bal. balance

Ba·laam (bā'ləm) *Bible* a prophet who was scolded by his donkey after he had beaten it for balking: Num. 22–24

Bal·a·kla·va (bäl'ə klä'və) seaport in the Crimea, U.S.S.R.: scene of the incident in the Crimean War celebrated in Tennyson's "Charge of the Light Brigade"

bal·a·lai·ka (bal'ə lī'kə) *n.* [Russ.] a Russian stringed instrument somewhat like a guitar, but with a triangular body

bal·ance (bal'əns) *n.* [OFr. < ML. < LL. *bilanx,* having two scales < L. *bis,* twice + *lanx,* a scale] **1.** an instrument for weighing, esp. one with two matched pans hanging from a bar supported in the middle; scales **2.** equality in weight, value, importance, etc., as between two things or the parts of a thing [to keep a *balance* between work and recreation] **3.** the ability to keep one's body steady without falling [Jo kept her *balance* on the tightrope] **4.** one's normal, steady state of mind **5.** the pleasing harmony of various elements in a work of art **6.** a weight, force, etc. that counteracts another or causes equilibrium **7.** the point along an object's length at which there is equilibrium: in full, **balance point 8.** *a)* equality between the amount of money one owes and the amount owed to one *b)* the difference between the amount of money one owes and the amount one has **9.** the amount still owed after part of a bill has been paid **10.** the part left over; remainder [the *balance* of the order will be delivered tomorrow] **11.** a balancing **12.** *same as* BALANCE WHEEL —*vt.* **-anced, -anc·ing 1.** to weigh in or as in a balance **2.** to compare as to relative importance, value, etc. **3.** to make up for by acting in an opposite way; counteract [his kind acts *balanced* his rough manner] **4.** to keep from falling, by holding steady [to *balance* oneself on stilts] **5.** to bring into proportion, harmony, etc. **6.** to make or be equal to in weight, force, etc. [*balance* both ends of the boat to keep from turning over] **7.** *a)* to find any difference in (an account) between the amount of money that one has or that is owed to one and the amount one owes or has spent; also, to make these amounts equal in [to

BALANCE
(sense 1)

balance a checking account] *b)* to settle (an account) by paying debts —*vi.* **1.** to be steady or stable [the dancer *balanced* on her toes] **2.** to be equal in value, weight, etc. [his virtues and his faults *balance*] **3.** to have the credit and debit sides equal [our account books *balance*] **4.** to waver slightly —see SYN. at SYMMETRY —**in the balance** in a critical, undecided state — **bal'ance·a·ble** *adj.* —**bal'anc·er** *n.*

balance beam a long, horizontal wooden beam raised about four feet above the floor, on which women gymnasts balance while performing jumps, turns, etc.

balance of (international) payments a balance estimated for a given period showing an excess or deficit in total payments of all kinds, including imports, exports, debt payments, etc., between one country and another country or other countries

balance of power 1. an even distribution of military and economic power among nations that keeps any one of them from being too strong or dangerous **2.** the power that a small group has to give control to either of two large groups in conflict by joining with one of them

balance of trade the difference in value between the imports and exports of a country

balance sheet a summarized statement showing the financial status of a business

balance wheel a wheel that swings back and forth to regulate the movement of a timepiece, etc.

bal·a·ta (bal'ə tə) *n.* [Sp. < Tupi] **1.** a tropical American tree **2.** its dried milky sap, a rubberlike gum used commercially, as for golf ball covers

bal·bo·a (bal bō'ə) *n.* [Sp., after BALBOA] *see* MONETARY UNITS, table (Panama)

Bal·bo·a (bal bō'ə; *Sp.* bäl bō'ä), **Vas·co Nú·ñez de** (väs'kô noo'nyeth the) 1475?–1517?; Sp. explorer: first European to discover the Pacific Ocean

bal·brig·gan (bal brig'ən) *n.* [after *Balbriggan,* in Ireland] a knitted cotton material used for hosiery, underwear, etc.

bal·co·ny (bal'kə nē) *n., pl.* **-nies** [< It. < Gmc., akin to OHG. *balcho,* a beam] **1.** a platform projecting from a building and enclosed by a balustrade **2.** an upper floor of rows of seats in a theater, etc., often jutting out over the main floor

bald (bôld) *adj.* [ME. *balled,* prob. < IE. base *bhel-,* gleaming, white] **1.** having white fur or feathers on the head, as some animals and birds **2.** having no hair on all or part of the scalp **3.** not covered by natural growth [*bald* hills] **4.** plain; unadorned [the *bald* facts] **5.** frank and blunt [a *bald* statement] —**bald'ly** *adv.* —**bald'ness** *n.*

bal·da·chin (bôl'də kin) *n.* [< It. < *Baldacco,* Baghdad, where the cloth was made] **1.** a rich brocade of silk and gold **2.** a canopy, orig. of this material, as over an altar or throne

☆**bald·cy·press** (bôld'sī'pris) *n.* a cone-bearing tree that grows in the swamps of the southeastern U.S. and sheds its needles in the fall

☆**bald eagle** a large, strong eagle of N. America: the adult has a white-feathered head and neck

Bal·der (bôl'dər) *Norse Myth.* the god of light, peace, virtue, and wisdom: also sp. **Baldr**

bal·der·dash (bôl'dər dash') *n.* [orig., a senseless mixture of liquids] nonsensical talk or writing

bald·faced (bôld'fāst') *adj.* ☆brazen; shameless [a *baldfaced* lie]

bald·head (-hed') *n.* **1.** a person who has a bald head **2.** any bird with a patch of white on the head —**bald'head'ed** *adj.*

bald·ing (bôl'diŋ) *adj.* becoming bald

bal·dric (bôl'drik) *n.* [< OFr. < L. *balteus,* BELT] a belt worn over one shoulder and across the chest to support a sword, etc.

Bald·win (bôld'win) [< OFr. < MHG. < OHG. *bald,* bold + *wini,* friend] **1.** a masculine name **2. James (Arthur),** 1924– ; U.S. writer —☆*n.* [after Col. L. *Baldwin* (1740–1807), Mass. apple grower] a moderately tangy, red winter apple

bale[1] (bāl) *n.* [OFr. < OHG. *balla,* a ball] a large bundle, esp. a standardized quantity, as of cotton, hay, or straw, tightly packed and wrapped for shipping —*vt.* **baled, bal'ing** to make into bales —**bal'er** *n.*

bale[2] (bāl) *n.* [OE. *bealu*] [Poet.] **1.** evil; disaster; harm **2.** sorrow; woe

Bal·e·ar·ic Islands (bal'ē er'ik) group of Sp. islands in the Mediterranean, east of Spain: see map at VALENCIA

ba·leen (bə lēn') *n.* [< OFr. < L. *ballaena,* a whale] *same as* WHALEBONE

BALE

bale·ful (bāl′fəl) *adj.* harmful or evil; sinister —**bale′ful·ly** *adv.* —**bale′ful·ness** *n.*

Ba·li (bä′lē, bal′ē) island of Indonesia, just off the eastern tip of Java: 2,100 sq. mi. —**Ba′li·nese′** (bä′lə nēz′, bal′ə-) *adj., n.*

balk (bôk) *n.* [OE. *balca*, a bank, ridge < IE. base *bhel-g̑-*, a beam, from which also come FULCRUM & PHALANX] 1. a ridge of unploughed land between furrows 2. a roughly cut piece of timber 3. something that blocks, hinders, defeats, etc. 4. *Baseball* an illegal motion by the pitcher, as an uncompleted motion to throw, entitling base runners to advance one base —*vt.* 1. to miss or let slip by 2. to bring to a stop; block *[the project was *balked* by a lack of funds]* —*vi.* 1. to stop and stubbornly refuse to move or act 2. to hesitate or recoil (*at*) *[she balked* at the idea of apologizing*]* 3. to make a balk in baseball —**balk′er** *n.*

Bal·kan (bôl′kən) *adj.* 1. of the Balkans, their people, etc. 2. of the Balkan Mountains

Bal·kan·ize (bôl′kə nīz′) *vt., vi.* **-ized′, -iz′ing** [*sometimes* b-] to break up into small political units that are hostile to one another, as the Balkans after World War I —**Bal′kan·i·za′tion** *n.*

Balkan Mountains mountain range extending across C Bulgaria, from Yugoslavia to the Black Sea

Balkan Peninsula peninsula in SE Europe, between the Adriatic and the Black seas

Bal·kans (bôl′kənz) the countries of the Balkan Peninsula (Yugoslavia, Albania, Bulgaria, Greece, & the European part of Turkey) & Romania: also **Balkan States**

BALKAN PENINSULA

balk·line (bôk′līn′) *n.* a line across one end of a billiard table, from behind which opening shots are made

balk·y (bôk′ē) *adj.* **balk′i·er, balk′i·est** stubbornly refusing to move or act —**balk′i·ness** *n.*

ball¹ (bôl) *n.* [ME. *bal* < IE. base *bhel-*, to swell, from which also come BOWL¹ & BLADDER] 1. any round object; sphere; globe 2. a planet or star, esp. the earth 3. *a)* a round or egg-shaped object used in various games *b)* any of several such games, esp. baseball 4. a throw or pitch of a ball *[a fast *ball]* 5. a solid missile for a cannon or firearm 6. a rounded part of the body *[the *ball* of the foot]* ☆7. *Baseball* a pitch that is wide of the plate or goes above the armpit or below the knee of the batter and is not struck at by the batter —*vi., vt.* to form into a ball —**ball up** [Slang] to confuse or mix up badly —☆**be on the ball** [Slang] to be alert; be efficient —☆**carry the ball** [Colloq.] to assume responsibility —☆**get (or keep) the ball rolling** [Colloq.] to start (or maintain) some action —☆**have something on the ball** [Slang] to have ability —**play ball** ☆1. to begin or resume playing a ball game ☆2. to begin or resume any activity ☆3. [Colloq.] to cooperate

ball² (bôl) *n.* [Fr. *bal* < OFr. < LL. *ballare*, to dance < Gr. *ballein*, to throw] 1. a formal social dance 2. [Slang] an enjoyable time or experience

bal·lad (bal′əd) *n.* [< OFr. *ballade*, dancing song, ult. < LL. *ballare*: see prec.] 1. a romantic or sentimental song with the same melody for each stanza 2. a song or poem, esp. one whose author is no longer known, that is passed down orally from one generation to the next, and that tells a story in short stanzas and simple words 3. a slow, sentimental popular song —**bal′lad·eer′** *n.* —**bal′lad·ry** *n.*

bal·lade (bə läd′) *n.* [Fr.: see prec.] 1. a verse form with three stanzas of eight or ten lines each and an envoy of four or five lines: the last line of each stanza and of the envoy are the same 2. a romantic musical composition

☆**ball and chain** 1. a heavy metal ball fastened by a chain to a prisoner's body to keep him from escaping 2. [Slang] one's wife

ball-and-sock·et joint (bôl′′n säk′it) a joint, as that of the hip, formed by a ball in a socket, allowing limited movement in any direction

bal·last (bal′əst) *n.* [LowG. < ODan. *barlast* < *bar*, bare + *last*, a load] 1. anything heavy carried in a ship, aircraft, or vehicle to keep it stable or in a balloon to help control altitude 2. anything that keeps a person's character, a relationship, etc. stable and firm 3. crushed rock or gravel, as that used to make a firm bed for railroad ties —*vt.* 1. to furnish with ballast; stabilize 2. to fill in (a railroad bed, etc.) with ballast

ball bearing 1. a bearing in which the moving parts revolve on freely rolling metal balls so that friction is reduced: see illustration at BEARING 2. any of these balls

BALL-AND-SOCKET JOINT

bal·le·ri·na (bal′ə rē′nə) *n.* [It. < LL. *ballare*: see BALL²] a woman ballet dancer

bal·let (bal′ā, ba lā′) *n.* [< Fr. < It. *balletto*, dim. < *ballo*, a dance: see BALL²] 1. *a)* a style of dancing performed on a stage, in which dancers in costume use pantomime and graceful, fixed movements to tell a story *b)* a single dance of this kind 2. a company of such dancers —**bal·let·ic** (ba let′ik) *adj.*

bal·lis·ta (bə lis′tə) *n., pl.* **-tae** (-tē) [L. < Gr. *ballein*, to throw] a device used in ancient warfare to hurl rocks, etc.

bal·lis·tic (bə lis′tik) *adj.* 1. having to do with ballistics 2. of the motion and force of a projectile

ballistic missile a long-range missile guided automatically in the first part of its flight, but free-falling as it nears its target

bal·lis·tics (bə lis′tiks) *n.pl.* [*with sing. v.*] 1. the science dealing with the motion and impact of projectiles, such as bullets, rockets, bombs, etc. 2. the study of the effects that firing has on a firearm or bullet, etc.

bal·loon (bə lōōn′) *n.* [< Fr. < It. *pallone* < *palla*, a ball] 1. a large, airtight bag that rises above the earth when filled with a gas lighter than air 2. a bag of this sort with an attached car for passengers or instruments 3. a small rubber bag blown up with air or gas and used as a toy 4. the outline enclosing spoken words in a comic strip —*vt.* to cause to swell like a balloon —*vi.* 1. to ride in a balloon 2. to swell; expand —*adj.* like a balloon —**bal·loon′ist** *n.*

bal·lot (bal′ət) *n.* [It. *ballotta, pallotta*, dim. of *palla*, a ball] 1. orig. a ball, now a ticket, paper, etc., by which a vote is registered 2. act or method of voting, esp. secret voting by the use of ballots or voting machines 3. the right to vote 4. the total number of votes cast in an election 5. a list of candidates for office; ticket —*vi.* to decide by means of the ballot; vote

☆**ball·park** (bôl′pärk′) *n.* a stadium in which baseball is played —*adj.* [Colloq.] reasonably accurate *[a ballpark estimate]* —**in the ballpark** [Colloq.] 1. reasonably accurate 2. fairly close to what is needed

ball·play·er (-plā′ər) *n.* a baseball player

☆**ball point pen** a pen having instead of a point a small ball bearing that rolls ink from a cartridge onto the writing surface: also **ball′-point′, ball′point′** *n.*

ball·room (-rōōm′) *n.* a large hall for social dances

ballroom dancing dancing in which two people dance as partners to a waltz, fox trot, etc.

☆**bal·ly·hoo** (bal′ē hōō′; *also for v.* bal′ē hōō′) *n.* [< ?] 1. loud talk; uproar 2. loud or sensational advertising or propaganda —*vt., vi.* **-hooed′, -hoo′ing** [Colloq.] to advertise or promote by sensational methods —**bal′ly·hoo′er** *n.*

balm (bäm) *n.* [< OFr. < L. < Gr. *balsamon*] 1. a sweet-smelling gum resin obtained from certain trees and plants and used as medicine; balsam 2. any fragrant ointment or oil 3. anything healing or soothing, esp. to the mind or temper *[sleep was a *balm* to his troubles]* 4. any of various sweet-smelling plants of the mint family 5. pleasant odor; fragrance

balm of Gilead 1. *a)* a small evergreen tree native to Asia and Africa *b)* a sweet-smelling ointment formerly prepared from its resin 2. anything healing or soothing ☆3. same as BALSAM FIR ☆4. a hybrid poplar of the northern U.S.

balm·y (bäm′ē) *adj.* **balm′i·er, balm′i·est** 1. having the qualities of balm; soothing, mild, pleasant, etc. *[a balmy day]* 2. [var. of BARMY] [Chiefly Brit. Slang] crazy or foolish —**balm′i·ly** *adv.* —**balm′i·ness** *n.*

☆**ba·lo·ney** (bə lō′nē) *n.* [altered < ? *bologna*, sausage] **1.** *same as* BOLOGNA **2.** [Slang] nonsense; foolishness —*interj.* [Slang] nonsense!

☆**bal·sa** (bôl′sə) *n.* [Sp.] **1.** a tropical American tree that yields an extremely light and buoyant wood used for rafts, etc. **2.** the wood **3.** a raft, esp. one made up of a frame on cylindrical floats

bal·sam (bôl′səm) *n.* [OE. < L.: see BALM] **1.** any of various sweet-smelling resins obtained from certain trees **2.** any of various sweet-smelling resinous oils or fluids, used in ointments, etc. **3.** anything healing or soothing; balm **4.** any of various trees that yield balsam, as the balsam fir **5.** any of various species of the impatiens —**bal·sam·ic** (bôl sam′ik) *adj.*

☆**balsam fir** an evergreen tree of Canada and the northern U.S. with a soft wood used for pulpwood: commonly used as a Christmas tree

Bal·tic (bôl′tik) *adj.* **1.** of the Baltic Sea **2.** of the Baltic States **3.** of a branch of Indo-European languages that includes Lithuanian, Latvian, and Old Prussian —*n.* the Baltic Sea

Baltic Sea sea in N Europe, south & east of Scandinavia & west of the U.S.S.R.

Baltic States former independent countries of Latvia, Lithuania, & Estonia

Bal·ti·more (bôl′tə môr′) [after Lord *Baltimore*, George Calvert (1580?–1632), Eng. founder of Md.] seaport in N Md., on Chesapeake Bay: pop. 906,000 (met. area 2,071,000)

☆**Baltimore oriole** [from the colors of the coat of arms of Lord *Baltimore*: see prec.] a N. American oriole that has an orange body with black on the head, wings, and tail

BALTIC SEA & STATES

Bal·to-Sla·vic (bôl′tō slä′vik) *n.* a group of Indo-European languages, including the Baltic and Slavic branches

Ba·lu·chi·stan (bə loo′chə stan′, -stän′) region in SW Pakistan & SE Iran

bal·us·ter (bal′əs tər) *n.* [< Fr. < It. < L. < Gr. *balaustion*, flower of the wild pomegranate: from similarity in shape] any of the small posts supporting a railing, as on a staircase

bal·us·trade (bal′ə strād′) *n.* a railing held up by balusters

Bal·zac (bál zàk′; *E.* bôl′zak), **Ho·no·ré de** (ô nô rā′ də) 1799–1850; Fr. novelist

Ba·ma·ko (bä mä kō′) capital of Mali, on the upper Niger River: pop. 170,000

bam·bi·no (bam bē′nō) *n., pl.* **-nos, -ni** (-nē) [It., dim. of *bambo*, childish] **1.** a child; baby **2.** any image of the infant Jesus

bam·boo (bam boo′) *n.* [Malay *bambu*] any of a number of treelike, semitropical or tropical grasses with springy, jointed, often hollow stems, sometimes growing to heights of 120 feet: the stems are used for furniture, canes, etc., and the young shoots of some species are eaten

bam·boo·zle (bam boo′z'l) *vt.* **-zled, -zling** [< ?] **1.** to deceive or cheat by trickery **2.** to confuse or puzzle [the riddle had us bamboozled] —**bam·boo·zle·ment** *n.* —**bam·boo·zler** *n.*

BAMBOO

ban[1] (ban) *vt.* **banned, ban′ning** [OE. *bannan*, to summon < IE. base *bha-*, to speak, from which also comes L. *fari*, to speak] to prohibit or forbid, as by official order [cars are *banned* on the island] —*n.* [< the *v.*; also < OFr. *ban*, decree < OHG. *bann*] **1.** an excommunication by church authorities **2.** a curse **3.** an official prohibition [a *ban* on traveling to certain countries] **4.** strong public disapproval **5.** a sentence of outlawry

ban[2] (bän) *n., pl.* **ba·ni** (bä′nē) *see* MONETARY UNITS, table (Romania)

ba·nal (bā′n'l; bə nal′, -näl′) *adj.* [Fr. < OFr., belonging to feudal serfs (hence common, ordinary) < *ban*: see BAN[1], *n.*] dull or stale because of overuse; trite; hackneyed [a speech full of *banal* jokes] —*see* SYN. at INSIPID —**ba·nal·i·ty** (bə nal′ə tē) *n., pl.* **-ties** —**ba·nal·ly** *adv.*

ba·nan·a (bə nan′ə) *n.* [Sp. & Port. < native name in W Africa] **1.** a treelike, tropical plant, with long, broad leaves and large clusters of edible fruit **2.** the fruit: it is narrow and somewhat curved, and has a sweet, creamy flesh covered by a yellow or reddish skin

BANANA

banana oil 1. a colorless liquid acetate with a bananalike odor, used in flavorings, in making lacquers, etc. **2.** [Old Slang] insincere talk

banana republic any small Latin American country whose one-crop economy is controlled by foreign capital

Ban·croft (ban′krôft, baŋ′-), **George** 1800–91; U.S. historian & statesman

band[1] (band) *n.* [ON.; also (in meaning "thin strip") < Fr. *bande* < OFr. < ML. < Goth. *binda* < *bindan*, to BIND] **1.** something that binds, ties together, restrains, etc. **2.** *a)* a strip or ring of wood, metal, rubber, etc. fastened around something to bind or tie it together *b)* a finger ring [a wedding *band*] **3.** a stripe [a chrome *band* along a car's side] **4.** a narrow strip of cloth used to line, decorate, etc. [*hatband*] **5.** [usually *pl.*] two strips hanging in front from the neck, as part of the dress of certain clergymen, judges, etc. **6.** a division on a long-playing phonograph record containing an individual selection **7.** a specific range of wavelengths or frequencies, as in radio broadcasting or sound or light transmission —*vt.* **1.** to put a band on or around ☆**2.** to put a band on in marking for identification [birds are *banded* to study their migrations]

band[2] (band) *n.* [Fr. *bande*, a troupe (orig., prob., those following the same sign) < It. *banda* < Goth. *bandwa*, a sign < *bindan*, to BIND] **1.** a group of people united for a common purpose **2.** a group of musicians playing together, esp. upon wind and percussion instruments [a marching *band*] —*vi., vt.* to unite for a common purpose (usually with *together*) —*see* SYN. at TROOP

band·age (ban′dij) *n.* [Fr. < *bande*, BAND[1]] a strip of cloth or other dressing used to bind or cover an injured part of the body —*vt.* **-aged, -ag·ing** to put a bandage on

☆**Band-Aid** (band′dād′) [BAND(AGE) + AID] *a trademark for* a small prepared bandage of gauze and adhesive tape —*n.* [b- a-] a bandage of this type: also **band′aid′**

ban·dan·na, ban·dan·a (ban dan′ə) *n.* [Hindi *bāndhnū*, method of dyeing] a large, colored handkerchief, usually with a printed pattern

band·box (band′bäks′) *n.* a light box of wood or pasteboard to hold hats, collars, etc.

ban·deau (ban dō′, ban′dō) *n., pl.* **-deaux** (-dōz′, -dō) [Fr.] **1.** a narrow ribbon, esp. one worn around the head to hold the hair in place **2.** a narrow brassiere giving little support

‡**ban·de·ril·la** (bän′de rēl′yä) *n.* [Sp., small banner] any of a number of barbed darts with little streamers attached, which are stuck into the neck and shoulders of the bull during a bullfight

ban·de·role, ban·de·rol (ban′də rōl′) *n.* [Fr. < It. dim. of *bandiera*, banner] a narrow flag or pennant, as one attached to a lance

ban·di·coot (ban′di kōōt′) *n.* [< Telugu *pandikokku*, pig rat] **1.** a very large rat found esp. in India and Ceylon **2.** a ratlike animal of Australia that carries its young in a pouch

ban·dit (ban′dit) *n., pl.* **-dits, ban·dit·ti** (ban dit′ē) [It. *bandito* < *bandire*, to outlaw, akin to OHG. *bann* (see BAN[1], *n.*)] **1.** a robber, esp. one who robs travelers on the road; brigand **2.** anyone who cheats, steals, etc. —**ban′dit·ry** *n.*

band·mas·ter (band′mas′tər) *n.* the leader or conductor of a military or brass band

ban·do·leer, ban·do·lier (ban′də lir′) *n.* [< Fr. < Sp. < *banda*, a scarf, a sash < Goth. *bandwa*: see BAND[2]] a broad shoulder belt with pockets for carrying ammunition, etc.

☆**band saw** a power saw consisting of an endless, toothed steel belt running over pulleys

band shell an outdoor platform for concerts, having a concave back serving as a sounding board

bands·man (bandz′mən) *n., pl.* **-men** a member of a band of musicians

band·stand (band′stand′) *n.* **1.** an outdoor, usually roofed platform for a band or orchestra **2.** any platform for a musical band, as in a ballroom

BANDOLEER

Ban·dung (bän′dooŋ, ban dooŋ′) city in W Java, Indonesia: pop. 973,000

☆**band·wag·on** (band′wag′ən) *n.* a wagon for the band to ride in, as in a parade —**on the bandwagon** [Colloq.] on the popular or apparently winning side, as in an election

band·width (-width′) *n.* the range of frequencies within a radiation band needed to transmit a particular signal

ban·dy[1] (ban′dē) *vt.* **-died, -dy·ing** [Fr. *bander*, to bandy at tennis] **1.** to toss or hit (a ball, etc.) back and forth **2.** to pass (gossip, etc.) about carelessly **3.** to exchange (words), as in arguing

ban·dy[2] (ban′dē) *adj.* [< Fr. pp. of *bander*, to bend (as a bow)] bent or curved outward

ban·dy·leg·ged (-leg′id, -legd′) *adj.* having bandy legs; bowlegged

bane (bān) *n.* [OE. *bana*, slayer < IE. base *bhen-*, to strike] **1.** [Poet.] ruin **2.** the cause of distress, death, or ruin [pollution, the *bane* of our existence] **3.** deadly poison: now obs. except in *ratsbane*, etc.

bane·ber·ry (bān′ber′ē) *n., pl.* **-ries 1.** any of a genus of plants of the buttercup family, with clusters of white or red berries, some of which are poisonous **2.** the berry of any of these plants

bane·ful (-fəl) *adj.* causing distress, death, or ruin; deadly; harmful —see *SYN.* at PERNICIOUS —**bane′ful·ly** *adv.*

Banff National Park (bamf) [after *Banff*, county in NE Scotland] Canadian National Park on the E slopes of the Rockies, in SW Alberta: 2,585 sq. mi.

bang[1] (baŋ) *vt.* [ON. *banga*, to pound] **1.** to hit hard and noisily **2.** to shut (a door, etc.) noisily **3.** to handle violently — *vi.* **1.** to make a sharp, loud noise **2.** to strike sharply (*against, into,* etc.) —*n.* **1.** a hard blow or loud knock **2.** a sudden, loud noise ☆**3.** *a*) [Colloq.] a display of enthusiasm or vigor [to start with a *bang*] *b*) [Slang] a thrill; excitement [Vi gets a *bang* out of skiing] —*adv.* **1.** hard, noisily, and suddenly [to run *bang* against a wall] **2.** suddenly or exactly [he stopped *bang* in the middle] —**bang up** to do physical damage to [who *banged up* the car?]

☆**bang**[2] (baŋ) *vt.* [< ?] to cut (hair) short and straight across — *n.* [usually *pl.*] banged hair worn across the forehead

Ban·ga·lore (baŋ′gə lôr′) city in S India: pop. 1,207,000

☆**bang·board** (baŋ′bôrd′) *n.* [BANG[1] + BOARD] a large board mounted along one side of a wagon, against which cornhuskers toss the ears of corn, causing them to rebound into the wagon

Bang·ka (bäŋ′kä) island of Indonesia, off the E coast of Sumatra: 4,610 sq. mi.

Bang·kok (baŋ′käk) capital of Thailand, a seaport in the S part: pop. 1,669,000

Bang·la·desh (bäŋ′glə desh′) country in S Asia, at the head of the Bay of Bengal: a member of the Commonwealth: 55,134 sq. mi.; pop. 50,840,000; cap. Dacca

ban·gle (baŋ′g'l) *n.* [Hindi *bangrī*, glass bracelet] **1.** a decorative bracelet, armlet, or anklet **2.** a disk-shaped ornament, as one hanging from a bracelet

bang·tail (baŋ′tāl′) *n.* ☆[Slang] a racehorse

Ban·gui (bäŋ gē′) capital of the Central African Republic, on the Ubangi River: pop. 150,000

bang-up (baŋ′up′) *adj.* [Colloq.] excellent

ban·ian[1] (ban′yən) *n. same as* BANYAN

ban·ian[2] (ban′yən) *n.* [Port., ult. < Sans. *vanij*, merchant] a Hindu merchant

ban·ish (ban′ish) *vt.* [< extended stem of OFr. *banir* < *ban:* see BAN[1]] **1.** to send into exile **2.** to send or put away; get rid of [to banish cares; to banish wrinkles] —**ban′ish·ment** *n.*
SYN. —**banish** means to force to leave a country (not necessarily one's own) as a punishment; **exile** implies being forced to leave one's own country, either because the government has ordered it or events have made it necessary; **expatriate** suggests more strongly exile by one's own choice and often implies the getting of citizenship in another country; to **deport** is to send (an alien) out of the country, because the alien either entered unlawfully or is considered undesirable

ban·is·ter (ban′əs tər) *n.* [altered < BALUSTER] **1.** [often *pl.*] a railing and the balusters supporting it, as on a staircase **2.** the railing itself

Ban·jer·ma·sin, Ban·jar·ma·sin (bän′jər mä′sin) seaport in S Borneo, Indonesia: pop. 214,000

☆**ban·jo** (ban′jō) *n., pl.* **-jos, -joes** [of Afr. origin] a stringed musical instrument having a long neck and a circular body covered with tightly stretched skin: the strings, usually four or five, are plucked with the fingers or a pick — **ban′jo·ist** *n.*

BANJO

Ban·jul (bän′jool′) capital of Gambia: pop. 40,000

bank[1] (baŋk) *n.* [< Fr. < It. *banca*, orig. a (moneylender's) table < OHG. *bank*, bench: see BANK[2]] **1.** *a*) an establishment for receiving, lending, or, sometimes, issuing money, and for making it easier to exchange funds, as by checks and notes *b*) its building **2.** *same as* PIGGY BANK **3.** the fund held, as by the dealer, in some gambling games **4.** *Med. a*) any place for gathering and distributing blood for transfusions or body parts for transplantation *b*) any reserve thus gathered —*vi.* **1.** to put money in or do business with a bank **2.** to manage a bank **3.** to keep the bank, as in some gambling games —*vt.* to deposit (money) in a bank —☆**bank on** [Colloq.] to depend on; rely on —☆**bank′a·ble** *adj.*

bank[2] (baŋk) *n.* [< ON. *bakki*, akin to OHG. *bank* & OE. *benc*, BENCH] **1.** a long mound or heap; ridge [a *bank* of earth] **2.** a steep slope, as of a hill **3.** a stretch of rising land at the edge of a stream, etc. **4.** a shoal or shallow place, as in a sea [the ship ran aground on a sand *bank*] **5.** the sloping of an airplane to one side to avoid slipping sideways on a turn **6.** the sloping of a road or racing track along a curve —*vt.* **1.** to heap dirt around (a plant, etc.) for protection from cold, etc. **2.** to cover (a fire) with ashes and fuel so that it will burn longer **3.** to pile up so as to form a bank [to *bank* snow along a road] **4.** to construct (a curve in a road, etc.) so that it slopes up from the inside edge **5.** to tilt (an airplane) sideways on a turn **6.** *Billiards* to stroke (a ball) so that it springs back from a cushion —*vi.* **1.** to take the form of a bank or banks **2.** to bank an airplane —see *SYN.* at SHOAL[2]

bank[3] (baŋk) *n.* [< OFr. < OHG. *bank:* see BANK[2]] **1.** a bench for rowers in a galley **2.** a row of oars **3.** a row or tier of objects **4.** a row of keys in a keyboard or console —*vt.* to arrange in a bank

☆**bank account** money deposited in a bank that can be withdrawn by the depositor

bank·book (baŋk′book′) *n.* the book in which the account of a depositor in a bank is recorded

bank·er (baŋ′kər) *n.* **1.** one who owns or manages a bank **2.** the keeper of the bank in some gambling games

bank·ing (-kiŋ) *n.* the business of managing a bank

bank note a promissory note issued by a bank, payable on demand: it is a form of paper money

☆**bank·roll** (baŋk′rōl′) *n.* a supply of money —*vt.* [Colloq.] to supply with money; finance

bank·rupt (baŋk′rupt′, -rəpt) *n.* [< Fr. < It. < *banca*, bench (see BANK[1]) + *rotta*, broken < L. pp. of *rumpere*, to break] a person legally declared unable to pay his debts: his property is divided among his creditors —*adj.* **1.** that is a bankrupt **2.** lacking in some quality [morally *bankrupt*] **3.** that has failed completely [a *bankrupt* foreign policy] —*vt.* to make bankrupt

bank·rupt·cy (-rupt′sē, -rəp sē) *n., pl.* **-cies 1.** the state or an instance of being bankrupt **2.** complete failure; ruin; destitution

ban·ner (ban′ər) *n.* [< OFr. *baniere* (< WGmc. *banda*, a sign), altered after *banir*, to announce (see BANISH)] **1.** a piece of cloth bearing a design, motto, etc., sometimes attached to a staff **2.** a flag **3.** a headline extending across a newspaper page —*adj.* foremost; leading [a *banner* year in sales]

ban·nock (ban′ək) *n.* [< Gael. *bannach*, a cake] [Scot.] a flat cake of oatmeal or barley meal

Ban·nock·burn (ban′ək burn′) town in C Scotland: site of a battle (1314) in which the Scots kept their independence

banns (banz) *n.pl.* [see BAN[1]] the public announcement, generally made in church on three successive Sundays, of an intended marriage

ban·quet (baŋ′kwit, ban′-) *n.* [Fr. < It. *banchetto*, dim. of *ban-*

ca: see BANK¹] **1.** an elaborate meal; feast **2.** a formal dinner for many people, usually with speeches —*vt.* to honor with a banquet —*vi.* to dine at a banquet —**ban′quet·er** *n.*

ban·quette (baŋ ket′) *n.* [Fr., dim. < Norm. *banque,* earthwork < Du. *bank,* BANK²] **1.** a gunners' platform along the inside of a trench or parapet ☆**2.** [South] a sidewalk **3.** an upholstered bench along a wall

Ban·quo (baŋ′kwō, ban′-) a character in Shakespeare's *Macbeth:* his ghost appears to Macbeth, who had ordered his murder

ban·shee, ban·shie (ban′shē) *n.* [< Ir. < *bean,* woman + *sith,* fairy] *Ir. & Scot. Folklore* a female spirit believed to wail outside a house to warn that someone in the family is about to die

ban·tam (ban′təm) *n.* [after *Bantam,* former Du. residency in Java] **1.** [*often* B-] any of various dwarf varieties of breeds of domestic fowl **2.** a small but aggressive person —*adj.* like a bantam; small and aggressive

ban·tam·weight (-wāt′) *n.* a boxer or wrestler between a flyweight and a featherweight (in boxing, 113–118 pounds)

ban·ter (ban′tər) *vt.* [17th-c. slang < ? BANDY¹] to tease in a playful way —*vi.* to exchange banter (*with* someone) —*n.* good-natured teasing or joking —**ban′ter·er** *n.* —**ban′ter·ing·ly** *adv.*

Ban·ting (ban′tiŋ), Sir **Frederick Grant** 1891–1941; Canad. physiologist: co-discoverer of insulin

bant·ling (bant′liŋ) *n.* [< G. *bänkling,* bastard < *bank,* a bench] [Archaic] a young child; brat

Ban·tu (ban′tōō) *n.* [Bantu *ba-ntu,* mankind] **1.** *pl.* **-tus, -tu** any member of a large group of Negroid tribes of equatorial and southern Africa **2.** any of the group of languages of these peoples —*adj.* of the Bantus or their languages

Ban·tu·stan (ban′tōō stan′) *n.* [BANTU + Per. *stän,* a place] any of several territories in South Africa set aside as reserves for native black peoples, supposedly with some self-government

ban·yan (ban′yən) *n.* [from a tree of this kind under which the *banians* (see BANIAN²) had built a pagoda] an East Indian fig tree whose branches grow shoots that take root and become new trunks

BANYAN

ban·zai (bän′zī′) *interj.* a Japanese greeting or shout, meaning "May you live ten thousand years!"

ba·o·bab (bä′ō bab′, bā′-) *n.* [prob. EAfr. native name] a tall tree of Africa and India, with a thick trunk and gourdlike, edible fruit: fiber from its bark is used in rope, paper, etc.

bap·tism (bap′tiz′m) *n.* [< OFr. < L. < Gr. *baptizein,* to immerse] **1.** the rite or sacrament of admitting a person into a Christian church by dipping him in water or by pouring or sprinkling water on him **2.** any experience that initiates, tests, or purifies —**bap·tis′mal** (-tiz′m'l) *adj.*

baptism of fire 1. the first time that a soldier is in combat **2.** any first test of one's courage, strength, etc.

bap·tist (bap′tist) *n.* **1.** a person who baptizes; specif., [B-] JOHN THE BAPTIST **2.** [B-] a member of a Protestant denomination holding that baptism should be given only to a person who has declared his faith and only by dipping the entire body in water

bap·tis·ter·y (bap′tis trē, -tis tər ē) *n., pl.* **-ter·ies** a place, esp. a part of a church, used for baptizing: also **bap′tis·try** (-trē), *pl.* **-tries**

bap·tize (bap′tīz, bap tīz′) *vt.* **-tized, -tiz·ing 1.** to take (a person) into a Christian church by baptism **2.** to initiate, purify, cleanse, etc. **3.** to give a first name to at a baptism; christen —*vi.* to administer baptism —**bap′tiz·er** *n.*

bar¹ (bär) *n.* [OFr. *barre* < ML. *barra,* barrier] **1.** any piece of wood, metal, etc. longer than it is wide or thick, often used as a barrier, lever, etc. **2.** *a)* an oblong piece [*bar* of soap] *b)* a small metal strip worn to show military or other rank **3.** anything that obstructs, hinders, or prevents [illiteracy is a *bar* to success] **4.** a strip, band, or broad line, as of light or color **5.** the part of a law court, enclosed by a railing, where the judges or lawyers sit, or where prisoners are brought to trial **6.** *a)* a law court *b)* any place of judgment [the *bar* of public opinion] **7.** *a)* lawyers as a group [the *bar* recommends him as a candidate] *b)* the legal profession [he is studying for the *bar*] **8.** *a)* a counter at which alcoholic drinks are served *b)* a place

with such a counter **9.** a handrail held onto while doing ballet exercises **10.** the mouthpiece of a horse's bit **11.** *Music a)* any of the vertical lines across a staff, dividing it into measures *b)* a measure —*vt.* **barred, bar′ring 1.** to fasten with or as with a bar [*bar* the door!] **2.** to obstruct; shut off; close [a fallen tree *bars* the path] **3.** to oppose, prevent, or forbid [the law *bars* convicts from voting] **4.** to keep out; exclude [he was *barred* from the contest] **5.** to set aside [*barring* certain possibilities] —*prep.* excluding; excepting [the best, *bar* none] —see SYN. at HINDER¹ and SHOAL² —**cross the bar** to die

bar² (bär) *n.* [G. < Gr. *baros,* weight: for IE. base see GRAVE¹] a metric unit of pressure equal to one million dynes per square centimeter

BAR Browning automatic rifle

bar. 1. barometer **2.** barrel **3.** barrister

barb¹ (bärb) *n.* [< OFr. < L. *barba,* BEARD] **1.** a beardlike growth near the mouth of certain animals **2.** a sharp point projecting backward from the main point of a fishhook, arrow, etc. **3.** a sarcastic remark **4.** any of the hairlike projections from the shaft of a feather —*vt.* to provide with a barb or barbs —**barbed** *adj.*

barb² (bärb) *n.* [< Fr. < It. < Ar. *Barbar,* Berber] a horse of a breed native to Barbary

Bar·ba·dos (bär bā′dōz, -dōs) country on the easternmost island of the West Indies, northeast of Trinidad: a member of the Commonwealth: 166 sq. mi.; pop. 253,000 —**Bar·ba′di·an** (-dē ən) *adj., n.*

Bar·ba·ra (bär′bər ə, -brə) [L., fem. of *barbarus* (see BARBAROUS), foreign, strange] a feminine name

bar·bar·i·an (bär ber′ē ən) *n.* [see BARBAROUS] **1.** orig., a foreigner; esp., in ancient times, a non-Greek, non-Roman, or non-Christian **2.** a member of a people with a civilization regarded as primitive, etc. **3.** a person who lacks culture **4.** a coarse or unmannerly person; boor **5.** a savage, cruel person; brute —*adj.* of or like a barbarian; esp., uncivilized, cruel, rude, etc. —**bar·bar′i·an·ism** *n.*

SYN.—**barbarian** simply refers to a primitive civilization, usually with no further connotation [the Anglo-Saxons were a *barbarian* people]; **barbaric** suggests the crudeness and wildness thought of as characteristic of primitive peoples [*barbaric* splendor]; **barbarous** emphasizes the cruelty and violent behavior thought of as characteristic of primitive peoples [*barbarous* warfare]; **savage** implies a more primitive civilization than **barbarian** and suggests even greater fierceness and cruelty [a *savage* inquisition] —ANT. **civilized**

bar·bar·ic (-ik) *adj.* **1.** of or like barbarians; uncivilized; primitive **2.** wild, crude, and without control —see SYN. at BARBARIAN —**bar·bar′i·cal·ly** *adv.*

bar·bar·ism (bär′bər iz'm) *n.* **1.** *a)* the use of words and expressions not standard in a language *b)* a word or expression of this sort (Ex.: "youse" for "you") **2.** the state of being primitive or uncivilized **3.** a barbarous act, custom, etc.

bar·bar·i·ty (bär ber′ə tē) *n., pl.* **-ties 1.** cruel or brutal behavior **2.** a cruel or brutal act **3.** a crude or coarse taste, manner, etc.

bar·bar·ize (bär′bə rīz′) *vt., vi.* **-rized′, -riz′ing** to make or become barbarous —**bar′ba·ri·za′tion** *n.*

Bar·ba·ros·sa (bär′bə räs′ə, -rōs′-), **Frederick** [It. < *barba,* beard + *rossa,* red: he had such a beard] *see* FREDERICK I

bar·ba·rous (bär′bər əs) *adj.* [< L. < Gr. *barbaros,* foreign; prob. < echoic word imitating unintelligible speech] **1.** orig., foreign or alien; esp., in the ancient world, non-Greek, non-Roman, or non-Christian **2.** using barbarisms in speaking or writing **3.** uncivilized **4.** uncultured, crude, coarse, etc. **5.** cruel; brutal —see SYN. at BARBARIAN —**bar′ba·rous·ly** *adv.* —**bar′ba·rous·ness** *n.*

Bar·ba·ry (bär′bər ē) region in N Africa, west of Egypt, inhabited chiefly by Berbers: its coast (**Barbary Coast**) was once a center of piracy

Barbary ape a tailless, apelike monkey of North Africa and Gibraltar

bar·bate (bär′bāt) *adj.* [< L. < *barba,* BEARD] bearded

bar·be·cue (bär′bə kyōō′) *n.* [< Sp. < Haitian Creole *barbacoa,* framework] **1.** orig., a framework for smoking, drying, or broiling meat **2.** a hog, steer, etc. roasted whole over an open fire **3.** any meat broiled over an open fire ☆**4.** a party or picnic at which such meat is served **5.** a portable outdoor grill —*vt.* **-cued′, -cu′ing 1.** to prepare (meat) outdoors by broiling on a spit or over a grill **2.** to cook (meat) with a highly seasoned sauce (**barbecue sauce**)

☆**barbed wire** twisted wire with sharp points all along it, used for fences or other barriers

bar·bel (bär′b'l) *n.* [OFr., ult. < L. *barba,* BEARD] **1.** a thread-like growth from the lips or jaws of certain fishes: it is an organ of touch **2.** any of several large European freshwater fishes with such growths

bar·bell (bär′bel′) *n.* [BAR¹ + (DUMB)BELL] a metal bar to which disks of varying weights are attached at each end, used for weight-lifting exercises: also **bar bell, bar-bell**

bar·ber (bär′bər) *n.* [OFr. *barbour,* ult. < L. *barba,* BEARD] a person whose work is cutting hair, shaving and trimming beards, etc. —*vt.* to cut the hair of, shave, etc. —*vi.* to work as a barber

BARBELS (on a channel catfish)

Bar·ber (bär′bər), **Samuel** 1910– ; U.S. composer

barber pole a pole with spiral stripes of red and white, a symbol of the barber's trade

bar·ber·ry (bär′ber′ē) *n., pl.* **-ries** [< ML. *barberis* < Ar. *barbāris*] **1.** a spiny shrub with sour, red berries and yellow flowers **2.** the berry

☆**bar·ber·shop** (bär′bər shäp′) *n.* a barber's place of business —*adj.* [Colloq.] designating, characterized by, or like the close harmony of male voices [a *barbershop* quartet]

bar·bette (bär bet′) *n.* [Fr. < *barbe,* BEARD] **1.** a platform for guns in a fort, from which they can be fired over the walls **2.** the armor around a gun platform on a warship

bar·bi·can (bär′bi kən) *n.* [< OFr., prob. < Per. *barbar-khānah,* house on a wall] a defensive tower at the gate or bridge leading into a town or castle

bar·bi·cel (bär′bə sel′) *n.* [< ModL. < L. *barba,* BEARD] any of the tiny, hairlike extensions growing from the barbules of a feather

☆**bar·bi·tal** (bär′bi tôl′) *n.* [BARBIT(URIC ACID) + -AL] a drug, $C_8H_{12}O_3N_2$, in the form of a white powder, used to induce sleep

bar·bi·tu·rate (bär bich′ər it, bär′bə tyoor′it) *n.* any salt or ester of barbituric acid, used as a sedative or to induce sleep

bar·bi·tu·ric acid (bär′bə tyoor′ik, -toor′-) [< G. *barbitur-säure* (< ModL. *Usnea barbata,* bearded moss + *urea,* UREA + *säure,* acid) + -IC] a crystalline acid, $C_4H_4O_3N_2$, from which drugs are produced that cause sleep

bar·bule (bär′byool) *n.* [< L. *barba,* BEARD] **1.** a very small barb **2.** any of the threadlike parts forming a fringe on each barb of a feather

barb·wire (bärb′wīr′) *n. same as* BARBED WIRE

bar·ca·role, bar·ca·rolle (bär′kə rōl′) *n.* [Fr. < It. < *barca,* boat] **1.** a song sung by Venetian gondoliers **2.** a piece of music imitating this

Bar·ce·lo·na (bär′sə lō′nə; *Sp.* bär′the lô′nä) seaport in NE Spain: pop. 1,697,000

bard (bärd) *n.* [Gael. & Ir.] **1.** an ancient Celtic poet and singer of epic poems **2.** any poet —**bard′ic** *adj.*

Bard of Avon William Shakespeare: so called from his birth-place, Stratford-on-Avon

bare¹ (ber) *adj.* **bar′er, bar′est** [OE. *bær*] **1.** *a)* without the customary covering [*bare* floors] *b)* without clothing; naked [*bare* legs] **2.** without equipment or furnishings; empty [a *bare* room] **3.** simple; plain [the *bare* facts] **4.** without tools or weapons [to use one's *bare* hands] **5.** worn down; threadbare [a *bare* rug] **6.** no more than; mere [a *bare* inch away] —*vt.* **bared, bar′ing** to make bare; uncover; strip —**lay bare** to uncover; expose —**bare′ness** *n.*

SYN.—**bare,** in this comparison, implies a lack of the usual or proper covering, esp. from some part of the body [*bare* legs; with the head *bare*]; **naked** implies a lack of clothing either entirely or from some part, and suggests a revealing of the body [a *naked* bosom]; **nude,** sometimes a euphemism for naked, is often applied to the unclothed human figure in art —**ANT.** covered, clothed

bare² (ber) *archaic pt. of* BEAR¹

bare·back (ber′bak′) *adv., adj.* on a horse with no saddle

bare·faced (-fāst′) *adj.* **1.** with the face uncovered or beardless **2.** unconcealed; open **3.** feeling or showing no shame; brazen [a *barefaced* lie] —**bare′fac·ed·ly** (-fās′id lē) *adv.* —**bare′fac·ed·ness** *n.*

bare·foot (-foot′) *adj., adv.* without shoes and stockings —**bare′foot·ed** *adj.*

bare·hand·ed (-han′did) *adj., adv.* **1.** with hands uncovered **2.** without weapons or other means

bare·head·ed (-hed′id) *adj., adv.* wearing no hat or other head covering

bare·leg·ged (-leg′id, -legd′) *adj., adv.* with the legs bare; without stockings on

bare·ly (ber′lē) *adv.* **1.** openly; plainly **2.** only just; no more than; scarcely [*barely* enough to eat] **3.** scantily [a *barely* furnished room]

Bar·ents Sea (ber′ənts, bär′-) part of the Arctic Ocean, north of Europe

☆**barf** (bärf) *vi., vt.* [echoic] [Slang] to vomit

☆**bar·fly** (bär′flī′) *n., pl.* **-flies′** [Slang] one who spends much time drinking in barrooms

bar·gain (bär′g'n) *n.* [< OFr. < *bargaignier,* to haggle < Frank. *borganjan,* to lend] **1.** a mutual agreement between parties on what should be given or done by each **2.** such an agreement in terms of its worth to one of the parties [a bad *bargain*] **3.** something sold at a price favorable to the buyer —*vi.* **1.** to talk over a transaction, contract, etc., trying to get the best possible terms **2.** to make a bargain —*vt.* to sell by bargaining; barter —**bargain for 1.** to try to get cheaply **2.** to expect; count on [more trouble than he had *bargained for*]: also **bargain on** —**into the bargain** in addition; besides —**bar′gain·er** *n.*

barge (bärj) *n.* [< OFr. < ML. *barga*] **1.** a large, flat-bottomed boat for carrying freight on rivers, etc.: it is usually towed or pushed **2.** a large pleasure boat, used for pageants, etc. **3.** a flagship's boat for use by flag officers —*vt.* **barged, barg′ing** to carry by barge —*vi.* **1.** to move slowly and clumsily **2.** to come or go (*in* or *into*) in a rude, abrupt way [he *barged* into the room without knocking] **3.** to collide clumsily (*into*) [in my confusion, I *barged* into the table]

BARGE

barge·man (bärj′mən) *n., pl.* **-men** a man who operates, or works on, a barge

bar graph a graph with parallel bars representing in proportional lengths the figures given in the data

Ba·ri (bä′rē) seaport in SE Italy, on the Adriatic: pop. 345,000

bar·ite (ber′īt) *n.* [< Gr. *barys,* weighty + -ITE] a white, crystalline mineral composed mainly of barium sulfate

bar·i·tone (bar′ə tōn′) *n.* [< It. < Gr. < *barys,* deep + *tonos,* tone] **1.** the range of a male voice between bass and tenor **2.** a voice or singer with such a range **3.** any wind instrument with a similar range **4.** a part for such a voice or instrument —*adj.* of, in, for, or having this range

bar·i·um (ber′ē əm) *n.* [ModL. < Gr. *barys,* heavy] a silver-white, metallic chemical element: symbol, Ba; at. wt., 137.34; at. no., 56

barium sulfate an odorless, tasteless, white powder, $BaSO_4$, that is opaque when swallowed and so helps in the examination of X-rays of the stomach and intestines

bark¹ (bärk) *n.* [ON. *borkr*] the outside covering of the stems and roots of trees and woody plants —*vt.* **1.** to tan (hides) with a bark infusion **2.** to take the bark off (a tree) **3.** [Colloq.] to scrape some skin off [to *bark* one's shin]

bark² (bärk) *vi.* [OE. *beorcan:* echoic] **1.** to make the sharp, abrupt cry of a dog **2.** to make a sound like this [the engine *barked*] **3.** to speak or shout sharply; snap **4.** [Colloq.] to cough ☆**5.** [Slang] to work as a barker —*vt.* to say with a bark or a shout —*n.* a sound made in barking —☆**bark up the wrong tree** to misdirect one's attack, energies, etc.

bark³ (bärk) *n.* [< Fr. < It. & L. *barca* < Gr. < Coptic *bari,* small boat] **1.** [Poet.] any boat, esp. a small sailing boat **2.** a sailing vessel with its two forward masts square-rigged and its rear mast rigged fore-and-aft

bar·keep·er (bär′kēp′ər) *n.* **1.** an owner or manager of a bar **2.** a bartender Also **bar′keep′**

☆**bark·en·tine** (bär′kən tēn′) *n.* [< BARK³ after BRIGANTINE] a sailing vessel with its foremast square-rigged and its other two masts rigged fore-and-aft

bark·er (bär′kər) *n.* one that barks; esp., a person in front of a sideshow, etc. who tries to attract customers by loud, lively talk about it

bar·ley (bär′lē) *n.* see PLURAL, II, D, 3 [< OE. *bærlic, adj.* < *bere,* barley] **1.** a cereal grass **2.** its grain, used in making malts, in soups, and as a feed for animals

bar·ley·corn (-kôrn′) *n.* barley or a grain of barley: see also JOHN BARLEYCORN

barm (bärm) *n.* [OE. *beorma:* for IE. base see BREATH] the foamy yeast that appears on the surface of fermenting malt liquors

bar·maid (bär′mād′) *n.* a waitress who serves alcoholic drinks in a bar

bar·man (-mən) *n., pl.* **-men** a bartender

Bar·me·cide feast (bär′mə sīd′) [< the name of a prince in *The Arabian Nights* who served such a feast] **1.** a pretended feast with no food **2.** any pretended hospitality

bar mitz·vah, bar miz·vah (bär mits′və) [Heb. *bar mitswāh,* son of the commandment] [*also* B- M-] **1.** a Jewish boy who has arrived at the age of religious responsibility, thirteen years **2.** the ceremony celebrating this event

barm·y (bär′mē) *adj.* **-i·er, -i·est 1.** full of barm; foamy **2.** [Brit. Slang] silly; idiotic

barn (bärn) *n.* [< OE. *bern, berern* < *bere,* barley + *ærn,* a building] a farm building for sheltering harvested crops, livestock, etc.

bar·na·cle (bär′nə k'l) *n.* [< Fr. *bernicle* & Bret. *bernik,* kind of shellfish] any of a number of saltwater shellfish that attach themselves to rocks, ship bottoms, etc. **—bar′na·cled** *adj.*

☆**barn dance** a party, originally one held in a barn, at which people dance square dances

barn owl a species of brown and gray owl with a spotted white breast, commonly found in barns

barn·storm (bärn′stôrm′) *vi., vt.* [BARN + STORM, *vi.* 3: from occas. use of barns as auditoriums] to tour in small towns and rural districts, performing plays, giving campaign speeches, etc. **—barn′storm′er** *n.* **—barn′storm′ing** *adj., n.*

barn swallow a common swallow with a long, deeply forked tail: it usually nests in barns

Bar·num (bär′nəm), **P(hineas) T(aylor)** 1810–91; U.S. showman & circus operator

barn·yard (bärn′yärd′) *n.* the yard or ground near a barn **—adj. 1.** of a barnyard **2.** like or fit for a barnyard; earthy, smutty, etc. [*barnyard* humor]

bar·o- [< Gr. *baros,* weight] *a prefix meaning* of pressure, esp. atmospheric pressure [*barograph*]

bar·o·graph (bar′ə graf′) *n.* a barometer that records changes in atmospheric pressure automatically on a revolving cylinder **—bar′o·graph′ic** *adj.*

ba·rom·e·ter (bə räm′ə tər) *n.* [BARO- + -METER] **1.** an instrument for measuring atmospheric pressure, as by a graduated glass tube (**mercury barometer**) in which a column of mercury rises or falls as the pressure changes (see also ANEROID BAROMETER): barometers are used in forecasting the weather or finding height above sea level **2.** anything that indicates change [the stock market is a *barometer* of business] **—bar·o·met·ric** (bar′ə met′rik), **bar′o·met′ri·cal** *adj.* **—bar′o·met′ri·cal·ly** *adv.*

barometric pressure the pressure of the atmosphere as indicated by a barometer: in a mercury barometer it averages 29.92 inches at sea level

bar·on (bar′ən) *n.* [OFr. < Frank. *baro,* freeman, man: for IE. base see BEAR[1]] **1.** a member of the lowest rank of the British nobility **2.** a European or Japanese nobleman of like rank ☆**3.** a powerful businessman or industrialist [an oil *baron*]

bar·on·age (bar′ə nij) *n.* **1.** barons as a class **2.** the peerage **3.** the rank, title, etc. of a baron

bar·on·ess (-nis) *n.* **1.** a baron's wife or widow **2.** a lady with a baron's rank

bar·on·et (-nit, -net′) *n.* a man holding the lowest hereditary British title, below a baron but above a knight **—bar′on·et·cy** (-sē) *n., pl.* **-cies**

ba·ro·ni·al (bə rō′nē əl) *adj.* of or fit for a baron [a *baronial* mansion]

bar·on·y (bar′ə nē) *n., pl.* **-on·ies 1.** a baron's lands **2.** the rank or title of a baron

ba·roque (bə rōk′) *adj.* [Fr. < Port. *barroco,* imperfect pearl] **1.** *a)* of or like a style of art and architecture with much ornamentation and curved forms rather than straight lines *b)* of or like a style of music with many grace notes, trills, etc. and much use of counterpoint and fugues **2.** of the period in which these styles flourished (from about 1550 to 1750) **3.** same as ROCOCO **4.** overdecorated, or too ornate **5.** irregular in shape: said of pearls **—n.** baroque style, baroque art, etc.

bar·o·scope (bar′ə skōp′) *n.* [BARO- + -SCOPE] an instrument indicating but not measuring changes in atmospheric pressure **—bar′o·scop′ic** (-skäp′ik) *adj.*

ba·rouche (bə rōōsh′) *n.* [< G. < It. < LL. *birotus* < *bi-,* two + *rota,* a wheel] a four-wheeled carriage with a collapsible hood, two double seats opposite each other, and a driver's seat in front

barque (bärk) *n.* same as BARK[3]

☆**bar·quen·tine** (bär′kən tēn′) *n.* same as BARKENTINE

Bar·qui·si·me·to (bär kē′sē mā′tô) city in NW Venezuela: pop. 235,000

bar·rack (bar′ik) *n.* [< Fr. < Sp. *barraca,* mud hut < *barro,* clay < VL. *barrum,* clay] [*pl., often with sing. v.*] **1.** a building or group of buildings for housing soldiers **2.** a large, plain, often temporary building for housing workmen, etc. **—vt., vi.** to house in barracks

barracks bag a large cloth bag to hold a soldier's equipment and personal possessions

bar·ra·cu·da (bar′ə kōō′də) *n., pl.* **-da, -das:** see PLURAL, II, D, 2 [Sp., prob. < native WInd. name] a fierce, pikelike fish of tropical seas

bar·rage (bə razh′, -räj′; *for n.* 3 bär′ij) *n.* [Fr. < *barrer,* to stop < *barre,* BAR[1]] **1.** a curtain of artillery fire laid down to keep enemy forces from moving, or to cover one's own forces, esp. in attack **2.** a heavy attack of words, blows, etc. **3.** a man-made barrier in a river; dam **—vi., vt. -raged′, -rag′ing** to lay down a barrage (against)

BARRACUDA
(to 10 ft. long)

bar·ran·ca (bə raŋ′kə) *n.* [Sp.] a deep ravine or a steep cliff: also **bar·ran′co** (-kō), *pl.* **-cos**

Bar·ran·qui·lla (bä′rän kē′yä) seaport in NW Colombia: pop. 498,000

bar·ra·tor, bar·ra·ter (bar′ə tər) *n.* [< OFr. *barater,* to cheat < *barate,* fraud < ON. *baratta,* quarrel] a person guilty of barratry

bar·ra·try (bar′ə trē) *n.* [see prec.] **1.** the crime of habitually bringing about quarrels or lawsuits **2.** fraud or negligence on the part of a ship's officers or crew that results in a loss to the owners **—bar′ra·trous** *adj.*

barred (bärd) *adj.* **1.** having bars or stripes [the *barred* owl has bars of brown feathers across the breast] **2.** closed off with bars [a *barred* door] **3.** forbidden or excluded

bar·rel (bar′əl) *n.* [< OFr. *baril* < ML. *barillus* < ?] **1.** a large, wooden, cylindrical container with slightly bulging sides and flat ends, made usually of staves bound together with hoops **2.** the amount that a standard barrel will hold (in the U.S., usually 31½ gal.) **3.** any somewhat similar cylinder, drum, etc. [the *barrel* of a windlass] **4.** the tube of a gun, through which the projectile is fired **5.** [Colloq.] a great amount [a *barrel* of fun] **—vt. -reled** or **-relled, -rel·ing** or **-rel·ling** to put or pack in a barrel or barrels **—**☆**vi.** [Slang] to go at a high speed **—**☆**have (someone) over a barrel** [Slang] to have (someone) completely at one's mercy

bar·rel-chest·ed (-ches′tid) *adj.* having an especially broad, deep chest for one's height

barrel organ a mechanical musical instrument having a revolving cylinder studded with pins which open pipe valves, producing a tune; hand organ

barrel roll a complete revolution made by an airplane around its longitudinal axis while in flight

bar·ren (bar′ən) *adj.* [< OFr. *baraigne,* orig. used of land] **1.** that cannot produce offspring; sterile [a *barren* cow] **2.** not producing crops or fruit; having little or no vegetation [*barren* soil] **3.** not productive; unprofitable [a *barren* plan] **4.** lacking appeal, interest, or meaning; dull; boring **5.** empty; devoid [*barren* of creative spirit] **—n. 1.** an area of unproductive land **2.** [*usually pl.*] land with shrubs, brush, etc. and sandy soil **—bar′ren·ly** *adv.* **—bar′ren·ness** *n.*

bar·rette (bə ret′, bä-) *n.* [Fr., dim. of *barre,* BAR[1]] a small bar or clasp for holding a girl's or woman's hair in place

bar·ri·cade (bar′ə kād′; *also, esp. for v.,* bar′ə kād′) *n.* [Fr. < It. pp. of *barricare,* to fortify < ? Sp. or Fr. *barrica,* barrel: casks were used as barriers] **1.** a barrier thrown up hastily for defense **2.** any barrier or obstruction **—vt. -cad′ed, -cad′ing 1.** to shut in or keep out with a barricade **2.** to put up barricades in; obstruct

Bar·rie (bar'ē), Sir **James M**(atthew) 1860–1937; Scot. novelist & playwright

bar·ri·er (bar'ē ər) *n.* [< OFr. < *barre,* BAR[1]] **1.** an obstruction, as a fence or wall **2.** anything that holds apart or separates [*racial barriers*] **3.** [*sometimes* B-] a part of the antarctic ice sheet reaching into the sea

barrier reef a long ridge of coral parallel to the coastline, separated from it by a lagoon

bar·ring (bär'iŋ) *prep.* unless there should be; excepting [*barring* rain, we leave tonight]

bar·ri·o (bär'ē ō) *n., pl.* **-os** [Sp. < Ar. < *barr,* open country] in Spanish-speaking countries, a district or suburb of a city

bar·ris·ter (bar'is tər) *n.* [< BAR[1] (*n.* 6) + *-ister,* as in MINISTER] in England, a lawyer who presents and pleads cases in court: distinguished from SOLICITOR —see SYN. at LAWYER

☆**bar·room** (bär'rōōm') *n.* a room with a bar at which alcoholic drinks are sold

bar·row[1] (bar'ō) *n.* [< OE. < *beran,* BEAR[1]] **1.** same as: *a)* HANDBARROW *b)* WHEELBARROW **2.** a small cart with two wheels, pushed by hand; pushcart

bar·row[2] (bar'ō) *n.* [OE. *beorg,* hill] **1.** a heap of earth or rocks marking an ancient grave **2.** a hill or mound: now used only in English place names

Bar·row (bar'ō), **Point** [after Sir J. *Barrow,* 19th-c. Eng. geographer] northernmost point of Alas.; cape on the Arctic Ocean

bar sinister *same as* BEND SINISTER

Bart. Baronet

☆**bar·tend·er** (bär'ten'dər) *n.* a man who mixes and serves alcoholic drinks at a bar

bar·ter (bär'tər) *vi.* [< OFr. *barater:* see BARRATOR] to trade by exchanging goods or services without using money —*vt.* to exchange (goods, etc.); trade —*n.* **1.** the act or practice of bartering **2.** anything bartered —**barter away** to give or trade for too small a return —**bar·ter·er** *n.*

Barth (bärt), **Karl** 1886–1968; Swiss theologian

Bar·thol·di (bär tôl dē'), **Fré·dé·ric Au·guste** (frā dā rēk' ô güst') 1834–1904; Fr. sculptor of the Statue of Liberty

Bar·thol·o·mew (bär thäl'ə myōō') [< LL. < Gr. *Bartholomaios* < Aram., lit., son of Talmai] **1.** a masculine name **2.** Saint, one of the twelve apostles

bar·ti·zan (bär'tə zən, bär'tə zan') *n.* [altered < ME. *bretasce,* a parapet < OFr., prob. < OHG. *bret,* a board] a small, overhanging turret on a tower or battlement

☆**Bart·lett pear** (bärt'lət) [after E. *Bartlett* of Roxbury, Mass., the distributor] a large, juicy variety of pear

Bar·tók (bär'tôk), **Bé·la** (bā'lä) 1881–1945; Hung. composer

Bar·ton (bär't'n), **Clara** 1821–1912; U.S. philanthropist: founder of the American Red Cross

bar·y·on (bar'ē än') *n.* [< Gr. *barys,* heavy + (ELECTR)ON] one of a class of heavy atomic particles, including the proton and neutron and the hyperons

ba·ry·tes (bə rit'ēz) *n. same as* BARITE

bar·y·tone (bar'ə tōn') *adj., n. same as* BARITONE

bas·al (bā's'l) *adj.* **1.** of, at, or forming the base **2.** basic; fundamental —**bas'al·ly** *adv.*

basal metabolism the quantity of energy used by any organism at rest, measured by the rate (**basal metabolic rate**) at which heat is given off by the organism: it is expressed in calories per hour per square meter of skin surface

ba·salt (bə sôlt'; bās'ôlt, bas'-) *n.* [< L. *basaltes,* a dark marble] a dark, tough volcanic rock occurring in lava flows —**ba·sal'tic** *adj.*

bas·cule (bas'kyōōl) *n.* [Fr.] any device balanced like a seesaw

bascule bridge a drawbridge counterweighted so that it can be raised and lowered easily

base[1] (bās) *n., pl.* **bas'es** (-əz) [< OFr. *bas* < L. *basis,* BASIS] **1.** the thing or part on which something rests; foundation **2.** the main part, as of a plan, system, etc., on which the rest depends **3.** the principal or essential ingredient [paint with an oil *base*] **4.** anything from which a start is made; basis **5.** a goal or place of safety in cer-

BASCULE BRIDGE

tain games, as baseball **6.** the point of attachment of a part of the body [the *base* of the thumb] **7.** a center of operations or source of supply; headquarters **8.** *Chem.* any compound that reacts with an acid to form a salt, produces hydroxyl ions in water solutions, and turns red litmus blue **9.** *Geom.* the line or plane upon which a figure is thought of as resting [the *base* of a triangle] **10.** *Linguis.* any morpheme to which prefixes, suffixes, etc. are added; stem or root **11.** *Math. a)* the number that is raised to various powers to produce the main counting units of a number system [10 is the *base* of the decimal system] *b)* the number that when raised to the logarithm of a given number produces the given number *c)* in business, etc., a figure or sum upon which certain calculations are made —*adj.* forming a base —*vt.* **based, bas'ing** **1.** to make or serve as a base for **2.** to put or rest (*on*) as a base or basis [to *base* a guess on logic] **3.** to place or station (*in* or *at* a base) —☆**off base** **1.** *Baseball* not touching the base **2.** [Slang] taking an unsound or wrong position, attitude, etc.

SYN.—**base** refers to a part or thing at the bottom, acting as a support [the *base* of a lamp]; **basis** conveys the same idea, but is the term preferred for nonphysical things [the *basis* of a theory]; **foundation** stresses that the supporting thing or part is solid and often suggests that the thing which is built on it will be permanent and stable [the *foundation* of a house; a constitution that is the *foundation* of a government]; **groundwork,** while close in meaning to **foundation,** is mainly applied to nonphysical things [the *groundwork* of a good education]

base[2] (bās) *adj.* [< OFr. < VL. *bassus,* low] **1.** with little or no honor, courage, or decency; mean; contemptible [a *base* informer] **2.** of a menial or degrading kind [*base* servitude] **3.** inferior in quality [a *base* substitute] **4.** of comparatively low worth [iron is a *base* metal, gold a precious one] **5.** debased or counterfeit [*base* coin] **6.** [Archaic] of servile or humble birth —**base'ly** *adv.* —**base'ness** *n.*

SYN.—**base** implies a putting of one's own interests ahead of all else, as because of greed or cowardice [*base* motives]; **mean** suggests a pettiness of character or conduct [his *mean* attempts to slander her]; **ignoble** suggests a lack of high moral qualities [to work for an *ignoble* end]; **abject** implies lowness of character and a lack of self-respect [an *abject* coward]; **sordid** suggests a depressing drabness of something mean or base [a *sordid* scheme to cheat others]; **vile** suggests disgusting foulness or wickedness [*vile* language]; **low** suggests coarseness and corruption, esp. in reference to taking unfair advantage [so *low* as to rob the poor] —*ANT.* noble, moral, virtuous

base·ball (bās'bôl') *n.* ☆**1.** a game played with a round, hide-covered ball and a bat by two opposing teams of nine players each, on a field with four bases forming a diamond ☆**2.** the ball used in this game

☆**base·board** (-bôrd') *n.* **1.** a board or molding covering the edge of a wall next to the floor **2.** any board at or forming a base

base·born (-bôrn') *adj.* **1.** of humble birth or origin **2.** born of parents not married to each other

☆**base·burn·er, base-burn·er** (-bʉr'nər) *n.* any stove, etc. in which more coal is fed automatically from above as the coal at the base is burned up

☆**base hit** *Baseball* a play in which the batter hits the ball and gets on base without benefit of an opponent's error and without forcing a runner

Ba·sel (bä'z'l) city in NW Switzerland, on the Rhine: pop. 212,000

base·less (bās'lis) *adj.* having no basis in fact; unfounded [a *baseless* rumor] —**base'less·ness** *n.*

base line **1.** a line serving as a base ☆**2.** *Baseball* the lane between any two consecutive bases **3.** *Tennis* the line at the back at either end of a court

☆**base·man** (-mən) *n., pl.* **-men** *Baseball* an infielder stationed at first, second, or third base

base·ment (bās'mənt) *n.* [BASE[1] + -MENT] **1.** the lower part of a wall or structure **2.** the lowest story of a building, below the main floor and wholly or partly below the surface of the ground

ba·sen·ji (bə sen'jē) *n.* [Bantu < *ba-,* plural prefix + *senji* < Fr. *singe,* a monkey] any of an African breed of small dog that has a reddish-brown coat and does not make a true barking sound

☆**base on balls** *Baseball same as* WALK

base pay the basic rate of pay for a particular job, not counting overtime pay, bonuses, etc.

☆**base runner** *Baseball* any member of the team at bat who is on base or is trying to reach a base

bas·es[1] (bās′ēz) *n. pl. of* BASE[1]

ba·ses[2] (bā′sēz) *n. pl. of* BASIS

bash (bash) *vt.* [echoic; akin to ON. *basca*, to strike] [Colloq.] to strike with a violent blow; smash (*in*) —*n.* 1. [Colloq.] a violent blow 2. [Slang] a gala event or party

bash·ful (bash′fəl) *adj.* [(A)BASH + -FUL] 1. timid, shy, and easily embarrassed 2. showing that one is embarrassed and shy [*a bashful smile*] —see SYN. at SHY[1] —**bash′ful·ly** *adv.* —**bash′ful·ness** *n.*

bas·ic (bā′sik) *adj.* 1. of, at, or forming a base; fundamental [*basic* principles] 2. introductory or elementary [*basic* training in the army] 3. *Chem.* of, having the nature of, or containing a base; alkaline —*n.* a basic principle, factor, etc.: *usually used in pl.* —**bas′i·cal·ly** *adv.*

Basic English a copyrighted simplified form of English for use as an international language and as an introduction to full English: it was developed by C. K. Ogden (1889–1957) and consists of a selected vocabulary of 850 essential words

ba·sic·i·ty (bə sis′ə tē) *n.* the quality, state, or degree of being a chemical base

ba·sid·i·o·my·cete (bə sid′ē ō mī sēt′) *n.* [< ModL. < Gr. *basis*, base + ModL. dim. suffix *-idium* + -MYCETE] any of a class of fungi, including the mushrooms, rusts, etc., that reproduce through spores borne on a club-shaped structure

bas·il (baz′′l, bā′z′l) *n.* [< OFr. < ML. < Gr. *basilikon* (*phyton*), lit., royal (plant) < *basileus*, king] a fragrant herb of the mint family, whose leaves are used for flavoring in cooking

bas·i·lar (bas′ə lər) *adj.* of or at the base, esp. of the skull: also **bas′i·lar′y** (-ler′ē)

ba·sil·i·ca (bə sil′i kə) *n.* [L. < Gr. *basilikē* (*stoa*), royal (portico): see BASIL] 1. in ancient Rome, a rectangular building with a broad nave having a row of columns at each side, used as a courtroom, etc. 2. a Christian church in this style — **ba·sil′i·can** *adj.*

bas·i·lisk (bas′ə lisk′) *n.* [< L. < Gr. dim. of *basileus*, king] 1. a mythical, lizardlike monster whose breath and glance were supposed to kill 2. a tropical American lizard with a crest on its back and tail

ba·sin (bās′′n) *n.* [< OFr. < VL. < *bacca*, water vessel] 1. *a*) a wide, shallow container, as for liquid *b*) its contents or capacity 2. a washbowl or sink 3. any shallow, esp. water-filled hollow, as a pond 4. a bay or harbor [yacht *basin*] 5. all the land drained by a river and its branches 6. a great hollow in the earth's surface filled by an ocean 7. *Geol.* a wide, depressed area in which the rock layers all incline toward a center

ba·sip·e·tal (bə sip′i t′l) *adj.* [< BASIC + PETAL] *Bot.* developing or moving from the apex toward the base of the stem

ba·sis (bā′sis) *n., pl.* **ba′ses** (-sēz) [L. < Gr., a base, pedestal < *bainein*, to go < IE. base *gwem-*, from which also come L. *venire* & COME] 1. the base or foundation [there is no *basis* for the rumor] 2. a principal constituent 3. the basic principle or theory, as of a system of knowledge —see SYN. at BASE[1]

bask (bask) *vi.* [ME. *basken*, to wallow (in blood) < ?] 1. to warm oneself pleasantly, as in sunlight 2. to enjoy any pleasant or warm feeling [he *basked* in her favor]

bas·ket (bas′kit) *n.* [ME. < ?] 1. a container made of interwoven cane, strips of wood, etc. and often having a handle or handles 2. the amount that a basket will hold 3. anything used or shaped like a basket [a metal wastepaper *basket*] 4. the structure hung from a balloon to carry persons, etc. ☆5. *Basketball a*) the goal, a round, open net hanging from a metal ring attached to a backboard *b*) a score made by tossing the ball through this net

☆**bas·ket·ball** (-bôl′) *n.* 1. a game played by two teams of five players each, in a zoned floor area: points are scored by tossing a ball through a basket at the opponent's end of the playing court 2. the round, inflated ball used in this game

basket case [Slang] 1. a person lacking all four limbs 2. any person unable to function because emotionally upset

Basket Maker any member of several early Indian peoples of the southwestern U.S. (c.100–700 A.D.), whose culture was characterized by great skill in basket making

bas·ket·ry (bas′kə trē) *n.* 1. the craft of making baskets 2. *same as* BASKETWORK

basket weave a weave of fabrics resembling the weave used in basketwork

bas·ket·work (bas′kit wurk′) *n.* work that is interlaced or woven like a basket; wickerwork

Basle (bäl) *older name for* BASEL

ba·so·phile (bā′sə fīl′, -fil′) *n.* [< BASIC + -PHILE] a cell or tissue that is readily stained with basic dyes: also **ba′so·phil′** (-fil′) —**ba′so·phil′ic** *adj.*

Basque (bask) *n.* 1. any member of a certain people living in the W Pyrenees 2. their language, which is unrelated to any other known language —*adj.* of the Basques, their language, culture, etc.

Basque Provinces region made up of three provinces in N Spain, inhabited by Basques

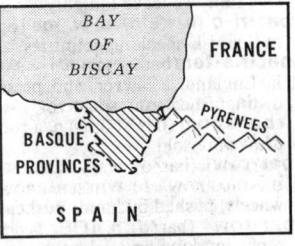
BASQUE PROVINCES

Bas·ra (bus′rə, buz′-) port in SE Iraq, on the Shatt-al-Arab: pop. 328,000

bas-re·lief (bä′rə lēf′) *n.* [Fr. < It. *basso-rilievo*: see BASSO & RELIEF] sculpture in which figures are carved in a flat surface so that they project only a little from the background

bass[1] (bās) *n.* [ME. *bas*, BASE[2]] 1. the range of the lowest male voice 2. a voice or singer with such a range 3. an instrument of the lowest range; specif., *same as* DOUBLE BASS 4. a part for such a voice or instrument —*adj.* of, in, for, or having this range

bass[2] (bas) *n., pl.* **bass**, **bass′es**: see PLURAL, II, D, 2 [OE. *bærs*: for IE. base see BRISTLE] a spiny-finned food and game fish of fresh or salt water

bass[3] (bas) *n. same as:* 1. BAST 2. BASSWOOD

bass clef (bās) *Music* a sign on a staff, indicating the position of F below middle C on the fourth line: see illustration at CLEF

bass drum (bās) the largest and lowest-toned of the double-headed drums

bas·set (bas′it) *n.* [OFr., orig., dim. of *bas*, BASE[2]] a kind of hunting hound with a long body, short legs, and long, drooping ears: also **basset hound**

bass horn (bās) *same as* TUBA

bas·si·net (bas′ə net′) *n.* [< Fr. *bercelonnette*, dim. of *berceau*, cradle] a basketlike bed for an infant: it is often hooded and set on a stand having casters

bass·ist (bās′ist) *n.* a person who plays the double bass

bas·so (bas′ō; It. bäs′sō) *n., pl.* **bas′sos**; It. **bas′si** (-sē) [It. < VL. *bassus*, low] a bass voice or singer

BASSETT
(11–15 in. high at shoulder)

bas·soon (bə sōōn′, ba-) *n.* [Fr. *basson* < It. *bassone* < prec.] a double-reed bass woodwind instrument with a long stem attached to the mouthpiece —**bas·soon′ist** *n.*

basso pro·fun·do (prə fun′dō, prō foon′dō) [< It. *basso*, low + *profundo*, deep] 1. a very deep bass voice 2. a man with such a voice

bas·so-re·lie·vo (bas′ō rə lē′vō) *n., pl.* **-vos** *same as* BAS-RELIEF

bass viol (bās) *same as:* 1. VIOLA DA GAMBA 2. DOUBLE BASS

☆**bass·wood** (bas′wood′) *n.* 1. any of several trees of the u.s. and canada, with fragrant, yellowish flowers and light, soft wood 2. the wood

BASSOON

bast (bast) *n.* [OE. *bæst*] 1. *same as* PHLOEM 2. fiber obtained from phloem, for making ropes, etc.

bas·tard (bas′tərd) *n.* [< OFr. < ?] 1. a person born of parents not married to each other 2. anything inferior, not genuine, or varying from standard 3. a person regarded with contempt, hatred, pity, etc. or, sometimes, with playful affection: a vulgar usage —*adj.* 1. *a*) born of parents not married to each other *b*) having an uncertain origin 2. of a size or shape not standard 3. not genuine or authentic; inferior; spurious —**bas′tard·ly** *adj.* —**bas′tard·y** *n., pl.* **-ies**

bas·tard·ize (bas′tər dīz′) *vt.* **-ized′**, **-iz′ing** 1. to make, declare, or show to be a bastard 2. to make corrupt or inferior

baste[1] (bāst) *vt.* **bast′ed**, **bast′ing** [< OFr. < OHG. *bastjan*, to sew with bast] to sew with long, loose stitches so as to keep the parts together until properly sewed —**bast′er** *n.*

baste[2] (bāst) *vt.* **bast′ed, bast′ing** [< OFr. < *bassiner*, to moisten < *bassin*, BASIN] to moisten (meat) with melted butter, drippings, etc. during roasting —**bast′er** *n.*

baste[3] (bāst) *vt.* **bast′ed, bast′ing** [ON. *beysta*] **1.** to beat soundly **2.** to attack with words; abuse

bas·tille, bas·tile (bas tēl′) *n.* [Fr. < OFr. *bastir*, to build: see BASTION] a prison —**the Bastille** a state prison in Paris until destroyed (July 14, 1789) in the French Revolution: July 14 is now observed in France as **Bastille Day**

bas·ti·na·do (bas′tə nā′dō, -nä′dō) *n., pl.* **-does** [< Sp. < *bastón*, a stick] **1.** a beating with a stick, usually on the soles of the feet, esp. as a punishment **2.** a rod or stick Also **bas′ti·nade′** (-nād′) —*vt.* **-doed, -do·ing** to punish with a bastinado

bast·ing (bās′tiŋ) *n.* **1.** the act of sewing with loose, temporary stitches **2.** loose, temporary stitches or the thread used for them

bas·tion (bas′chən) *n.* [Fr. < It. < *bastire*, to build < Gmc. *bastjan*, to make with bast, build] **1.** a projection from a fortification to give the defenders a wider firing range **2.** any strong defense or bulwark —**bas′tioned** *adj.*

bat[1] (bat) *n.* [< OE. *batt*, cudgel (prob. < W. *bat* < IE. base *bhat-*, to strike) & < OFr. *battre*, BATTER[1]] **1.** any stout club or stick **2.** a club used to strike the ball in baseball and cricket ☆**3.** a turn at batting, as in baseball [to be at *bat*] **4.** [Brit.] a batsman at cricket **5.** [Colloq.] a blow or hit ☆**6.** [Old Slang] a spree —*vt.* **bat′ted, bat′ting 1.** to strike with or as with a bat **2.** to have a batting average of [Hale is *batting* .285] —*vi.* to take a turn at batting —**bat around** [Slang] to consider or discuss (an idea, plan, etc.) —☆**go to bat for** [Colloq.] to support or defend, as in a conflict —☆**(right) off the bat** [Colloq.] immediately

bat[2] (bat) *n.* [altered < ME. *bakke* < Scand.] a mouselike mammal with a furry body and membranous wings, usually seen flying at night —**blind as a bat** quite blind —☆**have bats in the** (or one's) **belfry** [Slang] to be insane; have crazy notions

bat[3] (bat) *vt.* **bat′ted, bat′ting** [ME. *baten*, to flap (wings) < OFr. *battre*, BATTER[1]] [Colloq.] to wink; blink; flutter [to flirt by *batting* one's eyes] —**not bat an eye** (or **eyelash**) [Colloq.] not show surprise

Ba·ta·vi·a (bə tā′vē ə) *former name of* JAKARTA

batch (bach) *n.* [OE. *bacan*, BAKE] **1.** the amount (of bread, etc.) produced at one baking **2.** the quantity of anything needed for or made in one operation or lot [a *batch* of concrete] **3.** a number of things or persons taken as a group [a *batch* of test papers]

bate (bāt) *vt., vi.* **bat′ed, bat′ing** [< ABATE] to abate or lessen —**with bated breath** with the breath held in because of fear, excitement, etc.

☆**ba·teau** (ba tō′) *n., pl.* **-teaux′** (-tōz′) [Fr. < OFr. *batel* < OE. *bat*, boat] a lightweight, flat-bottomed river boat with tapering ends

bat·fish (bat′fish′) *n., pl.* **-fish′, -fish′es**: see FISH any of various strangely shaped marine fishes

Bath (bath) city in SW England: a health resort with hot springs: pop. 85,000

bath (bath) *n., pl.* **baths** (ba*th*z, baths) [OE. *bæth*: for IE. base see BAKE] **1.** a washing or dipping of a thing, esp. the body, in water or other liquid, steam, etc. **2.** water or other liquid for bathing, or for dipping, soaking, regulating temperature, etc. **3.** a container for such liquid **4.** a bathtub **5.** a bathroom **6.** a building or set of rooms for bathing **7.** [often *pl.*] a resort where bathing is part of the medical treatment; spa —*vt., vi.* [Brit.] *same as* BATHE

bathe (bā*th*) *vt.* **bathed, bath′ing** [OE. *bathian* < *bæth*, BATH] **1.** to put into a liquid; immerse **2.** to give a bath to; wash **3.** to wet or moisten [*sweat bathed* his brow] **4.** to cover as if with a liquid [trees *bathed* in moonlight] —*vi.* **1.** to take a bath **2.** to go into or be in water so as to swim, cool oneself, etc. **3.** to soak oneself in some substance or influence —*n.* [Brit.] a swim or dip —**bath·er** (bā*th*′ər) *n.*

BAT
(to 3½ in. long)

ba·thet·ic (bə thet′ik) *adj.* [< BATHOS, patterned after PATHETIC] characterized by bathos —**ba·thet′i·cal·ly** *adv.*

bath·house (bath′hous′) *n.* **1.** a public building where people can take baths ☆**2.** a building used by swimmers for changing clothes

bathing cap a tightfitting cap of rubber, etc., worn to keep the hair dry as while swimming

bathing suit a garment worn for swimming; swimsuit

bath·mat (bath′mat′) *n.* a mat used in or next to a bathtub, as to prevent slipping

ba·thos (bā′thäs, -thôs) *n.* [Gr., depth] **1.** an abrupt change from the lofty to the ordinary or trivial in writing or speech; anticlimax (Ex.: filled with love, devotion, and a hunger for candy) **2.** false pathos; sentimentality **3.** triteness

☆**bath·robe** (bath′rōb′) *n.* a long, loose coat for wear to and from the bath, in lounging, etc.

bath·room (-rōōm′) *n.* a room with a bathtub, toilet, washstand, etc.

Bath·she·ba (bath shē′bə, bath′shə bə) *Bible* a wife of King David and the mother of Solomon

☆**bath·tub** (-tub′) *n.* a tub, now usually a bathroom fixture, in which to take a bath

bath·y·scaph (bath′ə skaf′) *n.* [Fr. < Gr. *bathys*, deep + *skaphē*, boat] a deep-sea diving apparatus for reaching great depths without a cable: it consists of a steel observation cabin attached to a float filled with a fluid lighter than water: also **bath′y·scaphe′** (-skaf′, -skāf′)

☆**bath·y·sphere** (bath′ə sfir′) *n.* [< Gr. *bathys*, deep + -SPHERE] a round, watertight observation chamber lowered by cables into sea depths

ba·tik (bə tēk′, bat′ik) *n.* [Malay] **1.** a method of dyeing designs on cloth by coating with removable wax the parts not to be dyed **2.** cloth so decorated or a design made in this way —*adj.* of or like batik

BATHYSCAPH

ba·tiste (ba tēst′, bə-) *n.* [Fr. < OFr. *baptiste*: after the supposed original maker, *Baptiste* of Cambrai] a fine, thin cloth of cotton, linen, rayon, etc.

☆**bat mitz·vah, bat miz·vah** (bät mits′və) [Heb. *bat mitswāh*, daughter of the commandment] [*also* B- M-] **1.** a Jewish girl who undergoes a ceremony like that of a bar mitzvah **2.** the ceremony

ba·ton (bə tän′, ba-) *n.* [Fr. < OFr. < VL. *basto*, a stick] **1.** a staff serving as a symbol of office **2.** a slender stick used by a conductor in directing an orchestra, choir, etc. ☆**3.** a hollow metal rod twirled in a showy way, as by a drum majorette **4.** the short, light rod passed from one runner to the next in a relay race

Bat·on Rouge (bat′'n rōōzh′) [Fr. transl. of Choctaw *itúúma*, red (boundary) pole] capital of La., on the Mississippi: pop. 166,000

ba·tra·chi·an (bə trā′kē ən) *adj.* [< ModL. < Gr. < *batrachos*, frog] of, like, or concerning amphibians without tails, as frogs and toads —*n.* an amphibian without a tail; frog or toad

bats (bats) *adj.* [Slang] insane; crazy

bats·man (bats′mən) *n., pl.* **-men** the batter in cricket

bat·tal·ion (bə tal′yən) *n.* [< Fr. < It. < VL. *battalia*, BATTLE] **1.** a large group of soldiers arrayed for battle **2.** any large group joined together in some activity **3.** *U.S. Army* a tactical unit made up of three or more companies, batteries, or similar units

bat·ten[1] (bat′'n) *n.* [var. of BATON] **1.** a sawed strip of wood, flooring, etc. **2.** a strip of wood put over a seam between boards as a fastening or covering **3.** a strip used to fasten canvas over a ship's hatchways —*vt.* to fasten or supply with battens —**batten down the hatches** to fasten canvas over the hatches, esp. in preparing for a storm

bat·ten[2] (bat′'n) *vi.* [ON. *batna*, to improve: for IE. base see BEST] to grow fat; thrive —*vt.* to fatten up; overfeed

bat·ter[1] (bat′ər) *vt.* [< OFr. *batre, battre* < VL. < L. *battuere*, to beat; also, in part, < BAT[1], *v.*] **1.** to beat or strike with blow after blow; pound **2.** to injure by pounding, hard wear, or use [wearing a *battered* felt hat] —**vi.** to pound noisily and repeatedly

bat·ter[2] (bat′ər) *n.* the player who is batting in baseball or cricket

bat·ter[3] (bat′ər) *n.* [< OFr., prob. < *batre:* see BATTER[1]] a flowing mixture of flour, milk, eggs, etc. for making cakes, pancakes, etc.

bat·ter·ing ram (bat′ər iŋ ram′) **1.** an ancient military machine having a heavy wooden beam for battering down gates, walls, etc.: its iron end was sometimes shaped like a ram's head **2.** any bar, log, etc. used like this to force entrance

bat·ter·y (bat′ər ē, bat′rē) *n., pl.* **-ter·ies** [< Fr. < *battre:* see BATTER[1]] **1.** a battering or beating **2.** a group of similar things arranged, connected, or used together; set or series [a *battery* of microphones around the speaker] ☆**3.** *Baseball* the pitcher and the catcher **4.** *Elec.* a connected group of cells, or a single cell, storing an electrical charge and capable of furnishing a current **5.** *Law* any illegal beating or touching of another person: see ASSAULT AND BATTERY **6.** *Mil. a)* an emplacement or fortification equipped with heavy guns *b)* a set of heavy guns, rockets, etc. *c)* the men who operate such a set: usually the basic unit of artillery, like an infantry company

BATTERS (upper: baseball; lower: cricket)

bat·ting (bat′iŋ, bat′'n) *n.* [< BAT[1]] ☆fiber of cotton, wool, etc., wadded into sheets and used in bandages, quilts, etc.

☆**batting average 1.** a measure of a baseball player's batting effectiveness, figured by dividing the number of safe hits by the number of times at bat **2.** [Colloq.] the average level of skill or success reached in any activity

bat·tle (bat′'l) *n.* [< OFr. < VL. *battalia* < L. < *battuere:* see BATTER[1]] **1.** a large-scale fight between armed forces **2.** armed fighting; combat or war [wounded twice in *battle*] **3.** any fight or struggle; conflict [a *battle* of ideas] —**vt., vi.** **-tled, -tling** to oppose, fight, or struggle —**give** (or **do**) **battle** to engage in battle; fight —**bat′tler** *n.*

SYN.—**battle** refers to a conflict between armed forces in a war, and implies a large-scale contest that lasts for some time; **engagement** stresses the actual meeting of opposing forces; a **campaign** is a series of military actions having a particular goal and may involve a number of battles; **encounter** usually suggests a chance meeting of opposing forces; **skirmish** refers to a brief encounter between small groups

bat·tle-ax, bat·tle-axe (-aks′) *n.* **1.** a heavy ax formerly used as a weapon of war ☆**2.** [Slang] a woman who is harsh, domineering, etc.

battle cruiser a large warship that is faster and more easily maneuvered than a battleship, but is less heavily armored

battle cry a cry or slogan used to encourage those in a battle, struggle, contest, etc.

bat·tle·dore (bat′'l dôr′) *n.* [< ? Pr. *batedor,* beater] **1.** a paddle or racket used to hit a shuttlecock back and forth in a game (called **battledore and shuttlecock**) like badminton **2.** this game

battle fatigue *same as* COMBAT FATIGUE

bat·tle·field (bat′'l fēld′) *n.* **1.** the place where a battle is fought or was fought **2.** any area of conflict or struggle Also **bat′tle·ground′**

bat·tle·ment (-mənt) *n.* [< OFr. *batailler,* to fortify] **1.** a low wall, as on top of a tower, with open spaces for shooting **2.** an architectural decoration like this —**bat′tle·ment′ed** (-men′tid) *adj.*

battle royal *pl.* **battles royal 1.** a fight involving many contestants; free-for-all **2.** a bitterly fought battle **3.** a heated dispute

☆**bat·tle·ship** (-ship′) *n.* any of a class of large warships with the biggest guns and very heavy armor: also [Slang] **bat′-tle·wag′on**

bat·ty (bat′ē) *adj.* **-ti·er, -ti·est** [< BAT[2] + -Y[2]] [Slang] **1.** insane; crazy **2.** odd; eccentric

bau·ble (bô′b'l) *n.* [< OFr. *baubel, bel-bel,* prob. a doubling of *bel* < L. *bellus,* pretty] a showy but worthless thing; trinket, trifle, etc.

BATTLEMENTS

Baude·laire (bōd ler′), **(Pierre) Charles** (shàrl) 1821–67; Fr. poet & essayist

baulk (bôk) *n., vt., vi. same as* BALK

baux·ite (bôk′sīt, bō′zīt) *n.* [Fr. < (*Les*) *Baux,* town in SE France] the claylike ore from which aluminum is obtained

Ba·var·i·a (bə ver′ē ə) state of S West Germany: cap. Munich —**Ba·var′i·an** *adj., n.*

bawd (bôd) *n.* [< ? OFr. *baud,* gay, licentious (< Frank. *bald,* bold)] [Now Literary] **1.** a person, esp. a woman, who keeps a brothel **2.** a prostitute

bawd·ry (bôd′rē) *n.* [< OFr. *bauderie,* gaiety: see BAWD] obscene language; bawdiness

bawd·y (bô′dē) *adj.* **bawd′i·er, bawd′i·est** [see BAWD] indecent, obscene, coarsely humorous, etc. —**bawd′i·ly** *adv.* —**bawd′i·ness** *n.*

bawd·y·house (-hous′) *n.* a house of prostitution

bawl (bôl) *vi., vt.* [< ML. *baulare,* to bark & ? ON. *baula,* to low like a cow; both echoic] **1.** to shout or call out noisily; bellow **2.** to weep loudly —*n.* **1.** an outcry; bellow **2.** a noisy weeping —**bawl out** ☆[Slang] to scold angrily —**bawl′er** *n.*

bay[1] (bā) *n.* [< OFr. < ML. *baia*] a part of a sea or lake, that cuts into the shoreline; wide inlet

bay[2] (bā) *n.* [< OFr. *baer* < VL. *batare,* to gape] **1.** *a)* an opening or alcove set off from the rest of the room by columns, screens, etc. *b)* a recess in a wall, as for a window *c) same as* BAY WINDOW **2.** a wing of a building **3.** a compartment or space: see BOMB BAY **4.** *same as* SICK BAY

bay[3] (bā) *vi.* [< OFr., ult. < VL. *batare,* to gape] to bark with long, deep tones —*vt.* **1.** to bark at **2.** to bring to or hold at bay [hounds *baying* a raccoon in a tree] —*n.* **1.** the sound of baying **2.** the situation of or as of a hunted animal forced to turn and fight —**at bay 1.** with escape cut off; cornered **2.** held off [the bear kept the hunters *at bay*] —**bring to bay** to force into a situation that makes escape impossible

bay[4] (bā) *n.* [< OFr. < L. *baca,* berry] **1.** *same as* LAUREL (*n.* 1) **2.** [*pl.*] *a)* a wreath of bay leaves, a token of honor given to poets and conquerors, as by the ancient Greeks and Romans *b)* honor; fame

bay[5] (bā) *adj.* [< OFr. < L. *badius*] reddish-brown: said esp. of horses —*n.* **1.** a horse, etc. of this color **2.** reddish brown

Ba·ya·món (bä yä môn′) city in NE Puerto Rico, near San Juan: pop. 146,000

bay·ber·ry (bā′ber′ē) *n., pl.* **-ries** ☆**1.** *a)* any of several shrubs, as the wax myrtle, having a small, wax-covered, berry-like fruit *b)* this fruit **2.** a tropical American tree yielding an aromatic oil formerly used in bay rum

Bay·ern (bī′ərn) *Ger. name of* BAVARIA

bay leaf the aromatic leaf of the laurel, dried and used as a spice in cooking

☆**bay lynx** a common wildcat of N. America

bay·o·net (bā′ə nit, -net′; bā′ə net′) *n.* [< Fr. < *Bayonne,* city in France, where first made] a daggerlike blade that can be put on the muzzle end of a rifle, for hand-to-hand fighting —*vt., vi.* **-net′ed** or **-net′ted, -net′ing** or **-net′ting** to stab, prod, or kill with a bayonet

Ba·yonne (bā yōn′) [after a city in SW France] city in NE N.J.: pop. 73,000

☆**bay·ou** (bī′ōō, -ō) *n.* [AmFr. < Choctaw *bayuk,* small stream] in the southern U.S., a marshy inlet or outlet of a lake, river, etc.

bay rum an aromatic liquid formerly obtained from leaves of a bayberry tree, now made of certain oils, water, and alcohol: it is used in medicines and cosmetics

bay window 1. a window or set of windows jutting out from the wall of a building and forming an alcove inside ☆**2.** [Slang] a large, protruding belly

ba·zaar (bə zär′) *n.* [Per. *bāzār*] **1.** in Oriental countries, a market or street of shops **2.** a shop for selling various kinds of goods **3.** a sale of various articles, usually to raise money for a club, church, etc.

☆**ba·zoo·ka** (bə zōōk′ə) *n.* [term orig. coined for a comic musical horn] a weapon of metal tubing, for aiming and launching electrically fired rockets that can pierce tanks or other armor

BAY WINDOW

b.b., bb base on balls

B.B.A. Bachelor of Business Administration

BBC British Broadcasting Corporation

bbl. *pl.* **bbls.** barrel

☆**BB (shot)** [a designation of the size] a size of shot measuring .18 of an inch in diameter, fired from an air rifle (**BB gun**) or shotgun

B.C. **1.** before Christ **2.** British Columbia

B.C.E. before the Common Era

bch. *pl.* **bchs.** bunch

bd. *pl.* **bds.** **1.** board **2.** bond **3.** bound

B/D bank draft

B.D. Bachelor of Divinity

bd. ft. board foot (or feet)

bdl. *pl.* **bdls.** bundle

be (bē; *unstressed* bi) *vi.* **was** or **were, been, be′ing** [OE. *beon:* the forms of *be* come from three unrelated bases: 1) IE. *es-,* from which come *am, is, are;* 2) IE. *wes-,* to stay, remain, from which come *was, were;* 3) IE. *bheu-,* to grow, become, from which come *be, been*] **1.** to exist; live [Caesar *is* no more] **2.** to happen or occur [the party *is* tonight] **3.** to remain or continue [will he *be* here long?] **4.** to come to; belong [peace *be* with you] **5.** to have a place or position [the door *is* on your left] **NOTE:** *be* is often used to link its subject to a predicate nominative, adjective, or pronoun and is sometimes equivalent to the mathematical sign (=) (Ex.: he *is* brave, that hat *is* ten dollars, let x *be* y); *be* is also used as an auxiliary: (1) with the past participle of a transitive verb to form the passive voice [he will *be* paid] (2) with the past participle of certain intransitive verbs to form an archaic perfect tense [Christ *is* risen] (3) with the present participle of another verb to express continuation [the motor *is* running] (4) with the present participle or infinitive of another verb to express futurity, possibility, obligation, intention, etc. [he *is* going next week, she *is* to wash the dishes] *Be* is conjugated in the present indicative: (I) *am,* (he, she, it) *is,* (we, you, they) *are;* in the past indicative: (I, he, she, it) *was,* (we, you, they) *were;* archaic forms are (thou) *art, wert, wast;* the present subjunctive is *be,* the past subjunctive *were* —**be off** go away

be- [OE. < *be, bi,* about, near] *a prefix meaning:* **1.** around [besprinkle, beset] **2.** completely; thoroughly [bedeck, besmear] **3.** away [bereave, betake] **4.** about [bethink, bemoan] **5.** make [besot, bepretty] **6.** furnish with; affect by; treat as [befriend, bedizen, becloud] **7.** cover with; furnish with (to excess) [bemedaled, bewhiskered]

Be *Chem.* beryllium

B/E, b.e. bill of exchange

beach (bēch) *n.* [E. dial., orig., pebbles, shingles] **1.** a nearly level stretch of pebbles and sand beside a sea, lake, etc.; sandy shore **2.** an area of shore as for swimmers, sunbathers, etc. — *vt., vi.* to ground (a boat) on a beach —☆**on the beach** **1.** not aboard a ship **2.** unemployed

beach·comb·er (-kō′mər) *n.* **1.** a long wave rolling ashore; comber **2.** a man who loafs on beaches or wharves, living on what he can beg or find

beach·head (-hed′) *n.* **1.** a position established by invading troops on an enemy shore **2.** a position secured as a starting point for any action; foothold

bea·con (bēk′'n) *n.* [OE. *beacen* < IE. base *bha-,* to shine, from which also come FANTASY & PHENOMENON] **1.** a signal fire, esp. one on a hill, pole, etc. **2.** any light for warning or guiding [a *traffic* beacon] **3.** a lighthouse **4.** a radio transmitter that sends out signals for guiding aircraft, as at night **5.** a person or thing that warns, offers guidance, etc. —*vt.* **1.** to light up (darkness, etc.) **2.** to provide or mark with beacons —*vi.* to shine or serve as a beacon

Bea·cons·field (bēk′'nz fēld′), Earl of, *see* DISRAELI

bead (bēd) *n.* [ME. *bede,* prayer bead < OE. *bed* < *biddan,* to pray: see BID] **1.** a small, usually round piece of glass, wood, metal, etc., pierced for stringing **2.** [*pl.*] *a)* a string of beads; necklace *b)* a rosary **3.** any small, round object, as the front sight of a rifle **4.** a drop or bubble [beads of sweat on his forehead] **5.** foam, as on beer **6.** the inner edge of a rubber tire where it fits on the rim **7.** a narrow, half-round molding —*vt.* **1.** to decorate or string with beads **2.** to string like beads —*vi.* to form a bead or beads —☆**draw a bead on** to take careful aim at —**say** (or **tell** or **count**) **one's beads** to say prayers with a rosary —**bead′ed** *adj.*

bead·ing (-iŋ) *n.* **1.** beads or decorative work in beads, as on a dress or purse **2.** a molding or edge resembling a row of beads **3.** a narrow, half-round molding **4.** *a)* a narrow trimming of lacelike loops *b)* an openwork trimming through which a ribbon can be run

bea·dle (bē′d'l) *n.* [< OFr. < Frank. *bidal,* messenger] formerly, a minor parish officer in the Church of England, who kept order in church

beads·man (bēdz′mən) *n., pl.* **-men** [see BEAD] **1.** a person who prays for another's soul, esp. one hired to do so **2.** a person in a poorhouse —**beads′wom′an** *n.fem., pl.* **-wom′en**

bead·work (bēd′wurk′) *n. same as* BEADING (senses 1 & 2)

bead·y (bē′dē) *adj.* **bead′i·er, bead′i·est** **1.** small, round, and glittering like a bead [the *beady* eyes of a snake] **2.** decorated with beads

bea·gle (bē′g'l) *n.* [< ? Fr. *bégueule,* wide-throat] a small hound with a smooth coat, short legs, and drooping ears

beak (bēk) *n.* [< OFr. < L. *beccus* < Gaul.] **1.** a bird's bill, esp. the large, sharp, horny bill of a bird of prey **2.** a beaklike mouth, as of some insects, fishes, turtles, etc. **3.** the spout of a pitcher **4.** the metal-covered ram projecting from the prow of an ancient warship **5.** [Slang] the nose —**beak′less** *adj.* —**beak′like′** *adj.*

beaked (bēkt) *adj.* **1.** having a beak **2.** shaped like a beak [a *beaked* nose]

beak·er (bē′kər) *n.* [< ON. *bikarr,* a cup < VL. < LL. < L. *bacar,* wine glass] **1.** a large or ornate cup; goblet **2.** a jarlike container of glass or metal with a lip for pouring, used by chemists, druggists, etc. **3.** the contents or capacity of a beaker

BEAGLE
(13–15 in. high at shoulder)

beam (bēm) *n.* [< OE., akin to G. *baum,* a tree] **1.** a long, thick piece of wood, or of metal or stone, esp. one used as a horizontal support for a ceiling **2.** the part of a plow to which the handles, share, etc. are attached **3.** the crossbar of a balance, or the balance itself **4.** any of the heavy, horizontal crosspieces of a ship **5.** a ship's breadth at its widest point **6.** the side of a ship or the direction out sidewise from a ship **7.** a ray or stream of light or other radiation, as of X-rays **8.** a bright look, smile, etc. **9.** a stream of radio or radar signals sent continuously in one direction as a guide for aircraft or ships —*vt.* **1.** to give out (shafts of light); radiate **2.** to direct or aim (a radio signal, program, etc.) —*vi.* **1.** to shine brightly **2.** to smile warmly —**off the beam** **1.** not following a guiding beam, as an airplane ☆**2.** [Colloq.] wrong; incorrect —**on the beam** **1.** at right angles to the ship's keel **2.** following a guiding beam, as an airplane ☆**3.** [Colloq.] working or functioning well; alert, keen, quick, etc. —**beam′ing** *adj.* —**beam′ly·ly** *adv.*

beamed (bēmd) *adj.* having exposed beams [a *beamed* ceiling]

beam-ends (bēm′endz′) *n.pl.* the ends of a ship's beams —**on the beam-ends** **1.** tipping so far to the side as to be in danger of overturning **2.** having used up one's resources, money, etc.

beam·ish (bēm′ish) *adj.* [BEAM + -ISH: used by Lewis Carroll in *Through the Looking Glass*] shining; radiant; cheerful

bean (bēn) *n.* [OE. *bean*] **1.** any of various plants of the legume family, with smooth, kidney-shaped seeds that are cooked and eaten **2.** any such seed **3.** a pod with such seeds, eaten as a vegetable when still unripe **4.** any of various beanlike seeds [coffee *beans*] ☆**5.** [Slang] the head or brain ☆**6.** [*pl.*] [Slang] even a little amount [doesn't know *beans* about music] —☆*vt.* [Slang] to hit on the head, specif. with a pitched baseball —**full of beans** [Slang] **1.** lively; ebullient ☆**2.** mistaken; in error —☆**spill the beans** [Colloq.] to let secret information leak out —**bean′like′** *adj.*

☆**bean·bag** (bēn′bag′) *n.* a small cloth bag filled with beans, and thrown in some games

☆**bean ball** [Slang] *Baseball* a pitch aimed at the batter's head: such a pitch is against the rules

☆**bean·er·y** (bē′nər ē) *n., pl.* **-er·ies** [< baked *beans,* a chief dish] [Colloq.] a cheap restaurant

☆**bean·ie** (bē′nē) *n.* [Colloq.] any of various kinds of skullcap worn by children, etc.

☆**bean·pole** (bēn′pōl′) *n.* **1.** a thin pole for bean plants to climb on **2.** [Colloq.] a tall, lean person

bean·stalk (-stôk′) *n.* the main stem of a bean plant

bear¹ (ber) *vt.* **bore** or archaic **bare, borne** or **born** (see vt. 3),

bear'ing [OE. *beran* < IE. base *bher-*, to carry, bring, from which also come L. *ferre* & Gr. *pherein*, both meaning "to bear"] **1.** to carry; transport **2.** to have or show [the letter *bore* his signature] **3.** to give birth to: the passive past participle in this sense is **born** when *by* does not follow [three children were *borne* by the woman; when were you *born?*] **4.** to produce or yield [fruit-*bearing* trees] **5.** to support or sustain [a wall that *bears* some weight] **6.** to sustain the burden of [to *bear* the cost] **7.** to put up with; tolerate [to *bear* pain] **8.** to call for; require [his actions *bear* watching] **9.** to carry or conduct (oneself) **10.** to carry over or hold (a sentiment) [to *bear* a grudge] **11.** to bring and tell (a message, tales, etc.) **12.** to move or push as if carrying [the crowd *bore* us along] **13.** to give or supply [to *bear* witness] —*vi.* **1.** to be productive [the tree *bears* well] **2.** *a)* to lie or move in a given direction [*bear* right at the corner] *b)* to point toward (with *on* or *upon*) [the guns were set to *bear* on the fort] **3.** to have bearing (*on*); have a relation [his story *bears* on the crime] **4.** to tolerate; put up patiently (*with*) [*bear* with me another minute] **5.** to be oppressive; weigh [grief *bears* heavily on her] —**bear down 1.** to press or push down **2.** to make a strong effort —**bear down on 1.** to exert pressure on **2.** to make a strong effort toward accomplishing **3.** to approach —**bear out** to support or confirm —**bear up** to endure, as under a strain —**bring to bear on** (or **upon**) to cause to have an effect on [he *brought* his influence *to bear on* the lawmakers] **SYN.**—*bear* is the general word for putting up with something that annoys, pains, etc.; *suffer* suggests the quiet acceptance, without complaining, of that which is painful or unpleasant; *endure* stresses a holding up for a long time against continuing pain, distress, etc.; *tolerate* and the more informal *stand* both imply a deliberate holding back of one's opposition or reaction to something that one finds offensive or painful; *brook,* a literary word, is usually used in the negative, suggesting refusal to put up with what is unpleasant

bear² (ber) *n., pl.* **bears, bear:** see PLURAL, II, D, 1 [OE. *bera* < IE. base *bhero-s,* brown, brown animal, from which also come BEAVER¹ & BROWN] **1.** a large, heavy mammal with shaggy fur and a very short tail, native to temperate and arctic zones: bears walk flat on the soles of their feet and eat any sort of food **2.** [B-] either of two N constellations, the **Great Bear** and the **Little Bear 3.** a person who is clumsy, rude, etc. **4.** a person who believes prices on the stock market are going to drop and so sells shares in the hope of buying them back later at a lower price —*adj.* falling in price [a *bear* market] —**be a bear for punishment** to be able to withstand rough treatment, hardship, etc. —**bear'like'** *adj.*

bear·a·ble (-ə b'l) *adj.* that can be borne or endured; tolerable —**bear'a·bly** *adv.*

beard (bird) *n.* [OE. < IE. base *bhardha,* from which also come L. *barba* & G. *bart*] **1.** the hair growing on the lower part of a man's face; whiskers **2.** any beardlike part, as of certain animals **3.** a hairy outgrowth on the head of certain grains, etc.; awn **4.** anything that projects like a beard; barb or hook —*vt.* to face or oppose courageously, as if grasping by the beard; defy

Beard (bird) **1. Charles Austin,** 1874–1948; U.S. historian **2. Daniel Carter,** 1850–1941; U.S. author & illustrator: a founder of the Boy Scouts of America

beard·ed (bird'id) *adj.* having a beard

beard·less (bird'lis) *adj.* **1.** having no beard **2.** too young to have a beard **3.** young, callow, etc.

Beards·ley (birdz'lē), **Aubrey Vincent** 1872–98; Eng. artist & illustrator

bear·er (ber'ər) *n.* **1.** a person or thing that bears, carries, or supports **2.** a plant or tree that bears fruit **3.** a person presenting for payment a check, note, money order, etc. —*adj.* made out to the bearer [*bearer* bonds]

bear·ing (ber'iŋ) *n.* **1.** way of carrying and conducting oneself; carriage; manner [she walked with regal *bearing*] **2.** a support or supporting part **3.** *a)* the act, power, or period of producing young, fruit, etc. *b)* that which is produced, as a crop **4.** endurance **5.** *a)* [*sometimes pl.*] direction or position with reference to the compass, some known points, etc. *b)* [*pl.*] awareness of one's position or situation [to lose one's *bearings*] **6.** relevant meaning; application; relation [the evidence has no *bearing* on the case] **7.** *Heraldry* any figure in a coat of arms **8.** *Mech.* any part of a machine in or on which another part revolves, slides,

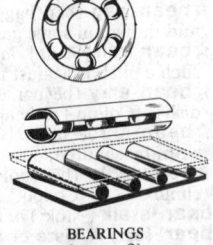

BEARINGS
(sense 8)

etc. —*adj.* that bears, or supports, weight [a *bearing* wall]

bear·ish (ber'ish) *adj.* **1.** bearlike; rough, surly, etc. **2.** expecting or causing a lowering of prices in the stock exchange —**bear'ish·ly** *adv.* —**bear'ish·ness** *n.*

bear·skin (ber'skin') *n.* **1.** the pelt or hide of a bear **2.** a rug, coat, etc. made of this **3.** a tall fur cap worn as part of some uniforms

beast (bēst) *n.* [< OFr. < L. *bestia*] **1.** orig., any animal except man **2.** any large, four-footed animal **3.** a person who is brutal, gross, vile, etc.

beast·ly (bēst'lē) *adj.* **-li·er, -li·est 1.** of or like a beast; bestial, brutal, etc. **2.** [Colloq.] disagreeable; unpleasant —*adv.* [Brit. Colloq.] very [*beastly* bad news] —**beast'li·ness** *n.*

beast of burden any animal used for carrying things

beast of prey any animal that kills other animals for food

beat (bēt) *vt.* **beat, beat'en, beat'ing** [OE. *beatan* < IE. base *bhau-, bhu-,* to strike, from which also come BEETLE² & BUTT¹ &²] **1.** to strike repeatedly; pound [to *beat* a drum] **2.** to punish by so striking; flog **3.** to dash repeatedly against [waves *beat* the shore] **4.** to form (a path, etc.) by repeated treading or riding **5.** to shape by hammering; forge [to *beat* copper into trays] **6.** to mix by stirring or striking repeatedly with a utensil; whip [to *beat* an egg] **7.** to move (esp. wings) up and down; flap **8.** to hunt through; search [the posse *beat* the countryside] **9.** to make or force, as by flailing or pounding [to *beat* one's way through a crowd] **10.** *a)* to defeat in a contest or struggle *b)* to outdo or surpass [nothing *beats* lemonade for quenching thirst] *c)* to act, arrive, or finish before [I'll *beat* you to the lake] **11.** to mark (time) by tapping, etc. **12.** to sound or signal, as by a drumbeat [to *beat* a retreat] **13.** [Colloq.] to baffle or puzzle [it *beats* me how she knew] ☆**14.** [Colloq.] to cheat or trick ☆**15.** [Slang] to avoid the penalties of (a charge, indictment, etc.); circumvent —*vi.* **1.** to strike repeatedly **2.** to move or sound rhythmically; throb, pulsate, etc. [my heart *beat* faster] **3.** to hunt through woods, etc. for game **4.** to take a beating or stirring [this cream doesn't *beat* well] **5.** to make a sound by being struck, as a drum **6.** [Colloq.] to win **7.** *Naut.* to progress by tacking into the wind —*n.* **1.** a beating, as of the heart **2.** any of a series of blows or strokes **3.** a pulsating movement or sound; throb **4.** a habitual route [a policeman's *beat*] **5.** *a)* the unit of musical rhythm [four *beats* to a measure] *b)* the accent in the rhythm of verse or music *c)* the gesture of the hand, baton, etc. used to mark this ☆**6.** *same as* BEATNIK ☆**7.** *Acoustics* the amplification of sound that keeps recurring and fading when two tones of nearly equal frequency are sounded together ☆**8.** *Journalism* a publishing of news before rival newspapers; scoop —*adj.* **1.** [Slang] tired out; exhausted ☆**2.** of or belonging to a group of young persons, esp. of the 1950's, rebelling against conventional attitudes, dress, speech, etc. —**beat about** to hunt or look through or around —**beat back** to force to retreat —**beat down 1.** to shine with dazzling light and intense heat **2.** to put down; suppress **3.** [Colloq.] to force to a lower price —☆**beat it!** [Slang] go away! —**beat off** to drive back; repel —☆**beat up (on)** [Slang] to give a beating to; thrash —**beat'er** *n.*

SYN.—*beat* is the general term for hitting or striking repeatedly, whether with the hands, feet, or some instrument; *pound* suggests heavier, more powerful blows than *beat* [to *pound* nails with a hammer]; *pummel* implies the beating of a person with the fists and suggests a continuous rain of damaging blows; *thrash,* originally referring to the beating of grain with a flail, suggests the same kind of broad, swinging strokes, as in striking a person over and over with a stick; *maul* implies a hitting with such heavy blows as to bruise or wound These terms are also used loosely, as in newspaper sports stories, in describing a decisive victory

beat·en (bēt'n) *adj.* **1.** struck with repeated blows; whipped **2.** shaped by hammering **3.** flattened by treading [a *beaten* path] **4.** *a)* defeated *b)* crushed in spirit by defeat **5.** tired out —**off the beaten track** (or **path**) unusual, unfamiliar, etc.

be·a·tif·ic (bē'ə tif'ik) *adj.* [see BEATIFY] **1.** making blissful or blessed **2.** full of bliss or joy [a *beatific* smile] —**be·a·tif·i·cal·ly** *adv.*

be·at·i·fi·ca·tion (bē at'ə fi kā'shən) *n.* [see BEATIFY] *R.C.Ch.* the process of declaring a certain dead person to be among the blessed in heaven and so entitled to public veneration

be·at·i·fy (bē at'ə fī') *vt.* **-fied', -fy'ing** [< Fr. < LL. *beatificare* < L. *beatus,* happy + *facere,* to make] **1.** to make blissfully happy **2.** *R.C.Ch.* to declare (a certain dead person) to have undergone beatification

beat·ing (bēt'iŋ) *n.* **1.** the act of one that beats **2.** a whipping or thrashing **3.** a throbbing; pulsation **4.** a defeat

be·at·i·tude (bē at′ə tōōd′, -tyōōd′) *n.* [< Fr. < L. < *beatus,* happy] perfect blessedness or happiness —**the Beatitudes** the blessings on the meek, the peacemakers, etc. in the Sermon on the Mount: Matt. 5:3–12

☆**beat·nik** (bēt′nik) *n.* [BEAT, *adj.* 2 + Russ. (via Yid.) *-nik,* equiv. to *-ER*] a member of the beat group

Be·a·trice (bē′ə tris) [It. < L. *beatrix,* she who makes happy < *beatus,* happy] a feminine name: var. *Beatrix*

☆**beat-up** (bēt′up′) *adj.* [Slang] in a worn-out condition; dilapidated, battered, shabby, etc.

beau (bō) *n., pl.* **beaus, beaux** (bōz) [Fr. < *beau,* pretty < L. *bellus,* pretty] the sweetheart or courter of a woman or girl

Beau Brum·mell (brum′əl) **1.** (*George Bryan Brummell*), 1778–1840; Eng. gentleman famous for his fashionable dress and manners **2.** any man who pays much attention to fashion in clothes and manners; dandy; fop

Beau·fort scale (bō′fərt) [after Sir Francis *Beaufort* (1774–1857), Brit. naval officer] *Meteorol.* a scale of wind force ranging from 0 (calm) to 17 (hurricane)

Beaufort Sea part of the Arctic Ocean, north of Alaska

‡**beau geste** (bō zhest′) *pl.* **beaux gestes** (bō zhest′) [Fr.] **1.** a fine gesture **2.** an act or offer that seems fine, noble, etc., but is empty

beau i·de·al (ī dē′əl) [Fr.] **1.** ideal beauty **2.** the perfect or ideal type (*of* something); model

Beau·mar·chais (bō már she′), **Pierre Au·gus·tin Ca·ron de** (pyer ō güs tan′ kä rōn′ də) 1732–99; Fr. dramatist

beau monde (bō′mänd′) [Fr.] fashionable society

Beau·mont (bō′mänt) [ult. < Fr., lit., beautiful hill] city in SE Tex.: pop. 116,000

☆**beaut** (byōōt) *n.* [Slang] one that is beautiful or superlative in some way: often used ironically [*a beaut* of an excuse]

beau·te·ous (byōōt′ē əs) *adj. same as* BEAUTIFUL —see SYN. at BEAUTIFUL —**beau′te·ous·ly** *adv.*

☆**beau·ti·cian** (byōō tish′ən) *n.* a person who does hair styling, manicuring, etc. in a beauty shop; cosmetologist

beau·ti·ful (byōōt′ə fəl) *adj.* having beauty; very pleasing to the eye, ear, etc. —**beau′ti·ful·ly** *adv.* —**beau′ti·ful·ness** *n.*
SYN. —**beautiful** is applied to that which gives the most pleasure and suggests that the thing that delights one comes close to one's ideal; **lovely** refers to that which delights by causing one to feel affection or warm admiration; **handsome** is used of that which attracts by its pleasing proportions, elegance, etc. and suggests a masculine quality; **pretty** implies daintiness or gracefulness and suggests a feminine quality; **comely** applies to persons only and suggests a wholesome attractiveness rather than great beauty; **fair** suggests beauty, esp. of complexion or features, that is fresh, bright, or perfect; **good-looking** generally equals either **handsome** or **pretty; beauteous,** a poetical synonym for **beautiful,** is now often used in a joking or belittling way —*ANT.* ugly

beau·ti·fy (byōōt′ə fī′) *vt., vi.* **-fied′, -fy′ing** to make or become beautiful or more beautiful —**beau′ti·fi·ca′tion** *n.* —**beau′ti·fi′er** *n.*

beau·ty (byōōt′ē) *n., pl.* **-ties** [< OFr. < L. *bellus,* pretty] **1.** the quality in someone or something that pleases the senses or mind, as by line, color, form, tone, behavior, etc. **2.** a thing having this quality **3.** good looks **4.** a very good-looking woman **5.** any very attractive feature

☆**beauty culture** the skill or work of a beautician

☆**beauty shop** (or **salon** or **parlor**) a place where women go for hair styling, manicuring, etc.

beauty spot 1. a tiny black patch formerly applied by women to the face or back to emphasize whiteness of skin **2.** a natural mark or mole on the skin **3.** any place noted for its beauty

beaux (bōz; Fr. bō) *n. alt. pl.* of BEAU

‡**beaux-arts** (bō zár′) *n., pl.* [Fr.] the fine arts

bea·ver[1] (bē′vər) *n.* [OE. *beofor:* for IE. base see BEAR[2]] **1.** *pl.* **-vers, -ver:** see PLURAL, II, D, 1 a large rodent with soft, brown fur, webbed hind feet, and a flat, broad tail: it can live on land or in water *b)* its fur **2.** a man's high silk hat **3.** a heavy cloth of felted wool ☆**4.** [Colloq.] a hard-working, painstaking person

BEAVER
(32–47 in. long, including tail)

bea·ver[2] (bē′vər) *n.* [OFr. *baviere,* ult. < *bave,* saliva] **1.** orig., a piece of armor to protect the mouth and chin **2.** the visor of a helmet: see illustration at ARMOR

☆**Bea·ver·board** (bē′vər bôrd′) *a trademark for* artificial board made of wood fiber, used for walls, etc. —*n.* [b-] fiberboard of this kind

be·calm (bi käm′) *vt.* **1.** to make calm **2.** to make (a sailing ship) motionless from lack of wind —**be·calmed′** *adj.*

be·came (bi kām′) *pt.* of BECOME

be·cause (bi kôz′, -kuz′) *conj.* [< ME. *bi,* by + *cause*] for the reason or cause that; since —**because of** by reason of; on account of

bé·cha·mel (bāsh′ə mel′) *n.* [Fr. < Louis de *Béchamel,* steward to Louis XIV] a white sauce made of cream, butter, flour, etc.

be·chance (bi chans′) *vt., vi.* **-chanced′, -chanc′ing** [Now Rare] to happen (to); befall

‡**bêche-de-mer** (besh də mer′) *n.* [Fr., worm of the sea < Port. *bicho do mar,* sea slug] **1.** *pl.* **bêches-de-mer′** (besh-) *same as* TREPANG **2.** a pidgin English spoken in island areas of the SW Pacific

Bech·u·a·na·land (bech′ōō wän′ə land′) *former name of* BOTSWANA

beck (bek) *n.* [< BECKON] a beckoning gesture of the hand, head, etc. —*vt., vi.* [Archaic] to beckon —**at the beck and call of** at the service of

Beck·et (bek′ət), **Saint Thomas à** 1118?–70; Eng. churchman; archbishop of Canterbury, who was murdered

Beck·ett (bek′ət), **Samuel** 1906– ; Ir. poet, novelist, & playwright in France, writing mostly in French

beck·on (bek′'n) *vt., vi.* [OE. *beacnian* < *beacen,* BEACON] **1.** to call or summon by a motion of the head or hand **2.** to seem attractive (to); lure [the woods *beckon*] —*n.* a summoning gesture

be·cloud (bi kloud′) *vt.* **1.** to cloud over; darken **2.** to confuse; muddle

be·come (bi kum′) *vi.* **-came′, -come′, -com′ing** [OE. *becuman:* see BE- & COME] **1.** to come to be [to *become* ill] **2.** to grow to be [the tadpole *becomes* a frog] —*vt.* **1.** to be right for or suitable to [that hat *becomes* you] —**become of** to happen to; be the fate of [whatever *became of* your plans?]

be·com·ing (bi kum′iŋ) *adj.* **1.** that is suitable or appropriate; fit [she answered with *becoming* modesty] **2.** suitable to the wearer [a *becoming* gown] —**be·com′ing·ly** *adv.*

Bec·que·rel (be krel′; E. bek′ə rel′) family of Fr. physicists: **1. A·lex·an·dre Ed·mond** (ȧ lek sän′dr′ ed môn′), 1820–91; father of *Antoine Henri* **2. An·toine Cé·sar** (än twän′ sä zȧr′), 1788–1878; father of *Alexandre* **3. Antoine Hen·ri** (än rē′), 1852–1908

bed (bed) *n.* [OE. < IE. base *bhedh-,* to dig, from which also come FOSSA & FOSSIL; orig. sense "a hollow in the ground for sleeping"] **1.** a piece of furniture for sleeping or resting on, consisting typically of a bedstead, spring, mattress, and bedding **2.** *same as* BEDSTEAD **3.** any place used for sleeping or reclining **4.** *a)* a plot of soil where plants are raised *b)* such plants **5.** *a)* the bottom of a river, lake, etc. *b)* a place on the ocean floor where things grow [oyster *bed*] **6.** rock, etc. in which something is firmly fixed **7.** any flat surface used as a base or support [mount the lathe on a *bed* of concrete] **8.** a pile or heap resembling a bed, esp. in softness or shape [a *bed* of leaves] **9.** a geological layer [a *bed* of coal] —*vt.* **bed′ded, bed′ding 1.** to provide with a sleeping place **2.** to put to bed **3.** to fix or place firmly; embed **4.** *a)* to plant in a bed of earth *b)* to make (earth) into a bed for plants **5.** to lay out flat like a bed; arrange in layers —*vi.* **1.** to go to bed; rest **2.** to form in layers —**bed and board** a place to sleep and meals **2.** the married state —☆**bed down** to prepare and use a sleeping place —**get up on the wrong side of the bed** to be cross or grouchy —**put to bed 1.** to get (a child, etc.) ready for sleep **2.** [Slang] to get (a newspaper, etc.) ready for the press —**take to one's bed** to go to bed because of illness, etc.

be·daub (bi dôb′) *vt.* **1.** to make daubs on; smear over [shoes *bedaubed* with mud] **2.** to overdecorate

be·daz·zle (bi daz′'l) *vt.* **-zled, -zling** to dazzle thoroughly; bewilder; confuse [*bedazzled* by all the neon signs]

bed·bug (bed′bug′) *n.* a small, wingless, reddish-brown, bloodsucking insect sometimes found in beds, etc. and active mainly at night

bed·cham·ber (-chām′bər) *n. same as* BEDROOM

bed·clothes (-klōz', -klō*thz*') *n.pl.* sheets, blankets, comforters, etc. used on a bed

bed·cov·er (-kuv'ər) *n.* a cover for a bed; coverlet; bedspread

bed·ding (-iŋ) *n.* 1. mattresses and bedclothes 2. straw, hay, etc., used to bed animals 3. a bottom layer 4. *Geol.* the arrangement of rocks in strata, or layers; stratification

Bede (bēd), Saint 673–735 A.D.; Eng. historian & theologian: called *the Venerable Bede*

be·deck (bi dek') *vt.* to cover with decorations; adorn —see SYN. at ADORN

be·dev·il (bi dev'l) *vt.* -iled or -illed, -il·ing or -il·ling 1. to trouble in a fiendish way; torment 2. to bewitch 3. to confuse completely; muddle [*bedeviled* by doubt] 4. to corrupt; spoil —**be·dev'il·ment** *n.*

be·dew (bi dōō', -dyōō') *vt.* to make wet with or as if with drops of dew

bed·fast (bed'fast') *adj. same as* BEDRIDDEN

bed·fel·low (-fel'ō) *n.* 1. a person who shares one's bed 2. an associate, ally, etc.

be·dight (bi dīt') *adj.* [pp. of obs. *bedight* < ME. < *bi-*, BE- + *dighten*, to set in order < OE. *dihtan*, to compose < L. *dictare*: see DICTATE] [Archaic or Poet.] bedecked; arrayed

be·dim (bi dim') *vt.* -dimmed', -dim'ming to make (the eyes or vision) dim; darken or obscure

be·di·zen (bi dī'z'n, -diz''n) *vt.* [BE- + DIZEN] to dress in a cheap, showy way —**be·di'zen·ment** *n.*

bed jacket a woman's short, loose upper garment sometimes worn in bed over a nightgown

bed·lam (bed'ləm) *n.* [< *Bedlam*, altered < (St. Mary of) *Bethlehem*, old insane asylum in London] 1. [Archaic] an insane asylum 2. any place or condition of noise and confusion —**bed'lam·ite'** (-īt') *n.*

bed linen bed sheets, pillowcases, etc.

bed of roses [Colloq.] a situation or position of ease and luxury

Bed·ou·in (bed'ōō win) *n.*, *pl.* -ins, -in [< Fr. < Ar. *badawīn*, dwellers in the desert] [*also* b-] 1. an Arab of any of the nomadic desert tribes of Arabia, Syria, or N Africa 2. any wanderer or nomad —*adj.* of or like the Bedouins

bed·pan (bed'pan') *n.* 1. *same as* WARMING PAN ☆2. a shallow pan for use as a toilet by a person confined to bed

bed·post (-pōst') *n.* any of the four posts at the corners of some beds

be·drag·gle (bi drag''l) *vt.* -gled, -gling to make wet, limp, and dirty, as by dragging through mud —**be·drag'gled** *adj.*

bed·rid·den (bed'rid'n) *adj.* having to stay in bed, usually for a long period, because of illness, weakness, etc.

☆**bed·rock** (-räk') *n.* 1. solid rock beneath the soil and surface rock 2. a strong foundation 3. the very bottom 4. basic principles and facts

☆**bed·roll** (-rōl') *n.* a portable roll of bedding, generally for sleeping outdoors

bed·room (-rōōm') *n.* a room to sleep in

bed·side (-sīd') *n.* the side of a bed; space beside a bed —*adj.* 1. beside a bed 2. in dealing with patients [a doctor's *bedside* manner]

bed·sore (-sôr') *n.* a sore on the body of a bedridden person, caused by chafing or pressure

☆**bed·spread** (-spred') *n.* a cover spread over the blanket on a bed when it is not being slept in

☆**bed·spring** (-spriŋ') *n.* 1. a framework of springs in a bed to support the mattress 2. any such spring

bed·stead (-sted') *n.* a framework for supporting the springs and mattress of a bed

bed·straw (-strô') *n.* [from its former use as straw for beds] a small plant of the madder family, with whorled leaves and small, white or colored flowers

bed·time (-tīm') *n.* one's usual time for going to bed

bedtime story 1. a story told to children at bedtime 2. an explanation that is not very convincing

bed·wet·ting (-wet'iŋ) *n.* urinating in bed

bee[1] (bē) *n.* [OE. *beo* < IE. base *bhei*-] a four-winged, hairy insect that gathers pollen and nectar: some bees live in organized colonies and make honey —**have a bee in one's bonnet** 1. to have an idea in one's mind that one cannot get rid of 2. to be not quite sane

bee[2] (bē) *n.* [ult. < OE. *ben*, compulsory service: for IE. base see BAN[1]] ☆a meeting of people to work together or to compete [a sewing *bee*, spelling *bee*]

bee·bread (bē'bred') *n.* a yellowish-brown mixture of pollen and honey, made and eaten by some bees

beech (bēch) *adj.* [OE. *bece*: see BOOK] designating a family of trees including the beeches, oaks, and chestnuts —*n.* 1. a tree of the beech family, with smooth bark, hard wood, dark-green leaves, and edible nuts 2. its wood —**beech'en** *adj.*

Bee·cher (bē'chər), **Henry Ward** 1813–87; U.S. clergyman & lecturer

beech·mast (bēch'mast') *n.* beechnuts, esp. as they lie on the ground: also **beech mast**

beech·nut (-nut') *n.* the small, three-cornered, edible nut of the beech tree

beech·wood (-wood') *n.* the wood of the beech tree

beef (bēf) *n.*, *pl.* **beeves**; also, and for 5 always, **beefs** [< OFr. *boef* < L. *bovis*, gen. of *bos*, ox < IE. base *gwou*-, from which also come COW[1] & BUFFALO] 1. a full-grown ox, cow, bull, or steer, esp. one bred for meat 2. meat from such an animal; specif., a dressed carcass 3. such animals as a group ☆4. [Colloq.] *a*) human flesh or muscle *b*) strength; brawn ☆5. [Slang] a complaint —☆*vi.* [Slang] to complain —**beef up** [Colloq.] to strengthen as by adding units [to *beef up* a sales force]

AMERICAN BEECH (tree, leaves, & nuts)

☆**beef cattle** cattle bred and fattened for meat

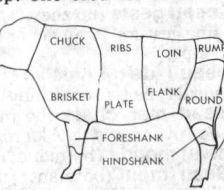

BEEF CUTS

beef·eat·er (-ēt'ər) *n.* 1. an eater of beef, generally thought of as a large, heavy, red-faced person 2. *same as* YEOMAN OF THE GUARD 3. a guard at the Tower of London 4. [Slang] an Englishman

beef·steak (-stāk') *n.* a slice of beef, esp. from the loin, cut thick for broiling or frying

beef tea a drink made from beef extract or by boiling lean strips of beef

beef·y (bēf'ē) *adj.* beef'i·er, beef'i·est fleshy and solid; very muscular; brawny

bee·hive (bē'hīv') *n.* 1. a box or other shelter for a colony of bees, where they make and store honey 2. a place of great activity

bee·keep·er (-kēp'ər) *n.* a person who keeps bees for producing honey —**bee'keep'ing** *n.*

☆**bee·line** (-līn') *n.* a straight, direct route —**make a beeline for** [Colloq.] to go straight toward

Be·el·ze·bub (bē el'zə bub') *Bible* the chief devil; Satan

☆**bee moth** a moth whose larvae, hatched in beehives, eat the wax of the honeycomb

been (bin, *chiefly Brit.* ben) *pp.* of BE

beep (bēp) *n.* [echoic] 1. the brief, high-pitched sound of a horn, as on an automobile 2. a brief, high-pitched electronic signal, used in warning, direction-finding, etc. —*vi., vt.* to make or cause to make such a sound

beer (bir) *n.* [OE. *beor*] 1. an alcoholic drink made from fermented grain, esp. malted barley, and flavored with hops 2. any of various soft drinks made from root and plant extracts [root *beer*]

Beer·she·ba (bir shē'bə) city in S Israel, in the Negev: pop. 70,000

beer·y (bir'ē) *adj.* beer'i·er, beer'i·est 1. of or like beer 2. showing the effects of drinking beer; drunken, maudlin, etc. —**beer'i·ness** *n.*

beest·ings (bēs'tiŋz) *n.pl.* [often with sing. v.] [OE. *bysting* < *beost*, beestings] the first milk of a cow after having a calf

bees·wax (bēz'waks') *n.* wax made and used by bees to build their honeycomb: see WAX[1] (sense 1)

beet (bēt) *n.* [< OE. < L. *beta*] 1. a plant with edible leaves and a thick, fleshy, white or red root 2. this root: some varieties are eaten as a vegetable, others are a source of sugar, and some are used as fodder

Bee·tho·ven (bā'tō vən), **Lud·wig van** (lōōt'viH vän) 1770–1827; Ger. composer

bee·tle[1] (bēt''l) *n.* [OE. *bitela < bitan*, to BITE] any of an order of insects with biting mouthparts and hard front wings that cover the membranous hind wings when these are folded

bee·tle[2] (bēt''l) *n.* [OE. *betel*: for IE. base see BEAT] 1. a heavy, wooden mallet 2. a household mallet or pestle for mashing or beating —*vt.* -tled, -tling to pound with a beetle

bee·tle[3] (bēt''l) *vi.* **-tled, -tling** [prob. < BEETLE-BROWED] to project or jut; overhang —*adj.* jutting; overhanging: also **bee′tling**

bee·tle-browed (bēt′'l broud′) *adj.* [ME. < ? *bitel*, sharp + *brouwe*, BROW] **1.** having bushy or overhanging eyebrows **2.** frowning; scowling

beet sugar sugar extracted from sugar beets

beeves (bēvz) *n. alt. pl. of* BEEF

be·fall (bi fôl′) *vi.* **-fell′, -fall′en, -fall′ing** [< OE. < *be-* + *feallan*, to FALL] [Archaic] to come to pass; happen —*vt.* to happen to [the disaster that *befell* us]

be·fit (bi fit′) *vt.* **-fit′ted, -fit′ting** to be suitable or proper for [as *befits* his position] —**be·fit′ting·ly** *adv.*

be·fog (bi fôg′, -fäg′) *vt.* **-fogged′, -fog′ging 1.** to cover with fog; make foggy **2.** to make obscure or muddled; confuse [to *befog* an issue]

BEETLE-BROWED
MAN

be·fore (bi fôr′) *adv.* [< OE. < *be-*, by + *foran*, before] **1.** ahead; in front [with an advance guard before] **2.** in the past; previously [I've seen him *before*] **3.** earlier; sooner [come at ten, not *before*] —*prep.* **1.** ahead of in time, space, rank, or importance [you go *before* me] **2.** just in front of [he paused *before* the door] **3.** in the sight, notice, presence, etc. of [to stand *before* a judge] **4.** being considered, judged, or decided by [the bill *before* the assembly] **5.** earlier than [he left *before* noon] **6.** in preference to [death *before* dishonor] **7.** still to be reached by [the years that lie *before* us] —*conj.* **1.** earlier than the time that [drop in *before* you go] **2.** rather than [I'd die *before* I'd tell]

be·fore·hand (-hand′) *adv., adj.* ahead of time; in advance [make your plans *beforehand*]

be·foul (bi foul′) *vt.* to dirty or sully; foul

be·friend (-frend′) *vt.* to act as a friend to; help

be·fud·dle (bi fud′'l) *vt.* **-dled, -dling 1.** to confuse (the mind, a person, etc.) **2.** to make dull or stupid with alcoholic liquor —**be·fud′dle·ment** *n.*

beg (beg) *vt.* **begged, beg′ging** [< Anglo-Fr. < OFr. *begard*, beggar < MDu. *beggaert*] **1.** to ask for as charity [he *begged* a dime] **2.** to ask for earnestly as a kindness or favor [I *beg* your permission to leave] —*vi.* **1.** to ask for charity **2.** to ask humbly; entreat —**beg off** to ask to be released from —**beg the question 1.** to use an argument that assumes as proved the very thing one is trying to prove **2.** loosely, to evade the issue —**go begging** to be unwanted

SYN.—**beg** implies being humble or earnest in asking for something [he *begged* me not to go]; **solicit** emphasizes being polite in a formal way in asking for something [we *solicit* your aid]; **entreat** implies using all of one's power to persuade; **beseech** suggests that there is much emotion in the asking and anxiety over what the result will be; **implore** is even stronger, suggesting that the asker is desperate or in great distress; **importune** suggests such persistence in asking as to become annoying

be·gan (bi gan′) *pt. of* BEGIN

be·get (bi get′) *vt.* **-got′** or archaic **-gat′** (-gat′), **-got′ten** or **-got′, -get′ting** [< OE. *begitan*, to acquire: see BE- & GET] **1.** to be the father of; procreate **2.** to bring into being; produce [tyranny *begets* rebellion] —**be·get′ter** *n.*

beg·gar (beg′ər) *n.* [< OFr. *begard*: see BEG] **1.** a person who begs; esp., one who lives by begging **2.** a very poor person; pauper **3.** a person; fellow [a cute little *beggar*] —*vt.* **1.** to make a beggar of; make poor **2.** to make seem inadequate or useless [her beauty *beggars* description] —**beg′gar·dom** (-dəm) *n.*

beg·gar·ly (-lē) *adj.* like or fit for a beggar; very poor, inadequate, etc. —**beg′gar·li·ness** *n.*

☆**beg·gar's-lice** (beg′ərz līs′) *n., pl.* **beg′gar's-lice 1.** any of various plants with dry, prickly fruits that stick to fur or clothing **2.** the fruit of such a plant Also called **beg′gar's-ticks′**

beg·gar·y (beg′ər ē) *n.* extreme poverty, or the condition of being a beggar

be·gin (bi gin′) *vi.* **be·gan′, be·gun′, be·gin′ning** [< OE. *beginnan*] **1.** to start doing something; get under way **2.** to come into being; arise [when did their quarrel *begin*?] **3.** to have a first part [the Bible *begins* with Genesis] **4.** to be or do

in the slightest degree [they don't *begin* to compare] —*vt.* **1.** to cause to start; commence **2.** to bring into being; originate **3.** to do or be the first part of [the case that *began* his career]

SYN.—**begin** is the general term for setting into motion some action or course [to *begin* eating]; **commence** is a more formal term, used with an elaborate course of action [to *commence* a court action]; **start** emphasizes the fact of leaving from some point in any motion or action [to *start* a journey; the boulder *started* a landslide]; **initiate** refers to the carrying out of the first steps in some course or process, without indicating what is to follow [to *initiate* peace talks] —*ANT.* end, finish, conclude

be·gin·ner (bi gin′ər) *n.* **1.** one who begins anything **2.** one just beginning to do or learn a thing; inexperienced person; novice

be·gin·ning (bi gin′iŋ) *n.* **1.** a starting or commencing **2.** the time or place of starting; birth; origin; source **3.** the first part [the *beginning* of a book] **4.** [*usually pl.*] an early stage [the *beginnings* of nuclear physics] —see *SYN.* at ORIGIN

be·gird (bi gurd′) *vt.* **-girt′** or **-gird′ed, -girt′, -gird′ing 1.** to bind around; gird **2.** to encircle

be·gone (bi gôn′, -gän′) *interj., vi.* (to) be gone; go away; get out: usually used in the imperative

be·gon·ia (bi gōn′yə) *n.* [after M. *Bégon* (1638-1710), Fr. governor of the Dominican Republic] a plant with showy flowers and ornamental leaves

be·got (bi gät′) *pt. & alt. pp. of* BEGET

be·got·ten (bi gät′'n) *alt. pp. of* BEGET

be·grime (bi grīm′) *vt.* **-grimed′, -grim′ing** to cover with grime; make dirty; soil

be·grudge (bi gruj′) *vt.* **-grudged′, -grudg′ing 1.** to feel envy or resentment because of (something possessed by another) [don't *begrudge* him his good fortune] **2.** to give with ill will or reluctance [he *begrudges* every cent he gives to charity] —see *SYN.* at ENVY —**be·grudg′ing·ly** *adv.*

be·guile (bi gīl′) *vt.* **-guiled′, -guil′ing 1.** to mislead by guile; deceive [he was *beguiled* into revealing secrets] **2.** to deprive (of or out of) by deceit; cheat [the carnival barker *beguiled* Tim out of his money] **3.** to pass (time) pleasantly; while away [he *beguiled* his day with reading] **4.** to charm or delight [her beauty *beguiled* us] —see *SYN.* at DECEIVE and LURE —**be·guile′·ment** *n.* —**be·guil′er** *n.* —**be·guil′ing·ly** *adv.*

be·guine (bi gēn′) *n.* [< Fr. *béguin*, infatuation] a native dance of Martinique or its music

be·gum (bē′gəm) *n.* [< Hindi *begam*, lady] in India, a Moslem lady of high rank

be·gun (bi gun′) *pp. of* BEGIN

be·half (bi haf′) *n.* [< OE. *be*, by + *healf*, side, half] support, interest, side, etc. [speak in his *behalf*] —**in** (or **on**) **behalf of** in the interest of; for —**on behalf of** speaking for; representing [wish her well *on behalf of* all of us]

be·have (bi hāv′) *vt., vi.* **-haved′, -hav′ing** [see BE- & HAVE] **1.** to conduct (oneself or itself) or act in a specified way [the car *behaved* well on the trip] **2.** to conduct (oneself) properly; do what is right [will the kids *behave* at a concert?]

be·hav·ior (bi hāv′yər) *n.* **1.** the way a person behaves or acts; conduct **2.** the way an organism, machine, element, etc. acts, responds, or functions —**be·hav′ior·al** *adj.* —**be·hav′ior·al·ly** *adv.*

behavioral science any of the sciences, as sociology, psychology, or anthropology, that study human behavior

☆**be·hav·ior·ism** (bi hāv′yər iz'm) *n.* the doctrine that the only valid data of psychology comes from objectively observing the behavior of people and animals —**be·hav′ior·ist** *n., adj.* —**be·hav′ior·is′tic** *adj.*

be·hav·iour (bi hāv′yər) *n. Brit. sp. of* BEHAVIOR

be·head (bi hed′) *vt.* to cut off the head of

be·held (bi held′) *pt. & pp. of* BEHOLD

be·he·moth (bi hē′məth, bē′ə-) *n.* [Heb. *behēmōth*, pl. of *behēmāh*, beast] **1.** *Bible* a huge animal, thought to have been the hippopotamus: Job 40:15-24 **2.** any huge animal or thing

be·hest (bi hest′) *n.* [OE. *behæs*, a vow: see BE- & HEST] an order, command, or request [I come at your *behest*]

be·hind (bi hīnd′) *adv.* [OE. *behindan*: see BE- & HIND[1]] **1.** in or to the rear or back [walk *behind*] **2.** in a former time, place, condition, etc. [the girl he left *behind*] **3.** into the state of being late or slow [to drop *behind* in one's studies] **4.** in or into arrears [to fall *behind* in one's dues] —*prep.* **1.** remaining after [the sons he left *behind* him] **2.** in back of [sit *behind* her] **3.** lower in rank, achievement, etc. than **4.** later than [*behind* schedule] **5.** on the other or farther side of [*behind* the hill] **6.** gone by or ended for [his schooling is *behind* him] **7.** supporting or advocating [Congress is *behind* the plan] **8.** hidden by; not yet revealed [the story *behind* the news] —*adj.* that follows [the person *behind*] —*n.* [Colloq.] the buttocks

be·hind·hand (-hand') *adv., adj.* **1.** behind in paying debts, rent, etc. **2.** behind time; late **3.** behind or slow in progress, advancement, etc.

be·hold (bi hōld') *vt.* **-held'**, **-held'** or archaic **-hold'en**, **-hold'ing** [OE. *bihealdan*, to hold: see BE- & HOLD[1]] to hold in view; look at; regard [I never *beheld* a lovelier sight] —*interj.* look! see! —see SYN. at SEE[1] —**be·hold'er** *n.*

be·hold·en (-ən) *adj.* obliged to feel grateful; owing thanks; indebted [she wants to be *beholden* to no one]

be·hoof (bi hōof') *n.* [OE. *behof*, profit: for IE. base see HAVE] behalf, benefit, interest, advantage, sake, etc.

be·hoove (-hōōv') *vt.* **-hooved'**, **-hoov'ing** [OE. *behofian*, to need < prec.] to be necessary for or be the duty of [it *behooves* us all to help in this crisis]

be·hove (-hōv') *vt.* **-hoved'**, **-hov'ing** *chiefly Brit. var. of* BE-HOOVE

beige (bāzh) *n.* [Fr.; < ? ML. *bambax*, cotton: see BOMBAST] **1.** a soft, unbleached and undyed, wool fabric **2.** its characteristic sandy color; grayish tan —*adj.* grayish-tan

be·ing (bē'iŋ) *n.* [see BE] **1.** existence; life [to come into *being*] **2.** basic or essential nature **3.** one that lives or exists, or is assumed to do so [a human *being*, a divine *being*] —**being as** (or **that**) [Dial.] since; because —**for the time being** for now

Bei·rut (bā rōōt', bā'rōōt) capital of Lebanon: pop. c. 500,000

be·jab·bers (bi jab'ərz) *interj.* [< *by Jesus*] an exclamation used to express surprise, pleasure, anger, etc.

be·jew·el (bi jōō'əl) *vt.* **-eled** or **-elled**, **-el·ing** or **-el·ling** to decorate with or as with jewels

☆**bel** (bel) *n.* [after A. G. BELL] a unit of power equal to 10 decibels

be·la·bor (bi lā'bər) *vt.* **1.** to beat severely **2.** to attack verbally **3.** *popularly, same as* LABOR, *vt.*

be·lat·ed (-lāt'id) *adj.* late or too late; tardy —**be·lat'ed·ly** *adv.* —**be·lat'ed·ness** *n.*

be·lay (bi lā') *vt., vi.* **-layed'**, **-lay'ing** [< OE. < *be-* + *lecgan*, to lay] **1.** to make (a rope) hold tight by winding around a pin (**belaying pin**), cleat, etc. **2.** to stop [*belay* there!] : sailor's informal term **3.** to make (a person or thing) firm or fast by a rope

bel can·to (bel' kän'tō) [It., lit., beautiful song] a style of singing in operas that stresses brilliant tones and singing technique

belch (belch) *vi., vt.* [OE. *bealcian*] **1.** to expel (gas) through the mouth from the stomach **2.** to utter (curses, etc.) violently **3.** to throw forth (its contents) violently [the volcano *belched* flame] —*n.* a belching

BELAYING PINS

bel·dam, bel·dame (bel'dəm) *n.* [*bel-* < Fr. *belle* (see BELLE) + DAME] an old woman; esp., a hideous old woman; hag

be·lea·guer (bi lē'gər) *vt.* [Du. *belegeren* < *legeren*, to camp < *leger* (akin to LAIR), a camp] **1.** to besiege by surrounding, as with an army **2.** to attack; harass

Be·lém (be len') seaport in NE Brazil: pop. 402,000

Bel·fast (bel'fast) seaport & capital of Northern Ireland: pop. 398,000

bel·fry (bel'frē) *n., pl.* **-fries** [altered (after BELL[1]) < OFr. *berfroi* < OHG. < *bergen*, to protect + *frid*, peace] **1.** a bell tower **2.** the part of a steeple that holds the bell or bells —**bel'fried** *adj.*

Belg. 1. Belgian **2.** Belgium

Bel·gian (bel'jən) *adj.* of Belgium, its people, etc. —*n.* a native or inhabitant of belgium

Belgian Congo former Belgian colony in C Africa, now the country of ZAIRE

Bel·gium (bel'jəm) kingdom in W Europe, on the North Sea: 11,779 sq. mi.; pop. 9,660,000; cap. Brussels: Fr. name **Belgique** (bel zhēk'); Fl. name **Bel·gi·ë** (bel'gē ə)

Bel·grade (bel'grād, -gräd; bel grād', -grād') capital of Yugoslavia, on the Danube: pop. 598,000

Be·li·al (bē'lē əl, bēl'yəl) *n.* [< LL. < Heb. *beliya'al*, worthlessness] *Bible* wickedness as an evil force (in the *New Testament*, personified as Satan)

be·lie (bi lī') *vt.* **-lied'**, **-ly'ing** **1.** to give a false idea of; misrepresent [his smile *belies* his anger] **2.** to leave unfulfilled [war *belied* hopes for peace] **3.** to show to be untrue [her cruelty *belied* her kind words] —**be·li'er** *n.*

be·lief (bə lēf') *n.* [ME. < *bi-*, BE- + *-leve* < OE. *geleafa*: see BELIEVE] **1.** the state of believing; acceptance that certain things are true or real [a *belief* in astrology] **2.** faith, esp. religious faith **3.** trust or confidence [I have *belief* in her ability] **4.** anything believed or accepted as true; esp., a creed, tenet, etc. **5.** an opinion; expectation [my *belief* is that he'll come] SYN. —**belief** is the general term for the acceptance of something as true, even without being completely certain; **faith** implies complete acceptance, even without proof and, esp., of something not supported by reason; **trust** implies assurance, often based on intuition, that someone or something is reliable; **confidence** also suggests such assurance, esp. when based on reason or proof —see also SYN. at OPINION —ANT. doubt, incredulity

be·lieve (bə lēv') *vt.* **-lieved'**, **-liev'ing** [ME. < *bi-*, BE- + *-leven* < OE. *geliefan* < IE. base *leubh-*, to like, desire, from which also come L. *libido* & LOVE, LIEF] **1.** to take as true, real, etc. [can we *believe* her story?] **2.** to have confidence in a statement or promise of (another person) **3.** to suppose or think [I *believe* that I'll have tea] —*vi.* **1.** to have trust or confidence (*in*), as being true, real, etc. **2.** to have religious faith —**be·liev'a·bil'i·ty** *n.* —**be·liev'a·ble** *adj.* —**be·liev'a·bly** *adv.* —**be·liev'er** *n.*

Be·lin·da (bə lin'də) [< Gmc. *Betlindis* < ?] a feminine name

☆**be·lit·tle** (bə lit'l) *vt.* **-tled**, **-tling** to make seem little, less important, etc.; depreciate [he tried to *belittle* her victory] —see SYN. at DISPARAGE —**be·lit'tle·ment** *n.* —**be·lit'tler** *n.*

Be·lize (bə lēz') **1.** self-governing Brit. territory in Central America: 8,867 sq. mi.; pop. 127,000 **2.** seaport on the Caribbean coast of this territory: pop. 39,000

bell[1] (bel) *n.* [OE. *belle* < IE. base *bhel-*, to sound, roar, from which also comes BELLOW] **1.** a hollow object, usually cuplike and of metal, which rings when struck, as by a clapper inside **2.** the sound made by a bell **3.** anything shaped like a bell, as a flower, the flare of a horn, etc. **4.** *Naut.* a stroke of a bell rung every half hour to mark the periods of the watch [eight *bells* mark the end of each four-hour watch, after which a new series is begun] —*vt.* **1.** to attach a bell to **2.** to shape like a bell —*vi.* to flare out like a bell [pants that *bell* at the cuffs]

bell[2] (bel) *n., vi., vt.* [OE. *bellan*: see BELL[1]] bellow; roar; bay

Bell (bel), **Alexander Graham** 1847–1922; U.S. inventor of the telephone, born in Scotland

bel·la·don·na (bel'ə dän'ə) *n.* [ModL. < It. *bella donna*, beautiful lady, a folk etym. for ML. *bladona*, nightshade] **1.** a poisonous plant with purplish, bell-shaped flowers and black berries; deadly nightshade **2.** *same as* ATROPINE

bell-bot·tom (bel'bät'əm) *adj.* designating trousers flaring at the ankles: also **bell'-bot'tomed**

☆**bell·boy** (-boi') *n. same as* BELLMAN (sense 2)

bell buoy a buoy with a warning bell rung by the motion of the waves

Belle (bel) [Fr.: see next entry] a feminine name

belle (bel) *n.* [Fr., fem. of *beau*: see BEAU] a pretty woman or girl; often, one who is the prettiest or most popular [the *belle* of the ball]

belles-let·tres (bel let'rə) *n.pl.* [Fr.] literature as a fine art; fiction, poetry, drama, etc. as distinguished from technical and scientific writings —**bel·let·rist** (bel let'rist) *n.* —**bel'le·tris'tic** (-lə tris'tik) *adj.*

Belle·vue (bel'vyōō') [Fr., lit., beautiful view] city in NW Wash.: suburb of Seattle: pop. 61,000

Bell·flow·er (bel'flou'ər) city in SW Calif.: suburb of Los Angeles: pop. 51,000

bell·flow·er (bel'flou'ər) *n.* a plant with showy, bell-shaped flowers of white, pink, or blue

☆**bell·hop** (bel'häp') *n. same as* BELLMAN (sense 2)

bel·li·cose (bel'ə kōs') *adj.* [< L. < *bellicus*, of war < *bellum*, war: see DUEL] of a quarrelsome nature; eager to fight; warlike —see SYN. at BELLIGERENT —**bel'li·cose'ly** *adv.* —**bel·li·cos·i·ty** (bel'ə käs'ə tē) *n.*

bel·lig·er·ence (bə lij'ər əns) *n.* belligerent or quarrelsome attitude or quality; readiness to fight

bel·lig·er·en·cy (bə lij'ər ən sē) *n.* **1.** the state of being at war or of being recognized as a belligerent **2.** *same as* BELLIGERENCE

bel·lig·er·ent (bə lij'ər ənt) *adj.* [< L. prp. of *belligerare* < *bellum*, war (see DUEL) + *gerere*, to carry on] **1.** recognized under international law as being at war **2.** of war; of fighting **3.** warlike **4.** showing readiness to fight or quarrel [a *belliger-*

ent gesture] —*n.* a belligerent person or nation —**bel·lig'er·ent·ly** *adv.*

SYN.—**belligerent** implies a taking part in war or fighting or in warlike actions [*belligerent* nations]; **bellicose** implies a warlike nature, suggesting a readiness to fight [a *bellicose* mood]; **pugnacious** and **quarrelsome** both suggest eagerness to start a fight, but **quarrelsome** more often suggests willingness to fight for no good reason; **contentious** suggests a readiness to keep on arguing or quarreling in an annoying way — **ANT. friendly, peaceful**

Bel·li·ni (bel lē′nē), **Gio·van·ni** (jô vän′nē) 1430?-1516; Venetian painter

bell jar a bell-shaped container or cover made of glass, used to keep air, moisture, etc. in or out: also **bell glass**

bell·man (bel′mən) *n., pl.* **-men** **1.** *same as* TOWN CRIER ☆**2.** a man employed by a hotel, club, etc. to carry luggage and do errands

bel·low (bel′ō) *vi.* [OE. *bylgan*: for IE. base see BELL¹] **1.** to roar with a loud, vibrating sound, as a bull **2.** to cry out loudly, as in anger or pain —*vt.* to utter loudly or powerfully —*n.* a bellowing sound; roar

Bel·low (bel′ō), **Saul** 1915– ; U.S. novelist

bel·lows (bel′ōz, -əz) *n. sing. & pl.* [ME. *belwes*, orig. pl. of *beli*: see BELLY] **1.** a device that produces a stream of air through a narrow tube when its sides are pumped together: used for blowing fires, in pipe organs, etc. **2.** anything like a bellows, as the folding part of some cameras

bell·weth·er (bel′weth′ər) *n.* a male sheep, usually wearing a bell, that leads the flock

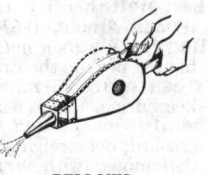

BELLOWS

bel·ly (bel′ē) *n., pl.* **-lies** [ME. *beli* < OE. *belg*, leather bag, bellows < IE. base *bhel-* (see BALL¹)] **1.** the lower front part of the human body between the chest and thighs; abdomen **2.** the underside of an animal's body **3.** the abdominal cavity **4.** the stomach **5.** the deep interior [the *belly* of a ship] **6.** any part or surface that curves outward or bulges [the *belly* of a sail] —*vt., vi.* **-lied, -ly·ing** to swell out; bulge

bel·ly·ache (-āk′) *n.* pain in the abdomen or bowels —☆*vi.* **-ached', -ach'ing** [Slang] to complain —**bel'ly·ach'er** *n.*

bel·ly·band (-band′) *n.* a band put around an animal's belly for keeping a saddle, etc. in place

bel·ly·but·ton (-but′'n) *n.* [Colloq.] the navel: also **belly button**

belly dance a dance originating in the Near East, done by twisting the abdomen, shaking the hips, etc. —**bel'ly-dance'** *vi.* **-danced', -danc'ing** —**belly dancer**

☆**bel·ly-flop** (-fläp′) *vi.* **-flopped', -flop'ping** [Colloq.] **1.** to dive awkwardly, with the belly striking flat against the water **2.** to throw oneself on a sled, with the belly downward, and coast, as down a hill Also **bel'ly-bump', bel'ly-whop', bel'ly-slam'**, etc.

bel·ly·ful (-fool′) *n.* **1.** enough or more than enough to eat **2.** [Slang] all that one can bear

☆**belly laugh** [Colloq.] a hearty laugh

Be·lo Ho·ri·zon·te (be′lô rē zôn′te) city in SE Brazil: pop. 1,233,000

be·long (bi lôŋ′) *vi.* [ME. < *be-*, intens. + OE. *langian*, belong] **1.** to have a proper or fitting place [the book *belongs* on her desk] **2.** to be part of; be related (*to*) [the orchard *belongs* to their farm] **3.** to be a member (with *to*) [does he *belong* to the glee club?] **4.** to be owned (with *to*) [that park does not now *belong* to the city] **5.** [Slang] to be the owner (with *to*) [who *belongs* to this hat?]

be·long·ing (-iŋ) *n.* **1.** a thing·that belongs to one **2.** [*pl.*] possessions; property **3.** close relationship; affinity [a sense of *belonging*]

be·lov·ed (bi luv′id, -luvd′) *adj.* dearly loved —*n.* a dearly loved person

be·low (bi lō′) *adv., adj.* [see BE- & LOW¹] **1.** in or to a lower place; beneath [look down *below*] **2.** in a lower place on the page or on a later page (of a book, etc.) [see the explanation *below*] **3.** in hell **4.** on earth **5.** on or to a lower floor or deck [he went to his bunk *below*] **6.** in or to a lesser rank, function, etc. —*prep.* **1.** lower than, as in position, rank, worth, etc. [a

price *below* $10] **2.** unworthy of [it is *below* her to do that]

Bel·shaz·zar (bel shaz′ər) *Bible* the last king of Babylon: Dan. 5

belt (belt) *n.* [OE., ult. < L. *balteus*, a belt] **1.** a band of leather, etc., worn about the waist to hold clothing up, support tools, etc., or as an ornament: see also SAFETY BELT **2.** any encircling thing like this **3.** an endless band for transferring motion from one wheel or pulley to another, or for carrying things **4.** an area or zone with some distinctive feature, product, crop, etc. [the corn *belt*] ☆**5.** an encircling road or route **6.** [Slang] a hard blow; cuff ☆**7.** [Slang] *a)* a drink or big gulp, esp. of liquor *b)* a thrill —*vt.* **1.** to surround or encircle as with a belt **2.** to fasten or attach as with a belt **3.** to hit hard, as with a belt ☆**4.** [Colloq.] to sing (*out*) strongly [to *belt* out a ballad] — **below the belt** unfair(ly); foul —**tighten one's belt** to live more thriftily —☆**under one's belt** [Colloq.] as part of one's experience [ten years at sea *under his belt*]

belt·ed (bel′tid) *adj.* **1.** wearing a belt, esp. as a mark of distinction **2.** marked by a band or stripe

belt·ing (-tiŋ) *n.* **1.** material for making belts **2.** belts collectively **3.** [Slang] a beating

be·lu·ga (bə lōō′gə) *n., pl.* **-ga, -gas**: see PLURAL, II, D, 2 [< Russ. < *byeli*, white] **1.** a large, white sturgeon of the Black and Caspian seas **2.** a large, white dolphin of northern seas; white whale

be·mire (bi mīr′) *vt.* **-mired', -mir'ing** **1.** to dirty as with mire **2.** to cause to bog down in mud

be·moan (bi mōn′) *vt., vi.* to moan about or lament (a loss, grief, etc.) [to *bemoan* one's fate]

be·muse (bi myōoz′) *vt.* **-mused', -mus'ing** [BE- + MUSE] **1.** to muddle, confuse, or stupefy **2.** to lose in thought; preoccupy [she sat *bemused* in the midst of the clamor] —**be·muse'ment** *n.*

Be·na·res (bə nä′rēz) *former name of* VARANASI

bench (bench) *n.* [OE. *benc* (see BANK²)] **1.** a long, hard seat for several persons, with or without a back **2.** the place where judges sit in a court **3.** [*sometimes* **B-**] *a)* the status or office of a judge *b)* judges as a group *c)* a law court ☆**4.** *a)* a seat on which the players on a sports team sit when not on the field *b)* substitute players as a group [a team with a strong *bench*] **5.** a stand for exhibiting a dog at a dog show **6.** a strong table on which work with tools is done; worktable —*vt.* **1.** to provide with benches **2.** to place on a bench, esp. an official one ☆**3.** *Sports* to keep (a player) out of a game —**on the bench 1.** serving as judge in a law court ☆**2.** *Sports* not taking part in the game, as a substitute player

bench mark 1. a surveyor's mark made on a permanent landmark whose altitude is known: it is used as a reference point in determining other altitudes **2.** a standard in judging quality, value, etc. Also **bench'mark'** *n.*

bench warrant an order issued by a judge or law court for the arrest of a person

bend¹ (bend) *vt.* **bent** or archaic **bend'ed, bend'ing** [OE. *bendan* (see BIND), to bind with a string; hence, to bend (a bow)] **1.** to force (an object) into a curved or crooked form, or (*back*) to its original form **2.** to turn from a straight line [to *bend* one's steps from a path] **3.** to make (someone) submit or give in, as to one's will **4.** to turn or direct (one's attention, etc. *to*) **5.** *Naut.* to fasten (sails or ropes) into position —*vi.* **1.** to turn or be turned as from a straight line **2.** to yield by curving or crooking, as from pressure [the saplings *bent* in the wind] **3.** to crook or curve the body; stoop (*over* or *down*) [can you *bend* down and touch your toes?] **4.** to give in; yield [he *bent* to her wishes] —*n.* **1.** a bending or being bent **2.** a bending or curving part, as of a river —**bend'a·ble** *adj.*

bend² (bend) *n.* [ME. < prec.] any of various knots used in tying one rope to another or to something else —☆**the bends** [Colloq.] *same as* DECOMPRESSION SICKNESS

bend³ (bend) *n.* [< OFr. < Goth. *bindan*, to BIND] *Heraldry* a diagonal band or stripe on a coat of arms

bend·er (ben′dər) *n.* **1.** a person or thing that bends ☆**2.** [Slang] a drinking spree

bend sinister *Heraldry* a band or stripe on a coat of arms, from the upper right to the lower left corner: a sign of bastardy in the family line

---

fat, āpe, cär, ten, ēven, is, bīte; gō, hôrn, tōol, look; oil, out; up, fur; get; joy; yet; chin; she; thin, then; zh, leisure; ŋ, ring; ə for a in ago, e in agent, i in sanity, o in comply, u in focus; ' as in able (ā′b'l); Fr. bal; ë, Fr. coeur; ö, Fr. feu; Fr. mon; δ, Fr. coq; ü, Fr. duc; r, Fr. cri; H, G. ich; kh, G. doch; ‡foreign; ☆ Americanism; < derived from. See inside front cover.

be·neath (bi nēth′) *adv., adj.* [< OE. < *be-* + *neothan,* down: see NETHER] **1.** in a lower place **2.** just below something; underneath [the top shelf and the one *beneath*] —*prep.* **1.** lower than; below **2.** directly under; underneath [*beneath* an umbrella] **3.** inferior to in rank, quality, worth, etc. **4.** unworthy of [it is *beneath* him to cheat]

ben·e·dic·i·te (ben′ə dis′ə tē′; *for n. 2 usually* bä′nä dē′chē tä′) *interj.* [L.] bless you! —*n.* **1.** the invocation of a blessing **2.** [B-] a canticle praising God

Ben·e·dict (ben′ə dikt′) [< L. *Benedictus,* blessed] **1.** a masculine name **2.** Saint, 480?–543? A.D.; It. monk: founder of the Benedictine order

ben·e·dict (ben′ə dikt′) *n.* [< *Benedick,* a bachelor in Shakespeare's *Much Ado About Nothing*] a newly married man, esp. one who seemed as though he would remain a bachelor

Ben·e·dic·tine (ben′ə dik′tin; *also, and for n. 2 usually,* -tēn) *adj.* **1.** of Saint Benedict **2.** designating or of the monastic order based on his teachings —*n.* **1.** a Benedictine monk or nun **2.** [b-] a liqueur, orig. made by Benedictine monks

ben·e·dic·tion (ben′ə dik′shən) *n.* [< L. < *bene,* well + *dicere,* to speak] **1.** a blessing **2.** a prayer asking for God's blessing, esp. at the end of a religious service **3.** blessedness — **ben′e·dic′to·ry** *adj.*

ben·e·fac·tion (ben′ə fak′shən, ben′ə fak′shən) *n.* [< LL. < L. *benefacere* < *bene,* well + *facere,* to do] **1.** the act of doing good or helping those in need **2.** money or help freely given

ben·e·fac·tor (ben′ə fak′tər) *n.* a person who has given help, esp. financial help; patron —**ben′e·fac′tress** (-tris) *n.fem.*

ben·e·fice (ben′ə fis) *n.* [OFr. < L. *beneficium,* a kindness: see BENEFACTION] **1.** a church office that provides a living for a vicar, rector, etc. **2.** its income —*vt.* **-ficed, -fic·ing** to provide with a benefice

be·nef·i·cence (bə nef′ə s′ns) *n.* [< L.: see BENEFACTION] **1.** the fact or quality of being kind or doing good **2.** a charitable act or generous gift

be·nef·i·cent (bə nef′ə s′nt) *adj.* **1.** showing beneficence; doing good **2.** resulting in benefit [*beneficent* criticism] Also **be·nef·ic** (bə nef′ik) —**be·nef′i·cent·ly** *adv.*

ben·e·fi·cial (ben′ə fish′əl) *adj.* producing benefits; advantageous [*beneficial* advice] —**ben′e·fi′cial·ly** *adv.*

ben·e·fi·ci·ar·y (ben′ə fish′ē er′ē, -fish′ər ē) *adj.* of or holding a benefice —*n., pl.* **-ar′ies 1.** a holder of a benefice **2.** anyone receiving benefit **3.** a person named in an insurance policy, will, etc. to receive the income or inheritance

ben·e·fit (ben′ə fit) *n.* [< OFr. < L.: see BENEFACTION] **1.** [Archaic] a charitable act **2.** anything helping to improve conditions; advantage [a paved road for the *benefit* of all the residents] **3.** [often *pl.*] payments made by an insurance company, public agency, etc. as during sickness, retirement, or unemployment **4.** a public performance, dance, etc. to raise money for a certain person, cause, etc. —*vt.* **-fit·ed, -fit·ing** to do good to or for; aid [a medical program to *benefit* everyone] —*vi.* to receive advantage; profit [she'll *benefit* from regular exercise]

benefit of clergy 1. the privilege that the medieval clergy had of being free from trial or punishment in any court except a church court **2.** the rites or approval of the church [marriage without *benefit of clergy*]

Be·ne·lux (ben′ə luks′) [< BE(LGIUM), NE(THERLANDS), LUX(EMBOURG)] economic union of Belgium, Netherlands, & Luxembourg formed in 1958: in full, **Benelux Economic Union**

Be·neš (ben′esh), **E·du·ard** (e′dōō ärt) 1884–1948; president of Czechoslovakia (1935–38; in exile 1939–45; 1946–48)

Be·nét (bə nā′), **Stephen Vincent** 1898–1943; U.S. writer

be·nev·o·lence (bə nev′ə ləns) *n.* [ME. & OFr. < L. < *bene,* well + *volens,* prp. of *velle,* to wish] **1.** a wanting to do good; kindliness **2.** a kindly, charitable act or gift; beneficence

be·nev·o·lent (-lənt) *adj.* **1.** doing or wanting to do good; kindly; charitable **2.** characterized by benevolence [a *benevolent* act] —see SYN. at KIND —**be·nev′o·lent·ly** *adv.*

Ben·gal (ben gôl′, beŋ-) **1.** region in the NE Indian peninsula, divided (1947) into **East Bengal** (now *Bangladesh*) and **West Bengal** (a state of India) **2. Bay of,** part of the Indian Ocean, east of India and west of Burma and the Malay Peninsula — **Ben′ga·lese′** (-gə lēz′) *adj., n., pl.* **-lese**

Ben·gal·i (ben gôl′ē, beŋ-) *n.* **1.** a native of Bengal **2.** the Indo-European, Indic language of Bengal —*adj.* of Bengal, its people, or their language

ben·ga·line (beŋ′gə lēn′, beŋ′gə lēn′) *n.* [Fr. < *Bengal*] a heavy, corded cloth of silk, rayon, etc. and either wool or cotton

Ben·gha·zi (ben gä′zē, beŋ-) seaport in Libya & one of its two capitals: pop. 140,000

be·night·ed (bi nīt′id) *adj.* **1.** surrounded by darkness or night **2.** intellectually or morally backward; ignorant —**be·night′ed·ness** *n.*

be·nign (bi nīn′) *adj.* [OFr. < L. < *bene,* well + *genus,* birth: see GENUS] **1.** good-natured; kindly [a *benign* smile] **2.** favorable; helpful [a *benign* climate] **3.** *med.* doing little or no harm; not malignant [a *benign* tumor] —see SYN. at KIND — **be·nign′ly** *adv.*

be·nig·nant (bi nig′nənt) *adj.* [< BENIGN, patterned after MALIGNANT] **1.** kindly or gracious, sometimes in a patronizing way **2.** favorable; helpful —**be·nig′nan·cy** *n., pl.* **-cies**

be·nig·ni·ty (bi nig′nə tē) *n., pl.* **-ties 1.** graciousness; kindliness **2.** a kind act; favor

Be·nin (be nēn′) country in WC Africa, on the Atlantic: 44,696 sq. mi.; pop. 3,112,000; cap. Porto Novo

ben·i·son (ben′ə z′n, -s′n) *n.* [< OFr. < L.: see BENEDICTION] a blessing; benediction

Ben·ja·min (ben′jə mən) [Heb. *binyāmīn,* lit., son of the right hand; hence, favorite son] **1.** a masculine name: dim. *Ben, Benjie, Benny* **2.** *Bible* a) Jacob's youngest son b) the tribe of Israel descended from him

Ben·nett (ben′it) [< BENEDICT] a masculine name **2.** (Enoch) **Arnold,** 1867–1931; Eng. novelist

Ben Ne·vis (ben nē′vis; nev′is) mountain in WC Scotland: highest peak in the British Isles: 4,406 ft.

☆**ben·ny** (ben′ē) *n., pl.* **-nies** [slang] an amphetamine pill, esp. benzedrine, used as a stimulant

bent[1] (bent) *pt. and pp. of* BEND —*adj.* **1.** made curved or crooked; not straight [use a *bent* pin for a fishhook] **2.** strongly determined (with *on*) [she is *bent* on going] **3.** set in a course; bound [westward *bent*] —*n.* **1.** an inclining; tendency **2.** a natural liking or skill; propensity [a *bent* for art] —**to** (or **at**) **the top of one's bent** to (or at) the limit of one's ability

bent[2] (bent) *n.* [OE. *beonot*] **1.** any of various wiry, low-growing grasses much used for lawns and golf greens: also called **bent′grass′ 2.** the stiff flower stalk of certain grasses

Ben·tham (ben′thəm), **Jeremy** 1748–1832; Eng. philosopher & economist

Ben·tham·ism (-iz'm) *n.* the philosophy of Jeremy Bentham, which holds that the greatest happiness of most people should be the main goal of society —**Ben′tham·ite′** (-īt′) *n.*

ben·thos (ben′thäs) *n.* [< Gr. *benthos,* ocean depths] all the plants and animals living at the bottom of a body of water, esp. the ocean

Ben·ton (ben′tən), **Thomas Hart** 1889–1975; U.S. painter

☆**ben·ton·ite** (ben′tə nīt′) *n.* [after Fort *Benton,* Montana, where found] a porous clay, formed as volcanic ash decomposes

bent·wood (bent′wood′) *adj.* designating furniture made of wood permanently bent into various forms after it has been softened by steaming

be·numb (bi num′) *vt.* **1.** to make numb **2.** to deaden the mind, will, or feelings of [benumbed by grief]

☆**Ben·ze·drine** (ben′zə drēn′) *a trademark for* AMPHETAMINE —*n.* [b-] this drug

ben·zene (ben′zēn, ben zēn′) *n.* [BENZ(OIC) + -ENE] a clear, flammable, poisonous liquid, C_6H_6, got from coal tar and used as a solvent for fats and in making varnishes, dyes, etc.

benzene ring a structural unit thought to exist in the molecules of benzene and derivatives of benzene, consisting of a ring of six carbon atoms with alternate single and double bonds between them

BENTWOOD CHAIR

ben·zine (ben′zēn, ben zēn′) *n.* [BENZ(OIC) + -INE[4]] a colorless, flammable liquid obtained in distilling petroleum and used as a motor fuel, a solvent in dry cleaning, etc.

ben·zo·ate (ben′zō āt′) *n.* a salt or ester of benzoic acid

ben·zo·caine (ben′zə kān′) *n.* [BENZO(IN) + (CO)CAINE] a white, odorless powder, $C_9H_{11}NO_2$, used in ointments as an anesthetic and to protect against sunburn

ben·zo·ic (ben zō′ik) *adj.* [BENZO(IN) + -IC] of or derived from benzoin

benzoic acid a white, crystalline organic acid, C_6H_5COOH, used as an antiseptic and to preserve foods

ben·zo·in (ben′zō in, -zoin) *n.* [< Fr. < It. *benzoino* < Ar. *lubān jāwi,* incense of Java] a sweet-smelling resin from certain tropical Asiatic trees, used in medicine, in making perfumes, and as incense

ben·zol (ben′zōl, -zôl) *n.* [BENZ(OIN) + -OL[1]] *same as* BENZENE: sometimes, a mixture distilling below 100°C that is 70 percent benzene

Be·o·wulf (bā′ə woolf′) the hero of an Old English folk epic written about 700 A.D.

be·queath (bi kwēth′, -kwēth′) *vt.* [OE. *becwethan*, to give by will < *be-* + *cwethan*, to say: see QUOTH] **1.** to leave (property) to another by last will and testament **2.** to hand down; pass on [legends *bequeathed* to us by our ancestors] —**be·queath′a·ble** *adj.* —**be·queath′al** (-əl) *n.*

be·quest (-kwest′) *n.* [< *be-* + OE. *cwis* < *cwethan*: see prec.] **1.** a bequeathing **2.** anything bequeathed

be·rate (bi rāt′) *vt.* **-rat′ed, -rat′ing** [BE- + RATE[2]] to scold harshly—see SYN. at SCOLD

Ber·ber (bur′bər) *n.* **1.** any of a Moslem people living in N Africa **2.** their language —*adj.* of the Berbers, their culture, or their language

ber·ceuse (ber sooz′) *n.* [Fr. < *bercer*, to rock] a lullaby, or a piece of music with the same lulling effect

be·reave (bi rēv′) *vt.* **-reaved′** or **-reft′** (-reft′), **-reav′ing** [OE. *bereafian* < *be-* + *reafian*, to ROB] **1.** to deprive or rob: now usually in the pp. (bereft) [*bereft* of hope] **2.** to leave in a sad or lonely state, as by death —**the bereaved** the survivors of a person who has recently died —**be·reave′ment** *n.*

be·ret (bə rā′) *n.* [< Fr. < Pr. < LL.: see BIRETTA] a soft, flat, round cap of felt, wool, etc.

berg (burg) *n. same as* ICEBERG

Berg (berkh; *E.* berg), **Al·ban** (äl′bän) 1885–1935; Austrian composer

ber·ga·mot (bur′gə mät′) *n.* [< Fr. < It. < Turk. *beg-armûdi*, prince's pear] **1.** *a)* a pear-shaped citrus fruit grown in S Europe for its oil, used in making perfume *b)* this oil ☆**2.** any of several sweet-smelling N. American herbs of the mint family

Ber·gen (ber′gən; *E.* bur′-) seaport in SW Norway: pop. 117,000

BERET

Ber·ge·rac (ber′zhə rak′), **Cy·ra·no de** (sir′ə nō′ də) 1619–55; Fr. writer and soldier: hero of a play (1897) by Edmond Rostand

Berg·son (berg sōn′; *E.* berg′sən), **Hen·ri** (än rē′) 1859–1941; Fr. philosopher —**Berg·so·ni·an** (berg sō′nē ən) *adj., n.* —**Berg′son·ism** *n.*

ber·i·ber·i (ber′ē ber′ē) *n.* [Sinh. *beri*, weakness] a disease caused by lack of thiamine (vitamin B₁) in the diet: it results in nerve disorders, swelling of the body, etc.

Ber·ing Sea (ber′iŋ, bir′-) part of the N Pacific Ocean, between NE Siberia & Alaska

Bering Standard Time *see* STANDARD TIME

Bering Strait strait between Siberia & Alaska: average width, c. 50 mi.

Berke·ley (bur′klē) [after G. BERKELEY] city in Calif., near Oakland: pop. 117,000

Berke·ley (bär′klē, bur′-), **George** 1685–1753; Ir. philosopher & bishop —**Berke′le·ian** (-klē ən, bər klē′ən) *adj.*

☆**berke·li·um** (bur′klē əm) *n.* [< U. of California at BERKELEY, where first isolated] a radioactive chemical element: symbol, Bk; at. wt., 248(?); at. no., 97

Berk·shire Hills (burk′shir, -shər) [after *Berkshire*, county in England] region of wooded hills and mountains in W Mass.: also **Berk′shires**

Ber·lin (bər lin′; *G.* ber lēn′) city in E Germany: capital of Germany (1871–1945): now divided into EAST BERLIN and WEST BERLIN

ber·lin (bər lin′, bur′lin) *n.* [after prec.] **1.** a four-wheeled, closed carriage with a footman's platform behind **2.** [*sometimes* B-] a fine, soft wool yarn: also called **Berlin wool**

Ber·li·oz (ber′lē ōz′; *Fr.* ber lyôz′), (**Louis**) **Hector** 1803–69; Fr. composer

berm, berme (burm) *n.* [Fr. < MDu. *baerm:* for IE. base see BRAMBLE] ☆a ledge or shoulder, as along the edge of a paved road

Ber·mu·da (bər myoo′də) self-governing Brit. colony on a group of islands in the W Atlantic, c. 580 mi. southeast of N.C.: 20 sq. mi.; pop. 52,000 —**Ber·mu′dan, Ber·mu′di·an** *adj., n.*

☆**Bermuda grass** a creeping grass grown in warm climates for lawns or pasture

☆**Bermuda onion** a large onion with a mild flavor, grown in Texas, California, etc.

☆**Bermuda shorts** short trousers extending to just above the knee

Bern, Berne (burn; *Fr.* bern) capital of Switzerland, in the WC part: pop. 167,000

Ber·nard (bər närd′, bur′nərd; *for 2* ber när′) [Fr. < OHG. *bero*, BEAR[2] + *hart*, bold, HARD] **1.** a masculine name: dim. **Bernie 2. Claude** (klōd), 1813–78; Fr. physiologist

Bernard of Clair·vaux (kler vō′), Saint 1090?–1153; Fr. Cistercian monk & religious leader —**Ber·nard·ine** (bur′nər din, -dēn′) *adj.*

Bern·hardt (burn′härt; *Fr.* ber när′), **Sarah** (born *Rosine Bernard*) 1844–1923; Fr. actress

Ber·nice (bər nēs′, bur′nis) [< L. < Gr. *Berenikē*, lit., victory-bringing] a feminine name: var. *Berenice*

Ber·ni·ni (ber nē′nē), **Gio·van·ni Lo·ren·zo** (jō vän′nē lô ren′tsō) 1598–1680; It. sculptor & architect

Ber·noul·li, Ber·nouil·li (ber noo′ yē′; *E.* ber noo′lē) family of Swiss mathematicians & scientists; esp., *a)* **Da·niel** (dä′nyel′), 1700–82: son of *Jean b)* **Jacques** (zhäk), 1654–1705: brother of *Jean c)* **Jean** (zhän), 1667–1748

ber·ret·ta (bə ret′ə) *n. same as* BIRETTA

ber·ry (ber′ē) *n., pl.* **-ries** [OE. *berie*] **1.** any small, juicy, fleshy fruit, as a raspberry, blueberry, etc. **2.** the dry seed or kernel of various plants, as a coffee bean **3.** an egg of a lobster, crayfish, etc. **4.** *Bot.* a fleshy fruit with a soft wall and thin skin, as the tomato, grape, banana, etc. —*vi.* **-ried, -ry·ing 1.** to bear berries **2.** to look for and pick berries —**ber′ry·like′** *adj.*

ber·serk (bər surk′, -zurk′; bur′sərk) *n. same as* BERSERKER —*adj., adv.* in or into a state of violent or destructive rage or frenzy [when he saw the destruction done to his village, he went *berserk*]

ber·serk·er (bər sur′kər, -zur′-; bur′sər kər) *n.* [ON. *berserkr*, warrior in bearskin < *ber*, a bear + *serkr*, coat] *Norse Legend* a warrior who worked himself into a frenzy before battle

berth (burth) *n.* [< base of BEAR[1]] **1.** *a)* enough space for a ship to keep clear of another ship, the shore, etc. *b)* space for anchoring *c)* a place of anchorage **2.** a position, office, job, etc. **3.** *a)* a built-in bed or bunk on a ship, train, etc. *b)* any sleeping place —*vt.* **1.** to put into a berth **2.** to furnish with a berth —*vi.* to come into or occupy a berth —**give a wide berth to** to stay well away from

Ber·tha (bur′thə) [G. < OHG. < *beraht*, shining] a feminine name

Ber·til·lon system (bur′tə län′; *Fr.* ber tē yōn′) [after A. *Bertillon* (1853–1914), Fr. anthropologist] a system of identifying people through records of measurements, coloring, fingerprints, etc.

Ber·tram (bur′trəm) [G. < OHG. < *beraht*, shining + *hraban*, raven] a masculine name

Ber·trand (bur′trənd) var. of BERTRAM

Ber·wyn (bur′win) [after *Berwyn* Mts., Wales] city in NE Ill., near Chicago: pop. 53,000

ber·yl (ber′əl) *n.* [< OFr. < L. < Gr. *bēryllos*] beryllium aluminum silicate, a very hard, crystalline mineral, usually blue, green, pink, or yellow in color: emerald and aquamarine are two varieties of beryl used as gems

be·ryl·li·um (bə ril′ē əm) *n.* [ModL. < prec.] a hard, rare, metallic chemical element, used in forming hard alloys and to control the speed of reactions in an atomic reactor: symbol, Be; at. wt., 9.0122; at. no., 4

Ber·ze·li·us (ber sā′lē oos; *E.* bər zē′lē əs), Baron **Jons Jakob** (yöns yä′kôp) 1779–1848; Swed. chemist

be·seech (bi sēch′) *vt.* **-sought′** or **-seeched′, -seech′ing** [< OE. *besecan* < *be-* & SEEK] **1.** to ask (someone) earnestly; implore [we *besought* him to stay] **2.** to ask for earnestly; beg for [I *beseech* your help]—see SYN. at BEG —**be·seech′ing·ly** *adv.*

BERING SEA

be·seem (bi sēm′) *vi.* to be suitable or appropriate (to) [in "it ill *beseems* him to ask," *him* is an indirect object]

be·set (bi set′) *vt.* -**set′**, -**set′ting** [< OE. *besettan:* see BE- & SET] 1. to set thickly with; stud [a crown *beset* with jewels] 2. to attack from all sides; harass or besiege [the worries that *beset* him] 3. to surround or hem in [a village *beset* with hills] —**be·set′ment** *n.*

be·set·ting (-iŋ) *adj.* constantly harassing or attacking [a *besetting* temptation]

be·shrew (bi shrōō′) *vt.* [< ME.: see BE- & SHREW] [Archaic] to curse: used mainly in mild oaths

be·side (bi sīd′) *prep.* [ME.: see BY & SIDE] 1. by or at the side of; alongside; near [sit *beside* me] 2. in comparison with [*beside* yours, my share seems small] 3. in addition to; besides [*beside* him, who is going?] 4. aside from; not pertinent to [*beside* the point] —*adv.* [Archaic] in addition —**beside oneself** wild with fear, rage, etc.

be·sides (-sīdz′) *adv.* [ME. < prec. + adv. gen. -(e)s] 1. in addition; as well [food and drink and entertainment *besides*] 2. except for that mentioned; else [he has a part-time selling job, but earns nothing *besides*] 3. moreover; furthermore [the book is well written, and *besides* I like mysteries] —*prep.* 1. in addition to; as well as [who's going *besides* you?] 2. other than; except [they lost no games *besides* the opener]

be·siege (bi sēj′) *vt.* -**sieged′**, -**sieg′ing** [ME. < *be-* + *segen*, to lay siege to < *sege*, SIEGE] 1. to hem in with armed forces and keep under attack so as to force a surrender 2. to close in on; crowd around [reporters *besieged* the returned astronauts] 3. to overwhelm or beset [the radio station was *besieged* with queries] —**be·sieg′er** *n.*

be·smear (bi smir′) *vt.* to smear over; soil

be·smirch (bi smurch′) *vt.* [BE- + SMIRCH] 1. to make dirty; soil 2. to bring dishonor to; sully [an act that *besmirched* his name]

be·som (bē′zəm) *n.* [< OE. *besma*, broom, rod] 1. a broom, esp. one made of twigs tied to a handle 2. *same as* BROOM (*n.* 1)

be·sot (bi sät′) *vt.* -**sot′ted**, -**sot′ting** 1. to make a sot of; stupefy, as with alcoholic drink 2. to make silly or foolish —**be·sot′ted** *adj.*

be·sought (bi sôt′) *alt. pt. and pp. of* BE-SEECH

be·span·gle (bi spaŋ′g'l) *vt.* -**gled**, -**gling** to cover with or as with spangles

be·spat·ter (bi spat′ər) *vt.* to spatter, as with mud or slander; soil or sully by spattering

be·speak (bi spēk′) *vt.* -**spoke′** (-spōk′) or archaic -**spake′** (-spāk′), -**spo′ken** or -**spoke′**, -**speak′ing** 1. to speak for or engage in advance; reserve [that room is *bespoken*] 2. to be an indication of; show [a mansion that *bespeaks* wealth] 3. to foreshadow; point to [her talent *bespeaks* success] 4. [Archaic or Poet.] to speak to; address

be·spec·ta·cled (bi spek′tə k'ld) *adj.* wearing eyeglasses

be·spread (bi spred′) *vt.* -**spread′**, -**spread′ing** to spread over or cover

be·sprin·kle (bi spriŋ′k'l) *vt.* -**kled**, -**kling** to sprinkle over (*with* something)

Bess (bes) a feminine name: see ELIZABETH

Bes·sa·ra·bi·a (bes′ə ra′bē ə) region in SW European Russia, mostly in the Moldavian S.S.R. —**Bes′sa·ra′bi·an** *adj., n.*

Bes·se·mer process (bes′ə mər) [after Sir Henry *Bessemer* (1813-98), Eng. engineer] a method of making steel by blasting air through molten pig iron in a large container (**Bessemer converter**) to burn away the carbon and other impurities

best (best) *adj. superl. of* GOOD [OE. *betst* < IE. base *bhad-*, good] 1. of the most excellent sort; above all others in worth or ability [the *best* play of the year] 2. most suitable, most desirable, etc. [the *best* time to plant corn] 3. being almost the whole; largest [the *best* part of an hour] —*adv. superl. of* WELL² 1. in the most excellent or most suitable manner [the first group sang *best*] 2. in the highest degree; most [I like the red one *best*] —*n.* 1. the person or people, thing, condition, action, etc. of the greatest excellence, worth, suitability, etc. [among the *best* in his profession] 2. the most that a person can do; utmost [he did his *best* to win] 3. one's finest clothes [dressed in her Sunday *best*] —*vt.* to win out over; defeat or outdo [they *bested* us at chess] —**all for the best** turning out to be fortunate after all —**as best one can** as well as one can —**at best** 1. under

BESOM

the most favorable conditions 2. at most [it will cost $10 *at best*] —**at one's best** in one's best mood, form, health, etc. —**get** (or **have**) **the best of** 1. to outdo or defeat 2. to outwit —**had best** ought to —**make the best of** to do as well as one can with —**with the best** as ably as anybody

be·stead (bi sted′) *adj.* [< ME. < *bi-*, be + *stad*, placed < ON. *staddr*, prp. of *stethja*, to place] [Archaic] situated; placed —*vt.* -**stead′ed**, -**stead′**, -**stead′ing** [Archaic] to help; avail

bes·tial (bes′chəl, -tyəl; bēs′-) *adj.* [OFr. < LL. *bestialis*] 1. of beasts 2. like a beast; brutish, savage, vile, etc. —**bes′tial·ly** *adv.*

bes·ti·al·i·ty (bes′chē al′ə tē, bēs′tē-) *n., pl.* -**ties** a bestial quality, character, or act; brutish behavior or practice

bes·tial·ize (bes′chə līz′, -tyə-; bēs′-) *vt.* -**ized**, -**iz′ing** to make bestial; brutalize

bes·ti·ar·y (bes′chē er′ē, bēs′tē-) *n., pl.* -**ar′ies** [< ML. < L. < *bestia*, beast] a type of medieval book on natural history, that told fables with morals about real and mythical animals

be·stir (bi stur′) *vt.* -**stirred′**, -**stir′ring** to stir to action; exert or busy (oneself) [she *bestirred* herself and made lunch]

☆**best man** the principal attendant of the bridegroom at a wedding

be·stow (bi stō′) *vt.* [see BE- & STOW] 1. to give or present as a gift (often with *on* or *upon*) [to *bestow* much time on a project] 2. to apply; devote [he *bestowed* millions of dollars on charities] 3. [Archaic] to put or place, as in storage 4. [Obs.] to give in marriage —see SYN. at GIVE —**be·stow′al** *n.*

be·strew (bi strōō′) *vt.* -**strewed′**, -**strewed′** or -**strewn′**, -**strew′ing** 1. to cover over (a surface); strew 2. to scatter or lie scattered over or about [leaves *bestrewed* the streets]

be·stride (bi strīd′) *vt.* -**strode′** (-strōd′), -**strid′den** (-strid′ 'n), -**strid′ing** 1. to sit on, mount, or stand over with a leg on each side; straddle [to *bestride* a horse or a ditch] 2. [Archaic] to stride over

☆**best seller** a book, phonograph record, etc. currently outselling most others

bet (bet) *n.* [prob. < ABET] 1. an agreement between two persons that the one proved wrong about the outcome of something will do or pay what is stipulated; wager 2. *a*) the thing or sum thus staked ☆*b*) the thing, contestant, etc. that something is staked on [this team is a poor *bet*] ☆3. a person, thing, or action likely to bring about a desired result [he's the best *bet* for the job] —*vt.* **bet** or **bet′ted**, **bet′ting** 1. to declare in or as in a bet [I *bet* he'll be late] 2. to stake (money, etc.) in a bet 3. to wager with (someone) —*vi.* to make a bet —☆**you bet** (**you**)! [Colloq.]

be·ta (bāt′ə; *chiefly Brit.* bēt′ə) *n.* [L. < Gr. *bēta* < Heb. *bēth*, lit., house; of Phoen. origin] 1. the second letter of the Greek alphabet (B, β) 2. the second of a group or series 3. the second brightest star in a constellation

be·take (bi tāk′) *vt.* -**took′**, -**tak′en**, -**tak′ing** 1. to take (oneself); go [he *betook* himself to his castle] 2. to direct or devote (oneself) [*betake* yourself to your studies]

beta particle an electron or positron ejected at high velocity from the nucleus of an atom undergoing radioactive disintegration

beta ray 1. *same as* BETA PARTICLE 2. a stream of beta particles

☆**be·ta·tron** (bāt′ə trän′) *n.* [BETA (RAY) + (ELEC)TRON] an electron accelerator that uses a rapidly changing magnetic field to accelerate the particles to high velocities

be·tel (bēt′'l) *n.* [Port. < Malay *vettilai*] a tropical Asian climbing plant of the pepper family, whose leaf is chewed by some Asian peoples

Be·tel·geuse, Be·tel·geux (bet′'l jōōz′, bēt′-) [< Fr. < Ar. *bayt al jauza*, lit., house of the twins] a very large, red, first-magnitude star, second brightest in the constellation Orion

betel nut the fruit of the betel palm, chewed together with lime and leaves of the betel (plant) by some Asian peoples

betel palm a palm grown in SE Asia

bête noire (bāt′ nwär′) *pl.* **bêtes noires** (bāt′ nwärz′) [Fr., lit., black beast] a person or thing feared, disliked, and avoided [science had become his *bête noire*]

beth (bāth, beth; *Heb.* bāt, bās) *n.* [Heb. *bēth:* see BETA] the second letter of the Hebrew alphabet

Beth·a·ny (beth′ə nē) ancient town in Palestine, near Jerusalem

Beth·el (beth′əl) ancient town in Palestine, just north of Jerusalem

beth·el (beth′əl) *n.* [LL. < Heb. *bēth 'ēl*, house of God] 1. a holy place ☆2. a church or other place of worship for seamen

be·think (bi thiŋk′) *vt.* **-thought′, -think′ing** to bring (oneself) to think of, consider, or recollect; remind (oneself) [he suddenly *bethought* himself of his obligations]

Beth·le·hem (beth′lə hem′, -lē əm) **1.** ancient town in Judea: birthplace of Jesus **2.** city in E Pa.: pop. 73,000

be·tide (bi tīd′) *vi., vt.* **-tid′ed, -tid′ing** [< ME. < *be-* + OE. *tidan,* to happen < *tid,* time: for IE. base see TIDE] to happen (to); befall: now mainly used in the phrase **woe betide (some-one),** may bad luck happen to (someone)

be·times (bi tīmz′) *adv.* [ME. < *bi-,* by + *time,* TIME] **1.** early or early enough [he awoke *betimes*] **2.** [Archaic] promptly or quickly

Bet·je·man (bech′ə mən), **John** 1906– ; Eng. poet

be·to·ken (bi tō′k′n) *vt.* [< ME. < *be-* + *toknen* < OE. *tacnian,* to mark < *tacen,* TOKEN] **1.** to be a token or sign of; show **2.** to show beforehand [clouds that *betoken* rain]

be·tray (bi trā′) *vt.* [< ME. < *be-* + *traien,* betray < OFr. < L. *tradere,* to hand over] **1.** to help the enemy of (one's country, cause, etc.); be a traitor to **2.** to break faith with; fail to uphold [to *betray* a trust] **3.** to lead astray; specif., to seduce and then desert **4.** to reveal unknowingly [his look *betrayed* his fear] **5.** to reveal or show signs of [the house *betrays* its age] **6.** to disclose (a secret, etc.) —see SYN. at DECEIVE and REVEAL —**be·tray′al** *n.* —**be·tray′er** *n.*

be·troth (bi trōth′, -trôth′) *vt.* [< ME. < *be-* + *treuthe* < OE. *treowth,* truth] **1.** to promise in marriage [to *betroth* a daughter] **2.** [Archaic] to promise to marry

be·troth·al (-əl) *n.* a betrothing or being betrothed; engagement to be married

be·trothed (bi trōthd′, -trôtht′) *adj.* engaged to be married —*n.* the person to whom one is betrothed

bet·ta (bet′ə) *n.* [ModL.] a brightly colored, tropical, freshwater fish of SE Asia: some species are kept in aquariums

bet·ted (bet′id) *alt. pt. and pp. of* BET

bet·ter (bet′ər) *adj. compar. of* GOOD [< OE. *betera:* see BEST] **1.** more excellent; above another or others in worth or ability [Bill is the *better* swimmer] **2.** more suitable, more desirable, etc. [a *better* time for the meeting] **3.** being more than half; larger [the *better* part of an hour] **4.** improved in health or disposition [the patient is getting *better*] —*adv. compar. of* WELL² **1.** in a more excellent or more suitable manner [she sings *better* now] **2.** in a higher degree [I like that one *better*] **3.** more [it took *better* than an hour] —*n.* **1.** a person higher in authority, position, etc. **2.** the thing, condition, etc. that is more excellent, etc. [her speech was the *better* of the two] —*vt.* **1.** to outdo; surpass [to *better* a record] **2.** to make better; improve [to *better* one's grades] —*vi.* to become better —see SYN. at IMPROVE —**better off 1.** in a better condition **2.** having more income, wealth, etc. —**for the better** to a better condition —**get (or have) the better of 1.** to outdo **2.** to outwit

better half [Slang] one's wife or, less often, one's husband

bet·ter·ment (-mənt) *n.* **1.** a making or being made better; improvement ☆**2.** *Law* an improvement, other than repairs, that increases the value of property

bet·tor, bet·ter (bet′ər) *n.* a person who bets

be·tween (bi twēn′) *prep.* [< OE. < *be,* by + *tweon(um),* by twos, in pairs: for IE. base see TWO] **1.** in or through the space that separates (two things) [the river *between* their farms] **2.** in or of the time, amount, or degree that separates (two things) [office hours *between* nine and five] **3.** that connects or relates to [a bond *between* friends] **4.** along a course that connects [a road *between* here and there] **5.** by the joint action of [*between* them they landed the fish] **6.** in or into the combined possession of [they had fifty dollars *between* them] **7.** from one or the other of [choose *between* love and duty] **8.** because of the combined effect of [*between* work and study he has no time left] **NOTE:** *among* is usually used of a relationship involving more than two [choose *among* the three of them], but *between* is sometimes used of more than two, if the relationship is thought of as involving each one with each of the others [a treaty *between* four powers] —*adv.* in an intermediate space, position, or function [with nothing *between*] —**between ourselves** in confidence; as a secret: also **between you and me** —**in between 1.** in an intermediate position **2.** in the midst of

be·tween·times (-tīmz′) *adv.* in the intervals

be·twixt (bi twikst′) *prep., adv.* [< OE. *betwix* < *be-* + a form related to *twegen,* TWAIN] between: now archaic except in **be-twixt and between,** neither altogether one nor altogether the other

Beu·lah (byōō′lə) [Heb. *be 'ūlāh,* married: a Biblical name for the land of Israel] a feminine name

bev, Bev (bev) *n., pl.* **bev, Bev** [B(ILLION) + E(LECTRON-)V(OLTS)] a unit of energy equal to one billion electron-volts

☆**bev·a·tron** (bev′ə trän′) *n.* [< BEV + (CYCLO)TRON] a synchrotron for accelerating atomic particles to an energy level of six or more bev

bev·el (bev′'l) *n.* [prob. < OFr. *baivel,* dim. < *baif,* gaping: see BAY²] **1.** a tool which is a rule with a movable arm, for measuring or marking angles, etc.: also **bevel square 2.** an angle other than a right angle **3.** a sloping edge between parallel surfaces —*adj.* sloped; beveled —*vt.* **-eled** or **-elled, -el·ing** or **-el·ling** to cut to an angle other than a right angle —*vi.* to slope at an angle

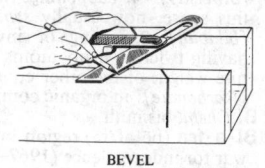
BEVEL

bevel gear a gearwheel meshed with another so that their shafts are at an angle

bev·er·age (bev′rij, -ər ij) *n.* [< OFr. < *bevre* < L. *bibere,* IMBIBE] any liquid for drinking, esp. other than plain water

Bev·er·ley, Bev·er·ly (bev′ər lē) [< ME. *bever,* BEAVER¹ + *ley,* lea] a feminine name

bev·y (bev′ē) *n., pl.* **bev′ies** [< Anglo-Fr. *bevée* < OFr., a drinking bout < *bevre:* see BEVERAGE] **1.** a group, esp. of girls or women **2.** a flock: now chiefly of quail —see SYN. at GROUP

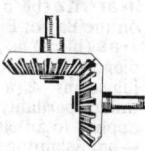
BEVEL GEAR

be·wail (bi wāl′) *vt.* to wail over or complain about; lament; mourn —**be·wail′er** *n.*

be·ware (bi wer′) *vi., vt.* **-wared′, -war′ing** [prob. < OE. < *be-* + *warian,* to be wary] to be wary of or careful (of); be on one's guard (against) [*beware* of ice on the road]

be·wigged (bi wigd′) *adj.* wearing a wig

be·wil·der (bi wil′dər) *vt.* [BE- + archaic *wilder,* to lose one's way] to confuse hopelessly, as by something complicated; puzzle [*bewildered* by the winding streets] —see SYN. at PUZZLE —**be·wil′dered** *adj.* —**be·wil′der·ing** *adj.* —**be·wil′der·ing·ly** *adv.* —**be·wil′der·ment** *n.*

be·witch (bi wich′) *vt.* [< ME. < *be-* + *wicchen* < OE. < *wicca:* see WITCH] **1.** to cast a spell over **2.** to charm and delight; fascinate [*bewitched* by the enchanting music] —**be·witch′ing** *adj.* —**be·witch′ing·ly** *adv.*

be·witch·ment (-mənt) *n.* **1.** power to bewitch **2.** a bewitching or being bewitched **3.** a spell that bewitches Also **be-witch′er·y** (-ər ē), *pl.* **-er·ies**

be·wray (bi rā′) *vt.* [< ME. < *be-* + OE. *wregan,* to inform] [Archaic] to divulge; reveal; betray

bey (bā) *n.* [Turk. *bey, beg*] **1.** in the Ottoman Empire, the governor of a Turkish province **2.** a Turkish title of respect and former title of rank **3.** the former native ruler of Tunis

be·yond (bi yänd′) *prep.* [< OE. < *be-* + *geond,* yonder] **1.** on or to the far side of; farther on than [*beyond* the hill] **2.** later than [*beyond* noon] **3.** outside the reach or under-standing of [*beyond* help] **4.** more or better than; exceeding [success *beyond* one's hopes] —*adv.* **1.** farther away [the meadow and the woods *beyond*] **2.** in addition; besides [room and board but nothing *beyond*] —**the (great) beyond** whatever follows death

bez·el (bez′'l) *n.* [< OFr. word thought to be *bisel* (Fr. *biseau*), sloping edge] **1.** a sloping surface, as the cutting edge of a chis-el **2.** the slanting faces of a cut jewel, esp. those of the upper half **3.** *a)* the groove and flange holding a gem or a watch crystal in place *b)* a movable rim on a watch or clock that can be rotated so that marks on it can record certain kinds of information

be·zique (bi zēk′) *n.* [Fr. *bésigue*] a card game resembling pinochle

bf, b.f. boldface

B/F brought forward

bg. *pl.* **bgs.** bag

---

fat, āpe, cär; ten, ēven; is, bīte; gō, hôrn, tōōl, lòòk; oil, out; up, fur; get; joy; yet; chin; she; thin, then; zh, leisure; ŋ, ring; ə for *a* in *ago, e* in *agent, i* in *sanity, o* in *comply, u* in *focus;* ' as in *able* (ā′b'l); Fr. bál; ë, Fr. coeur; ö, Fr. feu; ô, Fr. mon; ô̄, Fr. coq; ü, Fr. duc; r, Fr. cri; H, G. ich; kh, G. doch; ‡foreign; ☆ Americanism; < derived from. See inside front cover.

Bha·ga·vad-Gi·ta (bug′ə vəd gē′tə) *n.* a sacred Hindu philosophical writing, that is part of the MAHABHARATA

bhang (baŋ) *n.* [Hindi < Sans. *bhangā*, hemp] **1.** the hemp plant **2.** its dried leaves and flowers, or a preparation, such as hashish, made from these and used for its intoxicating properties

Bha·rat (bu′rut) *Hindu name for* INDIA (sense 2)

B-horizon *n.* see ABC SOIL

Bhu·tan (bōō tän′) country in the Himalayas: c. 18,000 sq. mi.; pop. 750,000 —**Bhu·tan·ese** (bōōt′'n ēz′) *adj., n., pl.* **-ese′**

bi- (bī) [L. *bi-* < OL. *dui-*, TWO] *a prefix meaning:* **1.** having two [*biangular*] **2.** doubly [*biconvex*] **3.** happening every two [*biennial*] **4.** happening twice during every [*bimonthly*]: in this sense, now usually *semi-* or *half-* **5.** using two or both [*bilabial*] **6.** joining or involving two [*bilateral*] **7.** *Chem.* having twice as many atoms or chemical equivalents for a definite weight of the other constituent of the compound [*sodium bicarbonate*]: in organic compounds, usually replaced by *di-*

Bi *Chem.* bismuth

Bi·a·fra (bē äf′rə) region in E Nigeria: fought an unsuccessful war for independence (1967–70)

bi·an·gu·lar (bī aŋ′gyoo lər) *adj.* having two angles

bi·an·nu·al (-an′yoo wəl, -yool) *adj.* coming twice a year; semiannual: see also BIENNIAL —**bi·an′nu·al·ly** *adv.*

Bi·ar·ritz (bē′ə rits′; *Fr.* byà rēts′) resort town in SW France, on the Bay of Biscay: pop. 25,000

bi·as (bī′əs) *n., pl.* **bi′as·es** [Fr. *biais*, a slant] **1.** a slanting or diagonal line, cut or sewn across the weave of cloth, as in making seams **2.** a mental leaning for or against someone or something; partiality; prejudice; bent **3.** *Radio* the fixed voltage applied to an electrode circuit to control the mode of operation —*adj.* slanting; diagonal —*adv.* diagonally —*vt.* **-ased** or **-assed, -as·ing** or **-as·sing** to cause to have a bias; prejudice [some men are *biased* against women] —see SYN. at PREJUDICE —**on the bias** diagonally; specif., cut or sewn diagonally across the weave

bi·ath·lon (bī ath′lən, -län) *n.* [BI- + Gr. *athlon*, a contest] in the winter Olympic games, an event combining a ski run and marksmanship

bi·ax·i·al (bī ak′sē əl) *adj.* having two axes, as some crystals —**bi·ax′i·al·ly** *adv.*

bib (bib) *n.* [< L. *bibere*, to drink] **1.** an apronlike cloth tied under a child's chin at meals **2.** the front upper part of an apron or overalls

Bib. **1.** Bible **2.** Biblical

bib and tucker [Colloq.] an outfit of clothes; esp., **best bib and tucker**, best, or most formal, clothes

☆**bibb lettuce** (bib) [after J. *Bibb* (1789–1884), Kentucky horticulturist] a kind of lettuce formed in loose heads of crisp, dark-green leaves

bib·cock (bib′käk′) *n.* a faucet whose nozzle is bent downward

‡**bi·be·lot** (bē blō′) *n.* [Fr. < OFr. < *belbel*, BAUBLE] a small object whose value lies in its beauty or rarity

Bibl., bibl. **1.** Biblical **2.** bibliographical

Bi·ble (bī′b'l) *n.* [< OFr. < ML. < Gr. *biblia*, collection of writings, pl. of *biblion*, book < *biblos*, papyrus] **1.** the sacred book of Christianity, consisting of an Old Testament and New Testament **2.** the Holy Scriptures of Judaism, that became the Old Testament of Christianity **3.** any collection of writings sacred to a religion [the Koran is the Moslem *Bible*] **4.** [**b-**] any book regarded as authoritative See also AUTHORIZED VERSION, REVISED STANDARD VERSION, DOUAY BIBLE, VULGATE, SEPTUAGINT, APOCRYPHA

Bib·li·cal (bib′li k'l) *adj.* [*also* **b-**] **1.** of or in the Bible **2.** in keeping with or according to the Bible; like that in the Bible —**Bib′li·cal·ly** *adv.*

Bib·li·cist (-sist) *n.* **1.** a person who takes the words of the Bible literally **2.** a specialist in Biblical literature —**Bib′li·cism** *n.*

bib·li·o- [< Gr. *biblion*: see BIBLE] *a combining form meaning:* **1.** book; of books [*bibliophile*] **2.** of the Bible [*bibliomancy*]

bib·li·og·ra·phy (bib′lē äg′rə fē) *n., pl.* **-phies** [< Gr.: see BIBLE & -GRAPHY] **1.** the study of the editions, dates, authorship, etc. of books and other writings **2.** a list of writings on a particular subject or by a particular author, etc. **3.** a list of the books, articles, etc. referred to by an author —**bib′li·og′ra·pher** *n.* —**bib′li·o·graph′ic** (-ə graf′ik), **bib′li·o·graph′i·cal** *adj.* —**bib′li·o·graph′i·cal·ly** *adv.*

bib·li·o·man·cy (bib′lē ə man′sē) *n.* [BIBLIO- + -MANCY] a way of trying to predict the future by choosing a Bible verse at random and interpreting it

bib·li·o·ma·ni·a (bib′lē ə mā′nē ə, -nyə) *n.* [BIBLIO- + -MANIA] a craze for collecting books, esp. rare ones —**bib′li·o·ma′ni·ac** *n., adj.*

bib·li·o·phile (bib′lē ə fīl′) *n.* [BIBLIO- + -PHILE] **1.** one who loves or admires books, esp. for their style of binding, printing, etc. **2.** a book collector —**bib′li·o·phil′ic** (-ə fil′ik) *adj.* —**bib′li·oph′i·lism** (-äf′ə liz′m), **bib′li·oph′i·ly** (-äf′ə lē) *n.*

bib·u·lous (bib′yoo ləs) *adj.* [< L. *bibere*, to drink: see IMBIBE] **1.** highly absorbent [a piece of *bibulous* terry cloth] **2.** fond of drinking alcoholic liquor —**bib′u·lous·ly** *adv.* —**bib′u·lous·ness** *n.*

bi·cam·er·al (bī kam′ər əl) *adj.* [< BI- + L. *camera*, a chamber] made up of or having two legislative chambers [the U.S. Congress is a *bicameral* legislature] —**bi·cam′er·al·ism** *n.*

bi·car·bon·ate (bī kär′bə nit, -nāt′) *n.* an acid salt of carbonic acid containing the radical HCO₃

bicarbonate of soda *same as* SODIUM BICARBONATE

bice (bīs) *n.* [ME. & OFr. *bis*, dusky, dark] **1.** a grayish blue, duller that azure **2.** a grayish-blue or green pigment

bi·cen·te·nar·y (bī′sen ten′ər ē, bī sen′tə ner′ē) *adj., n., pl.* **-nar·ies** *same as* BICENTENNIAL

bi·cen·ten·ni·al (bī′sen ten′ē əl) *adj.* **1.** happening once in a period of 200 years **2.** lasting for 200 years —☆*n.* a 200th anniversary or its celebration

bi·ceps (bī′seps) *n., pl.* **-ceps** or **-ceps·es** [L. < *bis*, two + *caput*, head] **1.** a muscle having two heads, or points of origin; esp., the large muscle in the front of the upper arm or the corresponding muscle at the back of the thigh **2.** strength or muscular development, esp. of the arm

bi·chlo·ride (bī klôr′īd) *n.* **1.** a binary compound containing two atoms of chlorine for each atom of another element **2.** *same as* MERCURIC CHLORIDE

bichloride of mercury *same as* MERCURIC CHLORIDE

bi·chro·mate (bī krō′māt) *n. same as* DICHROMATE

bick·er (bik′ər) *vi.* [ME. *bikeren*] **1.** to have a petty quarrel; squabble **2.** to move with quick, rippling noises [a *bickering* brook] **3.** to flicker, twinkle, etc. —*n.* a petty quarrel —**bick′er·er** *n.*

bi·col·or (bī′kul′ər) *adj.* of two colors: also **bi′col′ored**

bi·con·cave (bī′kän kāv′, bī kän′kāv) *adj.* concave on both surfaces [a *biconcave* lens]

bi·con·vex (bī′kän veks′, bī kän′veks) *adj.* convex on both surfaces [a *biconvex* lens]

bi·cus·pid (bī kus′pid) *adj.* [< BI- + L. *cuspis*, pointed end] having two points [a *bicuspid* tooth]: also **bi·cus′pi·date′** (-pi dāt′) —*n.* any of eight adult teeth with two-pointed crowns: there are two bicuspids on each side of both jaws, between the canines and the molars

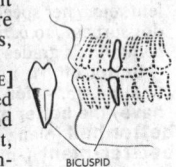

BICUSPID

bi·cy·cle (bī′si k'l) *n.* [Fr.: see BI- & CYCLE] a vehicle consisting of a metal frame mounted on two wheels, one behind the other, and equipped with handlebars, a saddlelike seat, and foot pedals or, sometimes, a gasoline engine —*vi., vt.* **-cled, -cling** to ride on a bicycle —**bi′cy·clist, bi′cy·cler** *n.*

bid (bid) *vt.* **bade** or **bid** or archaic **bad, bid′den** or **bid, bid′ding;** for vt. 2, 6, & for vi., the pt. & pp. are always **bid** [< OE. *biddan*, to urge (for IE. base see FAITH) & OE. *beodan*, to command < IE. base *bheudh-*, to be alert] **1.** to command, ask, or tell [the king *bade* him answer] **2.** to offer (a certain amount) as the price that one will pay or accept [to *bid* $20 for a lamp at an auction] **3.** to declare openly [to *bid* defiance] **4.** to express in greeting or taking leave [to *bid* farewell] **5.** [Archaic or Dial.] to invite **6.** *Card Games* to state (the number of tricks one expects to take) and declare (a suit or no-trump) —*vi.* to make a bid —*n.* **1.** a bidding of an amount **2.** the amount bid **3.** a chance to bid [it's your *bid*] **4.** an attempt or try [a *bid* for fame] ☆**5.** [Colloq.] an invitation, esp. to become a member **6.** *Card Games* a) the act of bidding b) the number of tricks stated c) a player's turn to bid —**bid fair** to seem likely [she *bids fair* to win the election] —☆**bid in** at an auction, to bid more than the best offer on one's own property in order to keep it —**bid up** to raise the amount bid

bid·da·ble (bid′ə b'l) *adj.* **1.** ready to obey orders; obedient; docile **2.** worth bidding on [a *biddable* bridge hand]

bid·der (bid′ər) *n.* a person who bids, as at an auction

bid·ding (bid′iŋ) *n.* **1.** a command or request **2.** an invitation or summons **3.** the bids or the making of bids in a card game or auction —**do the bidding of** to carry out the orders of

bid·dy (bid′ē) *n., pl.* **-dies 1.** a hen ☆**2.** [Slang] a woman, esp. an elderly, gossipy one

bide (bīd) *vi.* **bode** or **bid'ed, bid'ed, bid'ing** [OE. *bidan* < IE. base *bheidh-* (see BID)] [Archaic or Dial.] **1.** to stay; continue **2.** to dwell; reside **3.** to wait —*vt.* [Archaic or Dial.] to endure or tolerate —**bide one's time** *pt.* **bid'ed** to wait patiently for an opportunity

bi·den·tate (bī den'tāt) *adj.* having two teeth or toothlike parts

bi·det (bi dā') *n.* [Fr.] a low, bowl-shaped bathroom fixture equipped with running water, used for bathing the crotch

bi·en·ni·al (bī en'ē əl) *adj.* [< L. < *bis*, twice + *annus*, year + -AL] **1.** happening every two years **2.** lasting for two years —*n.* **1.** something that takes place every two years, as a convention **2.** *Bot.* a plant that lives two years, usually producing flowers and seed the second year —**bi·en'ni·al·ly** *adv.*

bier (bir) *n.* [OE. *beer*, a bed: for IE. base see BEAR[1]] **1.** a framework or stand on which a coffin or corpse is placed **2.** a coffin together with its stand

Bierce (birs), **Ambrose (Gwinett)** 1842–1914?; U.S. writer

biest·ings (bēs'tiŋz) *n.pl. same as* BEESTINGS

☆**biff** (bif) *n.* [prob. echoic] [Slang] a blow; strike; hit —*vt.* [Slang] to strike; hit

bi·fid (bī'fid) *adj.* [< L. < *bis*, twice+ *findere*, to cleave] divided into two equal parts by a cleft; forked [the *bifid* tongue of a snake] —**bi·fid'i·ty** (-ə tē) *n.* —**bi'fid·ly** *adv.*

☆**bi·fo·cal** (bī fō'k'l, bī'fō'k'l) *adj.* adjusted to two different focal lengths —*n.* a lens with one part ground to adjust the eyes for close focus, as for reading, and the rest ground for distant focus

☆**bi·fo·cals** (bī'fō'k'lz) *n.pl.* a pair of glasses with bifocal lenses

bi·fur·cate (bī'fər kāt', bī fur'kāt; *for adj. also* -kit) *adj.* [< ML. < L. < *bi-* + *furca*, FORK] having two branches; forked —*vt., vi.* -cat'ed, -cat'ing to divide into two branches —**bi'fur·cate·ly** *adv.* —**bi'fur·ca'tion** *n.*

BIFOCALS

big (big) *adj.* **big'ger, big'gest** [ME. < IE. base *b(e)u-, bh(e)u-*, to swell, from which also come L. *bucca*, puffed cheek & BOIL[1], POKE[2]] **1.** *a)* of great size, extent, or capacity; large [a *big* school; a *big* field; a *big* appetite] *b)* great in force or intensity [a *big* wind] **2.** *a)* full-grown [he's a *big* boy now] *b)* elder [his *big* sister] **3.** *a)* far advanced in pregnancy (*with*) [*big* with child] *b)* filled or swelling (*with*) **4.** loud [a *big* voice] **5.** important or outstanding [to do *big* things] **6.** boastful; extravagant [*big* talk] ☆**7.** generous; noble [a *big* heart] *Big* is much used in combination to form adjectives [*big*-bodied, *big*-souled] —*adv.* [Colloq.] **1.** pompously; boastfully [to talk *big*] **2.** impressively [to win *big*] **3.** in a broad way; showing imagination [think *big*!] —see SYN. at LARGE —**big'ness** *n.*

big·a·my (big'ə mē) *n., pl.* -**mies** [< OFr. < LL. < *bis*, twice + Gr. *gamos*, marriage] the act of marrying a second time while one is still married to another person: in most parts of the world, it is now illegal —**big'a·mist** *n.* —**big'a·mous** *adj.* —**big'a·mous·ly** *adv.*

big-bang theory a theory that the universe is constantly expanding and that the expansion of the universe began with a gigantic explosion

Big Ben **1.** the great bell in the Parliament clock tower in London **2.** the clock itself

Big Bend National Park national park in SW Texas, in the bend formed by the Rio Grande

☆**Big Board** **1.** the listing of the securities that are bought and sold on the New York Stock Exchange **2.** the New York Stock Exchange

big brother **1.** one's older brother **2.** [< such a situation in G. ORWELL's novel *1984*] [*usually* B- B-] the government, a business, etc. seen as invading people's privacy in trying to keep control over them

☆**Big Dipper** a dipper-shaped group of stars in the constellation Ursa Major (Great Bear)

bi·ge·ner·ic (bī'jə ner'ik) *adj.* designating or of hybrids that derive from two different genera

big game **1.** large wild animals hunted for sport, as lions, tigers, etc. **2.** the object of any important or dangerous undertaking

big·gish (big'ish) *adj.* somewhat big

big·heart·ed (big'här'tid) *adj.* quick to give or forgive; generous or magnanimous —**big'heart'ed·ly** *adv.*

☆**big·horn** (-hôrn') *n., pl.* -**horns'**, -**horn'**: see PLURAL, II, D, 1 an animal with large horns, esp. a large, wild, shaggy-haired sheep of the Rocky Mountains

☆**big house, the** [Old Slang] a penitentiary

bight (bīt) *n.* [ME. *byht* < base of *bugan* (see BOW[1])] **1.** a loop or slack part in a rope **2.** *a)* a curve in a river, coastline, etc. *b)* a bay formed by such a curve —*vt.* to fasten with a bight

☆**big-league** (big'lēg') *adj.* [after the *big* (i.e., major) *leagues* in professional baseball] [Colloq.] of or at the top level in one's work or profession [a *big-league* lawyer]

big lie, the a great distortion of facts, repeated over and over to make it seem believable: used for propaganda, as in politics

big mouth ☆[Slang] a person who talks too much, especially in a boastful or gossipy way

big·no·ni·a (big nō'nē ə) *n.* [after the Abbé *Bignon*, 18th-c. Fr. librarian] a tropical American vine with trumpet-shaped, yellow or reddish flowers

big·ot (big'ət) *n.* [Fr. < OFr., a term of insult used of Normans < ? ME. *bi god*, by God] a narrow-minded person who is prejudiced against other religions, opinions, races, etc. —**big'ot·ed** *adj.* —**big'ot·ed·ly** *adv.*

big·ot·ry (big'ə trē) *n., pl.* -**ries** the behavior, attitude, or beliefs of a bigot; prejudice

☆**big shot** [Slang] an important, influential person: also **big noise, big wheel,** etc.

☆**big stick** [from Theodore ROOSEVELT's phrase "speak softly and carry a big stick"] [*also* B- S-] the policy of negotiating by threatening to use force, esp. military action

☆**big time** [Slang] **1.** formerly, vaudeville in the top-ranking theatrical circuits **2.** the highest level in any profession, occupation, etc. —**big'-time'** *adj.*

☆**big top** [Colloq.] **1.** the main tent of a circus **2.** the life or work of circus performers

☆**big tree** a giant Sequoia tree related to the redwood and found in the high Sierras

big·wig (big'wig') *n.* [Colloq.] *same as* BIG SHOT

bi·jou (bē'zhōō) *n., pl.* -**joux** (-zhōōz) [Fr. < Bret. *bizou*, a ring < *biz*, a finger] **1.** a jewel **2.** something small and finely made, as an ornament or piece of jewelry

bi·ju·gate (bī'jo gāt', bī jōō'git) *adj.* [BI- + JUGATE] having two pairs of leaflets, as some pinnate leaves: also **bi'ju·gous** (-gəs)

☆**bike** (bīk) *n., vt., vi.* **biked, bik'ing** [< BICYCLE] [Colloq.] **1.** bicycle **2.** motorcycle

☆**bike·way** (bīk'wā') *n.* a path, lane, or route set aside for bicycle riders

bi·ki·ni (bi kē'nē) *n.* [< *Bikini*, atoll in the Marshall Islands] an extremely brief two-piece bathing suit for women

bi·la·bi·al (bī lā'bē əl) *adj.* **1.** *same as* BILABIATE **2.** made by stopping or partially stopping the airstream with the lips [*p* and *b* are *bilabial* sounds in English] —*n.* a bilabial sound

bi·la·bi·ate (bī lā'bē it, -āt') *adj.* [BI- + LABIATE] *Bot.* having two lips, as the corolla of some flowers

bi·lat·er·al (bī lat'ər əl) *adj.* [BI- + LATERAL] **1.** of, on, or having two sides, factions, etc. **2.** affecting both sides equally; reciprocal [a *bilateral* trade pact] **3.** having its parts arranged in a symmetrical way on both sides of an axis [a *bilateral* leaf]: see illustration on next page —**bi·lat'er·al·ism** *n.* —**bi·lat'er·al·ly** *adv.*

Bil·ba·o (bil bä'ō) seaport in N Spain: pop. 372,000

bil·ber·ry (bil'ber'ē) *n., pl.* -**ries** [ult. < ON. *bollr*, BALL[1] + *ber*, berry] a N. American blueberry or its fruit

BIGHORN
(3–4 ft. high
at shoulder)

BIKINI

bil·bo (bil′bō) *n., pl.* **-boes** [after BILBAO] **1.** [*pl.*] a long iron bar with shackles, for fettering a prisoner's feet **2.** [Archaic] a sword

bile (bīl) *n.* [Fr. < L. *bilis*] **1.** the bitter, yellow-brown or greenish fluid secreted by the liver and found in the gallbladder: it helps in digestion, esp. of fats **2.** [< ancient belief in bile as the humor causing anger] bitterness of spirit; anger

bilge (bilj) *n.* [var. of BULGE] **1.** the bulge of a cask **2.** the rounded, lower part of a ship's hold **3.** stagnant, dirty water that gathers there: also **bilge water 4.** [Slang] worthless talk or writing; nonsense —*vt., vi.* **bilged, bilg′ing** to break open in the bilge: said of a ship

bil·i·ar·y (bil′ē er′ē, bil′yər ē) *adj.* [Fr. *biliaire*] **1.** of or involving the bile **2.** bile-carrying **3.** bilious

bi·lin·gual (bī liŋ′gwəl) *adj.* [< L. < *bis*, two + *lingua*, tongue] **1.** of or in two languages [a bilingual poster] **2.** capable of using two languages, esp. with the ease of a native speaker —**bi·lin′gual·ism** *n.* —**bi·lin′gual·ly** *adv.*

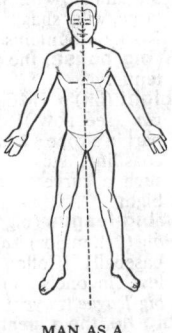

MAN AS A BILATERAL BEING

bil·ious (bil′yəs) *adj.* **1.** of the bile **2.** having, appearing to have, or resulting from some ailment of the bile or the liver **3.** bad-tempered; cross —**bil′ious·ly** *adv.* —**bil′ious·ness** *n.*

bilk (bilk) *vt.* [? altered < BALK] **1.** to cheat or swindle; defraud **2.** to get out of paying (a debt, etc.) **3.** to manage to get away from; elude [he *bilked* the police] —*n.* **1.** a bilking or being bilked **2.** a cheat or swindler —**bilk′er** *n.*

bill[1] (bil) *n.* [< Anglo-L. *billa*, altered < ML. *bulla*, sealed document < L. *bulla*, knob] **1.** a listing of money owed for goods or services; invoice [a garage *bill*] **2.** a list, as a menu, theater program, ship's roster, etc. **3.** a poster or handbill, esp. one announcing a circus, show, etc. **4.** the entertainment offered in a theater **5.** a proposed law to be voted on by a lawmaking body **6.** *same as* BILL OF EXCHANGE **7.** any promissory note ☆**8.** *a)* a bank note or piece of paper money *b)* [Slang] a hundred dollars or a hundred-dollar bill **9.** *Law* a written statement of charges against someone that is filed in a legal action —*vt.* **1.** to make out a bill of (items); list **2.** to present with a listing of money owed [the store *billed* me for the books] **3.** *a)* to advertise by bills or posters *b)* to book (a performer or performance) **4.** to post bills or placards throughout (a town, etc.) **5.** to enter on a bill of consignment; book for shipping —☆**fill the bill** [Colloq.] to meet the requirements; satisfy —**bill′a·ble** *adj.*

bill[2] (bil) *n.* [OE. *bile* < IE. base *bhei-*, to strike] **1.** the horny jaws of a bird, usually pointed; beak **2.** a beaklike mouthpart, as of a turtle ☆**3.** [Colloq.] the peak or visor of a cap —*vi.* **1.** to touch bills together **2.** to caress lovingly: now only in **bill and coo**, to kiss, talk softly, etc. in a loving way

bill[3] (bil) *n.* [OE. *bill*: for IE. base see BILL[2]] **1.** an ancient weapon having a hook-shaped blade with a spike at the back **2.** *same as* BILLHOOK

bill·a·bong (bil′ə bäŋ′) *n.* [native term < *billa*, water + ?] in Australia, **1.** a backwater channel that forms a lagoon or pool **2.** a river branch that reenters the main stream

☆**bill·board** (bil′bôrd′) *n.* a large signboard, usually outdoors, for posters used in advertising

bil·let[1] (bil′it) *n.* [< Anglo-Fr., dim. of *bille*, BILL[1]] **1.** *a)* a written order to provide lodging for military personnel, as in private buildings *b)* a place where such lodging is gotten *c)* the sleeping place assigned to a sailor on ship **2.** a position or job —*vt.* to assign to lodging by billet [the troops were *billeted* on nearby farms] —*vi.* to be billeted or quartered [who is *billeting* in the chateau?]

bil·let[2] (bil′it) *n.* [OFr. *billette*, dim. of *bille*, tree trunk] **1.** *a)* a short, thick piece of firewood *b)* [Obs.] a wooden club **2.** a small, unfinished metal bar, esp. of iron or steel

bil·let-doux (bil′ē dōō′) *n., pl.* **bil·lets-doux** (bil′ē dōōz′) [Fr., lit., sweet letter] a love letter

☆**bill·fold** (bil′fōld′) *n. same as* WALLET (sense 2)

bill·head (-hed′) *n.* a letterhead used for sending bills

bill·hook (-hŏŏk′) *n.* a tool with a curved or hooked blade at one end, for pruning and cutting

bil·liard (bil′yərd) *adj.* of or for billiards —*n.* a point scored in billiards by a carom

bil·liards (bil′yərdz) *n.* [Fr. *billard*; orig., a cue < *bille*: see BILLET[2]] any of several games played with hard balls on an oblong table covered with cloth and having raised, cushioned edges: a cue is used to hit and move the balls: see also POOL[2]

bill·ing (bil′iŋ) *n.* the listing or the order of listing of actors' names on a playbill, marquee, etc.

Bil·lings (bil′iŋz) [after F. *Billings* (1823–90), railroad executive] city in S Mont.: pop. 62,000

bil·lings·gate (bil′iŋz gāt′) *n.* [after a fish market in London, where such language was heard] foul, vulgar, abusive talk

bil·lion (bil′yən) *n.* [Fr. contr. < *bi-*, BI- + *million*] ☆**1.** a thousand millions (1,000,000,000) **2.** formerly, in Great Britain, a million millions (1,000,000,000,000) **3.** an indefinite but very large number —*adj.* amounting to one billion in number —**bil′lionth** *adj., n.*

bil·lion·aire (bil′yə ner′) *n.* one whose wealth comes to at least a billion dollars, pounds, etc.

bill of attainder a legislative act by which a person is declared guilty, without a trial, of some crime (esp. treason) and is punished by death and loss of property and civil rights: such bills are prohibited in the U.S. by the Constitution

bill of exchange a written order to pay a certain sum of money to the person named; draft

bill of fare a list of the foods served; menu

bill of goods a shipment of goods sent to an agent for sale —**sell (someone) a bill of goods** ☆[Colloq.] to deceive (someone) into accepting, believing, or doing something

bill of health a certificate stating whether there is infectious disease aboard a ship or in the port sailed from —**clean bill of health 1.** a bill of health certifying the absence of infectious disease **2.** [Colloq.] a good record; favorable report, as after an investigation

bill of lading a paper listing the goods received for shipment by a railroad, trucking company, etc. and promising their delivery

bill of rights 1. a list of the rights and freedoms regarded as essential to a people ☆**2.** [B- R-] the first ten amendments to the Constitution of the U.S., which guarantee certain rights to the people, as freedom of speech, assembly, and worship

bill of sale a paper showing that the buyer of something is now its legal owner

bil·low (bil′ō) *n.* [ON. *bylgja*: for IE. base see BALL[1]] **1.** a large wave; great swell of water **2.** any large, swelling mass or surge, as of smoke, sound, etc. —*vi., vt.* to surge, swell, or cause to swell like or in a billow

bil·low·y (bil′ə wē) *adj.* **-low·i·er, -low·i·est** swelling in or as in a billow —**bil′low·i·ness** *n.*

bill·post·er (bil′pōs′tər) *n.* a person hired to fasten advertisements on walls, billboards, etc.

bil·ly (bil′ē) *n., pl.* **-lies** [< BILLET[2]] a club or heavy stick, esp. one carried by a policeman

billy goat a male goat

bi·lo·bate (bī lō′bāt) *adj.* having or divided into two lobes: also **bi·lo′bat·ed, bi·lobed′**

bi·man·u·al (bī man′yŏŏ wəl) *adj.* using or requiring both hands —**bi·man′u·al·ly** *adv.*

bi·met·al (bī′met′'l) *adj. same as* BIMETALLIC —*n.* a bimetallic substance

bi·me·tal·lic (bī′mə tal′ik) *adj.* **1.** containing or using two metals, often two metals bonded together **2.** of or based on bimetallism

bi·met·al·lism (bī met′'l iz'm) *n.* the use of two metals, usually gold and silver, as the monetary standard, with fixed values in relation to each other —**bi·met′al·list** *n.*

bi·month·ly (bī munth′lē) *adj., adv.* **1.** once every two months **2.** twice a month: in this sense, *semimonthly* is the preferred term —*n., pl.* **-lies** a publication appearing once every two months

bin (bin) *n.* [OE., manger, crib] a box or crib for storing grain, coal, etc. —*vt.* **binned, bin′ning** to store in a bin

bi·na·ry (bī′nər ē) *adj.* [< L. < *bini*, two by two < *bis*, double] **1.** made up of two parts or things; twofold; double **2.** designating or of a number system that has 2 as its base **3.** *Chem.* composed of two elements or radicals or of one element and one radical [binary compounds] —*n., pl.* **-ries 1.** something made up of two parts or things **2.** *same as* BINARY STAR

binary star two stars revolving around a common center of gravity; double star

bi·nate (bī′nāt) *adj.* [see BINARY] *Bot.* occurring in pairs [binate leaves] —**bi′nate·ly** *adv.*

bi·na·tion·al (bī nash′ə n'l) *adj.* made up of or involving two nations or two nationalities

bin·au·ral (bī nôr′əl, bi-) *adj.* [< L. *bini* (see BINARY) & AURAL] **1.** having two ears **2.** involving the use of both ears *[binaural* hearing*]* **3.** of sound reproduction or transmission using at least two sources to give a stereophonic effect

bind (bīnd) *vt.* **bound, bind′ing** [< OE. *bindan* < IE. base *bhendh-,* from which also come BAND¹ & BEND¹] **1.** to tie together; make fast, as with a rope *[the thieves bound* her hands behind her back*]* **2.** to hold or restrain as if tied *[bound* by convention*]* **3.** to gird or encircle with a belt, etc. **4.** to bandage (often with *up*) *[to bind* up one's wounds*]* **5.** to make stick together *[used* mud to *bind* its nest*]* **6.** to constipate **7.** to strengthen or ornament the edges of by a band, as of tape **8.** to fasten together printed sheets of (a book) and enclose within a cover **9.** to secure or make firm (a bargain, contract, etc.) **10.** to obligate, as by duty *[I* felt *bound* to report it*]* **11.** to make do something, as because of an oath, law, or contract **12.** to make an apprentice of (often with *out* or *over*) **13.** to unite or hold, as by loyalty or love **—vi. 1.** to do the act of binding **2.** to be or become tight, hard, or stiff **3.** to be constricting *[the* smaller coat is likely to *bind]* **4.** to stick together **—n. 1.** anything that binds ☆**2.** [Colloq.] a difficult situation; jam —see **SYN.** at TIE **—bind over** to put under legal bond to appear, as before a law court

bind·er (bīn′dər) *n.* **1.** a person who binds; specif., a bookbinder **2.** a thing that binds; specif., *a)* a band, cord, etc. *b)* a substance, as tar, that binds things together *c)* a folder or cover for holding sheets of paper together ☆**3.** *a)* a device attached to a reaper, for tying grain in bundles *b)* a machine that reaps grain and then binds it **4.** *Law* a paper that makes an agreement binding until the formal contract can be drawn up

☆**bind·er·y** (bīn′dər ē, -drē) *n., pl.* **-er·ies** a place where books are bound

bind·ing (-diŋ) *n.* **1.** the action of one that binds **2.** a thing that binds, as *a)* the fastenings on a ski for the boot *b)* a band or bandage *c)* tape used in sewing for strengthening seams, edges, etc. *d)* the covers and backing of a book **—adj.** that binds; esp., that holds one to an agreement, promise, etc.

binding energy the energy needed to separate an atom into the neutrons and protons that make it up

bind·weed (bīnd′wēd′) *n.* any of a number of twining vines related to the morning glory

Bi·net-Si·mon test (bi nā′ sī′mən) [after its Fr. devisers, A. *Binet* (1857-1911) and T. *Simon* (1873-1961)] any of a series of tests seeking to measure intelligence in children: also **Binet test**

binge (binj) *n.* [? < dial. *binge,* to soak] [Colloq.] **1.** a drunken spree **2.** any wild, unrestrained action *[a* shopping *binge]*

Bing·ham·ton (biŋ′əm tən) [after W. *Bingham* (1752-1804), land donor] city in SC N.Y.: pop. 64,000

☆**bin·go** (biŋ′gō) *n.* [< ?] a gambling game resembling lotto

bin·na·cle (bin′ə k'l) *n.* [formerly *bittacle* < Port. < L. *habitaculum,* dwelling place < *habitare,* to inhabit] the case enclosing a ship's compass, usually located near the helm

bin·oc·u·lar (bī näk′yə lər; *also, esp. for n.,* bi-) *adj.* [< L. *bini,* double + *oculus,* an eye] using, or for the use of, both eyes at the same time **—n.** *[usually pl.]* a binocular instrument, as field glasses **—bin·oc′u·lar·ly** *adv.*

bi·no·mi·al (bī nō′mē əl) *n.* [< LL. < *bi-* + Gr. *nomos,* law + -AL] **1.** a mathematical expression consisting of two terms connected by a plus or minus sign *[2x* + 3y is a *binomial]* **2.** a two-word scientific name of a plant or animal, giving its genus and species *[the binomial* of the domesticated cat is *Felix catus]* **—adj. 1.** composed of two terms **2.** of binomials

BINOCULARS

binomial theorem a general formula for writing any power of a binomial without multiplying out *[Ex.:* $(a + b)^2 = a^2 + 2ab + b^2]$

bi·o (bī′ō) *n., pl.* **bi′os** [Colloq.] a biography, often a very brief one

bi·o- [Gr. < *bios,* life] *a combining form meaning* life, of living things, biological *[biography, biochemistry]*

bi·o·as·say (bī′ō as′ā, -a sā′) *n.* [BIO- + ASSAY] a way of test-

ing the strength of a drug, etc. by measuring its effect on a subject as compared with the effect of a standard substance

bi·o·as·tro·nau·tics (bī′ō as′trə nôt′iks) *n.pl.* [*with sing. v.*] the science dealing with the effects of space travel upon living organisms

bi·o·chem·is·try (-kem′is trē) *n.* the branch of chemistry that deals with plants and animals and their life processes; biological chemistry **—bi′o·chem′i·cal** *adj.* **—bi′o·chem′ist** *n.*

bi·o·cide (bī′ə sīd′) *n.* [BIO- + -CIDE] any substance that can kill living organisms

bi·o·de·grad·a·ble (bī′ō di grā′də b'l) *adj.* [BIO- + DEGRAD(E) + -ABLE] that can be readily decomposed by biological, esp. bacterial, action, as some detergents

bi·o·feed·back (bī′ō fēd′bak′) *n.* a method of trying to control one's emotions by training oneself, with the aid of electronic devices, to change one's heartbeat, blood pressure, etc.

bi·o·fla·vo·noid (bī′ō flā′və noid′) *n.* any of a group of substances found in plants, that can strengthen the walls of capillaries and help to prevent hemorrhaging

biog. 1. biographer **2.** biographical **3.** biography

bi·o·gen·e·sis (bī′ō jen′ə sis) *n.* [BIO- + GENESIS] the principle that living organisms derive only from other similar organisms **—bi′o·ge·net′ic** (-jə net′ik), **bi′o·ge·net′i·cal** *adj.*

bi·og·ra·phy (bī äg′rə fē, bē-) *n.* [< Gr.: see BIO- & -GRAPHY] **1.** *pl.* **-phies** an account of a person's life written by another; life story **2.** such writings, collectively, as a branch of literature **—bi·og′ra·pher** *n.* **—bi·o·graph·i·cal** (bī′ə graf′i k'l), **bi′o·graph′ic** *adj.* **—bi′o·graph′i·cal·ly** *adv.*

biol. 1. biological **2.** biologist **3.** biology

bi·o·log·i·cal (bī′ə läj′i k'l) *adj.* **1.** of or connected with biology; of plants and animals **2.** used in or produced by practical biology *[biological* drugs] Also **bi′o·log′ic** **—n.** a biological product **—bi′o·log′i·cal·ly** *adv.*

biological warfare the use of disease-spreading germs, toxins, etc. as a weapon of war: see also CHEMICAL WARFARE

bi·ol·o·gy (bī äl′ə jē) *n.* [BIO- + -LOGY] **1.** the science that deals with the origin, history, life processes, structure, etc. of plants and animals: it includes botany and zoology **2.** animal and plant life, as of a given area **—bi·ol′o·gist** *n.*

bi·ome (bī′ōm) *n.* [< BIO- + -ome, group < ModL. -oma] a major community of plants and animals whose makeup is determined by soil and climate *[a* desert *biome]*

bi·o·med·i·cine (bī′ō med′ə s'n) *n.* a branch of medicine that is combined with research in biology **—bi′o·med′i·cal** *adj.*

bi·o·met·rics (-met′riks) *n.pl.* [*with sing. v.*] the use of statistics in biological studies **—bi′o·met′ric, bi′o·met′ri·cal** *adj.* **—bi′o·met′ri·cal·ly** *adv.*

☆**bi·on·ic** (bī än′ik) *adj.* **1.** designating an artificial replacement for a part of the body **2.** furnished with such a replacement part or parts, chiefly in science fiction, so as to become exceptionally strong, skillful, etc.

☆**bi·on·ics** (bī än′iks) *n.pl.* [*with sing. v.*] [< Gr. *bion,* living + -ICS] the science of designing instruments or systems modeled after living organisms

bi·o·phys·ics (bī′ō fiz′iks) *n.pl.* [*with sing. v.*] the study of biological phenomena using the principles of physics **—bi′o·phys′i·cal** *adj.* **—bi′o·phys′i·cist** *n.*

bi·op·sy (bī′äp′sē) *n., pl.* **-sies** [< BIO- + Gr. *opsis,* a sight] the examination of bits of living tissue, fluids, etc. taken from the body, in making a diagnosis

bi·o·rhythm (bī′ō rith′'m, -rith′əm) *n.* any of three separate cycles during which, according to a theory, a person's physical, emotional, and intellectual energy levels rise and fall in regular patterns

bi·o·sat·el·lite (bī′ō sat′'l īt′) *n.* a spacecraft designed for studying the effects of space travel on plant and animal life

bi·os·co·py (bī äs′kə pē) *n.* [BIO- + -SCOPY] a medical examination to find out whether life is present

-bi·o·sis (bī ō′sis, bē-) [< Gr. *biōsis,* way of life < *bios,* life] *a combining form meaning* way of living *[symbiosis]*

bi·o·sphere (bī′ō sfir′) *n.* [BIO- + SPHERE] that portion of the earth and its atmosphere which contains living organisms

bi·o·syn·the·sis (bī ō sin′thə sis) *n.* the forming of chemical compounds by the cells of living organisms

bi·o·tin (bī′ə tin) *n.* [< Gr. *bios,* life + -IN¹] one of the vitamin

B group, found in liver, egg yolk, and yeast, that is important in growth

bi·par·ti·san (bī pär′tə z'n, -s'n) *adj.* of or representing two parties [a *bipartisan* policy] —**bi·par′ti·san·ship′** *n.*

bi·par·tite (bī pär′tīt) *adj.* [< L. < *bi-*, two + *partire*, to divide] **1.** having two (corresponding) parts **2.** with two involved [a *bipartite* alliance] **3.** *Bot.* divided in two nearly to the base, as some leaves —**bi·par′tite·ly** *adv.* —**bi·par·ti′tion** (-tish′ən) *n.*

bi·ped (bī′ped) *n.* [< L. < *bi-* + *pedis*, gen. of *pes*, FOOT] any two-footed animal —*adj.* two-footed: also **bi·ped′al**

bi·pet·al·ous (bī pet′'l əs) *adj.* having two petals

bi·pin·nate (bī pin′āt, -it) *adj.* having pinnate leaflets on stems that grow opposite each other on a main stem —**bi·pin′nate·ly** *adv.*

bi·plane (bī′plān′) *n.* an airplane with two sets of wings, one above the other

bi·po·lar (bī pō′lər) *adj.* **1.** of or having two poles **2.** of or at both of the earth's poles **3.** characterized by two opinions, natures, etc. that are opposed to each other —**bi·po·lar·i·ty** (bī′pō lar′ə tē) *n.*

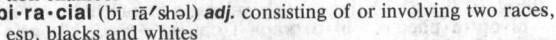

bi·pro·pel·lant (bī′prə pel′ənt) *n.* a rocket propellant consisting of a fuel and oxidizer that are brought together only in the combustion chamber

BIPINNATE
LEAF
(of acacia)

bi·ra·cial (bī rā′shəl) *adj.* consisting of or involving two races, esp. blacks and whites

birch (burch) *n.* [OE. *beorc* < IE. base *bhereg-*, to shine, white] **1.** a tree having smooth bark easily peeled off in thin sheets, and hard, closegrained wood **2.** this wood **3.** a birch rod or bunch of twigs used for whipping —*vt.* to beat with a birch —*adj.* of birch: also **birch′en**

bird (burd) *n.* [OE. *bridd*, young bird] **1.** any of a class of warmblooded, two-legged, egg-laying vertebrates with feathers and wings **2.** a small game bird **3.** same as CLAY PIGEON **4.** a shuttlecock ☆**5.** [Slang] a person, esp. an odd sort of person **6.** [Slang] a sound of disapproval made by fluttering the lips **7.** [Slang] a rocket or guided missile —*vi.* **1.** to shoot or catch birds **2.** to engage in bird watching —**bird in the hand** something sure because one already has it: opposed to **bird in the bush**, something unsure, etc. —**birds of a feather** people with the same characteristics or tastes —☆**for the birds** [Slang] ridiculous, worthless, etc. —**the birds and the bees** [Colloq.] the basic facts about sex —**bird′er** *n.*

BIRCH
(leaves & catkins)

☆**bird·bath** (burd′bath′) *n.* a basin of water set on a stand, as in a garden, for birds to bathe in

☆**bird·brain** (-brān′) *n.* [Colloq.] a stupid or silly person; nitwit

bird·call (-kôl′) *n.* **1.** the sound or song of a bird **2.** an imitation of this **3.** a device for imitating bird sounds Also **bird call**

☆**bird dog** (-kôl′) *n.* **1.** a dog trained for hunting birds, as a pointer **2.** [Colloq.] a person whose work is searching, as for missing persons, etc.

bird·ie (bur′dē) *n.* **1.** a small bird: child's word ☆**2.** *Golf* a score of one stroke under par for a hole

bird·lime (burd′līm′) *n.* **1.** a sticky substance spread on twigs to catch birds **2.** anything that snares —*vt.* **-limed′, -lim′ing** to catch with birdlime

bird of paradise **1.** any of a number of brightly colored birds found in and near New Guinea **2.** a tropical plant with brilliant orange and blue flowers that look like a bird in flight

bird of passage **1.** any bird that migrates with the change of season **2.** anyone who travels about constantly

bird of peace the dove

bird of prey any bird, as the hawk, owl, etc., that kills and eats mammals and other birds

bird·seed (-sēd′) *n.* seed for feeding caged birds

bird's-eye (burdz′ī′) *n.* a cotton or linen cloth with a woven pattern of small, diamond-shaped figures —*adj.* **1.** seen from above [a *bird's-eye* view] **2.** having markings like birds' eyes [*bird's-eye* maple]

bird's-foot (-foot′) *n., pl.* **-foots′** any of various plants whose leaves or flowers resemble a bird's foot, as a plant of the legume family (in full, **bird's-foot trefoil**) used for forage and hay

bird·shot (burd′shät′) *n.* small shot for shooting birds

bird watching the hobby of observing wild birds in their natural surroundings —**bird watcher**

bi·re·frin·gence (bī′ri frin′jəns) *n.* [< BI- + L. prp. of *refringere:* see REFRACT] the splitting of a light ray, generally by a crystal, into two components which travel at different velocities within the crystal —**bi·re·frin′gent** *adj.*

bi·reme (bī′rēm) *n.* [< L. < *bi-*, two + *remus*, oar] a galley having two rows of oars on each side

bi·ret·ta (bə ret′ə) *n.* [< It. < LL. dim. of L. *birrus*, a hood, cloak] a square cap with three projections and a tassel on top, worn by Roman Catholic clergy

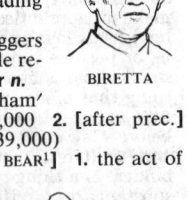

BIRETTA

Bir·ken·head (bur′k'n hed′) seaport in W England, at the mouth of the Mersey River: pop. 142,000

birl (burl) *vt., vi.* [? echoic, after WHIRL, PURL², etc.] ☆to revolve (a floating log) by treading on it

birl·ing (-iŋ) *n.* ☆a competition among loggers in which each tries to keep his balance while revolving a floating log with his feet —**birl′er** *n.*

Bir·ming·ham (bur′miŋ əm *for 1;* -miŋ ham′ *for 2)* **1.** city in C England: pop. 1,075,000 **2.** [after prec.] city in NC Ala.: pop. 301,000 (met. area 739,000)

birth (burth) *n.* [< OE. *byrde* < *beran*, to BEAR¹] **1.** the act of bringing forth offspring [she had an easy *birth* with her first child] **2.** the act of being born [his *birth* took place in Iowa] **3.** origin or descent [a Spaniard by *birth*] **4.** the beginning of anything [the *birth* of jazz in New Orleans] **5.** an inherited or natural talent [an actor by *birth*] —*vi., vt.* [Dial.] to give birth (to) —**give birth to 1.** to bring forth (offspring) **2.** to be the cause of; originate

BIRLING

☆**birth control** control of how many children a woman will have, as by contraception

birth·day (-dā′) *n.* **1.** the day of a person's birth or a thing's beginning **2.** the anniversary of this

birth·mark (-märk′) *n.* a skin blemish present at birth

birth·place (-plās′) *n.* **1.** the place of one's birth **2.** the place where something originated

birth·rate (-rāt′) *n.* the number of births per year per thousand of population in a given group: sometimes other units of time or population are used

birth·right (-rīt′) *n.* the rights that a person has because he was born in a certain family, nation, etc. or because he was the firstborn son

birth·stone (-stōn′) *n.* a precious or semiprecious gem that is used as a symbol of the month of one's birth

Bis·cay (bis′kā, -kē), **Bay of** part of the Atlantic, north of Spain & west of France

bis·cuit (bis′kit) *n., pl.* **-cuits, -cuit** [OFr. *bescuit* < ML. < L. *bis*, twice + *coctum*, pp. of *coquere*, to COOK] **1.** [Chiefly Brit.] a cracker or cookie ☆**2.** a quick bread baked in small pieces **3.** light brown; tan **4.** pottery after the first firing and before glazing

bi·sect (bī sekt′, bī′sekt) *vt.* [< ML. pp. of *bisecare* < L. *bi-*, two + *secare*, to cut] **1.** to cut in two **2.** *Geom.* to divide into two equal parts —*vi.* to divide; fork —**bi·sec′tion** *n.* —**bi·sec′tion·al** *adj.*

bi·sec·tor (bī sek′tər, bī′sek-) *n.* a thing that bisects; specif., a straight line that bisects an angle or line

bi·sex·u·al (bī sek′shoo wəl) *adj.* **1.** of both sexes **2.** having both male and female organs; hermaphroditic **3.** sexually attracted to both sexes —*n.* one that is bisexual —**bi·sex′u·al·i·ty** (-wal′ə tē), **bi·sex′u·al·ism** *n.* —**bi·sex′u·al·ly** *adv.*

bish·op (bish′əp) *n.* [< OE. *bisceop* < LL. < Gr. *episkopos*, overseer < *epi-*, upon + *skopein*, to look] **1.** a high-ranking Christian clergyman usually supervising a diocese or church district **2.** a chessman that can move only diagonally

bish·op·ric (bish′ə prik) *n.* the district, office, authority, or rank of a bishop

Bis·marck (biz′märk) [after Prince Otto von BISMARCK] capital of N.Dak., on the Missouri River: pop. 35,000

Bis·marck (biz′märk), Prince **Otto von** 1815–98; Prussian chancellor of Germany (1871–90)

bis·muth (biz′məth) *n.* [< G. *wismut* < ?] a hard, brittle, metallic chemical element used in making alloys of low melting point, medical compounds, etc.: symbol, Bi; at. wt., 208.980; at. no., 83

bi·son (bī′s'n, -z'n) *n., pl.* **bi′sons** [Fr. < L. < Gmc. *wisunt:* for IE. base see VIRUS] any of several mammals of the ox family, with a shaggy mane, short, curved horns, and a humped back, as the American buffalo

bisque[1] (bisk) *n.* [Fr.] **1.** a rich, thick, creamy soup made from shellfish or from rabbit, fowl, etc. **2.** a thick, strained, creamy vegetable soup

bisque[2] (bisk) *n.* [< BISCUIT] **1.** biscuit ceramic ware left unglazed in the finished state **2.** a red-yellow color

bis·ter, bis·tre (bis′tər) *n.* [Fr. *bistre*] **1.** a yellowish-brown to dark-brown pigment made from the soot of burned wood **2.** a color in this range

bis·tro (bis′trō, bēs′-) *n., pl.* **-tros** [Fr.] a small nightclub or bar

bi·sul·fate (bī sul′fāt) *n.* an acid sulfate; compound containing the monovalent HSO_4– radical

bi·sul·fide (bī sul′fīd) *n.* same as DISULFIDE

bit[1] (bit) *n.* [< OE. *bite,* a bite < *bitan,* to BITE] **1.** the metal mouthpiece on a bridle, used for controlling the horse **2.** anything that curbs or controls **3.** the part of a key that actually turns the lock **4.** the cutting part of any tool **5.** a drilling or boring tool for use in a brace, drill press, etc.: see illustration at BRACE AND BIT —*vt.* **bit′ted, bit′ting** to put a bit into the mouth of (a horse)

bit[2] (bit) *n.* [< OE. *bita,* a piece < *bitan,* to BITE] **1.** *a)* a small piece or quantity [a *bit* of candy] *b)* a limited degree: used as though it were an adverb meaning "somewhat" [a *bit* bored] *c)* a short time; moment [wait a *bit* longer] ☆**2.** [Colloq.] an amount equal to 12½ cents [a quarter is two *bits*] ☆**3.** a small part, as in a play —*adj.* very small [a *bit* role] —**bit by bit** little by little; gradually —**do one's bit** to do one's share —**every bit** altogether; entirely

bit[3] (bit) *n.* [b(*inary*) (d*ig*)it] **1.** a single character in a binary number system **2.** the smallest unit of information in a binary digital computer, expressed as the choice between two alternatives, such as "yes-no" or "off-on"

bitch (bich) *n.* [< OE. *bicce*] **1.** the female of the dog, wolf, etc. **2.** a bad-tempered, mean or spiteful woman: a coarse term of contempt ☆**3.** [Slang] a complaint —*vi.* ☆[Slang] to complain —**bitch′i·ness** *n.* —**bitch′y** *adj.* **bitch′i·er, bitch′i·est**

bite (bīt) *vt.* **bit** (bit), **bit·ten** (bit′'n) or **bit, bit′ing** [< OE. *bitan* < IE. base *bheid-,* to split, from which also come FISSURE & BITTER] **1.** to seize or cut with or as with the teeth [the dog *bit* his leg] **2.** to cut into, as with a sharp weapon **3.** to sting, as an insect **4.** to hurt in a sharp, stinging way [the cold wind *bites* my face] **5.** to eat into; corrode **6.** to seize or possess [bitten by a lust for fame] —*vi.* **1.** *a)* to press or snap the teeth or teethlike parts (*into, at,* etc.) [the trap *bit* into his foot] *b)* to have a tendency to do this [be careful of a dog that *bites*] **2.** to cause a biting sensation [a pepper that really *bites*] **3.** to press hard; grip [the tires *bit* into the snow] **4.** to seize a bait [the fish won't *bite*] **5.** to be caught, as by a trick —*n.* **1.** the act of biting **2.** biting quality; sting [his words have quite a *bite*] **3.** a wound or sting from biting [arms covered with mosquito *bites*] **4.** *a)* a mouthful [he took big *bites*] *b)* a light meal or snack **5.** a tight hold or grip **6.** the way the upper and lower teeth meet ☆**7.** [Colloq.] an amount removed [the tax takes quite a *bite* from his paycheck] —☆**put the bite on** [Slang] to press for a loan, gift, or bribe of money —**bit′er** *n.*

Bi·thyn·i·a (bə thin′ē ə) ancient kingdom in NW Asia Minor, in what is now Turkey

bit·ing (bīt′iŋ) *adj.* **1.** cutting; sharp [a *biting* frost] **2.** sarcastic [a *biting* comment] —**bit′ing·ly** *adv.*

bitt (bit) *n.* [< ?] *Naut.* any of the deck posts, usually in pairs, around which ropes or cables are fastened —*vt.* to wind around a bitt

bit·ten (bit′'n) *alt. pp. of* BITE

bit·ter (bit′ər) *adj.* [< OE. < base of *bitan,* to BITE] **1.** having a sharp, often unpleasant taste; acrid [*bitter* medicine] **2.** causing or showing sorrow, pain, etc. [*bitter* memories] **3.** sharp; harsh; piercing [a *bitter* wind] **4.** characterized by hatred, resentment, etc. [*bitter* enemies] —*adv.* in a bitter way [the night

was *bitter* cold] —*n.* **1.** something bitter [take the *bitter* with the sweet] **2.** [Brit.] bitter, strongly hopped ale: see also BITTERS —**bit′ter·ly** *adv.* —**bit′ter·ness** *n.*

bit·tern (bit′ərn) *n., pl.* **-terns, -tern:** see PLURAL, II, D, 1 [< OFr. *butor,* prob. < L. *butio*] a wading bird of the heron family, the male of which has a loud, deep, thumping call

bit·ter·root (bit′ər root′, -root′) *n.* a plant of western N. America having fleshy, edible roots and white or pink flowers

bit·ters (bit′ərz) *n.pl.* a liquor containing bitter herbs, roots, etc. and usually alcohol, used as a tonic and for flavoring in some cocktails

bit·ter·sweet (bit′ər swēt′) *n.* **1.** a N. American woody vine bearing clusters of small, orange fruits which open to expose the red seeds **2.** an old-world climbing vine of the nightshade family, with purple flowers and poisonous, red berries — *adj.* **1.** both bitter and sweet **2.** pleasant but with some sadness

bit·ty (bit′ē) *adj.* **-ti·er, -ti·est** [< BIT[2] + -Y[1]] ☆tiny: a playful term [a little *bitty* baby]

bi·tu·men (bi too′mən, bī-; -tyoo′-) *n.* [L. < Celt. < IE. base *gwet-,* resin, from which also comes CUD] any of several substances obtained in the process of distilling coal tar, petroleum, etc., or found naturally as asphalt —**bi·tu′mi·nous** *adj.*

bituminous coal coal that yields pitch or tar and produces much smoke when it burns; soft coal

bi·va·lent (bī vā′lənt, biv′ə-) *adj.* **1.** having two valences **2.** having a valence of two —**bi·va′lence, bi·va′len·cy** *n.*

bi·valve (bī′valv′) *n.* any mollusk having a shell of two parts, or valves, hinged together, as a mussel, clam, etc. —*adj.* having such a shell: also **bi′valved′**

biv·ou·ac (biv′wak, -oo wak′) *n.* [Fr. < OHG. *biwacht,* outpost < *bi-,* by + *wacht,* a guard] a temporary camp (esp. of soldiers) in the open, with little or no shelter —*vi.* **-acked, -ack·ing** to camp in the open

bi·week·ly (bī wēk′lē) *adj., adv.* **1.** once every two weeks **2.** twice a week: in this sense, *semiweekly* is the preferred term —*n., pl.* **-lies** a magazine, etc. that appears once every two weeks

bi·year·ly (bī yir′lē) *adj., adv.* **1.** once every two years; biennial(ly) **2.** twice a year: in this sense, *semiyearly, semiannual(ly),* or *biannual(ly)* is preferred

bi·zarre (bi zär′) *adj.* [Fr. < It. < Sp. *bizarro,* bold, knightly < Basque *bizar,* a beard] **1.** odd in manner, appearance, etc.; grotesque; queer; eccentric [wearing a *bizarre* costume] **3.** unexpected and unbelievable; fantastic [a *bizarre* chain of events] —see SYN. at FANTASTIC —**bi·zarre′ly** *adv.* —**bi·zarre′ness** *n.*

Bi·zet (bē zā′), **Georges** (zhôrzh) (born *Alexandre César Léopold Bizet*) 1838–75; Fr. composer

Bk *Chem.* berkelium

bk. *pl.* **bks. 1.** bank **2.** block **3.** book

bkg. banking

bkt. 1. basket(s) **2.** bracket

bl. 1. bale(s) **2.** barrel(s) **3.** black

B/L *pl.* **BS/L** bill of lading

B.L. Bachelor of Laws

blab (blab) *vt., vi.* **blabbed, blab′bing** [ME. *blabben:* see BLABBER] **1.** to give away (a secret) in idle chatter **2.** to chatter; prattle —*n.* **1.** loose chatter; gossip **2.** a person who blabs

blab·ber (-ər) *vt., vi.* [ME. *blabberen,* freq. of *blabben,* of echoic origin] [Dial. or Colloq.] to blab or babble —*n.* a person who blabs: also [Colloq.] **blab′ber·mouth′** (-mouth′)

black (blak) *adj.* [OE. *blæc* < IE. base *bhleg-* < *bhel-,* to burn, gleam: orig. sense of black was "covered with soot from flame"] **1.** opposite to white; of the color of coal: see COLOR **2.** having dark-colored skin and hair; esp., Negro **3.** without light; in complete darkness [lost in the *black* cave] **4.** without cream, milk, etc.: said of coffee **5.** soiled; dirty **6.** wearing black clothing **7.** evil; wicked [*black* deeds] **8.** disgraceful **9.** sad; dismal; gloomy [thinking *black* thoughts] **10.** sullen or angry [she gave him a *black* look] **11.** without hope [a *black* future] **12.** humorous or satirical in a despairing or cynical way [*black* comedy] —*n.* **1.** *a)* black color *b)* a black pigment, dye, etc.

BISON
(5½–6 ft. high at shoulder)

BITTERN
(to 31 in., including bill)

2. black clothes, esp. when worn in mourning 3. [*also* B-] a person with dark-colored skin; esp., a Negro: *black* is now the generally preferred term 4. complete darkness —*vt.*, *vi.* 1. to blacken 2. to polish with blacking —**black out** 1. to cover (writing, etc.) as with black pencil marks 2. to cause a blackout in 3. to lose consciousness —☆**in the black** operating at a profit —**black′ish** *adj.* —**black′ly** *adv.* —**black′ness** *n.*

black-and-blue (-ən bloo′) *adj.* discolored from blood congested under the skin; bruised

black and white 1. writing or print [to put an agreement down in *black and white*] 2. a drawing, photograph, etc. done in black and white

Black Angus *same as* ABERDEEN ANGUS

black art *same as* BLACK MAGIC

black·ball (-bôl′) *n.* [< the small, black ball once used to vote against something] a secret ballot or vote against a person or thing —*vt.* 1. to vote against; esp., to vote against letting (a person) join one's group 2. to ostracize

black bass (bas) any of various freshwater game fishes of N. America

black bear 1. the common N. American bear 2. any of several dark-colored bears of Asia

Black·beard (blak′bird′) (born *Edward Teach* or *Thatch*) ?-1718; Eng. pirate

black belt a black-colored belt awarded to an expert in judo or karate

black·ber·ry (-ber′ē) *n.*, *pl.* -ries 1. the fleshy, purple or black, edible fruit of various brambles of the rose family 2. a bush or vine bearing this fruit

black·bird (-burd′) *n.* any of various birds the male of which is almost entirely black, as the red-winged blackbird

black·board (-bôrd′) *n.* a smooth, usually dark surface of slate or other material on which to write or draw with chalk

black·bod·y (-bäd′ē) *n.* a surface or body that could, in theory, absorb all radiation striking it, with no reflection at all

black book a book with the names of those blacklisted

black·cap (-kap′) *n.* 1. a bird with a black crown, as the chickadee ☆2. same as BLACK RASPBERRY

black·cock (-käk′) *n.*, *pl.* -cocks′, -cock′: see PLURAL, II, D, 1 the male of the black grouse

black·damp (-damp′) *n.* a suffocating gas, a mixture of carbon dioxide and nitrogen, found in mines

Black Death a deadly disease, probably bubonic plague, which spread through Europe and Asia in the 14th cent. killing much of the population

black·en (blak′'n) *vi.* to become black or dark [rain clouds appeared and the sky *blackened*] —*vt.* 1. to make black; darken 2. to say bad things about; slander; defame [to *blacken* someone's reputation] —**black′en·er** *n.*

black eye 1. a bruise on the flesh surrounding an eye, resulting from a sharp blow or contusion ☆2. [Colloq.] bad reputation or dishonor, or a cause or source of this

☆**black-eyed pea** (blak′īd′) *same as* COWPEA (sense 2)

black-eyed Susan ☆a N. American wildflower with yellow ray flowers about a dark, cone-shaped center

black·face (blak′fās′) *adj.* having a black face —*n.* black makeup used by performers, as in minstrel shows, in gross caricature of Negroes

black·fish (-fish′) *n.*, *pl.* -fish′, -fish′es : see FISH ☆1. any of several small, black, toothed whales 2. any of various dark fishes, as the sea bass 3. a small freshwater fish of Siberia and Alaska that is said to revive after being frozen for some time

black flag the flag of piracy, usually with a white skull and crossbones on a black background

Black·foot (-foot′) *n.* 1. *pl.* -feet′, -foot′ any member of an Indian tribe consisting of three subtribes of Montana, Alberta, and Saskatchewan 2. their Algonquian language

Black Forest heavily wooded, mountainous region in SW Germany

black grouse a large grouse of Europe and Asia: the male is almost entirely black

black·guard (blag′ərd, -ärd) *n.* [BLACK + GUARD] a wicked person; scoundrel; villain —*adj.* vulgar, abusive, etc. —*vt.* to abuse with words; revile —**black′guard·ly** *adj.*, *adv.*

black·head (blak′hed′) *n.* 1. any of various birds having black feathers about the head and neck 2. a black-tipped bit of dried fatty matter clogging a skin pore

black·heart·ed (-här′tid) *adj.* wicked; evil

Black Hills mountainous region in SW S.Dak. & NE Wyo.

black hole any of a number of bodies that are thought to exist in outer space and are supposed to be invisible stars which

have collapsed and become so condensed that neither light nor matter can escape their gravitational field

black·ing (blak′iŋ) *n.* a black polish, as for shoes

black·jack (blak′jak′) *n.* ☆1. a small, leather-covered club with a flexible handle, used as a hitting weapon ☆2. the card game TWENTY-ONE — ☆*vt.* 1. to hit with a blackjack 2. to force by threatening; coerce

BLACKJACK

black lead graphite, used in lead pencils, etc.

black·leg (blak′leg′) *n.* 1. an infectious disease of young cattle and sheep, usually fatal 2. any of various diseases of certain plants 3. [Brit.] a strikebreaker; scab

black light ultraviolet or infrared radiation that is beyond the visible range of light

black·list (blak′list′) *n.* a list of censured persons who others think ought to be punished and who are being discriminated against, refused jobs, etc. —*vt.* to put on a blacklist

black lung (disease) a disease of the lungs caused by breathing in coal dust

black magic magic with an evil purpose; sorcery

black·mail (blak′māl′) *n.* [lit., black rent < OE. *mal*, lawsuit < ON. *mal*, discussion; infl. by OFr. *maille*, a coin] 1. payment gotten from someone by threatening to reveal information about him that could bring disgrace 2. the crime of forcing such payment —*vt.* 1. to get or try to get blackmail from 2. to force (*into* doing something) as by threats —**black′mail′er** *n.*

black mark an unfavorable item in one's record

black market a place or system for selling goods illegally, esp. in violation of rationing —**black′-mar′ket** *vt.*, *vi.* —**black marketeer (or marketer)**

☆**Black Muslim** a member of a sect practicing Islam in the U.S., made up chiefly of blacks: members of the sect call themselves simply *Muslims* (mooz′limz)

☆**black nationalism** a movement for establishing a separate nation of blacks within the U.S.

black nightshade a poisonous plant with white, star-shaped flowers and black berries

black·out (blak′out′) *n.* 1. a putting out of all stage lights to end a play or scene 2. a putting out or hiding of all lights that might be visible to enemy air raiders at night 3. a temporary loss of electric power in an area 4. a temporary loss of consciousness 5. a loss of memory of an event 6. a holding back of news by censorship

black pepper a hot seasoning made by grinding the whole dried, black berries of the pepper plant

Black·pool (blak′pool′) city in NW England, on the Irish Sea: pop. 148,000

☆**black power** political and economic power sought by black Americans in the struggle for civil rights

☆**black raspberry** a shrub of the rose family, bearing juicy, purple-black fruits

Black Sea sea surrounded by the European U.S.S.R., Asia Minor, & the Balkan Peninsula

black sheep a person regarded as not so respectable as the rest of his family or group

Black Shirt a member of any fascist organization (specif., of the Italian Fascist party) having a black-shirted uniform

black·smith (blak′smith′) *n.* a smith who works in iron, making and fitting horseshoes, etc.

☆**black·snake** (-snāk′) *n.* a slender, harmless, black or dark-colored snake of the U.S.

Black·stone (blak′stōn; *Brit.* -stən), Sir **William** 1723-80; Eng. jurist & writer on law

black·strap molasses (blak′strap′) ☆crude, dark molasses

black tea tea that has been left to ferment and wilt in the air before being dried by heating

black·thorn (-thôrn′) *n.* 1. a thorny shrub with blue-black, plumlike fruit; sloe 2. a walking stick made of its stem

black tie 1. a black bow tie, properly worn with a tuxedo 2. a tuxedo and the proper accessories

black·top (blak′täp′) *n.* a bituminous mixture, usually asphalt, used as a surface for roads, etc. —*vt.* -topped′, -top′ping to cover with blacktop

☆**black walnut** 1. a tall walnut tree of eastern N. America 2. its hard, heavy, dark-brown wood, used in making furniture, etc. 3. its edible, oily nut

☆**black widow** an American spider the female of which has a black body with red markings underneath, and a very poisonous bite: so called because the female sometimes eats its mate

blad·der (blad'ər) *n.* [OE. *blæddre:* for IE. base see BALL[1]] **1.** a bag of membranous tissue in the bodies of many animals, that can expand to receive and hold liquids or gases; esp., the **urinary bladder,** which holds urine flowing from the kidneys **2.** a bag, etc. resembling this [a football *bladder*] **3.** an air sac, as in some water plants —**blad'der·y** *adj.*

blad·der·wort (-wurt') *n.* a plant growing in or near water and having leaves with bladders on them that trap small insects and crustaceans

blade (blād) *n.* [OE. *blæd:* for IE. base see BLOOM] **1.** *a)* the leaf of a plant, esp. of grass *b)* the flat, expanded part of a leaf; lamina **2.** a broad, flat surface, as of an oar **3.** a flat bone [the shoulder *blade*] **4.** the cutting part of a knife, tool, etc. **5.** the metal runner of an ice skate **6.** a sword or a swordsman **7.** a lively, dashing young man **8.** *Phonet.* the flat part of the tongue, behind the tip —*adj.* designating or of various cuts of meat from the shoulder blade section —**blad'ed** *adj.*

☆**blah** (blä) *n., interj.* [Slang] nonsense —*adj.* [Slang] **1.** unappetizing **2.** dull, lifeless, etc.

blain (blān) *n.* [< OE. *blegen:* for IE. base see BALL[1]] an inflamed sore or swollen place; a pustule or blister

Blake (blāk), **William** 1757–1827; Eng. poet & artist

blam·a·ble, blame·a·ble (blām'ə b'l) *adj.* that deserves blame; culpable —**blam'a·bly** *adv.*

blame (blām) *vt.* **blamed, blam'ing** [< OFr. < LL. *blasphemare,* BLASPHEME] **1.** to accuse of being at fault; condemn (*for* something) [don't *blame* others for your own mistakes] **2.** to find fault with; criticize [I can't *blame* you for being angry] **3.** to put the responsibility of (an error, fault, etc. *on*) [they *blamed* the accident on Al] —*n.* **1.** a blaming; condemnation [a letter full of *blame*] **2.** responsibility for a fault or wrong [he accepted the *blame* for the mistake] **3.** [Archaic] fault —see SYN. at CRITICIZE —**be to blame** to deserve blame; be at fault —**blame'ful** *adj.* —**blame'ful·ly** *adv.* —**blame'ful·ness** *n.*

blame·less (blām'lis) *adj.* not deserving to be blamed; not responsible; innocent —**blame'less·ly** *adv.* —**blame'less·ness** *n.*

blame·wor·thy (blām'wur'thē) *adj.* deserving to be blamed — **blame'wor'thi·ness** *n.*

Blanc (blän), **Mont** (mōn) mountain in E France: highest peak in the Alps: 15,781 ft.: see map at SAVOY

blanch (blanch) *vt.* [OFr. *blanchir* < *blanc:* see BLANK] **1.** to make white; bleach **2.** to make pale [celery is *blanched* by covering the growing stalks with soil] **3.** to scald (vegetables, almonds, etc.), as for removing the skins —*vi.* to turn white or pale [he *blanched* at the news] —**blanch'er** *n.*

Blanche, Blanch (blanch) [Fr., lit., white, fem. of *blanc:* see BLANK] a feminine name

blanc·mange (blə mänzh', -mänj') *n.* [Fr. < *blanc,* white + *manger,* to eat] a sweet, molded, jellylike dessert made with starch or gelatin, milk, etc.

bland (bland) *adj.* [< L. *blandus,* mild, prob. < IE. base *mel-:* see MILL[1]] **1.** pleasantly smooth; agreeable; suave [a *bland* manner] **2.** mild and soothing; not sharp, harsh, etc. [*bland* medicine] *b)* tasteless, insipid, dull, etc. [a *bland* movie] —see SYN. at SOFT —**bland'ly** *adv.* —**bland'ness** *n.*

blan·dish (blan'dish) *vt., vi* [< OFr. < L. *blandiri,* to flatter < prec.] to flatter or coax in persuading; cajole

blan·dish·ment (blan'dish mənt) *n.* a flattering or coaxing act or remark, etc. meant to persuade: *usually used in pl.*

blank (blaŋk) *adj.* [OFr. *blanc,* white < Frank.: for IE. base see BLACK] **1.** *a)* not written on; not marked [a *blank* paper] *b)* having empty spaces to be filled in [a *blank* form] **2.** having an empty or vacant look; without interest or expression [his face remained *blank*] **3.** empty of thought [a *blank* mind] **4.** utter; complete [a *blank* denial] **5.** lacking certain elements or characteristics [a *blank* wall has no opening] —*n.* **1.** an empty space, esp. one to be filled out in a printed form **2.** such a printed form [an application *blank*] **3.** an empty place or time; void **4.** a piece of metal, etc. to be finished by stamping or marking **5.** a lottery ticket that fails to win **6.** a powder-filled cartridge without a bullet: in full, **blank cartridge** —*vt.* ☆to keep (an opponent) from scoring in a game —**blank out** to cross out or hide as by covering over —**draw a blank** [Colloq.] **1.** to be unsuccessful in an attempt **2.** to be unable to remember a particular thing —**blank'ly** *adv.* —**blank'ness** *n.*

blank check 1. a check carrying a signature only and allowing the bearer to fill in any amount **2.** permission to use as much money, authority, etc. as one wishes

blan·ket (blaŋ'kit) *n.* [< OFr. dim. of *blanc:* see BLANK] **1.** a large, soft piece of cloth used for warmth, esp. as a bed cover **2.** anything like a blanket [a *blanket* of leaves] —*adj.* ☆covering a group of conditions or items [a *blanket* insurance policy] —*vt.* **1.** to cover, as with a blanket **2.** to apply uniformly to: said of rates **3.** to hinder; obscure [a powerful radio station *blankets* a weaker one]

blank verse unrhymed verse; esp., unrhymed verse having five iambic feet per line, as in Shakespeare's plays

blare (bler) *vt., vi.* **blared, blar'ing** [ME. *bleren,* to bellow: for IE. base see BLEAR] **1.** to sound out with loud, harsh tones [car horns *blared* as traffic stalled] **2.** to exclaim loudly —*n.* **1.** a loud, brassy sound **2.** harsh brilliance or glare

blar·ney (blär'nē) *n.* [see BLARNEY STONE] smooth talk used in flattering or coaxing —*vt., vi.* **-neyed, -ney·ing** to use blarney (on)

Blarney stone a stone in Blarney Castle in the county of Cork, Ireland: it is said that those who kiss it become skilled at using blarney

bla·sé (blä zā', blä'zā) *adj.* [Fr., pp. of *blaser,* to satiate] bored with the pleasures of life; no longer surprised or pleased by experiences

blas·pheme (blas fēm', blas'fēm) *vt.* **-phemed', -phem'ing** [< OFr. < LL. < Gr. *blasphēmein,* to speak evil of] **1.** to speak with disrespect or scorn of or to (God or sacred things) **2.** to curse or abuse —*vi.* to utter blasphemy —**blas·phem'er** *n.*

blas·phe·my (blas'fə mē) *n., pl.* **-mies** [see prec.] words or action showing disrespect or scorn for God or anything held sacred —**blas'phe·mous** *adj.* —**blas'phe·mous·ly** *adv.*

blast (blast) *n.* [< OE. *blæst:* for IE. base see BALL[1]] **1.** a gust of wind; strong rush of air **2.** the sound of a sudden rush of air or gas, as through a trumpet **3.** the steady current of air forced into a blast furnace **4.** a sudden, damaging influence; esp., a sudden blight of a plant **5.** *a)* an explosion, as of dynamite *b)* a charge of explosive causing this ☆**6.** a strong, sudden outburst, as of criticism ☆**7.** [Slang] a gay, hilarious time; esp., a wild party —*vi.* **1.** to make a loud, harsh sound **2.** to set off explosives, gunfire, etc. **3.** to suffer from a blight —*vt.* **1.** to damage or destroy by or as if by a blight; wither **2.** to blow up with an explosive; explode ☆**3.** [Colloq.] to criticize sharply ☆**4.** *Sports* to hit (a ball) with great, driving force —(at) full **blast** at full speed or capacity —☆**blast off** to take off with explosive force and begin its flight, as a rocket or ballistic missile —**blast'er** *n.*

-blast (blast) [< Gr. *blastos,* a sprout] *a combining form meaning* of an embryo [*mesoblast*]

blast·ed (blas'tid) *adj.* **1.** blighted; withered; destroyed **2.** damned; confounded

blast furnace a smelting furnace into which a blast of air is forced from below for intense heat

☆**blast-off, blast-off** (blast'ôf') *n.* the launching of a rocket, space vehicle, etc.

blas·tu·la (blas'choo lə) *n., pl.* **-las, -lae'** (-lē') [ModL. dim. < Gr. *blastos,* a germ, sprout] an embryo at the stage of development in which it consists typically of a single layer of cells around a central cavity —**blas'tu·lar** *adj.*

☆**blat** (blat) *vi.* **blat'ted, blat'ting** [var. of BLEAT] to bleat —*vt.* to blurt out —*n.* a blatting sound

bla·tant (blāt''nt) *adj.* [coined by E. SPENSER, prob. < L. *blaterare,* to babble] **1.** disagreeably loud; noisy **2.** easily recognized or very obvious: said of something unpleasant [such *blatant* ignorance] —**bla'tan·cy** *n., pl.* **-cies** —**bla'tant·ly** *adv.*

blath·er (blath'ər) *n.* [ON. *blathr*] foolish talk —*vi., vt.* to chatter foolishly —**blath'er·er** *n.*

blath·er·skite (-skīt') *n.* a talkative, foolish person

blaze[1] (blāz) *n.* [< OE. *blæse:* for IE. base see BLACK] **1.** a brilliant burst of flame; strongly burning fire **2.** any very bright light or glare [in the *blaze* of the noonday sun] **3.** a sudden, showy outburst [a *blaze* of oratory] **4.** a brightness; vivid display [the garden was a *blaze* of color] —*vi.* **blazed, blaz'ing 1.** to burn rapidly or brightly **2.** to give off a strong light; glare **3.** to burst out with strong feeling [to *blaze* with anger] —**blaze away** to fire a gun rapidly several times

blaze[2] (blāz) *n.* [< ON. *blesi:* for IE. base see BLACK] **1.** a white spot on an animal's face ☆**2.** a mark made on a tree by cutting off a piece of bark, as for marking a trail —☆*vt.* **blazed, blaz'ing** to mark (a tree or trail) with blazes —☆**blaze a way** (or **path,** etc.) **in** to pioneer in (some activity)

blaze[3] (blāz) *vt.* **blazed, blaz'ing** [ME. *blasen,* to blow < OE. or ON.: for IE. base see BALL[1]] to make known publicly

blaz·er (blā'zər) *n.* [< BLAZE[1] + -ER] a lightweight sports jacket, often brightly colored or striped

bla·zon (blā'z'n) *n.* [OFr. *blason,* a shield] **1.** a coat of arms **2.** a description or illustration of a coat of arms **3.** showy display —*vt.* **1.** to make widely known; proclaim (often with *forth, out,* or *abroad*) **2.** to describe or illustrate (coats of arms) **3.** *a*) to portray in colors *b*) to adorn colorfully or showily —**bla'zon·er** *n.* —**bla'zon·ment** *n.* —**bla'zon·ry** *n., pl.* **-ries**

bldg. building

bleach (blēch) *vt., vi.* [OE. *blæcan < blac,* pale: for IE. base see BLACK] to make or become white or colorless by means of chemicals or by exposure to sunlight —*n.* **1.** a bleaching **2.** a substance used for bleaching —**bleach'er** *n.*

☆**bleach·ers** (-ərz) *n.pl.* [< prec., because the spectators are exposed to sunlight] a section of cheaper seats, usually without a roof, for spectators at sporting events

bleaching powder chloride of lime or any other powder used in bleaching

bleak (blēk) *adj.* [< ON. *bleikr,* pale: for IE. base see BLACK] **1.** exposed to wind and cold; unsheltered [the *bleak* plains] **2.** cold; harsh [a *bleak* wind] **3.** not cheerful or hopeful; gloomy [a *bleak* future] —**bleak'ly** *adv.* —**bleak'ness** *n.*

blear (blir) *adj.* [< ME. *bleren,* to have watery eyes < IE. base *bhle-,* to howl, weep, from which also come BLARE & BLEAT] **1.** made dim by tears, mucus, etc.: said of eyes **2.** blurred; dim —*vt.* **1.** to dim (the eyes) with tears, mucus, etc. **2.** to blur

blear·y (blir'ē) *adj.* **blear'i·er, blear'i·est 1.** dim or blurred **2.** having blurred vision —**blear'i·ly** *adv.* —**blear'i·ness** *n.*

blear·y-eyed (-īd') *adj.* having bleary eyes or blurred vision: also **blear'eyed'**

bleat (blēt) *vi.* [< OE. *blætan:* see BLEAR] **1.** to make the cry of a sheep, goat, or calf **2.** to make a sound like this cry —*vt.* to say in a bleating voice —*n.* a bleating cry or sound —**bleat'er** *n.*

bleed (blēd) *vi.* **bled** (bled), **bleed'ing** [< OE. *bledan < blod,* blood] **1.** to lose blood [the wound stopped *bleeding*] **2.** to suffer wounds or die in a battle or cause [he *bled* for his country] **3.** to feel pain, grief, or sympathy; suffer [her heart *bleeds* for the poor] **4.** to ooze sap, juice, etc., as bruised plants **5.** to run together, as dyes in wet cloth —*vt.* **1.** to draw blood from [doctors formerly *bled* patients] **2.** to empty of liquid, air, or gas [to *bleed* a tire] ☆**3.** to take sap or juice from **4.** [Colloq.] to extort money from, as by blackmail

bleed·er (-ər) *n.* a person who bleeds readily; hemophiliac

bleeding heart 1. a plant with fernlike leaves and drooping clusters of pink, heart-shaped flowers **2.** a person regarded as too sentimental or too liberal in his approach to social problems

bleep (blēp) *n., vi.* [echoic] *same as* BEEP —*vt.* to censor (something said), as in a telecast, by substituting a beep

blem·ish (blem'ish) *vt.* [< OFr. *blesmir,* to injure, akin to BLAZE[2]] to mar, as by some flaw or fault —*n.* **1.** a mark that mars the appearance, as a stain or nick **2.** any flaw or shortcoming [a *blemish* in his character] —see SYN. at DEFECT

blench[1] (blench) *vt., vi.* [var. of BLANCH] to make or become pale; whiten

blench[2] (blench) *vi.* [< OE. *blencan,* to deceive, ult. < IE. base of BLACK] to shrink back, as in fear; flinch

blend (blend) *vt.* **blend'ed** or **blent, blend'ing** [< OE. *blendan* & ON. *blanda,* to mix < IE. base *bhlendh-,* to glimmer dimly, from which also come BLIND & BLUNDER] **1.** to mix or mingle (varieties of tea, tobacco, etc.) **2.** to mix or fuse thoroughly, so the parts are no longer distinct [to *blend* paints on a palette] —*vi.* **1.** to mix or merge **2.** to shade gradually into each other, as colors **3.** to go well together; harmonize [a tie that *blends* with a suit] —*n.* **1.** a blending **2.** a mixture of varieties [a *blend* of coffee] ☆**3.** a word formed by combining parts of other words ["smog" is a *blend* of "smoke" and "fog"] —see SYN. at MIX —**blend'er** *n.*

blende (blend) *n.* [G. < *blenden,* to blind, deceive: so named because it falsely seems to contain lead] sphalerite or any of certain other sulfides

☆**blended whiskey** whiskey that is a blend of straight whiskey and neutral spirits or of two or more straight whiskeys

blen·ny (blen'ē) *n., pl.* **-nies, -ny:** see PLURAL, II, D, l [< L. < Gr. < *blenna,* slime] any of a number of small ocean fishes hav-

ing a tapering body covered with a slimy substance —**blen'ni·old'** (-ē oid') *adj.*

Blér·i·ot (bler'ē ō'; *Fr.* blā ryō'), **Louis** 1872–1936; *Fr.* designer of airplanes & pioneer in aviation

bless (bles) *vt.* **blessed** or **blest, bless'ing** [< OE. *bletsian,* orig. to consecrate with blood < *blod,* blood] **1.** to make or call holy; hallow **2.** to ask God's favor for [the minister *blessed* the congregation] **3.** to favor or endow (*with*) [blessed with health] **4.** to make happy or prosperous [God *bless* you!] **5.** to praise or glorify [to *bless* the Lord] **6.** to make the sign of the cross over **7.** to protect from evil, harm, etc. —**bless me** (or **you, him,** etc.)! an exclamation of surprise, dismay, etc.

bless·ed (bles'id; *occas.* blest) *adj.* **1.** holy; sacred **2.** blissful; fortunate **3.** of or in eternal bliss: a title applied to one who has been beatified **4.** bringing joy —**bless'ed·ly** *adv.* —**bless'ed·ness** *n.*

bless·ing (bles'iŋ) *n.* **1.** a prayer asking God's favor **2.** a grace said before or after eating **3.** the gift of divine favor **4.** good wishes or approval **5.** anything that brings joy or comfort [it's a *blessing* that she can live with them]

blest (blest) *alt. pt. & pp. of* BLESS —*adj.* blessed

bleth·er (bleth'ər) *n., vi., vt. same as* BLATHER

bleu cheese (blōō; *Fr.* blö) [Fr. *bleu,* blue] *same as* BLUE CHEESE

blew (blōō) *pt. of* BLOW[1] & BLOW[3]

blight (blīt) *n.* [? < ON. *blikja,* turn pale] **1.** any parasite, insect, etc. that destroys or stunts plants **2.** any of several plant diseases, as mildew **3.** anything that destroys, prevents growth, etc. [slums are a *blight* on a city] —*vt.* **1.** to wither **2.** to destroy or ruin [to *blight* someone's hopes] **3.** to frustrate —*vi.* to suffer blight

blimp (blimp) *n.* [echoic: from the sound made by thumping the airship bag] [Colloq.] a small, nonrigid or semirigid airship

blind (blīnd) *adj.* [OE.: see BLEND] **1.** without the power of sight; sightless **2.** of or for sightless persons **3.** not able or willing to notice or understand [I was *blind* to her faults] **4.** done without adequate directions or knowledge [a *blind* search] **5.** disregarding evidence, sound logic, etc. [*blind* faith] **6.** reckless; unreasonable [*blind* fury] **7.** hard to see; hidden [a *blind* driveway] **8.** closed at one end [a *blind* alley] **9.** not controlled by intelligence [*blind* destiny] **10.** *Aeron.* by the use of instruments only [*blind* flying] **11.** *Archit.* having no opening [a *blind* wall] —*vt.* **1.** to make sightless **2.** to dazzle [blinded by the oncoming headlights] **3.** to make unable to understand or judge well [his eagerness *blinded* him to the danger] —*n.* **1.** anything that hinders sight **2.** *a*) anything that keeps out light, as a window shade *b*) *same as* VENETIAN BLIND ☆**3.** a place of concealment [a *blind* from which to hunt ducks] **4.** a person or thing used to mislead; decoy —*adv.* **1.** blindly **2.** recklessly **3.** sight unseen [to buy a thing *blind*] —**the blind** blind people —**blind'ly** *adv.* —**blind'ness** *n.*

☆**blind date** [Colloq.] **1.** a social engagement arranged for a man and a woman who are strangers to each other **2.** either of these persons

blind·er (blīn'dər) *n.* either of two flaps on a horse's bridle that shut out the side view

blind·fold (blīnd'fōld') *vt.* [altered (after FOLD[1]) < ME. *blindfeld,* struck blind: see BLIND & FELL[2]] to cover the eyes of, as with a cloth —*n.* something used to cover the eyes —*adj.* **1.** with the eyes covered **2.** reckless

blind·man's buff (blīnd'manz buf') [buff, contr. < BUFFET[1]] a game in which a blindfolded player has to catch another player and tell who it is: also **blind'man's bluff'**

blind spot 1. the small area, insensitive to light, in the retina of the eye where the optic nerve enters: see illustration at EYE **2.** an area where vision is blocked **3.** a prejudice, or area of ignorance, that one has but is not aware of

BLINDERS

blind trust an arrangement by which a person, esp. a public official, tries to avoid a conflict of interest by putting certain personal assets under the control of an independent trustee, who manages them without letting the owner know the details of their management

blind·worm (blīnd'wurm') *n.* a lizard without legs, having a snakelike body and very small eyes

blink (bliŋk) *vi.* [ME. *blenken* (see BLENCH[2])] **1.** to wink quickly one or more times **2.** to flash on and off **3.** to look with half-shut, winking eyes —*vt.* to cause (eyes, light, etc.)

to wink or blink —*n.* **1.** a blinking **2.** a brief flash of light; glimmer —see SYN. at WINK —**blink at** to ignore or overlook (a mistake) —☆**on the blink** [Slang] not working right; out of order

blink·er (-ər) *n.* ☆**1.** a flashing warning light at crossings **2.** *same as* BLINDER

☆**blintz** (blints) *n.* [< Yid. < Russ. < *blin*, pancake] a thin pancake rolled with a filling of cottage cheese, etc.

blip (blip) *n.* [echoic of a brief sound] **1.** an image on an oscilloscope, as in a radar set **2.** a quick, sharp sound —*vt.* **blipped, blip′ping** *same as* BLEEP

bliss (blis) *n.* [OE. *bliths* < *blithe*, BLITHE] **1.** great joy or happiness **2.** spiritual joy —see SYN. at ECSTASY —**bliss′ful** *adj.* —**bliss′ful·ly** *adv.* —**bliss′ful·ness n.**

blis·ter (blis′tər) *n.* [< Du. *bluister* or OFr. *blestre* < ON. *blastr*: for IE. base see BALL¹] **1.** a raised patch of skin filled with watery matter and caused by burning or rubbing **2.** anything like a blister, as an air bubble on a painted surface —*vt.* **1.** to raise blisters on **2.** to attack strongly with words —*vi.* to form blisters —**blis′ter·y** *adj.*

blister beetle any of various small beetles whose dried and ground bodies were once used in medicine to form blisters on the skin

blithe (blīth, blith) *adj.* [OE.] gay; cheerful; carefree —**blithe′ly** *adv.* —**blithe′ness n.**

blith·er·ing (blith′ər iŋ) *adj.* [*blither*, var. of BLATHER] talking without sense; jabbering

blithe·some (blīth′səm, blith′-) *adj.* blithe; gay —**blithe′some·ly** *adv.* —**blithe′some·ness n.**

B.Litt., B.Lit. [L. *Baccalaureus Lit(t)erarum*] Bachelor of Letters (or Literature)

blitz (blits) *n.* [< BLITZKRIEG] a sudden, overwhelming attack —*vt.* to subject to a blitz; overwhelm

blitz·krieg (blits′krēg′) *n.* [G. < *blitz*, lightning + *krieg*, war] **1.** sudden, swift offensive warfare intended to win a quick victory **2.** any sudden, overwhelming attack

☆**bliz·zard** (bliz′ərd) *n.* [dial. *bliz*, violent blow (? akin to G. *blitz*, lightning) + -ARD] a violent storm with driving snow and very cold winds

blk. 1. black **2.** block **3.** bulk

bloat¹ (blōt) *adj.* [< ON. *blautr*, soaked, ult. < base of BALL¹] bloated; puffed up —*vt., vi.* **1.** to swell, as with water or air **2.** to puff up, as with pride —*n.* ☆a bloated person or thing

bloat² (blōt) *vt.* [< ME. *blote*, soft with moisture < ON. *blautr*: see prec.] to preserve (herring, etc.) by soaking in salt water and smoking

bloat·er (blōt′ər) *n.* a fat herring or mackerel that has been bloated

blob (bläb) *n.* [echoic] **1.** a small lump of something soft and moist [a *blob* of oatmeal] **2.** something of indefinite form [a *blob* of paint on a canvas] —*vt.* **blobbed, blob′bing** to splash or mark, as with blobs

bloc (bläk) *n.* [Fr. & OFr. < LowG. *block*, log] a group of legislators from different parties, or a group of nations, acting together in some common cause

Bloch (bläk; *G.* blôkh), **Ernest** 1880-1959; U.S. composer, born in Switzerland

block (bläk) *n.* [< MDu. or OFr. < LowG. *block:* see BLOC] **1.** any large, solid piece of wood, stone, or metal, often with flat surfaces **2.** a block-like stand on which chopping, etc. is done [a butcher's *block*] ☆**3.** an auctioneer's platform **4.** a mold upon which hats, etc. are shaped **5.** an obstruction or hindrance **6.** an interruption of a normal body function [a nerve *block*] **7.** a pulley in a frame **8.** a large, hollow building brick **9.** a child's wooden or plastic toy brick ☆**10.** a group of buildings ☆**11.** *a*) a city square *b*) one side of a city square **12.** any number of things regarded as a unit [a *block* of tickets] **13.** [Slang] a person's head **14.** *Printing* a piece of engraved wood, etc. with a design or picture **15.** *Psychiatry* a sudden interruption in speech or thought because of a deep emotional problem ☆**16.** *Sports* a legal hindering of an opponent's play or movement —*vt.* **1.** to hinder passage or progress in; obstruct [grease *blocked* the drain] **2.**

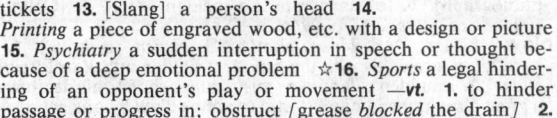

BLOCKS
(sense 7)

to stand in the way of [you're *blocking* my vision] **3.** to shape or mold on a block [to *block* a hat] **4.** to strengthen or support with blocks **5.** to sketch with little detail (often with *out*) **6.** *Med.* to deaden (a nerve), esp. by anesthesia **7.** *Sports* to hinder (an opponent or his play) —*vi.* to have a mental block (*on*) —see SYN. at HINDER¹ —☆**on the block** up for sale or auction —**block′age n.** —**block′er n.**

block·ade (blä kād′) *n.* [BLOCK + -ADE] **1.** a shutting off of a port or region by enemy troops or ships to prevent persons or supplies from moving in or out **2.** the troops or ships so used **3.** any barrier or obstacle —*vt.* -**ad′ed, -ad′ing** to put under a blockade —☆**run the blockade** to go through a blockade —**block·ad′er n.**

☆**blockade runner** a ship or person that tries to go through or past a blockade

block and tackle pulley blocks and ropes or cables, used for lifting or pulling large, heavy objects

block·bust·er (bläk′bus′tər) *n.* [Colloq.] **1.** a large, highly destructive aerial bomb ☆**2.** an expensive movie, novel, etc. that is intended to be widely popular

☆**block·bust·ing** (-bus′tiŋ) *n.* [Colloq.] the practice of causing the quick sale of homes by creating fear about a minority group moving into the neighborhood

block·head (-hed′) *n.* a stupid person

block·house (-hous′) *n.* **1.** formerly, a strong wooden fort with a projecting second story and openings in the walls to shoot from ☆**2.** any building of squared timber or logs **3.** *Mil.* a small structure of concrete for defense or from which to observe bomb tests, missile launchings, etc.

BLOCKHOUSE

block·ish (-ish) *adj.* stupid; dull —**block′ish·ly** *adv.*

block·y (bläk′ē) *adj.* **block′i·er, block′i·est 1.** having contrasting blocks, as of light and shade **2.** stocky; chunky —**block′i·ness n.**

Bloem·fon·tein (blōōm′fän tān′) city in C South Africa: pop. 146,000

bloke (blōk) *n.* [< ?] [Chiefly Brit. Slang] a fellow; chap

blond (bländ) *adj.* [Fr. < ? Gmc.] **1.** having yellow or yellowish-brown hair, often with fair skin and blue or gray eyes **2.** yellow or yellowish-brown: said of hair **3.** light-colored [*blond* furniture] —*n.* a blond person —**blond′ness n.**

blonde (bländ) *adj. same as* BLOND —*n.* a blond woman or girl

blood (blud) *n.* [< OE. *blod*] **1.** *a*) the fluid, usually red, circulating in the heart, arteries, and veins of vertebrates: it carries oxygen and cell-building material to the body tissues and carbon dioxide and waste matter away from them *b*) a similar fluid in invertebrates **2.** the spilling of blood; murder **3.** the essence of life; lifeblood **4.** the sap of a plant **5.** passion, temperament, or disposition [it made my *blood* boil] **6.** parental heritage; family line; lineage [fighting is in his *blood*] **7.** kinship; family relationship: from the false idea that the blood of related persons has some factor in common **8.** descent from nobility **9.** a descent from purebred stock **10.** a dandy [a young *blood*] **11.** people, esp. youthful people [new *blood* in the firm] —**bad blood** anger; hatred —**in cold blood 1.** with cruelty; unfeelingly **2.** on purpose, but without strong feeling —**make one's blood run cold** to terrify one

☆**blood bank 1.** a place where whole blood or plasma is stored for future use in transfusion **2.** any reserve of such blood

blood bath a massacre; slaughter

blood brother 1. a brother by birth **2.** a person bound to one by the ceremony of mixing together some of his blood with one's own —**blood brotherhood**

blood count the number of red corpuscles and white corpuscles in a given volume of blood

blood·cur·dling (-kurd′liŋ) *adj.* very frightening; causing terror or horror [a *bloodcurdling* sight]

blood·ed (blud′id) *adj.* **1.** having (a specified kind of) blood [hot-*blooded*] ☆**2.** of fine stock or breed [a *blooded* horse]

blood group any of several groups into which human blood is classified

blood·hound (-hound′) *n.* any of a breed of large dogs with a keen sense of smell, used in tracking fugitives, etc.

blood·less (blud′ləs) *adj.* 1. without blood 2. without bloodshed or killing [a *bloodless* revolution] 3. anemic or pale [his *bloodless* lips] 4. having little energy or vitality [*bloodless* writing] — **blood′less·ly** *adv.* — **blood′less·ness** *n.*

blood·let·ting (-let′iŋ) *n.* 1. the opening of a vein to remove blood; bleeding 2. *same as* BLOODSHED

☆**blood·mo·bile** (-mō bēl′, -mə-) *n.* [BLOOD + (AUTO)MOBILE] a traveling van with equipment for collecting blood from donors for blood banks

blood money 1. money paid to a hired killer 2. money paid to make up for a murder 3. money gotten ruthlessly through others' suffering

blood poisoning any of various diseases in which the blood contains microorganisms, their toxins, or other poisonous matter; septicemia

blood pressure the pressure of the blood against the inner walls of the arteries and other blood vessels: it varies with age, physical condition, etc.

blood pudding a large sausage made of pig's blood and suet, enclosed in a casing

blood·root (-root′, -root′) *n.* ☆a N. American wildflower of the poppy family, with a white flower and a rootstock that yields a red juice

blood·shed (-shed′) *n.* the shedding of blood; killing

blood·shot (-shät′) *adj.* red because the small blood vessels are swollen or broken: said of an eye

blood·stained (-stānd′) *adj.* 1. soiled or discolored with blood 2. guilty of murder

blood·stone (-stōn′) *n.* a dark-green variety of quartz spotted with red jasper, used as a gem

blood·stream (-strēm′) *n.* the blood flowing through the circulatory system of a body

blood·suck·er (-suk′ər) *n.* 1. an animal that sucks blood, esp. a leech 2. a person who ruthlessly takes from others all that he can —**blood′suck′ing** *adj., n.*

blood test an examination of a sample of a person's blood, as in order to classify it or to check for disease

blood·thirst·y (-thur′stē) *adj.* eager to kill; murderous; cruel —**blood′thirst′i·ly** *adv.* —**blood′thirst′i·ness** *n.*

blood type *same as* BLOOD GROUP

blood typing the classification of blood in finding the right types for transfusions

blood vessel a tube through which the blood circulates in the body; artery, vein, or capillary

blood·worm (blud′wurm′) *n.* any of various small, red annelid worms

blood·y (blud′ē) *adj.* **blood′i·er, blood′i·est** 1. of, like, or containing blood 2. covered or stained with blood [a *bloody* shirt] 3. involving bloodshed [a *bloody* fight] 4. bloodthirsty; cruel 5. [Brit. Slang] cursed; damned: not used in polite talk —*adv.* [Brit. Slang] very [he's not *bloody* likely to go]: not used in polite talk —*vt.* **blood′ied, blood′y·ing** to cover or stain with blood —**blood′i·ly** *adv.* —**blood′i·ness** *n.*

Bloody Mary ☆a drink of vodka with tomato juice

bloom (bloom) *n.* [< ON. *blomi,* flowers < IE. base *bhlo-* < *bhel-,* to spring up, sprout] 1. a flower; blossom 2. flowers collectively [the *bloom* of a plant] 3. the state or time of flowering [when lilacs are in *bloom*] 4. the state or time of most health, vigor, etc. 5. a youthful, healthy glow, as of the cheeks 6. *a*) the powdery coating on some fruits or leaves *b*) a similar coating, as on new coins —*vi.* 1. to bear flowers; blossom 2. to be at one's best, as in health, vigor, beauty, etc. 3. to glow as with health —**bloom′ing** *adj.*

bloom·er[1] (bloom′ər) *n.* 1. a plant in the way it blooms [an early *bloomer*] 2. a person when he is at his best

☆**bloom·er**[2] (bloom′ər) *n.* [after Amelia J. *Bloomer* (1818–94), U.S. feminist who was in favor of such a costume] 1. formerly, a woman's costume consisting of a short skirt and loose trousers gathered at the ankles 2. [*pl.*] *a*) baggy trousers gathered at the knee, formerly worn by women for athletics *b*) an undergarment somewhat like this

Bloom·ing·ton (bloom′miŋ tən) [? from the many flowering plants orig. found there] city in E Minn., near Minneapolis: pop. 82,000

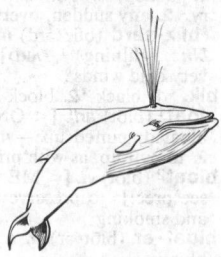
BLOODHOUND
(to 27 in. high at shoulder)

☆**bloop** (bloop) *vt.* [Slang] *Baseball* 1. to hit (a ball) as a blooper 2. to get (a hit) in this way

☆**bloop·er** (bloop′ər) *n.* [echoic of a vulgar noise] [Slang] 1. a stupid or foolish mistake; blunder 2. *Baseball* a ball batted so that it drops between the infield and outfield, usually for a hit

blos·som (bläs′əm) *n.* [< OE. *blostma:* for IE. base see BLOOM] 1. a flower or bloom, esp. of a fruit-bearing plant 2. a state or time of flowering [when cherries are in *blossom*] —*vi.* 1. to have or open into blossoms; bloom 2. to begin to thrive or develop [she's *blossoming* into a lovely woman] —**blos′som·y** *adj.*

blot (blät) *n.* [< ?] 1. a spot or stain, esp. of ink 2. anything that spoils or mars something [that shack is a *blot* on the landscape] 3. a moral stain; disgrace [a *blot* on his reputation] —*vt.* **blot′ted, blot′ting** 1. to make blots on; spot; stain 2. to erase or get rid of [memories *blotted* from one's mind] 3. to dry by soaking up the wet liquid, as with blotting paper —*vi.* 1. to make blots 2. to become blotted 3. to be absorbent — **blot out** 1. to darken or hide entirely 2. to kill or destroy

blotch (bläch) *n.* [? < BLOT] 1. a discolored patch or blemish on the skin 2. any large blot or stain —*vt.* to mark with blotches —**blotch′y** *adj.* **blotch′i·er, blotch′i·est**

blot·ter (blät′ər) *n.* 1. a piece of blotting paper ☆2. a book for recording events as they occur [a police *blotter* is a record of arrests, etc.]

blotting paper a thick, soft, absorbent paper used to dry a surface freshly written on by soaking up the ink

blouse (blous, blouz) *n.* [Fr., workman's or peasant's smock < ? Pr. (*lano*) *blouso,* short (wool)] 1. a loose, shirtlike garment extending to the waist, worn by women and children 2. the coat or jacket of a military uniform 3. a sailor's jumper —*vi., vt.* **bloused, blous′ing** to gather in and drape at the waist

blow[1] (blō) *vi.* **blew, blown, blow′ing** [< OE. *blawan:* for IE. base see BALL[1]] 1. to move with some force: said of the wind 2. to send forth air, as with the mouth [he *blew* on the soup to cool it] 3. to pant; be breathless 4. to make sound by blowing or being blown [the noon whistle is *blowing*] 5. to spout water and air, as whales do 6. to be carried by the wind [the paper *blew* away] 7. to be stormy 8. to burst suddenly, as a tire, or melt, as a fuse (often with *out*) 9. to lay eggs: said of flies 10. [Colloq.] to brag; boast ☆11. [Slang] to go away —*vt.* 1. to force air from (a bellows, etc.) 2. to send out (breath, etc.) from the mouth 3. to force air onto, into, or through 4. to drive by blowing [the fan *blew* the paper out the window] 5. *a*) to sound (a wind instrument) by blowing; hence, ☆[Slang] to play (any musical instrument) *b*) to make (a sound or signal) by blowing 6. to shape or form by blown air or gas [to *blow* bubbles] 7. to clear by blowing through [to *blow* one's nose] 8. to burst by an explosion [to *blow* a tire] 9. to cause (a horse) to pant 10. to melt (a fuse, etc.) 11. [Colloq.] *a*) to spend (money) freely or wastefully; squander *b*) to treat (to something) [they *blew* me to a movie] ☆12. [Colloq.] to forget (one's lines) in a show ☆13. [Slang] to go away from [he *blew* town] ☆14. [Slang] to bungle and fail in [we had our chance and *blew* it] —*n.* 1. a blowing 2. a blast of air 3. a strong wind; gale —**blow hot and cold** to be favorable toward and then opposed to; vacillate —☆**blow in** [Slang] to arrive —☆**blow one's stack** (or **top** or **lid**) [Slang] to lose one's temper —**blow out** 1. to put out or be put out by blowing [to *blow out* a candle] 2. to blow (*vi.* 8) 3. to dispel (itself) after a time: said of a storm —**blow over** 1. to move away, as rain clouds 2. to be forgotten —**blow up** 1. to fill with air or gas 2. to explode 3. to arise and become intense, as a storm 4. to enlarge (a photograph) 5. to exaggerate (an incident, etc.) 6. [Colloq.] to lose one's temper —**blow′er** *n.*

blow[2] (blō) *n.* [ME. *blowe,* akin to G. *bleuen,* to strike] 1. a hard hit or stroke, as with the fist 2. a sudden attack or forcible effort 3. a sudden calamity or misfortune; shock [his death was a great *blow* to the family] —**at a** (or **one**) **blow** by one action —**come to blows** to begin fighting

blow[3] (blō) *vi.* **blew, blown, blow′ing** [OE. *blowan:* for IE. base see BLOOM] [Poet.] to bloom; blossom —*n.* 1. a mass of blossoms 2. any splendid display

WHALE BLOWING

☆**blow·by** (blō′bī′) *adj.* designating or of a crankcase device that returns unburned gases to the engine for combustion so as to reduce air pollution

blow-by-blow (-bī′blō′) *adj.* told in great detail *[a blow-by-blow description]*

blow-dry (-drī′) *vt.* **-dried**′, **-dry′ing** to dry (wet hair) with an electric device (**blow′-dry′er**) that sends out a stream of heated air —*n.* the act of blow-drying the hair

☆**blow·fish** (-fish′) *n., pl.* **-fish**′, **-fish′es**: see FISH same as PUFFER (sense 2)

blow·fly (-flī′) *n., pl.* **-flies**′ [BLOW[1] (*vi.* 9) + FLY[2]] any of various flies that deposit eggs or larvae in meat, wounds, etc.

☆**blow·gun** (-gun′) *n.* a long, tubelike weapon through which darts or pellets are blown

☆**blow·hard** (-härd′) *n.* [Slang] a loudly boastful person

blow·hole (-hōl′) *n.* **1.** a nostril in the top of the head of whales, etc., used for breathing **2.** a hole through which gas or air can escape **3.** a hole in ice to which seals, etc. come for air

blown (blōn) *pp. of* BLOW[1] & BLOW[3] —*adj.* **1.** swollen or bloated **2.** out of breath, as from exertion **3.** made by blowing or by using a blowpipe, etc.

blow·out (blō′out′) *n.* **1.** the bursting of a tire **2.** the melting of an electric fuse **3.** [Slang] a party, celebration, etc.

blow·pipe (-pīp′) *n.* **1.** a tube for forcing air or gas into a flame to increase its heat **2.** a metal tube used in blowing glass **3.** *same as* BLOWGUN

☆**blow·torch** (-tôrch′) *n.* a small gasoline torch that shoots out a flame made hotter by a blast of air: used to melt metal, remove old paint, etc.

blow·up (-up′) *n.* **1.** an explosion **2.** an enlarged photograph **3.** [Colloq.] an angry or hysterical outburst

blow·y (blō′ē) *adj.* **blow′i·er, blow′i·est** windy

blowz·y (blou′zē) *adj.* **blowz′i·er, blowz′i·est** [< obs. *blouze*, wench] **1.** fat, ruddy, and coarse-looking **2.** slovenly; sloppy Also **blows′y**

bls. 1. bales **2.** barrels

B.L.S. Bachelor of Library Science

blub·ber[1] (blub′ər) *n.* [ME. *blober*, a bubble; prob. echoic] **1.** the fat of the whale and other sea mammals **2.** unsightly fat on the human body

blub·ber[2] (blub′ər) *vi.* [ME. *bloberen*, to bubble (see prec.)] to weep loudly, like a child —*vt.* to say while blubbering —*n.* loud weeping —*adj.* thick or swollen *[blubber* lips] —**blub′ber·er** *n.*

blub·ber·y (blub′ər ē) *adj.* **1.** of, full of, or like blubber **2.** swollen, as by blubbering

blu·cher (blōō′chər, -kər) *n.* [after G. L. von *Blücher* (1742-1819), Prussian field marshal] a kind of shoe in which the upper laps over the vamp, which is of one piece with the tongue

bludg·eon (bluj′n) *n.* [? altered < MFr. dim. of *bouge*, a club] a short club with a thick, heavy, or loaded end —*vt., vi.* **1.** to strike with or as with a bludgeon **2.** to bully or threaten

BLUCHER

blue (blōō) *adj.* [< OFr. *bleu* < Frank. *blao*, ult. < base of BLACK] **1.** having the color of the clear sky or the deep sea **2.** livid: said of the skin *[she turned blue* with cold] **3.** sad and gloomy; depressed or depressing **4.** puritanical; rigorous: see BLUE LAW **5.** [Colloq.] indecent; risqué *[a blue* joke] —*n.* **1.** the color of the clear sky or the deep sea **2.** any blue pigment or dye **3.** anything colored blue **4.** *a)* [*often* B-] one who wears a blue uniform *b)* [*pl.*] a sailor's blue uniform ☆**5.** [*pl.*] [Colloq.] a depressed, unhappy feeling (with *the*) ☆**6.** [*pl., also with sing. v.*] *a)* Negro folk music, or the jazz that grew from it, with minor harmonies, slow tempo, and melancholy words (often with *the*) *b)* a song in this style —*vt.* **blued, blu′ing** or **blue′ing 1.** to make blue **2.** to use bluing on or in —**once in a blue moon** very seldom —**out of the blue** as if from the sky; unexpected —**the blue 1.** the sky **2.** the sea —**blue′ness** *n.*

☆**blue baby** a baby born with cyanosis, as from a heart defect

Blue·beard (blōō′bird′) a character in an old legend who marries and murders one wife after another

blue·bell (-bel′) *n.* any of various plants with blue, bell-shaped flowers

blue·ber·ry (-ber′ē, -bər ē) *n., pl.* **-ries** ☆**1.** a shrub bearing small, edible, blue-black berries with tiny seeds ☆**2.** any of the berries

blue·bird (-burd′) *n.* ☆any of several small N. American songbirds: the male has a blue or bluish back and an orange or reddish breast

blue blood 1. the fact of being descended from nobles or royalty **2.** a person of such descent; aristocrat: also **blue′blood**′ *n.* —**blue′blood′ed** *adj.*

blue·bon·net (-bän′it) *n.* ☆**1.** a wildflower with blue blossoms, common in the southwestern U.S. **2.** [Chiefly Scot.] a cornflower with blue blossoms Also **blue bonnet**

blue book ☆**1.** a book listing socially prominent people ☆**2.** a blank booklet with a blue cover in which students write examination answers: also **blue′book**′ *n.*

blue·bot·tle (-bät′'l) *n.* **1.** any of several plants with blue, bottle-shaped flowers, as the cornflower, grape hyacinth, etc. **2.** a large blowfly with a steel-blue abdomen and a hairy body

blue cheese a cheese similar to Roquefort, but usually made of cow's milk

☆**blue-chip** (-chip′) *adj.* [after the high-value *blue chips* of poker] **1.** designating a high-priced stock that has a good record of earnings and keeps growing in value **2.** [Colloq.] excellent, valuable, etc.

blue·coat (-kōt′) *n.* ☆a policeman

☆**blue-col·lar** (-käl′ər) *adj.* [from the color of many work shirts] designating or of industrial workers, esp. those who are semiskilled or unskilled

☆**Blue Cross** a nonprofit health-insurance organization offering hospitalization, etc. to subscribers

☆**blue·fish** (-fish′) *n., pl.* **-fish**′, **-fish′es**: see FISH a bluish food fish, common along the Atlantic coast of N. America

blue flag ☆any iris with blue flowers

blue fox 1. an arctic fox that is a mutation, having a bluish or smoky-gray fur **2.** this fur

☆**blue·gill** (-gil′) *n.* a bluish, freshwater sunfish

☆**blue·grass** (-gras′) *n.* **1.** any of various forage grasses, as Kentucky bluegrass **2.** [*often* B-] Southern folk music played by string bands

blue-green algae (blōō′grēn′) any of various algae that contain a blue pigment that hides the chlorophyll

blue gum a large Australian tree, much grown in California, with aromatic leaves and a smooth bark that peels off in strips

blue·ing (-iŋ) *n. same as* BLUING

blue·ish (-ish) *adj. same as* BLUISH

blue·jack·et (-jak′it) *n.* an enlisted man in the U.S. or British navy

☆**blue jay** a noisy, often crested, American bird with a bluish upper part: also **blue′jay**′ *n.*

☆**blue law** a strict, puritanical law, esp. one that forbids dancing, sports, business, etc. on Sunday

blue·nose (-nōz′) *n.* ☆[Colloq.] a puritanical person

blue-pen·cil (-pen′s'l) *vt.* **-ciled** or **-cilled**, **-cil·ing** or **-cil·ling** to edit, cross out, etc. with or as with a blue pencil

☆**blue-plate special** (blōō′plāt′) an inexpensive restaurant meal served at a fixed price, orig. on a blue plate with compartments

☆**blue point** [< *Blue Point*, Long Island] a small oyster, usually eaten raw

blue·print (-print′) *n.* **1.** a photographic reproduction in white on a blue background, as of architectural plans **2.** any exact or detailed plan or outline —*vt.* to make a blueprint of

☆**blue racer** a long, blue-green N. American blacksnake, that can move very fast

blue-rib·bon (-rib′ən) *adj.* [Colloq.] **1.** outstanding of its kind ☆**2.** specially selected *[a blue-ribbon* jury]

blue ribbon first prize in a competition

Blue Ridge Mountains easternmost range of the Appalachians, extending from S Pa. to N Ga.

☆**blue-sky law** (blōō′skī′) [< the charge that some business groups were trying to "capitalize the blue skies"] a law to prevent fraud in the sale of stocks and bonds

BLUE JAY
(to 12 in. long)

blue·stock·ing (-stäk'iŋ) *n.* [from the informal blue stockings worn at literary meetings in 18th-c. London] a woman who has great interest in books and learning

☆**blue streak** [Colloq.] anything fast or vivid as a streak of lightning —**talk a blue streak** to talk much and fast

blu·et (blōō'it) *n.* [< Fr. dim. of *bleu*, blue] a small plant having little, pale-blue flowers

blue whale a whalebone whale with a dark blue-gray body: the largest animal that has ever lived

☆**bluff**[1] (bluf) *vt.*, *vi.* [prob. < Du. *bluffen*, to baffle] **1.** to mislead by falsely acting bold and confident **2.** to frighten or become frightened by threats that cannot be carried out **3.** to manage to get (one's way) by bluffing —*n.* **1.** a bluffing **2.** a person who bluffs —see **SYN.** at BLUNT —**bluff'er** *n.*

bluff[2] (bluf) *adj.* [< Du. *blaf*, flat] **1.** having a broad, flat front that slopes steeply [*bluff* river banks] **2.** rough and frank, but friendly —☆*n.* a high, steep bank or cliff —**bluff'ly** *adv.*

☆**blu·ing** (blōō'iŋ) *n.* a blue liquid, powder, etc. put in the rinse water of white fabrics to keep them from turning yellow

blu·ish (blōō'ish) *adj.* somewhat blue

blun·der (blun'dər) *vi.* [< ON. *blunda*, to shut the eyes: for IE. base see BLEND] **1.** to move clumsily or carelessly; flounder; stumble **2.** to make a foolish mistake —*vt.* to say stupidly or confusedly; blurt (*out*) —*n.* a foolish mistake —see **SYN.** at ERROR —**blun'der·er** *n.* —**blun'der·ing·ly** *adv.*

blun·der·buss (-bus') *n.* [Du. *donderbus*, thunder box: altered after prec.] **1.** an obsolete short gun with a broad muzzle, accurate only at close range **2.** a person who blunders

blunt (blunt) *adj.* [< ?] **1.** slow to feel or understand; dull **2.** having a dull edge or point **3.** plain-spoken and abrupt —*vt.* **1.** to make (a point or edge) dull **2.** to make less sensitive [wealth *blunted* her awareness of others' needs] **3.** to make less effective [to *blunt* an attack] —*vi.* to become dull —**blunt'ly** *adv.* —**blunt'ness** *n.*

SYN. —**blunt** implies a tactless honesty that does not spare the feelings of others ["I don't like you" was his *blunt* reply]; **bluff** suggests the good-natured frankness of one who is friendly but somewhat crude; **brusque** suggests the brisk abruptness of one who is more interested in speed and efficiency than in formal politeness [the secretary's *brusque* reply]; **curt** implies harsh abruptness that is almost rudeness and may suggest deliberate unkindness [her *curt* dismissal of my plea for help]; **gruff** indicates a rough, bad-tempered manner and often suggests also a harsh, hoarse tone of voice —see also **SYN.** at DULL

blur (blur) *vt.*, *vi.* **blurred, blur'ring** [? akin to BLEAR] **1.** to smear or smudge **2.** to make or become less distinct or clear [the fog *blurred* the view] **3.** to dim or dull [the medicine *blurred* his vision] —*n.* **1.** the state of being blurred **2.** an obscuring stain or blot **3.** anything indistinct to the sight or mind —**blur'ri·ness** *n.* —**blur'ry** *adj.*

☆**blurb** (blurb) *n.* [coined (c. 1907) by Gelett Burgess (1866–1951), U.S. humorist] [Colloq.] an advertisement, as on a book jacket, esp. one full of exaggerated praise

blurt (blurt) *vt.* [prob. echoic] to say suddenly, without stopping to think (with *out*) [to *blurt* out a confession]

blush (blush) *vi.* [< OE. *blyscan*, to shine: for IE. base see BLACK] **1.** to become red in the face from shame, embarrassment, etc. **2.** to be ashamed or embarrassed (*at* or *for*) [I *blush* for her rudeness] **3.** to be or become rosy —*n.* **1.** a reddening of the face, as from shame **2.** a rosy color [the *blush* of youth] —*adj.* rosy [*blush*-pink] —**at first blush** at first sight; without further thought —**blush'ful** *adj.* —**blush'ing·ly** *adv.*

blush·er (blush'ər) *n.* **1.** a person who blushes, esp. one who blushes readily **2.** any of various cosmetic powders, gels, creams, etc. applied to the face to give it color

blus·ter (blus'tər) *vi.* [< or akin to LowG. *blüstern*: for IE. base see BALL[1]] **1.** to blow stormily: said of wind **2.** to speak or behave in a noisy, boastful, or bullying way [he tries to hide his fear by *blustering*] —*vt.* to force by blustering —*n.* **1.** noisy commotion **2.** noisy swaggering or bullying talk —**blus'ter·er** *n.* —**blus'ter·ing·ly** *adv.* —**blus'ter·y, blus'ter·ous** *adj.*

blvd. boulevard

BM 1. bench mark **2.** [Colloq.] bowel movement

BMR basal metabolic rate

Bn., bn. battalion

BO, B.O. 1. body odor **2.** box office

b.o. 1. back order **2.** branch office

bo·a (bō'ə) *n.* [L.] **1.** any of a number of tropical snakes that crush their prey in their coils, as the anaconda, boa constrictor, etc. **2.** a woman's long, fluffy scarf, as of feathers

boa constrictor a species of boa which reaches a length of 10 to 15 feet

boar (bôr) *n.*, *pl.* **boars, boar:** see PLURAL, II, D 1 [OE. *bar*] **1.** an uncastrated male hog or pig **2.** a wild hog of Europe, Africa, and Asia

board (bôrd) *n.* [< OE. *bord*, plank & OFr. *bord*, side of a ship, both < IE. base *bheredh-*, to cut] **1.** a long, broad, flat piece of sawed wood ready for use **2.** a flat piece of wood or other material for some special use [a bulletin *board*, diving *board*] **3.** *a*) a construction material made in thin, flat, rectangular sheets [*fiberboard*] *b*) pasteboard or stiff paper, often used in book covers **4.** *a*) a table for meals *b*) food served at a table; esp., meals provided regularly for pay [room and *board* for $50 a week] **5.** a council table **6.** a group of administrators; council [a *board* of trustees] **7.** a stock exchange or its listings **8.** the side of a ship [*overboard*] **9.** a rim or border [*seaboard*] **10.** *Basketball* a backboard **11.** [*pl.*] *Hockey* the sideboards — *vt.* **1.** to cover or close (*up*) with boards [to *board up* a broken window] **2.** to provide with meals, or room and meals, regularly for pay **3.** to come onto the deck of (a ship) ☆**4.** to get on (an airplane, bus, etc.) —*vi.* to receive meals, or room and meals, regularly for pay —☆**across the board 1.** *Horse Racing* betting that a particular horse will win, place, or show **2.** including all classes or groups —**go by the board 1.** to be swept overboard **2.** to be got rid of, lost, etc. —**on board** on or in a ship, aircraft, bus, etc. —**the boards** the stage (of a theater)

BOAR
(to 36 in. high
at shoulder)

board·er (bôr'dər) *n.* **1.** one who boards at a boardinghouse, etc. **2.** one who boards a ship, etc., esp. a sailor who boards an enemy ship

☆**board foot** *pl.* **board feet** a unit of measure of lumber (**board measure**), equal to a board one foot square and one inch thick

board·ing·house (bôr'diŋ hous') *n.* a house where meals, or room and meals, can be had for pay: also **boarding house**

boarding school a school providing lodging and meals for the pupils

board of health a local government agency that supervises public health

☆**board·walk** (bôrd'wôk') *n.* a walk made of boards, esp. one along a beach

boast (bōst) *vi.* [< Anglo-Fr.] to talk about deeds, abilities, etc. with too much pride and satisfaction; brag [*boasting* of her son's high scores] —*vt.* **1.** to brag about **2.** to be proud of having or doing (something) [our city *boasts* a fine zoo] —*n.* **1.** the act of one who boasts **2.** anything boasted of —**boast'er** *n.* **boast'ing·ly** *adv.*

SYN. —**boast** suggests pride and pleasure, sometimes a little too great, in one's deeds or skills; **brag** suggests greater showiness and exaggeration in displaying such pride; **swagger** suggests a showing of one's feelings of being better than others, in a way that is crude and annoying; **crow** implies loud bragging that is in bad taste, as after a victory

boast·ful (bōst'fəl) *adj.* always ready to brag; boasting — **boast'ful·ly** *adv.* —**boast'ful·ness** *n.*

boat (bōt) *n.* [OE. *bat*: for IE. base see BITE] **1.** a small, open vessel or watercraft moved by oars, sails, or engine **2.** a large vessel; ship: a term in popular use, but not by sailors **3.** a boat-shaped dish [a gravy *boat*] —*vt.* to lay or carry in the boat [*boat* the oars] —*vi.* to row, sail, or travel in a boat —**in the same boat** in the same unfavorable situation —**miss the boat** [Colloq.] to fail to make the most of an opportunity —☆**rock the boat** [Colloq.] to disturb what seems to be a peaceful state of affairs —**boat'er** *n.*

boat·er (bōt'ər) *n.* [orig. worn when boating] a stiff hat of braided straw, with a flat crown and brim

boat·house (bōt'hous') *n.* a building for storing a boat or boats

boat·ing (-iŋ) *n.* rowing, sailing, or cruising

boat·load (-lōd') *n.* **1.** all the freight or passengers that a boat can carry or contain **2.** the load carried by a boat

boat·man (-mən) *n.*, *pl.* **-men** a man who operates, works on, rents, or sells boats

boat·swain (bō's'n) *n.* a ship's warrant officer or petty officer in charge of the deck crew, the rigging, anchors, boats, etc.

bob[1] (bäb) *n.* [ME. *bobbe*, hanging cluster; senses 4 & 5 < the *v.*] **1.** a knoblike weight hanging as at the end of a plumb line **2.** a docked tail, as of a horse **3.** a woman's or girl's short haircut **4.** a quick, jerky motion **5.** a float on a fishing line: now usually **bob'ber** —*vt.* **bobbed, bob'bing** [ME. *bobben*, to knock against] **1.** to move, esp. up and down, with short, jerky motions /she *bobbed* her head in quick approval/ **2.** to cut (hair, a tail, etc.) short —*vi.* **1.** to move with short, jerky motions /the little boat *bobbed* in the water/ **2.** to try to catch hanging or floating fruit with the teeth as a game /we *bobbed* for apples/—**bob up** to appear unexpectedly or suddenly

bob² (bäb) *n., pl.* **bob** [< ? *Bob*, nickname for ROBERT] [Brit. Slang] a shilling

bob·bin (bäb'in) *n.* [Fr. *bobine*] a reel or spool for thread or yarn, used in spinning, weaving, machine sewing, etc.

bob·bi·net (bäb'ə net') *n.* [< BOBBIN + NET¹] a kind of netting with a mesh of hexagons, made by machine

bob·ble (bäb''l) *n.* [< BOB¹, *v.*] **1.** a bobbing, up-and-down movement ☆**2.** [Colloq.] an awkward juggling of a ball in trying to catch it —*vi.* **-bled, -bling** to move jerkily; bob —☆ *vt.* [Colloq.] to deal with awkwardly; specif., to make a bobble with (a ball); muff; bungle

bob·by (bäb'ē) *n., pl.* **-bies** [after Sir Robert (*Bobby*) Peel (1788–1850), who reorganized the London police force] [Brit. Colloq.] a policeman

☆**bobby pin** [from use with *bobbed* hair] a metal hairpin with the sides pressing close together

☆**bobby socks** (or **sox**) [< BOB¹ (*vt.* 2)] [Colloq.] girls' socks that reach just above the ankle: term no longer used

☆**bob·cat** (bäb'kat') *n., pl.* **-cats', -cat':** see PLURAL, II, D, 1 [< its short tail] *same as* BAY LYNX

☆**bob·o·link** (bäb'ə liŋk') *n.* [echoic, after its call] a migratory songbird of N. American fields and meadows

☆**bob·sled** (-sled') *n.* a long sled with two sets of runners one behind the other, steering apparatus, and brakes: it is ridden by a team of four or two in races down a prepared run —*vi.* **-sled'ded, -sled'ding** to ride or race on a bobsled

bob·stay (-stā') *n.* a rope or chain for tying down a bowsprit to keep it from bobbing

BOBSLED

bob·tail (-tāl') *n.* **1.** a tail cut short; docked tail **2.** a horse or dog with a bobtail —*adj.* **1.** having a bobtail **2.** cut short; abbreviated —*vt.* **1.** to dock the tail of **2.** to cut short; curtail

☆**bob·white** (bäb'hwīt', -wīt') *n., pl.* **-whites', -white':** see PLURAL, II, D, 1 [echoic, after its call] a small N. American quail having markings of brown and white on a gray body

Boc·cac·cio (bō kä'chē ō'; *It.* bô kät'chô), **Gio·van·ni** (jō vän'nē) 1313–75; It. writer

Boc·che·ri·ni (bok'ke rē'nē; *E.* bōk'ə rē'nē), **Lu·i·gi** (lōō ē'jē) 1743–1805; It. composer

boc·cie, boc·ce, boc·ci (bäch'ē) *n.* [It. *bocce*] an Italian game similar to bowls, but played on a long clay court

☆**bock** (bäk) *n.* [G. < *bockbier* < *Einbecker bier* < *Einbeck*, Hanover, where first brewed] a dark beer traditionally drunk in the spring: also **bock beer**

BOD [b(iochemical) o(xygen) d(emand)] the amount of dissolved oxygen used by bacteria in decomposing organic matter in water: used as a measure of pollution

bode¹ (bōd) *vt.* **bod'ed, bod'ing** [< OE. < *boda*, messenger] to be an omen of; presage /a black cloud that *boded* rain/—**bode ill** (or **well**) to be a bad (or good) omen

bode² (bōd) *alt. pt. of* BIDE

bo·de·ga (bō dā'gə) *n.* [Sp. < L. *apotheca:* see APOTHECARY] **1.** a small grocery store **2.** a wine shop

bod·ice (bäd'is) *n.* [altered < *bodies*, pl. of BODY] **1.** the upper part of a woman's dress **2.** a kind of vest worn over a blouse or dress by women or girls, usually laced in front

bod·ied (bäd'ēd) *adj.* having a body of a specified kind /ablebodied/

bod·i·less (bäd'ē lis) *adj.* without a body; having no material substance; incorporeal

bod·i·ly (bäd''l ē) *adj.* of, in, by, or to the body /he did me no *bodily* harm/ —*adv.* **1.** in person; in the flesh /to be *bodily* present/ **2.** as a single body; in entirety /they walked *bodily* from the room/

SYN.—**bodily** refers to the human body as apart from the mind or spirit /*bodily* organs/; **physical** is often used like **bodily**, but may suggest less directly the organs or parts, etc. of the body /*physical* labor/; **corporeal** refers to the matter that makes up the body and is opposed to *spiritual* /her *corporeal* remains/; **corporal** refers to the effect of something upon

the body /*corporal* punishment/; **somatic** is the word used, as in a scientific description, to refer to the body as distinct from the mind /the *somatic* differences between individuals/

bod·kin (bäd'k'n) *n.* [ME. *boidekyn* < ?] **1.** a pointed instrument for making holes in cloth **2.** a long, ornamental hairpin **3.** a thick, blunt needle **4.** [Obs.] a dagger or stiletto

bod·y (bäd'ē) *n., pl.* **bod'ies** [< OE. *bodig*, trunk, orig. sense "cask"] **1.** the whole physical substance of a person, animal, or plant **2.** *a*) the trunk or torso of a man or animal /the boxer took several blows to the *body*/ *b*) the part of a garment that covers the trunk **3.** the flesh, as opposed to the spirit **4.** [Colloq.] a person /more than a *body* can stand/ **5.** a group of people or things regarded as a unit /an advisory *body*/ **6.** *a*) the main or central part of anything /the *body* of a document/ *b*) the part of a car, truck, etc. that holds the passengers or load **8.** a portion or mass of matter /a *body* of water/ **9.** density or consistency, as of a liquid, fabric, etc. /a silk with little *body* in it/ **10.** richness of tone or flavor /a wine with fine *body*/ —*vt.* **bod'ied, bod'y·ing** to give a body or substance to —**body forth** to give shape or form to —**keep body and soul together** to stay alive

☆**body English** [see ENGLISH (*n.* 4)] a follow-through motion of the body, as after bowling a ball, in a joking effort to control the ball's movement

bod·y·guard (bäd'ē gärd') *n.* a person or persons, usually armed, assigned to guard, or protect, someone

body language gestures, body movements, looks, etc. that tell something the way language does

body politic the people who collectively make up a political unit under a government

body snatcher formerly, a person who stole corpses from graves and sold them for dissection by those studying anatomy

☆**body stocking** a tightfitting garment, usually of one piece, that covers the torso and, sometimes, the legs

bod·y·suit (-sōōt') *n.* a one-piece, tightfitting garment that covers the torso, usually worn with slacks, a skirt, etc.

Boe·o·tia (bē ō'shə) region in EC Greece: in ancient times, a region dominated by Thebes —**Boe·o'tian** *adj., n.*

Boer (bôr, boor, bō'ər) *n.* [Du. *boer*, peasant: see BOOR] a South African whose ancestors were Dutch colonists

bog (bäg, bôg) *n.* [< Gael. & Ir. *bog*, soft, moist] wet, spongy ground; a small marsh or swamp —*vt., vi.* **bogged, bog'ging** to sink or become stuck in or as in a bog (often with *down*); mire /she got *bogged* down in a lot of petty details/ —**bog'gi·ness** *n.* —**bog'gy** *adj.* **-gi·er, -gi·est**

bo·gey (bō'gē) *n., pl.* **-geys 1.** *same as* BOGY ☆**2.** [after Colonel *Bogey*, imaginary first-rate golfer] *Golf* par or, now usually, one stroke more than par on a hole —☆ *vi.* **-geyed, -gey·ing** *Golf* to score one over par on (a hole)

bog·gle (bäg''l) *vi.* **-gled, -gling** [< Scot. *bogle*, specter; now associated with BUNGLE] **1.** to be startled or frightened (*at*); shy away **2.** to hesitate (*at*) /he *boggled* at telling a lie/ —*vt.* **1.** to bungle; botch **2.** to confuse or stagger (the mind)

bo·gie¹ (bō'gē) *n., pl.* **-gies 1.** *same as* BOGY ☆**2.** *same as* BOGEY (sense 2)

bo·gie² (bō'gē) *n., pl.* **-gies** [< Brit. Dial.] **1.** a swiveled undercarriage at either end of a railroad car **2.** any of the wheels supporting the weight on the inside of the tread of an armored tank

Bo·go·tá (bō'gō tä') capital of Colombia, in the central part: pop. 2,512,000

☆**bo·gus** (bō'gəs) *adj.* [< ?] not genuine; spurious; counterfeit — see SYN. at FALSE

bo·gy (bō'gē, boog'ē) *n., pl.* **-gies** [see BOGGLE] **1.** an imaginary evil spirit; goblin **2.** anything causing great, often needless, fear

bo·gy·man, bo·gey·man (bō'gē man', boog'ē-) *n., pl.* **-men'** (-men') an imaginary frightful being, esp. one used as a threat in disciplining children

Bo·he·mi·a (bō hē'mē ə) region and former province of W Czechoslovakia: earlier, a kingdom

Bo·he·mi·an (bō hē'mē ən) *n.* **1.** a native or inhabitant of bohemia **2.** *same as* CZECH (*n.* 2) **3.** a gypsy **4.** [*often* b-] an

BOGIES ON A TANK

fat, āpe, cär, ten, ēven, is, bīte; gō, hôrn, tōōl, look; oil, out; up, fur; get; joy; yet; chin; she; thin, *th*en; zh, leisure; ŋ, ring; ə for *a* in *ago*, *e* in *agent*, *i* in *sanity*, *o* in *comply*, *u* in *focus*; ' as in *able* (ā'b'l); Fr. bál; ë, Fr. coeur; ö, Fr. feu; Fr. mon; ő, Fr. coq; ü, Fr. duc; r, Fr. cri; H, G. ich; kh, G. doch; ‡foreign; ☆ Americanism; < derived from. See inside front cover.

artist, poet, etc. who lives in a free, unconventional way —*adj.*
1. of Bohemia, its people, or their language; Czech **2.** [*often* b-] like or characteristic of a Bohemian (*n.* 4) —**Bo·he'mi·an·ism** *n.*

Bohr (bôr), **Niels (Henrik David)** (nēlz) 1885–1962; Dan. physicist

boil[1] (boil) *vi.* [< OFr. < L. < *bulla*, a bubble, prob. < base of BIG] **1.** to bubble up and vaporize by being heated **2.** to seethe like boiling liquids **3.** to be agitated, as with rage [a retort that made him *boil*] **4.** to cook in boiling water or other liquid [let the peas *boil* a while] —*vt.* **1.** to heat to the boiling point **2.** to cook or process in boiling water, etc. [to *boil* potatoes] —*n.* the act or state of boiling —**boil away** to evaporate by boiling —**boil down 1.** to lessen in quantity by boiling **2.** to condense; summarize —**boil over 1.** to come to a boil and spill over the rim **2.** to lose one's temper

boil[2] (boil) *n.* [< OE. *byl* < base of BOIL[1]] an inflamed, painful, pus-filled swelling on the skin, caused by infection

boil·er (boi'lər) *n.* **1.** a container in which things are boiled or heated **2.** a tank in which water is turned to steam for heating or power **3.** a tank for heating water and storing it

boil·er·mak·er (-mā'kər) *n.* **1.** a worker who makes or repairs boilers ☆**2.** [Colloq.] a drink of whiskey in beer or with beer as a chaser

boiling point the temperature at which a particular liquid boils: water at sea level boils at 212°F or 100°C

Boi·se (boi'sē, -zē) [< Fr. *boisé*, wooded] capital of Ida.: pop. 75,000: also **Boise City**

bois·ter·ous (bois'tər əs) *adj.* [ME. *boistreous*, crude, coarse < *boistous*, violent] **1.** rough and stormy [the *boisterous* winds] **2.** *a)* noisy and unruly [a *boisterous* party] *b)* loud and exuberant [a *boisterous* greeting] —see SYN. at VOCIFEROUS —**bois'ter·ous·ly** *adv.* —**bois'ter·ous·ness** *n.*

bo·la (bō'la) *n.* [Sp., a ball < L. *bulla:* see BOIL[1]] a throwing weapon made of a long cord or thong with heavy balls at the ends: it winds around and entangles the animal at which it is thrown: also **bo'las** (-ləs)

bold (bōld) *adj.* [< OE. *beald:* for IE. base see BALL[1]] **1.** daring; fearless [a *bold* explorer] **2.** not polite or respectful; impudent ["who cares?" was her *bold* reply] **3.** steep or abrupt [a *bold* cliff] **4.** prominent and clear [a *bold* design] —see SYN. at BRAVE —**make bold** to dare (*to*) —**bold'ly** *adv.* —**bold'ness** *n.*

BOLA

bold·face (bōld'fās') *n.* a printing type with a heavy, dark face [the entry words in this dictionary are in **boldface**]

bold·faced (-fāst') *adj.* impudent; forward

bole (bōl) *n.* [ON. *bolr* < IE. base of BALL[1]] a tree trunk

bo·le·ro (bə ler'ō, bō-) *n., pl.* **-ros** [Sp. < *bola:* see BOLA] **1.** a Spanish dance in 3/4 time **2.** music for this **3.** a sleeveless or sleeved jacket that ends at the waist and is open in front

Bol·eyn (bool'in, bə lin'), **Anne** 1507?–36; 2d wife of Henry VIII of England: mother of ELIZABETH I

bo·li·var (bō lē'vär, bäl'ə vər) *n., pl.* **bo·li·va·res** (bō'li vä'res), **bo·li'vars** [after Simón BOLÍVAR] *see* MONETARY UNITS, table (Venezuela)

Bol·i·var (bäl'ə vər; *Sp.* bō lē'vär), **Si·món** (*Sp.* sē mōn') 1783–1830; S. American general & revolutionary leader

Bo·liv·i·a (bə liv'ē ə) country in WC S. America: 424,000 sq. mi.; pop. 4,804,000; capitals, La Paz & Sucre —**Bo·liv'i·an** *adj., n.*

boll (bōl) *n.* [OE. *bolla,* BOWL[1]] the roundish seed pod of a plant, esp. of cotton or flax

☆**boll weevil** a small, grayish weevil whose larvae destroy the cotton bolls in which they are hatched

bo·lo (bō'lō) *n., pl.* **-los** [Sp. < native name] a large, single-edged knife used in the Philippines

Bo·lo·gna (bō lō'nyä; *E.* bə lō'nə) city in NC Italy: pop. 485,000 —*n.* [*usually* b-] (bə lō'nē, -nyə, -nə) a large, smoked sausage of various meats: also **bologna sausage**

☆**bo·lo tie** (bō'lō) [altered from *bola tie:* see BOLA] a man's string tie held together with a slide device

Bol·she·vik (bōl'shə vik', bäl'-) *n., pl.* **-viks**, **Bol'she·vi'ki** (-vē'kē) [Russ. < *bolshe,* the majority] [*also* b-] **1.** orig., a member of a majority faction of the Social Democratic Party of Russia, which formed the Communist Party after seizing power in the 1917 Revolution **2.** a Communist, esp. of the Soviet Un-

ion **3.** loosely, any radical: hostile usage —*adj.* [*also* b-] of or like the Bolsheviks or Bolshevism —**Bol'she·vism** *n.* —**Bol'she·vist** *n., adj.*

bol·ster (bōl'stər) *n.* [OE. < base of BALL[1]] **1.** a long, narrow cushion or pillow **2.** a soft pad **3.** any bolsterlike object or support, as a piece that caps the top of a post supporting a beam —*vt.* to prop up as with a bolster; support (often with *up*) —**bol'ster·er** *n.*

bolt[1] (bōlt) *n.* [OE. < IE. base *bheld-,* to strike] **1.** an arrow with a thick, blunt head, shot from a crossbow **2.** a flash of lightning **3.** a sudden dash or movement **4.** a sliding bar for locking a door, etc. **5.** a similar bar in a lock, moved by a key **6.** a metal rod with a head, threaded and used with a nut to hold parts together **7.** a roll (*of* cloth, paper, etc.) of a given length ☆**8.** a withdrawal from one's party or group **9.** *Firearms* a sliding bar that pushes the cartridge into place and extracts the empty cartridge case after firing —*vt.* **1.** [Archaic] to shoot (an arrow, etc.) **2.** to say suddenly; blurt (*out*) **3.** to swallow (food) hurriedly; gulp down **4.** to fasten as with a bolt [to *bolt* a door] **5.** to roll (cloth, etc.) into bolts ☆**6.** to abandon (a party, group, etc.) —*vi.* **1.** to dash or spring away suddenly; dart [he *bolted* out of the room] ☆**2.** to withdraw support from a party, group, etc. —*adv.* straight; erectly [to sit *bolt* upright] —**shoot one's bolt** to do the most one is capable of —**bolt'er** *n.*

BOLTS

bolt[2] (bōlt) *vt.* [< OFr. *buleter* < ?] **1.** to sift (flour, grain, etc.) through a sieve **2.** to examine closely, as for separating good from bad —**bolt'er** *n.*

bo·lus (bō'ləs) *n., pl.* **bo'lus·es** [L. < Gr. *bólos,* a lump] **1.** a small, round lump or mass, as of chewed food **2.** a large pill, as one given to a horse

bomb (bäm) *n.* [< Fr. < It. < L. < Gr. *bombos,* hollow sound] **1.** a container filled with an explosive, incendiary, or other chemical, for dropping or hurling, or for detonating by a timing mechanism **2.** a sudden, surprising occurrence **3.** an aerosol container **4.** a shielded device containing radioactive material, used in the treatment of disease [a cobalt *bomb*] ☆**5.** [Slang] a complete failure: said esp. of a performance or show —*vt.* to attack or destroy with a bomb or bombs —*vi.* ☆[Slang] to have a complete failure

bom·bard (bäm bärd') *vt.* [< Fr. < *bombarde,* mortar < *bombe,* BOMB] **1.** to attack with artillery or bombs **2.** to keep attacking with questions, suggestions, etc. **3.** to direct a stream of particles, as neutrons, against —**bom·bard'ment** *n.*

bom·bar·dier (bäm'bə dir', -bər-) *n.* ☆the member of a bomber crew who aims and releases the bombs

bom·bast (bäm'bast) *n.* [< OFr. < ML. < *bambax,* cotton < LGr. < Per. *pambak,* cotton] **1.** orig., cotton, linen, etc. used for padding **2.** talk or writing that sounds grand but is empty or meaningless

bom·bas·tic (bäm bas'tik) *adj.* using or full of bombast —**bom·bas'ti·cal·ly** *adv.*

SYN.—**bombastic** refers to a padded, pompous style of writing or speaking and suggests the use of many words to say little of importance; **grandiloquent** suggests the use of grandiose words and hollow, high-sounding phrases, as by an old-fashioned orator; **flowery** language uses many similes and metaphors in an artificial way; **turgid** implies a wordy style that is not precise and is hard to understand

Bom·bay (bäm bā') seaport in W India, on the Arabian Sea: pop. 4,152,000

bomb bay a compartment in the fuselage of a bomber that can be opened to drop bombs

bom·ba·zine (bäm'bə zēn', bäm'bə zēn') *n.* [< Fr. < ML. < *bambax:* see BOMBAST] a twilled cloth of silk or rayon with worsted, often dyed black

bomb·er (bäm'ər) *n.* **1.** an airplane designed for dropping bombs **2.** a person who bombs

bomb·proof (bäm'prōōf') *adj.* strong enough to protect against the force of ordinary bombs

bomb·shell (-shel') *n.* same as BOMB (*n.* 1, 2)

bomb·sight (-sīt') *n.* an instrument on a bomber for aiming the bombs

bo·na fi·de (bō'nə fīd', bän'ə; bō'nə fī'dē) [L.] in good faith; without fraud or deceit; genuine; authentic

☆**bo·nan·za** (bə nan'zə, bō-) *n.* [Sp., fair weather, prosperity, ult. < Gr. *malakia,* a calm at sea] **1.** a rich vein of ore **2.** any source of wealth or profits

Bo·na·parte (bō′nə pärt′; *Fr.* bô nå pàrt′) Corsican family including NAPOLEON I & LOUIS NAPOLEON

bon·bon (bän′bän′) *n.* [Fr. *bon*, good] a small piece of candy, esp. one with a creamy filling

bond[1] (bänd) *n.* [ME. *bond, band:* see BAND[1]] **1.** anything that binds, fastens, or unites; specif., glue, solder, etc. **2.** [*pl.*] *a)* fetters; shackles *b)* [Archaic] imprisonment **3.** a binding or uniting force [a *bond* of loyalty] **4.** a binding agreement; covenant **5.** the status of goods kept in a warehouse until taxes are paid **6.** *same as* BOND PAPER **7.** *Chem.* the means by which atoms or groups of atoms are combined in molecules **8.** *Finance* a certificate issued by a government or business in return for a loan of money: it promises to pay the holder a specified sum, including interest, by a specified date **9.** *Law a)* a written obligation to pay specified sums, do or not do specified things, etc. *b)* an amount paid as surety or bail *c)* insurance by which an agency guarantees to pay a certain sum, as to an employer, in case of a loss resulting from the act of a particular person, as an employee *d)* [Archaic] a bondsman —*vt.* **1.** to fasten or unite as with a bond **2.** to furnish a bond, or bail, and thus become a surety for (someone) **3.** to place (goods) under bond **4.** to issue bonds (sense 8) on; mortgage **5.** to put under bonded debt —*vi.* to hold together by or as by a bond —**bottled in bond** bottled and stored in bonded warehouses for the length of time stated on the label, as some whiskey —**bond′a·ble** *adj.* —**bond′er** *n.*

bond[2] (bänd) *n.* [see BONDAGE] [Obs.] a serf or slave —*adj.* in serfdom or slavery

bond·age (bän′dij) *n.* [< Anglo-L. < OE. *bonda* < ON. *bonde* < *bua*, to inhabit < IE. base *bleu-*, to grow] **1.** serfdom; slavery **2.** the condition of being controlled by some force or influence

bond·ed (bän′did) *adj.* **1.** insured or protected by a bond or bonds **2.** placed in a warehouse under government care until taxes are paid

bond·hold·er (bänd′hōl′dər) *n.* an owner of bonds issued by a company, government, or person

bond·man (-mən) *n., pl.* **-men 1.** a feudal serf **2.** a male slave —**bond′maid** *n.fem.* —**bond′wom′an** *n.fem., pl.* **-wom′en**

☆**bond paper** a strong, superior stock of paper, esp. of rag pulp, used for documents, letterheads, etc.

bond·ser·vant (-sur′vənt) *n.* a slave

bonds·man (bändz′mən) *n., pl.* **-men 1.** *same as* BONDMAN **2.** a person who takes responsibility for another by furnishing a bond; surety

bone (bōn) *n.* [OE. *ban*] **1.** any of the pieces of hard tissue forming the skeleton of most vertebrate animals **2.** this hard tissue **3.** [*pl.*] *a)* the skeleton *b)* the body, living or dead [they laid his *bones* to rest] **4.** a bonelike substance or part, as whalebone **5.** a thing made of bone, plastic, etc.; specif., *a)* a corset stay *b)* [*pl.*] [Colloq.] dice **6.** *same as* BONE WHITE —*vt.* **boned, bon′ing 1.** to remove the bones from [to *bone* a fish] **2.** to put whalebone, etc. into to stiffen —*vi.* ☆[Slang] to study hard and hurriedly; cram (usually with *up*) [to *bone up* for a test] —☆**feel in one's bones** to be certain without any real reason —**have a bone to pick** to have something to quarrel about —**make no bones about** [Colloq.] **1.** to make no attempt to hide; admit freely **2.** to have no objection to or qualms about —**bone′like′** *adj.*

bone-dry (bōn′drī′) *adj.* dry as bone; very dry

☆**bone·fish** (-fish′) *n., pl.* **-fish′, -fish′es:** see FISH a silvery game and food fish that feeds on the bottom in shallow waters of tropical seas

☆**bone·head** (-hed′) *n.* [Slang] a stupid person

bone·less (-lis) *adj.* without bones; specif., with the bones removed [*boneless* sardines]

☆**bone meal** crushed or finely ground bones, used as feed for stock or as fertilizer

☆**bon·er** (bōn′ər) *n.* [Slang] a stupid blunder

☆**bone·set** (bōn′set′) *n.* a plant of the composite family, with flat clusters of white flowers: used in folk medicine

bone white any of various shades of grayish-white or yellowish-white

bon·fire (bän′fīr′) *n.* [ME. *banefyre*, bone fire; later, funeral pyre] a large fire built outdoors, as for a celebration

☆**bong** (bôŋ, bäŋ) *n.* [echoic] a deep, ringing sound, as of a large bell —*vi.* to make this sound

☆**bon·go** (bäŋ′gō) *n., pl.* **-gos** [AmSp. < ?] either of a pair of small joined drums, of different pitch, struck with the fingers: in full, **bongo drum**

bon·ho·mie, bon·hom·mie (bän′ə mē′) *n.* [Fr. < *bon*, good + *homme*, man] good nature; pleasant, friendly manner; amiability

bo·ni·to (bə nēt′ō) *n., pl.* **-tos, -toes, -to:** see PLURAL, II, D, 1 [Sp.] any of several saltwater fishes of the mackerel family, related to the tuna

‡**bon·jour** (bôn zhoor′) *interj.* [Fr.] good day; hello

bon mot (bôn′ mō′; *Fr.* bôn mō′) *pl.* **bons mots** (bôn′ mōz′; *Fr.* bôn mō′) [Fr., lit., good word] a clever or witty remark

Bonn (bän) capital of West Germany, on the Rhine: pop. 138,000

Bon·nard (bô när′), **Pierre** 1867-1947; Fr. painter

bon·net (bän′it) *n.* [OFr. *bonet* < ML. *abonnis*, kind of cap] **1.** a flat, brimless cap, worn by men and boys in Scotland **2.** *a)* a hat with a chin ribbon, worn by babies or girls *b)* [Colloq.] any hat for a woman or girl ☆**3.** *short for* WAR BONNET **4.** *a)* a metal covering, as over a fireplace *b)* [Brit.] an automobile hood —*vt.* to put a bonnet on

bon·ny, bon·nie (bän′ē) *adj.* **-ni·er, -ni·est** [< Fr. *bon*, good < L. *bonus*] [Now Chiefly Scot. or Eng. Dial.] **1.** handsome or pretty, with a healthy, cheerful glow **2.** fine; pleasant —**bon′ni·ly** *adv.* —**bon′ni·ness** *n.*

bon·sai (bän sī′) *n.* [Jpn., lit., tray arrangement] **1.** the art of growing dwarf trees or shrubs in shallow pots by pruning in a certain way, controlling fertilizer, etc. **2.** *pl.* **bon·sai′** such a tree or shrub

‡**bon·soir** (bôn swär′) *interj.* [Fr.] good evening

bo·nus (bō′nəs) *n., pl.* **bo′nus·es** [L., good] anything given or paid in addition to what is due or expected, as an incentive, reward, etc.

bon vi·vant (bän′ vi vänt′; *Fr.* bôn vē vän′) *pl.* **bons vi·vants** (bän′ vi vänts′; *Fr.* bôn vē vän′) [Fr.] one who enjoys good food and other luxuries

bon voy·age (bän′voi äzh′; *Fr.* bôn vwä yàzh′) [Fr.] pleasant journey: a farewell to a traveler

bon·y (bōn′ē) *adj.* **bon′i·er, bon′i·est 1.** of or like bone [a *bony* substance] **2.** having many bones [*bony* fish] **3.** having protruding bones [an old, *bony* horse] **4.** thin; emaciated —**bon′i·ness** *n.*

boo (boo) *interj., n., pl.* **boos** [echoic] a long, drawn-out sound made to show disapproval, scorn, etc., or a short sound like this made to startle someone —*vi., vt.* **booed, boo′ing** to make this sound —*vt.* to shout "boo" at

☆**boob** (boob) *n.* [Slang] a booby; foolish person

☆**boo-boo, boo·boo** (boo′boo′) *n., pl.* **-boos** [Slang] a stupid or foolish mistake

☆**boob tube** [Slang] television or a television set

boo·by (boo′bē) *n., pl.* **-bies** [prob. < Sp. *bobo*, stupid] **1.** a stupid or foolish person **2.** a tropical, diving sea bird related to the gannet

☆**booby prize** a prize, usually ridiculous, given in fun to whoever has done worst in a game, race, etc.

booby trap 1. any scheme or device for tricking a person who does not expect it **2.** a bomb set to be exploded as when it is touched by someone who does not suspect it —**boo′by-trap′** *vt.* **-trapped′, -trap′ping**

☆**boo·dle** (boo′d'l) *n.* [< Du. *boedel*, property] [Slang] **1.** the entire lot; caboodle **2.** something given as a bribe **3.** the loot taken in a robbery

☆**boo·gie-woo·gie** (boog′ē woog′ē) *n.* [? echoic of the characteristic "walking" bass] a style of jazz piano playing in which repeated bass figures in 8/8 rhythm accompany the melody and its variations

boo·hoo (boo′hoo′) *vi.* **-hooed′, -hoo′ing** [echoic] to weep noisily —*n., pl.* **-hoos′** noisy weeping

book (book) *n.* [OE. *boc*, pl. *bec*, akin to OE. *bece*, BEECH < IE. base *bhago-s*, beech: runes were first carved on beech tablets]

BONGO DRUMS

BONSAI

1. *a)* a number of sheets of paper, etc. with writing or printing on them, fastened together along one edge, usually between protective covers *b)* a relatively long piece of writing, as a novel, history, scientific work, etc. **2.** a main division of a literary work **3.** *a)* a number of blank or ruled sheets or printed forms bound together *[an account* book*] b)* a record or account kept in this **4.** the words of an opera, musical play, etc.; libretto **5.** a booklike package, as of matches or tickets **6.** a record of bets, as on horse races **7.** *Bridge,* etc. a specified number of tricks that must be won before scoring can take place —*vt.* **1.** to record in a book; list **2.** to engage (rooms, performers, etc.) ahead of time *[to* book *passage on a ship]* **3.** to record charges against on a police record *[he was* booked *for driving while drunk]* —*adj.* in, from, or according to books or accounts — **bring to book** to force to explain —**by the book** according to the rules —**close the books** *Bookkeeping* to make no further entries —**in one's book** in one's opinion —**keep books** to keep a record of business transactions —**know like a book** to know well or fully —☆**make book** [Slang] to make or accept bets —☆**one for the books** [Colloq.] something very surprising, unexpected, etc. —**on the books** **1.** recorded **2.** enrolled —**the Book** the Bible —☆**throw the book at** [Slang] **1.** to place all possible charges against (an accused person) **2.** to give the maximum punishment to —**book′er** *n.*

book·bind·ing (book′bīn′diŋ) *n.* the art, trade, or business of binding books —**book′bind′er** *n.* —**book′bind′er·y** *n.*, *pl.* **-er-ies**

book·case (-kās′) *n.* a set of shelves or a cabinet for holding books

book club ☆an organization that sells books, usually at reduced prices, to members who promise to buy a minimum number of them annually

book·end (-end′) *n.* a weight or bracket put at the end of a row of books to keep them upright

book·ie (-ē) *n.* [Slang] *same as* BOOKMAKER (sense 2)

book·ing (-iŋ) *n.* an engagement, as for a lecture, performance, etc.

book·ish (-ish) *adj.* **1.** of books **2.** spending much time reading and studying; scholarly **3.** having or showing mere book learning rather than actual experience; pedantic; stodgy — **book′ish·ness** *n.*

book·keep·ing (-kēp′iŋ) *n.* the work of keeping a record of business accounts —**book′keep′er** *n.*

book learning knowledge gotten from books or study rather than from practical experience: also **book′lore′** (-lôr′) *n.*

book·let (-lit) *n.* a small, often paper-covered book

book·mak·er (-māk′ər) *n.* **1.** a maker of books **2.** a person in the business of taking bets, as on horse races —**book′mak′-ing** *n.*

book·mark (-märk′) *n.* anything slipped between the pages of a book to mark a place

☆**book matches** safety matches made of paper and fastened into a small cardboard folder

☆**book·mo·bile** (-mō bēl′, -mə-) *n.* [BOOK + (AUTO)MOBILE] a traveling lending library moved from place to place in a truck

Book of Common Prayer the official book of services and prayers used in Anglican churches

book·plate (-plāt′) *n.* a label pasted in a book to identify its owner

book·rack (-rak′) *n.* **1.** a rack or shelf for books **2.** *same as* BOOKSTAND (sense 1)

book·rest (-rest′) *n.* *same as* BOOKSTAND (sense 1)

book review an article or talk in which a book is discussed and the reviewer's opinions about it are given

book·sell·er (-sel′ər) *n.* the owner or manager of a bookstore

book·shelf (-shelf′) *n.*, *pl.* **-shelves**′ a shelf on which books are kept

☆**book·stack** (-stak′) *n.* a series of bookshelves, one over the other, as in a library

book·stall (-stôl′) *n.* a stand, booth, or counter, often one outdoors, where books are sold

book·stand (-stand′) *n.* **1.** a stand for holding a book open before a reader **2.** *same as* BOOKSTALL

☆**book·store** (-stôr′) *n.* a store where books are sold: also **book′shop′**

book value the value as shown in account books; specif., the value of the capital stock of a business as shown by the excess of assets over liabilities

book·worm (-wurm′) *n.* **1.** an insect or insect larva that harms books by feeding on the binding, paste, etc. **2.** one who reads or studies a great deal

Bool·e·an algebra (boo′lē ən) [after George *Boole* (1815–64), Eng. mathematician] a system of mathematical logic in which all variables have the value of either 0 or 1 and the basic operators are "and," "or," "not," etc.: widely used in digital computers

boom[1] (boom) *vi.* [echoic] to make a deep, hollow, resonant sound —*vt.* to utter with such a sound —*n.* a booming sound, as of thunder, heavy guns, etc.

boom[2] (boom) *n.* [Du., a tree, BEAM] **1.** a spar extending from a mast to hold the bottom of a sail outstretched **2.** a long beam extending as from an upright to lift and guide something *[the* boom *of a derrick]* **3.** a barrier of chains or timbers placed in a harbor or river to keep ships out or to keep floating logs in —*vt.* to stretch out (sails) with a boom —*vi.* to sail or move at top speed (usually with *along*) —☆**lower the boom** [Colloq.] to act forcefully in punishing, criticizing, etc.

☆**boom**[3] (boom) *vi.* [< ? prec. *vi.*; later associated with BOOM[1]] to increase suddenly or grow swiftly; flourish *[business* boomed*]* —*vt.* **1.** to cause to flourish **2.** to promote with much effort; popularize *[they* boomed *him for mayor]* —*n.* a period of business prosperity, etc. —*adj.* of or resulting from a boom in business *[a* boom *town]*

boom·er·ang (boom′ə raŋ′) *n.* [< Australian native name] **1.** a flat, curved stick that can be thrown so that it will return to the thrower: used as a weapon by Australian aborigines **2.** something that goes against the expectation of the one who started it and ends up doing him harm —*vi.* to act as a boomerang

boon[1] (boon) *n.* [ON. *bon*, a petition: for IE. base see BAN[1]] **1.** a welcome benefit; blessing *[the new park was a* boon *to the whole neighborhood]* **2.** [Archaic] a request or favor

boon[2] (boon) *adj.* [< OFr. < L. *bonus*, good] **1.** [Archaic or Poet.] kind, generous, pleasant, etc. **2.** merry; convivial: now only in **boon companion**, a close friend who often joins one in seeking fun

boon·docks (boon′däks′) *n.pl.* [orig. military slang < Tag. *bundok*, mountain] [Colloq.] **1.** a wild, heavily wooded area; wilderness ☆**2.** any area far from cities or towns; hinterland Used with *the*

☆**boon·dog·gle** (boon′dôg′'l, -däg′-) *vi.* **-gled**, **-gling** [orig. sense, ornamental leather strap] [Colloq.] to do trivial or useless work —*n.* trivial or useless work or a useless project — **boon′dog′gler** *n.*

Boone (boon), **Daniel** 1734–1820; Am. frontiersman

boor (boor) *n.* [Du. *boer* < MDu. *gheboer*, fellow dweller < *ghe-*, with, CO- + *bouwen*, to cultivate: for IE. base see BONDAGE] **1.** orig., a peasant or farm worker **2.** a rude, awkward, or ill-mannered person

boor·ish (boor′ish) *adj.* like a boor; rude; ill-mannered —see SYN. at RUDE —**boor′ish·ly** *adv.* —**boor′ish·ness** *n.*

☆**boost** (boost) *vt.* [< ?] **1.** to raise by or as by a push from behind or below *[*boost *him up into the tree]* **2.** to urge others to support; promote *[to* boost *a candidate for mayor]* **3.** to increase in amount, power, etc. *[to* boost *the voltage in an electric line]* —*n.* **1.** a push to help a person or thing upward or forward **2.** an act that helps or promotes **3.** an increase in amount, power, etc. *[a* boost *in sales]*

☆**boost·er** (boos′tər) *n.* **1.** one who boosts; enthusiastic supporter **2.** any device providing added power, thrust, etc., as a device for making radio or TV signals stronger **3.** any of the early stages of a multistage rocket; also, a rocket system that launches a spacecraft, etc.: also **booster rocket**

☆**booster shot** (or **injection**) an injection of a vaccine given some time after the first series, to maintain immunity

boot[1] (boot) *n.* [OFr. *bote*] **1.** *a)* a protective covering of leather, rubber, etc. for the foot and part of the leg *b)* an overshoe **2.** an instrument of torture once used for crushing the leg **3.** a patch for the inner surface of an automobile tire **4.** [Brit.] the trunk of an automobile **5.** *a)* a kick *b)* [Colloq.] pleasurable excitement; thrill ☆**6.** [Slang] a navy or marine recruit —*vt.* **1.** to put boots on **2.** to kick **3.** [Slang] to dismiss ☆**4.** *Baseball* to fumble (a grounder) —**die with one's boots on** to die in action —☆**lick the boots of** to be servile or act humble toward —**the boot** [Slang] dismissal; discharge

boot[2] (boot) *n.*, *vt.*, *vi.* [OE. *bot*, advantage: for IE. base see BEST] [Archaic] profit —**to boot** besides; in addition *[she gave me the book and a pen* to boot*]*

boot·black (boot′blak′) *n.* a person whose work is shining shoes and boots

☆**boot camp** [Colloq.] a station where navy or marine recruits receive basic training

☆**boot·ee, boot·ie** (bōōt′ē, bōō tē′) *n.* **1.** a short boot or light overshoe worn by women and children **2.** a baby's soft, knitted or cloth shoe

Bo·ö·tes (bō ō′tēz) [L. < Gr. *boōtēs*, lit., plowman] a northern constellation including the star Arcturus

booth (bōōth) *n., pl.* **booths** (bōōthz) [< ON. *buth,* temporary dwelling < *bua,* to dwell, akin to BONDAGE] **1.** a stall for the sale or display of goods, as at a market **2.** a small enclosed space for voting at elections **3.** a small shelter, as for a public telephone, etc. **4.** a small, partially enclosed compartment with a table and seats, as in some restaurants

BOOTEE

Booth (bōōth), **1. Edwin (Thomas),** 1833–93; U.S. actor **2. John Wilkes** (wilks), 1838–65; U.S. actor, brother of *Edwin:* assassin of Abraham Lincoln **3. William,** 1829–1912; Eng. founder of the Salvation Army

☆**boot·leg** (bōōt′leg′) *vt., vi.* **-legged′, -leg′ging** [from the practice of hiding objects in the leg of a boot] to make, carry, or sell (esp. liquor) illegally —*adj.* bootlegged; illegal —*n.* bootlegged liquor —**boot′leg′ger** *n.*

boot·less (-lis) *adj.* [BOOT² + -LESS] useless —**boot′less·ly** *adv.* —**boot′less·ness** *n.*

☆**boot·lick** (-lik′) *vt., vi.* [Colloq.] to try to gain favor with (someone) by flattering, acting humble, etc. —**boot′lick′er** *n.*

boot·strap (-strap′) *n.* a strap on a boot for pulling it on —*adj.* undertaken without others' help *[a bootstrap operation]* —**lift (or raise) oneself by the (or one's own) bootstraps** to achieve success by one's own efforts, without help

boo·ty (bōōt′ē) *n., pl.* **-ties** [< MLowG. *bute;* infl. by BOOT²] **1.** goods taken from the enemy in war **2.** any loot

booze (bōōz) *vi.* **boozed, booz′ing** [< Du. *buizen*] [Colloq.] to drink too much alcoholic liquor —*n.* [Colloq.] alcoholic liquor —**booz′er** *n.* —**booz′y** *adj.* **-i·er, -i·est**

☆**bop** (bäp) *n., vt.* **bopped, bop′ping** [echoic] [Slang] hit; punch

bo·rac·ic (bə ras′ik) *adj. same as* BORIC

bor·age (bôr′ij, bur′-) *n.* [< OFr. < ML. < ? *burra,* coarse hair] an annual plant with brilliant blue flowers and hairy leaves, sometimes used in salads

bo·rane (bôr′ān) *n.* [BOR(ON) + -ANE] any of various compounds of boron and hydrogen, used as a rocket fuel, etc.

bo·rate (bôr′āt) *n.* a salt or ester of boric acid —*vt.* **-rat·ed, -rat·ing** to treat with borax or boric acid —**bo′rat·ed** *adj.*

bo·rax (bôr′aks) *n.* [< OFr. < ML. < Ar. < Per. *būrah*] a white, crystalline salt, Na₂B₄O₇, used as a flux and in glass, soaps, antiseptics, etc.

Bor·deaux (bôr dō′) seaport in SW France: pop. 267,000 —*n.* red or white wine from the region around Bordeaux

bor·der (bôr′dər) *n.* [< OFr. < OHG. *bord,* margin: see BOARD] **1.** an edge or a part near an edge; margin **2.** a dividing line between countries, etc.; frontier **3.** a narrow, ornamental strip along an edge —*vt.* **1.** to provide with a border *[a dress bordered* with lace*]* **2.** to lie along the edge of; bound *[lilies border* the drive*]* —*adj.* of, forming, or near a border —**border on (or upon) 1.** to be next to **2.** to be like; be nearly *[a mistake that bordered on* tragedy*]* —**bor′dered** *adj.*

bor·der·land (-land′) *n.* **1.** land forming near a border **2.** a vague, uncertain condition *[the borderland* between sleeping and waking*]*

bor·der·line (-līn′) *n.* a boundary —*adj.* on the boundary of what is acceptable, normal, etc.; not clearly one way or the other *[a borderline* case of heart disease*]*

bore¹ (bôr) *vt.* **bored, bor′ing** [< OE. < *bor,* auger < IE. base *bher-,* to cut] **1.** to make a hole in or through with a drill, etc. *[to bore* a plank*]* **2.** to make (a hole, tunnel, etc.) as by drilling **3.** to force (one's way), as through a crowd **4.** to make weary by being dull or uninteresting *[he bored* the children with stories of his youth*]* —*vi.* to bore a hole or passage —*n.* **1.** a hole made by or as by boring **2.** *a)* the hollow part of a tube, gun barrel, etc. *b)* its inside diameter; caliber **3.** a tiresome, dull person or thing

bore² (bôr) *n.* [< ON. *bara,* a billow] a high, forceful tidal wave that moves in quickly in a narrow channel

bore³ (bôr) *pt. of* BEAR¹

bo·re·al (bôr′ē əl) *adj.* [LL. *borealis* < BOREAS] **1.** northern **2.** of the northern zone of plant and animal life lying just below the tundra

Bo·re·as (bôr′ē əs) **1.** *Gr. Myth.* the god of the north wind **2.** the north wind thought of as a person

bore·dom (bôr′dəm) *n.* the condition of being bored or uninterested; ennui

bor·er (bôr′ər) *n.* **1.** a tool for boring **2.** an insect or worm that bores holes in trees, fruit, etc.

Bor·glum (bôr′gləm), **(John) Gut·zon** (gut′s'n) 1867–1941; U.S. sculptor

bo·ric (bôr′ik) *adj.* of or containing boron

boric acid a white, crystalline, weak acid, H₃BO₃, used as a mild antiseptic

Bor·is (bôr′is) [Russ., lit., fight] a masculine name

born (bôrn) *alt. pp. of* BEAR¹ —*adj.* **1.** brought into life or being **2.** by birth *[French-born]* **3.** being such naturally, as if from birth *[a born* athlete*]*

Born (bôrn), **Max** 1882–1970; Ger. nuclear physicist

born-a·gain (bôrn′ə gen′) *adj.* having a new, strong belief, esp. in the teaching that one can be saved by faith in Jesus

borne (bôrn) *alt. pp. of* BEAR¹

Bor·ne·o (bôr′nē ō) large island in the Malay Archipelago: the S part is in Indonesia & the N part is composed of Brunei & two states of Malaysia: 288,000 sq. mi.

Bo·ro·din (bôr′ə din; *Russ.* bô′rô dyēn′), **A·lek·san·dr** (ä′lyik sän′dr′) 1833–87; Russ. composer

Bor·o·di·no (bôr′ə dē′nō) Russian village near Moscow: site of a battle (1812) in which the Russian army was defeated by Napoleon's army

bo·ron (bôr′än) *n.* [< BOR(AX) + -on as in (CARB)ON] a nonmetallic chemical element occurring only in combination, as in borax: symbol, B; at. wt., 10.811; at. no., 5

boron carbide a compound of boron and carbon, B₄C, almost as hard as diamond: used as an abrasive and in control rods for nuclear reactors

bor·ough (bur′ō) *n.* [OE. *burg,* town, fortress < IE. base *bheregh-,* high] **1.** in certain States, a self-governing, incorporated town **2.** any of the five administrative units of New York City **3.** in England, *a)* a town with a municipal corporation granted by royal charter *b)* a town that sends representatives to Parliament

bor·row (bär′ō, bôr′ō) *vt., vi.* [OE. *borgian,* to borrow, lend] **1.** to take or receive (something) with the understanding that one will return it or something like it *[to borrow* a cup of sugar*]* **2.** to adopt (something) as one's own *[to borrow* a theory*]* **3.** to adopt (a word) from another language *[English borrowed* "tycoon" from Chinese*]* **4.** in subtraction, to take (a unit of ten) from the next higher denomination in the minuend and add it to the next lower —☆**borrow trouble** to worry before one has to —**bor′row·er** *n.*

borsch (bôrsh, bôrshch) *n.* [Russ. *borshch*] a Russian beet soup, served hot or cold, usually with sour cream: also **borsht** (bôrsht)

bort (bôrt) *n.* [< ? OFr. *bourt,* bastard] a poorly crystallized variety of diamond used as an abrasive: also **bortz** (bôrts)

bor·zoi (bôr′zoi) *n.* [Russ., swift] any of a breed of large dog with a narrow head, long legs, and silky coat; Russian wolfhound

bos·cage (bäs′kij) *n.* [OE. < Frank. *busk,* forest] a natural growth of trees or shrubs

Bosch (bäs, bôs), **Hier·on·y·mus** (hi rän′ə məs) 1450?–1516; Du. painter

bosh (bäsh) *n., interj.* [Turk., empty, worthless] [Colloq.] nonsense

bosk (bäsk) *n.* [ME. *bosk,* BUSH¹] a small wooded place; thicket

bosk·y (bäs′kē) *adj.* covered with trees or shrubs

BORZOI
(28–31 in. high at shoulder)

bo's'n (bōs′'n) *n. same as* BOATSWAIN

Bos·ni·a and Her·ce·go·vi·na (bäz′nē ə ənd hert′sə gō vē′nə) republic of Yugoslavia, in the C part: 19,745 sq. mi.; cap. Sarajevo

bos·om (booz′əm, bōō′zəm) *n.* [OE. *bosm*] **1.** the human breast; specif., a woman's breasts **2.** a thing thought of as like this /the *bosom* of the sea/ **3.** the breast regarded as the center of feelings **4.** the enclosing space formed by the breast and arms in embracing **5.** the inside; midst /in the *bosom* of one's family/ **6.** the part of a garment that covers the breast —*vt.* to conceal —*adj.* close; intimate /a *bosom* friend/

bos·om·y (-ē) *adj.* having large breasts

Bos·po·rus (bäs′pər əs) strait between the Black Sea & Sea of Marmara: also **Bos′pho·rus** (-fər əs) : see map at DARDANELLES

☆**boss**[1] (bôs, bäs) *n.* [Du. *baas,* a master] **1.** a person in charge of workers, as an employer or supervisor **2.** a person who controls a political organization: often **political boss** —*vt.* **1.** to act as boss of **2.** [Colloq.] to order (a person) about —*adj.* [Colloq.] chief

boss[2] (bôs, bäs) *n.* [< OFr. *boce,* a swelling] **1.** a raised part on a flat surface; esp., a decorative knob, stud, etc. **2.** the enlarged part of a machine shaft —*vt.* to decorate with knobs, studs, etc.

☆**boss·ism** (bôs′iz'm, bäs′-) *n.* control by political bosses

☆**boss·y**[1] (bôs′ē, bäs′ē) *adj.* **boss′i·er, boss′i·est** [BOSS[1] + -Y[2]] [Colloq.] acting like a boss, as by ordering people about; domineering —**boss′i·ly** *adv.* —**boss′i·ness** *n.*

boss·y[2] (bôs′ē, bäs′ē) *n. a pet name for* a cow

Bos·ton (bôs′t'n, bäs′-) [after *Boston,* port in NE England] capital of mass., on the atlantic: pop. 641,000 (met. area 2,754,000) —**Bos′to′ni·an** (-tō′nē ən) *adj., n.*

☆**Boston brown bread** a dark, steamed bread made of cornmeal, rye flour, etc. and molasses

☆**Boston cream pie** a cake of two layers with icing and a creamy filling

☆**Boston fern** a fern having drooping fronds of various forms, used as a house plant

☆**Boston ivy** a climbing vine of the grape family, with shield-shaped leaves and purple berries: often grown to cover walls

Boston Tea Party a protest (1773) against a British tax on tea imported by the American colonists, who boarded British ships in Boston harbor and dumped the tea overboard

☆**Boston terrier** any of a breed of small dog having a smooth, dark coat with white markings: also **Boston bull**

bo·sun (bōs′n) *n. same as* BOATSWAIN

Bos·well (bäz′wel, -wəl), **James** 1740–95; Scot. writer, who was a biographer of Samuel Johnson

bot (bät) *n.* [< ? Gael. < *boiteag,* maggot] the botfly larva

bot. **1.** botanical **2.** botanist **3.** botany

bo·tan·i·cal (bə tan′i k'l) *adj.* [< ML. < Gr. < *botanē,* a plant] **1.** of plants and plant life **2.** of. or connected with the science of botany Also **bo·tan′ic** —*n.* a vegetable drug prepared from bark, roots, herbs, etc. —**bo·tan′i·cal·ly** *adv.*

botanical garden a place where collections of plants and trees are kept for scientific study and for showing to visitors

bot·a·nize (bät′'n īz′) *vi.* **-nized′, -niz′ing** **1.** to gather plants for scientific study **2.** to study plants, esp. in their natural environment —*vt.* to study the plant life of (a region)

bot·a·ny (bät′'n ē) *n.* [BOTAN(ICAL) + -Y[3]] **1.** the science that deals with plants, their life, structure, growth, etc.: it is a branch of biology **2.** the plant life of an area **3.** the characteristics of a plant or plant group —**bot′a·nist** *n.*

Botany Bay bay on the SE coast of Australia, where the British formerly had a penal colony

botch (bäch) *vt.* [ME. *bocchen,* to repair < ? Du. *botsen,* to patch] **1.** to repair or patch clumsily **2.** to spoil by poor work; bungle —*n.* **1.** a badly patched place or part **2.** a bungled piece of work —**botch′er** *n.* —**botch′y** *adj.*

bot·fly (bät′flī′) *n., pl.* **-flies′** [see BOT] a fly whose larvae live as parasites in horses, sheep, etc.

both (bōth) *adj., pron.* [< OE. *ba tha,* both these] the two (of them) /use *both* hands; I ate *both* of the plums/ —*conj., adv.* together; equally; as well: used as a correlative with *and* /both tired *and* sick/

both·er (bäth′ər) *vt., vi.* [prob. Anglo-Ir. for POTHER] **1.** to worry, trouble, annoy, etc. /it *bothers* me when she is late/ **2.** to bewilder /all *bothered* by the change in plans/ **3.** to concern or trouble (oneself) /don't *bother* to reply/ —*n.* **1.** worry; trouble **2.** a person who gives trouble —*interj.* an expression of annoyance, etc.—see **SYN.** at ANNOY

both·er·a·tion (bäth′ə rā′shən) *n., interj.* [Colloq.] *same as* BOTHER

both·er·some (bäth′ər səm) *adj.* causing bother; annoying; troublesome; irksome

Both·ni·a (bäth′nē ə), **Gulf of** arm of the Baltic Sea, between Finland & Sweden

Bot·swa·na (bät swä′nə) country in S Africa: a member of the

Commonwealth: 222,000 sq. mi.; pop. 629,000; cap. Gaborone

bott (bät) *n. same as* BOT

Bot·ti·cel·li (bät′ə chel′ē), **San·dro** (sän′drō) 1445?–1510; It. Renaissance painter

bot·tle (bät′'l) *n.* [< OFr. < ML. *butticula,* a bottle < LL. *buttis,* a cask] **1.** a container, esp. for liquids, usually of glass or plastic and with a relatively narrow neck **2.** the amount that a bottle holds **3.** milk from an infant's nursing bottle —*vt.* **-tled, -tling** **1.** to put into a bottle or bottles **2.** to store under pressure in a cylinder, etc. /*bottled* gas/ —**bottle up** **1.** to shut in (enemy troops, etc.) **2.** to hold in or keep back (emotions) —☆**hit the bottle** [Slang] to drink much alcoholic liquor —**bot′tle·ful** *n., pl.* **-fuls′** —**bot′tler** *n.*

bot·tle·neck (bät′'l nek′) *n.* **1.** a place, as a narrow road, where traffic is slowed up or halted **2.** any point at which progress is slowed up /layoffs led to a production *bottleneck*/

bot·tle·nose (-nōz′) *n.* a kind of dolphin, gray or greenish, with a bottle-shaped snout

bot·tom (bät′əm) *n.* [< OE. *botm, bodan,* ground < IE. base *bhudh-*] **1.** the lowest part /the *bottom* of a page/ **2.** *a)* the lowest or last position /at the *bottom* of his class/ ☆*b) Baseball* the second half (*of* an inning) **3.** the part on which something rests; base **4.** the side or end that is underneath /the *bottom* of a crate/ **5.** the seat of a chair **6.** the ground beneath a body of water ☆**7.** [*often pl.*] *same as* BOTTOM LAND **8.** *a)* a ship's keel *b)* a ship **9.** [*usually pl.*] pajama trousers **10.** the true facts or the main reason; basis or cause /get to the *bottom* of the problem/ **11.** [Colloq.] the buttocks —*adj.* of, at, or on the bottom; lowest, last, etc. /on the *bottom* shelf/ —*vt.* **1.** to provide (a chair, etc.) with a bottom **2.** to understand; fathom **3.** to place or base (*on* or *upon*) —*vi.* **1.** to reach the bottom **2.** to be based —**at bottom** fundamentally; actually —**be at the bottom of** to be the real reason for —☆**bottom out** to level off at a low point, as prices —**bottoms up!** [Colloq.] drink deep!: a toast

☆**bottom land** low land through which a river flows: such land is rich in alluvial deposits

bot·tom·less (bät′əm lis) *adj.* **1.** having no bottom **2.** very deep, endless, etc.

☆**bottom line** **1.** the bottom line of the earnings report of a company, on which net profit per share of stock is shown **2.** [Colloq.] profits or losses **3.** [slang] the basic or most important factor, meaning, etc.

bot·tom·most (-mōst′) *adj.* at the very bottom; lowest, last, most basic, etc.

bot·u·lism (bäch′ə liz'm) *n.* [< G. < L. *botulus,* sausage + -*ismus,* -ISM: from early German cases involving sausages] poisoning resulting from the toxin produced by a certain bacillus sometimes found in foods that were not properly preserved

bou·clé, bou·cle (bōō klā′) *n.* [Fr., pp. of *boucler,* to buckle, curl] **1.** a curly yarn that gives the fabric made from it a tufted or knotted texture **2.** fabric made from this yarn

bou·doir (bōōd′wär) *n.* [Fr., lit., pouting place < *bouder,* to pout, sulk] a woman's bedroom, dressing room, or private sitting room

bouf·fant (bōō fänt′) *adj.* [Fr., prp. of *bouffer,* to puff out] puffed out; full, as a skirt, hairdo, etc.

bou·gain·vil·le·a, bou·gain·vil·lae·a (bōō′gən vil′ē ə) *n.* [ModL., after L. A. de *Bougainville* (1729–1811), Fr. explorer] a woody tropical vine having flowers with large, showy, purple or red bracts

bough (bou) *n.* [OE. *bog,* shoulder, hence branch] a branch of a tree, esp. a main branch

bought (bôt) *pt. & pp. of* BUY

bought·en (bôt′'n) *adj.* [Dial.] bought at a store and not homemade

bouil·la·baisse (bōōl′yə bäs′; Fr. bōō yä bes′) *n.* [Fr. < Pr. < *bouli,* to boil + *abaissa,* to settle] a chowder made with several kinds of fish and shellfish

bouil·lon (bōōl′yän, -yən; Fr. bōō yōn′) *n.* [Fr. < *bouillir,* BOIL[1]] a clear broth, esp. of beef

Boul·der (bōl′dər) [from the many large rocks found there] city in NC Colo.: pop. 67,000

boul·der (bōl′dər) *n.* [ME. *bulderstan* < Scand., as in Sw. *bullersten,* lit., noisy stone] any large rock made smooth and round by the action of weather and water

Boulder Dam *former name of* HOOVER DAM

boule (bōōl) *n.* [Fr., ball] **1.** [*usually pl.*] a French game similar to bowls **2.** a gambling game like roulette **3.** a small rounded mass, as of synthetic ruby, produced by the fusion of alumina

BOUFFANT HAIRDO

boul·e·vard (bool′ə värd′) *n.* [Fr., orig., the top of a rampart < MDu. *bolwerc*, BULWARK] ☆a broad street, often one lined with trees, plots of grass, etc.

bounce (bouns) *vt.* **bounced, bounc′ing** [akin to Du. *bonzen* & LowG. *bunsen*, to thump] **1.** orig., to bump or thump **2.** to cause to hit against a surface so as to spring back [to *bounce* a ball against a wall] ☆**3.** [Slang] *a*) to put (a person) out by force *b*) to discharge from a job; fire —*vi.* **1.** to spring back after striking a surface; rebound [to *bounce* on a trampoline] **2.** to jump; leap [*bounce* out of bed] ☆**3.** [Slang] to be returned to the payee by a bank: said of a worthless check —*n.* **1.** *a*) a bouncing; rebound *b*) a leap or jump **2.** capacity for bouncing [no *bounce* left in this ball] ☆**3.** [Colloq.] energy; zest —☆**bounce back** [Colloq.] to recover strength, spirits, etc. quickly —☆**the bounce** [Slang] a discharge from a job —**bounc′y** *adj.*

bounc·er (boun′sər) *n.* ☆[Slang] a man hired to remove disorderly people from a nightclub, etc.

bounc·ing (-siŋ) *adj.* big, healthy, strong, etc. [it's a *bouncing* baby boy]

bouncing Bet (bet) a perennial plant with clusters of pinkish flowers

bound[1] (bound) *vi.* [Fr. *bondir*, to leap, orig., to echo < LL. < L. *bombus*, a humming (see BOMB)] **1.** to move with a leap or series of leaps [kangaroos *bounding* across the plain] **2.** to bounce or rebound, as a ball —*n.* **1.** a jump; leap **2.** a bounce —see SYN. at SKIP[1]

bound[2] (bound) *pt. & pp.* of BIND —*adj.* **1.** confined by or as by being tied: often used in compounds [*snowbound*] **2.** closely connected **3.** certain; destined [*bound* to win] **4.** obliged [legally *bound* to pay] **5.** constipated **6.** provided with a binding [a *bound* book] **7.** designating a linguistic form, or morpheme, that never occurs by itself (Ex.: -*ing* in *walking* or *dis*- in *discredit*) **8.** [Colloq.] determined; resolved [a team *bound* on winning] —**bound up in** (or **with**) **1.** devoted to **2.** involved in

bound[3] (bound) *adj.* [ME. < *boun*, ready < ON. *buinn*, pp. of *bua*: see BONDAGE] going; headed [*bound* for home]

bound[4] (bound) *n.* [< OFr. < ML. *bodina*, boundary] **1.** a boundary **2.** [*pl.*] a place near or enclosed by a boundary —*vt.* **1.** to limit; confine **2.** to be a limit or boundary to ☆**3.** to name the boundaries of (a state, etc.) —*vi.* to have a boundary (*on* another country, etc.) —see SYN. at LIMIT —**out of bounds 1.** beyond the boundaries or limits, as of a playing field **2.** not to be entered or used; forbidden

-bound (bound) *a combining form meaning* going or headed in (a specified direction) [*southbound*]

bound·a·ry (boun′drē, -dər ē) *n., pl.* **-ries** [altered after BOUND[4] < ML. *bunnarium*] any line or thing marking a limit; bound; border [the Ohio River forms a *boundary* between Ohio and Kentucky]

bound·en (boun′dən) *adj.* [old pp. of BIND] **1.** under obligation **2.** that one is bound by; obligatory [his *bounden* duty]

bound·er (-dər) *n.* [BOUND[1] + -ER] [Chiefly Brit. Colloq.] a man who behaves in a dishonorable way; cad

bound·less (bound′lis) *adj.* having no bounds; unlimited [the *boundless* skies] —**bound′less·ly** *adv.* —**bound′less·ness** *n.*

boun·te·ous (boun′tē əs) *adj.* [< OFr. *bontive*: see BOUNTY] *same as* BOUNTIFUL —**boun′te·ous·ly** *adv.* —**boun′te·ous·ness** *n.*

boun·ti·ful (boun′tə f'l) *adj.* **1.** giving much in a gracious way; generous [a *bountiful* patron] **2.** more than just enough; plentiful [a *bountiful* harvest] —**boun′ti·ful·ly** *adv.* —**boun′ti·ful·ness** *n.*

boun·ty (boun′tē) *n., pl.* **-ties** [< OFr. < L. < *bonus*, good] **1.** generosity in giving **2.** a generous gift **3.** a reward or premium, as one given by a government for killing certain harmful animals, etc.

bou·quet (bō kā′; *also, & for 2 usually,* boo-) *n.* [Fr.] **1.** a bunch of cut flowers **2.** a fragrant smell or aroma, esp. of a wine or brandy

Bour·bon (boor′bən) the ruling family at various times of France, Spain, Naples, Sicily, etc. —*n.* [*also* b-] a political and social reactionary —☆**Bour′bon·ism** *n.* —**Bour′bon·ist** *n.*

bour·bon (bur′bən, boor′-) *n.* [< *Bourbon* County, Ky.] [*sometimes* B-] ☆a whiskey made from a mash of at least 51% corn and aged for not less than two years —*adj.* ☆of or made with such whiskey

bour·geois (boor zhwä′, boor′zhwä) *n., pl.* **-geois′** [Fr. < OFr. < ML. < LL. *burgus*, castle: for IE. base see BOROUGH] **1.** a shopkeeper **2.** a member of the bourgeoisie **3.** a person whose beliefs, attitudes, etc. are middle-class —*adj.* of or characteristic of the bourgeoisie; middle-class; specif., conventional, smug, materialistic, etc. —**bour·geoise′** (-zhwäz′) *n.fem.*

bour·geoi·sie (boor′zhwä zē′) *n.* [with sing. or pl. v.] **1.** the social class between the aristocracy or very wealthy and the working class; middle class **2.** in Marxist doctrine, capitalists as a social class opposed to the proletariat

bour·geon (bur′jən) *vi. same as* BURGEON

bourn[1], **bourne**[1] (bôrn, boorn) *n.* [OE. *burna*, a stream] a brook or stream

bourn[2], **bourne**[2] (bôrn, boorn) *n.* [< Fr. < OFr. < ML. *bodina*: see BOUND[4]] [Archaic] **1.** a limit; boundary **2.** a goal; objective **3.** a domain

Bourne·mouth (bôrn′məth, boorn′-) resort city in S England: pop. 151,000

bour·rée (boo rā′) *n.* [Fr. < *bourrir*, to whir] **1.** a lively, 17th-cent. French dance in duple time **2.** music for this

bourse (boors) *n.* [Fr., a purse < OFr. < ML. *bursa*, a bag < Gr. *byrsa*, a hide] a stock exchange; specif., [**B-**] the stock exchange of Paris

bout (bout) *n.* [for earlier *bought* < ME. *bught*] **1.** a struggle; contest or match [a boxing *bout*] **2.** a period of time taken up by some activity, illness, etc. [a *bout* of the flu]

bou·tique (boo tēk′) *n.* [Fr. < Gr. *apothēkē*: see APOTHECARY] a small shop, or a small department in a store, selling fashionable, expensive items

bou·ton·niere, bou·ton·nière (boot′'n ir′, -yer′) *n.* [Fr. *boutonnière*, a buttonhole] a flower or flowers worn in a buttonhole, as of a lapel

bou·var·di·a (boo vär′dē ə) *n.* [ModL., after C. *Bouvard*, 17th-c. Fr. physician] a plant of the madder family, having showy flowers often used in brides' bouquets

bou·zou·ki (boo zoo′kē) *n.* [< ModGr., prob. < Turk.] a stringed musical instrument of Greece, somewhat like a mandolin

BOUZOUKI

bo·vine (bō′vīn, -vin, -vēn) *adj.* [< LL. < L. *bovis*: see BEEF] **1.** of an ox or cow **2.** slow, dull, stupid, stolid, etc. —*n.* an ox, cow, etc.

bow[1] (bou) *vi.* [< OE. *bugan*, to bend < IE. base *bheugh*-] **1.** [Dial.] to bend or stoop **2.** to bend the head or body in respect, greeting, agreement, etc. **3.** to yield, as to authority [I *bow* to your wishes] —*vt.* **1.** [Dial.] to bend **2.** to bend (the head) in respect, prayer, shame, etc. **3.** to indicate (agreement, thanks, etc.) by bowing **4.** to weigh (*down*); overwhelm [*bowed* down by grief] —*n.* a bending of the head or body, as in respect, greeting, etc. —**bow and scrape** to be too polite or cringing —**bow out 1.** to leave or retire formally **2.** (or **in**) to usher out (or **in**) with a bow —**take a bow** to acknowledge applause, etc. as by bowing

bow[2] (bō) *n.* [< OE. *boga* < *bugan*, BOW[1]] **1.** anything curved or bent [a *rainbow*] **2.** a curve; bend **3.** a device for shooting arrows, made of a flexible, curved strip of wood, etc. with a taut cord connecting the two ends **4.** an archer **5.** a slender stick strung along its length with horsehairs, drawn across the strings of a violin, cello, etc. to play it **6.** *same as* BOWKNOT **7.** either of the sidepieces for the ears on a pair of glasses; temple —*vt., vi.* **1.** to bend or curve [the wall *bowed* outward] **2.** to play (a violin, etc.) with a bow

bow[3] (bou) *n.* [< LowG. or Scand.: akin to BOUGH] **1.** the front part of a ship, boat, etc.; prow **2.** the oarsman nearest the bow —*adj.* of or near the bow

bowd·ler·ize (boud′lə rīz′, bōd′-) *vt.* **-ized′, -iz′ing** [after Thomas *Bowdler*, who in 1818 published an expurgated Shakespeare] to remove passages thought to be obscene, improper, etc. from (a book, etc.); expurgate —**bowd′ler·ism** *n.* —**bowd′ler·i·za′tion** *n.*

bow·el (bou′əl, boul) *n.* [< OFr. < ML. < L. *botellus*, dim. of *botulus*, sausage] **1.** an intestine, esp. of a human being; gut; entrail: *usually used in pl.* **2.** [*pl.*] the inner part [the *bowels* of the earth] **3.** [*pl.*] [Archaic] tender emotions —*vt.* **-eled** or **-elled, -el·ing** or **-el·ling** to disembowel —**move one's bowels** to pass waste matter from the large intestine; defecate

bowel movement 1. the passing of waste matter from the large intestine; defecation **2.** waste matter so passed; feces

bow·er (bou'ər) *n.* [< OE. *bur*, a dwelling: for IE. base see BONDAGE] **1.** a place enclosed by overhanging boughs or by vines on a trellis; arbor **2.** [Archaic] a boudoir —*vt.* to enclose in a bower —**bow'er·y** *adj.*

Bow·er·y (bou'ər ē, bou'rē), the [Du. *bouwerij*, a farm] a street in New York City, or the district around this street, that is a center of cheap hotels, saloons, etc.

☆**bow·fin** (bō'fin') *n.* a primitive freshwater fish of eastern N. America, with a rounded tail fin

☆**bow·ie knife** (bōō'ē, bō'ē) [after Col. J. *Bowie*, Am. frontiersman] a long hunting knife with a single edge, carried in a sheath, as by frontiersmen

bow·knot (bō'nät') *n.* a knot tied with two loops that can be untied by pulling its two ends

bowl¹ (bōl) *n.* [OE. *bolla*: see BALL¹] **1.** a deep, hollow, rounded dish **2.** a large drinking cup **3.** a thing or part shaped like a bowl, as the hollowed-out part of a smoking pipe, the basin of a sink or toilet, or a hollow land formation ☆**4.** an amphitheater, or stadium **5.** the contents of a bowl —**bowl'like'** *adj.*

bowl² (bōl) *n.* [< OFr. < L. *bulla*, a bubble: see BOIL¹] **1.** a heavy ball used in the game of bowls **2.** a roll of the ball in bowling or bowls —*vi., vt.* **1.** to roll (a ball) or play at bowling or bowls **2.** to move or cause to move swiftly and smoothly, as on wheels [the car *bowled* along the highway] **3.** *Cricket* to throw (a ball) to the batsman —**bowl over 1.** to knock over **2.** [Colloq.] to astonish and confuse

bowl·der (bōl'dər) *n. same as* BOULDER

bow·leg (bō'leg') *n.* a leg that is bowed, or curved, outward

bow·leg·ged (-leg'id, -legd') *adj.* having legs that are bowed outward

bowl·er¹ (bōl'ər) *n.* a person who bowls

bowl·er² (bōl'ər) *n.* [< *Bowler*, name of 19th-c. London hat manufacturer] [Brit.] a derby hat

bow·line (bō'lin, -līn') *n.* [ME. *bouline*, prob. < Scand.] **1.** a rope used to keep the sail taut when sailing into the wind **2.** a knot used to tie off a loop: also **bowline knot:** see illustration at KNOT

bowl·ing (bōl'iŋ) *n.* **1.** a game in which a heavy ball is bowled along a wooden lane (**bowling alley**) in an attempt to knock over wooden pins, now usually ten, set upright at the far end **2.** *same as* BOWLS **3.** the playing of either game

bowls (bōlz) *n.* **1.** a game played on a smooth lawn (**bowling green**) with weighted wooden balls which are rolled in an attempt to make them stop near a target ball (the *jack*) **2.** ninepins, tenpins, or skittles

bow·man (bō'mən) *n., pl.* **-men** an archer

bow·sprit (bou'sprit, bō'-) *n.* [prob. < Du. < *boeg*, BOW³ + *spriet*, SPRIT] a large, tapered spar extending forward from the bow of a sailing vessel

bow·string (bō'striŋ') *n.* a cord stretched from one end of an archer's bow to the other

bow tie (bō) a small necktie tied in a bowknot

box¹ (bäks) *n.* [OE. < ML. *buxis* < L. < Gr. *pyxos*, boxwood] **1.** any of various kinds of containers made of cardboard, wood, or other stiff material and usually having a lid; case; carton **2.** the contents of a box [he ate two *boxes* of popcorn] **3.** [< the tool *box* under the seat] the driver's seat on a coach **4.** any boxlike thing, as *a)* a small, enclosed group of seats in a theater, stadium, etc. *b)* a small booth [a sentry's *box*] *c)* a large, enclosed stall, for a horse, etc.: in full, **box stall** *d)* a space for a certain person or group [a jury *box*] **5.** a short newspaper article enclosed in borders ☆**6.** *Baseball* any of the areas marked off for the batter, pitcher, catcher, and coaches **7.** *Mech.* a protective casing for a part [a journal *box*] —*vt.* to put into a box [to *box* a gift] —*adj.* **1.** shaped or made like a box [a *box* camera] **2.** packaged in a box [a *box* lunch] —**box in** (or **up**) to shut in or keep in —**box the compass 1.** to name the thirty-two points of the compass in order: compasses were kept in boxes **2.** to make a complete circuit —**in a box** [Colloq.] in a difficult situation —**box'like'** *adj.*

BOWSPRIT

box² (bäks) *n.* [< ?] a blow struck with the hand or fist, esp. on the ear —*vt.* **1.** to strike with such a blow **2.** to fight in a boxing match with —*vi.* to fight with the fists; engage in boxing

box³ (bäks) *n.* [OE. < L. *buxus* < Gr. *pyxos*] an evergreen shrub or small tree with small, leathery leaves

☆**box·car** (bäks'kär') *n.* a fully enclosed railroad freight car

☆**box elder** a fast-growing N. American maple with compound leaves

Box·er (bäk'sər) *n.* a member of a Chinese society that led an unsuccessful uprising (the **Boxer Rebellion,** 1900) against foreigners in China

box·er (bäk'sər) *n.* **1.** a man who boxes; pugilist; prizefighter **2.** a medium-sized dog with a sturdy body and a smooth, fawn or brindle coat

☆**boxer shorts** men's undershorts cut in a loose, full style and having an elastic waistband

box·ing (-siŋ) *n.* [< BOX²] the skill or sport of fighting with the fists, esp. in padded leather mittens (**boxing gloves**)

Boxing Day a holiday in England, Canada, etc., the first weekday after Christmas, when gifts are given to employees, postmen, etc.

box kite a kite with a long, box-shaped framework

box office 1. a place where admission tickets are sold, as in a theater ☆**2.** [Colloq.] the power of a show or performer to attract an audience

box pleat a double pleat with the under edges folded toward each other

☆**box score** a summary of a baseball game in the form of a chart, showing the hits, runs, errors, etc.

box seat a seat in a box at a theater, etc.

☆**box spring** a bedspring consisting of a boxlike frame containing rows of coil springs and enclosed in a cloth cover

☆**box turtle** a N. American land turtle with a hinged under shell that can be completely closed

box·wood (bäks'wood') *n.* **1.** the wood of the box (shrub or tree) **2.** the box (shrub or tree)

box·y (bäk'sē) *adj.* **-i·er, -i·est** like a box; square in shape, confining, etc.

boy (boi) *n.* [ME. *boie*] **1.** a male child from birth to manhood **2.** an immature or childish man **3.** any man; fellow [a night out with the *boys*] **4.** a man servant, porter, etc.: an impolite usage **5.** [Colloq.] a son —*interj.* [Slang] an exclamation of pleasure, surprise, etc.: often **oh, boy!** —**boy'ish** *adj.* —**boy'ish·ly** *adv.* —**boy'ish·ness** *n.*

boy·cott (boi'kät) *vt.* [after Captain C. C. *Boycott,* Irish land agent so treated in 1880] **1.** to join together in refusing to deal with, so as to punish, coerce, etc. **2.** to refuse to buy, sell, or use [to *boycott* a newspaper] —☆*n.* the act of boycotting

☆**boy·friend** (boi'frend') *n.* [Colloq.] **1.** a sweetheart or escort of a girl or woman **2.** a boy who is one's friend

boy·hood (-hood') *n.* [see -HOOD] **1.** the time or state of being a boy **2.** boys collectively

Boyle (boil), **Robert** 1627–91; Brit. chemist & physicist

Boyle's law [after R. BOYLE] the statement that for a body of gas at constant temperature the volume increases proportionally as the pressure decreases and vice versa

boy scout a member of the **Boy Scouts,** a worldwide boys' organization that stresses outdoor life and service to others

☆**boy·sen·ber·ry** (boi'z'n ber'ē) *n., pl.* **-ries** [after Rudolph *Boysen,* U.S. horticulturist] a large, purple berry, probably a cross of the raspberry, loganberry, and blackberry

bp. 1. birthplace: also **bpl. 2.** bishop

B/P, BP, b.p. bills payable

b.p. 1. below proof **2.** boiling point

Br *Chem.* bromine

Br. 1. Breton **2.** Britain **3.** British

br. 1. branch **2.** bronze **3.** brother **4.** brown

B/R, BR, b.r. bills receivable

☆**bra** (brä) *n.* [< BRA(SSIERE)] an undergarment worn by women to support and shape the breasts —**bra'less** *adj.*

brace (brās) *vt.* **braced, brac'ing** [< OFr. < L. *brachia,* pl. of *brachium,* an arm: see BRIEF] **1.** to tighten, esp. by stretching [to *brace* a drumhead] **2.** to strengthen or make firm by supporting the weight of, etc.; prop up [to *brace* a beam with a post] **3.** to make ready for an impact, shock, etc. [I *braced* myself for the crash] **4.** to stimulate; invigorate [*braced* by the cool, fresh wind] **5.** to get a firm hold with (the hands or feet) —*n.* **1.** a couple; pair [a *brace* of pistols] **2.** a device that clasps or connects; fastener **3.** [*pl.*] [Brit.] suspenders **4.** either of the signs { }, used to connect words, lines, or staves of music **5.** a device, as a beam, used as a support, to resist strain, etc.; prop **6.** *a)* any of various devices for supporting a weak or deformed part of the body *b)* [*often pl.*] a device worn on irregular teeth to force them to grow straight **7.** a tool for holding and rotating a drilling bit —☆**brace up** [Colloq.] to become strong or brave again, as after a defeat

brace and bit a tool for boring, consisting of a removable drill (*bit*) in a rotating handle (*brace*)

brace·let (brās′lit) *n.* [< OFr. < L. < *brachium*, an arm] **1.** an ornamental band or chain worn about the wrist or arm **2.** [Colloq.] a handcuff: *usually used in pl.* —**brace′let·ed** *adj.*

brac·er (brās′ər) *n.* **1.** a person or thing that braces ☆**2.** [Slang] a drink of alcoholic liquor

☆**bra·ce·ro** (brə ser′ō) *n., pl.* **-ros** [Sp. < *brazo*, an arm < L. *brachium*] a Mexican farm laborer brought into the U.S. temporarily for migrant work in harvesting crops

bra·chi·o- [< L. < Gr. *brachiōn*, an arm] *a combining form meaning* of an arm or the arms [*brachiopod*]: also **bra′chi-**

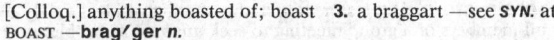

BRACE AND BIT

bra·chi·o·pod (brā′kē ə päd′, brak′ē-) *n.* [prec. + -POD] any of a number of related marine animals with hinged upper and lower shells and two armlike parts with tentacles

bra·chi·um (brā′kē əm, brak′ē-) *n., pl.* **-chi·a** (-ə) [L.] **1.** the part of the arm from the shoulder to the elbow **2.** *Biol.* any armlike part —**bra′chi·al** *adj.*

brach·y- [< Gr. *brachys*, short] *a combining form meaning* short [*brachycephalic*]

brach·y·ce·phal·ic (brak′i sə fal′ik) *adj.* [BRACHY- + -CEPHALIC] having a relatively short or broad head: also **brach′y·ceph′a·lous** (-sef′ə ləs): see CEPHALIC INDEX —**brach′y·ceph′a·ly** (-sef′ə lē) *n.*

brac·ing (brās′iŋ) *adj.* invigorating; refreshing [the *bracing* air at the seashore] —*n.* **1.** a device that braces **2.** a system of braces

brack·en (brak′'n) *n.* [< ON.] **1.** a large, coarse fern, as the brake **2.** a growth of such ferns

brack·et (brak′it) *n.* [< Fr. dim. of *brague*, knee pants, ult. < Gaul. *braca*, pants] **1.** a piece projecting from a wall and serving to support weight, as of a balcony **2.** any supporting piece, esp. one in the form of a right triangle **3.** a wall shelf held up by brackets **4.** a wall fixture, as for a small electric lamp **5.** either of the signs [ ], used to enclose words, figures, etc., such as those used for explanation **6.** the part of a classified grouping that falls within specified limits [a $5 to $10 price *bracket*] —*vt.* **1.** to support with brackets **2.** to enclose in brackets **3.** to classify or think of together [Grant and Lee are *bracketed* in history]

brack·ish (brak′ish) *adj.* [earlier Scot. *brack* < MDu. *brak*, salty + -ISH] **1.** somewhat salty, as water in some marshes near the sea **2.** having an unpleasant taste; nauseating —**brack′ish·ness** *n.*

bract (brakt) *n.* [L. *bractea*, thin metal plate] a modified leaf, usually small and scalelike, growing at the base of a flower or on its stalk —**brac·te·al** (brak′tē əl) *adj.* —**brac′te·ate** (-it) *adj.*

bract·let (brakt′lit) *n.* a secondary bract at the base of a flower: also **brac·te·ole** (brak′tē ōl′)

brad (brad) *n.* [ON. *broddr*, a spike] a thin wire nail with a small head, sometimes off-center —*vt.* **brad′ded, brad′ding** to fasten with brads

Brad·dock (brad′ək), **Edward** 1695-1755; Brit. general in the French and Indian War

Brad·ford (brad′fərd) city in N England, in Yorkshire: pop. 294,000

Brad·ford (brad′fərd), **William** 1590-1657; 2d governor of Plymouth Colony

Brad·street (brad′strēt′), **Anne** (born *Anne Dudley*) 1612?-72; Am. poet, born in England

Bra·dy (brā′dē), **Math·ew B.** (math′yoo) 1823?-96; U.S. photographer

brae (brā) *n.* [ON. *bra*, eyelid: for IE. base see BRAID] [Scot.] a sloping bank; hillside

brag (brag) *vt., vi.* **bragged, brag′ging** [prob. < OFr. *braguer*; ? akin to BRAY] to boast —*n.* **1.** boastful talk or manner **2.**

[Colloq.] anything boasted of; boast **3.** a braggart —see SYN. at BOAST —**brag′ger** *n.*

brag·ga·do·ci·o (brag′ə dō′shē ō, -dō′shō) *n., pl.* **-os** [coined by SPENSER < BRAG + It. ending] **1.** a braggart **2.** noisy boasting or bragging

brag·gart (brag′ərt) *n.* [< OFr.: see BRAG] a person who boasts to an annoying degree —*adj.* boastful

Bra·he (brä′ə), **Ty·cho** (tü′kō) 1546-1601; Dan. astronomer

Brah·ma (brä′mə; *for n.* brä′-) [Hindi < Sans. *brahman*, worship] *Hinduism* **1.** the supreme spirit of the universe **2.** the chief member of the trinity (Brahma, Vishnu, and Siva) and creator of the universe —☆*n. same as* BRAHMAN (sense 2)

Brah·man (brä′mən; *for 2* brä′-) *n., pl.* **-mans** [see prec.] **1.** a member of the priestly Hindu caste, the highest ☆**2.** a breed of domestic cattle developed from the zebu of India: it has a large hump over the shoulders —**Brah·man·ic** (brä man′ik), **Brah·man′i·cal** *adj.*

Brah·man·ism (brä′mən iz'm) *n.* the religious doctrines and system of the Brahmans

Brah·ma·pu·tra (brä′mə pōō′trə) river flowing through Tibet, India, & Bangladesh into the Bay of Bengal

Brah·min (brä′mən) *n.* **1.** *same as* BRAHMAN (sense 1) **2.** a cultured, upper-class person, esp. of New England, regarded as haughty or conservative —**Brah·min·ic** (brä min′ik) *adj.*

Brah·min·ism (-iz'm) *n.* **1.** *same as* BRAHMANISM **2.** the characteristic attitude, etc. of Brahmins

Brahms (brämz), **Jo·han·nes** (yō hän′əs) 1833-97; Ger. composer

braid (brād) *vt.* [< OE. *bregdan*, to move quickly < IE. base *bherek-*, to gleam] **1.** to interweave three or more strands of (hair, straw, etc.) **2.** to make by such interweaving [to *braid* a rug] **3.** to arrange (the hair) in a braid or braids **4.** to trim or bind with braid —*n.* **1.** a band or strip formed by braiding **2.** a length of braided hair **3.** a woven band of tape, ribbon, etc. used to bind or decorate clothing —**braid′er** *n.* —**braid′ing** *n.*

Braille (brāl) *n.* [after L. Braille (1809-52), Fr. teacher who devised it] [*also* b-] **1.** a system of printing and writing for the blind, using raised dots felt by the fingers **2.** the characters used in this system —*vt.* **Brailled, Brail′ling** [*also* b-] to print or write in such characters

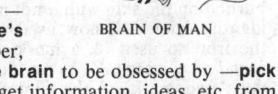

1	2	3	4	5	6	7
a	b	c	d	e	f	g
8	9	0				
h	i	j	k	l	m	n
o	p	q	r	s	t	
u	v	w	x	y	z	

BRAILLE ALPHABET
AND NUMBERS

brain (brān) *n.* [OE. *brægen*] **1.** the mass of nerve tissue in the skull of vertebrate animals, an extension of the spinal cord: it is the center of thought and receives and transmits impulses: see GRAY MATTER, WHITE MATTER **2.** *a)* [*often pl.*] intelligence; mental ability *b)* [Colloq.] a person of great intelligence *c)* [Colloq.] the main organizer of a group activity —*vt.* **1.** to dash out the brains of **2.** [Slang] to hit hard on the head —**beat (or rack, cudgel, etc.) one's brains** to try hard to remember, understand, etc. —**have on the brain** to be obsessed by —**pick (someone's) brains** [Slang] to get information, ideas, etc. from (someone) for one's own use

CEREBRUM
CEREBELLUM
MEDULLA
OBLONGATA
SPINAL CORD

BRAIN OF MAN

brain·child (-chīld′) *n.* [Colloq.] an idea, plan, etc. produced by one's mental labor

brain·less (-lis) *adj.* foolish or stupid —**brain′less·ly** *adv.* —**brain′less·ness** *n.*

brain·pan (-pan′) *n.* the part of the skull containing the brain

brain·pow·er (-pou′ər) *n.* mental ability

☆**brain·storm** (-stôrm′) *n.* [Colloq.] a sudden inspiration or idea —*vi.* to engage in brainstorming

☆**brain·storm·ing** (-stôr′miŋ) *n.* the offering of ideas freely by all members of a group meeting to seek answers to problems

☆**brain trust** a group of experts acting as advisers to a leader or administrator —**brain truster**

brain·wash (-wôsh′, -wäsh′) *vt.* ☆ [Colloq.] to teach doctrines or ideas to so thoroughly as to cause to undergo a radical change in beliefs

brain wave rhythmic electric impulses given off by nerve centers in the brain during rest

brain·y (-ē) *adj.* **brain′i·er, brain′i·est** [Colloq.] intelligent; mentally bright —**brain′i·ness** *n.*

braise (brāz) *vt.* **braised, brais′ing** [Fr. *braiser* < *braise* (< Gmc. *brasa*), live coals] to cook (meat) by browning in fat and then simmering in a covered pan with a little liquid

brake¹ (brāk) *n.* [prob. taken as sing. of BRACKEN] a large, coarse fern, a variety of bracken

brake² (brāk) *n.* [< MLowG. *brake* or ODu. *braeke* < *breken*, to break] **1.** a tool for beating flax or hemp so that the fiber can be separated **2.** any device for slowing or stopping the motion of a vehicle or machine, as by causing a block or band to press against a moving part —*vt.* **braked, brak′ing 1.** to break up (flax, etc.) into smaller pieces **2.** to slow down or stop as with a brake —*vi.* ☆**1.** to operate a brake **2.** to be slowed down or stopped by a brake —**brake′less** *adj.*

brake³ (brāk) *n.* [< or akin to MLowG. *brake*, stumps] a clump of brushwood, briers, etc.

brake⁴ (brāk) *archaic pt. of* BREAK

brake band a band with a lining (**brake lining**) of asbestos, fine wire, etc., that creates friction when tightened about the drum of a brake

brake drum the metal cylinder, as on the hub of a wheel, to which the brake band is applied in braking

☆**brake·man** (brāk′mən) *n., pl.* **-men** a railroad worker who operated the brakes on a train, but is now chiefly an assistant to the conductor

☆**brake shoe** a block curved to fit the shape of a wheel and forced against it to act as a brake

bram·ble (bram′b′l) *n.* [OE. *brǣmel* < *brom*, broom < IE. base *ph(e)rem-*, to form a point] **1.** any prickly shrub of the rose family, as the raspberry, blackberry, etc. **2.** any prickly shrub or vine —**bram′bly** *adj.* **-bli·er, -bli·est**

bran (bran) *n.* [OFr. *bren*] the skin or husk of grains of wheat, rye, oats, etc. separated from the flour, as by sifting

branch (branch) *n.* [< OFr. *brance* < LL. *branca*, a paw] **1.** any woody growth from the trunk or from a main limb of a tree or shrub **2.** anything like a branch, as a tine of a deer's antler ☆**3.** any of the streams into which a river may divide or which flow into it ☆**4.** *same as* BRANCH WATER **5.** *a)* a division of a body of learning [optics is a *branch* of physics] *b)* a division of a family descending from a certain ancestor *c)* a unit located away from the main unit [a *branch* of a library] —*vi.* **1.** to put forth or divide into branches; ramify [the road *branches* a mile from here] **2.** to come out (*from* the trunk or stem) as a branch —*vt.* to separate into branches —**branch off 1.** to separate into branches; fork **2.** to go off in another direction; diverge —**branch out 1.** to put forth branches **2.** to extend interests, activities, etc. —**branched** *adj.* —**branch′like′** *adj.*

bran·chi·ae (braŋ′ki ē′) *n.pl., sing.* **-chi·a** (-ə) [< L. < Gr. *branchia*, fins] the gills of a fish —**bran′chi·al** *adj.*

☆**branch water 1.** water from a small stream **2.** water as used for mixing with whiskey, etc.

brand (brand) *n.* [OE., flame, sword < base of *biernan*, BURN¹] **1.** a stick that is burning or partially burned **2.** *a)* a mark burned on the skin with a hot iron, formerly used to punish and identify criminals, now used on cattle to show ownership *b)* the iron so used **3.** a mark of disgrace; stigma [to bear the *brand* of coward] **4.** *a)* an identifying mark or label on products; trademark *b)* the kind or make of a commodity [a *brand* of cigars] *c)* a special kind [his own *brand* of nonsense] **5.** [Archaic] a sword —*vt.* **1.** to mark with or as with a brand **2.** to set apart as something shameful [they *branded* him a liar] —**brand′er** *n.*

Bran·deis (bran′dīs), **Louis Dem·bitz** (dem′bits) 1856–1941; U.S. Supreme Court justice (1916–39)

Bran·den·burg (bran′dən burg′; *G.* brän′dən boŏrk′) region in E Germany, in which Berlin is situated

bran·dish (bran′dish) *vt.* [< OFr. < Gmc. *brand*: see BRAND] to wave or shake in a menacing or showy way; flourish [to *brandish* a sword] —*n.* a brandishing of something

☆**brand name** the name by which a particular make of a product is known —**brand′name′** *adj.*

brand-new (brand′nōō′, -nyōō′) *adj.* [orig., fresh from the fire: see BRAND] **1.** entirely new; recently made and never used **2.** recently acquired [a *brand-new* baby]

bran·dy (bran′dē) *n., pl.* **-dies** [earlier *brandywine* < Du. *brandewijn*, lit., burnt (i.e., distilled) wine] **1.** an alcoholic liquor distilled from wine **2.** a similar liquor distilled from fermented fruit juice [cherry *brandy*] —*vt.* **-died, -dy·ing** to flavor, mix, or preserve with brandy

Bran·dy·wine (bran′dē wīn′) [< ?] creek in SE Pa. & N Del., near which the Americans suffered a defeat (1777) in the Revolutionary War

☆**bran·ni·gan** (bran′ə gən) *n.* [prob. < surname *Brannigan*] [Slang] a noisy quarrel or fight; brawl

brant (brant) *n., pl.* **brants, brant:** see PLURAL, II, D, 1 [< ?] any of a number of related small, dark wild geese of Europe and N. America

Brant (brant), **Joseph** (born *Thayendanegea*) 1742–1807; Mohawk Indian chief

Brant·ford (brant′fərd) city in SE Ontario, Canada: pop. 60,000

Braque (bräk), **Georges** (zhôrzh) 1882–1963; Fr. painter

brash (brash) *adj.* [< ?] **1.** acting too quickly; reckless; rash **2.** bold in a rude way; impudent —**brash′ly** *adv.* —**brash′ness** *n.*

bra·sier (brā′zhər) *n. same as* BRAZIER

Bra·sil (brä zēl′) *Port. sp. of* BRAZIL

Bra·sí·lia (brä zē′lyä) capital of Brazil, in the EC part: pop. 545,000

brass (bras) *n., pl.* **brass′es:** see PLURAL, II, D, 3 [OE. *brǣs*] **1.** a yellowish metal that is an alloy of copper and zinc **2.** things made of brass **3.** [*often pl.*] brass-wind musical instruments **4.** [Colloq.] bold impudence; effrontery ☆**5.** [*often with pl. v.*] [Slang] *a)* military officers of high rank: see BRASS HAT *b)* any high officials —*adj.* made of brass —see SYN. at TEMERITY

bras·sard (brə särd′, bras′ärd) *n.* [Fr., ult. < *bras*, an arm] **1.** armor for the upper arm: also **bras·sart** (bras′ärt) **2.** an arm band that serves as a badge or identification

brass band a band of mainly brass-wind instruments

brass hat [< the gold braid on the cap] [Slang] **1.** a military officer of high rank **2.** any high official

brass·ie (bras′ē) *n.* [orig. made with a *brass* sole] a golf club with a wooden head, used for long fairway shots: now usually called *number 2 wood*

bras·siere, bras·sière (brə zir′) *n.* [Fr., orig. arm guard < *bras*, an arm] *same as* BRA

☆**brass knuckles** linked metal rings or a metal bar with finger holes, worn for rough fighting

brass tacks ☆[Colloq.] basic facts; practical details: usually in **get** (or **come**) **down to brass tacks**

brass·ware (bras′wer′) *n.* articles made of brass

brass winds (windz) musical instruments made of coiled metal tubes and having a cup-shaped mouthpiece [the trumpet, trombone, and tuba are *brass winds*] —**brass′-wind′** *adj.*

brass·y (-ē) *adj.* **brass′i·er, brass′i·est 1.** of or decorated with brass **2.** like brass, as in color **3.** cheap and showy **4.** loud and blaring [a *brassy* voice] **5.** impudent; brazen —**brass′i·ly** *adv.* —**brass′i·ness** *n.*

brat (brat) *n.* [OE. *bratt*, a cloak < Gael. *bratt*, a cloth, rag < ?] a child, esp. one who is impudent or hard to manage: term sometimes used in a joking or playful way —**brat′ti·ness, brat′tish·ness** *n.* —**brat′ty, brat′tish** *adj.*

Bra·ti·sla·va (brä′ti slä′və) city in S Czechoslovakia, on the Danube: pop. 277,000

brat·wurst (brat′wərst; *G.* brät′vŏŏrsht) *n.* [G. < OHG. < *brato*, lean meat + *wurst*, sausage] highly seasoned, fresh sausage of veal and pork

bra·va·do (brə vä′dō) *n.* [< Sp. *bravada* < *bravo*, BRAVE] a pretending to be brave or bold when one is really afraid

brave (brāv) *adj.* [Fr. < It. *bravo*, brave, fine, orig., wild, savage < L. *barbarus*, BARBAROUS] **1.** not afraid; having courage; valiant **2.** fine; splendid [a *brave* new world] —*n.* **1.** any brave man **2.** a N. American Indian warrior —*vt.* **braved, brav′ing 1.** to face with courage [they *braved* the storm] **2.** to defy; dare —**brave′ly** *adv.* —**brave′ness** *n.*

SYN.—**brave** is the general term that implies fearlessness in meeting danger or difficulty; **courageous** suggests readiness to deal firmly with any dangerous situation because of self-discipline and strong convictions; **bold** stresses a daring nature, whether shown by courage, insolence, or defiance; **audacious** suggests reckless boldness; **valiant** emphasizes a heroic quality in the courage shown; **intrepid** implies absolute fearlessness in facing something new or unknown; **plucky** is usually used of someone who continues fighting even though at a disadvantage —*ANT.* **craven, cowardly**

brav·er·y (brā′vər ē) *n.* **1.** a being brave; courage; valor **2.** a showy display, as of clothes *[dressed in holiday bravery]*

bra·vo[1] (brä′vō) *interj.* [It.: see BRAVE, *adj.*] well done! very good! excellent! —*n., pl.* **-vos** a shout of "bravo!"

bra·vo[2] (brä′vō) *n., pl.* **-voes, -vos;** It. **-vi** (-vē) [It.: see BRAVE] a hired killer; assassin

bra·vu·ra (brə vyoor′ə) *n.* [It., spirit < *bravo*, BRAVE] **1.** a display of daring; dash **2.** *a)* a brilliant piece of music that shows off the performer's skill and technique *b)* brilliant musical technique

brawl (brôl) *vi.* [< ? Du. *brallen,* to boast] to quarrel or fight noisily —*n.* **1.** a noisy quarrel or fight; row **2.** [Slang] a noisy party —**brawl′er** *n.*

brawn (brôn) *n.* [< OFr. *braon,* muscular part < Frank. *brado,* meat, calf (of leg)] **1.** strong, well-developed muscles **2.** muscular strength *[a job that calls for brawn]* —**brawn′i·ness** *n.* — **brawn′y** *adj.* **brawn′i·er, brawn′i·est**

bray (brā) *vi.* [< OFr. < VL. *bragire,* to cry out] to make the loud, harsh cry of a donkey, or a sound, esp. a laugh, like this — *vt.* to utter loudly and harshly —*n.* the loud, harsh cry of a donkey, or a sound like this

braze[1] (brāz) *vt.* **brazed, braz′ing** [Fr. *braser,* to solder, var. of *braiser,* BRAISE] to solder with a metal having a high melting point, esp. with an alloy of zinc and copper —**braz′er** *n.*

braze[2] (brāz) *vt.* **brazed, braz′ing** [< OE. *bræsian* < *bræs,* BRASS] **1.** to make of, or coat with, brass **2.** to make hard like brass —**braz′er** *n.*

bra·zen (brā′z'n) *adj.* [OE. *bræsen* < *bræs,* BRASS] **1.** of brass **2.** like brass in color, etc. **3.** showing no shame; bold; impudent *[a brazen lie]* **4.** having the ringing sound of brass; harsh and piercing —**brazen it out** to act boldly as if one need not be ashamed —**bra′zen·ly** *adv.* —**bra′zen·ness** *n.*

bra·zen·faced (-fāst′) *adj.* shameless and impudent

bra·zier[1] (brā′zhər) *n.* [Fr. *brasier* < *braise:* see BRAISE] a metal pan, bowl, etc. to hold burning coals or charcoal

bra·zier[2] (brā′zhər) *n.* [see BRASS] a person who works in brass

Bra·zil (brə zil′) country in C & NE S. America: c. 3,287,000 sq. mi.; pop. 92,238,000; cap. Brasília —**Bra·zil′ian** (-yən) *adj., n.*

Brazil nut 1. a hard-shelled, three-sided, oily, edible seed of a tall S. American tree **2.** this tree, on which the seeds grow in capsules in clusters, like segments of an orange

Braz·za·ville (brä′zə vil′) capital of the Congo, on the Congo River: pop. 156,000

breach (brēch) *n.* [< OE. < *brecan,* to BREAK] **1.** orig., a breaking or being broken **2.** a failure to obey a law, keep a contract, follow the rules of etiquette, etc. **3.** an opening made by breaking through a wall, defense, etc. **4.** a break in friendly relations — *vt.* to make a breach in; break through

breach of promise a breaking of a promise to marry

BRAZIL NUTS

bread (bred) *n.* [OE. *bread,* crumb, morsel: see BURN[1]] **1.** a food baked from a leavened, kneaded dough made with flour or meal, water, yeast, etc. **2.** any baked food like bread but made with a batter *[quick breads, cornbread]* **3.** food generally **4.** one's livelihood *[to earn one's bread]* **5.** [Slang] money —*vt.* to cover with bread crumbs before cooking —**bread and butter** one's means of subsistence; livelihood — **break bread** to eat, esp. with someone else —**cast one's bread upon the waters** to do good deeds without expecting something in return —**know which side one's bread is buttered on** to know what is to one's best interest

bread-and-but·ter (bred′'n but′ər) *adj.* **1.** of one's means of livelihood **2.** basic, commonplace, everyday, etc. ☆**3.** expressing thanks, as a letter to one's host after a visit

bread·bas·ket (-bas′kit) *n.* **1.** a region supplying much grain **2.** [Slang] the stomach or abdomen

☆**bread·board** (-bôrd′) *n.* a board on which dough is kneaded or one on which bread is sliced

bread·fruit (-frōōt′) *n.* **1.** a large, round fruit with a starchy pulp, that is like bread when baked **2.** the tropical tree on which it grows

☆**bread line** a line of people waiting to be given food, either as government relief or from some charity

☆**bread-stuff** (-stuf′) *n.* ground grain or flour for bread

breadth (bredth) *n.* [OE. *brædu* < *brad,* broad + -TH[1]] **1.** the distance from side to side of a thing; width **2.** a piece of a given and regular width *[a breadth of linoleum]* **3.** lack of narrowness *[breadth of knowledge]*

breadth·ways (bredth′wāz′) *adv., adj.* in the direction of the breadth: also **breadth′wise′** (-wīz′)

bread·win·ner (bred′win′ər) *n.* a person who supports dependents by his earnings

break (brāk) *vt.* **broke, bro′ken, break′ing** [OE. *brecan* < IE. base *bhreg-,* from which also come L. *frangere* & BREACH, BREECH, FRAGILE] **1.** to cause to come apart by force; smash; burst *[the ball broke the window]* **2.** to cut open the surface of (soil, the skin, etc.) **3.** to cause the failure of by force *[to break a strike]* **4.** to make no longer usable *[to break a watch by overwinding it]* **5.** to tame (a horse, etc.) as with force **6.** *a)* to cause to get rid *(of a habit)* *[he broke himself of smoking]* *b)* to get rid of (a habit) **7.** to lower in rank or grade; demote *[to break a sergeant to private]* **8.** *a)* to reduce to poverty or bankruptcy *b)* to wreck the health, spirit, etc. of **9.** to surpass (a record) **10.** to violate (a law, agreement, etc.) **11.** to escape from by force *[to break prison]* **12.** to disrupt the order or completeness of *[to break ranks]* **13.** to interrupt (a journey, electric circuit, etc.) **14.** to reduce the force of by interrupting *[the awning broke her fall]* **15.** to bring to a sudden end *[to break a tie]* **16.** to penetrate (silence, darkness, etc.) **17.** to make known; disclose *[break the news to me gently]* **18.** *a)* to decipher (a code, etc.) *b)* to solve *[to break a criminal case]* **19.** to make (a will) invalid **20.** to prove (an alibi) false **21.** to exchange (a bill or coin) for smaller units *[can you break a dollar for me?]* —*vi.* **1.** to split into pieces; come apart; burst *[the cup broke when it fell]* **2.** to scatter; disperse *[break and run]* **3.** to force one's way *(through)* **4.** to stop associating *(with)* **5.** to become useless; go out of order *[my radio broke]* **6.** to change suddenly as by a sharp rise, fall, turn, shift, etc. *[her voice broke;* the hot spell *broke]* **7.** to move away suddenly *[he broke into the open]* **8.** to begin suddenly to perform, etc. *[break into song]* **9.** to come into being or general knowledge *[the story broke;* dawn was *breaking]* ☆**10.** to stop activity temporarily *[we broke for lunch]* **11.** to dash apart, as a wave on the shore ☆**12.** to curve near the plate: said of a pitched baseball **13.** [Colloq.] to happen in a certain way *[things were breaking badly]* —*n.* **1.** a breaking; breach; fracture **2.** *a)* a breaking in, out, or forth ☆*b)* a sudden move; rush; dash *[she made a break for the door]* **3.** a broken place; separation; crack **4.** a beginning or appearance *[break of day]* **5.** an interruption of something regular *[take a ten-minute break]* **6.** a gap; interval; omission **7.** a breach in friendly relations **8.** a sudden change ☆**9.** an escape, as from prison ☆**10.** a lowering or drop, as of prices ☆**11.** [Colloq.] an improper or untimely action or remark ☆**12.** [Slang] a chance piece of luck, specif. of good luck *[an actor waiting for a break]* **13.** *Music a)* the point where one register changes to another *b)* a phrase that joins two separate parts of a piece of jazz music —**break down 1.** to go out of working order **2.** to begin to cry or lose control of oneself **3.** to lose one's health and have a collapse **4.** to separate into parts for study; analyze —**break in 1.** to enter forcibly **2.** to interrupt **3.** to train (a beginner) ☆**4.** to work the stiffness out of (new equipment) —**break off 1.** to stop abruptly **2.** to stop being friendly —**break out 1.** to begin suddenly **2.** to escape **3.** to become covered with pimples or a rash **4.** to bring out for use *[break out the gear]* —**break up 1.** to disperse: also, esp. as a command, **break it up 2.** to take apart **3.** to put a stop to **4.** [Colloq.] to end a relationship ☆**5.** [Colloq.] to distress or upset ☆**6.** [Colloq.] to laugh or make laugh uncontrollably —**break′a·ble** *adj.*

SYN. —**break** expresses the general idea of separation into pieces as a result of force, stress, etc.; **smash** and **crash** add a sense of suddenness, violence, and noise; **crush** suggests a pressure that causes crumpling or powdering; **shatter** implies a sudden breaking up into pieces and a scattering of these pieces; **crack** implies incomplete separation of parts or a snapping noise in breaking; **split** describes separation lengthwise, as along the grain; **fracture** implies the breaking of a rigid substance, as bone or rock; **splinter** refers to the splitting of wood, etc. into thin, sharp pieces All of these terms are used figuratively [to break one's heart, smash one's hopes, crush the opposition, shatter one's nerves, etc.]

break·age (brāk′ij) n. **1.** a breaking **2.** things or quantity broken **3.** loss due to breaking, or the sum allowed for this

break·down (-doun′) n. **1.** a breaking down; specif., a) a failure to work properly [the breakdown of a machine, of authority, etc.] b) a failure of health c) decomposition d) a separating into parts; analysis [a breakdown of costs] **2.** a lively, shuffling dance

break·er (brāk′ər) n. a person or thing that breaks; specif., a wave that breaks into foam

break·fast (brek′fəst) n. [BREAK + FAST²] the first meal of the day —vi. to eat breakfast

break·front (brāk′frunt′) adj. having a front from which a section projects —n. a breakfront cabinet

breaking point the point at which material, or one's endurance, etc., breaks or gives way under strain

break·neck (brāk′nek′) adj. likely to cause an accident; highly dangerous [breakneck speed]

break·out (-out′) n. **1.** a sudden, forceful escape, as from prison **2.** a skin rash

break·through (-thrōō′) n. **1.** the act or place of breaking through against resistance **2.** an important discovery, as in some science, that solves a major problem

break·up (-up′) n. a breaking up; specif., a) a scattering b) a disintegration c) a collapse d) a stopping or ending

break·wa·ter (-wôt′ər, -wät′-) n. a barrier to break the force of waves, as before a harbor

bream (brēm; also, esp. for 2, brim) n., pl. bream, breams: see PLURAL, II, D, 2 [< OFr. bresme < Frank. brahsima: for IE. base see BRAID] **1.** a European freshwater fish related to the minnows **2.** any of various saltwater fishes ☆**3.** any of various freshwater sunfishes

breast (brest) n. [OE. breost < IE. base bhreus-, to swell] **1.** either of two milk-producing glands at the upper, front part of a woman's body **2.** a corresponding gland in other animals **3.** the upper, front part of the body; chest **4.** the part of a garment, etc. that is over the breast **5.** the breast regarded as the center of emotions **6.** anything likened to the breast [the breast of the sea] —vt. to face, esp. firmly; move forward against [to breast a tide of opposition] —**beat one's breast** to show in an exaggerated way that one has a feeling of guilt, etc. —**make a clean breast of** to confess (guilt, etc.) fully

breast·bone (brest′bōn′) n. the thin, flat bone to which most of the ribs are joined in the front of the chest; sternum

breast-feed (-fēd′) vt. -fed′ (-fed′), -feed′ing to feed (a baby) milk from the breast; suckle

breast·pin (-pin′) n. ☆an ornamental pin or brooch worn on a dress, near the throat

breast·plate (-plāt′) n. **1.** a piece of armor for the breast: see illustration at ARMOR **2.** an embroidered cloth worn on the breast of the ancient Jewish high priests

breast stroke a swimming stroke in which both arms are brought out sideways from a position in front of the head, while the legs are drawn up and then quickly extended backward

BREAST STROKE

breast·work (-wurk′) n. a low wall put up quickly as a defense, esp. to protect gunners

breath (breth) n. [OE. bræth, odor, exhalation < IE. base bher-, to boil up, from which also come FERMENT & BROOD] **1.** air taken into the lungs and then let out **2.** breathing; respiration **3.** the power to breathe easily and naturally [wait till I get my breath back] **4.** life or spirit [while there is breath in me, I will resist] **5.** air carrying fragrance or odor [the breath of spring] **6.** a puff or whiff, as of air; slight breeze **7.** moisture produced by a condensing of the breath, as in cold air [so cold that she could see her breath] **8.** a whisper or murmur [not a breath of scandal] **9.** a faint hint or indication [a breath of suspicion] **10.** Phonet. a voiceless letting out of the airstream, as in pronouncing (s) or (p) —**below** (or **under**) **one's breath** in a whisper or murmur —**catch one's breath 1.** to gasp or pant **2.** to pause or rest —**in the same breath** almost simultaneously —**out of breath** breathless, as from exertion —**save one's breath** to keep from talking when talk would be useless —**take one's breath away** to thrill

breathe (brēth) vi., vt. **breathed, breath′ing** [< ME. < breth, BREATH] **1.** to take (air) into the lungs and let it out again; inhale and exhale **2.** to live [while I breathe, you are safe] **3.** to give out the odor of [he breathed garlic in my face] **4.** to instill [to breathe confidence] **5.** to blow softly **6.** to speak or sing softly **7.** to give or take time to breathe; rest [to breathe a horse] **8.** to pant or cause to pant, as from exertion —**breathe again** (or **freely**) to have a feeling of relief or reassurance —**breathe one's last** to die —**breath·a·ble** (brē′thə b′l) adj.

breath·er (brē′thər) n. **1.** one who breathes in a certain way [a mouth breather] **2.** a small vent, as for releasing moisture **3.** [Colloq.] a pause as for rest

breath·ing (brē′thiŋ) adj. that breathes; living; alive —n. **1.** respiration **2.** the sound of h in hit, hope, etc.; aspirate

breathing space 1. enough space or time to breathe freely **2.** a chance to stop and think

breath·less (breth′lis) adj. **1.** without breath **2.** no longer breathing; dead **3.** out of breath; gasping **4.** unable to breathe easily because of excitement, fear, etc. **5.** still and heavy, as the air —**breath′less·ly** adv. —**breath′less·ness** n.

breath·tak·ing (-tāk′iŋ) adj. **1.** that takes one's breath away [a breathtaking climb to the fifth floor] **2.** very exciting; thrilling [a breathtaking view of the valley] —**breath′tak′ing·ly** adv.

breath·y (-ē) adj. with a loud letting out of breath [her breathy reply] —**breath′i·ly** adv. —**breath′i·ness** n.

brec·ci·a (brech′ē ə, bresh′-) n. [It.] rock consisting of sharp-cornered bits cemented together by sand, clay, or lime

Brecht (breHt; E. brekt), **Ber·tolt** (ber′tôlt) 1898–1956; Ger. playwright

bred (bred) pt. & pp. of BREED

breech (brēch) n. [< OE. brec, pl. of broc: for IE. base see BREAK] **1.** the buttocks; rump **2.** the lower or back part of a thing **3.** the part of a gun behind the barrel

☆**breech·cloth** (brēch′klôth′) n. a cloth worn about the loins; loincloth: also **breech′clout′** (-klout′)

breech·es (brich′iz) n.pl. [see BREECH] **1.** trousers reaching to the knees **2.** [Colloq.] any trousers

breech·es buoy (brēch′iz, brich′-) a device for rescuing people at sea, consisting of a pair of short canvas breeches hung from a life preserver that is run along a rope from ship to shore or to another ship

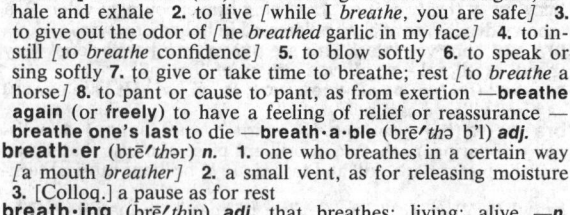

BREECH-ES

breech·ing (brich′iŋ, brēch′-) n. a harness strap around a horse's hindquarters

breech·load·er (brēch′lōd′ər) n. any gun loaded at the breech —**breech′-load′ing** adj.

breed (brēd) vt. bred, breed′ing [OE. bredan < brod, a hatching, fetus: see BROOD] **1.** to bring forth (offspring) **2.** to be the source of; produce [ignorance breeds prejudice] **3.** to cause to reproduce; raise [to breed dogs] **4.** to bring up or train [born and bred to be a teacher] **5.** to produce (fissionable material) in a breeder reactor —vi. **1.** to be produced; originate [crime breeds in slums] **2.** to reproduce —n. **1.** a stock of animals or plants descended from common ancestors [the Pekingese is a breed of dog] **2.** a kind; sort; type —**breed′er** n.

breeder reactor a nuclear reactor that produces more fissionable material than it uses up

breed·ing (brēd′iŋ) n. **1.** the producing of young **2.** the rearing of young **3.** good upbringing or training [concern for others is a sign of breeding] **4.** the producing of plants and animals, esp. so as to develop new or better types

breeze (brēz) n. [< Fr. brise, prob. < EFris. brisen, to blow fresh and strong] **1.** a wind, esp. a gentle wind **2.** [Brit. Colloq.] commotion ☆**3.** [Colloq.] a thing easy to do [the math test was a breeze] **4.** Meteorol. any wind ranging in speed from 4 to 31 miles per hour —vi. **breezed, breez′ing** ☆[Slang] to move or go quickly, briskly, etc. —☆**in a breeze** [Colloq.] easily —☆**shoot** (or **bat**) **the breeze** [Slang] to chat idly

☆**breeze·way** (brēz′wā′) n. a covered passageway, as between a house and garage

breez·y (brē′zē) adj. **breez′i·er, breez′i·est 1.** slightly windy **2.** lively and carefree [breezy talk] —**breez′i·ly** adv. —**breez′i·ness** n.

Bre·men (brem′ən; G. brā′mən) port in N West Germany: pop. 604,000

Bren·ner Pass (bren′ər) mountain pass across the Alps at the border between Italy & Austria

Bre·scia (bre′shä) city in N Italy, at the foot of the Alps: pop. 201,000

BREEZEWAY

Brest (brest) seaport in W France, on the Atlantic: pop. 154,000

breth·ren (breth′rən, -ərn) *n.pl.* brothers: now chiefly used of fellow members of a church

Bret·on (bret′'n) *adj.* [Fr., ult. same word as BRITON] of Brittany, its people, or their language —*n.* **1.** a native or inhabitant of Brittany **2.** the Celtic language of the Bretons

Breu·ghel (broi′gəl; *occas.* broi′-) *same as* BRUEGEL

breve (brev, brēv) *n.* [It. < L. *brevis*, BRIEF] a mark (ˇ) put over a short vowel or short or unstressed syllable

bre·vet (brə vet′; *chiefly Brit.* brev′it) *n.* [< OFr., a note < ML. *breve*, letter < L. *brevis*, BRIEF] *Mil.* a commission giving an officer a higher honorary rank without more pay —*adj.* held by brevet —*vt.* **-vet′ted** or **-vet′ed, -vet′ting** or **-vet′ing** to give a brevet to —*pl.* **-cies**

bre·vi·ar·y (brē′vē er′ē, brev′yər ē) *n.,* *pl.* **-ar·ies** [< ML. *breviarium*, abridgment, ult. < L. *brevis*, BRIEF] *R.C.Ch.* a book of the daily prayers, hymns, etc. to be said by priests and other clerics

brev·i·ty (brev′ə tē) *n.* [< L. < *brevis*, BRIEF] **1.** briefness of time **2.** shortness; conciseness [the *brevity* of his talk]

brew (broo) *vt.* [OE. *breowan*: see BURN[1]] **1.** to make (beer, ale, etc.) from malt and hops by steeping, boiling, and fermenting **2.** to make (tea, coffee, etc.) by steeping or boiling **3.** to plan (mischief, trouble, etc.); plot —*vi.* **1.** to brew beer, ale, etc. **2.** to begin to form: said of a storm, trouble, etc. —*n.* **1.** a brewed beverage **2.** an amount brewed —**brew′er** *n.*

brew·er·y (broo′ər ē) *n.,* *pl.* **-er·ies** an establishment where beer, ale, etc. are brewed

brew·ing (broo′iŋ) *n.* **1.** the preparation of a brew **2.** the amount of brew made at one time

Brezh·nev (brezh nyôf′; *E.* brezh′nef, -nev), **Le·o·nid I(lich)** (lā′ô nyēt′) 1906– ; general secretary of the Communist Party of the U.S.S.R. (1964–)

Bri·an (brī′ən) [Celt., ? strong] a masculine name

bri·ar[1] (brī′ər) *n.* *same as* BRIER[1] —**bri′ar·y** *adj.*

bri·ar[2] (brī′ər) *n.* **1.** *same as* BRIER[2] **2.** a tobacco pipe made of brierroot

bri·ar·root (-root′, -root′) *n.* *same as* BRIERROOT

bri·ar·wood (-wood′) *n.* *same as* BRIERWOOD

bribe (brīb) *n.* [< OFr., morsel of bread given to beggars < *briber*, to beg] anything given or promised to get a person to do something illegal or wrong or something that he does not want to do —*vt.* **bribed, brib′ing 1.** to offer or give a bribe to **2.** to get or influence by bribing —*vi.* to give bribes —**brib′a·ble** *adj.* —**brib′er** *n.*

brib·er·y (brī′bər ē) *n.,* *pl.* **-er·ies** the giving, offering, or taking of bribes

bric-a-brac (brik′ə brak′) *n.* [< Fr. < *à bric et à brac*, by hook or crook] small, rare, or artistic objects, or knickknacks, placed about a room for ornament

brick (brik) *n.* [< MDu. *bricke* & OFr. *brique*, a fragment] **1.** a substance made from clay molded into oblong blocks and baked, used in building, paving, etc. **2.** any of these blocks **3.** bricks collectively **4.** anything shaped like a brick [a *brick* of ice cream] **5.** [Colloq.] a fine fellow —*adj.* **1.** built or paved with brick **2.** like brick [*brick* red] —*vt.* to build or pave with brick —**brick up (or in)** to wall in with brick

brick·bat (brik′bat′) *n.* **1.** a piece of brick used as a missile **2.** an unfavorable or critical remark

☆**brick cheese** a ripened, semihard American cheese shaped like a brick

brick·lay·ing (-lā′iŋ) *n.* the act or work of building with bricks —**brick′lay′er** *n.*

brick red yellowish or brownish red —**brick′-red′** *adj.*

brick·work (-wurk′) *n.* **1.** anything built of bricks **2.** the work of bricklaying

☆**brick·yard** (-yärd′) *n.* a place where bricks are made or sold

brid·al (brīd′'l) *n.* [< OE. *bryd ealo*, marriage feast < *bryd*, bride + *ealo*, ale] a wedding —*adj.* **1.** of a bride [a *bridal* veil] **2.** of a wedding [a *bridal* feast]

bridal wreath ☆ a cultivated shrub of the rose family, with many small, white double flowers

bride (brīd) *n.* [OE. *bryd*] a woman who has just been married or is about to be married

bride·groom (brīd′groom′, -groom′) *n.* [< OE. *brydguma*, suit-or < *bryd*, bride + *guma*, man; altered by folk etym. after GROOM] a man who has just been married or is about to be married

brides·maid (brīdz′mād′) *n.* any of the young women who attend the bride at a wedding

bridge[1] (brij) *n.* [OE. *brycge*: for IE. base see BROW] **1.** a structure built over a river, railroad, etc. to provide a way across for vehicles or pedestrians **2.** a thing that provides connection or contact [a common language is a *bridge* between cultures] **3.** *a)* the upper, bony part of the nose *b)* the curved bow of a pair of glasses fitting over the nose **4.** the thin, arched piece over which the strings are stretched on a violin, etc. **5.** a raised platform on a ship for the commanding officer **6.** *Dentistry* a fixed or removable mounting for false teeth, attached to nearby teeth **7.** *Music* a connecting passage —*vt.* **bridged, bridg′ing 1.** to build a bridge on or over **2.** to provide a connection, transition, etc. across [he tried to *bridge* the generation gap] —**burn one's bridges (behind one)** to commit oneself to a course from which one cannot later retreat —**bridge′a·ble** *adj.*

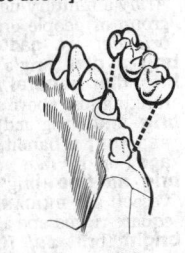

DENTAL BRIDGE

bridge[2] (brij) *n.* [earlier *biritch*, "Russian whist," altered after prec.; ? of Russ. origin] any of various card games that developed from whist: see AUCTION BRIDGE, CONTRACT BRIDGE

bridge·head (brij′hed′) *n.* **1.** a strong position set up by an attacking force on the enemy's side of a bridge, river, etc. **2.** *same as* BEACHHEAD (sense 2)

Bridge·port (brij′pôrt′) [after the bridge across a local river] seaport in SW Conn.: pop. 155,000

Bridg·es (brij′əz), **Robert (Seymour)** 1844–1930; Eng. poet; poet laureate (1913–30)

bridge·work (brij′wurk′) *n.* a dental bridge or bridges

bri·dle (brīd′'l) *n.* [< OE. < *bregdan*, to pull: see BRAID] **1.** a head harness for guiding a horse, including the bit and reins **2.** anything that controls or restrains [to remove the *bridle* of censorship] —*vt.* **-dled, -dling 1.** to put a bridle on **2.** to control as with a bridle [*bridle* your anger] —*vi.* **1.** to pull one's head back quickly with the chin drawn in, as in showing anger, scorn, etc. **2.** to take offense (*at*) [*bridled* at his remark] —see SYN. at RESTRAIN

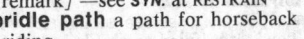

BROW BAND
CHEEK STRAP
NOSE BAND
BIT
REINS
BRIDLE

bridle path a path for horseback riding

brief (brēf) *adj.* [< OFr. *bref* < L. *brevis* < IE. base *mreghu-*, short, from which also come BRACE, PRETZEL, & MERRY] **1.** short in time or extent [a *brief* visit] **2.** not wordy; concise [a *brief* news report] **3.** curt or abrupt —*n.* **1.** a short statement; summary or abstract **2.** a statement of the main points of a law case for use in court **3.** [*pl.*] closefitting, legless underpants —*vt.* **1.** to summarize **2.** to supply with all the necessary instructions or information [to *brief* pilots before a flight] **3.** [Brit.] *a)* to furnish with a legal brief *b)* to hire as counsel —**hold a brief for** to argue for or be in favor of —**in brief** in a few words —**brief′ing** *n.* —**brief′ly** *adv.* —**brief′ness** *n.*

SYN.—**brief** and **short** are the opposites of *long* when applied to time [a *brief* or *short* interval], although **brief** often emphasizes being compact, concise, etc. [a *brief* review] and **short** often implies being incomplete or reduced [a *short* measure; to make *short* work of it]; **short** is usually used in referring to length, height, etc. [a *short* man]

brief·case (brēf′kās′) *n.* a flat, flexible case, usually of leather, for carrying papers, etc.

bri·er[1] (brī′ər) *n.* [< OE. *brer*] **1.** any thorny bush, as a bramble, wild rose, etc. **2.** a growth of such bushes —**bri′er·y** *adj.*

bri·er[2] (brī′ər) *n.* [Fr. *bruyère*, white heath] **1.** a heath native to S Europe **2.** its root, or a tobacco pipe made from the root: usually sp. **bri′ar**

bri·er·root (-root′, -root′) *n.* the root wood of the brier, or a pipe made of this

bri·er·wood (-wood′) *n.* *same as* BRIERROOT

brig[1] (brig) *n.* [< BRIGANTINE] a two-masted ship with square-rigged sails

☆**brig**[2] (brig) *n.* [< ?] **1.** a prison on a U.S. warship **2.** [Mil. Slang] the guardhouse; prison

bri·gade (bri gād′) *n.* [Fr. < It. *brigata*, troop < *brigare*, to contend < *briga*, strife] **1.** a large unit of soldiers **2.** *U.S. Army* a military unit composed of two or more battalions **3.** a group of people organized to work together as a unit [a fire *brigade*] —*vt.* **-gad′ed, -gad′ing** to organize into a brigade

brig·a·dier (brig′ə dir′) *n.* a brigade commander

brigadier general *pl.* **brigadier generals** *U.S. Mil.* an officer ranking just above a colonel: abbrev. **Brig. Gen.**

brig·and (brig′ənd) *n.* [< OFr. < It. *brigante* < *brigare:* see BRIGADE] a bandit, usually one of a roving band —**brig′and·age** (-ən dij) *n.*

brig·an·tine (brig′ən tēn′) *n.* [< Fr. < It. *brigantino*, pirate vessel: see BRIGAND] a two-masted ship with the foremast square-rigged and a fore-and-aft mainsail

bright (brīt) *adj.* [OE. *bryht*, earlier *beorht:* for IE. base see BIRCH] **1.** shining with light that is radiated or reflected; full of light [a *bright* room; a *bright* lamp] **2.** clear or brilliant in color or sound; vivid or intense [*bright* blue] **3.** lively or cheerful [a *bright* smile] **4.** mentally quick; clever [a *bright* child] **5.** full of happiness or hope; favorable [a *bright* future] —*adv.* in a bright manner [stars shining *bright*] —**bright′ly** *adv.* —**bright′ness** *n.*

SYN. —**bright** implies in a general way the giving forth or reflecting of light, or a being filled with light [a *bright* day, star, shield, etc.]; **radiant** emphasizes the sending out of rays of light; **shining** implies a steady, continuous brightness [the *shining* sun]; **brilliant** implies strong or flashing brightness [*brilliant* diamonds]; **luminous** is used of objects that are full of light or give off phosphorescent light; **lustrous** is used of objects whose surfaces gleam by reflected light and suggests glossiness [*lustrous* silk] —see also SYN. at INTELLIGENT —ANT. **dull, dim, dark**

bright·en (brīt′'n) *vt., vi.* **1.** to make or become bright or brighter **2.** to gladden; cheer up

Brigh·ton (brīt′'n) resort city in S England: pop. 165,000

Bright's disease (brīts) [after R. *Bright* (1789–1858), Eng. physician] a kidney disease in which albumin appears in the urine; chronic nephritis

brill (bril) *n., pl.* **brill, brills:** see PLURAL, II, D, 2 [< ?] an edible European flatfish related to the turbot

bril·liance (bril′yəns) *n.* great brightness, radiance, splendor, intelligence, etc.: also **bril′lian·cy**

bril·liant (bril′yənt) *adj.* [< Fr. prp. of *briller* < It. *brillare*, to sparkle] **1.** shining brightly; sparkling [her *brilliant* eyes] **2.** vivid; intense: said of color, musical tones, etc. **3.** very splendid or distinguished [a *brilliant* performance] **4.** highly intelligent, talented, or skillful [a *brilliant* student] —*n.* a gem, esp. a diamond, cut with many facets to increase its sparkle —see SYN. at BRIGHT and INTELLIGENT —**bril′liant·ly** *adv.*

brim (brim) *n.* [OE. *brim*, sea: for IE. base see BRAMBLE] **1.** the topmost edge of a cup, bowl, etc. [filled to the *brim*] **2.** a projecting rim or edge, as of a hat —*vt., vi.* **brimmed, brim′-ming** to fill or be full to the brim —**brim′less** *adj.*

brim·ful (brim′fool′) *adj.* full to the brim

brim·stone (brim′stōn′) *n.* [OE. *brynstan:* see BURN[1] & STONE] same as SULFUR

brin·dle (brin′d'l) *adj.* same as BRINDLED —*n.* **1.** a brindled color **2.** a brindled animal

brin·dled (-d'ld) *adj.* [prob. < ME. *brended* < *brennen*, BURN[1]] gray or tawny and streaked or spotted with a darker color [a *brindled* cow]

brine (brīn) *n.* [OE.; prob. < IE. base *bhrēi-*, to cut: orig. sense "cutting, sharp"] **1.** water full of salt **2.** *a)* the water of the sea *b)* the sea; ocean —*vt.* **brined, brin′ing** to soak in or treat with brine

bring (brin) *vt.* **brought, bring′ing** [OE. *bringan* < IE. base *bhrenk-*] **1.** to carry or lead (a person or thing) to the place thought of as "here" or to a place the speaker will be [*bring* him to my house for lunch] **2.** to cause to be, happen, appear, etc. [war *brings* death] **3.** to lead, persuade, or influence [I can't *bring* myself to tell her] **4.** to sell for [to *bring* a high price] **5.** *Law a)* to present in a law court [to *bring* charges] *b)* to put forward (evidence) —**bring about** to make happen; effect —**bring around** (or **round**) **1.** to persuade by arguing, urging, etc. **2.** to bring back to consciousness —**bring forth 1.** to produce (offspring, fruit, etc.) **2.** to make known; disclose —**bring forward** to introduce; show —**bring in 1.** to import **2.** to produce (income or revenue) —**bring off** to succeed in doing; accomplish —**bring on** to cause to be, happen, or appear —**bring out 1.** to reveal; make clear **2.** to publish (a book), produce (a

play), etc. **3.** to introduce (a girl) formally to society —**bring over** to convince or persuade —**bring to 1.** to revive (an unconscious person) **2.** to cause (a ship) to stop —**bring up 1.** to take care of during childhood; raise; rear **2.** to introduce, as into discussion **3.** to cough up **4.** to vomit **5.** to stop suddenly

SYN. —**bring** implies a carrying or leading of a thing or person to some place, and **take** implies similar action away from a place [*bring* the book to me; I will *take* it back to the library]; **fetch** implies a going after something, getting it, and bringing it back [he trained his dog to *fetch* his slippers]

brink (brink) *n.* [< MLowG. or Dan., shore, bank] **1.** the edge, esp. at the top of a steep place **2.** the point just short of [at the *brink* of war]

☆**brink·man·ship** (brink′mən ship′) *n.* [BRINK + -manship, as in *statesmanship*] the policy of following a dangerous course of action to the brink of disaster: also **brinks′man·ship′** (brinks′-)

brin·y (brīn′ē) *adj.* **brin′i·er, brin′i·est** of or like brine; very salty —**the briny** [Slang] the ocean —**brin′i·ness** *n.*

bri·oche (brē ōsh′, -ôsh′) *n.* [Fr.] a light, rich roll made with flour, butter, eggs, and yeast

bri·quette, bri·quet (bri ket′) *n.* [< Fr. dim. of *brique*, BRICK] a brick made of compressed coal dust, etc., used for fuel

Bris·bane (briz′bān, -bən) seaport on the E coast of Australia: pop. 833,000

brisk (brisk) *adj.* [< ? Fr. *brusque*, BRUSQUE] **1.** quick in manner or movement; energetic [we took a *brisk* walk] **2.** cool, dry, and bracing [*brisk* air] **3.** pungent, keen, sharp, etc. [a *brisk* flavor] **4.** active; busy [*brisk* trading] —**brisk′ly** *adv.* —**brisk′ness** *n.*

bris·ket (bris′kit) *n.* [ME. *brusket*, akin to Dan. *bryske:* for IE. base see BREAST] **1.** the breast of an animal **2.** meat cut from this part: see illustration at BEEF

bris·ling (bris′lin, briz′-) *n.* [Norw. dial. < older Dan. *bretling*] same as SPRAT (sense 1)

bris·tle (bris′'l) *n.* [< OE. *byrst* < IE. base *bhar-*, point, sharp] **1.** any short, stiff, prickly hair; esp., any of the hairs of a hog, etc., used for brushes **2.** an artificial hair, as of nylon, in a brush —*vi.* **-tled, -tling 1.** to become stiff and erect, like bristles **2.** to have the bristles become erect, as in fear [the cat *bristled* as the dog came near] **3.** to become tense with fear, anger, etc. **4.** to be thickly covered (*with*) [the battlefield *bristled* with guns] —*vt.* **1.** to make stand up like bristles **2.** to make bristly

bris·tle·tail (bris′'l tāl′) *n.* any of several wingless insects with bristles at the tail end, as the silverfish

bris·tly (bris′lē) *adj.* **-tli·er, -tli·est 1.** having bristles; rough with bristles [a *bristly* beard] **2.** bristlelike; prickly —**bris′tli·ness** *n.*

Bris·tol (bris′t'l) **1.** seaport in SW England: pop. 428,000 **2.** [after prec.] city in C Conn.: pop. 55,000

Bristol board [after BRISTOL, England] a fine, smooth pasteboard, used by artists, printers, etc.

Bristol Channel arm of the Atlantic, between S Wales & SW England

Brit. 1. Britain **2.** Britannia **3.** British

Brit·ain (brit′'n) same as GREAT BRITAIN

Bri·tan·ni·a (bri tan′yə, -tan′ē ə) **1.** *Roman name for* GREAT BRITAIN (sense 1), esp. the southern part **2.** same as BRITISH EMPIRE

britannia metal [also b-] an alloy of tin, copper, and antimony, used in tableware: it is like pewter but harder

Bri·tan·nic (bri tan′ik) *adj.* of Britain; British

britch·es (brich′iz) *n.pl.* [Colloq.] same as BREECHES (sense 2)

☆**Brit·i·cism** (brit′ə siz′m) *n.* a word, phrase, or idiom that is a special usage of British English: also **Brit′ish·ism**

Brit·ish (brit′ish) *adj.* [OE. *Bryttisc* < *Bret*, a Celtic inhabitant of Britain] **1.** of Great Britain or its people **2.** of the British Commonwealth —*n.* the English language as spoken and written in England: also called **British English** —**the British** the people of Great Britain

British Columbia province of SW Canada: 366,255 sq. mi.; pop. 2,467,000; cap. Victoria: abbrev. **B.C.**

British Commonwealth (of Nations) confederation of independent nations, with their dependencies, including the United Kingdom & other former parts of the British Empire, united under the British crown: official name, **the Commonwealth**

British Empire formerly, the United Kingdom and British dominions, colonies, etc.

☆**Brit·ish·er** (-ər) *n.* a native of Great Britain, esp. an Englishman

British Honduras *former name of* BELIZE

British Isles group of islands consisting of Great Britain, Ireland, & some smaller islands

British thermal unit the quantity of heat required to raise the temperature of one pound of water at its maximum density one degree Fahrenheit

British West Indies Brit. possessions in the West Indies, including the Bahamas, Antigua, etc.

Brit·on (brit′n) *n.* [< OFr. < L. *Brit(t)o*; of Celt. origin: see BRITISH] **1.** a member of an early Celtic people living in S Britain at the time of the Roman invasion **2.** a native or inhabitant of Great Britain, esp. an Englishman

Brit·ta·ny (brit′′n ē) peninsula & former province of NW France

Brit·ten (brit′′n), **(Edward) Benjamin** 1913–76; Eng. composer

brit·tle (brit′′l) *adj.* [< OE. *breotan*, to break] **1.** easily broken or shattered because hard and inflexible [older people tend to have *brittle* bones] **2.** having a sharp, hard quality [*brittle* tones] **3.** stiff and unbending in manner; lacking warmth [a *brittle* smile] —☆*n.* a brittle, crunchy candy with nuts in it [peanut *brittle*] —**brit′tle·ly, brit′tly** *adv.* —**brit′tle·ness** *n.*

Br·no (bur′nō) city in C Czechoslovakia: pop. 333,000

bro. *pl.* **bros.** brother

broach (brōch) *n.* [< OFr. < ML. *brocca*, a spike < L. *broccus*, with projecting teeth] **1.** a sharp-pointed rod to hold roasting meat **2.** a tapered bit for enlarging or shaping holes **3.** *same as* BROOCH —*vt.* **1.** to make a hole in so as to let out liquid [to *broach* a cask of wine] **2.** to start a discussion of; bring up [to *broach* a subject] —**broach′er** *n.*

BROACHES

broad (brôd) *adj.* [OE. *brad*] **1.** of large extent from side to side; wide [a *broad* street] **2.** having great extent; spacious [*broad* prairies] **3.** clear and open [*broad* daylight] **4.** easy to understand; obvious [a *broad* hint] **5.** strongly marked [a *broad* accent] **6.** crude or vulgar [a *broad* joke] **7.** tolerant; liberal [a *broad* view] **8.** wide in range; not limited [a *broad* survey] **9.** main or general; not detailed [in *broad* outline] **10.** *Phonet.* pronounced with the tongue held low and flat in the mouth; open, esp. as the (ä) of *father* —**broad′ly** *adv.* —**broad′ness** *n.*

SYN·—**broad** and **wide** both are applied to extent from side to side of surfaces having height or length, **wide** being preferred when the distance between limits is emphasized [two feet *wide*; a *wide* opening], and **broad**, when the full extent of surface is considered [*broad* hips; *broad* plains]; **deep**, in this connection, refers to distance backward, as from the front, an opening, etc. [a *deep* lot; a *deep* drawer]

broad·ax, broad·axe (brôd′aks′) *n.* an ax with a broad blade, used as a weapon or tool

broad·cast (-kast′) *vt.* **-cast′ed, -cast′ing 1.** to scatter (seed) widely **2.** to spread (information, etc.) widely **3.** to transmit by radio or TV —*vi.* to broadcast radio or TV programs —*adj.* **1.** widely scattered **2.** of, for, or by radio or TV broadcasting —*n.* **1.** a broadcasting **2.** a radio or TV program —*adv.* scattered about; far and wide [he sowed the grass seed *broadcast*] —**broad′cast′er** *n.*

Broad Church that group in the Anglican Church which is between High Church and Low Church in matters of doctrine —**Broad′-Church′** *adj.*

broad·cloth (-klôth′) *n.* **1.** a fine, smooth woolen cloth: it originally was made on broad looms **2.** a fine, smooth cotton or silk cloth, used for shirts, pajamas, etc.

broad·en (-′n) *vt., vi.* to widen; expand

broad gauge a width (between the rails of a railroad) greater than standard gauge or width (56¹/₂ inches) —**broad′-gauge′, broad′-gauged′** *adj.*

broad jump *earlier term for* LONG JUMP

broad·loom (-lōōm′) *adj.* woven on a broad loom, as in widths of 6, 9, 12, 15, or 18 feet [*broadloom* carpeting]

broad-mind·ed (-mīn′did) *adj.* tolerant of other people's opinions and behavior; not bigoted; liberal —**broad′-mind′ed·ly** *adv.* —**broad′-mind′ed·ness** *n.*

broad·side (-sīd′) *n.* **1.** the entire side of a ship above the waterline **2.** *a)* all the guns that can be fired from one side of a ship *b)* the firing at one time of all such guns **3.** a harsh attack in words **4.** a large sheet of paper printed as with advertising and often folded —*adv.* **1.** with the length turned (*to* an object) **2.** directly in the side [the train rammed the car *broadside*] **3.** without making distinctions [to level charges *broadside*]

broad-spec·trum (-spek′trəm) *adj.* effective against a wide variety of microorganisms, as some antibiotics

broad·sword (-sôrd′) *n.* a sword with a broad blade, for slashing rather than thrusting

broad·tail (-tāl′) *n.* **1.** *same as* KARAKUL (sense 1) **2.** the wavy pelt of the karakul lamb, esp. of one prematurely born

Broad·way (brôd′wā′) street in New York City, the center of the city's entertainment section

Brob·ding·nag (bräb′diŋ nag′) in Swift's *Gulliver's Travels,* a land of giants —**Brob′ding·nag′i·an** *adj., n.*

bro·cade (brō kād′) *n.* [Sp. *brocado* < It. pp. of *broccare,* to embroider: see BROACH] a rich cloth with a raised design, as of silk, velvet, gold, or silver, woven into it —*vt.* **-cad′ed, -cad′-ing** to weave a raised design into (cloth)

broc·co·li (bräk′ə lē) *n.* [It., pl. of *broccolo,* a sprout, dim. of *brocco:* see BROACH] a plant related to the cauliflower, whose tender shoots with greenish buds are cooked as a vegetable

bro·chette (brō shet′) *n.* [Fr., dim. of *broche:* see BROACH] a pin on which small pieces of meat and vegetables are fixed for broiling

bro·chure (brō shoor′) *n.* [Fr. < *brocher,* to stitch] a pamphlet, now esp. one advertising something

Brock·ton (bräk′tən) [after I. *Brock* (1769–1812), Lt. Gov. of Canada] city in E Mass.: pop. 89,000

bro·gan (brō′g'n) *n.* [Ir., dim. of *brog*] a heavy work shoe, fitting high on the ankle

brogue¹ (brōg) *n.* [prob. < Ir. *barrōg,* a hold, grip (esp. on the tongue)] the pronunciation of a particular dialect, esp. of English as spoken by the Irish

brogue² (brōg) *n.* [Gael. & Ir. *brōg,* a shoe] **1.** a coarse shoe of untanned leather, formerly worn in Ireland **2.** a man's heavy oxford shoe, usually a kind of blucher with perforations forming a decoration

broil¹ (broil) *vt.* [OFr. *bruillir,* prob. by confusion of *bruir,* to burn & *usler,* to singe] **1.** to cook by exposing to direct heat [to *broil* a steak over a charcoal fire] **2.** to make very hot —*vi.* **1.** to become broiled **2.** to become heated or angry —*n.* **1.** a broiling **2.** broiled meat

broil² (broil) *n.* [ME. *broilen,* to quarrel < OFr. *brouiller,* to dirty] a noisy or violent quarrel —*vi.* to take part in a broil

broil·er (broil′ər) *n.* ☆**1.** a pan, grill, etc. for broiling **2.** the part of a stove designed for broiling **3.** a young chicken suitable for broiling

broke (brōk) *pt. & archaic pp. of* BREAK —*adj.* [Colloq.] having no money; bankrupt —**go broke** [Colloq.] to become bankrupt —**go for broke** [Slang] to risk everything in a venture

bro·ken (brō′k'n) *pp. of* BREAK —*adj.* **1.** split or cracked into pieces; splintered, fractured, burst, etc. [a *broken* dish; a *broken* balloon] **2.** not in working condition [a *broken* watch] **3.** not kept or carried out [a *broken* promise] **4.** disturbed as by divorce [a *broken* home] **5.** sick, weakened, or beaten [a *broken* spirit] **6.** bankrupt **7.** not even; interrupted [*broken* sleep] **8.** not complete [*broken* sizes] **9.** imperfectly spoken, esp. as regards grammar and word order [*broken* English] **10.** subdued and trained; tamed [a *broken* horse] **11.** [Colloq.] demoted in rank   For phrases, see BREAK —**bro′ken·ly** *adv.* —**bro′ken·ness** *n.*

bro·ken-down (-doun′) *adj.* **1.** sick or worn out, as by old age or disease **2.** out of order; useless [a *broken-down* car]

bro·ken·heart·ed (-här′tid) *adj.* crushed by sorrow, grief, or disappointment; inconsolable

bro·ker (brō′kər) *n.* [< ONormFr. < OFr. *brochier,* to broach, tap; orig. sense "wine dealer"] **1.** a person hired to act for others in making contracts, buying or selling, etc. **2.** *same as* STOCKBROKER

bro·ker·age (-ij) *n.* **1.** the business of a broker **2.** a broker's fee

bro·mide (brō′mīd) *n.* [BROM(INE) + -IDE] **1.** a compound of bromine with another element or with a radical **2.** potassium bromide, KBr, used in medicine as a sedative ☆**3.** a trite saying; platitude

☆**bro·mid·ic** (brō mid′ik) *adj.* [see prec.] using or containing a trite remark or remarks; dull

bro·mine (brō′mēn) *n.* [Fr. *brome* < Gr. *brōmos*, stench + -INE⁴] a chemical element, usually a reddish-brown, corrosive liquid that gives off an irritating vapor: symbol, Br; at. wt., 79.909; at. no., 35

bron·chi (bräŋ′kī) *n. pl.* of BRONCHUS

bron·chi·al (bräŋ′kē əl) *adj.* of the bronchi or bronchioles

bronchial tubes the bronchi and the tubes branching from them

bron·chi·ole (bräŋ′kē ōl′) *n.* any of the small subdivisions of the bronchi

bron·chi·tis (bräŋ kīt′əs) *n.* [BRONCH(O)- + -ITIS] an inflammation of the mucous lining of the bronchial tubes —**bron·chit′ic** (-kit′ik) *adj.*

bron·cho- [< Gr. *bronchos*, windpipe] *a combining form meaning* having to do with the bronchi [*bronchoscope*]: also, before a vowel, **bronch-**

bron·cho·scope (bräŋ′kə skōp′) *n.* [BRONCHO- + -SCOPE] an instrument for examining the bronchi, or for removing foreign bodies from them

bron·chus (bräŋ′kəs) *n., pl.* **-chi** (-kī) [ModL. < Gr. *bronchos*, windpipe] either of the two main branches of the trachea, or windpipe

☆**bron·co** (bräŋ′kō) *n., pl.* **-cos** [MexSp. < Sp., rough] a wild or partially tamed horse or pony of the western U.S.: also sp. **bron′cho,** *pl.* **-chos**

☆**bron·co·bust·er** (-bus′tər) *n.* [Colloq.] a cowboy who tames broncos —**bron′co·bust′ing** *n.*

Bron·të (brän′tē) **1.** Charlotte, 1816–55; Eng. novelist **2. Emily Jane,** 1818–48; Eng. novelist: sister of *Charlotte*

☆**bron·to·sau·rus** (brän′tə sôr′əs) *n., pl.* **-sau·rus·es, -sau·ri** (-ī) [ModL. < Gr. *brontē*, thunder + -SAURUS] a huge, plant-eating American dinosaur of the Jurassic Period: also **bron′to·saur′** (-sôr′)

Bronx (bräŋks) [after J. *Bronck,* early settler] N borough of New York City: pop. 1,472,000

☆**Bronx cheer** [Slang] a noise made by vibrating the tongue placed between the lips, in showing scorn or contempt

BRONTOSAURUS
(to 75 ft. long)

bronze (bränz) *n.* [Fr. < It. *bronzo*] **1.** an alloy consisting chiefly of copper and tin **2.** an article, esp. a sculpture, made of bronze **3.** a reddish-brown color like that of bronze —*adj.* of or like bronze —*vt.* **bronzed, bronz′ing** to give a bronze color to —**bronz′y** *adj.*

Bronze Age a period of human culture (c. 3500–1000 B.C.) characterized by bronze tools and weapons

brooch (brōch, brōōch) *n.* [see BROACH] a large ornamental pin with a clasp, worn at the bosom or neck of a dress

brood (brōōd) *n.* [OE. *brod:* for IE. base see BREATH] **1.** a group of birds or fowl hatched at one time and cared for together **2.** all the children in a family **3.** a group of a particular breed or kind [*the new brood of poets*] —*vt.* **1.** to sit on and hatch (eggs) **2.** to hover over or protect (offspring.) —*vi.* **1.** to brood eggs or offspring **2.** to keep thinking about something in a troubled way; worry [often with *on, over,* or *about*] [are you still *brooding* over your loss?] —*adj.* kept for breeding [a *brood* mare] —**brood′ing·ly** *adv.*

brood·er (brōōd′ər) *n.* **1.** one that broods ☆**2.** a heated shelter for raising young chicks, ducklings, etc.

brood·y (brōōd′ē) *adj.* **brood′i·er, brood′i·est 1.** ready to brood, as poultry **2.** tending to brood over matters —**brood′i·ly** *adv.* —**brood′i·ness** *n.*

brook[1] (brook) *n.* [OE. *broc*] a small stream, usually not so large as a river

brook[2] (brook) *vt.* [OE. *brucan,* to use: for IE. base see FRUIT] to put up with; endure [he will *brook* no interference] —see SYN. at BEAR[1]

brook·let (brook′lit) *n.* a little brook

Brook·lyn (brook′lən) [< Du. *Bruijkleen; ?* after a village in the Netherlands] borough of New York City, on W Long Island: pop. 2,602,000 —**Brook′lyn·ite′** (-lə nīt′) *n.*

☆**brook trout** a spotted trout native to northeastern N. America, but introduced elsewhere as a game fish

broom (brōōm, broom) *n.* [OE. *brom:* see BRAMBLE] **1.** a shrub of the legume family, with many, usually yellow, flowers **2.** a bundle of long, stiff fibers or straws fastened to a long handle and used for sweeping: orig. made with twigs of the broom shrub —*vt.* to sweep as with a broom

☆**broom·corn** (brōōm′kôrn′, broom′-) *n.* a cultivated variety of sorghum: the stiff stems of the flower clusters are used in making brooms and brushes

broom·stick (-stik′) *n.* the handle of a broom

bros. brothers

broth (brôth) *n.* [OE.: for IE. base see BURN[1]] a clear, thin soup made by boiling meat, etc. in water

broth·el (brôth′əl, bräth′-) *n.* [ME., wretched person < OE. pp. of *breothan,* to go to ruin] a place to which men come for prostitutes

broth·er (bruth′ər) *n., pl.* **broth′ers;** in religious use, still often **breth′ren** [OE. *brothor* < IE. base *bhrater-*] **1.** a male as he is related to the other children of his parents **2.** a close friend who is like a brother **3.** a fellow man **4.** a fellow member of the same race, creed, profession, organization, etc. **5.** a lay member of a men's religious order —*vt.* to treat or address as a brother

broth·er·hood (-hood′) *n.* **1.** the state of being a brother or brothers; tie or bond that brothers feel [the *brotherhood* of man] **2.** an association of men united in a common interest, work, creed, etc.

broth·er·in·law (-in lô′) *n., pl.* **broth′ers·in·law′ 1.** the brother of one's husband or wife **2.** the husband of one's sister **3.** the husband of the sister of one's wife or husband

broth·er·ly (-lē) *adj.* **1.** of or like a brother **2.** friendly, kind, loyal, etc. [a little *brotherly* advice] —**broth′er·li·ness** *n.*

brougham (brōōm; brōō′əm, brō′-) *n.* [after Lord *Brougham* (1778–1868), Brit. statesman] **1.** a closed carriage with the driver's seat outside **2.** any of various styles of automobile

brought (brôt) *pt. & pp.* of BRING

brou·ha·ha (brōō′hä hä′) *n.* [Fr.] a noisy confusion; uproar; hubbub

brow (brou) *n.* [OE. *bru* < IE. base *bhru-,* eyebrow] **1.** the eyebrow **2.** the forehead **3.** the facial expression [an angry *brow*] **4.** a projecting top edge, as of a cliff

brow·beat (brou′bēt′) *vt.* **-beat′, -beat′en, -beat′ing** to frighten or force with harsh, stern looks and talk

brown (broun) *adj.* [OE. *brun:* for IE. base see BEAR[2]] **1.** having the color of chocolate or coffee, a mixture of red, black, and yellow **2.** tanned or dark-skinned —*n.* **1.** a brown color **2.** a brown pigment or dye —*vt., vi.* to make or become brown, as by exposure to sunlight or heat [to *brown* the turkey, remove the cover] —☆**do up brown** [Slang] to do completely or perfectly —**brown′ish** *adj.* —**brown′ness** *n.*

Brown, John 1800–59; U.S. abolitionist: hanged for raiding an arsenal at Harpers Ferry as part of a plan for an uprising among the slaves

brown algae a group of algae formed in cold seas, having a brown pigment that hides the green of the chlorophyll

brown bear a bear with brown fur; esp., a color variety of the N. American black bear

☆**brown bet·ty** (bet′ē) [*also* b- B-] a baked apple pudding made with bread crumbs, butter, etc.

brown bread 1. any bread made of dark flour **2.** *same as* BOSTON BROWN BREAD

brown coal *same as* LIGNITE

Browne (broun) **1. Charles Far·rar** (far′ər), *see* Artemus WARD **2. Sir Thomas,** 1605–82; Eng. physician & writer

brown fat a tissue stored in certain parts of the body by a bear or other animal that is hibernating: it produces heat and helps prevent freezing

Brown·i·an movement (broun′ē ən) [after R. *Brown* (1773–1858), Brit. botanist who described it] the random, zigzag movement of tiny particles suspended in a fluid: caused by the repeated collision of such particles with molecules of the fluid

brown·ie (broun′ē) *n.* **1.** a small, helpful, brown elf or goblin in folk tales **2.** [B-] a Girl Scout of the youngest group, those seven and eight years old ☆**3.** any of the small bars cut from a flat, rich chocolate cake with nuts in it

Brown·ing (broun′iŋ) **1. Elizabeth Bar·rett** (bar′it), 1806–61; Eng. poet **2. Robert,** 1812–89; Eng. poet: husband of *Elizabeth*

brown·out (-out′) *n.* a turning off of some lights in a city, as during an electric power shortage

brown rice rice that has not been polished

brown shirt 1. [*often* B- S-] a storm trooper in Nazi Germany **2.** any Nazi

brown·stone (-stōn′) *n.* ☆**1.** a reddish-brown sandstone, used for building ☆**2.** a house with a façade of brownstone

brown study [< early sense of BROWN, gloomy] a condition of being deep in thought; reverie

brown sugar soft sugar prepared so that the crystals retain a brown coating of dark syrup

Browns·ville (brounz′vil) [after a Major *Brown*, killed there] seaport in S Tex.: pop. 53,000

browse (brouz) *n.* [< OFr. < OS. *brustian*, to sprout] **1.** leaves, twigs, and young shoots of trees or shrubs, which animals feed on **2.** the act of browsing —*vt.* **browsed, brows′ing 1.** to nibble at (leaves, twigs, etc.) **2.** to graze on **3.** to examine casually —*vi.* **1.** to nibble at leaves, twigs, etc. **2.** to glance through a book, books, etc. casually, reading here and there **3.** to look casually over articles for sale —**brows′er** *n.*

Bruce (brōōs) [Scot. < Fr. *Brieuse*, locality in France] **1.** a masculine name **2. Robert (the),** 1274–1329; Scot. patriot &, as *Robert I*, king of Scotland (1306–29)

bru·cel·lo·sis (brōō′sə lō′sis) *n.* [after Sir David *Bruce* (1855–1931), Scot. physician + -OSIS] a disease, esp. in man and cattle, caused by bacteria: see UNDULANT FEVER

Bruck·ner (brook′nər), **An·ton** (än′tōn) 1824–96; Austrian composer

Brue·gel, Brue·ghel (brü′gəl; *occas.* broi′-), **Pie·ter** (pē′tər) 1522?–69; Fl. painter

Bru·in (brōō′ən) [Du., brown] [*also* b-] *a name for* the bear in fable and folklore

bruise (brōōz) *vt.* **bruised, bruis′ing** [ME. *bruisen* (infl. by OFr. *bruisier,* to break) < OE. *brysan,* to crush < IE. base *bhreus-*] **1.** to injure (body tissue) without breaking the skin but causing discoloration **2.** to injure the surface of (fruit, etc.) **3.** to crush as with a pestle in a mortar [to *bruise* peppermint leaves] **4.** to hurt (the feelings, spirit, etc.) —*vi.* to be or become bruised [she *bruises* at the slightest tap] —*n.* **1.** a bruised area of tissue, of a surface, etc. **2.** an injury to one's feelings, pride, etc.

bruis·er (brōōz′ər) *n.* a strong, pugnacious man; specif., a professional boxer

bruit (brōōt) *vt.* [< OFr. < *bruire,* to rumble, prob. < L. *rugire,* to roar] to spread (*about*) a rumor of

brunch (brunch) *n.* [BR(EAKFAST) + (L)UNCH] [Colloq.] a meal combining breakfast and lunch

Bru·nei (brōō nī′) sultanate under Brit. control on the NW coast of Borneo: 2,226 sq. mi.; pop. 116,000

bru·net (brōō net′) *adj.* [< OFr., dim. of *brun* < OHG. *brun,* BROWN] **1.** having black or dark-brown hair, often along with dark eyes and a dark complexion **2.** having a dark color: said of hair, eyes, or skin —*n.* a brunet person

bru·nette (-net′) *adj.* [Fr., fem. of prec.] *same as* BRUNET —*n.* a brunette woman or girl

Brun·hild (brōōn′hild) in the *Nibelungenlied,* a queen of Iceland: see also BRÜNNHILDE, BRYNHILD

Brünn·hil·de (brōōn hil′də; *G.* brün-) in Wagner's *Die Walküre,* a Valkyrie whom Siegfried releases from enchantment: see also BRUNHILD, BRYNHILD

Bru·no (brōō′nō) **1.** [OHG. < *brun,* BROWN] a masculine name **2. Gior·da·no** (jôr dä′nō), 1548–1600; It. philosopher

Bruns·wick (brunz′wik) **1.** region in C Germany **2.** city in this region: pop. 229,000

brunt (brunt) *n.* [< ? ON. *bruni,* heat] **1.** the shock (of an attack or impact (of a blow) **2.** the heaviest or hardest part [to bear the *brunt* of the blame]

brush¹ (brush) *n.* [OFr. *broce,* bush < VL. *bruscia* < Gmc. < IE. base *breus-,* to sprout] **1.** *same as* BRUSHWOOD ☆**2.** country covered with wild scrub growth, where few people live **3.** *a)* a device for cleaning, polishing, painting, etc., having bristles, hairs, or wires fastened into a back, with or without a handle *b)* a device of wires spread from a handle, used as on drums for a swishing effect **4.** the act of brushing **5.** a light, grazing stroke [a *brush* of the hand] **6.** a bushy tail, esp. that of a fox ☆**7.** [Slang] *same as* BRUSHOFF **8.** *Elec.* a piece or bundle of carbon, copper, etc. used as a conductor between an external

circuit and a revolving part, as in a motor —*vt.* **1.** to clean, polish, paint, etc. with a brush [to *brush* one's shoes] **2.** to apply, remove, etc. with a stroke or strokes as of a brush [*brush* the flies away] **3.** to touch or graze in passing [the tire *brushed* the curb] —*vi.* to graze past something [he *brushed* past the guard] —**brush aside** (or **away**) to refuse to think about; ignore — ☆**brush off** [Slang] to dismiss or get rid of abruptly —**brush up 1.** to clean up **2.** to refresh one's memory or skill (often with *on*)

brush² (brush) *vi.* [ME. *bruschen* < ?] to move with a rush; hurry —*n.* a short, quick fight or quarrel [the gang had several *brushes* with the police]

☆**brush fire** **1.** a fire in brushwood **2.** a sudden outburst, as of fighting, that threatens to spread or get stronger unless controlled

☆**brush·off** (brush′ôf′) *n.* [Slang] an abrupt dismissal: esp. in the phrase **give** (or **get**) **the brushoff**

brush·wood (-wood′) *n.* **1.** chopped-off or broken-off tree branches **2.** a thick growth of small trees and shrubs; underbrush

brush·work (-wurk′) *n.* the special way an artist has of applying paint with a brush [compare the *brushwork* of Renoir with that of Degas]

brush·y (brush′ē) *adj.* **brush′i·er, brush′i·est 1.** rough and bristly **2.** covered with brushwood or underbrush

brusque (brusk) *adj.* [Fr. < It. *brusco* < ML. *bruscus,* brushwood] rough and abrupt in manner or speech; curt: also **brusk** ["No, you can't" was his *brusque* reply] —see SYN. at BLUNT — **brusque′ly** *adv.* —**brusque′ness** *n.*

Brus·sels (brus′'lz) capital of Belgium, in the C part: pop. 1,079,000

Brussels sprouts **1.** a plant of the mustard family that bears miniature cabbagelike heads on a stiff stem **2.** these heads, cooked as a vegetable

bru·tal (brōōt′'l) *adj.* **1.** like a brute; savage, violent, ruthless, etc. **2.** very harsh [a *brutal* winter] **3.** plain and direct, but disturbing [*brutal* facts] —see SYN. at CRUEL —**bru′tal·ly** *adv.*

bru·tal·i·ty (brōō tal′ə tē) *n.* **1.** the quality of being brutal **2.** *pl.* **-ties** a brutal act

bru·tal·ize (brōōt′'l īz′) *vt.* **-ized′, -iz′ing 1.** to make brutal [war tends to *brutalize* men] **2.** to treat brutally [the guards *brutalized* the prisoners] —*vi.* to become brutal —**bru′tal·i·za′tion** *n.*

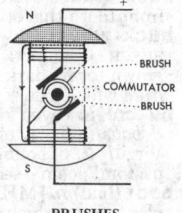

BRUSSELS SPROUTS

brute (brōōt) *adj.* [OFr. *brut* < L. *brutus,* irrational] **1.** lacking the ability to reason [a *brute* beast] **2.** lacking consciousness [the *brute* force of nature] **3.** of or like an animal; brutal, cruel, sensual, stupid, etc. —*n.* **1.** an animal **2.** a person who is brutal or stupid, sensual, etc.

brut·ish (brōōt′ish) *adj.* of or like a brute; savage, stupid, sensual, etc. —**brut′ish·ly** *adv.* —**brut′ish·ness** *n.*

Bru·tus (brōōt′əs), **(Marcus Junius)** 85?–42 B.C.; Rom. statesman who helped kill Julius Caesar

Bry·an (brī′ən), **William Jen·nings** (jen′ingz), 1860–1925; U.S. politician & orator

Bry·ant (brī′ənt) **1.** *var. of* BRIAN **2. William Cul·len** (kul′ən), 1794–1878; U.S. poet & journalist

Bryce Canyon National Park (brīs) [after E. *Bryce,* an early settler] national park in SW Utah

Bryn·hild (brin′hild) *Norse Legend* a Valkyrie awakened from an enchanted sleep by Sigurd: see also BRUNHILD, BRÜNNHILDE

bry·ol·o·gy (brī äl′ə jē) *n.* [< Gr. *bryon,* moss + -LOGY] the branch of botany dealing with bryophytes —**bry′o·log′i·cal** (-ə läj′i k'l) *adj.* —**bry·ol′o·gist** *n.*

bry·o·ny (brī′ə nē) *n., pl.* **-nies** [< L. < Gr. < *bryein,* to swell] a vine of the gourd family, with large, fleshy roots and greenish flowers

bry·o·phyte (brī′ə fīt′) *n.* [< Gr. *bryon,* moss + -PHYTE] any moss or liverwort —**bry′o·phyt′ic** (-fit′ik) *adj.*

bry·o·zo·an (brī′ə zō′ən) *n.* [< ModL. < Gr. *bryon,* moss + -ZO(A) + -AN] *same as* ECTOPROCT

BRUSHES
(sense 8)

N
+
BRUSH
COMMUTATOR
BRUSH
S

Bry·thon·ic (bri thän′ik) *adj., n.* [W., ult. < same word as BRITON] *see* CELTIC

B/s, b/s **1.** bags **2.** bales

B.S. Bachelor of Science

b.s. **1.** balance sheet **2.** bill of sale

B.S.A. Boy Scouts of America

B.Sc. [L. *Baccalaureus Scientiae*] Bachelor of Science

B.S.Ed. Bachelor of Science in Education

Bs/L bills of lading

Bt. Baronet

B.Th., B.T. [L. *Baccalaureus Theologiae*] Bachelor of Theology

btry battery (of artillery)

B.t.u. British thermal unit(s): also **B.T.U., b.t.u., Btu, btu**

bu. **1.** bureau **2.** bushel(s)

bub·ble (bub′'l) *n.* [echoic] **1.** a very thin film of liquid forming a ball around air or gas [soap *bubbles*] **2.** a tiny ball of air or gas in a liquid or solid [the *bubbles* in soda pop or in a piece of glass] **3.** anything shaped like a bubble, sphere, or hemisphere, as a transparent dome **4.** any scheme, etc. that turns out to be worthless or misleading **5.** the act or sound of bubbling —*vi.* **-bled, -bling** **1.** to rise in bubbles; boil; foam [water *bubbling* on the stove] **2.** to make a gurgling sound —*vt.* **1.** to form bubbles in; make bubble ☆**2.** to cause (a baby) to burp —**bubble over** **1.** to overflow, as boiling liquid **2.** to be unable to hold back one's enthusiasm, etc.

☆**bubble bath** **1.** a bath perfumed and softened by a solution, crystals, or powder that forms surface bubbles **2.** such a solution, powder, etc.

☆**bubble chamber** a container filled with a superheated, transparent liquid in which the behavior of charged atomic particles can be studied by photographing the tracks of bubbles that they create

☆**bubble gum** a kind of chewing gum that can be blown into large bubbles

bub·bly (bub′lē) *adj.* **1.** full of bubbles **2.** like a bubble —*n.* [Slang] champagne

bu·bo (byōō′bō, bōō′-) *n., pl.* **-boes** [< ML. < Gr. *boubōn,* groin] an inflamed swelling of a lymph gland, esp. in the armpit or groin —**bu·bon′ic** (-bän′ik) *adj.*

bubonic plague a contagious disease characterized by buboes, fever, and delirium: fleas from infected rats are the carriers

buc·cal (buk′'l) *adj.* [L. *bucca,* cheek + -AL] **1.** of the cheek or cheeks **2.** of the mouth

buc·ca·neer (buk′ə nir′) *n.* [Fr. *boucanier,* user of a *boucan,* native Brazilian grill for roasting meat; orig. applied to Fr. hunters in Haiti] a pirate, or sea robber

Bu·ceph·a·lus (byōō sef′ə ləs) the war horse of Alexander the Great

Bu·chan·an (byōō kan′ən), **James** 1791–1868; 15th president of the U.S. (1857–61)

Bu·cha·rest (bōō′kə rest′, byōō′-) capital of Romania, in the S part: pop. 1,415,000

Buch·en·wald (bōō′k'n wôld′; *G.* bōōkh′ən vält′) village in C Germany: site of a notorious Nazi concentration camp where many people were killed

buck[1] (buk) *n.* [OE. *bucca,* male goat < IE. base *bhugo-*] **1.** *pl.* **bucks, buck:** see PLURAL, II, D, 1 a male deer, goat, etc. ☆**2.** the act of bucking **3.** *same as* BUCKSKIN **4.** [Colloq.] a young man: a patronizing term —*vi.* ☆**1.** to rear upward and come down quickly with the back arched and forelegs stiff, in an attempt to throw off a rider: said of a horse, etc. **2.** to plunge forward with lowered head, as a goat ☆**3.** [Colloq.] to resist something as if plunging against it [to *buck* against a strong wind] ☆**4.** [Colloq.] to move jerkily —*vt.* ☆**1.** to charge against, as in football ☆**2.** to throw by bucking ☆**3.** [Colloq.] to resist stubbornly [to *buck* public opinion] —*adj.* **1.** male ☆**2.** of the lowest military rating [*buck* private, *buck* sergeant] —☆**buck for** [Slang] to work eagerly or too eagerly for (a promotion, etc.) —☆**buck up** [Colloq.] to cheer up —**buck′er** *n.*

☆**buck**[2] (buk) *n.* [< Du. *zaagbok*] a sawbuck; sawhorse

☆**buck**[3] (buk) *n.* [prob. < BUCKHORN: a knife with a buckhorn handle was used as a counter] **1.** *Poker* a counter placed

BUCKING HORSE

before a player as a reminder to deal next, etc. **2.** [Slang] a dollar —☆**pass the buck** [Colloq.] to seek to make someone else take the blame or responsibility

Buck (buk), **Pearl** 1892–1973; U.S. novelist

☆**buck and wing** a complicated, fast tap dance

☆**buck·a·roo** (buk′ə rōō′, buk′ə rōō′) *n., pl.* **-roos′** [prob. < Gullah *buckra,* white man, altered after Sp. *vaquero,* cowboy] a cowboy

☆**buck·board** (buk′bôrd′) *n.* [< ?] a four-wheeled, open carriage with the seat carried on a flooring of long, flexible boards whose ends rest directly on the axles

BUCKBOARD

buck·et (buk′it) *n.* [< Anglo-Fr. *buket,* dim. of OE. *buc,* pitcher] **1.** a round container with a flat bottom and a curved handle, for carrying water, coal, etc.; pail **2.** the amount held by a bucket: also **buck′et·ful′,** *pl.* **-fuls′** **3.** a thing like a bucket, as a scoop on a steam shovel —*vt., vi.* to carry or lift in a bucket —**kick the bucket** [? < obs. *bucket,* beam on which a slaughtered pig was hung] [Slang] to die

bucket seat a single contoured seat whose back can be tipped forward, as in some sports cars

☆**buck·eye** (buk′ī′) *n.* [BUCK[1] + EYE: from the appearance of the seed] **1.** a tree of the horse-chestnut family, with large, spiny capsules enclosing shiny brown seeds **2.** the seed **3.** [B-] [Colloq.] a native or inhabitant of Ohio (the **Buckeye State**)

☆**buck fever** the nervous excitement of inexperienced hunters when they see game for the first time

buck·horn (-hôrn′) *n.* the horn of a buck, used for knife handles, etc.

Buck·ing·ham Palace (buk′iŋ əm) the official residence in London of British sovereigns

buck·le[1] (buk′'l) *n.* [< OFr. < LL. < L. *buccula,* cheek strap of a helmet, dim. of *bucca,* cheek] **1.** a clasp for fastening one end of a strap, belt, etc. to the other **2.** a clasplike ornament, as for shoes —*vt., vi.* **-led, -ling** to fasten with a buckle —☆**buckle down** to set to work with real effort

buck·le[2] (buk′'l) *vt., vi.* **-led, -ling** [prob. < Du. *bukken,* to bend] to bend, warp, or crumple, as because of pressure or great heat —*n.* a bend, bulge, kink, etc. —**buckle under** to give in; yield; submit

buck·ler (buk′lər) *n.* [OFr. *bocler;* from the *bocle,* or boss, in its center] **1.** a small, round shield worn on the arm **2.** any protection or defense

buck·o (buk′ō) *n., pl.* **-oes** [< BUCK[1]] a bully

☆**buck-pass·er** (buk′pas′ər) *n.* [Colloq.] a person who regularly seeks to shift blame or responsibility to someone else —**buck′-pass′ing** *n.*

buck·ram (buk′rəm) *n.* [< OFr., prob. < *Bukhara,* in Uzbek S.S.R.] a coarse cloth stiffened with glue or other size, for use in bookbinding, for interlinings, etc. —*adj.* of or like buckram

☆**buck·saw** (buk′sô′) *n.* [see BUCK[2]] a saw set in a frame and held on one side with both hands in cutting wood

☆**buck·shot** (buk′shät′) *n.* a large lead shot for shooting deer and other large game

buck·skin (-skin′) *n.* **1.** a soft, usually napped, yellowish-gray leather made from the skins of deer or sheep **2.** [*pl.*] clothes or shoes made of buckskin —*adj.* made of buckskin

buck·thorn (-thôrn′) *n.* [BUCK[1] + THORN] **1.** a thorny tree or shrub with small, greenish flowers and purple drupes **2.** any of a genus of trees of the sapodilla family, native to the southern U.S.

buck·tooth (-tōōth′) *n., pl.* **-teeth′** [BUCK[1] + TOOTH] a large front tooth that sticks out —**buck′toothed′** *adj.*

buck·wheat (-hwēt′, -wēt′) *n.* [< ME. *bok-* (< OE. *boc-*), BEECH + WHEAT: from the beechnut-shaped seeds] **1.** a plant grown for its dark, triangular grains **2.** the grain of this plant, from which a dark flour is made ☆**3.** this flour

bu·col·ic (byōō käl′ik) *adj.* [< L. < Gr. < *boukolos,* herdsman < *bous,* ox] **1.** of shepherds; pastoral [the *bucolic* poems of Virgil] **2.** of country life; rustic [a quiet, *bucolic* scene] —*n.* a pastoral poem —see SYN. at RURAL —**bu·col′i·cal·ly** *adv.*

bud[1] (bud) *n.* [ME. *budde,* seedpod] **1.** *a)* a small swelling on a plant, from which a shoot, cluster of leaves, or flower develops *b)* a partly opened flower **2.** any immature person or thing **3.** a swelling on the body of a lower organism, that develops into a new individual —*vi.* **bud′ded, bud′ding** **1.** to put forth buds **2.** to begin to develop [a *budding* genius] —*vt.* **1.** to cause to bud **2.** to graft by inserting a bud of (a plant) into the bark of another sort of plant —**in bud** in the time or state of budding —**nip in the bud** to check at the earliest stage —**bud′der** *n.* —**bud′like′** *adj.*

☆**bud**[2] (bud) *n.* [Slang] *short for* BUDDY: used in addressing a man or boy

Bu·da·pest (boo͞o′də pest′) capital of Hungary, on the Danube: pop. 1,990,000

Bud·dha (bood′ə, boo͞o′də) [Sans., the enlightened one] Siddhartha Gautama, a religious philosopher who lived in India 563?–483? B.C. and was the founder of Buddhism

Bud·dhism (bood′iz′m, boo͞o′diz′m) *n.* a religion of central and eastern Asia, founded in India by Buddha: it teaches that by right living and right thinking, the soul can reach Nirvana, a state in which there is no pain, sorrow, or desire — **Bud′dhist** *n., adj.* —**Bud′dhis′tic** *adj.*

☆**bud·dy** (bud′ē) *n., pl.* -**dies** [< ? Brit. dial. *butty*, companion] [Colloq.] 1. companion; comrade 2. either of two persons paired off in an arrangement (**buddy system**) in which they help one another

☆**bud·dy-bud·dy** (bud′ē bud′ē) *adj.* [Slang] friendly or chummy, sometimes in an insincere way

CONVENTIONAL STATUE OF BUDDHA

budge (buj) *vt., vi.* **budged, budg′ing** [Fr. *bouger*, to move, ult. < L. *bulla*: see BOIL[1]] 1. to move even a little *[he was unable to budge the heavy desk]* 2. to yield or cause to yield *[all their pleas failed to budge her]*

budg·er·i·gar (buj′ə ri gär′) *n.* [native name] an Australian parakeet with a greenish-yellow body and bright blue on the cheeks and tail feathers

budg·et (buj′it) *n.* [< OFr. *bougette*, dim. of *bouge*, a bag < L. *bulga*, leather bag] 1. a careful plan for adjusting expenses to the income that is expected during a certain period 2. the estimated cost of living, operating, etc. 3. the amount of money needed for a specific use *[a budget of $10,000 for advertising]* —*vt.* 1. to put on or in a budget 2. to plan in detail; schedule *[budget your time]* —*vi.* to make a budget —**budg′et·ar′y** *adj.* —**budg′et·er** *n.*

budg·ie (buj′ē) *n.* [Colloq.] *same as* BUDGERIGAR

Bue·na Park (bwā′nə) [Sp. *buena*, good + PARK] city in SW Calif., near Los Angeles: pop. 64,000

Bue·nos Ai·res (bwā′nəs er′ēz, ī′rēz; *Sp.* bwe′nôs ī′res) capital of Argentina, on the Río de la Plata: pop. 2,967,000

buff[1] (buf) *n.* [earlier *buffe*, buffalo < It. *bufalo*, BUFFALO] 1. a heavy, soft, brownish-yellow leather made from the skin of a buffalo or from other animal hides 2. a military coat made of this leather 3. a stick, small block, or wheel (**buffing wheel**) covered with leather or cloth, used for cleaning or shining 4. a dull brownish yellow ☆5. [Colloq.] a devotee; fan *[a jazz buff]* —*adj.* 1. made of buff 2. of the color buff —*vt.* to shine with a buff —**in the buff** naked

buff[2] (buf) *vt.* [OFr. *buffe*: see BUFFET[1]] to lessen the force of —*vi.* to serve as a buffer

Buf·fa·lo (buf′ə lō′) [transl. of the name of a Seneca Indian who lived there] city in western N.Y., on Lake Erie: pop. 463,-000 (met. area 1,349,000)

buf·fa·lo (buf′ə lō′) *n., pl.* -**loes′, -los′, -lo′**: see PLURAL, II, D, 1 [It. *bufalo* < LL. < Gr. < *bous*, ox: see BEEF] 1. any of various wild oxen, sometimes domesticated, as the water buffalo of India, Cape buffalo of Africa, etc. ☆2. popularly, the American bison ☆3. any of several large freshwater fishes having a humped back: in full, **buffalo fish** —*vt.* -**loed′, -lo′ing** [Slang] to baffle, bluff, or overawe

Buffalo Bill nickname of William CODY

buffalo grass a low, creeping range grass of the Great Plains, used for forage

buff·er[1] (buf′ər) *n.* [BUFF[1], *v.* + -ER] a person or thing that buffs or polishes

WATER BUFFALO (55–70 in. high at shoulder)

buff·er[2] (buf′ər) *n.* [BUFF[2] + -ER] 1. a device to cushion the shock of a blow or bump 2. any person or thing that serves to lessen shock, as between opposing forces; specif., a small state (in full, **buffer state**) lying between two larger powers that are rivals 3. a substance that tends to stabilize the hydrogen ion concentration in a solution by neutralizing an added acid or alkali

buf·fet[1] (buf′it) *n.* [< OFr. < *buffe*, a blow] 1. a blow with the hand or fist 2. any blow or shock *[the buffets of misfortune]* —*vt.* 1. to punch or cuff 2. to thrust about *[the waves buffeted the boat]* 3. to struggle against *[a swimmer buffeting the waves]* —*vi.* to struggle

buf·fet[2] (bə fā′, boo-) *n.* [Fr. < OFr. *buffet*, a bench] 1. a piece of furniture with drawers and cupboards for dishes, table linen, silver, etc. 2. a counter where refreshments are served, or a restaurant with such a counter 3. a meal at which guests serve themselves as from a buffet

buff·ing wheel (buf′iŋ) a wheel covered with leather, cloth, etc., for buffing, or polishing, metal

☆**buf·fle·head** (buf′'l hed′) *n.* [< Fr. *buffle*, buffalo + HEAD] a small North American duck, black on top and white underneath

‡**buf·fo** (boo͞of′fô; *E.* boo͞o′fō) *n., pl.* -**fi** (-fē) [It., comic: see BUFFOON] an opera singer, generally a bass, who plays a comic role

buf·foon (bə foo͞on′) *n.* [< Fr. < It. < *buffare*, to jest] a person who is always clowning and trying to be funny —**buf·foon′er·y** *n.* —**buf·foon′ish** *adj.*

bug (bug) *n.* [prob. < W. *bwg*, hobgoblin] 1. any of various insects with sucking mouthparts and with forewings thickened toward the base 2. any insect or small, insectlike animal, specif. one regarded as a pest, as a louse, cockroach, etc. 3. [Colloq.] a germ or virus ☆4. [Slang] a tiny microphone hidden to record conversation secretly ☆5. [Slang] a defect, as in a machine *[to get the bugs out of a new invention]* ☆6. [Slang] a hobbyist or devotee *[he's a bug on chess]* —*vt.* **bugged, bug′ging** [Slang] 1. to hide a microphone in (a room, etc.) for secretly recording conversation 2. to annoy, anger, etc. —*vi.* [Slang] to bulge or open wide: said of the eyes

bug·a·boo (bug′ə boo͞o′) *n., pl.* -**boos′** a bugbear

bug·bear (bug′ber′) *n.* [BUG + BEAR[1]] 1. *same as* BOGYMAN 2. anything causing fear or anxiety for no good reason

☆**bug-eyed** (-īd′) *adj.* [Slang] with bulging eyes

bug·gy[1] (bug′ē) *n., pl.* -**gies** [< ?] 1. a light, one-horse carriage with one seat ☆2. *same as* BABY CARRIAGE

bug·gy[2] (bug′ē) *adj.* -**gi·er, -gi·est** 1. infested or swarming with bugs 2. [Slang] mentally ill

☆**bug·house** (-hous′) *n.* [Slang] an insane asylum —*adj.* [Slang] mentally ill

bu·gle (byoo͞o′g'l) *n.* [< OFr. < L. *buculus*, young ox, dim. of *bos*, ox: ox horns were made into hunting horns] a brass-wind instrument like a trumpet but smaller, and usually without keys or valves: used chiefly for military calls —*vi., vt.* -**gled, -gling** to call or signal by blowing a bugle —**bu′gler** *n.*

☆**bugs** (bugz) *adj.* [Slang] mentally ill

bug·shah (bug′shə, -shô) *n., pl.* -**shah, -shahs** see MONETARY UNITS, table (Yemen Arab Rep.)

build (bild) *vt.* **built** or archaic **build′ed, build′ing** [OE. *byldan* < base of *bold*, a house: for IE. base see BONDAGE] 1. to make, or direct the making of, by putting together materials, parts, etc.; construct *[to build a bridge or house]* 2. to make a basis for; establish *[to build a theory on facts]* 3. to create, develop, promote, strengthen, etc. (often with *up*) *[to build a business or build up one's body]* —*vi.* 1. *a)* to put up buildings *b)* to have a house, etc. built 2. to grow or intensify (often with *up*) *[his anger built up within him]* —*n.* form or figure *[a stocky build]* — **build up** 1. to make seem more attractive *[to build up a product by advertising]* 2. to erect many buildings in (an area)

build·er (bil′dər) *n.* 1. one that builds 2. a person in the business of constructing buildings

build·ing (bil′diŋ) *n.* 1. anything that is built with walls and a roof 2. the act, process, work, or business of constructing houses, ships, etc.

SYN.—**building** is the general term applied to a fixed structure in which people live, work, etc.; **edifice** implies a large or impressive building; **structure** also suggests an imposing building and is esp. used when the construction material is being emphasized *[a steel structure]*

☆**build·up, build-up** (bild′up′) *n.* [Colloq.] **1.** favorable publicity or praise that is meant to make someone or something popular or well-known **2.** growth or expansion [a military *buildup*]

built (bilt) *pt. & pp.* of BUILD

☆**built-in** (bilt′in′) *adj.* **1.** made as part of the building; not detachable [a *built-in* bathtub] **2.** intrinsic; inherent [*built-in* protection]

built-up (-up′) *adj.* **1.** made higher, stronger, etc. by the addition of parts [*built-up* heels] **2.** having many buildings on it: said of an area

Bu·jum·bu·ra (bōō′joom boor′ə) capital of Burundi, on Lake Tanganyika: pop. 70,000

bulb (bulb) *n.* [< L. < Gr. *bolbos*] **1.** an underground bud that sends down roots and has a very short stem covered with leafy scales, as in a lily, onion, etc. **2.** a corm, tuber, or tuberous root resembling a bulb, as in a crocus **3.** a plant that grows from a bulb **4.** anything shaped like a bulb [an electric light *bulb*] —**bulbed** *adj.*

bul·ba·ceous (bəl bā′shəs) *adj. same as* BULBOUS

bul·bar (bul′bər) *adj.* of a bulb or bulb-shaped part; esp., having to do with the medulla oblongata

bul·bous (bul′bəs) *adj.* **1.** of, having, or growing from bulbs **2.** shaped like a bulb [a *bulbous* nose]

Bul·gar·i·a (bəl ger′ē ə, bool-) country in SE Europe, on the Black Sea, south of Romania: 42,796 sq. mi.; pop. 8,436,000; cap. Sofia —**Bul·gar′i·an, Bul·gar** (bul′gär, bool′-) *adj., n.*

bulge (bulj) *n.* [ME., var. of *bouge:* see BUDGET] **1.** an outward swelling; protuberance [the candy made a *bulge* in his cheek] **2.** a projecting part, as in a rampart ☆**3.** [Colloq.] a sudden increase in size, value, etc. —*vi., vt.* **bulged, bulg′ing** to swell or bend outward; protrude [pockets *bulging* with papers] —see SYN. at PROJECTION —**bulg′y** *adj.*

bulk (bulk) *n.* [ON. *bulki,* a heap, cargo, prob. < IE. base of BALL¹] **1.** size, mass, or volume, esp. if great **2.** the main mass or body; largest part [the *bulk* of one's fortune] **3.** soft, bulky matter that passes through the intestines without being absorbed —*vi.* **1.** to form into a mass **2.** to increase in size, importance, etc. **3.** to have size or importance [a thought that *bulked* large in her mind] —*vt.* to cause to bulk; give more bulk to —*adj.* **1.** total; aggregate **2.** not put up in individual packages [*bulk* sugar] —**in bulk 1.** not put up in individual packages [to sell rice *in bulk*] **2.** in large amounts

SYN.—**bulk, mass,** and **volume** all refer to a quantity of matter or number of units making up a whole; **bulk** implies a body of great size, weight, or numbers [the lumbering *bulk* of an elephant; the *bulk* of humanity]; **mass** suggests a group or number of parts forming a single, unified body [an egg-shaped *mass;* the *mass* of workers]; **volume** implies a moving or flowing mass, often one that keeps changing [*volumes* of smoke; the *volume* of production]

bulk·head (bulk′hed′) *n.* [< ON. *balkr,* partition + HEAD] **1.** any of the upright partitions dividing a ship, airplane, etc. into compartments to protect against the spread of fire or water in case of an accident **2.** a wall or embankment for holding back earth, fire, water, etc. ☆**3.** a boxlike structure built over an opening, as at the head of a staircase, elevator shaft, etc.

bulk·y (bul′kē) *adj.* **bulk′i·er, bulk′i·est** *a)* having great bulk; large; massive *b)* relatively large for its weight **2.** awkwardly large; big and clumsy —**bulk′i·ly** *adv.* —**bulk′i·ness** *n.*

bull¹ (bool) *n.* [< OE. *bula,* a steer: for IE. base see BALL¹] **1.** the adult male of cattle, buffalo, etc., specif. one that has not been castrated **2.** the adult male of certain other large animals, as the elephant, moose, walrus, whale, etc. **3.** a person who believes prices on the stock market are going to rise and so buys shares in the hope of selling them later at a higher price **4.** a person regarded as like a bull in size, strength, etc. ☆**5.** [Slang] a policeman or detective ☆**6.** [Slang] foolish or insincere talk; nonsense —[**B-**] *same as* TAURUS —*vt.* ☆to make (one's way) with force —*adj.* **1.** male [a *bull* moose] **2.** like a bull in size, strength, etc. **3.** rising in price [a *bull* market] —☆**shoot the bull** [Slang] to talk idly —**take the bull by the horns** to deal boldly with a danger or difficulty —**bull′-like** *adj.*

bull² (bool) *n.* [< OFr. < LL. *bulla,* a seal (L., bubble)] an official document or decree from the Pope

bull³ (bool) *n.* [ult. < L. *bulla,* bubble] a mistake in statement that is foolish in an amusing way (Ex.: "If your parents had no children, you may not either")

bull- [< BULL¹] *a combining form meaning:* **1.** of a bull or bulls [*bullfight*] **2.** like a bull or bull's [*bullhead*] **3.** large or male [*bullfrog*]

bull. bulletin

bull·dog (bool′dôg′, -däg′) *n.* [BULL- + DOG] a short-haired, square-jawed, heavily built dog noted for its strong, stubborn grip —*adj.* like or characteristic of a bulldog —*vt.* **-dogged′, -dog′ging** to throw (a steer) by seizing its horns and twisting its neck

☆**bull·doze** (-dōz′) *vt.* **-dozed′, -doz′-ing** [< *bull* (Botany Bay slang), a flogging of 75 lashes + DOSE] **1.** [Colloq.] to force or frighten by threatening; intimidate **2.** to move, make level, dig out, etc. with a bulldozer

☆**bull·doz·er** (-dō′zər) *n.* **1.** a person who bulldozes **2.** a tractor with a large, shovellike blade on the front, for pushing or moving earth, debris, etc.

BULLDOG
(to 18 in. high
at shoulder)

bul·let (bool′it) *n.* [Fr. *boulette,* dim. of *boule,* a ball < L. *bulla:* see BULL²] **1.** a small ball or cone-shaped piece of lead, metal alloy, etc. to be shot from a firearm **2.** anything like a bullet in shape, action, etc.

bul·le·tin (bool′ət ′n) *n.* [Fr. < It. dim. of LL. *bulla:* see BULL²] **1.** a short report of the latest news [they interrupted the program with a *bulletin* on the tornado] **2.** a regular publication, as for members of a society —*vt.* to announce in a bulletin

☆**bulletin board** a board or wall area on which notices or displays are put up

bul·let·proof (bool′it prōōf′) *adj.* that bullets cannot pierce [a *bulletproof* car] —*vt.* to make bulletproof

☆**bull fiddle** [Colloq.] *same as* DOUBLE BASS

bull·fight (bool′fīt′) *n.* a public show in which a bull is first provoked in various ways and then usually killed with a sword by a matador —**bull′fight′er** *n.* —**bull′fight′ing** *n.*

bull·finch (-finch′) *n.* [BULL- + FINCH] **1.** a European songbird with a black head and white rump **2.** any of various other small songbirds

☆**bull·frog** (-frôg′, -fräg′) *n.* [BULL- + FROG] a large N. American frog with a deep, loud croak

bull·head (-hed′) *n.* [see BULL-] ☆**1.** any of various N. American freshwater catfishes **2.** any of various similar fishes of fresh or salt waters

bull·head·ed (-hed′id) *adj.* blindly stubborn; obstinate —**bull′head′ed·ly** *adv.* —**bull′head′ed·ness** *n.*

☆**bull·horn** (-hôrn′) *n.* [BULL- + HORN] a portable electronic device for amplifying the voice

bul·lion (bool′yən) *n.* [< Du. < OFr. *billon,* small coin < *bille,* a stick: see BILLET²] gold and silver as raw material; esp., bars of gold or silver before they have been made into coins

bull·ish (bool′ish) *adj.* **1.** of or like a bull **2.** expecting or causing a rise of prices in the stock exchange **3.** optimistic [he felt *bullish* about his chances] —**bull′ish·ly** *adv.* —**bull′ish·ness** *n.*

BULLHORN

Bull Moose a member of the Progressive Party led by Theodore Roosevelt in the presidential campaign of 1912

bull-necked (-nekt′) *adj.* having a short, thick neck

bull·ock (bool′ək) *n.* [< OE. *bulluc,* dim. of *bula:* see BULL¹] a castrated bull; steer

☆**bull·pen** (-pen′) *n.* **1.** a fenced enclosure for bulls **2.** [Colloq.] an enclosure in a jail, where prisoners are herded temporarily, as right after their arrest **3.** *Baseball* an area where relief pitchers practice and warm up

bull·ring (-riŋ′) *n.* an arena for bullfighting

Bull Run [< ?] small stream in NE Va.: site of two Union defeats (1861 & 1862) in the Civil War

☆**bull session** [Colloq.] an informal discussion or conversation among a small group

bull's-eye (boolz′ī′) *n.* **1.** a thick, circular glass in a roof, ship's deck, etc., for letting in light **2.** *a)* the central mark of a target *b)* a direct hit, as on such a mark **3.** *a)* a convex lens for concentrating light *b)* a lantern with such a lens **4.** a hard, round candy

bull terrier a strong, lean, white dog, developed by crossing the bulldog and the terrier

☆**bull·whip** (bool′hwip′, -wip′) *n.* [BULL- + WHIP] a long, heavy whip, formerly used by cattle drivers, etc. —*vt.* **-whipped′, -whip′ping** to whip with a bullwhip

bul·ly¹ (bool′ē) *n., pl.* **-lies** [orig., sweetheart < Du. < MHG.

buole (G. *buhle*), lover; later infl. by BULL¹] a person who hurts, frightens, or browbeats those who are smaller or weaker —**vt., vi.** **-lied, -ly·ing** to behave like a bully (toward) —**adj.** ☆[Colloq.] fine; very good —☆**interj.** [Colloq.] good! well done!

bul·ly² (bool′ē) n. [< Fr. < *bouillir*, BOIL¹] canned or corned beef: also **bully beef**

bul·rush (bool′rush′) n. [< OE. *bol*, BOLE + *risc*, a rush] 1. a marsh plant of the sedge family 2. the papyrus or other plant that grows in water like a bulrush

bul·wark (bool′wərk, bul′-) n. [< MDu. *bolwerc*: see BOLE & WORK] 1. an earthwork or defensive wall; rampart 2. a defense or protection [the Bill of Rights is a *bulwark* of our civil liberties] 3. [usually pl.] the part of a ship's side above the deck —**vt.** 1. to provide bulwarks for 2. to be a bulwark to

☆**bum** (bum) n. [prob. < G. *bummler*, loafer < *bummeln*, to go slowly] [Colloq.] 1. a vagrant, tramp, beggar, etc. 2. any irresponsible person who just loafs 3. any person who spends all of his time at some sport or game [a ski bum] —**vi.** **bummed, bum′ming** [Colloq.] 1. to live as a bum 2. to live by sponging on people —**vt.** [Slang] to get by begging; cadge [to bum a cigarette] —**adj.** **bum′mer, bum′mest** [Slang] 1. poor in quality [bum cooking] 2. false or not valid [a bum steer] 3. lame or ailing [a bum leg]—see SYN. at VAGRANT —**give** (or **get**) **the bum's rush** [Slang] to eject (or be ejected) forcibly —**on the bum** [Colloq.] 1. living as a vagrant 2. out of repair; broken

bum·ble·bee (bum′b'l bē′) n. [altered (after ME. *bomblen*, to buzz) < ME. *humbul-be*, bumblebee] a large, hairy, yellow-and-black bee that lives in colonies

bum·bling (bum′bliŋ) adj. [prp. of *bumble*, buzz: see prec.] self-important in a blundering way

☆**bum·mer** (bum′ər) n. 1. one that bums 2. [Slang] any unpleasant or unsatisfactory thing; esp., an unpleasant drug experience

bump (bump) vt. [echoic] 1. to hit against; collide lightly with [the boat *bumped* the pier] ☆2. [Slang] to displace, as from a job, plane reservation, etc. —**vi.** 1. to collide with a jolt 2. to move with jolts [an old truck *bumping* along the road] —**n.** 1. a light blow or jolt 2. a swelling or lump, esp. one caused by a blow —☆**bump into** [Colloq.] to meet unexpectedly —☆**bump off** [Slang] to murder

bump·er¹ (bum′pər) n. ☆a device for absorbing some of the shock of a collision; specif., a bar across the front or back of an automobile

bump·er² (bum′pər) n. [prob. < obs. *bombard*, liquor jug, altered after BUMP] 1. a cup or glass filled to the brim 2. [Colloq.] anything unusually large of its kind —**adj.** unusually abundant [a bumper crop]

☆**bumper sticker** a slogan, witty remark, etc. printed on gummed paper for sticking on an automobile bumper

bump·kin (bump′kən, bum′-) n. [prob. < MDu. *bommekijn*, small cask] an awkward or simple person from the country

bump·tious (bump′shəs) adj. [prob. < BUMP] disagreeably conceited, arrogant, or forward —**bump′tious·ly adv.** — **bump′tious·ness n.**

bump·y (bum′pē) adj. **bump′i·er, bump′i·est** full of bumps; rough [a bumpy road] —**bump′i·ly adv.** —**bump′i·ness n.**

bun (bun) n. [ME. *bunne*, wheat cake, prob. < OFr. *buigne*, a swelling] 1. a small roll, usually somewhat sweetened and often spiced 2. hair worn in a roll or knot on the back of the head

Bu·na (boo′nə, byoo′nə) [G. < *bu*(*tadien*), butadiene + *Na*, symbol for sodium] *a trademark for* a synthetic rubber made from butadiene

bunch (bunch) n. [ult. < Fl. *boudje*, dim. of *boud*, bundle] 1. a cluster of things growing together [a bunch of grapes] 2. a collection of things of the same kind fastened, grouped, or thought of together [a bunch of keys] 3. [Colloq.] a group of people —**vt., vi.** to gather together in a mass or in loose folds, wads, etc. (often with *up*) [his shirt *bunched* up at the waist] —**bunch′i·ness n.** — **bunch′y adj.**

Bunche (bunch), **Ralph Johnson** 1904-71; U.S. educator & diplomat

BUN

☆**bun·co** (buŋ′kō) n., pl. **-cos** [< Sp. *banca*, card game < It. *banca*, BANK¹] [Colloq.] a swindle, esp. at a card game or lottery; confidence game —**vt.** **-coed, -co·ing** [Colloq.] to swindle; cheat

☆**bun·combe** (buŋ′kəm) n. [< *Buncombe* county, N.C., whose Congressman (1819-21) regularly made "a speech for Buncombe"] [Colloq.] talk that is empty, insincere, or merely for effect; humbug

bun·dle (bun′d'l) n. [prob. < MDu. *bondel* < *binden*, BIND] 1. a number of things tied or wrapped together [a *bundle* of laundry] 2. a package or parcel 3. a bunch, collection, or group [a *bundle* of errors] 4. [Slang] a large amount of money 5. same as VASCULAR BUNDLE —**vt.** **-dled, -dling** 1. to make into a bundle; wrap or tie together 2. to send hastily (*away*, *off*, *out*, or *into*) [the children were *bundled* off to bed] —**vi.** 1. to move or go hastily; bustle 2. to lie in the same bed with one's sweetheart without undressing: a former courting custom, esp. in New England —**bundle up** to put on plenty of warm clothing — **bun′dler n.**

bung (buŋ) n. [< MDu. *bonge*] 1. a cork or other stopper for the hole in a barrel, cask, or keg 2. a bunghole —**vt.** 1. to close (a bunghole) with a stopper 2. to stop up 3. [Slang] to bruise or damage, as in a fight (with *up*)

bun·ga·low (buŋ′gə lō′) n. [< Hindi *bāṅglā*, thatched house, lit., Bengalese] a small house or cottage, usually of one story and an attic

bung·hole (buŋ′hōl′) n. a hole in a barrel or keg through which liquid can be drawn out

bun·gle (buŋ′g'l) vt. **-gled, -gling** [< ? Sw. *bangla*, to work ineffectually] to spoil by clumsy work; botch —**vi.** to do things badly or clumsily —**n.** 1. a bungling, or clumsy, act 2. a bungled piece of work —**bun′gler n.** —**bun′gling·ly adv.**

bun·ion (bun′yən) n. [prob. < ME. *boni*, swelling, boil < OFr. *buigne*: see BUN] an inflamed swelling at the base of the big toe, with a thickening of the skin

bunk¹ (buŋk) n. [prob. < Scand. word related to BENCH] 1. a shelflike bed or berth built into or against a wall, as in a ship 2. [Colloq.] any sleeping place, as a narrow cot —☆**vi.** 1. to sleep in a bunk 2. [Colloq.] to use a makeshift sleeping place [I'll *bunk* in the barn] —☆**vt.** to provide a sleeping place for

☆**bunk²** (buŋk) n. [Slang] *same as* BUNCOMBE

bunk bed a set of beds linked one above the other, often having a detachable ladder

bunk·er (buŋ′kər) n. [Scot. < ?] 1. a large bin or tank, as for a ship's fuel 2. a weapon emplacement of steel and concrete, often partly underground 3. a sand trap or mound of earth serving as an obstacle on a golf course —**vt.** 1. to supply (a ship) with fuel 2. *Golf* to hit (a ball) into a bunker

Bun·ker Hill (buŋ′kər) hill in Boston, Mass., near which a battle of the American Revolution was fought in 1775

bunk·house (buŋk′hous′) n. a barracks as for migratory workers on a ranch or farm

☆**bun·ko** (buŋ′kō) n., pl. **-kos, vt. -koed, -ko·ing** *same as* BUNCO

bun·kum (buŋ′kəm) n. *same as* BUNCOMBE

bun·ny (bun′ē) n., pl. **-nies** [dim. of dial. *bun*, rabbit] a rabbit: pet name used by children

Bun·sen burner (bun′s'n) [after R. W. *Bunsen*, 19th-c. Ger. chemist] a small, tubular gas burner that produces a hot, blue flame by letting air in near the bottom to mix with the gas: used in chemical laboratories, etc.

bunt¹ (bunt) vt., vi. [< ? base of Bret. *bounta*, to butt] 1. [Brit. Dial.] to strike or butt with or as with horns ☆2. *Baseball* to bat (a pitched ball) lightly without swinging so that it does not go beyond the infield, usually in attempting a sacrifice play —**n.** 1. a butt or shove ☆2. *Baseball* a) the act of bunting b) a bunted ball

bunt² (bunt) n. [< ?] a disease that destroys the grain of wheat, etc., caused by a fungus

bun·ting (bun′tiŋ) n. [< ME. *bonting*, sifting (cloth)] 1. a thin cloth used in making flags, etc. 2. flags, or strips of cloth in the colors of the flag, used as decorations ☆3. a baby's garment of soft, warm cloth made into a kind of hooded blanket that can be closed

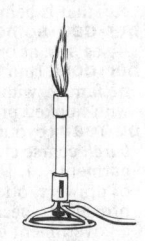

BUNSEN BURNER

bun·ting[2] (bun′tiŋ) *n.* [< ?] any of various small, brightly colored birds having a stout bill

bunt·line (bunt′lin, -līn′) *n.* [*bunt*, middle part of a sail + LINE[1]] one of the ropes attached to the foot of a square sail to prevent the sail from bellying when drawn up to be furled

Bun·yan (bun′yən) **1. John,** 1628–88; Eng. writer & preacher, who wrote *Pilgrim's Progress* **2.** see PAUL BUNYAN

Buo·na·par·te (bwȯ′nä pär′te) *It. sp. of* BONAPARTE

buoy (bōō′ē, boi; *for v., usually* boi) *n.* [< OFr. *buie,* chain < L. *boia,* fetter: prob. first applied to the chain anchoring the float] **1.** a floating object anchored in water to warn of rocks, shoals, etc. or to mark a channel **2.** *short for* LIFE BUOY —*vt.* **1.** to mark or provide with a buoy **2.** to keep afloat: usually with *up* **3.** to lift or keep up in spirits; encourage: usually with *up*

buoy·an·cy (boi′ən sē, bōō′yən-) *n.* [< BUOYANT] **1.** the ability or tendency to float or rise in liquid or air [balsa wood has much *buoyancy*] **2.** the power to keep something afloat [the thin air of the upper atmosphere has little *buoyancy*] **3.** a cheerful spirit not easily kept down

buoy·ant (boi′ənt, bōō′yənt) *adj.* [< ? Sp. < *boyar,* to float] having or showing buoyancy — **buoy′ant·ly** *adv.*

bur (bur) *n.* [ME. *burre* < Scand.] **1.** the rough, prickly seedcase or fruit of certain plants **2.** a weed or other plant with burs **3.** anything that clings like a bur **4.** *Dentistry* a cutting or drilling bit **5.** *same as* BURR[1] & BURR[2] —*vt.* **burred, bur′ring 1.** to remove burs from **2.** to burr

bur. bureau

Bur·bank (bur′baŋk) [after Dr. D. *Burbank,* one of the city planners] city in SW Calif.: suburb of Los Angeles: pop. 89,000

Bur·bank (bur′baŋk), **Luther** 1849–1926; U.S. horticulturist, who bred many new varieties of plants

bur·ble (bur′b'l) *vi.* **-bled, -bling** [echoic] **1.** to make a gurgling sound [a *burbling* brook] **2.** to babble as a child does

bur·bot (bur′bət) *n., pl.* **-bot, -bots:** see PLURAL, II, D, 2 [< OFr. *borbote,* ult. < L. *barba,* a beard] a freshwater fish of the cod family, with barbels on the nose and chin

bur·den[1] (burd′'n) *n.* [< OE. *byrthen* < base of *beran:* see BEAR[1]] **1.** anything that is carried; load **2.** a heavy load, as of work, responsibility, sorrow, etc. **3.** the carrying of loads [a beast of *burden*] **4.** the carrying capacity of a ship, or the weight of its cargo —*vt.* to put a burden on; load; oppress [he was *burdened* down with care]

bur·den[2] (burd′'n) *n.* [< OFr. *bourdon,* a humming < ML. *burdo,* DRONE[1], wind instrument] **1.** a chorus or refrain of a song **2.** a repeated, central idea; theme [the *burden* of a speech]

burden of proof the obligation to prove some statement, claim, etc. that is being challenged

bur·den·some (-səm) *adj.* hard to bear; heavy; oppressive —see SYN. at ONEROUS —**bur′den·some·ly** *adv.*

bur·dock (bur′däk′) *n.* [BUR + DOCK[3]] a plant of the composite family, with large leaves, and purple-flowered heads covered with hooked prickles

bu·reau (byoor′ō) *n., pl.* **-reaus, -reaux** (-ōz) [Fr., desk < OFr. *burel,* coarse cloth (as table cover) < LL. *burra,* ragged (woolen) garment] **1.** [Brit.] a desk with drawers for papers ☆**2.** a chest of drawers, often with a mirror, for clothing, etc. **3.** an agency providing specified services for clients [a travel *bureau*] ☆**4.** a government department or a subdivision of this

bu·reau·cra·cy (byoor räk′rə sē) *n., pl.* **-cies** [< Fr. *bureau* + *-cratie,* -CRACY] **1.** government by means of departments managed by officials who follow all rules without question and without exceptions **2.** such officials as a group **3.** the kind of fixed routine followed by such officials **4.** any similar system, as in a business, in which the fixed routines hold up action

bu·reau·crat (byoor′ə krat′) *n.* an official in a bureaucracy, esp. one who follows a routine in a narrow, mechanical way, insisting on proper forms, petty rules, etc. —**bu′reau·crat′ic** *adj.* —**bu′reau·crat′i·cal·ly** *adv.*

bu·reau·cra·tize (byoo räk′rə tīz′) *vt., vi.* **-tized′, -tiz′ing** to make or become bureaucratic —**bu·reau′cra·ti·za′tion** *n.*

bu·rette, bu·ret (byoo ret′) *n.* [Fr. < OFr. dim. of *buire,* flagon] a graduated glass tube with a stopcock at the bottom, for measuring small quantities of liquid or gas

burg (burg) *n.* [var. of BOROUGH] **1.** orig., a fortified town ☆**2.** [Colloq.] a city, town, or village, esp. one regarded as quiet, unexciting, etc.

-burg (burg) *a suffix meaning* burg or borough [*Vicksburg*]: also **-burgh** [*Pittsburgh*]

bur·geon (bur′jən) *vi.* [< OFr. < *burjon,* a bud] **1.** to put forth buds, shoots, etc. **2.** to grow or develop rapidly; flourish [the *burgeoning* suburbs]

☆**-burger** (bur′gər) [< (HAM)BURGER] *a combining form meaning:* **1.** sandwich of a patty of ground meat, fish, etc. [*turkeyburger*] **2.** hamburger and [*cheeseburger*]

Bur·ger (bur′gər), **Warren Earl** 1907– ; U.S. jurist; chief justice of the U.S. (1969–)

bur·gess (bur′jis) *n.* [OFr. *burgeis:* see BOURGEOIS] **1.** [Now Rare] a citizen or freeman of a British borough ☆**2.** a member of the lower house of the legislature of Md. or Va. before the American Revolution

burgh (burg; *Scot.* bu′rə) *n.* [Scot. var. of BOROUGH] **1.** [Brit.] a borough **2.** in Scotland, a chartered town

burgh·er (bur′gər) *n.* an inhabitant of a borough or town; now, esp., a middle-class townsman

bur·glar (bur′glər) *n.* [< Anglo-L. *burglator,* altered after L. *latro,* thief < OFr. *burgeor, burglar*] a person who commits burglary

bur·glar·i·ous (bər gler′ē əs) *adj.* of, like, or being burglary [a *burglarious* act] —**bur·glar′i·ous·ly** *adv.*

☆**bur·glar·ize** (bur′glər rīz′) *vt.* **-ized′, -iz′ing** [Colloq.] to commit burglary in or upon

bur·gla·ry (bur′glər ē) *n., pl.* **-ries** [BURGLAR + -Y[4]] **1.** the act of breaking into a house at night to steal or commit some other felony **2.** a breaking into any building at any time to steal, etc.

bur·gle (bur′g'l) *vt., vi.* **-gled, -gling** [< BURGLAR] [Colloq.] to burglarize or commit burglary

bur·go·mas·ter (bur′gə mas′tər) *n.* [< MDu. < *burg,* town + *meester,* master] the mayor or head magistrate of a city or town in the Netherlands, Flanders, Austria, or Germany

Bur·goyne (bər goin′, bur′goin), **John** 1722–92; Brit. general in the American Revolution

Bur·gun·dy (bur′gən dē) region in SE France, that was at various times a kingdom, province, & duchy —*n.* [*occas.* **b-**] *pl.* **-dies 1.** a kind of wine, either red or white, made in the Burgundy region **2.** a similar red wine made elsewhere —**Bur·gun·di·an** (bər gun′dē ən) *adj., n.*

bur·i·al (ber′ē əl) *n.* the burying of a dead body; interment —*adj.* of or connected with burial

burial ground a cemetery; graveyard

bu·rin (byoor′in) *n.* [Fr. < It. < Gmc. *boro,* borer] a pointed cutting tool used by engravers or marble workers

Burke (burk), **Edmund** 1729–97; Brit. statesman, orator, & writer, born in Ireland

burl (burl) *n.* [< OFr. < VL. < LL. *burra:* see BUREAU] **1.** a knot in wool, thread, yarn, etc. that gives a nubby appearance to cloth **2.** a kind of knot on some tree trunks **3.** veneer made from wood with burls in it —*vt.* to finish (cloth) by taking out the burls, loose threads, etc. —**burled** *adj.*

bur·lap (bur′lap) *n.* [< ? ME. *borel,* coarse cloth (< OFr. *burel:* see BUREAU) + *lappa,* LAP[1]] a coarse cloth made of jute or hemp, used for making sacks, etc.

bur·lesque (bər lesk′) *n.* [Fr. < It. < *burla,* a jest] **1.** any comic or satirical imitation of something serious; parody ☆**2.** a sort of vaudeville with skits of low comedy, striptease acts, etc. —*adj.* **1.** comically imitating; parodying ☆**2.** of or connected with burlesque (sense 2) —*vt., vi.* **-lesqued′, -lesqu′ing** to imitate comically, esp. in order to ridicule; parody —see SYN. at CARICATURE

☆**bur·ley** (bur′lē) *n.* [< ? a proper name] [*also* **B-**] a thin-leaved tobacco grown esp. in Kentucky

bur·ly (bur′lē) *adj.* **-li·er, -li·est** [ME. *borlich,* excellent, handsome < ? OE. *borlice,* very, excellently] **1.** big and strong; heavy and muscular **2.** rough and hearty in manner —**bur′li·ness** *n.*

Bur·ma (bur′mə) country in SE Asia, on the Indochinese peninsula: 261,789 sq. mi.; pop. 26,980,000; cap. Rangoon —**Burmese** (bər mēz′) *adj., n., pl.* **-mese′**

burn[1] (burn) *vt.* **burned** or **burnt, burn′ing** [< ON. & OE.: ON. *brenna,* to burn, light; OE. *biernan:* both < IE. base *bhereu-,* to well up, ferment, from which also come BREW & BREAD] **1.** to set on fire or cause to undergo combustion **2.** to destroy or consume by fire [to *burn* rubbish] **3.** to injure or damage by fire, friction, or acid; scorch, scald, etc. **4.** to consume as fuel [we *burn* oil in the furnace] **5.** to transform into energy by metabolism [to *burn* fat by exercise] **6.** to sunburn **7.** to cauterize **8.** to harden or glaze (bricks, pottery, etc.) by fire; fire **9.** to cause by fire, heat, etc. [to *burn* a hole in a coat] **10.** to cause a feeling of heat in [horseradish *burns* the throat] **11.** [Slang] to cheat, swindle, rob, etc.: usually used in the passive —*vi.* **1.** to be on fire; flame; blaze [the house *burned* for hours] **2.** to undergo combustion [asbestos doesn't *burn*] **3.** to give out light or heat; shine; glow [lamps *burning* in the window] **4.** to be destroyed by fire or heat **5.** to be injured or damaged by or as by fire or heat **6.** to feel hot [her cheeks were *burning*] **7.** to be excited or inflamed, as with anger or desire —*n.* **1.** an injury caused by fire, heat, wind, etc.: in medicine, burns are classified as **first-degree,** with reddened skin, **second-degree,** with blisters, and **third-degree,** with destruction of the skin and other tissues **2.** the process or result of burning, as in making bricks ☆**3.** a single firing of a rocket or thruster on a space vehicle —**burn down** to burn to the ground —**burn oneself out** to exhaust oneself by too much work or loose living —**burn out 1.** to stop burning because the fuel has run out **2.** to wear out by heat from friction, etc. [to *burn out* a bearing] **3.** to destroy the home, business, etc. of by fire —**burn up 1.** to burn completely ☆**2.** [Slang] to make or become angry

SYN.—*burn* is the general term in this comparison for any injury by fire, intense heat, friction, acid, etc. [a *burnt* log, *sunburn*, *windburn*]; **scorch** and **singe** both imply surface burns, **scorch** emphasizing a change of color or damage to texture [to *scorch* a shirt in ironing], and **singe,** the burning off of bristles, feathers, the ends of hair, etc.; **sear** implies the burning of animal tissue and is applied specifically to the quick browning of the outside of roasts, etc. in cooking to seal in the juices; **char** implies a changing to charcoal or carbon by burning. All of these terms are also used in a figurative way [a *burning* desire; a *scorching* criticism; a *singed* reputation; a soul-*searing* experience; *charred* hopes]

burn2 (bʉrn) *n.* [see BOURN1] [Scot.] a brook
burn·a·ble (bʉrn′ə b'l) *adj.* that can be burned [*burnable* rubbish] —*n.* something, esp. refuse, that can be burned
burn·er (bʉr′nər) *n.* **1.** the part of a stove, furnace, etc. from which the flame comes **2.** an apparatus for burning fuel or trash [early stoves were wood *burners*]
Bur·ney (bʉr′nē), **Fanny** (born *Frances*; married name *Madame d'Arblay*) 1752–1840; Eng. novelist & diarist
burn·ing (bʉr′niŋ) *adj.* **1.** that burns **2.** intense; critical [a *burning* issue]
burning glass a convex lens for focusing the sun's rays so as to set fire to something
bur·nish (bʉr′nish) *vt., vi.* [< OFr. *brunir*, to make brown < *brun*, BROWN] to make or become shiny by rubbing; polish —*n.* a gloss or polish —**bur′nish·er** *n.*
bur·noose, bur·nous (bər nōōs′, bʉr′nōōs) *n.* [< Fr. < Ar. *burnus*, prob. < Gr. *birros*, a cloak] a long cloak with a hood, worn by Arabs and Moors
Burns (bʉrnz), **Robert** 1759–96; Scot. poet
☆**burn·sides** (bʉrn′sīdz′) *n.pl.* [after A. E. *Burnside*, Union general in the Civil War] a style of beard with full side whiskers and mustache, but with the chin clean-shaven
burnt (bʉrnt) *alt. pt. and pp.* of BURN1
burnt sienna *see* SIENNA
burnt umber *see* UMBER
☆**burp** (bʉrp) *n., vi.* [echoic] [Colloq.] belch —*vt.* to help (a baby) to get rid of stomach gas, as by stroking its back
☆**burp gun** [echoic] [Mil. Slang] any of various automatic pistols or submachine guns
burr1 (bʉr) *n.* [var. of BUR] **1.** a rough edge left on metal, etc. by cutting or drilling **2.** *same as* BUR (senses 1, 2, 3) —*vt.* **1.** to form a rough edge on **2.** to remove burrs from (metal)
burr2 (bʉr) *n.* [prob. echoic] **1.** the trilling of the sound of *r*, with the uvula or tongue [a Scottish *burr*] **2.** a whirring sound —*vi.* **1.** to speak with a burr **2.** to make a whir —*vt.* to pronounce with a burr

BURNOOSE

Burr (bʉr), **Aaron** 1756–1836; U.S. political leader: killed Alexander Hamilton in a duel
bur·ro (bʉr′ō, boor′ō) *n., pl.* **-ros** [Sp. < LL. *burricus*, small horse] [Southwest] a donkey
Bur·roughs (bʉr′ōz) **1. Edgar Rice,** 1875–1950; U.S. writer, esp. of the Tarzan stories **2. John,** 1837–1921; U.S. naturalist & writer
bur·row (bʉr′ō, -ə) *n.* [see BOROUGH] **1.** a hole or tunnel dug in the ground by an animal **2.** any similar hole for shelter, refuge, etc. —*vi.* **1.** to make a burrow **2.** to live or hide in or as in a burrow **3.** to delve or search, as if by digging [to *burrow* into books for information] —*vt.* **1.** to make burrows in (the ground) **2.** to make by burrowing [to *burrow* a tunnel]
bur·ry1 (bʉr′ē) *adj.* **-ri·er, -ri·est 1.** full of burs **2.** like a bur or burs; prickly
bur·ry2 (bʉr′ē) *adj.* **-ri·er, -ri·est** having a burr in speech
Bur·sa (boor sä′) city in NW Turkey: pop. 212,000
bur·sa (bʉr′sə) *n., pl.* **-sae** (-sē), **-sas** [ML., a bag < Gr. *byrsa*, a hide] *Anat.* a sac or cavity, esp. one containing a fluid that reduces friction, as between a tendon and bone —**bur′sal** *adj.*
bur·sar (bʉr′sər) *n.* [ML. *bursarius* < *bursa*: see prec.] a treasurer, as of a college
bur·si·tis (bər sīt′əs) *n.* [< BURSA + -ITIS] inflammation of a bursa, often one near the shoulder or hip
burst (bʉrst) *vi.* **burst, burst′ing** [< OE. *berstan* & ON. *bresta*, both < IE. base *bhres-*, burst, break] **1.** to come apart suddenly and violently, as from pressure within; fly into pieces; explode [the balloon *burst*] **2.** to give sudden expression to some feeling; break [*into* tears, laughter, etc.] **3.** to go, come, start, etc. suddenly and with force [he *burst* into the room] **4.** *a*) to be as full or crowded as possible [a room *bursting* with visitors] *b*) to be filled (*with* anger, pride, etc.) —*vt.* to cause to burst —*n.* **1.** a bursting; explosion **2.** the result of a bursting; break **3.** a sudden, violent display of feeling [a *burst* of anger] **4.** a sudden action; spurt [a *burst* of speed] **5.** a single series of shots from an automatic firearm —**burst′er** *n.*
bur·then (bʉr′thən) *n., vt.* archaic var. of BURDEN1
Bur·ton (bʉr′tən), **Sir Richard Francis** 1821–90; Eng. writer, translator, & explorer
Bu·run·di (boo roon′dē, -run′-) country in EC Africa, east of Zaire: 10,745 sq. mi.; pop. 3,475,000; cap. Bujumbura —**Bu·run′di·an** *adj., n.*
bur·y (ber′ē) *vt.* **bur′ied, bur′y·ing** [OE. *byrgan*, akin to *beorgan* < IE. base *bhergh-*, to protect] **1.** to put (a dead body) into the earth, a tomb, the sea, etc.; inter **2.** *a*) to hide (something) in the ground *b*) to cover up so as to conceal [she *buried* her face in the pillow] **3.** to put away, as from one's mind [to *bury* a feud] **4.** to get deeply in [to *bury* oneself in one's work]
bus (bus) *n., pl.* **bus′es, bus′ses** [< (OMNI)BUS] **1.** a large motor coach for carrying many passengers, usually along a regular route; omnibus **2.** [Slang] an automobile **3.** *Elec.* a conductor used as a common connection for three or more circuits: in the form of a bar, also called **bus′bar′** —*vt.* **bused** or **bussed, bus′ing** or **bus′sing** to transport by bus —*vi.* **1.** to go by bus ☆**2.** to do the work of a busboy
bus. business
☆**bus·boy** (bus′boi′) *n.* a waiter's assistant who clears tables, brings water, etc.
bus·by (buz′bē) *n., pl.* **-bies** [prob. < the name *Busby*] a tall fur hat worn by hussars, British guardsmen, etc.
bush1 (boosh) *n.* [ME., of WGmc. orig.] **1.** a woody plant having many stems branching out low instead of one main stem; shrub **2.** anything resembling a bush; esp., a thickly furred tail ☆**3.** shrubby woodland or uncleared country —*vi.* to grow thickly or spread out like a bush —*vt.* to cover, bit bushes — **beat around the bush** to talk around a subject without getting to the point
bush2 (boosh) *n.* [MDu. *busse*, box < ML. *buxis*: see BOX1] *same as* BUSHING —*vt.* to fit with a bushing
bush baby any of various small mammals related to the lemurs and living in African forests

BUSBY

bushed (boosht) *adj.* ☆[Colloq.] very tired; fatigued

bush·el (boosh′'l) *n.* [OFr. *boissel* < *boisse,* grain measure] **1.** a unit of dry measure for grain, fruit, etc., equal to 4 pecks or 32 quarts **2.** a container holding one bushel; esp., a basket (**bush′el·bas′ket**) holding such an amount **3.** [Colloq.] a large amount Abbrev. **bu.**

Bu·shi·do (boo′shē dō′) *n.* [Jap., way of the warrior] [*also* b-] the code of chivalry practiced by the samurai of feudal Japan, in which death was chosen over dishonor

bush·ing (boosh′iŋ) *n.* [< BUSH²] a removable metal lining put into an opening of a machine part, as to reduce friction on a bearing or to lessen the size of the opening

☆**bush league** [Slang] *Baseball* a small or second-rate minor league —**bush′-league′** *adj.*

☆**bush leaguer** [Slang] **1.** a player in a bush league **2.** anyone whose attitude and performance are not professional

bush·man (boosh′mən) *n., pl.* -**men 1.** a person who lives in the Australian bush **2.** a backwoodsman **3.** [B-] a member of a nomadic people of SW Africa

bush·mas·ter (-mas′tər) *n.* a large, poisonous snake of Central and South America

bush·rang·er (-rān′jər) *n.* [< BUSH¹ (*n.* 3) + RANGER] **1.** a person who lives in the bush **2.** in Australia, an outlaw who makes the bush his hide-out

☆**bush·whack** (-hwak′, -wak′) *vi.* [prob. < BUSH¹ + WHACK] **1.** to beat or cut one's way through bushes **2.** to engage in guerrilla fighting, attacking from ambush —*vt.* to ambush —**bush′whack′er** *n.* —**bush′whack′ing** *n.*

bush·y (boosh′ē) *adj.* **bush′i·er, bush′i·est 1.** covered or overgrown with bushes **2.** thick and spreading out like a bush [a *bushy* tail] —**bush′i·ness** *n.*

bus·i·ly (biz′ə lē) *adv.* in a busy manner

busi·ness (biz′nis) *n.* [OE. *bisignes:* see BUSY & -NESS] **1.** one's work, occupation, or profession [her *business* is writing books] **2.** rightful concern or responsibility [no one's *business* but his own] **3.** a matter, affair, activity, etc. [what is your *business* with me?] **4.** the buying and selling of goods and services; commerce; trade **5.** a commercial or industrial establishment; store, factory, etc. **6.** action in a play, as during a pause in dialogue [she did the *business* of pouring tea] —*of* or for business [a *business* expense] —**business is business** sentiment, friendship, etc. cannot be allowed to interfere with profit making —**do business with 1.** to engage in commerce with **2.** to have dealings with —☆**give (someone) the business** [Slang] to subject (someone) to rough treatment, practical joking, etc. —**mean business** [Colloq.] to be in earnest

☆**business college** (or **school**) a school offering instruction in secretarial skills, business administration, etc.

busi·ness·like (-līk′) *adj.* having the qualities needed in business; efficient, methodical, etc.

busi·ness·man (-man′) *n., pl.* -**men′** (-men′) a man in business, esp. as an owner or executive —☆**busi′ness·wom′an** *n.fem., pl.* -**wom′en**

bus·ing, bus·sing (bus′iŋ) *n.* ☆the act of transporting children by bus to a school outside of their neighborhood, esp. in order to desegregate the school

bus·kin (bus′kin) *n.* [< ? OFr. < MDu. *brosekin,* small leather boot] **1.** a boot reaching to the calf or knee, worn long ago **2.** *a)* the high, thick-soled, laced boot worn by actors in ancient Greek and Roman tragedy *b)* tragic drama; tragedy —**bus′kined** *adj.*

bus·man (bus′mən) *n., pl.* -**men** the driver of a bus

busman's holiday a holiday in which one does as recreation what one usually does as one's work

buss (bus) *n., vt., vi.* [? akin to G. dial. (or W. & Gael.) *bus*] [Archaic or Dial.] kiss

bus·ses (bus′iz) *n. alt. pl. of* BUS

bust¹ (bust) *n.* [< Fr. < It. *busto*] **1.** a piece of sculpture representing a person's head, shoulders, and upper chest **2.** a woman's bosom

BUSKINS

bust² (bust) *vt., vi.* [var. of BURST] [Slang] **1.** to burst or break **2.** to make or become penniless or bankrupt ☆**3.** to demote or become demoted [to *bust* a sergeant to private] ☆**4.** to tame (esp. broncos) ☆**5.** to hit ☆**6.** to arrest —*n.* [Slang] ☆**1.** a failure ☆**2.** a business failure; depression; crash ☆**3.** a punch or blow ☆**4.** a spree ☆**5.** an arrest —**bust′ed** *adj.*

bus·tard (bus′tərd) *n.* [< OFr. < L. *avis tarda,* slow bird] a large, long-legged game bird of Europe, Asia, and Africa

bus·tle¹ (bus′'l) *vi., vt.* -**tled, -tling** [< ME. *busken,* to prepare < ON.] to hurry busily or with much fuss and bother —*n.* busy and noisy activity [the *bustle* of the farmers' market]

bus·tle² (bus′'l) *n.* [late 18th c. < ? G. *buschel,* a bunch, pad] a framework or padding worn at the back by women to puff out the skirt

bus·y (biz′ē) *adj.* **bus′i·er, bus′i·est** [OE. *bisig*] **1.** occupied; at work; not idle [she is *busy* at her desk] **2.** full of activity [a *busy* store] **3.** *a)* in use at the moment, as a telephone line *b)* indicating such use [the *busy* signal is a series of short buzzes] **4.** crowded with detail, colors, etc., esp. in a way that is not pleasing —*vt.* **bus′ied, bus′y·ing** to make or keep busy —**bus′y·ness** *n.*

BUSTLE

SYN.—*busy* suggests being taken up with some task or activity, either temporarily or steadily [I'm *busy* just now]; **industrious** suggests being steadily devoted to one's work or activity [an *industrious* salesclerk]; **diligent** suggests strict attention to what one is doing and implies enjoyment in the task itself [a *diligent* student of music]; **assiduous** suggests painstaking attention to the details of some task [*assiduous* study]; **sedulous** implies being steadily devoted to a task until the goal is reached [a *sedulous* investigation of the crime]

bus·y·bod·y (-bäd′ē) *n., pl.* -**bod′ies** one who mixes into other people's affairs; meddler

☆**bus·y·work, bus·y-work** (-wurk′) *n.* an activity, as an assignment in school, whose main purpose is to keep someone busy for a time

but (but; *unstressed* bət) *prep.* [< OE. *butan,* without < *be,* by + *utan,* out < *ut,* out] **1.** except; save [nobody came *but* me]: sometimes regarded as a conjunction [nobody came *but* I (came)] **2.** other than: used with an infinitive as the object [we cannot choose *but* (to) stay] —*conj.* **1.** yet; still; however [the story is long, *but* it is not dull] **2.** on the contrary [I am old, *but* you are young] **3.** except that; unless [it never rains *but* it pours] **4.** that [I don't question *but* you're right] **5.** that . . . not [I never think of London *but* I think of fog] —*adv.* **1.** only [if I had *but* known] **2.** merely [he is *but* a child] **3.** just [I heard it *but* now] **4.** [Slang] absolutely [do it *but* now!] —*pron.* who . . . not; which . . . not [not a man *but* felt it] —**but for** if it were not for —**but that 1.** about the fact that [I've no doubt *but that* he'll come] **2.** that there is not some chance that [we can't be sure *but that* she's right] Also [Colloq.] **but what**

bu·ta·di·ene (byoot′ə dī′ēn, -dī ēn′) *n.* [BUTA(NE) + DI-¹ + -ENE] a hydrocarbon, C_4H_6, used to make Buna

bu·tane (byoo′tān, byoo tān′) *n.* [BUT(YL) + -ANE] either of two gaseous hydrocarbons in the methane series, with the formula C_4H_{10}, used as a fuel, etc.

bu·ta·nol (byoo′tə nôl′, -nōl) *n.* [BUTAN(E) + -OL¹] same as BUTYL ALCOHOL

butch (booch) *adj.* [prob. < *Butch,* nickname for a boy] [Slang] ☆**1.** designating a man's close-cropped haircut ☆**2.** masculine in appearance, manner, etc.; mannish —*n.* [Slang] ☆a tough or rugged man or boy: chiefly a term of address

butch·er (booch′ər) *n.* [< OFr. < *bouc,* he-goat < Frank. *bukk;* for IE. base see BUCK¹] **1.** one whose work is killing animals or preparing their dead bodies for meat **2.** one who cuts up meat for sale **3.** anyone who kills as if slaughtering animals ☆**4.** one who sells candy, drinks, etc. in theaters, circuses, etc. —*vt.* **1.** to kill or prepare (animals) for meat **2.** to kill brutally or in large numbers; slaughter **3.** to mess up; botch

butch·er·bird (-burd′) *n.* a shrike which, after killing prey, hangs it on thorns

butch·er·y (-ē) *n., pl.* -**er·ies 1.** a slaughterhouse **2.** the work or business of a butcher **3.** brutal bloodshed **4.** the act or result of botching —see **SYN.** at SLAUGHTER

but·ler (but′lər) *n.* [< OFr. < *bouteille,* BOTTLE] a manservant, now usually the head servant of a household, in charge of wines, pantry, etc.

But·ler (but′lər), **Samuel** 1835–1902; Eng. novelist

butler's pantry a serving pantry between the kitchen and the dining room

but·ler·y (but′lər ē) *n., pl.* -**ler·ies** a butler's pantry; buttery

butt¹ (but) *n.* [< ? OFr. *bout,* end < *buter* (see BUTT²) or < ? ON. *būtr,* block of wood] **1.** the thick end of anything, as of a rifle stock **2.** a stub or stump, as of a partially smoked cigarette **3.** *a)* [? infl. by Fr. *butte,* mound] a mound of earth behind a target into which the fired rounds go *b)* a target *c)* [*pl.*] a target range **4.** an object of ridicule or criticism [Jo was the *butt* of their jokes*]* **5.** [Slang] a cigarette **6.** [Slang] the buttocks — *vt., vi.* to join end to end

butt² (but) *vt.* [< OFr. *buter* (< Frank. *botan*), to thrust against: for IE. base see BEAT] **1.** to ram with the head, as a goat does **2.** to strike against *[he butted his head against the wall]* **3.** to abut on — *vi.* **1.** to make a butting motion **2.** to stick out; project **3.** to abut — *n.* a thrust with the head or horns —☆**butt in** (or **into**) [Slang] to mix into (another's business, a conversation, etc.)

butt³ (but) *n.* [< OFr. *botte* < ML. < LL. *bottis*, cask] **1.** a large barrel or cask, as for wine or beer **2.** a measure of liquid capacity equal to 126 gallons or two hogsheads

butte (byōōt) *n.* [Fr., mound < OFr. *buter*: see BUTT²] a steep hill standing alone on a plain, esp. in the western U.S.; small mesa

but·ter (but′ər) *n.* [< OE. < L. *butyrum* < Gr. *boutyron* < *bous*, ox, cow + *tyros*, cheese] **1.** the solid, yellowish fat gotten by churning cream or whole milk and used as a spread on bread, in cooking, etc.

BUTTE

2. a substance somewhat like butter; specif., *a)* any of certain other spreads for bread *[peanut butter] b)* any of certain vegetable oils that are solid at ordinary temperatures *[cocoa butter]* **3.** [Colloq.] flattery —*vt.* **1.** to spread with butter **2.** [Colloq.] to flatter (often with *up*)

butter bean *same as:* **1.** LIMA BEAN **2.** WAX BEAN

but·ter·cup (-kup′) *n.* a yellow-flowered plant, common in meadows and wet places —*adj.* designating a large family of plants, including the peony, aconite, larkspur, etc.

but·ter·fat (-fat′) *n.* the fatty part of milk, from which butter is made

but·ter·fin·gers (-fiŋ′gərz) *n.* one who often fumbles and drops things —**but′ter·fin′gered** *adj.*

but·ter·fish (-fish′) *n., pl.* **-fish′, -fish′es:** see FISH any of various fishes with a slippery mucous coating

but·ter·fly (-flī′) *n., pl.* **-flies′** [OE. *buttorfleoge:* term first used of a yellow species] **1.** any of a large group of insects active by day, having a sucking mouthpart, slender body, and four broad, usually brightly colored wings **2.** a person, esp. a woman, thought of as flighty, frivolous, etc. —*adj.* like a butterfly in having parts spread out like wings *[a butterfly chair]*

butterfly stroke a swimming stroke done face down, in which the arms are thrust out at the sides, then brought forward and down through the water in a circular motion

butter knife a small, dull-edged knife for cutting or spreading butter

but·ter·milk (-milk′) *n.* the sour liquid left after churning butter from milk: now usually made by adding a culture of certain bacteria to skim milk

☆**but·ter·nut** (-nut′) *n.* **1.** a species of walnut of eastern N.America, with compound leaves and hard-shelled nuts **2.** the oily, edible nut of this tree

☆**butternut squash** a small, bell-shaped, smooth winter squash, with yellowish flesh

but·ter·scotch (-skäch′) *n.* a hard, sticky candy made with brown sugar, butter, etc. —*adj.* having the flavor of butterscotch

but·ter·y¹ (but′ər ē, but′rē) *n., pl.* **-ter·ies** [< OFr. < ML. *buteria*: see BUTT³] **1.** a storeroom for wine and liquor **2.** a pantry

but·ter·y² (but′ər ē) *adj.* **1.** like butter **2.** containing or spread with butter **3.** always flattering; adulatory

but·tock (but′ək) *n.* [< OE. *buttuc*, end, akin to BUTT¹] **1.** either of the two fleshy, rounded parts at the back of the hips **2.** *[pl.]* the rump; part on which one sits

but·ton (but′'n) *n.* [OFr. *boton*, a button < *buter*: see BUTT²] **1.** any small disk or knob used as a fastening, ornament, etc. on a garment, esp. one made for putting through a buttonhole **2.** anything small and shaped like a button; specif., *a)* a small emblem worn in the lapel, etc. *b)* a small knob for operating a doorbell, electric lamp, etc. *c)* a small mushroom ☆**3.** [Slang] the point of the chin —*vt., vi.* to fasten with buttons —☆**on the button** [Slang] exactly at the desired point, time, etc. —**but′ton·er** *n.* —**but′ton·less** *adj.* —**but′ton·like′** *adj.*

☆**but·ton-down** (-doun′) *adj.* designating a collar with points fastened down by small buttons

but·ton·hole (-hōl′) *n.* a slit or loop through which a button can be fastened —*vt.* **-holed′, -hol′ing** **1.** to make buttonholes in **2.** to make (a person) listen to one, as if by grasping his coat by a buttonhole —**but′ton·hol′er** *n.*

but·ton·hook (-hook′) *n.* a hook for pulling buttons through buttonholes, as in a former style of shoe

☆**but·ton·wood** (-wood′) *n. same as* PLANE¹

but·tress (but′ris) *n.* [< OFr. < *buter*: see BUTT²] **1.** a structure built against a wall to support or strengthen it: see FLYING BUTTRESS **2.** any support or prop *[her faith was a buttress in times of trouble]* —*vt.* **1.** to support or reinforce with a buttress **2.** to prop up or support *[to buttress an argument with facts]*

bu·tut (boo toot′) *n., pl.* **-tut′** [native term, lit., small] *see* MONETARY UNITS, table (Gambia)

bu·tyl (byoot′'l) *n.* [< L. *butyrum* (see BUTTER) + -YL] any of the four isomeric organic radicals C_4H_9

butyl alcohol any of four isomeric alcohols, C_4H_9OH, used as solvents and in organic synthesis

bu·tyr·ic (byoo tir′ik) *adj.* [< L. *butyrum* (see BUTTER) + -IC] **1.** of or obtained from butter **2.** of or pertaining to butyric acid

butyric acid a fatty acid, $C_3H_7CO_2H$, with a strong, stale smell, found in butter, etc.

bux·om (buk′səm) *adj.* [ME., humble, obedient < base of *bouen*, to BOW¹ + *-sum*, -SOME¹] healthy, attractive, plump, jolly, etc.; specif. now, having a shapely figure with a full bosom: said of a woman or girl —**bux′om·ly** *adv.* —**bux′om·ness** *n.*

Bux·te·hu·de (book′stə hoo′də), **Did·er·ik** (dē′də rik) 1637–1707; Dan. organist & composer, later in Germany

buy (bī) *vt.* **bought, buy′ing** [OE. *bycgan*, prob. < base of BOW¹] **1.** to get ownership of by paying money; purchase *[should we buy the car or lease it?]* **2.** to get by any exchange *[to buy time by negotiating]* **3.** to be the means of purchasing *[all that money can buy]* **4.** to bribe ☆**5.** [Slang] to accept as proper, agreeable, etc. *[I can't buy his excuse]* —*vi.* to buy things; be a buyer —*n.* **1.** a buying **2.** anything bought or buyable *[a good buy]* ☆**3.** [Colloq.] a bargain *[a real buy]* —**buy into** (or **in**) to pay money so as to get shares of, membership in, etc. —**buy off** to bribe —**buy out** to buy all the stock, rights, etc. of —**buy up** to buy all that is available of —**buy′a·ble** *adj.*

buy·er (bī′ər) *n.* **1.** one who buys; consumer **2.** one whose work is to buy merchandise for a retail store

buzz (buz) *vi.* [echoic] **1.** to make a long, steady *z* sound; hum like a bee **2.** to talk excitedly, esp. in low tones **3.** to gossip **4.** to move with a buzzing sound **5.** to be filled with noisy activity or talk *[the lunchroom was buzzing with the news]* —*vt.* **1.** to tell (rumors, etc.) in a buzzing manner **2.** to make (wings, etc.) buzz ☆**3.** to fly an airplane low over *[he was fined for buzzing the control tower]* **4.** to signal with a buzzer *[buzz me when you're ready]* **5.** [Colloq.] to telephone —*n.* **1.** a sound like a bee's hum **2.** a confused sound, as of many voices **3.** noisy activity **4.** a signal on a buzzer ☆**5.** [Colloq.] a telephone call *[I'll give you a buzz Friday]* —**buzz about** (or **around**) to scurry about —**buzz off** [Brit. Colloq.] to hurry away

buz·zard (buz′ərd) *n.* [< OFr. *busart* < *buse* (< L. *buteo*, kind of hawk) + *-art*, -ARD] **1.** any of various hawks that are slow and heavy in flight ☆**2.** *same as* TURKEY BUZZARD **3.** a person regarded as mean, grasping, etc.

buzz·er (buz′ər) *n.* an electrical device that makes a buzzing sound as a signal

☆**buzz saw** a circular saw rotated by machinery

bwa·na (bwä′nə) *n.* [Swahili < Ar. *abūna*, our father] *[often* B-] master; sir: native respectful term of address used in parts of Africa

B.W.I. British West Indies

bx. *pl.* **bxs.** box

by (bī) *prep.* [OE. *be, bi*] **1.** near or beside; at *[stand by the wall]* **2.** *a)* in or during *[to travel by night] b)* for a fixed time *[to work by the hour] c)* not later than *[be back by noon]* **3.** *a)* via; through *[to New Jersey by the Holland Tunnel] b)* past; beyond *[to march by the reviewing stand] c)* toward *[north by west]* **4.** in behalf of *[he did well by me]* **5.** through the means, work, or operations of *[made by hand]* **6.** *a)* according to *[by the book] b)* in *[to grow dark by degrees] c)* following in series *[march two by two]* **7.** with the sanction of *[by your leave]* **8.** *a)* in or to the amount or degree of *[apples by the peck] b)* and in another dimension *[two by* four] c) using (the given number) as multiplier or divisor [multiply (or divide) 6 *by* 3] —*adv.* **1.** close at hand; near [stand *by*] **2.** away; aside [put money *by*] **3.** past [cars sped *by*] ☆**4.** at someone's place [stop *by* on your way home] —*adj., n. same as* BYE —**by and by** after a while —☆**by and large** considering everything —**by oneself 1.** alone **2.** unaided —**by the by** incidentally

by- *a prefix meaning:* **1.** close by; near [*bystander*] **2.** on the side; secondary [*byproduct*]

by-and-by (bī'n bī') *n.* a future time ["in the sweet *by-and-by*"]

bye (bī) *n.* [see BY] **1.** something extra of lesser importance **2.** in sports in which competitors are paired, the status of any extra man, who advances to the next round without playing **3.** *Golf* any holes left unplayed at the end of a match —*adj.* extra and of lesser importance; incidental —**by the bye** incidentally; by the way

bye-bye (bī'bī', bī'bī') *n., interj.* goodbye

by-e-lec-tion (bī'i lek'shən) *n.* a special election between general elections, esp. in Great Britain

Bye-lo-rus-sian Soviet Socialist Republic (bye'lō rush'-ən) republic of the U.S.S.R., in the W part: 80,154 sq. mi.; pop. 9,000,000; cap. Minsk: also **Bye'lo-rus'sia** —**Bye'lo-rus'sian** *adj., n.*

by-gone (bī'gôn', -gän') *adj.* gone by; past —*n.* anything that is gone or past —**let bygones be bygones** to let past offenses be forgotten

by-law (bī'lô') *n.* [< ME. < *bi*, town (< ON. *byr* < *būa*, to dwell: see BONDAGE) + *laue*, LAW: meaning infl. by BY] any of a set of rules adopted by an organization for governing its own meetings or affairs

☆**by-line** (-līn') *n.* a line at the head of a newspaper or magazine article, telling who wrote it

by-pass (-pas') *n.* **1.** a way, path, pipe, channel, etc. between two points that avoids the main way, as in order to get around an obstacle; detour **2.** *Elec. same as* SHUNT (*n.* 3) —*vt.* **1.** to go around instead of through **2.** to furnish with a bypass **3.** to ignore, fail to consult, etc.

by-path, by-path (-path') *n.* a side path; byway

by-play (-plā') *n.* action, gestures, etc. going on aside from the main action, as in a play

by-prod-uct, by-prod-uct (-präd'əkt) *n.* anything produced in the course of making another thing; secondary product or result [glue is a *byproduct* of meatpacking]

Byrd (bửrd), **Richard Evelyn** 1888–1957; U.S. polar explorer

by-road (bī'rōd') *n.* a side road; byway

By-ron (bī'rən) [< Fr. < *Biron*, district in France] **1.** a masculine name **2. George Gordon,** 6th Baron Byron, 1788–1824; Eng. poet

By-ron-ic (bī rän'ik) *adj.* of, like, or characteristic of Byron or his writings; romantic, passionate, cynical, ironic, etc. —**By-ron'i-cal-ly** *adv.*

bys-sus (bis'əs) *n., pl.* **bys'sus-es, bys'si** (-ī) [L. < Gr. *byssos*, fine linen < Heb. *būs* < Egypt.] **1.** a linen cloth of ancient times, as that used to wrap Egyptian mummies **2.** a tuft of silk-like filaments in some mollusks, by which they attach themselves to objects

by-stand-er (bī'stan'dər) *n.* a person who stands near but does not take part in what is happening; onlooker

by-way (bī'wā') *n.* **1.** a path or road that is not a main road, esp. one not used very much **2.** a secondary activity, line of study, etc.

by-word (-wửrd') *n.* **1.** a familiar saying; proverb **2.** a person or thing considered typical of some bad or undesirable quality [his cruelty made him a *byword*] **3.** a favorite or pet word or phrase

By-zan-tine (biz'n tēn', -tīn'; bi zan'tin) *adj.* **1.** of or like Byzantium or the Byzantine Empire, its culture, etc. **2.** of or pertaining to the Orthodox Eastern Church **3.** *Archit.* designating or of a style developed in Byzantium, characterized by domes, round arches, mosaics, etc. —*n.* a native or inhabitant of Byzantium

Byzantine Empire empire (395–1453) in southeastern Europe & southwestern Asia, formed by the division of the Roman Empire: cap. Constantinople

BYZANTINE EMPIRE (12th cent.)

By-zan-ti-um (bi zan'shē-əm, -tē əm) *ancient name of* ISTANBUL (until 330 A.D.)

C

C, c (sē) *n., pl.* **C's, c's** **1.** the third letter of the English alphabet **2.** a sound of *C* or *c* **3.** *a symbol for* the third in a sequence or group

C (sē) *n.* **1.** a Roman numeral for 100: it subtracts one hundred units when placed before a larger numeral (for example, CM = 900) **2.** *Chem.* carbon ☆**3.** *Educ.* a grade indicating average work **4.** *Music* *a)* the first tone in the scale of C major *b)* the scale having this tone as the keynote

C- cargo transport

C, C. **1.** Celsius or centigrade **2.** Central

C. **1.** Catholic **2.** Church **3.** Congress **4.** Corps

C., c. **1.** capacitance **2.** carat **3.** catcher **4.** cathode **5.** cent **6.** center **7.** centimeter **8.** century **9.** *pl.* **CC.** chapter **10.** circa **11.** contralto **12.** copyright **13.** cubic **14.** cycle

Ca *Chem.* calcium

CA California

ca. **1.** cathode **2.** centiare **3.** circa

C.A. **1.** Central America **2.** Confederate Army

Caa·ba (kä′bə) *same as* KAABA

cab (kab) *n.* [< CABRIOLET] **1.** a horse-drawn carriage, esp. one that can be hired along with its driver **2.** *short for* TAXICAB **3.** the place in a locomotive, motor truck, crane, etc. where the operator sits

CAB Civil Aeronautics Board

ca·bal (kə bal′) *n.* [Fr., intrigue < ML. *cabbala*, CABALA] **1.** a small group of persons joined in a secret scheme or plot **2.** the scheme or plot of such a group —*vi.* **-balled′, -bal′ling** to join in a cabal; plot —see SYN. at PLOT

cab·a·la (kab′ə lə, kə bäl′ə) *n.* [< ML. < Heb. *qabbālāh*, received lore < *qābal*, to receive] **1.** a mystical philosophy of certain rabbis of the Middle Ages, based on a special interpretation of the Scriptures **2.** any esoteric or secret doctrine; occultism Also sp. **cab′ba·la** —**cab′a·lism** *n.* —**cab′a·list** *n.* —**cab′a·lis′tic** *adj.* —**cab′a·lis′ti·cal·ly** *adv.*

ca·bal·le·ro (kab′ə ler′ō, -əl yer′ō) *n., pl.* **-ros** [Sp. < LL. < L. *caballus*, horse] **1.** a Spanish gentleman or knight ☆**2.** [Southwest] *a)* a horseman *b)* a lady's escort

☆**ca·ba·na** (kə bän′ə, -bän′yə; -ban′-) *n.* [Sp. *cabaña* < LL. *capanna*, hut] **1.** a cabin or hut **2.** a small shelter or bathhouse for swimmers at a beach, pool, etc.

cab·a·ret (kab′ə rā′, kab′ə rā′) *n.* [Fr., pothouse, ult. < OFr. dim. of *cambre*, CHAMBER] **1.** a restaurant or café with dancing, singing, etc. as entertainment **2.** such entertainment

cab·bage (kab′ij) *n.* [OFr. *caboche*, ult. < ? L. *caput*, the head] a common vegetable of the mustard family, with thick leaves formed into a round, compact head on a short stalk

cabbage butterfly a common white butterfly whose green larvae feed on cabbage and related plants

cabbage palm **1.** any of several palms with buds used as a vegetable: also **cabbage tree** **2.** *see* PALMETTO

cab·driv·er (kab′drīv′ər) *n.* a person who drives a cab: also [Colloq.] **cab′by, cab′bie** (-ē), *pl.* **-bies**

cab·in (kab′n) *n.* [< OFr. < Pr. < LL. *capanna*, hut] **1.** a small house, built simply or crudely [a log *cabin*] ☆**2.** any simple, small structure designed for a brief stay [a tourist *cabin*] **3.** a private room on a ship, as a bedroom or office **4.** a roofed section of a small boat **5.** the enclosed section for passengers in an aircraft —*vt.* to confine in or as in a cabin; cramp

cabin boy a boy whose work is to serve and run errands for officers and passengers aboard a ship

☆**cabin cruiser** a motorboat with a cabin and all the equipment needed for living on board

cab·i·net (kab′ə nit, kab′nit) *n.* [Fr., dim. of *cabine* < ?] **1.** a case with drawers or shelves for holding or storing things [a filing *cabinet;* a medicine *cabinet*] **2.** a boxlike enclosure for a record player, radio, television, etc. **3.** formerly, a private council room ☆**4.** [often **C-**] a group of official advisers to a president, king, governor, etc.: in the U.S., the heads of certain governmental departments —*adj.* **1.** of a kind usually kept in a cabinet [*cabinet* curios] **2.** of a political cabinet

cab·i·net·mak·er (-māk′ər) *n.* a workman who makes fine furniture, etc. —**cab′i·net·mak′ing** *n.*

☆**cab·i·net·work** (-wurk′) *n.* **1.** articles made by a cabinetmaker **2.** the work or art of a cabinetmaker Also **cab′i·net·ry** (-rē)

ca·ble (kā′b'l) *n.* [OFr. < LL. *capulum* < L. *capere*, to take hold] **1.** a thick, heavy rope, now often of wire strands **2.** a ship's anchor chain **3.** *same as* CABLE LENGTH **4.** a bundle of insulated wires through which an electric current can be passed ☆**5.** *same as* CABLEGRAM —*vt.* **-bled, -bling** **1.** to fasten with a cable **2.** to send (a message) by undersea cable **3.** to send a cablegram to —*vi.* to send a cablegram

☆**cable car** a car drawn by a moving cable

☆**ca·ble·gram** (-gram′) *n.* a message sent by undersea cable

cable length a sailors' unit of measure variously equal to 720 feet (120 fathoms) or 600 feet (100 fathoms): also **cable's length**

☆**cable railway** a street railway on which cars are pulled by a continuously moving underground cable

cable stitch a type of raised stitch used in knitting: it resembles ropes twisted together

cab·man (kab′mən) *n., pl.* **-men** *same as* CABDRIVER

ca·bob (kə bäb′) *n. same as* KEBAB

cab·o·chon (kab′ə shän′) *n.* [Fr. < *caboche*, the head: see CABBAGE] any precious stone cut in a convex shape without facets and polished

☆**ca·boo·dle** (kə bōō′d'l) *n.* [prob. extended < BOODLE] [Colloq.] lot; group [the whole *caboodle*]

ca·boose (kə bōōs′) *n.* [< MDu. *kabuys, kambuis*, cabin house, ship's galley] **1.** [Brit.] a ship's galley or kitchen ☆**2.** the trainmen's car on a freight train, usually at the rear

Cab·ot (kab′ət), **John** (It. name *Giovanni Caboto*) 1450?-98; It. explorer in the service of England: discovered coast of N. America (1497)

ca·bret·ta (kə bret′ə) *adj.* [< Sp. *cabra*, goat + It. dim. suffix *-etta*] designating or of a soft leather made from a special kind of sheepskin

cab·ri·o·let (kab′rē ə lā′) *n.* [Fr., dim. of *cabriole*, a leap < It. *capriola*, CAPRIOLE] **1.** a light, two-wheeled carriage, usually

CABLES

with a hood that folds, drawn by one horse 2. a former style of automobile like a convertible coupe

cab·stand (kab'stand') *n.* a place where cabs are stationed while waiting to be hired

ca·ca·o (kə kā'ō, -kä'-) *n., pl.* **-ca'os** [Sp. < Nahuatl *cacauatl*, cacao seed] 1. a tropical American tree from whose seeds cocoa and chocolate are made 2. these seeds (**cacao beans**)

cac·cia·to·re (kach'ə tôr'ē) *adj.* [It., lit., a hunter < pp. of *cacciare*, to hunt] cooked in a casserole with olive oil and tomatoes, onions, spices, etc. [chicken *cacciatore*]

cach·a·lot (kash'ə lät', -lō') *n.* [Fr. < Sp. < ? Port. *cachola*, big head] *same as* SPERM WHALE

cache (kash) *n.* [Fr. < *cacher*, conceal < L. *coactare*, constrain] 1. a place in which stores of food, supplies, etc. are hidden 2. a safe place for hiding things 3. anything so hidden —*vt., vi.* **cached, cach'ing** to hide or store in a cache —see SYN. at HIDE[1]

cache·pot (kash'pät, -pō) *n.* [Fr., lit., hide-pot < *cacher*, to hide + *pot*, pot] a decorative pot, jar, etc., esp. for holding potted house plants: also **cache pot**

ca·chet (ka shā', kash'ā) *n.* [Fr. < *cacher*: see CACHE] 1. a seal or stamp on an official letter 2. *a)* a mark showing that something is genuine or of superior quality *b)* prestige 3. a commemorative design, slogan, etc. stamped on mail

ca·chex·i·a (kə kek'sē ə) *n.* [ModL. < Gr. < *kakos*, bad + *hexis*, habit] a weakened condition of the body, esp. as the result of a long illness —**ca·chec'tic** (-kek'tik) *adj.*

cach·in·nate (kak'ə nāt') *vi.* **-nat'ed, -nat'ing** [< L. pp. of *cachinnare*, prob. echoic] to laugh loudly or too much — **cach'in·na'tion** *n.*

ca·cique (kə sēk') *n.* [Sp. < native word] 1. in Spanish America, an Indian chief 2. in Spanish America and Spain, a local political boss

cack·le (kak'l) *vi.* **-led, -ling** [akin to Du. *kokkelen*, of echoic origin] 1. to make the shrill, broken, vocal sounds of a hen 2. to laugh or chatter with similar sounds —*vt.* to utter in a cackling manner —*n.* 1. the act or sound of cackling 2. cackling laughter or chatter

cac·o- [< Gr. *kakos*, bad, evil] *a combining form meaning* bad, poor, harsh [*cacography*]: also, before a vowel, **cac-**

ca·cog·ra·phy (kə käg'rə fē) *n.* [CACO- + -GRAPHY] 1. bad handwriting 2. incorrect spelling —**cac·o·graph·ic** (kak'ə graf'ik) *adj.*

☆**cac·o·mis·tle** (kak'ə mis''l) *n.* [AmSp. *cacomixtle* < Nahuatl] a slender, long-tailed animal of the southwestern U.S. and Mexico, like the raccoon: also **cac'o·mix'le** (-mis''l, -miks'l)

ca·coph·o·ny (kə käf'ə nē) *n., pl.* **-nies** [< ModL. < Gr. < *kakos*, bad + *phōnē*, voice] harsh, jarring sound; dissonance —**ca·coph'o·nous** *adj.* —**ca·coph'o·nous·ly** *adv.*

cac·tus (kak'təs) *n., pl.* **-tus·es, -ti** (-tī) [L. < Gr. *kaktos*, kind of thistle] any of various new-world desert plants with fleshy stems, bearing spines or scales instead of leaves, and often showy flowers

cad (kad) *n.* [< CADDIE & CADET] a man or boy whose behavior is not right or honorable

ca·dav·er (kə dav'ər) *n.* [L., prob. < *cadere*, to fall] a dead body, esp. of a person; corpse —**ca·dav'er·ic** *adj.*

ca·dav·er·ous (kə dav'ər əs) *adj.* of or like a cadaver; esp., pale, ghastly, or gaunt and haggard —**ca·dav'er·ous·ly** *adv.* —**ca·dav'er·ous·ness** *n.*

CACTUSES

cad·die (kad'ē) *n.* [Scot. form of Fr. *cadet*: see CADET] 1. a person whose work is helping a golf player, carrying the clubs, finding the balls, etc. 2. a small, wheeled cart —*vi.* **-died, -dy·ing** to act as a caddie

cad·dis fly (kad'is) [see CADDIS WORM] a small, mothlike insect with two pairs of wings, a soft body, and long legs

cad·dish (kad'ish) *adj.* like or characteristic of a cad; ungentlemanly —**cad'dish·ly** *adv.* —**cad'dish·ness** *n.*

cad·dis worm (kad'is) [< OFr. *cadas*, floss silk (with reference to the case)] the wormlike larva of the caddis fly that lives in fresh water in a case made of twigs, grains of sand, etc. cemented together with silk that it secretes: used as fishing bait

cad·dy[1] (kad'ē) *n., pl.* **-dies** [< Malay *kati*, weight equal to a little more than a pound] 1. a small container used for tea 2.

any of various devices for holding or storing certain articles [a letter *caddy*]

cad·dy[2] (kad'ē) *n., vi. same as* CADDIE

-cade (kād) [< (CAVAL)CADE] *a suffix meaning* procession, parade [*motorcade*]

ca·dence (kād'ns) *n.* [ult. < L. prp. of *cadere*, to fall] 1. fall of the voice in speaking 2. a change or variation in tone in speaking 3. a rhythmic flow of sound 4. measured movement, as in marching, or the beat of such movement 5. *Music* the final chords, trill, etc. of a phrase or movement Also **ca'den·cy** —**ca'denced** *adj.*

ca·den·za (kə den'zə) *n.* [It.: see prec.] 1. an elaborate musical passage played by the solo instrument in a concerto, usually near the end of the first movement: it is sometimes improvised by the performer 2. any brilliant flourish in an aria or solo passage

ca·det (kə det') *n.* [Fr. < dial. *capdet*, chief < Pr. < LL. dim. of L. *caput*: see CAPTAIN] 1. a younger son or brother 2. a student at an armed forces academy 3. a student at a military school ☆4. any trainee, as a practice teacher or a junior business associate —**ca·det'ship'** *n.*

cadge (kaj) *vt., vi.* **cadged, cadg'ing** [ME. *caggen*, to tie] to beg or get by begging; sponge —**cadg'er** *n.*

ca·di (kä'dē, kā'-) *n.* [Ar. *qādi*] a minor Moslem magistrate or judge

Cá·diz (kə diz', kā'diz; *Sp.* kä *thēth'*) seaport in SW Spain, on the Atlantic: pop. 133,000

Cad·me·an (kad mē'ən) *adj.* of or like Cadmus

Cadmean victory a victory won with great losses to the victors

cad·mi·um (kad'mē əm) *n.* [ModL. < L. *cadmia*, zinc ore < Gr. *kadmeia*] a blue-white, ductile, metallic chemical element occurring in zinc ores: it is used in some alloys, electroplating, etc.: symbol, Cd; at. wt., 112.40; at. no., 48 —**cad'mic** (-mik) *adj.*

Cad·mus (kad'məs) *Gr. Myth.* a Phoenician prince who killed a dragon and sowed its teeth, from which many armed men rose and fought: five survived to help him build Thebes

ca·dre (kad'rē) *n.* [Fr. < It. < L. *quadrum*, a square] 1. a framework 2. a small, experienced unit around which a larger group, as a military unit, can be built; nucleus

ca·du·ce·us (kə dōō'sē əs, -dyōō'-) *n., pl.* **-ce·i'** (-sē ī') [L.] 1. the staff of an ancient herald; esp., the winged staff with two serpents twined about it, supposedly carried by Mercury 2. a staff like this with one or two serpents twined about it, used as a symbol of the medical profession —**ca·du'ce·an** *adj.*

cae·cil·i·an (sē sil'ē ən, -sil'yən) *n.* [< L. *caecilia*, kind of lizard < *caecus*: see CECUM] a tropical amphibian that has no legs and resembles a worm

cae·cum (sē'kəm) *n., pl.* **-ca** (-kə) *same as* CECUM — **cae'cal** *adj.*

Caed·mon (kad'mən) first Eng. poet whose name is known: he lived in the late 7th cent. A.D.

Cae·sar (sē'zər), (Gaius) Julius [said to be < pp. of L. *caedere*, to cut (see CAESAREAN SECTION), but prob. of Etruscan origin] 100?–44 B.C.; Roman general & statesman —*n.* 1. the title of the Roman emperors from Augustus to Hadrian 2. any emperor or dictator

CADU-
CEUS

Caes·a·re·a (ses'ə rē'ə, sez'-; sē'zə-) ancient seaport in Israel, on the Mediterranean: it was the capital of Palestine under the Romans

Cae·sar·e·an, Cae·sar·i·an (si zer'ē ən) *adj.* of Julius Caesar or the Caesars —*n. same as* CAESAREAN SECTION

Caesarean section [after Julius *Caesar*, supposedly born in this way] [*also* **c- s-**] a surgical operation for removing a baby from the mother's uterus by cutting through the walls of the abdomen and uterus

cae·si·um (sē'zē əm) *n. same as* CESIUM

cae·su·ra (si zhoor'ə, -zyoor'ə) *n., pl.* **-ras, -rae** (-ē) [L., a cutting < pp. of *caedere*, to cut] 1. a break or pause in a line of verse, usually about the middle of the line (Ex.: "Whoever you are, ‖ to you endless announcements!") 2. a pause showing rhythmic division of a melody —**cae·su'ral** *adj.*

ca·fé, ca·fe (ka fā', kə-) *n.* [Fr. < It. *caffè*, COFFEE] 1. a coffeehouse 2. a small restaurant, esp. one serving alcoholic drinks and sometimes providing entertainment

‡**ca·fé au lait** (kà fā ō lā') [Fr.] 1. coffee with an equal part of hot milk 2. light brown

café curtains short, straight curtains, esp. for the lower part of a window, hung from a rod by sliding rings

‡**ca·fé noir** (kà fā nwàr') [Fr.] black coffee

☆**caf·e·te·ri·a** (kaf′ə tir′ē ə) *n.* [AmSp., coffee store] a restaurant in which food is displayed on counters, and patrons choose what they want and carry it to a table

caf·feine, caf·fein (kaf′ēn, -ē in; ka fēn′) *n.* [< G., ult. < It. *caffè*, COFFEE + *-in*, -INE⁴] an alkaloid, $C_8H_{10}N_4O_2$, present in coffee, tea, and kola: it is a stimulant to the heart and central nervous system

caf·tan (kaf′tən, käf tän′) *n.* [Turk. *qaftān*] a long-sleeved robe with a girdle, worn in eastern Mediterranean countries

cage (kāj) *n.* [OFr. < L *cavea*, hollow place < *cavus*, see CAVE] **1.** a box or structure of wires, bars, etc. for confining birds or animals **2.** any structure like this, as some elevator cars ☆**3.** *Baseball* a backstop used in batting practice, etc. ☆**4.** *Basketball* the basket **5.** *Hockey* the network frame that is the goal —*vt.* **caged, cag′ing** to put or confine, as in a cage

cage·ling (kāj′liŋ) *n.* a bird kept in a cage

cag·er (kā′jər) *n.* [Slang] ☆a basketball player

☆**ca·gey, ca·gy** (kā′jē) *adj.* **ca·gi·er, ca·gi·est** [< ?] [Colloq.] **1.** sly; tricky; cunning **2.** careful not to get caught or fooled —**ca′gi·ly** *adv.* —**ca′gi·ness** *n.*

Ca·glia·ri (kä′lyä rē′) capital of Sardinia; seaport on the S coast: pop. 216,000

Ca·guas (kä′gwäs) city in EC Puerto Rico: pop. 63,000

☆**ca·hoots** (kə hoots′) *n.pl.* [< ?] [Slang] partnership; league —**go cahoots** [Slang] to share alike —**in cahoots** [Slang] in league or partnership, esp. in doing something not quite proper or honest

cai·man (kā′mən) *n., pl.* **-mans** [Sp. < Carib native name] a reptile of Central or South America similar to the alligator and crocodile

Cain (kān) *Bible* the oldest son of Adam and Eve: he killed his brother Abel: Gen. 4 —*n.* any murderer —☆**raise Cain** [Slang] to cause a great commotion or much trouble

ca·ique, ca·ïque (kä ēk′) *n.* [Fr. < It. < Turk. *qayiq*] **1.** a light rowboat used on the Bosporus **2.** a sailboat used esp. in the eastern Mediterranean

cairn (kern) *n.* [Scot. < Gael. *carn*, an elevation] a heap of stones in the form of a cone, built as a monument or landmark

cairn·gorm (kern′gôrm′) *n.* [after *Cairngorm*, mountain in Scotland] a yellow or brown variety of quartz, used as a gem

cairn terrier [said to be so named because it burrows in cairns] a small, shaggy Scottish terrier

Cai·ro (kī′rō) capital of Egypt, at the head of the Nile delta: pop. 3,346,000

cais·son (kā′sän, kās′'n) *n.* [Fr. < It. < *cassa* < L. *capsa*, a box, CASE²] **1.** a chest for holding ammunition **2.** a two-wheeled wagon for transporting ammunition **3.** a watertight enclosure inside which men can do construction work under water **4.** a watertight, hollow box for floating sunken ships to the surface

☆**caisson disease** *same as* DECOMPRESSION SICKNESS

cai·tiff (kāt′if) *n.* [OFr. *caitif*, a captive < L. *captivus*, CAPTIVE] a mean, evil, or cowardly person —*adj.* mean, evil, or cowardly

ca·jole (kə jōl′) *vt., vi.* **-joled′, -jol′ing** [< Fr. < ? blend of OFr. *cage*, CAGE + *jaole, gaole*, prison: see JAIL] to coax with flattery and insincere talk; wheedle —**ca·jole′ment, ca·jol′er·y** *n.* —**ca·jol′er** *n.* —**ca·jol′ing·ly** *adv.*

☆**Ca·jun, Ca·jan** (kā′jən) *n.* [< Acadian Fr.] **1.** a native of Louisiana descended from French immigrants from Acadia **2.** the dialect of the Cajuns

cake (kāk) *n.* [< ON. *kaka*] **1.** a small, flat mass of dough or batter, or of some hashed food, that is baked or fried [wheat *cakes*, fish *cakes*] **2.** a mixture of flour, eggs, milk, sugar, etc. baked as in a loaf and often covered with icing [devil's-food *cake*] **3.** a shaped, solid mass, as of soap, ice, etc. **4.** a hard crust or deposit —*vt., vi.* **caked, cak′ing** to form into a hard mass or a crust [the mud had *caked* on his shoes] —**take the cake** [Slang] to win the prize; excel: usually used in an ironic way —**cak′y** *adj.* **cak′i·er, cak′i·est**

cakes and ale the good things of life

☆**cake·walk** (-wôk′) *n.* **1.** formerly, an elaborate walk performed by blacks in the South competing for the prize of a cake **2.** a strutting dance developed from this —*vi.* to do a cakewalk —**cake′walk·er** *n.*

Cal. 1. California **2.** large calorie(s)

cal. 1. calendar **2.** caliber **3.** small calorie(s)

cal·a·bash (kal′ə bash′) *n.* [< Fr. < Sp. *calabaza* < ?] **1.** a tropical American tree of the bignonia family, or its large, gourdlike fruit **2.** *a)* a tropical vine bearing white flowers, or its bottle-shaped gourd *b)* a large smoking pipe made from the neck of this gourd **3.** the dried, hollow shell of a calabash, used as a bowl, cup, etc.

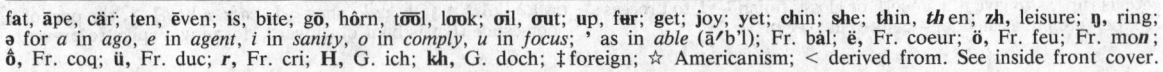

☆**cal·a·boose** (kal′ə boos′) *n.* [Sp. *calabozo*] [Slang] a prison; jail

Ca·la·bri·a (kə lā′brē ə; *It.* kä lä′bryä) region on the S coast of Italy, opposite Sicily

ca·la·di·um (kə lā′dē əm) *n.* [ModL. < Malay *kélády*, kind of plant] a tropical American plant of the arum family, with brilliantly colored leaves

Cal·ais (ka lā′, kal′ā) seaport in N France, on the Strait of Dover: pop. 75,000

cal·a·mine (kal′ə mīn′, -min) *n.* [Fr. < ML. *calamina* < L. *cadmia*: see CADMIUM] a pink powder consisting of zinc oxide mixed with a little ferric oxide, used in skin lotions and ointments

ca·lam·i·tous (kə lam′ə təs) *adj.* bringing or causing calamity —**ca·lam′i·tous·ly** *adv.* —**ca·lam′i·tous·ness** *n.*

ca·lam·i·ty (-tē) *n., pl.* **-ties** [< Fr. < L. *calamitas*: for IE. base see GLADIATOR] **1.** deep trouble or misery [the *calamity* of war] **2.** any great misfortune that brings loss and suffering; disaster

Calamity Jane (nickname of *Martha Jane Burke*) 1852–1903; Am. frontier woman, who was a famous marksman

ca·la·mon·din (kal′ə män′din) *n.* [Tag. *kalamunding*] a small, spicy orange of the Philippines

cal·a·mus (kal′ə məs) *n., pl.* **-mi′** (-mi′) [L. < Gr. *kalamos*, a reed < IE. base *kolem-*, a stalk] **1.** *same as* SWEET FLAG **2.** the quill of a feather

ca·lash (kə lash′) *n.* [Fr. *calèche* < G. < Czech *kolésa*; prob. < *kolo*, a wheel] **1.** a light, low-wheeled carriage, usually with a folding top **2.** a folding top of a carriage **3.** a folding hood or bonnet, worn by women in the 18th cent.

cal·ca·ne·us (kal kā′nē əs) *n., pl.* **-ne·i′** (-nē ī′) [LL. < L. < *calx*, the heel] the heel bone: also **cal·ca′ne·um** (-əm), *pl.* **-ne·a** (-ə) —**cal·ca′ne·al** *adj.*

cal·car·e·ous (kal ker′ē əs) *adj.* [< L. < *calx*, lime] of, like, or containing calcium carbonate, calcium, or lime —**cal·car′e·ous·ness** *n.*

cal·ces (kal′sēz) *n. alt. pl. of* CALX

cal·ci- [< L. *calx* (gen. *calcis*), lime] *a combining form meaning* calcium or lime [*calcify*]

cal·ci·cole (kal′sə kōl′) *n.* [< Fr. < L. *calx* (see CALCI-) + *colere*, to cultivate] a plant that grows well in limy soil

cal·cif·er·ol (kal sif′ə rôl′, -rōl′) *n.* [CALCIF(EROUS) + (ER-GOST)EROL] vitamin D₂: it is a crystalline alcohol, $C_{28}H_{43}OH$

cal·cif·er·ous (-ər əs) *adj.* [CALCI- + -FEROUS] producing or containing calcite

cal·ci·fuge (kal′sə fyooj′) *n.* [< Fr.: see CALCI- & -FUGE] a plant that does not grow well in limy soil

cal·ci·fy (kal′sə fī′) *vt., vi.* **-fied′, -fy′ing** [CALCI- + -FY] to change into a hard, stony substance by the deposit of lime or calcium salts —**cal′ci·fi·ca′tion** *n.*

cal·ci·mine (-mīn′, -min) *n.* [< L. *calx*, lime] a white or colored liquid of whiting or zinc white, glue, and water, used as a thin paint for plastered surfaces —*vt.* **-mined′, -min′ing** to cover with calcimine

cal·cine (kal′sīn, kal sīn′) *vt., vi.* **-cined, -cin·ing** [< OFr. < ML. *calcinare* (an alchemists' term)] **1.** to change to calx or powder by heat **2.** to burn to ashes or powder —**cal·ci·na·tion** (kal′sə nā′shən) *n.*

cal·cite (kal′sīt) *n.* calcium carbonate, $CaCO_3$, a mineral found as limestone, chalk, and marble

cal·ci·um (kal′sē əm) *n.* [ModL. < L. *calx*, lime] a soft, silver-white, metallic chemical element found in limestone, marble, chalk, etc.: symbol, Ca; at. wt., 40.08; at. no., 20

---

fat, āpe, cär; ten, ēven; is, bīte; gō, hôrn, tōol, look; oil, out; up, fur; get; joy; yet; chin; she; thin, then; zh, leisure; ŋ, ring; ə for a in ago, e in agent, i in sanity, o in comply, u in focus; ′ as in able (ā′b'l); Fr. bal; ë, Fr. coeur; ö, Fr. feu; Fr. mon; ô, Fr. coq; ü, Fr. duc; r, Fr. cri; H, G. ich; kh, G. doch; ‡foreign; ☆ Americanism; < derived from. See inside front cover.

calcium carbide a dark-gray, crystalline compound, CaC₂, used to produce acetylene, etc.

calcium carbonate a white powder or colorless, crystalline compound, $CaCO_3$, found mainly in limestone, marble, and chalk, and in bones, teeth, shells, and plant ash: used in making lime

calcium chloride a white, crystalline compound, $CaCl_2$, used in making ice, as a drying substance, etc.

calcium hydroxide slaked lime, $Ca(OH)_2$, a white, crystalline compound, used in making alkalies, bleaching powder, etc.

calcium light same as LIMELIGHT (sense 1)

calcium oxide a white, soft, caustic solid, CaO, prepared by heating calcium carbonate; lime: used in mortar and plaster, in ceramics, etc.

calcium phosphate any of a number of phosphates of calcium found in bones, teeth, etc. and used in enamels, glass, etc.

calc·spar (kalk´spär´) n. same as CALCITE

cal·cu·la·ble (kal´kyə lə b´l) adj. that can be calculated — **cal·cu·la·bil´i·ty** n. —**cal´cu·la·bly** adv.

cal·cu·late (kal´kyə lāt´) vt. -lat´ed, -lat´ing [< L. pp. of calculare, to reckon < calculus, pebble used in counting, dim. of calx, limestone] 1. to determine by using mathematics; compute [calculate the amount of lumber it will take] 2. to determine by reasoning; estimate [to calculate the effect of a decision] 3. to plan or intend [a tale calculated to fool us] ☆4. [Colloq.] to think; suppose —vi. 1. to make a computation 2. to rely or count (on)

SYN. —**calculate** refers to the use of mathematics, esp. higher mathematics, in finding a quantity, amount, etc. [to calculate distances in astronomy]; **compute** suggests simpler mathematics and implies an exact result [to compute the volume of a cylinder]; **estimate** refers to the judging, usually beforehand, of a quantity, cost, etc. and implies an approximate result [to estimate the cost of building a house]; **reckon**, an informal substitute for **compute**, suggests the use of such simple arithmetic as can be done in the mind [reckon up what I owe you]

cal·cu·lat·ed (kal´kyə lāt´id) adj. 1. undertaken after the probable results have been estimated [calculated risk] 2. deliberately planned [calculated cruelty] 3. apt or likely [a plan calculated to fail] —**cal´cu·lat´ed·ly** adv.

cal·cu·lat·ing (kal´kyə lāt´iŋ) adj. shrewd or scheming

cal·cu·la·tion (kal´kyə lā´shən) n. 1. a calculating 2. an answer found by calculating; estimate; plan 3. careful or deliberate planning, esp. when there is a selfish motive —**cal´cu·la´tive** adj.

cal·cu·la·tor (kal´kyə lāt´ər) n. 1. a person who calculates 2. a machine for doing rapid addition, subtraction, multiplication, and division: also **calculating machine**

cal·cu·lous (kal´kyə ləs) adj. Med. caused by or having a calculus or calculi

cal·cu·lus (kal´kyə ləs) n., pl. -li´ (-lī´), -lus·es [L.: see CALCULATE] 1. any abnormal stony substance formed in the body, as in a kidney 2. Math. a) a method of calculation using a special system of symbols b) a method of mathematical analysis using the combined methods of DIFFERENTIAL CALCULUS and INTEGRAL CALCULUS

Cal·cut·ta (kal kut´ə) seaport in NE India, in the Ganges delta: pop. 2,927,000

Cal·der (kôl´dər), **Alexander** 1898–1976; U.S. sculptor, esp. of mobiles and stabiles

cal·dron (kôl´drən) n. [< OFr. < L. caldaria, warm bath < calidus, warm < IE. base kel-, warm] a large kettle or boiler

Ca·leb (kā´ləb) [Heb. kālēb, lit., dog: hence, faithful] 1. a masculine name 2. Bible an Israelite leader who, with Joshua, was allowed to enter Canaan: see Num. 26:65

ca·lèche, ca·leche (kə lesh´) n. same as CALASH

Cal·e·do·ni·a (kal´ə dōn´yə, -dō´nē ə) [L.] poet. name for SCOTLAND —**Cal´e·do´ni·an** adj., n.

cal·en·dar (kal´ən dər) n. [L. kalendarium, account book < kalendae, CALENDS] 1. a system for arranging time into days, weeks, months, and years [the Gregorian calendar] 2. a table or chart that shows such an arrangement, usually for a single year 3. a list or schedule, as of court cases to be heard, bills to be discussed in a legislature, etc. —adj. of the kind that appears on popular calendars [calendar art] —vt. to enter in a calendar; schedule

calendar year the period of time from Jan. 1 through Dec. 31: distinguished from FISCAL YEAR

cal·en·der (kal´ən dər) n. [< Fr. < ML. < L. cylindrus, CYLINDER] a machine with rollers between which paper, cloth, etc. is run, as to give it a smooth or glossy finish —vt. to process (paper, etc.) in a calender —**cal´en·der·er** n.

cal·ends (kal´əndz) n.pl. [often with sing. v.] [< L. kalendae < calare, to proclaim < Gr. kalein] the first day of each month in the ancient Roman calendar

ca·len·du·la (kə len´jə lə) n. [ModL. < L. kalendae, calends: prob. because the plants flower in most months] any of a group of plants of the composite family, with yellow or orange flowers, esp. the pot marigold

ca·les·cent (kə les´'nt) adj. [< L. calescere, to grow warm] getting warm or hot —**ca·les´cence** n.

calf¹ (kaf) n., pl. **calves**; esp. for 3, **calfs** [< OE. cealf & ON. kalfr < IE. base geleb(h)-, to swell out, from which also come L. globus & CALF², CLUB] 1. a young cow or bull 2. the young of some other large animals, as the elephant, whale, hippopotamus, seal, etc. 3. leather from the hide of a calf; calfskin 4. [Colloq.] an awkward or silly youth —**kill the fatted calf** to make a feast of welcome: see Luke 15:23

calf² (kaf) n., pl. **calves** [ON. kalfi: see CALF¹] the fleshy back part of the leg below the knee

calf's-foot jelly (kafs´foot´) a gelatin food made by boiling calves' feet

calf·skin (kaf´skin´) n. 1. the skin of a calf 2. a soft, flexible leather made from this

Cal·ga·ry (kal´gər ē) city in S Alberta, Canada: pop. 470,000

Cal·houn (kal hoon´), **John Cald·well** (kôld´wel) 1782–1850; U.S. statesman; vice president (1825–32)

Ca·li (kä´lē) city in SW Colombia: pop. 638,000

Cal·i·ban (kal´ə ban) a deformed, savage creature in Shakespeare's The Tempest

cal·i·ber, cal·i·bre (kal´ə bər) n. [< Fr. & Sp. < calibo < Ar. qālib, a mold] 1. the size of a bullet or shell as measured by its diameter [a bullet of .45 caliber is 45/100 inch in diameter] 2. the diameter of the inside of a gun barrel measured in hundredths of an inch or in millimeters 3. the diameter of the inside of any cylinder 4. quality or ability [a statesman of high caliber]

cal·i·brate (-brāt´) vt. -brat´ed, -brat´ing 1. to find out the caliber of 2. to fix, check, or correct the scale of (a measuring instrument, as a thermometer) —**cal´i·bra´tion** n. —**cal´i·bra´tor** n.

cal·i·co (kal´ə kō´) n., pl. -coes´, -cos´ [< Calicut (now Kozhikode), city in India where first obtained] any of several kinds of cotton cloth, usually coarse and printed —adj. 1. of calico 2. spotted like calico [a calico cat]

☆**calico bass** same as CRAPPIE

Cal·i·for·ni·a (kal´ə fôr´nyə, -nē ə) [Sp., name of a fabled island] 1. State of the SW U.S., on the Pacific coast: 158,693 sq. mi.; pop. 19,953,000; cap. Sacramento: abbrev. **Calif.**, **CA**, **Cal.** 2. **Gulf of**, arm of the Pacific, between Baja California & the Mexican mainland —**Cal´i·for´ni·an** adj., n.

☆**cal·i·for·ni·um** (kal´ə fôr´nē əm) n. [< University of California] a radioactive chemical element produced synthetically from plutonium or curium: symbol, Cf; at. wt., 251(?); at. no., 98

Ca·lig·u·la (kə lig´yoo lə) (born Gaius Caesar) 12–41 A.D.; Roman emperor (37–41 A.D.)

cal·i·per (kal´ə pər) n. [var. of CALIBER] 1. [usually pl.] an instrument consisting of a pair of movable, curved legs fastened together at one end, used to measure the thickness or diameter of something: there are **inside calipers** and **outside calipers** 2. same as CALIPER RULE —vt., vi. to measure with calipers

caliper rule a rule marked off for measuring, with one sliding jaw and one that is stationary

ca·liph (kā´lif, kal´if) n. [< OFr. < Ar. khalīfa] supreme ruler: the title taken by Mohammed's successors as heads of Islam or of some Moslem states: also **ca'lif**

cal·iph·ate (kal´ə fāt´, -fit) n. the rank, reign, or territory of a caliph: also **cal'if·ate'**

cal·is·then·ics (kal´əs then´iks) n.pl. [< Gr. kallos, beauty + sthenos, strength] 1. exercises to develop a strong, trim body; simple gymnastics 2. [with sing. v.] the art of developing bodily strength and gracefulness by such exercises —**cal·is·then´ic, cal´is·then´i·cal** adj.

calk¹ (kôk) vt. same as CAULK —**calk´er** n.

calk² (kôk) n. [OE. calc, shoe < L. calx, a heel] 1. the part of a horseshoe that is bent downward, forming a spike to prevent

CALIPERS
(A, inside;
B, outside)

slipping ☆**2.** a metal plate with spurs, fastened to the sole of a shoe to prevent slipping —*vt.* to fasten calks on

call (kôl) *vt.* [< OE. *ceallian* & (or <) ON. *kalla* < IE. base *gal-*, to scream] **1.** to say or read in a loud tone; shout; announce [*call* the roll] **2.** to ask to come; summon [*call* a taxi for her] **3.** to summon to a specific duty, etc. [the army *called* him] **4.** to bring together persons for; convoke [to *call* a meeting] **5.** to give or apply a name to [*call* the baby Ann] **6.** to consider or declare to be as specified [I *call* it silly] **7.** to awaken [*call* me at six] **8.** to communicate with by telephone **9.** to give orders for [to *call* a strike] ☆**10.** to stop [game *called* because of rain] **11.** to demand payment of (a loan or bond issue) **12.** to utter directions for (a square dance) **13.** *a*) in pool, to describe (the shot one plans to make) *b*) to predict ☆**14.** *a*) *Poker* to force (a player) to show his hand by meeting his bet *b*) to expose (someone's bluff) by challenging him —*vi.* **1.** to speak in a loud tone; shout **2.** to utter its characteristic cry, as a bird or animal **3.** to telephone —*n.* **1.** an act or instance of calling **2.** a loud utterance; shout **3.** the distinctive cry of an animal or bird, or a device used in imitating this [a duck *call*] **4.** a summons to a meeting, etc. **5.** a signal on a bugle, etc. **6.** a market demand, as for a product [there isn't much *call* for buttonhooks these days] **7.** an inner urging toward a certain action or profession, esp. to be a priest, minister, etc. **8.** power to attract [the *call* of the wild] **9.** need; occasion [no *call* for tears] **10.** an order or demand for payment **11.** a brief visit, esp. a formal or professional visit [does your doctor make house *calls?*] **12.** *Sports* an official's decision —**call back 1.** to ask or command to come back **2.** to telephone again or in return —**call down 1.** to invoke ☆**2.** [Colloq.] to scold sharply —**call for 1.** to demand **2.** to come and get; stop for —**call forth** to bring into action or being —**call in 1.** to summon for help **2.** to take out of circulation, as coin —**call off 1.** to order away [*call off* your dog] **2.** to read aloud in order from a list [*call off* the roll] **3.** to cancel (a scheduled event) —**call on (or upon) 1.** to visit briefly **2.** to ask (a person) to speak —**call out 1.** to shout **2.** to summon into action [to *call out* the guard] —**call time** *Sports* to suspend play temporarily —**call up 1.** to make one remember **2.** to summon, esp. for military duty **3.** to telephone —**on call 1.** available when summoned **2.** payable on demand —**within call** close enough to hear if called **SYN.**—**call,** in this comparison, is the basic term for requesting someone to come somewhere [he *called* the waiter over]; **summon** is a more formal term and implies a request that is actually a command [to *summon* a witness]; **convene** and **convoke** refer to a calling together of a group for some purpose, but **convoke** suggests greater authority or more formal meeting [to *convene* a class; to *convoke* a congress]; **invite** suggests a polite request for someone's presence, esp. as a guest or participant, and usually implies that the person invited need come only if he wishes to

cal·la (kal′ə) *n.* [ModL. (named by Linnaeus) < L., a kind of plant] any of several plants of the arum family, with a large, white spathe surrounding a fleshy, yellow spike: also **calla lily**

Cal·la·o (kä yä′ō) seaport in W Peru: pop. 279,000

☆**call·board** (kôl′bôrd′) *n.* a bulletin board backstage in a theater for posting instructions, etc.

call·er (-ər) *n.* **1.** a person or thing that calls **2.** a person who makes a short visit

cal·lig·ra·phy (kə lig′rə fē) *n.* [< Gr. < *kallos*, beauty + *graphein*, to write] **1.** beautiful handwriting, esp. as an art **2.** handwriting; penmanship —**cal·lig′ra·pher** *n.* —**cal·li·graph·ic** (kal′ə graf′ik) *adj.*

call·ing (kôl′iŋ) *n.* **1.** the action of one that calls **2.** one's occupation, profession, or trade

☆**calling card** a small card with one's name and, sometimes, one's address, used in making visits

Cal·li·o·pe (kə lī′ə pē; *for n.*, also kal′ē ōp′) [L. < Gr. *Kalliopē* < *kallos*, beauty + *ops*, voice] *Gr. Myth.* the Muse of eloquence and epic poetry —☆*n.* [c-] a keyboard instrument like an organ, having a series of steam whistles

cal·li·per (kal′ə pər) *n., vt., vi.* same as CALIPER

cal·lis·then·ics (kal′əs then′iks) *n.pl. same as* CALISTHENICS —**cal′lis·then′ic** *adj.*

call letters the letters, and sometimes numbers, that identify a radio or TV transmitting station

☆**call loan** a loan that must be repaid on demand

☆**call number** the numbers and letters put on the spine of a book to show where it belongs in a library

cal·los·i·ty (ka läs′ə tē, kə-) *n.* **1.** the quality or state of being callous, hardened, or unfeeling **2.** *pl.* **-ties** a hardened, thickened place on skin or bark; callus

cal·lous (kal′əs) *adj.* [< L. < *callum*, hard skin] **1.** *a*) having calluses *b*) thick and hardened **2.** lacking pity, mercy, etc.; unfeeling; insensitive ["who cares?" was his *callous* reply —*vt., vi.* to make or become callous —**cal′lous·ly** *adv.* —**cal′lous·ness** *n.*

cal·low (kal′ō) *adj.* [< OE. *calu*, bald < IE. base *gal-*, naked] **1.** still lacking the feathers needed for flying [a *callow* eaglet] **2.** young and inexperienced; immature —**cal′low·ness** *n.*

call-up (kôl′up′) *n.* an order, as to those in the army reserves, to report for active duty

cal·lus (kal′əs) *n., pl.* **-lus·es** [L., var. of *callum*, hard skin] **1.** a hardened, thickened place on the skin **2.** the hard substance that forms at the break in a fractured bone so as to reunite the parts **3.** a mass of tissue that develops over cuts or wounds on plants as at the ends of leaf cuttings —*vi., vt.* to develop or cause to develop a callus

calm (käm; *occas.* kälm) *n.* [< OFr. < It. < LL. *cauma*, heat of the day (hence, in It., time to rest: cf. SIESTA) < Gr. *kauma*, heat] **1.** lack of wind or motion; stillness [the *calm* after a storm] **2.** lack of excitement; tranquillity; serenity —*adj.* **1.** without wind or motion; still; quiet **2.** not excited; tranquil —*vt., vi.* to make or become calm (often with *down*) —**calm′ly** *adv.* —**calm′ness** *n.*

SYN.—**calm,** basically applied to the weather, suggests a lack of movement or excitement [a *calm* sea; a *calm* reply]; **tranquil** implies a deeper or more permanent peace and quiet than calm [a *tranquil* old age]; **serene** suggests a dignified tranquillity, as of a person who is at peace with himself; **placid** implies total calmness, often to the point of being dull and uninteresting [she's as *placid* as a cow]; **peaceful** suggests freedom from disorder or from a show of strong feeling [a *peaceful* gathering] —*ANT.* stormy, agitated, excited

cal·o·mel (kal′ə mel′, -məl) *n.* [Fr. < Gr. *kalos*, beautiful + *melas*, black] mercurous chloride, HgCl, a white, tasteless powder, formerly used as a cathartic, for intestinal worms, etc.

ca·lor·ic (kə lôr′ik, -lär′-) *n.* [< Fr. < L. *calor*, heat] [Archaic] heat —*adj.* **1.** of heat **2.** of or having to do with calories —**ca·lor′i·cal·ly** *adv.*

cal·o·rie (kal′ə rē) *n.* [Fr. < L. *calor*, heat: for IE. base see CALDRON] **1.** the amount of heat needed to raise the temperature of one gram of water one degree centigrade: also **small calorie 2.** [*occas.* C-] the amount of heat needed to raise the temperature of one kilogram of water one degree centigrade: also **large calorie 3.** a unit equal to the large calorie, used for measuring energy produced by food in the body [one large egg produces about 100 *calories*] Also sp. **cal′o·ry,** *pl.* **-ries**

cal·o·rif·ic (kal′ə rif′ik) *adj.* [< Fr. < L. < *calor*, heat + *facere*, to make] producing heat

cal·o·rim·e·ter (kal′ə rim′ə tər) *n.* [< L. *calor*, heat + -METER] an apparatus for measuring amounts of heat produced, as in a chemical reaction

cal·o·rim·e·try (kal′ə rim′ə trē) *n.* [< L. *calor*, heat + -METRY] measurement of the quantity of heat —**cal·o·ri·met·ric** (kal′ə ri met′rik, kə lôr′ə-), **cal′o·ri·met′ri·cal** *adj.*

cal·u·met (kal′yə met′, kal′yə met′) *n.* [Fr.; ult. < L. *calamus*, CALAMUS] a long-stemmed pipe, smoked in a ceremony by N. American Indians as a token of peace

ca·lum·ni·ate (kə lum′nē āt′) *vt., vi.* **-at′ed, -at′ing** [< L. pp. of *calumniari*, to slander < *calumnia*, CALUMNY] to spread false and harmful statements about; slander —**ca·lum′ni·a′tion** *n.* —**ca·lum′ni·a′tor** *n.*

ca·lum·ni·ous (kə lum′nē əs) *adj.* full of calumnies; slanderous —**ca·lum′ni·ous·ly** *adv.*

CALUMET

CALLA LILY

cal·um·ny (kal′əm nē) *n., pl.* **-nies** [< Fr. < L. *calumnia,* trickery, slander (see CHALLENGE) < IE. base *kēl-,* to deceive] **1.** a false statement that is meant to hurt someone's reputation **2.** the uttering of such a statement; slander

Cal·va·ry (kal′vər ē) [< LL. < L. *calvaria,* skull; transl. of Aram. *gulgulthā,* Golgotha, lit., skull] *Bible* the place near Jerusalem where the crucifixion of Jesus took place: Luke 23:33, Matt. 27:33

calve (kav, käv) *vi., vt.* **calved, calv′ing** [OE. *cealfian* < *cealf,* CALF[1]] to give birth to (a calf)

calves (kavz, kävz) *n. pl. of* CALF

Cal·vin (kal′vin) [< ModL. < Fr., prob. < L. *calvus,* bald] **1.** a masculine name **2. John,** (born *Jean Cau(l)vin* or *Chauvin*) 1509–64; Fr. leader in the Protestant Reformation

Cal·vin·ism (-iz′m) *n.* the religious system of John Calvin and his followers, which teaches that everything depends on God, that man is sinful, and that only some people are chosen by God for salvation —**Cal′vin·ist** *n., adj.* —**Cal′vin·is′tic, Cal′vin·is′ti·cal** *adj.* —**Cal′vin·is′ti·cal·ly** *adv.*

calx (kalks) *n., pl.* **calx′es, cal·ces** (kal′sēz) [L., small stone, lime] the ashy powder left after a metal or mineral has been calcined

Ca·lyp·so (kə lip′sō) in Homer's *Odyssey,* a sea nymph who kept Odysseus on her island for seven years

ca·lyp·so (kə lip′sō) *adj.* [< ? prec.] designating or of lively ballads with a strong rhythm that are made up, as by natives of Trinidad, and deal in a satirical way with current topics —*n.* a calypso song or calypso music

ca·lyx (kā′liks, kal′iks) *n., pl.* **ca′lyx·es, ca·ly·ces** (kā′lə sēz′, kal′ə-) [L., outer covering, pod < Gr. *kalyx*] **1.** the outer whorl of protective leaves, or sepals, of a flower, usually green **2.** *Zool.* a cuplike part or cavity

cam (kam) *n.* [Du. *cam,* orig., a COMB] an irregular wheel or a projection on a wheel, which gives an irregular or back-and-forth motion as to a shaft, or receives such motion from it

ca·ma·ra·de·rie (käm′ə räd′ər ē, kam′-) *n.* [Fr. < *camarade,* COMRADE] loyalty and warm, friendly feeling among comrades; comradeship

☆**cam·ass, cam·as** (kam′əs) *n.* [Chinook < *chamas,* sweet] a N. American plant of the lily family, with sweet, edible bulbs and clusters of drooping, bluish flowers

cam·ber (kam′bər) *n.* [OFr., dial. var. of *chambre,* bent < L. *camur,* arched] **1.** a slight convex curve of a surface, as of a road, a beam, the deck of a ship, etc. **2.** a slight tilt given to each of a pair of automobile wheels by aligning them so that the bottoms are closer together than the tops **3.** *Aeron.* the arching curve of an airfoil from the leading edge to the trailing edge —*vt., vi.* to arch slightly

cam·bi·um (kam′bē əm) *n.* [LL., CHANGE] a layer of soft tissue between the wood and bark in woody plants, from which the cells of new wood and bark are developed

Cam·bo·di·a (kam bō′dē ə) *former name of* KAMPUCHEA —**Cam·bo′di·an** *adj., n.*

Cam·bri·a (kam′brē ə) *poet.* name for WALES

Cam·bri·an (-ən) *adj.* **1.** of Cambria; Welsh **2.** designating or of the first geological period in the Paleozoic Era —*n.* a native or inhabitant of Cambria; Welshman —**the Cambrian** the Cambrian Period or its rocks: see GEOLOGIC TIME CHART

CAMBER (A, perpendicular; B, degree of camber)

cam·bric (kām′brik) *n.* [< *Kambryk,* Fl. name of *Cambrai,* city in N France] **1.** a very fine, thin linen **2.** a cotton cloth like this

☆**cambric tea** a hot drink of milk, sugar, and water or, often, weak tea

Cam·bridge (kām′brij) **1.** city in EC England: pop. 100,000: site of Cambridge University **2.** city in E Mass., near Boston: pop. 100,000

Cam·den (kam′dən) [after C. Pratt, Earl of *Camden* (1714–94)] city in southwestern N.J.: pop. 103,000

came (kām) *pt. of* COME

cam·el (kam′l) *n.* [< OE. or OFr. < L. *camelus* < Gr. *kamēlos* < Heb. *gāmāl*] either of two species of large, domesticated, cud-chewing mammals with a humped back, long neck, and large, cushioned feet: it can store water in its body tissue and is

the common beast of burden in Asian and African deserts: see BACTRIAN CAMEL and DROMEDARY

cam·el·eer (kam′ə lir′) *n.* a camel driver

ca·mel·li·a (kə mēl′yə, -mē′lē ə) *n.* [after G. J. *Kamel* (1661–1706), Jesuit missionary to the Far East] **1.** any of a group of Asian evergreen trees and shrubs with glossy leaves and waxy, roselike flowers **2.** the flower

ca·mel·o·pard (kə mel′ə pärd′) *n.* [< LL. < L. < Gr. < *kamēlos,* camel + *pardalis,* leopard: from its camellike neck and leopardlike spots] *early name for the* GIRAFFE

Cam·e·lot (kam′ə lät′) the legendary English town where King Arthur had his court

camel's hair 1. the hair of the camel **2.** cloth made of this hair, sometimes mixed with wool, etc. —**cam′el's-hair′, cam′el-hair′** *adj.*

camel's-hair brush an artist's small brush, made of hair from a squirrel's tail

Cam·em·bert (cheese) (kam′əm ber′) [from *Camembert,* in Normandy] a soft, creamy, rich cheese

cam·e·o (kam′ē ō′) *n., pl.* **-os′** [< It. < ML. *camaeus* < ?] **1.** a carving in relief on certain gems or shells that come in layers, so that the raised design, often a head in profile, is usually in a layer of different color from its background **2.** a gem, shell, etc. so carved **3.** a choice minor role, esp. when played by a well-known actor

CAMEO

cam·er·a (kam′ər ə, kam′rə) *n., pl.* **-er·as;** also for 1, **-er·ae′** (-ə rē′) [L., a vault < Gr. *kamara,* vaulted chamber] **1.** a chamber; specif., the private office of a judge **2.** a device for taking photographs, consisting essentially of a closed box containing a plate or film sensitive to light, on which an image is formed when light enters the box through a lens **3.** *TV* that part of the transmitter which consists of a lens and a special cathode-ray tube containing a plate on which the image to be televised is projected and then changed into electrical signals for transmitting —**in camera** in privacy or secrecy

cam·er·a·man (-man′, -mən) *n., pl.* **-men′** (-men′, -mən) an operator of a camera, esp. of a movie or television camera

cam·er·a-shy (-shī′) *adj.* unwilling to be photographed

Cam·e·roons (kam′ə rōōnz′) region in W Africa, formerly made up of two trust territories (**French Cameroons** and **British Cameroons**), now divided between Cameroun and Nigeria

Cam·e·roun (kam′ə rōōn′) country in WC Africa, on the Atlantic: 183,000 sq. mi.; pop. 5,562,000; cap. Yaoundé: also sp. **Cameroon** —**Cam′e·roun′i·an** *adj., n.*

Ca·mille (kə mēl′) [Fr. < L. *camilla,* virgin of unblemished character] a feminine name: var. **Ca·mil′la** (-mil′ə)

cam·i·sole (kam′ə sōl′) *n.* [Fr. < Sp. dim. of *camisa,* shirt: see CHEMISE] **1.** a woman's sleeveless underwaist worn as under a sheer blouse **2.** a woman's short negligee

Ca·mões (kə moinsh′), **Lu·iz Vaz de** (lōō ēsh′ väzh də) 1524?-80; Port. poet: Eng. name **Cam·o·ëns** (kam′ō enz′)

cam·o·mile (kam′ə mīl′, -mēl′) *n.* same as CHAMOMILE

cam·ou·flage (kam′ə fläzh′, -fläj′) *n.* [Fr. < *camoufler,* to disguise] **1.** the disguising of troops, ships, guns, etc. to conceal them from the enemy, as by covering them with paint, nets, leaves, etc. to make them look like part of the background **2.** a disguise or concealment of this kind **3.** anything used to hide or mislead; deception *[his smile was mere camouflage covering hurt feelings]* —*vt., vi.* **-flaged′, -flag′ing** to disguise or conceal by camouflage —**cam′ou·flag′er** *n.*

camp (kamp) *n.* [< Fr. < It. < L. *campus:* see CAMPUS] **1.** *a)* a place where tents, huts, barracks, etc. are put up, as for soldiers in training or in bivouac *b)* military life **2.** *a)* a group of people who support some cause, opinion, etc. together *b)* the position taken by such a group **3.** a tent, cabin, etc., or a group of these, used for temporary lodging, as by hunters, fishermen, etc. **4.** a place in the country where people, esp. children, go for a vacation, with outdoor activities, often organized **5.** the people living in a camp ☆**6.** [Slang] the state of being camp or things that are camp —☆*adj.* [Slang] so artificial, trite, mediocre, etc. that a sophisticated person might find it interesting or amusing *[musical comedies of the 1930's are considered camp]* —*vi.* **1.** to set up a camp **2.** to live or stay in or as if in a camp (often with *out*) *[the children camped out in the backyard]* —**break camp** to pack up camping equipment and go away

cam·paign (kam pān′) *n.* [Fr. *campagne,* open country < It. <

LL. < L. *campus:* see CAMPUS] **1.** a series of connected military actions having some special goal, or objective **2.** a series of organized, planned actions for a particular purpose, as for electing a candidate —*vi.* to participate in, or go on, a campaign — see SYN. at BATTLE —**cam·paign'er** *n.*

Cam·pa·ni·a (kam pā'nē ə; *It.* käm pä'nyä) region in S Italy, on the Tyrrhenian Sea: chief city, Naples

cam·pa·ni·le (kam'pə nē'lē) *n., pl.* **-les, -li** (-lē) [It. < LL. *campana,* a bell] a bell tower, esp. one that stands apart from another building

cam·pa·nol·o·gy (kam'pə näl'ə jē) *n.* [< LL. *campana,* a bell + -LOGY] the art of bell ringing —**cam'pa·nol'o·gist** *n.*

cam·pan·u·la (kam pan'yoo lə) *n.* [ModL. < LL., dim. of *campana,* a bell] a plant with showy, bell-shaped flowers; bellflower

camp chair a lightweight folding chair

camp·craft (kamp'kraft') *n.* the art or practice of camping outdoors

cam·pea·chy wood (kam pē'chē) [< *Campeche,* state of SE Mexico] *same as* LOGWOOD (sense 1)

camp·er (kamp'ər) *n.* **1.** a person who vacations at a camp ☆**2.** any of various motor vehicles or trailers equipped for camping out

‡**cam·pe·si·ño** (käm'pe sē'nō) *n., pl.* **-nos** (-nōs) [Sp.] a peasant or farm worker

camp·fire (kamp'fīr') *n.* **1.** an outdoor fire at a camp **2.** a social gathering around such a fire

☆**campfire girl** a member of the **Camp Fire Girls,** a girls' organization, founded in 1910, with a program stressing health and the building of character

☆**camp·ground** (-ground') *n.* **1.** a place where a camp is set up **2.** a place where a camp meeting is held

cam·phor (kam'fər) *n.* [< OFr. < LL. < Ar. < Sans. *karpurah,* camphor tree] a crystalline substance, $C_{10}H_{16}O$, with a strong smell, derived chiefly from the wood of an Asian laurel (**camphor tree**): used as a moth repellent, in making cellulose plastics, and in liniments, etc. —**cam·phor'ic** (-fôr'ik) *adj.*

cam·phor·ate (kam'fə rāt') *vt.* **-at'ed, -at'ing** to put camphor in or on [*camphorated* oil]

camphor ball *same as* MOTHBALL

camphor ice an ointment made of white wax, camphor, spermaceti, and castor oil, used for dry, chapped skin

cam·pi·on (kam'pē ən) *n.* [prob. ult. < L. *campus,* field] any of various flowering plants of the pink family, with white or pink flowers

☆**camp meeting** a religious gathering held outdoors or in a tent, etc., usually lasting several days

☆**camp·o·ree** (kam'pə rē') *n.* [CAMP + (JAMB)OREE] a gathering of boy scouts of a particular region or district

☆**camp·site** (kamp'sīt') *n.* **1.** any site for a temporary camp **2.** an area in a park set aside for camping, often equipped with water, toilets, etc.

camp·stool (-stool') *n.* a light folding stool

☆**cam·pus** (kam'pəs) *n., pl.* **-pus·es** [L., a field < IE. *kamp-,* to bend] the grounds, sometimes including the buildings, of a school or college —*adj.* **1.** on or of the campus **2.** of a school or college [*campus* politics]

☆**camp·y** (kam'pē) *adj.* **camp'i·er, camp'i·est** [Slang] *same as* CAMP

cam·shaft (kam'shaft') *n.* a shaft to which a cam is fastened or of which a cam is an essential part

CAMPSTOOL

Ca·mus (ka mōō'; *Fr.* kà mü'), **Albert** 1913–60; Fr. writer

can[1] (kan; *unstressed* kən, k'n) *vi. pt.* **could** [< OE. < *cunnan,* to know, be able: for IE. base see KNOW] **1.** to know how to [*can* she read?] **2.** to be able to [I *can* lift it] **3.** to be likely to [*can* it be true?] **4.** to have the right to [anyone *can* attend the meeting] **5.** [Colloq.] to be permitted to; may [*can* I leave now?] —**can but** can only

SYN. —*can,* in formal use, refers to ability, either physical or mental [he *can* walk; I *can* understand you]; *may* refers to possibility [I *may* be sick]; *can* and *may* are both used to indicate permission, *may* in formal use [you *may* have a second helping], *can* in informal use, esp. in questions and negative statements [*can't* I go? you *cannot*]

can[2] (kan) *n.* [< OE. *canne,* a cup] **1.** a container of various kinds, usually made of metal or plastic with a separate cover [a milk *can,* a garbage *can*] ☆**2.** a container made of tinned iron or other metal, in which foods or other products that might spoil are sealed **3.** the contents of a can; canful ☆**4.** [Slang] *a)* a prison *b)* a toilet —*vt.* **canned, can'ning 1.** to put up in airtight cans or jars for preservation **2.** [Slang] to discharge (an employee); fire

Can. 1. Canada **2.** Canadian **3.** Canon

Ca·naan (kā'nən) Promised Land of the Israelites, between the Jordan & the Mediterranean

Ca·naan·ite (-īt') *n.* **1.** one of the inhabitants of Canaan before the Israelites settled there **2.** their Semitic language —**Ca'naan·it'ish** (-īt'ish), **Ca'naan·it'ic** (-it'ik) *adj.*

Canad. Canadian

Can·a·da (kan'ə də) country in N North America: a member of the Commonwealth: 3,852,000 sq. mi.; pop. 21,489,000; cap. Ottawa

CANAAN

Canada balsam a thick, yellow resin from the balsam fir, used as a cement on microscope slides

Canada goose a large wild goose of Canada and the northern U.S., gray, with black head and neck

Ca·na·di·an (kə nā'dē ən) *adj.* of Canada or its people —*n.* a native or inhabitant of canada

☆**Canadian bacon** cured, smoked pork cut from the loin of the pig in a boneless strip

Ca·na·di·an·ism (-iz'm) *n.* **1.** a custom, belief, etc. originating in Canada **2.** a word or phrase originating in or peculiar to Canadian English

ca·naille (kə nāl'; *Fr.* kà nä'y') *n.* [Fr. < It. *canaglia* < L. *canis,* a dog] the common people; rabble: a term showing contempt

ca·nal (kə nal') *n.* [< OFr. < L. *canalis,* a channel < *canna:* see CANE] **1.** an artificial waterway for ships or irrigation water **2.** a tubular passage or duct in the body —*vt.* **-nalled', -nalled', -nal'ling** or **-nal'ing** to build a canal through or across

ca·nal·boat (-bōt') *n.* a long, narrow boat for carrying freight on canals: also **canal boat**

can·a·lic·u·lus (kan'ə lik'yoo ləs) *n., pl.* **-li'** (-lī') [L., dim. of *canalis,* a groove: see CANAL] a very small groove, as in bone — **can'a·lic'u·late** (-lit, -lāt') *adj.*

ca·nal·i·za·tion (kə nal'ə zā'shən, kan'l ə-) *n.* **1.** the act of canalizing **2.** a system of canals or channels

ca·nal·ize (kə nal'īz, kan'ə līz') *vt.* **-ized, -iz·ing 1.** to make a canal through **2.** to change into or make like a canal

Canal Zone *former name of* the strip of land in Panama that extends about 5 miles on either side of the Panama Canal and was under lease to the U.S. from 1904 to 1979

ca·na·pé (kan'ə pē, -pā') *n.* [Fr., lit., upholstered sofa: see CANOPY] a small piece of bread or toast or a cracker spread with spiced meat, fish, cheese, etc., served as an appetizer

ca·nard (kə närd') *n.* [Fr., a duck, hoax] a false, harmful report made up and spread on purpose

ca·nar·y (kə ner'ē) *n., pl.* **-nar'ies** [after the CANARY ISLANDS] **1.** a small, yellow songbird of the finch family, native to the Canary Islands and often raised as a cage bird **2.** a light yellow: also **canary yellow 3.** a sweet wine like madeira, made in the Canary Islands

Canary Islands group of Sp. islands in the Atlantic, off the NW coast of Africa

ca·nas·ta (kə nas'tə) *n.* [Sp., basket] a card game like rummy for two to six players, played with two decks of cards

Ca·na·ver·al (kə nav'ər əl), **Cape** [Sp. *cañaveral,* canebrake] cape on the E coast of Fla.: U.S. proving ground for missiles and spacecraft

Can·ber·ra (kan'bər ə) capital of Australia, in the SE part: pop. 135,000

canc. 1. cancel **2.** canceled **3.** cancellation

can·can (kan′kan′) *n.* [Fr.] a lively dance with much high kicking performed by women entertainers, orig. in Paris dance halls in the late 19th cent.

can·cel (kan′s'l) *vt.* **-celed** or **-celled, -cel·ing** or **-cel·ling** [< Anglo-Fr. < L. *cancellare,* to draw lines like a lattice across < *cancer,* lattice] **1.** to cross out with lines or mark over, as in marking a postage stamp or check as used **2.** to make invalid; annul **3.** to do away with; abolish, withdraw, etc. [to *cancel* an order] **4.** to neutralize or balance; offset (often with *out*) [his gains and losses *cancel* each other out] **5.** *Math.* to remove (a common factor) from both terms of a fraction, (equivalents) from opposite sides of an equation, etc. —*vi.* to offset or cancel each other (with *out*) —*n.* a cancellation —**can′cel·er, can′cel·ler** *n.*

can·cel·la·tion (kan′sə lā′shən) *n.* **1.** the act of canceling **2.** something canceled **3.** the mark showing that something is canceled

can·cer (kan′sər) [< L., a crab; later, malignant tumor < IE. base *karkar-,* hard] **1.** [C-] a N constellation **2.** [C-] the fourth sign of the zodiac: see ZODIAC —*n.* **1.** a condition in which certain cells grow wild in the body, forming a malignant growth; also, such a growth: cancers tend to spread to other parts of the body: see also CARCINOMA, SARCOMA **2.** anything bad or harmful that spreads and destroys —**can′cer·ous** *adj.*

can·de·la (kan dē′lə) *n.* [L., candle] *same as* CANDLE (n. 3)

can·de·la·brum (kan′də lä′brəm, -lab′rəm, -lā′brəm) *n., pl.* **-bra** (-brə), **-brums** [L.: see CHANDELIER] a large candlestick with branches for several candles: also **can′de·la′bra,** *pl.* **-bras**

can·des·cent (kan des′'nt) *adj.* [< L. prp. of *candescere* < *candere,* to shine < IE. base *kand-,* to glow] glowing with heat; incandescent —**can·des′cence** *n.*

can·did (kan′did) *adj.* [L. *candidus,* white, sincere < *candere:* see prec.] **1.** very honest or frank in speech or writing [a *candid* opinion] **2.** unposed and informal [a *candid* photograph] —see SYN. at FRANK —**can′did·ly** *adv.* —**can′did·ness** *n.*

☆**can·di·da·cy** (kan′də də sē) *n., pl.* **-cies** the fact or state of being a candidate: also [Brit.] **can·di·da·ture** (-di chər, -dā′chər)

can·di·date (kan′də dāt′, -dit) *n.* [L. *candidatus,* white-robed < *candidus* (see CANDID): office seekers in Rome wore white gowns] **1.** a person who offers himself, or is nominated by others, for an office, an award, etc. **2.** a person or thing that seems destined for a certain end [a *candidate* for fame]

can·died (kan′dēd) *adj.* **1.** cooked in or with sugar or syrup, esp. to preserve or glaze [*candied* apples] **2.** crystallized into sugar [*candied* syrup]

can·dle (kan′d'l) *n.* [< OE. < L. *candela,* a torch < *candere:* see CANDESCENT] **1.** a cylinder or other form of tallow or wax with a wick through its center, which gives light when burned **2.** anything like this in form or use **3.** a unit of the intensity of light equal to 1/60 of the intensity of one square centimeter of a blackbody at the temperature at which platinum solidifies —*vt.* **-dled, -dling** to examine (eggs) for freshness, fertilization, etc. by holding in front of a light —**burn the candle at both ends** to work or, esp., play too much so that one's energy is used up —**not hold a candle to** to be not nearly so good as —**not worth the candle** not worth doing —**can′dler** *n.*

☆**can·dle·ber·ry** (kan′d'l ber′ē) *n., pl.* **-ries** *same as* BAYBERRY (sense 1)

can·dle·light (-līt′) *n.* **1.** soft light as given by candles **2.** twilight; evening

Can·dle·mas (kan′d'l məs) *n.* [< OE.: see CANDLE & MASS] a church feast, Feb. 2, commemorating the purification of the Virgin Mary: candles for sacred uses are blessed then: also **Candlemas Day**

can·dle·pow·er (-pou′ər) *n.* the intensity of light from a particular source, expressed in candles

can·dle·stick (-stik′) *n.* a device with a cup or spike for holding a candle

can·dor (kan′dər) *n.* [L., whiteness, openness < *candere:* see CANDESCENT] the quality of being honest, frank, or fair in expressing oneself: also, Brit. sp., **can′dour**

can·dy (kan′dē) *n., pl.* **-dies** [< *sugar candy* < OFr. < It. < Ar. < Per. *qand,* cane sugar] **1.** crystallized sugar made by evaporating boiled cane sugar, syrup, etc. **2.** *a)* a sweet food, usually made from sugar or syrup, in small pieces, with flavoring, fruit, chocolate, nuts, etc. added *b)* a piece of such food —*vt.* **-died, -dy·ing 1.** to cook in or with sugar or syrup, esp. so as to preserve or glaze **2.** to crystallize into sugar —*vi.* to become candied

can·dy-striped (-strīpt′) *adj.* having diagonal, colored stripes like those on a stick of candy

cane (kān) *n.* [< OFr. < It. < L. *canna,* a reed < Gr. *kanna*] **1.** the slender, jointed, usually flexible stem of any of certain plants, as bamboo, rattan, etc. **2.** any plant with such a stem, as sugar cane, sorghum, etc. **3.** the woody stem of certain plants, as the blackberry, rose, etc. **4.** a stick used for flogging **5.** *same as* WALKING STICK (sense 1) **6.** split rattan, used in weaving chair seats, etc. —*vt.* **caned, can′ing 1.** to flog with a cane **2.** to make or furnish (chair seats, etc.) with woven cane —**can′er** *n.*

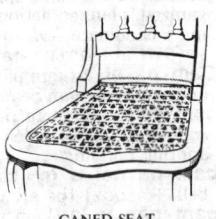

CANED SEAT

☆**cane·brake** (kān′brāk′) *n.* [CANE + BRAKE³] a dense growth of cane plants

cane sugar sugar (*sucrose*) from sugar cane

ca·nine (kā′nīn) *adj.* [L. *caninus* < *canis,* a dog < IE. base *kwon-,* dog, from which also come CYNIC & HOUND] **1.** of or like a dog **2.** of the family of animals that includes dogs, wolves, jackals, and foxes —*n.* **1.** a dog or other canine animal **2.** a sharp-pointed tooth on either side of the upper jaw and lower jaw, between the incisors and the bicuspids: in full, **canine tooth**

CANINE TOOTH

Ca·nis Ma·jor (kān′is mā′jər) [L., the Greater Dog] a southern constellation southeast of Orion, containing the Dog Star, Sirius

Canis Mi·nor (mī′nər) [L., the Lesser Dog] a northern constellation east of Orion, containing the bright star Procyon

can·is·ter (kan′is tər) *n.* [< L. *canistrum,* wicker basket < Gr. *kanistron* < *kanna:* see CANE] **1.** a small box or can for coffee, tea, etc. **2.** a vacuum cleaner whose motor, dust bag, etc. are enclosed in a boxlike container on wheels **3.** the part of a gas mask with chemicals for filtering the air

can·ker (kaŋ′kər) *n.* [< OFr. < L. *cancer:* see CANCER] **1.** an ulcerlike sore, esp. in the mouth, that spreads **2.** a disease of plants that causes decay **3.** anything that corrupts —*vt., vi.* to infect or become infected with canker —**can′ker·ous** *adj.*

can·ker·worm (-wʉrm′) *n.* ☆any of several moth larvae harmful to fruit and shade trees

can·na (kan′ə) *n.* [L.: see CANE] any of various tropical plants, often grown for their large, ornamental leaves and brilliant flowers

can·na·bis (kan′ə bis) *n.* [L., hemp < Gr. *kannabis*] **1.** *same as* HEMP **2.** the female flowering tops of the hemp

☆**canned** (kand) *adj.* **1.** preserved in cans or jars [*canned* peaches] **2.** [Slang] *a)* recorded to be played later on radio or TV [*canned* commercials] *b)* prepared for publication in all the newspapers of a chain [a *canned* editorial]

can·nel (coal) (kan′'l) [< ? *candle coal*] a variety of bituminous coal that burns with a bright, smoky flame

can·nel·lo·ni (kan′ə lō′nē) *n.* [It., pl. of *cannellone,* hollow noodle] macaroni in the form of large tubes, filled with ground meat, baked, and served in a tomato sauce

☆**can·ner·y** (kan′ər ē) *n., pl.* **-ner·ies** a factory where foods are canned

Cannes (kan, kanz; *Fr.* kån) city in SE France, on the Riviera: pop. 67,000

can·ni·bal (kan′ə b'l) *n.* [Sp. *canibal,* a savage (term used by Columbus) prob. < Carib *galibi,* lit., strong men] **1.** a person who eats human flesh **2.** an animal that eats its own kind —*adj.* of, resembling, or having the habits of, cannibals —**can′ni·bal·ism** *n.* —**can′ni·bal·is′tic** *adj.*

☆**can·ni·bal·ize** (-īz′) *vt., vi.* **-ized′, -iz′ing 1.** to take parts from (old or worn equipment) for use in other units **2.** to take persons or units from (one organization) for use in building up another —**can′ni·bal·i·za′tion** *n.*

can·ni·kin (kan′ə k'n) *n.* [< CAN² + -KIN] **1.** a small can; cup **2.** [Dial.] a wooden bucket

☆**can·ning** (kan′iŋ) *n.* the act, process, or work of preserving food in airtight cans or jars

can·non (kan′ən) *n., pl.* **-nons, -non:** see PLURAL, II, D, 4 [< OFr. < It. < L. *canna:* see CANE] **1.** *a)* a large, mounted piece of artillery; sometimes, specif., a large gun with a relatively short barrel, as a howitzer *b)* an automatic gun, now usually of 20-mm. caliber, mounted on an aircraft **2.** *same as* CANNON BONE —*vt., vi.* to cannonade

can·non·ade (kan′ə nād′) *n.* a continuous firing of artillery —*vi., vt.* **-ad′ed, -ad′ing** to fire artillery (at)

can·non·ball (kan′ən bôl′) *n.* **1.** a heavy ball, esp. of iron, formerly fired from cannons: also **cannon ball 2.** [Colloq.] a fast express train —*adj.* [Slang] fast; rapid —*vi.* [Slang] to move very rapidly

cannon bone the bone between the hock or knee and the fetlock in a four-legged, hoofed animal

can·non·eer (kan′ə nir′) *n.* an artilleryman

cannon fodder soldiers, sailors, etc. thought of as material to be used up (that is, killed or maimed) in war

can·non·ry (kan′ən rē) *n., pl.* **-ries 1.** cannons collectively; artillery **2.** cannon fire

can·not (kan′ät, -ət; kə nät′) can not —**cannot but** have no choice but to; must [*I cannot but* believe that he lied]

can·ny (kan′ē) *adj.* **-ni·er, -ni·est** [< CAN[1]] careful and shrewd in one's actions and dealings; clever and cautious [*a canny* bargainer] —**can′ni·ly** (-′l ē) *adv.* —**can′ni·ness** *n.*

ca·noe (kə nōo′) *n.* [< Sp. *canoa* < the Carib name] a narrow, light boat with its sides meeting in a sharp edge at each end: it is moved by a paddle or paddles —☆*vi.* **-noed′, -noe′ing** to paddle, or go in, a canoe —*vt.* to transport by canoe —**ca·noe′ist** *n.*

can·on[1] (kan′ən) *n.* [< OE. & OFr. < L., a rule < Gr. *kanōn*, rod, bar < *kanna:* see CANE] **1.** a law or body of laws of a church **2.** *a)* a basic or accepted rule, principle, or criterion [the *canons* of good taste] *b)* a body of rules, principles, criteria, etc. **3.** *a)* a list or books of the Bible officially accepted as genuine *b)* a list of the genuine works of an author [the Shakespearean *canon*] **4.** *a)* [*often* C-] *Eccles.* the fundamental, unchanging part of the Mass, having to do with the consecration of the Host *b)* an official list of saints, as in the Roman Catholic Church **5.** *Music* a composition for several voices in which one voice after another repeats the melody in the same or a related key

can·on[2] (kan′ən) *n.* [< OE. & OFr. < LL. *canonicus*, one living by the canon: see prec.] **1.** a member of a group of clergymen living according to a canon, or rule **2.** a clergyman serving in a cathedral or collegiate church

ca·ñon (kan′yən; *Sp.* kä nyôn′) *n.* same as CANYON

ca·non·ic (kə nän′ik) *adj.* **1.** *same as* CANONICAL **2.** of a musical canon

ca·non·i·cal (kə nän′i k′l) *adj.* **1.** of, according to, or ordered by church canon **2.** authoritative; accepted **3.** belonging to the canon of the Bible **4.** of a canon (clergyman) —**ca·non′i·cal·ly** *adv.*

canonical hour any of the seven periods of the day assigned to prayer and worship in some Christian churches

ca·non·i·cals (-k′lz) *n.pl.* the clothes that a clergyman is required to wear during church services

can·on·ic·i·ty (kan′ə nis′ə tē) *n.* the fact or condition of being canonical

can·on·ize (kan′ə nīz′) *vt.* **-ized′, -iz′ing** [< LL. *canonizare:* see CANON[1] + -IZE] **1.** to declare (a dead person) to be a saint; add to the official canon of saints **2.** to glorify **3.** to put in the Biblical canon —**can′on·i·za′tion** *n.*

canon law the laws governing the ecclesiastical affairs of a Christian church

can·o·py (kan′ə pē) *n., pl.* **-pies** [< ML. < L. < Gr. *kōnōpeion*, bed with mosquito nets, dim. of *kōnōps*, gnat] **1.** a covering of cloth, etc. fastened above a bed, throne, etc. or held on poles over a person or sacred thing **2.** canvas stretched over a framework to form a sheltered walk to a building entrance **3.** anything that covers or seems to cover like a canopy, as the sky **4.** a rooflike projection over a door, pulpit, etc. **5.** the part of a parachute that opens up and catches the air —*vt.* **-pied, -py·ing** to place or form a canopy over; cover; shelter

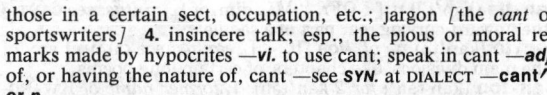

BED WITH A CANOPY

canst (kanst; *unstressed* kənst) *the archaic second person singular in the present tense of* CAN[1]: *used with* thou

cant[1] (kant) *n.* [< L. *cantus:* see CHANT] **1.** whining, singsong speech, esp. as used by beggars **2.** the secret slang of beggars, thieves, etc.; argot **3.** the special words and phrases used by those in a certain sect, occupation, etc.; jargon [the *cant* of sportswriters] **4.** insincere talk; esp., the pious or moral remarks made by hypocrites —*vi.* to use cant; speak in cant —*adj.* of, or having the nature of, cant —see SYN. at DIALECT —**cant′-er** *n.*

cant[2] (kant) *n.* [< OFr. < LL. < L. *cant(h)us*, tire of a wheel < Celt. < IE. base *kantho-*, a bend, corner] **1.** a slanting surface; beveled edge **2.** a sudden movement that causes tilting, turning, or overturning —*vt.* **1.** to give a sloping edge to; bevel **2.** to tilt or overturn —*vi.* **1.** to tilt or turn over **2.** to slant —*adj.* **1.** with canted sides or corners **2.** slanting

can't (kant) cannot

can·ta·bi·le (kän tä′bi lā′) *adj., adv.* [< It. < L. < *cantare:* see CHANT] *Music* in an easy, flowing manner; songlike —*n.* music in this style

Can·ta·brig·i·an (kan′tə brij′ē ən, -brij′ən) *adj.* [< ML. *Cantabrigia*, Cambridge] of Cambridge, England, or Cambridge University —*n.* **1.** a student or graduate of Cambridge University **2.** any inhabitant of Cambridge, England

can·ta·loupe, can·ta·loup (kan′tə lōp′) *n.* [< Fr. < It.< *Cantalupo*, near Rome, where first grown in Europe] a muskmelon with a hard, rough rind and sweet, juicy, orange-colored flesh

can·tan·ker·ous (kan taŋ′kər əs) *adj.* [prob. < ME. *contakour*, a troublemaker (< *contek*, strife) + -OUS] ready to quarrel or to oppose others; bad-tempered; quarrelsome —**can·tan′ker·ous·ly** *adv.* —**can·tan′ker·ous·ness** *n.*

can·ta·ta (kən tät′ə) *n.* [< It. pp. of *cantare:* see CHANT] a musical composition with vocal solos, choruses, etc. that tells a story, like an opera, but is not acted

can·teen (kan tēn′) *n.* [< Fr. < It. *cantina*, wine cellar: for IE. base see CANT[2]] **1.** *same as* POST EXCHANGE **2.** *a)* a place where refreshments can be obtained, as by employees or visitors *b)* such a place serving as a social center [a youth *canteen*] **3.** a small metal or plastic flask, usually covered with canvas, for carrying drinking water

can·ter (kan′tər) *n.* [contr. < *Canterbury gallop*, the riding pace of the medieval Canterbury pilgrims] a smooth, easy pace like a moderate gallop —*vi., vt.* to ride at a canter

Can·ter·bur·y (kan′tər ber′ē, -bər ē) city in SE England, that has a famous cathedral: pop. 33,000

Canterbury bells a cultivated bellflower with white, pink, or blue, cuplike flowers

cant hook [see CANT[2]] a pole with a movable hooked arm at or near one end, for catching hold of logs and rolling them

can·thus (kan′thəs) *n., pl.* **-thi** (-thī) [ModL. < Gr. *kanthos:* see CANT[2]] either corner of the eye, where the eyelids meet

can·ti·cle (kan′ti k′l) *n.* [< L. dim. of *canticum*, song < *cantus:* see CHANT] **1.** a song or chant **2.** a hymn with words from the Bible, used in church services

Can·ti·cles (kan′ti k′lz) *same as* SONG OF SOLOMON: also (in the Douay Bible) **Canticle of Canticles**

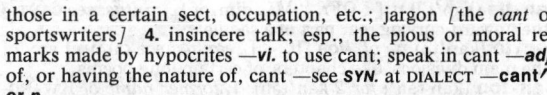

CANT HOOK

can·ti·le·na (kan′tə lē′nə) *n.* [It. < L., a song < *cantare*, to sing] a smooth, flowing, lyrical passage of vocal, or sometimes instrumental, music

can·ti·le·ver (kan′t'l ē′vər, -ev′ər) *n.* [as if < CANT[2] + LEVER] **1.** a large bracket or block projecting from a wall to support a balcony, cornice, etc. **2.** a projecting beam or structure that is anchored to a pier or wall at only one end —*vt.* to support by means of cantilevers —**can′ti·le′vered** *adj.*

CANTILEVER

cantilever bridge a bridge formed by two cantilevers that project toward each other and meet to form a span

can·til·la·tion (kan′t'l ā′shən) *n.* [< L. *cantillare*, to hum < *cantare:* see CHANT] in Jewish liturgy, a chanting with certain traditional musical phrases indicated by symbols over the syllables —**can′til·late′** (-āt′) *vt., vi.* **-lat·ed, -lat·ing**

---

fat, āpe, cär; ten, ēven; is, bīte; gō, hôrn, tōōl, look; oil, out; up, fur; get; joy; yet; chin; she; thin, then; zh, leisure; ŋ, ring; ə for *a* in *ago*, *e* in *agent*, *i* in *sanity*, *o* in *comply*, *u* in *focus*; ′ as in *able* (ā′b'l); Fr. bal; ë, Fr. coeur; ö, Fr. feu; Fr. mon; ô, Fr. coq; ü, Fr. duc; r, Fr. cri; H, G. ich; kh, G. doch; ‡foreign; ☆ Americanism; < derived from. See inside front cover.

can·tle (kan′t'l) *n.* [< OFr. < ML. dim. of L. *cantus*: see CANT²] the upward-curving rear part of a saddle

can·to (kan′tō) *n., pl.* **-tos** [It. < L. *cantus*: see CHANT] any of the main divisions, like chapters, of certain long poems

Can·ton (kan tän′; *for 2* kan′tən) **1.** *former name of* KWANG-CHOW **2.** [prob. named after the city in China] city in EC Ohio: pop. 110,000

can·ton (kan′tən, -tän; kan tän′; *for vt. 2* kan tän′, -tōn′) *n.* [Fr. < It. < LL. *cantus*, corner: see CANT²] any of certain political divisions of a country; specif., any of the states in the Swiss Republic —*vt.* **1.** to divide into cantons **2.** to assign quarters to (troops, etc.) —**can′ton·al** *adj.*

Can·ton·ese (kan′tə nēz′) *adj.* of Canton, China, or its people —*n.* **1.** *pl.* **-ese** a native or inhabitant of Canton **2.** the Chinese dialect spoken in and around Canton

can·ton·ment (kan tän′mənt, -tōn′-) *n.* [< Fr.: see CANTON] **1.** the assigning of troops to temporary quarters **2.** the place to which they are assigned

can·tor (kan′tər) *n.* [L., singer < *canere*: see CHANT] **1.** a church choir leader **2.** a singer who leads the congregation in prayer in a synagogue —**can·to′ri·al** (-tôr′ē əl) *adj.*

☆**Ca·nuck** (kə nuk′) *n.* [< ?] [Colloq.] a Canadian; orig., specif., a French Canadian

Ca·nute (kə nōōt′, -nyōōt′) 994?–1035; Dan. king of England (1017–35) & of Denmark (1018–35) & of Norway (1028–35): also called **Canute the Great**

can·vas (kan′vəs) *n.* [< OFr. < It. < L. *cannabis*, hemp] **1.** a closely woven, coarse cloth of hemp, cotton, or linen, used for tents, sails, etc. **2.** a sail or set of sails **3.** *a)* a specially prepared piece of canvas on which an oil painting is made *b)* such a painting **4.** any loosely woven, coarse cloth for embroidery, etc. —**the canvas** the canvas-covered floor of a boxing or wrestling ring —**under canvas** **1.** in tents [a circus *under canvas*] **2.** with sails unfurled

☆**can·vas·back** (-bak′) *n., pl.* **-backs′, -back′:** see PLURAL, II, D,1 a large, N. American wild duck with a brownish-red head and dark back

can·vass (kan′vəs) *vt.* [< *canvas*: ? because canvas was used for sifting] **1.** to examine or discuss in detail [*to canvass* ways of raising money] **2.** to go through (places) or among (people) asking for (votes, opinions, orders, etc.) [she *canvassed* the suburbs for her candidate] —*vi.* to try to get votes, orders, etc. —*n.* the act of canvassing, esp. in trying to estimate the outcome of an election, sales campaign, etc. —**can′vass·er** *n.*

☆**can·yon** (kan′yən) *n.* [Sp. *cañón*, a canyon, tube < L. *canna*, a reed: see CANE] a long, narrow valley between high cliffs, often with a stream flowing through it

Can·yon·lands National Park (kan′yən landz′) national park along the Colorado River, in SE Utah

caou·tchouc (kou chōōk′, kōō′chook) *n.* [Fr. < obs. Sp. *cauchuc* < Quechua] crude, natural rubber

cap (kap) *n.* [OE. *cæppe* < LL. *cappa*, a cloak] **1.** any closefitting head covering that has only a visor or no brim at all **2.** *a)* a head covering worn to show one's occupation, rank, etc. [a cardinal's *cap*] *b)* a mortarboard (sense 2) **3.** a caplike part or thing; cover or top [the *cap* on a bottle of soda pop] **4.** *same as* PERCUSSION CAP —*vt.* **capped, cap′ping 1.** to put a cap on **2.** to present with a cap, as at a graduation ceremony [to *cap* a nurse] **3.** to cover the top or end of [snow *capped* the hills] **4.** to match, surpass, or top [can you *cap* the winning time of 10.6 seconds?] **5.** to bring to a high point; climax [they *capped* the evening with a string quartet] —**cap the climax** to be or do more than could be expected or believed

CAP, C.A.P. Civil Air Patrol

cap. 1. capacity **2.** *pl.* **caps.** capital **3.** capitalize **4.** capitalized

ca·pa·bil·i·ty (kā′pə bil′ə tē) *n., pl.* **-ties 1.** the quality of being capable; ability **2.** the possibility of being used or developed [the *capability* of a plastic for being molded] **3.** [*pl.*] abilities, features, etc. not yet developed

ca·pa·ble (kā′pə b'l) *adj.* [Fr. < LL. *capabilis* < L. *capere*: see CAPTURE] having ability; able; skilled [a *capable* lawyer] —**capable of 1.** admitting of; open to [a situation *capable* of improvement] **2.** having the qualities necessary for [a table *capable* of seating ten] **3.** able or ready to [*capable* of telling a lie] —see SYN. at ABLE —**ca′pa·bly** *adv.*

ca·pa·cious (kə pā′shəs) *adj.* [< L. *capax* (gen. *capacis*) < *capere* (see CAPTURE) + -OUS] able to contain or hold much; roomy; spacious [a *capacious* trunk] —**ca·pa′cious·ly** *adv.* —**ca·pa′cious·ness** *n.*

ca·pac·i·tance (kə pas′ə təns) *n.* [CAPACIT(Y) + -ANCE] *Elec.* the quantity of electric charge that can be stored in a capacitor: it is expressed in farads and is the ratio of the charge to the potential difference between the plates —**ca·pac′i·tive** *adj.*

ca·pac·i·tor (-tər) *n. Elec.* a device consisting of two or more conducting plates separated by insulating material and used for storing an electric charge; condenser

ca·pac·i·ty (kə pas′ə tē) *n., pl.* **-ties** [< OFr. < L. < *capax*: see CAPACIOUS] **1.** the ability to contain, absorb, or receive [a theater with a *capacity* of 300 persons] **2.** the amount of space that can be filled; content or volume [a jar with a *capacity* of 2 quarts] **3.** mental ability **4.** aptitude; capability; potentiality [the *capacity* to be an actor] **5.** maximum producing ability [a factory with a *capacity* of 10,000 units a day] **6.** position, function, status, etc. [acting in the *capacity* of adviser] **7.** *Elec. same as* CAPACITANCE —see SYN. at FUNCTION

cap and bells a cap with bells on it, once worn by jesters

cap and gown a flat cap (MORTARBOARD) and a long robe, worn at graduation, etc. at schools and colleges

ca·par·i·son (kə par′ə s'n) *n.* [< Fr. < Pr. *caparasso*, large cloak < CAPE¹] **1.** an ornamented covering for a horse; trappings **2.** clothing, equipment, and ornaments; outfit —*vt.* to adorn, as with trappings or rich clothing

cape¹ (kāp) *n.* [Fr. < Pr. *capa* < LL. *cappa*, mantle, cloak] a sleeveless garment fastened at the neck and hanging over the back and shoulders

cape² (kāp) *n.* [OFr. < ML. *caput*, headland < L., HEAD] a piece of land projecting into a body of water —**the Cape** *short for:* **1.** Cape of GOOD HOPE **2.** Cape COD

Cape Breton Island island of NE Nova Scotia: 3,975 sq. mi.

Ča·pek (chä′pek), **Ka·rel** (kär′əl) 1890–1938; Czech playwright & novelist

ca·per¹ (kā′pər) *vi.* [prob. < CAPRIOLE] to skip about in a playful manner —*n.* **1.** a gay, playful jump or leap **2.** a wild, foolish action or prank ☆**3.** [Slang] a criminal act, esp. a robbery —**cut a caper** (or **capers**) **1.** to caper **2.** to play tricks

ca·per² (kā′pər) *n.* [< L. < Gr. *kapparis*] **1.** a prickly, trailing Mediterranean bush whose green flower buds are pickled and used to flavor sauces, etc. **2.** any of these buds

cap·er·cail·lie (kap′ər kāl′yē) *n.* [< Gael. *capull* (< L. *caballus*, horse) + *coille*, (of the) forest] the largest European grouse

Ca·per·na·um (kə pur′nē əm) city in ancient Palestine, on the Sea of Galilee

Ca·pe·tian (kə pē′shən) *adj.* the French dynasty (987–1328 A.D.) founded by **Hugh Ca·pet** (kā′pit, kap′it), king of France (987–996) —*n.* a member of this dynasty

Cape Town seaport of South Africa, where the legislature meets: pop. 807,000: also, esp. formerly, **Cape′town′**

Cape Verde country on a group of islands in the Atlantic, west of Cape Verde, Senegal: 1,557 sq. mi.; pop. 294,000

cap·ful (kap′fool′) *n., pl.* **-fuls** as much as the cap of the bottle can hold

ca·pi·as (kā′pē əs, kap′ē-) *n.* [< ML. < L., you may take < *capere*, to take] *Law* a writ issued by a court, directing an officer to arrest the person named

cap·il·lar·i·ty (kap′ə ler′ə tē) *n.* **1.** the state of being capillary **2.** the property of having capillary attraction **3.** *same as* CAPILLARY ATTRACTION

cap·il·lar·y (kap′ə ler′ē) *adj.* [< L. < *capillus*, hair] **1.** of or like a hair; very slender **2.** having a very small bore **3.** in or of capillaries —*n., pl.* **-lar′ies 1.** a tube with a very small bore: also **capillary tube 2.** any of the tiny blood vessels connecting the arteries with the veins

capillary attraction a force that causes the surface of a liquid in a capillary tube to rise or be depressed in the tube depending on whether cohesion or adhesion is the greater force: also **capillary action**

cap·i·tal¹ (kap′ə t'l) *adj.* [< OFr. < L. < *caput*, HEAD] **1.** that can be punished by death [a *capital* offense] **2.** most important or most serious; principal; chief [a *capital* virtue] **3.** being the seat of government [a *capital* city] **4.** of or having to do with capital, or wealth [*capital* assets] **5.** first-rate; excellent [a *capital* idea] See also CAPITAL LETTER —*n.* **1.** *same as* CAPITAL LETTER **2.** a city or town that is the official seat of government of a state, nation, etc. **3.** a city where a certain industry, etc. is centered [Akron is the rubber *capital*] **4.** money or property owned or used in business by a person, corporation, etc. **5.** an accumulation of such wealth, or its value **6.** wealth used to produce more wealth **7.** [*often* C-] capitalists as a group: distinguished from LABOR —**make capital of** to make the most of; exploit

cap·i·tal² (kap′ə t′l) *n.* [< OFr. < L. dim. of *caput*, HEAD] the top part of a column or pilaster

capital expenditure money spent to replace or improve business facilities

☆**capital gain** profit from the sale of stocks, real estate, etc., taxed at a lower rate than other income

capital goods goods, such as raw materials and machinery, used in producing other goods

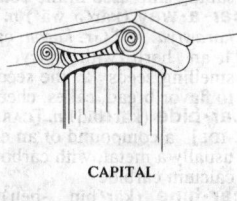

CAPITAL

cap·i·tal·ism (kap′ə t′l iz′m) *n.*
1. the economic system in which the means of producing and distributing goods are privately owned and operated for profit, originally with full competition in a free market 2. the principles, power, etc. of capitalists

cap·i·tal·ist (-ist) *n.* 1. a person who has capital; owner of wealth used in business 2. a person who is in favor of capitalism —*adj.* capitalistic

☆**cap·i·tal·is·tic** (kap′ə t′l is′tik) *adj.* 1. of or characteristic of capitalists or capitalism 2. practicing or supporting capitalism —**cap′i·tal·is′ti·cal·ly** *adv.*

cap·i·tal·i·za·tion (kap′ə t′l ə zā′shən) *n.* 1. the act or process of capitalizing something 2. the total amount of money used as capital by a corporation and represented by stocks, bonds, etc. ☆3. the act or system of using capital letters in writing and printing

cap·i·tal·ize (kap′ə t′l īz′) *vt.* **-ized′, -iz′ing** 1. to change into capital, or wealth to be used in business ☆2. to supply capital to or for (an enterprise) ☆3. to print or write (a word or words) in capital letters [*capitalize* the entire heading] ☆4. to begin (a word) with a capital letter [we usually *capitalize* a proper name] —**capitalize on (something)** to use (something) to one's own advantage [to *capitalize on* someone's error]

capital letter a large letter of a kind used to begin a sentence or proper name, as A, B, C

cap·i·tal·ly (kap′ə t′l ē) *adv.* in an excellent or admirable manner; very well

capital punishment penalty of death for a crime

capital ship formerly, an armored warship carrying guns of more than a specified caliber

capital stock the capital, or usable wealth, of a corporation, divided into shares that can be bought and sold

cap·i·ta·tion (kap′ə tā′shən) *n.* [< LL. < L. *caput*, HEAD] a fixed tax levied on each head, or person

Cap·i·tol (kap′ə t′l) [< OFr. < L. *Capitolium*, the temple of Jupiter] 1. the temple of Jupiter in Rome ☆2. the building in which the U.S. Congress meets, in Washington, D.C. —*n.* ☆[*usually* **c-**] the building in which a State legislature meets

Cap·i·to·line (kap′ə t′l īn′) one of the SEVEN HILLS OF ROME —*adj.* 1. of this hill 2. of the temple of Jupiter which stood there

ca·pit·u·late (kə pich′ə lāt′) *vi.* **-lat′ed, -lat′ing** [< LL. pp. of *capitulare*, to draw up in heads or chapters < L. *capitulum*: see CAPITULUM] 1. to give up (*to* an enemy) on certain conditions 2. to give up; stop resisting —see SYN. at YIELD

ca·pit·u·la·tion (kə pich′ə lā′shən) *n.* 1. a statement of the main parts of a subject 2. a capitulating; surrender on certain conditions 3. a document containing terms of surrender, etc.

ca·pit·u·lum (kə pich′ə ləm) *n., pl.* **-la** (-lə) [L., dim. of *caput*, HEAD] 1. a knoblike part, as at the end of some bones 2. *same as* HEAD (*n.* 16 *a*)

ca·po (kä′pō) *n., pl.* **-pos** [short for *capotasto* < It., lit., chief key] a device fastened over the fingerboard as of a guitar to shorten all the strings at the same time and make a change of key easy

ca·pon (kā′pän, -pən) *n.* [< OE. & OFr. < L. *capo*: for IE. base see SHAPE] a rooster that is castrated and fattened for eating —**ca′pon·ize′** (-pə nīz′) *vt.* **-ized′, -iz′ing**

ca·pote (kə pōt′) *n.* [Fr., dim. of *cape*, CAPE¹] a long cloak, usually with a hood

Cap·pa·do·ci·a (kap′ə dō′shē ə,

CAPO

-shə) ancient kingdom, later a Roman province, in E Asia Minor

Ca·pri (ka prē′, kä′prē) island near the entrance to the Bay of Naples: 5 sq. mi.

ca·pric·ci·o (kə prē′chē ō; *It.* kä prēt′chô) *n., pl.* **-ci·os**; *It.* **-pric′ci** (-chē) [It.: see CAPRICE] 1. a whim; caprice 2. a lively musical composition in a free form

ca·price (kə prēs′) *n.* [Fr. < It. *capriccio*, a shivering, whim < *capo*, head + *riccio*, curl] 1. a sudden change in thought or action that seems to have no reason; whim 2. a tendency to have such changes 3. *Music same as* CAPRICCIO

ca·pri·cious (kə prish′əs) *adj.* full of caprices; likely to change suddenly and for no apparent reason; flighty [*capricious* in his choice of reading matter] —**ca·pri′cious·ly** *adv.* —**ca·pri′cious·ness** *n.*

Cap·ri·corn (kap′rə kôrn′) [< OFr. < L. < *caper*, goat + *cornu*, a horn] 1. a S constellation 2. the tenth sign of the zodiac: see ZODIAC

cap·ri·ole (kap′rē ōl′) *n.* [Fr. < It., ult. < L. *caper*, goat] 1. a caper; leap 2. an upward leap made by a horse without going forward —*vi.* **-oled′, -ol′ing** to make a capriole

caps. capitals (capital letters)

cap·si·cum (kap′sə kəm) *n.* [ModL. < L. *capsa*, a box] 1. any of various red peppers whose sharp-tasting, fleshy pods are known as chili peppers, cayenne peppers, etc. 2. these pods prepared for use as seasoning

cap·size (kap′sīz, kap sīz′) *vt., vi.* **-sized, -siz·ing** [? < Sp. *cabezar*, lit., to sink by the head] to overturn or upset: said esp. of a boat

cap·stan (kap′stən) *n.* [Fr. & Pr. *cabestan* < ? L. < *capere*: see CAPTURE] an upright cylinder around which cables or hawsers are wound, by machinery or by hand, for hoisting anchors, etc. on a ship

capstan bar any of the poles inserted in a capstan and used as levers in turning it by hand

cap·stone (kap′stōn′) *n.* the top stone of a structure

cap·su·lar (kap′sə lər, -syoo-) *adj.*
1. having the nature of a capsule 2. of or in a capsule

CAPSTAN

cap·su·late (-lāt′, -lit) *adj.* contained in or formed into a capsule: also **cap′su·lat·ed**

cap·sule (kap′s′l, -syool) *n.* [Fr. < L. dim. of *capsa*, CASE²] ☆1. a small, soluble gelatin container for enclosing a dose of medicine ☆2. *a)* an airplane cockpit that can be ejected in an emergency *b)* a closed compartment to hold and protect men, instruments, etc. in a rocket, that can be separated in flight: in full, **space capsule** 3. *Anat.* a sac or membrane enclosing an organ or part 4. *Bot.* a case, pod, or fruit containing seeds, spores, or carpels, esp. one that bursts when ripe —☆*adj.* in a small or concise form [a *capsule* biography] —*vt.* **-suled, -sul·ing** to condense

cap·sul·ize (-īz′) ☆*vt.* **-ized′, -iz′ing** 1. to enclose in a capsule 2. to put in a brief form; condense

Capt. Captain

cap·tain (kap′tən) *n.* [< OFr. < LL. < L. *caput*, HEAD] 1. a chief or leader 2. the head of a group or division; esp., *a)* U.S. Mil. an officer ranking above a first lieutenant *b)* U.S. Navy an officer ranking above a commander *c)* the commander or master of a ship *d)* the chief pilot of a commercial airplane *e)* the leader of a team, as in sports ☆*f)* a precinct commander in a police or fire department —*vt.* to be captain of [who will *captain* the football team?] —**cap′tain·cy** (-sē), *pl.* **-cies, cap′tain·ship′** *n.*

cap·tion (kap′shən) *n.* [< OFr. < L. < pp. of *capere*: see CAPTURE] ☆1. a heading, as of a newspaper article, or a title, as under an illustration 2. *same as* SUBTITLE (*n.* 2) —*vt.* to supply a caption for

cap·tious (kap′shəs) *adj.* [< L. *captiosus* < prec.] 1. made only for the sake of arguing or finding fault [*captious* criticism] 2. quick to find fault in others; quibbling —see SYN. at CRITICAL —**cap′tious·ly** *adv.* —**cap′tious·ness** *n.*

cap·ti·vate (kap′tə vāt′) *vt.* **-vat′ed, -vat′ing** [< LL., ult. < L. *captivus*, CAPTIVE] 1. orig., to take captive; capture 2. to cap-

---

fat, āpe, cär; ten, ēven; is, bīte; gō, hôrn, tōol, look; oil, out; up, fur; get; joy; yet; chin; she; thin, then; zh, leisure; ŋ, ring; ə for *a* in *ago*, *e* in *agent*, *i* in *sanity*, *o* in *comply*, *u* in *focus*; ′ as in *able* (ā′b'l); Fr. bál; ë, Fr. coeur; ö, Fr. feu; Fr. mon; ô, Fr. coq; ü, Fr. duc; r, Fr. cri; H, G. ich; kh, G. doch; ‡ foreign; ☆ Americanism; < derived from. See inside front cover.

ture the attention or affection of, as by beauty, excellence, etc.; fascinate; charm [he was *captivated* by her lovely voice] —see SYN. at ATTRACT —**cap′ti·vat′ing·ly** *adv.* —**cap′ti·va′tion** *n.* — **cap′ti·va′tor** *n.*

cap·tive (kap′tiv) *n.* [L. *captivus* < pp. of *capere*: see CAPTURE] **1.** a person caught and held prisoner, as in war **2.** a person captivated, as by someone's beauty —*adj.* **1.** *a)* taken or held prisoner *b)* unable to act independently [a *captive* nation] ☆*c)* forced to listen whether wanting to or not [a *captive* audience] **2.** captivated **3.** of captivity

cap·tiv·i·ty (kap tiv′ə tē) *n., pl.* **-ties** the condition or time of being captive; imprisonment

cap·tor (kap′tər) *n.* [L.] a person who captures

cap·ture (kap′chər) *n.* [Fr. < L. *captura* < pp. of *capere*, to take: for IE. base see HAVE] **1.** a taking or being taken by force, surprise, or skill [the *capture* of a fort; the *capture* of a pawn in chess] **2.** that which is thus taken **3.** the absorption of a bombarding particle by an atomic nucleus, often causing radiation —*vt.* **-tured, -tur·ing** **1.** to take or seize by force, surprise, or skill [to *capture* a ship; to *capture* someone's attention] **2.** to represent (something fleeting) in more or less permanent form [he *captured* the mood of the party in his letter]

Cap·u·chin (kap′yoo shin, -chin; kə pyōō′-) *n.* [< Fr. *capucin*, monk who wears a cowl < *capuce* (It. *cappuccio*), a cowl] **1.** a monk of a strict branch of the Franciscan order **2.** [c-] a woman's cloak with a hood **3.** [c-] a new-world monkey with a hoodlike crown of hair

cap·y·ba·ra (kap′ə bär′ə) *n.* [Port. *capibara* < native name, lit., one who eats grass] a S. American animal, the largest of the existing rodents, which reaches a length of over four feet, has partially webbed feet, and lacks a tail

car (kär) *n.* [< ONormFr. < LL. < L. *carrus*, two-wheeled chariot < Gaul. *carros*] **1.** any vehicle on wheels **2.** [Poet.] a chariot ☆**3.** a vehicle that moves on rails, as a streetcar **4.** an automobile ☆**5.** the part of an elevator in which people ride **6.** the part of a balloon or airship for carrying people and equipment

ca·ra·bao (kär′ə bou′) *n., pl.* **-baos′, -bao′:** see PLURAL, II, D, 1 [Sp. < Malay *karbau*] *same as* WATER BUFFALO

car·a·bi·neer, car·a·bi·nier (kär′ə bə nir′) *n.* [Fr. *carabinier*] a cavalryman armed with a carbine

Car·a·cal·la (kar′ə kal′ə) (born *Marcus Aurelius Antoninus*) 188–217 A.D.; Roman emperor (211–217)

ca·ra·ca·ra (kär′ə kär′ə) *n.* [Sp. < native name] a large hawk of S. America, that looks like a vulture

Ca·ra·cas (kə räk′əs, -rak′-; *Sp.* kä rä′käs) capital of Venezuela, in the NC part: pop. 1,000,000

car·a·cole (kar′ə kōl′) *n.* [Fr. < Walloon < Sp. *caracol*, shell of a snail < Fr. *escargot*, snail] a half turn to the right or left made by a horse with a rider —*vi.* **-coled, -col′ing** to make a caracole or caracoles

car·a·cul (kar′ə kəl) *n. same as* KARAKUL

ca·rafe (kə raf′, -räf′) *n.* [Fr. < It. *caraffa*, prob. < Ar. *gharafa*, to draw water] a glass or metal bottle for serving water, coffee, or wine

ca·ra·ga·na (kar′ə gän′ə) *n.* [< Kirghiz *karaghan*, the Siberian pea shrub] a hardy shrub of the legume family, grown for its showy golden flowers and often as a windbreak in dry climates

☆**ca·ram·ba** (kä räm′bä) *interj.* [AmSp. < Sp., euphemism for *carajo*, penis] [Southwest] an exclamation of surprise, dismay, etc.

car·a·mel (kar′ə m'l, -mel′; kär′m'l) *n.* [Fr. < OFr., ult. < L. *canna mellis*, sugar cane] **1.** burnt sugar used to color or flavor food **2.** a chewy candy made from sugar, milk, etc.

car·a·mel·ize (kar′ə mə līz′, kär′mə-) *vt., vi.* **-ized′, -iz′ing** to turn into caramel

car·a·pace (kar′ə pās′) *n.* [Fr. < Sp. *carapacho*] an upper case or shell, as of the turtle

car·at (kar′ət) *n.* [Fr. < It. < Ar. < Gr. *keration*, carat, dim. of *keras*, HORN] **1.** a unit of weight for precious stones, equal to 200 milligrams **2.** *same as* KARAT

Ca·ra·vag·gio (kä′rä väd′jô), **(Michelangelo da)** (born *Michelangelo Merisi*) 1573–1610; It. painter

car·a·van (kar′ə van′) *n.* [< Fr. < OFr. < Per. *kārwān*, caravan] **1.** a company of merchants, pilgrims, etc. traveling together for safety, as through a desert **2.** a number of vehicles traveling together **3.** a large covered vehicle for passengers, circus animals, etc.; van **4.** [Brit.] a trailer (sense 3)

car·a·van·sa·ry (kar′ə van′sə rē) *n., pl.* **-ries** [< Fr. < Per. *kārwān*, caravan + *sarāī*, palace] in the Orient, a kind of inn with a large central court, where caravans stop for the night

car·a·vel (kar′ə vel′) *n.* [< Fr. < Port. < LL. < Gr. *karabos*, kind of light ship] a fast, small sailing ship used in the 16th cent.

car·a·way (kar′ə wā′) *n.* [< Ar. *karawiyā′* < ? Gr. *karon*, caraway] **1.** an herb with spicy, strong-smelling seeds **2.** the seeds, used to flavor bread, cakes, cheese, etc.

car·bide (kär′bīd) *n.* [CARB(O)- + -IDE] a compound of an element, usually a metal, with carbon; esp., calcium carbide

car·bine (kär′bīn, -bēn) *n.* [< Fr., ult. < *scarabée*, a beetle] **1.** a rifle with a short barrel ☆**2.** *U.S. Armed Forces* a semiautomatic or automatic .30-caliber rifle

CARAVEL

car·bi·neer (kär′bə nir′) *n. same as* CARABINEER

car·bo- *a combining form meaning* carbon: also, before a vowel, **carb-**

car·bo·hy·drate (kär′bə hī′drāt) *n.* [CARBO- + HYDRATE] any of a group of organic compounds, including the sugars and starches, composed of carbon, hydrogen, and oxygen: carbohydrates form an important class of foods

car·bo·lat·ed (kär′bə lāt′id) *adj.* containing or treated with carbolic acid

car·bol·ic acid (kär bäl′ik) [CARB(O)- + -OL¹ + -IC] *same as* PHENOL (sense 1)

car·bo·lize (kär′bə līz′) *vt.* **-lized′, -liz′ing** [see prec.] to treat or sterilize with phenol

car·bon (kär′bən) *n.* [< Fr. < L. *carbo*, coal] **1.** a nonmetallic chemical element found in many inorganic compounds and all organic compounds: diamond and graphite are pure carbon; carbon is also present in coal, coke, etc.: symbol, C; at. wt., 12.01115; at. no., 6: a radioactive isotope (**carbon 14**) is used in dating fossils and other matter containing carbon by measuring the degree to which it has decayed, etc. **2.** a sheet of carbon paper **3.** a copy, as of a letter, made with carbon paper: in full, **carbon copy** —*adj.* of carbon

car·bo·na·ceous (kär′bə nā′shəs) *adj.* of, consisting of, or containing carbon

car·bon·ate (kär′bə nit; *also, and for v. always,* -nāt′) *n.* a salt or ester of carbonic acid —*vt.* **-at′ed, -at′ing** **1.** to charge with carbon dioxide so as to make bubbly [carbonated drinks] **2.** to form into a carbonate —**car′bon·a′tion** *n.*

carbon black finely divided carbon produced by the incomplete burning of oil or gas, used esp. in rubber and ink

car·bon-date (kär′bən dāt′) *vt.* **-dat′ed, -dat′ing** to establish the approximate age of (fossils, etc.) by measuring the degree to which the carbon 14 in it has decayed

carbon dioxide a colorless, odorless gas, CO_2: it passes out of the lungs in respiration, and is absorbed by plants in photosynthesis

carbon disulfide a highly flammable, poisonous, colorless liquid, CS_2, used as a solvent, preservative, insecticide, etc.

car·bon·ic (kär bän′ik) *adj.* of, containing, or obtained from carbon or carbon dioxide

carbonic acid a weak, colorless acid, H_2CO_3, formed by dissolving carbon dioxide in water

car·bon·if·er·ous (kär′bə nif′ər əs) *adj.* [< CARBON + -FEROUS] **1.** producing or containing carbon or coal **2.** [C-] designating or of a great coal-making period of the Paleozoic Era: the warm, damp climate produced great forests, which later formed rich coal seams —**the Carboniferous 1.** the Carboniferous Period **2.** the rock and coal strata formed then See GEOLOGIC TIME CHART

car·bon·ize (kär′bə nīz′) *vt.* **-ized′, -iz′ing** **1.** to change into carbon, as by partial burning [to *carbonize* wood into charcoal] **2.** to treat, cover, or combine with carbon —*vi.* to become carbonized —**car′bon·i·za′tion** *n.*

carbon monoxide a colorless, odorless, highly poisonous gas, CO, produced when carbon is not completely burned, as in an automobile engine

carbon paper very thin paper coated on one side with a carbon preparation: it is placed between sheets of paper, so that the pressure of typing or writing on the upper sheet makes a copy on the lower

carbon tet·ra·chlo·ride (tet′rə klôr′īd) a nonflammable, colorless liquid, CCl_4, used in fire extinguishers, cleaning mixtures, etc.

☆**Car·bo·run·dum** (kär′bə run′dəm) [CARB(ON) + (C)ORUNDUM] *a trademark for* a very hard, abrasive substance, esp. a carbide of silicon, used in grindstones, abrasives, etc. —**n.** [c-] such a substance

car·box·yl (kär bäk′s′l) **n.** [CARB(ON) + OX(YGEN) + -YL] the univalent radical COOH, occurring in organic acids —**car′·box·yl′ic** (-sil′ik) **adj.**

car·boy (kär′boi) **n.** [< Per. qarābah] a large glass bottle protected in basketwork or in a wooden crate: used as a container for acids and the like

car·bun·cle (kär′buŋ k′l) **n.** [< OFr. < L. dim. of carbo, coal] 1. a smooth garnet cut in a convex shape 2. a painful inflammation of the tissue beneath the skin, filled with pus: it is more severe than a boil and has several openings —**car·bun′cu·lar** (-kyoo lər) **adj.**

car·bu·ret (kär′bə rāt′, -ret′; -byoo-) **vt.** -**ret′ed** or -**ret′ted**, -**ret′ing** or -**ret′ting** [< obs. carburet, carbide] 1. to combine chemically with carbon 2. to mix or charge (gas or air) with volatile carbon compounds —**car′bu·re′tion** (-rā′shən) **n.**

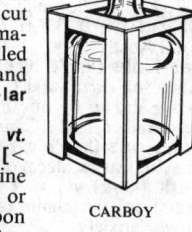

CARBOY

car·bu·ret·or (kär′bə rāt′ər, -byoo-) **n.** a device in which air is mixed with gasoline spray to make an explosive mixture in an internal-combustion engine: Brit. sp. **car′bu·ret′tor** (-byoo-ret′ər)

☆**car·ca·jou** (kär′kə joo′, -zhoo′) **n.** [CanadFr. < Algonquian] same as WOLVERINE

car·cass (kär′kəs) **n.** [< OFr. & Fr. < ?] 1. the dead body of an animal, esp. of an animal slaughtered and cleaned for use as meat 2. the human body, living or dead: a mocking or joking usage 3. the worthless remains of something [the carcass of an empire] 4. a framework or shell [the carcass of a ship] Also, Brit. var., **car′case** (-kəs)

car·cin·o·gen (kär sin′ə jən) **n.** [< CARCINOMA + -GEN] any substance that produces cancer —**car·ci·no·gen·e·sis** (kär′sə nō jen′ə sis) **n.** —**car·ci·no·gen′ic adj.**

car·ci·no·ma (kär′sə nō′mə) **n.,** pl. -**mas**, -**ma·ta** (-mə tə) [L. < Gr. karkinōma, cancer < karkinos, a crab, CANCER] a growth that is a cancer and is made up of epithelial cells —**car′ci·nom′a·tous** (-näm′ə təs, -nō′mə-) **adj.**

☆**car coat** a short overcoat, reaching midway down the thigh

card[1] (kärd) **n.** [< OFr. < L. charta < Gr. chartēs, leaf of paper] 1. a flat, stiff piece of thick paper or thin pasteboard, usually rectangular; specif., a) one of a pack of playing cards: see also CARDS ☆b) a pasteboard with small articles attached for sale [a card of thumbtacks] c) same as CALLING CARD, COMPASS CARD, POSTAL CARD, SCORE CARD d) a card bearing a message or greeting [a birthday card] e) a card identifying a person as an agent, member, patron, etc. f) any of a series of cards on which information is recorded [a file card] ☆2. a series of events making up a program, as in boxing 3. [Colloq.] a comical person —**vt.** 1. to provide with a card 2. to put or list on a card or cards —**card up one's sleeve** a plan or help kept secret or held back for use if others fail —**in** (or **on**) **the cards** that seems likely to happen, as if by fate —**put** (or **lay**) **one's cards on the table** to be frank in telling one's plans, feelings, etc.

card[2] (kärd) **n.** [< Fr. < Pr. < L. carere, to card; sp. influenced by L. carduus, thistle] 1. a metal comb or wire brush, as for combing fibers of wool, cotton, etc. 2. a machine with rollers covered with wire teeth, used to brush, clean, and straighten such fibers —**vt.** to use a card on (fibers) in preparation for spinning —**card′er n.** —**card′ing n., adj.**

car·da·mom (kär′də məm) **n.** [< L. < Gr. < kardamon, cress + amōmon, spice plant] 1. an Asiatic plant with fragrant, spicy seeds 2. its seeds, used in medicine and as a spice Also **car′da·mon** (-mən)

card·board (kärd′bôrd′) **n.** stiff, thick paper, or pasteboard, used for cards, boxes, etc.

☆**card file** cards containing data or records, arranged in a systematic way, usually alphabetically: also **card catalog**

car·di·ac (kär′dē ak′) **adj.** [< Fr. < L. < Gr. < kardia, HEART] 1. of, near, or affecting the heart 2. of the part of the stomach where it is connected with the esophagus —**n.** a person with a heart disorder

Car·diff (kär′dif) seaport in SE Wales, on the Bristol Channel: pop. 287,000

car·di·gan (kär′də gən) **n.** [after 7th Earl of Cardigan (1797–1868), Eng. general] a sweater or jacket, usually knitted, that opens down the front: also **cardigan sweater** (or **jacket**)

car·di·nal (kärd′n əl) **adj.** [< OFr. < L. cardinalis, chief < cardo, hinge] 1. of main importance; principal; chief [one of his cardinal beliefs] 2. bright-red —**n.** 1. one of the Roman Catholic officials appointed by the Pope to his council (COLLEGE OF CARDINALS) 2. bright red ☆3. a crested American songbird related to the finch: in full, **cardinal bird** 4. same as CARDINAL NUMBER —**car′di·nal·ly adv.** ☆3. **car′di·nal·ship′ n.**

CARDIGAN

car·di·nal·ate (-āt′) **n.** the position, dignity, or rank of a cardinal

☆**cardinal flower** 1. the bright-red flower of a N. American plant that grows in damp, shady places or in shallow water 2. this plant

cardinal number any number used in counting or showing how many (e.g., two, forty, 627, etc.): distinguished from ORDINAL NUMBER

cardinal points the four principal points of the compass; north, south, east, and west

cardinal virtues the four main virtues taught in ancient Greek philosophy: justice, prudence, fortitude, and temperance: see also THEOLOGICAL VIRTUES

☆**card index** same as CARD FILE

car·di·o- [< Gr. kardia, HEART] a combining form meaning of the heart: also, before a vowel, **cardi-**

car·di·o·gram (kär′dē ə gram′) **n.** same as ELECTROCARDIOGRAM —**car′di·o·graph′** (-graf′) **n.** —**car′di·og′ra·phy** (-äg′rə fē) **n.**

car·di·ol·o·gy (kär′dē äl′ə jē) **n.** the branch of medicine dealing with the heart, its functions, and its diseases —**car′di·ol′o·gist n.**

car·di·o·vas·cu·lar (kär′dē ō vas′kyoo lər) **adj.** of the heart and the blood vessels regarded as a unified system

car·di·tis (kär dīt′əs) **n.** [ModL. < Gr. kardia, HEART + -ITIS] inflammation of the heart

cards (kärdz) **n.pl.** 1. a game or games played with a deck of cards, as bridge, rummy, poker, etc. 2. the playing of such games; card playing

☆**card shark** [Colloq.] 1. an expert card player 2. same as CARDSHARP

☆**card·sharp** (kärd′shärp′) **n.** [Colloq.] a person who makes a living by cheating at cards: also **card′sharp′er**

care (ker) **n.** [< OE. caru, sorrow < IE. base gar-, to cry out] 1. a) worry or concern [a mind filled with care for their safety] b) a cause of this [the cares of parenthood] 2. close attention or careful heed [drive with care] 3. a liking or regard (for) [to show no care for others] 4. charge; protection; custody [his books were left in a friend's care] 5. something to watch over or attend to [a sick pet is a great care] —**vi.** cared, car′ing 1. to have objection, worry, regret, etc.; mind [do you care if I go?] 2. to feel concern or interest [to care about the effects of pollution] 3. to feel love or a liking (for) 4. to look after; provide (for) 5. to wish (for); want [do you care for more pie?] —**vt.** 1. to feel concern about or interest in [I don't care what you did] 2. to wish or desire [do you care to eat now?] —**care of** at the address of —**have a care** to be careful: also **take care** ☆**take care of** 1. to be responsible for; attend to 2. to provide for

SYN.—**care** suggests an uneasy or troubled state of mind caused by great responsibilities [worn out by the cares of the day]; **concern** implies such a state of mind over someone for whom one feels affection or something in which one has great interest [she felt concern when her father didn't arrive]; **worry** suggests a great troubling of the mind over some problem [his chief worry was that he might fail]; **anxiety** refers to an uneasy feeling over some bad but indefinite thing that might happen [he viewed the world situation with anxiety]; **solicitude** implies a being thoughtful, often in an anxious way, over the welfare or comfort of another [she showed great solicitude when I tripped and fell] —**ANT. unconcern, indifference**

☆**CARE** (ker) Cooperative for American Relief Everywhere, Inc.

ca·reen (kə rēn′) **vt.** [< Fr. < It. < L. carina, keel] 1. to cause (a ship) to lean or lie on one side, as for repairs 2. to cause to lean sideways; tip; tilt —**vi.** 1. to lean sideways, as a sailing ship before a high wind **2.** to lurch from side to side, esp. while moving rapidly —*n.* a careening

ca·reer (kə rir′) *n.* [Fr. *carrière*, racecourse < It. < *carro*, CAR] **1.** a swift course [the sun in its *career* through the sky] **2.** one's progress through life or in one's work [she had a long *career* in politics] **3.** a profession or occupation [will he make music his *career*?] —☆*adj.* making a career of what is normally a temporary job [a *career* soldier] —*vi.* to move at full speed; rush wildly —**in full career** at full speed

ca·reer·ist (-ist) *n.* a person interested chiefly in succeeding in his career, so that he neglects other things —**ca·reer′ism** *n.*

☆**career woman** [Colloq.] a woman who has a career in business or a profession, sometimes giving up marriage for this

care·free (ker′frē′) *adj.* free from troubles or worry

care·ful (-fəl) *adj.* **1.** acting or working in a thoughtful way, with attention to details [a *careful* accountant] **2.** cautious or wary [be *careful* as you cross the street] **3.** accurately or thoroughly done [a *careful* analysis] —**care′ful·ly** *adv.* —**care′ful·ness** *n.*

care·less (-lis) *adj.* **1.** carefree; untroubled [with a *careless* wave of his hand] **2.** not paying enough attention; not thinking before one acts or speaks [it was *careless* of me to lock the car with my keys still in it] **3.** done without enough attention, precision, etc. [a *careless* piece of writing] —**care′less·ly** *adv.* —**care′less·ness** *n.*

ca·ress (kə res′) *vt.* [< Fr. < It., ult. < L. *carus*, dear] to touch or stroke lovingly or gently; also, to embrace or kiss —*n.* an affectionate touch or gesture —**ca·ress′er** *n.* —**ca·ress′ing·ly** *adv.* —**ca·res′sive** *adj.* —**ca·res′sive·ly** *adv.*

car·et (kar′it, ker′-) *n.* [L., lit., there is lacking] a mark (∧) used in writing or in correcting proof, to show where something is to be added

care·tak·er (ker′tāk′ər) *n.* a person hired to take care of something, as a house, estate, etc.

care·worn (-wôrn′) *adj.* showing the effects of troubles and worry; haggard [a *careworn* face]

☆**car·fare** (kär′fer′) *n.* the price of a ride on a streetcar, bus, etc.

car·go (kär′gō) *n., pl.* **-goes, -gos** [< Sp. < *cargar*, to load < VL. *carricare*: see CHARGE] the load of goods carried by a ship, airplane, truck, etc.; freight

☆**car·hop** (kär′häp′) *n.* [CAR + (BELL)HOP] one who serves customers in cars at a drive-in restaurant

Car·i·a (ker′ē ə) ancient region in SW Asia Minor

Car·ib (kar′ib) *n.* [< Sp. *caribal*, altered < *canibal*: see CANNIBAL] **1.** a member of an Indian people of the S West Indies and the N coast of S. America **2.** the family of languages of the Caribs —**Car′ib·an** *adj., n.*

Car·ib·be·an (kar′ə bē′ən, kə rib′ē ən) *same as* CARIBBEAN SEA —*adj.* **1.** of the Caribs, their language, culture, etc. **2.** of the Caribbean Sea, its islands, etc. —*n. same as* CARIB (sense 1)

Car·ib·be·an Sea (kar′ə bē′ən, kə rib′ē ən) part of the Atlantic, bounded by the West Indies, Central America, & South America

ca·ri·be (kə rē′bā) *n.* [AmSp., lit., Carib (see CANNIBAL)] *same as* PIRANHA

☆**car·i·bou** (kar′ə boo′) *n., pl.* **-bous′, -bou′:** see PLURAL, II, D, 1 [CanadFr. < Algonquian name] a large, northern N. American deer closely related to the reindeer

car·i·ca·ture (kar′ə kə chər, -choor′) *n.* [Fr. < It. *caricare*, to load, exaggerate] **1.** a picture or imitation of a person, writing style, etc. that exaggerates certain characteristics in a satirical way **2.** the art of making caricatures **3.** a poor imitation [he is just a *caricature* of a statesman] —*vt.* **-tured, -tur·ing** to picture or describe as a caricature —**car′i·ca·tur·ist** *n.*

SYN.—caricature refers to an imitation or drawing of a person, as in a cartoon, that exaggerates outstanding features in a comical way; **burlesque** implies the handling of a serious subject in a light and flippant way or of a trivial subject in a way that pretends to be serious; a **parody** imitates the style of a writer or of some writing very closely, but makes fun of it by using an absurd subject or a nonsensical approach; a **travesty**, on the other hand, deals with the same subject as the original but in a ridiculous style or laughable language; **satire** refers to writing in which evil, stupid, or wicked persons or institutions are ridiculed or dealt with sarcastically

car·ies (ker′ēz) *n.* [L., decay] decay of bones, or, esp., of teeth [a tooth cavity is caused by *caries*]

car·il·lon (kar′ə län′) *n.* [Fr., chime of (orig. four) bells, ult. < L. *quattuor*, four] **1.** a set of stationary bells, each producing a different tone, used in playing melodies by means of a keyboard **2.** a melody played on such bells **3.** an organ stop producing a sound like that of such bells

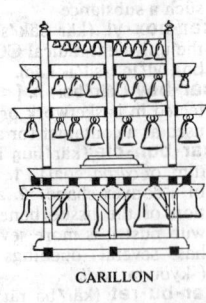
CARILLON

car·il·lon·neur (kar′ə lə nur′) *n.* [Fr.] a carillon player

Ca·rin·thi·a (kə rin′thē ə) province of S Austria

car·i·ole (kar′ē ōl′) *n.* [< Fr. < It. dim. of *carro*, CAR] **1.** a small carriage drawn by one horse **2.** a light, covered cart **3.** [Canad.] a dog sled

car·i·ous (kar′ē əs) *adj.* [L. *cariosus*] having caries; decayed —**car′i·os′i·ty** (-äs′ə tē) *n.*

cark (kärk) *vt., vi.* [< ONormFr. var. of OFr. *chargier*: see CHARGE] [Archaic] to worry or be worried —*n.* [Archaic] distress; anxiety

Carl (kärl) *var. of* CHARLES

☆**car·load** (kär′lōd′) *n.* a load that fills a car, esp. a freight car

☆**car·load·ings** (-iŋz) *n.pl.* the number of railroad carloads shipped within a given period

Car·lot·ta (kär lät′ə) *var. of* CHARLOTTE

Carls·bad Caverns National Park (kärlz′bad) national park in SE New Mexico, with large limestone caverns

Car·lyle (kär līl′, kär′līl), **Thomas** 1795–1881; Brit. writer, born in Scotland

car·ma·gnole (kär′mən yōl′) *n.* [Fr., altered < older *carmignole*, kind of cap] **1.** the costume worn by French Revolutionaries (1792) **2.** a song and dance popular during the French Revolution

Car·mel (kär′m'l), **Mount** mountain ridge in NW Israel; highest peak, c. 1800 ft.

Car·mel·ite (kär′mə līt′) *n.* a friar or nun of the order of Our Lady of Mount Carmel, founded in Syria about 1160 —*adj.* of this order

car·min·a·tive (kär min′ə tiv) *adj.* [ModL. < L. pp. of *carminare*, to card, cleanse] causing gas to be expelled from the stomach and intestines —*n.* a medicine that expels gas

car·mine (kär′min, -mīn) *n.* [< Fr. < ML. *carminium* < Ar. *qirmiz*, crimson (see KERMES); altered after L. *minium*, cinnabar red] **1.** a red or purplish-red pigment obtained mainly from cochineal **2.** its color —*adj.* red or purplish-red; crimson

car·nage (kär′nij) *n.* [< Fr. < It., ult. < L. *carnis*, genitive of *caro*, flesh (s)ker-, to cut, from which also come SHEAR & HARVEST] bloody slaughter of many people, esp. in battle; massacre; bloodshed —see SYN. at SLAUGHTER

car·nal (kär′n'l) *adj.* [OFr. < LL. *carnalis* < L. *caro*: see prec.] **1.** in or of the flesh or material world; not spiritual **2.** sensual; sexual [*carnal* desires] —**have carnal knowledge of** to have sexual intercourse with —**car·nal·i·ty** (kär nal′ə tē) *n., pl.* **-ties** —**car′nal·ly** *adv.*

car·na·tion (kär nā′shən) *n.* [Fr. < LL. *carnatio* < *caro*: see CARNAGE] **1.** formerly, rosy pink; now, deep red **2.** a plant of the pink family, with white, pink, or red flowers that smell like cloves

car·nau·ba (kär nô′bə, -nou′-) *n.* [Braz. Port. < Tupi native name] a Brazilian palm yielding a hard wax used in polishes, lipsticks, etc.

Car·ne·gie (kär′nə gē′, kär nā′gē), **Andrew** 1835–1919; U.S. industrialist & philanthropist, born in Scotland

car·nel·ian (kär nēl′yən) *n.* [altered (after L. *caro*: see CARNAGE) < CORNELIAN] a red variety of chalcedony, used in jewelry

car·ni·val (kär′nə vəl) *n.* [< Fr. or It. < ML. *carnem levare*, to remove meat (see CARNAGE & LEVER)] **1.** the period of feasting and merrymaking just before Lent, with parades, masquerades, etc. **2.** any merrymaking, or reveling **3.** an entertainment that travels from place to place, setting up sideshows, rides, etc. **4.** a program of contests, etc. [a winter sports *carnival*]

car·ni·vore (kär′nə vôr′) *n.* [Fr.: see CARNIVOROUS] **1.** any of a large group of flesh-eating mammals, including the dog, wolf, cat, lion, bear, seal, etc.: opposed to HERBIVORE **2.** a plant that uses insects for its food

car·niv·o·rous (kär niv′ə rəs) *adj.* [< L. < *caro* (see CARNAGE) + *vorare*, to eat] **1.** *a*) flesh-eating: opposed to HERBIVOROUS *b*) insect-eating, as certain plants **2.** of the carnivores —**car·niv′o·rous·ly** *adv.* —**car·niv′o·rous·ness** *n.*

CARIBOU
(40–55 in. high at shoulder)

Car·ol (kar′əl) *var. of:* **1.** CAROLINE **2.** CHARLES

car·ol (kar′əl) *n.* [< OFr. < L. < Gr. < *choros*, dance + *aulein*, to play on the flute] a song of joy or praise; esp., a Christmas song —*vi.* -**oled** or -**olled**, -**ol·ing** or -**ol·ling** **1.** to sing in joy; warble **2.** to sing carols, esp. Christmas carols —*vt.* **1.** to sing (a tune, etc.) **2.** to praise in song —**car′ol·er, car′ol·ler** *n.*

Car·o·li·na¹ (kar′ə li′nə) [L. fem. adj. of *Carolus* (see CARO-LINE), in honor of CHARLES I] English colony including what is now N.Carolina, S.Carolina, Ga., & N Fla. —**the Carolinas** N.Carolina & S.Carolina

Ca·ro·li·na² (kä′rô lē′nä) city in NE Puerto Rico, near San Juan: pop. 95,000

Car·o·line (kar′ə līn′, -lən) [G. & Fr. < It. *Carolina*, fem. < ML. *Carolus*, CHARLES] a feminine name —*adj.* of Charles I or Charles II of England or the period in which they lived

Caroline Islands group of islands in the W Pacific: see Trust Territory of the PACIFIC ISLANDS

Car·o·lin·gi·an (kar′ə lin′jē ən) *adj.* designating or of the second Frankish dynasty, founded in 751 A.D. by a son of Charles MARTEL —*n.* a member of this dynasty

Car·o·lin·i·an (kar′ə lin′ē ən) *adj.* of North Carolina or South Carolina —*n.* a native or inhabitant of North Carolina or South Carolina

Car·o·lyn (kar′ə lin) *var. of* CAROLINE

car·om (kar′əm) *n.* [< Fr. < Sp. *carambola*] **1.** *Billiards* a shot in which the cue ball hits the two object balls, one after the other ☆**2.** a hitting and rebounding, as of a ball striking a surface — ☆*vi.* **1.** to make a carom **2.** to hit and rebound

car·o·tene (kar′ə tēn′) *n.* [< L. *carota*, CARROT + -ENE] any of three red or orange-colored hydrocarbons, C₄₀H₅₆, found in carrots and some other vegetables, and changed into vitamin A in the body: also **car′o·tin** (-tin)

ca·rot·e·noid, ca·rot·i·noid (kə rät′'n oid′) *n.* any of several red and yellow pigments related to and including carotene —*adj.* **1.** of or like carotene **2.** of the carotenoids

ca·rot·id (kə rät′id) *adj.* [Gr. *karōtides*, the carotids < *karoun*, to plunge into sleep: compressing of these arteries causes unconsciousness] designating, of, or near either of the two principal arteries, one on each side of the neck, that carry the blood to the head —*n.* a carotid artery

ca·rous·al (kə rou′zəl) *n. same as* CAROUSE

ca·rouse (kə rouz′) *vi.* -**roused′**, -**rous′ing** [< Fr. < G. *gar aus*(*trinken*), (to drink) up entirely] to drink much alcoholic liquor, esp. along with others having a noisy, merry time —*n.* a noisy, merry drinking party —**ca·rous′er** *n.*

car·ou·sel (kar′ə sel′, -zel′) *n.* ☆*same as* CARROUSEL

carp¹ (kärp) *n., pl.* **carp, carps:** *see* PLURAL, II, D, 2 [OFr. *carpe* < Gmc. *carpa*] **1.** any of a group of edible freshwater fishes living in ponds or lakes **2.** any of various similar or related fishes, as the goldfish

carp² (kärp) *vi.* [< ON. *karpa*, to brag] to find fault in a petty or nagging way —**carp′er** *n.*

-carp (kärp) [< Gr. *karpos*, fruit] *a combining form meaning* fruit [*endocarp*]

car·pal (kär′pəl) *adj.* [ModL. *carpalis*] of the carpus —*n.* a bone of the carpus: also **car·pa′le** (-pā′lē), *pl.* -**li·a** (-lē ə)

Car·pa·thi·an Mountains (kär pā′thē ən) mountain system in C Europe, extending from S Poland into NE Romania: also **Car·pa′thi·ans**

‡**car·pe di·em** (kär′pe dē′em, dī′-) [L., lit., seize the day] make the most of present opportunities

car·pel (kär′pəl) *n.* [ModL. dim. < Gr. *karpos*, fruit] a simple pistil of a flower, or any of the segments of a compound pistil: it is the part in which the seeds grow —**car′pel·lar′y** (-pə ler′ē) *adj.* —**car′pel·late′** (-pə lāt′) *adj.*

CARPEL

car·pen·ter (kär′pən tər) *n.* [Anglo-Fr. < LL. *carpentarius* < L. *carpentum*, a cart < Gaul.] a workman who builds and repairs wooden articles, buildings, etc. —*vi.* to do a carpenter's work —*vt.* to make or repair as by carpentry

car·pen·try (-trē) *n.* the work or trade of a carpenter

car·pet (kär′pit) *n.* [< OFr. < ML. *car-*

pita, woolen cloth < L. pp. of *carpere*, to card: see EXCERPT] **1.** a heavy fabric for covering a floor, stairs, etc. **2.** anything that covers like a carpet [a *carpet* of snow] —*vt.* to cover as with a carpet —**on the carpet 1.** under consideration **2.** being, or about to be, scolded or criticized

car·pet·bag (-bag′) *n.* an old-fashioned type of traveling bag, made of carpeting —☆*vi.* -**bagged′**, -**bag′ging** to act as a carpet-bagger

☆**car·pet·bag·ger** (-bag′ər) *n.* [< the *carpetbags* they often carried] a Northern politician or adventurer who went South after the Civil War to profit from the confusion there

carpet beetle (or **bug**) a small beetle whose larvae feed on furs and woolens, esp. carpets

car·pet·ing (-iŋ) *n.* carpets or carpet fabric

☆**carpet sweeper** a device with a revolving brush, pushed by hand for sweeping up dirt from carpets and rugs

-car·pic (kär′pik) *same as* -CARPOUS

carp·ing (kär′piŋ) *adj.* tending to carp, or find fault; captious —see SYN. at CRITICAL —**carp′ing·ly** *adv.*

car·po- [< Gr. *karpos*, fruit] *a combining form meaning* fruit, seeds

☆**car pool** an arrangement by a group to take turns in using their cars to drive the group to work, school, etc.

☆**car·port** (kär′pôrt′) *n.* a shelter for an automobile, consisting of a roof reaching out from the side of a building, sometimes with an additional wall

-car·pous (kär′pəs) [< Gr. *karpos*, fruit] *a combining form meaning* fruited; having (a certain number of) fruits or (a certain kind of) fruit

car·pus (kär′pəs) *n., pl.* -**pi** (-pī) [ModL. < Gr. *karpos*, wrist] the wrist, or the wrist bones

car·rack (kar′ək) *n.* [< OFr. < Sp. < Ar. pl. of *qurqūr*, merchant ship] *same as* GALLEON

car·ra·geen, car·ra·gheen (kar′ə gēn′) *n.* [< *Carragheen*, Ireland] a brownish-purple seaweed found on rocky shores of N Europe and N. America: used in jellies, lotions, etc.

Car·ra·ra (kə rä′rə) city in NW Italy: a fine, white marble (**Carrara marble**) is quarried in nearby mountains: pop. 67,000

car·rel, car·rell (kar′əl) *n.* [< ML. *carula*, small study in a cloister] a small enclosure in a library, for privacy in studying or reading

car·riage (kar′ij; *for 2, usually* kar′ē-ij) *n.* [< Anglo-Fr. < *carier*, CARRY] **1.** a carrying; transportation **2.** the cost of carrying **3.** manner of carrying the head and body; posture [a man of stately *carriage*] **4.** *a)* a four-wheeled passenger vehicle, usually horse-drawn *b) same as* BABY CARRIAGE **5.** a wheeled support [a gun *carriage*] **6.** a moving part (as on a typewriter) for supporting and shifting something

CARREL

car·rick bend (kar′ik) a kind of knot for joining two ropes

Car·rie (kar′ē) [< CAROLINE] a feminine name

car·ri·er (kar′ē ər) *n.* **1.** a person or thing that carries something [a mailman, paperboy, bus, and airplane are all *carriers*] **2.** one in the transportation business **3.** a messenger or porter **4.** something in or on which something else is carried or conducted, as a water conduit **5.** *same as* AIRCRAFT CARRIER **6.** a person or animal that carries and passes on disease germs, esp. a person who is himself immune to the germs **7.** *Electronics* the steady transmitted wave whose strength, frequency, etc. are varied by the signal

carrier pigeon 1. a homing pigeon used to carry written messages fastened to its leg **2.** any of a breed of large pigeons with big wattles

car·ri·ole (kar′ē ōl′) *n. same as* CARIOLE

car·ri·on (kar′ē ən) *n.* [< Anglo-Fr., ult. < L. *caro:* see CAR-NAGE] **1.** the decaying flesh of a dead body **2.** anything very repulsive —*adj.* **1.** of or like carrion **2.** feeding on carrion [a *carrion* crow]

carrion crow the common crow of Europe

Car·roll (kar′əl), **Lewis** *pen name of* Charles Lutwidge DODGSON

car·rom (kar′əm) *n., vi. same as* CAROM

car·rot (kar′ət) *n.* [< Fr. < L. < Gr. *karōton*] **1.** a plant of the parsley family, with a fleshy, orange-red root eaten as a vegetable **2.** the root

car·rot·y (-ē) *adj.* orange-red, like carrots

car·rou·sel (kar′ə sel′, -zel′) *n.* [Fr. < It. dial. *carusiello*, prob. < *carro*, CAR] ☆a merry-go-round

car·ry (kar′ē) *vt.* **-ried, -ry·ing** [< Anglo-Fr. *carier* < VL. *carricare:* see CHARGE] **1.** to hold or support while moving /help me *carry* this box out/ **2.** to take from one place to another; transport, as in a vehicle /ships *carrying* oil/ **3.** to hold, and direct the motion of; convey /a pipe *carrying* water/ **4.** to cause to go; lead /ambition that *carried* him to the top/ **5.** to transmit /air *carries* sound/ **6.** to transfer or extend /to *carry* a pipe to a sewer/ **7.** to transfer (a figure, entry, etc.) from one column, time, etc. to the next **8.** to bear the weight of /this wall helps *carry* the roof/ **9.** to be pregnant with **10.** to have as a quality, consequence, etc. /to *carry* a guarantee/ **11.** to keep with one /to *carry* a watch/ **12.** to hold or conduct (oneself) in a specified way ☆**13.** to include as part of its contents or program: said of a newspaper, TV station, etc. **14.** to have or keep on a list or register **15.** to capture (a fortress, etc.) **16.** to win over or influence (a group) **17.** *a)* to win (an election, argument, etc.) *b)* to gain a majority of the votes in (a district, state, etc.) **18.** *Commerce a)* to keep in stock /do you *carry* textbooks?/ *b)* to keep on one's account books, etc. **19.** *Music* to sing the notes of (a melody or part) accurately /he can't *carry* a tune/ —*vi.* **1.** to act as a bearer, conductor, etc. /he'll fetch and *carry* for you/ **2.** to have or cover a range /her voice *carries* well/ **3.** to have an intended effect **4.** to win approval /the motion *carried*/ —*n., pl.* **-ries** **1.** the range or distance covered by a gun, golf ball, etc. **2.** a carrying ☆**3.** a portage between two bodies of water **3.** a carrying —**be** (or **get**) **carried away** to be moved by such strong feelings that one does not think clearly —**carry forward** to make progress with —**carry off** **1.** to kill /disease *carries off* many/ **2.** to win (a prize, etc.) **3.** to handle (a situation), esp. with success —**carry on** **1.** to engage in; conduct **2.** to continue as before **3.** [Colloq.] to behave in a wild, childish, or improper way —**carry out** **1.** to put (plans, etc.) into practice **2.** to get done; accomplish —**carry over** **1.** to have or be remaining **2.** to transfer or hold over **3.** to postpone; continue —**carry through** **1.** to get done; accomplish **2.** to keep (a person) going; sustain

☆**car·ry·all**[1] (-ôl′) *n.* [< Fr. *carriole* (see CARIOLE)] a light, covered carriage with seats for several people

☆**car·ry·all**[2] (-ôl′) *n.* a large bag, basket, etc.

☆**carrying charge** interest paid on the amount still owed for something bought on a charge account

car·ry·ings-on (kar′ē iŋz än′) *n.pl.* [Colloq.] wild behavior

car·ry-on (kar′ē än′) *adj.* designating luggage designed to be carried onto an airplane by a passenger, esp. if small enough to fit under an airplane seat —*n.* such a piece of luggage

☆**car·ry·out** (kar′ē out′) *adj.* designating a service, as of a restaurant, by which food and beverages may be taken out to be eaten and drunk elsewhere

car·ry-o·ver (-ō′vər) *n.* something carried or left over

car·sick (kär′sik′) *adj.* nauseated from riding in an automobile, bus, etc. —**car′sick′ness** *n.*

Car·son (kär′s'n) [after Kit CARSON] city in SW Calif.: suburb of Los Angeles: pop. 71,000

Car·son (kär′s'n) **1. Kit** (kit), (born *Christopher Carson*) 1809–68; U.S. frontiersman **2. Rachel** (**Louise**), 1907–64; U.S. biologist & science writer

Carson City [after Kit CARSON] capital of Nev., near Lake Tahoe: pop. 15,000

cart (kärt) *n.* [< ON. *kartr* < IE. base *ger-*, to twist] **1.** a small, strong, two-wheeled vehicle drawn by a horse, etc. **2.** a small, wheeled vehicle, drawn or pushed by hand —*vt., vi.* to carry or deliver, as in a cart, truck, etc. —**put the cart before the horse** to do things backwards —**cart′er** *n.*

cart·age (kär′tij) *n.* **1.** the act or work of carting **2.** the charges made for carting

Car·ta·ge·na (kär′tə jē′nə, -gä′-; *Sp.* kär′tä hā′nä) **1.** seaport in NW Colombia, on the Caribbean: pop. 319,000 **2.** seaport in NE Spain, on the Mediterranean: pop. 147,000

carte blanche (kärt′ blänsh′, blänch′) *pl.* **cartes blanches** (kärts′ blänsh′, kärt blän′shəz) [Fr., lit., white (i.e., blank) card] **1.** full authority **2.** freedom to do as one thinks best

car·tel (kär tel′) *n.* [Fr. < It. *cartello*, dim. of *carta*, CARD[1]] **1.** a written challenge, as to a duel **2.** a written agreement between nations at war, esp. as to exchange of prisoners **3.** [G. *kartell* < Fr.] a group of business firms who have established a national or international monopoly in order to fix prices and get rid of competition —see **SYN.** at MONOPOLY

Car·ter (kär′tər), **Jim·my** (jim′ē) (full name *James Earl Carter, Jr.*) 1924– ; 39th president of the U.S. (1977–)

Car·te·sian (kär tē′zhən) *adj.* [< *Cartesius*, Latinized form of DESCARTES] of Descartes or his ideas, methods, etc.

Cartesian coordinates a pair of numbers that locate a point by its distances from two lines intersecting usually at right angles: each distance is measured along a parallel to the other line

Car·thage (kär′thij) ancient city-state in N Africa, founded by the Phoenicians near the site of modern Tunis: destroyed by the Romans, 146 B.C. —**Car′tha·gin′i·an** (-thə jin′ē ən) *adj., n.*

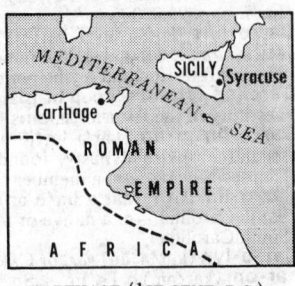

CARTHAGE (1ST CENT. B.C.)

Car·thu·sian (kär thōō′zhən, -thyōō′-) *n.* [< ML. < L. name for Chartreuse] a monk or nun of a very strict order founded at Chartreuse, France, in 1084 —*adj.* of the Carthusians

Car·tier (kár tyā′), **Jacques** (zhäk) 1491–1557; Fr. explorer in North America

car·ti·lage (kärt′'l ij) *n.* [OFr. < L. *cartilago*] **1.** a tough, elastic, whitish tissue forming part of the skeleton; gristle /the tough part of the outer ear is *cartilage*/ **2.** a part or structure consisting of cartilage

car·ti·lag·i·nous (kärt′'l aj′ə nəs) *adj.* **1.** of or like cartilage; gristly **2.** having a skeleton made up mainly of cartilage

car·tog·ra·phy (kär täg′rə fē) *n.* [< Fr. < ML. *carta* (see CARD[1]) + -GRAPHY] the art or work of making maps or charts —**car·tog′ra·pher** *n.* —**car·to·graph·ic** (kär′tə graf′ik) *adj.*

car·ton (kärt′'n) *n.* [Fr. < It. *cartone* < *carta:* see CARD[1]] **1.** a cardboard box or container **2.** a full carton or its contents

car·toon (kär tōōn′) *n.* [Fr. *carton* < It. *cartone:* see prec.] **1.** a drawing that is a caricature, often a satirical one, of some news event, person, etc. **2.** the original full-size sketch of a design or picture which is then copied in a fresco, tapestry, etc. **3.** *a)* a humorous drawing, often with a caption ☆*b)* same as COMIC STRIP ☆**4.** same as ANIMATED CARTOON —☆*vt.* to draw a cartoon of —☆*vi.* to draw cartoons —**car·toon′ist** *n.*

car·tridge (kär′trij) *n.* [altered < Fr. *cartouche* < It. < *carta:* see CARD[1]] **1.** a tube of cardboard, metal, etc. containing the charge and primer, and usually the bullet or shot, for a firearm **2.** a small container holding a supply of material for insertion into a larger device /an ink *cartridge* for a pen/ **3.** a protected roll of camera film **4.** a replaceable unit in a phonograph pickup, that contains the stylus, or needle

cartridge clip a metal container for cartridges, inserted in certain types of firearms

cart·wheel (kärt′hwēl′, -wēl′) *n.* **1.** a kind of handspring performed sidewise ☆**2.** [Old Slang] a silver dollar

car·un·cle (kar′əŋ k'l, kə ruŋ′k'l) *n.* [< Fr. < L. *caruncula*, dim. of *caro*, flesh] **1.** a growth of flesh, as the comb of a rooster **2.** a swelling at the base of a seed

Ca·ru·so (kə rōō′sō; *It.* kä rōō′zō), **En·ri·co** (en rē′kō) 1873–1921; It. operatic tenor

carve (kärv) *vt.* **carved, carv′ing** [< OE. *ceorfan* < IE. base *gerebh-*, to scratch] **1.** to make or shape by or as by cutting, chipping, etc. /carve a statue, *carve* a career/ **2.** to decorate the surface of with cut designs **3.** to divide by cutting; slice /to *carve* meat/ —*vi.* **1.** to carve statues or designs **2.** to carve meat —**carv′er** *n.*

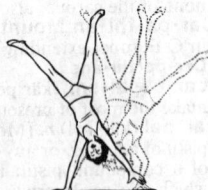

CARTWHEEL

carv·en (kär′v'n) *adj.* [Archaic or Poet.] carved

Car·ver (kär′vər), **George Washington** 1864–1943; U.S. botanist & chemist

carv·ing (kär′viŋ) *n.* **1.** the work or art of a person who carves **2.** a carved figure or design

carving knife a large knife for carving meat, used with a large, two-tined fork (**carving fork**)

☆**car·wash** (kär′wôsh′, -wäsh′) *n.* a place where automobiles are washed as a business, often with automatic equipment

car·y·at·id (kar′ē at′id) *n., pl.* **-ids, -i·des′** (-ə dēz′) [< L. < Gr. *karyatides*, priestesses at Karyai, in Macedonia] a supporting column that has the form of a woman in draped robes

car·y·o- *same as* KARYO-

ca·sa·ba (kə sä′bə) *n.* [< *Kassaba*, town near Smyrna, Asia Minor] a cultivated melon with a hard, yellow rind and sweet, usually white flesh

Ca·sa·blan·ca (kas′ə blaŋ′kə, kä′sə bläŋ′kə) seaport in NW Morocco: pop. 1,177,000

Ca·sals (kə sälz′, -salz′), **Pa·blo** (päb′lō) 1876–1973; Sp. cellist who exiled himself from Spain

Ca·sa·no·va (kas′ə nō′və; *It.* kä′zä nô′vä), **Gio·van·ni** (**Jacopo**) (jô vän′nē) 1725–98; It. adventurer, noted for his *Memoirs*

cas·bah (käz′bä, kas′-) *n.* [Fr. < Ar. dial. + *qasba* < Ar. *qasaba*, fortress] **1.** in N Africa, a fortress **2.** the old, crowded quarter of a N African city, esp. [C-] of Algiers

cas·cade (kas kād′) *n.* [< It. *cascata* < L. *cadere*, to fall] **1.** a small, steep waterfall, esp. one of a series **2.** a shower of sparks, or rippling fall of lace, etc. —*vt., vi.* **-cad′ed, -cad′ing** to fall or drop in a cascade

Cascade Range [after cascades on the Columbia River] mountain range extending from N Calif., through Oreg. and Wash., into British Columbia

☆**cas·car·a** (kas ker′ə) *n.* [Sp. *cáscara*, bark] **1.** a small buckthorn of the U.S. Pacific coast **2.** a laxative made from its bark: in full, **cascara sa·gra·da** (sə grä′də, -grä′-)

case[1] (kās) *n.* [< OFr. *cas*, an event < L. *casus*, an accident, pp. of *cadere*, to fall < IE. base *kad-*, to fall] **1.** an example or instance [a *case* of measles] **2.** a person being treated or helped, as by a doctor or social worker **3.** any matter undergoing observation, study, etc., as by the police [ten *cases* of stolen cars] **4.** a statement of the facts, as in a law court [the *case* for the defendant] **5.** convincing arguments [she has no *case*] **6.** a lawsuit **7.** the actual state of affairs; real condition [such was not the *case*] **8.** *Gram. a)* an inflected form taken by a noun, pronoun, or adjective to show its relationship to other words in the sentence [*"him"* is the objective *case* of "he"] *b)* such relationship —*vt.* **cased, cas′ing** ☆[Slang] to look (a house, store, etc.) over carefully, esp. for an intended robbery —see SYN. at INSTANCE —**in any case** anyhow —**in case** in the event that; if —**in case of** in the event of —**in no case** by no means; never

case[2] (kās) *n.* [< ONormFr. < L. *capsa*, a box < *capere*, to hold: for IE. base see HAVE] **1.** a container, as a box, sheath, folder, etc. **2.** a protective cover [a *watchcase*] **3.** a full box or its contents [we drank two *cases* of soda pop] **4.** a set or pair [a *case* of pistols] **5.** a frame, as for a window **6.** *Printing* a shallow tray in which type is kept: the **upper case** is for capitals, the **lower case** for small letters —*vt.* **cased, cas′ing 1.** to put in a container **2.** to cover or enclose

ca·se·fy (kā′sə fī′) *vt., vi.* **-fied′, -fy′ing** [< L. *caseus*, CHEESE[1] + -FY] to make or become like cheese

case·hard·en (kās′här′d'n) *vt.* **1.** *Metallurgy* to form a hard, thin surface on (an iron alloy) **2.** to make callous or unfeeling —**case′hard′ened** *adj.*

case history (or **study**) collected information about an individual or group, for use in sociological, medical, or psychiatric studies

ca·se·in (kā′sē in, kā′sēn) *n.* [< L. *caseus*, CHEESE[1] + -IN[1]] one of the chief proteins of milk, that is the basis of cheese: used in making plastics, glues, etc.

case knife 1. *same as* SHEATH KNIFE **2.** a table knife

case law law based on earlier court decisions or on precedents: distinguished from STATUTE LAW

case·load (kās′lōd′) *n.* the number of cases being handled by a court, a social or welfare agency, a caseworker, etc.

case·mate (kās′māt′) *n.* [Fr. < It. < Gr. *chasmata*, pl. of *chasma*, CHASM] a protected enclosure with openings for guns, as in a fortress or on a warship —**case′mat′ed** *adj.*

case·ment (kās′mənt) *n.* [< OFr. *encassement*, a frame: see CASE[2]] **1.** a hinged window frame that opens outward: a **casement window** often has two such frames, opening like French doors **2.** a casing; covering —**case′ment·ed** *adj.*

ca·se·ous (kā′sē əs) *adj.* [< L. *caseus*, CHEESE[1]] of or like cheese

ca·sern, ca·serne (kə zurn′) *n.* [< Fr. < Pr. *cazerna*, small hut < LL. *quaterna*, four each < *quattuor*, FOUR] formerly, a military barracks in a fortified town

case·work (kās′wurk′) *n.* social work in which the worker studies cases of personal or family problems and helps to find solutions —**case′work′er** *n.*

cash[1] (kash) *n.* [< Fr. *caisse*, money box < Pr. < L. *capsa*: see CASE[2]] **1.** money that a person actually has; esp., ready money **2.** bills and coins **3.** money, a check, etc. paid at the time of purchase [to buy a car for *cash* instead of on credit] —*vt.* to give or get cash for [to *cash* a check] —*adj.* of, for, or requiring cash [a *cash* sale] —☆**cash in 1.** to exchange for cash **2.** [Slang] to die —☆**cash in on** to get profit or profitable use from

cash[2] (kash) *n., pl.* **cash** [Port. *caixa* < Tamil *kasu* < Sans. *karṣa*] any of several Chinese or Indian coins of small value

☆**cash-and-car·ry** (kash′ən kar′ē) *adj.* with cash payments and no deliveries

cash·book (-book′) *n.* a book containing a record of all money received and paid

cash discount a discount that a purchaser gets for paying his bill within a certain period

cash·ew (kash′ōō, kə shōō′) *n.* [< Fr. < Port. < Tupi *acajú*] **1.** a tropical tree bearing edible, kidney-shaped nuts **2.** the nut: also **cashew nut**

cash flow the pattern of expenses and income of a company, government, etc., that determines how much cash, if any, is available at any given time

cash·ier[1] (ka shir′) *n.* [< Fr. *caissier*] one who takes in or pays out money, as in a bank, store, etc.

cash·ier[2] (ka shir′) *vt.* [< MDu. < OFr. < LL. *cassare* (see QUASH[1]) & L. *quassare* (see QUASH[2])] to punish by removing in disgrace from a position of command, trust, etc.

☆**cashier's check** a check drawn by a bank on its own funds and signed by the cashier

CASHEW
(blossom & nut)

cash·mere (kazh′mir, kash′-) *n.* [< KASHMIR] **1.** a fine carded wool from goats of Kashmir and Tibet **2.** a soft, twilled cloth of this or similar wool **3.** a cashmere shawl, sweater, etc.

☆**cash register** a business machine, usually with a drawer for money, that registers and shows the amount of each sale

cas·ing (kās′iŋ) *n.* **1.** a protective covering; specif., ☆*a)* a membrane used as the skin of a wiener, salami, etc. *b)* the outer part of a rubber tire not counting the tread, ☆*c)* the steel pipe used to line an oil or gas well ☆**2.** a frame, as of a window

ca·si·no (kə sē′nō) *n., pl.* **-nos** [It., dim. of *casa*, house < L., hut] **1.** a room or building for dancing, or, esp., gambling **2.** *same as* CASSINO

cask (kask, käsk) *n.* [< Fr. *casque* < Sp. *casco*, ult. < L. *quassare*: see QUASH[2]] **1.** a barrel of any size, made of staves, esp. one for liquids **2.** the contents of a full cask; barrelful

cas·ket (kas′kit) *n.* [prob. < OFr. dim. of *casse* (see CASE[2])] **1.** a small box or chest, as for valuables ☆**2.** a coffin —*vt.* to put into a casket

Cas·pi·an Sea (kas′pē ən) inland sea between Caucasia and Asiatic U.S.S.R. —**Cas′pi·an** *adj.*

casque (kask) *n.* [Fr.: see CASK] a helmet —**casqued** (kaskt) *adj.*

cas·sa·ba (kə sä′bə) *n. same as* CASABA

Cas·san·dra (kə san′drə) *Gr. Myth.* Priam's daughter: Apollo gave her the power to make prophecies but decreed that no one should believe them —*n.* a person whose warnings of misfortune are ignored

Cas·satt (kə sat′), **Mary** 1845–1926; U.S. painter

CASPIAN SEA

---

fat, āpe, cär, ten, ēven, is, bīte; gō, hôrn, tōōl, look; oil, out; up, fur; get; joy; yet; chin; she; thin, then; zh, leisure; ŋ, ring; ə for *a* in *ago*, *e* in *agent*, *i* in *sanity*, *o* in *comply*, *u* in *focus*; ′ as in *able* (ā′b'l); Fr. bâl; ë, Fr. coeur; ö, Fr. feu; Fr. mon; ô, Fr. coq; ü, Fr. duc; r, Fr. cri; H, G. ich; kh, G. doch; ‡foreign; ☆ Americanism; < derived from. See inside front cover.

cas·sa·va (kə säʹvə) *n.* [< Fr. < Sp. < native Indian *casávi*]
1. any of several tropical American plants with edible starchy
roots **2.** a starch taken from the root, used to make bread and
tapioca

cas·se·role (kasʹə rōlʹ) *n.* [Fr., dim. of *casse*, a bowl < Pr. <
VL. < Gr. dim. of *kyathos*, a bowl] **1.** an earthenware or glass
baking dish, often with a cover, in which food can be cooked
and then served **2.** the food baked and served in such a dish,
usually a mixture of meat or fish with rice, vegetables, macaroni,
etc.

cas·sette (ka setʹ, kə-) *n.* [Fr., dim. < ONormFr. *casse*, a
CASE²] **1.** a case with roll film in it, for
loading a camera quickly and easily **2.**
a similar case with magnetic tape, for
use in a tape recorder

cas·sia (kashʹə) *n.* [< L. < Gr. *kasia*,
kind of cinnamon < Heb. *qeṣīʹāh*] **1.**
a) the bark (**cassia bark**) of a tree native to southeastern Asia: used as a
source of cinnamon *b)* this tree **2.** *a)*
any of several plants of the legume
family, common in tropical countries:
the pods (**cassia pods**) of some of these
plants have a pulp (**cassia pulp**) used as
a mild laxative; from others the drug
senna is extracted *b)* cassia pods *c)*
cassia pulp

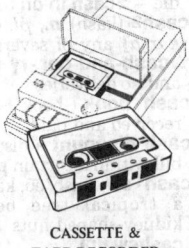

CASSETTE &
TAPE RECORDER

cas·si·mere (kasʹə mirʹ) *n.* [var. of CASHMERE] a woolen
cloth, twilled or plain, used for men's suits

cas·si·no (kə sēʹnō) *n.* [see CASINO] a simple card game for
two to four players

Cas·si·o·pe·ia (kasʹē ə pēʹə) **1.** *Gr. Myth.* the mother of
Andromeda **2.** a N constellation near Andromeda

Cassiopeia's Chair five stars in the constellation Cassiopeia,
supposedly outlining a chair

Cas·si·us (Longinus) (kashʹəs, kasʹē əs), (Gaius) ?–42 B.C.;
Rom. general & conspirator against Caesar

cas·sock (kasʹək) *n.* [< Fr. < Per. *kazhāghand*, a jacket < *kazh*,
raw silk] a long, closefitting garment, usually
black, worn by some clergymen, choristers, etc.

cas·so·war·y (kasʹə werʹē) *n., pl.* **-war·ies**
[Malay *kasuārī*] a large, flightless bird of Australia and New Guinea, somewhat like the ostrich, but smaller

CASSOCK

cast (kast) *vt.* **cast, cast·ing** [< ON. *kasta*, to
throw] **1.** to throw with force; fling; hurl **2.**
to deposit (a ballot or vote) **3.** *a)* to cause to
fall or turn; direct [to *cast* one's eyes on a
thing] *b)* to give forth [to *cast* light, gloom,
etc.] **4.** to throw out or drop (a net, anchor,
etc.) at the end of a rope or cable **5.** to throw
out (a fly, etc.) at the end of a fishing line **6.** to
draw (lots) or shake (dice) out of a container **7.** to throw off;
shed [the snake *casts* its skin] **8.** to add up (accounts) **9.** to
calculate (a horoscope, tides, etc.) **10.** to arrange in some form
or system; formulate [to *cast* a dictionary entry] **11.** *a)* to form
(molten metal, plastic, etc.) by pouring or pressing into a mold
b) to make by such a method [to *cast* a pair of bookends] **12.**
a) to choose actors for (a play or movie) *b)* to select (an actor)
for (a role) —*vi.* **1.** to throw dice **2.** to throw out a fly, etc. on
a fishing line —*n.* **1.** a casting; a throw; specif., *a)* a throw of
dice; also, the number thrown *b)* a turn of the eye; glance;
look *c)* a throw of a fishing line, net, etc. **2.** a quantity or
thing cast in a certain way; specif., *a)* something formed in a
mold, as a statue; also, the mold *b)* a mold taken of an object
c) a plaster form to keep a broken arm, leg, etc. in place while it
heals *d)* the set of actors in a play or movie **3.** the form in
which a thing is cast; specif., *a)* an appearance [the handsome
cast of his face] *b)* kind; quality [of an aristocratic *cast*] *c)* a
tinge; shade [a reddish *cast*] *d)* a turn or twist to one side *e)*
a slight turning in or out of the eye; squint —see SYN. at THROW
—**cast about 1.** to search (*for*) **2.** to make plans; devise —
cast aside (or **away**) to discard; abandon —**cast back** to refer
to something past —**cast down 1.** to turn downward **2.** to
sadden; discourage —**cast off 1.** to discard; disown **2.** to set
free **3.** to free a ship from a dock, quay, etc., as by releasing the
lines **4.** *Knitting* to make the last row of stitches —**cast on**
Knitting to make the first row of stitches —**cast out** to force to
go away; expel —**cast up 1.** to throw up; vomit **2.** to turn
upward **3.** to add up; total **4.** to construct by digging [to *cast
up* earthworks]

cas·ta·nets (kasʹtə netsʹ) *n.pl.* [< Fr. < Sp. *castañeta*, dim. <
L. *castanea*, chestnut: from the shape] a pair of
small, hollowed pieces of hard wood, ivory, etc.
held in the hand and clicked together in time to
music, esp. in Spanish dances

cast·a·way (kasʹtə wāʹ) *n.* **1.** a person or
thing cast out or off, esp. an outcast **2.** a shipwrecked person —*adj.* **1.** thrown away; discarded **2.** stranded, as by shipwreck

caste (kast) *n.* [Fr. < Port. *casta*, a breed < L.
castus, pure, orig. cut off: for IE. base see CAS-
TRATE] **1.** any of the distinct social classes into
which Hindus are born: castes were kept, by
tradition, from social dealings with one another,
but officially no distinctions now exist **2.** any exclusive social
class or group based on wealth, occupation, etc. **3.** any social
system in which the society is divided into such classes **4.** any
of the distinct types of social insects in a colony —**lose caste** to
lose the status or rank that upper classes usually have

CASTANETS

cas·tel·lat·ed (kasʹtə lātʹid) *adj.* [< ML. < L, *castellum*,
CASTLE] built with turrets and battlements, like a castle —**casʹ-
tel·laʹtion** *n.*

cast·er (kasʹtər) *n.* **1.** a person or thing that casts **2.** *a)* a
small bottle or container for serving vinegar, salt, etc. at the table ☆*b)* a stand for holding such containers **3.** a wheel or
freely rolling ball set in a swivel frame and attached to each leg
or bottom corner of a piece of furniture, etc. so that it can be
moved easily

cas·ti·gate (kasʹtə gātʹ) *vt.* **-gat·ed, -gat·ing** [< L. pp. of *castigare*, to purify, chastise < *castus*: see CASTE] to punish or
scold severely, esp. by criticizing publicly —**casʹti·gaʹtion** *n.*
—**casʹti·gaʹtor** *n.* —**casʹti·ga·toʹry** (-gə tôrʹē) *adj.*

Cas·tile (kas tēlʹ) region and former kingdom in N and C
Spain

Castile soap [< *Castile*,
where first made] [*also* c-
s-] a fine, mild, hard soap
made from olive oil and sodium hydroxide

Cas·til·ian (kas tilʹyən)
adj. of Castile, its people,
language, or culture —*n.* **1.**
a native or inhabitant of Castile **2.** the dialect spoken in
Castile, now the standard
form of Spanish

cast·ing (kasʹtiŋ) *n.* **1.** the
action of one that casts **2.**
anything, esp. of metal, that
has been cast in a mold **3.**
Zool. anything thrown off,
excreted, etc.

CASTILE (c. 12th cent.)

casting vote (or **voice**) the deciding vote cast by the presiding
officer to break a tie vote

cast-i·ron (kastʹīʹərn) *adj.* **1.** made of cast iron **2.** very
hard, rigid, strong, healthy, etc. [a *cast-iron* stomach]

cast iron a hard, brittle alloy of iron used for casting: it has a
high proportion of carbon

cas·tle (kasʹl) *n.* [< OE. & Anglo-Fr. < L. *castellum*, dim. of
castrum, fort] **1.** a large building or group of buildings fortified
with thick walls, turrets, and often a moat: castles were strong-
holds for noblemen in the Middle Ages **2.** any very large and
solid house like this **3.** *Chess* same as ROOK² —*vt.* **-tled, -tling**
1. to furnish with a castle **2.** *Chess* to move (a king) two
squares to either side and then, in the same move, set the castle
in the square skipped by the king —*vi.* *Chess* to castle a king

castle in the air an imaginary scheme that is not likely to come
true; daydream: also **castle in Spain**

cast·off (kastʹôfʹ) *adj.* thrown away; discarded —*n.* a person or
thing cast off

Cas·tor (kasʹtər) **1.** *Gr. & Rom. Myth.* the mortal twin of Pollux **2.** one of the two bright stars in the constellation Gemini

cas·tor¹ (kasʹtər) *n.* [< L. < Gr. *kastōr*, beaver] **1.** a
strong-smelling, oily substance obtained from the beaver, used
in making perfumes: also **cas·to·re·um** (-tôrʹē əm) **2.** a hat
of beaver or rabbit fur

cas·tor² (kasʹtər) *n.* same as CASTER (senses 2 & 3)

cas·tor-oil plant (kasʹtər oilʹ) a tropical plant with large,
beanlike seeds (**castor beans**) from which oil (**castor oil**) is extracted: this oil is used as a cathartic and lubricant

cas·trate (kasʹtrāt) *vt.* **-trat·ed, -trat·ing** [< L. *castratus*, pp.

of *castrare* < IE. base *kes-*, to cut] **1.** to remove the testicles of; emasculate; geld **2.** to cause to lose strength or meaning, as by removing important parts [a play *castrated* by the censors] **—cas·tra′tion** *n.*

Cas·tro (kas′trō; *Sp.* käs′trô), **Fi·del** (fē del′) 1927?- ; Cuban revolutionary leader; prime minister (1959–)

cast steel steel formed by casting, not by rolling or forging — **cast′-steel′** *adj.*

cas·u·al (kazh′ŏō wəl) *adj.* [< OFr. < LL. *casualis*, by chance < L. *casus*, chance: see CASE[1]] **1.** happening by chance; not planned [a *casual* visit] **2.** happening, active, etc. at irregular intervals; occasional [a *casual* worker] **3.** slight or superficial [a *casual* acquaintance] **4.** careless or nonchalant [a *casual* remark; a *casual* wave of the hand] **5.** *a)* informal or relaxed [a *casual* atmosphere] *b)* designed for informal occasions or use [*casual* clothes] **—n. 1.** one who does something only occasionally or temporarily, esp. a casual worker **2.** [*pl.*] shoes, clothes, etc. for informal occasions **3.** *Mil.* a person temporarily attached to a unit —see SYN. at ACCIDENTAL and RANDOM **—cas′u·al·ly** *adv.* **—cas′ual·ness** *n.*

cas·u·al·ty (kazh′əl tē, -ōō wəl-) *n., pl.* **-ties** [see prec.] **1.** an accident, esp. a fatal one **2.** a member of the armed forces killed, wounded, captured, etc. **3.** anyone hurt or killed in an accident **4.** anything lost or ruined by some unfortunate happening [his business was a *casualty* of the depression]

cas·u·ist (kazh′ŏō wist) *n.* [< Fr. < L. *casus*, CASE[1]] a person who is an expert in casuistry or uses it often **—cas′u·is′tic, cas′u·is′ti·cal** *adj.* **—cas′u·is′ti·cal·ly** *adv.*

cas·u·ist·ry (kazh′ŏō wis trē) *n., pl.* **-ries** [prec. + -RY] **1.** the deciding of questions of right and wrong in conduct by applying general principles of ethics **2.** clever but misleading or false reasoning, esp. about moral issues; sophistry

‡ca·sus bel·li (kā′səs bel′ī) [L.] an event causing war or used as an excuse to make war

cat (kat) *n., pl.* **cats, cat:** see PLURAL, II, D, 1 [OE.] **1.** any of a family of flesh-eating mammals, including the lion, tiger, leopard, etc.; specif., a small, lithe, soft-furred animal of this family, often kept as a pet or for killing mice **2.** a woman who makes spiteful remarks **3.** *same as* CAT-O'-NINE-TAILS **4.** a catfish ☆**5.** [C-] *same as* CATERPILLAR (tractor) ☆**6.** [Slang] *a)* a jazz musician or enthusiast *b)* any person, esp. a man **7.** *Naut.* tackle to hoist an anchor to the cathead **—vt. cat′ted, cat′ting** to hoist (an anchor) to the cathead **—let the cat out of the bag** to let a secret be found out

cat. 1. catalog **2.** catechism

cat·a- (kat′ə) [< Gr. *kata*, down] *a prefix meaning:* **1.** down, downward [*catabolism*] **2.** away, completely [*catalysis*] **3.** against [*catapult*] Also, before a vowel, **cat-**

ca·tab·o·lism (kə tab′ə liz'm) *n.* [< CATA- + Gr. *ballein*, to throw + -ISM] the process in a plant or animal by which living tissue is changed into waste products of a simpler composition; destructive metabolism: opposed to ANABOLISM **—cat·a·bol·ic** (kat′ə bäl′ik) *adj.* **—cat·a·bol′i·cal·ly** *adv.*

ca·tab·o·lize (-līz′) *vi., vt.* **-lized′, -liz′ing** to change by catabolism

cat·a·chre·sis (kat′ə krē′sis) *n., pl.* **-ses** (-sēz) [L. < Gr. < *kata-*, against + *chrēsthai*, to use] incorrect use of a word or words **—cat′a·chres′tic** (-kres′tik), **cat′a·chres′ti·cal** *adj.*

cat·a·clysm (kat′ə kliz'm) *n.* [< L. < Gr. < *kata-*, down + *klyzein*, to wash] **1.** a great flood; deluge **2.** any great upheaval or sudden, violent change, as an earthquake, war, etc. **— cat′a·clys′mic** (-kliz′mik), **cat′a·clys′mal** *adj.*

cat·a·comb (kat′ə kōm′) *n.* [< LL. *catacumba* < L. < *cata* (< Gr. *kata*), by + *tumba*, TOMB] any of a series of galleries in an underground burial place: *usually used in pl.*

cat·a·falque (kat′ə falk′, -fôlk′) *n.* [Fr. < It. < L. *cata* (< Gr. *kata*), by + *fala*, a scaffold] a wooden framework, usually draped, on which the body in a coffin is sometimes placed for a period before the funeral

Cat·a·lan (kat′'l an′, -'l ən) *adj.* of Catalonia, its people, or their language **—n. 1.** a native or inhabitant of Catalonia **2.** the Romance language of Catalonia, related to Provençal

cat·a·lep·sy (kat′'l ep′sē) *n.* [< LL. < Gr. *katalēpsis*, a seizing < *kata-*, down + *lambanein*, to seize] a condition in which a person suddenly loses consciousness and feeling for a time and the muscles become rigid: it may occur in epilepsy,

schizophrenia, etc. **—cat′a·lep′tic** *adj., n.*

☆**cat·a·lo** (kat′'l ō′) *n., pl.* **-loes′, -los′** [CAT(TLE) + (BUFF)ALO] an animal bred by crossing the American buffalo, or bison, with domestic cattle

cat·a·log, cat·a·logue (kat′'l ôg′, -äg′) *n.* [Fr. < LL. *catalogus*, list < Gr. < *kata*, down + *legein*, to count] a complete list; esp., ☆*a)* an alphabetical card file, as of the books in a library *b)* a list of things exhibited, articles for sale, school courses offered, etc., usually with some description and illustrations *c)* a book or pamphlet with such a list **—vt., vi. -loged′** or **-logued′, -log′ing** or **-logu′ing 1.** to enter in a catalog [to *catalog* a book] **2.** to make a catalog of [to *catalog* items for a rummage sale] **—cat′a·log′er** or **cat′a·logu′er, cat′a·log′ist** or **cat′a·logu′ist** *n.*

Cat·a·lo·ni·a (kat′'l ō′nē ə) region in NE Spain, on the Mediterranean **—Cat′a·lo′ni·an** *adj., n.*

☆**ca·tal·pa** (kə tal′pə) *n.* [< AmInd. (Creek) *kutuhlpa*] a tree of America and Asia with large, heart-shaped leaves, showy, trumpet-shaped flowers, and slender, beanlike pods

ca·tal·y·sis (kə tal′ə sis) *n., pl.* **-ses′** (-sēz′) [Gr. *katalysis*, dissolution < *kata-*, down + *lyein*, to loose] the speeding up or, sometimes, slowing down of a chemical reaction by adding a substance which itself is not changed chemically

cat·a·lyst (kat′'l ist) *n.* **1.** any substance that causes catalysis **2.** a person or thing that causes something to happen or speed up [*Uncle Tom's Cabin* was a *catalyst* in the antislavery movement] **—cat′a·lyt′ic** *adj., n.* **—cat′a·lyt′i·cal·ly** *adv.*

catalytic converter a device that is part of the exhaust system of an automobile or truck and contains a chemical catalyst to reduce the gases that pollute the air

cat·a·lyze (kat′'l īz′) *vt.* **-lyzed′, -lyz′ing** to change or bring about as a catalyst

cat·a·ma·ran (kat′ə mə ran′) *n.* [Tamil *kattumaram* < *kattu*, tie + *maram*, log, tree] **1.** a narrow log raft or float propelled by sails or paddles **2.** a boat with two parallel hulls

cat·a·mount (kat′ə mount′) *n.* [< CAT + obs. *a*, of + MOUNT(AIN)] any of various wildcats; esp., ☆*a)* the puma; cougar ☆*b)* the lynx

Ca·ta·nia (kä tä′nyä; *E.* kə tän′yə) seaport on the E coast of Sicily: pop. 407,000

cat·a·pult (kat′ə pult′, -poolt′) *n.* [< L. < Gr. *katapeltēs* < *kata-*, down + *pallein*, to hurl] **1.** an ancient military device for throwing or shooting stones, spears, etc. ☆**2.** a slingshot **3.** a mechanism for launching an airplane, rocket, etc., as from a ship's deck **—vt.** to shoot from or as from a catapult; hurl **—vi.** to be catapulted; move quickly; leap [she *catapulted* into fame with just one novel]

cat·a·ract (kat′ə rakt′) *n.* [< L. *cataracta* < Gr. *kataraktēs* < *kata-*, down + *rhēgnynai*, to break] **1.** a large waterfall **2.** any strong flood or rush of water **3.** *a)* an eye disease in which the crystalline lens or its capsule becomes opaque, causing partial or total blindness *b)* the opaque area

ca·tarrh (kə tär′) *n.* [< Fr. < LL. < Gr. < *kata-*, down + *rhein*, to flow] a condition in which a mucous membrane, esp. of the nose or throat, becomes inflamed, causing a heavy flow of mucus: an old-fashioned term **—ca·tarrh′al, ca·tarrh′ous** *adj.*

ca·tas·tro·phe (kə tas′trə fē) *n.* [< L. < Gr. *katastrophē*, an overthrowing < *kata-*, down + *strephein*, to turn] **1.** a final scene of a drama, esp. of a tragedy, by which the plot is resolved **2.** a disastrous end **3.** any great and sudden loss, suffering, or damage; terrible disaster **4.** a total failure; fiasco **—cat·a·stroph·ic** (kat′ə sträf′ik) *adj.* **—cat′a·stroph′i·cal·ly** *adv.*

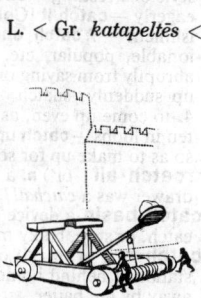

CATALPA
(tree, leaves
& pods)

CATAPULT

cat·a·ton·ic (kat′ə tän′ik) *adj.* [< CATA- + Gr. *tonos*, tension] of or in a condition of stupor in which the body remains in a fixed position

Ca·taw·ba (kə tô′bə) *n.* [after name of a Choctaw Indian tribe] [*often* c-] **1.** a reddish grape of the eastern U.S. **2.** a wine made from this grape

☆**cat·bird** (kat′burd′) *n.* a slate-gray N. American songbird with a black crown and tail: its call sounds like the mewing of a cat

cat·boat (-bōt′) *n.* a sailboat with a single sail on a mast set forward in the bow

☆**cat brier** a thorny climbing vine of the lily family, with oval leaves and black berries

cat burglar [Slang] a burglar who climbs up to openings in upper stories, roofs, etc. to enter

cat·call (-kôl′) *n.* a shrill shout or whistle expressing contempt or disapproval, as of a speaker, actor, etc. —*vt., vi.* to make catcalls (at)

catch (kach, kech) *vt.* **caught, catch′ing** [< Anglo-Fr. *cachier* < VL. < L. *captare*, to try to seize < pp. of *capere*: see CAPTURE] **1.** to seize and hold, as after a chase; capture **2.** to take by or as by a trap, snare, etc. [to *catch* a fish] **3.** to deceive; ensnare **4.** to surprise in the act [to be *caught* stealing] **5.** to hit [the blow *caught* him in the eye] **6.** to get to in time [to *catch* a train] **7.** to lay hold of; grab [to *catch* a ball] **8.** *a)* to get as by chance or quickly [to *catch* a glimpse] *b)* [Colloq.] to manage to see, hear, etc. [to *catch* a newscast] **9.** to get as by being exposed to someone who is infected [to *catch* the mumps] **10.** *a)* to understand; apprehend [I *catch* what you mean] *b)* to show an understanding of by depicting [the statue *catches* her beauty] **11.** to captivate; charm **12.** to cause to be entangled [to *catch* one's heel in a rug] ☆**13.** *Baseball* to act as catcher for (a specified pitcher) —*vi.* **1.** to become held, fastened, or entangled [her heel *caught* in the rug] **2.** to take fire or start burning [the damp wood didn't *catch*] **3.** to take and keep hold, as a lock **4.** to act as a catcher —*n.* **1.** the act of catching [he made a great *catch*] **2.** a thing that catches or holds, as a fastening on a gate **3.** the person or thing caught **4.** the amount caught **5.** a person worth catching, esp. as a husband or wife **6.** a snatch, scrap, or bit [*catches* of old tunes] **7.** an emotional break in the voice ☆**8.** a simple game of throwing and catching a ball ☆**9.** [Colloq.] a hidden qualification; tricky condition [a *catch* in his offer] **10.** *Music* a round for three or more voices **11.** *Sports* a catching of a ball in a specified manner —*adj.* tricky; deceptive [a *catch* question on an exam] —**catch as catch can** with any hold, approach, etc.: orig. said of a style of wrestling —**catch at 1.** to try to catch **2.** to reach for eagerly —**catch it** [Colloq.] to receive a scolding or other punishment —☆**catch on 1.** to understand **2.** to become fashionable, popular, etc. —**catch oneself** to hold oneself back abruptly from saying or doing something —**catch up 1.** to take up suddenly; snatch **2.** to show to be in error **3.** to heckle **4.** to come up even, as by hurrying or by extra work **5.** to fasten in loops —**catch up on** to engage in more (work, sleep, etc.) so as to make up for some that was lost

☆**catch·all** (-ôl′) *n.* a place for holding all sorts of things [one drawer was a *catchall*]

catch basin a device like a sieve at the opening of a sewer to catch, or stop, bulky matter

catch·er (-ər) *n.* **1.** one that catches ☆**2.** *Baseball* the player stationed behind home plate, who catches pitched balls not hit away by the batter

catch·fly (-flī′) *n., pl.* **-flies′** same as CAMPION

catch·ing (-iŋ) *adj.* **1.** contagious; infectious [measles are *catching*] **2.** attractive; catchy

catch·pen·ny (-pen′ē) *adj.* cheap and flashy; worthless —*n., pl.* **-nies** a catchpenny article

catch phrase a phrase that catches or is meant to catch popular attention

catch·up (kech′əp, kach′-) *n.* same as KETCHUP

catch·word (kach′wurd′, kech′-) *n.* **1.** a word placed to catch attention and be a guide, as either of the words at the top of this page **2.** a word or phrase repeated so often that it becomes a slogan

catch·y (-ē) *adj.* **catch′i·er, catch′i·est 1.** catching attention; arousing interest [a *catchy* ad] **2.** easily taken up and remembered [a *catchy* tune] **3.** meant to trick [a *catchy* question] **4.** spasmodic —**catch′i·ness** *n.*

cat·e·chet·i·cal (kat′ə ket′i k'l) *adj.* **1.** of or like a catechism **2.** teaching by questions and answers Also **cat′e·chet′ic** —**cat′e·chet′i·cal·ly** *adv.*

cat·e·chism (kat′ə kiz′m) *n.* [< LL. < Gr. < *katēchizein*, to catechize < *kata-*, thoroughly + *ēchein*, to sound] **1.** a handbook of questions and answers for teaching the principles of a religion **2.** any similar handbook for teaching any subject **3.** a series of questions; close questioning —**cat′e·chis′mal** *adj.* —**cat′e·chis′tic** (-kis′tik), **cat′e·chis′ti·cal** *adj.*

cat·e·chist (-kist) *n.* a person who catechizes

cat·e·chize (-kīz′) *vt.* **-chized′, -chiz′ing** [see CATECHISM] **1.** to teach (someone), esp. religion, by the use of questions and answers **2.** to question closely Also sp. **cat′e·chise′** —**cat′e·chi·za′tion** *n.* —**cat′e·chiz′er** *n.*

cat·e·chu (kat′ə chōō′) *n.* [Malay *kachu*] an astringent substance obtained from several Asiatic trees: used in dyeing, tanning, etc.

cat·e·chu·men (kat′ə kyōō′mən) *n.* [< LL. < Gr. *katēchoumenos*: see CATECHISM] a person, esp. an adult, being taught the basic principles of Christianity before baptism or confirmation

cat·e·gor·i·cal (kat′ə gôr′i k'l, -gär′-) *adj.* **1.** unqualified; unconditional; absolute; positive [a *categorical* denial] **2.** of, as, or in a category Also **cat′e·gor′ic** —**cat′e·gor′i·cal·ly** *adv.*

cat·e·go·rize (kat′ə gə rīz′) *vt.* **-rized′, -riz′ing** to place in a category —**cat′e·go·ri·za′tion** *n.*

cat·e·go·ry (kat′ə gôr′ē) *n., pl.* **-ries** [< LL. < Gr. < *katēgorein*, to accuse < *kata-*, against + *agoreuein*, to declaim] **1.** a class or division in a system of classification [biology is divided into two *categories*, zoology and botany] **2.** *Logic* any of the basic concepts into which knowledge is classified

cat·e·nate (kat′'n āt′) *vt.* **-nat′ed, -nat′ing** [< L. < *catena*, CHAIN] to form into a chain or linked series; link —**cat′e·na′tion** *n.*

ca·ter (kā′tər) *vi.* [< OFr. < *achater*, to buy, ult. < L. *ad-*, to + *capere*, to take] **1.** to provide food; act as a caterer **2.** to try hard to supply what another needs or desires (with *to*) [a restaurant that *caters* to businessmen] —*vt.* to serve as caterer for (a banquet, party, etc.)

cat·er-cor·nered (kat′ē kôr′nərd, kit′-) *adj.* [ME. *cater*, four (ult. < L. *quattuor*, FOUR) + CORNERED] diagonal —*adv.* diagonally Also **cat′er-cor′ner**

ca·ter·er (kā′tər ər) *n.* one who caters; esp., one whose business is providing food and service as for parties

cat·er·pil·lar (kat′ər pil′ər, kat′ə-) *n.* [< ONormFr. *catepilose* < L. *catta pilosa*, hairy cat] the wormlike larva of various insects, esp. of a butterfly or moth —☆[C-] a trademark for a tractor having on each side an endless belt rolling over toothed wheels, for moving over rough or muddy ground

cat·er·waul (kat′ər wôl′) *vi.* [ME. *cater* (prob. < MDu. *kater*, tomcat) + *w(r)awlen*, v., prob. echoic] to make a shrill, howling sound like that of a cat; wail; scream —*n.* such a sound

cat·fish (kat′fish′) *n., pl.* **-fish′, -fish′es:** see FISH ☆any of a group of scaleless fishes with long barbels about the mouth

cat·gut (-gut′) *n.* [CAT + GUT: reason for *cat* is uncertain] a tough string or thread made from the dried intestines of sheep, horses, etc. and used for surgical sutures, musical instruments, etc.

cath- (kath) same as CATA-: used before an aspirate

Cath. 1. Catholic **2.** [*also* c-] cathedral

ca·thar·sis (kə thär′sis) *n.* [ModL. < Gr. *katharsis* < *katharos*, pure] **1.** an emptying of the bowels **2.** a relieving of the emotions, esp. by art, as by watching a tragic play **3.** *Psychiatry* the relieving of fears, problems, etc. by bringing them to the conscious mind

ca·thar·tic (kə thär′tik) *adj.* of or causing catharsis; purging: also **ca·thar′ti·cal** —*n.* a medicine to make the bowels move; purgative

Ca·thay (ka thā′, kə-) *poet. or archaic name of* CHINA

cat·head (kat′hed′) *n.* a projecting beam near the bow of a ship, to which the anchor is fastened

ca·the·dra (kə thē′drə, kath′i-) *n.* [LL. < L. < Gr. *kathedra*, a seat < *kata-*, down + *hedra*, a seat] **1.** the bishop's throne in a cathedral **2.** the episcopal see See also EX CATHEDRA

ca·the·dral (kə thē′drəl) *n.* **1.** the main church of a bishop's see, containing the cathedra **2.** loosely, any large, imposing church —*adj.* **1.** of, like, or containing a cathedra **2.** official **3.** of or like a cathedral

CATFISH
(to 12 ft. long)

Cath·er (kath′ər), **Wil·la** (**Sibert**) (wil′ə) 1873–1947; U.S. writer

Cath·er·ine (kath′rin, -ər in) [Fr. < L. *Catharina* < Gr. *Aikaterinē*; infl. by *katharos*, pure] **1.** a feminine name: dim. *Cathy, Kate, Kit, Kitty* **2. Catherine II** 1729–96; German-born empress of Russia (1762–96): called **Catherine the Great**

cath·e·ter (kath′ə tər) *n.* [LL. < Gr. *kathetēr* < *kata-*, down + *hienai*, to send] a slender tube inserted into a body passage, blood vessel, etc. for passing fluids, making examinations, etc., esp. for draining urine from the bladder

cath·e·ter·ize (-īz′) *vt.* **-ized′, -iz′ing** to insert a catheter into —**cath′e·ter·i·za′tion** *n.*

cath·ode (kath′ōd) *n.* [< Gr. *kathodos*, descent < *kata-*, down + *hodos*, way] **1.** in an electrolytic cell, the negative electrode, from which current flows **2.** in a vacuum tube, the negatively charged electron emitter **3.** the positive terminal of a battery

cathode rays streams of electrons projected from the surface of a cathode in a vacuum tube: cathode rays produce X-rays when they strike solids

cathode-ray tube a vacuum tube in which the electrons can be focused on a fluorescent screen, producing lighted traces that can be seen on the outside surface of the tube: used as oscilloscopes, television picture tubes, etc.

cath·o·lic (kath′ə lik, kath′lik) *adj.* [L. *catholicus*, universal < Gr. < *kata-*, completely + *holos*, whole] **1.** including many or all kinds; universal; broad; liberal [she has *catholic* tastes in music] **2.** [*often* **C-**] of the Christian church as a whole; specif., of the ancient, undivided Christian church **3.** [**C-**] of the Christian church headed by the Pope; Roman Catholic —*n.* **1.** [*often* **C-**] a member of the Christian church as a whole **2.** [**C-**] *same as* ROMAN CATHOLIC —**ca·thol·i·cal·ly** (kə thäl′i k'l ē, -ik lē) *adv.*

Ca·thol·i·cism (kə thäl′ə siz'm) *n.* the doctrine, practice, etc. of a Catholic church, esp. of the Roman Catholic Church

cath·o·lic·i·ty (kath′ə lis′ə tē) *n.* **1.** the fact of including many or all kinds; broadness; liberality **2.** [**C-**] Catholicism

cat·i·on (kat′ī′ən) *n.* [coined by Faraday < Gr. < *kata,* down + *ion*, prp. of *ienai*, to go] a positive ion: in electrolysis, cations move toward the cathode —**cat·i·on·ic** (kat′ī än′ik) *adj.*

cat·kin (kat′kin) *n.* [< Du. dim. of *katte*, cat] a drooping, scaly spike of small, crowded flowers, as on poplars or walnuts; ament

☆**cat·nap** (kat′nap′) *n.* a short, light sleep; doze —*vi.* **-napped′, -nap′ping** to take a catnap

☆**cat·nip** (-nip′) *n.* [CAT + nip (dial. for *catnip*) < L. *nepeta*] a plant of the mint family, with downy leaves and bluish flowers: cats like its odor

Ca·to (kāt′ō) **1.** (**Marcus Porcius**), 234–149 B.C.; Rom. statesman: called *the Elder* **2.** (**Marcus Porcius**), 95–46 B.C.; Rom. statesman & philosopher: great-grandson of *prec.*: called *the Younger*

cat-o'-nine-tails (kat′ə nīn′tālz′) *n., pl.* **-tails′** a whip made of nine knotted cords tied to a handle, formerly used for flogging

cat rig a rig, esp. of a catboat, consisting of one large sail on a mast well forward in the bow —**cat′rigged′** (-rigd′) *adj.*

CAT scan (kat) [*c*(omputerized) *a*(xial) *t*(omography)]: tomography is an X-ray photography technique] **1.** a method for diagnosing disorders of the soft tissues of the body, esp. of the brain: it uses a computerized combination of many X-rays to form an image **2.** the image so formed —**CAT scanner**

cat's cradle a child's game in which a string looped over the fingers is shifted back and forth on the hands of the players to form designs

cat's-eye (kats′ī′) *n.* any gem, stone, shell, etc. that reflects light in such a way as to look like a cat's eye

Cats·kill Mountains (kat′skil′) [Du., *cat stream*] mountain range in southeastern N.Y.: also **Cats′kills′**

cat's-paw (kats′pô′) *n.* **1.** [from the tale of the monkey who used the cat's paw to rake chestnuts out of the fire] a

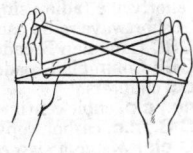

CATKIN
(of the aspen)

CAT'S CRADLE

person used by another to do for him something wrong or dangerous; dupe **2.** a light breeze rippling the surface of water

cat·sup (kech′əp, kach′-; kat′səp) *n. same as* KETCHUP

cat·tail (kat′tāl′) *n.* a tall marsh plant with reedlike leaves and long, brown, fuzzy, cylindrical flower spikes

☆**cat·ta·lo** (kat′'l ō′) *n., pl.* **-loes′, -los′** *same as* CATALO

cat·tish (kat′ish) *adj.* **1.** like a cat; feline **2.** *same as* CATTY —**cat′tish·ly** *adv.* —**cat′tish·ness** *n.*

cat·tle (kat′'l) *n.* [< Anglo-Fr. *catel* < ML. *captale,* property < L. < *caput,* HEAD; orig. used in the sense of CHATTEL] **1.** [Archaic] farm animals **2.** domesticated bovine animals as a group; cows, bulls, steers, or oxen

☆**cat·tle·man** (-mən) *n., pl.* **-men** a man who tends cattle or raises them for market

cat·ty (kat′ē) *adj.* **-ti·er, -ti·est 1.** of or like a cat **2.** spiteful, mean, malicious, etc. —**cat′ti·ly** *adv.* —**cat′ti·ness** *n.*

cat·ty-cor·nered (kat′ē kôr′nərd, kit′-) *adj., adv. same as* CATER-CORNERED: also **cat′ty-cor′ner**

Ca·tul·lus (kə tul′əs), (**Gaius Valerius**) 87?-55? B.C.; Rom. lyric poet

CATV community antenna television

cat·walk (kat′wôk′) *n.* a high, narrow walk, as along the edge of a bridge or over an engine room

Cau·ca·sia (kô kā′zhə) *same as* CAUCASUS (sense 1)

Cau·ca·sian (kô kā′zhən) *adj.* **1.** of the Caucasus, its people, their languages, etc. **2.** *same as* CAUCASOID Also **Cau·cas′ic** (-kas′ik) —*n.* **1.** a native of the Caucasus **2.** *same as* CAUCASOID **3.** the Caucasian languages; Circassian, Georgian, etc.

Cau·ca·soid (kôk′ə soid′) *adj.* [from the incorrect notion that this group originated in the Caucasus] designating or of one of the major groups of mankind that includes the native peoples of Europe, North Africa, the Near East, India, etc.: loosely called the *white race,* although skin color varies —*n.* a member of the Caucasoid group

Cau·ca·sus (kôk′ə səs) **1.** region in SE European U.S.S.R., between the Black Sea and the Caspian: often called **the Caucasus 2.** mountain range in this region: in full, **Caucasus Mountains**

☆**cau·cus** (kôk′əs) *n.* [< ? *Caucus* Club, 18th-c. social and political club; ult. < MGr. *kaukos,* drinking cup] a private meeting of leaders or a committee of a political party or faction to decide on policy, candidates, etc., esp. before the main meeting — *vi.* **-cused** or **-cussed, -cus·ing** or **-cus·sing** to hold, or take part in, a caucus

CAUCASUS

cau·dal (kôd′'l) *adj.* [< L. *cauda,* tail] **1.** of or like a tail [a *caudal* fin] **2.** at or near the tail [the *caudal* area]

cau·date (kô′dāt) *adj.* [< L. *cauda,* tail] having a tail or tail-like part: also **cau′dat·ed**

cau·dle (kôd′'l) *n.* [< Anglo-Fr., ult. < L. *cal(i)dus,* warm] a warm drink for invalids; esp., a thin gruel with sugar, spice, and wine or ale added

caught (kôt) *pt. & pp. of* CATCH

caul (kôl) *n.* [OE. *cawl,* basket, net] a membrane sometimes surrounding the head of a child at birth: in earlier superstition it was thought to bring good luck

caul·dron (kôl′drən) *n. same as* CALDRON

cau·li·flow·er (kôl′ə flou′ər, käl′-) *n.* [< It. *cavolfiore,* after L. *caulis,* cabbage] **1.** a variety of cabbage with a firm, white head of fleshy flower stalks **2.** the head of this plant, eaten as a vegetable

☆**cauliflower ear** an ear that has been deformed by injuries from repeated blows, as in boxing

cau·lis (kô′lis) *n., pl.* **-les** (-lēz) [L., akin to Gr. *kaulos*] *bot.* the main stem of a plant

CAULIFLOWER

caulk (kôk) **vt.** [< OFr. < L. *calcare*, to tread < *calx*, a heel] **1.** to make (a boat, etc.) watertight by filling the seams or cracks with oakum, tar, etc. **2.** to stop up (cracks of window frames, etc.) with a filler —**caulk'er n.**

caus·al (kôz'l) **adj. 1.** of, like, or being a cause **2.** relating to cause and effect [a *causal* relationship] **3.** expressing a cause or reason —**caus'al·ly adv.**

cau·sal·i·ty (kô zal'ə tē) **n.,** *pl.* **-ties 1.** causal quality or agency **2.** the relation between cause and effect; principle that nothing can exist or happen without a cause

cau·sa·tion (kô zā'shən) **n. 1.** the act of causing **2.** anything producing an effect; cause **3.** causality

caus·a·tive (kôz'ə tiv) **adj. 1.** producing an effect; causing **2.** expressing causation [fell is a *causative* verb, meaning "to cause to fall"] —**n.** a causative word or form —**caus'a·tive·ly adv.**

cause (kôz) **n.** [< OFr. < L. *causa*] **1.** anything producing an effect or result [God is sometimes called the First *Cause*] **2.** a person or thing that brings about an effect or result [a spark was the *cause* of the fire] **3.** a reason for some action, feeling, etc.; esp., sufficient reason [he has no *cause* for complaint] **4.** any objective or movement that a person or group is interested in and supports, esp. one involving social reform [the *cause* of peace] **5.** *Law* an action or question to be resolved by a court of law —**vt. caused, caus'ing** to be the cause of; bring about; effect, produce, compel, etc. [what *caused* the laughter?] —**make common cause with** to join forces with —**caus'a·ble adj.** —**cause'less adj.** —**caus'er n.**

SY —**cause** refers to something that produces an effect or result [carelessness is often a *cause* of accidents]; **reason** implies thinking that is engaged in to explain some act or idea [she had a *reason* for laughing]; a **motive** is a thought, emotion, or desire that leads to action [the *motive* for the crime]; an **antecedent** is an event or thing that comes before, and is responsible for, a later event or thing [war always has its *antecedents*]; an **occasion** is a situation or event that allows a cause to have an effect [the court case was an *occasion* for stating a new legal principle]

‡**cause cé·lèb·re** (kōz' sā leb'r'; *E.* kôz' sə leb') **[Fr.]** a famous law case, trial, or controversy

cause of action *Law* the right by which a party seeks a remedy against another in a court of law

cau·se·rie (kō'zə rē') **n.** [Fr. < *causer*, to chat < VL. < L. *causari*, to plead < *causa*, cause] **1.** an informal talk; chat **2.** a short piece of writing in an informal style

cause·way (kôz'wā') **n.** [< Brit. dial. *causey*, ult. < L. *calx*, limestone + WAY] **1.** a raised path or road, as across a marsh or shallow water **2.** a paved way or road; highway

caus·tic (kôs'tik) **adj.** [< L. < Gr. *kaustikos* < *kaiein*, to burn] **1.** that can burn or destroy tissue by chemical action; corrosive **2.** very sarcastic; sharp or biting [*caustic* comments] —**n.** any caustic substance —see **SYN.** at SARCASTIC —**caus'ti·cal·ly adv.** —**caus·tic'i·ty** (-tis'ə tē) **n.**

caustic potash same as POTASSIUM HYDROXIDE

caustic soda same as SODIUM HYDROXIDE

cau·ter·ize (kôt'ər īz') **vt. -ized', -iz'ing** [< LL. < Gr. *kautērion*, branding iron < *kaiein*, to burn] to burn with a hot iron or needle, or with a caustic substance, so as to destroy dead tissue, etc. —**cau'ter·i·za'tion n.**

cau·ter·y (kôt'ər ē) **n.,** *pl.* **-ter·ies 1.** an instrument or substance for cauterizing: also **cau'ter·ant 2.** the act of cauterizing

cau·tion (kô'shən) **n.** [< L. *cautio* < same base as *cavere*, to be wary] **1.** a warning; admonition [a word of *caution*] **2.** a word, sign, etc. by which warning is given [a yellow *caution* light warns of oncoming traffic] **3.** the act or practice of being cautious; wariness [use *caution* in handling acids] ☆**4.** [Colloq.] a remarkable person or thing —**vt.** to urge to be cautious; warn

cau·tion·ar·y (-er'ē) **adj.** urging caution or intended to warn; warning

cau·tious (kô'shəs) **adj.** full of caution; careful to avoid danger or mistakes; wary [a *cautious* chess player] —**cau'tious·ly adv.** —**cau'tious·ness n.**

cav·al·cade (kav''l kād', kav''l kād') **n.** [Fr. < It. < *cavalcare*, to ride, ult. < L. *caballus*, horse, nag] **1.** a procession of horsemen or carriages **2.** *a)* any procession *b)* a series or sequence [a *cavalcade* of events]

cav·a·lier (kav'ə lir') **n.** [Fr. < It. *cavaliere* < LL. < L. *caballus*, horse, nag] **1.** an armed horseman; knight **2.** a gallant gentleman, esp. one serving as a lady's escort **3.** [C-] a supporter of Charles I of England in his struggles with Parliament (1641–49); Royalist —**adj. 1.** [C-] of the Cavaliers **2.** *a)* free and easy; gay [*cavalier* wit] *b)* paying little attention to matters of some importance [a *cavalier* attitude] *c)* haughty; arro-

gant; scornful [*cavalier* contempt] —**cav'a·lier'ly adv., adj.**

cav·al·ry (kav''l rē) **n.,** *pl.* **-ries** [< Fr. < It. < *cavaliere:* see CAVALIER] combat troops mounted originally on horses but now often riding in motorized armored vehicles —**cav'al·ry·man** (-mən) **n.,** *pl.* **-men**

cave (kāv) **n.** [< OFr. < L. < *cavus*, hollow < IE. base *keu-*, a swelling, arch] a hollow place inside the earth; cavern; often, an opening extending back into a hillside —**vt. caved, cav'ing** to make a hollow in —**vi.** [Colloq.] **1.** to cave in **2.** to explore caves —**cave in 1.** to collapse **2.** to make collapse **3.** [Colloq.] to give way; give in; yield —**cav'er n.**

ca·ve·at (kā'vē at', kav'ē-; kä'vē ät') **n.** [L., let him beware] **1.** *Law* a notice that an interested party files with the proper officers directing them to stop an action until he can be heard **2.** a warning

caveat emp·tor (emp'tôr) **[L.]** let the buyer beware (i.e., one buys at his own risk)

cave-in (kāv'in') **n. 1.** a caving in **2.** a place where the ground, a mine, etc. has caved in

cave man 1. a prehistoric human being of the Stone Age who lived in caves: also **cave dweller 2.** a man who acts in a rough, crude way, esp. toward women

Cav·en·dish (kav''n dish), **Henry** 1731–1810; Eng. chemist & physicist

cav·ern (kav'ərn) **n.** [< Fr. < L. *caverna* < *cavus:* see CAVE] a cave, esp. a large cave —**vt. 1.** to enclose in or as in a cavern **2.** to hollow (*out*)

cav·ern·ous (kav'ər nəs) **adj. 1.** full of caverns [*cavernous* hills] **2.** full of cavities; porous **3.** like a cavern; deep-set, hollow, etc. [*cavernous* cheeks] —**cav'ern·ous·ly adv.**

cav·i·ar, cav·i·are (kav'ē är', käv'-; kav'ē är') **n.** [Fr. < It. < Turk. < Per. *khāviyār*] the salted eggs of sturgeon, salmon, etc. eaten as an appetizer

cav·il (kav''l) **vi. -iled or -illed, -il·ing or -il·ling** [< OFr. < L. *cavillari* < *cavilla*, a jest] to object when there is little reason to do so; criticize minor details; carp (*at* or *about*) —**n.** a trivial objection; quibble —**cav'il·er, cav'il·ler n.**

cav·i·ty (kav'ə tē) **n.,** *pl.* **-ties** [< Fr. < LL. *cavitas* < L. *cavus:* see CAVE] **1.** a hole or hollow place, as one caused by decay in a tooth **2.** a natural hollow place within the body [the abdominal *cavity*]

☆**ca·vort** (kə vôrt') **vi.** [< ?] **1.** to leap about; prance or caper **2.** to romp about happily; frolic

Ca·vour (kä vōōr'), **Conte Ca·mil·lo Ben·so di** (kä mēl'lō ben'sô dē) 1810–61; It. statesman who helped unify Italy

ca·vy (kā'vē) **n.,** *pl.* **-vies** [< Carib *cabiai*] any of several short-tailed S. American rodents, as the guinea pig

caw (kô) **n.** [echoic] the harsh cry of a crow or raven —**vi.** to make this sound

Cax·ton (kak'stən), **William** 1422?–91; 1st Eng. printer

cay (kā, kē) **n.** [Sp. *cayo:* see KEY²] a low island, coral reef, or sandbank off a mainland

Cay·enne (kī en', kā-) seaport & chief town of French Guiana: pop. 25,000

cay·enne (kī en', kā-) **n.** [< Tupi *kynnha*] a very hot red pepper made from the dried fruit of a pepper plant, esp. of the capsicum: also **cayenne pepper**

cay·man (kā'mən) **n.,** *pl.* **-mans** same as CAIMAN

Ca·yu·ga (kā yōō'gə, kī-) **n. 1.** *pl.* **-gas, -ga** any member of a tribe of Iroquoian Indians who lived around Cayuga Lake and Seneca Lake in N.Y.: see FIVE NATIONS **2.** their Iroquoian dialect

Cay·use (kī'ōōs, kī ōōs') **n.,** *pl.* **-us·es; for 1 *a*, also -use 1.** *a)* a member of a tribe of Oregonian Indians *b)* their language **2.** [c-] a small Western horse used by cowboys

CB (sē'bē') **adj.** [CITIZENS' BAND] that is or has to do with shortwave radio using citizens' band frequencies —**n.,** *pl.* **CB's** a shortwave radio using citizens' band frequencies

CBC Canadian Broadcasting Corporation

CBS Columbia Broadcasting System

cc. chapters

cc., c.c. cubic centimeter(s)

C.C., c.c. carbon copy

C clef *Music* a sign on a staff indicating that C is the note on the third line (*alto clef*) or on the fourth line (*tenor clef*)

Cd *Chem.* cadmium

CD, C.D. Civil Defense

cd. cord(s)

CDR, Cdr. Commander

Ce *Chem.* cerium

C.E. 1. Church of England **2.** Civil Engineer **3.** Common Era

cease (sēs) *vt., vi.* **ceased, ceas′ing** [< OFr. < L. *cessare* < *cedere*, to yield] to bring or come to an end; stop; discontinue —*n.* a ceasing: chiefly in **without cease** —see SYN. at STOP

cease-fire (sēs′fīr′) *n.* a temporary stopping of warfare by mutual agreement of the participants

cease·less (-lis) *adj.* going on and on; unceasing; continual —**cease′less·ly** *adv.*

Ce·bu (sā bōō′) **1.** seaport on an island in the SC Philippines: pop. 351,000 **2.** this island

Ce·cil (sēs′'l, ses′'l) [L. *Caecilius*, prob. < *caecus*, dim-sighted, blind] a masculine name

Ce·cil·ia (sə sēl′yə) [L. < fem. of *Caecilius*: see prec.] a feminine name: var. **Cecile, Cecily**

☆**ce·cro·pi·a moth** (si krō′pē ə) [< *Cecrops*, legendary Gr. king] the largest moth of the U.S., having wide wings, each with a crescent-shaped spot

ce·cum (sē′kəm) *n., pl.* **-ca** (-kə) [< L. (*intestinum*) *caecum*, blind (intestine)] the pouch that is the beginning of the large intestine —**ce′cal** *adj.*

ce·dar (sē′dər) *n.* [< OFr. < L. < Gr. *kedros*] **1.** any of certain cone-bearing trees of the pine family, having durable, fragrant wood, as the **cedar of Lebanon 2.** any of various trees like this **3.** the wood of any of these, often used to make chests and closets for storing clothes —*adj.* of cedar

CECROPIA MOTH
(wingspread to 6 in.)

Cedar Rapids [after the rapids of nearby Cedar River] city in EC Iowa: pop. 109,000

☆**cedar waxwing** a brownish-gray, crested American bird, with red, waxlike tips on its secondary wing feathers: also **ce′dar·bird′** *n.*

cede (sēd) *vt.* **ced′ed, ced′ing** [< Fr. < L. *cedere*, to yield (< IE. base *ke-*, HERE), akin to *sedere*, SIT] **1.** to give up one's rights in; surrender [Spain *ceded* Puerto Rico to the U.S. in 1898] **2.** to transfer the title or ownership of

ce·di (sā′dē) *n., pl.* **-dis** [< native word *sedie*, cowrie, formerly used as money] *see* MONETARY UNITS, table (Ghana)

ce·dil·la (si dil′ə) *n.* [< Fr. < Sp. *cedilla*, dim. of *zeda* (< Gr. *zēta*, zeta)] a hooklike mark put under *c* in some French words (Ex.: *façade*) to show that it is to be sounded like an *s*

Ced·ric (sed′rik, sē′drik) [< ? Celt.] a masculine name

ceil (sēl) *vt.* [< OFr. < L. *celare*, to hide; prob. influenced by L. *caelum*, heaven] to build a ceiling in or over

ceil·ing (sēl′iŋ) *n.* [< prec.] **1.** the inside top part of a room, opposite the floor **2.** an upper limit set on anything [a ceiling on prices] **3.** *Aeron. a)* a covering of clouds that limits visibility, or the height of the lower surface of such a covering *b)* the maximum height at which an aircraft can normally fly — ☆**hit the ceiling** [Slang] to lose one's temper

cel·an·dine (sel′ən dīn′, -dēn′) *n.* [< OFr. < L. < Gr. < *chelidōn*, a swallow] **1.** a weedy plant related to the poppy, with yellow flowers **2.** a plant of the buttercup family, with yellow flowers

-cele (sēl) [< Gr. *kēlē*] **1.** *a combining form meaning* tumor, hernia, or swelling **2.** *same as* -COELE

Cel·e·bes (sel′ə bēz′, sə lē′bēz) island of Indonesia, east of Borneo: 69,277 sq. mi.

cel·e·brant (sel′ə brənt) *n.* [see CELEBRATE] **1.** a person who performs a religious rite, as the priest officiating at Mass **2.** one who celebrates

cel·e·brate (-brāt′) *vt.* **-brat′ed, -brat′ing** [< L. pp. of *celebrare*, to frequent, honor < *celeber*, much frequented, famous] **1.** to perform (a ritual, etc.) publicly and formally; solemnize **2.** to observe (an anniversary, holiday, etc.) in some special way **3.** to honor or praise publicly **4.** to mark (a happy occasion) with a pleasurable activity [let's *celebrate* her promotion by going to a concert] —*vi.* **1.** to observe a holiday, anniversary, etc. with festivities **2.** to perform a religious ceremony **3.** [Colloq.] to have a good time —**cel′e·bra′tor** *n.* —**ce·leb·ra·to·ry** (sə leb′rə tôr′ē) *adj.*

SYN.—**celebrate** implies the marking of an occasion or event, esp. a joyous one, with some kind of ceremony or merrymaking [to *celebrate* Thanksgiv-

ing with a family dinner]; to **commemorate** is to honor the memory of some person or event by a ceremony [to *commemorate* Lincoln's birthday by reading the Gettysburg Address]; **observe** and **keep**, which is less formal, suggest the respectful marking of a day or occasion by following traditional rituals [to *observe*, or *keep*, a religious holiday]; **solemnize** suggests the use of formal ritual in observing an event, esp. one of a religious nature [to *solemnize* a marriage]

cel·e·brat·ed (-id) *adj.* famous; renowned —see SYN. at FAMOUS

cel·e·bra·tion (sel′ə brā′shən) *n.* **1.** the act or an instance of celebrating **2.** that which is done to celebrate

ce·leb·ri·ty (sə leb′rə tē) *n.* **1.** wide recognition; fame [he seeks *celebrity*] **2.** *pl.* **-ties** a famous person

ce·ler·i·ac (sə ler′ē ak′) *n.* [altered < CELERY] a variety of celery grown for its edible root, that is like a turnip

ce·ler·i·ty (sə ler′ə tē) *n.* [< Fr. < L. *celeritas* < *celer*, swift] swiftness in acting or moving; speed

cel·er·y (sel′ər ē, sel′rē) *n.* [Fr. *céleri* < It. < Gr. *selinon*, parsley] a plant of the parsley family, with long, crisp leafstalks eaten as a vegetable

celery salt a seasoning made of powdered celery seed and salt

ce·les·ta (sə les′tə) *n.* [< Fr. < *céleste*, celestial] a small keyboard instrument with hammers that strike metal plates to make bell-like tones

Ce·leste (sə lest′) [Fr. *Céleste*: see prec.] a feminine name

ce·les·tial (sə les′chəl) *adj.* [OFr. < L. *caelestis* < *caelum*, heaven: for IE. base see CHINTZ] **1.** of the heavens, or sky [the stars are *celestial* bodies] **2.** *a)* of heaven; divine [*celestial* beings] *b)* highest; perfect [*celestial* bliss] —**ce·les′tial·ly** *adv.*

celestial equator the great circle of the celestial sphere formed by projecting the plane of the earth's equator on the celestial sphere

celestial sphere an imaginary sphere whose diameter is infinite and on which all celestial bodies appear to be projected

Cel·ia (sēl′yə) [L. fem. of *Caelius*, name of a Roman clan] a feminine name

ce·li·ac (sē′lē ak′) *adj.* [L. *coeliacus* < Gr. *koilia*: see -COELE] of or in the abdominal cavity

cel·i·ba·cy (sel′ə bə sē) *n.* [see CELIBATE] **1.** the state of being unmarried; esp., the life of a person under a vow not to marry **2.** the condition of never having sexual intercourse

cel·i·bate (sel′ə bət, -bāt′) *adj.* [< L. *caelebs*, unmarried] of or in a state of celibacy —*n.* a celibate person

cell (sel) *n.* [< OFr. *celle* < L. *cella* < IE. base *kel-*, to conceal, from which also come HALL, HELL & HULL[1]] **1.** a small room or cubicle, as in a convent or prison **2.** a very small hollow, cavity, or enclosed space, as in a honeycomb, or in a plant ovary **3.** any of the smallest organizational units of a group or movement, as of a Communist party **4.** *Biol.* a small unit of protoplasm, usually with a nucleus, cytoplasm, and an enclosing membrane: all plants and animals are made up of one or more cells **5.** *Elec.* a container holding electrodes and an electrolyte, used either for generating electricity by chemical reactions or for decomposing compounds by electrolysis —**celled** *adj.*

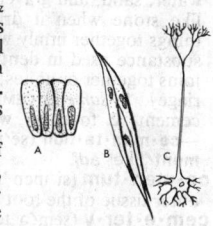

CELLS
(A, epithelial;
B, smooth muscle;
C, nerve)

cel·lar (sel′ər) *n.* [< OFr. < L. *cellarium* < *cella*: see CELL] **1.** a room or rooms below ground level and usually under a building, often used for storing fuel, provisions, wines, etc. **2.** a stock of wines kept in a cellar —*vt.* to store in a cellar — ☆**the cellar** [Colloq.] the lowest position in the standings of the teams in a league

cel·lar·age (-ij) *n.* **1.** space of or in a cellar **2.** the fee for storage in a cellar

cel·lar·et (sel′ə ret′) *n.* [CELLAR + -ET] a cabinet for bottles of wine or liquor, glasses, etc.

Cel·li·ni (chə lē′nē), **Ben·ve·nu·to** (ben′və nōō′tō) 1500–71; It. sculptor & goldsmith

cel·list (chel′ist) *n.* a person who plays the cello; violoncellist: also sp. **'cel′list**

cel·lo (chel′ō) *n., pl.* **-los, -li** (-ē) [< VIOLONCELLO] an instrument of the violin family, between the viola and double bass in size and pitch; violoncello: also sp. **'cel′lo**

cel·lo·phane (sel′ə fān′) *n.* [< CELLULOSE + Gr. *phainein*, appear] a thin, transparent material made from cellulose, used as moistureproof wrapping for foods, etc.

cel·lu·lar (sel′yoo lər) *adj.* of, like, or containing a cell or cells —**cel′lu·lar′i·ty** (-lar′ə tē) *n.*

cel·lule (sel′yool) *n.* [L. *cellula*] a very small cell

☆**Cel·lu·loid** (sel′yoo loid′) [CELLUL(OSE) + -OID] *a trademark for* a flammable substance made from pyroxylin and camphor, used, esp. before the development of plastics, for various articles —*n.* [c-] **1.** this substance **2.** motion pictures: celluloid was formerly used for photographic film

CELLO

cel·lu·lose (sel′yoo lōs′) *n.* [Fr.: see CELLULE & -OSE¹] the chief constituent of the cell walls or fibers of all plant tissue: used in the manufacture of paper, textiles, explosives, etc. —**cel′lu·los′ic** (-lō′sik) *adj., n.*

cellulose acetate a cellulose resin used in making acetate fiber, plastics, lacquers, etc.

ce·lom (sē′ləm) *n. same as* COELOM

Cel·si·us (sel′sē əs) *adj.* [after A. *Celsius* (1701-44), Swed. astronomer] designating or of a thermometer on which 0° is the freezing point and 100° is the boiling point of water; centigrade: abbrev. C: the formula for changing a Celsius temperature to Fahrenheit is C° = 5/9(F°-32)

Celt (selt, kelt) *n.* [< Fr. < L. *Celta*, pl. *Celtae* (Gr. *Keltoi*), the Gauls] **1.** a person who speaks Celtic: the Bretons, Irish, Welsh, and Highland Scots are Celts **2.** an ancient Gaul or Briton

Cel·tic (sel′tik, kel′-) *adj.* of the Celts, their languages, culture, etc. —*n.* an Indo-European subfamily of languages with a Goidelic branch (Irish Gaelic, Scottish Gaelic, Manx) in Ireland, the Scottish Highlands, and the Isle of Man, and a Brythonic branch (Welsh, Breton, and the extinct Cornish) in Wales and Brittany

ce·ment (si ment′) *n.* [< OFr. < L. *caementum*, rough stone < *caedere*, to cut] **1.** a powdered substance made of burned lime and clay, mixed with water and sand to make mortar or with water, sand, and gravel to make concrete: the mixture hardens like stone when it dries **2.** any soft substance that fastens things together firmly when it hardens, as glue **3.** a cementlike substance used in dentistry as to fill cavities **4.** anything that joins together or unites; bond [love was the *cement* of their marriage] **5.** *same as* CEMENTUM —*vt.* **1.** to join or unite as with cement **2.** to cover with cement —*vi.* to become cemented —**ce·men·ta′tion** (sē′men tā′shən) *n.* —**ce·ment′er** *n.* —**ce·ment′like′** *adj.*

ce·men·tum (si men′təm) *n.* [< L.: see prec.] the hard, bony outer tissue of the root of a tooth

cem·e·ter·y (sem′ə ter′ē) *n., pl.* **-ter′ies** [< LL. < Gr. *koimētērion* < *koiman*, to put to sleep] a place for the burial of the dead; graveyard

cen·o·bite (sen′ə bīt′, sē′nə-) *n.* [< LL. *coenobita* < Gr. < *koinos*, common + *bios*, life] a member of a religious order in a monastery or convent —**cen′o·bit′ic** (-bit′ik), **cen′o·bit′i·cal** *adj.* —**cen′o·bit·ism** (-bit iz′m) *n.*

cen·o·taph (sen′ə taf′) *n.* [< Fr. < L. < Gr. < *kenos*, empty + *taphos*, a tomb] a monument honoring a dead person whose body is somewhere else

Ce·no·zo·ic (sē′nə zō′ik, sen′ə-) *adj.* [< Gr. *kainos*, recent + ZO- + -IC] designating or of the geologic era following the Mesozoic and including the present: it is the era during which mammals became highly developed —**the Cenozoic** the Cenozoic Era or its rocks: see GEOLOGIC TIME CHART

cen·ser (sen′sər) *n.* [< OFr. < *encens*: see INCENSE¹] a container in which incense is burned, esp. in religious rites

cen·sor (sen′sər) *n.* [L. < *censere*, to tax, value < IE. base *kens-*, to announce] **1.** in ancient Rome, one of two officials who took the census and guarded the morals of the people **2.** a government official who has the power to examine books, newspapers, magazines, movies, mail, etc. and to remove or forbid anything considered to be obscene, critical of the government, etc. —*vt.* to examine (a book, letter, movie, etc.) as a censor —**cen·so·ri·al** (sen sôr′ē əl) *adj.*

cen·so·ri·ous (sen sôr′ē əs) *adj.* [see prec.] inclined to find fault; harshly critical —**cen·so′ri·ous·ly** *adv.* —**cen·so′ri·ous·ness** *n.*

cen·sor·ship (sen′sər ship′) *n.* **1.** the act or a system of censoring **2.** the work or position of a censor

cen·sure (sen′shər) *n.* [L. *censura* < *censor*, CENSOR] **1.** a blaming of someone or a finding fault; strong disapproval **2.** an official expression of disapproval, specif. as passed by a legislature —*vt.* **-sured, -sur·ing** to blame or find fault with (someone); express strong disapproval of [the senator was *censured* for taking bribes] —see SYN. at CRITICIZE —**cen′sur·a·ble** *adj.* —**cen′sur·a·bly** *adv.* —**cen′sur·er** *n.*

cen·sus (sen′səs) *n.* [L., orig. pp. of *censere*: see CENSOR] **1.** in ancient Rome, the act of counting the people and putting a value on their property in order to tax it **2.** an official counting of all the people in a country or area to find out how many there are and of what sex, age, occupation, etc. [the U.S. *census* has been taken every ten years since 1790]

cent (sent) *n.* [< OFr. < L. *centum*, a hundred < IE. base *kmto-*, hundred] ☆**1.** a 100th part of a dollar, or a coin of this value; penny: symbol, ¢ **2.** a 100th part of a rupee, piaster, etc.: see MONETARY UNITS, table

cent. 1. centigrade **2.** centimeter **3.** century

cen·tare (sen′ter, -tär) *n. same as* CENTIARE

cen·taur (sen′tôr) *n.* [< L. < Gr. *Kentauros*] **1.** *Gr. Myth.* any of a race of monsters with a man's head, trunk, and arms, and a horse's body and legs **2.** [C-] *same as* CEN-TAURUS

Cen·tau·rus (sen tôr′əs) [L. < Gr.] a southern constellation near the Southern Cross: its brightest star (**alpha Centauri**) is nearer the earth than any other known star

cen·ta·vo (sen tä′vō) *n., pl.* **-vos** [Sp. < L. *centum*: see CENT] a unit of currency equal to 1/100 of a peso in Mexico, the Philippines, etc. and to 1/100 of a Brazilian cruzeiro, a Portuguese escudo, etc.: see MONETARY UNITS, table

CENTAUR

cen·te·nar·i·an (sen′tə ner′ē ən) *adj.* **1.** of 100 years; of a centenary **2.** of a centenarian —*n.* a person at least 100 years old

cen·te·nar·y (sen ten′ər ē, sen′tə ner′ē) *adj.* [< L. < *centum*: see CENT] **1.** of a century, or period of 100 years **2.** of a centennial —*n., pl.* **-nar·ies** **1.** a century; period of 100 years **2.** *same as* CENTENNIAL

cen·ten·ni·al (sen ten′ē əl) *adj.* [< L. *centum* (see CENT) + *annus*, year + -AL] **1.** of 100 years **2.** happening once in 100 years **3.** 100 years old **4.** of a 100th anniversary —*n.* a 100th anniversary or its celebration —**cen·ten′ni·al·ly** *adv.*

cen·ter (sen′tər) *n.* [< OFr. < L. *centrum* < Gr. *kentron*, sharp point < IE. base *kent-*, to prick] **1.** a point that is the same distance from all points on the circumference of a circle or surface of a sphere **2.** the point around which anything revolves; pivot [the *center* of a wheel] **3.** a place where an activity or group of activities is carried on [a shopping *center*] or where certain ideas, influences, etc. get their start [Paris, the fashion *center*] **4.** a person or thing to which many people are attracted [he always wants to be the *center* of attention] **5.** the middle point, place, or part of anything [the *center* of town] **6.** a group of nerve cells regulating a particular function **7.** in football, basketball, etc., a player whose position at the start of play is near the center of the line or playing area: the center often puts the ball or puck into play **8.** [*often* C-] *Politics* a position or party between the left (radicals and liberals) and the right (conservatives and reactionaries) —*vt.* **1.** to place in, at, or near the center [*center* the picture on the wall] **2.** to draw or gather to one center; concentrate; focus [her energy is *centered* on her career] **3.** *Football* to pass (the ball) back to a player in the backfield: said of the center —*vi.* to be centered; be concentrated or focused [his interests *center* around his church]

☆**cen·ter·board** (-bôrd′) *n.* a movable board, like a keel, that is lowered through a slot in the floor of a sailboat to prevent drifting to leeward

☆**cen·ter·fold** (-fōld′) *n.* **1.** the center facing pages of a magazine, given over to a single photograph or other pictured material **2.** a person, often a young woman or man photographed in the nude, whose picture appears on a centerfold

center of gravity that point in a body or system around which its weight is evenly distributed or balanced

cen·ter·piece (sen′tər pēs′) *n.* an ornament, bowl of flowers, etc. for the center of a table

center punch a steel punch for marking a spot where a hole is to be drilled

cen·tes·i·mal (sen tes′ə məl) *adj.* [< L. *centesimus* < *centum*: see CENT] **1.** hundredth **2.** of or divided into hundredths — **cen·tes′i·mal·ly** *adv.*

cen·tes·i·mo (sen tes′ə mō′; *Sp.* -ē mō′; *It.* chen te′sē mō′) *n., pl.* **-mos′** (-mōz′; *Sp.* -mòs′); It. **-mi′** (-mē′) [It. & Sp. < L.: see prec.] a unit of currency equal to 1/100th of an Italian lira, a Uruguayan peso, etc.: see MONETARY UNITS, table

cen·ti- [L. < *centum*: see CENT] *a combining form meaning:* **1.** hundred or hundredfold [*centipede*] **2.** a 100th part of; the factor 10^{-2} [*centigram*]

cen·ti·are (sen′tē er′, -är′) *n.* [Fr.: see CENTI- & ARE²] a 100th part of an are; unit of land measure, equal to one square meter

cen·ti·grade (sen′tə grād′) *adj.* [Fr. < L. *centum* (see CENT) + *gradus*, a degree] **1.** consisting of or divided into 100 degrees **2.** *same as* CELSIUS: the preferred term until *Celsius* was adopted in 1948 by international agreement

cen·ti·gram (-gram′) *n.* [Fr.: see CENTI- & GRAM] a unit of weight, equal to 1/100 gram: also, chiefly Brit. sp., **cen′ti·gramme′**: abbrev. **cg., cgm.**

cen·ti·li·ter (sen′tə lēt′ər) *n.* [Fr.: see CENTI- & LITER] a unit of capacity, equal to 1/100 liter: also, chiefly Brit. sp., **cen′ti·li′tre:** abbrev. **cl.**

cen·time (sän′tēm; *Fr.* sän tēm′) *n.* [Fr. < L.: see CENTESIMAL] the 100th part of a franc, the Algerian dinar, etc.: see MONETARY UNITS, table

cen·ti·me·ter (sen′tə mēt′ər) *n.* [< Fr.: see CENTI- & METER¹] a unit of measure, equal to 1/100 meter: also, chiefly Brit. sp., **cen′ti·me′tre:** abbrev. **cm., c., C., cent.**

cen·ti·me·ter-gram-sec·ond (-gram′sek′ənd) *adj.* designating or of a system of measurement in which the centimeter, gram, and second are used as the units of length, mass, and time, respectively

cen·ti·mo (sen′tə mō′) *n., pl.* **-mos′** [see CENTIME] the 100th part of a Spanish peseta, a Venezuelan bolívar, etc.: see MONETARY UNITS, table

cen·ti·pede (sen′tə pēd′) *n.* [Fr. < L. < *centum* (see CENT) + *pes* (gen. *pedis*), a foot] a wormlike animal with many segments and a pair of legs to each segment: the front pair are poison claws

CENTIPEDE
(to 6 in. long)

cen·tral (sen′trəl) *adj.* [L. *centralis*] **1.** in, at, or near the center [*the central* part of the city] **2.** of or forming the center [*a central* point] **3.** at about the same distance from various points [we chose her house as a *central* meeting place] **4.** main; most important; principal [*loving is *central* to living*] **5.** of or having to do with a single source that controls all activity in an organization or system [*a central* office] **6.** designating or of that part of the nervous system consisting of the brain and spinal cord —**cen·tral′i·ty** (-tral′ə tē) *n.* —**cen′tral·ly** *adv.*

Central African Republic country in C Africa, south of Chad: 238,224 sq. mi.; pop. 2,370,000; cap. Bangui

Central America part of N. America between Mexico and S. America —**Central American**

central city the principal city of a metropolitan area, surrounded by suburbs; esp., the crowded, industrial, often run-down area of such a city

cen·tral·ism (sen′trəl iz′m) *n.* the principle or system of concentrating power or authority, as of a government, in a central organization —**cen′tral·ist** *adj., n.* —**cen′tral·is′tic** *adj.*

cen·tral·ize (sen′trə līz′) *vt.* **-ized′, -iz′ing** to organize under one control [all government power is *centralized* under the president] *vi.* to become centralized —**cen′tral·i·za′tion** *n.*

Central Powers in World War I, Germany, Austria-Hungary, Turkey, and Bulgaria

☆**Central Standard Time** *see* STANDARD TIME

cen·tre (sen′tər) *n., vt., vi.* **-tred, -tring** *chiefly Brit. sp.* of CENTER

cen·tri- *same as* CENTRO-

cen·tric (sen′trik) *adj.* **1.** in, at, or near the center; central **2.** of or having a center Also **cen′tri·cal** —**cen′tri·cal·ly** *adv.* — **cen·tric′i·ty** (-tris′ə tē) *n.*

-cen·tric (sen′trik) *a combining form meaning:* **1.** having a center or centers (of a specified kind or number) [*polycentric*] **2.** having (a specified thing) as its center [*geocentric*]

cen·trif·u·gal (sen trif′yə gəl, -ə gəl) *adj.* [< ModL. < CENTRI- + L. *fugere*, to flee + -AL] **1.** moving or tending to move away from a center **2.** using or acted on by centrifugal force — ☆*n.* a centrifuge —**cen·trif′u·gal·ly** *adv.*

centrifugal force the force tending to pull a thing outward when it is rotating rapidly around a center

cen·trif·u·gal·ize (-īz′) *vt.* **-ized′, -iz′ing** to whirl in or as if in a centrifuge —**cen·trif′u·gal·i·za′tion** *n.*

cen·tri·fuge (sen′trə fyōōj′) *n.* a machine in which something can be whirled so that centrifugal force will separate heavier particles from lighter ones, as cream from milk —*vt.* **-fuged′, -fug′ing** to whirl in a centrifuge

cen·tri·ole (sen′trē ōl′) *n.* [altered (after CENTRI-) < G. *zentriol* < *zentrum*, CENTER] a small, dense structure in the middle of a centrosome: it doubles before mitosis and each part forms the center of an aster at mitosis

cen·trip·e·tal (sen trip′ət 'l) *adj.* [< ModL. < CENTRI- + L. *petere*, to seek + -AL] **1.** moving or tending to move toward a center **2.** using or acted on by centripetal force

centripetal force the force tending to pull a thing inward when it is rotating rapidly around a center

cen·trist (sen′trist) *n.* a member of a political party of the center

cen·tro- [< L. *centrum*, CENTER] *a combining form meaning* center [*centrosome*]

cen·tro·mere (sen′trə mir′) *n.* [CENTRO- +-MERE] a structure in a chromosome to which spindle-shaped fibers become attached during mitosis

cen·tro·some (sen′trə sōm′) *n.* [CENTRO- + -SOME³] a very small body near the nucleus in most animal cells: it divides in mitosis —**cen′tro·som′ic** (-säm′ik, -sōm′-) *adj.*

cen·tu·ri·on (sen tyoor′ē ən, -toor′-) *n.* [< L. < *centuria*: see CENTURY] the commander of a Roman military company

cen·tu·ry (sen′chər ē) *n., pl.* **-ries** [L. *centuria* < *centum*, a hundred: see CENT] **1.** any period of 100 years, as from 1776 to 1876 **2.** any of the 100-year periods counted forward or backward from the beginning of the Christian era [1801 A.D. through 1900 A.D. is the 19th *century*, 400 B.C. through 301 B.C. is the 4th *century* B.C.] **3.** in ancient Rome *a)* a military unit, originally made up of 100 men *b)* any of a number of political divisions, each of which had one vote —**cen·tu·ri·al** (sen tyoor′ē əl, -toor′-) *adj.*

☆**century plant** a tropical American agave having fleshy leaves and a tall stalk that bears greenish flowers only once after 10 to 30 years and then dies: mistakenly thought to bloom only once a century

ce·phal·ic (sə fal′ik) *adj.* [< L. < Gr. < *kephalē*, the head: for IE. base see GABLE] **1.** of the head, skull, or cranium **2.** in, on, near, or toward the head —**ce·phal′i·cal·ly** *adv.*

-ce·phal·ic (sə fal′ik) *a combining form meaning* head or skull [*dolichocephalic*]

cephalic index a number used to indicate the shape of a human head, arrived at by dividing its breadth by its length and multiplying by 100

ceph·a·lo- [see CEPHALIC] *a combining form meaning* the head, skull, or brain [*cephalopod*] : also, before a vowel, **cephal-**

Ceph·a·lo·ni·a (sef′ə lō′nē ə) Gr. island in the Ionian Sea, off the W coast of Greece: 289 sq. mi.

ceph·a·lo·pod (sef′ə lə päd′) *n.* [CEPHALO- + -POD] any of those mollusks, such as the octopus, squid, and cuttlefish, that have a head with a beak and strong, armlike growths around the mouth, usually with suckers on them

ceph·a·lo·tho·rax (sef′ə lə thôr′aks) *n.* the head and thorax united as a single part, in certain crustaceans and arachnids

-ceph·a·lous (sef′əl əs) [see CEPHALIC] *a combining form meaning* -headed [*microcephalous*]

---

fat, āpe, cär, ten, ēven, is, bīte; gō, hôrn, tōōl, look; oil, out; up, fur; get; joy; yet; chin; she; thin, *th*en; zh, leisure; ŋ, ring; ə for *a* in *ago*, *e* in *agent*, *i* in *sanity*, *o* in *comply*, *u* in *focus*; ′ as in *able* (ā′b'l); Fr. bàl; ë, Fr. coeur; ö, Fr. feu; Fr. mon; ô, Fr. coq; ü, Fr. duc; r, Fr. cri; H, G. ich; kh, G. doch; ‡foreign; ☆ Americanism; < derived from. See inside front cover.

ceph·e·id (**variable**) (sef′ē id, sē′fē-) [< *Cepheus*, a N constellation] any of a class of stars whose light varies in brightness in regular periods

Ce·ram (si ram′) one of the Molucca Islands, in Indonesia: 6,622 sq. mi.

ce·ram·ic (sə ram′ik) *adj.* [< Gr. *keramos*, clay, pottery] **1.** of pottery, earthenware, tile, porcelain, etc. **2.** of ceramics —*n.* **1.** [*pl.*, *with sing. v.*] the art or work of making objects of baked clay **2.** such an object —**ce·ram·ist** (sə ram′ist, ser′ə mist), **ce·ram′i·cist** (-ə sist) *n.*

Cer·ber·us (sur′bər əs) *Gr. & Rom. Myth.* the three-headed dog guarding the gate of Hades

cer·ca·ri·a (sər ker′ē ə) *n.*, *pl.* **-ri·ae** (-i ē′) [ModL. < Gr. *kerkos*, tail] the free-swimming larval form of a fluke, having a forked tail

cer·cus (sur′kəs) *n.*, *pl.* **cer′ci** (-sī) [ModL. < Gr. *kerkos*, tail] either of a pair of feelerlike growths at the hind end of the abdomen of many insects

cere (sir) *n.* [< Fr. < L. < Gr. *kēros*, wax] a waxy, fleshy area at the base of the beak of some birds, as the parrot, eagle, etc.: it contains the nostrils —*vt.* **cered, cer′ing** to wrap in a cerecloth

ce·re·al (sir′ē əl) *adj.* [< L. *Cerealis*, of Ceres < IE. base *ker-*, to grow] of grain or the grasses producing grain —*n.* **1.** any grain used for food, as wheat, oats, rice, etc. **2.** any grass producing such grain ☆**3.** food made from grain, esp. breakfast food, as oatmeal or cornflakes

cer·e·bel·lum (ser′ə bel′əm) *n.*, *pl.* **-lums, -la** (-ə) [L., dim. of *cerebrum*, the brain: for IE. base see HORN] the section of the brain behind and below the cerebrum: it is the center that controls muscular movement: see illustration at BRAIN

cer·e·bral (ser′ə brəl, sə rē′-) *adj.* of the brain or the cerebrum —**cer′e·bral·ly** *adv.*

cerebral palsy a condition caused by damage to the brain, esp. before or during birth, in which there is difficulty in moving or speaking

cer·e·brate (ser′ə brāt′) *vi.* **-brat′ed, -brat′ing** [< L. *cerebrum* (see CEREBELLUM) + -ATE[1]] to use one's brain; think —**cer′e·bra′tion** *n.*

cer·e·bro- [< L. *cerebrum*: see CEREBELLUM] a combining form meaning the brain (and); cerebrum (and) [*cerebrospinal*]

cer·e·bro·spi·nal (ser′ə brō spī′n'l, sə rē′brō-) *adj.* of or affecting the brain and the spinal cord

cer·e·brum (ser′ə brəm, sə rē′-) *n.*, *pl.* **-brums, -bra** (-brə) [L.: see CEREBELLUM] the upper, main part of the brain of animals with backbones, consisting of two equal segments: in human beings the cerebrum is the largest part of the brain: see illustration at BRAIN

cere·cloth (sir′klôth′) *n.* [< *cered cloth*: see CERE] cloth treated with wax or a similar substance, formerly used to wrap a dead person for burial

cer·e·ment (ser′ə mənt, sir′mənt) *n.* [see CERE] **1.** a cerecloth; shroud **2.** [*usually pl.*] clothes put on a person to be buried

cer·e·mo·ni·al (ser′ə mō′nē əl, -nyəl) *adj.* of, for, or consisting of ceremony; ritual; formal —*n.* **1.** an established system of rites or formal actions connected with an occasion; ritual **2.** a rite or ceremony —**cer′e·mo′ni·al·ism** *n.* —**cer′e·mo′ni·al·ist** *n.* —**cer′e·mo′ni·al·ly** *adv.*

cer·e·mo·ni·ous (-nē əs, -nyəs) *adj.* **1.** ceremonial **2.** full of ceremony **3.** very polite in conventional or formal ways —**cer′e·mo′ni·ous·ly** *adv.* —**cer′e·mo′ni·ous·ness** *n.*

cer·e·mo·ny (ser′ə mō′nē) *n.*, *pl.* **-nies** [L. *caerimonia*] **1.** a formal act or set of formal acts established as proper to a special occasion, such as a wedding, religious rite, etc. **2.** a conventionally courteous act **3.** very polite behavior that follows strict etiquette; formality [a dinner served with great *ceremony*] —**stand on ceremony** to behave with ceremony or formality or insist on it

Ce·res (sir′ēz) **1.** *Rom. Myth.* the goddess of agriculture: identified with the Greek goddess Demeter **2.** the first asteroid discovered (1801)

ce·re·us (sir′ē əs) *n.* [L., wax taper: from its shape] any of various cactuses of the southwestern U.S. and Mexico, esp. certain kinds that bloom at night

ce·rise (sə rēs′, -rēz′) *n.*, *adj.* [Fr.: see CHERRY] bright red

ce·ri·um (sir′ē əm) *n.* [after the asteroid *Ceres*] a gray, metallic chemical element: symbol, Ce; at. wt., 140.12; at. no., 58

cer·met (sur′met) *n.* [CER(AMIC) + MET(AL)] a mixture of ceramic material and a metal that is tough and heat-resistant; used in gas turbines, rocket motors, etc.

ce·ro- [< L. < Gr. *kēros*, wax] a combining form meaning wax

ce·rog·ra·phy (si räg′rə fē) *n.* [CERO- + -GRAPHY] the process of engraving on a wax-covered metal plate from which a printing surface is prepared by electrotyping

cert. 1. certificate **2.** certified

cer·tain (surt′'n) *adj.* [< OFr. < L. *certus*, determined < *cernere*, to decide: for IE. base see CARNAGE] **1.** fixed, settled, or determined [he was promised a *certain* share] **2.** sure (to happen, etc.); inevitable [to risk *certain* death] **3.** not to be doubted [the evidence is *certain*] **4.** reliable; dependable [a *certain* cure] **5.** that will not miss; controlled [his aim is *certain*] **6.** sure; positive [I'm *certain* he's here] **7.** not named or described, though perhaps known [a *certain* person was just here —guess who] **8.** some, but not very much; appreciable [to a *certain* extent] —see SYN. at SURE —**for certain** without doubt; surely [do you know *for certain*?]

cer·tain·ly (-lē) *adv.* beyond a doubt; surely

cer·tain·ty (-tē) *n.* **1.** the condition or quality of being certain; sureness [success cannot be predicted with *certainty*] **2.** *pl.* **-ties** anything certain; definite fact

SYN.—**certainty** suggests a firm belief that something is true [he knew for a *certainty* that she stole it]; **certitude** implies an unquestioning faith in something that cannot be proved [the *certitude* of a theist]; **assurance** suggests confidence or trust in something expected [the candidate has *assurance* of the labor vote]; **conviction** suggests a being convinced by reasons or proof that overcome any doubts one may have had [no one could shake her *conviction* that her son was innocent]

cer·tes (sur′tēz) *adv.* [< OFr. < L. *certus*, CERTAIN] [Archaic] certainly; verily

cer·tif·i·cate (sər tif′ə kit; *for v.* -kāt′) *n.* [< OFr. < ML. < LL. pp. of *certificare*, CERTIFY] a written or printed statement that can be used as proof of something because it is official [a birth *certificate* proves where and when one was born; a stock *certificate* proves that one owns shares of stock] —*vt.* **-cat′ed, -cat′ing** to issue a certificate to —**cer·tif′i·ca·to·ry** (-kə tôr′ē) *adj.*

cer·ti·fi·ca·tion (sur′tə fi kā′shən) *n.* **1.** a certifying or being certified **2.** a certified statement

cer·ti·fied (sur′tə fīd′) *adj.* **1.** vouched for; guaranteed **2.** having a certificate that is proof that requirements, standards, etc. have been met

☆**certified check** a check drawn by a depositor on his checking account, which his bank then certifies to be genuine and on which it guarantees payment

☆**certified mail** a postal service which provides a receipt to the sender of first-class mail and a record of its delivery; also, mail sent by this service

☆**certified public accountant** a public accountant certified by a State examining board after meeting the requirements of State law

cer·ti·fy (sur′tə fī′) *vt.* **-fied′, -fy′ing** [< OFr. < LL. *certificare* < L. *certus*, CERTAIN + *facere*, to make] **1.** to declare (a thing) to be true, genuine, accurate, certain, etc. by formal statement; verify [these papers *certify* that the horse is a Thoroughbred] **2.** to declare by official, legal action (a person) to be insane ☆**3.** to guarantee; vouch for [the bank *certified* his check] **4.** to issue a certificate to [the State *certified* her as a teacher] **5.** [Archaic] to assure; make certain —*vi.* to testify (*to*) —see SYN. at APPROVE —**cer′ti·fi′a·ble** *adj.* —**cer′ti·fi′a·bly** *adv.* —**cer′ti·fi′er** *n.*

cer·ti·o·ra·ri (sur′shē ə rer′ē, -rär′-) *n.* [LL., to be made more certain] *Law* a writ from a higher court to a lower one, or to a board or official with judicial power, requesting the record of a case for review

cer·ti·tude (sur′tə tōōd′, -tyōōd′) *n.* [< OFr. < LL. *certitudo*] **1.** a feeling absolutely sure or certain **2.** a being absolutely sure or certain —see SYN. at CERTAINTY

ce·ru·le·an (sə rōō′lē ən) *adj.* [< L., prob. < dim. of *caelum*, heaven] sky-blue; azure

ce·ru·men (sə rōō′mən) *n.* [< L. *cera*, wax, after ALBUMEN] *same as* EARWAX

Cer·van·tes (**Saavedra**) (thər vän′tes; *E.* sər van′tēz), **Miguel de** (mē gel′ *the*) 1547–1616; Sp. writer: author of *Don Quixote*

cer·vi·cal (sur′vi kəl) *adj.* of the neck or cervix

cer·vix (sur′viks) *n.*, *pl.* **-vi·ces′** (sur′və sēz′, sər vī′sēz), **-vix·es** [L., the neck] **1.** the neck, esp. the back of the neck **2.** a necklike part, esp. of the uterus

Ce·sar·e·an, Ce·sar·i·an (si zer′ē ən) *adj.*, *n. same as* CAESAREAN

ce·si·um (sē′zē əm) *n.* [ModL., neut. of L. *caesius*, bluish-gray] a soft, silver-white, ductile, metallic chemical element, used in photoelectric cells: symbol, Cs; at. wt., 132.905; at. no., 55

ces·sa·tion (se sā'shən) *n.* [< L. < pp. of *cessare,* CEASE] a ceasing or stopping, either forever or for some time [there was a *cessation* of work during the holidays]

ces·sion (sesh'ən) *n.* [OFr. < L. < pp. of *cedere,* to yield] a ceding or giving up (of rights, territory, etc.) to another [the *cession* of Guam to the U.S. by Spain took place in 1898]

cess·pool (ses'pool') *n.* [< It. *cesso,* privy < L. *secessus,* place of retirement: see SECEDE] **1.** a tank or deep hole in the ground to receive drainage or sewage from the sinks, toilets, etc. of a house **2.** a center of moral filth and corruption

ces·ta (ses'tə) *n.* [Sp., basket] the narrow, curved, basketlike racket strapped to the forearm in jai alai

‡c'est la vie (se lä vē') [Fr.] that's life; such is life

ces·tus (ses'təs) *n.* [L. *caestus* < *caedere,* to strike] a device of leather straps, sometimes weighted with metal, worn on the hand by boxers in ancient Rome

ce·su·ra (si zhoor'ə, -zyoor'ə) *n., pl.* **-ras, -rae** (-ē) *same as* CAESURA

CESTUS

CETA Comprehensive Employment Training Act

ce·ta·cean (si tā'shən) *n.* [L. *cetus,* whale < Gr. *kētos*] any of a group of nearly hairless, fishlike water mammals with paddlelike forelimbs, including whales, porpoises, and dolphins —*adj.* of the cetaceans: also **ce·ta'ceous** (-shəs)

ce·vi·tam·ic acid (sē'vī tam'ik, -vi-) [< C + VITAM(IN) + -IC] *same as* ASCORBIC ACID

Cey·lon (sə län', sā-, sē-) *former name of* SRI LANKA —**Cey·lo·nese** (sel'ə nēz') *adj., n.*

Cé·zanne (sā zàn'), **Paul** 1839–1906; Fr. impressionist & postimpressionist painter

Cf *Chem.* californium

cf. 1. *Baseball* center field (or center fielder): also **cf 2.** [L. *confer*] compare

CG, C.G. Coast Guard

cg, cg., cgm, cgm. centigram(s)

cgs, c.g.s., C.G.S. centimeter-gram-second

Ch. 1. Chaldean **2.** China **3.** Chinese

Ch., ch. 1. chain **2.** champion **3.** chapter **4.** child; children **5.** church

Cha·blis (shab'lē; *Fr.* shà blē') *n.* a dry, white Burgundy wine, originally from the region of Chablis, France

☆**cha-cha** (chä'chä) *n.* [AmSp., of echoic origin] a ballroom dance of Latin-American origin, with a repeating three-beat rhythm —*vi.* to dance the cha-cha Also **cha'-cha'-cha'**

Cha·co (chä'kð) large lowland plain in Argentina, Paraguay, & Bolivia: c.300,000 sq. mi.

cha·conne (shä kôn', -kôn') *n.* [Fr. < Sp. *chacona*] **1.** a slow, stately dance of Spanish or Moorish origin, popular in 17th- and 18th-cent. Europe **2.** music for this dance, or a musical form based on this dance

Chad (chad) **1.** country in NC Africa, south of Libya: 495,000 sq. mi.; pop. 3,361,000; cap. Fort Lamy **2. Lake,** lake at the juncture of the Chad, Niger, and Nigeria borders —**Chad'i·an** *adj., n.*

Chaer·o·ne·a (ker'ə nē'ə) ancient Greek town in Boeotia: site of a Macedonian victory (338 B.C.) over the Greeks

chafe (chāf) *vt.* **chafed, chaf'ing** [< OFr. *chaufer,* to warm < L. < *calere,* to be warm + *facere,* to make] **1.** to rub so as to make warm **2.** to wear away by rubbing **3.** to make sore by rubbing **4.** to annoy; irritate —*vi.* **1.** to rub (*on* or *against*) **2.** to be or become irritated or annoyed —*n.* an injury or irritation caused by rubbing —**chafe at the bit** to be impatient, as from having to wait: originally said of horses

chaf·er (chāf'ər) *n.* [OE. *ceafor*] any of various beetles that feed on plants

chaff (chaf) *n.* [OE. *ceaf*] **1.** the husks of wheat or other grain separated in threshing or winnowing **2.** anything worthless **3.** good-natured teasing; banter —*vt., vi.* to tease or ridicule in a good-natured way —**chaff'y** *adj.* **chaff'i·er, chaff'i·est**

chaf·finch (chaf'finch') *n.* [OE. *ceaffinc:* see CHAFF + FINCH: it eats chaff] a small European songbird, often kept in a cage as a pet

chaf·ing dish (chāf'iŋ) [see CHAFE] a pan with a heating apparatus beneath it, to cook food at the table or to keep food hot

Cha·gall (shä gäl'), **Marc** 1889– ; Russ. painter, esp. in France

cha·grin (shə grin') *n.* [Fr., grief, prob. < OFr. *graignier,* to sorrow < Gmc. *gram,* sorrow] a feeling of embarrassment and annoyance because one has failed or has been disappointed —*vt.* **-grined', -grin'ing** to embarrass and annoy [he was *chagrined* when the guest of honor failed to appear]

CHAFING DISH

chain (chān) *n.* [OFr. *chaine* < L. *catena,* a chain < IE. base *kat-,* to twist] **1.** a number of loops or links joined together in a line that can be bent [a *chain* of gold around her neck] **2.** [*pl.*] *a)* anything that holds someone prisoner, as bonds, shackles, etc. *b)* bondage, captivity, or slavery **3.** a chain of metal links used for measuring length: a *surveyor's chain* is 66 feet; an *engineer's chain* is 100 feet **4.** a series of things joined together [a *chain* of events; a mountain *chain*] ☆**5.** a number of stores, restaurants, etc. owned by one company **6.** *Chem.* a linking of atoms in a molecule —*vt.* **1.** to fasten or shackle with chains **2.** to hold down, restrain, confine, etc. —see SYN. at SERIES

chain gang a gang of prisoners chained together, as when working

chain letter a letter to be circulated among many people by being copied and passed to others

chain mail flexible armor made of metal links joined together

chain reaction a series of actions, changes, or events, each of which in turn starts another [atomic energy is produced by a *chain reaction* in which some atomic particles are set free to strike other atoms in a mass, freeing more particles that strike other atoms, and so forth]

☆**chain saw** a portable power saw with an endless chain that carries cutting teeth

chain-smoke (-smōk') *vt., vi.* **-smoked', -smok'ing** to smoke (cigarettes) one right after the other — **chain smoker, chain'-smok'er** *n.*

chain stitch a fancy stitch in which the loops are connected in a chainlike way, as in crocheting —**chain'-stitch'** *vt.*

☆**chain store** any of a chain of retail stores

chair (cher) *n.* [OFr. *chaiere* < L. *cathedra:* see CATHEDRA] **1.** a piece of furniture for one person to sit on, having a back and, usually, four legs **2.** a seat of authority or dignity [the *chair* of a bishop] **3.** the position of a player in a certain section of instruments in a symphony orchestra [he has the first *chair* in the violin section] **4.** an important or official position, as a professorship [Professor Jones holds the *chair* of literature] **5.** a person who presides over a meeting; chairman [address your remarks to the *chair*] **6.** *same as: a)* SEDAN CHAIR ☆*b)* ELECTRIC CHAIR —*vt.* **1.** to place in a chair; seat **2.** to place in authority **3.** to preside over as chairman —**take the chair** to preside as chairman

☆**chair·lift** (cher'lift') *n.* a line of seats suspended from a power-driven endless cable, used esp. to carry skiers up a slope

chair·man (-mən) *n., pl.* **-men** a person who presides at a meeting or heads a committee, board, etc. —*vt.* **-maned** or **-manned, -man·ing** or **-man·ning** to preside over as chairman —**chair'man·ship'** *n.* —**chair'wom'an** *n.fem., pl.* **-wom'en**

chair·per·son (-pur's'n) *n. same as* CHAIRMAN: preferred by some as a neutral term that does not suggest a man

chaise (shāz) *n.* [Fr., var. of *chaire,* CHAIR] **1.** a lightweight carriage, esp. one with a folding top and two or four wheels **2.** *same as* CHAISE LONGUE

chaise longue (shāz' lôṇ'; *often also* lounj' —*see next entry*) *pl.* **chaise** (or **chaises**) **longues** (shāz' lôṇz'; loun'jəz) [Fr., lit., long chair] a couchlike chair with a support for the back and a seat long enough to support the sitter's outstretched legs

chaise lounge (lounj) *pl.* **chaise lounges** [by folk etym. < prec.] *same as* CHAISE LONGUE

CHAIN SAW

cha·la·za (kə lā′zə) *n., pl.* **-zae** (-zē), **-zas** [ModL. < Gr. *chalaza*, hailstone] either of the spiral bands of dense albumen extending from the yolk toward the lining membrane at each end of a bird's egg: it keeps the yolk suspended near the center of the albumen: see illustration at EGG

chal·ced·o·ny (kal sed′'n ē, kal′sə dō′nē) *n., pl.* **-nies** [< OFr. < LL. < Gr. *chalkēdōn*, a precious stone < ?] a kind of quartz, such as onyx, agate, jasper, etc., that has the luster of wax

Chal·de·a, Chal·dae·a (kal dē′ə) ancient province of Babylonia, at the head of the Persian Gulf —**Chal·de′an, Chal·dae′an, Chal·da′ic** (-dā′ik), **Chal′dee** (-dē) *adj., n.*

cha·let (sha lā′, shal′ē) *n.* [Swiss-Fr., prob. ult. < L. *casa*, a house] **1.** a herdsman's hut or cabin in the Swiss Alps **2.** *a)* a type of Swiss house, with balconies and overhanging eaves *b)* any building in this style

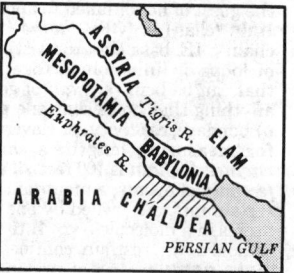

CHALDEA

chal·ice (chal′is) *n.* [OFr. < L. *calix*, a cup] **1.** a cup; goblet **2.** the cup for the wine of Holy Communion **3.** a cup-shaped flower

chalk (chôk) *n.* [OE. *cealc* < L. *calx*, limestone] **1.** a white or gray limestone that is soft and easily crushed into a powder **2.** any substance like chalk **3.** a piece of chalk, often colored, used for writing on a blackboard, etc. —*adj.* made or drawn with chalk —*vt.* **1.** to rub or smear with chalk **2.** to make pale **3.** to write, draw, or mark with chalk —*vi.* to become chalky or powdery —**chalk out 1.** to mark out as with chalk **2.** to outline; plan —**chalk up 1.** to score, get, or achieve **2.** to charge or credit —**walk a chalk line** [Colloq.] to behave in a very proper way —**chalk′i·ness** *n.* —**chalk′y** *adj.* **chalk′i·er, chalk′i·est**

☆**chalk·board** (chôk′bôrd′) *n.* a blackboard, esp. a light-colored one

☆**chalk talk** a talk given by a person who draws pictures, diagrams, etc. in chalk on a blackboard to explain his talk

chal·lenge (chal′ənj) *n.* [< OFr. < L. *calumnia*, CALUMNY] **1.** a demand that someone identify himself [a sentry gave the *challenge*] **2.** a demand that something be proved, explained, etc. [a *challenge* to an assertion] **3.** a call or dare to take part in a fight, contest, etc. **4.** anything, as a difficult task, that calls for special effort ☆**5.** a questioning of someone's right to vote or of his vote **6.** *Law* a formal rejection of a person chosen as a prospective juror —*vt.* **-lenged, -leng·ing 1.** to call to a halt and make (someone) identify himself **2.** *a)* to call to account *b)* to demand an explanation of or proof for **3.** to call or dare to take part in a fight, contest, etc.; defy **4.** to call for; make demands on [the test *challenged* his ability] **5.** to reject (a vote or voter) as not being valid or qualified **6.** *Law* to reject formally (a prospective juror) —*vi.* to issue or offer a challenge —**chal′lenge·a·ble** *adj.* —**chal′leng·er** *n.*

chal·lis, chal·lie (shal′ē) *n.* [< ?] a soft, lightweight cloth of wool, cotton, etc., usually printed with a pattern

cha·lyb·e·ate (kə lib′ē ət, -āt′) *adj.* [< L. *chalybs* < Gr. *chalyps*, steel] **1.** containing salts of iron **2.** tasting like iron —*n.* a chalybeate liquid

cham (kam) *n. archaic var. of* KHAN[1]

cham·ber (chām′bər) *n.* [< OFr. < LL. < L. *camera*: see CAMERA] **1.** a room in a house, esp. a bedroom **2.** [*pl.*] [Brit.] a suite of rooms used by one person **3.** [*pl.*] a judge's office near the courtroom **4.** a large meeting room **5.** an official group of judges or lawmakers [the *Chamber* of Deputies] **6.** a council or board [a *chamber* of commerce] **7.** an enclosed space in the body of a plant or animal [a *chamber* of the heart] **8.** a compartment; specif., the part of a gun that holds the charge or cartridge —*vt.* to provide a chamber or chambers for —**cham′bered** *adj.*

cham·ber·lain (chām′bər lin) *n.* [< OFr. < OHG. < *chamara* (< L. *camera*) + dim. suffix *-linc*: see CAMERA & -LING] **1.** an officer in charge of the household of a ruler or lord; steward **2.** a high official in certain royal courts **3.** [Brit.] a treasurer

Cham·ber·lain (chām′bər lin), **(Arthur) Neville** 1869–1940; Brit. statesman; prime minister (1937–40)

cham·ber·maid (chām′bər mād′) *n.* a woman whose work is taking care of bedrooms, as in hotels

chamber music music that is meant to be played by a small group, orig. in a small hall [trios, sonatas, and quartets are forms of *chamber music*]

chamber of commerce an association established to further the business interests of its community

chamber pot a portable container kept in a bedroom and used as a toilet

☆**cham·bray** (sham′brā) *n.* [var. of CAMBRIC] a smooth cotton cloth made by weaving white or unbleached threads across colored ones

cha·me·le·on (kə mēl′yən, -mē′lē ən) *n.* [< L. < Gr. < *chamai*, on the ground + *leōn*, lion] **1.** any of various lizards that can change the color of their skin **2.** a person who keeps changing his opinions and attitudes

cham·fer (cham′fər) *n.* [< Fr. < OFr. < L. *cantum frangere*: see CANT[2] & FRAGILE] a beveled edge or corner, esp. one cut at a 45° angle —*vt.* **1.** to cut a chamfer on; bevel **2.** to make a groove or fluting in

CHAMELEON
(to 24 in. long,
including tail)

cham·ois (sham′ē) *n., pl.* **-ois** [Fr. < VL. *camox*] **1.** a small, goatlike antelope of the mountains of Europe and the Caucasus **2.** *a)* a soft leather made from the skin of chamois, or of sheep, deer, goats, etc. *b)* a piece of this leather, used as a polishing cloth: also **cham·my** (sham′ē), *pl.* **-mies** —*adj.* **1.** made of chamois **2.** yellowish-brown —*vt.* **cham′oised** (-ēd), **cham′ois·ing** (-ē iŋ) to polish with a chamois skin

cham·o·mile (kam′ə mīl′, -mēl′) *n.* [< OFr. < L. < Gr. *chamaimēlon* < *chamai*, on the ground + *mēlon*, apple] any of several plants with strong-smelling leaves; esp., a plant whose dried flower heads have been used in a medicinal tea

champ[1] (champ) *vt., vi.* [earlier *cham*: prob. echoic] to chew hard and noisily; munch —*n.* the act of champing —**champ at the bit 1.** to bite upon its bit repeatedly and restlessly: said of a horse **2.** to be restless

☆**champ**[2] (champ) *n.* [Slang] *same as* CHAMPION

CHAMOIS
(30–32 in. high
at shoulder)

cham·pagne (sham pān′) *n.* **1.** orig., any of various wines produced in Champagne, a region in NE France **2.** now, any white wine that bubbles like soda water: a symbol of luxurious living **3.** pale, tawny yellow

Cham·paign (sham pān′) [see CHAMPAIGN (flat country)] city in EC Ill.: pop. 57,000

cham·paign (sham pān′) *n.* [< OFr. *champaigne*: see CAMPAIGN] a broad plain; flat, open country —*adj.* of or like a champaign

cham·pi·on (cham′pē ən) *n.* [< OFr. < LL. *campio*, gladiator < L. *campus*, a field: see CAMPUS] **1.** a person who fights for another or for a cause; defender; supporter [a *champion* of the poor] **2.** a winner of first place in a competition [a tennis *champion*] —*adj.* winning first place; excelling over all others [a *champion* bull] —*vt.* to fight for; defend; support [to *champion* women's rights]

cham·pi·on·ship (-ship′) *n.* **1.** the act of championing; defense; support **2.** the position or title of a champion

Cham·plain (sham plān′), **Lake** [after S. de *Champlain*, 17th-c. Fr. explorer] lake between N.Y. and Vt.

Champs É·ly·sées (shän zā lē zā′) [Fr., lit., Elysian fields] famous avenue in Paris

Chan., Chanc. 1. Chancellor **2.** Chancery

chan. channel

chance (chans) *n.* [< OFr. < ML. < L. prp. of *cadere*, to fall: see CASE[1]] **1.** the happening of events by accident; luck [to leave things to *chance*] **2.** something that happens by accident **3.** a risk or gamble [take a *chance*] **4.** a ticket in a lottery or raffle **5.** an opportunity [a *chance* to go] **6.** a possibility or probability [a *chance* that he will live] ☆**7.** *Baseball* an opportunity to field the ball —*adj.* happening by chance; accidental [a *chance* meeting] —*vi.* **chanced, chanc′ing 1.** to have the fortune (to) **2.** [Archaic] to happen by chance —*vt.* to leave to chance; risk [let's *chance* it] —see SYN. at RANDOM —**by chance 1.** as it may happen **2.** accidentally —**chance on** (or **upon**) to find by chance —**on the (off) chance** relying on the (remote) possibility; in case

chan·cel (chan's'l) *n.* [< OFr. < LL. < L. *cancelli*, *pl.*, lattices: see CANCEL] that part of a church around the altar, reserved for the clergy and the choir: it is sometimes set off by a railing

chan·cel·ler·y (chan'sə lə rē, -slə rē) *n.*, *pl.* **-ler·ies** 1. the position of a chancellor 2. a chancellor's office or the building that houses it 3. the office of an embassy or consulate Also sp. **chan·cel·lor·y**

chan·cel·lor (-lər) *n.* [< OFr. < LL. *cancellarius*, keeper of the barrier: see CANCEL] 1. [*usually* C-] any of several high officials in the British government 2. the title of the president or a high officer in some universities 3. the prime minister in certain countries ☆4. a chief judge of a court of chancery or equity in some States of the U.S. 5. a high church official —**chan'cel·lor·ship'** *n.*

chance-med·ley (chans'med'lē) *n.* [see CHANCE & MEDDLE] 1. accidental homicide 2. any unplanned or random act

chan·cer·y (chan'sər ē) *n.*, *pl.* **-cer·ies** [< OFr. < ML. *cancellaria*: see CHANCELLOR] 1. a division of the High Court of Justice in England and Wales 2. a court of equity or its system of law 3. an office for public documents 4. *same as* CHANCELLERY (senses 2 & 3) 5. *R.C.Ch.* the diocesan office in charge of certain documents, secretarial services, etc. for the bishop —**in chancery** 1. engaged in a law suit in a court of equity 2. in a helpless situation

chan·cre (shaŋ'kər) *n.* [Fr.: see CANCER] a venereal sore or ulcer, esp. one caused by syphilis —**chan'crous** (-krəs) *adj.*

chan·croid (shaŋ'kroid) *n.* [CHANCR(E) + -OID] a venereal ulcer not caused by syphilis: also called **soft chancre**

chanc·y (chan'sē) *adj.* **chanc'i·er**, **chanc'i·est** risky; uncertain

chan·de·lier (shan'də lir') *n.* [Fr. < OFr. < L. *candelabrum* < *candela*, CANDLE] a lighting fixture hanging from a ceiling, with branches for candles, electric bulbs, etc.

chan·dler (chan'dlər) *n.* [< OFr. < L. *candela*, CANDLE] 1. a maker or seller of candles 2. a retailer of supplies, equipment, etc. of a certain kind [a ship *chandler* sells provisions for ships] —**chan'dler·y** (-ē) *n.*, *pl.* **-dler·ies**

Chang·chun (chäŋ'choon') city in NE China: pop. 1,800,000

change (chānj) *vt.* **changed**, **chang'ing** [< OFr. < LL. < L. *cambire*, to barter < Celt. < IE. base *kamb-*, to bend] 1. to put or take (a thing) in place of something else; substitute [to *change* one's clothes] 2. to give for (another thing in return); exchange [let's *change* seats] 3. *a*) to make different; alter [success *changed* him] *b*) to become different in [leaves *change* color] 4. to give or receive for (a coin or bank note) the same amount in smaller coins or bills or in foreign money 5. to put a fresh sheet, diaper, etc. on [to *change* a bed; *change* the baby] —*vi.* 1. *a*) to alter; vary [the scene *changes*] *b*) to be altered or replaced [the price *changes* at 6:00 P.M.] 2. to become lower in range, as the male voice at puberty 3. to leave one train, bus, etc. and board another 4. to put on other clothes 5. to make an exchange —*n.* 1. the act or process of changing in some way 2. absence of monotony; variety 3. something of the same kind but new or fresh 4. another set of clothes, esp. a clean, fresh set 5. *a*) money returned as the difference between the purchase price and the larger sum given in payment [it cost 45 cents and he got back 55 cents as *change* from his dollar] *b*) a number of coins or bills whose total value equals a single larger coin or bill [give me *change* for a dollar bill] *c*) small coins 6. a place where merchants meet to do business; exchange: also **'change** 7. [*usually pl.*] *Bell Ringing* any order in which the bells may be rung —**change off** to take turns —**ring the changes** 1. to ring a set of bells with all possible variations 2. to do or say a thing in many and various ways —**change'ful** *adj.* —**change'ful·ly** *adv.* —**change'ful·ness** *n.* —**chang'er** *n.*
SYN.—**change** refers to a making or becoming different in character or a replacing or being replaced with something else [the quiet town *changed* into a busy city; go *change* your shoes]; **alter** implies a partial change, as in the way something looks [the suit was *altered* to fit his son]; **vary** suggests changing from one thing to another from time to time [to *vary* your diet, try rice instead of potatoes]; **modify** implies minor change, often so as to limit or restrict [the union *modified* its demands for wage increases]; **transform** implies a change in form and, now, usually a change in what something is or the way it works [to *transform* matter into energy]; **convert** suggests a change made to suit a different purpose [to *convert* a barn into a house]

change·a·ble (chān'jə b'l) *adj.* 1. *a*) that can change or be changed; alterable *b*) likely or tending to change; fickle 2. having a changing appearance or color; iridescent —**change'a·bil'i·ty, change'a·ble·ness** *n.* —**change'a·bly** *adv.*

change·less (chānj'lis) *adj.* that does not change or cannot be changed; unchanging —**change'less·ly** *adv.* —**change'less·ness** *n.*

change·ling (-liŋ) *n.* a child secretly put in the place of another, esp., in folk tales, by fairies

change of life *same as* MENOPAUSE

change·o·ver (-ō'vər) *n.* a complete change, as in goods produced, equipment, etc.

change ringing the art of ringing a series of unrepeated changes on a set of bells tuned together

chan·nel (chan''l) *n.* [< OFr.: see CANAL] 1. the bed of a river, etc. 2. the deeper part of a river, harbor, etc. 3. a body of water joining two larger bodies of water 4. any tube or groove through which a liquid flows 5. any means by which something moves or passes 6. [*pl.*] the proper or official course of action [to make a request through army *channels*] 7. a long groove or furrow 8. the band of frequencies within which a radio or television transmitting station must keep its signal —*vt.* **-neled** or **-nelled**, **-nel·ing** or **-nel·ling** 1. to make a channel in 2. to send through or direct into a channel

Channel Islands group of Brit. islands in the English Channel, off the coast of Normandy

‡**chan·son** (shän sōn'; *E.* shan'sən) *n.*, *pl.* **-sons'** (-sōn'; *E.* -sənz) [Fr.] a song

chant (chant) *n.* [Fr. < L. *cantus*, song < the *v.*] 1. a song; melody 2. *a*) a simple song in which a series of syllables or words is sung to each tone *b*) words, as of a psalm, to be sung in this way 3. *a*) a singsong way of speaking *b*) anything uttered in this way —*vi.* [< OFr. < L. *cantare*, freq. of *canere*, to sing] 1. to sing a chant; intone 2. to say the same thing over and over —*vt.* 1. to sing a chant 2. to praise in song 3. to sing or recite in the manner of a chant —**chant'er** *n.*

chan·teuse (shan tooz') *n.* [Fr.] a woman singer

chan·tey (shan'tē, chan'tē) *n.*, *pl.* **-teys** [< ? Fr.: see CHANT] a song that sailors sing in rhythm with their motions while working: also **chan'ty**, *pl.* **-ties**

chan·ti·cleer (chan'tə klir') *n.* [< OFr.: see CHANT & CLEAR] a rooster: name used in fable and folklore

Cha·nu·kah (khä'noo kä') *n. same as* HANUKA

cha·os (kā'äs) *n.* [L. < Gr. *chaos*, space, chaos (sense 1) < IE. base *gheu-*, to gape] 1. the disorder that is supposed to have existed before the universe came into being 2. extreme confusion or disorder —see SYN. at CONFUSION

cha·ot·ic (kā ät'ik) *adj.* in a state of chaos; in a completely confused or disordered condition —**cha·ot'i·cal·ly** *adv.*

chap[1] (chäp, chap) *n.* [prob. < ME. *cheppe* < ?] *same as* CHOP[2]

chap[2] (chap) *n.* [< CHAPMAN] [Colloq.] a man or boy; fellow

chap[3] (chap) *vt.*, *vi.* **chapped** or **chapt**, **chap'ping** [ME. *chappen*, var. of *choppen* (see CHOP[1])] to crack open; make or become rough [the cold wind *chapped* his skin] —*n.* a chapped place in the skin

chap. 1. chaplain 2. chapter

☆**cha·pa·re·jos, cha·pa·ra·jos** (chap'ə rā'hōs, shap'-) *n.pl.* [MexSp.] [Southwest] *same as* CHAPS[1]

☆**chap·ar·ral** (chap'ə ral', shap'-) *n.* [Sp. < *chaparro*, evergreen oak] [Southwest] a thicket of shrubs, thorny bushes, etc., orig. of evergreen oaks

chap·book (chap'book') *n.* [< CHAP(MAN): chapmen peddled such books] a small book or pamphlet of poems, ballads, religious tracts, etc.

cha·peau (sha pō') *n.*, *pl.* **-peaus'**, **-peaux'** (-pōz') [Fr. < OFr. < VL. *capellus*, dim. of LL. *cappa*: see CAPE[1]] a hat

chap·el (chap''l) *n.* [< OFr. < ML. < VL. (see prec.): orig. sanctuary in which cloak of St. Martin was preserved] 1. a place of Christian worship smaller than a church 2. a room or building used as a place of worship, as in a school 3. a small room in a church, having its own altar 4. a religious service, as in a chapel 5. in Great Britain, any place of worship for those who are not members of an established church

chap·er·on, chap·er·one (shap'ə rōn') *n.* [Fr. < OFr., hood (hence, protector) < *chape*, COPE[2]] a person, esp. an older or married woman, who goes along with young unmarried people to a party, dance, etc. to see that they behave properly —**vt., vi.** -oned', -on'ing to act as chaperon (to) —**chap'er·on·age** n.

chap·fall·en (chǎp'fô'lən, chǎp'-) **adj.** [CHAP[1] + FALLEN] **1.** having the lower jaw hanging down, as from fatigue **2.** disheartened, depressed, or humiliated

chap·lain (chǎp'lən) **n.** [< OFr. < ML.: see CHAPEL] **1.** a clergyman attached to a chapel, as of a royal court **2.** a minister, priest, or rabbi who serves in the armed forces as a clergyman, or in a prison, hospital, etc. **3.** a person chosen to conduct religious services for an organization, club, etc. —**chap'lain·cy,** pl. -cies, **chap'lain·ship'** n.

chap·let (chǎp'lit) **n.** [< OFr. dim. of chapel < VL. capellus: see CHAPEAU] **1.** a garland for the head **2.** a) a string of prayer beads one third the length of a full rosary b) the prayers said with such beads **3.** any string of beads —**chap'let·ed** adj.

Chap·lin (chǎp'lin), Sir **Charles Spencer** 1889–1977; Eng. motion-picture actor & producer, in the U.S. (1910–52)

chap·man (chǎp'mən) **n.,** pl. -men [< OE. < ceap, trade + man] [Brit.] a peddler; hawker

Chap·man (chǎp'mən), **George** 1559?-1634; Eng. poet, playwright, & translator of Homer

☆**chaps**[1] (chaps, shaps) **n.pl.** [< CHAPAREJOS] leather trousers without a seat, worn over ordinary trousers by cowboys to protect their legs

chaps[2] (chǎps, chaps) **n.pl.** [see CHAP[1]] same as CHOPS

chap·ter (chǎp'tər) **n.** [< OFr. chapitre < L. capitulum, dim. of caput, HEAD] **1.** a main division, as of a book **2.** a thing like a chapter; part; episode [a chapter of one's life] **3.** a) a formal meeting of canons of a church or of the members of a religious order b) the group of such canons, etc. ☆**4.** a local branch of a club, fraternity, etc. —**vt.** to divide into chapters

Cha·pul·te·pec (chə pool'tə pek', -pul'-) fortress near Mexico City: captured by U.S. forces in the Mexican War

char[1] (chär) **vt., vi.** charred, char'ring [< CHARCOAL] **1.** to burn so as to make charcoal **2.** to scorch —**n.** anything charred; charcoal — see **SYN.** at BURN[1]

CHAPS

char[2] (chär) **n.** [< CHARWOMAN] [Brit.] a charwoman —**vi.** charred, char'ring [Chiefly Brit.] to work as a charwoman

char[3] (chär) **n.,** pl. chars, char: [< PLURAL, II, D, 1 [< Gael. ceara, red] a kind of trout with small scales and a red belly

char·a·banc, char-à-banc (shar'ə baŋk', -baŋ) **n.** [Fr., lit., car with bench] [Brit.] a sightseeing bus

char·ac·ter (kar'ik tər) **n.** [< OFr. < L. < Gr. charaktēr, an engraving instrument < charattein, to engrave] **1.** any figure, letter, or symbol used in writing and printing **2.** the basic quality or qualities that make up something **3.** the pattern of behavior or personality found in an individual or group **4.** moral strength; self-discipline, courage, etc. **5.** a) reputation b) good reputation [left without a shred of character] **6.** position or role [in his character as a son] **7.** a person in a play, novel, etc. **8.** [Colloq.] an odd or peculiar person **9.** a special trait or characteristic **10.** Genetics the color, shape, etc. caused in an individual by the action of one or more genes —see **SYN.** at DISPOSITION and QUALITY —**in** (or **out of**) **character** in keeping with (or not in keeping with) the role or general character

character actor an actor who plays roles with strong or peculiar characteristics —**character actress** fem.

char·ac·ter·is·tic (kar'ik tə ris'tik) **adj.** that gives the basic quality or character to someone or something [the characteristic sound made by an owl] —**n. 1.** a trait, feature, etc. that makes a person or thing different from others **2.** the whole number, or integral part, of a logarithm, as 4 in the logarithm 4.7193: see also MANTISSA —**char'ac·ter·is'ti·cal·ly** adv.

SYN. —**characteristic** suggests a quality that is typical of, and helps identify, a certain person or thing [her characteristic honesty; the characteristic taste of honey]; **individual** and **distinctive** refer to a quality that makes something different from others of its kind, **distinctive** often implying excellence [an individual, or distinctive, style]

char·ac·ter·ize (kar'ik tə rīz') **vt.** -ized', -iz'ing **1.** to describe or show as having particular qualities or traits [Tennyson characterized King Arthur as wise and brave] **2.** to be the distinctive character of; distinguish [bribery characterized her term in office] —**char'ac·ter·i·za'tion** n.

character sketch a short piece of writing describing a person or type of person

cha·rade (shə rād') **n.** [Fr. < Pr. charrada < charrar, to gossip] [often pl.] **1.** a game in which the players try to guess a

word or phrase that another player is acting out without speaking, often syllable by syllable **2.** an action, show of feeling, etc. that is easily seen as misleading or insincere

char·coal (chär'kōl') **n.** [ME. char cole, prob. < charren, to char + cole, coal] **1.** a form of carbon produced by partially burning wood or other organic matter in large closed containers from which air is kept out **2.** a pencil made of this substance **3.** a drawing made with such a pencil **4.** a very dark gray or brown, almost black —**vt.** to draw with charcoal

chard (chärd) **n.** [Fr. carde < L. carduus, thistle] a kind of beet whose large leaves and thick stalks are used as food

Char·din (shär dan'), **1. Jean Si·mé·on** (sē mā ōn'), 1699–1779; Fr. painter **2. Teilhard de,** see TEILHARD DE CHARDIN

chare (cher) **n.** [OE. cierr, a turn, job < cierran, to turn] a chore, esp. a household chore —**vi.** chared, char'ing **1.** to do chores **2.** same as CHAR[2]

charge (chärj) **vt.** charged, charg'ing [< OFr. chargier < VL. carricare, to load < L. carrus, CAR, wagon] **1.** to load or fill with the required material [a firearm charged with gunpowder] **2.** to saturate with another substance [air charged with steam] **3.** to add carbon dioxide to (water, etc.) ☆**4.** to add an electrical charge to (a battery, etc.) **5.** to give as a task, duty, etc. to [the nurse is charged with giving medicine to the patients] **6.** to give instructions to or command authoritatively [the judge charged the jury] **7.** to accuse of wrongdoing; censure [the state charged her with murder] **8.** to set as a price or fee [barbers used to charge a dollar for a haircut] **9.** to have recorded as a debt one is to pay later [he charged his purchases] **10.** to attack vigorously [our troops charged the enemy] —**vi. 1.** to ask payment (for) [to charge for a service] **2.** to attack vigorously or move forward as if attacking —**n. 1.** the amount, as of fuel, gunpowder, etc., used to load or fill something **2.** a) the amount of chemical energy stored in a battery to be a source of electrical energy b) a change from the condition of electrical neutrality by the gaining of electrons (negative charge) or by the loss of electrons (positive charge) ☆**3.** [Slang] a thrill **4.** responsibility or duty (of) [she took charge of the finances] **5.** care or custody (of) **6.** a person or thing entrusted to someone's care [the children were the nurses' charges] **7.** instruction or command, esp. instructions given by a judge to a jury **8.** accusation; indictment [charges of cruelty] **9.** the cost or price of an article, service, etc. **10.** a debt or expense ☆**11.** same as CHARGE ACCOUNT **12.** a) an attack, as by troops b) the signal for this **13.** Heraldry a bearing —see **SYN.** at COMMAND —**charge off 1.** to regard as a loss **2.** to think of as due to a certain cause; ascribe [charge off her mistake to inexperience] —**in charge (of)** having the responsibility or control (of) —**in the charge of** in the care of or under the control of —**charge·a·ble** (chär'jə b'l) **adj.** ☆**charge account** a business arrangement by which a customer may pay for purchases within a specified future period

charge card (or **plate**) a thin plastic card embossed with the owner's name, account number, etc., for stamping bills when purchases are charged

char·gé d'af·faires (shär zhā' də fer') pl. **char·gés d'af·faires** (shär zhāz' də fer', shär zhā') [Fr.] **1.** a diplomat temporarily substituting for a minister or ambassador **2.** a diplomat ranking below an ambassador or minister

charg·er[1] (chär'jər) **n. 1.** one that charges **2.** a horse ridden in battle **3.** an apparatus for charging storage batteries

charg·er[2] (chär'jər) **n.** [ME. chargeour] [Archaic] a large, flat dish; platter

char·i·ly (cher'ə lē) **adv.** in a chary manner

char·i·ness (-ē nis) **n.** the quality of being chary

char·i·ot (char'ē ət) **n.** [< OFr. < VL. carricare: see CHARGE] a horse-drawn, two-wheeled cart used in ancient times for war, racing, etc. —**vt., vi.** to drive or ride in a chariot

char·i·ot·eer (char'ē ə tir') **n.** a chariot driver

cha·ris·ma (kə riz'mə) **n.,** pl. -ma·ta (-mə tə) [< Gr., favor, grace] **1.** Christian Theol. a divinely inspired gift or talent, as for prophesying **2.** a special quality of leadership that captures the imagination of many people and inspires great devotion

CHARIOT

char·is·mat·ic (kar'iz mat'ik) **adj. 1.** having or resulting from charisma **2.** describing any religious group that believes that God may directly give people certain powers, as to heal

char·i·ta·ble (char′i tə b'l) *adj.* **1.** kind and generous in giving help to those in need **2.** for the poor and sick and others needing help [a *charitable* institution] **3.** kind and forgiving in judging others; lenient —**char′i·ta·ble·ness** *n.* —**char′i·ta·bly** *adv.*

char·i·ty (char′ə tē) *n., pl.* **-ties** [< OFr. < L. *caritas*, affection < *carus*, dear < IE. base *karo-*, to like, desire] **1.** *Christian Theol.* the love of God for man or of man for his fellow men **2.** an act or feeling of good will; benevolence **3.** kindness in judging others **4.** a giving of money or help to those in need **5.** a welfare institution, organization, etc.

char·la·tan (shär′lə t'n) *n.* [Fr. < It. *ciarlatano* < LL. *cerretanus*, seller of papal indulgences] one who pretends to have expert knowledge or skill that he does not have; fake; mountebank —**char′la·tan·ism, char′la·tan·ry,** *pl.* **-ries** *n.*

Char·le·magne (shär′lə mān′) 742–814 A.D.; king of the Franks (768–814); emperor of the Holy Roman Empire (800–814): also called **Charles the Great**

Charles (chärlz) [Fr. < ML. *Carolus* (or) < Gmc. *Karl;* lit., full-grown] **1.** a masculine name: dim. *Charley, Charlie* **2. Charles I** *a)* 1600–49; king of England, Scotland, & Ireland (1625–49) *b) same as* CHARLEMAGNE **3. Charles II** 1630–85; king of England, Scotland, and Ireland (1660–85): son of *Charles I* **4. Charles V** 1500–58; Holy Roman Emperor (1519–56) *&* as **Charles I,** king of Spain (1516–56)

Charles's law (chärl′ziz) the statement that for a body of ideal gas at constant pressure the volume is directly proportional to the absolute temperature: first stated by J. Charles (1746–1823), Fr. physicist

Charles's Wain (chärl′ziz) [Brit.] *same as* BIG DIPPER

Charles·ton (chärl′stən) [after CHARLES I of England] **1.** capital of W.Va., in the W part: pop. 72,000 **2.** seaport in S.C.: pop. 67,000 —*n.* [< the seaport] a lively dance in 4/4 time, popular during the 1920's

☆**char·ley horse** (chär′lē) [Colloq.] a cramp in the leg or arm muscles, caused by strain

char·lock (chär′lək) *n.* [OE. *cerlic*] a weed of the mustard family, with yellow flowers

Char·lotte (shär′lət) [Fr., fem. of *Charlot,* dim. of *Charles*] **1.** a feminine name **2.** [after Queen *Charlotte,* wife of GEORGE III] city in southern N.C.: pop. 241,000

char·lotte (shär′lət) *n.* [Fr. < prec.] a dessert made of fruit, gelatin, custard, etc. in a mold lined with strips of bread, cake, etc.

Charlotte A·ma·lie (ə mäl′yə, ə mäl′ē) capital of the Virgin Islands of the U.S.: pop. 12,000

charlotte russe (rōōs) [Fr., lit., Russian charlotte] a dessert made of whipped cream, custard, etc. in a mold lined with spongecake

Char·lotte·town (shär′lət toun′) capital of Prince Edward Island, Canada: pop. 18,000

charm (chärm) *n.* [< OFr. < L. *carmen,* song, charm] **1.** a chanted word, phrase, etc., an action, or an object assumed to have magic power to help or hurt **2.** a trinket on a bracelet, watch chain, etc. **3.** a quality or feature that attracts or delights [her *charm* won her friends] —*vt.* **1.** to act on or protect as though by magic [he led a *charmed* life] **2.** to attract or please greatly; fascinate; delight —*vi.* to be charming —see SYN. at ATTRACT —**charm′er** *n.*

charm·ing (chärm′iŋ) *adj.* attractive; fascinating; delightful —**charm′ing·ly** *adv.*

char·nel (chär′n'l) *n.* [OFr. < LL. *carnale,* graveyard; neut. of *carnalis,* CARNAL] a building or place where corpses or bones are deposited: in full, **charnel house** —*adj.* of, like, or fit for a charnel

Cha·ron (ker′ən) *Gr. Myth.* the boatman who ferried souls of the dead across the river Styx to Hades

Char·pen·tier (shàr päⁿ tyā′), **Gus·tave** (güs tàv′) 1860–1956; Fr. composer

charr (chär) *n., pl.* **charrs, charr:** see PLURAL, II, D, 1 *same as* CHAR³

chart (chärt) *n.* [OFr. < ML. < L. *charta:* see CARD¹] **1.** a map, esp. one used in navigating a ship or airplane **2.** an outline map on which special information, as on weather conditions, is plotted **3.** *a)* a group of facts set up in the form of a diagram, graph, etc. *b)* such a diagram, graph, etc., or a sheet with diagrams, etc. ☆**4.** [Colloq.] *a)* an arrangement of a musical composition, as for a jazz band *b)* a list of the best-selling phonograph recordings for a given period: *usually used in pl.* —*vt.* **1.** to make a chart of **2.** to plan (a course of action) **3.** to show by, on, or as by, a chart —**chart′less** *adj.*

char·ter (chär′tər) *n.* [< OFr. < L. dim. of *charta:* see CARD¹] **1.** a document in which specified rights are given by a government or ruler to a person, corporation, etc. **2.** *a)* a document setting forth the aims and principles of a united group, as of nations *b)* the constitution of a city, setting forth its governmental organization and powers **3.** a document authorizing the organization of a local chapter of a society **4.** the hire or lease of a ship, bus, etc. —*vt.* **1.** to grant a charter to **2.** to hire for the special use of a group —see SYN. at HIRE —**char′ter·er** *n.*

☆**charter member** one of the founders or original members of an organization

Char·tres (shàr′tr′; *E.* shärt) city in NC France: site of a Gothic cathedral: pop. 31,000

char·treuse (shär trōōz′, -trōōs′; *Fr.* shàr trôz′) *n.* [Fr., Carthusian] **1.** a yellow, pale-green, or white liqueur made by Carthusian monks **2.** pale, yellowish green

char·wom·an (chär′woom′ən) *n., pl.* **-wom′en** [see CHARE, CHORE] a woman who does cleaning or scrubbing, as in office buildings

char·y (cher′ē, char′ē) *adj.* **char′i·er, char′i·est** [OE. *cearig* < *cearu,* care] **1.** not taking chances; cautious [be *chary* of offending others] **2.** not giving freely; sparing [*chary* of his favors to friends]

Cha·ryb·dis (kə rib′dis) whirlpool off the NE coast of Sicily: see SCYLLA

chase¹ (chās) *vt.* **chased, chas′ing** [< OFr. *chacier, cachier:* see CATCH] **1.** to follow quickly or without stopping so as to catch or harm **2.** to run after; follow **3.** to make move away; drive [using his hand to *chase* flies away] —*vi.* **1.** to go in pursuit [*chase* after him] **2.** [Colloq.] to go hurriedly; rush [to *chase* around town on errands] —*n.* **1.** a chasing; pursuit **2.** the hunting of game for sport (often with *the*) —**give chase** to chase

chase² (chās) *n.* [OFr. *châsse,* a frame, ult. < L. *capsa:* see CASE²] **1.** a groove; furrow **2.** a rectangular metal frame in which pages or columns of type are locked —*vt.* **chased, chas′ing** to make a groove or furrow in; indent

chase³ (chās) *vt.* **chased, chas′ing** [< Fr. *enchâsser,* enshrine] to ornament (metal) by engraving, embossing, etc.

chas·er (chā′sər) *n.* **1.** one that chases; pursuer ☆**2.** [Colloq.] a mild drink, as water, taken after or with whiskey, rum, etc.

chasm (kaz′'m) *n.* [L. & Gr. *chasma* < Gr. *chainein,* to gape: for IE. base see CHAOS] **1.** a deep crack in the earth's surface; abyss; gorge **2.** any break or gap **3.** a wide difference in feelings, interests, etc.

chas·seur (sha sur′) *n.* [Fr.] **1.** a hunter **2.** a soldier, esp. one of certain French infantrymen or cavalrymen, trained for rapid action **3.** a uniformed attendant

Chas·sid·im (has′i dim; *Heb.* khä sē′-) *n.pl., sing.* **Chas′sid** *same as* HASIDIM —**Chas·sid′ic** *adj.* —**Chas′sid·ism** *n.*

chas·sis (chas′ē, shas′ē) *n., pl.* **-sis** (-ēz) [Fr. *châssis:* see CHASE²] **1.** the frame, wheels, etc. of a motor vehicle, but not the body and engine **2.** the frame supporting the body of an airplane **3.** *Radio & TV a)* the framework to which the parts of a receiver, amplifier, etc. are attached *b)* the assembled frame and parts ☆**4.** [Slang] the body; figure

chaste (chāst) *adj.* [OFr. < L. *castus,* pure: see CASTE] **1.** not indulging in unlawful sexual activity; virtuous: said esp. of women **2.** not indulging in any sexual activity; celibate **3.** pure; decent; modest **4.** restrained and simple in style —**chaste′ly** *adv.* —**chaste′ness** *n.*

chas·ten (chās′'n) *vt.* [< OFr. < L. *castigare,* to punish < *castus,* pure + *agere,* to lead] **1.** to punish so as to correct; chastise **2.** to make less intense, lively, extreme, etc.; subdue [with his enthusiasm *chastened* by criticism] —**chas′ten·er** *n.*

chas·tise (chas tīz′, chas′tīz) *vt.* **-tised′, -tis′ing** [< OFr.: see CHASTEN] **1.** to punish, esp. by beating **2.** to scold or condemn sharply —see SYN. at PUNISH —**chas·tise′ment** *n.* —**chas·tis′er** *n.*

chas·ti·ty (chas′tə tē) *n.* [see CHASTE] the quality or state of being chaste, virtuous, celibate, etc.

chas·u·ble (chaz′yoo b′l, chas′-) *n.* [OFr. < ML. *casubla*, hooded garment, prob. < L. dim. of *casa*, house] a sleeveless outer vestment worn over the alb by priests at Mass

chat (chat) *vi.* **chat′ted, chat′ting** [< CHATTER] to talk or converse in a light, easy, informal way —*n.* **1.** a light, easy, informal conversation **2.** any of various birds with a chattering call

châ·teau (sha tō′) *n., pl.* **-teaux′** (-tōz′, -tō′), **-teaus′** [Fr. < OFr. < L. *castellum*, CASTLE] **1.** a French feudal castle of the Middle Ages **2.** a large country house, esp. in France Also **cha·teau′**

CHASUBLE

cha·teau·bri·and (shà tō brē än′) *n.* [after F. R. de *Chateaubriand* (1768–1848), Fr. statesman] a thick beef fillet from the center of the tenderloin

chat·e·laine (shat′'l ān′) *n.* [Fr., ult. < L. *castellum*, CASTLE] **1.** the mistress of a castle or of any large household **2.** a woman's ornamental chain or clasp, esp. for the waist, with keys, a watch, etc. fastened to it

Chat·ta·noo·ga (chat′ə nōō′gə) [< AmInd.] city in SE Tenn., on the Ga. border: pop. 119,000

chat·tel (chat′'l) *n.* [OFr. *chatel:* see CATTLE] **1.** *a*) a movable item of personal property, rather than real estate or other real property: in full, **chattel personal** [furniture is *chattel*] *b*) any interest in real estate less than a freehold: in full, **chattel real 2.** [Archaic] a slave

chattel mortgage a mortgage on personal property

chat·ter (chat′ər) *vi.* [echoic] **1.** to make short, indistinct sounds in rapid succession [birds and apes *chatter*] **2.** to talk fast and foolishly, without stopping **3.** to click together rapidly, as the teeth do when one is frightened or cold —*n.* **1.** the act or sound of chattering **2.** rapid, foolish talk —**chat′ter·er** *n.*

chat·ter·box (-bäks′) *n.* a person who talks all the time

chat·ty (chat′ē) *adj.* **-ti·er, -ti·est 1.** fond of chatting **2.** friendly and informal [a *chatty* letter] —**chat′ti·ly** *adv.* — **chat′ti·ness** *n.*

Chau·cer (chô′sər), **Geoffrey** 1340?–1400; Eng. poet: author of *The Canterbury Tales* —**Chau·ce′ri·an** (-sir′ē ən) *adj.*

chauf·feur (shō′fər, shō fur′) *n.* [Fr., lit., stoker < *chauffer*, to heat: see CHAFE] a person hired to drive a private automobile for someone else —*vt.* to act as chauffeur to

chaunt (chônt) *n., vt., vi. archaic var.* of CHANT

☆**chau·tau·qua** (shə tô′kwə) *n.* [< the summer schools first held at Chautauqua, N.Y., in 1874] an educational and recreational assembly with a program of lectures, concerts, etc.

chau·vin·ism (shō′və niz′m) *n.* [< Fr. < N. *Chauvin*, Napoleonic soldier, notorious for his fanatical patriotism] **1.** militant, boastful, and fanatical patriotism **2.** unreasoning devotion to one's race, sex, etc., with contempt for other races, the opposite sex, etc. —**chau′vin·ist** *n., adj.* —**chau·vin·is′tic** *adj.* —**chau·vin·is′ti·cal·ly** *adv.*

chaw (chô) *n. dial. var.* of CHEW (*n.* 2)

cheap (chēp) *adj.* [< *good cheap*, good bargain < OE. *ceap*, a bargain, ult. < L. *caupo*, a trader] **1.** low in price; not expensive **2.** charging low prices [a *cheap* hotel] **3.** worth more than the price [that suit would be *cheap* at twice the price] **4.** gotten with little effort or trouble [a *cheap* victory] **5.** of little or no value **6.** not deserving respect **7.** [Colloq.] stingy; miserly **8.** lowered in buying power or available at low interest rates: said of money —*adv.* at low cost —**cheap′ly** *adv.* — **cheap′ness** *n.*

SYN.—**cheap** and **inexpensive** both mean low in cost or price, but **inexpensive** suggests that something bought costs less than others of the same kind [a durable, *inexpensive* skillet], whereas **cheap** is used of something that is very inexpensive and a bargain [woolens are *cheap* in Scotland, but expensive when imported]; **cheap** may also imply that something is of inferior quality, flashy but shoddy, unworthy, etc. [*cheap* jewelry; to feel *cheap*] —**ANT.** costly, expensive

cheap·en (chēp′'n) *vt., vi.* to make or become cheap or cheaper —**cheap′en·er** *n.*

cheap-jack (-jak′) *adj.* [CHEAP + JACK] cheap, inferior, base, etc.

☆**cheap·skate** (-skāt′) *n.* [Slang] a person who does not like to spend money; stingy person

cheat (chēt) *n.* [< ME. *eschete*: see ESCHEAT] **1.** a fraud; deception **2.** one who deceives or defrauds others; swindler —*vt.* **1.** to deal with dishonestly in order to gain something for oneself; defraud; swindle [to *cheat* a person out of his savings] **2.** to deceive by trickery; fool [lighting effects which *cheat* the

eye] **3.** to foil or escape by tricks or good luck [to *cheat* death] —*vi.* **1.** to practice fraud or deception ☆**2.** [Slang] to be sexually unfaithful (often with *on*) —**cheat′er** *n.* —**cheat′ing·ly** *adv.*

SYN.—**cheat** implies the use of dishonesty in dealing with someone, in order to get something he has; **defraud** stresses the use of deliberate deception in taking away a person's rights, property, etc. in a way that is against the law; **swindle** stresses the winning of a person's trust in order to cheat or defraud him of money, etc.; **trick** implies the use of a clever scheme or device to mislead someone, but does not necessarily suggest dishonesty; **dupe** suggests the tricking of someone who is foolish and too willing to trust others; **hoax** implies the use of a complicated scheme to dupe others, often simply in fun

check (chek) *n.* [OFr. *eschec*, a check at chess < ML. *scaccus* < Per. *shāh*, king] **1.** a sudden stop **2.** any restraint or control put upon action **3.** a person or thing that restrains or controls [price control acts as a *check* on inflation] **4.** a test, comparison, etc. to see if something is as it should be [add the figures again as a *check* on your addition] **5.** a mark (✔) to show that something is right or to call attention to something ☆**6.** a token or ticket that shows one's right to claim an article left in a checkroom, etc. [a hat *check*] ☆**7.** one's bill at a restaurant or bar **8.** a written order to a bank to pay to someone the stated amount from one's account **9.** *a*) a pattern of small squares like that of a chessboard *b*) one of these squares **10.** a fabric with such a pattern **11.** a small split or crack **12.** *Chess* the condition of a king that is in danger and must be put into a safe position **13.** *Hockey* a blocking of an opponent's play or movement —*interj.* ☆**1.** [Colloq.] agreed! right! OK! **2.** *Chess* a call meaning the opponent's king is in check —*vt.* **1.** to make stop suddenly **2.** to hold back; restrain **3.** to rebuff, repulse, or rebuke **4.** to test, measure, verify, or control by investigation or examination [*check* the tires for leaks] **5.** to mark with a check (✔) **6.** to mark with a pattern of squares ☆**7.** to put in a checkroom, safe, etc. for a time ☆**8.** to get (esp. luggage) cleared for shipment **9.** to make chinks or cracks in **10.** *Chess* to place (an opponent's king) in check **11.** *Hockey* to block the play or movement of (an opponent) —*vi.* ☆**1.** to agree with one another, item for item [does his story *check* with hers?] ☆**2.** to investigate so as to determine the condition, truth, etc. of something (often with *on*) **3.** to crack in small checks [old paint may *check*] **4.** *Chess* to place an opponent's king in check —*adj.* **1.** used to check or verify **2.** having a crisscross pattern; checked —see SYN. at RESTRAIN —☆**check in 1.** to register at a hotel, convention, etc. **2.** [Colloq.] to report, as by presenting oneself [*check in* at the office] —**check off** to mark as verified, examined, etc. —☆**check out 1.** to settle one's bill and leave a hotel, etc. **2.** to add up the prices of (purchases) and collect the total: said of a cashier, as in a supermarket **3.** to examine and verify or approve **4.** to prove to be accurate, in sound condition, etc. upon examination **5.** to record certain information in borrowing or lending (a library book, factory tool, etc.) —☆**check up on** to examine or investigate —**in check** in restraint; under control

☆**check·book** (chek′book′) *n.* a book containing detachable forms for writing checks drawn on one's checking account

checked (chekt) *adj.* having a pattern of squares

check·er[1] (chek′ər) *n.* [OFr. *eschekier*, a chessboard < *eschec:* see CHECK] **1.** a small square, as on a chessboard **2.** a pattern of such squares **3.** *a*) [*pl.*, *with sing. v.*] a game played on a checkerboard by two players, each with twelve round, flat pieces to move *b*) any of these pieces —*vt.* to mark off in squares of different colors or shades

check·er[2] (chek′ər) *n.* **1.** a person who examines or makes a check, test, etc. ☆**2.** a person who checks hats, luggage, etc. ☆**3.** a cashier, as in a supermarket

☆**check·er·ber·ry** (-ber′ē) *n., pl.* **-ries 1.** same as WINTERGREEN (sense 1) **2.** the edible, red, berrylike fruit of the wintergreen

check·er·board (-bôrd′) *n.* a board with 64 squares of two alternating colors, used in checkers and chess

check·ered (-ərd) *adj.* **1.** having a pattern of squares **2.** varied in color and shading **3.** full of changes, varied activities, etc. [Churchill's *checkered* career]

☆**checking account** a bank account against which the depositor can draw checks at any time

☆**check·list** (chek′list′) *n.* a list of things to be checked off or referred to: also **check list**

check·mate (-māt′) *n.* [OFr. *eschec mat*, ult. < Per. *shāh māt*, lit., the king is dead] **1.** *Chess a*) the winning move that checks the opponent's king so that it cannot be put into safety *b)* the king's position after this move **2.** complete defeat, frustration, etc. —*interj. Chess* a call indicating checkmate —*vt.* **-mat′ed, -mat′ing** to place in checkmate; defeat completely

☆**check·off** (-ôf′) *n.* an arrangement by which dues of trade-union members are withheld from wages and turned over to the union by the employer

☆**check·out** (-out′) *n.* **1.** the act or place of checking out purchases, as in a supermarket **2.** the time by which one must check out of a hotel, etc. **3.** a testing, esp. of a machine, as for accuracy Also **check′-out′**

check·point (-point′) *n.* a place where traffic is stopped by authorities, as for inspection

check·rein (-rān′) *n.* a short rein attached to the bridle to keep a horse's head up

☆**check·room** (-rōōm′, -room′) *n.* a room where hats, coats, parcels, etc. may be left in safekeeping for a time

☆**check·up** (-up′) *n.* an examination or investigation, esp. a general medical examination

Ched·dar (cheese) (ched′ər) [< *Cheddar,* Somersetshire, England, where orig. made] [*often* c-] a variety of hard, smooth cheese

cheek (chēk) *n.* [OE. *ceoke,* jaw, jawbone] **1.** either side of the face, below the eye **2.** either of two sides of a thing, as the jaws of a vise: *usually used in pl.* **3.** either of the buttocks **4.** [Colloq.] sauciness; impudence —see SYN. at TEMERITY —**cheek by jowl** close together; intimately —**(with) tongue in cheek** in a humorously mocking or insincere way

cheek·bone (chēk′bōn′) *n.* the bone of the upper cheek, just below the eye

cheek pouch a pouchlike swelling in the cheek of certain rodents, monkeys, etc., used for holding food

cheek·y (chēk′ē) *adj.* **cheek′i·er, cheek′i·est** [CHEEK + -Y²] [Colloq.] saucy; impudent; insolent —**cheek′i·ly** *adv.* —**cheek′i·ness** *n.*

cheep (chēp) *n.* [echoic] the short, faint, shrill sound of a young bird; peep —*vt., vi.* to make, or utter with, such a sound —**cheep′er** *n.*

cheer (chir) *n.* [< OFr. *chiere* < LL. *cara,* the head < Gr. *kara:* for IE. base see HORN] **1.** state of mind or of feeling; spirit: now in **be of good cheer, with good cheer,** etc. **2.** glad feelings; joy [*her visit brought* cheer *to the invalid*] **3.** festive food or entertainment **4.** encouragement **5.** *a)* a shout of welcome, approval, encouragement, etc. [*the crowd gave him three* cheers] *b)* a jingle, etc. shouted in unison in rooting for a team —*vt.* **1.** to fill with joy and hope; gladden; comfort (often with *up*) **2.** to urge on or encourage by cheers **3.** to greet or applaud with cheers —*vi.* **1.** to be or become cheerful; feel encouraged (usually with *up*) **2.** to shout cheers

☆**cheer·lead·er** (-lē′dər) *n.* one who leads others in cheering for a football team, etc.

cheer·ful (chir′fəl) *adj.* **1.** full of cheer; joyful **2.** bright and attractive [*a* cheerful *room*] **3.** willing [*a* cheerful *helper*] —see SYN. at HAPPY —**cheer′ful·ly** *adv.* —**cheer′ful·ness** *n.*

cheer·i·o (-ē ō′) *interj., n., pl.* **-os′** [Brit. Colloq.] **1.** goodbye **2.** good health: a toast

cheer·less (-lis) *adj.* not cheerful; dismal; joyless —**cheer′·less·ly** *adv.* —**cheer′less·ness** *n.*

cheers (chirz) *interj.* [Chiefly Brit.] good health: a toast

cheer·y (chir′ē) *adj.* **cheer′i·er, cheer′i·est** *same as* CHEERFUL (senses 1 & 2) —**cheer′i·ly** *adv.* —**cheer′i·ness** *n.*

cheese¹ (chēz) *n.* [OE. *cyse,* akin to L. *caseus* < IE. base *kwat-,* to ferment] **1.** a solid food made by pressing together curds of soured milk **2.** a shaped mass of this

cheese² (chēz) *n.* [Hindi *chīz* (< Per. *čiz*), thing] [slang] an important person or thing

cheese·burg·er (chēz′bur′gər) *n.* [CHEESE¹ + -BURGER] a hamburger topped with melted cheese

cheese·cake (-kāk′) *n.* **1.** a kind of cake made of cottage cheese or cream cheese, eggs, sugar, etc., usually baked with a bottom crust of crumbs ☆**2.** [Slang] display of the figure, esp. the legs, of a pretty girl, as in some newspaper photographs

cheese·cloth (-klôth′) *n.* [from use as cheese wrapping] a thin cotton cloth with a loose weave

chees·y (-ē) *adj.* **chees′i·er, chees′i·est** **1.** like cheese in consistency, smell, etc. **2.** [Slang] inferior; poor —**chees′i·ness** *n.*

chee·tah (chēt′ə) *n.* [Hindi *chītā* < Sans. *citra:* see CHINTZ] a swift, leopardlike animal of Africa and southern Asia, with a small head, long legs, and a black-spotted, tawny coat: it can be trained to hunt

chef (shef) *n.* [Fr. < *chef de cuisine,* lit., head of the kitchen: see CHIEF] **1.** a head cook, as in a restaurant **2.** any cook

‡**chef-d'oeu·vre** (she dë′vr′) *n., pl.* **chefs-d'oeu′vre** (she dë′vr′) [Fr., principal work] a masterpiece, as in art or literature

CHEETAH
(to 7 ft. long,
including tail)

Che·khov (chek′ôf; *Russ.* chekh′ôf), **An·ton (Pavlovich)** (än tôn′) 1860–1904; Russ. dramatist & short-story writer: also sp. **Chekov**

che·la (kē′lə) *n., pl.* **-lae** (-lē) [ModL. < Gr. *chēlē,* claw] a pincerlike claw of a crab, lobster, scorpion, etc.

che·late (kē′lāt) *adj.* resembling or having chelae —*n. Chem.* a compound in which a central atom (usually a metal ion) is attached to at least two other atoms by bonds so as to form a ring structure —*vt.* **-lat·ed, -lat·ing** to cause (a metal ion) to react with another molecule to form a chelate —**che·la′tion** *n.*

che·lic·er·a (kə lis′ə rə) *n., pl.* **-er·ae** (-ə rē′) [ModL. < Gr. *chēlē,* claw + *keras,* HORN] either of a pair of clawlike organs found on spiders and other arachnids

che·loid (kē′loid) *n. same as* KELOID

che·lo·ni·an (ki lō′nē ən) *adj.* [< ModL. *Chelonia* < Gr. *chelōnē*] of, like, or being a turtle or tortoise —*n.* a turtle or tortoise

Chel·ya·binsk (chi lyä′binsk) city in the southwestern R.S.F.S.R., in the S Urals: pop. 874,000

chem. 1. chemical(s) **2.** chemist **3.** chemistry

chem·ic (kem′ik) *adj.* [Now Poet.] chemical

chem·i·cal (kem′i k'l) *adj.* **1.** of or having to do with chemistry **2.** involving the use of chemicals —*n.* any substance used in or obtained by a chemical process —**chem′i·cal·ly** *adv.*

chemical engineering the science or profession of applying chemistry to industrial uses

chemical warfare warfare using poisonous gases, flame throwers, incendiary bombs, etc.: see also BIOLOGICAL WARFARE

chem·i·lu·mi·nes·cence (kem′i lōō′mə nes′'ns) *n.* visible light chemically produced without heat

che·mise (shə mēz′) *n.* [OFr. < VL. *camisia,* shirt < Gaul.] **1.** a woman's undergarment somewhat like a loose, short slip **2.** a straight, loose dress

chem·ist (kem′ist) *n.* [< (AL)CHEMIST] **1.** an expert or specialist in chemistry **2.** [Brit.] a pharmacist, or druggist

chem·is·try (kem′is trē) *n., pl.* **-tries** [prec. + -RY] **1.** the science dealing with the composition and properties of substances, and with the reactions by which they are combined or separated to form other substances **2.** the application of this to a specified subject or field of activity **3.** the chemical properties, composition, reactions, and uses of a substance

chem·o- *a combining form meaning* of, with, or by chemicals or chemistry [*chemotherapy*]

chem·o·re·cep·tor (kem′ō ri sep′tər, kē′mō-) *n.* a nerve ending or sense organ that can respond to chemical stimuli, as a taste bud —**chem′o·re·cep′tion** *n.*

chem·o·sur·ger·y (-sur′jər ē) *n.* the use of chemicals to remove tumors or diseased tissue

chem·o·ther·a·py (-ther′ə pē) *n.* the prevention or treatment of infection or disease by doses of chemical drugs: also **chem′o·ther′a·peu′tics** (-ther′ə pyōōt′iks) —**chem′o·ther′·a·peu′tic** *adj.* —**chem′o·ther′a·pist** *n.*

chem·ur·gy (kem′ər jē) *n.* [CHEM(O)- + -URGY] the branch of chemistry dealing with the use in industry of organic products, esp. from farms (for example, the use of soybeans as a base for plastics) —**chem·ur·gic** (kem ur′jik) *adj.*

Che·nab (chi näb′) river rising in Kashmir & flowing southwest into the Sutlej River in Pakistan

Cheng·tu (chuŋ′dōō′) city in SC China: pop. 1,135,000

che·nille (shi nēl′) *n.* [Fr., lit., hairy caterpillar < L. *canicula,* little dog] **1.** a tufted, velvety yarn used for trimming, embroidery, etc. **2.** a fabric filled or woven with this, used for bedspreads, rugs, etc.

che·ong·sam, che·ong·sam (chē ôŋ′säm′) *n.* [Chin.] a high-necked, closefitting Chinese dress with the skirt slit part way up the sides

Che·ops (kē′äps) *Gr. name of* KHUFU

cheque (chek) *n. Brit. sp. of* CHECK (*n.* 8)

cheq·uer (chek′ər) *n., vt. Brit. sp. of* CHECKER¹

Cher·bourg (sher′boorg; *Fr.* sher boor′) seaport in NW France, on the English Channel: pop. 37,000

cher·ish (cher′ish) *vt.* [< OFr. < *cher*, dear < L. *carus*: see CHARITY] **1.** to hold dear; feel or show love for [to *cherish* one's family] **2.** to take good care of; protect; foster [to *cherish* one's rights] **3.** to cling to the idea or feeling of [to *cherish* a hope] —see SYN. at APPRECIATE

Cher·o·kee (cher′ə kē′) *n.* [prob. < Choctaw *chiluk-ki*, "cave people"] **1.** *pl.* **-kees′, -kee′** a member of a tribe of Iroquoian Indians, most of whom were moved from the southeastern U.S. to Oklahoma **2.** their Iroquoian language

☆**Cherokee rose** an evergreen climbing rose with fragrant, large, white flowers and glossy leaves, native to China but now growing wild in the southern U.S.

che·root (shə root′) *n.* [< Tamil *churuttu*, a roll] a cigar with both ends cut square

cher·ry (cher′ē) *n., pl.* **-ries** [Anglo-Fr. *cherise* < OFr. < VL. < Gr. *kerasion* < *kerasos*, cherry tree] **1.** a small, fleshy fruit, yellow to dark red, with a smooth, hard pit **2.** any tree of the rose family which bears this fruit, or its wood **3.** the bright-red color of certain cherries —*adj.* **1.** bright-red **2.** of cherry wood **3.** made with cherries

cherry bomb a round, red, powerful firecracker

☆**cher·ry·stone** (-stōn′) *n.* a small quahog, a variety of clam: also **cherrystone clam**

chert (churt) *n.* [< ?] a very fine-grained, tough rock composed mainly of silica —**chert′y** (-ē) *adj.* **chert′i·er, chert′i·est**

cher·ub (cher′əb) *n., pl.* **-ubs**; for 1–3 usually **-u·bim** (-ə bim, -yoo bim) or (KJV) **-u·bims** [< LL. < Heb. *kerūbh*] **1.** *Bible* one of certain winged heavenly beings: Ezek. 10 **2.** *Christian Theol.* any of the second order of angels, just below the seraphim **3.** a representation of a cherub, now usually as a chubby, rosy-faced child with wings **4.** a person, esp. a child, with a sweet, innocent face —**che·ru·bic** (chə roo′bik) *adj.* —**che·ru′bi·cal·ly** *adv.*

cher·vil (chur′vəl) *n.* [< OE. < L. < Gr. < *chairein*, to rejoice + *phyllon*, leaf] a plant of the parsley family, with leaves used to flavor soups, etc.

Ches·a·peake (ches′ə pēk′) [see next entry] city in SE Va., at the base of Chesapeake Bay: pop. 90,000

Chesapeake Bay [*Chesapeake* < Algonquian, lit., country on a big river] arm of the Atlantic, extending north into Va. and Md.

Chesh·ire cat (chesh′ir, -ər) a proverbial grinning cat from Cheshire, a county of western England, esp. one described in Lewis Carroll's *Alice's Adventures in Wonderland*

Chesh·van (khesh′vän) *n. same as* HESHVAN

chess (ches) *n.* [< OFr. *esches*, pl. of *eschec*: see CHECK] a game for two, each with 16 pieces moved variously on a chessboard, the object being to checkmate the opponent's king

chess·board (ches′bôrd′) *n.* a board with 64 squares of two alternating colors, for chess and checkers

chess·man (-man′, -mən) *n., pl.* **-men** (-men′, -mən) any of the pieces used in chess

chest (chest) *n.* [< OE. < L. < Gr. *kistē*, a box] **1.** a box with a lid and, often, a lock, for storing or shipping things **2.** a public fund [community *chest*] **3.** *same as* CHEST OF DRAWERS **4.** a cabinet for medicines, toiletries, etc. **5.** *a)* the part of the body enclosed by the ribs; thorax *b)* the outside front of this —**get (something) off one's chest** [Colloq.] to unburden oneself of (some trouble, etc.) by talking about it

chest·ed (ches′tid) *adj.* having a (specified kind of) chest, or thorax [hollow-*chested*]

Ches·ter (ches′tər) [< OE. < L. *castra*, a camp] **1.** a masculine name **2.** [after *Chester*, city in W England] seaport in SE Pa., near Philadelphia, on the Delaware River: pop. 56,000

Ches·ter·field (ches′tər fēld′), 4th Earl of (*Philip Dormer Stanhope*) 1694–1773; Eng. statesman & writer: called *Lord Chesterfield*

ches·ter·field (ches′tər fēld′) *n.* [after a 19th-c. Earl of *Chesterfield*] **1.** a single-breasted topcoat, usually with a velvet collar **2.** a sofa with upright ends

CHEONGSAM

Ches·ter·ton (ches′tər tən), **G(ilbert) K(eith)** 1874–1936; Eng. writer

Chester White [after *Chester* County, Pa.] a variety of large, white hog

chest·nut (ches′nut′, -nət) *n.* [< OFr. < L. < Gr. *kastaneia*] **1.** the smooth-shelled, sweet, edible nut of certain trees of the beech family **2.** one of these trees, or the wood **3.** *same as* HORSE CHESTNUT **4.** reddish brown **5.** a reddish-brown horse ☆**6.** [Colloq.] *a)* a very old, stale joke or phrase; cliché *b)* a familiar story, piece of music, etc., repeated too often —*adj.* reddish-brown

chest of drawers a set of drawers within a frame, as for keeping clothing in a bedroom; bureau

☆**chest-on-chest** (chest′än chest′) *n.* a chest of drawers fitted onto another, somewhat larger one

chest·y (ches′tē) *adj.* **chest′i·er, chest′i·est** [Colloq.] **1.** having a large chest, or thorax **2.** bosomy ☆**3.** boastful, proud, or conceited

che·val-de-frise (shə val′də frēz′) *n., pl.* **che·vaux′-de-frise** (shə vō′-) [Fr., lit., horse of Friesland, which had no cavalry] **1.** a piece of wood with projecting spikes, formerly used to hinder enemy horsemen **2.** a row of spikes or jagged glass set into the masonry on top of a wall to prevent people from going over it

che·val glass (shə val′) [Fr. *cheval*, horse, support + GLASS] a full-length mirror on swivels in a frame

chev·a·lier (shev′ə lir′; *for 1, often* shə val′yā′) *n.* [see CAVALIER] **1.** a member of the lowest rank of the French Legion of Honor **2.** an honorable, courteous man; gallant **3.** [Archaic] a knight

Chev·i·ot (chev′ē ət; *also, and for 2 always,* shev′-) *n.* [after the *Cheviot Hills,* between England and Scotland] **1.** any of a breed of sheep with short, dense wool **2.** [*usually* c-] *a)* a rough wool fabric in a twill weave *b)* a cotton cloth resembling this

chev·ron (shev′rən) *n.* [< OFr., rafter (from its shape), ult. < L. *capra,* she-goat] a V-shaped bar or bars worn on the sleeve, as of a military uniform, to show rank or service

chew (choo) *vt.* [< OE. *ceowan* < IE. base *gjeu-*] **1.** to bite and crush with the teeth **2.** *a)* to think over *b)* to discuss ☆**3.** [Slang] to rebuke severely (often with *out*) —*vi.* to chew something; ☆sometimes specif., [Colloq.] to chew tobacco —*n.* **1.** a chewing **2.** something chewed or for chewing, as a portion of tobacco —**chew the rag (or fat)** [Slang] to converse idly —**chew′er** *n.*

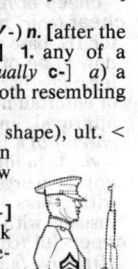

☆**chew·ing gum** (choo′iŋ) a gummy substance, such as chicle, flavored and sweetened for chewing

☆**che·wink** (chi wiŋk′) *n.* [echoic of its note] the eastern towhee of N. America, with the iris of the eye bright red

chew·y (choo′ē) *adj.* **chew′i·er, chew′i·est** needing much chewing —**chew′i·ness** *n.*

Chey·enne¹ (shī en′, -an′) *n.* [Dakota *shaiyena* < *shaia,* to speak gibberish] **1.** *pl.* **-ennes′, -enne′** a member of a tribe of Algonquian Indians now of Montana and Oklahoma but originally of Minnesota **2.** their language

Chey·enne² (shī an′, -en′) [< prec.] capital of Wyo., in the SE part: pop. 41,000

‡**chez** (shā) *prep.* [Fr.] by; at; at the home of

chg. *pl.* **chgs.** charge

chgd. charged

chi (kī) *n.* [Gr.] the 22d letter of the Greek alphabet (X, χ)

Chiang Kai-shek (chaŋ′kī shek′; *Chin.* jyäŋ′-) (born *Chiang Chung-chen*) 1888–1975; Chin. generalissimo & head of government on Taiwan (1950–75)

Chi·an·ti (kē än′tē, -an′-) *n.* [It.] a dry, red wine, orig. made in Tuscany

chi·a·ro·scu·ro (kē är′ə skyoor′ō) *n., pl.* **-ros** [It. < L. *clarus,* clear + *obscurus,* dark] **1.** the treatment of light and shade in a painting, drawing, etc., as to make it look as if it has depth **2.** a style or a painting, drawing, etc. using this —**chi·a·ro·scu′rist** *n.*

AMERICAN CHESTNUT (tree, leaves & nuts)

CHEVRON

chic (shēk) *n.* [Fr. < MLowG. *schick*, order, skill] smart elegance of style and manner —☆*adj.* **chic·quer** (shēk'ər), **chic'·quest** (-ist) stylish in a smart, pleasing way

Chi·ca·go (shə kä'gō, -kô'-) [< Fr. < Algonquian, lit., place of the wild onion] city in NE Ill., on Lake Michigan: pop. 3,367,000 (met. area 6,979,000) —**Chi·ca'go·an** *n.*

chi·cane (shi kān', chi-) *n.* [Fr. < *chicaner*, to quibble < MLowG. *schikken*, to arrange] *same as* CHICANERY

chi·can·er·y (-kān'ər ē) *n., pl.* **-er·ies** **1.** the use of clever but tricky talk or action to deceive, evade, etc. **2.** an instance of this

☆**Chi·ca·no** (chi kä'nō) *n., pl.* **-nos** [altered < AmSp. (*Mé*)*jicano*, a Mexican] [*also* c-] [Southwest] a U.S. citizen or inhabitant of Mexican descent

chi·chi, chi-chi (shē'shē, chē'chē) *adj.* [Fr.] extremely chic; very elegant, esp. in a showy way

chick (chik) *n.* [< CHICKEN] **1.** a young chicken **2.** any young bird **3.** a child: term of affection ☆**4.** [Slang] a young woman

☆**chick·a·dee** (chik'ə dē') *n.* [echoic of its call] any of various small birds closely related to the titmice, with black, gray, and white feathers

☆**chick·a·ree** (chik'ə rē') *n.* [echoic of its cry] a reddish squirrel of the western U.S.

Chick·a·saw (chik'ə sô') *n.* **1.** *pl.* **-saws', -saw'** a member of a tribe of Muskogean Indians now of Oklahoma but formerly of Mississippi and Tennessee **2.** their Muskogean dialect

chick·en (chik'ən) *n.* [< OE. *cycen*, lit., little cock] **1.** a common farm bird raised for its edible eggs or flesh; hen or rooster, esp. a young one **2.** its flesh **3.** any young bird **4.** a young or inexperienced person **5.** [Slang] a timid or cowardly person —*adj.* **1.** made of chicken **2.** small and tender [a *chicken* lobster] **3.** [Slang] timid or cowardly —☆*vi.* [Slang] to lose courage and abandon a plan, action, etc. (usually with *out*)

☆**chicken feed** [Slang] a petty sum of money

☆**chick·en-fried** (-frīd') *adj.* coated with seasoned flour or batter and fried [*chicken-fried* steak]

☆**chicken hawk** a hawk preying on barnyard fowl

chick·en-heart·ed (-här'tid) *adj.* timid; cowardly: also **chick'en-liv'ered**

chicken pox a contagious disease, usually of young children, in which there is a mild fever and small blisters form on the skin

☆**chicken wire** light, pliable wire fencing, used esp. for enclosing chicken coops

chick·pea (chik'pē') *n.* [for *chich pea*, ult. < L. *cicer*, pea] **1.** a bushy annual plant of the legume family, with short, hairy pods containing usually two seeds **2.** the edible seed

chick·weed (-wēd') *n.* any of several low-growing plants of the pink family, often found as weeds

☆**chic·le** (chik'l) *n.* [AmSp. < Nahuatl *chictli*] a gumlike substance made from the milky juice of the sapodilla tree, used in making chewing gum

Chic·o·pee (chik'ə pē) [< AmInd., lit., swift river] city in SW Mass.: pop. 67,000

chic·o·ry (chik'ə rē) *n., pl.* **-ries** [< OFr. < L. < Gr. *kichora*] **1.** a weedy plant of the composite family, with blue flowers: the leaves are used in salads **2.** its root, roasted and ground for mixing with coffee or for use as a coffee substitute

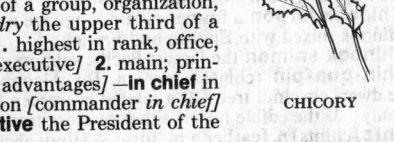
CHICORY

chide (chīd) *vt., vi.* **chid'ed** or **chid** (chid), **chid'ed** or **chid** or **chid·den** (chid''n), **chid'ing** [OE. *cidan*] to scold, esp. in a mild way —**chid'ing·ly** *adv.*

chief (chēf) *n.* [< OFr. < L. *caput*, the head: for IE. base see HEAD] **1.** the head or leader of a group, organization, etc. **2.** *Heraldry* the upper third of a shield —*adj.* **1.** highest in rank, office, etc. [the *chief* executive] **2.** main; principal [the *chief* advantages] —**in chief** in the chief position [commander *in chief*]

☆**Chief Executive** the President of the U.S.

chief justice the presiding judge of a court made up of several judges

chief·ly (chēf'lē) *adv.* **1.** most of all; above all [*chiefly* in-terested in science] **2.** mainly; mostly [a melon is *chiefly* water] —*adj.* of or like a chief

chief of staff the head member of the staff officers of a division or higher unit in the armed forces, or of the Departments of the Army or Air Force

chief·tain (-tən) *n.* [< OFr. < LL. < L. *caput*: see CHIEF] a leader, esp. of a clan or tribe —**chief'tain·cy,** *pl.* **-cies, chief'·tain·ship'** *n.*

chif·fon (shi fän', shif'än) *n.* [Fr., dim. of *chiffe*, a rag] a sheer, lightweight fabric of silk, nylon, etc. —*adj.* **1.** made of chiffon **2.** *Cooking* made light and porous as by adding beaten egg whites [lemon *chiffon* pie]

chif·fo·nier, chif·fon·nier (shif'ə nir') *n.* [Fr., orig., rag-picker < prec.] a narrow, high bureau or chest of drawers, often with a mirror

chig·ger (chig'ər) *n.* [of Afr. origin] ☆**1.** the tiny, red larva of certain mites, whose bite causes severe itching **2.** *same as* CHIGOE

chi·gnon (shēn'yän) *n.* [Fr. < OFr. < L. *catena*: see CHAIN] a coil of hair sometimes worn at the back of the neck by women

chig·oe (chig'ō) *n., pl.* **-oes** (-ōz) [? via Fr. *chique* < WInd. native name] **1.** a flea of tropical S. America and Africa: the female burrows into the skin, causing painful sores **2.** *same as* CHIGGER

Chi·hua·hua (chi wä'wä) city in NC Mexico: pop. 364,000 —☆*n.* any of an ancient Mexican breed of very small dog with large, pointed ears

chil·blain (chil'blān') *n.* [CHIL(L) + BLAIN] a painful swelling or sore on the foot or hand, caused by exposure to cold —**chil'·blained'** *adj.*

child (chīld) *n., pl.* **chil'dren** [< OE. *cild*, pl. *cildru* < IE. base *gel-*, rounded (sense development: swelling—womb—fetus—offspring)] **1.** an infant; baby **2.** an unborn offspring **3.** a boy or girl in the period before puberty **4.** a son or daughter **5.** a descendant **6.** a person like a child; immature or childish adult **7.** a person or thing viewed as produced by a certain place, time, source, etc. [a *child* of the Renaissance] —**with child** pregnant —**child'less** *adj.* —**child'less·ness** *n.*

child·bear·ing (chīld'ber'iŋ) *n.* the act of giving birth to children; parturition

child·bed (-bed') *n.* the condition of a woman giving birth to a child

child·birth (-burth') *n.* the act of giving birth to a child; parturition

child·hood (-hood') *n.* **1.** the time or state of being a child; esp., the period from infancy to puberty **2.** an early stage of development

child·ish (-ish) *adj.* **1.** of or like a child **2.** not fit for an adult; immature; silly —see SYN. at CHILDLIKE —**child'ish·ly** *adv.* —**child'ish·ness** *n.*

child labor the regular, full-time employment in factories, stores, offices, etc. of children who are less than a legally defined age: in the U.S., it is against Federal law to employ children under the age of 16 (or under 18 in dangerous occupations)

child·like (-līk') *adj.* like a child, esp. in being innocent, trusting, etc. —**child'like'ness** *n.*

SYN. —**childlike** and **childish** are both applied to persons of any age in referring to qualities considered typical of a child, **childlike** suggesting the favorable qualities such as innocence, honesty, curiosity, zest, etc., and **childish** the unfavorable ones such as immaturity, foolishness, lack of self-control, self-centeredness, etc.

chil·dren (chil'drən) *n. pl. of* CHILD

children of Israel the Jews; Hebrews

child's play (chīldz) anything simple to do

Chil·e (chil'ē; Sp. chē'le) country on the SW coast of S. America: 286,397 sq. mi.; pop. 9,780,000; cap. Santiago —**Chil'·e·an** *adj., n.*

☆**chil·e** (chil'ē) *n. same as* CHILI

☆**chil·e con car·ne** (chil'ē kən kär'nē, kän') *same as* CHILI CON CARNE

Chile saltpeter native sodium nitrate, esp. as found naturally in Chile and Peru

☆**chil·i** (chil'ē) *n., pl.* **chil'ies** [MexSp. < Nahuatl *chilli*] **1.** the dried pod of red pepper, a very hot seasoning **2.** the tropical American plant, of the nightshade family, that bears this pod **3.** *same as* CHILI CON CARNE

---

fat, āpe, cär, ten, ēven, is, bīte; gō, hôrn, tōol, look; oil, out; up, fur; get; joy; yet; chin; she; thin, *then*; zh, leisure; ŋ, ring; ə for *a* in *ago*, *e* in *agent*, *i* in *sanity*, *o* in *comply*, *u* in *focus*; ' as in *able* (ā'b'l); Fr. bål; ë, Fr. coeur; ö, Fr. feu; Fr. mon; ð, Fr. coq; ü, Fr. duc; r, Fr. cri; H, G. ich; kh, G. doch; ‡foreign; ☆ Americanism; < derived from. See inside front cover.

☆**chil·i con car·ne** (chil′ē kən kär′nē, kän′) [< MexSp., lit., red pepper with meat] a highly seasoned dish with beef ground or in bits, chilies or chili powder, beans, and often tomatoes

☆**chili powder** a powder of dried chili pods, herbs, etc.

☆**chili sauce** a spiced sauce of chopped tomatoes, green and red sweet peppers, onions, etc.

chill (chil) n. [OE. *ciele*] **1.** a feeling of coldness that makes one shiver **2.** a moderate coldness **3.** a discouraging influence **4.** a feeling of sudden fear **5.** unfriendliness —*adj.* same as CHILLY —*vi.* to become cool or cold —*vt.* **1.** to make cool or cold **2.** to cause a chill in **3.** to check (enthusiasm, etc.); discourage **4.** *Metallurgy* to harden (metal) on the surface by rapid cooling —**chill′er** n. —**chill′ing·ly** adv. —**chill′ness** n.

chill factor the combined effect of low temperature and high winds in making the body lose heat

chil·li (chil′ē) n., pl. -**lies** same as CHILI

chill·y (chil′ē) adj. **chill′i·er, chill′i·est 1.** moderately cold; uncomfortably cool **2.** cool in manner; unfriendly [a *chilly* smile] —**chill′i·ly** adv. —**chill′i·ness** n.

Chi·mae·ra (ki mir′ə, kī-) same as CHIMERA

chime[1] (chīm) n. [< OFr. < L. *cymbalum*, CYMBAL] **1.** [*usually pl.*] a) a tuned set of bells or metal tubes b) the sounds produced by these **2.** a single bell in a clock, etc. **3.** harmony; agreement —*vi.* **chimed, chim′ing 1.** to sound as a chime **2.** to sound in harmony, as bells **3.** to harmonize; agree —*vt.* **1.** to ring (a bell, set of bells, etc.) **2.** to indicate (time) by chiming —**chime in 1.** to join in or interrupt a conversation, etc. **2.** to agree

chime[2] (chīm) n. [ME. *chimb* < OE. *cimb*- (only in compounds)] the extended rim at each end of a cask or barrel

Chi·me·ra (ki mir′ə, kī-) [< OFr. < L. < Gr. *chimaira*, she-goat] *Gr. Myth.* a fire-breathing monster with a lion's head, goat's body, and serpent's tail —*n.* [c-] **1.** any similar unreal monster **2.** an impossible or foolish idea **3.** *Biol.* an organism that has tissues that come from two or more species, sometimes as the result of grafting

chi·mere (chi mir′, shi-) n. [< OFr. < Sp. < Ar. *sammūr*, sable] a loose robe sometimes worn by Anglican bishops: also **chim′er** (chim′ər, shim′-)

chi·mer·i·cal (ki mir′i k'l, -mer′-; kī-) adj. [see CHIMERA] **1.** imaginary; unreal **2.** absurd; impossible **3.** visionary Also **chi·mer′ic** —**chi·mer′i·cal·ly** adv.

chim·ney (chim′nē) n., pl. -**neys** [< OFr. < LL. *caminata*, fireplace < L. *caminus* < Gr. *kaminos*, oven] **1.** the passage through which smoke escapes from a fire; flue **2.** a structure containing a flue and extending above the roof **3.** a glass tube around the flame of a lamp, etc. **4.** a fissure or vent, as in a cliff or volcano

chimney corner 1. a large opening with seats at the sides of an old-fashioned fireplace **2.** a place near the fire

chimney pot a short pipe on a chimney top to carry the smoke away and increase the draft

chimney sweep a person whose work is cleaning the soot from chimneys

☆**chimney swift** a sooty-brown N. American bird resembling the swallow: so called from its habit of making a nest in an unused chimney: also **chimney swallow**

chimp (chimp) n. [Colloq.] a chimpanzee

chim·pan·zee (chim′pan zē′, chim pan′zē) n. [< Fr. < Bantu *kampenzi*] an anthropoid ape of Africa, with black hair and large ears: it is smaller than a gorilla and is noted for its intelligence

chin (chin) n. [OE. *cin* < IE. base *genu*-] the part of the face below the lower lip; projecting part of the lower jaw —*vt.* **chinned, chin′ning** ☆to pull (oneself) up, while hanging by the hands from a bar, until the chin is just above the level of the bar —☆*vi.* **1.** to chin oneself **2.** [Slang] to chat, gossip, etc. —**keep one's chin up** to face trouble, sorrow, etc. bravely

CHIMPANZEE
(35–60 in. high)

Chin. 1. China **2.** Chinese

Chi·na (chī′nə) country in E Asia, south and east of the U.S.S.R.: 3,691,000 sq. mi.; pop. 732,000,000; cap. Peking: see also TAIWAN

chi·na (chī′nə) n. **1.** a fine porcelain, originally imported from China **2.** dishes, ornaments, etc. of this **3.** any earthenware dishes or crockery

China aster an annual garden flower of the composite family, with large blooms of various colors

☆**chi·na·ber·ry** (chī′nə ber′ē) n., pl. -**ries 1.** a tree, orig. of tropical Asia, bearing yellow, beadlike fruit: also **China tree 2.** a tree of Mexico and the southwestern U.S., with an orange-brown fruit formerly used as soap **3.** either fruit

☆**Chi·na·town** (-toun′) n. the Chinese quarter of a city, as in San Francisco

chi·na·ware (-wer′) n. same as CHINA

☆**chin·ca·pin** (chiŋ′kə pin) n. same as CHINQUAPIN

chinch (chinch) n. [Sp. *chinche* < L. *cimex*, bug] same as: **1.** BEDBUG ☆**2.** CHINCH BUG

☆**chinch bug** a small, white-winged, black bug that damages grain plants

chin·chil·la (chin chil′ə) n. [Sp., prob. dim. of *chinche*: see CHINCH] **1.** a small rodent of the Andes, bred for its fur **2.** its expensive, soft, pale-gray fur **3.** a heavy, nubby wool cloth

chine (chīn) n. [< OFr. *eschine* < Frank. *skina*, small bone, shin-bone] **1.** the backbone; spine **2.** a cut of meat containing part of the backbone **3.** a ridge

Chi·nese (chī nēz′, -nēs′; *for adj.*, often chī′nēz′) **1.** pl. -**nese** a native of China or a person of Chinese descent **2.** the standard language of the Chinese; Mandarin **3.** any Chinese language —*adj.* of China, its people, languages, etc.

Chinese cabbage any of several vegetables of the mustard family, with long, narrow leaves in loose, cylindrical heads and a cabbagelike taste

Chinese checkers [< ?] a game like checkers for two to six players, using marbles on a board with holes in a star-shaped pattern

Chinese Empire China from the founding of its first dynasty (c. 2200 B.C.) to the revolution of 1911

Chinese lantern a lantern of brightly colored paper, made so that it can be folded up

Chi·nese-lan·tern plant a perennial plant of the nightshade family that has a red calyx shaped like a lantern and is used in winter bouquets

Chinese puzzle any puzzle that is hard to solve

Chinese red a brilliant orange-red

Chinese Revolution a revolution (1911) in which the Manchu dynasty was overthrown and a republic set up in China

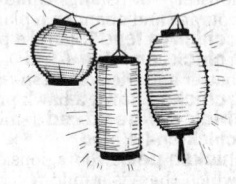

CHINESE LANTERNS

chink[1] (chiŋk) n. [OE. *cine*] a narrow opening; crack —*vt.* to close up the chinks in

chink[2] (chiŋk) n. [echoic] a sharp, clinking sound, as of coins striking together —*vi., vt.* to make or cause to make a sharp, clinking sound

☆**chin·ka·pin** (chiŋ′kə pin) n. same as CHINQUAPIN

☆**chi·no** (chē′nō, shē′-) n. [< ?] **1.** a strong, twilled cotton cloth **2.** [pl.] pants of chino

Chi·no- (chī′nō) a combining form meaning Chinese and [*Chino*-Soviet]

chin·oise·rie (shin′wäz rē′) n. [Fr. < *Chinois*, Chinese + -erie, -ERY] **1.** an ornate decorative style, esp. in 18th-cent. Europe, that has or suggests a Chinese style **2.** furniture, textiles, designs, etc. in this style

Chi·nook (chi nōok′, -nook′; *for 4, usually* shi-) n. **1.** pl. -**nooks′, -nook′** any of a family of Indian tribes, formerly of the Columbia River valley **2.** their language **3.** same as CHINOOK JARGON **4.** [*usually* c-] a warm, moist southwest wind blowing from the sea onto the coast of the northwestern U.S. and southwestern Canada in winter and spring; also, a dry wind blowing down the eastern slope of the Rocky Mountains: in full, **chinook wind** —☆**chinook′an** (-ən) adj., n.

☆**Chinook jargon** a former pidgin language made up of simple Chinook mixed with English and French

☆**chinook salmon** the largest Pacific salmon

☆**chin·qua·pin** (chiŋ′kə pin′) n. [of Algonquian origin] **1.** the dwarf chestnut tree **2.** a related evergreen tree of the beech family **3.** the edible nut of either of these trees

chintz (chints) n. [earlier *pl. form* < Hindi *chhīnt* < Sans. *citra*, spotted, bright < IE. base (s)*kai*-, bright] a cotton cloth printed in colors and usually glazed

chintz·y (chint′sē) adj. **chintz′i·er, chintz′i·est 1.** like chintz ☆**2.** [Colloq.] cheap, stingy, etc.

Chi·os (kī′äs) same as KHÍOS

chip (chip) vt. **chipped, chip′ping** [< OE. *cippian*] **1.** a) to break or cut a small piece or thin slice from b) to break or cut off (a small piece or pieces) **2.** to shape by cutting or chopping *[chip a hole in the ice]* —*vi.* **1.** to break off into small pieces *[this glass chips easily]* **2.** *Golf* to make a chip shot —*n.* **1.** a small, thin piece of wood, etc. cut or broken off **2.** a place where a small piece has been chipped off ☆**3.** a fragment of dried animal dung, sometimes used for fuel **4.** a small, round disk used in gambling games in place of money **5.** *a)* a thin slice or shaving of food *[potato chips]* *b)* *[pl.]* *[Brit.]* French fried potatoes **6.** *Electronics a)* a semiconductor body for an integrated circuit *b) same as* INTEGRATED CIRCUIT **7.** *Golf same as* CHIP SHOT —☆**chip in** [Colloq.] **1.** to share in giving money or help **2.** to add one's comments —**chip off the old block** a person much like his father —☆**chip on one's shoulder** [Colloq.] an inclination to fight —☆**in the chips** [Slang] rich; wealthy —**let the chips fall where they may** whatever the consequences may be —☆**when the chips are down** when something is really at stake

chip·munk (chip′muŋk′) *n.* [of Algonquian origin] a small N. American squirrel with striped markings on its back: it lives mainly on the ground

☆**chipped beef** shavings of dried or smoked beef, usually prepared with a cream sauce

Chip·pen·dale (chip′'n dāl′) *adj.* [after T. *Chippendale* (1718?–79), Eng. cabinet-maker] designating or of an 18th-cent. Eng. style of furniture with graceful lines and, often, rococo carving

chip·per (chip′ər) *adj.* [< northern Brit. *kipper*] [Colloq.] cheerful and energetic *[feeling chipper after a good night's rest]*

Chip·pe·wa (chip′ə wô′, -wä′, -wə, -wā′) *n.*, *pl.* **-was**, **-wa** *var.* of OJIBWA: also **Chip′pe·way′** (-wā′)

☆**chip·ping sparrow** (chip′iŋ) [< *chip*, echoic of its cry] a small N. American sparrow with a reddish-brown crown

chip shot *Golf* a short shot hit in a high curve, esp. one made from just off the green

chi·ro- [< Gr. *cheir*, the hand] *a combining form meaning hand* *[chiromancy]*

chi·rog·ra·phy (kī räg′rə fē) *n.* [CHIRO- + -GRAPHY] handwriting; penmanship —**chi·rog′ra·pher** *n.* —**chi·ro·graph·ic** (kī′rə graf′ik), **chi′ro·graph′i·cal** *adj.*

chi·ro·man·cy (kī′rə man′sē) *n.* [CHIRO- + -MANCY] *same as* PALMISTRY —**chi′ro·man′cer** *n.*

chi·rop·o·dy (kə räp′ə dē, kī-) *n.* [CHIRO- + -POD + -Y³] *same as* PODIATRY —**chi·rop′o·dist** *n.*

☆**chi·ro·prac·tor** (kī′rə prak′tər) *n.* [< CHIRO- + Gr. *praktikos*, practical] a person who practices a system of treating diseases by pressing and moving the spine and joints of the body with the hands —**chi·ro·prac·tic** (kī′rə prak′tik, kī′rə prak′-tik) *n.*, *adj.*

chirp (churp) *vi.* [echoic] **1.** to make the short, shrill sound of some birds or insects **2.** to speak in a lively, shrill way —*vt.* to utter in a sharp, shrill tone —*n.* a short, shrill sound

chirr (chur) *n.* [echoic] a shrill, trilled sound, as of some insects or birds —*vi.* to make such a sound

chir·rup (chur′əp, chir′-) *vi.* [var. of CHIRP] to chirp repeatedly —*n.* a chirruping sound

chi·rur·geon (kī rur′jən) *n.* *archaic var.* of SURGEON —**chi·rur′ger·y** (-jər ē) *n.*

chis·el (chiz′'l) *n.* [ONormFr. < VL. < L. pp. of *caedere*, to cut] a tool having a strong blade with a sharp edge for cutting or shaping wood, stone, or metal —*vi.*, *vt.* **-eled** or **-elled**, **-el·ing** or **-el·ling** **1.** to cut or shape with or as with a chisel *[finely chiseled features]* **2.** [Colloq.] *a)* to take advantage of (someone) by cheating, sponging, etc. *b)* to get (something) in this way —**chisel in** [Colloq.] to force oneself upon others without being asked or welcomed — **chis′el·er**, **chis′el·ler** *n.*

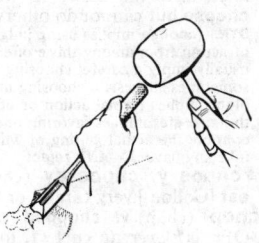

WOOD CHISEL

CHIPMUNK
(to 9 in. long, including tail)

Chis·holm Trail (chiz′əm) [after J. *Chisholm* (1806?–68), Am. frontier scout] cattle trail from San Antonio, Tex., to Abilene, Kans.: important from 1865 until the 1880's

chit¹ (chit) *n.* [ME. *chitte*, prob. var. of *kitte*, for kitten] **1.** a child **2.** an immature or childish girl

chit² (chit) *n.* [< Hindi < Sans. *citra*] **1.** [Chiefly Brit.] a short note or letter **2.** a bill for a small sum owed for drink, food, etc., esp. one signed on a charge account

chit·chat (chit′chat′) *n.* [< CHAT] **1.** light talk about common, everyday things; small talk **2.** gossip

chi·tin (kīt′'n) *n.* [Fr. *chitine* < Gr.: see CHITON] a tough, horny substance forming the outer covering of insects, crustaceans, etc. —**chi′tin·ous** *adj.*

chit·lins, chit·lings (chit′lənz) *n.pl. dial. var.* of CHITTERLINGS

chi·ton (kīt′'n, kī′tän) *n.* [Gr. *chitōn*, garment, tunic < Sem.] a loose garment similar to a tunic, worn by both men and women in ancient Greece

chit·ter·lings (chit′lənz; *now chiefly Brit.* chit′ər liŋz) *n.pl.* [ME. *chiterling*: for IE. base see COVE] the small intestines of pigs, used for food

chiv·al·ric (shi val′rik, shiv′'l rik) *adj.* **1.** of chivalry **2.** *same as* CHIVALROUS

chiv·al·rous (shiv′'l rəs) *adj.* **1.** having the noble qualities knights of old were supposed to have; gallant, courteous, honorable, etc. *[it was chivalrous of him to offer her his coat when it started to rain]* **2.** having to do with chivalry; chivalric —see SYN. at CIVIL —**chiv′al·rous·ly** *adv.* —**chiv′al·rous·ness** *n.*

chiv·al·ry (shiv′'l rē) *n.* [< OFr. *chivalerie* < *chevaler*, a knight: doublet of CAVALRY] **1.** a group of knights or gallant gentlemen **2.** the way of life followed by the knights of the Middle Ages **3.** the noble qualities a knight was supposed to have, such as courage, honor, and a readiness to help the weak and protect women **4.** action displaying any of these qualities

chives (chīvz) *n.pl.* [< OFr. < L. *cepa*, onion] *[often with sing. v.]* a plant with small and slender hollow leaves that have a mild onion odor and are chopped up for use as flavoring

chiv·y, chiv·vy (chiv′ē) *vt.*, *vi.* [< hunting cry] **chiv′ied** or **chiv′vied**, **chiv′y·ing** or **chiv′vy·ing** **1.** to nag or pester **2.** to get, put, etc. by skillful handling; manipulate

chla·mys (klā′məs, klam′əs) *n.*, *pl.* **chla′mys·es**, **chlam·y·des** (klam′ə dēz′) [L. < Gr. *chlamys*] a short cloak fastened at the shoulder, worn by men in ancient Greece

chlo·ral (klôr′əl) *n.* [CHLOR(O)- + AL(COHOL)] a thin, oily, colorless liquid, CCl_3CHO, with a sharp smell, prepared by the action of chlorine on alcohol: a drug made with chloral (**chloral hydrate**) is used to cause sleep

chlor·am·phen·i·col (klôr′am fen′ə kôl′, -kōl′) *n.* [CHLOR(O)- + AM(IDE) + PHE(NO)- + NI(TRO)- + (GLY)COL] an antibiotic drug, $C_{11}H_{12}Cl_2N_2O_5$, used against many bacteria and some viruses

chlo·rate (klôr′āt, -it) *n.* a salt of chloric acid

☆**chlor·dane** (klôr′dān) *n.* [CHLOR(O)- + (in)dane, a coal-tar derivative] a poisonous, vaporizing oil, $C_{10}H_6Cl_8$, used as an insecticide: also **chlor′dan** (-dan)

chlo·rel·la (klə rel′ə) *n.* [ModL. < CHLOR(O)- + *-ella*, fem. dim. suffix] any of a group of one-celled green algae that are rich sources of proteins, carbohydrates, and fats

chlo·ric (klôr′ik) *adj.* **1.** of or containing chlorine with a higher valence than in corresponding chlorous compounds **2.** designating or of a colorless acid, $HClO_3$, whose salts are chlorates

chlo·ride (klôr′īd) *n.* a compound of chlorine with another element or radical *[salts of hydrochloric acid are chlorides]*

chloride of lime a white powder, $CaOCl_2$, obtained by treating slaked lime with chlorine and used for disinfecting and bleaching

chlo·ri·nate (klôr′ə nāt′) *vt.* **-nat·ed**, **-nat·ing** to treat or combine (a substance) with chlorine; esp., to add chlorine to in order to make pure *[chlorinate drinking water]* —**chlo′ri·na′tion** *n.* —**chlo′ri·na′tor** *n.*

chlo·rine (klôr′ēn, -in) *n.* [CHLOR(O)- + -INE⁴] a greenish-yellow, poisonous gas that is a chemical element: it is used in

CHLAMYS

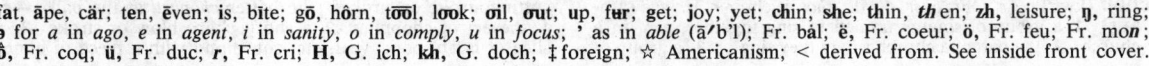

fat, āpe, cär; ten, ēven; is, bīte; gō, hôrn, tōōl, look; oil, out; up, fur; get; joy; yet; chin; she; thin, *th*en; zh, leisure; ŋ, ring; ə for a in ago, e in agent, i in sanity, o in comply, u in focus; ′ as in able (ā′b'l); Fr. bal; ë, Fr. coeur; ö, Fr. feu; Fr. mon; ô, Fr. coq; ü, Fr. duc; r, Fr. cri; H, G. ich; kh, G. doch; ‡foreign; ☆ Americanism; < derived from. See inside front cover.

bleaches, for making water pure, etc.: symbol, Cl; at. wt., 35.453; at. no., 17

chlo·rite (-īt) *n.* a salt of chlorous acid

chlo·ro- [< Gr. *chlōros*, pale green] *a combining form meaning:* **1.** green [*chlorophyll*] **2.** having chlorine in the molecule [*chloroform*] Also, before a vowel, **chlor-**

chlo·ro·form (klôr′ə fôrm′) *n.* [see CHLORO- & FORMIC] a sweetish, colorless liquid, CHCl₃, that changes into a vapor easily: it is used as a general anesthetic and as a solvent —*vt.* **1.** to make unconscious by giving chloroform to **2.** to kill with chloroform [a butterfly collector who *chloroforms* his specimens]

☆**Chlo·ro·my·ce·tin** (klôr′ə mī sēt′′n) [< CHLORO- + -MY-CETE + -IN¹] *a trademark for* CHLORAMPHENICOL

chlo·ro·phyll, chlo·ro·phyl (klôr′ə fil′) *n.* [< Fr. < Gr. *chloros*, green + *phyllon*, a leaf] the green coloring matter of plants: sunlight causes it to change carbon dioxide and water into the carbohydrates that are the food of the plant: see also PHOTOSYNTHESIS —**chlo′ro·phyl′lose** (-ōs), **chlo′ro·phyl′lous** (-əs) *adj.*

chlo·ro·plast (klôr′ə plast′) *n.* [CHLORO- + Gr. *plastos*, formed] any of the oval bits of protoplasm that contain chlorophyll in the cells of green plants

☆**chlo·ro·prene** (klôr′ə prēn′) *n.* [CHLORO- + (ISO)PRENE] a colorless liquid made from acetylene, used to form the synthetic rubber neoprene

chlo·ro·sis (klə rō′sis) *n.* [see CHLORO- + -OSIS] **1.** a condition of plants in which the green parts whiten or yellow as a result of disease or lack of light **2.** an anemia of some girls at puberty, in which the skin turns greenish

chlo·rous (klôr′əs) *adj.* **1.** of or containing chlorine with a lower valence than in corresponding chloric compounds **2.** designating or of an unstable acid, HClO₂, a strong oxidizing agent whose salts are chlorites

chlor·prom·a·zine (klôr präm′ə zēn′) *n.* a synthetic drug, C₁₇H₁₉N₂SCl, used as a tranquilizer

☆**chlor·tet·ra·cy·cline** (klôr′tet′rə sī′klēn, -klin) *n.* a yellow antibiotic, C₂₂H₂₃ClN₂O₈, used against many bacteria and some viruses

chm., chmn. chairman

chock (chäk) *n.* [ONormFr. *choque*, a block] **1.** a block or wedge placed under a wheel, barrel, etc. to keep it from rolling **2.** *Naut.* a block with two hornlike projections curving inward, through which a rope may be run —*vt.* to put a chock under as a wedge —*adv.* as close or tight as can be

chock·a·block (chäk′ə bläk′) *adj.* **1.** pulled so tight as to have the blocks touching: said of a hoisting tackle **2.** crowded —*adv.* tightly together

chock-full (chäk′fool′, chuk′-) *adj.* as full as possible; filled to capacity [a carton *chock-full* of books]

choc·o·late (chôk′lət, chäk′-; -ə lət) *n.* [< Fr. < Sp. < Nahuatl *chocolatl*] **1.** a paste, powder, etc. made from cacao seeds that have been roasted and ground **2.** a drink made of chocolate, hot milk or water, and sugar **3.** a candy made of or coated with chocolate **4.** reddish brown —*adj.* **1.** made of or flavored with chocolate **2.** reddish-brown

Choc·taw (chäk′tô) *n.* [< tribal name *Chata* < ?] **1.** *pl.* **-taws,** **-taw** a member of a tribe of Muskogean Indians who once lived in the Southeast but now live in Oklahoma **2.** their Muskogean dialect

choice (chois) *n.* [< OFr. < *choisir*, to choose < Goth. *kausjan*, to taste: for IE. base see CHOOSE] **1.** a choosing; selection [he read a book of his own *choice*] **2.** the right or power to choose; option [you have a *choice* as to where you will sit] **3.** a person or thing chosen [he is my *choice* for captain] **4.** the best [the *choice* of the litter] **5.** a variety from which to choose [we have a *choice* of three movies to see] **6.** an alternative [he had no *choice* but to leave] —*adj.* **choic′er, choic′est** **1.** of special excellence; very good [*choice* fruits] **2.** carefully chosen [expressed in *choice* words] —**of choice** that is preferred [the medical treatment *of choice*] —**choice′ly** *adv.* —**choice′ness** *n.* **SYN.**—**choice** implies the chance, right, or power to choose, usually by freely using one's judgment [a bachelor by *choice*]; **option** suggests a right to choose that has been given to one by someone who has the power to do so [*local option* on liquor sales]; **alternative** refers to a choice to be made from two possibilities or, less strictly, from more than two [the *alternative* of paying a fine or serving 30 days]; **preference** suggests a particular liking that would help determine one's choice [a *preference* for striped ties]

choir (kwīr) *n.* [< OFr. *cuer* < ML. *chorus*, choir < L.: see CHO-RUS] **1.** a group of singers trained to sing together, esp. in a church **2.** the part of a church where they sing ☆**3.** a group of

instruments of the same kind in an orchestra [the brass *choir*] **4.** an organized group, as of dancers

choir·mas·ter (kwīr′mas′tər) *n.* the director of a choir

choke (chōk) *vt.* **choked, chok′ing** [< OE. *aceocian*] **1.** to keep from breathing by blocking the windpipe or squeezing the throat of; strangle; suffocate **2.** to block up; obstruct by clogging [garbage *choked* the drain in the kitchen sink] **3.** to hold back the growth or action of [weeds are *choking* the grass in the lawn] **4.** to fill up [the store's shelves were *choked* with canned goods] **5.** to cut off some air from the carburetor of (a gasoline engine) so as to make a richer gasoline mixture ☆**6.** to hold (a bat, golf club, etc.) closer toward the middle of the handle —*vi.* **1.** to be suffocated; have a hard time breathing **2.** to be blocked up; be obstructed **3.** to become strained with emotion [a *choking* voice] —*n.* **1.** the act or sound of choking **2.** the valve that chokes a carburetor —**choke back** to hold back (feelings, sobs, etc.) —**choke down** to swallow with difficulty —**choke off** to bring to an end; end the growth of —**choke up 1.** to block up; clog **2.** to fill too full ☆**3.** [Colloq.] to be unable to speak or act normally because of fear, tension, etc.

choke·bore (chōk′bôr′) *n.* **1.** a shotgun bore that becomes smaller toward the muzzle to keep the shot closely bunched **2.** a gun with such a bore

☆**choke·cher·ry** (-cher′ē) *n., pl.* **-ries 1.** a N. American wild cherry tree **2.** its bitter fruit

choke·damp (chōk′damp′) *n.* same as BLACKDAMP

chok·er (chōk′ər) *n.* **1.** a person or thing that chokes **2.** a closely fitting necklace

chok·y (-ē) *adj.* **chok′i·er, chok′i·est** **1.** inclined to choke **2.** suffocating; stifling Also sp. **chok′ey**

chol·e- *same as* CHOLO-: also, before a vowel, **chol-**

chol·er (käl′ər) *n.* [< OFr. < L. *cholera*: see CHOLERA] **1.** [Obs.] bile: in medieval times yellow bile was thought to be the cause of anger and irritability **2.** [Now Rare] anger or bad temper

chol·er·a (käl′ər ə) *n.* [L., jaundice < Gr. *cholera*, nausea < *cholē*, bile: for IE. base see GOLD] any of several diseases of the intestines; esp., ASIATIC CHOLERA

chol·er·ic (käl′ər ik, kə ler′ik) *adj.* [see CHOLER] showing a quick temper; easily made angry —see SYN. at IRRITABLE

cho·les·ter·ol (kə les′tə rōl′, -rôl′) *n.* [< CHOLE- + Gr. *stereos*, solid + -OL¹] a crystalline fatty alcohol, C₂₇H₄₅OH, found esp. in animal fats, blood, etc.: thought to be a cause of hardening of the arteries

cho·line (kō′lēn, käl′ēn) *n.* [CHOL(O)- + -INE⁴] a liquid, C₅H₁₅O₂N, found in many animal and vegetable tissues, important in fat metabolism: a vitamin of the B complex

chol·o- [< Gr. *cholē*: see CHOLERA] *a combining form meaning* bile, gall

chomp (chämp) *vt., vi.* [dial. var. of CHAMP¹] **1.** to chew hard and noisily **2.** to bite down (on) repeatedly and restlessly [a cigar-*chomping* general] —*n.* the act or sound of chomping —**chomp′er** *n.*

chon (chän) *n., pl.* **chon** see MONETARY UNITS, table (Korea)

choose (chōz) *vt.* **chose, cho′sen** or obs. **chose, choos′ing** [OE. *ceosan* < IE. base *geus-*, to enjoy, taste] **1.** to pick out; take as a choice; select [he *chose* a career in law] **2.** to decide or prefer [to *choose* to remain] —*vi.* **1.** to make one's selection **2.** to have the desire or wish [do as you *choose*] —**cannot choose but** cannot do otherwise than —**choos′er** *n.* **SYN.**—**choose** implies using judgment in deciding upon a thing or course of action from among those offered; **select**, and the more informal **pick**, usually imply a careful choosing from a large number available, but **pick** sometimes suggests a choosing at random [pick a number from 1 to 10]; **elect** implies formal action or official procedure in choosing a person or thing; **prefer** implies favoring one thing over another but does not always connote the actual getting of what one chooses [I prefer vanilla but will take any flavor] —ANT. reject

☆**choos·y, choos·ey** (chōō′zē) *adj.* **choos′i·er, choos′i·est** [Colloq.] very careful or fussy in choosing

chop¹ (chäp) *vt.* **chopped, chop′ping** [ME. *choppen*, prob. < OFr. *c(h)oper*, to cut] **1.** to cut by blows with an ax or other sharp tool **2.** to cut into small bits; mince [to *chop* up an onion] **3.** to hit with a short, sharp stroke —*vi.* to make a quick, cutting stroke or strokes [the batter *chopped* at the ball] —*n.* **1.** the act of chopping **2.** a short, sharp blow or stroke **3.** a slice of lamb, pork, veal, etc. cut, along with a piece of bone,

CHOKER

from the rib, loin, or shoulder **4.** a short, broken movement of waves

chop² (chäp) *n.* [var. of CHAP¹] **1.** a jaw **2.** a cheek See CHOPS

chop³ (chäp) *vi.* **chopped, chop′ping** [OE. *ceapian,* to bargain: see CHEAP] to shift or veer suddenly, as the wind

chop·fall·en (chäp′fô′lən) *adj.* same as CHAPFALLEN

chop·house (-hous′) *n.* a restaurant that specializes in chops and steaks

Cho·pin (shō′pan; *Fr.* shô pan′), **Fré·dé·ric Fran·çois** (frä dä rĕk′ frän swä′) 1810–49; Pol. composer & pianist, in France after 1831

chop·per (chäp′ər) *n.* **1.** a person or thing that chops **2.** [*pl.*] [Slang] teeth, esp. false teeth ☆**3.** [Colloq.] a helicopter

chop·py¹ (-ē) *adj.* **-pi·er, -pi·est** [< CHOP³ + -Y²] shifting constantly and abruptly, as the wind —**chop′pi·ness** *n.*

chop·py² (-ē) *adj.* **-pi·er, -pi·est** [< CHOP¹ + -Y²] **1.** rough with short, broken waves, as the sea **2.** making abrupt starts and stops; jerky —**chop′pi·ly** *adv.* —**chop′pi·ness** *n.*

chops (chäps) *n.pl.* [see CHAP¹] **1.** the jaws **2.** the mouth and lower cheeks ☆**3.** [Slang] technical skill, as of a jazz musician

chop·sticks (chäp′stiks′) *n.pl.* [pidgin Eng. for Chin. *k'wai-tsze,* the quick ones] **1.** two small sticks held together in one hand and used in some Asian countries to lift food to the mouth **2.** [*with sing. v.*] a short, choppy tune played on a piano

CHOPSTICKS

☆**chop su·ey** (chäp′ sōō′ē) [altered < Chin. *tsa-sui,* lit., various pieces] a Chinese-American dish of meat, bean sprouts, celery, mushrooms, etc. cooked together in a sauce and served with rice

cho·ral (kôr′əl) *adj.* [Fr.] of, for, sung by, or recited by a choir or chorus — **cho′ral·ly** *adv.*

cho·rale, cho·ral (kə ral′, kô-) *n.* [< G. *choral* (*gesang*), choral (song)] **1.** a hymn tune **2.** a choral composition based on such a tune **3.** a group of singers; choir

chord¹ (kôrd) *n.* [altered (after L. *chorda*) < CORD] **1.** a feeling or emotion thought of as being played on like the string of a harp [to strike a sympathetic *chord*] **2.** *Anat.* same as CORD (sense 5) **3.** *Engineering* a main horizontal section in a rigid framework, as of a bridge **4.** *Geom.* a straight line joining any two points on an arc, curve, or circumference

chord² (kôrd) *n.* [altered (after L. *chorda*) < ME. *cord* < *accord,* ACCORD] *Music* a combination of three or more tones that make harmony when sounded together — *vi., vt.* **1.** to harmonize **2.** to play chords on (a piano, guitar, etc.) —**chord′al** *adj.*

CHORDS (AC, AO)

chor·date (kôr′dāt) *n.* [L. *chorda* (see CORD) + -ATE¹] any of a large group of animals having at some stage of development a notochord and a nerve cord along the back: vertebrates, tunicates, and lancelets are all chordates

chore (chôr) *n.* [< OE. *cierr:* see CHARE] **1.** a common, everyday task, as on a farm or in the home [his *chores* included washing the dishes and vacuuming] : *often used in pl.* **2.** any hard or unpleasant task [writing letters is a real *chore* for her]

cho·re·a (kô rē′ə) *n.* [ModL. < L. < Gr. *choreia,* choral dance] a nervous disorder in which jerking movements are caused by uncontrollable contractions of the muscles; Saint Vitus' dance

chor·e·o·graph (kôr′ē ə graf′) *vt., vi.* [< CHOREOGRAPHY] to design or plan the movements of (a dance, esp. a ballet) — **chor′e·og′ra·pher** (-äg′rə fər) *n.*

chor·e·og·ra·phy (kôr′ē äg′rə fē) *n.* [Gr. *choreia,* dance + -GRAPHY] **1.** dancing, esp. ballet dancing **2.** the arrangement of the movements of a dance **3.** the art of planning dances, esp. ballets —**chor′e·o·graph′ic** (-ə graf′ik) *adj.*

cho·ric (kôr′ik) *adj.* of, for, or like a chorus, esp. in an ancient Greek play

cho·ri·on (kôr′ē än′) *n.* [ModL. < Gr. *chorion,* membrane] the outermost of the two membranes that enclose a fetus

chor·is·ter (kôr′is tər) *n.* [< OFr. *cueristre:* see CHOIR] a member of a choir, esp. a boy who sings in one

C-horizon *n.* see ABC SOIL

cho·roid (kôr′oid) *adj.* [< Gr. < *chorion,* CHORION + *eidos,* form] designating or of certain membranes containing many blood vessels —*n.* the dark membrane of this kind between the sclera and retina of the eye: see illustration at EYE Also **cho′ri·oid′** (-ē oid′)

chor·tle (chôr′t'l) *vi., vt.* **-tled, -tling** [coined by Lewis Carroll, prob. < CHUCKLE + SNORT] to make, or utter with, a gleeful chuckling or snorting sound —*n.* such a sound —**chor′tler** *n.*

cho·rus (kôr′əs) *n.* [L. < Gr. *choros,* a dance, chorus] **1.** in ancient Greek drama, a group whose singing, dancing, and reciting help to explain the play, carry along its mood, etc. **2.** the singers and dancers who work together as a group and not as soloists in a musical show, opera, etc. **3.** the part of a drama, song, etc. performed by a chorus **4.** a group trained to sing or speak something together **5.** a number of voices speaking at once [a *chorus* of protest] **6.** music written for group singing **7.** *a)* the part of a song that is repeated after each verse; refrain *b)* the main tune, as of a jazz piece, following the introduction —*vt., vi.* to sing, speak, or say together or at the same time —**in chorus** all at once; together

chorus girl (or **boy**) a woman (or man) singing or dancing in the chorus of a musical show

chose (chōz) *pt. & obs. pp.* of CHOOSE

cho·sen (chō′z'n) *pp.* of CHOOSE —*adj.* picked out by preference; selected

Chou (jō) a Chinese dynasty (1122? to 256? B.C.)

Chou En-lai (jō′ en′lī′) 1898–1976; Chin. Communist leader; prime minister (1949–76)

chow (chou) *n.* [< Chin. dial. form akin to Cantonese *kaú,* a dog] **1.** any of a breed of dog, originally from China, with a thick, brown or black coat and a black tongue: official name **chow chow** ☆**2.** [Slang] food or mealtime

chow-chow (chou′chou′) *n.* [PidE. < Chin.] ☆pickled vegetables chopped up in a highly seasoned mustard sauce

☆**chow·der** (chou′dər) *n.* [Fr. *chaudière,* a pot < LL. *caldaria:* see CALDRON] a thick soup usually made with clams or fish along with onions, potatoes, and milk or corn, tomatoes, etc.

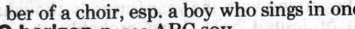

CHOW (to 20 in. high at shoulder)

☆**chow mein** (chou mān′) [Chin. *ch'ao,* to fry + *mien,* flour] a Chinese-American dish consisting of a thick stew of meat, celery, bean sprouts, etc., served with fried noodles and usually soy sauce

Chr. 1. Christ **2.** Christian **3.** Chronicles

chrism (kriz′m) *n.* [< OE. < LL. < Gr. *chrisma,* an anointing < *chriein:* see CHRIST] consecrated oil used in baptism and other sacraments in certain churches —**chris′mal** *adj.*

Christ (krīst) [< LL. < Gr. *christos,* the anointed (in NT., MESSIAH) < *chriein,* to anoint < IE. base *ghrei-,* to smear] Jesus of Nazareth, regarded by Christians as the Messiah prophesied in the Old Testament

Christ·church (krīst′church′) city on the E coast of South Island, New Zealand: pop. (of urban area) 256,000

chris·ten (kris′'n) *vt.* [OE. *cristnian*] **1.** to take into a Christian church by baptism; baptize **2.** to give a name to at baptism **3.** to give a name to (a ship being launched, etc.) **4.** [Colloq.] to make use of for the first time —**chris′ten·ing** *n.*

Chris·ten·dom (kris′'n dəm) *n.* **1.** Christians as a group **2.** those parts of the world where most of the inhabitants declare belief in Christianity

Chris·tian (kris′chən) a masculine name —*n.* [OE. *cristen,* ult. < Gr. *christos:* see CHRIST] **1.** a person declaring belief in Jesus as the Christ, or in the religion based on his teachings **2.** [Colloq.] a decent, respectable person —*adj.* **1.** of Jesus Christ or his teachings **2.** of or declaring belief in the religion based on these teachings **3.** having or showing the qualities that Christians are supposed to have, as kindness, charity, and humbleness **4.** of or representing Christians or Christianity —**Chris′tian·ly** *adj., adv.*

fat, āpe, cär, ten, ēven, is, bīte; gō, hôrn, tōōl, look; oil, out; up, fur; get; joy; yet; chin; she; thin, *then*; zh, leisure; ŋ, ring; ə for *a* in *ago, e* in *agent, i* in *sanity, o* in *comply, u* in *focus*; ′ as in *able* (ā′b'l); Fr. bál; ë, Fr. coeur; ö, Fr. feu; Fr. mon; ծ, Fr. coq; ü, Fr. duc; r, Fr. cri; H, G. ich; kh, G. doch; ‡foreign; ☆ Americanism; < derived from. See inside front cover.

Christian Era the era beginning with the year formerly thought to be that of the birth of Jesus Christ (born probably c. 8–4 B.C.): *A.D.* marks dates in this era, *B.C.* marks dates before it

Chris·ti·a·ni·a (kris′chē an′ē ə, -tē än′-) *former name of* OSLO —*n.* [*also* **c-**] *same as* CHRISTIE

Chris·ti·an·i·ty (kris′chē an′ə tē) *n.* **1.** Christians as a group **2.** the Christian religion **3.** the state of being a Christian

Chris·tian·ize (kris′chə nīz′) *vt.* **-ized′, -iz′ing** **1.** to convert to Christianity **2.** to make Christian in character —**Chris′tian·i·za′tion** *n.* —**Chris′tian·iz′er** *n.*

Christian name the baptismal name or given name, as distinguished from the surname or family name

Christian Science ☆a religion and system of healing founded by Mary Baker Eddy c. 1866: official name, CHURCH OF CHRIST, SCIENTIST —**Christian Scientist**

chris·tie, chris·ty (kris′tē) *n., pl.* **-ties** [< CHRISTIANIA] Skiing a turn at high speed to change direction, stop, etc., made by shifting weight, with skis usually kept parallel

Chris·tine (kris tēn′) [< LL. fem. of CHRISTIAN] a feminine name: var. *Christina*

Christ·like (krīst′līk′) *adj.* like Jesus Christ, esp. in character or spirit —**Christ′like′ness** *n.*

Christ·ly (-lē) *adj.* of Jesus Christ; Christlike —**Christ′li·ness** *n.*

Christ·mas (kris′məs) *n.* [OE. *Cristesmæsse:* see CHRIST & MASS] **1.** a holiday on Dec. 25 celebrating the birth of Jesus Christ: also **Christmas Day** **2.** *same as* CHRISTMASTIDE

Christmas Eve the evening before Christmas Day

Christmas Island **1.** island in the Indian Ocean, south of Java: under Australian administration: 55 sq. mi. **2.** Brit. island in the Gilbert and Ellice Islands: 222 sq. mi.

Christ·mas·tide (-tīd′) *n.* Christmas time, from Christmas Eve through New Year's Day or to Epiphany (Jan. 6)

☆**Christmas tree** an evergreen tree or artificial tree hung with decorations and lights at Christmas time

Chris·tophe (krēs tôf′), **Hen·ri** (än rē′) 1767–1820; Haitian revolutionary leader; king of Haiti (1811–20)

Chris·to·pher (kris′tə fər) [< LL. < Gr. *Christophoros,* lit., bearing Christ] **1.** a masculine name: dim. *Chris* **2.** Saint, 3d cent. A.D.?; patron saint of travelers

chro·mate (krō′māt) *n.* a salt of chromic acid

chro·mat·ic (krō mat′ik) *adj.* [< LL. < Gr. *chrōmatos,* genitive of *chrōma,* color < IE. base *ghreu-,* to rub, crumble, from which also come GRIT & GREAT] **1.** of or having color or colors **2.** *Music* a) using or progressing by semitones, or halftones: the chromatic scale has thirteen successive halftones to the octave b) using tones not in the key of a work [*chromatic* harmony] —*n. Music* a tone modified by an accidental, as by a sharp or flat —**chro·mat′i·cal·ly** *adv.* —**chro·mat′i·cism** (-ə siz′m) *n.*

chromatic aberration a property of lenses that causes the various colors in a beam of light to be focused at different points, thus forming a border of colors around the edges of the image

chro·mat·ics (krō mat′iks) *n.pl.* [*with sing. v.*] the scientific study of colors

chro·ma·tin (krō′mə tin) *n.* [< Gr. *chrōma* (see CHROMATIC) + -IN[1]] the substance in the nucleus of living cells that readily takes a deep stain and forms the chromosomes

chro·ma·to- [< Gr. *chrōma:* see CHROMATIC] a combining form meaning: **1.** color or pigmentation **2.** chromatin Also, before a vowel, **chromat-**

chrome (krōm) *n.* [Fr. < Gr. *chrōma:* see CHROMATIC] **1.** chromium or chromium alloy, esp. as used for plating **2.** any of certain salts of chromium, used in dyeing and tanning **3.** a chromium coloring matter —*vt.* **chromed, chrom′ing** **1.** to plate with chromium **2.** to treat with a salt of chromium, as in dyeing

-chrome (krōm) [< Gr. *chrōma:* see CHROMATIC] a combining form meaning color or coloring agent [*monochrome*]

chro·mic (krō′mik) *adj.* designating or of compounds containing chromium with a valence of three

chromic acid an acid, H_2CrO_4, existing only in solution or known in the form of its salts

chro·mi·um (krō′mē əm) *n.* [< CHROME] a very hard metal that is a chemical element: chromium does not rust easily and is used in steel alloys and as a plating for metals: symbol, Cr; at. wt., 51.996; at. no., 24

chromium steel a very strong, hard alloy steel containing chromium: also **chrome steel**

☆**chro·mo** (krō′mō) *n., pl.* **-mos** *short for* CHROMOLITHOGRAPH

chro·mo- [< Gr. *chrōma:* see CHROMATIC] a combining form meaning color or coloring matter [*chromosome*]: also, before a vowel, **chrom-**

chro·mo·lith·o·graph (krō′mō lith′ə graf′) *n.* a color lithograph: an earlier term

chro·mo·some (krō′mə sōm′) *n.* [CHROMO- + -SOME[3]] any of the microscopic rod-shaped bodies into which the chromatin of a cell nucleus separates during mitosis: chromosomes carry the genes, which are the units of heredity and are always the same in number for a particular species —**chro′mo·so′mal** *adj.*

chro·mo·sphere (-sfir′) *n.* [CHROMO- + -SPHERE] the layer of gases around the sun between the photosphere and the corona

chro·mous (krō′məs) *adj.* designating or of compounds containing chromium with a valence of two

Chron. Chronicles

chron. **1.** chronological **2.** chronology

chron·ic (krän′ik) *adj.* [< Fr. < L. < Gr. < *chronos,* time] **1.** lasting a long time or coming back again and again: said of a disease, and distinguished from ACUTE **2.** having been such for a long time; constant or habitual [a *chronic* invalid; a *chronic* complainer; a *chronic* worry] —**chron′i·cal·ly** *adv.*

SYN.—**chronic** implies a condition that goes on and on or keeps coming back and is used especially of diseases that are very hard to cure [a *chronic* cough]; **inveterate** suggests that a habit, practice, etc. has become firmly established over a long period of time [an *inveterate* liar]; **confirmed** suggests being fixed in some condition or practice, often a more deeply felt dislike of changing [a *confirmed* bachelor]; **hardened** implies having fixed tendencies and an unfeeling indifference to emotional or moral matters [a *hardened* criminal]

chron·i·cle (krän′i k'l) *n.* [< Anglo-Fr. < OFr. < L. < Gr. *chronika,* annals: see prec.] a history or story; esp., a record or tale of things that happened, in the order in which they happened —*vt.* **-cled, -cling** to tell or write the history or story of; put into a chronicle —**chron′i·cler** (-klər) *n.*

Chron·i·cles (-k'lz) either of two books of the Bible, I and II Chronicles

chro·no- [Gr. < *chronos,* time] a combining form meaning time: also, before a vowel, **chron-**

chron·o·graph (krän′ə graf′, krō′nə-) *n.* [CHRONO- + -GRAPH] an instrument for showing or recording to the fraction of a second the time it takes for something to happen

chron·o·log·i·cal (krän′ə läj′i k'l) *adj.* **1.** arranged in the order in which things happened **2.** having to do with chronology Also **chron′o·log′ic** —**chron′o·log′i·cal·ly** *adv.*

chro·nol·o·gy (krə näl′ə jē) *n., pl.* **-gies** [CHRONO- + -LOGY] **1.** the science of measuring time and of dating events in proper order **2.** an arrangement or list of events, dates, etc. in the order of occurrence —**chro·nol′o·gist, chro·nol′o·ger** *n.*

chro·nom·e·ter (krə näm′ə tər) *n.* [CHRONO- + -METER] a very accurate clock or watch, as for scientific use

chro·nom·e·try (krə näm′ə trē) *n.* the scientific measurement of time

chrys·a·lid (kris′'l id) *n. same as* CHRYSALIS —*adj.* of a chrysalis

chrys·a·lis (kris′'l əs) *n., pl.* **chry·sal·i·des** (kri sal′ə dēz′), **chrys·a·lis·es** [< L. < Gr. *chrysallis,* golden-colored chrysalis < *chrysos,* gold] **1.** the pupa of a butterfly, the form of the insect between the time when it is a larva and the time when it is a winged adult **2.** a stage of development when something or someone is still protected

chrys·an·the·mum (kri san′thə məm) *n.* [L. < Gr. < *chrysos,* gold + *anthemon,* a flower] **1.** a late-blooming plant of the composite family, with showy flowers, grown in a wide variety of sizes and colors **2.** any of these flowers

CHRYSALIS
(as seen
from front
and side)

chrys·o·lite (kris′ə līt′) *n.* [< OFr. < L. < Gr. < *chrysos,* gold + *lithos,* stone] *same as* OLIVINE

chrys·o·prase (-prāz′) *n.* [< OFr. < L. < Gr. < *chrysos,* gold + *prason,* leek] a light-green variety of chalcedony sometimes used as a semiprecious stone

Chrys·os·tom (kris′əs təm, kri säs′-), **Saint John** 347?–407 A.D.; Gr. priest & church father

chub (chub) *n., pl.* **chubs, chub:** see PLURAL, II, D, 1 [ME. *chub-be*] ☆any of several small, freshwater fishes related to the minnows and carp

chub·by (chub′ē) *adj.* **-bi·er, -bi·est** [< prec.] round and plump —**chub′bi·ness** *n.*

chuck[1] (chuk) *vt.* [< ? Fr. *choquer,* to strike against] **1.** to tap or pat gently, esp. under the chin, as a playful gesture **2.** to throw with a quick, short movement; toss **3.** [Slang] *a)* to throw out; get rid of ☆**b)** to quit (as one's job) ☆**c)** to vomit (often with *up*) —*n.* **1.** a light tap or squeeze under the chin **2.** a toss **3.** [Chiefly Western] food

chuck² (chuk) *n.* [prob. var. of CHOCK] **1.** a cut of beef including the parts around the neck and the shoulder blade: see illustration at BEEF **2.** a clamplike device, as on a lathe, by which the tool or work is held

chuck³ (chuk) *vi., n.* [echoic] *same as* CLUCK

☆**chuck-a-luck** (chuk′ə luk′) *n.* [< CHUCK¹ + LUCK] a gambling game using three dice: also called **chuck′-luck′**

chuck-full (chuk′fool′) *adj. same as* CHOCK-FULL

☆**chuck-hole** (chuk′hōl′) *n.* [< dial. *chock*, a bump + HOLE] a rough hole in a road, made by wear and weathering

CHUCK (of a drill)

chuck-le (chuk′'l) *vi.* **-led, -ling** [prob. CHUCK³ + -LE²] to laugh softly in a low tone, often to oneself, as when one is amused by something —*n.* a soft laugh —see SYN. at LAUGH —**chuck′ler** *n.*

chuck-le-head (-hed′) *n.* [Colloq.] a stupid person

☆**chuck wagon** [CHUCK¹, *n.* 3 + WAGON] [Slang] a wagon equipped as a kitchen for feeding cowboys or other outdoor workers

chuff (chuf) *vi., n.* [echoic] *same as* CHUG

☆**chug** (chug) *n.* [echoic] any of a series of short, puffing or explosive sounds, as of a steam engine —*vi.* **chugged, chug′ging** to make, or move with, such sounds

Chu Kiang (chōō′jyäŋ′) river in SE China, forming an estuary between Macao & Hong Kong

chuk-ka (boot) (chuk′ə) [< CHUKKER] a man's ankle-high bootlike shoe, often fleece-lined, with two pairs of eyelets

chuk-ker, chuk-kar (chuk′ər) *n.* [Hindi *chakar* < Sans. *cakra,* wheel] any of the periods of play, 7½ minutes each, of a polo match

Chu-la Vis-ta (chōō′lə vis′tə) [AmSp., lit., beautiful view] city in SW Calif.: suburb of San Diego: pop. 68,000

chum (chum) *n.* [17th-c. slang; prob. < *chamber* in *chamber mate*] [Colloq.] a close friend —*vi.* **chummed, chum′ming** [Colloq.] to be close friends

chum-my (chum′ē) *adj.* **-mi-er, -mi-est** [Colloq.] like a chum; intimate; friendly —**chum′mi-ly** *adv.* —**chum′mi-ness** *n.*

chump (chump) *n.* [< ? CHUCK² or CHUNK + LUMP¹] **1.** a heavy block of wood **2.** a thick, blunt end **3.** [Colloq.] a foolish, stupid, or gullible person

Chung-king (choōŋ′kiŋ′; *Chin.* jooŋ′chiŋ′) city in SC China, on the Yangtze: pop. 4,070,000

chunk (chuŋk) *n.* [< ? CHUCK²] **1.** a short, thick piece, as of meat, wood, etc. **2.** a sizable part [taxes take a *chunk* out of a person's paycheck] ☆**3.** a stocky animal, esp. a horse

☆**chunk-y** (chuŋ′kē) *adj.* **chunk′i-er, chunk′i-est** **1.** short and thick **2.** stocky; thickset **3.** containing chunks —**chunk′i-ness** *n.*

church (church) *n.* [< OE. *cirice,* ult. < LGr. *kyriakē* (*oikia*), Lord's (house) < Gr. *kyros,* supreme power] **1.** a building for public worship, esp. one for Christian worship **2.** public worship; religious service **3.** [*usually* C-] all Christians as a group, or a particular sect or denomination of Christians **4.** church government, or its power, as opposed to civil government **5.** the profession of the clergy **6.** a group of worshipers —*adj.* of a church or of organized Christian worship —**church′less** *adj.*

church-go-er (church′gō′ər) *n.* a person who attends church, esp. regularly —**church′go′ing** *n., adj.*

Church-ill (church′chil), Sir **Win-ston** (**Leonard Spencer**) (win′stən) 1874-1965; Brit. statesman & writer; prime minister (1940-45; 1951-55)

church-ly (church′lē) *adj.* of, fit for, or belonging to a church —**church′li-ness** *n.*

church-man (-mən) *n., pl.* **-men** **1.** a clergyman **2.** a member of a church

Church of Christ, Scientist *see* CHRISTIAN SCIENCE

Church of England the episcopal church of England; Anglican Church: it is an established church with the sovereign as its head

Church of Jesus Christ of Latter-day Saints *see* MORMON

church-ward-en (-wôr′d'n) *n.* a lay officer chosen annually in every parish of the Church of England or of the Protestant Episcopal Church to attend to certain matters of business, etc.

church-wom-an (-woom′ən) *n., pl.* **-wom′en** (-wim′in) a woman member of a church

church-yard (-yärd′) *n.* the yard around a church, often used as a place of burial

churl (church) *n.* [OE. *ceorl,* freeman: for IE. base see CORN¹] **1.** a peasant or rustic; specif., a freeman of the lowest class in England long ago **2.** a person who is mean, rude, surly, etc.; boor —**churl′ish** *adj.* —**churl′ish-ly** *adv.* —**churl′ish-ness** *n.*

churn (churn) *n.* [OE. *cyrne:* for IE. base see CORN¹] **1.** a container or machine in which milk or cream is beaten and shaken to form butter **2.** violent motion or stirring —*vt.* **1.** to beat and shake (milk or cream) in a churn **2.** to make (butter) in a churn **3.** to stir up vigorously **4.** to make (foam, etc.) by stirring vigorously —*vi.* **1.** to use a churn in making butter **2.** to move as if in a churn; seethe [ideas *churning* in his brain]

churr (churr) *n., vi. same as* CHIRR

☆**chute¹** (shoot) *n.* [Fr., a fall, ult. < L. *cadere,* to fall] **1.** a waterfall or rapids in a river **2.** an inclined or vertical trough or passage down which something may slide or be slid or dropped

chute² (shoot) *n. short for* PARACHUTE —**chut′ist** *n.*

chut-ney (chut′nē) *n., pl.* **-neys** [Hindi *chatnī*] a relish made of fruits, spices, and herbs: also sp. **chut′nee**

CHURN

chutz-pah, chutz-pa (hoots′pə, khoots′-; -pä) *n.* [Heb. via Yid.] [Colloq.] boldness that shows no shame or respect; impudence; brass

chyle (kīl) *n.* [LL. < Gr. *chylos* < *cheein,* to pour: for IE. base see FOUND³] a milky fluid made up of lymph and emulsified fats: it is formed from chyme in the small intestine and is passed into the blood through the thoracic duct —**chy-la-ceous** (kī lā′shəs), **chy′lous** *adj.*

chyme (kīm) *n.* [< LL. < Gr. *chymos,* juice < *cheein:* see prec.] the thick, flowing mass resulting from gastric digestion of food: see CHYLE —**chy′mous** *adj.*

CIA, C.I.A. Central Intelligence Agency

‡**ciao** (chou) *interj.* [It.] an informal expression of greeting or farewell

ci-bo-ri-um (si bôr′ē əm) *n., pl.* **-ri-a** (-ə) [ML. < L., a cup < Gr. *kibōrion,* seed vessel of the Egyptian waterlily, hence, a cup] **1.** a canopy covering an altar **2.** a covered cup for holding the consecrated wafers of the Eucharist

ci-ca-da (si kā′də, -kä′-) *n., pl.* **-das, -dae** (-dē) [L.] a large flylike insect with transparent wings: the male makes a loud, shrill sound by vibrating a special organ on its underside

cic-a-trix (sik′ə triks) *n., pl.* **cic-a-tri-ces** (si-kat′rə sēz′, sik′ə trī′sēz) [L.] **1.** *Med.* the scar at the place where a wound has healed **2.** *Bot.* the scar left where a branch, leaf, seed, etc. was once attached or where a wound has healed Also **cic′a-trice** (-tris) —**cic′a-tri′cial** (-trish′əl) *adj.*

cic-a-trize (sik′ə trīz′) *vt., vi.* **-trized′, -triz′ing** to heal with the formation of a scar —**cic′a-tri-za′-tion** *n.*

Cic-er-o (sis′ə rō′) [after CICERO, the orator] city in NE Ill.: suburb of Chicago: pop. 67,000

Cic-er-o (sis′ə rō′), (**Marcus Tullius**) 106-43 B.C.; Rom. statesman & orator —**Cic′e-ro′ni-an** *adj.*

ci-ce-ro-ne (sis′ə rō′nē; *It.* chē che rô′ne) *n., pl.* **-nes**; *It.* **-ni** (-nē) [It. < L. *Cicero,* the orator] a guide who explains the history and chief features of a place to sightseers

Cid (sid; *Sp.* thēth), **the** [Sp. < Ar. *sayyid,* a lord] (born Rodrigo, or Ruy, *Díaz de Bivar*) 1040?-99; Sp. hero and soldier of fortune

-cide (sīd) [< Fr. *-cide* or L. *-cida* < L. *caedere,* to kill] *a suffix* meaning: **1.** killer [*pesticide*] **2.** killing [*genocide*]

ci-der (sī′dər) *n.* [< OFr. < LL. < Gr. *sikera* < Heb. *shēkār,* strong drink] the juice pressed from apples, used as a beverage or for making vinegar: **sweet cider** is unfermented, **hard cider** is fermented

C.I.F., c.i.f. cost, insurance, and freight

CICADA (1-2 inches)

ci·gar (si gär′) *n.* [Sp. *cigarro*, prob. < Maya *sicar*, to smoke < *sic̆*, tobacco] tobacco leaves formed into a tight roll for smoking

cig·a·rette, cig·a·ret (sig′ə ret′, sig′ə ret′) *n.* [Fr., dim. of *cigare*, cigar] a small roll of finely cut tobacco wrapped in thin paper for smoking

cig·a·ril·lo (sig′ə ril′ō) *n., pl.* **-los** [Sp., dim. of *cigarro*, CIGAR] a small, thin cigar

cil·i·a (sil′ē ə) *n.pl., sing.* **-i·um** (-əm) [L.] **1.** the eyelashes **2.** fine hairlike parts growing out from some plant and animal cells: certain one-celled animals, as protozoa, move by waving their cilia, and many higher forms have ducts lined with cilia that act to move fluids through **—cil′i·ate** (-it, -āt′), **cil′i·at′ed** *adj.*

cil·i·ar·y (sil′ē er′ē) *adj.* of, like, or having cilia

Ci·li·cia (sə lish′ə) ancient region in SE Asia Minor, on the Mediterranean **—Ci·li′cian** *adj., n.*

Cim·ar·ron (sim′ə rōn′, -rän′) [AmSp. *cimarrón*, wild, unruly] river flowing from NE N.Mex. to the Arkansas River in Okla.: 600 mi.

cim·ba·lom, cym·ba·lom (sim′bə ləm) *n.* [< Hung. < L. *cymbalum*, cymbal] a type of large dulcimer much used in playing Hungarian folk music

Cim·me·ri·an (si mir′ē ən) *n. Gr. Myth.* any of a people living in a land of perpetual mist and darkness **—adj.** dark; gloomy

☆**cinch** (sinch) *n.* [< Sp. < L. *cingulum*, a girdle < *cingere*, to encircle < IE. base *kenk-*, to gird] **1.** a girth for holding a saddle or pack in place **2.** [Colloq.] a firm grip **3.** [Slang] a sure or easy thing **—vt. 1.** to fasten (a saddle) on (a horse, burro, etc.) with a cinch **2.** [Slang] *a)* to get a firm hold on *b)* to make sure of

cin·cho·na (sin kō′nə, siŋ-) *n.* [ModL., after the Countess del *Chinchón*, wife of a 17th-c. Peruv. viceroy, who was treated with the bark] **1.** a tropical S. American tree from the bark of which quinine is obtained **2.** the bitter bark of this tree **—cin·chon′ic** (-kän′ik) *adj.*

Cin·cin·nat·i (sin′sə nat′ē, -ə) [ult. after *Cincinnatus*, Rom. general of 5th c. B.C.] city in SW Ohio, on the Ohio River: pop. 453,000 (met. area 1,385,000)

cinc·ture (siŋk′chər) *n.* [L. *cinctura*, a girdle < *cingere:* see CINCH] **1.** an encircling or girding **2.** anything that encircles, as a belt or girdle **—vt. -tured, -tur·ing** to encircle with or as with a cincture

cin·der (sin′dər) *n.* [OE. *sinder*] **1.** slag, as from the smelting of ores **2.** any matter, as coal or wood, partly burned but not all the way to ashes **3.** a tiny piece of such matter **4.** a coal that is still burning but not flaming **5.** [*pl.*] ashes from coal or wood **—cin′der·y** *adj.*

☆**cinder block** a building block, usually hollow, made of concrete and fine cinders

Cin·der·el·la (sin′də rel′ə) the title character of a fairy tale, a household drudge who, with the help of a fairy godmother, marries a prince

‡**cin·é·aste** (sē nā äst′; *E.* sin′ē ast′) *n.* [Fr. < *ciné(matographe)*, CINEMATOGRAPH + (*enthousi*)*aste*, enthusiast] a person very involved in watching or making motion pictures

cin·e·ma (sin′ə mə) *n.* [< CINEMA(TOGRAPH)] [Chiefly Brit.] **1.** a motion picture **2.** a motion-picture theater **—the cinema 1.** the art or business of making motion pictures **2.** motion pictures; the movies **—cin′e·mat′ic** (-mat′ik) *adj.* **—cin′e·mat′i·cal·ly** *adv.*

cin·e·mat·o·graph (sin′ə mat′ə graf) *n.* [< Fr. < Gr. *kinēma*, motion + *graphein*, to write] [Chiefly Brit.] a motion-picture projector, camera, theater, etc.

cin·e·ma·tog·ra·pher (sin′ə mə täg′rə fər) *n.* [Chiefly Brit.] the person who directs the photography in making a motion picture

cin·e·ma·tog·ra·phy (-fē) *n.* the art of photography in making motion pictures **—cin′e·mat′o·graph′ic** (-mat′ə graf′ik), **cin′e·mat′o·graph′i·cal** *adj.* **—cin′e·mat′o·graph′i·cal·ly** *adv.*

‡**cin·é·ma vér·i·té** (sē nā mä′ vä rē tā′) [Fr., lit., truth cinema] a form of documentary film in which a small camera and simple techniques are used to record scenes so that they seem as natural and spontaneous as possible

cin·e·rar·i·a (sin′ə rer′ē ə) *n.* [ModL. < L. *cinis*, ashes: the leaves have an ash-colored down] a common hothouse plant of the composite family, with heart-shaped leaves and colorful flowers

cin·e·rar·i·um (sin′ə rer′ē əm) *n., pl.* **-rar′i·a** (-ə) [L. < *cinis*, ashes] a place to keep the ashes of cremated bodies **—cin′e·rar′y** *adj.*

cin·er·a·tor (sin′ə rāt′ər) *n.* [< CINERARIUM] a furnace for cremation; crematory

cin·na·bar (sin′ə bär′) *n.* [< L. < Gr. *kinnabari* < ? Per. *šangarf*] **1.** mercuric sulfide, HgS, a heavy, bright-red mineral, the main ore of mercury **2.** artificial mercuric sulfide, used as a red coloring matter **3.** brilliant red; vermilion

cin·na·mon (sin′ə mən) *n.* [< OFr. < L. < Gr. < Heb. *qinnāmōn*] **1.** the yellowish-brown spice made from the dried inner bark of a laurel tree or shrub native to the East Indies and southeastern Asia **2.** this bark **3.** any tree or shrub from which it is obtained **4.** yellowish brown **—adj. 1.** yellowish-brown **2.** made or flavored with cinnamon

cinque·foil (siŋk′foil′) *n.* [< OFr. < It. < L. < *quinque*, five + *folium*, leaf] **1.** a plant of the rose family with a fruit like a dry strawberry: some species have compound leaves with five leaflets **2.** *Archit.* a circular design of five arcs joined together

CIO, C.I.O. Congress of Industrial Organizations: see AFL-CIO

CINQUEFOIL

ci·on (sī′ən) *n. same as* SCION (sense 1)

Ci·pan·go (si paŋ′gō) *old name for* JAPAN

ci·pher (sī′fər) *n.* [< OFr. < ML. < Ar. *ṣifr*, nothing < *ṣafare*, to be empty] **1.** the symbol 0; zero **2.** a person or thing of no importance or value; nonentity **3.** *a)* a system of secret writing based on a key *b)* a message in such writing *c)* the key to such a system See also CODE **4.** a monogram **5.** an Arabic numeral **—vt., vi. 1.** [Now Rare] to do, or solve by, arithmetic **2.** to write in cipher, or secret writing

cir., circ. 1. circa **2.** circulation **3.** circumference

cir·ca (sur′kə) *prep.* [L.] about: used before an approximate date, figure, etc. [*circa* 1650]

cir·ca·di·an (sər kā′dē ən) *adj.* [coined < L. *circa*, about + acc. sing. of *dies*, day] designating or of certain rhythms of life, as the times of sleeping, eating, etc. in the 24-hour daily cycle

Cir·cas·si·a (sər kash′ə, -kash′ē ə) region of the U.S.S.R., in the NW Caucasus **—Cir·cas′si·an** *adj., n.*

Cir·ce (sur′sē) in Homer's *Odyssey*, an enchantress who turned men into swine **—Cir·ce·an** (sər sē′ən, sur′sē ən) *adj.*

cir·cle (sur′k'l) *n.* [< OFr. < L. *circulus*, dim. of *circus*: see CIRCUS] **1.** a plane figure bounded by a single curved line every point of which is the same distance from the point at the center **2.** the line bounding such a figure; circumference **3.** anything shaped like a circle, as a ring, crown, etc. **4.** the orbit of a heavenly body **5.** a section of seats in a theater, as in a balcony [the dress *circle*] **6.** any series that ends the way it began or is repeated over and over; cycle; period [a *circle* of events] **7.** a group of people bound together by common interests; group; coterie [a small *circle* of friends] **8.** range or extent, as of influence or interest; scope **—vt. -cled, -cling 1.** to form a circle around; encompass; surround [the children *circled* the Maypole] **2.** to move around, as in a circle [the planets *circle* the sun] **—vi.** to go around in a circle; revolve **—see** SYN. at COTERIE **—come full circle** to return to an original position or state after going through a series or cycle **—cir′cler** *n.*

cir·clet (sur′klit) *n.* **1.** a small circle **2.** a circular band worn as an ornament, esp. on the head

cir·cuit (sur′kit) *n.* [OFr. < L. *circuitus* < *circum*, around + *ire*, to go] **1.** the line or length of the line forming the boundaries of an area **2.** the area bounded **3.** a going around something; course or journey around [the moon's *circuit* of the earth takes about 28 days] **4.** *a)* the regular journey through a fixed district of a person performing his duties, as of a circuit court judge *b)* such a district **5.** a chain or group of theaters, resorts, etc. at which plays, movies, entertainers, etc. appear in turn **6.** *Elec. a)* a complete or partial path over which current may flow *b)* a hookup that is connected into this path, as for radio, television, etc. **—vi.** to go in a circuit **—vt.** to make a circuit about **—cir′cuit·al** *adj.*

☆**circuit breaker** a device that automatically interrupts the flow of an electric current

☆**circuit court** a State court having original jurisdiction in several counties or a district

cir·cu·i·tous (sər kyōō′ə təs) *adj.* [see CIRCUIT] roundabout; indirect; devious **—cir·cu′i·tous·ly** *adv.* **—cir·cu′i·tous·ness, cir·cu′i·ty** *n., pl.* **-ties**

☆**circuit rider** a minister who travels from place to place in his circuit to preach

cir·cuit·ry (sur′kə trē) *n.* the scheme, system, or components of an electric circuit

cir·cu·lar (sur'kyə lər) *adj.* [L. *circularis*] **1.** in the shape of a circle; round **2.** relating to a circle **3.** moving in a circle or spiral **4.** roundabout; circuitous **5.** intended for circulation among a number of people —*n.* a circular advertisement, letter, etc. —see SYN. at ROUND —**cir'cu·lar'i·ty** (-ler'ə tē) *n.* —**cir'cu·lar·ly** *adv.*

cir·cu·lar·ize (-lə rīz') *vt.* **-ized', -iz'ing 1.** to make circular **2.** to send circulars to **3.** to canvass for opinions, support, etc. —**cir'cu·lar·i·za'tion** *n.* —**cir'cu·lar·iz'er** *n.*

circular measure a system for measuring circles and angles: see TABLES OF WEIGHTS AND MEASURES in Supplements

circular saw a saw in the form of a disk with a toothed edge, rotated at high speed by a motor

cir·cu·late (sur'kyə lāt') *vi.* **-lat'ed, -lat'ing** [< L. pp. of *circulari*, to form a circle] **1.** to move in a circle or circuit and return to the same point, as blood through the body **2.** to go from person to person or from place to place; specif., *a)* to move about freely, as air *b)* to move about in society, at a party, etc. *c)* to be made widely known [that rumor has been *circulating* around town] *d)* to be distributed to a mass of readers —*vt.* to cause to circulate —**cir'cu·la'tor** *n.* —**cir'cu·la·to·ry** (-lə tôr'ē), **cir'cu·la'tive** (-lā'tiv) *adj.*

CIRCULAR SAW

circulating decimal *same as* REPEATING DECIMAL

circulating library a library from which books can be borrowed, sometimes for a small daily fee

cir·cu·la·tion (sur'kyə lā'shən) *n.* **1.** a circulating or moving around, often specif. in a complete circuit, as of air in ventilating or of blood through the arteries and veins **2.** the passing of something, as money, news, etc., from person to person **3.** *a)* the distribution of newspapers, magazines, etc. *b)* the average number of copies of a magazine or newspaper sold in a given period

cir·cum- [< L. *circum*, around, about: for IE. base see CIRCUS] *a prefix meaning* around, surrounding, on all sides

cir·cum·am·bi·ent (sur'kəm am'bē ənt) *adj.* [CIRCUM- + AMBIENT] extending all around; surrounding —**cir'cum·am'bi·ence, cir'cum·am'bi·en·cy** *n.*

cir·cum·cise (sur'kəm sīz') *vt.* **-cised', -cis'ing** [< OFr. < L. pp. of *circumcidere* < *circum-*, around + *caedere*, to cut] to cut off the foreskin of —**cir'cum·ci'sion** (-sizh'ən) *n.*

cir·cum·fer·ence (sər kum'fər əns, -frəns) *n.* [< L. prp. of *circumferre* < *circum-*, around + *ferre*, to carry] **1.** the line bounding a circle or other rounded surface or area **2.** the distance measured by this line —**cir'cum'fer·en'tial** (-fə ren'shəl) *adj.* —**cir'cum'fer·en'tial·ly** *adv.*

cir·cum·flex (sur'kəm fleks') *n.* [< L. pp. of *circumflectere* < *circum-*, around + *flectere*, to bend] a mark (∧, ^, ~) used over certain vowels in some languages to indicate a specific sound, or as a diacritical mark in some pronunciation systems: also **circumflex accent** —*adj.* **1.** of or marked by a circumflex **2.** bending around; curved —*vt.* **1.** to bend around; curve **2.** to write with a circumflex —**cir'cum·flex'ion** *n.*

cir·cum·flu·ent (sər kum'floo wənt) *adj.* [< L. prp. of *circumfluere* < *circum-*, around + *fluere*, to flow] flowing around; surrounding: also **cir·cum'flu·ous**

cir·cum·fuse (sur'kəm fyooz') *vt.* **-fused', -fus'ing** [< L. pp. of *circumfundere* < *circum-*, around + *fundere*, to pour] **1.** to pour or spread (a fluid) around; diffuse **2.** to surround (*with* a fluid); suffuse (*in*) —**cir'cum·fu'sion** *n.*

cir·cum·lo·cu·tion (sur'kəm lō kyoo'shən) *n.* [< L.: see CIRCUM- & LOCUTION] a roundabout, indirect, or lengthy way of expressing something ["to become the recipient of" is a *circumlocution* for "to get"] —**cir'cum·loc'u·to·ry** (-läk'yə tôr'ē) *adj.*

cir·cum·nav·i·gate (-nav'ə gāt') *vt.* **-gat'ed, -gat'ing** [< L. pp. of *circumnavigare*: see CIRCUM- & NAVIGATE] to sail or fly around (the earth, an island, etc.) —**cir'cum·nav'i·ga'tion** *n.* —**cir'cum·nav'i·ga'tor** *n.*

cir·cum·po·lar (-pō'lər) *adj.* around either pole of the earth or the heavens

cir·cum·scribe (sur'kəm skrīb', sur'kəm skrīb') *vt.* **-scribed', -scrib'ing** [< L. < *circum-*, around + *scribere*, to write] **1.** to trace a line around; encircle **2.** *a)* to limit; bound *b)* to restrict in scope, activity, etc. [his interests were *circumscribed* until he went away to college] **3.** *Geom.* *a)* to draw a figure around (another figure) so as to touch it at as many points as possible *b)* to be thus drawn around —see SYN. at LIMIT —**cir'cum·scrib'a·ble** *adj.* —**cir'cum·scrib'er** *n.* —**cir'cum·scrip'tion** (-skrip'shən) *n.*

cir·cum·spect (sur'kəm spekt') *adj.* [< L. pp. of *circumspicere* < *circum-*, around + *specere*, to look] careful to consider all related circumstances before acting, deciding, etc.; cautious and prudent [be *circumspect* in finding out where he has been] —**cir'cum·spec'tion** *n.* —**cir'cum·spect'ly** *adv.*

cir·cum·stance (-stans', -stəns) *n.* [< OFr. < L. < *circum-*, around + *stare*, to STAND] **1.** a fact or event connected with or forming part of a situation [what were the *circumstances* that led up to his arrest?] **2.** [*pl.*] conditions affecting a person, esp. financial conditions [in comfortable *circumstances*] **3.** chance; luck; fate [as *circumstance* would have it, I was unable to attend] **4.** ceremony; show [pomp and *circumstance*] —*vt.* **-stanced', -stanc'ing** to place in certain circumstances —see SYN. at OCCURRENCE —**under no circumstances** under no conditions; never —**under the circumstances** conditions being what they are or were —**cir'cum·stanced'** *adj.*

cir·cum·stan·tial (sur'kəm stan'shəl) *adj.* **1.** having to do with, or depending on, circumstances **2.** not of primary importance; incidental **3.** full or complete in detail **4.** ceremonial —**cir'cum·stan'ti·al'i·ty** (-shē al'ə tē) *n.*, *pl.* **-ties** —**cir'cum·stan'tial·ly** *adv.*

circumstantial evidence *Law* evidence offered to prove certain circumstances from which the existence of the fact at issue may be inferred; indirect evidence

cir·cum·stan·ti·ate (sur'kəm stan'shē āt') *vt.* **-at'ed, -at'ing** to give detailed proof or support of —**cir'cum·stan'ti·a'tion** *n.*

cir·cum·vent (sur'kəm vent') *vt.* [< L. pp. of *circumvenire* < *circum-*, around + *venire*, to COME] **1.** to surround or circle around **2.** to surround with evils, enmity, etc.; entrap **3.** to get the better of or prevent from happening by sly or tricky methods [to *circumvent* taxes by using loopholes in the law] —**cir'cum·ven'tion** *n.*

cir·cus (sur'kəs) *n.* [L. < or akin to Gr. *kirkos*, a circle < IE. base (s)*ker-*, to turn, bend] **1.** in ancient Rome, an oval or oblong arena with tiers of seats around it, used for games, races, etc. **2.** a show, esp. a traveling show, held in tents or in a hall, with acrobats, trained animals, clowns, etc. ☆**3.** [Colloq.] any riotously entertaining person, event, etc.

ci·ré (sə rā') *adj.* [Fr., lit., waxed, ult. < Gr. *kēros*, wax] having a smooth, glossy finish as by treatment with wax —*n.* a ciré silk, straw, etc.

cirque (surk) *n.* [< Fr. < L. *circus*: see CIRCUS] **1.** a circular space or arrangement **2.** *Geol.* a deep hollow high on a mountainside, caused by a glacier

cir·rho·sis (sə rō'sis) *n.* [ModL. < Gr. *kirrhos*, tawny + -OSIS: after the yellowish color of the diseased liver] a disease of the liver, in which connective tissue forms and the liver cells degenerate —**cir·rhot'ic** (-rät'ik) *adj.*

cir·ri- [< L. *cirrus*] *a combining form meaning* curl, ringlet: also **cir'ro-, cir'rhi-, cir'rho-**

cir·ri·ped (sir'ə ped') *n.* [< ModL.: see CIRRI- & -PEDE] any of a group of crustaceans, including the barnacles, that are attached or parasitic as adults

cir·ro·cu·mu·lus (sir'ō kyoo'myə ləs) *n.* a high formation of clouds in small, white puffs, flakes, or streaks

cir·ro·stra·tus (-strāt'əs, -strat'-) *n.* a high formation of clouds in a thin, whitish veil

cir·rus (sir'əs) *n.*, *pl.* **-ri** (-ī); for 2 **-rus** [L., a curl] **1.** *a)* a plant tendril *b)* a flexible, threadlike appendage, as a feeler in certain organisms *c)* a cluster of fused cilia as in some infusorians **2.** a high formation of clouds in wispy filaments or feathery tufts

cis- [< L. *cis*, on this side] *a prefix meaning:* **1.** on this side of **2.** subsequent to

cis·al·pine (sis al'pīn, -pin) *adj.* [< L.: see CIS- & ALPINE] on this (the Roman, or southern) side of the Alps

☆**cis·co** (sis'kō) *n.*, *pl.* **-co, -coes, -cos:** see PLURAL, II, D, 2 [< CanadFr. < Algonquian] a fish related to the whitefish, found in the colder lakes of the northeastern U.S. and of Canada

---

fat, āpe, cär; ten, ēven; is, bīte; gō, hôrn, too͞l, loo͝ok; oil, out; up, fur; get; joy; yet; chin; she; thin, *th*en; zh, leisure; ŋ, ring; ə for *a* in *ago*, *e* in *agent*, *i* in *sanity*, *o* in *comply*, *u* in *focus*; ' as in *able* (ā'b'l); Fr. bal; ë, Fr. coeur; ö, Fr. feu; ô, Fr. mon; ô, Fr. coq; ü, Fr. duc; r, Fr. cri; H, G. ich; kh, G. doch; ‡foreign; ☆ Americanism; < derived from. See inside front cover.

cis·lu·nar (sis loo'nər) *adj.* [CIS- + LUNAR] on this side of the moon, between the moon and the earth

Cis·ter·cian (sis tur'shən) *adj.* [< OFr. < ML. *Cistercium* (now *Cîteaux*, France)] designating or of a monastic order following the Benedictine rule strictly —*n.* a Cistercian monk or nun

cis·tern (sis'tərn) *n.* [< OFr. < L. < *cista*, CHEST] **1.** a large tank, usually underground, for storing water, esp. rain water **2.** *Anat.* a sac or cavity containing a natural body fluid: also **cis·ter'na** (-tur'nə), *pl.* **-nae** (-nē) —**cis·ter'nal** *adj.*

cit. **1.** citation **2.** cited **3.** citizen **4.** citrate

cit·a·del (sit'ə d'l, -del') *n.* [< Fr. < It. dim. of *cittade*, city < L. *civitas*, CITY] **1.** a fortress on a commanding height for defense of a city **2.** a fortified place; stronghold **3.** a place of safety; refuge

ci·ta·tion (sī tā'shən) *n.* [< OFr. < L. pp. of *citare*: see CITE] **1.** a summons to appear before a court of law **2.** a citing; quoting **3.** a passage cited; quotation **4.** a reference to a legal statute, a previous law case, etc. ☆**5.** *a)* official honorable mention for meritorious service in the armed forces *b)* a formal statement honoring a person —**ci'ta·tor** *n.* —**ci·ta·to·ry** (sīt'ə tôr'ē) *adj.*

cite (sīt) *vt.* **cit'ed, cit'ing** [< OFr. < L. *citare*, to summon < *ciere*, to rouse < IE. base *kei*-] **1.** to summon to appear before a court of law **2.** to quote (a passage, book, writer, etc.) **3.** to refer to or mention by way of example, proof, etc. ☆**4.** to mention in a citation (sense 5) —**cit'a·ble, cite'a·ble** *adj.*

cith·a·ra (sith'ə rə) *n.* [L. < Gr. *kithara*] an ancient musical instrument somewhat like a lyre

cith·er (sith'ər) *n.* [< Fr. < prec.] *same as* CITTERN: also **cith'ern** (-ərn)

☆**cit·i·fied** (sit'i fīd') *adj.* having the manners, dress, etc. of city people

cit·i·zen (sit'ə zən) *n.* [Anglo-Fr. *citizein* < OFr. < *cite*: see CITY] **1.** formerly, an inhabitant of a town or city **2.** a member of a state or nation who owes allegiance to it by birth or naturalization and is entitled to full civil rights **3.** a civilian, as distinguished from a soldier, policeman, etc.

SYN.—**citizen** refers especially to a member of a state or nation having a republican form of government; **subject** is the term used when the government is headed by a monarch or other sovereign; **national** is applied to a person living away from the country in which he is a citizen or subject [French *nationals* in the U.S.]; **native** is used in referring to a person in connection with his place or country of birth [a *native* of Ohio]

cit·i·zen·ry (-rē) *n.* all citizens as a group

citizen's arrest an arrest made under common law or statutory right by a citizen of a person he sees committing a felony

☆**citizens' band** either of two bands of shortwave radio frequencies for local use at low power by private persons

cit·i·zen·ship (-ship') *n.* **1.** the status or condition of a citizen, or his duties, rights, and privileges **2.** one's conduct as a citizen

cit·rate (sī'trāt, sī'-) *n.* [CITR(US) + -ATE²] a salt or ester of citric acid

cit·ric (si'trik) *adj.* [CITR(US) + -IC] **1.** of or from lemons, oranges, or similar fruits **2.** designating or of an acid, $C_6H_8O_7$, obtained from such fruits, used in making dyes, citrates, etc.

☆**cit·ri·cul·ture** (si'trə kul'chər) *n.* the cultivation of citrus fruits

cit·rine (si'trin, -trēn, -trīn) *adj.* [< OFr. < ML. < L. *citrus*, CITRUS] of the yellow color of a lemon —*n.* **1.** lemon yellow **2.** a yellow quartz

cit·ron (si'trən) *n.* [Fr., lemon < It. *citrone* < L. *citrus*, CITRUS] **1.** a yellow, thick-skinned fruit resembling a lemon but larger and less acid **2.** the semitropical tree bearing this fruit **3.** the candied rind of this fruit, used in fruitcake, etc. ☆**4.** *same as* CITRON MELON

cit·ron·el·la (si'trə nel'ə) *n.* [ModL. < prec.] **1.** a sharp-smelling oil that vaporizes easily, used in perfume, soap, insect repellents, etc.: also **citronella oil** **2.** a grass of southern Asia from which it is derived

☆**citron melon** a kind of watermelon with hard, white flesh, used only candied or preserved

cit·rus (si'trəs) *n.* [L., citron tree (whence Gr. *kitron*)] **1.** any of a genus of trees and shrubs that bear oranges, lemons, limes, or other such fruit —*adj.* of these trees or shrubs: also **cit'rous** (-trəs)

cit·tern (sit'ərn) *n.* [< CITHER, prob. infl. by ME. *giterne*, GITTERN] a stringed instrument of the guitar family, popular in the 16th & 17th cent.

CITTERN

cit·y (sit'ē) *n., pl.* **cit'ies** [< OFr. *cite* < L. *civitas*, orig. citizenship < *civis*, citizen < IE. base *kei*-, to lie, camp, from which also comes HOME] **1.** a center of population larger or more important than a town or village **2.** in the U.S., a municipality whose boundaries and powers of self-government are defined by a charter from its State **3.** in Canada, a large urban municipality within a province **4.** all the people of a city —*adj.* of or in a city —**the City** the financial and commercial district of London

☆**city chicken** skewered pieces of pork or veal breaded and cooked by braising or baking

☆**city editor** a newspaper editor who handles local news and assignments to reporters

☆**city fathers** the important officials of a city

☆**cit·y·fied** (sit'i fīd') *adj. same as* CITIFIED

☆**city hall** **1.** a building housing the offices of a municipal government **2.** a municipal government —**fight city hall** to fight in vain against petty or impersonal bureaucracy

☆**city manager** the head of a city government appointed by a city council on a professional basis, with tenure free from public elections

City of Seven Hills Rome

cit·y·scape (sit'ē skāp') *n.* [CITY + (LAND)SCAPE] **1.** a painting, photograph, etc. of a section of a city **2.** a view of a section of a city, esp. of buildings silhouetted against the horizon

cit·y·state (-stāt') *n.* a state made up of an independent city and the territory directly controlled by it, as in ancient Greece

Ciu·dad Juá·rez (syoo thäth' hwä'res) city in N Mexico, on the Rio Grande: pop. 522,000

civ. **1.** civil **2.** civilian

civ·et (siv'it) *n.* [< Fr. < It. *zibetto* < Ar. *zabād*] **1.** a yellowish substance with a musklike scent, secreted by a gland of the civet cat and used in making some perfumes **2.** the civet cat or its fur

civet cat a catlike, flesh-eating mammal of Africa and southern Asia, with spotted, yellowish fur

civ·ic (siv'ik) *adj.* [L. *civicus* < *civis*: see CITY] **1.** of a city [plans for *civic* development] **2.** of citizens or citizenship [voting is a *civic* duty] —**civ'i·cal·ly** *adv.*

☆**civ·ics** (siv'iks) *n.pl.* [with sing. v.] the branch of political science dealing with civic affairs and the duties and rights of citizenship

civ·ies (siv'ēz) *n.pl.* [Colloq.] *same as* CIVVIES

civ·il (siv''l) *adj.* [OFr. < L. *civilis* < *civis*: see CITY] **1.** of a citizen or citizens [civil rights] **2.** of a community of citizens, their government, or their interrelations **3.** civilized **4.** polite or courteous, esp. in a merely formal way **5.** not military or religious [civil marriage] **6.** *Law* relating to private rights and legal actions involving these

SYN.—**civil** implies merely a trying not to be rude [give me a *civil* answer]; **polite** and **courteous** both express in a positive way the showing of good manners, **courteous** sometimes stressing thoughtfulness of others as part of one's nature [it is not *polite* to interrupt; he was *courteous* to visitors even when they came without being invited]; **chivalrous** implies a noble, selfless quality in one's behavior, especially in a man's behavior toward women [he was *chivalrous* in her defense]; **gallant** suggests a very attentive and courtly manner in a man's behavior toward women

civil defense a system of warning devices, air-raid or fallout shelters, etc. for defense of a population against enemy attack

civil disobedience nonviolent opposition to a government policy or law by refusing to comply with it, on the grounds of conscience: see also NONCOOPERATION, PASSIVE RESISTANCE

civil engineering the branch of engineering dealing with the design and construction of highways, bridges, harbors, etc. —**civil engineer**

ci·vil·ian (sə vil'yən) *n.* [< OFr. < L.: see CIVIL] a person not an active member of the armed forces or of an official force having police power —*adj.* of or for civilians; nonmilitary

ci·vil·i·ty (sə vil'ə tē) *n., pl.* **-ties** **1.** politeness, esp. of a merely formal kind **2.** a civil, or polite, act or remark

civ·i·li·za·tion (siv'ə lə zā'shən) *n.* **1.** a civilizing or becoming civilized **2.** the condition of being civilized; social organization of a high order, in which the arts, sciences, government, etc.

are developed **3.** the total culture of a people, nation, period, etc. **4.** the countries and peoples considered to have reached a high stage of social and cultural development **5.** intellectual and cultural refinement **6.** the comforts of civilized life

civ·i·lize (siv′ə līz′) **vt. -lized′, -liz′ing** [< Fr. < L.: see CIVIL & -IZE] **1.** to bring out of a primitive or savage condition and educate in the arts, sciences, government, etc. **2.** to improve in habits or manners; cause to be refined, smoothly polite, sophisticated, etc. [let's stop arguing and be *civilized* about the matter] —**civ′i·liz′a·ble** *adj.* —**civ′i·lized′** *adj.*

civil law the body of law of a nation or state concerning private rights and obligations

civil liberties the right to think, speak, and act as one chooses without interference by the government, as long as one does not interfere with the rights of others

civ·il·ly (siv′'l ē) *adv.* **1.** with civility; politely **2.** in relation to civil law, civil rights, etc.

civil marriage a marriage performed by a public official, not by a clergyman

civil rights ☆the rights of all individuals, regardless of race, religion, sex, etc., to receive equal treatment with regard to the enjoyment of life, liberty, and property and to equal protection of the law: such rights are guaranteed by the U.S. Constitution

civil service 1. all those employed in government work except those in the armed forces or those elected or appointed to office **2.** a system under which government jobs are gotten by those who score highest on examinations open to everyone —**civil servant**

civil war war between different sections or factions of the same nation —**the Civil War** the war between the North (the Union) and the South (the Confederacy) in the U.S. (1861–1865)

civ·vies (siv′ēz) *n.pl.* [Colloq.] civilian clothes, as distinguished from a military uniform; mufti

ck. *pl.* **cks. 1.** cask **2.** check

Cl *Chem.* chlorine

cl. 1. centiliter(s) **2.** claim **3.** class **4.** clause

c.l. 1. carload **2.** carload lots

clab·ber (klab′ər) *n.* [Ir. *clabar*] [Dial.] thickly curdled sour milk —*vi., vt.* [Dial.] to curdle

clack (klak) *vi.* [prob. < ON. *klaka*, of echoic origin] **1.** to make a sudden, sharp sound [high heels *clacking*] **2.** to chatter —*vt.* to cause to make a sudden, sharp sound —*n.* **1.** a clacking sound **2.** chatter —**clack′er** *n.*

clad (klad) *alt. pt. & pp. of* CLOTHE —*adj.* **1.** clothed; dressed **2.** having a layer of another metal or of an alloy bonded to it [*clad* steel]

clad·ding (klad′iŋ) *n.* [see prec.] **1.** a layer of some metal or alloy bonded to another **2.** the process of bonding such materials

clad·o·phyll (klad′ə fil′) *n.* [< Gr. *klados*, a branch + *phyllon*, leaf] a flattened branch arising from the axil of a leaf, with the shape and functions of a foliage leaf: also **clad·ode** (-ōd)

claim (klām) *vt.* [< OFr. < L. *clamare*: see CLAMOR] **1.** to demand as rightfully belonging to one; assert one's right to (a title, possession, etc) [he *claimed* the package at the post office] **2.** to call for; require; deserve [problems *claiming* our attention] ☆**3.** to state as a fact or as one's belief; assert [he *claimed* that he had been cheated] —*n.* **1.** a demand for something rightfully due **2.** a right or title to something **3.** something claimed, as land staked out by a settler ☆**4.** a statement as a fact of something that may be called into question; assertion [false *claims* as sometimes made about used cars] —**claim′a·ble** *adj.* —**claim′er** *n.*

claim·ant (klā′mənt) *n.* one who makes a claim

Claire (kler) [Fr., equiv. of CLARA] a feminine name

clair·voy·ance (kler voi′əns) *n.* [Fr. < CLAIRVOYANT] **1.** the supposed ability to see things that are not in sight or that cannot be seen **2.** keen perception or insight

clair·voy·ant (-ənt) *adj.* [Fr. < *clair*, clear + prp. of *voir*, to see] **1.** of or seeming to have clairvoyance **2.** having keen insight —*n.* a clairvoyant person —**clair·voy′ant·ly** *adv.*

clam (klam) *n., pl.* **clams, clam:** see PLURAL, II, D, 1 [< OE. *clamm*, fetter, in reference to the action of the shells: for IE. base see CLAW] **1.** any of certain mollusks with a soft body enclosed in two hard shells hinged together: clams live in the sand of shores of seas, lakes, etc. **2.** the flesh of these mollusks, somewhat firmer than that of oysters ☆**3.** *same as* CLAMSHELL (sense

2) —*vi.* **clammed, clam′ming** to dig, or go digging, for clams —☆**clam up** [Colloq.] to refuse to talk

☆**clam·bake** (klam′bāk′) *n.* **1.** a feast or picnic at which clams are steamed or baked with lobster, chicken, corn, etc. **2.** the food so prepared

clam·ber (klam′bər) *vi., vt.* [ME. *clambren:* for IE. base see CLAW] to climb clumsily or with effort, using both hands and feet —*n.* a hard or clumsy climb —**clam′ber·er** *n.*

clam·my (klam′ē) *adj.* **-mi·er, -mi·est** [prob. < OE. *clam*, CLAY] unpleasantly moist, cold, and sticky —**clam′mi·ly** *adv.* —**clam′mi·ness** *n.*

clam·or (klam′ər) *n.* [< OFr. < L. < *clamare*, to cry out < IE. base *kel-*, from which also comes LOW²] **1.** a loud outcry; uproar **2.** a strong, insistent public demand or complaint **3.** a loud, sustained noise —*vi.* to make a clamor; cry out, demand, or complain noisily —*vt.* to express in clamor Also, Brit. sp., **clam′our** —see SYN. at NOISE —**clam′or·er** *n.*

clam·or·ous (-əs) *adj.* **1.** loud and confused; noisy **2.** loudly demanding or complaining —see SYN. at VOCIFEROUS —**clam′or·ous·ly** *adv.* —**clam′or·ous·ness** *n.*

clamp (klamp) *n.* [< MDu. *klampe:* for IE. base see CLAW] a device for clasping or fastening things together; esp., an appliance with two parts brought together, usually by a screw, to grip something —*vt.* **1.** to grip, fasten, or brace with a clamp ☆**2.** to put into effect forcefully [to *clamp* a curfew on the town] —☆**clamp down (on)** to become more strict (with)

☆**clamp·down** (klamp′doun′) *n.* a clamping down; sudden strict action, as in censoring, enforcing rules, etc.

CLAMP

clam·shell (klam′shel′) *n.* **1.** the shell of a clam ☆**2.** a dredging bucket, hinged like the shell of a clam

clan (klan) *n.* [Gael. & Ir. *clann*, offspring < L. *planta*, offshoot: see PLANT] **1.** a social group, as in the Scottish Highlands, composed of several families descended from a common ancestor **2.** a group of people with interests in common **3.** a division of a primitive tribe descended from a common ancestor **4.** [Colloq.] family (sense 3)

clan·des·tine (klan des′t'n) *adj.* [< Fr. < L. *clandestinus* < *clam*, secret] kept secret or hidden, esp. for some purpose; not proper or lawful; surreptitious [a *clandestine* meeting] —see SYN. at SECRET —**clan·des′tine·ly** *adv.*

clang (klaŋ) *vi., vt.* [echoic] to make or cause to make a loud, sharp, ringing sound, as by striking metal —*n.* a clanging sound or cry

clan·gor (klaŋ′ər) *n.* [L. < *clangere*, to clang] a clanging sound, esp. a continued clanging —*vi.* to make a clangor Also, Brit. sp., **clan′gour** —**clan′gor·ous** *adj.* —**clan′gor·ous·ly** *adv.*

clank (klaŋk) *n.* [echoic] a sharp, metallic sound, not so resonant as a clang —*vi.* to make, or move with, a clank —*vt.* to cause to clank

clan·nish (klan′ish) *adj.* **1.** of a clan **2.** sticking closely to one's own group and avoiding others —**clan′nish·ly** *adv.* —**clan′nish·ness** *n.*

clans·man (klanz′mən) *n., pl.* **-men** a member of a clan —**clans′wom′an** *n.fem., pl.* **-wom′en**

clap¹ (klap) *vi.* **clapped** or archaic **clapt, clap′ping** [OE. *clæppan*, to beat] **1.** to make a sudden, explosive sound, as of two flat surfaces being struck together **2.** to strike the hands together, as in applauding —*vt.* **1.** to strike together briskly and loudly **2.** to strike with the palm of the hand ["Good work!" he said, *clapping* me on the shoulder] **3.** to put, move, etc. swiftly [*clapped* into jail] **4.** to put together hastily [to *clap* together a makeshift stage] —*n.* **1.** the sudden, loud sound of clapping [a *clap* of thunder] **2.** the act of striking the hands together **3.** a sharp slap, as in hearty greeting —**clap eyes on** [Colloq.] to catch sight of; see

clap² (klap) *n.* [< ME. *claper*, brothel, orig. rabbit burrow < OFr. *clapier*] [Slang] gonorrhea: with *the*

clap·board (klab′ərd, klap′bôrd′) *n.* [partial transl. of MDu. *klapholt* < *klappen*, to fit + *holt*, wood] ☆a thin board with one edge thicker than the other, used as siding —☆*vt.* to cover with clapboards

clap·per (klap'ər) *n.* **1.** a person who claps **2.** a thing that makes a clapping noise, as the tongue of a bell or, jokingly, that of a person

clap·trap (-trap') *n.* [CLAP¹ + TRAP¹] showy, insincere, empty talk, etc. intended only to get applause or attention —*adj.* showy and cheap

claque (klak) *n.* [Fr. < *claquer*, to clap] **1.** a group of people paid to go to a play, opera, etc. and applaud **2.** a group of fawning followers

Clar·a (klar'ə) [< L. fem. of *clarus*, bright] a feminine name: var. *Clare, Clara, Clarissa*

Clar·ence (klar'əns) [< name of Eng. dukedom of *Clarence*] a masculine name

clar·et (klar'it) *n.* [< OFr. dim. of *cler* < L. *clarus*, CLEAR] **1.** a dry red wine, esp. red Bordeaux **2.** purplish red: also **claret red** —*adj.* purplish-red

clar·i·fy (klar'ə fī') *vt., vi.* **-fied', -fy'ing** [< OFr. < L. < *clarus*, CLEAR + *facere*, to make] **1.** to make or become clear and free from impurities: said esp. of liquids **2.** to make or become easier to understand [*clarify* your meaning] —**clar'i·fi·ca'tion** *n.* —**clar'i·fi'er** *n.*

clar·i·net (klar'ə net', klar'ə nit') *n.* [Fr. *clarinette*, dim. of *clarine*, little bell < ML. *clario*: see CLARION] a single-reed, woodwind instrument with a long wooden or metal tube and a flaring bell, played by means of holes and keys —**clar'i·net'ist, clar'i·net'tist** *n.*

clar·i·on (klar'ē ən) *n.* [OFr. < ML. *clario* < L. *clarus*, CLEAR] **1.** a trumpet of the Middle Ages producing clear, sharp, shrill tones **2.** [Poet.] a sound of or like a clarion —*adj.* clear, sharp, and ringing [a *clarion* call] —*vt.* to announce forcefully or loudly

clar·i·ty (klar'ə tē) *n.* [OFr. *clarte* < L. *claritas* < *clarus*, CLEAR] the quality or condition of being clear; clearness

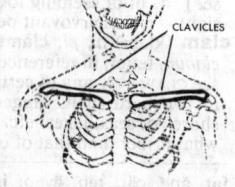

CLARINET

Clark (klärk) [< OFr. & OE.: see CLERK] **1.** a masculine name **2.** William, 1770–1838; Am. explorer: see Meriwether LEWIS

clash (klash) *vi.* [echoic] **1.** to collide with a loud, harsh, metallic noise **2.** *a)* to come into conflict; disagree sharply [they *clashed* in debate] *b)* to fail to harmonize [*clashing* color] —*vt.* to strike together, shut, etc. with a loud, harsh noise —*n.* **1.** the sound of clashing **2.** *a)* conflict *b)* lack of harmony —**clash'er** *n.*

clasp (klasp) *n.* [ME. *claspe*] **1.** a fastening, as a hook or catch, to hold two things or parts together **2.** a grasping; embrace **3.** a grip of the hand —*vt.* **1.** to fasten with a clasp **2.** to grasp firmly; embrace **3.** to grip with the hand **4.** to cling to —**clasp'er** *n.*

clasp knife a large pocketknife, esp. one with blades which, when open, can be secured by a catch

class (klas) *n.* [< Fr. < L. *classis*, prob. akin to *calare*, to call] **1.** a number of people or things grouped together because of certain likenesses; kind; sort **2.** a group of people of the same social or economic status [the middle *class*] **3.** high social rank or caste **4.** the division of society into ranks or castes ☆**5.** *a)* a group of students taught together *b)* a meeting of such a group *c)* a group of students graduating together [the *class* of 1977] **6.** grade or quality [travel first *class*] **7.** [Slang] excellence, as of style **8.** *Biol.* a group of animals or plants ranking below a phylum and above an order —*vt.* to put in a class; classify —*vi.* to be classed —**in a class by itself (or oneself)** unique

class. **1.** classic **2.** classical **3.** classification **4.** classified

☆**class book** a book published by a school or college class, containing pictures of students and teachers, an account of student activities, etc.

class consciousness a sense of belonging to and identifying with a certain economic class —**class'-con'scious** *adj.*

☆**class day** the day on which special ceremonies are held by the senior class at a school or college to celebrate its coming graduation

clas·sic (klas'ik) *adj.* [L. *classicus*, superior < *classis*, CLASS] **1.** of the highest class; being a model of its kind; standard [a *classic* example of Tudor architecture] **2.** *a)* of the art, literature, and culture of the ancient Greeks or Romans, or their writers, artists, etc. *b)* derived from their literary and artistic standards **3.** balanced, formal, objective, restrained, regular, etc. in style **4.** famous as traditional or typical [a *classic* court case] ☆**5.** [Colloq.] simple in style and continuing in fashion: said of an article of apparel —*n.* **1.** a writer, artist, etc., or a literary or artistic work, recognized as excellent, authoritative,

etc. ☆**2.** a famous traditional event [the Kentucky Derby is a racing *classic*] ☆**3.** [Colloq.] a suit, dress, etc. that is classic (sense 5) ☆**4.** [Colloq.] an automobile of the period 1925–42 —**the classics** literature regarded as classic (senses 1, 2)

clas·si·cal (klas'i k'l) *adj.* **1.** *same as* CLASSIC (senses 1, 2, 3) **2.** versed in and devoted to Greek and Roman culture, literature, etc. **3.** designating or of music that follows certain established standards of form and is not folk music, popular music, or the like [the works of Haydn are *classical*] **4.** traditional rather than new and experimental [*classical* economics] —**clas·si·cal'i·ty** (-kal'ə tē), **clas'si·cal·ness,** *n.* —**clas'si·cal·ly** *adv.*

clas·si·cism (klas'ə siz'm) *n.* **1.** the aesthetic principles or qualities of ancient Greece and Rome; formality, balance, simplicity, restraint, etc. **2.** adherence to such principles **3.** knowledge of the literature and art of ancient Greece and Rome **4.** a Greek or Latin idiom or expression Also **clas'si·cal·ism** —**clas'si·cist** *n.*

clas·si·cize (-sīz') *vt.* **-cized', -ciz'ing** to make classic —*vi.* to use a classic style

clas·si·fi·ca·tion (klas'ə fi kā'shən) *n.* **1.** an arrangement according to some systematic division into classes or groups **2.** such a class or group **3.** *Biol.* same as TAXONOMY —**clas·si·fi·ca·to·ry** (klas'ə fi kā'tər ē, -kə tôr'ē) *adj.*

☆**classified advertising** advertising, as in newspaper columns, under such listings as *help wanted, for sale*, etc.

clas·si·fy (klas'ə fī') *vt.* **-fied', -fy'ing** **1.** to arrange in classes according to some system or principle **2.** to place in a category **3.** to designate (government documents, etc.) as secret or confidential —**clas'si·fi'a·ble** *adj.* —**clas'si·fi'er** *n.*

class·less (klas'lis) *adj.* having no distinct social or economic classes [a *classless* society]

☆**class·mate** (-māt') *n.* a member of the same class at a school or college

☆**class·room** (-rōōm') *n.* a room in a school or college in which classes are taught

class·y (-ē) *adj.* **class'i·er, class'i·est** [Slang] first-class, esp. in style or manner —**class'i·ness** *n.*

clas·tic (klas'tik) *adj.* [< Gr. < *klan*, to break: for IE. base see GLADIATOR] *Geol.* consisting of fragments of older rocks

clat·ter (klat'ər) *vi.* [ME. *clateren*: for IE. base see CALL] **1.** to make, or move with, a rapid succession of loud, sharp noises, as dishes rattling **2.** to chatter noisily —*vt.* to cause to clatter —*n.* **1.** a rapid succession of loud, sharp noises **2.** a tumult; hubbub **3.** noisy chatter —**clat'ter·er** *n.* —**clat'ter·ing·ly** *adv.*

Claude (klôd) [Fr. < L. *Claudius*, name of a Roman gens] a masculine name

Clau·di·a (klô'dē ə) [L., fem. of prec.] a feminine name

Clau·di·us I (klô'dē əs) (*Tiberius Claudius Drusus Nero Germanicus*) 10 B.C.–54 A.D.; Roman emperor (41–54)

clause (klôz) *n.* [OFr. < ML. *clausa* < L. pp. of *claudere*, to CLOSE²] **1.** a group of words containing a subject and verb, usually forming part of a compound or complex sentence: cf. MAIN CLAUSE, SUBORDINATE CLAUSE **2.** a particular article, stipulation, or provision in a formal or legal document —**claus'al** (klô'z'l) *adj.*

Clau·se·witz (klou'zə vits), **Karl von** (fôn) 1780–1831; Prussian army officer & writer on military strategy

claus·tro·pho·bi·a (klôs'trə fō'bē ə) *n.* [< L. *claustrum* (see CLOISTER) + -PHOBIA] an abnormal fear of being in an enclosed or confined place —**claus'tro·pho'bic** *adj.*

cla·vate (klā'vāt) *adj.* [< L. *clava*, a club + -ATE¹] club-shaped —**cla'vate·ly** *adv.* —**cla·va'tion** *n.*

clave (klāv) *archaic pt. of* CLEAVE¹ & CLEAVE²

clav·i·chord (klav'ə kôrd') *n.* [< ML. < L. *clavis*, a key + *chorda*, a string] a stringed musical instrument with a keyboard, replaced by the piano

clav·i·cle (klav'i k'l) *n.* [< Fr. < L. *clavicula*, dim. of *clavis*, a key: for IE. base see CLOSE²] a bone connecting the breastbone with the shoulder blade; collarbone —**cla·vic·u·lar** (kla vik'yoo lər) *adj.*

cla·vier (klə vir'; *for 1, also* klav'ē ər) *n.* [Fr., keyboard < L. *clavis*, see CLAVICLE] **1.** the keyboard of an organ, piano, etc. **2.** any stringed instrument that has a keyboard

claw (klô) *n.* [OE. *clawu* < IE. base *gel-*, to make round, clench (as a fist), from which also come CLING & CLIMB] **1.** a sharp, hooked nail on the foot of a bird and of

CLAVICLES

many reptiles and mammals **2.** a foot with such nails **3.** a pincer, or chela, of a lobster, crab, etc. **4.** anything regarded as or resembling a claw, as a hammer (**claw hammer**) with one end forked and curved, used to pull nails —*vt., vi.* to scratch, clutch, pull, dig, or tear with or as with claws —**clawed** (klôd) *adj.*

clay (klā) *n.* [OE. *clæg*: for IE. base see CLAW] **1.** a stiff, sticky earth, mostly aluminum silicates, that becomes hard when it is baked: used in the manufacture of bricks, pottery, etc. **2.** *a)* earth *b)* the human body —**clay′ey** *adj.* **clay′i·er, clay′i-est** —**clay′ish** *adj.*

Clay (klā), **Henry** 1777–1852; U.S. statesman

clay·more (klā′môr′) *n.* [Gael. *claidheamhmor*, great sword] **1.** a large, two-edged broadsword formerly used by Scottish Highlanders **2.** a broadsword with a basket hilt worn by Highland regiments

☆**clay pigeon** a disk as of baked clay, tossed into the air from a trap as a target in trapshooting

clean (klēn) *adj.* [OE. *clæne* < IE. base *gel-*, to gleam] **1.** free from dirt or impurities; unsoiled; unstained ☆**2.** having less radioactive fallout at the time of explosion than other nuclear bombs **3.** recently laundered; fresh **4.** *a)* morally pure [he led a *clean* life] *b)* not obscene or indecent [a *clean* joke] **5.** sportsmanlike; fair [a *clean* fight] **6.** keeping oneself or one's surroundings neat and tidy **7.** shapely or trim [*clean* lines] **8.** skillful; deft [a *clean* stroke] **9.** complete; thorough [a *clean* sweep] **10.** empty [a *clean* sheet of paper] ☆**11.** [Slang] not guilty of an illegal act; innocent —*adv.* **1.** in a clean manner **2.** completely [*clean* forgotten] —*vt.* **1.** to make clean **2.** to remove (dirt, impurities, etc.) **3.** to empty or clear **4.** to prepare (fish, fowl, etc.) for cooking ☆**5.** [Slang] to take away or use up the money, etc. of (often with *out*) —*vi.* **1.** to clean something **2.** to be made clean [this rug *cleans* easily] —**clean out 1.** to empty so as to make clean **2.** to empty —**clean up 1.** to make clean or neat **2.** to get washed, combed, etc. **3.** [Colloq.] to finish ☆**4.** [Slang] to make much profit —☆**clean up on** [Slang] to defeat; beat —☆**come clean** [Slang] to confess; tell the truth —**clean′a·ble** *adj.* —**clean′ness** *n.*

SYN.—**clean** is the general term for doing away with dirt or impurities, as by washing, scrubbing, etc. [to *clean* one's house]; **cleanse** suggests more specifically a thorough cleaning or purifying and is often used in connection with the spirit or conscience [to feel *cleansed* of sin] —ANT. soil, dirty

clean-cut (klēn′kut′) *adj.* **1.** having a clear, sharp outline **2.** good-looking, trim, neat, etc. [a *clean-cut* young man]

clean·er (klēn′ər) *n.* a person or thing that cleans; specif., *a)* one who dry-cleans *b)* a preparation for removing dirt, stains, etc.

clean·hand·ed (-han′did) *adj.* innocent; blameless

clean·limbed (-limd′) *adj.* having shapely limbs

clean·ly[1] (klen′lē) *adj.* **-li·er, -li·est 1.** keeping oneself or one's surroundings clean **2.** always kept clean —**clean′li·ly** *adv.* —**clean′li·ness** *n.*

clean·ly[2] (klēn′lē) *adv.* in a clean manner

☆**clean room** a room or other enclosed space in which the air can be kept almost 100% free of dust, pollen, bacteria, etc.: used in the manufacture of spacecraft, in hospitals, etc.

cleanse (klenz) *vt.* **cleansed, cleans′ing** [OE. *clænsian* < *clæne*, CLEAN] to make clean, pure, etc.; purge —see SYN. at CLEAN

cleans·er (klen′zər) *n.* a preparation for cleansing, esp. a powder for scouring pots, sinks, etc.

clean·shav·en (klēn′shā′v'n) *adj.* having all the hair shaved off; specif., wearing no beard or mustache

clean·up (klēn′up′) *n.* **1.** a cleaning up ☆**2.** elimination of crime, vice, etc. ☆**3.** [Slang] profit; gain —☆*adj.* Baseball designating the fourth batter in a team's lineup

clear (klir) *adj.* [< OFr. < L. *clarus*, orig., clear-sounding: for IE. base see CLAMOR] **1.** free from clouds or mist; bright; light [a *clear* day] **2.** transparent; not opaque, cloudy, etc. [*clear* glass] **3.** having no blemishes [a *clear* skin] **4.** sharp and distinct; not dim or blurred [a *clear* outline; *clear* tones] **5.** able to see or think well [a *clear* eye; a *clear* mind] **6.** serene and calm **7.** not obscure; easily understood **8.** obvious [a *clear* case of neglect] **9.** certain; positive [to be *clear* on a point] **10.** free from guilt; innocent **11.** free from charges or deductions; net [a *clear* profit of $10,000] **12.** free from debt or other complications [a *clear* title to property] **13.** absolute;

complete [a *clear* majority] **14.** free from being blocked; open [a *clear* passage] **15.** free from contact **16.** emptied of freight or cargo —*adv.* **1.** in a clear manner; so as to be clear **2.** all the way; completely [it sank *clear* to the bottom] —*vt.* **1.** to make clear or bright **2.** to free from impurities, muddiness, blemishes, etc. **3.** *a)* to make easy to understand *b)* to decode or decipher **4.** to unblock; open **5.** to get rid of; remove **6.** to empty or unload **7.** to free (a person or thing) *of* or *from* something **8.** to free from guilt or blame **9.** to pass over, under, by, etc. with space to spare [will this truck *clear* the bridge?] **10.** to discharge (a debt) by paying it **11.** to give or get clearance for **12.** to be passed or approved by [the bill *cleared* Congress] **13.** to make (a given amount) as profit; net **14.** *Banking* to pass (a check, etc.) through a clearinghouse —*vi.* **1.** to become clear, unclouded, etc. **2.** to pass away; vanish **3.** to get clearance, as a ship leaving port **4.** *Banking* to exchange checks, etc., and balance accounts, through a clearinghouse —*n.* a clear space —see SYN. at EVIDENT —**clear away 1.** to take away so as to leave a cleared space **2.** to go away —**clear off 1.** to clear away **2.** to remove things from (a surface) —**clear out 1.** to clear by emptying ☆**2.** [Colloq.] to depart —**clear the air** (or **atmosphere**) to get rid of hurt or bitter feelings, misunderstandings, etc. —**clear up 1.** to make or become clear **2.** to make orderly **3.** to explain **4.** to cure or become cured —**in the clear 1.** in the open **2.** [Colloq.] free from suspicion, guilt, etc. —**clear′a·ble** *adj.* —**clear′er** *n.* —**clear′ly** *adv.* —**clear′ness** *n.*

clear·ance (klir′əns) *n.* **1.** a making clear **2.** the clear space between things, or between a moving object and that which it passes by, through, over, under, etc. **3.** official authorization to see classified documents, work on secret projects, etc. **4.** *Banking* the adjustment of accounts in a clearinghouse **5.** *Naut.* a certificate authorizing a ship to enter or leave port: also called **clearance papers**

clearance sale a sale to get rid of old merchandise and make room for new

clear-cut (-kut′) *adj.* **1.** clearly and sharply outlined **2.** distinct; definite; certain [a *clear-cut* victory]

clear·head·ed (-hed′id) *adj.* having a clear mind; unconfused —**clear′head′ed·ly** *adv.* —**clear′head′ed·ness** *n.*

clear·ing (klir′iŋ) *n.* **1.** a making clear or being cleared ☆**2.** an area of land cleared of trees **3.** *Banking a)* same as CLEARANCE *b)* [*pl.*] the amount of the balances settled in clearance

clear·ing·house (-hous′) *n.* **1.** an office maintained by a group of banks as a center for exchanging checks, balancing accounts, etc. **2.** a central office for getting and giving information, etc.

clear·sight·ed (klir′sīt′id) *adj.* **1.** seeing clearly **2.** understanding or thinking clearly —**clear′sight′ed·ly** *adv.* —**clear′sight′ed·ness** *n.*

clear·sto·ry (-stôr′ē) *n., pl.* **-ries** same as CLERESTORY

Clear·wa·ter (klir′wôt′ər, -wät′-) city in WC Fla., on the Gulf of Mexico: suburb of St. Petersburg: pop. 52,000

cleat (klēt) *n.* [< OE. hyp. *cleat*, a lump: for IE. base see CLAW] **1.** a piece of wood or metal, often wedge-shaped, fastened to something to strengthen it or give secure footing [golf shoes have *cleats* on the soles] **2.** *Naut.* a small piece of wood or metal with projecting ends on which a rope can be fastened —*vt.* to fasten to or with a cleat

cleav·age (klē′vij) *n.* **1.** a cleaving, splitting, or dividing **2.** the manner in which a thing splits **3.** a cleft; fissure **4.** the hollow between a woman's breasts, as exposed by a low-cut neckline **5.** *Biol.* cell division that transforms the fertilized ovum into the earliest embryonic stage

cleave[1] (klēv) *vt.* **cleaved** or **cleft** or **clove, cleaved** or **cleft** or **clo′ven, cleav′ing** [OE. *cleofan* < IE. base *gleubh-*, to cut] **1.** to divide by a blow, as with an ax; split **2.** to pierce **3.** to sever; disunite —*vi.* **1.** to split; separate **2.** to make one's way by or as by cutting —**cleav′a·ble** *adj.*

cleave[2] (klēv) *vi.* **cleaved, cleav′ing** [OE. *cleofian*: for IE. base see CLAW] **1.** to adhere; cling (*to*) **2.** to be faithful (*to*)

cleav·er (klēv′ər) *n.* a heavy cleaving tool with a broad blade, used by butchers

cleav·ers (-ərz) *n., pl.* **-ers** [< CLEAVE[2]] a plant of the madder family, with stalkless leaves, clusters of small flowers, and prickly stems

---

fat, āpe, cär; ten, ēven; is, bīte; gō, hôrn, tool, look; oil, out; up, fur; get; joy; yet; chin; she; thin, then; zh, leisure; ŋ, ring; ə for *a* in *ago*, *e* in *agent*, *i* in *sanity*, *o* in *comply*, *u* in *focus*; ′ as in *able* (ā′b'l); Fr. bal; ë, Fr. coeur; ö, Fr. feu; Fr. mon; ô, Fr. coq; ü, Fr. duc; r, Fr. cri; H, G. ich; kh, G. doch; ‡foreign; ☆ Americanism; < derived from. See inside front cover.

clef (klef) *n.* [Fr. < L. *clavis*, a key: see CLOSE²] a symbol used in music to indicate the pitch of the notes on the staff: there are three clefs: G (treble), F (bass), and C (tenor or alto)

cleft¹ (kleft) *n.* [< OE. hyp. *clyft* < *cleofan*, CLEAVE¹] an opening or hollow made by or as by cleaving; crack; crevice [a *cleft* in the rocks; a *cleft* in the chin]

cleft² *alt. pt. & pp. of* CLEAVE¹ —*adj.* split; divided [a *cleft* palate]

cleis·tog·a·my (klīs täg′ə mē) *n.* [< Gr. *kleistos*, closed + -GAMY] self-fertilization within certain unopened flowers, as in the violet —**cleis·tog′a·mous** (-məs) *adj.*

clem·a·tis (klem′ə tis, klə mat′is) *n.* [L. < Gr. < *klēma*, vine, twig] a perennial plant or woody vine of the buttercup family, with bright-colored flowers

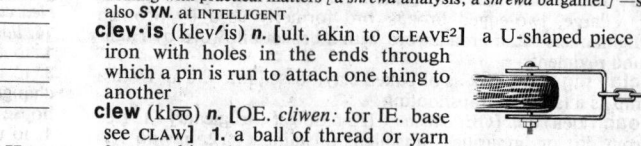

G CLEF   F CLEF

C CLEFS

TYPES OF CLEF

Cle·men·ceau (klā män sō′; E. klem′ən sō′), **Georges (Benjamin Eugène)** (zhôrzh) 1841–1929; Fr. statesman; premier of France (1906–09; 1917–20)

clem·en·cy (klem′ən sē) *n., pl.* -**cies** [< L. < *clemens*, merciful] **1.** kindness in judging or punishing someone; mercy **2.** mildness, as of weather

Clem·ens (klem′ənz), **Samuel Lang·horne** (laŋ′hôrn) (pseud. *Mark Twain*) 1835–1910; U.S. writer & humorist

Clem·ent (klem′ənt) [L. < *clemens*, mild, gentle] a masculine name: dim. *Clem*

clem·ent (klem′ənt) *adj.* [L. *clemens*] **1.** showing mercy; lenient; merciful **2.** mild, as weather —**clem′ent·ly** *adv.*

Clem·en·tine (klem′ən tīn′, -tēn′) [< CLEMENT] a feminine name

clench (klench) *vt.* [< OE. -*clencan* (in *beclencan*), lit., to make cling: for IE. base see CLAW] **1.** to clinch (a nail, etc.) **2.** to bring together tightly; close (the teeth or fist) firmly **3.** to grip tightly —*n.* **1.** a firm grip **2.** a device that clenches —**clench′er** *n.*

Cle·o·pa·tra (klē′ə pat′rə, -pā′trə, -pä′trə) 69?–30 B.C.; queen of Egypt (51–49; 48–30)

clep·sy·dra (klep′si drə) *n., pl.* -**dras** or -**drae** (-drē′) [L. < Gr. < *kleptein*, to steal + *hydōr*, WATER] *same as* WATER CLOCK

clep·to·ma·ni·a (klep′tə mā′nē ə) *n. same as* KLEPTOMANIA

clere·sto·ry (klir′stôr′ē) *n., pl.* -**ries** [< ME. < *cler*, CLEAR + *storie*, STORY²] **1.** the wall of a church rising above the roofs of the side aisles and containing windows for lighting the central part of the structure **2.** any similar windowed wall

cler·gy (klur′jē) *n., pl.* -**gies** [< OFr. < LL. *clericus*: see CLERK] ministers, priests, rabbis, etc. as a group

cler·gy·man (-mən) *n., pl.* -**men** a member of the clergy; minister, priest, rabbi, etc.

cler·ic (kler′ik) *n.* [LL. *clericus*: see CLERK] a clergyman —*adj.* of a clergyman or the clergy

cler·i·cal (kler′i k'l) *adj.* [LL. *clericalis* < *clericus*: see CLERK] **1.** relating to a clergyman or the clergy **2.** relating to office clerks or their work **3.** favoring clericalism —*n.* **1.** a clergyman **2.** [*pl.*] clergymen's garments **3.** one who favors clericalism —**cler′i·cal·ly** *adv.*

clerical collar a stiff, white collar buttoned at the back, worn by certain clergymen

cler·i·cal·ism (-iz'm) *n.* political influence or power of the clergy, or a policy or principles favoring this —**cler′i·cal·ist** *n.*

clerk (klurk; Brit. klärk) *n.* [< OFr. & OE. < LL. *clericus* < Gr. *klērikos*, priest < *klēros*, lot, inheritance (later, clergy): for IE. base see GLADIATOR] **1.** a layman who has minor duties in a church **2.** an office worker who keeps records, types letters, does filing, etc. **3.** an official in charge of records, etc. of a court, town, etc. ☆**4.** a hotel employee who keeps the register, assigns guests to rooms, etc. ☆**5.** a person who sells in a store; salesclerk **6.** [Archaic] *a)* a clergyman *b)* a scholar —*vi.* ☆to work as a clerk, esp. a salesclerk —**clerk′ly** *adj., adv.* —**clerk′ship′** *n.*

Cleve·land (klēv′lənd) [after M. *Cleaveland*, 18th-c. Conn. surveyor] city in NE Ohio, on Lake Erie: pop. 751,000 (met. area 2,064,000)

Cleve·land (klēv′lənd), **(Stephen) Gro·ver** (grō′vər) 1837–1908; 22d and 24th president of the U.S. (1885–89; 1893–97)

Cleveland Heights city in NE Ohio: suburb of Cleveland: pop. 61,000

clev·er (klev′ər) *adj.* [prob. < EFris. *klüfer* or Norw. *klöver*, skillful] **1.** skillful in doing something; adroit; dexterous [magicians are *clever* with their hands] **2.** intelligent, quick-witted, witty, smart, etc. **3.** showing quick, often showy, intelligence [a *clever* book] —**clev′er·ly** *adv.* —**clev′er·ness** *n.*

SYN.—*clever* implies a quickness of mind or wit, as in solving a problem, in conversation, etc. [a *clever* idea; a *clever* reply]; **cunning** implies cleverness of a sly, tricky, or crafty kind [*cunning* as a fox]; **ingenious** suggests cleverness in thinking up or inventing something [an *ingenious* explanation; an *ingenious* designer]; **shrewd** suggests cleverness or sharpness in dealing with practical matters [a *shrewd* analysis; a *shrewd* bargainer]—see also **SYN.** at INTELLIGENT

clev·is (klev′is) *n.* [ult. akin to CLEAVE²] a U-shaped piece of iron with holes in the ends through which a pin is run to attach one thing to another

CLEVIS

clew (kloo) *n.* [OE. *cliwen*: for IE. base see CLAW] **1.** a ball of thread or yarn **2.** something that leads out of a maze or helps to solve a problem: usually sp. **clue 3.** *Naut. a)* a lower corner of a square sail *b)* the lower corner aft of a fore-and-aft sail *c)* a metal loop in the corner of a sail —*vt.* **1.** to wind (*up*) into a ball **2.** *same as* CLUE —**clew down** (or *up*) to lower (or raise) a sail by the clews

cli·ché (klē shā′) *n.* [Fr. < *clicher*, to stereotype] an expression or idea that has become stale from too much use [“As old as the hills” is a *cliché*]

click (klik) *n.* [echoic] **1.** a slight, sharp sound like that of a door latch snapping into place **2.** a mechanical device, as a catch or pawl, that clicks into position **3.** *Phonet.* a sound made by drawing the breath into the mouth and snapping the tongue from the roof of the mouth —*vi.* **1.** to make a click **2.** [Colloq.] *a)* to be suddenly understood *b)* to work or get along together successfully *c)* to be a success —*vt.* to cause to click —**click′er** *n.*

click beetle a kind of beetle that rights itself with a clicking sound after being on its back

click·e·ty-clack (klik′ə tē klak′) *n.* [echoic] a rhythmic, metallic sound, as that made by the wheels of a moving train

cli·ent (klī′ənt) *n.* [OFr. < L. *cliens*, follower < IE. base *klei-*, to lean] **1.** a person or company for whom a lawyer, accountant, etc. is acting **2.** a customer —**cli·en·tal** (klī en′t'l) *adj.*

cli·en·tele (klī′ən tel′; also, chiefly Brit., klē′än-) *n.* [< Fr. < L. *clientela*: see CLIENT] all one's clients or customers, as a group: also **cli·ent·age** (klī′ən tij)

cliff (klif) *n.* [OE. *clif*] a high, steep face of rock that comes down sharply with little or no slope —**cliff′y** *adj.*

☆**cliff dweller** a member of a race of ancient American Indians of the Southwest, who lived in hollows or caves in cliffs: they were ancestors of the Pueblo Indians —**cliff′-dwell′ing** *adj.*

☆**cliff-hang·er, cliff-hang′er** (klif′haŋ′ər) *n.* any story, situation, etc. that seems as full of suspense as the old movie serials, which sometimes ended an episode with the hero hanging from a cliff —**cliff′hang′ing, cliff′-hang′ing** *adj.*

Clif·ford (klif′ərd) [< CLIFF + FORD, hence, lit., ford at the cliff] a masculine name: dim. *Cliff*

☆**cliff swallow** a N. American swallow that builds its bottle-shaped nest of mud, grass, etc. against cliffs or under eaves

Clif·ton (klif′tən) [< CLIFF + -*ton*, town] **1.** a masculine name **2.** [< its location at the foot of a mountain] city in northeastern N.J.: pop. 82,000

cli·mac·ter·ic (klī mak′tər ik, klī′mak ter′ik) *n.* [< L. < Gr. < *klimax*: see CLIMAX] **1.** a time in the life of a mature person when an important change takes place in the functioning of the body, esp. the menopause **2.** any turning point or crucial time —*adj.* of or like a climacteric: also **cli′mac·ter′i·cal**

cli·mac·tic (klī mak′tik) *adj.* of or forming a climax: also **cli·mac′ti·cal** —**cli·mac′ti·cal·ly** *adv.*

cli·mate (klī′mət) *n.* [< OFr. < L. < Gr. *klima*, region: for IE. base see CLIENT] **1.** the average weather conditions of a place over a period of years [Arizona has a mild, dry *climate*, but its weather last week was bad] **2.** a region with particular weather conditions [to move to a warm *climate*] **3.** the trend of conditions or influences of a particular time or place [a favorable *climate* of opinion] —**cli·mat·ic** (klī mat′ik) *adj.* —**cli·mat′i·cal·ly** *adv.*

cli·ma·tol·o·gy (klī′mə täl′ə jē) *n.* the science dealing with climate and climate phenomena —**cli′ma·to·log′i·cal** (-tə läj′i k'l) *adj.* —**cli′ma·tol′o·gist** *n.*

cli·max (klī′maks) *n.* [L. < Gr. *klimax,* ladder: for IE. base see CLIENT] **1.** formerly, an arrangement of ideas, images, etc. with the most forceful last **2.** the final and strongest idea or event in a series; highest point, as of interest, excitement, etc.; specif., *a)* the decisive turning point of the action, as in a drama *b)* an orgasm **3.** *Ecol.* a community of plants or animals that has reached its fullest development and will live on as long as the same conditions of climate and soil prevail —*vi., vt.* to reach, or bring to, a climax —see SYN.at SUMMIT

climb (klīm) *vi., vt.* climbed *or archaic* clomb, **climb′ing** [OE. *climban:* for IE. base see CLAW] **1.** to go up by using the feet and often the hands **2.** to rise or ascend gradually; mount **3.** to move (*down, over, along,* etc.) using the hands and feet **4.** *Bot.* to grow upward on (a wall, trellis, etc.) by winding around or clinging with tendrils —*n.* **1.** a climbing; rise; ascent **2.** a thing or place to be climbed —**climb′a·ble** *adj.*

climb·er (klīm′ər) *n.* **1.** one that climbs ☆**2.** *same as* LINEMEN'S CLIMBER ☆**3.** [Colloq.] one who tries to get ahead socially or in business **4.** *Bot.* a climbing plant or vine

climbing iron *same as* LINEMEN'S CLIMBER

clime (klīm) *n.* [L. *clima:* see CLIMATE] [Poet.] a region, esp. with regard to its climate

clinch (klinch) *vt.* [var. of CLENCH] **1.** to fasten (a nail, bolt, etc. driven through something) by bending or flattening the end that sticks out **2.** to fasten together by this means **3.** *a)* to settle (an argument, deal, etc.) definitely *b)* to make sure of winning —*vi.* ☆**1.** *Boxing* to grip the opponent's body with the arms ☆**2.** [Slang] to embrace —*n.* **1.** *a)* a clinching, as with a nail *b)* a clinched nail, bolt, etc. *c)* the part clinched ☆**2.** *Boxing* an act of clinching ☆**3.** [Slang] an embrace

clinch·er (klin′chər) *n.* **1.** a tool for clinching nails **2.** a decisive point, argument, act, etc.

cling (kliŋ) *vi.* clung, **cling′ing** [OE. *clingan:* for IE. base see CLAW] **1.** to hold fast by or as by embracing, entwining, or sticking; adhere *[a* child *clinging* to his mother; a vine *clinging* to the wall] **2.** *a)* to be or stay near, as if holding fast [the tobacco smell *clinging* to the curtains] *b)* to be tied to by habit, strong feelings, etc. [to *cling* to a custom] —☆*adj., n. same as* CLINGSTONE —**cling′er** *n.* —**cling′ing·ly** *adv.* —**cling′y** *adj.*

☆**cling·stone** (kliŋ′stōn′) *adj.* having a stone that clings to the fleshy part: said of some peaches —*n.* a peach of this sort

clin·ic (klin′ik) *n.* [L. *clinicus,* physician who attends persons sick in bed < Gr. *klinikos,* of a bed < *klinē,* a bed] **1.** the teaching of medicine by examining and treating patients while students watch **2.** a class so taught **3.** a place where patients are examined or treated by doctors who are specialists and are practicing as a group **4.** a department of a hospital or medical school where outpatients are treated, sometimes free or for a small fee **5.** an organization that offers some kind of advice, treatment, or instruction *[a* maternal health *clinic]*

clin·i·cal (klin′i k'l) *adj.* **1.** of or connected with a clinic **2.** having to do with the treatment and observation of patients, as distinguished from experimental or laboratory study **3.** objective and impersonal in a scientific way **4.** austere, antiseptic, etc., like a medical clinic —**clin′i·cal·ly** *adv.*

clinical thermometer a thermometer with which the body temperature is measured

cli·ni·cian (kli nish′ən) *n.* an expert in or practitioner of clinical medicine, psychology, etc.

clink (kliŋk) *vi., vt.* [< MDu. *klinken:* echoic] to make or cause to make a slight, sharp sound, as of glasses striking together —*n.* **1.** such a sound **2.** [< name of an 18th-c. London prison] [Colloq.] a jail; prison

clink·er (kliŋk′ər) *n.* [Du. *klinker,* vitrified brick < *klinken,* to ring] **1.** a stony mass or lump of fused matter formed in a furnace, as from impurities in the coal **2.** [Slang] *a)* a mistake; error *b)* a total failure —*vi.* to form clinkers in burning

clink·er-built (-bilt′) *adj.* [*clinker* < *clink,* dial. var. of CLENCH] built with overlapping boards or plates, as a boat

cli·nom·e·ter (klī näm′ə tər) *n.* [< Gr. *klinein,* to slope + -METER] an instrument for measuring angles of slope or inclination —**cli′no·met′ric** (klī′nō met′rik) *adj.*

Clin·ton (klin′t'n) [Eng. place name < ?] **1.** a masculine name **2. De Witt** (də wit′), 1769–1828; U.S. statesman

Cli·o (klī′ō) [L. < Gr. < *kleos,* fame] *Gr. Myth.* the Muse of history

cli·o·met·rics (klī′ō met′riks) *n.pl.* [with sing v.] [< prec. + Gr. *metron,* measure] the use of mathematics, statistics, and often computers, in trying to examine and explain historical events —**cli′o·met′ric** *adj.* —**cli′o·me·tri′cian** (-mə trish′ən) *n.*

clip¹ (klip) *vt.* clipped, **clip′ping** [< ON. *klippa*] **1.** to cut or cut off as with shears **2.** to cut (an item) out of (a newspaper, etc.) **3.** *a)* to cut short *b)* to shorten by omitting syllables, etc. **4.** to cut the hair of **5.** [Colloq.] to hit with a quick, sharp blow ☆**6.** [Slang] to cheat, esp. by overcharging —*vi.* **1.** to clip something **2.** to move rapidly —*n.* **1.** the act of clipping **2.** a thing clipped; specif., *a)* the amount of wool clipped from sheep at one time *b)* a sequence clipped from a movie film **3.** a rapid pace **4.** [Colloq.] a quick, sharp blow **5.** *same as* CLIPPED FORM

clip² (klip) *vi., vt.* clipped, **clip′ping** [OE. *clyppan,* to embrace: for IE. base see CLAW] **1.** to grip tightly; fasten ☆**2.** *Football* to block (an opponent who is not carrying the ball) from behind: an illegal act —*n.* **1.** any device that clips or fastens **2.** *same as* CARTRIDGE CLIP ☆**3.** *Football* an act of clipping

☆**clip·board** (klip′bôrd′) *n.* a portable writing board with a hinged clip at the top to hold papers

clipped form (or **word**) a shortened form of a word, as *pike* (for *turnpike*) or *fan* (for *fanatic*)

clip·per (klip′ər) *n.* [ME. < *clippen,* CLIP¹] **1.** a person who cuts, trims, etc. **2.** [*usually pl.*] a tool for cutting or trimming ☆**3.** a sharp-bowed, narrow-beamed sailing ship built for great speed

CLIPBOARD

clip·ping (-iŋ) *n.* **1.** something cut out or trimmed off ☆**2.** an item clipped from a newspaper, magazine, etc.

clique (klēk, klik) *n.* [Fr. < *cliquer,* to make a noise] a small, exclusive circle of people; snobbish or narrow coterie —see SYN.at COTERIE —**cliqu′ish, cliqu′ey, cliqu′y** *adj.* —**cliqu′ish·ly** *adv.* —**cliqu′ish·ness** *n.*

clit·o·ris (klit′ər əs, klīt′-) *n.* [ModL. < Gr. *kleitys,* hill] a small, sensitive, sexual organ at the upper end of the vulva —**clit′o·ral** (-ər əl), **cli·tor·ic** (klī tôr′ik) *adj.*

Clive (klīv) [< the surname] **1.** a masculine name **2. Robert,** Baron Clive of Plassey, 1725–74; Brit. soldier & statesman in India

CLIPPER SHIP

clo·a·ca (klō ā′kə) *n., pl.* **-cae** (-sē, -kē), **-cas** [L. < *cluere,* to cleanse] **1.** a sewer or cesspool **2.** *Zool.* the cavity that is the opening for the intestines and the urinary and genital tracts in reptiles, birds, amphibians, and many fishes —**clo·a′cal** *adj.*

cloak (klōk) *n.* [< OFr. < ML. *clocca* (see CLOCK¹), a bell, cloak: so called from its bell-like appearance] **1.** a loose, usually sleeveless outer garment **2.** something that covers or conceals —*vt.* **1.** to cover as with a cloak **2.** to conceal; hide

cloak-and-dag·ger (-ən dag′ər) *adj.* of or like spies and spying, esp. as described in fiction in an exaggerated way

cloak·room (-rōōm′) *n.* a room where hats, coats, umbrellas, etc. can be left for a time

clob·ber (kläb′ər) *vt.* [< ?] [Slang] **1.** to beat or hit repeatedly; maul **2.** to defeat finally

cloche (klōsh) *n.* [Fr. < ML. *clocca:* see CLOCK¹] a closefitting, bell-shaped hat for women

clock¹ (kläk) *n.* [ME. *clokke,* orig., clock with bells < ML. *clocca,* bell < Celt. < ? IE. base of CLAMOR] **1.** a device for measuring and showing the passing of time, as by pointers moving around a dial: clocks, unlike watches, are not carried on one's person ☆**2.** *same as* TIME CLOCK —*vt.* **1.** to measure or record the time of (a race, runner, etc.) with a stopwatch, etc. **2.** to register (an amount, etc.) on a meter —**around the clock** day and night, without stopping

clock² (kläk) *n.* [< ? prec., because orig. bell-shaped] a woven or embroidered ornament on a sock, going up from the ankle

clock·like (-līk′) *adj.* as precise or regular as a clock

☆**clock radio** a radio with a built-in clock that can be set to turn the radio on or off

clock·wise (-wīz′) *adv., adj.* in the direction in which the hands of a clock rotate

clock·work (-wʉrk′) *n.* **1.** the mechanism of a clock **2.** any similar mechanism, consisting of springs and gears, as in some mechanical toys —**like clockwork** very regularly and evenly

clod (kläd) *n.* [OE.: for IE. base see CLAW] **1.** a lump, esp. of earth, clay, loam, etc. **2.** earth; soil **3.** a dull, stupid fellow; dolt —**clod′dish** *adj.* —**clod′dish·ly** *adv.* —**clod′dish·ness** *n.*

clod·hop·per (-häp′ər) *n.* [CLOD + HOPPER] **1.** a plowman **2.** a clumsy, stupid fellow; lout **3.** a coarse, heavy shoe

clog (kläg) *n.* [ME. *clogge*, a lump of wood] **1.** a weight fastened to an animal's leg to hinder motion **2.** anything that blocks up or gets in the way **3.** a shoe with a thick, usually wooden sole: light clogs are used in clog dancing **4.** *same as* CLOG DANCE —*vt.* **clogged, clog′ging 1.** to slow up; hinder; impede **2.** to block or stop up, as with thick, sticky matter —*vi.* **1.** to become stopped up **2.** to do a clog dance —**clog′gy** *adj.*

clog dance a dance in which clogs are worn to beat out the rhythm —**clog dancer** —**clog dancing**

cloi·son·né (kloi′zə nā′) *adj.* [Fr., lit., partitioned] being a kind of enamel work in which enamel is set into hollows formed by thin strips of wire welded in a decorative pattern to a metal plate —*n.* cloisonné enamel

clois·ter (klois′tər) *n.* [< OFr. < L. *claustrum*, bolt, place shut in < pp. of *claudere*, CLOSE²] **1.** a place of religious isolation; monastery or convent **2.** monastic life **3.** any peaceful place where one may get away from people **4.** a covered walk along the inside walls of a monastery, convent, etc., with a columned opening along one side —*vt.* **1.** to isolate or confine as in a cloister **2.** to furnish with a cloister —**clois′-tered** *adj.* —**clois′tral** *adj.*

CLOISTER

clomb (klōm) *archaic pt. & pp. of* CLIMB

clomp (klämp) *vi.* to walk heavily or noisily; clump

☆**clone** (klōn) *n.* [< Gr. *klōn*, a twig] **1.** *Bot.* all the descendants derived asexually from a single individual by cuttings, bulbs, etc. **2.** an individual produced by cloning—**clon′al** *adj.*

☆**clon·ing** (klōn′iŋ) *n.* the technique of producing an exact duplicate of an individual organism by replacing the nucleus of an unfertilized ovum with the nucleus of a body cell from the organism

clonk (kläŋk) *n., vi., vt. same as* CLUNK

clo·nus (klō′nəs) *n.* [ModL. < Gr. *klonos*, turmoil] a series of spasms in which the muscles tighten

clop (kläp) *n.* [echoic] a sharp, clattering sound, like hoofbeats on a pavement —*vi.* **clopped, clop′ping** to make, or move with, such a sound

close¹ (klōs) *adj.* **clos′er, clos′est** [< OFr. *clos*, pp. of *clore*: see CLOSE²] **1.** shut; not open **2.** enclosed or enclosing **3.** confined or confining; narrow [*close* quarters] **4.** carefully guarded [in *close* custody] **5.** hidden; secluded **6.** secretive; not frank [he is *close* about his future plans] **7.** miserly; stingy [she is *close* with her money] **8.** restricted, as in membership **9.** warm and stuffy, as stale air **10.** not readily available [credit is *close*] **11.** with little space between; near together **12.** compact; dense [a *close* weave] **13.** fitting tightly [a *close* coat] **14.** *a)* down or near to the surface [a *close* shave] *b)* nearby [a *close* neighbor] **15.** very near in interests, affection, etc.; intimate [a *close* friend] **16.** very nearly like the original [a *close* translation] **17.** strict; thorough; careful [*close* attention] **18.** *a)* compactly expressed; concise [a *close* description] *b)* accurate; precise [*close* reasoning] **19.** nearly equal or alike [*close* in age] **20.** nearly even [a *close* contest] —*adv.* in a close manner —**close to the wind** *Naut.* heading as closely as possible in the direction from which the wind blows —**close′ly** *adv.* —**close′ness** *n.*

SYN.—**close** suggests something whose parts are near together with little space between [*close* formation]; **dense** suggests such a crowding together of parts as to form an almost solid mass [a *dense* fog]; **compact** suggests close and firm packing and usually implies neatness and order in the arrangement of parts [a *compact* bundle]; **thick**, in this synonymy, suggests a great number of parts formed into a tight mass [*thick* fur] —see also SYN. at STINGY —**ANT.** open, dispersed

close² (klōz) *vt.* **closed, clos′ing** [< OFr. < *clore* < L. *claudere*, to close < IE. base *kleu-*, a hook, close with a hook, from which also come L. *clavis*, key & LOT] **1.** to shut (a door, lid, etc.) **2.** to block up or stop (an opening, passage, etc.) **3.** to bring together; unite [*close* forces] **4.** to bring to an end; finish [they

closed discussion with a vote] **5.** to stop the operation of (a school, business, etc.) **6.** to complete or make final (a sale, agreement, etc.) —*vi.* **1.** to undergo shutting [the door *closes* quietly] **2.** to come to an end [the movie *closed* abruptly] **3.** to end or suspend operations [the store *closes* at noon]; specif., in the stock exchange, to show an indicated price level at day's end [steel *closed* high] **4.** to become joined together [the wound has *closed*] **5.** to come together [the ranks *closed*] **6.** to take hold [her hand *closed* on the package] **7.** to throng closely [his friends *closed* about him] **8.** to lessen the distance between [*closing* on the leading runner] **9.** to come close in order to fight —*n.* **1.** a closing or being closed **2.** the final part; end —**close down** ☆**1.** to shut or stop entirely ☆**2.** to settle down (on), as darkness or fog —**close in** to surround, cutting off escape —☆**close out** to sell out (goods), as in ending a business —**close up 1.** to draw nearer together **2.** to shut or stop up entirely **3.** to heal, as a wound does —**clos′er** *n.*

SYN.—**close** suggests a coming or bringing to a stop, as if by shutting something that can be open or has been open [nominations are now *closed*]; to **conclude** is to bring or come to a formal end, often by reaching an agreement [to *conclude* negotiations]; **finish** emphasizes the bringing to a desired end of that which one has set out to do, esp. by adding perfecting touches [to *finish* a painting]; **complete** may suggest a finishing by filling in the missing or needed parts [this volume will *complete* the set] or a finishing of some project [the scientist *completed* his experiment]; **end** and **terminate** both suggest the stopping of something going on or existing, whether or not it has been satisfactorily completed, or the setting or reaching of some limit [let's *end* this argument; the company *terminated* his contract] —**ANT.** begin, start, commence

close³ (klōs) *n.* [< OFr. *clos* < L. *clausum*, neut. pp. of *claudere*: see prec.] [Chiefly Brit.] **1.** an enclosed place **2.** enclosed grounds around or beside a building [a cathedral *close*] **3.** a narrow street or passageway

☆**close call** (klōs) [Colloq.] a narrow escape from danger: also **close shave**

closed (klōzd) *adj.* **1.** not open; shut [a *closed* door] **2.** covered over or enclosed [a *closed* wagon] **3.** functioning independently; not depending on outside help [a *closed* economic system] **4.** not open to new ideas, discussion, etc. [a *closed* mind] **5.** restricted to certain persons; exclusive [a *closed* meeting] **6.** *Math. a)* of a curve whose ends are joined *b)* of a surface whose plane sections are closed curves *c)* of a set in which an operation on pairs of its elements always produces an element of the set **7.** *Phonet.* ending in a consonant sound [a *closed* syllable]

closed chain the structural form of certain molecules, pictured as a ring of atoms

closed circuit a system for transmitting a telecast over cables to a limited number of television receivers connected to a circuit —**closed′-cir′cuit** *adj.*

☆**closed-end** (-end′) *adj.* of an investment company issuing a fixed number of shares traded on the open market

☆**closed primary** *see* DIRECT PRIMARY ELECTION

☆**closed shop** a factory, business, etc. operating under a contract with a labor union by which only members of the union may be employed

close·fist·ed (klōs′fis′tid) *adj.* stingy; miserly

close·fit·ting (-fit′iŋ) *adj.* fitting tightly, esp. so as to show the shape of the body

close·grained (-grānd′) *adj.* having a fine grain with the fibers, layers, etc. close together, as certain kinds of wood

close harmony (klōs) *Music* harmony in which the chords have all four tones within the range of an octave

close·hauled (-hôld′) *adj.* with the sails set for heading as nearly as possible into the wind

close·mouthed (-mouthd′, -moutht′) *adj.* not talking much; telling little: also **close′lipped′** (-lipt′)

close order an arrangement of troops in compact units at close intervals and distances

clos·et (kläz′it) *n.* [OFr., dim. of *clos*: see CLOSE³] **1.** a small room or cupboard for clothes, supplies, etc. **2.** a small, private room for reading, consultation, etc. **3.** *same as* WATER CLOSET —*adj.* private or secret —*vt.* to shut up in a private room for confidential discussion

closet drama drama written mainly to be read, not staged

☆**close-up** (klōs′up′) *n.* a photograph, or a movie or TV shot, made at very close range

clos·trid·i·um (kläs trid′ē əm, klōs-) *n., pl.* **-trid′i·a** (-ə) [ModL. < Gr. *klōstēr*, a spindle,

WIND

CLOSEHAULED

rod + ModL. *-idium*, dim. suffix] any of a group of rod-shaped bacteria: one kind causes tetanus

clo·sure (klō′zhər) *n.* [OFr. < L. *clausura* < pp. of *claudere*, CLOSE²] **1.** a closing or being closed **2.** a finish; end; conclusion **3.** anything that closes **4.** *same as* CLOTURE **5.** *Math.* the union of a set and all the points that limit a sequence of points of the given set —*vt.* **-sured, -sur·ing** *same as* CLOTURE

clot (klät) *n.* [OE. *clott:* for IE. base see CLAW] a soft, thickened area or lump formed on or within a liquid [a blood *clot*] —*vt., vi.* **clot′ted, clot′ting** to thicken or form into a clot or clots; coagulate

cloth (klôth, kläth) *n., pl.* **cloths** (klôthz, kläthz; *also* klôths, kläths *for "kinds of cloth"*) [OE. *clath*] **1.** a woven, knitted, or pressed fabric of fibrous material, as cotton, wool, silk, hair, synthetic fibers, etc. **2.** a piece of such fabric for a special use [*tablecloth, washcloth*] —*adj.* made of cloth —**the cloth 1.** a kind of clothing worn to show what one's profession is **2.** the clergy as a group

clothe (klōth) *vt.* **clothed** or **clad, cloth′ing** [OE. *clathian* < prec.] **1.** to put clothes on; dress **2.** to provide with clothes [*give money to *clothe* the poor*] **3.** to cover over as if with a garment [*hills *clothed* in snow*]

clothes (klōz, klōthz) *n.pl.* [OE. *clathas*, pl. of *clath*, CLOTH] **1.** articles, usually of cloth, to cover the body; apparel; garments; dresses, suits, etc. **2.** *same as* BEDCLOTHES

clothes·horse (-hôrs′) *n.* **1.** a frame on which to hang clothes, etc. for airing or drying **2.** [Slang] a person who pays too much attention to his clothes

clothes·line (-līn′) *n.* a rope or wire on which clothes, etc. are hung for airing or drying

clothes moth *see* MOTH

☆**clothes·pin** (-pin′) *n.* a small clip, as of wood or plastic, for fastening clothes on a line

clothes·press (-pres′) *n.* a closet, wardrobe, or chest in which to keep clothes

☆**clothes tree** an upright pole with branching hooks or pegs near the top to hold coats and hats

cloth·ier (klōth′yər, klō′thē ər) *n.* **1.** a person who makes or sells clothes **2.** a dealer in cloth

cloth·ing (klō′thiŋ) *n.* **1.** wearing apparel; clothes; garments **2.** a covering

Clo·tho (klō′thō) *Gr. & Rom. Myth.* that one of the three Fates, who spins the thread of human life

clo·ture (klō′chər) *n.* [Fr. < OFr. < ML. < L. *clausura:* see CLOSURE] a way of ending further debate or discussion about a matter in a legislature so that it can be voted on —*vt.* **-tured, -tur·ing** to use cloture on (a debate, bill, etc.)

cloud (kloud) *n.* [OE. *clud*, mass of rock: for IE. base see CLAW] **1.** a mass of fine drops of water floating in the air above the earth **2.** a mass of smoke, dust, steam, etc. **3.** a great number of moving things close together [*a *cloud* of locusts*] **4.** a murkiness or dimness, as in a liquid **5.** a dark marking, as in marble **6.** anything that darkens, obscures, threatens, or makes gloomy [*he is under a *cloud* of suspicion*] —*vt.* **1.** to cover with clouds **2.** to make muddy or foggy **3.** to darken; obscure **4.** to make gloomy or troubled **5.** to sully (a reputation, etc.) —*vi.* **1.** to become cloudy **2.** to become gloomy or troubled [*her face *clouded* with worry*] —**in the clouds 1.** high up in the sky **2.** not practical; fanciful **3.** having a daydream —**under a cloud 1.** under suspicion of wrongdoing **2.** troubled; depressed

☆**cloud·burst** (-burst′) *n.* a sudden, very heavy rain

cloud chamber a closed chamber with much more water vapor inside than is normal so that one can see the movement of charged particles that ionize the vapor

cloud·less (-lis) *adj.* free from clouds; clear; bright —**cloud′-less·ly** *adv.* —**cloud′less·ness** *n.*

cloud·let (-lit) *n.* a small cloud

☆**cloud nine** [Slang] a state of great joy or bliss

cloud·y (-ē) *adj.* **cloud′i·er, cloud′i·est 1.** covered with clouds; overcast **2.** of or like clouds **3.** streaked, as marble **4.** opaque, muddy, or foggy [*a *cloudy* liquid*] **5.** not clear; obscure; vague [*cloudy* ideas] **6.** troubled; gloomy —**cloud′i·ly** *adv.* —**cloud′i·ness** *n.*

clout (klout) *n.* [OE. *clut:* for IE. base see CLAW] **1.** [Archaic] a piece of cloth **2.** a blow, as with the hand; rap ☆**3.** [Colloq.]

a) a long hit in baseball *b)* power or influence; esp., political power —*vt.* **1.** [Colloq.] to strike, as with the hand ☆**2.** [Slang] to hit (a ball) a far distance

clove¹ (klōv) *n.* [OFr. *clou* < L. *clavus*, nail: from its shape] **1.** the dried flower bud of a tropical evergreen tree of the myrtle family: it is used as a strong, fragrant spice **2.** the tree

clove² (klōv) *n.* [OE. *clufu*, akin to *cleofan*, CLEAVE¹] a section of a bulb, as of garlic

clove³ (klōv) *alt. pt. of* CLEAVE¹

clove hitch a kind of knot for fastening a rope around a pole, spar, etc.: see illustration at KNOT

clo·ven (klō′v′n) *alt. pp. of* CLEAVE¹ —*adj.* divided; split

cloven foot (or **hoof**) a foot divided by a hollow space, as in the ox, deer, and sheep: used as a symbol of the Devil, usually pictured with such hoofs —**clo′ven-foot′ed, clo′ven-hoofed′** *adj.*

clo·ver (klō′vər) *n.* [< OE. *clafre*] **1.** any of a group of low-growing plants of the legume family, with leaves of three leaflets and small flowers in dense heads **2.** any similar plant: see SWEET CLOVER —**in clover** living a pleasant, easy life

clo·ver·leaf (-lēf′) *n., pl.* **-leafs′** ☆a multiple highway interchange in the form of a four-leaf clover, which, by means of an overpass with curving ramps, permits traffic to move or turn in any of four directions with little interference —*adj.* in the shape of a leaf of clover

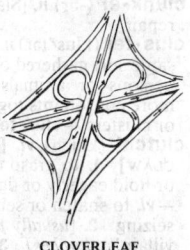

CLOVERLEAF

clown (kloun) *n.* [altered < ? Fr. *colon*, farmer < L. *colonus:* see COLONY] **1.** orig., a peasant; rustic **2.** a clumsy, rude person **3.** a performer who entertains, as in a circus, by doing comical tricks and silly stunts **4.** a person who plays the fool; buffoon —*vi.* **1.** to perform as a clown **2.** to play practical jokes, act silly, etc. —**clown′er·y** *n.* —**clown′ish** *adj.* —**clown′ish·ly** *adv.* —**clown′ish·ness** *n.*

cloy (kloi) *vt., vi.* [< OFr. *encloyer*, to fasten with a nail, hinder < *clou:* see CLOVE¹] to make weary or displeased by too much of something, esp. something sweet, rich, etc. —see SYN. at SATIATE —**cloy′ing·ly** *adv.*

club (klub) *n.* [< ON. *klumba*, mass of something, CLUMP] **1.** *a)* a heavy stick, usually thinner at one end, used as a weapon *b)* anything used to threaten **2.** any stick or bat used to strike a ball in a game [*a golf *club*] **3.** *same as* INDIAN CLUB **4.** a group of people who have come together for some special purpose [*a social *club*] **5.** the room, building, etc. used by such a group **6.** *same as* NIGHTCLUB **7.** *a)* [*pl.*] a suit of playing cards marked with a black cloverleaf figure (♣) *b)* a card of this suit —*vt.* **clubbed, club′bing 1.** to strike as with a club or with the butt of a rifle, etc. **2.** to unite for a common purpose **3.** to pool (resources, etc.) —*vi.* to unite or combine for a common purpose

☆**club car** a railroad lounge car, usually with a bar

club·foot (-foot′) *n.* **1.** a twisted or clublike deformity of the foot, caused by faulty development of the fetus before birth; talipes **2.** *pl.* **-feet′** a foot so deformed —**club′foot′ed** *adj.*

club·house (-hous′) *n.* **1.** a building occupied by a club ☆**2.** a locker room for an athletic team

club·man (-mən, -man′) *n., pl.* **-men** (-mən, -men′) a man who is a member of a private club or clubs, or spends much time there —**club′wom′an** *n.fem., pl.* **-wom′en**

club moss any of various flowerless plants, with small, scalelike leaves, a mosslike appearance, and club-shaped cones containing spores

☆**club sandwich** a sandwich of several layers, often toasted, containing chicken, bacon, lettuce, etc.

club soda *same as* SODA WATER

☆**club steak** a small beefsteak cut from the loin tip

cluck (kluk) *vi.* [< OE. *cloccian:* orig. echoic] to make a low, sharp, clicking sound, as of a hen calling her chickens —*vt.* to utter with such a sound —*n.* **1.** the sound of clucking ☆**2.** [Slang] a dull, stupid person; dolt

clue (klōō) *n.* a clew; esp., a fact, object, etc. that helps solve a mystery or problem —*vt.* **clued, clu′ing 1.** to indicate by or as by a clue ☆**2.** [Colloq.] to provide with necessary information (often with *in*)

Cluj (klōozh) city in northwestern Romania: pop. 203,000

clum·ber (**spaniel**) (klum'bər) [<*Clumber*, estate of the Duke of Newcastle] [*also* **C-**] a short-legged spaniel with a thick coat of straight, white hair marked with yellow or orange

clump (klump) *n.* [< Du. *klomp* or LowG. *klump:* for IE. base see CLAW] **1.** a lump; mass **2.** a cluster, as of trees **3.** the sound of heavy footsteps —*vi.* **1.** to tramp heavily **2.** to form clumps —*vt.* **1.** to group together in a cluster **2.** to cause to form clumps

clump·y (klum'pē) *adj.* clump'i·er, clump'i·est **1.** full of or like clumps **2.** heavy and clumsy: also **clump'ish**

clum·sy (klum'zē) *adj.* -si·er, -si·est [ME. *clumsid*, numb with cold < ON. base as in CLAM] **1.** lacking grace or skill; awkward [the *clumsy* boy dropped his fork] **2.** awkwardly shaped or made; ill-constructed [a *clumsy* shelter of old boards] **3.** crude; inelegant [a *clumsy* style] —**clum'si·ly** *adv.* —**clum'si·ness** *n.*

clung (kluŋ) *pt. & pp. of* CLING

clunk (kluŋk) *n.* [echoic] **1.** a dull, metallic sound **2.** [Colloq.] a heavy blow **3.** [Slang] a dull or stupid person —*vi., vt.* to move or strike with a clunk or clunks

clunk·er (-ər) *n.* [Slang] an old machine or automobile in poor repair

clus·ter (klus'tər) *n.* [OE. *clyster*] **1.** a number of things of the same sort gathered or growing together; bunch **2.** a number of persons or animals grouped together **3.** *Linguistics* two or more consonants together —*vi., vt.* to gather or grow in a cluster or clusters —**clus'ter·y** *adj.*

clutch[1] (kluch) *vt.* [OE. *clyccan*, to clench: for IE. base see CLAW] **1.** to grasp or snatch with a hand or claw **2.** to grasp or hold eagerly or tightly [the child *clutched* his mother's sleeve] —*vi.* to snatch or seize (*at*) *n.* **1.** a claw or hand in the act of seizing **2.** [*usually pl.*] power; control [the heroine was in the villain's *clutches*] **3.** *a*) a clutching *b*) a grasp; grip **4.** *a*) a mechanical device, as in an automobile, for putting the motor into or out of gear *b*) the lever or pedal that operates this **5.** a device for gripping **6.** a woman's small handbag with no handle or strap: also **clutch bag** ☆**7.** [Colloq.] an emergency [dependable in the *clutch*]

clutch[2] (kluch) *n.* [< ME. *clekken* (< ON. *klekja*), to hatch] **1.** a nest of eggs **2.** a brood of chicks **3.** a cluster of persons, animals, or things

clut·ter (klut'ər) *n.* [< CLOT] **1.** a number of things scattered in confusion or disorder; jumble **2.** *dial. var. of* CLATTER **3.** the traces on a radarscope caused by hills, buildings, etc. —*vt.* to make confused or untidy; jumble (often with *up*) —*vi.* [Dial.] to make a clatter —**clut'ter·y** *adj.*

Clyde (klīd) [< ?] **1.** a masculine name **2.** river in S Scotland, flowing, through an estuary (**Firth of Clyde**), into the North Channel

Clydes·dale (klīdz'dāl') *n.* [orig. from *Clydesdale*, Scotland] any of a breed of strong draft horse

clyp·e·ate (klip'ē it, -āt') *adj.* [< L. < *clypeus*, a shield] *Biol.* **1.** shaped like a round shield **2.** having a shieldlike part that sticks out Also **clyp'e·at'ed**

clys·ter (klis'tər) *n.* [< L. < Gr. *klystēr* < *klyzein*, to wash] same *as* ENEMA

Cly·tem·nes·tra, Cly·taem·nes·tra (klīt'əm nes'trə) *Gr. Myth.* the wife of Agamemnon: see ELECTRA

Cm *Chem.* curium

cm, cm. centimeter; centimeters

cmdg. commanding

Cmdr. Commander

cml. commercial

Cnos·sus (näs'əs) ancient city in N Crete: center of ancient Minoan civilization

☆**C-note** (sē'nōt') *n.* [for CENTURY-note] [Slang] a one-hundred-dollar bill

co- **1.** *a prefix shortened from* COM- *meaning: a*) together with [*cooperation*] *b*) joint [*co-owner*] *c*) equally [*coextensive*] **2.** *a prefix meaning* complement of [*cosine*]

Co *Chem.* cobalt

CO Colorado

Co., co. *pl.* **Cos., cos.** **1.** company **2.** county

C/O, co. **1.** care of **2.** carried over

CLYDESDALE

C.O., CO **1.** Commanding Officer **2.** conscientious objector

coach (kōch) *n.* [< Fr. < G. < Hung. *kocsi* (*szekér*), (carriage of) Kócs, village in Hungary] **1.** a large, covered, four-wheeled carriage with an open, raised seat in front for the driver; stagecoach ☆**2.** a railroad passenger car with the lowest-priced seats **3.** the lowest-priced class of seats on some airlines **4.** a bus **5.** an enclosed automobile, usually a two-door sedan **6.** a private tutor who prepares a student as for an examination **7.** an instructor or trainer, as of athletes, singers, etc. **8.** *Sports* a person in charge of a team or of some aspect of team play or practice —*vt.* **1.** to instruct by private tutoring **2.** to instruct and train (athletes, actors, etc.) —*vi.* to act as a coach

coach dog same *as* DALMATIAN

coach·man (kōch'mən) *n., pl.* **-men** the driver of a coach or carriage

co·ad·ju·tor (kō aj'ə tər; *also, and for 2 usually,* kō'ə jōot'ər) *n.* [< OFr. < L. < *co-*, together + *adjuvare*, to help] **1.** an assistant; helper **2.** a bishop appointed to assist a bishop

co·ag·u·la·ble (kō ag'yoo lə b'l) *adj.* that can be coagulated —**co·ag'u·la·bil'i·ty** *n.*

co·ag·u·late (kō ag'yoo lāt') *vt.* **-lat'ed, -lat'ing** [< L. pp. of *coagulare* < *coagulum*, coagulating agent < *cogere*, to curdle: see COGENT] to cause (a liquid) to become a soft, semisolid mass; curdle; clot —*vi.* to become coagulated —**co·ag'u·lant** *n.* —**co·ag'u·la'tion** *n.* —**co·ag'u·la'tive** *adj.* —**co·ag'u·la'tor** *n.*

coal (kōl) *n.* [OE. *col*, a live coal, charcoal] **1.** a black, burnable, mineral solid resulting from the partial breaking down of vegetable matter away from air and under high heat and great pressure over millions of years: used as a fuel and to produce coke and many coal-tar compounds **2.** a piece of this substance, or a number of pieces **3.** an ember **4.** charcoal —*vt.* to provide with coal —*vi.* to take in a supply of coal —**haul** (or **rake, drag, call**) **over the coals** to criticize sharply; censure — **heap coals of fire on** (**someone's**) **head** to cause (someone) to feel guilt by returning good for his evil —**coal'y** *adj.*

coal·er (-ər) *n.* a ship, railroad freight car (also ☆**coal car**), etc. that transports or supplies coal

co·a·lesce (kō'ə les') *vi.* **-lesced', -lesc'ing** [< L. *coalescere* < *co-*, together + *alescere*, to grow up] **1.** to grow together **2.** to unite or merge into a single body, group, or mass —**co'a·les'cence** *n.* —**co'a·les'cent** *adj.*

coal gas **1.** a gas formed from the vapors given off when soft coal is burned: used for lighting and heating **2.** a poisonous gas given off by burning coal

co·a·li·tion (kō'ə lish'ən) *n.* [< ML. < LL., orig. pp. of *coalescere:* see COALESCE] **1.** a combination; union **2.** a temporary alliance of political parties, nations, etc. for some specific purpose —see SYN. at ALLIANCE —**co'a·li'tion·ist** *n.*

coal measures coal beds or strata

☆**coal oil** **1.** kerosene **2.** crude petroleum

coal tar a black, thick liquid formed from the vapors given off when soft coal is burned: many synthetic compounds have been developed from it, including dyes, medicines, explosives, and perfumes

coam·ing (kō'miŋ) *n.* [< ?] a raised border around a hatchway, etc. to keep out water

coarse (kôrs) *adj.* [var. of COURSE in sense of "ordinary or usual order," as in *of course*] **1.** of inferior or poor quality; common [food of a *coarse* kind] **2.** consisting of rather large particles [*coarse* sand] **3.** not fine in texture, form, etc.; rough [*coarse* cloth] **4.** for rough work or results [a *coarse* file] **5.** not refined; crude; vulgar; offensive [a *coarse* joke] —**coarse'ly** *adv.* —**coarse'ness** *n.*

SYN.—**coarse**, in this synonymy, implies being so crude in manners or speech as to be offensive to good taste or one's moral sense [*coarse* laughter]; **gross** suggests being very crude or rough [*gross* table manners]; **indelicate** suggests being almost improper or immodest [an *indelicate* remark]; **vulgar** emphasizes a lack of proper training, culture, or good taste [*vulgar* decorations]; **obscene** is used of that which seems indecent or immodest and lewd [*obscene* gestures]; **ribald** suggests such mild indecency or lewdness as might make those laugh who enjoy lusty humor [*ribald* jokes] —**ANT. refined**

coarse-grained (-grānd') *adj.* **1.** having a coarse texture **2.** not delicate or refined; crude

coars·en (kôrs''n) *vt., vi.* to make or become coarse

coast (kōst) *n.* [< OFr. < L. *costa*, a rib, side] **1.** land alongside the sea; seashore ☆**2.** [< CanadFr., hillside, slope] a hill down which a slide is taken ☆**3.** a slide or ride downhill, as on a sled —*vi.* **1.** to sail near or along a coast ☆**2.** to go down a hill on a sled ☆**3.** to continue to move along even after the driving power has stopped [the car ran out of gas and *coasted* to a stop] ☆**4.** to let one's past efforts carry one along —*vt.* to sail along or near the coast of —**the Coast** ☆[Colloq.] in the U.S., the Pacific coast —**the coast is clear** there is nothing or no one to stop or hinder one

coast·al (-'l) *adj.* of, at, near, or along a coast

coast·er (kōs'tər) *n.* **1.** a person or thing that coasts **2.** a ship that travels from port to port along a coast ☆**3.** a sled or wagon for coasting **4.** a small tray, mat, disk, etc. placed under a glass or bottle to protect a table or other surface

☆**coaster brake** a brake in the hub of the rear wheel of a bicycle, worked by pressing backward on the pedals: it also permits free coasting

coast guard 1. a group of people employed by the government to defend a nation's coasts, prevent smuggling, aid vessels in distress, etc.; specif., [C- G-] such a branch of the U.S. armed forces, normally under the control of the Department of Transportation **2.** a member of a coast guard —**coast guards'man, coast guard'man,** *pl.* **-men**

coast·land (kōst'land') *n.* land along a coast

coast·line (-līn') *n.* the outline of a coast

Coast Ranges series of mountain ranges along the W coast of N. America, extending from Alas. to Baja California

coast·ward (-wərd) *adj., adv.* toward the coast: also **coast'-wards** *adv.*

coast·wise (-wīz') *adv., adj.* along the coast: also **coast'ways'** (-wāz') *adv.*

coat (kōt) *n.* [< OFr. < ML. *cot(t)a*, a tunic < Frank. *kotta*, coarse cloth] **1.** an outer garment with sleeves, that opens down the front, as a suit jacket or an overcoat **2.** the natural covering of an animal, as of skin, fur, wool, etc. **3.** any outer covering, as of a plant **4.** a layer of some substance, as paint, over a surface —*vt.* to provide or cover with a coat or layer of something *[the street is coated with ice]* —**coat'ed** *adj.* —**coat'less** *adj.*

co·a·ti (kō ät'ē) *n., pl.* **-tis** [Tupi < *cua*, a cincture + *tim*, the nose] a small, flesh-eating mammal that lives in trees in Mexico and Central and South America, like the raccoon but with a long snout Also **co·a·ti·mun·di** (-mun'dē)

coat·ing (kōt'iŋ) *n.* **1.** a coat or layer over a surface **2.** cloth for making coats

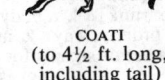

COATI
(to 4½ ft. long,
including tail)

coat of arms [after Fr. *cotte d'armes*, light garment worn over armor, and blazoned with one's heraldic arms] a group of emblems and figures (heraldic bearings) usually arranged on and around a shield to serve as the special mark of a family, etc.

coat of mail *pl.* **coats of mail** a suit of armor made of linked metal rings or overlapping plates

coat·tail (-tāl') *n.* the back part of a coat below the waist; esp., either half of this part when divided —☆**ride** (or **hang**, etc.) **on (someone's) coattails** to have one's own success depend on another's

co·au·thor (kō ô'thər) *n.* either of two authors working together

coax (kōks) *vt.* [< obs. slang *coax, cokes,* a fool] **1.** to persuade or urge by soothing words, flattery, etc.; wheedle **2.** to get by coaxing —*vi.* to use gentle persuasion, urging, etc. —**coax'er** *n.* —**coax'ing** *adj., n.* —**coax'ing·ly** *adv.*

co·ax·i·al (kō ak'sē əl) *adj.* [CO- + AXIAL] **1.** having a common axis: also **co·ax'al 2.** that is a compound loudspeaker consisting of a smaller unit mounted within a larger one and connected to it on a common axis ☆**3.** that is a high-frequency transmission cable or line for telephone, telegraph, television, etc.: its outer conductor tube surrounds an insulated central conductor

cob (käb) *n.* [prob. < LowG.] **1.** [Brit. Dial.] *a)* a lump *b)* a leader; chief ☆**2.** a corncob **3.** a male swan **4.** a short, stout horse

co·balt (kō'bôlt) *n.* [G. *kobalt* < *kobold,* goblin, demon of the mines] a hard, shiny, steel-gray metallic chemical element, used in alloys, inks, paints, etc.: symbol, Co; at. wt., 58.9332; at. no., 27: a radioactive isotope (**cobalt 60**) is used in the treatment of cancer, in research, etc. —**co·bal'tic** *adj.* —**co·bal'tous** *adj.*

cobalt blue 1. a dark blue coloring matter made from cobalt and aluminum oxides **2.** dark blue

cob·ble[1] (käb''l) *vt.* **-bled, -bling** [prob. akin to COB] **1.** to mend (shoes, etc.) **2.** to mend or put together clumsily or crudely

cob·ble[2] (käb''l) *n.* [prob. < COB] *same as* COBBLESTONE —*vt.* **-bled, -bling** to pave with cobblestones

☆**cob·bler**[1] (käb'lər) *n.* [of U.S. origin < ?] **1.** an iced drink of wine, whiskey, or rum, an orange or lemon slice, sugar, etc. **2.** a deep-dish fruit pie

cob·bler[2] (käb'lər) *n.* **1.** a person whose work is mending shoes **2.** [Archaic] a clumsy workman

cob·ble·stone (käb''l stōn') *n.* [COBBLE[2] + STONE] a rounded stone of a kind formerly much used for paving streets

cob coal coal in large, rounded lumps

co·bel·lig·er·ent (kō'bə lij'ər ənt) *n.* a nation associated but not formally allied with another or others in waging war

☆**co·bi·a** (kō'bē ə) *n.* [< ?] a large game fish of warm seas

co·bra (kō'brə) *n.* [< Port. *cobra (de capello),* serpent (of the hood)] a very poisonous snake of Asia and Africa: loose skin around the neck expands into a hood when the snake is excited

INDIAN COBRA
(to 6 ft. long)

cob·web (käb'web') *n.* [< ME. *coppe,* spider + WEB] **1.** a web spun by a spider **2.** a single thread of such a web **3.** anything that is thin or slight, or that traps like a spider's web —*vt.* **-webbed', -web'bing** to cover as with cobwebs —**cob'web'by** *adj.*

co·ca (kō'kə) *n.* [Quechuan *cuca*] **1.** any of certain S. American shrubs, esp. a species whose dried leaves are the source of cocaine and some other alkaloids **2.** these dried leaves

co·caine, co·cain (kō kān', kō'kān) *n.* [COCA + -INE[4]] a crystalline alkaloid, $C_{17}H_{21}NO_4$, obtained from dried coca leaves: it is a narcotic and local anesthetic

-coc·cal (käk''l) *a combining form meaning* of or produced by a (specified kind of) coccus *[staphylococcal]:* also **-coc'cic** (-sik)

coc·cus (käk'əs) *n., pl.* **coc·ci** (käk'sī) [ModL. < Gr. *kokkos,* a berry] a bacterium in the shape of a sphere: see illustration at BACTERIA —**coc'coid** (-oid) *adj.*

-coc·cus (käk'əs) *a combining form meaning* coccus: used in names of various bacteria *[gonococcus]*

coc·cyx (käk'siks) *n., pl.* **coc·cy·ges** (käk si'jēz) [L. < Gr. *kokkyx,* cuckoo: from its shape like a cuckoo's beak] a small, triangular bone at the lower end of the backbone —**coc·cyg'e·al** (-sij'ē əl) *adj.*

Co·chin (kō'chin', käch'in) *n.* [first bred in COCHIN CHINA] *[also* c-*]* a large domestic fowl with thickly feathered legs: also **Cochin China**

Cochin China, Cochin-China region & former Fr. colony in S Indochina: now part of South Vietnam

coch·i·neal (käch'ə nēl', käch'ə nēl') *n.* [< Fr. < It. < L. *coccinus,* scarlet-colored < *coccum,* a berry] a red dye made from the dried bodies of female cochineal insects: used, esp. formerly, in coloring foods and in cosmetics and as a dye

cochineal insect a scale insect having a brilliant red body fluid and feeding on cactus: it is found chiefly in Mexico and is a source of cochineal

coch·le·a (käk'lē ə) *n., pl.* **-le·ae'** (-ē'), **-le·as** [L. < Gr. *kochlias,* snail] the spiral-shaped part of the internal ear, containing the nerve endings for the sense of hearing: see illustration at EAR —**coch'le·ar** *adj.*

coch·le·ate (-it, -āt') *adj.* [< L.: see prec.] shaped like a snail shell: also **coch'le·at'ed**

cock[1] (käk) *n.* [OE. *coc*] **1.** *a)* the male of the chicken; rooster *b)* the male of certain other birds **2.** a weathercock **3.** a leader or chief **4.** a faucet or valve for regulating the flow of liquid or gas **5.** the hammer of a firearm, or the position of the hammer set for firing **6.** a jaunty, erect position *[the cock of a hat]* —*vt.* **1.** to tilt to one side; tilt *[he cocked his hat over his ear]* **2.** to raise up; erect *[a dog cocks his ears]* **3.** to turn (the eye or ear) toward something **4.** *a)* to set the hammer of (a gun) in firing position *b)* to set (a tripping device, as for a camera shutter) **5.** to draw back (one's fist, etc.) ready to strike —*vi.* to turn up or stick up

cock² (käk) *n.* [ME. *cokke:* for IE. base see COVE] a small, cone-shaped pile, as of hay —*vt.* to pile in cocks

cock·ade (kä kād′) *n.* [Fr. *cocarde* < *coq*, a cock] a rosette, knot of ribbon, etc. worn on the hat as a badge

☆**cock·a·ma·mie** (käk′ə mā′mē) *adj.* [alteration of DECAL-COMANIA] [Slang] of poor quality; inferior

cock-and-bull story (käk′'n bool′) [< Fr. *coq à l'âne*] an absurd, unlikely story

cock·a·teel, cock·a·tiel (käk′ə tēl′) *n.* [< Du. dim. of *kaketoe:* see COCKATOO] a small, crested, Australian parrot with a long tail and yellow head

cock·a·too (käk′ə tōō′, käk′ə tōō′) *n., pl.* **-toos′** [Du. *kaketoe* < Malay *kakatua;* prob. echoic] a crested parrot of Australia and the East Indies, with white plumage tinged with yellow or pink

cock·a·trice (käk′ə tris′) *n.* [< OFr. < L. *calcare*, to tread < *calx*, the heel] a legendary serpent supposedly hatched from a cock's egg and having power to kill by a look

cock·boat (käk′bōt′) *n.* [< ME. < *cok*, ship's boat + *bote*, BOAT] a small boat, esp. one used as a ship's tender

cock·chaf·er (käk′chāf′ər) *n.* [COCK¹ (? because of size) + CHAFER] a large European beetle whose grubs feed on the roots of plants

Cock·croft (kō′krôft, käk′rôft), Sir **John Douglas** 1897–1967; Eng. nuclear physicist

cock·crow (käk′krō′) *n.* the time when roosters begin to crow; dawn: also **cock′crow′ing**

cocked hat **1.** a three-cornered hat with a turned-up brim **2.** a peaked hat pointed in front and in back —**knock into a cocked hat** [Slang] to damage or spoil completely; ruin

cock·er·el (käk′ər əl, käk′rəl) *n.* [dim. of COCK¹] a young rooster, less than a year old

cock·er (spaniel) (käk′ər) [from its use in hunting woodcock] a small spaniel with a compact body, long, silky hair, and long, drooping ears

cock·eye (käk′ī′) *n.* [COCK¹, *vi.* + EYE] a squinting eye

cock·eyed (-īd′) *adj.* **1.** cross-eyed **2.** [Slang] *a)* tilted; crooked; awry *b)* silly; foolish *c)* drunk

cock·fight (-fīt′) *n.* a fight between gamecocks, usually wearing metal spurs —**cock′fight′ing** *n.*

cock·horse (-hôrs′) *n.* [16th c., toy horse] *same as* ROCKING HORSE or HOBBYHORSE (sense 1)

cock·le¹ (käk′'l) *n.* [< OFr. *coquille*, a shell < L. < Gr. < *konchē*, CONCH] **1.** a shellfish that is used for food and has two heart-shaped, hinged shells with ridges **2.** a cockleshell **3.** a wrinkle; pucker —*vi., vt.* **-led, -ling** to wrinkle; pucker —**cockles of one's heart** one's deepest feelings or emotions

cock·le² (käk′'l) *n.* [< OE. *coccel*, tares] any of various weeds that grow in grainfields

☆**cock·le·bur** (-bur′) *n.* a coarse plant of the composite family, bearing burs, that grows as a weed

cock·le·shell (-shel′) *n.* **1.** the shell of a cockle **2.** loosely, a scallop shell, etc. **3.** a small boat

cock·ney (käk′nē) *n., pl.* **-neys** [ME. *cokenei*, spoiled child; understood as *coken-ey*, lit., cock's egg; ? infl. by Fr. *acoquiné*, idle < *coquin*, rascal] [*often* C-] **1.** a native of the East End of London, England, speaking the dialect heard in that district **2.** this dialect [*in cockney*, the "h" sound is often dropped, so that "his" sounds like "is"]: also **cock′ney·ese′** (-ēz′) —*adj.* [*often* C-] of or like cockneys or their dialect —**cock′ney·ish** *adj.* —**cock′ney·ism** *n.*

cock of the walk the person who is the leader of a group, esp. one who is overbearing

cock·pit (käk′pit′) *n.* **1.** an enclosed space for cockfighting **2.** in small decked vessels, a sunken space toward the stern used by the steersman, etc. **3.** the space in a small airplane for the pilot and, sometimes, passengers, or in a large airplane for the pilot and copilot or crew

cock·roach (-rōch′) *n.* [Sp. *cucaracha*, altered after COCK¹ + ROACH²] an insect with long feelers, and a flat, soft body: a common pest in some kitchens, etc.

cocks·comb (käks′kōm′) *n.* **1.** the red, fleshy growth on the head of a rooster **2.** *same as* COXCOMB **3.** a plant related to the amaranth, with red or yellow flower heads

COCKATOO (12–20 in. long)

COCKROACH (to 1½ in. long)

cock·sure (käk′shoor′, -shur′) *adj.* [COCK¹ (see COCKY) + SURE] **1.** absolutely sure **2.** self-confident and overbearing —**cock′sure′ness** *n.*

cock·swain (käk′s′n, -swān′) *n. same as* COXSWAIN

cock·tail (-tāl′) *n.* [< ?] ☆**1.** an alcoholic drink, usually iced, made of a distilled liquor mixed with a wine, fruit juice, etc. ☆**2.** an appetizer, as fruit juice, diced fruits, or seafood

☆**cocktail table** a low table for serving refreshments, etc., esp. in a living room

cock·y (käk′ē) *adj.* **cock′i·er, cock′i·est** [COCK¹ + -Y²] [Colloq.] conceited; self-confident in a rude or bold way —**cock′i·ly** *adv.* —**cock′i·ness** *n.*

co·co (kō′kō) *n., pl.* **-cos** [Sp. & Port. < L. *coccum*, a seed < Gr. *kokkos*, a berry] **1.** *same as* COCONUT PALM **2.** its fruit; coconut —*adj.* made of the fiber from coconut husks

co·coa (kō′kō) *n.* [Sp. & Port. *cacao* < Nahuatl *cacauatl*] **1.** powder made from cacao seeds that have been roasted and ground **2.** a drink made by adding sugar and hot water or milk to this powder **3.** a reddish-yellow brown

cocoa butter a yellowish fat prepared from cacao seeds: used in pharmacy and in cosmetics

co·co·nut, co·coa·nut (kō′kə nut′) *n.* the large, round fruit of the coconut palm: inside its thick, brown husk and hard shell is a layer of white meat that can be eaten, and in the hollow center is a sweet, milky fluid called **coconut milk**

coconut oil oil obtained from the dried meat of coconuts, used for making soap, etc.

coconut palm (or **tree**) a tall palm tree that bears coconuts and grows in the tropics: also **coco palm**

co·coon (kə kōōn′) *n.* [< Fr. < Pr. *coucoun*, egg shell, ult. < ML. *coco*, shell] **1.** the silky case which the larvae of certain insects spin about themselves for shelter during the pupa stage **2.** any protective cover like this

cod (käd) *n., pl.* **cod, cods:** see PLURAL, II, D, 2 [ME.] an important food fish, with firm flesh, found in northern seas

C.O.D., c.o.d. cash (or collect) on delivery

Cod (käd), **Cape** peninsula in E Mass.

co·da (kō′də) *n.* [It. < L. *cauda*, a tail] *Music* a passage formally ending a composition or section

cod·dle (käd′'l) *vt.* **-dled, -dling** [prob. < CAUDLE] **1.** to cook (esp. eggs) gently in water not quite boiling **2.** to treat (an invalid, child, etc.) tenderly; pamper

code (kōd) *n.* [OFr. < L. *codex*, wooden tablet for writing, orig., tree trunk] **1.** a body of laws of a nation, city, etc. arranged in an orderly way **2.** any set of principles [*a moral code*] **3.** *a)* a set of signals for sending messages, as by telegraph, flags, etc. *b)* any set of signals, as that (**genetic code**) in the chromosomes determining the pattern of growth, etc. **4.** *a)* a system of symbols used in secret writing, in processing information, etc., in which letters, figures, etc. are given certain meanings *b)* the symbols used —*vt.* **cod′ed, cod′ing** to put in the form or symbols of a code —**cod′er** *n.*

co·de·fend·ant (kō′di fen′dənt) *n.* a person who is a defendant jointly with another

co·deine (kō′dēn, -dē in) *n.* [< Gr. *kōdeia*, poppy head + -INE⁴] an alkaloid gotten from opium and resembling morphine: used for relieving pain and in cough medicines: also **co′dein, co·de·ia** (kō dē′ə)

co·dex (kō′deks) *n., pl.* **co·di·ces** (kō′də sēz′, käd′ə-) [L.: see CODE] **1.** orig., a code, or body of laws **2.** a manuscript volume, esp. of the Scriptures or of a classic text

cod·fish (käd′fish′) *n., pl.* **-fish, -fish′es:** see FISH *same as* COD

codg·er (käj′ər) *n.* [prob. var. of CADGER] [Colloq.] an odd or queer fellow, esp. one who is old

cod·i·cil (käd′i s'l, -sil′) *n.* [< L. dim. of *codex:* see CODE] **1.** *Law* an addition to a will to change, revoke, or add sections **2.** an appendix or supplement —**cod′i·cil·la·ry** (-sil′ər ē) *adj.*

cod·i·fy (käd′ə fī′, kō′də-) *vt.* **-fied, -fy′ing** [see CODE & -FY] to arrange (laws, etc.) in an orderly way —**cod′i·fi·ca′tion** *n.* —**cod′i·fi′er** *n.*

cod·ling¹ (käd′liŋ) *n., pl.* **-ling, -lings:** see PLURAL, II, D, 2 a young cod

cod·ling² (käd′liŋ) *n.* [ult. < Fr. *coeur de lion*, lit., heart of lion] **1.** a variety of long, narrow apple **2.** a small, unripe apple Also **cod′lin** (-lin)

codling (or **codlin**) **moth** a small moth whose larva destroys apples, pears, quinces, etc.

cod-liv·er oil (käd′liv′ər) oil obtained from the liver of the cod and related fishes: it is rich in vitamins A and D

Co·dy (kō′dē), **William Frederick** 1846–1917; U.S. plainsman & showman: called *Buffalo Bill*

☆**co·ed, co-ed** (kō′ed′) *n.* [Colloq.] a girl attending a coeducational college or university —*adj.* [Colloq.] **1.** coeducational **2.** of a coed

☆**co·ed·u·ca·tion** (kō′ej ə kā′shən) *n.* [CO- + EDUCATION] the educational system in which students of both sexes attend classes together at a school or college —**co′ed·u·ca′tion·al** *adj.* —**co′ed·u·ca′tion·al·ly** *adv.*

co·ef·fi·cient (kō′ə fish′ənt) *n.* [CO- + EFFICIENT] **1.** a factor that contributes to produce a result **2.** *Math.* a number, symbol, etc. used as a multiplier [6 is a *coefficient* in 6*ab*] **3.** *Physics* a number, constant for a given substance, used as a multiplier in measuring the change in some property of the substance under given conditions [the *coefficient* of expansion]

coe·la·canth (sē′lə kanth′) *n.* [ModL. < Gr. *koilos* (see -COELE) + *akantha*, point] any of a group of primitive fishes that were possibly ancestors to land animals: there are only a few coelacanths alive today

-coele, -coel (sēl) [< Gr. *koilia*, body cavity < *koilos*, hollow; for IE. base see CAVE] *a combining form meaning* cavity, chamber of the body

coe·len·ter·ate (si len′tə rāt′, -tər it) *n.* [ult. < Gr. *koilos* (see prec.) + *enteron*, intestine] any of a large group of sea animals, as the hydroids, jellyfishes, corals, etc., which have a large central cavity with a single opening

coe·li·ac (sē′lē ak′) *adj. same as* CELIAC

coe·lom (sē′ləm) *n.* [< Gr. < *koilos*: see -COELE] the main body cavity of most higher animals, in which the visceral organs are found

coe·no- [< Gr. *koinos*, common] *a combining form meaning* common: also, before a vowel, **coen-**

coe·no·bite (sē′nə bīt′, sen′ə-) *n. same as* CENOBITE

co·e·qual (kō ē′kwəl) *adj., n.* equal —**co′e·qual′i·ty** (-i kwäl′ə tē) *n.* —**co·e′qual·ly** *adv.*

co·erce (kō urs′) *vt.* -**erced′**, -**erc′ing** [< OFr. < L. *coercere* < *co-*, together + *arcere*, to confine] **1.** to restrain or constrain by force; curb **2.** to force or compel into doing something [he was *coerced* by threats into helping them] **3.** to enforce —see SYN. at FORCE —**co·erc′er** *n.* —**co·er′ci·ble** *adj.* —**co·er′ci·bly** *adv.*

co·er·cion (kō ur′shən, -zhən) *n.* **1.** the act or power of coercing **2.** government by force

co·er·cive (-siv) *adj.* of coercion or tending to coerce —**co·er′cive·ly** *adv.* —**co·er′cive·ness** *n.*

co·e·val (kō ē′v'l) *adj.* [< LL. < L. *co-*, together + *aevum*, age + -AL] of the same age or period; contemporary —*n.* a contemporary —see SYN. at CONTEMPORARY —**co·e′val·ly** *adv.*

co·ex·ec·u·tor (kō′ig zek′yoo tər) *n.* a person acting as executor jointly with another

co·ex·ist (-ig zist′) *vi.* **1.** to exist together, at the same time, or in the same place **2.** to live together without hostility or conflict despite differences, as in political systems —**co′ex·ist′ence** *n.* —**co′ex·ist′ent** *adj.*

co·ex·tend (-ik stend′) *vt., vi.* to extend equally in space or time —**co′ex·ten′sion** *n.* —**co′ex·ten′sive** *adj.* —**co′ex·ten′sive·ly** *adv.*

C. of C. Chamber of Commerce

cof·fee (kôf′ē, käf′ē) *n.* see PLURAL, II, D, 3 [< It. *caffè* < Turk. *qahwe* < Ar. *qahwa*, coffee, orig., wine] **1.** a dark-brown, aromatic drink made by brewing in water the roasted and ground beanlike seeds of a tall tropical shrub of the madder family **2.** these seeds: also **coffee beans 3.** the shrub **4.** the color of coffee with milk or cream in it; brown

☆**coffee break** a brief rest from work when coffee or other refreshment may be taken

☆**cof·fee·cake** (-kāk′) *n.* a kind of cake or roll, often nut-filled, coated with icing, etc., to be eaten with coffee or the like

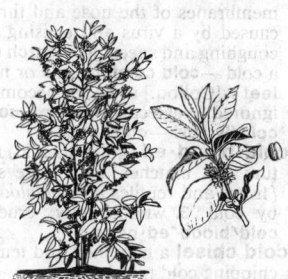

COFFEE
(plant, 5–10 ft. high;
branch; berry)

cof·fee·house (-hous′) *n.* a place where coffee and other refreshments are served and people gather for conversation, entertainment, etc.

☆**coffee klatch** (or **klatsch**) *same as* KAFFEEKLATSCH

coffee mill a machine for grinding roasted coffee beans

cof·fee·pot (-pät′) *n.* a container with a lid and spout, for making and serving coffee

coffee shop an informal restaurant, as in a hotel, where light refreshments or meals are served

☆**coffee table** a low table, usually in a living room, for serving refreshments

cof·fer (kôf′ər, käf′-) *n.* [< OFr. < L. *cophinus*: see COFFIN] **1.** a chest or strongbox for keeping valuables **2.** [*pl.*] a treasury; funds [he emptied his *coffers* to pay his taxes] **3.** a decorative sunken panel in a vault, dome, etc. **4.** a cofferdam **5.** a lock in a canal —*vt.* **1.** to enclose in a coffer **2.** to furnish with coffers (*n.* 3)

cof·fer·dam (-dam′) *n.* [prec. + DAM¹] **1.** a watertight temporary structure in a river, lake, etc. to keep the water from an enclosed area that has been pumped dry so that dams, etc. may be constructed **2.** a watertight box attached to the side of a ship so that repairs can be made below the waterline

cof·fin (kôf′in, käf′-) *n.* [< OFr. < L. *cophinus* < Gr. *kophinos*, basket] the case or box in which a dead body is buried

☆**coffin nail** [Old Slang] a cigarette

cog¹ (käg) *n.* [< Scand.] **1.** *a)* any of a series of teeth on the rim of a wheel, for passing on or receiving motion by fitting between the teeth of another wheel; gear tooth *b)* a cogwheel ☆**2.** [Colloq.] a person thought of as one small part in the working of a business, etc. —**cogged** *adj.*

cog² (käg) *n.* [altered (after prec.) < earlier *cock*, to secure] a part that sticks out from a beam so as to fit into a matching groove or notch in another beam, making a joint —*vt., vi.* **cogged**, **cog′ging** to join by a cog or cogs

co·gent (kō′jənt) *adj.* [< L. prp. of *cogere*, to collect < *co-*, together + *agere*, to drive] forceful and to the point, as a reason or argument; compelling —**co′gen·cy** *n.* —**co′gent·ly** *adv.*

cog·i·tate (käj′ə tāt′) *vi., vt.* -**tat′ed**, -**tat′ing** [< L. pp. of *cogitare*, to ponder] to think seriously and deeply (about); ponder; consider —see SYN. at THINK¹ —**cog′i·ta·ble** *adj.* —**cog′i·ta′tion** *n.* —**cog′i·ta′tor** *n.*

co·gnac (kōn′yak, kän′-, kôn′-) *n.* [Fr.] **1.** a French brandy distilled from wine near Cognac, France **2.** loosely, any brandy

cog·nate (käg′nāt) *adj.* [L. *cognatus* < *co-*, together + pp. of (g)*nasci*, to be born: for IE. base see GENUS] **1.** related by family **2.** coming from a common original form [French and Italian are *cognate* languages] **3.** having the same nature or quality —*n.* **1.** a person related to another through common ancestry **2.** a cognate word, language, or thing —**cog·na′tion** *n.*

cog·ni·tion (käg nish′ən) *n.* [L. *cognitio*, knowledge < pp. of *cognoscere* < *co-*, together + (g)*noscere*, KNOW] **1.** the process of knowing in the broadest sense, including perception, memory, judgment, etc. **2.** the result of such a process; perception, etc. —**cog·ni′tion·al** *adj.* —**cog′ni·tive** *adj.*

cog·ni·za·ble (käg′ni zə b'l, käg niz′-; *occas.* kän′ə-) *adj.* **1.** that can be known or perceived **2.** *Law* within the jurisdiction of a court

cog·ni·zance (käg′nə zəns, kän′ə-) *n.* [< OFr. *conoissance*, knowledge < L. *cognoscere*: see COGNITION] **1.** the fact of being aware or knowing; perception; knowledge **2.** official observation **3.** *Heraldry* a distinguishing crest or mark **4.** *Law a)* a court hearing *b)* the right or power of dealing with a matter judicially —**take cognizance of** to notice or recognize

cog·ni·zant (-zənt) *adj.* having cognizance; aware or informed (*of* something) —see SYN. at AWARE

cog·no·men (käg nō′mən) *n., pl.* -**no′mens**, -**nom′i·na** (-näm′i nə) [L. < *co-*, with + *nomen*, NAME] **1.** the third or family name of an ancient Roman **2.** any family name; surname **3.** any name; esp., a nickname —**cog·nom′i·nal** (-näm′i n'l) *adj.*

cog·no·vit (käg nō′vit) *n.* [< L. *cognovit actionem*, lit., he has acknowledged the action] a legal paper, esp. a note (**cognovit note**) signed by a debtor that permits any attorney to collect the debt without a formal trial

cog·wheel (käg′hwēl′) *n.* a wheel with a rim notched into teeth which mesh with those of another wheel or of a rack to pass on or receive motion

COGWHEELS

co·hab·it (kō hab′it) *vi.* [< LL. < L. *co-*, together + *habitare*, to dwell] 1. to live together as husband and wife, esp. when not legally married 2. [Archaic] to live together —**co·hab′it·ant** *n.* —**co·hab′i·ta′tion** *n.*

co·heir (kō′er′) *n.* a person who inherits jointly with another or others —**co′heir′ess** *n.fem.*

co·here (kō hir′) *vi.* -hered′, -her′ing [< L. < *co-*, together + *haerere*, to stick] 1. to stick together, as parts of a mass 2. to be connected naturally or logically [the ideas in his article do not *cohere*] 3. to be in accord [his account *coheres* with hers]

co·her·ence (kō hir′əns) *n.* 1. the condition of cohering 2. the quality of being logically consistent and intelligible [his story lacked *coherence*] 3. *Physics* the mutual relationship between sets of waves in which their amplitudes are identical and rise and fall together Also, for senses 1 & 2, **co·her′en·cy**

co·her·ent (-ənt) *adj.* 1. sticking together; having cohesion 2. having all parts connected in a way that makes sense; consistent [the old man's rambling stories were not *coherent*] 3. able to think, speak, etc. in a way that makes sense 4. *Physics* exhibiting coherence —**co·her′ent·ly** *adv.*

co·he·sion (kō hē′zhən) *n.* 1. the act or condition of cohering; tendency to stick together 2. *Bot.* the union of flower parts that are alike 3. *Physics* the force by which the molecules of a substance are held together: distinguished from ADHESION —**co·he′sive** (-hēs′iv) *adj.* —**co·he′sive·ly** *adv.* —**co·he′sive·ness** *n.*

co·ho (kō′hō) *n., pl.* -ho, -hos: see PLURAL, II, D, 2 [< ?] a small Pacific salmon, now a freshwater game fish in the northern U.S.: also **coho salmon**

co·hort (kō′hôrt) *n.* [< L. *cohors*, enclosure, crowd] 1. an ancient Roman military unit of 300–600 men, one tenth of a legion 2. a band of soldiers 3. any group or band 4. an associate, colleague, or supporter

coif (koif; *for n. 2 & vt. 2, usually* kwäf) *n.* [< OFr. < LL. *cofea*, a cap, hood] 1. a cap that fits the head closely, as that once worn under a hood of mail 2. [< COIFFURE] a style of arranging the hair —*vt.* **coifed, coif′ing**; also, and for 2 usually, **coiffed, coif′fing** 1. to cover as with a coif 2. *a)* to style (the hair) *b)* to give a coiffure to

coif·feur (kwä fur′; *Fr.* kwȧ fër′) *n.* [Fr. < *coiffer*, to dress the hair < prec.] a male hairdresser

coif·fure (kwä fyoor′, -fyur′; *Fr.* kwȧ für′) *n.* [Fr. < *coiffe*, COIF] 1. a headdress 2. a style of arranging the hair —*vt.* **-fured′, -fur′ing** to coif (sense 2)

coign of vantage (koin) [archaic var. of *coin* (QUOIN)] a good position from which to see or do something

coil (koil) *vt.* [< OFr. < L. *colligere*: see COLLECT²] to wind or gather (rope, etc.) into a circular or spiral form —*vi.* 1. to wind around and around [vines *coiled* around the tree] 2. to move in a winding course [smoke *coiled* from the chimney] —*n.* 1. anything wound into a series of rings or a spiral 2. such a series of rings or a spiral 3. a single turn of a coiled figure 4. a series of connected pipes in rows or coils 5. *Elec.* a spiral of wire, etc. used as an inductor, resistor, heating element, etc.

coin (koin) *n.* [< OFr. < L. *cuneus*, a wedge] 1. *archaic var. of* QUOIN 2. *a)* a piece of metal with a distinctive stamp, issued by a government as money *b)* money made of metal; coins 3. [Slang] money —*vt.* 1. *a)* to make (coins) by stamping metal *b)* to make (metal) into coins 2. to invent (a new word or phrase) —*vi.* to make coins —**coin money** [Colloq.] to earn money rapidly —**coin′er** *n.*

coin·age (koi′nij) *n.* 1. the act or process of coining 2. metal money 3. a system of metal currency 4. an invented word or expression [*laser* is a recent *coinage*]

co·in·cide (kō′in sīd′) *vi.* -cid′ed, -cid′ing [< Fr. < ML. < L. *co-*, together + *incidere*, to fall upon: see INCIDENT] 1. to take up the same place in space 2. to occur at the same time [our birthdays *coincide*] 3. to hold equivalent positions, as on a scale 4. to be the same; correspond exactly [our interests *coincide*] 5. to be in accord; agree —see SYN. at AGREE

co·in·ci·dence (kō in′sə dəns) *n.* 1. the fact or condition of coinciding 2. an accidental and remarkable occurrence of events, ideas, etc. at the same time, without one seeming to cause the other

co·in·ci·dent (-dənt) *adj.* 1. occurring at the same time 2. in the same position in space at the same time 3. in agree-

ment; identical [desire *coincident* with need] —**co·in′ci·dent·ly** *adv.*

co·in·ci·den·tal (kō in′sə den′t'l) *adj.* being a coincidence; happening by accident [our meeting was purely *coincidental*] —**co·in′ci·den′tal·ly** *adv.*

coir (koir) *n.* [< Port., ult. < Tamil *kayaru*, to be twisted] the prepared fiber of the husks of coconuts, used to make rope, etc.

co·i·tus (kō′it əs, kō ēt′əs) *n.* [L. < *co-*, together + *ire*, to go] sexual intercourse: also **co·i·tion** (kō ish′ən) —**co′i·tal** *adj.*

coke¹ (kōk) *n.* [< ME. *colke*, core, charcoal] coal from which most of the gases have been removed by heating: it burns with intense heat and little smoke, and is used as an industrial fuel —*vt., vi.* **coked, cok′ing** to change into coke

☆**coke²** (kōk) *n.* [short for COCAINE] [Slang] cocaine

coke oven an oven in which coke is made

col (käl) *n.* [Fr. < L. *collum*, the neck] 1. a gap between mountain peaks 2. a low-pressure area between two anticyclones

col- *see* COM-

Col. 1. Colombia 2. Colonel 3. Colossians

col. 1. collected 2. collector 3. college 4. colony 5. color(ed) 6. column

co·la (kō′lə) *n.* [< WAfr. name] 1. an African tree whose nuts yield an extract with caffeine, used in soft drinks and medicine 2. a sweet, carbonated soft drink flavored with this extract

col·an·der (kul′ən dər, käl′-) *n.* [prob. ult. < L. *colare*, to strain < *colum*, strainer] a pan with many small holes in the bottom to drain off liquids, as in washing vegetables

COLANDER

col·chi·cine (käl′chə sēn′, -ki sin) *n.* [< COLCHICUM + -INE⁴] a poisonous alkaloid, $C_{22}H_{25}O_6N$, extracted from colchicum, used to treat gout and to produce chromosome doubling in plants for greater growth and fertile hybrids

col·chi·cum (-kəm) *n.* [L. < Gr. *kolchikon*, plant with a poisonous root] 1. a plant of the lily family, with crocuslike flowers usually blooming in the fall 2. its dried seeds or corm

Col·chis (käl′kis) ancient country south of the Caucasus Mountains, on the Black Sea, in what is now the Georgian S.S.R.

cold (kōld) *adj.* [OE. *cald*; for IE. base see COOL] 1. of a temperature much lower than that of the human body; very chilly; frigid [cold weather] 2. without the proper heat or warmth [this soup is *cold*] 3. dead 4. feeling chilled [if you are *cold*, put on your coat] 5. without warmth of feeling; not cordial; unfriendly [a *cold* personality] 6. not easily aroused sexually 7. depressing or saddening [the *cold* truth] 8. not involving one's feelings; detached [*cold* logic] 9. designating or having colors that suggest cold, as tones of blue, green, or gray 10. still far from what one is trying to discover [guess again, you are *cold*] 11. faint or stale [a *cold* scent] 12. [Colloq.] with little or no preparation [to enter a game *cold*] ☆13. [Slang] completely mastered [the actor had his lines down *cold*] ☆14. [Slang] unconscious [knocked *cold*] —*adv.* wholly; completely [*cold* sober] —*n.* 1. *a)* absence of heat; lack of warmth [the intense *cold* of the arctic regions] *b)* a low temperature, esp. one below freezing 2. the sensation produced by a loss or absence of heat 3. cold weather 4. an illness in which the mucous membranes of the nose and throat are inflamed, thought to be caused by a virus and causing a discharge from the nose and coughing and sneezing —**catch (or take) cold** to become ill with a cold —**cold comfort** little or no comfort —**have (or get) cold feet** ☆[Colloq.] to be (or become) timid or fearful —**in the cold** ignored; neglected —**throw cold water on** to discourage —**cold′ly** *adv.* —**cold′ness** *n.*

cold·blood·ed (kōld′blud′id) *adj.* 1. having a body temperature that matches that of the surrounding air, land, or water [fishes and reptiles are *coldblooded* animals] 2. easily affected by cold 3. without pity; cruel —**cold′blood′ed·ly** *adv.* —**cold′blood′ed·ness** *n.*

cold chisel a hardened and tempered steel chisel for cutting or chipping cold metal

cold cream a creamy, soothing preparation for softening and cleansing the skin

cold cuts slices of cold meats and, often, cheeses

cold duck [transl. of G. *kalte ente* < ?] a drink made from equal parts of sparkling burgundy and champagne

cold frame an unheated, boxlike, glass-covered structure for protecting young plants

cold front *Meteorol.* the forward edge of a cold air mass advancing into a warmer air mass

cold·heart·ed (-här′tid) *adj.* lacking sympathy or kindness; unfeeling —**cold′heart′ed·ly** *adv.* —**cold′heart′ed·ness** *n.*

cold pack a process of canning foodstuffs in which the raw products are placed in jars first and then subjected to heat —**cold′-pack′** *vt.*

cold shoulder [Colloq.] deliberate indifference; slight or snub: often with *the* —**cold′-shoul′der** *vt.*

☆**cold snap** a sudden, brief spell of cold weather

cold sore *same as* HERPES SIMPLEX

☆**cold turkey** [Slang] **1.** the abrupt, total withdrawal of drugs from an addict **2.** in a frank, blunt way [to talk *cold turkey*] **3.** without preparation [take a test *cold turkey*]

cold war sharp conflict in diplomacy, economics, etc. between states, without actual warfare

☆**cold wave 1.** a period of weather colder than is normal **2.** a permanent wave in which the hair is set with a liquid preparation instead of heat

cole (kōl) *n.* [OE. *cal* < L. *caulis, colis,* a cabbage] any of various plants of the mustard family, to which cabbage belongs; esp., rape

co·le·op·ter·an (kō′lē äp′tər ən, käl′ē-) *n.* [< ModL. < Gr. < *koleos,* sheath + *pteron,* wing] any of a large group of insects, including beetles and weevils, with the front wings forming a horny covering for the membranous hind wings —**co′le·op′ter·ous** *adj.*

co·le·op·ter·on (kō′lē äp′tər än′, käl′ē-) *n., pl.* -**ter·a** (-ə) any coleopterous insect: also **co′le·op′ter·an** (-ən)

Cole·ridge (kōl′rij, -ər ij), **Samuel Taylor** 1772–1834; Eng. poet & critic

☆**cole·slaw** (kōl′slô′) *n.* [< Du. *kool,* cabbage (akin to COLE) + *sla,* for *salade,* salad] a salad made of shredded raw cabbage: also **cole slaw**

co·le·us (kō′lē əs) *n.* [ModL. < Gr. *koleos,* a sheath] a plant of the mint family, grown for its showy, bright-colored leaves

cole·wort (kōl′wurt′) *n.* [COLE + WORT²] any cabbage whose leaves do not form a compact head

col·ic (käl′ik) *n.* [< OFr. < L. < Gr. < *kolon,* colon] sharp pain in the bowels —**col′ick·y** *adj.*

co·li·form (kō′lə fôrm′, käl′ə-) *adj.* being or like the aerobic bacillus normally found in the colon: a coliform count is used to show whether fecal matter is present in a water supply

Co·lin (kō′lin, käl′in) [prob. < L. *columba,* a dove] a masculine name

col·i·se·um (käl′ə sē′əm) [see COLOSSEUM] [C-] *same as* COLOSSEUM —*n.* a large building or stadium for sports events, shows, etc.

co·li·tis (kō līt′is) *n.* [ModL. < Gr. *kolon,* colon + -ITIS] an illness in which the large intestine is inflamed

coll. 1. collect **2.** collection **3.** college

col·lab·o·rate (kə lab′ə rāt′) *vi.* -**rat′ed, -rat′ing** [< L. pp. of *collaborare* < *com-,* with + *laborare,* to work] **1.** to work together, esp. in some literary, artistic, or scientific undertaking **2.** to cooperate with an enemy invader —**col·lab′o·ra′tion** *n.* —**col·lab′o·ra′tive** *adj.* —**col·lab′o·ra′tor** *n.*

col·lab·o·ra·tion·ist (kə lab′ə rā′shən ist) *n.* a person who cooperates with an enemy invader

col·lage (kə läzh′) *n.* [Fr. < *colle,* paste < Gr. *kolla*] **1.** an art form in which bits of objects, as newspaper, cloth, leaves, etc., are pasted together on a surface **2.** a composition so made

col·la·gen (käl′ə jen) *n.* [< Gr. *kolla,* glue + -GEN] a fibrous protein found in connective tissue, bone, and cartilage —**col′la·gen′ic** *adj.*

col·lapse (kə laps′) *vi.* -**lapsed′, -laps′ing** [< L. pp. of *collabi* < *com-,* together + *labi,* to fall] **1.** to fall down or fall to pieces; cave in [hurricane winds made the houses *collapse*] **2.** to break down suddenly; fail; give way [her career *collapsed* because of the scandal] **3.** *a)* to break down suddenly in health *b)* to fall down, as from a blow or exhaustion *c)* to fold or drop severely, as in value, force, etc. [stock prices *collapsed*] **4.** to fold or come together compactly [a convertible automobile has a top that *collapses*] —*vt.* to cause to collapse —*n.* the act of collapsing; a falling in or together; failure or breakdown, as in business, health, etc. —**col·laps′i·bil′i·ty** *n.* —**col·laps′i·ble** *adj.*

col·lar (käl′ər) *n.* [< OFr. < L. < *collum,* the neck < IE. base *kwel-,* to turn, from which also comes WHEEL] **1.** the part of a garment that fits around the neck **2.** a cloth band attached to the neck of a garment **3.** a band of leather or metal for the neck of a dog, cat, etc. **4.** the part of the harness that fits over the neck of a horse **5.** a ring or flange, as on rods or pipes, to prevent sideward motion, connect parts, etc. **6.** a band of contrasting color, etc. on an animal's neck —*vt.* **1.** to put a collar on **2.** to seize, as by the collar [the police *collared* the thief]

col·lar·bone (-bōn′) *n.* a slender bone joining the breastbone to the shoulder blade; clavicle

col·lard (käl′ərd) *n.* [contr. < COLEWORT] a kind of kale whose coarse leaves are borne in tufts

collat. collateral

col·late (kä lāt′, kə-; käl′āt) *vt.* -**lat′ed, -lat′ing** [< L. *collatus,* pp. of *conferre* < *com-,* together + *ferre,* to BEAR] **1.** to compare (texts, data, etc.) in order to note how they are alike, different, etc. **2.** *a)* to gather (the sections of a book) together in proper order for binding *b)* to examine (such sections) to see that all pages are present and in proper order —**col·la′tor** *n.*

col·lat·er·al (kə lat′ər əl) *adj.* [< ML. *collateralis* < L. *com-,* together + *lateralis,* LATERAL] **1.** side by side; parallel **2.** that goes along with the main thing but in a less important way; additional or secondary [*collateral* evidence] **3.** having the same ancestors but in a different line [your cousins are your *collateral* relatives] **4.** *a)* designating or of security given as a pledge that something will be done *b)* secured by stocks, bonds, etc. [a *collateral* loan] —*n.* ☆stocks, bonds, or other property given as a pledge that a loan will be repaid —**col·lat′er·al·ly** *adv.*

col·la·tion (kä lā′shən, kə-) *n.* **1.** the act, process, or result of collating **2.** a light meal

col·league (käl′ēg) *n.* [< Fr. < L. *collega* < *com-,* with + *legare,* to appoint as deputy: see LEGATE] a fellow worker in the same profession or in the same office —see *SYN.* at ASSOCIATE

col·lect¹ (kə lekt′) *vt.* [< OFr. < L. *collectus:* see COLLECT²] **1.** to gather together; assemble **2.** to gather (stamps, books, etc.) for a hobby **3.** to call for and receive (money) for (rent, a fund, taxes, bills, etc.) **4.** to regain control of (oneself or one's wits) —*vi.* **1.** to gather; assemble [a crowd *collected*] **2.** to accumulate [water *collects* in the basement] **3.** to collect payments, etc. —*adj., adv.* ☆with payment to be made by the receiver [telephone her *collect*] —see *SYN.* at GATHER

col·lect² (käl′ekt) *n.* [< OFr., ult. < L. *collectus,* pp. of *colligere* < *com-,* together + *legere,* to gather: for IE. base see LOGIC] [*also* C-] a short prayer used in certain church services

col·lect·ed (kə lek′tid) *adj.* **1.** gathered together; assembled [the *collected* works of Poe] **2.** in control of oneself; calm —see *SYN.* at COOL —**col·lect′ed·ly** *adv.* —**col·lect′ed·ness** *n.*

col·lect·i·ble, col·lect·a·ble (-tə b'l) *adj.* **1.** that can be collected **2.** suitable for people to collect as a hobby —*n.* any of a class of old things that people collect as a hobby although they are not antiques and usually have little value otherwise

col·lec·tion (kə lek′shən) *n.* **1.** the act or process of collecting **2.** things collected [a *collection* of stamps] **3.** a mass or pile; accumulation **4.** money collected, as during a church service

col·lec·tive (kə lek′tiv) *adj.* **1.** formed by collecting; gathered into a whole **2.** of or as a group; of or by the individuals in a group acting together [the *collective* effort of the students] **3.** designating or of any enterprise in which people work together as a group, esp. under a system of collectivism [a *collective* farm] **4.** *Gram.* that is a noun which is singular in form but is the name for a collection of individuals (e.g., *army, crowd*): it is treated as singular when the collection is thought of as a whole and as plural when the individual members are thought of as acting separately —*n.* **1.** *a)* any collective enterprise; specif., a collective farm *b)* the people involved **2.** *Gram.* a collective noun —**col·lec′tive·ly** *adv.* —**col·lec·tiv·i·ty** (käl′ek tiv′ə tē, kə lek′-) *n.*

collective bargaining a bargaining between organized workers and their employer or employers concerning wages, hours, and working conditions

collective security a system of security in which a group of nations agree to take joint action against a nation that attacks any one of the group

col·lec·tiv·ism (kə lek′tə viz′m) *n.* the ownership and control of the means of production and distribution by all the people rather than by a few people —**col·lec′tiv·ist** *n., adj.* —**col·lec′-tiv·is·tic** *adj.*

col·lec·tiv·ize (-tə vīz′) *vt.* **-ized′, -iz′ing** to establish or organize under a system of collectivism —**col·lec′ti·vi·za′tion** *n.*

☆**collect on delivery** payment in cash when a purchase or shipment is delivered

col·lec·tor (kə lek′tər) *n.* a person or thing that collects; specif., *a*) a person whose work is collecting taxes, overdue bills, etc. *b*) a person who collects stamps, etc. as a hobby

Col·leen (käl′ēn, kə lēn′) [see next entry] a feminine name

col·leen (käl′ēn, kə lēn′) *n.* [< Ir., dim. of *caile*] [Irish] a girl

col·lege (käl′ij) *n.* [< OFr. < L. *collegium*, a society, guild < *collega*, COLLEAGUE] **1.** a group of persons having certain powers, duties, etc. [the electoral *college*] **2.** an institution of higher education that grants degrees; specif., *a*) any of the schools of a university granting degrees in any of certain courses of study, as in law or medicine *b*) the undergraduate division of a university, which offers a general four-year course leading to the bachelor's degree **3.** a school offering training in some occupation [a secretarial *college*] **4.** the buildings, students, faculty, or administrators of a college

College of Cardinals the cardinals of the Roman Catholic Church, serving as a privy council to the Pope and electing his successor

col·le·gi·al (kə lē′jē əl) *adj.* **1.** with authority shared equally among colleagues **2.** same as COLLEGIATE

col·le·gi·al·i·ty (kə lē′jē al′ə tē) *n.* **1.** the sharing of authority among colleagues **2.** *R.C.Ch.* the principle that authority is shared by the Pope and the bishops

col·le·gian (kə lē′jən) *n.* a college student

col·le·giate (-jət, -jē ət) *adj.* of or like a college or college students

collegiate church a church with a chapter of canons although it is not a bishop's see

col·lide (kə līd′) *vi.* **-lid′ed, -lid′ing** [L. *collidere* < *com-*, together + *laedere*, to strike] **1.** to come into violent contact; strike violently against each other; crash [the car *collided* with a train] **2.** to come into conflict; clash [our views *collide* on the subject]

col·lie (käl′ē) *n.* [< ? *coaly*, from black coat of earlier collies] a large, long-haired dog with a long, narrow head: first bred in Scotland to herd sheep

col·lier (käl′yər) *n.* [see COAL & -IER] [Chiefly Brit.] **1.** a coal miner **2.** a ship for carrying coal

col·lier·y (-ē) *n., pl.* **-lier·ies** [Chiefly Brit.] a coal mine and its buildings, equipment, etc.

col·li·mate (käl′ə māt′) *vt.* **-mat′ed, -mat′ing** [< false reading of L. *collineare* < *com-*, with + *lineare*, to make straight < *linea*, a line] **1.** to make (light rays, etc.) parallel **2.** to adjust the line of sight of (a telescope, etc.) —**col′li·ma′tion** *n.*

col·li·ma·tor (-māt′ər) *n.* [see prec.] a small telescope fixed to another telescope, surveying instrument, etc. for adjusting the line of sight

col·lin·e·ar (kə lin′ē ər) *adj.* [COL- (see COM-) + LINEAR] in the same straight line

Col·lins (käl′inz) *n.* ☆an iced drink made with gin (*Tom Collins*), or vodka, rum, whiskey, etc., mixed with soda water, lime or lemon juice, and sugar

Col·lins (käl′inz) **1. Michael,** 1890–1922; Ir. revolutionary leader **2. (William) Wil·kie** (wil′kē), 1824–89; Eng. novelist **3. William,** 1721–59; Eng. poet

col·li·sion (kə lizh′ən) *n.* **1.** a colliding, or coming together with sudden, violent force **2.** a clash or conflict of opinions, interests, etc.

col·lo·cate (käl′ə kāt′) *vt.* **-cat′ed, -cat′ing** [< L. pp. of *collocare*: see LOCATE] to arrange or place together, esp. side by side —**col′lo·ca′tion** *n.*

☆**col·lo·di·on** (kə lō′dē ən) *n.* [< Gr. < *kolla*, glue + *eidos*, form] a highly flammable solution of nitrated cellulose that dries quickly, forming a tough, elastic film: used to protect wounds, in photographic films, etc.

col·loid (käl′oid) *n.* [< Gr. *kolla*, glue + -OID] a thick substance formed when very fine particles (such as large molecules) that cannot be dissolved stay scattered throughout a liquid, solid, or gas without sinking —**col·loi′dal** *adj.*

COLLIE
(24–26 in. high at shoulder)

colloq. 1. colloquial **2.** colloquialism **3.** colloquially

col·lo·qui·al (kə lō′kwē əl) *adj.* [see COLLOQUY] **1.** having to do with or like conversation **2.** being or containing the words, phrases, and idioms that are commonly used in informal speech and writing; informal: the label [Colloq.] is used throughout this dictionary in this sense, and does not suggest that any word or term so labeled is below standard ["John is on the beam" is a *colloquial* way of saying "John is alert and keen"] —**col·lo′qui·al·ly** *adv.*

col·lo·qui·al·ism (-iz′m) *n.* **1.** colloquial quality, style, or usage **2.** a colloquial word or expression

col·lo·qui·um (kə lō′kwē əm) *n., pl.* **-qui·a** (-ə), **-qui·ums** [L.: see COLLOQUY] an organized gathering of a number of scholars or experts to discuss a particular subject or problem

col·lo·quy (käl′ə kwē) *n., pl.* **-quies** [L. *colloquium*, conversation < *com-*, together + *loqui*, to speak] a conversation, esp. a formal discussion; conference —**col′lo·quist** *n.*

col·lude (kə lōōd′) *vi.* **-lud′ed, -lud′ing** [< L. < *com-*, with + *ludere*, to play] to act in collusion or conspire, esp. in order to cheat someone out of something —**col·lud′er** *n.*

col·lu·sion (kə lōō′zhən) *n.* [see prec.] a secret agreement for doing something that is illegal or meant to defraud someone; conspiracy —**col·lu′sive** (-siv) *adj.* —**col·lu′sive·ly** *adv.*

col·ly·wob·bles (käl′ē wäb′lz) *n.pl.* [often with sing. v.] [prob. < COLIC + WOBBLE] [Colloq.] pain in the abdomen; bellyache: usually with *the*

Colo. Colorado

Co·logne (kə lōn′) city in W West Germany, on the Rhine: pop. 854,000

co·logne (kə lōn′) *n.* same as EAU DE COLOGNE

Co·lom·bi·a (kə lum′bē ə; *Sp.* kô lôm′byä) country in NW S. America: 455,335 sq. mi.; pop. 20,463,000; cap. Bogotá —**Co·lom′bi·an** *adj., n.*

Co·lom·bo (kə lum′bō) capital of Ceylon: seaport on the W coast: pop. 512,000

Co·lón (kə lōn′) seaport in Panama, at the Caribbean entrance to the Panama Canal: pop. 64,000

co·lon[1] (kō′lən) *n.* [L. < Gr. *kōlon*, member, limb] a mark of punctuation (:) used before a long quotation, explanation, example, series, etc., and after the salutation of a formal letter

co·lon[2] (kō′lən) *n., pl.* **-lons, -la** (-lə) [L. < Gr. *kolon*] that part of the large intestine extending from the cecum to the rectum: see illustration at INTESTINE —**co·lon·ic** (kə län′ik) *adj.*

co·lon[3] (kō′lən′; *Sp.* kô lôn′) *n., pl.* **-lons, Sp. -lon′es** (-lô′nes) [AmSp. *colón* < Sp. *Colón*, COLUMBUS] see MONETARY UNITS, table (Costa Rica, El Salvador)

co·lo·nel (kʉr′n'l) *n.* [earlier *coronel* < Fr. < It. < *colonna*, (military) column < L. *columna*, COLUMN] **1.** a military officer ranking above a lieutenant colonel ☆**2.** an honorary, nonmilitary title in some southern or western States —**colo′nel·cy** (-sē) *n., pl.* **-cies**

co·lo·ni·al (kə lō′nē əl) *adj.* **1.** of or living in a colony or colonies **2.** [often C-] of or in the thirteen British colonies that became the U.S., or of their period **3.** made up of or having colonies —*n.* a person who lives in a colony —**co·lo′ni·al·ly** *adv.*

co·lo·ni·al·ism (-iz′m) *n.* the system or policy by which a country holds onto foreign colonies, esp. in order to make as much money from them as possible —**co·lo′ni·al·ist** *n., adj.*

☆**col·o·nist** (käl′ə nist) *n.* **1.** any of the original settlers of a colony **2.** a person who lives in a colony

col·o·nize (käl′ə nīz′) *vt., vi.* **-nized, -niz′ing 1.** to found or establish a colony or colonies (in) **2.** to settle (persons) in a colony —**col′o·ni·za′tion** *n.* —**col′o·niz′er** *n.*

col·on·nade (käl′ə nād′) *n.* [Fr. < It. < L. *columna*, COLUMN] a series of columns set at regular intervals, usually supporting a roof or series of arches of a building —**col′on·nad′ed** *adj.*

col·o·ny (käl′ə nē) *n., pl.* **-nies** [< L. < *colonus*, farmer < *colere*, CULTIVATE] **1.** *a*) a group of people who settle in a distant land but are still under the control of their native land *b*) the region thus settled **2.** a territory distant from the state having control over it **3.** [C-] [pl.] the thirteen British colonies in N. America that became the U.S. **4.** a community of people having the same nationality or pursuits and concentrated in a particular place [an artists' *colony*] **5.** *Bacteriology* a group of similar bacteria growing in a culture medium **6.** *Biol.* a group of similar plants or animals living or growing together

COLONNADE

7. *Zool.* a compound organism of incompletely separated individuals, as in corals, hydroids, etc.

col·o·phon (käl′ə fän′, -fən) *n.* [LL. < Gr. *kolophōn*, summit, top, end] **1.** a note in a book giving facts about its production ☆**2.** the distinctive emblem of the publisher, as on the title page of a book

col·or (kul′ər) *n.* [< OFr. < L. < OL. *colos*, orig., a covering: for IE. base see CELL] **1.** the sensation or effect that light rays of certain lengths have on the retina of the eye **2.** the property of reflecting light of a particular wavelength: the distinct colors of the spectrum are red, orange, yellow, green, blue, indigo, and violet; the *primary colors* of the spectrum are red, green, and blue **3.** any coloring matter; dye; pigment; paint: the *primary colors* (red, yellow, and blue) and *secondary colors* formed from these (green, orange, purple, etc.) are sometimes distinguished from black, white, and gray (*achromatic colors*) **4.** color of the face; esp., a healthy rosiness or a blush **5.** the color of the skin of a person, as a black, who is not Caucasoid **6.** [*pl.*] a colored badge, costume, etc. worn by someone to show who or what he is **7.** [*pl.*] *a)* a flag of a country, regiment, etc. *b)* the armed forces of a country, symbolized by the flag [to serve with the *colors*] **8.** [*pl.*] one's position or opinion [stick to your *colors*] **9.** outward appearance or semblance; plausibility **10.** appearance of truth; justification [the news lent *color* to the rumor] **11.** general nature; character [the *color* of his mind] **12.** vivid quality, as in a personality, literary work, etc. **13.** *Art* the way of using color —*vt.* **1.** to give color to; paint, stain, or dye [Jimmy *colored* the drawings red] **2.** to change the color of [the rosy dawn *colored* the clouds] **3.** to alter or influence, as by distortion [prejudice *colored* his views] —*vi.* **1.** to become colored **2.** to change in color **3.** to blush or flush [the fever made him *color*] —**call to the colors 1.** call or order to serve in the armed forces **2.** *Mil.* a bugle call for the daily flag-raising and flag-lowering ceremonies —**change color 1.** to become pale **2.** to blush or flush —**lose color** to become pale —**col′or·er** *n.*

col·or·a·ble (-ə b'l) *adj.* **1.** capable of being colored **2.** that seems to be but really is not true, right, etc.; deceptive

Col·o·ra·do (käl′ə rad′ō, -rä′dō) **1.** [after the river] Mountain State of the U.S.: 104,247 sq. mi.; pop. 2,207,000; cap. Denver: abbrev. **Colo., CO 2.** [< Sp. *Río Colorado*, Red River] river flowing from N Colo. southwest into the Gulf of California —**Col′o·rad′an, Col′o·rad′o·an** *adj., n.*

col·o·rad·o (käl′ə rad′ō, -rä′dō) *adj.* [Sp., red] of medium strength and color: said of cigars

☆**Colorado beetle** a widely distributed black-and-yellow beetle that is a destructive pest of potatoes and other plants

Colorado Springs city in C Colo.: pop. 135,000

☆**col·or·ant** (kul′ər ənt) *n.* [Fr. < prp. of *colorer*, to color] anything used to give color to something else; pigment, dye, etc.

col·or·a·tion (kul′ə rā′shən) *n.* **1.** a being colored **2.** the way a thing is colored **3.** the technique of using colors, as in painting

col·o·ra·tu·ra (kul′ər ə toor′ə, -tyoor′-) *n.* [It. < L. pp. of *colorare*, to color] **1.** brilliant runs, trills, etc., used to display a singer's skill **2.** music containing such ornamentation **3.** a soprano who sings such music: in full, **coloratura soprano**

col·or·blind (kul′ər blīnd′) *adj.* unable to perceive colors or to distinguish between certain colors, as red and green —**col′or·blind′ness** *n.*

col·or·cast (-kast′) *n.* [COLOR + (TELE)CAST] a television broadcast in color —*vt., vi.* **-cast′** or **-cast′ed, -cast′ing** to televise in color

col·ored (kul′ərd) *adj.* **1.** having color **2.** of a (specified) color **3.** of a group of mankind other than the Caucasoid; specif., black (or Negro) **4.** [-C-] in South Africa, of racially mixed parentage: usually **Coloured 5.** of or having to do with colored persons **6.** altered, distorted, or exaggerated [remarks *colored* by prejudice] —**the colored** colored persons

col·or·fast (kul′ər fast′) *adj.* that will keep its color without fading or running —**col′or·fast′ness** *n.*

color filter a screen of colored glass, dyed gelatin, etc. used in photography to control or produce certain color or light effects

col·or·ful (-fəl) *adj.* **1.** full of vivid colors [*colorful* wallpaper] **2.** full of interest or variety; picturesque; vivid [a story full of *colorful* details] —**col′or·ful·ly** *adv.* —**col′or·ful·ness** *n.*

☆**color guard** the persons carrying and escorting the colors (flag) in a parade, ceremony, etc.

col·or·im·e·ter (kul′ə rim′ə tər) *n.* [< COLOR + -METER] an instrument for determining the intensity and hue of a color by comparing it with standard colors —**col′or·i·met′ric** (-ər ə me′trik) *adj.* —**col′or·im′e·try** *n.*

col·or·ing (kul′ər iŋ) *n.* **1.** the act or art of applying colors **2.** anything applied to impart color; pigment, dye, stain, etc. **3.** *same as* COLORATION **4.** skin color **5.** deceptive or false appearance **6.** alteration or influence

col·or·ist (-ist) *n.* **1.** a person who uses colors **2.** an artist skillful in the use of colors

col·or·less (-lis) *adj.* **1.** without color [*colorless* glass] **2.** dull in color; gray or pallid **3.** lacking interest; dull [a *colorless* novel] —**col′or·less·ly** *adv.* —**col′or·less·ness** *n.*

☆**color line** social, political, and economic restrictions as when imposed on blacks or other nonwhites —**draw the color line** to impose or accept such restrictions

Co·los·sae (kə läs′ē) city in ancient Phrygia, SW Asia Minor —**Co·los′sian** (-läsh′ən) *adj., n.*

co·los·sal (kə läs′'l) *adj.* **1.** like a colossus in size; huge; gigantic **2.** [Colloq.] extraordinary [a *colossal* fool; a *colossal* production] —see SYN. at ENORMOUS —**co·los′sal·ly** *adv.*

Col·os·se·um (käl′ə sē′əm) [L., neut. of *colosseus*, gigantic: see COLOSSUS] an amphitheater in Rome, built c. 75–80 A.D.: much of it is still standing —*n.* [c-] *same as* COLISEUM

Co·los·sians (kə läsh′ənz) a book of the New Testament: an epistle from the Apostle Paul to the Christians of Colossae

co·los·sus (kə läs′əs) *n., pl.* **-los′si** (-ī), **-los′sus·es** [L. < Gr. *kolossos*] **1.** a gigantic statue; esp., [C-] that of Apollo set at the entrance to the harbor of Rhodes c. 280 B.C. **2.** any huge or important person or thing

co·los·to·my (kə läs′tə mē) *n., pl.* **-mies** [COLO(N)² + -STOMY] the surgical operation of forming an artificial anal opening in the colon

col·our (kul′ər) *n., vt., vi. Brit. sp.* of COLOR

-co·lous (kə ləs) [< base of L. *colere*, CULTIVATE + -OUS] a combining form meaning growing (or living) in or among

colt (kōlt) *n.* [OE.] **1.** a young horse, donkey, zebra, etc.; specif., a male racehorse four years of age or under **2.** a young, inexperienced person

col·ter (kōl′tər) *n.* [< OFr. or OE., both < L. *culter*, plowshare] a blade or disk on a plow, for making vertical cuts in the soil

colt·ish (kōl′tish) *adj.* of or like a colt; esp., frisky, frolicsome, etc. —**colt′ish·ly** *adv.*

colts·foot (kōlts′foot′) *n., pl.* **-foots′** a plant of the composite family, with yellow flowers and large leaves suggesting the print of a colt's foot

Col·um (käl′əm), **Pad·raic** (pô′thrig) 1881–1972; Ir. poet & playwright, in the U.S.

☆**Co·lum·bi·a** (kə lum′bē ə, -byə) [after Christopher COLUMBUS] **1.** [Poet.] the U.S. personified as a woman **2.** capital of S.C.: pop. 114,000 **3.** city in C Mo.: pop. 59,000 **3.** river flowing from SE British Columbia, through Wash., into the Pacific —**Co·lum′bi·an** *adj.*

col·um·bine (käl′əm bīn′) *n.* [OFr. < ML. < L. *columbinus*, dovelike < *columba*, dove] a plant of the buttercup family, with showy, spurred flowers of various colors

Co·lum·bus (kə lum′bəs) [after Christopher COLUMBUS] **1.** capital of Ohio, in the C part: pop. 540,000 (met. area 916,000) **2.** city in W Ga.: pop. 154,000

Co·lum·bus (kə lum′bəs), **Christopher** (It. name *Cristoforo Colombo;* Sp. name *Cristóbal Colón*) 1451?–1506; It. explorer in the service of Spain: discovered America (1492)

Columbus Day a legal holiday in the U.S. commemorating the discovery of America by Columbus in 1492, observed on the second Monday in October

col·umn (käl′əm) *n.* [< OFr. < L. *columna:* for IE. base see HILL] **1.** a slender upright structure, generally a round shaft with a base and a capital; pillar: a single column may be part of a monument or a number may be used to hold up a roof or ceiling **2.** anything like a column in shape or use [the spinal *column*] **3.** a formation

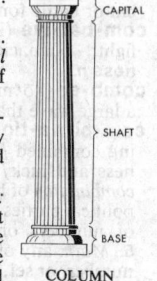

COLUMN

of troops, ships, etc. in a file **4.** any of the vertical sections of printed matter lying side by side on a page and separated by a line or blank space **5.** a series of feature articles that appear regularly in a newspaper or magazine and are written by a special writer or on a certain subject —**co·lum·nar** (kəlum′nər), **col′umned** *adj.*

co·lum·ni·a·tion (kə lum′nē ā′shən) *n.* the architectural use or arrangement of columns

☆**col·um·nist** (käl′əm nist, -ə mist) *n.* a person who writes or conducts a column, as in a newspaper

col·za (käl′zə) *n.* [Fr. < Du. < *kool*, a cabbage + *zaad*, a seed] **1.** any of several plants of the mustard family, esp. rape, whose seeds yield an oil used in lubricants, etc. **2.** this oil: in full, **colza oil**

com- [L. *com-* < OL. *com* (L. *cum*), with] *a prefix meaning:* **1.** with or together [*combine*] **2.** very or very much [*command*] It is changed to **col-** before *l*; **cor-** before *r*; **con-** before *c, d, g, j, n, q, s, t*, and *v*; and **co-** before *h, w*, and all vowels

Com. **1.** Commander **2.** Commission(er) **3.** Committee

com. **1.** commerce **2.** commercial **3.** common **4.** communication

co·ma[1] (kō′mə) *n.* [ModL. < Gr. *koma*, deep sleep] **1.** a condition like a deep, long sleep, when one is made unconscious by injury or disease **2.** a condition of stupor or lethargy

co·ma[2] (kō′mə) *n., pl.* **-mae** (-mē) [L. < Gr. *komē*, hair] **1.** *Astron.* a globular, cloudlike mass around the nucleus of a comet **2.** *a)* a bunch of branches, as on the top of some palms *b)* a tuft of hairs at the end of certain seeds —**co′mate** (-māt) *adj.*

co·make (kō′māk′) *vt.* **-made′, -mak′ing** same as COSIGN — **co′mak·er** *n.*

Co·man·che (kə man′chē) *n.* [MexSp. < Ute *komanchi*, stranger] **1.** *pl.* **-ches, -che** any member of a tribe of N. American Indians who ranged from the Platte River to the Mexican border and now live in Oklahoma **2.** their Shoshonean dialect of Uto-Aztecan

co·ma·tose (kō′mə tōs′, käm′ə-) *adj.* **1.** of, like, or in a coma or stupor **2.** as if in a coma; torpid; lethargic

comb (kōm) *n.* [OE. *camb* < IE. base *gombho-s*, tooth] **1.** a thin strip of hard rubber, plastic, metal, etc. with teeth, passed through the hair to arrange or clean it, or set in the hair to hold it in place **2.** anything like a comb in form or function; specif., *a)* a currycomb *b)* a tool for cleaning and straightening wool, flax, etc. *c)* a red, fleshy outgrowth on the top of the head, as of a rooster *d)* a thing like a rooster's comb in position or appearance, as a helmet crest **3.** a honeycomb —*vt.* **1.** to clean or arrange with a comb **2.** to remove with or as with a comb; separate (often with *out*) ☆**3.** to search thoroughly; look everywhere in [we've *combed* the house for that book] —☆*vi.* to roll over; break: said of waves

com·bat (for *v.*, kəm bat′, käm′bat; *for n. & adj.*, käm′bat, kum′-) *vi.* **-bat′ed** or **-bat′ted, -bat′ing** or **-bat′ting** [< Fr. < VL. < L. *com-*, with + *battuere*, to beat] to fight, contend, or struggle —*vt.* to fight or struggle against; oppose; resist, or seek to get rid of [laws to *combat* racism] —*n.* **1.** armed fighting; battle [he was killed in *combat*] **2.** any struggle or conflict; strife —*adj. Mil.* of or for combat

com·bat·ant (käm′bə tənt, kəm bat′′nt) *adj.* **1.** fighting **2.** ready or prepared to fight —*n.* a person who engages in combat; fighter

combat fatigue a neurotic condition in which one is anxious, irritable, depressed, etc., often as a result of having been in combat or battle for a long time

com·bat·ive (kəm bat′iv, käm′bə tiv) *adj.* ready or eager to fight; pugnacious —**com·bat′ive·ly** *adv.* —**com·bat′ive·ness** *n.*

comb·er (kō′mər) *n.* **1.** one that combs wool, flax, etc. ☆**2.** a large wave that breaks as on a beach

com·bi·na·tion (käm′bə nā′shən) *n.* **1.** a combining or being combined [his success came from a *combination* of cleverness and luck] **2.** a thing formed by combining [green is a *combination* of blue and yellow] **3.** a number of persons, firms, political parties, etc. united for a common purpose **4.** the series of numbers or letters used in opening a combination lock **5.** *Math.* any of the various groupings, or subsets, into which a number, or set, of units may be arranged without regard to order —**com′bi·na′tion·al, com′bi·na′tive** *adj.*

☆**combination lock** a lock operated by a dial that must be turned in the right order to a set series of numbers or letters to work the mechanism that opens it

com·bine (kəm bīn′; *for n. & v.* 3, käm′bīn) *vt., vi.* **-bined′, -bin′ing** [< OFr. < LL. *combinare* < L. *com-*, together + *bini*,

two by two: see BI-] **1.** to come or bring into union; act or mix together; unite; join [to *combine* work with pleasure] **2.** to unite to form a chemical compound ☆**3.** to harvest and thresh with a combine —*n.* ☆**1.** a machine for harvesting and threshing grain ☆**2.** a group of persons, corporations, etc. joined together for business or political purposes, usually to benefit themselves only —see SYN. at JOIN —**com·bin′a·ble** *adj.* —**com·bin′er** *n.*

comb·ings (kō′miŋz) *n.pl.* loose hair, wool, etc. removed in combing

combining form a word form that occurs only in compounds or derivatives, and that can combine with other such forms or with affixes to form a word (Ex.: *cardio-* and *-graph* in *cardiograph*)

com·bo (käm′bō) *n., pl.* **-bos** [Colloq.] a combination; specif., a small jazz ensemble

com·bus·ti·ble (kəm bus′tə b'l) *adj.* [see COMBUSTION] **1.** that catches fire and burns easily; flammable [a *combustible* cleaning fluid] **2.** easily aroused; fiery [he has a *combustible* temper] —*n.* a flammable substance —**com·bus′ti·bil′i·ty** *n.* —**com·bus′ti·bly** *adv.*

com·bus·tion (-chən) *n.* [< OFr. < LL. < L. pp. of *comburere* < *com-*, very much + *urere*, to burn] **1.** the act or process of burning **2.** rapid oxidation accompanied by heat and, usually, light **3.** slow oxidation accompanied by relatively little heat and no light **4.** violent excitement; tumult —**com·bus′tive** *adj.*

☆**com·bus·tor** (-tər) *n.* the chamber in a jet engine, gas turbine, etc. in which combustion occurs

Comdr. Commander

Comdt. Commandant

come (kum) *vi.* **came, come, com′ing** [OE. *cuman*: for IE. base see BASIS] **1.** to move from a place thought of as "there" to a place thought of as "here" [please come to our party] **2.** to approach by moving toward **3.** to arrive or appear [help will *come*] **4.** to extend; reach [his hair *came* to his shoulders] **5.** to take place; happen [success *came* to him] **6.** to take form in the mind [her name *came* to him] **7.** to occur in a certain place or order [after 9 *comes* 10] **8.** to become actual; evolve; develop [will peace *come*?] **9.** *a)* to be derived or descended [he *comes* from a large family] *b)* to be a resident or former resident (with *from*) **10.** to be caused; result [no good will *come* of it] ☆**11.** to be due or owed (*to*): used in the participle [to get what is *coming* to one] **12.** to pass as by inheritance **13.** to get to be; become [it *came* loose] **14.** to be available [this dress *comes* in four sizes] **15.** to amount; add up (*to*) [the bill *comes* to $5.85] —*interj.* look! see here! stop! —**come about 1.** to happen; occur **2.** to turn about **3.** to change from one tack to another in sailing —**come across 1.** to find by chance **2.** [Colloq.] to be effective, etc. ☆**3.** [Slang] to give, do, or say what is wanted —**come again?** ☆[Colloq.] what did you say? —**come and get it!** [Colloq.] the meal is ready! —**come around** (or **round**) **1.** to revive; recover **2.** to make a turn **3.** to concede or yield —**come at 1.** to reach; attain **2.** to approach angrily or swiftly —**come back 1.** to return ☆**2.** [Colloq.] to make a comeback —**come between** to separate and make unfriendly; divide —**come by 1.** to get; gain ☆**2.** to pay a visit —**come down** to suffer loss in status, wealth, etc. —**come down on** (or **upon**) to scold; criticize harshly —**come in 1.** to enter **2.** to come into fashion **3.** to finish in a contest [he *came* in fifth] —**come in for** [Colloq.] to get; acquire —**come into 1.** to enter into **2.** to inherit [he *came into* a fortune] —**come off 1.** to become detached **2.** to occur **3.** [Colloq.] to prove successful, etc. —**come on 1.** to make progress **2.** to find **3.** to appear, make an entrance, etc. —**come on!** [Colloq.] **1.** get started! hurry! **2.** stop behaving like that! —**come one's way** to yield or become agreeable —**come out 1.** to be disclosed **2.** to be offered for public sale, etc. [the new cars *came out*] **3.** to make a debut **4.** to end up; turn out —**come out for** to support; endorse —☆**come out with 1.** to disclose **2.** to say; publish **3.** to offer for public sale, etc. —**come over** to happen to [what's *come over* you?] —**come through** ☆**1.** to complete or endure something successfully ☆**2.** [Slang] to do or give what is wanted —**come to 1.** to become conscious again **2.** to bring the ship's head nearer the wind; also, to anchor —**come up 1.** to arise or be mentioned, as in discussion **2.** to rise, as in status **3.** to be put forward, as for a vote —**come upon** to find by chance —**come up to 1.** to reach **2.** to equal —☆**come up with** to propose, produce, find, etc. —☆**how come?** [Colloq.] how is it that?

come·back (kum′bak′) *n.* [Colloq.] **1.** a return to a previous state or position, as of success ☆**2.** a witty answer ☆**3.** ground for complaint [he was paid well, so he has no *comeback*]

co·me·di·an (kə mē′dē ən) *n.* **1.** an actor who plays comic parts **2.** an entertainer who tells jokes, sings comic songs, etc. **3.** a person who amuses others by doing or saying things that make them laugh

co·me·di·enne (kə mē′dē en′) *n.* a woman comedian

com·e·do (käm′ə dō′) *n., pl.* **com′e·do′nes** (-dō′nēz), **com′e·dos′** [< L. < *comedere:* see COMESTIBLE] *same as* BLACKHEAD (sense 2)

☆**come·down** (kum′doun′) *n.* a fall to a lower status or position, as of power, wealth, etc.

com·e·dy (käm′ə dē) *n., pl.* **-dies** [< OFr. < L. < Gr. *kōmōidia* < *kōmos,* festival + *aeidein,* to sing] **1.** orig., a drama or narrative with a happy ending or nontragic theme **2.** *a)* any of various types of play or motion picture with a humorous treatment of characters and situation and a happy ending *b)* the branch of drama having to do with such plays **3.** a novel or any narrative having a comic theme, tone, etc. **4.** the comic element in a literary work, or in life —**cut the comedy** [Slang] to stop joking —**co·me·dic** (kə mē′dik, -med′ik) *adj.*

comedy of manners a type of comedy satirizing the manners and customs of fashionable society

come-hith·er (kum′hith′ər) *adj.* [Colloq.] flirtatious or inviting [a *come-hither* look]

come·ly (kum′lē) *adj.* **-li·er, -li·est** [OE. *cymlic* < *cyme,* delicate, orig., feeble] **1.** pleasant to look at; attractive **2.** [Archaic] seemly; proper —see SYN. at BEAUTIFUL —**come′li·ness** *n.*

☆**come-on** (kum′än′) *n.* [Slang] **1.** an inviting look or gesture **2.** an inducement [the gift is a *come-on* to attract new customers] **3.** a swindler

com·er (-ər) *n.* **1.** a person who comes [a contest open to all *comers*] ☆**2.** [Colloq.] a person or thing that shows promise of being a success

co·mes·ti·ble (kə mes′tə b'l) *adj.* [Fr. < L. pp. of *comedere* < *com-,* very much + *edere,* to EAT] [Rare] eatable; edible —*n.* [usually *pl.*] food

com·et (käm′ət) *n.* [< OE. < L. *cometa* < Gr. < *komē,* hair] a heavenly body having a starlike center with a shining mass (*coma*) around it, and, usually, a long, fiery tail: comets move in orbits around the sun —**com′et·ar′y** (-ə ter′ē), **co·met·ic** (kä·met′ik) *adj.*

☆**come·up·pance** (kum′up′'ns) *n.* [< COME + UP¹ + -ANCE] [Colloq.] deserved punishment; retribution [the bully got his *comeuppance* when my older brother roughed him up]

com·fit (kum′fit, käm′-) *n.* [< OFr. < L. *conficere:* see CONFECT] a candy or sweetmeat, as a candied fruit

com·fort (kum′fərt) *vt.* [< OFr. < LL. < L. *com-,* very + *fortis,* strong] **1.** to make feel less sad or sorrowful; soothe; console [she *comforted* the widow] **2.** to give a sense of ease to [to *comfort* one's aching back with a hot bath] —*n.* **1.** aid; encouragement: now only in **aid and comfort 2.** relief from distress, grief, etc. [sympathy from friends gives *comfort*] **3.** a person or thing that comforts [TV is a *comfort* to shut-ins] **4.** a state of, or thing that provides, ease and quiet enjoyment [to live in *comfort*] ☆**5.** a quilted bed covering —**com′fort·ing** *adj.* —**com′fort·ing·ly** *adv.* —**com′fort·less** *adj.*

SYN.—**comfort** suggests any attempt to make someone less sorrowful or unhappy as by trying to cheer him up or inspire him with hope; **console** suggests the offering of help or relief to someone who has lost someone or something or has been disappointed [to *console* someone whose best friend has died]; **solace** suggests anything or any action that makes a person less sad, depressed, bored, lonely, etc. [he *solaced* himself by playing the guitar]; **relieve** suggests the easing, often just for a time, of misery or discomfort so that one can bear it more easily [to *relieve* the poor on welfare]; **soothe** implies trying to calm or lessen pain or distress [she *soothed* the child with a lullaby] —**ANT. afflict, distress**

com·fort·a·ble (kumf′tər b'l, kum′fər tə b'l) *adj.* **1.** giving comfort or ease [*comfortable* shoes] **2.** at ease in body or mind; contented **3.** [Colloq.] enough to satisfy one's needs or desires [a *comfortable* salary] —**com′fort·a·ble·ness** *n.* —**com′fort·a·bly** *adv.*

com·fort·er (kum′fər tər, -fə tər) *n.* **1.** a person or thing that comforts ☆**2.** a quilted bed covering —**the Comforter** *Bible* the Holy Spirit: John 14:26

☆**comfort station** a public toilet or restroom

com·fy (kum′fē) *adj.* **-fi·er, -fi·est** [contr. < COMFORTABLE] [Colloq.] comfortable

com·ic (käm′ik) *adj.* [< L. < Gr. *kōmikos*] **1.** of or having to do with comedy **2.** amusing; humorous; funny **3.** of comic strips or cartoons —*n.* **1.** a comedian **2.** the humorous element in art or life ☆**3.** *a)* same as COMIC STRIP or COMIC BOOK *b)* [*pl.*] a section of comic strips, as in a newspaper —see SYN. at FUNNY

com·i·cal (käm′i k'l) *adj.* causing amusement; humorous; funny —see SYN. at FUNNY —**com′i·cal·i·ty** (-kal′ə tē), **com′i·cal·ness** *n.* —**com′i·cal·ly** *adv.*

☆**comic book** a paper booklet of comic strips, sometimes sensational or violent

comic opera opera with humorous situations, a story that ends happily, and some spoken dialogue

☆**comic strip** a series of cartoons, as in a newspaper, telling a story that is humorous or full of adventure

com·ing (kum′iŋ) *adj.* **1.** approaching; next [this *coming* Tuesday] **2.** showing promise of being successful, etc. [the *coming* thing] —*n.* arrival; advent

Com·in·tern (käm′in turn′) *n.* [< *Com*(*munist*) *Intern*(*ational*)] the international organization (*Third International*) of Communist parties (1919–43)

com·i·ty (käm′ə tē) *n., pl.* **-ties** [< L. *comitas* < *comis,* polite, kind] **1.** courteous behavior; politeness **2.** agreement among Christian denominations to avoid having more churches, missions, etc. than are needed in specific areas

comity of nations the respect that peaceful nations show for each other's laws and institutions

comm. 1. commander **2.** commission **3.** committee **4.** commonwealth

com·ma (käm′ə) *n.* [L. < Gr. *komma,* clause, that which is cut off < *koptein,* to cut off: for IE. base see SHAPE] a mark of punctuation (,) used to show a pause that is shorter than the pause at the end of a sentence, as in setting off nonrestrictive or parenthetical elements, quotations, items in a series, etc.

comma bacillus the bacillus causing Asiatic cholera

com·mand (kə mand′) *vt.* [< OFr. < VL. < L. *com-,* very much + *mandare:* see MANDATE] **1.** to give an order to; direct with authority [the police *commanded* the thief to halt] **2.** to have authority over; control [he *commands* a large crew] **3.** to have ready for use [to *command* a large vocabulary] **4.** to deserve and get; require as due [to *command* respect] **5.** to control or overlook from a higher position [the fort *commands* the harbor] —*vi.* to exercise authority; be in control; act as commander —*n.* **1.** an order; direction; mandate **2.** authority to command **3.** power to control by position **4.** range of view **5.** ability to use; mastery [his *command* of English is poor] **6.** *a)* a military or naval force, organization, or district, under a specified authority *b)* same as AIR COMMAND **7.** the post where the person in command is stationed

SYN.—**command,** when it has to do with giving orders, suggests a doing so with the absolute authority of a king, dictator, general, etc.; **order** often stresses the bullying or browbeating of others, and sometimes the use of threats to force others to do as one wishes [he was *ordered* to report for duty]; **direct** and **instruct** are both used in connection with management or supervision, as in a business firm, **instruct** perhaps more often stressing the giving of directions clearly and in detail; **enjoin** suggests a directing along with strong warning [he *enjoined* them to keep it a secret] and sometimes involves the prohibiting of some action by legal order; **charge** often involves the giving to someone of some task that should or must be done —see also SYN. at POWER

com·man·dant (käm′ən dant′, -dänt′) *n.* a commanding officer of a fort, a school for military personnel, etc.

com·man·deer (käm′ən dir′) *vt.* [< Du. or Afrik. < Fr. *commander,* to command] **1.** to force into military service **2.** to seize (property) for military or governmental use [the army *commandeered* the church as a barracks] **3.** [Colloq.] to take by force

com·mand·er (kə man′dər) *n.* **1.** a person who commands; leader **2.** *same as* COMMANDING OFFICER **3.** *U.S. Navy* an officer ranking above a lieutenant commander —**com·mand′er·ship′** *n.*

commander in chief *pl.* **commanders in chief 1.** the supreme commander of the armed forces of a nation, as, in the U.S., the President **2.** an officer in command of all armed forces in a certain theater of war

commanding officer the officer in command of any of certain military units or installations

com·mand·ment (kə mand′mənt) *n.* a command or order backed by authority; mandate; precept; specif., any of the Ten Commandments

com·man·do (kə man′dō) *n., pl.* **-dos, -does** [Afrik. < Port., lit., party commanded] **1.** orig., in South Africa, a force of Boer troops **2.** *a)* a small group of soldiers trained to make surprise raids inside enemy territory *b)* a member of such a group

command performance a performance, as of a play, put on at the command or request of a ruler, etc.

command post the field headquarters of a military unit, where the commander directs operations

‡**com·me·dia del·l'ar·te** (kŏm mā′dyä del lär′te) [It., lit., comedy of art] a type of Italian comedy of the 16th century, having a plot well-known to the audience and dialogue that is made up by stock characters, such as Harlequin, Pantaloon, etc.

‡**comme il faut** (kô mēl fō′) [Fr.] as it should be; proper

com·mem·o·rate (kə mem′ə rāt′) *vt.* **-rat′ed, -rat′ing** [< L. pp. of *commemorare* < *com-*, very much + *memorare*, to remind: see MEMORY] **1.** to honor the memory of, as by a ceremony [Memorial Day *commemorates* dead soldiers] **2.** to serve as a memorial to [a plaque *commemorating* his service] —see SYN. at CELEBRATE —**com·mem′o·ra′tion** *n.* —**com·mem′o·ra·tive** (-ər ə tiv, -ə rāt′iv), **com·mem′o·ra·to·ry** *adj.* —**com·mem′o·ra·tive·ly** *adv.* —**com·mem′o·ra′tor** *n.*

com·mence (kə mens′) *vi., vt.* **-menced′, -menc′ing** [< OFr. < L. *com-*, together + *initiare*, to INITIATE] to begin; start; originate —see SYN. at BEGIN —**com·menc′er** *n.*

com·mence·ment (-mənt) *n.* **1.** the act or time of commencing; beginning; start **2.** the ceremonies at which degrees or diplomas are given out at a school or college

com·mend (kə mend′) *vt.* [< L. *commendare* < *com-* + *mandare*: see COMMAND] **1.** to put in the care of another; entrust [we *commended* our safety into his hands] **2.** to mention as worthy; recommend [he was *commended* in the report for his bravery] **3.** to express approval of; praise ["all our swains *commend* her"] —**com·mend′a·ble** *adj.* —**com·mend′a·bly** *adv.*

com·men·da·tion (käm′ən dā′shən) *n.* a commending; esp., recommendation or praise

com·men·da·to·ry (kə men′də tôr′ē) *adj.* **1.** expressing praise or approval **2.** recommending

com·men·sal (kə men′səl) *n. Biol.* either of the organisms living in commensalism —*adj.* of, like, or being a commensal —**com·men′sal·ly** *adv.*

com·men·sal·ism (-iz′m) *n.* [< ML. < L. *com-*, together + *mensa*, table] the relationship between two kinds of organisms living together in which one benefits, as by the food or protection it gains, while the other is neither hurt nor helped

com·men·su·ra·ble (kə men′shər ə b'l, -sər-) *adj.* [LL. *commensurabilis* < L. *com-*, together + *mensurare*: see COMMENSURATE] **1.** measurable by the same standard or measure [quarts and gallons are *commensurable*] **2.** *same as* COMMENSURATE (sense 2) —see SYN. at PROPORTIONATE —**com·men′su·ra·bil′i·ty** *n.* —**com·men′su·ra·bly** *adv.*

com·men·su·rate (-shər it, -sər-) *adj.* [< LL. < *com-*, with + pp. of *mensurare*, to measure < L. *mensura*, MEASURE] **1.** equal in measure or extent **2.** in the proper proportion; proportionate [his punishment is not *commensurate* with his crime] **3.** *same as* COMMENSURABLE (sense 1) —see SYN. at PROPORTIONATE —**com·men′su·rate·ly** *adv.* —**com·men′su·ra′tion** (-ā′shən) *n.*

com·ment (käm′ent) *n.* [OFr. < L. < pp. of *comminisci*, to contrive < *com-*, very much + base of *meminisse*, to remember] **1.** a note or remark that explains, criticizes, or gives an opinion about something written, said, or done; talk; gossip [his absence caused much *comment*] —*vi.* [< OFr. < L. *commentari*, to consider thoroughly] to make a comment or comments (*on* or *upon*); make remarks —see SYN. at REMARK

com·men·tar·y (käm′ən ter′ē) *n., pl.* **-tar′ies 1.** a series of comments or notes on a book, etc. [a *commentary* on Milton's poems] **2.** a series of remarks or observations **3.** something having the force of a comment or remark [his abrupt departure was a sharp *commentary* on the lecture] **4.** [*usually pl.*] a personal report of events; memoir [Caesar's *Commentaries*] —**com·men·tar′i·al** *adj.*

com·men·tate (-tāt′) *vt.* **-tat′ed, -tat′ing** [back-formation from COMMENTATOR] to give a commentary on —*vi.* to perform as a commentator (sense 2)

com·men·ta·tor (-ər) *n.* **1.** a person who gives a commentary **2.** a person who reports and analyzes news, sports, etc., as on radio and TV

com·merce (käm′ərs) *n.* [Fr. < L. *commercium* < *com-*, together + *merx* (gen. *mercis*), merchandise] **1.** the buying and selling of goods, as between cities, states, or countries; trade **2.** dealings or relations of any kind; relationship

com·mer·cial (kə mur′shəl) *adj.* **1.** of or connected with commerce or trade [*commercial* relations between countries] **2.** of or having to do with stores, office buildings, etc. [*commercial* property] **3.** of a lower grade, or for use in large quantities in industry [*commercial* sulfuric acid] **4.** in, for, or concerned with the making of profit [the book was an artistic success but a *commercial* failure] [a *commercial* course at high school] **6.** *Radio & TV* paid for by sponsors —*n. Radio & TV* a paid advertisement —**com·mer′cial·ly** *adv.*

commercial bank a bank that accepts demand deposits that are used as checking accounts

com·mer·cial·ism (-iz′m) *n.* the practices and spirit of commerce or business, esp. in seeking profits —**com·mer′cial·ist** *n.* —**com·mer′cial·is′tic** *adj.*

com·mer·cial·ize (-īz′) *vt.* **-ized, -iz′ing 1.** to use commercial or business methods on, esp. so as to make a profit [radio and television in the U.S. are largely *commercialized*] **2.** to cause to be affected by commercialism [she was a fine singer but has become *commercialized*] —**com·mer′cial·i·za′tion** *n.*

☆**commercial paper** legally transferable documents, such as promissory notes and bills of exchange

commercial traveler *same as* TRAVELING SALESMAN

Com·mie (käm′ē) *adj., n.* [*sometimes* c-] [Colloq.] Communist: an unfriendly usage

com·min·gle (kə miŋ′g'l) *vt., vi.* **-gled, -gling** to mingle together; intermix; blend

com·mi·nute (käm′ə nōōt′, -nyōōt′) *vt.* **-nut′ed, -nut′ing** [< L. pp. of *comminuere* < *com-*, very much + *minuere*, to make small] to crush, grind, etc. into powder or small particles; pulverize —**com′mi·nu′tion** *n.*

com·mis·er·ate (kə miz′ə rāt′) *vi.* **-at′ed, -at′ing** [< L. pp. of *commiserari* < *com-*, very much + *miserari*, to pity] to feel or show sorrow or pity for another's troubles; sympathize (*with*) [his friends *commiserated* with him on his loss] —**com·mis′er·a′tion** *n.* —**com·mis′er·a′tive** (-ə rāt′iv, -ər ə tiv) *adj.* —**com·mis′er·a′tive·ly** *adv.*

com·mis·sar (käm′ə sär′) *n.* [< Russ. < ML. *commissarius*: see COMMISSARY] the head of a commissariat (sense 2); since 1946, called *minister*

com·mis·sar·i·at (käm′ə ser′ē ət) *n.* **1.** the branch of an army which provides food and supplies for the troops **2.** formerly, a government department in the U.S.S.R.: since 1946, called *ministry*

com·mis·sar·y (käm′ə ser′ē) *n., pl.* **-sar′ies** [ML. *commissarius* < L. pp. of *committere*: see COMMIT] **1.** a deputy assigned to some duty **2.** formerly, an army officer in charge of providing food and supplies ☆**3.** a store in a lumber camp, army camp, etc. handling food and supplies ☆**4.** a restaurant in a movie or TV studio —**com·mis·sar′i·al** *adj.*

com·mis·sion (kə mish′ən) *n.* [OFr. < ML. < L. pp. of *committere*: see COMMIT] **1.** the right to perform certain duties or to take on certain powers **2.** a document giving this right **3.** the condition of having such a right **4.** the right to act for another **5.** that which one is given the right to do for another **6.** a committing or doing, as of a crime **7.** *a)* a group of people officially appointed to perform specified duties *b)* an administrative agency of the government [the Interstate Commerce *Commission*] **8.** a percentage of the money taken in on sales, paid to the salesclerk or agent, often in addition to salary or wages **9.** *a)* an official certificate giving a person a rank of officer in the armed forces *b)* the rank given —*vt.* **1.** to give a commission to **2.** to authorize (a person) to do a particular thing **3.** to order (a thing to be made or done) [to *commission* a portrait] **4.** *Naut.* to put (a ship) into service —**in** (or **out of**) **commission 1.** in (or not in) use **2.** in (or not in) working order

commissioned officer an officer in the armed forces holding rank by a commission

com·mis·sion·er (-ə nər) *n.* **1.** a member of a commission (sense 7) **2.** an official in charge of a certain government bureau, commission, etc. **3.** an official appointed to administer a territory, province, etc.: usually **high commissioner** ☆**4.** a man selected to regulate and control a professional sport

com·mit (kə mit′) *vt.* **-mit′ted, -mit′ting** [L. *committere* < *com-*, together + *mittere*, to send] **1.** to give in charge or trust; consign [we *commit* his fame to posterity] **2.** to put officially in custody or confinement [*committed* to prison] **3.** to hand over or set apart for some purpose [to *commit* something to the trash heap] **4.** to do or perpetrate (an offense or crime) **5.** to bind as by a promise; pledge [*committed* to the struggle] **6.** to make known the opinions or views of [to *commit* oneself on an issue] **7.** to refer (a bill, etc.) to a committee to be considered —**commit to memory** to learn by heart; memorize —**commit to paper** (or **writing**) to write down —**com·mit′ta·ble** *adj.*

SYN.—**commit** implies the giving of a person or thing into the care or keeping of another; **entrust** implies such giving based on trust and confidence [*entrusted* with investing his friend's money]; **confide** emphasizes the private nature of information entrusted to another, as to a close friend or relative; **consign** suggests formal action in transferring something to another's possession or control [*consigned* to the care of a trustee]

com·mit·ment (-mənt) *n.* **1.** a committing or being committed **2.** official delivery by court order of a person to prison, to a mental hospital, etc. **3.** a pledge or promise Also **com·mit′tal**

com·mit·tee (kə mit′ē) *n.* [< Anglo-Fr. < L. *committere:* see COMMIT] **1.** a group of people chosen, as in a legislature or club, to consider or act on some matter **2.** a group of people organized to support some cause —**in committee** under consideration by a committee, as a resolution or bill

com·mit·tee·man (-mən) *n., pl.* **-men** **1.** a member of a committee ☆**2.** a ward or precinct leader for a political party —**com·mit′tee·wom′an** *n.fem., pl.* **-wom′en**

☆**committee of the whole** a committee consisting of all the members of a legislative body, etc. under more informal rules than usual

com·mix (kə miks′, kä-) *vt., vi.* to mix together; blend —**com·mix′ture** (-chər) *n.*

com·mode (kə mōd′) *n.* [Fr. < L. *commodus,* suitable: see COM- & MODE] **1.** a chest of drawers **2.** a small, low table with drawers or cabinet space: also **commode table** **3.** a movable washstand **4.** a kind of chair enclosing a chamber pot **5.** a toilet bowl

com·mo·di·ous (kə mō′dē əs) *adj.* [ME., convenient < L.: see prec.] spacious; roomy; not crowded [a *commodious* house] —**com·mo′di·ous·ly** *adv.* —**com·mo′di·ous·ness** *n.*

com·mod·i·ty (kə mäd′ə tē) *n., pl.* **-ties** [< OFr. < L. < *commodus:* see COMMODE] **1.** any useful thing **2.** anything bought and sold; any article of commerce; often, specif., [*pl.*] basic or staple products, as of agriculture

com·mo·dore (käm′ə dôr′) *n.* [prob. via Du. *kommandeur* < Fr. *commandeur:* see COMMAND] **1.** *U.S. Navy* formerly, an officer ranking just above a captain: the rank was temporarily restored in World War II **2.** *Brit. Navy* a title for a captain temporarily heading a squadron or division of a fleet **3.** a courtesy title, as of the president of a yacht club

com·mon (käm′ən) *adj.* [< OFr. < L. *communis,* shared by all or many] **1.** belonging equally to, or shared by all [*groups* joining together because of *common* interests] **2.** of or belonging or relating to the community at large; public [*common* carriers] **3.** of, from, by, or to all [the *common* good] **4.** widely but unfavorably known [a *common* criminal] **5.** often seen, heard, used, etc.; widespread; familiar; usual [a *common* sight; a *common* saying; *common* salt] **6.** not of the upper classes; of the masses [the *common* people] **7.** having no rank [a *common* soldier] **8.** below ordinary; inferior [*rough common* linens] **9.** vulgar; low; coarse [*common* manners] **10.** *Gram. a)* designating a noun that refers to any of a group or class, as *book, apple, street:* opposed to PROPER *b)* either masculine or feminine [the word *child* is of *common* gender] **11.** *Math.* belonging equally to two or more quantities [a *common* denominator] —*n.* ☆[*sometimes pl.*] land owned or used by all the inhabitants of a place —**in common** owned, used, or shared equally by all —**com′mon·ness** *n.*

com·mon·al·i·ty (käm′ə nal′ə tē) *n.* **1.** same as COMMONALTY **2.** a sharing of common features, etc.

com·mon·al·ty (käm′ən əl tē) *n., pl.* **-ties** **1.** the common people **2.** the members of a group generally **3.** a corporation or its membership

common carrier a person or company in the business of transporting people or goods for a fee, at a uniform rate available to all persons

common cold *same as* COLD (*n.* 4)

common denominator **1.** a common multiple of the denominators of two or more fractions **2.** a quality, trait, etc. held in common

common divisor (or **factor**) a number or quantity that divides two or more numbers or quantities without a remainder [6 is a *common divisor* of 6, 12, and 36]

com·mon·er (-ər) *n.* one of the common people

Common Era *same as* CHRISTIAN ERA

common fraction a fraction whose numerator and denominator are both whole numbers

common law the law of a country or state based on custom, usage, and the decisions of law courts, as apart from STATUTE LAW

com·mon-law marriage (käm′ən lô′) *Law* a marriage without a religious or civil ceremony, in which a man and woman agree to live together as man and wife and do so

common logarithm *Math.* a logarithm having 10 for its base

com·mon·ly (-lē) *adv.* **1.** in a common manner **2.** as a general rule; usually; ordinarily

common market an association of countries formed to bring about a closer economic union, esp. by lowering or doing away with tariffs among themselves; specif., [C- M-] the European Economic Community

common multiple a multiple of each of two or more numbers or quantities [12 is a *common multiple* of 2, 3, 4, and 6]

com·mon·place (-plās′) *n.* **1.** a trite or obvious remark; truism; platitude **2.** anything common or ordinary —*adj.* neither new nor interesting; obvious or ordinary —see **SYN.** at TRITE —**com′mon·place′ness** *n.*

common pleas *Law* ☆in some States, a court having general and original jurisdiction over civil and criminal trials: in full, **court of common pleas**

com·mons (käm′ənz) *n.pl.* **1.** the common people **2.** [*often with sing. v.*] [C-] *same as* HOUSE OF COMMONS **3.** [*often with sing. v.*] food provided for meals in common for a whole group, or a dining room where such food is served, as at a college

common sense ordinary good sense or sound practical judgment —**com′mon-sense′, com′mon-sen′si·cal** (-sen′si k'l) *adj.*

☆**common stock** ordinary capital stock in a company without a definite dividend rate or the privileges of preferred stock, but usually with voting rights at shareholders' meetings

common time *Music* a meter of four beats to the measure; 4/4 time: also **common measure**

com·mon·weal (käm′ən wēl′) *n.* the public good; the general welfare

com·mon·wealth (-welth′) *n.* **1.** the people of a nation or state **2.** *a)* a democracy or republic *b)* a federation of states [the *Commonwealth* of Australia] *Commonwealth* is also the official designation of Puerto Rico in its special status under the U.S. government ☆**3.** loosely, any State of the U.S.; strictly, Kentucky, Massachusetts, Pennsylvania, or Virginia **4.** a group of people united by common interests —**the Commonwealth 1.** the government in England under the Cromwells and Parliament (1649-1660) **2.** *current name of the* BRITISH COMMONWEALTH (OF NATIONS)

com·mo·tion (kə mō′shən) *n.* [< L. pp. of *commovere* < *com-,* together + *movere,* to MOVE] **1.** violent motion; turbulence **2.** a noisy rushing about; confusion; bustle

com·mu·nal (käm′yoon 'l, kə myoon′'l) *adj.* **1.** of a commune or communes **2.** of or belonging to the community; public [the park is *communal* property] **3.** designating or of social or economic organization in which there is common ownership of property —**com·mu′nal·ly** *adv.*

com·mu·nal·ism (-iz'm) *n.* **1.** a theory or system of government in which communes or local communities have virtual autonomy within a federated state **2.** communal organization —**com·mu′nal·ist** *n., adj.* —**com·mu′nal·is′tic** *adj.*

com·mu·nal·ize (-īz′) *vt.* **-ized′, -iz′ing** to make communal —**com·mu′nal·i·za′tion** *n.*

Com·mu·nard (käm′yoo närd′) *n.* [Fr.] a person who supported or took part in the Commune of Paris of 1871

com·mune¹ (kə myoon′; *for n.* käm′yoon) *vi.* **-muned′, -mun′ing** [< OFr. *comuner,* to share < *comun* (see COMMON)] **1.** to talk, meet, or deal with in close understanding [to *commune* with nature] **2.** to receive Holy Communion —*n.* [Poet.]

converse; communion —**commune with oneself** to ponder

com·mune[2] (kəm′yōōn, kə myōōn′) *n.* [< OFr., ult. < L. *communis,* COMMON] **1.** a community; specif., the smallest administrative district of local government in France, Belgium, and some other European countries **2.** a collective farm, as in China ☆**3.** a small group of people living together and sharing in work, earnings, etc. —**the Commune** the revolutionary government of Paris from 1792 to 1794 or the one in 1871

com·mu·ni·ca·ble (kə myōō′ni kə b′l) *adj.* **1.** that can be communicated, as an idea **2.** that can be transmitted, as a disease —**com·mu′ni·ca·bil′i·ty** *n.* —**com·mu′ni·ca·bly** *adv.*

com·mu·ni·cant (-kənt) *n.* a person who receives Holy Communion or belongs to a church celebrating this sacrament

com·mu·ni·cate (-kāt′) *vt.* **-cat′ed, -cat′ing** [< L. pp. of *communicare* < *communis,* COMMON] **1.** to pass along; impart; transmit (heat, motion, a disease, etc.) **2.** to make known; give (information, etc.) —*vi.* **1.** to receive Holy Communion **2.** *a*) to give or exchange information, as by talk, writing, etc. *b*) to have a sympathetic personal relationship **3.** to be connected [*communicating* rooms] —**com·mu′ni·ca′tor** *n.*

com·mu·ni·ca·tion (kə myōō′nə kā′shən) *n.* **1.** a transmitting **2.** *a*) a giving or exchanging of information, etc. by talk, writing, etc. *b*) the information so given **3.** close, sympathetic relationship **4.** a means of communicating; specif., *a*) [*pl.*] a system for sending and receiving messages, as by telephone or radio *b*) [*pl.*] a system as of routes for moving troops and materiel *c*) a passage for getting from one place to another **5.** [*often pl., with sing. v.*] *a*) the art of expressing ideas, esp. in speech and writing *b*) the science of transmitting information

com·mu·ni·ca·tive (kə myōō′nə kāt′iv, -ni kə tiv) *adj.* **1.** giving information readily; talkative **2.** of communication — **com·mu′ni·ca′tive·ly** *adv.* —**com·mu′ni·ca′tive·ness** *n.*

com·mun·ion (kə myōōn′yən) *n.* [OFr. < L. < *communis,* COMMON] **1.** a sharing; possession in common [*a communion* of interests] **2.** a sharing of one's thoughts and emotions **3.** a close relationship with deep understanding **4.** a Christian religious body **5.** [C-] a sharing in, or celebrating of, Holy Communion: see HOLY COMMUNION

com·mu·ni·qué (kə myōō′nə kā′; kə myōō′nə kā′) *n.* [Fr.] an official communication or bulletin

com·mu·nism (käm′yə niz′m) *n.* [< Fr.: see COMMON & -ISM] **1.** a theory or system based on the ownership of all property by the community as a whole **2.** [*often* C-] *a*) a hypothetical stage of socialism, as formulated by Marx, Engels, Lenin, etc., to be characterized by a classless and stateless society and the equal distribution of economic goods *b*) the form of government in the U.S.S.R., China, etc., professing to be working toward this stage **3.** [*often* C-] *a*) a political movement for establishing a communist system *b*) the doctrines, methods, etc. of the Communist parties See also SOCIALISM

com·mu·nist (-nist) *n.* **1.** an advocate or supporter of communism **2.** [C-] a member of a Communist Party —*adj.* **1.** of, characteristic of, or like communism or communists **2.** advocating or supporting communism **3.** [C-] designating or of a political party advocating Communism —**com′mu·nis′tic** *adj.* —**com′mu·nis′ti·cal·ly** *adv.*

com·mu·ni·ty (kə myōō′nə tē) *n., pl.* **-ties** [< L. *communitas* < *communis,* COMMON] **1.** *a*) all the people living in a particular district, city, etc. *b*) the district, city, etc. where they live **2.** a group of people living together as a smaller social unit within a larger one, and having interests, work, etc. in common [a college *community*] **3.** a group of nations associated because of common traditions or for mutual advantage [the Atlantic *community*] **4.** society in general; the public [the values of the *community*] **5.** ownership or sharing in common [*community* property; a *community* of interests] **6.** similarity; likeness [a *community* of tastes] **7.** friendly association; fellowship [a feeling of *community*] **8.** *Ecology* a group of animals and plants living together in close relationship

☆**community center** a meeting place in a community for cultural, recreational, or social activities

☆**community chest** (or **fund**) a fund collected annually in many cities and towns by private contributions for certain local welfare agencies

☆**community college** a junior college serving a certain community and supported by it in part

com·mu·nize (käm′yə nīz′) *vt.* **-nized′, -niz′ing 1.** to subject to communal ownership and control **2.** to make communistic —**com′mu·ni·za′tion** *n.*

com·mu·tate (käm′yə tāt′) *vt.* **-tat′ed, -tat′ing** [backformation < COMMUTATION] to change the direction of

(an electric current); esp., to change (alternating current) to direct current

com·mu·ta·tion (käm′yə tā′shən) *n.* [< OFr. < L. < pp. of *commutare,* COMMUTE] **1.** an exchange; substitution **2.** the substitution of one kind of payment for another ☆**3.** the act of traveling as a commuter **4.** *Elec.* change of the direction of a current by a commutator **5.** *Law* a change of a sentence or punishment to one that is *less* severe —**com·mu·ta·tive** (käm′yə tāt′iv, kə myōōt′ə tiv) *adj.*

com·mu·ta·tor (käm′yə tāt′ər) *n.* **1.** a device for commutating an electric current **2.** in a dynamo or motor, a revolving part that collects the current from the brushes or distributes it to them: see illustration at BRUSH[1]

com·mute (kə myōōt′) *vt.* **-mut′ed, -mut′ing** [< L. *commutare* < *com-,* very much + *mutare,* to change] **1.** to exchange; substitute **2.** to change (an obligation, punishment, etc.) to one that is less severe —*vi.* to be a substitute ☆**2.** to travel as a commuter —**com·mut′a·ble** *adj.*

☆**com·mut·er** (-ər) *n.* a person who travels daily or regularly, esp. by train, bus, etc., between two points at some distance

Com·o·ros (käm′ə rōs′) country on a group of islands in the Indian Ocean, between Mozambique and Madagascar: 700 sq. mi.; pop. 292,000

☆**comp**[1] (kämp) *vi.* [< ACCOMPANY] [Colloq.] *Jazz* to play an accompaniment: said of a pianist, guitarist, etc.

comp[2] (kämp) *n.* [< COMPLIMENTARY] [Slang] a free theater ticket, book, etc. given usually for publicity

comp. 1. comparative **2.** compare **3.** compiled **4.** composition **5.** compositor **6.** compound

com·pact (kəm pakt′; *also for adj., and for n. always,* käm′-pakt) *adj.* [< L. pp. of *compingere* < *com-,* together + *pangere,* to fasten: for IE. base see PEACE] **1.** closely and firmly packed; dense; solid **2.** taking little space because parts are arranged in a close, orderly way [a *compact* kitchen] **3.** not wordy; concise **4.** made up or composed (*of*) ☆**5.** designating or of a small, light, economical model of automobile —*vt.* **1.** to pack or join firmly together **2.** to make by putting together [a report *compacted* of lies and half-truths] **3.** to make more dense; compress; condense —*n.* **1.** a small cosmetic case, usually containing face powder and a mirror ☆**2.** a compact automobile **3.** [< L. pp. of *compacisci,* to agree together] an agreement; covenant, as between persons or states —see SYN.at CLOSE[1] —**com·pact′ly** *adv.* —**com·pact′ness** *n.*

☆**com·pac·tor** (kəm pak′tər) *n.* a device for pressing trash into small bundles that can be got rid of easily

com·pan·ion[1] (kəm pan′yən) *n.* [< OFr. < VL. *companio,* messmate < L. *com-,* with + *panis,* bread] **1.** one who spends much time with another or others in work, play, etc.; associate; comrade **2.** a person employed to live or travel with another **3.** a thing that matches another in sort, color, etc. —*vt.* to accompany —see SYN.at ASSOCIATE —**com·pan′ion·ship′** *n.*

com·pan·ion[2] (kəm pan′yən) *n.* [< Du. < OFr. < It. (*camera della*) *compagna,* (room of the) company, crew] *Naut.* **1.** the covering at the head of a companionway **2.** a companionway

com·pan·ion·a·ble (-ə b′l) *adj.* having the qualities of a good companion; friendly; sociable —**com·pan′ion·a·bil′i·ty** *n.* —**com·pan′ion·a·bly** *adv.*

com·pan·ion·ate (-it) *adj.* of or characteristic of companions

com·pan·ion·way (-wā′) *n.* a stairway leading from the deck of a ship to the cabins or space below

com·pa·ny (kum′pə nē) *n., pl.* **-nies** [< OFr. < VL. *compania,* lit., group sharing bread: see COMPANION[1]] **1.** a being together as companions; companionship; society [neighbors who enjoy each other's *company*] **2.** a group of people; specif., *a*) a group gathered for social purposes [he's shy in *company*] *b*) a group associated for some purpose [a theatrical *company;* a business *company*] **3.** the partners whose names are not given in the title of a firm [John Smith and *Company*] **4.** a guest or guests [we had *company* for dinner] **5.** the people who are one's companions [a man is judged by the *company* he keeps] **6.** *Mil.* a body of troops, normally composed of two or more platoons **7.** *Naut.* the whole crew of a ship, including officers: in full, **ship's company** —see SYN.at TROOP —**keep (a person) company** to stay with (a person) and provide companionship —**keep company 1.** to associate (*with*) **2.** to go together, as a couple intending to marry —**part company 1.** to stop associating (*with*) **2.** to separate and go in different directions

compar. 1. comparative **2.** comparison

com·pa·ra·ble (käm′pər ə b′l; *occas.* kəm par′ə b′l) *adj.* **1.** that can be compared; having features in common [Rugby is a game *comparable* with football] **2.** worthy of comparison [no one is *comparable* to her in charm] —**com′pa·ra·bil′i·ty, com′-pa·ra·ble·ness** *n.* —**com′pa·ra·bly** *adv.*

com·par·a·tive (kəm par′ə tiv) *adj.* **1.** that compares; involving comparison as a method [*comparative* linguistics] **2.** judged by comparison with others; relative [*comparative* joy] **3.** being the form of adjectives and adverbs that shows a greater but not the greatest degree in meaning: the comparative degree is usually indicated by the suffix -*er* (*harder*) or by the use of *more* (*more beautiful, more beautifully*) —*n. Gram.* **1.** the comparative degree **2.** a word or form in this degree —**com·par′a·tive·ly** *adv.* —**com·par′a·tive·ness** *n.*

com·pare (kəm per′) *vt.* -**pared′**, -**par′ing** [< OFr. < L. *com-parare* < *com-*, with + *par*, equal] **1.** to regard as similar; liken (*to*) [he *compared* the sound of thunder to the roll of drums] **2.** to examine in order to observe similarities or differences (often followed by *with*) [*compare* their voting records] **3.** *Gram.* to form the positive, comparative, and superlative degrees of (an adjective or adverb) —*vi.* **1.** to be worthy of comparison (*with*) [the movie *compares* favorably with the novel] **2.** to be regarded as similar or equal [few dogs can *compare* with the Great Dane in size] —*n.* [Poet.] comparison —**beyond** (or **past** or **without**) **compare** without equal

SYN.—**compare** implies a noting of likenesses and differences and an examining of features side by side to see how they are alike or different [to *compare* Shaw with Chekhov]; **contrast** implies a comparing for the express purpose of showing differences [to *contrast* city life with living in the country]

com·par·i·son (kəm par′ə s'n) *n.* **1.** a comparing or being compared; estimation of similarities and differences **2.** likeness; similarity [no *comparison* between the two] **3.** *Gram.* change in an adjective or adverb to show the positive, comparative, and superlative degrees (Ex.: *long, longer, longest; good, better, best; slowly, more slowly, most slowly*) —**in comparison with** compared with

com·part·ment (kəm pärt′mənt) *n.* [< Fr. < It. < LL. < L. *com-*, very much + *partiri*, to divide < *pars*, PART] **1.** any of the parts into which an enclosed space is divided **2.** a separate section, part, division, or category —*vt.* same as COMPARTMENTALIZE —**com·part′men′tal** (-men′t'l) *adj.* —**com·part′ment·ed** *adj.*

com·part·men·tal·ize (kəm pärt′men′tə līz′) *vt.* -**ized′**, -**iz′ing** to put into separate compartments, divisions, or categories —**com·part′men′tal·i·za′tion** *n.*

com·pass (kum′pəs) *vt.* [< OFr., ult. < L. *com-*, together +

 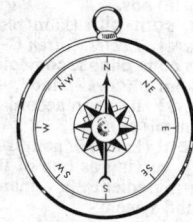

DRAWING COMPASS DIRECTIONAL COMPASS

passus, a step] **1.** to go around; circle **2.** to surround; encircle [a medieval town *compassed* by a wall] **3.** to understand; comprehend [more than his mind could *compass*] **4.** to achieve; accomplish [to *compass* one's purpose] **5.** to plot or contrive (something harmful) —*n.* **1.** [often pl.] an instrument consisting of two hinged legs, used for drawing arcs or circles or for taking measurements: also called **pair of compasses 2.** a boundary; circumference **3.** full extent or range; reach; scope [within the *compass* of one's experience; the *compass* of a singer's voice] **4.** an instrument for showing direction, esp. one consisting of a magnetic needle swinging freely on a pivot and pointing to the magnetic north —*adj.* round; circular or semicircular —see SYN. at RANGE —**com′pass·a·ble** *adj.*

compass card the circular card mounted on a free pivot inside a compass and marked with points of direction and, often, the degrees of the circle

com·pas·sion (kəm pash′ən) *n.* [OFr. < LL. *compassio*, ult. < L. *com-*, together + *pati*, to suffer] sorrow for the sufferings or trouble of another, with the urge to help; deep sympathy; pity —see SYN. at PITY

com·pas·sion·ate (-it) *adj.* feeling or showing compassion; sympathizing deeply —**com·pas′sion·ate·ly** *adv.*

com·pat·i·ble (kəm pat′ə b'l) *adj.* [< ML. < LL.: see COM-PASSION] **1.** capable of living together in harmony or getting along well together; in agreement [violence is not *compatible* with reason] **2.** that can be mixed without bad effects: said of drugs, etc. —**com·pat′i·bil′i·ty, com·pat′i·ble·ness** *n.* —**com·pat′i·bly** *adv.*

com·pa·tri·ot (kəm pā′trē ət; *chiefly Brit.* -pat′rē-) *n.* [< Fr. < LL. *compatriota*: see COM- & PATRIOT] **1.** a fellow countryman **2.** a colleague —*adj.* of the same country —**com·pa′tri·ot·ism** *n.*

com·peer (käm′pir, kəm pir′) *n.* [< OFr. < L. < *com-*, with + *par*, equal] **1.** an equal; peer **2.** a companion; comrade

com·pel (kəm pel′) *vt.* -**pelled′**, -**pel′ling** [< OFr. < L. *com-pellere* < *com-*, together + *pellere*, to drive] **1.** to force or oblige to do something **2.** to get or bring about by force [a bully cannot *compel* respect] —see SYN. at FORCE —**com·pel′la·ble** *adj.* —**com·pel′ler** *n.* —**com·pel′ling·ly** *adv.*

com·pen·di·ous (kəm pen′dē əs) *adj.* [L. *compendiosus:* see COMPENDIUM] containing all the essentials in a brief form; concise but comprehensive —**com·pen′di·ous·ly** *adv.* —**com·pen′di·ous·ness** *n.*

com·pen·di·um (-əm) *n., pl.* -**di·ums, -di·a** (-ə) [L., an abridgment < *com-*, together + *pendere*, to weigh] a summary containing the essential information in a brief form; concise but comprehensive treatise: also **com·pend** (käm′pend)

com·pen·sa·ble (kəm pen′sə b'l) *adj.* entitling to compensation

com·pen·sate (käm′pən sāt′) *vt.* -**sat′ed, -sat′ing** [< L. pp. of *compensare* < *com-*, with + *pensare*, var. of *pendere*, to weigh] **1.** to make up for; balance in weight, force, effect, etc. **2.** to repay (a person) for a loss, injury, service, etc.; recompense [to *compensate* an owner for land taken by a city] —*vi.* to make or serve as compensation or amends [hard study can *compensate* for slow learning] —see SYN. at PAY¹ —**com·pen·sa·tive** (käm′pən sāt′iv, kəm pen′sə tiv) *adj.* —**com′pen·sa′tor** *n.* —**com·pen·sa·to·ry** (kəm pen′sə tôr′ē) *adj.*

com·pen·sa·tion (käm′pən sā′shən) *n.* **1.** a compensating or being compensated **2.** *a)* anything given as an equivalent, or to make up for a loss, injury, etc. *b)* payment for services; esp., wages **3.** the counterbalancing of a defect by a greater activity or development of some other part, quality, etc. —**com′pen·sa′tion·al** *adj.*

com·pete (kəm pēt′) *vi.* -**pet′ed, -pet′ing** [< L. *competere* < *com-*, together + *petere*, to seek] to enter into or be in rivalry; contend; vie (*in* a contest, etc.) [nations *compete* for markets]

com·pe·tence (käm′pə təns) *n.* [< Fr. < L. < prp. of *com-petere:* see prec.] **1.** sufficient means for one's needs **2.** ability or fitness for some task, work, etc. **3.** power or right to do something legally or officially Also **com′pe·ten·cy**

com·pe·tent (-tənt) *adj.* [< OFr. < L. prp. of *competere:* see COMPETE] **1.** well qualified; capable; fit [a *competent* doctor] **2.** sufficient; adequate [a *competent* understanding of law] **3.** legally qualified or fit —see SYN. at ABLE —**com′pe·tent·ly** *adv.*

com·pe·ti·tion (käm′pə tish′ən) *n.* **1.** a competing; rivalry **2.** a contest, or match **3.** rivalry in business, as for customers or markets **4.** the person or persons against whom one competes **5.** *Ecology* the struggle among individual organisms for a limited supply of food, water, space, etc.

SYN.—**competition** denotes a striving for the same object, position, prize, etc., usually following certain fixed rules; **rivalry** implies keen competition between opponents more or less evenly matched, and often suggests unfriendliness or even enmity —ANT. cooperation

com·pet·i·tive (kəm pet′ə tiv) *adj.* of, involving, or based on competition [*competitive* sports]: also **com·pet′i·to·ry** (-tôr′ē) —**com·pet′i·tive·ly** *adv.* —**com·pet′i·tive·ness** *n.*

com·pet·i·tor (-tər) *n.* a person who competes, as a business rival

com·pi·la·tion (käm′pə lā′shən) *n.* **1.** a compiling **2.** something compiled [an almanac is a *compilation* of many facts]

com·pile (kəm pīl′) *vt.* -**piled′**, -**pil′ing** [< OFr. < L. *compilare* < *com-*, together + *pilare*, to compress] **1.** to gather together (statistics, facts, etc.) in an orderly form **2.** to put together (a book, etc.) of materials gathered from various sources —**com·pil′er** n.

com·pla·cen·cy (kəm plās′'n sē) n. [< LL. < L.: see COMPLACENT] quiet satisfaction; contentment; often, a condition of self-satisfaction, or smugness: also **com·pla′cence**

com·pla·cent (-'nt) adj. [< L. prp. of complacere < com-, very much + placere, to PLEASE] self-satisfied; smug [a complacent team will often lose a game] —**com·pla′cent·ly** adv.

com·plain (kəm plān′) vi. [< OFr. < VL. complangere < L. com-, very much + plangere, to strike (the breast)] 1. to express pain, displeasure, etc. 2. to find fault [she complained about our lack of neatness] 3. to make an accusation or a formal charge [we complained to the police about the noise] —**com·plain′er** n. —**com·plain′ing·ly** adv.

com·plain·ant (-ənt) n. Law one who files a charge or makes the complaint in court; plaintiff

com·plaint (kəm plānt′) n. 1. a complaining; utterance of pain, displeasure, annoyance, etc. 2. a subject or cause for complaining 3. an illness; ailment 4. Law a formal charge

com·plai·sant (kəm plā′z'nt, -s'nt) adj. [< Fr. prp. of complaire < L. complacere: see COMPLACENT] willing to please; affably agreeable; obliging —**com·plai′sance** n. —**com·plai′sant·ly** adv.

com·pleat (kəm plēt′) adj. archaic sp. of COMPLETE

☆**com·plect·ed** (kəm plek′tid) adj. [altered < COMPLEXIONED] [Dial. or Colloq.] same as COMPLEXIONED

com·ple·ment (käm′plə mənt; for v. -ment′) n. [L. complementum < complere: see COMPLETE] 1. that which completes or brings to perfection [wines to complement a formal dinner] 2. the amount needed to fill or complete 3. the full number needed [the ship has a complement of 300 men] 4. either of two parts that complete each other 5. Gram. a word or words that complete the meaning of the predicate (Ex.: foreman in make him foreman, paid in he expects to get paid) 6. Math. a) the number of degrees which together with a given angle or arc equal 90 degrees b) the set of all elements in a designated group that are not members of the given set —vt. to make complete; be a complement to [a bright scarf to complement your black dress]—

COMPLEMENT
(arc YM, complement of arc WY; angle YXM, complement of angle WXY)

com·ple·men·ta·ry (käm′plə men′tər ē) adj. 1. acting as a complement; completing 2. making up what is lacking in one another Also **com′ple·men′tal** —**com′ple·men·tar′i·ty** (-tər′ə tē) n.

complementary angle either of two angles that together form a 90° angle

complementary colors any two colors of the spectrum that combine to form white light

com·plete (kəm plēt′) adj. [< OFr. < L. pp. of complere < com-, very much + plere, to fill: for IE. base see FULL¹] 1. lacking no part; entire; whole [a complete deck of cards] 2. ended; finished [no one's education is ever really complete] 3. thorough; absolute [she has complete confidence in her doctor] —vt. -plet′ed, -plet′ing 1. to end; finish [he completed his homework on time] 2. to make whole, full, or perfect [the building was completed last month] —see SYN. at CLOSE² —**com·plete′ly** adv. —**com·plete′ness** n.

com·ple·tion (kəm plē′shən) n. 1. a completing, or finishing 2. the state of being completed

com·plex (kəm pleks′; also, and for n. always, käm′pleks) adj. [< L. pp. of complecti < com-, with + plectere, to weave] 1. consisting of two or more related parts; not simple; complicated —n. 1. a group of related ideas, activities, things, etc. that form a single whole [the complex of expressways in a State] 2. Psychoanalysis a) a group of largely unconscious ideas and feelings related to a particular object, activity, etc., strongly influencing the individual's behavior [the Oedipus complex] b) popularly, an exaggerated dislike or fear [a complex about traveling in airplanes] —**com·plex′ly** adv. —**com·plex′ness** n.

SYN.—**complex** refers to that which is made up of many related and connected parts, so that much study or knowledge is needed to understand or operate it [a computer is a complex mechanism]; **complicated** is applied to that which is highly complex and thus very difficult to analyze, solve, or understand [a complicated problem]; **intricate** specifically suggests a complicated interweaving of parts that is very puzzling and difficult to follow [an intricate maze]; **involved** is applied to situations, ideas, etc. whose parts are thought of as twisting together in a complicated, often disordered way [an involved argument] —ANT. simple

complex fraction a fraction with a fraction in its numerator or denominator, or in both

com·plex·ion (kəm plek′shən) n. [OFr. < L. < complexus: see COMPLEX] 1. the color, texture, etc. of the skin, esp. of the face 2. general appearance or nature; character; aspect [the complexion of their lives was changed by war] —**com·plex′ion·al** adj.

com·plex·ioned (-shənd) adj. having a (specified) complexion [light-complexioned]

com·plex·i·ty (kəm plek′sə tē) n. 1. a complex condition or quality 2. pl. -ties anything complex or intricate; complication

complex sentence a sentence consisting of a main clause and one or more subordinate clauses

com·pli·ance (kəm plī′əns) n. 1. a complying by giving in to a request, demand, etc. or following a rule or requirement 2. a tendency to give in readily to others Also **com·pli′an·cy** —**in compliance with** complying with

com·pli·ant (-ənt) adj. complying; yielding; submissive —see SYN. at OBEDIENT —**com·pli′ant·ly** adv.

com·pli·cate (käm′plə kāt′) vt., vi. -cat′ed, -cat′ing [< L. pp. of complicare < com-, together + plicare, to fold < IE. base plek-, to braid] to make or become difficult, mixed-up, or involved [heavy debts have complicated his life]

com·pli·cat·ed (-kāt′id) adj. quite involved; hard to untangle, solve, analyze, etc. —see SYN. at COMPLEX —**com′pli·cat′ed·ly** adv. —**com′pli·cat′ed·ness** n.

com·pli·ca·tion (käm′plə kā′shən) n. 1. a complicating 2. a complicated condition or structure 3. a complicating factor, as in the plot of a story 4. Med. a second disease or abnormal condition occurring during the course of a primary disease

com·plic·i·ty (kəm plis′ə tē) n., pl. -ties [< Fr. < L. complicis, genitive of complex: see COMPLEX] the fact or state of being involved with another in wrongdoing

com·pli·ment (käm′plə mənt; for v. -ment′) n. [Fr. < It., ult. < L. complere, to COMPLETE] 1. a formal act of courtesy or respect [the audience paid him the compliment of standing up when he entered] 2. something said in praise 3. [pl.] courteous greetings; respects [sent with our compliments] —vt. 1. to pay a compliment to 2. to present something to (a person) to show respect

com·pli·men·ta·ry (käm′plə men′tər ē) adj. 1. paying or containing a compliment 2. given free as a courtesy [a complimentary ticket] —**com·pli·men·tar′i·ly** (-men ter′ə lē, -men′tər ə lē) adv.

com·pline, com·plin (käm′plən) n. [< OFr. < L. completus: see COMPLETE] Eccles. [often C-] the last of the seven canonical hours: also **com′plines, com′plins** (-plənz)

com·ply (kəm plī′) vi. -plied′, -ply′ing [< OFr. < L. complere: see COMPLETE] to act in accordance (with a request, order, rule, etc.) —**com·pli′er** n.

com·po·nent (kəm pō′nənt) adj. [< L. prp. of componere: see COMPOSITE] serving as one of the parts of a whole —n. 1. an element or ingredient 2. a main constituent part, as of a high-fidelity sound system

com·port (kəm pôrt′) vt. [< OFr. < L. comportare < com-, together + portare, to bring] to behave (oneself) in a specified manner —vi. to agree or fit in [his comic remarks did not comport with the seriousness of the matter] —**com·port′ment** n.

com·pose (kəm pōz′) vt. -posed′, -pos′ing [< OFr. composer < com-, with + poser, to place] 1. to make up; constitute [mortar is composed of lime, sand, and water] 2. to put together in proper order or form [the figures in this painting are well composed] 3. to create (a musical or literary work) 4. to adjust or settle [to compose differences] 5. to calm (oneself, one's mind, etc.); quiet 6. Printing to set (type) —vi. 1. to create musical or literary works 2. to set type

com·posed (-pōzd′) adj. calm; tranquil; self-controlled; not excited, confused, etc. —see SYN. at COOL —**com·pos′ed·ly** (-pō′zid lē) adv. —**com·pos′ed·ness** n.

com·pos·er (-pō′zər) n. a person who composes, esp. one who composes music

com·pos·ite (kəm päz′it) adj. [< L. pp. of componere < com-, together + ponere, to put] 1. formed of distinct parts put together [a composite photograph in which a farmhouse is shown with skyscrapers in the background] 2. designating a large family of plants, as the daisy, chrysanthemum, etc., having flower heads composed of dense clusters of small flowers 3. [C-] Archit. designating the classic order which combines features of the Ionic and Corinthian capitals —n. 1. a thing formed of distinct parts **2.** a composite plant —**com·pos′ite·ly** *adv.*

com·po·si·tion (käm′pə zish′ən) *n.* **1.** a composing; specif., *a)* the art of writing *b)* the creation of musical works **2.** the makeup of a thing or person; the parts or materials of a thing and the way they are put together; constitution **3.** that which is composed; specif., *a)* a mixture of several parts or ingredients *b)* a work of music, literature, or art *c)* an exercise in writing done as schoolwork **4.** a unified arrangement of parts in a work of art, as in a painting **5.** an agreement, or settlement, often by compromise **6.** *Printing* the work of setting type — **com·po·si·tion·al** *adj.*

com·pos·i·tor (kəm päz′ə tər) *n.* a person who sets type; typesetter

com·pos men·tis (käm′pəs men′tis) [L.] *Law* of sound mind; sane

com·post (käm′pōst) *n.* [< OFr. < L.: see COMPOSITE] **1.** a compound **2.** a mixture of rotting vegetation, manure, etc. for fertilizing soil

com·po·sure (kəm pō′zhər) *n.* [COMPOS(E) + -URE] calmness; tranquillity; self-control —see SYN. at EQUANIMITY

com·pote (käm′pōt) *n.* [Fr.: see COMPOST] **1.** a dish of fruits stewed in a syrup ☆**2.** a long-stemmed dish for serving candy, fruit, etc.

com·pound¹ (käm pound′, kəm-; *for n. and, usually, for adj.,* käm′pound) *vt.* [< OFr. < L. *componere:* see COMPOSITE] **1.** to mix or combine **2.** to make by combining parts [to *compound* a medical prescription] **3.** to settle by mutual agreement; specif., to settle (a debt) by compromise payment **4.** to make greater by adding new elements [to *compound* a problem] **5.** to compute (interest) as compound interest —*vi.* to agree or compromise —*adj.* made up of two or more separate parts or elements —*n.* **1.** a thing formed by the combination of parts **2.** a substance containing two or more elements chemically combined in fixed proportions: distinguished from MIXTURE in that a compound has characteristics different from those of its constituents **3.** a word composed of two or more bases that are words themselves (Ex.: *blackbird*) —**compound a felony** (or **crime**) to agree, for payment, not to inform about or prosecute for a felony (or crime)

COMPOTE

com·pound² (käm′pound) *n.* [Anglo-Ind. < Malay *kampong*] **1.** in the Orient, an enclosed space with a building or group of buildings in it, esp. if occupied by foreigners **2.** any similar space

compound eye an eye, as in most insects, made up of numerous simple eyes, each having light-sensing cells and a refractive system that can form a part of an image

compound fraction *same as* COMPLEX FRACTION

compound fracture a bone fracture in which broken ends of bone have pierced the skin

compound interest interest paid on both the principal and the accumulated unpaid interest

compound leaf a leaf divided into two or more leaflets with a common leafstalk

compound microscope a microscope having a set of lenses built into the objective and another set in the eyepiece

compound number a quantity expressed in two or more sorts of related units (Ex.: 4 ft., 7 in.)

compound sentence a sentence consisting of two or more independent, coordinate clauses

com·pre·hend (käm′prə hend′) *vt.* [< L. *comprehendere* < *com-,* with + *prehendere,* to seize: see PREHENSILE] **1.** to grasp mentally; understand **2.** to include; comprise; take in —see SYN. at INCLUDE and UNDERSTAND —**com′pre·hend′ing·ly** *adv.*

com·pre·hen·si·ble (-hen′sə b′l) *adj.* that can be comprehended; intelligible; understandable —**com′pre·hen′si·bil′i·ty** *n.* —**com′pre·hen′si·bly** *adv.*

com·pre·hen·sion (-hen′shən) *n.* **1.** the fact of including or comprising; inclusiveness **2.** the act of understanding or the power to understand

com·pre·hen·sive (-hen′siv) *adj.* **1.** including much; inclusive [a *comprehensive* survey] **2.** able to comprehend fully [a *comprehensive* mind] —**com′pre·hen′sive·ly** *adv.* —**com′pre·hen′sive·ness** *n.*

com·press (kəm pres′; *for n.* käm′pres) *vt.* [< OFr. < LL. < L. pp. of *comprimere* < *com-,* together + *premere,* to PRESS¹] to press together; make more compact as by pressure [to *compress* medicine into tablets; to *compress* a long treatise into a brief summary] —*n.* **1.** a pad of folded cloth, often medicated or wet, for applying pressure, heat, cold, etc. to a part of the body ☆**2.** a machine for compressing cotton into bales —see SYN. at CONTRACT —**com·pressed′** *adj.* —**com·pres′si·bil′i·ty** *n.* —**com·pres′si·ble** *adj.* —**com·pres′sive** *adj.* —**com·pres′sive·ly** *adv.*

compressed air air held under pressure in a container: its force on expanding can operate machines

com·pres·sion (kəm presh′ən) *n.* **1.** a compressing or being compressed **2.** the compressing of a working fluid in an engine, as of the mixture in an internal-combustion engine just before ignition

com·pres·sor (-pres′ər) *n.* **1.** one that compresses **2.** a muscle that compresses a part **3.** a machine for compressing air, gas, etc.

com·prise (kəm prīz′) *vt.* **-prised′, -pris′ing** [< OFr. pp. of *comprendre:* see COMPREHEND] **1.** to include; contain **2.** to consist of [a nation *comprising* fifty States] **3.** to make up; form [a nation *comprised* of fifty States]: in this sense regarded by some as a loose usage —see SYN. at INCLUDE —**com·pris′a·ble** *adj.* —**com·pris′al** *n.*

com·pro·mise (käm′prə mīz′) *n.* [< OFr. < LL. < L. pp. of *compromittere* < *com-,* together + *promittere,* to PROMISE] **1.** a settlement in which each side gives up part of what it wants **2.** the result of such a settlement **3.** something midway between two other things in quality, effect, etc. **4.** *a)* exposure, as of one's reputation, to danger, suspicion, or disgrace *b)* a weakening, as of one's principles —*vt.* **-mised′, -mis′ing** **1.** to settle by a compromise **2.** to lay open to danger, suspicion, or disgrace **3.** to weaken (one's principles, etc.) in order to gain something —*vi.* to make a compromise —**com′pro·mis′er** *n.*

Comp·ton (kämp′tən) [after G. *Compton,* a founder of the U. of S Cal.] city in SW Calif.: suburb of Los Angeles: pop. 79,000

Comp·ton (kämp′tən) **1. Arthur Hol·ly** (häl′ē), 1892–1962; U.S. physicist **2. Karl Taylor,** 1887–1954; U.S. physicist: brother of *Arthur*

comp·trol·ler (kən trō′lər) *n.* [altered (after Fr. *compte,* an account) < CONTROLLER] *same as* CONTROLLER (sense 1) —**comp·trol′ler·ship′** *n.*

com·pul·sion (kəm pul′shən) *n.* [< LL. < L. pp. of *compellere,* COMPEL] **1.** a compelling or being compelled; coercion [under *compulsion* by oath to tell the truth] **2.** a driving force **3.** *Psychol.* a repeated, senseless impulse to do a particular thing that a person is unable to resist

com·pul·sive (-siv) *adj.* of, having to do with, or resulting from compulsion —**com·pul′sive·ly** *adv.* —**com·pul′sive·ness** *n.*

com·pul·so·ry (-sər ē) *adj.* **1.** that must be done; necessary; required [English is a *compulsory* subject in our school] **2.** compelling; coercive —**com·pul′so·ri·ly** *adv.* —**com·pul′so·ri·ness** *n.*

com·punc·tion (kəm puŋk′shən) *n.* [< OFr. < LL. *compunctio,* a pricking (of conscience) < L. *com-,* very much + *pungere,* to prick] **1.** a sharp feeling of uneasiness brought on by a sense of guilt; remorse **2.** a feeling of slight regret for something done —see SYN. at PENITENCE and QUALM —**com·punc′tious** *adj.* —**com·punc′tious·ly** *adv.*

com·pu·ta·tion (käm′pyoo tā′shən) *n.* **1.** a computing; calculation **2.** a method of computing **3.** a computed amount —**com′pu·ta′tion·al** *adj.*

com·pute (kəm pyoot′) *vt., vi.* **-put′ed, -put′ing** [L. *computare* < *com-,* with + *putare,* to reckon] to determine (an amount, etc.) by arithmetic; calculate —see SYN. at CALCULATE —**com·put′a·bil′i·ty** *n.* —**com·put′a·ble** *adj.*

com·put·er (kəm pyoot′ər) *n.* a person or thing that computes; specif., an electronic machine used as a calculator or to store and select data: see also ANALOG COMPUTER, DIGITAL COMPUTER

com·put·er·ize (-īz′) *vt.* **-ized′, -iz′ing** to equip with or operate by electronic computers [a bank's *computerized* accounting system] —**com·put′er·i·za′tion** *n.*

Comr. Commissioner

com·rade (käm′rad, -rəd) *n.* [< Fr. < Sp. *camarada,* chamber mate < L. *camera:* see CAMERA] **1.** a close friend; companion **2.** one who shares interests and activities in common with others; associate **3.** [C-] [Colloq.] a Communist —see SYN. at ASSOCIATE —**com′rade·ly** *adj.* —**com′rade·ship′** *n.*

comrade in arms a fellow soldier

☆**com·rade·ry** (-rē) *n. same as* CAMARADERIE

Com·stock Lode (käm′stäk′) [after H. *Comstock* (1820-70), who held first claim to it] rich deposits of silver and gold discovered in 1859 in W Nev.: virtually depleted by 1890

‡**comte** (kônt) *n.* [Fr.] *same as* COUNT² —**com·tesse** (kôn tes′) *n.fem.*

Comte (kônt; *E.* kōmt), (**Isidore**) **Au·guste** (ō güst′) 1798-1857; Fr. philosopher: founder of positivism —**Com·ti·an, Com·te·an** (käm′tē ən, kōm′-) *adj.*

con¹ (kän) *adv.* [< L. *contra,* against] against; in opposition [to argue pro and *con*] —*n.* a reason, vote, position, etc. in opposition

con² (kän) *vt.* **conned, con′ning** [ME. *connen,* to be able: see CAN¹] to study or learn carefully

con³ (kän) *vt., n. same as* CONN

☆**con**⁴ (kän) *adj.* [Slang] confidence [a *con* man] —*vt.* **conned, con′ning** [Slang] **1.** to swindle (a victim) by first gaining his confidence **2.** to trick or fool, esp. by smooth, persuasive talk

☆**con**⁵ (kän) *n.* [Slang] a convict

con- see COM-

con. **1.** concerto **2.** conclusion **3.** consolidated

Con·a·kry (kän′ə krē′) capital of Guinea; seaport on the Atlantic: pop. 120,000

con a·mo·re (kän′ ə môr′ē; *It.* kôn′ ä mô′re) [It.] with love; tenderly: a direction in music

Conan Doyle, Sir Arthur *see* DOYLE

con bri·o (kän brē′ō, kōn) [It.] with spirit; spiritedly: a direction in music

con·cat·e·nate (kän kat′'n āt′, kən-) *adj.* [< LL. pp. of *concatenare* < L. < *com-,* together + *catenare* < *catena,* a CHAIN] linked together; connected —*vt.* **-nat′ed, -nat′ing** to link or join, as in a chain

con·cat·e·na·tion (kän kat′'n ā′shən, kən-) *n.* **1.** a linking together or being linked together **2.** a connected series [a *concatenation* of events]

con·cave (kän kāv′; *also, and for n. usually,* kän′kāv) *adj.* [< OFr. < L. < *com-,* very + *cavus:* see CAVE] hollow and curved like the inside half of a hollow ball —*n.* a concave surface, line, object, etc. —*vt.* **-caved′, -cav′ing** to make concave —**con·cave′ly** *adv.* —**con·cave′ness** *n.*

con·cav·i·ty (kän kav′ə tē) *n.* **1.** the quality or condition of being concave **2.** *pl.* **-ties** a concave surface, line, etc.

con·ca·vo-con·cave (kän kā′vō kän kāv′) *adj.* concave on both sides, as some lenses

con·ca·vo-con·vex (-kän veks′) *adj.* concave on one side and convex on the other

con·ceal (kən sēl′) *vt.* [< OFr. < L. *concelare* < *com-,* together + *celare,* to hide: for IE. base see CELL] **1.** to put out of sight; hide [*concealed* weapons] **2.** to keep from another's knowledge; keep secret [to *conceal* one's amusement] —see SYN. at HIDE¹ —**con·ceal′ment** *n.*

con·cede (kən sēd′) *vt.* **-ced′ed, -ced′ing** [L. *concedere* < *com-,* with + *cedere,* to CEDE] **1.** to admit as true; acknowledge [to *concede* a point in argument] **2.** to admit as certain [to *concede* victory to an opponent] **3.** to grant as a right [to *concede* autonomy to local governments] —*vi.* **1.** to make a concession ☆**2.** to acknowledge defeat in an election —**con·ced′er** *n.*

con·ceit (kən sēt′) *n.* [see CONCEIVE] **1.** orig., an idea **2.** an exaggerated opinion of oneself, one's merits, etc.; vanity **3.** a fanciful or witty expression or notion **4.** a flight of imagination

con·ceit·ed (-id) *adj.* having an exaggerated opinion of oneself, one's merits, etc.; vain —**con·ceit′ed·ly** *adv.* —**con·ceit′ed·ness** *n.*

con·ceiv·a·ble (kən sē′və b'l) *adj.* that can be conceived, understood, imagined, or believed [he had no *conceivable* reason for lying] —**con·ceiv′a·bil′i·ty** *n.* —**con·ceiv′a·bly** *adv.*

con·ceive (kən sēv′) *vt.* **-ceived′, -ceiv′ing** [< OFr. < L. *concipere,* to receive < *com-,* together + *capere,* to take: for IE. base see HAVE] **1.** to become pregnant with **2.** to form in the mind [I have *conceived* a plan for action] **3.** to hold as one's opinion; think; imagine **4.** to understand [she can't *conceive* how this machine works] **5.** to express in words —*vi.* **1.** to become pregnant **2.** to form an idea (*of*)

con·cel·e·brate (kän sel′ə brāt′) *vt.* **-brat′ed, -brat′ing** [< L. pp. of *concelebrare:* see COM- & CELEBRATE] to celebrate (the

Eucharistic liturgy) jointly: said of two or more priests —**con′cel·e·bra′tion** *n.*

con·cen·ter (kən sen′tər) *vt., vi.* [< Fr. < L. *com-,* together + *centrum,* CENTER] to bring or come to a common center; concentrate or converge

con·cen·trate (kän′sən trāt′) *vt.* **-trat′ed, -trat′ing** [< prec. + -ATE¹] **1.** to bring to a common center; mass in one place [the troops were *concentrated* at the border] **2.** to focus (one's thoughts, efforts, etc.) **3.** to increase the strength, density, or intensity of [to *concentrate* soup by boiling it down] —*vi.* **1.** to come to a common center **2.** to fix one's attention (*on* or *upon*) —*n.* a substance that has been concentrated —*adj.* concentrated —**con′cen·tra′tive** *adj.* —**con′cen·tra′tor** *n.*

con·cen·tra·tion (kän′sən trā′shən) *n.* **1.** a concentrating or being concentrated **2.** close or fixed attention **3.** strength or density, as of a solution

concentration camp a prison camp in which political dissenters, members of minority ethnic groups, etc. are confined

con·cen·tric (kən sen′trik) *adj.* [< OFr. < ML. < L. *com-,* together + *centrum,* CENTER] having a center in common [*concentric* circles] —**con·cen′tri·cal·ly** *adv.* —**con·cen·tric·i·ty** (kän′sen tris′ə tē) *n.*

Con·cep·ción (kən sep′sē ōn′; *Sp.* kôn sep′syôn′) seaport on a river in SC Chile: pop. 202,000

con·cept (kän′sept) *n.* [< L. pp. of *concipere:* see CONCEIVE] an idea or thought, esp. a general idea of what a thing or class of things is [Jefferson's *concept* of democracy differed from Hamilton's] —see SYN. at IDEA

con·cep·tion (kən sep′shən) *n.* **1.** a conceiving or being conceived in the womb **2.** an embryo or fetus **3.** the conceiving or forming of an idea **4.** a general idea; concept **5.** an original or particular idea, design, plan, etc. [Shakespeare's *conception* of Richard II; the architect's *conception* of an industrial park] —see SYN. at IDEA —**con·cep′tion·al** *adj.*

con·cep·tu·al (kən sep′choo wəl) *adj.* of conception or concepts —**con·cep′tu·al·ly** *adv.*

con·cep·tu·al·ize (-īz′) *vt.* **-ized′, -iz′ing** to form a concept or idea of; conceive —**con·cep′tu·al·i·za′tion** *n.*

con·cern (kən surn′) *vt.* [< ML. < L. *com-,* with + *cernere,* to sift] **1.** to have a relation to; deal with [a book *concerning* foreign affairs] **2.** to involve; be a proper affair of [this matter *concerns* all men] **3.** to make uneasy or anxious [his depressions *concern* me] —*n.* **1.** a matter of importance to one; affair **2.** interest in or regard for a person or thing **3.** worry; anxiety **4.** a business firm —see SYN. at CARE —**as concerns** in regard to —**concern oneself 1.** to busy oneself (*with, about, over, in* something) **2.** to be worried or anxious

con·cerned (-surnd′) *adj.* **1.** involved or interested (often with *in*) **2.** uneasy or anxious

con·cern·ing (-sur′niŋ) *prep.* relating to; having to do with; in regard to; about

con·cern·ment (-surn′mənt) *n.* [Rare] *same as* CONCERN

con·cert (kən surt′; *for n. & adj.* kän′sərt) *vt., vi.* [Fr. < It. < *concertare* < *com-,* with + *certare,* to strive] to plan together; devise —*n.* **1.** mutual agreement **2.** musical harmony **3.** a program of vocal or instrumental music —*adj.* of or for concerts —**in concert** in unison or in agreement; all together

con·cert·ed (kən sur′tid) *adj.* **1.** arranged or agreed upon by all; done together [we made a *concerted* effort to surround them] **2.** *Music* arranged in parts —**con·cert′ed·ly** *adv.*

concert grand (piano) the largest size of grand piano, for concert performance

con·cer·ti·na (kän′sər tē′nə) *n.* [CONCERT + -INA: a coinage] a small musical instrument similar to an accordion, with buttons instead of a keyboard

con·cert·ize (kän′sər tīz′) *vi.* **-ized′, -iz′ing** to perform as a soloist in concerts

con·cert·mas·ter (kän′sərt mas′tər) *n.* [transl. of G. *konzertmeister*] the leader of the first violins of a symphony orchestra, often an assistant to the conductor: also **con′cert·meis′ter** (-mīs′-)

con·cer·to (kən cher′tō) *n., pl.* **-tos, -ti** (-tē) [It.: see CONCERT] a composition, usually in three movements in

CONCENTRIC
CIRCLES

CONCERTINA

symphonic form, for one or more solo instruments and an orchestra

con·certo gros·so (grō′sō) *pl.* **concerti gros′si** (-sē) [It., lit., big concerto] a concerto for a small group of solo instruments and a full orchestra

con·ces·sion (kən sesh′ən) *n.* **1.** a conceding, or giving in **2.** a thing conceded [a ruthless invader unwilling to make any *concessions* to a people suing for peace] **3.** a privilege granted by a government, company, etc.; esp., *a)* the right to use land for some purpose ☆*b)* the right to sell food, parking space, etc. on the lessor's premises —**con·ces′sive** (-ses′iv) *adj.*

con·ces·sion·aire (kən sesh′ə ner′) *n.* [Fr. *concessionnaire*] the holder of a concession granted by a government, company, etc.: also ☆**con·ces′sion·er**

conch (käŋk, känch) *n., pl.* **conchs** (käŋks), **conch·es** (kän′chəz) [< L. < Gr. *konchē*] **1.** the large spiral shell of any of various sea mollusks **2.** such a mollusk, often edible

con·chol·o·gy (käŋ käl′ə jē) *n.* [see prec. & -LOGY] the branch of zoology that deals with mollusks and shells — **con·chol′o·gist** *n.*

con·cierge (kän′sē urzh′; *Fr.* kōn syerzh′) *n.* [Fr.] **1.** a doorkeeper **2.** a custodian or head porter, as of an apartment house or hotel

CONCH

con·cil·i·ar (kən sil′ē ər) *adj.* [< L. *concilium*, COUNCIL] of, from, or by means of a council

con·cil·i·ate (kən sil′ē āt′) *vt.* **-at′ed, -at′ing** [< L. pp. of *conciliare* < *concilium*, COUNCIL] **1.** to win over; make friendly; placate [William Penn was notable among the colonizers for his efforts to *conciliate* the Indians] **2.** [Archaic] to reconcile; make consistent —see SYN. at PACIFY —**con·cil′i·a′tion** *n.* — **con·cil′i·a′tor** *n.*

con·cil·i·a·to·ry (-ə tôr′ē) *adj.* tending to conciliate or reconcile: also **con·cil′i·a′tive** (-āt′iv)

con·cise (kən sīs′) *adj.* [< L. pp. of *concidere* < *com-*, very much + *caedere*, to cut] brief and to the point; short and clear —**con·cise′ly** *adv.* —**con·cise′ness, con·ci′sion** (-sizh′ən) *n.*
SYN.—**concise** stresses briefness in speaking or writing so that no more words are used than are needed to express something clearly [a *concise* statement]; **terse** suggests extremely clipped and abrupt expression, as when one must be brief and to the point [the captain's *terse* command]; **laconic** implies a very brief, sometimes vague statement, as by someone who habitually says very little [the cowboy's *laconic* reply]; **succinct** indicates very brief, clear, and compact expression in which only what is essential is dealt with [a *succinct* record of the proceedings]; **pithy** suggests that what is stated in highly compressed form is important and full of meaning [a *pithy* proverb] —**ANT.** redundant, prolix

con·clave (kän′klāv, kän′-) *n.* [OFr. < L., a room, closet < *com-*, with + *clavis*, a key] **1.** R.C.Ch. *a)* the private meeting of the cardinals to elect a pope *b)* the cardinals as a group **2.** any private or secret meeting

con·clude (kən klōōd′) *vt.* **-clud′ed, -clud′ing** [< L. *concludere* < *com-*, together + *claudere*, to shut] **1.** to bring to a close; end; finish [he *concluded* the speech with a call for unity] **2.** to decide by reasoning; infer; deduce [from what you say, I *conclude* that no one person is to blame] **3.** to decide; determine [we *concluded* that he would go with us] **4.** to settle; come to an agreement about [to *conclude* a treaty with France] —*vi.* **1.** to come to a close; end; finish **2.** to come to an agreement —see SYN. at CLOSE², DECIDE, and INFER

con·clu·sion (kən klōō′zhən) *n.* **1.** the end or last part; as, *a)* the last section of a long, formal speech, etc. *b)* the last step in a reasoning process; judgment formed after thought *c)* the last of a chain of events; outcome **2.** a concluding (of a treaty, etc.) —**in conclusion** lastly; in closing

con·clu·sive (-siv) *adj.* that settles a question; final; decisive —**con·clu′sive·ly** *adv.* —**con·clu′sive·ness** *n.*

con·coct (kən käkt′, kän-) *vt.* [< L. pp. of *concoquere* < *com-*, together + *coquere*, to COOK] **1.** to make by combining ingredients [to *concoct* a stew from leftovers] **2.** to devise; make up [to *concoct* an excuse] —**con·coct′er** *or* **con·coc′tion** *n.*

con·com·i·tance (kən käm′ə təns, kän-) *n.* the fact of being concomitant: also **con·com′i·tan·cy**

con·com·i·tant (-käm′ə tənt) *adj.* [< L. prp. of *concomitari* <

com-, together + *comitari*, to accompany < *comes*, companion] accompanying; attendant [*concomitant* events] —*n.* an accompanying or attendant condition, circumstance, or thing —**con·com′i·tant·ly** *adv.*

Con·cord (käŋ′kôrd; *for 2 & 3 & n.* käŋ′kərd) **1.** city in W Calif., near Oakland: pop. 85,000 **2.** capital of N.H., in the SC part: pop. 30,000 **3.** town in E Mass., near Boston: site of one of the first battles of the Revolutionary War: pop. 16,000 —*n.* ☆**1.** a large, dark-blue grape: in full, **Concord grape** ☆**2.** a wine made from it

con·cord (kän′kôrd, käŋ′-) *n.* [< OFr. < L. < *concordis*, genitive of *concors*, of the same mind < *com-*, together + *cor*, heart] **1.** agreement; harmony **2.** *a)* peaceful relations, as between nations *b)* a treaty establishing this

con·cord·ance (kən kôr′d'ns, kän-) *n.* [see prec.] **1.** agreement; harmony **2.** an alphabetical list of the words used in a book or by an author, with references to the passages in which they occur [a Bible *concordance*]

con·cord·ant (-d'nt) *adj.* agreeing; consonant; harmonious — **con·cord′ant·ly** *adv.*

con·cor·dat (kən kôr′dat, kän-) *n.* [Fr. < ML. < L. pp. of *concordare*, to agree < *concors*: see CONCORD] **1.** a compact; formal agreement **2.** an agreement between a pope and a government concerning church affairs

con·course (kän′kôrs, käŋ′-) *n.* [< OFr. < L. < *concurrere*: see CONCUR] **1.** a coming or flowing together **2.** a crowd; throng ☆**3.** a large open space where crowds gather, as in a park or airport terminal **4.** a broad boulevard

con·crete (kän krēt′; *also, and for n. & vt. 2 usually,* kän′krēt) *adj.* [< L. pp. of *concrescere* < *com-*, together + *crescere*, to grow] **1.** formed into a solid mass; coalesced **2.** existing in reality or in material form; real; actual [to offer *concrete* help] **3.** specific, not general or abstract [a *concrete* example of his selfishness] **4.** made of concrete **5.** designating a thing or class of things that are real or exist in material form; not abstract [″tree″ is a *concrete* noun] —*n.* **1.** a concrete thing, idea, etc. **2.** a building material of sand and gravel bonded with cement into a hard substance: used in making bridges, road surfaces, etc. —*vt.* **-cret′ed, -cret′ing** **1.** to form into a mass; solidify **2.** to make of, or cover with, concrete —*vi.* to solidify —**con·crete′ly** *adv.* —**con·crete′ness** *n.*

con·cre·tion (kän krē′shən) *n.* [see prec.] **1.** a solidifying or being solidified **2.** a solidified mass

con·cre·tize (kän′krə tīz′, käŋ′-) *vt.* **-tized′, -tiz′ing** to make (something) concrete; make specific; give definite form to

con·cu·bine (käŋ′kyə bīn′, kän′-) *n.* [< OFr. < L. < *concumbere* < *com-*, with + *cubare*, to lie down] a woman who cohabits with a man although not legally married to him, specif., in some societies, as a secondary wife, of inferior status [″And he had seven hundred wives, princesses, and three hundred *concubines*″—I Kings 11:3] —**con·cu·bi·nage** (kän kyōō′bə nij) *n.*

con·cu·pis·cence (kän kyōō′pə s'ns) *n.* [OFr. < LL. < L. prp. of *concupiscere* < *com-*, very much + *cupere*, to desire] sexual desire; lust —**con·cu′pis·cent** *adj.*

con·cur (kən kur′) *vi.* **-curred′, -cur′ring** [< L. *concurrere* < *com-*, together + *currere*, to run] **1.** to occur at the same time **2.** to combine in having an effect; act together [several events *concurred* to bring about this result] **3.** to agree (*with*); be in accord (*in* an opinion, etc.) —see SYN. at CONSENT

con·cur·rence (-əns) *n.* **1.** a coming or happening together **2.** a combining to bring about something **3.** agreement; accord [We are in complete *concurrence*] Also **con·cur′ren·cy**

con·cur·rent (-ənt) *adj.* **1.** occurring or existing at the same time [*concurrent* investigations by local and federal authorities] **2.** converging or meeting at a point **3.** acting together [*concurrent* causes] **4.** in agreement **5.** *Law* exercised equally over the same area [*concurrent* jurisdiction] —**con·cur′rent·ly** *adv.*

☆**concurrent resolution** a resolution passed by one legislative branch and concurred in by the other, indicating opinion but not having the force of law: see also JOINT RESOLUTION

con·cuss (kən kus′) *vt.* to give a concussion to

con·cus·sion (kən kush′ən) *n.* [L. *concussio* < pp. of *concutere* < *com-*, together + *quatere*, to shake] **1.** a violent shaking or jarring; shock, as from impact **2.** *Med.* a hurt suffered by the brain, as a result of a blow on the head, causing unconsciousness, vomiting, etc. —**con·cus′sive** (-kus′iv) *adj.*

---

fat, āpe, cär; ten, ēven; is, bīte; gō, hôrn, tōōl, lŏŏk; oil, out; up, fur; get; joy; yet; chin; she; thin, then; zh, leisure; ŋ, ring; ə for *a* in *ago*, *e* in *agent*, *i* in *sanity*, *o* in *comply*, *u* in *focus*; ′ as in *able* (ā′b'l); Fr. bäl; ë, Fr. coeur; ö, Fr. feu; ô, Fr. mon; ô̜, Fr. coq; ü, Fr. duc; r, Fr. cri; H, G. ich; kh, G. doch; ‡foreign; ☆ Americanism; < derived from. See inside front cover.

con·demn (kən dem′) *vt.* [< OFr. < L. *condemnare* < *com-*, very much + *damnare,* to harm, condemn: for IE. base see DAMN] **1.** to disapprove of strongly; censure [an educator who *condemns* formal methods of teaching] **2.** *a)* to declare guilty of wrongdoing; convict *b)* to inflict a penalty upon [to *condemn* a man to death] *c)* to doom [she seems *condemned* to a life of drudgery] ☆**3.** to declare (property) legally appropriated for public use **4.** to declare unfit for use or service [to *condemn* a slum tenement] —see SYN. at CRITICIZE —**con·dem′na·ble** (-dem′nə b′l, -ə b′l) *adj.* —**con·demn′er** *n.*

con·dem·na·tion (kän′dem nā′shən, -dəm-) *n.* **1.** a condemning or being condemned **2.** a reason for condemning —**con·dem·na·to·ry** (kən dem′nə tôr′ē) *adj.*

con·den·sate (kän′dən sāt′, kən den′sāt) *n.* a substance formed by condensation

con·den·sa·tion (kän′dən sā′shən) *n.* **1.** a condensing or being condensed **2.** anything condensed [to read the *condensation* of a novel]

con·dense (kən dens′) *vt.* **-densed′, -dens′ing** [< Fr. < L. < *com-*, very + *densus,* dense] **1.** to make more dense or compact; compress **2.** to express in fewer words; make concise; abridge **3.** to change (a substance) to a denser form, as from a gas to a liquid —*vi.* to become condensed [steam *condenses* to water when it strikes a cold surface] —see SYN. at CONTRACT —**con·dens·a·bil·i·ty, con·dens′i·bil′i·ty** *n.* —**con·dens′a·ble, con·dens′i·ble** *adj.*

☆**condensed milk** a thick milk made by evaporating part of the water from cow's milk and adding sugar

con·dens·er (kən den′sər) *n.* a person or thing that condenses; specif., *a)* an apparatus for converting gases or vapors to a liquid state *b)* a lens or series of lenses for concentrating light rays on an area *c) Elec.* same as CAPACITOR

con·de·scend (kän′də send′) *vi.* [< OFr. < LL. *condescendere* < L. *com-*, together + *descendere,* DESCEND] **1.** to descend to the level of the person that one is dealing with; be politely willing to do something thought to be beneath one's dignity [the judge *condescended* to join in the game] **2.** to deal with others in a patronizing manner —see SYN. at STOOP —**con′de·scend′ing** *adj.* —**con′de·scend′ly** *adv.* —**con′de·scen′sion** (-sen′shən), **con′de·scend′ence** *n.*

con·dign (kən dīn′) *adj.* [< OFr. < L. *condignus* < *com-*, very + *dignus,* worthy] deserved; suitable: said esp. of punishment —**con·dign′ly** *adv.*

con·di·ment (kän′də mənt) *n.* [< OFr. < L. *condimentum,* a spice < *condire,* to pickle] a seasoning or relish for food, as pepper, mustard, sauces, etc.

con·di·tion (kən dish′ən) *n.* [< OFr. < L. *condicio,* agreement < *com-*, together + *dicere,* to speak] **1.** anything required before the performance or completion of something else; provision; stipulation [*conditions* set for a cease-fire] **2.** prerequisite [some consider wealth a *condition* of happiness] **3.** anything that has an effect on the nature of something else; circumstance [*conditions* were favorable for business] **4.** manner or state of being [a house in a dilapidated *condition*] **5.** *a)* state of health [the patient's *condition*] *b)* [Colloq.] an illness; ailment [a lung *condition*] **6.** a proper or healthy state [athletes out of *condition*] **7.** social position; rank; station ☆**8.** the requirement that a student make up deficiencies in a subject in order to pass it **9.** *Law* a clause in a contract, will, etc. that revokes or modifies all or part of it if a certain thing happens —*vt.* **1.** to impose a condition or conditions on **2.** to be a condition of; determine, modify, or influence [factors which *condition* our lives] **3.** to bring into a proper or desired condition [training camps help to *condition* a team] **4.** *Psychol. a)* to develop a conditioned reflex or behavior pattern in *b)* to cause to become accustomed (*to*) [to *condition* people to change] —see SYN. at STATE —**on condition that** provided that —**con·di′tion·er** *n.*

con·di·tion·al (-′l) *adj.* **1.** containing or dependent on a condition; qualified [a *conditional* award] **2.** expressing a condition [a *conditional* clause] —**con·di′tion·al′i·ty** (-al′ə tē) *n.* —**con·di′tion·al·ly** *adv.*

conditioned reflex (or **response**) a reflex in which the response (e.g., secretion of saliva in a dog) is occasioned by a secondary stimulus (e.g., the ringing of a bell) repeatedly associated with the primary stimulus (e.g., the sight of meat)

☆**con·do** (kän′dō) *n., pl.* **-dos, -does** *clipped form of* CONDOMINIUM (sense 2)

con·dole (kən dōl′) *vi.* **-doled′, -dol′ing** [< LL. *condolere* < L. *com-*, with + *dolere,* to grieve] to express sympathy; mourn in sympathy [to *condole* with the widow] —**con·do′la·to·ry** (-dō′lə tôr′ē) *adj.* —**con·dol′er** *n.*

con·do·lence (kən dō′ləns) *n.* [often *pl.*] expression of sympathy with another in grief: also **con·dole′ment**

con·dom (kun′dəm, kän′-) *n.* [supposedly from the name of a 17th-c. Brit. colonel] a thin sheath, esp. of rubber, for the penis, used to prevent venereal disease or as a contraceptive

con·do·min·i·um (kän′də min′ē əm) *n.* [ModL. < L. *com-*, together + *dominium,* dominion] **1.** joint rule by two or more states ☆**2.** *pl.* **-i·ums, -i·a** (-ə) an apartment building or multiple-unit dwelling in which each tenant holds full title to his or her unit and joint ownership in the common grounds

con·done (kən dōn′) *vt.* **-doned′, -don′ing** [< L. *condonare* < *com-*, very much + *donare,* to give] to forgive, pardon, or overlook (an offense) —**con·don′a·ble** *adj.* —**con·do·na·tion** (kän′dō nā′shən, -də-) *n.* —**con·don′er** *n.*

con·dor (kän′dər) *n.* [Sp. < Quechua *cuntur*] **1.** a very large vulture of the S. American Andes, with a bare head and a neck ruff of downy white feathers **2.** a similar vulture of southern Calif. **3.** *pl.*

con·dor·es (kän dō′res) any of various S. American gold coins

CONDOR
(wingspread to 12 ft.)

con·duce (kən dōōs′, -dyōōs′) *vi.* **-duced′, -duc′ing** [< L. *conducere* < *com-*, together + *ducere,* to lead] to tend or lead (*to* an effect); contribute

con·du·cive (-dōō′siv, -dyōō′-) *adj.* conducing; tending or leading (*to*) [soft music is *conducive* to sleep] —**con·du′cive·ness** *n.*

con·duct (kän′dukt′; *for v.* kən dukt′) *n.* [< L. pp. of *conducere:* see CONDUCE] **1.** management; handling [the *conduct* of the war] **2.** the way that one acts; behavior —*vt.* **1.** to lead; guide [*conduct* her to a seat] **2.** to manage, control, or direct [to *conduct* a meeting] **3.** to direct (an orchestra, choir, etc.) **4.** to behave (oneself) [he *conducted* himself like a gentleman] **5.** to be able to transmit [copper *conducts* electricity] —*vi.* to act as a conductor —**con·duct′i·bil′i·ty** *n.* —**con·duct′i·ble** *adj.*

SYN. —**conduct,** in this comparison, implies supervision by one with some skill or experience in carrying out plans, projects, etc. [to *conduct* a sales campaign]; **direct** suggests supervision by one who has overall authority but is not concerned with actual details [to *direct* a nation's economic policy]; **manage** implies supervision that involves the personal handling of all details [to *manage* a baseball team]; **control** suggests firm overall supervision, often by one who has complete authority to direct others [the superintendent of schools *controls* the system]

con·duct·ance (kən duk′təns) *n.* the ability of a component to conduct electricity, measured by the ratio of the current to applied electromotive force

con·duc·tion (kən duk′shən) *n.* **1.** a conveying, as of liquid through a channel **2.** the transmission of nerve impulses **3.** *Physics a)* transmission (*of* electricity, heat, etc.) by the passage of energy from particle to particle *b)* same as CONDUCTIVITY: see also CONVECTION, RADIATION

con·duc·tive (-tiv) *adj.* having conductivity

con·duc·tiv·i·ty (kän′duk tiv′ə tē) *n.* the property of conducting heat, electricity, etc.

con·duc·tor (kən duk′tər) *n.* **1.** a person who conducts; leader; guide **2.** the director of an orchestra, choir, etc. ☆**3.** one who has charge of the passengers and collects fares on a train, streetcar, or bus **4.** a thing that conducts electricity, heat, etc. —**con·duc·to·ri·al** (kän′duk tôr′ē əl) *adj.*

con·duit (kän′dit, -dōō wit) *n.* [< OFr. < L. pp. of *conducere:* see CONDUCE] **1.** a pipe or channel for carrying fluids **2.** a tube for protecting electric wires or cables

cone (kōn) *n.* [< L. < Gr. *kōnos*] **1.** *a)* a solid with a circle for its base and a curved surface tapering evenly to a point *b)* a surface described by a moving straight line passing through a fixed point and tracing a fixed curve, as a circle or ellipse, at another point **2.** any object shaped like a cone, as a shell of pastry for holding ice cream, the peak of a volcano, etc. **3.** a reproductive structure of certain lower plants, with an elongated central axis bearing overlapping scales, bracts, etc. which produce pollen, spores, or ovules **4.** *Zool.* any of the flask-shaped cells in the retina, sensitive to light and color —*vt.* **coned**, **con′ing** to shape like a cone

CONES
(A, longleaf pine;
B, piñon;
C, blue spruce)

☆**Con·es·to·ga wagon** (kän′ə stō′gə) [after *Conestoga* Valley, Pa.] a broad-wheeled covered wagon used by American pioneers crossing the prairies

co·ney (kō′nē) *n.*, *pl.* **-neys**, **-nies** [< OFr. < L. *cuniculus*, rabbit] **1.** a rabbit, esp. the European rabbit **2.** rabbit fur **3.** *Bible* a small animal, probably the hyrax **4.** *same as* PIKA

CONESTOGA WAGON

Co·ney Island (kō′nē) [< Du. *Konynen Eyland*, rabbit island] beach & amusement park in Brooklyn, N.Y., at the SW end of Long Island

conf. 1. conference **2.** confessor

con·fab (kän′fab′; *for v. usually* kən fab′) *n.* [Colloq.] a confabulation; talk or discussion —*vi.* **-fabbed′, -fab′bing** [Colloq.] to confabulate; talk together

con·fab·u·late (kən fab′yə lāt′) *vi.* **-lat′ed, -lat′ing** [< L. pp. of *confabulari* < *com-*, together + *fabulari*, to talk: see FABLE] to talk together —**con·fab′u·la′tion** *n.*

con·fect (kən fekt′) *vt.* [< L. pp. of *conficere* < *com-*, with + *facere*, to make, DO¹] to prepare or make, esp. by mixing or combining

con·fec·tion (kən fek′shən) *n.* [< OFr. < L. < pp. of *conficere* < *com-*, with + *facere*, to make, DO¹] a confecting of something or the thing confected; specif., any candy or other sweet preparation, as ice cream —**con·fec′tion·ar′y** *adj.*

con·fec·tion·er (-ər) *n.* one whose work or business is making or selling confectionery

☆**confectioners' sugar** very fine powdered sugar

con·fec·tion·er·y (-er′ē) *n.*, *pl.* **-er′ies 1.** confections or candy and other sweets **2.** the business, work, or shop of a confectioner

Confed. 1. Confederate **2.** Confederation

con·fed·er·a·cy (kən fed′ər ə sē) *n.*, *pl.* **-cies** [see CONFEDERATE] **1.** people, nations, etc. united for some common purpose **2.** a league or alliance formed by them —see SYN. at ALLIANCE —☆**the Confederacy** the league of Southern States that seceded from the U.S. in 1860 & 1861: official name **Confederate States of America**

con·fed·er·ate (kən fed′ər it; *for v.* -ə rāt′) *adj.* [< LL. pp. of *confoederare*, to unite by a league < *foedus*, a league: for IE. base see FAITH] **1.** united in a confederacy or league ☆**2.** [C-] of the Confederacy —*n.* **1.** a person, group, or state united with another or others for a common purpose; ally **2.** an associate in crime; accomplice ☆**3.** [C-] any Southern supporter of the Confederacy —*vt., vi.* **-at′ed, -at′ing** to unite in a confederacy; ally —see SYN. at ASSOCIATE

con·fed·er·a·tion (kən fed′ə rā′shən) *n.* **1.** a uniting or being united in a league or alliance **2.** nations or states joined in a league, as for common defense —☆**the Confederation** the United States of America (1781–1789) under the ARTICLES OF CONFEDERATION —see SYN. at ALLIANCE —**con·fed′er·al** *adj.* —**con·fed′er·a′tive** *adj.*

con·fer (kən fur′) *vt.* **-ferred′, -fer′ring** [< L. *conferre* < *com-*, together + *ferre*, to BEAR¹] to give, grant, or bestow [to *confer* a medal upon the hero] —*vi.* to have a conference; meet for discussion —see SYN. at GIVE —**con·fer′ment, con·fer′ral** *n.* —**con·fer′ra·ble** *adj.* —**con·fer′rer** *n.*

☆**con·fer·ee** (kän′fə rē′) *n.* **1.** one who takes part in a conference **2.** a person on whom an honor, degree, favor, etc. is conferred

con·fer·ence (kän′fər əns, -frəns) *n.* **1.** a conferring or consulting on a serious matter **2.** a formal meeting of a number of people for discussion, as of committees from both branches of a legislature to work out differences between their bills **3.** [often C-] the governing body of some churches **4.** an association, as of colleges or athletic teams —**con·fer·en·tial** (kän′fə ren′shəl) *adj.*

con·fess (kən fes′) *vt.* [< OFr. < L. pp. of *confiteri* < *com-*, together + *fateri*, to acknowledge] **1.** *a)* to admit (a fault, crime, etc.) *b)* to acknowledge (an opinion, etc.) [I *confess* that operas bore me] **2.** *a)* to tell (one's sins), esp. to a priest in the sacrament of penance *b)* to hear the confession of (a person): said of a priest —*vi.* **1.** to admit a fault or crime **2.** *a)* to make one's confession to a priest *b)* to hear such con-

fessions —see SYN. at ACKNOWLEDGE —**confess to** to admit or admit having —**stand confessed as** to be revealed as

con·fess·ed·ly (-id lē) *adv.* admittedly

con·fes·sion (kən fesh′ən) *n.* **1.** a confessing; specif., *a)* an admission of guilt, as by a person charged with a crime *b)* a confessing of sins to a priest in the sacrament of penance **2.** something confessed **3.** *a)* a statement of religious beliefs: in full, **confession of faith** *b)* a church having such a confession; communion

con·fes·sion·al (-'l) *n.* a small, enclosed place in a church, where a priest hears confessions —*adj.* of or for a confession

con·fes·sor (kən fes′ər) *n.* **1.** one who confesses **2.** *R.C.Ch.* a male saint who was not a martyr **3.** a priest who hears confessions

con·fet·ti (kən fet′ē) *n.pl.* [*with sing. v.*] [It., pl. of *confetto*, sweetmeat: candies were formerly so scattered] bits of colored paper scattered about at carnivals and other celebrations

con·fi·dant (kän′fə dant′, -dänt′; kän′fə dant′, -dänt′) *n.* a close, trusted friend to whom one confides personal secrets —**con′fi·dante′** *n.fem.*

con·fide (kən fīd′) *vi.* **-fid′ed, -fid′ing** [L. *confidere* < *com-*, very much + *fidere*, to trust: see FAITH] to trust (in someone), esp. by sharing secrets or discussing private affairs —*vt.* **1.** to tell or talk about as a secret [to *confide* one's troubles to a friend] **2.** to entrust (a duty, person, etc.) *to* someone —see SYN. at COMMIT —**con·fid′er** *n.*

con·fi·dence (kän′fə dəns) *n.* **1.** firm belief; trust; reliance [having *confidence* in his skill] **2.** certainty; assurance [to recommend him with *confidence*] **3.** belief in one's own abilities; self-confidence **4.** a relationship as confidant [take me into your *confidence*] **5.** the belief that another will keep a secret [told in strict *confidence*] **6.** something told as a secret — ☆*adj.* swindling or used to swindle —see SYN. at BELIEF

☆**confidence game** a swindle carried out by one who first gains the confidence of his victim

☆**confidence man** a swindler who first tries to gain the confidence of his victim

con·fi·dent (-dənt) *adj.* full of confidence; specif., *a)* assured; certain [*confident* of victory] *b)* sure of oneself; self-confident; bold [a *confident* boy] —*n. same as* CONFIDANT —see SYN. at SURE —**con′fi·dent·ly** *adv.*

con·fi·den·tial (kän′fə den′shəl) *adj.* **1.** told in confidence; secret [a *confidential* report] **2.** of or showing confidence or trust [to get *confidential* with a new friend] **3.** entrusted with private or secret matters [a *confidential* agent] —**con′fi·den′tial·ly** *adv.*

con·fid·ing (kən fīd′iŋ) *adj.* trustful or inclined to trust —**con·fid′ing·ly** *adv.*

con·fig·u·ra·tion (kən fig′yə rā′shən) *n.* [< L. *configurare* < *com-*, together + *figurare*: see FIGURE] **1.** arrangement of parts **2.** form, outline, or structure as determined by the arrangement of parts —**con·fig′u·ra′tion·al** *adj.* —**con·fig′u·ra′tive** *adj.*

con·fine (kən fīn′; *for n.* kän′fīn′) *n.* [< OFr. < L. *confinium*, boundary < *com-*, with + *finis*, an end, limit] a boundary or limit: *usually used in pl.* [the *confines* of the park] —*vt.* **-fined′, -fin′ing 1.** to keep within limits; restrict [to *confine* a talk to ten minutes] **2.** to keep shut up, as in prison, in bed because of illness, indoors, etc. —**con·fin′a·ble, con·fine′a·ble** *adj.*

con·fine·ment (kən fīn′mənt) *n.* **1.** a confining or being confined; specif., *a)* imprisonment *b)* limitation; restriction; restraint **2.** childbirth; lying-in

con·firm (kən furm′) *vt.* [< OFr. < L. *confirmare* < *com-*, very much + *firmare*, to strengthen < *firmus*, firm] **1.** to make firm; strengthen; establish [the propaganda he read *confirmed* him in his prejudices] **2.** to make valid by formal approval; ratify [to *confirm* a treaty] **3.** to prove the truth or validity of; verify **4.** to cause to undergo religious confirmation —**con·firm′a·ble** *adj.*

SYN.—to **confirm** is to establish the truth of something that was doubtful or uncertain [to *confirm* a rumor]; **substantiate** suggests the producing of evidence that proves an earlier statement [census figures *substantiate* his claim]; **corroborate** suggests the strengthening of one statement by another [two other witnesses *corroborated* her testimony]; to **verify** is to prove the truth or accuracy of something by investigation or by comparison with a standard or the facts [to *verify* an account]; **authenticate** implies proof of genuineness by an expert [to *authenticate* a painting]; **validate** implies the confirming of something officially to be valid [to *validate* a will] —**ANT.** contradict, disprove

con·fir·mand (kän′fər mand′, kän′fər mand′) *n.* a person who is to be confirmed in a religious ceremony

con·fir·ma·tion (kän′fər mā′shən) *n.* **1.** a confirming or being confirmed; ratification; verification **2.** something that confirms or proves **3.** *a)* a Christian ceremony admitting a person to full church membership ☆*b)* a Jewish ceremony in which young people reaffirm their belief in Judaism

con·fir·ma·to·ry (kən fur′mə tôr′ē) *adj.* confirming or tending to confirm: also **con·firm′a·tive**

con·firmed (kən furmd′) *adj.* **1.** firmly established, as in a habit or condition [a *confirmed* bachelor] **2.** proved to be true [a *confirmed* theory] **3.** having accepted religious confirmation —see SYN. at CHRONIC —**con·firm′ed·ly** *adv.*

con·fis·ca·ble (kän fis′kə b'l) *adj.* liable to be confiscated: also **con·fis·cat·a·ble** (kän′fə skāt′ə b'l)

con·fis·cate (kän′fə skāt′) *vt.* **-cat′ed, -cat′ing** [< L. pp. of *confiscare*, to lay up in a chest < *com-*, together + *fiscus*, money chest, treasury] **1.** to seize (private property) for the public treasury, usually as a penalty [to *confiscate* smuggled goods] **2.** to seize as by authority; appropriate [the teacher *confiscated* the comic books] —**con′fis·ca′tion** *n.* —**con′fis·ca′tor** *n.*

con·fis·ca·to·ry (kən fis′kə tôr′ē) *adj.* **1.** of, constituting, or bringing about confiscation [a *confiscatory* tax] **2.** confiscating

con·fit·e·or (kən fit′ē ôr′) *n.* [< LL., I confess] a formal prayer in which sins are confessed

con·fla·gra·tion (kän′flə grā′shən) *n.* [< L. < pp. of *conflagrare* < *com-*, very much + *flagrare*, to burn: for IE. base see BLACK] a big fire that does great damage

con·flict (kən flikt′; *for n.* kän′flikt) *vi.* [< L. pp. of *confligere* < *com-*, together + *fligere*, to strike] **1.** orig., to fight **2.** to disagree sharply; be antagonistic, incompatible, or contradictory; clash [his ideas *conflict* with mine] —*n.* **1.** a fight or struggle **2.** sharp disagreement or opposition, as of interests or ideas **3.** emotional disturbance resulting from opposing impulses —**con·flic′tion** *n.* —**con·flic′tive** *adj.*

conflict of interest a conflict between one's obligation to the public and one's self-interest, as in the case of an elected official who owns stock in a company seeking government contracts

con·flu·ence (kän′floo əns) *n.* [OFr. < LL. < L. prp. of *confluere* < *com-*, together + *fluere*, to flow] **1.** a flowing together, esp. of two or more streams **2.** the place where they join, or a stream formed in this way **3.** a coming together as of people; crowd; throng —**con′flu·ent** *adj.*

con·form (kən fôrm′) *vt.* [< OFr. < L. *conformare* < *com-*, together + *formare*, to FORM] **1.** to make the same or similar **2.** to bring into harmony or agreement; adapt —*vi.* **1.** to be or become the same or similar [the routes did not *conform* with those shown on the map] **2.** to be in accord or agreement [the house *conforms* to specifications] **3.** to accept without question customs, traditions, prevailing opinion, etc. and behave the way most people do —see SYN. at ADAPT and AGREE —**con·form′er** *n.* —**con·form′ism** *n.* —**con·form′ist** *n.*

con·form·a·ble (-fôr′mə b'l) *adj.* **1.** that conforms; specif., *a)* similar *b)* in harmony or agreement *c)* suited; adapted **2.** quick to conform; obedient; submissive —**con·form′a·bil′i·ty** *n.* —**con·form′a·bly** *adv.*

con·form·ance (-fôr′məns) *n.* same as CONFORMITY

con·for·ma·tion (kän′fôr mā′shən) *n.* **1.** a symmetrical formation and arrangement of the parts of a thing **2.** the structure or form of a thing as determined by the arrangement of its parts [an earthquake changed the *conformation* of the land]

con·form·i·ty (kən fôr′mə tē) *n., pl.* **-ties** **1.** the condition or fact of being in harmony or agreement; correspondence [in *conformity* with humanitarian principles] **2.** action in accordance with customs, rules, popular opinion, etc. [extreme *conformity* often prevents original thought]

con·found (kən found′, kän-; *for 3, usually* kän′-) *vt.* [< OFr. < L. *confundere* < *com-*, together + *fundere*, to pour: see FOUND³] **1.** to mix up or lump together in a confused way [to *confound* the good with the bad] **2.** to make feel confused; bewilder [*confounded* by all the problems he faced] **3.** to damn: used as a mild oath [*confound* it!] **4.** [Archaic] to defeat or destroy —see SYN. at PUZZLE

con·found·ed (-id) *adj.* **1.** confused; bewildered **2.** damned: a mild oath —**con·found′ed·ly** *adv.*

con·fra·ter·ni·ty (kän′frə tur′nə tē) *n., pl.* **-ties** [< ML.: see COM- & FRATERNITY] **1.** brotherhood **2.** a group of men associated for some purpose, often religious

con·frere (kän′frer, kōn′-) *n.* [OFr. *confrère*] a fellow member or worker; colleague

con·front (kən frunt′) *vt.* [Fr. < ML. *confrontare* < L. *com-*, together + *frons*, forehead: see FRONT] **1.** to stand or meet face to face [let us solve the problems *confronting* us] **2.** to face or oppose boldly or defiantly [to *confront* an enemy] **3.** to bring face to face (*with*) [to *confront* him with the facts] —**con·fron·ta·tion** (kän′frən tā′shən), **con·front′al** *n.*

Con·fu·cian·ism (kən fyōō′shən iz'm) *n.* the ethical teachings of Confucius, emphasizing devotion to family and friends, ancestor worship, and the maintenance of justice and peace — **Con·fu′cian·ist** *n., adj.*

Con·fu·cius (kən fyōō′shəs) (L. name of *K'ung Fu-tse*) 551?–479? B.C.; Chin. philosopher & teacher —**Con·fu′cian** (-shən) *adj., n.*

con·fuse (kən fyōōz′) *vt.* **-fused′, -fus′ing** [< OFr. < L. pp. of *confundere*: see CONFOUND] **1.** to mix up; jumble together; put into disorder [papers on the desk in a *confused* heap] **2.** to mix up mentally; specif., *a)* to bewilder; perplex [the complicated instructions *confused* me] *b)* to embarrass; disconcert [*confused* by the praise, he blushed and stammered] *c)* to fail to distinguish between; mistake the identity of [don't *confuse* wisdom and knowledge] —see SYN. at PUZZLE —**con·fus′ed·ly** (-fyōōz′id lē) *adv.* —**con·fus′ing** *adj.* —**con·fus′ing·ly** *adv.*

con·fu·sion (kən fyōō′zhən) *n.* a confusing or being confused; specif., *a)* state of disorder *b)* bewilderment *c)* embarrassment *d)* failure to distinguish between things [his *confusion* of colors comes from color blindness] —**covered with confusion** greatly embarrassed —**con·fu′sion·al** *adj.*

SYN.—**confusion** suggests such a mixing together of things that it is hard to recognize the individual parts [the hall was a *confusion* of languages]; **disorder** and **disarray** imply a disturbance of the proper order or arrangement of parts [the *disorder* in the room following the burglary; high winds left her hair in *disarray*]; **chaos** implies such a total lack of organization that putting things straight seems impossible [the *chaos* left in the wake of the hurricane]; **jumble** suggests a confused mixture of unlike things [her purse was a *jumble* of cosmetics, papers, earrings, and change]; **muddle** implies a tangled confusion resulting from bungling or lack of skill [the young accountant made a *muddle* of the company's books] —*ANT.* order, system

con·fute (kən fyōōt′) *vt.* **-fut′ed, -fut′ing** [L. *confutare*: for IE. base see BEAT] **1.** to prove (a person, statement, etc.) to be in error or false; overcome by argument or proof [the old deed *confutes* the squatter's claim to the property] —see SYN. at DISPROVE —**con·fu·ta·tion** (kän′fyoo tā′shən) *n.* —**con·fut′er** *n.*

Cong. **1.** Congress **2.** Congressional

con·ga (käŋ′gə) *n.* [AmSp., ult. < CONGO] **1.** a Latin American dance in which the dancers form a winding line **2.** syncopated music for this dance

con·gé (kän′zhā, -jā′; *Fr.* kōn zhā′) *n.* [Fr. < OFr. < L. < *com-*, to and fro + *meare*, to go] **1.** a curt dismissal **2.** a formal farewell

con·geal (kən jēl′) *vt., vi.* [< OFr. < L. *congelare* < *com-*, together + *gelare*, to freeze: for IE. base see COOL] **1.** to solidify or thicken by cooling or freezing **2.** to thicken; coagulate; jell —**con·geal′a·ble** *adj.* —**con·geal′ment** *n.*

con·gen·er (kän′jə nər) *n.* [L. < *com-*, together + *generis*, genitive of *genus*, race, kind] a person or thing of the same kind, class, genus, etc. —**con·ge·ner′ic** (-ner′ik), **con·gen·er·ous** (kən jen′ər əs) *adj.*

con·gen·ial (kən jēn′yəl) *adj.* [see COM- & GENIAL] **1.** similar; compatible [our tastes are *congenial*] **2.** having the same tastes and temperament; sympathetic [*congenial* friends] **3.** suited to one's needs, mood, or nature; agreeable [*congenial* work] — **con·ge·ni·al·i·ty** (-jēn′ē al′ə tē) *n.* —**con·gen′ial·ly** *adv.*

con·gen·i·tal (kən jen′ə t'l) *adj.* [< L.: see COM- & GENITAL] **1.** existing as such at birth, or from the period in the womb [a *congenital* disease] **2.** as if from birth; inherent [a *congenital* liar] —**con·gen′i·tal·ly** *adv.*

con·ger (eel) (käŋ′gər) [< OFr. < L. < Gr. *gongros*] a large, edible saltwater eel

con·ge·ries (kän′jə rēz′, kän jir′ēz) *n., pl.* **con·ge·ries′** [L. < *congerere*: see CONGEST] a collection of things or parts massed together; heap; pile

con·gest (kən jest′) *vt.* [< L. pp. of *congerere*, to pile up < *com-*, together + *gerere*, to carry] **1.** to cause too much blood to collect in the vessels of (a part of the body) **2.** to make too full; overcrowd; clog [a *congested* highway] —*vi.* to become congested —**con·ges′tion** (-jes′chən) *n.* —**con·ges′tive** (₋tiv) *adj.*

con·glo·bate (kän glō′bāt; kän′glō bāt′, käŋ′-) *vt., vi.* **-bat′ed, -bat′ing** [< L.: see COM- & GLOBE & -ATE¹] to form into a ball or rounded mass: also **con·globe** (kən glōb′) —*adj.* formed into a ball —**con′glo·ba′tion** *n.*

con·glom·er·ate (kən gläm′ə rāt′; *for adj. & n.* -ər it) *vt., vi.* **-at·ed, -at·ing** [< L. pp. of *conglomerare* < *com-*, together + *glomerare* < *glomus*, a ball: for IE. base see CLAW] to form or collect into a rounded or compact mass —*adj.* **1.** formed into a rounded or compact mass; clustered **2.** made up of separate substances collected into a single mass **3.** *Geol.* made up of rock fragments or pebbles cemented together by clay, silica, etc.: also **con·glom′·er·at′ic** (-ə rat′ik), **con·glom′er·it′ic** (-ə·rit′ik) —*n.* **1.** a conglomerate mass; cluster ☆**2.** a large corporation formed by merging many companies in various industries **3.** *Geol.* a conglomerate rock —**con·glom′·er·a′tion** *n.*

CONGLOMERATE ROCK

Con·go (käŋ′gō) **1.** river in C Africa, flowing through Zaire into the Atlantic **2.** country in WC Africa, west of Zaire: 132,046 sq. mi.; pop. 826,000; cap. Brazzaville **3.** *former name of* ZAIRE —**Con′go·lese′** (-gə lēz′) *adj., n.*

☆**congo eel** (or **snake**) an eellike animal of the southeastern U.S. that can live on land and in water: it has two pairs of small, weak legs

con·grat·u·late (kən grach′ə lāt′) *vt.* **-lat·ed, -lat·ing** [< L. pp. of *congratulari* < *com-*, together + *gratulari*, to wish joy < *gratus*, agreeable] to express to (a person) one's pleasure at his good fortune, success, etc. [his fellow students *congratulated* him when he won the scholarship] —**con·grat′u·la′tor** *n.* — **con·grat′u·la·to′ry** (-lə tôr′ē) *adj.*

con·grat·u·la·tion (kən grach′ə lā′shən) *n.* **1.** a congratulating **2.** [*pl.*] expressions of pleasure and good wishes at another's fortune or success

con·gre·gate (käŋ′grə gāt′; *for adj.* -git) *vt., vi.* **-gat·ed, -gat·ing** [< L. pp. of *congregare* < *com-*, together + *gregare*, to gather < *grex*, a flock] to gather into a mass or crowd; collect; assemble [we *congregated* around the piano] —*adj.* **1.** assembled; collected **2.** collective —**con′gre·ga′tive** *adj.* —**con′gre·ga′tor** *n.*

con·gre·ga·tion (käŋ′grə gā′shən) *n.* **1.** a congregating or being congregated **2.** a gathering of people or things; assemblage **3.** a group of people meeting for religious worship **4.** the members of a particular place of worship **5.** *R.C.Ch.* a religious community not necessarily under solemn vows but bound by a common rule

con·gre·ga·tion·al (-'l) *adj.* **1.** of or like a congregation **2.** [C-] of Congregationalism or Congregationalists

con·gre·ga·tion·al·ism (-'l iz′m) *n.* **1.** a form of church organization in which each local congregation is self-governing **2.** [C-] the faith and form of organization of a Protestant denomination in which each member church is self-governing —**Con′gre·ga′tion·al·ist** *n., adj.*

con·gress (käŋ′grəs) *n.* [< L. pp. of *congredi* < *com-*, together + *gradi*, to walk < *gradus*, a step] **1.** a coming together; meeting **2.** an association or society **3.** an assembly or conference **4.** any of various legislatures, esp. the national legislature of a republic ☆**5.** [C-] *a)* the legislature of the U.S., consisting of the Senate and the House of Representatives *b)* a session of this legislature *c)* the body of Senators and Representatives during any of the two-year terms of Representatives

☆**con·gres·sion·al** (kən gresh′ən 'l) *adj.* **1.** of a congress **2.** [C-] of Congress —**con·gres′sion·al·ly** *adv.*

☆**Congressional district** any of the districts into which a State is divided for electing members of the U.S. House of Representatives

☆**con·gress·man** (käŋ′grəs mən) *n., pl.* **-men** [often C-] a member of Congress, esp. of the House of Representatives: also, for a woman member, often **con′gress·wom′an**

Con·greve (kän′grēv, käŋ′-), **William** 1670–1729; Eng. Restoration playwright

con·gru·ence (käŋ′groo wəns, kən groo′əns) *n.* **1.** the state or quality of being congruent, or in agreement, coinciding, etc. **2.** *Math.* the relation between two numbers each of which, when divided by a third, leaves the same remainder Also **con′gru·en·cy**

con·gru·ent (-wənt, -ənt) *adj.* [< L. prp. of *congruere*, to come together, agree] **1.** in agreement; harmonious **2.** *Geom.* of the same shape and size: congruent figures, if placed one upon

another, coincide exactly in all their parts **3.** *Math.* in congruence [*congruent* numbers] —**con′gru·ent·ly** *adv.*

con·gru·i·ty (kən groo′ə tē) *n., pl.* **-ties 1.** the condition or fact of being congruous or congruent; specif., *a)* agreement; harmony *b)* fitness; appropriateness *c) Geom.* exact coincidence (of two or more figures) **2.** an instance of agreement

con·gru·ous (käŋ′groo wəs) *adj.* **1.** *same as* CONGRUENT **2.** corresponding to what is right, proper, or reasonable; fitting; suitable; appropriate [her low, rasping voice was not *congruous* with her delicate appearance] —**con′gru·ous·ly** *adv.* —**con′gru·ous·ness** *n.*

con·ic (kän′ik) *adj. same as* CONICAL —*n. same as* CONIC SECTION

con·i·cal (kän′i k'l) *adj.* **1.** of a cone **2.** resembling or shaped like a cone —**con′i·cal·ly** *adv.*

conic section a curve, as an ellipse, circle, parabola, or hyperbola, formed by the intersection of a plane with a cone

co·nid·i·um (kə nid′ē əm) *n., pl.* **-i·a** (-ə) [ModL. < Gr. *konis*, dust] a small asexual spore of certain fungi —**co·nid′i·al, co·nid′i·an** *adj.*

co·ni·fer (kän′ə fər, kō′nə-) *n.* [L. < *conus*, a cone + *ferre*, to BEAR¹] any of a large group of trees and shrubs, mostly evergreens, that bear cones, as the pine, spruce, fir, cedar, yew, etc. —**co·nif·er·ous** (kə·nif′ər əs) *adj.*

CONIC SECTIONS
(A, circle; B, hyperbola; C, parabola; D, ellipse)

conj. 1. conjugation **2.** conjunction

con·jec·tur·al (kən jek′chər əl) *adj.* based on or involving conjecture [a highly *conjectural* theory] —**con·jec′tur·al·ly** *adv.*

con·jec·ture (kən jek′chər) *n.* [< L. *conjectura* < pp. of *conicere*, to guess < *com-*, together + *jacere*, to throw] **1.** a guessing, judging, or predicting from incomplete evidence; guesswork **2.** a guess, judgment, or prediction based on this —*vt., vi.* **-tured, -tur·ing** to arrive at or propose (something) by conjecture; guess —see SYN. at GUESS —**con·jec′tur·a·ble** *adj.* —**con·jec′tur·er** *n.*

con·join (kən join′) *vt., vi.* [< OFr. < L. *conjungere* < *com-*, together + *jungere*, JOIN] to join together; unite; combine [events *conjoining* to bring about his downfall] —**con·join′er** *n.*

con·joint (-joint′) *adj.* [see prec.] **1.** joined together; united; combined **2.** of or involving two or more combined; joint —**con·joint′ly** *adv.*

con·ju·gal (kän′jə gəl, kən joo′-) *adj.* [< L. < *conjunx*, spouse < *com-*, together + base akin to *jugum*, YOKE] of marriage or the relation between husband and wife; matrimonial —**con′ju·gal′i·ty** (-jə gal′ə tē) *n.* —**con′ju·gal·ly** *adv.*

con·ju·gate (kän′jə gət; *also, and for v. always,* -gāt′) *adj.* [< L. pp. of *conjugare* < *com-*, together + *jugare*, to join < *jugum*, YOKE] **1.** joined together, esp. in a pair; coupled **2.** derived from the same base and, usually, related in meaning: said of words —*n.* a conjugate word —*vt.* **-gat·ed, -gat·ing 1.** [Archaic] to join together; couple **2.** *Gram.* to inflect (a verb) in a systematic way, giving its different forms according to voice, mood, tense, number, and person —*vi. Gram.* **1.** to conjugate a verb **2.** to be conjugated —**con′ju·ga′tive** *adj.* —**con′ju·ga′tor** *n.*

con·ju·ga·tion (kän′jə gā′shən) *n.* **1.** a conjugating or being conjugated; union **2.** *Gram. a)* a systematic presentation of the inflected forms of a verb *b)* a class of verbs with similar inflected forms —**con′ju·ga′tion·al** *adj.* —**con′ju·ga′tion·al·ly** *adv.*

con·junct (kən juŋkt′; *also, and for n. always,* kän′juŋkt) *adj.* [see CONJOIN] joined together; joint; associated —*n.* a person or thing joined or associated with another

con·junc·tion (kən juŋk′shən) *n.* [see CONJOIN] **1.** a joining together or being joined together; union; combination [a nation acting in *conjunction* with its allies] **2.** an occurring together [the *conjunction* of events] **3.** *Astrol., Astron. a)* the apparent closeness of two or more heavenly bodies *b)* the condition of being in the same celestial longitude [planets in *conjunction*] **4.** *Gram.* an uninflected word used to connect words, phrases, clauses, or sentences; connective: conjunctions may be coordinating (e.g., *and*, *but*, *or*), subordinating (e.g., *if*, *when*, *as*, *because*, *though*), or correlative (e.g., *either . . . or*, *both . . . and*) —con·junc′tion·al *adj.*

con·junc·ti·va (kän′jəŋk tī′və, kən juŋk′ti və) *n.*, *pl.* -vas, -vae (-vē) [< ModL. (*membrana*) *conjunctiva*, connecting (membrane)] the mucous membrane lining the inner surface of the eyelids and covering the front part of the eyeball: see illustration at EYE —con′junc·ti′val *adj.*

con·junc·tive (kən juŋk′tiv) *adj.* 1. serving to join together; connective 2. united; combined; joint 3. *Gram.* used as a conjunction [a *conjunctive* adverb] —n. *Gram.* a conjunctive word; esp., a conjunction —con·junc′tive·ly *adv.*

con·junc·ti·vi·tis (kən juŋk′tə vīt′is) *n.* [see -ITIS] inflammation of the conjunctiva

con·junc·ture (kən juŋk′chər) *n.* [< ML.: see CONJOIN] a combination of events or circumstances, esp. one creating a crisis

con·ju·ra·tion (kän′jə rā′shən) *n.* 1. a conjuring; invocation 2. a magic spell; incantation

con·jure (kän′jər, kun′-; *for vt. 1* kən joor′) *vi.* -jured, -jur·ing [< OFr. *conjurare* < *com*-, together + *jurare*, to swear] 1. to summon a demon, spirit, etc. by a magic spell 2. to practice magic —*vt.* 1. to appeal to or plead with solemnly [I *conjure* you to keep your vow] 2. to summon (a devil, etc.) by a magic spell —**conjure away** to cause to go away as by magic —**conjure up** 1. to cause to appear as by magic 2. to call to mind [the music *conjured* up memories]

con·jur·er, con·ju·ror (kän′jər ər, kun′-) *n.* a magician

conk (käŋk, kôŋk) *n.* [< CONCH] [Slang] a blow on the head —*vt.* [Slang] to hit on the head —**conk out** [Slang] 1. to stop working suddenly, as a motor 2. to become very tired and, usually, fall asleep

☆**con man** [Slang] *same as* CONFIDENCE MAN

conn (kän) *vt.* conned, con′ning [< OFr. < L. *conducere*: see CONDUCE] *Naut.* to direct the course of (a ship) —*n.* control of a ship's movements

Conn. Connecticut

con·nect (kə nekt′) *vt.* [< L. *connectere* < *com*-, together + *nectere*, to fasten] 1. to join (two things together, or one thing *with* or *to* another); link; couple 2. to show or think of as related; associate [the first man to *connect* bacteria with disease] 3. to plug into an electrical circuit —*vi.* 1. to be joined or be related ☆2. to meet so that passengers can transfer promptly: said of buses, airplanes, etc. 3. [Colloq.] *Sports* to hit a ball, target, etc. solidly —see SYN. at JOIN —con·nec′tor, con·nect′er *n.*

Con·nect·i·cut (kə net′ə kət) [< Algonquian, lit., place of the long river] New England State of the U.S.: 5,009 sq. mi.; pop. 3,032,000; cap. Hartford: abbrev. **Conn.**, **CT**

connecting rod a rod connecting by reciprocating motion two or more moving parts of a machine

con·nec·tion (kə nek′shən) *n.* 1. a joining or being joined; coupling; union 2. a thing that joins; means of joining 3. a relation; association [knowing the *connection* between lightning and thunder; having nothing to say in that *connection*; having no business *connections* abroad] 4. *a)* a relative, esp. by marriage *b)* a business associate, friend, etc., esp. an influential one: *usually used in pl.* ☆5. [*usually pl.*] the act or means of transferring from one bus, airplane, etc. to another 6. a group of people associated in some way ☆7. [Slang] a person who sells narcotics illegally 8. *Elec.*, etc. a circuit [to break a telephone *connection*] Brit. sp. con·nex′ion —**in connection with** 1. together with 2. with reference to —con·nec′tion·al *adj.*

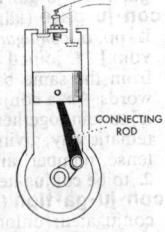

CONNECTING ROD

con·nec·tive (kə nek′tiv) *adj.* connecting or serving to connect —n. something that connects, esp. a word that connects words, phrases, or clauses, as a conjunction or relative pronoun —con·nec′tive·ly *adv.* —con·nec·tiv·i·ty (kän′ek tiv′ə tē) *n.*

connective tissue body tissue that connects and supports other tissues and organs in the body

conn·ing tower (kän′iŋ) [prp. of CONN] 1. an armored pilothouse on the deck of a warship 2. on submarines, a low observation tower serving also as an entrance to the interior

☆con·nip·tion (kə nip′shən) *n.* [pseudo-Latin] [Colloq.] [*often pl.*] a fit of anger, hysteria, etc.: also **conniption fit**

con·niv·ance (kə nī′vəns) *n.* a conniving, esp. in wrongdoing

con·nive (kə nīv′) *vi.* -nived′, -niv′ing [< L. *conivere*, to wink, connive] 1. to pretend not to see or look (*at* something wrong or evil), thus seeming to give one's consent 2. *a)* to cooperate secretly (*with* someone), esp. in wrongdoing *b)* to scheme underhandedly —con·niv′er *n.*

con·nois·seur (kän′ə sur′, -soor′) *n.* [< Fr. < OFr. < L. *cognoscere*, to know: see COGNITION] one who has expert knowledge and a sure sense of what is best in some field, esp. in the fine arts

con·no·ta·tion (kän′ə tā′shən) *n.* 1. the act or process of connoting 2. any idea suggested by or associated with a word, phrase, etc. in addition to its basic or literal meaning, or denotation —con·no·ta·tive (kän′ə tāt′iv, kə nōt′ə tiv), con′no·ta′tion·al *adj.* —con′no·ta′tive·ly *adv.*

con·note (kə nōt′) *vt.* -not′ed, -not′ing [< ML. *connotare* < L. *com*-, together + *notare*, to mark: see NOTE] to suggest (related ideas, feelings, etc.) in addition to the basic, or denoted, meaning [the word "brother" means "male sibling," but it usually *connotes* fellowship, loving concern, helpfulness, etc.]

con·nu·bi·al (kə nōo′bē əl, -nyoo′-) *adj.* [< L. < *conubium*, marriage < *com*-, together + *nubere*, to marry] of marriage or the state of being married; conjugal —con·nu′bi·al′i·ty (-bē·al′ə tē) *n.* —con·nu′bi·al·ly *adv.*

co·noid (kō′noid) *adj.* cone-shaped: also co·noi′dal —*n.* a cone-shaped thing

con·quer (käŋ′kər) *vt.* [< OFr. < VL. *conquarere* < L. *com*-, very much + *quaerere*, to seek] 1. to get possession or control of by or as by winning a war 2. to overcome by physical, mental, or moral force; defeat —*vi.* to be victorious; win —con′quer·a·ble *adj.* —con′quer·or *n.*

SYN.—**conquer** implies gaining mastery over something or someone by physical, intellectual, or moral force [to *conquer* bad habits]; **vanquish** suggests a thorough overpowering, often in a sharp struggle [a *vanquished* foe]; to **defeat** is to get the better of, often only for a time [the *defeated* team went on to win in the playoffs]; **overcome** implies the overpowering of an opponent or a dealing successfully with difficulties [to *overcome* a tendency to stutter]; to **subdue** is to conquer so completely that the desire to fight back is lost; **overthrow** suggests a victory in which a person, party, etc. is thrown from power by force; to **rout** is to defeat in an overwhelming, humiliating way, as by causing the enemy to flee in confusion

con·quest (käŋ′kwest, kän′-) *n.* [< OFr. < ML. < L. pp. of *conquirere*, to procure] 1. the act of conquering 2. something conquered 3. *a)* a winning of someone's love *b)* one whose love has been won

con·quis·ta·dor (kän kwis′tə dôr′, -kēs′-; käŋ-) *n.*, *pl.* -dors′, -dores′ [Sp., conqueror] any of the Spanish conquerors of Mexico, Peru, or other parts of America in the 16th century

Con·rad (kän′rad) [< G. or Fr. < OHG. < *kuon*, bold, wise + *rat*, counsel] 1. a masculine name 2. **Joseph**, (born *Józef Teodor Konrad Nalecz Korzeniowski*) 1857–1924; Eng. novelist, born in Poland

cons. 1. consolidated 2. consonant 3. consulting

cons., **Cons.** 1. constitution 2. consul

con·san·guin·e·ous (kän′saŋ gwin′ē əs, -san-) *adj.* [see COM- & SANGUINE] having the same ancestor; related by blood: also con·san′guine (-saŋ′gwin) —con′san·guin′e·ous·ly *adv.* —con′san·guin′i·ty *n.*

con·science (kän′shəns) *n.* [OFr. < L. < prp. of *conscire* < *com*-, with + *scire*, to know] a knowledge or sense of right and wrong, with an urge to do right; moral judgment that keeps one from violating one's ethical principles and that leads one to have guilt feelings if one does —**in (all) conscience** in fairness —**on one's conscience** causing one to feel guilty —con′science·less *adj.*

conscience money money one pays to relieve one's conscience, as for some former dishonesty

con·science-strick·en (-strik′ən) *adj.* feeling guilty or remorseful because of having done some wrong

con·sci·en·tious (kän′shē en′shəs, -chəs) *adj.* [see CONSCIENCE] 1. controlled by, or done according to, what one knows is right; scrupulous [a *conscientious* worker] 2. showing care and exactness; painstaking [*conscientious* work] —con′sci·en′tious·ly *adv.* —con′sci·en′tious·ness *n.*

conscientious objector a person who for reasons of conscience refuses to take part in warfare

con·scious (kän′shəs) *adj.* [< L. *conscius* < *conscire*: see CONSCIENCE] 1. having a feeling or knowledge (*with of* or *that*); aware; cognizant [*conscious* of a slight noise] 2. able to feel and think; in the normal waking state [to become *conscious* after having fainted] 3. aware of oneself as a thinking being 4. *same as* SELF-CONSCIOUS 5. done with awareness or on purpose;

intentional [*conscious* humor] **6.** known to or felt by oneself [*conscious* guilt] —see SYN. at AWARE —**con′scious·ly** *adv.*

con·scious·ness (-nis) *n.* **1.** the state of being conscious; awareness of one's own feelings, what is happening around one, etc. **2.** all of one's thoughts, feelings, and impressions; conscious mind [the memory of the event was gone from his *consciousness*]

☆**con·script** (kən skript′; *for adj. & n.* kän′skript) *vt.* [< the *adj.*] **1.** to force to serve in the armed forces; draft **2.** to force (labor, capital, etc.) to serve for the government —*adj.* [< L. pp. of *conscribere*, enroll < *com-*, with + *scribere*, to write] conscripted —*n.* a conscripted person; draftee —**con·scrip′tion** *n.*

con·se·crate (kän′sə krāt′) *vt.* -crat′ed, -crat′ing [< L. pp. of *consecrare* < *com-*, together + *sacrare*, to make holy < *sacer*, sacred] **1.** to set apart as holy; make or declare sacred for religious use **2.** to devote entirely; dedicate [to *consecrate* one's life to art] **3.** to cause to be revered; hallow [ground *consecrated* by their martyrdom] —see SYN. at HOLY —**con′se·cra′tion** *n.* —**con′se·cra′tor** *n.* —**con′se·cra·to·ry** (-krə tôr′ē) *adj.*

con·sec·u·tive (kən sek′yə tiv) *adj.* [< Fr. < ML. < pp. of L. *consequi:* see CONSEQUENCE] **1.** following in order, without interruption; successive [losing four *consecutive* games] **2.** proceeding from one part or idea to the next in logical order [*consecutive* arguments in a debate] —**con·sec′u·tive·ly** *adv.* —**con·sec′u·tive·ness** *n.*

con·sen·su·al (kən sen′shoo wəl) *adj.* [< CONSENSUS + -AL] *Law* existing by mutual consent, as a contract

con·sen·sus (kən sen′səs) *n.* [L. < pp. of *consentire*, to CONSENT] **1.** an opinion held by all or most **2.** general agreement, esp. in opinion

con·sent (kən sent′) *vi.* [< OFr. < L. *consentire* < *com-*, with + *sentire*, to feel: for IE. base see SEND] **1.** to agree (*to* do something) **2.** to give permission or approval —*n.* **1.** permission, approval, or assent [". . . by and with the advice and *consent* of the Senate . . ."] **2.** agreement [by common *consent*] —**con·sent′er** *n.*

SYN.—**consent** implies giving in to something proposed or requested when one has the power to do so or not [to *consent* to serve as chairman]; to **assent** is to express one's acceptance or approval of something [he *assented* to the plan favored by the others]; **agree** implies accord reached by settling differences of opinion or overcoming resistance [to *agree* on a fair price for the property]; **concur** implies agreement arrived at formally on a specific matter, often with regard to a line of action [all the doctors *concurred* in the decision to operate]; to **accede** is to yield one's assent to a proposal [he *acceded* to the union's request for arbitration]; **acquiesce** implies a giving in quietly when one may have some doubts —**ANT.** dissent, refuse, deny

con·se·quence (kän′sə kwens′, -kwəns) *n.* [OFr. < L. < prp. of *consequi* < *com-*, with + *sequi*, to follow] **1.** a result of an action, process, etc.; effect **2.** a logical result or conclusion; inference [it follows as a *consequence* that he is guilty] **3.** importance as a cause [a matter of slight *consequence*] **4.** importance in rank; influence [a person of *consequence*] —see SYN. at EFFECT and IMPORTANCE —**in consequence (of)** as a result (of) —**take the consequences** to accept the results of one's actions

con·se·quent (-kwent′, -kwənt) *adj.* **1.** following as a result; resulting [his trial and *consequent* imprisonment] **2.** proceeding in logical order —*n.* anything that follows —**consequent on** (or **upon**) **1.** following as a result of **2.** inferred from

con·se·quen·tial (kän′sə kwen′shəl) *adj.* **1.** following as an effect **2.** self-important [a *consequential* manner] —**con′se·quen′ti·al·i·ty** (-shē al′ə tē), **con′se·quen′tial·ness** *n.* —**con′se·quen′tial·ly** *adv.*

con·se·quent·ly (kän′sə kwent′lē, -kwənt-) *adv.* as a result; by logical inference; therefore

con·ser·van·cy (kən sur′vən sē) *n.* conservation of natural resources —*adj.* set apart for the protection of natural resources, as a State district

con·ser·va·tion (kän′sər vā′shən) *n.* **1.** a conserving; protection from loss, waste, etc. **2.** the official care and protection of natural resources, as forests —**con′ser·va′tion·al** *adj.* —**con′ser·va′tion·ist** *n.*

conservation of energy (or **matter**, or **mass**) the principle that energy (or matter, or mass) is never used up but only changes form: it is now recognized that energy can be changed into matter, and matter into energy, but the total of energy and matter in a closed system remains constant

con·ser·va·tism (kən sur′və tiz'm) *n.* the principles and practices of a conservative person or party; tendency to oppose change, esp. in political and social matters

con·ser·va·tive (-tiv) *adj.* **1.** conserving or tending to conserve; preservative **2.** tending to uphold established institutions or methods and to resist or oppose any changes in these [*conservative* politics; *conservative* art] **3.** [-C-] designating or of the major right-wing political party of Great Britain or of Canada **4.** [C-] designating or of a movement in Judaism that keeps much of the tradition while adapting to modern conditions ☆**5.** moderate; cautious; safe [a *conservative* estimate] —*n.* **1.** a conservative person **2.** [C-] a member of a Conservative party —**con·ser′va·tive·ly** *adv.* —**con·ser′va·tive·ness** *n.*

con·ser·va·toire (kən sur′və twär′, -sur′və twär′) *n.* [Fr.] *same as* CONSERVATORY (n. 2)

con·ser·va·tor (kän′sər vāt′ər, kən sur′və tər) *n.* [see CONSERVE] a protector, guardian, or custodian

con·ser·va·to·ry (kən sur′və tôr′ē) *n., pl.* -ries [see CONSERVE] **1.** a room enclosed in glass, for growing and showing plants; noncommercial greenhouse **2.** a school, or academy, of music, art, etc.

con·serve (kən surv′; *for n., usually* kän′sərv) *vt.* -served′, -serv′ing [< OFr. < L. *conservare* < *com-*, with + *servare:* see OBSERVE] **1.** to keep from being damaged, lost, or wasted; save [to *conserve* one's energy] **2.** to make (fruit) into preserves —*n.* [*often pl.*] a kind of jam made of two or more fruits —**con·serv′a·ble** *adj.* —**con·serv′er** *n.*

con·sid·er (kən sid′ər) *vt.* [< OFr. < L. *considerare*, to observe < *com-*, with + *sidus*, a star] **1.** to think about in order to understand or decide; ponder [to *consider* a problem] **2.** to keep in mind; take into account [her health is good if you *consider* her age] **3.** to be thoughtful of (others, their feelings, etc.) **4.** to regard as; think to be [I *consider* him an expert] —*vi.* to think carefully; reflect

SYN.—**consider** implies a turning of one's mind to something in order to understand it or to make a decision about it; **study** implies a deeper concentration of the mind and a careful attention to details [the committee *studied* ways and means to raise money]; **contemplate** implies long, but relaxed consideration [the retired couple *contemplated* a move to a warmer climate]; **weigh** suggests a balancing of opposing information, conflicting opinions, or possible results, in reaching a decision; **reflect**, suggesting a turning of one's thoughts back to something, implies quiet, serious consideration [*reflecting* on the successes of the past year]

con·sid·er·a·ble (-ə b'l) *adj.* **1.** worth considering; important [a *considerable* criticism; a *considerable* poet] **2.** much or large [*considerable* success] —*n.* ☆[*Chiefly Dial.*] a large amount; much: used chiefly in the phrases **a considerable of, by considerable** —**con·sid′er·a·bly** *adv.*

con·sid·er·ate (-it) *adj.* [see CONSIDER] having or showing regard for others and their feelings; thoughtful —see SYN. at THOUGHTFUL —**con·sid′er·ate·ly** *adv.* —**con·sid′er·ate·ness** *n.*

con·sid·er·a·tion (kən sid′ə rā′shən) *n.* **1.** the act of considering; careful thought [after long *consideration*, he decided to run for mayor] **2.** *a)* thoughtful or sympathetic regard for others *b)* esteem **3.** something considered in making a decision [past debts were a *consideration* in accepting the offer] **4.** a thought or opinion produced by considering **5.** something paid for a favor or service —**in consideration of 1.** because of **2.** in return for —**take into consideration** to keep in mind; take into account —**under consideration** being thought over

con·sid·ered (kən sid′ərd) *adj.* arrived at after careful thought [her *considered* opinion]

con·sid·er·ing (-ər iŋ) *prep.* in view of; taking into account [*considering* his age, he is quite spry] —*adv.* [Colloq.] taking everything into account [things turned out quite well, *considering*]

con·sign (kən sīn′) *vt.* [L. *consignare*, to seal < *com-*, together + *signare* < *signum*, SIGN] **1.** to hand over; deliver [*consigned* to jail] **2.** to put in the care of another; entrust [*consign* the orphan to her uncle's care] **3.** to assign to an undesirable position or place; relegate [*consigned* to oblivion] **4.** to send or deliver (goods) [a shipment *consigned* to the Detroit branch] —see SYN. at COMMIT —**con·sign′a·ble** *adj.* —**con·sign·ee** (kän′sī nē′, kən sī′nē′) *n.* —**con·sign′or, con·sign′er** *n.*

con·sign·ment (-mənt) *n.* **1.** a consigning or being consigned **2.** something consigned; esp., a shipment of goods sent to an agent for sale or safekeeping —**on consignment** shipped or turned over to an agent for sale, with payment to follow sale

con·sist (kən sist′) *vi.* [L. *consistere* < *com-*, together + *sistere*, to cause to stand < *stare*, to STAND] **1.** to be formed or composed (*of*) [water *consists* of hydrogen and oxygen] **2.** to be contained or inherent (*in* something) as a cause, quality, etc. [*wisdom does not consist* only in knowing facts]

con·sis·ten·cy (kən sis′tən sē) *n., pl.* -**cies** **1.** *a*) firmness or thickness, as of a liquid *b*) degree of this [oil of the wrong *consistency*] **2.** agreement; harmony [arguments lacking *consistency*] **3.** a being consistent in practice or principle [he is unpredictable because he lacks *consistency*] Also **con·sis′tence**

con·sis·tent (-tənt) *adj.* [see CONSIST] **1.** [Rare] firm; solid **2.** in agreement or harmony; compatible [deeds not *consistent* with his words] **3.** holding always to the same principles or practice [*consistent* behavior] —**con·sis′tent·ly** *adv.*

con·sis·to·ry (kən sis′tər ē) *n., pl.* -**ries** [< L. *consistorium*, place of assembly < *consistere*: see CONSIST] **1.** a church council or court, as the papal senate **2.** a session of such a body —**con·sis·to·ri·al** (kän′sis tôr′ē əl) *adj.*

con·so·la·tion (kän′sə lā′shən) *n.* **1.** a consoling or being consoled; comfort; solace **2.** a person or thing that consoles or comforts

consolation prize a prize given to a contestant who does well but does not win

con·sol·a·to·ry (kən sōl′ə tôr′ē, -säl′-) *adj.* consoling or tending to console; comforting

con·sole¹ (kən sōl′) *vt.* -**soled′**, -**sol′ing** [< Fr. < L. *consolari* < *com-*, with + *solari*, to solace] to make feel less sad or disappointed; comfort [*consoling* words to the losers] —see SYN. at COMFORT —**con·sol′a·ble** *adj.* —**con·sol′er** *n.* —**con·sol′ing·ly** *adv.*

con·sole² (kän′sōl) *n.* [Fr.] **1.** an ornamental bracket for supporting a shelf, bust, cornice, etc. **2.** *same as* CONSOLE TABLE **3.** the part of an organ at which the player sits, containing the keys, stops, pedals, etc. **4.** a radio, television, or phonograph cabinet that stands on the floor ☆**5.** an instrument panel or unit, containing the controls for operating aircraft, computers, etc.

CONSOLE
(of an organ)

console table a small table with legs resembling consoles, or brackets, placed against a wall

con·sol·i·date (kən säl′ə dāt′) *vt., vi.* -**dat′ed**, -**dat′ing** [< L. pp. of *consolidare* < *com-*, together + *solidare* < *solidus*, solid] **1.** to combine into a single whole; merge; unite [a corporation formed by *consolidating* several companies] **2.** to make or become strong, stable, etc. [the troops *consolidated* their position] **3.** to make or become solid or compact —see SYN. at JOIN —**con·sol′i·da′tion** *n.* —**con·sol′i·da′tor** *n.*

☆**consolidated school** a public school attended by pupils from several nearby districts, esp. rural ones

con·sols (kən sälz′, kän′sälz) *n.pl.* [< *consolidated annuities*] British government bonds

con·som·mé (kän′sə mā′) *n.* [Fr., orig. pp. of *consommer*, CONSUMMATE, confused with *consumer*, CONSUME] a clear soup made by boiling meat, and sometimes vegetables, in water and straining

con·so·nance (kän′sə nəns) *n.* [OFr. < L. < prp. of *consonare* < *com-*, with + *sonare*, to SOUND¹] **1.** harmony or agreement of elements or parts; accord [deeds in *consonance* with words] **2.** harmony of musical tones Also **con′so·nan·cy**

con·so·nant (kän′sə nənt) *adj.* [see prec.] **1.** in harmony or agreement; in accord [policies not *consonant* with democratic principles] **2.** harmonious in tone: opposed to DISSONANT **3.** consonantal —*n.* **1.** any speech sound made by stopping or partly stopping the breath with the tongue, teeth, or lips, as the sounds of p, t, k, m, l, f, etc.: see also VOWEL **2.** a letter or symbol representing such a sound —**con′so·nant·ly** *adv.*

con·so·nan·tal (kän′sə nant′'l) *adj.* of, being, or having a consonant or consonants

con·sort (kän′sôrt; *for v.* kən sôrt′) *n.* [< OFr. < L. *consortis*, genitive of *consors* < *com-*, with + *sors*, a share] **1.** orig., a partner; companion **2.** a wife or husband; spouse, esp. of a reigning king or queen **3.** a ship that travels along with another —*vi.* **1.** to keep company; associate [she *consorts* with snobs] **2.** to agree; be in accord —*vt.* to associate; join

con·sor·ti·um (kən sôr′shē əm) *n., pl.* -**ti·a** (-ə) [L., community of goods: see prec.] **1.** an alliance, as of two or more business firms in some venture **2.** an international banking agreement or association

con·spe·cif·ic (kän′spə sif′ik) *adj.* [< CON- + SPECIES, after SPECIFIC] belonging to the same species

con·spec·tus (kən spek′təs) *n.* [L., a view, pp. of *conspicere*: see CONSPICUOUS] **1.** a general view; survey **2.** a summary; synopsis; digest

con·spic·u·ous (kən spik′yōō wəs) *adj.* [< L. < *conspicere*, to look at < *com-*, very much + *specere*, to see (see SPY)] **1.** easy to see or perceive; obvious [a *conspicuous* poster] **2.** attracting attention by being outstanding; striking [*conspicuous* bravery, *conspicuous* folly] —see SYN. at NOTICEABLE —**con·spic′u·ous·ly** *adv.* —**con·spic′u·ous·ness** *n.*

con·spir·a·cy (kən spir′ə sē) *n., pl.* -**cies** **1.** a conspiring, esp. in an unlawful or harmful plot **2.** such a plot **3.** the group taking part in such a plot **4.** a combining or working together [the *conspiracy* of events] —see SYN. at PLOT

con·spir·a·tor (-tər) *n.* a person who takes part in a conspiracy —**con·spir·a·to·ri·al** (kən spir′ə tôr′ē əl) *adj.* —**con·spir′a·to′ri·al·ly** *adv.*

con·spire (kən spīr′) *vi.* -**spired′**, -**spir′ing** [< OFr. < L. *conspirare* < *com-*, together + *spirare*, to breathe] **1.** to plan and act together secretly, esp. in order to commit a crime **2.** to combine or work together for any purpose or effect [events *conspired* to ruin him]

con spi·ri·to (kän spir′i tō′) [It.] *Music* with spirit or vigor

con·sta·ble (kän′stə b'l, kun′-) *n.* [< OFr. < LL. *comes stabuli*, lit., count of the stable] **1.** in the Middle Ages, the highest ranking official of a royal household, court, etc. **2.** a peace officer in a town or village **3.** [Chiefly Brit.] a policeman

Con·sta·ble (kun′stə b'l, kän′-), **John** 1776–1837; Eng. landscape painter

con·stab·u·lar·y (kən stab′yə ler′ē) *n., pl.* -**lar·ies** all the constables, as of a district or country; police force —*adj.* of constables or a constabulary: also **con·stab′u·lar** (-lər)

Con·stance (kän′stəns) [Fr. < L. *Constantia*, lit., constancy] a feminine name

con·stan·cy (kän′stən sē) *n.* a staying the same; firmness, faithfulness, steadiness, regularity, etc.

con·stant (kän′stənt) *adj.* [< OFr. < L. prp. of *constare* < *com-*, together + *stare*, to STAND] **1.** not changing; remaining the same; specif., *a*) remaining firm in purpose; resolute [he was *constant* in his opposition] *b*) loyal; faithful [a *constant* friend] *c*) regular; stable; unvarying [at a *constant* speed] **2.** going on all the time; continual; persistent [*constant* interruptions] —*n.* **1.** anything that does not change or vary **2.** *Math., Physics a*) a quantity (**absolute constant**) that always has the same value *b*) a quantity or factor (**arbitrary constant**) assumed to have one value throughout a particular discussion or investigation: symbol, c (or k): opposed to VARIABLE —see SYN. at CONTINUAL and FAITHFUL —**con′stant·ly** *adv.*

Con·stan·tine I (kän′stən tēn′, -tīn′) 280?–337 A.D.; emperor of Rome (306–337): called *the Great*

Con·stan·ti·no·ple (kän′stan tə nō′p'l) former name (330 A.D.–1930) of ISTANBUL

con·stel·late (kän′stə lāt′) *vi., vt.* -**lat′ed**, -**lat′ing** to unite in a constellation or cluster

con·stel·la·tion (kän′stə lā′shən) *n.* [< OFr. < LL. < L. *com-*, with + pp. of *stellare*, to shine < *stella*, STAR] **1.** *a*) a particular group of fixed stars, usually named after some object, animal, or mythological being that they supposedly suggest in outline *b*) the part of the heavens occupied by such a group **2.** any brilliant cluster, gathering, or collection **3.** a group of related ideas, feelings, etc.

con·ster·nate (kän′stər nāt′) *vt.* -**nat′ed**, -**nat′ing** to overcome with consternation; dismay

con·ster·na·tion (kän′stər nā′shən) *n.* [< L. < *consternare*, to terrify] great fear or shock that makes one feel helpless or bewildered

con·sti·pate (kän′stə pāt′) *vt.* -**pat′ed**, -**pat′ing** [< L. pp. of *constipare* < *com-*, together + *stipare*, to cram] to cause constipation in

con·sti·pa·tion (kän′stə pā′shən) *n.* [see prec.] a condition in which waste matter from the bowels is hard and does not empty easily or often enough

con·stit·u·en·cy (kən stich′oo wən sē) *n., pl.* -**cies** [< CONSTITUENT + -CY] **1.** all the people, esp. voters, served by a particular elected official **2.** the district of such a group of voters, etc. **3.** a group of clients, supporters, etc.

con·stit·u·ent (-oo wənt) *adj.* [< L. prp. of *constituere*, CON-STITUTE] **1.** necessary in forming a whole; component [a *constituent* part] **2.** that can appoint or elect **3.** authorized to make or revise a constitution or establish a government [a *constituent* assembly] —*n.* **1.** a person who appoints another as his representative **2.** a member of a constituency, esp. any of the voters represented by a particular official **3.** a necessary part or element; component **4.** *Linguistics* an element of a construction: in "they painted signs" the main elements *they* and *painted signs* are called *immediate constituents*

con·sti·tute (kän'stə toot', -tyoot') *vt.* -tut'ed, -tut'ing [< L. pp. of *constituere* < *com-*, together + *statuere*, to set] **1.** to establish (a law, government, institution, etc.) **2.** to set up (an assembly, proceeding, etc.) in a legal form **3.** to give a certain office or function to [we *constitute* you our spokesman] **4.** to make up; form; compose [twelve people *constitute* a jury]

con·sti·tu·tion (kän'stə too'shən, -tyoo'-) *n.* **1.** a constituting; establishment, appointment, or formation **2.** the way a thing is made up; structure; organization **3.** the physical make-up of a person [a man of strong *constitution*] **4.** *a)* the system of fundamental laws and principles of a government, state, society, etc. *b)* a document in which these are written down; specif., [**C-**] such a document of the U.S.: it consists of seven articles and twenty-five amendments, and has been the supreme law of the nation since its adoption in 1789

con·sti·tu·tion·al (-əl) *adj.* **1.** of or in the constitution of a person or thing; basic; essential [a *constitutional* weakness] **2.** for improving a person's constitution **3.** of or in accordance with the constitution of a nation, society, etc. [*constitutional* rights] **4.** upholding the constitution —*n.* a walk or other exercise taken for one's health —**con'sti·tu'tion·al'i·ty** (-shə-nal'ə tē) *n.* —**con'sti·tu'tion·al·ly** *adv.*

con·sti·tu·tive (kän'stə toot'iv, -tyoot'-) *adj.* **1.** having power to establish, appoint, or enact **2.** making a thing what it is; basic **3.** forming a part (*of*); constituent

constr. **1.** construction **2.** construed

con·strain (kən strān') *vt.* [< OFr. < L. *constringere* < *com-*, together + *stringere*, to draw tight] **1.** to hold back or in by force or strain; restrain **2.** to force; compel [*constrained* to agree] —see SYN. at FORCE

con·strained (-strānd') *adj.* **1.** compelled; forced **2.** forced and unnatural [a *constrained* laugh] —**con·strain'ed·ly** (-strā'nid lē) *adv.*

con·straint (-strānt') *n.* **1.** a constraining or being constrained; specif., *a)* confinement or restriction *b)* compulsion or coercion **2.** forced, unnatural manner

con·strict (kən strikt') *vt.* [< L. pp. of *constringere*: see CONSTRAIN] **1.** to make smaller or narrower by binding, squeezing, etc.; contract [the tight belt *constricted* her waist] **2.** to hold in; limit; restrict [a *constricted* outlook] —**con·stric'tive** *adj.*

con·stric·tion (-strik'shən) *n.* **1.** a constricting or being constricted **2.** a feeling of tightness or pressure, as in the chest **3.** something that constricts **4.** a constricted part

con·stric·tor (-strik'tər) *n.* that which constricts; specif., *a)* a muscle that contracts an opening or compresses an organ *b)* a snake that kills by coiling around its prey and squeezing

con·struct (kən strukt'; *for n.* kän'strukt) *vt.* [< L. pp. of *construere* < *com-*, together + *struere*, to pile up] **1.** to build, form, or devise by fitting parts or elements together systematically [to *construct* a house, a theory, a sentence, etc.] **2.** *Geom.* to draw (a figure) so as to meet the specified requirements —*n.* **1.** something built or put together systematically **2.** a concept or theory developed to put together in an orderly way the varied data on a phenomenon: also **logical construct** **3.** *Linguistics* a grammatical pattern consisting of two or more immediate constituents: see CONSTITUENT, *n.* 4 —see SYN. at MAKE —**con·struc'tor, con·struct'er** *n.*

con·struc·tion (kən struk'shən) *n.* **1.** the act or process of constructing **2.** the way in which something is constructed **3.** something constructed; structure; building **4.** an explanation or interpretation, as of a statement **5.** the arrangement and relation of words in a phrase, clause, or sentence **6.** a three-dimensional work of art of various materials —**con·struc'tion·al** *adj.* —**con·struc'tion·al·ly** *adv.*

con·struc·tion·ist (-ist) *n.* [see prec., sense 4] a person who interprets a law, document, etc. in a specified way

con·struc·tive (kən struk'tiv) *adj.* **1.** helping to construct; leading to improvements [*constructive* criticism] **2.** of construction or structure **3.** inferred or implied by legal or judicial interpretation —**con·struc'tive·ly** *adv.* —**con·struc'tive·ness** *n.*

con·strue (kən stroo') *vt.* -strued', -stru'ing [< L. *construere*: see CONSTRUCT] **1.** to analyze (a sentence, clause, etc.) so as to show its construction and meaning **2.** to translate **3.** to explain or deduce the meaning of; interpret [her silence was *construed* as agreement] **4.** *Gram.* to combine in syntax [the verb "let," unlike "permit," is *construed* with an infinitive omitting the "to"] —see SYN. at EXPLAIN —**con·stru'a·ble** *adj.*

con·sul (kän's'l) *n.* [< OFr. < L. < *consulere*, to deliberate] **1.** either of the two chief magistrates of the ancient Roman republic **2.** any of the three highest officials of the French republic from 1799 to 1804 **3.** a government official appointed to live in a foreign city and serve his country's citizens and business interests there —**con'sul·ar** (-ər) *adj.* —**con'sul·ship'** *n.*

consular agent an official serving as a consul at a place not very important commercially

con·sul·ate (-it) *n.* **1.** the position, powers, and duties of a consul **2.** the office or residence of a consul **3.** the term of office of a consul **4.** government by consuls; specif., [**C-**] the government of France from 1799 to 1804

consul general *pl.* **consuls general, consul generals** a consul in a principal commercial city, who supervises other consuls within his district

con·sult (kən sult') *vi.* [L. *consultare* < pp. of *consulere*, to deliberate] to talk things over in order to decide something; confer [to *consult* with a specialist] —*vt.* **1.** *a)* to ask the advice of [to *consult* a lawyer] *b)* to refer to, esp. for information [to *consult* a map] **2.** to keep in mind; consider [*consult* your own wishes in the matter] —**con·sult'er** *n.*

con·sult·ant (kən sul't'nt) *n.* **1.** a person who consults with another **2.** an expert called on for professional or technical advice or opinions

con·sul·ta·tion (kän's'l tā'shən) *n.* **1.** the act of consulting **2.** a meeting to discuss, decide, or plan something —**con·sul·ta·tive** (kən sul'tə tiv, kän's'l tā'-), **con·sul·ta·to·ry** (-tôr'ē) *adj.*

con·sult·ing (kən sul'tiŋ) *adj.* consulted for professional or technical advice; advisory [a *consulting* engineer]

con·sume (kən soom', -syoom') *vt.* -sumed', -sum'ing [< OFr. < L. *consumere* < *com-*, together + *sumere*, to take < *sub-*, under + *emere*, to buy] **1.** to destroy, as by fire **2.** to use up; spend or waste (time, energy, money, etc.) **3.** to eat or drink up; devour **4.** to absorb completely or obsess [*consumed* with envy; a *consuming* interest] —**con·sum'a·ble** *adj.*

con·sum·ed·ly (-id lē) *adv.* very much or too much

con·sum·er (kən soo'mər, -syoo'-) *n.* a person or thing that consumes; specif., a person who buys goods or services for his own needs and not for resale or to use in the production of other goods for resale: opposed to PRODUCER

☆**consumer credit** credit to consumers through installment plans, charge accounts, short-term loans, etc.

consumer goods goods, such as food, clothing, etc., for satisfying people's needs rather than for producing other goods or services

con·sum·er·ism (-iz'm) *n.* **1.** the movement for consumer protection in connection with defective and unsafe products, misleading business practices, etc. **2.** the consumption of goods and services

con·sum·mate (kən sum'it; *for v.* kän'sə māt') *adj.* [< L. pp. of *consummare*, to sum up < *com-*, together + *summa*, a SUM] **1.** complete or perfect [*consummate* happiness] **2.** highly expert [a *consummate* liar] —*vt.* -mat'ed, -mat'ing **1.** to make complete; fulfill; finish [to *consummate* a project] **2.** to make (a marriage) complete by sexual intercourse —**con·sum'mate·ly** *adv.* —**con·sum·ma·tive** (kän'sə māt'iv) *adj.* —**con'sum·ma'tor** *n.*

con·sum·ma·tion (kän'sə mā'shən) *n.* **1.** a consummating or being consummated **2.** an end; outcome

con·sump·tion (kən sump'shən) *n.* **1.** *a)* a consuming or being consumed; specif., the using up of goods or services *b)* the amount consumed **2.** tuberculosis of the lungs: an old-fashioned term

---

con·sump·tive (-tiv) *adj.* **1.** consuming or tending to consume; destructive; wasteful **2.** of, having, or relating to tuberculosis of the lungs: an old-fashioned term —*n.* a person who has tuberculosis of the lungs: an old-fashioned term —**con·sump′tive·ly** *adv.*

cont. **1.** containing **2.** contents **3.** continent **4.** continue **5.** continued **6.** contra

con·tact (kän′takt) *n.* [< L. pp. of *contingere* < *com-*, together + *tangere*, to touch < IE. base *tag-*, to touch] **1.** the act or state of touching or meeting [two surfaces in *contact*] **2.** the state or fact of being in touch, communication, or association (*with*) [to come into *contact* with new ideas] ☆**3.** *a*) an acquaintance, esp. one who is influential *b*) a connection with such a person [his *contacts* at city hall] **4.** *Elec.* *a*) a connection between two conductors in a circuit *b*) a device for opening and closing such a connection **5.** *Med.* a person who may have caught a disease from an infected person —*vt.* **1.** to place or come in contact with ☆**2.** to get in touch or communication with —*vi.* to be in or come into contact —*adj.* of, involving, or relating to contact

☆**contact flying** the setting of one's course and altitude in flying an airplane by observing landmarks

contact lens a tiny, thin lens of glass or plastic placed in the fluid over the cornea of the eye, used for correcting faulty vision

con·tac·tor (kän′tak tər) *n. Elec.* a device, usually automatic, for making and breaking a circuit repeatedly

contact print a photographic print made with the negative pressed against a photosensitive surface

con·ta·gion (kən tā′jən) *n.* [L. *contagio*, a touching < *contingere*: see CONTACT] **1.** the spreading of disease by contact **2.** a contagious disease **3.** the agent causing a communicable disease; germ, virus, etc. **4.** *a*) the spreading of a feeling, idea, etc. from person to person [the *contagion* of laughter] *b*) the feeling, idea, etc. so spread

con·ta·gious (-jəs) *adj.* [< OFr. < LL. *contagiosus*] **1.** spread by contact: said of diseases **2.** carrying the agent causing such a disease **3.** quickly spreading from person to person [*contagious* laughter] —**con·ta′gious·ly** *adv.* —**con·ta′gious·ness** *n.*

con·tain (kən tān′) *vt.* [< OFr. < L. *continere* < *com-*, together + *tenere*, to hold: see TENANT] **1.** to have in it; hold, enclose, or include [the can *contains* tea; the list *contains* 10 items] **2.** to have the capacity for holding **3.** to be equal to [a gallon *contains* four quarts] **4.** to hold back or within fixed limits; specif., *a*) to hold back (one's feelings, oneself, etc.) *b*) to check the power or spread of [to try to *contain* a forest fire] **5.** to be divisible by, esp. without a remainder [10 *contains* 5 and 2] —**con·tain′a·ble** *adj.*

SYN.—**contain**, in narrow usage, means to enclose within or include as a component, part, etc. and **hold** means to contain to the greatest possible degree [the bottle *contains* two ounces of liquid, but it *holds* a pint]; to **accommodate** is to hold comfortably without crowding [a restaurant built to *accommodate* 250 people]

con·tain·er (-ər) *n.* a thing for containing something; box, can, jar, etc.

con·tain·er·ize (-ər īz′) *vt.* **-ized′, -iz′ing** to pack (cargo) in large, standardized containers that can be easily transferred in shipping, as from trucks to trains —**con·tain′er·i·za′tion** *n.*

con·tain·ment (-mənt) *n.* the policy of attempting to prevent the influence of an opposing nation or political system from spreading

con·tam·i·nant (kən tam′ə nənt) *n.* a substance that contaminates another substance, the air, water, etc.

con·tam·i·nate (kən tam′ə nāt′) *vt.* **-nat′ed, -nat′ing** [< L. pp. of *contaminare*, to defile < *contamen*, contact < *com-*, together + base of *tangere*, to touch: see CONTACT] to make impure, infected, corrupt, radioactive, etc. by contact with or addition of something; pollute; defile; sully; taint —**con·tam′i·na′tion** *n.* —**con·tam′i·na′tive** *adj.* —**con·tam′i·na′tor** *n.*

contd. continued

‡**con·te** (kôn′te) *n.* [It.] *same as* COUNT[2] —**con·tes·sa** (kôn tes′sä) *n.fem.*

con·temn (kən tem′) *vt.* [< OFr. < L. *contemnere* < *com-*, very much + *temnere*, to scorn] to treat with contempt; scorn —**con·temn′er, con·tem′nor** (-tem′ər, -tem′nər) *n.*

con·tem·plate (kän′təm plāt′) *vt.* **-plat′ed, -plat′ing** [< L. pp. of *contemplari*, to observe (orig., in augury, to mark out a space for observation) < *com-* + *templum*, TEMPLE[1]] **1.** to look at intently; gaze at **2.** to think about intently; study carefully; consider [the Council *contemplated* its money crisis] **3.** to expect or intend [I *contemplate* leaving tomorrow] —*vi.* to meditate or muse —see SYN. at CONSIDER —**con′tem·pla′tor** *n.*

con·tem·pla·tion (kän′təm plā′shən) *n.* a contemplating; specif., *a*) thoughtful study *b*) religious or mystical meditation *c*) expectation or intention

con·tem·pla·tive (kən tem′plə tiv, kän′təm plāt′iv) *adj.* of or given to contemplation; thoughtful; meditative —*n.* a member of a religious order dedicated to contemplation —see SYN. at PENSIVE—**con·tem′pla·tive·ly** *adv.* —**con·tem′pla·tive·ness** *n.*

con·tem·po·ra·ne·ous (kən tem′pə rā′nē əs) *adj.* [< L. < *com-*, with + *temporis*, genitive of *tempus*, time] existing or happening in the same period of time —see SYN. at CONTEMPORARY —**con·tem′po·ra·ne′i·ty** (-pər ə nē′ə tē), **con·tem′po·ra′ne·ous·ness** *n.* —**con·tem′po·ra′ne·ous·ly** *adv.*

con·tem·po·rar·y (kən tem′pə rer′ē) *adj.* [< L. *com-*, with + *temporarius* < *tempus*: see prec.] **1.** living or happening in the same period **2.** of about the same age **3.** of or in the style of the present or recent times; modern [*contemporary* art] —*n.*, *pl.* **-rar′ies** a person or thing of the same period or about the same age as another or others

SYN.—**contemporary** and **contemporaneous** both mean existing or happening at the same period of time, **contemporary** referring more often to persons or their works, and **contemporaneous**, to events [Longfellow was *contemporary* with Dickens; the emancipation of slaves in the U.S. was *contemporaneous* with that of serfs in Russia]; **coeval** implies extension over the same period of time when a far-off time or very long length of time is involved [*coeval* empires]; **synchronous** implies exact agreement in time of occurrence or rate of movement [*synchronous* oscillations]; **simultaneous** implies occurrence at the same point or brief interval of time [*simultaneous* translations at a world conference]

con·tem·po·rize (kən tem′pə rīz′) *vt., vi.* **-rized′, -riz′ing** to make or be contemporary

con·tempt (kən tempt′) *n.* [OFr. < L. pp. of *contemnere*: see CONTEMN] **1.** the feeling of a person toward someone or something he considers worthless or beneath notice; scorn [to feel *contempt* for a cheat] **2.** the condition of being despised or scorned [to be held in *contempt*] **3.** *Law* a showing disrespect for the authority or dignity of a court (or legislature): in full, **contempt of court** (or **congress**, etc.)

con·tempt·i·ble (kən temp′tə b'l) *adj.* deserving contempt or scorn; despicable [a *contemptible* liar] —**con·tempt′i·bil·i·ty, con·tempt′i·ble·ness** *n.* —**con·tempt′i·bly** *adv.*

con·temp·tu·ous (kən temp′choo wəs) *adj.* full of contempt; scornful; disdainful [a *contemptuous* sneer] —**con·temp′tu·ous·ly** *adv.* —**con·temp′tu·ous·ness** *n.*

con·tend (kən tend′) *vi.* [< L. *contendere* < *com-*, together + *tendere*, to stretch] **1.** to strive in combat; fight; struggle [to *contend* with greed and envy] **2.** to strive in debate; argue **3.** to strive in competition; compete [to *contend* for a prize] —*vt.* to hold to be a fact; assert [we *contend* that he is guilty] —**con·tend′er** *n.*

con·tent¹ (kən tent′) *adj.* [< OFr. < L. pp. of *continere*: see CONTAIN] happy enough with what one has or is; satisfied [*content* with living on a farm] —*vt.* to make content; satisfy [I must *content* myself with reading about travel] —*n.* a being contented or satisfied [a sigh of *content*] —see SYN. at SATISFY

con·tent² (kän′tent) *n.* [< L. pp. of *continere*: see CONTAIN] **1.** [usually *pl.*] *a*) all that is contained in something [the *contents* of a trunk] *b*) all that is dealt with in a writing or speech [a table of *contents*] **2.** *a*) all that is dealt with in an area of study, work of art, discussion, etc. *b*) meaning or substance [the *content* of a poem as distinguished from its form] **3.** the amount contained [iron with a high carbon *content*]

con·tent·ed (kən ten′tid) *adj.* having or showing no desire for something more or different; satisfied —**con·tent′ed·ly** *adv.* —**con·tent′ed·ness** *n.*

con·ten·tion (kən ten′shən) *n.* [see CONTEND] **1.** the act of contending; strife, struggle, competition, dispute, quarrel, etc. [*contention* about a point of law; in *contention* for the title] **2.** a statement or point that one argues for as true or valid [it was his *contention* that we should all pay] —see SYN. at DISCORD

con·ten·tious (-ten′shəs) *adj.* **1.** always ready to argue; quarrelsome **2.** of or marked by contention —see SYN. at BELLIGERENT —**con·ten′tious·ly** *adv.* —**con·ten′tious·ness** *n.*

con·tent·ment (kən tent′mənt) *n.* the state, quality, or fact of being contented

con·ter·mi·nous (kən tur′mə nəs, kän-) *adj.* [< L. < *com-*, together + *terminus*, an end] **1.** having a common boundary; contiguous **2.** contained within the same boundaries or limits [forty-eight States of the U.S. are *conterminous*] —**con·ter′mi·nous·ly** *adv.*

con·test (kən test′; *for n.* kän′test) *vt.* [< Fr. < L. *contestari* < *com-*, together + *testari*, to bear witness < *testis*, a witness]

1. to try to prove that (something) is not true, right, or lawful; dispute [to *contest* a will] **2.** to fight for; struggle to win or keep [to *contest* every inch of ground in a battle] —*vi.* to struggle (*with* or *against*); contend —*n.* **1.** a fight, struggle, or controversy **2.** any race, game, etc. in which individuals or teams compete to determine the winner —**con·test′a·ble** *adj.* —**con·test′er** *n.*

con·test·ant (kən tes′tənt) *n.* [Fr.] **1.** one that competes in a contest **2.** one who contests a claim, decision, etc.

con·text (kän′tekst) *n.* [< L. pp. of *contexere* < *com-*, together + *texere*, to weave] **1.** the words just before and after a certain word, sentence, etc., that help make clear what it means [a remark taken out of *context* may be misunderstood] **2.** the circumstances or conditions surrounding a particular thing —**con·tex·tu·al** (kən teks′choo wəl) *adj.* —**con·tex′tu·al·ly** *adv.*

contg. containing

con·ti·gu·i·ty (kän′tə gyoo′ə tē) *n., pl.* **-ties** the state of being contiguous; nearness or contact

con·tig·u·ous (kən tig′yoo wəs) *adj.* [< L. *contiguus* < base of *contingere*: see CONTACT] **1.** touching along all or most of one side [the U.S. is *contiguous* with Canada] **2.** near, next, or adjacent [*contiguous* houses] —see SYN. at ADJACENT —**con·tig′u·ous·ly** *adv.* —**con·tig′u·ous·ness** *n.*

con·ti·nence (känt′'n əns) *n.* [see CONTINENT] self-restraint; specif., a refraining from all sexual activity

con·ti·nent (känt′'n ənt) *adj.* [< OFr. < L. prp. of *continere*: see CONTAIN] self-restrained; specif., practicing sexual continence —*n.* any of the main large land areas of the earth (Africa, Asia, Australia, Europe, N. America, S. America, and, sometimes, Antarctica) —**the Continent** all of Europe except the British Isles —**con′ti·nent·ly** *adv.*

con·ti·nen·tal (känt′'n en′t'l) *adj.* **1.** of a continent **2.** [*sometimes* C-] European ☆**3.** [C-] of the American colonies at the time of the American Revolution —*n.* **1.** [*usually* C-] a European ☆**2.** [C-] a soldier of the American army during the Revolution ☆**3.** a piece of paper money issued by the Continental Congress: it became almost worthless before the end of the war, hence the phrases **not care** (or **give**), or **not worth, a continental** —**con′ti·nen′tal·ly** *adv.*

Continental Congress either of the two assemblies of representatives from the American colonies during the Revolutionary period: the second issued the Declaration of Independence (1776)

Continental Divide ridge of the Rocky Mountains forming a watershed that separates rivers flowing in an easterly direction from those flowing in a westerly direction

continental drift the theory of the drifting of continents due to currents in the molten rocks of the earth's mantle

continental shelf the gradually sloping shelf of land under water that borders a continent and ends in a steep descent (**continental slope**) to the deep ocean

con·tin·gen·cy (kən tin′jən sē) *n., pl.* **-cies** **1.** a contingent quality or condition; esp., dependence on chance or uncertain conditions **2.** a possible, unforeseen, or accidental happening [be prepared for any *contingency*] **3.** some thing or event which depends on or is incidental to another [the *contingencies* of war] Also **con·tin′gence**

con·tin·gent (-jənt) *adj.* [< L. prp. of *contingere*: see CONTACT] **1.** that may or may not happen; possible [*contingent* events] **2.** happening by chance; accidental **3.** dependent (*on* or *upon* an uncertainty); conditional [his promotion is *contingent* on his passing the final test] —*n.* **1.** a chance happening **2.** a group forming part of a larger group; esp., one's share or quota, as of troops, laborers, delegates, etc. [the Iowa *contingent* at the convention]

con·tin·u·al (kən tin′yoo wəl) *adj.* **1.** happening over and over again; repeated often [his *continual* jokes] **2.** going on without stopping; continuous [the *continual* roar of the waterfall] —**con·tin′u·al·ly** *adv.*

SYN.—**continual** applies to that which happens again and again or goes on without stopping over a long period of time [*continual* arguments]; **continuous** applies to that which goes on without a break in either space or time [a *continuous* area of land]; **constant** stresses being steady or regular in happening or happening again and again [the *constant* beat of the heart]; **incessant** implies activity that goes on without being stopped or interrupted [*incessant* chatter]; **perpetual** applies to that which lasts or remains for an indefinitely long period of time [a *perpetual* nuisance]; **eter-**

nal stresses an endless or timeless quality [the *eternal* truths] —*ANT.* intermittent, interrupted

con·tin·u·ance (kən tin′yoo wəns) *n.* **1.** the act or process of continuing, or going on [a treaty ensuring the *continuance* of trade] **2.** the time during which an action or state lasts; duration **3.** the fact of remaining (*in* a place or condition); stay **4.** *Law* postponement or adjournment to a later date [asking for a *continuance* of the trial]

con·tin·u·ant (-yə wənt) *n.* a speech sound that can be prolonged during a breath, including *fricatives* (s, f, th, etc.), *nasals* (m, n, ŋ), *liquids* (l, r), or *vowels*: distinguished from STOP

con·tin·u·a·tion (kən tin′yoo wā′shən) *n.* **1.** a keeping up or going on without stopping **2.** a beginning again after an interruption; resumption [a *continuation* of the meeting after lunch] **3.** a part or thing by which something is continued, as a sequel to a story or an extension of a highway

con·tin·ue (kən tin′yoo, -yoo) *vi.* **-ued, -u·ing** [< OFr. < L. *continuare*, to join < *continere*: see CONTAIN] **1.** to remain in existence or effect; last; endure [the war *continued* for five years] **2.** to go on in a specified course of action or condition; persist [he *continued* ailing] **3.** to go on or extend [the road *continues* to the highway] **4.** to stay in the same place or position [he *continued* in office for another year] **5.** to go on again after an interruption; resume [after a sip of water, the speaker *continued*] —*vt.* **1.** to go on with; carry on; keep up [despite the noise, he *continued* reading] **2.** to extend **3.** to go on with (an activity, story, etc.) again after stopping; resume **4.** to cause to remain; retain [to *continue* someone in office] **5.** *Law* to postpone or adjourn to a later date —**con·tin′u·a·ble** *adj.* —**con·tin′u·er** *n.*

SYN.—**continue** implies a going on in a specified course or condition and stresses uninterrupted existence rather than duration; **last** stresses duration, either for the specified time or for a long time beyond that which is usual; **endure** implies a holding up under suffering, hardship, etc.; **abide** is applied to that which remains stable and steadfast, esp. in contrast to that which is changing or temporary; **persist** implies continued existence beyond the expected or normal time —*ANT.* stop, cease

con·ti·nu·i·ty (kän′tə noo′ə tē, -nyoo′-) *n., pl.* **-ties** **1.** the state or quality of being continuous **2.** an unbroken, connected whole ☆**3.** the script or scenario for a motion picture, radio or television program, etc. **4.** a series of comments connecting the parts of a radio or television program

con·tin·u·ous (kən tin′yoo wəs) *adj.* [L. *continuus*: see CONTINUE] going on or extending without interruption or break; unbroken; connected [a *continuous* line of trees] —see SYN. at CONTINUAL —**con·tin′u·ous·ly** *adv.*

con·tin·u·um (-yoo wəm) *n., pl.* **-u·a** (-wə), **-u·ums** [L.] a continuous whole, quantity, or series

con·tort (kən tôrt′) *vt., vi.* [< L. pp. of *contorquere* < *com-*, together + *torquere*, to twist] to twist or wrench out of its usual form; distort violently [a face *contorted* with pain]

con·tor·tion (kən tôr′shən) *n.* **1.** a contorting or being contorted, esp. of the face or body **2.** a contorted condition or position —**con·tor′tive** *adj.*

con·tor·tion·ist (kən tôr′shən ist) *n.* a person who can twist his body into unnatural positions

con·tour (kän′toor) *n.* [Fr. < It. < LL. *contornare* < L. *com-*, very much + *tornare*, to turn: see TURN] the outline of a figure, land, etc. —*vt.* **1.** to represent in contour **2.** to shape or mold to the contour of something [a chair *contoured* to the body] — *adj.* **1.** made so as to conform to the shape of something [*contour* sheets for a bed] **2.** characterized by the making of furrows along the natural contour lines so as to keep the land from eroding [*contour* farming]

contour map a map with lines (**contour lines**) connecting all points of the same elevation

contr. **1.** contract **2.** contraction **3.** contrary

con·tra- [< L. *contra*, against] *a prefix meaning*: **1.** against, opposite, opposed to [*contradict*] **2.** lower in musical pitch [*contrabassoon*]

con·tra·band (kän′trə band′) *n.* [< Sp. < It. < *contra-*, against + *bando* < VL. *bannum* (akin to BAN[1])] **1.** unlawful or prohibited trade **2.** smuggled goods, forbidden by law to be imported or exported **3.** *same as* CONTRABAND OF WAR —*adj.*

CONTOUR MAP

---

fat, āpe, cär; ten, ēven; is, bīte; gō, hôrn, tōol, lŏok; oil, out; up, fur; get; joy; yet; chin; she; thin, *th*en; zh, leisure; ŋ, ring; ə for *a* in ago, *e* in agent, *i* in sanity, *o* in comply, *u* in focus; ′ as in able (ā′b'l); Fr. bal; ë, Fr. coeur; ö, Fr. feu; Fr. mon; ô, Fr. coq; ü, Fr. duc; r, Fr. cri; H, G. ich; kh, G. doch; ‡foreign; ☆ Americanism; < derived from. See inside front cover.

forbidden by law to be imported or exported —**con·tra·band·ist** *n.*

contraband of war war materiel which, by international law, may be seized by a belligerent nation when shipped to its enemy by a neutral country

con·tra·bass (kän′trə bās′) *adj.* [see CONTRA- & BASS¹] having its pitch an octave lower than the normal bass —*n.* *same as* DOUBLE BASS —**con′tra·bass′ist** *n.*

con·tra·bas·soon (kän′trə bə sōōn′) *n.* the double bassoon, which is larger than the ordinary bassoon and an octave lower in pitch

con·tra·cep·tion (kän′trə sep′shən) *n.* [CONTRA- + (CON)CEPTION] the prevention of the female ovum from being fertilized by the male sperm, as by the use of special devices, drugs, etc.

con·tra·cep·tive (-tiv) *adj.* of or used for contraception —*n.* any contraceptive device or agent

con·tract (kän′trakt *for n. & usually for vt. 1 & vi. 1;* kən trakt′ *for v. generally*) *n.* [OFr. < L. pp. of *contrahere* < *com-*, together + *trahere*, to DRAW] 1. an agreement to do something, esp. one in writing that can be enforced by law 2. a formal agreement of marriage or betrothal 3. a document containing the terms of an agreement 4. *Bridge a)* the number of tricks bid by the highest bidder *b)* *same as* CONTRACT BRIDGE —*vt.* 1. to enter upon, or undertake, by contract 2. to get or acquire [to *contract* a disease, debts, etc.] 3. to reduce in size; draw together; shrink [cold *contracts* metals] 4. to narrow in scope; restrict 5. *Gram.* to shorten (a word or phrase) by the omission of a letter or sound, as in *I'm, e'er, can't* —*vi.* 1. to make a contract 2. to become reduced in size or bulk —**contract out** to assign (a job) by contract —**con·tract′i·bil′i·ty** *n.* —**con·tract′i·ble** *adj.* SYN.—**contract** implies a drawing together of surfaces or parts and a resulting decrease in size, bulk, or extent; to **shrink** is to contract so as to be short of the normal or required length, amount, extent, etc. [those shirts have *shrunk*]; **condense** suggests a reducing of something into a more compact or more dense form without loss of essential content [*condensed* milk]; to **compress** is to press or squeeze into a more compact, orderly form [a lifetime's work *compressed* into one volume] —ANT. expand, inflate

con·tract bridge (kän′trakt) a form of auction bridge in which only the tricks bid may be counted toward a game

con·trac·tile (kən trak′t'l) *adj.* 1. having the power of contracting [*contractile* tissue] 2. producing contraction —**con·trac·til·i·ty** (kän′trak til′ə tē) *n.*

con·trac·tion (-shən) *n.* 1. a contracting or being contracted 2. the drawing up and thickening of a muscle in action 3. *Gram. a)* the shortening of a word or phrase *b)* a word form resulting from this (Ex.: *aren't* for *are not*) —**con·trac′tion·al** *adj.* —**con·trac′tive** (-tiv) *adj.*

con·trac·tor (kän′trak tər, kən trak′-) *n.* 1. one of the parties to a contract 2. one who contracts to supply certain materials or do certain work for a specified sum; esp., one who does so in the building trades 3. a muscle that contracts

con·trac·tu·al (kən trak′chōō wəl) *adj.* of, or having the nature of, a contract —**con·trac′tu·al·ly** *adv.*

con·tra·dance (kän′trə dans′) *n. same as* CONTREDANSE

con·tra·dict (kän′trə dikt′) *vt.* [< L. pp. of *contradicere* < *contra-*, against + *dicere*, to speak: see DICTION] 1. *a)* to assert the opposite of (a statement) *b)* to deny the statement of (a person) 2. to be contrary or opposed to; go against [the facts *contradict* his theory] —**con′tra·dict′a·ble** *adj.* —**con′tra·dic′tor, con′tra·dict′er** *n.*

con·tra·dic·tion (-dik′shən) *n.* 1. a contradicting or being contradicted 2. a statement in opposition to another; denial 3. a condition in which things tend to be contrary to each other; inconsistency; discrepancy

con·tra·dic·to·ry (-dik′tər ē) *adj.* 1. involving a contradiction; inconsistent [*contradictory* statements] 2. inclined to contradict or deny Also **con′tra·dic′tive** —**con′tra·dic′to·ri·ly** *adv.* —**con′tra·dic′to·ri·ness** *n.*

con·tra·dis·tinc·tion (-dis tiŋk′shən) *n.* distinction by contrast [tolerance in *contradistinction* to love] —**con′tra·dis·tinc′tive** *adj.* —**con′tra·dis·tinc′tive·ly** *adv.*

☆**con·trail** (kän′trāl′) *n.* [CON(DENSATION) + TRAIL] a white trail of condensed water vapor that sometimes forms in the wake of an aircraft

con·tral·to (kən tral′tō) *n., pl.* -tos, -ti (-tē) [It.: see CONTRA- & ALTO] 1. the range of the lowest female voice 2. a voice, singer, or part with such range —*adj.* of or for a contralto

con·trap·tion (kən trap′shən) *n.* [< ? CON(TRIVE) + TRAP¹ + -TION] [Colloq.] a device that seems to one to be put together in a complicated way; contrivance; gadget

con·tra·pun·tal (kän′trə pun′t'l) *adj.* [< It. *contrappunto* (see COUNTERPOINT) + -AL] 1. of or using counterpoint 2. according to the principles of counterpoint —**con′tra·pun′tal·ly** *adv.* —**con′tra·pun′tist** *n.*

con·tra·ri·e·ty (kän′trə rī′ə tē) *n.* 1. the condition or quality of being contrary 2. *pl.* **-ties** anything that is contrary; inconsistency

con·trar·i·wise (kän′trer ē wīz′; *for 3, often* kən trer′-) *adv.* 1. on the contrary; from the opposite point of view 2. in the opposite way, order, direction, etc. 3. stubbornly contrary; perversely

con·trar·y (kän′trer ē; *for adj. 4, often* kən trer′ē) *adj.* [< OFr. < L. *contrarius* < *contra*, against] 1. being or acting against; opposed [*contrary* to the rules] 2. opposite in nature, order, direction, etc.; altogether different [*contrary* opinions] 3. unfavorable [*contrary* winds] 4. inclined to oppose stubbornly; perverse [a *contrary* child] —*n., pl.* **-trar·ies** the opposite; thing that is the opposite of another —*adv.* in a contrary way —see SYN. at OPPOSITE —**on the contrary** as opposed to what has been said —**to the contrary** to the opposite effect —**con′trar·i·ly** *adv.* —**con′trar·i·ness** *n.*

con·trast (kən trast′; *for n.* kän′trast) *vt.* [< Fr. < It. & VL. < L. *contra*, against + *stare*, to STAND] to compare so as to point out the differences; set off against one another [to *contrast* two systems] —*vi.* to show differences when compared [their methods *contrast* sharply with ours] —*n.* 1. a contrasting or being contrasted 2. a difference, esp. a striking difference, between things being compared or parts that are adjacent [the *contrast* between air and rail travel; color *contrast* in a painting] 3. a person or thing showing differences when compared with another [the tall, lean man is quite a *contrast* to his short, stout wife] —see SYN. at COMPARE —**con·trast′a·ble** *adj.* —**con·trast′ive** *adj.*

con·tra·vene (kän′trə vēn′) *vt.* **-vened′, -ven′ing** [< Fr. < LL. < L. *contra*, against + *venire*, to come (see BASIS)] 1. to go against; oppose; violate [practices *contravening* an ethical code] 2. to disagree with; contradict [a truth that cannot be *contravened*] —**con′tra·ven′er** *n.* —**con′tra·ven′tion** (-ven′shən) *n.*

con·tre·danse (kän′trə dans′, kōn′trə däns′) *n.* [Fr., altered (after *contre*, opposite) < COUNTRY-DANCE] a folk dance with the partners in two facing lines

con·tre·temps (kōn′trə tän′, kän′-) *n., pl.* **-temps′** (-tän′, -tänz′) [Fr., ult. < OFr. prp. of *contrester*, CONTRAST] a happening coming at a poor time and causing embarrassment

con·trib·ute (kən trib′yōōt, -yoot) *vt., vi.* **-ut·ed, -ut·ing** [< L. pp. of *contribuere*: see COM- & TRIBUTE] 1. to give (money, etc.) jointly with others to a common fund, as for charity, education, etc. 2. to write (an article, poem, etc.) for a magazine, newspaper, etc. 3. to furnish (knowledge, ideas, etc.) —**contribute to** to have a share in bringing about [his jokes *contributed to* our fun] —**con·trib′u·tive** *adj.* —**con·trib′u·tor** *n.*

con·tri·bu·tion (kän′trə byōō′shən) *n.* 1. a contributing 2. something contributed, as money to a charity or a poem to a magazine 3. [Archaic] a special levy or tax

con·trib·u·to·ry (kən trib′yoo tôr′ē) *adj.* 1. helping to bring something about; contributing [a *contributory* factor to our victory] 2. involving a contribution —*n., pl.* **-ries** a person or thing that contributes

con·trite (kən trīt′, kän′trīt) *adj.* [OFr. < LL. < L. pp. of *conterere*, to grind < *com-*, together + *terere*: see TRITE] 1. feeling deep sorrow or remorse for having sinned or done wrong 2. showing or resulting from remorse or guilt [a *contrite* apology] —**con·trite′ly** *adv.* —**con·trite′ness** *n.*

con·tri·tion (kən trish′ən) *n.* a feeling of remorse for sins or wrongdoing; earnest repentance —see SYN. at PENITENCE

con·triv·ance (kən trī′vəns) *n.* 1. the act, way, or power of contriving 2. something contrived, as an invention, mechanical device, plan, etc.

con·trive (kən trīv′) *vt.* **-trived′, -triv′ing** [< OFr. *controver*, to find out < VL. *contropare*, to compare] 1. to think up; devise; plan [to *contrive* a way to help] 2. to construct skillfully or ingeniously; fabricate [he *contrived* a new kind of car] 3. to bring about, as by a scheme [he *contrived* to get in] —*vi.* to form plans; scheme —**con·triv′a·ble** *adj.* —**con·triv′er** *n.*

con·trived (-trīvd′) *adj.* not spontaneous or natural; too obvious as being planned [a *contrived* ending to a play]

con·trol (kən trōl′) *vt.* **-trolled′, -trol′ling** [< Anglo-Fr. < Fr. < ML. *contrarotulus*, a register < L. *contra*, against + *rotulus*: see ROLL] 1. to have the power of ruling, guiding, or managing; direct or regulate [a thermostat *controls* the heat; the FCC *controls* the licensing of radio and TV stations/ **2.** to hold back; curb; restrain /*control* your temper/ **—n. 1.** power to direct or regulate /she has no *control* over her children/ **2.** the condition of being directed; restraint /the car went out of *control*/ **3.** a means of controlling; check /wage and price *controls*/ **4.** a standard of comparison for checking the findings of an experiment **5.** [*usually pl.*] an apparatus to regulate a mechanism —see **SYN.** at CONDUCT and POWER **—con·trol′la·bil′i·ty** *n.* **—con·trol′la·ble** *adj.*

control experiment an experiment in which one factor after another is varied while the other factors are controlled

con·trol·ler (kən trōl′ər) *n.* **1.** a person in charge of the finances of a business, government, etc., including keeping track of income, expenses, etc.: in government usage *comptroller* is the usual spelling **2.** a person or device that controls **—con·trol′ler·ship′** *n.*

control tower a tower at an airport, from which air traffic is directed

con·tro·ver·sial (kän′trə vur′shəl) *adj.* of, subject to, or stirring up controversy; debatable /a *controversial* book/ **—con′tro·ver′sial·ist** *n.* **—con′tro·ver′sial·ly** *adv.*

con·tro·ver·sy (kän′trə vur′sē) *n., pl.* **-sies** [< L. < *contra*, against + pp. of *vertere*, to turn: see VERSE] **1.** a discussion of a question in which opposing opinions clash; debate **2.** a quarrel or dispute —see **SYN.** at ARGUMENT

con·tro·vert (kän′trə vurt′, kän′trə vurt′) *vt.* [back-formation < prec.] **1.** to argue or reason against; dispute or deny /his report *controverts* the candidate's claims/ **2.** to argue about; debate; discuss **—con′tro·vert′i·ble** *adj.* **—con′tro·vert′i·bly** *adv.*

con·tu·ma·cious (kän′tŏŏ mā′shəs, -tyŏŏ-) *adj.* [< CONTUMACY] stubbornly resisting authority; disobedient — **con′tu·ma′cious·ly** *adv.*

con·tu·ma·cy (kän′tŏŏ mə sē, -tyŏŏ-; kən tŏŏ′-) *n., pl.* **-cies** [< L. < *contumax*, stubborn < *com-*, very much + *tumere*, to swell up] stubborn refusal to submit to authority; disobedience

con·tu·me·ly (kän′tŏŏ mə lē, -mē′-, -tyŏŏ-; kən tŏŏ′-) *n., pl.* **-lies** [< OFr. < L. *contumelia*, reproach, prob. akin to prec.] **1.** insulting words or acts; humiliating treatment **2.** a scornful insult **—con′tu·me′li·ous** (-mē′lē əs) *adj.* **—con′tu·me′li·ous·ly** *adv.*

con·tuse (kən tŏŏz′, -tyŏŏz′) *vt.* **-tused′, -tus′ing** [< L. pp. of *contundere* < *com-*, very much + *tundere*, to beat] to bruise without breaking the skin

con·tu·sion (-tŏŏ′zhən, -tyŏŏ′-) *n.* a bruise

co·nun·drum (kə nun′drəm) *n.* [16th-c. Oxford University L. slang] **1.** a riddle whose answer contains a pun (Ex.: "What's the difference between a jeweler and a jailer?" "One sells watches and the other watches cells.") **2.** any puzzling question or problem

con·ur·ba·tion (kän′ər bā′shən) *n.* [< CON- + L. *urbs*, city + -ATION] a densely populated urban area, including suburbs and towns around a large city

con·va·lesce (kän′və les′) *vi.* **-lesced′, -lesc′ing** [< L. *convalescere* < *com-*, very + *valescere*, to grow strong < *valere*, to be strong] to recover gradually from illness; get back strength and health

con·va·les·cence (-les′′ns) *n.* [see prec.] **1.** a gradual recovery of health after illness **2.** the period of such recovery

con·va·les·cent (-les′′nt) *adj.* **1.** getting back health and strength after illness **2.** of or having to do with convalescence /a *convalescent* diet/ **—n.** a convalescent person

con·vec·tion (kən vek′shən) *n.* [< L. < pp. of *convehere* < *com-*, together + *vehere*, to carry] **1.** a transmitting or conveying **2.** *a)* the movement of parts of a fluid within the fluid because of differences in the density, temperature, etc. of the parts *b)* the transference of heat by such movement, as by the upward movement of a warm, light air current **—con·vec′tion·al** *adj.* **—con·vec′tive** *adj.* **—con·vec′tive·ly** *adv.* **—con·vec′tor** *n.*

con·vene (kən vēn′) *vi., vt.* **-vened′, -ven′ing** [< OFr. < L. *convenire* < *com-*, together + *venire*, to come (see BASIS)] to come or call together for a meeting; assemble /Congress regularly *convenes* in January; in a crisis, the President can convene Congress for a special session/ —see **SYN.** at CALL **—con·ven′er** *n.*

con·ven·ience (kən vēn′yəns) *n.* [< L. < *convenire*, CONVENE] **1.** the quality or condition of being convenient **2.** personal comfort /this telephone is for the *convenience* of customers/ **3.** anything that adds to one's comfort or saves work /cars, refrigerators, and other modern *conveniences*/ **—at one's convenience** at a time, place, etc. that suits one

☆**convenience food** packaged food sold in a prepared or partly prepared form, as frozen dinners, dry cake mixes, etc.

con·ven·ient (-yənt) *adj.* **1.** favorable to one's comfort; easy to do, use, or get to; handy /a *convenient* time and place for the meeting/ **2.** [Colloq.] easily accessible (*to*); near (*to*) **—con·ven′ient·ly** *adv.*

con·vent (kän′vənt, -vent) *n.* [< OFr. < L. *conventus*, assembly, orig. pp. of *convenire*, CONVENE] **1.** a community of nuns or, sometimes, monks, living under strict religious vows **2.** the building or buildings occupied by such a group

con·ven·ti·cle (kən ven′ti k'l) *n.* [< OFr. < L. dim. of prec.] **1.** a religious assembly, esp. an illegal or secret one **2.** a place where such an assembly meets

con·ven·tion (kən ven′shən) *n.* [< L. < pp. of *convenire*, CONVENE] **1.** a meeting of members or delegates from various places, held every year or so /a political *convention*, lawyers' *convention*/ **2.** *a)* an agreement between persons, nations, etc. /the Geneva *Convention*/ *b)* general agreement on the usages and practices of social life **3.** a customary practice, rule, method, etc. /it is a *convention* to say "How do you do?" on being introduced to someone/

con·ven·tion·al (-'l) *adj.* **1.** having to do with a convention **2.** of, sanctioned by, or growing out of custom or usage; customary /"hello" is a *conventional* greeting in answering a telephone/ **3.** *a)* conforming to accepted rules or standards; formal; not natural, original, or spontaneous /*conventional* attitudes, behavior, etc./ *b)* not unusual; ordinary /a *conventional* business suit/ **4.** stylized; conventionalized /a *conventional* portrait/ **5.** nonnuclear /*conventional* weapons/ **—con·ven′tion·al·ism** *n.* **—con·ven′tion·al·ist** *n.* **—con·ven′tion·al·ly** *adv.*

con·ven·tion·al·i·ty (kən ven′shə nal′ə tē) *n., pl.* **-ties 1.** the quality, fact, or condition of being conventional **2.** conventional behavior or act **3.** a conventional form or rule

con·ven·tion·al·ize (kən ven′shən 'l īz′) *vt.* **-ized′, -iz′ing 1.** to make conventional **2.** *Art* to treat in a conventional manner **—con·ven′tion·al·i·za′tion** *n.*

conventional wisdom the belief that most people have about some matter

☆**con·ven·tion·eer** (kən ven′shə nir′) *n.* a delegate or member attending a convention

con·ven·tu·al (kən ven′chŏŏ wəl) *adj.* of or like a convent **—n.** a member of a convent

con·verge (kən vurj′) *vi.* **-verged′, -verg′ing** [< LL. *convergere* < L. *com-*, together + *vergere*, to turn: see VERGE²] **1.** to come together or tend to come together at a point /*converging* lines/ **2.** to move or be directed toward each other or toward the same place, purpose, or result /the crowds *converged* on the stadium/ **—vt.** to cause to converge

con·ver·gence (-vur′jəns) *n.* **1.** the act, fact, or condition of converging **2.** the point at which things converge Also **con·ver′gen·cy,** *pl.* **-cies —con·ver′gent** *adj.*

con·vers·a·ble (kən vur′sə b'l) *adj.* **1.** easy to talk to; affable **2.** liking to converse or talk

con·ver·sant (kən vur′s'nt, kän′vər-) *adj.* [see CONVERSE¹] familiar or acquainted (*with*), esp. as a result of study or experience; versed (*in*) **—con·ver′sance, con·ver′san·cy** *n.* **—con·ver′sant·ly** *adv.*

con·ver·sa·tion (kän′vər sā′shən) *n.* [see CONVERSE¹] a talking together; specif., *a)* familiar talk; spoken exchange of ideas, opinions, etc. *b)* an informal conference by representatives of governments, factions, etc.

con·ver·sa·tion·al (-'l) *adj.* **1.** of, like, or for conversation /a *conversational* style in her letters/ **2.** given to conversation; liking to talk with others **—con·ver·sa′tion·al·ist, con′ver·sa′tion·ist** *n.* **—con′ver·sa′tion·al·ly** *adv.*

conversation piece an unusual article of furniture, bric-a-brac, etc. that attracts attention or invites comment

con·verse¹ (kən vurs′; *for n.* kän′vərs) *vi.* **-versed′, -vers′ing** [< OFr. < L. *conversari*, to live with, ult. < *convertere*: see CON-

VERT] to hold a conversation; talk —*n.* informal talk; conversation —see SYN. at SPEAK —**con·vers′er** *n.*

con·verse[2] (kän′vərs; *also, for adj.,* kən vurs′) *adj.* [< L. pp. of *convertere:* see CONVERT] reversed in position, order, etc.; opposite; contrary —*n.* a thing related in a converse way; the opposite —**con·verse′ly** *adv.*

con·ver·sion (kən vur′zhən, -shən) *n.* a converting or being converted, as from one form to another, from one religion to another, etc. —**con·ver′sion·al, con·ver′sion·ar′y** *adj.*

con·vert (kən vurt′; *for n.* kän′vərt) *vt.* [< OFr. < L. *convertere < com-,* together + *vertere,* to turn: see VERSE] 1. to change from one form or use to another; transform [*convert* grain into flour] 2. to cause to change from one belief, religion, etc. to another 3. to exchange for something equal in value 4. *Finance* to change (a security, currency, etc.) into an equivalent of another form 5. *Law* to take and use (another's property) unlawfully —*vi.* 1. to be converted ☆2. *Bowling* to knock down all of the standing pins on the second bowl, scoring a spare ☆3. *Football* to score the extra point or points after a touchdown —*n.* a person converted, as to a religion —see SYN. at CHANGE and TRANSFORM

con·vert·er (kən vur′tər) *n.* a person or thing that converts; specif., *a)* a furnace for converting pig iron into steel *b) Elec.* a device for converting alternating current into direct current: see INVERTER *c) Radio & TV* any device for adapting a receiver to added frequencies or modulations Also sp. **con·ver′tor**

converter reactor a nuclear reactor that produces less fissionable material than it consumes

con·vert·i·ble (kən vur′tə b'l) *adj.* that can be converted —*n.* 1. a thing that can be converted ☆2. an automobile with a top that can be folded back —**con·vert′i·bil′i·ty** *n.* —**con·vert′i·bly** *adv.*

con·vex (kän veks′, kən-; *also, & for n. usually,* kän′veks) *adj.* [< L. *convexus,* pp. of *convehere < com-,* together + *vehere,* to bring] curving outward like the surface of a sphere —*n.* a convex surface, line, object, etc. —**con·vex′i·ty** *n., pl.* **-ties** —**con·vex′ly** *adv.*

con·vex·o·con·cave (kən vek′sō kän kāv′) *adj.* convex on one side and concave on the other

con·vex·o·con·vex (-kän veks′) *adj.* convex on both sides, as some lenses

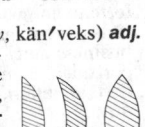

CONVEX LENSES
(A, plano-convex;
B, convexo-concave;
C, convexo-convex)

con·vey (kən vā′) *vt.* [< Anglo-Fr. *conveier,* to escort < L. *com-,* together + *via,* way] 1. to take from one place to another; transport; carry [the cattle were *conveyed* in trucks to the market] 2. to serve as a channel or medium for; transmit [a pipeline to *convey* oil] 3. to make known; communicate [writing a note to *convey* his sympathy] 4. to transfer, as title to property, to another person —**con·vey′a·ble** *adj.*

con·vey·ance (-əns) *n.* 1. a conveying 2. a means of conveying, esp. a vehicle 3. *a)* the transfer of the ownership of real property from one person to another *b)* the document showing this; deed —**con·vey′anc·er** *n.* —**con·vey′anc·ing** *n.*

con·vey·or, con·vey·er (-ər) *n.* one that conveys; esp., a mechanical contrivance, as a continuous chain or belt (**conveyor belt**) for conveying something

con·vict (kən vikt′; *for n.* kän′vikt) *vt.* [< L. pp. of *convincere:* see CONVINCE] 1. to prove (a person) guilty [*convicted* by the evidence] 2. to judge and find guilty of an offense charged [the jury *convicted* him of theft] —*n.* 1. one found guilty of a crime and sentenced by a court 2. one serving a sentence in prison

con·vic·tion (kən vik′shən) *n.* 1. a convicting or being convicted 2. the state or appearance of being convinced, as of the truth of a belief [to speak with *conviction*] 3. a strong belief —see SYN. at CERTAINTY and OPINION —**con·vic′tive** *adj.*

con·vince (kən vins′) *vt.* **-vinced′, -vinc′ing** [L. *convincere < com-,* very much + *vincere,* to conquer] to overcome the doubts of; persuade [by argument or evidence; make feel sure [I'm *convinced* he is telling the truth] —**con·vinc′er** *n.* —**con·vin′ci·ble** *adj.* —**con·vinc′ing·ly** *adv.*

con·viv·i·al (kən viv′ē əl) *adj.* [< L. < *convivium,* a feast < *com-,* together + *vivere,* to live] 1. having to do with a feast or festive activity 2. fond of eating, drinking, and good company; sociable; jovial [*convivial* fellows] —**con·viv′i·al′i·ty** *n.* —**con·viv′i·al·ly** *adv.*

con·vo·ca·tion (kän′və kā′shən) *n.* 1. a convoking 2. a group that has been convoked; esp., an ecclesiastical or academic assembly —**con′vo·ca′tion·al** *adj.*

con·voke (kən vōk′) *vt.* **-voked′, -vok′ing** [< Fr. < L. *convocare < com-,* together + *vocare,* to call] to call together for a meeting; summon to assemble; convene —see SYN. at CALL —**con·vok′er** *n.*

con·vo·lute (kän′və loot′) *adj.* [< L. pp. of *convolvere:* see CONVOLVE] rolled up in a spiral with the coils falling one upon the other; coiled —*vt., vi.* **-lut′ed, -lut′ing** to wind around; coil —**con′vo·lute′ly** *adv.*

con·vo·lut·ed (-id) *adj.* 1. having convolutions; coiled 2. involved; intricate; complicated [*convoluted* reasoning]

con·vo·lu·tion (kän′və loo′shən) *n.* 1. a twisting, coiling, or winding together 2. a convoluted condition 3. a fold, twist, or coil of something convoluted; specif., any of the irregular folds or ridges on the surface of the brain

con·volve (kən välv′) *vt., vi.* **-volved′, -volv′ing** [< L. *convolvere < com-,* together + *volvere,* to roll] to roll, coil, or twist together

CONVOLUTIONS
(of the brain)

con·vol·vu·lus (kən väl′vyə ləs) *n., pl.* **-lus·es, -li′** (-lī′) [L., bindweed: see prec.] any of a genus of trailing or twining plants related to the morning glory

con·voy (kän′voi; *also for v.* kən voi′) *vt.* [< OFr. *convoier,* CONVEY] to go along with as an escort, esp. in order to protect —*n.* 1. the act of convoying 2. a protecting escort, as for ships or troops 3. a group of ships, vehicles, etc. traveling together for mutual protection

con·vulse (kən vuls′) *vt.* **-vulsed′, -vuls′ing** [< L. *convulsus,* pp. of *convellere < com-,* together + *vellere,* to pluck] 1. to shake or disturb violently; agitate 2. to cause convulsions, or spasms, in 3. to cause to shake with laughter, rage, grief, etc. —**con·vul′sive** *adj.* —**con·vul′sive·ly** *adv.*

con·vul·sion (-vul′shən) *n.* 1. a violent, uncontrollable contraction or spasm of the muscles: *often used in pl.* 2. a violent fit of laughter 3. any violent disturbance, as an earthquake or a riot —**con·vul′sion·ar′y** *adj.*

co·ny (kō′nē) *n., pl.* **-nies** same as CONEY

coo (koo) *vi.* [echoic] 1. to make the soft, murmuring sound of pigeons or doves or a sound like this 2. to speak gently and lovingly: see BILL[2], *vi.* 2 —*vt.* to express lovingly, as with a coo —*n.* a cooing sound —**coo′ing·ly** *adv.*

cook (kook) *n.* [OE. *coc* < L. < *coquere,* to cook < IE. base *pekw-,* to cook] a person who prepares food for eating —*vt.* 1. to prepare (food) for eating by boiling, baking, frying, etc. 2. to apply heat to or treat in some way suggestive of this, as in industry 3. [Slang] to spoil; ruin —*vi.* 1. to act as a cook 2. to undergo cooking —**cook up** [Colloq.] to think up; concoct; devise [he *cooked up* an alibi] —☆**what's cooking?** [Slang] what's happening? —**cook′er** *n.*

Cook (kook), **James** 1728–79; Eng. naval officer & explorer: explored Australia, New Zealand, etc.

Cook, Mount highest mountain in New Zealand, on South Island: 12,349 ft.

☆**cook·book** (kook′book′) *n.* a book with recipes and other information about preparing food

cook·er·y (-ər ē) *n.* [Chiefly Brit.] the art, practice, or work of cooking

cook·ie, cook·y (kook′ē) *n., pl.* **-ies** [prob. Du. *koekje,* dim. of *koek,* a cake] ☆1. a small, sweet cake, usually flat ☆2. [Slang] a person, esp. one described as "tough, smart, etc."

☆**cook·out** (kook′out′) *n.* a meal prepared on an outdoor grill, etc. and eaten outdoors

☆**cook·stove** (-stōv′) *n.* a stove for cooking

Cook Strait strait between North Island & South Island, New Zealand

cook·ware (-wer′) *n.* utensils in which food is cooked; pots, pans, casseroles, etc.

cool (kool) *adj.* [OE. *col* < IE. base *gel-,* cold, to freeze] 1. moderately cold; neither warm nor very cold 2. tending to lessen discomfort in hot weather [*cool* clothes] 3. *a)* not excited; calm; composed [to keep *cool* in an emergency] *b)* [Old Slang] not letting one's feelings become involved; dispassionate 4. not friendly or interested; showing dislike or indifference [he passed me on the street with a *cool* "hello"] 5. calmly impudent or bold [a *cool* stare] 6. not suggesting warmth [blue and green are *cool* colors] 7. [Colloq.] all of; no less than [a *cool* thousand dollars] ☆8. [Slang] pleasing; excellent —*adv.* in a cool manner —*n.* 1. a cool place, time, thing, etc. ☆2. [Slang] cool, dispassionate attitude or manner —*vt., vi.* to make or become cool —**cool off** 1. to calm down 2. to lose enthusiasm, interest, etc. —☆**play it cool** [Slang] to control or not show one's feelings; stay aloof —**cool′ish** *adj.* —**cool′ly** *adv.* —**cool′ness** *n.*

SYN.—**cool**, in this comparison, implies freedom from the heat of emotion or excitement, suggesting a calm attitude or a controlled alertness in difficult circumstances; **composed** suggests readiness to meet a trying situation through self-possession or the disciplining of one's feelings [although the caterers were late in arriving, the hostess remained *composed*]; **collected** stresses a being in full command of one's faculties or feelings in a distracting situation [the theater manager was calm and *collected* in restoring order after the false fire alarm]; **unruffled** suggests a keeping of one's poise or composure in the face of something that might upset or embarrass one [he was *unruffled* by the criticism]; **nonchalant** stresses a casual lack of concern, as in an embarrassing situation —**ANT.** excited, agitated

cool·ant (kool′ənt) *n.* a substance, usually a fluid, used to remove heat as from a nuclear reactor, an internal-combustion engine, etc.

cool·er (-ər) *n.* **1.** a device, container, or room for cooling things or keeping them cool **2.** anything that cools ☆**3.** [Slang] a jail

cool·head·ed (-hed′id) *adj.* not easily excited or flustered; calm —**cool′head′ed·ness** *n.*

Coo·lidge (kool′lij), **(John) Calvin** 1872–1933; 30th president of the U.S. (1923–29)

coo·lie (kool′lē) *n.* [Hindi *qūlī*, hired servant] **1.** an unskilled native laborer, esp. formerly, in China, India, etc. **2.** any person doing heavy labor for little pay

☆**coon** (koon) *n. shortened form of* RACCOON

☆**coon cat** [Colloq.] *same as* CACOMISTLE

☆**coon·skin** (koon′skin′) *n.* the skin of a raccoon, used as a fur —*adj.* made of coonskin

coop (koop) *n.* [ult. < L. *cupa*, tub, cask < IE. base *keu-*, bend, hollow] **1.** a small cage, pen, or building for poultry, etc. **2.** any place of confinement; specif., [Slang] a jail —*vt.* to confine in or as in a coop (usually with *up* or *in*) —☆**fly the coop** [Slang] to escape, as from a jail

co-op (kō′äp) *n.* [Colloq.] a cooperative

co-op., coop. cooperative

coop·er (koop′ər, koop′-) *n.* [< MDu. < LL. *cuparius* < L. *cupa*, a cask: see COOP] a person whose work is making or repairing barrels and casks —*vt., vi.* to make or repair (barrels and casks)

Coop·er (koop′ər, koop′-), **James Fen·i·more** (fen′ə môr′) 1789–1851; U.S. novelist

coop·er·age (-ij) *n.* **1.** the work or workshop of a cooper: also **coop′er·y**, *pl.* **-ies** **2.** the price for such work

co·op·er·ate, co-op·er·ate (kō äp′ə rāt′) *vi.* **-at′ed**, **-at′ing** [< LL. pp. of *cooperari* < L. *co-*, with + *operari*, to work < *opus*, work] to act or work together for some purpose [if we all *cooperate*, we can finish sooner; the sunshine *cooperated* with the warmth to make an ideal day for the picnic]: also **co·öp′er·ate′** —**co·op′er·a′tor, co-op′er·a′tor** *n.*

co·op·er·a·tion, co-op·er·a·tion (kō äp′ə rā′shən) *n.* **1.** a cooperating; joint effort or operation **2.** the association of a number of people in an enterprise so that they all benefit Also **co·öp′er·a′tion**

co·op·er·a·tive, co-op·er·a·tive (kō äp′ər ə tiv, -ər āt′iv; -äp′rə tiv) *adj.* **1.** cooperating or willing to cooperate **2.** designating or of an organization (as for the production or marketing of goods), an apartment house, store, etc. owned collectively by members who share in its benefits —*n.* a cooperative society, store, etc. Also **co·öp′er·a·tive** —**co·op′er·a·tive·ly, co-op′er·a·tive·ly** *adv.* —**co·op′er·a·tive·ness, co-op′er·a·tive·ness** *n.*

co-opt (kō äpt′) *vt.* [< L. < *co-*, with + *optare*, to choose] **1.** to add (a person or persons) to a group by the vote of those already members **2.** to persuade or lure (someone with a different view) to join one's own group, system, party, etc.: also **co·öpt′** —**co′-op·ta′tion, co-op′tion** *n.* —**co-op′ta·tive, co-op′tive** *adj.*

co·or·di·nate, co-or·di·nate (kō ôr′d'n it; *also, and for v. always*, -də nāt′) *adj.* [< ML. pp. of *coordinare* < L. *co-*, with + *ordinare*, to arrange < *ordo* (gen. *ordinis*), order] **1.** of equal order, rank, or importance [the *coordinate* main clauses in a compound sentence] **2.** of or involving coordination or coordinates —*n.* **1.** a coordinate person or thing **2.** any of two or more numbers or magnitudes used to define the position of a

point, line, curve, or plane [locating a city on a map by the *coordinates* of latitude and longitude]: see also CARTESIAN COORDINATES —*vt.* **-nat′ed**, **-nat′ing** **1.** to make coordinate **2.** to bring into proper order or relation; adjust [to *coordinate* all the work on an assembly line] —*vi.* to become coordinate Also **co·ör′di·nate** —**co·or′di·nate·ly, co-or′di·nate·ly** *adv.* —**co·or′di·na·tive, co-or′di·na·tive** (-nə tiv, -nāt′iv) *adj.* —**co·or′di·na′tor, co-or′di·na′tor** *n.*

coordinating conjunction a conjunction that connects coordinate words, phrases, or clauses (Ex.: *and, but, for, or, nor, yet*)

co·or·di·na·tion, co-or·di·na·tion (kō ôr′d'n ā′shən) *n.* **1.** a coordinating or being coordinated **2.** harmonious or coordinated action, as of muscles [*coordination* of both hands is important in playing the piano] Also **co·ör′di·na′tion**

coot (koot) *n., pl.* **coots**: also for 1 & 2 **coot**: see PLURAL, II, D, 1 [< ? MDu. *koet*] **1.** a ducklike, freshwater bird of the rail family, with unwebbed toes ☆**2.** *same as* SCOTER **3.** [Colloq.] a foolish, stupid, or senile person

coot·ie (koot′ē) *n.* [Polynesian *kutu*] [Slang] a louse

cop (käp) *vt.* **copped**, **cop′ping** [< obs. *cap*, to seize; ? ult. < L. *capere*, to take] [Slang] to seize, capture, win, steal, etc. —☆*n.* [Slang] a policeman —☆**cop out** [Slang] **1.** to confess to the police **2.** *a)* to go back (*on* a promise, commitment, etc.); back down; renege *b)* to give up; quit

co·pal (kō′pəl, -pal) *n.* [Sp. < Nahuatl *copalli*, resin] a hard resin from tropical trees, used in varnishes

co·part·ner (kō pärt′nər) *n.* a partner, or associate, as in business —**co·part′ner·ship** *n.*

cope¹ (kōp) *vi.* **coped**, **cop′ing** [OFr. *couper*, to strike < *coup*, COUP] **1.** to fight or contend (*with*) successfully or on equal terms [to *cope* with the enemy] **2.** to deal (*with* problems, troubles, etc.): now often used without the preposition [he was no longer able to *cope*]

cope² (kōp) *n.* [< ML. *capa*, var. of *cappa*: see CAP] **1.** a large, capelike vestment worn by priests at certain ceremonies **2.** anything that covers like a cope, as a canopy —*vt.* **coped**, **cop′ing** to cover with a cope or coping

cope³ (kōp) *vt.* **coped**, **cop′ing** [< COPING] to cut so as to fit against a coping or molding with curves, angles, etc.

co·peck (kō′pek) *n. same as* KOPECK

Co·pen·hag·en (kō′pən hā′gən, -hä′-) capital of Denmark, on the E coast of Zealand & on an adjacent island: pop. 874,000 (met. area 1,378,000)

Copernican system the theory of Copernicus that the planets revolve around the sun and that the earth rotates: basis of modern astronomy

COPE

Co·per·ni·cus (kō pur′ni kəs), **Nic·o·la·us** (nik′ə lā′əs) (L. form of *Mikołaj Kopernik*) 1473–1543; Pol. astronomer —**Co·per′ni·can** *adj., n.*

cope·stone (kōp′stōn′) *n.* **1.** the top stone of a wall; stone in a coping **2.** a finishing touch

cop·i·er (käp′ē ər) *n.* **1.** one who copies; imitator, transcriber, etc. **2.** a duplicating machine

co·pi·lot (kō′pī′lət) *n.* the assistant pilot of an aircraft, who aids or relieves the pilot

cop·ing (kō′piŋ) *n.* [< fig. use of COPE²] the top layer of a masonry wall, usually sloped

coping saw a saw with a narrow blade in a U-shaped frame, esp. for cutting curved outlines

co·pi·ous (kō′pē əs) *adj.* [< L. < *copia*, abundance] **1.** plentiful; abundant [a *copious* supply of food] **2.** wordy; profuse or diffuse [*copious* praise] **3.** full of information —see SYN. at PLENTIFUL —**co′pi·ous·ly** *adv.* —**co′pi·ous·ness** *n.*

co·pla·nar (kō plā′nər) *adj. Math.* in the same plane

Cop·land (kōp′lənd), **Aaron** 1900– ; U.S. composer

Cop·ley (käp′lē), **John Sin·gle·ton** (siŋ′g'l tən) 1738–1815; Am. painter, in England after 1775

COPING SAW

co·pol·y·mer (kō päl′ə mər) *n.* a compound produced by the polymerization of two or more unlike molecules —**co·po·lym·er·i·za·tion** (kō′pə lim′ər i zā′shən, kō päl′ə mər i-) *n.* — **co′po·lym′er·ize** (-īz′) *vt., vi.* -**ized′, -iz′ing**

☆**cop-out** (käp′out′) *n.* [Slang] a copping out, as by confessing, backing down, quitting, etc.

cop·per[1] (käp′ər) *n.* see PLURAL, II, D, 3 [OE. *coper* < LL. *cuprum,* contr. < *Cyprium (aes),* Cyprian (brass), copper < Gr. *Kyprios,* Cyprus, noted for its copper mines] 1. a reddish-brown metal that is a chemical element: it is easily beaten or stretched into various shapes and is an excellent conductor of electricity and heat; symbol, Cu; at. wt., 63.546; at. no., 29 2. [Now chiefly Brit.] a copper coin, as a penny 3. the color of copper; reddish brown —*adj.* 1. of copper 2. reddish-brown —*vt.* to cover with copper —**cop′per·y** *adj.*

cop·per[2] (käp′ər) *n.* [prob. < COP] [Slang] a policeman

cop·per·as (käp′ər əs) *n.* [< OFr. < ML. *(aqua) cuprosa,* lit., copper (water)] ferrous sulfate, $FeSO_4 \cdot 7H_2O$, a green, crystal-line compound used in dyeing, the making of ink, etc.

☆**cop·per·head** (-hed′) *n.* 1. a poisonous N. American pit vi-per with a copper-colored head 2. [C-] a Northerner who sym-pathized with the South during the Civil War: so called in the North

cop·per·plate (-plāt′) *n.* 1. a sheet of copper etched or en-graved for printing 2. a print made from this 3. copperplate printing or engraving

cop·per·smith (-smith′) *n.* a person whose work is making utensils, etc. out of copper

copper sulfate a blue, crystalline substance, $CuSO_4 \cdot 5H_2O$: used in making pigments, batteries, etc.

cop·pice (käp′is) *n.* [< OFr. *copeis* < *couper,* to cut: see COUP] *same as* COPSE

co·pra (kō′prə, käp′rə) *n.* [Port. < Malayalam < Hindi *khoprā*] dried coconut meat, the source of coconut oil

cop·ro- [< Gr. *kopros,* dung] *a combining form meaning* dung, feces: also, before a vowel, **copr-**

cop·ro·lite (käp′rə līt′) *n.* [COPRO- + -LITE] fossilized animal dung —**cop′ro·lit′ic** (-lit′ik) *adj.*

cop·roph·a·gous (käp räf′ə gəs) *adj.* [COPRO- + -PHAGOUS] feeding on dung, as some beetles —**cop·roph′a·gy** (-jē) *n.*

cop·ro·phil·i·a (käp′rə fil′ē ə) *n.* [COPRO- + -PHILIA] *Psychol.* an abnormal interest in feces

copse (käps) *n.* [< COPPICE] a thicket of small trees or shrubs; coppice

Copt (käpt) *n.* 1. a native of Egypt descended from the ancient inhabitants of that country 2. a member of the Coptic Church

☆**cop·ter** (käp′tər) *n. shortened form of* HELICOPTER

Cop·tic (käp′tik) *adj.* [< ModL. < Ar. *Quft,* the Copts < Gr. *Aigyptios,* Egyptian] 1. of the Copts, their language, etc. 2. of the Coptic Church —*n.* the Afro-Asiatic language of the Copts, derived from ancient Egyptian and now used only in the ritual of the Coptic Church

Coptic Church the native Christian church of Egypt and of Ethiopia

cop·u·la (käp′yə lə) *n., pl.* -**las** [L., a link < *co-,* together + OL. *apere,* to join] something that connects or links together; specif., *same as* LINKING VERB —**cop′u·lar** *adj.*

cop·u·late (-lāt′) *vi.* -**lat′ed, -lat′ing** [< L. pp. of *copulare,* to couple < *copula:* see prec.] to have sexual intercourse —**cop′u·la′tion** *n.* —**cop′u·la·to·ry** (-lə tôr′ē) *adj.*

cop·u·la·tive (-lāt′iv, -lə tiv) *adj.* 1. joining together; cou-pling 2. *Gram. a)* connecting coordinate words, phrases, or clauses *b)* involving connected words or clauses *c)* being a copula [a *copulative* verb] 3. of or for copulating —*n.* a copulative word —**cop′u·la′tive·ly** *adv.*

cop·y (käp′ē) *n., pl.* **cop′ies** [< OFr. < ML. *copia,* copious transcript < L. *copia,* plenty] 1. a thing made just like another; imitation 2. any of a number of books, magazines, engravings, etc. printed from the same plates or having the same printed matter 3. material to be set in type or printed 4. subject mat-ter for a writer 5. the words of an advertisement —*vt., vi.* **cop′ied, cop′y·ing** 1. to make a copy or copies of; reproduce 2. to act or be the same as; imitate

SYN.—**copy** is the broadest of the terms here referring to anything that is made to be like the original or patterned after it [a carbon *copy,* a *copy* of a designer's dress]; **reproduction** implies a close imitation of the original, often, however, with differences, as of material, size, or quality [a *reproduction* of a painting]; a **facsimile** is an exact reproduction, sometimes only differing in scale [a photostated *facsimile* of a document]; a **duplicate** is a double, or counterpart, of something, serving all the purposes of the origi-nal [all the books of a single printing are *duplicates*]; a **replica** is an exact reproduction of a work of art

cop·y·book (-book′) *n.* a book with models of handwriting, for-merly used in teaching penmanship —*adj.* ordinary; trite [*copy-book* maxims]

☆**cop·y·cat** (-kat′) *n.* a person who imitates or mimics others: a child's term

☆**copy desk** the desk in a newspaper office where copy is edited and headlines are written

cop·y·ist (-ist) *n.* 1. a person who makes written copies; tran-scriber 2. a person who imitates

☆**cop·y·read·er** (-rē′dər) *n.* a person whose work is editing articles or other copy for publication

cop·y·right (-rīt′) *n.* [COPY + RIGHT] the exclusive right to the publication, production, or sale of the rights of a literary, musi-cal, or artistic work, granted by law for a specified period of time to an author, composer, etc. —*vt.* to protect (a book, etc.) by copyright —*adj.* protected by copyright —**cop′y·right′a·ble** *adj.* —**cop′y·right′er** *n.*

cop·y·writ·er (-rīt′ər) *n.* a writer of copy for advertising or pro-motional material

co·quet (kō ket′) *vi.* -**quet′ted, -quet′ting** [< Fr. < dim. of *coq,* a rooster: see COCK[1]] 1. to behave as a coquette; flirt 2. to trifle or dally (*with* an idea, offer, etc.) —*adj.* coquettish —**co·quet·ry** (kōk′ə trē, kō ket′rē) *n., pl.* -**ries**

co·quette (kō ket′) *n.* [Fr.: see prec.] a girl or woman who tries to get men to notice and admire her; flirt —*vi.* -**quet′ted, -quet′ting** to behave as a coquette; flirt —**co·quet′tish** *adj.* —**co·quet′tish·ly** *adv.* —**co·quet′tish·ness** *n.*

☆**co·qui·na** (kō kē′nə) *n.* [Sp., shellfish < L. *concha:* see CONCH] 1. a soft, whitish limestone made up of broken sea-shells and corals 2. a small saltwater clam

cor- *see* COM-

Cor. 1. Corinthians 2. Coroner

cor. 1. corner 2. cornet 3. correct 4. correction 5. correla-tive 6. correspondence

Cor·a (kôr′ə) [L. < Gr. *Korē,* lit., maiden] a feminine name

cor·a·cle (kôr′ə k'l, kär′-) *n.* [< W. < *corwg,* orig., leather-covered boat] a small boat of waterproof material stretched over a wooden frame

cor·a·coid (kôr′ə koid′) *adj.* [< Gr. < *korax,* raven + *eidos,* form] of a bony process of the shoulder blade in mammals, or a bone in many other vertebrates that extends from the shoulder blade to the breastbone —*n.* this process or bone

cor·al (kôr′əl, kär′-) *n.* [OFr. < L. < Gr. *korallion* < ? Heb. *gōrāl,* pebble] 1. the hard, stony skeleton of some marine polyps, often in masses forming reefs and atolls in tropical seas 2. any of such polyps, living singly or in large colonies 3. a piece of coral 4. yel-lowish red or yellowish pink: also **coral red** or **coral pink** —*adj.* 1. made of coral 2. coral-red or coral-pink

coral reef a reef made up chiefly of coral

cor·al·root (-root′, -root′) *n.* a brownish orchid with corallike rootstocks and no leaves

Coral Sea part of the S Pacific, northeast of Australia & south of the Solomon Is-lands

coral snake ☆a small, poisonous snake with coral-red, yellow, and black bands around its body, found in the southern U.S.

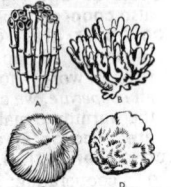

CORAL
(A, organ-pipe; B, reef; C, mush-room; D, Bermuda)

cor·bel (kôr′bəl) *n.* [OFr. < L. *corvus,* raven] a bracket of stone, wood, etc. projecting from a wall to support a cornice, etc. —*vt.* -**beled, -beling** or -**belled, -bel·ling** to provide or support with a corbel or corbels

cor·bie (kôr′bē) *n., pl.* -**bies** [see prec.] [Scot.] a crow or raven

Corbusier, Le *see* LE CORBUSIER

cord (kôrd) *n.* [< OFr. < L. < Gr. *chordē* < IE. base *gher-,* intestine] 1. (a) thick string or thin rope 2. any force acting as a tie or bond 3. [from cord used in measuring] a measure of wood cut for fuel (128 cubic feet) 4. *a)* a rib on the surface of a fabric *b)* cloth with a ribbed surface; corduroy *c)* [*pl.*] corduroy trousers 5. *Anat.* any part like a cord [the spinal *cord;* vocal *cords*]: also CHORD[1] 6. *Elec.* a slender, insulated ca-ble fitted with a plug or plugs —*vt.* 1. to fasten or provide with a cord or cords 2. to stack (wood) in cords

CORBEL

cord·age (kôrd′ij) *n.* 1. cords and ropes, esp. the ropes in a ship's rigging 2. the amount of wood, in cords, in a given area

cor·date (kôr′dāt) *adj.* [< ModL. < L. *cordis*, genitive of *cor*, heart] heart-shaped —**cor′date·ly** *adv.*

cord·ed (kôr′did) *adj.* **1.** fastened with cords **2.** made of cords **3.** that looks like a tight cord, as a muscle **4.** having a ribbed surface, as corduroy **5.** stacked in cords, as wood

cor·dial (kôr′jəl) *adj.* [< ML. < L. *cordis*, genitive of *cor*, HEART] **1.** [Rare] invigorating **2.** warm and friendly; hearty; sincere —*n.* **1.** [Rare] a stimulating medicine, food, or drink **2.** a flavored, syrupy alcoholic drink; liqueur —see SYN. at AMIABLE —**cor′dial·ly** *adv.* —**cor′dial·ness** *n.*

cor·di·al·i·ty (kôr′jē al′ə tē, kôr jal′-) *n.* **1.** a cordial quality; warm, friendly feeling **2.** *pl.* **-ties** a cordial act or remark

cor·dil·le·ra (kôr′dil yer′ə, kôr dil′ər ə) *n.* [Sp. < dim. of *cuerda*, rope < L. *chorda*, CORD] a chain of mountains; esp., the principal mountain range of a continent —**cor·dil·le·ran** *adj.*

Cor·dil·le·ras (kôr′dil yer′əz, kôr dil′ər əz) **1.** mountain system of western N. America, including all mountains between the Rockies & the Pacific coast **2.** mountain system of western S. America; Andes

cord·ing (kôr′diŋ) *n.* the ribbed surface of corded cloth

cord·ite (-dīt) *n.* [CORD + -ITE: from its stringiness] a smokeless explosive made of nitroglycerin, guncotton, petroleum jelly, and acetone

☆**cord·less** (kôrd′lis) *adj.* operated by batteries and not by a cord going to an electric outlet [a *cordless* electric shaver]

Cór·do·ba (kôr′də bə, -və; *Sp.* kôr′thō bä) **1.** city in NC Argentina: pop. 589,000 **2.** city in S Spain: pop. 220,000

cor·do·ba (kôr′də bə) *n.* [after F. F. de *Córdoba*, 16th-cent. Sp. explorer] *see* MONETARY UNITS, table (Nicaragua)

cor·don (kôr′d'n) *n.* [Fr., dim. of *corde*: see CORD] **1.** a line or circle of police, ships, etc. stationed around an area to guard it **2.** a cord, ribbon, or braid worn as a decoration or badge —*vt.* to encircle or shut (*off*) with a cordon

‡**cor·don bleu** (kôr dōn blö′) [Fr., lit., blue ribbon] **1.** a very high honor or distinction **2.** any person highly distinguished in his field; specif., an expert chef

Cor·do·va (kôr′də və) *Eng.* name of CÓRDOBA

cor·do·van (kôr′də vən) *adj.* [< Sp. < CÓRDOBA, Spain, noted for its fine leather] made of cordovan —*n.* **1.** a fine-grained, colored leather, usually of split horsehide **2.** [*pl.*] shoes made of this leather

cor·du·roy (kôr′də roi′) *n.* [prob. < CORD + obs. *duroy*, a coarse fabric] **1.** a heavy cotton fabric with a velvety surface, ribbed vertically **2.** [*pl.*] trousers made of this —*adj.* **1.** made of, or ribbed like, corduroy ☆**2.** made of logs laid crosswise [a *corduroy* road]

cord·wain·er (kôrd′wān′ər) *n.* [see CORDOVAN] [Archaic] a shoemaker

cord·wood (kôrd′wood′) *n.* wood stacked or sold in cords

core (kôr) *n.* [< OFr., prob. < L. *cor*, heart] **1.** the hard, central part of an apple, pear, etc., containing the seeds **2.** the central part of anything [the *core* of a boil] **3.** the most important part; essence; pith [the *core* of a problem] **4.** in foundry work, that part of a mold forming the interior of a hollow casting **5.** a sample section of the earth's strata from underground, obtained with a hollow drill **6.** the center of a nuclear reactor that contains the fissionable fuel **7.** *Chem.* the nucleus of an atom with its electron shells **8.** *Elec.* a bar of iron inside a wire coil: it strengthens the magnetic field resulting from the current in the coil —*vt.* **cored**, **cor′ing** to cut out the core of —**cor′er** *n.*

co·re·li·gion·ist (kō′ri lij′ə nist) *n.* a person of the same religion or religious denomination

Co·rel·li (kô rel′ē; *It.* kô rel′lē), **Ar·can·ge·lo** (är kän′je lô) 1653–1713; It. composer & violinist

☆**co·re·op·sis** (kôr′ē äp′sis) *n.* [ModL. < Gr. *koris*, bug + *opsis*, appearance: from the shape of the fruit] a plant of the composite family, with showy flowers of yellow, crimson, or maroon

co·re·spond·ent (kō′ri spän′dənt) *n.* [CO- + RESPONDENT] *Law* a person charged with having committed adultery with the wife or husband from whom a divorce is being sought —**co′re·spond′en·cy** *n.*

Cor·fu (kôr′foo, kôr foo′, -fyoo′) Gr. island in the Ionian Sea, off the W coast of Greece: 229 sq. mi.

cor·gi (kôr′gē) *n.* same as WELSH CORGI

co·ri·an·der (kôr′ē an′dər) *n.* [< OFr. < L. < Gr. *koriandron*] **1.** a European herb of the parsley family **2.** its strong-smelling, seedlike fruit, used in flavoring food and liqueurs

Co·rinne (kə rin′, kôr ēn′) [Fr. < L. < Gr. *Korinna*, ? dim. of *Korē*: see CORA] a feminine name

Cor·inth (kôr′inth, kär′-) ancient city in the NE Peloponnesus, Greece: noted for its luxury *See map at* GREECE

Co·rin·thi·an (kə rin′thē ən) *adj.* **1.** of Corinth, its people, or culture **2.** designating or of the most elaborate of the three orders of Greek architecture, having a bell-shaped capital with a design of acanthus leaves: see also DORIC and IONIC —*n.* a native or inhabitant of Corinth

CORINTHIAN CAPITAL

Co·rin·thi·ans (-ənz) either of two books of the New Testament, epistles from the Apostle Paul to the Christians of Corinth

Cor·i·o·lis force (kô′rē ō′lis) [after G. de *Coriolis*, 19th-c. Fr. mathematician] the force, caused by the earth's rotation, that produces the deflection (**Coriolis effect**) of a moving body, as wind or water, to the right in the Northern Hemisphere and to the left in the Southern

co·ri·um (kôr′ē əm) *n., pl.* **-ri·a** (-ə) [L., skin: for IE. base see CARNAGE] *same as* DERMIS

Cork (kôrk) seaport in S Ireland: pop. 122,000

cork (kôrk) *n.* [< Sp. *corcho*, ult. (via ? Ar.) < L. *quercus*, oak] **1.** the light, thick, elastic outer bark of an oak tree, the **cork oak**, of the Mediterranean area **2.** a piece of cork; esp., a stopper for a bottle, cask, etc. **3.** any stopper, as one of rubber, etc. **4.** the outer bark of the stems of woody plants —*adj.* made of cork —*vt.* **1.** to stop or seal with a cork [to *cork* a bottle] **2.** to hold back; check [anger kept *corked* up inside him] **3.** to blacken with burnt cork [actors in minstrel shows *corked* their faces]

cork cambium *Bot.* the tissue between the cork and the cortex, from which the protective outer layer is formed

cork·er (kôr′kər) *n.* **1.** a worker or device that corks bottles **2.** [Slang] *a*) a remarkable person or thing *b*) the capping argument, etc. *c*) an absurd lie

cork·ing (-kiŋ) *adj., adv., interj.* [Chiefly Brit. Slang] very good; excellent

cork·screw (kôrk′skroo′) *n.* a spiral-shaped device for pulling corks out of bottles —*adj.* shaped like a corkscrew —*vi., vt.* to move in a spiral; twist

cork·wood (-wood′) *n.* **1.** any of several trees whose wood is very light **2.** the wood of any of these trees

cork·y (kôr′kē) *adj.* **cork′i·er**, **cork′i·est** **1.** of or like cork **2.** tasting of the cork: said of wine

corm (kôrm) *n.* [< Gr. *kormos*, a lopped tree trunk < *keirein*, to cut off] the fleshy, scaly, underground stem of certain plants, as the gladiolus: it differs from a bulb in having more stem tissue and fewer scale leaves

cor·mel (kôr′məl) *n.* a new, small corm

cor·mo·rant (kôr′mə rənt) *n.* [< OFr. < L. < *corvus*, raven + *marinus*, MARINE] **1.** a large sea bird that is greedy for food and dives for the fish it eats: it is used by fishermen in the Orient to catch fish **2.** a greedy person

corn¹ (kôrn) *n.* see PLURAL, II, D, 3 [OE. < IE. base *ger-*, to ripen, grow old from which also come L. *granum*, GRAIN, CHURL & CHURN] **1.** a small, hard seed, esp. a seed or grain of a cereal grass; kernel: chiefly in compounds, as peppercorn, barleycorn, etc. ☆**2.** *a*) a cultivated American cereal plant, with the grain growing on cobs enclosed in husks; maize; Indian corn *b*) the ears or kernels of this plant **3.** [Brit.] the seeds of all cereal grasses; grain; specif., the leading cereal crop (in England, wheat; in Scotland, oats) ☆**4.** [Colloq.] corn whiskey ☆**5.** [Slang] ideas, music, etc. considered old-fashioned, trite, sentimental, etc. —*vt.* to preserve or pickle (meat, etc.) with salt granules or in brine —**corned** *adj.*

corn² (kôrn) *n.* [< OFr. < L. *cornu*, HORN] a hard, thick, painful growth of skin, esp. on a toe

☆**corn·ball** (kôrn′bôl′) *adj.* [CORN¹, *n.* 5 + (SCREW)BALL] [Slang] unsophisticated; corny —*n.* [Slang] a person or thing that is corny

CORMORANT
(to 3 ft. long)

☆**Corn Belt** plains region in the NC part of the Middle West where much corn and cornfed livestock are raised

☆**corn borer** a moth larva that feeds on corn, etc.

☆**corn bread** a bread made with cornmeal

☆**corn·cake** (-kāk′) *n. same as* JOHNNYCAKE

☆**corn·cob** (-käb′) *n.* **1.** the woody core of an ear of corn **2.** a tobacco pipe with a bowl made of a hollowed, dried piece of such a core: in full, **corncob pipe**

corn cockle a tall weed of the pink family, with pink flowers, often found in grainfields

☆**corn·crib** (-krib′) *n.* a small, ventilated structure for storing ears of corn

cor·ne·a (kôr′nē ə) *n.* [< ML. < L. *cornea* (*tela*), horny (tissue) < *cornu*, HORN] the transparent outer coat of the eyeball, covering the iris and pupil: see illustration at EYE —**cor′ne·al** *adj.*

Cor·neille (kôr nā′y′), **Pierre** 1606–84; Fr. dramatist

cor·nel (kôr′n'l, -nel) *n.* [< OFr. < VL. < L. *cornus*] any of a genus of shrubs and small trees with very hard wood, including the dogwoods

cor·nel·ian (kôr nēl′yən) *n.* [< OFr. *corneola*, prob. < VL. *cornea*: see CORNEL] *same as* CARNELIAN

cor·ne·ous (kôr′nē əs) *adj.* [< L. < *cornu*, HORN] horny; hornlike

cor·ner (kôr′nər) *n.* [< OFr. < ML. < *cornu*, HORN] **1.** the point or place where lines or surfaces join and form an angle **2.** the space within the angle formed at the joining of lines or surfaces [a chair in the *corner* of the room] **3.** the area at the tip of any angle formed at a street intersection [the drugstore on the *corner*] **4.** something used to form, mark, protect, or decorate a corner [leather *corners* on a book] **5.** a remote, secret, or secluded spot **6.** region; quarter [every *corner* of America] **7.** an awkward position from which escape is difficult [driven into a *corner*] ☆**8.** a monopoly acquired on a stock or commodity to raise the price [to have a *corner* in wheat] —*vt.* ☆**1.** to force into a corner or awkward position, so that escape is difficult ☆**2.** to get a monopoly on (a stock or commodity) —*vi.* **1.** to meet at or abut (*on*) a corner: said of buildings, etc. **2.** to turn corners [this car *corners* easily] —*adj.* **1.** at or on a corner [a *corner* store] **2.** used in a corner [a *corner* table] — **around the corner** in the immediate vicinity or future; imminent —☆**cut corners 1.** to take a direct route by going across corners **2.** to cut down expenses, time, labor, etc. —**turn the corner** to get safely past the critical point

☆**cor·ner·back** (-bak′) *n. Football* a player of the defensive backfield between the line of scrimmage and the safety men

cor·nered (kôr′nərd) *adj.* having (a specified number or type of) corners [a three-*cornered* hat]

cor·ner·stone (-stōn′) *n.* **1.** a stone laid in the corner of a building, esp. at a ceremony for the beginning of building **2.** the basic part; foundation

cor·ner·wise (-wīz′) *adv.* **1.** with the corner to the front **2.** from one corner to an opposite corner; diagonally Also **cor′ner·ways′**

cor·net (kôr net′) *n.* [< OFr. < L. *cornu*, HORN] **1.** a brass-wind musical instrument like the trumpet but with a shorter tube **2.** *a)* a cone-shaped paper for holding candy, etc. *b)* a cone-shaped pastry —☆**cor·net′ist, cor·net′tist** *n.*

☆**corn·fed** (kôrn′fed′) *adj.* **1.** fed on corn **2.** [Slang] robust from living in the country and simple, unsophisticated, etc.

corn·field (-fēld′) *n.* a field in which corn is grown

CORNET

☆**corn·flakes** (kôrn′flāks′) *n.pl.* a breakfast cereal of crisp flakes made from hulled corn and served cold, as with milk: also **corn flakes**

corn·flow·er (-flou′ər) *n.* a plant of the composite family, with white, pink, or blue flowers

☆**corn·husk·ing** (-hus′kiŋ) *n.* a gathering of friends and neighbors for husking corn —**corn′husk′er** *n.*

cor·nice (kôr′nis) *n.* [Fr. < It. < L. < Gr. *korōnis*, a wreath] **1.** a horizontal molding projecting along the top of a wall, building, etc. **2.** the top part of an entablature: see illustration at ENTABLATURE **3.** a decorative strip above a window for hiding a curtain rod —*vt.* -**niced**, -**nic·ing** to top as with a cornice

Cor·nish (kôr′nish) *adj.* of Cornwall, its people, or culture —*n.* **1.** the Brythonic Celtic language spoken in Cornwall until c. 1800 **2.** *pl.* **Cor′nish** *a)* a British breed of chicken *b)* a

breed of miniature chicken crossbred from these and Plymouth Rocks: also **Cornish hen** or **Rock Cornish (hen)**

Cor·nish·man (-mən) *n., pl.* -**men** a native or inhabitant of Cornwall

corn·meal (kôrn′mēl′) *n.* ☆meal made from corn (maize)

☆**corn pone** [Chiefly Southern] a kind of corn bread baked in small, oval loaves (*pones*)

☆**corn silk** the long, silky fibers that hang in a tuft from the husk of an ear of corn

☆**corn·stalk** (-stôk′) *n.* a stalk of corn (maize)

☆**corn·starch** (-stärch′) *n.* a starch made from corn and used in cooking and to make corn syrup, etc.

☆**corn sugar** a dextrose made from cornstarch

☆**corn syrup** a syrup made from cornstarch

cor·nu·co·pi·a (kôr′nə kō′pē ə, -nyoo-) *n.* [L. *cornu copiae*, horn of plenty] **1.** a representation in painting, sculpture, etc. of a horn overflowing with fruits, flowers, and grain; horn of plenty **2.** an abundance **3.** any cone-shaped container

Corn·wall (kôrn′wôl; *chiefly Brit.* -wəl) county at the SW tip of England: 1,357 sq. mi.

Corn·wal·lis (kôrn wôl′is, -wäl′is), **Charles,** 1st Marquis Cornwallis, 1738–1805; Eng. general: a commander of British forces in the American Revolution

☆**corn whiskey** whiskey made from corn (maize)

CORNUCOPIA

corn·y (kôr′nē) *adj.* **corn′i·er, corn′i·est 1.** of corn ☆**2.** [Colloq.] unsophisticated, old-fashioned, trite, sentimental in a foolish way, etc. —**corn′i·ness** *n.*

corol., coroll. corollary

co·rol·la (kə räl′ə, -rōl′ə) *n.* [L., dim. of *corona*, CROWN] the petals, or inner floral leaves, of a flower —**cor·ol·late** (kôr′ə lāt′, kär′-), **cor′ol·lat′ed** *adj.*

cor·ol·lar·y (kôr′ə ler′ē, kär′-) *n., pl.* -**lar′ies** [< LL. *corollarium*, a deduction < L., a gift < *corolla*: see prec.] **1.** a proposition that follows from another that has been proved [if two angles of a triangle are equal, it follows as a *corollary* that two of its sides are equal] **2.** an inference or deduction **3.** anything that follows as a normal result [reduced tariffs bring free trade as a *corollary*]

Cor·o·man·del Coast (kôr′ə man′d'l, kär′-) coastal region of SE India

co·ro·na (kə rō′nə) *n., pl.* -**nas, -nae** (-nē) [L., CROWN] **1.** a crown or something like a crown **2.** a long cigar with blunt ends **3.** *Anat.* the crown of a tooth, of a skull, etc. **4.** *Astron. a)* the outermost part of the sun's atmosphere, seen during a total solar eclipse *b)* a ring of colored light seen around a luminous body, as the sun or moon, as a result of diffraction by mist, dust, etc. **5.** *Bot.* the cuplike part on the inner side of the corolla of certain flowers, as the daffodil **6.** *Elec.* a sometimes visible electric discharge around a conductor at high potential —**co·ro′nal** *adj.*

cor·o·nach (kôr′ə nəkh, kär′-) *n.* [Scot. & Ir.] a dirge

Co·ro·na·do (kôr′ə nä′dō; *Sp.* kô′rô nä′thô), **Fran·cis·co Vás·quez de** (frän thes′kô väs′keth the) 1510?–54?; Sp. explorer of SW N. America

cor·o·nar·y (kôr′ə ner′ē, kär′-) *adj.* [see CORONA] **1.** of, or in the form of, a crown **2.** *Anat.* designating or of either of two arteries branching from the aorta and supplying blood directly to the heart muscle —☆*n., pl.* -**nar′ies** *same as* CORONARY THROMBOSIS

☆**coronary thrombosis** the formation of a clot that blocks a coronary artery: also **coronary occlusion**

cor·o·na·tion (kôr′ə nā′shən, kär′-) *n.* [< OFr. < L. pp. of *coronare* < *corona*, CROWN] the act or ceremony of crowning a king, queen, emperor, etc.

cor·o·ner (kôr′ə nər, kär′-) *n.* [ME., officer of the crown < Anglo-Fr. < L. *corona*, CROWN] a public officer whose chief duty is to determine by inquest, sometimes with the aid of a jury, the cause of any death that does not seem to be due to natural causes

cor·o·net (kôr′ə net′, kär′-) *n.* [< OFr. dim. of *corone*, CROWN] **1.** a small crown worn by princes and others of high rank **2.** an ornamental band, as of gold, jewels, or flowers, worn around the head —**cor′o·net′ed, cor′o·net′ted** *adj.*

Co·rot (kə rō′; *Fr.* kô rō′), **Jean Bap·tiste Ca·mille** (zhän bä·tēst′ kä mē′y′) 1796–1875; Fr. painter

corp., corpn. corporation

cor·po·ral[1] (kôr′pər əl) n. [< Fr. < It. < capo, chief < L. caput, the head] the lowest-ranking noncommissioned officer, just below a sergeant; specif., an enlisted man or woman in the fourth grade in the U.S. Army and Marine Corps: abbrev. **Corp., Cpl** —**cor′po·ral·cy**, pl. **-cies, cor′po·ral·ship′** n.

cor·po·ral[2] (kôr′pər əl) adj. [< L. corporalis < corporis, genitive of corpus, body: see CORPUS] of the body; bodily —see SYN. at BODILY —**cor′po·ral′i·ty** (-pə ral′ə tē) n. —**cor′po·ral·ly** adv.

cor·po·ral[3] (kôr′pər əl) n. [OFr. < ML. corporalis (palla), body (cloth): see prec.] Eccles. a small, linen altar cloth on which the bread and chalice are placed for the Eucharist

corporal punishment punishment inflicted directly on the body, as flogging

cor·po·rate (kôr′pər it) adj. [< L. pp. of corporare, to make into a body < corpus: see CORPORAL[2]] **1.** formed into a corporation; incorporated **2.** of a corporation [corporate debts] **3.** shared by all in a group; common; joint [corporate blame] —**cor′po·rate·ly** adv.

cor·po·ra·tion (kôr′pə rā′shən) n. **1.** a group of people who get a charter granting them as a body certain of the legal powers, rights, and liabilities of an individual **2.** a group of people, as the mayor and aldermen of an incorporated town, legally authorized to act as an individual —**cor′po·ra·tive** adj.

cor·po·re·al (kôr pôr′ē əl) adj. [< L. < corpus: see CORPORAL[2]] **1.** of or for the body; bodily [corporeal appetites] **2.** material; physical; tangible [corporeal property] —see SYN. at BODILY and MATERIAL —**cor·po′re·al′i·ty** (-al′ə tē) n. —**cor·po′re·al·ly** adv.

corps (kôr) n., pl. **corps** (kôrz) [< OFr. corps, cors < L. corpus, body: see CORPUS] **1.** a body of people associated in some work, organization, etc. [the press corps covering the UN] **2.** Mil. a) a branch of the armed forces with some specialized function [Signal Corps] b) a tactical subdivision of an army, composed of two or more divisions

corps de bal·let (kôr′ də ba lā′) [Fr.] all the dancers of a ballet company except the featured dancers

corpse (kôrps) n. [var. of CORPS] **1.** a dead body, esp. a person **2.** something lifeless and of no use

corps·man (kôr′mən) n., pl. **-men** same as AIDMAN

cor·pu·lence (kôr′pyoo ləns) n. [OFr. < L. corpulentia < corpus, body: see CORPUS] fatness or stoutness of body; obesity: also **cor′pu·len·cy** —**cor′pu·lent** adj. —**cor′pu·lent·ly** adv.

cor·pus (kôr′pəs) n., pl. **cor′po·ra** (-pər ə) [L., body < IE. base krep-] **1.** a human or animal body; esp., a dead one: now mainly a facetious usage **2.** a complete collection, as of laws or writings of a specified type **3.** the main body or substance of anything

Corpus Christ·i (kris′tē) [L., Body of Christ] **1.** R.C.Ch. a festival celebrated on the Thursday after Trinity Sunday, in honor of the Eucharist **2.** city in SE Tex., on the Gulf of Mexico: pop. 205,000

cor·pus·cle (kôr′pəs 'l, -pus′'l) n. [< L. dim. of corpus, body] **1.** a very small particle **2.** Anat. a cell with a special function; esp., any of the red blood cells (erythrocytes) or white blood cells (leukocytes) in the bloodstream: also **cor·pus·cule** (kôr pus′kyōol) —**cor·pus′cu·lar** (-kyoo lər) adj.

corpus de·lic·ti (di lik′tī) [ModL., lit., body of the crime] **1.** the facts showing or proving a crime has been committed **2.** loosely, the body of a murder victim

corpus ju·ris (joor′is) [L., body of law] a collection of all the laws of a nation or district

corpus lu·te·um (lōo′tē əm) pl. **cor·po·ra lu·te·a** (kôr′pər ə lōo′tē ə) [ModL., lit., yellow body] a mass of yellow tissue, formed in the ovary after ovulation, that secretes progesterone if fertilization occurs

corr. **1.** corrected **2.** correspondence

☆**cor·ral** (kə ral′) n. [Sp. < corro, a circle < L. currere, to run] a place fenced in for holding or capturing horses, cattle, etc.; pen —vt. **-ralled′, -ral′ling** **1.** to drive into or confine in a corral **2.** to surround or capture; round up **3.** [Slang] to take possession of; lay hold of

cor·rect (kə rekt′) vt. [< L. pp. of corrigere < com-, together + regere, to lead straight] **1.** to make right; change from wrong to right [the proofreader corrected the spellings] **2.** to mark the errors or faults of [correcting students' test papers] **3.** to make

conform to a standard [to correct the bathroom scales] **4.** to scold or punish for one's mistakes or faults **5.** to cure or counteract (a fault, disease, etc.) [braces on one's teeth to correct one's bite] —vi. to make corrections or an adjustment to compensate (for an error, etc.) —adj. **1.** conforming to an established standard; proper [the correct way to dress for an occasion] **2.** conforming to fact or logic; true; accurate; right [a correct statement of the facts] **3.** equal to the required number, amount, etc. [the correct postage for the parcel] —**cor·rect′a·ble** adj. —**cor·rect′ly** adv. —**cor·rect′ness** n. —**cor·rec′tor** n.

SYN.—**correct** implies the absence of error [a correct answer] or a conforming to what is proper [correct behavior]; **accurate** suggests the care taken not to stray from the facts or not to be in error [how accurate is his report of the events?]; **exact** stresses perfect conformity to fact, truth, or some standard [the exact time; an exact quotation]; **precise** suggests an exactness in every detail and often connotes an attitude that is finicky or too fastidious [precise in all his habits] —see also SYN. at PUNISH —ANT. wrong, false

cor·rec·tion (kə rek′shən) n. **1.** a correcting or being corrected **2.** a change that corrects a mistake; rectification **3.** punishment or scolding to correct faults —**cor·rec′tion·al** adj.

cor·rec·tive (-tiv) adj. tending or meant to correct or improve; remedial [corrective lenses] —n. something corrective; remedy —**cor·rec′tive·ly** adv.

Cor·reg·gio (kə rej′ō), (Antonio Allegri da) 1494?–1534; It. painter

cor·re·late (kôr′ə lāt′, kär′-) n. [cor- (see COM-) + L. relatus: see RELATE] either of two interrelated things —adj. closely and naturally related —vi. **-lat′ed, -lat′ing** to be mutually related (to or with) —vt. to bring (a thing) into mutual relation (with another); calculate or show the relation between [to correlate crime with poverty; to correlate history, geography, etc. in social studies]

cor·re·la·tion (kôr′ə lā′shən, kär′-) n. [see prec.] **1.** a mutual relationship or connection [the correlation between ignorance and prejudice] **2.** the degree of relative correspondence between two sets of data [a correlation of 75%] **3.** a correlating or being correlated —**cor′re·la′tion·al** adj.

cor·rel·a·tive (kə rel′ə tiv) adj. **1.** having a mutual relationship; reciprocally dependent [correlative rights and duties] **2.** Gram. expressing mutual relation and used in pairs [neither . . . nor are correlative conjunctions] —n. **1.** a thing closely related to something else **2.** a correlative word —**cor·rel′a·tive·ly** adv. —**cor·rel′a·tiv′i·ty** n.

cor·re·spond (kôr′ə spänd′, kär′-) vi. [< Fr. < ML. correspondere < L. com-, together + respondere, to answer] **1.** to be in agreement (with something); conform (to something); match [her opinions correspond with mine] **2.** to be similar, analogous, or equal (to something) [a general in the army corresponds to an admiral in the navy] **3.** to communicate (with someone) by letters, esp. regularly —see SYN. at AGREE —**cor′re·spond′ing·ly** adv.

cor·re·spond·ence (-spän′dəns) n. [see prec.] **1.** agreement; conformity **2.** similarity; analogy **3.** a) communication by exchange of letters b) the letters written or received

☆**correspondence school** a school that gives courses of instruction (**correspondence courses**) by mail

cor·re·spond·ent (kôr′ə spän′dənt, kär′-) adj. corresponding; agreeing; matching —n. **1.** a thing that corresponds **2.** a person who exchanges letters with another or writes a letter to another **3.** a person hired as by a newspaper to send news regularly from a distant city or country

cor·ri·dor (kôr′ə dər, kär′-; -dôr′) n. [Fr. < It. < L. currere, to run: see CURRENT] **1.** a long passageway or hall **2.** a strip of land that goes through land held by another country, as one that is a passageway from a country to its seaport

cor·ri·gen·dum (kôr′ə jen′dəm, kär′-) n., pl. **-da** (-də) [L., gerundive of corrigere: see CORRECT] an error to be corrected in a printed work, or [pl.] a list of such errors with their corrections, inserted in the work

cor·ri·gi·ble (kôr′i jə b'l, kär′-) adj. [< OFr. < ML. < L. corrigere: see CORRECT] capable of being corrected, improved, or reformed —**cor′ri·gi·bil′i·ty** n. —**cor′ri·gi·bly** adv.

cor·rob·o·rate (kə räb′ə rāt′) vt. **-rat′ed, -rat′ing** [< L. pp. of corroborare < com-, very much + roborare < robur, strength]

---

fat, āpe, cär; ten, ēven; is, bīte; gō, hôrn, tōol, look; oil, out; up, fur; get; joy; yet; chin; she; thin, then; zh, leisure; ŋ, ring; ə for a in ago, e in agent, i in sanity, o in comply, u in focus; ′ as in able (ā′b'l); Fr. bal; ë, Fr. coeur; ö, Fr. feu; Fr. mon; ô, Fr. coq; ü, Fr. duc; r, Fr. cri; H, G. ich; kh, G. doch; ‡ foreign; ☆ Americanism; < derived from. See inside front cover.

to give proof of; confirm; bolster; support [a witness *corroborated* his story]—see SYN. at CONFIRM **—cor·rob′o·ra′tion** *n.* **—cor·rob′o·ra′tor** *n.*

cor·rob·o·ra·tive (kə räb′ə rāt′iv, -ər ə tiv) *adj.* corroborating; confirmatory: also **cor·rob′o·ra·to·ry** (-ər ə tôr′ē) **—cor·rob′o·ra′tive·ly** *adv.*

cor·rode (kə rōd′) *vt.* **-rod′ed, -rod′ing** [< OFr. < L. *corrodere* < *com-*, very much + *rodere*, to gnaw] **1.** to eat into or wear away gradually, as by rusting or by the action of chemicals **2.** to have a bad effect on little by little [a town *corroded* by corruption] *—vi.* to become corroded **—cor·rod′i·ble** *adj.*

cor·ro·sion (kə rō′zhən) *n.* **1.** a corroding or being corroded **2.** a substance formed by corroding

cor·ro·sive (kə rōs′iv) *adj.* [< OFr. < ML. *corrosivus*] causing corrosion *—n.* something causing corrosion **—cor·ro′sive·ly** *adv.* **—cor·ro′sive·ness** *n.*

corrosive sublimate *same as* MERCURIC CHLORIDE

cor·ru·gate (kôr′ə gāt′, kär′-; -yoo-) *vt., vi.* **-gat′ed, -gat′ing** [< L. pp. of *corrugare* < *com-*, very much + *rugare*, to wrinkle] to put grooves and ridges in, so as to make look wavy; make wrinkles in [*corrugated* iron, *corrugated* paper]

CORRUGATED SURFACE

cor·ru·ga·tion (kôr′ə gā′shən, kär′-; -yoo-) *n.* **1.** a corrugating or being corrugated **2.** any ridge or groove of a corrugated surface

cor·rupt (kə rupt′) *adj.* [< L. pp. of *corrumpere*, to ruin < *com-*, together + *rumpere*, to break: see RUPTURE] **1.** orig., spoiled; rotten **2.** changed from good to bad; having become evil, depraved, dishonest, etc. [accepting bribes made him a *corrupt* official] **3.** containing alterations or errors [a *corrupt* edition of *Hamlet*] *—vt., vi.* to make or become corrupt—see SYN. at DEBASE **—cor·rupt′er, cor·rup′tor** *n.* **—cor·rup′tive** *adj.* **—cor·rupt′ly** *adv.* **—cor·rupt′ness** *n.*

cor·rupt·i·ble (kə rup′tə b′l) *adj.* that can be corrupted, esp. so as to change from good to bad **—cor·rupt′i·bil′i·ty** *n.* **—cor·rupt′i·bly** *adv.*

cor·rup·tion (kə rup′shən) *n.* **1.** a making, becoming, or being corrupt **2.** evil or wicked ways **3.** bribery or dishonest dealings **4.** decay; rottenness **5.** something corrupted

corrupt practices acts laws limiting the amount of money that can be contributed to election campaigns or spent on them and making illegal certain methods of influencing voters, etc.

cor·sage (kôr säzh′, -säj′) *n.* [Fr., bodice: see CORPS & -AGE] ☆a small bouquet for a woman to wear, as at the waist or shoulder

cor·sair (kôr′ser) *n.* [< Fr. < Pr. < It. < L. *cursus*, a COURSE] **1.** a privateer **2.** a pirate **3.** a pirate ship

corse (kôrs) *n.* [Archaic or Poet.] a corpse

corse·let (kôrs′lət; *for 2* kôr′sə let′) *n.* [OFr., dim. of *cors*: see CORPS] **1.** a medieval piece of body armor: also sp. **cors′let 2.** a woman's lightweight corset: also sp. **cor′se·lette**

cor·set (kôr′sit) *n.* [OFr., dim. of *cors*: see CORPS] [*sometimes pl.*] a closefitting undergarment, often strengthened with stays, worn, chiefly by women, to give support to or shape the torso *—vt.* to dress in, or fit with, a corset

Cor·si·ca (kôr′si kə) Fr. island in the Mediterranean, north of Sardinia: 3,367 sq. mi.; pop. 270,000; chief city, Ajaccio: see map at LIGURIA **—Cor′si·can** *adj., n.*

cor·tege, cor·tège (kôr tezh′, -tāzh′) *n.* [Fr. < It. *corteggio*, retinue < L. *cohors*: see COURT] **1.** a group of attendants; retinue **2.** a solemn parade or procession, as at a funeral

Cor·tés (kôr tez′; *Sp.* kôr tes′), **Her·nan·do** (hər nan′dō) or **Her·nán** (er nän′) 1485–1547; Sp. explorer: conqueror of Mexico: also sp. **Cortez**

cor·tex (kôr′teks) *n., pl.* **-ti·ces** (-tə sēz′) [L., bark of a tree: for IE. base see CARNAGE] **1.** *a)* the outer part of an internal organ, as of the kidney *b)* the outer layer of gray matter over most of the brain **2.** a layer of tissue under the epidermis in plant roots and stems **3.** the bark or rind of a plant **—cor′ti·cal** (-ti k′l) *adj.* **—cor′ti·cal·ly** *adv.*

cor·ti·cate (kôr′ti kit, -kāt′) *adj.* [L. *corticatus* < *cortex*, CORTEX] covered with bark: also **cor′ti·cat′ed, cor′ti·cose′** (-kōs′)

cor·ti·co·ste·roid (kôr′ti kō stir′oid) *n.* [< L. *cortex*, bark + STEROID] any of a group of steroid hormones secreted by the adrenal cortex that are active in protein metabolism and that increase the glycogen in the tissues

cor·ti·sol (kôr′tə sōl′) *n.* [CORTIS(ONE) + -OL¹] an adrenal-gland hormone that regulates carbohydrate metabolism

☆**cor·ti·sone** (kôrt′ə sōn′, -zōn′) *n.* [< *corticosterone*, a hormone] a hormone, $C_{21}H_{28}O_5$, secreted by the cortex of the adrenal glands or made synthetically and used in treating various inflammations and allergies

co·run·dum (kə run′dəm) *n.* [Tamil *kurundam* < Sans. *kuruvinda*, ruby] a hard mineral, aluminum oxide, Al_2O_3, used for grinding and polishing: the ruby, sapphire, etc. are precious varieties

cor·us·cate (kôr′əs kāt′, kär′-) *vt.* **-cat′ed, -cat′ing** [< L. pp. of *coruscare* < *coruscus*, vibrating] to give off flashes of light; glitter; sparkle **—co·rus·cant** (kə rus′kənt) *adj.* **—cor′us·ca′tion** *n.*

cor·vette (kôr vet′) *n.* [Fr., prob. ult. < L. *corbita* (*navis*), cargo (ship) < *corbis*, basket] **1.** formerly, a sailing warship smaller than a frigate **2.** a small, fast British warship used for antisubmarine and convoy duty

cor·vine (kôr′vīn, -vin) *adj.* [< L. < *corvus*, a raven] of or like a crow or raven

Cor·y·bant (kôr′ə bant′) *n., pl.* **-bants′, Cor′y·ban′tes** (-ban′tēz) **1.** *a)* Gr. *Myth.* an attendant of the goddess Cybele at her orgiastic revelries *b)* a priest of Cybele **2.** [c-] a reveler **—Cor′y·ban′tic, Cor′y·ban′tian** (-ban′shən) *adj.*

cor·ymb (kôr′im, -imb; kär′-) *n.* [< Fr. < L. *corymbus*, flower cluster < Gr. *korymbos*] a broad, flat cluster of flowers in which the outer stems are longer than the ones toward the center **—co·rym·bose** (kə rim′bōs), **co·rym′bous** *adj.*

co·ry·za (kə rī′zə) *n.* [ModL. < LL. < Gr. *koryza*, catarrh] a cold in the head; acute nasal congestion

cos cosine

Cos., cos. 1. companies **2.** counties

cosec cosecant

co·se·cant (kō sē′kənt, -kant) *n. Trigonometry* the ratio between the hypotenuse and the side opposite a given acute angle in a right triangle

co·sign (kō′sīn′) *vt., vi.* **1.** to sign (a promissory note) in addition to the maker, thus becoming responsible for the obligation if the maker should default **2.** to sign jointly **—co′sign′er** *n.*

co·sig·na·to·ry (kō sig′nə tôr′ē) *adj.* signing jointly *—n., pl.* **-ries** one of two or more joint signers

co·sine (kō′sīn) *n. Trigonometry* the ratio between the side adjacent to a given acute angle in a right triangle and the hypotenuse

cos·met·ic (käz met′ik) *adj.* [< Gr. *kosmētikos*, skilled in arranging < *kosmos*, order] **1.** designed to beautify the complexion, hair, etc. **2.** for improving the appearance by correcting deformities, esp. of the face *—n.* any cosmetic preparation for the skin, hair, etc. **—cos·met′i·cal·ly** *adv.*

cos·me·tol·o·gy (käz′mə täl′ə jē) *n.* the work of applying cosmetics to women, as in a beauty shop **—cos′me·tol′o·gist** *n.*

cos·mic (käz′mik) *adj.* [Gr. *kosmikos* < *kosmos*, order] **1.** of the cosmos; relating to the universe as an orderly whole **2.** of the universe but not including the earth [*cosmic* dust] **3.** vast; enormous **—cos′mi·cal·ly** *adv.*

cosmic dust small particles falling from interstellar space to the earth

☆**cosmic rays** streams of charged particles, such as protons, that bombard the earth from outer space

cos·mo- [see COSMOS] *a combining form meaning* world, universe [*cosmology*]

cos·mog·o·ny (käz mäg′ə nē) *n.* [< Gr. < *kosmos*, universe + *gignesthai*, to produce] **1.** the origin of the universe **2.** *pl.* **-nies** a theory or account of this **—cos′mo·gon′ic** (-mə gän′ik), **cos′mo·gon′i·cal, cos·mog′o·nal** *adj.* **—cos·mog′o·nist** *n.*

cos·mog·ra·phy (-rə fē) *n.* [< LL. < Gr.: see COSMO- & -GRAPHY] the science dealing with the structure of the universe as a whole **—cos·mog′ra·pher** *n.* **—cos′mo·graph′ic** (-mə graf′ik), **cos′mo·graph′i·cal** *adj.* **—cos′mo·graph′i·cal·ly** *adv.*

cos·mol·o·gy (käz mäl′ə jē) *n.* [COSMO- + -LOGY] the study of the universe as a whole and of its form, nature, etc. as a physical system **—cos′mo·log′i·cal** (-mə läj′ə k′l) *adj.* **—cos′mo·log′i·cal·ly** *adv.* **—cos·mol′o·gist** *n.*

cos·mo·naut (käz′mə nôt′, -nät′) *n.* [Russ. *kosmonaut* < *kosmo-*, COSMO-, + -*naut* < Gr. *nautēs*, sailor (see NAUTICAL)] *same as* ASTRONAUT

cos·mo·pol·i·tan (käz′mə päl′ə t′n) *adj.* [COSMOPOLIT(E) + -AN] **1.** representative of all the world or many parts of it **2.** not bound by local or national habits or customs; at home in all

CORYMB

countries or places —*n.* a cosmopolitan person —**cos′mo·pol′i·tan·ism** *n.*

cos·mop·o·lite (käz mäp′ə līt′) *n.* [< Gr. < *kosmos*, world + *politēs*, citizen < *polis*, city] **1.** a cosmopolitan person **2.** a plant or animal common to all or most parts of the world

cos·mos (käz′məs; *for 1 & 2 also* -mōs) *n.* [Gr. *kosmos*, universe, harmony] **1.** the universe considered as a harmonious and orderly system **2.** any complete and orderly system **3.** *pl.* **cos′mos** a tropical American plant of the composite family, with featherlike leaves and white, pink, or purple flower heads

co·spon·sor (kō′spän′sər) *n.* a joint sponsor, as of a proposed piece of legislation —*vt.* to be a cosponsor of —**co′spon′sor·ship′** *n.*

Cos·sack (käs′ak, -ək; kô′sak) *n.* [Russ. *kozak* < Turk.] a member of a people of southern Russia, famous as horsemen —*adj.* of the Cossacks

cos·set (käs′it) *n.* [< ? OE. *cot-sæta*, cot dweller] a pet lamb, or any small pet —*vt.* to make a pet of; fondle, pamper, etc.

cost (kôst) *vt.* **cost** or, *for 2*, **cost′ed, cost′ing** [< OFr. < ML. *costare* < L. < *com-*, together + *stare*, to STAND] **1.** *a)* to be obtained for or sold for [it *costs* a dime] *b)* to cause the giving up of or the loss of [the flood *cost* many lives] Regarded as a *vi.* when used with an adverb [it *cost* him dearly] **2.** *Business* to estimate the cost of producing (often with *out*) —*n.* **1.** *a)* the amount asked or paid for a thing *b)* the amount spent in producing a commodity **2.** *a)* the amount of money, effort, etc. required to achieve an end *b)* loss; sacrifice [to smoke at the *cost* of one's health] **3.** [*pl.*] *Law* court expenses of a lawsuit —**at all costs** regardless of the cost or difficulty involved: also **at any cost**

cos·tal (käs′t'l) *adj.* [Fr. < ML. < L. *costa*, a rib] of or near a rib or the ribs

Cos·ta Me·sa (kōs′tə mā′sə) [Sp., lit., coast plateau] city in SW Calif., near Long Beach: pop. 73,000

Cos·ta Ri·ca (käs′tə rē′kə, kôs′-, kōs′-) country in Central America: 19,575 sq. mi.; pop. 1,685,000; cap. San José —**Cos′ta Ri′can**

cos·ter·mon·ger (käs′tər muŋ′gər, kôs′-) *n.* [< *costard*, a kind of apple + MONGER] [Brit.] a person who sells fruit or vegetables from a cart or street stand: also **cos′ter**

cos·tive (käs′tiv, kôs′-) *adj.* [< OFr. pp. of *costever* < L. *constipare*: see CONSTIPATE] constipated or constipating —**cos′tive·ly** *adv.* —**cos′tive·ness** *n.*

cost·ly (kôst′lē) *adj.* **-li·er, -li·est** **1.** *a)* costing much; expensive; dear *b)* at the cost of great effort, damage, etc. [a *costly* victory] **2.** magnificent; sumptuous —**cost′li·ness** *n.*
SYN.—**costly** refers to something that costs much and usually implies richness, magnificence, rareness, etc. [*costly* gems]: it is often applied to that which it would cost much in money or effort to correct or replace [a *costly* error]; **expensive** implies a price that is greater than the article is worth or more than the purchaser is able to pay [an *expensive* dress]; **dear** implies a very high price or one considerably beyond the normal or fair price [meat is so *dear* these days] —ANT. **cheap**

cost of living the average cost of the necessities of life, as food, shelter, and clothes

☆**cost-plus** (kôst′plus′) *adj.* with the price for goods or services set at the cost of materials, labor, etc. plus a specified amount of profit

cos·tume (käs′tōōm, -tyōōm) *n.* [< Fr. < It. < L. *consuetudo*, CUSTOM] **1.** *a)* the style of dress typical of a certain period, people, etc. *b)* a set of such clothes as worn in a play or at a masquerade **2.** a set of outer clothes for some occasion, esp. one worn by a woman —*vt.* **-tumed, -tum·ing** to provide with a costume

☆**costume jewelry** relatively inexpensive jewelry

☆**cos·tum·er** (-ər) *n.* one who makes, sells, or rents costumes, as for masquerades, theaters, etc.: also **cos·tum·ier** (käs-tōōm′yər, -tyōōm′-)

co·sy (kō′zē) *adj.* **-si·er, -si·est** & *n., pl.* **-sies** *same as* COZY — **co′si·ly** *adv.* —**co′si·ness** *n.*

cot¹ (kät) *n.* [Anglo-Ind. < Hindi *khāṭ* < Sans.] a narrow bed, as one made of canvas on a frame that can be folded up

cot² (kät) *n.* [OE.] **1.** [Poet.] a cottage **2.** a cote **3.** a sheath, as for a hurt finger

cot cotangent

co·tan·gent (kō tan′jənt) *n.* *Trigonometry* the ratio between the side adjacent to a given acute angle in a right triangle and the side opposite

cote (kōt) *n.* [ME., COT²] **1.** a small shelter for sheep, doves, etc. **2.** [Dial.] a cottage

co·ten·ant (kō ten′ənt) *n.* one of two or more tenants who share a place —**co·ten′an·cy** *n.*

co·te·rie (kōt′ər ē) *n.* [Fr., orig., organization of feudal tenants < OFr. *cotier*, COTTER¹] a close circle of friends with common interests
SYN.—a **coterie** is a small, select group of people associated for social or other reasons [a literary *coterie*]; **circle** suggests any group of people having some interest or pursuit in common [in music *circles*]; **set** refers to a group, usually larger and, hence, less exclusive than a coterie, having a common background, interest, etc. [the sporting *set*]; **clique** refers to a small, highly exclusive group, often within a larger one, and implies snobbery

co·ter·mi·nous (kō tur′mə nəs) *adj.* *same as* CONTERMINOUS: also **co·ter′mi·nal** —**co·ter′mi·nous·ly** *adv.*

co·til·lion (kō til′yən, kə-) *n.* [Fr. *cotillon*, orig., petticoat < OFr. *cotte*, a COAT] **1.** a dance with many intricate figures and the continual changing of partners **2.** a formal ball, esp. one at which debutantes are presented Also sp. **co·til′lon**

cot·tage (kät′ij) *n.* [< ML. *cotagium* < OFr. *cote* or ME. *cot*, hut] **1.** a small house, as one in which a peasant lives ☆**2.** a house at a resort or in the country, used for vacation ☆**3.** any of the separate dwelling units for small groups in certain institutions, etc.

☆**cottage cheese** a soft, white cheese made by straining and seasoning the curds of sour milk

☆**cottage pudding** cake covered with a sweet sauce

cot·tag·er (kät′ij ər) *n.* **1.** a person who lives in a cottage **2.** [Brit.] a farm laborer **3.** [Canad.] a summer resident

cot·ter¹, cot·tar (kät′ər) *n.* [< OFr. *cotier* < OE. *cot*, COT²] **1.** a cottager **2.** [Scot.] a tenant farmer

cot·ter² (kät′ər) *n.* [< ?] **1.** a bolt or wedge put through a slot to hold together parts of machinery **2.** *same as* COTTER PIN

cotter pin a split pin used as a cotter, fastened by spreading apart its ends after it is put in place

cot·ton (kät′'n) *n.* [< OFr. < Ar. *quṭun*] **1.** the soft, white, hairy fibers around the seeds inside the pods of various shrubby plants of the mallow family **2.** a plant or plants producing this material **3.** the crop of such plants **4.** thread or cloth made of cotton fibers —*adj.* of cotton —**cotton to** [Colloq.] **1.** to take a liking to **2.** to become aware of (a situation) —**cotton up to** [Colloq.] to try to make friends with —**cot′ton·y** *adj.*

COTTER PIN

☆**cotton batting** thin, pressed layers of fluffy, absorbent cotton, used for surgical dressing, etc.

☆**Cotton Belt** region in southern U.S. where much cotton is grown

☆**cotton candy** a cottony candy consisting of threadlike fibers of melted sugar spun into a fluffy mass around a paper cone

cotton flannel a soft, fleecy cotton cloth

☆**cotton gin** [see GIN²] a machine for separating cotton fibers from the seeds

☆**cot·ton·mouth** (-mouth′) *n.* [from its whitish mouth] *same as* WATER MOCCASIN

☆**cot·ton-pick·ing** (-pik′'n) *adj.* [Slang] worthless, damned, hateful, etc.

cot·ton·seed (-sēd′) *n.* the seed of the cotton plant, from which an oil (**cottonseed oil**) is pressed for use in margarine, cooking oil, etc.

☆**cot·ton·tail** (-tāl′) *n.* a common American rabbit with a short, fluffy tail

☆**cot·ton·wood** (-wood′) *n.* **1.** a poplar that has seeds covered with cottony hairs **2.** its wood

cotton wool raw cotton or cotton batting

cot·y·le·don (kät′'l ēd′'n) *n.* [L. < Gr. *kotylē*, a cavity] the first single leaf or either of the first pair of leaves produced by the embryo of a flowering plant —**cot′y·le′don·ous, cot′y·le′don·al** *adj.*

couch (kouch) *n.* [< OFr.: see the *v.*] ☆**1.** an article of furniture on which one may sit or lie down; sofa **2.** any resting place —**vt.** [< OFr. *coucher,* to lie down < L. *collocare* < *com-,* together + *locare,* to place] **1.** to place as on a couch [*to couch* oneself or be *couched* in comfort] **2.** to bring down; esp., to lower (a spear, etc.) to an attacking position **3.** to put in words; express —**vi. 1.** to lie down on a bed; recline **2.** to lie in hiding or ambush

couch·ant (-ənt) *adj.* [see prec.] *Heraldry* lying down, but keeping the head up [*a lion couchant*]

couch grass (kouch) [var. of QUITCH] a weedy grass that spreads rapidly by its underground stems

cou·gar (kōō′gər, -gär) *n., pl.* **-gars, -gar**: see PLURAL, II, D, 1 [< Fr. < Port. *cuçuarana* < Tupi < *su-usú,* deer + *rana,* false] a large, tawny-brown animal of the cat family, with a long, slender body

COUGAR
(to 8 ft. long,
including tail)

cough (kôf) *vi.* [ME. *coughen*] to force air suddenly and noisily from the lungs through the glottis, as to clear the throat —**vt.** to expel by coughing —**n. 1.** a coughing **2.** a condition, as of the lungs or throat, causing frequent coughing —**cough up 1.** to bring up (phlegm, etc.) by coughing ☆**2.** [Slang] to hand over (money, etc.) —**cough′er** *n.*

☆**cough drop** a small, flavored, medicated tablet for the relief of coughs, hoarseness, etc.

could (kŏŏd) *v.* [< OE. *cuthe,* pt. of *cunnan:* see CAN[1]] **1.** *pt. of* CAN[1] **2.** a helping verb used in verb phrases that has the same meaning as *can* and is used in the same ways, esp. if one wants to show a bit more doubt [it *could* be done; I *could* do it tomorrow]

could·n't (-'nt) could not

couldst (kŏŏdst) *archaic second person singular in the past tense of* CAN[1]: *used with* thou

cou·lee (kōō′lē) *n.* [Fr. < *couler,* to flow < L. < *colum,* a strainer] **1.** a stream or sheet of lava ☆**2.** [Northwest] a deep gulch or ravine, usually dry in summer

cou·lomb (kōō läm′, kōō′läm) *n.* [after C. A. de *Coulomb* (1736-1806), Fr. physicist] the meter-kilogram-second unit of electric charge; charge transported through a conductor by a current of one ampere flowing for one second

coul·ter (kōl′tər) *n.* same as COLTER

coun·cil (koun′s'l) *n.* [< OFr. < L. *concilium,* meeting < *com-,* with + *calere,* to call (for IE. base see CLAMOR)] **1.** a group of people called together to plan or discuss something or give advice **2.** a group of people chosen to serve officially as administrators or advisers, as to a ruler **3.** the lawmaking body of a city or town **4.** a church assembly to discuss points of doctrine, etc. **5.** any of various organizations or societies

Council Bluffs [scene of councils with Indians by LEWIS & CLARK] city in SW Iowa: pop. 60,000

coun·cil·man (-mən) *n., pl.* **-men** a member of a council, esp. of a city or town —**coun′cil·man′ic** (-man′ik) *adj.*

coun·ci·lor (koun′sə lər) *n.* [< COUNSELOR] a member of a council: also [Chiefly Brit.] **coun′cil·lor** —**coun′ci·lor·ship′** *n.*

coun·sel (koun′s'l) *n.* [< OFr. < L. *consilium*] **1.** a talking together in order to exchange ideas, opinions, etc.; discussion **2.** *a)* advice resulting from such an exchange *b)* any advice **3.** *a)* a lawyer or group of lawyers giving legal advice to clients or working for them *b)* a consultant —**vt. -seled** or **-selled, -sel·ing** or **-sel·ling 1.** to give advice to; advise **2.** to urge the acceptance of (a plan, etc.); recommend —**vi.** to give or take advice —see SYN. at LAWYER —**keep one's own counsel** to keep one's thoughts, plans, etc. to oneself —**take counsel** to consult; exchange advice, opinions, etc.

coun·se·lor, coun·sel·lor (-ər) *n.* **1.** a person who counsels; adviser **2.** a lawyer, esp. one who handles cases in court: in full, **counselor-at-law 3.** a person in charge of children at a camp —see SYN. at LAWYER —**coun′se·lor·ship′, coun′sel·lor·ship′** *n.*

count[1] (kount) *vt.* [< OFr. < L. *computare,* COMPUTE] **1.** to name numbers in regular order to (a certain number) [I'll *count* five] **2.** to add up, one by one, by units or groups, so as to get a total [*to count* the people] **3.** to check by numbering off; inventory [*to count* the cans on the shelf] **4.** to take account of; include [ten, *counting* you] **5.** to believe to be; consider [*to count* oneself lucky] —**vi. 1.** to name numbers or items in order [that little boy can *count* to ten] **2.** to be taken into account; have importance, value, etc. [every bit of help *counts*] **3.** to have a specified value (often with *for*) [a touchdown *counts* for

six points] **4.** to rely or depend (*on* or *upon*) [you can *count* on him in a crisis] —*n.* **1.** a counting, or adding up **2.** the number or a total reached by counting **3.** a reckoning or accounting ☆**4.** *Baseball* the number of balls and strikes that have been pitched to the batter **5.** *Boxing* the counting of seconds up to ten, during which a boxer who has been knocked down must rise or lose the match **6.** *Law* any of the charges or crimes listed in an indictment [he was found guilty on two *counts*] —☆**count in** to include —**count off** to separate into equal divisions by counting —**count out 1.** to disregard; omit ☆**2.** *Boxing* to declare (a boxer) defeated when he has remained down for a count of ten —**count′a·ble** *adj.*

count[2] (kount) *n.* [< OFr. < L. *comes* (gen. *comitis*), companion < *com-,* with + *ire,* to go] a European nobleman equal in rank to an English earl

☆**count·down** (kount′doun′) *n.* the schedule of operations just before the firing of a rocket, etc.; also, the counting off, in reverse order, of units of time in such a schedule

coun·te·nance (koun′tə nəns) *n.* [< OFr. < L. *continentia,* bearing < *continere,* CONTAIN] **1.** the look on a person's face that shows his nature or feelings [a friendly *countenance*] **2.** the face; facial features [a smile spread over his *countenance*] **3.** *a)* a look of approval *b)* approval; support [to give *countenance* to a plan] **4.** calm control; composure —**vt. -nanced, -nanc·ing** to give support to; approve [I will not *countenance* such rudeness] —see SYN. at FACE —**in countenance** calm; composed —**put out of countenance** to disconcert; embarrass

count·er[1] (koun′tər) *n.* [see COUNT[1]] **1.** a person or thing that counts or keeps count **2.** a small piece of metal, wood, etc., used in some games, esp. for keeping score **3.** an imitation coin, or token **4.** a long table, board, cabinet top, etc., as in a store or kitchen for the display of goods, serving or preparing of food, etc. —**over the counter** sold directly, not through a stock exchange —**under the counter** in a secret, stealthy way: said of illegal sales

coun·ter[2] (koun′tər) *adv.* [< Fr. < L. *contra,* against] in the opposite direction, manner, etc. [the committee vote went *counter* to my wishes] —*adj.* acting in opposition or in an opposite direction [a *counter* statement] —*n.* **1.** the opposite; contrary **2.** an opposing action **3.** a stiff leather piece around the heel of a shoe **4.** the part of a ship's stern between the waterline and the curved part **5.** *Boxing a)* a blow given while parrying an opponent's blow *b)* a giving of such a blow —**vt., vi. 1.** to oppose or check (a person or thing) **2.** to say or do (something) in reply or defense **3.** *Boxing* to strike one's opponent while parrying (his blow)

coun·ter- [< Fr. < L. *contra-,* against] *a combining form meaning:* **1.** opposite, contrary to [*counterclockwise*] **2.** in opposition or in return [*counterplot*] **3.** that is like something else [*counterpart*]

coun·ter·act (koun′tər akt′) *vt.* to act against; undo the effect of with opposing action [medicines to *counteract* diseases] —**coun′ter·ac′tion** *n.* —**coun′ter·ac′tive** *adj., n.*

coun·ter·at·tack (koun′tər ə tak′; *for v.,* usually koun′tər ə tak′) *n.* an attack made in opposition to another attack —**vt., vi.** to attack so as to offset the enemy's attack

coun·ter·bal·ance (koun′tər bal′əns; *for v.,* usually koun′tər bal′əns) *n.* **1.** a weight used to balance another weight **2.** any force or influence that balances or offsets another —**vt. -anced, -anc·ing** to be a counterbalance to; offset

coun·ter·charge (koun′tər chärj′; *for v.,* usually koun′tər chärj′) *n.* **1.** a charge made in answer to another charge or against the accuser **2.** an attack made in return —**vt. -charged′, -charg′ing 1.** to attack in return **2.** to accuse in return

coun·ter·check (koun′tər chek′; *for v.,* usually koun′tər chek′) *n.* **1.** anything that checks, restrains, etc. **2.** a double-check to be sure —**vt. 1.** to check or counteract **2.** to check again to be sure

☆**counter check** a check obtained at a bank by a depositor making a withdrawal

coun·ter·claim (koun′tər klām′; *for v.,* usually koun′tər klām′) *n.* an opposing claim to offset another —**vt., vi.** to make a counterclaim (of) —**coun′ter·claim′ant** *n.*

coun·ter·clock·wise (koun′tər kläk′wīz) *adj., adv.* in a direction opposite to that in which the hands of a clock move

coun·ter·cul·ture (koun′tər kul′chər) *n.* the culture of the young people of the 1960's and 1970's with a life style opposed to the prevailing culture

coun·ter·es·pi·on·age (coun′tər es′pē ə näzh′, -näj′, -nij) *n.* actions to prevent or thwart enemy espionage

coun·ter·feit (koun′tər fit) *adj.* [< OFr. pp. of *contrefaire*, to imitate < *contre-*, counter- + *faire* (< L. *facere*), to make] **1.** made in imitation of something genuine so as to fool or cheat people [*counterfeit* money] **2.** pretended; sham; feigned [*counterfeit* grief] —*n.* **1.** an imitation made to deceive **2.** something so much like something else as to mislead —*vt., vi.* **1.** to make an imitation of (money, pictures, etc.) in order to cheat **2.** to pretend; feign [to *counterfeit* affection] **3.** to resemble (something) closely —see SYN. at FALSE —**coun′ter·feit′er** *n.*

coun·ter·foil (-foil′) *n.* [COUNTER- + FOIL²] the stub of a check, receipt, etc. kept as a record by the one who writes it

coun·ter·in·sur·gen·cy (koun′tər in sur′jən sē) *n.* military and political action carried on to put down a revolt

coun·ter·in·tel·li·gence (-in tel′ə jəns) *n.* actions to counter enemy intelligence or espionage activity carried on by the enemy or to prevent sabotage, etc.

coun·ter·ir·ri·tant (-ir′ə tənt) *n.* anything used to produce a slight irritation to relieve more serious inflammation elsewhere

count·er·man (koun′tər man′, -mən) *n., pl.* **-men** (-men′, -mən) a man whose work is serving customers at a counter as of a lunchroom

coun·ter·mand (koun′tər mand′; *also, and for n. always,* koun′tər mand′) *vt.* [< OFr. < L. *contra*, against + *mandare*: see MANDATE] **1.** to cancel or revoke (a command or order) **2.** to call back or order back by a contrary order —*n.* a command or order canceling another

coun·ter·march (koun′tər märch′; *for v., also* koun′tər·märch′) *n.* a march back or in the opposite direction —*vi., vt.* to march back

coun·ter·meas·ure (-mezh′ər, -mā′zhər) *n.* an action taken in order to counter or oppose something

coun·ter·move (koun′tər mōōv′) *n.* a move made in order to counter or oppose something

coun·ter·of·fen·sive (koun′tər ə fen′siv) *n.* a strong attack made by troops who have been defending a position

coun·ter·of·fer (-ôf′ər) *n.* an offer proposed in response to one regarded as unsatisfactory

coun·ter·pane (koun′tər pān′) *n.* [altered < ME. *countrepoint*, quilt < OFr. < L. *culcita puncta*, pricked (i.e., embroidered) quilt] a bedspread

coun·ter·part (-pärt′) *n.* **1.** a person or thing that is or looks very much like another **2.** a thing that completes something else or goes with it to make a set **3.** a copy or duplicate, as of a lease

coun·ter·plot (koun′tər plät′; *for v., also* koun′tər plät′) *n.* a plot to defeat another plot —*vt., vi.* **-plot′ted, -plot′ting** to plot against (a plot); defeat (a plot) with another

coun·ter·point (-point′) *n.* [< Fr. < It. *contrappunto*, lit., pointed against: see COUNTER- & POINT, *n.*] **1.** a melody accompanying another melody note for note **2.** *a)* the art of adding related but independent melodies to a basic melody, in accordance with the fixed rules of harmony *b)* this kind of composition

coun·ter·poise (-poiz′) *n.* [< ONormFr.: see COUNTER² & POISE] **1.** *same as* COUNTERBALANCE **2.** a state of balance or equilibrium —*vt.* **-poised′, -pois′ing** *same as* COUNTERBALANCE

coun·ter·pro·duc·tive (-prə duk′tiv) *adj.* bringing about effects or results that are the opposite of those intended

coun·ter·pro·po·sal (-prə pō′z'l) *n.* a proposal in response to one regarded as unsatisfactory

Counter-Reformation the reform movement in the Roman Catholic Church in the 16th cent., following in reaction to the Protestant Reformation

coun·ter·rev·o·lu·tion (koun′tər rev′ə lōō′shən) *n.* **1.** a political movement to overthrow a government or social system set up by a previous revolution **2.** a movement to combat revolutionary tendencies —**coun′ter·rev′o·lu′tion·ar′y** *adj., n.* —**coun′ter·rev′o·lu′tion·ist** *n.*

coun·ter·shaft (koun′tər shaft′) *n.* a connecting shaft that passes motion from the main shaft of a machine along to a working part

coun·ter·sign (koun′tər sīn′; *for v., also* koun′tər sīn′) *n.* **1.** a signature added to a document to confirm that a signature already on it is genuine **2.** *Mil.* a secret word or signal which must be given to a sentry by someone wishing to pass; password —*vt.* to add one's signature as a countersign to (a document) —**coun′ter·sig′na·ture** (-sig′nə chər) *n.*

coun·ter·sink (koun′tər siŋk′; *for v., also* koun′tər siŋk′) *vt.* **-sunk′, -sink′ing 1.** to enlarge the top part of (a hole in metal, wood, etc.) to make the head of a bolt, screw, etc. fit into it **2.** to sink (a bolt, screw, etc.) into such a hole —*n.* **1.** a tool for countersinking holes **2.** a countersunk hole

COUNTERSUNK SCREW

coun·ter·spy (-spī′) *n.* a spy engaged in counterespionage

coun·ter·ten·or (-ten′ər) *n.* **1.** the range of the highest mature male voice, above tenor **2.** a voice, singer, or part with such a range

coun·ter·vail (koun′tər vāl′) *vt.* [< OFr. < *contre* (see COUNTER²) + *valoir*, to avail < L. *valere*, to be strong] **1.** to make up for; compensate **2.** to counteract; avail against —*vi.* to avail (*against*)

coun·ter·weigh (-wā′) *vt. same as* COUNTERBALANCE —**coun′ter·weight′** *n.*

counter word any word freely used as a general term of approval or disapproval without reference to its more exact meaning, as *nice* or *terrible*

count·ess (koun′tis) *n.* **1.** the wife or widow of a count or earl **2.** a noblewoman whose rank is equal to that of a count or earl

count·ing·house (koun′tiŋ hous′) *n.* [Now Rare] an office where a firm keeps accounts, etc.

count·less (kount′lis) *adj.* too many to count; innumerable; myriad

coun·tri·fied (kun′tri fīd′) *adj.* **1.** rural; rustic **2.** having the appearance, actions, etc. that country people are thought to have Also sp. **coun′try·fied′**

coun·try (kun′trē) *n., pl.* **-tries** [< OFr. < VL. *contrata*, that which is beyond < L. *contra*, opposite] **1.** an area of land; region [wooded *country*] **2.** the whole territory of a nation **3.** the people of a nation [a broadcast to the whole *country*] **4.** the land where one was born or is a citizen ["my *country*, 'tis of thee"] **5.** land with farms and small towns; rural region —*adj.* **1.** of, in, or from a rural district **2.** like that of the country; rustic [*country* music]

☆**country club** a social club in the outskirts of a city, equipped with a clubhouse, golf course, etc.

country cousin a person from a rural region who is confused or excited by city life when he comes to the city

coun·try-dance (-dans′) *n.* an English folk dance, esp. one in which partners form two facing lines

coun·try·man (-mən) *n., pl.* **-men 1.** a man who lives in the country; rustic **2.** a man of one's own country; compatriot —**coun′try·wom′an** *n.fem., pl.* **-wom′en**

☆**country mile** [Colloq.] a very long way or distance

country music folk music of rural regions, esp. folk music of the Southern highlands and backwoods, or a commercialized variety of this

coun·try·seat (-sēt′) *n.* a rural mansion or estate

coun·try·side (-sīd′) *n.* a rural region or its inhabitants

coun·ty (koun′tē) *n., pl.* **-ties** [< OFr. < ML. *comitatus*, jurisdiction of a count < L. *comes*: see COUNT²] **1.** a small administrative district; esp., ☆*a)* the largest local administrative subdivision of most States *b)* any of the chief administrative and judicial districts into which Great Britain and Ireland are divided **2.** the people in a county

☆**county agent** a specialist employed by the government to inform farmers and rural families in a county of improved practices in agriculture and home economics

county commissioner ☆a member of an elected governing board in the counties of certain States

☆**county seat** a town or city that is the seat of government of a county

coup (kōō) *n., pl.* **coups** (kōōz; *Fr.* kōō) [Fr., a blow < VL. < L. *colaphus*, a box on the ear < Gr. *kolaphos*] **1.** a sudden, successful move or action; brilliant stroke **2.** *same as* COUP D'ÉTAT

‡**coup de grâce** (kōō də gräs′) [Fr., lit., stroke of mercy] **1.** the blow, shot, etc. that brings death to a sufferer **2.** a finishing stroke

‡**coup de main** (man′) [Fr., lit., stroke of hand] a surprise attack or movement, as in war

---

fat, āpe, cär; ten, ēven; is, bīte; gō, hôrn, tōōl, look; oil, out; up, fur; get; joy; yet; chin; she; thin, *th*en; zh, leisure; ŋ, ring; ə for *a* in *ago*, *e* in *agent*, *i* in *sanity*, *o* in *comply*, *u* in *focus*; ' as in *able* (ā′b'l); Fr. bál; ë, Fr. coeur; ö, Fr. feu; Fr. mon; ō̆, Fr. coq; ü, Fr. duc; r, Fr. cri; H, G. ich; kh, G. doch; ‡foreign; ☆ Americanism; < derived from. See inside front cover.

‡**coup d'é·tat** (dā´tä´) [Fr., lit., stroke of state] a sudden, forceful stroke in politics, esp. the sudden overthrow of a government, as by means of a military plot

‡**coup d'oeil** (kōō´dě´y´) [Fr., lit., stroke of eye] a rapid glance; quick view or survey

coupe (kōōp; *orig., but now rarely,* kōō pā´) *n.* [< COUPÉ] a closed, two-door automobile with a body smaller than that of a sedan

cou·pé (kōō pā´) *n.* [Fr., pp. of *couper,* to cut] 1. a closed carriage seating two passengers, with a seat outside for the driver 2. same as COUPE

Cou·perin (kōō pran´), **Fran·çois** (frän swà´) 1668-1733; Fr. composer & organist

cou·ple (kup´'l) *n.* [< OFr. < L. *copula:* see COPULA] 1. anything joining two things together; bond; link 2. two things or persons of the same sort that are somehow associated 3. a man and a woman who are engaged, married, or partners in a dance, etc. 4. [Colloq.] a few; several: now often used like an adjective [a *couple* ideas] —*vt.* -**pled, -pling** to join together; link; connect [to *couple* railroad cars] —*vi.* 1. to come together; unite 2. to copulate

cou·pler (kup´lər) *n.* a person or thing that couples; specif., same as COUPLING (sense 3)

cou·plet (kup´lit) *n.* [Fr., dim. of *couple,* COUPLE] 1. two lines of poetry, one after the other, esp. two of the same length that rhyme 2. [Rare] a couple

cou·pling (kup´liŋ) *n.* 1. a joining together 2. a mechanical device for joining parts together 3. a device for joining railroad cars 4. a method or device for joining two electric circuits to transfer energy from one to the other

COUPLING

cou·pon (kōō´pän, kyōō´-) *n.* [Fr. < *couper,* to cut] 1. a printed statement on a bond which can be cut off at certain times and turned in, in order to collect interest 2. a certificate or ticket that gives the holder a specified right [the *coupon* on the cereal box is worth 10¢ toward buying another box] 3. a part of a printed advertisement for use in ordering goods, etc.

cour·age (kur´ij) *n.* [< OFr. < L. *cor,* HEART] a willingness to face and deal with danger, trouble, or pain; fearlessness; bravery; valor —**the courage of one's convictions** the courage to do what one thinks is right

cou·ra·geous (kə rā´jəs) *adj.* having or showing courage; brave —see SYN. at BRAVE —**cou·ra´geous·ly** *adv.* —**cou·ra´geous·ness** *n.*

cou·rante (kōō ränt´) *n.* [Fr. < prp. of *courir,* to run < L. *currere,* to run] 1. an old, lively French dance with running steps 2. the music for this dance Also **cou·rant´** (-ränt´)

Cour·bet (kōōr be´), **Gus·tave** (güs täv´) 1819-77; Fr. painter

cou·ri·er (koor´ē ər, kur´-) *n.* [< OFr., ult. < L. *currere:* see COURSE] a messenger sent in haste or on a regular schedule with important or urgent messages

course (kôrs) *n.* [< OFr. *cours* < L. pp. of *currere,* to run: see CURRENT] 1. an onward movement; progress [the *course* of history] 2. a way, path, or channel of movement; specif., same as: a) [Brit.] RACECOURSE b) GOLF COURSE 3. the direction taken, as by a ship or plane [a *course* due south] 4. a) a regular manner of proceeding [the law must take its *course*] b) a way of behaving; mode of conduct [our wisest *course*] 5. a) a series of like things in some regular order b) a particular succession of events or actions 6. natural development [the *course* of true love] 7. a part of a meal served at one time [the main *course* was roast beef] 8. a horizontal layer, as of bricks, in the face of a building 9. *Educ.* a) a complete series of studies leading to graduation, a degree, etc. b) any of the separate units of instruction in a subject —*vt.* **coursed, cours'ing** 1. to chase after; pursue 2. to cause (esp. hunting hounds) to chase 3. to run through; traverse —*vi.* 1. to run or race [blood *coursing* through the veins] 2. to hunt with hounds —**in due course** in the usual or proper sequence (of events) —**in the course of** in the process of; during —**of course** 1. as is or was to be expected; naturally 2. certainly —**on** (or **off**) **course** moving (or not moving) in the intended direction

cours·er[1] (kôr´sər) *n.* [< OFr. < *cours,* COURSE] [Poet.] 1. a graceful, spirited, or swift horse 2. a war horse; charger

cours·er[2] (kôr´sər) *n.* 1. a person or thing that courses 2. a dog for coursing

cours·ing (-siŋ) *n.* 1. the action of a person or thing that courses 2. hunting with hounds trained to follow game by sight rather than scent

court (kôrt) *n.* [OFr. < LL. < L. *cohors:* see COHORT] 1. an uncovered space wholly or partly surrounded by buildings or walls 2. a short street, often closed at one end 3. a) an area for playing any of several ball games [a tennis *court*] b) a part of such an area ☆4. a motel: in full, **motor court** 5. a) the palace of a sovereign b) the family, advisers, etc. of a sovereign, as a group c) a sovereign and his councilors as a governing body d) any formal gathering held by a sovereign 6. attention paid to someone in order to get something 7. courtship; wooing 8. a) a person or persons appointed to examine and decide law cases, make investigations, etc.; judge or judges b) a place where trials are held, investigations made, etc. c) an assembly or meeting of the judge or judges, the lawyers, and the jury in a law court —*vt.* 1. to pay attention to (a person) in order to get something 2. to try to get the love of; woo 3. to try to get; seek [to *court* favor] 4. to make oneself open to [to *court* insults] —*vi.* to woo —*adj.* of or fit for a court —**out of court** without a trial —**pay court to** to court, as for favor or love —**court´er** *n.*

cour·te·ous (kur´tē əs) *adj.* [< OFr. *courteis* < *court:* see COURT & -EOUS] polite and gracious; considerate of others; well-mannered —see SYN. at CIVIL —**cour´te·ous·ly** *adv.* —**cour´te·ous·ness** *n.*

cour·te·san (kôr´tə z'n, kur´-) *n.* [< Fr. < It. *cortigiana,* court lady < *corte,* COURT] a prostitute; esp., formerly, a mistress of a king, nobleman, etc.: also **cour´te·zan**

cour·te·sy (kur´tə sē) *n., pl.* -**sies** [< OFr. *curteisie:* see COURTEOUS] 1. courteous behavior; gracious politeness 2. a polite or considerate act or remark 3. an act or usage intended to honor or compliment [a title of *courtesy*]

☆**courtesy card** a card entitling the bearer to special privileges, as at a hotel, bank, etc.

court·house (kôrt´hous´) *n.* 1. a building in which law courts are held ☆2. a building that houses the offices of a county government

cour·ti·er (kôr´tē ər, -tyər) *n.* 1. an attendant at a royal court 2. a person who flatters other people or tries to please them in order to get something or to win their favor

court·ly (kôrt´lē) *adj.* -**li·er, -li·est** 1. suitable for a king's court; dignified, elegant, etc. [*courtly* manners] 2. flattering, esp. in a fawning or humble way —*adv.* in a courtly manner —**court´li·ness** *n.*

court-mar·tial (-mär´shəl) *n., pl.* **courts´-mar´tial;** for 2, now often **court´-mar´tials** 1. a court of personnel in the armed forces for the trial of persons accused of breaking military law 2. a trial by a court-martial —*vt.* -**tialed** or **-tialled, -tial·ing** or **-tial·ling** to try by a court-martial

☆**court of appeals** [*often* C- A-] 1. a State court to which appeals are taken from the trial courts 2. any of the Federal appellate courts, between the U.S. district courts and the Supreme Court

Court of St. James [< *St. James's Palace,* former royal residence] the British royal court

court plaster [from former use by court ladies for beauty spots] cloth covered with an adhesive material, formerly used to protect minor skin wounds

court·room (kôrt´rōōm´) *n.* a room in which a law court is regularly held

court·ship (-ship´) *n.* the act, process, or period of courting, or wooing

court tennis *see* TENNIS

court·yard (-yärd´) *n.* an open space with buildings or walls around it

cous·cous (kōōs´kōōs, kōōs kōōs´) *n.* [Fr. < Berber < Ar. < *kaskasa,* to grind] a N. African dish of crushed grain, usually steamed and served with meat

cous·in (kuz´'n) *n.* [< OFr. < L. < *com-,* with + *sobrinus,* maternal cousin < *soror,* sister] 1. the son or daughter of one's uncle or aunt: also called **first** (or **full**) **cousin** or **cous´in-ger´man** (-jur´mən): one's **second cousin** is a child of one's parent's first cousin; one's **first cousin once removed** is a child of one's first cousin 2. loosely, any relative by blood or marriage 3. a person thought of as related to another 4. a title of address used by one sovereign to another or to a nobleman —**cous´in·ly** *adj., adv.* —**cous´in·ship´** *n.*

cou·ture (kōō tōōr´) *n.* [Fr., sewing < L. pp. of *consuere* < *com-,* together + *suere,* to SEW] the work or business of designing new fashions in women's clothes

‡**cou·tu·rier** (kōō tü ryā´; E. kōō toor´ē ä´) *n.* [Fr.] a man engaged in couture —**cou·tu·rière** (-tü ryer´; E. -toor´ē er´) *n.fem.*

co·va·lence (kō vā′ləns) *n.* the number of pairs of electrons an atom can share with neighboring atoms —**co·va′lent** *adj.*

cove (kōv) *n.* [< OE. *cofa,* cave, cell < IE. base *gew-,* to bend, arch] **1.** a sheltered nook or recess, as in cliffs **2.** a small bay or inlet ☆**3.** a small valley **4.** a concave molding, esp. one where the wall meets the ceiling or floor **5.** a concave arch or vault **6.** a trough for concealed lighting on a wall near a ceiling —*vt., vi.* **coved, cov′ing** to curve with a concave form

cov·en (kuv′ən, kō′vən) *n.* [< OFr. < L. *convenire,* CONVENE] a gathering or meeting, esp. of witches

cov·e·nant (kuv′ə nənt) *n.* [OFr. < L. *convenire,* CONVENE] **1.** a binding agreement made by two or more individuals, parties, etc. to do or keep from doing a specified thing; compact **2.** *Law* a formal, sealed contract **3.** *Theol.* the promises made by God to man, as recorded in the Bible —*vt., vi.* to promise by or in a covenant —**cove′e·nan′tal** (-nan′t'l) *adj.* —**cov′e·nant·er, cov′e·nan·tor** (-nan tər) *n.*

Covenant of the League of Nations the first section of the Treaty of Versailles (1919): it was the constitution of the League of Nations

Cov·ent Garden (kuv′nt, käv′-) **1.** a market area in London **2.** a theater, the Royal Opera House, in this area

Cov·en·try (kuv′ən trē, käv′-) city in C England: pop. 335,000 —*n.* the condition of someone who is avoided by people or banished; ostracism [to send someone to *Coventry*]

cov·er (kuv′ər) *vt.* [< OFr. < L. < *co-,* very much + *operire,* to hide] **1.** to place something on, over, or in front of [*cover* the table with a cloth] **2.** to extend over; overlay [ice *covers* the pond] **3.** to mate with (a mare): said of a stallion **4.** to clothe **5.** to coat, sprinkle, etc. thickly [*covered* with mud] **6.** to sit on (eggs); brood **7.** to conceal by hiding or screening [*cover* the hole with a patch] **8.** to protect as by shielding [*covered* by secret service men] **9.** to take into account [the law *covers* such cases] **10.** *a)* to protect (someone or something) against financial loss, or make up for (a loss, etc.), as by insurance *b)* to be sufficient for payment of (a debt, etc.) ☆*c)* to buy stock to replace (shares borrowed from a broker to effect a short sale) **11.** to accept (a bet) **12.** to travel over [to *cover* a distance] **13.** to be responsible for (an area or range of activity) **14.** to deal with [to *cover* a subject] **15.** to point a firearm at ☆**16.** *Journalism* to get news, pictures, etc. of [to *cover* a train wreck] ☆**17.** *Sports* to guard or obstruct (an opponent, position, etc.) —*vi.* **1.** to spread over a surface, as a liquid does **2.** to put on a cap, hat, etc. ☆**3.** to provide an alibi or excuse (*for* another) —*n.* **1.** anything that covers, as a binding, lid, top, etc. **2.** a protective shelter or a hiding place **3.** a tablecloth and a place setting for one person **4.** *same as* COVER-UP **5.** an envelope, wrapping, etc. for mail —**break cover** to come out of protective shelter —**cover up 1.** to cover entirely; envelop; wrap **2.** to keep blunders, crimes, etc. from being known —**take cover** to seek protective shelter —**under cover** in secrecy or concealment —**cov′er·er** *n.*

☆**cov·er·age** (-ij) *n.* **1.** the amount, extent, etc. covered by something **2.** *Insurance* all the risks covered by an insurance policy

cov·er·all (-ôl′) *n.* [*usually pl.*] a one-piece garment with sleeves and legs, worn like overalls

☆**cover charge** a fixed charge added to the cost of food and drink, as at a nightclub or restaurant

cover crop a crop, as vetch or clover, grown to protect soil from erosion and to keep it fertile

Cov·er·dale (kuv′ər dāl′), **Miles** 1488–1568; Eng. clergyman & translator of the Bible (1535)

☆**covered wagon** a large wagon with an arched cover of canvas, used by American pioneers

☆**cover girl** [Colloq.] a girl model whose picture is often put on magazine covers, etc.

cov·er·ing (kuv′ər iŋ) *n.* anything that covers

covering letter (or **note,** etc.) a letter (or note, etc.) sent along with a package, another letter, etc. to explain it

cov·er·let (kuv′ər lit) *n.* [< Anglo-Fr. < OFr. *covrir,* COVER + *lit,* a bed < L. *lectus*] **1.** a bedspread **2.** any covering Also [Dial.] **cov′er·lid**

cov·ert (kuv′ərt, kō′vərt) *adj.* [OFr., pp. of *covrir,* COVER] concealed, hidden, or disguised [a *covert* look at his neighbor's

COVERALLS

test paper] —*n.* **1.** a covered or protected place; shelter **2.** a hiding place for game animals **3.** any of the small feathers covering the bases of the larger feathers of a bird's wing and tail —see SYN. at SECRET —**cov′ert·ly** *adv.* —**cov′ert·ness** *n.*

covert (cloth) a smooth, twilled, lightweight cloth, usually of wool, used for suits, topcoats, etc.

cov·er·ture (kuv′ər chər) *n.* **1.** a covering **2.** a refuge **3.** a concealment or disguise

cov·er-up (kuv′ər up′) *n.* something used for hiding one's real activities, intentions, etc.

cov·et (kuv′it) *vt., vi.* [< OFr. < L. *cupiditas:* see CUPIDITY] to want greedily (esp., something that another has); long for with envy —see SYN. at ENVY —**cov′et·a·ble** *adj.* —**cov′et·er** *n.*

cov·et·ous (-əs) *adj.* greedy to have what another has; avaricious —see SYN. at GREEDY —**cov′et·ous·ly** *adv.* —**cov′et·ous·ness** *n.*

cov·ey (kuv′ē) *n., pl.* **-eys** [< OFr. < *cover,* to hatch < L. *cubare,* to lie down] **1.** a small flock of birds, esp. partridges or quail **2.** a small group of people or, sometimes, things —see SYN. at GROUP

cov·in (kuv′in) *n.* [OFr., fraud < LL. < L. *convenire,* CONVENE] *Law* a plot by two or more people to cheat or injure another or others

cov·ing (kōv′iŋ) *n.* a concave molding or arch; cove

Cov·ing·ton (kuv′iŋ tən) [after Gen. L. *Covington,* 1768–1813] city in N Ky.: pop. 53,000

cow[1] (kou) *n., pl.* **cows;** archaic **kine** (kīn) [OE. *cu:* for IE. base see BEEF] **1.** the full-grown female of domestic cattle, valued for its milk, or of certain other animals, as the buffalo, elephant, etc.: the male of such animals is called a *bull* ☆**2.** [Western] any domestic bovine animal, whether a steer, bull, cow, or calf: *usually used in pl.*

cow[2] (kou) *vt.* [< ON. *kūga,* to subdue] to make timid and meek by filling with fear or awe

cow·ard (kou′ərd) *n.* [< OFr. < *coe* < L. *cauda,* tail] one who lacks courage or is full of cowardice —*adj.* cowardly

cow·ard·ice (-is) *n.* lack of courage; esp., great fear of danger, difficulty, etc. that makes one feel ashamed

cow·ard·ly (-lē) *adj.* of or like a coward —*adv.* in the manner of a coward —**cow′ard·li·ness** *n.*

cow·bane (kou′bān′) *n.* [COW[1] + BANE] a plant of the parsley family with very poisonous roots and clusters of small white flowers

cow·bell (kou′bel′) *n.* a bell hung from a cow's neck so she can be found by its clanking

cow·ber·ry (-ber′ē) *n., pl.* **-ries 1.** a low creeping shrub with white or pink flowers and dark-red, acid berries **2.** its berry

☆**cow·bird** (-burd′) *n.* a small American blackbird often seen near cattle

cow·boy (-boi′) *n.* ☆**1.** a ranch worker who rides horseback on his job of herding cattle; also **cow′hand**′ **2.** a performer in a rodeo ☆**3.** in novels, movies, etc., any Western character who rides a horse and carries a gun —☆**cow′girl**′ *n.fem.*

☆**cow·catch·er** (-kach′ər, -kech′ər) *n.* a metal frame on the front of a locomotive or streetcar to remove obstructions from the tracks

cow·er (kou′ər) *vi.* [ME. *couren,* prob. < ON.: for IE. base see COVE] **1.** to crouch or huddle up, as from fear **2.** to shrink and tremble, as from someone's anger, threats, or blows; cringe —**cow′er·ing·ly** *adv.*

cow·fish (kou′fish′) *n., pl.* **-fish**′, **-fish′es:** see FISH **1.** any of several small sea animals related to the whale, as the grampus **2.** any of several fishes with hornlike growths on the head

cow·herd (kou′hurd′) *n.* a person whose work is looking after grazing cattle

cow·hide (-hīd′) *n.* **1.** the hide of a cow **2.** leather made from it ☆**3.** a whip made of this leather —*vt.* **-hid′ed, -hid′ing** to flog with a cowhide

☆**cow killer** a large, wingless, antlike wasp of the southern U.S. that gives a severe sting

COWCATCHER

cowl (koul) *n.* [< OE. < LL. < L. *cucullus*, hood] **1.** *a)* a monk's hood *b)* a monk's cloak with a hood **2.** something shaped like a cowl; esp., *a)* a cover for the top of a chimney, to increase the draft *b)* the top front part of an automobile body, to which the windshield and dashboard are fastened *c)* a cowling —*vt.* to cover as with a cowl —**cowled** *adj.*

COWL

cow·lick (kou′lik) *n.* [from the notion that the hair looks as if it has been licked by a cow] a tuft of hair on the head that cannot easily be combed flat

cowl·ing (kou′liŋ) *n.* [see COWL] a metal covering for an airplane engine, etc. that can be removed if necessary

☆**cow·man** (kou′mən) *n., pl.* **-men** **1.** the owner or operator of a cattle ranch **2.** one who tends cattle

co-work·er (kō′wur′kər) *n.* a fellow worker

cow parsnip a plant of the parsley family, with flat clusters of white or purple flowers and thick stems

☆**cow·pea** (kou′pē′) *n.* **1.** a bushlike annual plant of the legume family, with seeds in slender pods, grown in the southern U.S. for forage **2.** its edible seed, cooked as a vegetable

Cow·per (koo′pər, koop′ər; *now occas.* kou′pər), **William** 1731–1800; Eng. poet

☆**cow·poke** (kou′pōk′) *n.* [see COWPUNCHER] [Colloq.] same as COWBOY

☆**cow pony** a horse used by a cowboy in herding cattle

cow·pox (kou′päks′) *n.* a contagious disease of cows that causes pustules on the udders: smallpox vaccine is made from the virus

☆**cow·punch·er** (-pun′chər) *n.* [from prodding the animals in herding] [Colloq.] same as COWBOY

cow·rie, cow·ry (kou′rē) *n., pl.* **-ries** [< Hindi < Sans. *kaparda*] **1.** any of certain gastropods having brightly colored shells and living in warm seas **2.** the shell of such a mollusk, esp. of the **money cowrie**, formerly used as currency in parts of Africa and southern Asia

cow·shed (kou′shed′) *n.* a shelter for cows

cow·slip (-slip′) *n.* [< OE., lit., cow dung < *cu*, cow + *slyppe*, paste] **1.** a European primrose with yellow or purple flowers ☆**2.** same as: *a)* MARSH MARIGOLD *b)* VIRGINIA COWSLIP

COWRIE SHELLS

cox (käks) *n., pl.* **cox′es** [Colloq.] a coxswain —*vt., vi.* to be coxswain for (a boat or crew)

cox·a (käk′sə) *n., pl.* **cox′ae** (-sē) [L.] **1.** the hip or hip joint **2.** the basal segment of an arthropod leg —**cox′al** *adj.*

cox·al·gi·a (käk sal′jē ə, -jə) *n.* [see prec. & -ALGIA] pain in, or disease of, the hip or hip joint: also **cox·al′gy** (-jē) —**cox·al′gic** *adj.*

cox·comb (käks′kōm′) *n.* [for *cock's comb*] **1.** a cap topped with a notched strip of red cloth like a cock's comb, formerly worn by jesters **2.** a silly, vain, foppish fellow; dandy —**cox′comb′ry** (-kōm′rē) *n., pl.* **-ries**

cox·swain (käk′s'n, -swān′) *n.* [< COCK(BOAT) + SWAIN] **1.** a person in charge of a ship's boat and acting as its steersman **2.** the man who steers a racing shell and calls out the rhythm for the oarsmen's stroke

coy (koi) *adj.* [< OFr. < LL. < L. *quietus*: see QUIET] **1.** bashful; shy **2.** pretending to be innocent or shy, esp. in a flirting way **3.** unwilling to express one's views, plans, etc. [the mayor was *coy* in answering questions] —**coy′ly** *adv.* —**coy′ness** *n.*

☆**coy·o·te** (kī ōt′ē, kī′ōt) *n., pl.* **coy·o′tes, coy·o′te**: see PLURAL, II, D, 1 [AmSp. < Nahuatl *coyotl*] a small wolf of western N. American prairies

☆**coy·o·til·lo** (koi′ə tēl′yō, -til′ō; kī′-) *n., pl.* **-los** [AmSp., dim. of COYOTE] a thorny, poisonous shrub found in Mexico and in the Southwest

coy·pu (koi′poo) *n., pl.* **-pus, -pu**: see PLURAL, II, D, 1 [< AmSp. < native name] same as NUTRIA

coz (kuz) *n.* [Colloq.] cousin

coz·en (kuz′'n) *vt., vi.* [< ME. *cosin*, fraud < ?] to cheat, defraud, or deceive —**coz′en·age** *n.*

co·zy (kō′zē) *adj.* **-zi·er, -zi·est** [Scot., prob. < Scand.] warm and comfortable; snug —*n., pl.* **-zies** a knitted or padded cover for a teapot, to keep the tea hot —

COYOTE
(to 4 ft. long, including tail)

☆**cozy up to** [Colloq.] to try to make oneself liked by being nice to (someone) —☆**play it cozy** [Slang] to act cautiously —**co′zi·ly** *adv.* —**co′zi·ness** *n.*

CP Command Post

cp candlepower

cp. compare

C.P. **1.** Common Pleas **2.** Common Prayer **3.** Communist Party

c.p. chemically pure

CPA, C.P.A. Certified Public Accountant

cpd. compound

Cpl, Cpl. Corporal

cpm, c.p.m. cycles per minute

CPO, C.P.O. Chief Petty Officer

cps, c.p.s. cycles per second

cpt. counterpoint

CQ amateur radio operators' signal inviting a reply

Cr *Chem.* chromium

cr. **1.** credit **2.** creditor **3.** crown

C.R. Costa Rica

crab[1] (krab) *n.* [OE. *crabba*: for IE. base see CARVE] **1.** any of various crustaceans with four pairs of legs, one pair of pincers, a flattish shell, and a short, broad abdomen folded under its thorax **2.** any of several similar animals **3.** same as CRAB LOUSE **4.** a machine for hoisting heavy weights —[**C-**] Cancer, the constellation and zodiac sign —*vi.* **crabbed, crab′bing** to fish for or catch crabs —**catch a crab** *Rowing* to unbalance the boat by a faulty stroke —**crab′ber** *n.*

EDIBLE CRAB
(to 7 in. in diameter)

crab[2] (krab) *n.* [akin ? to Scot. *scrabbe*, Sw. dial. *scrabba*, wild apple] **1.** same as CRAB APPLE **2.** a person who is always cross and complaining —*adj.* of a crab apple —*vi.* **crabbed, crab′bing** [Colloq.] to complain and find fault [they *crabbed* about the food in the cafeteria] —☆**crab one's act (the deal,** etc.) [Colloq.] to spoil one's scheme (the deal, etc.) —**crab′ber** *n.*

crab apple **1.** a small, very sour apple, used for jellies, etc. **2.** a tree bearing crab apples: also **crab tree**

crab·bed (krab′id) *adj.* [< CRAB (APPLE)] **1.** peevish; cross **2.** hard to understand; intricate **3.** hard to read; illegible [*crabbed* handwriting] —**crab′bed·ly** *adv.* —**crab′bed·ness** *n.*

crab·by (-ē) *adj.* **-bi·er, -bi·est** [see prec.] cross and complaining; peevish —**crab′bi·ly** *adv.* —**crab′bi·ness** *n.*

☆**crab cactus** a common house plant with flat, fleshy stems and red flowers

crab grass ☆a coarse, weedy annual grass that spreads rapidly because of its freely rooting stems

crab louse a louse, like a crab in shape, that fastens itself in the groin, armpits, etc.

crack (krak) *vi.* [< OE. *cracian*, to resound: for IE. base see CRANE] **1.** to make a sudden, sharp breaking noise [the whip *cracked* over the lion's head] **2.** to break or split, usually without complete separation of parts [leather *cracks* if it isn't oiled] **3.** to become rasping or change pitch suddenly, as the voice [his voice *cracked* when he hit high C] **4.** [Colloq.] to break down [he *cracked* under the strain] —*vt.* **1.** to cause to make a sharp, sudden noise [she *cracked* the ruler against the desk] **2.** to cause to break or split [to *crack* the shells of peanuts] **3.** to destroy or impair [to *crack* his resistance] ☆**4.** to subject (as petroleum) to cracking: see CRACKING[2] **5.** to hit or strike with a sudden, sharp blow or impact [he *cracked* his shin on the table] **6.** to manage to solve [to *crack* a code] **7.** [Colloq.] *a)* to break open or into (a safe, etc.) *b)* to open and read or study (a book) **8.** [Slang] to make (a joke) —*n.* **1.** a sudden, sharp noise [the *crack* of a whip] **2.** a break, usually with the parts still staying together ☆**3.** a narrow opening [the *cracks* between the floorboards] **4.** a cracking of the voice **5.** a moment; instant [at the *crack* of dawn] **6.** [Colloq.] a sudden, sharp blow [a *crack* on the head] ☆**7.** [Colloq.] an attempt; try [to take a *crack* at solving a puzzle] ☆**8.** [Slang] a joke or mocking remark —*adj.* [Colloq.] excelling in skill; first-rate [*crack* troops] —see SYN. at BREAK —**crack a smile** [Slang] to relax enough to smile —☆**crack down (on)** to become strict or stricter (with) —☆**cracked up to be** [Colloq.] said or believed to be —**crack up** **1.** to crash, as (in) an airplane **2.** [Colloq.] *a)* to break down physically or mentally *b)* to break into a fit of laughter or tears —**get cracking** [Colloq.] to start moving, working, etc. rapidly

crack·brained (krak′brānd′) *adj.* crazy or insane

☆**crack·down** (-doun′) *n.* a using of strict or stricter measures of discipline or punishment

cracked (krakt) *adj.* **1.** broken, usually without complete separation of parts **2.** harsh [a *cracked* voice] **3.** [Colloq.] crazy

cracked wheat coarsely milled wheat particles

crack·er (krak′ər) *n.* **1.** one that cracks **2.** a firecracker **3.** a little paper roll used as a party favor: it contains candy, etc. and pops open when the ends are pulled **4.** a thin, crisp wafer

crack·er·bar·rel (-bar′əl) *adj.* [< the large barrel of soda crackers formerly found in general stores] [Colloq.] of or like the informal discussions that persons gathered at a country store have

☆**crack·er·jack** (krak′ər jak′) *adj.* [extension of CRACK, *adj.* + JACK (nickname)] [Slang] excellent —*n.* [Slang] an excellent person or thing

crack·ers (krak′ərz) *adj.* [altered < CRACKED] [Chiefly Brit. Slang] crazy or insane

crack·ing[1] (krak′iŋ) *adj.* [Colloq.] excellent; fine —*adv.* [Colloq.] very [a *cracking* good time]

crack·ing[2] (krak′iŋ) *n.* ☆the process of breaking down heavier hydrocarbons, as by heat and pressure, into lighter hydrocarbons, as in producing gasoline

crack·le (krak′'l) *vi.* **-led, -ling** [CRACK + -LE[2]] **1.** to make slight, sharp popping sounds, as of dry wood burning **2.** to be bursting with energy, etc. **3.** to develop a finely cracked surface —*vt.* **1.** to crush or break with crackling sounds **2.** to produce a finely cracked surface on [pottery *crackled* with age] —*n.* **1.** crackling sounds **2.** fine, irregular surface cracks, as on old oil paintings **3.** crackleware

crack·le·ware (krak′'l wer′) *n.* pottery, porcelain, etc. with a finely cracked surface

crack·ling (krak′liŋ; *for 2, usually* -lin) *n.* **1.** the making of slight, sharp popping sounds **2.** *a)* the browned, crisp rind of roast pork *b)* [*pl.*] crisp bits left when hog fat is rendered

crack·ly (-lē) *adj.* that crackles; crackling

crack of doom [phrase in *Macbeth* IV, i] the signal for the beginning of Judgment Day

crack·pot (-pät′) *n.* [Colloq.] a crazy or peculiar person —*adj.* [Colloq.] crazy or peculiar

crack·up (krak′up′) *n.* **1.** a crash, as of an airplane **2.** [Colloq.] a mental or physical collapse

-cra·cy (krə sē) [< Fr. < ML. < Gr. -*kratia* < *kratos*, rule] *a combining form meaning* a (specified) type of government; rule by [*democracy* is government by the people]

cra·dle (krā′d'l) *n.* [OE. *cradol:* for IE. base see CART] **1.** a baby's small bed, usually on rockers **2.** the time when one is a baby; infancy **3.** the place of a thing's beginning **4.** anything cradlelike; specif., *a)* a framework to hold or lift a boat, aircraft, etc. being built or repaired *b)* the support for the handset of a telephone (**cradle telephone**) *c)* *Agric.* a frame on a scythe (**cradle scythe**) for laying the grain evenly as it is cut ☆*d)* *Mining* a boxlike device on rockers for washing gold out of sand —*vt.* **-dled, -dling** **1.** to rock or hold in or as in a cradle ☆**2.** *Mining* to wash (sand) in a cradle

cra·dle·song (-sôŋ′) *n.* a lullaby

craft (kraft) *n.* [OE. *cræft*, strength, power: for IE. base see CART] **1.** a special skill or art **2.** an occupation requiring special skill or training, esp. in the use of the hands **3.** the members of a skilled trade **4.** skill in deceiving; slyness **5.** *pl.* **craft** a boat, ship, or aircraft —*vt.* to make with skill as a craftsman does: usually in pp. [handsomely *crafted* jewelry]

-craft (kraft) [< prec.] *a combining form meaning* the work, skill, or practice of [*witchcraft*]

crafts·man (krafts′mən) *n., pl.* **-men** **1.** a skilled workman, esp. one trained in a skilled trade **2.** a skillful artist —**crafts′-man·ship′** *n.*

craft union a labor union to which only workers in a certain trade, craft, or occupation can belong: distinguished from INDUSTRIAL UNION

craft·y (kraf′tē) *adj.* **craft′i·er, craft′i·est** sly; cunning —see SYN. at SLY —**craft′i·ly** *adv.* —**craft′i·ness** *n.*

crag (krag) *n.* [< Celt.] a steep, rugged rock that rises above other rocks or juts out from a rock mass

crag·gy (krag′ē) *adj.* **-gi·er, -gi·est** having many crags; steep and rugged —**crag′gi·ness** *n.*

crake (krāk) *n., pl.* **crakes, crake:** see PLURAL, II, D, 1 [< ON. *kraka,* crow: for IE. base see CRANE] any of several rails with long legs and a short bill

cram (kram) *vt.* **crammed, cram′ming** [OE. *crammian,* to stuff < IE. base *ger-,* to collect, from which also come CONGREGATE, SEGREGATE, etc.] **1.** to pack full or too full [to *cram* a cupboard with dishes] **2.** to stuff; force [to *cram* papers into a drawer] **3.** to feed to excess **4.** to review (a subject) for an examination in a hurried, intensive way —*vi.* **1.** to eat too much or too quickly **2.** to study a subject in a hurried, intensive way, for an examination —*n.* a cramming for an examination —**cram′mer** *n.*

cramp[1] (kramp) *n.* [< OFr. *crampe,* bent, twisted < Frank.: for IE. base see CART] **1.** a sudden, painful tightening of a muscle due to chill, strain, etc. **2.** a condition in which muscles become paralyzed for a time because of overuse **3.** [usually *pl.*] sharp pains in the belly —*vt.* to cause a cramp in

cramp[2] (kramp) *n.* [MDu. *krampe,* lit., bent in] **1.** a metal bar bent at each end at a right angle, for holding together timbers, etc.: also **cramp iron** **2.** a clamp **3.** anything that confines or hampers —*vt.* **1.** to fasten as with a cramp **2.** to confine or hamper [his tight suit *cramps* his movements] —**cramp one's style** [Slang] to hamper one's skill, confidence, etc. in doing something

cramped (krampt) *adj.* **1.** confined; restricted [living in *cramped* quarters] **2.** irregular and crowded, as some handwriting

cramp·fish (kramp′fish′) *n., pl.* **-fish′, -fish′es:** see FISH same as ELECTRIC RAY

cram·pon (kram′pän, -pən) *n.* [Fr., akin to CRAMP[2]] **1.** either of a pair of iron hooks for raising heavy weights **2.** either of a pair of spiked iron plates fastened on shoes to prevent slipping

CRAMPON

Cra·nach (krä′näkh), **Lu·cas** (lōō′-käs) 1472–1553; Ger. painter & engraver

☆**cran·ber·ry** (kran′ber′ē, -bər ē) *n., pl.* **-ries** [< Du. *kranebere,* LowG. *kraanbere,* lit., crane berry] **1.** a firm, sour, red berry that grows on an evergreen shrub and can be eaten **2.** this shrub

crane (krān) *n.* [OE. *cran* < IE. base *ger-,* to cry hoarsely] **1.** *pl.* **cranes, crane:** see PLURAL, II, D, 1 *a)* a large wading bird with very long legs and neck, and a long, straight bill *b)* popularly, any of various herons or storks **2.** a machine for lifting or moving heavy weights by means of a long, movable arm or of a device that travels on an overhead track **3.** any device with a swinging arm fixed on an upright support, as to hold a kettle —*vt., vi.* **craned, cran′ing** **1.** to raise or move as by a crane **2.** to stretch (the neck), as in trying to see over something

Crane (krān) **1.** (Harold) **Hart,** 1899–1932; U.S. poet **2. Stephen,** 1871–1900; U.S. writer

crane fly any of various two-winged, slender flies with very long legs

cranes·bill, crane's·bill (krānz′bil′) *n. a popular name for* GERANIUM (sense 1)

cra·ni·al (krā′nē əl) *adj.* of or from the cranium

cranial nerve any of the pairs of nerves, twelve in man, connected directly with the brain

cra·ni·o- [Gr. *kranio-* < *kranion:* see CRANIUM] *a combining form meaning* of the head, cranial

cra·ni·ol·o·gy (krā′nē äl′ə jē) *n.* the scientific study of skulls, esp. human skulls

cra·ni·om·e·try (-äm′ə trē) *n.* the science of measuring skulls; cranial measurement

cra·ni·ot·o·my (-ät′ə mē) *n., pl.* **-mies** the surgical operation of opening the skull

cra·ni·um (krā′nē əm) *n., pl.* **-ni·ums, -ni·a** (-ə) [ML. < Gr. *kranion:* for IE. base see HORN] **1.** the skull **2.** the bones that form an outer covering for the brain

crank (kraŋk) *n.* [< OE. *cranc-,* as in *crancstæf,* yarn comb: for IE. base see CART] **1.** a handle or arm bent at right angles and connected to a shaft of a machine, in order to turn it or make it go **2.** [Colloq.] ☆*a*) an odd or queer person *b*) an irritable, complaining person —*vt.* to start or operate by a crank —*vi.* to turn a crank —**crank up** [Colloq.] to get started or get moving faster

crank·case (kraŋk′kās′) *n.* the metal casing around the crankshaft of an internal-combustion engine

crank·shaft (-shaft′) *n.* a shaft having one or more cranks for transmitting motion

crank·y (kraŋ′kē) *adj.* **crank′i·er, crank′i·est 1.** in poor working order **2.** irritable; cross **3.** queer; eccentric —see SYN. at IRRITABLE —**crank′i·ly** *adv.* —**crank′i·ness** *n.*

Cran·mer (kran′mər), **Thomas** 1489–1556; Eng. churchman; archbishop of Canterbury

CRANKSHAFT

cran·ny (kran′ē) *n., pl.* **-nies** [OFr. *cran* < OIt. < LL. *crena,* a notch] a small, narrow opening; crack, as in a wall —**cran′nied** (-ēd) *adj.*

Cran·ston (kran′stən) [after S. *Cranston,* 18th-c. colonial governor] city in east central R.I.: pop. 73,000

☆**crap**[1] (krap) *n.* [see CRAPS] **1.** *same as* CRAPS **2.** a losing throw at craps —**crap out 1.** to make a losing throw at craps **2.** [Slang] to fail, give up, etc. because one is worn out, very tired, etc.

crap[2] (krap) *n.* [< OFr., ordure] [Vulgar Slang] ☆**1.** nonsense, falseness, insincerity, etc. ☆**2.** trash; junk —**crap′py** *adj.* **-pi·er, -pi·est**

crape (krāp) *n.* [Fr. *crêpe:* see CREPE] **1.** *same as* CREPE (sense 1) **2.** a piece of black crepe as a sign of mourning

☆**crape·hang·er** (-haŋ′ər) *n.* [Slang] a person with a gloomy outlook; pessimist

☆**crape myrtle** [so named because of its crepelike flowers] an ornamental shrub with usually pink flowers, widely grown in the southern U.S.

☆**crap·pie** (krap′ē) *n., pl.* **-pies, -pie:** see PLURAL, II, D, 1 [< ?] a small sunfish of the eastern and central U.S.

☆**craps** (kraps) *n.pl.* [with sing. v.] [Fr. *crabs, craps* < obs. E. *crabs,* lowest throw at hazard, two aces] a gambling game played with two dice, in which, for example, a first throw of seven or eleven wins

☆**crap·shoot·er** (krap′shōōt′ər) *n.* a gambler at craps —**crap′shoot′ing** *n.*

crap·u·lence (krap′yoo ləns) *n.* [see CRAPULOUS] **1.** sickness from excess in drinking or eating **2.** extreme intemperance, esp. in drinking —**crap′u·lent** *adj.*

crap·u·lous (-ləs) *adj.* [< LL. < L. *crapula,* drunkenness < Gr. *kraipalē,* drunken headache] **1.** intemperate, esp. in drinking **2.** sick from such intemperance

crash[1] (krash) *vi.* [ME. *crashen,* prob. echoic var. of *craken,* CRACK] **1.** to fall, collide, or break with force and with a loud, smashing noise **2.** *a)* to make a sudden, loud noise *b)* to move with such a noise **3.** to fall and be damaged or destroyed: said of aircraft **4.** to collapse, as a business —*vt.* **1.** to break into pieces; smash **2.** to cause (a car, etc.) to crash **3.** to force or impel with a crashing noise (with *in, out,* etc.) ☆**4.** [Colloq.] to get into (a party, theater, etc.) without an invitation, ticket, etc. —*n.* **1.** a loud, smashing noise **2.** a crashing **3.** a sudden collapse, as of a business —*adj.* [Colloq.] using all possible resources, effort, and speed [a *crash* program] —see SYN. at BREAK

crash[2] (krash) *n.* [prob. < Russ. *krashenina,* colored linen] a coarse cloth of plain, loose weave

Crash·aw (krash′ô), **Richard** 1613?–49; Eng. religious poet

crash dive an emergency dive by a submarine to escape from attack —**crash′-dive′** *vi.* **-dived′, -div′ing**

crash helmet a thickly padded, protective helmet worn by motorcyclists, racing-car drivers, etc.

crash·ing (krash′iŋ) *adj.* [Colloq.] thorough; complete [a *crashing* bore]

crash-land (krash′land′) *vt., vi.* to bring (an airplane) down in a forced landing, with some damage —**crash landing**

crass (kras) *adj.* [L. *crassus,* gross] very stupid or coarse —**crass′ly** *adv.* —**crass′ness** *n.*

-crat (krat) [< Fr. < Gr. *-kratēs* < *kratos,* rule] *a combining form meaning* participant in or supporter of (a specified kind of) government or ruling body [*democrat, aristocrat*]

CRASH HELMET

crate (krāt) *n.* [L. *cratis,* wickerwork < IE. base *kert-,* to weave] **1.** a box or case made of wood slats, for shipping or storing things **2.** [Slang] an old, worn-out automobile or airplane — ☆*vt.* **crat′ed, crat′ing** to pack in a crate

cra·ter (krāt′ər) *n.* [L. < Gr. *kratēr*] **1.** in ancient Greece, a kind of bowl or jar **2.** a bowl-shaped cavity, as at the mouth of a volcano or on the moon **3.** any pit like this, as one made by an exploding bomb

Crater Lake National Park national park in SW Oreg., containing a lake (**Crater Lake**) in the crater of an extinct volcano

cra·vat (krə vat′) *n.* [< Fr. < *Cravate,* Croat: referring to scarves worn by Croatian soldiers] **1.** a neckerchief or scarf **2.** a necktie

crave (krāv) *vt.* **craved, crav′ing** [OE. *crafian* < base of *cræft:* see CRAFT] **1.** to ask for earnestly; beg [to *crave* pardon] **2.** to long for; desire strongly [to *crave* freedom] **3.** to want or need greatly [to *crave* sweets] —*vi.* to have a longing or strong desire (*for*) —see SYN. at DESIRE —**crav′er** *n.*

cra·ven (krā′vən) *adj.* [< OFr. < L. *crepare,* to creak] very cowardly —*n.* a thorough coward —**cra′ven·ly** *adv.* —**cra′ven·ness** *n.*

crav·ing (krā′viŋ) *n.* an intense desire or longing, as for affection or a food, drug, etc.

craw (krô) *n.* [ME. *craue*] **1.** the crop of a bird or insect **2.** the stomach of any animal —**to stick in the** (or **one's**) **craw** to be unacceptable to one

☆**craw·dad** (krô′dad′) *n.* [< CRAWFISH] [Dial.] *same as* CRAYFISH

craw·fish (krô′fish′) *n., pl.* **-fish′, -fish′es:** see FISH *same as* CRAYFISH —☆*vi.* [Colloq.] to withdraw from a position; back down

crawl[1] (krôl) *vi.* [< ON. *krafla:* for IE. base see CARVE] **1.** to move slowly by drawing the body along the ground, as a worm does **2.** to go on hands and knees **3.** to move slowly [trucks *crawled* up the steep hill] **4.** to behave in a cringing, overly humble way **5.** to swarm (*with* crawling things) [a log *crawling* with ants] **6.** to feel as if insects were crawling on the skin [stories that made her flesh *crawl*] —*n.* **1.** a crawling **2.** an overarm swimming stroke, face downward —**crawl′er** *n.*

crawl[2] (krôl) *n.* [WInd.Du. *kraal* < Sp. *corral:* see CORRAL] an enclosure in shallow water for confining fish, turtles, etc.

☆**crawler tractor** a tractor equipped on each side with a continuous roller belt over cogged wheels, for moving over rough or muddy ground

☆**crawl space** a narrow space, as under a roof or floor, allowing access to wiring, plumbing, etc.

crawl·y (krôl′ē) *adj.* **crawl′i·er, crawl′i·est** *same as* CREEPY

cray·fish (krā′fish′) *n., pl.* **-fish′, -fish′es:** see FISH [< OFr. *crevice* < OHG.] ☆**1.** any of certain small, lobster-shaped freshwater crustaceans **2.** *same as* SPINY LOBSTER

cray·on (krā′ən, -än′) *n.* [Fr. < *craie,* chalk < L. *creta*] **1.** a small stick of chalk, charcoal, or colored wax, used for drawing, coloring, or writing **2.** a drawing made with crayons —*vt.* to draw or color with crayons —**cray′on·ist** *n.*

craze (krāz) *vt.* **crazed, craz′ing** [ME. *crasen,* to crack < Scand.] **1.** to make mentally ill or insane **2.** to produce small cracks in the surface or glaze of (pottery, etc.) —*vi.* to become finely cracked, as pottery glaze —*n.* **1.** a mania **2.** a fad **3.** a crack in the glaze of pottery, etc.

cra·zy (krā′zē) *adj.* **-zi·er, -zi·est** [< CRAZE] **1.** flawed, cracked, or rickety **2.** mentally unbalanced or insane **3.** [Colloq.] foolish, wild, fantastic, etc. [a *crazy* idea] **4.** [Colloq.] very enthusiastic or eager [*crazy* about movies] ☆**5.** [Slang] excellent, thrilling, etc. —☆*n., pl.* **-zies** [Slang] a mentally unbalanced person —**cra′zi·ly** *adv.* —**cra′zi·ness** *n.*

☆**crazy bone** *same as* FUNNY BONE

☆**crazy quilt** a quilt made up of pieces of cloth of various colors, patterns, shapes, and sizes

creak (krēk) *vi., vt.* [ME. *creken:* for IE. base see CRANE] to make, cause to make, or move with a harsh, shrill, grating, or squeaking sound, as rusted hinges or old floorboards —*n.* such a sound

creak·y (krēk′ē) *adj.* **creak′i·er, creak′i·est** creaking or apt to creak —**creak′i·ly** *adv.* —**creak′i·ness** *n.*

cream (krēm) *n.* [OFr. *cresme,* prob. a blend of LL. *chrisma* (see CHRISM) & VL. *crama,* cream] **1.** the oily, yellowish part of milk, which rises to the top **2.** any food made of cream or having a creamy consistency [ice *cream*] **3.** a creamy cosmetic or emulsion **4.** the best part [the *cream* of the crop] **5.** yellowish white —*adj.* of, with, or like cream; creamy, cream-colored, etc. —*vi.* to form cream or a creamy foam —*vt.* **1.** to take the cream from **2.** to add cream to **3.** to cook with cream or a cream sauce **4.** to make creamy by beating, etc. ☆**5.** [Slang] *a)* to strike with great force and hurt, damage, etc. *b)* to defeat soundly —**cream of** creamed purée of [*cream of* tomato soup]

cream cheese a soft, white cheese made of cream or of milk enriched with cream

cream-col·ored (-kul′ərd) *adj.* yellowish-white

cream·er (krēm′ər) *n.* ☆**1.** a small pitcher for cream **2.** a device for separating cream from milk

☆**cream·er·y** (-ər ē) *n., pl.* -**er·ies** **1.** a place where milk and cream are pasteurized, separated, and bottled, and butter and cheese are made **2.** a shop where dairy products are sold

cream of tartar a white, acid, crystalline substance, $KHC_4H_4O_6$, used in baking powder

☆**cream puff** a round shell of pastry filled with whipped cream or custard

cream sauce a sauce made of butter and flour cooked together with milk or cream

☆**cream soda** soda pop, usually colorless, that is flavored with vanilla

cream·y (-ē) *adj.* **cream′i·er**, **cream′i·est** **1.** of, like, or full of cream; yellowish white, soft, rich, smooth, etc. **2.** like cream in consistency or color —**cream′i·ness** *n.*

crease[1] (krēs) *n.* [earlier *creaste*, lit., ridge < ME. *creste*, crest < OFr. *creste:* see CREST] **1.** a line, mark, or ridge made by folding and pressing cloth, paper, etc. **2.** a fold or wrinkle [*creases* in an old man's face] —*vt.* **1.** to make a crease in ☆**2.** to graze with a bullet —*vi.* to become creased —**creas′er** *n.* —**creas′y** *adj.*

crease[2] (krēs) *n.* same as KRIS

cre·ate (krē āt′) *vt.* -**at′ed**, -**at′ing** [< L. pp. of *creare*, to create: for IE. base see CEREAL] **1.** to bring into being; originate, design, invent, etc. [Raphael *created* many works of art] **2.** to bring about; cause [new industries *create* new jobs] **3.** to give a new rank, function, etc. to [the President *created* two new generals]

cre·a·tion (-ā′shən) *n.* **1.** a creating or being created **2.** the whole universe **3.** anything created; esp., something original created by the imagination —**the Creation** *Theol.* God's creating of the world

cre·a·tive (-āt′iv) *adj.* **1.** creating or able to create **2.** showing imagination and ability [a *creative* mind] **3.** stimulating the ability to create or invent [a *creative* environment] **4.** stimulating the inventive powers —**cre·a′tive·ly** *adv.* —**cre·a′tive·ness** *n.*

cre·a·tiv·i·ty (krē′ā tiv′ə tē) *n.* creative ability, esp. in an artistic or intellectual way

cre·a·tor (krē āt′ər) *n.* **1.** one who creates **2.** [C-] God

crea·ture (krē′chər) *n.* [< OFr. < L. *creatura*] **1.** anything created, living or not living **2.** a living being; esp., ☆*a)* a domestic animal *b)* a human being: often used to show contempt, pity, etc. **3.** one completely dominated by another or dependent on another —**crea′tur·al**, **crea′ture·ly** *adj.*

creature comfort anything providing bodily comfort, as food, clothing, or shelter

crèche (kresh, krāsh) *n.* [Fr. < Frank. word thought to be *kripja*, crib: for IE. base see CART] **1.** a display of a stable with figures, representing a scene at the birth of Jesus **2.** an institution for foundlings **3.** [Chiefly Brit.] a day nursery

cre·dal (krēd′'l) *adj.* of a creed

cre·dence (krēd′'ns) *n.* [< OFr. < ML. < L. prp. of *credere:* see CREED] **1.** belief, esp. in another's reports or testimony [to give *credence* to rumors] **2.** *Eccles.* a small side table for the Eucharistic wine, etc.

cre·den·tials (kri den′shəlz, -chəlz) *n.pl.* a letter or certificate showing that one has a right to a certain position or authority

cre·den·za (kri den′zə) *n.* [It.] a type of buffet, or sideboard

cred·i·ble (kred′ə b'l) *adj.* [< L. < *credere:* see CREED] that can be believed; believable —see SYN. at PLAUSIBLE —**cred′i·bil′i·ty** *n.* —**cred′i·bly** *adv.*

cred·it (kred′it) *n.* [< Fr. < It. < L. pp. of *credere:* see CREED] **1.** belief or trust; confidence [he places *credit* in what she says] **2.** *a)* good reputation *b)* one's influence based on one's reputation **3.** praise or approval [to deserve *credit* for trying] **4.** a person or thing that gets approval or honor [he is a *credit* to the team] **5.** acknowledgment of work done or help given;

specif., [*pl.*] a list of such acknowledgments in a movie, TV show, etc. **6.** *a)* the amount in a bank account, etc. *b)* a sum made available by a bank for someone named to withdraw **7.** *Accounting a)* acknowledgment of a payment on a debt by entry of the amount in an account *b)* the right-hand side of an account, where such entries are made *c)* an entry, or the sum of entries, made there *d)* a deduction from a debt or an addition (as to a bank account) in making an adjustment **8.** *Business a)* trust that a person will be able and willing to make payments when due *b)* time allowed for payment ☆**9.** *a)* an official record that one has successfully completed a unit or course of study in a school, etc. *b)* a unit so recorded —*vt.* **1.** to believe in the truth, reliability, etc. of; trust [he wouldn't *credit* my excuse] **2.** to give credit to or deserved commendation for **3.** to give credit in a bank account, etc. [*credit* her with $5.00] **4.** *Accounting* to enter on the credit side ☆**5.** to enter credits on the record of (a student) in a school, etc. —**credit one with** to believe that someone has (some quality) [to *credit* him with honesty] —**do credit to** to bring approval or honor to —**give credit to 1.** to trust; believe **2.** to commend —**give one credit for 1.** to commend one for **2.** to believe or recognize that one has —**on credit** by agreeing to pay later [to buy a car *on credit*] —**to one's credit** bringing approval or honor to one

cred·it·a·ble (-ə b'l) *adj.* **1.** deserving credit or praise **2.** thought of as belonging (*to*) —**cred′it·a·bly** *adv.*

☆**credit bureau** an agency supplying information on the credit rating of individuals or firms

☆**credit card** a card allowing a person to charge bills at certain restaurants, gas stations, hotels, etc.

☆**credit line** an acknowledgment of work done or help given, as in the credits for a movie, TV show, etc.

cred·i·tor (kred′it ər) *n.* a person who extends business credit or one to whom money is owed

☆**credit rating** the rating of an individual or firm as a credit risk, based on past records of debt repayment, financial status, etc.

☆**credit union** a cooperative association for pooling savings of members and making loans to them at a low rate of interest

cre·do (krē′dō, krā′dō) *n., pl.* -**dos** [L., I believe: see CREED] **1.** same as CREED **2.** [usually C-] the Apostles' Creed or the Nicene Creed

cre·du·li·ty (krə dōō′lə tē, -dyōō′-) *n.* a tendency to believe too readily, even without proof

cred·u·lous (krej′oo ləs) *adj.* [L. *credulus* < *credere:* see CREED] **1.** tending to believe too readily **2.** resulting from or indicating credulity —**cred′u·lous·ly** *adv.* —**cred′u·lous·ness** *n.*

Cree (krē) *n.* [< AmInd.] **1.** *pl.* **Crees**, **Cree** a member of a tribe of Algonquian Indians of central Canada **2.** the Algonquian language of this tribe

creed (krēd) *n.* [< OE. < L. *credo*, lit., I believe < *credere*, to trust < IE. base *kred-dhe-*, to believe] **1.** a brief statement of the main beliefs of a religion **2.** any statement of belief, opinions, etc. —**creed′al** *adj.*

Creek (krēk) *n.* [from the many creeks in their territory] **1.** *pl.* **Creeks**, **Creek** an American Indian of any of several tribes, mainly Muskogean, orig. in the southeastern U.S., now in Oklahoma **2.** their language

creek (krēk, krik) *n.* [ME. *creke* < ON. *-kriki*, a winding: for IE. base see CART] ☆**1.** a small stream, somewhat larger than a brook **2.** [Now chiefly Brit.] a narrow inlet or bay —☆**up the creek** [Slang] in trouble

creel (krēl) *n.* [< OFr. *grail:* see GRIDDLE] a wicker basket for holding fish, often worn by fishermen

creep (krēp) *vi.* **crept**, **creep′ing** [OE. *creopan:* for IE. base see CART] **1.** to move along with the body close to the ground, as on hands and knees **2.** to move slowly, stealthily, etc. [cars *crept* along in the heavy traffic] **3.** to come on gradually [old age *crept* up on him] **4.** to grow along the ground, etc., as some plants **5.** to change position or shape slightly —*n.* **1.** a creeping ☆**2.** [Slang] a person regarded as very annoying, disgusting, etc. —**make one's flesh** (or **skin**) **creep** to give one a feel-

CREEL

ing of fear, disgust, etc., as if insects were creeping on one's skin —**the creeps** [Colloq.] a feeling of fear, disgust, etc.

creep·age (krēp′ij) *n.* a gradual creeping movement

creep·er (krēp′ər) *n.* 1. a person, animal, or thing that creeps 2. a plant whose stem puts out tendrils or rootlets for creeping along a surface 3. the lowest gear in a truck, as for use on steep grades: in full, **creeper gear** ☆4. [*pl.*] a baby's one-piece garment, combining pants and shirt

creeping bent grass a low-growing grass which roots along the stem: see BENT[2]

creep·y (krēp′ē) *adj.* **creep′i·er, creep′i·est** 1. creeping; moving slowly 2. having or causing fear or disgust, as if insects were creeping on one's skin —**creep′i·ly** *adv.* —**creep′i·ness** *n.*

creese (krēs) *n. same as* KRIS

cre·mate (krē′māt, kri māt′) *vt.* **-mat·ed, -mat·ing** [< L. pp. of *cremare*, to burn < IE. base *ker-*, to burn, from which also comes HEARTH] 1. to burn up; esp., to burn (a dead body) to ashes —**cre·ma′tion** *n.* —**cre′ma·tor** *n.*

cre·ma·to·ry (krē′mə tôr′ē; *chiefly Brit.* krem′ə-) *n., pl.* **-ries** 1. a furnace for cremating 2. a building with such a furnace in it Also **cre′ma·to′ri·um** (-ē əm), *pl.* **-ri·ums, -ri·a** (-ə) —*adj.* of or for cremation: also **cre′ma·to′ri·al**

crème (krem, krēm) *n.* [Fr.] 1. cream 2. a thick liqueur

crème de ca·ca·o (də kə kā′ō, -kā′ō; də kō′kō) [Fr.] a sweet, chocolate-flavored liqueur

crème de menthe (də mänt′, menth′, mint′) [Fr.] a sweet, mint-flavored liqueur, green or colorless

Cre·mo·na (kri mō′nə) *n.* any famous violin formerly made in Cremona, Italy, as by Stradivari

cre·nate (krē′nāt) *adj.* [< ModL. < VL. *crena*, a notch] having a scalloped edge, as certain leaves: also **cre′nat·ed** —**cre′-nate·ly** *adv.* —**cre·na′tion** *n.*

cren·el (kren′l) *n.* [OFr. < VL. *crena*, a notch] any of the indentations in the top of a battlement or wall

cren·el·ate, cren·el·late (kren′l āt′) *vt.* **-el·at′ed or -el·lat′ed, -el·at′ing or -el·lat′ing** to furnish with battlements or crenels, or with squared notches —**cren′el·a′tion, cren′el·la′tion** *n.*

cren·u·late (kren′yoo lit, -lāt′) *adj.* [see CRENATE] having tiny scallops along the edge, as certain leaves: also **cren′u·lat′ed**

Cre·ole, cre·ole (krē′ōl) *n.* [< Fr. < Sp. *criollo* < Port. < *criar*, to rear < L. *creare*, to create] 1. orig., a person born in Latin America or the Gulf States of parents who came from Europe 2. *a)* a descendant of such persons, ☆esp. of French settlers in Louisiana or of Spanish settlers in the Gulf States ☆*b)* a person of both Creole and Negro descent ☆3. French as spoken by Creoles —*adj.* 1. of Creoles or their languages ☆2. [*usually* *c-*] made with sautéed tomatoes, green peppers, onions, etc.

cre·o·sol (krē′ə sōl′, -sōl′) *n.* [CREOS(OTE) + -OL[1]] a colorless, oily, antiseptic liquid, $C_8H_{10}O_2$, obtained esp. from beech tar

cre·o·sote (krē′ə sōt′) *n.* [< Gr. *kreas*, flesh + *sōzein*, to save] a transparent, oily liquid with a sharp smell, that is distilled from wood tar or coal tar: used as an antiseptic and to preserve wood —*vt.* **-sot′ed, -sot′ing** to treat with creosote

crepe, crêpe (krāp; *for 3, also* krep) *n.* [Fr. *crêpe* < L. *crispus*: see CRISP] 1. a thin, crinkled cloth, as of silk or wool; crape 2. *same as: a)* CRAPE (sense 2) *b)* CREPE PAPER *c)* CREPE RUBBER 3. a very thin pancake, generally rolled up or folded with a filling: usually **crêpe**

crepe paper thin paper crinkled like crepe

crepe rubber soft rubber in sheets with a wrinkled surface, used for some shoe soles

crêpes su·zette (krāp′ soo zet′; *Fr.* krep sü-) [Fr.] crêpes in a hot, orange-flavored sauce, usually served in flaming brandy

crep·i·tate (krep′ə tāt′) *vi.* **-tat·ed, -tat·ing** [< L. pp. of *crepitare* < *crepare*, to creak] to crackle —**crep′i·tant** *adj.* —**crep′-i·ta′tion** *n.*

crept (krept) *pt. & pp. of* CREEP

cre·pus·cu·lar (kri pus′kyoo lər) *adj.* [< L. *crepusculum*, twilight < *creper*, dark] of, like, or active at, twilight

cre·scen·do (krə shen′dō) *adj., adv.* [It. < L. *crescere*: see CRESCENT] *Music* gradually getting louder: symbol < —*n., pl.* **-dos** 1. a gradual increase in loudness or intensity 2. a passage played crescendo —*vi.* **-doed, -do·ing** to get louder gradually

cres·cent (kres′nt) *n.* [< OFr. < L. *crescere*, to grow: for IE. base see CEREAL] 1. the moon in its first or last quarter, when one edge looks concave and the other looks convex 2. the shape of the moon at this time 3. anything of similar shape, as

a curved roll 4. [*also* C-] [< the Turkish crescent emblem] Turkish or Moslem power —*adj.* 1. [Poet.] increasing; growing 2. shaped like a crescent

cre·sol (krē′sōl, -sōl) *n.* [< CREOSOTE + -OL[1]] any of three colorless, oily liquids or solids, C_7H_8O, distilled from coal tar and used in disinfectants, etc.

cress (kres) *n.* [OE. *cressa*, lit., ? creeper] a plant of the mustard family, as watercress, with pungent leaves used in salads and as garnishes

cres·set (kres′it) *n.* [< OFr.] a metal container for burning oil, wood, etc., used as a torch or lantern

Cres·si·da (kres′i də) in a legend of the Middle Ages, a Trojan woman who was the unfaithful lover of Troilus

crest (krest) *n.* [< OFr. < L. *crista*] 1. a comb, tuft, etc. on the heads of some animals or birds 2. a plume or emblem on a helmet 3. a helmet 4. a heraldic device placed above the shield in a coat of arms or used on silverware, note paper, etc. 5. top; ridge [a mountain *crest*] 6. the highest point or level —*vt.* 1. to provide with a crest 2. to reach the top of [we *crested* the hill] —*vi.* 1. to form or reach a crest [the flooded river *crested* at thirty feet]

crest·ed (kres′tid) *adj.* having a crest

crest·fall·en (krest′fôl′ən) *adj.* 1. with drooping crest or bowed head 2. made sad or humble [the team is *crestfallen* at losing the game]

cre·ta·ceous (kri tā′shəs) *adj.* [< L. < *creta*: see CRAYON] 1. of, like, or containing chalk 2. [C-] designating or of the third geological period of the Mesozoic Era —**the Cretaceous** the Cretaceous Period or its rocks: see GEOLOGIC TIME CHART

Crete (krēt) Greek island in the E Mediterranean: 3,218 sq. mi.; pop. 483,000 —**Cre′tan** *adj., n.*

cre·tin (krēt′n) *n.* [< Fr. dial. form of *chrétien*, Christian, hence human being] a person suffering from cretinism —**cre′-ti·nous** *adj.*

cre·tin·ism (-iz′m) *n.* [see prec.] a thyroid deficiency that a person is born with, causing him to be deformed and mentally retarded

cre·tonne (krē′tän, kri tän′) *n.* [Fr. < *Creton*, village in Normandy] a heavy, unglazed cotton or linen cloth, printed with a design and used for curtains, etc.

cre·vasse (kri vas′) *n.* [Fr. < OFr. *crevace*, CREVICE] 1. a deep crack or fissure, esp. in a glacier ☆2. a break in a levee, as of a river

Crève·coeur (krev koor′; *Fr.* krev kër′), **St. John de** (born *Michel Guillaume Jean de Crèvecoeur*) 1735–1813; Fr. essayist & agriculturist in America

crev·ice (krev′is) *n.* [< OFr. < L. *crepare*, to creak] a narrow opening caused by a crack or split; fissure; cleft —**crev′iced** *adj.*

crew[1] (kroo) *n.* [OFr. *creue*, growth < L. *crescere* (see CRESCENT)] 1. a group of people associating or working together or classed together; company, set, gang, etc. 2. all the men serving on a ship, usually excepting the officers 3. all the men manning an aircraft 4. a rowing team for a racing shell, usually of eight men —*vt., vi.* to serve (on) as a crew member —**crew′man** (-mən) *n., pl.* **-men**

crew[2] (kroo) *alt. pt. of* CROW[2] (sense 1)

☆**crew cut** a style of man's haircut in which the hair is cut close to the head

crew·el (kroo′əl) *n.* [LME. *crule* < ?] a fine worsted yarn used in needlework and embroidery —**crew′el·work′** *n.*

☆**crew neck** a round, closefitting neckline

crib (krib) *n.* [OE.: for IE. base see CART] 1. a rack, trough, or box for fodder; manger 2. a small, crude house or room 3. a small bed with high sides, for a baby 4. a framework of bars for support or strengthening 5. a framework or bin as for storing grain ☆6. a structure anchored under water, serving as a pier, water intake, etc. 7. [Colloq.] *a)* a petty theft *b)* the passing off of another's ideas, etc. as one's own *c)* a translation, another's notes, etc. used, often dishonestly, in doing schoolwork —*vt.* **cribbed, crib′bing** 1. to shut up as in a crib 2. to provide with a crib 3. [Colloq.] *a)* to steal *b)* to pass off (another's ideas, etc.) as one's own —*vi.* [Colloq.] to do schoolwork dishonestly, as by using a crib —**crib′ber** *n.*

CREW CUT

crib·bage (krib′ij) *n.* [< prec. + -AGE] a card game for two, three, or four players, in which the object is to form various combinations that count for points: score is kept by moving pegs on a small board

crib biting a habit some horses have of biting the feeding trough and swallowing air —**crib′·bite′** *vi.* -**bit′**, -**bit′ten** or -**bit′**, -**bit′·ing**

crick¹ (krik) *n.* [< ? ON.] a painful cramp in the neck, back, etc. —*vt.* to cause a crick in

crick² (krik) *n.* [Dial.] ☆ *same as* CREEK (sense 1)

Crick (krik), **Francis H(arry) C(ompton)** 1916– ; Eng. scientist: helped determine the structure of DNA

crick·et¹ (krik′it) *n.* [< OFr. < *criquer*, to creak] **1.** a leaping insect related to the locusts and grasshoppers: the males make a chirping noise by rubbing their forewings together **2.** a small toy or device pressed to make a clicking sound

crick·et² (krik′it) *n.* [< OFr.; prob. < MDu. *cricke*, a stick] **1.** an outdoor game played by two teams of eleven men each, in which a ball, bats, and wickets are used: popular mainly in England **2.** [Colloq.] fair play; sportsmanship —**crick′et·er** *n.*

crick·et³ (krik′it) *n.* [< ?] a wooden footstool

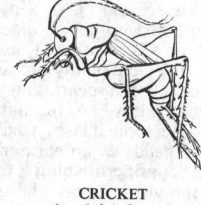
CRICKET
(to 1 in. long)

cried (krīd) *pt. & pp. of* CRY

cri·er (krī′ər) *n.* **1.** a person who cries **2.** an officer who makes announcements, as in a court **3.** *same as* TOWN CRIER

crim. criminal

crime (krīm) *n.* [OFr. < L. *crimen*, verdict, offense] **1.** the doing of something that is against the law, esp. a serious wrongdoing that is a felony or misdemeanor **2.** an evil act; sin; wrong **3.** all crimes or criminal acts, as a group **4.** [Colloq.] something to be regretted; shame [it's a *crime* he didn't finish school]

Cri·me·a (krī mē′ə, krə-) peninsula in southwestern U.S.S.R., extending into the Black Sea —**Cri·me′an** *adj.*

crim·i·nal (krim′ə n'l) *adj.* **1.** having the nature of crime; being a crime [*criminal* acts] **2.** relating to or dealing with crime [*criminal* law] **3.** guilty of crime **4.** [Colloq.] that is regretted; deplorable —*n.* a person guilty of a crime or convicted of a crime —**crim′i·nal′i·ty** (-ə tē) *n.* —**crim′i·nal·ly** *adv.*

criminal law law dealing with crime

criminal lawyer a lawyer who is hired for the most part to defend those accused of crime

crim·i·nate (krim′ə nāt′) *vt.* -**nat′ed**, -**nat′ing** [< L. pp. of *criminari* < *crimen*: see CRIME] **1.** to accuse of a crime **2.** to incriminate —**crim′i·na′tion** *n.* —**crim′i·na′tive, crim′i·na′to·ry** (-ə tôr′ē) *adj.*

crim·i·nol·o·gy (krim′ə näl′ə jē) *n.* [< L. *crimen* (gen. *criminis*): see CRIME & -LOGY] the scientific study and investigation of crime —**crim′i·no·log′i·cal** (-nə läj′i k'l) *adj.* —**crim′i·no·log′i·cal·ly** *adv.* —**crim′i·nol′o·gist** *n.*

crimp¹ (krimp) *vt.* [< OE. (*ge*)*crympan*, to curl & MDu. *crimpen*, to wrinkle] **1.** to press into narrow, regular folds; pleat **2.** to make (hair, etc.) wavy or curly **3.** to pinch together ☆**4.** [Colloq.] to hamper —*n.* **1.** a crimping **2.** a fold, pleat, or wave ☆**3.** a wavy condition —☆**put a crimp in** [Colloq.] to hamper —**crimp′er** *n.*

crimp² (krimp) *n.* [< CRIMP¹: orig. name of a card game] a person who gets men by force or trickery to serve as sailors or soldiers —*vt.* to get (men) thus into such service

crimp·y (krim′pē) *adj.* **crimp′i·er**, **crimp′i·est** [< CRIMP¹] curly; wavy; frizzly —**crimp′i·ness** *n.*

crim·son (krim′z'n) *n.* [< ML., ult. < Ar. *qirmiz*: see CARMINE] **1.** deep red **2.** deep-red coloring matter —*adj.* **1.** deep-red **2.** bloody —*vt., vi.* to make or become crimson

cringe (krinj) *vi.* **cringed**, **cring′ing** [OE. *cringan*, to fall (in battle): for IE. base see CRANK] **1.** to draw back, crouch, etc., as when afraid; cower [the dog *cringed*, then slunk away] **2.** to act in a timid or fawning manner [the king's courtiers *cringed* in his presence] —*n.* a cringing —**cring′er** *n.*

crin·gle (kriŋ′g'l) *n.* [< ON. *kringla*, circle, or MDu. *kringel*, ring: for IE. base see CART] a small ring or loop of rope or metal on the edge of a sail, for inserting a rope to fasten a sail

crin·kle (kriŋ′k'l) *vi., vt.* -**kled**, -**kling** [OE. *crincan*, var. of *cringan*: see CRINGE] **1.** to be or make full of wrinkles or ripples **2.** to rustle, as paper when crushed —*n.* **1.** a wrinkle, twist, or ripple **2.** a rustling sound —**crin′kly** *adj.* -**kli·er**, -**kli·est**

cri·noid (krī′noid, krin′oid) *adj.* [< Gr. < *krinon*, lily + -*eidēs*, -OID] **1.** lily-shaped **2.** designating or of a class of marine animals that are flowerlike and anchored by a stalk or that are free-swimming —*n.* such an animal

crin·o·line (krin′'l in) *n.* [Fr. < It. < L. *crinis*, hair + *linum*, thread] **1.** a coarse, stiff cloth, originally made of horsehair and linen, used as lining to stiffen garments **2.** a petticoat of this, worn to puff out a skirt **3.** *same as* HOOP SKIRT

crip·ple (krip′'l) *n.* [< OE. < base of *creopan*, to CREEP] a person or animal that is lame or disabled so that it cannot move in a normal way —*vt.* -**pled**, -**pling** to lame or disable —**crip′pler** *n.*

cri·sis (krī′sis) *n., pl.* -**ses** (-sēz) [L. < Gr. < *krinein*, to separate: for IE. base see CARNAGE] **1.** the turning point in a disease, when it becomes clear whether the patient will recover or die **2.** any turning point, as in history **3.** a time of great danger or trouble

crisp (krisp) *adj.* [OE. < L. *crispus*, curly] **1.** easily broken or crumbled; brittle [*crisp* bacon] **2.** fresh and firm, as celery **3.** fresh and tidy, as a uniform **4.** sharp, clear, brisk, lively, etc., as talk **5.** invigorating [*crisp* air] **6.** closely curled and wiry [*crisp* hair] —*n.* something crisp —*vt., vi.* to make or become crisp —**crisp′ly** *adv.* —**crisp′ness** *n.*

crisp·er (kris′pər) *n.* a compartment in a refrigerator for keeping vegetables crisp

crisp·y (kris′pē) *adj.* **crisp′i·er**, **crisp′i·est** *same as* CRISP —**crisp′i·ness** *n.*

criss·cross (kris′krôs′) *n.* [earlier Christ's cross, for the symbol X, abbrev. of Christ] a pattern of crossed lines —*adj.* marked with or moving in crossing lines —*vt., vi.* **1.** to mark with crossing lines **2.** to cross back and forth [railroad tracks *crisscross* the valley] —*adv.* crosswise

crit. **1.** critical **2.** criticism

cri·te·ri·on (krī tir′ē ən) *n., pl.* -**i·a** (-ē ə), -**i·ons** [< Gr. < *kritēs*, judge: see CRITIC] a standard, rule, or test by which something can be judged [what *criteria* should one use in buying a car?] —see SYN. at STANDARD

crit·ic (krit′ik) *n.* [< L. < Gr. *kritikos*, orig., able to discern, akin to *krinein*: see CRISIS] **1.** a person who forms and expresses judgments of people or things; specif., one who writes judgments of books, plays, music, etc., as for a newspaper **2.** a person who is quick to find fault

crit·i·cal (krit′i k'l) *adj.* **1.** tending to find fault; censorious **2.** based on or showing sound, careful judgment [a good *critical* mind] **3.** of critics or criticism **4.** of or forming a crisis; decisive [the *critical* stage of a disease] **5.** dangerous or risky [in a *critical* financial condition] **6.** designating or of supplies subject to increased production and restricted distribution, as in wartime **7.** designating or of the point at which some quality, property, or condition undergoes a change or at which a nuclear chain reaction becomes self-sustaining —**crit′i·cal·ly** *adv.*

SYN.—**critical**, in its strictest use, implies an attempt to analyze something carefully so as to discover both its merits and flaws, but it often suggests (as **hypercritical** always does) an emphasis on faults or shortcomings; **faultfinding** implies a habitual or unreasonable seeking out of faults or defects; **captious** suggests a small-minded tendency to find fault with even the most minor mistakes; **carping** implies a tendency to find fault in a harsh, nagging, disagreeable way —see also SYN. at ACUTE

crit·i·cism (krit′ə siz′m) *n.* **1.** the act, art, or principles of criticizing, esp. of criticizing literary or artistic work **2.** a comment, review, article, etc. by a critic **3.** faultfinding; disapproval

crit·i·cize (-sīz′) *vi., vt.* -**cized′**, -**ciz′ing** **1.** to analyze and judge as a critic **2.** to find fault (with) —**crit′i·ciz′a·ble** *adj.* —**crit′i·ciz′er** *n.*

SYN.—**criticize**, in this comparison, is the general term for finding fault with or disapproving of a person or thing; **reprehend** suggests severe disapproval, usually of faults, errors, etc. rather than of people; **blame** stresses the fixing of responsibility for an error, fault, etc. [don't *blame* your laziness on the heat]; **censure** implies the expression of severe criticism or disapproval as by a person in authority; **condemn** suggests the passing of harsh final judgment on a person or thing considered guilty or to blame; **denounce** implies a speaking out publicly against persons or actions thought to be immoral, corrupt, evil, etc. —ANT. praise

cri·tique (kri tēk′) *n.* [Fr.] a critical analysis or evaluation of a subject, situation, book, etc.

crit·ter, crit·tur (krit′ər) *n. dial. var. of* CREATURE

croak (krōk) *vi.* [< OE. < *cræcettan*: for IE. base see CRANE]

1. to make a deep, hoarse sound, as that of a frog **2.** to talk dismally; grumble **3.** [Slang] to die —*vt.* **1.** to utter in deep, hoarse tones **2.** [Slang] to kill —*n.* a croaking sound —**croak′y** (-ē) *adj.* **croak′i·er, croak′i·est**

croak·er (-ər) *n.* **1.** an animal or fish that makes croaking sounds **2.** a foreteller of evil; grumbler

Cro·at (krō′at, -ət; krōt) *n.* **1.** a native or inhabitant of Croatia **2.** *same as* CROATIAN (*n.* 2) —*adj. same as* CROATIAN

Cro·a·tia (krō ā′shə) republic of Yugoslavia, in the NW part: 21,830 sq. mi.; cap. Zagreb

Cro·a·tian (-shən) *adj.* of Croatia, its people, language, etc. —*n.* **1.** a Croat **2.** the South Slavic language of the Croats: see SERBO-CROATION

Cro·ce (krō′che; *E.* krō′chē), **Be·ne·det·to** (be′ne det′tô) 1866–1952; It. philosopher & critic

cro·chet (krō shā′) *n.* [Fr., small hook: see CROTCHET] needlework in which loops of thread or yarn are interwoven with a hooked needle (**crochet hook**) —*vi.,* *vt.* **-cheted** (-shād′), **-chet′ing** to do crochet or make by crochet —**cro·chet′er** (-shā′ər) *n.*

crock[1] (kräk) *n.* [OE. *crocca*: for IE. base see CART] **1.** an earthenware pot or jar ☆**2.** [Slang] something absurd; nonsense

crock[2] (kräk) *n.* [< ON. *kraki*, bent object] [Slang] anyone or anything worthless or useless, as from age

crocked (kräkt) *adj.* ☆[Slang] drunk; intoxicated

crock·er·y (kräk′ər ē) *n.* [CROCK[1] + -ERY (sense 5)] earthenware pots, jars, dishes, etc.

Crock·ett (kräk′it), **David** (called *Davy Crockett*) 1786–1836; Am. frontiersman & politician

croc·o·dile (kräk′ə dīl′) *n.* [< OFr. < ML. < L. < Gr. *krokodilos* < ? *krokē*, pebble + *drilos*, worm] **1.** a large, flesh-eating, lizardlike reptile of tropical streams, with a thick, horny skin, long tail, and long, narrow head with massive jaws **2.** leather made from a crocodile's hide

crocodile tears tears shed or grief expressed in an insincere way

croc·o·dil·i·an (kräk′ə dil′ē ən) *adj.* **1.** of or like a crocodile **2.** of a group of reptiles including the crocodile, alligator, cayman, and gavial —*n.* any reptile of this group

cro·cus (krō′kəs) *n., pl.* **cro′cus·es, cro′ci** (-sī) [L. < Gr. *krokos*, saffron, via Sem. ult. < Sans.] a small plant with a fleshy corm and a yellow, purple, or white flower that blooms early in spring

Croe·sus (krē′səs) fl. 6th cent. B.C.; last king of Lydia (560–546), noted for his great wealth —*n.* a very rich man

croft (krôft) *n.* [OE.: for IE. base see CART] [Brit.] **1.** a small enclosed field **2.** a small farm, esp. one worked by a renter —**croft′er** *n.*

crois·sant (krə sänt′) *n.* [Fr., lit., CRESCENT] a rich, flaky bread roll in the shape of a crescent

‡croix de guerre (krwä də ger′) [Fr., cross of war] a French military decoration for bravery

Cro-Ma·gnon (krō mag′nən, -man′yən) *adj.* [after the *Cro-Magnon* cave in SW France, where remains were found] belonging to a prehistoric, Caucasoid type of man, tall and erect, who lived on the European continent —*n.* a member of this group

crom·lech (kräm′lek) *n.* [W. < *crom*, bent + *llech*, flat stone] **1.** *same as* DOLMEN **2.** an ancient monument of monoliths, arranged in a circle around a mound or dolmen

Crom·well (kräm′wel, -wəl) **1. Oliver,** 1599–1658; Eng. revolutionary leader & Protector of the Commonwealth (1653–58) **2. Richard,** 1626–1712; Protector of the Commonwealth (1658–59): son of *Oliver*

crone (krōn) *n.* [< Anglo-Fr. *carogne* (see CARRION) or via MDu. *kronje,* old ewe] an ugly, withered old woman; hag

Cro·nus (krō′nəs) *Gr. Myth.* a Titan who overthrew his father, Uranus, and was himself overthrown by his son Zeus: identified with the Roman Saturn

cro·ny (krō′nē) *n., pl.* **-nies** [Brit. university slang < ? Gr. *chronios*, long-continued (hence "old friend")] a close companion

crook (krook) *n.* [< ON. *krōkr,* hook: for IE. base see CART] **1.** a hooked, bent, or curved thing or part; hook **2.** *a)* a shepherd's staff, with a hook at one end *b)* a crosier **3.** a bend or curve ☆**4.** [Colloq.] one who steals or cheats; swindler or thief —*vt., vi.* **crooked** (krookt), **crook′ing** to bend or curve

crook·ed (krook′t; *for 2 & 3* krook′id) *adj.* **1.** having a crook or hook **2.** not straight; bent; curved ☆**3.** dishonest; swindling —**crook′ed·ly** *adv.* —**crook′ed·ness** *n.*

Crookes (krooks), Sir **William** 1832–1919; Eng. chemist & physicist

☆**crook·neck** (krook′nek′) *n.* a squash with a long, tapering, curved neck

croon (kroon) *vi., vt.* [< MDu. *cronen,* to growl: for IE. base see CRANE] **1.** to sing or hum in a low, gentle tone ☆**2.** to sing (popular songs) in a soft, sentimental manner —*n.* a low, gentle singing or humming —**croon′er** *n.*

crop (kräp) *n.* [OE. *croppa,* cluster, flower, crop of bird: for IE. base see CART] **1.** a pouch in a bird's gullet, in which food is softened up before digestion; craw: see illustration at GIZZARD **2.** any farm product, growing or harvested, as wheat, fruit, etc. **3.** the yield of any product in one season or place **4.** a group or collection appearing together [a new *crop* of students; a *crop* of complaints] **5.** the handle or butt of a whip **6.** a short whip with a looped lash, used in horseback riding **7.** hair cut close to the head **8.** an earmark on an animal, made by clipping —*vt.* **cropped, crop′ping 1.** to cut off or bite off the tops or ends of [the goat *cropped* the grass] **2.** to grow or harvest as a crop **3.** to cut short [to *crop* hair] —*vi.* **1.** to plant, grow, or bear crops **2.** to feed by grazing —**crop out** (or **up**) **1.** to appear unexpectedly **2.** to appear at the surface, as a rock formation

crop-dust·ing (kräp′dust′iŋ) *n.* the spraying of growing crops with pesticides from an airplane —**crop′-dust′** *vi., vt.* —**crop′-dust′er** *n.*

crop·per (-ər) *n.* **1.** a person or thing that crops **2.** a sharecropper —**come a cropper** [Colloq.] **1.** to fall heavily or headlong **2.** to fail

☆**crop·pie** (kräp′ē) *n., pl.* **-pies, -pie:** see PLURAL, II, D, 1 *same as* CRAPPIE

crop rotation a system of growing in turn crops that have different food requirements, to keep the soil fertile, break up a disease cycle, etc.

cropt (kräpt) *occas. pt. & pp. of* CROP

cro·quet (krō kā′) *n.* [Fr., dial. form of *crochet:* see CROTCHET] an outdoor game in which the players use mallets to drive a wooden ball through a series of hoops placed in the ground

cro·quette (krō ket′) *n.* [Fr. < *croquer,* to crunch] a small mass of chopped, cooked meat, fish, etc., coated with crumbs and fried in deep fat

cro·sier (krō′zhər) *n.* [< OFr. < *croce* < ML. *crocia* < Frank. word thought to be *krukja,* crutch: for IE. base see CART] a staff with a crook at the top, carried by or before a bishop or abbot as a symbol of his office

cross (krôs) *n.* [< OE. *cros* & ON. *kross,* both < OIr. *cros* < L. *crux* (gen. *crucis*), a cross: for IE. base see CIRCUS] **1.** an upright post with a bar across it near the top, on which the ancient Romans fastened convicted persons to die **2.** a representation of a cross, used as a badge, crossroad marker, etc. **3.** a representation of a cross as a symbol of the crucifixion of Jesus, and hence of the Christian religion **4.** any trouble or affliction that one has to bear or that hinders one **5.** any mark made by intersecting lines or surfaces **6.** such a mark (X) made as a signature by one who cannot write **7.** *a)* a crossing of varieties or breeds; hybridization *b)* the result of such mixing; hybrid [a bull terrier is a *cross* between a bulldog and a terrier **8.** something that combines the qualities of two different things or types [a *cross* between a smile and a sneer] **9.** [Slang] a dishonest act, event, etc. —*vt.* **1.** to make the sign of the cross over or upon **2.** to place across or crosswise [*cross* your fingers] **3.** to lie or cut across; intersect [where two streets *cross* one another] **4.** to draw a line or lines across [*cross* your t's] **5.** to pass over; go across [to *cross* the ocean] **6.** to carry or lead across [the guard *crossed* the schoolchildren] **7.** to extend across [the bridge *crosses* a river] **8.** to bring into contact, causing electrical interference [the wires were *crossed*] **9.** to go against; oppose [no one likes to be *crossed*] **10.** to interbreed (animals or plants); hybridize —*vi.* **1.** to lie across; intersect **2.** to go or extend from one side to the other: often with *over* **3.** to pass each other while moving in opposite directions [our letters *crossed* in the mail] **4.** to interbreed —*adj.* **1.** lying or

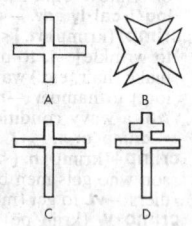

CROSSES
(A, Greek; B, Maltese; C, Latin; D, Patriarchal)

passing across; crossing; transverse [*cross* street; *cross* ventilation] **2.** going counter; contrary; opposed [at *cross* purposes] **3.** ill-tempered; cranky; irritable **4.** of mixed variety or breed; hybrid —*adv.* crosswise —see SYN. at IRRITABLE —**cross off** (or **out**) to cancel by or as by drawing lines across —**cross one's mind** to come suddenly or briefly to one's mind —**cross one's palm** to pay one money, esp. as a bribe —**cross one's path** to meet one —**cross up 1.** to confuse or disorder **2.** to deceive or double-cross —**the Cross 1.** the cross on which Jesus was put to death **2.** the suffering and death or Atonement of Jesus **3.** Christianity or Christendom —**cross'ly** *adv.* —**cross'ness** *n.*

cross·bar (krôs′bär′) *n.* a bar, line, or stripe placed crosswise —*vt.* **-barred′, -bar′ring** to furnish with crossbars

cross·beam (-bēm′) *n.* a beam placed across another or from one wall to another

cross·bill (-bil′) *n.* a finch having a bill with curving points that cross

cross·bones (-bōnz′) *n. see* SKULL AND CROSSBONES

cross·bow (-bō′) *n.* a medieval weapon consisting of a bow set across on a wooden stock: the stock was grooved to direct an arrow or stone —**cross′bow′man** *n., pl.* **-men**

CROSSBOW

cross·bred (-bred′, -bred′) *adj.* produced by the interbreeding of different varieties or breeds —*n.* a crossbred plant or animal; hybrid; mongrel

cross·breed (-brēd′, -brēd′) *vt., vi.* **-bred** (-bred′, -bred′), **-breed′ing** *same as* HYBRIDIZE —*n. same as* HYBRID (sense 1)

cross-check (-chek′, -chek′) *vt., vi.* to check or verify in several ways or against several sources —*n.* a cross-checking

cross-coun·try (-kun′trē) *adj., adv.* **1.** across open country or fields, not by roads **2.** across a country —*n.* cross-country footracing

cross·cur·rent (-kʉr′ənt) *n.* **1.** a current flowing at an angle to the main current **2.** an opposing opinion, influence, or tendency

cross·cut (-kut′) *adj.* **1.** made or used for cutting across [a *crosscut* saw] **2.** cut across —*n.* **1.** a cut across **2.** something that cuts across **3.** *Mining* a cutting made across a vein —*vt., vi.* **-cut′, -cut′ting** to cut across

crosse (krôs) *n.* [Fr.: see CROSIER] the pouched racket used in playing lacrosse

cross-ex·am·ine (krôs′ig zam′in) *vt., vi.* **-ined, -in·ing 1.** to question closely **2.** *Law* to question (a witness already questioned by the opposing side) in order to check the earlier answers —**cross′-ex·am′i·na′tion** *n.* —**cross′-ex·am′in·er** *n.*

cross-eye (krôs′ī′) *n.* an abnormal condition in which the eyes are turned toward each other —**cross′-eyed′** (-īd′) *adj.*

cross-fer·ti·lize (-fʉrt′'l īz′) *vt., vi.* **-lized′, -liz′ing** to fertilize or be fertilized by pollen from another plant or variety of plant —**cross′-fer′ti·li·za′tion** *n.*

cross-file (-fīl′) *vi.* **-filed′, -fil′ing** ☆to file as a candidate in the primary elections of two or more parties

cross fire 1. *Mil.* a firing at an objective from two or more positions so that the lines of fire cross **2.** any group of opposing forces, opinions, etc.

cross-grained (-grānd′) *adj.* **1.** having the grain irregular or running across: said of wood **2.** stubbornly disagreeable; contrary; perverse; cantankerous

cross·hatch (-hach′) *vt., vi.* to shade with two sets of crossing parallel lines —**cross′hatch′ing** *n.*

cross·ing (-iŋ) *n.* **1.** the act of passing across, opposing, interbreeding, etc. **2.** an intersection, as of lines, streets, etc. **3.** a place where a street, river, etc. may be crossed

cross·ing-o·ver (-ō′vər) *n.* a mutual exchange of equivalent parts between homologous chromosomes during meiosis: also **cross′o′ver**

cross-leg·ged (-leg′id, -legd′) *adj., adv.* with ankles crossed, or with one leg crossed over the other

CROSS-HATCHING

cross·patch (-pach′) *n.* [CROSS + dial. *patch*, fool] [Old Colloq.] a cross, bad-tempered person

cross·piece (-pēs′) *n.* a piece lying across another

cross·pol·li·nate (krôs′päl′ə nāt′) *vt., vi.* **-nat′ed, -nat′ing** to transfer pollen from the anther of (one flower) to the stigma of (another) —**cross′-pol′li·na′tion** *n.*

cross·pur·pose (krôs′pʉr′pəs) *n.* a contrary or conflicting purpose —**at cross-purposes** having a misunderstanding as to each other's purposes

cross·ques·tion (-kwes′chən) *vt.* to cross-examine —*n.* a question asked in cross-examination

cross·re·fer (-ri fʉr′) *vt., vi.* **-ferred′, -fer′ring** to refer from one part to another

cross·ref·er·ence (-ref′ər əns, -ref′rəns) *n.* a reference from one part of a book, catalog, index, etc. to another part —*vt., vi.* **-enced, -enc·ing 1.** to provide (an index, reference book, etc.) with systematic cross-references **2.** *same as* CROSS-REFER

cross·road (-rōd′) *n.* **1.** a road that crosses another **2.** a road that connects main roads **3.** [*usually pl.*] *a)* the place where roads intersect, often the site of a rural settlement *b)* any center to which people come from a wide area to carry on some activity —**at the crossroads** at the point where one must choose between different courses of action

cross·ruff (-ruf′) *n. Card Games* a sequence of plays in which each of two partners in turn leads a card which the other can trump

cross section 1. *a)* a cutting through something, esp. straight across *b)* a piece so cut off *c)* a drawing of a surface as exposed by such a cutting **2.** a sample with enough of each kind to show what the whole is like [the newspaper polled a *cross section* of the city's voters] —**cross′-sec′tion** *vt.* —**cross′-sec′tion·al** *adj.*

cross·stitch (-stich′) *n.* **1.** a stitch made by crossing two stitches diagonally in the form of an X **2.** needlework made with this stitch —*vt., vi.* to sew or embroider with this stitch

cross talk *Radio, etc.* interference in one channel from another or others

cross·tie (-tī′) *n.* a beam, rod, etc. placed crosswise to give support; ☆specif., any of the timbers lying across and supporting a railroad track

☆**cross·town** (-toun′) *adj.* going across the main avenues or transportation lines of a city [*cross-town* bus lines]

cross·trees (-trēz′) *n.pl.* two short, horizontal bars across a ship's masthead, which spread the rigging that supports the mast

☆**cross·walk** (-wôk′) *n.* a lane marked off for pedestrians to use in crossing a street

cross·way (-wā′) *n. same as* CROSSROAD

cross·wise (-wīz′) *adv.* so as to cross; across: also **cross′ways′** (-wāz′)

☆**cross·word puzzle** (-wʉrd′) an arrangement of numbered squares to be filled in with words, a letter to each square, so that a letter in a horizontal word is usually also part of a vertical word: numbered synonyms, definitions, etc. are given as clues for the words

crotch (kräch) *n.* [ME. *croche*, var. of *crucche*, CRUTCH] **1.** a pole forked on top **2.** a forked place, as where a tree trunk divides into two branches **3.** the place where the legs fork from the human body **4.** the place where the legs of a pair of pants, etc. meet —**crotched** *adj.*

crotch·et (kräch′it) *n.* [OFr. *crochet*, dim. < *croc*, a hook: for IE. base see CART] **1.** a queer or stubborn notion **2.** [Brit.] *same as* QUARTER NOTE

crotch·et·y (-ē) *adj.* full of queer or stubborn notions; cantankerous [a *crotchety* old fellow] —**crotch′et·i·ness** *n.*

cro·ton (krōt′'n) *n.* [ModL. < Gr. *kroton*] any of a large group of tropical shrubs or trees of the spurge family: one species yields an oil (**croton oil**) formerly used in medicine

☆**Croton bug** [< *Croton* Aqueduct in New York City] a small cockroach

crouch (krouch) *vi.* [< OFr. *crochir* < *croc*: see CROTCHET] to stoop low with the limbs close to the body, as an animal ready to pounce or cowering in fear —*n.* the act or position of crouching

croup[1] (krōōp) *n.* [< obs. or dial. *croup*, to speak hoarsely, of

TULIP IN CROSS SECTION

echoic origin] an inflammation of the breathing passages that causes hard breathing and hoarse coughing —**croup′y** *adj.*

croup[2] (kro͞op) *n.* [OFr. *coupe* < Frank.] the rump of a horse, etc.

crou·pi·er (kro͞o′pē ā′, -ər) *n.* [Fr., orig., one who rides on the croup: see prec.] a person in charge of a gambling table, who rakes in and pays out the money

crou·ton (kro͞o′tän, kro͞o tän′) *n.* [< Fr. *croûte* < L. *crusta*: see CRUST] a small piece of toasted or fried bread, often served in soup or salads

Crow (krō) *n.* [transl., via Fr., of their native name, *Absaroke*, crow people] **1.** *pl.* **Crows, Crow** a member of a tribe of Siouan Indians living near the Yellowstone River **2.** their Siouan language

crow[1] (krō) *n.* [OE. *crawa*: for IE. base see CRANE] a large bird with glossy black plumage and a typical harsh call: the raven, rook, and jackdaw are crows —**as the crow flies** in a direct line —☆**eat crow** [Colloq.] to be humiliated by having to admit that one was wrong

crow[2] (krō) *vi.* **crowed** or, for 1, chiefly Brit., **crew** (kro͞o), **crowed, crow′ing** [OE. *crawan*: see CROW[1]] **1.** to make the shrill cry of a rooster **2.** to boast in triumph; exult [to *crow* over a victory] **3.** to make a sound expressing pleasure, as a baby does —*n.* a crowing sound —see SYN. at BOAST

crow·bar (krō′bär′) *n.* a long metal bar, like a chisel at one end, used as a lever for prying, etc.

crowd[1] (kroud) *vi.* [OE. *crudan* < IE. base *greut-*, to press] **1.** to press, push, or squeeze [they all *crowded* into one car] **2.** to push one's way [forward, into, etc.] **3.** to come together in a large group; throng [people *crowded* to see the show] —*vt.* **1.** to press, push, or shove **2.** to press closely together; cram [he *crowded* them into the room] **3.** to fill too full [the room was *crowded* with furniture] **4.** to be or press very near to; specif., ☆*Baseball* to stand very close to the plate in batting **5.** [Colloq.] to put (a person) under pressure, as by dunning —*n.* **1.** a large number of people or things gathered closely together **2.** the common people; the masses ☆**3.** [Colloq.] a set or clique [he goes around with an older *crowd*] —**crowd (on) sail** to put up more sails so as to increase the ship's speed —**crowd out** to exclude because of insufficient space or time —**crowd′ed** *adj.*

SYN.—**crowd** is applied to a large group of persons or things gathered or packed tightly together and may suggest lack of order, loss of personal identity, etc. [*crowds* lined the street]; **throng** suggests a moving crowd of people pushing one another [*throngs* of celebrators at Times Square]; **swarm** suggests a large, continuously moving group [*swarms* of sightseers]; **mob**, properly applied to a disorderly or lawless crowd, is a term of abuse when used to describe the masses or any specific group of people; **host** refers to any sizable group as a whole [he has a *host* of friends]; **horde** suggests a large, threatening, often disorganized, band [a *horde* of office seekers]

crowd[2] (kroud) *n.* [W. *crwth*] an obsolete Celtic musical instrument somewhat like a violin but with a flat, broad body

crow·foot (krō′foot′) *n., pl.* **-foots′** a plant of the buttercup family, with leaves somewhat resembling a crow's foot

crown (kroun) *n.* [< OFr. < L. *corona*, a garland < Gr. *korōnē*, wreath: for IE. base see CIRCUS] **1.** a garland or wreath worn on the head as a sign of honor, victory, etc. **2.** a reward or honor given for merit; specif., a sports championship **3.** the gold, jeweled headdress of a monarch that is an emblem of his power **4.** [*often* C-] *a*) the power or dominion of a monarch *b*) the monarch as head of the state **5.** anything serving to adorn or honor like a crown **6.** a thing like a crown in shape, position, etc., as the top of the head, of a hat, etc. **7.** *a*) orig., any coin bearing the figure of a crown *b*) a British coin equal to five shillings **8.** the highest point, as of an arch **9.** the highest quality, state, etc. of anything **10.** *a*) the part of a tooth that sticks out from the gum line: see illustration at TOOTH *b*) an artificial substitute for this **11.** the lowest point of an anchor, between the arms —*vt.* **1.** *a*) to put a crown on the head of *b*) to enthrone [Elizabeth I was *crowned* in 1558] **2.** to honor or reward as with a crown [the victor was *crowned* with glory] **3.** to be the crown or highest part of [woods *crowned* the hill] **4.** to complete successfully; put the finishing touch on [success *crowned* his efforts] **5.** to cover (a tooth) with an artificial crown **6.** [Slang] to hit on the head **7.** *Checkers* to make a king of —**crown′er** *n.*

☆**crown cap** a cork-lined metal stopper whose edges are crimped over the mouth of the bottle

crown colony a British colony directly under the control of the home government in London

crown glass a very clear optical glass

crown prince the prince who is heir apparent to a throne

crown princess 1. the wife of a crown prince **2.** a female heir presumptive to a throne

crown saw a saw in the form of a hollow cylinder with teeth on the bottom edge, for cutting circles

crow's-foot (krōz′foot′) *n., pl.* **-feet′** any of the wrinkles that often develop at the outer corners of the eyes: *usually used in pl.*

crow's-nest (-nest′) *n.* **1.** a small, partly enclosed platform close to the top of a ship's mast, used by the lookout **2.** any platform like this

cro·zier (krō′zhər) *n.* same as CROSIER

cru·ces (kro͞o′sēz) *n.* alt. pl. of CRUX

cru·cial (kro͞o′shəl) *adj.* [Fr. < L. *crux*, CROSS] of supreme importance; decisive; critical [a *crucial* experiment] —see SYN. at ACUTE —**cru′cial·ly** *adv.*

cru·ci·ble (kro͞o′sə b'l) *n.* [< ML. *crucibulum*, lamp] **1.** a container made of a heat-resistant substance, as graphite, for melting ores, metals, etc. **2.** a severe test or trial

cru·ci·fix (kro͞o′sə fiks′) *n.* [< OFr. or ML., orig. pp. of LL. *crucifigere*, CRUCIFY] **1.** a representation of a cross with the figure of Jesus crucified on it **2.** the cross as a Christian symbol

CROW'S-NEST

cru·ci·fix·ion (kro͞o′sə fik′shən) *n.* **1.** a crucifying or being crucified **2.** [C-] the crucifying of Jesus, or a representation of this in painting, statuary, etc.

cru·ci·form (kro͞o′sə fôrm′) *adj.* [< L. *crux*, CROSS + -FORM] cross-shaped —**cru′ci·form·ly** *adv.*

cru·ci·fy (kro͞o′sə fi′) *vt.* **-fied′, -fy′ing** [< OFr. < LL. *crucificare*, for *crucifigere* < L. *crux*, CROSS + *figere*, FIX] **1.** to execute by nailing or binding to a cross and leaving to die of exposure **2.** to treat cruelly; torment; torture —**cru′ci·fi′er** *n.*

crud[1] (krud) *vt., vi.* **crud′ded, crud′ding** [ME. *crud*: see CURD] [Dial.] to curdle —*n.* [Slang] **1.** any coagulated substance, caked deposit, dregs, filth, etc. **2.** a worthless, disgusting, or contemptible person or thing —**crud′dy** *adj.* **-di·er, -di·est**

crud[2] (krud) *n.* [< ? W. *cryd*, plague] [Slang] an imaginary or vaguely identified disease or ailment

crude (kro͞od) *adj.* [L. *crudus*, raw, rough < IE. base *krew-*, congealed (blood)] **1.** in a raw or natural condition; not refined or processed [*crude* oil] **2.** lacking grace, taste, etc.; uncultured [a *crude* remark] **3.** not carefully made or done; rough [a *crude* drawing] **4.** stark and bare [*crude* reality] —**crude′ly** *adv.* —**crude′ness** *n.*

cru·di·ty (kro͞o′də tē) *n.* **1.** a crude condition or quality **2.** *pl.* **-ties** a crude action, remark, etc.

cru·el (kro͞o′əl) *adj.* [OFr. < L. *crudelis* < *crudus*: see CRUDE] **1.** liking to make others suffer; having no mercy or pity **2.** causing, or of a kind to cause, pain, distress, etc. [*cruel* insults; a *cruel* winter] —**cru′el·ly** *adv.* —**cru′el·ness** *n.*

SYN.—**cruel** implies lack of concern for the suffering of others or a being inclined to cause it for others [*cruel* fate; a *cruel* taskmaster]; **brutal** implies a savage cruelty that is altogether unfeeling [a *brutal* beating]; **inhuman** stresses the complete absence of those qualities expected of a civilized human being, such as sympathy, mercy, or kindness; **pitiless** implies a callous refusal to be moved or influenced by the suffering of those one has wronged; **ruthless** implies a cruel and contemptuous disregard for the rights or welfare of others, while pursuing a goal [a *ruthless* tyrant] —**ANT.** humane, kind

cru·el·ty (-tē) *n.* **1.** the quality of being cruel; inhumanity; hardheartedness **2.** *pl.* **-ties** a cruel action, remark, etc. **3.** *Law* willful mistreatment seriously harmful to life or to health

cru·et (kro͞o′it) *n.* [< Anglo-Fr. dim. of OFr. *crue*, earthen pot < Gmc.: for IE. base see CART] a small glass bottle, as for holding vinegar, oil, etc., for the table

Cruik·shank (krook′shaŋk), **George** 1792–1878; Eng. caricaturist & illustrator

cruise (kro͞oz) *vi.* **cruised, cruis′ing** [< Du. *kruisen*, to cross < *kruis* < L. *crux*, CROSS] **1.** to sail from place to place, as for pleasure or in search of something **2.** to go or drive about in a similar manner [a taxi *cruises* to pick up passengers] **3.** to move at the most efficient speed for sustained travel [the airplane *cruised* at 400 miles per hour] —*vt.* to sail, journey, or move over or about [to *cruise* the Caribbean] —*n.* the action of cruising; esp., a cruising voyage

---

CROWBAR

cruis·er (-ər) *n.* **1.** one that cruises, as an airplane, squad car, etc. **2.** a fast warship somewhat smaller than a battleship and having less armor and fire power **3.** *same as* CABIN CRUISER

☆**crul·ler** (krul′ər) *n.* [Du. < *krullen*, to CURL] a kind of twisted doughnut made with a rich dough

crumb (krum) *n.* [OE. *cruma*: for IE. base see CART] **1.** a very small piece broken off something, as of bread or cake **2.** any bit or scrap [*crumbs* of knowledge] **3.** the soft, inner part of bread ☆**4.** [Slang] a worthless or disgusting person: also **crum′bum′** —*vt.* **1.** to clear (a table, etc.) of crumbs **2.** *Cooking* to cover or thicken with crumbs

crum·ble (krum′b'l) *vt.* -bled, -bling [CRUMB + -LE²] to break into crumbs or small pieces [he *crumbled* crackers into his soup] —*vi.* to fall to pieces; decay; disintegrate [*crumbling* plaster; *crumbling* hopes]

crum·bly (-blē) *adj.* -bli·er, -bli·est apt to crumble; easily crumbled —**crum′bli·ness** *n.*

crumb·y (krum′ē) *adj.* **crumb′i·er, crumb′i·est** **1.** full of crumbs **2.** soft, as the inner part of bread ☆**3.** [Slang] *same as* CRUMMY —**crumb′i·ness** *n.*

crum·my (krum′ē) *adj.* -mi·er, -mi·est [< CRUM(B) + -Y²] [Slang] **1.** dirty, cheap, shabby, etc. **2.** inferior, worthless, contemptible, etc. —**crum′mi·ness** *n.*

crum·pet (krum′pit) *n.* [prob. < ME. *crompid* < OE. *crompeht*, flat cake] a batter cake baked on a griddle: it is usually toasted before serving

crum·ple (krum′p'l) *vt., vi.* -pled, -pling [ME. *crumplen*, var. of *crimplen*, to wrinkle < *crimpen*, CRIMP¹] **1.** to crush or become crushed together into wrinkles **2.** to break down; collapse —*n.* a crease or wrinkle —**crum′ply** *adj.*

crunch (krunch) *vi., vt.* [of echoic origin] **1.** to chew with a noisy, crackling sound **2.** to press, grind, tread, etc. with a noisy, crushing sound —*n.* **1.** the act or sound of crunching ☆**2.** [Slang] *a)* a showdown *b)* a tight situation [a housing *crunch*]

crunch·y (krun′chē) *adj.* **crunch′i·er, crunch′i·est** making a crunching sound, as when chewed —**crunch′i·ness** *n.*

crup·per (krup′ər, kroop′-) *n.* [< OFr. *cropiere* < *crope*, rump] **1.** a leather strap attached to a saddle or harness and passed under the horse's tail **2.** a horse's rump; croup

cru·ral (kroor′əl) *adj.* [L. *cruralis* < *crus*, leg, shank] *Anat.* of the leg or thigh

cru·sade (kroo sād′) *n.* [< Sp. *cruzada* & Fr. *croisade*, both < ML. pp. of *cruciare*, to mark with a cross < L. *crux*, CROSS] **1.** [sometimes C-] any of the military expeditions which Christians of western Europe undertook from the 11th to the 13th cent. to capture the Holy Land from the Moslems **2.** any fight for a cause thought to be good or against something thought to be bad [a *crusade* for better housing; a *crusade* against cancer] —*vi.* -sad·ed, -sad·ing to engage in a crusade —**cru·sad′er** *n.*

cruse (krooz, kroos) *n.* [OE. *cruse*] a small container for water, oil, honey, etc.

crush (krush) *vt.* [< OFr. *croisir*, to break < Frank. *krostjan*, to gnash] **1.** to press or squeeze with force so as to break, hurt, or put out of shape; crumple [he *crushed* the walnut in his hand] **2.** to grind or pound into small particles [this machine *crushes* rocks] **3.** to put down by or as by force; subdue; overwhelm [the government *crushed* the rebellion] **4.** to extract by pressing or squeezing —*vi.* **1.** to be or become crushed **2.** to press forward; crowd (*into*, etc.) —*n.* **1.** a crushing; severe pressure **2.** a crowded mass of people ☆**3.** [Colloq.] a strong attraction toward someone; infatuation —see SYN. at BREAK —**crush′a·ble** *adj.* —**crush′er** *n.*

Cru·soe (kroo′sō), **Robinson** *see* ROBINSON CRUSOE

crust (krust) *n.* [< OFr. *crouste* < L. *crusta*: for IE. base see CRUDE] **1.** *a)* the hard, outer part of bread *b)* a piece of this *c)* any dry, hard piece of bread **2.** the pastry shell of a pie **3.** any hard surface layer, as of snow, soil, etc. **4.** *same as* SCAB (*n.* 1). **5.** [Slang] impudent boldness; audacity; insolence **6.** *Geol.* the solid outer shell of the earth —*vt., vi.* **1.** to cover or become covered with a crust **2.** to harden into a crust —**crus·tal** (krus′t'l) *adj.* —**crust′ed** *adj.*

crus·ta·cean (krus tā′shən) *n.* [< ModL. < *crustaceus*, having a crust < L. *crusta*, CRUST] any of a class of arthropods, including shrimps, crabs, barnacles, and lobsters, that usually live in water and breathe through gills: they have a hard outer shell and

jointed appendages and bodies —*adj.* of crustaceans: also **crus·ta′ceous**

crust·y (krus′tē) *adj.* **crust′i·er, crust′i·est** **1.** having, forming, or resembling a crust **2.** rudely abrupt or surly; bad-tempered —**crust′i·ly** *adv.* —**crust′i·ness** *n.*

crutch (kruch) *n.* [OE. *crycce*, staff: for IE. base see CART] **1.** a device used by lame people as an aid in walking, as a staff having a crosspiece that fits under the armpit or a metal ring that fits around the forearm **2.** anything relied on for support; prop **3.** any device that resembles a crutch —*vt.* to support with or as with a crutch; prop up

crux (kruks) *n., pl.* **crux′es, cru·ces** (kroo′sēz) [L., CROSS] **1.** a difficult problem; puzzling thing **2.** the essential or deciding point

cru·zei·ro (kroo zā′rō; *Port.* kroo zā′roo) *n., pl.* **-ros** [Port.< *cruz*, a cross < L. *crux*, CROSS] *see* MONETARY UNITS, table (Brazil)

crwth (krooth) *n.* [W.] *same as* CROWD²

cry (krī) *vi.* **cried, cry′ing** [OFr. *crier* < L. *quiritare*, to wail] **1.** to make a loud sound with the voice; call out or shout [to *cry* out in fright; to *cry* for help] **2.** to sob and shed tears in expressing sorrow, pain, etc.; weep **3.** *a)* to plead or clamor (*for*) *b)* to show a great need (*for*) [problems *crying* for solution] **4.** to utter its characteristic call: said of an animal —*vt.* **1.** to plead or beg for [to *cry* quarter] **2.** to utter loudly; shout ["Help! Help!" he *cried*] **3.** to call out (wares for sale, etc.) **4.** to bring into a specified condition by crying [she *cried* herself to sleep] —*n., pl.* **cries** **1.** a loud sound made in expressing pain, anger, etc. **2.** any loud utterance; shout [a *cry* of "Gangway!"] **3.** an announcement called out publicly **4.** an urgent appeal; plea **5.** rallying call; slogan **6.** public outcry [the *cry* for tax reform] **7.** a fit of weeping **8.** the characteristic sound uttered by an animal **9.** the baying of hounds in the chase —**a far cry** a great distance or difference —**cry down** to belittle; disparage —**cry one's eyes out** to weep much and bitterly —**cry out** **1.** to shout; yell **2.** to complain loudly —**cry up** to praise highly —**in full cry** in eager pursuit

☆**cry·ba·by** (krī′bā′bē) *n., pl.* **-bies** **1.** a child who cries often or with little cause **2.** a person who complains when he fails to win or get his own way

cry·ing (-iŋ) *adj.* **1.** that cries **2.** demanding immediate notice [a *crying* need] —**for crying out loud** [Slang] an exclamation of annoyance, surprise, etc.

cry·o- [< Gr. *kryos*, cold: for IE. base see CRUDE] a combining form meaning cold or freezing [*cryolite*]

cry·o·gen (krī′ə jen) *n.* [CRYO- + -GEN] a refrigerant

cry·o·gen·ics (krī′ə jen′iks) *n.pl.* [with sing. v.] [CRYOGEN + -ICS] the science that deals with the effects of very low temperatures on the properties of matter —**cry·o·gen′ic** (-ik) *adj.*

cry·o·lite (krī′ə līt′) *n.* [CRYO- + -LITE] a fluoride of sodium and aluminum, Na_3AlF_6, used in the production of aluminum

cry·o·sur·ger·y (krī′ə sur′jə rē) *n.* [CRYO- + SURGERY] surgery in which tissues are destroyed by freezing: also **cryogenic surgery**

crypt (kript) *n.* [< L. < Gr. < *kryptein*, to hide] an underground chamber; esp., a vault under the main floor of a church, used as a burial place

cryp·tic (krip′tik) *adj.* [< LL. < Gr.: see prec.] **1.** having a hidden meaning; mysterious [a *cryptic* answer] **2.** obscure and curt in the way one expresses oneself Also **cryp′ti·cal** —see SYN. at OBSCURE —**cryp′ti·cal·ly** *adv.*

cryp·to- *a combining form meaning:* **1.** secret or hidden [*cryptogram*] **2.** being such secretly [a *crypto*-Fascist] Also, before a vowel, **crypt-**

cryp·to·gam (krip′tə gam′) *n.* [< Fr. < Gr. *kryptos*, hidden + *gamos*, marriage] a plant that bears no flowers or seeds but reproduces by means of spores, as algae, mosses, ferns, etc. —**cryp′to·gam′ic, cryp·tog′a·mous** (-täg′ə məs) *adj.*

cryp·to·gram (krip′tə gram′) *n.* [CRYPTO- + -GRAM] something written in code or cipher: also **cryp′to·graph′** (-graf′) —**cryp′to·gram′ic** *adj.*

cryp·tog·ra·phy (krip täg′rə fē) *n.* [CRYPTO- + -GRAPHY] **1.** the art of writing or deciphering messages in code **2.** a code system —**cryp·tog′ra·pher, cryp·tog′ra·phist** *n.* —**cryp·to·graph·ic** (krip′tə graf′ik) *adj.* —**cryp′to·graph′i·cal·ly** *adv.*

cryst. **1.** crystalline **2.** crystallized

---

fat, āpe, cär; ten, ēven; is, bīte; gō, hôrn, tōol, look; oil, out; up, fur; get; joy; yet; chin; she; thin, *th*en; zh, leisure; ŋ, ring; ə for *a* in *ago*, *e* in *agent*, *i* in *sanity*, *o* in *comply*, *u* in *focus*; ′ as in *able* (ā′b'l); Fr. bal; ë, Fr. coeur; ö, Fr. feu; Fr. mon; ô, Fr. coq; ü, Fr. duc; r, Fr. cri; H, G. ich; kh, G. doch; ‡foreign; ☆ Americanism; < derived from. See inside front cover.

crys·tal (kris′t′l) *n.* [< OE. & OFr. < L. < Gr. *krystallos*, ice < *kryos*, frost: see CRYO-] **1.** *a)* a clear, transparent quartz *b)* a piece of this cut in the form of an ornament **2.** *a)* a very clear, brilliant glass *b)* an article or articles made of such glass, as goblets, bowls, etc. ☆**3.** the transparent covering over the face of a watch **4.** anything clear and transparent like crystal **5.** a solidified form of a substance made up of plane faces in three dimensions in a symmetrical arrangement [salt *crystals*] **6.** a piezoelectric material, as quartz, used to produce or control very precisely a desired frequency, as in radio transmitters, etc. —*adj.* **1.** of or composed of crystal **2.** like crystal; clear and transparent **3.** using a crystal (sense 6)

crystal detector a detector that uses a crystal diode to extract the audio or video signal from a carrier wave

crystal gazing the practice of gazing into a large glass ball (**crystal ball**) and claiming to see images, esp. of future events —**crystal gazer**

crys·tal·line (kris′tə lin) *adj.* **1.** consisting or made of crystal or crystals **2.** like crystal; clear and transparent **3.** having the character or structure of a crystal

crystalline lens the lens of the eye, serving to focus light on the retina

crys·tal·lize (kris′tə līz′) *vt.* -lized′, -liz′ing **1.** to cause to form crystals **2.** to give a definite form to **3.** to coat with sugar [*crystallized* fruit] —*vi.* **1.** to become crystalline in form [boil the maple syrup until it will *crystallize*] **2.** to take on a definite form [their customs *crystallized* into law] —**crys′tal·liz′a·ble** *adj.* —**crys′tal·li·za′tion** *n.*

crys·tal·lo- [< Gr. *krystallos*, CRYSTAL] *a combining form meaning* crystal: also, before a vowel, **crys·tall-**

crys·tal·log·ra·phy (kris′tə läg′rə fē) *n.* [prec. + -GRAPHY] the science of the form, structure, properties, and classification of crystals —**crys′tal·lo·graph′ic** (-lə graf′ik), **crys′tal·lo·graph′i·cal** *adj.*

crys·tal·loid (kris′tə loid′) *adj.* **1.** like a crystal **2.** having the nature of a crystalloid —*n.* a substance, usually crystallizable, which, when in solution, readily passes through vegetable and animal membranes —**crys′tal·loi′dal** *adj.*

crystal pickup a piezoelectric vibration pickup, often used on electric phonographs

crystal set an early type of radio receiver with a crystal, instead of an electron tube, detector

Cs *Chem.* cesium

cs. case; cases

C.S. Christian Science

C.S., c.s. **1.** capital stock **2.** civil service

C.S.A. Confederate States of America

CSC Civil Service Commission

csc cosecant

CST, C.S.T. Central Standard Time

CT Connecticut

ct. **1.** *pl.* **cts.** cent **2.** court

cte·noid (ten′oid, tē′noid) *adj.* [< Gr. *ktenos*, genitive of *kteis*, comb + -OID] having an edge with projecting parts like the teeth of a comb, as the scales and teeth of certain fishes

cten·o·phore (ten′ə fôr′) *n.* [see CTENOID & -PHORE] any of a group of sea animals with an oval, transparent, jellylike body bearing eight rows of comblike plates that aid in swimming — **cte·noph·o·ran** (ti näf′ə rən) *adj., n.*

ctn **1.** carton: also **ctn. 2.** cotangent

ctr. center

cts. **1.** centimes **2.** cents

Cu [L. *cuprum*] *Chem.* copper

cu. cubic

cub (kub) *n.* [< ? OIr. *cuib*, whelp] **1.** the young of certain mammals, as the fox, bear, lion, whale, etc. **2.** an inexperienced or immature person, esp. a beginning reporter — **cub′bish** *adj.* —**cub′bish·ness** *n.*

Cu·ba (kyōō′bə; *Sp.* kōō′bä) island country in the West Indies, south of Fla.: 44,218 sq. mi.; pop. 8,074,000; cap. Havana — **Cu′ban** *adj., n.*

cub·age (kyōō′bij) *n.* [CUB(E) + -AGE] cubic content

cub·by·hole (kub′ē hōl′) *n.* [< Brit. dial. *cub*, little shed + HOLE] a small, snug room, closet, or compartment

cube (kyōōb) *n.* [Fr. < L. < Gr. *kybos*, a cube, die: for IE. base see COOP] **1.** a solid with six equal, square sides **2.** anything having more or less this shape [an ice *cube*] **3.** the product ob-

tained by multiplying a given number or quantity by its square; third power [the *cube* of 3 is 27 (3x3x3)] —*vt.* **cubed, cub′ing 1.** to raise to the third power **2.** to cut or shape into cubes [*cube* the vegetables] **3.** to score (meat) in a crisscross pattern in order to tenderize it —**cub′er** *n.*

cu·beb (kyōō′beb) *n.* [< Fr. < ML. < Ar. *kababa*] the spicy berry of an East Indian vine, formerly used medicinally in cigarettes

cube root the number or quantity of which a given number or quantity is the cube [the *cube root* of 8 is 2]

cu·bic (kyōō′bik) *adj.* **1.** having the shape of a cube **2.** having three dimensions, or having the volume of a cube whose length, width, and depth each measure the given unit [a *cubic* foot] **3.** designating a crystal form that has three equal axes at right angles to one another: see illustration at CRYSTAL **4.** relating to the cubes of numbers or quantities Also, esp. for 1, **cu′bi·cal** (-bi k′l) —**cu′bi·cal·ly** *adv.*

cu·bi·cle (kyōō′bi k′l) *n.* [L. *cubiculum* < *cubare*, to lie down] **1.** a small sleeping compartment, as in a dormitory **2.** any small compartment

cubic measure a system of measuring volume in cubic units, esp. that in which 1,728 cubic inches = 1 cubic foot and 1,000 cubic millimeters = 1 cubic centimeter: see TABLE OF WEIGHTS AND MEASURES in Supplements

cu·bi·form (kyōō′bə fôrm′) *adj.* cube-shaped

cub·ism (kyōō′biz′m) *n.* a movement in art, esp. of the early 20th century, characterized by a separation of the subject into cubes and other geometric forms in abstract arrangements rather than by a realistic representation of nature —**cub′ist** *n., adj.* —**cu·bis′tic** *adj.*

cu·bit (kyōō′bit) *n.* [< OE. < L. *cubitum*, the elbow, cubit] an ancient measure of length, about 18–22 inches; orig., the length of the arm from the end of the middle finger to the elbow

cu·boid (kyōō′boid) *adj.* cube-shaped: also **cu·boi′dal** —*n.* a six-sided figure with all faces rectangular

Cub Scout a member of a division of the Boy Scouts for boys eight through ten years old

cuck·ing stool (kuk′iŋ) [ME. *coking-stole*, lit., toilet seat, which it was made to resemble] a chair in which disorderly women, scolds, cheats, etc. were fastened and exposed to public ridicule or sometimes ducked in water

cuck·old (kuk′′ld) *n.* [< OFr. *cucuault* < *cucu*, CUCKOO, the female of which is said to change mates often] a man whose wife has committed adultery —*vt.* to make a cuckold of — **cuck′old·ry** (-rē) *n.*

cuck·oo (kōō′kōō′, kook′ōō) *n., pl.* **cuck′oos** [< OFr. *coucou, cucu*, echoic of its cry] **1.** any of a family of grayish-brown birds with a long, slender body: the European species lays eggs in the nests of other birds, but the American varieties hatch their own young **2.** the call of a cuckoo, which sounds somewhat like its name **3.** an imitation of this **4.** [Slang] a crazy or foolish person —*vi.* to utter or imitate the call of a cuckoo —*adj.* [Slang] crazy; silly

cuckoo clock a clock with a toy bird that pops out and cuckoos to mark intervals of time

cuckoo spit (or **spittle**) a froth produced on plants by the nymphs of certain insects

cu·cul·late (kyōō′kə lāt′, kyōō kul′it) *adj.* [< L. *cucullus*, hood] shaped like a hood, as the leaves of violets: also **cu′cul·lat′ed**

cu·cum·ber (kyōō′kum bər) *n.* [< OFr. < L. *cucumis* (gen. *cucumeris*)] **1.** an annual vine of the gourd family, grown for its edible fruit **2.** the long fruit, with a green rind and firm, white flesh, used in salads or preserved as pickles — **cool as a cucumber 1.** comfortably cool **2.** calm and self-possessed

cud (kud) *n.* [OE. *cudu:* see BITUMEN] a mouthful of swallowed food brought back from the first stomach of cattle and other ruminants and chewed slowly a second time —**chew the cud** to recall and think over something; ruminate; ponder

CUCKOO CLOCK

cud·dle (kud′′l) *vt.* **-dled, -dling** [? < ME. *couthelen* < *couth*, known, hence comfortable with + -LE²] to hold lovingly and gently in one's arms; embrace and fondle —*vi.* to lie close and snug; nestle —*n.* **1.** a cuddling **2.** an embrace; hug —**cud′-dle·some** (-səm), **cud′dly** *adj.* **-dli·er, -dli·est**

cudg·el (kuj′əl) *n.* [OE. *cycgel*] a short, thick stick or club —*vt.* **-eled** or **-elled, -el·ing** or **-el·ling** to beat with a cudgel —**cudgel one's brains** to think hard —**take up the cudgels (for)** to come to the defense (of)

CRYSTALS (A, cubic; B, monoclinic; C, triclinic)

cue[1] (kyōō) *n.* [< *q*, *Q* (? for L. *quando*, when) found in 16th-c. plays to mark actors' entrances] **1.** a bit of dialogue, action, or music that is a signal for an actor's entrance or speech, or for lights, sound effects, etc. **2.** anything serving as a signal to do something **3.** an indirect suggestion; hint [unsure of what fork to use, he took a *cue* from his host] —*vt.* **cued, cu'ing** or **cue'-ing** to give a cue to

cue[2] (kyōō) *n.* [var. of QUEUE] **1.** *same as* QUEUE **2.** a long, tapering rod used in billiards, pool, etc. to strike the cue ball **3.** a long, shovellike stick used in shuffleboard to push the disks —*vt.* **cued, cu'ing** or **cue'ing** to strike (a cue ball, etc.) with a cue

cue ball the ball, usually white, that a player strikes with his cue in billiards or pool

cuff[1] (kuf) *n.* [< ME. *cuffe*, glove] **1.** a fixed or detachable band or fold at the end of a sleeve **2.** a turned-up fold at the bottom of a trouser leg **3.** the part of a glove covering the wrist or forearm **4.** a handcuff —*vt.* to put a cuff on —☆**off the cuff** [Slang] without preparation; in an offhand manner —☆**on the cuff** [Slang] on credit

cuff[2] (kuf) *vt.* [< ? CUFF[1] (in orig. sense "glove")] to strike, esp. with the open hand; slap —*n.* a slap or blow

cuff link a pair of linked buttons or any similar small device for keeping a shirt cuff closed

cui·rass (kwi ras') *n.* [< Fr. < It. < L. (*vestis*) *coriacea*, leather (clothing) < *corium*, leather] **1.** a piece of closefitting armor for protecting the breast and back, orig. made of leather **2.** the breastplate of such armor —*vt.* to cover as with a cuirass

cui·ras·sier (kwir'ə sir') *n.* [Fr.] a cavalryman wearing a cuirass

cui·sine (kwi zēn') *n.* [Fr. < LL. *coquina*, kitchen < L. *coquere*, to COOK] **1.** style of cooking or preparing food [Italian *cuisine*] **2.** the food prepared, as at a restaurant

cuisse (kwis) *n.* [< OFr. < L. *coxa*, hip] a piece of armor to protect the thigh: also **cuish** (kwish): see illustration at ARMOR

cul-de-sac (kul'də sak', kool'-; *Fr.* küt såk') *n.*, *pl.* **cul'-de-sacs'**; *Fr.* **culs-de-sac** (küt såk') [Fr., lit., bottom of a sack] **1.** a passage or position with only one outlet; blind alley **2.** a situation from which there is no escape

-cule (kyōōl, kyool) [< Fr. or L.] *a suffix meaning* small, little [*animalcule*]

cu·lex (kyōō'leks) *n.* [L., a gnat] any of a large group of mosquitoes including many of the most common species found in N. America and Europe

cu·li·nar·y (kyōō'lə ner'ē, kul'ə-) *adj.* [< LL. < L. *culina*, kitchen] of or for the kitchen or cooking [the *culinary* art; *culinary* aids]

cull (kul) *vt.* [< OFr. < L. *colligere*: see COLLECT[2]] **1.** to pick out; select and gather [to *cull* the facts needed from an almanac] **2.** to look over in order to select or reject [to *cull* a cornfield for ripe ears] —*n.* something picked out; esp., something rejected as not being up to standard

culm[1] (kulm) *n.* [< ME. *colme* < ? OE. *col*, coal] waste material from coal screenings or washings

culm[2] (kulm) *n.* [L. *culmus*, a stem] the jointed stem of various grasses, usually hollow —*vi.* to grow or develop into a culm

cul·mi·nate (kul'mə nāt') *vi.* **-nat'ed, -nat'ing** [< ML. pp. of *culminare* < L. *culmen* (gen. *culminis*), peak: for IE. base see HILL] to reach its highest point or climax; result (*in*) [his career *culminated* in his being elected President] —*vt.* to bring to its climax —**cul'mi·nant** *adj.*

cul·mi·na·tion (kul'mə nā'shən) *n.* **1.** a culminating **2.** the highest point; climax

cu·lotte (koo lät', kyoo-) *n.* [Fr. < *cul*, posterior < L. *culus*] [often *pl.*] trousers made full in the legs to resemble a skirt, worn by women and girls

cul·pa·ble (kul'pə b'l) *adj.* [< OFr. < L. < *culpa*, fault, blame] deserving blame; blameworthy —**cul'pa·bil'i·ty, cul'pa·ble·ness** *n.* —**cul'pa·bly** *adv.*

cul·prit (kul'prit) *n.* [< Anglo-Fr. *cul.*, contr. for *culpable*, guilty + *prit*, ready (i.e., to prove guilt)] **1.** *orig.*, a person accused of a crime, as in a court **2.** a person guilty of a crime or offense; offender

cult (kult) *n.* [< L. *cultus*, care, orig. pp. of *colere*, to till: for IE. base see COLLAR] **1.** a system of religious worship or ritual [a *cult* of snake worshipers] **2.** *a)* great devotion to, or ad-

miration for, a person or thing, esp. when thought of as a fad [the *cult* of nudism] *b)* the object of such attachment [a rock singer that has become a *cult*] **3.** a group of followers; sect [a Zen *cult* that meets weekly] —**cult'ic** *adj.* —**cult'ism** *n.* —**cult'ist** *n.*

cul·ti·gen (kul'ti jən) *n.* [CULTI(VATED) + -GEN] a plant, as maize, not known in any wild form but only as cultivated

cul·ti·va·ble (kul'tə və b'l) *adj.* that can be cultivated: also **cul'ti·vat'a·ble** (-vāt'ə b'l) —**cul'ti·va·bil'i·ty** *n.*

☆**cul·ti·var** (kul'ti vär', -ver') *n.* [CULTI(VATED) VAR(IETY)] a variety of a plant that has been developed in cultivation

cul·ti·vate (kul'tə vāt') *vt.* **-vat'ed, -vat'ing** [< ML. < LL. *cultivus*, tilled < L. *cultus*: see CULT] **1.** to prepare and use (land) for growing crops; till **2.** to break up the surface soil around (plants) in order to kill weeds, save moisture, etc. **3.** to grow (plants or crops) **4.** to develop (plants) by various horticultural techniques **5.** to develop or improve by care, training, etc.; refine [to *cultivate* one's mind] **6.** to seek to become familiar with [to *cultivate* a person]

cul·ti·vat·ed (-id) *adj.* **1.** prepared and used for growing crops; tilled [*cultivated* land] **2.** grown by cultivation: opposed to WILD **3.** trained and developed; refined; cultured [a *cultivated* person]

cul·ti·va·tion (kul'tə vā'shən) *n.* **1.** the act of cultivating (in various senses) **2.** the result of improving one's mind, tastes, and manners; refinement; culture

cul·ti·va·tor (kul'tə vāt'ər) *n.* **1.** one who cultivates **2.** a tool or machine for loosening the earth and destroying weeds around growing plants

cul·tur·al (kul'chər əl) *adj.*, of culture; specif., of the training and refinement of the mind, tastes, skills, arts, etc. —**cul'tur·al·ly** *adv.*

cul·ture (kul'chər) *n.* [< L. *cultura* < *colere*: see CULT] **1.** cultivation of the soil **2.** the raising or improving of a particular plant or animal **3.** a growth of bacteria, etc. in a specially prepared nourishing substance (**culture medium**) **4.** *a)* development, improvement, or refinement of the mind, manners, taste, etc. *b)* the result of this **5.** development or improvement of physical qualities by special training or care [*body culture*] **6.** the ideas, customs, skills, arts, etc. of a given people in a given period; civilization [the *culture* of the Aztecs] —*vt.* **-tured, -tur·ing** **1.** to cultivate **2.** to grow (microorganisms) in a specially prepared medium —**cul'tur·ist** *n.*

cul·tured (-chərd) *adj.* **1.** produced by cultivation **2.** refined in speech, behavior, etc.

cultured pearl any of the pearls from oysters in tended oyster beds whose growth was started by such a method as the insertion of a bead of mother-of-pearl

culture medium a nutrient substance sterilized and prepared for the controlled growth of microorganisms

cul·tus (kul'təs) *n.* [L.] a religious cult

cul·vert (kul'vərt) *n.* [< ?] a drain or waterway passing under a road, through an embankment, etc.

CULVERT

cum (kum, koom) *prep.* [L.] with in the sense of "combined with," "plus": chiefly in hyphenated compounds [*nurse-cum-cook*]

Cu·mae (kyōō'mē) ancient Greek city in SW Italy, near Naples: known in legend for its sibyl —**Cu·mae'an** *adj.*

cum·ber (kum'bər) *vt.* [< OFr. *encombrer* < *en-* (see EN-[1]) + *combre*, obstruction] to hinder, burden, or trouble; encumber

Cum·ber·land (kum'bər lənd) [after the Duke of *Cumberland* (1721–65), Eng. general] river in S Ky. & N Tenn., flowing west into the Ohio

Cumberland Gap pass in the W Appalachians, at the juncture of the Va., Ky., & Tenn. borders

Cumberland Plateau (or **Mountains**) division of the W Appalachians, extending from southern W.Va. to northern Ala.: highest peak, 4,150 ft.

cum·ber·some (kum'bər səm) *adj.* hard to handle or deal with, as because of size, weight, or many parts; burdensome; unwieldy; clumsy —see SYN. at HEAVY —**cum'ber·some·ly** *adv.* —**cum'ber·some·ness** *n.*

---

fat, āpe, cär; ten, ēven; is, bīte; gō, hôrn, tōōl, look; oil, out; up, fur; get; joy; yet; chin; she; thin, then; zh, leisure; ŋ, ring; ə for *a* in *ago*, *e* in *agent*, *i* in *sanity*, *o* in *comply*, *u* in *focus*; ' as in *able* (ā'b'l); Fr. bål; ë, Fr. coeur; ö, Fr. feu; Fr. mon; ô, Fr. coq; ü, Fr. duc; *r*, Fr. cri; H, G. ich; kh, G. doch; ‡foreign; ☆ Americanism; < derived from. See inside front cover.

cum·brous (-brəs) *adj.* same as CUMBERSOME —**cum′brous·ly** *adv.* —**cum′brous·ness** *n.*

cum·in (kum′in) *n.* [< OFr. < L. < Gr. < Sem., as in Heb. *kammōn,* Ar. *kammūn*] 1. a small plant of the parsley family 2. its spicy fruits that look like seeds, used for flavoring pickles, soups, etc. Also sp. **cum′min**

‡**cum lau·de** (koom lou′de, kum lô′dē) [L.] with praise: phrase used to note graduation with honors from a college or university

cum·mer·bund (kum′ər bund′) *n.* [Hindi & Per. *kamarband,* loin band] a wide sash worn as a waistband, esp. with men's formal dress

Cum·mings (kum′iŋz), **E(dward) E(stlin)** 1894-1962; U.S. poet

cum·quat (kum′kwät) *n.* same as KUMQUAT

cu·mu·late (kyoom′yə lāt′) *vt., vi.* **-lat′ed, -lat′ing** [< L. pp. of *cumulare,* to heap up < *cumulus:* see CUMULUS] same as ACCUMULATE —**cu′mu·la′tion** *n.*

cu·mu·la·tive (kyoom′yə lāt′iv, -lə tiv) *adj.* [see prec.] increasing in effect, size, quantity, etc. by successive additions; accumulated *[cumulative* interest is interest added to the principal and drawing additional interest] —**cu′mu·la·tive·ly** *adv.* —**cu′mu·la·tive·ness** *n.*

cu·mu·lo·nim·bus (kyoom′yoo lō nim′bəs) *n.* a dense and very high cloud type, usually producing heavy rain

cu·mu·lus (-yə ləs) *n., pl.* **-li′** (-lī′) [L., a heap: for IE. base see CAVE] 1. a heap 2. a thick cloud type with a dark, horizontal base and upper parts resembling domes —**cu′mu·lous** *adj.*

cu·ne·ate (kyoo′nē it, -āt′) *adj.* [< L. < *cuneus,* a wedge] wedge-shaped; tapering, as some leaves: also **cu′ne·al, cu′ne·at′ed** (-āt′id), **cu′ne·at′ic** (-at′ik) —**cu′ne·ate·ly** *adv.*

cu·ne·i·form (kyoo nē′ə fôrm′, kyoo′nē ə-) *adj.* [< L. *cuneus* (see prec.) + -FORM] wedge-shaped; esp., designating the characters used in ancient Assyrian, Babylonian, and Persian inscriptions, or such inscriptions —*n.* cuneiform characters or inscriptions

GOD   SUN   MAN

CUNEIFORM CHARACTERS

cun·ner (kun′ər) *n.* [< ?] a small, brownish-blue fish used for food, found along the Atlantic coast of N. America

cun·ning (kun′iŋ) *adj.* [ME. < prp. of *cunnen,* to know: see CAN¹] 1. [Now Rare] skillful or clever 2. skillful in deception; sly; crafty 3. made or done with skill or ingenuity ☆4. pleasing or pretty in a delicate way; cute *[a cunning child]* —*n.* 1. [Now Rare] skill 2. skill in deception; slyness; craftiness —see SYN. at CLEVER and SLY —**cun′ning·ly** *adv.* —**cun′ning·ness** *n.*

cup (kup) *n.* [OE. *cuppe* < LL. *cuppa* < L. *cupa,* tub: for IE. base see COVE] 1. a small, bowl-shaped container for beverages, often with a handle 2. the bowl part of a drinking utensil 3. a cup and its contents 4. the amount a cup holds; cupful: see CUPFUL 5. anything shaped like a cup 6. an inscribed cup, as of silver, given as a prize 7. the wine chalice at Communion; also, the wine 8. one's portion, share, or allotment *[a full cup* of happiness] 9. something served in a cup *[a fruit cup* for dessert] 10. *Golf* the hole in each putting green —*vt.* **cupped, cup′ping** 1. to shape like a cup *[cup* your hands] 2. to take in or put into a cup 3. *Med.* to subject to cupping —**in one's cups** drunk —**cup′like′** *adj.*

cup·bear·er (cup′ber′ər) *n.* a person who fills and serves the wine cups, as in a king's palace

cup·board (kub′ərd) *n.* a closet or cabinet with shelves for holding cups, plates, food, etc.

☆**cup·cake** (kup′kāk′) *n.* a little cake for one person, baked in a cup-shaped mold

cu·pel (kyoo′pəl, kyoo pel′) *n.* [<Fr. < ML. *cupella,* dim. < L. *cupa:* see CUP] a small cup used in assaying gold, silver, etc. —*vt.* **-peled** or **-pelled, -pel·ing** or **-pel·ling** to assay in a cupel

cup·ful (kup′fool′) *n., pl.* **-fuls′** as much as a cup will hold: a standard measuring cup holds eight ounces

Cu·pid (kyoo′pid) [< OFr. < L. < *cupido,* desire] the Roman god of love, son of Venus: identified with the Greek god Eros —*n.* [c-] a representation of Cupid as a naked, winged cherub with bow and arrow

cu·pid·i·ty (kyoo pid′ə tē) *n.* [< Anglo-Fr. < L. < *cupere,* to desire] strong desire for wealth; greed

cup of tea [Colloq.] a favorite thing, activity, etc. *[golf isn't his cup of tea]*

CUMMERBUND

cu·po·la (kyoo′pə lə) *n.* [It. < L. dim. of *cupa:* see CUP] 1. a rounded roof or ceiling 2. a small dome or similar structure on a roof —**cu′po·laed** (-ləd) *adj.*

cup·ping (kup′iŋ) *n.* the use of a glass cup (**cupping glass**) from which the air has been removed, to draw blood to the surface of the skin: used, esp. formerly, in medicine —**cup′per** *n.*

cu·pre·ous (kyoo′prē əs) *adj.* [< L.: see COPPER¹] of, like, or containing copper

cu·pric (kyoo′prik) *adj.* [CUPR(O)- + -IC] *Chem.* of or containing copper with a valence of two

cu·pro- [< L. *cuprum:* see COPPER¹] a combining form meaning copper (and): also **cu·pri-, cupr-**

cu·pro·nick·el (kyoo′prō nik′'l) *n.* an alloy of copper and nickel, used in condenser tubes, some coins, etc.

cu·prous (kyoo′prəs) *adj.* [CUPR(O)- + -OUS] *Chem.* of or containing copper with a valence of one

cur (kur) *n.* [prob. < ON. *kurra* or MLowG. *korren,* to growl] 1. a dog of mixed breed; mongrel 2. a mean, contemptible, or cowardly person

cur. 1. currency 2. current

cur·a·ble (kyoor′ə b'l) *adj.* that can be cured —**cur′a·bil′i·ty** *n.*

Cu·ra·çao (kyoor′ə sō′, kyoor′ə sou′) largest island of the Netherlands Antilles, off the N coast of Venezuela —*n.* [c-] a liqueur flavored with orange peel

cu·ra·cy (kyoor′ə sē) *n., pl.* **-cies** the position, office, or work of a curate

cu·ra·re, cu·ra·ri (kyoo rä′rē, koo-) *n.* [< Port. or Sp. < native (Tupi) name] 1. a black, resinous substance prepared from the juices of certain S. American plants, used as an arrow poison by some Indians and in medicine to relax muscles 2. any of the plants from which this is prepared

cu·rate (kyoor′it) *n.* [< ML. < L. pp. of *curare:* see CURATOR] a clergyman who assists a vicar or rector

cur·a·tive (kyoor′ə tiv) *adj.* curing or having the power to cure —*n.* a thing that cures; remedy

cu·ra·tor (kyoo rāt′ər, kyoor′āt′ər, -ə tər) *n.* [L. < *curare,* take care of < *cura:* see CURE] a person in charge of a museum, library, etc. —**cu·ra·to·ri·al** (kyoor′ə tôr′ē əl) *adj.* —**cu·ra′tor·ship′** *n.*

curb (kurb) *n.* [< OFr. < L. *curvus:* see CURVE] 1. a chain or strap passed around a horse's lower jaw and attached to the bit, used to check the horse 2. anything that checks, holds back, or subdues *[fear of punishment is often a curb* to wrongdoing] 3. a raised margin along an edge, to strengthen or confine 4. the stone or concrete edging forming a gutter along a street 5. a market dealing in stocks and bonds not listed on the stock exchange —*vt.* 1. to hold back; keep in check; control *[try to curb* your temper] 2. to lead (a dog) to the curb to pass its waste matter 3. to provide with a curb —see SYN. at RESTRAIN

curb bit a horse's bit with a curb

curb·ing (kurb′iŋ) *n.* 1. material for a curb 2. a curb (sense 4)

curb roof same as MANSARD ROOF or GAMBREL ROOF

☆**curb service** service offered to customers who wish to stay in their cars, as at a drive-in restaurant

curb·stone (-stōn′) *n.* any of the stones, or a row of stones, making up a curb

cur·cu·li·o (kər kyoo′lē ō′) *n., pl.* **-li·os′** [L., weevil] any of a family of weevils with long snouts: some are harmful to fruit

curd (kurd) *n.* [< ME. *crud,* orig., any coagulated substance: for IE. base see CROWD¹] [often pl.] the thick, clotted part of soured milk, from which cheese is made: distinguished from whey, the watery part —*vt., vi.* to curdle —**curd′y** *adj.*

cur·dle (kur′d'l) *vt., vi.* **-dled, -dling** [CURD + -LE²] to form into curd; coagulate; congeal —**curdle one's blood** to horrify or terrify one

cure (kyoor) *n.* [OFr. < L. *cura,* care < IE. base *kois-,* be concerned] 1. a getting or bringing back to a healthy or sound condition 2. a medicine or treatment for restoring health; remedy 3. a method or course of treating a disease, ailment, etc. 4. same as CURACY 5. a process for curing meat, fish, tobacco, etc. —*vt.* cured, cur′ing 1. to restore to health or a sound condition; heal 2. to get rid of (an ailment, evil, etc.) 3. to get rid of an undesirable condition in (with *of*) *[cured* him of lying] 4. *a)* to preserve (meat, fish, etc.), as by salting or smoking *b*) to process (tobacco, leather, etc.), as by drying or aging —*vi.* **1.** to bring about a cure **2.** to undergo curing, preserving, or processing —**cure′less** *adj.* —**cur′er** *n.*

SYN.—**cure** and **heal** both imply a restoring to health or soundness, **cure** specifically suggesting the doing away with of disease, distress, evil, etc., and **heal**, the making or becoming whole of a wound, sore, etc. or, figuratively, the mending of a break in relations, agreement, etc.; **remedy** suggests the use of some corrective treatment in relieving disease, injury, distress, etc.

cu·ré (kyoo rā′) *n.* [Fr.] in France, a parish priest

cure-all (kyoor′ôl′) *n.* ☆something supposed to cure all ailments or evils; panacea

cu·ret, cu·rette (kyoo ret′) *n.* [Fr. < *curer,* to cleanse] a spoon-shaped surgical instrument for the removal of tissue from the walls of body cavities —*vt.* **-ret′-ted, -ret′ting** to clean or scrape with a curet

CURET

cu·ret·tage (kyoor′ə täzh′, kyoo-ret′ij) *n.* [Fr.: see prec.] the process of curetting

cur·few (kur′fyoo) *n.* [< OFr. *covrefeu* < *covrir,* to COVER + *feu,* fire < L. *focus,* fireplace] **1.** *a*) in the Middle Ages, the ringing of a bell every evening as a signal for people to cover fires, put out lights, and retire *b*) the bell *c*) the time at which it was rung **2.** *a*) a time in the evening set as a deadline beyond which children, etc. may not appear on the streets *b*) the regulation establishing this time

cu·ri·a (kyoor′ē ə) *n., pl.* **-ri·ae** (-ē′) [L.] **1.** in ancient Rome, *a*) any of the ten political subdivisions into which the Latin, Sabine, and Etruscan tribes were each divided *b*) the senate house at Rome **2.** a medieval law court or council held in the king's name **3.** [C-] the administrative body of the Roman Catholic Church, consisting of various departments, courts, officials, etc. under the authority of the Pope: in full, **Curia Roma·na** (rō mä′nə, -mä′-) —**cu′ri·al** *adj.*

Cu·rie (kyoo rē′, kyoor′ē; *Fr.* kü rē′), **Marie** (born *Marie Sklodowska*) 1867–1934; Pol. chemist & physicist in France: discoverer, with her husband **Pierre** (1859–1906), of polonium & radium

cu·rie (kyoor′ē, kyoo rē′) *n.* [after Marie CURIE] the unit used in measuring radioactivity

cu·ri·o (kyoor′ē ō′) *n., pl.* **-os′** [contr. of CURIOSITY] any unusual or rare article

cu·ri·os·i·ty (kyoor′ē äs′ə tē) *n., pl.* **-ties** [< OFr. < L. *curiositas* < *curiosus:* see CURIOUS] **1.** a desire to learn or know [*a baby's curiosity* is his best teacher] **2.** a desire to learn about things that do not properly concern one [*curiosity* killed the cat] **3.** anything unusual, rare, or strange [a fire engine pulled by horses is now a *curiosity*]

cu·ri·ous (kyoor′ē əs) *adj.* [OFr. < L. *curiosus,* careful, akin to *cura:* see CURE] **1.** eager to learn or know [a *curious* scholar] **2.** inquisitive; prying [too *curious* for her own good] **3.** arousing attention or interest because unusual or strange [a *curious* combination of colors] —**cu′ri·ous·ly** *adv.* —**cu′ri·ous·ness** *n.*

SYN.—**curious,** in this comparison, implies eagerness or anxiousness to find out things and may suggest a wholesome desire to be informed [*curious* about how computers are programmed]; **inquisitive** implies a habitual tendency to be curious, esp. about matters that do not concern one, and an attempt to get information by continual questioning [a gossipy, *inquisitive* neighbor]; **prying** suggests an inquisitiveness that is very rude and meddlesome and is not easily turned aside —**ANT.** incurious, uninterested, indifferent

☆**cu·ri·um** (kyoor′ē əm) *n.* [ModL., after Marie & Pierre CURIE] a radioactive chemical element made from plutonium by nuclear bombardment: symbol, Cm; at. wt., 247(?); at. no., 96

curl (kurl) *vt.* [ME. *curlen* < *crul,* curly: for IE. base see CART] **1.** to wind (esp. hair) into ringlets or coils **2.** to cause to bend around [the dampness *curled* the pages of the book] **3.** to raise the upper corner of (the lip), as in showing scorn —*vi.* **1.** to become curled **2.** to form, or move in, a spiral or curve [the fog *curled* around our feet] **3.** to play the game of curling —*n.* **1.** a ringlet of hair **2.** anything with a curled shape; coil [a *curl* of smoke from the chimney] **3.** a curling or being curled —**curl up 1.** to gather into spirals or curls; roll up **2.** to sit or lie with

the legs drawn up [I *curled up* on the sofa] —**in curl** curled —**curl′er** *n.*

cur·lew (kur′loo, -lyoo) *n., pl.* **-lews, -lew:** see PLURAL, II, D, 1 [< OFr. *corlieu,* of echoic origin] a large, brownish wading bird with long legs

curl·i·cue (kur′li kyoo′) *n.* [< CURLY + CUE²] a fancy curve, flourish, etc., as in a design or in handwriting

curl·ing (kur′lin) *n.* a game played on ice by sliding a heavy disk (**curling stone**) toward a target circle

curling iron (or **irons**) a metal rod heated for curling or waving hair rolled around it

curl·y (kur′lē) *adj.* **curl′i·er, curl′i·est 1.** curling or tending to curl **2.** having curls **3.** having a wavy grain, as certain woods —**curl′i·ness** *n.*

CURLEW
(length to 19 in.; wingspread to 33 in.)

cur·mudg·eon (kər muj′ən) *n.* [< ?] a surly, ill-mannered person; cantankerous fellow

cur·rant (kur′ənt) *n.* [< Anglo-Fr. (*raisins de*) *Corauntz,* lit., (raisins of) Corinth] **1.** a small, seedless raisin from the Mediterranean region **2.** *a*) the sour and red, white, or black berry of several species of hardy shrubs, used for jellies and jams *b*) a shrub bearing this fruit

cur·ren·cy (kur′ən sē) *n., pl.* **-cies** [< L. *currens:* see CURRENT] **1.** a continual passing from hand to hand or person to person; circulation ☆**2.** the money in circulation in any country; often, specif., paper money **3.** common acceptance or use; prevalence [slang words usually lose *currency* quickly]

cur·rent (kur′ənt) *adj.* [< OFr. < L. *currere,* to run < IE. base *kers-,* to run] **1.** *a*) now in progress; now going on [his *current* job] *b*) at the present time; contemporary [*current* fashions] *c*) of most recent date [the *current* edition] **2.** passing from person to person; circulating [*current* rumors] **3.** commonly used or accepted; prevalent [a *current* term] —*n.* **1.** a flow of water or air in a definite direction; specif., such a flow within a larger body of water or mass of air **2.** a general tendency or drift, as of opinion; course **3.** *Elec.* the flow or rate of flow of electric charge in a conductor —see **SYN.** at PREVAILING and TENDENCY —**cur′rent·ly** *adv.*

cur·ri·cle (kur′i k'l) *n.* [< L.: see CURRICULUM] a two-wheeled carriage drawn by two horses abreast

cur·ric·u·lum (kə rik′yə ləm) *n., pl.* **-u·la** (-lə), **-u·lums** [L., a course, race < *currere:* see CURRENT] **1.** a series of studies required, as for graduation **2.** all of the courses offered in a school, college, etc., or in a particular subject —**cur·ric′u·lar** *adj.*

cur·rish (kur′ish) *adj.* like a cur; mean; ill-bred —**cur′rish·ly** *adv.*

cur·ry¹ (kur′ē) *vt.* **-ried, -ry·ing** [< OFr. *correier,* to put in order] **1.** to rub down and clean the coat of (a horse, etc.) with a currycomb or brush **2.** to prepare (tanned leather) by soaking, cleaning, beating, etc. —**curry favor** to try to win favor by flattery, fawning, etc. —**cur′ri·er** *n.*

cur·ry² (kur′ē) *n., pl.* **-ries** [Tamil *kari,* sauce] **1.** *same as* CURRY POWDER **2.** a sauce made with curry powder **3.** a kind of stew prepared with curry —*vt.* **-ried, -ry·ing** to prepare with curry powder

cur·ry·comb (kur′ē kōm′) *n.* a comb with rows of teeth or ridges, to curry a horse —*vt.* to curry with this

curry powder a seasoning prepared from turmeric and various spices and herbs

curse (kurs) *n.* [Late OE. *curs, n., cursian, v.*] **1.** a calling on God or the gods to send evil or injury to some person or thing **2.** a word or words used in swearing at someone; profane oath **3.** a thing that has been cursed **4.** evil or injury that seems to come in answer to a curse **5.** any cause of evil or injury [not sure whether atomic power is a blessing or a *curse*] —*vt.* **cursed** or **curst, curs′ing 1.** to call evil or injury down on; damn **2.** to swear at; use profane language against **3.** to bring evil or injury on; afflict —*vi.* to utter curses; swear; blaspheme —**be cursed with** to suffer from —**curs′er** *n.*

CURRYCOMB

curs·ed (kur′sid, kurst) *adj.* **1.** under a curse **2.** deserving to be cursed; specif., *a)* evil; wicked *b)* hateful —**curs′ed·ly** *adv.* —**curs′ed·ness** *n.*

cur·sive (kur′siv) *adj.* [ML. *cursivus* < L. pp. of *currere*: see CURRENT] designating or of writing in which the letters are joined in each word —*n.* **1.** a cursive character or script **2.** *Printing* a typeface that looks like handwriting —**cur′sive·ly** *adv.* —**cur′sive·ness** *n.*

cur·so·ri·al (kər sôr′ē əl) *adj.* [see CURSORY & -AL] having legs adapted for running [the road runner is a *cursorial* bird]

cur·so·ry (kur′sər ē) *adj.* [< L. < *cursor*, runner < pp. of *currere*: see CURRENT] done rapidly with little attention to detail; hurried [a *cursory* inspection] —see SYN. at SUPERFICIAL —**cur′so·ri·ly** *adv.* —**cur′so·ri·ness** *n.*

curt (kurt) *adj.* [L. *curtus*: for IE. base see CARNAGE] **1.** orig., short or shortened **2.** so short or abrupt as to seem rude; brusque [a *curt* reply] —see SYN. at BLUNT —**curt′ly** *adv.* —**curt′ness** *n.*

cur·tail (kər tāl′) *vt.* [< OFr. *curtald*, shortened < L. *curtus*, short: see CURT] to cut short; reduce [to *curtail* expenses] —see SYN. at SHORTEN —**cur·tail′er** *n.* —**cur·tail′ment** *n.*

cur·tain (kur′t'n) *n.* [< OFr. < LL. *cortina*, circle of a theater < L. *cohors*, a COURT] **1.** a piece of cloth, etc. (often one that can be drawn up or sideways) hung, as at a window, to decorate, cover, or conceal **2.** anything that covers, conceals, or shuts off [a *curtain* of fog] **3.** *Theater a)* the drape at the front of the stage, which is drawn up or aside to reveal the stage *b)* the opening or the closing of the curtain for a play, act, or scene ☆**4.** [*pl.*] [Slang] death; the end —*vt.* to provide or shut off as with a curtain —**draw (or drop) the curtain** on **1.** to end **2.** to conceal —**lift (or raise) the curtain on 1.** to begin **2.** to reveal

curtain call 1. a call, usually by continued applause, for the performers to return to the stage **2.** such a return, acknowledging the applause

curtain raiser 1. a short play or skit presented before a longer production **2.** any brief preliminary event

curtain wall an independently supported outer wall bearing only its own weight

Cur·tis (kur′tis) [< ONormFr. *curteis*, courteous] a masculine name

curt·sey (kurt′sē) *n., pl.* **-seys,** *vi.* **-seyed, -sey·ing** *same as* CURTSY

curt·sy (kurt′sē) *n., pl.* **-sies** [var. of COURTESY] a gesture of greeting, respect, etc. made, esp. formerly, by girls and women and characterized by a bending of the knees and a slight lowering of the body —*vi.* **-sied, -sy·ing** to make a curtsy

cur·va·ceous (kər vā′shəs) *adj.* [CURV(E) + -ACEOUS] [Colloq.] having a full, shapely figure: said of a woman

cur·va·ture (kur′və chər) *n.* **1.** a curving or being curved **2.** a curve; curved part of anything **3.** *Geom.* the rate of deviation of a curve from a straight line tangent to it **4.** *Med.* an abnormal curving of a part [*curvature* of the spine]

CURTSY

curve (kurv) *n.* [L. *curvus*, bent: for IE. base see CIRCUS] **1.** a line having no straight part; bend with no angles, as an arc, parabola, etc. **2.** a thing or part with the shape of a curve **3.** a curving, or the extent of this **4.** a curved line, as on a graph, indicating variations, as in prices ☆**5.** *Baseball* a pitched ball thrown so that it curves before crossing the plate —*vt., vi.* **curved, curv′ing 1.** to form a curve by bending [the trail *curves* to the left] **2.** to move in a curve

cur·vet (kur′vit; *for v., usually* kər vet′) *n.* [< It. dim. < *corvo* < L. *curvus*: see CURVE] an upward leap by a horse, in which it raises its hind legs just before its forelegs come down again —*vi.* **-vet′ted** *or* **-vet′ed, -vet′ting** *or* **-vet′ing 1.** to make a curvet **2.** to leap; frolic —*vt.* to cause to curvet

cur·vi·lin·e·ar (kur′və lin′ē ər) *adj.* consisting of or enclosed by a curved line or lines: also **cur′vi·lin′e·al**

curv·y (kur′vē) *adj.* **curv′i·er, curv′i·est 1.** having curves or a curve **2.** [Colloq.] curvaceous

cu·sec (kyoo′sek′) *n.* a unit for measuring volume of flow, equal to one cubic foot per second

cush·ion (koosh′ən) *n.* [< OFr. *coissin* < ML. *coxinum* (infl. by L. *coxa*, hip) < L. *culcita*] **1.** a pillow or pad for sitting or kneeling on, or reclining against **2.** a thing like this in shape or use **3.** anything serving to absorb shock, as air or steam in

some machines, the elastic inner rim of a billiard table, or a soft, padded insole **4.** anything that relieves distress, provides comfort, etc. —*vt.* **1.** to provide with a cushion **2.** to seat or set on a cushion **3.** to absorb (shock or noise) **4.** to act as a cushion as in protecting from injury, relieving distress, etc. [grass *cushioned* his fall]

Cush·it·ic (kush it′ik, koosh-) *adj.* [< *Cush*, son of HAM] designating or of a group of languages spoken in Ethiopia and eastern Africa —*n.* this group of languages

cush·y (koosh′ē) *adj.* **cush′i·er, cush′i·est** [orig. Brit. army slang < Hindi *khush*, pleasant < Per.] [Slang] easy; comfortable [a *cushy* job] —**cush′i·ly** *adv.* —**cush′i·ness** *n.*

cusp (kusp) *n.* [L. *cuspis*, a point] **1.** a pointed end; peak **2.** any of the high points on the chewing surface of a tooth **3.** any triangular fold of a heart valve **4.** either horn of a crescent, as of the moon **5.** *Geom.* a point formed where two curves that are tangent to each other meet

cus·pid (kus′pid) *n.* a canine tooth: see CANINE

cus·pi·date (kus′pə dāt′) *adj.* **1.** having a cusp or cusps **2.** having a short, abrupt point, as some leaves

☆**cus·pi·dor** (kus′pə dôr′) *n.* [< Port. < *cuspir*, to spit < L. < *com-*, very much + *spuere*, to spit out] *same as* SPITTOON

cuss (kus) *n.* [< CURSE] [Colloq.] **1.** a curse ☆**2.** a person or animal regarded as queer or annoying —*vt., vi.* [Colloq.] to curse

cuss·ed (kus′id) *adj.* [Colloq.] **1.** cursed **2.** perverse; stubborn —**cuss′ed·ly** *adv.* —**cuss′ed·ness** *n.*

cus·tard (kus′tərd) *n.* [< L. *crusta*, CRUST] **1.** a mixture of eggs, milk, flavoring, and, often, sugar, either boiled or baked **2.** a similar mixture frozen like ice cream: in full, **frozen custard**

cus·tard-ap·ple (-ap′'l) *n.* **1.** any of several tropical trees with edible, heart-shaped fruits **2.** the fruit

Cus·ter (kus′tər), **George Armstrong** 1839–76; U.S. army officer: killed in a battle with Sioux Indians

cus·to·di·an (kəs tō′dē ən) *n.* **1.** one who has the custody or care of something; keeper [the *custodian* of the club's records] **2.** one whose work is to take care of a building; janitor —**cus·to′di·an·ship′** *n.*

cus·to·dy (kus′tə dē) *n., pl.* **-dies** [< L. < *custos*, a guard] a guarding or keeping safe; care [tax records in the *custody* of the county auditor; a child in the *custody* of a guardian] —**in custody** in the keeping of the police; under arrest —**take into custody** to arrest —**cus·to′di·al** (-tō′dē əl) *adj.*

cus·tom (kus′təm) *n.* [< OFr. < L. *consuetudo* < *com-*, very much + *suere*, to be accustomed] **1.** a usual practice or habitual way of behaving; habit [it is his *custom* to have tea after dinner] **2.** *a)* a social practice carried on by tradition [the *custom* of eating turkey on Thanksgiving] *b)* such practices taken together **3.** [*pl.*] *a)* duties or taxes imposed by a government on imported goods *b)* [*with sing. v.*] the agency in charge of collecting these duties **4.** the regular business given to a store, etc. by its customers [that baker has had our family's *custom* for years] **5.** *Law* a usage that by common consent and long-established practice has taken on the force of law —*adj.* **1.** made or done to order or as if to order [*custom* shoes] **2.** making things to order, or dealing in such things [a *custom* tailor] —see SYN. at HABIT

cus·tom·ar·y (kus′tə mer′ē) *adj.* **1.** in keeping with custom, or usage; usual [it is *customary* to tip waiters] **2.** *Law* holding or held by custom —see SYN. at USUAL —**cus′tom·ar′i·ly** *adv.* —**cus′tom·ar′i·ness** *n.*

☆**cus·tom-built** (kus′təm bilt′) *adj.* built to order, according to the customer's specifications

cus·tom·er (kus′tə mər) *n.* [see CUSTOM] **1.** a person who buys, esp. one who buys at a particular store, etc. regularly **2.** [Colloq.] any person with whom one has dealings [a rough *customer*]

cus·tom·house (kus′təm hous′) *n.* a building or office where customs or duties are paid, and ships cleared for entering or leaving: also **cus′toms·house′**

☆**cus·tom·ize** (-īz′) *vt., vi.* **-ized′, -iz′ing** [CUSTOM + -IZE] to make or build according to individual specifications —**cus′tom·iz′er** *n.*

☆**cus·tom-made** (-mād′) *adj.* made to order, according to the customer's specifications

cut (kut) *vt.* **cut, cut′ting** [ME. *cutten* < a Scand. base] **1.** to make an opening in as with a sharp-edged instrument; pierce, gash, wound, etc. [he *cut* his chin while shaving] **2.** to strike, constrict, etc. in a piercing or painful way [the shoe is *cutting* her in the instep] **3.** to hurt the feelings of [the insult *cut* him deeply] **4.** to grow (a new tooth making its way through the gum) **5.** to divide into parts with a sharp-edged instrument;

sever [will you *cut* the cake?] **6.** to carve (meat) **7.** to cause to fall by severing; fell; hew **8.** to mow or reap **9.** to pass through or across; intersect [the path *cuts* the meadow] **10.** to divide (a pack of cards) at random before dealing **11.** to stop photographing (a motion-picture scene) **12.** to reduce; lessen; curtail [to *cut* salaries] **13.** to make shorter by trimming (hair, branches, etc.) ☆**14.** to dilute (alcohol, etc.) **15.** to dissolve the fat globules of [lye *cuts* grease] **16.** to make or do by or as by cutting; specif., *a)* to make (an opening, clearing, channel, etc.), as by drilling or excavating *b)* to type or otherwise mark (a stencil) for mimeographing *c)* to cut cloth so as to form the parts for (a garment) *d)* to perform [to *cut* a caper] *e)* to hit, drive, or throw (a ball) so that it spins or glances off *f)* to cause (a wheel) to turn sharply ☆*g)* to edit (movie film) as by deleting scenes ☆*h)* to make a recording of (a speech, music, etc.) on (a phonograph record) **17.** [Colloq.] to pretend not to see or know (a person); snub **18.** [Colloq.] to stay away from (a school class, etc.) without being excused ☆**19.** [Slang] to stop; discontinue —*vi.* **1.** to do the work of a sharp-edged instrument; pierce, sever, gash, etc. **2.** to work as a cutter **3.** to take cutting [pine *cuts* easily] **4.** to use an instrument that cuts **5.** to cause pain by sharp, piercing strokes [the wind *cut* through his coat] **6.** to swing a bat, etc. (at a ball) **7.** to move swiftly **8.** to make a sudden shift to another scene, as in a movie —*adj.* **1.** that has or have been cut [cut flowers] **2.** made or formed by cutting **3.** reduced; lessened [cut prices] —*n.* **1.** a cutting or being cut **2.** a stroke or blow with a sharp-edged instrument, whip, etc. **3.** a stroke taken at a ball, esp. one that makes it spin **4.** an opening, wound, etc. made by a sharp-edged instrument **5.** the leaving out of a part **6.** a piece or part cut off or out, as from a meat animal ☆**7.** *a)* the amount cut, as of timber *b)* a reduction; decrease [a *cut* in pay] **8.** the shortest way across: usually **short cut 9.** a passage or channel cut out or worn away **10.** the style in which a thing is cut; fashion [a stylish *cut*] **11.** an act, remark, etc. that hurts one's feelings **12.** a block or plate engraved for printing, or the impression made from it **13.** [Colloq.] the act of snubbing or ignoring ☆**14.** [Colloq.] an unauthorized absence from school, etc. ☆**15.** [Slang] a share, as of profits or loot —**a cut above** [Colloq.] somewhat better than —**cut across** to take a shorter course by going straight across —**cut a figure** to attract attention or make a (certain kind of) impression —**cut and dried 1.** arranged beforehand; routine **2.** lifeless; dull; boring —**cut back 1.** to make shorter by cutting off the end **2.** to reduce or discontinue (production, etc.) ☆**3.** to go back to earlier narrative events, as in a novel ☆**4.** to change direction suddenly, as a runner in football —**cut dead** [Colloq.] to snub completely —**cut down 1.** to make fall by cutting **2.** to kill **3.** to reduce; lessen —**cut in 1.** to move in suddenly, as into a small opening in a lane of traffic **2.** to interrupt ☆**3.** to interrupt a couple dancing in order to dance with one of them **4.** to make a connection, as in an electrical circuit **5.** to give a share to —**cut it fine** [Colloq.] to make exact calculations or distinctions —**cut it out** [Colloq.] to stop what one is doing —**cut loose** ☆[Colloq.] to act without self-control —☆**cut no ice** [Colloq.] to make no impression —**cut off 1.** to separate from other parts by cutting; sever **2.** to stop abruptly **3.** to shut off **4.** to interrupt **5.** to intercept **6.** to disinherit —**cut one's teeth on** to learn or use at an early age —**cut out 1.** to remove by cutting **2.** to remove; omit **3.** to eliminate and take the place of (a rival) **4.** to make or form as by cutting ☆**5.** [Colloq.] to discontinue; stop **6.** [Slang] to leave abruptly —**cut out for** fitted for; suited for —**cut short** to stop abruptly before the end —**cut up 1.** to cut into pieces **2.** to inflict cuts on **3.** [Colloq.] *a)* to criticize harshly *b)* to cause to be dejected or distressed ☆**4.** [Slang] to clown, joke, etc. to attract attention

cu·ta·ne·ous (kyōo tā′nē əs) *adj.* [< ML. < L. *cutis:* see CUTICLE] of, on, or affecting the skin

cut·a·way (kut′ə wā′) *n.* a man's formal coat for daytime wear, with the front of the skirt cut so as to curve back to the tails: also **cutaway coat** —*adj.* having outer parts cut away so as to show the inside [a *cutaway* diagram or model]

cut·back (kut′bak′) *n.* a cutting back; specif., a reduction, as of production, personnel, etc.

☆**cute** (kyōot) *adj.* **cut′er, cut′est** [< ACUTE] [Colloq.] **1.** clever; sharp; shrewd [a *cute* trick] **2.** pretty or pleasing, esp.

in a dainty way **3.** straining for effect; artificial —**cute′ly** *adv.* —**cute′ness** *n.*

cut glass glass, esp. flint glass, shaped or ornamented by grinding and polishing —**cut′-glass′** *adj.*

cut·i·cle (kyōōt′i k'l) *n.* [L. *cuticula*, skin, dim. < *cutis*, skin: for IE. base see HIDE] **1.** the outer layer of skin; epidermis **2.** hardened skin at the base and sides of a fingernail or toenail **3.** *Zool.* the tough, nonliving outer structure secreted by the epidermis in many invertebrates, as insects

☆**cu·tie** (kyōōt′ē) *n.* [CUT(E) + -IE] [Slang] **1.** an attractive girl **2.** a shrewd or clever person, act, etc.

cu·tin·i·za·tion (kyōōt′'n ə zā′shən) *n.* [< L. *cutis*, skin] a process in which the outermost plant cells become thickened and covered with a varnishlike material (**cutin**), making them waterproof —**cu′tin·ize′** (-īz′) *vi., vt.* **-ized′, -iz′ing**

cu·tis (kyōōt′is) *n.* [L.: see CUTICLE] **1.** the vertebrate skin, including both the dermis and the epidermis **2.** the dermis only

cut·lass, cut·las (kut′ləs) *n.* [< Fr. < It. < L. < *culter*, a knife < IE. base *skel-*, to cut] a short, thick, curved sword with a single cutting edge, formerly used esp. by sailors

cut·ler (kut′lər) *n.* [< Anglo-Fr. < OFr. < ML. < L. < *culter*: see CUTLASS] a person who makes, sells, or repairs knives and other cutting tools

cut·ler·y (kut′lər ē) *n.* **1.** the work or business of a cutler **2.** cutting instruments, such as knives and scissors; often, specif., such implements used in preparing and eating food

cut·let (kut′lit) *n.* [< Fr. *côtelette* < OFr. dim. of *coste*, a rib < L. *costa*] **1.** a small slice of meat from the ribs or leg, often breaded and fried, etc. **2.** a small, flat cake of chopped meat or fish

CUTLASS

cut·off (kut′ôf′) *n.* **1.** the act of cutting off; esp., the limit set for a process, activity, etc. **2.** a road or passage that is a short cut **3.** the act of stopping steam, etc. from entering the cylinder of an engine **4.** any device for cutting off the flow of a fluid, a connection, etc. —*adj.* of an arbitrary limit [*cutoff* date]

cut·out (-out′) *n.* **1.** a device for breaking or closing an electric circuit **2.** a device for letting the exhaust gases of an internal-combustion engine pass directly into the air instead of through a muffler **3.** a design to be cut out

☆**cut·o·ver** (-ō′vər) *adj.* cleared of trees [*cutover* land]

cut·purse (-purs′) *n.* **1.** orig., a thief who cut purses from belts **2.** a pickpocket

☆**cut-rate** (-rāt′) *adj.* selling or on sale at a lower price [a *cut-rate* drugstore]

cut·ter (kut′ər) *n.* **1.** a device for cutting **2.** a person whose work is cutting, as the parts for a garment **3.** a small, swift ship or boat; specif., *a)* a small, armed, engine-powered ship, used by the Coast Guard: also **Coast Guard cutter** *b)* a single-masted sailboat with two headsails ☆**4.** a small, light sleigh, usually drawn by one horse

cut·throat (kut′thrōt′) *n.* a murderer —*adj.* **1.** murderous **2.** merciless; ruthless

cut·ting (kut′iŋ) *n.* **1.** the act of one that cuts **2.** a piece cut off **3.** [Brit.] a newspaper clipping **4.** a shoot cut away from a plant for rooting or grafting —*adj.* **1.** that cuts; sharp **2.** chilling or piercing [a *cutting* wind] **3.** wounding the feelings; sarcastic [a *cutting* remark] —**cut′ting·ly** *adv.*

cut·tle·bone (kut′'l bōn′) *n.* the internal shell of cuttlefish, used as food for caged birds and, when powdered, as a polishing agent

cut·tle·fish (-fish′) *n., pl.* **-fish′, -fish′es:** see FISH [OE. *cudele*] a squidlike sea mollusk with ten sucker-bearing arms and a hard internal shell: when in danger, some cuttlefish eject an inky fluid: also **cuttle**

☆**cut-up** (kut′up′) *n.* [Colloq.] a person who clowns, plays practical jokes, etc. to attract attention

cut·wa·ter (-wôt′ər, -wät′ər) *n.* the fore part of a ship's prow

cut·worm (-wurm′) *n.* any of a number of caterpillars that feed on young plants of cabbage, corn, etc., cutting them off at ground level

CUTTLEFISH
(to 18 in. long)

Cu·vier (kü vyā′; *E.* kōō′vē ā′), Baron **Georges** (**Léopold Chrétien Frédéric Dagobert**) (zhôrzh) 1769–1832; Fr. naturalist

Cuy·a·ho·ga Falls (kī′ə hō′gə, -hô′-) [< Iroquois name] city in NE Ohio: suburb of Akron: pop. 50,000

Cuz·co (kōōs′kō) city in S Peru: capital of the former Inca empire: pop. 93,000

CWO Chief Warrant Officer

C.W.O., c.w.o. cash with order

cwt. hundredweight

-cy (sē, si) [< OFr. *-cie*, L. *-cia*, Gr. *-kia*] *a suffix meaning:* 1. quality, condition, state, or fact of being [*hesitancy*] 2. position, rank, or office of [*captaincy*]

cy·a·nate (sī′ə nāt′) *n.* a salt of cyanic acid

cy·an·ic (sī an′ik) *adj.* 1. of or containing cyanogen 2. blue

cyanic acid a colorless, poisonous acid, HOCN

cy·a·nide (sī′ə nīd′, -nid) *n.* a compound containing the cyanogen radical, –CN; esp., potassium cyanide, KCN, or sodium cyanide, NaCN, highly poisonous compounds with many industrial uses —*vt.* **-nid′ed, -nid′ing** to treat with cyanide

cy·an·o·gen (sī an′ə jən) *n.* [< Gr. *kyanos*, blue + -GEN] 1. a colorless, poisonous, flammable gas, C$_2$N$_2$ 2. the univalent radical –CN, in cyanides

cy·a·no·sis (sī′ə nō′sis) *n.* [ModL. < Gr. < *kyanos*, blue] a bluish coloration of the skin caused by lack of oxygen in the blood —**cy·a·not′ic** (-nät′ik) *adj.*

Cyb·e·le (sib′ə lē′) a nature goddess of ancient Asia Minor: identified with the Greek goddess Rhea

☆**cy·ber·na·tion** (sī′bər nā′shən) *n.* [CYBERN(ETICS) + -ATION] the use of computers in connection with automated equipment —**cy′ber·nate′** *vt.* **-nat′ed, -nat′ing**

☆**cy·ber·net·ics** (sī′bər net′iks) *n.pl.* [*with sing. v.*] [< Gr. *kybernētēs*, helmsman + -ICS] the comparative study of the operations of complex electronic computers and the human nervous system —**cy′ber·net′ic** *adj.*

cyc. 1. cyclopedia 2. cyclopedic

cy·cad (sī′kad) *n.* [ModL. *Cycas* < Gr. *kykas*, erroneous pl. of *koïx*, a palm] a tropical shrub or tree resembling a thick-stemmed palm, with a crown of leathery, fernlike leaves

Cyc·la·des (sik′lə dēz′) group of Greek islands in the S Aegean: 995 sq. mi.

cy·cla·mate (sī′klə māt′, sik′lə-) *n.* a complex organic compound with an extremely sweet taste

cyc·la·men (sī′klə mən, sik′lə-) *n., pl.* **-mens** [< L. < Gr. *kyklaminos*] a plant of the primrose family, having heart-shaped leaves and white, pink, or red flowers with twisted petals

cy·cle (sī′k'l) *n.* [< LL. *cyclus* < Gr. *kyklos*, a circle: for IE. base see COLLAR] 1. *a)* a complete set or series of events or changes that happen over and over again in the same order [the life *cycle* of the frog] *b)* the time it takes for one complete set to take place [the yearly *cycle* of the seasons] 2. a very long period of time; an age 3. all the traditional or legendary poems, songs, etc. connected with a hero or an event [the Charlemagne *cycle*] 4. a series of poems or songs on the same theme 5. a bicycle, tricycle, or motorcycle 6. *Elec.* one complete period of the reversal of an alternating current from positive to negative and back again —*vi.* **-cled, -cling** 1. to occur in cycles; pass through a cycle 2. to ride a bicycle, tricycle, or motorcycle

cy·clic (sī′klik, sik′lik) *adj.* 1. of, or having the nature of, a cycle; moving or occurring in cycles 2. *Chem.* arranged in a ring or closed-chain structure: said of atoms Also **cy′cli·cal** —**cy′cli·cal·ly** *adv.*

cy·clist (sī′klist) *n.* a person who rides a bicycle, motorcycle, etc.

cy·clo- [< Gr. *kyklos*, a circle: see CYCLE] *a combining form meaning* of a circle or wheel, circular: also, before a vowel, **cycl-**

cy·cloid (sī′kloid) *n.* [< Gr. *kyklos* (see CYCLE) + *eidos*, form] *Geom.* a curve traced by any point on the circumference, or on a radius, of a circle which rolls through one complete revolution along a straight line in a single plane —*adj.* 1. circular: also **cy·cloi′dal** (sī kloi′d'l) 2. *same as* CYCLOTHYMIC

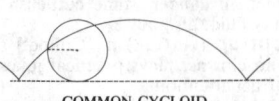

COMMON CYCLOID

cy·clom·e·ter (sī kläm′ə tər) *n.* [CYCLO- + -METER] an instrument that records the revolutions of a wheel, for measuring distance traveled

cy·clone (sī′klōn) *n.* [< Gr. *kykloein*, to whirl < *kyklos:* see CYCLE] 1. loosely, a violent, whirling windstorm; tornado or hurricane 2. *Meteorol.* a storm with strong winds rotating about a moving center of low atmospheric pressure —**cy·clon·ic** (sī klän′ik) *adj.* —**cy·clon′i·cal·ly** *adv.*

☆**cyclone cellar** a deep cellar for shelter during a cyclone or heavy windstorm

Cy·clo·pe·an (sī′klə pē′ən) *adj.* 1. of the Cyclopes 2. [c-] huge; gigantic; enormous

cy·clo·pe·di·a, cy·clo·pae·di·a (sī′klə pē′dē ə) *n. same as* ENCYCLOPEDIA —**cy′clo·pe′dic, cy′clo·pae′dic** *adj.* —**cy′clo·pe′dist, cy′clo·pae′dist** *n.*

Cy·clops (sī′kläps) *n., pl.* **Cy·clo·pes** (sī klō′pēz) [L. < Gr. < *kyklos*, a circle + *ōps*, an eye] *Gr. Myth.* any of a race of giants who had only one eye, centered in the forehead

cy·clo·ra·ma (sī′klə ram′ə) *n.* [CYCLO- + Gr. *horama*, sight] 1. a series of large pictures, as of a landscape, put on the wall of a circular room so as to suggest natural perspective to a viewer 2. a large, curved curtain or screen used as a background for stage sets —**cy′clo·ram′ic** *adj.*

cy·clo·sis (sī klō′sis) *n.* [ModL. < Gr. < *kyklos:* see CYCLE] regular circulation of protoplasm in certain cells

cy·clo·stome (sī′klə stōm′) *n.* [CYCLO- + -STOME] any of a group of eellike parasitic fishes with a circular, sucking mouth and no jaws, as the lamprey —**cy·clos′to·mate** (sī kläs′tə māt′) *adj.*

cy·clo·thy·mic (sī′klə thī′mik) *adj.* [ModL. < CYCLO- + Gr. *thymos*, spirit + -IC] of or having an emotional condition in which high periods of elation are followed by low periods of depression —**cy′clo·thy′mi·a** (-mē ə) *n.*

☆**cy·clo·tron** (sī′klə trän′) *n.* [CYCLO- + (ELEC)TRON] an apparatus for giving high energy to particles, usually protons, deuterons, and helium ions, so as to produce nuclear changes or radioactivity in a target element

cyg·net (sig′nət) *n.* [dim. < Fr. *cygne*, swan < VL. < Gr. *kyknos*, swan] a young swan

Cyg·nus (sig′nəs) [L. < *cygnus*, a swan < Gr. *kyknos*] a N constellation, the Swan, in the Milky Way

cyl. 1. cylinder 2. cylindrical

cyl·in·der (sil′ən dər) *n.* [< Fr. < L. < Gr. < *kylindein*, to roll < IE. base (*s*)*kel*-, to bend] 1. *Geom.* a solid figure described by the edge of a rectangle rotated around the parallel edge as axis: the ends of a cylinder are parallel and equal circles 2. anything, hollow or solid, with the shape of a cylinder; specif., *a)* the turning part of a revolver, containing chambers for cartridges *b)* the chamber in which the piston of an engine moves up and down *c)* the barrel of a pump

cylinder head the closed end, usually detachable, of a cylinder in an internal-combustion engine

CYLINDER

cy·lin·dri·cal (sə lin′dri k'l) *adj.* 1. having the shape of a cylinder 2. of a cylinder Also **cy·lin′dric** —**cy·lin′dri·cal·i·ty** (-kal′ə tē) *n.* —**cy·lin′dri·cal·ly** *adv.*

Cym. Cymric

cym·bal (sim′b'l) *n.* [< OFr. & OE. < L. < Gr. < *kymbē*, hollow of a vessel: for IE. base see COOP] a circular, slightly concave brass plate used as a percussion instrument: it is struck with a drumstick, brush, etc. or used in pairs which are struck together to produce a crashing, ringing sound —**cym′bal·ist** *n.*

CYMBALS

cym·bid·i·um (sim bid′ē əm) *n., pl.* **-i·ums, -i·a** (-ə) [ModL. < L. *cymba*, a boat (< Gr. *kymbē:* see CYMBAL) + ModL. *-idium*, dim. suffix] any of various tropical Asiatic orchids with sprays of white, pink, yellow, or maroon flowers

cyme (sīm) *n.* [< L. < Gr. *kyma*, swelling < *kyein*, to be pregnant: for IE. base see CAVE] a flat-topped flower cluster in which the central flower blooms first, followed by the outer ones —**cy·mose** (sī′mōs, sī mōs′) *adj.*

Cym·ric (kim′rik; *occas.* sim′-) *adj.* [< W. < *Cymru*, Wales] 1. of the Celtic people of Wales 2. of their language —*n.* Brythonic: see CELTIC

Cym·ry (-rē) *n.pl.* the Cymric Celts; the Welsh

cyn·ic (sin′ik) *n.* [see CYNICAL] 1. [C-] a member of a school of ancient Greek philosophers who held virtue to be the only good, and stressed independence from worldly needs and pleasures: they became critical of the social values of comfort, pleasure, and wealth **2.** a cynical person —*adj.* **1.** [C-] of or like the Cynics or their doctrines **2.** *same as* CYNICAL

cyn·i·cal (sin′i k′l) *adj.* [< L. < Gr. *kynikos,* canine < *kyōn,* dog: for IE. base see CANINE] **1.** doubting the sincerity of people's motives and actions, or the value of living **2.** sarcastic, sneering, etc. **3.** [C-] *same as* CYNIC —**cyn′i·cal·ly** *adv.* —**cyn′i·cal·ness** *n.*

cyn·i·cism (sin′ə siz′m) *n.* **1.** [C-] the philosophy of the Cynics **2.** the attitude or beliefs of a cynical person **3.** a cynical remark, idea, or action

cy·no·sure (sī′nə shoor′, sin′ə-) [L. < Gr. *kynosoura,* dog's tail < *kyōn* (see CYNICAL) + *oura,* a tail] [C-] *an old name for:* **1.** URSA MINOR **2.** NORTH STAR —*n.* any person or thing that is a center of attention or interest

Cyn·thi·a (sin′thē ə) [L. < Gr. *Kynthia,* epithet of Artemis] **1.** a feminine name **2.** Artemis, goddess of the moon **3.** the moon personified

CYO, C.Y.O. Catholic Youth Organization

cy·pher (sī′fər) *n., vt., vi.* Brit. var. of CIPHER

cy·press (sī′prəs) *n.* [< OFr. < L. *cupressus* < Gr. *kyparissos*] **1.** any of a group of cone-bearing evergreens with scalelike leaves, native to N. America, Europe, and Asia **2.** any of a number of related trees **3.** the wood of any of these **4.** cypress branches used as a symbol of mourning

cyp·ri·noid (sip′rə noid′) *adj.* [< Gr. *kyprinos,* carp + -OID] of or like the fishes of the carp family —*n.* any of a family of freshwater fishes, including the carps, minnows, dace, etc. Also **cyp′ri·nid** (-nid)

cyp·ri·pe·di·um (sip′rə pē′dē əm) *n., pl.* **-di·ums, -di·a** (-ə) [ModL. < Gr. *Kypris,* Venus + *podion,* slipper] *same as* LADY-SLIPPER

CYPRESS
(tree, branch & cones)

Cy·prus (sī′prəs) country on an island at the E end of the Mediterranean: a member of the Commonwealth: 3,572 sq. mi.; pop. 630,000; cap. Nicosia —**Cyp·ri·ot** (sip′rē ət) *adj., n.*

Cyr·e·na·i·ca (sir′ə nā′i kə, sī′rə-) ancient Greek kingdom, later a Roman province, on the N coast of Africa

Cy·ril (sir′əl) [< Gr. < *kyrios,* lord] a masculine name

Cy·ril·lic (sə ril′ik) *adj.* designating or of the Slavic alphabet attributed to Saint Cyril, 9th-cent. apostle to the Slavs: it is used in Russia, Bulgaria, and other Slavic countries

Cy·rus (sī′rəs) [L. < Gr. < OPer. *Kūrush*] **1.** a masculine name **2.** ?–529 B.C.; king of the Medes & Persians: founded Persian Empire: called *the Great*

cyst (sist) *n.* [ModL. *cystis* < Gr. *kystis,* sac] **1.** any of certain saclike structures in plants or animals; specif., such a structure when abnormal and filled with fluid or diseased matter **2.** a protective membrane surrounding certain organisms in a resting stage —**cyst′ic** *adj.* —**cyst′oid** *adj., n.*

-cyst (sist) [see prec.] *a suffix meaning* sac, pouch, bladder *[encyst]*

cys·ti·cer·cus (sis′tə sur′kəs) *n., pl.* **-cer′ci** (-sī) [ModL. < *cysti-* (see CYST) + Gr. *kerkos,* tail] the larva of certain tapeworms having the head and neck partly enclosed in a bladderlike cyst

cystic fibrosis a congenital disease of children, characterized by fibrosis and malfunctioning of the pancreas, and frequent respiratory infections

cys·ti·tis (sis tīt′is) *n.* [CYST(O)- + -ITIS] an inflammation of the urinary bladder

cys·to- [see CYST] *a combining form meaning* of or like a bladder or sac: also **cyst-, cysti-**

cys·to·scope (sis′tə skōp′) *n.* [CYSTO- + -SCOPE] an instrument for visually examining the interior of the urinary bladder —*vt.* **-scoped′, -scop′ing** to examine with a cystoscope —**cys′to·scop′ic** (-skäp′ik) *adj.*

cys·tos·co·py (sis täs′kə pē) *n., pl.* **-pies** examination of the urinary bladder with the aid of a cystoscope

-cyte (sīt) [< Gr. *kytos,* a hollow] *a combining form meaning* a cell *[lymphocyte]*

Cyth·e·re·a (sith′ə rē′ə) *same as* APHRODITE —**Cyth′e·re′an** *adj.*

cy·to- [see -CYTE] *a combining form meaning* of a cell or cells: also, before a vowel, **cyt-**

cy·to·ge·net·ics (sīt′ō jə net′iks) *n.pl.* [with sing. v.] the science correlating cytology and genetics with regard to heredity and variation —**cy′to·ge·net′ic, cy′to·ge·net′i·cal** *adj.* —**cy′to·ge·net′i·cal·ly** *adv.* —**cy′to·ge·net′i·cist** *n.*

cy·tol·o·gy (sī täl′ə jē) *n.* [CYTO- + -LOGY] the branch of biology dealing with the structure, function, pathology, and life history of cells —**cy·to·log·ic** (sī′tə läj′ik), **cy′to·log′i·cal** *adj.* —**cy′to·log′i·cal·ly** *adv.* —**cy·tol′o·gist** *n.*

cy·to·plasm (sīt′ə plaz′m) *n.* [CYTO- + -PLASM] the protoplasm of a cell, exclusive of the nucleus —**cy′to·plas′mic** *adj.*

cy·to·sine (sīt′ə sēn′) *n.* [G. *zytosin*] a nitrogenous base, $C_4H_5N_3O$, a constituent of DNA and other nucleic acids

C.Z., CZ Canal Zone

czar (zär) *n.* [< Russ. < OSlav. via Goth. < L. *Caesar*] **1.** an emperor: title of any of the former emperors of Russia ☆**2.** an absolute ruler; despot —**czar′dom** *n.* —**czar′ism** *n.* —**czar′ist** *adj., n.*

czar·das (chär′dəsh, -däsh) *n.* [Hung. *csárdás*] **1.** a Hungarian dance with fast and slow sections **2.** music for this dance

czar·e·vitch (zär′ə vich′) *n.* [< Russ.] the eldest son of a czar of Russia

cza·ri·na (zä rē′nə) *n.* [< G. < Russ. *tsaritsa*] the wife of a czar; empress of Russia: also **cza·rit′za** (-rit′sə)

Czech (chek) *n.* **1.** a Bohemian, Moravian, or Silesian Slav of Czechoslovakia **2.** the West Slavic language of the Czechs **3.** loosely, a native or inhabitant of Czechoslovakia —*adj.* of Czechoslovakia, its people, or their language: also **Czech′ish**

Czech·o·slo·vak (chek′ə slō′väk) *adj.* of Czechoslovakia or its people —*n.* a Czech or Slovak living in Czechoslovakia Also **Czech′o·slo·va′ki·an** (-slō vä′kē ən)

Czech·o·slo·va·ki·a (chek′ə slō vä′kē ə) country in C Europe, east of Germany: 49,367 sq. mi.; pop. 14,445,000; cap. Prague

D

D, d (dē) *n., pl.* **D's, d's 1.** the fourth letter of the English alphabet **2.** the sound of *D* or *d* **3.** *a symbol for* the fourth in a sequence or group

D (dē) *n.* **1.** a Roman numeral for 500 **2.** *Chem.* deuterium ☆**3.** *Educ.* a grade indicating below-average work, or merely passing **4.** *Music a)* the second tone in the ascending scale of C major *b)* the scale having this tone as the keynote **5.** *Physics the symbol for* density

D. 1. December **2.** Democrat(ic) **3.** Dutch

d. 1. daughter **2.** day(s) **3.** dead **4.** delete **5.** diameter **6.** died **7.** dose **8.** dyne **9.** [L. *denarius,* pl. *denarii*] penny; pence

'd 1. *contraction of* had or would (used as auxiliaries) [*I'd, they'd*] **2.** *contraction of* -ed [*foster'd*]

D.A. District Attorney

dab[1] (dab) *vt., vi.* **dabbed, dab'bing** [ME. *dabben,* to strike] **1.** to touch lightly and quickly **2.** to pat with something soft or moist **3.** to put on (paint, etc.) with light, quick strokes —*n.* **1.** a light, quick stroke; tap; pat **2.** a bit, esp. of a soft or moist thing [*a dab of rouge*] —**dab'ber** *n.*

dab[2] (dab) *n.* [ME. *dabbe* < ?] **1.** any of several flounders of coastal waters **2.** any small flatfish

dab·ble (dab'l) *vt.* **-bled, -bling** [Du. *dabbelen* < *dabben,* to strike, DAB[1]] **1.** to dip lightly in and out of a liquid **2.** to spatter or splash —*vi.* **1.** to play in water, as with the hands **2.** to do something superficially, not seriously (with *in* or *at*) [*to dabble in art*] —**dab'bler** *n.*

dab·chick (dab'chik') *n.* [DAB[1] + CHICK] either of two small water birds of the grebe family, found in Europe and the Americas

‡**da ca·po** (dä kä'pō) [It.] *Music* from the beginning: a direction to repeat

Dac·ca (dak'ə, däk'ə) capital of Bangladesh, in the EC part: pop. 557,000

dace (dās) *n., pl.* **dace, dac'es:** see PLURAL, II, D, 2 [< OFr. *dars* < VL. *darsus*] a small freshwater fish of the carp family

‡**da·cha** (dä'chə) *n.* [Russ.] a country house or cottage used as a summer home

Da·chau (dä'khou) city in S Germany: site of a Nazi concentration camp where many were murdered

dachs·hund (däks'hoond, -hoont; dash'hund) *n.* [G. *dachs,* a badger + *hund,* a dog] a small dog of German breed, with a long body and short legs

Da·cia (dā'shə) ancient kingdom in SE Europe, corresponding approximately to modern Romania: see map at ROMAN EMPIRE

☆**Da·cron** (dā'krän, dak'rän) [arbitrary coinage, after (NYL)ON] *a trademark for* a synthetic polyester fiber or a washable, wrinkle-resistant fabric made from it —*n.* [*also* d-] this fiber or fabric

DACHSHUND
(8–10 in. high
at shoulder)

dac·tyl (dak't'l) *n.* [< L. < Gr. *daktylos,* a finger or (by analogy with a finger's three joints) a dactyl] a metrical foot of three syllables, the first accented and the others unaccented, as in English verse (Ex.: "táke hĕr ŭp/ téndĕrlў") —**dac·tyl'ic** *adj.*

dad (dad) *n.* [< child's cry *dada*] [Colloq.] father

da·da (dä'dä, -də) *n.* [Fr., lǐt., hobbyhorse < baby talk] [*also* D-] a movement (1916–22) in art and literature characterized by fantastic, abstract, or nonsensical creations that satirized the conventions in art and society: also **da'da·ism** —**da'da·ist** *adj., n.* —**da·da·is'tic** *adj.*

dad·dy (dad'ē) *n., pl.* **-dies** [see DAD] [Colloq.] father

dad·dy-long·legs (dad'ē lôŋ'legz') *n., pl.* **-long'legs'** *same as:* **1.** HARVESTMAN (sense 2) **2.** CRANE FLY

da·do (dā'dō) *n., pl.* **-does** [< It. < L. *datum,* a die] **1.** the part of a pedestal between the cap and the base **2.** the lower part of the wall of a room if decorated differently from the upper part **3.** *a)* a rectangular groove cut in the side of one board so that another board may be fitted into it, usually at right angles *b)* the joint thus made: in full, **dado joint** —*vt.* **-doed, -do·ing 1.** to furnish with a dado **2.** to fit into a dado groove

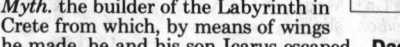

CAP

DADO

BASE

Daed·a·lus (ded''l əs, dēd'-) *Gr. Myth.* the builder of the Labyrinth in Crete from which, by means of wings he made, he and his son Icarus escaped —**Dae·da·li·an, Dae·da·le·an** (di dāl'yən, -ē ən) *adj.*

dae·mon (dē'mən) *n.* [L. < Gr. *daimōn*] **1.** *Gr. Myth.* any of the secondary divinities ranking below the gods **2.** a guardian spirit or inner, inspiring spirit **3.** *same as* DEMON —**dae·mon·ic** (di män'ik) *adj.*

daf·fo·dil (daf'ə dil') *n.* [< ML. < L. < Gr. *asphodelos*] **1.** any of several hardy kinds of narcissus, typically having a single, yellow flower with a trumpetlike corona **2.** the flower

daf·fy (daf'ē) *adj.* **-fi·er, -fi·est** [see DAFT] [Colloq.] **1.** crazy; foolish; silly **2.** playful in a giddy way —**daf'fi·ness** *n.*

daft (daft) *adj.* [< OE. *(ge)dæfte,* mild, gentle] **1.** silly; foolish **2.** insane; crazy —**daft'ly** *adv.* —**daft'ness** *n.*

da Gam·a (də gam'ə; *Port.* dä gä'mä), **Vas·co** (väs'kō) 1469?–1524; Port. navigator: discovered the sea route around Africa to India

dag·ger (dag'ər) *n.* [< ML. *daggarius*] **1.** a weapon with a short, pointed blade, used for stabbing **2.** *Printing* a reference mark (†) —*vt.* **1.** to stab with a dagger **2.** to mark with a dagger —**look daggers at** to look at with anger

Da·gon (dā'gän) [< LL. < LGr. < Heb.] the main god of the ancient Philistines, represented as half man and half fish

☆**da·guerre·o·type** (də ger'ə tīp') *n.* [after L. J. M. *Daguerre* (1789–1851), Fr. inventor] **1.** a photograph made by an early method on a plate of chemically treated metal or glass **2.** this method —*vt.* **-typed', -typ'ing** to photograph by this method —**da·guerre'o·typ'y** *n.*

☆**Dag·wood** (**sandwich**) (dag'wood') [after such sandwiches eaten by a comic-strip character] a tall sandwich with a variety of fillings, often ones that are not usually eaten together

dahl·ia (dal'yə, däl'-; *chiefly Brit.* dāl'-) *n.* [after A. *Dahl,* 18th-c. Swed. botanist] **1.** a perennial plant of the composite family, with tuberous roots and large, showy flowers **2.** the flower

Da·ho·mey (də hō'mē) *former name of* BENIN

Dail Eir·eann (dôl'er'ən) [Ir. *dáil,* assembly + *Eireann,* genitive of *Eire,* Ireland] the lower house of the legislature of Ireland

dai·ly (dā'lē) *adj.* **1.** relating to, done, happening, or published every day or every weekday **2.** calculated by the day [*daily rate*] —☆*n., pl.* **-lies** a daily newspaper —*adv.* every day; day after day

daily double a betting procedure or bet, the success of which depends on choosing both winners in two specified races on the same program

☆**daily dozen** [Colloq.] gymnastic setting-up exercises (originally twelve) done daily

dai·mio, dai·myo (dī′myō) *n.*, *pl.* **-mio, -mios** [Jap. < Chin. *dai*, great + *mio*, name] a feudal nobleman of an earlier time in Japan

dain·ty (dān′tē) *n.*, *pl.* **-ties** [< OFr. *deinté*, worth, delicacy < L. *dignitas*, worth, DIGNITY] a choice food; delicacy —*adj.* **1.** delicious and choice [a *dainty* morsel] **2.** delicately pretty or lovely [a *dainty* lace handkerchief] **3.** *a*) of or showing delicate and refined taste [a *dainty* appetite] *b*) fussy; squeamish —**dain′ti·ly** *adv.* —**dain′ti·ness** *n.*

☆**dai·qui·ri** (dak′ər ē, dīk′-) *n.* [after *Daiquirí*, village in Cuba] a cocktail made of rum, sugar, and lime or lemon juice

dair·y (der′ē) *n.*, *pl.* **dair′ies** [ME. *daierie* < *daie*, dairymaid < OE. *dæge*, bread maker: for IE. base see DOUGH] **1.** a room, building, etc. where milk and cream are kept and butter, cheese, etc. are made **2.** a farm (**dairy farm**) in the business of producing milk and milk products **3.** *a*) a commercial establishment that processes and distributes milk and milk products *b*) a retail store where these are sold —*adj.* of milk, cream, butter, cheese, etc.

dairy cattle cows raised mainly for their milk

dair·y·ing (-iŋ) *n.* the business of producing or selling dairy products

dair·y·maid (-mād′) *n.* a girl or woman who milks cows or works in a dairy

dair·y·man (-mən) *n.*, *pl.* **-men** a man who works in or for a dairy or who owns a dairy

da·is (dā′is, dī′-) *n.*, *pl.* **da′is·es** [< OFr. < ML. *discus*, table < L. *discus*, DISCUS] a platform raised above the floor at one end of a hall or room, as for seats of honor, a speaker's stand, etc.

Dai·sy (dā′zē) [< DAISY] a feminine name

dai·sy (dā′zē) *n.*, *pl.* **-sies** [< OE. *dæges eage*, lit., day's eye] ☆**1.** a plant of the composite family, bearing flowers with white rays around a yellow disk **2.** any similar member of the composite family **3.** the flower of any of these plants —**push up (the) daisies** [Slang] to be dead and buried

Da·kar (dä kär′, dak′är) capital of Senegal, at the westernmost point of Africa: pop. 474,000

Da·ko·ta[1] (də kō′tə) *n.* [< Dakota *dakóta*, allies] **1.** *pl.* **-tas, -ta** a member of a group of Indian tribes (also called *Sioux*) of the northern plains of the U.S. and adjacent southern Canada **2.** their Siouan language —*adj.* **1.** of the Dakota Indians or their language **2.** of North Dakota, South Dakota, or both —**the Dakotas** North Dakota and South Dakota —**Da·ko′tan** *adj., n.*

Da·ko·ta[2] (də kō′tə) [< prec.] former U.S. territory from which N.Dak. & S.Dak. were formed in 1889

Da·lai La·ma (dä lī′ lä′mə) [Mongol. *dalai*, ocean + *blama*: see LAMA] the traditional high priest of the Lamaist religion: see LAMAISM

da·la·si (dä′lä sē) *n.*, *pl.* **-si** [native term, lit., complete] *see* MONETARY UNITS, table (Gambia)

dale (dāl) *n.* [OE. *dæl*] a valley

d'A·lem·bert (dà län ber′), **Jean le Rond** (zhän lə rōn′) 1717–83; Fr. philosopher & editor of an encyclopedia

Da·li (dä′lē), **Sal·va·dor** (sal′və dôr′) 1904– ; Sp. surrealist painter, in U.S. since 1940

Dal·las (dal′əs) [after G. *Dallas* (1792–1864), U.S. vice president (1845–49)] city in NE Tex.: pop. 844,000 (met. area 1,556,000)

dal·li·ance (dal′ē əns) *n.* the act of dallying; flirting, toying, trifling, etc.

dal·ly (dal′ē) *vi.* **-lied, -ly·ing** [< OFr. *dalier*, to converse, trifle] **1.** to make love in a playful way **2.** to deal lightly or carelessly (*with*); trifle; toy [to *dally* with an idea] **3.** to waste time; loiter —see SYN. at LOITER and TRIFLE —**dally away** to waste (time) in trifling activities

Dal·ma·tia (dal mā′shə) region along the Adriatic coast of Yugoslavia: part of Croatia

DAISY

Dal·ma·tian (-shən) *adj.* of Dalmatia or its people —*n.* **1.** a native of Dalmatia **2.** a large, short-haired dog with dark spots on a white coat

dal·mat·ic (dal mat′ik) *n.* [< OFr. < LL. *dalmatica* (*vestis*), Dalmatian garment] **1.** a short-sleeved garment worn at Mass as by a deacon or bishop **2.** a similar robe worn by a British monarch during coronation

‡**dal se·gno** (däl se′nyô) [It.] *Music* from the sign: a direction to return and repeat from the sign 𝄋

Dal·ton (dôl′t'n), **John** 1766–1844; Eng. chemist & physicist —**Dal·to·ni·an** (dôl tō′nē ən) *adj.*

Da·ly City (dā′lē) [after a prominent citizen, J. *Daly*] city in W Calif.: suburb of San Francisco: pop. 67,000

dam[1] (dam) *n.* [< Gmc. base seen in ON. *dammr*, to stop up: for IE. base see DO[1]] **1.** a barrier built to hold back flowing water **2.** the water thus kept back **3.** any barrier like a dam —*vt.* **dammed, dam′ming 1.** to build a dam in **2.** to keep back or confine as by a dam (usually with *up*) [to *dam* up one's energies]

dam[2] (dam) *n.* [ME., var. of *dame*, DAME] **1.** the female parent of any four-legged animal **2.** [Archaic] a mother

dam·age (dam′ij) *n.* [OFr. < L. *damnum*: see DAMN] **1.** injury or harm to something that makes it less valuable, useful, etc. [the tornado caused *damage* to his house] **2.** [pl.] *Law* money claimed by, or ordered paid to, a person to make up for injury, loss, etc. that is another's fault **3.** [Colloq.] cost or expense —*vt.* **-aged, -ag·ing** to do damage to [frost *damaged* the orange crop] —*vi.* to incur damage —see SYN. at INJURE —**dam′age·a·ble** *adj.*

Dam·a·scene (dam′ə sēn′, dam′ə sēn′) *adj.* [L. *Damascenus*, of Damascus] **1.** of Damascus, its people, etc. **2.** [d-] of damascening or damask —*n.* **1.** a native or inhabitant of Damascus **2.** [d-] damascened work —*vt.* **-scened′, -scen′ing** [d-] to decorate (steel, etc.) with wavy markings or with inlaid patterns of gold or silver

Da·mas·cus (də mas′kəs) capital of Syria, a very ancient city in the SC part: pop. 557,000

Damascus steel a hard, flexible steel decorated with wavy lines, originally made in Damascus and used for sword blades: also **damask steel**

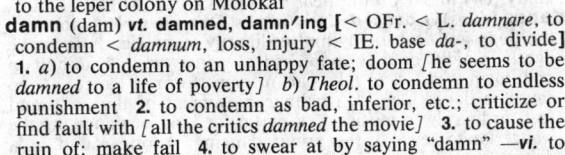

DALMATIAN
(19–23 in. high
at shoulder)

DAMASCENE

dam·ask (dam′əsk) *n.* [< It. < L. *Damascus* (the city)] **1.** a durable, lustrous fabric as of silk or linen, decorated with woven designs, used for table linen, upholstery, etc. **2.** *a*) same as DAMASCUS STEEL *b*) the wavy markings of such steel **3.** deep pink or rose —*adj.* **1.** orig., of or from Damascus **2.** made of damask **3.** like damask **4.** deep-pink or rose —*vt.* **1.** to ornament with flowered designs or wavy lines **2.** to make deep-pink or rose

damask rose a very fragrant rose important as a source of attar of roses

dame (dām) *n.* [OFr. < L. *domina*, lady, fem. of *dominus*: see DOMINATE] **1.** orig., a title given to the woman in charge of a household **2.** an elderly woman **3.** [D-] in Great Britain *a*) the legal title of the wife of a knight or baronet *b*) the title of a woman who has received an order of knighthood **4.** [Slang] any woman

Da·mi·en (de Veuster) (dā′mē ən; Fr. dà myaⁿ′), **Father (Joseph)** 1840–89; Belgian Roman Catholic priest & missionary to the leper colony on Molokai

damn (dam) *vt.* **damned, damn′ing** [< OFr. < L. *damnare*, to condemn < *damnum*, loss, injury < IE. base *da-*, to divide] **1.** *a*) to condemn to an unhappy fate; doom [he seems to be *damned* to a life of poverty] *b*) *Theol.* to condemn to endless punishment **2.** to condemn as bad, inferior, etc.; criticize or find fault with [all the critics *damned* the movie] **3.** to cause the ruin of; make fail **4.** to swear at by saying "damn" —*vi.* to

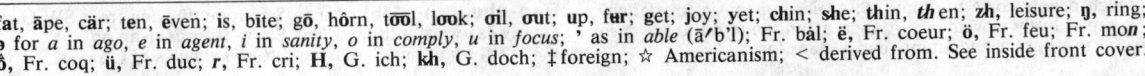

fat, āpe, cär; ten, ēven; is, bīte; gō, hôrn, tōōl, look; oil, out; up, fur; get; joy; yet; chin; she; thin, then; zh, leisure; ŋ, ring; ə for a in ago, e in agent, i in sanity, o in comply, u in focus; ′ as in able (ā′b'l); Fr. bâl; ë, Fr. coeur; ö, Fr. feu; Fr. mon; ô, Fr. coq; ü, Fr. duc; r, Fr. cri; H, G. ich; kh, G. doch; ‡foreign; ☆ Americanism; < derived from. See inside front cover.

swear or curse; say "damn," etc. —*n.* the saying of "damn" as a curse —*adj., adv.* [Colloq.] *clipped form of* DAMNED —*interj.* an expression of anger, annoyance, etc. —**damn with faint praise** to praise so unenthusiastically as, in effect, to condemn —**not give** (or **care**) **a damn** [Colloq.] not care at all —**not worth a damn** [Colloq.] worthless

dam·na·ble (dam′nə b'l) *adj.* deserving to be damned; very bad; outrageous; execrable —**dam′na·bly** *adv.*

dam·na·tion (dam nā′shən) *n.* a damning or being damned — *interj.* an expression of anger, annoyance, etc.

dam·na·to·ry (dam′nə tôr′ē) *adj.* **1.** threatening with damnation; damning **2.** condemning *[damnatory* evidence*]*

damned (damd; *occas.* dam′nid) *adj.* **1.** condemned or deserving condemnation **2.** [Colloq.] deserving cursing; outrageous: now often only for emphasis *[a damned* shame*]* —*adv.* [Colloq.] very *[a damned* good job*]* —**do** (or **try**) **one's damnedest** (or **damndest**) [Colloq.] to do or try one's utmost —**the damned** *Theol.* souls doomed to eternal punishment

Dam·o·cles (dam′ə klēz′) a courtier of ancient Syracuse who, according to legend, was given a lesson in the perils to a ruler's life when the king seated him at a feast under a sword hanging by a hair —**sword of Damocles** any danger that seems about to happen

dam·oi·selle, dam·o·sel, dam·o·zel (dam′ə zel′) *n.* [Archaic or Poet.] a damsel

Da·mon and Pyth·i·as (dā′mən ən pith′ē əs) *Classical Legend* friends so devoted to each other that when Pythias, who had been condemned to death, wanted time to arrange his affairs, Damon pledged his life that his friend would return

damp (damp) *n.* [MDu., vapor < IE. base *dhem-*, to smoke, mist] **1.** a slight wetness; moisture *[rains* caused *damp* in the basement*]* **2.** any harmful gas in a mine; firedamp, blackdamp, etc. —*adj.* somewhat moist or wet; humid —*vt.* **1.** to make damp; moisten **2.** to reduce or check (energy, action, etc., as fire in a furnace or the vibration of a piano string) —see SYN. at WET —**damp′ish** *adj.* —**damp′ly** *adv.* —**damp′ness** *n.*

☆**damp-dry** (damp′drī′) *vt.* -dried′, -dry′ing to dry (laundry) so that some moisture is left in it —*adj.* designating or of laundry so dried

damp·en (dam′pən) *vt.* **1.** to make damp; moisten **2.** to deaden, depress, reduce, or lessen *[the* sad news *dampened* our spirits*]* —*vi.* to become damp —**damp′en·er** *n.*

damp·er (-pər) *n.* [see DAMP] **1.** anything that deadens or depresses **2.** a plate or valve in the flue of a stove or furnace that can be turned to control the draft **3.** a device to check vibration in the strings of a piano, etc. **4.** a device for lessening the oscillation of a magnetic needle, a moving coil, etc.

Dam·pier (dam′pyer, -pē ər, -pir) **Walter** 1652–1715; Eng. explorer & pirate

dam·sel (dam′z'l) *n.* [< OFr. *dameisele* < L. *domina:* see DAME] [Archaic or Poet.] a girl; maiden

DAMPER

dam·son (dam′z'n, -s'n) *n.* [< OFr. < L. *Damascenus,* (plum) of Damascus] **1.** a variety of small, purple plum **2.** the tree on which it grows

Dan (dan) **1.** *Bible a)* the fifth son of Jacob *b)* the tribe of Israel descended from him **2.** village in northeastern Israel: site of an ancient town at the northernmost edge of Israelite territory

Dan. 1. Daniel **2.** Danish

Da·na (dā′nə), **Richard Henry** 1815–82; U.S. writer & lawyer

Da·na·i·des, Da·na·ï·des (də nā′ə dēz′) *n.pl. Gr. Myth.* the fifty daughters of Danaus, a king of Argos: forty-nine murdered their husbands at their father's command and were condemned in Hades to keep drawing water with a sieve

Da Nang (dä′ näŋ′) seaport in N South Vietnam, on the South China Sea: pop. 144,000: also sp. **Da′nang′**

Dan·bur·y (dan′ber′ē, -bər ē) [after *Danbury,* town in England] city in SW Conn., near Bridgeport: pop. 51,000

dance (dans) *vi.* **danced, danc′ing** [< OFr. *danser*] **1.** to move the body and feet in rhythm, ordinarily to music **2.** to move lightly, rapidly, or gaily about, as leaves in a wind **3.** to bob up and down —*vt.* **1.** to take part in or perform (a dance) **2.** to cause to dance —*n.* **1.** rhythmic movement of the body and feet, ordinarily to music **2.** a particular kind of dance, as the waltz, tango, etc. **3.** the art of dancing **4.** one round of a dance *[may* I have the next *dance* with you?*]* **5.** a party to which people come to dance **6.** a piece of music for dancing **7.** rapid, lively movement —**dance attendance on** to stay near so as to be polite and attentive to —**danc′er** *n.*

dance of death a symbolic portrayal, esp. in medieval art, of Death· whirling persons away in a dance as each dies

D and C dilatation (of the cervix) and curettage (of the uterus)

dan·de·li·on (dan′də lī′ən, -dē-) *n.* [< OFr. *dent de lion* < L. *dentis,* genitive of *dens,* tooth + *de,* of + *leo,* lion] a common weed with jagged leaves, often eaten as greens, and yellow flowers

dan·der (dan′dər) *n.* [< ?] ☆[Colloq.] anger or temper —**get one's dander up** [Colloq.] to become or make angry

DANCE OF DEATH

dan·di·fy (dan′də fī′) *vt.* -fied′, -fy′ing to dress up like a dandy —**dan′di·fi·ca′tion** *n.*

dan·dle (dan′d'l) *vt.* -dled, -dling [< ? OIt. *dandolare,* to dally] **1.** to move (a child) up and down on the knee or in the arms **2.** to fondle; pet

dan·druff (dan′drəf) *n.* [< earlier *dandro* (< ?) + dial. *hurf,* scab] little scales or flakes of dead skin formed on the scalp —**dan′druff·y** *adj.*

dan·dy (dan′dē) *n., pl.* -dies [Scot. var. of *Andy* < *Andrew* (see MERRY-ANDREW)] **1.** a man who is very fussy about his clothes and appearance; fop ☆**2.** [Colloq.] something very good or first-rate —*adj.* -di·er, -di·est ☆[Colloq.] very good; first-rate —**dan′dy·ish** *adj.* —**dan′dy·ism** *n.*

Dane (dān) *n.* a native or inhabitant of Denmark

Dane·law, Dane·lagh (dān′lô′) *n.* the law code enforced in northeastern England by Danish invaders in the 9th and 10th cent. A.D.; also, this part of England

dan·ger (dān′jər) *n.* [< OFr. < L. < *dominus,* a master] **1.** a condition in which there could be injury, damage, loss, or pain *[to* live in constant *danger]* **2.** a thing that may cause injury, pain, etc. *[the* dangers faced by a fireman*]*

SYN.—**danger** is the general word for any kind of exposure to injury, loss, etc. *[the* danger of falling on icy walks*]*; **peril** suggests great danger that is near at hand *[flood* waters put the town in *peril]*; **jeopardy** emphasizes exposure to extreme danger *[reckless* driving puts one's life in *jeopardy]*; **hazard** implies danger of which one may be aware but over which one has little control *[the* hazards of combat duty*]*; **risk** implies willingness to take a dangerous chance *[he* saved the dog at the *risk* of his life*]* —ANT. safety, security

dan·ger·ous (-əs) *adj.* full of danger; unsafe; perilous — **dan′ger·ous·ly** *adv.* —**dan′ger·ous·ness** *n.*

dan·gle (daŋ′g'l) *vi.* -gled, -gling [< Scand.] **1.** to hang loosely so as to swing back and forth **2.** to be a hanger-on; follow (*after*) **3.** *Gram.* to lack clear connection, as one sentence element modifying another *[in* "while crossing the street, the light changed," the participle "crossing" *dangles]* —*vt.* to cause to dangle —**dan′gler** *n.*

Dan·iel (dan′yəl) [Heb. *dānī'ēl,* lit., God is my judge] **1.** a masculine name: dim. *Dan* **2.** *Bible a)* a Hebrew prophet whose faith saved him in the lions' den *b)* the book containing his story

da·ni·o (dā′nē ō′) *n., pl.* -os [ModL. < old name in East India] a brightly colored tropical fish: often kept in aquariums

Dan·ish (dā′nish) *adj.* of Denmark, the Danes, or their language —*n.* **1.** the language of the Danes **2.** [*also* d-] clipped form of DANISH PASTRY

Danish pastry [*also* d- p-] a rich, flaky pastry of raised dough filled with fruit, cheese, etc. and usually topped with icing

dank (daŋk) *adj.* [ME., akin to ON. *dǫkk,* marsh: for IE. base see DAMP] disagreeably damp; moist and chilly —see SYN. at WET —**dank′ly** *adv.* —**dank′ness** *n.*

D'An·nun·zio (dä nōōn′tsyô), **Ga·bri·e·le** (gä′brē e′le) 1863–1938; It. poet, writer, & political adventurer

dan·seuse (dän sooz′; *Fr.* dän söz′) *n., pl.* -seus′es (-sooz′əz; *Fr.* -söz′) [Fr.] a girl or woman dancer, esp. a ballet dancer

Dan·te (Alighieri) (dän′tā, -tē; dan′tē; *It.* dän′te) 1265–1321; It. poet: wrote *The Divine Comedy* —**Dan′te·an** *adj., n.* —**Dan·tesque′** (-tesk′) *adj.*

Dan·ton (dän tôn′), **Georges Jacques** (zhôrzh zhäk) 1759–94; Fr. Revolutionary leader

Dan·ube (dan′yōōb) river in S Europe, flowing from SW Germany eastward into the Black Sea —**Da·nu′bi·an** *adj.*

Dan·zig (dan′sig; *G.* dän′tsiH) *German name of* GDAŃSK

Daph·ne (daf′nē) [L. < Gr. *daphnē*, the laurel tree] **1.** a feminine name **2.** *Gr. Myth.* a nymph who escaped from Apollo by becoming a laurel tree

dap·per (dap′ər) *adj.* [< ? MDu. *dapper*, nimble] **1.** small and active **2.** trim, neat, and dressed with care —**dap′per·ly** *adv.*

dap·ple (dap′'l) *adj.* [< ON. *depill*, a spot < *dapi*, a pool] marked with spots; mottled: also **dap′pled** —*n.* **1.** a spotted condition **2.** an animal whose skin is spotted —*vt., vi.* **-pled, -pling** to cover or become covered with spots

dap·ple-gray (-grā′) *adj.* gray spotted with darker gray —*n.* a dapple-gray horse

DAR, D.A.R. Daughters of the American Revolution

Dar·by and Joan (där′bē ən jōn′) [< an 18th-cent. song] an old married couple devoted to each other

d'Arc, Jeanne (zhän därk′) *see* JOAN OF ARC

Dar·da·nelles (där′də nelz′) strait between the Aegean Sea & the Sea of Marmara

dare (der, dar) *vi.* **dared** or archaic **durst** (durst), **dared, dar′ing;** 3d pers. sing. pres. indic., **dare** or **dares** [< OE. *dear*, 1st pers. sing. of *durran*, to dare < IE. base *dhers-*] to be brave or bold enough to do a certain thing [criticize him if you *dare*] —*vt.* **1.** to have courage for; venture upon **2.** to oppose and defy [he *dared* the wrath of the tyrant] **3.** to challenge (someone) to do something hard or dangerous as a test of courage —*n.* a challenge to do a hard, dangerous, or rash thing as a test of courage —**dare say** to think likely or probable; suppose [I *dare* say he's right] —**dar′er** *n.*

DARDANELLES

dare·dev·il (-dev′'l) *adj.* bold and reckless —*n.* a bold, reckless person —**dare′dev′il·ry, dare′dev′il·try** *n.*

Dar es Sa·laam (där′ es sə läm′) capital of Tanzania, on the Indian Ocean: pop. 373,000

dar·ing (der′iŋ, dar′-) *adj.* having or showing a bold willingness to take risks; fearless —*n.* bold courage —**dar′ing·ly** *adv.*

Da·ri·us I (də rī′əs) 550?–486? B.C.; king of Persia (521–486?): called *the Great*

Dar·jee·ling (där jē′liŋ) *n.* a fine variety of tea from Darjeeling, a district in northeastern India

dark (därk) *adj.* [< OE. *deorc* < IE. base *dher-*, dirty, somber] **1.** entirely or partly without light **2.** neither giving nor receiving light ☆**3.** giving no performance [this theater is *dark* tonight] **4.** *a)* almost black *b)* not light in color; deep in shade [a *dark* green] **5.** not fair in complexion; brunet **6.** hidden; secret **7.** not easily understood **8.** gloomy; dismal [always looking on the *dark* side of things] **9.** angry or sullen [responding to my criticism with *dark* looks] **10.** evil; sinister [Satan's *dark* powers] **11.** ignorant; unenlightened —*n.* **1.** the state of being dark **2.** night; nightfall **3.** a dark color or shade [the contrast of lights and *darks* in the picture] —**in the dark** uninformed; ignorant —**keep dark** to keep secret or hidden —**dark′ish** *adj.* —**dark′ly** *adv.* —**dark′ness** *n.*

SYN.—**dark,** the general word in this comparison, indicates absence of light, either total or partial [a *dark* night]; **dim** implies faint light in which it is difficult to see things [seated at the table in *dim* candlelight]; **dusky** suggests the grayish, shadowy light of twilight [a *dusky* winter evening]; **murky** suggests the thick, heavy darkness of fog or smoke-filled air [a *murky* alley near a factory]; **gloomy** suggests darkness that is associated with feelings of sadness or hopelessness [a *gloomy* dungeon] —**ANT.** light, bright

Dark Ages, dark ages the Middle Ages; esp., the early part from 476 A.D. to the late 10th cent.

Dark Continent Africa: so called because it was little known until the late 19th cent.

dark·en (där′kən) *vt., vi.* to make or become dark or darker —**not darken one's door** (or **doorway**) not come to one's home —**dark′en·er** *n.*

dark horse [Colloq.] **1.** an unexpected winner in a horse race, thought beforehand to have very little chance **2.** a contestant regarded as not likely to win ☆**3.** *Politics* a person who gets or may get the nomination unexpectedly, often by a compromise

dark lantern a lantern with a shutter that can hide the light

dark·ling (därk′liŋ) *adv.* [DARK + -LING[2]] [Poet.] in the dark —*adj.* [Poet.] dark, dim, obscure, etc.

dark·room (därk′rōōm′) *n.* a room from which all actinic rays are excluded, so that photographs can be developed in it

dark·some (-səm) *adj.* [Poet.] **1.** dark; darkish **2.** dismal; gloomy

Dar·ling (där′liŋ) river in SE Australia, flowing southwest into the Murray River

dar·ling (där′liŋ) *n.* [OE. *deorling*, dim. of *deore*, DEAR] **1.** a person much loved by another **2.** a favorite or a lovable person —*adj.* **1.** very dear; beloved **2.** [Colloq.] cute; attractive [a *darling* dress]

Darm·stadt (därm′stat; *G.* därm′shtät) city in SW West Germany: pop. 141,000

darn[1] (därn) *vt., vi.* [< MFr. dial. *darner*, to mend < Bret. *darn*, a piece: for IE. base see TEAR[1]] to mend (cloth, etc.) or repair (a hole in cloth) by sewing a network of stitches across the gap —*n.* a darned place in fabric —**darn′er** *n.*

darn[2] (därn) *vt., vi., n., adj., adv., interj.* [Colloq.] *a word used in place of* DAMN (the curse) —**darned** *adj., adv.*

dar·nel (där′n'l) *n.* [< Fr. dial. *darnelle*] a weedy rye grass often found in grainfields: a certain fungus can make the seeds poisonous

darn·ing (där′niŋ) *n.* **1.** a mending with interlaced stitches **2.** clothes to be darned

darning needle 1. a large needle for darning **2.** *same as* DRAGONFLY

Dar·row (dar′ō), **Clarence (Seward)** 1857–1938; U.S. lawyer

dart (därt) *n.* [< OFr.] **1.** a short arrow with a sharp point that is thrown as a weapon, or at a target in games **2.** a sudden, quick movement **3.** a short, tapered, stitched fold in a garment to make it fit more closely **4.** [*pl.*, *with sing. v.*] a game in which a number of darts (sense 1) are thrown at a target —*vt., vi.* **1.** to throw, shoot, send out, etc. suddenly and fast [he *darted* a look at her] **2.** to move suddenly and fast [birds *darting* through the trees]

GAME OF DARTS

dart·er (där′tər) *n.* **1.** a thing or animal that darts ☆**2.** a tropical diving bird with a long, pointed bill and a long neck ☆**3.** any of various small, brightly colored freshwater fishes of N. America

Dart·mouth (därt′məth) city in S Nova Scotia, Canada, near Halifax: pop. 59,000

☆**Dar·von** (där′vän) a trademark for a pain-killing drug containing aspirin, etc.

Dar·win (där′win) seaport on the NW coast of Australia; capital of the Northern Territory: pop. 21,000

Dar·win (där′win), **Charles Robert** 1809–82; Eng. naturalist —**Dar·win′i·an** (-win′ē ən) *adj., n.*

Darwinian theory Darwin's theory of evolution, which holds that all species of plants and animals develop from earlier forms by the inheritance of slight variations from earlier generations, and that the forms which survive are those that are best adapted to the environment (see NATURAL SELECTION): also called **Dar′-win·ism** —**Dar′win·ist** *adj., n.*

dash (dash) *vt.* [< Scand., as in Sw. *daska*, to slap] **1.** to throw so as to break; smash [he *dashed* the plate to the floor] **2.** to throw, thrust, etc. (with *away, against*, etc.) **3.** to splash (liquid) on (someone or something) [we *dashed* water in his face] **4.** to destroy; frustrate [to *dash* one's hopes] **5.** to depress; discourage —*vi.* **1.** to strike violently (*against* or *on*) [waves *dashed* against the rocks] **2.** to move swiftly; rush —*n.* **1.** the sound of smashing **2.** a bit of something added [a *dash* of salt] **3.** a sudden rush ☆**4.** a short, fast run or race [a 100-yard *dash*] **5.** vigor; verve **6.** showy appearance **7.** *short for* DASHBOARD (sense 2) **8.** the mark (—), used in printing and writing to indicate a sudden break in a sentence, as for something added or left out **9.** a long sound or signal, as in Morse code: see also DOT[1] —**dash off 1.** to do, write, etc. hastily **2.** to rush away

dash·board (dash′bôrd′) *n.* **1.** a screen at the front or side of a carriage, boat, etc., for protection against splashing   **2.** a panel with instruments and gauges on it, as in an automobile

dash·er (-ər) *n.* **1.** a person or thing that dashes   **2.** a rotating device, as the agitator in a churn

☆**da·shi·ki** (dä shē′kē) *n.* [coined by its U.S. manufacturer] a loose-fitting, usually brightly colored robe or tunic modeled after an African tribal garment

dash·ing (-iŋ) *adj.* **1.** full of dash or spirit; lively   **2.** showy; stylish [a *dashing* costume] —**dash′ing·ly** *adv.*

dash light a light to light up a dashboard (sense 2)

das·tard (das′tərd) *n.* [ME., prob. < Scand. base] a sneaky, cowardly evildoer

das·tard·ly (-lē) *adj.* [see prec.] mean, sneaky, cowardly, etc. —**das′tard·li·ness** *n.*

das·y·ure (das′ē yoor′) *n.* [< Gr. *dasys*, hairy + *oura*, tail] a small tree-dwelling marsupial of Australia

dat. dative

da·ta (dāt′ə, dat′ə) *n.pl.* [often with *sing.* v.] [L., things given < pp. of *dare*, to give] things known or assumed; facts or figures from which conclusions can be drawn; information: the *sing.* form is *datum*

data processing the recording and handling of information by means of mechanical or electronic equipment

date[1] (dāt) *n.* [< OFr. < L. *data*, as in *data Romae*, etc., lit., given at Rome, etc., formula used in letters for place and date] **1.** a statement on a writing, coin, etc. of when it was made **2.** the time at which a thing happens or is done   **3.** the time that anything lasts   **4.** the day of the month   ☆**5.** *a)* an appointment for a set time; specif., a social engagement with a person of the opposite sex   *b)* the person with whom one has such an engagement —*vt.* **dat′ed, dat′ing**   **1.** to mark (a letter, etc.) with a date   **2.** to determine when something happened or was done or made [art experts trying to *date* a painting]   **3.** to assign a date to   **4.** *a)* to show or reveal as typical of a certain period or age   *b)* to make seem old-fashioned or out of date [wearing that style *dates* her]   **5.** to reckon by dates   ☆**6.** to have a social engagement with —*vi.* to belong to, or have origin in, a definite period in the past (usually with *from*) [a vase that *dates* from the 5th century B.C.] —**out of date** no longer in use; old-fashioned —**to date** until now; as yet —**up to date** in or into agreement with the latest facts, ideas, etc. [bringing a reference book *up to date*] —**dat′a·ble, date′a·ble** *adj.* —**dat′er** *n.*

date[2] (dāt) *n.* [< OFr. < L. < Gr. *daktylos*, a date, lit., a finger] **1.** the sweet, fleshy fruit of a cultivated palm (**date palm**)   **2.** the tree itself

date·less (dāt′lis) *adj.* **1.** without a date   **2.** without limit or end   **3.** too old for its date to be fixed   **4.** still good or interesting though old

date·line (-līn′) *n.* ☆**1.** the date and place where something was written or issued, as given in a line in a newspaper, a dispatch, etc.   **2.** *same as* DATE LINE —☆*vt.* **-lined′, -lin′ing** to furnish with a dateline

date line an imaginary line drawn north and south through the Pacific Ocean, largely along the 180th meridian: at this line, by international agreement, each calendar day begins at midnight, so that when it is Sunday just west of the line, it is Saturday just east of it

da·tive (dāt′iv) *adj.* [L. *dativus*, of giving < *datus*, pp. of *dare*, to give] designating, of, or in that case of a noun, pronoun, or adjective which expresses the indirect object of a verb and, in many languages, approach toward something —*n.* **1.** the dative case: in English, the dative is expressed by *to* or by word order (Ex.: I gave the book *to him*, I gave *him* the book)   **2.** a word or phrase in the dative case —**da·ti·val** (dā tī′v'l) *adj.* —**da′tive·ly** *adv.*

da·tum (dāt′əm, dat′-) *n. sing.* of DATA

dau. daughter

daub (dôb) *vt., vi.* [< OFr. < L. *dealbare*, to whitewash < *de-*, entirely + *albus*, white] **1.** to cover or smear with sticky, soft

INTERNATIONAL DATE LINE

matter [to *daub* a wound with salve]   **2.** to smear on (grease, plaster, etc.)   **3.** to paint coarsely and unskillfully —*n.* **1.** anything daubed on [*daubs* of plaster]   **2.** a daubing stroke or splash   **3.** a poorly painted picture —**daub′er** *n.* —**daub′er·y** *n.*

Dau·det (dō dā′), **Al·phonse** (àl fôns′) 1840–97; Fr. novelist

daugh·ter (dôt′ər) *n.* [< OE. *dohtor*] **1.** a girl or woman as she is related to a parent or to both parents: sometimes also used of animals   **2.** a female descendant   **3.** *a)* a daughter-in-law   *b)* a stepdaughter   **4.** a female thought of as having been influenced by something as a child is by a parent [a *daughter* of France] —**daugh′ter·li·ness** *n.* —**daugh′ter·ly** *adj.*

daughter cell *Biol.* either of the cells that result from the division of a cell, as in mitosis

daugh·ter-in-law (-in lô′) *n., pl.* **daugh′ters-in-law′** the wife of one's son

Dau·mier (dō myā′), **Ho·no·ré** (ô nô rā′) 1809–79; Fr. painter & caricaturist

daunt (dônt, dänt) *vt.* [< OFr. < L. < *domare*, to tame] to make afraid or discouraged; intimidate; dishearten [she was never *daunted* by misfortune] —see SYN. at DISMAY

daunt·less (dônt′lis, dänt′-) *adj.* that cannot be daunted, frightened, or discouraged; fearless —**daunt′less·ly** *adv.*

dau·phin (dô′fin; *Fr.* dō fan′) *n.* [Fr., lit., DOLPHIN: orig. a proper name] the eldest son of the king of France: a title used from 1349 to 1830

Da·vao (dä vou′) seaport in the Philippines, on the SE coast of Mindanao: pop. 315,000

Dav·en·port (dav′ən pôrt′) [after Col. G. *Davenport*, 19th-c. fur trader] city in E Iowa, on the Mississippi: pop. 98,000

dav·en·port (dav′ən pôrt′) *n.* [< ?] ☆a large sofa

Da·vid (dā′vid) [Heb. *dāvīd*, lit., beloved] **1.** a masculine name: dim. *Dave, Davy*   *Bible* the second king of Israel, succeeded by his son Solomon   **3.** (dà vēd′), **Jacques Louis** (zhàk lwē), 1748–1825; Fr. painter

da Vin·ci (də vin′chē; *It.* dä vēn′chē), **Le·o·nar·do** (lē′ə när′dō; *It.* le′ô när′dô) 1452–1519; It. painter, sculptor, architect, & scientist

Da·vis (dā′vis), **Jefferson** 1808–89; U.S. statesman; president of the Confederacy (1861–65)

Davis Strait arm of the Atlantic between Baffin Island, Canada, and W Greenland

dav·it (dav′it) *n.* [< OFr. dim. of *David*] either of a pair of uprights that stick out over the side of a ship for holding, lowering, or raising a boat

Da·vy (dā′vē), **Sir Humphry** 1778–1829; Eng. chemist

Da·vy Jones (dā′vē jōnz′) the spirit of the sea: humorous name given by sailors

Davy Jones's locker (jōn′ziz, jōnz) the bottom of the sea; grave of those drowned or buried at sea

daw (dô) *n.* [ME. *dawe*] *same as* JACKDAW

daw·dle (dôd′'l) *vi., vt.* **-dled, -dling** [< ?] to waste (time) in pointless activity or by being slow; loiter (often with *away*) [he *dawdled* away the afternoon] —see SYN. at LOITER —**daw′dler** *n.*

dawn (dôn) *vi.* [< OE. < *dagian*, to become day < *dæg*, DAY] **1.** to begin to be day; grow light [day is *dawning*]   **2.** to begin to appear, develop, etc. [the age of the computer had *dawned*]   **3.** to begin to be understood or felt (usually with *on* or *upon*) [the truth just *dawned* on me] —*n.* **1.** daybreak   **2.** the beginning (of something) [the *dawn* of a new era]

dawn redwood a cone-bearing tree of China that is like a California redwood and is now grown in the U.S.

Daw·son (dô′s'n) city in W Yukon Territory, Canada, on the Yukon River: pop. 900

day (dā) *n.* [< OE. *dæg*] **1.** *a)* the period of light between sunrise and sunset   *b)* daylight   *c)* sunshine   **2.** *a)* the time (24 hours) that it takes the earth to revolve once on its axis: the civil day is from midnight to midnight   *b)* *Astron.* the time that it takes any celestial body to revolve once on its axis   **3.** [often D-] a particular or specified day [Memorial *Day*]   **4.** [also *pl.*] a period of time; era [the best writer of his *day*, in *days* of old]   **5.** a time of power, glory, success, etc. [he has had his *day*]   **6.** a struggle or contest [to win or carry the *day*]   **7.** the time one works each day [an eight-hour *day*]   **8.** an unspecified time [one of these *days*]   **9.** [*pl.*] one's lifetime [to spend one's *days* in study] —**call it a day** [Colloq.] to stop working for the day —**day after day** every day —**day by day** each day —**day in, day**

out every day —**from day to day** 1. from one day to the next 2. without particular concern about the future

Day·ak (dī′ak) *n. same as* DYAK

day·bed (-bed′) *n.* a couch that can also be used as a bed

day·book (-book′) *n.* 1. a diary or journal 2. *Bookkeeping* a book used for recording the transactions of each day as they occur

day·break (-brāk′) *n.* the time in the morning when light first appears; dawn

day-care center (-ker′) *same as* DAY NURSERY

day·dream (-drēm′) *n.* 1. a pleasant, dreamlike thinking or wishing; reverie 2. something pleasant to think about that one will probably never have —*vi.* to have daydreams —**day′- dream′er** *n.*

☆**Day-Glo** (dā′glō′) *a trademark for* a coloring agent added to pigments, dyes, etc. to produce any of a variety of brilliant, fluorescent colors —*adj.* of or like such a color or colors

day laborer a unskilled worker paid by the day

☆**day letter** a telegram with a minimum charge for fifty words or fewer, sent in the daytime: it is cheaper but slower than a regular telegram

Day Lewis, C(ecil) 1904–72; Brit. poet & novelist, born in Ireland

day·light (-līt′) *n.* 1. the light of day; sunlight 2. dawn; daybreak 3. daytime 4. full understanding or knowledge of something hidden or obscure 5. the approaching end of a task, etc. [to see *daylight*] 6. [*pl.*] [Slang] orig., the eyes; hence, the state of being awake or conscious: often used to suggest a violent or shocking effect, as in **scare** (or **beat, knock,** etc.) **the daylights out of**

day·light-sav·ing time (-sā′vin) time that is one hour later than standard time, generally used in the summer to give an hour more of daylight at the end of the usual working day

day lily 1. a plant of the lily family, with showy flowers, usually opening for a single day 2. *same as* PLANTAIN LILY

day·long (dā′lôn′) *adj., adv.* during the whole day

☆**day nursery** a nursery school for the daytime care and training of preschool children, as of working mothers

Day of Atonement *same as* YOM KIPPUR

day room a room for recreation, reading, etc., as in a barracks, institution, or the like

days (dāz) *adv.* on every day or most days

day school 1. a school that has classes only in the daytime 2. a private school whose students live at home and attend classes daily

days of grace extra time allowed, as for payment of an insurance premium after it is due

day·star (dā′stär′) *n.* 1. the morning star 2. [Poet.] the sun

day·time (dā′tīm′) *n.* the period of daylight

day-to-day (dā′tə dā′) *adj.* everyday; daily

Day·ton (dāt′n) [after Gen. E. *Dayton* (1737–1807)] city in SW Ohio: pop. 244,000 (met. area 850,000)

day·work (dā′wurk′) *n.* work done (esp. by a domestic worker) and paid for on a daily basis

daze (dāz) *vt.* **dazed, daz′ing** [< ON. *dasast*, to become weary < *dasi*, tired] 1. to stun or bewilder, as by a shock or blow [he was *dazed* by the news of his defeat] 2. to dazzle —*n.* a dazed condition; bewilderment —**daz′ed·ly** *adv.*

daz·zle (daz′'l) *vt.* **daz′zled, daz′zling** [< DAZE, *vt.* + -LE²] 1. to make nearly blinded with very bright light or moving lights [the headlights of oncoming cars *dazzled* our driver] 2. to be so brilliant and splendid as to cause great surprise or admiration [the pianist's skill *dazzled* the audience] —*vi.* 1. to be overpowered by glare 2. to arouse great surprise or admiration by brilliant display —*n.* 1. a dazzling 2. something that dazzles —**daz′zle·ment** *n.* —**daz′zler** *n.* —**daz′zling·ly** *adv.*

db decibel; decibels

D.Bib. Douay Bible

dbl. double

DC, D.C., d.c. direct current

D.C., DC 1. District of Columbia 2. *da capo*

dd., d/d delivered

D.D. [L. *Divinitatis Doctor*] Doctor of Divinity

D-day (dē′dā′) *n.* the day for beginning a military operation; specif., June 6, 1944, the day Allied forces invaded western Europe in World War II

☆**DDD** a colorless, crystalline substance for killing insects, related to DDT but considered to be less toxic to animals

D.D.S. Doctor of Dental Surgery

DDT a powerful chemical compound for killing insects

de- [< Fr. *dé-* or L. *de* < L. *dis-*: see DIS-] *a prefix meaning:* 1. away from, off [*derail*] 2. down [*decline*] 3. wholly, entirely [*defunct*] 4. reverse the action of; undo [*defrost, decode*]

dea·con (dēk′n) *n.* [OE. < LL. < Gr. *diakonos*, servant] 1. a clergyman ranking just below a priest in the Roman Catholic and Anglican churches 2. in certain other Christian churches, a church officer who helps the minister, esp. in matters not having to do with worship

dea·con·ess (dēk′n is) *n.* a woman appointed as an assistant in a church, as for helping with the care of the sick and poor of a parish

de·ac·ti·vate (dē ak′tə vāt′) *vt.* **-vat′ed, -vat′ing** 1. to make (an explosive, chemical, etc.) unable to have its expected effect or action 2. *Mil.* to place (troops, etc.) on nonactive status —**de·ac′ti·va′tion** *n.*

dead (ded) *adj.* [OE. < IE. base *dheu-*, to die] 1. no longer living; having died 2. without life; inanimate [*dead* stones] 3. as in death; deathlike [a *dead* faint] 4. lacking vitality, interest, variety, warmth, brilliance, etc. [a *dead* party; a *dead* white] 5. without feeling, motion, or power [his arm hung *dead* at his side] 6. *a)* no longer burning [*dead* coals] *b)* extinct [a *dead* volcano] 7. motionless, slack, stagnant, etc. [*dead* water] 8. not working or usable [a *dead* telephone; a *dead* tennis ball] 9. no longer used or significant; obsolete [*dead* languages] 10. barren or unprofitable [*dead* soil] 11. unerring; sure [a *dead* shot] 12. exact; precise [*dead* center] 13. complete; absolute [a *dead* stop] 14. [Colloq.] very tired; exhausted 15. *Elec. a)* without current [a *dead* wire] *b)* having lost its charge [a *dead* battery] 16. *Sports* no longer in play [a *dead* ball] —*n.* the time of greatest darkness, most intense cold, etc. [the *dead* of night, the *dead* of winter] —*adv.* 1. completely; absolutely [*dead* right] 2. directly [*dead* ahead] —**the dead** those who have died —**dead′ness** *n.*

SYN.—**dead** is the general word for a person or thing that was alive but is no longer alive; **deceased** and **departed** are both used when one wants to avoid using the word when mentioning someone who has recently died, but **deceased** is primarily a legal term and **departed** suggests religious notions; **late** is often used before the name or title of one who has recently died [the *late* president]; **defunct** is applied to something that has failed and thus no longer exists [a *defunct* magazine] and is not used of a dead person except in a joking way —**ANT. alive, living**

dead·beat (ded′bēt′) ☆*n.* [Slang] 1. a person who evades paying his debts 2. a lazy, idle person

dead duck (or **pigeon**) ☆[Slang] a person or thing that is ruined or certain to be ruined or to fail or die

dead·en (ded′'n) *vt.* 1. to lessen the vigor or intensity of; dull [heavy curtains *deadened* the noise] 2. to make numb [the dentist *deadened* the nerve] —*vi.* to lose vigor, intensity, etc.

dead-end (-end′) *adj.* 1. having only one outlet [a *dead-end* street] 2. giving no opportunity for progress [a *dead-end* plan]

dead end 1. an end of a street, etc. that has no regular exit 2. a situation from which there seems to be no way to escape

dead·eye (-ī′) *n.* 1. a round, flat wooden block with three holes in it for the lanyard, used on a ship to fasten the shrouds 2. [Slang] an accurate marksman

dead·fall (-fôl′) *n.* a trap arranged so that a heavy weight is dropped on the prey

dead·head (-hed′) *n.* ☆1. a person using a free ticket as to get into a show ☆2. a vehicle traveling without cargo or passengers ☆3. a floating log, mostly underwater ☆4. [Slang] a dull or stupid person —☆*vi.* to make a trip without cargo or passengers —☆*adv.* without passengers or cargo

dead heat a race in which two or more contestants reach the finish line at exactly the same time; tie

dead letter 1. a law, practice, etc. no longer enforced or in effect but not formally done away with 2. a letter that cannot be delivered or returned, as because of a wrong address

DEADEYES

fat, āpe, cär; ten, ēven; is, bīte; gō, hôrn, tool, look; oil, out; up, fur; get; joy; yet; chin; she; thin, then; zh, leisure; ŋ, ring; ə for a in ago, e in agent, i in sanity, o in comply, u in focus; ′ as in able (ā′b'l); Fr. bal; ë, Fr. coeur; ö, Fr. feu; Fr. mon; ô, Fr. coq; ü, Fr. duc; r, Fr. cri; H, G. ich; kh, G. doch; ‡foreign; ☆ Americanism; < derived from. See inside front cover.

dead·line (-līn′) *n.* ☆the latest time by which something must be done or completed [a *deadline* for paying a bill]

dead·lock (-läk′) *n.* **1.** a complete stop that results when equal forces are opposed to each other **2.** a tie between opponents **3.** a lock with a bolt that is moved not by a spring but only by turning the key or knob —*vt., vi.* to bring or come to a deadlock

dead·ly (-lē) *adj.* **-li·er, -li·est 1.** causing or likely to cause death [a *deadly* poison] **2.** to the death; mortal [*deadly* combat] **3.** as in death [*deadly* pallor] **4.** very harmful **5.** extreme or excessive [*deadly* silence] **6.** oppressively tiresome [a *deadly* bore] **7.** perfectly accurate [*deadly* aim] **8.** *Theol.* causing spiritual death [*deadly* sins] —*adv.* **1.** as if dead [to lie *deadly* still] **2.** extremely or excessively [*deadly* serious] —see *SYN.* at FATAL —**dead′li·ness** *n.*

deadly nightshade *same as* BELLADONNA (sense 1)

deadly sins *Theol.* the seven most serious sins (pride, covetousness, lust, anger, gluttony, envy, and sloth): so called because regarded as causing spiritual death

dead march funeral music in slow march tempo

☆**dead·pan** (-pan′) *n.* [Slang] an expressionless face, or a person with such a face —*adj., adv.* [Slang] without expression or show of emotion

dead reckoning [< ? *ded* (for *deduced*) *reckoning*] the finding of a ship's position by an estimate based on data recorded in the log, such as the time spent on a specified course, speed, etc., rather than by taking observations of the sun and stars

Dead Sea inland body of salt water between Israel and Jordan: c. 1,290 ft. below sea level

Dead Sea Scrolls scrolls dating from 100? B.C.–70? A.D. discovered since 1947 in caves near the Dead Sea: they contain Jewish Scriptural writings, etc.

☆**dead soldier** [Slang] an emptied bottle, as of liquor

dead weight 1. the weight of an inert person or thing **2.** the weight of a vehicle without a load

dead·wood (-wood′) *n.* **1.** dead wood on trees ☆**2.** a useless or burdensome person or thing

deaf (def) *adj.* [OE.: for IE. base see DOWN²] **1.** totally or partially unable to hear **2.** unwilling to hear or listen [*deaf* to her pleas] —**deaf′ly** *adv.* —**deaf′ness** *n.*

deaf-and-dumb (def′'n dum′) *adj.* **1.** deaf-mute **2.** of or for deaf-mutes Now regarded as a term showing contempt

deaf·en (-'n) *vt.* **1.** to make deaf **2.** to make so much noise that it becomes hard to hear —**deaf′en·ing** *adj., n.*

deaf-mute (-myoot′) *n.* a person who is deaf, esp. from birth, and unable to speak: most deaf-mutes, having the necessary vocal organs, can be taught to speak —*adj.* of or being a deaf-mute

deal¹ (dēl) *vt.* **dealt, deal′ing** [OE. *dælan*] **1.** to portion out or distribute **2.** to give or deliver (a blow) —*vi.* **1.** to have to do (*with*) [books *dealing* with fish] **2.** to act or conduct oneself (followed by *with*) [*deal* fairly with others] **3.** to consider or attend to; cope (*with*) [to *deal* with a problem] **4.** to do business; trade (*with* or *in*) [to *deal* in hardware] **5.** to hand playing cards, one by one, to the players —*n.* **1.** *a)* the act of dealing playing cards *b)* cards dealt *c)* a player's turn to deal *d)* the playing of one deal of cards **2.** a business transaction ☆**3.** a bargain or agreement, esp. when secret or underhanded ☆**4.** *a)* [Colloq.] behavior or conduct toward another; treatment [a square *deal*] *b)* a particular plan, policy, etc. [the New *Deal*] —**big deal** [Colloq.] ☆a very important or impressive thing — ☆**make a big deal out of** [Colloq.] to make a big fuss about —**deal′er** *n.*

deal² (dēl) *n.* [OE. *dæl,* a part] an indefinite or considerable amount [a *deal* of trouble] —**a good** (or **great**) **deal 1.** a large amount **2.** very much

deal³ (dēl) *n.* [MDu. *dele*] **1.** a fir or pine board **2.** fir or pine wood —*adj.* made of deal

☆**deal·er·ship** (dēl′ər ship′) *n.* a franchise to market a product in an area, or a distributor holding this

deal·ing (dēl′iŋ) *n.* **1.** distribution **2.** way of acting toward others **3.** [*usually pl.*] transactions or relations [business *dealings*]

dealt (delt) *pt. and pp. of* DEAL¹

dean (dēn) *n.* [< OFr. < LL. *decanus,* head of ten soldiers or monks < L. *decem,* TEN] **1.** *a)* the presiding official of a cathedral or collegiate church *b)* R.C.Ch. a priest chosen by his bishop to supervise a number of parishes within the diocese ☆**2.** a college or university official in charge of a school or faculty, or of the students **3.** the oldest or most outstanding member of a particular group [the *dean* of U.S. poets] —**dean′ship′** *n.*

dean·er·y (dēn′ər ē) *n., pl.* **-er·ies 1.** the rank or authority of a dean **2.** the residence of a dean

☆**dean's list** a list of students with the highest grades, issued periodically at certain colleges

dear (dir) *adj.* [OE. *deore*] **1.** much loved; beloved **2.** much valued; esteemed: a polite form of address [*Dear* Sir] **3.** *a)* high-priced *b)* charging high prices **4.** earnest [our *dearest* wish] —*adv.* **1.** with deep affection **2.** at a high cost —*n.* a loved or lovable person —*interj.* an expression of surprise, pity, etc. —see *SYN.* at COSTLY —**dear′ly** *adv.* —**dear′ness** *n.*

Dear·born (dir′bərn, -bôrn′) [after Gen. H. *Dearborn,* U.S. Secretary of War (1801–09)] city in SE Mich.: suburb of Detroit: pop. 104,000

Dearborn Heights city in SE Mich.: suburb of Detroit: pop. 80,000

dearth (dʉrth) *n.* [see DEAR & -TH¹] **1.** scarcity of food; famine **2.** any scarcity or lack [a *dearth* of good books]

dear·y, dear·ie (dir′ē) *n., pl.* **-ies** [Colloq.] dear; darling: now often used when being sarcastic or humorous

death (deth) *n.* [OE.: for IE. base see DEAD] **1.** the act or fact of dying; permanent ending of life **2.** [D-] the personification of death, usually as a skeleton holding a scythe **3.** the state of being dead **4.** any end that is like dying [the *death* of fascism] **5.** any experience thought of as like dying or being dead **6.** the cause of death [smoking will be the *death* of him] **7.** murder or bloodshed —**at death's door** nearly dead —**put to death** to kill; execute —**to death** very much [worried *to death*] —**to the death 1.** to the very end of (a struggle, etc.) **2.** always —**death′like′** *adj.*

death·bed (deth′bed′) *n.* **1.** the bed on which a person dies **2.** the last hours of a person's life —*adj.* done or made in one's last hours of life [a *deathbed* confession]

death·blow (-blō′) *n.* **1.** a blow that kills **2.** a thing destructive or fatal (*to* something)

death cup a deadly mushroom with a white cap and a cuplike structure around the base of the stalk

death duty [Brit.] *same as* INHERITANCE TAX

☆**death house** a cell block, etc. where prisoners condemned to die are kept until their execution

death·less (-lis) *adj.* that cannot die; immortal [the poet's *deathless* lines] —**death′less·ly** *adv.* —**death′less·ness** *n.*

death·ly (-lē) *adj.* **1.** causing death; deadly **2.** like death or as in death [a *deathly* stillness] —*adv.* **1.** in a deathlike way **2.** extremely [*deathly* ill]

death mask a cast of a dead person's face

death rate the number of deaths per year per thousand of population: sometimes other units of time or population are used

☆**death row** *same as* DEATH HOUSE

death's-head (deths′hed′) *n.* a human skull or a representation of it, symbolizing death

death tax *same as* INHERITANCE TAX

☆**death·trap** (deth′trap′) *n.* **1.** an unsafe building, vehicle, etc. **2.** any very dangerous place or situation

Death Valley dry, hot desert basin in E Calif. & S Nev.: 282 ft. below sea level

death warrant 1. an official order to put a person to death **2.** anything that makes the destruction or end of a person or thing something that cannot be avoided

death·watch (-wäch′, -wôch′) *n.* **1.** a vigil kept beside a dead or dying person **2.** a beetle that burrows into wood and makes a tapping sound superstitiously regarded as an omen of death

☆**deb** (deb) *n.* [Colloq.] *short for* DEBUTANTE

deb. debenture

de·ba·cle (di bäk′'l, -bak′-; dā-) *n.* [< Fr. < *débâcler,* to break up] **1.** a breaking up of ice in a river, etc. **2.** a rush of debris-filled waters **3.** an overwhelming defeat or rout **4.** a total, often ludicrous, collapse or failure

de·bar (dē bär′) *vt.* **-barred′, -bar′ring** [< Anglo-Fr.: see DE- & BAR¹] **1.** to keep (*from* some right or privilege); bar [he was *debarred* from voting] **2.** to prevent or prohibit —**de·bar′ment** *n.*

de·bark (di bärk′) *vt., vi.* [< Fr.: see DE- & BARK³] to unload from or leave a ship or aircraft —**de·bar·ka·tion** (dē′bär kā′shən) *n.*

de·base (di bās′) *vt.* **-based′, -bas′ing** [DE- + (A)BASE] to make lower in value, quality, character, dignity, etc.; cheapen —**de·base′ment** *n.* —**de·bas′er** *n.*

SYN.—**debase** implies generally a lowering in quality, value, character, etc. [to *debase* oneself by telling lies]; **deprave** suggests influences that

DEATH CUP

cause a change in character to wickedness, immorality, etc. [he was *depraved* by evil men]; **corrupt** implies a loss of soundness as the result of some destructive influence [an official *corrupted* by bribery]; **debauch** suggests a loss of moral purity as the result of overindulgence in drinking, gambling, etc.; **pervert** implies a turning or leading astray from what is considered good, natural, or true [objective news reporting *perverted* into propaganda] —see also SYN. at DEGRADE —*ANT.* **elevate, improve**

de·bat·a·ble (di bāt′ə b'l) *adj.* **1.** that can be debated; having strong points on both sides [a *debatable* question] **2.** that can be questioned or disputed; questionable

de·bate (di bāt′) *vi.* **-bat′ed, -bat′ing** [< OFr. *debatre*, to fight: see DE- & BATTER¹] **1.** to discuss opposing reasons; argue **2.** to take part in a formal discussion or a debate (*n.* 2) —*vt.* **1.** to dispute about, esp. in a meeting or legislature [the Senate *debated* the foreign aid bill] **2.** to argue (a question) or argue with (a person) formally **3.** to consider reasons for and against (*with* oneself or *in* one's own mind) [he *debated* with himself what to do] —*n.* **1.** discussion or consideration of opposing reasons **2.** a formal contest of skill in reasoned argument, with two teams taking opposite sides of a question **3.** the art or study of formal debate —see SYN. at DISCUSS —**de·bat′er** *n.*

de·bauch (di bôch′) *vt.* [< Fr. < OFr. *desbaucher*, to seduce] to lead astray morally into evil ways; corrupt —*vi.* to indulge in debauchery; dissipate —*n.* **1.** *same as* DEBAUCHERY **2.** an orgy —see SYN. at DEBASE —**de·bauch′er** *n.* —**de·bauch′-ment** *n.*

deb·au·chee (di bôch·ē′; deb′ô chē′, -shē′) *n.* one who indulges in debauchery; dissipated person

de·bauch·er·y (di bôch′ər ē) *n.,* pl. **-er·ies** **1.** the satisfying of one's desires and appetites in a bad or wild way; dissipation **2.** [*pl.*] orgies **3.** a leading astray morally

de·ben·ture (di ben′chər) *n.* [< ML. < L. *debentur*, there are owing < *debere:* see DEBT] **1.** a voucher stating that a debt is owed by the signer **2.** an interest-bearing bond issued by a corporation or governmental unit, often without security

de·bil·i·tate (di bil′ə tāt′) *vt.* **-tat′ed, -tat′ing** [< L. pp. of *debilitare,* to weaken < *debilis,* weak] to make weak or feeble; enervate [bodies *debilitated* by starvation] —see SYN. at WEAKEN —**de·bil′i·ta′tion** *n.*

de·bil·i·ty (-tē) *n.,* pl. **-ties** [< OFr. < L. *debilitas* < *debilis,* weak] weakness or feebleness, esp. of one's body

deb·it (deb′it) *n.* [< OFr. < L. *debitum,* what is owing: neut. pp. of *debere:* see DEBT] **1.** an entry on the left-hand side of an account, as of money owed **2.** the total of such entries —*vt.* to enter as a debit or debits

deb·o·nair, deb·o·naire (deb′ə ner′) *adj.* [< OFr. < *de bon aire,* lit., of good breed] **1.** friendly in a cheerful way; genial; affable **2.** carefree in manner; jaunty —**deb′o·nair′ly** *adv.*

Deb·o·rah (deb′ə rə, deb′rə) [Heb. *debōrāh,* lit., a bee] a feminine name: dim. *Debby*

de·bouch (di boosh′) *vi.* [< Fr. < *dé-,* DE- + *bouche,* the mouth < L. *bucca,* cheek] **1.** *Mil.* to come forth from a narrow or shut-in place into open country **2.** to come forth; emerge —**de·bouch′ment** *n.*

dé·bride·ment (di brēd′mənt; *Fr.* dā brēd män′) *n.* [Fr. < *débrider,* to cut away tissue] *Surgery* the cutting away of dead tissue from a wound to prevent infection

de·brief (dē brēf′) *vt.* [DE- + BRIEF] to question (a pilot, emissary, etc.) just after he has returned from a flight, mission, etc. and, often, tell him what he may say about it publicly —**de·brief′ing** *n.*

de·bris, dé·bris (də brē′; *also, esp. Brit. & Canad.,* de′brē, dā′-) *n.* [Fr. < OFr. *desbrisier,* to break apart] **1.** broken pieces of stone, wood, glass, etc. left after the destruction caused by a storm, explosion, etc.; rubble **2.** bits of rubbish; litter [*debris* along the road] **3.** a heap of rock fragments, as from a glacier

Debs (debz), **Eugene Victor** 1855–1926; U.S. labor leader & Socialist candidate for president

debt (det) *n.* [< OFr. < L. *debitum,* neut. pp. of *debere,* to owe < *de-,* from + *habere,* to have: see HABIT] **1.** something owed by one person to another **2.** an obligation or liability to pay or return something **3.** the condition of owing [to be in *debt*] **4.** *Theol.* a sin

debt of honor a gambling or betting debt

debt·or (det′ər) *n.* one that owes a debt

de·bug (dē bug′) *vt.* **-bugged′, -bug′ging** [DE- + BUG] **1.** to remove insects from **2.** [Slang] to find and correct defects,

faults, etc. in **3.** [Slang] to find and remove hidden electronic listening devices from (a room, etc.)

☆**de·bunk** (di buŋk′) *vt.* [DE- + BUNK²] [Colloq.] to expose the false claims of; show or tell the real truth about —**de·bunk′er** *n.*

De·bus·sy (də bü sē′; *E.* deb′yoo sē′, də byoo′sē), **(Achille) Claude** 1862–1918; Fr. composer

de·but, dé·but (di byoo′, dā-; dā′byoo) *n.* [Fr. < *débuter,* to lead off < (*jouer*) *de but,* (to play) for the mark] **1.** the first appearance before the public, as of an actor **2.** the formal introduction of a girl into society **3.** the beginning of a career, course, etc.

deb·u·tante (deb′yoo tänt′, deb′yoo tänt′) *n.* [< Fr. fem. of *débutant,* prp. of *débuter,* to make a DEBUT] a girl making a debut, esp. into society

Dec. December

dec. **1.** deceased **2.** decimeter **3.** declension **4.** decrease

dec·a- [< Gr. *deka,* TEN] *a combining form meaning* ten, the factor 10¹ [*decagon, decameter*]: also, before a vowel, **dec-**

dec·ade (dek′ād) *n.* [< OFr. < L. < Gr. *deka,* TEN] **1.** a group of ten **2.** a period of ten years

dec·a·dence (dek′ə dəns, di kā′d'ns) *n.* [< Fr. < ML. < prp. of VL. *decadere* < L. *de-,* from + *cadere,* to fall] a decadent process, condition, or period, as in morals, art, literature, etc.; deterioration; decay

dec·a·dent (-dənt) *adj.* that is becoming bad, immoral, wicked, etc.; marked by decadence [a *decadent* society] —*n.* a decadent person, esp. a decadent writer or artist —**dec′a·dent·ly** *adv.*

dec·a·gon (dek′ə gän′) *n.* [see DECA- & -GON] a plane figure with ten sides and ten angles —**de·cag·o·nal** (di kag′ə nəl) *adj.*

dec·a·gram (-gram′) *n.* [see DECA- & GRAM] a measure of weight, equal to 10 grams: also, chiefly Brit., **dec′a·gramme′** (-gram′)

dec·a·he·dron (dek′ə hē′drən) *n.,* pl. **-drons, -dra** (-drə) [see DECA- & -HEDRON] a solid figure with ten plane surfaces —**dec′a·he′dral** (-drəl) *adj.*

de·cal (di kal′, dē′kal) *n. same as* DECALCOMANIA

DECAGON

de·cal·ci·fy (dē kal′sə fī′) *vt.* **-fied′, -fy′ing** to remove calcium or lime from (bones, etc.) —**de·cal′ci·fi·ca′tion** *n.* —**de·cal′ci·fi′er** *n.*

de·cal·co·ma·ni·a (di kal′kə mā′nē ə) *n.* [< Fr. < *dé-,* DE- + *calquer,* to copy + *manie,* mania] **1.** the process of transferring decorative pictures or designs from specially prepared paper onto glass, wood, etc. **2.** a picture or design of this kind

dec·a·li·ter (dek′ə lēt′ər) *n.* [see DECA- & LITER] a measure of capacity, equal to 10 liters: also, chiefly Brit., **dec′a·li′tre** (-lēt′ər)

Dec·a·logue, Dec·a·log (dek′ə lôg′, -läg′) *n.* [< LL. < Gr. *dekalogos:* see DECA- & -LOGUE] [*sometimes* d-] *same as* TEN COMMANDMENTS

dec·a·me·ter (dek′ə mēt′ər) *n.* [see DECA- & METER¹] a measure of length, equal to 10 meters: also, chiefly Brit., **dec′a·me′tre** (-mēt′ər)

de·camp (di kamp′) *vi.* [< Fr.: see DE- & CAMP] **1.** to break or leave camp **2.** to go away suddenly and secretly; run away [the treasurer *decamped* with the tax money] —**de·camp′ment** *n.*

de·cant (di kant′) *vt.* [< Fr. < ML. < L. *de-,* from + *canthus,* rim, edge] to pour off (a liquid) gently, as into another container, without stirring up the sediment [to *decant* wine] —**de·can·ta·tion** (dē′kan tā′shən) *n.*

de·cant·er (-ər) *n.* a decorative glass bottle, used for serving wine, etc.

de·cap·i·tate (di kap′ə tāt′) *vt.* **-tat′ed, -tat′ing** [< Fr. < ML. pp. of *decapitare* < L. *de-,* off + *caput,* the HEAD] to cut off the head of; behead —**de·cap′i·ta′tion** *n.*

dec·a·pod (dek′ə päd′) *adj.* [see DECA- & -POD] ten-legged —*n.* **1.** any crustacean with ten legs, as a lobster, shrimp, crab, etc. **2.** any cephalopod with ten arms, as a squid —**de·cap·o·dal** (di kap′ə d'l), **de·cap′o·dous** (-dəs) *adj.* —**de·cap′o·dan** (-dən) *adj., n.*

de·car·bon·ate (dē kär′bə nāt′) *vt.* **-at′ed,**

DECANTER

-at'ing to remove carbon dioxide or carbonic acid from —**de·car'bon·a'tion** n.

de·car·bon·ize (-nīz') vt. **-ized', -iz'ing** to remove carbon from: also **de·car'bu·rize'** (-bə rīz', -byōō-) **-rized', -riz'ing** —**de·car'bon·i·za'tion** n.

de·car·box·y·la·tion (dē'kär bäk'sə lā'shən) n. the removal of a carboxyl group from an organic acid —**de'car·box'y·late'** vt., vi. **-lat'ed, -lat'ing**

dec·a·syl·la·ble (dek'ə sil'ə b'l) n. a line of verse with ten syllables —**dec'a·syl·lab'ic** (-si lab'ik) adj.

de·cath·lon (di kath'län, -lən) n. [DEC(A)- + Gr. athlon, a contest] an athletic contest consisting of ten events in track and field sports: the contestant receiving the highest total of points wins

De·ca·tur (di kāt'ər) [after S. DECATUR] city in C Ill.: pop. 90,000

De·ca·tur (di kāt'ər), **Stephen** 1779–1820; U.S. naval officer

de·cay (di kā') vi. [< Anglo-Fr. & OFr. < VL. decadere: see DECADENCE] **1.** to become gradually no longer strong, powerful, healthy, sound, rich, beautiful, etc.; waste away [Spain's power decayed after her fleet was destroyed] **2.** to rot by the action of bacteria **3.** to undergo decay (n. 4) —vt. to cause to decay —n. **1.** a gradual decline or wasting away **2.** a rotting, as of vegetable matter **3.** a) rottenness b) rotted matter **4.** a) the continuing disintegration of radioactive atoms that results in a decrease in their number b) the continuing disintegration of a particle or nucleus, as a meson, until a more stable state is formed

SYN.—**decay** implies a gradual, often natural, change for the worse from a sound or normal condition [his teeth have begun to decay]; **rot** refers to the decay of organic, esp. vegetable, matter, caused by bacteria, fungi, etc. [apples rotting on the ground]; **putrefy** suggests rotting that produces foul odors and causes feelings of disgust [bodies putrefying in the fields]; **spoil** is the common, informal word for the decay of foods [fish spoils quickly in summer]; **molder** suggests a slow decaying and crumbling into dust [an abandoned cabin moldering away]; **decompose**, which suggests the breaking up of something into its basic parts, is often used as a polite substitute for rot and putrefy

Dec·can Plateau (dek'ən) triangular tableland occupying most of the peninsula of India, south of the Narbada River

de·cease (di sēs') n. [< OFr. < L. decessus, pp. of decedere < de-, from + cedere, to go] death —vi. **-ceased', -ceas'ing** to die —see SYN. at DIE[1]

de·ceased (di sēst') adj. dead —see SYN. at DEAD —the **deceased** the dead person or persons

de·ce·dent (di sēd''nt) n. Law a deceased person

de·ceit (di sēt') n. [< OFr. pp. of deceveir: see DECEIVE] **1.** the act of deceiving or lying **2.** a dishonest action or trick; lie **3.** the quality of being deceitful

de·ceit·ful (-fəl) adj. **1.** tending to deceive; apt to lie or cheat **2.** intended to deceive; deceptive; false —**de·ceit'ful·ly** adv. —**de·ceit'ful·ness** n.

de·ceive (di sēv') vt. **-ceived', -ceiv'ing** [< OFr. deceveir < L. decipere, to ensnare < de-, from + capere, to take] to make (a person) believe what is not true; mislead —vi. to be deceitful —**de·ceiv'a·ble** adj. —**de·ceiv'er** n. —**de·ceiv'ing·ly** adv.

SYN.—**deceive** implies a deliberate telling of lies or acting dishonestly, usually by one who expects to gain something for himself [he was deceived by the salesman into paying too much for the car]; to **mislead** is to cause to follow the wrong course or do the wrong thing, although not always on purpose [misled by the sign into going to the wrong floor]; **beguile** implies the use of charm, tempting promises, etc. in deceiving or misleading [she beguiled him into believing her lies]; to **delude** is to fool someone so completely that he accepts as true or real something that is false; **betray** implies a breaking of faith while seeming to be loyal, true, or friendly

de·cel·er·ate (dē sel'ə rāt') vt., vi. **-at'ed, -at'ing** [DE- + (AC)CELERATE] to slow down —**de·cel'er·a'tion** n. —**de·cel'er·a'tor** n.

De·cem·ber (di sem'bər) n. [< OFr. < L. < decem, TEN: the early Romans reckoned from March] the twelfth and last month of the year, having 31 days: abbrev. **Dec., D.**

de·cem·vir (di sem'vər) n., pl. **-virs, -vir·i·** (-və rī') [L. < decem, TEN + vir, a man] a member of a council of ten magistrates in ancient Rome

de·cen·cy (dē's'n sē) n., pl. **-cies** **1.** a being decent; propriety; proper behavior, modesty, good taste, etc. [he hasn't the decency to say he's sorry] **2.** [pl.] socially proper actions **3.** [pl.] things needed, as food and shelter, in order to have a decent standard of living

de·cen·ni·al (di sen'ē əl) adj. [< L. decem, TEN + annus, year + -AL] **1.** of or lasting ten years **2.** occurring every ten years —n. a tenth anniversary —**de·cen'ni·al·ly** adv.

de·cent (dē's'nt) adj. [< L. prp. of decere, to befit: for IE. base see DIGNITY] **1.** proper and fitting [a decent burial] **2.** not immodest; not obscene [decent language] **3.** conforming to approved social standards; respectable [decent apparel] **4.** reasonably good; adequate [decent wages] **5.** fair and kind [decent treatment] **6.** [Colloq.] adequately clothed for propriety —**de'cent·ly** adv.

de·cen·tral·ize (dē sen'trə līz') vt. **-ized', -iz'ing** to break up (governmental authority, industry, etc.) in a main center as by spreading it to local groups or to many places —**de·cen'tral·i·za'tion** n.

de·cep·tion (di sep'shən) n. [< OFr. < L. pp. of decipere: see DECEIVE] **1.** a deceiving or being deceived **2.** something that deceives, as an illusion, or is meant to deceive, as a fraud

de·cep·tive (-tiv) adj. deceiving or meant to deceive —**de·cep'tive·ly** adv. —**de·cep'tive·ness** n.

dec·i- [Fr. < L. < decem, TEN] a combining form meaning one tenth, the factor 10^{-1} [decigram]

dec·i·bel (des'ə bel', -b'l) n. [DECI- + bel (after A. G. Bell)] **1.** a unit of the relative loudness of a sound **2.** a unit of the relative power level of an electrical signal

de·cide (di sīd') vt. **-cid'ed, -cid'ing** [< L. decidere < de-, off + caedere, to cut] **1.** to end (a contest, dispute, etc.) by giving one side the victory [a jury will decide the case] **2.** to reach a decision about; make up one's mind about [he can't decide what to do] **3.** to cause to reach a decision [the offer of a better job decided her to move] —vi. to arrive at a judgment or decision —**de·cid'a·ble** adj. —**de·cid'er** n.

SYN.—**decide** implies the bringing to an end of wavering, doubt, dispute, etc. by making up one's mind about something to be done or a judgment to be made; **determine** suggests coming to a decision after much thought or investigation [the club decided to sponsor a lecture series and appointed a committee to determine the details of speakers, meeting place, etc.]; **settle** emphasizes finality in a decision, often one arrived at by a judge, referee, etc., and implies that all doubt or controversy has been ended; to **conclude** is to decide after careful investigation or reasoning; **resolve** implies firmness of intention to carry through a decision [he resolved to read a book every week]

de·cid·ed (di sīd'id) adj. **1.** definite; clear-cut [a decided change] **2.** free from hesitation; determined [a decided manner of speaking] —**de·cid'ed·ly** adv.

de·cid·u·ous (di sij'oo wəs) adj. [L. deciduus < de-, off + cadere, to fall] **1.** falling off at a certain season or stage of growth, as the leaves of some trees **2.** shedding its leaves every year: opposed to EVERGREEN [elms are deciduous trees] —**de·cid'u·ous·ly** adv. —**de·cid'u·ous·ness** n.

dec·i·gram (des'ə gram') n. [see DECI- & GRAM] a metric weight, equal to 1/10 gram: also, chiefly Brit., **dec'i·gramme'**

dec·i·li·ter (des'ə lēt'ər) n. [see DECI- & LITER] a metric measure of volume, equal to 1/10 liter: also, chiefly Brit., **dec'i·li'tre**

de·cil·lion (di sil'yən) n. [DEC(A)- + (M)ILLION] ☆**1.** in the U.S. and France, the number written as 1 followed by 33 zeros **2.** in England and Germany, the number written as 1 followed by 60 zeros —adj. amounting to one decillion in number

dec·i·mal (des'ə m'l) adj. [OFr. < ML. decimalis < L. < decem, TEN] of or based on the number 10; progressing by tens —n. a fraction with an unwritten denominator of 10, or of 100 or 1,000, etc.: it is shown by a point (**decimal point**) before the numerator (Ex.: .5 = 5/10); in full, **decimal fraction**

☆**decimal classification** a system used in libraries for classifying books by use of numbers with decimals

dec·i·mal·ize (des'ə m'l īz') vt. **-ized', -iz'ing** **1.** to adopt a decimal system for (currency, etc.) **2.** to change into decimals —**dec'i·mal·i·za'tion** n.

dec·i·mal·ly (-ē) adv. **1.** by tens **2.** in decimals

decimal system **1.** a system for computing or measuring based on the number ten ☆**2.** same as DECIMAL CLASSIFICATION

dec·i·mate (des'ə māt') vt. **-mat'ed, -mat'ing** [< L. pp. of decimare < decem, TEN] **1.** orig., to pick out by casting lots and kill every tenth one of (a group) **2.** to destroy or kill a large part of —**dec'i·ma'tion** n. —**dec'i·ma'tor** n.

dec·i·me·ter (des'ə mēt'ər) n. [see DECI- & METER[1]] a metric measure of length, equal to 1/10 meter: also, chiefly Brit., **dec'i·me'tre**

de·ci·pher (di sī'fər) vt. [DE- + CIPHER] **1.** to translate (a message in secret writing or code) into ordinary language; decode **2.** to make out the meaning of (scrawled or blurred writing) —**de·ci'pher·a·ble** adj. —**de·ci'pher·ment** n.

de·ci·sion (di sizh'ən) n. **1.** the act of deciding something **2.** a judgment or conclusion reached or given [the decision of the judges will be final] **3.** determination; firmness of mind [a man of *decision*] **4.** *Boxing* a victory on points instead of by a knockout —**de·ci′sion·al** *adj.*

de·ci·sive (di sī′siv) *adj.* **1.** that settles a dispute, question, etc.; conclusive [a *decisive* battle in a war] **2.** critically important; crucial [a *decisive* moment in his career] **3.** showing firmness or determination [a *decisive* tone of voice] —**de·ci′sive·ly** *adv.* —**de·ci′sive·ness** *n.*

dec·i·stere (des′ə stir′) *n.* [see DECI- & STERE] a metric measure of volume, 1/10 cubic meter

deck¹ (dek) *n.* [prob. < MLowG. *verdeck* (< *ver-*, prefix + *deck-en*, to cover)] **1.** a roof over a section of a ship's hold, serving as a floor **2.** any platform or floor like a ship's deck **3.** a pack of playing cards —*vt.* ☆[Slang] to knock down —**clear the decks** to get ready for action —☆**hit the deck** [Slang] **1.** to get out of bed **2.** to get ready for action **3.** to throw oneself to the ground, as to avoid injury **4.** to be knocked down —☆**on deck** [Colloq.] **1.** ready; on hand **2.** ready to take one's turn

deck² (dek) *vt.* [MDu. *decken*, to cover] **1.** to cover or clothe with fine clothes or ornaments; adorn [she *decked* herself out in expensive furs] **2.** to furnish (a ship, etc.) with a deck

deck chair a folding chair, usually with a leg rest

-deck·er (dek′ər) *a combining form meaning* having (a specified number of) decks, layers, etc. [two-*decker*]

☆**deck·hand** (dek′hand′) *n.* a common sailor

deck·le edge (dek′'l) [G. dim. of *decke*, a cover] a rough, irregular edge sometimes given to a sheet of paper

DECK CHAIR

de·claim (di klām′) *vi., vt.* [< L. < *de-*, very much + *clamare*, to shout] **1.** to recite (a speech, poem, etc.) or speak (anything) in a loud and showy or affected way **2.** to deliver a violent speech (against) —**de·claim′er** *n.*

dec·la·ma·tion (dek′lə mā′shən) *n.* **1.** the act or art of declaiming **2.** a speech, poem, etc. that is or can be declaimed

de·clam·a·to·ry (di klam′ə tôr′ē) *adj.* **1.** of or fit for declaiming [a *declamatory* poem] **2.** speaking in a loud and showy or affected way

de·clar·a·ble (di klar′ə b'l, -kler′-) *adj.* that can be or must be declared so that it can be taxed

dec·la·ra·tion (dek′lə rā′shən) *n.* **1.** the act of declaring; announcement [his *declaration* that he was innocent] **2.** a thing declared **3.** a formal statement [the *Declaration* of Independence] **4.** a statement of taxable goods **5.** the winning bid in a game of bridge

Declaration of Independence a formal statement adopted July 4, 1776, by the Second Continental Congress, declaring the thirteen American colonies free and independent of Great Britain

de·clar·a·tive (di klar′ə tiv, -kler′-) *adj.* making a statement, specif. a positive statement: also **de·clar′a·to·ry** (-ə tôr′ē) —**de·clar′a·tive·ly** *adv.*

de·clare (di kler′) *vt.* **-clared′, -clar′ing** [< OFr. < L. < *de-*, entirely + *clarare* < *clarus*, CLEAR] **1.** to make clearly known; announce openly, formally, etc. [only Congress can *declare* war] **2.** to show or reveal **3.** to say emphatically **4.** to tell that one is bringing (some taxable article) into a country [he *declared* to the customs officer the camera he bought in Canada] **5.** to authorize payment of (a dividend, etc.) **6.** *Card Games* to establish (trump or no-trump) by a successful bid —*vi.* **1.** to make a declaration **2.** to state openly a choice, opinion, etc. (for or against) [the editor *declared* for the liberal candidate] —**declare oneself 1.** to state strongly one's opinion **2.** to reveal one's true character, etc. —**I declare!** I am surprised, startled, etc. —**de·clar′er** *n.*

de·clar·ed·ly (-id lē) *adv.* openly or admittedly

de·clas·si·fy (dē klas′ə fī′) *vt.* **-fied′, -fy′ing** ☆to remove (governmental documents, reports, etc.) from secret or restricted classifications and make available to the public

de·clen·sion (di klen′shən) *n.* [< OFr. < L. < pp. of *de-clinare*: see DECLINE] **1.** a sloping; descent **2.** a declining or wasting away **3.** *Gram. a)* a class of nouns, pronouns, or adjectives having the same or a similar system of endings or other

changes to show case *b)* such change in the form of words [in English only the pronouns show *declension*, as in *he, his, him*] —**de·clen′sion·al** *adj.*

dec·li·na·tion (dek′lə nā′shən) *n.* **1.** a bending or sloping downward **2.** a slanting variation from a definite direction **3.** the angle formed by a magnetic needle with the line pointing to true north **4.** a polite refusal **5.** *Astron.* the angular distance of a heavenly body north or south from the celestial equator

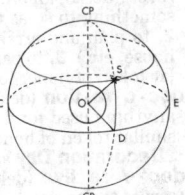

DECLINATION
(CP, celestial poles; CE, celestial equator; O, observer, or center of earth; DS, or angle DOS, declination of star S)

de·cline (di klīn′) *vi.* **-clined′, -clin′-ing** [< OFr. < L. < *de-*, from + *-clinare*, to bend: for IE. base see CLIENT] **1.** to bend or slope downward or aside **2.** to sink, as the setting sun **3.** to approach the end; wane [the day is *declining*] **4.** to become less, smaller, or weaker; decay [strength usually *declines* in old age] **5.** to descend to base or immoral behavior **6.** to refuse to do something —*vt.* **1.** to cause to bend or slope downward or aside **2.** to refuse, esp. politely [he *declined* the invitation] **3.** *Gram.* to give the different case forms of (a noun, pronoun, or adjective) —*n.* **1.** a declining or becoming less, smaller, etc.; decay [a *decline* in employment] **2.** a failing of health, etc. **3.** a period of decline **4.** the last part [the *decline* of life] **5.** a downward slope [he skied down the *decline*] —**de·clin′a·ble** *adj.* —**de·clin′er** *n.*

SYN.—**decline** implies being courteous in not accepting an invitation, proposal, etc. [he *declined* the nomination]; **refuse** is a more direct, sometimes even rude term, implying an emphatic denial of a request, demand, etc. [to *refuse* a person money]; **reject** emphasizes a negative or hostile attitude and implies definite refusal to accept, use, believe, etc. [they *rejected* the peace treaty]; to **spurn** is to refuse or reject with contempt or scorn [she *spurned* his attentions] —**ANT.** accept

de·cliv·i·tous (di kliv′ə təs) *adj.* fairly steep

de·cliv·i·ty (-tē) *n., pl.* **-ties** [< L. < *de-*, down + *clivus*, a slope: for IE. base see CLIENT] a downward slope of the ground

de·coct (di käkt′) *vt.* [< L. pp. of *decoquere* < *de-*, down + *co-quere*, to COOK] to draw out the essence, flavor, etc. of by boiling —**de·coc′tion** *n.*

de·code (dē kōd′) *vt.* **-cod′ed, -cod′ing** to translate (a coded message) into ordinary, understandable language —**de·cod′-er** *n.*

de·col·le·tage (dā käl′ə tazh′; *Fr.* dā kôl tazh′) *n.* [Fr.: see DÉCOLLETÉ] **1.** the neckline or top of a dress cut low so as to bare the neck and shoulders **2.** a décolleté dress, etc.

dé·col·le·té (dā kal′ə tā′; *Fr.* dā kôl tā′) *adj.* [Fr., ult. < L. *de*, from + *collum*, the neck] **1.** cut low so as to bare the neck and shoulders **2.** wearing a décolleté dress, etc.

de·col·o·ni·za·tion (dē käl′ə nə zā′shən) *n.* a freeing or being freed from colonialism or colonial status —**de·col′o·nize′** (-nīz′) *vt., vi.* **-nized′, -niz′ing**

de·col·or·ize (dē kul′ər īz′) *vt.* **-ized′, -iz′ing** to take the color out of, as by bleaching —**de·col′or·i·za′tion** *n.*

de·com·pen·sa·tion (dē käm′pən sā′shən) *n.* same as HEART FAILURE

de·com·pose (dē′kəm pōz′) *vt., vi.* **-posed′, -pos′ing** [< Fr.: see DE- & COMPOSE] **1.** to break up or separate into its separate basic parts [electrolysis will *decompose* water into hydrogen and oxygen] **2.** to rot —see SYN. at DECAY —**de′com·pos′a·ble** *adj.* —**de′com·po·si′tion** (-käm pə zish′ən) *n.*

de·com·press (dē′kəm pres′) *vt.* to free from pressure —**de′-com·pres′sion** *n.*

☆**decompression sickness** a condition caused by the formation of nitrogen bubbles in the blood or body tissues as a result of a sudden lowering of air pressure, resulting in collapse in severe cases

de·con·gest·ant (dē′kən jes′tənt) *n.* a medication that relieves congestion, as in the nasal passages

de·con·tam·i·nate (dē′kən tam′ə nāt′) *vt.* **-nat′ed, -nat′ing** to rid of a harmful substance, as radioactive products —**de′con·tam′i·na′tion** *n.*

de·con·trol (dē′kən trōl′) *vt.* **-trolled′, -trol′ling** to free from controls —*n.* withdrawal of controls

dé·cor, de·cor (dā kôr′, dā′kôr) *n.* [Fr. < L. < *decere*, to befit: see DECENT] **1.** decoration **2.** the decorative scheme of a room, stage set, etc.

dec·o·rate (dek′ə rāt′) *vt.* **-rat′ed, -rat′ing** [< L. pp. of *decorare* < *decus*, an ornament: for IE. base see DIGNITY] **1.** to add something to so as to make more attractive; adorn; ornament **2.** to plan and arrange the colors, furnishings, etc. of (a room, house, etc.) **3.** to paint or wallpaper **4.** to give a medal or similar token of honor to —see SYN. at ADORN

dec·o·ra·tion (dek′ə rā′shən) *n.* **1.** the act of decorating **2.** anything used for decorating; ornament **3.** a medal, badge, or similar token of honor

☆**Decoration Day** same as MEMORIAL DAY

dec·o·ra·tive (dek′ər ə tiv, -ə rāt′iv; dek′rə tiv) *adj.* that serves to decorate; ornamental —**dec′o·ra·tive·ly** *adv.* —**dec′o·ra·tive·ness** *n.*

dec·o·ra·tor (dek′ə rāt′ər) *n.* a person who decorates; specif., a specialist whose work is decorating and furnishing rooms

dec·or·ous (dek′ər əs, di kôr′əs) *adj.* [L. *decorus*, becoming < *decor*: see DÉCOR] having or showing dignity or good taste; behaving well —**dec′o·rous·ly** *adv.* —**dec′o·rous·ness** *n.*

de·co·rum (di kôr′əm) *n.* [L., neut. of *decorus*: see prec.] **1.** proper and dignified behavior, speech, dress, etc. that is in good taste [her rudeness to guests shows a lack of *decorum*] **2.** an act or requirement of polite behavior: *often used in pl.*

de·cou·page, dé·cou·page (dā′kōō pązh′) *n.* [Fr., a cutting up] the mounting of decorative paper cutouts on a surface over which coats of shellac, etc. are usually applied

de·coy (dē koi′; *for n.* also dē′koi) *n.* [< Du. *de kooi*, the cage < L. *cavea*, CAGE] **1.** a place into which wild ducks, etc. are lured for capture **2.** an artificial bird or animal used to lure game to a place where it can be shot, or one that is alive and trained to do this **3.** a thing or person used to lure others into a trap —*vt.,* *vi.* to lure or be lured into a trap, danger, etc.—see SYN. at LURE

DECOY

de·crease (di krēs′; *also, & for n. usually,* dē′krēs) *vi., vt.* **-creased′, -creas′ing** [< OFr. < L. < *de-,* from + *crescere,* to grow: for IE. base see CEREAL] to become or cause to become gradually less, smaller, etc.; diminish [the number of students at the school has *decreased*] —*n.* **1.** a decreasing; lessening [a *decrease* in enrollment] **2.** amount of decreasing [a *decrease* in sales of 25%] —**on the decrease** decreasing —**de·creas′ing·ly** *adv.*

SYN. —**decrease** and **dwindle** suggest a growing gradually smaller in bulk, size, volume, or number, but **dwindle** emphasizes a wasting away to the point of disappearance [his hopes *decreased* as his fortune *dwindled* away to nothing]; **lessen** is equivalent to **decrease**, except that it does not imply any particular rate of decline [his influence *lessened* overnight]; **diminish** emphasizes a taking away from the whole, often over a period of time [disease had *diminished* their ranks]; **reduce** implies a lowering, or bringing down [to *reduce* prices] —**ANT. increase**

de·cree (di krē′) *n.* [< OFr. < L. *decretum* < *de-,* from + *cernere,* to decide: see CERTAIN] an official order or decision, as of a government or court —*vt.* **-creed′, -cree′ing** to order, decide, or appoint by decree —*vi.* to issue a decree

de·crep·it (di krep′it) *adj.* [< OFr. < L. < *de-,* very much + pp. of *crepare,* to creak] broken down or worn out by old age, illness, or long use —see SYN. at WEAK —**de·crep′it·ly** *adv.*

de·crep·i·tude (di krep′ə tōōd′, -tyōōd′) *n.* a decrepit condition; feebleness or infirmity

de·cre·scen·do (dē′krə shen′dō, dā′-) *adj., adv.* [It.] *Music* with a gradual decrease in loudness —*n., pl.* **-dos** *Music* **1.** a gradual decrease in loudness: symbol > **2.** a decrescendo passage

de·cre·tal (di krēt′'l) *adj.* [< LL. *decretalis*] of or containing a decree —*n.* **1.** a decree **2.** *R.C.Ch.* a decree issued by the Pope on some matter of discipline in the church

☆**de·crim·i·nal·ize** (dē krim′ə n'l īz′) *vt.* **-ized′, -iz′ing** to remove the legal penalties for (a particular crime); make no longer a crime

de·cry (di krī′) *vt.* **-cried′, -cry′ing** [< Fr. < OFr. *descrier:* see DE-, & CRY] **1.** to speak out against strongly and openly; denounce [they *decried* the tax increase] **2.** to depreciate (money, etc.) officially —**de·cri′al** *n.* —**de·cri′er** *n.*

de·cum·bent (di kum′bənt) *adj.* [< L. prp. of *decumbere* < *de-,* down + *-cumbere, cubare,* to recline] **1.** lying down **2.** *Bot.* trailing on the ground and rising at the tip, as some stems

de·cus·sate (di kus′it, di kus′āt) *adj.* [< L. pp. of *decussare,* to form an X, ult. < *decem,* TEN] *Bot.* arranged in pairs growing at right angles to those above and below: said of leaves or branches —**de·cus′sate·ly** *adv.*

ded·i·cate (ded′ə kāt′) *vt.* **-cat′ed, -cat′ing** [< L. pp. of *dedicare* < *de-,* entirely + *dicare,* to proclaim < *dicere,* to speak] **1.** to devote to a sacred purpose [a temple *dedicated* to Venus] **2.** to devote to some work, duty, etc. **3.** to state at the beginning of (a book, artistic performance, etc.) that it is in honor of someone ☆**4.** to open formally (a public building, etc.) —**ded′i·ca′tor** *n.*

ded·i·ca·tion (ded′ə kā′shən) *n.* **1.** a dedicating or being dedicated **2.** an inscription, as in a book, dedicating it to someone **3.** wholehearted devotion —**ded′i·ca·to′ry, ded′i·ca′tive** *adj.*

de·dif·fer·en·ti·a·tion (dē dif′ə ren′shē ā′shən) *n.* a reversal of cell development, esp. in plants, so that the cell becomes more generalized in structure

de·duce (di dōōs′, -dyōōs′) *vt.* **-duced′, -duc′ing** [< L. < *de-,* down + *ducere,* to lead] **1.** to trace the course or origin of **2.** to figure out by logical reasoning; conclude from known facts or general principles [the detective *deduced* who did the crime] —see SYN. at INFER —**de·duc′i·ble** *adj.*

de·duct (di dukt′) *vt.* [L. *deductus,* pp. of *deducere:* see prec.] to take away or subtract (a quantity)

de·duct·i·ble (-ə b′l) *adj.* **1.** that can be deducted **2.** that is allowed as a deduction in computing income tax

de·duc·tion (di duk′shən) *n.* **1.** a deducting or being deducted; subtraction **2.** the amount deducted **3.** *Logic a)* reasoning from known facts or general principles to a logical conclusion [detectives in stories solve crimes by *deduction*] *b)* a conclusion so deduced Opposed to INDUCTION —**de·duc′tive** *adj.* —**de·duc′tive·ly** *adv.*

deed (dēd) *n.* [OE. *ded, dæd:* for IE. base see DO[1]] **1.** a thing done or an act, esp. one that shows courage, skill, etc. **2.** action; actual performance **3.** *Law* an official paper drawn up according to law that hands over a property from one owner to another —☆*vt.* to hand over (property) by such a paper —**in deed** in fact; really

☆**dee·jay** (dē′jā′) *n.* [D(ISC) J(OCKEY)] [Colloq.] same as DISC JOCKEY

deem (dēm) *vt., vi.* [OE. *deman,* to judge < base of *dom,* DOOM] to think, believe, or judge [he is *deemed* likely to win]

de·em·pha·size (dē em′fə sīz′) *vt.* **-sized′, -siz′ing** to lessen the importance given to [this school *de-emphasizes* football] —**de·em′pha·sis** (-sis) *n.*

deep (dēp) *adj.* [OE. *deop* < IE. base *dheub-,* deep, hollow] **1.** extending far downward from the top, inward from the surface, or backward from the front [a *deep* lake] **2.** extending down, back, or in a specified distance [two feet *deep*] **3.** *a)* located far down or back [*deep* in the outfield] *b)* coming from or going far down or back [a *deep* breath] **4.** hard to understand; abstruse [a *deep* book] **5.** extremely grave or serious [in *deep* trouble] **6.** strongly felt [*deep* love] **7.** intellectually profound [a *deep* discussion] **8.** tricky and sly *b)* carefully guarded [a *deep* secret] **9.** dark and rich [a *deep* red] **10.** absorbed by [*deep* in thought] **11.** *a)* intense [*deep* joy] *b)* heavy and unbroken [a *deep* sleep] **12.** much involved [*deep* in debt] **13.** of low pitch [a *deep* voice] —*n.* **1.** a deep place **2.** the middle part; part that is darkest, etc. [the *deep* of the night] —*adv.* in a deep way; far down, far back, far on, etc. [to dig *deep*] —see SYN. at BROAD —**go off the deep end** [Colloq.] **1.** to become deeply involved **2.** to become angry or excited —**in deep water** in trouble or difficulty —**the deep** [Poet.] the sea or ocean —**deep′ly** *adv.* —**deep′ness** *n.*

deep-chest·ed (dēp′ches′tid) *adj.* having a thick chest, or coming as from a thick chest [a *deep-chested* roar]

☆**deep-dish pie** (dēp′dish′) a pie baked in a deep dish and having only a top crust

deep·en (dēp′n) *vt., vi.* to make or become deep or deeper

☆**Deep·freeze** (dēp′frēz′) *a trademark for* a deep freezer —*n.* [d-] **1.** storage in a deep freezer **2.** a condition during which some activity is halted for a time —*vt.* [d-] **-froze′** or **-freezed′, -fro′zen** or **-freezed′, -freez′ing 1.** to subject (foods) to sudden freezing so as to preserve and store **2.** to store in a deep freezer

DECUSSATE LEAVES

☆**deep freezer** any freezer for quick-freezing and storing food

deep-fry (-frī′) vt. -fried′, -fry′ing to fry in a deep pan of boiling fat or oil

deep-root·ed (-rōōt′id, -root′id) adj. 1. having deep roots 2. firmly fixed; hard to remove [deep-rooted prejudice]

deep-seat·ed (-sēt′id) adj. 1. placed or coming from far beneath the surface 2. firmly fixed

deep-set (-set′) adj. 1. deeply set 2. firmly fixed

deer (dir) n., pl. **deer**, occas. **deers** [OE. deor, wild animal: for IE. base see DOWN²] any of a family of cud-chewing animals with hoofs, including the moose, reindeer, caribou, etc.: the males usually have antlers that are shed every year

deer·hound (dir′hound′) n. any of a Scottish breed of large, shaggy-haired dog, orig. used in hunting deer

☆**deer mouse** 1. a white-footed mouse of N. America 2. a light-brown mouse of the southwestern U.S.

deer·skin (-skin′) n. 1. the hide of a deer 2. leather or a garment made from this —adj. made of deerskin

deer·stalk·er (-stôk′ər) n. a hunter's cap with a low crown, and a visor in front and in back

☆**de·es·ca·late** (dē es′kə lāt′) vi., vt. -lat′ed, -lat′ing to reduce or lessen in size, extent, importance, etc. [efforts to de-escalate the war] —de·es·ca·la′tion n.

def. 1. defendant 2. defense 3. deferred 4. defined 6. definite 6. definition

DEERSTALKER

de·face (di fās′) vt. -faced′, -fac′ing [< OFr. desfacier: see DE- & FACE] to spoil or mar the surface or appearance of [to deface a picture by writing on it] —de·face′ment n. —de·fac′er n.

de fac·to (di fak′tō, dā) [L.] existing in actual fact though not by official recognition, etc. [a de facto government]: see DE JURE

de·fal·cate (di fal′kāt, -fôl′-) vi. -cat·ed, -cat·ing [< ML. pp. of defalcare, to cut off < L. de-, from + falcis, genitive of falx, sickle] to steal or misuse funds entrusted to one's care; embezzle —de·fal·ca′tion (dē′fal kā′shən, -fôl-) n. —de·fal′ca·tor n.

def·a·ma·tion (def′ə mā′shən) n. a defaming or being defamed; slander or libel

de·fame (di fām′) vt. -famed′, -fam′ing [< OFr. or ML. < L. < dis-, from + fama, FAME] to attack the reputation of; slander or libel —def·a·ma·to·ry (di fam′ə tôr′ē) adj. —de·fam′er n.

de·fault (di fôlt′) n. [< OFr. defaute < L. de-, away + fallere, to fail, deceive] failure to do or appear as required; specif., a) failure to pay money due b) failure to appear in court to defend or prosecute a case c) failure to take part in or finish a contest [he couldn't play and so lost the game by default] —vi. 1. to fail to do or appear as required; specif., a) to fail to make payment when due b) to fail to appear in court c) to fail to take part in or finish a contest 2. to lose by default —vt. 1. to fail to do, pay, finish, etc. (something) when required 2. to lose (a contest, etc.) by default —in default of through lack of —de·fault′er n.

de·feat (di fēt′) vt. [< OFr. < ML. < L. dis-, from + facere, to DO¹] 1. to win victory over; overcome; beat [to defeat the enemy] 2. to bring to nothing; make fail; frustrate [his hopes were defeated] —n. a defeating or being defeated —see SYN. at CONQUER

de·feat·ist (-ist) n. a person who too readily accepts defeat or gives up without trying —adj. of or like a defeatist —de·feat′ism n.

def·e·cate (def′ə kāt′) vt. -cat·ed, -cat·ing [< L. pp. of defaecare < de-, from + faecis, genitive of faex, dregs] to remove impurities from; refine —vi. 1. to become free from impurities 2. to move one's bowels —def′e·ca′tion n. —def′e·ca′tor n.

de·fect (dē′fekt; also, and for v. always, di fekt′) n. [< L. pp. of deficere, to fail < de-, from + facere, to DO¹] 1. lack of something necessary for completeness 2. an imperfection; fault; blemish —vi. to desert a cause, political party, etc. that one has been supporting —de·fec′tor n.

SYN.—defect implies that something missing or wrong keeps a thing from

being complete or perfect [a defect in vision]; an **imperfection** is any faulty detail that takes away from perfection [tiny bubbles are imperfections in glass]; a **blemish** is an imperfection on the surface that spoils the looks of something or someone [skin blemishes]; a **flaw** is an imperfection, such as a crack or gap, that spoils the structure or substance of something and keeps it from being whole or acceptable [a flaw in the pipe made it leak]

de·fec·tion (di fek′shən) n. 1. a deserting or becoming disloyal 2. a failure

de·fec·tive (-tiv) adj. 1. having a defect or defects; faulty 2. Gram. lacking some of the usual grammatical forms ["ought" is a defective verb] 3. subnormal in intelligence —n. ☆a person with some bodily or mental defect —de·fec′tive·ly adv. —de·fec′tive·ness n.

de·fence (di fens′) n. Brit. sp. of DEFENSE

de·fend (di fend′) vt. [< OFr. < L. defendere < de-, away + fendere, to strike < IE. base gwhen-, to strike] 1. to guard from attack; protect [guns defending the harbor] 2. to support, maintain, or justify [can you defend your rudeness?] 3. Law a) to oppose (an action, etc.) b) to act as lawyer for (an accused person) —vi. to make a defense —de·fend′a·ble adj. —de·fend′er n.

SYN.—defend implies an active effort to drive back an actual attack, threat, or invasion [to defend oneself in court]; **guard** suggests a watching over to keep safe from any possible attack or harm [to guard a coastline]; **protect** and **shield** imply a keeping safe from harm or injury by putting a barrier between [he built a fence to protect his garden], but **shield** also suggests protection against something attacking or about to attack or harm [to shield one's eyes against a glare]; **preserve** implies a keeping safe from being wasted, spoiled, ruined, etc. [to preserve one's freedom] —ANT. attack

de·fend·ant (di fen′dənt) adj. defending —n. Law the person in a law court who is being sued or accused

de·fense (di fens′, dē′fens) n. [OFr. < LL. < L. pp. of defendere, DEFEND] 1. a defending or being defended against attack or danger [to spend millions for defense] 2. means of protection [levees as defenses against flooding] 3. justification or support by speech or writing 4. self-protection, as by boxing 5. the side that is defending in any contest 6. a) the arguments of the defendant in contesting a case ☆b) the defendant and his lawyer or lawyers, as a group

de·fense·less (-lis) adj. lacking defense; helpless; unprotected —de·fense′less·ly adv. —de·fense′less·ness n.

defense mechanism Psychiatry any behavior that a person uses without being aware of it in order to protect himself against painful feelings, impulses, etc. that he wants to ignore

de·fen·si·ble (di fen′sə b'l) adj. that can be defended or justified —de·fen′si·bil′i·ty, de·fen′si·ble·ness n. —de·fen′si·bly adv.

de·fen·sive (-siv) adj. 1. defending 2. of or for defense 3. Psychol. feeling under attack and hence quick to justify one's actions —n. a position of defense: chiefly in the phrase on the defensive, in a position that makes defense necessary —de·fen′sive·ly adv. —de·fen′sive·ness n.

de·fer¹ (di fur′) vt., vi. -ferred′, -fer′ring [< OFr. differer: see DIFFER] 1. to put off until a later time; postpone; delay [to defer paying a bill] 2. to postpone the induction of (a person) into compulsory military service —de·fer′ment, de·fer′ral n. —de·fer′rer n.

de·fer² (di fur′) vi. -ferred′, -fer′ring [< OFr. < L. < de-, down + ferre, to BEAR¹] to give in or yield to the wish or judgment of another, as in showing respect —see SYN. at YIELD

def·er·ence (def′ər əns) n. 1. a yielding in one's opinion, judgment, etc. to another's 2. courteous regard or respect for the wishes or opinions of others —see SYN. at HONOR —in deference to out of regard for (a person, his wishes, etc.)

def·er·en·tial (def′ə ren′shəl) adj. showing deference; very respectful: also **def·er·ent** (def′ər ənt) —def′er·en′tial·ly adv.

de·fi·ance (di fī′əns) n. 1. a defying or opposing boldly a powerful person or thing 2. a challenge —in defiance of in spite of

de·fi·ant (-ənt) adj. full of defiance; openly and boldly resisting —de·fi′ant·ly adv.

de·fib·ril·late (di fib′rə lāt′) vt. -lat′ed, -lat′ing to stop fibrillation of (the heart), as by electric current —de·fib′ril·la′tion n. —de·fib′ril·la′tor n.

de·fi·cien·cy (di fish′ən sē) n. 1. the quality or state of being deficient; absence of an essential; incompleteness 2. pl. -cies a) a shortage b) the amount of shortage; deficit

---

fat, āpe, cär; ten, ēven; is, bīte; gō, hôrn, tōōl, look; oil, out; up, fur; get; joy; yet; chin; she; thin, then; zh, leisure; ŋ, ring; ə for a in ago, e in agent, i in sanity, o in comply, u in focus; ' as in able (ā′b'l); Fr. bâl; ë, Fr. coeur; ö, Fr. feu; Fr. mon; ô, Fr. coq; ü, Fr. duc; r, Fr. cri; H, G. ich; kh, G. doch; ‡foreign; ☆ Americanism; < derived from. See inside front cover.

deficiency disease a disease, as rickets, caused by lack of vitamins, minerals, etc. in the diet

de·fi·cient (di fish′ənt) *adj.* [< L. *deficiens*, prp. of *deficere*: see DEFECT] **1.** lacking in something essential; incomplete; defective **2.** not sufficient in amount, quality, degree, etc. —*n.* a deficient person or thing —**de·fi′cient·ly** *adv.*

def·i·cit (def′ə sit) *n.* [L., it is lacking < *deficere*: see DEFECT] the amount by which a sum of money is less than the required amount, as an excess of spending over income

de·fi·er (di fī′ər) *n.* a person who defies

de·file[1] (di fīl′) *vt.* **-filed′, -fil′ing** [< OFr. *defouler*, to tread underfoot (infl. by OE. *fylan*, make foul)] **1.** to make dirty or filthy; pollute [water *defiled* with sewage] **2.** to make impure; corrupt **3.** to profane or disgrace (a person's name, etc.) **4.** [Archaic] to violate the chastity of —**de·file′ment** *n.* —**de·fil′·er** *n.*

de·file[2] (di fīl′, dē′fīl) *vi.* **-filed′, -fil′ing** [< Fr. < *dé-* (L. *de*), from + *filer*, to form a line] to march in single file or by files —*n.* **1.** a narrow passage through which troops must defile **2.** any narrow valley or mountain pass

de·fine (di fīn′) *vt.* **-fined′, -fin′ing** [< OFr. < L. *definire*, to limit < *de-*, from + *finis*, boundary] **1.** to determine the boundaries of **2.** to describe the extent and nature of [*define* your duties] **3.** to state the meaning or meanings of (a word, etc.) —*vi.* to prepare definitions, as of words —**de·fin′a·ble** *adj.* —**de·fin′er** *n.*

def·i·nite (def′ə nit) *adj.* [< L. pp. of *definire*: see prec.] **1.** having exact limits [a *definite* boundary] **2.** exact and clear in meaning; explicit [*definite* orders] **3.** certain; positive [it's *definite* that he'll go] **4.** *Gram.* limiting or specifying ["the" is the *definite* article] —**def′i·nite·ly** *adv.* —**def′i·nite·ness** *n.*

def·i·ni·tion (def′ə nish′ən) *n.* **1.** a defining or being defined **2.** a statement of the meaning of a word, phrase, etc. **3.** *a)* a putting or being in clear, sharp outline *b)* a making or being definite or explicit **4.** the power of a lens to show (an object) in clear, sharp outline **5.** *Radio & TV* the clearness with which sounds or images are reproduced —**def′i·ni′tion·al** *adj.*

de·fin·i·tive (di fin′ə tiv) *adj.* **1.** that decides or settles in a final way; decisive; conclusive [a *definitive* answer] **2.** most nearly complete and accurate [a *definitive* biography] **3.** serving to define precisely [*definitive* details] **4.** *Biol.* fully developed —**de·fin′i·tive·ly** *adv.* —**de·fin′i·tive·ness** *n.*

de·flate (di flāt′) *vt., vi.* **-flat′ed, -flat′ing** [DE- + (IN)FLATE] **1.** to collapse by letting out air or gas [to *deflate* a tire] **2.** to make or become smaller or less important [he felt *deflated* when no one said hello] **3.** to cause deflation of (money, prices, etc.) Opposed to INFLATE —**de·fla′tor** *n.*

de·fla·tion (di flā′shən) *n.* **1.** a deflating or being deflated **2.** a lessening of the amount of money in circulation that causes a rise in its value and a fall in prices —**de·fla′tion·ar′y** *adj.*

de·flect (di flekt′) *vt., vi.* [< L. < *de-*, from + *flectere*, to bend] to bend or turn to one side; swerve [adjust the louvers to *deflect* the air] —**de·flec′tion** or Brit. **de·flex′ion** *n.* —**de·flec′tive** *adj.* —**de·flec′tor** *n.*

de·flow·er (di flou′ər) *vt.* [see DE- & FLOWER] **1.** to cause (a woman) to be no longer a virgin **2.** to ruin or spoil **3.** to remove flowers from (a plant) —**def·lo·ra·tion** (def′lə rā′shən) *n.*

De·foe (di fō′), **Daniel** 1660?–1731; Eng. writer

☆**de·fo·li·ant** (dē fō′lē ənt) *n.* a chemical spray that strips growing plants of their leaves

de·fo·li·ate (-āt′) *vt.* **-at′ed, -at′ing** [< LL. pp. of *defoliare* < L. *de-*, from + *folium*, a leaf] **1.** to strip (trees, etc.) of leaves ☆**2.** to use defoliants on —**de·fo′li·a′tion** *n.* —**de·fo′li·a′tor** *n.*

de·for·est (dē fôr′ist, -fär′-) *vt.* to clear (land) of forests or trees —☆**de·for′est·a′tion** *n.*

De For·est (di fôr′ist, fär′-), **Lee** 1873–1961; U.S. inventor of radio devices, etc.

de·form (di fôrm′) *vt.* [< OFr. < L. < *de-*, from + *forma*, form] **1.** to damage the form or shape of [a tree *deformed* by disease] **2.** to make ugly; disfigure [a face *deformed* by greed] **3.** *Physics* to change the shape of by pressure or stress —*vi.* to become deformed —**de·form′a·ble** *adj.* —**de·for·ma·tion** (dē′fôr mā′shən, def′ər-) *n.*

de·formed (di fôrmd′) *adj.* changed as in form or shape, esp. so as to be misshapen, ugly, etc.

de·form·i·ty (di fôr′mə tē) *n., pl.* **-ties** **1.** the condition of being deformed **2.** a deformed or disfigured part of the body **3.** ugliness or depravity **4.** anything deformed or disfigured

de·fraud (di frôd′) *vt.* [< OFr. < L. *defraudare* < *de-*, from + *fraus*, FRAUD] to take or hold back property, rights, etc. from

by fraud; cheat —see SYN. at CHEAT —**de·frau·da·tion** (dē′frô dā′shən) *n.* —**de·fraud′er** *n.*

de·fray (di frā′) *vt.* [< Fr. < OFr., prob. < L. *de*, from + *fractum*, neut. pp. of *frangere*, to BREAK] to pay (the cost or expenses) —**de·fray′a·ble** *adj.* —**de·fray′al, de·fray′ment** *n.*

de·frost (di frôst′) *vt.* **1.** to remove frost or ice from by thawing **2.** to cause (frozen foods) to become unfrozen —*vi.* to become defrosted

de·frost·er (-ər) *n.* a device for melting ice and frost, as on a windshield

deft (deft) *adj.* [see DAFT] skillful in a quick, sure, and easy way —see SYN. at DEXTEROUS —**deft′ly** *adv.* —**deft′ness** *n.*

de·funct (di funkt′) *adj.* [< L. *defunctus*, pp. of *defungi*, to finish, die < *de-*, from, off + *fungi*, to perform: see FUNCTION] no longer living or existing; dead or extinct —see SYN. at DEAD

de·fy (di fī′; *also for n.* dē′fī) *vt.* **-fied′, -fy′ing** [< OFr. *defier* < L. *dis-*, from + *fidus*, faithful] **1.** to resist or oppose boldly or openly [to *defy* the law] **2.** to resist completely in a confusing way [the puzzle *defied* solution] **3.** to dare (someone) to do or prove something —☆*n., pl.* **-fies** [Colloq.] a defiance or challenge

deg. degree; degrees

de·gas (dē gas′) *vt.* **-gassed′, -gas′sing** to remove gas from

De·gas (də gä′), **(Hilaire Germain) Ed·gar** (ed gär′) 1834–1917; Fr. painter

de Gaulle (də gôl′; *Fr.* gōl′), **Charles** 1890–1970; Fr. general; president of France (1959–69)

de·gauss (di gous′) *vt.* [DE- + GAUSS] to demagnetize (as a ship) by passing an electric current through a coil along or around the edge in order to neutralize the surrounding magnetic field —**de·gauss′er** *n.*

de·gen·er·a·cy (di jen′ər ə sē) *n.* **1.** the state of being degenerate **2.** degenerate behavior

de·gen·er·ate (-ər it; *for v.* -ə rāt′) *adj.* [L. pp. of *degenerare*, ult. < *de-*, from + *genus*, race: see GENUS] **1.** having sunk below a former or normal condition, etc.; deteriorated **2.** morally corrupt; depraved [the *degenerate* life of drug addicts] —*n.* a degenerate person, esp. one who is morally corrupt or sexually perverted —*vi.* **-at′ed, -at′ing** **1.** to lose former normal or higher qualities [the neighborhood *degenerated* into a slum] **2.** to become less moral, cultured, etc. [they *degenerated* into barbarians] **3.** *Biol.* to undergo degeneration —**de·gen′er·ate·ly** *adv.* —**de·gen′er·ate·ness** *n.* —**de·gen′er·a·tive** *adj.* —**de·gen′er·a·tive·ly** *adv.*

de·gen·er·a·tion (di jen′ə rā′shən) *n.* **1.** the process of degenerating **2.** a degenerate condition **3.** *Biol.* deterioration or loss of a function or structure in the course of evolution **4.** *Med.* deterioration in structure or function of cells, tissues, or organs, as in disease or aging

de·grade (di grād′) *vt.* **-grad′ed, -grad′ing** [< OFr. < LL. *degradare* < L. *de-*, down + *gradus*: see GRADE] **1.** to bring down to a lower rank or status, as in punishing; demote **2.** to make lower or corrupt in quality, moral character, etc.; make lose respect; disgrace; dishonor [he *degraded* himself by taking bribes] **3.** *Chem.* to convert (an organic compound) into a simpler compound **4.** *Geol.* to lower (a land surface) by erosion —**de·grad′a·ble** *adj.* —**deg·ra·da·tion** (deg′rə dā′shən) *n.* —**de·grad′er** *n.*

SYN.—degrade literally means to lower in grade or rank, but it commonly implies a lowering or corrupting of moral character, self-respect, etc.; **abase** suggests a loss of dignity, respect, etc., often a temporary loss that one brings on himself [he *abased* himself before his employer]; **debase** implies a decline in value, quality, character, etc. [a *debased* mind]; to **humble** is to lower the pride or increase the humility, esp. of another, and suggests that the lowering is deserved unless it is said not to be [humbled by the frightening experience]; to **humiliate** is to humble or shame (another) painfully and in public [humiliated by their laughter] —**ANT. exalt, dignify**

de·grad·ed (di grād′id) *adj.* disgraced, debased, depraved, etc. —**de·grad′ed·ly** *adv.* —**de·grad′ed·ness** *n.*

de·grad·ing (-iŋ) *adj.* that degrades; debasing —**de·grad′ing·ly** *adv.*

de·gree (di grē′) *n.* [< OFr. < LL. *degradare*: see DEGRADE] **1.** any of the successive steps or stages in a process or series [advancing by *degrees*] **2.** a step in the direct line of descent [a cousin in the second *degree*] **3.** social or official rank [a man of low *degree*] **4.** relative condition; manner or respect [each helping the cause in his *degree*] **5.** extent, amount, or relative intensity [hungry to a slight *degree*] **6.** *Algebra* rank as determined by the sum of a term's exponents [a^3c^2 and x^5 are each of the fifth *degree*] **7.** *Educ.* a rank given by a college or university to a student who has completed a required course of study, or to an outstanding person as an honor [a B.A. *degree*] **8.** *Gram.* any of the three forms that an adjective or adverb takes when it is compared [the superlative *degree* of "good" is "best"] ☆**9.** *Law* the seriousness of a crime [murder in the first *degree*] **10.** *Math., Astron., Geog.,* etc. a unit of measure for angles or arcs [there are 360 *degrees* in the circumference of a circle] **11.** *Music* a) a line or space on the staff b) an interval between two such lines or spaces **12.** *Physics* a unit of measure on a scale, as for temperature: the symbol for degree is ° [at sea level, water boils at 100°C] —**by degrees** step by step; gradually —**to a degree** somewhat

de·hisce (di his′) *vi.* **-hisced′, -hisc′ing** [< L. < *de-*, off + *hiscere*, to gape] to burst or split open, as a seedpod —**de·his′·cence** *n.* —**de·his′cent** *adj.*

☆**de·horn** (dē hôrn′) *vt.* to remove the horns from

de·hu·man·ize (dē hyōō′mə nīz′) *vt.* **-ized′, -iz′ing** to deprive of human qualities, such as individuality, creativity, etc.; make inhuman or machinelike [long hours of boring work *dehumanize* people] —**de·hu′man·i·za′tion** *n.*

de·hu·mid·i·fy (dē′hyōō mid′ə fī′) *vt.* **-fied′, -fy′ing** to remove moisture from (the air, etc.) —**de′hu·mid′i·fi·ca′tion** *n.* —**de′hu·mid′i·fi′er** *n.*

de·hy·drate (dē hī′drāt) *vt.* **-drat·ed, -drat·ing** to remove water from (a compound, body tissues, etc.); dry [powdered milk is milk that has been *dehydrated*] —*vi.* to lose water; become dry —**de′hy·dra′tion** *n.* —**de·hy′dra·tor** *n.*

☆**de·hy·dro·gen·ase** (dē hī′drə jə nās′, dē′hī dräj′ə nās′) *n.* [DE- + HYDROGEN + -ASE] an enzyme that helps cause oxidation in certain compounds by removing hydrogen

de·hy·dro·gen·ate (dē hī′drə jə nāt′) *vt.* **-at·ed, -at′ing** to remove hydrogen from: also **de·hy′dro·gen·ize′** (-nīz′) **-ized′, -iz′ing** —**de·hy′dro·gen·a′tion** *n.*

de-ice (dē īs′) *vt.* **-iced′, -ic′ing** to melt ice from or keep free of ice —**de-ic′er** *n.*

de·i·fy (dē′ə fī′) *vt.* **-fied′, -fy′ing** [< OFr. < LL. < L. *deus*, god + *facere*, to make] **1.** to make a god of; rank among the gods **2.** to look upon or worship as a god or as if a god; glorify; adore —**de·if′ic** (-if′ik) *adj.* —**de′i·fi·ca′tion** (-ə fi kā′shən) *n.* —**de′i·fi′er** *n.*

deign (dān) *vi.* [< OFr. < L. *dignare* < *dignus*, worthy] to think of as not being beneath one's dignity (*to do* something); condescend [the queen *deigned* to shake hands with him] —see SYN. at STOOP[1]

de·i·on·ize (dē ī′ə nīz′) *vt.* **-ized′, -iz′ing** to remove ions from (water)

de·ism (dē′iz'm) *n.* [< Fr. < L. *deus*, god] the doctrine that God created the world and its natural laws, but takes no personal interest in the world or its creatures —**de′ist** *n.* —**de·is′tic, de·is′ti·cal** *adj.* —**de·is′ti·cal·ly** *adv.*

de·i·ty (dē′ə tē) *n., pl.* **-ties** [< OFr. < LL. < L. *deus*, god < IE. base *dei-*, from which also comes L. *dies*, day] **1.** the state of being a god; divine nature [for the ancient Greeks, Apollo had *deity*] **2.** a god or goddess [nymphs and other minor deities] —**the Deity** God

‡**dé·jà vu** (dā zhà vü′) [Fr., lit., already seen] *Psychol.* the illusion that one has already lived through an experience that is actually new to one

de·ject (di jekt′) *vt.* [< L. pp. of *dejicere* < *de-*, down + *jacere*, to throw: see JET[1]] to dishearten; depress

de·ject·ed (di jek′tid) *adj.* in low spirits; depressed; disheartened; sad —see SYN. at SAD —**de·ject′ed·ly** *adv.* —**de·ject′ed·ness** *n.*

de·jec·tion (di jek′shən) *n.* a being dejected or sad; depression

de ju·re (dē joor′ē, dā) [L.] by right or legal establishment [de jure government]: see DE FACTO

dek·a- *same as* DECA-: also, before a vowel, **dek-**

de Koon·ing (də kō′niŋ), **Wil·lem** (wil′əm) 1904– ; U.S. painter, born in the Netherlands

de Kruif (də krīf), **Paul (Henry)** 1890– ; U.S. bacteriologist & writer

del. **1.** delegate **2.** delegation **3.** delete

De·la·croix (də là krwä′), **(Ferdinand Victor) Eu·gène** (ö zhen′) 1798–1863; Fr. painter

Del·a·ware (del′ə wer′, -war′) [after Baron *De La Warr*, colonial gov. of Va. (1610–11)] **1.** E State of the U.S., on the Atlantic: 2,057 sq. mi.; pop. 548,000; cap. Dover: abbrev. **Del.,**

DE 2. river flowing southward from southern N.Y. into the Atlantic —*n.* **1.** *pl.* **-wares′, -ware′** a member of a tribe of Indians who lived in the Delaware River valley **2.** their Algonquian language —**Del′a·war′e·an** *adj., n.*

de·lay (di lā′) *vt.* [< OFr. < *de-*, entirely + *laier*, to leave, let < L. *laxare*: see RELAX] **1.** to put off to a later time; postpone [his illness will *delay* the concert] **2.** to make late; detain [I was *delayed* by the storm] —*vi.* to stop for a while; linger —*n.* **1.** a delaying or being delayed **2.** the period of time for which something is delayed [a month's *delay* in filling the order] —**de·lay′er** *n.*

de·le (dē′lē) *vt.* **-led, -le·ing** [L., imperative sing. of *delere*: see DELETE] to take out (a letter, word, etc.) in printed matter; delete —*n.* a mark (⸜) used in deleting a letter, word, etc.

de·lec·ta·ble (di lek′tə b'l) *adj.* [OFr. < L. < *delectare*: see DELIGHT] very pleasing; delightful; now, esp., pleasing to the taste; delicious —**de·lec′ta·bil′i·ty, de·lec′ta·ble·ness** *n.* —**de·lec′ta·bly** *adv.*

de·lec·ta·tion (dē′lek tā′shən, di lek′-) *n.* [OFr. < L. < *delectare*: see DELIGHT] delight; entertainment

del·e·gate (del′ə gāt′; *also for n.* -git) *n.* [< ML. < L. pp. of *delegare* < *de-*, from + *legare*, to send] **1.** a person sent to speak and act for his group or organization; representative, as at a convention ☆**2.** a member of a House of Delegates —*vt.* **-gat′ed, -gat′ing** **1.** to send or appoint as a representative or deputy **2.** to entrust (authority, power, etc.) to a person acting as one's representative [the voters *delegate* power to their congressmen to make laws]

del·e·ga·tion (del′ə gā′shən) *n.* **1.** a delegating or being delegated **2.** a group of delegates [the Iowa *delegation* voted as a unit] Also **del·e·ga·cy** (del′ə gə sē) *pl.* **-cies**

de·lete (di lēt′) *vt.* **-let·ed, -let′ing** [< L. *deletus*, pp. of *delere*, to destroy < *de-*, from + base of *linere*, to smear < IE. base *lei-*, slimy] to take out (a printed or written letter, word, etc.); cross out —**de·le′tion** *n.*

del·e·te·ri·ous (del′ə tir′ē əs) *adj.* [Gr. *dēlētērios* < *dēleisthai*, to injure] harmful to health, well-being, etc.; injurious —see SYN. at PERNICIOUS —**del′e·te′ri·ous·ly** *adv.* —**del′e·te′ri·ous·ness** *n.*

delft·ware (delft′wer′) *n.* **1.** glazed earthenware, usually blue and white, which originated in Delft, a city in western Netherlands **2.** any similar ware Also **delft, delf** (delf)

Del·hi (del′ē) city in N India: pop. 2,062,000: see also NEW DELHI

del·i (del′ē) *n. shortened form of* DELICATESSEN

Del·ia (dēl′yə) [L., fem. of *Delius*, of Delos, a Greek island] a feminine name

de·lib·er·ate (di lib′ər it; *for v.* -āt′) *adj.* [< L. pp. of *deliberare* < *de-*, entirely + *librare*, to weigh < *libra*, a scales] **1.** carefully thought out and formed, or done on purpose [a *deliberate* refusal] **2.** careful in considering choices; not rash or hasty [he was very *deliberate* in choosing a partner] **3.** unhurried and methodical [deliberate aim] —*vi.* **-at′ed, -at′ing** to think or consider carefully and fully; esp., to consider reasons for and against a thing in order to make up one's mind —*vt.* to consider carefully —see SYN. at THINK[1] and VOLUNTARY —**de·lib′er·ate·ly** *adv.* —**de·lib′er·ate·ness** *n.* —**de·lib′er·a′tor** *n.*

de·lib·er·a·tion (di lib′ə rā′shən) *n.* **1.** a deliberating, or considering carefully **2.** [*often pl.*] consideration and discussion before reaching a decision **3.** carefulness; slowness

de·lib·er·a·tive (di lib′ə rāt′iv, -ər ə tiv) *adj.* **1.** of or for deliberating [a *deliberative* assembly] **2.** showing or using deliberation —**de·lib′er·a′tive·ly** *adv.* —**de·lib′er·a′tive·ness** *n.*

De·libes (də lēb′), **(Clément Philibert) Lé·o** (lā ō′) 1836–91; Fr. composer

del·i·ca·cy (del′i kə sē) *n., pl.* **-cies** **1.** a delicate quality, as in taste, texture, etc. **2.** graceful slightness, softness, etc.; fineness [the *delicacy* of a rose petal] **3.** weakness of constitution or health **4.** a need for careful and deft handling [negotiations of great *delicacy*] **5.** fineness of feeling or appreciation [delicacy of musical taste] **6.** fineness of touch, skill, etc. **7.** a fine regard for the feelings of others **8.** a sensitive distaste for what is considered improper or offensive **9.** a choice food [caviar and other *delicacies*]

del·i·cate (del′i kit) *adj.* [L. *delicatus*, delightful < OL. *deli-*

cere: see DELIGHT] **1.** pleasing in its lightness, mildness, etc. [a *delicate* flavor, color, etc.] **2.** beautifully fine in texture, workmanship, etc. [*delicate* linen] **3.** slight and subtle [a *delicate* difference] **4.** easily damaged, disordered, spoiled, etc.; fragile [a *delicate* vase] **5.** frail in health **6.** *a)* needing careful handling, tact, etc. [a *delicate* situation] *b)* showing tact, consideration, etc. **7.** finely sensitive [a *delicate* ear for music; a *delicate* gauge] **8.** finely skilled **9.** having a sensitive distaste for what is considered offensive or improper —**del′i·cate·ly** *adv.* —**del′i·cate·ness** *n.*

☆**del·i·ca·tes·sen** (del′i kə tes′′n) *n.* [G. pl. < Fr. *délicatesse,* delicacy] **1.** prepared cooked meats, smoked fish, cheeses, salads, relishes, etc., as a group **2.** a shop where such foods are sold

de·li·cious (di lish′əs) *adj.* [< OFr. < L. < *deliciae,* delight < OL. *delicere:* see DELIGHT] **1.** very enjoyable; delightful **2.** very pleasing to taste or smell —☆*n.* [D-] a sweet, red or yellow winter apple —**de·li′cious·ly** *adv.* —**de·li′cious·ness** *n.*

de·light (di līt′) *vt.* [< OFr. < L. *delectare,* to delight < OL. *delicere < de-,* from + *lacere,* to entice] to give great pleasure to —*vi.* **1.** to give great pleasure **2.** to be highly pleased [we *delighted* in our good fortune] —*n.* **1.** great pleasure **2.** something giving great pleasure —see SYN. at PLEASURE —**de·light′ed** *adj.* —**de·light′ed·ly** *adv.* —**de·light′ed·ness** *n.*

de·light·ful (-fəl) *adj.* giving delight; very pleasing; charming: also [Archaic] **de·light′some** (-səm) —**de·light′ful·ly** *adv.* —**de·light′ful·ness** *n.*

De·li·lah (di lī′lə) [Heb. *delîlāh,* lit., delicate] **1.** a feminine name **2.** *Bible* the mistress of Samson, who betrayed him to the Philistines: Judg. 16 —*n.* a seductive, treacherous woman

de·lim·it (di lim′it) *vt.* to set the limits or boundaries of: also **de·lim′i·tate′** (-ə tāt′) -tat′ed, -tat′ing —**de·lim′i·ta′tion** *n.* —**de·lim′i·ta′tive** *adj.*

de·lin·e·ate (di lin′ē āt′) *vt.* -at′ed, -at′ing [< L. < *de-,* from + *linea,* LINE[1]] **1.** to trace the outline of **2.** to draw; depict **3.** to describe in words —**de·lin′e·a′tion** *n.* —**de·lin′e·a′tive** *adj.* —**de·lin′e·a′tor** *n.*

de·lin·quen·cy (di liŋ′kwən sē) *n., pl.* **-cies** **1.** failure or neglect to do what duty or law requires ☆**2.** an overdue debt, tax, etc. **3.** a fault; misdeed ☆**4.** antisocial or illegal behavior, esp. by the young: see JUVENILE DELINQUENCY

de·lin·quent (-kwənt) *adj.* [< L. *delinquens,* prp. of *delinquere < de-,* from + *linquere,* to leave: for IE. base see LOAN] **1.** failing or neglecting to do what duty or law requires ☆**2.** overdue [*delinquent* taxes] —*n.* a delinquent person; esp., a juvenile delinquent —**de·lin′quent·ly** *adv.*

del·i·quesce (del′ə kwes′) *vi.* -quesced′, -quesc′ing [< L. *deliquescere < de-,* from + *liquere,* to be liquid] **1.** to melt away **2.** to become liquid by absorbing moisture from the air —**del′i·ques′cence** *n.* —**del′i·ques′cent** *adj.*

de·lir·i·ous (di lir′ē əs) *adj.* **1.** in a state of delirium **2.** of or caused by delirium **3.** wildly excited —**de·lir′i·ous·ly** *adv.* —**de·lir′i·ous·ness** *n.*

de·lir·i·um (-ē əm) *n., pl.* **-i·ums, -i·a** (-ə) [L. < *delirare,* to rave, lit., to turn the furrow awry in plowing < *de-,* from + *lira,* a line] **1.** a temporary state of extreme mental excitement, marked by confused speech and hallucinations: it sometimes occurs during a fever, in some forms of insanity, etc. **2.** uncontrollably wild excitement

delirium tre·mens (trē′mənz) [ModL., lit., trembling delirium] a violent delirium resulting chiefly from excessive drinking of alcoholic liquor

De·li·us (dē′lē əs, dēl′yəs), **Frederick** 1862-1934; Eng. composer

de·liv·er (di liv′ər) *vt.* [< OFr. < VL. < L. *de-,* from + *liberare,* to free < *liber,* free] **1.** to set free or save from evil, danger, etc. [*delivered* from slavery] **2.** to assist (a female) at the birth of (offspring) **3.** to express in words; utter [to *deliver* a speech] **4.** to hand over; transfer [to *deliver* a prisoner into custody] **5.** to distribute [*deliver* the mail] **6.** to strike (a blow) **7.** to throw (a ball, etc.) —*vi.* to make deliveries, as of merchandise —**be delivered of** to give birth to —**deliver oneself of** to express; utter —**de·liv′er·a·ble** *adj.* —**de·liv′er·er** *n.*

de·liv·er·ance (-əns) *n.* **1.** a freeing or being freed **2.** an opinion, etc. publicly expressed

de·liv·er·y (-ē) *n., pl.* **-er·ies** **1.** a handing over; transfer **2.** a distributing, as of mail **3.** a giving birth; childbirth **4.** any giving forth **5.** the act or manner of giving a speech, striking a blow, throwing a ball, etc. **6.** something delivered

dell (del) *n.* [OE. *del*] a small, secluded valley or glen, usually a wooded one

del·la Rob·bia (del′lä rôb′byä; *E.* del′ə rō′bē ə), **Lu·ca** (lōō′kä) 1400?-82; Florentine sculptor

Del·mar·va Peninsula (del mär′və) peninsula in the eastern U.S., between Chesapeake Bay & the Atlantic: it consists of Delaware & parts of Maryland & Virginia

De·los (dē′läs) small island of the Cyclades in the Aegean

de·louse (dē lous′, -louz′) *vt.* -loused′, -lous′ing to rid of lice —**de·lous′er** *n.*

Del·phi (del′fī) ancient city in C Greece, on the slopes of Mount Parnassus: see map at GREECE

Del·phic (del′fik) *adj.* **1.** of Delphi **2.** designating or of the oracle of Apollo at Delphi in ancient times Also **Del′phi·an** (-fē ən)

del·phin·i·um (del fin′ē əm) *n.* [ModL. < Gr. < *delphin,* DOLPHIN: its nectary resembles a dolphin] a plant of the buttercup family, bearing spikes of spurred, irregular flowers, usually blue, on tall stalks: some are poisonous

del·ta (del′tə) *n.* [L. < Gr.] **1.** the fourth letter of the Greek alphabet (Δ, δ) **2.** a deposit of sand and soil, usually triangular, formed at the mouth of some rivers —**del·ta·ic** (del tā′ik) *adj.*

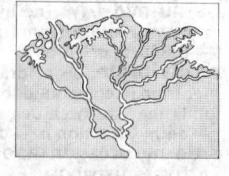

delta ray an electron ejected by the passage of a primary ionizing particle through matter

delta wing the triangular shape of certain jet aircraft —**del′ta-wing′, del′ta-winged′** *adj.*

DELTA

del·toid (del′toid) *adj.* **1.** shaped like a delta; triangular **2.** designating or of a large, triangular muscle of the shoulder —*n.* the deltoid muscle

de·lude (di lōōd′) *vt.* -lud′ed, -lud′ing [< L. < *de-,* from + *ludere,* to play] to fool, as by false promises; mislead; trick —see SYN. at DECEIVE —**de·lud′er** *n.*

del·uge (del′yōōj) *n.* [< OFr. < L. *diluvium < dis-,* off + *lavere,* to wash: for IE. base see LATHER] **1.** a great flood **2.** a heavy rainfall **3.** an overwhelming, floodlike rush of anything [a *deluge* of questions followed his talk] —*vt.* -uged, -ug·ing **1.** to flood **2.** to overwhelm —**the Deluge** *Bible* the great flood in Noah's time: Gen. 7

de·lu·sion (di lōō′zhən) *n.* **1.** a deluding or being deluded **2.** a false belief or opinion **3.** *Psychiatry* a false, continuing belief not supported by objective evidence —**de·lu′sion·al** *adj.*

SYN.—**delusion** implies belief in something that is contrary to fact or reality, resulting from trickery, a misunderstanding, or a mental disorder [to have *delusions* of grandeur]; an **illusion** suggests or gives an appearance of something real by copying it or making something that looks like it [movies give us the *illusion* of seeing and hearing real people]; a **hallucination** gives one the impression of experiencing, as though it were real, something that is not actually there, as when one is drugged or has a mental disorder

de·lu·sive (di lōō′siv) *adj.* **1.** tending to delude; misleading **2.** unreal Also **de·lu′so·ry** (-lōō′sə rē) —**de·lu′sive·ly** *adv.* —**de·lu′sive·ness** *n.*

de·luxe (di luks′, -lŏoks′, -lōoks′) *adj.* [Fr., lit., of luxury] of extra fine quality; luxurious; elegant [the *deluxe* edition of the book is bound in leather] —*adv.* in a deluxe manner

delve (delv) *vi.* delved, delv′ing [OE. *delfan*] **1.** [Archaic] to dig with a spade **2.** to investigate for information; search [into books, the past, etc.) —**delv′er** *n.*

Dem. **1.** Democrat **2.** Democratic

de·mag·net·ize (dē mag′nə tīz′) *vt.* -ized′, -iz′ing to deprive of magnetism —**de·mag′net·i·za′tion** *n.* —**de·mag′net·iz′er** *n.*

dem·a·gog·ic (dem′ə gäj′ik, -gäg′-, -gō′jik) *adj.* of, like, or characteristic of a demagogue or demagogy: also **dem′a·gog′i·cal** —**dem′a·gog′i·cal·ly** *adv.*

dem·a·gogue, dem·a·gog (dem′ə gäg′, -gôg′) *n.* [< Gr. < *dēmos,* the people + *agōgos,* leader < *agein,* to lead] a person who tries to stir up the people by appeals to emotion, prejudice, etc. in order to win them over quickly and so gain power —*vi.* -gogued′ or -goged′, -gogu′ing or -gog′ing to behave as a demagogue

dem·a·gog·y (dem′ə gō′jē, -gäg′ē, -gôg′ē) *n.* the methods or practices of a demagogue: also ☆**dem′a·gog′uer·y** (-gäg′ər ē, -gôg′-)

de·mand (di mand′) *vt.* [< OFr. < L. < *de-,* from + *mandare,* to entrust: see MANDATE] **1.** to ask for boldly or urgently **2.** to ask for as a right or with authority [the police *demanded* entry] **3.** to ask to know or be informed of [they *demanded* the cause of her behavior] **4.** to require; need [the work *demands* time] —**vi.** to make a demand —**n.** **1.** a demanding **2.** a thing demanded **3.** a strong request **4.** an urgent requirement or claim [this job makes *demands* on my time] **5.** *a)* the desire for a certain product by buyers who are ready to buy at the stated price *b)* the amount people are ready to buy at a certain price —**in demand** asked for —**on demand** when presented for payment —**de·mand′a·ble** *adj.* —**de·mand′er** *n.*

☆**demand deposit** *Banking* a deposit that may be withdrawn on demand, without advance notice

de·mand·ing (-iŋ) *adj.* making demands on one's patience, energy, etc. —**de·mand′ing·ly** *adv.*

de·mar·cate (di mär′kāt, dē′mär kāt′) *vt.* **-cat·ed, -cat·ing** [shortened < DEMARCATION] **1.** to mark the limits of **2.** to distinguish; separate Also **de·mark′**

de·mar·ca·tion, de·mar·ka·tion (dē′mär kā′shən) *n.* [Sp. < *de-* (L. *de*), from + *marcar*, to mark] **1.** the act of setting and marking boundaries **2.** a limit or boundary **3.** a separation

dé·marche (dā märsh′) *n.* [Fr.: see DE- & MARCH¹] a step, procedure, or maneuver, esp. in diplomacy

de·mean¹ (di mēn′) *vt.* [DE- + MEAN², after DEBASE] to make low or cheap; degrade; humble [to *demean* oneself by lying]

de·mean² (di mēn′) *vt.* [see DEMEANOR] to behave or conduct (oneself)

de·mean·or (-ər) *n.* [< OFr. < *de-* (L. *de*), from + *mener*, to lead < LL. *minare*, to drive (animals) < L. *minari*, to threaten] outward behavior; conduct; deportment: also, Brit. sp., **de·mean′our**

de·ment·ed (di ment′id) *adj.* [< L. < *dementis*, genitive of *de-mens*, mad: see DEMENTIA] mentally sick; insane —**de·ment′ed·ly** *adv.*

de·men·tia (di men′shə) *n.* [L. < *de-*, out from + *mens*, MIND] loss or weakening of mental powers due to organic causes: see AMENTIA —see SYN. at INSANITY

dementia prae·cox (prē′käks) [ModL.: see prec. & PRECOCIOUS] *obs. term for* SCHIZOPHRENIA

de·mer·it (di mer′it) *n.* [< OFr. < ML. < L. *demerere*, to deserve well, with prefix *de-*, entirely, mistaken as negative in ML.] **1.** a fault; defect ☆**2.** a mark recorded against a student, trainee, etc. for poor conduct or work

☆**Dem·e·rol** (dem′ə rōl′, -rôl′) *a trademark for* MEPERIDINE

de·mesne (di mān′, -mēn′) *n.* [OFr. *demeine* < L. *dominium*: see DOMAIN] **1.** *Law* possession (of real estate) in one's own right **2.** the land around a mansion **3.** a region or domain: also used figuratively

De·me·ter (di mēt′ər) *Gr. Myth.* the goddess of agriculture: identified with the Roman goddess Ceres

dem·i- [OFr. < L. < *dis-*, apart + *medius*, middle] *a prefix meaning:* **1.** half [*demisemiquaver*] **2.** less than usual in size, power, etc. [*demigod*]

dem·i·god (dem′ē gäd′) *n.* **1.** *Myth. a)* a minor god *b)* the offspring of a human being and a god or goddess **2.** a god-like person

dem·i·john (-jän′) *n.* [Fr. *dame-jeanne*] a large bottle of glass or earthenware, with a narrow neck and a wicker casing and handle

de·mil·i·ta·rize (dē mil′ə tə rīz′) *vt.* **-rized′, -riz′ing** to free from military control or activity, or from militarism —**de·mil′i·ta·ri·za′tion** *n.*

dem·i·mon·daine (dem′ē män dān′) *n.* [Fr.] a woman of the demimonde

dem·i·monde (dem′ē mänd′, dem′ē mänd′) *n.* [Fr. < *demi-*, DEMI- + *monde* (< L. *mundus*), world] the class of women who have lost social standing because of sexual promiscuity

DEMIJOHN

de·mise (di mīz′) *n.* [< Fr. fem. pp. of *démettre*, to dismiss < L. < *de-*, down + *mittere*, to send: see MISSION] **1.** *Law* a transfer of an estate by lease **2.** the transfer of sovereignty by death or abdication **3.** death —*vt.* **-mised′, -mis′ing** **1.** to give or transfer (an estate) by lease **2.** to transfer (sovereignty) by death or abdication

dem·i·sem·i·qua·ver (dem′ē sem′ē kwā′vər) *n.* [Brit.] *same as* THIRTY-SECOND NOTE

dem·i·tasse (dem′ē tas′, -täs′) *n.* [Fr. < *demi-*, DEMI- + *tasse*, a cup] a small cup of or for after-dinner black coffee

de·mob (dē mäb′) *vt.* **-mobbed′, -mob′bing** [Brit. Colloq.] to demobilize

de·mo·bi·lize (dē mō′bə līz′) *vt.* **-lized′, -liz′ing** **1.** to disband (troops) **2.** to discharge (a person) from the armed forces —**de·mo′bi·li·za′tion** *n.*

de·moc·ra·cy (di mäk′rə sē) *n., pl.* **-cies** [< Fr. < ML. *democratia* < Gr. < *dēmos*, the people + *kratein*, to rule] **1.** government in which the people hold the ruling power either directly or through elected representatives **2.** a country, state, etc. with such government **3.** majority rule **4.** the principle of equality of rights, opportunity, etc., or the practice of this principle

dem·o·crat (dem′ə krat′) *n.* **1.** a person who believes in and upholds government by the people **2.** a person who believes in and practices the principle of equality of rights, opportunity, etc. ☆**3.** [D-] a member of the Democratic Party

dem·o·crat·ic (dem′ə krat′ik) *adj.* **1.** of, belonging to, or upholding democracy [a *democratic* nation] **2.** of or for all or most people [a *democratic* cultural program] **3.** treating people of all classes in the same way [a *democratic* employer] ☆**4.** [D-] of or belonging to the Democratic Party —**dem′o·crat′i·cal·ly** *adv.*

☆**Democratic Party** one of the two major political parties in the U.S., developed (c. 1830) from the Republican Party led by Thomas Jefferson

de·moc·ra·tize (di mäk′rə tīz′) *vt., vi.* **-tized′, -tiz′ing** to make or become democratic —**de·moc′ra·ti·za′tion** *n.*

De·moc·ri·tus (di mäk′rə təs) 460?-370? B.C.; Gr. philosopher

de·mod·u·late (dē mäj′oo lāt′) *vt.* **-lat·ed, -lat·ing** to cause to undergo demodulation

de·mod·u·la·tion (dē mäj′oo lā′shən) *n. Radio* the recovery, at the receiver, of a signal that has been modulated on a carrier wave

de·mod·u·la·tor (dē mäj′oo lāt′ər) *n. Radio* a device used in demodulation

de·mog·ra·phy (di mäg′rə fē) *n.* [< Gr. *dēmos*, the people + -GRAPHY] the study of human populations that seeks to determine the numbers of people in various localities and their percentages by age, sex, occupation, etc. —**de·mog′ra·pher** *n.* —**de·mo·graph·ic** (dē′mə graf′ik, dem′ə-) *adj.* —**de′mo·graph′i·cal·ly** *adv.*

dem·oi·selle (dem′wə zel′) *n.* [Fr.] **1.** a damsel **2.** a small crane of Africa, Asia, and Europe

de·mol·ish (di mäl′ish) *vt.* [< Fr. < L. *demoliri*, to destroy < *de-*, down + *moliri*, to build < *moles*, a mass] **1.** to tear down or smash to pieces (a building, etc.) **2.** to destroy; ruin [the evidence *demolishes* his argument] —see SYN. at DESTROY —**de·mol′ish·er** *n.* —**de·mol′ish·ment** *n.*

dem·o·li·tion (dem′ə lish′ən, dē′mə-) *n.* a demolishing or being demolished; often, specif., destruction by explosives

de·mon (dē′mən) *n.* [L. *daemon*: see DAEMON] **1.** *same as* DAEMON **2.** a devil; evil spirit **3.** a person or thing thought of as being evil, cruel, etc. [the *demon* of jealousy] **4.** a person who has great energy or skill [a *demon* at golf] —**de·mon·ic** (di män′ik) *adj.* —**de·mon′i·cal·ly** *adv.*

de·mon·e·tize (dē män′ə tīz′) *vt.* **-tized′, -tiz′ing** **1.** to deprive (currency) of its standard value **2.** to stop using (silver or gold) as a monetary standard —**de·mon′e·ti·za′tion** *n.*

de·mo·ni·ac (di mō′nē ak′) *adj.* **1.** possessed or influenced by a demon **2.** of a demon or demons **3.** like or characteristic of a demon; fiendish Also **de·mo·ni·a·cal** (dē′mə nī′ə k′l) —*n.* a person supposedly possessed by a demon —**de′mo·ni′a·cal·ly** *adv.*

de·mon·ism (dē′mən iz'm) *n.* belief in demons

de·mon·o- *a combining form meaning* demon: also, before a vowel, **demon-**

de·mon·ol·a·try (dē′mə näl′ə trē) *n.* worship of demons —**de′mon·ol′a·ter** *n.*

de·mon·ol·o·gy (-jē) *n.* the study of demons or of beliefs about them —**de′mon·ol′o·gist** *n.*

de·mon·stra·ble (di män′strə b'l, dem′ən-) *adj.* that can be demonstrated, or proved —**de·mon′stra·bil′i·ty** *n.* —**de·mon′stra·bly** *adv.*

DEMOISELLE
(to 3 ft. high)

dem·on·strate (dem′ən strāt′) *vt.* **-strat′ed, -strat′ing** [< L. pp. of *demonstrare* < *de-*, from + *monstrare*, to show] **1.** to show by reasoning; prove **2.** to explain by using examples, experiments, etc. [we can *demonstrate* the laws of heredity by breeding fruit flies] **3.** to show the operation or working of [the salesman *demonstrated* the vacuum cleaner to the housewife] **4.** to show (feelings) plainly as by one's actions [he *demonstrated* his love by the sacrifices he made] —*vi.* to show one's feelings or views by taking part in a public meeting, parade, etc.

dem·on·stra·tion (dem′ən strā′shən) *n.* **1.** a making evident or proving **2.** an explanation by example, experiment, etc. **3.** a practical showing of how something works or is used **4.** a display or outward show [a *demonstration* of grief] **5.** a public show of opinion, etc., as by a mass meeting

de·mon·stra·tive (di män′strə tiv) *adj.* **1.** giving convincing evidence or proof (usually with *of*) **2.** having to do with demonstration **3.** showing feelings openly and frankly **4.** *Gram.* pointing out ["this" is a *demonstrative* pronoun] —*n. Gram.* a demonstrative pronoun or adjective —**de·mon′stra·tive·ly** *adv.* —**de·mon′stra·tive·ness** *n.*

dem·on·stra·tor (dem′ən strāt′ər) *n.* [L.] **1.** one that demonstrates; specif., a person who takes part in a public demonstration ☆**2.** a product, as an automobile, used for demonstration

☆**de·mor·al·ize** (di môr′ə līz′) *vt.* **-ized′, -iz′ing** **1.** [Now Rare] to corrupt the morals of **2.** to lower the morale of; weaken the spirit or discipline of **3.** to throw into confusion —**de·mor′al·i·za′tion** *n.* —**de·mor′al·iz′er** *n.*

De·mos·the·nes (di mäs′thə nēz′) 384?–322 B.C.; Athenian orator & statesman

☆**de·mote** (di mōt′) *vt.* **-mot′ed, -mot′ing** [DE- + (PRO)MOTE] to reduce to a lower grade or rank —**de·mo′tion** *n.*

de·mot·ic (di mät′ik) *adj.* [< ML. < Gr. *dēmotes*, one of the people < *dēmos*, the people] **1.** of the people; popular; specif., vernacular (sense 2) **2.** designating or of a simplified system of ancient Egyptian writing

de·mul·cent (di mul′s'nt) *adj.* [< L. prp. of *demulcere* < *de-*, down + *mulcere*, to stroke] soothing —*n.* a medicine or ointment that soothes irritated mucous membrane

de·mur (di mur′) *vi.* **-murred′, -mur′ring** [OFr. *demorer* < L. < *de-*, from + *morari*, to delay < *mora*, a delay] **1.** to be unwilling because of doubts or objections; object **2.** *Law* to enter a demurrer —*n.* **1.** a demurring **2.** an objection raised or exception taken Also **de·mur′ral** *n.*

DEMOTIC WRITING

de·mure (di myoor′) *adj.* [< ME. < *de-*, entirely + *mur* < OFr. *mëur*, ripe < L. *maturus*, MATURE] **1.** modest; reserved **2.** modest or shy, or pretending to be so; coy —see SYN. at SHY[1] —**de·mure′ly** *adv.* —**de·mure′ness** *n.*

de·mur·rage (di mur′ij) *n.* [< OFr. < *demorer*: see DEMUR] **1.** the delaying of a ship, freight car, etc., as by failure to load, unload, or sail within the time allowed **2.** the compensation paid for this

de·mur·rer (-ər) *n.* [OFr. *demorer*, to DEMUR] **1.** a plea for the dismissal of a lawsuit, as on the grounds that the pleading of the opposition is legally faulty **2.** an objection; demur **3.** a person who demurs

den (den) *n.* [OE. *denn*] **1.** the cave or other lair of a wild animal **2.** a retreat or headquarters, as of thieves **3.** a small, cozy room where a person can be alone to read, work, etc. —*vi.* **denned, den′ning** to live or hide as in a den

Den. Denmark

de·nar·i·us (di nar′ē əs, -ner′-) *n., pl.* **-nar′i·i′** (-ī′) [< L. < *deni*, by tens < *decem*, TEN] **1.** an ancient Roman silver coin, the penny of the New Testament **2.** an ancient Roman gold coin

de·na·tion·al·ize (dē nash′ə n'l īz′) *vt.* **-ized′, -iz′ing** **1.** to deprive of national rights or status **2.** to place (an industry controlled by the government) under private ownership —**de·na′tion·al·i·za′tion** *n.*

de·nat·u·ral·ize (dē nach′ər ə līz′) *vt.* **-ized′, -iz′ing** **1.** to make unnatural **2.** to take citizenship away from —**de·nat′u·ral·i·za′tion** *n.*

de·na·ture (dē nā′chər) *vt.* **-tured, -tur·ing** **1.** to change the nature of **2.** to make (alcohol, etc.) unfit for drinking without spoiling for other uses **3.** to change the composition of (a protein) by heat, acids, etc. —**de·na′tur·ant** *n.* —**de·na′tur·a′tion** *n.*

den·drite (den′drīt) *n.* [< Gr. < *dendron*: see DENDRO-] the branched part of a nerve cell that carries impulses toward the cell body —**den·drit′ic** (-drit′ik), **den·drit′i·cal** *adj.*

den·dro- [< Gr. *dendron*: for IE. base see TREE] *a combining form meaning* tree: also **dendri-** or, before a vowel, **dendr-**

den·drol·o·gy (den dräl′ə jē) *n.* the scientific study of trees —**den′dro·log′ic** (-drə läj′ik), **den′dro·log′i·cal** *adj.* —**den·drol′o·gist** *n.*

-den·dron (den′drən) [see DENDRO-] *a combining form meaning* tree or treelike structure

☆**den·gue** (deŋ′gē, -gā) *n.* [WIndSp. < Swahili *dinga*, a cramp, infl. by Sp. *dengue*, contortion] an infectious tropical disease transmitted by mosquitoes and characterized by severe pain in the joints and back, fever, and rash

de·ni·a·ble (di nī′ə b'l) *adj.* that can be denied

de·ni·al (di nī′əl) *n.* **1.** a denying; saying "no" (to a request, etc.) **2.** a statement in opposition to another [the *denial* of the rumor] **3.** a disowning; refusal to recognize as one's own [the *denial* of one's family] **4.** a refusal to believe or accept (a doctrine, etc.) **5.** *same as* SELF-DENIAL

de·nic·o·tin·ize (dē nik′ə tin īz′) *vt.* **-ized′, -iz′ing** to remove nicotine from (tobacco) —**de·nic′o·tin′i·za′tion** *n.*

de·nier[1] (den′yər) *n.* [< OFr. < L. *denarius*, DENARIUS] a unit of weight for measuring the fineness of threads of silk, nylon, etc.

de·nier[2] (di nī′ər) *n.* a person who denies

den·i·grate (den′ə grāt′) *vt.* **-grat′ed, -grat′ing** [< L. pp. of *denigrare* < *de-*, entirely + *nigrare*, to blacken < *niger*, black] to belittle or disparage the character of; defame —**den′i·gra′tion** *n.* —**den′i·gra′tor** *n.*

den·im (den′əm) *n.* [< Fr. (*serge*) *de Nîmes*, (serge) of Nîmes, Fr. town] a coarse, twilled cotton cloth used for jeans, overalls, uniforms, etc.

Den·is (den′is) [Fr. < L. *Dionysius*] **1.** a masculine name: also sp. **Den′nis 2.** Saint, 3d cent. A.D.; patron saint of France

de·ni·tri·fy (dē nī′trə fī′) *vt.* **-fied′, -fy′ing** **1.** to remove nitrogen from **2.** to reduce (nitrates or nitrites) to compounds of lower oxidation —**de·ni′tri·fi·ca′tion** *n.*

den·i·zen (den′ə zən) *n.* [< Anglo-Fr. < VL. < L. *de intus*, from within] **1.** *a)* an inhabitant *b)* one who frequents a particular place **2.** an animal, plant, etc. that has become naturalized

Den·mark (den′märk) country in Europe, on the peninsula of Jutland & several nearby islands: 16,615 sq. mi.; pop. 4,870,000; cap. Copenhagen

☆**den mother** a woman who supervises meetings of a small group (den) of Cub Scouts

de·nom·i·nate (di näm′ə nāt′) *vt.* **-nat′ed, -nat′ing** [< L. pp. of *denominare* < *de-*, entirely + *nominare*: see NOMINATE] to give a specified name to; call —*adj.* specifying a quantity in some unit of measure [3 lb. and 15 ft. are *denominate* numbers]

de·nom·i·na·tion (di näm′ə nā′shən) *n.* **1.** the act of denominating **2.** a name, esp. of a class of things **3.** a class or kind (esp. of units in a system) with a specific name or value [coins of different *denominations*] **4.** a particular religious sect or body [Protestant *denominations*]

de·nom·i·na·tion·al (-'l) *adj.* of, or under the control of, a religious denomination —**de·nom′i·na′tion·al·ism** *n.* —**de·nom′i·na′tion·al·ly** *adv.*

de·nom·i·na·tive (di näm′ə nə tiv) *adj.* **1.** denominating; naming **2.** *Gram.* formed from a noun or adjective stem ["to eye" is a *denominative* verb] —*n.* a denominative word, esp. a verb

de·nom·i·na·tor (-nāt′ər) *n.* [ML.] the term below the line in a fraction, indicating the number of equal parts into which the whole is divided [in the fraction 2/5, 5 is the *denominator*]

de·no·ta·tion (dē′nō tā′shən) *n.* **1.** a denoting **2.** the basic or literal meaning or reference of a word or term: see CONNOTATION **3.** an indication or sign

de·note (di nōt′) *vt.* **-not′ed, -not′ing** [< Fr. < L. < *de-*, down + *notare*, to mark < *nota*, NOTE] **1.** to be a sign of; indicate [dark clouds *denote* rain] **2.** to signify or refer to in its basic or literal meaning; mean: see CONNOTE —**de·no·ta·tive** (dē′nō tāt′iv, di nōt′ə tiv) —**de′no·ta′tive·ly** *adv.*

de·noue·ment, dé·noue·ment (dā nōō′män; *Fr.* dā nōō·män′) *n.* [Fr. < *dé-* (L. *dis-*), out + *nouer*, to tie < L. < *nodus*, a knot] **1.** the outcome, solution, or unraveling of a plot in a drama, story, etc. **2.** any final revelation or outcome

de·nounce (di nouns′) *vt.* **-nounced′, -nounc′ing** [< OFr. < L. *denuntiare*: see DENUNCIATION] **1.** to accuse publicly; inform against **2.** to condemn strongly as evil **3.** to give formal notice of the ending of (a treaty, armistice, etc.) —see SYN. at CRITICIZE —de·nounce′ment n. —de·nounc′er n.

‡de no·vo (dē nō′vō) [L.] once more; anew

dense (dens) adj. dens′er, dens′est [L. densus, compact] 1. having its parts close together; crowded, compact, etc. [dense shrubbery; a dense population area] 2. difficult to get through, penetrate, etc. [a dense fog; dense ignorance] 3. stupid 4. Photog. opaque, with good contrast in light and shade: said of a negative —see SYN. at CLOSE¹ and STUPID —dense′ly adv. —dense′ness n.

den·si·ty (den′sə tē) n., pl. -ties 1. the quality or condition of being dense, thick, or crowded 2. quantity or number per unit, as of area [the density of population] 3. Physics the ratio of the mass of a substance to its volume [the density of a metal expressed in grams per cubic centimeter]

dent (dent) n. [ME., var. of DINT] 1. a slight hollow made in a surface by a blow or pressure 2. a noticeable effect —vt. to make a dent in —vi. to become dented

den·tal (den′t'l) adj. [ModL. < L. dentis, genitive of dens, a tooth] 1. of or for the teeth or dentistry 2. Phonet. formed by placing the tip of the tongue against or near the upper front teeth —n. Phonet. a dental consonant (th, th)

☆dental floss thin, strong thread for removing food particles from between the teeth

☆dental hygienist a dentist's assistant, who cleans teeth, takes dental X-rays, etc.

den·tate (den′tāt) adj. [< L. < dens: see DENTAL] having teeth or toothlike projections; toothed or notched —den′tate·ly adv. —den·ta′tion n.

den·ti- [< L. dens: see DENTAL] a combining form meaning tooth or teeth: also dento- or, before a vowel, dent-

den·ti·frice (den′tə fris) n. [< L. < dens (see DENTAL) + fricare, to rub] any substance for cleaning teeth, as a powder, paste, or liquid

den·til (den′til) n. [< MFr. < L. dens: see DENTAL] Archit. any of a series of small rectangular blocks projecting like teeth, as from under a cornice

den·tin (den′tin) n. [< L. dens: see DENTAL] the hard, bony tissue forming the body of a tooth, under the enamel: see illustration at TOOTH: also den′tine (-tēn, -tin)

DENTILS

den·tist (den′tist) n. [< Fr. < ML. < L. dens: see DENTAL] one whose profession is the care of teeth and surrounding tissues, the replacement of missing teeth with artificial ones, etc.

den·tist·ry (-rē) n. the profession or work of a dentist

den·ti·tion (den tish′ən) n. [< L. < dentire, to cut teeth < dens: see DENTAL] 1. the teething process 2. the number and kind of teeth and their arrangement

den·ture (den′chər) n. [Fr. < L. dens: see DENTAL] a fitting for the mouth, with artificial teeth, often a full set

de·nu·cle·ar·ize (dē no̅o̅′klē ə rīz′, -nyo̅o̅′-) vt. -ized′, -iz′ing to prohibit the possession of nuclear weapons in (an area or nation) —de·nu′cle·ar·i·za′tion n.

de·nude (di no̅o̅d′, -nyo̅o̅d′) vt. -nud′ed, -nud′ing [L. denudare, de-, off + nudare, to strip] 1. to make bare; strip 2. to destroy all life in (an area) 3. to lay bare as by erosion —de·nu·da·tion (dē′no̅o̅ dā′shən, -nyo̅o̅-; den′yo̅o̅-) n.

de·nun·ci·ate (di nun′sē āt′) vt. -at′ed, -at′ing same as DENOUNCE —de·nun′ci·a′tor n.

de·nun·ci·a·tion (di nun′sē ā′shən) n. [< L. pp. of denuntiare < de-, entirely + nuntiare, ANNOUNCE] the act of denouncing; a condemning, informing against, etc. —de·nun′ci·a·to′ry (-ə tôr′ē), de·nun′ci·a′tive (-āt′iv) adj.

Den·ver (den′vər) [after J. Denver (1817-94), gov. of Kans.] capital of Colo., in the NC part: pop. 515,000 (met. area 1,228,000)

de·ny (di nī′) vt. -nied′, -ny′ing [< OFr. < L. < de-, entirely + negare, to deny] 1. to declare (a statement) untrue [he denied the charge] 2. to refuse to accept as true or right [he denied the possibility] 3. to refuse to recognize as one's own; repudiate [to deny one's religion] 4. to refuse the use of [to deny lockers to all except members] 5. to refuse to give [to deny permission] —deny oneself to do without desired things

de·o·dar (dē′ə där′) n. [Hindi < Sans. dēvadāru, lit., tree of the gods] 1. a Himalayan cedar with fragrant, light-red wood 2. the wood

de·o·dor·ant (dē ō′dər ənt) adj. that prevents, destroys, or masks undesired odors —n. any deodorant preparation, esp. one used on the body

de·o·dor·ize (dē ō′də rīz′) vt. -ized′, -iz′ing to remove or mask the odor of or in —de·o′dor·i·za′tion n. —de·o′dor·iz′er n.

de·ox·i·dize (dē äk′sə dīz′) vt. -dized′, -diz′ing to remove oxygen, esp. chemically combined oxygen, from —de·ox′i·diz′er n.

de·ox·y·gen·ate (dē äk′sə jə nāt′) vt. -at′ed, -at′ing to remove oxygen, esp. free oxygen, from (water, air, etc.)

de·ox·y·ri·bo·nu·cle·ic acid (dē äk′si rī′bō no̅o̅ klē′ik, -nyo̅o̅-) an essential component of all living matter and a basic material in the chromosomes of the cell nucleus: it contains the genetic code and transmits the hereditary pattern: commonly called DNA

dep. 1. department 2. deposit 3. deputy

de·part (di pärt′) vi. [< OFr. departir < VL. < L. < dis-, apart + partire, to divide < pars, a PART] 1. to go away (from); leave 2. to set out; start [the bus will depart on time] 3. to die 4. to turn aside (from something) [to depart from custom] —vt. to leave: now only in depart this life, to die —see SYN. at GO

de·part·ed (-id) adj. 1. gone away; past [the departed years] 2. dead [our departed ancestors] —see SYN. at DEAD —the departed the dead person or persons

de·part·ment (di pärt′mənt) n. [see DEPART] 1. a separate part or division, as of a government, business, or school [the State Department; the police department; the sales department] 2. a field of knowledge or activity [keeping the records is her department] 3. an administrative district in France or in certain Latin American countries —de·part·men·tal (di pärt′men′t'l, dē′pärt-) adj. —de·part′men′tal·ly adv.

de·part·men·tal·ize (di pärt′men′tə līz′, dē′pärt-) vt. -ized′, -iz′ing to organize into departments —de·part′men′tal·i·za′tion n.

☆department store a large retail store for the sale of many kinds of goods arranged in departments

de·par·ture (di pär′chər) n. 1. a departing, or going away 2. a starting out, as on a trip or new course of action 3. a deviation or turning aside (from something) 4. [Archaic] death

de·pend (di pend′) vi. [< OFr. < L. < de-, down + pendere, to hang] 1. to be influenced or controlled by something else; be contingent (on) [the attendance at the game depends on the weather] 2. to be sure of; rely (on) [you certainly can't depend on the weather] 3. to rely (on) for support or aid [he depends on his brother for money] 4. [Archaic] to hang down

de·pend·a·ble (di pen′də b'l) adj. that can be depended on; reliable —see SYN. at RELIABLE —de·pend′a·bil′i·ty n. —de·pend′a·bly adv.

de·pend·ence (di pen′dəns) n. 1. the condition or fact of being dependent; specif., a) a being influenced or controlled by something else b) reliance (on another) for support or aid 2. reliance; trust [I place dependence in his word] Also sp. de·pend′ance

de·pend·en·cy (-dən sē) n., pl. -cies 1. same as DEPENDENCE 2. something dependent or subordinate 3. a land or territory geographically separate from the country governing it

de·pend·ent (-dənt) adj. 1. influenced or controlled by something else 2. relying (on another) for support or aid 3. subordinate —n. a person who depends on someone else for support, etc. Also sp., esp. for n., de·pend′ant

dependent clause same as SUBORDINATE CLAUSE

de·per·son·al·ize (dē pur′s'n ə līz′) vt. -ized′, -iz′ing 1. to deprive of individuality; treat impersonally 2. to cause to lose one's sense of personal identity [to become a depersonalized employee of a large corporation] —de·per′son·al·i·za′tion n.

de·pict (di pikt′) vt. [< L. pp. of depingere < de-, entirely + pingere, to PAINT] 1. to represent in a drawing, sculpture, etc. 2. to picture in words; describe [his novel depicts life in a small town] —de·pic′tion n. —de·pic′tor n.

dep·i·late (dep′ə lāt′) vt. -lat′ed, -lat′ing [< L. pp. of depilare < de-, from + pilus, hair] to remove hair from (a part of the body) —dep′i·la′tion n.

de·pil·a·to·ry (di pil′ə tôr′ē) adj. serving to remove unwanted hair —*n., pl.* **-ries** a depilatory substance, as in cream form

de·plane (dē plān′) *vi.* **-planed′, -plan′ing** to get out of an airplane after it lands

de·plete (di plēt′) *vt.* **-plet′ed, -plet′ing** [< L. pp. of *deplere* < *de-*, from + *plere*, to fill] 1. to make less by gradually using up (funds, energy, etc.) 2. to empty wholly or partly —**de·ple′tion** *n.*

de·plor·a·ble (di plôr′ə b'l) *adj.* 1. that can or should be deplored; regrettable [a *deplorable* oversight] 2. very bad; wretched [*deplorable* living conditions in the slums] —**de·plor′a·bly** *adv.*

de·plore (di plôr′) *vt.* **-plored′, -plor′ing** [< Fr. < L. < *de-*, entirely + *plorare*, to weep] 1. to be regretful or sorry about; lament 2. to regard as unfortunate or wretched

de·ploy (dē ploi′) *vt., vi.* [< Fr. < OFr. *desployer* < L. *displicare*, to scatter, unfold: see DISPLAY] *Mil.* 1. to spread out (troops, etc.) so as to form a wider front 2. to station or move in accordance with a plan —**de·ploy′ment** *n.*

de·po·lar·ize (dē pō′lə rīz′) *vt.* **-ized′, -iz′ing** to destroy or counteract the polarization of —**de·po·lar·i·za′tion** *n.*

de·po·lit·i·cize (dē′pə lit′ə sīz′) *vt.* **-cized′, -ciz′ing** to remove from political influence: also **de·po·lit′i·cal·ize′ -ized′, -iz′ing**

de·pol·lute (dē′pə loot′) *vt.* to free from pollution [plans to *depollute* the Great Lakes] —**de·pol·lu′tion** *n.*

de·pon·ent (di pō′nənt) *adj.* [< L. prp. of *deponere*, to set down: see DEPOSIT] *L. & Gr. Gram.* denoting a verb that has a passive-voice form and an active meaning —*n.* 1. a deponent verb 2. *Law* a person who gives written testimony under oath

de·pop·u·late (dē päp′yə lāt′) *vt.* **-lat′ed, -lat′ing** to reduce the population of, esp. by violence, disease, etc. —**de·pop′u·la′tion** *n.* —**de·pop′u·la′tor** *n.*

de·port (di pôrt′) *vt.* [< OFr. < L. < *de-*, from + *portare*, to carry: for IE. base see FARE] 1. to behave (oneself) in a specified way 2. to carry or send away; specif., to force (an alien) to leave a country by official order —see SYN. at BANISH —**de·port′a·ble** *adj.*

de·por·ta·tion (dē′pôr tā′shən) *n.* a deporting or expulsion, as of an undesirable alien, from a country

de·port·ment (di pôrt′mənt) *n.* the way a person behaves himself; behavior

de·pose (di pōz′) *vt.* **-posed′, -pos′ing** [< OFr. < de- (L. *de*), from + *poser* < L. *pausare*, to cease: confused with L. *deponere*: see DEPOSIT] 1. to remove from office or a position of power, esp. from a throne; oust 2. *Law* to state or testify under oath but out of court —*vi.* to bear witness —**de·pos′al** *n.*

de·pos·it (di päz′it) *vt.* [< L. *depositus*, pp. of *deponere*, to put down < *de-*, down + *ponere*, to put: see POSITION] 1. to place or entrust, as for safekeeping [to *deposit* money in a bank] 2. to give as a pledge or partial payment 3. to put or set down 4. to leave (sediment, etc.) lying —*n.* 1. something placed for safekeeping; specif., money put in a bank 2. a pledge or part payment 3. a depository 4. something left lying, as sand or clay deposited by the action of wind, water, etc. —**on deposit** placed or entrusted for safekeeping

de·pos·i·tar·y (di päz′ə ter′ē) *n., pl.* **-tar′ies** 1. a person, firm, etc. entrusted with something for safekeeping; trustee 2. a storehouse; depository

dep·o·si·tion (dep′ə zish′ən) *n.* 1. a deposing or being deposed, as from office 2. a testifying 3. a depositing or being deposited 4. something deposited 5. *Law* the written testimony of a witness, made under oath, to be used in court

de·pos·i·tor (di päz′ə tər) *n.* a person who deposits something, esp. money in a bank

de·pos·i·to·ry (di päz′ə tôr′ē) *n., pl.* **-ries** 1. a place where things are put for safekeeping; storehouse 2. a trustee; depositary

de·pot (dē′pō; *military & Brit.* dep′ō) *n.* [Fr. *dépôt*, a storehouse < L. *depositum:* see DEPOSIT] 1. a storehouse; warehouse ☆2. a railroad or bus station 3. *Mil. a)* a storage place for supplies *b)* a station for bringing together new soldiers or combat replacements

de·prave (di prāv′) *vt.* **-praved′, -prav′ing** [< OFr. < L. < *de-*, entirely + *pravus*, crooked] to make morally bad; corrupt [he had become *depraved* by associating with criminals] —see SYN. at DEBASE —**dep·ra·va·tion** (dep′rə vā′shən) *n.*

de·prav·i·ty (di prav′ə tē) *n.* 1. a depraved condition; corruption; wickedness 2. *pl.* **-ties** a depraved act or practice

dep·re·cate (dep′rə kāt′) *vt.* **-cat′ed, -cat′ing** [< L. pp. of *deprecari* < *de-*, off + *precari*, PRAY] 1. to feel and express

disapproval of [he *deprecated* our lack of interest] 2. to depreciate; belittle [to be self-*deprecating*] —**dep′re·cat′ing·ly** *adv.* —**dep′re·ca′tion** *n.* —**dep′re·ca′tor** *n.*

dep·re·ca·to·ry (-kə tôr′ē) *adj.* deprecating; disapproving, belittling, etc.: also **dep′re·ca′tive** (-kāt′iv)

de·pre·ci·ate (di prē′shē āt′) *vt.* **-at′ed, -at′ing** [< L. pp. of *depretiare* < *de-*, from + *pretiare*, to value < *pretium*, a PRICE] 1. to reduce in value or price 2. to make seem unimportant; belittle; disparage [she shouldn't *depreciate* her own abilities] —☆*vi.* to drop in value or price [an automobile *depreciates* with age] —see SYN. at DISPARAGE —**de·pre′ci·a·to·ry** (-shē ə tôr′ē, -shə tôr′ē) *adj.*

de·pre·ci·a·tion (di prē′shē ā′shən) *n.* ☆1. a decrease in value of property through wear, aging, etc. ☆2. a decrease in the purchasing power of money 3. a belittling; disparagement

dep·re·da·tion (dep′rə dā′shən) *n.* [< LL. pp. of *depraedari* < L. *de-*, entirely + *praedari*, to plunder < *praeda*, PREY] a robbing, plundering, or laying waste

de·press (di pres′) *vt.* [< OFr. < L. *depressus*, pp. of *deprimere* < *de-*, down + *premere*, to PRESS¹] 1. to press down; lower [*depress* the gas pedal slowly] 2. to lower in spirits; make gloomy; sadden 3. to decrease the activity of; weaken [high tariffs have *depressed* world trade] 4. to lower in value, price, or amount 5. *Music* to lower the pitch of —**de·press′ing** *adj.* —**de·press′ing·ly** *adv.*

de·pres·sant (di pres′ənt) *adj.* slowing up the activity of the muscles, nervous system, etc. —*n.* a depressant medicine, drug, etc.; sedative

de·pressed (di prest′) *adj.* 1. pressed down 2. lowered in position, intensity, amount, etc. 3. flattened or hollowed, as if pressed down 4. gloomy; dejected; sad 5. characterized by widespread unemployment, poverty, etc. [a *depressed* area] 6. *Bot.* flattened vertically, as if from downward pressure —see SYN. at SAD

de·pres·sion (di presh′ən) *n.* 1. a depressing or being depressed 2. a hollow or low place 3. sadness; dejection 4. a decrease in activity, amount, etc. ☆5. a period marked by less business activity, much unemployment, falling prices and wages, etc. 6. *Psychol.* an emotional condition characterized by feelings of hopelessness, inadequacy, etc.

de·pres·sive (di pres′iv) *adj.* 1. tending to depress 2. characterized by psychological depression —**de·pres′sive·ly** *adv.* —**de·pres′sive·ness** *n.*

de·pres·sor (-ər) *n.* 1. one that depresses 2. a muscle that draws down a part of the body 3. an instrument for pressing a part out of the way, as during a medical examination [a tongue *depressor*]

dep·ri·va·tion (dep′rə vā′shən) *n.* a depriving or being deprived: also [Rare] **de·priv·al** (di prī′v'l)

de·prive (di prīv′) *vt.* **-prived′, -priv′ing** [< ML. < L. *de-*, entirely + *privare*, to separate] 1. to take something away from by force [the Indians were *deprived* of their lands] 2. to keep from having, using, or enjoying [*deprived* of the comforts of life by poverty]

dept. 1. department 2. deputy

depth (depth) *n.* [ME. *depthe:* see DEEP & -TH¹] 1. *a)* the distance from the top downward, or from front to back *b)* perspective, as in a painting 2. the condition of being deep; deepness; specif., *a)* intensity, as of colors, emotion, etc. *b)* profoundness of thought *c)* lowness of pitch 3. the middle part [the *depth* of winter] 4. [usually *pl.*] the inmost part [the *depths* of a wood] 5. [usually *pl.*] the deep or deepest part, as of the sea 6. [usually *pl.*] the extreme degree, as of despair 7. reserve strength, as of suitable substitute players for a team —**in depth** in a thorough way [analysis *in depth*] —**out of** (or **beyond**) **one's depth** 1. in water too deep for one 2. past one's ability or understanding

depth charge (or **bomb**) an explosive charge that explodes under water: used esp. against submarines

depth perception ability to see objects in perspective

dep·u·ta·tion (dep′yoo tā′shən) *n.* 1. a deputing or being deputed 2. a group of persons, or one person, appointed to represent others; delegation

de·pute (di pyoot′) *vt.* **-put′ed, -put′ing** [< OFr. < L. < *de-*, from + *putare*, lit., to cleanse] 1. to give (authority, etc.) to someone else as deputy 2. to appoint as one's substitute, agent, etc.

dep·u·tize (dep′yə tīz′) *vt.* **-tized′, -tiz′ing** to appoint as deputy —*vi.* to act as deputy (for another)

dep·u·ty (dep′yə tē) *n., pl.* **-ties** [see DEPUTE] 1. a person appointed to substitute for, or to assist, another [a sheriff's *deputy*]

2. a member of a legislature called a Chamber of Deputies — *adj.* acting as deputy

De Quin·cey (də kwin′sē), **Thomas** 1785–1859; Eng. essayist & critic

de·rac·i·nate (di ras′ə nāt′) *vt.* **-nat′ed, -nat′ing** [< Fr. < *dé-* (L. *dis-*), from + *racine*, a root < LL. < L. *radix*, ROOT¹] to pull up by or as by the roots; uproot —**de·rac′i·na′tion** *n.*

de·rail (di rāl′) *vi., vt.* to go or cause to go off the rails: said of a train, etc. —**de·rail′ment** *n.*

de·range (di rānj′) *vt.* **-ranged′, -rang′ing** [< Fr. < OFr. < *des-* (L. *dis-*), apart + *rengier*: see RANGE] **1.** to upset the order or working of **2.** to make insane —**de·range′ment** *n.*

Der·by (dur′bē; *chiefly Brit.* där′bē) city in C England: pop. 221,000 —*n., pl.* **-bies 1.** an annual race for three-year-old horses at Epsom Downs, begun by the Earl of Derby in 1780 **2.** any similar horse race, esp. the one (**Kentucky Derby**) run in Louisville, Kentucky ☆**3.** [d-] a stiff felt hat with a round crown and curved brim

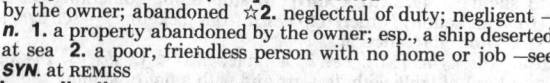

DERBY

☆**de·reg·u·late** (dē reg′yə lāt′) *vt.* **-lat′ed, -lat′ing** to remove the regulations that control [to *deregulate* the price of natural gas] —**de·reg′u·la′tion** *n.*

der·e·lict (der′ə likt′) *adj.* [< L. pp. of *derelinquere*, to abandon < *de-*, entirely + *relinquere*: see RELINQUISH] **1.** deserted by the owner; abandoned ☆**2.** neglectful of duty; negligent — *n.* **1.** a property abandoned by the owner; esp., a ship deserted at sea **2.** a poor, friendless person with no home or job —see SYN. at REMISS

der·e·lic·tion (der′ə lik′shən) *n.* **1.** an abandoning or being abandoned **2.** a neglect of, or failure in, duty; a being remiss

de·ride (di rīd′) *vt.* **-rid′ed, -rid′ing** [< L. < *de-*, down + *ridere*, to laugh] to laugh at in contempt or scorn; ridicule —see SYN. at RIDICULE —**de·rid′er** *n.* —**de·rid′ing·ly** *adv.*

‡**de ri·gueur** (də rē gër′) [Fr.] **1.** required by etiquette; according to good form **2.** fashionable

de·ri·sion (di rizh′ən) *n.* a deriding or being derided; contempt or ridicule

de·ri·sive (di rī′siv) *adj.* showing derision; ridiculing: also **de·ri′so·ry** (-sə rē) —**de·ri′sive·ly** *adv.* —**de·ri′sive·ness** *n.*

deriv. 1. derivation **2.** derivative **3.** derived

der·i·va·tion (der′ə vā′shən) *n.* **1.** a deriving or being derived **2.** something derived **3.** *a)* the source or origin of something [a Roman myth of Greek *derivation*] *b)* the etymology of a word **4.** the forming of words from bases, as by adding affixes —**der′i·va′tion·al** *adj.*

de·riv·a·tive (də riv′ə tiv) *adj.* derived from something else; not original —*n.* **1.** something derived **2.** a word formed by derivation **3.** *Chem.* a substance derived from another by chemical change, esp. by the substitution of one or more elements or radicals **4.** *math.* the instantaneous rate of change of one variable with respect to another —**de·riv′a·tive·ly** *adv.*

de·rive (di rīv′) *vt.* **-rived′, -riv′ing** [< OFr. < L. *derivare*, to divert a stream < *de-*, from + *rivus*, a stream] **1.** to get or receive (*from* a source) [we *derive* gasoline from petroleum; many people *derive* pleasure from music] **2.** to get by reasoning; deduce or infer **3.** to trace from or to a source; show the derivation of **4.** *Chem.* to obtain (a compound) from another compound by replacing one element with one or more other elements —*vi.* to come (*from* a source) [our laws *derive* from those of England] —**de·riv′a·ble** *adj.*

-derm (durm) [see DERMA¹] a suffix meaning skin or covering [*endoderm*]

der·ma¹ (dur′mə) *n.* [ModL. < Gr. *derma*, the skin] same as DERMIS —**der′mal, der′mic** *adj.*

der·ma² (dur′mə) *n.* [< Yid. pl. of *darm*, gut, ult. < OHG. *daram*] beef casing stuffed with bread crumbs, seasoning, etc. and roasted

der·ma·ti·tis (dur′mə tīt′is) *n.* [< DERMATO- + -ITIS] inflammation of the skin

der·ma·to- [Gr. < *derma* (gen. *dermatos*)] a combining form meaning skin: also **dermat-, dermo-, derm-**

der·ma·tol·o·gy (dur′mə täl′ə jē) *n.* [DERMATO- + -LOGY] the branch of medicine dealing with the skin, its functions, and

its diseases —**der′ma·to·log′i·cal** (-tə läj′ə k′l) *adj.* —**der′ma·tol′o·gist** *n.*

der·mis (dur′mis) *n.* [ModL. < LL. *epidermis*, EPIDERMIS] the layer of skin just below the epidermis

der·o·gate (der′ə gāt′) *vt., vi.* **-gat′ed, -gat′ing** [< L. pp. of *derogare* < *de-*, from + *rogare*, to ask] **1.** [Archaic] to take away (*from*) so as to impair **2.** to disparage; belittle —**der′o·ga′tion** *n.*

de·rog·a·to·ry (di räg′ə tôr′ē) *adj.* **1.** tending to lessen or impair; detracting **2.** disparaging; belittling [*derogatory* remarks] Also **de·rog′a·tive** —**de·rog′a·to′ri·ly** *adv.*

der·rick (der′ik) *n.* [orig., a gallows, after T. *Derrick*, 17th-c. London hangman] **1.** a large apparatus with tackle and beams, for lifting and moving heavy objects ☆**2.** a tall, tapering framework, as over an oil well, to support drilling machinery, etc.

DERRICK
(for oil well)

der·ri·ère (der′ē er′) *n.* [Fr., back part < LL. < L. *de*, from + *retro*, back] the buttocks

der·ring-do (der′iŋ dōō′) *n.* [ME. *derrynge do*, daring to do] daring action; reckless courage

☆**der·rin·ger** (der′in jər) *n.* [after H. *Deringer*, 19th-cent. U.S. gunsmith] a small, short-barreled pistol of large caliber

der·vish (dur′vish) *n.* [Turk. < Per. *darvēsh*, beggar] a member of any of various Moslem orders dedicated to poverty and chastity: some dervishes practice whirling, howling, etc. as religious acts

de·sal·i·na·tion (dē sal′ə nā′shən) *n.* [DE- + SALIN(E) + -ATION] the removal of salt, esp. from sea water to make it drinkable: also **de·sal′i·ni·za′tion** —**de·sal′i·nate′** *vt.* **-nat′ed, -nat′ing**

☆**de·salt** (dē sôlt′) *vt.* to remove salt from (esp. sea water)

des·cant (des′kant; *for vi., also* des kant′) *n.* [< Anglo-Fr. < L. *dis-*, apart + *cantus*, song] **1.** *Medieval Music a)* singing in which there is a fixed melody and a subordinate melody added above *b)* this added melody **2.** a comment; discourse —*vi.* **1.** to talk at length; discourse (*on* or *upon*) **2.** to sing or play a descant **3.** to sing

Des·cartes (dā kärt′), **Re·né** (rə nā′) 1596–1650; Fr. philosopher & mathematician

de·scend (di send′) *vi.* [< OFr. < L. < *de-*, down + *scandere*, to climb] **1.** to move from a higher to a lower place; come or go down **2.** to pass from an earlier to a later time, from greater to less, etc. [prices have *descended* during the past month] **3.** to slope downward **4.** to come down (*from* a source, as *from* an ancestor) [she is *descended* from pioneers] **5.** to pass by inheritance or heredity [estates *descending* from father to son] **6.** to stoop (*to* some act regarded as unworthy of one) **7.** to make a sudden visit or attack (*on* or *upon*) [the marauders *descended* upon the village] **8.** *Astron.* to move toward the horizon —*vt.* to move down or down along [to *descend* a staircase] —**de·scend′i·ble** *adj.*

de·scend·ant (-ənt) *adj.* descending: also **de·scend′ent** —*n.* **1.** one who is descended from a certain ancestor, family, group, etc. **2.** something derived from an earlier form

de·scent (di sent′) *n.* **1.** a descending; coming or going down **2.** lineage; ancestry [she is of French *descent*] **3.** one generation (in a specified lineage) **4.** a way or slope downward [a steep *descent* down the mountain] **5.** a sudden raid or attack (*on* or *upon*) **6.** a decline; fall [a sharp *descent* in prices] **7.** a lowering oneself; stooping (*to* an act) **8.** *Law* transference of property) to heirs

de·scribe (di skrīb′) *vt.* **-scribed′, -scrib′ing** [< OFr. < L. < *de-*, from + *scribere*: see SCRIBE] **1.** to tell or write about; give a detailed account of [to *describe* a trip one has taken] **2.** to picture in words [*describe* your house] **3.** to trace the outline of [her hand *described* a circle in the air] —**de·scrib′a·ble** *adj.* —**de·scrib′er** *n.*

de·scrip·tion (di skrip′shən) *n.* **1.** the act, process, or technique of describing **2.** that which is said or written to describe something [a *description* of the lost articles] **3.** sort or variety [books of every *description*]

de·scrip·tive (-tiv) *adj.* of or characterized by description; that describes [*descriptive* writing; a *descriptive* adjective] —**de·scrip′tive·ly** *adv.* —**de·scrip′tive·ness** *n.*

de·scry (di skrī′) *vt.* -**scried′**, -**scry′ing** [< OFr. *descrier*, to proclaim < *des-*, from + *crier*: see CRY] **1.** to catch sight of (distant or obscure objects) [to *descry* a ship on the horizon] **2.** to look for and discover; detect

Des·de·mo·na (dez′də mō′nə) *see* OTHELLO

des·e·crate (des′ə krāt′) *vt.* -**crat′ed**, -**crat′ing** [< DE- + (CON)SECRATE] to violate or insult the sacredness of; profane [to *desecrate* a holy place, the memory of a revered person, etc.] —**des′e·crat′er**, **des′e·cra′tor** *n.* —**des′e·cra′tion** *n.*

de·seg·re·gate (dē seg′rə gāt′) *vt.*, *vi.* -**gat′ed**, -**gat′ing** to stop racial segregation in (public schools, etc.) —**de·seg′re·ga′tion** *n.*

de·sen·si·tize (dē sen′sə tīz′) *vt.* -**tized′**, -**tiz′ing** to make insensitive or less sensitive [*desensitized* to an allergen] —**de·sen′si·ti·za′tion** *n.* —**de·sen′si·tiz′er** *n.*

de·sert¹ (di zurt′) *vt.* [< Fr. < LL. *desertare* < L. pp. of *deserere*, lit., to disjoin < *de-*, from + *serere*, to join < IE. base *ser-*, to line up] **1.** to leave (someone or something that one ought not to leave); abandon; forsake [he *deserted* his wife] **2.** to leave (one's post, etc.) without permission —**vi.** to leave one's post, etc. without permission and with no intent to return or, in war, to avoid hazardous duty —*see* SYN. at ABANDON —**de·sert′er** *n.*

des·ert² (dez′ərt) *n.* [< OFr. < LL. *desertum*, a desert < L. pp. of *deserere*: see prec.] **1.** an uncultivated region without inhabitants; wilderness **2.** a dry, sandy region with little or no plant life —*adj.* **1.** of a desert **2.** wild and uninhabited [a *desert* island] —*see* SYN. at WASTE

de·sert³ (di zurt′) *n.* [< OFr. < *deservir*, DESERVE] **1.** the fact of deserving reward or punishment **2.** [*often pl.*] deserved reward or punishment [to get one's just *deserts*]

de·ser·tion (di zur′shən) *n.* a deserting or being deserted

de·serve (di zurv′) *vt.* -**served′**, -**serv′ing** [< OFr. *deservir* < L. < *de-*, entirely + *servire*, to SERVE] to be worthy of (reward, punishment, etc.); have a right to; merit [he *deserves* a scolding; this *deserves* our attention] —*vi.* to be worthy

de·served (-zurvd′) *adj.* rightfully earned or merited; just —**de·serv′ed·ly** (-zur′vid lē) *adv.*

de·serv·ing (-zur′viŋ) *adj.* **1.** having merit; worthy of help, etc. [a *deserving* student] **2.** worthy (*of* reward, punishment, etc.) —**de·serv′ing·ly** *adv.*

des·ha·bille (dez′ə bēl′, des′-) *n.* same as DISHABILLE

des·ic·cant (des′i kənt) *adj.* [see DESICCATE] drying —*n.* a substance used as a drying agent

des·ic·cate (-kāt′) *vt.* -**cat′ed**, -**cat′ing** [< L. pp. of *desiccare* < *de-*, entirely + *siccare* < *siccus*, dry] **1.** to dry completely **2.** to preserve (food) by drying —*vi.* to become completely dry —**des′ic·ca′tion** *n.* —**des′ic·ca′tor** *n.*

de·sid·er·ate (di sid′ə rāt′) *vt.* -**at′ed**, -**at′ing** [< L. pp. of *desiderare*: see DESIRE] to want; need —**de·sid′er·a′tion** *n.* —**de·sid′er·a′tive** *adj.*

de·sid·er·a·tum (di sid′ə rāt′əm, -zid′-; -rät′-) *n.*, *pl.* -**ta** (-ə) [L., neut. pp. of *desiderare*: see DESIRE] something needed and wanted

de·sign (di zīn′) *vt.* [< L. < *de-*, out + *signare* < *signum*, a mark, SIGN] **1.** to make preliminary sketches of; plan [to *design* a new model of car] **2.** to form (plans, etc.) in the mind; contrive **3.** to plan and work out (something) creatively; devise [who *designed* this book?] **4.** to intend for some purpose [this chair was not *designed* for hard use] —*vi.* to make original plans, patterns, etc. —*n.* **1.** a plan or purpose [it was his *design* to study law] **2.** [*pl.*] a secret, usually dishonest or selfish scheme (often with *on* or *upon*) [he had *designs* on her money] **3.** a plan or sketch to work from; pattern [the *designs* for a house] **4.** the art of making designs or patterns [a student in *design*] **5.** the arrangement of parts, form, color, etc.; pattern [the *design* in a rug] **6.** a finished artistic work or decoration —*see* SYN. at INTEND and PLAN —**by design** purposely

des·ig·nate (dez′ig nāt′; *for adj., also* -nit) *adj.* [see prec.] named for an office, etc. but not yet in it [ambassador *designate*] —*vt.* -**nat′ed**, -**nat′ing** **1.** to point out; indicate; specify [cities are *designated* on this map by dots] **2.** to give a name to; call [the top grade of beef is *designated* as "prime"] **3.** to name for an office or duty; appoint [we have *designated* Smith to be chairman] —**des′ig·na′tive** *adj.* —**des′ig·na′tor** *n.*

designated hitter *Baseball* a player without a fielding position in the game but named to bat in the regular lineup in place of the pitcher, who does not necessarily leave the game

des·ig·na·tion (dez′ig nā′shən) *n.* **1.** a pointing out or marking out **2.** appointment to an office, post, etc. **3.** a distinguishing name, title, etc.

de·sign·ed·ly (di zīn′id lē) *adv.* purposely

de·sign·er (di zī′nər) *n.* a person who designs, or makes original sketches, patterns, etc. [a dress *designer*]

de·sign·ing (-niŋ) *adj.* **1.** that designs or makes plans, patterns, etc. **2.** scheming; crafty —*n.* the art or work of creating designs, patterns, etc.

de·sir·a·ble (di zīr′ə b'l) *adj.* worth wanting or having; pleasing, excellent, etc. —**de·sir′a·bil′i·ty** *n.* —**de·sir′a·bly** *adv.*

de·sire (di zīr′) *vt.* -**sired′**, -**sir′ing** [< OFr. < L. *desiderare* < *de-*, from + *sideris*, genitive of *sidus*, a star] **1.** to wish or long for; crave **2.** to ask for; request **3.** to want sexually —*vi.* to have a desire —*n.* **1.** a strong wish or craving **2.** sexual appetite **3.** a request **4.** anything desired

SYN.—**desire**, which can generally be used in place of the other words here in the sense of "to long for," emphasizes strong feeling [to *desire* success]; **wish** is not so strong a term as **desire** and has special use when an unrealistic longing is meant [he *wished* summer were here]; **want** specifically suggests a longing for something lacking or needed, but in general use is just a more informal equivalent of **wish** [she *wants*, or *wishes*, to go with us]; **crave** suggests desire to satisfy a physical appetite or an urgent need [to *crave* affection]

de·sir·ous (di zīr′əs) *adj.* desiring; having or characterized by desire [to be *desirous* of learning]

de·sist (di zist′) *vi.* [< OFr. < L. < *de-*, from + *sistere*, to cause to stand < *stare*, to STAND] to stop doing something; cease (*from* an action) [ordered to *desist* from picketing] —*see* SYN. at STOP —**de·sist′ance** *n.*

desk (desk) *n.* [ML. *desca*, a table, ult. < L. *discus*, DISCUS] **1.** a kind of table with drawers and with a flat or sloping top for writing, etc. **2.** the place in a hotel where guests register, check out, etc.

Des Moines (də moin′) [Fr., lit., of the monks] capital of Iowa, in the C part: pop. 201,000

des·o·late (des′ə lit; *for v.* -lāt′) *adj.* [< L. pp. of *desolare* < *de-*, entirely + *solare*, to make lonely < *solus*, alone] **1.** lonely; solitary [a *desolate* tree on a rocky crag] **2.** uninhabited; deserted [a *desolate* wilderness] **3.** ruined or destroyed [the *desolate* farms in a drought area] **4.** very unhappy; miserable [her death left him *desolate*] —*vt.* -**lat′ed**, -**lat′ing** **1.** to rid of inhabitants **2.** to lay waste; devastate **3.** to forsake; abandon **4.** to make unhappy, miserable, etc. —**des′o·late·ly** *adv.* —**des′o·late·ness** *n.* —**des′o·la′tor**, **des′o·lat′er** *n.*

des·o·la·tion (des′ə lā′shən) *n.* **1.** a making desolate **2.** a desolate condition **3.** lonely grief; misery **4.** loneliness **5.** a desolate place

De So·to (di sōt′ō), **Her·nan·do** (hər nan′dō) 1500?-42; Sp. explorer in America: also **de Soto**

de·spair (di sper′) *vi.* [< OFr. < L. < *de-*, without + *sperare*, to hope < *spes*, hope] to lose hope; be without hope (usually with *of*) [the prisoner *despaired* of ever being free again] —*n.* **1.** a despairing; loss of hope **2.** a person or thing causing despair

de·spair·ing (-iŋ) *adj.* feeling or showing despair; hopeless —*see* SYN. at HOPELESS —**de·spair′ing·ly** *adv.*

des·patch (di spach′) *vt.*, *n.* var. sp. of DISPATCH

des·per·a·do (des′pə rä′dō, -rā′-) *n.*, *pl.* -**does**, -**dos** [OSp. < L. *desperare*: see DESPAIR] a dangerous, reckless criminal; bold outlaw

des·per·ate (des′pər it) *adj.* [< L. pp. of *desperare*: see DESPAIR] **1.** reckless or violent because one has lost hope [a *desperate* criminal] **2.** having a very great desire, need, etc. [*desperate* for affection] **3.** causing one to lose hope; extremely dangerous or serious [a *desperate* illness] **4.** extreme; drastic [in *desperate* need] —*see* SYN. at HOPELESS —**des′per·ate·ly** *adv.*

des·per·a·tion (des′pə rā′shən) *n.* **1.** the state of being desperate **2.** recklessness caused by despair [in *desperation*, the hunted deer leaped over the chasm]

des·pi·ca·ble (des′pik ə b'l, di spik′-) *adj.* deserving to be despised; contemptible [a *despicable* bully] —**des′pi·ca·ble·ness** *n.* —**des′pi·ca·bly** *adv.*

de·spise (di spīz′) *vt.* -**spised′**, -**spis′ing** [< OFr. < L. *despicere* < *de*, down + *specere*, to look at: see SPECTACLE] **1.** to look down on with contempt and scorn [the general *despised* cowards] **2.** to regard with extreme dislike [he *despised* having to work nights] —*see* SYN. at HATE

de·spite (di spīt′) *n.* [< OFr. < L. pp. of *despicere*: see prec.] **1.** malice; spite **2.** [Archaic] contempt; scorn —*prep.* in spite of; notwithstanding —**in despite of** in spite of

Des Plaines (des plānz′) [prob. < Miss. Valley Fr. *plaines*, sugar maples, once growing there] city in NE Ill.: suburb of Chicago: pop. 57,000

de·spoil (di spoil′) *vt.* [< OFr. < L. < *de-*, entirely + *spoliare*, to plunder: see SPOIL] to deprive (*of* something) by force; rob; plunder —**de·spoil′er** *n.* —**de·spoil′ment** *n.*

de·spo·li·a·tion (di spō′lē ā′shən) *n.* a despoiling or being despoiled; pillage

de·spond (di spänd′) *vi.* [L. *despondere*, to give up < *de*, from + *spondere*, to promise] to lose courage or hope; become disheartened —*n.* despondency: now chiefly in **slough of despond** —**de·spond′ing·ly** *adv.*

de·spond·en·cy (di spän′dən sē) *n.* [see prec.] loss of courage or hope; dejection: also **de·spond′ence**

de·spond·ent (-dənt) *adj.* filled with despondency; dejected; discouraged [he was *despondent* over the loss of his job] —see SYN. at HOPELESS —**de·spond′ent·ly** *adv.*

des·pot (des′pət, -pät) *n.* [< OFr. < Gr. *despotēs*, a master] 1. an absolute ruler; autocrat 2. anyone in charge who acts like a tyrant

des·pot·ic (de spät′ik) *adj.* of or like a despot; autocratic; tyrannical [a *despotic* foreman] —**des·pot′i·cal·ly** *adv.*

des·pot·ism (des′pə tiz′m) *n.* 1. rule by a despot; autocracy 2. the methods of a despot; tyranny

des·qua·mate (des′kwə māt′) *vi.* -mat·ed, -mat·ing [< L. pp. of *desquamare* < *de-*, off + *squama*, a scale] to fall off in scales; peel off —**des′qua·ma′tion** *n.*

des·sert (di zurt′) *n.* [< OFr. < *desservir*, to clear the table < *des-* (L. *de*), from + *servir* < L. *servire*, to SERVE] ☆1. a course of pie, cake, ice cream, or the like, served at the end of a meal 2. [Brit.] uncooked fruit and nuts served after the sweet course

de·sta·bi·lize (dē stā′bə līz′) *vt.* -lized′, -liz′ing to upset the stability of; unbalance

de Staël, Madame *see* STAËL

des·ti·na·tion (des′tə nā′shən) *n.* 1. the end for which something or someone is destined 2. the place toward which someone or something is going or sent

des·tine (des′tin) *vt.* -tined, -tin·ing [< OFr. < L. *destinare*, to secure, fix < *de-*, entirely + base of *stare*, to STAND] 1. to determine beforehand, as by fate [he seemed *destined* to succeed] 2. to set apart for a certain purpose; intend —**destined for** 1. bound for [*destined for* home] 2. intended for [*destined for* leadership]

des·ti·ny (des′tə nē) *n.*, *pl.* -ies [see DESTINE] 1. a series of events that follow one another in a way that seems inevitable 2. what will necessarily happen to any person or thing; (one's) fate 3. that which determines events —see SYN. at FATE

des·ti·tute (des′tə tōōt′, -tyōōt′) *adj.* [< L. pp. of *destituere*, to forsake < *de-*, down + *statuere*, to set: see STATUE] 1. not having; lacking (with *of*) [*destitute* of trees] 2. living in complete poverty —see SYN. at POOR

des·ti·tu·tion (des′tə tōō′shən, -tyōō′-) *n.* the state of being destitute; esp., utter poverty —see SYN. at POVERTY

de·stroy (di stroi′) *vt.* [< OFr. < L. < *de-*, down + *struere*, to build] 1. to tear down; demolish 2. to spoil completely; ruin 3. to put an end to 4. to kill 5. to undo or neutralize the effect of [the sharp spices *destroy* the delicate flavor of the herbs] 6. to make useless —*vi.* to bring about destruction

SYN.—**destroy** implies a tearing down or bringing to an end in any of various ways, as by wrecking, spoiling, ruining, killing, etc. [to *destroy* a civilization; to *destroy* weeds; to *destroy* one's plans]; **demolish** implies such destructive force as to completely smash to pieces [the bombs *demolished* the factories]; **raze** means to level to the ground, either destructively or by systematic wrecking with a salvaging of useful parts [they *razed* the old mansion to make room for a parking lot]; **annihilate** is to destroy so completely as to wipe out of existence [an atomic war could *annihilate* whole nations]

de·stroy·er (-ər) *n.* 1. a person or thing that destroys 2. a small, fast, heavily armed warship

destroying angel *same as* DEATH CUP

☆**de·struct** (di strukt′, dē′strukt′) *n.* [back-formation < DESTRUCTION] the deliberate destruction of a malfunctioning missile, rocket, etc. after its launch —*vi.* to be automatically destroyed —**de·struc′tor** *n.*

de·struc·ti·ble (di struk′tə b'l) *adj.* that can be destroyed —**de·struct′i·bil′i·ty** *n.*

de·struc·tion (di struk′shən) *n.* [< OFr. < L. pp. of *destruere*: see DESTROY] 1. a destroying or being destroyed; ruin [the earthquake caused much *destruction*] 2. the cause or means of destroying

de·struc·tive (di struk′tiv) *adj.* 1. tending or likely to cause destruction 2. causing destruction; destroying 3. merely negative; not helpful [*destructive* criticism] —**de·struc′tive·ly** *adv.* —**de·struc′tive·ness, de·struc′tiv′i·ty** *n.*

destructive distillation the decomposition of coal, wood, etc. by heat in the absence of air, and the recovery of the volatile products, as by condensation

des·ue·tude (des′wi tōōd′, -tyōōd′) *n.* [< L. < pp. of *desuescere* < *de-*, from + *suescere*, to be accustomed] the condition of being no longer used; disuse [laws fallen into *desuetude*]

de·sul·fur·ize (dē sul′fə rīz′) *vt.* -ized′, -iz′ing to remove sulfur from: also **de·sul′fur** —**de·sul′fur·i·za′tion** *n.*

de·sul·to·ry (des′l tôr′ē) *adj.* [< L. < *desultor*, vaulter < pp. of *desilire* < *de-*, from + *salire*, to leap: see SALIENT] 1. passing from one thing to another in an aimless way; disconnected; not methodical [a *desultory* conversation] 2. random [a *desultory* observation] —see SYN. at RANDOM —**des′ul·to′ri·ly** *adv.* —**des′ul·to′ri·ness** *n.*

de·tach (di tach′) *vt.* [Fr. *détacher* < OFr. < *de-*, off + *estachier*, to ATTACH] 1. to unfasten or separate and remove; disconnect [to *detach* freight cars from a train] 2. to send (troops, ships, etc.) on a special mission —**de·tach′a·bil′i·ty** *n.* —**de·tach′a·ble** *adj.*

de·tached (di tacht′) *adj.* 1. not connected; separate [a *detached* garage] 2. not taking sides or having feelings one way or the other; impartial; aloof [a *detached* observer] —see SYN. at INDIFFERENT —**de·tach′ed·ly** (-tach′id lē) *adv.* —**de·tach′ed·ness** *n.*

de·tach·ment (di tach′mənt) *n.* 1. a detaching; separation 2. *a)* the sending of troops or ships on special service *b)* a unit of troops assigned to some special task 3. the state of being disinterested, impartial, or aloof

de·tail (di tāl′, dē′tāl) *n.* [< Fr. < *dé-* (L. *de*), from + *tailler*, to cut] 1. a dealing with things item by item [the *detail* of business] 2. a minute account [to go into *detail*] 3. any of the small parts that go to make up something; an item or particular [the *details* of a plan] 4. a small part of a whole structure, design, etc. [a *detail* of a façade, of a mural, etc.] 5. *a)* one or more soldiers, sailors, etc. chosen for a particular task *b)* the task itself —*vt.* 1. to give the particulars of; tell, item by item [the salesman had to *detail* all expenses in his report] 2. to choose for a particular task [*detail* a man for sentry duty] —**in detail** item by item; with particulars

de·tailed (di tāld′, dē′tāld) *adj.* marked by careful attention to detail [a *detailed* plan]

de·tain (di tān′) *vt.* [< OFr. < L. < *de-*, off + *tenere*, to hold] 1. to keep in custody; confine [*detained* by government agents on a charge of smuggling] 2. to keep from going on; hold back [*detained* at the office by some unexpected business] —**de·tain′er** *n.* —**de·tain′ment** *n.*

☆**de·tas·sel** (dē tas′'l) *vt.* -seled or -selled, -sel·ing or -sel·ling to remove tassels from (corn), thus forcing cross-pollination

de·tect (di tekt′) *vt.* [< L. *detectus*, pp. of *detegere* < *de-*, from + *tegere*, to cover] 1. to catch or discover, as in a misdeed 2. to discover (something hidden or not easily noticed) [to *detect* a slight flaw in an argument] 3. *Radio* same as DEMODULATE —**de·tect′a·ble, de·tect′i·ble** *adj.*

de·tec·tion (di tek′shən) *n.* 1. a finding out or being found out 2. *same as* DEMODULATION

de·tec·tive (-tiv) *adj.* 1. of or for detection 2. of detectives and their work —*n.* a person, usually on a police force, whose work is trying to solve crimes, getting secret information, etc.

de·tec·tor (-tər) *n.* 1. a person or thing that detects 2. *same as* DEMODULATOR

de·tent (di tent′, dē′tent) *n.* [< Fr. < *détendre*, to slacken; ult. < L. *dis-*, from + *tendere*, to stretch out] a catch or pawl that stops or releases a movement

dé·tente, de·tente (dā tänt′) *n.* [Fr.: see DETENT] a lessening of tension or hostility, esp. between nations

de·ten·tion (di ten′shən) *n.* a detaining or being detained; specif., *a)* a keeping in custody; confinement *b)* an enforced delay

☆**detention home** a place where juvenile offenders or delinquents are held in custody, esp. temporarily

de·ter (di tʉr′) *vt.* **-terred′, -ter′ring** [< L. < *de-*, from + *terrere*, to frighten] to keep or discourage (a person) from doing something by instilling fear, anxiety, doubt, etc. [does capital punishment *deter* crime?] —**de·ter′ment** *n.*

de·terge (di tʉrj′) *vt.* **-terged′, -terg′ing** [< L. < *de-*, off + *tergere*, to wipe: for IE. base see TRITE] to cleanse, as a wound —**de·ter′gen·cy, de·ter′gence** *n.*

de·ter·gent (di tʉr′jənt) *adj.* [see prec.] cleansing —*n.* a cleansing substance that is like soap but is made from certain chemical compounds and not from fats and lye

de·te·ri·o·rate (di tir′ē ə rāt′) *vt., vi.* **-rat′ed, -rat′ing** [< LL. pp. of *deteriorare* < L. *deterior*, worse] to make or become worse; lower in quality or value; depreciate [*deteriorating* property, health, etc.] —**de·te′ri·o·ra′tion** *n.* —**de·te′ri·o·ra′tive** *adj.*

de·ter·mi·na·cy (di tʉr′mi nə sē) *n.* **1.** the state or quality of being determinate **2.** the condition of being determined, as in being caused or in having predictable results

de·ter·mi·nant (-nənt) *adj.* determining —*n.* a thing or factor that determines

de·ter·mi·nate (-nit) *adj.* [see DETERMINE] **1.** having exact limits; definite; fixed **2.** settled; conclusive **3.** *Bot.* having a flower at the end of the primary axis and of each secondary axis —**de·ter′mi·nate·ly** *adv.* —**de·ter′mi·nate·ness** *n.*

de·ter·mi·na·tion (di tʉr′mə nā′shən) *n.* **1.** a determining or being determined **2.** a firm intention **3.** firmness of purpose

de·ter·mi·na·tive (di tʉr′mə nā′tiv, -nə tiv) *adj.* determining —*n.* a thing that determines —**de·ter′mi·na·tive·ly** *adv.* —**de·ter′mi·na·tive·ness** *n.*

de·ter·mine (di tʉr′mən) *vt.* **-mined, -min·ing** [< OFr. < L. < *de-*, from + *terminare*, to set bounds < *terminus*, an end: for IE. base see TERM] **1.** to set limits to; bound; define **2.** to settle (a dispute, question, etc.) conclusively; decide **3.** to reach a decision about; decide upon [to *determine* which career to follow] **4.** to establish or affect the nature, kind, or quality of [genes *determine* heredity] **5.** to find out exactly; calculate precisely [*determine* the ship's position] **6.** to give a definite aim to; direct [a boy's hobbies often *determine* his choice of a career] —*vi.* **1.** to decide; resolve **2.** *Law* to come to an end —see SYN. at DECIDE and LEARN —**de·ter′mi·na·ble** *adj.* —**de·ter′min·er** *n.*

de·ter·mined (-mənd) *adj.* **1.** having one's mind made up; resolved [*determined* to succeed] **2.** resolute; unwavering [a *determined* knock on the door] —**de·ter′mined·ly** *adv.* —**de·ter′mined·ness** *n.*

de·ter·min·er (di tʉr′mən ər) *n.* anything that determines, as, specif., a word, such as *the, a, an,* or *this,* that determines the use of a noun without modifying it in a descriptive way

de·ter·min·ism (-mə niz′m) *n.* the doctrine that everything, esp. one's choice of action, is determined by a sequence of causes independent of one's will —**de·ter′min·ist** *n., adj.* —**de·ter′min·is′tic** *adj.*

de·ter·rence (di tʉr′əns) *n.* the act of deterring

de·ter·rent (di tʉr′ənt) *adj.* deterring or tending to deter —*n.* a thing or factor that deters; hindrance

de·test (di test′) *vt.* [< Fr. < L. *detestari*, to curse by calling the gods to witness < *de-*, down + *testis*, a witness] to dislike intensely; hate; abhor —see SYN. at HATE —**de·test′er** *n.*

de·test·a·ble (di tes′tə b'l) *adj.* that is or should be detested; hateful; odious —**de·test′a·bil′i·ty, de·test′a·ble·ness** *n.* —**de·test′a·bly** *adv.*

de·tes·ta·tion (dē′tes tā′shən) *n.* **1.** intense dislike or hatred; loathing **2.** a detested person or thing

de·throne (dē thrōn′) *vt.* **-throned′, -thron′ing** to remove from a throne or from any high position; depose —**de·throne′ment** *n.* —**de·thron′er** *n.*

det·o·nate (det′'n āt′) *vi., vt.* **-nat′ed, -nat′ing** [< L. pp. of *detonare* < *de-*, entirely + *tonare*, to THUNDER] to explode noisily [to *detonate* a bomb] —**det′o·na′tion** *n.*

det·o·na·tor (-āt′ər) *n.* **1.** a fuse, percussion cap, etc. for setting off explosives **2.** an explosive

de·tour (dē′toor, di toor′) *n.* [< Fr. < *détourner*, to turn aside < OFr. < *des-* (L. *dis-*), from + *tourner*, see TURN] **1.** a roundabout way **2.** a route used when the regular route is closed to traffic —*vi., vt.* to go or cause to go by way of a detour

de·tox·i·fy (dē tăk′sə fī′) *vt.* **-fied′, -fy′ing** [DE- + TOXI(N) + -FY] to remove a poison or poisonous effect from

de·tract (di trakt′) *vt.* [< L. pp. of *detrahere* < *de-*, from + *trahere*, to DRAW] to take or draw away —*vi.* to take something

desirable away (*from*) [frowning *detracts* from her beauty] —**de·trac′tion** *n.* —**de·trac′tive** *adj.* —**de·trac′tor** *n.*

de·train (dē trān′) *vi., vt.* to get off or remove from a railroad train —**de·train′ment** *n.*

det·ri·ment (det′rə mənt) *n.* [OFr. < L. *detrimentum*, damage < pp. of *deterere* < *de-*, off + *terere*, to rub: see TRITE] **1.** damage; injury; harm [keeping late hours to the *detriment* of his health] **2.** anything that causes damage or injury

det·ri·men·tal (det′ri men′t'l) *adj.* [DETRIMENT + -AL] damaging; harmful —see SYN. at PERNICIOUS —**det′ri·men′tal·ly** *adv.*

de·tri·tus (di trīt′əs) *n.* [L., pp. of *deterere*: see prec.] fragments of rock, etc. produced by breaking up or wearing away; debris

De·troit (di troit′) [< Fr. *détroit*, strait] **1.** river flowing south from Lake St. Clair into Lake Erie **2.** city in SE Mich., on this river: pop. 1,511,000 (met. area 4,200,000)

‡**de trop** (də trō′) [Fr.] too much; superfluous

deuce[1] (dōōs, dyōōs) *n.* [< OFr. < L. acc. of *duo*, TWO] **1.** a playing card with two spots **2.** the side of a die bearing two spots, or a throw of the dice totaling two **3.** *Tennis* a score of 40 each (or five games each) after which one side must get two successive points (or games) to win the game (or set)

deuce[2] (dōōs, dyōōs) *n., interj.* [< OFr. *dieu* & L. *deus* (see DEITY): also infl. by DEUCE[1], in reference to low score at dice] bad luck, the devil, etc.: a mild oath or exclamation of annoyance, surprise, etc.

deu·ced (dōō′sid, dyōō′-; dōōst, dyōōst) *adj.* **1.** devilish; confounded **2.** extreme Used in mild oaths —*adv.* extremely; very: also **deu′ced·ly**

‡**De·us** (dā′ōōs, dē′əs) [L.] God

‡**de·us ex ma·chi·na** (eks′ mak′i nə) [L., god from a machine: the device used in classical plays] something abruptly brought into the plot of a story, play, etc. to make everything come out all right

Deut. Deuteronomy

☆**deu·te·ri·um** (dōō tir′ē əm, dyōō-) *n.* [ModL. < Gr. *deuteros*, second] the hydrogen isotope having an atomic weight of 2.0141 and boiling point of −249.7°C; heavy hydrogen: symbol, D: with oxygen it forms deuterium oxide, D_2O (heavy water)

deu·ter·o-, deu·ter- [< Gr. *deuteros*, second] *a combining form meaning* second, secondary

☆**deu·ter·on** (dōōt′ər än′, dyōōt′-) *n.* the nucleus of an atom of deuterium

Deu·ter·on·o·my (dōōt′ər än′ə mē, dyōōt′-) [< LL. < Gr. < DEUTERO- + *nomos*, law: in this book the law received by Moses appears for the second time] the fifth book of the Pentateuch in the Bible

deut·sche mark (doi′chə) *pl.* **mark,** Eng. **marks** *see* MONETARY UNITS, table (West Germany)

Deutsch·land (doich′länt′) [G.] *Ger. name of* GERMANY

De Va·le·ra (dev′ə ler′ə, -lir′ə), **Ea·mon** (ā′mən) 1882– ; Ir. statesman, born in U.S.

de·val·ue (dē val′yōō) *vt.* **-ued, -u·ing** **1.** to lessen the value of **2.** to lower the exchange value of (a currency) in relation to other currencies Also **de·val′u·ate′** (-yōō wāt′) **-at′ed, -at′ing** —**de·val′u·a′tion** *n.*

dev·as·tate (dev′əs stāt′) *vt.* **-tat′ed, -tat′ing** [< L. pp. < *de-*, entirely + *vastare*, to make empty < *vastus*, empty] **1.** to lay waste; make desolate; ravage; destroy [the invaders *devastated* the land] **2.** to make helpless; overwhelm [a *devastating* criticism] —**dev′as·tat′ing·ly** *adv.* —**dev′as·ta′tion** *n.* —**dev′as·ta′tor** *n.*

de Vega, Lope *see* Lope de VEGA

de·vel·op (di vel′əp) *vt.* [< Fr. < *dé-* (L. *dis-*), apart + OFr. *voloper*, to wrap] **1.** to cause to become gradually fuller, larger, better, stronger, etc. [to *develop* one's muscles; to *develop* a business] **2.** *a)* to bring into being [to *develop* a theory, a cure for cancer, etc.] *b)* to come to have [the hinges *developed* a squeak; he *developed* ulcers] **3.** to cause (one's personality, a bud, etc.) to unfold or evolve gradually **4.** to make (housing, highways, etc.) more available or extensive **5.** to elaborate (a theme) in music **6.** *a)* to put (an exposed film, plate, or printing paper) in various chemical solutions in order to make the photograph visible *b)* to show or work out by degrees; make known gradually [to *develop* a plot in a novel skillfully] **8.** to explain more clearly [to *develop* a thesis] —*vi.* **1.** to come into being or activity **2.** to become larger, fuller, better, etc.; make progress; grow or evolve ☆**3.** to become known or be disclosed [it *developed* that he was using an alias] —**de·vel′op·a·ble** *adj.*

de·vel·op·er (-ər) *n.* a person or thing that develops; esp., *a)* a person in the business of developing real estate *b) Photog.* a chemical used to develop film, plates, etc.

de·vel·op·ment (-mənt) *n.* **1.** a developing or being developed **2.** a stage in growth, advancement, etc. **3.** an event or happening [an unexpected *development* in a case] **4.** a thing that is developed, as a tract of land with newly built homes, etc. —**de·vel·op·men·tal** (-men′t'l) *adj.* —**de·vel·op′men·tal·ly** *adv.*

de·vi·ant (dē′vē ənt) *adj.* [< LL. prp. of *deviare*] deviating, esp. from what is considered normal in a group or for a society —*n.* a person whose behavior is deviant —**de·vi′an·cy, de·vi′ance** *n.*

de·vi·ate (dē′vē āt′; *for adj. & n.* -it) *vi., vt.* -at′ed, -at′ing [< LL. pp. of *deviare* < *de*-, from + *via*, road] to turn aside (*from* a course, direction, standard, etc.) [to *deviate* from the truth] —*adj. same as* DEVIANT —*n.* a deviant; esp., one with deviant sexual behavior —**de·vi′a·tor** *n.*

SYN.—**deviate** suggests a turning aside, often to only a slight degree, from the correct or prescribed course, standard, doctrine, etc. [to *deviate* from the truth]; **swerve** implies a sudden or sharp turning from a path, course, etc. [the car *swerved* to avoid hitting us; he never *swerved* from the plan he outlined to reach his goal]; **veer**, originally used of ships and wind, suggests a turning or series of turnings so as to change direction [the road *veered* to the left; some people *veer* in their opinions as the times change]

de·vi·a·tion (dē′vē ā′shən) *n.* **1.** a deviating or being deviant, as in behavior, political ideology, etc. **2.** *Statistics* the difference between a particular number in a set and some fixed value, usually the mean —**de·vi·a′tion·ism** *n.* —**de·vi·a′tion·ist** *adj., n.*

de·vice (di vīs′) *n.* [< OFr. *devis*, division < *deviser*: see DEVISE] **1.** something made or invented for some special use; tool, machine, appliance, etc. **2.** a plan that has been worked out to bring about a certain result; scheme [the errand was a *device* to get him out of the house] **3.** something used for artistic effect [rhetorical *devices*] **4.** an ornamental figure or design **5.** a design or emblem, often with a motto, on a coat of arms **6.** any motto or emblem —**leave to one's own devices** to allow to do as one wishes

dev·il (dev′'l) *n.* [OE. *deofol* < LL. < Gr. *diabolos*, slanderous (in N.T., devil) < *dia*-, across + *ballein*, to throw] **1.** [*often* D-] *Theol. a)* the chief evil spirit; Satan (with *the*): typically depicted as a man with horns, a tail, and cloven feet *b)* any demon of hell **2.** a wicked or cruel person **3.** one who is mischievous, reckless, etc. **4.** an unlucky, unhappy person [that poor *devil*] **5.** anything hard to operate, control, etc. **6.** any machine for tearing paper, rags, etc. to bits —*vt.* -iled *or* -illed, -il·ing *or* -il·ling **1.** to prepare (food, often finely chopped) with hot seasoning ☆**2.** to annoy; torment; tease —**a devil of a** an extreme example of a —**between the devil and the deep (blue) sea** between equally unpleasant alternatives —**give the devil his due** to acknowledge the good qualities of even a wicked or disliked person —**go to the devil** to fall into bad habits: also used as a curse —**play the devil with** [Colloq.] to disturb; upset —**the devil!** [Colloq.] an exclamation of anger, surprise, etc. —**the devil take the hindmost** leave the last, slowest, or least able to his fate without bothering about him —**the devil to pay** trouble as a consequence

dev·il·fish (-fish′) *n., pl.* -fish′, -fish′es: see FISH **1.** a large ray whose pectoral fins are hornlike when rolled up **2.** an octopus

dev·il·ish (dev′'l ish, dev′lish) *adj.* **1.** of, like, or characteristic of a devil; diabolical **2.** mischievous; reckless **3.** [Colloq.] *a)* extremely bad *b)* extreme —*adv.* [Colloq.] extremely; very —**dev′il·ish·ly** *adv.* —**dev′il·ish·ness** *n.*

dev·il-may-care (dev′'l mā ker′) *adj.* reckless or careless; happy-go-lucky

dev·il·ment (dev′'l mənt) *n.* **1.** [Archaic] evil behavior **2.** mischief or mischievous action

dev·il·ry (-rē) *n., pl.* -ries [Chiefly Brit.] **1.** witchcraft **2.** evil behavior **3.** *same as* DEVILTRY

devil's advocate 1. *R.C.Ch.* an official selected to raise objections in the case of one named for beatification or canoniza-

DEVILFISH
(to 20 ft. across)

tion **2.** one who upholds the wrong side, as for argument's sake

dev·il's-darn·ing-nee·dle (dev′'lz där′niŋ nē′d'l) *n. same as* DRAGONFLY

☆**dev·il's-food cake** (dev′'lz food′) a rich cake made with chocolate or cocoa and baking soda

Devil's Island Fr. island off the coast of French Guiana: site of a former penal colony

dev·il·try (dev′'l trē) *n., pl.* -tries **1.** reckless mischief, fun, etc. **2.** *same as* DEVILRY

de·vi·ous (dē′vē əs) *adj.* [< L. *devius* < *de*-, off, from + *via*, road] **1.** roundabout; winding [a *devious* route] **2.** going astray **3.** not straightforward or frank; deceiving [*devious* behavior] —**de′vi·ous·ly** *adv.* —**de′vi·ous·ness** *n.*

de·vise (di vīz′) *vt., vi.* -vised′, -vis′ing [< OFr. *deviser*, to distribute, direct < L. pp. of *dividere*, to divide] **1.** to work out (something) by thinking; plan; invent [to *devise* a filing system] **2.** *Law* to bequeath (real property) by will —*n. Law* **1.** a gift of real property by will **2.** a will, or clause in a will, granting such a gift —**de·vis′a·ble** *adj.* —**de·vis′al** *n.* —**de·vis′er,** *Law* **de·vi′sor** *n.*

de·vi·tal·ize (dē vīt′'l īz′) *vt.* -ized′, -iz′ing to lower the vitality of —**de·vi′tal·i·za′tion** *n.*

de·void (di void′) *adj.* [< OFr. < *des*- (L. *dis*-), from + *vuidier*: see VOID] completely without; empty (*of*) [a man *devoid* of enthusiasm]

de·volve (di välv′) *vt., vi.* -volved′, -volv′ing [< L. < *de*-, down + *volvere*, to roll: for IE. base see WALK] to pass (*on*) to another; said of duties, responsibilities, etc. —**dev·o·lu′tion** (dev′ə loo′shən) *n.* —**de·volve′ment** *n.*

De·vo·ni·an (di vō′nē ən) *adj.* [after *Devonshire*, county in England, where the rocks were first studied] designating or of the period after the Silurian in the Paleozoic Era —**the Devonian** the Devonian Period or its rocks: see GEOLOGIC TIME CHART

de·vote (di vōt′) *vt.* -vot′ed, -vot′ing [< L. pp. of *devovere* < *de*-, from + *vovere*, to vow] **1.** to set apart for a special use or service; dedicate **2.** to give up (oneself or one's time, energy, etc.) to some purpose, activity, or person

de·vot·ed (-id) *adj.* **1.** dedicated; consecrated **2.** very loving, loyal, or faithful —**de·vot′ed·ly** *adv.* —**de·vot′ed·ness** *n.*

dev·o·tee (dev′ə tē′, -tā′) *n.* a person strongly devoted to someone or to something [a *devotee* of religion; a *devotee* of ballet]

de·vo·tion (di vō′shən) *n.* **1.** a devoting or being devoted **2.** piety **3.** religious worship **4.** [*pl.*] prayers **5.** loyalty or deep affection

de·vo·tion·al (-'l) *adj.* of or characterized by devotion —☆*n.* a brief worship service —**de·vo′tion·al·ly** *adv.*

de·vour (di vour′) *vt.* [< OFr. < L. < *de*-, thoroughly + *vorare*, to swallow: see VORACIOUS] **1.** to eat (up) hungrily or greedily **2.** to consume or destroy with great force **3.** to take in greedily with the eyes, ears, or mind [to *devour* novels] **4.** to absorb; engross [*devoured* by curiosity] **5.** to swallow up; engulf —**de·vour′er** *n.*

de·vout (di vout′) *adj.* [< OFr. < L. *devotus*: see DEVOTE] **1.** very religious; pious **2.** showing reverence **3.** earnest; sincere; heartfelt [a *devout* admirer] —**de·vout′ly** *adv.* —**de·vout′ness** *n.*

De Vries (də vrēs′), **Hugo** 1848-1935; Du. botanist

dew (doo, dyoo) *n.* [OE. *deaw*] **1.** the moisture that condenses after a warm day and appears during the night in little drops on cool surfaces **2.** anything regarded as refreshing, pure, etc., like dew **3.** any moisture in small drops —*vt.* [Poet.] to wet as with drops of dew

dew·ber·ry (doo′ber′ē, dyoo′-) *n., pl.* -ries **1.** any of various trailing blackberry plants of the rose family **2.** the fruit of any of these plants

dew·claw (-klô′) *n.* **1.** a functionless digit on the foot of some animals, as on the inner side of a dog's leg **2.** the claw or hoof on such a digit

dew·drop (-dräp′) *n.* a drop of dew

Dew·ey (doo′ē, dyoo′ē) **1. George,** 1837-1917; U.S. admiral in the Spanish-American War **2. John,** 1859-1952; U.S. philosopher & educator **3. Melvil,** 1851-1931; U.S. librarian: originated **Dewey Decimal System** for book classification in libraries

---

fat, āpe, cär; ten, ēven; is, bīte; gō, hôrn, tool, look; oil, out; up, fur; get; joy; yet; chin; she; thin, *th*en; zh, leisure; ŋ, ring; ə for *a* in *ago, e* in *agent, i* in *sanity, o* in *comply, u* in *focus*; ' as in *able* (ā′b'l); Fr. bál; ë, Fr. coeur; ö, Fr. feu; Fr. mo*n*; ô, Fr. coq; ü, Fr. duc; *r*, Fr. cri; H, G. ich; kh, G. doch; ‡foreign; ☆ Americanism; < derived from. See inside front cover.

dew·lap (do͞o′lap′, dyo͞o′-) *n.* [< ME. < *dew*, prob. dew + *lappe*, a fold < OE. *læppa*] **1.** a loose fold of skin hanging from the throat of cattle and certain other animals **2.** a similar loose fold under the chin of an elderly person —**dew′lapped′** (-lapt′) *adj.*

☆**DEW line** (do͞o, dyo͞o) [*D*(*istant*) *E*(*arly*) *W*(*arning*)] a line of radar stations near the 70th parallel in N. America

dew point the temperature at which dew starts to form or vapor to condense into liquid

dew·y (do͞o′ē, dyo͞o′-) *adj.* **dew′i·er, dew′i·est** **1.** wet or damp with or as with dew **2.** of dew **3.** [Poet.] dewlike; refreshing, etc. —**dew′i·ly** *adv.* —**dew′i·ness** *n.*

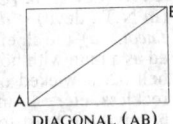

DEWLAP

dex·ter (dek′stər) *adj.* [L., right] of or on the right-hand side (on a coat of arms, the left of the viewer)

dex·ter·i·ty (dek ster′ə tē) *n.* [< L. < *dexter:* see prec.] **1.** skill in using one's hands or body; adroitness **2.** skill in using one's mind; cleverness

dex·ter·ous (dek′strəs, -stər əs) *adj.* [DEXTER + -OUS] **1.** having or showing skill in the use of the hands or body **2.** having or showing mental skill —**dex′ter·ous·ly** *adv.* —**dex′ter·ous·ness** *n.*

SYN.—**dexterous** implies an ability to do things with skill and precision [a *dexterous* weaver]; **adroit** adds to this the idea of cleverness, now esp. in dealing with people, ideas, etc. [they admired her *adroit* handling of an awkward situation]; **deft** suggests a nimbleness and sureness of touch [a seamstress *deft* with the needle]; **handy** suggests skill, usually without training, at a large variety of tasks [he is very *handy* around the house] — **ANT.** clumsy, awkward, inept

dex·tral (dek′strəl) *adj.* [< L. *dextra*, right-hand side] **1.** on the right-hand side; right **2.** right-handed —**dex·tral′i·ty** (-stral′ə tē) *n.* —**dex′tral·ly** *adv.*

dex·trin (dek′strin) *n.* [< Fr. < L. *dexter*, right: it turns the plane of polarized light to the right] a soluble, gummy substance obtained from starch and used as adhesive, sizing, etc.: also **dex′trine** (-strēn, -strən)

dex·tro- [< L. *dexter*, right] *a combining form meaning:* **1.** toward the right; clockwise [*dextrorotatory*] **2.** dextrorotatory [*dextrose*] Also, before a vowel, **dextr-**

dex·tro·ro·ta·to·ry (dek′strō rōt′ə tôr′ē) *adj.* **1.** turning to the right, in a clockwise direction **2.** turning the plane of polarized light clockwise: said of certain crystals, solutions, etc.

dex·trorse (dek′strôrs) *adj.* [< L. < *dexter*, right + *versus*, pp. of *vertere*, to turn] *Bot.* twining upward to the right, as the stem of the hop

DEXTRORSE VINE

dex·trose (dek′strōs) *n.* [DEXTR(O)- + -OSE¹] dextrorotatory glucose, $C_6H_{12}O_6$, found in plants and animals

dex·trous (-strəs) *adj.* same as DEXTEROUS

DF, D/F, D.F. *Radio* direction finder

dg. decigram; decigrams

dh *Baseball* designated hitter

‡**dhar·ma** (dur′mə, där′-) *n.* [Sans., law] *Hinduism, Buddhism* **1.** cosmic order or law, including the natural and moral principles that apply to all beings and things **2.** observance of this law in one's life

dhow (dou) *n.* [Ar. *dawa*] a single-masted ship with a lateen sail, used along the Indian Ocean coasts

di-¹ [Gr. *di-* < *dis*, twice < base of TWO] *a prefix meaning:* **1.** twice, double, twofold **2.** *Chem.* having two atoms, molecules, radicals, etc.

di-² same as DIS-

di-³ same as DIA-

di., dia. diameter

di·a- [< Gr.] *a prefix meaning:* **1.** through, across [*diaphragm, diagonal*] **2.** apart, between [*diagnose*]

di·a·be·tes (dī′ə bēt′is, -ēz) *n.* [L. < Gr. *diabētēs*, a siphon < *dia-*, through + *bainein*, to go] any of various diseases characterized by an excessive discharge of urine; esp., DIABETES MEL-LITUS

DHOW

diabetes mel·li·tus (mə līt′is) [ModL., lit., honey diabetes] a chronic form of diabetes involving an insulin deficiency and characterized by excess of sugar in the blood and urine, hunger, thirst, etc.

di·a·bet·ic (dī′ə bet′ik) *adj.* of or having diabetes —*n.* a person who has diabetes

di·a·bol·ic (dī′ə bäl′ik) *adj.* [< Fr. < LL. < Gr. *diabolos:* see DEVIL] **1.** of the Devil or devils **2.** very wicked or cruel; fiendish Also **di′a·bol′i·cal** —**di′a·bol′i·cal·ly** *adv.*

di·ac·o·nal (dī ak′ə n′l) *adj.* of a deacon or deacons

di·ac·o·nate (-nit) *n.* **1.** the rank, office, or tenure of a deacon **2.** a group of deacons

di·a·crit·ic (dī′ə krit′ik) *adj.* [Gr. *diakritikos* < *dia-*, across + *krinein*, to separate] *same as* DIACRITICAL —*n. same as* DIACRITICAL MARK

di·a·crit·i·cal (-i k′l) *adj.* **1.** serving to distinguish **2.** able to distinguish —**di′a·crit′i·cal·ly** *adv.*

diacritical mark a mark, as a macron or a cedilla, added to a letter or symbol to show its pronunciation or to distinguish it in some way

di·a·dem (dī′ə dem′, -dəm) *n.* [< OFr. < L. < Gr. *diadēma* < *dia-*, through + *dein*, to bind] **1.** a crown **2.** an ornamental cloth headband worn as a crown **3.** royal power or authority —*vt.* to put a diadem on; crown

di·aer·e·sis (dī er′ə sis) *n., pl.* **-ses**′ (-sēz′) *same as* DIERESIS

diag. **1.** diagonal **2.** diagram

Dia·ghi·lev (dyä′gi lyef; *E.* -lef), **Ser·gei (Pavlovich)** (syer-gyā′i) 1872–1929; Russ. ballet producer

di·ag·nose (dī′əg nōs′, -nōz′) *vt., vi.* **-nosed**′ **-nos′ing** to make a diagnosis of (a disease, a problem, etc.)

di·ag·no·sis (dī′əg nō′sis) *n., pl.* **-ses** (-sēz) [ModL. < Gr. < *dia-*, between + *gignōskein*, KNOW] **1.** the act or process of deciding the nature of a diseased condition by examination of the symptoms **2.** a careful analysis of the facts in order to explain something [a *diagnosis* of the economy] **3.** a decision based on such an examination or analysis —**di′ag·nos′tic** (-näs′tik) *adj.* —**di′ag·nos′ti·cal·ly** *adv.* —**di′ag·nos·ti′cian** (-näs tish′-ən) *n.*

di·ag·o·nal (dī ag′ə n′l) *adj.* [L. *diagonalis* < Gr. < *dia-*, through + *gōnia*, an angle] **1.** slanting from one corner to the opposite corner, as of a rectangle **2.** having a slanting direction or slanting markings, lines, etc. —*n.* **1.** *a)* a diagonal line or plane *b) same as* VIRGULE **2.** any diagonal course, row, part, etc. —**di′ag·o·nal·ly** *adv.*

DIAGONAL (AB)

di·a·gram (dī′ə gram′) *n.* [Gr. *diagramma* < *dia-*, across + *graphein*, to write: for IE. base see CARVE] a drawing, plan, or chart that explains a thing, as by showing its parts and their relationships, workings, etc. —*vt.* **-gramed**′ or **-grammed**′, **-gram′ing** or **-gram′ming** to show or explain by means of a diagram; make a diagram of —**di′a·gram·mat′ic** (-grə mat′ik), **di′a·gram·mat′i·cal** *adj.* —**di′a·gram·mat′i·cal·ly** *adv.*

di·al (dī′əl, dīl) *n.* [< ML. *dialis*, daily < L. *dies*, day: for IE. base see DEITY] **1.** a sundial **2.** the face of a watch or clock **3.** the face of a meter, gauge, etc. on which a pointer moves to show an amount, degree, etc. **4.** a marked disk or strip on a radio or television set, for tuning in stations or channels ☆**5.** a rotating disk on a telephone, used in making connections automatically —*vt., vi.* **-aled** or **-alled, -al·ing** or **-al·ling** **1.** to measure, regulate, etc. with a dial **2.** to tune in (a radio station, television channel, program, etc.) ☆**3.** to call on a telephone by using a dial or similar automatic device

dial. **1.** dialect(al) **2.** dialectic(al)

di·a·lect (dī′ə lekt′) *n.* [< L. < Gr. *dialektos*, discourse < *dia-*, between + *legein*, to talk: see LOGIC] **1.** *a)* any of the forms of a language spoken in a particular region or community or by a specified social group *b)* loosely, any such form regarded as differing significantly from the form of the language that is considered standard **2.** any language as a member of a group or family of languages [English is a West Germanic *dialect*] —*adj.* of or in dialect —**di′a·lec′tal** *adj.* —**di′a·lec′tal·ly** *adv.*

SYN.—**dialect** refers to a form of the language of a locality or group that differs from the standard language in certain matters of pronunciation, grammar, and vocabulary; **vernacular** refers to the variety of a language in common, everyday use, as distinguished from the formal or literary variety; **jargon** is applied, esp. by outsiders, to the specialized vocabulary of people in the same work, way of life, etc. [medical *jargon*]; **cant** and **argot** are both applied to jargon of various sorts, originally to the secret jargon of thieves, beggars, etc., but popularly **cant** is often used of insincere, trite talk that is pious or moralizing

di·a·lec·tic (dī′ə lek′tik) *n.* [< OFr. < L. < Gr. < *dialektikos:* see prec.] **1.** [*often pl.*] the art or practice of examining ideas logically, often by question and answer, so as to determine their validity **2.** logical argumentation **3.** [*often pl.*] the method of logic used by Hegel and adapted by Marx to observable social and economic processes: its basic principle is that every idea, event, etc. has its opposite and the conflict between the two leads to a resolution —*adj. same as* DIALECTICAL

di·a·lec·ti·cal (-ti k′l) *adj.* **1.** of or using dialectic or dialectics **2.** of or characteristic of a dialect; dialectal —**di·a·lec′ti·cal·ly** *adv.*

dialectical materialism the philosophy stemming from Marx and Engels which applies Hegel's dialectical method to observable social processes

di·a·lec·ti·cian (dī′ə lek tish′ən) *n.* **1.** an expert in dialectic; logician **2.** a specialist in dialects

di·a·logue, di·a·log (dī′ə lôg′, -läg′) *n.* [OFr. < L. < Gr. *dialogos* < *dialegein:* see DIALECT] **1.** a talking together; conversation **2.** open and frank discussion of ideas, as in seeking to understand each other better **3.** a written work in the form of a conversation **4.** the passages of talk in a play, story, etc. —*vi.* **-logued′, -logu′ing** to hold a conversation —*vt.* to express in dialogue —**di·a·log·ist** (dī al′ə jist, dī′ə lôg′ist) *n.*

Dialogue Mass *R.C.Ch.* a Low Mass at which the congregation, following an earlier custom now revived, makes the responses aloud and in unison

☆**dial tone** a low buzzing sound indicating to the user of a dial telephone that the line is open and a number may be dialed

di·al·y·sis (dī al′ə sis) *n., pl.* **-ses′** (-sēz′) [L. < Gr. < *dia-,* apart + *lyein,* to loose] the separation of crystalloids from colloids in solution through a semipermeable membrane, as in a mechanical apparatus to clear the blood of impurities during kidney failure —**di·a·lyt·ic** (dī′ə lit′ik) *adj.* —**di·a·lyt′i·cal·ly** *adv.*

di·a·lyze (dī′ə līz′) *vt.* **-lyzed′, -lyz′ing** to apply dialysis to or separate by dialysis —*vi.* to undergo dialysis —**di′a·lyz′er** *n.*

diam. diameter

di·a·mag·net·ic (dī′ə mag net′ik) *adj.* having diamagnetism —*n.* a diamagnetic substance, as bismuth or zinc: also **di′a·mag′net**

di·a·mag·net·ism (-mag′nə tiz′m) *n.* the property that certain substances have of being repelled by both poles of a magnet

di·a·man·té (dē′ə män tā′, -män′tā) *adj.* [Fr.] decorated with rhinestones or other glittering bits of material —*n.* glittering ornamentation

di·am·e·ter (dī am′ət ər) *n.* [< OFr. < ML. < L. < Gr. < *dia-,* through + *metron,* a measure: for IE. base see MEASURE] **1.** a straight line passing through the center of a circle, sphere, etc. from one side to the other **2.** the length of such a line; width through the center

di·a·met·ri·cal (dī′ə met′ri k′l) *adj.* **1.** of or along a diameter **2.** designating an opposite, a difference, etc. that is wholly so [*diametrical* opposites]: also **di′a·met′ric** —**di′a·met′ri·cal·ly** *adv.*

di·a·mond (dī′mənd, -ə mənd) *n.* [< OFr. < ML. *diamas* (gen. *diamantis*) < L. < Gr. *adamas,* ADAMANT, diamond] **1.** a mineral consisting of nearly pure carbon in crystalline form: it is the hardest mineral known and has great brilliance: unflawed stones are cut into precious gems; less perfect forms are used for phonograph-needle tips, cutting tools, abrasives, etc. **2.** a gem cut from this mineral **3.** *a)* a lozenge-shaped plane figure (◇) *b)* a red mark like this on a suit of playing cards *c)* [*pl.*] this suit *d)* a card of this suit ☆**4.** *Baseball a)* the infield *b)* the whole playing field —*adj.* of, like, or set with a diamond —**diamond in the rough 1.** a diamond in its natural state **2.** a person or thing of fine quality but lacking polish

diamond anniversary the sixtieth, or sometimes seventy-fifth, anniversary: also **diamond jubilee**

di·a·mond·back (-bak′) *adj.* having diamond-shaped markings on the back —*n.* ☆**1.** a large, poisonous rattlesnake native to the southern U.S. ☆**2.** an edible turtle found in coastal salt marshes from Cape Cod to Mexico: in full, **diamondback terrapin 3.** a small, brown and white moth

Di·an·a (dī an′ə) [ML. < L., ult. < *divus,* divine] **1.** a feminine name: var. *Diane* **2.** *Rom. Myth.* the virgin goddess of the moon and of hunting: identified with the Greek goddess Artemis

di·a·pa·son (dī′ə pāz′′n, -pās′-) *n.* [< L. < Gr. contr. < *dia,* through + *pason,* gen. pl. of *pas,* all (notes)] **1.** *a)* the entire range of a musical instrument or voice *b)* the entire range of some activity, emotion, etc. **2.** one of the principal stops of an organ covering the instrument's complete range **3.** a swelling burst of harmony

di·a·per (dī′pər, dī′ə pər) *n.* [< OFr. *diapre* < ML. *diasprum,* flowered cloth] **1.** *a)* orig., cloth or fabric with a pattern of repeated small figures, such as diamonds *b)* such a pattern, as in art **2.** a soft, absorbent cloth folded and arranged between the legs and around the waist of a baby —*vt.* **1.** to decorate with a diaper design **2.** to put a fresh diaper on (a baby)

di·aph·a·nous (dī af′ə nəs) *adj.* [< ML. < Gr. < *dia-,* through + *phainein,* to show] **1.** so fine or gauzy in texture as to be transparent or translucent [*diaphanous* cloth] **2.** vague or indistinct —**di·aph′a·nous·ly** *adv.*

di·a·pho·re·sis (dī′ə fə rē′sis) *n.* [LL. < Gr. < *dia-,* through + *pherein,* BEAR¹] perspiration, esp. when profuse —**di′a·pho·ret′ic** (-ret′ik) *adj., n.*

di·a·phragm (dī′ə fram′) *n.* [< LL. < Gr. < *dia-,* through + *phragma,* a fence < *phrassein,* enclose] **1.** the partition of muscles and tendons between the chest cavity and the abdominal cavity; midriff **2.** any separating membrane or device; specif., ☆a contraceptive device for the vagina **3.** a device to regulate the amount of light entering a camera lens, etc. **4.** a thin, vibrating disk or cone that produces electrical signals, as in a microphone, or sound waves, as in a loudspeaker —**di′a·phrag·mat′ic** (-frag mat′ik) *adj.* —**di′a·phrag·mat′i·cal·ly** *adv.*

di·aph·y·sis (dī af′ə sis) *n., pl.* **-ses′** (-sēz′) [ModL. < Gr. < *dia-,* through + *phyein,* to produce] the shaft of a long bone —**di·a·phys·e·al, di·a·phys·i·al** (dī′ə fiz′ē əl) *adj.*

di·a·rist (dī′ə rist) *n.* a person who keeps a diary

di·ar·rhe·a, di·ar·rhoe·a (dī′ə rē′ə) *n.* [< OFr. & LL. < Gr. < *dia-,* through + *rhein,* to flow] a condition in which bowel movements come too often and are too loose —**di′ar·rhe′al, di′ar·rhe′ic** *adj.*

di·a·ry (dī′ə rē) *n., pl.* **-ries** [L. *diarium* < *dies,* day: for IE. base see DEITY] **1.** a daily written record, esp. of the writer's own experiences, thoughts, etc. **2.** a book for keeping such a record

Di·as (dē′äsh; *E.* -əs), **Bar·tho·lo·me·u** (bär′too̅ loo̅ me′oo̅) 1450?-1500; Port. navigator & explorer: also sp. **Diaz**

Di·as·po·ra (dī as′pə rə) *n.* [< Gr. < *dia-,* across + *speirein,* to sow] **1.** *a)* the scattering of the Jews after the Babylonian exile *b)* the Jews scattered throughout the world **2.** [**d-**] any scattering of people with a common origin, background, beliefs, etc.

di·a·stase (dī′ə stās′) *n.* [Fr. < Gr. *diastasis,* separation < *dia-,* apart + *histanai,* to stand] an enzyme, occurring in the seed of grains and malt, that changes starches into maltose and later into dextrose —**di′a·stat′ic** (-stat′ik) *adj.*

di·as·to·le (dī as′tə lē′) *n.* [LL. < Gr. *diastolē,* expansion < *dia-,* apart + *stellein,* to put] the usual rhythmic dilatation of the heart, esp. of the ventricles, during which the chambers fill with blood —**di·a·stol·ic** (dī′ə stäl′ik) *adj.*

di·as·tro·phism (dī as′trə fiz′m) *n.* [< Gr. < *dia-,* aside + *strephein,* to turn + -ISM] the process by which the earth's surface is reshaped by rock movements —**di·a·stroph·ic** (dī′ə sträf′ik) *adj.*

di·a·ther·my (dī′ə thur′mē) *n.* [ModL. < Gr. *dia-,* through + *thermē,* heat] medical treatment in which heat is produced in the tissues beneath the skin by a high-frequency electric current —**di′a·ther′mic** *adj.*

di·a·tom (dī′ə täm′, -ət əm) *n.* [ModL. < Gr. < *dia-,* through + *temnein,* to cut] any of a number of related microscopic algae whose cell walls contain silica: diatoms are a source of food for marine life —**di·a·to·ma·ceous** (dī′ət ə mā′shəs, dī at′ə-) *adj.*

di·a·ton·ic (dī′ə tän′ik) *adj.* [Fr. < LL. < Gr. *diatonikos,* stretched through (the notes) < *dia-,* through + *teinein,* to stretch] *Music* designating, of, or using any standard major or minor scale of eight tones without the chromatic intervals —**di′a·ton′i·cal·ly** *adv.*

di·a·tribe (dī′ə trīb′) *n.* [Fr. < L. < Gr. *diatribē,* a wearing away < *dia-,* through + *tribein,* to rub: for IE. base see TRITE] a speech or writing that attacks some person or thing in a very harsh way

di·bas·ic (dī bās′ik) *adj.* denoting or of an acid with two hydrogen atoms which may be replaced by basic radicals or atoms to form a salt

dib·ble (dib′'l) *n.* [ME. *dibbel*, prob. < *dibben*, to dip] a pointed tool used to make holes in the soil for seeds, bulbs, or young plants: also called **dib′ber** —*vt.* **-bled, -bling** **1.** to make a hole in (the soil) with a dibble **2.** to plant with a dibble —*vi.* to use a dibble

dib·buk (dib′ək) *n. same as* DYBBUK

dibs (dibz) *n.pl.* [< *dibstone*, a jack in a children's game] ☆[Colloq.] a claim to a share of, or rights in, something wanted — ☆*interj.* an exclamation announcing such a claim: chiefly a child's term

dice (dīs) *n.pl., sing.* **die** or **dice** [ME. *dis,* pl.: see DIE[2]] **1.** small cubes of bone, plastic, etc. marked on each side with from one to six spots and used, usually in pairs, in games of chance **2.** [*with sing. v.*] a gambling game played with dice **3.** any small cubes —*vi.* **diced, dic′-ing** to play or gamble with dice —*vt.* to cut (vegetables, etc.) into small cubes —**no dice** [Colloq.] **1.** no: used in refusing a request **2.** no success, luck, etc. —**dic′er** *n.*

DICE

di·chlo·ride (dī klôr′īd, -id) *n.* any chemical compound in which two atoms of chlorine are combined with an element or radical

di·chot·o·mize (dī kät′ə mīz′) *vt.* **-mized′, -miz′ing** [see DICHOTOMY] to divide or separate into two parts

di·chot·o·my (dī kät′ə mē) *n., pl.* **-mies** [< Gr. < *dicha*, in two + *temnein*, to cut] **1.** division into two usually opposed parts or groups **2.** *Biol., Bot.* a dividing or branching into two parts, esp. when repeated —**di·chot′o·mous** (-məs) *adj.*

di·chro·mate (dī krō′māt) *n.* any salt of dichromic acid

di·chro·mat·ic (dī′krō mat′ik) *adj.* [DI-[1] + CHROMATIC] **1.** having two colors **2.** *Biol.* having two varieties of coloration independent of sex or age, as some insects, owls, parrots, etc.—**di·chro′ma·tism** *n.*

di·chro·mic (dī krō′mik) *adj.* **1.** *same as* DICHROMATIC **2.** *Chem.* designating a hypothetical acid, $H_2Cr_2O_7$, from which dichromates are formed

Dick (dik) [< RICHARD] a masculine name —*n.* [d-] [Slang] a detective

☆**dick·cis·sel** (dik sis′'l) *n.* [echoic of its cry] an American bunting with a black throat and yellow breast, living in prairie regions

dick·ens (dik′'nz) *n., interj.* [prob. < nickname for RICHARD] [Colloq.] devil; deuce: a mild oath

Dick·ens (dik′'nz), **Charles** (pseud. *Boz*) 1812-70; Eng. novelist —**Dick·en·si·an** (di ken′zē ən) *adj.*

☆**dick·er** (dik′ər) *vi., vt.* [< *dicker*, ten, ten hides (as a unit of barter), ult. < L. *decem,* TEN] to trade by bargaining, esp. on a small scale; barter or haggle —*n.* the act of bargaining or haggling

dick·ey (dik′ē) *n., pl.* **-eys** [< DICK] **1.** a man's detachable, or false, shirt front **2.** a woman's detachable collar or blouse front **3.** a small bird: also **dickey bird** Also sp. **dick′y,** pl. **dick′ies**

Dick·in·son (dik′in s'n), **Emily (Elizabeth)** 1830-86; U.S. poet

di·cli·nous (dī klī′nəs) *adj.* [< DI-[1] + Gr. *klinē,* bed + -OUS] *Bot.* having the stamens and pistils in separate flowers —**di·cli·nism** (dī′klī niz'm), **di′cli·ny** (-nē) *n.*

di·cot·y·le·don (dī′kät 'l ēd′'n, dī kät′'l-) *n.* a flowering plant with two seed leaves (cotyledons) —**di′cot·y·le′don·ous** *adj.*

di·cou·ma·rin (dī kōō′mər in) *n.* [DI-[1] + *coumarin,* a plant extract] a chemical compound, $C_{19}H_{12}O_6$, used as an anticoagulant

dict. **1.** dictator **2.** dictionary

dic·ta (dik′tə) *n. alt. pl. of* DICTUM

☆**Dic·ta·phone** (dik′tə fōn′) [DICTA(TE) + -PHONE] *a trademark for* a machine that records spoken words so that they can be played back later, as for typing —*n.* this machine

dic·tate (dik′tāt; *also for v.* dik tāt′) *vt., vi.* **-tat·ed, -tat·ing** [< L. pp. of *dictare* < *dicere:* see DICTION] **1.** to speak or read (something) aloud for someone else to write down [to *dictate* a letter to a secretary] **2.** to give (orders) with authority or in an arbitrary way; command or order —*n.* **1.** an order or command given with authority [a *dictate* of the court] **2.** a guiding principle [the *dictates* of conscience]

dic·ta·tion (dik tā′shən) *n.* **1.** the dictating of words for another to write down **2.** the words so spoken or read **3.** the giving of authoritative orders or commands —**dic·ta′tion·al** *adj.*

dic·ta·tor (dik′tāt ər, dik tāt′-) *n.* **1.** a ruler with absolute power and authority, esp. a tyrant or despot **2.** a person who is domineering or arbitrary in giving orders, etc. **3.** one who dictates words for another to write down —**dic·ta′tor·ship′** *n.*

dic·ta·to·ri·al (dik′tə tôr′ē əl) *adj.* of, like, or characteristic of a dictator; autocratic; tyrannical; domineering —**dic·ta·to′-ri·al·ly** *adv.*

SYN.—**dictatorial** implies the overbearing or tyrannical methods or manner of a dictator [a *dictatorial* foreman]; **arbitrary** suggests the use of one's power or authority so as to suit only one's own will or judgment [an *arbitrary* decision]; **dogmatic** suggests the attitude of a religious teacher who presents certain doctrines as absolute truths not to be doubted [the scientific method is not *dogmatic*]; **doctrinaire** implies a sticking stubbornly to doctrines or theories without regard to practical problems in applying them

dic·tion (dik′shən) *n.* [< L. pp. of *dicere,* to say < IE. base *deik-,* to point out] **1.** the way in which something is put into words; choice and arrangement of words [the *diction* of everyday talk is different from that of a formal essay] **2.** a way of speaking or pronouncing words; enunciation [an actor must have good, clear *diction*]

dic·tion·ar·y (dik′shə ner′ē) *n., pl.* **-ar′ies** [ML. *dictionarium* < LL. *dictio:* see prec.] **1.** a book of words in a language in alphabetical order, with their definitions, etymologies, pronunciations, etc.; lexicon **2.** such a book of words in one language explained in the words of another [a Spanish-English *dictionary*] **3.** any alphabetically arranged list of words or articles relating to a special subject [a medical *dictionary*]

dic·tum (dik′təm) *n., pl.* **-tums, -ta** (-tə) [L., neut. pp. of *dicere:* see DICTION] a formal statement of fact, opinion, principle, etc.; pronouncement [the business *dictum* "grow or die"]

☆**Di·cu·ma·rol** (dī kōō′mə rôl′, -kyōō′-) *a collective trademark for* DICOUMARIN

did (did) *pt. of* DO[1]

☆**di·dact** (dī′dakt) *n.* a didactic person

di·dac·tic (dī dak′tik) *adj.* [Gr. *didaktikos* < *didaskein,* to teach] **1.** used or intended for teaching or instruction [a *didactic* mock trial at law school] **2.** morally instructive [*didactic* fables] **3.** too much inclined to teach others; boringly pedantic or moralistic Also **di·dac′ti·cal** —**di·dac′ti·cal·ly** *adv.* —**di·dac′ti·cism** (-tə siz'm) *n.*

di·dac·tics (-tiks) *n.pl.* [*usually with sing. v.*] the art or science of teaching; pedagogy

did·dle[1] (did′'l) *vi., vt.* **-dled, -dling** [Eng. dial. *duddle, diddle,* to totter] [Colloq.] to move back and forth jerkily; jiggle —**did′-dler** *n.*

did·dle[2] (did′'l) *vt., vi.* **-dled, -dling** [ult. < OE. *dyderian,* to fool] [Colloq.] **1.** to cheat or swindle **2.** to waste (time) in trifling —**did′dler** *n.*

Di·de·rot (dē′də rō′; *Fr.* dē drō′), **Denis** 1713-84; Fr. encyclopedist & philosopher

did·n't (did′'nt) did not

Di·do (dī′dō) *Rom. Legend* queen of Carthage, who kills herself when her lover Aeneas leaves her

di·do (dī′dō) *n., pl.* **-does, -dos** [< ?] [Colloq.] a mischievous trick; prank; caper

didst (didst) *archaic second person singular in the past tense of* DO[1]: *used with* thou

☆**di·dy** (dī′dē) *n., pl.* **-dies** [< DIAPER] [Colloq.] a diaper (sense 2)

di·dym·i·um (dī dim′ē əm) *n.* [< Gr. *didymos,* twin] a mixture of certain rare earths

die[1] (dī) *vi.* **died, dy′ing** [< ON. *deyja:* for IE. base see DEAD] **1.** to stop living; become dead **2.** to suffer the agony of, or like that of, death **3.** to cease existing or stop going, moving, acting, etc.; end **4.** to lose force or vitality; fade away [a dying culture] **5.** [Colloq.] to want very much; yearn [she's *dying* to tell] **6.** *Theol.* to suffer death of the spirit —**die away** (or **down**) to become weaker and cease gradually —**die back** (or **down**) to wither to the roots or woody part —**die hard** to resist to the last —**die off** to die one by one until all are gone —**die out** to go out of existence

SYN.—**die** is the basic, simple, direct word meaning to stop living or become dead; **decease** and **pass away** (or **pass on**) are euphemisms for the word **die**, **decease** being also the legal term and **pass away** and **pass on** being more common in informal usage; **perish** implies death by a violent means or in a disaster [twenty people *perished* in the fire]; **expire** means literally to breathe one's last breath

DICKEY

die[2] (dī) *n., pl.,* for 1 **dice** (dīs); for 2 **dies** (dīz) [< OFr. *de* < L. pp. of *dare,* to give] **1.** a small, marked cube used in games of chance: see also DICE **2.** any of various tools or devices for molding, stamping, cutting, or shaping, as the part of a stamping machine into which the punch is pressed —*vt.* **died, die′ing** to mold, stamp, cut, or shape with a die —**the die is cast** the decision has been made and cannot be changed

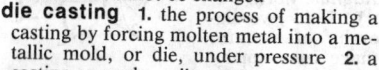

PUNCH
DIE

die casting 1. the process of making a casting by forcing molten metal into a metallic mold, or die, under pressure **2.** a casting so made —**die caster**

dief·fen·bach·i·a (dēf′n bak′ē ə) *n.* [ModL. < E. *Dieffenbach* (19th-c. Ger. botanist)] a tropical plant of the arum family, with large leaves

die-hard, die·hard (dī′härd′) *adj.* extremely stubborn in resisting; unwilling to give in —*n.* a stubborn or resisting person, esp. an extreme conservative

☆**diel·drin** (dēl′drin) *n.* a highly toxic, long-lasting insecticide, $C_{12}H_8OCl_6$

di·e·lec·tric (dī′ə lek′trik) *n.* [< DI(A)- + ELECTRIC] a substance, as air, rubber, glass, etc., that does not conduct electricity and that can sustain an electric field: used in capacitors, etc. —*adj.* having the properties or function of a dielectric

di·er·e·sis (dī er′ə sis) *n., pl.* -**ses′** (-sēz′) [LL. < Gr. *diairesis,* division < *dia-,* apart + *hairein,* to take] a mark (¨) placed over the second of two consecutive vowels to show that it is pronounced in a separate syllable: now usually replaced by a hyphen (*reënter, re-enter*), or simply omitted (*cooperate, naive*) The mark is also used, as in this dictionary, to show a certain pronunciation of a vowel (ä)

die·sel (dē′z'l, -s'l) *n.* [after R. *Diesel* (1858–1913), Ger. inventor] [*often* D-] **1.** a type of internal-combustion engine that burns fuel oil: the ignition is brought about by heat resulting from air compression, instead of by an electric spark as in a gasoline engine: also **diesel engine** (or **motor**) **2.** a locomotive, truck, etc. with such an engine

die·sink·er (dī′siŋ′kər) *n.* a maker of dies used in stamping or shaping —**die′sink′ing** *n.*

‡**Di·es I·rae** (dē′ez ir′ā, dē′äs ir′ē) [L., Day of Wrath] a medieval Latin hymn about Judgment Day, beginning *Dies Irae,* a part of the Requiem Mass

di·e·sis (dī′ə sis) *n., pl.* -**ses′** (-sēz′) [L. < Gr. < *diienai,* to send through] a reference mark (‡) used in printing: also called DOUBLE DAGGER

die·stock (dī′stäk′) *n.* a frame to hold dies for cutting threads on water pipes, screws, bolts, etc.

di·et[1] (dī′ət) *n.* [< OFr. < ML. < L. < Gr. *diaita,* way of life] **1.** *a)* what a person or animal usually eats and drinks; daily fare *b)* what a person regularly reads, listens to, does, etc. **2.** a special or limited selection of food and drink, chosen or prescribed for health or to gain or lose weight —*vi.* to eat special or limited food, esp. for losing weight —**di′et·er** *n.*

di·et[2] (dī′ət) *n.* [< OFr. < ML. < L. *dies,* day: for IE. base see DEITY] **1.** a formal assembly, as formerly of princes, electors, etc. of the Holy Roman Empire **2.** in some countries, a national or local legislative assembly

di·e·tar·y (dī′ə ter′ē) *n., pl.* -**ies 1.** a system of diet **2.** daily food allowance or ration —*adj.* of diet [the *dietary* laws of the Moslems]

di·e·tet·ic (dī′ə tet′ik) *adj.* of, relating to, or designed for a particular diet of food and drink: also **di′e·tet′i·cal** —**di′e·tet′i·cal·ly** *adv.*

di·e·tet·ics (-iks) *n.pl.* [*with sing. v.*] the study of the kinds and quantities of food needed for health

☆**di·e·ti·tian, di·e·ti·cian** (dī′ə tish′ən) *n.* an expert in dietetics; specialist in planning meals or diets

dif- *same as* DIS-: used before *f*

dif·fer (dif′ər) *vi.* [< OFr. < L. *differre* < *dis-,* apart + *ferre,* to BEAR[1]] **1.** to be unlike; be not the same (often with *from*) **2.** to be of opposite or unlike opinions; disagree [we *differed* about the meaning of the poem]

dif·fer·ence (dif′ər əns, dif′rəns) *n.* [see prec.] **1.** condition or quality of being different **2.** the way in which people or things are different **3.** a differing in opinion; disagreement or point of disagreement; dispute [friends in spite of their *differences* over politics] **4.** the amount by which one quantity is greater or less than another —**make a difference 1.** to have an effect; matter **2.** to change the situation —**split the difference 1.** to share equally what is left over **2.** to make a compromise —**what's the difference** [Colloq.] what does it matter?

dif·fer·ent (dif′ər ənt, dif′rənt) *adj.* [see DIFFER] **1.** not alike; dissimilar (with *from,* or, esp. colloquially, *than,* and, in Brit. usage, *to*) **2.** not the same; distinct; separate; other **3.** various **4.** unlike most others; unusual [their house is really *different*] —**dif′fer·ent·ly** *adv.*

SYN.—different implies a distinct separateness [there are three *different* colleges in the city] or contrast [the twins wore *different* hats]; **diverse** more forcefully sets apart the things referred to [the *diverse* cultures of the Aztecs and their Spanish conquerors]; **divergent** suggests a branching off in different directions with an ever-widening distance between [*divergent* schools of thought; *divergent* opinions]; **distinct** stresses that each of two or more things has a different identity and is unmistakably separate from the others, whether or not they are similar in kind, class, etc. [he was charged with two *distinct* offenses]; **dissimilar** stresses the lack of similarity in appearance, properties, or nature [*dissimilar* techniques]; **disparate** implies complete difference [*disparate* concepts] —**ANT.** alike, similar

dif·fer·en·ti·a (dif′ə ren′shē ə, -shə) *n., pl.* -**ti·ae′** (-shi ē′) a distinguishing characteristic

dif·fer·en·tial (dif′ə ren′shəl) *adj.* **1.** of, showing, or depending on a difference [*differential* rates] **2.** constituting a specific difference; distinguishing [*differential* qualities] **3.** having different effects or making use of differences [a *differential* gear] **4.** *Math.* of or involving differentials —*n.* **1.** a differentiating amount, degree, factor, etc. [*differentials* in salary] **2.** *Math. a)* an infinitesimal difference between two consecutive values of a variable quantity *b)* the derivative of a function multiplied by the increment of the independent variable **3.** *Mech.* same as DIFFERENTIAL GEAR —**dif′fer·en′tial·ly** *adv.*

differential calculus the branch of higher mathematics which deals with derivatives and their applications

differential gear (or **gearing**) an arrangement of gears connecting two axles in the same line and allowing one axle to turn faster than the other: used in the rear axles of automobiles to permit a difference in axle speeds while turning curves

dif·fer·en·ti·ate (-shē āt′) *vt.* -**at′ed, -at′ing 1.** to be or make a difference in or between [what *differentiates* the Bactrian camel from the dromedary?] **2.** to tell or see the difference in; distinguish between [he could *differentiate* colors at the age of two] **3.** *Math.* to work out the differential or derivative of —*vi.* **1.** to become different or differentiated [the ectoderm of the embryo *differentiates* into skin, hair, etc.] **2.** to tell or see the difference [to *differentiate* between the real and the fake] —see SYN. at DISTINGUISH —**dif′fer·en′ti·a′tion** *n.*

dif·fi·cult (dif′i kəlt, -kult′) *adj.* **1.** hard to do, make, understand, etc. [this math problem is *difficult*] **2.** hard to satisfy, persuade, etc. [he was a *difficult* employer] —see SYN. at HARD —**dif′fi·cult·ly** *adv.*

dif·fi·cul·ty (dif′i kul′tē, -kəl-) *n., pl.* -**ties** [< OFr. < L. *difficultas* < *dis-,* not + *facilis,* easy: see FACILE] **1.** the condition or fact of being difficult **2.** something difficult; an obstacle or objection [the pioneers faced many *difficulties* as they moved west] **3.** trouble or the cause of trouble [he had *difficulty* starting the car] **4.** a disagreement or quarrel —**in difficulties** in trouble, esp. because of a lack of money

SYN.—difficulty is applied to anything hard to deal with, regardless of the kind of problem or of how hard it is; **hardship** suggests suffering, want, or trouble that is extremely hard to bear [the *hardships* of poverty]; **rigor** suggests severe hardship that is usually brought on by outside circumstances beyond one's control [the *rigors* of winter]; **vicissitude** suggests a difficulty that is likely to occur in the course of something, often one that is part of the situation [the *vicissitudes* of political life]

dif·fi·dent (dif′ə dənt) *adj.* [< L. prp. of *diffidere* < *dis-,* not + *fidere,* to trust: for IE. base see FAITH] lacking confidence in oneself; hesitant to assert oneself; shy —see SYN. at SHY[1] —**dif′fi·dence** *n.* —**dif′fi·dent·ly** *adv.*

dif·fract (di frakt′) *vt.* [< L. pp. of *diffringere* < *dis-,* apart + *frangere,* to BREAK] to break into parts; specif., to subject to diffraction

dif·frac·tion (di frak′shən) *n.* **1.** the breaking up of a ray of light into dark and light bands or into the colors of the spectrum

2. a similar breaking up of other waves, as of sound or electricity —**dif·frac′tive** (-tiv) *adj.* —**dif·frac′tive·ly** *adv.*

dif·fuse (di fyōōs′; *for v.* -fyōōz′) *adj.* [< L. pp. < *dis-*, apart + *fundere*, to pour: see FOUND³] **1.** spread out; not centered in one place [this lamp gives *diffuse* light] **2.** using more words than are needed [a *diffuse* style] —*vt., vi.* -**fused′, -fus′ing 1.** to pour or spread out in every direction; scatter widely [to *diffuse* light, heat, etc.] **2.** *Physics* to mix by diffusion, as gases, liquids, etc.—see SYN. at WORDY —**dif·fuse′ly** *adv.* —**dif·fuse′ness** *n.* —**dif·fus′er, dif·fu′sor** (-fyōō′zər) *n.* —**dif·fus′i·bil′i·ty** *n.* —**dif·fus′i·ble** *adj.*

dif·fu·sion (di fyōō′zhən) *n.* **1.** a diffusing or being diffused; specif., *a*) a spreading about, as of news *b*) a scattering of light rays, as by reflection; also, the spreading and softening of light, as by using frosted glass *c*) a mixing together of the molecules of liquids, gases, etc. **2.** wordiness

dif·fu·sive (-siv) *adj.* **1.** tending to diffuse **2.** marked by diffusion **3.** diffuse —**dif·fu′sive·ly** *adv.* —**dif·fu′sive·ness** *n.*

dig (dig) *vt.* **dug** *or archaic & poet.* **digged, dig′ging** [< OFr. *digue*, dike < Du. *dijk* < IE. base *dheigw-*, to pierce] **1.** to break and turn up or remove (ground, etc.) with a spade or other tool, or with hands, claws, etc. **2.** to make (a hole, cellar, etc.) as by doing this **3.** to get from the ground in this way [to *dig* potatoes] ☆**4.** to find out, as by careful study; unearth (usually with *up* or *out*) [to *dig* out the truth] **5.** to jab or prod ☆**6.** [Slang] *a*) to understand *b*) to approve of or like —*vi.* **1.** to dig the ground **2.** to make a way by or as by digging (*through, into, under*) ☆**3.** [Colloq.] to work or study hard —*n.* **1.** the act of digging **2.** [Colloq.] *a*) a poke, nudge, etc. *b*) a sarcastic comment; taunt **3.** an archaeological excavation **4.** [*pl.,* often with *sing. v.*] [Colloq.] living quarters —**dig in 1.** to dig trenches for cover **2.** to establish oneself safely **3.** [Colloq.] *a*) to begin to work hard *b*) to begin eating —**dig into** [Colloq.] to work hard at

di·gest (dī′jest; *for v.* di jest′, dī-) *n.* [< L. pp. of *digerere,* to separate < *di-,* apart + *gerere,* to bear] **1.** a short account or report of a longer story, article, etc.; summary or synopsis **2.** a book, periodical, etc. consisting of such summaries [a *digest* of recent law cases] —*vt.* **1.** *a*) to arrange according to a system, usually in condensed form *b*) to condense and summarize (a piece of writing) **2.** to change (food), esp. in the stomach and intestines, into a form that can be used by the body **3.** to aid the digestion of (food) **4.** to think over so as to understand [read and *digest* that article] **5.** to soften or dissolve soluble material in, esp. with liquid —*vi.* to be digested [milk usually *digests* easily] —see SYN. at ABRIDGMENT —**di·gest′er** *n.*

di·gest·i·ble (di jes′tə b'l) *adj.* that can be digested —**di·gest′i·bil′i·ty** *n.* —**di·gest′i·bly** *adv.*

di·ges·tion (-chən) *n.* **1.** the act or process of digesting food **2.** the ability to digest food **3.** the digesting of ideas, as from books **4.** decomposition of sewage by bacteria

di·ges·tive (-tiv) *adj.* of, for, or aiding digestion —*n.* any substance or drink that aids digestion —**di·ges′tive·ly** *adv.* —**di·ges′tive·ness** *n.*

dig·ger (dig′ər) *n.* **1.** one that digs **2.** a tool or machine for digging ☆**3.** [D-] a member of any of several tribes of Indians in western North America who dug roots for food **4.** *same as* DIGGER WASP **5.** [D-] [Slang] an Australian or New Zealander

digger wasp any of various wasps that dig a nest in the ground

dig·gings (dig′iŋz) *n.pl.* **1.** materials dug out **2.** [*often with sing. v.*] a place where digging or mining is carried on **3.** [Slang] one's lodgings

dight (dīt) *vt.* **dight** *or* **dight′ed, dight′ing** [< OE. *dihtan,* to arrange < L. *dictare:* see DICTATE] [Archaic or Poet.] **1.** to adorn **2.** to equip

dig·it (dij′it) *n.* [L. *digitus,* a finger, toe: for IE. base see DICTION] **1.** a finger or toe **2.** any numeral from 0 to 9

dig·it·al (-'l) *adj.* **1.** of, like, or constituting a digit **2.** having digits **3.** performed with the finger **4.** using numbers that are digits to represent all the variables involved in calculation **5.** showing the time, temperature, etc. by a row of digits rather than by numbers on a dial, etc. [a *digital* watch] —*n.* **1.** a finger **2.** a key played with a finger, as on the piano —**dig′it·al·ly** *adv.*

☆**digital computer** a computer that uses numbers to perform calculations, usually in a binary system

dig·i·tal·is (dij′ə tal′is) *n.* [ModL. < L.: see DIGIT: from its flowers] **1.** any of a genus of plants of the figwort family, with long spikes of thimblelike flowers **2.** the dried leaves of the purple foxglove **3.** a medicine made from these leaves, used to stimulate the heart

dig·i·tate (dij′ə tāt′) *adj.* [see DIGIT] **1.** having separate fingers or toes **2.** fingerlike **3.** *Bot.* having fingerlike divisions, as some leaves Also **dig′i·tat′ed** —**dig′i·tate′ly** *adv.* —**dig′i·ta′tion** *n.*

DIGITATE LEAF

dig·ni·fied (dig′nə fīd′) *adj.* having or showing dignity; noble; stately —**dig′ni·fied′ly** *adv.*

dig·ni·fy (dig′nə fī′) *vt.* -**fied′, -fy′ing** [< OFr. < ML. < L. *dignus,* worthy + *facere,* to make, DO¹] **1.** to give dignity to; make worthy of esteem; honor **2.** to make seem worthy or noble [to *dignify* a politician by calling him a statesman]

dig·ni·tar·y (-ter′ē) *n., pl.* -**tar′ies** [< L. *dignitas,* dignity + -ARY] a person holding a high, dignified position or office —*adj.* of a dignitary

dig·ni·ty (dig′nə tē) *n., pl.* -**ties** [< OFr. < L. < *dignus,* worthy < IE. base *dek-,* to receive, be fitting, from which also come DECENT & DOCILE] **1.** the quality of being worthy of esteem or honor [she respects the *dignity* of all people] **2.** high repute; honor **3.** the degree of worth, repute, or honor [the post of chancellor has increased in *dignity*] **4.** a high position, rank, or title [the *dignity* of our courts must be upheld] **5.** a noble or stately appearance or manner [the *dignity* with which swans move in water] **6.** proper pride and self-respect [it is beneath my *dignity* to notice his rudeness]

di·graph (dī′graf) *n.* [DI-¹ + -GRAPH] a combination of two letters to express a simple sound (Ex.: read, show, graphic) —**di·graph′ic** *adj.*

di·gress (dī gres′, di-) *vi.* [< L. pp. of *digredi* < *dis-,* apart + *gradi,* to go, step: see GRADE] to wander for a time from the subject one has been talking or writing about —**di·gres′sion** (-gresh′ən) *n.*

di·gres·sive (-gres′iv) *adj.* tending to digress —**di·gres′sive·ly** *adv.* —**di·gres′sive·ness** *n.*

di·he·dral (dī hē′drəl) *adj.* [< DI-¹ + Gr. *hedra,* a seat] **1.** having or formed by two intersecting plane faces [a *dihedral* angle] **2.** *a*) inclined to each other at a dihedral angle, as some airplane wings *b*) having such wings —*n.* a dihedral angle

Di·jon (dē zhōn′) city in EC France: pop. 145,000

dik-dik (dik′dik′) *n.* [< the Ethiopian native name] any of several small antelopes found in E Africa

dike (dīk) *n.* [< OE. *dic* & ON. *diki:* for IE. base see DIG] **1.** [Brit. Dial.] a ditch or channel for water **2.** an embankment or dam made to prevent flooding as by the sea **3.** a protective barrier **4.** *Geol.* igneous rock solidified as a flat body in a vertical fissure —*vt.* **diked, dik′ing 1.** to protect with a dike **2.** to drain by a ditch

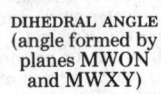
DIHEDRAL ANGLE (angle formed by planes MWON and MWXY)

☆**Di·lan·tin** (**Sodium**) (di lan′tin, dī-) *a trademark for* a drug, $C_{15}H_{11}N_2O_2Na$, used in the treatment of epileptic attacks —*n.* [d-] this substance

di·lap·i·date (di lap′ə dāt′) *vi., vt.* -**dat′ed, -dat′ing** [< L. pp. of *dilapidare,* to demolish < *dis-,* apart + *lapidare,* to throw stones at < *lapis,* a stone] to become or make partially ruined and in need of repairs, as through neglect —**di·lap′i·da′tion** *n.*

di·lap·i·dat·ed (-id) *adj.* falling to pieces; broken down; shabby and neglected

dil·a·ta·tion (dil′ə tā′shən, dī′lə-) *n.* **1.** *same as* DILATION **2.** *Med.* the act of making a cavity, opening of the body, etc. larger than it is normally —**dil′a·ta′tion·al** *adj.*

di·late (dī lāt′, di-; dī′lāt) *vt.* -**lat′ed, -lat′ing** [L. *dilatare* < *dis-,* apart + *latus,* wide] to make wider or larger; cause to expand or swell —*vi.* **1.** to become wider or larger; swell **2.** to speak or write in detail (*on* or *upon* a subject) —see SYN. at EXPAND —**di·lat′a·ble** *adj.* —**di·lat′ive** *adj.* —**di·la′tor** *n.*

di·la·tion (dī lā′shən, di-) *n.* **1.** a dilating or being dilated **2.** a dilated part

dil·a·to·ry (dil′ə tôr′ē) *adj.* [< LL. < L. < *dilatus,* pp. of *differre,* DEFER¹] **1.** causing or tending to cause delay **2.** inclined to delay; slow; tardy —**dil′a·to′ri·ly** *adv.* —**dil′a·to′ri·ness** *n.*

di·lem·ma (di lem′ə) *n.* [LL. < LGr. < *di-,* two + *lēmma,* proposition] an argument or a situation in which one must choose between things equally unpleasant or dangerous

dil·et·tante (dil′ə tänt′, -tän′tē, -tan′tē; dil′ə tänt′) *n., pl.* **-tantes′, -tan′ti** (-tän′tē, -tan′tē) [It. < prp. of *dilettare* < L. *delectare*, to delight] **1.** a person who loves the fine arts **2.** a person who is interested in an art or science in a superficial way —*adj.* of or like a dilettante —**dil′et·tant′ish** *adj.* —**dil′et·tant′ism, dil′et·tan′te·ism** *n.*

dil·i·gence[1] (dil′ə jəns) *n.* [OFr. < L. < prp. of *diligere*, to esteem highly < *di-*, apart + *legere*, to choose: for IE. base see LOGIC] a being diligent; constant, careful effort; perseverance; industry

dil·i·gence[2] (dil′ə jəns; *Fr.* dē lē zhäns′) *n.* [Fr.] a public stagecoach, esp. as formerly used in France

dil·i·gent (dil′ə jənt) *adj.* [OFr. < L.: see DILIGENCE[1]] **1.** working hard and carefully; industrious **2.** done with careful, steady effort; painstaking —see SYN. at BUSY —**dil′i·gent·ly** *adv.*

dill (dil) *n.* [OE. *dile*] **1.** a plant of the parsley family, with bitter seeds and spicy leaves, used to flavor pickles, etc. **2.** the seeds or leaves

☆**dill pickle** a cucumber pickle flavored with dill

☆**dil·ly** (dil′ē) *n., pl.* **-lies** [< ? DEL(IGHTFUL) + -Y[1]] [Slang] a surprising or remarkable person or thing

dil·ly·dal·ly (dil′ē dal′ē) *vi.* **-lied, -ly·ing** [< repetition of sounds of DALLY] to waste time in hesitation; loiter or dawdle

di·lute (di loot′, dī-) *vt.* **-lut′ed, -lut′ing** [< L. pp. of *diluere* < *dis-*, off + *-luere* < *lavare*, to wash: for IE. base see LATHER] **1.** to thin down or weaken by mixing with water or other liquid [to *dilute* condensed milk] **2.** to change or weaken (in brilliance, force, effect, etc.) by mixing with something else [his use of too many words *dilutes* the force of what he has to say] —*vi.* to become diluted —*adj.* diluted —**di·lute′ness** *n.* —**di·lut′er, di·lu′tor** *n.*

di·lu·tion (-loo′shən) *n.* **1.** a diluting or being diluted **2.** something diluted

di·lu·vi·al (di loo′vē əl) *adj.* [< LL. < L. *diluvium*, a DELUGE] of or caused by a flood, esp. the Deluge Also **di·lu′vi·an**

dim (dim) *adj.* **dim′mer, dim′mest** [OE. *dimm*: for IE. base see DAMP] **1.** not bright; somewhat dark; dull [the *dim* twilight] **2.** not clear or distinct; lacking definition, strength, etc. [a *dim* sound in the distance] **3.** not clearly seen, heard, or understood; vague [a *dim* memory] **4.** not clearly seeing, hearing, or understanding [his eyes are *dim*] **5.** not likely to turn out well [*dim* prospects] —*vt., vi.* **dimmed, dim′ming** to make or grow dim —*n.* **1.** [Poet.] dim light; dusk **2.** a dim headlight on an automobile: usually used in *pl.* —see SYN. at DARK —**take a dim view of** to view without hope, enthusiasm, etc. —**dim′ly** *adv.* —**dim′ness** *n.*

dim., dimin. **1.** diminuendo **2.** diminutive

dime (dīm) *n.* [< OFr. < L. *decimus*, a tenth < *decem*, TEN] ☆a coin of the U.S. and of Canada equal to ten cents; tenth of a dollar —☆**a dime a dozen** [Colloq.] very abundant or cheap

di·men·hy·dri·nate (dī′men hī′drə nāt′) *n.* a white, crystalline solid, $C_{24}H_{28}ClN_5O_3$, used to control nausea and vomiting, as in motion sickness

☆**dime novel** a very cheap, melodramatic novel

di·men·sion (də men′shən) *n.* [L. *dimensio* < pp. of *dimetiri* < *dis-*, off + *metiri*, to MEASURE] **1.** any measurable extent, as length, width, depth, etc.: see also FOURTH DIMENSION **2.** [*pl.*] measurements in length and width, and often depth **3.** [often *pl.*] size or importance [a project of vast *dimensions*] —**di·men′sion·al** *adj.* —**di·men′sion·al·ly** *adv.* —**di·men′sion·less** *adj.*

dim·er·ous (dim′ər əs) *adj.* [< ModL.: see DI-[1] & -MEROUS] having two parts

☆**dime store** same as FIVE-AND-TEN-CENT STORE

dim·e·ter (dim′ə tər) *n.* [LL. < Gr. < *di-*, two + *metron*, a measure] **1.** a line of verse containing two metrical feet **2.** verse consisting of dimeters —*adj.* consisting of two metrical feet

di·min·ish (də min′ish) *vt.* [a blend of ME. *diminuen* (ult. < L. *deminuere*, to make smaller) & *minishen* (ult. < L. *minutus*, MINUTE[2])] **1.** to make, or make seem, smaller; reduce in size, degree, importance, etc. [war *diminished* the male population] **2.** *Music* to reduce (a minor interval) by a semitone —*vi.* to become smaller or less —see SYN. at DECREASE —**di·min′ish·a·ble** *adj.* —**di·min′ished** *adj.*

di·min·u·en·do (də min′yoo wen′dō) *adj., adv., n., pl.* **-dos** [It. < L. *diminuere*, make smaller] same as DECRESCENDO

dim·i·nu·tion (dim′ə nyoo′shən, -noo′-) *n.* a diminishing or being diminished; lessening; decrease

di·min·u·tive (də min′yoo tiv) *adj.* **1.** very small; tiny **2.** *Gram.* expressing smallness or diminution [a *diminutive* suffix] —*n.* **1.** a very small person or thing **2.** *a)* a word or name formed from another by the addition of a suffix expressing smallness and, sometimes, affection or condescension, as *ringlet*, *Jackie*, *sonny b)* such a suffix —see SYN. at SMALL —**di·min′u·tive·ly** *adv.* —**di·min′u·tive·ness** *n.*

dim·i·ty (dim′ə tē) *n., pl.* **-ties** [< ML. < MGr. *dimitos*, double-threaded < *dis-*, two + *mitos*, a thread] a thin, often corded or patterned cotton cloth, used for curtains, dresses, etc.

dim·mer (dim′ər) *n.* **1.** a person that dims **2.** a device for dimming an electric light, as in automobile headlights or theater stage lights

di·mor·phism (dī môr′fiz′m) *n.* [< Gr. *di-*, two + *morphē*, form + -ISM] **1.** *Bot.* the state of having two different kinds of leaves, flowers, etc. on the same plant **2.** *Zool.* the occurrence of two types of individuals in the same species —**di·mor′phic** (-fik), **di·mor′phous** (-fəs) *adj.*

dim·out (dim′out′) *n.* a dimming or reduction of the night lighting in a city, etc., to make it less easily visible, as to enemy aircraft

dim·ple (dim′p'l) *n.* [ME. *dimpel*: for IE. base see DEEP] **1.** a small, natural hollow spot, as on the cheek or chin **2.** any little hollow, as on water —*vt.* **-pled, -pling** to make dimples in —*vi.* to show or form dimples

☆**dim·wit** (dim′wit′) *n.* [Slang] a stupid person; simpleton —**dim′wit′ted** *adj.* —**dim′wit′ted·ly** *adv.* —**dim′wit′ted·ness** *n.*

din (din) *n.* [OE. *dyne*] a loud, continuous noise; confused clamor or uproar —*vt.* **dinned, din′ning** **1.** to attack with a din **2.** to repeat or say again and again [to *din* an idea into one's head] —*vi.* to make a din —see SYN. at NOISE

Di·nah (dī′nə) [Heb. *dīnāh*, lit., judged] a feminine name

di·nar (di när′) *n.* [< Ar. < L. *denarius*: see DENARIUS] the monetary unit of Algeria, Iraq, Jordan, Libya, Tunisia, etc., and a coin of Iran: see MONETARY UNITS, table

dine (dīn) *vi.* **dined, din′ing** [< OFr. *disner*, ult. < L. *dis-*, away + *jejunus*, fasting] to eat dinner —*vt.* to provide a dinner for, or entertain at dinner —**dine out** to dine away from home

din·er (dī′nər) *n.* **1.** a person eating dinner ☆**2.** *same as* DINING CAR ☆**3.** a small restaurant built to look like a dining car

☆**din·ette** (dī net′) *n.* **1.** an alcove or small room used as a dining room **2.** a set of tables and chairs for such a space [a five-piece *dinette*]

ding (diŋ) *vi.* [< Scand. (as in ON. *dengja*, to hammer)] to make a sound like that of a bell; ring —*n.* the sound of a bell

☆**ding-a-ling, ding·a·ling** (diŋ′ə liŋ′) *n.* [Slang] a person who seems crazy, silly, eccentric, etc.

ding-dong (diŋ′dôŋ′, -däŋ′) *n.* [echoic] the sound of a bell struck repeatedly —*adj.* [Colloq.] carried out, as a contest, with one side in the lead and then the other —*vi.* to sound with a ding-dong

din·ghy (diŋ′gē, diŋ′ē) *n., pl.* **-ghies** [Hindi *ḍiṅgī*] **1.** orig., a rowboat used on the rivers of India **2.** any small boat used as a tender to a yacht, etc. **3.** a small, single-masted racing boat **4.** an inflatable life raft Also sp. **din′gey**

din·gle (diŋ′g'l) *n.* [ME. *dingel*, abyss] a small, deep, wooded valley

din·go (diŋ′gō) *n., pl.* **-goes** [native name] the Australian wild dog

ding·us (diŋ′əs) *n.* [Du. *dinges* (or G. *dings*), orig. gen. of *ding*, THING[1]] [Colloq.] any device; gadget: humorous substitute for a name not known or temporarily forgotten

din·gy (din′jē) *adj.* **-gi·er, -gi·est** [orig. dial. var. of DUNGY] **1.** dirty-colored; not bright or clean **2.** dismal; shabby —**din′gi·ly** *adv.* —**din′gi·ness** *n.*

☆**dining car** a railroad car equipped to serve meals to passengers

dining room a room where meals are eaten

din·key (diŋ′kē) *n., pl.* **-keys** [< DINKY] [Colloq.] ☆**1.** a small locomotive for hauling cars, etc. in a railroad yard **2.** a small trolley car

DILL

din·ky (diŋ′kē) *adj.* **-ki·er, -ki·est** [< Scot. *dink*, trim + -Y²] [Colloq.] small and unimportant; of no consequence —*n., pl.* **-kies** *same as* DINKEY

din·ner (din′ər) *n.* [< OFr. *disner*, to dine: the infinitive used as a *n.*: see DINE] **1.** the chief meal of the day, whether eaten in the evening or about noon **2.** a banquet in honor of some person or event **3.** a complete meal at a set price with no course omitted; table d'hôte

dinner jacket a tuxedo jacket

din·ner·ware (-wer′) *n.* plates, cups, saucers, etc. for use when eating

di·no·flag·el·late (dī′nə flaj′ə lit, -lāt′) *n.* [< ModL. < Gr. *dinos*, rotation + ModL. *flagellum*, a whip] any of certain single-celled organisms found mainly in the ocean: some cause the red tides dangerous to ocean life

di·no·saur (dī′nə sôr′) *n.* [< Gr. *deinos*, terrible + *sauros*, lizard] any of a large group of extinct, four-limbed reptiles of the Mesozoic Era, including some almost 100 ft. long —**di′no·sau′ri·an** *adj.*

dint (dint) *n.* [OE. *dynt*, a blow] **1.** force; exertion [by *dint* of great effort he won] **2.** a dent

dioc. **1.** diocesan **2.** diocese

di·oc·e·san (dī äs′ə s'n) *adj.* of a diocese —*n.* the bishop of a diocese

di·o·cese (dī′ə sis, -sēs′) *n.* [< OFr. < L. < Gr. *dioikēsis*, administration < *dioikein*, to keep house < *dia-*, through + *oikos*, a house] the church district under a bishop's control

Di·o·cle·tian (dī′ə klē′shən) (L. name *Gaius Aurelius Valerius Diocletianus*) 245-313 A.D.; Rom. emperor (284-305)

di·ode (dī′ōd) *n.* [DI-¹ + -ODE] an electron tube or semiconductor device having two terminals and conducting electricity in only one direction

di·oe·cious (dī ē′shəs) *adj.* [< DI-¹ + Gr. *oikos*, a house + -OUS] *Biol.* having the male reproductive organs in one individual and the female organs in another —**di·oe′cious·ly** *adv.* —**di·oe′cism** (-siz'm) *n.*

Di·og·e·nes (dī äj′ə nēz′) 412?-323? B.C.; Gr. Cynic philosopher

Di·o·ny·sian (dī′ə nish′ən, -nis′ē ən, -nī′sē ən) *adj.* [< DIONYSUS] wild, frenzied, and sensuous

Di·o·ny·si·us (dī′ə nish′əs, -nis′ē əs, -nī′sē əs) 430?-367 B.C.; Gr. tyrant of ancient Syracuse

Di·o·ny·sus, Di·o·ny·sos (dī′ə nī′səs) *Gr. Myth.* the god of wine and merrymaking; Bacchus

di·op·ter, di·op·tre (dī äp′tər) *n.* [< L. < Gr. *dioptra*, leveling instrument < *dia-*, through + base of *opsis*, sight] a unit of measure of the refractive power of a lens, equal to the power of a lens with a focal distance of one meter —**di·op′tral** *adj.*

di·o·ra·ma (dī′ə ram′ə) *n.* [< DI(A)- + (PAN)ORAMA] **1.** a picture painted on a set of transparent curtains and looked at through a small opening **2.** a miniature scene showing three-dimensional figures in a realistic setting **3.** a museum display of a preserved or reconstructed specimen, as of wildlife in a setting that suggests its native environment

di·ox·ide (dī äk′sīd) *n.* an oxide containing two atoms of oxygen per molecule

dip (dip) *vt.* **dipped, dip′ping** [OE. *dyppan*: for IE. base see DEEP] **1.** to put into liquid for a moment and then quickly take out **2.** to dye in this way **3.** to baptize by immersion **4.** to bathe and clean (sheep or hogs) in disinfectant **5.** to make (a candle) by putting a wick repeatedly in melted tallow or wax **6.** to take out as by scooping up with a container, the hand, etc. **7.** to lower and immediately raise again [*dip* the flag in salute] —*vi.* **1.** to go down as into a liquid and quickly come up again **2.** to sink or seem to sink suddenly [the sun *dips* into the ocean] **3.** to undergo a slight decline [sales *dipped* in May] **4.** to slope downward, as a road **5.** to lower a container, the hand, etc. into liquid, a receptacle, etc., esp. in order to take something out: often used as a figure of speech [to *dip* into one's savings] **6.** to read or study casually or superficially (with *into*) [to *dip* into a book] **7.** *Aeron.* to drop suddenly before climbing —*n.* **1.** a dipping or being dipped **2.** *a)* a brief plunge into a liquid *b)* a brief swim **3.** a liquid into which something is dipped, as for dyeing **4.** whatever is removed by dipping **5.** a candle made by dipping **6.** *a)* a downward slope or inclination or a deviation *b)* the amount of

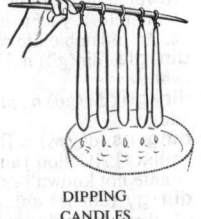

DIPPING CANDLES

this **7.** a slight hollow **8.** a short downward plunge, as of an airplane **9.** *a)* a sweet liquid sauce for desserts ☆*b)* a thick, creamy sauce into which one dips crackers or other appetizers **10.** [Slang] a pickpocket

di·phase (dī′fāz′) *adj.* [DI-¹ + PHASE] having two phases: also **di·pha′sic** (-fā′zik)

diph·the·ri·a (dif thir′ē ə, dip-) *n.* [ModL. < Fr. < Gr. *diphthera*, leather < *dephein*, to tan hides] an acute infectious disease that causes a sore throat, high fever, and the formation in the air passages of a membrane that can block breathing —**diph·the′ri·al** *adj.* —**diph′the·rit′ic** (-thə rit′ik), **diph·ther′ic** *adj.*

diph·thong (dif′thôŋ, dip′-) *n.* [< LL. < Gr. < *di-*, two + *phthongos*, sound] *Phonet.* a complex vowel sound made by gliding continuously from the position for one vowel to that for another within the same syllable, as (ou) in *down*, (oi) in *boy* —**diph·thon′gal** (-thôŋ′g'l) *adj.*

diph·thong·ize (-īz′) *vt.* **-ized′, -iz′ing** to pronounce (a simple vowel) as a diphthong —*vi.* to become a diphthong —**diph′thong·i·za′tion** *n.*

di·ple·gi·a (dī plē′jē ə) *n.* [ModL.: see DI-¹ & -PLEGIA] paralysis of similar parts on both sides of the body

dip·loid (dip′loid) *adj.* [< Gr. *diploos*, double + -OID] **1.** twofold or double **2.** *Biol.* having twice the number of chromosomes normally occurring in a mature germ cell: most somatic cells are diploid: see HAPLOID —**dip·loi′dy** (-loi′dē) *n.*

di·plo·ma (di plō′mə) *n.* [L. < Gr. *diplōma*, folded letter < *diploos*, double] **1.** a certificate granting honors, privileges, etc. **2.** a certificate recording the graduation of a student from a school, college, or university, or granting a degree

di·plo·ma·cy (di plō′mə sē) *n., pl.* **-cies** [< Fr.: see DIPLOMAT] **1.** (skill in) conducting relations between nations **2.** tact in dealing with people

dip·lo·mat (dip′lə mat′) *n.* [< Fr., ult. < L. *diploma*, DIPLOMA] **1.** a representative of a government who conducts relations with another government in the interests of his own country **2.** a person skilled in dealing with other people; tactful person Also **di·plo·ma·tist** (di plō′mə tist)

dip·lo·mat·ic (dip′lə mat′ik) *n.* **1.** of or connected with diplomacy **2.** tactful and skillful in dealing with people —**dip·lo·mat′i·cal·ly** *adv.*

diplomatic immunity freedom from local taxes, court action, etc. in a foreign country, granted to all members of a diplomatic service

di·plo·pi·a (di plō′pē ə) *n.* [ModL. < Gr. *diploos*, double + *ōps*, eye] eye trouble in which a single object is seen as double: also called **double vision**

di·pole (dī′pōl′) *n.* **1.** *Physics* any system having two equal but opposite electric charges or magnetic poles separated by a small distance **2.** an antenna usually separated at the center by an insulator and fed by a balanced transmission line: in full, **dipole antenna** —**di·po′lar** *adj.*

dip·per (dip′ər) *n.* **1.** a person whose work is dipping something in liquid ☆**2.** a container for dipping; esp., a long-handled cup ☆**3.** [D-] either of two groups of stars in the shape of a dipper: see BIG DIPPER, LITTLE DIPPER **4.** any of certain songbirds, as the water ouzel, which wade and submerge in streams in search of insects, etc. —**dip′per·ful′** *n., pl.* **-fuls′**

dip·so·ma·ni·a (dip′sə mā′nē ə, -nyə) *n.* [ModL. < Gr. *dipsa*, thirst + -MANIA] a craving for alcoholic drink that is not normal and cannot be satisfied —**dip′so·ma′ni·ac′** (-ak′) *n.* —**dip′so·ma·ni′a·cal** (-mə nī′ə k'l) *adj.*

DIPPER

dip·stick (dip′stik′) *n.* a rod marked in degrees for measuring the depth of a substance in its container

dip·ter·an (dip′tər ən) *n.* [see DIPTEROUS] any of a large group of insects, including the housefly, gnat, etc., having one pair of wings and usually a second, undeveloped pair

dip·ter·ous (-əs) *adj.* [< ModL. < Gr. < *di-*, two + *pteron*, a wing] **1.** having two wings or two winglike parts **2.** of the dipterans

dip·tych (dip′tik) *n.* [< LL. < Gr. < *di-*, twice + *ptychē*, a fold] **1.** an ancient writing tablet made up of a hinged pair of wooden or ivory pieces **2.** a picture painted or carved on two hinged tablets

Di·rac (di rak′), **Paul A·dri·en Maurice** (ā′drē ən) 1902- ; Eng. mathematician & nuclear physicist

dire (dīr) *adj.* **dir′er, dir′est** [L. *dirus*] **1.** arousing terror; dreadful; terrible [a *dire* misfortune] **2.** calling for quick action; urgent [a *dire* need] —**dire′ly** *adv.* —**dire′ness** *n.*

di·rect (di rekt′, dī-) *adj.* [< L. pp. of *dirigere*, to lay straight < *dis-*, apart + *regere*, to rule: for IE. base see REGAL] **1.** by the shortest way; not roundabout; straight [a *direct* route] **2.** honest and straightforward; frank [a *direct* answer] **3.** with nothing or no one between; immediate [*direct* contact] **4.** traced in an unbroken line through a parent, grandparent, etc.; lineal [a *direct* descendant] **5.** exact; complete [the *direct* opposite] **6.** in the exact words of the speaker [a *direct* quotation] **7.** by action of the people through popular vote instead of through representatives **8.** *Math.* designating or of a relationship between variables in which one increases or decreases with the other [a *direct* proportion] —*vt.* **1.** to manage the affairs or action of; guide; conduct [to *direct* the building of a bridge] **2.** to order or command with authority [he was *directed* to appear in court] **3.** to turn or point (a person or thing) toward an object or goal; aim; head **4.** to tell (a person) the way to a place **5.** to address (words, etc.) to a specific person or persons [his remarks were *directed* at you] **6.** to write the name and address on (a letter, etc.) **7.** *a)* to plan and supervise the action of (a play, motion picture, etc.) or of (the actors, etc.) *b)* to rehearse and conduct the performance of (a choir, band, etc.) —*vi.* **1.** to give directions **2.** to be a director —*adv.* directly —see SYN. at COMMAND and CONDUCT —**di·rect′ness** *n.*

direct current an electric current flowing in one direction

di·rect·ed (də rek′tid, dī-) *adj.* indicated as positive or negative, as a number, angle, or line segment

di·rec·tion (də rek′shən, dī-) *n.* **1.** the act of directing; management; supervision [the choir is under his *direction*] **2.** [usually *pl.*] instructions for doing, using, etc. [*directions* for driving to New York] **3.** an authoritative order or command **4.** the point toward which one faces or line along which one moves or lies ["North," "up," "left," and "forward" are *directions*] **5.** a way, trend, or line of development [research in new *directions*]

di·rec·tion·al (-'l) *adj.* **1.** of, aimed at, or indicating (a specific) direction **2.** designed for radiating or receiving radio signals most effectively in one or more particular directions [a *directional* antenna] **3.** designed to pick up or send out sound most efficiently in one direction —**di·rec′tion·al′i·ty** *n.* —**di·rec′tion·al·ly** *adv.*

direction finder a device for finding out the direction from which radio waves or signals are coming

di·rec·tive (də rek′tiv, dī-) *adj.* **1.** directing **2.** indicating direction —*n.* a general instruction or order issued authoritatively

di·rect·ly (-rekt′lē) *adv.* **1.** in a direct way or line; straight [the town is *directly* east of here] **2.** with nothing coming between [he is *directly* responsible to the president] **3.** exactly [*directly* opposite] **4.** right away [he'll come *directly*] —*conj.* [Chiefly Brit.] as soon as

☆**direct mail** mail sent directly to a large number of individuals to promote a product, institution, etc., and ask for orders, donations, etc.

direct object the word or words that tell who or what receives the action of a transitive verb (Ex.: *ball* in *he hit the ball*)

di·rec·tor (di rek′tər) *n.* a person or thing that directs; specif., *a)* the supervisor of a bureau, school, etc. *b)* a member of a board chosen to direct the affairs of a corporation or institution ☆*c)* a person who directs the production of a play, motion picture, etc. *d)* *Music* a conductor —**di·rec·to·ri·al** (də rek′tôr′ē əl, dī-) *adj.* —**di·rec′tor·ship′** *n.* —**di·rec′tress** (-tris) [Now Rare] *n.fem.*

di·rec·tor·ate (-it) *n.* **1.** the position of director **2.** a board of directors

di·rec·to·ry (də rek′tə rē, dī-) *adj.* directing or advising —*n., pl.* **-ries 1.** a book of directions **2.** a book listing the names, addresses, etc. of a specific group of persons **3.** a directorate

☆**direct primary election** a preliminary election at which candidates for public office are chosen by direct vote of the people instead of by delegates at a convention: in **closed primary elections** voters may vote only for candidates of their party

di·rec·trix (də rek′triks, dī-) *n., pl.* **-trix·es, -tri·ces** (dī′rek trī′sēz) *Geom.* a fixed line such that the distance of any point on a conic from the fixed point is in a constant ratio to its distance from the fixed line

direct tax a tax collected directly from the person who is to pay it, as an income tax or property tax

dire·ful (dīr′fəl) *adj.* dreadful; terrible —**dire′ful·ly** *adv.* —**dire′ful·ness** *n.*

dirge (durj) *n.* [< L. *dirige* (imper. of *dirigere*, to direct), first word of an antiphon in the Office of the Dead] **1.** a funeral hymn **2.** a slow, sad song, poem, etc. expressing grief, esp. for the dead

dir·ham (dir ham′) *n.* [Ar. < L. *drachma*, DRACHMA] *see* MONETARY UNITS, table (Morocco, Qatar)

dir·i·gi·ble (dir′i jə b'l, də rij′ə-) *adj.* [ML. *dirigibilis*: see DIRECT & -IBLE] that can be directed or steered —*n. same as* AIRSHIP

dirk (durk) *n.* [earlier *dork, durk* < ?] a short, straight dagger —*vt.* to stab with a dirk

dirn·dl (durn′d'l) *n.* [G., dial. dim. of *dirne*, girl] **1.** a kind of dress with a full skirt, gathered waist, and closefitting bodice **2.** a full skirt with a gathered waist: also **dirndl skirt**

dirt (durt) *n.* [ME. < *drit* < ON. *dritr*, excrement] **1.** any unclean matter, as mud, trash, etc.; filth **2.** earth or garden soil **3.** dirtiness, nastiness, wicked behavior, etc. ☆**4.** obscene writing, speech, etc. ☆**5.** talk or gossip intended to harm ☆**6.** *Gold Mining* the gravel, soil, etc. from which gold is separated by washing or panning —*adj.* ☆surfaced with earth firmly packed together [a *dirt* road] —☆**do one dirt** [Slang] to harm one —**hit the dirt** [Slang] to drop to the ground

DIRNDL

dirt-cheap (durt′chēp′) *adj.* [Colloq.] as cheap as dirt; very inexpensive

☆**dirt farmer** [Colloq.] a farmer who works his own land

dirt·y (-ē) *adj.* **dirt′i·er, dirt′i·est 1.** soiled or soiling with dirt; unclean **2.** muddy or clouded [a *dirty* green] **3.** obscene; pornographic [*dirty* jokes] **4.** not nice; mean; nasty [a *dirty* coward] **5.** unfair; dishonest [a *dirty* player] ☆**6.** producing much fallout: said of nuclear weapons **7.** revealing anger or irritation [a *dirty* look] **8.** *Naut.* stormy; rough [*dirty* weather] —*vt., vi.* **dirt′ied, dirt′y·ing** to make or become dirty; soil; stain —**a dirty shame** a very unfortunate circumstance —**dirty linen** (or **wash**) private matters that could cause gossip —☆**dirty pool** [Slang] unfair or dishonest tactics —**dirt′i·ly** *adv.* —**dirt′i·ness** *n.*

Dis (dis) *Rom. Myth.* **1.** the god of the lower world: identified with the Greek god Pluto **2.** Hades

dis- [< OFr. or L.; OFr. *des-* < L. *dis-*: see DE-] *a prefix meaning:* **1.** *a)* away, apart [*dismiss*] *b)* deprive of, expel from [*disbar*] *c)* cause to be the opposite of [*disable*] *d)* fail, cease, refuse to [*dissatisfy*] or do the opposite of [*disjoin*] **2.** not, un- [*dishonest*] **3.** opposite of, lack of [*disunion*]

dis·a·bil·i·ty (dis′ə bil′ə tē) *n., pl.* **-ties 1.** a disabled condition **2.** that which disables, as an illness or injury **3.** a legal disqualification **4.** a limitation or disadvantage

dis·a·ble (dis ā′b'l) *vt.* **-bled, -bling 1.** to make unable to move, act, or work in a normal way; cripple; incapacitate [she is *disabled* by arthritis] **2.** to disqualify legally —**dis·a′ble·ment** *n.*

dis·a·buse (dis′ə byōōz′) *vt.* **-bused′, -bus′ing** to free from false ideas; put right [he *disabused* her of her notion that he was a hero]

di·sac·cha·ride (dī sak′ə rīd′) *n.* [DI-¹ + SACCHARIDE] any of a group of sugars, as sucrose, maltose, and lactose, which can be broken down into two monosaccharides

dis·ad·van·tage (dis′əd van′tij) *n.* **1.** anything that hinders success; unfavorable situation; drawback; handicap [it was a *disadvantage* to have no friends] **2.** harm or injury to one's interests [his rudeness worked to his *disadvantage*] —*vt.* **-taged, -tag·ing** to work against the interests of —**at a disadvantage** in an unfavorable situation

dis·ad·van·taged (-tijd) *adj.* not having a decent standard of living, education, etc. because one is poor and has had no advantages; underprivileged

dis·ad·van·ta·geous (dis ad′vən tā′jəs) *adj.* causing disadvantage; unfavorable; adverse —**dis·ad′van·ta′geous·ly** *adv.*

dis·af·fect (dis′ə fekt′) *vt.* to make unfriendly, discontented, or disloyal, as toward the government —**dis′af·fect′ed** *adj.* — **dis′af·fec′tion** *n.*

dis·af·fil·i·ate (-ə fil′ē āt′) *vt.*, *vi.* **-at·ed, -at·ing** to end an affiliation (with) —**dis′af·fil′i·a′tion** *n.*

dis·af·firm (dis′ə furm′) *vt.* **1.** to deny (a former statement) **2.** *Law a)* to refuse to abide by (an agreement, etc.) *b)* to set aside (a former decision) —**dis′af·firm′ance, dis′af·fir·ma′tion** (-af ər mā′shən) *n.*

dis·a·gree (-ə grē′) *vi.* **-greed′, -gree′ing 1.** to fail to agree; be different [his story of the accident *disagreed* with hers] **2.** to differ in opinion; often, specif., to quarrel or dispute [to *disagree* on politics] **3.** to be harmful or make sick [corn *disagrees* with me]

dis·a·gree·a·ble (-ə b′l) *adj.* **1.** not to one's taste; unpleasant; offensive **2.** hard to get along with; quarrelsome —**dis′a·gree′a·ble·ness** *n.* —**dis′a·gree′a·bly** *adv.*

dis·a·gree·ment (-mənt) *n.* **1.** refusal to agree **2.** failure to agree; difference; discrepancy **3.** difference of opinion **4.** a quarrel or dispute

dis·al·low (dis′ə lou′) *vt.* to refuse to allow; reject as invalid or illegal —**dis′al·low′ance** *n.*

dis·ap·pear (-ə pir′) *vi.* **1.** to stop being seen; go out of sight **2.** to stop being; become lost or extinct [dinosaurs *disappeared* millions of years ago] —**dis′ap·pear′ance** *n.*

dis·ap·point (-ə point′) *vt.* **1.** to fail to satisfy the hopes or expectations of; leave unsatisfied **2.** to frustrate (hopes, etc.) —**dis′ap·point′ing·ly** *adv.*

dis·ap·point·ment (-mənt) *n.* **1.** a disappointing or being disappointed [our *disappointment* over not winning] **2.** a person or thing that disappoints

dis·ap·pro·ba·tion (dis ap′rə bā′shən) *n.* disapproval

dis·ap·prov·al (dis′ə prōōv′'l) *n.* failure or refusal to approve; unfavorable opinion

dis·ap·prove (-ə prōōv′) *vt.* **-proved′, -prov′ing 1.** to have or express an unfavorable opinion of [the war was *disapproved* by the people] **2.** to refuse to approve; reject [the Senate *disapproved* the treaty] —*vi.* to feel or express disapproval (*of*) [Quakers *disapprove* of any violence] —**dis′ap·prov′ing·ly** *adv.*

dis·arm (dis ärm′) *vt.* **1.** to take away weapons or armaments from [police *disarmed* the gunman] **2.** to make harmless, friendly, or no longer hostile [his charm *disarmed* me] —*vi.* **1.** to lay down arms **2.** to reduce or do away with armed forces and armaments [the two nations agreed to *disarm*]

dis·ar·ma·ment (-är′mə mənt) *n.* **1.** the act of disarming **2.** the reduction of armed forces and armaments, as to a limitation set by treaty

dis·arm·ing (-är′miŋ) *adj.* removing suspicions, fears, or hostility —**dis·arm′ing·ly** *adv.*

dis·ar·range (dis′ə rānj′) *vt.* **-ranged′, -rang′ing** to upset the order or arrangement of; make less neat; disorder —**dis′ar·range′ment** *n.*

dis·ar·ray (-ə rā′) *vt.* **1.** to throw into disorder or confusion; upset **2.** [Archaic] to undress —*n.* **1.** an untidy condition; disorder; confusion **2.** a state of untidy or insufficient dress —see **SYN.** at CONFUSION

dis·as·sem·ble (-ə sem′b'l) *vt.* **-bled, -bling** ☆to take apart [to *disassemble* a motor] —☆**dis′as·sem′bly** *n.*

dis·as·so·ci·ate (-ə sō′shē āt′, -sē-) *vt.* **-at·ed, -at·ing** to break off association with; separate; dissociate —**dis′as·so′ci·a′tion** *n.*

dis·as·ter (di zas′tər) *n.* [< OFr. < It. < L. *dis-* + *astrum* < Gr. *astron*, a star: see ILL-STARRED] any happening that causes great harm or damage, as an earthquake; serious or sudden misfortune; calamity

dis·as·trous (-trəs) *adj.* of the nature of a disaster; causing great harm, damage, grief, etc.; calamitous —**dis·as′trous·ly** *adv.*

dis·a·vow (dis′ə vou′) *vt.* to deny any knowledge or approval of, or responsibility for; disclaim; repudiate [he can never *disavow* the letter he wrote] —**dis′a·vow′al** *n.*

dis·band (dis band′) *vt.* **1.** to break up (an association or organization) **2.** to dismiss (a military force) from service —*vi.* to stop existing as an organization; scatter; disperse —**dis·band′ment** *n.*

dis·bar (-bär′) *vt.* **-barred′, -bar′ring** to expel (a lawyer) from the bar; deprive of the right to practice law —**dis·bar′ment** *n.*

dis·be·lief (dis′bə lēf′) *n.* refusal to believe; absence of belief

dis·be·lieve (-lēv′) *vt.* **-lieved′, -liev′ing** to refuse to believe; reject as untrue —*vi.* to refuse to believe (*in*) —**dis′be·liev′er** *n.*

dis·bur·den (dis bur′d'n) *vt.* to relieve or rid of a burden, as of something weighing on one's mind

dis·burse (-burs′) *vt.* **-bursed′, -burs′ing** [< OFr. *desbourser:* see DIS- & BOURSE] to pay out (money, funds, etc.); expend —**dis·burs′a·ble** *adj.* —**dis·burse′ment** *n.* —**dis·burs′er** *n.*

disc (disk) *n.* **1.** same as DISK **2.** a phonograph record ☆**3.** any of the sharp, circular blades on a disc harrow **4.** *Biol.* any disk-shaped part or structure: see DISK

disc. **1.** discount **2.** discovered

dis·card (dis kärd′; *for n.* dis′kärd) *vt.* [< OFr.: see DIS- & CARD¹] **1.** *Card Games* to remove (a card or cards) from the hand dealt **2.** to get rid of or throw away as no longer valuable, useful, or wanted [to *discard* old letters] —*vi. Card Games* to make a discard —*n.* **1.** a discarding or being discarded **2.** something discarded **3.** *Card Games* the card or cards discarded

disc brake a brake, as on an automobile, that causes two friction pads to press on either side of a disc rotating along with the wheel

dis·cern (di surn′, -zurn′) *vt.* [< OFr. < L. < *dis-*, apart + *cernere*, to separate] **1.** to recognize as separate or different [to *discern* good from evil] **2.** to perceive or recognize; make out clearly [I can't *discern* his features in the dim light] —*vi.* to perceive or recognize the difference —**dis·cern′i·ble** *adj.* —**dis·cern′i·bly** *adv.*

SYN.—**discern** implies a making out of something or recognizing it clearly with the eyes or in the mind [to *discern* one's motives]; **perceive** implies a recognizing by means of any of the senses, and often, in addition, implies keen understanding or insight [to *perceive* differences in pitch; to *perceive* a change in attitude]; **distinguish** implies a perceiving clearly by sight, hearing, etc. [he *distinguished* the voices of men and women down the hall]; **observe** and **notice** both connote paying attention to some degree, and usually suggest use of the sense of sight [to *observe* an eclipse; to *notice* a sign]

dis·cern·ing (-iŋ) *adj.* having or showing good judgment or understanding —**dis·cern′ing·ly** *adv.*

dis·cern·ment (-mənt) *n.* **1.** a discerning **2.** keen perception or judgment; insight; acumen

dis·charge (dis chärj′; *for n. usually* dis′chärj) *vt.* **-charged′, -charg′ing** [< OFr. < L. *dis-*, from + *carrus*, wagon, CAR] **1.** to relieve of or release from something that burdens or holds in; specif., *a)* to remove the cargo of (a ship) *b)* to release the charge of (a gun) *c)* to release (a soldier, jury, etc.) from duty *d)* to dismiss from a job; fire *e)* to release (a prisoner) from jail, (a patient) from a hospital, (a debtor or bankrupt person) from obligations, etc. **2.** to release or remove (that by which one is burdened or held in); specif., *a)* to unload (a cargo) *b)* to shoot (a projectile) **3.** to relieve oneself or itself of (a burden, load, etc.); specif., *a)* to let out or give off; emit [to *discharge* pus] *b)* to pay (a debt) or perform (a duty) ☆**4.** to use up the electrical charge in (a battery or capacitor) —*vi.* **1.** to get rid of a burden, load, charge, etc. **2.** to be released or thrown off **3.** to go off: said of a gun, etc. **4.** to give off waste matter: said of a wound, etc. —*n.* **1.** a′discharging or being discharged **2.** that which discharges, as a certificate showing one's dismissal from military service, etc. **3.** that which is discharged, as pus from a sore **4.** a flow of electric current across a gap, as in a spark or arc —**dis·charge′a·ble** *adj.* —**dis·charg′er** *n.*

discharge tube a device in which a gas or metal vapor conducting an electric discharge is the source of light, as in a mercury-vapor lamp

☆**disc harrow** a harrow with sharp, revolving circular blades used to break up the soil for sowing

dis·ci·ple (di sī′p'l) *n.* [< OFr. & OE., both < L. *discipulus*, pupil < *dis-*, apart + *capere*, to hold] **1.** a pupil or follower of any teacher or school **2.** an early follower of Jesus, esp. one of the Apostles —see **SYN.** at FOLLOWER —**dis·ci′ple·ship′** *n.*

DISC HARROW

dis·ci·pli·nar·i·an (dis′ə pli ner′ē ən) *n.* a person who believes in strict discipline or enforces it

dis·ci·pli·nar·y (dis′ə pli ner′ē) *adj.* **1.** of or having to do with discipline **2.** that enforces discipline by punishing or correcting [to take *disciplinary* action]

dis·ci·pline (dis′ə plin) *n.* [< OFr. < L. *disciplina* < *discipulus*: see DISCIPLE] **1.** a branch of knowledge or learning [his *discipline* is science] **2.** *a)* training that develops self-control or orderliness and efficiency *b)* strict control to enforce obedience [the *discipline* of the army] **3.** the result of such training or control; orderly conduct, obedience, etc. [the perfect *discipline* of the pupils studying] **4.** a system of rules, as for those belonging to a monastic order **5.** treatment that corrects or punishes [for *discipline* he had to stay after school] —*vt.* **-plined,**

-plin·ing 1. to train in discipline *[soldiers disciplined to obey commands]* **2.** to punish —see **SYN.** at PUNISH —**dis·ci·plin·a·ble** *adj.* —**dis'ci·plin·al** *adj.* —**dis'ci·plin·er** *n.*

☆**disc jockey** a person who conducts a radio program of recorded music mixed with chatter, commercials, etc., or one who plays recorded music at a disco

dis·claim (dis klām') *vt.* **1.** to give up any claim to or connection with *[to disclaim one's rights to property]* **2.** to refuse to acknowledge or admit; repudiate *[to disclaim knowledge of a crime]* —*vi.* to make a denial

dis·claim·er (-ər) *n.* **1.** a disclaiming, denial, or renunciation, as of a claim, title, etc. **2.** a refusal to accept responsibility

dis·close (dis klōz') *vt.* **-closed', -clos'ing 1.** to bring into view; uncover *[the curtain rose to disclose the stage]* **2.** to reveal; make known *[to disclose a secret]* —see **SYN.** at REVEAL — **dis·clos'er** *n.*

dis·clo·sure (-klō'zhər) *n.* **1.** a disclosing or being disclosed **2.** a thing disclosed; revelation

☆ **dis·co** (dis'kō) *n.* [DISCO(THÈQUE)] **1.** *pl.* **-cos** a nightclub or other public place for dancing to recorded music **2.** a kind of popular dance music combining soul music, a strong Latin American beat, and simple, repeated lyrics, usually accompanied by flashing lights, etc. —*adj.* of discos, their music, etc. —*vi.* **-coed, -co·ing** to dance at a disco

dis·cog·ra·phy (dis käg'rə fē) *n., pl.* **-phies** [< L. *discus,* a disk + (BIBLIO)GRAPHY] **1.** the systematic cataloging of phonograph records **2.** a list of the recordings of a particular performer, composer, composition, etc. —**dis·cog'ra·pher** *n.*

dis·coid (dis'koid) *adj.* [< LL. < Gr. < *diskos,* a disk + *eidos,* form] shaped like a disk: also **dis·coi'dal** —*n.* anything shaped like a disk

dis·col·or (dis kul'ər) *vt., vi.* to change in color by fading, streaking, or staining *[the drapes were discolored]*

dis·col·or·a·tion (-kul'ə rā'shən) *n.* **1.** a discoloring or being discolored **2.** a discolored spot or mark

☆**dis·com·bob·u·late** (dis'kəm bäb'yoo lāt') *vt.* **-lat'ed, -lat'ing** [prob. a humorous changing of DISCOMFIT] [Colloq.] to upset the calmness of; disconcert

dis·com·fit (dis kum'fit) *vt.* [< OFr. < L. *dis- + conficere:* see CONFECT] **1.** orig., to defeat **2.** to frustrate the plans or expectations of **3.** to make uneasy; disconcert —see **SYN.** at EMBARRASS —**dis·com'fi·ture** (-fi chər) *n.*

dis·com·fort (dis kum'fərt) *n.* **1.** lack of comfort; uneasiness **2.** anything causing this —*vt.* to cause discomfort to

dis·com·mode (dis'kə mōd') *vt.* **-mod'ed, -mod'ing** [< DIS- + L. *commodare,* to make suitable] to cause bother to; inconvenience

dis·com·pose (-kəm pōz') *vt.* **-posed', -pos'ing** to disturb the calm or poise of; fluster —**dis'com·po'sure** (-pō'zhər) *n.*

dis·con·cert (-kən surt') *vt.* **1.** to upset or frustrate (plans, etc.) **2.** to upset the calmness of; embarrass *[to be disconcerted by a sudden change in plans]* —see **SYN.** at EMBARRASS —**dis'con·cert'ing** *adj.* —**dis'con·cert'ing·ly** *adv.*

dis·con·nect (-kə nekt') *vt.* to break or undo the connection of; separate, detach, unplug, etc. —**dis'con·nec'tion** *n.*

dis·con·nect·ed (-nek'tid) *adj.* **1.** separated, detached, etc. *[a disconnected stove]* **2.** broken up into unrelated parts; incoherent *[a disconnected plot]* —**dis'con·nect'ed·ly** *adv.* —**dis'con·nect'ed·ness** *n.*

dis·con·so·late (dis kän'sə lit) *adj.* [< ML. < L.: see DIS- & CONSOLE¹] **1.** so unhappy that nothing will comfort one; dejected *[Anne is disconsolate because her bicycle was stolen]* **2.** causing sadness; cheerless —**dis·con'so·late·ly** *adv.* —**dis·con'so·late·ness, dis·con'so·la'tion** (-lā'shən) *n.*

dis·con·tent (dis'kən tent') *adj. same as* DISCONTENTED —*n.* desire for something more or different; lack of contentment; dissatisfaction: also **dis'con·tent'ment** —*vt.* to make discontented

dis·con·tent·ed (-id) *adj.* not contented; wanting something more or different —**dis'con·tent'ed·ly** *adv.* —**dis'con·tent'ed·ness** *n.*

dis·con·tin·ue (dis'kən tin'yoo) *vt.* **-ued, -u·ing 1.** to stop using, doing, etc.; cease; give up *[his father discontinued smoking]* **2.** *Law* to stop (a suit) before trial —*vi.* to stop; end —see **SYN.** at STOP —**dis'con·tin'u·ance** (-yoo wəns), **dis'con·tin'u·a'tion** (-yoo wā'shən) *n.*

dis·con·tin·u·ous (-yoo wəs) *adj.* not continuous; broken up by interruptions —**dis·con·ti·nu·i·ty** (dis kän'tə noo'ə tē, dis'kän-; -nyoo'-) *n.* —**dis'con·tin'u·ous·ly** *adv.*

dis·cord (dis'kôrd; *for v., usually* dis kôrd') *n.* [< OFr. < L. < *discors* (gen. *discordis*), discordant < *dis-,* apart + *cor,* HEART] **1.** disagreement **2.** a harsh noise, as the sound of battle **3.** *Music* a lack of harmony in tones sounded together

SYN.—**discord** denotes disagreement or lack of harmony and may imply quarreling between persons, conflicting qualities in things, dissonance in sound, etc.; **strife** emphasizes the struggle to win out where there is a conflict or disagreement; **contention** suggests strife or quarreling among persons as expressed in argument, controversy, dispute, etc.; **dissension** implies difference of opinion, usually suggesting conflict between opposing groups within a larger group —**ANT.** harmony, agreement

dis·cord·ant (dis kôr'd'nt) *adj.* **1.** not in accord; disagreeing; conflicting *[he and she hold discordant opinions]* **2.** not in harmony; dissonant; clashing *[discordant music]* —**dis·cord'ance, dis·cord'an·cy** *n.* —**dis·cord'ant·ly** *adv.*

☆**dis·co·thèque** (dis'kə tek) *n.* [Fr. < *disque,* record + *bibliothèque,* library] *the full name* of DISCO (*n.* 1.)

dis·count (dis'kount; *for v., also* dis kount') *n.* [< OFr. < ML. *discomputare:* see DIS- & COMPUTE] **1.** *a)* a reduction from the usual price or a list price *[sold at a 10% discount]* *b)* a deduction from a debt, allowed for prompt or cash payment **2.** the interest deducted in advance by one who lends money on a promissory note, etc. **3.** the rate of interest (**discount rate**) charged for this **4.** a discounting —*vt.* **1.** to pay or receive the value of (a promissory note, etc.), minus the discount (sense 2) **2.** to deduct an amount or percent from (a bill, price, etc.) **3.** to sell at less than the regular price **4.** *a)* to believe (a story, etc.) only in part, allowing for exaggeration, bias, etc. *b)* to disbelieve or disregard entirely **5.** to lessen the effect of by anticipating; reckon with in advance —*vi.* to lend or sell with discounts —**at a discount 1.** below the regular price **2.** worth little —**dis'count·a·ble** *adj.*

dis·coun·te·nance (dis koun'tə nəns) *vt.* **-nanced, -nanc·ing 1.** to make ashamed or embarrassed; disconcert **2.** to refuse approval or support to

☆**discount house** (or **store**) a retail store that sells goods for less than regular or list prices

dis·cour·age (dis kur'ij) *vt.* **-aged, -ag·ing** [OFr. *descoragier*] **1.** to cause to lose courage or confidence; dishearten *[the singer was discouraged by the lack of applause]* **2.** to advise or persuade (a person) to keep from doing something *[we discouraged her from risking her money]* **3.** to prevent or try to prevent by disapproving *[the law discourages hitchhiking]* —*vi.* to become discouraged —**dis·cour'age·ment** *n.* —**dis·cour'ag·ing** *adj.* —**dis·cour'ag·ing·ly** *adv.*

dis·course (dis'kôrs; *also, and for v. usually,* dis kôrs') *n.* [< OFr. < L. pp. < *dis-,* from + *currere,* to run: see CURRENT] **1.** communication of ideas, information, etc., esp. by talking; conversation **2.** a formal treatment of a subject, in speech or writing —*vi.* **-coursed', -cours'ing 1.** to converse; talk **2.** to speak or write (*on* or *upon* a subject) formally —see **SYN.** at SPEAK

dis·cour·te·ous (dis kur'tē əs) *adj.* not courteous; impolite; ill-mannered —see **SYN.** at RUDE —**dis·cour'te·ous·ly** *adv.* —**dis·cour'te·ous·ness** *n.*

dis·cour·te·sy (-tə sē) *n.* **1.** lack of courtesy; impoliteness; rudeness **2.** *pl.* **-sies** a rude or impolite act or remark

dis·cov·er (dis kuv'ər) *vt.* [< OFr. < LL. *discooperire:* see DIS- & COVER] **1.** *a)* to be the first to find, see, or know about *[the Curies discovered radium]* *b)* to be the first non-native person to come to or see (a continent, river, etc.) **2.** to find out; learn of the existence of **3.** [Archaic] *a)* to reveal *b)* to uncover —see **SYN.** at LEARN —**dis·cov'er·a·ble** *adj.* —**dis·cov'er·er** *n.*

dis·cov·er·y (-ər ē) *n., pl.* **-er·ies 1.** a discovering **2.** anything discovered **3.** [Archaic] a revealing

dis·cred·it (dis kred'it) *vt.* **1.** to reject as untrue **2.** to cast doubt on *[his earlier lies discredit anything he may say]* **3.** to damage the reputation of; disgrace *[the judge discredited himself by taking bribes]* —*n.* **1.** loss of belief or trust; doubt **2.** damage to one's reputation; disgrace *[she lied, much to her discredit]* **3.** something that causes disgrace —**dis·cred'it·a·ble** *adj.* —**dis·cred'it·a·bly** *adv.*

dis·creet (dis krēt') *adj.* [< OFr. < L. pp. of *discernere:* see DISCERN] careful about what one says or does; prudent; esp.,

fat, āpe, cär, ten, ēven, is, bīte; gō, hôrn, tōōl, look; oil, out; up, fur; get; joy; yet; chin; she; thin, *th*en; zh, leisure; ŋ, ring; ə for *a* in *ago, e* in *agent, i* in *sanity, o* in *comply, u* in *focus;* ' as in *able* (ā'b'l); Fr. bál; ë, Fr. coeur; ö, Fr. feu; Fr. mon; ổ, Fr. coq; ü, Fr. duc; r, Fr. cri; H, G. ich; kh, G. doch; ‡foreign; ☆ Americanism; < derived from. See inside front cover.

keeping secrets when necessary —**dis·creet′ly** *adv.* —**dis·creet′ness** *n.*

dis·crep·an·cy (dis krep′ən sē) *n., pl.* **-cies** [< OFr. < L. < prp. of *discrepare*, to sound differently < *dis-*, from + *crepare*, to rattle] lack of agreement, or an instance of this; difference; inconsistency —**dis·crep′ant** *adj.* —**dis·crep′ant·ly** *adv.*

dis·crete (dis krēt′) *adj.* [< L.: see DISCREET] **1.** separate and distinct; not attached to others; unrelated **2.** made up of distinct parts; discontinuous —**dis·crete′ly** *adv.* —**dis·crete′ness** *n.*

dis·cre·tion (dis kresh′ən) *n.* **1.** the freedom or power to make decisions and choices [use your own *discretion* in choosing a topic] **2.** the quality of being discreet or careful about what one does; prudence [she used *discretion* in handling complaints] —**at one's discretion** as one wishes

dis·cre·tion·ar·y (-er′ē) *adj.* left to one's judgment or choice: also **dis·cre′tion·al**

dis·crim·i·na·ble (dis krim′ə nə b'l) *adj.* that can be discriminated or distinguished

dis·crim·i·nant (-nənt) *n. Math.* an expression whose sign serves to classify observations into two separate classes

dis·crim·i·nate (dis krim′ə nāt′; *for adj.* -nit) *vt.* **-nat′ed, -nat′ing** [< L. pp. of *discriminare* < *discrimen*, division < *discernere:* see DISCERN] to make or see the difference between; distinguish [abilities which *discriminate* one person from another] —*vi.* **1.** to see the difference (*between* things); distinguish **2.** to be discerning **3.** to show favoritism or prejudice [he *discriminated* in favor of a relative; they *discriminate* against no one in hiring] —*adj.* distinguishing carefully —see SYN. at DISTINGUISH —**dis·crim′i·na′tor** *n.*

dis·crim·i·nat·ing (-nāt′iŋ) *adj.* **1.** that discriminates **2.** able to make or see fine distinctions; discerning **3.** *same as* DISCRIMINATORY Also **dis·crim′i·na′tive** (-nāt′iv, -nə tiv) —**dis·crim′i·nat′ing·ly** *adv.*

dis·crim·i·na·tion (dis krim′ə nā′shən) *n.* **1.** the act of discriminating, or distinguishing differences **2.** the ability to do this **3.** a showing of favoritism or prejudice in treatment; specif., policies directed against the welfare of minority groups

dis·crim·i·na·to·ry (-krim′ə nə tôr′ē) *adj.* **1.** practicing discrimination, or showing prejudice **2.** discriminating, or distinguishing

dis·cur·sive (dis kur′siv) *adj.* [< ML. < L.: see DISCOURSE] **1.** wandering from one topic to another; rambling; digressive **2.** *Philos.* going from premises to conclusions in a series of logical steps —**dis·cur′sive·ly** *adv.* —**dis·cur′sive·ness** *n.*

dis·cus (dis′kəs) *n., pl.* **dis′cus·es, dis·ci** (dis′ī) [L. < Gr. *diskos*] **1.** a heavy disk of metal and wood thrown for distance in a contest of strength and skill **2.** such a contest: in full, **discus throw**

DISCUS THROWER

dis·cuss (dis kus′) *vt.* [< L. pp. of *discutire* < *dis-*, apart + *quatere*, to shake] to talk or write about; consider and argue the pros and cons of —**dis·cuss′a·ble, dis·cuss′i·ble** *adj.* —**dis·cuss′er** *n.*

SYN.—**discuss** implies a talking about something in a calm, informal way, with varying opinions offered rationally in an attempt to reach a satisfactory decision; **argue** suggests either the giving of reasons or evidence to support or disprove a statement, belief, etc., or a taking part in an emotional, quarrelsome, or angry exchange of opinion; **debate** implies a formal argument between opposing groups, usually concerning a matter of public interest; **dispute** suggests an angry or heated clash of opposing opinions

☆**dis·cuss·ant** (dis kus′ənt) *n.* a person taking part in an organized discussion

dis·cus·sion (dis kush′ən) *n.* talk or writing in which the pros and cons or various aspects of a subject are considered —**under discussion** being discussed

dis·dain (dis dān′) *vt.* [< OFr. < L. *dis-*, not + *dignari*, DEIGN] to regard as beneath one's dignity; specif., to refuse or reject with aloof contempt or scorn —*n.* aloof contempt or scorn [his *disdain* as a dog owner for those who keep cats]

dis·dain·ful (-fəl) *adj.* scornful and aloof —see SYN. at PROUD —**dis·dain′ful·ly** *adv.*

dis·ease (di zēz′) *n.* [OFr. *desaise* < *des-*, DIS- + *aise*, EASE] **1.** a condition of not being healthy; illness in general **2.** a particular destructive process in an organ or organism; specific illness **3.** a harmful condition, as of society —*vt.* **-eased′, -eas′ing** to cause disease in; infect —**dis·eased′** *adj.*

dis·em·bark (dis′im bärk′) *vt.* to unload (passengers or goods) from a ship, aircraft, etc. —*vi.* to go ashore from a ship or leave an aircraft, etc. —**dis·em·bar·ka·tion** (dis′em bär kā′shən) *n.*

dis·em·bar·rass (-im bar′əs) *vt.* to rid or relieve of something embarrassing, annoying, entangling, perplexing, or burdensome

dis·em·bod·y (-im bäd′ē) *vt.* **-bod′ied, -bod′y·ing** to separate (a spirit, etc.) from the body —**dis·em·bod′ied** *adj.* —**dis·em·bod′i·ment** *n.*

dis·em·bow·el (-im bou′əl) *vt.* **-eled** or **-elled, -el·ing** or **-el·ling** to take out the bowels, or entrails, of; eviscerate —**dis·em·bow′el·ment** *n.*

dis·em·ployed (-im ploid′) *adj.* out of work, esp. because of lack of training or education, rather than because work is unavailable —**dis′em·ploy′ment** *n.*

dis·en·chant (-in chant′) *vt.* to set free from an enchantment or illusion; disillusion —**dis·en·chant′ment** *n.*

dis·en·cum·ber (-in kum′bər) *vt.* to relieve of a burden; free from a hindrance or annoyance

dis·en·fran·chise (-in fran′chīz) *vt.* **-chised, -chis·ing** *same as* DISFRANCHISE —**dis·en·fran′chise·ment** *n.*

dis·en·gage (-in gāj′) *vt.* **-gaged′, -gag′ing** to release or loosen from something that binds, holds, entangles, etc.; detach —*vi.* to release oneself or itself —**dis·en·gage′ment** *n.*

dis·en·tan·gle (-in taŋ′g'l) *vt.* **-gled, -gling 1.** to free from something that entangles, confuses, etc.; extricate **2.** to straighten out (anything tangled, confused, etc.); untangle —*vi.* to get free from a tangle —**dis·en·tan′gle·ment** *n.*

dis·e·qui·lib·ri·um (dis ē′kwə lib′rē əm) *n., pl.* **-ri·ums, -ri·a** (-ə) lack or destruction of equilibrium, esp. in the economy

dis·es·tab·lish (dis′ə stab′lish) *vt.* **1.** to deprive of the status of being established **2.** to deprive (a state church) of official sanction and support by the government —**dis′es·tab′lish·ment** *n.*

dis·es·teem (-ə stēm′) *vt.* to hold in low esteem; dislike; slight —*n.* lack of esteem; disfavor

dis·fa·vor (dis fā′vər) *n.* **1.** an unfavorable opinion; dislike; disapproval [to view the idea with *disfavor*] **2.** the state of being disliked or disapproved of [to fall into *disfavor*] **3.** an unkind act; disservice —*vt.* to regard or treat unfavorably; slight

dis·fig·ure (dis fig′yər) *vt.* **-ured, -ur·ing** to hurt the appearance or attractiveness of; deface; mar —**dis·fig′ure·ment, dis·fig′u·ra′tion** *n.*

dis·fran·chise (-fran′chīz) *vt.* **-chised, -chis·ing 1.** to deprive of the rights of citizenship, esp. of the right to vote **2.** to deprive of a privilege, right, or power —**dis·fran′chise·ment** *n.*

dis·gorge (-gôrj′) *vt., vi.* **-gorged′, -gorg′ing** [< OFr.: see DIS- & GORGE] **1.** to vomit **2.** to give up (something) against one's will **3.** to pour forth (its contents)

dis·grace (dis grās′) *n.* [< Fr. < It. < *dis-* (L. *dis-*), not + *grazia*, favor < L. *gratia:* see GRACE] **1.** a being in disfavor as because of bad conduct [he is in *disgrace* because he cheated] **2.** loss of respect; public dishonor; shame **3.** a person or thing that brings shame (*to* one) [air pollution is a *disgrace* to our cities] —*vt.* **-graced′, -grac′ing** to bring shame or dishonor upon; be a discredit to

SYN.—**disgrace** refers to the loss of other people's respect and a feeling of hurt pride brought about by one's own or another's misconduct [the son's crime brought *disgrace* on his family]; **dishonor** implies a loss of honor and self-respect as the result of one's own actions; **shame** emphasizes the pain a person feels when he believes he is being looked down upon by others because of improper or foolish behavior [he blushed with *shame* when the teacher laughed at him]; **infamy** stresses the widespread bad reputation that results from extreme misconduct; **ignominy** stresses the contemptible nature of that which caused disgrace; **odium** refers to the disgrace or infamy brought about by an especially disgusting or hateful action; **scandal** stresses the severe criticism, gossip, etc. brought on by a shameful or wicked act —ANT. honor, respect, esteem

dis·grace·ful (-grās′fəl) *adj.* causing or characterized by disgrace; shameful —**dis·grace′ful·ly** *adv.* —**dis·grace′ful·ness** *n.*

dis·grun·tle (dis grun′t'l) *vt.* **-tled, -tling** [DIS- + obs. *gruntle* < GRUNT + -LE²] to make peevishly discontented; displease and make sulky —**dis·grun′tle·ment** *n.*

dis·guise (dis gīz′) *vt.* **-guised′, -guis′ing** [< OFr.: see DIS- & GUISE] **1.** to make appear, sound, etc. different from usual so as to be unrecognizable [to *disguise* her voice] **2.** to hide so as to keep from being known [to *disguise* his fears] —*n.* **1.** any clothes, equipment, manner, etc. used for disguising **2.** the state of being disguised **3.** the act or practice of disguising —**dis·guis′ed·ly** *adv.*

dis·gust (dis gust′) *n.* [< MFr. < *des-* (see DIS-) + L. *gustus*, taste] a sickening distaste or dislike; deep aversion; repugnance —*vt.* to cause to feel disgust; be sickening or repulsive to —**dis·gust′ed** *adj.* —**dis·gust′ed·ly** *adv.* —**dis·gust′ful** *adj.* —**dis·gust′ing·ly** *adv.*

dish (dish) *n.* [OE. *disc*, dish, ult. < L. *discus*, DISCUS] **1.** *a)* any container, generally shallow and concave, for food *b)* [*pl.*] plates, bowls, cups, etc. as a group [wash the *dishes*] **2.** *a)* the food in a dish *b)* a particular kind of food [hash is his favorite *dish*] **3.** a dishful **4.** a dish-shaped object or concavity ☆**5.** [Slang] *a)* a pretty girl or woman *b)* a favorite thing: also **dish of tea** —*vt.* **1.** to serve (food) in a dish (usually with *up* or *out*) **2.** to make concave —☆**dish it out** [Slang] to scold, harass, etc.

dis·ha·bille (dis′ə bēl′) *n.* [< Fr. < *dés-* (see DIS-) + *habiller*, to dress] the state of being dressed only partially or in night clothes

dish antenna a radio transmitting or receiving antenna with a dish-shaped reflector

dis·har·mo·ny (dis här′mə nē) *n.* lack of harmony; discord — **dis·har·mo·ni·ous** (-mō′nē əs) *adj.*

dish·cloth (dish′klôth′, -kläth′) *n.* a cloth for washing dishes

dis·heart·en (dis härt′'n) *vt.* to discourage; depress —**dis·heart′en·ing** *adj.* —**dis·heart′en·ing·ly** *adv.* —**dis·heart′en·ment** *n.*

di·shev·el (di shev′'l) *vt.* **-eled** or **-elled, -el·ing** or **-el·ling** [< OFr. < *des-*, DIS- + *chevel*, hair < L. *capillus*] **1.** to cause (hair, clothing, etc.) to become mussed and untidy; rumple **2.** to cause the hair or clothes of (a person) to become rumpled —**di·shev′eled, di·shev′elled** *adj.* —**di·shev′el·ment** *n.*

dish·ful (dish′fool′) *n., pl.* **-fuls′** as much as a dish holds

dis·hon·est (dis än′ist) *adj.* not honest; lying, cheating, etc. —**dis·hon′est·ly** *adv.*

dis·hon·es·ty (-ist ē) *n.* **1.** the quality of being dishonest **2.** *pl.* **-ties** a dishonest act or statement; fraud, lie, etc.

dis·hon·or (dis än′ər) *n.* **1.** *a)* loss of honor, respect, etc. *b)* state of shame; disgrace **2.** a cause of dishonor; discredit **3.** a refusal or failure to pay a check, draft, etc. —*vt.* **1.** to treat disrespectfully **2.** to disgrace **3.** to refuse or fail to pay (a check, draft, etc.) —see SYN. at DISGRACE

dis·hon·or·a·ble (-ər ə b'l) *adj.* causing or deserving dishonor; shameful; disgraceful —**dis·hon′or·a·ble·ness** *n.* —**dis·hon′or·a·bly** *adv.*

☆**dish·pan** (dish′pan′) *n.* a pan in which dishes, cooking utensils, etc. are washed

☆**dish·rag** (-rag′) *n. same as* DISHCLOTH

☆**dish towel** a towel for drying dishes

☆**dish·wash·er** (-wôsh′ər, -wäsh′-) *n.* a person or machine that washes dishes, cooking utensils, etc.

dish·wa·ter (-wôt′ər, -wät′-) *n.* water in which dishes, cooking utensils, etc. are washed or have been washed

dis·il·lu·sion (dis′i loo′zhən) *vt.* **1.** to free from illusion or false ideas **2.** to take away the idealism of and make disappointed, bitter, etc. [a sad young man *disillusioned* by his experiences] —*n.* a disillusioning or being disillusioned: also **dis′il·lu′sion·ment**

dis·in·cli·na·tion (dis in′klə nā′shən) *n.* a dislike or unwillingness; aversion; reluctance

dis·in·cline (dis′in klīn′) *vt.* **-clined′, -clin′ing** to make unwilling —see SYN. at RELUCTANT

dis·in·fect (-in fekt′) *vt.* to destroy the harmful bacteria, viruses, etc. in or on —**dis′in·fec′tion** *n.*

dis·in·fect·ant (-ənt) *adj.* disinfecting —*n.* anything that disinfects

dis·in·gen·u·ous (dis′in jen′yoo wəs) *adj.* not straightforward; not frank; insincere —**dis′in·gen′u·ous·ly** *adv.* —**dis′in·gen′u·ous·ness** *n.*

dis·in·her·it (-in her′it) *vt.* **1.** to take away the right of (someone) to inherit **2.** to take any right or privilege away from —**dis′in·her′it·ance** *n.*

dis·in·te·grate (dis in′tə grāt′) *vt., vi.* **-grat′ed, -grat′ing** **1.** to separate into parts or fragments; break up [the bomb explosion *disintegrated* the building] **2.** to undergo or cause to undergo a nuclear transformation —**dis·in′te·gra′tion** *n.* — **dis·in′te·gra′tive** *adj.* —**dis·in′te·gra′tor** *n.*

dis·in·ter (dis′in tur′) *vt.* **-terred′, -ter′ring** **1.** to remove from a grave, tomb, etc.; dig up; exhume **2.** to bring (something hidden) to light —**dis′in·ter′ment** *n.*

dis·in·ter·est (dis in′trist, -tər ist) *n.* **1.** lack of personal or selfish interest **2.** lack of interest

dis·in·ter·est·ed (-id) *adj.* **1.** not influenced by personal interest or selfish motives; impartial [a *disinterested* judge picked the winner] **2.** uninterested: a revival of an obsolete meaning —see SYN. at INDIFFERENT —**dis·in′ter·est·ed·ly** *adv.* —**dis·in′ter·est·ed·ness** *n.*

dis·join (-join′) *vt.* to separate or detach

dis·joint (-joint′) *vt.* **1.** to put out of joint; dislocate **2.** to cut or tear apart at the joints; dismember [to *disjoint* a duck]

dis·joint·ed (-id) *adj.* **1.** out of joint **2.** dismembered **3.** disconnected; not clear or orderly [speaking in short, *disjointed* sentences] —**dis·joint′ed·ly** *adv.* —**dis·joint′ed·ness** *n.*

dis·junc·tion (-juŋk′shən) *n.* **1.** a disjoining or being disjoined; separation: also **dis·junc′ture** (-chər) **2.** *a)* the relation between alternatives of a disjunctive proposition *b)* a disjunctive proposition

dis·junc·tive (-tiv) *adj.* **1.** disjoining; separating or causing to separate **2.** *Gram.* indicating a contrast or an alternative between words, clauses, etc. ["or" and "but" are *disjunctive* conjunctions] **3.** *Logic* presenting alternatives [a *disjunctive* proposition] —*n.* **1.** *Gram.* a disjunctive conjunction **2.** *Logic* a disjunctive proposition —**dis·junc′tive·ly** *adv.*

disk (disk) *n.* [< L. *discus*, DISCUS] **1.** any thin, flat, circular thing **2.** anything like this in form [the moon's *disk*] **3.** *same as* DISC; specif., *a)* the disk-shaped center of certain composite flowers *b)* a layer of fibrous connective tissue, with some cartilage, occurring between vertebrae

disk flower any of the tubular flowers in the central disk of the flower head of a composite plant

☆**disk harrow** *same as* DISC HARROW

☆**disk jockey** *same as* DISC JOCKEY

disk wheel a wheel made solid from rim to hub, without spokes

dis·like (dis līk′) *vt.* **-liked′, -lik′ing** to have a feeling of not liking; feel aversion to —*n.* a feeling of not liking; distaste; aversion —**dis·lik′a·ble, dis·like′a·ble** *adj.*

dis·lo·cate (dis′lō kāt′, dis lō′kāt) *vt.* **-cat′ed, -cat′ing** **1.** to put out of place; specif., to displace (a bone) from its proper position at a joint **2.** to disrupt; disturb [normal traffic movement *dislocated* by stalled cars] —**dis′lo·ca′tion** *n.*

dis·lodge (dis läj′) *vt., vi.* **-lodged′, -lodg′ing** to force or be forced from a position or place where lodged, hiding, etc. —**dis·lodg′ment** *n.*

dis·loy·al (-loi′əl) *adj.* not loyal or faithful; faithless —see SYN. at FAITHLESS —**dis·loy′al·ly** *adv.*

dis·loy·al·ty (-tē) *n.* **1.** the quality of being disloyal **2.** *pl.* **-ties** a disloyal act

dis·mal (diz′m'l) *adj.* [ME., originally a noun, evil days < OFr. < ML. *dies mali*] **1.** causing gloom or misery [*dismal* news] **2.** dark and gloomy; bleak; dreary [a *dismal* room] **3.** depressed; miserable —**dis′mal·ly** *adv.*

Dismal Swamp marshy region between Norfolk, Va., & Albemarle Sound, N.C.

dis·man·tle (dis man′t'l) *vt.* **-tled, -tling** [< OFr. *desmanteller*: see DIS- & MANTLE] **1.** to strip of covering **2.** to strip (a house, ship, etc.) of furniture, equipment, etc. **3.** to take apart; disassemble —**dis·man′tle·ment** *n.*

dis·may (dis mā′) *vt.* [< Anglo-Fr. < OFr. *des-*, thoroughly + *esmayer*, to deprive of power] to make discouraged at the prospect of trouble; fill with alarm; daunt —*n.* a loss of courage when faced with trouble or danger

SYN.—dismay suggests fear or (in

DISLOCATED HIPBONE

DISMAL SWAMP

modern usage) discouragement in the face of a difficulty one does not quite know how to deal with [*dismayed* by the complexity of his new job]; **appall** suggests terror or (now more commonly) dismay at a shocking situation that it seems cannot be changed [the *appalling* highway death rate]; **horrify** suggests horror or loathing or (in a weakened sense) irritation at that which shocks or offends one [*horrified* at the suggestion]; **daunt** implies a becoming disheartened while performing an act that requires courage [the captain, not *daunted* by the storm, sailed on]

dis·mem·ber (dis mem′bər) *vt.* [< OFr.: see DIS- & MEMBER] **1.** to remove the limbs of by cutting or tearing [to *dismember* a body] **2.** to pull or cut to pieces; divide up or mutilate [to *dismember* a conquered nation] —**dis·mem′ber·ment** *n.*

dis·miss (-mis′) *vt.* [< ML. pp. of *dismittere*, for L. *dimittere* < *dis-*, from + *mittere*, to send] **1.** to send away; cause or allow to leave [to *dismiss* a class] **2.** to remove or discharge from an office, employment, etc. **3.** to put out of one's mind [to *dismiss* one's fears] **4.** *Law* to reject (a claim or action) —**dis·miss′al** *n.*

dis·mount (-mount′) *vi.* to get off, as from a horse or bicycle —*vt.* **1.** to remove (a thing) from its mounting or setting **2.** to cause to dismount **3.** to take apart; dismantle

Dis·ney (diz′nē), **Walt(er Elias)** 1901-66; U.S. motion-picture producer, esp. of animated cartoons

dis·o·be·di·ence (dis′ə bē′dē əns) *n.* refusal to obey; failure to follow commands; insubordination —**dis′o·be′di·ent** *adj.* —**dis′o·be′di·ent·ly** *adv.*

dis·o·bey (dis′ə bā′) *vt., vi.* to refuse to obey or fail to obey

dis·o·blige (-ə blīj′) *vt.* -**bliged′**, -**blig′ing 1.** to refuse to oblige, or do a favor for **2.** to slight; offend —**dis′o·blig′ing** *adj.* —**dis′o·blig′ing·ly** *adv.*

dis·or·der (dis ôr′dər) *n.* **1.** a lack of order; confusion **2.** a breach of public peace; riot **3.** an upset of normal function; ailment [a nervous *disorder*] —*vt.* to cause disorder in —see SYN. at CONFUSION —**dis·or′dered** *adj.*

dis·or·der·ly (-lē) *adj.* **1.** not orderly; untidy; unsystematic [a *disorderly* desk] **2.** unruly; riotous **3.** *Law* violating public peace, safety, or order [arrested for *disorderly* conduct] —**dis·or′der·li·ness** *n.*

dis·or·gan·ize (dis ôr′gə nīz′) *vt.* -**ized′**, -**iz′ing** to break up the order, arrangement, or system of; throw into disorder [the unexpected guests *disorganized* the party] —**dis·or′gan·i·za′tion** *n.*

dis·o·ri·ent (-ôr′ē ent′) *vt.* **1.** to cause to lose one's bearings **2.** to confuse mentally Also **dis·o′ri·en·tate′** (-ən tāt′) -**tat′ed**, -**tat′ing** —**dis·o′ri·en·ta′tion** *n.*

dis·own (-ōn′) *vt.* to refuse to acknowledge as one's own; refuse to have anything further to do with; cast off [to *disown* one's family]

dis·par·age (dis par′ij) *vt.* -**aged**, -**ag·ing** [< OFr. *desparagier*, to marry one of inferior rank < *des-* (see DIS-) + *parage*, rank < *per*, PEER¹] **1.** to lower in esteem; discredit **2.** to speak slightingly of; belittle —**dis·par′age·ment** *n.* —**dis·par′ag·ing** *adj.* —**dis·par′ag·ing·ly** *adv.*

SYN.—to **disparage** is to cast doubt on the worth or reputation of someone or something, often in subtle ways, as by praising with little enthusiasm or making an unfair comparison [to *disparage* a modern dramatist by comparing him with Shakespeare]; to **depreciate** is to suggest that something has less value than it is generally supposed to have; to **belittle** is to indicate, often spitefully or scornfully, one's low opinion of something's or someone's worth [always *belittling* his fellow scientist's achievements]; to **minimize** is to make seem as small as possible [a biased biographer who *minimized* his subject's faults] —**ANT. extol, praise, magnify**

dis·pa·rate (dis′pər it) *adj.* [< L. pp. of *disparare* < *dis-*, apart, not + *parare*, to make equal < *par*, equal: see PAR] distinct or different in kind; unequal —see SYN. at DIFFERENT —**dis′pa·rate·ly** *adv.* —**dis′pa·rate·ness** *n.*

dis·par·i·ty (dis par′ə tē) *n., pl.* -**ties** inequality or difference, as in rank, quality, amount, etc. [a great *disparity* in the pay the two men received]

dis·pas·sion·ate (-pash′ən it) *adj.* free from passion, emotion, or bias; calm; impartial —see SYN. at FAIR¹ —**dis·pas′sion** *n.* —**dis·pas′sion·ate·ly** *adv.*

dis·patch (-pach′) *vt.* [< Sp. & It. < OFr. *despeechier*, ult. < L. *dis-*, not + LL. *impedicare*, to entangle < L. < *pes*, FOOT] **1.** to send off or out promptly on a specific errand or official business; specif., to send out (trains, buses, etc.) according to a schedule **2.** to kill **3.** to finish quickly or promptly [to *dispatch* one's business] —*n.* **1.** a sending out or off **2.** efficient speed; promptness [working with great *dispatch*] **3.** a message, esp. an official message **4.** a news story sent to a newspaper, TV station, etc., as by a special reporter or news agency —see SYN. at HASTE —**dis·patch′er** *n.*

dis·pel (dis pel′) *vt.* -**pelled′**, -**pel′ling** [< L. *dispellere* < *dis-*, away + *pellere*, to drive] to scatter and drive away; disperse [wind *dispelled* the fog] —see SYN. at SCATTER

dis·pen·sa·ble (dis pen′sə b′l) *adj.* **1.** that can be dispensed or dealt out **2.** that can be dispensed with —**dis·pen·sa·bil′i·ty** *n.*

dis·pen·sa·ry (dis pen′sə rē) *n., pl.* -**ries** a room or place, as in a school or factory, where medicines and first aid are available

dis·pen·sa·tion (dis′pən sā′shən, -pen-) *n.* **1.** a dispensing; distribution **2.** anything distributed **3.** an administrative system; management **4.** a release from an obligation **5.** *R.C.Ch.* an exemption from a specific church law **6.** *Theol. a)* the ordering of events under divine authority *b)* any religious system —**dis′pen·sa′tion·al** *adj.*

dis·pen·sa·to·ry (dis pen′sə tôr′ē) *n., pl.* -**ries** a handbook on medicines; pharmacopeia

dis·pense (-pens′) *vt.* -**pensed′**, -**pens′ing** [< OFr. < L. *dispensare* < pp. of *dispendere* < *dis-*, out + *pendere*, to weigh] **1.** to give or deal out; distribute **2.** to prepare and give out (medicines, prescriptions, etc.) **3.** to administer [to *dispense* the law] —**dispense with 1.** to get rid of; do away with **2.** to do without

dis·pen·ser (-pen′sər) *n.* one that dispenses; specif., a container designed to dispense its contents in handy units or portions

dis·perse (-purs′) *vt.* -**persed′**, -**pers′ing** [< L. pp. of *dispergere* < *dis-*, out + *spargere*, to strew] **1.** to break up and scatter in all directions; distribute widely [police *dispersed* the mob] **2.** to dispel (mist, etc.) **3.** to break up (light) into its component colored rays —*vi.* to break up and move in different directions; scatter [the crowd *dispersed* after his speech] —see SYN. at SCATTER —**dis·per′sal** *n.* —**dis·pers′i·ble** *adj.* —**dis·per′sive** (-pur′siv) *adj.*

dis·per·sion (dis pur′zhən, -shən) *n.* **1.** a dispersing or being dispersed **2.** the breaking up of light into component colored rays, as by a prism **3.** a colloidal system with its dispersed particles and the medium in which these are suspended

dis·pir·it (di spir′it) *vt.* to make sad or discouraged; depress —**dis·pir′it·ed** *adj.* —**dis·pir′it·ed·ly** *adv.*

dis·place (dis plās′) *vt.* -**placed′**, -**plac′ing 1.** to move from its usual or proper place **2.** to take the place of; replace [a ship *displaces* a certain amount of water] —see SYN. at REPLACE

displaced person a person forced from his country, esp. in war, and left homeless elsewhere

dis·place·ment (-mənt) *n.* **1.** a displacing or being displaced **2.** *a)* the weight or volume of a fluid displaced by a floating object; specif., the weight of water displaced by a ship *b)* the volume displaced by a piston

dis·play (dis plā′) *vt.* [< OFr. < L. *displicare* < *dis-*, apart + *plicare*, to fold: for IE. base see COMPLICATE] **1.** to put or spread out to be seen; exhibit [many families *display* the flag on holidays] **2.** to disclose; reveal [to *display* great courage] —*n.* **1.** a displaying; exhibition **2.** anything displayed; exhibit **3.** showy exhibition; ostentation **4.** *a)* a manifestation [a *display* of courage] *b)* a mere show of something that is not genuine [a *display* of sympathy] —*adj.* designating printing type in larger sizes, used for headings, advertisements, etc. —see SYN. at SHOW —**dis·play′er** *n.*

dis·please (-plēz′) *vt., vi.* -**pleased′**, -**pleas′ing** to fail to please; annoy; offend

dis·pleas·ure (-plezh′ər) *n.* **1.** the fact or feeling of being displeased; dissatisfaction, annoyance, etc. **2.** [Archaic] discomfort, trouble, etc. —see SYN. at OFFENSE

dis·port (dis pôrt′) *vi.* [< OFr. < *des-* (see DIS-) + *porter* < L. *portare*, to carry] to play; frolic —*vt.* to amuse or divert (oneself)

dis·pos·a·ble (dis pō′zə b′l) *adj.* **1.** that can be thrown away after use [*disposable* bottles] **2.** that can be disposed as one wishes

dis·pos·al (-pō′z′l) *n.* **1.** a disposing; specif., *a)* arrangement in a particular order [the *disposal* of furniture in a room] *b)* a dealing with matters; settling of affairs [the *disposal* of a lawsuit] *c)* a giving away; transfer [the *disposal* of property] *d)* a getting rid of [the *disposal* of garbage] **2.** the power to dispose **3.** *same as* DISPOSER (sense 2) —**at one's disposal** available to be used as one wishes

dis·pose (-pōz′) *vt.* -**posed′**, -**pos′ing** [< OFr. < L. pp. of *disponere*: see DIS- & POSITION] **1.** to place in a certain order; arrange [to *dispose* the chairs in a circle] **2.** to make willing; incline [not *disposed* to help] **3.** to make susceptible or liable [hot weather *disposes* me to laziness] —*vi.* to have the power to arrange or settle affairs —**dispose of 1.** to deal with; settle

2. to give away or sell **3.** to throw away; get rid of **4.** to eat or drink up

dis·pos·er (-pō′zər) *n.* **1.** one that disposes ☆**2.** a device installed in the drain of a kitchen sink to grind up garbage that is then flushed away

dis·po·si·tion (dis′pə zish′ən) *n.* **1.** arrangement [the *disposition* of chairs in the room] **2.** management or settlement of affairs **3.** a selling, giving away, etc. of something **4.** the power to dispose; control **5.** an inclination or tendency [a *disposition* to be helpful] **6.** one's general nature or mood [a happy *disposition*]
SYN.—disposition refers to one's usual mood in response to people and things [a sunny *disposition*]; **temperament** refers to the balance of traits revealed by one's habitual ways of behaving or thinking [an artistic *temperament*]; **temper** refers to one's basic emotional nature, esp. with regard to the likelihood of one's becoming angry [a hot *temper*; an even *temper*]; **character** is applied to the sum of moral qualities making one person different from another [a weak *character*] and, when used without an adjective, suggests moral strength, self-discipline, etc. [a man of *character*]; **personality** is applied to the blend of physical, emotional, and mental qualities that makes one person different from another and is important in determining how others feel about him [a cold, negative *personality*] and, when used without an adjective, suggests attractiveness or charm [a good man but without much *personality*]

dis·pos·sess (-pə zes′) *vt.* to deprive of the possession of land, a house, etc.; oust [to *dispossess* him of his farm] **—dis·pos·ses′sion** (-zesh′ən) *n.* **—dis·pos·ses′sor** *n.*

dis·praise (dis prāz′) *vt.* **-praised′, -prais′ing** to speak of with disapproval; disparage; censure **—n.** a dispraising; blame **—dis·prais′ing·ly** *adv.*

dis·proof (-prōof′) *n.* **1.** a disproving; refutation **2.** evidence that disproves

dis·pro·por·tion (dis′prə pôr′shən) *n.* lack of proportion; lack of symmetry **—vt.** to cause to be disproportionate **—dis′pro·por′tion·al** *adj.* **—dis′pro·por′tion·al·ly** *adv.*

dis·pro·por·tion·ate (-it) *adj.* not proportionate; not in proportion; too great or too small [taking up a *disproportionate* amount of space] **—dis′pro·por′tion·ate·ly** *adv.*

dis·prove (dis prōov′) *vt.* **-proved′, -prov′ing** to prove to be false or in error
SYN.—disprove implies the presentation of evidence or logical arguments that show a statement, theory, etc. to be false or in error; **refute** implies a more thorough gathering of evidence and a more careful development of argument and thus suggests that the proof against a statement, theory, etc. is completely convincing; **confute** suggests the silencing of a person or the overwhelming of his arguments by proof or counter-argument

dis·pu·ta·ble (dis pyōot′ə b'l, dis′pyōot-) *adj.* that can be disputed; debatable **—dis·pu·ta·bil′i·ty** *n.* **—dis·pu′ta·bly** *adv.*

dis·pu·tant (dis pyōot′'nt, dis′pyōo tənt) *adj.* disputing **—n.** one who disputes, or debates

dis·pu·ta·tion (dis′pyōo tā′shən) *n.* **1.** a disputing; dispute **2.** discussion marked by formal debate

dis·pu·ta·tious (-shəs) *adj.* inclined to dispute; fond of arguing: also **dis·pu·ta·tive** (dis pyōot′ə tiv) **—dis′pu·ta′tious·ly** *adv.* **—dis′pu·ta′tious·ness** *n.*

dis·pute (dis pyōot′) *vi.* **-put′ed, -put′ing** [< OFr. < L. *disputare* < *dis-*, apart + *putare*, to think] **1.** to argue; debate **2.** to quarrel **—vt.** **1.** to argue or debate (a question) **2.** to question the truth of; doubt [doctors *dispute* the claims made for certain patent medicines] **3.** to oppose in any way; resist **4.** to fight for; contest [the retreating army *disputed* every foot of ground] **—n.** **1.** a disputing; argument; debate **2.** a quarrel **—beyond dispute** **1.** not open to dispute; settled **2.** indisputably **—in dispute** still being argued about; not settled **—see SYN.** at ARGUMENT and DISCUSS **—dis·put′er** *n.*

dis·qual·i·fy (-kwäl′ə fī′) *vt.* **-fied′, -fy′ing** **1.** to make unfit or unqualified **2.** to say or declare that (someone) is unfit or forbidden to participate further in a sport, hold an office, etc. **—dis·qual′i·fi·ca′tion** (-fi kā′shən) *n.*

dis·qui·et (-kwī′ət) *vt.* to make anxious or uneasy; disturb **—n.** uneasiness; anxiety **—dis·qui′et·ing** *adj.* **—dis·qui′et·ing·ly** *adv.*

dis·qui·e·tude (-kwī′ə tōod′, -tyōod′) *n.* a disturbed or uneasy condition; restlessness; anxiety

dis·qui·si·tion (dis′kwə zish′ən) *n.* [< L. < pp. of *disquirere* < *dis-*, apart + *quaerere*, to seek] a formal discussion of some subject; treatise

Dis·rae·li (diz rā′lē), **Benjamin,** 1st Earl of Beaconsfield, 1804–81; Eng. prime minister

dis·re·gard (dis′ri gärd′) *vt.* **1.** to pay little or no attention to [the hunters *disregarded* the no trespassing sign] **2.** to treat without due respect; slight **—n.** **1.** lack of attention **2.** lack of due regard or respect [with shocking *disregard* for the law]

dis·re·pair (-ri per′) *n.* the condition of needing repairs; state of neglect; dilapidation [an old house in *disrepair*]

dis·rep·u·ta·ble (dis rep′yoo tə b'l) *adj.* **1.** not reputable; having or causing a bad reputation **2.** not fit to be seen; shabby, dirty, etc. **—dis·rep′u·ta·bly** *adv.*

dis·re·pute (dis′ri pyōot′) *n.* lack or loss of repute; bad reputation; disgrace; disfavor

dis·re·spect (-ri spekt′) *n.* lack of respect or esteem; discourtesy **—dis′re·spect′ful** *adj.* **—dis′re·spect′ful·ly** *adv.* **—dis′re·spect′ful·ness** *n.*

dis·robe (dis rōb′) *vt., vi.* **-robed′, -rob′ing** to undress

dis·rupt (dis rupt′) *vt., vi.* [< L. pp. of *disrumpere* < *dis-*, apart + *rumpere*, to break: see RUPTURE] **1.** to break apart; split up **2.** to disturb the orderly course of (a meeting, etc.) **—dis·rupt′er, dis·rup′tor** *n.* **—dis·rup′tion** *n.* **—dis·rup′tive** *adj.*

dis·sat·is·fac·tion (dis sat′is fak′shən) *n.* the condition of being dissatisfied; discontent

dis·sat·is·fac·to·ry (-tə rē) *adj.* not satisfactory

dis·sat·is·fy (dis sat′is fī′) *vt.* **-fied′, -fy′ing** to fail to satisfy; make discontented; displease

dis·sect (di sekt′, dī-) *vt.* [< L. pp. of *dissecare* < *dis-*, apart + *secare*, to cut: for IE. base see SAW¹] **1.** to cut apart piece by piece; separate into parts, as a body for purposes of study **2.** to examine or analyze closely **—dis·sec′tion** *n.* **—dis·sec′tor** *n.*

dis·sect·ed (-id) *adj.* **1.** cut up into parts **2.** *Bot.* consisting of many lobes and segments, as some leaves **3.** *Geol.* cut by erosion into valleys and hills

dis·sem·ble (di sem′b'l) *vt.* **-bled, -bling** [< OFr. < *des-*, DIS- + *sembler* < L. *simulare*, SIMULATE] **1.** to conceal under a false appearance [to *dissemble* fear by smiling] **2.** to make a false show of; feign [to *dissemble* innocence] **—vi.** to conceal the truth, or one's true feelings, motives, etc., by pretense **—dis·sem′blance** *n.* **—dis·sem′bler** *n.*

dis·sem·i·nate (di sem′ə nāt′) *vt.* **-nat′ed, -nat′ing** [< L. pp. of *disseminare* < *dis-*, apart + *seminare*, to sow < *semen*, seed] to scatter far and wide; spread widely [books *disseminate* ideas] **—dis·sem′i·na′tion** *n.* **—dis·sem′i·na′tive** *adj.* **—dis·sem′i·na′tor** *n.*

dis·sen·sion (di sen′shən) *n.* a dissenting in opinion; disagreement or, esp., violent quarreling or wrangling **—see SYN.** at DISCORD

dis·sent (di sent′) *vi.* [< L. *dissentire* < *dis-*, apart + *sentire*, to feel: for IE. base see SEND] **1.** to differ in belief or opinion; disagree **2.** to reject the doctrines and forms of an established church **—n.** a dissenting; specif., *a*) a minority opinion in the decision of a law case *b*) religious nonconformity **—dis·sent′er** *n.* **—dis·sent′ing** *adj.*

dis·sen·tient (di sen′shənt) *adj.* dissenting, esp. from the majority opinion **—n.** one who dissents

dis·ser·ta·tion (dis′ər tā′shən) *n.* [< L. < pp. of *dissertare*, to discuss < *disserere* < *dis-*, apart + *serere*, to join: see DESERT¹] a long, formal report on some subject, esp. one written in order to get the degree of doctor from a university

dis·serv·ice (dis sur′vis) *n.* harmful action; injury [to do someone a *disservice*]

dis·sev·er (di sev′er) *vt.* **1.** to sever; separate **2.** to divide into parts **—vi.** to separate; disunite **—dis·sev′er·ance, dis·sev′er·ment** *n.*

dis·si·dence (dis′ə dəns) *n.* [< L. < prp. of *dissidere* < *dis-*, apart + *sedere*, SIT] disagreement; dissent

dis·si·dent (-dənt) *adj.* not agreeing; dissenting **—n.** a dissident person; dissenter **—dis′si·dent·ly** *adv.*

dis·sim·i·lar (di sim′ə lər) *adj.* not similar or alike; different **—see SYN.** at DIFFERENT **—dis·sim′i·lar′i·ty** *n.,* pl. **-ties** **—dis·sim′i·lar·ly** *adv.*

dis·sim·i·la·tion (di sim′ə lā′shən) *n.* **1.** a making or becoming dissimilar **2.** the replacement or disappearance of a phoneme when it recurs in the same word (Ex.: Eng. ma*r*ble < OFr. ma*r*bre)

---

fat, āpe, cär; ten, ēven; is, bīte; gō, hôrn, tōol, look; oil, out; up, fur; get; joy; yet; chin; she; thin, then; zh, leisure; ŋ, ring; ə for a in ago, e in agent, i in sanity, o in comply, u in focus; ′ as in able (ā′b'l); Fr. bàl; ë, Fr. coeur; ö, Fr. feu; Fr. mon; ô, Fr. coq; ü, Fr. duc; r, Fr. cri; H, G. ich; kh, G. doch; ‡ foreign; ☆ Americanism; < derived from. See inside front cover.

dis·si·mil·i·tude (dis'si mil'ə tōōd', -tyōōd') *n.* dissimilarity; difference

dis·sim·u·late (di sim'yə lāt') *vt., vi.* -lat'ed, -lat'ing [< L. pp. of *dissimulare*: see DIS- & SIMULATE] to hide (one's feelings, motives, etc.) by pretending to have different ones; dissemble —**dis·sim'u·la'tion** *n.* —**dis·sim'u·la'tor** *n.*

dis·si·pate (dis'ə pāt') *vt.* -pat'ed, -pat'ing [< L. pp. of *dissipare* < *dis-*, apart + *supare*, to throw] **1.** to scatter; disperse **2.** to drive completely away; make disappear [the music *dissipated* his sadness] **3.** to waste or squander [to *dissipate* a fortune] —*vi.* **1.** to be dispelled; vanish **2.** to indulge in pleasure to the point of harming oneself —see SYN. at SCATTER —**dis'si·pat'er, dis'si·pa'tor** *n.* —**dis'si·pa'tive** *adj.*

dis·si·pat·ed (-id) *adj.* **1.** scattered **2.** squandered or wasted **3.** showing the harmful effects of too much drinking, gambling, etc.; dissolute

dis·si·pa·tion (dis'ə pā'shən) *n.* a dissipating or being dissipated; dispersion, squandering, dissoluteness, etc.

dis·so·ci·ate (di sō'shē āt', -sē-) *vt.* -at'ed, -at'ing [< L. pp. of *dissociare* < *dis-*, apart + *sociare*, to join < *socius*, companion] **1.** to break the ties between; sever association with; separate; disunite **2.** to cause to undergo dissociation —*vi.* to undergo dissociation —**dissociate oneself from** to deny or refuse to have any connection with

dis·so·ci·a·tion (di sō'sē ā'shən, -shē-) *n.* **1.** a dissociating or being dissociated **2.** *Chem.* the breaking up of a compound into simpler components **3.** *Psychol.* a split in one's individual consciousness that makes a certain group of mental activities seem to be those of another person —**dis·so'ci·a'tive** *adj.*

dis·sol·u·ble (di säl'yoo b'l) *adj.* that can be dissolved —**dis·sol'u·bil'i·ty** *n.*

dis·so·lute (dis'ə lōōt') *adj.* [< L. pp. of *dissolvere*: see DISSOLVE] dissipated and immoral; debauched —**dis'so·lute'ly** *adv.* —**dis'so·lute'ness** *n.*

dis·so·lu·tion (dis'ə lōō'shən) *n.* a dissolving or being dissolved; specif., *a)* a breaking up or into parts; disintegration [the *dissolution* of an empire] *b)* the termination or ending of something [the *dissolution* of a friendship] *c)* death *d)* the dismissal of an assembly or adjournment of a meeting

dis·solve (di zälv', -zôlv') *vt., vi.* -solved', -solv'ing [< L. *dissolvere* < *dis-*, apart + *solvere*, to loosen: see SOLVE] **1.** to make or become liquid; melt [ice *dissolving* in the sun] **2.** to merge with a liquid; pass or make pass into solution [to *dissolve* sugar in water] **3.** to break up; decompose **4.** to end as by breaking up; terminate [to *dissolve* a partnership] **5.** to disappear or make disappear ☆**6.** *Motion Pictures & TV* to fade out by means of a lap dissolve —☆*n. Motion Pictures & TV* same as LAP DISSOLVE —**dissolved in tears** weeping —**dis·solv'a·ble** *adj.* —**dis·solv'er** *n.*

dis·so·nance (dis'ə nəns) *n.* [< LL. < L. prp. of *dissonare* < *dis-*, apart + *sonare*, to SOUND] **1.** an inharmonious combination of sounds; discord **2.** any lack of harmony or agreement; incongruity **3.** *Music* a chord that sounds harsh and incomplete

dis·so·nant (-nənt) *adj.* **1.** characterized by or constituting a dissonance **2.** opposing in opinion, temperament, etc.; incompatible —**dis'so·nant·ly** *adv.*

dis·suade (di swād') *vt.* -suad'ed, -suad'ing [L. *dissuadere* < *dis-*, away + *suadere*, to persuade] to turn (a person) aside (*from* a course of action, etc.) by persuasion or advice —**dis·suad'er** *n.* —**dis·sua'sion** *n.* —**dis·sua'sive** *adj.*

dis·syl·la·ble (dis'sil'ə b'l) *n.* same as DISYLLABLE —**dis·syl·lab·ic** (dis'si lab'ik) *adj.*

dist. **1.** distance **2.** distinguish **3.** district

dis·taff (dis'taf) *n.* [< OE. < *dis-*, flax + *stæf*, a STAFF] **1.** a staff on which flax, wool, etc. is wound for use in spinning **2.** woman's work or concerns **3.** woman, or women in general —*adj.* female; specif., designating the maternal side of a family

dis·tal (dis't'l) *adj.* [DIST(ANT) + -AL] *Anat.* farthest from the center or the point of attachment or origin —**dis'tal·ly** *adv.*

dis·tance (dis'təns) *n.* [< OFr. < L. < prp. of *distare* < *dis-*, apart + *stare*, to STAND] **1.** the fact or condition of being separated in space or time; remoteness [*distance* lends charm even to ugly objects] **2.** a space between two points **3.** an interval between two points in time **4.** the length of a line between two points [the *distance*

DISTAFF

between Boston and Chicago is 851 miles] **5.** a remoteness in relationship [the *distance* between his views and those of his parents] **6.** a remote point in space or time [viewing things from a *distance*] —*vt.* -tanced, -tanc·ing to leave behind; outdistance —**go the distance** to last through an activity —**keep at a distance** to treat in a cool or unfriendly way —**keep one's distance** to be cool or unfriendly

dis·tant (-tənt) *adj.* **1.** having a space between; separated **2.** widely separated; far apart in space or time **3.** away [ten miles *distant*] **4.** far apart in relationship [a *distant* cousin] **5.** cool in manner; aloof **6.** from or at a distance [a *distant* sound] **7.** faraway or dreamy [a *distant* look] —**dis'tant·ly** *adv.*

dis·taste (dis tāst') *n.* dislike or aversion (*for*)

dis·taste·ful (-fəl) *adj.* **1.** unpleasant to taste **2.** causing distaste; unpleasant; disagreeable —**dis·taste'ful·ly** *adv.* —**dis·taste'ful·ness** *n.*

dis·tem·per¹ (dis tem'pər) *vt.* [< OFr. < ML. *distemperare*, to disorder < L. *dis-*, apart + *temperare*, to mix in proportion] to upset the functions of; derange; disorder —*n.* **1.** a mental or physical disorder; disease **2.** an infectious virus disease of young dogs

dis·tem·per² (dis tem'pər) *n.* [< OFr. < ML. < L. *dis-*, thoroughly + *temperare*: see prec.] [Chiefly Brit.] any of various water-based paints, as for walls, etc.

dis·tend (dis tend') *vt., vi.* [< L. *distendere* < *dis-*, apart + *tendere*, to stretch: see TEND²] **1.** to stretch out **2.** to expand; make or become swollen [a rubber balloon *distended* with air] —see SYN. at EXPAND —**dis·ten'si·ble** *adj.* —**dis·ten'tion, dis·ten'sion** *n.*

dis·tich (dis'tik) *n.* [< L. < Gr. < *di-*, two + *stichos*, a row] two lines of verse one after the other; couplet

dis·tich·ous (-ti kəs) *adj.* [< LL. < Gr.: see DISTICH & -OUS] *Bot.* arranged in two vertical rows, as leaves on opposite sides of a stem —**dis'tich·ous·ly** *adv.*

dis·till, dis·til (dis til') *vi.* -tilled', -till'ing [< OFr. < L. *destillare* < *de-*, down + *stillare*, to drip < *stilla*, a drop] **1.** to fall in drops; drip **2.** to undergo distillation **3.** to be produced as the essence of something —*vt.* **1.** to let fall in drops **2.** to subject to distillation [to *distill* ocean water for drinking] **3.** to remove, extract, etc. by distillation [to *distill* alcohol from fermented grain] **4.** to purify, refine, or concentrate as by distillation

dis·til·late (dis'tə lāt', -t'l it) *n.* **1.** a liquid obtained by distilling **2.** the essence of anything

dis·til·la·tion (dis'tə lā'shən) *n.* **1.** a distilling **2.** the process of heating a mixture to separate out the parts easily turned to vapor, and condensing the resulting vapor to produce a more nearly pure substance **3.** a distillate

dis·tilled (dis tild') *adj.* produced by distillation

dis·till·er (dis til'ər) *n.* **1.** a person or apparatus that distills **2.** a person, company, etc. in the business of distilling alcoholic liquors

dis·till·er·y (-til'ər ē) *n., pl.* -er·ies a place where alcoholic liquors are distilled

dis·tinct (dis tiŋkt') *adj.* [OFr. < L. pp. of *distinguere*: see DISTINGUISH] **1.** not alike; different [brothers with *distinct* personalities] **2.** separate; individual [divided into four *distinct* parts] **3.** easily seen, heard, etc.; plain [a *distinct* image] **4.** well-defined; unmistakable [a *distinct* success] —see SYN. at DIFFERENT —**dis·tinct'ly** *adv.* —**dis·tinct'ness** *n.*

dis·tinc·tion (-tiŋk'shən) *n.* **1.** the act of making or keeping distinct [open to all, without *distinction*] **2.** the condition of being different **3.** a quality or feature that differentiates [the *distinctions* between two breeds of dog] **4.** fame; eminence [a singer of *distinction*] **5.** the quality that makes one seem superior [to serve with *distinction*] **6.** a mark or sign of special recognition or honor

dis·tinc·tive (-tiŋk'tiv) *adj.* making distinct or different from others; characteristic [the *distinctive* markings of a skunk] —see SYN. at CHARACTERISTIC —**dis·tinc'tive·ly** *adv.* —**dis·tinc'tive·ness** *n.*

dis·tin·gué (dis taŋ gā') *adj.* [Fr.] having an air of distinction; distinguished: also, sometimes, **dis·tin·guée'** *fem.*

dis·tin·guish (dis tiŋ'gwish) *vt.* [< L. *distinguere* < *dis-*, apart + *-stinguere*, to prick (for IE. base see STICK): see -ISH, 2] **1.** to perceive or show the difference in; differentiate [to *distinguish* right from wrong] **2.** to characterize [a mammal *distinguished* by its ability to fly] **3.** to recognize plainly by any of the senses [to *distinguish* a faint odor of gas] **4.** to separate and classify **5.** to make famous or eminent [to *distinguish* oneself as a poet]

—*vi.* to make a distinction (*between* or *among*) —**dis·tin′guish-a·ble** *adj.* —**dis·tin′guish·a·bly** *adv.*

SYN.—**distinguish** implies a recognizing or setting apart from others by means of special features or characteristic qualities [to *distinguish* the Asian elephant from the African elephant]; **discriminate** suggests a distinguishing of minute or subtle differences between similar things [to *discriminate* between synonyms]; **differentiate** suggests noticing or pointing out specific differences between things by comparing them in detail [his duties as a son as *differentiated* from those as a brother] —see also **SYN.** at **DISCERN**

dis·tin·guished (-gwisht) *adj.* **1.** celebrated; famous **2.** having an air of distinction —see **SYN.** at **FAMOUS**

dis·tort (dis tôrt′) *vt.* [< L. pp. of *distorquere* < *dis-*, thoroughly + *torquere*, to twist: see **TORT**] **1.** to twist out of its usual shape or look **2.** to misrepresent; pervert [to *distort* the facts] **3.** to modify (a sound, signal, etc.) so that in reproduction it is different —**dis·tort′er** *n.* —**dis·tor′tion** *n.*

dis·tract (dis trakt′) *vt.* [< L. pp. of *distrahere* < *dis-*, apart + *trahere*, to **DRAW**] **1.** to draw (the mind, etc.) away in another direction; divert **2.** to create conflict and confusion in —**dis·tract′ed** *adj.* —**dis·tract′ed·ly** *adv.* —**dis·tract′i·ble** *adj.* —**dis·tract′ing** *adj.* —**dis·tract′ing·ly** *adv.*

dis·trac·tion (-trak′shən) *n.* **1.** a distracting or being distracted; confusion **2.** anything that distracts; specif., *a)* a cause of mental confusion [her constant interruptions were a great *distraction*] *b)* anything that gives mental relaxation [crossword puzzles were the general's favorite *distraction*] **3.** great mental distress or disturbance [to drive a person to *distraction*] —**dis·trac′tive** *adj.*

dis·train (dis trān′) *vt., vi.* [< OFr. < ML. *distringere* < L. < *dis-*, apart + *stringere*, to stretch] *Law* to seize and hold (property) as security or indemnity for a debt —**dis·traint′** *n.*

dis·trait (dis trā′) *adj.* [< OFr. < L. *distrahere*: see **DISTRACT**] absent-minded; inattentive

dis·traught (-trôt′) *adj.* [var. of prec.] **1.** very troubled or confused **2.** driven mad; crazed —see **SYN.** at **ABSENT-MINDED**

dis·tress (dis tres′) *vt.* [< OFr. < ML. < L. pp. of *distringere*: see **DISTRAIN**] to cause sorrow, worry, or suffering to; pain; trouble **2.** to weaken with strain —*n.* **1.** the state of being distressed; pain, suffering, etc. **2.** anything that distresses; affliction **3.** a state of danger [a ship in *distress*] **4.** *Law a)* distraint *b)* the property distrained —**dis·tress′ful** *adj.* —**dis·tress′ful·ly** *adv.* —**dis·tress′ing** *adj.* —**dis·tress′ing·ly** *adv.*

SYN.—**distress** implies mental or physical strain caused by pain, trouble, worry, etc. and usually suggests that the strain could be relieved [*distress* caused by famine]; **suffering** stresses the actual enduring of pain or misery [the *suffering* of the wounded]; **agony** suggests mental or physical torment so intense that it can hardly be endured [in mortal *agony*]; **anguish** is usually applied to extreme mental torment or suffering [the *anguish* she felt when her whole family died]

dis·tressed (-trest′) *adj.* **1.** full of distress; anxious, troubled, etc. **2.** given an antique appearance, as by having the finish marred [*distressed* walnut] **3.** designating an area in which there is much poverty, unemployment, etc. **4.** designating repossessed goods sold at low prices

dis·trib·ute (dis trib′yoot) *vt.* **-ut·ed, -ut·ing** [< L. pp. of *distribuere* < *dis-*, apart + *tribuere*, to allot] **1.** to divide and give out in shares; allot [to *distribute* food to the starving] **2.** to scatter or spread out, as over a surface [*distribute* the paint evenly] **3.** to classify **4.** to put (things) in various distinct places [to *distribute* shrubs in rows along the driveway] —**dis·trib′ut-a·ble** *adj.*

dis·tri·bu·tion (dis′trə byoo′shən) *n.* **1.** a distributing or being distributed; specif., *a)* apportionment by law (*of* funds, etc.) *b)* the process by which commercial products get to consumers *c)* frequency of occurrence or extent of existence **2.** anything distributed; portion; share **3.** *Statistics* the arrangement of a set of numbers classified according to some property, as frequency, or to some other criterion, as time or location —**dis′tri·bu′tion·al** *adj.*

dis·trib·u·tive (dis trib′yoo tiv) *adj.* **1.** distributing or tending to distribute **2.** relating to distribution **3.** *Gram.* referring to each member of a group regarded individually ["each" is a *distributive* word] **4.** *Math.* of the principle in multiplication that allows the multiplier to be used separately with each term of the multiplicand —*n.* a distributive word —**dis·trib′u·tive·ly** *adv.*

dis·trib·u·tor (-tər) *n.* a person or thing that distributes; specif., ☆*a)* an agent or business firm that distributes goods to consumers or dealers ☆*b)* a device for distributing electric current to the spark plugs of a gasoline engine —**dis·trib′u·tor·ship′** *n.*

ENGINE DISTRIBUTOR

dis·trict (dis′trikt) *n.* [Fr. < ML. < L. pp. of *distringere*: see **DISTRAIN**] **1.** a geographical or political division made for a specific purpose [a school *district*] **2.** any region; part of a country, city, etc. —☆*vt.* to divide into districts

☆**district attorney** a lawyer serving in a specified judicial district as a prosecutor for the State or Federal government in criminal cases

☆**district court** **1.** the Federal trial court sitting in each district of the U.S. **2.** in some States, the court of general jurisdiction in each judicial district

District of Columbia [after Christopher **COLUMBUS**] Federal district of the U.S., on the Potomac: 69 sq. mi.; pop. 757,000; the city of Washington takes up the entire area: abbrev. **D.C., DC**

dis·trust (dis trust′) *n.* a lack of trust or of confidence; doubt; suspicion —*vt.* to have no trust or confidence in; doubt; suspect —**dis·trust′ful** *adj.* —**dis·trust′ful·ly** *adv.* —**dis·trust′ful·ness** *n.*

dis·turb (dis tʉrb′) *vt.* [< OFr. < L. *disturbare* < *dis-*, thoroughly + *turbare*, to disorder < *turba*, a mob: see **TURBID**] **1.** to break up the quiet or calm of; agitate [the roar of motorcycles *disturbed* the peace] **2.** to upset mentally or emotionally; make uneasy or anxious [she is *disturbed* by her parents' divorce] **3.** to break up the settled order of **4.** to break in on; interrupt [don't *disturb* him at work] **5.** to inconvenience —**dis·turb′er** *n.*

dis·turb·ance (-əns) *n.* **1.** *a)* a disturbing or being disturbed *b)* any departure from normal **2.** anything that disturbs **3.** commotion; disorder

di·sul·fide (dī sul′fīd) *n.* a chemical compound of two sulfur atoms united with a single radical or with a single atom of an element

dis·un·ion (dis yoon′yən) *n.* **1.** the ending of union; separation **2.** lack of unity; discord

dis·u·nite (dis′yoo nīt′) *vt.* **-nit′ed, -nit′ing** to destroy the unity of; separate —*vi.* to become separated or divided —**dis·u′ni·ty** (-yoo′nə tē) *n.*

dis·use (dis yooz′; *for n.* -yoos′) *vt.* **-used′, -us′ing** to stop using —*n.* lack of use [skills can be lost through *disuse*]

di·syl·la·ble (dī sil′ə b'l, di-; dī′sil′-) *n.* [< Fr. < L. < Gr. < *di-*, two + *syllabē*, **SYLLABLE**] a word of two syllables —**di·syl·lab·ic** (dī′si lab′ik, di′-) *adj.*

ditch (dich) *n.* [OE. *dic:* for IE. base see **DIG**] a long, narrow channel dug into the earth, as a trough for drainage or irrigation —*vt.* **1.** to make a ditch in ☆**2.** to cause (a car, etc.) to go into a ditch **3.** to set (a disabled aircraft) down on water and abandon it ☆**4.** [Slang] to get rid of or get away from —*vi.* **1.** to dig a ditch **2.** to ditch a disabled plane

dith·er (dith′ər) *vi.* [prob. akin to ME. *daderen*, **DODDER**[1]] to be nervously excited or confused —*n.* a nervously excited or confused condition

dith·y·ramb (dith′ə ram′, -ramb′) *n.* [< L. < Gr. *dithyrambos*] **1.** in ancient Greece, a wild choric hymn in honor of Dionysus **2.** any wildly emotional speech or writing —**dith′y·ram′bic** *adj., n.*

dit·to (dit′ō) *n., pl.* **-tos** [It. < L. *dictum*, a saying: see **DICTUM**] **1.** the same (as something stated above or before) **2.** a duplicate **3.** *same as* **DITTO MARK** —*adv.* as said before; likewise —*vt.* **-toed, -to·ing** **1.** to duplicate or make copies of **2.** to indicate repetition of by using ditto marks **3.** to repeat

ditto mark a mark (″) used in lists or tables to show that the item above it is to be repeated

Example: 2 pounds of cheese at $1.25 a pound
3 ″ ″ ham at $1.49 ″ ″

dit·ty (dit′ē) *n., pl.* **-ties** [< OFr. < L. pp. of *dictare*: see **DICTATE**] a short, simple song

ditty bag (or **box**) [< ? obs. *dutty*, coarse calico, orig. Anglo-Ind.] a small bag (or box) used as by sailors for carrying sewing equipment, toilet articles, etc.

---

fat, āpe, cär; ten, ēven; is, bīte; gō, hôrn, tōōl, lookook; oil, out; up, fʉr; get; joy; yet; chin; she; thin, then; zh, leisure; ŋ, ring; ə for *a* in *ago*, *e* in *agent*, *i* in *sanity*, *o* in *comply*, *u* in *focus*; ′ as in *able* (ā′b'l); Fr. bâl; ë, Fr. coeur; ö, Fr. feu; Fr. mon; ô, Fr. coq; ü, Fr. duc; r, Fr. cri; H, G. ich; kh, G. doch; ‡foreign; ☆ Americanism; < derived from. See inside front cover.

di·u·ret·ic (dī′yoo ret′ik) *adj.* [< LL. < Gr. < *dia-*, through + *ourein*, to urinate] increasing the secretion and flow of urine — *n.* a diuretic drug or other substance —**di′u·ret′i·cal·ly** *adv.*

di·ur·nal (dī ur′n'l) *adj.* [< L. < *diurnus* < *dies*, day: see DEITY] 1. happening each day; daily 2. of or in the daytime: opposed to NOCTURNAL —**di·ur′nal·ly** *adv.*

div. 1. dividend 2. division 3. divorced

di·va (dē′və) *n., pl.* **-vas**; It. **-ve** (-ve) [It. < L., goddess: see DEITY] a leading woman singer in grand opera

di·va·gate (dī′və gāt′) *vi.* **-gat′ed, -gat′ing** [< LL. < L. *dis-*, from + *vagari*, to wander] 1. to wander about 2. to stray from the subject; digress —**di′va·ga′tion** *n.*

di·va·lent (dī vā′lənt) *adj. Chem.* same as BIVALENT

di·van (dī′van, di van′) *n.* [< Turk. *dīwān* < Per.] a large, low couch or sofa, usually without armrests or back

dive (dīv) *vi.* **dived** or **dove, dived, div′ing** [OE. *dyfan:* for IE. base see DEEP] 1. to plunge headfirst into water 2. to go under water; submerge, as a submarine 3. to plunge the hand or body suddenly into something [to *dive* into a foxhole] 4. to bring oneself zestfully into something [to *dive* into one's work] 5. to make a steep, sudden descent, as an airplane —*vt.* 1. to cause to dive; specif., to send (one's airplane) into a dive —*n.* 1. a plunge into water 2. any sudden plunge 3. a sharp descent, as of an airplane ☆4. [Colloq.] a cheap, disreputable bar, nightclub, etc. —☆**take a dive** [Slang] to lose a prizefight purposely by pretending to get knocked out

dive bomber an airplane designed to release bombs while diving at a target —**dive′bomb′** *vt., vi.*

div·er (dīv′ər) *n.* one that dives; specif., *a)* one who works or explores under water *b)* any of several diving water birds, esp. the loon

di·verge (də vurj′, dī-) *vi.* **-verged′, -verg′ing** [ML. *divergere* < L. *dis-*, apart + *vergere*, to turn: see VERGE²] 1. to branch off or go in different directions from a common point or from each other [paths *diverge*] 2. to take on gradually a different form [customs *diverge*] 3. to depart from a given viewpoint, practice, etc.; differ

di·ver·gence (-vur′jəns) *n.* 1. a diverging, or branching off 2. a becoming different in form or kind 3. departure from a particular viewpoint, practice, etc. 4. difference of opinion; disagreement Also **di·ver′gen·cy**, *pl.* **-cies**

di·ver·gent (-vur′jənt) *adj.* 1. diverging 2. varying from one another or from a norm; different 3. causing divergence —see SYN. at DIFFERENT —**di·ver′gent·ly** *adv.*

di·vers (dī′vərz) *adj.* [OFr.: see DIVERSE] several; various

di·verse (dī vurs′, də-; dī′vurs) *adj.* [OFr. < L. pp. of *divertere* < *dis-*, apart + *vertere*, to turn: see VERSE] 1. different; dissimilar [the *diverse* customs of the two countries] 2. varied; diversified [the great woman's *diverse* career] —see SYN. at DIFFERENT —**di·verse′ly** *adv.* —**di·verse′ness** *n.*

di·ver·si·fy (də vur′sə fī′) *vt.* **-fied′, -fy′ing** [see prec. & -FY] 1. to make diverse; give variety to; vary [the program of studies is *diversified*] 2. to divide up (investments, liabilities, etc.) among different companies, securities, etc. 3. to expand (a business, etc.) by adding different kinds of products, services, etc. —*vi.* to take on different kinds of businesses or ventures: said esp. of a corporation —**di·ver′si·fi·ca′tion** *n.*

di·ver·sion (də vur′zhən, dī-) *n.* 1. a diverting, or turning aside 2. distraction of attention 3. a pastime or amusement

di·ver·sion·ar·y (-er′ē) *adj.* serving to divert or distract [*diversionary* military tactics]

di·ver·si·ty (də vur′sə tē, dī-) *n., pl.* **-ties** 1. a being diverse; difference 2. variety

di·vert (də vurt′) *vt.* [< OFr. < L. *divertere:* see DIVERSE] 1. to turn aside; deflect [to *divert* the creek into a new channel] 2. to amuse; entertain —see SYN. at AMUSE —**di·vert′ing** *adj.* —**di·vert′ing·ly** *adv.*

di·ver·tic·u·li·tis (dī′vər tik′yoo līt′əs) *n.* [see -ITIS] inflammation of a diverticulum

di·ver·tic·u·lum (dī′vər tik′yoo ləm) *n., pl.* **-la** (-lə) [L. < *devertere* < *de-*, from + *vertere*, to turn] *Anat.* a normal or abnormal pouch or sac opening out from a tubular organ or main cavity

di·ver·ti·men·to (di ver′ti men′tō) *n., pl.* **-ti** (-tē), **-tos** [It.] any of various light, melodic instrumental compositions in several movements

‡di·ver·tisse·ment (dē ver tēs män′; E. di vurt′is mənt) *n.* [Fr.] 1. a diversion; amusement 2. a short ballet, etc. performed between acts of a play or opera

di·vest (də vest′, dī-) *vt.* [altered < earlier *devest*, ult. < L. *devestire* < *dis-*, from + *vestire*, to dress] 1. to strip (of cloth-

ing, etc.) 2. to take away from; deprive [the officer was *divested* of his rank] —**di·vest′i·ture** (-ə chər), **di·vest′ment, di·ves′ture** *n.*

di·vide (də vīd′) *vt.* **-vid′ed, -vid′ing** [< L. *dividere*] 1. to separate into parts; split up 2. to separate into groups; classify [organisms are *divided* into plants and animals] 3. to make or keep separate as by a partition 4. to give out in shares; apportion [*divide* the pie among them] 5. to cause to disagree [the members are *divided* on this issue] 6. *Math.* to separate into equal parts by a divisor 7. *Mech.* to mark off the divisions of; graduate —*vi.* 1. to be or become separate; part 2. to disagree 3. to separate into groups in voting on a question 4. to share 5. *Math.* to do division —*n.* ☆a ridge that divides two drainage areas; watershed —**di·vid′a·ble** *adj.*

di·vid·ed (-id) *adj.* 1. *a)* separated into parts *b)* having a median strip separating traffic [a *divided* highway] *c)* having indentations reaching to the base or midrib, as some leaves 2. disagreeing

div·i·dend (div′ə dend′) *n.* [< L.] 1. the number or quantity to be divided [in 6 ÷ 3, the number 6 is the *dividend*] 2. *a)* a sum of money to be divided among stockholders, creditors, etc. *b)* a single share of this 3. a bonus

di·vid·er (də vīd′ər) *n.* a person or thing that divides; specif., *a)* [*pl.*] an instrument for dividing lines, measuring distances, etc.; compasses *b)* a set of shelves, etc. used to separate a room into distinct areas

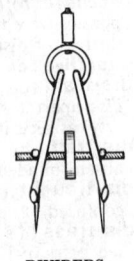

DIVIDERS

div·i·na·tion (div′ə nā′shən) *n.* [< L. < pp. of *divinare:* see DIVINE] 1. the act or practice of trying to foretell the future or the unknown by magic, astrology, etc. 2. a prophecy; augury 3. a successful guess

di·vine (də vīn′) *adj.* [< OFr. < L. *divinus* < *divus*, a god, DEITY] 1. of or like God or a god 2. given or inspired by God; holy; sacred [*divine* scripture] 3. devoted to God; religious [*divine* worship] 4. supremely great, good, etc. 5. [Colloq.] very pleasing, attractive, etc. —*n.* 1. a clergyman 2. a theologian —*vt.* **-vined′, -vin′ing** 1. to prophesy 2. to guess; conjecture 3. to find out by intuition —*vi.* 1. to engage in divination 2. to use a divining rod —see SYN. at HOLY —**di·vine′ly** *adv.* —**di·vin′er** *n.*

Divine Comedy a long narrative poem in Italian, written (c. 1307–1321) by Dante Alighieri

Divine Office the prayers said for each of the canonical hours

divine right of kings the God-given right of kings to rule, as formerly believed

div·ing bell (dīv′iŋ) a large, hollow, air-filled apparatus in which divers can work under water

☆**diving board** a springboard projecting over a swimming pool, lake, etc., for use in diving

diving suit a heavy, waterproof garment worn by divers working under water: it has a detachable helmet into which air is pumped through a hose

divining rod a forked stick alleged to reveal hidden water or minerals by dipping downward

di·vin·i·ty (də vin′ə tē) *n., pl.* **-ties** 1. the quality or condition of being divine 2. a god; deity 3. a divine power, virtue, etc. 4. the study of religion; theology —**the Divinity** God

DIVING SUIT

di·vis·i·ble (də viz′ə b'l) *adj.* that can be divided, esp. without leaving a remainder —**di·vis′i·bil′i·ty** *n.*

di·vi·sion (də vizh′ən) *n.* 1. a dividing or being divided 2. a sharing or distribution 3. a difference of opinion; disagreement 4. a separation into groups in voting 5. anything that divides; partition; boundary 6. anything separated or distinguished from the larger unit of which it is a part; a section, group, rank, segment, etc. 7. the process of finding how many times a number (the *divisor*) is contained in another (the *dividend*): the answer is the *quotient* 8. *Mil.* a major tactical or administrative unit under one command; specif., an army unit larger than a regiment and smaller than a corps —see SYN. at PART —**di·vi′sion·al** *adj.*

division sign (or **mark**) the symbol (÷), indicating that the preceding number is to be divided by the following number (Ex.: 8 ÷ 4 = 2)

di·vi·sive (də vī′siv, -vis′iv) *adj.* causing division; esp., causing disagreement or dissension —**di·vi′sive·ly** *adv.* —**di·vi′sive·ness** *n.*

di·vi·sor (də vī′zər) *n.* [L.] the number or quantity by which the dividend is divided to produce the quotient [in 6 ÷ 3, the number 3 is the *divisor*]

di·vorce (də vôrs′) *n.* [OFr. < L. *divortium* < *divertere*: see DIVERSE] 1. the ending of a marriage in a legal way 2. any complete separation or disunion —*vt.* **-vorced′, -vorc′ing** 1. to end the marriage between in a legal way 2. to separate from (one's spouse) by divorce 3. to separate; disunite —*vi.* to get a divorce —**di·vorce′ment** *n.*

☆**di·vor·cé** (də vôr′sā′, -sē′; -vôr′sā, -sē) *n.* [Fr.] a divorced man

☆**di·vor·cée, di·vor·cee** (də vôr′sā′, -sē′; -vôr′sā, -sē) *n.* [Fr.] a divorced woman

div·ot (div′ət) *n.* [Scot. dial. < ?] *Golf* a lump of turf dislodged in making a stroke

di·vulge (də vulj′) *vt.* **-vulged′, -vulg′ing** [< L. *divulgare* < *dis-*, apart + *vulgare*, to make public < *vulgus*, the common people] to make known; reveal [to *divulge* a secret] —see SYN. at REVEAL —**di·vul′gence** (-vul′jəns), **di·vulge′ment** *n.*

div·vy (div′ē) *vt., vi.* **-vied, -vy·ing** [< DIVIDE] [Slang] to share; divide (*up*) —*n.* [Slang] a division

Dix·ie (dik′sē) *n.* [< title of song (1859) by D.D. Emmett, ult. < proper name] the Southern States of the U.S., as a group

☆**Dixie Cup** *a trademark for* a small, paper drinking cup —[**d- c-**] such a cup

Dix·ie·land (-land′) *adj.* in, of, or like a style of jazz modified by white New Orleans musicians, with a fast, ragtime tempo —*n.* 1. the South; Dixie: also **Dixie Land** 2. Dixieland jazz

diz·en (diz′n, dī′z′n) *vt.* [MDu. *disen*, to put flax on a distaff < LowG. *diesse*, bunch of flax] [Archaic or Poet.] *same as* BEDIZEN

diz·zy (diz′ē) *adj.* **-zi·er, -zi·est** [OE. *dysig*, foolish: for IE. base see DOWN²] 1. feeling giddy or unsteady 2. causing or likely to cause giddiness [*dizzy* heights] 3. confused; bewildered 4. [Colloq.] silly —*vt.* **-zied, -zy·ing** to make dizzy —**diz′zi·ly** *adv.* —**diz′zi·ness** *n.*

D.J., DJ disc jockey

Dja·kar·ta (jə kär′tə) capital of Indonesia, on the NW coast of Java: pop. 4,750,000

Dji·bou·ti (ji boot′ē) country in E Africa, on the Gulf of Aden: 8,500 sq. mi.; pop. 180,000

dkg. decagram; decagrams

dkl. decaliter; decaliters

dkm. decameter; decameters

dl, dl. deciliter; deciliters

D layer the lowest layer of the ionosphere, below the E layer

DM deutsche mark

dm. decimeter; decimeters

DMZ demilitarized zone

DNA deoxyribonucleic acid

Dne·pr (nē′pər; *Russ.* dnye′pər) river in western U.S.S.R., flowing south & southwest into the Black Sea

Dne·pro·pe·trovsk (dnye′prô pye trôfsk′) city in the Ukrainian S.S.R., on the Dnepr: pop. 863,000

Dnes·tr (nēs′tər; *Russ.* dnyes′tər) river in southwestern U.S.S.R., flowing southeast into the Black Sea

do¹ (doo) *vt.* **did, done, do′ing** [OE. *don* < IE. base *dhe-*, to put, set, from which also comes L. *facere*, to do] 1. *a)* to perform (an action, etc.) [*do* great deeds] *b)* to carry out 2. to bring to completion; finish [dinner has been *done* for an hour] 3. to bring about; cause [it *does* no harm] 4. to exert (efforts, etc.) [*do* your best] 5. to deal with as is required; attend to [*do* the ironing] 6. to have as one's occupation; work at 7. to work out; solve [*do* a problem] 8. to produce (a play, etc.) [we *did* Hamlet] 9. to play the role of [she *did* Juliet] 10. to write (a book), compose (a musical score), etc. 11. *a)* to cover (distance) [to *do* a mile in four minutes] *b)* to move along at a speed of [to *do* 60 miles an hour] 12. to give; render [*do* honor to the dead] 13. to be convenient to; suit [this will *do* me very well] 14. [Colloq.] to cheat; swindle [you've been *done*] 15. [Colloq.] to serve (a jail term) —*vi.* 1. to behave [he *does* well when praised] 2. to be active; work [*do;* don't talk] 3. to get along; fare [the patient is *doing* well] 4. to be adequate or suitable [that necktie will *do*] 5. to take place [anything *doing* tonight?] *Do* is also used: 1. to give emphasis [please *do* stay] 2. to ask a question [*did* you write?] 3. to help express negation [*do* not go] 4. to take the place of another verb [love me as I *do* (love) you] 5. to form constructions with the word order shifted after some adverbs [little *did* she realize] —*n., pl.* **do's** or **dos** 1. [Colloq.] a party or social event 2. something to be done —**do by** to act toward or for —**do for** [Colloq.] to ruin; destroy —**do in** [Slang] to kill —**do over** [Colloq.] to redecorate —**do up** [Colloq.] 1. to clean and prepare (laundry, etc.) 2. to wrap up; tie up 3. to arrange (the hair) off the neck and shoulders 4. to tire out; exhaust —**do with** to make use of —**do without** to get along without —**have to do with** 1. to be related to or connected with 2. to deal with —**make do** to get along with what is available —**to do** 1. for keeping one occupied 2. that needs to be done

do² (dō) *n.* [It.: used instead of earlier *ut:* see GAMUT] *Music* a syllable representing the first or last tone of the diatonic scale

do. ditto

D.O. Doctor of Osteopathy

DOA, D.O.A. dead on arrival

do·a·ble (doo′ə b′l) *adj.* that can be done

dob·bin (däb′in) *n.* [< *Dobbin,* nickname for ROBERT (sense 1)] a horse, esp. a plodding, patient one

Do·ber·man pin·scher (dō′bər mən pin′shər) [< G.] a breed of large dog, with smooth, dark hair and tan markings

☆**dob·son·fly** (däb′s′n flī′) *n., pl.* **-flies′** a large insect whose larvae live in water: some males develop huge mandibles

☆**doc** (däk) *n.* [Slang] doctor: often used as a general term of address like *Mac, Bud, Jack,* etc.

doc. document

doc·ile (däs′′l) *adj.* [Fr. < L. *docilis* < *docere,* to teach: for IE. base see DIGNITY] 1. [Now Rare] easy to teach 2. easy to manage or discipline; tractable —see SYN. at OBEDIENT —**doc′·ile·ly** *adv.* —**do·cil·i·ty** (dä sil′ə tē) *n.*

dock¹ (däk) *n.* [< MDu. *docke,* channel < It. *doccia:* see DOUCHE] 1. a large excavated basin with floodgates, for receiving ships between voyages 2. ☆*a)* a landing pier; wharf *b)* the water between two piers ☆3. a platform at which trucks or freight cars are loaded and unloaded ☆4. a building or area for servicing aircraft —*vt.* 1. to pilot (a ship) to a dock ☆2. to join (vehicles) together in outer space —*vi.* 1. to come into a dock ☆2. to join up with another vehicle in outer space

dock² (däk) *n.* [< Fl. *dok,* cage] the place where the accused stands or sits in court

dock³ (däk) *n.* [OE. *docce*] a coarse weed of the buckwheat family, with large leaves

dock⁴ (däk) *n.* [< OE. *-docca* or ON. *dockr*] 1. the solid part of an animal's tail 2. an animal's bobbed tail —*vt.* 1. to cut off the end of (a tail); bob 2. to bob the tail of 3. to deduct from (wages, etc.) 4. to deduct from the wages of 5. to remove part of —**dock′er** *n.*

dock·age¹ (däk′ij) *n.* 1. docking accommodations 2. the fee for this 3. the docking of ships

dock·age² (däk′ij) *n.* a docking, or cutting off

dock·et (däk′it) *n.* [earlier *doggette,* register] 1. a summary, as of legal decisions ☆2. a list of cases to be tried by a law court 3. any list of things to be done or considered; agenda 4. a label listing the contents of a package, directions, etc. —*vt.* ☆1. to enter in a docket 2. to put a docket on; label

dock·side (däk′sīd′) *n.* the area alongside a dock

dock·yard (-yärd′) *n.* a place with docks, machinery, etc. for repairing or building ships

doc·tor (däk′tər) *n.* [< OFr. or < L. *doctor,* teacher < pp. of *docere,* to teach: for IE. base see DIGNITY] 1. orig., a teacher or learned man 2. a person to whom a university or college has granted one of its highest degrees [*Doctor* of Philosophy] 3. a physician or surgeon (M.D.) 4. a person licensed to practice any of the healing arts, as an osteopath, dentist, veterinarian, etc. 5. a witch doctor or medicine man —*vt.* [Colloq.] 1. to try to heal; apply medicine to 2. to repair; mend 3. to tamper with or change in order to deceive [to *doctor* the accounts] —*vi.* [Colloq.] 1. to practice medicine ☆2. to undergo medical treatment, take medicine, etc. —**doc′tor·al** (-əl) *adj.*

doc·tor·ate (-it) *n.* the degree or status of doctor granted by a university or college

---

fat, āpe, cär, ten, ēven, is, bīte; gō, hôrn, tōōl, look; oil, out; up, fur; get; joy; yet; chin; she; thin, *then;* zh, leisure; ŋ, ring; ə for *a* in *ago, e* in *agent, i* in *sanity, o* in *comply, u* in *focus;* ′ as in *able* (ā′b′l); Fr. bàl; ë, Fr. coeur; ö, Fr. feu; Fr. mon; ô, Fr. coq; ü, Fr. duc; r, Fr. cri; H, G. ich; kh, G. doch; ‡foreign; ☆ Americanism; < derived from. See inside front cover.

doc·tri·naire (däk′trə ner′) *n.* [Fr.] a person who insists on applying certain theories regardless of whether they fit the circumstances —*adj.* sticking to a doctrine or theory in a stubborn, unyielding way —see SYN. at DICTATORIAL —**doc′tri·nair′ism** *n.*

doc·trine (däk′trən) *n.* [< L. *doctrina* < *doctor:* see DOCTOR] 1. something taught; teachings 2. something taught as the principles of a religion, political party, etc.; tenet or tenets; dogma 3. a principle of law ☆4. a statement of basic policy [the Monroe *Doctrine*] —**doc′tri·nal** *adj.* —**doc′tri·nal·ly** *adv.*
SYN.—**doctrine** refers to a theory based on carefully worked out principles and taught or advocated by those who believe in it [scientific or social *doctrines*]; **dogma** refers to a belief or doctrine that is handed down by an authority as true and not to be doubted, and often suggests arbitrariness, arrogance, etc. [religious *dogma*]; **tenet** emphasizes the maintenance or defense of a theory or principle rather than the teaching of it [the *tenets* of a political party]

doc·u·ment (däk′yə mənt; *for v.* -ment′) *n.* [OFr. < L. *documentum*, lesson, proof < *docere:* see DOCTOR] 1. anything printed, written, etc. that is relied upon to record or prove something, as a birth certificate 2. anything serving as proof —*vt.* 1. to provide (a book, etc.) with documents or supporting references 2. to prove or support as by reference to documents [these papers *document* his claim] —**doc′u·men′tal** *adj.*

doc·u·men·ta·ry (däk′yə men′tə rē) *adj.* 1. of, in, supported by, or serving as a document or documents 2. dramatically showing or analyzing news events, social conditions, etc., with little or nothing added that is not based on fact —*n., pl.* -**ries** a documentary film, TV show, etc.

doc·u·men·ta·tion (-mən tā′shən, -men-) *n.* 1. the supplying of documents or supporting references 2. the documents or references supplied 3. the collecting, abstracting, and coding of printed or written information for future reference

dod·der[1] (däd′ər) *vi.* [ME. *daderen*] 1. to shake or tremble, as from old age 2. to be unsteady; totter —**dod′der·ing** *adj.*

dod·der[2] (däd′ər) *n.* [ME. *doder*] any of a large group of plants that have no leaves, roots, and chlorophyll and are parasites on other plants

do·dec·a- [< Gr. *dōdeka*, twelve] *a prefix meaning* twelve: also, before a vowel, **do·dec-**

do·dec·a·gon (dō dek′ə gän′) *n.* [< Gr.: see DODECA- & -GON] a plane figure with twelve angles and twelve sides

do·dec·a·he·dron (dō′dek ə hē′drən) *n., pl.* -**drons**, -**dra** (-drə) [< Gr.: see DODECA- & -HEDRON] a solid figure with twelve plane faces —**do·dec·a·he′dral** *adj.*

Do·dec·a·nese (dō dek′ə nēz′, -nēs′) group of Greek islands in the Aegean

dodge (däj) *vi.* **dodged**, **dodg′ing** [? akin to Scot. *dod*, to jog] 1. to move or twist quickly aside, as to avoid a blow 2. to use tricks or evasions —*vt.* 1. to avoid by moving quickly aside 2. to evade by trickery, cleverness, etc. [to *dodge* a question] 3. to avoid meeting —*n.* 1. a dodging 2. a trick used in evading or cheating —**dodg′y** *adj.* **dodg′i·er**, **dodg′i·est**

dodg·er (däj′ər) *n.* 1. a person who dodges 2. a tricky, dishonest person ☆3. a small handbill

Dodg·son (däj′s'n), **Charles Lut·widge** (lut′wij) (pen name *Lewis Carroll*) 1832–98; Eng. writer and mathematician, who wrote *Alice's Adventures in Wonderland*

do·do (dō′dō) *n., pl.* -**dos**, -**does** [Port. *doudo*, lit., foolish, stupid] 1. a large bird, now extinct, that had wings that were too small to be used for flying: formerly found on Mauritius 2. an old-fashioned person; fogy

Doe a name (*John Doe*) used in legal papers, etc. to refer to any person whose name is unknown

doe (dō) *n., pl.* **does**, **doe**: see PLURAL, II, D, 1 [OE. *da*] the female of the deer, or of the antelope, rabbit, or almost any other animal the male of which is called a buck

do·er (dōō′ər) *n.* 1. a person who does something 2. a person who gets things done

DODO
(2 ft. high)

does (duz) *third person singular in the present tense of* DO[1]

doe·skin (dō′skin′) *n.* 1. the skin of a female deer 2. leather made from this or, now usually, from lambskin 3. a fine, soft, smooth woolen cloth

does·n't (duz′′nt) does not

do·est (dōō′ist) *archaic second person singular in the present tense of* DO[1]: *used with* thou

do·eth (-ith) *archaic third person singular in the present tense of* DO[1]: *used with* thou

doff (däf, dôf) *vt.* [ME. *doffen* < *don of:* see DO[1] & OFF] 1. to take off (clothes, etc.); esp., to remove or raise (one's hat) 2. to put aside or discard

dog (dôg, däg) *n., pl.* **dogs**, **dog**: see PLURAL, II, D, 1 [OE. *docga* < ?] 1. any of a large group of animals related to the fox, wolf, jackal, etc. and raised as pets or trained to hunt or herd other animals 2. the male of any of these 3. a mean or bad fellow; scoundrel 4. a prairie dog, dogfish, or other animal thought to resemble a dog 5. an andiron 6. [Colloq.] a boy or man [lucky *dog*] ☆7. [*pl.*] [Slang] feet 8. [Slang] *a)* an unattractive or unpopular person ☆*b)* an unsatisfactory thing or a failure 9. [D-] *Astron.* either of the constellations Great Dog or Little Dog 10. *Mech.* a device for holding or grappling —*vt.* **dogged**, **dog′ging** to follow or hunt like a dog —*adv.* very; completely [*dog*-tired] —**a dog's age** [Colloq.] a long time —**a dog's life** a wretched existence —**dog eat dog** ruthless competition —**dog in the manger** a person who keeps others from using something which he cannot or will not use —**go to the dogs** [Colloq.] to become worse; deteriorate —☆**put on the dog** [Slang] to make a show of being very elegant, wealthy, etc.

dog·bane (dôg′bān′, däg′-) *n.* a plant with small pink or white flowers and milky juice

dog biscuit a hard biscuit containing ground bones, meat, etc., for feeding dogs

dog·cart (-kärt′) *n.* 1. a small, light cart drawn by dogs 2. a small, light, open carriage having two seats arranged back to back

☆**dog·catch·er** (-kach′ər) *n.* a local official whose work is catching and locking up stray animals

dog days the hot, humid days in July and August

doge (dōj) *n.* [It. < L. *dux*, leader: see DUKE] the chief official of either of the former republics of Venice and Genoa

dog·ear (dôg′ir′, däg′-) *n.* a turned-down corner of the leaf of a book —*vt.* to turn down the corner or corners of (a leaf in a book) —**dog′eared′** *adj.*

☆**dog·face** (-fās′) *n.* [Slang] an enlisted man in the army, esp. an infantryman

dog·fight (-fit′) *n.* a rough, violent fight, as between dogs; specif., *Mil.* combat as between fighter planes at close quarters

dog·fish (-fish′) *n., pl.* -**fish′**, -**fish′es**: see FISH 1. any of various small sharks 2. any of several other fishes, as the bowfin

dog·ged (dôg′id, däg′-) *adj.* [see DOG] not giving in readily; persistent; stubborn —see SYN. at STUBBORN —**dog′ged·ly** *adv.* —**dog′ged·ness** *n.*

dog·ger·el (dôg′ər əl, däg′-) *n.* [prob. < It. *doga*, barrel stave] light verse, usually of a comic sort, with a regular rhythm and simple ideas —*adj.* designating or of such verse Also **dog′grel** (-rəl)

☆**dog·gie bag** (dôg′ē, däg′-) a bag supplied to a patron of a restaurant, in which he may place leftovers as to take to his dog

dog·gish (-ish) *adj.* of or like a dog —**dog′gish·ly** *adv.* —**dog′gish·ness** *n.*

dog·gone (dôg′gôn′, däg′gän′) *interj.* damn! darn! —*vt.* -**goned′**, -**gon′ing** [Colloq.] to damn —*n.* [Colloq.] a damn —*adj.* [Colloq.] damned: also **dog′goned′**

dog·gy, **dog·gie** (-ē) *n., pl.* -**gies** a little dog: a child's word —*adj.* -**gi·er**, -**gi·est** 1. of or like a dog ☆2. [Colloq.] stylish and showy

dog·house (-hous′) *n.* a dog's shelter; kennel —☆**in the doghouse** [Slang] in disfavor

☆**do·gie**, **do·gy** (dō′gē) *n., pl.* -**gies** [< ?] in the western U.S., a stray or motherless calf

dog·leg (dôg′leg′, däg′-) *n.* a sharp angle or bend like that formed by a dog's hind leg, as in a golf fairway

dog·ma (dôg′mə, däg′-) *n., pl.* -**mas**, -**ma·ta** (-mə tə) [L. < Gr. < *dokein*, to think] 1. a belief that a church holds and teaches to be truth, not to be doubted; also, all such beliefs of any particular church 2. any belief held as a truth not to be questioned [a matter of scientific *dogma*] —see SYN. at DOCTRINE

dog·mat·ic (dôg mat′ik, däg-) *adj.* 1. of or like dogma 2. said without any proof being offered 3. stating opinion in a positive or arrogant manner: also **dog·mat′i·cal** —see SYN. at DICTATORIAL —**dog·mat′i·cal·ly** *adv.*

dog·ma·tism (dôg′mə tiz′m, däg′-) *n.* the giving of an opinion in a dogmatic way, usually without any evidence being offered —**dog′ma·tist** *n.*

dog·ma·tize (-tīz′) *vi.* -**tized′**, -**tiz′ing** to speak or write dogmatically —*vt.* to formulate or express as dogma —**dog′ma·tiz′er** *n.*

☆**dog·nap** (dôg′nap′, däg′-) *vt.* **-napped′** or **-naped′, -nap′ping** or **-nap′ing** [DOG + (KID)NAP] to steal (a dog), esp. in order to sell it to a medical research laboratory —**dog′nap′per, dog′nap′er** *n.*

☆**do-good·er** (dōō′good′ər) *n.* [Colloq.] a person who seeks to correct social ills in an idealistic, but usually impractical or superficial way —**do′-good′, do·good′ing** *adj.* —**do′-good′ism** *n.*

dog rose a European wild rose with single, pink flowers and hooked spines

dog sled (or **sledge**) a sled (or sledge) drawn by dogs

Dog Star 1. the brightest star in the constellation Canis Major; Sirius 2. Procyon

dog tag 1. a license tag or other tag on a dog to identify it ☆2. [Slang] a tag worn about the neck to identify a member of the armed forces

DOG SLED

dog·tooth (dôg′tōōth′, däg′-) *n.*, *pl.* **-teeth′** a canine tooth

dogtooth violet ☆1. a small American plant of the lily family, with a yellow or white flower 2. a European plant with a purple or rose flower Also **dog′s-tooth violet**

dog·trot (-trät′) *n.* a slow, easy trot

dog·watch (-wäch′, -wôch′) *n.* *Naut.* a duty period, either from 4 to 6 P.M. or from 6 to 8 P.M.

dog·wood (-wood′) *n.* 1. a small tree of eastern U.S., with groups of small flowers surrounded by four large white or pink bracts 2. its hard wood

Do·ha (dō′hə) capital of Qatar, on the Persian Gulf: pop. 100,000

doi·ly (doi′lē) *n.*, *pl.* **-lies** [after name of a 17th-c. London draper] a small mat, as of lace or paper, used to protect or decorate a surface

do·ings (dōō′iŋz) *n.pl.* things done; actions, events, etc.

☆**do-it-your·self** (dōō′it yoor self′) *n.* the practice of constructing, repairing, redecorating, etc. by oneself instead of hiring another to do it —*adj.* of, used for, or engaged in do-it-yourself

dol. *pl.* **dols.** dollar

dol·drums (däl′drəmz, dōl′-) *n.pl.* [< ? ME. *dul*, DULL] 1. low spirits; dull, listless feeling 2. sluggishness; stagnation 3. equatorial ocean regions noted for dead calms and light, fluctuating winds

dole[1] (dōl) *n.* [OE. *dal*] 1. a giving out of money or food to those in need 2. that which is thus given out 3. anything given out sparingly 4. a form of payment by a government to the unemployed —*vt.* **doled, dol′ing** to give out in small amounts or as a dole [the cashier *doled* out my change coin by coin] —**on the dole** receiving a dole (sense 4)

dole[2] (dōl) *n.* [see DOLEFUL] [Archaic] sorrow

dole·ful (dōl′fəl) *adj.* [< OFr. < VL. < L. *dolere*, to suffer + *-ful*, -FUL] full of sorrow or sadness; mournful: also [Rare] **dole′some** —see SYN. at SAD —**dole′ful·ly** *adv.* —**dole′ful·ness** *n.*

dol·i·cho·ce·phal·ic (däl′i kō′sə fal′ik) *adj.* [< Gr. *dolichos*, long + -CEPHALIC] having a relatively long head: also **dol′i·cho·ceph′a·lous** (-sef′ə ləs): see CEPHALIC INDEX —**dol′i·cho·ceph′a·ly** (-ə lē) *n.*

doll (däl) *n.* [< *Doll*, nickname for DOROTHY] 1. a child's toy made to resemble a human being 2. a pretty but silly young woman 3. a pretty child 4. [Slang] *a)* any young woman *b)* any lovable person —*vt.*, *vi.* [Colloq.] to dress stylishly or showily (with *up*)

dol·lar (däl′ər) *n.* [< LowG. & Early ModDu. < G. *thaler*, contr. < *Joachimsthaler*, coin made at *Joachimstal*, Bohemia] ☆1. the monetary unit of the U.S., equal to 100 cents: symbol, $ 2. the monetary unit of various other countries, as of Canada, Australia, Ethiopia, etc.: see MONETARY UNITS, table 3. a monetary unit used only in trade, as the British Hong Kong dollar 4. a coin or paper bill of the value of a dollar

☆**dollar diplomacy** the use of the economic power of a govern-

ment to promote in other countries the business interests of its corporations, etc.

☆**dollar sign** (or **mark**) a symbol, $, for dollar(s)

dol·lop (däl′əp) *n.* [< ?] 1. a soft mass, as of some food 2. a splash, jigger, etc. of liquid 3. a small amount [the story has a *dollop* of wit]

dol·ly (däl′ē) *n.*, *pl.* **-lies** 1. a doll: child's word ☆2. any of several kinds of low, flat, wheeled frames or platforms for moving heavy objects —*vi.* **-lied, -ly·ing** to move a camera on a dolly (*in*, *out*, etc.) as in televising —*vt.* to move on a dolly

dol·man sleeve (däl′mən, dōl′-) [< Fr. < Turk. *dolama*, long robe] a kind of sleeve for a woman's coat or dress, tapering from a wide opening at the armhole to a narrow one at the wrist

dol·men (däl′mən, dōl′-) *n.* [Fr. < Bret. *taol*, a table + *men*, stone] a prehistoric monument formed by a large, flat stone laid across upright stones

do·lo·mite (dō′lə mīt′, däl′ə-) *n.* [after the Fr. geologist *Dolomieu* (1750–1801)] a common rock-forming mineral, $CaMg(CO_3)_2$

do·lor (dō′lər) *n.* [< OFr. < L. *dolor* < *dolere*, to suffer] [Poet.] sorrow; grief

Do·lor·es (də lôr′əs) [Sp. < *Maria de los Dolores*, lit., Mary of the sorrows] a feminine name

do·lor·ous (dō′lər əs, däl′ər-) *adj.* 1. sorrowful or sad; mournful 2. painful —**do′lor·ous·ly** *adv.*

DOLMAN SLEEVE

dol·phin (däl′fən, dôl′-) *n.* [< OFr. < L. < Gr. *delphis* (gen. *delphinos*)] 1. any of several water-dwelling mammals with numerous teeth and often a beaklike snout 2. either of two ocean fishes that change to bright colors out of water

dolt (dōlt) *n.* [prob. < ME. pp. of *dullen*, to DULL] a stupid, slow-thinking person; blockhead —**dolt′ish** *adj.* —**dolt′ish·ly** *adv.* —**dolt′ish·ness** *n.*

-dom (dəm) [OE. *dom*, state: see DOOM] a suffix meaning: 1. the rank, position, or dominion of [*kingdom*] 2. fact or state of being [*martyrdom*] 3. a total of all who are [*officialdom*]

dom. 1. domestic 2. dominion

do·main (dō mān′, də-) *n.* [< MFr. < L. < *dominus*, a lord: see DOMINATE] 1. territory under one government or ruler 2. land belonging to one person; estate 3. field or sphere of activity or influence [the *domain* of science] 4. *Math.* the set of possible values that the independent variable of a function can take on

BOTTLE-NOSED DOLPHIN
(70–160 in. long)

dome (dōm) *n.* [< Fr. < Pr. < LL. < Gr. *dōma*, housetop, house < IE. base *dem-*, to build] 1. a round roof shaped more or less like half a globe 2. any dome-shaped structure 3. [Slang] the head —*vt.* **domed, dom′ing** 1. to cover as with a dome 2. to form into a dome —*vi.* to swell out like a dome

do·mes·tic (də mes′tik) *adj.* [< OFr. < L. *domesticus* < *domus*, house: see prec.] 1. of the home or family [*domestic* joys] 2. of one's own country or the country referred to [Canada's *domestic* affairs] 3. made in the home country; native [*domestic* wine] 4. domesticated; tame: said of animals 5. devoted to home and family life —*n.* a servant for the home, as a maid —**do·mes′ti·cal·ly** *adv.*

do·mes·ti·cate (də mes′tə kāt′) *vt.* **-cat′ed, -cat′ing** 1. to accustom to home life; make domestic 2. *a)* to tame (wild animals) *b)* to adapt and cultivate (wild plants) for human use 3. to naturalize (a custom, word, etc.) from another country —*vi.* to become domestic —**do·mes′ti·ca′tion** *n.*

do·mes·tic·i·ty (dō′mes tis′ə tē) *n.*, *pl.* **-ties** 1. home life; family life 2. devotion to home and family life 3. [*pl.*] household affairs

☆**domestic science** same as HOME ECONOMICS

dom·i·cile (däm′ə sīl′, -sil; dō′mə-) *n.* [OFr. < L. < *domus*, house: see DOME] a customary dwelling place; one's house or home; residence —*vt.* **-ciled′, -cil′ing** to establish (oneself or another) in a domicile —**dom′i·cil′i·ar′y** (-sil′ē er′ē) *adj.*

dom·i·nance (däm′ə nəns) *n.* a dominating; being dominant; control; authority: also **dom′i·nan·cy**

dom·i·nant (-nənt) *adj.* **1.** dominating; ruling; prevailing /the *dominant* idea of a speech/ **2.** *Genetics* designating or of that one of any pair of allelic characters which, when both are presents in the germ plasm, dominates over the other and appears in the organism: opposed to RECESSIVE **3.** *Music* of or based upon the fifth note of a diatonic scale —*n.* **1.** *Genetics* a dominant character or factor **2.** *Music* the fifth note of a diatonic scale —**dom′i·nant·ly** *adv.*

dom·i·nate (-nāt′) *vt., vi.* -**nat′ed, -nat′ing** [< L. pp. of *dominari,* to rule < *dominus,* a master: for IE. base see DOME] **1.** to rule or control by superior power or influence /small nations *dominated* by superpowers/ **2.** to tower over; rise high above (the surroundings, etc.) /that building *dominates* the city/ —**dom′i·na′tion** *n.* —**dom′i·na′tor** *n.*

dom·i·neer (däm′ə nir′) *vi., vt.* [< Du. < Fr. < L.: see prec.] to rule (*over*) in a harsh or bullying way; tyrannize

dom·i·neer·ing (-iŋ) *adj.* overbearing; tyrannical; bullying —see SYN. at MASTERFUL —**dom′i·neer′ing·ly** *adv.*

Dom·i·nic (däm′ə nik) [L. *Dominicus,* lit., belonging to a lord < *dominus,* a master] **1.** a masculine name **2.** Saint, 1170–1221; Sp. priest: founder of the Dominican order

Dom·i·ni·ca (däm′ə nē′kə, də min′i kə) a country that is an island in the Windward group of the West Indies: 290 sq. mi.; pop. 80,000

Do·min·i·can (də min′i kən) *adj.* **1.** of Saint Dominic or of a religious order founded by him **2.** of the Dominican Republic —*n.* **1.** a friar or nun of one of the Dominican orders **2.** a native or inhabitant of the Dominican Republic

Dominican Republic country occupying the E part of Hispaniola, in the West Indies: 18,816 sq. mi.; pop. 4,188,000; cap. Santo Domingo

dom·i·nie (däm′ə nē) *n.* [< vocative case (*domine*) of L. *dominus:* see DOMINATE] **1.** in Scotland, a schoolmaster **2.** [Colloq.] a clergyman

do·min·ion (də min′yən) *n.* [< ML. *dominio* < L. *dominus:* see DOMINATE] **1.** rule or power to rule; sovereignty **2.** a governed territory or country **3.** [D-] formerly, any of certain self-governing member nations of the Commonwealth —see SYN. at POWER

Dominion Day in Canada, July 1, a legal holiday, the anniversary of the proclamation in 1867 of the establishment of the Dominion of Canada

dom·i·no (däm′ə nō′) *n., pl.* -**noes, -nos′** [Fr. & It. < dat. of L. *dominus:* see DOMINATE] **1.** a loose cloak with wide sleeves, hood, and mask, worn at masquerades **2.** a small mask for the eyes; half mask **3.** one dressed in such a cloak or mask **4.** a small, oblong piece of wood, etc. marked with dots **5.** [*pl.,* with sing. *v.*] a game played with a number of such pieces, usually 28

☆**domino theory** the theory that a certain result (**domino effect**) will follow a certain cause, as a row of dominoes standing on

DOMINOES

edge will fall if the first is pushed; specif., the theory that if a nation becomes a Communist state, the nations nearby will also

Don (dän; *Russ.* dôn) river of the C European R.S.F.S.R., flowing south into the Sea of Azov

don1 (dän) *n.* [Sp. < L. *dominus:* see DOMINATE] **1.** [D-] Sir; Mr.: a Spanish title of respect **2.** a Spanish nobleman or gentleman **3.** a distinguished man **4.** [Colloq.] a head, tutor, or fellow of any college of Oxford or Cambridge

don2 (dän) *vt.* **donned, don′ning** [contr. of *do on*] to put on (a garment, etc.)

‡**Do·ña** (dô′nyä) *n.* [Sp. < L. *domina,* mistress] **1.** Lady; Madam: a Spanish title of respect **2.** [d-] a Spanish lady

Don·ald (dän′ld) [Ir. *Donghal,* lit., brown stranger (or ? Gael. *Domhnall,* lit., world ruler)] a masculine name: dim. *Don*

☆**do·nate** (dō′nāt, dō nāt′) *vt., vi.* -**nat·ed, -nat·ing** [prob. back-formation < DONATION] to give or contribute, as to some cause —**do′na·tor** *n.*

Do·na·tel·lo (dän′ə tel′ō) (born *Donato di Niccolò di Betto Bardi*) 1386?–1466; It. sculptor

do·na·tion (dō nā′shən) *n.* [< L. < pp. of *donare* < *donum,* gift] **1.** the act of donating **2.** a gift or contribution —see SYN. at PRESENT

done (dun) *pp. of* DO1 —*adj.* **1.** completed **2.** sufficiently cooked **3.** socially acceptable —**done (for)** [Colloq.] dead,

ruined, finished, etc. —**done in** [Colloq.] exhausted; worn out

do·nee (dō nē′) *n.* one who receives a donation

Do·nets (də nets′; *Russ.* dô nyets′) river in SW European U.S.S.R., flowing into the Don

Do·netsk (dô nyetsk′) city in SE Ukrainian S.S.R., in the Donets River valley: pop. 855,000

dong1 (dôŋ, däŋ) *n.* [echoic] the sound of a large bell

dong2 (dôŋ) *n. see* MONETARY UNITS, table (Vietnam)

Don·i·zet·ti (dän′ə zet′ē), **Ga·e·ta·no** (gä′e tä′nō) 1797–1848; It. composer of operas

don·jon (dun′jən, dän′-) *n.* [old sp. of DUNGEON] the heavily fortified inner tower of a castle

Don Ju·an (dän′ jōō′ən, dän′ wän′; *Sp.* dôn Hwän′) **1.** *Sp. Legend* a dissolute nobleman and seducer of women **2.** any man who seduces women; libertine

don·key (däŋ′kē, dôŋ′-, duŋ′-) *n., pl.* -**keys** [< ? DUNCAN or < ? DUN1] **1.** a domesticated ass: see ASS (sense 1) **2.** a stupid or stubborn person **3.** a small steam engine: in full, **donkey engine**

Don·na (dän′ə) [It. < L. *domina,* mistress] a feminine name —*n.* (It. dôn′nä) **1.** Lady; Madam: an Italian title of respect **2.** [d-] an Italian lady

Donne (dun), **John** 1573–1631; Eng. poet

don·nish (dän′ish) *adj.* of or like a university don; esp., learned but boring —**don′nish·ly** *adv.* —**don′nish·ness** *n.*

don·ny·brook (dän′ē brook′) *n.* [< a fair formerly held at *Donnybrook,* Ireland: scene of many fights] [Colloq.] a rough, rowdy fight or free-for-all

do·nor (dō′nər) *n.* [< Anglo-Fr. < L. *donator*] **1.** one who donates something; giver **2.** one from whom blood for transfusion, tissue for grafting, etc. is taken

Don Qui·xo·te (dän′ kē hōt′ē, dän′ kwik′sət; *Sp.* dôn′ kē Hō′te) **1.** a satirical romance by Cervantes **2.** the chivalrous hero of this romance, who does mad, foolish things trying to help those in need and to fight evil

don't (dōnt) **1.** do not **2.** does not /"he *don't,*" "she *don't,*" and "it *don't*" are not now considered to be standard/

do·nut (dō′nut′) *n. informal sp. for* DOUGHNUT

☆**doo·dad** (dōō′dad′) *n.* [fanciful extension of DO1] [Colloq.] **1.** a trinket **2.** any small object or device whose name one does not or cannot recall

doo·dle (dōōd′'l) *vi.* -**dled, -dling** [G. *dudeln,* to play (the bagpipe), hence to trifle] ☆to scribble or draw aimlessly, esp. when one's attention is elsewhere —*n.* ☆a mark, design, etc. made in doodling —**doo′dler** *n.*

☆**doo·dle·bug** (-bug′) *n.* [prec. + BUG] *same as* ANT LION (sense 1)

☆**doo·hick·ey** (dōō′hik′ē) *n.* [fanciful extension of DO1] [Colloq.] any small object or device whose name one does not know or cannot quite remember

doom (dōōm) *n.* [OE. *dom,* lit., decree: for IE. base see DO1] **1.** a judgment; esp., a sentence that condemns a guilty person to some punishment /the judge pronounced her *doom*/ **2.** destiny or fate; esp., a tragic fate that brings ruin or death /its *doom* was sealed when the dog started chasing cars/ —*vt.* **1.** to pass judgment on; condemn /Louis XVI was *doomed* to the guillotine/ **2.** to destine to a tragic fate or to disaster, etc. /his plans are *doomed* to failure/ —see SYN. at FATE

dooms·day (dōōmz′dā′) *n.* **1.** *same as* JUDGMENT DAY **2.** any day of judgment

door (dôr) *n.* [OE. *dor, duru* < IE. base *dhiver-,* door] **1.** a structure of boards, panels, etc. for opening or closing an entrance, as to a building, room, closet, etc.: most doors turn on hinges, slide in grooves, or revolve on an axis **2.** the room or building to which a particular door belongs /the class meets two *doors* down the hall/ **3.** *same as* DOORWAY —**lay at the door of** to blame (a person) for —**out of doors** outdoors —**show (someone) the door** to command (someone) to leave

door·bell (dôr′bel′) *n.* a bell rung by someone wishing to enter a building or room

door·jamb (-jam′) *n.* a vertical piece of wood, etc. forming the side of a doorway: also **door′post** (-pōst′)

door·keep·er (-kēp′ər) *n.* a person guarding the entrance of a house, hotel, etc.; porter

door·knob (-näb′) *n.* a small knob or lever on a door, usually for releasing the latch

door·man (-man′, -mən) *n., pl.* -**men** (-men′, -mən) a man whose work is opening the door of a building for those who enter or leave, hailing taxicabs, etc.

door·mat (-mat′) *n.* a mat to wipe the shoes on before entering a house, room, etc.

door·nail (-nāl′) *n.* a large-headed nail used in studding some doors —**dead as a doornail** dead beyond a doubt

door·plate (-plāt′) *n.* a plate on an entrance door, bearing the number, a name, etc.

☆**door prize** a prize given by lottery to one or more of those attending some gathering

door·sill (-sil′) *n.* a length of wood, masonry, etc. fastened to the floor beneath a door; threshold

door·step (-step′) *n.* a step that leads from an outer door to a path, lawn, etc.

door·stop (-stäp′) *n.* any device for controlling or stopping the closing of a door

☆**door-to-door** (-tə dôr′) *adj., adv.* from one home to the next, calling on each in turn [a *door-to-door* salesman]

door·way (-wā′) *n.* **1.** an opening in a wall that can be closed by a door **2.** any way to go in or out; passage; access

☆**door·yard** (-yärd′) *n.* a yard onto which a door of a house opens

☆**doo·zy** (dōō′zē) *n., pl.* **-zies** [< ?] [Slang] anything outstanding of its kind

☆**do·pa·mine** (dō′pə mēn′, -min) *n.* an amine whose presence in the brain is important to normal nerve activity

☆**dope** (dōp) *n.* [Du. *doop*, sauce < *doopen*, to dip: for IE. base see DEEP] **1.** any thick liquid or paste used to lubricate or absorb something **2.** a varnish or filler, as for protecting the cloth covering of airplane wings **3.** any additive, as a food preservative **4.** [Slang] any drug or narcotic, or such drugs as a group **5.** [Slang] a slow-witted or stupid person **6.** [Slang] information, esp. as used for predicting **7.** *Photog.* a developer —*vt.* **doped, dop′ing 1.** to give dope to **2.** to drug or stupefy **3.** to add an adulterant or impure substance to (another substance) —**dope out** [Colloq.] to figure out or work out —**dop′er** *n.*

☆**dope·ster** (dōp′stər) *n.* [Colloq.] a person who analyzes or predicts trends in politics, sports, etc.

☆**dop·ey, dop·y** (dō′pē) *adj.* **dop′i·er, dop′i·est** [Slang] **1.** under the influence of a narcotic **2.** mentally confused **3.** dull, sluggish, or stupid —**dop′i·ness** *n.*

Dor·a (dôr′ə) [dim. of DOROTHEA] a feminine name

Dor·dogne (dôr dōn′y′) river in SW France, uniting with the Garonne to form the Gironde estuary

Do·ré (dô rā′), (**Paul**) **Gus·tave** (güs tàv′) 1832?–83; Fr. artist

Dor·ic (dôr′ik, där′-) *adj.* [< L. < Gr. *Dorikos*, of *Dōris*: see DORIS] designating or of the simplest of the three orders of Greek architecture, having fluted, heavy columns with simple capitals: see also CORINTHIAN and IONIC

Dor·is (dôr′is, där′-) [L. < Gr. *Dōris*] **1.** a feminine name **2.** ancient mountainous region in what is now WC Greece: see map at GREECE —**Do·ri·an** (dôr′ē ən) *adj., n.*

☆**dorm** (dôrm) *n.* [Colloq.] same as DORMITORY

dor·mant (dôr′mənt) *adj.* [OFr. prp. of *dormir* < L. *dormire*, to sleep] **1.** sleeping **2.** as if asleep; quiet; still **3.** inactive or not moving or growing, as some animals or plants in winter —**dor′man·cy** (-mən sē) *n.*

dor·mer (dôr′mər) *n.* [< OFr. < L. *dormitorium*: see DORMITORY] **1.** a window set upright in a sloping roof **2.** the roofed projection in which this window is set Also **dormer window**

dor·mi·to·ry (dôr′mə tôr′ē) *n., pl.* **-ries** [L. *dormitorium* < pp. of *dormire*, to sleep] **1.** a large room with beds for a number of people **2.** a building with many rooms for a number of people to sleep in and live in, as at a college

dor·mouse (dôr′mous′) *n., pl.* **-mice′** (-mīs′) [? altered by folk etym. (after *mous*, MOUSE) < OFr. *dormeuse*, sleepy < *dormir*: see DORMANT] a small, old-world rodent that resembles a squirrel

Dor·o·the·a (dôr′ə thē′ə, där′-) [L. < Gr. *Dōrothea*, lit., gift of God < *dōron*, gift + *theos*, God] a feminine name: dim. *Dolly, Dora, Dotty*

Dor·o·thy (dôr′ə thē, där′-) [< DOROTHEA] a feminine name

dor·sal (dôr′s′l) *adj.* [< ML. < L. *dorsum*, the back] of, on, or near the back —**dor′sal·ly** *adv.*

Dort·mund (dôrt′mŏŏnt; *E.* dôrt′mənd) city in W West Germany: pop. 649,000

DORMER

do·ry (dôr′ē) *n., pl.* **-ries** [AmInd. (Central America) *dori*, a dugout] a small, flat-bottomed fishing boat with high sides

dos·age (dōs′ij) *n.* **1.** a dosing or being dosed **2.** the system to be followed in taking doses, as of medicine [the prescribed *dosage* is one teaspoon every 4 hours] **3.** the amount used in a dose

dose (dōs) *n.* [OFr. < ML. < Gr. *dosis*, orig., a giving < *didonai*, to give] **1.** an amount of medicine to be taken at one time or at stated intervals **2.** amount of a punishment or other unpleasant experience undergone at one time **3.** the amount of ionizing radiation delivered to a specified area or body part —*vt.* **dosed, dos′ing** to give doses of medicine to —*vi.* to take a dose of medicine

do·sim·e·ter (dō sim′ə tər) *n.* [see DOSE & -METER] a small device for measuring the radiation a person has absorbed

dos·si·er (däs′ē ā′, dôs′-) *n.* [Fr. < *dos*, the back: so named because labeled on the back] a collection of documents about some person or matter

dost (dust) *archaic second person singular in the present tense of* DO[1]: *used with* thou (chiefly as an auxiliary)

Dos·to·ev·ski (dôs′tô yef′skē), **Feo·dor** (**Mikhailovich**) (fyô′dôr) 1821–81; Russ. novelist

dot[1] (dät) *n.* [OE. *dott*, head of boil] **1.** a tiny spot, speck, or mark; point; as, *a)* the mark placed above an *i* or *j b) Music* a point after a note, increasing its time value by one half; also, a point above or below a note to show it is staccato **2.** any small, round spot **3.** a short sound or click, as in Morse code —*vt.* **dot′ted, dot′ting 1.** to mark with a dot or dots **2.** to cover as with dots [trees *dotted* the landscape] —*vi.* to make a dot or dots —**dot one's i's and cross one's t's** to be minutely correct —**on the dot** [Colloq.] at the exact time —**dot′ter** *n.*

dot[2] (dät) *n.* [Fr. < L. *dos* (gen. *dotis*) < *dare*, to give] a woman's marriage dowry —**do·tal** (dōt′′l) *adj.*

dot·age (dōt′ij) *n.* [ME. < *doten*, DOTE] **1.** feeble and childish state due to old age; senility **2.** a doting; foolish or excessive affection

dot·ard (-ərd) *n.* [ME. < *doten*, DOTE] a foolish and doddering old person

dote (dōt) *vi.* **dot′ed, dot′ing** [ME. *doten*] **1.** to be foolish or weak-minded, esp. because of old age **2.** to be excessively or foolishly fond (with *on* or *upon*) —**dot′er** *n.* —**dot′ing** *adj.* —**dot′ing·ly** *adv.*

doth (duth) *archaic third person singular in the present tense of* DO[1] (chiefly in auxiliary uses)

dot·ter·el (dät′ər əl) *n., pl.* **-els, -el:** see PLURAL, II, D, 1 [< DOTE, because easy to catch] a European and Asian plover with a short bill

dot·tle, dot·tel (dät′′l) *n.* [< ME. var. of *dosel*, a plug] the tobacco plug left in the bowl of a pipe after it has been smoked

dot·ty (dät′ē) *adj.* **-ti·er, -ti·est 1.** covered with dots; dotted **2.** [Colloq.] feeble; unsteady **3.** [Colloq.] feeble-minded or crazy

Dou·ay Bible (dōō ā′) [< *Douai*, in France, where it was published in part (1609–10)] an English translation of the Bible from the Vulgate, for Roman Catholics: also **Douay Version**

dou·ble (dub′′l) *adj.* [OFr. < L. *duplus*, lit., twofold] **1.** having two parts that are alike; twofold; duplex [a *double* house] **2.** having two layers; folded in two **3.** having two of one kind; repeated [a *double* consonant] **4.** being of two kinds; dual [a *double* standard] **5.** having two meanings; ambiguous **6.** twice as much, as many, as large, etc. [a *double* portion] **7.** of extra size, value, strength, etc. **8.** made for two [a *double* bed] **9.** two-faced; deceiving [to live a *double* life] **10.** having a tone an octave lower [*double* bass] **11.** *Bot.* having more than one set of petals —*adv.* **1.** twofold **2.** two together; in a pair [to ride *double* on a horse] —*n.* **1.** anything twice as much, as many, or as large as normal **2.** a person or thing looking very much like another; duplicate; counterpart **3.** a stand-in, as in motion pictures **4.** a fold; second ply **5.** a sharp shift of direction **6.** a trick; shift **7.** [*pl.*] a game of tennis, handball, etc. with two players on each side ☆**8.** *Baseball* a hit on which the batter reaches second base **9.** *Bridge a)* the doubling of an opponent's bid *b)* a hand that makes this possible —*vt.* **-bled, -bling 1.** to make twice as much or many [to *double* the recipe] **2.** to fold **3.** to repeat or duplicate **4.** to be the double of ☆**5.** *Baseball a)* to put out (the second runner) in executing a

double play *b*) to advance (a runner) by hitting a double **6.** *Bridge* to increase the point value or penalty of (an opponent's bid) **7.** *Naut.* to sail around [they *doubled* Cape Horn] —*vi.* **1.** to become double **2.** to turn sharply backward [the animal *doubled* on its tracks] **3.** to serve as a double [the living room *doubles* as a dining area] **4.** to serve an additional purpose or function ☆**5.** [Colloq.] to double-date ☆**6.** *Baseball* to hit a double —**double back 1.** to fold back **2.** to turn back in the direction from which one came —**double up 1.** to fold completely; clench (one's fist) **2.** to bend over, as in laughter or pain **3.** to share a room, etc. with someone —**on** (or **at**) **the double** [Colloq.] **1.** in double time **2.** quickly —**dou′bler** *n.*

double agent a spy who secretly gets into an enemy espionage organization in order to betray it

dou·ble-bar·reled (dub′'l bar′əld) *adj.* **1.** having two barrels, as a kind of shotgun **2.** having a double purpose or meaning [a *double-barreled* remark]

double bass (bās) the largest and deepest-toned instrument of the violin family (orig. of the viol family), with a range of approximately three octaves

double bassoon *same as* CONTRABASSOON

☆**double boiler** a utensil consisting of two pans, one of which fits over the other; food is cooked in the upper one by water boiling in the lower

dou·ble-breast·ed (-bres′tid) *adj.* overlapping across the breast and having a double row of buttons, as a coat

☆**dou·ble-check** (-chek′) *vt., vi.* to check again; verify —*n.* the act of double-checking

double chin a fold of flesh beneath the chin

dou·ble-cross (-krôs′) *vt.* [Colloq.] to betray (a person) by not doing what one has promised or, esp., by doing the opposite —**dou′ble-cross′er** *n.*

double cross [Colloq.] a double-crossing; treachery

double dagger a mark (‡) used in printing and writing to indicate a note or cross-reference

☆**dou·ble-date** (-dāt′) *vi., vt.* -**dat′ed**, -**dat′ing** [Colloq.] to go out on a double date (*with*)

☆**double date** [Colloq.] a social engagement shared by two couples

dou·ble-deal·ing (-dēl′iŋ) *n.* the act of doing the opposite of what one pretends to do; duplicity —**dou′ble-deal′er** *n.*

dou·ble-deck·er (-dek′ər) *n.* **1.** any structure or vehicle with two levels ☆**2.** [Colloq.] a sandwich with two layers of filling

dou·ble-edged (-ejd′) *adj.* **1.** having two cutting edges **2.** that can be used either for or against, as an argument

dou·ble-en·ten·dre (dōō′blän tän′dr∂, dub′'l än-) *n.* [Fr. (now obs.), double meaning] a word or phrase with two meanings, esp. when one of them is risqué or indecent

double entry a system of bookkeeping in which each transaction is entered as a debit and a credit

double exposure *Photog.* **1.** the making of two exposures on the same film or plate **2.** a photograph resulting from this

dou·ble-faced (dub′'l fāst′) *adj.* **1.** having two faces or aspects **2.** hypocritical; insincere

☆**double feature** two full-length motion pictures on the same program

☆**dou·ble-head·er** (-hed′ər) *n.* two games played one after the other on the same day, esp. baseball games

☆**double indemnity** a clause in some insurance policies providing for the payment of twice the face value of the contract for accidental death

☆**double jeopardy** *Law* the jeopardy in which a defendant is placed by a second prosecution for the same offense: prohibited by the U.S. Constitution

dou·ble-joint·ed (-join′tid) *adj.* having joints that permit limbs, fingers, etc. to bend at other than the usual angles

dou·ble-knit (-nit′) *adj.* knit with a double stitch, which gives extra thickness to the fabric

☆**dou·ble-park** (-pärk′) *vt., vi.* to park (a vehicle) parallel to another parked alongside a curb

☆**double play** *Baseball* a play in which two players are put out

double pneumonia pneumonia of both lungs

dou·ble-quick (-kwik′) *adj.* very quick —*n.* a very quick marching pace; specif., *same as* DOUBLE TIME (sense 2) —*vi., vt.* to march at such a pace —*adv.* at this pace

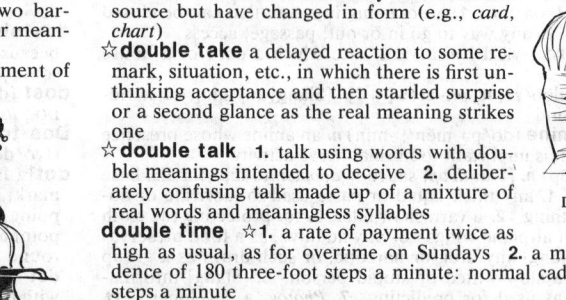

DOUBLE BASS

dou·ble-reed (-rēd′) *adj.* designating or of a group of woodwind instruments, as the oboe or bassoon, having two reeds separated by a narrow opening —*n.* a double-reed instrument

dou·ble-space (-spās′) *vt., vi.* -**spaced′**, -**spac′ing** to type (copy) so as to leave a full space between lines

double standard a system, code, etc. applied unequally; specif., one that is stricter for women than for men, esp. in matters of sex

double star *same as* BINARY STAR

dou·blet (dub′lit) *n.* [OFr., dim. of *double*, orig., something folded] **1.** a man's short, closefitting jacket of the 14th to the 16th cent. **2.** either of a pair of similar things **3.** a pair; couple **4.** either of two words that derive ultimately from the same source but have changed in form (e.g., *card, chart*)

☆**double take** a delayed reaction to some remark, situation, etc., in which there is first unthinking acceptance and then startled surprise or a second glance as the real meaning strikes one

☆**double talk 1.** talk using words with double meanings intended to deceive **2.** deliberately confusing talk made up of a mixture of real words and meaningless syllables

DOUBLET

double time ☆**1.** a rate of payment twice as high as usual, as for overtime on Sundays **2.** a marching cadence of 180 three-foot steps a minute: normal cadence is 120 steps a minute

☆**dou·ble·tree** (dub′'l trē′) *n.* [DOUBLE + (SINGLE)TREE] a crossbar on a wagon, plow, etc., to each end of which the singletrees are attached for harnessing two horses abreast

dou·bloon (du blōōn′) *n.* [< Fr. < Sp. < L. *duplus*, double] an obsolete Spanish gold coin

dou·bly (dub′lē) *adv.* **1.** twice **2.** two at a time

doubt (dout) *vi.* [< OFr. < L. *dubitare*] to be uncertain in opinion or belief; be undecided —*vt.* **1.** to be uncertain about; question [he *doubted* that he would win] **2.** to be inclined to disbelieve [he *doubted* his good fortune] **3.** [Archaic] to be fearful of —*n.* **1.** *a*) a lack of conviction; uncertainty *b*) lack of trust **2.** a condition of uncertainty [the outcome was in *doubt*] **3.** an unsettled point or matter; difficulty —see SYN. at UNCERTAINTY —**beyond** (or **without**) **doubt** certainly —**no doubt 1.** certainly **2.** probably —**doubt′a·ble** *adj.* —**doubt′er** *n.*

doubt·ful (dout′fəl) *adj.* **1.** in doubt; not sure or certain **2.** causing doubt; questionable, as in reputation **3.** feeling doubt; unsettled in opinion or belief —**doubt′ful·ly** *adv.* —**doubt′ful·ness** *n.*

SYN.—**doubtful** implies strong uncertainty as to the probability, value, honesty, validity, etc. of something [a *doubtful* remedy]; **dubious** is less strong, suggesting merely vague suspicion or a hesitant attitude [*dubious* about the future]; **questionable** suggests that there is some reason for doubt, and·it is often used in a polite way to imply that one suspects or is almost certain that someone or something is immoral, dishonest, etc. [a *questionable* reputation]; **problematic** implies only being uncertain without suggesting a moral question [a *problematic* success] —ANT. **certain, sure**

doubt·ing Thomas (-iŋ) [after the apostle THOMAS] a person who is in the habit of having doubts

doubt·less (-lis) *adj.* [Rare] free from doubt —*adv.* **1.** without doubt; certainly **2.** probably —**doubt′less·ly** *adv.* —**doubt′less·ness** *n.*

douche (dōōsh) *n.* [Fr. < It. *doccia*, shower, orig., conduit, ult. < L. *ductus*, pp. of *ducere*: see DUKE] **1.** a stream of liquid applied externally or internally to some part of the body **2.** a bath or treatment of this kind **3.** a device for douching —*vt., vi.* **douched, douch′ing** to apply a douche (to)

dough (dō) *n.* [OE. *dag* < IE. base *dheigh-*, to knead, form] **1.** a mixture of flour, liquid, and other ingredients, worked into a soft, thick mass for baking into bread, pastry, etc. **2.** any pasty mass like this ☆**3.** [Slang] money

dough·boy (dō′boi′) *n.* ☆[Colloq.] a U.S. infantryman, esp. of World War I

dough·nut (-nut′) *n.* a small, usually ring-shaped cake, fried in deep fat

dough·ty (dout′ē) *adj.* -**ti·er**, -**ti·est** [< OE. < *dugan*, to avail] [Now Rare] valiant; brave —**dough′ti·ly** *adv.*

dough·y (dō′ē) *adj.* **dough′i·er, dough′i·est** of or like dough; soft, pasty, etc. —**dough′i·ness** *n.*

Doug·las (dug′ləs) [< Gael., lit., black stream] **1.** a masculine name: dim. *Doug* **2.** Stephen A(rnold), 1813–61; U.S. politician

Douglas fir (or **spruce, pine, hemlock**) [after David *Douglas*, 19th-c. Scot. botanist in U.S.] a tall evergreen tree of the pine family, found in western N. America and valued for its wood

Doug·lass (dug′ləs), Frederick 1817?–95; U.S. Negro leader, journalist, & statesman

dour (door, d‾oor, dour) *adj.* [< L. *durus*, hard] **1.** [Scot.] stern; severe **2.** [Scot.] obstinate **3.** sullen; gloomy —**dour′ly** *adv.* —**dour′ness** *n.*

Dou·ro (d‾o′r‾oo) river flowing from NC Spain across N Portugal into the Atlantic

douse¹ (dous) *vt.* **doused, dous′ing** [< ?] **1.** *Naut.* to lower (sails) quickly **2.** [Colloq.] to put out (a light or fire) quickly

douse² (dous) *vt.* **doused, dous′ing** [< ? prec.] **1.** to plunge or thrust suddenly into liquid **2.** to pour liquid over; drench —*n.* an immersion or drenching

douse³ (douz) *vi.* **doused, dous′ing** same as DOWSE²

dove¹ (duv) *n.* [< ? ON. *dūfa*: for IE. base see DOWN²] **1.** a bird of the pigeon family, esp. any of the smaller ones, with a full-breasted body and short legs: a symbol of peace ☆**2.** an advocate of the use of peaceful means to solve international conflicts **3.** a person regarded as gentle or innocent —**dov′ish** *adj.*

dove² (dōv) *alt. pt. of* DIVE

dove·cote (duv′kōt′, -kät′) *n.* [DOVE¹ + COTE] a small house or box with compartments for nesting pigeons: also **dove′cot′** (-kät′)

Do·ver (dō′vər) **1.** seaport in SE England, on the Strait of Dover: pop. 36,000 **2.** capital of Del.: pop. 17,000 **3. Strait** (or **Straits) of,** strait between France and England

dove·tail (duv′tāl′) *n.* **1.** a thing shaped like a dove's tail; specif., a projecting, wedge-shaped part that fits into a corresponding cut-out space to form a joint **2.** a joint thus formed —*vt.* **1.** to join together by means of dovetails **2.** to piece together (facts, etc.) so as to make them seem logically connected —*vi.* to fit together closely or logically

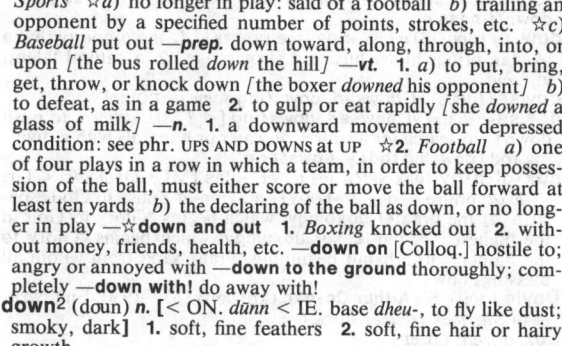

DOVETAIL

dow·a·ger (dou′ə jər) *n.* [< OFr. < *douage*, dowry, ult. < L. *dos*: see DOT²] **1.** a widow with a title or property received from her dead husband **2.** an elderly woman of wealth and dignity

dow·dy (dou′dē) *adj.* **-di·er, -di·est** [< ME. *doude*, unattractive woman] not neat or not stylish in looks or dress; shabby —*n., pl.* **-dies** a dowdy woman —**dow′di·ly** *adv.* —**dow′di·ness** *n.* —**dow′dy·ish** *adj.*

dow·el (dou′əl) *n.* [ME. *doule*] a peg or pin of wood, metal, etc., usually fitted into corresponding holes in two pieces to fasten them together —*vt.* **-eled** or **-elled, -el·ing** or **-el·ling** to fasten with dowels

dow·er (dou′ər) *n.* [< OFr. < ML. *dotarium* < L. *dos*: see DOT²] **1.** that part of a man's property which his widow inherits for life **2.** same as DOWRY (sense 1) **3.** a natural talent, gift, etc. —*vt.* **1.** to give a dower to **2.** to endow or provide (with)

DOWEL

dow·er·y (-ē) *n., pl.* **-er·ies** same as DOWRY

down¹ (doun) *adv.* [< OE. *adune*, from the hill < *a-*, off + *dune*, hill] **1.** from a higher to a lower place [leaves falling *down*] **2.** in or on a lower position or level [to lie *down*] **3.** *a)* in or to a place thought of as lower; often, specif., southward *b)* out of one's hands [put it *down*] **4.** below the horizon [the sun went *down*] **5.** from an earlier to a later period or person [*down* through the years; passed *down* from father to son] **6.** into a low physical or emotional condition [to break *down* in body or mind] **7.** in a lesser position or condition [held *down* by harsh laws] **8.** to a lower amount or bulk [to come *down* in price] **9.** into a quiet or less excited state [to settle *down*] **10.** seriously; earnestly [get *down* to work] **11.** completely [loaded *down*] **12.** in cash or when bought [$5 *down* and $5 a week] **13.** in writing; on record [take *down* his name] —*adj.* **1.** directed toward a lower position **2.** in a lower place **3.** gone, brought, pulled, etc. down **4.** sad or discouraged **5.** prostrate; ill [he is *down* with the flu] **6.** completed [four *down*, six to go] ☆**7.**

in cash, as part of the purchase price [a *down* payment] **8.** *Sports* ☆*a)* no longer in play: said of a football *b)* trailing an opponent by a specified number of points, strokes, etc. ☆*c) Baseball* put out —*prep.* down toward, along, through, into, or upon [the bus rolled *down* the hill] —*vt.* **1.** *a)* to put, bring, get, throw, or knock down [the boxer *downed* his opponent] *b)* to defeat, as in a game **2.** to gulp or eat rapidly [she *downed* a glass of milk] —*n.* **1.** a downward movement or depressed condition: see phr. UPS AND DOWNS at UP ☆**2.** *Football a)* one of four plays in a row in which a team, in order to keep possession of the ball, must either score or move the ball forward at least ten yards *b)* the declaring of the ball as down, or no longer in play —☆**down and out 1.** *Boxing* knocked out **2.** without money, friends, health, etc. —**down on** [Colloq.] hostile to; angry or annoyed with —**down to the ground** thoroughly; completely —**down with!** do away with!

down² (doun) *n.* [< ON. *dūnn* < IE. base *dheu-*, to fly like dust; smoky, dark] **1.** soft, fine feathers **2.** soft, fine hair or hairy growth

down³ (doun) *n.* [OE. *dun*, a hill] a large area of open, high, grassy land: *usually used in pl.*

down·beat (doun′bēt′) *n. Music* a downward stroke made by a conductor to show the first beat of each measure

down·cast (-kast′) *adj.* **1.** directed downward [*downcast* eyes] **2.** unhappy or discouraged; dejected [a *downcast* expression]

Dow·ney (dou′nē) [after J. *Downey*, gov. of Calif., 1860–62] city in SW Calif.: suburb of Los Angeles: pop. 88,000

down·fall (doun′fôl′) *n.* **1.** *a)* a sudden loss of wealth or power; ruin *b)* the cause of this **2.** a sudden, heavy fall, as of snow —**down′fall′en** *adj.*

☆**down·grade** (-grād′) *n.* a downward slope, esp. in a road —*adv., adj.* downhill; downward —*vt.* **-grad′ed, -grad′ing 1.** to reduce to a less skilled job at lower pay **2.** to lower in importance, value, etc. **3.** to belittle —**on the downgrade** losing status, influence, health, etc.; declining

down·heart·ed (-här′tid) *adj.* sad or discouraged; dejected —**down′heart′ed·ly** *adv.*

down·hill (-hil′) *adv.* **1.** toward the bottom of a hill **2.** to a poorer condition, status, etc. —*adj.* **1.** sloping or going downward **2.** of or having to do with skiing downhill

Down·ing Street (doun′iŋ) [after Sir G. *Downing* (1623–84), who owned property there] **1.** street in the West End of London, location of some important government offices **2.** the British government

down·pour (doun′pôr′) *n.* a heavy rain

☆**down·range** (-rānj′) *adv., adj.* along the course away from the launching site, as of a rocket

down·right (-rīt′) *adv.* thoroughly; completely —*adj.* **1.** absolute; thoroughgoing; complete [a *downright* fool] **2.** straightforward; plain; frank

☆**down·spout** (-spout′) *n.* a vertical pipe for carrying rain water from a roof gutter to ground level

Down's syndrome (dounz) [after J.L.H. *Down* (1828–96), Eng. physician] a congenital disease in which there is mental deficiency and a characteristic broad face, with slanting eyes, etc.

down·stairs (doun′sterz′) *adv.* **1.** down the stairs **2.** on or to a lower floor —*adj.* situated on a lower floor —*n.* a lower floor or floors

☆**down·state** (-stāt′) *n.* that part of a State farther to the south —*adj., adv.* in, to, or from downstate

down·stream (-strēm′) *adv., adj.* in the direction in which a stream is flowing

down·swing (-swiŋ′) *n.* a downward trend, as in business: also **down′turn′** (-turn′)

down-to-earth (-tə urth′) *adj.* realistic or practical

☆**down·town** (-toun′) *adj., adv.* of, in, like, to, or toward the lower part or main business section of a city or town —*n.* the downtown section

down·trod·den (-träd′'n) *adj.* **1.** trampled on or down **2.** forced to live in poverty or slavery; oppressed

down under [Colloq.] Australia or New Zealand

down·ward (-wərd) *adv., adj.* **1.** toward a lower place, state, etc. **2.** from an earlier to a later time Also **down′wards** *adv.* —**down′ward·ly** *adv.*

down·wind (-wind′) *adv., adj.* in the direction in which the wind is blowing or usually blows

---

fat, āpe, cär; ten, ēven; is, bīte; gō, hôrn, t‾ool, l‾ook; oil, out; up, fur; get; joy; yet; chin; she; thin, *th*en; zh, leisure; ŋ, ring; ə for *a* in *ago*, *e* in *agent*, *i* in *sanity*, *o* in *comply*, *u* in *focus*; ′ as in *able* (ā′b'l); Fr. bal; ë, Fr. coeur; ö, Fr. feu; Fr. mon; ô, Fr. coq; ü, Fr. duc; r, Fr. cri; H, G. ich; kh, G. doch; ‡foreign; ☆ Americanism; < derived from. See inside front cover.

down·y (-ē) *adj.* **down′i·er, down′i·est** **1.** of or covered with soft, fine feathers or hair **2.** soft and fluffy, like down — **down′i·ness** *n.*

dow·ry (dou′rē) *n., pl.* **-ries** [see DOWER] **1.** the property that a woman brings to her husband at marriage **2.** a natural talent, gift, etc.

dowse[1] (dous) *vt.* **dowsed, dows′ing** *same as* DOUSE[1]

dowse[2] (douz) *vi.* **dowsed, dows′ing** [< ? ME. *dushen*, to push down] to search for a source of water or minerals with a divining rod (**dowsing rod**) —**dows′er** *n.*

dox·ol·o·gy (däk säl′ə jē) *n., pl.* **-gies** [ML. *doxologia* < Gr. < *doxa*, praise + -*logia*, -LOGY] a hymn of praise to God; specif., *a)* the **greater doxology**, which begins "Glory to God in the highest" *b)* the **lesser doxology**, which begins "Glory to the Father" *c)* a hymn beginning "Praise God from whom all blessings flow"

Doyle (doil), Sir **Arthur Co·nan** (kō′nən) 1859–1930; Eng. writer of *Sherlock Holmes* stories

doz. dozen; dozens

doze (dōz) *vi.* **dozed, doz′ing** [prob. < Scand.] to sleep lightly or fitfully; be half asleep —*vt.* to spend (time) in dozing —*n.* a light sleep; nap —**doze off** to fall into a light sleep —**doz′er** *n.*

doz·en (duz′'n) *n., pl.* **-ens** or, esp. after a number, **-en** [< OFr. < *douze*, twelve < L. < *duo*, TWO + *decem*, TEN] a set of twelve —**doz′enth** *adj.*

doz·y (dō′zē) *adj.* **doz′i·er, doz′i·est** sleepy; drowsy —**doz′i·ly** *adv.* —**doz′i·ness** *n.*

DP, D.P. displaced person

dpt. **1.** department **2.** deponent

Dr. **1.** Doctor **2.** Drive

dr. **1.** debit **2.** debtor **3.** drachma(s) **4.** dram(s)

drab[1] (drab) *n.* [< Fr. *drap*, cloth < VL. *drappus*] a dull yellowish brown —*adj.* **drab′ber, drab′best** **1.** of a dull yellowish-brown color **2.** not bright or lively; dull; monotonous — **drab′ly** *adv.* —**drab′ness** *n.*

drab[2] (drab) *n.* [< Celt. as in Ir. *drabog*, slattern] a dirty and untidy woman

drachm (dram) *n. same as:* **1.** DRACHMA **2.** DRAM

drach·ma (drak′mə) *n., pl.* **-mas, -mae** (-mē), **-mai** (-mī) [L. < Gr. *drachmē*, lit., a handful < *drassesthai*, to grasp] **1.** an ancient Greek silver coin **2.** the monetary unit of modern Greece: see MONETARY UNITS, table

draft (draft) *n.* [ME. *draught*, a drawing < OE. *dragan*, DRAW] **1.** *a)* a drawing, as of a vehicle or load *b)* the thing, quantity, or load pulled **2.** *a)* a drawing in of a fish net *b)* the amount of fish caught in one draw **3.** *a)* a drinking *b)* the amount taken at one drink **4.** *a)* a drink; specif., a dose of medicine *b)* [Colloq.] a portion of beer, ale, etc. drawn from a cask **5.** *a)* a drawing into the lungs, as of air *b)* the amount of air, etc. drawn in **6.** a rough sketch of a writing **7.** a plan or drawing of a work to be done **8.** a current of air, as in a room **9.** a device for controlling the current of air in a heating system **10.** a written order from one person, firm, etc., directing the payment of money to another; check **11.** a demand or drain made on something **12.** *a)* the taking of persons for a special purpose, esp. compulsory military service ☆*b)* those so taken **13.** *Naut.* the depth of water to which a ship sinks, esp. when loaded ☆**14.** *Sports* a system of allotting to each team in a professional league exclusive rights to certain new players —*vt.* **1.** to choose from a group and order to serve in the armed forces **2.** to choose for some special work or position [they *drafted* him to act as chairman] **3.** to draw off or away **4.** to make a preliminary sketch of or working plans for [to *draft* a speech] —*adj.* **1.** used for pulling loads [*draft* animals] **2.** drawn from a cask on order [*draft* beer] **3.** in a preliminary or rough form [a *draft* resolution] —**on draft** ready to be drawn directly from the cask —**draft′a·ble** *adj.* —**draft′er** *n.*

☆**draft board** any of the boards of civilians having official power by law to draft persons into the U.S. armed forces

draft dodger ☆a person who tries to keep from being drafted into the armed forces

☆**draft·ee** (draf tē′) *n.* a person drafted, esp. for service in the armed forces

drafts·man (drafts′mən) *n., pl.* **-men** **1.** a person who draws plans of structures or machinery **2.** a person who draws up legal documents, speeches, etc. **3.** an artist skillful in drawing — **drafts′man·ship** *n.*

draft·y (draf′tē) *adj.* **draft′i·er, draft′i·est** letting in, having, or exposed to a draft or drafts of air —**draft′i·ly** *adv.* —**draft′i·ness** *n.*

drag (drag) *vt.* **dragged, drag′ging** [< OE. *dragan* or ON.

draga: see DRAW] **1.** to pull, draw, or move with effort, esp. along the ground; haul **2.** to force into some action, etc. [he was *dragged* into the scandal] **3.** to pull a grapnel, net, etc. over the bottom of (a river, etc.) in searching for something; dredge **4.** to draw a harrow over (land) **5.** to draw (something) out over a period of time **6.** to bring (a subject) into a conversation, piece of writing, etc. —*vi.* **1.** to be dragged along the ground; trail **2.** to lag behind [he was just *dragging* along] **3.** to move or pass too slowly [time *dragged* as he waited] **4.** to search a body of water with a grapnel, net, etc. **5.** [Slang] to draw (on) a cigarette, etc. **6.** [Slang] to take part in a drag race —*n.* **1.** something dragged along the ground; specif., *a)* a harrow *b)* a heavy sledge or sled **2.** a grapnel, dragnet, etc. **3.** anything that hinders [a *drag* on his resources] **4.** a dragging; slow, heavy movement ☆**5.** [Slang] influence that gains special favors; pull ☆**6.** [Slang] a puff of a cigarette, etc. **7.** [Slang] street; road [the main *drag*] ☆**8.** [Slang] a dull or boring person, situation, etc. **9.** [Slang] clothing of the opposite sex, esp. as worn by a male homosexual **10.** *Aeron.* a resisting force exerted on an aircraft, tending to hold back its motion —see SYN. at PULL —**drag on** (or **out**) to extend or be extended boringly —☆**drag one's feet** (or **heels**) [Slang] to be uncooperative —**drag′ger** *n.* —**drag′gy** *adj.* **-gi·er, -gi·est**

drag·gle (drag′'l) *vt., vi.* **-gled, -gling** [< DRAG + -LE[2]] to make or become wet or dirty by dragging in mud or water

drag·net (-net′) *n.* **1.** a net dragged along the bottom of a river, lake, etc. for catching fish **2.** a net for catching small game ☆**3.** an organized system or network for catching criminals, etc.

drag·o·man (drag′ə mən) *n., pl.* **-mans, -men** [< OFr. < It. < MGr. *dragomanos* < Ar. *tarǧumān*] in the Near East, an interpreter or guide for travelers

drag·on (drag′ən) *n.* [< OFr. < L. < Gr. *drakōn* < *derkesthai*, to see] **1.** a mythical monster, usually shown as a large reptile with wings and claws, breathing out fire and smoke **2.** a fierce person, esp. a strict chaperon

drag·on·fly (-flī′) *n., pl.* **-flies** a large, harmless insect having narrow, transparent, net-veined wings: it feeds mostly on flies, etc.

dra·goon (drə gōōn′) *n.* [Fr. *dragon:* see DRAGON] a heavily armed cavalryman —*vt.* **1.** to torment or persecute by dragoons **2.** to force (into doing) [he was *dragooned* into doing his homework]

☆**drag race** a race between automobiles to test which can get away faster from a complete stop, specif. between hot-rod cars (**dragsters**) on a short, straight course (**drag strip**) — **drag′-race′** *vi.* **-raced′, -rac′ing**

DRAGONFLY
(to 5 in. long)

drain (drān) *vt.* [< OE. *dreahnian* < base of *dryge*, DRY] **1.** to draw off (liquid) gradually **2.** to draw liquid from gradually [to *drain* a swamp] **3.** to receive the waters of [the St. Lawrence *drains* the Great Lakes] **4.** to drink all the liquid from (a cup, etc.) **5.** to exhaust (strength, emotions, or resources) gradually —*vi.* **1.** to flow off gradually **2.** to become dry by the drawing or flowing off of liquid **3.** to disappear gradually [his courage *drained* away] **4.** to flow (into) [the Ohio River *drains* into the Mississippi] —*n.* **1.** a channel, pipe, tube, etc. for carrying off water, sewage, pus, etc. **2.** a draining **3.** that which gradually exhausts strength, etc. [war is a *drain* on a nation's youth] — **down the drain** lost in a wasteful, careless way —**drain′er** *n.*

drain·age (drān′ij) *n.* **1.** the act, process, or method of draining **2.** a system of pipes, etc. for carrying off waste matter **3.** that which is drained off **4.** an area drained, as by a river

☆**drainage basin** the land drained by a river system

drain·pipe (-pīp′) *n.* a large pipe used to carry off water, sewage, etc.

drake (drāk) *n.* [< WGmc. word thought to be *drako*, male] a male duck

Drake (drāk), Sir **Francis** 1540?–96; Eng. admiral, navigator, & buccaneer

dram (dram) *n.* [< OFr. < ML. < L. *drachma:* see DRACHMA] **1.** *Apothecaries' Weight* a unit equal to 1/8 ounce **2.** *Avoirdupois Weight* a unit equal to 1/16 ounce **3.** *same as* FLUID DRAM **4.** a small drink of alcoholic liquor **5.** a small amount of anything

dra·ma (drä′mə, dram′ə) *n.* [LL. < Gr., a deed, drama < *dran*, to do] **1.** a literary composition that tells a story by means of dialogue and action, to be performed by actors; play **2.** the art or profession of writing, acting, or producing plays (often with *the*) **3.** plays as a group [Greek *drama*] **4.** a series of events as interesting, exciting, etc. as a play [the *drama* of the Civil War] **5.** the quality of being dramatic

☆**Dram·a·mine** (dram′ə mēn′) *a trademark for* DIMENHYDRI-NATE —*n.* [d-] this substance

dra·mat·ic (drə mat′ik) *adj.* **1.** of or connected with drama **2.** *a*) like a play *b*) full of action; vivid, striking, exciting, etc. — **dra·mat′i·cal·ly** *adv.*

dra·mat·ics (-iks) *n.pl.* **1.** [*usually with sing. v.*] the art of performing or producing plays **2.** plays presented by amateurs **3.** dramatic effect; esp., exaggerated emotional behavior

dram·a·tis per·so·nae (dram′ə tis pər sō′nē) [ModL.] the characters in a play

dram·a·tist (dram′ə tist) *n.* a playwright

dram·a·tize (dram′ə tīz′) *vt.* **-tized′, -tiz′ing 1.** to make into a drama; adapt (a story, events, etc.) for performance on the stage, screen, etc. **2.** to regard or present (actions, oneself, etc.) in a dramatic manner; make seem very exciting or tense —*vi.* **1.** to be capable of being dramatized **2.** to dramatize oneself — **dram′a·ti·za′tion** *n.* —**dram′a·tiz′er** *n.*

dram·a·tur·gy (-tur′jē) *n.* [< G. < Gr. *dramatourgia* < *drama*, DRAMA + *ergon*, WORK] the art of writing or producing plays —**dram′a·tur′gic, dram′a·tur′gi·cal** *adj.* —**dram′a·tur′gi·cal·ly** *adv.* —**dram′a·tur′gist, dram′a·turge′** *n.*

drank (draŋk) *pt. & often colloq. pp. of* DRINK

drape (drāp) *vt.* **draped, drap′ing** [< OFr. < *drap*, cloth: see DRAB[1]] **1.** to cover, hang, or decorate as with cloth or clothes in loose folds **2.** to arrange (a garment, cloth, etc.) artistically in folds or hangings —*vi.* to hang or fall in folds —*n.* cloth hanging in loose folds; esp., a drapery: *usually used in pl.*

drap·er (drā′pər) *n.* [Brit.] a dealer in dry goods

drap·er·y (drā′pər ē) *n., pl.* **-er·ies 1.** *a*) hangings, etc. arranged in loose folds *b*) an artistic arrangement of such hangings **2.** [*pl.*] curtains of heavy material

dras·tic (dras′tik) *adj.* [Gr. *drastikos*, active < *dran*, to do] acting with force; having a violent effect; severe; harsh —**dras′ti·cal·ly** *adv.*

draught (draft) *n., vt., adj.* now chiefly Brit. sp. *of* DRAFT

draughts (drafts) *n.pl.* [Brit.] the game of checkers

draughts·man (drafts′mən) *n., pl.* **-men** Brit. sp. *of* DRAFTS-MAN —**draughts′man·ship′** *n.*

draught·y (draf′tē) *adj.* **draught′i·er, draught′i·est** Brit. sp. *of* DRAFTY —**draught′i·ness** *n.*

Dra·vid·i·an (drə vid′ē ən) *n.* **1.** any of a group of intermixed races chiefly in southern India and northern Ceylon **2.** the family of non-Indo-European languages spoken by these races, including Tamil, Malayalam, etc. —*adj.* of the Dravidians or their languages: also **Dra·vid′ic**

draw (drô) *vt.* **drew, drawn, draw′ing** [< OE. *dragan* < IE. base *dherəgh-*, to pull, from which also comes L. *trahere*] **1.** to make move toward one or along with one; pull; drag [the horse *drew* the cart] **2.** to pull up, down, in, across, back, etc. [to *draw* the drapes] **3.** to need (a specified depth of water) to float in: said of a ship **4.** to attract; charm [to *draw* a large audience] **5.** to breathe in; inhale **6.** to bring forth; elicit [her challenge *drew* no reply] **7.** to bring on; provoke [to *draw* enemy fire] **8.** to pull out; extract (a cork, sword, etc.) **9.** *a*) to remove (liquid) by sucking, draining, etc. *b*) to bring up [to *draw* water from a well] *c*) to cause (liquid) to flow [to *draw* a bath, *draw* blood] **10.** to remove the bowels of **11.** *a*) to get from some source [to *draw* a salary] *b*) to get or pick (a number, prize, etc.) at random **12.** to withdraw (money) held in an account **13.** to have accruing to it [savings *draw* interest] **14.** to write (a check or draft) **15.** to reach (a conclusion, etc.); deduce **16.** to bring (a game or contest) to a tie **17.** to stretch tautly or to full length [to *draw* a rope tight] **18.** to pull out of shape; distort [a face *drawn* with fear] **19.** to flatten or shape (metal) by die stamping, hammering, etc. **20.** to make (metal) into wire by pulling it through holes **21.** to make (lines, pictures, etc.) as with a pencil, pen, brush, etc. **22.** to describe in words [he *drew* a glowing picture of the future] **23.** to make

DRAPED TOGA

(comparisons, etc.); formulate —*vi.* **1.** to draw something (in various senses of the *vt.*) **2.** to be drawn or have a drawing effect **3.** to come; move [to *draw* near] **4.** to shrink; contract **5.** to allow a draft, as of smoke, to move through [the chimney *draws* well] **6.** to attract audiences —*n.* **1.** a drawing or being drawn (in various senses) **2.** the result of drawing **3.** a thing drawn **4.** the cards dealt as replacement in draw poker **5.** a tie; stalemate [the game ended in a *draw*] **6.** a thing that attracts interest, audiences, etc. ☆**7.** the movable part of a draw-bridge **8.** a gully or ravine that water drains into —see SYN.at PULL —**draw away** to move away or ahead —**draw on** (or **nigh**) to approach —**draw out 1.** to extend; lengthen [to *draw* out a story] **2.** to take out; extract **3.** to get (a person) to talk — **draw up 1.** to arrange in order **2.** to compose (a document) in proper form **3.** to stop

draw·back (drô′bak′) *n.* anything that makes something or someone less satisfactory; disadvantage; shortcoming

draw·bridge (-brij′) *n.* a bridge that can be raised, lowered, or moved to one side

draw·ee (drô′ē′) *n.* the party that the drawer directs, by a draft, etc., to pay money over to a third party (called *payee*)

draw·er (drô′ər; *for 4* drôr) *n.* **1.** a person or thing that draws **2.** one who draws an order for the payment of money **3.** a draftsman **4.** a sliding box in a table, chest, bureau, etc., that can be drawn out and then pushed back into place

drawers (drôrz) *n.pl. same as* UNDERPANTS

draw·ing (drô′iŋ) *n.* **1.** the act of one that draws; specif., the art of representing something by lines made on a surface with a pencil, pen, etc. **2.** a picture, design, etc. thus made **3.** a lottery

☆**draw·ing card** an entertainer, speaker, show, etc. that normally draws a large audience

drawing room [< earlier *withdrawing room*, to which guests withdrew after dinner] **1.** a room where guests are received or entertained; parlor ☆**2.** a private compartment on a railroad sleeping car

draw·knife (drô′nīf′) *n., pl.* **-knives** (-nīvz′) a knife with a handle at each end: the user draws it toward him in shaving a surface: also **drawing knife, draw′shave′** (-shāv′)

drawl (drôl) *vt., vi.* [prob. < DRAW] to speak slowly, drawing out the vowels —*n.* a slow manner of speech in which vowels are drawn out — **drawl′er** *n.* —**drawl′ing·ly** *adv.*

drawn (drôn) *pp. of* DRAW —*adj.* **1.** pulled out of the sheath **2.** even or tied, as a game **3.** having had the bowels removed **4.** having a worn-out look

DRAWKNIFE

☆**drawn butter** melted butter, sometimes thickened and seasoned, used as a sauce

drawn·work (-wurk′) *n.* ornamental work done on textiles by pulling out threads to produce a lacelike design

☆**draw poker** a form of poker in which each player is dealt five cards face down, and may be dealt other cards for unwanted cards (usually three or fewer)

draw·string (drô′striŋ′) *n.* a string that tightens or closes an opening, as of a bag, when drawn

dray (drā) *n.* [< OE. *dræge*, lit., something drawn < *dragan*, to DRAW] a low, sturdy cart with detachable sides, for carrying heavy loads —*vt.* to carry or haul on a dray —*vi.* to drive a dray

dray·age (drā′ij) *n.* **1.** the hauling of a load by dray ☆**2.** the charge made for this

dray·man (-mən) *n., pl.* **-men** the driver of a dray

dread (dred) *vt.* [OE. *drædan*] to anticipate with great fear, worry, doubt, or distaste —*n.* **1.** intense fear, esp. of something which may happen **2.** fear mixed with awe **3.** something dreaded —*adj.* **1.** dreaded or dreadful **2.** inspiring awe or reverence; awesome

dread·ful (dred′fəl) *adj.* **1.** inspiring dread; terrible or awesome **2.** [Colloq.] very bad, offensive, disagreeable, etc. — **dread′ful·ness** *n.*

dread·ful·ly (-fəl ē) *adv.* **1.** in a dreadful manner **2.** [Colloq.] very; extremely [*dreadfully* tired]

---

fat, āpe, cär, ten, ēven, is, bīte; gō, hôrn, tōōl, look; oil, out; up, fur; get; joy; yet; chin; she; thin, then; zh, leisure; ŋ, ring; ə for a in ago, e in agent, i in sanity, o in comply, u in focus; ′ as in able (ā′b'l); Fr. bâl; ë, Fr. coeur; ö, Fr. feu; Fr. mon; δ, Fr. coq; ü, Fr. duc; r, Fr. cri; H, G. ich; kh, G. doch; ‡foreign; ☆ Americanism; < derived from. See inside front cover.

dread·nought, dread·naught (-nôt′, -nät′) *n.* a large, heavily armored battleship with big guns

dream (drēm) *n.* [form < OE. *dream*, joy, music; sense < ON. *draumr*, a dream] **1.** a series of sensations, images, thoughts, etc. passing through a sleeping person's mind **2.** a fanciful vision of the conscious mind; daydream; reverie **3.** the state in which such a daydream occurs **4.** a fond hope or strong desire **5.** anything so lovely, temporary, etc. as to seem dreamlike —*vi.* **dreamed** (drēmd, dremt) or **dreamt** (dremt), **dream′ing 1.** to have dreams **2.** to have daydreams **3.** to think (*of*) as at all possible [I wouldn't *dream* of going] —*vt.* **1.** *a)* to have (a dream or dreams) *b)* to have a dream of **2.** to spend in dreaming (with *away* or *out*) **3.** to imagine as possible; suppose —*adj.* ideal [her *dream* house] —**dream up** [Colloq.] to conceive of, imagine, or devise —**dream′er** *n.* —**dream′ful** *adj.* —**dream′less** *adj.* —**dream′like′** *adj.*

dream·y (drē′mē) *adj.* **dream′i·er, dream′i·est 1.** filled with dreams **2.** fond of daydreaming; visionary; impractical **3.** like something in a dream; misty, vague, etc. **4.** lulling; soothing [*dreamy* music] ☆**5.** [Slang] delightful —**dream′i·ly** *adv.* —**dream′i·ness** *n.*

drear (drir) *adj.* [Poet.] dreary; melancholy

drear·y (drir′ē) *adj.* **drear′i·er, drear′i·est** [< OE. *dreorig*, sad, orig., bloody, gory: for IE. base see DRIP] gloomy; cheerless; depressing; dismal; dull —**drear′i·ly** *adv.* —**drear′i·ness** *n.*

dredge[1] (drej) *n.* [prob. < MDu. *dregge*, akin to DRAG] **1.** a net attached to a frame, dragged along the bottom of a river, bay, etc. to gather shellfish, etc. **2.** an apparatus for scooping or sucking up mud, sand, etc., as in deepening or clearing channels, harbors, etc. **3.** a barge or other boat with a dredge on it —*vt.* **dredged, dredg′ing 1.** to gather (*up*) with or as with a dredge **2.** to enlarge or clean out (a river channel, harbor, etc.) with a dredge —*vi.* **1.** to use a dredge **2.** to search as with a dredge —**dredg′er** *n.*

dredge[2] (drej) *vt.* **dredged, dredg′ing** [< ME. *dragge*, sweetmeat, ult. < Gr. *tragēma*, dessert: for IE. base see TRITE] **1.** to coat (food) with flour or the like, as by sprinkling [*dredge* the chicken in cornmeal before frying] **2.** to sprinkle (flour, etc.) —**dredg′er** *n.*

dregs (dregz) *n.pl.* [< ON. *dregg*: for IE. base see DARK] **1.** solid bits that settle to the bottom in a liquid; lees **2.** the most worthless part [*dregs* of society] —**dreg′gi·ness** *n.* —**dreg′gy** *adj.* **-gi·er, -gi·est**

Drei·ser (drī′sər, -zər), **Theodore (Herman Albert)** 1871–1945; U.S. novelist

drench (drench) *vt.* [< OE. *drencan*, to make drink < *drincan*, to drink] **1.** to make (a horse, cow, etc.) swallow a medicinal liquid **2.** to make wet all over; soak or saturate —*n.* **1.** a large liquid dose, esp. for a sick animal **2.** a drenching; soaking **3.** a solution for soaking —see SYN. at SOAK

Dres·den (drez′dən) city in SC East Germany, on the Elbe: pop. 500,000 —*n.* a fine porcelain or chinaware made near Dresden —*adj.* designating or of such porcelain or chinaware

dress (dres) *vt.* **dressed** or **drest, dress′ing** [< OFr. *drecier*, to arrange < L. *directus*: see DIRECT] **1.** to put clothes on; clothe **2.** to provide with clothing **3.** to decorate; trim; adorn **4.** to arrange a display in [to *dress* a store window] **5.** to arrange or do up (the hair) **6.** to arrange (troops, etc.) in straight lines **7.** to apply medicines and bandages to (a wound, etc.) **8.** to treat in preparing for use, grooming, etc.; esp., *a)* to clean and remove the bowels of (a fowl, etc.) *b)* to cultivate (fields or plants) *c)* to smooth or finish (leather, stone, etc.) —*vi.* **1.** to put on or wear clothes **2.** to dress in formal clothes **3.** to get into a straight line: said of soldiers —*n.* **1.** clothes; clothing; apparel **2.** the usual outer garment of women, generally of one piece with a skirt **3.** formal clothes **4.** external covering or appearance —*adj.* **1.** of or for dresses [*dress* material] **2.** worn on formal occasions [a *dress* suit] **3.** requiring formal clothes [a *dress* occasion] —**dress down** to scold severely; reprimand —**dress up** **1.** to dress in formal clothes, or in clothes more elegant, showy, etc. than usual **2.** to improve the appearance of, as by decorating

dres·sage (drə säzh′) *n.* [Fr., training] exhibition horsemanship in which the horse is controlled by very slight movements of the rider

dress circle a section of seats in a theater or concert hall, usually a mezzanine, where formal dress was formerly customary

dress·er[1] (dres′ər) *n.* **1.** a person who dresses people, as actors in their costumes, or things, as store windows, leather, wounds, etc. **2.** one who dresses elegantly or in a certain way [a fancy *dresser*]

dress·er[2] (dres′ər) *n.* [< OFr. *dreceur*] **1.** formerly, a table on which food was prepared for serving **2.** a kitchen cupboard ☆**3.** a chest of drawers for clothes, usually with a mirror; bureau

dress·ing (-iŋ) *n.* **1.** the act of one that dresses **2.** that which is used to dress something (as manure applied to soil, bandages applied to a wound, etc.) **3.** a sauce for salads, etc.: see also SALAD DRESSING **4.** a stuffing, as of bread and seasoning, for roast chicken, turkey, etc.

dress·ing-down (-doun′) *n.* a severe scolding

dressing gown a loose robe for wear when one is undressed or lounging

dressing room a room for getting dressed in, esp. backstage in a theater

dressing table a low table with a mirror, for use while putting on cosmetics, grooming the hair, etc.

dress·mak·er (dres′māk′ər) *n.* one who makes women's dresses, suits, etc. to order —☆*adj.* designating a woman's suit, coat, etc. not cut on severe, mannish lines: see also TAILORED —**dress′mak′ing** *n.*

☆**dress parade** a military parade in dress uniform

dress rehearsal a final rehearsal, as of a play, performed exactly as it is to take place

dress suit a man's formal suit for evening wear

dress uniform a military uniform worn on formal occasions

dress·y (-ē) *adj.* **dress′i·er, dress′i·est 1.** showy or fancy in dress or appearance **2.** stylish, elegant, etc. —**dress′i·ly** *adv.* —**dress′i·ness** *n.*

drew (drōō) *pt. of* DRAW

Drey·fus (drā′fəs, drī′-; *Fr.* dre füs′), **Alfred** 1859–1935; Fr. army officer convicted of treason and imprisoned but later declared blameless when proved to be the victim of anti-Semitism and conspiracy

drib (drib) *vi., vt.* **dribbed, drib′bing** [< DRIP] [Obs.] to fall, or let fall, in driblets —**dribs and drabs** small amounts

drib·ble (drib′'l) *vi., vt.* **-bled, -bling** [< DRIB + -LE[2]] **1.** to flow, or let flow, in drops or driblets; trickle **2.** to come forth or let out a little at a time **3.** to let (saliva) drip from the mouth; drool **4.** in certain games, to move (the ball or puck) along by rapid, repeated bounces, short kicks, or light taps —*n.* **1.** a small drop, or a flowing in small drops **2.** a very small amount **3.** the act of dribbling a ball or puck **4.** a drizzling rain —**drib′bler** *n.*

drib·let (-lit) *n.* [dim. of DRIBBLE] a small amount

dried (drīd) *pt. & pp. of* DRY

dri·er (drī′ər) *n.* **1.** a substance added to paint, varnish, etc. to make it dry fast **2.** *same as* DRYER —*adj. compar. of* DRY

dri·est (-ist) *adj. superl. of* DRY

drift (drift) *n.* [< OE. *drifan*, to DRIVE] **1.** a being driven or carried along, as by a current of air or water or by force of circumstances **2.** the course on which something is directed **3.** the turning aside of a ship or aircraft from its course, caused by side currents or winds **4.** *a)* a slow ocean current *b)* a gradual shifting **5.** a tendency or trend [the nation's *drift* toward war] **6.** general meaning; tenor [I got the *drift* of his speech] **7.** *a)* something driven, as rain or snow before the wind *b)* a heap of snow, sand, etc. piled up by the wind, or floating matter washed ashore **8.** *Geol.* gravel, boulders, etc. moved and deposited by a glacier or water **9.** *Mining* a horizontal passageway, as along the path of a vein —*vi.* **1.** to be carried along as by a current [the log *drifted* downstream] **2.** to go along aimlessly [he *drifted* from job to job] **3.** to wander about from place to place, etc. **4.** to pile up in heaps by force of wind or water [the snow *drifted* against the door] **5.** to move gradually away from a set position —*vt.* **1.** to cause to drift **2.** to cover with drifts —see SYN. at TENDENCY —**drift′er** *n.*

drift·age (drift′ij) *n.* **1.** a drifting **2.** the turning aside caused by drifting **3.** that which has drifted

drift·wood (-wood′) *n.* wood drifting in the water, or that has been washed ashore

drill[1] (dril) *n.* [Du. *dril* < *drillen*, to bore: for IE. base see TRITE] **1.** a tool or apparatus for boring holes in wood, metal, etc. ☆**2.** a snail that bores into the shells of oysters and kills them **3.** military or physical training, esp. of a group, as in marching, the handling of

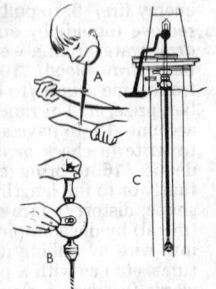

DRILLS
(A, bow; B, hand; C, rotary oil)

weapons, or gymnastic exercises **4.** the process of training or teaching by the repetition of an exercise **5.** a single exercise in drilling —**vt. 1.** to bore (a hole) in (something) with or as with a drill **2.** to train in military or physical exercises **3.** to teach by having do repeated exercises **4.** to instill (ideas, etc. *into*) by repetition ☆**5.** [Colloq.] to cause to move swiftly and directly *[he drilled the ball past me]* ☆**6.** [Slang] to penetrate with bullets —**vi. 1.** to bore a hole or holes **2.** to engage in military, physical, or mental exercises, or be put through such exercises —**drill′er** *n.*

drill² (dril) *n.* [< ? prec.] **1.** a furrow in which seeds are planted **2.** a row of planted seeds **3.** a machine for making holes or furrows, dropping seeds into them, and covering them —**vt. 1.** to sow (seeds) in rows **2.** to plant (a field) in drills

drill³ (dril) *n.* [< earlier *drilling*, ult. < L. < *tri-*, TRI- + *licium*, a thread] a coarse linen or cotton twill, used for work clothes, linings, etc.

drill⁴ (dril) *n.* [< ? Fr. *drill*, a soldier] a bright-cheeked monkey native to western Africa

drill·mas·ter (-mas′tər) *n.* **1.** an instructor in military drill **2.** one who teaches by drilling

drill press a machine tool for drilling holes

dri·ly (drī′lē) *adv. same as* DRYLY

drink (driŋk) *vt.* **drank** or archaic **drunk, drunk** or now colloq. **drank** or archaic **drunk′en, drink′ing** [OE. *drincan*] **1.** to swallow (liquid) **2.** to soak up or draw in; absorb (liquid or moisture) **3.** to swallow the contents of *[he drank three glasses of milk]* **4.** to join in (a toast) **5.** to bring (oneself) into a specified condition by drinking *[he drank himself to death]* **6.** to use (*up*) or spend by drinking alcoholic liquor *[they drank up all the profits]* —*vi.* **1.** to swallow liquid **2.** to absorb anything as if in drinking **3.** to drink alcoholic liquor, or to drink it to excess —*n.* **1.** any liquid for drinking; beverage **2.** alcoholic liquor **3.** too much or constant use of alcoholic liquor —**drink in** to take in eagerly with the senses or with the mind —**drink to** to drink a toast to —☆**the drink** [Colloq.] a body of water, esp. the ocean —**drink′a·ble** *adj.* —**drink′er** *n.*

drinking fountain a device for providing a jet or flow of drinking water, as in a public place

drip (drip) *vi.* **dripped** or **dript, drip′ping** [OE. *dryppan* < IE. base *dhreub-*, to drop, crumble] **1.** to fall in drops **2.** to let drops of liquid fall *[the faucet dripped all night]* —*vt.* to let fall in drops —*n.* **1.** a falling in drops **2.** liquid falling in drops, or the sound made by this **3.** a projecting part of a sill, etc. that sheds rain water **4.** [Slang] a person regarded as dull, uninteresting, etc.

drip-dry (-drī′) *adj.* designating or of fabrics or garments that dry quickly when hung soaking wet and require little or no ironing —*vi.* **-dried′, -dry′ing** to launder as a drip-dry fabric does

drip·pings (drip′iŋz) *n.* the fat and juices that drip from roasting meat

drip·py (-ē) *adj.* **-pi·er, -pi·est 1.** characterized by dripping water, rain, etc. **2.** [Slang] overly sentimental, stupid, etc.

drive (drīv) *vt.* **drove, driv′en, driv′ing** [OE. *drifan* < IE. base *dhreibh-*, to push] **1.** to force to go; push forward *[drive the cows into the barn]* **2.** to force into or from a state or act *[he drove her mad]* **3.** to force to work, usually too much **4.** *a)* to force as by a blow *b)* to hit or cast (a ball) hard and swiftly **5.** to cause to go into or through; make penetrate *[to drive a nail in the wall]* **6.** to produce by penetrating *[to drive a hole through metal]* **7.** to control the movement of (a vehicle) **8.** to transport in a vehicle **9.** to cause to function **10.** to push (a bargain, etc.) through —*vi.* **1.** to advance violently; dash **2.** to work or try hard **3.** to drive a blow, ball, etc. **4.** to be driven; operate: said of a motor vehicle **5.** to be carried in a vehicle **6.** to operate a motor vehicle —*n.* **1.** a driving **2.** a trip in a vehicle **3.** *a)* a road for automobiles, etc. *b)* a driveway ☆**4.** *a)* a rounding up of animals as for branding *b)* the animals rounded up **5.** a hard, swift blow, thrust, etc., as of a ball in a game ☆**6.** an organized movement to achieve some purpose; campaign *[a drive to collect money for charity]* ☆**7.** the power or energy to get things done; aggressive vigor **8.** that which is urgent, as a basic biological urge ☆**9.** a collection of logs floating down a river **10.** *a)* the mechanism of a motor vehicle, machine, etc. that makes it go *[a gear drive]* *b)* that arrangement

in an automatic transmission of a motor vehicle allowing forward speeds —**drive at 1.** to aim at **2.** to mean; intend —**drive in 1.** to force in, as by a blow ☆**2.** *Baseball* to cause (a runner) to score or (a run) to be scored, as by getting a hit —**let drive** to hit or aim

☆**drive-in** (-in′) *adj.* designating or of a restaurant, movie theater, bank, etc. that provides its services to persons who drive up and remain seated in their cars —*n.* such a restaurant, theater, etc.

driv·el (driv′'l) *vi.* **-eled** or **-elled, -el·ing** or **-el·ling** [< OE. *dreflian:* for IE. base see DARK] **1.** to let saliva flow from one's mouth; slobber **2.** to speak in a silly or stupid manner —*vt.* to say in a silly, stupid, or nonsensical manner —*n.* silly, stupid talk; childish nonsense —**driv′el·er, driv′el·ler** *n.*

driv·en (driv′'n) *pp. of* DRIVE —*adj.* moved along and piled up by the wind *[driven snow]*

driv·er (drī′vər) *n.* **1.** a person who drives; specif., *a)* one who drives an automobile, etc. *b)* one who herds cattle *c)* one who makes those under him work hard **2.** a thing that drives; specif., *a)* a mallet, hammer, etc. *b)* a wooden-headed golf club used in hitting the ball from the tee: also called **number 1 wood** *c)* any machine part that passes on motion —**the driver's seat** the position of control or dominance

drive shaft a shaft that passes on motion or power, as from the transmission to the rear axle in an automobile

☆**drive·way** (drīv′wā′) *n.* a path for cars, leading from a street to a garage, house, etc.

driz·zle (driz′'l) *vi., vt.* **-zled, -zling** [prob. < ME. word thought to be *drisnen*, to fall as dew: for IE. base see DRIP] to rain or let fall in fine, mistlike drops —*n.* a fine, mistlike rain —**driz′zly** *adj.*

drogue (drōg) *n.* [prob. < Scot. *drug*, DRAG] **1.** *same as* SEA ANCHOR **2.** a funnel-shaped device towed behind an aircraft for its drag effect (also **drogue parachute**), or as a target, etc.

droll (drōl) *adj.* [< Fr. < MDu. *drol*, short, stout fellow] amusing in an odd or ironic way —see SYN. at FUNNY —**droll′ness** *n.* —**drol′ly** *adv.*

droll·er·y (drōl′ər ē) *n., pl.* **-er·ies 1.** a droll act, remark, picture, story, etc. **2.** the act of joking **3.** quaint or ironic humor

-drome (drōm) [< Gr. *dromos*, a running] *a suffix meaning* running, racecourse *[hippodrome]*

drom·e·dar·y (dräm′ə der′ē) *n., pl.* **-dar′ies** [< OFr. < LL. < L. < Gr. < *dramein*, to run] the one-humped camel, found from northern Africa to India and trained for fast riding

drone¹ (drōn) *n.* [< OE. *dran*] **1.** a male honeybee: it has no sting and does no work **2.** an idle person who is supported by others; parasite or loafer **3.** an airplane that has no pilot and is directed by remote control —*vi.* **droned, dron′ing** to live in idleness; loaf

drone² (drōn) *vi.* **droned, dron′ing** [LME. *dronen* < prec.] **1.** to make a continuous humming sound **2.** to talk on and on in a dull, monotonous way —*vt.* to utter in a dull, monotonous tone —*n.* **1.** a continuous humming sound **2.** *a)* a bagpipe *b)* any of the pipes of fixed tone in a bagpipe

DROMEDARY
(70–80 in. high
at shoulder)

drool (drool) *vi.* [< DRIVEL] **1.** to let saliva flow from one's mouth; drivel **2.** to flow from the mouth, as saliva **3.** [Slang] to speak in a silly or stupid way **4.** [Slang] to be greatly enthusiastic, eager, desiring, etc. —*vt.* to let drivel from the mouth —*n.* saliva running from the mouth

droop (droop) *vi.* [< ON. *drupa:* for IE. base see DRIP] **1.** to sink, hang, or bend down **2.** to lose energy or strength; become weak, tired, etc. **3.** to become depressed, sad, etc. —*vt.* to let sink or hang down —*n.* a drooping

droop·y (droop′ē) *adj.* **droop′i·er, droop′i·est 1.** tending to droop **2.** [Colloq.] tired or depressed —**droop′i·ly** *adv.* —**droop′i·ness** *n.*

drop (dräp) *n.* [OE. *dropa:* for IE. base see DRIP] **1.** a small quantity of liquid that is rounded in shape, as when falling **2.** a very small quantity of liquid **3.** [*pl.*] liquid medicine taken in drops **4.** a very small quantity of anything *[he hasn't a drop of pity]* **5.** a thing like a drop in shape, size, etc. *[a chocolate drop]* **6.** a dropping; sudden fall, descent, slump, etc. *[a drop* in prices] **7.** *same as* AIRDROP **8.** anything that drops or is used for dropping, as a drop curtain, a trapdoor, a slot for depositing letters, etc. **9.** the distance between a higher and lower level [a *drop* of five feet to the ground] —*vi.* **dropped** *or*, occas., **dropt, drop′ping 1.** to fall in drops **2.** to fall; come down [the ripe apples *dropped* from the tree] **3.** to fall exhausted, wounded, or dead **4.** to pass into a specified state [to *drop* off to sleep] **5.** to come to an end [let the matter *drop*] **6.** to become lower or less, as temperature, prices, etc. **7.** to move down with a current of water or air —*vt.* **1.** to let or make fall; release hold of **2.** to give birth to: said of animals **3.** to utter (a hint, etc.) casually **4.** to send (a letter) **5.** to cause to fall, as by wounding, killing, etc. **6.** *a)* to stop or have done with [let's *drop* this argument] *b)* to dismiss [he was *dropped* from his job] **7.** to lower or lessen **8.** to make (the voice) less loud **9.** *same as* AIRDROP **10.** to omit (a letter or sound) in a word **11.** [Colloq.] to leave (a person or thing) at a specified place **12.** [Slang] to lose (money or a game) —☆**at the drop of a hat** immediately —**drop back 1.** to move back; retreat **2.** to fall behind; lag: also **drop behind** —**drop in (or over, by,** etc.**)** to pay a casual or unexpected visit —**drop off 1.** to decline; decrease **2.** [Colloq.] to fall asleep —**drop out** to stop being a member or participant —☆**get (or have) the drop on** [Slang] **1.** to draw and aim one's gun at (another) faster than he can **2.** to get (or have) any advantage over

☆**drop·cloth** (dräp′klôth′, -kläth′) *n.* a large piece of cloth, plastic, etc. for protection against dripping paint

☆**drop cookie** a cookie made from batter dropped onto a baking sheet as by teaspoonfuls

drop curtain a theater curtain that is lowered and raised rather than drawn

drop-forge (-fôrj′) *vt.* **-forged′, -forg′ing** to pound or shape (heated metal) between dies with a drop hammer or a press — **drop′-forg′er** *n.*

drop forging a product made by drop-forging

☆**drop hammer 1.** a machine for pounding metal into shape, with a heavy weight that is raised and then dropped on the metal **2.** this weight

drop kick *Football* a kick in which the ball is dropped and kicked just as it bounces from the ground —**drop′-kick′** *vt., vi.* —**drop′-kick′er** *n.*

☆**drop leaf** a board attached by hinges to the side or to the end of a table and raised to form an extra part of the table top — **drop′-leaf′** *adj.*

drop·let (-lit) *n.* a very small drop

☆**drop·light** (-līt′) *n.* a light arranged to hang from a fixture so that it can be raised or lowered

☆**drop·out** (-out′) *n.* a person who withdraws from school, esp. high school, before graduating

drop·per (-ər) *n.* **1.** a person or thing that drops ☆**2.** a small tube of glass, plastic, etc. with a hollow rubber bulb at one end, used to measure out a liquid in drops

☆**drop press** *same as* DROP HAMMER

drop·sy (dräp′sē) *n.* [< OFr. < L. < Gr. *hydrōps* < *hydōr*, WATER] an earlier term for EDEMA —**drop′si·cal** (-si k'l), **drop′-sied** *adj.* —**drop′si·cal·ly** *adv.*

dropt (dräpt) *occas.* pt. & pp. of DROP

drosh·ky (dräsh′kē, drôsh′-) *n., pl.* **-kies** [Russ. *drozhki*] a low, open, four-wheeled Russian carriage: also **dros′ky** (dräs′-, drôs′-) *pl.* **-kies**

dro·soph·i·la (drə säf′ə lə, drō-) *n., pl.* **-lae′** (-lē′) [ModL. < Gr. *drosos*, dew + fem. of *philos*, loving] a tiny fly used in laboratory experiments in heredity; fruit fly

dross (drôs, dräs) *n.* [OE. *dros*, DREGS] **1.** a scum formed on the surface of molten metal **2.** waste matter; rubbish —**dross′i·ness** *n.* —**dross′y** *adj.* **dross′i·er, dross′i·est**

drought (drout, drouth) *n.* [OE. *drugoth*, dryness < *drugian*, to dry up] **1.** a long period of dry weather; lack of rain **2.** a serious shortage or deficiency —**drought′y** *adj.* **drought′i·er, drought′i·est**

drouth (drouth, drout) *n.* same as DROUGHT

drove[1] (drōv) *n.* [OE. *draf* < *drifan*, DRIVE] **1.** a number of cattle, sheep, etc. driven or moving as a group; flock; herd **2.** a moving crowd of people —see SYN. at GROUP

drove[2] (drōv) *pt.* of DRIVE

drov·er (drō′vər) *n.* a person who herds droves of animals, esp. to market

drown (droun) *vi.* [prob. < var. of ON. *drukna*] to die by being kept under water or other liquid so that one cannot breathe —*vt.* **1.** to kill by causing to drown **2.** *a)* to cover with water; flood *b)* to overwhelm **3.** to be so loud as to overcome (another

sound): usually with *out* [the rock band *drowned* out all conversation] **4.** to get rid of [to *drown* one's sorrow in drink]

drowse (drouz) *vi.* **drowsed, drows′ing** [< OE. *drusian*, to become sluggish: for IE. base see DRIP] to sleep lightly; doze —*vt.* to spend (time) in drowsing —*n.* the act or an instance of drowsing; doze

drow·sy (drou′zē) *adj.* **-si·er, -si·est 1.** *a)* sleepy or half asleep *b)* making sleepy [*drowsy* music] **2.** brought on by sleepiness **3.** peacefully quiet or inactive [a *drowsy* village] — **drow′si·ly** *adv.* —**drow′si·ness** *n.*

drub (drub) *vt.* **drubbed, drub′bing** [< ? Turk. *durb* < Ar. *darb*, a beating] **1.** to beat as with a stick; cudgel **2.** to defeat thoroughly in a fight, contest, etc. —*vi.* to drum or tap —*n.* a blow as with a club —**drub′ber** *n.*

drub·bing (drub′iŋ) *n.* a thorough beating or defeat

drudge (druj) *n.* [prob. < OE. *dreogan*, to suffer] a person who does hard and tiresome work —*vi.* **drudged, drudg′ing** to do such work

drudg·er·y (druj′ər ē) *n., pl.* **-er·ies** work that is hard and tiresome

drug (drug) *n.* [< OFr. *drogue*] **1.** any substance used as or in a medicine **2.** a substance that has a narcotic effect, gives one hallucinations, etc., esp. when habit-forming —*vt.* **drugged, drug′ging 1.** to put a harmful drug in (a drink, etc.) **2.** to give a drug to, esp. so as to put to sleep or make unconscious **3.** to make feel dull or dazed as with a drug —**drug on the market** something that is available in a large quantity but that few people want

drug addict a person who uses narcotics so much that it is a habit he cannot break without great effort or help

drug·gist (drug′ist) *n.* **1.** a dealer in drugs, medical equipment, etc. **2.** a person authorized to fill prescriptions; pharmacist ☆**3.** an owner or manager of a drugstore

☆**drug·store** (-stôr′) *n.* a store where drugs and medical supplies are sold: most drugstores also sell many other articles

dru·id (drōō′id) *n.* [< Fr. < L. *druides*, pl. < Celt.: for IE. base see TREE] [*often* D-] a member of a Celtic religious order in ancient Britain, Ireland, and France —**dru·id′ic, dru·id′i·cal** *adj.* —**dru′id·ism** *n.*

drum (drum) *n.* [< Du. *trom*] **1.** a percussion instrument consisting of a hollow cylinder or hemisphere with a membrane stretched tightly over the end or ends **2.** the sound made by beating a drum, or any sound like this **3.** any drumlike object; specif., *a)* a metal cylinder around which cable, etc. is wound in a machine *b)* a barrellike metal container for oil, etc. ☆**4.** any of various fishes that make a drumming sound **5.** *Anat.* same as: *a)* MIDDLE EAR *b)* EARDRUM —*vi.* **drummed, drum′ming 1.** to beat a drum **2.** to beat or tap continually, as with the fingers —*vt.* **1.** to beat out (a tune, etc.) as on a drum **2.** to beat or tap continually **3.** to assemble by beating a drum **4.** to put (ideas, facts, etc. *into*) by repeating again and again —☆**beat the drum for** [Colloq.] to try to arouse enthusiasm for —**drum out of** to expel from in disgrace —**drum up 1.** to summon as by beating a drum **2.** to get (business) by asking or appealing

drum·beat (drum′bēt′) *n.* a sound made by beating a drum

☆**drum·fish** (-fish′) *n., pl.* **-fish′, -fish′es** see FISH *same as* DRUM (*n.* 4)

drum·head (-hed′) *n.* the membrane stretched over the open end or ends of a drum

drum·lin (drum′lin) *n.* [< Ir. *druim*, a ridge + *-lin*, dim. suffix] a long ridge formed of matter deposited by a glacier

drum major a person who leads or precedes a marching band, often twirling a baton and prancing —☆**drum majorette** *fem.*

drum·mer (-ər) *n.* **1.** a drum player **2.** an animal that makes a drumming sound **3.** [see phrase *drum up* at DRUM] [Colloq.] a traveling salesman

drum·stick (-stik′) *n.* **1.** a stick for beating a drum **2.** the lower half of the leg of a cooked fowl

drunk (druŋk) *pp.* & *archaic pt.* of DRINK —*adj.* [*usually used in the predicate:* see also DRUNKEN] **1.** having lost control of oneself from drinking alcoholic liquor; intoxicated [he was *drunk* on beer] **2.** overcome by any powerful emotion [*drunk* with ecstasy] **3.** [Colloq.] *same as* DRUNKEN (sense 2) —*n.* [Slang] **1.** a drunken person **2.** a drinking spree

drunk·ard (druŋ′kərd) *n.* a person who often gets drunk; sot; inebriate

drunk·en (-kən) *archaic pp.* of DRINK —*adj.* [*used before the noun:* see also DRUNK] **1.** drunk, or intoxicated; esp., drunk very often [a *drunken* bum] **2.** caused by being drunk [a *drunken* rage] —**drunk′en·ly** *adv.* —**drunk′en·ness** *n.*

drupe (droop) *n.* [< ModL. *drupa* < L. *drupa* (*oliva*), overripe (olive) < Gr. *dryppa*, olive] any fruit with a soft, fleshy part around an inner stone that contains the seed, as an apricot, cherry, plum, etc. —**dru·pa·ceous** (droo pā′shəs) *adj.*

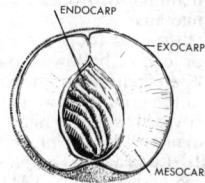

ENDOCARP
EXOCARP
MESOCARP

DRUPE (of peach)

drupe·let (droop′lit) *n.* a small drupe: a single blackberry consists of many drupelets

druth·ers (druth′ərz) *n.* [contr. < *I'd rather*] ☆[Dial. or Colloq.] a choice or preference [if I had my *druthers*]

dry (drī) *adj.* **dri′er, dri′est** [OE. *dryge*] **1.** not under water [*dry* land] **2.** having no moisture; not wet or damp [*wipe with a *dry* cloth*] **3.** not shedding tears [with *dry* eyes] **4.** lacking rain [a *dry* summer] **5.** *a*) having lost water or moisture; arid, withered, dehydrated, etc. *b*) empty of water or other liquid [a *dry* well] **6.** thirsty **7.** not yielding milk [a *dry* cow] **8.** without butter, jam, etc. [*dry* toast] **9.** solid; not liquid [*dry* measure] **10.** not sweet [*dry* wine] **11.** having no mucous or watery discharge [a *dry* cough] ☆**12.** prohibiting or opposed to the sale of alcoholic liquors [a *dry* town] **13.** plain or sober [*dry* facts] **14.** funny in a quiet but sharp way [*dry* wit] **15.** dull or boring [a *dry* lecture] —*n., pl.* **drys** ☆[Colloq.] a prohibitionist —*vt., vi.* **dried, dry′ing** to make or become dry —**dry up** **1.** to make or become thoroughly dry **2.** to make or become unproductive, uncreative, etc. ☆**3.** [Slang] to stop talking —**not dry behind the ears** [Colloq.] immature; inexperienced

dry·ad (drī′əd, -ad) *n., pl.* **-ads, -ad·es′** (-ə dēz′) [L. *dryadis* < Gr. *drys*, an oak, TREE] [*also* D-] Gr. & Rom. *Myth.* any nymph living in a tree; wood nymph

dry battery **1.** an electric battery made up of several connected dry cells **2.** a dry cell

dry cell a voltaic cell containing a substance to absorb the chemicals that might otherwise spill

dry-clean (drī′klēn′) *vt.* to clean (garments, etc.) with some solvent other than water, as naphtha, gasoline, etc. —**dry cleaner** —**dry cleaning**

Dry·den (drīd′'n), **John** 1631–1700; Eng. poet, critic, & playwright

dry-dock (drī′däk′) *vt., vi.* to place or go into a dry dock

dry dock a dock from which the water can be emptied, used for building and repairing ships

dry·er (-ər) *n.* **1.** a person or thing that dries; specif., an apparatus for drying by heating or blowing air, esp. an appliance for drying clothes **2.** *same as* DRIER

dry-eyed (-īd′) *adj.* shedding no tears

☆**dry farming** farming in an almost rainless region without irrigation: done by conserving moisture already in the soil and by planting crops that resist drought —**dry′-farm′** *vt., vi.* —**dry farmer**

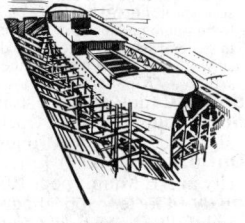

DRY DOCK

dry goods cloth, cloth products, thread, etc.

☆**dry ice** carbon dioxide in the solid form of snowlike cakes, used as a refrigerant: it evaporates instead of melting

dry·ly (-lē) *adv.* in a dry manner; matter-of-factly

dry measure a system of measuring the volume of dry things, as grain, vegetables, etc.; esp., the system in which 2 pints = 1 quart, 8 quarts = 1 peck, and 4 pecks = 1 bushel: see TABLE OF WEIGHTS AND MEASURES in Supplements

dry·ness (-nis) *n.* the quality or state of being dry

dry point **1.** a needle for engraving lines on a copper plate without using acid **2.** a print from such a plate **3.** this way of engraving

dry rot **1.** a fungous decay causing seasoned timber to crumble to powder **2.** a similar fungous disease of plants, fruits, etc. — **dry′-rot′** *vi., vt.* **-rot′ted, -rot′ting**

☆**dry run** **1.** [Mil. Slang] practice in firing without using live ammunition **2.** [Slang] a rehearsal

dry socket a painful condition in a tooth socket when a blood clot does not properly form after the tooth has been extracted

dry wall **1.** a wall of rocks or stones with no mortar ☆**2.** a wall constructed of wallboard, plasterboard, etc. without using wet plaster —**dry′wall′** *adj.*

☆**dry wash** laundry washed and dried but not ironed

D.S., d.s. [It. *dal segno*] (repeat) from this sign

D.S., D.Sc. Doctor of Science

D.S.C., DSC Distinguished Service Cross

D.S.M., DSM Distinguished Service Medal

D.S.O., DSO Distinguished Service Order

D.S.T., DST Daylight Saving Time

D.T.'s, d.t.'s (dē′tēz′) [Slang] *same as* DELIRIUM TREMENS

Du. 1. Duke **2.** Dutch

du·al (doo′əl, dyoo′-) *adj.* [L. *dualis* < *duo*, TWO] **1.** of or for two [a car with *dual* controls] **2.** having or composed of two parts or kinds, like or unlike; double; twofold [a *dual* nature] —*n. Linguis.* **1.** *same as* DUAL NUMBER **2.** a word having dual number —**du·al′i·ty** (-al′ə tē) *n.* —**du′al·ly** *adv.*

du·al·ism (-iz'm) *n.* **1.** the state of being dual; duality **2.** any theory or doctrine based on a twofold distinction, as the doctrine that man has two natures, physical and spiritual —**du′al·ist** *n.* —**du′al·is′tic** *adj.* —**du′al·is′ti·cal·ly** *adv.*

du·al·ize (-īz′) *vt.* **-ized′, -iz′ing** to make, or consider as, dual

dual number in some languages, a grammatical number indicating *two, a pair:* distinguished from *singular* and *plural*

du·al-pur·pose (-pur′pəs) *adj.* having, or meant to have, two uses [a *dual-purpose* hall]

dub[1] (dub) *vt.* **dubbed, dub′bing** [< OE. *dubbian*, to strike] **1.** to confer knighthood on by tapping on the shoulder with a sword **2.** to confer a title, name, or nickname upon [as a boy, he was *dubbed* "Slim"] **3.** to make smooth, as by hammering, scraping, or rubbing **4.** [Slang] to bungle (a golf stroke, etc.) —☆*n.* [Slang] a clumsy, unskillful person —**dub′ber** *n.*

☆**dub**[2] (dub) *vt.* **dubbed, dub′bing** [contr. < DOUBLE] to insert (dialogue, music, etc.) in a film or recording (often with *in*) —*n.* dialogue, music, etc. so inserted —**dub′ber** *n.*

du Bar·ry (doo bar′ē; *Fr.* dü ba rē′) comtesse (born *Marie Jeanne Bécu*) 1743?–93; mistress of Louis XV of France

du·bi·e·ty (doo bī′ə tē, dyoo-) *n.* [LL. *dubietas*] **1.** a being dubious; doubtfulness **2.** *pl.* **-ties** a doubtful thing —see SYN. at UNCERTAINTY

du·bi·ous (doo′bē əs, dyoo′-) *adj.* [< L. < *dubius*, uncertain] **1.** causing doubt; ambiguous [a *dubious* answer] **2.** feeling doubt; skeptical **3.** uncertain [*dubious* battle] **4.** probably bad or immoral; questionable [a *dubious* character] —see SYN. at DOUBTFUL —**du′bi·ous·ly** *adv.* —**du′bi·ous·ness** *n.*

Dub·lin (dub′lən) capital of Ireland; seaport on the Irish Sea: pop. 569,000

Du Bois (doo bois′), **W(illiam) E(dward) B(urghardt)** 1868–1963; U.S. historian & Negro leader

Du·buque (də byook′) [after J. *Dubuque*, early lead miner] city in E Iowa, on the Mississippi: pop. 62,000

du·cal (doo′k'l, dyoo′-) *adj.* [see DUKE] of a duke or dukedom —**du′cal·ly** *adv.*

duc·at (duk′ət) *n.* [OFr. < It. *ducato*, coin with image of a duke < LL. *ducatus:* see DUCHY] **1.** any of several former European coins of gold or silver **2.** [Slang] a ticket

‡**du·ce** (doo′che) *n.* [It. < L. *dux:* see DUKE] chief; leader: title (**Il Duce**) taken by Benito MUSSOLINI

Du·champ (dü shän′), **Marcel** 1887–1968; U.S. painter, born in France

duch·ess (duch′is) *n.* **1.** the wife or widow of a duke **2.** a woman who, like a duke, rules a duchy

duch·y (duch′ē) *n., pl.* **duch′ies** [< OFr. < LL. *ducatus*, military command < L. *dux:* see DUKE] the territory ruled by a duke or duchess; dukedom

duck[1] (duk) *n.* [< OE. *duce*, lit., diver < base of DUCK[2]] **1.** *pl.* **ducks, duck:** see PLURAL, II, D, 1 a wild or domestic swimming bird with a flat bill, short neck and legs, and webbed feet **2.** a female duck: opposed to DRAKE **3.** the flesh of a duck as food ☆**4.** [Slang] a person [an odd *duck*] —**like water off a duck's back** with no effect or reaction

duck[2] (duk) *vt., vi.* [ME. *douken* < OE. *ducan*, to dive] **1.** to plunge or dip under water for a moment **2.** to lower or move (the head, body, etc.) suddenly, as in avoiding a blow or in hiding ☆**3.** [Colloq.] to try to keep away from (a task, person, question, etc.) **4.** [Slang] to run (*in* or *out*) —*n.* a ducking

---

fat, āpe, cär; ten, ēven; is, bīte; gō, hôrn, tōōl, look; oil, out; up, fur; get; joy; yet; chin; she; thin, *th*en; zh, leisure; ŋ, ring; ə for *a* in *ago*, *e* in *agent*, *i* in *sanity*, *o* in *comply*, *u* in *focus*; ' as in *able* (ā′b'l); Fr. bál; ë, Fr. coeur; ö, Fr. feu; Fr. mon; ô, Fr. coq; ü, Fr. duc; r, Fr. cri; H, G. ich; kh, G. doch; ‡foreign; ☆ Americanism; < derived from. See inside front cover.

duck³ (duk) *n.* [Du. *doek*] **1.** a cotton or linen cloth like canvas but finer and lighter in weight **2.** [*pl.*] [Colloq.] trousers made of this cloth

duck⁴ (duk) *n.* [altered (after DUCK¹) < *DUKW*, code name] [Mil. Slang] an amphibious motor vehicle

duck·bill (duk/bil′) *n.* same as PLATYPUS

duck·ling (-liŋ) *n.* a young duck

duck·pins (-pinz′) *n.pl.* **1.** [*with sing. v.*] a game like bowling or tenpins, played with smaller pins and balls **2.** the pins used

☆**duck soup** [Slang] something that is easy to do

duck·weed (-wēd′) *n.* a minute flowering plant that floats in colonies on ponds and sluggish streams: often eaten by ducks

duck·y (-ē) *adj.* **duck/i·er, duck/i·est** [Old Slang] pleasing, delightful, darling, etc.

duct (dukt) *n.* [< ML. < L. *ductus*, pp. of *ducere*, to lead: see DUKE] **1.** a tube or channel through which a fluid moves [air ducts from a furnace] **2.** a tube in the body for excretions or secretions to move through [a bile duct] **3.** a pipe or conduit enclosing wires —**duct/less** *adj.*

duc·tile (duk/t′l) *adj.* [see prec.] **1.** that can be stretched, drawn, or hammered thin without breaking [gold is a *ductile* metal] **2.** easily molded; pliant, as clay **3.** easily led; tractable —see SYN. at PLIABLE—**duc·til/i·ty** (-til′ə tē) *n.*

ductless gland an endocrine gland

dud (dud) *n.* [prob. < Du. *dood*, dead] [Colloq.] **1.** a bomb or shell that fails to explode **2.** a person or thing that fails —*adj.* [Colloq.] worthless

☆**dude** (dōōd) *n.* [< ?] **1.** a dandy; fop **2.** [Western Slang] a city fellow or tourist, esp. one from the East **3.** [Slang] any man or boy; fellow —**dud/ish** *adj.* —**dud/ish·ly** *adv.*

☆**dude ranch** a ranch or farm operated as a vacation resort, with horseback riding, etc.

dudg·eon (duj/ən) *n.* [prob. < Anglo-Fr. *en digeon*, at the dagger hilt] anger or resentment: now chiefly in **in high dudgeon**, very angry, offended, or resentful

duds (dudz) *n.pl.* [prob. < ON. < *dutha*, to wrap up, swathe] [Colloq.] **1.** clothes **2.** belongings

due (dōō) *adj.* [< OFr. *deu*, pp. of *devoir*, to owe < L. *debere*: see DEBT] **1.** owed or owing as a debt, right, etc.; payable [a payment is *due* in May] **2.** suitable; proper [*due* respect] **3.** enough; adequate [*due* care] **4.** expected or scheduled to arrive or be ready [the plane is *due* now] —*adv.* exactly; directly [*due* west] —*n.* anything due; specif., *a*) deserved recognition [give the man his *due*] *b*) [*pl.*] fees, taxes, or other charges [membership *dues*] —**become** (or **fall**) **due** to become payable as previously arranged —☆**due to 1.** caused by; resulting from [deaths *due to* cancer] **2.** [Colloq.] because of [*due to* his help, we won]

☆**due bill** a paper acknowledging a debt to a person but not payable to his order: due bills can often be exchanged only for merchandise or services

du·el (dōō/əl) *n.* [< ML. < OL. *duellum* (L. *bellum*), war < IE. base *dau-*, to injure, burn] **1.** a formal fight according to fixed rules between two persons armed with deadly weapons, watched by witnesses **2.** any contest suggesting such a fight [a verbal *duel*] —*vi., vt.* **-eled** or **-elled, -el·ing** or **-el·ling** to fight a duel (with) —**du/el·ist** or **du/el·list, du/el·er** or **du/el·ler** *n.*

du·en·na (dōō en/ə, dyōō-) *n.* [Sp. *dueña* < L. *domina*, mistress] **1.** an elderly woman who has charge of the young unmarried women of a Spanish or Portuguese family **2.** a chaperon or governess

due process (of law) the legal system set up by a country to protect the rights of the individual

du·et (dōō et′, dyōō-) *n.* [< It. < L. *duo*, TWO] *Music* **1.** a composition for two voices or instruments **2.** the two performers of such a composition

duff (duf) *n.* [dial. var. of DOUGH] a thick flour pudding boiled in a cloth bag

duf·fel, duf·fle (duf/′l) *n.* [Du. < *Duffel*, town in N Belgium] **1.** a coarse woolen cloth ☆**2.** clothing and equipment carried by a camper, soldier, etc. ☆**3.** same as DUFFEL BAG

☆**duffel (or duffle) bag** a large, cylindrical cloth bag for carrying clothing and personal belongings

duf·fer (duf/ər) *n.* [< thieves' slang *duff*, to fake] [Slang] an incompetent or stupid person; specif., a golfer without much skill

Du·fy (dü fē′), **Ra·oul** (Ernest Joseph) (rä ōōl′) 1877–1953; Fr. painter

dug¹ (dug) *pt. & pp. of* DIG

dug² (dug) *n.* [< same base as Dan. *dægge*, to suckle] a nipple, teat, or udder

du·gong (dōō/gôŋ, -gäŋ) *n.* [Malay *dūyung*] a large, whalelike mammal of tropical seas, like the manatee

☆**dug·out** (dug/out′) *n.* **1.** a boat or canoe hollowed out of a log **2.** a shelter, as in warfare, dug in the ground or in a hillside **3.** a covered shelter near a baseball diamond for the players to sit in

dui·ker (dik/ər) *n., pl.* **-kers, -ker:** see PLURAL, II, D, 1 [Du.] any of several small, African antelopes

Duis·burg (düs/boork) city in W West Germany, on the Rhine: pop. 458,000

DUGONG
(to 8 ft. long)

duke (dōōk, dyōōk) *n.* [< OFr. < L. *dux*, leader < *ducere*, to lead < IE. base *deuk-*, to pull, from which also come TEAM & TUG] **1.** the ruler of an independent duchy **2.** a nobleman of the highest hereditary rank below that of a prince —**duke/dom** *n.*

dukes (dōōks, dyōōks) *n.pl.* [< *duke*, short for *Duke of York*, used as a slang rhyme for *fork*, meaning "fingers"] [Slang] the fists or hands

dul·cet (dul/sit) *adj.* [< OFr. < L. *dulcis*, sweet] soothing or pleasant to hear; melodious

dul·ci·mer (dul/sə mər) *n.* [< OFr. < Sp. < L. < *dulce*, sweet + *melos* < Gr. *melos*, a song] **1.** a musical instrument with metal strings, which are struck with two small hammers by the player ☆**2.** a violin-shaped stringed instrument of the southern Appalachians, plucked with a plectrum or a goose quill: also **dul/ci·more** (-môr′, -mər)

dull (dul) *adj.* [OE. *dol*, stupid: for IE. base see DOWN²] **1.** mentally slow; stupid **2.** lacking sensitivity; unfeeling [*dull* to grief] **3.** physically slow; sluggish **4.** lacking spirit; listless **5.** not active; slack [a *dull* business period] **6.** causing boredom; tedious [a *dull* party] **7.** not sharp; blunt [a *dull* knife] **8.** not felt keenly [a *dull* headache] **9.** not vivid [a *dull* color] **10.** not glossy [a *dull* finish] **11.** not distinct [a *dull* thud] **12.** gloomy; cloudy [a *dull* day] —*vt., vi.* to make or become dull —**dull/ish** *adj.* —**dull/ness, dul/ness** *n.* —**dul/ly** *adv.*

SYN.—**dull** is applied to a tip or edge that has lost the sharpness it once had [a *dull* pencil, a *dull* knife] and in general use suggests a lack of keenness, zest, spirit, intensity, etc. [a *dull* book, a *dull* pain]; **obtuse** applies literally to an angle greater than 90°, suggesting a point that is not very sharp, and in general use refers to great dullness of understanding or a lack of sensitivity [too *obtuse* to grasp the meaning of her remark] See also SYN. at STUPID —ANT. sharp, keen

dull·ard (dul/ərd) *n.* a stupid person

dulse (duls) *n.* [Ir. & Gael. *duileasq*] any of several edible sea algae with large, red fronds

Du·luth (də lōōth′) [after D. *Du Lhut*, 17th-c. Fr. explorer] city in NE Minn.: pop. 101,000

du·ly (dōō/lē, dyōō/-) *adv.* in due manner; specif., *a*) as due; rightfully [he was *duly* grateful] *b*) when due; at the right time [you will be *duly* notified] *c*) as required [after the matter was *duly* considered]

Du·ma (dōō/mä) *n.* [Russ. < Gmc., as in OE. *dom*, judgment] the parliament of czarist Russia (1905–17)

Du·mas (dü mà′; *E.* dōō/mä) **1. Alexandre,** 1802–70; Fr. novelist & playwright: called *Dumas père* **2. Alexandre,** 1824–95; Fr. playwright & novelist: son of *prec.*: called *Dumas fils*

dumb (dum) *adj.* [OE.: for IE. base see DOWN²] **1.** lacking the power of speech; mute [a *dumb* animal] **2.** unwilling to talk; silent **3.** not accompanied by speech [*dumb* sorrow] **4.** temporarily unable to speak [struck *dumb* with fear] ☆**5.** [G. *dumm*] [Colloq.] stupid; moronic —see SYN. at VOICELESS —**dumb/ly** *adv.* —**dumb/ness** *n.*

dumb·bell (dum/bel′) *n.* **1.** a device consisting of round weights joined by a short bar, usually used in pairs to exercise the muscles ☆**2.** [Slang] a dumb or stupid person

dumb·found, dum·found (dum/-found′) *vt.* [DUMB + (CON)FOUND] to make speechless by shocking; amaze; astonish

dumb show 1. formerly, a part of a play done in pantomime **2.** gestures without speech

DUCALMER

DUMBBELL

dumb·wait·er (dum/wāt/ər) *n.* **1.** a small, portable stand for serving food ☆**2.** a small elevator for sending food, trash, etc. from one floor to another

dum·dum (bullet) (dum/dum/) [< *Dumdum*, arsenal near Calcutta, India] a soft-nosed bullet that expands when it hits, inflicting a large wound

dum·my (dum/ē) *n., pl.* **-mies 1.** *an impolite term for* MUTE **2.** a figure made in human form, as for displaying clothing, practicing tackling in football, etc. **3.** an imitation or sham **4.** a person secretly acting for another while seeming to be acting in his own interests **5.** [Slang] a stupid person **6.** *Bridge, Whist*, etc. *a)* the declarer's partner, whose hand is exposed on the board and played by the declarer *b)* such a hand **7.** a model copy, as of a book, with blank pages or areas upon which the format is laid out —*adj.* **1.** imitation; sham [a *dummy* gun] **2.** secretly acting as a front for another [a *dummy* corporation] **3.** *Bridge,* etc. played with a dummy —**dummy up, -mied, -my·ing** [Slang] to refuse to talk

dump¹ (dump) *vt.* [prob. < ON.: for IE. base see DEEP] **1.** to empty out or unload as in a heap or mass [*dump* the topsoil in the yard] **2.** *a)* to throw away (rubbish, etc.) esp. in or at a dump *b)* to get rid of abruptly or roughly **3.** to sell (a commodity) in a large quantity at a low price, esp. abroad —*vi.* **1.** to fall or drop suddenly **2.** to unload rubbish **3.** to dump commodities —*n.* **1.** a rubbish pile ☆**2.** a place for dumping rubbish, etc. **3.** *Mil.* a temporary storage center, as for ammunition ☆**4.** [Slang] a place that is unpleasant, ugly, run-down, etc. —**dump/er** *n.*

dump² (dump) *n.* [< ? Du. *domp*, haze] [Obs.] a sad song — **(down) in the dumps** in low spirits; depressed

dump·ling (dump/liŋ) *n.* [< Brit. *dump*, lump + -LING¹] **1.** a small piece of dough, steamed or boiled and served with meat or soup **2.** a crust of dough filled with fruit and steamed or baked

☆**dump truck** a truck that is unloaded by tilting the truck bed backward with the tailgate open

dump·y¹ (dump/pē) *adj.* **dump/i·er, dump/i·est 1.** short and thick; squat **2.** [Slang] ugly, run-down, etc. —**dump/i·ly** *adv.* —**dump/i·ness** *n.*

dump·y² (dump/pē) *adj.* **dump/i·er, dump/i·est** [see DUMP²] melancholy; depressed

dun¹ (dun) *adj.* [OE.] dull grayish-brown —*n.* **1.** a dull grayish brown **2.** a dun horse

dun² (dun) *vt., vi.* **dunned, dun/ning** [? dial. var. of DIN] to ask (a debtor) again and again for payment —*n.* a repeated demand for payment of a debt

Dun·bar (dun/bär), **Paul Laurence** 1872–1906; U.S. poet

Dun·can (duŋ/kən) [Gael. *Donnchadh*, lit., brown warrior] **1.** a masculine name **2. Isadora** 1878–1927; U.S. dancer

dunce (duns) *n.* [< *Dunsmen* or *Dunces*, followers of DUNS SCOTUS, who were considered foes of new ideas] **1.** a dull, ignorant person **2.** a person slow at learning

dunce cap a cone-shaped hat which children slow at learning were formerly forced to wear in school

Dun·dee (dun dē/) seaport in E Scotland, on the North Sea: pop. 182,000

dun·der·head (dun/dər hed/) *n.* [< Du. *donder*, thunder, influenced by BLUNDER] a stupid person; dunce

dune (dōōn, dyōōn) *n.* [Fr. < ODu. *duna:* for IE. base see DOWN²] a rounded hill or ridge of sand heaped up by the wind

☆**dune buggy** [from orig. use on sand dunes] a small, light automobile made from a standard, compact chassis and a prefabricated body

Dun·e·din (də nē/d'n) city on the SE coast of South Island, New Zealand: pop. 110,000

dung (duŋ) *n.* [OE.] **1.** waste matter dropped by animals; manure **2.** filth —*vt.* to spread with dung, as in fertilizing

dun·ga·ree (duŋ/gə rē/) *n.* [Hindi *dungrī*] **1.** a coarse cotton cloth; specif., blue denim **2.** [*pl.*] work trousers or overalls of this cloth

dun·geon (dun/jən) *n.* [< OFr. *donjon*] **1.** *same as* DONJON **2.** a dark, underground cell or prison

dung·hill (duŋ/hil/) *n.* **1.** a heap of dung **2.** anything filthy or disgusting

dung·y (duŋ/ē) *adj.* **dung/i·er, dung/i·est** of, like, or soiled with dung; filthy; vile

☆**dunk** (duŋk) *vt.* [G. *tunken*, to dip < OHG. *dunchôn*] **1.** to dip (bread, cake, etc.) into coffee or other liquid before eating it **2.** to plunge into liquid for a short time

Dun·kirk (dun/kərk) seaport in N France, where Allied troops were evacuated under fire (1940): Fr. name **Dun·kerque** (dön kerk/)

dun·lin (dun/lin) *n., pl.* **-lins, -lin:** see PLURAL, II, D, 1 [< DUN¹ + -LING¹] a small sandpiper with a reddish back and a black patch on its belly

dun·nage (dun/ij) *n.* [< ML. *dennagium* < ?] **1.** a loose packing of any bulky material put around cargo to protect it from damage **2.** personal baggage or belongings

Duns Sco·tus (dunz skōt/əs), **John** 1265?–1308; Scot. scholastic philosopher & theologian

du·o (dōō/ō, dyōō/ō) *n., pl.* **du/os, du/i** (-ē) [It.] **1.** *same as* DUET (esp. sense 2) **2.** a pair; couple

du·o- [< L. *duo*, TWO] *a combining form meaning* two, double [*duologue*]

du·o·dec·i·mal (dōō/ə des/ə m'l, dyōō/-) *adj.* [< L. < *duo*, TWO + *decem*, TEN + -AL] **1.** relating to twelve or twelfths **2.** consisting of or counting by twelves —*n.* **1.** one twelfth **2.** [*pl.*] *Math.* a system of numbering that has twelve as its base

du·o·dec·i·mo (-mō/) *n., pl.* **-mos/** [< L. *in duodecimo*, in twelve] **1.** a page size (about 5 by 7½ in.), 1/12 of a printer's sheet **2.** a book with pages of this size Also called *twelvemo*, and written *12mo* or *12°* —*adj.* with pages of this size

du·o·de·num (dōō/ə dē/nəm, dyōō/-; dōō äd/'n əm) *n., pl.* **-de/na** (-nə), **-de/nums** [< ML. < L. *duodeni*, twelve each: its length is about twelve fingers' breadth] the first section of the small intestine, between the stomach and the jejunum: see illustration at INTESTINE —**du·o·de/nal** *adj.*

du·op·o·ly (dōō äp/ə lē, dyōō-) *n., pl.* **-lies** [DUO- + (MONO)POLY] control of a particular market by only two suppliers

dup. duplicate

dupe (dōōp, dyōōp) *n.* [Fr. < OFr. < L. *upupa*, hoopoe, stupid bird] a person easily tricked or fooled —*vt.* **duped, dup/ing** to deceive or cheat —see SYN. at CHEAT —**dup/a·ble** *adj.* —**dup/er** *n.* —**dup/er·y** *n., pl.* **-er·ies**

du·ple (dōō/p'l, dyōō/-) *adj.* [L. *duplus:* see DOUBLE] **1.** double; twofold **2.** *Music* having two (or a multiple of two) beats to the measure [*duple* time]

du·plex (dōō/pleks, dyōō/-) *adj.* [L. < *duo*, TWO + -*plex*, -fold, akin to *plaga*, area] **1.** double; twofold **2.** having two units operating in the same way or simultaneously —☆*n. same as* DUPLEX HOUSE or DUPLEX APARTMENT —**du·plex/i·ty** *n.*

☆**duplex apartment** an apartment with rooms on two floors and a private inner stairway

☆**duplex house** a house consisting of two separate family units

du·pli·cate (dōō/plə kit, dyōō/-; *for v.* -kāt/) *adj.* [< L. pp. of *duplicare*, to double: see DUPLEX] **1.** double **2.** having two similar parts **3.** exactly like another or like each other [make a set of *duplicate* keys] **4.** designating a game of bridge, etc. in which the same hands are played off again by other players to compare scores —*n.* an exact copy; replica; facsimile [the original letter and two *duplicates*] —*vt.* **-cat/ed, -cat/ing 1.** to make double or twofold **2.** to make an exact copy of **3.** to make, do, or cause to happen again [I'll try to *duplicate* my score] —see SYN. at COPY —**in duplicate** in two identical copies —**du/pli·ca·ble, du/pli·cat/a·ble** *adj.* —**du/pli·ca/tion** *n.* —**du/pli·ca/tive** *adj.*

duplicating machine a machine for making exact copies of a letter, photograph, drawing, etc.: also **du/pli·ca/tor** *n.*

du·plic·i·ty (dōō plis/ə tē, dyōō-) *n., pl.* **-ties** [< OFr. < LL. *duplicitas:* see DUPLEX] tricky or dishonest dealing, esp. by doing the opposite of what one pretends to do; double-dealing

dur·a·ble (door/ə b'l, dyoor/-) *adj.* [OFr. < L. < *durare*, to last, harden < *durus*, hard] **1.** lasting in spite of hard wear or frequent use [*durable* shoes] **2.** continuing to exist; stable [a *durable* society] —*n.* [*pl.*] *same as* DURABLE GOODS —**du/ra·bil/i·ty** *n.* —**du/ra·bly** *adv.*

durable goods goods usable for a relatively long time, as machinery, cars, or home appliances

du·ral·u·min (doo ral/yoo m'n, dyoo-) *n.* [DUR(ABLE) + ALU·MIN(UM)] a strong, lightweight alloy of aluminum with copper, manganese, magnesium, and silicon

---

fat, āpe, cär; ten, ēven; is, bīte; gō, hôrn, tōōl, look; oil, out; up, fur; get; joy; yet; chin; she; thin, *th*en; zh, leisure; ŋ, ring; ə for *a* in *ago, e* in *agent, i* in *sanity, o* in *comply, u* in *focus;* ' as in *able* (ā/b'l); Fr. bàl; ë, Fr. coeur; ö, Fr. feu; Fr. mon; ô, Fr. coq; ü, Fr. duc; r, Fr. cri; H, G. ich; kh, G. doch; ‡foreign; ☆ Americanism; < derived from. See inside front cover.

du·ra ma·ter (door′ə māt′ər, dyoor′-) [ML., lit., hard mother < an Ar. term] the outermost and toughest of the three membranes covering the brain and spinal cord: also **du′ra** n. —**du′ral** adj.

du·ra·men (doo rā′mən, dyoo-) n. [L. < durare: see DURABLE] same as HEARTWOOD

dur·ance (door′əns, dyoor′-) n. [< OFr. < L. durans, prp. of durare: see DURABLE] imprisonment: mainly in the phrase **in durance vile**, meaning "imprisoned"

du·ra·tion (doo rā′shən, dyoo-) n. [< ML. < pp. of L. durare: see DURABLE] 1. continuance in time [an illness of long duration] 2. the time that a thing continues or lasts [for the duration of the school year]

Dur·ban (dur′bən) seaport in Natal, on the E coast of South Africa: pop. 663,000

dur·bar (dur′bär) n. [Hindi < Per. < dar, portal + bär, court] 1. formerly in India or Africa, a reception or audience held by a native prince or British governor 2. the place where this was held

Dü·rer (dü′rər; E. dyoor′ər), **Al·brecht** (äl′breHt) 1471–1528; Ger. painter & wood engraver

du·ress (doo res′, dyoo-; door′is, dyoor′-) n. [< OFr. < L. duritia, hardness < durus, hard: for IE. base see TREE] 1. imprisonment 2. the use of force or threats [a confession signed under duress has no legal force]

Dur·ham (dur′əm) [after Durham County, England] city in north central N.C.: pop. 95,000 —n. one of a breed of short-horned beef cattle, orig. bred in Durham County, England

dur·ing (door′iŋ, dyoor′-) prep. [ME. originally prp. of duren, to last < OFr. < L.: see DURABLE] 1. throughout the entire time of; all through [the lake was frozen during the whole winter] 2. at some point in the entire time of; in the course of [he left during the night]

☆**Du·roc-Jer·sey** (door′äk jur′zē, dyoor′-) n. any of a breed of large, red hog: also **Du′roc**

dur·ra (door′ə) n. [Ar. dhurah] a kind of grain sorghum

durst (durst) archaic pt. of DARE

du·rum (wheat) (door′əm, dyoor′-) [L., neut. of durus, hard] a hard wheat from which is made flour and semolina used in macaroni, spaghetti, etc.

Du·shan·be (doo shän′be) capital of the Tadzhik S.S.R., in the W part: pop. 374,000

dusk (dusk) adj. [< OE. dox, dark-colored] [Poet.] dark in color; dusky —n. 1. the dim part of twilight just before the dark of night 2. gloom; dusky quality —vt., vi. to make or become dusky or shadowy

dusk·y (dus′kē) adj. **dusk′i·er, dusk′i·est** 1. somewhat dark in color; esp., having a dark skin; swarthy 2. lacking light; dim 3. gloomy —see SYN. at DARK —**dusk′i·ly** adv. —**dusk′i·ness** n.

Düs·sel·dorf (düs′əl dôrf′) city in W West Germany, on the Rhine: pop. 689,000

dust (dust) n. [OE.] 1. powdery earth or any finely powdered matter 2. a cloud of such matter [let the dust settle] 3. confusion; turmoil 4. a) earth b) the remains of a human being after death 5. a humble or abject condition 6. anything worthless ☆7. same as GOLD DUST —vt. 1. to sprinkle with dust, powder, etc. 2. to sprinkle (powder, etc.) on something 3. to rid of dust, as by brushing or wiping —vi. to remove dust, as from furniture —**bite the dust** to be killed, esp. in battle —**dust off** ☆[Slang] to pitch a baseball deliberately close to (the batter) —**shake the dust off one's feet** to leave a place feeling scorn or contempt —**throw dust in (someone's) eyes** to mislead or deceive (someone) —**dust′less** adj.

dust·bin (dust′bin′) n. [Brit.] a container for rubbish

☆**dust bowl** a region where topsoil has eroded and is blown away by winds during droughts

dust devil a small whirlwind that raises dust and litter in a narrow column

dust·er (dus′tər) n. 1. a person or thing that dusts; specif., a) a brush or cloth for removing dust from furniture, etc. b) a device for sprinkling a powder ☆2. a short, loose, lightweight housecoat

dust jacket a paper cover for protecting the binding of a book from dirt or scratches

dust·man (-mən) n., pl. **-men** [Brit.] a man whose work is removing rubbish, ashes, garbage, etc.

dust·pan (-pan′) n. a pan like a small shovel into which dust or debris is swept from a floor

☆**dust storm** a windstorm that sweeps up clouds of dust when passing over a dry region

dust-up (-up′) n. [Slang] a commotion or fight

dust·y (-ē) adj. **dust′i·er, dust′i·est** 1. covered with or full of dust [dusty shoes] 2. like dust; powdery [dusty sand] 3. of the color of dust; grayish —**dust′i·ly** adv. —**dust′i·ness** n.

Dutch (duch) adj. [< MDu. Duutsch, Dutch, German] 1. of the Netherlands, its people, language, or culture ☆2. of the Pennsylvania Dutch 3. [Slang] German —n. 1. the language of the Netherlands 2. [Slang] German —**beat the Dutch** [Colloq.] to be very unusual —☆**go Dutch** [Colloq.] to have each pay his own expenses —☆**in Dutch** [Colloq.] in trouble or disfavor —**the Dutch** 1. the people of the Netherlands ☆2. the Pennsylvania Dutch

☆**Dutch bob** a haircut with bangs and a straight, even bob that covers the ears

Dutch door a door with upper and lower halves that can be opened separately

Dutch East Indies same as NETHERLANDS (EAST) INDIES

☆**Dutch elm disease** [from its first appearance in the Netherlands] a widespread fungous disease of elms that causes the tree to die

Dutch Guiana former name of SURINAM

Dutch·man (-mən) n., pl. **-men** 1. a native or inhabitant of the Netherlands 2. a Dutch ship 3. [Slang] a German

Dutch·man's-breech·es (-mənz brich′iz) n., pl. **-breech′es** a spring wildflower with pinkish, double-spurred flowers, found in the eastern U.S.

Dutch oven 1. a heavy metal pot with a high, arched lid, for cooking pot roasts, etc. 2. a metal container for roasting meats, etc., with an open side placed toward the fire 3. a brick oven in which the heat comes from the walls, which have been heated earlier

☆**Dutch treat** [Colloq.] any entertainment, etc. at which each participant pays his own expenses

Dutch uncle [Colloq.] a person who bluntly and sternly lectures or scolds someone else

Dutch West Indies former name of NETHERLANDS ANTILLES

du·te·ous (doot′ē əs, dyoot′-) adj. dutiful; obedient —**du′te·ous·ly** adv. —**du′te·ous·ness** n.

du·ti·a·ble (doot′ē ə b'l, dyoot′-) adj. requiring payment of a duty or tax, as imported goods

du·ti·ful (doot′ə fəl, dyoot′-) adj. 1. showing, or resulting from, a sense of duty [her dutiful reply] 2. having a proper sense of duty; obedient [a dutiful son] —**du′ti·ful·ly** adv. —**du′ti·ful·ness** n.

du·ty (doot′ē, dyoot′-) n., pl. **-ties** [< Anglo-Fr. dueté, what is due: see DUE & -TY¹] 1. obedience or respect that is due to parents, older people, etc. 2. something that one ought to do because it is thought to be morally right or necessary [the duty of a citizen to vote] 3. any action required by one's occupation or position [her duties include writing the reports] 4. a sense of obligation [duty calls] 5. service, esp. military service 6. a payment due to the government, esp. a tax on imports, exports, etc. 7. service or use: see HEAVY-DUTY —**on** (or **off**) **duty** at (or having time off from) one's work or duty

SYN.—duty refers to what one must do because of one's sense of what is right, just, or moral [he always carried out his duty to his fellow men]; **obligation** refers to what one is bound to do to carry out a contract, promise, or social requirement [a man's obligation to support his family]; **responsibility** refers to a particular task or trust which one is expected to take care of [the garden is his responsibility; her education will be my responsibility] See also SYN. at FUNCTION

du·um·vir (doo um′vər, dyoo-) n., pl. **-virs, -vi·ri′** (-və rī′) [L. < duo, TWO + vir, a man] either of two magistrates in ancient Rome who together held a single office

du·um·vi·rate (-və rit) n. 1. a single governmental position held by two men 2. two such men

Dvo·řák (dvôr′zhäk, -zhak), **An·ton** (än′tôn) 1841–1904; Czech composer

dwarf (dwôrf) n., pl. **dwarfs, dwarves** (dwôrvz) [OE. dweorg] 1. a person, animal, or plant much smaller than the usual size of its kind 2. Folklore an ugly little being with supposed magic powers 3. a star of relatively small mass and low luminosity: in full, **dwarf star** —vt. 1. to stunt the growth of 2. to make seem small by comparison [the redwood dwarfs other trees]

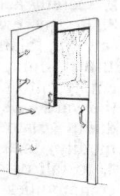

DUTCH DOOR

DUTCHMAN'S-BREECHES

—vi. to become stunted or dwarfed **—adj.** undersized; stunted [a *dwarf* plum tree] **—dwarf'ish** *adj.* **—dwarf'ish·ness** *n.* **—dwarf'ism** *n.*

SYN. —dwarf refers to an individual that is much smaller than the usual kind and sometimes implies that the parts are deformed or not in normal proportion; **midget** refers to a very small human being who has normal form and proportions; **Pygmy,** in strict use, refers to a member of any of several small-sized African or Asian peoples, but it is sometimes used (written **pygmy**) as a synonym for **dwarf** or **midget**

dwell (dwel) *vi.* **dwelt** or **dwelled, dwell'ing** [OE. *dwellan,* to lead astray, hinder: for IE. base see DOWN²] to make one's home; reside; live: no longer used in ordinary speech or writing **—dwell on** (or **upon**) to think about or discuss for a long time **—dwell'er** *n.*

dwell·ing (dwel'iŋ) *n.* a place to live in; residence; house; abode: also **dwelling place**

DWI, D.W.I. driving while intoxicated

Dwight (dwīt) [a surname < ?] a masculine name

dwin·dle (dwin'd'l) *vi., vt.* **-dled, -dling** [< ME. *dwinen* < OE. *dwinan,* to wither: for IE. base see DEAD] to become or make smaller or less; diminish; shrink [his profits are *dwindling*] **—** see SYN. at DECREASE

dwt. [*d*(*enarius*) *w*(*eigh*)*t*] pennyweight(s)

DX, D.X. *Radio* **1.** distance **2.** distant

Dy *Chem.* dysprosium

Dy·ak (dī'ak) *n.* [Malay *dayak,* savage] **1.** a member of an aboriginal people of Borneo **2.** their Indonesian language

dyb·buk (dib'ək) *n.* [Heb. *dibbūq* < *dābhaq,* to cleave] *Jewish Folklore* the spirit of a dead person that is supposed to enter the body of a living person

dye (dī) *n.* [OE. *deag*] **1.** color produced in fabric, hair, etc. by wetting it down with a coloring agent dissolved in liquid; tint; hue **2.** any such coloring agent or a solution containing it **—vt. dyed, dye'ing** to color as with a dye **—vi.** to take on color in dyeing [does this fabric *dye* easily?] **—of (the) deepest dye** of the worst sort **—dy'er** *n.*

dyed-in-the-wool (dīd'n *th*ə wool') *adj.* **1.** dyed before being woven ☆**2.** thoroughgoing; unchanging [a *dyed-in-the-wool* pessimist]

dye·ing (dī'iŋ) *prp.* of DYE **—n.** the process or work of coloring fabrics, hair, etc. with dyes

dye·stuff (dī'stuf') *n.* any substance used as a dye or from which a dye is obtained

dy·ing (dī'iŋ) *prp.* of DIE¹ **—adj. 1.** about to die or end [a *dying* culture] **2.** of or at the time of death [her *dying* words] **—n.** a ceasing to live or exist; death

dyke (dīk) *n., vt. same as* DIKE

dy·nam·ic (dī nam'ik) *adj.* [< Fr. < Gr. < *dynamis,* power < *dynasthai,* to be able] **1.** relating to energy or physical force in motion: opposed to STATIC **2.** relating to dynamics **3.** energetic; vigorous; forceful **4.** relating to change Also **dy·nam'i·cal** **—n.** *same as* DYNAMICS (sense 2*a*) **—dy·nam'i·cal·ly** *adv.*

dy·nam·ics (-iks) *n.pl.* [with sing. v. for 1, 2*c,* & 3] **1.** the branch of mechanics dealing with the motions of material bodies under the action of given forces; kinetics **2.** *a*) the various forces, physical, moral, economic, etc., operating in any field [the *dynamics* of politics] *b*) the way such forces work in relation to one another *c*) the study of such forces **3.** the effect of changing the degrees of loudness and softness in performing music

dy·na·mism (dī'nə miz'm) *n.* **1.** any theory that makes force

or energy the main principle of the universe **2.** a dynamic quality **—dy'na·mis'tic** *adj.*

dy·na·mite (dī'nə mīt') *n.* [coined by A. NOBEL < Gr. *dynamis:* see DYNAMIC] a powerful explosive made of nitroglycerin soaked into an absorbent material **—vt. -mit·ed, -mit·ing** to blow up or destroy with dynamite **—☆adj.** [Slang] excellent; very exciting, effective, etc. **—dy'na·mit'er** *n.*

dy·na·mo (dī'nə mō') *n., pl.* **-mos'** [< *dynamoelectric machine*] **1.** a machine that generates electricity: see GENERATOR **2.** a forceful, dynamic person

dy·na·mo- [< Gr. *dynamis:* see DYNAMIC] *a combining form meaning* power [*dynamoelectric*]

dy·na·mo·e·lec·tric (dī'nə mō i lek'trik) *adj.* having to do with the production of electrical energy from mechanical energy, or the reverse process: also **dy'na·mo·e·lec'tri·cal**

dy·na·mom·e·ter (-mäm'ə tər) *n.* an apparatus for measuring force or power, esp. mechanical power **—dy'na·mo·met'ric** (-mō met'rik) *adj.* **—dy'na·mom'e·try** *n.*

dy·na·mo·tor (dī'nə mōt'ər) *n.* a generator and motor combined in one machine, for transforming current from one voltage to another

dy·nast (dī'nast, -nəst) *n.* [< L. < Gr. < *dynasthai,* to be strong] a ruler, esp. a hereditary ruler

dy·nas·ty (dī'nəs tē) *n., pl.* **-ties** [see prec.] **1.** a series of rulers who are members of the same family **2.** the period during which a certain family reigns **—dy·nas·tic** (dī nas'tik), **dy·nas'ti·cal** *adj.* **—dy·nas'ti·cal·ly** *adv.*

dyne (dīn) *n.* [Fr. < Gr. *dynamis,* power] the amount of force that causes a mass of one gram to accelerate at the rate of one centimeter per second per second

☆**Dy·nel** (dī nel') *a trademark for* a synthetic fiber **—n.** [d-] this fiber, used for making artificial hair and fur

dys- [Gr.] *a prefix meaning* bad, ill, abnormal, impaired, difficult, etc. [*dysfunction*]

dys·en·ter·y (dis'n ter'ē) *n.* [< OFr. < L. < Gr. < *dys-,* bad + *entera,* bowels] a painful disease of the intestines that causes diarrhea with a discharge of blood and mucus **—dys'en·ter'ic** *adj.*

dys·func·tion (dis fuŋk'shən) *n.* abnormal or faulty functioning, as of a body organ or part **—dys·func'tion·al** *adj.*

dys·pep·si·a (dis pep'shə, -sē ə) *n.* [L. < Gr. < *dys-,* bad + *pepsis,* cooking < *peptein,* to digest] faulty digestion; indigestion: also [Dial.] **dys·pep'sy** (-sē)

dys·pep·tic (-tik) *adj.* **1.** of, causing, or having dyspepsia **2.** gloomy; grouchy **—n.** a person who has dyspepsia **—dys·pep'ti·cal·ly** *adv.*

dys·pla·si·a (dis plā'zhē ə, -plā'zhə) *n.* [ModL.: see DYS- & -PLASIA] a faulty development or growth of body tissues or parts **—dys·plas'tic** (-plas'tik) *adj.*

dysp·ne·a (disp'nē ə, disp nē'ə) *n.* [< L. < Gr. < *dys-,* hard + *pnoē* < *pnein,* to breathe] difficult or painful breathing **— dysp·ne'al, dysp·ne'ic** *adj.*

dys·pro·si·um (dis prō'sē əm, -zē-, -shē-) *n.* [< Gr. *dysprositos,* difficult to get] a chemical element of the rare-earth group: symbol, Dy; at. wt., 162.50; at. no., 66: it is one of the most magnetic of all known substances

dys·tro·phy (dis'trə fē) *n.* [ModL. *dystrophia:* see DYS- & -TROPHY] **1.** faulty nutrition **2.** faulty development, or a wasting away: see also MUSCULAR DYSTROPHY **—dys·tro'phic** (-träf'ik, -trō'fik) *adj.*

dz. dozen; dozens

E

E, e (ē) *n., pl.* **E's, e's** **1.** the fifth letter of the English alphabet **2.** a sound of *E* or *e*

E (ē) *n.* **1.** *Educ. a)* a grade indicating below-average work *b)* occas., a grade meaning *excellent* **2.** *Music a)* the third tone in the ascending scale of C major *b)* the scale having this tone as the keynote **3.** *Physics the symbol for: a)* energy *b)* electromotive force

e **1.** *Physics* erg **2.** *Math.* the number used as the base of a system of logarithms, approximately 2.71828: written *e*

e- *a prefix meaning* out, from, etc.: see EX-

E, E., e, e. **1.** east **2.** eastern

E. **1.** Earl **2.** Easter **3.** English

E., e. **1.** earth **2.** engineer(ing) **3.** *Baseball* errors

ea. each

each (ēch) *adj., pron.* [< OE. *ælc*] every one of two or more considered separately [*each* (one) of you will be notified] —*adv.* apiece [ten cents *each*] —**each other** each one the other; one another: some use *each other* only of two and *one another* of more than two, but in common use no distinction is made [help *each other*]

ea·ger (ē′gər) *adj.* [< OFr. *aigre* < L. *acer*, sharp: for IE. base see ACID] feeling or showing keen desire; impatient or anxious to do or get [*eager* for success] —**ea′ger·ly** *adv.* —**ea′ger·ness** *n.*

☆**eager beaver** [Slang] a person who seems too eager to get things done or to advance himself

ea·gle (ē′g'l) *n.* [< OFr. *aigle* < L. *aquila*] **1.** a large, strong bird of prey that feeds on other birds and animals and has sharp vision and powerful wings **2.** a representation of the eagle as a symbol of a nation, etc.; esp., ☆the national emblem of the U.S. ☆**3.** a former U.S. gold coin worth $10 **4.** *Golf* a score of two under par on any hole

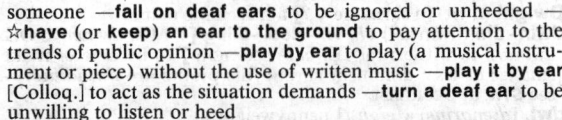

EAGLE
(wingspread
to 8 ft.)

ea·gle-eyed (-īd′) *adj.* having keen vision

☆**Eagle Scout** a boy scout in the highest rank

ea·glet (ē′glit) *n.* a young eagle

Ea·kins (ā′kinz), **Thomas** 1844-1916; U.S. painter

-e·an (ē′ən) [< L. & Gr.] *a suffix meaning* of, belonging to, like [European]

ear¹ (ir) *n.* [OE. *eare* < IE. base *ous-*] **1.** the part of the body through which sound is heard; organ of hearing **2.** the visible, external part of the ear **3.** the sense of hearing **4.** the ability to recognize slight differences in sound, esp. in musical tones [he has a good *ear* for speech sounds] **5.** anything shaped or placed like an ear [the *ear* of a pitcher] —**be all ears** to listen attentively or eagerly —☆**bend someone's ear** [Slang] to talk too much to

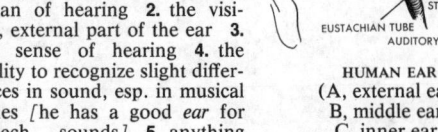

AUDITORY CANAL
SEMICIRCULAR CANAL
HAMMER ANVIL
VESTIBULE
COCHLEA
STAPES
EUSTACHIAN TUBE
AUDITORY NERVES

HUMAN EAR
(A, external ear;
B, middle ear;
C, inner ear)

someone —**fall on deaf ears** to be ignored or unheeded —☆**have (or keep) an ear to the ground** to pay attention to the trends of public opinion —**play by ear** to play (a musical instrument or piece) without the use of written music —**play it by ear** [Colloq.] to act as the situation demands —**turn a deaf ear** to be unwilling to listen or heed

ear² (ir) *n.* [< OE. *ær:* for IE. base see ACID] the spike of a cereal plant on which the grain grows [an *ear* of corn] —*vi.* to sprout ears

ear·ache (ir′āk′) *n.* an ache or pain in the ear

ear·drum (-drum′) *n.* same as: **1.** TYMPANIC MEMBRANE **2.** MIDDLE EAR

☆**ear·ful** (-fool′) *n.* [Colloq.] talk listened to that is especially gossipy, scolding, tedious, etc.

Earl, Earle (url) [see next entry] a masculine name

earl (url) *n.* [OE. *eorl*, warrior, nobleman] a British nobleman ranking above a viscount and below a marquess —**earl′dom** *n.*

ear·lap (ir′lap′) *n.* **1.** the ear lobe **2.** the external ear

ear·ly (ur′lē) *adv., adj.* **-li·er, -li·est** [< OE. < *ær*, before (see ERE) + *-lice* (see -LY²)] **1.** near the beginning of a given period of time or of a series, as of events [*early* in his career] **2.** before the expected or usual time [let's have an *early* lunch] **3.** in the far distant past [*early* man] **4.** in the near future; before long [we hope for an *early* reply] —**early on** [Chiefly Brit.] at any early stage —**ear′li·ness** *n.*

early bird [Colloq.] a person who arrives early or gets up early in the morning

Early Modern English English as spoken and written from about 1450 to about 1750

ear·mark (ir′märk′) *n.* **1.** an identification mark put on the ear of an animal to show ownership **2.** an identifying mark or feature; sign [she has all the *earmarks* of a good teacher] —*vt.* **1.** to mark the ears of (livestock) for identification **2.** to reserve or set aside for a special purpose [money *earmarked* for research]

☆**ear·muffs** (-mufs′) *n.pl.* cloth or fur coverings for the ears in cold weather

earn (urn) *vt.* [OE. *earnian*, to gain, lit., to harvest] **1.** to receive (salary, wages, etc.) for one's labor or service **2.** to get or deserve as a result of something done [you've *earned* our thanks for all your help] **3.** to gain (interest, etc.) as profit ☆**4.** *Baseball* to score (a run not a result of an error) against a pitcher [he's given up five *earned* runs in two games] —**earn′er** *n.*

Ear·nest (ur′nist) [var. of ERNEST] a masculine name

ear·nest¹ (ur′nist) *adj.* [OE. *eornoste*] **1.** serious and intense; not joking; zealous and sincere **2.** not petty; important —see SYN. at SERIOUS —**in earnest 1.** serious **2.** in a determined manner —**ear′nest·ly** *adv.* —**ear′nest·ness** *n.*

ear·nest² (ur′nist) *n.* [< OFr. *erres* < L. *arrae*, pl. < Gr. *arrabōn* < Heb. *'ērābōn*] **1.** money given as a part payment and pledge in binding a bargain: in full, **earnest money 2.** something given or done as an indication of what is to come; token —see SYN. at PLEDGE

earn·ings (ur′ninz) *n.pl.* **1.** wages or other payment for work done **2.** profits, interest, dividends, etc.

ear·phone (ir′fōn′) *n.* a receiver for radio, telephone, etc. held to or put into the ear

ear·plug (-plug′) *n.* a plug inserted in the outer ear, as to keep out sound or water

ear·ring (-rin′) *n.* a ring or other small ornament worn on the lobe of the ear

ear·shot (-shät′) *n.* the distance within which a sound, esp. that of the unaided human voice, can be heard [if you stay within *earshot*, you won't get lost]

earth (urth) *n.* [OE. *eorthe*] 1. the planet that we live on: it is the fifth largest planet of the solar system and the third in distance from the sun: diameter, 7,927 mi. 2. the world we know, as distinguished from heaven and hell 3. all the people on the earth 4. land, as distinguished from sea or sky 5. soil; ground 6. [Poet.] *a)* the human body *b)* worldly matters 7. the hole of a burrowing animal 8. *Chem.* any of the metallic oxides which are reduced with difficulty, as alumina 9. *Elec.* [Brit.] *same as* GROUND¹ —*vt.* to cover (*up*) with soil for protection, as seeds or plants —**come back** (or **down**) **to earth** to return to reality —**down to earth** practical; realistic —**on earth** of all things, persons, places, etc.: used to give force to an interrogative pronoun [what *on earth* is that?] —**run to earth** 1. to hunt down 2. to find by search

earth·bound (urth′bound′) *adj.* 1. confined to or by the earth or earthly things 2. headed for the earth [an *earthbound* spaceship]

earth·en (ur′thən) *adj.* 1. made of earth or of baked clay 2. earthly

earth·en·ware (-wer′) *n.* the coarser sort of dishes, jars, vases, etc. made of baked clay

earth·ly (urth′lē) *adj.* 1. of the earth; specif., *a)* terrestrial *b)* worldly; not spiritual *c)* temporal or secular 2. conceivable; possible [advice that was of no *earthly* use] —**earth′li·ness** *n.*

SYN.—**earthly** is applied to that which belongs to the earth or to the present life, esp. in contrast to *heavenly* [all his *earthly* possessions]; **terrestrial**, the opposite of *celestial*, is mainly a formal and scientific usage [a *terrestrial* globe; *terrestrial* magnetism]; **worldly** suggests the material things and goals that people concern themselves with and is used in contrast to *spiritual* [*worldly* cares; *worldly* wisdom]; **mundane**, although often used as a close synonym of **worldly**, emphasizes everyday practical matters [the *mundane* affairs of business]

earth·man (-man′) *n., pl.* **-men′** (-men′) a person on or from the planet earth, as in science fiction

☆**earth·mov·er** (-mōōv′ər) *n.* a bulldozer or other large machine for moving or digging out large quantities of earth

earth·nut (-nut′) *n.* the root, tuber, or underground pod of various plants, as the peanut

earth·quake (-kwāk′) *n.* a shaking of the crust of the earth, caused by underground volcanic forces or by shifting of rock

earth·shak·ing (-shā′kiŋ) *adj.* having or likely to have enormous importance or effect; momentous [an *earthshaking* event]

earth·ward (-wərd) *adv., adj.* toward the earth: also **earth′wards** *adv.*

earth·work (-wurk′) *n.* 1. an embankment made by piling up earth, esp. one made for defense against attack 2. *Engineering* the work of excavating or building embankments

earth·worm (-wurm′) *n.* a round worm with a body in segments, that burrows in the soil

earth·y (ur′thē) *adj.* **earth′i·er, earth′i·est** 1. of or like earth or soil [an *earthy* smell] 2. *a)* coarse; unrefined [a crude, *earthy* joke] *b)* simple and natural [her *earthy* wisdom] —**earth′i·ness** *n.*

ear trumpet a trumpet-shaped tube formerly used as a hearing aid by the partially deaf

ear·wax (ir′waks′) *n.* the yellowish, waxlike substance that is secreted in the canal of the outer ear; cerumen

ear·wig (-wig′) *n.* [< OE. < *eare*, EAR¹ + *wicga*, beetle, worm: it was once thought to seek out the human ear to crawl into] an insect with short, horny forewings and a pair of forceps at the tail end

ease (ēz) *n.* [< OFr. *aise* < L. *adjacens*, lying nearby: see ADJACENT] 1. freedom from pain or trouble; comfort [your assurance has given me *ease* of mind] 2. a natural, relaxed manner; poise 3. freedom from difficulty or a need for great effort [to write with *ease*] 4. freedom from poverty or hardship [a life of *ease*] —*vt.* **eased, eas′ing** 1. to free from pain or trouble; comfort [his kind words *eased* the upset girl] 2. to lessen (pain, anxiety, etc.) 3. to make easier; facilitate [that will *ease* your task] 4. to reduce the strain or pressure of; loosen: often with *away, down, up,* or *off* 5. to move by careful shifting, etc. [to *ease* a piano into place] —*vi.* 1. to move or be moved by careful shifting, etc. [the boat *eased* into the dock] 2. to lessen in

tension, speed, pain, pressure, etc.: often with *up* or *off* [the soreness began to *ease up*] —**at ease** 1. without pain, anxiety, etc. 2. *Mil.* in a relaxed position, but keeping silent and staying in place —**take one's ease** to relax in comfort —**ease′ful** *adj.* —**ease′ful·ly** *adv.*

ea·sel (ē′z'l) *n.* [< Du. *ezel* (G. *esel*), ass, ult. < L. *asinus*, ASS¹] an upright frame or tripod to hold an artist's canvas, a picture on display, etc.

ease·ment (ēz′mənt) *n.* 1. an easing or being eased 2. a comfort, relief, or convenience 3. *Law* a right that one may have in another's land, as the right to pass through

eas·i·ly (ē′z'l ē) *adv.* 1. in an easy way; with no great effort, trouble, etc. [he solved it *easily*] 2. by far [*easily* the best] 3. very likely [it may *easily* rain]

eas·i·ness (ē′zē nis) *n.* the quality or state of being easy to do or get, or of being at ease

EASEL

east (ēst) *n.* [OE. *east*] 1. the direction to the right of a person facing north; direction in which sunrise occurs (90° on the compass, opposite west) 2. a region or district in or toward this direction 3. [E-] Asia and the nearby islands; the Orient —*adj.* 1. in, of, to, or toward the east 2. from the east [an *east* wind] 3. [E-] designating the eastern part of a country, etc. [*East* Africa] —*adv.* in or toward the east —**the East** ☆the eastern part of the U.S., esp. from Maine through Maryland

East Berlin E section of Berlin; capital of East Germany: pop. 1,084,000: see BERLIN

☆**east·bound** (ēst′bound′) *adj.* going eastward

East China Sea part of the Pacific Ocean east of China and west of Kyushu, Japan

East·er (ēs′tər) *n.* [< OE. < *Eastre*, dawn goddess: her pagan festival took place at the same time as the Christian festival] 1. an annual Christian festival celebrating the resurrection of Jesus, held on the first Sunday after the first full moon on or after March 21 2. this Sunday: also **Easter Sunday**

Easter egg a colored egg or an egg-shaped candy, etc., used as an Easter gift or ornament

Easter Island [discovered *Easter* day, 1722] Chilean island in the South Pacific, c. 2,000 mi. west of Chile: 64 sq. mi.

east·er·ly (ēs′tər lē) *adj., adv.* 1. toward the east 2. from the east [an *easterly* wind]

east·ern (ēs′tərn) *adj.* 1. in, of, or toward the east [the *eastern* sky] 2. from the east [an *eastern* wind] 3. [E-] of or characteristic of the East

Eastern Church 1. *a)* orig., the Christian Church in eastern Europe, western Asia, and Egypt *b)* those churches descended from this church and in union with Rome but having their own rite (**Eastern Rite**) 2. *same as* ORTHODOX EASTERN CHURCH

east·ern·er (-ər) *n.* a native or inhabitant of the east, specif. ☆[E-] of the eastern part of the U.S.

Eastern Hemisphere that half of the earth that includes Europe, Africa, Asia, and Australia

east·ern·most (-mōst′) *adj.* farthest east

Eastern Orthodox Church *same as* ORTHODOX EASTERN CHURCH

Eastern Roman Empire Byzantine Empire, esp. so called until 476 A.D.: see WESTERN ROMAN EMPIRE

Eastern Shore E shore of Chesapeake Bay, including all of Md. and Va. east of the Bay

☆**Eastern Standard Time** *see* STANDARD TIME

East·er·tide (ēs′tər tīd′) *n.* the period from Easter to Ascension Day, Whitsunday, or Trinity Sunday

East Germany a country in NC Europe: 41,800 sq. mi.; pop. 17,084,000; cap. East Berlin: see GERMANY

East Indies 1. Malay Archipelago; esp., the islands of Indonesia 2. formerly, India, the Indochinese peninsula, the Malay Peninsula, and the Malay Archipelago —**East Indian**

east-north·east (ēst′nôrth′ēst′, -nôr′-) *n.* the direction halfway between due east and northeast; 22°30′ north of due east —*adj., adv.* 1. in or toward this direction 2. from this direction

East Orange city in northeastern N.J., adjoining Newark: pop. 75,000

fat, āpe, cär; ten, ēven; is, bīte; gō, hôrn, tōōl, lŏŏk; oil, out; up, fur; get; joy; yet; chin; she; thin, then; zh, leisure; ŋ, ring; ə for *a* in *ago*, *e* in *agent*, *i* in *sanity*, *o* in *comply*, *u* in *focus*; ′ as in *able* (ā′b'l); Fr. bal; ë, Fr. coeur; ö, Fr. feu; ô, Fr. coq; ü, Fr. duc; r, Fr. cri; H, G. ich; kh, G. doch; ‡foreign; ☆ Americanism; < derived from. See inside front cover.

East Prussia former province of NE Germany, on the Baltic Sea: since 1945, in Poland & the U.S.S.R.

East River strait in southeastern N.Y., separating Manhattan Island from Long Island

east·south·east (ēst′south′ēst′, -sou′-) *n.* the direction halfway between due east and southeast; 22°30′ south of due east —*adj., adv.* **1.** in or toward this direction **2.** from this direction

East St. Louis city in SW Ill., on the Mississippi, opposite St. Louis: pop. 70,000

east·ward (ēst′wərd) *adj., adv.* toward the east: also **east′-wards** *adv.* —*n.* an eastward direction, point, or region

east·ward·ly (-lē) *adv., adj.* **1.** toward the east **2.** from the east [an *eastwardly* wind]

eas·y (ē′zē) *adj.* **eas′i·er, eas′i·est** [< OFr. *aisé* < *aise:* see EASE] **1.** that can be done, got, etc. with ease; not difficult [an *easy* job] **2.** free from trouble, anxiety, pain, etc. [an *easy* life] **3.** providing comfort or rest [an *easy* chair] **4.** fond of comfort or ease [an *easy* disposition] **5.** not stiff or awkward [an *easy* manner] **6.** not strict; lenient [an *easy* boss] **7.** ready to agree or accept; not doubting or refusing anyone [an *easy* mark] **8.** *a*) unhurried [an *easy* pace] *b*) gradual [an *easy* descent] —*adv.* [Colloq.] **1.** easily **2.** slowly and carefully —**easy does it** be careful —☆**go easy on** [Colloq.] **1.** to use sparingly [go *easy* on the paper] **2.** to deal with leniently [to go *easy* on traffic violators] —☆**on easy street** well-to-do —**take it easy** [Colloq.] **1.** to try not to be angry, hasty, etc. **2.** to relax; rest

SYN.—easy is the general term applied to that which calls for little effort or offers little difficulty [*easy* work; an *easy* problem]; **facile** means happening, moving, working, etc. easily and quickly, but sometimes suggests a lack of thoroughness or depth [a *facile* style]; **effortless**, on the other hand, is applied to something done with no seeming effort because of expert skill or knowledge [the *effortless* grace of the skater]; **smooth** is used of something easily achieved because there are no interruptions, obstacles, or difficulties [a *smooth* path to success]; **simple**, in this comparison, is applied to something easy to understand because it is not complicated or highly detailed —**ANT. hard, difficult**

easy chair a stuffed or padded armchair

eas·y·go·ing (-gō′iŋ) *adj.* **1.** not hurried or worried **2.** not strict; lenient

eat (ēt) *vt.* **ate** (āt; *Brit.* et) or archaic & dial. **eat** (et, ēt), **eat·en** (ēt′'n) or archaic **eat** (et, ēt), **eat′ing** [OE. *etan* < IE. base *ed-*, to eat] **1.** to chew and swallow (food) **2.** to use up or destroy as by eating; consume or ravage (usually with *away* or *up*) [inflation has *eaten* up their savings] **3.** to penetrate and destroy [hinges *eaten* away by rust] **4.** to make by or as by eating [acid *ate* holes in the cloth] **5.** to bring (oneself) into a specified condition by eating [he *ate* himself sick] ☆**6.** [Slang] to worry or bother [what's *eating* him?] —*vi.* **1.** to eat food; have a meal or meals **2.** to destroy or use up something gradually (often with *into*) [the acid *ate* into the paint] —**eat one's words** to take back something said earlier —**eat′er** *n.*

eat·a·ble (ēt′ə b'l) *adj.* fit to be eaten; edible —*n.* a thing fit to be eaten: *usually used in pl.*

☆**eat·er·y** (-ər ē) *n., pl.* **-er·ies** [Colloq.] a restaurant

eat·ing (-iŋ) *n.* **1.** the action of one that eats **2.** food, with reference to its quality [that dinner was good *eating*] —*adj.* **1.** that eats **2.** good for eating uncooked [*eating* apples]

☆**eats** (ēts) *n.pl.* [Colloq.] food; meals

eau de Co·logne (ō′də kə lōn′) [Fr., lit., water of Cologne] a perfumed toilet water made of alcohol and aromatic oils: usually shortened to *cologne*

eaves (ēvz) *n.pl., sing.* **eave** [orig. sing., OE. *efes*] the lower edge or edges of a roof, usually projecting beyond the sides of a building

eaves·drop (ēvz′dräp′) *vi.* **-dropped′, -drop′ping** [prob. backformation < *eavesdropper*, lit., one who stands under the eaves to listen] to listen secretly to a private conversation —**eaves′drop′per** *n.*

ebb (eb) *n.* [OE. *ebba*] **1.** the flow of water back toward the sea, as the tide falls **2.** a weakening or lessening; decline [the *ebb* of one's hopes] —*vi.* **1.** to flow back; recede, as the tide **2.** to weaken or lessen; decline [our hopes for victory *ebbed*] —see SYN. at WANE

ebb tide the outgoing or falling tide

eb·on (eb′ən) *adj., n.* [< L. *ebenus* < Gr. *ebenos* < Egypt. *hbnj* (Heb. *hobnim*)] [Poet.] *same as* EBONY

eb·on·ite (-īt′) *n.* [EBON(Y) + -ITE] *same as* VULCANITE

eb·on·ize (-īz′) *vt.* **-ized′, -iz′ing** to finish (wood, etc.) to look like ebony

eb·on·y (-ē) *n., pl.* **-on·ies** [< LL. *ebenius* < *ebenus:* see EBON] **1.** the hard, heavy, dark, durable wood of certain tropical trees, used in decorative woodwork, etc. **2.** such a tree —*adj.* **1.** made of ebony **2.** like ebony, esp. in color; dark; black

E·bro (ā′brō; *E.* ē′brō) river in N Spain, flowing southeastward into the Mediterranean

e·bul·lient (i bool′yənt, -bul′-) *adj.* [< L. prp. of *ebullire* < *e-*, out + *bullire*, to BOIL[1]] **1.** bubbling **2.** overflowing with enthusiasm, etc.; exuberant —**e·bul′lience, e·bul′lien·cy** *n.* —**e·bul′lient·ly** *adv.*

e·bul·li·tion (eb′ə lish′ən) *n.* **1.** a boiling or bubbling up **2.** a sudden outburst, as of emotion

Ec·bat·a·na (ek bat′'n ə) capital of ancient Media

ec·cen·tric (ik sen′trik) *adj.* [< ML. < LL. < Gr. < *ek-*, out of + *kentron*, CENTER] **1.** not having the same center, as two circles one inside the other: opposed to CONCENTRIC **2.** not having the axis exactly in the center; off center [an *eccentric* wheel] **3.** not exactly circular in shape or motion **4.** not usual or normal in behavior; odd; unconventional —*n.* **1.** a disk set off center on a shaft in an apparatus for converting circular motion into back-and-forth motion **2.** an eccentric person —**ec·cen′tri·cal·ly** *adv.*

ec·cen·tric·i·ty (ek′sen tris′ə tē, -sən-) *n., pl.* **-ties** **1.** the state, quality, or amount of being eccentric **2.** unusual or odd behavior, or a peculiar habit —see SYN. at IDIOSYNCRASY

eccl., eccles. ecclesiastical

Eccles., Eccl. Ecclesiastes

Ec·cle·si·as·tes (i klē′zē as′tēz) [LL. < Gr. *ekklēsia*, assembly: transl. of Heb. *qōheleth*, speaker before an assembly] a book of the Bible, written as though by Solomon

ec·cle·si·as·tic (-tik) *adj.* [< LL. < Gr. < *ekklēsia*, assembly, ult. < *ek-*, out + *kalein*, to call] *same as* ECCLESIASTICAL —*n.* a clergyman

ec·cle·si·as·ti·cal (-ti k'l) *adj.* of the church or the clergy —**ec·cle′si·as′ti·cal·ly** *adv.*

Ec·cle·si·as·ti·cus (-ti kəs) [LL.] a book of proverbs in the Apocrypha: abbrev. **Ecclus.**

ec·dy·sis (ek′də sis) *n.* [ModL. < Gr. < *ekdein*, to strip off < *ek-*, out of + *dyein*, to enter] the shedding of an outer layer of skin, as by snakes, insects, etc.

ECG electrocardiogram

ech·e·lon (esh′ə län′) *n.* [< Fr. < OFr. *eschelle* < L. *scala*, ladder] **1.** a steplike formation of ships, aircraft, or troops **2.** a section of a military force in its relation to others [rear *echelon;* command *echelon*] —*vt., vi.* to assemble in echelon

e·chid·na (i kid′nə) *n.* [ModL. < L. < Gr. *echidna*, adder] a small, egg-laying Australasian mammal with a long snout and a spiny coat: it feeds on ants

e·chi·no·derm (i kī′nə durm′, ek′ə-) *n.* [< ModL. < Gr. *echinos*, sea urchin, hedgehog + *derma*, skin] any of a group of sea animals with a hard, spiny skeleton and radial body, as a starfish

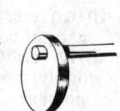

ECCENTRIC
CIRCLES AND
WHEEL

ECHIDNA
(14-21 in. long)

ech·o (ek′ō) *n., pl.* **-oes** [< L. < Gr. *ēchō*] **1.** *a*) the repetition of a sound that occurs when sound waves are reflected from a surface *b*) a sound so made **2.** *a*) any repetition or imitation of the words, ideas, etc. of another *b*) a person who repeats or imitates in this way **3.** sympathetic response **4.** a radar wave reflected from an object, appearing as a spot of light on a radarscope —[E-] *Gr. Myth.* a nymph who pined away for Narcissus until only her voice remained —*vi.* **-oed, -o·ing** **1.** to be filled with echoes [the long hall *echoed* with their laughter] **2.** to be repeated as an echo [his words *echoed* in the valley] —*vt.* **1.** to repeat (the words, ideas, etc.) of (another) **2.** to repeat or reflect (sound) from a surface

☆**echo chamber** a room, or now often a device, used in recording and broadcasting to make sounds more resonant or to produce an echo effect

e·cho·ic (e kō′ik) *adj.* **1.** having the nature of an echo **2.** imitating the sound of the thing or action described; onomatopoeic [the words *clash, buzz,* and *meow* are *echoic*] —**ech′o·ism** *n.*

ech·o·lo·ca·tion (ek′ō lō kā′shən) *n.* the method used by bats, in radar, etc. of finding an object's position by sending out sound waves which are reflected back to the sender —**ech′o·lo′cate** *vt., vi.* **-cat·ed, -cat·ing**

echo sounding a method of measuring the depth of water or underwater distances by a device (**echo sounder**) that measures the time it takes for a sound wave to be reflected

é·clair (ā kler′, ē-, i-) *n.* [Fr., lit., lightning] a small, oblong pastry shell filled with flavored custard or whipped cream and covered with frosting

é·clat (ā klä′, i-) *n.* [Fr. < *éclater*, to burst (out)] **1.** brilliant success **2.** approval; acclaim **3.** fame; renown

ec·lec·tic (i klek′tik, e-) *adj.* [< Gr. < *ek-*, out + *legein*, to pick] **1.** selecting from various systems, doctrines, or sources [an *eclectic* philosopher] **2.** made up of parts chosen from various sources [an *eclectic* reader] —*n.* one who uses eclectic methods —**ec·lec′ti·cal·ly** *adv.* —**ec·lec′ti·cism** (-siz′m) *n.*

e·clipse (i klips′, ē-) *n.* [< OFr. < L. < Gr. *ekleipsis* < *ek-*, out + *leipein*, to leave: for IE. base see LOAN] **1.** a partial or total hiding of the sun when the moon comes between it and the earth (**solar eclipse**), or of the moon when the earth's shadow is cast upon it (**lunar eclipse**) **2.** a dimming or destroying, as of fame —*vt.* **e·clipsed′, e·clips′ing 1.** to cause an eclipse of **2.** to overshadow or surpass [a record that has *eclipsed* all others]

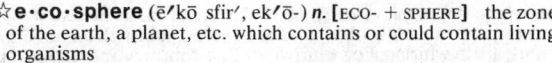

SUN
MOON PENUMBRA
UMBRA
EARTH
ECLIPSE
(of the sun)

e·clip·tic (i klip′tik, ē-) *n.* the path that the sun appears to travel annually on the celestial sphere —*adj.* of eclipses or the ecliptic

ec·logue (ek′lôg, -läg) *n.* [< Fr. < L. < Gr. < *eklegein:* see ECLECTIC] a short pastoral poem, usually a dialogue between two shepherds

e·co- [< LL. < Gr. < *oikos*, house] *a combining form meaning* environment or habitat [*ecosystem*]

☆**e·co·cide** (ē′kō sīd′, ek′ō-) *n.* the destruction of the environment or of ecosystems, as by pollution

ecol. 1. ecological **2.** ecology

e·col·o·gy (ē käl′ə jē) *n.* [< G. < Gr. *oikos*, house + *-logia*, -LOGY] **1.** the science that deals with the relations between living things and their environment **2.** any particular instance of such relations —**ec·o·log·i·cal** (ek′ə läj′i k'l, ē′kə-), **ec′o·log′ic** *adj.* —**ec′o·log′i·cal·ly** *adv.* —**e·col′o·gist** *n.*

econ. 1. economic **2.** economics **3.** economy

e·con·o·met·rics (i kän′ə met′riks) *n.pl.* [with *sing. v.*] [< ECONOMY + METER² + -ICS] the use of statistical methods in developing economic theories and checking their accuracy —**e·con′o·met′ric** *adj.* —**e·con′o·me·tri′cian** (-mə trish′ən) *n.*

e·co·nom·ic (ē′kə näm′ik, ek′ə-) *adj.* **1.** of the management of the income and expenses of a business, community, etc. **2.** of the science of economics

e·co·nom·i·cal (-i k'l) *adj.* **1.** not wasting money, time, material, etc.; thrifty or efficient [an *economical* person; an *economical* stove] **2.** expressed or done with economy, using few lines, words, etc. [an *economical* style] **3.** of economics —see SYN. at THRIFTY —**e′co·nom′i·cal·ly** *adv.*

e·co·nom·ics (-iks) *n.pl.* [with *sing. v.*] **1.** the science dealing with the production, distribution, and consumption of wealth and with the various related problems of labor, finance, taxation, etc. **2.** economic factors or relationships

e·con·o·mist (i kän′ə mist) *n.* a specialist in economics

e·con·o·mize (-mīz′) *vi.* **-mized′, -miz′ing** to avoid waste or reduce expenses —*vt.* to manage or use with thrift —**e·con′o·miz′er** *n.*

e·con·o·my (-mē) *n., pl.* **-mies** [< L. < Gr. < *oikonomos*, manager < *oikos*, house + *nomos*, managing < *nemein*, to distribute] **1.** management of income, expenses, etc. **2.** *a)* careful management of wealth, resources, etc.; thrift *b)* controlled or efficient use of one's materials, techniques, etc., as in the arts [there is an *economy* of line in his drawings] **3.** an orderly arrangement or management of parts [the *economy* of the human body] **4.** an economic system of a specified kind, place, era, or condition [an agricultural *economy*]

☆**e·co·sphere** (ē′kō sfir′, ek′ō-) *n.* [ECO- + SPHERE] the zone of the earth, a planet, etc. which contains or could contain living organisms

e·co·sys·tem (ē′kō sis′təm, ek′ō-) *n.* [ECO- + SYSTEM] a community of animals, plants, and bacteria forming a complete system with the physical and chemical environment in which it exists

ec·ru (ek′rōō, ā′krōō) *adj., n.* [Fr. *écru*, unbleached < OFr. < *es-* (L. *ex-*), thoroughly + *cru*, raw < L. *crudus*] light tan

ec·sta·sy (ek′stə sē) *n., pl.* **-sies** [< OFr. < L. < Gr. *ekstasis*, distraction < *ek-*, out + *histanai*, to place] **1.** an overpowering feeling of joy or delight; state of rapture **2.** a trance, as one caused by strong religious feeling

SYN.—ecstasy implies very strong feeling, now usually intense delight, that overpowers one's senses and lifts one into a kind of trance; **bliss** implies a state of happiness and contentment so great as to suggest the joys of heaven; **rapture** now generally suggests the intense feeling one has when something causing great joy or pleasure captures all of one's attention; **transport** implies a being carried away by any powerful feeling

ec·stat·ic (ik stat′ik, ek-) *adj.* of, feeling, causing, or caused by ecstasy —**ec·stat′i·cal·ly** *adv.*

ec·to- [ModL. < Gr. *ektos*, outside] *a combining form meaning* outside, external: also, before a vowel, **ect-**

ec·to·derm (ek′tə durm′) *n.* [ECTO- + -DERM] the outer layer of cells of an embryo, from which the skin, hair, etc. develop —**ec′to·der′mal, ec′to·der′mic** *adj.*

ec·to·mor·phic (ek′tə môr′fik) *adj.* [ECTO- + -MORPHIC] designating a type of body build that is slender and light and in which the structures developed from the ectoderm are most prominent —**ec′to·morph′** *n.*

-ec·to·my (ek′tə mē) [< Gr. < *ek-*, out + *temnein*, to cut] *a combining form meaning* a surgical operation [*appendectomy*]

ec·to·plasm (ek′tə plaz′m) *n.* [ECTO- + -PLASM] **1.** the outer cytoplasm of a cell **2.** a glowing vapor supposedly given off by the body of a medium in a spiritualistic trance —**ec′to·plas′mic** *adj.*

ec·to·proct (-präkt) *n.* [< ModL. < *ecto-* (see ECTO-) + Gr. *prōktos*, anus] any of various minute water animals that form mosslike colonies and reproduce by budding —**ec′to·proc′tan** *adj.*

Ec·ua·dor (ek′wə dôr′) country on the NW coast of S. America: 104,506 sq. mi.; pop. 5,840,000; cap. Quito —**Ec′ua·do′re·an, Ec′ua·do′ri·an, Ec′ua·dor′an** *adj., n.*

ec·u·men·i·cal (ek′yōō men′i k'l) *adj.* [< LL. < Gr. < *oikoumenē* (*gē*), the inhabited (world) < *oikein*, to inhabit < *oikos*, house] **1.** general, or universal; esp., of the Christian church as a whole **2.** *a)* encouraging the joining together or cooperation of Christian churches *b)* promoting better understanding among differing religious groups Also **ec′u·men′ic** —**ec′u·men′i·cal·ism** *n.* —**ec′u·men′i·cal·ly** *adv.*

ec·u·men·i·cism (-i siz′m) *n. same as* ECUMENISM

ec·u·men·ism (ek′yōō mə niz′m, e kyōō′-) *n.* **1.** any ecumenical movement **2.** ecumenical principles or practice Also **ec′u·me·nic′i·ty** (-nis′ə tē) —**ec′u·men·ist** *n.*

ec·ze·ma (ek′sə mə, eg′zə-; ig zē′mə) *n.* [ModL. < Gr. < *ek-*, out of + *zein*, to boil] a disorder of the skin in which it becomes inflamed, scaly, and very itchy —**ec·zem·a·tous** (ig zem′ə təs, -zē′mə-) *adj.*

-ed (id, əd; d, t) [< OE.] **1.** *a suffix used: a)* to form the past tense and past participle of weak verbs [*wanted*] *b)* to form adjectives from nouns or verbs [*cultured*] or from adjectives ending in *-ate* [*serrated*] **2.** *a suffix added to nouns, meaning* having [*bearded*]

ed. 1. edited **2.** *pl.* **eds.** *a)* edition *b)* editor **3.** education

E·dam (cheese) (ē′dəm, -dam) [orig. made in the Du. town of *Edam*] a round, mild, yellow cheese, usually coated with red paraffin

Ed.B. Bachelor of Education

Ed.D. Doctor of Education

Ed·da (ed′ə) [ON.] either of two early Icelandic literary works: *a)* the **Prose**, or **Younger, Edda** (c. 1230), a collection of Norse myths *b)* the **Poetic**, or **Elder, Edda** (c. 1200), a collection of Old Norse poetry —**Ed·dic** (ed′ik), **Ed·da·ic** (i-dā′ik) *adj.*

Ed·ding·ton (ed′iŋ tən), Sir **Arthur Stanley** 1882–1944; Eng. astronomer & astrophysicist

---

fat, āpe, cär; ten, ēven; is, bīte; gō, hôrn, tōōl, look; oil, out; up, fur; get; joy; yet; chin; she; thin, then; zh, leisure; ŋ, ring; ə for *a* in *ago*, *e* in *agent*, *i* in *sanity*, *o* in *comply*, *u* in *focus*; ′ as in *able* (ā′b'l); Fr. bál; ë, Fr. coeur; ö, Fr. feu; Fr. mon; ô, Fr. coq; ü, Fr. duc; r, Fr. cri; H, G. ich; kh, G. doch; ‡foreign; ☆ Americanism; < derived from. See inside front cover.

ed·dy (ed′ē) *n., pl.* **-dies** [prob. < ON. *itha*] **1.** a current of air, water, etc. moving with a circular motion against the main current; little whirlpool or whirlwind **2.** a contrary movement or trend of little importance —*vi.* **-died, -dy·ing** to move in an eddy; whirl

Ed·dy (ed′ē), **Mary Baker** 1821–1910; U.S. founder of Christian Science

e·del·weiss (ā′d'l vīs′) *n.* [G. < *edel*, noble + *weiss*, white] a small plant of the composite family, native to the high mountains of Europe and C Asia, esp. the Alps, with white, woolly leaves and bracts

e·de·ma (i dē′mə) *n., pl.* **-mas, -ma·ta** (-mə tə) [ModL. < Gr. *oidēma*, a swelling] **1.** an abnormal accumulation of fluid in tissues, cells, or cavities of the body, causing swelling **2.** a similar swelling in plants —**e·dem·a·tous** (i dem′ə təs, i dē′mə-) *adj.*

E·den (ē′d'n) [LL. < Heb. *'ēdhen*, lit., delight] *Bible* the garden where Adam and Eve first lived; Paradise —*n.* any delightful place or state

EDELWEISS

e·den·tate (ē den′tāt) *adj.* [< L. pp. of *edentare*, to make toothless < *e-*, out + *dens*, TOOTH] **1.** without teeth **2.** of the edentates —*n.* any of a group of mammals with molars only or no teeth at all, as sloths and anteaters

Ed·gar (ed′gər) [< OE. < *ead*, riches + *gar*, a spear] a masculine name: dim. *Ed*

edge (ej) *n.* [OE. *ecg*: for IE. base see ACID] **1.** the sharp, cutting part of a blade **2.** sharpness; keenness [there is an *edge* to her humor] **3.** a projecting ledge, as of a cliff **4.** the line or part where something begins or ends; border; margin **5.** the line formed by two intersecting plane faces of a solid **6.** the verge or brink, as of a condition [on the *edge* of disaster] ☆**7.** [Colloq.] advantage [you have the *edge* on me] —*vt.* **edged, edg′ing 1.** *a)* to put an edge on [to *edge* a pocket with braid] *b)* to trim the edge of [to *edge* a lawn] **2.** to make (one's way) sideways **3.** to move gradually or cautiously [he *edged* the car seat forward] **4.** [Colloq.] to defeat by a small margin [we *edged* South High 84 to 83] —*vi.* to move sideways or gradually or cautiously —**on edge** irritable or impatient —**set one's teeth on edge 1.** to give a sensation of tingling discomfort **2.** to irritate; provoke —**take the edge off** to dull the intensity or pleasure (of) —**edg′er** *n.*

edge·ways (-wāz′) *adv.* with the edge foremost; on, by, or toward the edge: also **edge′wise′** (-wīz′) —**get a word in edgeways** to manage to say something in a conversation in which someone else is doing all the talking

edg·ing (ej′iŋ) *n.* something forming an edge

edg·y (ej′ē) *adj.* **edg′i·er, edg′i·est 1.** having an edge; sharp **2.** irritable; on edge —**edg′i·ly** *adv.* —**edg′i·ness** *n.*

ed·i·ble (ed′ə b'l) *adj.* [LL. *edibilis* < L. *edere*, EAT] fit to be eaten —*n.* anything fit to be eaten; food: *usually used in pl.* —**ed′i·bil′i·ty** (-bil′ə tē), **ed′i·ble·ness** *n.*

e·dict (ē′dikt) *n.* [< L. pp. of *edicere*, to proclaim < *e-*, out + *dicere*, to say: see DICTION] an official public order or law put forth by a ruler or other authority; decree

ed·i·fice (ed′ə fis) *n.* [< OFr. < L. *aedificium*, a building < *aedificare*: see EDIFY] **1.** a building, esp. one that is large or looks important **2.** any complicated organization —see SYN.at BUILDING

ed·i·fy (ed′ə fī′) *vt.* **-fied′, -fy′ing** [< OFr. < L. *aedificare*, to build < *aedes*, a house (for IE. base see ETHER) + *-ficare* < *facere*, to make] to teach or instruct so as to improve in morals or character; enlighten —**ed′i·fi·ca′tion** (-fi kā′shən) *n.* —**ed′·i·fi′er** *n.*

e·dile (ē′dīl) *n. same as* AEDILE

Ed·in·burgh (ed′'n bur′ə, -ō) capital of Scotland, on the Firth of Forth: pop. 468,000

Ed·i·son (ed′ə s'n), **Thomas Al·va** (al′və) 1847–1931; U.S. inventor

ed·it (ed′it) *vt., vi.* [back-formation < EDITOR] **1.** to prepare (an author's works, a manuscript, etc.) for publication by selecting, arranging, revising, etc. **2.** to be in charge of what is printed in (a newspaper or periodical) ☆**3.** to prepare (a film, tape, or recording) for presentation by cutting, rearranging, etc. —☆**edit out** to delete in editing

edit. 1. edited **2.** edition **3.** editor

E·dith (ē′dith) [< OE. < *ead*, riches + *guth*, battle] a feminine name

e·di·tion (i dish′ən) *n.* [< L. *editio*, a publishing < *edere*: see EDITOR] **1.** the size, style, or form in which a book, etc. is published [a pocket *edition*] **2.** *a)* the total number of identical copies of a book, etc. published at about the same time [her book went through six *editions*] *b)* one of these copies [he has a first *edition* of Tom Sawyer]

ed·i·tor (ed′i tər) *n.* [< L. pp. of *edere*, to publish < *e-*, out + *dare*, to give] **1.** a person who edits ☆**2.** the head of a department of a newspaper, magazine, etc. ☆**3.** a device used to edit (sense 3) —**ed′i·tor·ship′** *n.*

ed·i·to·ri·al (ed′ə tôr′ē əl) *adj.* of, by, or characteristic of an editor or editors —☆*n.* a statement of opinion in a newspaper, etc. or on radio or TV that gives the views of the owner, publisher, etc. —**ed′i·to′ri·al·ly** *adv.*

☆**ed·i·to·ri·al·ist** (-ist) *n.* an editorial writer

☆**ed·i·to·ri·al·ize** (-īz′) *vt., vi.* **-ized′, -iz′ing 1.** to express editorial opinions about (something) **2.** to put editorial opinions into (a news article, etc.) —**ed′i·to′ri·al·i·za′tion** *n.* —**ed′i·to′ri·al·iz′er** *n.*

editor in chief *pl.* **editors in chief** the editor who heads the editorial staff of a publication

Ed·mon·ton (ed′mən tən) capital of Alberta, Canada, in the C part: pop. 461,000

Ed·mund, Ed·mond (ed′mənd) [< OE. < *ead*, riches + *mund*, protection] a masculine name

Ed·na (ed′nə) [Gr. < Heb. *'ēdnāh*, rejuvenation] a feminine name

E·dom (ē′dəm) ancient kingdom in SW Asia, south of the Dead Sea —**E′dom·ite′** (-īt′) *n.*

EDP electronic data processing

ed·u·ca·ble (ej′ə kə b'l) *adj.* that can be educated or trained —**ed′u·ca·bil′i·ty** *n.*

ed·u·cate (ej′ə kāt′) *vt.* **-cat′ed, -cat′ing** [< L. pp. of *educare*, to train < *educere* < *e-*, out + *ducere*, to lead: see DUKE] **1.** to train, teach, instruct, or develop, esp. by formal schooling **2.** to pay for the schooling of (a person) —see SYN.at TEACH

ed·u·cat·ed (-kāt′id) *adj.* **1.** having, or showing the results of, much education ☆**2.** based on knowledge or experience [an *educated* guess]

ed·u·ca·tion (ej′ə kā′shən) *n.* **1.** an educating or a being educated **2.** knowledge, ability, etc. developed by being educated or trained **3.** *a)* formal schooling *b)* a stage of this [a high-school *education*] **4.** study of the methods and theories of teaching and learning

ed·u·ca·tion·al (-'l) *adj.* **1.** relating to education [*educational* theories] **2.** that teaches or informs [an *educational* film] —**ed′u·ca′tion·al·ly** *adj.*

ed·u·ca·tion·ist (-ist) *n.* an educator; esp., an authority on educational theory: often used as a term to belittle: also **ed′u·ca′tion·al·ist**

ed·u·ca·tive (ej′ə kāt′iv) *adj.* **1.** educating or tending to educate **2.** of education; educational

ed·u·ca·tor (ej′ə kāt′ər) *n.* **1.** a person whose work is to educate others; teacher **2.** a specialist in educational methods, theories, etc., who helps train teachers

e·duce (i doos′, ē-; -dyoos′) *vt.* **-duced′, -duc′ing** [L. *educere*: see EDUCATE] **1.** to draw out; bring forth; elicit **2.** *same as* DEDUCE —see SYN.at EXTRACT —**e·duc′i·ble** *adj.* —**e·duc·tion** (i duk′shən, ē-) *n.*

Ed·ward (ed′wərd) [< OE. < *ead*, riches + *weard*, guardian] **1.** a masculine name **2.** name of eight kings of England: *a)* **Edward I** 1239–1307; king (1272–1307) *b)* **Edward II** 1284–1327; king (1307–27) *c)* **Edward III** 1312–77; king (1327–77) *d)* **Edward IV** 1442–83; king (1461–70; 1471–83) *e)* **Edward V** 1470–83; king (1483): murdered *f)* **Edward VI** 1537–53; king (1547–53) *g)* **Edward VII** 1841–1910; king (1901–10) *h)* **Edward VIII** *see* Duke of WINDSOR

Ed·ward·i·an (ed wär′dē ən, -wôr′-) *adj.* designating or of the reign of any of the English kings named Edward, specif. of Edward VII

Ed·wards (ed′wərdz), **Jonathan** 1703–58; Am. theologian

Edward the Confessor 1004?–66; king of England (1042–66)

Ed·win (ed′win) [< OE. < *ead*, riches + *wine*, friend] a masculine name

-ee (ē) [< OFr. *-é*, orig. masc. ending of pp. of verbs in *-er*] *a suffix meaning:* **1.** the person who receives a specified action or benefit [*appointee, mortgagee*] **2.** a person in a specified condition [*absentee, employee*]

E.E. Electrical Engineer

E.E.C. European Economic Community: see COMMON MARKET

EEG electroencephalogram

eel (ēl) *n., pl.* **eels, eel:** see PLURAL, II, D, 1 [OE. *æl*] a snakelike fish with a long, slippery body and no pelvic fins —**eel′like′, eel′y** *adj.*

☆**eel·grass** (ēl′gras′) *n.* an underwater flowering plant with long, grasslike leaves

eel·pout (-pout′) *n., pl.* **-pout′, -pouts′:** see PLURAL, II, D, 2 [OE. *ælepute*] **1.** a saltwater fish resembling the blenny **2.** *same as* BURBOT

eel·worm (-wurm′) *n.* any of various nematode worms: some live as parasites on plants

EEL
(to 5 ft. long)

e'en (ēn) *adv.* [Poet.] even —*n.* [Poet. or Dial.] even(ing)

e'er (er, ar) *adv.* [Poet.] ever

-eer (ir) [Fr. *-ier* < L. *-arius*] **1.** *a suffix forming nouns meaning* one that has to do with [*mountaineer*] or one that writes, makes, etc. [*pamphleteer*] **2.** *a suffix forming verbs meaning* to have to do with [*electioneer*]

ee·rie, ee·ry (ir′ē) *adj.* **-ri·er, -ri·est** [prob. ult. < OE. *earg*, timid] weird or uncanny, esp. in a frightening way [the *eerie* echoes in the cave] —see SYN. at WEIRD —**ee′ri·ly** *adv.* —**ee′ri·ness** *n.*

ef·face (i fās′, e-) *vt.* **-faced′, -fac′ing** [Fr. *effacer* < *e-* (L. *ex*, out) + *face:* see FACE] **1.** to rub out or wipe out; erase [to *efface* a memory] **2.** to keep (oneself) from being noticed —see SYN. at ERASE —**ef·face′a·ble** *adj.* —**ef·face′ment** *n.* —**ef·fac′er** *n.*

ef·fect (ə fekt′, i-) *n.* [< OFr. < L. pp. of *efficere* < *ex-*, out + *facere*, DO¹] **1.** anything brought about by a cause; result **2.** the power to produce results; efficacy [scolding has no *effect* on him] **3.** influence or action [the drug had a cathartic *effect*] **4.** general meaning; purport [he spoke to this *effect*] **5.** *a)* the impression produced, as by artistic design, a way of speaking, acting, etc. [his angry words were just for *effect*] *b)* something that makes such an impression [cloud *effects*] **6.** the condition or fact of being in force [a law now in *effect*] **7.** [*pl.*] belongings; property [personal *effects*] —*vt.* to bring about; cause; accomplish [the treatment *effected* a cure] —**give effect to** to put into practice or operation —**in effect 1.** in result; actually **2.** in essence; virtually **3.** in operation; in force —**take effect** to begin to produce results; become operative —**to the effect** with the general meaning —**ef·fect′er** *n.*

SYN.—effect is used of that which is the direct result of some action, process, or agent [he always looks for cause and *effect*]; **consequence** is used of that which follows something else on which it depends in some way, but is not as closely connected as an effect is with the cause [their decision to stay had a number of *consequences*]; **result** is applied to that which is the final effect or consequence of an action, process, etc. [the *result* of Fleming's experiments was the discovery of penicillin]; **outcome** refers to the result of something that was in doubt [the *outcome* of a war] —see also SYN. at PERFORM —*ANT.* cause

ef·fec·tive (ə fek′tiv, i-) *adj.* **1.** having an effect **2.** producing a desired effect [an *effective* remedy] **3.** in effect; operative **4.** actual, not merely theoretical **5.** making a striking impression [an *effective* speaker] **6.** equipped and ready for combat [an *effective* unit] —*n.* a combat-ready soldier, unit, etc. —**ef·fec′tive·ly** *adv.* —**ef·fec′tive·ness** *n.*

ef·fec·tu·al (ə fek′chōō wəl, i-) *adj.* **1.** producing, or able to produce, the desired effect [an *effectual* plan] **2.** having legal force; valid —**ef·fec′tu·al′i·ty** (-wal′ə tē) *n.* —**ef·fec′tu·al·ly** *adv.*

ef·fec·tu·ate (-wāt′) *vt.* **-at′ed, -at′ing** to bring about; effect —**ef·fec′tu·a′tion** *n.*

ef·fem·i·nate (i fem′ə nit) *adj.* [< L. pp. of *effeminare* < *ex-*, out + *femina*, woman: see FEMALE] having or showing qualities that have been thought of as more characteristic of women than of men, as weakness, delicacy, etc.; unmanly: term used only of men or boys —**ef·fem′i·na·cy** (-nə sē) *n.* —**ef·fem′i·nate·ly** *adv.*

ef·fen·di (i fen′dē) *n., pl.* **-dis** [< Turk. < ModGr. < Gr. *authentēs*, a master] Sir; Master: former Turkish title of respect

ef·fer·ent (ef′ər ənt) *adj.* [< L. prp. of *efferre* < *ex-*, out + *ferre*, BEAR¹] *Physiol.* carrying away from a central part; specif., designating nerves that carry impulses away from a nerve center: opposed to AFFERENT

ef·fer·vesce (ef′ər ves′) *vi.* **-vesced′, -vesc′ing** [< L. < *ex-*, out + *fervescere*, to begin to boil < *fervere*, to boil: see FERVENT] **1.** to give off gas bubbles, as soda water; bubble **2.** to be lively and full of high spirits —**ef′fer·ves′cence** *n.* —**ef′fer·ves′cent** *adj.* —**ef′fer·ves′cent·ly** *adv.*

ef·fete (e fēt′, i-) *adj.* [L. *effetus*, exhausted by bearing < *ex-*, out + *fetus*, productive: for IE. base see FEMALE] **1.** no longer able to produce; worn out and sterile [an *effete* writer] **2.** decadent, soft, etc. [an *effete* society] —**ef·fete′ly** *adv.* —**ef·fete′ness** *n.*

ef·fi·ca·cious (ef′ə kā′shəs) *adj.* [L. *efficax* < *efficere* (see EFFECT) + *-ous*] producing or capable of producing the desired effect; effective —**ef′fi·ca′cious·ly** *adv.* —**ef′fi·ca′cious·ness** *n.*

ef·fi·ca·cy (ef′i kə sē) *n., pl.* **-cies** [see prec.] power to produce effects or results; effectiveness [the *efficacy* of a treatment]

ef·fi·cien·cy (ə fish′ən sē, i-) *n., pl.* **-cies 1.** ability to produce a desired effect with the least effort or waste; a being efficient **2.** the ratio of effective work to energy used in producing it: said of a machine, etc. ☆**3.** *same as* EFFICIENCY APARTMENT

☆**efficiency apartment** a one-room apartment having a kitchenette and a bathroom

ef·fi·cient (-ənt) *adj.* [< L. prp. of *efficere:* see EFFECT] **1.** directly producing an effect or result; effective [illness was the *efficient* cause of her loss of weight] **2.** producing a desired effect with the least effort or waste [an *efficient* production method] —**ef·fi′cient·ly** *adv.*

ef·fi·gy (ef′ə jē) *n., pl.* **-gies** [< Fr. < L. *effigies* < *ex-*, out + *fingere*, to form: for IE. base see DOUGH] a statue or other likeness; often, a crude figure of a hated person —**burn (or hang) in effigy** to burn (or hang) a hated person's effigy in public as a way of showing protest

ef·flo·resce (ef′lō res′, -lə-) *vi.* **-resced′, -resc′ing** [< L. < *ex-*, out + *florescere*, to blossom < *flos*, a FLOWER] **1.** to blossom out; flower **2.** *Chem. a)* to change from crystals to a powder through loss of the water of crystallization *b)* to develop a powdery crust, as of salts, by evaporation or chemical change [stone walls often *effloresce*]

ef·flo·res·cence (-res′'ns) *n.* **1.** a flowering **2.** the time of flowering **3.** *Chem. a)* an efflorescing *b)* the resulting powder or crust **4.** *Med.* an eruption on the skin; rash —**ef′flo·res′cent** *adj.*

ef·flu·ence (ef′lōō wəns) *n.* [< L. prp. of *effluere* < *ex-*, out + *fluere*, to flow] **1.** a flowing out or forth **2.** a thing that flows out or forth; emanation

ef·flu·ent (-wənt) *adj.* [see EFFLUENCE] flowing out or forth —*n.* a thing that flows out or forth; specif., *a)* a stream flowing out of a body of water *b)* matter flowing out of a sewer, etc.

ef·flu·vi·um (e flōō′vē əm, i-) *n., pl.* **-vi·a** (-ə), **-vi·ums** [L., a flowing out: see prec.] **1.** something that flows out in the form of a vapor or invisible stream, or is thought to flow out in this way **2.** a bad-smelling vapor —**ef·flu′vi·al** *adj.*

ef·fort (ef′ərt) *n.* [Fr. < OFr. < *esforcier*, to make an effort, ult. < L. *ex-*, thoroughly + *fortis*, strong] **1.** use of energy to do something; a trying hard physically or mentally [rowing takes great *effort*] **2.** a try; attempt [he made no *effort* to be friendly] **3.** a result of working or trying; achievement [her early *efforts* at poetry were not published]

SYN.—effort refers to an active attempt to do something [make some *effort* to be friendly]; **exertion** implies the general use of much energy, power, or strength in doing something [she feels faint after any *exertion*]; **endeavor** suggests a serious, continued attempt to get something done, usually something deserving praise [a life spent in the *endeavor* to help others]; **pains** suggests taking the trouble to do something in a steady, careful way [to take *pains* with one's work] —*ANT.* ease

ef·fort·less (-lis) *adj.* making, needing, or showing almost no effort [she skates in an *effortless* way] —see SYN. at EASY —**ef′fort·less·ly** *adv.* —**ef′fort·less·ness** *n.*

ef·fron·ter·y (e frun′tər ē, i-) *n., pl.* **-ter·ies** [< Fr. < L. *effrons*, shameless, barefaced < *ex-*, from + *frons*, forehead] unashamed boldness; impudence; audacity [he had the *effrontery* to criticize the press for exposing his dishonesty] —see SYN. at TEMERITY

ef·ful·gence (e ful′jəns, i-) *n.* [< L. prp. of *effulgere* < *ex-*, forth + *fulgere*, to shine: for IE. base see BLACK] great brightness; radiance —**ef·ful′gent** *adj.*

ef·fuse (e fyō̅o̅z′, i-) **vt., vi. -fused′, -fus′ing** [< L. pp. of *effundere* < *ex-*, out + *fundere*, to pour] to pour, or spread, out or forth

ef·fu·sion (e fyō̅o̅′zhən, i-) **n.** [see prec.] **1.** a pouring forth of liquid **2.** uncontrolled expression of feeling or thought [an *effusion* of joy]

ef·fu·sive (-siv) **adj.** overflowing with words or feelings; gushy [*effusive* praise] —**ef·fu′sive·ly adv.** —**ef·fu′sive·ness n.**

eft (eft) **n.** [OE. *efeta*] *same as* NEWT

eft·soon (eft sō̅o̅n′) **adv.** [OE. < *eft*, again + *sona*, soon] [Archaic] soon after: also **eft·soons′** (-sō̅o̅nz′)

Eg. **1.** Egypt **2.** Egyptian **3.** Egyptology

e.g. [L. *exempli gratia*] for example

e·gad (i gad′, ē-) **interj.** [prob. < *oh God*] a mild oath

e·gal·i·tar·i·an (i gal′ə ter′ē ən, ē-) **adj.** [< Fr. < *égalité*, equality + -IAN] of or for equal political, social, and economic rights for all —**n.** an advocate of equal rights —**e·gal′i·tar′i·an·ism n.**

Eg·bert (eg′bərt) 775?–839 A.D.; first king of all England (829–839)

egg¹ (eg) **n.** [ON.] **1.** an oval or round body laid by a female bird, fish, insect, etc., containing within a shell or membrane the germ of a new individual and food for its development: fully formed young eventually are hatched from eggs **2.** a female reproductive cell; ovum: also called **egg cell 3.** a hen's egg, raw or cooked **4.** something egg-like, esp. in shape **5.** [Slang] a person [he's a good *egg*] —☆**lay an egg** [Slang] to fail, as a performance

egg² (eg) **vt.** [< ON. *eggja*, lit., to give edge to (< *egg*, edge] to urge or incite (with *on*) [he wouldn't have jumped if they hadn't *egged* him on]

☆**egg·beat·er** (eg′bēt′ər) **n.** **1.** a kitchen utensil for beating eggs, etc. **2.** [Slang] a helicopter

☆**egg foo yong** (or **young**) (eg′ fō̅o̅ yuŋ′) a Chinese-American dish made of beaten eggs mixed with bean sprouts, onions, minced meat, etc. and fried like an omelet

☆**egg·head** (-hed′) **n.** [Slang] an intellectual: a term of mild contempt as used by those who are anti-intellectual

☆**egg·nog** (-näg′) **n.** [EGG¹ + NOG] a drink of beaten eggs, milk, sugar, and nutmeg, often with alcoholic liquor

egg·plant (-plant′) **n.** **1.** a plant of the nightshade family, with a large, somewhat egg-shaped, usually purple-skinned fruit eaten as a cooked vegetable **2.** the fruit

☆**egg roll** a Chinese-American dish made by wrapping thin, flat egg dough around minced vegetables, meat, shrimp, etc. in a small roll, which is then fried

egg·shell (-shel′) **n.** the shell of an egg; esp., the hard, brittle covering of a bird's egg —**adj.** **1.** fragile and thin, like an eggshell **2.** yellowish-white

e·gis (ē′jis) **n.** *same as* AEGIS

eg·lan·tine (eg′lən tīn′, -tēn′) **n.** [< Fr. < OFr. *aiglent* < L. *aculeus*, a sting, dim. of *acus*, a point] a European rose with hooked spines, sweet-scented leaves, and usually pink flowers; sweetbrier

e·go (ē′gō; *chiefly Brit.* eg′ō) **n.,** *pl.* **e′gos** [L., I] **1.** the self; the individual as aware of himself **2.** egotism; conceit **3.** *Psychoanalysis* the part of the psyche that is thought of as settling conflicts in a conscious, reasoning way between the id and the superego

e·go·cen·tric (ē′gō sen′trik; *chiefly Brit.* eg′ō-) **adj.** viewing everything in relation to oneself; self-centered —**n.** an egocentric person —**e′go·cen′tri·cal·ly adv.** —**e′go·cen·tric′i·ty** (-tris′ə tē) **n.** —**e′go·cen′trism n.**

e·go·ism (ē′gō iz′m; *chiefly Brit.* eg′ō-) **n.** **1.** the tendency to be self-centered, or to consider only one's own interests **2.** self-conceit; egotism

e·go·ist (-ist) **n.** **1.** a person who is self-centered **2.** a conceited person; egotist

e·go·is·tic (ē′gō is′tik; *chiefly Brit.* eg′ō-) **adj.** **1.** thinking only about one's own interests; self-centered **2.** egotistic; conceited Also **e′go·is′ti·cal** —**e′go·is′ti·cal·ly adv.**

e·go·ma·ni·a (ē′gō mā′nē ə, -mān′yə) **n.** egotism so great as

to be a form of mental illness —**e′go·ma′ni·ac′** (-ak′) **n.** —**e′go·ma·ni′a·cal** (-mə nī′ə k′l) **adj.**

e·go·tism (ē′gə tiz′m; *chiefly Brit.* eg′ə-) **n.** **1.** a thinking, talking, or writing too much about oneself; excessive use of *I, me*, etc. **2.** too high an opinion of oneself; self-conceit *Egotism* is generally considered a term showing more contempt than *egoism* —**e′go·tist n.** —**e′go·tis′tic, e′go·tis′ti·cal adj.** —**e′go·tis′ti·cal·ly adv.**

☆**ego trip** **1.** an experience, activity, etc. that one uses for self-fulfillment, self-expression, etc. **2.** anything that serves to increase one's vanity, self-conceit, etc. —**e′go-trip′ vi. -tripped′, -trip′ping** —**e′go-trip′per n.**

e·gre·gious (i grē′jəs, -jē əs) **adj.** [L. *egregius*, apart from the herd, outstanding < *e-*, out + *grex*, a herd: for IE. base see CRAM] remarkably bad; flagrant [an *egregious* error] —**e·gre′gious·ly adv.** —**e·gre′gious·ness n.**

e·gress (ē′gres) **n.** [< L. pp. of *egredi* < *e-*, out + *gradi*, to step, go: see GRADE] **1.** a going out; emergence [the blockade prevented the *egress* of ships from the harbor] **2.** the right to go out **3.** a way to go out; exit

e·gret (ē′grit, eg′rit) **n.** [< OFr. *aigrette* < Pr. < *aigron*, a heron < Frank.] **1.** *pl.* **-grets, -gret:** see PLURAL, II, D, 1 a heronlike wading bird, usually with long, white plumes, esp. the **American egret** of temperate and tropical America **2.** an aigrette (sense 1)

E·gypt (ē′jipt) country in NE Africa, on the Mediterranean and Red seas: c. 386,000 sq. mi.; pop. 34,583,000; cap. Cairo

Egypt. Egyptian

E·gyp·tian (i jip′shən, ē-) **adj.** of Egypt, its people, etc. —**n.** **1.** a native or inhabitant of Egypt **2.** the language of the ancient Egyptians

E·gyp·tol·o·gy (ē′jip täl′ə jē) **n.** the study of ancient Egyptian culture, language, architecture, etc. —**E′gyp·tol′o·gist n.**

eh (ā, e, en) **interj.** a sound expressing: **1.** surprise **2.** doubt or a question, meaning: *a)* "What did you say?" *b)* "Don't you agree?"

EHF extremely high frequency

Ehr·lich (er′lik; *G.* er′liH), **Paul** 1854–1915; Ger. bacteriologist & immunologist

ei·der (ī′dər) **n.** [ult. < ON. *æthr*] **1.** *pl.* **-ders, -der:** see PLURAL, II, D, 1 a large sea duck of northern regions: often **eider duck** **2.** *same as* EIDERDOWN

ei·der·down (-doun′) **n.** **1.** the soft, fine breast feathers, or down, of the eider duck, used to stuff quilts, pillows, etc. **2.** a quilt so stuffed

ei·det·ic (ī det′ik) **adj.** [< Gr. < *eidos*, what is seen] produced by the mind in an unusually sharp and accurate way [an *eidetic* memory] —**ei·det′i·cal·ly adv.**

Eif·fel Tower (ī′f′l) [after A. G. *Eiffel* (1832–93), Fr. engineer] tower of iron framework in Paris, built for the 1889 Exposition: 984 ft. high

eight (āt) **adj.** [OE. *eahta*] totaling one more than seven —**n.** **1.** the cardinal number between seven and nine; 8; VIII **2.** anything having eight units or members, or numbered eight, or shaped like 8; specif., an eight-cylinder engine or automobile

☆**eight ball** a black ball with the number eight on it, used in playing pool —**behind the eight ball** [Slang] in a very unfavorable position

eight·een (ā′tēn′) **adj.** [OE. *eahtatiene*] eight more than ten —**n.** the cardinal number between seventeen and nineteen; 18; XVIII

eight·eenth (ā′tēnth′) **adj.** **1.** coming after seventeen others in a series; 18th **2.** designating any of the eighteen equal parts of something —**n.** **1.** the one following the seventeenth **2.** any of the eighteen equal parts of something; 1/18

eight·fold (āt′fōld′) **adj.** [see -FOLD] **1.** having eight parts **2.** having eight times as much or as many —**adv.** eight times as much or as many

eighth (ātth, āth) **adj.** [< OE.: see EIGHT & -TH²] **1.** coming after seven others in a series; 8th **2.** designating any of the eight equal parts of something —**n.** **1.** the one following the seventh **2.** any of the eight equal parts of something; 1/8 **3.** *Music* the interval of an octave

eighth note *Music* a note held for one eighth as long as a whole note: see illustration at NOTE

EIFFEL TOWER

HEN'S EGG
(A, yolk; B, air space; C, white; D, outer shell membrane; E, inner shell membrane; F, chalaza-bearing membrane; G, chalaza; H, shell)

EGGPLANT

eight·i·eth (āt'ē ith) *adj.* **1.** coming after seventy-nine others in a series; 80th **2.** designating any of the eighty equal parts of something —*n.* **1.** the one following the seventy-ninth **2.** any of the eighty equal parts of something; 1/80

eight·y (āt'ē) *adj.* [OE. (*hund*)*eahtatig*] eight times ten —*n., pl.* **eight'ies** the cardinal number between seventy-nine and eighty-one; 80; LXXX —**the eighties** the numbers or years, as of a century, from eighty through eighty-nine

ei·kon (ī'kän) *n.* same as ICON

Ei·leen (ī lēn', ā-) [Ir. *Eibhlin*] a feminine name

Eind·ho·ven (īnt'hō'vən) city in S Netherlands: pop. 185,000

Ein·stein (īn'stīn), **Albert** 1879–1955; U.S. physicist, born in Germany: he developed the theory of relativity —**Ein·stein'i·an** (-stī'nē ən) *adj.*

☆**ein·stein·i·um** (īn stī'nē əm) *n.* [after prec.] a radioactive chemical element produced artificially from plutonium: symbol, Es; at. wt., 252(?); at. no., 99

Eir·e (er'ə) *Gaelic name of* IRELAND (sense 2)

Ei·sen·how·er (ī'z'n hou'ər), **Dwight David** 1890–1969; U.S. general & 34th president of the U.S. (1953–61)

ei·ther (ē'thər, ī'-) *adj.* [OE. *æghwæther* < *a* (æ), always (see AYE[1]) + *gehwæther*, each of two (see WHETHER)] **1.** one or the other (of two) [*use either hand*] **2.** each (of two) [*doors open at either end of the room*] —*pron.* one or the other (of two) —*conj.* a word used along with *or*, implying a choice of alternatives [*either* go or stay] —*adv.* **1.** any more than the other; also: used after a negative statement [if he won't, she won't *either*] **2.** [Colloq.] certainly; indeed: used to strengthen a negative statement ["It's his." "It isn't *either!*]

e·jac·u·late (i jak'yə lāt') *vt., vi.* **-lat'ed, -lat'ing** [< L. pp. of *ejaculari* < *e-*, out + *jaculari*, to throw < *jaculum*, a dart < *jacere*, to throw] **1.** to eject or discharge (esp. semen) **2.** to say suddenly and sharply; exclaim —**e·jac'u·la'tor** *n.*

e·jac·u·la·tion (i jak'yə lā'shən) *n.* **1.** a sudden discharge of fluid, esp. of semen, from the body **2.** something said suddenly and sharply; exclamation

e·jac·u·la·to·ry (i jak'yə lə tôr'ē) *adj.* **1.** of or for ejaculation [an *ejaculatory* duct] **2.** like an ejaculation; exclamatory [*ejaculatory* words]

e·ject (i jekt', ē-) *vt.* [< L. pp. of *ejicere* < *e-*, out + *jacere*, to throw: see JET[1]] **1.** to throw out; expel; discharge [the chimney *ejects* smoke] **2.** to drive out; evict [to *eject* a heckler from the stands] —**e·ject'a·ble** *adj.* —**e·jec'tion** *n.* —**e·jec'tive** *adj.* —**e·jec'tor** *n.*

SYN.—**eject** implies generally a throwing or casting out from within [to *eject* saliva from the mouth]; **expel** suggests a driving out, as by force, specif., a forcing out of a country, organization, etc., often in disgrace [*expelled* from school]; **evict** refers to a forcing out by the use of legal means [to *evict* a tenant]; **oust** implies the getting rid of something that is not wanted, as by the use of force or the action of the law [to *oust* corrupt officials]

eke[1] (ēk) *vt.* **eked, ek'ing** [OE. *eacan & eacian:* for IE. base see AUGMENT] [Archaic or Dial.] to increase —**eke out 1.** to add to so as to have enough; supplement [to *eke out* one's income with a second job] **2.** to make (a living) with difficulty **3.** to use (a supply) carefully, without waste

eke[2] (ēk) *adv., conj.* [OE. *eac*] [Archaic] also

EKG electrocardiogram

☆**e·kis·tics** (i kis'tiks) *n.pl.* [with sing. v.] [< Gr. *oikos*, house + -ICS] the science dealing with the planning and development of cities and towns and concerning itself with the problems of transportation, communication, education, etc. —**e·kis'ti·cal** *adj.*

el (el) *n.* **1.** same as ELL[1] ☆**2.** [< el(evated)] [Colloq.] an elevated railway

e·lab·o·rate (i lab'ər it; *for v.* -ə rāt') *adj.* [< L. pp. of *elaborare* < *e-*, out + *laborare* < *labor*, LABOR] **1.** developed in great detail [an *elaborate* plan] **2.** complicated and very ornate [the *elaborate* decoration on her costume] —*vt.* **-rat'ed, -rat'ing 1.** to produce by effort **2.** to work out in careful detail [to *elaborate* a theory] **3.** to change (food or substances in the body) into compounds that can be assimilated, etc. —*vi.* to state something in detail or add more details (usually with *on* or *upon*) [please *elaborate* on your answer] —**e·lab'o·rate·ly** *adv.* —**e·lab'o·rate·ness** *n.* —**e·lab'o·ra'tion** *n.* —**e·lab'o·ra'tive** *adj.* —**e·lab'o·ra'tor** *n.*

E·laine (i lān', ē-) [OFr., equiv. of HELEN] a feminine name

E·lam (ē'ləm) ancient kingdom of SW Asia, on the Persian Gulf —**E'lam·ite'** (-īt') *adj., n.*

é·lan (ā län'; *Fr.* -län') *n.* [Fr. < *élancer*, to dart] much spirit or enthusiasm; liveliness

ELAM (8th cent. B.C.)

e·land (ē'lənd) *n., pl.* **e'land, e'lands:** see PLURAL, II, D, 2 [Afrik. < Du., elk] either of two large, ox-like African antelopes with spirally twisted horns

e·lapse (i laps') *vi.* **e·lapsed', e·laps'ing** [< L. pp. of *elabi* < *e-*, out + *labi*, to glide: for IE. base see LAP[1]] to slip by; pass: said of time

e·las·mo·branch (i laz'mə braŋk', -las'-) *adj.* [< ModL. < Gr. *elasmos*, beaten metal + L. *branchia*, gills] of a group of fishes with horny scales, no air bladders, and skeletons made up of cartilage —*n.* any fish of this class, as the shark, ray, etc.

e·las·tic (i las'tik) *adj.* [< ModL. < LGr. *elastikos* < Gr. *elaunein*, to drive] **1.** able to spring back to its original size, shape, or position after being stretched, squeezed, etc.; springy [an *elastic* rubber ball] **2.** able to recover easily from gloominess, fatigue, etc.; buoyant **3.** easily changed to fit the circumstances —*n.* **1.** *a)* an elastic fabric loosely woven with strands of rubber, etc. running through it *b)* a band, garter, etc. made of this **2.** a rubber band —**e·las'ti·cal·ly** *adv.*

e·las·tic·i·ty (i las'tis'ə tē, ē'las-) *n., pl.* **-ties** the quality or condition of being elastic; specif., *a)* springiness; flexibility *b)* lightness of spirit *c)* adaptability

e·las·ti·cize (i las'tə sīz') *vt.* **-cized', -ciz'ing** to make (fabric) elastic

☆**e·las·to·mer** (i las'tə mər) *n.* [< ELAST(IC) + (POLY)MER] a rubberlike synthetic polymer, as silicone rubber —**e·las'to·mer'ic** (-mer'ik) *adj.*

e·late (i lāt', ē-) *vt.* **-lat'ed, -lat'ing** [< L. *elatus*, pp. of *efferre* < *ex-*, out + *ferre*, BEAR[1]] to raise the spirits of; make very proud, happy, joyful, etc. —**e·lat'ed·ly** *adv.* —**e·lat'ed·ness** *n.*

e·la·tion (i lā'shən, ē-) *n.* high spirits

E layer a layer of the ionosphere at an altitude of about 60 miles that can reflect radio waves

El·ba (el'bə) It. island between Corsica & Italy: site of Napoleon's first exile (1814–15)

El·be (el'bə, elb) river flowing from NW Czechoslovakia through Germany into the North Sea

El·bert (el'bərt), **Mount** [after S. H. *Elbert*, governor of Colo. (1873–74)] highest peak of the Rocky Mountains in the U.S., in C Colo.: 14,431 ft.

el·bow (el'bō) *n.* [OE. *elboga*] **1.** the joint between the upper and lower arm; esp., the outer part of the angle made by a bent arm **2.** anything bent like an elbow, as a pipe fitting —*vt., vi.* **1.** to shove or jostle with the elbow **2.** to push (one's way) by shoving with the elbow —**out at (the) elbows** shabby or poor —**rub elbows with** to mingle with (famous people)

ELBOW (sense 2)

elbow grease [Colloq.] hard work or effort

el·bow·room (-rōōm', -room') *n.* room enough to move or work in; sufficient space

El·brus (el'brōōs, -brōōz'), **Mount** mountain of the Caucasus range, in the Georgian S.S.R.: highest peak in Europe, 18,481 ft.: also sp. **El'brus**

El·burz Mountains (el boorz') mountain range in N Iran, along the Caspian Sea

El Ca·jon (el kə hōn') [Sp., the box] city in S Calif.: suburb of San Diego: pop. 52,000

eld (eld) *n.* [< OE. < base of *ald*, OLD] [Archaic] **1.** old age **2.** ancient times; days of yore

eld·er[1] (el'dər) *adj.* [OE. *eldra*, compar. < base of *ald*, OLD] **1.** born or brought forth earlier than another or others; senior; older [the *elder* son] **2.** earlier; former [in *elder* times] —*n.*

1. an older or aged person **2.** a person with some authority in a tribe or community because of age or experience **3.** an ancestor ☆**4.** one of the higher order of priests in the Mormon Church **5.** in some Protestant churches, a minister; also, a member of the ruling body —**eld′er·ship′** *n.*

el·der² (el′dər) *n.* [OE. *ellern*] a shrub or tree with flat-topped clusters of small, white flowers and red or purple berries

el·der·ber·ry (-ber′ē) *n., pl.* **-ries 1.** *same as* ELDER² **2.** its berry, used in making wines, etc.

eld·er·ly (-lē) *adj.* somewhat old; approaching old age —**eld′er·li·ness** *n.*

elder statesman any elderly retired statesman who from time to time is asked for advice on matters of government

eld·est (el′dist) *adj.* [OE. superl. of *ald*, old] oldest; esp., first-born or oldest surviving

El Do·ra·do, El·do·ra·do (el′də rä′dō, -rā′dō, -rad′ō) *pl.* **-dos** [Sp., the gilded] **1.** a legendary country in S. America, supposed to be rich in gold and jewels ☆**2.** any place that is, or is supposed to be, rich in gold, opportunity, etc.

El·ea·nor (el′ə nər, -nôr′) [var. of HELEN] a feminine name

elec., elect. 1. electric **2.** electrical **3.** electricity

e·lect (i lekt′) *adj.* [< L. pp. of *eligere* < *e-*, out + *legere*, to choose: for IE. base see LOGIC] **1.** chosen; given preference **2.** elected but not yet installed in office [the mayor-*elect*] **3.** *Theol.* chosen by God for salvation and eternal life —*n.* a person who is elect —*vt.* **1.** to select for some office by voting **2.** to choose or decide [we *elected* to stay] —*vi.* to make a choice; choose [do as you *elect*] —see SYN. at CHOOSE —**the elect 1.** persons belonging to a specially privileged group **2.** *Theol.* those who are elect

e·lec·tion (i lek′shən) *n.* **1.** a choosing or choice **2.** a choosing or being chosen for office by vote **3.** *Theol.* the selection by God of certain people for salvation and eternal life

e·lec·tion·eer (i lek′shə nir′) *vi.* to try to get votes for a candidate, party, etc. in an election —**e·lec′tion·eer′ing** *n.*

e·lec·tive (i lek′tiv) *adj.* **1.** *a)* filled by election [an *elective* office] *b)* chosen by election [*elective* officials] **2.** of or based on election **3.** having the power to choose **4.** that may be chosen but is not required; optional [music and art are usually *elective* subjects in high school] —☆*n.* an elective subject or course in a school or college curriculum —**e·lec′tive·ly** *adv.*

e·lec·tor (-tər) *n.* **1.** one who elects; specif., a qualified voter **2.** a member of the electoral college **3.** [*usually* E-] any of the German princes of the Holy Roman Empire who took part in the election of the emperor —**e·lec′tor·al** *adj.*

electoral college ☆an assembly elected by the voters to perform the formal duty of electing both the president and the vice president of the United States

e·lec·tor·ate (-tər it) *n.* all those qualified to vote in an election

E·lec·tra (i lek′trə) *Gr. Myth.* a daughter of Agamemnon and Clytemnestra: she encouraged her brother, Orestes, to kill their mother and their mother's lover, to avenge Agamemnon's murder

e·lec·tric (i lek′trik) *adj.* [ModL. *electricus*, orig., produced from amber by rubbing < ML. < L. *electrum*, amber < Gr. *ēlektron*] **1.** of, charged with, or conducting electricity [an *electric* wire] **2.** producing, or produced by, electricity [an *electric* generator] **3.** operated by electricity [an *electric* iron] **4.** very tense or exciting; electrifying [an *electric* situation] —*n.* ☆a train, car, etc. operated by electricity

e·lec·tri·cal (-tri k'l) *adj.* **1.** *same as* ELECTRIC **2.** connected with the science or use of electricity [an *electrical* engineer]

e·lec·tri·cal·ly (-trik lē, -tri k'l ē) *adv.* by or with electricity

electric blue a bright, metallic blue

☆**electric chair 1.** a chair used in electrocuting persons sentenced to death **2.** the death sentence by electrocution

electric eel a large, eel-shaped fish of northern S. America, with special organs that can give electric shocks

☆**electric eye** *same as* PHOTOELECTRIC CELL

electric field that space around an electrically charged body within which there is an electric force exerted on every charged particle

electric guitar a guitar whose tones are transmitted to an amplifier and loudspeaker through an electrical pickup attached to the instrument

☆**e·lec·tri·cian** (i lek′trish′ən) *n.* a

ELECTRIC
GUITAR

person whose work is the construction, repair, or installation of electric apparatus

e·lec·tric·i·ty (i lek′tris′ə tē) *n.* **1.** a property of certain fundamental particles of all matter, as electrons (negative charges) and protons or positrons (positive charges) that have a field of force associated with them: it can be generated by friction, induction, or chemical change and is used as a source of energy **2.** *a)* an electric current: see CURRENT (*n.* 3) *b)* an electric charge: see CHARGE (*n.* 2) **3.** the branch of physics dealing with electricity **4.** electric current as supplied for lighting, heating, etc. **5.** strong emotional tension, excitement, etc.

electric needle a slender, pointed electrode used in surgery to cut and cauterize tissue, etc.

electric ray a fish with a broad, flat body and electric organs that can stun enemies or prey

e·lec·tri·fy (i lek′trə fī′) *vt.* **-fied′, -fy′ing 1.** to charge with electricity **2.** to give an electric shock to **3.** to give a shock of excitement to; thrill [to *electrify* an audience] **4.** to equip for the use of electricity; provide with electric power [to *electrify* rural areas] —**e·lec′tri·fi·ca′tion** *n.* —**e·lec′tri·fi′er** *n.*

e·lec·tro (i lek′trō) *n., pl.* **-tros** *short for:* **1.** ELECTROTYPE **2.** ELECTROPLATE

e·lec·tro- *a combining form meaning:* **1.** electric [*electromagnet*] **2.** electrically [*electrocute*] **3.** electricity [*electrostatics*]

e·lec·tro·car·di·o·gram (i lek′trō kär′dē ə gram′) *n.* a tracing showing the changes in electric potential produced by contractions of the heart

e·lec·tro·car·di·o·graph (-dē ə graf′) *n.* an instrument for making an electrocardiogram —**e·lec′tro·car′di·o·graph′ic** (-dē ə graf′ik) *adj.* —**e·lec′tro·car′di·og′ra·phy** (-äg′rə fē) *n.*

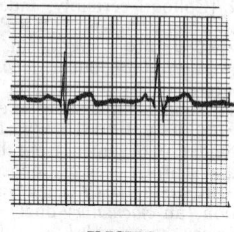

ELECTRO-
CARDIOGRAM

e·lec·tro·chem·is·try (-kem′is trē) *n.* the science dealing with the use of electrical energy to bring about a chemical reaction or with the generation of electrical energy by means of chemical action —**e·lec′tro·chem′i·cal** *adj.* —**e·lec′tro·chem′i·cal·ly** *adv.*

☆**e·lec·tro·cute** (i lek′trə kyōōt′) *vt.* **-cut′ed, -cut′ing** [ELECTRO- + (EXE)CUTE] to kill with a charge of electricity; specif., to execute in the electric chair —**e·lec′tro·cu′tion** *n.*

e·lec·trode (i lek′trōd) *n.* [ELECTR(O)- + -ODE] any terminal that conducts an electric current into or away from various conducting substances in a circuit, as the anode or cathode in a battery, or that emits, collects, or controls the flow of electrons in an electron tube, as the cathode, plate, or grid

e·lec·tro·de·pos·it (i lek′trō di päz′it) *vt.* to deposit (a metal, etc.) electrolytically —*n.* a deposit thus made, as in electroplating —**e·lec′tro·dep′o·si′tion** (-dep′ə zish′ən) *n.*

e·lec·tro·dy·nam·ics (i lek′trō dī nam′iks) *n.pl.* [*with sing. v.*] the branch of physics dealing with the phenomena of electric currents and associated magnetic forces —**e·lec′tro·dy·nam′ic** *adj.* —**e·lec′tro·dy·nam′i·cal·ly** *adv.*

e·lec·tro·en·ceph·a·lo·gram (-en sef′ə lə gram′) *n.* a tracing showing the changes in electric potential produced by the brain

e·lec·tro·en·ceph·a·lo·graph (-en sef′ə lə graf′) *n.* an instrument for making electroencephalograms —**e·lec′tro·en·ceph′a·lo·graph′ic** *adj.* —**e·lec′tro·en·ceph′a·log′ra·phy** (-ə läg′rə fē) *n.*

e·lec·tro·ki·net·ics (-ki net′iks) *n.pl.* [*with sing. v.*] the branch of electrodynamics dealing with electricity in motion, or electric currents

e·lec·trol·y·sis (i lek′träl′ə sis) *n.* [ELECTRO- + -LYSIS] **1.** the decomposition of an electrolyte by the action of an electric current passing through it **2.** the removal of unwanted hair from the body by destroying the hair roots with an electrified needle

e·lec·tro·lyte (i lek′trə līt′) *n.* [ELECTRO- + -LYTE] any substance which in solution can conduct an electric current by the movement of its positive ions to the negative electrode and negative ions to the positive electrode: the ions are deposited as a coating, set free as a gas, etc. —**e·lec′tro·lyt′ic** (-lit′ik) *adj.* —**e·lec′tro·lyt′i·cal·ly** *adv.*

e·lec·tro·lyze (i lek′trə līz′) *vt.* **-lyzed′, -lyz′ing** to subject to electrolysis

e·lec·tro·mag·net (i lek′trō mag′nit) *n.* a soft iron core surrounded by a coil of wire, that temporarily becomes a magnet when an electric current flows through the wire

e·lec·tro·mag·net·ic (-mag net′ik) *adj.* of, prod..ed by, or having to do with electromagnetism or an electromagnet — **e·lec′tro·mag·net′i·cal·ly** *adv.*

electromagnetic spectrum the complete range of frequencies of electromagnetic waves, including, in order of increasing frequencies and decreasing wavelengths, those of radio waves, infrared light, visible light, ultraviolet light, X-rays, gamma rays, and cosmic rays

electromagnetic wave a wave propagated through space or matter by the oscillating electric and magnetic field generated by an oscillating electric charge

e·lec·tro·mag·net·ism (-mag′nə tiz'm) *n.* **1.** magnetism produced by an electric current **2.** the branch of physics dealing with the relations between electricity and magnetism

e·lec·trom·e·ter (i lek′träm′ə tər) *n.* a device for detecting or measuring differences of potential by means of electrostatic or mechanical forces

e·lec·tro·mo·tive (i lek′trə mōt′iv) *adj.* **1.** producing an electric current through difference in potential **2.** relating to electromotive force

electromotive force the force that causes a current to flow in a circuit, equivalent to the potential difference between the terminals and commonly measured in volts

e·lec·tron (i lek′trän) *n.* [arbitrary coinage < ELECTR(IC) + -ON] any of the negatively charged particles that form a part of all atoms: the number of electrons circulating around a nucleus is equal to the number of positive charges on the nucleus

e·lec·tro·neg·a·tive (i lek′trō neg′ə tiv) *adj.* **1.** having a negative electrical charge; tending to move to the positive electrode, or anode, in electrolysis **2.** able to attract electrons, esp. in forming a chemical bond

e·lec·tron·ic (i lek′trän′ik) *adj.* **1.** of electrons **2.** operating, produced, or done by the action of electrons or by devices dependent on such action —**e·lec·tron′i·cal·ly** *adv.*

electronic data processing data processing by means of electronic equipment, esp. computers

electronic music music in which the sounds are made or changed by electronic devices, and arranged and recorded on tape for presentation

☆**electronic organ** a musical instrument with a console like that of a pipe organ, but producing tones by means of electronic devices instead of pipes

e·lec·tron·ics (-iks) *n.pl.* [with sing. v.] the science that deals with the action and control of electrons in vacuums and gases, and with the use of electron tubes, transistors, etc.

electron microscope an instrument for focusing a beam of electrons, using electric or magnetic fields, to form an enlarged image of an object on a fluorescent screen or photographic plate: it is much more powerful than any optical microscope

electron tube a sealed glass or metal tube having a gas or vacuum inside and two or more electrodes, used to control the flow of electrons

e·lec·tron-volt (-vōlt′) *n.* a unit of energy equal to that gained by an electron when it passes through a potential difference of one volt

e·lec·tro·pho·re·sis (i lek′trō fə rē′sis) *n.* [ModL. < ELECTRO- + Gr. *phorēsis* < *pherein*, BEAR¹] the movement of colloidal particles through a fluid in an electric field to the electrodes

e·lec·troph·o·rus (i lek′träf′ər əs) *n., pl.* -ri′ (-ī′) [ModL. < ELECTRO- + Gr. *phoros* < *pherein*, BEAR¹] an apparatus consisting of a resin disk and a metal plate, for producing static electricity by induction

e·lec·tro·plate (i lek′trə plāt′) *vt.* -plat′ed, -plat′ing to deposit a coating of metal on by electrolysis —*n.* anything so plated

e·lec·tro·pos·i·tive (i lek′trə päz′ə tiv) *adj.* **1.** having a positive electrical charge; tending to move to the negative electrode, or cathode, in electrolysis **2.** able to give up electrons, esp. in forming a chemical bond

e·lec·tro·scope (i lek′trə skōp′) *n.* [ELECTRO- + -SCOPE] an instrument for detecting very small charges of electricity, as by the repulsion between electrically charged strips of gold leaf — **e·lec′tro·scop′ic** (-skäp′ik) *adj.*

e·lec·tro·shock therapy (-shäk′) *see* SHOCK THERAPY

e·lec·tro·stat·ics (i lek′trə stat′iks) *n.pl.* [with sing. v.] the branch of physics dealing with electric charges at rest, or static electricity —**e·lec′tro·stat′ic** *adj.* —**e·lec′tro·stat′i·cal·ly** *adv.*

e·lec·tro·ther·a·py (-ther′ə pē) *n.* the treatment of disease by means of electricity, as by diathermy —**e·lec′tro·ther′a·pist** *n.*

e·lec·tro·type (i lek′trə tīp′) *n. Printing* **1.** a printing plate made by electroplating a wax or plastic impression of the surface to be reproduced **2.** a print made from such a plate **3.** *same as* ELECTROTYPY —*vt., vi.* -typed′, -typ′ing to make an electrotype or electrotypes (of) —**e·lec′tro·typ′er** *n.*

e·lec·tro·typ·y (-tīp′ē) *n.* the process of making electrotypes

e·lec·trum (i lek′trəm) *n.* [L. < Gr. *ēlektron:* see ELECTRIC] a light-yellow alloy of gold and silver

e·lec·tu·ar·y (i lek′choo wer′ē) *n., pl.* -ar′ies [< LL. < Gr. < *ek-*, out + *leichein*, to lick] a medicine mixed with honey or syrup to form a paste

el·ee·mos·y·nar·y (el′i mäs′ə ner′ē, el′ē ə-) *adj.* [< ML. < LL. < Gr. *eleēmosynē*, pity (in N.T., alms) < *eleos*, mercy] **1.** of or for charity; charitable **2.** supported by or dependent on charity **3.** given as charity; free

el·e·gance (el′ə gəns) *n.* **1.** the quality of being elegant **2.** anything elegant Also, esp. for sense 2, **el′e·gan·cy**, *pl.* -cies

el·e·gant (-gənt) *adj.* [< Fr. < L. *elegans* < *e-*, out + word thought to be *legare*, var. of *legere*, to choose: see LOGIC] **1.** having a dignified richness and grace, as of design, dress, style, etc.; tastefully luxurious **2.** very refined in manners and tastes **3.** [Colloq.] excellent; fine —**el′e·gant·ly** *adv.*

el·e·gi·ac (el′ə jī′ak, i lē′jē ak′) *adj.* **1.** of or composed in dactylic hexameter couplets, the second line having only an accented syllable in the third and sixth feet: the form was used for Greek and Latin elegies, etc. **2.** of, like, or fit for an elegy **3.** sad; mournful Also **el′e·gi′a·cal** —*n.* **1.** an elegiac couplet **2.** [*pl.*] a poem or poems written in such couplets

el·e·gize (el′ə jīz′) *vi.* -gized′, -giz′ing to write elegies —*vt.* to lament as in an elegy

el·e·gy (-jē) *n., pl.* -gies [< Fr. < L. < Gr. *elegeia* < *elegos*, a lament] **1.** a poem or song of lament and praise for the dead **2.** any poem in elegiac verse **3.** a poem, song, etc. in a mournful, serious tone —**el′e·gist** *n.*

elem. 1. element(s) **2.** elementary

el·e·ment (el′ə mənt) *n.* [OFr. < L. *elementum*] **1.** any of the four substances (earth, air, fire, and water) formerly believed to make up all physical matter **2.** the natural or suitable environment, situation, etc. for a person or thing [he's in his *element* only when he's in the woods] **3.** *a)* a component part or quality, often one that is basic or essential [an *element* of suspense in a story] *b)* a group of a specified kind in a whole [the criminal *element* in a city] **4.** *Chem.* any substance that cannot be separated into different substances by ordinary chemical methods: all matter is composed of such substances: elements can be changed into other elements by radioactive decay or by nuclear reactions: see table of CHEMICAL ELEMENTS on page 309 **5.** [*pl.*] *Eccles.* the bread and wine of Communion **6.** *Elec.* the wire coil, etc. that becomes glowing hot, as in an electric oven —**the elements 1.** the first or basic principles; rudiments [the *elements* of grammar] **2.** wind, rain, and the other forces of nature that make the weather

el·e·men·tal (el′ə men′t'l) *adj.* **1.** of the four elements (sense 1) **2.** of or like the forces of nature **3.** basic and powerful; primal [hunger is an *elemental* drive] **4.** *same as* ELEMENTARY (sense 2 *a*) **5.** being an essential part or parts **6.** being a chemical element in uncombined form —*n.* a basic principle: *usually used in pl.* —**el′e·men′tal·ly** *adv.*

el·e·men·ta·ry (-tər ē, -trē) *adj.* **1.** *same as* ELEMENTAL **2.** *a)* of first principles or fundamentals; introductory; basic *b)* of or having to do with the formal instruction of children in basic subjects —**el′e·men′ta·ri·ly** *adv.* —**el′e·men′ta·ri·ness** *n.*

elementary particle a particle that is smaller than an atom and is capable of independent existence, as a neutron, proton, electron, etc.

elementary school a school of the first six grades (sometimes, first eight grades), where basic subjects are taught

---

fat, āpe, cär; ten, ēven; is, bīte; gō, hôrn, tōōl, lŏŏk; oil, out; up, fur; get; joy; yet; chin; she; thin, then; zh, leisure; ŋ, ring; ə for *a* in *ago*, *e* in *agent*, *i* in *sanity*, *o* in *comply*, *u* in *focus*; ′ as in *able* (ā′b'l); Fr. bál; ë, Fr. coeur; ö, Fr. feu; Fr. mon; ô, Fr. coq; ü, Fr. duc; r, Fr. cri; H, G. ich; kh, G. doch; ‡foreign; ☆ Americanism; < derived from. See inside front cover.

el·e·phant (el'ə fənt) *n., pl.* **-phants, -phant:** see PLURAL, II, D, 1 [< L. < Gr. *elephantos,* genitive of *elephas,* elephant, ivory] a huge, thick-skinned mammal, the largest of the four-footed animals, with a long, flexible snout (called a *trunk*) and, usually, two ivory tusks: the **African elephant** has a flatter head and larger ears than the **Asian** (or **Indian**) **elephant**

el·e·phan·ti·a·sis (el'ə fən tī'ə sis) *n.* a chronic disease of the skin characterized by the enlargement of the legs or other parts, and by the hardening of the skin: it is caused by obstruction of the lymphatic vessels, esp. by filarial worms

el·e·phan·tine (el'ə fan'tēn, -tīn, -tin) *adj.* **1.** of an elephant or elephants **2.** like an elephant in size or gait; huge, heavy, slow, clumsy, etc.

El·eu·sin·i·an (el'yoo sin'ē ən) *adj.* [after *Eleusis,* ancient Gr. city near Athens, where celebrated] of the secret religious rites (**Eleusinian mysteries**) anciently celebrated in honor of Demeter and Persephone

elev. elevation

el·e·vate (el'ə vāt') *vt.* **-vat'ed, -vat'ing** [< L. pp. of *elevare* < *e-,* out + *levare,* to lift < *levis,* LIGHT²] **1.** to lift up; raise **2.** to raise in rank or position **3.** to raise to a higher intellectual or moral level **4.** to raise the spirits of; elate; exhilarate —see SYN. at LIFT

el·e·vat·ed (-vāt'id) *adj.* **1.** lifted up; raised; high **2.** exalted; dignified; lofty **3.** high-spirited; exhilarated —☆ *n.* a railway elevated above street level: in full, **elevated railway** (or **railroad**)

el·e·va·tion (el'ə vā'shən) *n.* **1.** an elevating or being elevated **2.** a high place or position **3.** height above the surface of the earth **4.** dignity; loftiness **5.** a flat scale drawing of the front, rear, or side of a building, etc. **6.** *Astron.* altitude **7.** *Geog.* height above sea level; altitude

el·e·va·tor (el'ə vāt'ər) *n.* **1.** a person or thing that raises or lifts up ☆**2.** a cage or car for hoisting or lowering people or things, attached by cables to a machine that moves it in a shaft ☆**3.** a machine, usually consisting of buckets or scoops fastened to an endless belt, for hoisting grain, etc. ☆**4.** a warehouse for storing, hoisting, and discharging grain **5.** a movable airfoil like a horizontal rudder, for making an aircraft go up or down

e·lev·en (i lev'ən) *adj.* [OE. *endleofan,* lit., one left over (ten)] totaling one more than ten —*n.* **1.** the cardinal number between ten and twelve; 11; XI **2.** a football or cricket team

e·lev·enth (-ənth) *adj.* **1.** preceded by ten others in a series; 11th **2.** designating any of the eleven equal parts of something —*n.* **1.** the one following the tenth **2.** any of the eleven equal parts of something; 1/11 —**at the eleventh hour** at the last possible time

elf (elf) *n., pl.* **elves** (elvz) [OE. *ælf*] **1.** *Folklore* a tiny, often prankish fairy **2.** a mischievous, small child or being —**elf'ish** *adj.* —**elf'ish·ly** *adv.* —**elf'ish·ness** *n.* —**elf'like'** *adj.*

elf·in (elf'in) *adj.* of or like an elf; full of strange charm [*elfin* laughter] —*n.* an elf

elf·lock (elf'läk') *n.* a tangled, matted lock of hair

El·gar (el'gər, -gär), Sir **Edward** (**William**) 1857-1934; Eng. composer

El·gin (el'jən) [after *Elgin,* city in Scotland] city in NE Ill., near Chicago: pop. 56,000

El Grec·o (el grek'ō) (born *Domenikos Theotokopoulos*) 1541?-1614?; painter in Italy & Spain, born in Crete

E·li (ē'lī) [Heb. *'ēlī,* lit., high] a masculine name

e·lic·it (i lis'it) *vt.* [< L. pp. of *elicere* < *e-,* out + *lacere,* to entice] **1.** to draw forth; evoke [to *elicit* laughter] **2.** to cause to be revealed [to *elicit* the true facts] —see SYN. at EXTRACT — **e·lic'i·ta'tion** *n.* —**e·lic'i·tor** *n.*

e·lide (i līd') *vt.* **e·lid'ed, e·lid'ing** [< L. *elidere* < *e-,* out + *laedere,* to strike] **1.** to leave out; suppress; omit **2.** to leave out or slur over (a vowel, syllable, etc.) in pronouncing a word, phrase, etc. —**e·lid'i·ble** *adj.*

el·i·gi·ble (el'i jə b'l) *adj.* [< ML. < L. *eligere:* see ELECT] **1.** fit to be chosen; qualified by law, rules, etc. [*eligible* to hold office] **2.** desirable, esp. for marriage [an *eligible* bachelor] —*n.*

an eligible person —**el'i·gi·bil'i·ty** *n.* —**el'i·gi·bly** *adv.*

E·li·jah (i lī'jə) [Heb. *'ēlīyāhū,* lit., Jehovah is God] **1.** a masculine name **2.** a prophet of Israel in the 9th century B.C.: I Kings 17-19; II Kings 2:1-11 Also **E·li·as** (i lī'əs)

e·lim·i·nate (i lim'ə nāt') *vt.* **-nat'ed, -nat'ing** [< L. pp. of *eliminare* < *e-,* out + *limen,* threshold] **1.** to take out; get rid of [to *eliminate* errors] **2.** to leave out of consideration; reject; omit [a possibility that cannot be *eliminated*] **3.** to drop (a person, team, etc. losing a round or match) from further competition **4.** *Algebra* to get rid of (an unknown quantity) by combining equations **5.** *Physiol.* to expel (waste products) from the body; excrete —**e·lim'i·na'tion** *n.* —**e·lim'i·na'tive** *adj.* —**e·lim'i·na'tor** *n.* —**e·lim'i·na·to·ry** *adj.*

El·i·ot (el'ē ət, el'yət) [dim. of ELLIS] **1.** a masculine name **2.** **George,** (pseud. of *Mary Ann Evans*) 1819-80; Eng. novelist **3.** **T(homas) S(tearns)** 1888-1965; Brit. poet & critic, born in the U.S.

E·lis (ē'lis) ancient country in the W Peloponnesus, in which Olympia was located: see map at GREECE

E·li·sha (i lī'shə) [Heb. *elīshā',* lit., God is salvation] **1.** a masculine name **2.** *Bible* a prophet of Israel, who succeeded Elijah: II Kings 2

e·li·sion (i lizh'ən) *n.* **1.** the eliding of a vowel, syllable, etc. in pronunciation (Ex.: it's, they'd, we've) **2.** any leaving out of parts [*elisions* made in a two-hour version of *Hamlet*]

e·lite, é·lite (i lēt', ā-) *n.* [< Fr., ult. < L. *eligere:* see ELECT] **1.** [*also used with pl. v.*] the group or part of a group selected or regarded as the finest, best, most powerful, etc. **2.** a size of type for typewriters, measuring 12 characters to the inch —*adj.* of, forming, or for an elite

e·lit·ism (-iz'm) *n.* government or control by an elite, or advocacy of such control —**e·lit'ist** *adj., n.*

e·lix·ir (i lik'sər) *n.* [< ML. < Ar. *al-iksīr,* prob. < Gr. *xērion,* powder for drying wounds < *xēros,* dry] **1.** an imaginary substance sought for by medieval alchemists to change base metals into gold or (in full, **elixir of life**) to keep people alive forever **2.** a supposed remedy for all ailments; cure-all **3.** a medicine of drugs in alcoholic solution, usually sweetened

Eliz. **1.** Elizabeth **2.** Elizabethan

E·liz·a·beth¹ (i liz'ə bəth) [< LL. < Gr. < Heb. *elīsheba',* lit., God is (my) oath] **1.** a feminine name: dim. *Bess, Beth, Betsy, Betty, Elsie;* var. *Elisabeth, Eliza* **2.** **Elizabeth I** 1533-1603; queen of England (1558-1603): daughter of HENRY VIII **3.** **Elizabeth II** 1926- ; queen of Great Britain & Northern Ireland (1952-): daughter of GEORGE VI

E·liz·a·beth² (i liz'ə bəth) [after wife of Sir G. Carteret, proprietor] city in northeastern N.J., adjacent to Newark: pop. 113,000

E·liz·a·be·than (i liz'ə bē'thən, -beth'ən) *adj.* of or characteristic of the time when Elizabeth I was queen of England —*n.* an English person, esp. writer, of the time of Queen Elizabeth I

Elizabethan sonnet same as SHAKESPEAREAN SONNET

elk (elk) *n., pl.* **elk, elks:** see PLURAL, II, D, 2 [OE. *eolh*] **1.** a large, mooselike deer of N Europe and Asia, with broad antlers ☆**2.** same as WAPITI

ell¹ (el) *n.* something L-shaped; specif., ☆an extension or wing at right angles to the main structure

ell² (el) *n.* [OE. *eln*] a former English measure of length, mainly for cloth, equal to 45 in.

El·la (el'ə) [dim. of ELEANOR] a feminine name

El·len (el'ən) [var. of HELEN] a feminine name

Elles·mere Island (elz'mir) island in the Arctic Ocean, Northwest Territories, Canada, west of NW Greenland

El·lice Islands (el'is) former name of TUVALU

El·li·ot, El·li·ott (el'ē ət) [var. of ELIOT] a masculine name

el·lipse (i lips', ə-) *n., pl.* **-lip'ses** (-lip'siz) [< ModL. < Gr. *elleipein,* to fall short (of a perfect circle): for IE. base see LOAN] *Geom.* the path of a point moving so that the sum of its distances from two fixed points (called *foci*) is constant

el·lip·sis (i lip'sis, ə-) *n., pl.* **-ses** (-sēz) [see ELLIPSE] **1.** *Gram.* the omission of a word or words necessary for complete grammatical construction but understood in the context (Ex.: "if possible" for "if it is possible") **2.** *Writing & Printing a)* a mark (... or formerly ***) indicating an intentional omission of words or letters, a lapse of time, etc. *b)* the use of such marks

ELEPHANTS
(shoulder height:
African, 10-13 ft.;
Indian, 8½-10 ft.)

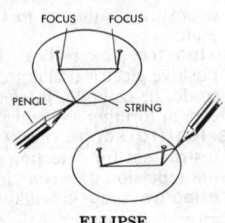

ELLIPSE

CHEMICAL ELEMENTS
With International Atomic Weights. Carbon at 12 is the standard.

	Symbol	Atomic Number	Atomic Weight		Symbol	Atomic Number	Atomic Weight
actinium	Ac	89	227(?)	mercury	Hg	80	200.59
aluminum	Al	13	26.9815	molybdenum	Mo	42	95.94
americium	Am	95	243.13	neodymium	Nd	60	144.24
antimony	Sb	51	121.75	neon	Ne	10	20.183
argon	Ar	18	39.948	neptunium	Np	93	237.00
arsenic	As	33	74.9216	nickel	Ni	28	58.71
astatine	At	85	210(?)	niobium	Nb	41	92.906
barium	Ba	56	137.34	nitrogen	N	7	14.0067
berkelium	Bk	97	248(?)	nobelium	No	102	255(?)
beryllium	Be	4	9.0122	osmium	Os	76	190.2
bismuth	Bi	83	208.980	oxygen	O	8	15.9994
boron	B	5	10.811	palladium	Pd	46	106.4
bromine	Br	35	79.909	phosphorus	P	15	30.9738
cadmium	Cd	48	112.40	platinum	Pt	78	195.09
calcium	Ca	20	40.08	plutonium	Pu	94	239.05
californium	Cf	98	251(?)	polonium	Po	84	210.05
carbon	C	6	12.01115	potassium	K	19	39.102
cerium	Ce	58	140.12	praseodymium	Pr	59	140.907
cesium	Cs	55	132.905	promethium	Pm	61	145(?)
chlorine	Cl	17	35.453	protactinium	Pa	91	231.10
chromium	Cr	24	51.996	radium	Ra	88	226.00
cobalt	Co	27	58.9332	radon	Rn	86	222.00
copper	Cu	29	63.546	rhenium	Re	75	186.2
curium	Cm	96	247(?)	rhodium	Rh	45	102.905
dysprosium	Dy	66	162.50	rubidium	Rb	37	85.47
einsteinium	Es	99	252(?)	ruthenium	Ru	44	101.07
erbium	Er	68	167.28	samarium	Sm	62	150.35
europium	Eu	63	151.96	scandium	Sc	21	44.956
fermium	Fm	100	257(?)	selenium	Se	34	78.96
fluorine	F	9	18.9984	silicon	Si	14	28.086
francium	Fr	87	223(?)	silver	Ag	47	107.868
gadolinium	Gd	64	157.25	sodium	Na	11	22.9898
gallium	Ga	31	69.72	strontium	Sr	38	87.62
germanium	Ge	32	72.59	sulfur	S	16	32.064
gold	Au	79	196.967	tantalum	Ta	73	180.948
hafnium	Hf	72	178.49	technetium	Tc	43	97(?)
helium	He	2	4.0026	tellurium	Te	52	127.60
holmium	Ho	67	164.930	terbium	Tb	65	158.924
hydrogen	H	1	1.00797	thallium	Tl	81	204.37
indium	In	49	114.82	thorium	Th	90	232.038
iodine	I	53	126.9044	thulium	Tm	69	168.934
iridium	Ir	77	192.2	tin	Sn	50	118.69
iron	Fe	26	55.847	titanium	Ti	22	47.90
krypton	Kr	36	83.80	tungsten	W	74	183.85
lanthanum	La	57	138.91	uranium	U	92	238.03
lawrencium	Lr	103	256(?)	vanadium	V	23	50.942
lead	Pb	82	207.19	xenon	Xe	54	131.30
lithium	Li	3	6.939	ytterbium	Yb	70	173.04
lutetium	Lu	71	174.97	yttrium	Y	39	88.905
magnesium	Mg	12	24.312	zinc	Zn	30	65.37
manganese	Mn	25	54.9380	zirconium	Zr	40	91.22
mendelevium	Md	101	258(?)				

el·lip·soid (-soid) *n. Geom.* a solid whose plane sections are all ellipses or circles —*adj.* shaped like an ellipsoid: also **el·lip′soi′-dal**

el·lip·ti·cal (i lip′ti k'l, ə-) *adj.* **1.** of, or having the form of, an ellipse **2.** of or marked by ellipsis; with a word or words omitted Also **el·lip′tic** —**el·lip′ti·cal·ly** *adv.*

El·lis (el′is) [var. of ELISHA] **1.** a masculine name **2.** (**Henry**) **Have·lock** (hav′läk, -lək), 1859–1939; Eng. psychologist & writer

Ellis Island [after S. *Ellis*, former owner] small island in New York Bay: former examination center for immigrants seeking to enter the U.S.

elm (elm) *n.* [OE.] **1.** a tall, hardy shade tree growing largely in the North Temperate Zone **2.** the hard, heavy wood of this tree

El·mer (el′mər) [< ? OE. < *æthel*, noble or *egil-* (< *ege*, awe) + *mære*, famous] a masculine name

Elm·hurst (elm′hurst) [after *elm* + *hurst*, grove] city in NE Ill.: suburb of Chicago: pop. 51,000

El Mon·te (el män′te) [Sp., lit., the thicket] city in SW Calif.: suburb of Los Angeles: pop. 70,000

el·o·cu·tion (el′ə kyōō′shən) *n.* [< L. < pp. of *eloqui*: see ELOQUENT] the art or style of giving talks or readings in public, esp. an older style now thought of as showy and not natural —**el′o·cu′tion·ar′y** *adj.* —**el′o·cu′-tion·ist** *n.*

El·o·ise (el′ə wēz′, el′ə wēz′) [var. of LOUISE] a feminine name

e·lon·gate (i lôŋ′gāt) *vt., vi.* **-gat·ed, -gat·ing** [< LL. pp. of *elongare*, to prolong < L. *e-*, out + *longus*, LONG] to make or become longer; stretch —*adj.* **1.** lengthened; stretched **2.** *Bot.* long and narrow —see SYN. at EXTEND —**e·lon·ga·tion** (i-lôŋ′gā′shən, ē′lôŋ-) *n.*

e·lope (i lōp′, ə-) *vi.* **e·loped′, e·lop′ing** [Anglo-Fr. *aloper*, prob. < ME. < OE. < *a-*, away + *hleapan*, to run] **1.** to run away secretly, esp. in order to get married: said of lovers **2.** to run away; escape —**e·lope′ment** *n.* —**e·lop′er** *n.*

el·o·quence (el′ə kwəns) *n.* **1.** speech or writing that can stir people's feelings or influence their thinking **2.** the art or manner of such speech or writing **3.** persuasive power

el·o·quent (-kwənt) *adj.* [OFr. < L. prp. of *eloqui* < *e-*, out + *loqui*, to speak] **1.** having eloquence; forceful and persuasive [an *eloquent* plea] **2.** expressing much feeling [he gave an *eloquent* sigh] —**el′o·quent·ly** *adv.*

El Pas·o (el pas′ō) [Sp., the ford] city in westernmost Tex., on the Rio Grande: pop. 322,000

El·sa (el′sə) [G. < ?] a feminine name

El Sal·va·dor (el sal′və dôr′; *Sp.* säl′vä thôr′) country in Central America, on the Pacific: 8,260 sq. mi.; pop. 3,541,000; cap. San Salvador

else (els) *adj.* [OE. *elles*, orig. the genitive of a noun meaning "other"] **1.** different; other [somebody *else*] **2.** in addition; more [is there anything *else*?] The adjective *else* comes after the word it modifies, and in the possessive case *else*, rather than the pronoun it follows, takes the possessive form [anybody *else's*] —*adv.* **1.** in a different or additional time, place, or manner; otherwise [where *else* can I go?] **2.** if not [study, (or) *else* you will fail]

else·where (els′hwer′, -wer′) *adv.* in or to some other place; somewhere else

El·sie (el′sē) [dim. of ELIZABETH¹] a feminine name

e·lu·ci·date (i lōō′sə dāt′, ə-) *vt., vi.* **-dat·ed, -dat·ing** [< LL. pp. of *elucidare* < L. *e-*, out + *lucidus*, clear < *lux*, LIGHT¹] to make clear (esp. something hard to understand); explain —see SYN. at EXPLAIN —**e·lu′ci·da′tion** *n.* —**e·lu′ci·da′tive** *adj.* —**e·lu′ci·da′tor** *n.*

e·lude (i lōōd′) *vt.* **e·lud′ed, e·lud′ing** [< L. *eludere* < *e-*, out + *ludere*, to play] **1.** to avoid or escape from by quickness, cunning, etc.; evade [to *elude* the police] **2.** to keep from being seen, understood, or remembered by [his name *eludes* me] —see SYN. at ESCAPE —**e·lud′er** *n.* —**e·lu·sion** (i lōō′zhən, ə-) *n.*

El·ul (el′ōol) *n.* [Heb.] *see* JEWISH CALENDAR

e·lu·sive (i lōō′siv) *adj.* **1.** tending to elude; hard to catch, discover, etc. [an *elusive* burglar] **2.** hard to understand or keep clearly in mind; puzzling Also, rarely, **e·lu′so·ry** (-sə rē) —**e·lu′sive·ly** *adv.* —**e·lu′sive·ness** *n.*

el·ver (el′vər) *n.* [for *eelfare*, migration of eels] a young eel

elves (elvz) *n. pl. of* ELF

elv·ish (el′vish) *adj.* of or like an elf —**elv′ish·ly** *adv.*

E·lyr·i·a (i lir′ē ə, ə-) [after J. *Ely*, proprietor, & *Maria*, his wife] city in N Ohio, near Cleveland: pop. 53,000

E·ly·si·um (i lizh′ē əm, -liz′-) [L. < Gr.] *Gr. Myth.* the dwelling place of virtuous people after death —*n.* any place or condition of ideal bliss or complete happiness; paradise Also **Elysian Fields** —**E·ly·sian** (-ly′shən, -ē ən) *adj.*

em (em) *n.* **1.** the letter M, m **2.** *Printing* a square of any type body, used as a unit of measure, as of column width; esp., an em pica, about 1/6 in.

'em (əm, 'm) *pron.* [Colloq.] them

em- *same as* EN-: used before *p*, *b*, or *m*

e·ma·ci·ate (i mā′shē āt′, -sē-) *vt.* **-at·ed, -at·ing** [< L. pp. of *emaciare* < *e-*, out + *macies*, leanness < *macer*, MEAGER] to make very thin; cause to lose much flesh or weight, as by starvation or disease —**e·ma′ci·a′tion** *n.*

em·a·nate (em′ə nāt′) *vi.* **-nat·ed, -nat·ing** [< L. pp. of *emanare* < *e-*, out + *manare*, to flow] to come forth; issue [the smell of food *emanated* from the kitchen; the order *emanated* from headquarters] —*vt.* to send forth; emit

em·a·na·tion (em′ə nā′shən) *n.* **1.** an emanating **2.** something that comes forth from a source —**em′a·na′tive** *adj.*

e·man·ci·pate (i man′sə pāt′) *vt.* **-pat·ed, -pat·ing** [< L. pp. of *emancipare* < *e-*, out + *mancipare*, to deliver up as property, ult. < *manus*, the hand + *capere*, to take] **1.** to set free (a slave, etc.); release from bondage or serfdom **2.** to free from anything that restrains or controls [an *emancipated* woman in Victorian England] —**e·man′ci·pa′tion** *n.* —**e·man′ci·pa′tive, e·man′ci·pa·to′ry** (-pə tôr′ē) *adj.* —**e·man′ci·pa′tor** *n.*

e·mas·cu·late (i mas′kyə lāt′) *vt.* **-lat·ed, -lat·ing** [< L. pp. of *emasculare* < *e-*, out + *masculus*, MASCULINE] **1.** to remove the testicles of; castrate **2.** to destroy the strength or force of; weaken [an anti-gambling law *emasculated* by lowering fines] —**e·mas′cu·la′tion** *n.* —**e·mas′cu·la·tive, e·mas′cu·la·to′ry** (-lə tôr′ē) *adj.* —**e·mas′cu·la′tor** *n.*

em·balm (im bäm′) *vt.* [< OFr. *embaumer*: see EN- & BALM] **1.** to treat (a dead body) with various chemicals to keep it from decaying rapidly **2.** to preserve in memory **3.** to make fragrant; perfume —**em·balm′er** *n.* —**em·balm′ment** *n.*

em·bank (im baŋk′) *vt.* to protect, support, or enclose with a bank of earth, rubble, etc.

em·bank·ment (-mənt) *n.* **1.** the act or process of embanking **2.** a bank of earth, rubble, etc. used to keep back water, hold up a roadway, etc.

☆**em·bar·ca·der·o** (em bär′kə der′ō) *n., pl.* **-der′os** [Sp. < pp. of *embarcar*, EMBARK] a wharf, dock, or pier

em·bar·go (im bär′gō) *n., pl.* **-goes** [Sp., ult. < L. *in-*, in, on + ML. *barra*, BAR¹] **1.** a government order prohibiting the entry or departure of commercial ships at its ports **2.** any restriction, restraint, or prohibition, esp. one imposed on commerce by law —*vt.* **-goed, -go·ing** to put an embargo on

em·bark (im bärk′) *vt.* [< Fr. < Sp. or OPr. < *em-* (L. *in-*) + L. *barca*, BARK³] to put or take (passengers or goods) aboard a ship, airplane, etc. —*vi.* **1.** to go aboard a ship, airplane, etc. **2.** to begin a journey **3.** to get started in an enterprise —**em·bar·ka·tion** (em′bär kā′shən), **em·bark′ment** *n.*

em·bar·rass (im bar′əs) *vt.* [< Fr. < Sp. < It. < *imbarrare*, to impede < *in-* (L. *in-*) + *barra*, BAR¹] **1.** to cause to feel self-conscious, confused, and ill at ease **2.** to cause difficulties to; hinder [his campaign was *embarrassed* by lack of party support] **3.** to cause to be in debt; cause financial difficulties to **4.** to complicate —**em·bar′rass·ing** *adj.* —**em·bar′rass·ing·ly** *adv.* —**em·bar′rass·ment** *n.*

SYN.—**embarrass** implies an uncomfortable feeling that one gets because of a sense of shyness, modesty, good manners, etc. [flattery *embarrasses* him]; **abash** suggests embarrassment that results from being ashamed of oneself [she was *abashed* by his kindness after she had insulted him]; **discomfit** implies that one's plans or hopes have been upset, resulting in a feeling of humiliation, embarrassment, etc. [*discomfited* when his proposals were rejected]; **disconcert** implies a sudden loss of poise that results in a confused state of mind [his interruptions were *disconcerting*]; **rattle** and **faze** are informal equivalents for **disconcert**, **faze** being commonly used in the negative [the barrage of criticism did not *faze* him] —**ANT. compose, assure**

em·bas·sy (em′bə sē) *n., pl.* **-sies** [< MFr. < OIt. < Pr. < *ambaissa*: see AMBASSADOR] **1.** the position or functions of an ambassador **2.** the official residence or offices of an ambassador **3.** an ambassador and his staff **4.** a person or group sent on an official mission to a foreign government **5.** any important or official mission or errand

ELM
(tree, leaves & samaras)

em·bat·tle[1] (im bat′′l) *vt.* **-tled, -tling** to provide with battlements; build battlements on

em·bat·tle[2] (im bat′′l) *vt.* **-tled, -tling** [Rare, except in pp.] to prepare or set in line for battle

em·bed (im bed′) *vt.* **-bed′ded, -bed′ding** **1.** to set or fix firmly in a surrounding mass [to *embed* tiles in cement] **2.** to fix in the mind, memory, etc. —**em·bed′ment** *n.*

em·bel·lish (im bel′ish) *vt.* [< OFr. *embelir* < *em-* (L. *in*) + *bel* < L. *bellus*, beautiful] **1.** to decorate; ornament; adorn **2.** to improve (a story, etc.) by adding details, often of a fictitious kind; touch up —see SYN. at ADORN —**em·bel′lish·ment** *n.*

em·ber[1] (em′bər) *n.* [< OE. *æmerge*] **1.** a glowing piece of coal, wood, etc. from a fire **2.** [*pl.*] the smoldering remains of a fire

em·ber[2] (em′bər) *adj.* [< OE. < *ymbryne* < *ymb*, round + *ryne*, a running] [*often* E-] designating or of three days (Wednesday, Friday, and Saturday) set aside for prayer and, sometimes, fasting in a specified week of each season of the year: observed in the Roman Catholic Church and certain other churches

em·bez·zle (im bez′′l) *vt.* **-zled, -zling** [< Anglo-Fr. < OFr. *en-* (see EN-) + *besillier*, to destroy] to steal (money, etc. entrusted to one's care); take by fraud for one's own use [the bank manager *embezzled* $50,000] —**em·bez′zle·ment** *n.* —**em·bez′zler** *n.*

em·bit·ter (im bit′ər) *vt.* to cause to have bitter or more bitter feelings —**em·bit′ter·ment** *n.*

em·bla·zon (im blā′z′n) *vt.* [see BLAZON] **1.** to decorate (*with* coats of arms, etc.) **2.** to display brilliantly; decorate with bright colors **3.** to praise; celebrate [deeds *emblazoned* in legend] —**em·bla′zon·ment** *n.*

em·blem (em′bləm) *n.* [orig., inlaid work < L. < Gr. *emblēma*, insertion < *en-*, in + *ballein*, to throw] **1.** a visible symbol of a thing, idea, etc.; object that stands for or suggests something else [the cross is an *emblem* of Christianity] **2.** a sign, badge, or device

em·blem·at·ic (em′blə mat′ik) *adj.* of, containing, or serving as an emblem; symbolic: also **em·blem·at′i·cal** —**em·blem·at′i·cal·ly** *adv.*

em·bod·i·ment (im bäd′ē mənt) *n.* **1.** an embodying or being embodied **2.** that in which some idea, quality, etc. is embodied [she is the *embodiment* of virtue]

em·bod·y (-bäd′ē) *vt.* **-bod′ied, -bod′y·ing** **1.** to give bodily form to; incarnate **2.** to give definite or visible form to; make concrete [a speech *embodying* democratic ideals] **3.** to bring together into, or make part of, an organized whole; incorporate [the latest findings *embodied* in the new book]

em·bold·en (im bōl′d′n) *vt.* to give courage to; cause to be bold or bolder

em·bo·lism (em′bə liz′m) *n. Med.* the obstruction of a blood vessel by an embolus

em·bo·lus (-ləs) *n., pl.* **-li**′ (-lī′) [ModL. < Gr. < *en-*, in + *ballein*, to throw] any foreign matter, as a blood clot or air bubble, carried in the bloodstream —**em·bol′ic** (-bäl′ik) *adj.*

em·bos·om (im booz′əm, -boo′zəm) *vt.* **1.** to embrace; cherish **2.** to enclose; surround; shelter

em·boss (im bôs′, -bäs′) *vt.* [< OFr.: see EN- & BOSS[2]] **1.** to decorate with designs, etc. raised above the surface [wallpaper *embossed* with a leaf design] **2.** to make stand out from the surface; raise in relief [Lincoln's head is *embossed* on the penny] —**em·boss′er** *n.* —**em·boss′ment** *n.*

em·bou·chure (äm′boo shoor′, äm′boo shoor′) *n.* [Fr. < *emboucher*, to put into the mouth < L. *in*, in + *bucca*, the cheek] **1.** the mouth of a river **2.** *Music a)* the mouthpiece of a wind instrument *b)* the method of applying the lips and tongue to the mouthpiece of a wind instrument

em·bow·er (im bou′ər) *vt.* to enclose or shelter in or as in a bower

em·brace (im brās′) *vt.* **-braced′, -brac′ing** [< OFr. < L. *im-*, in + *brachium*, an arm] **1.** to clasp in the arms lovingly or affectionately; hug **2.** to accept readily [to *embrace* an opportunity] **3.** to take up or adopt, esp. eagerly or seriously [to *embrace* a new profession] **4.** to encircle; surround [an isle *embraced* by the sea] **5.** to include; contain [biology *embraces* botany and zoology] —*vi.* to clasp each other in the arms —*n.* an embracing; hug —see SYN. at INCLUDE —**em·brace′a·ble** *adj.* —**em·brace′ment** *n.* —**em·brac′er** *n.*

em·bra·sure (im brā′zhər) *n.* [Fr. < obs. *embraser*, to widen an opening] **1.** an opening (for a door, window, etc.) with the sides slanted so that it is wider on the inside than on the outside **2.** an opening, as in a parapet, with the sides slanting outward to increase the angle of fire of a gun

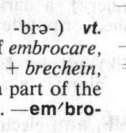

EMBRASURE

em·bro·cate (em′brō kāt′, -brə-) *vt.* **-cat′ed, -cat′ing** [< LL. pp. of *embrocare*, to foment < L. < Gr. < *en-*, in + *brechein*, to wet] to moisten and rub (a part of the body) with an oil, liniment, etc. —**em′bro·ca′tion** *n.*

em·broi·der (im broi′dər) *vt.* [< OFr. *en-*, in + *brosder*, to embroider] **1.** to ornament (fabric) with a design in needlework **2.** to make (a design, etc.) on fabric with needlework **3.** to embellish (a story, etc.); exaggerate —*vi.* **1.** to do embroidery **2.** to exaggerate —**em·broi′der·er** *n.*

em·broi·der·y (-ē) *n., pl.* **-der·ies** **1.** the art or work of ornamenting fabric with needlework **2.** embroidered work or fabric **3.** embellishment, as of a story **4.** an unnecessary but attractive addition

em·broil (im broil′) *vt.* [< Fr.: see EN- & BROIL[2]] **1.** to confuse (affairs, etc.); mix up; muddle **2.** to draw into a conflict or fight; involve in trouble [she refused to become *embroiled* in her neighbors' disputes] —**em·broil′ment** *n.*

em·bry·o (em′brē ō′) *n., pl.* **-os**′ [ML. < Gr. *embryon* < *en-*, in + *bryein*, to swell] **1.** an animal that is in the earliest stages of its development in the uterus: the human organism up to the third month after conception is called an *embryo*, thereafter a *fetus* **2.** *a)* an early or undeveloped stage of something *b)* anything in such a stage **3.** the rudimentary plant contained in a seed —*adj.* same as EMBRYONIC

em·bry·o- *a combining form meaning* embryo, embryonic

em·bry·ol·o·gy (em′brē äl′ə jē) *n.* [EMBRYO- + -LOGY] the branch of biology dealing with the formation and development of embryos —**em′bry·o·log′ic** (-ə läj′ik), **em′bry·o·log′i·cal** *adj.* —**em′bry·o·log′i·cal·ly** *adv.* —**em′bry·ol′o·gist** *n.*

EMBRYO
(at 2 months)

em·bry·on·ic (-än′ik) *adj.* **1.** of or like an embryo **2.** in an early stage; undeveloped [*embryonic* plans]

☆**em·cee** (em′sē′) *vt., vi.* **-ceed′, -cee′ing** [< M.C., sense 1] [Colloq.] to act as master of ceremonies (for) —*n.* [Colloq.] a master of ceremonies

e·meer (ə mir′) *n.* same as EMIR —**e·meer′ate** *n.*

e·mend (i mend′) *vt.* [L. *emendare*, to correct < *e-*, out + *mendum*, a fault] to make scholarly corrections or improvements in (a text)

e·men·date (ē′mən dāt′) *vt.* **-dat′ed, -dat′ing** same as EMEND —**e′men·da′tor** *n.* —**e·men′da·to·ry** (i men′də tôr′ē) *adj.*

e·men·da·tion (ē′mən dā′shən, em′ən-) *n.* **1.** an emending **2.** correction or change made in a text, as in attempting to restore the original reading

em·er·ald (em′ər əld, em′rəld) *n.* [< OFr. < VL. *smaraldus* < L. < Gr. *smaragdos*] **1.** a bright-green, transparent precious stone; green variety of beryl **2.** a similar variety of corundum **3.** bright green —*adj.* **1.** bright-green **2.** made of or with an emerald or emeralds

Emerald Isle [< its green landscape] Ireland

e·merge (i murj′) *vi.* **e·merged′, e·merg′ing** [L. *emergere* < *e-*, out + *mergere*, to dip] **1.** to rise as from a fluid **2.** *a)* to come forth into view; become visible [a bear *emerged* from the woods] *b)* to become known [the true story *emerged* later] **3.** to develop as something new, improved, etc. [a strong breed *emerged*] —**e·mer′gence** *n.* —**e·mer′gent** *adj.*

e·mer·gen·cy (i mur′jən sē) *n., pl.* **-cies** [orig. sense, an emerging] a sudden happening or unforeseen situation that needs immediate action or attention [the *emergency* created by the floods] —*adj.* for use in case of sudden necessity [an *emergency* exit]

e·mer·i·tus (i mer′ə təs) *adj.* [L., pp. of *emereri* < *e-*, out +

mereri, to serve] retired from active service, usually for age, but keeping one's rank or title [*professor* emeritus]

e·mer·sion (ē mur′zhən, -shən) *n.* an emerging

Em·er·son (em′ər sən), **Ralph Waldo** 1803–82; U.S. essayist, philosopher, & poet

em·er·y (em′ər ē, em′rē) *n.* [< Fr. < OFr. < It. < MGr. *smeri,* for Gr. *smyris,* emery] a dark, impure variety of corundum used in solid, crushed, or powdered form for grinding, polishing, etc.

e·met·ic (i met′ik) *adj.* [< L. < Gr. *emetikos* < *emein,* to vomit] causing vomiting —*n.* an emetic medicine or other substance

E.M.F., e.m.f., EMF, emf electromotive force

-e·mi·a (ēm′ē ə, ēm′yə) [ModL. < Gr. < *haima,* blood] *a suffix meaning* a (specified) condition or disease of the blood [*leukemia*]

em·i·grant (em′ə grənt) *adj.* **1.** emigrating **2.** of emigrants or emigration —*n.* one who emigrates

em·i·grate (-grāt′) *vi.* **-grat′ed, -grat′ing** [< L. pp. of *emigrare* < *e-,* out + *migrare,* MIGRATE] to leave one country or region to settle in another [*emigrating* from Italy to the U.S.] —**em′i·gra′tion** *n.*

é·mi·gré, e·mi·gré (em′ə grā′, ā′mə grā′) *n.* [Fr.] **1.** an emigrant **2.** a person forced to flee his country for political reasons

E·mil (ā′m'l, ē′-; em′'l) [G. < Fr. < L. *aemulus:* see EMULATE] a masculine name

Em·i·ly (em′'l ē) [fem. of EMIL] a feminine name

em·i·nence (em′ə nəns) *n.* [< OFr. < L. < prp. of *eminere,* to stand out: see MOUNT¹] **1.** a high or lofty place, thing, etc., as a hill **2.** *a)* superiority in rank, position, etc.; greatness [Einstein's *eminence* in science] *b)* a person of eminence **3.** [E-] *R.C.Ch.* a title of honor used in speaking to or of a cardinal, preceded by *His* or *Your*

em·i·nent (-nənt) *adj.* [< L.: see prec.] **1.** rising high above others; high; lofty **2.** projecting; prominent **3.** standing high by comparison with others; exalted; distinguished [an *eminent* poet] **4.** outstanding; noteworthy [a man of *eminent* courage] —see SYN. at FAMOUS —**em′i·nent·ly** *adv.*

eminent domain *Law* ☆the right of a government to take private property for public use, fair payment usually being given to the owner

e·mir (i mir′) *n.* [Ar. *amir,* commander] **1.** in certain Moslem countries, a ruler, prince, or commander **2.** a title given Mohammed's descendants through his daughter Fatima — **e·mir′ate** (-it, -āt) *n.*

em·is·sar·y (em′ə ser′ē) *n., pl.* **-sar′ies** [< L. < pp. of *emittere:* see EMIT] a person or agent sent on a specific mission, often in secret —*adj.* of, or serving as, an emissary or emissaries

e·mis·sion (i mish′ən) *n.* **1.** an emitting; issuance **2.** something emitted; discharge —**e·mis′sive** *adj.*

e·mit (i mit′) *vt.* **e·mit′ted, e·mit′ting** [< L. *emittere* < *e-,* out + *mittere,* to send: see MISSION] **1.** to send out; give forth [the kettle *emitted* steam] **2.** to utter (sounds, etc.) **3.** to transmit (a signal) as by radio waves **4.** to give off (electrons) under the influence of heat, radiation, etc. —**e·mit′ter** *n.*

Em·ma (em′ə) [G. < *Erma* < names beginning with *Erm-:* see IRMA] a feminine name

Em·man·u·el (i man′yoo wəl) [< Gr. < Heb. *'immānūēl,* lit., God with us] **1.** a masculine name: var. *Emanuel* **2.** the Messiah: see IMMANUEL

Em·my (em′ē) *n., pl.* **-mys** [altered < *Immy,* slang for a kind of TV camera] ☆[Slang] any of the statuettes awarded annually in the U.S. for special achievement in television programming, acting, etc.

EmnE., EMnE. Early Modern English

e·mol·li·ent (i mäl′yənt) *adj.* [< L. prp. of *emollire* < *e-,* out + *mollire,* to soften < *mollis,* MILD] softening; soothing —*n.* an emollient preparation, esp. for the surface tissues of the body, as a lotion for the skin

e·mol·u·ment (i mäl′yoo mənt) *n.* [< L. < *emolere* < *e-,* out + *molere,* to grind] gain from employment or position; salary, wages, fees, etc.

☆**e·mote** (i mōt′) *vi.* **e·mot′ed, e·mot′ing** [< EMOTION, by analogy with DEVOTE] [Colloq.] to express emotion in an affected or exaggerated way

e·mo·tion (i mō′shən) *n.* [Fr. (prob. after *motion*) < L. *emovere* < *e-,* out + *movere,* MOVE] **1.** strong feeling; excitement [a voice choked with *emotion*] **2.** any specific feeling, as love, hate, fear, anger, etc.

e·mo·tion·al (-'l) *adj.* **1.** of the emotions or feelings [emo-

tional problems] **2.** showing emotion, esp. strong emotion [an *emotional* look] **3.** having feelings that are easily stirred; quick to cry, be angry, etc. [an *emotional* person] **4.** appealing to or stirring the emotions [an *emotional* call to arms] —**e·mo′tion·al·ly** *adv.*

e·mo·tion·al·ism (-'l iz'm) *n.* **1.** the tendency to be emotional **2.** display of emotion **3.** an appeal to emotion, esp. to sway an audience

e·mo·tion·al·ize (-'l īz′) *vt.* **-ized′, -iz′ing** to deal with in an emotional way; give an emotional quality to —**e·mo′tion·al·i·za′tion** *n.*

e·mo·tive (i mōt′iv) *adj.* **1.** expressing or producing emotion **2.** relating to the emotions

Emp. 1. Emperor **2.** Empire **3.** Empress

em·pan·el (im pan′'l) *vt.* **-eled** or **-elled, -el·ing** or **-el·ling** *same as* IMPANEL

em·pa·thy (em′pə thē) *n.* [< Gr. < *en-,* in + *pathos,* feeling] the ability to share in another's emotions, thoughts, or feelings —**em·path·ic** (im path′ik), **em·pa·thet·ic** (em′pə thet′ik) *adj.*

Em·ped·o·cles (em ped′ə klēz′) 495?–435? B.C.; Gr. philosopher

em·pen·nage (em′pə näzh′, em′pə nij′) *n.* [Fr.] the tail assembly of an aircraft

em·per·or (em′pər ər) *n.* [< OFr. < L. *imperator* < pp. of *imperare,* to command < *in-,* in + *parare,* to set in order] the supreme ruler of an empire

em·pha·sis (em′fə sis) *n., pl.* **-ses** (-sēz′) [L. < Gr. < *emphainein,* to indicate < *en-,* in + *phainein,* to show: for IE. base see BEACON] **1.** force of expression, feeling, action, etc. **2.** special force given to a syllable, word, phrase, etc. in speaking **3.** special attention given to something so as to make it stand out; importance; stress [to put less *emphasis* on athletics]

em·pha·size (-sīz′) *vt.* **-sized′, -siz′ing** to give emphasis, or special force, to; stress

em·phat·ic (im fat′ik) *adj.* **1.** expressed, felt, or done with emphasis **2.** using emphasis in speaking, expressing, etc. **3.** very striking; forcible; definite [an *emphatic* defeat] **4.** *Gram.* designating or of a present tense or past tense in which a form of *do* is used as an auxiliary for emphasis (Ex.: I *do* care) —**em·phat′i·cal·ly** *adv.*

em·phy·se·ma (em′fə sē′mə) *n.* [Gr. < *en-,* in + *physaein,* to blow] abnormal swelling of the alveoli, or air cells, of the lungs, accompanied by loss of elasticity in the tissues and difficulty in breathing

em·pire (em′pīr; *for adj. usually* äm pir′) *n.* [< OFr. < L. < *imperare:* see EMPEROR] **1.** supreme rule; absolute power or authority **2.** government by an emperor or empress **3.** *a)* a group of states or territories under the rule of an emperor or empress *b)* a state uniting many territories and peoples under one ruler **4.** an extensive social or economic organization under the control of a single person, family, or corporation —*adj.* [E-] of or in the style of the first French Empire (1804–15) under Napoleon [*Empire* furniture; an *Empire* gown with a short, low-cut bodice and a long, flowing skirt]

em·pir·ic (em pir′ik) *n.* [< L. < Gr. < *empeiria,* experience < *en-,* in + *peira,* a trial] a person who relies solely on practical experience rather than on scientific principles —*adj.* empirical

em·pir·i·cal (-i k'l) *adj.* [see prec.] **1.** relying or based solely on experiment and observation rather than theory [the *empirical* method] **2.** relying or based on practical experience without reference to scientific principles [an *empirical* remedy] —**em·pir′i·cal·ly** *adv.*

em·pir·i·cism (-ə siz'm) *n.* **1.** experimental method; search for knowledge by observation and experiment **2.** *a)* a disregarding of scientific methods and relying solely on experience *b)* quackery **3.** *Philos.* the theory that experience is the only source of knowledge —**em·pir′i·cist** *n.*

em·place (im plās′) *vt.* **-placed′, -plac′ing** to place in position

em·place·ment (-mənt) *n.* **1.** an emplacing; placement **2.** the position in which something is placed; specif., *Mil.* the prepared position from which a heavy gun or guns are fired

em·plane (im plān′) *vi.* **-planed′, -plan′ing** *same as* ENPLANE

em·ploy (im ploi′) *vt.* [< OFr. < L. *implicare,* to enfold: see IMPLY] **1.** to make use of; use [he *employs* skill in his work] **2.** to keep busy or occupied [she needs something to *employ* her mind] **3.** to provide work and pay for [mining *employs* fewer men now] **4.** to engage the services or labor of for pay; hire —*n.* the state of being employed; paid service; employment [he is no longer in our *employ*] —see SYN. at USE —**em·ploy′a·ble** *adj.*

em·ploy·ee, em·ploy·e (im ploi′ē, em′ploi ē′) *n.* a person hired by another, or by a business firm, etc., to work for wages or salary

em·ploy·er (im ploi′ər) *n.* one who employs; esp., a person, business firm, etc. that hires one or more persons to work for wages or salary

em·ploy·ment (-mənt) *n.* **1.** an employing or being employed **2.** the thing at which one is employed; work; occupation; job **3.** the number or percentage of persons gainfully employed

em·po·ri·um (em pôr′ē əm) *n., pl.* **-ri·ums, -ri·a** (-ə) [L. < Gr. < *emporos*, traveler < *en-*, in + *poros*, way] **1.** a place of commerce; trading center; marketplace **2.** a large store with a wide variety of things for sale: an old-fashioned term

em·pow·er (im pou′ər) *vt.* **1.** to give power to; authorize [Congress is *empowered* to levy taxes] **2.** to enable; permit —**em·pow′er·ment** *n.*

em·press (em′pris) *n.* **1.** the wife of an emperor **2.** a woman ruler of an empire

emp·ty (emp′tē) *adj.* **-ti·er, -ti·est** [< OE. æmettig, unoccupied < æmetta, leisure + -ig, -y²] **1.** containing nothing; having nothing in it **2.** having no one in it; unoccupied [an *empty* house] **3.** worthless; unsatisfying [*empty* pleasures] **4.** meaningless; insincere; vain [*empty* promises] **5.** [Colloq.] hungry —*vt.* **-tied, -ty·ing** **1.** to make empty **2.** to pour out or remove (the contents) of something **3.** to unburden or discharge (oneself or itself) —*vi.* **1.** to become empty **2.** to pour out; discharge [the river *empties* into the sea] —*n., pl.* **-ties** an empty freight car, truck, bottle, etc. —**empty of** lacking; without; devoid of —**emp′ti·ly** *adv.* —**emp′ti·ness** *n.*

SYN.—**empty** means having nothing or no one in it [an *empty* box, street, stomach, etc.]; **vacant** means lacking that which properly or usually occupies or fills it [a *vacant* apartment, position, etc.]; **void** emphasizes total emptiness [a heart *void* of pity]—see also SYN. at VAIN —**ANT. full**

emp·ty-hand·ed (-han′did) *adj.* bringing or carrying away nothing

emp·ty-head·ed (-hed′id) *adj.* silly and light-minded

em·pur·ple (im pur′p'l) *vt., vi.* **-pled, -pling** to make or become purple

em·pyr·e·al (em pir′ē əl; em′pī rē′əl, -pə-) *adj.* [< LL. < Gr. *empyrios*, fiery < *en-*, in + *pyr*, a fire] of the empyrean; heavenly; sublime

em·py·re·an (em′pī rē′ən, -pə-; em pir′ē ən) *n.* [see prec. & -AN] **1.** the highest heaven: among the ancients, the sphere of pure light or fire **2.** the sky; the firmament —*adj. same as* EMPYREAL

e·mu (ē′myōō) *n.* [prob. < Port. *ema*, a crane] a large Australian bird, like the ostrich unable to fly but smaller

E.M.U., e.m.u., emu electromagnetic units

em·u·late (em′yə lāt′) *vt.* **-lat′ed, -lat′ing** [< L. pp. of *aemulari* < *aemulus*, trying to equal] **1.** to try to equal or surpass [a new shopping center *emulating* the neighboring ones] **2.** to imitate (a person or thing admired) [the younger Dumas *emulated* his father, the novelist] **3.** to rival successfully —**em′u·la′tion** *n.* —**em′u·la′tive** *adj.* —**em′u·la′tor** *n.*

em·u·lous (em′yə ləs) *adj.* having or showing a desire to emulate —**em′u·lous·ly** *adv.* —**em′u·lous·ness** *n.*

EMU
(to 5 ft. high)

e·mul·si·fy (i mul′sə fī′) *vt., vi.* **-fied′, -fy′ing** to form into an emulsion —**e·mul′si·fi′a·ble** *adj.* —**e·mul′si·fi·ca′tion** *n.* —**e·mul′si·fi′er** *n.*

e·mul·sion (i mul′shən) *n.* [< ModL. < L. pp. of *emulgere* < *e-*, out + *mulgere*, to milk] **1.** a mixture of liquids, as oil and water, in which very fine drops of one stay evenly scattered throughout the other [homogenized milk is an *emulsion*]: sometimes a gummy or soapy substance is used as an emulsifier **2.** *Photog.* a suspension of a light-sensitive salt of silver in gelatin, used to coat plates and film —**e·mul′sive** *adj.*

en (en) *n.* **1.** the letter N, n **2.** *Printing* a space half the width of an em

en- (in, en) [OFr. < L. *in-* < *in*, IN] **1.** *a prefix meaning: a)* to put or get into or on [*entrain*] *b)* to cover with [*enrobe*] *c)* to make, cause to be [*enfeeble*] *d)* in or into [*enclose*] **2.** *a prefix used to add emphasis* [*enliven*] *en-* is changed to *em-* before

p, b, m Many words with *en-* are also spelled *in-* (Ex.: *enquire, inquire*)

-en (ən, 'n) [< OE. suffixes *-nian, -an, -en*] *any of several suffixes:* **1.** *meaning: a)* to become or cause to be [*darken, weaken*] *b)* to come to have, cause to have [*strengthen*] **2.** *meaning* made of [*woolen*] **3.** *used to form the pp. of strong verbs* [*risen*] **4.** *used to form plurals* [*children*] **5.** *used to form diminutives* [*chicken*]

en·a·ble (in ā′b'l) *vt.* **-bled, -bling** **1.** to make able; provide with means, opportunity, power, or authority (*to* do something) [a loan *enabled* him to finish college] **2.** to make possible

en·act (in akt′) *vt.* **1.** to make (a bill, etc.) into a law; pass (a law); decree; ordain **2.** to represent or perform in or as in a play; act out —**en·ac′tive** *adj.* —**en·ac′tor** *n.*

en·act·ment (-mənt) *n.* **1.** an enacting or being enacted **2.** something enacted, as a law

en·am·el (i nam′'l) *n.* [see the *v.*] **1.** a glassy, colored, opaque substance fused to surfaces, as of metals, to form a coating that protects or decorates **2.** any smooth, hard, glossy coating like enamel **3.** the hard, white, glossy coating of the crown of a tooth **4.** anything enameled **5.** paint or varnish with a smooth, hard, glossy surface when it dries —*vt.* **-eled** or **-elled, -el·ing** or **-el·ling** [< Anglo-Fr. < *en-* (see EN-) + *amayl* < OFr. *esmail*, enamel] **1.** to inlay or cover with enamel **2.** to decorate in various colors, as if with enamel **3.** to form an enamel-like surface on —**en·am′el·er, en·am′el·ler, en·am′el·ist, en·am′el·list** *n.*

en·am·el·ware (-wer′) *n.* kitchen utensils, etc. made of enameled metal

en·am·or (in am′ər) *vt.* [< OFr. < *en-*, in + *amour* < L. *amor*, love] to fill with love and desire; charm; captivate: now mainly in the passive voice, with *of* [much *enamored* of her]

en bloc (en bläk′; Fr. än blôk′) [Fr., lit., in a block] in one lump; as a whole; all together

enc., encl. enclosure

en·camp (in kamp′) *vi.* to set up a camp [the army *encamped* in the valley] —*vt.* **1.** to put in a camp **2.** to form into a camp

en·camp·ment (-mənt) *n.* **1.** an encamping or being encamped **2.** a camp or campsite

en·cap·su·late (in kap′sə lāt′, -syoo-) *vt.* **-lat′ed, -lat′ing** **1.** to enclose in or as if in a capsule **2.** to put in concise form; condense Also **en·cap′sule** (-s'l, -syool) **-suled, -sul·ing** —**en·cap′su·la′tion** *n.*

en·case (in kās′) *vt.* **-cased′, -cas′ing** **1.** to cover completely; enclose **2.** to put into a case or cases —**en·case′ment** *n.*

en cas·se·role (en cas′ə rōl′; Fr. än kàs rôl′) [Fr.] (baked and served) in a casserole

en·caus·tic (en kôs′tik) *adj.* [< L. < Gr. < *en-*, in + *kaiein*, to burn] done by a process of burning in or applying heat [*encaustic* tile] —*n.* a method of painting in which colors in wax are fused to a surface with hot irons —**en·caus′ti·cal·ly** *adv.*

-ence (əns, 'ns) [< OFr. *-ence* & L. *-entia* (see -ENT + -IA)] *a suffix meaning* act, fact, quality, state, result, or degree [*conference, excellence*]

‡en·ceinte (än sant′; E. än sānt′) *adj.* [Fr., ult. < L. *in-*, not + pp. of *cingere*, to gird] pregnant

en·ceph·a·li·tis (en sef′ə līt′is, en′sef-) *n.* [< ENCEPHAL(O)- + -ITIS] inflammation of the brain —**en·ceph′a·lit′ic** (-lit′ik) *adj.*

en·ceph·a·lo- [< Gr. *enkephalos*, the brain] *a combining form meaning* of the brain: also **en·ceph′al-**

en·ceph·a·lo·gram (en sef′ə lō gram′) *n. shortened form of:* **1.** ELECTROENCEPHALOGRAM **2.** PNEUMOENCEPHALOGRAM

en·ceph·a·lon (en sef′ə län′) *n., pl.* **-la** (-lə) [ModL. < Gr. < *en-*, in + *kephalē*: for IE. base see GABLE] *Anat.* the brain —**en·ce·phal·ic** (en′sə fal′ik) *adj.*

en·chain (in chān′) *vt.* **1.** to bind with chains **2.** to hold fast; captivate —**en·chain′ment** *n.*

en·chant (in chant′) *vt.* [< OFr. < L. *incantare*, to bewitch: see INCANTATION] **1.** to cast a spell over, as by magic; bewitch **2.** to charm greatly; delight [his garden *enchants* me] —see SYN. at ATTRACT —**en·chant′er** *n.* —**en·chant′ress** *n.fem.*

en·chant·ing (-iŋ) *adj.* **1.** charming; delightful **2.** bewitching; fascinating —**en·chant′ing·ly** *adv.*

en·chant·ment (-mənt) *n.* **1.** an enchanting or being enchanted **2.** a magic spell or charm **3.** something that charms greatly **4.** great delight

en·chase (in chās′) *vt.* **-chased′, -chas′ing** [< OFr. *enchasser*: see CHASE³] **1.** to put in a setting **2.** to ornament by engraving, inlaying with gems, etc. **3.** to carve (designs, etc.)

☆**en·chi·la·da** (en′chə lä′də) *n.* [AmSp.] a tortilla usually rolled with meat inside and served with a chili-flavored sauce

en·cir·cle (in sur′k′l) *vt.* **-cled, -cling 1.** to make a circle around; surround [hills *encircle* the valley] **2.** to move in a circle around [the earth *encircles* the sun] —**en·cir′cle·ment** *n.*

en·clave (en′klāv) *n.* [Fr. < OFr. < L. *in*, in + *clavis*, a key: see CLOSE²] **1.** a territory surrounded by the territory of a foreign country **2.** a minority culture group within a larger group

en·clit·ic (en klit′ik) *adj.* [< LL. < Gr. < *enklinein*, to lean toward] *Gram.* dependent for its stress on the preceding word, often one with which it has combined (Ex.: *man* in *layman*) — *n.* any such word or particle

en·close (in klōz′) *vt.* **-closed′, -clos′ing 1.** to shut in all around; surround [high walls *enclose* the garden] **2.** to insert in an envelope, wrapper, etc., often along with something else [to *enclose* a check with one's order] **3.** to contain

en·clo·sure (-klō′zhər) *n.* **1.** an enclosing or being enclosed **2.** something that encloses, as a fence **3.** something enclosed; specif., *a*) an enclosed place *b*) a document, money, etc. enclosed as with a letter

en·code (in kōd′) *vt.* **-cod′ed, -cod′ing** to put (information, etc.) into code —**en·cod′er** *n.*

en·co·mi·ast (en kō′mē ast′) *n.* [< Gr. < *enkōmiazein*, to praise] a person who speaks or writes encomiums; eulogist — **en·co′mi·as′tic** *adj.*

en·co·mi·um (en kō′mē əm) *n., pl.* **-mi·ums, -mi·a** (-ə) [L. < Gr. *enkōmion*, song of praise < *en-*, in + *kōmos*, a revel] a formal expression of high praise; eulogy —see SYN.at TRIBUTE

en·com·pass (in kum′pəs) *vt.* **1.** to shut in all around; surround **2.** to contain; include [the information *encompassed* in an encyclopedia] **3.** to bring about; achieve [to *encompass* its destruction] —**en·com′pass·ment** *n.*

en·core (äŋ′kôr, än kôr′) *interj.* [Fr., yet, again] again; once more —*n.* **1.** a demand by the audience, shown by applause, for further performance **2.** the performance or piece performed in answer to such a demand —*vt.* **-cored, -cor·ing** to demand further performance of or by

en·coun·ter (in koun′tər) *vt.* [< OFr. < L. *in*, in + *contra*, against] **1.** to meet unexpectedly; come upon [she *encountered* a former classmate on vacation] **2.** to meet in conflict or battle **3.** to face (difficulties, trouble, etc.) —*n.* **1.** a direct meeting, as in conflict or battle **2.** an unexpected meeting —*adj.* designating or of a small group meeting to explore personal relationships through an open exchange of intimate feelings, release of inhibitions, etc. —see SYN.at BATTLE

en·cour·age (in kur′ij) *vt.* **-aged, -ag·ing 1.** to give courage, hope, or confidence to; hearten [her praise *encouraged* me to go on] **2.** to give support to; foster; help [warm weather *encourages* ice cream sales] —**en·cour′ag·ing** *adj.* —**en·cour′ag·ing·ly** *adv.*

en·cour·age·ment (-mənt) *n.* **1.** an encouraging or being encouraged **2.** something that encourages

en·croach (in krōch′) *vi.* [< OFr. *encrochier*, to seize upon < *en-*, in + *croc*, a hook] **1.** to trespass or intrude (*on* or *upon* the rights, property, etc. of another) **2.** to go beyond the proper, original, or usual limits [the lake has *encroached* upon the shoreline] —**en·croach′ment** *n.*

en·crust (in krust′) *vt., vi. same as* INCRUST —**en′crus·ta′tion** *n.*

en·cum·ber (in kum′bər) *vt.* [< OFr.: see EN- & CUMBER] **1.** to hold back the motion or action of, as with a burden; hinder [a hiker *encumbered* with a heavy knapsack] **2.** to fill so as to obstruct or block up [a hallway *encumbered* with furniture] **3.** to load or weigh down, as with claims, debts, etc.; burden

en·cum·brance (-brəns) *n.* **1.** something that encumbers; hindrance; burden **2.** *Law same as* INCUMBRANCE

-en·cy (ən sē, 'n sē) [L. *-entia*] a suffix meaning act, fact, quality, state, result, or degree [*dependency, emergency, efficiency*]

ency., encyc., encycl. encyclopedia

en·cyc·li·cal (in sik′li k′l, -sī′kli-) *adj.* [LL. *encyclicus* < Gr. < *en-*, in + *kyklos*, a circle: for IE. base see COLLAR] for general circulation: also **en·cyc′lic** —*n. R.C.Ch.* a letter from the Pope to the bishops, usually dealing with matters of doctrine

en·cy·clo·pe·di·a, en·cy·clo·pae·di·a (en sī′klə pē′dē ə) *n.* [ModL. < Gr. *enkyklopaideia* < *enkyklios*, general + *paideia*, education] a book or set of books giving information on all or many branches of knowledge, or on one field of study, generally in articles alphabetically arranged

en·cy·clo·pe·dic, en·cy·clo·pae·dic (-pē′dik) *adj.* of or like an encyclopedia; esp., giving information about many subjects; comprehensive in scope —**en·cy′clo·pe′di·cal·ly, en·cy′clo·pae′di·cal·ly** *adv.*

en·cy·clo·pe·dist, en·cy·clo·pae·dist (-pē′dist) *n.* a person who compiles or helps compile an encyclopedia

en·cyst (en sist′) *vt., vi.* to enclose or become enclosed as in a cyst —**en·cyst′ment, en′cys·ta′tion** (-sis tā′shən) *n.*

end (end) *n.* [OE. *ende*] **1.** a limit or limiting part; boundary [the north *end* of the town] **2.** the last part of anything; final point; finish; conclusion [the *end* of the day; the *end* of a story] **3.** a ceasing to exist; death or destruction [he met his *end* in battle] **4.** the part at or near either extremity of anything; tip [the *end* of a rope] **5.** a purpose; intention; object [to achieve one's *ends*] **6.** an outcome; result; consequence [what will the *end* of the matter be?] **7.** a piece left over; remnant [odds and *ends*] **8.** the reason for being [happiness should be the *end* of government] ☆**9.** *Football a*) a player at either end of the line *b*) his position —*vt.* **1.** to bring to an end; finish; stop **2.** to form the end of —*vi.* **1.** to come to an end; terminate: often with *up* **2.** to die —*adj.* at the end; final [end product] —see SYN.at CLOSE² —**ends of the earth** remote regions —**make an end of 1.** to finish; stop **2.** to do away with —**make (both) ends meet** to keep one's expenses within one's income —**no end** [Colloq.] very much or very many —**on end 1.** in an upright position **2.** without interruption [for days *on end*] —**put an end to 1.** to stop **2.** to do away with —**to end** that goes beyond or exceeds [a trip *to end* all trips]

en·da·moe·ba (en′də mē′bə) *n.* [see ENDO- & AMOEBA] any of certain parasitic amoebas, including the species that causes amoebic dysentery in man: also sp. **en′da·me′ba**

en·dan·ger (in dān′jər) *vt.* to expose to danger, harm, or loss; imperil [to *endanger* one's life] —**en·dan′ger·ment** *n.*

en·dan·gered species (-jərd) a species of animal or plant in danger of becoming extinct

en·dear (in dir′) *vt.* to make dear or beloved

en·dear·ing (-iŋ) *adj.* **1.** that makes dear or well liked **2.** expressing affection [*endearing* tones]

en·dear·ment (-mənt) *n.* **1.** warm liking; affection **2.** a word or act expressing affection

en·deav·or (in dev′ər) *vi.* [< *en-* + OFr. *deveir*, duty < L. *debere*, to owe] to make an earnest attempt —*vt.* **1.** [Archaic] to try to achieve **2.** to try (*to* do something) —*n.* an earnest attempt or effort Also, Brit. sp., **en·deav′our** —see SYN.at EFFORT and TRY

En·de·cott (en′di kät′, -kət), **John** 1588?-1665; English Puritan; 1st governor of Massachusetts Bay colony: also sp. **Endicott**

en·dem·ic (en dem′ik) *adj.* [Fr. < Gr. < *en-*, in + *dēmos*, the people] **1.** native to a particular country, region, etc.: said of plants and animals **2.** regularly present in a particular region or people: said of a disease: also **en·dem′i·cal** [black lung disease is *endemic* among coal miners] —*n.* **1.** an endemic plant or animal **2.** an endemic disease —see SYN.at NATIVE —**en·dem′i·cal·ly** *adv.* —**en·de·mic·i·ty** (en′də mis′ə tē) *n.*

end·ing (en′diŋ) *n.* **1.** *a*) the last part; finish *b*) death **2.** *Gram.* the final letter or letters added to a word base to make a derivative or an inflectional form [*-ed* is the *ending* in *wanted*]

en·dive (en′dīv, än′dēv) *n.* [OFr. < ML. < MGr. < L. *intibus* < Gr. *entybon*] **1.** *a*) a cultivated plant of the composite family, with curled, narrow leaves used in salads *b*) another form of this with wide, smooth leaves; escarole. esp. when blanched like celery for salads **2.** the young leaves of chicory

end·less (end′lis) *adj.* **1.** having no end; going on forever; eternal; infinite [*endless* space] **2.** lasting too long [an *endless* speech] **3.** continual [*endless* interruptions] **4.** with the ends joined to form a closed unit that can move continuously over wheels, etc. [an *endless* belt] —**end′less·ly** *adv.* —**end′less·ness** *n.*

end·most (-mōst′) *adj.* at the end; farthest; last

en·do- [< Gr. *edon*, within] *a combining form meaning* within, inner [*endoderm*] : also, before a vowel, **end-**

en·do·blast (en′də blast′) *n. same as* ENDODERM

en·do·car·di·tis (en′dō kär dīt′is) *n.* [ModL. < ENDO- + Gr. *kardia*, heart + -ITIS] inflammation of the thin membrane lining the heart cavities

ENDIVE
(sense 1b)

en·do·carp (en′də kärp′) *n.* the inner layer of the wall of a ripened ovary or fruit, as the pit around the seed of a plum

en·do·crine (en′də krin, -krīn′, -krēn′) *adj.* [ENDO- + Gr. *krinein,* to separate: see CRISIS] **1.** designating or of any gland producing one or more internal secretions that, introduced into the bloodstream, are carried to other parts of the body whose functions they regulate [the thyroid, adrenal, and pituitary glands are *endocrine* glands] **2.** designating or of such a secretion —*n.* any such gland or its secretion

en·do·cri·nol·o·gy (en′dō kri näl′ə jē, -krī-) *n.* the branch of medicine dealing with the endocrine glands and the internal secretions of the body —**en′do·cri′no·log′i·cal** (-nə läj′ə k′l) *adj.* —**en′do·cri·nol′o·gist** *n.*

en·do·derm (en′də durm′) *n.* the inner layer of cells of the embryo, from which is formed the lining of the digestive tract, of other internal organs, and of certain glands —**en′do·der′mal, en′do·der′mic** *adj.*

en·dog·a·my (en däg′ə mē) *n.* [ENDO- + -GAMY] **1.** the custom of marrying only within one's own tribe, clan, etc.; inbreeding **2.** cross-pollination among flowers of the same plant —**en·dog′a·mous, en·do·gam·ic** (en′də gam′ik) *adj.*

en·dog·e·nous (en däj′ə nəs) *adj.* **1.** developing from the inside; originating internally **2.** *Biol.* growing or developing from or on the inside —**en·dog′e·nous·ly** *adv.*

en·do·mor·phic (en′də môr′fik) *adj.* [ENDO- + -MORPHIC] designating a fleshy or heavy type of body build, in which the structures developed from the endoderm are most prominent —**en′do·morph′** *n.*

en·do·plasm (en′də plaz′m) *n.* the inner part of the cytoplasm of a cell —**en′do·plas′mic** *adj.*

end organ any structure at the end of a nerve fiber that either receives a sensation or sends an impulse to a muscle

en·dorse (in dôrs′) *vt.* **-dorsed′, -dors′ing** [< OFr. < ML. < L. *in,* on + *dorsum,* the back] **1.** to write on the back of (a document); specif., to sign (one's name) as payee on the back of (a check, etc.) **2.** to give approval to; support; sanction [to *endorse* a candidate] —see SYN. at APPROVE —**en·dors′a·ble** *adj.* —**en·dors′er** *n.*

en·dor·see (in dôr′sē′, en′dôr sē′) *n.* the person to whom a check, etc. is made over by endorsement

en·dorse·ment (in dôrs′mənt) *n.* **1.** an endorsing **2.** something written in endorsing; specif., *a)* the signature of a payee on the back of a check, etc. *b)* a statement endorsing a person, product, etc.

en·do·skel·e·ton (en′də skel′ə t′n) *n.* the internal bony, supporting framework in vertebrates

en·do·sperm (en′də spurm′) *n.* [ENDO- + SPERM¹] a tissue which surrounds the developing embryo of a seed and provides food for its growth; albumen —**en′do·sper′mic** *adj.*

en·dow (in dou′) *vt.* [< Anglo-Fr. < OFr. < *en-,* in + *douer* < L. *dotare,* to endow] **1.** to provide with some talent, quality, etc. [*endowed* with courage] **2.** to think of as having some quality or characteristic [to *endow* gods with human traits] **3.** to give money or property so as to provide an income for the support of (a college, hospital, etc.)

en·dow·ment (-mənt) *n.* **1.** an endowing **2.** that with which something is endowed; bequest **3.** a gift of nature; talent, ability, etc.

☆**endowment policy** an insurance policy by which a stated amount is paid to the insured after the period of time specified in the contract, or to the beneficiaries if the insured dies during that time

end·pa·per (end′pā′pər) *n.* a folded sheet of paper one half of which is pasted to the inside of either cover of a book, the other half to the inside edge of the first (or last) page

end product the final result of any series of changes, processes, or chemical reactions

☆**end table** a small table placed beside a chair, etc.

en·due (in dōō′, -dyōō′) *vt.* **-dued′, -du′ing** [< OFr. < L. *inducere:* see INDUCE] to provide (*with* something); specif., to endow (*with* qualities, talents, etc.)

en·dur·ance (in door′əns, -dyoor′-) *n.* **1.** an enduring **2.** ability to last, continue, or remain **3.** ability to stand pain, distress, fatigue, etc.; fortitude **4.** duration

en·dure (in door′, -dyoor′) *vt.* **-dured′, -dur′ing** [< OFr. < LL. < L. < *in-,* in + *durare,* to harden < *durus,* hard] **1.** to hold up under (pain, fatigue, etc.); bear **2.** to put up with; tolerate —*vi.* **1.** to continue in existence; last; remain [his fame will *endure* for ages] **2.** to bear pain, etc. without flinching; hold out —see SYN. at BEAR¹ and CONTINUE —**en·dur′a·ble** *adj.* —**en·dur′a·bly** *adv.*

en·dur·ing (-iŋ) *adj.* lasting; permanent; durable —**en·dur′ing·ly** *adv.* —**en·dur′ing·ness** *n.*

end·ways (end′wāz′) *adv.* **1.** on end; upright **2.** with the end foremost **3.** lengthwise **4.** end to end Also **end′wise′** (-wīz′)

En·dym·i·on (en dim′ē ən) *Gr. Myth.* a beautiful young shepherd loved by Selene

☆**end zone** *Football* the area between the goal line and the end boundary (**end line**) ten yards behind it, at each end of the playing field

-ene (ēn) [after L. *-enus,* Gr. *-ēnos,* adj. suffix] a suffix used: **1.** *Chem.* to form names for some hydrocarbons [*propylene, benzene*] **2.** to form some commercial names

ENE, E.N.E., e.n.e. east-northeast

en·e·ma (en′ə mə) *n.* [LL. < Gr. < *en-,* in + *hienai,* to send] **1.** a liquid injected into the colon through the anus, for making the bowels move, as a medicine, etc. **2.** such an injection

en·e·my (en′ə mē) *n., pl.* **-mies** [< OFr. < L. *inimicus* < *in-,* not + *amicus,* friend] **1.** a person who hates another, and wishes or tries to harm him; foe **2.** *a)* a nation or force hostile to another *b)* troops, fleet, ship, member, etc. of a hostile nation **3.** a person hostile to an idea, cause, etc. [an *enemy* of slavery] **4.** anything injurious or harmful [he is his own greatest *enemy*] —*adj.* of an enemy —see SYN. at OPPONENT

en·er·get·ic (en′ər jet′ik) *adj.* of, having, or showing energy; vigorous; forceful —**en·er·get′i·cal·ly** *adv.*

en·er·gize (en′ər jīz′) *vt.* **-gized′, -giz′ing** **1.** to give energy to; make active; invigorate **2.** *Elec.* to apply a source of voltage or current to (a circuit, etc.) —**en′er·giz′er** *n.*

en·er·gy (en′ər jē) *n., pl.* **-gies** [< LL. < Gr. *energeia* < *en-,* in + *ergon,* work] **1.** power to work or be active, or such power used in a vigorous way; force; vigor [a man of great *energy;* to scrub with *energy*] **2.** *Physics* the capacity for doing work and overcoming resistance [electricity and heat are forms of *energy*]

en·er·vate (en′ər vāt′; *for adj.* i nur′vit) *vt.* **-vat′ed, -vat′ing** [< L. pp. of *enervare* < *e-,* out + *nervus,* a nerve, sinew] to deprive of strength, force, vigor, etc.; debilitate —*adj.* enervated; weakened —see SYN. at WEAKEN —**en′er·va′tion** *n.* —**en′er·va′tor** *n.*

E·ne·sco (i nes′kō), **Georges** (zhôrzh) 1881-1955; Romanian violinist, composer, & conductor

‡**en fa·mille** (än fà mē′y) [Fr.] **1.** with one's family; at home **2.** in an informal way

‡**en·fant ter·ri·ble** (än fän te rē′bl′) [Fr.] **1.** an unmanageable, mischievous child **2.** a person who says or does things that shock and embarrass others

en·fee·ble (in fē′b′l) *vt.* **-bled, -bling** to make feeble —**en·fee′ble·ment** *n.*

en·fi·lade (en′fə lād′, en′fə lād′) *n.* [Fr. < *enfiler,* to thread < *en-* (L. *in*), in + *fil* (L. *filum*), a thread] **1.** gunfire directed from either side along the length of a line of troops **2.** a placement of troops that makes them open to such fire —*vt.* **-lad′ed, -lad′ing** to direct such gunfire at (a column, etc.)

en·fold (in fōld′) *vt.* **1.** to wrap in folds; envelop **2.** to embrace —**en·fold′ment** *n.*

en·force (in fôrs′) *vt.* **-forced′, -forc′ing** **1.** to give force to [to *enforce* an argument by giving facts] **2.** to bring about or impose by force [to *enforce* one's will on a child] **3.** to force observance of (a law, etc.) —**en·force′a·ble** *adj.* —**en·force′ment** *n.* —**en·forc′er** *n.*

en·fran·chise (in fran′chīz) *vt.* **-chised, -chis·ing** **1.** to free from slavery, bondage, etc. **2.** to give a franchise to; specif., to admit to citizenship, esp. to the right to vote —**en·fran′chise·ment** (-chiz mənt, -chīz-) *n.* —**en·fran′chis·er** *n.*

Eng. 1. England **2.** English

eng. 1. engineer(ing) **2.** engraved **3.** engraving

en·gage (in gāj′) *vt.* **-gaged′, -gag′ing** [< OFr. *engagier:* see EN- & GAGE¹] **1.** to bind (oneself) by a promise; pledge; specif. (now only in the passive), to bind by a promise of marriage; betroth [he is *engaged* to Ann] **2.** to hire; employ [to *engage* a lawyer] **3.** to arrange for the use of; reserve [to *engage* a hotel room*]* **4.** to draw into; involve, as in conversation **5.** to attract and hold (the attention, etc.) **6.** to keep busy; occupy *[reading engages his spare time]* **7.** to enter into conflict with (the enemy) **8.** to interlock with; mesh together *[engage the gears]* —*vi.* **1.** to pledge oneself; promise; undertake *[to engage to do something]* **2.** to involve oneself; be active *[to engage in dramatics]* **3.** to enter into conflict **4.** to interlock

en·gaged (-gājd*´*) *adj.* **1.** pledged; esp., pledged in marriage; betrothed **2.** occupied or busy **3.** involved in combat, as troops **4.** attached to or partly set into a wall, etc. *[engaged columns]* **5.** in gear; interlocked; meshed

en·gage·ment (-gāj*´*mənt) *n.* **1.** an engaging or being engaged; specif., *a)* a betrothal *b)* an appointment to meet someone or go somewhere *c)* employment or period of employment, esp. in the performing arts *d)* a conflict; battle *e)* *[usually pl.]* financial obligations *f)* state of being in gear **2.** something that engages —see SYN. at BATTLE

en·gag·ing (-gāj*´*iŋ) *adj.* attractive; winning; charming —**en·gag´ing·ly** *adv.*

‡**en garde** (äⁿ gård*´*) [Fr.] *Fencing* on guard: the opening position in which the fencer is prepared either to attack or defend

En·gels (eŋ*´*əls), **Frie·drich** (frē*´*driH) 1820–95; Ger. socialist writer (with Karl Marx)

en·gen·der (in jen*´*dər) *vt.* [< OFr. < L. < *in-*, in + *generare*, GENERATE] to bring into being; cause; produce *[militarism engenders war]*

engin. **1.** engineer **2.** engineering

en·gine (en*´*jən) *n.* [< OFr. < L. *ingenium*, genius < *in-*, in & base of *gignere*, to produce: see GENUS] **1.** any machine that uses energy to develop mechanical power; esp., a machine for starting motion in some other machine **2.** a railroad locomotive **3.** any instrument or machine; apparatus *[engines of torture]* **4.** *same as* FIRE ENGINE

en·gi·neer (en*´*jə nir*´*) *n.* **1.** a person skilled in some branch of engineering *[a mechanical engineer]* **2.** *a)* an operator of engines or technical equipment *[a locomotive engineer, radio engineer]* *b)* a specialist in planning or directing operations in some technical field **3.** a skillful or clever manager **4.** *Mil.* a member of that branch of the armed forces concerned with the building and blowing up of bridges, roads, etc. —*vt.* **1.** to plan, construct, or manage as an engineer ☆**2.** to plan and direct skillfully *[to engineer a business merger]*

en·gi·neer·ing (-iŋ) *n.* **1.** *a)* the science concerned with putting scientific knowledge to practical uses, divided into different branches, as civil, electrical, mechanical, or chemical engineering *b)* the planning, designing, construction, or management of machinery, roads, bridges, buildings, waterways, etc. **2.** a maneuvering or managing

Eng·land (iŋ*´*glənd) **1.** division of the United Kingdom, occupying most of the S part of Great Britain: 50,331 sq. mi.; pop. 47,023,000; cap. London **2.** *same as* UNITED KINGDOM

Eng·lish (iŋ*´*glish) *adj.* [OE. *Englisc*, lit., of the Angles] **1.** of England, its people, their culture, etc. **2.** of their language —*n.* **1.** the language of the people of England, the official language of the Commonwealth, the U.S., Liberia, etc. **2.** the English language of a specific period: see OLD ENGLISH, MIDDLE ENGLISH, MODERN ENGLISH **3.** a school course in the English language or its literature ☆**4.** *[sometimes* e-*] Billiards, Bowling,* etc. a spinning motion given to a ball, as by striking it on one side —*vt.* **1.** to translate into English **2.** to Anglicize (a foreign word) —**the English** the people of England

English Channel arm of the Atlantic, between England & France: 21–150 mi. wide

English horn a double-reed instrument of the woodwind family, similar to the oboe but larger and a fifth lower in pitch

☆**English ivy** *same as* IVY (sense 1)

Eng·lish·man (-mən) *n., pl.* **-men** a native or inhabitant of England, esp. a man — **Eng´lish·wom´an** *n.fem., pl.* **-wom´en**

☆**English muffin** a large, flat yeast roll, often baked on a griddle, and served split and toasted

English setter any of a breed of setter with a white, long-haired coat with black, yellow, or orange spots

English sonnet *same as* SHAKESPEAREAN SONNET

☆**English sparrow** the common sparrow, a small brownish-gray, finchlike bird of European origin

ENGLISH HORN

☆**English walnut** **1.** an Asiatic walnut tree now grown in Europe and N. America **2.** its nut

en·gorge (in gôrj*´*) *vt., vi.* **-gorged´, -gorg´ing** **1.** to eat greedily; gorge; glut **2.** *Med.* to congest with blood or other fluid —**en·gorge´ment** *n.*

engr. **1.** engineer **2.** engraved **3.** engraver

en·graft (in graft*´*) *vt.* **1.** to graft (a shoot, etc.) from one plant onto another **2.** to establish firmly; implant —**en·graft´ment** *n.*

en·grave (in grāv*´*) *vt.* **-graved´, -grav´ing** [< Fr. < *en-*, in + *graver*, to incise, ult. < Gr. *graphein*, to write: see GRAPHIC] **1.** to cut or etch (letters, designs, etc.) in or on (a surface) or into (a metal plate, wooden block, etc. for printing) **2.** to print by means of such a plate, block, etc. **3.** to impress deeply on the mind or memory —**en·grav´er** *n.*

en·grav·ing (-iŋ) *n.* **1.** the act, process, or art of one who engraves **2.** an engraved plate, design, etc. **3.** a print made from an engraved surface

en·gross (in grōs*´*) *vt.* [< OFr.: see EN- & GROSS] **1.** *a)* to write in the large letters once used for legal documents *b)* to make a final fair copy of (a document) **2.** to express formally or in legal form **3.** to take the entire attention of; occupy wholly; absorb *[engrossed in a book]* —**en·gross´er** *n.* —**en·gross´ing** *adj., n.* —**en·gross´ment** *n.*

en·gulf (in gulf*´*) *vt.* **1.** to swallow up; overwhelm *[a huge wave engulfed the swimmer]* **2.** to plunge, as into a gulf —**en·gulf´ment** *n.*

en·hance (in hans*´*) *vt.* **-hanced´, -hanc´ing** [< Anglo-Fr. < OFr. *enhaucier*, ult. < L. *in*, in + *altus*, high] to make greater, as in value, attractiveness, etc.; heighten *[the soft music enhanced the scene]* —*vi.* to increase, as in value or price —**en·hance´ment** *n.* —**en·hanc´er** *n.*

en·har·mon·ic (en*´*här män*´*ik) *adj. Music* relating to tones that are nearly identical in pitch, as E♭ and D♯, and that on the piano and similar keyed instruments are made identical

e·nig·ma (ə nig*´*mə) *n., pl.* **-mas** [< L. < Gr. *ainigma* < *ainissesthai*, to speak in riddles < *ainos*, tale] **1.** a puzzling, usually ambiguous, statement; riddle **2.** a puzzling or baffling matter, person, etc. —see SYN. at MYSTERY[1]

e·nig·mat·ic (en*´*ig mat*´*ik, ē*´*nig-) *adj.* of or like an enigma; puzzling; mysterious: **e´nig·mat´i·cal** —see SYN. at OBSCURE — **e´nig·mat´i·cal·ly** *adv.*

en·isle (in īl*´*) *vt.* **-isled´, -isl´ing** **1.** to make an island of **2.** to place on or as on an island; isolate

en·jamb·ment, en·jambe·ment (in jam*´*mənt) *n.* [Fr.] the running over of a sentence from one line or couplet of poetry to the next, with little or no pause

en·join (in join*´*) *vt.* [< OFr. < L. < *in-*, in + *jungere*, JOIN] **1.** to order or command *[to enjoin silence]* **2.** to prohibit, esp. by legal injunction; forbid *[the court enjoined the union from picketing]* **3.** to order (someone) to do something, esp. by legal injunction —see SYN. at COMMAND

en·joy (in joi*´*) *vt.* [< OFr. *enjoir* < *en-*, in + *joir* < L. *gaudere*, to be glad: see JOY] **1.** to get joy or pleasure from; relish *[to enjoy family life, movies, teasing people, etc.]* **2.** to have the use or benefit of *[the book enjoyed large sales]* —**enjoy oneself** to have a good time

en·joy·a·ble (-ə b'l) *adj.* giving or capable of giving enjoyment; pleasurable —see SYN. at PLEASANT —**en·joy´a·ble·ness** *n.* —**en·joy´a·bly** *adv.*

en·joy·ment (-mənt) *n.* **1.** an enjoying **2.** something enjoyed **3.** pleasure; gratification; joy —see SYN. at PLEASURE

en·kin·dle (en kin*´*d'l) *vt.* **-dled, -dling** **1.** to set on fire; make blaze up **2.** to stir up; arouse

enl. **1.** enlarge **2.** enlisted

en·lace (in lās*´*) *vt.* **-laced´, -lac´ing** **1.** to wind about as with a lace; encircle; enfold **2.** to entangle; interlace —**en·lace´ment** *n.*

en·large (in lärj*´*) *vt.* **-larged´, -larg´ing** **1.** to make larger; increase in size, volume, extent, etc.; expand **2.** *Photog.* to reproduce on a larger scale —*vi.* **1.** to become larger; increase **2.** to discuss at greater length or in greater detail (with *on* or *upon*) —see SYN. at INCREASE —**en·large´ment** *n.* —**en·larg´er** *n.*

en·light·en (in līt*´*'n) *vt.* **1.** to give the light of knowledge to; free from ignorance, prejudice, or superstition **2.** to make clear to (a person) the true facts or nature of something; inform —**en·light´en·er** *n.*

en·light·en·ment (-mənt) *n.* an enlightening or being enlightened —**the Enlightenment** an 18th-cent. European philosophical and social movement characterized by rationalism

en·list (in list′) *vt.* **1.** to enroll in some branch of the armed forces **2.** to win the support of; get the help or services of [to *enlist* men in a cause] **3.** to get (another's help, support, etc.) —*vi.* **1.** to join some branch of the armed forces **2.** to join or support a cause or movement (with *in*) —**en·list′ee′** *n.*

enlisted man any man in the armed forces who is not a commissioned officer or warrant officer

en·list·ment (-mənt) *n.* **1.** an enlisting or being enlisted ☆**2.** the period for which one enlists

en·liv·en (in lī′v'n) *vt.* to make active, lively, interesting, or cheerful; liven up or brighten [to *enliven* a party by playing games] —**en·liv′en·er** *n.* —**en·liv′en·ment** *n.*

en masse (en mas′; *Fr.* än màs′) [Fr., lit., in mass] in a group; as a whole; all together

en·mesh (en mesh′) *vt.* to catch in or as in the meshes of a net; entangle

en·mi·ty (en′mə tē) *n., pl.* **-ties** [< OFr. < L. *inimicus,* ENEMY] the bitter attitude or feelings of an enemy or mutual enemies; hostility
SYN.—**enmity** denotes a strong, fixed feeling of hatred, whether hidden or openly shown; **hostility** suggests open enmity shown in active opposition, attacks, etc.; **animosity** suggests bitterness of feeling, usually in personal relationships, that tends to break out in open hostility; **antagonism** stresses the opposition of persons, forces, etc. that compete or work against each other

en·no·ble (i nō′b'l) *vt.* **-bled, -bling** **1.** to raise to the rank of nobleman **2.** to give a noble quality to; dignify —**en·no′ble·ment** *n.* —**en·no′bler** *n.*

en·nui (än wē′; *Fr.* än nwē′) *n.* [Fr.: see ANNOY] a feeling of being very bored and tired of everything; boredom

e·nor·mi·ty (i nôr′mə tē) *n., pl.* **-ties** [< Fr. < L. < *enormis,* irregular, immense < *e-,* out + *norma,* rule: for IE. base see KNOW] **1.** great wickedness [the *enormity* of a crime] **2.** a very wicked crime **3.** enormous size or extent: generally considered a loose usage

e·nor·mous (i nôr′məs) *adj.* [see prec.] **1.** very large or very great; huge **2.** [Archaic] very wicked; outrageous —**e·nor′mous·ly** *adv.* —**e·nor′mous·ness** *n.*
SYN.—**enormous** implies a going far beyond what is normal in size, amount, or degree [an *enormous* room; *enormous* expenses]; **immense** implies size beyond the usual measurements but suggests that great size is normal for the thing described [redwoods are *immense* trees]; **huge** usually suggests a great mass or bulk [a *huge* building; *huge* profits]; **gigantic,** **colossal,** and **mammoth** originally implied a likeness to a *giant,* the *Colossus* of Rhodes, and an extinct elephant (the *mammoth*), and therefore these words emphasize the idea of great size, force, importance, etc., now often in an exaggerated way; **tremendous** literally suggests that which causes awe or amazement because of its great size

e·nough (i nuf′) *adj.* [OE. *genoh*] as much or as many as needed or wanted; sufficient [*enough* money to pay the bills] —*n.* the amount or number needed or wanted —*adv.* **1.** as much or as often as necessary; sufficiently [the stew is not cooked *enough*] **2.** fully; quite [oddly *enough*] **3.** just adequately; tolerably; fairly [he played well *enough*]

e·now (i nou′) *adj., n., adv.* [Archaic] enough

en·plane (en plān′) *vi.* **-planed′, -plan′ing** to board an airplane

en·quire (in kwīr′) *vt., vi.* **-quired′, -quir′ing** same as INQUIRE —**en·quir′y** *n., pl.* **-quir′ies**

en·rage (in rāj′) *vt.* **-raged′, -rag′ing** to put into a rage; make very angry; infuriate —**en·rage′ment** *n.*

‡**en rap·port** (än rà pôr′) [Fr.] in harmony; in sympathy; in accord

en·rapt (in rapt′) *adj.* enraptured; rapt

en·rap·ture (-rap′chər) *vt.* **-tured, -tur·ing** to fill with great pleasure or delight: also **en·rav′ish**

en·rich (in rich′) *vt.* to make rich or richer; specif., *a)* to give more wealth to *b)* to give greater value or effectiveness to [to *enrich* a curriculum] *c)* to decorate; adorn *d)* to fertilize (soil) *e)* to add vitamins, minerals, etc. to (bread, etc.) for more food value —**en·rich′ment** *n.*

en·roll, en·rol (in rōl′) *vt.* **-rolled′, -roll′ing** **1.** to record in a list **2.** to enlist **3.** to accept as a member —*vi.* to enroll oneself or become enrolled; register; become a member —**en·roll′ee′** *n.*

en·roll·ment, en·rol·ment (-mənt) *n.* **1.** an enrolling or being enrolled **2.** a list of those enrolled **3.** the number of those enrolled

en route (än rōōt′, en) [Fr.] on or along the way

Ens. Ensign

En·sche·de (en′skhə dā′) city in E Netherlands, near the German border: pop. 136,000

en·sconce (in skäns′) *vt.* **-sconced′, -sconc′ing** [EN- + *sconce,* a small fort] **1.** [Now Rare] to hide; conceal; shelter **2.** to place or settle snugly [to *ensconce* oneself in an armchair]

en·sem·ble (än säm′b'l) *n.* [Fr. < OFr. < L. < *in-,* in + *simul,* at the same time] **1.** all the parts considered as a whole; total effect **2.** a whole costume, esp. of matching or complementary articles of dress **3.** a company of actors, dancers, etc. **4.** *Music* *a)* a small group of musicians performing together *b)* their instruments or voices *c)* the performance together of such a group, or of an orchestra, chorus, etc.

en·shrine (in shrīn′) *vt.* **-shrined′, -shrin′ing** **1.** to enclose in or as in a shrine **2.** to hold as sacred; cherish [*enshrined* in memory] —**en·shrine′ment** *n.*

en·shroud (-shroud′) *vt.* to cover as if with a shroud; hide; veil; obscure [towers *enshrouded* in mist]

en·sign (en′sīn; *also, and for 4 always,* -s'n) *n.* [< OFr. < L. < *insignia:* see INSIGNIA] **1.** a badge, symbol, or token of office or authority **2.** a flag or banner; specif., a national flag, as one displayed on a ship **3.** *Brit. Army* formerly, a commissioned officer who served as standard-bearer ☆**4.** *U.S. Navy* a commissioned officer of the lowest rank, ranking below a lieutenant junior grade —**en′sign·ship′, en′sign·cy** *n.*

en·si·lage (en′s'l ij) *n.* [Fr.] **1.** the preserving of green fodder by storage in a silo **2.** green fodder so preserved; silage

en·sile (en sīl′) *vt.* **-siled′, -sil′ing** [Fr. *ensiler*] to store (green fodder) in a silo

en·slave (in slāv′) *vt.* **-slaved′, -slav′ing** **1.** to put into slavery; make a slave of **2.** to keep complete control over; dominate; subjugate [she was *enslaved* by her work] —**en·slave′ment** *n.* —**en·slav′er** *n.*

en·snare (-sner′) *vt.* **-snared′, -snar′ing** to catch in or as in a snare; trap —**en·snare′ment** *n.*

en·snarl (-snärl′) *vt.* to draw into a snarl or tangle

en·sue (in sōō′, -syōō′) *vi.* **-sued′, -su′ing** [< OFr., ult. < L. *insequi* < *in-,* in + *sequi,* to follow] **1.** to come afterward; follow immediately [we met and a long friendship *ensued*] **2.** to happen as a consequence; result [the damage that *ensued* from the flood] —see SYN. at FOLLOW

en·sure (in shoor′) *vt.* **-sured′, -sur′ing** [< Anglo-Fr. *enseurer:* see EN- & SURE] **1.** to make sure; guarantee [measures to *ensure* accuracy] **2.** to make safe; protect [safety devices to *ensure* workers against accidents]

-ent (ənt, 'nt) [< OFr. *-ent,* L. *-ens* (gen. *-entis),* stem ending of certain present participles] **1.** *a suffix meaning* that has, shows, or does [*insistent*] **2.** *a suffix meaning* a person or thing that [*superintendent, solvent*]

en·tab·la·ture (en tab′lə chər) *n.* [MFr. < It. *intavolatura* < *in-,* in + *tavola* < L. *tabula,* TABLE] *Archit.* **1.** a horizontal structure supported by columns and composed of architrave, frieze, and cornice **2.** any structure like this

en·tail (in tāl′) *vt.* [< ME. < *en-,* in + *taile,* an agreement < OFr. < *taillier,* to cut: see TAILOR] **1.** *Law* to limit the inheritance of (real property) to a specific line or class of heirs **2.** to have as a necessary part or result; involve; require [the plan *entails* work] —*n.* **1.** an entailing or being entailed **2.** an entailed inheritance **3.** the order of descent for an entailed inheritance —**en·tail′ment** *n.*

en·ta·moe·ba (en′tə mē′bə) *n.* same as ENDAMOEBA

en·tan·gle (in taŋ′g'l) *vt.* **-gled, -gling** **1.** to make tangled, or catch in a tangle; ensnare or ensnarl [the fishing lines became *entangled*] **2.** to involve in difficulty [they *entangled* him in a bad business deal] **3.** to confuse; perplex —**en·tan′gle·ment** *n.*

en·tente (än tänt′) *n.* [Fr. < OFr. < *entendre,* to understand] **1.** an understanding or agreement, as between nations **2.** the nations, etc. having such an understanding

en·ter (en′tər) *vt.* [< OFr. *entrer* < L. *intrare* < *intra,* within < IE. base *en-,* in] **1.** to come or go in or into **2.** to force a way into; penetrate [the bullet *entered* his leg] **3.** to put into; insert **4.** to write down in a record, list, etc. **5.** *a)* to list as a participant in a competition, race, etc. *b)* to become a participant in (a contest) **6.** to join; become a member of (a school, club, etc.) **7.** to get (someone) admitted **8.** to start upon; begin (a career, etc.) **9.** to submit [to *enter* a protest] **10.** to register (a ship or cargo) at a customhouse **11.** *Law* to place on record before a court [to *enter* a plea of guilty] —*vi.* **1.** to come or go into some place **2.** to pierce; penetrate —**enter into 1.** to engage in; take part in **2.** to form a part of; be a factor in **3.** to deal with; discuss —**enter on** (or **upon**) **1.** to begin; start **2.** to begin to possess or enjoy

en·ter·ic (en ter′ik) *adj.* [see ENTERO-] *same as* INTESTINAL

en·ter·o- [< Gr. *enteron*, intestine] *a combining form meaning* intestine: also **enter-**

en·ter·prise (en′tər prīz′) *n.* [< OFr. < *entreprendre*, to undertake < *entre-* (L. *inter*), in + *prendre* (L. *prehendere*), to take] **1.** an undertaking; project; specif., *a)* a bold, difficult, dangerous, or important undertaking *b)* a business venture or company **2.** willingness to undertake new or risky projects; energy and initiative [a young man lacking in *enterprise*] **3.** a taking part actively in projects

en·ter·pris·ing (-prī′ziŋ) *adj.* showing enterprise; willing to start and try new projects; venturesome —**en′ter·pris·ing·ly** *adv.*

en·ter·tain (en′tər tān′) *vt.* [< OFr. *entre* (< L. *inter*), between + *tenir* (L. *tenere*), to hold] **1.** to hold the interest of and give pleasure to; divert; amuse **2.** to give hospitality to; have as a guest **3.** to have in mind; consider [to *entertain* the idea of buying a car] —*vi.* to have guests [it's expensive to *entertain* often] —see SYN. at AMUSE

en·ter·tain·er (-ər) *n.* a person who entertains; esp., a popular singer, dancer, comedian, etc.

en·ter·tain·ing (-iŋ) *adj.* interesting and pleasurable; amusing —**en′ter·tain′ing·ly** *adv.*

en·ter·tain·ment (-mənt) *n.* **1.** an entertaining or being entertained **2.** something that entertains; interesting, diverting, or amusing thing; esp., a show or performance

en·thrall, en·thral (in thrôl′) *vt.* **-thralled′, -thrall′ing** [see EN- & THRALL] **1.** [Now Rare] to enslave **2.** to hold as if in a spell; captivate; fascinate [the exciting story *enthralled* us] —**en·thrall′ment, en·thral′ment** *n.*

en·throne (in thrōn′) *vt.* **-throned′, -thron′ing 1.** to place on a throne; make a king, etc. of **2.** to place in a high position; exalt —**en·throne′ment** *n.*

☆**en·thuse** (in thōōz′, -thyōōz′) *vi.* **-thused′, -thus′ing** [back-formation < ENTHUSIASM] [Colloq.] to express enthusiasm —*vt.* [Colloq.] to make enthusiastic

en·thu·si·asm (in thōō′zē az′m, -thyōō′-) *n.* [< Gr. < *enthous*, possessed by a god, inspired < *en-*, in + *theos*, god] **1.** intense or eager interest; zeal; fervor **2.** something arousing this —see SYN. at PASSION

en·thu·si·ast (-ast′) *n.* a person full of enthusiasm; an ardent supporter, a devotee, etc. —see SYN. at ZEALOT

en·thu·si·as·tic (in thōō′zē as′tik, -thyōō′-) *adj.* of, having, or showing enthusiasm; ardent [an *enthusiastic* follower; *enthusiastic* applause] —**en·thu′si·as′ti·cal·ly** *adv.*

en·tice (in tīs′) *vt.* **-ticed′, -tic′ing** [< OFr. *enticier*, to set afire, excite, prob. ult. < L. *in*, in + *titio*, a firebrand] to attract by offering hope of reward or pleasure; tempt —see SYN. at LURE —**en·tice′ment** *n.* —**en·tic′er** *n.* —**en·tic′ing·ly** *adv.*

en·tire (in tīr′) *adj.* [< OFr. *entier* < L. *integer*, untouched, whole: for IE. base see CONTACT] **1.** *a)* not lacking any of the parts; whole [the *entire* class attended] *b)* complete; absolute [to give one's *entire* attention] **2.** being wholly of one piece **3.** *Bot.* having a margin without notches or indentations, as some leaves —**en·tire′ness** *n.*

en·tire·ly (-lē) *adv.* **1.** wholly; completely; totally [*entirely* forgotten] **2.** solely; only [depending *entirely* on me]

en·tire·ty (-tē) *n., pl.* **-ties 1.** the state or fact of being entire; wholeness; completeness **2.** an entire thing; whole —**in its entirety** as a whole

en·ti·tle (in tīt′'l) *vt.* **-tled, -tling 1.** to give a title or name to [a poem *entitled* "Dover Beach"] **2.** to give a right or legal title to [a ticket that *entitles* him to sit in the press box]

en·ti·ty (en′tə tē) *n., pl.* **-ties** [< Fr. or < ML. *entitas* < L. prp. of *esse*, to be] **1.** being; existence **2.** a thing that has definite, individual existence in reality or in the mind

en·to- [ModL. < Gr. *entos*, within] *a combining form meaning* within or inner

entom., entomol. entomology

en·tomb (in tōōm′) *vt.* to place in a tomb or grave; bury —**en·tomb′ment** *n.*

en·to·mo- [Fr. < Gr. *entoma* (*zōa*), lit., notched animals] *a combining form meaning* insect or insects

en·to·mol·o·gy (en′tə mäl′ə jē) *n.* [ENTOMO- + -LOGY] the branch of zoology that deals with insects —**en′to·mo·log′i·cal** (-mə läj′i k'l), **en′to·mo·log′ic** *adj.* —**en′to·mo·log′i·cal·ly** *adv.* —**en′to·mol′o·gist** *n.*

en·tou·rage (än′tōō räzh′) *n.* [Fr. < *entourer*, to surround] a group of accompanying attendants, assistants, or associates; retinue

en·tr'acte (än trakt′, än′trakt) *n.* [Fr. < *entre-*, between + *acte*, an act] **1.** the interval between two acts of a play, opera, etc.; intermission **2.** music, a dance, etc. performed during this interval

en·trails (en′trālz, -trəlz) *n.pl.* [< OFr. < ML. *intralia* < L. < *interaneus*, internal < *inter*, between: for IE. base see ENTER] **1.** the inner organs of men or animals; specif., the intestines; viscera; guts **2.** the inner parts of a thing

en·train (in trān′) *vt.* to put aboard a train —*vi.* to go aboard a train —**en·train′ment** *n.*

en·trance[1] (en′trəns) *n.* **1.** the act or point of entering **2.** a place for entering; door, gate, etc. **3.** permission or right to enter; admission [the college *entrance* exams]

en·trance[2] (in trans′) *vt.* **-tranced′, -tranc′ing 1.** to put into a trance **2.** to enchant; charm; enrapture —**en·trance′ment** *n.* —**en·tranc′ing·ly** *adv.*

en·trant (en′trənt) *n.* a person who enters, esp. one who enters a contest

en·trap (in trap′) *vt.* **-trapped′, -trap′ping 1.** to catch as in a trap **2.** to trick into doing something wrong [he was *entrapped* into telling a lie] —**en·trap′ment** *n.*

en·treat (in trēt′) *vt.* [< Anglo-Fr. < OFr. < *en-*, in + *traiter*: see TREAT] to ask earnestly; beg; beseech; implore —*vi.* to make an earnest appeal; plead —see SYN. at BEG —**en·treat′ing·ly** *adv.*

en·treat·y (-ē) *n., pl.* **-treat′ies** an earnest request; plea

en·tre·chat (än′trə shä′) *n.* [Fr.] *Ballet* a leap straight upward during which the dancer crosses his legs or strikes his heels together a number of times

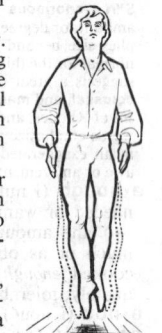

ENTRECHAT

en·tree, en·trée (än′trā; *Fr.* än trā′) *n.* [< Fr. < OFr. *entrer*, ENTER] **1.** *a)* the act of entering *b)* the right or freedom to enter, use, or take part in; access **2.** *a)* the main course of a meal *b)* formerly, and still in some countries, a dish served before the roast or between the main courses

en·trench (in trench′) *vt.* **1.** to surround or fortify with a trench or trenches **2.** to establish securely [an official *entrenched* in office] —*vi.* to encroach or infringe (*on* or *upon*) —**en·trench′ment** *n.*

en·tre·pre·neur (än′trə prə nur′, -noor′, -nyoor′) *n.* [Fr. < OFr. *entreprendre*: see ENTERPRISE] a person who organizes and manages a business undertaking, assuming the risk for the sake of profit

en·tro·py (en′trə pē) *n.* [G. *entropie*, arbitrary use of Gr. *entropē*, a turning toward] a measure of the amount of energy unavailable for work in a thermodynamic system: entropy keeps increasing and available energy diminishing in a closed system, as the universe

en·trust (in trust′) *vt.* **1.** to charge with a trust or duty [to *entrust* a lawyer with the responsibility] **2.** to assign the care of; turn over for safekeeping [*entrust* the key to me] —see SYN. at COMMIT —**en·trust′ment** *n.*

en·try (en′trē) *n., pl.* **-tries** [< OFr. < *entrer*, ENTER] **1.** *a)* the act of entering; entrance *b)* the right or freedom to enter; entree **2.** a way or passage by which to enter; door, hall, etc. **3.** *a)* the recording of an item or note in a list, journal, etc. *b)* an item thus recorded **4.** the registration of a ship or cargo at a customhouse **5.** one entered in a race, competition, etc. **6.** *a) Law* the taking possession of buildings, land, etc. by entering them *b)* the entering upon premises with the intention of committing a crime

☆**en·try·way** (-wā′) *n.* a way or passage by which to enter

en·twine (in twīn′) *vt., vi.* **-twined′, -twin′ing** to twine or twist together or around

e·nu·mer·ate (i nōō′mə rāt′, -nyōō′-) *vt.* **-at′ed, -at′ing** [< L. pp. of *enumerare* < *e-*, out + *numerare*, to count < *numerus*, a number] **1.** to determine the number of; count **2.** to name one by one; specify, as in a list *[he enumerated his objections to the plan]* **—e·nu′mer·a′tion** *n.* **—e·nu′mer·a·tive** *adj.* **—e·nu′mer·a′tor** *n.*

e·nun·ci·ate (i nun′sē āt′, -shē-) *vt.* **-at′ed, -at′ing** [< L. pp. of *enuntiare* < *e-*, out + *nuntiare*, ANNOUNCE] **1.** to state definitely; announce *[to enunciate a theory]* **2.** to pronounce (words) —*vi.* to pronounce words, esp. clearly; articulate **—e·nun′ci·a′tion** *n.* **—e·nun′ci·a′tor** *n.*

en·u·re·sis (en′yoo rē′sis) *n.* [ModL. < Gr. *enourein*, to urinate in] inability to control one's urination; esp., bed-wetting **—en′u·ret′ic** (-ret′ik) *adj.*

en·vel·op (in vel′əp) *vt.* [< OFr. *envoluper*: see EN- & DEVELOP] **1.** to wrap up; cover completely *[enveloped in blankets]* **2.** to conceal; hide *[enveloped in a mist]* **—en·vel′op·ment** *n.*

en·ve·lope (en′və lōp′, än′-) *n.* [< Fr. < OFr.: see prec.] **1.** a thing that envelops; wrapper; covering **2.** a folded paper container for letters, etc., usually with a gummed flap **3.** the bag that contains the gas in a dirigible or balloon **4.** any enclosing membrane, skin, etc.

en·ven·om (in ven′əm) *vt.* **1.** to put venom or poison on or into **2.** to fill with hate; embitter

en·vi·a·ble (en′vē ə b'l) *adj.* good enough to be envied or desired **—en′vi·a·bly** *adv.*

en·vi·ous (-əs) *adj.* [< OFr. < L. < *invidia*, ENVY] feeling or showing envy **—en′vi·ous·ly** *adv.* **—en′vi·ous·ness** *n.*

en·vi·ron (in vī′rən) *vt.* [< OFr. < *environ*, about: see ENVIRONS] to form a ring around; surround

en·vi·ron·ment (in vī′rən mənt, -ərn mənt) *n.* [ENVIRON + -MENT] **1.** surroundings **2.** all the conditions, circumstances, and influences surrounding an organism or group of organisms and affecting its development **—en·vi′ron·men′tal** (-men′t'l) *adj.* **—en·vi′ron·men′tal·ly** *adv.*

☆**en·vi·ron·men·tal·ist** (in vī′rən men′t'l ist) *n.* a person working to solve environmental problems, such as air and water pollution, the careless use of natural resources, uncontrolled population growth, etc.

en·vi·rons (in vī′rəns, -ərnz; en′vər ənz) *n.pl.* [< OFr. < *en-*, in + *viron*, a circuit < *virer*, to turn] **1.** the districts surrounding a city; suburbs or outskirts **2.** surrounding area; vicinity

en·vis·age (en viz′ij) *vt.* **-aged, -ag·ing** [< Fr.: see EN- & VISAGE] to form an image of in the mind; imagine

en·vi·sion (en vizh′ən) *vt.* to imagine (something not yet in existence)

en·voi (en′voi, än′-) *n.* [Fr.] **1.** *same as* ENVOY² **2.** a remark made in farewell or conclusion

en·voy¹ (en′voi, än′-) *n.* [< Fr. < *envoyer*, to send < OFr. < *en-* (L. *in*), in + *voie* (L. *via*), way] **1.** a messenger; agent **2.** an official sent by his government or ruler to handle diplomatic business in a foreign country: an **envoy extraordinary** ranks just below an ambassador

en·voy² (en′voi, än′-) *n.* [< OFr. *envoy*, lit., a sending: see prec.] a postscript to a poem, essay, or book, containing a dedication, explanation, etc.

en·vy (en′vē) *n., pl.* **-vies** [< OFr. < L. < *invidia* < *invidere*, to look askance at < *in-*, upon + *videre*, to look: see WISE¹] **1.** a feeling of discontent and ill will because another has advantages, possessions, etc. that one would like to have **2.** an object of this envious feeling *[her new car is the envy of the neighborhood]* —*vt.* **-vied, -vy·ing** to feel envy toward, at, or because of **—en′vi·er** *n.* **—en′vy·ing·ly** *adv.*

SYN. —to **envy** someone is to feel ill will, jealousy, or discontent at his possession of something that one keenly desires for oneself; to **begrudge** someone something is to feel annoyed, displeased, or resentful at his having something one is unwilling for him to have even though he needs or deserves it; to **covet** is to have a strong desire to possess something that rightfully belongs to another

en·wrap (en rap′) *vt.* **-wrapped′, -wrap′ping** to wrap; envelop

en·wreathe (en rēth′) *vt.* **-wreathed′, -wreath′ing** to encircle with or as with a wreath

en·zyme (en′zīm) *n.* [< G. < LGr. *enzymos*, leavened < Gr. *en-*, in + *zymē*, leaven] a proteinlike substance, formed in plant and animal cells, that acts as a catalyst in starting or speeding up specific chemical changes in other substances *[pepsin is an enzyme that helps to digest food]* **—en′zy·mat′ic** (-zī mat′ik, -zi-), **en·zy′mic** *adj.*

e·o- [< Gr. *ēōs*, dawn] a prefix meaning early, early part of a period *[Eocene]*

E·o·cene (ē′ə sēn′) *adj.* [EO- + Gr. *kainos*, new] designating or of the second and longest epoch of the Tertiary Period in the Cenozoic Era **—the Eocene** the Eocene Epoch or its rocks: see GEOLOGIC TIME CHART

e·o·hip·pus (ē′ō hip′əs) *n.* [ModL. < EO- + Gr. *hippos*, horse] an extinct ancestor of the modern horse: it was about the size of a fox and had four toes on the front feet and three on the hind

E·o·li·an (ē ō′lē ən) *adj., n. same as* AEOLIAN

e·o·lith·ic (ē′ə lith′ik) *adj.* [EO- + -LITHIC] designating or of the early part of the Stone Age, during which crude stone tools were first used

e·on (ē′ən, ē′än) *n.* [LL. < Gr. *aiōn*, an age, lifetime] an extremely long, indefinite period of time

EOHIPPUS (11 in. high at shoulder)

E·os (ē′äs) [see EO-] *Gr. Myth.* the goddess of dawn: identified with the Roman goddess Aurora

e·o·sin (ē′ə sin) *n.* [< Gr. *ēōs*, dawn + -IN¹] a rose-colored dye, $C_{20}H_8O_5Br_4$, used as an industrial pigment and as a biological stain: also **e′o·sine** (-sin, -sēn′) **—e′o·sin′ic** *adj.*

-e·ous (ē əs) [< L. *-eus* + -OUS] a suffix meaning having the nature of, like *[beauteous]*

EPA Environmental Protection Agency

ep·au·let, ep·au·lette (ep′ə let′) *n.* [< Fr. < OFr. < L. *spatula*: see SPATULA] a shoulder ornament, as on military uniforms

e·pee, é·pée (e pā′, ā-) *n.* [Fr. < OFr. < L. < Gr. *spathē*, blade] a sword, esp. a thin, pointed fencing sword with no cutting edge **—e·pee′ist, é·pée′ist** *n.*

Eph. Ephesians: also **Ephes.**

e·phah, e·pha (ē′fə) *n.* [< LL. < Heb. *'ēphāh*] an ancient Hebrew dry measure, estimated at from 1/3 bushel to a little over one bushel

EPAULETS

e·phed·rine (i fed′rin) *n.* [< ModL. *Ephedra*, genus name of the plants < L. < Gr. *ephedra*, the horsetail] an alkaloid, $C_{10}H_{15}NO$, derived from certain asiatic plants or synthesized, used to relieve nasal congestion and asthma

e·phem·er·al (i fem′ər əl) *adj.* [< Gr. < *epi-*, upon + *hēmera*, a day + -AL] **1.** lasting only one day **2.** short-lived; transitory *[ephemeral pleasures]* —*n.* an ephemeral thing —see SYN. at TRANSIENT **—e·phem′er·al·ly** *adv.*

e·phem·er·id (-id) *n.* [see prec. & -ID] *same as* MAYFLY

e·phem·er·is (-is) *n., pl.* **eph·e·mer·i·des** (ef′ə mer′ə dēz′) [see EPHEMERAL] a table giving the daily positions of a heavenly body for a given period

E·phe·sians (i fē′zhənz) a book of the New Testament: an epistle of the Apostle Paul to the Christians of Ephesus

Eph·e·sus (ef′ə səs) ancient Greek city in W Asia Minor **—E·phe·sian** (i fē′zhən) *adj., n.*

eph·od (ef′äd, -əd) *n.* [< LL. < Heb. < *āphad*, to put on] an outer vestment worn by ancient Jewish priests

eph·or (ef′ôr, -ər) *n., pl.* **-ors, -or·i′** (-ə rī′) [< L. < Gr. *epi-*, over + *horan*, to see] a magistrate of ancient Sparta

E·phra·im (ē′frē əm) [LL. < Gr. < Heb. *ephrayim*, lit., very fruitful] **1.** a masculine name **2.** *Bible a)* the younger son of Joseph *b)* the tribe of Israel descended from this son *c)* the kingdom of Israel

ep·i- [< Gr. *epi*, at, on, upon, etc.] a prefix meaning on, upon, over, on the outside, anterior, beside *[epiglottis, epidemic, epidermis]* : also **ep-** (before a vowel)

ep·ic (ep′ik) *n.* [< L. < Gr. *epos*, a word, song] **1.** a long narrative poem in a dignified, formal style, about the deeds of a traditional or historical hero or heroes, as the *Iliad* and *Odyssey* **2.** a prose narrative, play, etc. regarded as having the style and importance of an epic **3.** a series of events regarded as a proper subject for an epic —*adj.* of, or having the nature of, an epic; heroic; grand; majestic: also **ep′i·cal** *[the epic westward march of the pioneers]* **—ep′i·cal·ly** *adv.*

---

fat, āpe, cär, ten, ēven, is, bīte; gō, hôrn, too̅l, look; oil, out; up, fur; get; joy; yet; chin; she; thin, then; zh, leisure; ŋ, ring; ə for *a* in *ago, e* in *agent, i* in *sanity, o* in *comply, u* in *focus*; ′ as in *able* (ā′b'l); Fr. bal; ë, Fr. coeur; ö, Fr. feu; Fr. mon; ổ, Fr. coq; ü, Fr. duc; r, Fr. cri; H, G. ich; kh, G. doch; ‡foreign; ☆ Americanism; < derived from. See inside front cover.

ep·i·ca·lyx (ep'ə kā'liks, -kal'iks) *n., pl.* **-lyx·es, -ly·ces'** (-lə-sēz') [EPI- + CALYX] a ring of small leaves (called *bracts*) at the base of certain flowers, resembling an extra outer calyx

EPICALYX

ep·i·can·thus (ep'ə kan'thəs) *n.* [EPI- + CANTHUS] a small fold of skin sometimes covering the inner corner of the eye, as in many Asian peoples —**ep'i·can'thic** *adj.*

ep·i·car·di·um (ep'ə kär'dē əm) *n., pl.* **-di·a** (-ə) [ModL. < EPI- + Gr. *kardia*, HEART] the innermost layer of the pericardium —**ep'i·car'di·al** *adj.*

ep·i·carp (ep'ə kärp') *n.* [EPI- + -CARP] *same as* EXOCARP

ep·i·cene (ep'ə sēn') *adj.* [< L. < Gr. < *epi-*, to + *koinos*, common] belonging to one sex but having characteristics of the other, or of neither; specif., effeminate; unmanly

ep·i·cen·ter (ep'ə sen'tər) *n.* **1.** the area of the earth's surface directly above the place of origin, or focus, of an earthquake: also **ep'i·cen'trum** (-trəm), *pl.* **-tra** (-trə) **2.** a focal or central point —**ep'i·cen'tral** *adj.*

Ep·ic·te·tus (ep'ik tēt'əs) 50?–135? A.D.; Gr. Stoic philosopher

ep·i·cure (ep'i kyoor') *n.* [< L. < Gr.: see EPICURUS] **1.** a person who knows much about fine foods and drinks and enjoys them greatly **2.** [Archaic] a person who is especially fond of luxury and sensuous pleasure —**ep'i·cur·ism** *n.*

SYN.—an **epicure** is a person whose taste in food and drink is highly refined and who takes great pleasure in eating and drinking good things; a **gourmet** is one who is very fond of fine things to eat and drink, has expert knowledge about their selection and preparation, and takes pride in his ability to appreciate subtle differences in flavor and quality; **gourmand**, occasionally used to mean the same thing as **gourmet**, is more often applied to a person who has such a hearty appetite for good food that he tends to overeat

Ep·i·cu·re·an (ep'i kyoo rē'ən, -kyoor'ē ən) *adj.* **1.** of Epicurus or his philosophy **2.** [e-] *a)* fond of luxury and sensuous pleasure, esp. that of eating and drinking *b)* suited to or characteristic of an epicure —*n.* **1.** a follower of Epicurus or his philosophy **2.** [e-] an epicure —**Ep'i·cu·re'an·ism, ep'i·cu·re'an·ism** *n.*

Ep·i·cu·rus (ep'ə kyoor'əs) 341?–270 B.C.; Gr. philosopher: he held that man should lead a life of pleasure but in a calm, moral, and temperate way

ep·i·dem·ic (ep'ə dem'ik) *adj.* [< Fr. < *épidémie* < ML. < Gr. < *epi-*, among + *dēmos*, people] affecting many individuals in a community at the same time and spreading rapidly, as a contagious disease —*n.* **1.** an epidemic disease **2.** the epidemic spreading of a disease **3.** the rapid, widespread occurrence of a fad, fashion, etc. —**ep'i·dem'i·cal·ly** *adv.*

ep·i·de·mi·ol·o·gy (-dē'mē äl'ə jē, -dem'ē-) *n.* [< Gr. (see prec.) + -LOGY] **1.** the branch of medicine concerned with the causes and control of epidemics **2.** all the factors that tend to make a disease occur or not occur among a group of people —**ep'i·de'mi·o·log'ic** (-mē ə läj'ik), **ep'i·de'mi·o·log'i·cal** *adj.* —**ep'i·de'mi·ol'o·gist** *n.*

ep·i·der·mis (ep'ə dur'mis) *n.* [LL. < Gr. < *epi-*, upon + *derma*, the skin] **1.** the outermost layer of skin in vertebrates **2.** the outermost layer of cells covering seed plants and ferns **3.** any of various other outer coverings —**ep'i·der'mal, ep'i·der'mic** *adj.*

ep·i·der·moid (-dur'moid) *adj.* like epidermis: also **ep'i·der·moi'dal**

ep·i·glot·tis (ep'ə glät'is) *n.* [see EPI- & GLOTTIS] the thin, triangular, lidlike piece of cartilage that folds back over the opening of the windpipe during swallowing, thus preventing food, etc. from entering the lungs —**ep'i·glot'tal, ep'i·glot'tic** *adj.*

PHARYNX
EPIGLOTTIS
LARYNX
TRACHEA
ESOPHAGUS

ep·i·gram (ep'ə gram') *n.* [< OFr. < L. < Gr. *epigramma* < *epi-*, upon + *graphein*, to write] **1.** a short, witty or satirical poem **2.** any brief, witty, pointed statement, often with a clever twist in thought (Ex.: "Experience is the name everyone gives to his mistakes") —see **SYN.** at SAYING —**ep·i·gram·mat·ic** (ep'i grə mat'ik), **ep'i·gram·mat'i·cal** *adj.* —**ep'i·gram·mat'i·cal·ly** *adv.* —**ep'i·gram'ma·tist** *n.*

ep·i·graph (ep'ə graf') *n.* [Gr. *epigraphē*, inscription < *epigraphein*: see EPIGRAM] **1.** an inscription on a building, monu-ment, etc. **2.** a motto or quotation at the beginning of a book, chapter, etc.

ep·i·graph·ic (ep'ə graf'ik) *adj.* of an epigraph or epigraphy: also **ep'i·graph'i·cal** —**ep'i·graph'i·cal·ly** *adv.*

e·pig·ra·phy (i pig'rə fē) *n.* [see EPIGRAPH] **1.** inscriptions as a group **2.** the study that deals with deciphering, interpreting, and classifying inscriptions, esp. ancient inscriptions —**e·pig'ra·phist, e·pig'ra·pher** *n.*

ep·i·lep·sy (ep'ə lep'sē) *n.* [< OFr. < LL. < Gr. *epilēpsia* < *epi-*, upon + *lambanein*, to seize] a chronic disease of the nervous system, that may cause convulsions and unconsciousness: see GRAND MAL, PETIT MAL

ep·i·lep·tic (ep'ə lep'tik) *adj.* of or having epilepsy —*n.* a person who has epilepsy

ep·i·logue (ep'ə lôg', -läg') *n.* [< OFr. < L. < Gr. *epilogos*, conclusion < *epi-*, upon + *legein*, to say: see LOGIC] **1.** a closing section added to a novel, play, etc., providing further comment or information **2.** a short speech or poem spoken to the audience by one of the actors at the end of a play **3.** the actor speaking this

☆**ep·i·neph·rine** (ep'ə nef'rin, -rēn) *n.* [EPI- + NEPHR(O)- + -INE[4]] a hormone secreted by the adrenal gland, that stimulates the heart, increases muscular strength, etc.: it is taken from the adrenal glands of animals or prepared synthetically for human use

E·piph·a·ny (i pif'ə nē) *n., pl.* **-nies** [< OFr. < LL. < Gr. *epiphaneia*, appearance < *epi-*, upon + *phainein*, to show] in many Christian churches, a yearly festival (January 6) commemorating both the revealing of Jesus as the Christ to the Magi and the baptism of Jesus

e·piph·y·sis (i pif'ə sis) *n., pl.* **-ses'** (-sēz') [ModL. < Gr. < *epi-*, upon + *phyein*, to grow] the end part of a long bone which is at first separated from the main part by cartilage, but later fuses with it when the cartilage becomes bone

ep·i·phyte (ep'ə fīt') *n.* [EPI- + -PHYTE] a nonparasitic plant that grows on another plant, producing its own food by photosynthesis, as certain orchids, mosses, and lichens; air plant —**ep'i·phyt'ic** (-fit'ik) *adj.* —**ep'i·phyt'i·cal·ly** *adv.*

E·pi·rus (i pī'rəs) ancient kingdom on the Ionian Sea, in what is now S Albania & NW Greece: see map at GREECE

Epis. Epistle

Epis., Episc. **1.** Episcopal **2.** Episcopalian

e·pis·co·pa·cy (i pis'kə pə sē) *n., pl.* **-cies** [< LL. < *episcopus*, BISHOP] **1.** the system by which churches are governed by bishops **2.** *same as* EPISCOPATE

e·pis·co·pal (-kə pəl) *adj.* [see prec.] **1.** of or governed by bishops **2.** [E-] designating or of any of various churches governed by bishops, as the Protestant Episcopal or the Anglican Church —**e·pis'co·pal·ly** *adv.*

E·pis·co·pa·li·an (i pis'kə pāl'yən, -pā'lē ən) *adj. same as* EPISCOPAL —*n.* ☆a member of the Protestant Episcopal Church —**E·pis'co·pa'li·an·ism** *n.*

e·pis·co·pate (i pis'kə pit, -pāt') *n.* **1.** the position, rank, or term of office of a bishop **2.** a bishop's see **3.** bishops as a group

ep·i·sode (ep'ə sōd') *n.* [< Gr. < *epeisodios*, following upon the entrance < *epi-*, upon + *eis-*, into + *hodos*, a way] **1.** in a novel, poem, etc., any part of the story that is complete in itself; incident **2.** in a musical composition, any minor passage not based on the main theme **3.** any event or series of events complete in itself but forming part of a larger one [an *episode* in the war] **4.** any installment of a serialized story or drama —see **SYN.** at OCCURRENCE

ep·i·sod·ic (ep'ə säd'ik) *adj.* **1.** having the nature of an episode; incidental **2.** made up of episodes, esp. episodes which have no clear connection with each other Also **ep'i·sod'i·cal** —**ep'i·sod'i·cal·ly** *adv.*

e·pis·te·mol·o·gy (i pis'tə mäl'ə jē) *n., pl.* **-gies** [< Gr. *epistēmē*, knowledge + -LOGY] the study or theory of the origin, nature, methods, and limits of knowledge —**e·pis'te·mo·log'i·cal** (-mə läj'i k'l) *adj.* —**e·pis'te·mo·log'i·cal·ly** *adv.* —**e·pis'te·mol'o·gist** *n.*

e·pis·tle (i pis''l) *n.* [< OFr. < L. < Gr. *epistolē* < *epi-*, to + *stellein*, to send] **1.** a letter, esp. a long, formal, instructive letter: now used humorously **2.** [E-] *a)* any of the letters of the Apostles in the New Testament *b)* a selection from these Epistles, read as part of Mass, Communion, etc. in various churches —**e·pis'tler** *n.*

e·pis·to·lar·y (i pis'tə ler'ē) *adj.* [see EPISTLE] **1.** of or suitable to letters or letter writing **2.** contained in, conducted by, or made up of letters

ep·i·taph (ep′ə taf′) *n.* [< OFr. < L. *epitaphium*, eulogy < Gr. < *epi-*, upon + *taphos*, tomb] an inscription, as on a tomb, in memory of the person buried there

ep·i·tha·la·mi·um (ep′ə thə lā′mē əm) *n., pl.* **-mi·ums**, **-mi·a** (-ə) [< L. < Gr. < *epi-*, at + *thalamos*, bridal chamber] a song or poem in honor of a bride or bridegroom, or of both: also **ep′i·tha·la′mi·on** (-ən), *pl.* **-mi·a** (-ə)

ep·i·the·li·um (ep′ə thē′lē əm) *n., pl.* **-li·ums**, **-li·a** (-ə) [ModL. < Gr. *epi-*, upon + *thēlē*, nipple] cellular tissue covering surfaces, forming glands, and lining most cavities of the body —**ep′i·the′li·al** *adj.*

ep·i·thet (ep′ə thet′, -thət) *n.* [< L. < Gr. *epitheton* < *epi-*, on + *tithenai*, to put, DO¹] **1.** a word or phrase used to suggest some quality or feature of a person or thing, often in a mocking way (Ex.: "egghead" for an intellectual) **2.** a descriptive name or title (Ex.: Philip the Fair) —**ep′i·thet′i·cal, ep′i·thet′ic** *adj.*

e·pit·o·me (i pit′ə mē) *n., pl.* **-mes** [L. < Gr. *epitomē*, abridgment < *epi-*, upon + *temnein*, to cut] **1.** a short statement giving the main points of a book, report, etc.; abstract; summary **2.** a person or thing that shows all the typical qualities of something [she is the *epitome* of motherhood]

e·pit·o·mize (-mīz′) *vt.* **-mized′, -miz′ing** to make or be an epitome of —**e·pit′o·miz′er** *n.*

ep·i·zo·ot·ic (ep′ə zō ät′ik) *adj.* [< Fr. < Gr. *epi-*, upon + *zōion*, animal] epidemic among animals —*n.* an epizootic disease

‡ plu·ri·bus u·num (ē′ ploor′ə bəs yōō′nəm) [L.] out of many, one: a motto of the U.S.

ep·och (ep′ək; *Brit. & Canad., usually* ē′päk) *n.* [< ML. < Gr. *epochē*, a pause < *epi-*, upon + *echein*, to hold: for IE. base see SCHOOL¹] **1.** the beginning of a new and important period in the history of anything [the first earth satellite marked a new *epoch* in man's study of the universe] **2.** a period of time considered in terms of noteworthy events, developments, persons, etc. [an *epoch* of social revolution] **3.** *Astron.* the time at which observations are made, as of the positions of planets or stars **4.** *Geol.* a subdivision of a geologic period [the Eocene *Epoch*] —**ep′och·al** *adj.* —**ep′och·al·ly** *adv.*

ep·ode (ep′ōd) *n.* [MFr. < L. < Gr. *epōidos*, aftersong < *epi-*, upon + *aeidein*, to sing] the final stanza in certain lyric odes, following the strophe and antistrophe

ep·o·nym (ep′ə nim′) *n.* [< Gr. < *epi-*, upon + *onyma*, NAME] a real or mythical person from whose name the name of a nation, race, etc. comes [William *Penn* is the *eponym* of *Penn*sylvania] —**e·pon·y·mous** (i pän′ə məs) *adj.*

ep·ox·y (e päk′sē) *adj.* [EP(I)- + OXY(GEN)] designating or of a compound in which an oxygen atom is joined to two carbon atoms in a chain to form a bridgelike connection; specif., designating a tough resin formed by polymerization, used in glues, etc. —*n., pl.* **-ox′ies** an epoxy resin

ep·si·lon (ep′sə län′, -lən) *n.* [Gr.] the fifth letter of the Greek alphabet (E, ε)

Ep·som (ep′səm) town in England, near London: site of **Epsom Downs**, where the Derby is run

Epsom salts (or **salt**) [< EPSOM, famous for its mineral springs] a white, bitter, crystalline salt, magnesium sulfate, MgSO₄·7H₂O, used in medicine

Ep·stein (ep′stīn), Sir **Jacob** 1880–1959; Brit. sculptor; born in the U.S.

eq. 1. equal **2.** equation **3.** equivalent

eq·ua·ble (ek′wə b'l, ē′kwə-) *adj.* [< L. < *aequare*, to make equal < *aequus*: see EQUAL] **1.** not varying or fluctuating much; steady; uniform [an *equable* temperature] **2.** even; serene [an *equable* temperament] —see SYN. at STEADY —**eq′ua·bil′i·ty** *n.* —**eq′ua·bly** *adv.*

e·qual (ē′kwəl) *adj.* [< L. < *aequus*, plain, even, flat] **1.** of the same quantity, size, number, value, degree, etc. [*equal* pay for the same work] **2.** having the same rights, ability, rank, etc. [to make women *equal* with men] **3.** evenly proportioned; being balanced or uniform [*equal* justice for all] **4.** having the necessary ability, power, courage, etc. (to) [he is *equal* to the challenge] **5.** [Archaic] fair; just —*n.* any thing or person that is equal [to be the *equal* of another] —*vt.* **e′qualed** or **e′qualled, e′qual·ing** or **e′qual·ling 1.** to be equal to; match in value [six minus two *equals* four] **2.** to do or make something equal to [you can *equal* his score easily] —see SYN. at SAME

e·qual-ar·e·a (ē′kwəl er′ē ə) *adj.* designating any of several map projections in which areas enclosed between corresponding meridians and parallels are proportionally equal to areas on the earth's surface

e·qual·i·tar·i·an (i kwäl′ə ter′ē ən, -kwôl′-) *adj., n. same as* EGALITARIAN —**e·qual′i·tar′i·an·ism** *n.*

e·qual·i·ty (i kwäl′ə tē, -kwôl′-) *n., pl.* **-ties** state or instance of being equal, esp. of having the same political, economic, and social rights

e·qual·ize (ē′kwə līz′) *vt.* **-ized′, -iz′ing 1.** to make equal **2.** to make uniform —**e′qual·i·za′tion** *n.* —**e′qual·iz′er** *n.*

e·qual·ly (ē′kwə lē) *adv.* in an equal manner; to an equal degree; uniformly, impartially, etc.

equal sign (or **mark**) the arithmetical sign (=), indicating that the terms on either side of it are equal (Ex.: 2 + 2 = 4)

e·qua·nim·i·ty (ek′wə nim′ə tē, ē′kwə-) *n.* [< L. < *aequus*, even + *animus*, the mind] calmness of mind; evenness of temper; composure

SYN.—**equanimity** implies a natural evenness of temper, a basically calm, unexcitable disposition; **composure** suggests a calm, dignified manner resulting from a successful effort to control one's feelings in a trying situation; **serenity** implies deep inner tranquility and genuine peace of mind which remain undisturbed in the face of stress or excitement; **nonchalance** suggests carefree lack of concern or anxiety about situations which might be expected to disturb one emotionally; **sang-froid** implies great coolness and the ability to think clearly and act quickly in dangerous or difficult circumstances

e·quate (i kwāt′) *vt.* **e·quat′ed, e·quat′ing** [< L. pp. of *aequare*, to make equal < *aequus*, plain, even] **1.** *a)* to make equal or equivalent *b)* to treat, regard, or think of as equal, equivalent, or closely related [to *equate* wealth with happiness] **2.** *Math.* to state the equality of; put in the form of an equation —**e·quat′a·ble** *adj.*

e·qua·tion (i kwā′zhən) *n.* **1.** an equating or being equated **2.** a complex whole [the human *equation*] **3.** a statement of equality between two quantities, as shown by the equal sign (=) [a quadratic *equation*] **4.** an expression in which symbols and formulas are used to represent a chemical reaction (Ex.: $H_2SO_4 + 2NaCl = 2HCl + Na_2SO_4$) —**e·qua′tion·al** *adj.*

e·qua·tor (i kwāt′ər) *n.* [< ML. < LL. *aequator* < L. *aequare*: see EQUATE] **1.** an imaginary circle around the earth, equally distant from the North Pole and the South Pole: it divides the earth into the Northern Hemisphere and the Southern Hemisphere **2.** any circle that divides a sphere, etc. into two equal parts **3.** *same as* CELESTIAL EQUATOR

e·qua·to·ri·al (ē′kwə tôr′ē al, ek′wə-) *adj.* **1.** of or near the earth's equator **2.** of any equator **3.** like or characteristic of conditions near the earth's equator [*equatorial* heat]

Equatorial Guinea country in C Africa, including a mainland section & two islands in the Gulf of Guinea: 10,832 sq. mi.; pop. 286,000; cap. Santa Isabel

eq·uer·ry (ek′wər ē; *also, esp. Brit.,* i kwer′i) *n., pl.* **-ries** [altered (after L. *equus*, horse) < Fr. < OFr. *escuerie*, status of a squire] **1.** formerly, an officer in charge of the horses of a royal or noble household **2.** an officer who is a personal attendant on some member of a royal family

e·ques·tri·an (i kwes′trē ən) *adj.* [< L. *equestris* < *eques*, horseman < *equus*, horse] **1.** of horses, horsemen, or horsemanship **2.** on horseback [an *equestrian* statue] —*n.* a rider on horseback, as in a circus —**e·ques′tri·an·ism** *n.* —**e·ques′tri·enne′** (-trē en′) *n.fem.*

e·qui- [< L. *aequus*, equal] *a combining form meaning* equal, equally [*equidistant*]

e·qui·an·gu·lar (ē′kwə aŋ′gyə lər) *adj.* having all angles equal

e·qui·dis·tant (-dis′tənt) *adj.* equally distant —**e′qui·dis′tance** *n.* —**e′qui·dis′tant·ly** *adv.*

e·qui·lat·er·al (-lat′ər əl) *adj.* [< LL. < L. *aequus*, equal + *latus*, side] having all sides equal [an *equilateral* triangle] —*n.* **1.** a figure having equal sides **2.** a side exactly equal to another

e·quil·i·brant (i kwil′ə brənt) *n.* [< Fr. < L. *aequilibrium*, EQUILIBRIUM] *Physics* a force or combination of forces that can balance another

e·quil·i·brate (i kwil′ə brāt′, ē′kwə li′brāt) *vt., vi.* **-brat′ed, -brat′ing** to bring into or be in equilibrium; balance or counterbalance —**e·quil′i·bra′tion** *n.* —**e·quil′i·bra′tor** *n.*

---

fat, āpe, cär; ten, ēven; is, bīte; gō, hôrn, tōōl, lōōk; oil, out; up, fur; get; joy; yet; chin; she; thin, then; zh, leisure; ŋ, ring; ə for *a* in *ago, e* in *agent, i* in *sanity, o* in *comply, u* in *focus;* ′ as in *able* (ā′b'l); Fr. bál; ë, Fr. coeur; ö, Fr. feu; Fr. mon; ô, Fr. coq; ü, Fr. duc; r, Fr. cri; H, G. ich; kh, G. doch; ‡foreign; ☆ Americanism; < derived from. See inside front cover.

e·qui·lib·ri·um (ē′kwə lib′rē əm) *n., pl.* **-ri·ums, -ri·a** (-ə) [L. *aequilibrium* < *aequus*, equal + *libra*, a balance] **1.** a state of balance or equality between opposing forces **2.** a state of balance or adjustment of conflicting desires, interests, etc. **3.** *a*) bodily balance *b*) mental or emotional stability

e·quine (ē′kwīn, ek′wīn) *adj.* [< L. < *equus*, a horse] of, like, or characteristic of a horse —*n.* a horse

e·qui·noc·tial (ē′kwə näk′shəl) *adj.* **1.** relating to either of the equinoxes **2.** occurring at about the time of an equinox [an *equinoctial* storm] **3.** equatorial —*n.* **1.** *same as* CELESTIAL EQUATOR **2.** an equinoctial storm

equinoctial circle (or **line**) *same as* CELESTIAL EQUATOR

e·qui·nox (ē′kwə näks′) *n.* [< OFr. < ML. < L. < *aequus*, equal + *nox*, night] **1.** the time when the sun crosses the equator, making night and day of equal length in all parts of the earth: the **vernal equinox** occurs about March 21, the **autumnal equinox** about September 22 **2.** either of the two points on the celestial equator where the sun crosses it on these dates: also **equinoctial point**

e·quip (i kwip′) *vt.* **e·quipped′, e·quip′ping** [< Fr. < OFr. *es-quiper*, embark, prob. < OE. < *scip*, a ship; or < ? ON. *skipa*, to arrange] **1.** to provide with what is needed; outfit [to *equip* a ship for Arctic duty] **2.** to prepare by training, instruction, etc. [poorly *equipped* to earn a living] —see SYN. at FURNISH — **e·quip′per** *n.*

eq·ui·page (ek′wə pij) *n.* **1.** the equipment of a ship, army, expedition, etc. **2.** a carriage, esp. one with horses, coachmen, and other servants

e·quip·ment (i kwip′mənt) *n.* **1.** an equipping or being equipped **2.** whatever one is equipped with for some purpose; supplies, furnishings, apparatus, etc. [camping *equipment*] **3.** one's abilities, knowledge, etc.

eq·ui·poise (ek′wə poiz′, ē′kwə-) *n.* [EQUI- + POISE] **1.** equal distribution of weight; state of balance, or equilibrium **2.** a weight or force that balances another

eq·ui·se·tum (ek′wə sēt′əm) *n., pl.* **-tums, -ta** (-tə) [ModL. < L. *equus*, horse + *saeta*, bristle] *same as* HORSETAIL (sense 2)

eq·ui·ta·ble (ek′wit ə b′l) *adj.* **1.** characterized by equity; fair; just [an *equitable* share] **2.** *Law a*) having to do with equity, as distinguished from common or statute law *b*) valid in equity —**eq′ui·ta·ble·ness** *n.* —**eq′ui·ta·bly** *adv.*

eq·ui·ta·tion (ek′wə tā′shən) *n.* [< L. pp. of *equitare*, to ride < *eques*: see EQUESTRIAN] the art of riding on horseback; horsemanship

eq·ui·ty (ek′wət ē) *n., pl.* **-ties** [< OFr. < L. *aequitas*, equality < *aequus*, equal] **1.** fairness; impartiality; justice **2.** anything that is fair or equitable ☆**3.** the value of property beyond the total amount owed on it in mortgages, liens, etc. **4.** *Law a*) a system of rules and doctrines, as in the U.S., supplementing common and statute law and superseding such law when it proves inadequate for just settlement *b*) a right or claim recognized in a court of equity

☆**equity capital 1.** funds contributed by the owners of a business **2.** assets minus liabilities; net worth

equiv. equivalent

e·quiv·a·lence (i kwiv′ə ləns) *n.* the condition of being equivalent; equality of quantity, value, meaning, etc.: also **e·quiv′a·len·cy**

e·quiv·a·lent (-lənt) *adj.* [< OFr. < LL. < L. *aequus*, equal + *valere*, to be strong] **1.** equal in quantity, value, force, meaning, etc. **2.** *Chem.* having the same valence **3.** *Geom.* equal in area or volume but not of the same shape —*n.* **1.** an equivalent thing [what is the *equivalent* of six feet in the metric system?] **2.** *Chem.* the quantity by weight (of a substance) that combines with one gram of hydrogen or eight grams of oxygen —see SYN. at SAME —**e·quiv′a·lent·ly** *adv.*

e·quiv·o·cal (i kwiv′ə k′l) *adj.* [< LL. *aequivocus* (see EQUIVOCATE & -AL)] **1.** having two or more meanings; purposely vague or ambiguous [an *equivocal* reply] **2.** uncertain; doubtful [an *equivocal* outcome] **3.** suspected of being immoral, dishonest, etc.; suspicious; questionable [*equivocal* conduct] —see SYN. at OBSCURE —**e·quiv′o·cal′i·ty** (-kal′ə tē), **e·quiv′o·cal·ness** *n.* —**e·quiv′o·cal·ly** *adv.*

e·quiv·o·cate (-kāt′) *vi.* **-cat′ed, -cat′ing** [< LL. *aequivocus*, of like sound < L. *aequus*, equal + *vox*, voice] to say things that have more than one meaning in order to deceive, mislead, hedge, etc. —see SYN. at LIE² —**e·quiv′o·ca′tion** *n.* —**e·quiv′o·ca′tor** *n.*

er (*variously* u, ə, ä, *etc.*; ur, ər *are spelling pronunciations*) *interj.* a conventionalized representation of a sound often made by a speaker when hesitating briefly

-er (ər) *a suffix of various origins and meanings:* **1.** [OE. *-ere*] *a*) a person having to do with [*hatter*] : see also -IER, -YER *b*) a person living in [*New Yorker*] *c*) a thing or action connected with [*diner*] *d*) a person or thing that [*sprayer, roller*] **2.** [OE. *-ra*] more: *added to many adjectives and adverbs to form the comparative degree* [*greater, later*] **3.** [< Anglo-Fr. inf. suffix] the action of: *used in legal language* [*demurrer, waiver*] **4.** [OE. *-rian*] repeatedly [*flicker*]

Er *Chem.* erbium

e·ra (ir′ə; *now often* er′ə) *n.* [LL. *aera*, era, earlier sense, "counters" < pl. of L. *aes*, brass] **1.** a system of reckoning time by numbering the years from some given date [the Christian *Era*] **2.** an event or date that marks the beginning of a new period in the history of something **3.** a period of time measured from an important event or date **4.** a period of time considered in terms of noteworthy and typical events or people [an *era* of progress] **5.** any of the five main divisions of geologic time [the Paleozoic *Era*] : see also EPOCH, PERIOD, AGE

ERA Equal Rights Amendment

e·ra·di·ate (ē rā′dē āt′) *vi., vt.* **-at′ed, -at′ing** *same as* RADIATE —**e·ra′di·a′tion** *n.*

e·rad·i·cate (i rad′ə kāt′) *vt.* **-cat′ed, -cat′ing** [< L. pp. of *eradicare*, to root out < *e-*, out + *radix*, ROOT¹] **1.** to tear out by the roots; uproot **2.** to get rid of; wipe out; destroy [to *eradicate* slums] —see SYN. at EXTERMINATE —**e·rad′i·ca·ble** (-kə b′l) *adj.* —**e·rad′i·ca′tion** *n.* —**e·rad′i·ca′tor** *n.*

e·rase (i rās′) *vt.* **e·rased′, e·ras′ing** [< L. pp. of *eradere* < *e-*, out + *radere*, to scrape: see RAZE] **1.** to rub, scrape, or wipe out (esp. writing or printing); efface **2.** to remove (something recorded) from (magnetic tape) **3.** to remove any sign of; obliterate, as from the mind **4.** [Slang] to kill —**e·ras′a·ble** *adj.*

SYN.—**erase** means simply a rubbing or wiping out of something written or drawn; **efface** implies a complete or partial rubbing out from a surface of all recognizable marks and may suggest a slow process of wearing away; to **expunge** is to remove or wipe out completely; **obliterate** suggests the forceful and total blotting out of something so that all visible traces of it are removed

e·ras·er (i rā′sər) *n.* a thing that erases; specif., a device made of rubber for erasing ink or pencil marks, or a pad of felt or cloth for removing chalk marks from a blackboard

E·ras·mus (i raz′məs), **Des·i·der·i·us** (des′ə dir′ē əs) (born *Gerhard Gerhards*) 1466?-1536; Du. humanist & scholar —**E·ras′mi·an** (-mē ən) *adj., n.*

e·ra·sure (i rā′shər; *chiefly Brit.* -zhər) *n.* **1.** an erasing **2.** an erased word, mark, etc. **3.** the place on a surface where something has been erased

Er·a·to (er′ə tō′) *Gr. Myth.* the Muse of love poetry

er·bi·um (ur′bē əm) *n.* [ModL. < (*Ytt*)*erby*, Sw. town where first found] a metallic chemical element of the rare-earth group: symbol, Er; at. wt., 167.28; at. no., 68

ere (er) *prep.* [< OE. *ær*] [Archaic or Poet.] before (in time) [would she had come *ere* now] —*conj.* [Archaic or Poet.] **1.** before **2.** sooner than; rather than

Er·e·bus (er′ə bəs) **1.** *Gr. Myth.* the dark place under the earth through which the dead passed before entering Hades **2.** **Mount,** volcanic mountain on an island in the Pacific, just off the coast of Antarctica: over 13,000 ft.

e·rect (i rekt′) *adj.* [< L. *erectus*, pp. of *erigere* < *e-*, up + *regere*, to make straight: for IE. base see REGAL] **1.** upright; vertical **2.** sticking out or up; bristling; stiff —*vt.* **1.** to raise or construct (a building, etc.) **2.** to set up; cause to arise [to *erect* social barriers] **3.** to set in an upright position; raise [to *erect* goal posts] **4.** to put together; assemble **5.** [Archaic] to establish; found **6.** *Geom.* to construct or draw (a perpendicular, figure, etc.) upon a base line —**e·rect′ly** *adv.* —**e·rect′ness** *n.* —**e·rec′tor** *n.*

e·rec·tile (i rek′t′l; *chiefly Brit.* -tīl′) *adj.* that can become erect: used esp. of tissue that becomes swollen and rigid when filled with blood —**e·rec′til′i·ty** (-til′ə tē) *n.*

e·rec·tion (i rek′shən) *n.* **1.** an erecting or being erected **2.** something erected, as a building **3.** an erectile condition

ere·long (er′lôn′) *adv.* [Archaic or Poet.] before long; soon

er·e·mite (er′ə mīt′) *n.* [< OFr. or LL.: see HERMIT] a religious recluse; hermit —**er′e·mit′ic** (-mit′ik), **er′e·mit′i·cal** *adj.*

e·rep·sin (i rep′sin) *n.* [G. < L. pp. of *eripere* < *e-*, out + *rapere*, to snatch + G. *pepsin*, PEPSIN] an enzyme mixture secreted by the intestine and involved in the breaking down of proteins into their component amino acids

Er·furt (er′foort) city in SW East Germany: pop. 193,000

erg (urg) *n.* [< Gr. *ergon*, work] *Physics* the unit of work or energy in the cgs (metric) system, being the work done by one dyne acting through a distance of one centimeter

er·go (ur′gō, er′-) *conj., adv.* [L.] therefore

er·gos·ter·ol (ər gäs′tə rōl′) *n.* [< ERGOT + STEROL] an alcohol, $C_{28}H_{44}O$, formerly prepared from ergot but now chiefly from yeast: when exposed to ultraviolet rays it produces a vitamin (D_2) used to prevent or cure rickets

er·got (ur′gət) *n.* [Fr. < OFr. *argot*, a rooster's spur: from the shape of the growth] **1.** a fungous growth that invades the kernels of rye, or of other cereal plants **2.** the disease in which this occurs **3.** an extract of the dried rye fungus, used as a drug to contract the blood vessels and the smooth muscle tissue

er·got·a·mine (ər gät′ə mēn′) *n.* [ERGOT + AMINE] an alkaloid isolated from ergot and used esp. in the treatment of migraine headaches

Er·ic (er′ik) [Scand. < ON. *Eirikr*, lit., honorable ruler] a masculine name

Er·ics·son (er′ik sən), **Leif** (lāf) fl. 1000;. Norw. explorer: discovered what is now believed to be part of N. America: son of ERIC THE RED Also sp. **Ericson**

Eric the Red fl. 10th cent.; Norw. explorer: discovered & colonized Greenland

Er·ie[1] (ir′ē) *n., pl.* **Er′ies, Er′ie** [AmFr. < Huron *yĕñresh*, wildcat + -′e, at the place of] a member of a tribe of Iroquoian Indians who lived in an area east and southeast of Lake Erie

Er·ie[2] (ir′ē) [after prec.] **1.** port on Lake Erie, in NW Pa.: pop. 129,000 **2. Lake,** one of the Great Lakes, between Lake Huron & Lake Ontario: 9,914 sq. mi.; 241 mi. long

Erie Canal canal between Buffalo, on Lake Erie, and Albany, on the Hudson: completed 1825: part of the New York State Barge Canal

Er·in (er′in) [OIr.] *poet. name for* IRELAND

E·rin·y·es (i rin′ē ēz′) *n.pl., sing.* **E·rin·ys** (i rin′is, -rī′nis) *Gr. Myth. same as* FURIES

E·ris (ir′is, er′-) *Gr. Myth.* the goddess of strife and discord

Er·i·tre·a (er′ə trē′ə) province of Ethiopia, on the Red Sea: 45,000 sq. mi. —**Er′i·tre′an** *adj., n.*

ERIE CANAL

Er·len·mey·er flask (ur′lən mī′ər, er′-) [after E. *Erlenmeyer* (1825–1909), Ger. chemist] [*also* **e-**] a cone-shaped laboratory flask with a flat bottom and a short neck

er·mine (ur′mən) *n., pl.* **-mines, -mine:** see PLURAL, II, D, 1 [OFr.; prob. < MHG. < OHG. *harmo,* weasel] **1.** a weasel of northern regions whose fur is brown in summer but white with a black-tipped tail in winter **2.** the soft, white fur of this animal **3.** the position, rank, or functions of some European judges or peers, whose state robe is trimmed with ermine —**er′mined** *adj.*

ERMINE
(body 5–10 in. long;
tail 1–6 in. long)

erne, ern (urn) *n.* [OE. *earn*] the European white-tailed eagle, which lives near the sea

Er·nest (ur′nəst) [< G. < OHG. *Ernust*, lit., resolute < *ernust,* seriousness] a masculine name

Er·nes·tine (ur′nəs tēn′) [G., fem. of ERNEST] a feminine name

Ernst (ernst), **Max** (mäks) 1891–1976; Ger. surrealist painter, in France & the U.S.

e·rode (i rōd′) *vt.* **e·rod′ed, e·rod′ing** [< Fr. < L. < *e-,* out, off + *rodere,* to gnaw: see RODENT] **1.** to eat into; wear away; disintegrate [acid *erodes* metal] **2.** to form by wearing away gradually [the stream *eroded* a gully] **3.** to cause to deteriorate, decay, or vanish —*vi.* to become eroded —**e·rod′i·ble** *adj.*

e·rog·e·nous (i räj′ə nəs) *adj.* [< Gr. *erōs,* love + -GENOUS] *same as* EROTOGENIC

E·ros (er′äs, ir′-) *Gr. Myth.* the god of love, son of Aphrodite: identified with the Roman god Cupid

e·ro·sion (i rō′zhən) *n.* an eroding or being eroded —**e·ro′sion·al** *adj.* —**e·ro′sive** *adj.*

e·rot·ic (i rät′ik) *adj.* [Gr. *erōtikos* < *erōtos,* genitive of *erōs,* love] of, having, or arousing sexual feelings or desires; having to do with sexual love; amatory —**e·rot′i·cal·ly** *adv.*

e·rot·i·ca (-i kə) *n.pl.* [*often with sing. v.*] erotic books, pictures, etc.

e·rot·i·cism (-ə siz′m) *n.* **1.** erotic quality or character **2.** sexual excitement or behavior **3.** a great interest in sexual matters Also, and for 2 now usually, **er·o·tism** (er′ə tiz′m)

e·ro·to·gen·ic (i rät′ə jen′ik; er′ə tə-) *adj.* [*eroto-* (< Gr.), sexual desire + -GENIC] designating or of those areas of the body that are particularly sensitive to sexual stimulation

err (ur, er) *vi.* [< OFr. *errer* < L. *errare,* to wander: for IE. base see RACE[1]] **1.** to be wrong or mistaken; fall into error [she *erred* in calling Columbus a Spaniard] **2.** to do something that is morally wrong ["To *err* is human, to forgive divine"]

er·ran·cy (er′ən sē) *n., pl.* **-cies 1.** the state or an instance of erring **2.** a tendency to err

er·rand (er′ənd) *n.* [OE. *ærende*] **1.** a short trip to do a definite thing, often for someone else **2.** the thing to be done or such a trip; purpose or object for which one goes or is sent

er·rant (er′ənt) *adj.* [OFr., prp. of *errer,* to travel, ult. < L. *iter,* a journey] **1.** roving or wandering, esp. in search of adventure [a knight-*errant*] **2.** *a)* [see ERR] erring or straying from what is right *b)* shifting about [an *errant* wind] —**er′rant·ly** *adv.*

er·rant·ry (-rē) *n.* the condition or behavior of a knight-errant; spirit or deeds of chivalry

er·ra·ta (e rät′ə, -rāt′-, -rat′-) *n.* **1.** *pl.* of ERRATUM **2.** a list of errors with their corrections, inserted on a separate page of a published book, magazine, etc.

er·rat·ic (i rat′ik) *adj.* [< OFr. < L. *erraticus* < pp. of *errare:* see ERR] **1.** having no fixed course; irregular in action or behavior **2.** eccentric; queer —*n.* an erratic person —**er·rat′i·cal·ly** *adv.*

er·ra·tum (e rät′əm, -rāt′-, -rat′-) *n., pl.* **-ta** (-ə) [L., neut. pp. of *errare:* see ERR] an error in printing or writing

er·ro·ne·ous (ə rō′nē əs, e-) *adj.* containing error or based on error; mistaken; wrong [an *erroneous* belief] —**er·ro′ne·ous·ly** *adv.*

er·ror (er′ər) *n.* [< OFr. < L. *error* < *errare:* see ERR] **1.** the state of believing what is untrue or incorrect [to be in *error*] **2.** a wrong belief; incorrect opinion **3.** something done incorrectly as through carelessness; mistake **4.** transgression; wrongdoing; sin **5.** the amount by which something deviates from what is required or correct ☆**6.** *Baseball* any misplay in fielding a ball which allows a player who should have been out to reach a base safely or remain at bat, or which permits a runner to advance —**er′ror·less** *adj.*

SYN. —**error** is a broad term covering any failure to be true, accurate, correct, etc., whether accidental or deliberate [an *error* in judgment]; **mistake** suggests an error resulting from carelessness, misunderstanding, etc. and does not in itself strongly imply criticism [a *mistake* in reading a blueprint]; **blunder** implies stupidity, clumsiness, etc. and strongly suggests criticism [his *blunder* in driving caused the accident]; a **slip** is a minor mistake made accidentally in speaking or writing; a **faux pas** is a social blunder or error in etiquette that causes embarrassment

er·satz (ur′zäts, er′-) *n., adj.* [G.] substitute or synthetic: the word is usually used of something considered to be inferior

Erse (urs) *adj., n.* [ME. *Erish,* var. of *Irisc,* Irish] *same as* GAELIC, *adj.* 2, *n.* 2

erst (urst) *adv.* [OE. *ærest,* superl. of *ær,* ere] [Archaic] formerly —*adj.* [Obs.] first

erst·while (urst′hwīl′) *adv.* [Archaic] some time ago; formerly —*adj.* former [my *erstwhile* friend]

e·ruct (i rukt′) *vt., vi.* [< L. *eructare* < *e-,* out + *ructare,* to belch] to belch —**e·ruc·ta·tion** (i ruk′tā′shən, ē′ruk-) *n.*

er·u·dite (er′yoo dīt′, -oo-) *adj.* [< L. pp. of *erudire,* to instruct < *e-,* out + *rudis,* RUDE] learned; scholarly —**er′u·dite′ly** *adv.*

er·u·di·tion (er′yoo dish′ən, -oo-) *n.* learning acquired by reading and study; scholarship—see **SYN.** at INFORMATION

e·rupt (i rupt′) *vi.* [< L. *eruptus,* pp. of *erumpere* < *e-,* out + *rumpere,* to break: see RUPTURE] **1.** to burst forth or out, as from some restraint [the lava *erupted,* a riot *erupted*] **2.** to throw forth lava, water, steam, etc., as a volcano **3.** to break out in a rash **4.** to break through the gums, as a new tooth —*vt.* to cause to burst forth —**e·rupt′i·ble** *adj.*

e·rup·tion (i rup′shən) *n.* **1.** a bursting forth or out **2.** a throwing forth of lava, water, steam, etc. **3.** *Med.* *a)* a breaking out in a rash *b)* a rash —**e·rup′tive** *adj.* —**e·rup′tive·ly** *adv.*

Er·win (ur′win) [G. < OHG. *hari*, host + *wini*, friend] a masculine name

-er·y (ər ē) [< OFr. *-erie* < LL. *-aria*, or < OFr. *-ier* + *-ie* (L. *-ia*)] *a suffix meaning:* **1.** a place to [*tannery*] **2.** a place for [*nunnery*] **3.** the practice, act, or occupation of [*surgery*] **4.** the product or goods of [*pottery*] **5.** a collection of [*crockery*] **6.** the state or condition of [*drudgery*] **7.** the behavior or qualities of [*tomfoolery*]

er·y·sip·e·las (er′ə sip′′l əs, ir′-) *n.* [< L. < Gr. < *erythros*, red + *-pelas* (L. *pellis*), skin] an acute infectious disease of the skin or mucous membranes caused by a streptococcus and causing inflammation and fever

e·ryth·ro- [< Gr. *erythros*, red] *a combining form meaning:* **1.** red [*erythrocyte*] **2.** erythrocyte

e·ryth·ro·cyte (i rith′rə sīt′) *n.* [ERYTHRO- + -CYTE] a red blood corpuscle: it is a very small, circular disk and contains hemoglobin, which carries oxygen to the body tissues — **e·ryth′ro·cyt′ic** (-sit′ik) *adj.*

☆**e·ryth·ro·my·cin** (i rith′rə mī′sin) *n.* [< ERYTHRO- + Gr. *mykēs*, fungus + -IN¹] an antibiotic derived from a soil bacterium, used to treat various bacterial diseases

Es *Chem.* einsteinium

-es (iz, əz, z) [variously < OE. *-as*, *-s*] *a suffix used:* **1.** to form the plural of some nouns, as in *fishes:* see PLURAL **2.** to form the third person singular in the present tense of verbs, as in (he) *kisses:* see also -s

E·sau (ē′sô) [L. < Gr. < Heb. *'ēsāw*, lit., hairy] *Bible* the son of Isaac and Rebekah, who sold his birthright to his younger twin brother, Jacob: Gen. 25:21–34, 27

es·ca·drille (es′kə dril′; *Fr.* es kȧ drē′y) *n.* [Fr. < Sp. < *escuadra*, squad] a squadron of airplanes, as in the French armed forces of World War I

es·ca·lade (es′kə lād′, es′kə lād′) *n.* [< Fr. < It. < *scalare*, to climb < L. *scala*, ladder] the act of climbing the walls of a fortified place by ladders —*vt.* **-lad′ed**, **-lad′ing** to climb (a wall, etc.) or enter (a fortified place) by ladders

☆**es·ca·late** (es′kə lāt′) *vi.* **-lat′ed**, **-lat′ing** [back-formation < ESCALATOR] **1.** to rise as on an escalator **2.** to expand, as from a limited conflict into a general war **3.** to increase rapidly, as prices —*vt.* to cause to escalate —**es′ca·la′tion** *n.*

☆**es·ca·la·tor** (-ər) *n.* [< ESCALA(DE) + -*tor*, as in (ELEVA)TOR] a moving stairway consisting of treads linked in an endless belt

☆**escalator clause** a clause in a contract by which wages, etc. are adjusted to cost of living, etc.

es·cal·lop, es·cal·op (e skäl′əp, -skal′-) *n., vt.* [< OFr.: see SCALLOP] *same as* SCALLOP

es·ca·pade (es′kə pād′) *n.* [Fr., ult. < Sp. < *escapar*, to ESCAPE] a wild or reckless adventure or prank

es·cape (ə skāp′, e-) *vi.* **-caped′**, **-cap′ing** [< ONormFr. < L. *ex-*, out of + *cappa*, cloak (i.e., leave one's cloak)] **1.** to get free; get away; break loose, as from prison **2.** to avoid an illness, accident, pain, etc. [two were injured, but he *escaped*] **3.** to flow, drain, or leak away [gas *escaping* from a pipe] **4.** to slip away; disappear [the image *escaped* from her memory] —*vt.* **1.** to get away from; flee from [to *escape* pursuers] **2.** to manage to keep away from; avoid [to *escape* punishment] **3.** to come from without being intended [a scream *escaped* her lips] **4.** to slip away from; be missed or forgotten by [his name *escapes* me] —*n.* **1.** an escaping or the state of having escaped **2.** a means of escape [a fire *escape*] **3.** an outward flow or leakage [an *escape* in the gas line] **4.** a way of avoiding worry or boredom for a while [movies are her *escape*] —*adj.* **1.** giving escape (*n.* 4) [detective stories are *escape* reading] **2.** *a)* making escape possible [an *escape* hatch] *b)* providing a basis for avoiding a claim, responsibility, etc. [an *escape* clause] —**es·cap′a·ble** *adj.* —**es·cap′er** *n.*

SYN.—**escape** implies a getting out of, a keeping away from, or simply a remaining unaffected by a danger, evil, confinement, etc. that is present or about to happen [to *escape* death, criticism, etc.]; **avoid** suggests the display of conscious effort in keeping clear of something undesirable or harmful [to *avoid* crowds during a flu epidemic]; to **evade** is to escape or avoid by being clever, tricky, or cunning [to *evade* pursuit, one's duty, etc.]; to **elude** is to escape being caught, as by using clever or sly tricks [the criminal *eluded* the police] or to escape the grasp or understanding of someone, as by being baffling or confusing [success *eluded* him; the meaning *eluded* her]

es·cap·ee (ə skā′pē′, e-) *n.* a person who has escaped, esp. from confinement

es·cape·ment (ə skāp′mənt, e-) *n.* **1.** [Rare] a means of escape **2.** the part in a clock or watch that controls the speed and regularity of the balance wheel or pendulum by means of a notched wheel (**escape wheel**), one tooth of which is allowed to escape from the holding catch at a time **3.** a ratchet mechanism, esp. on a typewriter to regulate the horizontal movement of the carriage

ESCAPEMENT

escape velocity the minimum speed required for a particle, spacecraft, etc. to escape permanently from the gravitational field of a planet, star, etc.

es·cap·ism (ə skāp′iz′m, e-) *n.* a tendency to escape from reality, the responsibilities of real life, etc., esp. by having fantasies, daydreams, etc. —**es·cap′ist** *adj., n.*

es·ca·role (es′kə rōl′) *n.* [Fr. < ML. < L. < *esca*: see ESCULENT] *same as* ENDIVE (sense 1 *b*)

es·carp·ment (e skärp′mənt) *n.* [< Fr.: see SCARP] **1.** a steep slope or cliff formed by erosion or by faulting **2.** ground formed into a steep slope on the exterior of a fortification See also SCARP

-es·cence (es′ns) *a suffix used to form nouns from adjectives ending in* -ESCENT [*obsolescence*]

-es·cent (es′nt) [< L. *-escens, -escentis*, prp. ending] *a suffix meaning:* **1.** starting to be; being or becoming [*convalescent*] **2.** giving off or reflecting light, or exhibiting a play of color [*phosphorescent*]

es·cheat (es chēt′) *n.* [< OFr. < pp. of *escheoir*, to fall to one's share < VL. < L. *ex-*, out + *cadere*, to fall] *Law* **1.** the turning over of property to the lord of the manor, to the crown, or to the government when there are no legal heirs **2.** property so turned over —*vt., vi.* to take or be taken by escheat —**es·cheat′a·ble** *adj.*

es·chew (es chōō′) *vt.* [< Anglo-Fr. < OFr. < OHG. *sciuhan*, to fear] to keep away from (something harmful or disliked); shun —**es·chew′al** *n.*

es·cort (es′kôrt; *for v.* i skôrt′) *n.* [< Fr. < It. < *scorta* < *scorgere*, to lead < L. *ex-*, out + *corrigere*, to CORRECT] **1.** one or more persons (or cars, ships, airplanes, etc.) accompanying another or others to give protection or show honor **2.** a man or boy accompanying a woman or girl, as to a party **3.** accompaniment by an escort —*vt.* to go with as an escort

es·cri·toire (es′krə twär′) *n.* [< OFr. < LL. < pp. of L. *scribere*, to write] a writing desk or table; secretary

es·crow (es′krō; *chiefly Brit.* es krō′) *n.* [OFr. *escroue*, scroll] *Law* a written agreement, as a bond or deed, put in the care of a third party until certain conditions are fulfilled —☆**in escrow** *Law* so put in the care of a third party

es·cu·do (es kōō′dō) *n., pl.* **-dos** [Sp., a shield < L. *scutum*] **1.** any of several obsolete coins of Spain and Portugal **2.** the monetary unit of Chile and Portugal: see MONETARY UNITS, table

es·cu·lent (es′kyoo lənt) *adj.* [< L. < *esca*, food: for IE. base see EAT] fit for food; eatable; edible —*n.* something fit for food, esp. a vegetable

es·cutch·eon (i skuch′ən) *n.* [ONormFr. < L. *scutum*, shield] a shield or shield-shaped surface on which a coat of arms is displayed —**a blot on one's escutcheon** a disgrace to one's honor or reputation

ESCUTCHEON

Es·dra·e·lon (ez′drə ē′lən, es′-) plain in N Israel, extending from the Jordan River valley to Mt. Carmel

Es·dras (ez′drəs) *Douay Bible* name for EZRA

-ese (ēz, ēs) [< OFr. & It. < L. *-ensis*] *a suffix meaning:* **1.** (a native or inhabitant) of [*Javanese*] **2.** (in) the language or dialect of [*Cantonese*] **3.** (in) the style of [*journalese*]

ESE, E.S.E., e.s.e. east-southeast

Es·fa·hán (es′fä hän′) city in WC Iran: pop. 575,000

Es·ki·mo (es′kə mō′) *n.* [< Fr. < Algonquian: lit., eater of raw flesh] **1.** *pl.* **-mos′**, **-mo′** a member of a group of native N. American people living in Greenland, northern Canada and Alaska, and the northeastern tip of Asia **2.** either of the two languages of the Eskimos —*adj.* of the Eskimos, their language, or their culture —**Es′ki·mo′an** *adj.*

Eskimo dog a strong breed of dog with grayish, shaggy fur, used by the Eskimos to pull sleds

e·soph·a·gus (i säf′ə gəs) *n., pl.* **-a·gi′** (-jī′) [< OFr. < ML. < Gr. *oisophagos* < *oisein*, future inf. of *pherein*, to carry + *phagein*, to eat] the tube through which food passes from the pharynx to the stomach: see illustration at EPIGLOTTIS —e·soph·a·ge·al (i säf′ə jē′əl) *adj.*

es·o·ter·ic (es′ə ter′ik) *adj.* [< Gr. < *esōteros*, inner, compar. of *esō*, within] **1.** *a)* understood by only a chosen few, as an inner group of disciples or initiates: said of ideas, literature, etc. *b)* beyond the understanding or knowledge of most people; abstruse **2.** confidential; private [an *esoteric* plan] —es′o·ter′i·cal·ly *adv.*

ESP extrasensory perception

esp., espec. especially

es·pa·drille (es′pə dril′) *n.* [Fr. < Sp. *esparto*, ESPARTO] a shoe for casual wear, with a canvas upper and a sole of twisted rope or of rubber, etc.

es·pal·ier (es pal′yər) *n.* [Fr. < It. *spalliera*, support < *spalla*, the shoulder < L. *spatula*: see SPATULA] **1.** a lattice or trellis on which trees and shrubs are trained to grow flat **2.** a plant, tree, etc. so trained —*vt.* **1.** to train as or on an espalier **2.** to provide with an espalier

Es·pa·ña (es pä′nyä) *Sp.* name of SPAIN

es·par·to (es pär′tō) *n.* [Sp. < L. *spartum* < Gr. *sparton*] a long, coarse grass of Spain and northern Africa, used to make rope, shoes, etc.: also **esparto grass**

es·pe·cial (ə spesh′əl, es pesh′-) *adj.* special; particular; outstanding —see SYN. at SPECIAL

ESPALIER

es·pe·cial·ly (-ē) *adv.* particularly; mainly; to a marked degree; unusually

Es·pe·ran·to (es′pə rän′tō, -ran′-) *n.* [after pseudonym of Dr. L. L. Zamenhof (1859–1917), its inventor] an artificial language for international (chiefly European) use, based on word bases common to the main European languages

es·pi·al (ə spī′əl, es pī′-) *n.* **1.** an espying or being espied; observation **2.** discovery

es·pi·o·nage (es′pē ə näzh′, -nij′) *n.* [< Fr. < *espion*, a spy < It. *spione* < *spia*, a SPY] **1.** the act of spying **2.** the use of spies by a government to learn the military secrets of other nations

es·pla·nade (es′plə nād′, -näd′) *n.* [Fr. < It. < *spianare* < L. *explanare*, to level: see EXPLAIN] a level, open space of ground; esp., a public walk or roadway, often along a shore; promenade

es·pous·al (i spou′z’l) *n.* **1.** [*often pl.*] *a)* an engagement to marry; betrothal *b)* a wedding **2.** an espousing (of some cause, idea, etc.); advocacy

es·pouse (i spouz′) *vt.* **-poused′, -pous′ing** [< OFr. < LL. *sponsare* < L. *sponsus*: see SPOUSE] **1.** to marry; esp., to take as a wife **2.** to take up, support, or advocate (some cause, idea, etc.)

es·pres·so (es pres′ō) *n., pl.* **-sos** [It. (*caffè*) *espresso*, pressed-out (coffee)] coffee prepared in a special machine by forcing steam through finely ground coffee beans

es·prit (es prē′) *n.* [Fr.] **1.** spirit **2.** lively intelligence or wit

es·prit de corps (es prē′ də kôr′) [Fr.] group spirit; sense of pride, honor, etc. shared by those in the same group or undertaking

es·py (ə spī′, es pī′) *vt.* **-pied′, -py′ing** [< OFr. *espier*: see SPY] to catch sight of; spy

Esq., Esqr. Esquire

-esque (esk) [Fr. < It. *-esco*] *a suffix meaning:* **1.** in the manner or style of [Romanesque] **2.** having the quality of [picturesque]

Es·qui·mau (es′kə mō′) *n., pl.* **-maux′** (-mō′, -mōz′), **-mau′** [Fr.] *same as* ESKIMO

es·quire (es′kwīr, ə skwīr′) *n.* [< OFr. < LL. *scutarius*, a shield-bearer < L. *scutum*, a shield] **1.** formerly, a candidate for knighthood, acting as attendant for a knight **2.** in England, a member of the gentry ranking just below a knight **3.** [E-] a title of courtesy, usually abbrev. *Esq., Esqr.*, placed after a man's surname [Samuel Johnson, *Esq.*]

ess (es) *n., pl.* **ess′es** **1.** the letter S, s **2.** something shaped like an S

-ess (is, əs; *occas.* es) [< OFr. < LL. *-issa* < Gr.] *a suffix meaning female* [lioness]: in referring to persons (*poetess*, etc.), now often avoided as showing contempt

es·say (e sā′; *for n.* 1 *usually, and for n.* 2 *always,* es′ā) *vt.* [< OFr. < LL. *exagium*, a weighing < *ex-*, out of + *agere*, to do: see ACT] to try; attempt —*n.* **1.** an attempt; trial **2.** a

short piece of writing in which the writer attempts to analyze or interpret something in a personal way —see SYN. at TRY —es·say′er *n.*

es·say·ist (es′ā ist) *n.* a writer of essays

Es·sen (es′'n) city in W West Germany, in the Ruhr valley: pop. 697,000

es·sence (es′'ns) *n.* [< OFr. & < L. *essentia* < *esse*, to be: for IE. base see IS] **1.** something that exists; entity **2.** that which makes something what it is; fundamental nature or most important quality (of something) [the *essence* of law is justice] **3.** *a)* a substance that keeps, in a strong, pure form, the flavor, fragrance, etc. of the plant, drug, food, etc. from which it is taken *b)* a solution of such a substance in alcohol *c)* a perfume

Es·sene (es′ēn, ə sēn′) *n.* [< L. < Gr. *Essēnoi*] a member of a mystical Jewish sect, existing from the 2d century B.C. to the 2d century A.D.

es·sen·tial (ə sen′shəl) *adj.* **1.** of or constituting the essence of something; basic; inherent [kindness was an *essential* part of his character] **2.** absolutely necessary; indispensable [it is *essential* for guards on duty to stay awake] —*n.* something necessary, fundamental, or indispensable —es·sen·ti·al·i·ty (i sen′shē al′ə tē) *n.* —es·sen′tial·ly *adv.* —es·sen′tial·ness *n.*
SYN.—**essential** is applied to that which is the basic essence or fundamental nature of a thing and therefore must be present for the thing to exist, function, etc. [food is *essential* to life]; an **indispensable** person or thing cannot be done without if the specified purpose is to be achieved; **requisite** is applied to that which is required by the circumstances or for the purpose and often suggests a requirement that is demanded or insisted upon [the *requisite* skills for the job]; **necessary** implies an urgent or pressing need but not always for something that is indispensable

es·sen·tial·ism (-iz′m) *n. Philos.* a theory which stresses essence as opposed to existence

essential oil any volatile oil that gives a plant, flower, or fruit its characteristic odor, flavor, etc.

Es·sex (es′iks), 2d Earl of (*Robert Devereux*) 1566–1601; Eng. soldier & courtier

-est (ist, əst) [< OE. *-est, -ost, -ast*] *a suffix used to form:* **1.** the superlative degree of adjectives and adverbs [greatest, soonest] **2.** the archaic second person singular of verbs, in the present tense [thou goest]

EST, E.S.T. Eastern Standard Time

est. **1.** established **2.** estimate **3.** estimated

es·tab·lish (ə stab′lish) *vt.* [< OFr. *establir* < L. < *stabilis*, STABLE¹] **1.** to make stable; settle [to establish a habit] **2.** to order, ordain, or enact (a law, statute, etc.) permanently **3.** to set up (a nation, business, etc.); found **4.** to cause to be; bring about [to establish good relations] **5.** to settle in an office, or set up in business or a profession **6.** to make (a particular church or religion) the official one of a state or nation **7.** to cause (a precedent, theory, etc.) to be accepted or recognized **8.** to prove; demonstrate (a case at law) —es·tab′lish·er *n.*

established church the only church officially recognized and supported by a government; specif., [E- C-] the Church of England

es·tab·lish·ment (-mənt) *n.* **1.** an establishing or being established **2.** a thing established, as a business, military organization, household, etc. —**the Establishment** the ruling inner circle of any nation, institution, etc.

es·tate (ə stāt′) *n.* [< OFr. *estat*, STATE] **1.** *a)* condition or state [to restore the theater to its former *estate*] *b)* stage of life [boys finally come to man's *estate*] *c)* social status or rank **2.** formerly, any of the three social classes having specific political powers: the clergy (**first estate**), the nobility (**second estate**), and the commons, or bourgeoisie (**third estate**) **3.** property; possessions **4.** landed property; individually owned piece of land containing a residence, esp. one that is large and maintained by great wealth **5.** *Law a)* the degree, nature, and extent of ownership that one has in land or other property *b)* all the property, real or personal, owned by one, or left by a dead person —**the fourth estate** [see sense 2] journalism or journalists

es·teem (ə stēm′) *vt.* [< OFr. < L. *aestimare*, to value, estimate] **1.** to have great regard for; value highly; respect [he *esteemed* her love for him] **2.** to hold to be; consider [we *esteem* it an honor to be invited] —*n.* favorable opinion; high regard [their gift to him is a sign of their *esteem*] —see SYN. at APPRECIATE and REGARD

Es·tel·la (e stel′ə) [Sp. < L. *Stella*, lit., star] a feminine name: var. *Estelle*

es·ter (es′tər) *n.* [G., contr. < *essig*, vinegar + *äther*, ETHER] an organic compound, comparable to an inorganic salt, formed by the reaction of an acid and an alcohol, or a phenol: the organic radical of the alcohol or phenol replaces the acid hydrogen of the acid

es·ter·ase (-ās′) *n.* [ESTER + -ASE] any of certain enzymes that can speed up the hydrolysis or synthesis of esters

Es·ther (es′tər) [< LL. < Gr. < Heb. *estēr*, prob. < Bab. *Ishtar*, Ishtar] **1.** a feminine name **2.** *Bible a)* the Jewish wife of a Persian king: she saved her people from slaughter *b)* the book telling her story: abbrev. **Esth.**

es·thete (es′thēt) *n.* same as AESTHETE —**es·thet·ic** (-thet′ik) *adj.* —**es·thet′i·cal·ly** *adv.* —**es·thet′i·cism** (-ə siz′m) *n.*

es·thet·ics (es thet′iks) *n.pl.* same as AESTHETICS

es·ti·ma·ble (es′tə mə b′l) *adj.* worthy of esteem —**es′ti·ma·ble·ness** *n.* —**es′ti·ma·bly** *adv.*

es·ti·mate (es′tə māt′; *for n.* -mit) *vt.* -**mat′ed**, -**mat′ing** [< L. pp. of *aestimare*: see ESTEEM] **1.** to form an opinion about [to *estimate* the merits of a movie] **2.** to make a general but careful guess about (size, value, cost, etc.) [he *estimated* the size of the crowd to be 300] —*vi.* to make an estimate —*n.* **1.** a general calculation of size, value, etc.; esp., an approximate figuring of the probable cost of a piece of work made by a person undertaking to do the work **2.** an opinion or judgment [this is a good book in my *estimate*] —**es′ti·ma′tive** *adj.* —**es′ti·ma′tor** *n.*
SYN.—**estimate** refers generally to the forming of a personal opinion or judgment; **appraise** implies the intention of giving an accurate or expert judgment, as of value or worth [to *appraise* a new house]; **evaluate** also connotes an attempt at an exact judgment, but rarely with reference to value in terms of money [let us *evaluate* the evidence]; **rate** implies the comparing of one person or thing with another or others as to value, quality, etc. [he is *rated* the best in his field] —see also SYN. at CALCULATE

es·ti·ma·tion (es′tə mā′shən) *n.* **1.** an estimating **2.** an opinion or judgment **3.** esteem; regard; respect [he is held in *estimation* by his fellow workers]

es·ti·val (es′tə v′l, es tī′-) *adj.* [< L. < *aestivus* < *aestas*, summer: for IE. base see ETHER] of or for summer

es·ti·vate (es′tə vāt′) *vi.* -**vat′ed**, -**vat′ing** [< L. pp. of *aestivare* < *aestas*: see ESTIVAL] **1.** to spend the summer **2.** to pass the summer in a dormant state, as snails: compare HIBERNATE —**es′ti·va′tion** *n.*

Es·to·ni·a (es tō′nē ə) republic of the U.S.S.R., in NE Europe, on the Baltic Sea: 17,410 sq. mi.; pop. 1,357,000; cap. Tallinn: in full, **Estonian Soviet Socialist Republic** —**Es·to′ni·an** *adj., n.*

es·top (e stäp′) *vt.* -**topped′**, -**top′ping** [< Anglo-Fr. & OFr. < L. *stuppa*, oakum] *Law* to stop or prevent (a person) from contradicting a previous statement

es·trange (ə strānj′) *vt.* -**tranged′**, -**trang′ing** [OFr. *estranger* < ML. < L. *extraneus*, STRANGE] **1.** to remove; keep apart or away **2.** to turn (a person) from an affectionate or friendly attitude to an indifferent, unfriendly, or hostile one; alienate the affections of —**es·trange′ment** *n.*

es·tro·gen (es′trə jən) *n.* [< ESTRUS + -GEN] any of several female sex hormones or synthetic compounds used in place of these —**es′tro·gen′ic** (-jen′ik) *adj.*

estrous cycle the regular reproductive cycle in most female mammals: it is controlled by hormones and includes a period of heat

es·trus (es′trəs, ēs′-) *n.* [ModL. < L. *oestrus* < Gr. *oistros*, frenzy] the periodic sexual excitement, or heat, of most female mammals, or the period of this Also **es′trum** (-trəm) —**es′trous** *adj.*

es·tu·ar·y (es′choo wer′ē) *n., pl.* -**ar′ies** [< L. < *aestus*, the tide, akin to *aestas*: see ESTIVAL] an inlet or arm of the sea; esp., the wide mouth of a river, where the tide meets the current —**es′tu·ar′i·al**, **es′tu·ar·ine** (-wər in, -īn′) *adj.*

-et (it, ət) [< OFr. -*et*, masc., -*ete* (Fr. -*ette*), fem.] a suffix added to nouns, meaning little [islet]

e·ta (āt′ə, ēt′ə) *n.* the seventh letter of the Greek alphabet (H, η)

‡é·ta·gère (ā tä zher′) *n.* [Fr.] a stand with open shelves like a whatnot, for displaying small art objects, ornaments, etc.

et al. 1. [L. *et alibi*] and elsewhere **2.** [L. *et alii*] and others

etc. et cetera

et cet·er·a (et set′ər ə, set′rə) [L.] and others; and the like; and the rest; and so forth

et·cet·er·as (-əz, -rəz) *n.pl.* additional things or persons; customary extras

etch (ech) *vt.* [< Du. < G. < MHG. *etzen*, to cause to eat: for

IE. base see EAT] **1.** to make (a drawing, design, etc.) on metal, glass, etc. by the action of an acid, esp. by coating the surface with wax and letting the acid eat into lines and areas laid bare with a needle **2.** to engrave (a metal plate, glass, etc.) in this way for use in printing such drawings, etc. **3.** to picture or impress sharply and distinctly [the adventure is *etched* in his memory] —*vi.* to make etchings —**etch′er** *n.*

etch·ing (ech′iŋ) *n.* **1.** an etched plate, drawing, or design **2.** a print made from an etched plate **3.** the art of making such drawings, etc.

e·ter·nal (i tur′n′l) *adj.* [< OFr. < LL. *aeternalis* < L. < *aevum*, an age: for IE. base see AGE] **1.** without beginning or end; everlasting **2.** of eternity **3.** forever the same; unchanging [eternal truths] **4.** never stopping or ending; perpetual [eternal fame] **5.** seeming never to stop; continual [eternal bickering] **6.** timeless —**the Eternal God** —see SYN. at CONTINUAL —**e·ter′nal·ly** *adv.* —**e·ter′nal·ness** *n.*

e·ter·ni·ty (i tur′nə tē) *n., pl.* -**ties 1.** the quality, state, or fact of being eternal; continuance without end **2.** infinite time; time without beginning or end **3.** a long period of time that seems endless [an *eternity* of waiting] **4.** the endless time after death

e·ter·nize (-nīz) *vt.* -**nized**, -**niz·ing 1.** to make eternal **2.** to make famous forever; immortalize Also **e·ter′nal·ize′ -ized′, -iz′ing** —**e·ter′ni·za′tion** *n.*

-eth¹ (əth, ith) same as -TH² [fortieth, sixtieth, etc.]

-eth² (ith, əth) [< OE. -(*a*)*th*] archaic ending of the third person singular of verbs, in the present tense [asketh, bringeth]: see also -TH³

Eth. 1. Ethiopia **2.** Ethiopian **3.** Ethiopic

E·than (ē′thən) [LL. < Heb. *ēthān*, strength] a masculine name

eth·ane (eth′ān) *n.* [ETH(YL) + -ANE] an odorless, colorless, gaseous hydrocarbon, C_2H_6: it is found in natural gas and used as a fuel, etc.

eth·a·nol (eth′ə nôl′, -nōl) *n.* [ETHAN(E) + -OL¹] same as ALCOHOL (sense 1)

Eth·el (eth′əl) [< OE. < *æthel*, noble] a feminine name

Eth·el·red II (eth′əl red′) 968–1016; king of England (978–1016): called *the Unready*

eth·ene (eth′ēn) *n.* same as ETHYLENE

e·ther (ē′thər) *n.* [< L. < Gr. *aithēr* < *aithein*, to kindle, burn < IE. base *aidh-*, to burn] **1.** the upper regions of space; clear sky **2.** *Chem.* a volatile, colorless, highly flammable liquid, $(C_2H_5)_2O$: it is used as an anesthetic and a solvent for resins and fats **3.** *Physics* an invisible substance thought of (in older theory) as filling all space and serving as the medium for the transmission of radiant energy, as light waves

e·the·re·al (i thir′ē əl) *adj.* **1.** of or like the ether, or upper regions of space **2.** very light; airy; delicate [ethereal music] **3.** heavenly —**e·the′re·al′i·ty** (-al′ə tē), **e·the′re·al·ness** *n.* —**e·the′re·al·ly** *adv.*

e·the·re·al·ize (-ə līz′) *vt.* -**ized′, -iz′ing** to make, or treat as being, ethereal —**e·the′re·al·i·za′tion** *n.*

e·ther·ize (ē′thə rīz′) *vt.* -**ized′, -iz′ing** ☆to anesthetize as by causing to inhale ether fumes —**e′ther·i·za′tion** *n.*

eth·ic (eth′ik) *n.* **1.** ethics or a system of ethics [the humanist *ethic*] **2.** any single element in a system of ethics —*adj.* same as ETHICAL

eth·i·cal (-i k′l) *adj.* [< L. < Gr. *ēthikos* < *ēthos*, character, custom + -AL] **1.** having to do with ethics or morality; of or conforming to moral standards [ethical principles] **2.** conforming to professional standards of conduct [ethical medical practice] **3.** designating or of a drug available only on a doctor's prescription —see SYN. at MORAL —**eth′i·cal′i·ty** (-kal′ə tē), **eth′i·cal·ness** *n.* —**eth′i·cal·ly** *adv.*

eth·ics (eth′iks) *n.pl.* [with sing. v. in 1 & 2, and occas. 3] [see prec.] **1.** the study of standards of conduct and moral judgment **2.** a treatise on this study **3.** the system or code of morals of a particular person, religion, group, profession, etc. [legal *ethics*]

E·thi·o·pi·a (ē′thē ō′pē ə) **1.** ancient kingdom in NE Africa, corresponding to modern Sudan & N Ethiopia (sense 2) **2.** country in E Africa, on the Red Sea: 457,000 sq. mi.; pop. 25,248,000; cap. Addis Ababa —**E′thi·o′pi·an** *adj., n.*

E·thi·op·ic (-äp′ik, -ō′pik) *adj.* **1.** same as ETHIOPIAN **2.** of the Semitic languages of the Ethiopians —*n.* **1.** the classical Semitic language of Ethiopia, used in the liturgy of the Christian church in Ethiopia **2.** the group of languages spoken by Ethiopians, belonging to the Semitic branch of the Afro-Asiatic language family

eth·moid (eth′moid) *adj.* [< Gr. < *ēthmos*, strainer + *eidos*, form] designating or of any of the bones forming the nose that have holes through which the olfactory nerves pass —*n.* an ethmoid bone

eth·nic (eth′nik) *adj.* [< LL. < Gr. *ethnikos*, national < *ethnos*, nation] designating or of any of the basic groups or divisions of mankind or of a mixed population, set apart by its customs, attitudes, language, etc.; ethnological Also **eth′ni·cal** —*n.* a member of an ethnic group, esp. one belonging to a minority or nationality group in a larger community, who clings to the customs, attitudes, etc. of his group —**eth′ni·cal·ly** *adv.*

eth·no- [< Gr. *ethnos*, nation] *a combining form meaning* ethnic group or division; people or peoples [*ethnology*]: also, before a vowel, **ethn-**

eth·no·cen·trism (eth′nə sen′triz′m) *n.* the emotional attitude that one's own ethnic group, nation, or culture is superior to all others —**eth′no·cen′tric** *adj.* —**eth′no·cen′tri·cal·ly** *adv.*

eth·nog·ra·phy (eth näg′rə fē) *n.* the branch of anthropology concerned with describing specific cultures, esp. those of nonliterate peoples —**eth·nog′ra·pher** *n.* —**eth′no·graph′ic** (-nə-graf′ik), **eth′no·graph′i·cal·ly** *adv.*

eth·nol·o·gy (eth näl′ə jē) *n.* the branch of anthropology that deals with the comparative cultures of various peoples, including their distribution, characteristics, folkways, etc. —**eth·no·log·i·cal** (-nə läj′i k'l), **eth′no·log′ic** *adj.* —**eth′no·log′i·cal·ly** *adv.* —**eth·nol′o·gist** *n.*

e·thol·o·gy (e thäl′ə jē, ē-) *n.* [L. *ethologia*, character portrayal < Gr.: see ETHOS & -LOGY] *Biol.* the scientific study of the characteristic behavior patterns of animals —**e·tho·log·i·cal** (eth′ə läj′i k'l, ē′thə-) *adj.* —**e·thol′o·gist** *n.*

e·thos (ē′thäs) *n.* [Gr. *ēthos*, character] the characteristic attitudes, habits, beliefs, etc. of an individual or group

eth·yl (eth′'l) *n.* [ETH(ER) + -YL] the monovalent hydrocarbon radical, C_2H_5, which forms the base of common alcohol, ether, and many other compounds

ethyl alcohol *same as* ALCOHOL (sense 1)

☆**eth·yl·ene** (eth′ə lēn′) *n.* [ETHYL + -ENE] a colorless, flammable, gaseous hydrocarbon, C_2H_4, used as a fuel and anesthetic, in hastening the ripening of fruits, and to form polyethylene

☆**ethylene glycol** a colorless, viscous alcohol, $C_2H_6O_2$, used as an antifreeze or solvent, in resins, etc.

e·ti·ol·o·gy (ē′tē äl′ə jē) *n., pl.* **-gies** [< LL. < Gr. < *aitia*, cause + -LOGY] **1.** the finding of a cause, or the cause found [the *etiology* of a folkway] **2.** the science of causes or origins **3.** *Med.* the causes of a disease —**e′ti·o·log′ic** (-ə läj′ik), **e′ti·o·log′i·cal** *adj.* —**e′ti·o·log′i·cal·ly** *adv.*

et·i·quette (et′i kət, -ket′) *n.* [Fr. *étiquette*, a ticket] the forms, manners, and ceremonies established by general agreement as acceptable or required in social relations

Et·na (et′nə) volcanic mountain in E Sicily

E·ton (ēt′'n) town in SC England, near London: site of a private preparatory school for boys (**Eton College**) —**E·to·ni·an** (ē tō′nē ən) *adj., n.*

Eton collar a broad, white linen collar worn with an Eton jacket, or a collar like this

Eton jacket (or **coat**) a black, waist-length jacket with broad lapels, left open in front, as that worn by students at Eton

E·tru·ri·a (i troor′ē ə) ancient country in what is now WC Italy

E·trus·can (i trus′kən) *adj.* of Etruria, its people, their language, or culture —*n.* **1.** a native or inhabitant of Etruria **2.** the language of the ancient Etruscans Also **E·tru·ri·an** (i troor′ē ən)

et seq. 1. [L. *et sequens*] and the following **2.** [L. *et sequentes* or *et sequentia*] and those that follow

Et·ta (et′ə) [dim. of HENRIETTA] a feminine name

-ette (et) [Fr.: see -ET] *a suffix meaning:* **1.** little

ETRURIA (8th cent. B.C.)

[*statuette*] ☆**2.** female [*majorette*] **3.** a substitute for [*leatherette*]

é·tude (ā′tōōd, -tyōōd; *Fr.* ā tüd′) *n.* [Fr., STUDY] a musical composition for a solo instrument, designed to give practice in some special point of technique, but often performed for its artistic worth

ETV educational television

ety., etym., etymol. 1. etymological **2.** etymology

et·y·mo·log·i·cal (et′ə mə läj′ə k'l) *adj.* of or according to the etymology, or to the principles of etymology —**et′y·mo·log′i·cal·ly** *adv.*

et·y·mol·o·gist (et′ə mäl′ə jist) *n.* an expert in etymology

et·y·mol·o·gize (-jīz′) *vt., vi.* **-gized′, -giz′ing** to trace the etymology of (a word or words)

et·y·mol·o·gy (et′ə mäl′ə jē) *n., pl.* **-gies** [< OFr. < L. < Gr. < *etymon*, literal sense of a word, neut. of *etymos*, true + -LOGY] the origin and development of a word, affix, phrase, etc.; the tracing of a word or words back as far as possible, or the branch of linguistics dealing with this

eu- [Fr. < Gr.] *a prefix meaning* good, well [*eulogy, eugenic*]: opposed to DYS-, CACO-

Eu *Chem.* europium

Eu·boe·a (yōō bē′ə) *former name of* EVVOIA: see map at GREECE

eu·ca·lyp·tus (yōō′kə lip′təs) *n., pl.* **-tus·es, -ti** (-tī) [ModL. < EU- + Gr. *kalyptos*, covered (from the covering of the buds) < *kalyptein*, to cover] a tall evergreen tree of the myrtle family, found chiefly in Australia and valued for its timber, gum, and oil: also **eu′ca·lypt′**

EUCALYPTUS
(tree and leaves)

eucalyptus oil an oil taken from eucalyptus leaves that is used as an antiseptic

Eu·cha·rist (yōō′kə rist) *n.* [< OFr. < LL. < Gr. *eucharistia*, gratitude < *eu-*, well + *charis*, favor] **1.** *same as* HOLY COMMUNION **2.** the consecrated bread and wine used in Holy Communion —**Eu′cha·ris′tic** *adj.*

☆**eu·chre** (yōō′kər) *n.* [earlier *yuker, uker* < ?] **1.** a card game for two, three, or four players, played with thirty-two cards **2.** a euchring or being euchred —*vt.* **-chred, -chring 1.** to prevent (the trump-declaring opponent at euchre) from taking the required three tricks **2.** [Colloq.] to outwit

Eu·clid¹ (yōō′klid) fl. 300 B.C.; Gr. mathematician: author of a basic work in geometry —**Eu·clid′e·an, Eu·clid′i·an** (-ē ən) *adj.*

Eu·clid² (yōō′klid) [so named (after prec.) by its surveyors] city in NE Ohio: suburb of Cleveland: pop. 72,000

Eu·gene¹ (yōō′jēn; *for 2, Fr.* ö zhen′) **1.** [< Fr. < L. *Eugenius* < Gr. < *eugenēs*, well-born] a masculine name **2.** Prince, (*François Eugène de Savoie-Carignan*) 1663–1736; Austrian general, born in France

Eu·gene² (yōō jēn′) [after *Eugene* Skinner, early settler] city in W Oreg.: pop. 76,000

Eu·ge·ni·a (yōō jē′nē ə, -jēn′yə) [L., fem. of *Eugenius*: see EUGENE¹] a feminine name

eu·gen·ic (yōō jen′ik) *adj.* [< Gr.: see EU- & GENESIS] **1.** relating to the bearing of healthy offspring **2.** of, relating to, or improved by eugenics Also **eu·gen′i·cal** —**eu·gen′i·cal·ly** *adv.*

eu·gen·i·cist (-ə sist) *n.* a specialist in or advocate of eugenics: also **eu·gen·ist** (yōō′jə nist, yōō jen′ist)

eu·gen·ics (yōō jen′iks) *n.pl.* [*with sing. v.*] the movement devoted to improving the human species by control of hereditary factors in mating

Eu·gé·nie (yōō jē′nē; *Fr.* ö zhā nē′), Empress (*Eugénie Marie de Montijo de Guzmán*) 1826–1920; wife of Louis Napoleon & empress of France (1853–71), born in Spain

eu·gle·na (yōō glē′nə) *n.* [ModL. < EU- + Gr. *glenē*, pupil of the eye] any of a group of green protozoans with a single flagellum and a red pigment spot

Eu·ler (oi′lər), **Le·on·hard** (lā′ôn härt′) 1707–83; Swiss mathematician

eu·lo·gis·tic (yōō′lə jis′tik) *adj.* of or expressing eulogy; praising highly —**eu′lo·gis′ti·cal·ly** *adv.*

eu·lo·gi·um (yōō lō′jē əm) *n., pl.* **-gi·ums, -gi·a** (-ə) [ML.] *same as* EULOGY

eu·lo·gize (yōō′lə jīz′) *vt.* **-gized′, -giz′ing** to praise as in a eulogy; say very good things about —see SYN.at PRAISE —**eu′lo·gist, eu′lo·giz′er** *n.*

eu·lo·gy (-jē) *n., pl.* **-gies** [< ML. < Gr. < *eulegein,* to speak well of] **1.** speech or writing in praise of a person or thing; esp., a funeral oration **2.** high praise —see SYN.at TRIBUTE

Eu·men·i·des (yōō men′ə dēz′) *n.pl.* [L. < Gr. *Eumenidēs,* lit., gracious ones: so called to win their favor] *same as* FURIES

Eu·nice (yōō′nis) [LL. < Gr. *Eunikē* < *eu-,* well + *nikē,* victory] a feminine name

eu·nuch (yōō′nək) *n.* [< L. < Gr. *eunouchos,* bed guardian < *eunē,* bed + *echein,* to keep] a castrated man; esp., one in charge of a harem or employed as a chamberlain in an Oriental palace

eu·pep·si·a (yōō pep′shə, -sē ə) *n.* [ModL. < Gr. *eupepsia,* digestibility] good digestion —**eu·pep′tic** *adj.*

eu·phe·mism (yōō′fə miz′m) *n.* [< Gr. < *eu-,* good + *phēmē,* voice < *phanai,* to speak: for IE. base see BAN¹] **1.** the use of a word or phrase that is less expressive or direct but considered less distasteful or offensive than another **2.** a word or phrase so substituted (Ex.: *remains* for *corpse*) —**eu′phe·mist** *n.* —**eu′phe·mis′tic, eu′phe·mis′ti·cal** *adj.* —**eu′phe·mis′ti·cal·ly** *adv.*

eu·phe·mize (-mīz′) *vt., vi.* **-mized′, -miz′ing** to use euphemisms in speaking or writing (of)

eu·phon·ic (yōō fän′ik) *adj.* **1.** of euphony **2.** *same as* EUPHONIOUS Also **eu·phon′i·cal** —**eu·phon′i·cal·ly** *adv.*

eu·pho·ni·ous (yōō fō′nē əs) *adj.* characterized by euphony; having a pleasant sound; harmonious —**eu·pho′ni·ous·ly** *adv.* —**eu·pho′ni·ous·ness** *n.*

eu·pho·ni·um (-əm) *n.* a brass-wind instrument like the baritone but having a more mellow tone

eu·pho·ny (yōō′fə nē) *n., pl.* **-nies** [< LL. < Gr. < *eu-,* well + *phōnē,* voice: for IE. base see BAN¹] the quality of having a pleasing sound; pleasant combining of agreeable sounds in spoken words

eu·phor·bi·a (yōō fôr′bē ə) *n.* [< L. < *Euphorbus,* physician of 1st cent. A.D.] *same as* SPURGE

eu·pho·ri·a (yōō fôr′ē ə) *n.* [ModL. < Gr. < *eu-,* well + *pherein,* BEAR¹] a feeling of well-being or high spirits, specif. *Psychol.* a feeling of this sort that seems exaggerated and without cause —**eu·phor′ic** *adj.*

eu·pho·tic (yōō fōt′ik) *adj.* [< EU- + Gr. *phōtos,* genitive of *phōs,* a light + -IC] *Ecol.* of or pertaining to the upper portion of a body of water, which receives enough light for photosynthesis and plant growth

Eu·phra·tes (yōō frāt′ēz) river flowing from EC Turkey through Syria & Iraq, joining the Tigris to form the Shatt-al-Arab

eu·phu·ism (yōō′fyōō wiz′m) *n.* [< *Euphues,* fictitious character in two works by J. LYLY < Gr. *euphyēs,* graceful < *eu-,* well + *phyē,* growth] **1.** an artificial, affected style of speaking or writing, esp. such a style of the late 16th cent., using alliteration, balanced sentences, farfetched figures of speech, etc. **2.** an instance of this —**eu′phu·ist** *n.* —**eu′phu·is′tic, eu′phu·is′ti·cal** *adj.* —**eu′phu·is′ti·cal·ly** *adv.*

Eur. **1.** Europe **2.** European

Eur·a·sia (yōō rā′zhə; *chiefly Brit.* -shə) land mass made up of the continents of Europe & Asia

Eur·a·sian (-zhən; *chiefly Brit.* -shən) *adj.* **1.** of Eurasia **2.** of mixed European and Asian descent —*n.* a person with one European parent and one Asian parent, or of mixed European and Asian descent

Eur·a·tom (yoor′ə täm′) European Atomic Energy Community, an agency of the European Economic Community

eu·re·ka (yōō rē′kə) *interj.* [Gr. *heurēka*] I have found (it): an exclamation of triumphant achievement

eu·rhyth·mics (yōō rith′miks) *n.pl. same as* EURYTHMICS — **eu·rhyth′mic** *adj.* —**eu·rhyth′my** *n.*

Eu·rip·i·des (yōō rip′ə dēz′) 479?–406? B.C.; Gr. writer of tragedies —**Eu·rip′i·de′an** (-dē′ən) *adj.*

Eu·ro·com·mu·nism (yoor′ə käm′yə niz′m) *n.* a policy of some European Communist parties of remaining independent of the U.S.S.R., supporting democratic political systems, etc. — **Eu′ro·com′mu·nist** *n., adj.*

Eu·ro·mart (yoor′ə märt′) *n. same as* EUROPEAN ECONOMIC COMMUNITY: also **Eu′ro·mar′ket** (-mär′kit)

Eu·ro·pa (yōō rō′pə) *Gr. Myth.* a Phoenician princess loved by Zeus: disguised as a white bull, he carried her off to Crete

Eu·rope (yoor′əp) continent between Asia (or the Ural Mountains) & the Atlantic Ocean: c.3,750,000 sq. mi.; pop. c.647,837,000 —**Eu′ro·pe′an** (-ə pē′ən) *adj., n.*

European Economic Community the European common market formed in 1958 by Belgium, France, West Germany, Italy, Luxembourg, and the Netherlands, and joined, in 1973, by Denmark, Ireland, and the United Kingdom

☆**European plan** a system of hotel operation in which the charge to guests covers rooms and service but not meals: distinguished from AMERICAN PLAN

eu·ro·pi·um (yōō rō′pē əm) *n.* [ModL. < EUROPE] a chemical element of the rare-earth group: symbol, Eu; at. wt., 151.96; at. no., 63

Eu·ryd·i·ce (yōō rid′ə sē′) *Gr. Myth.* the wife of Orpheus: see ORPHEUS

eu·ryth·mics (yōō rith′miks) *n.pl.* [*with sing. v.*] [< L. < Gr. < *eu-,* well + *rhythmos,* RHYTHM] the art of performing various bodily movements in rhythm, usually to musical accompaniment —**eu·ryth′mic, eu·ryth′mi·cal** *adj.*

Eu·sta·chi·an tube (yōō stā′shən, -shē ən, -kē ən) [after B. *Eustachio* (1520–1574), It. anatomist] a slender tube between the middle ear and the pharynx, which serves to make air pressure equal on both sides of the eardrum: see illustration at EAR

Eu·ter·pe (yōō tur′pē) *Gr. Myth.* the Muse of music and lyric poetry

eu·tha·na·si·a (yōō′thə nā′zhə, -zhē ə) *n.* [< Gr. < *eu-,* well + *thanatos,* death] **1.** an easy and painless death **2.** act or method of causing death painlessly to end suffering: advocated by some in cases of incurable, painful diseases

☆**eu·then·ics** (yōō then′iks) *n.pl.* [*with sing. v.*] [< Gr. *euthēnein,* to flourish + -ICS] the movement devoted to improving species and breeds, esp. the human species, by control of environmental factors

eu·troph·ic (yōō träf′ik, -trō′fik) *adj.* [< EU- + Gr. *trophikos* < *trophē,* food] designating or of a lake, pond, etc. rich in mineral and plant nutrients but often lacking in oxygen —**eu′troph·i·ca′tion** *n.*

Eux·ine Sea (yōōk′sən, -sīn) *ancient name of the* BLACK SEA

ev, EV electron-volt

E·va (ē′və, ev′ə) [var. of EVE] a feminine name

EVA extravehicular activity

e·vac·u·ate (i vak′yōō wāt′) *vt.* **-at′ed, -at′ing** [< L. pp. of *evacuare* < *e-,* out + *vacuare,* to make empty < *vacuus,* empty] **1.** to make empty; remove the contents of; specif., to remove the air from **2.** to discharge (bodily waste, esp. feces) **3.** to remove (inhabitants, troops, etc.) from (a place or area), as for protective purposes —*vi.* **1.** to withdraw, as from a danger area **2.** to discharge bodily waste —**e·vac′u·a′tion** *n.* —**e·vac′u·a′tive** *adj.* —**e·vac′u·a′tor** *n.*

e·vac·u·ee (i vak′yōō wē′, i vak′yōō wē′) *n.* a person evacuated from an area of danger

e·vade (i vād′) *vi.* **e·vad′ed, e·vad′ing** [< Fr. < L. < *e-,* out, from + *vadere,* to go] to be tricky or clever in avoiding or escaping something —*vt.* **1.** to avoid or escape from by means of tricks or cleverness **2.** to avoid doing or answering directly [*to evade tax payment*] —see SYN.at ESCAPE —**e·vad′er** *n.*

e·val·u·ate (i val′yōō wāt′) *vt.* **-at′ed, -at′ing** [< Fr. < *é-* (L. *ex-*), out + *valuer,* to VALUE] **1.** to find the value or amount of [*he evaluated the cost of repairs*] **2.** to judge or determine the worth or quality of; appraise [*critics evaluate new books*] —see SYN.at ESTIMATE —**e·val′u·a′tion** *n.* —**e·val′u·a′tive** *adj.*

Ev·an (ev′ən) [W., var. of JOHN] a masculine name

ev·a·nesce (ev′ə nes′) *vi.* **-nesced′, -nesc′ing** [< L. < *e-,* out + *vanescere,* to vanish < *vanus,* empty] to fade from sight like mist or smoke; vanish

ev·a·nes·cent (-nes′nt) *adj.* tending to fade away; vanishing; fleeting —see SYN.at TRANSIENT —**ev′a·nes′cence** *n.* — **ev′a·nes′cent·ly** *adv.*

e·van·gel (i van′jəl) *n.* [< OFr. < LL. < Gr. *euangelos,* bringing good news < *eu-,* well + *angelos,* messenger] **1.** the gospel **2.** [E-] any of the four Gospels **3.** an evangelist

e·van·gel·i·cal (ē′van jel′i k′l, ev′ən-) *adj.* **1.** in, of, or according to the Gospels or the New Testament **2.** of those Protestant churches, as the Methodist and Baptist, that emphasize salvation by faith in the atonement of Jesus **3.** *same as* EVANGELISTIC Also **e′van·gel′ic** —*n.* a member of an evangelical church —**e′van·gel′i·cal·ism** *n.* —**e′van·gel′i·cal·ly** *adv.*

e·van·gel·ism (i van′jə liz′m) *n.* **1.** a preaching of the gospel, or an enthusiastic effort to spread the gospel, as in revival meetings **2.** any enthusiastic effort in propagandizing for a cause —**e·van′gel·is′tic** *adj.* —**e·van′gel·is′ti·cal·ly** *adv.*

e·van·gel·ist (-list) *n.* **1.** [E-] any of the four writers of the Gospels; Matthew, Mark, Luke, or John **2.** anyone who evangelizes; esp., a traveling preacher; revivalist

e·van·gel·ize (-līz′) *vt.* **-ized′, -iz′ing 1.** to preach the gospel to **2.** to convert to Christianity —*vi.* to preach the gospel —**e·van′gel·i·za′tion** *n.*

Ev·ans·ton (ev′ən stən) [after Dr. J. *Evans*, local philanthropist] city in NE Ill.: suburb of Chicago: pop. 80,000

Ev·ans·ville (ev′ənz vil′) [after Gen. R. *Evans*, who served in the War of 1812] city in SW Ind., on the Ohio River: pop. 139,000

e·vap·o·rate (i vap′ə rāt′) *vt.* **-rat′ed, -rat′ing** [< L. pp. of *evaporare* < *e-*, out + *vapor*, vapor] **1.** to change (a liquid or solid) into vapor **2.** to remove moisture from (milk, vegetables, etc.), as by heating, so as to get a concentrated product —*vi.* **1.** to become vapor [the perfume in the bottle has *evaporated*] **2.** to give off vapor **3.** to disappear; vanish [his courage *evaporated* when he saw the lion] —**e·vap′o·ra·bil′i·ty** *n.* —**e·vap′o·ra·ble** *adj.* —**e·vap′o·ra′tion** *n.* —**e·vap′o·ra′tive** *adj.* —**e·vap′o·ra′tor** *n.*

☆**evaporated milk** unsweetened milk thickened by evaporation to about half its weight, and then canned: see also CONDENSED MILK

e·va·sion (i vā′zhən) *n.* **1.** an evading; specif., an avoiding of a duty, question, etc. by means of tricks or cleverness **2.** a way of doing this; subterfuge

e·va·sive (-siv) *adj.* **1.** tending or seeking to evade; not straightforward; tricky **2.** hard to catch, grasp, etc.; elusive —**e·va′sive·ly** *adv.* —**e·va′sive·ness** *n.*

Eve (ēv) [< LL. < Heb. *ḥawwāh*, lit., ? life] **1.** a feminine name **2.** *Bible* Adam's wife, the first woman: Gen. 3:20

eve (ēv) *n.* [ME., var. of *even* < OE. *æfen*, EVENING] **1.** [Poet.] evening **2.** [often E-] the evening or day before a holiday [Christmas *Eve*] **3.** the period immediately before some event [on the *eve* of victory]

Ev·e·line (ev′ə lin′, -lēn′) [ONormFr. < *Aveline*, prob. ult. < Gmc.] a feminine name: var. *Evelina*

Ev·e·lyn (ev′ə lin′; *Brit. usually* ēv′lin) [see prec.] a feminine and masculine name

e·ven¹ (ē′vən, -v'n) *adj.* [OE. *efne, efen*] **1.** flat; level; smooth [*even* country] **2.** not varying; constant [an *even* tempo] **3.** calm; tranquil [an *even* disposition] **4.** in the same plane or line [the water is *even* with the rim] **5.** equally balanced **6.** *a)* owing and being owed nothing *b)* with neither a profit nor a loss **7.** revenged for a wrong, insult, etc. [he got *even* with his tormentors] **8.** just; fair [an *even* exchange] **9.** equal or identical in number, quantity, etc. **10.** exactly divisible by two [the *even* numbers are 2, 4, 6, 8, etc.] **11.** exact [an *even* mile] —*adv.* **1.** moreover; however improbable; indeed; fully [*even* a fool could do it] **2.** exactly; just [it happened *even* as I expected] **3.** just as; while [*even* as he spoke, she entered] **4.** comparatively; still; yet [an *even* worse mistake] —*vt., vi.* to make, become, or be even; level (*off*) —see SYN. at STEADY —☆**break even** [Colloq.] to finish as neither a winner nor a loser —**even if** in spite of the fact that; though —**e′ven·ly** *adv.* —**e′ven·ness** *n.*

e·ven² (ē′vən) *n.* [see EVE] [Poet.] evening

e·ven·fall (ē′vən fôl′) *n.* [Poet.] twilight; dusk

e·ven·hand·ed (-han′did) *adj.* not favoring one side more than another; impartial; fair —**e′ven·hand′ed·ly** *adv.* —**e′ven·hand′ed·ness** *n.*

eve·ning (ēv′niŋ) *n.* [< OE. < *æfnian*, to become evening < *æfen*, evening] **1.** the last part of the day and early part of night **2.** in some parts of the South, the period from noon through sunset **3.** the last period, as of life, a career, etc. —*adj.* in, for, or of the evening [*evening* dress or clothes]

evening primrose a plant having yellow flowers that open in the evening

eve·nings (-niŋz) *adv.* during every evening or most evenings

evening star a bright planet, esp. Venus, seen in the western sky soon after sunset

even money equal stakes in betting, with no odds

e·ven·song (ē′vən sôŋ′) *n.* **1.** *R.C.Ch.* vespers (see VESPER, sense 2*a*) **2.** *Anglican Ch.* the worship service assigned to the evening

e·ven·ste·ven, e·ven·ste·phen (ē′v'n stē′v'n) *adj.* [rhyming slang < EVEN¹ + STEVEN] [Colloq.] same as EVEN¹ (senses 4–9): also **even steven, even stephen**

e·vent (i vent′) *n.* [OFr. < L. pp. of *evenire*, to happen < *e-*, out + *venire*, COME] **1.** a happening or occurrence, esp. when important **2.** a result; outcome **3.** a particular contest or item in a program of sports [the final *event* in the track meet was the pole vault] —see SYN. at OCCURRENCE —**in any event** no matter what happens; anyhow: also **at all events** —**in the event of** in case of —**in the event that** if it should happen that

e·ven-tem·pered (ē′vən tem′pərd) *adj.* not quickly angered or excited; placid; calm

e·vent·ful (i vent′fəl) *adj.* **1.** full of outstanding events [an *eventful* year] **2.** having an important outcome [an *eventful* conversation] —**e·vent′ful·ly** *adv.* —**e·vent′ful·ness** *n.*

e·ven·tide (ē′vən tīd′) *n.* [Archaic] evening

e·ven·tu·al (i ven′choo wəl) *adj.* **1.** [Archaic] depending on events; contingent **2.** happening in the end; ultimate; final [*eventual* success] —**e·ven′tu·al·ly** *adv.*

e·ven·tu·al·i·ty (i ven′choo wal′ə tē) *n., pl.* **-ties** a possible event, outcome, or condition; contingency

☆**e·ven·tu·ate** (i ven′choo wāt′) *vi.* **-at′ed, -at′ing** to happen in the end; result (often with *in*)

ev·er (ev′ər) *adv.* [< OE. *æfre*] **1.** at all times; always [lived happily *ever* after] **2.** at any time [have you *ever* seen her?] **3.** at all; by any chance; in any way [how can I *ever* repay you?] **4.** [Colloq.] truly; indeed [was she *ever* tired!] —**ever so** [Colloq.] very —**for ever and a day** always: also **for ever and ever**

Ev·er·est (ev′ər ist, ev′rist), **Mount** peak of the Himalayas, on the border of Nepal & Tibet: highest known mountain in the world: 29,028 ft. See map at HIMALAYAS

Ev·er·ett (ev′ər it, ev′rit) [< Du. < OFr. < OHG. < *ebur*, wild boar + *harto*, strong] **1.** a masculine name **2.** [after *Everett* Colby, son of a founder] port in NW Wash., near Seattle: pop. 54,000

☆**ev·er·glade** (ev′ər glād′) *n.* swampland —**the Everglades** large tract of swampland in S Fla., part of which forms a national park (**Everglades National Park**)

ev·er·green (ev′ər grēn′) *adj.* having green leaves throughout the year: opposed to DECIDUOUS —*n.* **1.** an evergreen plant or tree, as a pine, spruce, etc. **2.** [*pl.*] the branches and twigs of evergreens, used for decoration

ev·er·last·ing (ev′ər las′tiŋ) *adj.* **1.** lasting forever; eternal **2.** going on for a long time **3.** going on too long; seeming never to stop [*everlasting* complaints] —*n.* **1.** eternity **2.** *a)* any of various plants whose blossoms keep their color and shape when dried; esp., an annual with pink, lilac, or white flowers *b)* the blossom of such a plant —**the Everlasting** God —**ev′er·last′ing·ly** *adv.*

THE EVERGLADES

ev·er·more (-môr′) *adv.* **1.** forever; constantly **2.** [Poet.] for all future time —**for evermore** forever

e·ver·sion (ē vur′zhən, -shən) *n.* an everting or being everted

e·vert (ē vurt′) *vt.* [L. *evertere* < *e-*, out + *vertere*: see VERSE] to turn outward or inside out, as an eyelid

ev·er·y (ev′rē; *occas.* -ər ē) *adj.* [< OE. *æfre ælc*, lit., ever each] **1.** each, individually and separately [*every* man among you] **2.** the fullest possible; all that there could be [he was given *every* chance] **3.** each group or interval of (a specified number or time) [take a pill *every* three hours] —**every now and then** from time to time; occasionally: also [Colloq.] **every so often** —**every other** each alternate, as the first, third, fifth, etc. —☆**every which way** [Colloq.] in complete disorder

ev·er·y·bod·y (-bäd′ē, -bud′ē) *pron.* every person; everyone

ev·er·y·day (-dā′) *adj.* **1.** daily [one's *everyday* routine] **2.** suitable for ordinary days [*everyday* shoes] **3.** usual; common [an *everyday* occurrence]

ev·er·y·one (-wən, -wun′) *pron.* every person; everybody

every one every person or thing of those named [remind *every one* of the students]

ev·er·y·thing (-thiŋ′) *pron.* 1. every thing; all 2. all things relating to a specified matter 3. the most important thing [money isn't *everything*]

ev·er·y·where (-hwer′, -wer′) *adv.* in or to every place

e·vict (i vikt′) *vt.* [< L. *evictus*, pp. of *evincere*: see EVINCE] to force (a person) by law to move from a house, apartment, etc. he has rented or leased, as for not paying his rent —see SYN. at EJECT —**e·vic′tion** *n.*

ev·i·dence (ev′ə dəns) *n.* 1. the condition of being evident 2. something that makes another thing evident; indication; sign [the clear, sunny sky gave *evidence* of a pleasant day] 3. something that tends to prove [one's fingerprints on an object are *evidence* that one has used it] 4. *Law* something presented before a court, as a statement of a witness, an object, etc., which is related to or establishes the point in question —*vt.* -**denced**, -**denc·ing** 1. to make evident; indicate; show 2. to bear witness to; attest —**in evidence** easily seen; in plain sight

ev·i·dent (-dənt, -dent′) *adj.* [< OFr. < L. *evidens*, clear < *e-*, from + prp. of *videre*, to see: see VISION] easy to see or perceive; clear; obvious; plain —**ev′i·dent·ly** *adv.*

SYN.—**evident** and **apparent** apply to that which can be easily recognized or inferred, but **evident** implies that something is real, true, genuine, etc. [his frown showed his *evident* disapproval] and **apparent** suggests that something may or may not be what it seems to be [we were deceived by his *apparent* friendliness]; **manifest** applies to that which is immediately clear to the understanding; **obvious** refers to that which is so noticeable that no one can fail to see or understand it; **palpable** applies especially to that which can be noticed or understood through some other sense than that of sight [palpable signs of fever]; **clear** implies that there is no confusion or vagueness to hinder understanding [clear proof]; **plain** implies being so simple or uncomplicated as to be easily seen or understood [the plain facts are these]

ev·i·den·tial (ev′ə den′shəl) *adj.* of, serving as, or providing evidence —**ev′i·den′tial·ly** *adv.*

e·vil (ē′v'l) *adj.* [OE. *yfel*: for IE. base see UP¹] 1. *a)* morally bad or wrong; wicked; depraved *b)* resulting from conduct regarded as immoral [an evil *reputation*] 2. harmful; injurious; troublesome [an evil *rumor*] 3. offensive or disgusting [an evil *odor*] 4. unlucky; disastrous; unfortunate [an evil *hour*] —*n.* 1. wickedness; depravity; sin 2. anything that causes harm, pain, trouble, disaster, etc. —**the Evil One** the Devil —**e′vil·ly** *adv.* —**e′vil·ness** *n.*

e·vil·do·er (-dōo′ər) *n.* a person who does evil; wicked person —**e′vil·do′ing** *n.*

evil eye a look which, in superstitious belief, is able to harm or bewitch the one stared at; also, the supposed power to cast such a look: with *the*

e·vil-mind·ed (-mīn′did) *adj.* having an evil mind; specif., *a)* intentionally harmful or wicked *b)* tending to think of things as being wicked, immoral, obscene, etc. even when they are not —**e′vil-mind′ed·ly** *adv.* —**e′vil-mind′ed·ness** *n.*

e·vince (i vins′) *vt.* **e·vinced′**, **e·vinc′ing** [< L. < *ex-*, thoroughly + *vincere*, to conquer: see VICTOR] to show plainly; make clear; esp., to show that one has (a specified quality, feeling, etc.) [he *evinced* interest in getting a scholarship] —**e·vin′ci·ble** *adj.* —**e·vin′cive** *adj.*

e·vis·cer·ate (i vis′ə rāt′) *vt.* -**at·ed**, -**at·ing** [< L. pp. of *eviscerare* < *e-*, out + *viscera*, VISCERA] 1. to remove the intestines and other internal organs from 2. to take away a vital part of —**e·vis′cer·a′tion** *n.*

ev·o·ca·ble (ev′ə kə b'l, i vō′kə b'l) *adj.* that can be evoked

ev·o·ca·tion (ev′ə kā′shən, ē′vō-) *n.* an evoking, or calling forth —**e·voc·a·tive** (i väk′ə tiv) *adj.* —**e·voc′a·tive·ly** *adv.* —**e·voc′a·tive·ness** *n.* —**ev′o·ca′tor** *n.*

e·voke (i vōk′) *vt.* **e·voked′**, **e·vok′ing** [< Fr. < L. < *e-*, out + *vocare*, to call < *vox*, VOICE] 1. to call forth (a spirit, etc.) 2. to call forth or draw out (some memory, idea, response, etc.) —see SYN. at EXTRACT —**e·vok′er** *n.*

ev·o·lu·tion (ev′ə lōo′shən) *n.* [< L. pp. of *evolvere*: see EVOLVE] 1. a process of gradual change taking place as something develops into a different or more complex form [the *evolution* of the automobile from the buggy] 2. a result of this; thing evolved 3. a movement that is part of a series or pattern, as in dancing 4. a setting free or giving off, as of gas in a chemical reaction 5. *Biol.* *a)* the development of a species, organism, or organ from its original to its present state *b)* a theory that all species of plants and animals developed from earlier forms: see DARWINIAN THEORY 6. *Math.* the extracting of a root 7. *Mil.* any of various maneuvers by which troops, ships, etc. change

formation —**ev′o·lu′tion·al** *adj.* —**ev′o·lu′tion·al·ly** *adv.* —**ev′o·lu′tion·ar′y** *adj.*

ev·o·lu·tion·ist (-ist) *n.* a person who accepts the principles of evolution, esp. in biology —*adj.* 1. of the theory of evolution 2. of evolutionists —**ev′o·lu′tion·ism** *n.* —**ev′o·lu′tion·is′tic** *adj.* —**ev′o·lu′tion·is′ti·cal·ly** *adv.*

e·volve (i välv′) *vt.* **e·volved′**, **e·volv′ing** [< L. < *e-*, out + *volvere*, to roll: for IE. base see WALK] 1. to develop by gradual changes; work out [to *evolve* a new theory] 2. to set free or give off (gas, heat, etc.) 3. to produce or change by evolution —*vi.* 1. to develop gradually by a process of growth and change [chemistry *evolved* from alchemy] ☆2. to become known; unfold —**e·volve′ment** *n.*

Ev·voi·a (ev′ē ə) large Greek island in the Aegean Sea, off the E coast of Greece

ewe (yōo; *dial.* yō) *n.* [OE. *eowu*] a female sheep

ew·er (yōo′ər) *n.* [< Anglo-Fr. < OFr. *evier*, ult. < L. *aquarius*: see AQUARIUM] a large water pitcher with a wide mouth

ex (eks) *prep.* [L.] without; exclusive of [ex interest] —*n., pl.* **ex′es** [Colloq.] one's divorced husband or wife

EWER

ex- [< OFr. or L., akin to Gr. *ex-*, *exō-*] 1. *a prefix meaning: a)* from, out [expel] *b)* beyond [excess] *c)* out of [expatriate] *d)* thoroughly [exterminate] *e)* upward [exalt] It is changed to *ef-* before *f; e-* before *b, d, g, l, m, n, r,* and *v;* and, often, *ec-* before *c* or *s* 2. *a prefix meaning* former, previously [ex-president]

Ex. Exodus

ex. 1. examined 2. example 3. except(ed) 4. express 5. extra

ex·ac·er·bate (ig zas′ər bāt′) *vt.* -**bat·ed**, -**bat·ing** [< L. pp. of *exacerbare* < *ex-*, thoroughly + *acerbus*, harsh, sour] 1. to make more intense or sharp; make worse; aggravate (disease, pain, feelings, etc.) 2. to irritate —**ex·ac′er·ba′tion** *n.*

ex·act (ig zakt′) *adj.* [< L. pp. of *exigere*, to measure < *ex-*, out + *agere*, to do: see ACT] 1. having, requiring, or capable of accuracy of detail; very accurate; correct [an *exact* science] 2. without variation; precise [an *exact* replica; the *exact* amount] 3. being the very (one specified or understood) [the *exact* spot where I put it] 4. strict; severe; rigorous [exact in enforcing rules] —*vt.* 1. to demand and get by authority or force [to *exact* high fees; to *exact* obedience] 2. to make necessary; require [the work *exacts* close attention] —see SYN. at CORRECT —**exact′a·ble** *adj.* —**ex·act′ness** *n.* —**ex·ac′tor, ex·act′er** *n.*

ex·act·ing (-iŋ) *adj.* 1. making severe demands; not easily satisfied; strict [an *exacting* teacher] 2. demanding great care, effort, etc.; arduous [an *exacting* job] —see SYN. at ONEROUS —**ex·act′ing·ly** *adv.* —**ex·act′ing·ness** *n.*

ex·ac·tion (ig zak′shən) *n.* 1. an exacting, as of money, time, etc. 2. an excessive demand; extortion 3. an exacted fee, tax, etc.

ex·ac·ti·tude (ig zak′tə tōod′, -tyōod′) *n.* the quality of being exact; precision; accuracy

ex·act·ly (ig zakt′lē) *adv.* in an exact manner; accurately; precisely: also used as a comment or reply to mean "I agree," "quite true"

ex·ag·ger·ate (ig zaj′ə rāt′) *vt.* -**at·ed**, -**at·ing** [< L. pp. of *exaggerare* < *ex-*, out + *aggerare*, to heap up < *agger*, a heap] 1. to think, speak, or write of as greater than is really so; overstate [he *exaggerated* the seriousness of the situation] 2. to increase or enlarge to an abnormal degree [in a caricature, distinctive features are *exaggerated*] —*vi.* to give an exaggerated account —**ex·ag′ger·at′ed·ly** *adv.* —**ex·ag′ger·a′tion** *n.* —**ex·ag′ger·a′tive** *adj.* —**ex·ag′ger·a′tor** *n.*

ex·alt (ig zôlt′) *vt.* [< OFr. < LL. *exaltare* < *ex-*, out, up + *altus*, high] to lift up; specif., *a)* to raise in status, dignity, power, wealth, etc. *b)* to praise; glorify; extol *c)* to fill with joy, pride, etc.; elate [they were *exalted* by the music; an *exalting* effect] *d)* to heighten or intensify the action or effect of —**ex·alt′ed·ly** *adv.* —**ex·alt′er** *n.*

ex·al·ta·tion (eg′zôl tā′shən) *n.* 1. an exalting or being exalted 2. a feeling of great joy, pride, etc.; elation; rapture

ex·am (ig zam′) *n.* [Colloq.] examination

ex·am·i·na·tion (ig zam′ə nā′shən) *n.* 1. an examining or being examined; investigation, inquiry, inspection, etc. 2. means or method of examining 3. a set of questions asked in testing; test —**ex·am′i·na′tion·al** *adj.* —**ex·am′i·na·to′ri·al** (-nə tôr′ē əl) *adj.*

ex·am·ine (ig zam′ən) *vt.* -**ined**, -**in·ing** [< OFr. < L. < *examen*, tongue of a balance, examination] 1. to look at or into closely and carefully to find out the facts, condition, etc. of; investigate; inspect [to *examine* the heart for defects; to *examine* the records] **2.** to test by questioning to find out the knowledge, skill, etc. of [to *examine* a witness in court] —**ex·am'i·na·ble** *adj.* —**ex·am'in·er, ex·am'i·nant** *n.*

ex·am·i·nee (ig zam'ə nē') *n.* a person being examined

ex·am·ple (ig zam'p'l) *n.* [< OFr. < L. *exemplum* < *eximere*, to take out < *ex-*, out + *emere*, to buy] **1.** something selected to show the nature or character of the rest; sample [he gave a few *examples* of what he meant] **2.** a case that serves as a warning or caution [to fine a speeder as an *example* to others] **3.** a person or thing to be imitated; model [her generosity is a good *example* for others] **4.** a problem, as in mathematics, that illustrates a principle or method —see SYN. at INSTANCE —**set an example** to behave so as to be a pattern or model for others —**without example** having no precedent

ex·as·per·ate (ig zas'pə rāt') *vt.* -at'ed, -at'ing [< L. pp. of *exasperare* < *ex-*, out + *asperare*, to roughen < *asper*, rough] to make angry; irritate or annoy very much; vex —see SYN. at IRRITATE —**ex·as'per·at'ing·ly** *adv.* —**ex·as'per·a'tion** *n.*

Ex·cal·i·bur (eks kal'ə bər) *n. Arthurian Legend* King Arthur's sword

ex ca·the·dra (eks' kə thē'drə, kath'i drə) [ModL., lit., from the chair] with the authority that comes from one's rank or office: often used of certain authoritative papal pronouncements on faith or morals

ex·ca·vate (eks'kə vāt') *vt.* -vat'ed, -vat'ing [< L. pp. of *excavare* < *ex-*, out + *cavare*, to make hollow < *cavus*, hollow: see CAVE] **1.** to make a hole or cavity in, as by digging; hollow out [to *excavate* a hill in building a tunnel] **2.** to form by hollowing out [to *excavate* a tunnel] **3.** to uncover by digging; unearth [to *excavate* ancient ruins] **4.** to dig out (earth, soil, etc.) —**ex'ca·va'tor** *n.*

ex·ca·va·tion (eks'kə vā'shən) *n.* **1.** an excavating or being excavated **2.** a hole made by excavating

ex·ceed (ik sēd') *vt.* [< OFr. < L. < *ex-*, out + *cedere*, to go] **1.** to go or be beyond (a limit, measure, etc.) [to *exceed* a speed limit] **2.** to be more than or greater than; surpass [to *exceed* one's hopes] —*vi.* to be better than others, as in quality or quantity

ex·ceed·ing (-iŋ) *adj.* more than usual; extraordinary; extreme —*adv.* [Archaic] same as EXCEEDINGLY

ex·ceed·ing·ly (-iŋ lē) *adv.* very; extremely

ex·cel (ik sel') *vi., vt.* -celled', -cel'ling [< OFr. < L. < *ex-*, out of + *-cellere*, to rise] to be better or greater than (another or others)

ex·cel·lence (ek's'l əns) *n.* **1.** the fact or condition of excelling; superiority **2.** something in which a person or thing excels **3.** [E-] same as EXCELLENCY

ex·cel·len·cy (-ən sē) *n., pl.* -cies **1.** [E-] a title of honor applied to various persons of high position, as an ambassador, bishop, etc. **2.** same as EXCELLENCE

ex·cel·lent (-ənt) *adj.* outstandingly good of its kind; of exceptional merit, virtue, etc. —**ex'cel·lent·ly** *adv.*

☆**ex·cel·si·or** (ek sel'sē ôr'; *for n.* ik sel'sē ər) *adj., interj.* [L., compar. of *excelsus*, high < *excellere*, EXCEL] higher; always upward —*n.* long, thin wood shavings used for packing or as stuffing

ex·cept (ik sept') *vt.* [< OFr. < L. < pp. of *excipere* < *ex-*, out + *capere*, to take] to leave out or take out; exclude; omit [he *excepted* Jones from his criticism] —*vi.* to take exception (with *to* or *against*); object —*prep.* leaving out; other than; but [to everyone *except* me] —*conj.* **1.** [Archaic] unless **2.** [Colloq.] were it not that [I'd quit *except* I need the money] —**except for** if it were not for

ex·cept·ing (-iŋ) *prep., conj.* same as EXCEPT

ex·cep·tion (ik sep'shən) *n.* **1.** an excepting or being excepted; exclusion **2.** anything that is excepted; specif., *a)* a case to which a rule, principle, etc. does not apply *b)* a person or thing different from others of the same class **3.** an objection —**take exception 1.** to object **2.** to resent; feel offended —**ex·cep'tion·less** *adj.*

ex·cep·tion·a·ble (-ə b'l) *adj.* liable or open to exception or objection —**ex·cep'tion·a·bly** *adv.*

ex·cep·tion·al (-əl) *adj.* **1.** being an exception; not ordinary or average; esp., much above average in quality, ability, etc.

☆**2.** *Educ.* needing special attention because mentally gifted or, esp., because mentally or physically handicapped —**ex·cep'·tion·al·ly** *adv.*

ex·cerpt (ik sʉrpt'; *also, and for n. always*, ek'sʉrpt') *vt.* [< L. pp. of *excerpere* < *ex-*, out + *carpere*, to pick] to select or quote (passages from a book, etc.); extract —*n.* a passage selected or quoted from a book, article, etc.; extract —**ex·cerp'·tion** *n.*

ex·cess (ik ses'; *also, and for adj. usually*, ek'ses') *n.* [< OFr. < L. pp. of *excedere*: see EXCEED] **1.** action or conduct that goes beyond the usual, reasonable, or lawful limit **2.** lack of moderation; intemperance; overindulgence **3.** an amount or quantity greater than is necessary, desirable, etc. **4.** the amount or degree by which one thing exceeds another; surplus —*adj.* extra or surplus —**in excess of** more than —**to excess** too much

ex·ces·sive (ik ses'iv) *adj.* characterized by excess; being too much or too great; immoderate —**ex·ces'sive·ly** *adv.* —**ex·ces'sive·ness** *n.*

SYN.—**excessive** applies to that which goes beyond what is needed, right, or usual [*excessive* demands]; **exorbitant** is applied esp. to charges, prices, etc. that are unreasonably or unfairly high [*exorbitant* profits]; **extravagant** and **immoderate** both imply excessiveness resulting from a lack of control or careful judgment [*extravagant* praise; *immoderate* smoking]; **inordinate** implies a going beyond the orderly limits of convention or good taste [his *inordinate* pride]

ex·change (iks chānj') *vt.* -changed', -chang'ing [< OFr. < VL. *excambiare*: see EX- & CHANGE] **1.** *a)* to give or transfer (for another thing in return) *b)* to receive or give another thing for (something returned) **2.** to give each other (similar things) [to *exchange* gifts] **3.** to give up for a substitute or alternative [to *exchange* honor for wealth] —*vi.* **1.** to make an exchange; barter **2.** *Finance* to pass in exchange [currency that *exchanges* at par value] —*n.* **1.** a giving or taking of one thing for another; barter **2.** a giving to one another of similar things [an *exchange* of greetings] **3.** the substituting of one thing for another [an *exchange* of tears for smiles] **4.** a thing given or received in exchange **5.** a place for exchanging; esp., a place where trade is carried on by brokers, merchants, etc. [a stock *exchange*] ☆**6.** a central office in a telephone system, serving a certain area **7.** *Commerce, Finance a)* the payment of debts by negotiable drafts or bills of exchange *b)* a bill of exchange *c)* a fee paid for settling accounts or collecting a draft, bill of exchange, etc. *d)* an exchanging of a sum of money of one country for the equivalent in the money of another country *e)* the rate of exchange; value of one currency in terms of the other —*adj.* **1.** exchanged [an *exchange* student] **2.** having to do with an exchange [an *exchange* broker] —**ex·change'a·bil'i·ty** *n.* —**ex·change'a·ble** *adj.* —**ex·chang'er** *n.*

ex·cheq·uer (iks chek'ər, eks'chek ər) *n.* [< OFr. *eschekier:* see CHECKER[1]] **1.** [often E-] the British state department in charge of the national revenue **2.** the funds in the British treasury **3.** a treasury, as of a country or organization **4.** money in one's possession; funds

ex·cis·a·ble (ik sī'zə b'l, ek'sī-) *adj.* **1.** subject to an excise tax **2.** that can be cut out

ex·cise[1] (ek'sīz, -sīs; *for v.* ik sīz') *n.* [< MDu. < OFr. *assise:* see ASSIZE] a tax on the making, selling, or using of certain goods within a country, as liquor, tobacco, etc.: also **excise tax** —*vt.* -cised', -cis'ing to put an excise on

ex·cise[2] (ik sīz') *vt.* -cised', -cis'ing [< L. pp. of *excidere* < *ex-*, out + *caedere*, to cut] to remove (a tumor, etc.) by cutting out or away —**ex·ci'sion** (-sizh'ən) *n.*

ex·cise·man (ik sīz'mən) *n., pl.* -men (-mən) in Great Britain, an official who collects excises

ex·cit·a·ble (ik sīt'ə b'l) *adj.* that can be excited; easily excited —**ex·cit'a·bil'i·ty** *n.* —**ex·cit'a·bly** *adv.*

ex·ci·ta·tion (ek'sī tā'shən, -si-) *n.* an exciting or being excited (esp. in senses 4, 5, 6)

ex·cite (ik sīt') *vt.* -cit'ed, -cit'ing [< OFr. < L. *excitare* < *ex-*, out + pp. of *ciere*, to call] **1.** to put into motion or activity; stir up [tapping on the hive *excited* the bees] **2.** to call forth; arouse; provoke [to *excite* pity] **3.** to arouse the feelings of [the news *excited* us] **4.** *Elec.* to supply electric current to, as to produce a magnetic field **5.** *Physics* to raise (a nucleus, atom, etc.) to a higher energy state **6.** *Physiol.* to produce the

---

fat, āpe, cär; ten, ēven; is, bīte; gō, hôrn, tool, look; oil, out; up, fʉr; get; joy; yet; chin; she; thin, then; zh, leisure; ŋ, ring; ə for *a* in *ago*, *e* in *agent*, *i* in *sanity*, *o* in *comply*, *u* in *focus*; ' as in *able* (ā'b'l); Fr. bál; ë, Fr. coeur; ö, Fr. feu; Fr. mon; ô, Fr. coq; ü, Fr. duc; *r*, Fr. cri; H, G. ich; kh, G. doch; ‡foreign; ☆ Americanism; < derived from. See inside front cover.

response of (an organ, tissue, etc.) to a proper stimulus —**ex·cit′a·tive** (-ə tiv), **ex·cit′a·to·ry** (-ə tôr′ē) *adj.* —**ex·cit′er, ex·ci′tor** *n.*

ex·cit·ed (-id) *adj.* emotionally stirred up —**ex·cit′ed·ly** *adv.*

ex·cite·ment (-mənt) *n.* **1.** an exciting or being excited; agitation **2.** something that excites

ex·cit·ing (-iŋ) *adj.* causing excitement; stirring, thrilling, etc. —**ex·cit′ing·ly** *adv.*

ex·claim (iks klām′) *vi., vt.* [< Fr. < L. *exclamare* < *ex-*, out + *clamare*, to shout: see CLAMOR] to cry out; speak or say suddenly and excitedly, as in surprise, anger, etc. —**ex·claim′er** *n.*

ex·cla·ma·tion (eks′klə mā′shən) *n.* **1.** the act of exclaiming **2.** something exclaimed; interjection [*"oh!" and "watch out!" are exclamations*]

☆**exclamation mark** (or **point**) a mark (!) used after a word or sentence in writing or printing to express surprise, strong feeling, etc.

ex·clam·a·to·ry (iks klam′ə tôr′ē) *adj.* showing or using exclamation [*an exclamatory sentence, style, etc.*]

ex·clave (eks′klāv) *n.* [EX- + (EN)CLAVE] a territory (of a nearby specified country) surrounded by foreign territory [*East Prussia was an exclave of Germany*]

ex·clude (iks klōōd′) *vt.* -**clud′ed**, -**clud′ing** [< L. *excludere* < *ex-*, out + *claudere*, CLOSE[2]] **1.** to refuse to admit, consider, include, etc.; shut out; reject; bar [*you should not exclude the possibility of failure*] **2.** to put out; force out; expel [*he was excluded from the club*] —**ex·clud′a·ble** *adj.* —**ex·clud′er** *n.*

ex·clu·sion (-klōō′zhən) *n.* **1.** an excluding or being excluded **2.** a thing excluded —**to the exclusion of** so as to keep out, bar, etc. —**ex·clu′sion·ar′y** *adj.*

ex·clu·sive (-klōō′siv) *adj.* **1.** excluding all others; shutting out other considerations, happenings, etc. [*an exclusive interest in sports*] **2.** excluding all but what is specified [*"only" is an exclusive particle*] **3.** not shared or divided; sole [*an exclusive right to dig for oil on this land*] **4.** *a)* excluding certain people or groups, as for social or economic reasons [*an exclusive club*] *b)* snobbish; undemocratic **5.** dealing only in costly items [*an exclusive shop*] —**exclusive of** not including or allowing for —**ex·clu′sive·ly** *adv.* —**ex·clu′sive·ness** *n.*

ex·clu·siv·i·ty (eks′klōō siv′ə tē) *n.* the condition or practice of being exclusive; esp., clannishness or isolationism: also **ex·clu′siv·ism** —**ex·clu′siv·ist** *n., adj.* —**ex·clu′siv·is′tic** *adj.*

ex·com·mu·ni·cate (eks′kə myōō′nə kāt′; *for adj. and n.*, *usually* -kit) *vt.* -**cat′ed**, -**cat′ing** to exclude, by ecclesiastical authority, from the sacraments, privileges, etc. of a church; condemn by cutting off from communion with a church —*adj.* excommunicated —*n.* an excommunicated person —**ex′com·mu′ni·ca′tion** *n.*

ex·co·ri·ate (ik skôr′ē āt′) *vt.* -**at′ed**, -**at′ing** [< L. pp. of *excoriare* < *ex-*, off + *corium*, the skin] **1.** to strip, scratch, or rub off the skin of **2.** to condemn strongly and harshly —**ex·co′ri·a′tion** *n.*

ex·cre·ment (eks′krə mənt) *n.* [< Fr. < L. < *excretus*: see EX-CRETE] waste matter from the bowels; feces —**ex′cre·men′tal** (-men′t'l) *adj.*

ex·cres·cence (iks kres′'ns) *n.* [< OFr. < L. < *ex-*, out + *crescere*, to grow] **1.** [Now Rare] a normal outgrowth, as a fingernail **2.** an abnormal or disfiguring outgrowth, as a bunion

ex·cres·cen·cy (-'n sē) *n.* **1.** the condition of being excrescent **2.** *pl.* -**cies** *same as* EXCRESCENCE

ex·cres·cent (-'nt) *adj.* **1.** forming an excrescence; growing abnormally **2.** *Phonetics* designating or of an unhistorical sound or letter in a word, as the *b* in *mumble* or the extra syllable in the pronunciation (ath′ə lēt′) for *athlete*

ex·cre·ta (eks krēt′ə) *n.pl.* waste matter excreted from the body, esp. sweat or urine —**ex·cre′tal** *adj.*

ex·crete (iks krēt′) *vt., vi.* -**cret′ed**, -**cret′ing** [< L. *excretus*, pp. of *excernere* < *ex-*, out of + *cernere*, to sift] to separate (waste matter) from the blood or tissue and eliminate from the body —**ex·cre′tive** *adj.*

ex·cre·tion (-krē′shən) *n.* **1.** the act or process of excreting **2.** waste matter excreted; sweat, urine, etc.

ex·cre·to·ry (eks′krə tôr′ē) *adj.* of or for excreting —*n., pl.* -**ries** an excretory organ

ex·cru·ci·ate (iks krōō′shē āt′) *vt.* -**at′ed**, -**at′ing** [< L. pp. of *excruciare* < *ex-*, thoroughly + *cruciare*, to crucify < *crucis*, genitive of *crux*, a CROSS] **1.** to cause great bodily pain to; torture **2.** to subject to mental suffering; torment —**ex·cru′ci·a′tion** *n.*

ex·cru·ci·at·ing (-āt′iŋ) *adj.* **1.** causing great pain or suffering; agonizing **2.** intense or extreme [*excruciating care*] —**ex·cru′ci·at′ing·ly** *adv.*

ex·cul·pate (eks′kəl pāt′, ik skul′pāt) *vt.* -**pat′ed**, -**pat′ing** [< L. *ex*, out + pp. of *culpare*, to blame < *culpa*, fault] to free from blame; declare or prove guiltless —**ex·cul·pa·ble** (ik-skul′pə b'l) *adj.* —**ex·cul′pa′tion** *n.* —**ex·cul′pa·to′ry** *adj.*

ex·cur·sion (ik skur′zhən) *n.* [< L. < pp. of *excurrere* < *ex-*, out + *currere*, to run] **1.** a short trip for pleasure **2.** a round trip (on a train, bus, etc.) at special reduced rates **3.** a group taking such a trip **4.** a turning aside for a time; deviation or digression [*an excursion into politics*] **5.** [Obs.] a military raid —*adj.* of or for an excursion —**ex·cur′sion·ist** *n.*

ex·cur·sive (-siv) *adj.* departing from the subject; rambling; digressive —**ex·cur′sive·ly** *adv.* —**ex·cur′sive·ness** *n.*

ex·cuse (ik skyōōz′; *for n.* -skyōōs′) *vt.* -**cused′**, -**cus′ing** [< OFr. < L. *excusare* < *ex-*, from + *causa*, a charge] **1.** to give reasons in defense of (oneself or another) [*excusing himself for being late*] **2.** to try to pardon (a fault); apologize or give reasons for [*excusing the oversight as due to haste*] **3.** to think of (an offense or fault) as not important; overlook; pardon [*excuse my rudeness*] **4.** to release from an obligation, promise, etc. [*he was excused from jury duty*] **5.** to permit to leave [*she was excused from the table*] **6.** to serve as an explanation or justification for; justify; absolve [*nothing can excuse such selfishness*] —*n.* **1.** a plea in defense of some action; apology **2.** a release from obligation, duty, etc. **3.** something that excuses; justifying factor **4.** a pretended reason; pretext —**a poor** (or **bad**, etc.) **excuse for** a very inferior example of —**excuse oneself 1.** to apologize **2.** to ask for permission to leave —**ex·cus′a·ble** *adj.* —**ex·cus′a·bly** *adv.* —**ex·cus′er** *n.*

ex·ec (ig zek′) *n.* [Colloq.] an executive officer

exec. 1. executive **2.** executor

ex·e·cra·ble (ek′si krə b'l) *adj.* [L. *execrabilis*] that deserves to be hated or detested; very bad [*an execrable betrayal; execrable taste*] —**ex′e·cra·bly** *adv.*

ex·e·crate (-krāt′) *vt.* -**crat′ed**, -**crat′ing** [< L. pp. of *execrare*, to curse < *ex-*, out + *sacrare*, to consecrate < *sacer*, sacred] **1.** orig., to call down evil upon; curse **2.** to condemn strongly and harshly **3.** to hate very much; detest —*vi.* to curse —**ex′e·cra′tive, ex′e·cra·to′ry** (-krə tôr′ē) *adj.* —**ex′e·cra′tor** *n.*

ex·e·cra·tion (ek′si krā′shən) *n.* **1.** a cursing, condemning, etc. **2.** a curse **3.** a thing cursed or hated

ex·e·cute (ek′sə kyōōt′) *vt.* -**cut′ed**, -**cut′ing** [< OFr. < L. pp. of *ex(s)equi* < *ex-*, thoroughly + *sequi*, to follow] **1.** to carry out; do; perform [*to execute another's orders*] **2.** to carry into effect; administer (laws, etc.) [*the President "shall take care that the laws be faithfully executed"*] **3.** to put to death in accordance with a legally imposed sentence [*to execute a criminal*] **4.** to create in accordance with an idea, plan, etc. [*to execute a statue*] **5.** to perform (a piece of music, etc.) **6.** *Law* to make valid (a deed, contract, etc.) as by signing, sealing, and delivering —see SYN. at PERFORM —**ex′e·cut′a·ble** *adj.* —**ex′e·cut′er** *n.*

ex·e·cu·tion (ek′sə kyōō′shən) *n.* **1.** the act of executing; specif., *a)* a carrying out, doing, etc. *b)* a putting to death in accordance with a legally imposed sentence **2.** the manner of doing or producing something, as of performing a piece of music **3.** *Law* a writ, issued by a court, giving authority to put a judgment into effect

ex·e·cu·tion·er (-ər) *n.* a person who carries out the death penalty imposed by a court

ex·ec·u·tive (ig zek′yə tiv) *adj.* **1.** of, capable of, or concerned with, managing affairs, as in a business **2.** given the power and required to administer (laws, government affairs, etc.) [*the executive branch of government*] **3.** of management personnel or functions —*n.* **1.** the person, group, or branch of government given the power and required to administer the laws and affairs of a nation **2.** a person whose function is to administer or manage affairs, as of a corporation

☆**Executive Mansion 1.** the White House (in Washington, D.C.), official home of the President of the U.S. **2.** the official home of the governor of a State

executive officer *Mil.* an officer who is chief assistant to the commanding officer

ex·ec·u·tor (ek′sə kyōōt′ər; *for 2* ig zek′yə tər) *n.* **1.** a person who gets something done or produced **2.** a person appointed to carry out the provisions and directions of another person's will —**ex·ec′u·to′ri·al** (-tôr′ē əl), **ex·ec′u·to′ry** *adj.* —**ex·ec′u·trix** (-triks) *n.fem., pl.* -**trix·es, -tri′ces** (-trī′sēz)

ex·e·ge·sis (ek′sə jē′sis) *n., pl.* -**ge′ses** (-sēz) [< Gr. < *ex-*, out + *hēgeisthai*, to guide] analysis or explanation of a word, passage, etc., esp. of the Bible —**ex′e·get′ic** (-jet′ik), **ex′e·get′i·cal** adj. —**ex′e·get′i·cal·ly** adv.

ex·e·gete (ek′sə jēt′) n. an expert in exegesis

ex·em·plar (ig zem′plär, -plər) n. [< OFr. < LL. < L. exemplum, EXAMPLE] 1. one that is considered worthy of imitation; model 2. a typical specimen or example

ex·em·pla·ry (-plə rē) adj. 1. serving as a model or example; worth imitating [exemplary behavior] 2. serving as a warning [exemplary punishment] 3. serving as a sample; illustrative [exemplary selections from his writings] —**ex·em·pla·ri·ly** (eg′zəm pler′ə lē) adv. —**ex·em′pla·ri·ness** n.

exemplary damages Law damages beyond the actual loss, imposed as a punishment

ex·em·pli·fy (ig zem′plə fī′) vt. -fied′, -fy′ing [< OFr. < ML. < L. exemplum, an example + facere, to make] 1. to show by example; serve as an example of [Da Vinci exemplifies the Renaissance man] 2. to make a certified copy of (a document, etc.) under seal —**ex·em′pli·fi·ca′tion** n.

ex·empt (ig zempt′) vt. [< Anglo-Fr. < L. pp. of eximere: see EXAMPLE] to free from a rule or obligation which applies to others; excuse; release —adj. not subject to or bound by a rule, obligation, tax, etc. —n. an exempted person —**ex·empt′i·ble** adj.

ex·emp·tion (ig zemp′shən) n. 1. an exempting or being exempted; freedom from a liability, obligation, etc. 2. a certain sum of money earned, on which income tax is not paid [an exemption is given for each person supported]

ex·er·cise (ek′sər sīz′) n. [< OFr. < L. < pp. of exercere, to drive out (farm animals to work) < ex-, out + arcere, to enclose] 1. active use or operation [the exercise of wit] 2. performance (of duties, etc.) 3. activity for training or developing the body or mind; esp., bodily exertion for the sake of health [he walked for exercise] 4. a series of movements done regularly to strengthen or develop some part of the body [an exercise to slim the hips; setting-up exercises] 5. a problem or task to be worked on in order to develop some skill [math exercises; piano exercises] ☆6. [pl.] a set program of formal ceremonies, speeches, etc., as at a graduation —vt. -cised′, -cis′ing 1. to put into action; employ [to exercise self-control] 2. to put (the body, mind, etc.) into use so as to develop or train 3. to give exercise or exercises to; drill, train, etc. 4. to engage the attention and energy of, esp. so as to worry or bother [greatly exercised over their refusal to help] 5. to exert or have (influence, control, etc.) —vi. to take exercise; do exercises —**ex′er·cis′a·ble** adj. —**ex′er·cis′er** n.

ex·ert (ig zurt′) vt. [< L. < exserere, to stretch out < ex-, out + serere, to join] 1. to put into action or use [exert your will] 2. to apply (oneself) with great energy or effort —**ex·er′tive** adj.

ex·er·tion (ig zur′shən) n. 1. the act, fact, or process of exerting [the exertion of skill] 2. the use of power and strength; effort [the swimmer was worn out by his exertions] —see SYN. at EFFORT

ex·e·unt (ek′sē ənt, -oont) [L.] they (two or more characters) leave the stage: a stage direction

exeunt om·nes (äm′nēz) [L.] all (of the characters who are on stage) leave: a stage direction

ex·fo·li·ate (eks fō′lē āt′) vt., vi. -at′ed, -at′ing [< LL. pp. of exfoliare, to strip of leaves < ex-, out + folium, a leaf] to cast or come off in flakes, scales, or layers, as skin, bark, etc. —**ex·fo′li·a′tion** n. —**ex·fo′li·a′tive** adj.

ex·ha·la·tion (eks′hə lā′shən, ek′sə-) n. 1. an exhaling or being exhaled 2. something exhaled, as air, vapor, or an odor

ex·hale (eks hāl′, ek sāl′) vi. -haled′, -hal′ing [< Fr. < L. exhalare < ex-, out + halare, to breathe] 1. to breathe out 2. to rise into the air as vapor; evaporate —vt. 1. to breathe out (air, cigarette smoke, etc.) 2. to give off (vapor, fumes, etc.)

ex·haust (ig zôst′) vt. [< L. pp. of exhaurire < ex-, out + haurire, to draw] 1. to draw off or let out completely (air, gas, etc.), as from a container 2. to use up; expend completely [to exhaust one's resources] 3. to empty completely; drain [to exhaust a well] 4. to drain of power, resources, etc. [war exhausts nations] 5. to tire out; weaken [tennis exhausts her] 6. to deal with or study completely and thoroughly [to exhaust a subject] —vi. to be let out, as gas or steam from an engine —n. 1. the withdrawing of air, gas, etc. from a container or enclo-

sure, as by means of a fan or pump 2. a) the discharge of used steam, gas, etc. from the cylinders of an engine at the end of every working stroke of the pistons b) the pipe through which such steam, gas, etc. is released 3. something given off, as fumes from a gasoline engine —see SYN. at TIRED —**ex·haust′ed** adj. —**ex·haust′i·bil′i·ty** n. —**ex·haust′i·ble** adj. —**ex·haust′less** adj.

ex·haus·tion (ig zôs′chən) n. 1. an exhausting, or using up 2. the state of being exhausted; esp., a) a being very tired; great weariness b) a being used up; complete consumption

ex·haus·tive (ig zôs′tiv) adj. 1. exhausting or tending to exhaust 2. leaving nothing out; covering every possible detail; thorough [exhaustive research] —**ex·haus′tive·ly** adv. —**ex·haus′tive·ness** n.

ex·hib·it (ig zib′it) vt. [< L. pp. of exhibere < ex-, out + habere, to hold, have] 1. to show; display [an act that exhibits courage] 2. to show to the public [to exhibit paintings at an art gallery] 3. Law to present (evidence, etc.) officially to a court —vi. to put pictures, wares, etc. on public display —n. 1. a show; display 2. an object or objects displayed publicly 3. Law an object produced as evidence in a court —see SYN. at SHOW —**ex·hib′i·tor, ex·hib′it·er** n.

ex·hi·bi·tion (ek′sə bish′ən) n. 1. the act or fact of exhibiting 2. the thing or things exhibited 3. a public show or display, as of art

ex·hi·bi·tion·ism (-iz′m) n. 1. a tendency to call attention to oneself or show off one's talents, skill, etc. 2. Psychol. a tendency to expose parts of the body that are normally concealed —**ex′hi·bi′tion·ist** n. —**ex′hi·bi′tion·is′tic** adj.

ex·hib·i·tive (ig zib′ə tiv) adj. serving or tending to exhibit (usually with of)

ex·hil·a·rate (ig zil′ə rāt′) vt. -rat′ed, -rat′ing [< L. pp. of exhilarare < ex-, thoroughly + hilarare, to gladden < hilaris, glad] 1. to make merry or lively 2. to invigorate or stimulate —**ex·hil′a·ra′tive** adj.

ex·hil·a·ra·tion (ig zil′ə rā′shən) n. 1. an exhilarating 2. an exhilarated feeling; liveliness; high spirits

ex·hort (ig zôrt′) vt., vi. [< L. exhortari < ex-, out + hortari, to urge] to urge strongly by advice, warning, etc. (to do what is proper or required); entreat —see SYN. at URGE —**ex·hor′ta·to′ry** (-tə tôr′ē), **ex·hor′ta·tive** adj. —**ex·hort′er** n.

ex·hor·ta·tion (eg′zôr tā′shən, ek′sər-) n. 1. an exhorting 2. a plea, sermon, etc. that exhorts

ex·hume (ig zyōōm′, iks hyōōm′) vt. -humed′, -hum′ing [< ML. exhumare < L. ex, out + humus, the ground] 1. to dig out of the earth; remove from the grave 2. to reveal —**ex·hu·ma·tion** (eks′hyoo mā′shən) n.

ex·i·gen·cy (ek′sə jən sē) n., pl. -cies [see EXIGENT] 1. urgency 2. a situation calling for immediate action or attention 3. [pl.] urgent needs; demands [the exigencies of a situation] Also **ex′i·gence** —see SYN. at NEED

ex·i·gent (ek′sə jənt) adj. [< L. prp. of exigere: see EXACT] 1. calling for immediate action or attention; urgent 2. requiring more than is reasonable; exacting —**ex′i·gent·ly** adv.

ex·ig·u·ous (eg zig′yoo wəs) adj. [< L. < exigere: see EXACT] scanty; little; small; meager —**ex·i·gu·i·ty** (ek′sə gyoo′ə tē) n.

ex·ile (eg′zīl, ek′sīl) n. [< OFr. < L. exilium < exul, an exile] 1. a living away from one's country, community, etc. because one has been or feels forced to leave 2. a person in exile —vt. -iled, -il·ing to force (a person) to leave his country, community, etc.; banish —see SYN. at BANISH —**ex·il·ic** (ig zil′ik, ik sil′ik) adj.

ex·ist (ig zist′) vi. [< Fr. < L. existere < ex-, forth + sistere, to cause to stand] 1. to have reality or actual being; be [the unicorn never really existed] 2. to occur or be present [the qualities that exist in a person] 3. to continue being; live [fish cannot exist long out of water]

ex·ist·ence (-əns) n. 1. the act of existing; state or fact of being 2. a continuing of being; life; living 3. an occurring or being present 4. a manner of existing [a happy existence] 5. a being; entity; thing that exists

ex·ist·ent (-ənt) adj. 1. having existence or being; existing 2. existing now; present

ex·is·ten·tial (eg′zis ten′shəl, ek′sis-) adj. 1. of, based on, or expressing existence 2. of, relating to, or based on existentialism

ex·is·ten·tial·ism (-shəl iz'm) *n.* a philosophical and literary movement which emphasizes existence rather than essence and holds that man is totally free and responsible for his acts, and that this responsibility causes man's fear and anxiety —**ex'is·ten'tial·ist** *n.*

ex·it (eg'zit, ek'sit) *n.* [L. *exitus,* orig. pp. of *exire* < *ex-,* out + *ire,* to go] **1.** an actor's departure from the stage **2.** a going out; departure **3.** a way or passage out **4.** [L., 3d person singular, present indicative, of *exire*] he (or she) leaves: a stage direction —*vi.* to leave a place; depart

‡**ex li·bris** (eks lē'bris, li'-) [L.] **1.** from the library of: an inscription on bookplates **2.** a bookplate

ex·o- [< Gr. *exō,* without] *a prefix meaning* outside, outer, outer part

ex·o·bi·ol·o·gy (ek'sō bī äl'ə jē) *n.* [EXO- + BIOLOGY] the study of the possible existence of living organisms elsewhere in the universe than on earth —**ex'o·bi'o·log'i·cal** *adj.* —**ex'o·bi·ol'o·gist** *n.*

ex·o·carp (ek'sō kärp') *n.* [EXO- + -CARP] the outer layer of a ripened ovary or fruit, as the skin of a plum

ex·o·crine (ek'sə krin, -krīn', -krēn') *adj.* [EXO- + (ENDO)-CRINE] designating or of a gland secreting externally, either directly or through a duct —*n.* any such gland, as a sweat gland, or its secretion

Exod. Exodus

ex·o·dus (ek'sə dəs) *n.* [< LL. < Gr. < *ex-,* out + *hodos,* way] a going out or forth, esp. in a large group —[**E-**] **1.** the departure of the Israelites from Egypt (with *the*) **2.** the second book of the Bible, which describes this

ex of·fi·ci·o (eks' ə fish'ē ō') [L., lit., from office] because of one's office, or position [the president of the company was, *ex officio,* on the board of directors]

ex·og·a·my (ek säg'ə mē) *n.* [EXO- + -GAMY] the custom of marrying only outside one's own tribe, clan, etc.; outbreeding —**ex·og'a·mous, ex·o·gam·ic** (ek'sə gam'ik) *adj.*

ex·og·e·nous (ek säj'ə nəs) *adj.* [EXO- + -GENOUS] **1.** developing from the outside; originating externally **2.** *Biol.* of or relating to external factors, as food, light, etc., that have an effect on an organism —**ex·og'e·nous·ly** *adv.*

ex·on·er·ate (ig zän'ə rāt') *vt.* -**at·ed,** -**at·ing** [< L. pp. of *exonerare* < *ex-,* out + *onerare,* to load < *onus,* a burden] to free from a charge of guilt; declare or prove blameless [the accused was *exonerated* by the testimony of two witnesses] —*SYN.* at ABSOLVE —**ex·on'er·a'tion** *n.* —**ex·on'er·a'tive** *adj.* —**ex·on'er·a'tor** *n.*

ex·oph·thal·mos (ek'säf thal'məs) *n.* [< Gr. < *ex-,* out + *ophthalmos,* an eye] abnormal bulging out of the eyeball, caused by disease: also **ex'oph·thal'mus, ex'oph·thal'mi·a** (-mē ə) —**ex'oph·thal'mic** *adj.*

ex·or·bi·tant (ig zôr'bə tənt) *adj.* [< L. prp. of *exorbitare* < *ex-,* out + *orbita,* a track, ORBIT] going beyond what is reasonable, fair, usual, etc., as a price; excessive; extravagant —*see SYN.* at EXCESSIVE —**ex·or'bi·tance, ex·or'bi·tan·cy** *n.* —**ex·or'bi·tant·ly** *adv.*

ex·or·cise, ex·or·cize (ek'sôr sīz') *vt.* -**cised'** or -**cized',** -**cis'ing** or -**ciz'ing** [< LL. < Gr. < *ex-,* out + *horkizein,* to make one swear < *horkos,* an oath] **1.** to drive (an evil spirit) out or away by ritual prayers, chants, etc., in accordance with certain religious beliefs and practices **2.** to free thus from such a spirit —**ex'or·cis'er, ex'or·ciz'er** *n.*

ex·or·cism (-siz'm) *n.* **1.** the act of exorcising **2.** a formula or ritual used in exorcising —**ex'or·cist** *n.*

ex·or·di·um (ig zôr'dē əm) *n., pl.* -**di·ums, -di·a** (-ə) [< L. < *ex-,* from + *ordiri,* to begin] **1.** a beginning **2.** the opening part of a speech, treatise, etc.

ex·o·skel·e·ton (ek'sō skel'ə t'n) *n. Zool.* any hard, external supporting structure, as the shell of an oyster —**ex'o·skel'e·tal** *adj.*

ex·o·ter·ic (ek'sə ter'ik) *adj.* [LL. < Gr. *exōterikos,* external < compar. of *exō,* outside: see EX-] **1.** of the outside world; external **2.** not limited to a chosen few **3.** that can be understood by the public; popular —**ex'o·ter'i·cal·ly** *adv.*

ex·ot·ic (ig zät'ik) *adj.* [< L. < Gr. *exōtikos* < *exō,* outside] **1.** foreign; not native **2.** strangely beautiful, attractive, etc. —*n.* **1.** a foreign or imported thing **2.** a plant that is not native —**ex·ot'i·cal·ly** *adv.* —**ex·ot'i·cism** (-ə siz'm) *n.*

exp. **1.** expenses **2.** export **3.** express

ex·pand (ik spand') *vt.* [< L. < *ex-,* out + *pandere,* to spread] **1.** to spread out; open out; stretch out; unfold [the eagle *expanded* its wings] **2.** to make greater in size, scope, etc.; enlarge; dilate [he *expanded* his horizons] **3.** to enlarge upon (a

topic, idea, etc.); develop in detail or fully —*vi.* to spread out, unfold, enlarge, etc. —**ex·pand'er** *n.*

SYN.—**expand** implies an increasing in size, scope, or extent by adding, spreading, puffing out, etc. [the nation *expanded* westward; *expand* your chest with a deep breath]; **swell** implies expansion beyond the normal limits or size [his sprained ankle *swelled* up; the heavy rains *swelled* the rivers]; **distend** implies a swelling as a result of pressure from within that forces a bulging outward [the balloon was *distended* with gas]; **dilate** suggests a widening or stretching of something circular [atropine *dilates* the pupils] —*ANT.* contract

expanded metal sheet metal stretched out in latticelike strips, used as lath for plastering, etc.

ex·panse (ik spans') *n.* a large, open area or unbroken surface; wide extent; great breadth [an *expanse* of desert]

ex·pan·si·ble (ik span'sə b'l) *adj.* that can be expanded: also **ex·pand'a·ble** —**ex·pan'si·bil'i·ty** *n.*

ex·pan·sile (-s'l) *adj.* **1.** tending to expand **2.** of expansion

ex·pan·sion (ik span'shən) *n.* **1.** an expanding or being expanded; enlargement **2.** an expanded thing or part **3.** the extent or degree of expansion **4.** a development or full treatment, as of a topic

ex·pan·sion·ar·y (ik span'shən er'ē) *adj.* directed toward expansion

expansion bolt a bolt with an attachment that expands so as to anchor as it is screwed inward

ex·pan·sion·ism (-iz'm) *n.* the policy of expanding a nation's territory or its sphere of influence, usually at the expense of other nations —**ex·pan'sion·ist** *adj., n.* —**ex·pan'sion·is'tic** *adj.*

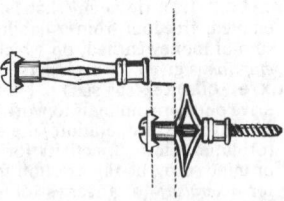
EXPANSION BOLT

ex·pan·sive (ik span'siv) *adj.* **1.** tending or being able to expand **2.** of, or working by means of, expansion **3.** spread over a wide area; broad; extensive **4.** having a free and generous nature; sympathetic; demonstrative [an *expansive* person] —**ex·pan'sive·ly** *adv.* —**ex·pan'sive·ness** *n.*

ex par·te (eks pärt'ē) [< L.] of or from one side or party only; one-sided

ex·pa·ti·ate (ik spā'shē āt') *vi.* -**at·ed,** -**at·ing** [< L. pp. of *expatiari,* to wander < *ex-,* out + *spatiari,* to walk < *spatium,* space] to speak or write in great detail [to *expatiate* on a subject] —**ex·pa'ti·a'tion** *n.*

ex·pa·tri·ate (eks pā'trē āt'; *for adj. & n., usually* -it) *vt.* -**at·ed,** -**at·ing** [< ML. pp. of *expatriare* < L. *ex,* out of + *patria,* fatherland < *pater,* FATHER] **1.** to drive (a person) from his native land; exile or banish **2.** to withdraw (oneself) from one's native land —*adj.* expatriated —*n.* an expatriated person —*see SYN.* at BANISH —**ex·pa'tri·a'tion** *n.*

ex·pect (ik spekt') *vt.* [< L. < *ex-,* out + *spectare,* to look] **1.** to look for as likely to occur or appear; look forward to; anticipate [I *expected* you sooner] **2.** to look for as due, proper, or necessary [to *expect* a reward] **3.** [Colloq.] to suppose; presume; guess —**be expecting** [Colloq.] to be pregnant —**ex·pect'a·ble** *adj.*

SYN.—**expect** implies confidence that a particular thing will happen [to *expect* guests for dinner]; **anticipate** implies a looking forward to something with some idea of the pleasure or pain it promises, or a realizing of something in advance, and a taking of steps to meet it [to *anticipate* trouble]; **hope** implies a desire for something to happen or be as one wishes [to *hope* for the best]; **await** implies a waiting for, or a being ready for, a person or thing [a hearty welcome *awaits* you]

ex·pect·an·cy (ik spek'tən sē) *n., pl.* -**cies** **1.** an expecting or being expected; expectation **2.** that which is expected, esp. on a statistical basis [life *expectancy*] Also **ex·pect'ance**

ex·pect·ant (-tənt) *adj.* *a)* expecting; specif., *a)* having or showing expectation *b)* waiting, as for a position, the birth of a child, etc. —*n.* a person who expects something —**ex·pect'ant·ly** *adv.*

ex·pec·ta·tion (ek'spek tā'shən) *n.* **1.** a looking forward to; anticipation **2.** a looking for as due, proper, or necessary **3.** a thing looked forward to **4.** [also *pl.*] a reason for looking forward to something; prospect of future success, prosperity, etc. —**in expectation** in the state of being looked for —**ex·pec·ta·tive** (ik spek'tə tiv) *adj.*

ex·pec·to·rant (ik spek'tər ənt) *adj.* causing or easing the bringing up of phlegm, mucus, etc. from the lungs, throat, etc. —*n.* an expectorant medicine

ex·pec·to·rate (-tə rāt') *vt., vi.* -**rat·ed,** -**rat·ing** [< L. pp. of *expectorare* < *ex-,* out + *pectus* (gen. *pectoris*), breast] **1.** to cough up and spit out (phlegm, mucus, etc.) **2.** to spit —**ex·pec'to·ra'tion** *n.*

ex·pe·di·en·cy (ik spē'dē ən sē) *n., pl.* **-cies 1.** the quality or state of being expedient; a being right or useful for a given purpose [sent by messenger as a matter of *expediency*] **2.** the doing of what is of use or advantage rather than what is right or just; self-interest [political *expediency* determined the Senator's vote] **3.** an expedient Also **ex·pe'di·ence**

ex·pe·di·ent (-dē ənt) *adj.* [< OFr. < L. prp. of *expedire*: see EXPEDITE] **1.** useful for bringing about a desired result; suited to the circumstances; convenient **2.** based on what is of use or advantage rather than what is right or just; guided by self-interest —*n.* an expedient thing; means to an end —see SYN. at RESOURCE —**ex·pe'di·ent·ly** *adv.*

ex·pe·dite (ek'spə dīt') *vt.* **-dit'ed, -dit'ing** [< L. pp. of *expedire*, lit., to free one caught by the feet < *ex-*, out + *pedis*, genitive of *pes*, FOOT] **1.** to speed up or make easy the progress or action of; facilitate [we *expedited* the loading by adding men to the crew] **2.** to do quickly

ex·pe·dit·er (-ər) *n.* a person who expedites; esp., one employed, as in industry, to expedite urgent or involved projects

ex·pe·di·tion (ek'spə dish'ən) *n.* [< OFr. < L. pp. of *expedire*: see EXPEDITE] **1.** *a)* a journey, voyage, etc., as for exploration or battle *b)* the people, ships, etc. on such a journey **2.** speed or quickness with little effort or waste —see SYN. at HASTE and TRIP —**ex·pe·di'tion·ar'y** *adj.*

ex·pe·di·tious (ek'spə dish'əs) *adj.* efficient and speedy; prompt —**ex·pe·di'tious·ly** *adv.*

ex·pel (ik spel') *vt.* **-pelled', -pel'ling** [< L. *expellere* < *ex-*, out + *pellere*, to thrust] **1.** to drive out by force; force out; eject [harmful gases *expelled* through the exhaust pipe] **2.** to dismiss or send away by authority [he was *expelled* from school for misconduct —see SYN. at EJECT —**ex·pel'la·ble** *adj.* —**ex·pel·lee** (ek'spel ē') *n.* —**ex·pel'ler** *n.*

ex·pend (ik spend') *vt.* [< L. *expendere*, to pay out < *ex-*, out + *pendere*, to weigh] **1.** to spend **2.** to consume by using; use up —**ex·pend'er** *n.*

ex·pend·a·ble (ik spen'də b'l) *adj.* **1.** that can be expended **2.** *Mil.* designating equipment (and hence, men) expected to be used up (or sacrificed) in service —*n.* a person or thing considered expendable —**ex·pend'a·bil'i·ty** *n.* —**ex·pend'a·bly** *adv.*

ex·pend·i·ture (-də chər) *n.* **1.** an expending; a spending or using up of money, time, etc. **2.** the amount of money, time, etc. expended

ex·pense (ik spens') *n.* [< Anglo-Fr. < LL. *expensa* (pecunia), paid out (money) < L. pp. of *expendere*: see EXPEND] **1.** financial cost; fee **2.** any cost or sacrifice [the battle was won at terrible *expense*] **3.** [pl.] *a)* charges met with in doing one's work, etc. *b)* money to pay for these charges [the salesman got traveling *expenses*] **4.** a cause of spending [a car can be a great *expense*] —**at the expense of** with the payment, loss, sacrifice, etc. of

☆**expense account 1.** an arrangement whereby certain expenses of an employee related to his work are paid for by his employer **2.** a record of these expenses

ex·pen·sive (ik spen'siv) *adj.* requiring or involving much expense; high-priced; dear —see SYN. at COSTLY —**ex·pen'sive·ly** *adv.* —**ex·pen'sive·ness** *n.*

ex·pe·ri·ence (ik spir'ē əns) *n.* [< OFr. < L. < prp. of *experiri*, to try < *ex-*, out + base as in *peritus*, experienced] **1.** the act of living through an event or events [*experience* teaches us much] **2.** anything or everything observed or lived through [an *experience* he'll never forget] **3.** effect on one of anything or everything that has happened to him **4.** *a)* activity that includes training, practice, and work *b)* the period of such activity *c)* knowledge, skill, or practice resulting from this [an actor with much *experience*] —*vt.* **-enced, -enc·ing** to have experience of; undergo

ex·pe·ri·enced (-ənst) *adj.* **1.** having had much experience **2.** having learned from experience; made wise, competent, etc. by experience

ex·pe·ri·en·tial (ik spir'ē en'shəl) *adj.* of or based on experience —**ex·pe'ri·en'tial·ly** *adv.*

ex·per·i·ment (ik sper'ə mənt; *for v., also* -ment') *n.* [< OFr. < L. *experimentum* < *experiri*: see EXPERIENCE] **1.** a test or trial of something; specif., any action or process undertaken to dis-

cover something not yet known or to demonstrate or test something known **2.** the conducting of such tests or trials —*vi.* to make an experiment —see SYN. at TRIAL —**ex·per'i·ment'er** *n.*

ex·per·i·men·tal (ik sper'ə men't'l) *adj.* **1.** of or based on experience rather than on theory or authority **2.** based on, tested by, or having the nature of, experiment [an *experimental* science] **3.** being an experiment; testing; trial [a baby's first, *experimental* steps] **4.** of or used for experiments [an *experimental* farm] —**ex·per'i·men'tal·ly** *adv.*

ex·per·i·men·ta·tion (ik sper'ə mən tā'shən, -men-) *n.* the act or practice of experimenting

ex·pert (ek'spərt; *also, for adj.,* ik spurt') *adj.* [< OFr. < L. pp. of *experiri*: see EXPERIENCE] **1.** very skillful; having much training and knowledge in some special field **2.** of or from an expert [an *expert* opinion] —*n.* a person who is very skillful or highly trained and informed in some special field —**ex'pert·ly** *adv.* —**ex'pert·ness** *n.*

ex·per·tise (ek'spər tēz') *n.* [Fr.] the skill, knowledge, judgment, etc. of an expert

ex·pi·ate (ek'spē āt') *vt.* **-at'ed, -at'ing** [< L. pp. of *expiare* < *ex-*, out + *piare*, to appease < *pius*, devout] to make amends for (wrongdoing or guilt); atone for; pay the penalty for [he *expiated* his sins by doing good works] —**ex'pi·a·ble** (-ə b'l) *adj.* —**ex'pi·a'tion** *n.* —**ex'pi·a'tor** *n.*

ex·pi·a·to·ry (ek'spē ə tôr'ē) *adj.* that expiates or is meant to expiate

ex·pi·ra·tion (ek'spə rā'shən) *n.* **1.** a breathing out, as of air from the lungs **2.** something breathed out **3.** a breathing one's last; dying **4.** a coming to an end; close [the *expiration* of a term of office] —**ex·pir·a·to·ry** (ik spīr'ə tôr'ē) *adj.*

ex·pire (ik spīr') *vt.* **-pired', -pir'ing** [< L. *exspirare* < *ex-*, out + *spirare*, to breathe] to breathe out (air from the lungs) —*vi.* **1.** to breathe out air **2.** to breathe one's last breath; die **3.** to come to an end; terminate [the lease has *expired*] —see SYN. at DIE[1]

ex·plain (ik splān') *vt.* [< L. < *ex-*, out + *planare*, to make level < *planus*, level] **1.** to make plain or understandable; give details of [*explain* the new plan] **2.** to give the meaning or interpretation of; expound [*explain* the allegory] **3.** to account for; state reasons for [*explain* your absence] —*vi.* to give an explanation —**explain away** to state reasons for so as to justify —**explain oneself 1.** to make clear what one means **2.** to give reasons justifying one's conduct —**ex·plain'a·ble** *adj.* —**ex·plain'er** *n.*

SYN.—**explain** implies a making clear of something that is not known or understood [to *explain* how a machine operates]; **expound** implies an orderly and thorough explanation, often one made by a person having expert knowledge [to *expound* a theory]; **explicate** implies a scholarly analysis or explanation that is developed in detail [the *explication* of a Biblical passage]; **elucidate** implies a shedding light upon by clear and specific explanation, illustration, etc. [to *elucidate* the country's foreign policy]; to **interpret** is to bring out meanings not immediately clear, as by translation, personal insight, or special knowledge [how do you *interpret* his silence?]; **construe** suggests a particular interpretation of something that can be understood in several ways [his statement is not to be lightly *construed*]

ex·pla·na·tion (eks'plə nā'shən) *n.* **1.** an explaining **2.** something that explains **3.** the interpretation, meaning, etc. given in explaining

ex·plan·a·to·ry (ik splan'ə tôr'ē) *adj.* explaining or intended to explain: also **ex·plan'a·tive** —**ex·plan'a·to'ri·ly** *adv.*

ex·plant (eks plant') *vt.* [EX- + PLANT, *v.*] to transfer (living tissue) for culture in an artificial medium

ex·ple·tive (eks'plə tiv) *n.* [< LL. < L. pp. of *explere* < *ex-*, out + *plere*, to fill] **1.** an oath or exclamation ["hell!" and "wow!" are *expletives*] **2.** a word, phrase, etc. used merely to fill out a sentence or metrical line [there in "there is nothing left" is an *expletive*] —*adj.* used to fill out a sentence, line, etc.: also **ex'ple·to·ry** (-tôr'ē)

ex·pli·ca·ble (eks'pli kə b'l, iks plik'ə b'l) *adj.* that can be explained

ex·pli·cate (eks'pli kāt') *vt.* **-cat'ed, -cat'ing** [< L. pp. of *explicare* < *ex-*, out + *plicare*, to fold] to make clear or explicit (something unclear or implied); explain fully —see SYN. at EXPLAIN —**ex'pli·ca'tion** *n.* —**ex'pli·ca'tive** (-kāt'iv, ik splik'ə-) *adj.*, **ex'pli·ca·to'ry** (-kə tôr'ē, ik splik'ə-) *adj.* —**ex'pli·ca'tor** *n.*

ex·plic·it (ik splis'it) *adj.* [< ML. < L. pp. of *explicare*: see prec.] **1.** clearly stated or expressed, with no doubt as to mean-

---

ing; definite [he gave his *explicit* approval] **2.** saying what is meant, without holding anything back; outspoken [he was *explicit* about the need for tax reform] **3.** plain to see —**ex·plic′it·ly** *adv.* —**ex·plic′it·ness** *n.*

ex·plode (ik splōd′) *vt.* **-plod′ed, -plod′ing** [orig., to drive off the stage by clapping and hooting < L. *explodere* < *ex-*, off + *plaudere*, to applaud] **1.** to show to be false or foolish; discredit [to *explode* a theory] **2.** to make burst with a loud noise; blow up **3.** to cause a rapid, violent change in by chemical reaction or by nuclear fission or fusion —*vi.* **1.** to burst noisily and violently **2.** to break forth noisily [to *explode* with anger] **3.** to increase very rapidly [an *exploding* population] —**ex·plod′a·ble** *adj.* —**ex·plod′er** *n.*

exploded view a photograph or drawing showing separately but in their proper relationship the various parts of something

ex·ploit (eks′ploit; *also, and for v. usually,* ik sploit′) *n.* [< OFr. < L. pp. of *explicare*: see EX-PLICATE] a daring act or bold deed —*vt.* **1.** to make use of; utilize productively [to *exploit* the water power of a river] **2.** to make use of or profit from the labor of (others) in an unethical way [talented children are sometimes *exploited* by their parents] **3.** to promote or further the sales of (a product, etc.) —**ex·ploit′a·ble** *adj.* —**ex′ploi·ta′tion** *n.* —**ex·ploit′a·tive, ex·ploi′tive** *adj.* —**ex·ploit′er** *n.*

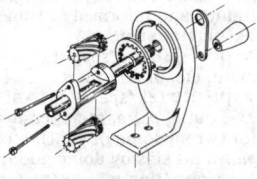
EXPLODED VIEW
(of pencil sharpener)

ex·plo·ra·tion (eks′plə rā′shən, -plô-) *n.* an exploring or being explored —**ex·plor·a·to·ry** (ik splôr′ə tôr′ē), **ex·plor′a·tive** (-tiv) *adj.*

ex·plore (ik splôr′) *vt.* **-plored′, -plor′ing** [L. *explorare*, to search out < *ex-*, out + *plorare*, to cry out] **1.** to look into or examine carefully [to *explore* ways and means of raising money] **2.** to travel in (a region previously unknown or little known) for discovery **3.** *Med.* to examine (an organ, etc.) by operation, probing, etc., as in order to make a diagnosis —*vi.* to explore new regions, etc. —**ex·plor′er** *n.*

ex·plo·sion (ik splō′zhən) *n.* **1.** an exploding; esp., a blowing up; detonation **2.** the noise made by exploding **3.** a noisy outburst [an *explosion* of temper] **4.** a sudden, rapid, and widespread increase [the population *explosion*]

ex·plo·sive (-siv) *adj.* **1.** of, causing, or having the nature of, an explosion **2.** tending to explode; esp., tending to burst forth noisily **3.** *same as* PLOSIVE —*n.* **1.** a substance that can explode, as gunpowder **2.** *same as* PLOSIVE —**ex·plo′sive·ly** *adv.* —**ex·plo′sive·ness** *n.*

ex·po·nent (ik spō′nənt; *for n. 3, usually* ek′spō′nənt) *adj.* [< L. prp. of *exponere*: see EXPOUND] explaining, interpreting, or expounding —*n.* **1.** a person who explains, interprets, or promotes (principles, methods, etc.) [an *exponent* of modern music] **2.** a person or thing that is an example or symbol (*of* something) **3.** *Math.* a small figure or symbol placed at the upper right of another figure or symbol to show how many times the latter is to be multiplied by itself (Ex.: $b^2 = b \times b$)

ex·po·nen·tial (eks′pō nen′shəl) *adj. Math.* **1.** of an exponent **2.** involving a variable or unknown quantity as an exponent —**ex′po·nen′tial·ly** *adv.*

ex·port (ik spôrt′; *also, and for n. & adj. always,* eks′pôrt) *vt.* [< L. < *ex-*, out + *portare*, to carry] **1.** to carry or send (goods, etc.) to other countries, esp. for purposes of sale **2.** to carry or send (ideas, culture, etc.) from one place to another —*n.* **1.** something exported **2.** an exporting Also **ex′por·ta′tion** —*adj.* of or for exporting or exports —**ex·port′a·ble** *adj.* —**ex·port′er** *n.*

ex·pose (ik spōz′) *vt.* **-posed′, -pos′ing** [< OFr. < L. pp. of *exponere*: see EXPOUND] **1.** *a)* to lay open (*to* danger, attack, ridicule, etc.); leave unprotected *b)* to make open or subject (*to* an influence or action) **2.** to leave out in the open, as to die **3.** to allow to be seen; reveal; display [he removed the bandage and *exposed* the wound] **4.** *a)* to make (a crime, fraud, etc.) known *b)* to make known the crimes, etc. of **5.** *Photog.* to let light rays, X-rays, etc. fall on (a sensitized film or plate) so as to record a picture —see SYN. at SHOW —**ex·pos′er** *n.*

ex·po·sé (eks′pō zā′) *n.* [Fr., pp. of *exposer*, to expose] a public uncovering of a scandal, crime, etc.

ex·po·si·tion (eks′pə zish′ən) *n.* [< OFr. < L. pp. of *exponere*: see EXPOUND] **1.** a setting forth of facts, ideas, etc.; detailed explanation **2.** writing or speaking that sets forth or

explains **3.** a large public exhibition or show **4.** the first section of certain musical forms, introducing the main theme or themes

ex·pos·i·tor (ik späz′ə tər) *n.* one that expounds or explains

ex·pos·i·to·ry (-ə tôr′ē) *adj.* of, like, or containing exposition; that serves to explain: also **ex·pos′i·tive** (-ə tiv)

ex post fac·to (eks pōst fak′tō) [L., from (the thing) done afterward] done or made afterward, esp. when having retroactive effect [an *ex post facto* law]

ex·pos·tu·late (ik späs′chə lāt′) *vi.* **-lat′ed, -lat′ing** [< L. pp. of *expostulare* < *ex-*, intens. + *postulare*, to demand] to reason with a person earnestly, objecting to his actions or intentions; remonstrate (*with*) —see SYN. at OBJECT —**ex·pos′tu·la′tion** *n.* —**ex·pos′tu·la′tor** *n.* —**ex·pos′tu·la·to·ry** (-lə tôr′ē) *adj.*

ex·po·sure (ik spō′zhər) *n.* **1.** an exposing or being exposed **2.** a location, as of a house, in relation to the sun, winds, etc. [an eastern *exposure*] **3.** appearance or appearances before the public, as on TV, etc. **4.** a being exposed, when helpless, to the sun, storms, etc. **5.** *Photog. a)* the exposing of a film or plate to light, etc. *b)* a film section for making one picture *c)* the time during which film is exposed

ex·pound (ik spound′) *vt.* [< OFr. < L. < *ex-*, out + *ponere*, to put] **1.** to set forth; state in detail **2.** to explain or interpret —see SYN. at EXPLAIN —**ex·pound′er** *n.*

ex·press (ik spres′) *vt.* [< ML. *expressus*, pp. of *exprimere* < *ex-*, out + *premere*: see PRESS¹] **1.** to press out or squeeze out (juice, etc.) **2.** to put into words; state **3.** to make known; show [his face *expressed* joy] **4.** to represent in art, music, etc. **5.** to show by a sign; symbolize [the sign + *expresses* addition] ☆**6.** to send by express —*adj.* **1.** *a)* expressed and not implied; explicit [to give *express* orders] *b)* specific [his *express* reason for going] **2.** fast, direct, and making few stops [an *express* train] **3.** *a)* for fast driving [an *express* highway] *b)* having to do with express (*n.* 2) —*adv.* by express —*n.* **1.** an express train, bus, elevator, etc. ☆**2.** *a)* a method or service for transporting goods rapidly: express is usually more expensive than freight *b)* the things sent by express **3.** any method or means of swift transmission —**express oneself 1.** to state one's thoughts **2.** to give expression to one's feelings, imagination, talents, etc. —**ex·press′er** *n.* —**ex·press′i·ble** *adj.*

ex·pres·sion (ik spresh′ən) *n.* **1.** a pressing out or squeezing out, as of juice **2.** a putting into words **3.** a representing in art, music, etc. **4.** a manner of expressing; esp., a way of speaking, singing, etc. something that gives it real meaning or feeling [to read with *expression*] **5.** a particular word or phrase [a trite *expression*] **6.** a showing of feeling, character, etc. [laughter is an *expression* of joy] **7.** a look, intonation, etc. that shows meaning or feeling [a sad *expression* on his face] **8.** a symbol or set of symbols expressing some mathematical fact **9.** a showing by a symbol, sign, figures, etc. —**ex·pres′sion·less** *adj.* —**ex·pres′sion·less·ly** *adv.*

ex·pres·sion·ism (-iz′m) *n.* an early 20th-cent. movement in art, drama, etc., in which reality, form, etc. were distorted so as to express the artist's or writer's feelings and thoughts in a striking, forceful way —**ex·pres′sion·ist** *adj., n.* —**ex·pres′sion·is′tic** *adj.* —**ex·pres′sion·is′ti·cal·ly** *adv.*

ex·pres·sive (ik spres′iv) *adj.* **1.** of or characterized by expression **2.** that expresses; indicative (*of*) [a song *expressive* of joy] **3.** full of meaning or feeling [an *expressive* nod] —**ex·pres′sive·ly** *adv.* —**ex·pres′sive·ness** *n.*

ex·press·ly (ik spres′lē) *adv.* **1.** plainly; definitely; explicitly [I *expressly* told him not to go] **2.** especially; particularly [she went to school *expressly* to become a nurse]

☆**ex·press·man** (-mən) *n., pl.* **-men** a person employed by an express company; esp., a driver of an express truck, who collects and delivers packages

ex·pres·so (ek spres′ō) *n. same as* ESPRESSO

☆**ex·press·way** (ik spres′wā′) *n.* a divided highway for high-speed, through traffic, with controlled access and generally with overpasses or underpasses at intersections

ex·pro·pri·ate (eks prō′prē āt′) *vt.* **-at′ed, -at′ing** [< ML. pp. of *expropriare* < L. *ex-*, out + *proprius*, one's own] to take (land, property, etc.) from its owner, esp. for public use —**ex·pro′pri·a′tion** *n.* —**ex·pro′pri·a′tor** *n.*

ex·pul·sion (ik spul′shən) *n.* an expelling, or forcing out, or the condition of being expelled —**ex·pul′sive** (-siv) *adj.*

ex·punge (ik spunj′) *vt.* **-punged′, -pung′ing** [L. *expungere* < *ex-*, out + *pungere*, to prick] to erase or remove completely [to *expunge* names from a record] —see SYN. at ERASE

ex·pur·gate (eks′pər gāt′) *vt.* **-gat′ed, -gat′ing** [< L. pp. of *expurgare* < *ex-*, out + *purgare*, PURGE] to remove passages considered obscene or otherwise objectionable from (a book, etc.) —**ex′pur·ga′tion** *n.* —**ex′pur·ga′tor** *n.*

ex·qui·site (eks′kwi zit, ik skwiz′it) *adj.* [< L. pp. of *exquirere,* to search out < *ex-,* out + *quaerere,* to ask] **1.** carefully done or elaborately made [an *exquisite* design] **2.** very beautiful, esp. in a delicate or carefully wrought way [an *exquisite,* lacy leaf] **3.** of highest quality; consummate [*exquisite* technique] **4.** highly sensitive; keenly discriminating [an *exquisite* ear for music] **5.** sharply intense; keen [*exquisite* pain] —*n.* one who makes a great show of being refined and fastidious in his tastes, etc. —**ex′qui·site·ly** *adv.* —**ex′qui·site·ness** *n.*

ext. **1.** extension **2.** external **3.** extra **4.** extract

ex·tant (ek′stənt, ik stant′) *adj.* [< L. prp. of *exstare* < *ex-,* out + *stare,* STAND] still existing [one of the few *extant* copies of the book]

ex·tem·po·ra·ne·ous (ik stem′pə rā′nē əs) *adj.* [< LL.: see EXTEMPORE] **1.** made, done, or spoken without any preparation; offhand **2.** spoken with some preparation but not written out or memorized: see IMPROMPTU **3.** speaking or skilled at speaking without preparation —**ex·tem′po·ra·ne·ous·ly** *adv.*

ex·tem·po·rar·y (ik stem′pə rer′ē) *adj. same as* EXTEMPORANEOUS —**ex·tem′po·rar′i·ly** *adv.*

ex·tem·po·re (ik stem′pə rē) *adv., adj.* [L. < *ex,* out of + *tempore,* abl. of *tempus,* time] without preparation; offhand [to speak *extempore*]

ex·tem·po·rize (-rīz′) *vi., vt.* **-rized′, -riz′ing** **1.** to speak, perform, or compose extempore; improvise **2.** to make (something), or manage to get along, by using what is available —**ex·tem′po·ri·za′tion** *n.* —**ex·tem′po·riz′er** *n.*

ex·tend (ik stend′) *vt.* [L. *extendere* < *ex-,* out + *tendere,* to stretch: see TEND²] **1.** *a)* to stretch out or draw out *b)* to draw out or lengthen in time or space; prolong [cleaning *extends* the life of a rug] **2.** to enlarge in area, scope, influence, etc.; expand; spread [to *extend* a nation's power] **3.** to stretch forth; hold out [to *extend* one's hand in greeting] **4.** to offer; accord; grant [to *extend* congratulations to the winner] **5.** to straighten out (a flexed limb of the body) **6.** to make (oneself) work or try hard **7.** to increase the bulk of (a substance) by adding another substance, usually one cheaper or inferior —*vi.* **1.** to be extended **2.** to reach or stretch [the fence *extends* to the meadow]

SYN.—**extend** and **lengthen** both imply a making longer in space or time, but **extend** also may refer to an enlarging in area, scope, influence, etc.; **elongate** indicates a stretching out in space to unusual length; **prolong** and **protract** both imply an extending in time, with **prolong** suggesting a going on beyond the usual or expected limit and **protract** suggesting a being drawn out in a needless or tiring way

ex·tend·ed (ik sten′did) *adj.* **1.** stretched out; spread out **2.** drawn out in time; prolonged **3.** enlarged in influence, meaning, scope, etc.; widespread

ex·tend·er (-dər) *n.* **1.** a substance added to another to give more bulk or body or to adulterate or dilute it **2.** a part added or attached, for lengthening

ex·ten·si·ble (ik sten′sə b'l) *adj.* that can be extended: also **ex·tend′i·ble** —**ex·ten′si·bil′i·ty** *n.*

ex·ten·sion (ik sten′shən) *n.* **1.** an extending or being extended **2.** range; extent **3.** a part that forms a continuation or addition [building an *extension* onto the library] **4.** an extra period of time allowed a debtor for making payment **5.** a branch of a university located away from its main campus **6.** an extra telephone on the same line as the main telephone **7.** *Physics* that property of a body by which it occupies space —☆*adj.* designating a device that can be extended or that extends something else [extension ladder, extension cord] —**ex·ten′sion·al** *adj.*

EXTENSION LADDER

ex·ten·sive (ik sten′siv) *adj.* **1.** of great extent, or area, amount, length, etc.; vast [the *extensive* jungles of Brazil] **2.** broad in scope, influence, etc.; far-reaching [making *extensive* changes in the law] —**ex·ten′sive·ly** *adv.* —**ex·ten′sive·ness** *n.*

ex·ten·sor (ik sten′sər) *n.* a muscle that extends or straightens some part of the body, esp. a flexed arm or leg

ex·tent (ik stent′) *n.* **1.** the space, amount, or degree to which a thing extends; length; breadth **2.** range or limits; scope; coverage [to the full *extent* of the law] **3.** an extended space; vast area [an *extent* of woodland]

ex·ten·u·ate (ik sten′yōō wāt′) *vt.* **-at′ed, -at′ing** [< L. pp. of *extenuare* < *ex-,* out + *tenuare,* to make thin < *tenuis,* THIN] to lessen or seem to lessen the seriousness of (an offense, guilt, etc.) by giving excuses or serving as an excuse [*extenuating* circumstances] —**ex·ten′u·a′tion** *n.*

ex·te·ri·or (ik stir′ē ər) *adj.* [L., compar. of *exter(us),* on the outside: see EXTERNAL] **1.** *a)* on the outside; outer; outermost [an *exterior* wall] *b)* for use on the outside [*exterior* paint] **2.** acting or coming from without [*exterior* forces] —*n.* **1.** an outside or outside surface **2.** an outward appearance [misled by his calm *exterior*] ☆**3.** a picture, view, setting, etc. of an outdoor scene —**ex·te′ri·or·ly** *adv.*

exterior angle any of the four angles formed on the outside of two straight lines by a straight line cutting across them

ex·te·ri·or·ize (-ə rīz′) *vt.* **-ized′, -iz′ing** *same as* EXTERNALIZE —**ex·te′ri·or·i·za′tion** *n.*

ex·ter·mi·nate (ik stur′mə nāt′) *vt.* **-nat′ed, -nat′ing** [< L. pp. of *exterminare,* to drive out, destroy < *ex-,* out + *terminus,* a boundary] to destroy or get rid of entirely, as by killing; wipe out; annihilate —**ex·ter′mi·na′tion** *n.*

EXTERIOR ANGLES (CEL, LER, ADT, TDF)

SYN.—**exterminate** implies the complete destruction of living beings or things that one wants to get rid of [to *exterminate* the ants in the kitchen]; **extirpate** and **eradicate** both imply the complete rooting out of something, **extirpate** suggesting an act that is swift, forceful, thorough, etc. [to *extirpate* a tumor; to *extirpate* the traffic in drugs] and **eradicate** suggesting a process that takes time and planning [to *eradicate* illiteracy in a nation]

ex·ter·mi·na·tor (-nāt′ər) *n.* a person or thing that exterminates; specif., ☆*a)* one whose work is exterminating rats, cockroaches, and other vermin ☆*b)* any of various powders, liquids, etc. for exterminating vermin

ex·tern (ek′stərn) *n.* [< Fr. < L. *externus:* see EXTERNAL] a person working in an institution but not living in it, as a non-resident doctor in a hospital

ex·ter·nal (ik stur′n'l) *adj.* [< L. *externus* < *exter(us),* on the outside, compar. form < *ex,* out of (see EX-) + -AL] **1.** that is on the outside; outer; exterior **2.** on, or for use on, the outside of the body [a medicine for *external* use only] **3.** *a)* outwardly visible [all *external* signs indicated that he was healthy] *b)* existing apart from the mind; material **4.** acting or coming from without [an *external* force] **5.** *a)* for outward appearance or show; superficial [mere *external* politeness] *b)* not basic or essential [*external* factors] **6.** having to do with foreign countries [a nation's *external* affairs] —*n.* **1.** an outside or outward surface or part **2.** [*pl.*] outward appearance or behavior [to judge by *externals*] —**ex·ter·nal·i·ty** (eks′tər nal′ə tē) *n., pl.* **-ties** —**ex·ter′nal·ly** *adv.*

ex·ter·nal·ize (-īz′) *vt.* **-ized′, -iz′ing** to make, or think of as being, external —**ex·ter′nal·i·za′tion** *n.*

ex·tinct (ik stiŋkt′) *adj.* [< L. pp. of *exstinguere:* see EXTINGUISH] **1.** no longer active [an *extinct* volcano] **2.** no longer living; having died out [an *extinct* species]

ex·tinc·tion (ik stiŋk′shən) *n.* **1.** a putting out or being put out, as of a fire **2.** a destroying or being destroyed **3.** the fact or state of being or becoming extinct; dying out, as of a species of animal

ex·tin·guish (ik stiŋ′gwish) *vt.* [< L. *exstinguere* < *ex-,* out + *stinguere,* to extinguish] **1.** to put out (a fire, light, etc.) **2.** to put an end to; destroy [to *extinguish* all hope] **3.** to eclipse; obscure —**ex·tin′guish·a·ble** *adj.* —**ex·tin′guish·er** *n.* —**ex·tin′guish·ment** *n.*

ex·tir·pate (ek′stər pāt′, ik stur′pāt) *vt.* **-pat′ed, -pat′ing** [< L. pp. of *ex(s)tirpare* < *ex-,* out + *stirps,* root: for IE. base see STARE] **1.** to pull up by the roots **2.** to destroy completely; abolish —see SYN. at EXTERMINATE —**ex′tir·pa′tion** *n.* —**ex′tir·pa′tive** *adj.* —**ex′tir·pa′tor** *n.*

ex·tol, ex·toll (ik stōl′) *vt.* **-tolled′, -tol′ling** [< L. *extollere* < *ex-*, up + *tollere*, to raise] to praise highly; laud —see SYN. at PRAISE —**ex·tol′ler** *n.* —**ex·tol′ment, ex·toll′ment** *n.*

ex·tort (ik stôrt′) *vt.* [< L. pp. of *extorquere* < *ex-*, out + *torquere*, to twist: see TORT] to get (money, a confession, a promise, etc.) by force, threats, misuse of authority, etc.; exact (*from*) —**ex·tort′er** *n.* —**ex·tor′tive** *adj.*

ex·tor·tion (ik stôr′shən) *n.* **1.** an extorting: sometimes applied to the demanding of too high a price **2.** *Law* the offense of an official who extorts **3.** something extorted

ex·tor·tion·ate (-it) *adj.* **1.** using extortion **2.** excessive; exorbitant [an *extortionate* price]

ex·tor·tion·er (-ər) *n.* a person guilty of extortion: also **extor′tion·ist**

ex·tra (eks′trə) *adj.* [contr. < EXTRAORDINARY; also < L. < *extra*, *adv.*, more than, outside: see EXTRA-] **1.** more, larger, or better than is normal, expected, necessary, etc.; additional [carrying *extra* fuel] **2.** to be paid for by an added charge [such services are *extra*] —*n.* an extra person or thing; specif., *a*) an additional charge ☆*b*) formerly, a special edition of a newspaper, covering unusually important news *c*) an extra benefit or feature *d*) a spare copy *e*) an extra worker *f*) *Motion Pictures* an actor hired by the day to play a minor part —*adv.* more than usually [*extra* hot]

ex·tra- [L. < *exter(us)*: see EXTERNAL] *a prefix meaning* outside, outside the scope of, beyond, as in the following list:

extrafamilial extramarital
extragovernmental extraofficial
extrajudicial extraterrestrial

☆**ex·tra-base hit** (-bās′) *Baseball* any hit greater than a single; double, triple, or home run

ex·tract (ik strakt′; *for n.* eks′trakt) *vt.* [< L. pp. of *extrahere* < *ex-*, out + *trahere*, to DRAW] **1.** to draw out by effort; pull out [to *extract* teeth, to *extract* a promise] **2.** to separate (metal) from ore **3.** to obtain by pressing, distilling, using a solvent, etc. [to *extract* juice from fruit] **4.** to deduce, derive, or elicit (meaning, information, pleasure, etc.) **5.** to copy out or quote (a passage from a book, etc.) **6.** *Math.* to find (the root of a quantity) —*n.* something extracted; specif., *a*) a concentrated form of a food, flavoring, etc. [vanilla *extract*] *b*) a quotation from a book, etc. —**ex·tract′a·ble, ex·tract′i·ble** *adj.* —**extrac′tive** *adj.* —**ex·trac′tor** *n.*

SYN.—**extract** implies a drawing out of something, as if by pulling [to *extract* testimony from an unwilling witness]; **educe** suggests a bringing out or evolving of something that is undeveloped [to *educe* a theory from the known facts]; **elicit** suggests difficulty or skill in drawing forth something [his jokes *elicited* laughter from the angry crowd]; **evoke** implies a calling forth, as of a mental image, by stimulating the mind or emotions [the odor *evoked* a memory of childhood]

ex·trac·tion (ik strak′shən) *n.* **1.** an extracting; specif., the extracting of a tooth **2.** origin; lineage; descent [a man of French *extraction*]

☆**ex·tra·cur·ric·u·lar** (eks′trə kə rik′yə lər) *adj.* not part of the required curriculum or course of studies [dramatics, athletics, and other *extracurricular* school activities]

ex·tra·dite (eks′trə dīt′) *vt.* **-dit′ed, -dit′ing** [back-formation < EXTRADITION] **1.** to turn over (an alleged criminal, fugitive, etc.) to the jurisdiction of another country, State, etc. **2.** to obtain the extradition of —**ex′tra·dit′a·ble** *adj.*

ex·tra·di·tion (eks′trə dish′ən) *n.* [Fr. < L. *ex*, out + *traditio*, a surrender: see TRADITION] the turning over of an alleged criminal, fugitive, etc. by one country, State, etc. to another

ex·tra·dos (eks′trə däs′, -dōs′; ik strā′däs) *n.* [Fr. < L. *extra*, beyond + Fr. *dos* < L. *dorsum*, back] *Archit.* the outside curved surface of an arch

EXTRADOS

ex·tra·le·gal (eks′trə lē′g'l) *adj.* outside of legal control or authority; not regulated by law —**ex′tra·le′gal·ly** *adv.*

ex·tra·ne·ous (ik strā′nē əs) *adj.* [< L. *extraneus* < *extra*: see EXTRA-] **1.** coming from outside; foreign [filtered to remove *extraneous* matter] **2.** not essential or not pertinent —see SYN. at EXTRINSIC —**ex·tra′ne·ous·ly** *adv.* —**ex·tra′ne·ous·ness** *n.*

ex·traor·di·nar·y (ik strôr′d'n er′ē; *for 3* eks′trə ôr′-) *adj.* [< L. < *extra ordinem*, out of the usual order] **1.** not according to the usual custom or regular plan [an *extraordinary* session of Congress] **2.** very unusual; exceptional; remarkable [her *extraordinary* poise] **3.** outside of the regular staff; sent on a special errand [an envoy *extraordinary*] —**ex·traor′di·nar′i·ly** *adv.* —**ex·traor′di·nar′i·ness** *n.*

ex·trap·o·late (ik strap′ə lāt′) *vt., vi.* **-lat′ed, -lat′ing** [L. *extra* (see EXTRA-) + (INTER)POLATE] **1.** to estimate (a value, quantity, etc. beyond the known range) on the basis of certain known variables **2.** to arrive at (conclusions) by speculating on the basis of (known facts) —*n.* an instance of excess in extrapolating —**ex·trap′o·la′tion** *n.* —**ex·trap′o·la′tive** *adj.* —**ex·trap′o·la′tor** *n.*

ex·tra·sen·so·ry (eks′trə sen′sər ē) *adj.* seeming to occur apart from the normal working of the senses of sight, hearing, etc. [*extrasensory* perception]

ex·tra·ter·ri·to·ri·al (-ter′ə tôr′ē əl) *adj.* **1.** outside the territorial limits or jurisdiction of the country, State, etc. **2.** of extraterritoriality

ex·tra·ter·ri·to·ri·al·i·ty (-tôr′ē al′ə tē) *n.* **1.** freedom from the jurisdiction of a country: a privilege of foreign diplomats, etc. **2.** jurisdiction of a country over its citizens in foreign lands

ex·trav·a·gance (ik strav′ə gəns) *n.* **1.** a going beyond reasonable or proper limits; excess **2.** a spending of more than is reasonable or necessary **3.** an instance of excess in spending, behavior, or speech Also **ex·trav′a·gan·cy**, *pl.* **-cies**

ex·trav·a·gant (-gənt) *adj.* [< Anglo-Fr. < ML. prp. of *extravagari* < L. *extra*, beyond + *vagari*, to wander] **1.** going beyond reasonable limits; excessive or unrestrained [*extravagant* praise] **2.** too ornate or showy [*extravagant* designs] **3.** costing or spending too much —see SYN. at EXCESSIVE —**ex·trav′a·gant·ly** *adv.*

ex·trav·a·gan·za (ik strav′ə gan′zə) *n.* [< It. *estravaganza*, extravagance] **1.** a literary, musical, or dramatic fantasy characterized by a loose structure and farce **2.** a spectacular, elaborate theatrical show, as some musicals

ex·trav·a·sate (ik strav′ə sāt′) *vi., vt.* **-sat′ed, -sat′ing** [L. *extra* (see EXTRA-) + *vas*, a vessel + -ATE[1]] to escape or force to flow into surrounding tissue, as blood, lymph, etc. —**ex·trav′a·sa′tion** *n.*

☆**ex·tra·ve·hic·u·lar** (eks′trə vē hik′yoo lər) *adj.* designating or of activity by an astronaut outside a vehicle in space

ex·tra·ver·sion (eks′trə vur′zhən) *n.* same as EXTROVERSION —**ex′tra·vert′** (-vurt′) *n., adj.*

ex·treme (ik strēm′) *adj.* [OFr. < L. *extremus*, superl. of *exterus*, outer: see EXTERNAL] **1.** at the end or outermost point; farthest away [the *extreme* limits of outer space] **2.** to the greatest or an excessive degree; very great [*extreme* pain] **3.** very unusual or unconventional [*extreme* styles] **4.** furthest from a central or moderate view; specif., furthest to the right or left in politics **5.** very severe; drastic [*extreme* measures] —*n.* **1.** either of two things that are as different or as far as possible from each other **2.** an extreme degree **3.** an extreme act, expedient, etc. **4.** an extreme state **5.** *Math.* the first or last term of a proportion —**go to extremes** to do or say more than is reasonable or proper —**in the extreme** to the utmost degree —**ex·treme′ly** *adv.* —**ex·treme′ness** *n.*

extremely high frequency any radio frequency between 30,000 and 300,000 megahertz

extreme unction same as ANOINTING OF THE SICK

ex·trem·ist (ik strēm′ist) *n.* **1.** one who goes to extremes **2.** a person who holds extreme views, as in politics —*adj.* of extremists or extreme views, actions, etc. —**ex·trem′ism** *n.*

ex·trem·i·ty (ik strem′ə tē) *n., pl.* **-ties** **1.** the outermost or utmost point or part; end [the eastern *extremity* of the island] **2.** the greatest degree [an *extremity* of grief] **3.** a state of extreme necessity, danger, etc. [the surrounded troops realized the *extremity* of their position] **4.** the end of life; dying **5.** an extreme measure; strong action: *usually used in pl.* [to resort to *extremities* in an emergency] **6.** *a*) a body limb *b*) [*pl.*] the hands and feet

ex·tri·cate (eks′trə kāt′) *vt.* **-cat′ed, -cat′ing** [< L. pp. of *extricare* < *ex-*, out + *tricae*, hindrances, vexations] to set free; disentangle (*from* a net, difficulty, embarrassment, etc.) —**ex′tri·ca·ble** (-kə b'l) *adj.* —**ex′tri·ca′tion** *n.*

ex·trin·sic (ek strin′sik) *adj.* [< Fr. < L. *extrinsecus*, from without < *exter*, without + *secus*, following] **1.** not really belonging to the thing with which it is connected; not inherent **2.** being, coming, or acting from the outside; extraneous —**ex·trin′si·cal·ly** *adv.*

SYN.—**extrinsic** refers to that which may be connected with something else but is not an essential part of it [much of the discussion was *extrinsic* to the main issue]; **extraneous** also implies that something is not essential and often that it can be easily done without [in his second portrait, the artist left out *extraneous* details]; **foreign** refers to something regarded as not belonging in or with something else because it is very different [bragging is *foreign* to his nature; *foreign* matter in a solution] **alien** suggests something so different that it cannot or should not be associated with something else [a practice *alien* to our tradition]

ex·trorse (eks trôrs′) *adj.* [ult. < L. *extra*, outside + *vertere*, to turn] *Bot.* turned outward or away from the axis of growth —**ex·trorse′ly** *adv.*

ex·tro·ver·sion (eks′trə vur′zhən) *n.* [< G. < L. *extra*- (see EXTRA-) + ML. *versio*, a turning: see VERSION] *Psychol.* an attitude in which a person directs his interest to things outside himself and to other people rather than to his own experiences and feelings: opposed to INTROVERSION

ex·tro·vert (eks′trə vurt′) *n. Psychol.* a person who is interested in other people and things rather than just in his own thoughts and feelings: opposed to INTROVERT —*adj.* showing extroversion; outgoing: usually **ex′tro·vert′ed**

ex·trude (ik strōōd′) *vt.* **-trud′ed, -trud′ing** [L. *extrudere* < *ex-*, out + *trudere*, to THRUST] **1.** to push or force out **2.** to force (metal, plastic, etc.) through a die or very small holes to give it a certain shape —*vi.* to be extruded; esp., to protrude —**ex·trud′er** *n.* —**ex·tru′sion** (-strōō′zhən) *n.* —**ex·tru′sive** *adj.*

ex·u·ber·ance (ig zōō′bər əns, -zyōō′-) *n.* [< Fr. < L. < prp. of *exuberare* < *ex-*, intens. + *uberare*, to bear abundantly < *uber*, udder] **1.** the state or quality of being exuberant; great abundance **2.** an instance of this; esp., action or speech showing high spirits Also **ex·u′ber·an·cy,** *pl.* **-cies**

ex·u·ber·ant (-ənt) *adj.* **1.** growing thickly and in great quantity; luxuriant [*exuberant* foliage] **2.** full of life, vitality, or high spirits **3.** overflowing, unrestrained, lavish, etc. —**ex·u′ber·ant·ly** *adv.*

ex·ude (ig zōōd′, -zyōōd′) *vt., vi.* **-ud′ed, -ud′ing** [< L. < *ex-*, out + *sudare*, to sweat < *sudor*, SWEAT] **1.** to pass out in drops through pores, an incision, etc.; ooze **2.** to spread out in every direction [to *exude* joy] —**ex·u·da·tion** (eks′yə dā′shən) *n.*

ex·ult (ig zult′) *vi.* [< Fr. < L. *ex(s)ultare,* to leap for joy < *ex-*, thoroughly + *saltare* < *salire:* see SALIENT] to rejoice greatly; be jubilant; glory —**ex′ul·ta′tion** *n.*

ex·ult·ant (-′nt) *adj.* exulting; triumphant; jubilant —**ex·ult′ant·ly** *adv.*

☆**ex·ur·bi·a** (eks ur′bē ə) *n.* [EX- + (SUB)URBIA] the small, semirural communities beyond the suburbs, lived in by upper-income people who work in the city —**ex·ur′ban** (-bən) *adj.* —**ex·ur′ban·ite′** (-bə nīt′) *n., adj.*

ex·u·vi·ate (ig zōō′vē āt′) *vt., vi.* **-at′ed, -at′ing** [< L. < *exuere,* to strip off + -ATE¹] to cast off (a skin, shell, etc.); molt —**ex·u′vi·a′tion** *n.*

-ey (ē, i) *same as* -Y²: used esp. after words ending in *y* [*clayey*]

eye (ī) *n.* [OE. *eage* < IE. base *okw-*, to see, from which also come Gr. *ōps* & L. *oculus*] **1.** the organ of sight in man and animals **2.** *a)* the eyeball *b)* the iris [brown *eyes*] **3.** the area around the eye [to get a black *eye*] **4.** [often *pl.*] sight; vision [weak *eyes*] **5.** a look; glance [cast an *eye* over here] **6.** attention; observation [under the *eye* of the guards] **7.** the power of judging, estimating, etc. by eyesight [a good *eye* for distances] **8.** [often *pl.*] judgment; opinion [in the *eyes* of the law] **9.** a thing like an eye in shape or function, as a bud of a potato, the hole of a needle, a loop of metal or thread, any primitive, light-sensitive organ, etc. **10.** *Meteorol.* the calm, low-pressure center (of a hurricane), around which the winds whirl —*vt.* **eyed, eye′ing** or **ey′ing** to look at; observe [he *eyed* the stranger suspiciously] —**all eyes** extremely attentive —**an eye for an eye** punishment in return as great as the injury suffered —**catch one's eye** to attract one's attention —☆**easy on the eyes** [Slang] attractive —**feast one's eyes on** to look at with pleasure —**have an eye for** to have a keen appreciation of —**have eyes for** [Colloq.] to be interested in and want —**in the public eye** often brought to public attention —**keep an**

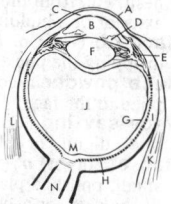

HUMAN EYE
(A, conjunctiva; B, anterior chamber; C, cornea; D, iris; E, ciliary body; F, lens; G, retina; H, choroid; I, sclera; J, vitreous body; K, lateral rectus muscle; L, medial rectus muscle; M, blind spot; N, optic nerve)

eye on to look after; watch carefully —☆**keep an eye out for** to be watchful for —**keep one's eyes open** (or **peeled** or **skinned**) to be watchful —**lay** (or **set** or **clap**) **eyes on** to see; look at —**make eyes at** to look at flirtatiously; ogle —**open one's eyes** to make one aware of the facts —**run one's eye over** to glance over —**see eye to eye** to agree completely —**shut one's eyes to** to refuse to see or think about —**with an eye to** paying attention to

eye·ball (ī′bôl′) *n.* the ball-shaped part of the eye, enclosed by the socket and eyelids —☆*vt., vi.* [Slang] to look at closely or carefully

eye·brow (-brou′) *n.* **1.** the bony arch over each eye **2.** the arch of hair growing on this —**raise** (or **lift**) **an eyebrow** to show doubt, surprise, etc.

☆**eye-catch·er** (-kach′ər) *n.* something that especially attracts one's attention —**eye′-catch′ing** *adj.*

☆**eye·cup** (-kup′) *n.* a small cup used in applying medicine to the eyes or washing them

eyed (īd) *adj.* having eyes (of a specified kind) [blue-*eyed*]

☆**eye·drop·per** (ī′dräp′ər) *n. same as* DROPPER (*n.* 2)

eye·ful (-fool′) *n.* **1.** a quantity of something in the eye **2.** a full look at something **3.** [Slang] a person or thing that looks striking or unusual

eye·glass (-glas′) *n.* **1.** a lens to help faulty vision; monocle **2.** [*pl.*] a pair of such lenses, usually in a frame; glasses **3.** *same as* EYEPIECE

eye·hole (-hōl′) *n.* **1.** the socket for the eyeball **2.** a peephole **3.** *same as* EYELET (sense 1)

eye·lash (-lash′) *n.* **1.** any of the hairs on the edge of the eyelid **2.** a fringe of these hairs

eye·less (-lis) *adj.* without eyes; blind

eye·let (-lit) *n.* [< OFr. dim. of *oeil* < L. *oculus*, eye] **1.** a small hole for a cord, hook, etc. to pass through **2.** a metal ring or short tube for lining such a hole **3.** a small hole edged by stitching in embroidered work —*vt.* to provide with eyelets

eye·lid (-lid′) *n.* either of the two folds of skin that cover and uncover the front of the eyeball

eye liner a cosmetic preparation applied in a thin line on the eyelid at the base of the eyelashes

☆**eye-o·pen·er** (-ō′p'n ər) *n.* **1.** a surprising piece of news, sudden realization, etc. **2.** [Colloq.] an alcoholic drink, esp. one taken early in the day

eye·piece (-pēs′) *n.* in a telescope, microscope, etc., the lens or lenses nearest the viewer's eye

☆**eye shadow** a cosmetic preparation, usually green or blue, applied to the upper eyelids

eye·shot (-shät′) *n.* range of vision

eye·sight (-sīt′) *n.* **1.** the power of seeing; sight; vision **2.** the range of vision

eye·sore (-sôr′) *n.* a thing that is unpleasant to look at

eye·spot (-spät′) *n.* a small spot of pigment sensitive to light, found in many invertebrates

eye·strain (-strān′) *n.* a tired or strained condition of the eye muscles, caused by too much use or an incorrect use of the eyes

eye·tooth (-tōōth′) *n., pl.* **-teeth′** a canine tooth of the upper jaw —**cut one's eyeteeth** to become experienced or sophisticated

eye·wash (-wôsh′, -wäsh′) *n.* **1.** a lotion for the eyes **2.** [Slang] *a)* nonsense *b)* flattery *c)* something done only to impress an observer

eye·wit·ness (-wit′nis) *n.* **1.** a person who sees something happen, as an accident, crime, etc. **2.** a person who testifies to what he has seen

ey·rie, ey·ry (er′ē, ir′-) *n., pl.* **-ries** *same as* AERIE

ey·rir (ā′rir) *n., pl.* **au·rar** (ou′rär) [Ice. < ON., a coin < L. *aureus*, a gold coin: see AUREATE] *see* MONETARY UNITS, table (Iceland)

E·zek·i·el (i zē′kē əl, -kyəl) [< LL. < Gr. < Heb. *yehezq'ēl*, lit., God strengthens] **1.** a masculine name **2.** *Bible a)* a Hebrew prophet of the 6th cent. B.C. *b)* the book containing his prophetic writings: abbrev. **Ezek.**

Ez·ra (ez′rə) [LL. < Heb. *ezrā*, lit., help] **1.** a masculine name **2.** *Bible a)* a Hebrew scribe, prophet, and religious reformer of the 5th cent. B.C. *b)* the book telling of his life and teachings: abbrev. **Ez., Ezr.**

---

fat, āpe, cär; ten, ēven; is, bīte; gō, hôrn, tōol, look; oil, out; up, fur; get; joy; yet; chin; she; thin, then; zh, leisure; ŋ, ring; ə for *a* in *ago, e* in *agent, i* in *sanity, o* in *comply, u* in *focus;* ′ as in *able* (ā′b'l); Fr. bäl; ë, Fr. coeur; ö, Fr. feu; Fr. mon; ô, Fr. coq; ü, Fr. duc; r, Fr. cri; H, G. ich; kh, G. doch; ‡foreign; ☆ Americanism; < derived from. See inside front cover.

F

F, f (ef) *n., pl.* **F's, f's** **1.** the sixth letter of the English alphabet **2.** the sound of *F* or *f*

F (ef) *n.* **1.** *Chem.* fluorine **2.** *Educ. a)* a grade meaning *failing b)* sometimes, a grade meaning *fair* **3.** *Music a)* the fourth tone in the ascending scale of C major *b)* the scale having this tone as the keynote

F **1.** Fahrenheit **2.** farad **3.** fathom

F/, f/, f:, f. f-number

F- fighter (plane)

F. **1.** Fahrenheit **2.** February **3.** Fellow **4.** French **5.** Friday

F., f. **1.** farad **2.** farthing **3.** fathom **4.** feminine **5.** fluid **6.** folio(s) **7.** following **8.** *Music* forte **9.** franc(s)

fa (fä) *n.* [< ML. < *fa*(*muli*): see GAMUT] *Music* a syllable representing the fourth tone of the diatonic scale

FAA Federal Aviation Administration

Fa·bi·an (fā′bē ən) *adj.* [< L. < *Fabius*, Roman general of 3d cent. B.C.] ☆**1.** using a cautious strategy of delay and avoidance of battle **2.** designating or of an English socialist organization (**Fabian Society**) advocating gradual reforms —*n.* a member of the Fabian Society —**Fa′bi·an·ism** *n.*

fa·ble (fā′b'l) *n.* [< OFr. < L. *fabula*, a story < *fari:* see BAN¹] **1.** a fictitious story meant to teach a moral lesson: the characters are usually talking animals **2.** a myth or legend **3.** a story that is not true; a falsehood or fiction —*vi., vt.* **-bled, -bling** to write or tell (fables) —**fa′bler** *n.*

fa·bled (-b'ld) *adj.* **1.** told of in fables or legends; legendary **2.** unreal; fictitious

Fa·bre (fà′br′), **Jean Hen·ri** (zhän än rē′) 1823–1915; Fr. entomologist

fab·ric (fab′rik) *n.* [< MFr. < L. *fabrica*, a workshop < *faber*, a workman] **1.** *a)* anything made of parts put together *b)* the basic structure of anything [the *fabric* of society] **2.** the style or plan of construction **3.** a material made from fibers or threads by weaving, knitting, etc., as any cloth, felt, lace, etc.

fab·ri·cate (fab′rə kāt′) *vt.* **-cat′ed, -cat′ing** [< L. pp. of *fabricari*, to build < *fabrica:* see prec.] **1.** to make, build, construct, etc., esp. by assembling parts; manufacture **2.** to make up (a story, lie, etc.); invent —see SYN. at MAKE —**fab′ri·ca′tion** *n.* —**fab′ri·ca′tor** *n.*

☆**Fab·ri·koid** (fab′rə koid′) [see FABRIC & -OID] *a trademark for* a fabric made to resemble leather

fab·u·list (fab′yoo list) *n.* **1.** a person who writes or tells fables **2.** a liar

fab·u·lous (-ləs) *adj.* [< L. < *fabula:* see FABLE] **1.** of or like a fable; imaginary [the centaur is a *fabulous* monster] **2.** incredible; astounding [to spend a *fabulous* amount of money] **3.** [Colloq.] very good; wonderful —**fab′u·lous·ly** *adv.* —**fab′u·lous·ness** *n.*

fa·çade, fa·cade (fə säd′) *n.* [Fr. < It. < VL. *facia:* see FACE] **1.** the front of a building **2.** an outward appearance that is false or misleading

face (fās) *n.* [< OFr. < VL. *facia* < L. *facies*, the face: for IE. base see DO¹] **1.** the front of the head, where the eyes, nose, and mouth are **2.** a look that shows meaning or feeling [a sad *face*] **3.** a surface of a thing; esp., *a)* the main surface or side *b)* the front, upper, or outer surface *c)* any of the surfaces of a crystal **4.** the side or sur-

FAÇADE

face that is marked or intended to be seen, as of a clock, playing card, etc. **5.** the appearance; outward aspect **6.** [< Chin. idiom] dignity; self-respect; reputation: in **lose** (or **save**) **face 7.** the topography (of an area) **8.** the working or striking surface (of a tool, etc.) **9.** [Colloq.] impudence; audacity **10.** *Typography a)* the printing surface of a letter or plate *b)* the design of type —*vt.* **faced, fac′ing** **1.** to turn, or have the face turned, toward [the house *faces* the park] **2.** to meet face to face **3.** to meet or oppose with boldness, courage, etc. [to *face* danger] **4.** to put another material on the surface of [to *face* the building with brick] **5.** to sew a facing to (a collar, etc.) **6.** to put a smooth surface on (a stone, tool, etc.) —*vi.* **1.** to turn, or have the face turned, toward a specified thing or in a specified direction **2.** *Mil.* to pivot in a specified direction [right *face!*] —**face down** to overcome or make ill at ease by a bold, confident manner —**face off** *Hockey* to start play with a face-off —**face to face** **1.** with each facing the other **2.** very close; in the presence of: followed by *with* —**face up to** **1.** to confront and resist **2.** to realize and be ready to meet [to *face up to* the unpleasant facts] —**in the face of** **1.** in the presence of **2.** in spite of —**make a face** to twist the face; grimace —**on the face of it** apparently —**pull** (or **wear**) **a long face** to look sad, glum, disapproving, etc. —**to one's face** in one's presence; openly —**faced** *adj.*

SYN. —**face** is the basic word for the front of the head; **countenance** refers to the face as it shows the feelings or emotions [his happy *countenance*]; **visage** refers to the shape, proportions, and expression of the face, esp. as they show a person's usual disposition [a stern *visage*]; **physiognomy** refers to the features of a person's face supposedly showing the person's character [the *physiognomy* of an honest man]

face card any king, queen, or jack in a deck of cards

face·less (fās′lis) *adj.* **1.** lacking a face **2.** lacking a distinct, individual character; anonymous

☆**face lifting** **1.** plastic surgery for removing wrinkles, sagging flesh, etc. from the face **2.** an altering, cleaning, etc., as of the exterior of a building Also **face lift** —**face′-lift′** *vt.*

face-off (-ôf′) *n.* *Hockey* the starting of play by the referee's dropping the puck between two opposing players

face powder a cosmetic powder, as of flesh-colored talc, applied to the face

face-sav·ing (-sā′viŋ) *adj.* preserving or intended to preserve one's dignity or self-respect

fac·et (fas′it) *n.* [Fr. dim. of *face:* see FACE] **1.** any of the small, polished plane surfaces of a cut gem **2.** any of the sides or aspects, as of a personality —*vt.* **-et-ed** or **-et·ted, -et·ing** or **-et·ting** to cut or make facets on

fa·ce·tious (fə sē′shəs) *adj.* [< Fr. < L. < *facetus*, witty] joking or trying to be humorous, esp. at the wrong time —see SYN. at WITTY —**fa·ce′tious·ly** *adv.* —**fa·ce′tious·ness** *n.*

FACETS OF A GEM

face value **1.** the value printed or written on a bill, bond, etc. **2.** the seeming value [to take a promise at *face value*]

fa·cial (fā′shəl) *adj.* of or for the face —☆*n.* a cosmetic treatment intended to improve the appearance of the skin of the face —**fa′cial·ly** *adv.*

☆**facial tissue** a sheet of soft tissue paper used for cleansing, or as a handkerchief, etc.

-fa·cient (fā′shənt) [< L. prp. of *facere*, to make, DO¹] *a suffix meaning* making or causing to become [liquefacient]

fa·ci·es (fā′shē ēz′) *n., pl.* **fa′ci·es′** [L., FACE] **1.** the general appearance of anything **2.** *Geol.* the characteristics of a rock body, part of a rock body, etc. that differentiate it from others, as in appearance or composition

fac·ile (fas′′l) *adj.* [Fr. < L. *facilis* < *facere*, to make, DO¹] **1.** not hard to do; easy **2.** acting, working, or done quickly and smoothly; fluent; ready [a *facile* wit] **3.** not sincere or profound; superficial [a *facile* answer to a serious, complex question] —see SYN. at EASY —**fac′ile·ly** *adv.*

fa·cil·i·tate (fə sil′ə tāt′) *vt.* **-tat′ed, -tat′ing** [< Fr. < It. < L. *facilis* (see prec.) + -ATE¹] to make easy or easier [methods that will *facilitate* the learning process] —**fa·cil′i·ta′tion** *n.* —**fa·cil′i·ta′tive** *adj.*

fa·cil·i·ty (fə sil′ə tē) *n., pl.* **-ties** [< OFr. < L. < *facilis*, FACILE] **1.** ease; absence of difficulty **2.** a ready ability; skill; fluency [reading French with great *facility*] **3.** [*usually pl.*] the means by which something can be done [with no *facilities* for washing clothes] **4.** a building, room, etc. for some activity [to build a new athletic *facility*]

fac·ing (fās′iŋ) *n.* **1.** a lining, often decorative, sewn on a collar, cuff, etc. **2.** any material used for this **3.** a covering of contrasting material, for decorating or protecting a surface [a marble *facing* on a building]

fac·sim·i·le (fak sim′ə lē) *n.* [L. *fac*, imper. of *facere*, DO¹ + *simile*, SIMILAR] **1.** an exact reproduction or copy **2.** the transmission and reproduction of printed matter, photographs, etc. by radio or telegraph —*adj.* of or like a facsimile —see SYN. at COPY

fact (fakt) *n.* [L. *factum*, deed < *facere*, DO¹] **1.** a deed; act: now esp. "a criminal deed" in **before** (or **after**) **the fact** [an accessory *after the fact*] **2.** a thing that has actually happened or is true **3.** the state of things as they are; reality; truth [based on *fact*, not fantasy] **4.** something said to have occurred or supposed to be true [check the accuracy of your *facts*] —**as a matter of fact** in reality; really: also **in fact, in point of fact** — ☆**the facts of life 1.** basic information about life, esp. about sexual reproduction **2.** the harsh, unpleasant facts one must face in life or in some situation

fac·tion (fak′shən) *n.* [< Fr. < L. *factio*, a making < pp. of *facere:* see FACT] **1.** a group of people inside a political party, club, etc. working together against other such groups for its own ideas or goals **2.** partisan conflict within an organization or country; dissension [a nation torn by *faction*] —**fac′tion·al** *adj.* —**fac′tion·al·ism** *n.* —**fac′tion·al·ist** *n., adj.* —**fac′tion·al·ly** *adv.*

fac·tious (fak′shəs) *adj.* **1.** producing or tending to produce faction, or dissension **2.** produced or characterized by faction — **fac′tious·ly** *adv.* —**fac′tious·ness** *n.*

fac·ti·tious (fak tish′əs) *adj.* [< L. < pp. of *facere*, DO¹] not genuine or spontaneous; forced or artificial [*factitious* needs created by advertising] —**fac·ti′tious·ly** *adv.* —**fac·ti′tious·ness** *n.*

fac·tor (fak′tər) *n.* [< OFr. < L. < pp. of *facere*, DO¹] **1.** a person who carries on business transactions for another; agent **2.** any of the circumstances, conditions, etc. that bring about a result [the hot climate was a *factor* in his decision to move north] **3.** *Biol.* same as GENE **4.** *Math.* any of two or more quantities which form a product when multiplied together —*vt. Math.* to find the factors of —**fac′tor·a·ble** *adj.* —**fac′tor·ship′** *n.*

fac·to·ri·al (fak tôr′ē əl) *n. Math.* the product of a given series of consecutive whole numbers beginning with 1 [the *factorial* of 4 is $1 \times 2 \times 3 \times 4$, or 24] —*adj.* of factors or factorials

fac·to·ry (fak′tə rē, -trē) *n., pl.* **-ries** [see FACTOR] a building or buildings in which things are manufactured; manufacturing plant

fac·to·tum (fak tōt′əm) *n.* [ModL. < L. *fac*, imper. of *facere*, DO¹ + *totum*, all] a person hired to do all sorts of work; handyman

fac·tu·al (fak′chōō wəl) *adj.* [FACT + (ACT)UAL] **1.** of or containing facts **2.** having the nature of fact; real; actual —**fac′tu·al·ly** *adv.*

fac·ul·ty (fak′′l tē) *n., pl.* **-ties** [< OFr. < L. < *facilis:* see FACILE] **1.** formerly, the ability to perform an action **2.** any natural or specialized power of a living organism [the *faculty* of speech] **3.** special aptitude or skill; knack [the *faculty* of remembering names] ☆**4.** all the teachers of a school, college,

or university or of one of its divisions **5.** all the members of any profession **6.** *Psychol.* any of the powers formerly thought of as composing the mind, such as will, reason, etc. —see SYN. at TALENT

fad (fad) *n.* [< Brit. Midland dial.] a custom, style, etc. that many people are interested in for a short time; craze —see SYN. at FASHION —**fad′dish** *adj.* —**fad′dish·ly** *adv.* —**fad′dish·ness** *n.* —**fad′dism** *n.* —**fad′dist** *n.*

fade (fād) *vi.* **fad′ed, fad′ing** [< OFr. *fader* < *fade*, pale] **1.** to become less distinct; lose color, brilliance, intensity, etc. [the painting has *faded* with age] **2.** to lose freshness or strength; wither; wane [the roses *faded* and lost their petals] **3.** to disappear slowly; die out [the music *faded* away] —*vt.* to cause to fade —☆**fade back** *Football* to move back from the line of scrimmage, as in order to throw a forward pass —☆**fade in** (or **out**) *Motion Pictures, Radio & TV* to appear (or disappear) gradually or cause to do so; become or make more (or less) distinct

☆**fade-in** (fād′in′) *n. Motion Pictures, Radio & TV* a fading in of a scene or sound

☆**fade-out** (-out′) *n. Motion Pictures, Radio & TV* a fading out of a scene or sound

fae·ces (fē′sēz) *n.pl.* same as FECES —**fae′cal** (-k′l) *adj.*

fa·er·ie, fa·er·y (fer′ē; *also, for 1,* fā′ər ē) *n.* [Archaic] **1.** fairyland **2.** *pl.* **-ies** a fairy —*adj.* [Archaic] fairy Also written **faërie, faëry**

Faer·oe Islands (fer′ō) group of Danish islands in the N Atlantic, north of the British Isles

Faer·o·ese (fer′ə wēz′) *n.* **1.** *pl.* **Faer′o·ese′** a native or inhabitant of the Faeroe Islands **2.** the North Germanic language of the Faeroe Islands —*adj.* of the Faeroe Islands, their people, language, etc.

fag¹ (fag) *vi.* **fagged, fag′ging** [< ?] **1.** to work hard and become very tired **2.** [Brit. Colloq.] to serve as a fag —*vt.* to make tired by hard work —*n.* [Brit. Colloq.] a boy in an English public school who acts as a servant for another boy in a higher form, or class

fag² (fag) *n.* [< FAG END] [Old Slang] a cigarette

fag end [< ME. *fagge*, broken thread] **1.** *a)* the last part or coarse end of a piece of cloth *b)* the frayed, untwisted end of a rope **2.** the last and worst part of anything

fag·ot, fag·got (fag′ət) *n.* [< OFr., ult. < Gr. *phakelos*, a bundle] **1.** a bundle of sticks or twigs, esp. for use as fuel **2.** *Metallurgy* a stack of iron or steel pieces to be welded into bars —*vt.* **1.** to form a fagot of **2.** to decorate with fagoting

fag·ot·ing, fag·got·ing (-iŋ) *n.* **1.** a kind of drawnwork or hemstitch with wide spaces **2.** openwork decoration in which the thread is drawn in crisscross or barlike stitches across the open seam

Fah., Fahr. Fahrenheit

Fahr·en·heit (fer′ən hīt′, fär′-) *adj.* [after G. D. *Fahrenheit*, 18th-c. G. physicist] designating or of a thermometer on which 32° is the freezing point and 212° the boiling point of water: abbrev. **F**

FAGOTING
(A, bar; B, crisscross)

fa·ience (fī äns′, fā-) *n.* [Fr. < *Faenza*, Italy] earthenware having a colorful, opaque glaze

fail (fāl) *vi.* [< OFr. < L. *fallere*, to deceive] **1.** to be lacking or insufficient; fall short; default [the water supply is *failing*] **2.** to lose power or strength; weaken; die away [his health *failed*] **3.** to stop functioning [the brakes *failed*] **4.** to be unsuccessful in obtaining a desired end [to *fail* as a singer] **5.** to become bankrupt [the business *failed*] **6.** *Educ.* to get a grade of failure —*vt.* **1.** to be of no help to; disappoint [don't *fail* us in our time of need] **2.** to leave; abandon [his courage *failed* him] **3.** to miss, neglect, or omit [to *fail* to go] **4.** *Educ. a)* to give a grade of failure to *b)* to get a grade of failure in —*n.* failure: now only in **without fail**, without failing (to occur, do something, etc.) —**fail of** to fail to achieve

fail·ing (fāl′iŋ) *n.* **1.** a failure **2.** a slight fault or defect; weakness [my worst *failing* is that I talk too much] —*prep.* without; lacking [*failing* some rain soon, the crops will wither] —see SYN. at FAULT

faille (fīl, fāl) *n.* [Fr.] a ribbed, soft fabric of silk or rayon, for dresses, etc.

fail-safe (fāl′sāf′) *adj.* [FAIL, *v.* + SAFE, *adj.*] designed to prevent damage in case of failure of a system or to prevent the accidental or unauthorized use of bombs, rockets, etc. [a fail-safe device, control, etc.]

fail·ure (fāl′yər) *n.* [see FAIL] **1.** the act or fact of failing, or falling short, losing strength, breaking down, going bankrupt, not doing or succeeding, etc. **2.** a person or thing that fails **3.** *Educ. a)* a failing to pass ☆*b)* a grade or mark (usually F) indicating a failing to pass

fain (fān) *adj.* [OE. *fægen*, glad] [Archaic] **1.** glad; ready **2.** reluctantly willing **3.** eager —*adv.* [Archaic] gladly or willingly [she would *fain* stay]

faint (fānt) *adj.* [< OFr. *feint*, sluggish, orig. pp. of *feindre*: see FEIGN] **1.** without strength; weak; feeble [a *faint* whisper] **2.** without courage; timid [*faint* heart never won fair lady] **3.** done without vigor or enthusiasm [a *faint* effort] **4.** feeling weak and dizzy, as if about to swoon **5.** dim; indistinct [*faint* shadows] **6.** slight [a *faint* hope] —*n.* a condition in which one becomes unconscious because not enough blood reaches the brain, as in sudden shock —*vi.* to fall into a faint; swoon — **faint′ly** *adv.* —**faint′ness** *n.*

faint·heart·ed (fānt′här′tid) *adj.* cowardly; timid —**faint′heart′ed·ly** *adv.* —**faint′heart′ed·ness** *n.*

fair[1] (fer) *adj.* [OE. *fæger*] **1.** beautiful [a *fair* maiden] **2.** unblemished; clean [a *fair* name] **3.** light in color; blond [*fair* hair] **4.** clear and sunny [*fair* weather] **5.** easy to read; clear [a *fair* hand] **6.** just and honest; impartial; specif., free from discrimination based on race, religion, sex, etc. [*fair* employment practices; *fair* housing] **7.** according to the rules [a *fair* blow] **8.** likely; promising [in a *fair* way to benefit] **9.** pleasant and courteous, often falsely smooth [the traitor's *fair* words] **10.** favorable; helpful [a *fair* wind] **11.** of moderately good size **12.** neither very bad nor very good; average [a *fair* chance of winning] —*adv.* **1.** in a fair manner [play *fair*] **2.** straight; squarely [struck *fair* in the face] —**fair and square** [Colloq.] with justice and honesty —**fair to middling** [Colloq.] moderately good; passable; adequate —**fair′ish** *adj.* —**fair′ness** *n.*

SYN.—**fair** implies the treating of both or all sides alike, without showing preference for any side [a *fair* hearing]; **just** implies judgment according to a fixed standard of what is right or lawful [a *just* decision]; **impartial** and **unbiased** both stress being open-minded and free from prejudice for or against any side [an *impartial* referee; an *unbiased* account]; **dispassionate** implies the absence of strong feelings and, hence, suggests cool, reasoning judgment [a *dispassionate* critic]; **objective** implies the viewing of persons or things according to the facts as they really are [an *objective* study of the problems] Basic to all these synonyms is the idea of making judgments without being influenced by one's own feelings or interests —see also *SYN.* at BEAUTIFUL —*ANT.* prejudiced, biased

fair[2] (fer) *n.* [< OFr. < ML. < LL. < L. *feriae*, pl., festivals] **1.** orig., a gathering of people at regular times for barter and sale of goods **2.** a carnival where there is entertainment and things are sold, often for charity; bazaar ☆**3.** an exhibition, often competitive (**county fair, state fair**), of farm, household, and manufactured products, or of international displays (**world's fair**), with amusement areas and educational displays; exposition

☆**fair ball** *Baseball* a batted ball that first strikes the ground in the infield and either stops there or passes first or third base inside the foul line, or one that first strikes the ground inside the foul line beyond first or third base

Fair·banks (fer′baŋks′) [after C. W. *Fairbanks,* prominent political figure] city in EC Alas.: pop. 15,000

☆**fair catch** *Football* a catch of a punted ball by a player who has given a signal indicating that no attempt will be made to run with the ball

fair game 1. game that may lawfully be hunted **2.** any legitimate object of attack or pursuit

fair·ground (fer′ground′) *n.* [often *pl.*] an open space where fairs are held

fair-haired (-herd′) *adj.* **1.** having blond hair ☆**2.** [Colloq.] favorite [mother's *fair-haired* boy]

fair·ly (-lē) *adv.* **1.** in a fair manner; justly; equitably **2.** to a fair degree; moderately; somewhat [*fairly* hot] **3.** completely or really [his voice *fairly* rang]

fair-mind·ed (-mīn′did) *adj.* just; impartial —**fair′-mind′ed·ly** *adv.* —**fair′-mind′ed·ness** *n.*

fair play an abiding by the rules in sports or any other activity; dealing fairly with competitors, customers, etc.

fair sex women collectively: used with *the*

☆**fair shake** [Colloq.] fair, just, or impartial treatment; square deal

fair-spo·ken (-spō′kən) *adj.* speaking or spoken politely and pleasantly or smoothly and plausibly

fair-trade (-trād′) *adj.* ☆designating or of an agreement whereby a seller is to charge no less than the minimum price set by the manufacturer —*vt.* -**trad′ed,** -**trad′ing** to sell (a commodity) under a fair-trade agreement

fair·way (-wā′) *n.* **1.** a navigable channel in a river, harbor, etc. **2.** the mowed part of a golf course that lies between a tee and a green

fair-weath·er (-weth′ər) *adj.* **1.** suitable only for fair weather **2.** unreliable in times of distress or need [*fair-weather* friends]

fair·y (fer′ē) *n., pl.* **fair′ies** [< OFr. *faerie* < *fée*: see FAY] a tiny, graceful, delicate imaginary being in human form, supposed to have magic powers —*adj.* **1.** of fairies **2.** like a fairy; graceful; delicate

fair·y·land (-land′) *n.* **1.** the imaginary land where the fairies live **2.** a lovely, enchanting place

fairy tale 1. a story about fairies, magic deeds, etc. **2.** an unbelievable or untrue story; lie

‡**fait ac·com·pli** (fe tà kôn plē′) [Fr., lit., an accomplished fact] a thing already done, so that opposition or argument is useless

Faith (fāth) [see the next entry] a feminine name

faith (fāth) *n.* [< OFr. < L. *fides* < *fidere*, to trust < IE. base *bheidh-*, be convinced] **1.** unquestioning belief that does not require proof [his *faith* in the goodness of man] **2.** unquestioning belief in God, religious doctrines, etc. **3.** a particular religion [the Catholic *faith*] **4.** anything believed **5.** complete trust or confidence [to have *faith* in one's doctor] **6.** loyalty; allegiance [knights pledged their *faith* to the king] —*interj.* indeed —see *SYN.* at BELIEF —**bad faith** insincerity; dishonesty —**break** (or **keep**) **faith 1.** to be disloyal (or loyal) to one's principles **2.** to break (or keep) a promise —**good faith** sincerity; honesty —**in faith** indeed; really

☆**faith cure** *same as* FAITH HEALING

faith·ful (fāth′fəl) *adj.* **1.** remaining loyal; constant [*faithful* friends] **2.** showing a strong sense of duty; conscientious [*faithful* attendance] **3.** accurate; exact [a *faithful* copy] —**the faithful** the true believers or loyal followers —**faith′ful·ly** *adv.* —**faith′ful·ness** *n.*

SYN.—**faithful** implies steadiness and reliability in staying true to a person or thing that one is bound to by an oath, duty, obligation, etc. [a *faithful* wife]; **loyal** implies unswerving devotion to a person, cause, etc. which one feels morally bound to support or defend [a *loyal* friend]; **constant** stresses steadfastness in one's affections or loyalties [constant in her devotion to duty]; **staunch** suggests very strong, firm loyalty or support [a *staunch* defender of freedom] —*ANT.* faithless

☆**faith healing** a trying to cure disease by religious faith, praying, etc. —**faith healer**

faith·less (-lis) *adj.* **1.** not keeping faith; dishonest; disloyal **2.** unreliable; undependable —**faith′less·ly** *adv.* —**faith′less·ness** *n.*

SYN.—**faithless** implies failure to do what is required by an oath, obligation, etc. [a *faithless* wife]; **false** implies a being unfaithful while pretending to be faithful or loyal [a *false* friend]; **disloyal** implies failure in the allegiance owed to a person, cause, institution, etc. [*disloyal* to one's family]; **traitorous** strictly implies the deliberate committing of an act of treason, as against one's country; **treacherous** suggests a tendency to betray someone who trusts one and **perfidious** suggests a deliberate intention to do so —*ANT.* faithful

fake (fāk) *vt., vi.* **faked, fak′ing** [< ? G. *fegen*, to clean, sweep] to practice deception by giving a false indication or appearance of (something); feign [he *faked* a cold and stayed home] —*n.* anything or anyone not genuine; fraud —*adj.* fraudulent; sham; false [a *fake* diamond] —see *SYN.* at FALSE —**fake** (**someone**) **out** [Colloq.] to deceive (someone) by a feint, bluff, etc. —**fak′er** *n.* —**fak′er·y** *n., pl.* -**er·ies**

fa·kir (fə kir′) *n.* [Ar. *faqīr,* lit., poor] **1.** a member of a Moslem holy sect who lives by begging **2.** a Hindu ascetic Also sp. **fa·keer′**

Fa·lange (fā′lanj; *Sp.* fä län′he) *n.* [Sp. < L. *phalanx,* PHALANX] a fascist organization that became the only official political party of Spain under Franco following the Spanish civil war (1936–39) —**Fa·lang·ist** (fə lan′jist) *n.*

fal·cate (fal′kāt) *adj.* [< L. *falcis,* genitive of *falx,* a sickle] sickle-shaped; curved; hooked

fal·chion (fôl′chən, -shən) *n.* [< OFr. < L. *falx:* see prec.] **1.** a medieval sword with a short, broad, slightly curved blade **2.** [Poet.] any sword

fal·con (fal′kən, fôl′-, fô′-) *n.* [< OFr. < LL. *falconis*, genitive of *falco*, derived by folk etym. < L. *falx*: see FALCATE] **1.** any hawk trained to hunt and kill small game **2.** a hawklike bird with long, pointed wings and a short, curved, notched beak

fal·con·ry (-rē) *n.* **1.** the art of training falcons to hunt game **2.** the sport of hunting with falcons —**fal′con·er** *n.*

fal·de·ral (fôl′də rôl′) *n.* [nonsense syllables] **1.** a showy but worthless trinket **2.** mere nonsense

Falk·land Islands (fôk′lənd) group of Brit. islands, east of the southern tip of S. America

FALCON
(PEREGRINE)
(to 16 in. long;
wingspread
to 3½ ft.)

fall (fôl) *vi.* fell, fall′en, fall′ing [OE. *feallan* < IE. base *phol-*] **1.** to come down by the force of gravity, as when detached, pushed, dropped, etc. [apples *fall* from the tree] **2.** to come down suddenly from a standing or sitting position; tumble [he slipped and *fell* on the ice] **3.** to be wounded or killed in battle **4.** to collapse [the building *fell*] **5.** to hang down [hair *falling* about her shoulders] **6.** to strike; hit [the arrow *fell* wide of the mark] **7.** to take a downward direction [land *falling* away to the sea] **8.** to become lower in amount, degree, etc.; drop; abate [prices *fell*] **9.** to lose power [the government *fell*] **10.** to lose status, reputation, dignity, etc. **11.** *a)* to do wrong; sin *b)* to lose one's chastity **12.** to be captured or conquered [Berlin *fell* to the Allies] **13.** to take on a dejected look [his face *fell*] **14.** to become lower in pitch or volume [her voice *fell*] **15.** to take place; occur [the meeting *fell* on a Friday] **16.** to come by lot, inheritance, etc. [the estate *falls* to the son] **17.** to pass into a specified condition; become [to *fall* ill] **18.** to come at a specified place [the accent *falls* on the third syllable] **19.** to be directed by chance [his eye *fell* on us] **20.** to be spoken suddenly, almost without thought [an oath *fell* from his lips] **21.** to be divided (*into*) [to *fall* into two classes] —*n.* **1.** a dropping; descending **2.** a coming down suddenly from a standing or sitting position **3.** a hanging down, or a part hanging down **4.** a downward direction or slope **5.** a becoming lower or less; reduction in value, price, degree, etc. [a *fall* in the temperature] **6.** a capture; overthrow; ruin **7.** a loss of status, reputation, etc. **8.** something that has fallen [a *fall* of leaves] **9.** autumn **10.** the amount of what has fallen [a six-inch *fall* of snow] **11.** the distance that something falls **12.** [*usually pl.*, *often with sing. v.*] water falling over a cliff, etc.; cascade **13.** a long tress of hair, often synthetic, used by women to fill out their coiffure **14.** *a)* in wrestling, the throwing of an opponent on his back so that both shoulders touch the floor *b)* a division of a wrestling match —*adj.* of, for, or in the autumn —☆**fall (all) over oneself** [Colloq.] to behave in too eager or zealous a manner —**fall away 1.** to take away friendship, support, etc.; desert **2.** to become less in size, strength, etc.; specif., to grow thin and weak —**fall back** to withdraw; give way; retreat —**fall back on** (or **upon**) to turn, or return, to for help —☆**fall down on** [Slang] to fail or be unsuccessful in (a job, etc.) —**fall flat** to fail to have the desired effect —☆**fall for** [Colloq.] **1.** to fall in love with **2.** to be tricked by —**fall in 1.** to agree **2.** *Mil.* to line up in proper formation —**fall off** to become smaller, less, worse, etc. —**fall on** (or **upon**) **1.** to attack **2.** to be the duty of —**fall out 1.** to quarrel **2.** to happen; result **3.** *Mil.* to leave one's place in a formation —**fall through** to come to nothing; fail —**fall to 1.** to begin; start **2.** to start attacking **3.** to start eating —**fall under 1.** to come under (an influence, etc.) **2.** to be classified as —**the Fall (of Man)** *Christian Theol.* Adam's sin of yielding to temptation in eating the forbidden fruit

fal·la·cious (fə lā′shəs) *adj.* **1.** containing a fallacy **2.** misleading, deceptive, or causing disappointment —**fal·la′cious·ly** *adv.* —**fal·la′cious·ness** *n.*

fal·la·cy (fal′ə sē) *n., pl.* -cies [< OFr. < L. *fallacis*, genitive of *fallax* < *fallere*, to deceive] **1.** aptness to mislead or deceive [the *fallacy* of the senses] **2.** a false or mistaken idea, opinion, etc.; error **3.** an error in reasoning; specif., *Logic* an argument based on incorrect demonstration, as a vicious circle

fall·en (fôl′ən) *adj.* **1.** having come down; dropped **2.** on the ground; prostrate **3.** degraded **4.** captured; overthrown **5.** ruined **6.** dead

☆**fall guy** [Slang] a person left to face the consequences, as of a scheme that has miscarried

fal·li·ble (fal′ə b'l) *adj.* [< ML. < L. *fallere*, to deceive] **1.** liable to be mistaken or deceived **2.** liable to be wrong or inaccurate —**fal′li·bil′i·ty** *n.* —**fal′li·bly** *adv.*

fall·ing-out (fôl′iŋ out′) *n.* a quarrel

falling sickness *former name for* EPILEPSY

falling star *same as* METEOR (sense 1)

☆**fall-off** (fôl′ôf′) *n.* the act or an instance of becoming less or worse; decline

Fal·lo·pi·an tube (fə lō′pē ən) [after G. *Fallopio*, It. anatomist (1523–62)] either of two slender tubes that carry ova from the ovaries to the uterus

fall·out (fôl′out′) *n.* ☆**1.** the descent to earth of radioactive particles, as after a nuclear explosion ☆**2.** these particles **3.** whatever comes as a result without being planned

fal·low[1] (fal′ō) *n.* [< OE. *fealh*] **1.** land plowed but not seeded for one or more seasons, to kill weeds, enrich the soil, etc. **2.** the plowing of land to be left idle thus —*adj.* **1.** left uncultivated or unplanted **2.** untrained; inactive: said esp. of the mind —*vt.* to leave (land) unplanted after plowing —**lie fallow** to remain uncultivated, unused, etc. for a time —**fal′low·ness** *n.*

fal·low[2] (fal′ō) *adj.* [< OE. *fealo*] pale-yellow

fallow deer a small European deer having a yellowish coat spotted with white in summer

Fall River [transl. of Algonquian name of local river] seaport in SE Mass.: pop. 97,000

false (fôls) *adj.* fals′er, fals′est [< OFr. < L. pp. of *fallere*, to deceive] **1.** not true; in error; incorrect; wrong [a *false* argument] **2.** untruthful; lying [to give *false* testimony] **3.** disloyal; unfaithful [a *false* friend] **4.** deceiving; misleading [a *false* scent] **5.** not real; artificial; counterfeit [*false* teeth] **6.** not properly so named [*false* jasmine] **7.** based on mistaken ideas [*false* pride] **8.** temporary, nonessential, or added on for protection, disguise, etc. [a *false* drawer] **9.** *Music* pitched inaccurately —*adv.* in a false manner —**play (a person) false** to deceive or betray (a person) —**false′ly** *adv.* —**false′ness** *n.*

SYN.—**false** refers to anything that is not basically what it seems to be and may or may not suggest something intended to deceive others [*false* teeth]; **sham** refers to an imitating or pretending to be something, usually with the intention of deceiving others [*sham* piety]; **counterfeit** and the colloquial **bogus** refer to a very careful imitation and always imply an intention of deceiving or defrauding others [*counterfeit*, or *bogus*, money]; **fake** is a less formal term for any person or thing that is not genuine [a *fake* doctor, *fake* tears] See also SYN. at FAITHLESS —**ANT. genuine, real**

false arrest *Law* any arrest that involves the forceful and unlawful restraint of a person by another

false fruit *Bot.* a fruitlike structure formed from the separate carpels of one flower or from the uniting of a cluster of flowers, as a fruit of the strawberry plant

false·heart·ed (fôls′här′tid) *adj.* disloyal; deceitful

false·hood (-hood′) *n.* **1.** lack of accuracy or truth; falsity **2.** the telling of lies; lying **3.** a false statement; lie **4.** a false belief, theory, idea, etc.

false imprisonment *Law* the unlawful arrest or imprisonment of a person

false ribs the five lower ribs on each side of the body: so called because not directly attached to the breastbone

false step 1. a misstep; stumble **2.** a social blunder

fal·set·to (fôl set′ō) *n., pl.* -tos [It. dim. < L.: see FALSE] **1.** *a)* an artificial way of singing or speaking, in a voice that is much higher than one's usual or natural voice *b)* this voice **2.** a person using falsetto: also **fal·set′tist** —*adj.* of or singing in falsetto —*adv.* in falsetto

fal·si·fy (fôl′sə fī′) *vt.* -fied′, -fy′ing [< OFr. < ML. < L. *falsus*, FALSE + *facere*, to make, DO[1]] **1.** to make false; specif., *a)* to give an untrue account of *b)* to alter (a record, etc.) in order to deceive or defraud **2.** to prove or show to be unfounded [to *falsify* their hopes] —*vi.* to tell falsehoods; lie —**fal′si·fi·ca′tion** *n.* —**fal′si·fi′er** *n.*

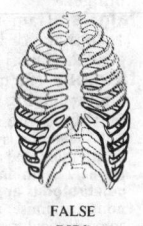

FALSE
RIBS

fal·si·ty (fôl′sə tē) *n., pl.* -ties **1.** the condition or quality of being false; specif., *a)* incorrectness *b)* dishonesty *c)* deceitfulness *d)* disloyalty 2. something false; esp., a lie

Fal·staff (fôl'staf, -stäf), Sir **John** a fat, jovial, witty knight that is a character in some of Shakespeare's plays —**Fal·staff'i·an** *adj.*

falt·boat (falt'bōt') *n.* [G. *faltboot* < *falten,* FOLD¹ + *boot,* BOAT] *same as* FOLDBOAT

fal·ter (fôl'tər) *vi.* [ME. *faltren,* prob. < ON.] 1. to move uncertainly or unsteadily; stumble 2. to stumble in speech; stammer 3. to act hesitantly; show uncertainty; waver 4. to lose strength; weaken [the economy *faltered*] —*vt.* to say hesitatingly or timidly —*n.* 1. a faltering 2. a faltering sound —see SYN. at HESITATE —**fal'ter·er** *n.* —**fal'ter·ing·ly** *adv.*

fame (fām) *n.* [< OFr. < L. *fama,* fame, akin to *fari:* see BAN¹] 1. [Archaic] public report; rumor 2. reputation, esp. for good 3. the state of being well known or much talked about; renown

famed (fāmd) *adj.* much talked about or widely known; famous; renowned (*for* something)

fa·mil·ial (fə mil'yəl) *adj.* of, involving, or common to a family

fa·mil·iar (fə mil'yər) *adj.* [< OFr. < L. < *familia,* FAMILY] 1. friendly, informal, or intimate 2. too friendly; intimate in a bold way [she was annoyed by his *familiar* manner] 3. knowing about; closely acquainted (*with*) [he is *familiar* with the Bible] 4. well-known; common [a *familiar* sight] —*n.* 1. a close friend 2. in superstitious belief, a spirit acting as servant to a witch —**fa·mil'iar·ly** *adv.*

fa·mil·i·ar·i·ty (fə mil'yar'ə tē, -mil'ē ar'-) *n., pl.* **-ties** 1. intimacy 2. free and intimate behavior 3. intimacy that is too bold or unwelcome 4. a highly intimate act, remark, etc.; specif., a caress 5. the fact of being closely acquainted (*with* something) [his *familiarity* with the subject makes him an expert]

fa·mil·iar·ize (fə mil'yə rīz') *vt.* **-ized', -iz'ing** 1. to make commonly known [a song *familiarized* by much playing] 2. to make (another or oneself) accustomed or fully acquainted [he *familiarized* himself with the city] —**fa·mil'iar·i·za'tion** *n.*

fam·i·ly (fam'ə lē, fam'lē) *n., pl.* **-lies** [L. *familia,* household < *famulus,* servant] 1. orig., all the people living in the same house; household 2. *a)* a social unit consisting of parents and their children *b)* the children of the same parents 3. a group of people related by ancestry or marriage; relatives 4. all those claiming descent from a common ancestor; tribe or clan; lineage 5. a group of things having a common source or similar features; specif., *a) Biol.* a category that is used in classifying plants or animals and that ranks above a genus and below an order *b) Linguis.* a group of languages having a common ancestral language *c) Math.* a set of curves, etc. with some shared property —*adj.* of or for a family

family man 1. a man who has a wife and children 2. a man devoted to his family and home

family name a surname

family planning *same as* BIRTH CONTROL

☆**family style** a way of serving food so that each person at the table helps himself from large dishes

family tree 1. all the ancestors and descendants in a family 2. a chart showing their relationship

fam·ine (fam'ən) *n.* [< OFr., ult. < L. *fames,* hunger] 1. an acute shortage of food that causes starving throughout a wide area, or a period of this 2. any acute and widespread shortage [the steel *famine* during the war] 3. [Archaic] starvation; great hunger

fam·ish (fam'ish) *vt., vi.* [< OFr. < L. *ad,* to + *fames,* hunger] 1. to make or be very hungry; make or become weak from hunger 2. [Obs.] to starve to death

fa·mous (fā'məs) *adj.* [< L. < *fama,* FAME] 1. much talked about; having fame, or celebrity; renowned 2. [Colloq.] excellent; first-rate —**fa'mous·ly** *adv.*

SYN.—*famous* is applied to persons or things that have received wide public attention and are much talked about; **renowned** suggests a being named publicly again and again for some outstanding quality, achievement, etc.; **celebrated** is applied to persons or things that have received much public honor or praise; **noted** implies a being brought to public notice because of some particular quality or characteristic [*noted* for his strength]; **notorious** suggests a being widely known, but for something bad [a *notorious* liar]; **distinguished** implies a being noted as superior in its class or of its kind [a *distinguished* performance]; **eminent** more strongly stresses the outstanding superiority of persons or things [an *eminent* statesman]; **illustrious** suggests a reputation based on brilliance of achievement or splendidness of character [an *illustrious* career] —**ANT.** obscure, unknown

fan¹ (fan) *n.* [OE. *fann* < L. *vannus,* basket for winnowing grain < IE. base *we-,* to blow, from which also come WIND² & WEATHER] 1. orig., a device for winnowing grain 2. any device used to move the air in a room, etc. so as to change the air or make things cool; specif., *a)* any flat surface moved by hand *b)* a folding device of paper, cloth, etc. that opens up in the shape of a half circle *c)* a motor-driven device with blades revolving around a hub 3. anything in the shape of a fan (sense 2 *b)* —*vt.* **fanned, fan'ning** 1. to move or agitate (air) as with a fan 2. to direct a current of air toward with or as with a fan; blow on [she *fanned* herself with a magazine] 3. to stir up; excite [to *fan* a revolt] 4. to blow or drive away with a fan 5. to spread out into the shape of a fan (*n.* 2 *b)* 6. to separate (grain) from chaff ☆7. [Slang] to fire (a pistol) several times quickly by slapping the hammer back between shots ☆8. *Baseball* to strike (a batter) out —*vi.* ☆*Baseball* to strike out —**fan out** to scatter or spread out like an open fan [the police *fanned out* to search the field] —**fan'like'** *adj.* —**fan'ner** *n.*

fan² (fan) *n.* [< FANATIC] [Colloq.] a person enthusiastic about a specified sport, pastime, or performer; devotee [a baseball *fan*]

fa·nat·ic (fə nat'ik) *adj.* [< L. < *fanum,* a temple] enthusiastic in an unreasonable or unbalanced way; overly zealous: also **fa·nat'i·cal** —*n.* a person who is fanatic in his zeal, piety, etc.; zealot —see SYN. at ZEALOT —**fa·nat'i·cal·ly** *adv.* —**fa·nat'i·cism** (-ə siz'm) *n.*

fan·cied (fan'sēd) *adj.* imaginary; imagined

fan·ci·er (fan'sē ər) *n.* a person who has a special interest in something, particularly plant or animal breeding, and knows a great deal about it [a dog *fancier*]

fan·ci·ful (fan'si fəl) *adj.* 1. full of fancy; having or showing a playful imagination [*fanciful* costumes] 2. not real, practical, etc.; imaginary [a *fanciful* tale] —see SYN. at IMAGINARY —**fan'·ci·ful·ly** *adv.* —**fan'ci·ful·ness** *n.*

fan·cy (fan'sē) *n., pl.* **-cies** [contr. < FANTASY] 1. imagination, now esp. light, whimsical, or playful imagination 2. a mental image 3. an impulsive idea; notion; caprice; whim [he had a sudden *fancy* to fly to Paris] 4. an inclination, liking, or fondness, often for a brief time [to take a *fancy* to someone] —*adj.* **-ci·er, -ci·est** 1. very high; extravagant [a *fancy* price] 2. not plain; decorated, elaborate, ornamental, etc. [a *fancy* necktie] 3. showing expert skill [*fancy* diving] 4. of superior quality and therefore more expensive [a *fancy* grade of tuna] 5. bred for some special feature —*vt.* **-cied, -cy·ing** 1. to form an idea of; imagine [I can't *fancy* you as an actor] 2. to have a liking for 3. to think or suppose without being sure [he *fancied* that she loved him] —*fancy* (**that**)! can you imagine (that)! — **fan'ci·less** *adj.* —**fan'ci·ly** *adv.* —**fan'ci·ness** *n.*

fan·cy-free (-frē') *adj.* 1. free to fall in love; not married, engaged, etc. 2. carefree

fan·cy·work (-wurk') *n.* embroidery, crocheting, and other ornamental needlework

fan·dan·go (fan daŋ'gō) *n., pl.* **-gos** [Sp.] 1. a lively Spanish dance in rhythm varying from slow to quick 3/4 time 2. music for this

fane (fān) *n.* [L. *fanum*] [Archaic or Poet.] a temple or church

Fan·euil Hall (fan'əl, -yəl) [after P. *Faneuil* (1700-43), its builder] old market building & public hall in Boston, Mass.

fan·fare (fan'fer') *n.* [Fr., prob. < *fanfaron,* braggart] 1. a loud flourish of trumpets 2. noisy or showy display

fang (faŋ) *n.* [OE. < base of *fon,* to seize: for IE. base see PEACE] 1. *a)* one of the long, pointed teeth with which meat-eating animals seize and tear their prey *b)* one of the long, hollow or grooved teeth through which poisonous snakes inject their venom 2. the pointed part of something —**fanged** (faŋd) *adj.*

FANGS

fan·jet (fan'jet') *n.* a jet aircraft with a turbofan engine

fan·light (fan'līt') *n.* a window in the shape of a half circle, often with sash bars in a fanlike arrangement, over a door or larger window

☆**fan mail** letters of praise or adulation from fans or devoted followers of a well-known person

Fan·nie, Fan·ny (fan'ē) [dim. of FRANCES] a feminine name

fan·tail (fan'tāl') *n.* 1. a part, tail, or end spread out like an opened fan 2. *Naut.* the part of the main deck at the stern 3. *Zool.* a variety of domestic pigeon, a breed of goldfish, etc. with a fanlike tail

fan-tan (fan'tan') *n.* [< Chin. *fan,* number of times + *t'an,* apportion] 1. a Chinese gambling game 2. a card game in which the players seek to discard all their cards in proper sequence Also **fan tan**

fan·ta·si·a (fan tā'zhə, -zē ə; fan'tə zē'ə) *n.* [It. < L.: see

FANTASY] **1.** a musical composition having no fixed form **2.** a medley of familiar tunes

fan·ta·size (fan′tə sīz′) *vt., vi.* **-sized′, -siz′ing** [FANTAS(Y) + -IZE] to create or imagine (something) in a fantasy; have daydreams (about) —**fan′ta·sist** *n.*

fan·tas·tic (fan tas′tik) *adj.* [< OFr. < ML. < LL. < Gr. *phantastikos*, able to present to the mind < *phainein*: see FANTASY] **1.** imaginary; unreal [*fantastic* terrors] **2.** having a strange, grotesque, or odd look [*fantastic* designs] **3.** strange and unusual; extravagant; capricious; eccentric [a *fantastic* plan] **4.** seemingly impossible; incredible [*fantastic* progress] Also **fan·tas′ti·cal** —**fan·tas′ti·cal·ly** *adv.* —**fan·tas′ti·cal·ness** *n.*
SYN.—**fantastic** implies a completely free use of the imagination, and suggests that which is unreal or dreamlike in a striking way [*fantastic* stage sets]; **bizarre** suggests that which is extremely strange or unusual because it is startling or unexpected [a *bizarre* combination of costumes]; **grotesque** suggests something that appears comic or frightening because it is a distortion of the real or natural [pain twisted his face into a *grotesque* mask] See also **SYN.** at IMAGINARY

fan·ta·sy (fan′tə sē, -zē) *n., pl.* **-sies** [< OFr. < L. < Gr. *phantasia*, appearance < *phainein*, to show: see BEACON] **1.** imagination or fancy; esp., wild, visionary fancy **2.** an unnatural or very strange mental image **3.** an odd notion; whim; caprice **4.** a highly imaginative poem, play, etc. **5.** *same as* FANTASIA **6.** a daydream or daydreaming, esp. about something one would like to do or have —*vt.* **-sied, -sy·ing** to form fantasies about —*vi.* to have fantasies, as by daydreaming

FAO Food and Agriculture Organization (of the UN)

far (fär) *adj.* **far′ther, far′thest:** see also FURTHER, FURTHEST [OE. *feorr* < IE. base *per-*, forward, beyond] **1.** distant in space, time, or degree; not near [he is *far* from home] **2.** extending a long way [a *far* journey] **3.** more distant [the *far* side of the room] **4.** very different in quality or nature [*far* from poor] —*adv.* **1.** at a great distance in space, time, or degree [the play is set *far* in the future] **2.** to or from a great distance in time or position [he has traveled *far*] **3.** very much [*far* better] **4.** to a certain distance or degree [how *far* did you go?] —*n.* a distant place [to come from *far*] —**as far as 1.** to the distance, extent, or degree that **2.** [Colloq.] with reference to; as for —**by far** very much: also **far and away** —**far and near** (or **wide**) everywhere —**far be it from me** I would not dare or wish —**far gone** close to ruin, death, the end, etc. —**far out** ☆*same as* FAR-OUT (see below) —**few and far between** scarce; rare —**go far 1.** to cover much extent; last long **2.** to have a strong tendency **3.** to accomplish much —**in so far as** to the extent or degree that —**so far** up to this place, time, or degree —**so far as** to the extent or point that —**so far, so good** up to this point everything is all right —**far′ness** *n.*

far·ad (far′ad, -əd) *n.* [after M. FARADAY] a unit of capacitance, equal to the amount that permits the storing of one coulomb of charge for each volt of applied potential

Far·a·day (far′ə dā′), **Michael** 1791-1867; Eng. scientist: noted esp. for his work in electricity

far·a·way (fär′ə wā′) *adj.* **1.** distant in time or place **2.** seeming to be distant; dreamy [a *faraway* look]

farce (färs) *n.* [Fr. < L. *farcire*, to stuff: early farces were used to fill interludes between acts] **1.** an exaggerated comedy based on highly unlikely situations that are broadly humorous **2.** broad humor of the kind found in such plays **3.** an action, situation, etc. that is ridiculous or unbelievable

far·ci·cal (fär′si k'l) *adj.* of, or having the nature of, a farce; absurd, ridiculous, etc. —see **SYN.** at FUNNY —**far′ci·cal·i·ty** (-kal′ə tē) *n.* —**far′ci·cal·ly** *adv.*

far·del (fär′d'l) *n.* [OFr.] [Archaic] a burden

fare (fer) *vi.* **fared, far′ing** [OE. *faran*, to go, wander < IE. base *per-*, to come over] **1.** [Poet.] to travel; go **2.** to happen; result [how did it *fare* with him?] **3.** to be in a specified condition; get on [he *fared* well on his trip] **4.** to eat or be given food —*n.* **1.** money paid for a trip in a train, taxi, plane, etc. **2.** a passenger who pays a fare **3.** *a)* food *b)* the usual diet

Far East E Asia, including China, Japan, Korea, & Mongolia, &, sometimes, Indochina

fare-thee-well (fer′thē wel′) *n.* ☆the highest or ultimate degree: usually in the phrase **to a fare-thee-well:** also **fare′-you-well′**

fare·well (fer′wel′; *for adj.* -wel′) *interj.* [FARE (imperative) + WELL²] goodbye —*n.* **1.** parting words; good wishes at parting **2.** a leaving or going away —*adj.* parting; last; final [a *farewell* gesture]

far-fetched (fär′fecht′) *adj.* resulting or introduced in a forced, or unnatural, way; strained [a *far-fetched* example]

far-flung (-fluŋ′) *adj.* extending over a wide area

Far·go (fär′gō) [after W. *Fargo* of Wells, Fargo & Co., shippers] city in eastern N.Dak.: pop. 53,000

fa·ri·na (fə rē′nə) *n.* [L. < *far*, kind of grain] flour or meal made from cereal grains (esp. whole wheat), potatoes, nuts, etc., eaten as a cooked cereal

far·i·na·ceous (far′ə nā′shəs) *adj.* [see prec.] **1.** containing, consisting of, or made from flour or meal **2.** like meal **3.** containing starch

☆**far·kle·ber·ry** (fär′k'l ber′ē) *n., pl.* **-ries** [< ?] a shrub or small tree of the southern U.S., with round, black berries

farm (färm) *n.* [< OFr. < ML. *firma*, fixed payment < *firmare*, to lease < L. *firmus*, steadfast] **1.** a piece of land (with house, barns, etc.) on which crops or animals are raised; orig., such land let out or leased to tenants **2.** any place where certain things are raised [a tract of water for raising fish is a fish *farm*] ☆**3.** *Baseball* a minor-league team, esp. one owned by a major-league team: in full, **farm club** (or **team**) —*vt.* **1.** to cultivate (land) **2.** to collect and keep (taxes, fees, etc.) by paying a fixed amount for the privilege **3.** to turn over to another for a fee —*vi.* to work on or operate a farm; raise crops or animals on a farm —**farm out 1.** to rent (land, a business, etc.) for a fixed payment **2.** to send (work) from a shop, office, etc. to workers on the outside **3.** to let out the labor of (a convict, etc.) for a fixed amount ☆**4.** *Baseball* to send to a farm (*n.* 3)

farm·er (fär′mər) *n.* **1.** a person who earns his living by farming; esp., one who manages or operates a farm **2.** a person who pays for a right, as, formerly, to collect and keep taxes **3.** a person who contracts to do something for a fixed price

farm·hand (färm′hand′) *n.* a hired farm laborer

farm·house (-hous′) *n.* a house on a farm; esp., the main dwelling house on a farm

farm·ing (fär′miŋ) *adj.* of or for agriculture —*n.* **1.** the business of operating a farm **2.** the letting out to farm of land, revenue, etc.

farm·stead (färm′sted′) *n.* the land and buildings of a farm

farm·yard (-yärd′) *n.* the yard surrounding or enclosed by the farm buildings

far·o (fer′ō) *n.* [Fr. *pharaon* < ? *Pharaoh*] a gambling game in which players bet on the cards to be turned up from the top of the dealer's pack

far-off (fär′ôf′) *adj.* distant; remote

far-out (fär′out′) *adj.* ☆[Colloq.] very advanced, experimental, or nonconformist; esp., avant-garde

Far·quhar (fär′kwər, -kər), **George** 1678-1707; Brit. playwright, born in Ireland

far·ra·go (fə rä′gō, -rā′-) *n., pl.* **-goes** [L., mixed fodder, mixture < *far*: see FARINA] a confused mixture; jumble

Far·ra·gut (far′ə gət), **David Glasgow** (born *James Glasgow Farragut*) 1801-70; U.S. admiral

far-reach·ing (fär′rēch′iŋ) *adj.* having a wide range, extent, influence, or effect

far·ri·er (far′ē ər) *n.* [< OFr. < ML. < L. *ferrum*, iron] [Brit.] a blacksmith who shoes horses; also, sometimes, one who treats their diseases —**far′ri·er·y,** *n., pl.* **-er·ies**

far·row (far′ō) *n.* [< OE. *fearh*, young pig] a litter of pigs —*vt., vi.* to give birth to (a litter of pigs)

far·see·ing (fär′sē′iŋ) *adj.* *same as* FARSIGHTED (senses 1 & 2)

far·sight·ed (-sīt′id) *adj.* **1.** capable of seeing far **2.** able to look ahead and plan for the future **3.** able to see things that are far away more clearly than those that are close —**far′sight′ed·ly** *adv.* —**far′sight′ed·ness** *n.*

far·ther (fär′thər) *adj. compar. of* FAR [ME. *ferther,* var. of *further,* FURTHER] **1.** more distant [Chicago is *farther* from New York than Detroit is] **2.** additional; further —*adv. compar. of* FAR **1.** at or to a greater distance or more remote point [Bob swam *farther* than Tim] **2.** to a greater degree; further **3.** in addition; further In sense 2 of the *adj.* and senses 2 and 3 of the *adv.,* FURTHER is more commonly used

far·ther·most (-mōst′) *adj.* most distant; farthest

far·thest (fär′thist) *adj. superl. of* FAR [ME. *farthest:* see FAR-THER] most distant [*the farthest regions*] —*adv. superl. of* FAR 1. at or to the greatest distance or most remote point [who can throw *farthest?*] 2. to the greatest degree

far·thing (fär′thiŋ) *n.* [OE. *feorthing,* dim. of *feortha,* FOURTH] 1. a former small British coin, equal to one fourth of a penny 2. a thing of little value; the least amount

far·thin·gale (fär′thiŋ gāl′) *n.* [OFr. *verdugalle* < Sp. < *verdugo,* tree shoot, rod < *verde* < L. *viridis,* green] a hoop skirt worn by women in the 16th and 17th centuries

fas·ces (fas′ēz) *n.pl.* [L., pl. of *fascis,* a bundle] a bundle of rods bound about an ax, carried before ancient Roman magistrates as a symbol of authority: later the symbol of Italian fascism

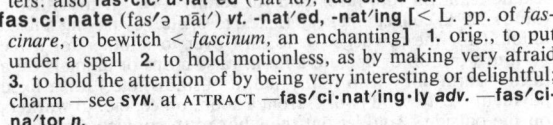

FASCES

fas·ci·a (fash′ē ə, fash′ə) *n., pl.* -ci·ae′ (-ē′), -ci·as [L., a band] 1. a flat strip; band 2. *Anat.* a thin layer of connective tissue —**fas′ci·al** *adj.*

fas·ci·cle (fas′i k'l) *n.* [< OFr. < L. dim. of *fascis:* see FASCES] 1. a single section of a book published in installments 2. a small bundle or cluster, as of leaves, stems, etc. —**fas′ci·cled** *adj.*

fas·cic·u·late (fə sik′yoo lit, -lāt′) *adj.* [see prec.] formed of, or growing in, bundles or clusters: also **fas·cic′u·lat·ed** (-lāt′id), **fas·cic′u·lar**

fas·ci·nate (fas′ə nāt′) *vt.* -nat′ed, -nat′ing [< L. pp. of *fascinare,* to bewitch < *fascinum,* an enchanting] 1. orig., to put under a spell 2. to hold motionless, as by making very afraid 3. to hold the attention of by being very interesting or delightful; charm —see SYN. at ATTRACT —**fas′ci·nat′ing·ly** *adv.* —**fas′ci·na′tor** *n.*

fas·ci·na·tion (fas′ə nā′shən) *n.* 1. a fascinating or being fascinated 2. charm; allure

fas·cism (fash′iz'm) *n.* [It. *fascismo* < L. *fascis:* see FASCES] 1. [F-] the doctrines, methods, or movement of the Fascisti 2. a system of government in which a dictator and a single party have absolute power over the politics, industry, etc. of a country, and seek to stay in power by promoting nationalism, racism, and militarism, as in Italy under Mussolini and in Nazi Germany

fas·cist (-ist) *n.* 1. [F-] *a)* a member of the Fascisti *b)* a member of some similar party; Nazi, Falangist, etc. 2. a supporter of fascism —*adj.* 1. [F-] of Fascists or Fascism 2. of, believing in, or practicing fascism —**fa·scis′tic** (fa shis′tik) *adj.* —**fa·scis′ti·cal·ly** *adv.*

Fa·scis·ti (fa shis′tē) *n.pl.* [It., pl. of *fascista,* a Fascist < L. *fascis:* see FASCES] an Italian political organization which seized power and set up a fascist dictatorship (1922–43) under Mussolini

fash·ion (fash′ən) *n.* [< OFr. *faceon* < L. *factio:* see FACTION] 1. the make, form, or shape of a thing 2. [Now Rare] kind; sort 3. way; manner 4. the current style of dress, conduct, etc. [will the *fashion* to wear wigs last?] 5. something in the current style [the store carries the latest *fashions* in shoes] 6. fashionable society [a man of *fashion*] —*vt.* 1. to make or form in a certain way; shape [to *fashion* artificial flowers] 2. to fit; accommodate (*to*) 3. [Archaic] to contrive —**after** (or **in**) **a fashion** to some extent, but not very well —**fash′ion·er** *n.*

SYN.—**fashion** refers to what has been made popular in the dress, manners, speech, art, literature, etc. of a particular place or time by leaders in society and various fields; **style** suggests a distinct fashion, esp. a way of dressing, living, etc. that is established by persons with money and taste; **mode,** the French word expressing this idea, suggests the highest fashions in dress, behavior, etc. at any particular time; **vogue** stresses the general acceptance or great popularity of a certain fashion; **fad** stresses the impulsive enthusiasm with which a fashion is taken up for a short time See also SYN. at MAKE and METHOD

fash·ion·a·ble (-ə b'l) *adj.* 1. in fashion; stylish 2. of, characteristic of, or used by people who follow fashion —*n.* a fashionable person —**fash′ion·a·ble·ness** *n.* —**fash′ion·a·bly** *adv.*

☆**fashion plate** 1. a picture showing a current style in dress 2. a fashionably dressed person

fast¹ (fast) *adj.* [OE. *fæst*] 1. firm, fixed, or stuck [the car is *fast* in the mud] 2. firmly fastened or shut [make the shutters *fast*] 3. loyal; devoted [*fast* friends] 4. that will not fade [*fast* colors] 5. swift; quick; speedy 6. permitting swift movement [a *fast* highway] 7. lasting a short time [a *fast* lunch] 8. showing a time that is ahead of the correct time [his watch is *fast*] 9. *a)* reckless; wild [a *fast* crowd] *b)* sexually promiscuous ☆10. [Colloq.] glib and deceptive [a *fast* talker] 11. [Slang] acting, gotten, done, etc. quickly and often dishonestly [out for a *fast* buck] 12. *Photog.* adapted to very short exposure

time [*fast* film] 13. [Dial.] complete; sound [a *fast* sleep] —*adv.* 1. firmly; fixedly 2. thoroughly; soundly [*fast* asleep] 3. rapidly; swiftly 4. ahead of time 5. in a reckless, dissipated way; wildly 6. [Obs.] close; near [*fast* by the river] —☆**a fast one** [Slang] a deceptive act [to pull *a fast one*] —**play fast and loose** to behave in a reckless and dishonest or insincere way

SYN.—**fast** and **rapid** are both used to express the idea of a relatively high rate of movement or action, but **fast** more often refers to the person or thing that moves or acts, and **rapid** to the action [a *fast* typist; *rapid* transcription]; **swift** implies great rapidity, but in addition often connotes smooth, easy movement; **fleet** suggests a nimbleness or lightness in that which moves swiftly; **quick** implies promptness of action, or occurrence in a brief space of time, rather than a high rate of speed [*quick* to take offense; a *quick* reply]; **speedy** intensifies the idea of quickness, but may also connote rapid motion [a *speedy* recovery; a *speedy* flight]; **hasty** suggests hurried action, and may connote carelessness, rashness, or impatience —ANT. slow

fast² (fast) *vi.* [OE. *fæstan*] 1. to go without all or certain foods, as in observing a holy day 2. to eat very little or nothing —*n.* 1. the act of fasting 2. a period of fasting —**break one's fast** to eat food for the first time after fasting, or for the first time in the day

fast day a holy day, etc. observed by fasting

fas·ten (fas′'n) *vt.* [OE. *fæstnian* < base of *fæst,* FAST¹] 1. to join (one thing *to* another); attach 2. to make stay closed or in place, as by locking, buttoning, etc. [*fasten* the door] 3. to hold or direct (the attention, etc.) steadily (*on*) 4. to cause to be connected with [to *fasten* a crime on someone] 5. to force (oneself *on* or *upon* another) in an annoying way —*vi.* 1. to become attached or joined 2. to take a firm hold (*on* or *upon*); seize 3. to concentrate (*on* or *upon*) —see SYN. at TIE —**fas′ten·er** *n.*

fas·ten·ing (-iŋ) *n.* anything used to fasten; bolt, clasp, hook, lock, button, etc.

☆**fast-food** (fast′food′) *adj.* designating a business, as a hamburger stand, that offers food prepared and served quickly

fas·tid·i·ous (fas tid′ē əs, fas-) *adj.* [< L. *fastidium,* a loathing < *fastus,* disdain + *taedium:* see TEDIUM] 1. not easy to please; very critical 2. daintily refined; easily disgusted —**fas·tid′i·ous·ly** *adv.* —**fas·tid′i·ous·ness** *n.*

fast·ness (fast′nis) *n.* 1. the quality or condition of being fast 2. a secure place; stronghold

fast time *same as* DAYLIGHT-SAVING TIME

fat (fat) *adj.* **fat′ter, fat′test** [OE. *fætt,* pp. of *fætan,* to fatten: for IE. base see PINE¹] 1. containing or full of fat; oily; greasy 2. *a)* fleshy; plump *b)* too plump; obese 3. thick; broad [a *fat* book] 4. fertile; productive [*fat* land] 5. profitable; lucrative [a *fat* job] 6. prosperous 7. plentiful; ample 8. stupid; dull 9. [Slang] large or important [a *fat* role in a play] —*n.* 1. any of various oily or greasy materials found in solid or semisolid form in animal tissue and in plant seeds 2. fleshiness; corpulence 3. the richest part of anything 4. anything unnecessary that can be trimmed away 5. *Chem.* a class of esters of fatty acids, insoluble in water —*vt., vi.* **fat′ted, fat′ting** to make or become fat: now usually FATTEN —☆**a fat chance** [Slang] very little or no chance —**chew the fat** [Slang] to talk together; chat —**the fat of the land** the best things obtainable; great luxury —**fat′ly** *adv.* —**fat′ness** *n.*

fa·tal (fāt′'l) *adj.* [OFr. < L. *fatalis* < *fatum,* FATE] 1. fateful; decisive [the *fatal* day arrived] 2. resulting in death 3. very destructive; most unfortunate —**fa′tal·ly** *adv.* —**fa′tal·ness** *n.* SYN.—**fatal** implies that death or disaster has occurred or will surely occur [a *fatal* disease; a *fatal* mistake]; **deadly** is applied to a thing that can and probably will cause death [a *deadly* poison]; **mortal** is applied to that which has just caused or will soon cause death [a *mortal* wound]; **lethal** is applied to that which is intended or designed to cause death [a *lethal* weapon]

fa·tal·ism (-iz'm) *n.* 1. the belief that all events are determined by fate and cannot be prevented from happening 2. acceptance of every event as something that cannot be avoided —**fa′tal·ist** *n.* —**fa′tal·is′tic** *adj.* —**fa′tal·is′ti·cal·ly** *adv.*

fa·tal·i·ty (fə tal′ə tē, fā-) *n., pl.* -ties 1. fate or necessity; subjection to fate 2. something caused by fate 3. a strong likelihood of ending in disaster 4. a tendency to cause death; deadliness [the *fatality* of a disease] 5. a death caused by a disaster, as in an accident, war, etc.

☆**fat·back** (fat′bak′) *n.* 1. fat from a hog's back, usually dried and salted in strips 2. *same as* MENHADEN

☆**fat cat** [Slang] a wealthy, influential person

fate (fāt) *n.* [< L. *fatum,* oracle < neut. pp. of *fari,* to speak: see BAN¹] 1. the power that is supposed to settle ahead of time what will happen [what does *fate* hold for us?] 2. *a)* something supposedly controlled by this power *b)* a person's lot or fortune *[it was his fate to die young]* **3.** the way things turn out in the end; final outcome *[what was the fate of the ship in the storm?]* **4.** death; destruction —*vt.* **fat′ed, fat′ing** to destine: now usually in the passive —**the Fates** *Gr. & Rom. Myth.* the three goddesses who control human destiny and life: see CLOTHO, LACHESIS, and ATROPOS

SYN.—**fate** and **destiny** both imply belief in a godlike power that decides how things will happen before they happen, but **destiny** often implies that things will turn out happily *[it was her destiny to be a famous singer]*; **portion** and **lot** usually suggest how a particular individual or group shares in the way things are decided by fate, but **portion** implies a sharing that seems fair and just and **lot** implies a sharing that occurs more by chance and may seem unfair; **doom** always suggests a fate or ending that brings death, disaster, etc.

fat·ed (fāt′id) *adj.* **1.** decided by fate; destined **2.** destined to destruction; doomed

fate·ful (-fəl) *adj.* **1.** telling what is to come; prophetic *[the fateful words of the oracle]* **2.** having important results *[a fateful decision]* **3.** controlled as if by fate **4.** bringing death or destruction *[the fateful explosion]* —see **SYN.** at OMINOUS — **fate′ful·ly** *adv.* —**fate′ful·ness** *n.*

fat·head (fat′hed′) *n.* [Slang] a stupid person —**fat′head′ed** *adj.*

fa·ther (fä′thər) *n.* [OE. fæder < IE. base *pəter*] **1.** a male parent; esp., a man as he is related to his child or children **2.** *a)* a stepfather *b)* a father-in-law **3.** a man thought of as a parent or protector **4.** [F-] God, or God as the first person of the Trinity **5.** a forefather; ancestor **6.** a man who is the originator, founder, or inventor of something **7.** any of the leaders of a city, assembly, etc.: *usually used in the pl.* **8.** [*often* F-] *a)* any of the important early Christian religious writers *b)* a Christian priest: used esp. as a title —*vt.* **1.** to be the father of; beget **2.** to care for as a father does; protect, rear, etc. **3.** to found, originate, or invent —**fa′ther·hood′** *n.* —**fa′ther·less** *adj.*

father confessor 1. a priest who hears confessions **2.** a person to whom one is in the habit of telling one's private affairs

father figure a person that one thinks of as if he were one's father

fa·ther-in-law (-ən lô′) *n., pl.* **fa′thers-in-law′** the father of one's wife or husband

fa·ther·land (-land′) *n.* a person's native land or, sometimes, the land of his ancestors

fa·ther·ly (-lē) *adj.* of or like a father; kindly; protective — **fa′ther·li·ness** *n.*

☆**Father's Day** the third Sunday in June, a day set aside (in the U.S.) in honor of fathers

Father Time time personified as a very old man carrying a scythe and an hourglass

fath·om (fath′əm) *n.* [OE. fæthm, the two arms outstretched (to measure, etc.): for IE. base see PETAL] a unit of length, equal to 6 feet, used mainly for measuring the depth of water —*vt.* **1.** to measure the depth of; sound **2.** to understand thoroughly *[I can't fathom the mystery]* —**fath′om·a·ble** *adj.*

☆**Fa·thom·e·ter** (fath äm′ə tər) *a trademark for* a sonar device used to measure depth of oceans, etc. —*n.* [f-] such a device

fath·om·less (fath′əm lis) *adj.* **1.** too deep to be measured **2.** too mysterious to understand —**fath′om·less·ness** *n.*

FATHER TIME

fa·tigue (fə tēg′) *n.* [Fr. < L. fatigare, to weary] **1.** a tired feeling, as from hard work; physical or mental exhaustion; weariness **2.** *a)* manual labor or menial duty, other than drill or instruction, required of soldiers: in full, **fatigue duty** *b)* [*pl.*] sturdy work clothing worn on fatigue duty: also **fatigue clothes** (or **clothing**) **3.** the tendency of a metal or other material to crack under continued stress —*vt., vi.* **-tigued′, -tigu′ing** **1.** to make or become tired; weary **2.** to subject to or undergo fatigue —see **SYN.** at TIRED —**fat′i·ga·bil′i·ty** *n.* —**fat·i·ga·ble** (fat′i gə b'l) *adj.*

Fat·i·ma (fat′i mə, fät′-; fə tē′mə) 606?-632 A.D.; daughter of Mohammed

fat·ling (fat′liŋ) *n.* a calf, lamb, kid, or young pig fattened before being slaughtered

fat·sol·u·ble (fat′säl′yə b'l) *adj.* soluble in fats or in solvents for fats

fat·ten (fat′'n) *vt., vi.* to make or become fat —**fat′ten·er** *n.*

fat·tish (-ish) *adj.* somewhat fat

fat·ty (-ē) *adj.* **-ti·er, -ti·est** **1.** of or containing fat **2.** very plump **3.** resembling fat; greasy; oily —*n.* [Colloq.] a fat person —**fat′ti·ness** *n.*

fatty acid 1. any of a series of saturated organic acids having the general formula $C_nH_{2n+1}COOH$ **2.** any of a number of saturated or unsaturated organic acids usually having an even number of carbon atoms in a straight chain and occurring naturally in the form of glycerol esters in fats and oils

fa·tu·i·ty (fə tōō′ə tē, -tyōō′-; fa-) *n., pl.* **-ties** **1.** a being fatuous **2.** a fatuous remark, act, etc. —**fa·tu′i·tous** *adj.*

fat·u·ous (fach′ōō wəs) *adj.* [L. fatuus, foolish: for IE. base see BAT¹] stupid or foolish in a smug or complacent way —see **SYN.** at SILLY —**fat′u·ous·ly** *adv.* —**fat′u·ous·ness** *n.*

fau·ces (fô′sēz) *n.pl.* [L., throat] the passage leading from the back of the mouth into the pharynx

fau·cet (fô′sit) *n.* [< OFr., prob. < *faulser*, to breach, falsify < LL. < L. *falsus*, FALSE] a device with a valve that can be turned on or off to control the flow of a liquid from a pipe, etc.; tap

Faulk·ner (fôk′nər), **William** 1897-1962; U.S. novelist

fault (fôlt) *n.* [< OFr. faulte, ult. < L. falsus, FALSE] **1.** a thing that mars or makes something imperfect; flaw; defect **2.** *a)* a misdeed; offense *b)* an error; mistake **3.** responsibility for something wrong; blame *[it's my fault that he's late]* **4.** *Geol.* a fracture or zone of fractures in rock strata along with a shifting of the strata **5.** *Tennis, Squash,* etc. an error in service —*vt.* **1.** to find fault with; blame **2.** *Geol.* to cause a fault in —*vi.* **1.** to commit a fault in tennis, etc. **2.** *Geol.* to develop a fault —**at fault** guilty of error; deserving blame —**find fault (with)** to seek and point out faults (of) —**to a fault** too much; excessively

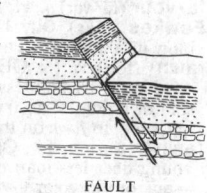
FAULT
(sense 4)

SYN.—**fault** refers to a definite imperfection in character, but not one which is strongly condemned *[her only fault is stubbornness]*; **failing** implies an even less serious shortcoming, usually one that many people have *[tardiness was one of his failings]*; **weakness** applies to a minor shortcoming that results from a lack of perfect self-control *[talking too much is his weakness]*; **foible** refers to a slight weakness that is regarded more as an amusing peculiarity than an actual defect in character *[eating desserts first is one of his foibles]*; **vice,** although it implies the doing of something morally wrong, does not suggest a serious moral weakness or shortcoming when used as a synonym for any of the preceding terms *[a little gambling is his only vice]* —**ANT.** virtue

fault·find·ing (-fīn′diŋ) *n., adj.* finding fault; calling attention to defects —see **SYN.** at CRITICAL —**fault′find′er** *n.*

fault·less (-lis) *adj.* without any fault; perfect —**fault′less·ly** *adv.* —**fault′less·ness** *n.*

fault·y (-ē) *adj.* **fault′i·er, fault′i·est** having a fault or faults; imperfect —**fault′i·ly** *adv.* —**fault′i·ness** *n.*

faun (fôn) *n.* [< L. < Faunus, a Roman nature god] any of a class of minor Roman deities, usually represented as having the body of a man, but the horns, ears, tail, and hind legs of a goat

fau·na (fô′nə) *n., pl.* **-nas, -nae** (-nē) [ModL. < LL. Fauna, Roman goddess] the animals of a specified region or time —**fau′nal** *adj.*

Fau·ré (fô rā′), **Gabriel** 1845-1924; Fr. composer

Faust (foust) the hero of a medieval legend, and later literary and operatic works, who sells his soul to the devil to gain knowledge and power: also **Faus′tus** (fôs′təs, fous′-) —**Faust′i·an** *adj.*

FAUN

fau·vism (fō′viz'm) *n.* [< Fr. < *fauve*, wild beast] [*often* F-] a French form of expressionist painting making use of bold distortions and strong, pure color —**fauve** (fōv), **fau′vist** *n., adj.*

faux pas (fō′ pä′) *pl.* **faux pas** (fō′ päz′) [Fr., lit., false step] a social blunder; error in etiquette —see **SYN.** at ERROR

fa·vor (fā'vər) *n.* [< OFr. < L. < *favere*, to favor] **1.** friendly regard; good will [his gifts won her *favor*] **2.** unfair partiality; favoritism [a good umpire shows no *favor* to either team] **3.** a kind or friendly act [to do someone a *favor*] **4.** a small gift, souvenir, or token —*vt.* **1.** to regard with favor; approve or like [do you *favor* his plan?] **2.** to be partial to; prefer unfairly [the teacher tends to *favor* the boys in her class] **3.** to support; advocate [the group *favors* radical change] **4.** to make easier; help [rain *favored* his escape] **5.** to do a kindness for [the manager *favored* us with free tickets] **6.** to look like; resemble [to *favor* one's mother] **7.** to use gently; spare [to *favor* an injured leg] —**find favor** to be pleasing —**in favor of 1.** approving; supporting **2.** to the advantage of **3.** payable to, as a check —**in one's favor** to one's advantage —**fa'vor·er** *n.*

fa·vor·a·ble (-ə b'l) *adj.* **1.** approving or supporting [a *favorable* opinion] **2.** helpful or advantageous [*favorable* winds] **3.** pleasing or desirable [a *favorable* impression] —**fa'vor·a·ble·ness** *n.* —**fa'vor·a·bly** *adv.*

fa·vored (fā'vərd) *adj.* **1.** treated with favor; specially privileged [a *favored* customer] **2.** having (specified) features of the face [ill-*favored*]

fa·vor·ite (fā'vər it, fāv'rit) *n.* **1.** a person or thing regarded with special liking; specif., a person granted special privileges, as by a king, etc. **2.** a contestant regarded as most likely to win —*adj.* held in special regard; best liked; preferred

fa·vor·it·ism (-iz'm) *n.* the showing of more kindness and help to some person or persons than to others

fa·vour (fā'vər) *n., vt. Brit. var.* of FAVOR

Fawkes (fôks), **Guy** 1570–1606; Eng. conspirator in a plot to blow up the king & Parliament

fawn[1] (fôn) *vi.* [< OE. *fagnian* < *fagen*, var. of *fægen*, fain] **1.** to show friendliness by licking hands, wagging its tail, etc.: said of a dog **2.** to try to gain favor by acting humble, flattering, etc. [to *fawn* on the rich] —**fawn'er** *n.* —**fawn'ing·ly** *adv.*

fawn[2] (fôn) *n.* [< OFr. *faon*, ult. < L. *fetus*, FETUS] **1.** a young deer less than one year old **2.** a pale, yellowish brown —*adj.* of this color —*vi., vt.* to bring forth (young): said of deer

Fay, Faye (fā) [< ? ME. *faie*, FAY or ? ME. *fei*, FAITH] a feminine name

fay (fā) *n.* [< OFr. < VL. < L. *fatum*, FATE] a fairy

Fay·ette·ville (fā'ət vil') [after Marquis de (LA)FAYETTE] city in south central N.C.: pop. 54,000

faze (fāz) *vt.* **fazed, faz'ing** [< OE. *fesan*, to drive] [Colloq.] to disturb; disconcert —see SYN. at EMBARRASS

FBI, F.B.I. Federal Bureau of Investigation

FCC, F.C.C. Federal Communications Commission

F clef *same as* BASS CLEF

FDA, F.D.A. Food and Drug Administration

FDIC, F.D.I.C. Federal Deposit Insurance Corporation

Fe [L. *ferrum*] *Chem.* iron

fe·al·ty (fē'əl tē) *n., pl.* **-ties** [< OFr. *feauté* < L. *fidelitas*, FIDELITY] **1.** the loyalty owed by a vassal to his feudal lord **2.** [Archaic] loyalty —see SYN. at ALLEGIANCE

fear (fir) *n.* [OE. *fær*, danger: for IE. base see FARE] **1.** anxiety and agitation caused by the presence of danger, evil, pain, etc.; fright **2.** awe; reverence **3.** a feeling of uneasiness or apprehension; concern [a *fear* that it will rain] **4.** a cause for fear, or concern; chance [there is no *fear* of his losing] —*vt.* **1.** to be afraid of [do you *fear* death?] **2.** to feel reverence or awe for **3.** to expect with misgiving [I *fear* I am late] —*vi.* **1.** to feel fear **2.** to be uneasy or anxious —**for fear of** in order to avoid or prevent —**fear'less** *adj.* —**fear'less·ly** *adv.* —**fear'less·ness** *n.*

Fear (fir), **Cape** cape on an island off the SE coast of N.C.

fear·ful (fir'fəl) *adj.* **1.** causing fear or terror [a *fearful* tale] **2.** feeling fear; afraid **3.** showing fear [a *fearful* look] **4.** [Colloq.] very bad, great, etc. [a *fearful* liar] —see SYN. at AFRAID —**fear'ful·ly** *adv.* —**fear'ful·ness** *n.*

fear·some (-səm) *adj.* **1.** causing fear; frightening [a *fearsome* noise] **2.** frightened; timid —**fear'some·ly** *adv.* —**fear'some·ness** *n.*

fea·si·ble (fē'zə b'l) *adj.* [< OFr. < *faire*, to make, do < L. *facere*: see FACT] **1.** capable of being done with conditions as they are; possible [a *feasible* scheme] **2.** within reason; likely; probable [a *feasible* story] **3.** capable of being used successfully; suitable [land *feasible* for cultivation] —see SYN. at POSSIBLE —**fea'si·bil'i·ty** *pl.* **-ties, fea'si·ble·ness** *n.* —**fea'si·bly** *adv.*

feast (fēst) *n.* [< OFr. < VL. *festa* < pl. of L. *festum* < *festus*, festal] **1.** a festival; esp., a religious festival honoring a god, saint, event, etc. **2.** a rich and elaborate meal; banquet **3.** anything that gives pleasure by its abundance or richness —*vi.*

1. to eat a rich, elaborate meal **2.** to have a special treat —*vt.* **1.** to entertain at a feast or banquet **2.** to give pleasure to; delight [to *feast* one's eyes on a sight] —**feast'er** *n.*

feat (fēt) *n.* [< Anglo-Fr. < OFr. < L. *factum*, a deed < pp. of *facere*: see FACT] an act or deed showing unusual daring, skill, etc.

feath·er (feth'ər) *n.* [OE. *fether* < IE. base *pet-*, to fly] **1.** any of the growths covering the body of a bird and making up a large part of the wing surface **2.** anything like a feather in appearance, lightness, etc. **3.** [*pl.*] *a)* plumage *b)* attire **4.** class; kind [birds of a *feather*] —*vt.* **1.** to provide or adorn as with feathers **2.** to give a featheredge to **3.** to join by inserting a wedge-shaped part into a groove **4.** to turn the edge of (the blade of an oar or propeller) toward the line of movement so as to offer the least resistance —*vi.* **1.** to grow feathers **2.** to move, grow, or look like feathers **3.** to feather an oar or propeller —**feather in one's cap** an achievement one can be proud of —**feather one's (own) nest** to provide for one's own comfort or security —**in feather** feathered —**in fine (or high or good) feather** in very good humor, health, or form —**feath'ered** *adj.* —**feath'er·ing** *n.* —**feath'er·less** *adj.*

feather bed a strong cloth container thickly filled with feathers or down, used as a mattress

☆**feath·er·bed·ding** (-bed'iŋ) *n.* the practice of limiting output or requiring extra workers, as by union contract, in order to provide more jobs —**feath'er·bed'** *adj., vi., vt.* **-bed'ded, -bed'ding**

feath·er·brain (-brān') *n.* a silly, foolish, or frivolous person —**feath'er·brained'** *adj.*

feath·er·edge (-ej') *n.* a very thin edge, easily broken or curled —*vt.* **-edged', -edg'ing** to give such an edge to

feath·er·stitch (-stich') *n.* an embroidery stitch forming a zigzag line —*vt., vi.* to embroider with such a stitch

feath·er·weight (-wāt') *n.* **1.** any person or thing of light weight or small size **2.** a boxer who weighs over 118 but not over 126 pounds **3.** a wrestler who weighs over 123 but not over 134 pounds —*adj.* **1.** of featherweights **2.** light or trivial

feath·er·y (-ē) *adj.* **1.** covered with or as with feathers **2.** resembling feathers; soft, light, etc. —**feath'er·i·ness** *n.*

FEATHER-STITCH

fea·ture (fē'chər) *n.* [< OFr. < L. *factura*, a making < pp. of *facere*: see FACT] **1.** orig., the make, form, or appearance of a person or thing **2.** *a)* [*pl.*] the form or look of the face *b)* any of the parts of the face, as the eyes, nose, mouth, etc. **3.** a distinct or outstanding part or quality of something ☆**4.** a prominently displayed or publicized attraction at an entertainment, sale, etc. ☆**5.** a special story, article, etc. in a newspaper or magazine ☆**6.** a full-length motion picture —*vt.* **-tured, -tur·ing** ☆**1.** to give prominence to; make a feature of **2.** to sketch or show the features of **3.** to be a feature of ☆**4.** [Slang] to conceive of —☆*vi.* to have a prominent part —**fea'ture·less** *adj.*

fea·tured (-chərd) *adj.* **1.** having (a specified kind of) facial features [broad-*featured*] ☆**2.** given special prominence as a main attraction

feaze (fēz, fāz) *vt.* **feazed, feaz'ing** *var.* of FAZE

Feb. February

feb·ri- [< L. *febris*, FEVER] *a combining form meaning* fever [*febrifuge*]

feb·ri·fuge (feb'rə fyoōj') *n.* [< Fr.: see FEBRI- & -FUGE] any substance for reducing fever —*adj.* reducing fever

fe·brile (fē'brəl, feb'rəl) *adj.* [< Fr. < L. *febris*, fever] of, having, or like fever; feverish

Feb·ru·ar·y (feb'rə wer'ē, feb'yoo wer'ē) *n.* [L. *Februarius* < *februa*, Roman festival of purification held Feb. 15] the second month of the year, having 28 days (or 29 days in leap years): abbrev. **Feb., F.**

fe·cal (fē'kəl) *adj.* of or consisting of feces

fe·ces (fē'sēz) *n.pl.* [< L. *faeces*, dregs] waste matter expelled from the bowels; excrement

feck·less (fek'lis) *adj.* [Scot. < *feck* (< EFFECT) + -LESS] **1.** weak; ineffective **2.** careless; irresponsible —**feck'less·ly** *adv.* —**feck'less·ness** *n.*

fe·cund (fē'kənd, fek'ənd) *adj.* [< OFr. < L. *fecundus*, fruitful: for IE. base see FEMALE] fruitful or fertile; productive —see SYN. at FERTILE

fe·cun·date (fē'kən dāt', fek'ən-) *vt.* **-dat'ed, -dat'ing** [< L. pp. of *fecundare* < *fecundus*: see prec.] **1.** to make fecund **2.** to fertilize; impregnate; pollinate —**fe'cun·da'tion** *n.*

fed[1] (fed) *pt. & pp. of* FEED —**fed up** [Colloq.] having had enough to become disgusted, bored, etc.

fed[2] (fed) *n.* [*often* F-] ☆[Slang] a Federal agent or officer

Fed. **1.** Federal **2.** Federated **3.** Federation

fed·a·yeen (fed′ä yēn′) *n.pl.* [Ar., lit., those who sacrifice themselves] Arab guerrillas in the Middle East

fed·er·al (fed′ər əl, fed′rəl) *adj.* [< L. *foedus* (gen. *foederis*), a league: for IE. base see FAITH] **1.** of or formed by an agreement; specif., designating or of a union of states, groups, etc. in which each member subordinates its governmental power to a central authority in certain common affairs **2.** designating or of a central government in such a union; specif., ☆[*usually* F-] of the central government of the U.S. ☆**3.** [F-] of the Federalist Party ☆**4.** [F-] of or supporting the U.S. government in the Civil War; Union —*n.* ☆**1.** [F-] a Federalist ☆**2.** [F-] a supporter or soldier of the U.S. government in the Civil War ☆**3.** [F-] a Federal agent or officer —**fed′er·al·ly** *adv.*

☆**Federal Bureau of Investigation** a branch of the U.S. Department of Justice whose duty is to investigate violations of Federal laws

☆**Federal Communications Commission** a Federal agency which regulates communication by wire and radio, including licensing of radio and TV stations

fed·er·al·ism (-iz′m) *n.* **1.** the federal principle of government or organization ☆**2.** [F-] the principles of the Federalist Party

fed·er·al·ist (-ist) *n.* **1.** one who believes in or supports federalism ☆**2.** [F-] a member or supporter of the Federalist Party —*adj.* **1.** of or supporting federalism ☆**2.** [F-] of or supporting the Federalist Party or its principles Also **fed′er·al·is′tic**

☆**Federalist** (or **Federal**) **Party** a political party in the U.S. (1789–1816) which advocated the adoption of the Constitution and the establishment of a strong, centralized government

fed·er·al·ize (fed′ər ə līz′, fed′rə-) *vt.* **-ized′, -iz′ing** **1.** to unite (states, etc.) in a federal union **2.** to put under the authority of a federal government —**fed′er·al·i·za′tion** *n.*

☆**Federal Reserve Bank** any of the twelve district banks of the Federal Reserve System

☆**Federal Reserve note** any piece of U.S. paper currency issued by the individual Federal Reserve Banks

☆**Federal Reserve System** a centralized banking system in the U.S., with supervisory powers over Federal Reserve Banks and about 6,000 member banks

☆**Federal Trade Commission** a Federal agency whose duty is to investigate and stop unfair methods of competition in business, fraudulent advertising, etc.

fed·er·ate (fed′ər it; *for v.* -ə rāt′) *adj.* [< L. pp. of *foederare* < *foedus*: see FEDERAL] united by common agreement under a central government or authority —*vt., vi.* **-at′ed, -at′ing** to unite in a federation

fed·er·a·tion (fed′ə rā′shən) *n.* **1.** the act of uniting or of forming a union of states, groups, etc. by agreement of each member to subordinate its power to a central authority in common affairs **2.** an organization formed thus; a federal union, as of states —see SYN. at ALLIANCE —**fed′er·a′tive** *adj.*

☆**fe·do·ra** (fə dôr′ə) *n.* [Fr. < *Fédora* (1882), play by V. Sardou, Fr. dramatist] a soft felt hat with the crown creased lengthwise and a curved brim

fee (fē) *n.* [< Anglo-Fr. *fee* & < OE. *feoh*, cattle, property < IE. base *pek-*, wealth] **1.** orig., a fief **2.** a payment asked or given for professional services, admissions, licenses, tuition, etc.; charge **3.** *Law* an inheritance in land: a person who holds land in **fee simple** has the right to sell or give it to anyone; if he holds it in **fee tail** he can give it only to a certain specified class of heirs —see SYN. at WAGE

FEDORA

fee·ble (fē′b'l) *adj.* **-bler, -blest** [< OFr. < L. *flebilis*, to be wept over < *flere*, to weep: for IE. base see BLEAR] weak; not strong; specif., *a)* infirm [a *feeble* old man] *b)* without force or effectiveness [a *feeble* attempt] *c)* easily broken; frail [a *feeble* barrier] —see SYN. at WEAK —**fee′ble·ness** *n.* —**fee′bly** *adv.*

fee·ble·mind·ed (-mīn′did) *adj.* mentally retarded: term no longer used in psychology —**fee′ble·mind′ed·ly** *adv.* —**fee′ble·mind′ed·ness** *n.*

feed (fēd) *vt.* **fed, feed′ing** [< OE. *fedan* < base of *foda*, FOOD] **1.** to give food to; provide food for [to *feed* oats to horses] *b)* to serve as food for **3.** to provide something necessary for the growth or existence of; nourish [to *feed* one's anger] **4.** to provide (material to be used up, processed, etc.) [to *feed* coal into a stove] **5.** to provide with material [*feed* the stove] **6.** to provide satisfaction for; gratify [to *feed* one's vanity] **7.** *Sports* to pass (the ball, puck, etc.) to (a teammate ready to try for a shot, goal, etc.) **8.** *Theater* to supply (an actor) with (cue lines) —*vi.* **1.** to eat: said chiefly of animals **2.** to flow steadily, as into a machine for use, processing, etc. —*n.* **1.** *a)* food given to animals; fodder *b)* the amount of fodder given at one time **2.** *a)* the material fed into a machine *b)* the part of the machine supplying this material *c)* the supplying of this material **3.** [Colloq.] a meal —**feed on** (or **upon**) to be nourished or gratified by —**off one's feed** [Slang] lacking appetite; somewhat sick —**feed′er** *n.*

feed·back (-bak′) *n.* **1.** *Elec.* the transfer of part of the output back to the input: it may be an unwanted effect or one desired, as to reduce distortion **2.** a process in which the result modifies the factors producing the result

☆**feed bag** a bag filled with grain, fastened over a horse's muzzle for feeding

feel (fēl) *vt.* **felt, feel′ing** [OE. *felan*] **1.** to touch; examine by touching or handling **2.** to be aware of through physical sensation [to *feel* rain on the face] **3.** *a)* to experience (an emotion or condition) *b)* to be emotionally moved by [to *feel* a death keenly] **4.** to be aware of mentally [to *feel* the weight of an argument] **5.** to think or believe, often for emotional reasons [he *feels* that we should go] —*vi.* **1.** to have physical sensation **2.** to appear to be to the senses, esp. to the sense of touch [the water *feels* warm] **3.** to have the indicated effect [it *feels* good to be home] **4.** to search by touching; grope (*for*) **5.** to be aware of being [to *feel* sad] **6.** to be moved to sympathy, pity, etc. (*for*) —*n.* **1.** the act of feeling **2.** the sense of touch **3.** the nature of a thing perceived through touch [the *feel* of wet sawdust] **4.** an emotional sensation [the *feel* of happiness] **5.** instinctive ability or appreciation [a *feel* for design] —☆**feel (a person) out** to try cautiously to find out the opinions of (a person) —☆**feel like** [Colloq.] to have a desire for —**feel one's way** to move cautiously, as if by groping —**feel up to** [Colloq.] to feel able to

feel·er (fēl′ər) *n.* **1.** a person or thing that feels **2.** a specialized organ of touch in an animal or insect, as an antenna **3.** a remark, question, offer, etc. made to feel out another

feel·ing (-iŋ) *adj.* sensitive and sympathetic —*n.* **1.** the sense of touch, through the skin, by which one can tell whether something is rough or smooth, hot or cold, painful or pleasant, etc. **2.** the ability to experience these physical sensations **3.** an awareness; sensation [a *feeling* of pain] **4.** an emotion [to control one's *feelings*] **5.** sympathy or pity [he spoke with *feeling* about human suffering] **6.** an opinion or belief [I have a *feeling* that he is right] **7.** a forewarning; premonition [a *feeling* of doom] **8.** air; atmosphere [the lonely *feeling* of the city] **9.** a natural ability or sensitive appreciation [a *feeling* for music] **10.** the emotional quality in a work of art —**hurt one's feelings** to make one unhappy or angry —**feel′ing·ly** *adv.*

feet (fēt) *n. pl. of* FOOT —**have one's feet on the ground** to be practical, realistic, etc. —**on one's feet** **1.** firmly established **2.** in a healthy condition **3.** alert or alertly —**sit at the feet of** to be an admiring disciple or pupil of —**stand on one's own (two) feet** to be independent —**sweep** (or **carry**) **off one's feet** **1.** to fill with enthusiasm **2.** to impress deeply

feign (fān) *vt.* [< OFr. *feindre* < L. *fingere*, to shape: for IE. base see DOUGH] **1.** to make up (a story, excuse, etc.); fabricate **2.** to make a false show of; pretend [to *feign* illness] —*vi.* to pretend; dissemble —**feigned** *adj.* —**feign′er** *n.* —**feign′ing·ly** *adv.*

Fei·ning·er (fī′niŋ ər), **Ly·o·nel** (**Charles Adrian**) (lī′ə n′l) 1871–1956; U.S. painter

feint (fānt) *n.* [< Fr. pp. of *feindre*: see FEIGN] **1.** a false show; sham [to make a *feint* of working] **2.** a pretended blow or attack intended to take the opponent off his guard, as in boxing or fencing —*vi., vt.* to deliver (such a blow or attack)

---

fat, āpe, cär; ten, ēven; is, bīte; gō, hôrn, tōōl, lŏŏk; oil, out; up, fur; get; joy; yet; chin; she; thin, *th*en; zh, leisure; ŋ, ring; ə for *a* in *ago*, *e* in *agent*, *i* in *sanity*, *o* in *comply*, *u* in *focus*; ′ as in *able* (ā′b'l); Fr. bål; ë, Fr. coeur; ö, Fr. feu; Fr. mon; ô, Fr. coq; ü, Fr. duc; r, Fr. cri; H, G. ich; kh, G. doch; ‡foreign; ☆ Americanism; < derived from. See inside front cover.

☆**feist·y** (fīst′ē) *adj.* **feist′i·er, feist′i·est** [< ME. *fist*, a breaking of wind + -y²] [Colloq. or Dial.] **1.** lively; energetic **2.** quarrelsome; belligerent —**feist′i·ness** *n.*

feld·spar (feld′spär′, fel′-) *n.* [< G. < *feld*, field + *spat(h)*, spar] any of several crystalline minerals made up of aluminum silicates with sodium, potassium, or calcium, usually glassy and moderately hard, found in igneous rocks —**feld·spath′ic** (-spa′thik) *adj.*

Fe·li·ci·a (fə lish′ē ə) [fem. of FELIX] a feminine name

fe·lic·i·tate (fə lis′ə tāt′) *vt.* **-tat′ed, -tat′ing** [< L. pp. of *felicitare* < *felix*, happy] to wish happiness to —**fe·lic′i·ta′tion** *n.* —**fe·lic′i·ta′tor** *n.*

fe·lic·i·tous (-təs) *adj.* [< FELICITY + -OUS] **1.** used or expressed in a way suitable to the occasion; appropriate **2.** having the knack of appropriate and pleasing expression —**fe·lic′i·tous·ly** *adv.* —**fe·lic′i·tous·ness** *n.*

fe·lic·i·ty (-tē) *n., pl.* **-ties** [< OFr. < L. < *felix* (gen. *felicis*), happy: for IE. base see FEMALE] **1.** happiness; bliss **2.** anything producing happiness **3.** a way of writing or speaking, or a remark, that is pleasing and just right for the occasion

fe·line (fē′līn) *adj.* [< L. < *felis*, cat] **1.** of a cat or the cat family **2.** catlike; esp., *a)* sly, stealthy, etc. *b)* sleekly graceful —*n.* any animal of the cat family, including the cat, lion, panther, tiger, etc. —**fe′line·ly** *adv.* —**fe′line·ness, fe·lin·i·ty** (fi lin′ə tē) *n.*

Fe·lix (fē′liks) [L., lit., happy] a masculine name

fell[1] (fel) *pt. of* FALL

fell[2] (fel) *vt.* [OE. *fellan:* for IE. base see FALL] **1.** to make fall; knock down [*he felled* his opponent with a blow] **2.** to cut down (a tree) **3.** to turn over (the rough edge of a seam) and sew down flat on the underside —*n.* **1.** the trees cut down in one season **2.** a felled seam —**fell′a·ble** *adj.* —**fell′er** *n.*

fell[3] (fel) *adj.* [< OFr. < ML. *fello:* see FELON¹] **1.** fierce; terrible; cruel [a *fell* blow] **2.** [Archaic] causing death; deadly [a *fell* plague] —**fell′ness** *n.*

fell[4] (fel) *n.* [OE. *fel*] an animal's hide or skin

fell[5] (fel) *n.* [< Scand.] [Brit.] a moor; down

fel·lah (fel′ə) *n., pl.* **fel′lahs;** Ar. **fel·la·heen, fel·la·hin** (fel′ə hēn′) [< Ar. < *falāḥa*, to plow] a peasant or farm laborer in Egypt or some other countries where Arabic is spoken

fel·loe (fel′ō) *n.* same as FELLY

fel·low (fel′ō, -ə) *n.* [< Late OE. *feolaga*, partner < *feoh* (see FEE) + *laga*, a laying down] **1.** a companion; associate [his *fellows* in crime] **2.** one of the same class or rank; equal **3.** either of a pair of things that match; mate [I lost the *fellow* to this shoe] **4.** a graduate student holding a fellowship in a university or college **5.** a member of a learned society **6.** at some British and U.S. universities, a member of the governing body **7.** [Colloq.] *a)* a man or boy *b)* a person; one [a *fellow* must eat] **8.** [Colloq.] a suitor; beau —*adj.* having the same ideas, position, work, etc.; associated [*fellow* workers]

fel·low·ship (-ship′) *n.* **1.** companionship; friendly association **2.** a mutual sharing, as of activity, etc. **3.** a group of people with the same interests **4.** an endowment, or a sum of money paid from it, for the support of a graduate student, scholar, etc. doing advanced study **5.** the rank or position of a fellow in a university or college

fellow traveler a person who advocates the cause of a party without being a member

fel·ly (fel′ē) *n., pl.* **-lies** [OE. *felg*] the rim of a spoked wheel, or a segment of the rim

fel·on[1] (fel′ən) *n.* [< OFr. < ML. *felo*, earlier *fello* < ?] *Law* a person guilty of a major crime; criminal —*adj.* [Poet.] wicked; base

fel·on[2] (fel′ən) *n.* [< ?] a painful, pus-producing infection at the end of a finger or toe, near the nail

fe·lo·ni·ous (fə lō′nē əs) *adj.* **1.** [Poet.] wicked; base **2.** *Law* of, like, or being a felony —**fe·lo′ni·ous·ly** *adv.* —**fe·lo′ni·ous·ness** *n.*

fel·o·ny (fel′ə nē) *n., pl.* **-nies** [< OFr. < ML. < *felo*, FELON¹] a major crime, as murder, arson, rape, etc., for which statute provides a greater punishment than for a misdemeanor

fel·spar (fel′spär′) *n.* same as FELDSPAR

felt[1] (felt) *n.* [OE. < IE. base *pel-*, to beat] **1.** a fabric of wool, often mixed with fur, cotton, rayon, etc., the fibers being worked together by pressure, heat, chemical action, etc.: also **felt′ing 2.** anything like felt, with a fuzzy, springy surface **3.** anything made of felt —*adj.* made of felt —*vt.* **1.** *a)* to make into felt *b)* to cover with felt **2.** to mat (fibers) together —*vi.* to become matted together

felt[2] (felt) *pt. and pp. of* FEEL

fe·luc·ca (fə luk′ə, -l⊙⊙′kə) *n.* [< It. *feluca*, prob. < Ar.] a small, narrow ship propelled by oars or lateen sails, used esp. in the Mediterranean

FELUCCA

fem. feminine

fe·male (fē′māl) *adj.* [< OFr. < L. dim. of *femina*, a woman < IE. base *dhe-*, to suck, suckle] **1.** designating or of the sex that produces ova and bears offspring **2.** of, like, or suitable to members of this sex; feminine **3.** of women or girls **4.** having a hollow part shaped to receive a part (called *male*) designed to fit into it: said of electric sockets, etc. **5.** *Bot.* having a pistil and no stamen —*n.* a female person, animal, or plant —**fe′male·ness** *n.*

SYN.—**female** is the basic term applied to members of the sex that is biologically different from the male sex, esp. in the role that each sex plays in reproduction; **feminine** is now the preferred term in referring to qualities that women are conventionally thought of as having, such as delicacy, gentleness, etc.; **womanly** suggests those qualities traditionally associated with a mature, responsible woman, usually a wife and mother or homemaker; **womanish** is a term applied, usually in an unflattering way, to any woman or man regarded as being weak, passive, timid, frivolous, etc. —see also **SYN.** at WOMAN —**ANT.** male, masculine, manly, mannish

fem·i·nine (fem′ə nin) *adj.* [< OFr. < L. < *femina:* see FEMALE] **1.** of women or girls **2.** having qualities thought of as those that women and girls have, as gentleness, delicacy, etc. **3.** suitable to or for a woman **4.** effeminate: said of a man **5.** *Gram.* designating or of the gender of words referring to females or things originally thought of as female **6.** *Poetry* designating or of a rhyme of two or three syllables with only the first stressed (Ex.: danger, stranger) —*n. Gram.* **1.** the feminine gender **2.** a word or form in this gender —see **SYN.** at FEMALE —**fem′i·nine·ly** *adv.* —**fem′i·nin′i·ty, fem′i·nine·ness** *n.*

fem·i·nism (fem′ə niz′m) *n.* **1.** the principle that women should have political, economic, and social rights equal to those of men **2.** the movement to win these rights —**fem′i·nist** *n., adj.* —**fem′i·nis′tic** *adj.*

fem·i·nize (fem′ə nīz′) *vt., vi.* **-nized′, -niz′ing** to make or become feminine or effeminate —**fem′i·ni·za′tion** *n.*

femme (fem; Fr. fàm) *n., pl.* **femmes** (femz; Fr. fàm) [Fr.] [Slang] a woman or wife

fem·to- (fem′tō) [< Dan. *femten*, fifteen] a combining form meaning one quadrillionth; the factor 10^{-15} [*femtosecond*]

fe·mur (fē′mər) *n., pl.* **fe′murs, fem·o·ra** (fem′ər ə) [ModL. < L., thigh] same as THIGHBONE —**fem′o·ral** *adj.*

fen[1] (fen) *n.* [OE.] an area of low, flat, marshy land; swamp; bog —**fen′ny** *adj.*

fen[2] (fen) *n. see* MONETARY UNITS, table (China)

fe·na·gle (fə nā′g'l) *vi., vt.* **-gled, -gling** same as FINAGLE —**fe·na′gler** *n.*

fence (fens) *n.* [ME. *fens*, short for *defens*, DEFENSE] **1.** a barrier of posts, wire, rails, etc., used as a boundary or means of protection or confinement **2.** the art of self-defense with foil, saber, etc.; fencing **3.** *a)* one who buys and sells stolen goods *b)* a place for such dealings —*vt.* **fenced, fenc′ing 1.** to enclose, restrict, etc. with or as with a fence (with *in, off,* etc.) **2.** to keep (*out*) by or as by a fence —*vi.* **1.** to practice the art of fencing **2.** to avoid giving a direct reply; be evasive (with) **3.** to buy or sell stolen goods —☆**mend (one's) fences** to engage in politicking; look after one's political interests: said esp. of a legislator —☆**on the fence** not taking one side or the other; uncommitted —**fence′less** *adj.* —**fenc′er** *n.*

fenc·ing (fen′siŋ) *n.* **1.** the art of fighting with a foil or other sword **2.** *a)* material for making fences *b)* a system of fences

fend (fend) *vt.* [ME. *fenden*, short for *defenden*, DEFEND] [Archaic] to defend —*vi.* to resist; parry —**fend for oneself** to get along without help from others —**fend off** to keep off; turn aside

FENCING

fend·er (fen′dər) *n.* anything that fends off or protects something else; specif., ☆*a)* any one of the metal frames over the wheels of an automobile or other vehicle to protect against splashing mud, etc. ☆*b)* a device on the front of a streetcar or locomotive to catch or push aside anything on the track *c)* a screen or guard placed in front of a fireplace

fen·es·tra·tion (fen′ə strā′shən) *n.* [ult. < L. *fenestra*, window] **1.** the arrangement of windows and doors in a building **2.** the surgical operation of making an opening into the inner ear in certain cases of otosclerosis

Fe·ni·an (fē′nē ən, fēn′yən) *n.* [< pl. of Ir. Gael. *Fiann*, the old militia of Ireland] ☆a member of a secret Irish revolutionary group formed in New York about 1858 to free Ireland from English rule —*adj.* of the Fenians —**Fe′ni·an·ism** *n.*

fen·nel (fen′'l) *n.* [< OE. < L. *feniculum*, dim. of *fenum*, hay] a tall herb of the parsley family, with yellow flowers: its aromatic seeds are used as a seasoning and in medicine

feoff (fef, fēf) *vt.* [< Anglo-Fr. < OFr. < *fieu*, fief] to give or sell a fief to —*n.* a fief —**feoff′ment** *n.* —**feof′for, feoff′er** *n.*

FEP Fair Employment Practice(s)

-fer (fər) [< Fr. or L. < L. *ferre*, BEAR[1]] *a suffix meaning* bearer, producer [*conifer*]

fe·ral (fir′əl) *adj.* [< L. < *ferus*, fierce + -AL] **1.** untamed; wild **2.** savage; brutal

fer-de-lance (fer′də läns′) *n.* [Fr., iron tip of a lance] a large, poisonous pit viper, related to the rattlesnake, found in tropical America

Fer·di·nand (fur′d'n and′) [Fr., prob. < Gmc. bases meaning "bold in peace"] **1.** a masculine name **2. Ferdinand I** 1000?–65; king of Castile (1033–65) & of León (1037–65): called *the Great* **3. Ferdinand V** 1452–1516; king of Castile (1474–1504): husband of ISABELLA I

FER-DE-LANCE
(to 8 ft. long)

fer·ma·ta (fer mät′ə) *n.* [It. < *fermare*, to stop] *Music* **1.** the holding of a tone or rest beyond its written value, at the performer's discretion **2.** the sign (⌢) or (⌣) indicating this

fer·ment (fur′ment; *for v.* fər ment′) *n.* [< OFr. < L. *fermentum* < *fervere*, to boil; see BREATH] **1.** a substance or organism causing fermentation, as yeast, bacteria, etc. **2.** *same as* FERMENTATION **3.** a state of excitement or agitation —*vt.* **1.** to cause fermentation in **2.** to excite; agitate —*vi.* **1.** to be in the process of fermentation **2.** to be excited or agitated —**fer·ment′a·ble** *adj.*

fer·men·ta·tion (fur′mən tā′shən, -men-) *n.* **1.** the breakdown of complex molecules in organic compounds, caused by a ferment [*bacteria curdle milk by fermentation*] **2.** excitement; agitation —**fer·ment·a·tive** (fər men′tə tiv) *adj.*

Fer·mi (fer′mē), **En·ri·co** (en rē′kō) 1901–54; It. nuclear physicist, in the U.S. after 1938

☆**fer·mi·um** (fer′mē əm) *n.* [after E. FERMI] a radioactive chemical element: symbol, Fm; at. wt., 257(?); at. no., 100

fern (furn) *n.* [OE. *fearn*] any of a group of nonflowering plants having roots, stems, and fronds, and reproducing by spores instead of by seeds —**fern′y** *adj.*

fern·er·y (fur′nər ē) *n., pl.* **-er·ies** a place where ferns are grown; collection of growing ferns

fe·ro·cious (fə rō′shəs) *adj.* [< L. *ferox* (gen. *ferocis*) < *ferus*, fierce + -OUS] **1.** fierce; savage; violently cruel **2.** [Colloq.] very great [*a ferocious appetite*] —**fe·ro′cious·ly** *adv.* —**fe·ro′cious·ness** *n.*

fe·roc·i·ty (fə räs′ə tē) *n., pl.* **-ties** wild force or cruelty; ferociousness

-fer·ous (fər əs) [L. *-fer* < *ferre*, BEAR[1] + -OUS] *a suffix meaning* bearing, producing [*coniferous*]

Fer·ra·ra (fə rär′ə) city in NC Italy: pop. 156,000

fer·ret (fer′it) *n.* [< OFr. < LL. dim. of *furo* < L. *fur*, thief: for IE. base see BEAR[1]] a small, weasellike animal, easily tamed and used for hunting rabbits, rats, etc. —*vt.* **1.** to force out of hiding as with a ferret **2.** to search for persistently and discover (facts, etc.); search (*out*) —*vi.* **1.** to hunt with ferrets **2.** to search around —**fer′ret·er** *n.*

fer·ri- *a combining form meaning* containing ferric iron: see FERRO-

fer·ric (fer′ik) *adj.* [FERR(O)- + -IC] **1.** of, containing, or derived from iron **2.** *Chem.* designating or of iron with a valence of three, or compounds containing such iron

ferric oxide a brown or reddish oxide of iron, Fe_2O_3: used as a pigment, in magnetic tapes, etc.

☆**Fer·ris wheel** (fer′is) [after G. *Ferris* (1859–1896), U.S. engineer who invented it] a large, upright wheel revolving on a fixed axle and having seats hanging from the frame around the rim of the wheel: used as an amusement ride

fer·ro- [< L. *ferrum*, iron] *a combining form meaning:* **1.** iron [*ferromagnetic*] **2.** iron and [*ferromanganese*] **3.** containing ferrous iron

fer·ro·al·loy (fer′ō al′oi) *n.* any of various alloys of iron used in the manufacture of steel

fer·ro·con·crete (fer′ō kän′krēt, -kän krēt′) *n. same as* REINFORCED CONCRETE

fer·ro·mag·net·ic (-mag net′ik) *adj.* designating a material, as iron, nickel, or cobalt, that is easily magnetized —**fer′ro·mag′net·ism** *n.*

fer·ro·man·ga·nese (-maŋ′gə nēs′, -nēz′) *n.* an alloy of iron and manganese, used for making hard steel

fer·rous (fer′əs) *adj.* [< L. *ferrum*, iron + -OUS] **1.** of, containing, or derived from iron **2.** *Chem.* designating or of iron with a valence of two, or compounds containing it

fer·ru·gi·nous (fə rōō′ji nəs) *adj.* [< L. < *ferrugo*, iron rust < *ferrum*, iron] **1.** of or containing iron **2.** having the color of iron rust; reddish-brown

fer·rule (fer′əl, -ool) *n.* [< OFr. < L. *viriola*, dim. of *viriae*, bracelets < IE. base *wei-*, to bend] a metal ring or cap put around the end of a cane, tool handle, etc. to give added strength —*vt.* **-ruled, -rul·ing** to furnish with a ferrule

fer·ry (fer′ē) *vt.* **-ried, -ry·ing** [OE. *ferian*, to carry] **1.** to take across a river, etc. in a boat **2.** to cross (a river, etc.) on a ferry **3.** to deliver (airplanes) by flying to the destination —*vi.* to cross a river, etc. by ferry —*n., pl.* **-ries** **1.** a system for carrying people, cars, or goods across a river, etc. by boat **2.** a boat (**fer′ry·boat′**) used for this, or the place where it docks on either shore **3.** the delivery of airplanes to their destination by flying them —**fer′ry·man** *n., pl.* **-men**

fer·tile (fur′t'l; *chiefly Brit.* -tīl) *adj.* [< OFr. < L. *fertilis* < stem of *ferre*, BEAR[1]] **1.** producing abundantly; rich in resources or invention; fruitful [*fertile* soil; a *fertile* imagination] **2.** able to produce young, seeds, fruit, etc. [*fertile* cattle] **3.** capable of developing into a new individual; fertilized [*fertile* eggs] —**fer′tile·ly** *adv.* —**fer′tile·ness** *n.*

SYN.—**fertile** implies a producing, or power of producing, fruit or offspring, and may be used in speaking of a mind or imagination that produces many new ideas, stories, inventions, etc.; **fecund** implies the abundant production of offspring or fruit, or suggests the productivity of a highly creative writer, inventor, etc.; **fruitful** specifically suggests the bearing of much fruit, but it is also used to imply fertility (of soil), favorable results, profitableness, etc.; **prolific**, a close synonym for **fecund**, also suggests the sometimes undesirable results of producing many things or offspring very rapidly.—**ANT. sterile, barren**

fer·til·i·ty (fər til′ə tē) *n.* the quality, state, or degree of being fertile; fecundity

fer·til·ize (fur′t'l īz′) *vt.* **-ized′, -iz′ing** **1.** to make fertile; make fruitful or productive **2.** to spread fertilizer on [to *fertilize* a lawn] **3.** to make (the female reproductive cell or female individual) fruitful by bringing the male germ cell to the female; impregnate —**fer′til·iz′a·ble** *adj.* —**fer′til·i·za′tion** *n.*

fer·til·iz·er (-ī′zər) *n.* one that fertilizes; specif., manure, chemicals, etc. put in soil in order to make more plants grow or make the plants more productive

fer·ule (fer′əl, -ool) *n.* [L. *ferula*, rod] a flat stick or ruler used for punishing children —*vt.* **-uled, -ul·ing** to strike with a ferule

fer·vent (fur′vənt) *adj.* [< L. prp. of *fervere*, to glow, boil: for IE. base see BURN[1]] **1.** hot; burning; glowing [*fervent* rays of the sun] **2.** having or showing great warmth of feeling; intensely earnest [a *fervent* appeal for help] —see SYN. at PASSIONATE —**fer′ven·cy** (-vən sē) *n.* —**fer′vent·ly** *adv.*

fer·vid (fur′vəd) *adj.* [< L. < *fervere*: see prec.] **1.** hot; glowing **2.** impassioned; fervent; ardent [*fervid* hatred] —see SYN. at PASSIONATE —**fer′vid·ly** *adv.* —**fer′vid·ness** *n.*

fer·vor (fur′vər) *n.* [< OFr. < L. < *fervere*: see FERVENT] **1.** intense heat **2.** great warmth of emotion; ardor; zeal Brit. sp. **fer′vour** —see SYN. at PASSION

fes·cue (fes′kyōō) *n.* [< OFr. < L. *festuca*, a straw] a tough grass used for pasture or lawns

fess, fesse (fes) *n.* [< OFr. < L. *fascia*, a band] *Heraldry* a horizontal band forming the middle third of an escutcheon

☆**-fest** (fest) [< G. *fest*, a celebration < L. *festum*, feast] *an informal combining form meaning* an occasion of much [*funfest*]

fes·tal (fes′t′l) *adj.* [< L. *festum*, feast] of or like a joyous celebration; festive —**fes′tal·ly** *adv.*

fes·ter (fes′tər) *n.* [< OFr. < L. *fistula*, ulcer] a small sore filled with pus —*vi.* **1.** to form pus **2.** to cause irritation; rankle **3.** to decay —*vt.* **1.** to cause pus to form in **2.** to make angry or bitter

fes·ti·val (fes′tə v′l) *n.* [< OFr. < ML. < L. *festivus* < *festum*, feast] **1.** a time or day of feasting or celebrating [the Mardi gras is a colorful *festival*] **2.** a celebration or a planned series of performances, shows, exhibits, etc. of a certain kind [many music students will perform in the Bach *festival*] **3.** merrymaking; festivity —*adj.* of, for, or fit for a festival

fes·tive (fes′tiv) *adj.* [< L. *festivus* < *festum*, feast] of or for a feast or festival; merry; joyous —**fes′tive·ly** *adv.* —**fes′tive·ness** *n.*

fes·tiv·i·ty (fes tiv′ə tē) *n.*, *pl.* **-ties 1.** merrymaking; gaiety **2.** *a)* a festival *b)* [*pl.*] festive proceedings; things done in celebration

fes·toon (fes tōōn′) *n.* [< Fr. < It. *festone* < *festa*, feast] **1.** an arrangement of flowers, leaves, etc. hanging in a loop or curve **2.** any molding or decoration like this —*vt.* to decorate with, form into, or join by festoons —**fes·toon′er·y** *n.*

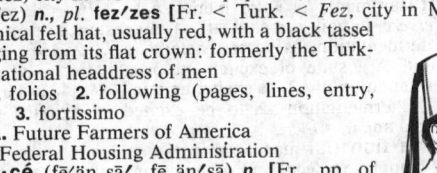
FESTOON
(sense 2)

fet·a (**cheese**) (fet′ə) [< ModGr. < It. *fetta*, a slice, ult. < L. *offa*, a piece] a white, soft cheese made in Greece from ewe's milk or goat's milk

fe·tal (fēt′l) *adj.* of or like a fetus

fetch (fech) *vt.* [OE. *feccan*: for IE. base see FOOT] **1.** to go after and come back with; bring; get [the dog *fetched* my slippers] **2.** to cause to come; produce [his joke *fetched* laughter] **3.** to draw (a breath) or heave (a sigh, groan, etc.) **4.** to bring as a price; sell for [the sofa *fetched* $50] **5.** [Colloq.] to attract; charm **6.** [Colloq.] to deliver or deal (a blow, etc.) —*vi.* to go and bring them back —*n.* **1.** a fetching **2.** a trick; dodge —see SYN. at BRING —**fetch up 1.** [Colloq.] to reach; stop **2.** [Dial.] to raise (a child, pet, etc.)

fetch·ing (fech′iŋ) *adj.* attractive; charming —**fetch′ing·ly** *adv.*

fete, fête (fāt) *n.* [Fr. < OFr.: see FEAST] a festival; entertainment; esp., a gala entertainment held outdoors —*vt.* **fet′ed** or **fêt′ed, fet′ing** or **fêt′ing** to celebrate or honor with a fete; entertain

fet·id (fet′id, fēt′-) *adj.* [< L. *f(o)etidus* < *f(o)etere*, to stink] having a bad smell, as of decay; stinking —see SYN. at STINKING —**fet′id·ly** *adv.* —**fet′id·ness** *n.*

fet·ish (fet′ish, fēt′-) *n.* [< Fr. < Port. *feitiço*, a charm < L. *facticius*, FACTITIOUS] **1.** any object believed by superstitious people to have magical power **2.** any thing or activity to which one is unreasonably devoted [he makes a *fetish* of watching football on TV] **3.** *Psychiatry* any nonsexual object that brings forth fetishism Also sp. **fet′ich**

fet·ish·ism (-iz′m) *n.* **1.** worship of fetishes or belief in fetishes **2.** *Psychiatry* an abnormal condition in which erotic feelings are excited by a nonsexual object, as a foot, glove, etc. Also sp. **fet′ich·ism** —**fet′ish·ist** *n.* —**fet′ish·is′tic** *adj.*

fet·lock (fet′läk′) *n.* [ME. *fitlok* < MDu. or MLowG.] **1.** a tuft of hair on the back of the leg of a horse, donkey, etc., just above the hoof **2.** the joint or projection bearing this tuft

FETLOCK

fet·ter (fet′ər) *n.* [OE. *feter* < base of *fot*, FOOT] **1.** a shackle or chain for the feet **2.** anything that holds in check; restraint —*vt.* **1.** to bind with fetters; shackle; chain **2.** to hold in check; restrain

fet·tle (fet′l) *vt.* **-tled, -tling** [ME. *fetlen*, to make ready, prob. < OE. *fetel*, belt] [Dial.] to arrange —*n.* condition of body and mind [in fine *fettle*]

fe·tus (fēt′əs) *n.*, *pl.* **-tus·es** [L., a bringing forth: for IE. base see FEMALE] the unborn young of an animal while still in the uterus or egg, esp. in its later stages: see EMBRYO

feud[1] (fyōōd) *n.* [OFr. *faide* < Frank. *faida* < IE. base *peik-*, hostile] a bitter, long-continued, and deadly quarrel, esp. between clans or families —*vi.* to carry on a feud; quarrel —☆**feud′ist** *n.*

feud[2] (fyōōd) *n.* [< ML. *feodum* < OHG. *feho*, cattle + *od*, wealth] land held from a feudal lord in return for service

feu·dal (fyōōd′'l) *adj.* **1.** of a feud (land) **2.** of or like feudalism —**feu′dal·ly** *adv.*

feu·dal·ism (-iz′m) *n.* the economic, political, and social system (**feudal system**) in medieval Europe, in which land, worked by serfs who were bound to it, was held by vassals in exchange for military and other services given to overlords —**feu′dal·ist** *n.* —**feu′dal·is′tic** *adj.*

feu·da·to·ry (fyōō′də tôr′ē) *n.*, *pl.* **-ries 1.** a feudal vassal **2.** a feudal estate; fief —*adj.* **1.** of the feudal relationship between vassal and lord **2.** owing feudal allegiance (*to*)

fe·ver (fē′vər) *n.* [< OE. *fefer* & OFr. *fievre*, both < L. *febris*] **1.** a state of abnormally increased body temperature, often accompanied by a quickened pulse, delirium, etc. **2.** any of various diseases in which there is a high fever **3.** a condition of nervousness —*vt.* to cause fever in —**fe′vered** *adj.*

fever blister (or **sore**) *same as* HERPES SIMPLEX

fe·ver·few (fē′vər fyōō′) *n.* [< OE., ult. < L. *febris*, fever + *fugia* < *fugare*, to drive away] a bushy plant of the composite family, with small, white heads of flowers

fe·ver·ish (fē′vər ish) *adj.* **1.** having fever, esp. slight fever **2.** of, like, or caused by fever **3.** causing fever **4.** greatly excited or nervous Also **fe′ver·ous** —**fe′ver·ish·ly** *adv.* —**fe′ver·ish·ness** *n.*

few (fyōō) *adj.* [OE. *feawe, pl.* < IE. base *pou-*, small, little] not many; a small number of [*few* seats were left; a *few* people came] —*pron., n.* not many; a small number [many left, *few* stayed; a *few* of the men wore hats] —☆**quite a few** [Colloq.] a rather large number —**the few** a small limited group —**few′ness** *n.*

fey (fā) *adj.* [OE. *fæge*, fated: for IE. base see FEUD[1]] **1.** [Archaic or Scot.] *a)* fated to die *b)* highly excited **2.** strange, as in being eccentric, full of mischief, visionary, etc.

Fez (fez) city in NC Morocco: pop. 249,000

fez (fez) *n.*, *pl.* **fez′zes** [Fr. < Turk. < *Fez*, city in Morocco] a conical felt hat, usually red, with a black tassel hanging from its flat crown: formerly the Turkish national headdress of men

ff. 1. folios **2.** following (pages, lines, entry, etc.) **3.** fortissimo

F.F.A. Future Farmers of America

FHA Federal Housing Administration

fi·an·cé (fē′än sā′, fē än′sā) *n.* [Fr., pp. of *fiancer* < OFr. *fiance*, a promise: for IE. base see FAITH] the man to whom a woman is engaged to be married

FEZ

fi·an·cée (fē′än sā′, fē än′sā) *n.* [Fr., fem. pp. of *fiancer*: see prec.] the woman to whom a man is engaged to be married

fi·as·co (fē as′kō) *n.*, *pl.* **-coes, -cos** [Fr. < It. (*far*) *fiasco*, to fail < *fiasco*, bottle] a complete failure; esp., a project with great plans that ends as a ridiculous failure

fi·at (fī′at, -ət) *n.* [L., let it be done] **1.** an order backed up by legal authority; decree **2.** a sanction; permission; authorization **3.** any order based on one's personal wishes or whim

☆**fiat money** paper currency made legal tender by law or fiat, although not backed by gold or silver and not necessarily convertible into coin

fib (fib) *n.* [? ult. < *fable*] a lie about something unimportant —*vi.* **fibbed, fib′bing** to tell such a lie or lies —see SYN. at LIE[2] —**fib′ber** *n.*

fi·ber, fi·bre (fī′bər) *n.* [< Fr. < L. *fibra*] **1.** *a)* a slender, threadlike structure that combines with others to form animal or vegetable tissue *b)* the tissue so formed [muscle *fiber*] **2.** *a)* any substance that can be separated into threadlike structures for weaving, etc. [cotton or wool *fiber*] *b)* such a threadlike structure [cotton or wool *fibers*] *c)* a threadlike structure made from a mineral or synthetically [rayon *fibers*] **3.** a threadlike root **4.** the texture of something [a fabric of coarse *fiber*] **5.** character or nature [a man of strong moral *fiber*] —**fi′ber·like′** *adj.*

☆**fi·ber·board** (-bôrd′) *n.* a flexible boardlike material made from pressed fibers of wood, etc., used in building

☆**Fi·ber·glas** (-glas′) *a trademark for* finely spun threads of glass made into textiles, used as insulation, etc. —*n.* [f-] this substance: usually **fiberglass, fiber glass,** or **fiber-glass**

fi·bril (fī′brəl) *n.* **1.** a small fiber **2.** a root hair —**fi′bril·lar** (-brə lər), **fi′bril·lar′y** (-brə ler′ē) *adj.* —**fi′bril·lose′** (-brə lōs′) *adj.*

fi·bril·la·tion (fib′rə lā′shən, fī′brə-) *n.* [< FIBRIL +

-ATION] a rapid series of contractions of the heart, causing weak and irregular heartbeats

fi·brin (fī′brən) *n.* [FIBR(E) + -IN¹] an elastic, threadlike, insoluble protein formed in the clotting of blood —**fi′brin·ous** *adj.*

fi·bro- [< L. *fibra,* fiber] *a combining form meaning* of fibrous matter or structure: also, before a vowel, **fibr-**

fi·broid (fī′broid) *adj.* [FIBR(O)- + -OID] like, made up of, or forming fibrous tissue [*fibroid* tumors]

fi·bro·sis (fī brō′sis) *n.* [FIBR(O)- + -OSIS] an abnormal increase in the amount of fibrous connective tissue in an organ or tissue —**fi·brot′ic** (-brät′ik) *adj.*

fi·brous (fī′brəs) *adj.* 1. containing or made up of fibers 2. like fiber

fib·u·la (fib′yoo lə) *n., pl.* **-lae′** (-lē′), **-las** [L., a clasp] 1. the long, thin, outer bone of the human leg between the knee and the ankle 2. a similar bone in the hind leg of other animals —**fib′u·lar** *adj.*

-fic (fik) [< Fr. < *-fique* < L. *-ficus* < *facere,* to make] *a suffix meaning* making, creating [*terrific*]

FICA Federal Insurance Contributions Act

-fi·ca·tion (fi kā′shən) [< Fr. & L., ult. < L. *facere,* to make] *a suffix meaning* a making, creating, causing [*glorification*]

Fich·te (fiH′tə), **Jo·hann Gott·lief** (yō′hän gôt′lēp) 1762–1814; Ger. philosopher

fich·u (fish′ōō) *n.* [Fr.] a three-cornered lace or muslin cape for women, worn with the ends fastened or crossed in front

fick·le (fik′'l) *adj.* [OE. *ficol:* for IE. base see FEUD¹] changeable or unstable in affection, interest, etc. —**fick′le·ness** *n.*

fic·tion (fik′shən) *n.* [< OFr. < L. *fictio,* a making < pp. of *fingere:* see FIGURE] 1. anything made up or imagined, as a statement, story, etc. 2. *a)* any literary work about imaginary characters and events, as a novel, story, or play *b)* such works as a group 3. *Law* something accepted as fact for convenience, although not necessarily true —**fic′tion·al, fic′tive** *adj.* —**fic′tion·al·ly** *adv.*

fic·tion·al·ize (-'l īz′) *vt.* **-ized′, -iz′ing** to deal with (historical events, etc.) as fiction: also **fic′tion·ize′** —**fic′tion·al·i·za′tion** *n.*

fic·tion·ist (-ist) *n.* a writer of fiction

fic·ti·tious (fik tish′əs) *adj.* 1. of or like fiction; imaginary [a *fictitious* character in a play] 2. not real; pretended [*fictitious* joy] 3. that one takes to disguise oneself or deceive others [a *fictitious* name] —**fic·ti′tious·ly** *adv.* —**fic·ti′tious·ness** *n.*

fid (fid) *n.* [< ?] 1. a hard, tapering pin for separating the strands of rope in splicing 2. a bar or pin for supporting something; specif., a square bar for supporting a topmast

-fid (fid) [< L. < *findere,* to cleave] *a combining form meaning* split or separated into parts

fid·dle (fid′'l) *n.* [OE. *fithele*] any stringed instrument played with a bow, esp. the violin —*vt.* **-dled, -dling** [Colloq.] to play (a tune) on a fiddle —*vi.* 1. [Colloq.] to play on a fiddle 2. to toy or play (*with*), esp. in a nervous way —**fiddle around** [Colloq.] to pass time aimlessly —**fiddle away** to waste (time) —**fit as a fiddle** in excellent health —**fid′dler** *n.*

☆fiddler (crab) a small, burrowing crab, the male of which has one claw much larger than the other

fid·dle·stick (fid′'l stik′) *n.* 1. the bow for a fiddle 2. a trifle; mere nothing

fid·dle·sticks (-stiks) *interj.* nonsense!

fi·del·i·ty (fə del′ə tē, fī-) *n., pl.* **-ties** [< OFr. < L. < *fides,* FAITH] 1. faithful devotion to duty, obligations, or vows 2. accuracy of a description, translation, sound reproduction, etc. —see SYN. at ALLEGIANCE

fidg·et (fij′it) *n.* [< ? ON. *fikja*] 1. a being restless, nervous, or uneasy 2. a fidgety person —*vi.* to move about in a restless, nervous, or uneasy way —*vt.* to make restless or uneasy —**the fidgets** restless, uneasy feelings or movements

fidg·et·y (-ē) *adj.* nervous; uneasy —**fidg′et·i·ness** *n.*

fi·du·ci·ar·y (fi dōō′shē er′ē, -shə rē) *adj.* [< L. < *fiducia,*

FICHU

FIDDLER CRAB
(width to 1-2/3 in.;
length to 1 in.)

trust < *fidere:* see FAITH] 1. designating or of one who holds something in trust for another [a *fiduciary* guardian for a child] 2. held in trust [*fiduciary* property] 3. valuable only because the public has confidence in it: said of certain paper money —*n., pl.* **-ar′ies** a trustee

fie (fī) *interj.* [< OFr., of echoic origin] for shame!: now often used in a joking way

fief (fēf) *n.* [Fr.: see FEE] 1. under feudalism, land held from a lord in return for service 2. the right to hold such land

field (fēld) *n.* [OE. *feld* < IE. base *pele-,* flat and broad] 1. a wide stretch of open land; plain 2. a piece of cleared land for raising crops or pasturing livestock 3. a piece of land for some particular purpose [a landing *field*] 4. an area of land producing some natural resource [a gold *field*] 5. any wide, flat space [a *field* of ice] 6. *a)* a battlefield *b)* a battle 7. an area of military operations 8. *a)* an area where practical work is done, away from the central office, laboratory, etc. *b)* an area of knowledge or of special work [the *field* of electronics] 9. an area that is observed, as in a microscope, or that is viewed, as by a TV camera 10. the background, as on a flag or coin 11. *a)* an area where athletic events are held *b)* the part of such an area, usually inside a closed racing track, where contests in jumping, shot put, pole vault, etc. are held ☆*c)* in baseball, the outfield *d)* all those entered in a contest 12. *Math.* a set of numbers or other algebraic elements for which arithmetic operations (except by zero) are defined in a consistent manner to produce another element of the set 13. *Physics* a space within which magnetic or electrical lines of force are active: in full, **field of force** —*adj.* 1. of, operating in, or held on the field or fields 2. living or growing in fields —*vt. Baseball,* etc. 1. to stop or catch or to catch and throw (a ball) in play 2. to put (a player) into a field position —*vi. Baseball,* etc. to play as a fielder —☆**play the field** to explore every chance one has —**take (or leave) the field** to begin (or withdraw from) activity in a game, military operation, etc.

field artillery movable artillery capable of accompanying an army into battle

☆**field corn** corn (maize) grown to feed livestock

field day 1. a day of military exercises and display, or of athletic events 2. a day of enjoyably exciting events or highly successful activity

field·er (fēld′ər) *n. Baseball,* etc. a player in the field

☆**fielder's choice** *Baseball* an attempt by a fielder to retire a runner already on base rather than the batter

field event any of the contests held on the field in a track meet, as the high jump, shot put, etc.

field glass a small, portable, binocular telescope: *usually used in pl.* (**field glasses**): see illustration at BINOCULAR

☆**field goal** 1. *Basketball* a basket toss made from play, scoring two points 2. *Football* a goal kicked from the field, scoring three points

☆**field hand** a hired farm laborer

field hockey *same as* HOCKEY (sense 2)

☆**field house** 1. a building near an athletic field, with lockers, showers, etc. for the athletes' use 2. a large building for indoor sports events

Field·ing (fēl′diŋ), **Henry** 1707–54; Eng. novelist

field magnet the magnet used to create and maintain the magnetic field in a motor or generator

field marshal in some armies, an officer of the highest rank

field officer a colonel, lieutenant colonel, or major in the army

field·piece (fēld′pēs′) *n.* a mobile artillery piece

☆**field-strip** (-strip′) *vt.* **-stripped′, -strip′ping** to take apart (a firearm) for cleaning and inspection

☆**field-test** (-test′) *vt.* to test (a device, method, etc.) under actual operating conditions

field trip a trip away from the classroom to permit the gathering of data at first hand

field·work (-wurk′) *n.* 1. any temporary fortification made by troops in the field 2. the work of collecting scientific data in the field, as by a geologist —**field′work′er** *n.*

fiend (fēnd) *n.* [OE. *feond:* for IE. base see FEUD¹] 1. an evil spirit; devil 2. an inhumanly wicked or cruel person ☆3. [Colloq.] *a)* a person addicted to some activity, habit, etc. [a fresh-air *fiend*] *b)* one who is excellent at some activity [a *fiend* at tennis] —**the Fiend** the Devil —**fiend′like′** *adj.*

fat, āpe, cär; ten, ēven; is, bīte; gō, hôrn, tōōl, look; oil, out; up, fur; get; joy; yet; chin; she; thin, then; zh, leisure; ŋ, ring; ə for *a* in *ago, e* in *agent, i* in *sanity, o* in *comply, u* in *focus;* ′ as in *able* (ā′b'l); Fr. bál; ë, Fr. coeur; ö, Fr. feu; Fr. mon; ô, Fr. coq; ü, Fr. duc; r, Fr. cri; H, G. ich; kh, G. doch; ‡ foreign; ☆ Americanism; < derived from. See inside front cover.

fiend·ish (fēn′dish) *adj.* **1.** of or like a fiend; devilish; inhumanly wicked or cruel **2.** extremely troublesome or difficult —**fiend′ish·ly** *adv.* —**fiend′ish·ness** *n.*

fierce (firs) *adj.* **fierc′er, fierc′est** [< OFr. < L. *ferus,* wild] **1.** of a violently cruel nature; savage [a *fierce* dog] **2.** violent; uncontrolled [a *fierce* storm] **3.** very eager; intense [a *fierce* effort] ☆**4.** [Colloq.] very distasteful, bad, etc. [a *fierce* headache] —**fierce′ly** *adv.* —**fierce′ness** *n.*

fi·er·y (fī′ər ē) *adj.* **-er·i·er, -er·i·est** [ME. *firi*] **1.** containing or consisting of fire **2.** like fire; glaring, hot, etc. [the *fiery* sun] **3.** showing strong emotion; intense [*fiery* words] **4.** easily stirred up; excitable [a *fiery* nature] **5.** inflamed [a *fiery* sore] —**fi′er·i·ly** *adv.* —**fi′er·i·ness** *n.*

☆**fi·es·ta** (fē es′tə) *n.* [Sp. < VL. *festa:* see FEAST] **1.** a religious festival; esp., a saint's day **2.** any festive celebration

fife (fīf) *n.* [< G. < MHG. < OHG. *pfifa*] a small, shrill-toned musical instrument resembling a flute —*vt., vi.* **fifed, fif′ing** to play on a fife —**fif′er** *n.*

fif·teen (fif′tēn′) *adj.* [OE. *fiftene*] five more than ten —*n.* the cardinal number between fourteen and sixteen; 15; XV

FIFE

fif·teenth (-tēnth′) *adj.* **1.** coming after fourteen others in a series; 15th **2.** designating any of the fifteen equal parts of something —*n.* **1.** the one following the fourteenth **2.** any of the fifteen equal parts of something; 1/15

fifth (fifth) *adj.* [< OE. < *fif,* FIVE] **1.** coming after four others in a series; 5th **2.** designating any of the five equal parts of something —*n.* **1.** the one following the fourth **2.** any of the five equal parts of something; 1/5 ☆**3.** a fifth of a gallon **4.** *Music a)* the fifth tone of an ascending diatonic scale, or a tone four degrees above or below a given tone *b)* the interval between two such tones, or a combination of them —**fifth′ly** *adv.*

☆**Fifth Amendment** the fifth amendment to the U.S. Constitution; specif., the clause protecting a person from being forced to be a witness against himself

fifth column [orig. (1936) applied to Franco sympathizers inside Madrid, then besieged by four of his columns on the outside] a group of people who give aid and support to the enemy from within their own country —**fifth columnist**

fifth wheel any unnecessary person or thing

fif·ti·eth (fif′tē ith) *adj.* **1.** coming after forty-nine others in a series; 50th **2.** designating any of the fifty equal parts of something —*n.* **1.** the one following the forty-ninth **2.** any of fifty equal parts of something; 1/50

fif·ty (fif′tē) *adj.* [OE. *fiftig:* see FIVE & -TY²] five times ten —*n., pl.* **-ties** the cardinal number between forty-nine and fifty-one; 50; L —**the fifties** the numbers or years, as of a century, from fifty through fifty-nine

☆**fif·ty-fif·ty** (fif′tē fif′tē) *adj.* [Colloq.] equal; even —*adv.* [Colloq.] equally

fig (fig) *n.* [< OFr., ult. < L. *ficus*] **1.** a small, hollow, pear-shaped fruit with sweet, seed-filled flesh **2.** a tree bearing this fruit **3.** a little bit [not worth a *fig*]

fig. **1.** figurative(ly) **2.** figure(s)

fig·eat·er (fig′ēt′ər) *n.* ☆a large, green beetle that feeds on ripe fruit: the June bug of the southeastern U.S.

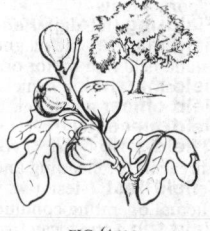

FIG (tree, leaves & fruit)

fight (fīt) *vi.* **fought, fight′ing** [OE. *feohtan:* for IE. base see FEE] **1.** to take part in a physical struggle or battle, specif. in a boxing match **2.** to struggle or work hard in trying to overcome or to win; contend [to *fight* for one's rights] —*vt.* **1.** to oppose physically, as with fists in boxing or in battle with weapons, etc. **2.** to struggle against or contend with, as by argument **3.** to engage in or carry on (a war, conflict, etc.) **4.** to gain by struggle [he *fought* his way up] **5.** to cause to fight; manage (a boxer, etc.) —*n.* **1.** a physical struggle; battle; combat **2.** any struggle, contest, or quarrel **3.** power or readiness to fight [full of *fight*] —**fight it out** to fight until one side is defeated —**fight off** to struggle to avoid

fight·er (-ər) *n.* **1.** one that fights or is inclined to fight **2.** a boxer; prizefighter **3.** a small, fast airplane easy to maneuver in fighting enemy aircraft

fig·ment (fig′mənt) *n.* [< L. *figmentum* < *fingere:* see FIGURE] something merely imagined or made up in the mind

fig·u·ra·tion (fig′yə rā′shən) *n.* **1.** a forming; shaping **2.** form; appearance **3.** a representing by figures or ornamenting with figures —**fig′u·ra′tion·al** *adj.*

fig·u·ra·tive (fig′yər ə tiv) *adj.* **1.** representing by means of a figure or symbol **2.** not in its usual, literal, or exact meaning or reference; representing one thing in terms of another that may be thought of as similar to it; metaphorical [in "screaming headlines," the word "screaming" is a *figurative* use] **3.** containing or using figures of speech —**fig′u·ra·tive·ly** *adv.* —**fig′u·ra·tive·ness** *n.*

fig·ure (fig′yər; *chiefly Brit.* fig′ər) *n.* [< OFr. < L. *figura* < *fingere,* to form: for IE. base see DOUGH] **1.** the outline or shape of something; form **2.** the human form **3.** a person seen or thought of in a specified way [a great social *figure*] **4.** a likeness of a person or thing **5.** an illustration; diagram; picture **6.** an artistic design in fabrics, etc.; pattern **7.** *a)* the symbol for a number [the *figure* 5] *b)* [pl.] arithmetic [very good at *figures*] **8.** a sum of money [that sold at a high *figure*] **9.** *Dancing & Skating* a series or pattern of steps or movements **10.** *Geom.* a surface or space bounded on all sides by lines or planes **11.** *Music* a series of tones or chords that follow in order and form a distinct group **12.** *Rhetoric* same as FIGURE OF SPEECH —*vt.* **-ured, -ur·ing** **1.** to represent in definite form **2.** to represent mentally; imagine **3.** to ornament with a design **4.** to arrive at by using arithmetic [to *figure* the cost] **5.** [Colloq.] to believe, think, decide, etc. [I *figure* he will win] —*vi.* **1.** to appear prominently; be conspicuous [a good marriage *figured* in his success] **2.** to do arithmetic ☆**3.** [Colloq.] to be as expected [that *figures*] —**figure in** ☆to add in; include —☆**figure on** to plan or depend on —☆**figure out** **1.** to solve; compute **2.** to understand; reason out —☆**figure up** to add; total —**fig′ur·er** *n.*

fig·ured (-yərd) *adj.* **1.** shaped; formed **2.** having a design or pattern **3.** *Music* with numbers to indicate accompanying chords: said of the bass

fig·ure·head (fig′yər hed′) *n.* **1.** a carved figure on the bow of a ship **2.** a person holding a high position but having no real power or authority

fig·ure-of-eight knot (-əv āt′) a kind of knot: see illustration at KNOT

FIGUREHEAD

figure of speech an expression, as a metaphor or simile, using words in a meaning that is not the literal or usual meaning in order to add vividness, etc. to what is said

figure skating ice skating in which the performer traces various elaborate figures on the ice

fig·u·rine (fig′yə rēn′) *n.* [Fr. < It. *figurina*] a small sculptured or molded figure; statuette

fig·wort (fig′wurt′) *n.* designating a large family of plants including the foxglove, snapdragon, etc. —*n.* a plant of the figwort family, with square stems and small flowers

Fi·ji (fē′jē) country on a group of islands (**Fiji Islands**) in the SW Pacific, north of New Zealand: a member of the Commonwealth: c.7,000 sq. mi.; pop. 535,000; cap. Suva — **Fi′ji·an** *adj., n.*

fil·a·ment (fil′ə mənt) *n.* [Fr. < ML. < VL. < L. *filum:* see FILE¹] **1.** a very slender thread or threadlike part; specif., *a)* the fine metal wire in a light bulb which is made incandescent by an electric current *b)* the wire cathode of a thermionic tube **2.** *Bot.* the stalk of a stamen bearing the anther —**fil′a·men′ta·ry** (-men′tər ē) *adj.* —**fil′a·men′tous** *adj.*

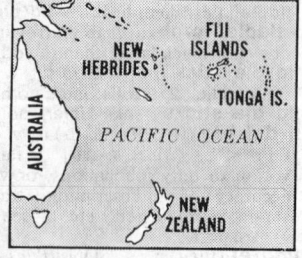

FIJI ISLANDS

fi·lar·i·a (fi ler′ē ə) *n., pl.* **fi·lar′i·ae′** (-ē ē′) [ModL. < L. *filum:* see FILE¹] any of several kinds of threadlike parasitic worms that live in the blood and tissues of vertebrate animals —**fi·lar′i·al, fi·lar′i·an** *adj.*

fil·a·ri·a·sis (fil′ə rī′ə sis) *n.* a disease caused by filarial worms transmitted by mosquitoes: the worms cause swelling, esp. in the lower parts of the body

fil·bert (fil′bərt) *n.* [ult. < St. *Philibert*, whose feast came in the nutting season] **1.** the edible nut of a cultivated European hazel tree **2.** a tree bearing this nut **3.** *same as* HAZELNUT

filch (filch) *vt.* [ME. *filchen*] to steal (esp. something small or petty); pilfer —**filch′er** *n.*

file¹ (fīl) *vt.* **filed**, **fil′ing** [Fr. < OFr. *filer*, to string papers on a thread < VL. *filare*, to spin < L. *filum*, a thread < IE. base *gwhislo*-] **1.** to arrange (papers, etc.) in order for future reference ☆**2.** to send out (a news story) to a newspaper office **3.** to register (an application, etc.) **4.** to put (a legal document) on public record **5.** to start (a legal action) —*vi.* **1.** to move in a line [the children *filed* out of the school] ☆**2.** to register as a candidate (*for* a political office) **3.** to apply (*for*) —*n.* **1.** a folder, cabinet, etc. for keeping papers in order **2.** an orderly arrangement of papers, cards, etc., as for reference **3.** a line of persons or things, one behind another —**on file** kept as in a file for reference —**file′a·ble** *adj.* —**fil′er** *n.*

file² (fīl) *n.* [OE. *feol*] a steel tool with a rough, ridged surface for smoothing or grinding down something —*vt.* **filed**, **fil′ing** to smooth or grind down with a file —*fil′er n.*

file clerk a person hired to keep office files in order

file·fish (fīl′fish′) *n., pl.* -**fish′**, -**fish′es**: see FISH a fish with very small, rough scales

fi·let (fi lā′, fil′ā) *n.* [see FILLET] **1.** a net or lace with a simple pattern on a square mesh background **2.** *same as* FILLET (*n.* 3) —*vt.* -**leted′** (-lād′), -**let′ing** (-lā′iŋ) *same as* FILLET (*vt.* 2)

fi·let mi·gnon (fi lā′ min yōn′, -yän′; Fr. fē le mē nyōn′) [Fr., lit., tiny fillet] a thick, round cut of lean beef tenderloin broiled, usually with mushrooms and bacon

fil·i·al (fil′ē əl, fil′yəl) *adj.* [< LL. < L. *filius*, son, *filia*, daughter: for IE. base see FEMALE] **1.** of, suitable to, or expected from a son or daughter [*filial* devotion] **2.** *Genetics* of the indicated generation (i.e., F₁, F₂, etc.) following the parental —**fil′i·al·ly** *adv.*

fil·i·bus·ter (fil′ə bus′tər) *n.* [< Sp. < MDu. *vrijbuiter*, freebooter] **1.** an adventurer who engages in unauthorized warfare against another country; freebooter ☆**2.** a member of a legislative body who blocks the passage of a bill by making long speeches, talking about other matters, etc.: also **fil′i·bus·ter·er** ☆**3.** the use of such methods to block a bill —*vi.* **1.** to engage in unauthorized warfare as a freebooter ☆**2.** to engage in a filibuster —*vt.* ☆to block the passage of (a bill) by a filibuster

fil·i·gree (fil′ə grē′) *n.* [< earlier *filigrain* < Fr. < It. < L. *filum*, a thread + *granum*, grain] **1.** lacelike ornamental work of intertwined wire of gold, silver, etc. **2.** any delicate work or design like this —*adj.* like, made of, or made into filigree —*vt.* -**greed′**, -**gree′ing** to ornament with filigree

fil·ing (fīl′iŋ) *n.* a small piece, as of metal, scraped off with a file: *usually used in pl.*

Fil·i·pine (fil′ə pēn′) *adj. same as* PHILIPPINE

Fil·i·pi·no (fil′ə pē′nō) *n.* [Sp.] **1.** *pl.* -**nos** a native or citizen of the Philippines **2.** *var. form of* PILIPINO —*adj.* Philippine

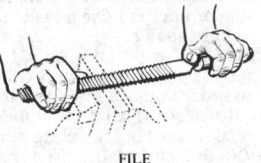

FILIGREE EARRINGS

fill (fil) *vt.* [OE. *fyllan* < base of *full*, FULL¹] **1.** *a)* to put as much as possible into; make full *b)* to put a great amount of something into [to *fill* the tub for a bath] **2.** *a)* to take up or occupy all or nearly all the capacity or extent of [the crowd *filled* the room] *b)* to spread throughout [smoke *filled* the house] **3.** *a)* to occupy (an office, position, etc.) *b)* to put a person into (an office, position, etc.) ☆**4.** to fulfill (an engagement to perform, etc.) ☆**5.** *a)* to supply the things called for in (an order, prescription, etc.) *b)* to satisfy (a need, requirement, etc.) **6.** *a)* to close or plug (holes, cracks, etc.) *b)* to put a filling in (a tooth) **7.** to satisfy the hunger or desire of [the cookies *filled* them] —*vi.* to become full —*n.* **1.** all that is needed to make full **2.** all that is needed to satisfy [to drink one's *fill*] ☆**3.** anything that fills; esp., earth, gravel, etc. used for filling holes, etc. —**fill in 1.** to fill with some substance **2.** to complete by

supplying (something) ☆**3.** to be a substitute —☆**fill one in on** [Colloq.] to provide one with additional details about —**fill out 1.** to make or become rounder, shapelier, etc. ☆**2.** to complete (a document, etc.) by writing in information —**fill up** to make or become completely full

fill·er (fil′ər) *n.* a person or thing that fills; specif., *a)* matter added to increase bulk, solidity, etc. *b)* a preparation used to fill in cracks, etc. *c)* the tobacco inside a cigar *d)* a short, space-filling item in a newspaper *e)* the paper for a loose-leaf notebook

fil·lér (fel′er) *n., pl.* -**lér**, -**lérs** see MONETARY UNITS, table (Hungary)

fil·let (fil′it; *for n.* 3 & *vt.* 2, *usually* fil′ā, fi lā′) *n.* [< OFr. dim. of *fil* < L. *filum*: see FILE¹] **1.** a narrow band worn around the head as to hold the hair in place **2.** a thin strip or band **3.** a boneless, lean piece of meat or fish —*vt.* **1.** to bind or decorate with a band, molding, etc. **2.** to remove the bone from and slice (meat or fish)

fill·ing (fil′iŋ) *n.* **1.** a thing used to fill something else; specif., *a)* the metal, plastic, etc. that a dentist puts into a cavity he has cleaned out by drilling *b)* the foodstuff used in a pastry shell, etc. ☆**2.** the woof in a woven fabric

☆**filling station** *same as* SERVICE STATION

fil·lip (fil′əp) *n.* [echoic extension of FLIP¹] **1.** the snap made by a finger held down by the thumb and then suddenly released **2.** a light tap given in this way **3.** anything that stimulates or livens up [salads give a *fillip* to meals] —*vt.* **1.** to strike or snap with a fillip **2.** to stimulate or liven up —*vi.* to make a fillip

FILLIP

Fill·more (fil′môr), **Mill·ard** (mil′ərd) 1800–74; 13th president of the U.S. (1850–53)

fil·ly (fil′ē) *n., pl.* -**lies** [ON. *fylja*: for IE. base see FEW] **1.** a young female horse, specif. one under five years of age **2.** [Colloq.] a lively girl

film (film) *n.* [OE. *filmen*] **1.** a fine, thin skin or coating **2.** a flexible cellulose material covered with a substance sensitive to light and used in taking photographs or making motion pictures **3.** a haze or blur, as over the eyes **4.** a motion picture or motion pictures **5.** a gauzy web —*vt.* **1.** to cover as with a film **2.** to take a photograph of **3.** to make a motion picture of (a novel, play, etc.) —*vi.* **1.** to become covered with a film **2.** *a)* to make a motion picture *b)* to be filmed or suitable for filming [this novel won't *film* well] —**film′er** *n.*

film·ic (fil′mik) *adj.* of motion pictures or the art of making them

film·strip (film′strip′) *n.* a length of film containing still photographs arranged so that they can be projected one after the other and used in teaching, etc.

film·y (fil′mē) *adj.* **film′i·er**, **film′i·est** **1.** of or like a film; hazy, gauzy, etc. **2.** covered as with a film —**film′i·ly** *adv.* —**film′i·ness** *n.*

fils (fēls, fils) *n., pl.* **fils** [< Ar. < LGr. *phollis*, a small coin] see MONETARY UNITS, table (Bahrain, Iraq, Jordan, Kuwait, Yemen)

fil·ter (fil′tər) *n.* [< OFr. < ML. *filtrum*, *feltrum*, FELT¹ (used for filters)] **1.** a device for straining a fluid through a porous substance so as to remove solid particles, impurities, etc. **2.** any porous substance so used, as sand, charcoal, etc. **3.** *a)* a device that allows only certain frequencies of electricity to pass *b)* a device that absorbs certain light rays [a color *filter* for a camera lens] —*vt.* **1.** to pass (a fluid) through a filter **2.** to remove (solid particles, etc.) from a fluid with a filter —*vi.* **1.** to pass through or as if through a filter **2.** to pass slowly [the news *filtered* through town]

fil·ter·a·ble (-ə b'l) *adj.* that can be filtered: also **fil′tra·ble** (-trə b'l) —**fil′ter·a·bil′i·ty** *n.*

filterable virus any virus: so called because most viruses can pass through fine filters that bacteria cannot pass through

filter paper porous paper for filtering liquids

filth (filth) *n.* [OE. *fylthe* < base of *ful*, FOUL + -TH¹] **1.** dirt, garbage, etc. that is foul or disgusting **2.** anything thought to be immoral or obscene [novels filled with *filth* and violence]

filth·y (fil′thē) *adj.* **filth′i·er**, **filth′i·est** **1.** full of filth; disgusting; foul **2.** obscene; indecent [*filthy* talk] **3.** morally bad;

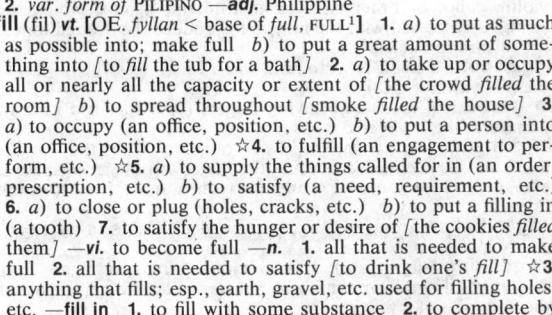

FILE

dishonest, corrupt, etc. [he has lived a *filthy* life] —**filth′i·ly** *adv.* —**filth′i·ness** *n.*

fil·trate (fil′trāt) *vt.* **-trat·ed, -trat·ing** to filter —*n.* a filtered liquid —**fil·tra′tion** *n.*

fim·bri·a (fim′brē ə) *n., pl.* **-bri·ae** (-brē ē) [L., fringe] *Biol.* a fringe of hairs, fibers, etc., esp. at the opening of an oviduct in mammals —**fim′bri·ate** (-āt) *adj.* —**fim′bri·a′tion** *n.*

fin[1] (fin) *n.* [OE. *finn*] **1.** any of several organs shaped like fans that stick out from the body of a fish, dolphin, etc. and are used in swimming and balancing: see illustration at FISH **2.** anything like a fin, as certain parts used for balancing an aircraft or boat

☆**fin**[2] (fin) *n.* [< Yid. < MHG. < OHG. *fimf*, FIVE] [Slang] a five-dollar bill

fin. **1.** finance **2.** financial **3.** finis

fi·na·gle (fə nā′g'l) *vt.* **-gled, -gling** [< ?] to get or arrange by cleverness, persuasion, etc., or esp. by craftiness or trickery [he *finagled* a date with my girlfriend] —*vi.* to use craftiness or trick-ery —**fi·na′gler** *n.*

fi·nal (fī′n'l) *adj.* [< OFr. < L. *finalis* < *finis:* see FINISH] **1.** of or coming at the end; last; concluding [the *final* chapter] **2.** allowing no further change; deciding; conclusive [a *final* de-cree] **3.** having to do with the ultimate purpose or goal [God is sometimes described as the *final* cause of all things] —*n.* **1.** anything final **2.** [pl.] the last of a series of contests **3.** a final examination —see SYN. at LAST[1]

fi·na·le (fə nä′lē, -nal′ē) *n.* [It.] **1.** the concluding part of a piece of music, a revue, an opera, etc. **2.** the conclusion or last part; end

fi·nal·ist (fī′n'l ist) *n.* a contestant who participates in the final, deciding contest of a series

fi·nal·i·ty (fī nal′ə tē) *n.* **1.** the quality or condition of being final, settled, or complete; conclusiveness [the *finality* of a cour. decision] **2.** *pl.* **-ties** anything final

☆**fi·nal·ize** (fī′n'l īz′) *vt.* **-ized′, -iz′ing** [FINAL + -IZE] to make final or complete; finish [to *finalize* an agreement] —**fi′-nal·i·za′tion** *n.*

fi·nal·ly (-ē) *adv.* **1.** at the end; in conclusion **2.** decisively; conclusively [the matter must be settled *finally*]

fi·nance (fə nans′, fī′nans) *n.* [< OFr. < *finer*, to end, settle accounts < *fin* < L. *finis*, an end: see FINISH] **1.** [pl.] the money, income, etc. that a nation, organization, or person has and can use **2.** the managing or science of managing money matters —*vt.* **-nanced′, -nanc′ing** to supply or obtain money or credit for [loans to *finance* new business]

☆**finance company** a company that lends money to individu-als, extends credit to businesses, etc.

fi·nan·cial (fə nan′shəl, fī-) *adj.* of finance, finances, or finan-ciers —**fi·nan′cial·ly** *adv.*

SYN.—**financial** is used of money matters, esp. where large amounts are involved [a *financial* success]; **fiscal** refers to the income, spending, etc. of a government or a large corporation or organization [a *fiscal* year]; **pecuniary** refers to the use of money in practical ways or by an individual [a student seeking *pecuniary* assistance]

fin·an·cier (fin′ən sir′) *n.* [Fr.] **1.** a person skilled in finance **2.** a person who spends or invests large sums of money in busi-ness dealings

☆**fin·back** (fin′bak′) *n.* a large whalebone whale of the eastern coast of the U.S., with a large dorsal fin

finch (finch) *n.* [OE. *finc*] any of a large group of small song-birds with short beaks, including the bunting, canary, cardinal, and sparrow

find (fīnd) *vt.* **found, find′ing** [OE. *findan* < IE. base *pent-*, to walk] **1.** to happen on; discover by chance [I sometimes *find* violets in the woods] **2.** to get by searching or by making an effort [*find* the answer] **3.** to come to know; perceive; learn [I *find* that I was wrong] **4.** to experience or feel [to *find* pleasure in music] **5.** *a)* to recover (something lost) [to *find* a missing book] *b)* to get or recover the use of [we *found* our sea legs] **6.** to consider; think [he *finds* TV boring] **7.** to get to; reach [the arrow *found* its mark] **8.** to declare after careful thought [to *find* him guilty] —*vi.* to announce a decision [the jury *found* for the accused] —*n.* **1.** a finding **2.** something found, esp. something valuable —**find oneself 1.** to learn what one's real talents are and begin to apply them **2.** to become aware of be-ing [to *find oneself* in trouble] —**find out 1.** to discover; learn **2.** to learn what (someone or something) really is

find·er (fīn′dər) *n.* **1.** a person or thing that finds **2.** a camera device that shows what will appear in the photograph **3.** a small telescope attached to, and used to locate objects for closer view with, a larger, more powerful one

‡**fin de siè·cle** (fant sye′kl′) [Fr., end of the century] of or like the last years of the 19th century: now usually used to sug-gest a lack of vigor, moral strength, etc.

find·ing (fīn′diŋ) *n.* **1.** the act of one who finds; discovery **2.** something found or discovered **3.** [often pl.] the conclusion reached by a judge, scholar, etc. after thinking carefully about the facts

fine[1] (fīn) *adj.* **fin′er, fin′est** [< OFr. < ML. *finus*, for L. *finis:* see FINISH] **1.** orig., finished; perfected **2.** superior in quality, character, ability, etc.; excellent [a *fine* report; a *fine* teacher] **3.** with no impurities; refined [*fine* gold] **4.** containing a spec-ified proportion of pure metal: said of gold or silver **5.** clear and bright [a *fine* spring day] **6.** having small particles or grains [*fine* sand] **7.** *a)* very thin [*fine* thread] *b)* very small [*fine* print] **8.** sharp; keen [a knife with a *fine* edge] **9.** hav-ing to do with small, subtle differences [the *fine* distinction be-tween pity and sympathy] **10.** having a delicate texture [*fine* china] **11.** calling for great accuracy [a *fine* adjustment] **12.** too elegant; showy [*fine* writing] —*adv.* **1.** same as FINELY **2.** [Colloq.] very well —*vt., vi.* **fined, fin′ing** to make or become fine or finer [to *fine* a blade until it can cut the toughest leather] —**fine′ness** *n.*

fine[2] (fīn) *n.* [< OFr. *fin* < L. *finis:* see FINISH] a sum of money paid as punishment for breaking a law or rule —*vt.* **fined, fin′ing** to order to pay a fine —**in fine 1.** in conclusion **2.** in brief

fi·ne[3] (fē′nä) *n.* [It. < L. *finis:* see FINISH] *Music* the end: a di-rection marking the close of a repetition

fine art any of the art forms that include drawing, painting, sculpture, and ceramics, or, occasionally, architecture, litera-ture, music, dramatic art, or dancing: *usually used in pl.*

fine-drawn (fīn′drôn′) *adj.* **1.** drawn out until very fine, as wire **2.** very subtle: said of reasoning, arguments, etc.

fine-grained (-grānd′) *adj.* having a fine, smooth grain, as some wood, leather, etc.

fine·ly (-lē) *adv.* in a fine manner

fin·er·y (fīn′ər ē) *n., pl.* **-er·ies** showy, elaborate decoration, esp. bright, decorative clothes, jewelry, etc.

fine·spun (fīn′spun′) *adj.* **1.** delicate; fragile [*finespun* lace] **2.** extremely or overly subtle [*finespun* reasoning]

fi·nesse (fi nes′) *n.* [Fr. < OFr. *fin*, FINE[1]] **1.** skillfulness and delicacy of performance [the *finesse* with which the artist drew a portrait] **2.** the ability to handle difficult situations with tact and skill [to show *finesse* in dealing with customers] **3.** *Bridge* an attempt to take a trick with a lower card while holding a higher card not in sequence with it —*vt., vi.* **-nessed′, -ness′ing 1.** to manage by or use finesse **2.** *Bridge* to make a finesse with (a card)

☆**fine-toothed comb** (fīn′tōōtht′) a comb with fine teeth set close together: also **fine-tooth comb** —**go over with a fine-toothed comb** to examine very thoroughly

fin·ger (fiŋ′gər) *n.* [OE.] **1.** any of the five parts at the end of the hand, esp. any of these other than the thumb **2.** the part of a glove covering a finger **3.** anything like a finger in shape or use ☆**4.** a unit of measurement based on the breadth of a finger (about 3/4 inch) or the length of a finger (about 4½ inches) —*vt.* **1.** to touch or handle with the fingers **2.** to play (an instru-ment) by using the fingers on strings, keys, etc. ☆**3.** [Slang] to point out; identify; specif., to inform on —*vi.* to be fingered, as a violin —**have a finger in the pie** to help do something —**put one's finger on** to point out or find out exactly

fin·ger·board (-bôrd′) *n.* a strip of hard wood in the neck of a violin, cello, or other stringed instrument, against which the strings are pressed with the fingers to produce the desired tones: see illustration at VIOLIN

finger bowl a small bowl to hold water for rinsing the fingers at the table after a meal

fin·gered (fiŋ′gərd) *adj.* having fingers (of a specified kind or number) [thick-*fingered*]

fin·ger·ing (fiŋ′gər iŋ) *n.* **1.** a touching with the fingers **2.** *Music a)* technique of using the fingers on the strings, keys, etc. to produce tones *b)* directions on a score for using the fingers

Finger Lakes group of long, narrow glacial lakes in west cen-tral N.Y.

fin·ger·ling (-liŋ) *n.* a small fish about as long as a finger

fin·ger·nail (-nāl′) *n.* the horny substance on the upper part of the end joint of a finger

☆**finger painting** the act or method of painting by using the fingers or hand to spread paints made of starch, glycerin, and pigments (**finger paints**) on moistened paper —**fin′ger-paint′** (-pānt′) *vi., vt.*

finger post a post with a sign, often shaped like a pointing finger, showing a direction

fin·ger·print (-print′) *n.* a mark left when the tip of a finger is pressed against a flat surface: it can be used to identify a person —*vt.* to make an inked impression of the finger tips of

finger tip the tip of a finger —**have at one's finger tips 1.** to have available for instant use **2.** to be completely familiar with —**to one's** (or **the**) **finger tips** entirely; altogether [a lady *to her finger tips*]

fin·i·al (fin′ē əl) *n.* [ME., originally an adj., FINAL] a decorative part at the tip of a spire, lamp shade support, etc., or projecting upward from the top of a cabinet, etc.

fin·i·cal (fin′i k'l) *adj.* [< FINE¹] *same as* FINICKY —**fin′i·cal·ly** *adv.*

fin·ick·y (fin′i kē′) *adj.* [< FINICAL] too particular; overly critical; fussy [*finicky* about what he eats]: also **fin′ick·ing, fin′nick·y** —**fin′ick·i·ness** *n.*

fi·nis (fin′is, fī′nis) *n., pl.* **-nis·es** [L.: see FINISH] the end, as of a book; conclusion

fin·ish (fin′ish) *vt.* [< OFr. < L. *finire* < *finis*, an end: for IE. base see DIG] **1.** *a)* to bring to an end; complete [to *finish* the work] *b)* to come to the end of [to *finish* reading a book] **2.** to use up; consume entirely [*finish* your milk] **3.** to give final touches to [to *finish* a room by putting up molding] **4.** to give (cloth, wood, etc.) a desired surface effect [to *finish* the walls in gray] **5.** *a)* to cause the defeat, death, etc. of *b)* to make worthless, useless, etc. [the long march *finished* the troops] —*vi.* **1.** to come to an end [the game *finished* early] **2.** to complete something being done [my horse *finished* first in the race] —*n.* **1.** the last part; end [we stayed to the *finish*] **2.** anything used to give a desired surface effect, as varnish, wax, etc. **3.** completeness; perfection [a good poem, but lacking in *finish*] **4.** the manner or method of completion **5.** the way in which the surface, as of furniture, is finished **6.** polish or refinement in manners, speech, etc. **7.** defeat, collapse, etc. or that which brings it about —see SYN. at CLOSE² —**finish off 1.** to end or complete **2.** to kill or destroy —**finish up 1.** to end or complete **2.** to use all of —**finish with 1.** to end or complete **2.** to end relations with; become indifferent to —**in at the finish** being present or taking part at the conclusion, as of a contest —**fin′ish·er** *n.*

fin·ished (fin′isht) *adj.* **1.** ended **2.** completed **3.** highly skilled or polished [a *finished* performer] **4.** given a certain kind of surface, as of paint

finishing school a private school for girls that specializes in teaching social poise and good manners

fi·nite (fī′nīt) *adj.* [< L. *finitus*, pp. of *finire*, FINISH] **1.** having measurable limits; not infinite [*finite* distances] **2.** *Gram.* having limits of person, number, and tense: said of a verb that can be used in a predicate **3.** *Math.* capable of being reached, completed, or surpassed by counting: said of numbers or sets —**fi′nite·ly** *adv.* —**fi′nite·ness** *n.*

fin·i·tude (fin′ə tood′, fī′nə-; -tyood′) *n.* the state or quality of being finite

☆**fink** (fiŋk) *n.* [< ?] [Slang] **1.** an informer or strikebreaker **2.** a person thought of as annoying or unpleasant

Fin·land (fin′lənd) **1.** country in N Europe, northeast of the Baltic Sea: 130,119 sq. mi.; pop. 4,650,000; cap. Helsinki **2. Gulf of,** arm of the Baltic Sea, between Finland & the U.S.S.R.

Finn (fin) *n.* a native or inhabitant of Finland

Finn. Finnish

fin·nan had·die (fin′ən had′ē) [prob. < *Findhorn* (Scot. fishing port) *haddock*] smoked haddock: also **finnan haddock**

Finn·ish (fin′ish) *adj.* **1.** of Finland **2.** of the Finns, their language, or culture —*n.* the Finno-Ugric language of the Finns

Fin·no- *a combining form meaning* Finn, Finnish

Fin·no-U·gric (fin′ō oo′grik, -yoo′-) *adj.* designating or of a subfamily of the Uralic languages spoken in northeastern Europe, western Siberia, and Hungary: it includes Finnish, Estonian, Hungarian, etc. —*n.* this subfamily of languages Also **Fin′no-U′gri·an** (-grē ən)

fin·ny (fin′ē) *adj.* **1.** *a)* having fins *b)* like a fin **2.** of, being, or full of fish

FINGERPRINT

fiord (fyôrd) *n.* [< Norw. < ON. *fjörthr*] a narrow inlet of the sea bordered by steep cliffs, esp. in Norway

fir (fur) *n.* [< OE. *fyrh*] **1.** an evergreen tree of the pine family, having woody cones **2.** its wood

fire (fīr) *n.* [OE. *fyr* < IE. base *pewor*-] **1.** the heat and light of something burning **2.** something burning, as fuel in a furnace **3.** a destructive burning [a forest *fire*] **4.** anything like fire in heat, brilliance, etc. **5.** great suffering or distress that tests one's endurance and self-control **6.** strong feeling; enthusiasm, passion, etc. [a speech full of *fire*] **7.** *a)* a shooting of firearms or artillery *b)* a great number of questions, complaints, etc. coming quickly one after another [he resigned under the *fire* of criticism] —*vt.* **fired, fir′ing 1.** to make burn; ignite **2.** to supply with fuel [to *fire* a furnace] **3.** to bake (bricks, pottery, etc.) in a kiln **4.** to dry by heat **5.** to stimulate, inspire, excite, etc. [to *fire* one's imagination] **6.** to shoot or discharge (a gun, bullet, etc.) **7.** to throw or direct with force [to *fire* questions] ☆**8.** to dismiss from a job; discharge —*vi.* **1.** to start burning; flame **2.** to tend a fire **3.** to become excited or aroused **4.** to shoot a firearm **5.** to discharge a projectile [the gun *fired*] —**between two fires** shot at, criticized, etc. from both sides —**catch (on) fire** to begin burning —**fire up** to start a fire, as in a furnace —**miss fire 1.** to fail to fire, as a gun **2.** to fail in an attempt See also MISFIRE —**on fire 1.** burning **2.** greatly excited —**open fire 1.** to begin to shoot **2.** to begin; start —**play with fire** to do something risky —**set fire to** to make burn; ignite —**take fire 1.** to begin to burn **2.** to become excited —**under fire 1.** under attack, as by gunfire **2.** being criticized —**fir′er** *n.*

fire·arm (fīr′ärm′) *n.* any weapon from which a shot is fired by explosive force; esp., such a weapon that is small enough to be carried, as a rifle

☆**fire·base** (-bās′) *n.* a military base in a combat zone, from which artillery, rockets, etc. are fired

☆**fire·boat** (-bōt′) *n.* a boat equipped with firefighting equipment, used in harbors, etc.

fire·bomb (-bäm′) *n.* a bomb intended to start a fire; incendiary bomb —*vt.* to attack with a firebomb or firebombs

fire·box (-bäks′) *n.* the place for the fire in a furnace, etc.

fire·brand (-brand′) *n.* **1.** a piece of burning wood **2.** a person who stirs up a revolt, etc.

fire·break (-brāk′) *n.* a strip of land cleared to stop the spread of fire, as in a forest

fire·brick (-brik′) *n.* a brick made to withstand great heat, used to line furnaces, etc.

☆**fire·bug** (-bug′) *n.* [Colloq.] a person who purposely sets fire to buildings, etc.; pyromaniac

☆**fire chief** the officer in charge of a fire department

fire·clay (-klā′) *n.* a clay that can resist intense heat, used to make firebricks, furnace linings, etc.

☆**fire·crack·er** (-krak′ər) *n.* a roll of paper that contains an explosive and an attached fuse: it goes off with a loud noise and is used at celebrations, in play, etc.

fire·damp (-damp′) *n.* a gas, largely methane, that is formed in coal mines: it is explosive when mixed with a certain proportion of air

☆**fire department** a municipal department whose work is fighting fires and preventing their occurrence

fire·dog (-dôg′) *n. same as* ANDIRON

fire door ☆a door of metal or other fire-resistant material designed to keep a fire from spreading

fire-eat·er (-ēt′ər) *n.* **1.** an entertainer who pretends to eat fire **2.** a person who is always ready to quarrel or fight

fire engine 1. a motor truck equipped to spray water, chemicals, etc. on fires to put them out **2.** loosely, any motor truck for carrying firemen and equipment to a fire

fire escape a stairway, ladder, etc. down an outside wall, for escape from a burning building

fire extinguisher a portable device holding chemicals that can be sprayed on a fire to put it out

fire·fight·er (-fīt′ər) *n. same as* FIREMAN (sense 1)

FIORD

fire·fly (-flī′) *n., pl.* **-flies**′ a small, flying beetle whose lower body glows with a light that goes off and on

☆**fire·house** (-hous′) *n. same as* FIRE STATION

fire insurance insurance against loss or damage resulting from fire

fire·light (-līt′) *n.* light from an open fire

fire·man (-mən) *n., pl.* **-men** 1. a man whose work is fighting fires 2. a man who tends a fire in a furnace, locomotive engine, etc. ☆3. *U.S. Navy* a nonrated enlisted man whose duties are concerned with the ship's engines, etc. ☆4. [Slang] *Baseball* a relief pitcher

FIREFLY
(to ½ in. long)

Fi·ren·ze (fē ren′dze) *It. name of* FLORENCE, Italy

fire·place (fīr′plās′) *n.* a place for a fire, esp. an open place built in a wall, at the base of a chimney

fire·plug (-plug′) *n.* a street hydrant to which a hose can be attached for fighting fires

fire·pow·er (-pou′ər) *n. Mil.* 1. the effectiveness of a weapon in terms of its accuracy and the number of shots it can fire 2. the number of shots a given unit can fire in a short time

fire·proof (-prōōf′) *adj.* that does not burn or is not easily destroyed by fire —*vt.* to make fireproof

☆**fire sale** a sale of goods damaged in a fire

fire·side (-sīd′) *n.* 1. the part of a room near a fireplace; hearth 2. home or home life

fire station the place where fire engines are kept and where firemen stay when on duty

fire·storm (-stôrm′) *n.* an intense fire over a large area, as one caused by an atomic explosion

fire tower a tower, usually in a forest, where a lookout is posted to watch for fires and give the alarm

fire·trap (-trap′) *n.* a building that would be unsafe in case of fire because it will burn easily or does not have enough exits

☆**fire wall** a fireproof wall for preventing the spread of fire, as from one room to the next

☆**fire·wa·ter** (-wôt′ər, -wät′ər) *n.* [prob. transl. of AmInd. term] alcoholic liquor: now humorous

☆**fire·weed** (-wēd′) *n.* any of various plants that grow readily on cleared or burned-over land

fire·wood (-wood′) *n.* wood used as fuel

fire·works (-wurks′) *n.pl.* 1. firecrackers, rockets, etc. used, as in celebrations, to produce loud noises or a fancy show of lights: *sometimes used in sing.* 2. a display of or as of fireworks [the speaker's verbal *fireworks*]

firing line 1. the line from which gunfire is directed against the enemy 2. the front position in any kind of activity

firing squad 1. a group of soldiers assigned to shoot someone sentenced to death by a military court 2. a group assigned to fire a volley of shots as a military tribute

fir·kin (fur′kin) *n.* [< MDu. dim. of *vierdel*, a fourth] 1. a small wooden tub for butter, lard, etc. 2. a unit of measure equal to 1/4 barrel

firm[1] (furm) *adj.* [< OFr. < L. *firmus*] 1. not giving way easily under pressure; solid [*firm* muscles] 2. not moved or shaken easily; fixed; stable [he stood as *firm* as a rock] 3. remaining the same; steady [a *firm* friendship] 4. unchanging; constant [a *firm* faith] 5. showing determination, strength, etc. [a *firm* command] 6. formally settled; definite; final [a *firm* contract] —*vt., vi.* to make or become firm: often with *up* [exercise will *firm* up flabby muscles] —**firm′ly** *adv.* —**firm′ness** *n.*

SYN.—**firm** refers to something whose parts hold together so tightly that it does not give way easily under pressure or springs back into shape after being pressed [*firm* flesh]; **hard** is applied to that which is so firm that it is not easily cut into or crushed [*hard* as rock]; **solid** refers to something which is firm or hard and suggests that it is heavy or has its parts packed close together [*solid* muscle]; **stiff** is used of that which is not easily bent or stretched [a *stiff* collar]

firm[2] (furm) *n.* [It. *firma*, signature < L. < *firmus*, FIRM[1]] a business company or partnership

fir·ma·ment (fur′mə mənt) *n.* [< OFr. < LL. < L. *firmare*, to strengthen < *firmus*, FIRM[1]] the sky thought of as if it were a solid arch

first (furst) *adj.* [< OE. *fyrst*: for IE. base see FAR] 1. before any others; 1st: used as the ordinal of ONE [the *first* volume in the series] 2. happening or acting before all others; earliest [the *first* snow of winter] 3. foremost in rank, quality, importance, etc. [*first* prize] 4. *Music* playing or singing the part

highest in pitch or the leading part —*adv.* 1. *a)* before any other person or thing [guests are served *first*] *b)* before doing anything else [*first* we had soup] 2. as the first point [*first*, let me say this] 3. for the first time [I *first* met him yesterday] 4. sooner; preferably [when told to beg, he said he'd starve *first*] —*n.* 1. the first person, thing, class, place, etc. 2. the first day of the month 3. the beginning; start [at *first*, I believed him] 4. a first happening or thing of its kind 5. [pl.] the best quality of merchandise 6. the winning place, as in a race 7. the first or lowest forward gear ratio of a motor vehicle

first aid emergency treatment for injury or sudden illness, given while waiting for regular medical care —**first′-aid′** *adj.*

☆**first base** *Baseball* the base on the pitcher's left, the first of the four bases a runner must touch in succession to score a run

first·born (furst′bôrn′) *adj.* born first in a family; oldest —*n.* the firstborn child

first-class (-klas′) *adj.* 1. of the highest class, rank, quality, etc.; excellent 2. of the most expensive kind [a *first-class* cabin on a ship] ☆3. designating or of mail that is sealed and that carries the highest regular postage rates —*adv.* 1. with the most expensive accommodations [traveling *first-class*] 2. as or by first-class mail

first cousin the son or daughter of one's aunt or uncle

first finger the finger next to the thumb

first·hand (-hand′) *adj., adv.* from the original producer or source; direct [a *firsthand* report]

☆**first lady** [often F- L-] the wife of the U.S. president

first lieutenant a U.S. military officer ranking above a second lieutenant

first·ling (-liŋ) *n.* 1. the first of a kind 2. the first fruit, produce, offspring, etc.

first·ly (-lē) *adv.* in the first place; first

first mate a merchant ship's officer next in rank below the captain: also **first officer**

first offender a person found guilty for the first time of breaking the law

first person that form of a pronoun (as *I* or *we*) or verb (as *do*) which refers to the speaker or speakers

first-rate (-rāt′) *adj.* of the highest class, rank, or quality; excellent —*adv.* [Colloq.] very well [I feel *first-rate*]

☆**first sergeant** *U.S. Army & Marine Corps* the noncommissioned officer, usually a master sergeant, serving as chief assistant to the commander of a company, battery, etc.

☆**first-string** (-striŋ′) *adj.* [Colloq.] *Sports* that is the first choice for regular play at a specified position [our *first-string* quarterback]

first water the best quality [a pearl of the *first water*]

firth (furth) *n.* [< ON. *fjörthr*] a narrow arm of the sea; estuary

fis·cal (fis′kəl) *adj.* [Fr. < LL. < L. *fiscus*, money basket: for IE. base see FAITH] 1. having to do with the public treasury or revenues 2. financial —see SYN. at FINANCIAL —**fis′cal·ly** *adv.*

☆**fiscal year** the twelve-month period between settlements of financial accounts: the U.S. government fiscal year legally ends June 30

fish (fish) *n., pl.* **fish**; in referring to different species, **fish′es**: see PLURAL, II, D, 2 [OE. *fisc* < IE. base *pisk-*] 1. any of a large group of coldblooded animals living in water and having backbones, gills for breathing, fins, and, usually, scales 2. loosely, any animal living in water only, as a crab, oyster, etc. 3. the flesh of a fish used as food 4. [Colloq.] a person thought of as like a fish in being easily lured, lacking emotion, etc. —[F-] the constellation Pisces —*vi.* 1. to catch or try to catch fish 2. *a)* to grope or feel about for something [she *fished* for the key in her purse] *b)* to try to get something in a roundabout way [to *fish* for compliments] —*vt.* 1. to fish in (a stream, lake, etc.) 2. to grope for, find, and pull out [he *fished* a coin out of his pocket] —*adj.* 1. of fish or fishing 2. selling fish —**drink like a fish** to drink heavily, esp. alcoholic liquor —**like a fish out of water** in a situation in which one does not know how to act or what to do —**other fish to fry** other, more important things to do —**fish′a·ble** *adj.* —**fish′like′** *adj.*

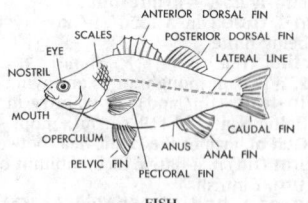
FISH
ANTERIOR DORSAL FIN
POSTERIOR DORSAL FIN
LATERAL LINE
SCALES
EYE
NOSTRIL
MOUTH
OPERCULUM
PELVIC FIN
PECTORAL FIN
ANUS
ANAL FIN
CAUDAL FIN

fish and chips [Chiefly Brit.] fried fillets of fish served with French fried potatoes

fish·er (fish′ər) *n.* **1.** a fisherman **2.** *pl.* -ers, -er: see PLURAL, II, D, 1 a flesh-eating animal related to the marten, like a weasel but larger

fish·er·man (-mən) *n.*, *pl.* -men **1.** a person who fishes for sport or for a living **2.** a ship used in fishing

fish·er·y (-ē) *n.*, *pl.* -er·ies **1.** the business of catching fish **2.** a place where fish are caught **3.** a place where fish are bred

fish-eye lens (fish′ī′) a camera lens designed to record a 180-degree field of vision

fish hawk *same as* OSPREY

fish·hook (-hook′) *n.* a hook, usually a barbed hook, for catching fish

fish·ing (-iŋ) *n.* the catching of fish for sport or for a living

☆**fishing pole** a simple device for fishing, consisting of a pole, line, and hook

fishing rod a slender pole with an attached line, hook, and usually a reel, used in fishing

☆**fish ladder** a series of pools arranged so that fish swimming upstream can pass around a dam or waterfall

fish meal ground, dried fish, used as fertilizer or as food for animals

fish·mon·ger (-muŋ′gər, -mäŋ′-) *n.* one who sells fish

fish·plate (fish′plāt′) *n.* [prob. < Fr. *fiche*, means of fixing] either of a pair of steel plates bolting two rails together lengthwise, as on a railroad

☆**fish story** [Colloq.] an unbelievable story

fish·wife (-wīf′) *n.*, *pl.* -wives′ (-wīvz′) **1.** a woman who sells fish **2.** a coarse, scolding woman

FISHPLATE

fish·y (-ē) *adj.* **fish′i·er**, **fish′i·est** **1.** of or full of fish **2.** like a fish in odor, taste, etc. **3.** dull or without expression [a *fishy* stare] **4.** [Colloq.] causing doubt or suspicion; questionable; odd [a *fishy* story] —**fish′i·ly** *adv.* —**fish′i·ness** *n.*

fis·sile (fis′'l) *adj.* [< L. < *fissus*, pp. of *findere*, to split: for IE. base see BITE] **1.** that can be split **2.** *same as* FISSIONABLE —**fis·sil·i·ty** (fi sil′ə tē) *n.*

fis·sion (fish′ən) *n.* [< L. < *fissus*: see prec.] **1.** a splitting apart; division into parts **2.** *same as* NUCLEAR FISSION **3.** *Biol.* a form of asexual reproduction in which the parent organism divides into two or more parts, each becoming an independent individual —*vi.*, *vt.* to undergo or cause to undergo nuclear fission

fis·sion·a·ble (-ə b'l) *adj.* that can undergo fission

fis·sure (fish′ər) *n.* [< OFr. < L. *fissura* < *fissus*: see FISSILE] **1.** a long, narrow, deep opening or crack **2.** a dividing or breaking into parts —*vt.*, *vi.* -sured, -sur·ing to crack or split apart

fist (fist) *n.* [< OE. *fyst*] **1.** a hand with the fingers closed tightly into the palm **2.** [Colloq.] *a)* a hand *b)* the grasp **3.** *Printing* the sign (☞), used to direct special attention to something

fist·ic (fis′tik) *adj.* having to do with boxing; fought with the fists; pugilistic

fist·i·cuffs (fis′ti kufs′) *n.pl.* [< FIST + CUFF²] **1.** a fight with the fists **2.** the science of boxing

fis·tu·la (fis′chōō lə) *n.*, *pl.* -las, -lae′ (-lē′) [< OFr. < L., a pipe, ulcer] an abnormal passage from an abscess, cavity, or hollow organ to the skin or to another abscess, cavity, or organ —**fis′tu·lous**, **fis′tu·lar** *adj.*

fit¹ (fit) *vt.* **fit′ted** or **fit**, **fit′ted**, **fit′ting** [ME. *fitten* < ? ON. *fitja*, to knit, tie] **1.** to be suitable or adapted to [let the punishment *fit* the crime] **2.** to be the proper size, shape, etc. for [the coat *fits* me] **3.** *a)* to make or alter so as to fit [his new suit has to be *fitted*] *b)* to measure (a person) for something that must be fitted [*fit* her for new shoes] **4.** to make suitable or qualified [his training *fits* him for the job] **5.** *a)* to insert [to *fit* a key into a lock] *b)* to make a place for (with *in* or *into*) [to *fit* another passenger into the car] **6.** to equip; outfit (often with *out*) [to *fit* out a ship for a voyage] —*vi.* **1.** to go along well with something else; be in harmony (often with *in* or *into*) [it *fits* in with my plans] **2.** to have the proper size or shape for a particular figure, space, etc. [his coat *fits* well] —*adj.* **fit′ter**, **fit′test** **1.** adapted, qualified, or suited to some purpose, function, etc. [food not *fit* to be eaten] **2.** proper; right [it is not *fit*

for you to show fear] **3.** in good physical condition; healthy [still *fit* in her eighties] —*n.* **1.** a fitting or being fitted **2.** the manner of fitting [a tight *fit*] **3.** anything that fits —☆**fit to be tied** [Colloq.] frustrated or angry —**fit′ly** *adv.* —**fit′ness** *n.*

SYN.—**fit** is used of that which has the characteristics needed in some situation or activity or for some purpose [a meal *fit* for a king]; **suitable** is applied to that which is right or useful for a certain occasion or set of circumstances [a car *suitable* for mountain driving]; **proper** refers to that which is, by its nature, correct or which good judgment indicates is suitable [*proper* respect for one's elders]; that is **appropriate** which is especially fit or suitable [he could think of nothing *appropriate* to say]; **fitting** is applied to that which goes along very well with the character or spirit of something [business is not a *fitting* subject of conversation at a party]; **apt**, in this connection, is used of that which suits the purpose exactly [an *apt* time to ask her to help]

fit² (fit) *n.* [OE. *fitt*, conflict] **1.** any sudden, uncontrolled attack [a *fit* of coughing] **2.** a sharp, brief display of feeling [a *fit* of anger] **3.** a temporary bursts of activity **4.** *Med.* a sudden attack in which one loses consciousness or has convulsions or both —**by fits (and starts)** in an irregular way; in bursts of activity followed by periods of inactivity —**have** (or ☆**throw**) **a fit** [Colloq.] to become very angry or upset

fitch (fich) *n.* [< OFr. < MDu. *vitsche*] *same as* POLECAT (sense 1): also **fitch′et** (-it), **fitch′ew** (-ōō)

Fitch (fich), **John** 1743–98; U.S. inventor of a steamboat

fit·ful (fit′fəl) *adj.* happening or done only from time to time; not regular or steady [*fitful* breezes] —**fit′ful·ly** *adv.* —**fit′ful·ness** *n.*

fit·ted (fit′id) *adj.* designed to take on the shape of that which it covers

fit·ter (-ər) *n.* **1.** a person who alters or adjusts garments to fit **2.** a person who installs or adjusts machinery, pipes, etc.

fit·ting (-iŋ) *adj.* suitable; proper; appropriate —*n.* **1.** an adjustment or trying on of clothes, etc. for fit **2.** a part used to join, adjust, or adapt other parts, as in a system of pipes **3.** [*pl.*] the fixtures, furnishings, or decorations of a house, automobile, office, etc. —see **SYN.** at FIT¹ —**fit′ting·ly** *adv.* —**fit′ting·ness** *n.*

Fitz·Ger·ald (fits jer′əld), **Edward** (born *Edward Purcell*) 1809–83; Eng. poet & translator of Omar Khayyam's *The Rubáiyát*: also written **Fitzgerald**

Fitz·ger·ald (fits jer′əld), **F(rancis) Scott (Key)** 1896–1940; U.S. author

Fiu·me (fyōō′me) *former* (*It.*) *name of* RIJEKA

five (fīv) *adj.* [< OE. *fif* < IE. base *penkue-*] totaling one more than four —*n.* **1.** the cardinal number between four and six; 5; V **2.** anything having five units or members, or numbered five; specif., ☆*a)* a basketball team ☆*b)* [Colloq.] a five-dollar bill

☆**five-and-ten-cent store** (fīv′'n ten′sent′) a store that sells a wide variety of inexpensive merchandise: also **five′-and-ten′**, **five′-and-dime′**

five·fold (-fōld′) *adj.* [see -FOLD] **1.** having five parts **2.** having five times as much or as many —*adv.* five times as much or as many

☆**Five Nations** a league of Iroquoian Indians, including the Mohawks, Oneidas, Onondagas, Cayugas, and Senecas

fix (fiks) *vt.* [< L. *fixus*, pp. of *figere*, to fasten: for IE. base see DIG] **1.** *a)* to make firm, stable, or secure [to *fix* the post in the ground] *b)* to fasten firmly [an aerial *fixed* to the chimney] **2.** to set firmly in the mind **3.** to direct steadily [to *fix* the eyes on a spot] **4.** to make rigid or stiff [a jaw *fixed* in determination] **5.** to make permanent or lasting [color is *fixed* in dyeing] **6.** to establish definitely; set or determine [to *fix* the date of a wedding] **7.** to set in order; adjust [to *fix* one's hair] **8.** to repair, mend, etc. [he *fixed* the broken chair] **9.** to prepare (food or meals) ☆**10.** [Colloq.] to influence the result or action of (a race, election, etc) by bribery, trickery, etc. ☆**11.** [Colloq.] to get even with; punish **12.** [Colloq.] to spay or castrate **13.** *Chem. a)* to make solid or nonvolatile *b)* to cause (nitrogen in the atmosphere) to combine with other elements or compounds to form nitrates, ammonia, etc. **14.** *Photog.* to make (a film, print, etc.) permanent by washing in a chemical solution —*vi.* **1.** to become fixed, firm, or stable **2.** [Colloq. or Dial.] to prepare or intend [I'm *fixing* to go] —*n.* **1.** the position of a ship or aircraft determined from the bearings of two or more known points or from radio signals ☆**2.** [Colloq.] a difficult or awkward situation; predicament ☆**3.** [Slang] *a)* the fixing of the outcome of a contest, situation, etc. *b)* a contest, situation, etc. that has been fixed **4.** [Slang] an injection of a narcotic, as heroin —**fix on** (or **upon**) to choose —**fix up** [Colloq.] **1.** to repair, mend, etc. **2.** to set in order **3.** to make arrangements for —**fix′a·ble** *adj.* —**fix′er** *n.*

fix·ate (fik′sāt) *vt., vi.* **-at·ed, -at·ing 1.** to make or become fixed **2.** *Psychoanalysis* to have or cause to have a fixation

fix·a·tion (fik sā′shən) *n.* **1.** a fixing or being fixed, as in chemistry, photography, etc. **2.** popularly, an overly strong interest or concern; obsession [she has a *fixation* about germs] **3.** *Psychoanalysis* an emotional attachment to an object or person associated with an earlier stage of psychosexual development [a father *fixation*]

fix·a·tive (fik′sə tiv) *adj.* that is able or tends to make permanent, prevent fading, etc. —*n.* a fixative substance, as a mordant used in dyeing

fixed (fikst) *adj.* **1.** firmly placed or attached; not movable **2.** established; set [a *fixed* price] **3.** steady; unchanging [a *fixed* purpose] **4.** staying in the mind and tending to control one's thoughts and actions; obsessive [a *fixed* idea] ☆**5.** [Colloq.] supplied with something, specif. money [comfortably *fixed* for life] ☆**6.** [Slang] with the outcome dishonestly arranged beforehand [a *fixed* race] **7.** *Chem. a)* nonvolatile [*fixed* oils] *b)* taken from its free state and made a part of a stable compound [*fixed* nitrogen] —**fix·ed·ly** (fik′sid lē) *adv.* —**fix′ed·ness** *n.*

fixed star a star so far from the earth that it appears to keep the same position in relation to other stars

fix·ings (fik′siŋz) *n.pl.* ☆[Colloq.] all the things that usually go with the main thing; trimmings [roast turkey and all the *fixings*]

fix·i·ty (-sə tē) *n.* the quality or state of being fixed; steadiness or permanence [great *fixity* of purpose]

fixt (fikst) *poet. pt. and pp. of* FIX

fix·ture (fiks′chər) *n.* [< LL. *fixura* < L. *fixus* (see FIX): form infl. by MIXTURE] **1.** anything firmly in place **2.** any of the firmly attached fittings of a house, store, etc. [bathroom *fixtures*] **3.** a person or thing that has been in a place or job so long as to seem fixed there

fizz (fiz) *n.* [echoic] **1.** a hissing, sputtering sound, as of a carbonated drink **2.** a drink made with carbonated water [a gin *fizz*] —*vi.* **1.** to make a hissing or bubbling sound **2.** to give off gas bubbles; effervesce

fiz·zle (fiz′'l) *vi.* -zled, -zling [ME. *fesilen*, to break wind silently] **1.** to make a hissing or sputtering sound **2.** [Colloq.] to fail, esp. after a successful beginning —*n.* **1.** a hissing or sputtering sound **2.** [Colloq.] a failure

fizz·y (fiz′ē) *adj.* fizz′i·er, fizz′i·est fizzing; effervescent

fjord (fyôrd) *n. same as* FIORD

FL Florida

Fl. 1. Flanders **2.** Flemish

fl. 1. [L. *floruit*] (he or she) flourished **2.** fluid

Fla. Florida

flab (flab) *n.* [back-formation < FLABBY] [Colloq.] soft, sagging flesh

flab·ber·gast (flab′ər gast′) *vt.* [< ? FLABBY + AGHAST] to make speechless with amazement; astonish

flab·by (flab′ē) *adj.* -bi·er, -bi·est [var. of *flappy* < FLAP] **1.** lacking firmness; limp and soft [*flabby* muscles] **2.** lacking force; weak [a *flabby* style] —**flab′bi·ly** *adv.* —**flab′bi·ness** *n.*

flac·cid (flak′sid, flas′id) *adj.* [L. *flaccidus* < *flaccus*, flabby] **1.** soft and limp; flabby **2.** weak; feeble —**flac·cid′i·ty** *n.* —**flac′cid·ly** *adv.*

‡**fla·con** (flà kôn′; *E.* flak′'n) *n.* [Fr.: see FLAGON] a small bottle with a stopper, as for perfume

flag¹ (flag) *n.* [< ? FLAG⁴, in obs. sense "to flutter"] **1.** a piece of cloth with colors, patterns, or devices, used as a national or state symbol or as a signal; banner; standard **2.** the tail of a deer **3.** the bushy tail of certain dogs, as setters **4.** *Music* any of the lines extending from a stem, indicating whether the note is an eighth, sixteenth, etc. —*vt.* **flagged, flag′ging 1.** to decorate or mark with flags **2.** to signal with or as with a flag; esp., to signal to stop (often with *down*) —**flag′ger** *n.*

flag² (flag) *n.* [ON. *flaga*, slab of stone: for IE. base see FLAKE] *same as* FLAGSTONE —*vt.* **flagged, flag′ging** to pave with flagstones

flag³ (flag) *n.* [ME. *flagge*, akin ? to FLAG⁴] **1.** any of various wild irises, with sword-shaped leaves and blue, white, or yellow flowers **2.** *same as* SWEET FLAG

flag⁴ (flag) *vi.* **flagged, flag′ging** [< ? ON. *flakka*, to flutter] to lose strength; grow weak or tired [his enthusiasm *flagged*]

☆**Flag Day** June 14, anniversary of the day in 1777 when the U.S. flag was adopted

flag·el·lant (flaj′ə lənt) *n.* a person who whips; specif., one who whips himself or has himself whipped as for religious discipline —*adj.* engaging in flagellation

flag·el·late (flaj′ə lāt′) *vt.* -lat′ed, -lat′ing [< L. < *flagellare*, to whip < *flagellum*, a whip] to whip; flog —*adj.* **1.** having a flagellum or flagella: also **flag′el·lat′ed 2.** shaped like a flagellum —**flag′el·la′tor** *n.*

flag·el·la·tion (flaj′ə lā′shən) *n.* a whipping or flogging, esp. as a religious discipline

fla·gel·lum (flə jel′əm) *n., pl.* **-la** (-ə), **-lums** [L., a whip] **1.** *Biol.* a part shaped like a whip, serving certain cells, bacteria, protozoans, etc. as a means of moving about **2.** *Bot.* a long, thin shoot or runner

flag·eo·let (flaj′ə let′) *n.* [Fr., dim. of OFr. *flageol*, a flute < L. *flare*, to blow] a small wind instrument similar to the recorder

flag·ging¹ (flag′iŋ) *adj.* [prp. of FLAG⁴] weakening or drooping [our *flagging* hopes] —**flag′ging·ly** *adv.*

flag·ging² (flag′iŋ) *n.* flagstones or a pavement made of flagstones

fla·gi·tious (flə jish′əs) *adj.* [< L. < *flagitium*, shameful act < *flagitare*, to demand] shamefully wicked; vile and scandalous —**fla·gi′tious·ly** *adv.* —**fla·gi′tious·ness** *n.*

flag·man (flag′mən) *n., pl.* **-men** a person whose work is signaling with a flag or lantern

flag officer ☆*U.S. Navy* any officer above the rank of captain

FLAGEOLET

flag·on (flag′ən) *n.* [< OFr. *flacon* < LL. < *flasca*, flask] **1.** a container for liquids, with a handle, a spout, and, often, a lid **2.** the contents of a flagon

flag·pole (flag′pōl′) *n.* a pole on which a flag is flown: also **flag′staff′** (-staf′)

fla·gran·cy (flā′grən sē) *n.* the quality or state of being flagrant: also **fla′grance**

fla·grant (flā′grənt) *adj.* [< L. prp. of *flagrare*, to blaze: for IE. base see BLACK] clearly bad; notorious; outrageous —**fla′grant·ly** *adv.*

SYN.—**flagrant** applies to anything that is so clearly bad or wrong that it deserves to be criticized or condemned [a *flagrant* violation of the law]; **glaring** is used of something bad that stands out even more clearly so that it is noticed immediately [a *glaring* error in arithmetic]; **gross** implies badness or wrongness which is so extreme or disgusting that it cannot be excused or forgiven [*gross* neglect of a child] —see also SYN. at OUTRAGEOUS

‡**fla·gran·te de·lic·to** (flə gran′tē di lik′tō) [L.] *same as* IN FLAGRANTE DELICTO

flag·ship (flag′ship′) *n.* **1.** the ship carrying the commander of a fleet or squadron and displaying his flag **2.** the finest, largest, or newest ship of a steamship line

flag·stone (flag′stōn′) *n.* **1.** any hard stone that splits into flat pieces used to pave walks, terraces, etc. **2.** a piece of such stone

flag·wav·ing (flag′wā′viŋ) *n.* an emotional appeal meant to stir up intense patriotic feelings

flail (flāl) *n.* [OFr. *flaiel* < L. *flagellum*, a whip] a farm tool having a free-swinging stick attached to a long handle, used to thresh grain by hand —*vt., vi.* **1.** to thresh with a flail **2.** to beat as with a flail **3.** to move (one's arms) about like flails [kicking and *flailing* about in the water]

flair (fler) *n.* [< OFr. < *flairer*, ult. < L. *fragare*, to give off a smell] **1.** keen, natural judgment or understanding **2.** a natural talent or ability; aptitude; knack [a *flair* for the dramatic] **3.** [Colloq.] a sense of what is stylish; dash [she dresses with great *flair*]

flak (flak) *n.* [G. < Fl(ieger)-a(bwehr)k(anone), antiaircraft gun] **1.** the fire of antiaircraft guns **2.** [Slang] sharp or angry criticism

flake (flāk) *n.* [< Scand., as in Norw. *flak*, ice floe, ON. *flackna*, to flake off < IE. base *plak-*, flat] **1.** a small, thin mass [a *flake* of snow] **2.** a thin piece or layer split or peeled off from anything; chip —*vt., vi.* **flaked, flak′ing 1.** to form into flakes **2.** to chip or peel off in flakes [plaster *flaking* off the walls]

FLAIL

3. to make or become spotted with flakes [his collar was *flaked* with dandruff] —**flak′er** *n.*

flak·y (flāk′ē) *adj.* **flak/i·er, flak/i·est** **1.** containing or made up of flakes **2.** breaking easily into flakes ☆**3.** [Slang] odd; eccentric —**flak/i·ly** *adv.* —**flak/i·ness** *n.*

‡**flam·bé** (flän bā′) *adj.* [Fr., lit., flaming] served with a flaming sauce containing brandy, rum, etc.

flam·beau (flam′bō) *n., pl.* **-beaux** (-bōz), **-beaus** [Fr., dim. of OFr. *flambe,* FLAME] a lighted torch

flam·boy·ant (flam boi′ənt) *adj.* [Fr. < OFr. < *flambe,* FLAME] **1.** highly decorated, with curving designs that look somewhat like flames, as late French Gothic architecture **2.** flamelike or brilliant [*flamboyant* autumn leaves] **3.** too showy or ornate [a *flamboyant* costume] —**flam·boy′ance, flam·boy′an·cy** *n.*

flame (flām) *n.* [< OFr. < L. < *flamma* < *flagrare:* see FLA-GRANT] **1.** the burning gas of a fire, seen as a flickering light; blaze **2.** a tongue of light rising from a fire **3.** the state of burning with a blaze of light [to burst into *flame*] **4.** a thing like a flame in heat, etc. **5.** an intense emotion **6.** a sweetheart: now usually humorous —*vi.* **flamed, flam′ing 1.** to burst into flame; blaze **2.** to grow red or hot [her face *flamed* with embarrassment] **3.** to become very excited [he *flamed* with anger] —*vt.* to treat with flame —**flame up** (or **out**) to burst out in or as in flame

flame cell a special, hollow cell in many lower animals, as flatworms, used in excretion

fla·men·co (flə meŋ′kō) *n.* [Sp., Flemish < DuFl. *Flaming,* a Fleming] **1.** the energetic, emotional style of Spanish gypsy dance or music **2.** *pl.* **-cos** a song or dance in this style

flame·out (flām′out′) *n.* ☆the ceasing of combustion in a jet engine, due to an abnormal flight condition

flame thrower a military weapon for shooting a stream of flaming gasoline, etc.

flam·ing (flā′miŋ) *adj.* **1.** burning with flames; blazing **2.** like a flame in brilliance or heat [*flaming* colors] **3.** very emotional; ardent; passionate —**flam′ing·ly** *adv.*

fla·min·go (flə miŋ′gō) *n., pl.* **-gos, -goes** [Port. < Sp. *flamenco,* lit., Flemish: infl. by *flama,* FLAME] a tropical wading bird with long legs, a long neck, and bright pink or red feathers

flam·ma·ble (flam′ə b'l) *adj.* easily set on fire: term now usually used rather than INFLAMMABLE in commerce, industry, etc. —**flam′ma·bil/i·ty** *n.*

Flan·ders (flan′dərz) region in NW Europe, on the North Sea, including W Belgium & a part of NW France & a part of SW Netherlands

flange (flanj) *n.* [< ? ME. *flaunch,* an outer edge of a coat of arms] a projecting rim or collar on a wheel, pipe, etc., to hold it in place, give it strength, or attach it to something else —*vt.* **flanged, flang′ing** to put a flange on

flank (flaŋk) *n.* [< OFr. *flanc:* for IE. base see LANK] **1.** the fleshy part of the side of a person or animal between the ribs and the hip **2.** a cut of beef from this part **3.** the side of anything **4.** *Mil.* the right or left side of a formation —*adj.* of or having to do with the flank —*vt.* **1.** to be at the side of [fountains *flank* the statue on either side] **2.** to place at the side, or on either side, of **3.** *a)* to attack the side of (an enemy unit) *b)* to pass around the side of (an enemy unit) —*vi.* to be located at the side (with *on* or *upon*)

flank·er (flaŋk′ər) *n.* one that flanks; specif., ☆*Football* an offensive back who takes a position closer to the sidelines than the rest of the team

flan·nel (flan′'l) *n.* [< W. *gwlanen* < *gwlan,* WOOL] **1.** a soft, lightweight, loosely woven woolen cloth **2.** *same as* COTTON FLANNEL **3.** [*pl.*] *a)* trousers etc. made of light flannel *b)* heavy woolen underwear —**flan′nel·ly** *adj.*

flan·nel·ette, flan·nel·et (flan′ə let′) *n.* a soft cotton cloth like cotton flannel but lighter

FLAMINGO
(to 4 ft. high; wingspread 5–6 ft.)

FLANGE

---

flap (flap) *n.* [ME. *flappe* < v. *flappen:* prob. echoic] **1.** anything flat and broad that is attached at one end and hangs loose or covers an opening [the *flap* of a pocket] **2.** the motion or slapping sound of a swinging flap [the *flap* of the awning woke her] **3.** a hinged section of an airplane wing, used in landing and taking off **4.** [Slang] a confused, excited, or worried state; fuss [the storm forecast had us all in a *flap*] **5.** *Phonet.* a sound made by slapping the tongue against the roof of the mouth —*vt.* **flapped, flap′ping 1.** to slap with something flat and broad **2.** to move back and forth or up and down [the bird *flapped* its wings] —*vi.* **1.** to move back and forth or up and down, as in the wind; flutter **2.** to fly or try to fly by flapping the wings —**flap′py** *adj.*

flap·jack (flap′jak′) *n.* a pancake or griddlecake

flap·per (flap′ər) *n.* **1.** one that flaps **2.** [Colloq.] in the 1920's, a young woman considered bold or unconventional in the way she acted and dressed

flare (fler) *vi.* **flared, flar′ing** [ME. *fleare* < ?] **1.** to blaze up brightly or burn unsteadily **2.** to burst out suddenly in anger, etc. (often with *up* or *out*) **3.** to curve or spread outward, as the bell of a trumpet —*vt.* to make flare —*n.* **1.** a bright, brief, unsteady blaze of light **2.** a very bright light used as a distress signal, etc. **3.** a sudden, brief outburst, as of emotion or sound **4.** *a)* a curving or spreading outward, as of a skirt *b)* a part that curves or spreads outward **5.** a brief outburst of brightness on the sun

flare-up (fler′up′) *n.* a sudden outburst of flame or of anger, trouble, etc.

flar·ing (fler′iŋ) *adj.* **1.** blazing brightly for a little while **2.** curving or spreading outward —**flar′ing·ly** *adv.*

flash (flash) *vi.* [ME. *flaschen,* to splash: echoic] **1.** to send out a sudden, brief light, esp. at intervals **2.** to sparkle or gleam [eyes *flashing* with anger] **3.** to speak abruptly, esp. in anger (usually with *out*) **4.** to come or pass swiftly and suddenly [the train *flashed* by] —*vt.* **1.** to send out (light, etc.) in sudden, brief spurts **2.** to cause to flash **3.** to signal with light **4.** to send (news, etc.) swiftly or suddenly **5.** [Colloq.] to show briefly or in a way meant to be impressive [to *flash* a roll of money] —*n.* **1.** *a)* a sudden, brief light *b)* a sudden burst of flame or heat **2.** a brief time; moment [I'll be there in a *flash*] **3.** a sudden, brief display [a *flash* of wit] ☆**4.** a brief item of news sent by telegraph or radio **5.** a showy display **6.** anything that flashes; specif., [Colloq.] a person very quick or skillful at something —*adj.* **1.** happening swiftly or suddenly [a *flash* flood] **2.** working along with a flash of light [a *flash* camera] —**flash in the pan** [orig. of powder in pan of a flintlock] **1.** a sudden, seemingly skillful effort that fails **2.** one that fails after such an effort —**flash′er** *n.* —**flash′ing·ly** *adv.*

SYN.—flash implies a sudden, brief, brilliant light; **gleam** suggests a steady, narrow ray of light shining through darkness; **sparkle** implies a number of brief, bright flashes from many points of light; **glitter** implies the reflection of such bright flashes, as from metal or a jewel; **glisten** suggests the reflection of a bright light, as from a wet surface; **shimmer** refers to a soft, wavering reflection of light, as from the surface of gently moving water

☆**flash·back** (flash′bak′) *n.* **1.** an interruption in the regular flow of events in a story, play, etc. by the introduction of an episode that took place earlier **2.** such an episode

flash·bulb (-bulb′) *n.* an electric light bulb giving a brief, dazzling light, used in taking photographs

☆**flash·card** (-kärd′) *n.* any of a set of cards with words, numbers, etc. on them, flashed one by one before a class in a drill

☆**flash·cube** (-kyo̅o̅b′) *n.* a small, rotating cube containing a flashbulb in each of four sides

flash gun a device that sets off a flashbulb and works the camera shutter at the same time

flash·ing (-iŋ) *n.* sheets of metal, etc. used to weatherproof joints, edges, etc., esp. of a roof

flash·light (-līt′) *n.* ☆**1.** a portable electric light, usually operated by batteries **2.** a brief, dazzling light for taking photographs at night or indoors

flash point the lowest temperature at which the vapor of a volatile oil will ignite with a flash

FLASHCUBE

flash·y (-ē) *adj.* **flash′i·er, flash′i·est** **1.** dazzling or bright for a little while **2.** too showy or fancy —see SYN. at GAUDY —**flash′i·ly** *adv.* —**flash′i·ness** *n.*

flask (flask) *n.* [< ML. *flasco* & OE. *flasce* < LL. < *flasca*] **1.** any small bottle with a narrow neck, used in laboratories, etc. **2.** a small, flat container for liquor, etc., to be carried in the pocket

flat[1] (flat) *adj.* **flat′ter, flat′test** [< ON. *flatr*: for IE. base see PLANT] **1.** having a smooth, level surface [a *flat* stretch of land] **2.** *a)* lying spread out at full length [to lie *flat* on the floor] *b)* spread out smooth and level **3.** *a)* broad, even, and not very thick [a penny is *flat*] *b)* having a flat heel or no heel [*flat* shoes] **4.** almost straight or level [a *flat* trajectory or flight] **5.** definite; positive [a *flat* denial] **6.** not varying [a *flat* rate] **7.** having little or no sparkle or taste [a *flat* drink] **8.** monotonous; dull [a *flat* voice] **9.** not clear or full [a *flat* sound] ☆**10.** emptied of air [a *flat* tire] **11.** not shiny or glossy [*flat* paint] **12.** *Art a)* not seeming to have depth; lacking perspective *b)* having the same tint or shade throughout **13.** *Music a)* below the true pitch *b)* lower in pitch by a half step [D *flat*] **14.** *Phonet.* designating the vowel *a* sounded with the tongue in a flat position, as in *can* —*adv.* **1.** in a flat manner **2.** in a flat position **3.** *a)* exactly; precisely [in ten seconds *flat*] *b)* bluntly; abruptly [she left him *flat*] **4.** *Music* below the true pitch —*n.* **1.** a flat surface or part [the *flat* of the hand] **2.** an area of level land **3.** a low-lying marsh **4.** a shallow; shoal **5.** a shallow box, as for growing seedlings **6.** a piece of theatrical scenery on a flat frame ☆**7.** a deflated tire **8.** [*pl.*] flat-heeled shoes **9.** *Music a)* a note or tone one half step below another *b)* the symbol (♭) indicating such a note —*vt.* **flat′ted, flat′ting** *Music* to make flat —*vi. Music* to sing or play below the true pitch —see SYN. at INSIPID —**fall flat** to fail to have the effect that is wanted —**flat out 1.** at full speed, with maximum effort, etc. **2.** [Colloq.] clear or clearly; definite or definitely —**flat′ly** *adv.* —**flat′ness** *n.* —**flat′tish** *adj.*

flat[2] (flat) *n.* [altered < Scot. dial. *flet* (OE. *flet*), a floor of a dwelling] an apartment or suite of rooms on one floor of a building

flat·bed, flat-bed (flat′bed′) *adj.* ☆designating or of a truck, trailer, etc. having a bed or platform without sides or stakes —*n.* ☆a flatbed truck, trailer, etc.

flat·boat (-bōt′) *n.* a flat-bottomed boat for carrying freight in shallow waters or on rivers

☆**flat·car** (-kär′) *n.* a railroad car without sides or a roof, for carrying certain kinds of freight

flat·fish (-fish′) *n., pl.* -**fish′, -fish′es**: see FISH a fish with a flat body and both eyes on the top side, as the flounder, halibut, etc.

flat·foot (-foot′) *n.* **1.** a condition in which the bottom of the foot is flat instead of being curved by the arch ☆**2.** [Slang] a policeman

flat-foot·ed (-foot′id) *adj.* **1.** having flatfoot ☆**2.** [Colloq.] plain and firm [his *flat-footed* refusal to join us] —☆**catch flat-footed** [Colloq.] to take by surprise; catch unprepared —**flat′-foot′ed·ly** *adv.* —**flat′-foot′ed·ness** *n.*

flat·i·ron (-ī′ərn) *n.* an iron for pressing clothes

☆**flat silver** silver knives, forks, spoons, etc.

flat·ten (-'n) *vt., vi.* **1.** to make or become flat or flatter **2.** to knock (someone or something) down —**flat′ten·er** *n.*

flat·ter (flat′ər) *vt.* [< OFr. *flater*, to smooth < Frank. *flat*] **1.** to praise too much or insincerely, as to win favor **2.** to try to please, or get the favor of, as by praise and attention **3.** to make seem more attractive than is so [his portrait *flatters* him] **4.** to make feel pleased or honored [I'm *flattered* that you remember me] —*vi.* to use flattery —**flatter oneself** to hold the pleasing or foolish belief (*that*) [don't *flatter yourself* that he will forgive you] —**flat′ter·er** *n.* —**flat′ter·ing·ly** *adv.*

flat·ter·y (flat′ər ē) *n., pl.* -**ter·ies** **1.** a flattering **2.** too much praise, or praise that is not sincere

☆**flat·top** (-täp′) *n.* [Slang] something with a flat or level surface, as an aircraft carrier

flat·u·lent (flach′ə lənt, -yōo-) *adj.* [Fr. < ModL. < L. < *flare*, to blow] **1.** of, having, or producing gas in the stomach or intestines **2.** windy or empty in speech; pompous; pretentious —**flat′u·lence, flat′u·len·cy** *n.* —**flat′u·lent·ly** *adv.*

flat·ware (flat′wer′) *n.* relatively flat tableware; ☆specif., knives, forks, and spoons

☆**flat·work** (-wurk′) *n.* sheets, napkins, and other flat pieces that can be pressed in a mangle

flat·worm (-wurm′) *n. same as* PLATYHELMINTH

Flau·bert (flō ber′), **Gus·tave** (güs tàv′) 1821–80; Fr. novelist

flaunt (flônt) *vi.* [prob. < dial. *flant*, to strut coquettishly] **1.** to make a gaudy or impudent display **2.** to flutter freely —*vt.* to show off proudly or impudently [to *flaunt* one's wealth] —see SYN. at SHOW —**flaunt′ing·ly** *adv.*

flau·tist (flôt′ist, flout′-) *n.* [It. *flautista* < *flauto*, flute] *same as* FLUTIST

fla·vin (flā′vin, flav′in) *n.* [< L. *flavus*, yellow + -IN[1]] **1.** a complex ketone, $C_{10}H_6N_4O_2$ **2.** any of a group of natural or synthetic yellow pigments that form enzymes important in tissue respiration Also **fla·vine** (flā′vēn, flav′ēn)

fla·vor (flā′vər) *n.* [< OFr. *flaur* < L. *flatare* < *flare*, to blow: for IE. base see BALL[1]] **1.** *a)* the combined taste and smell of something *b)* taste in general [a soup lacking *flavor*] **2.** *same as* FLAVORING **3.** characteristic quality [the *flavor* of adventure] —*vt.* to give flavor to —**fla′vor·ful** *adj.* —**fla′vor·less** *adj.*

fla·vor·ing (-iŋ) *n.* an essence, extract, etc. added to a food or drink to give it a certain taste [vanilla *flavoring*]

fla·vour (flā′vər) *n., vt. Brit. sp. of* FLAVOR

flaw[1] (flô) *n.* [prob. < Scand.: see FLAKE] **1.** a break, scratch, crack, etc. that spoils something; blemish [a *flaw* in a diamond] **2.** a defect; fault; error [a *flaw* in his reasoning] —*vt., vi.* to make or become faulty —see SYN. at DEFECT —**flaw′less** *adj.* —**flaw′less·ly** *adv.* —**flaw′less·ness** *n.*

flaw[2] (flô) *n.* [prob. < ON. *flaga*, sudden onset] a sudden, brief gust of wind; squall

flax (flaks) *n.* [OE. *fleax*: for IE. base see COMPLICATE] **1.** a slender, erect plant with delicate blue flowers and narrow leaves: the seed (**flax′seed′**) yields linseed oil, and the fibers of the stem are spun into linen thread **2.** these fibers

flax·en (flaks′'n) *adj.* **1.** of or made of flax **2.** like flax in color; pale-yellow: also **flax′y**

flay (flā) *vt.* [OE. *flean*: see FLESH] **1.** to strip off the skin or hide of, as by whipping **2.** to criticize or scold mercilessly **3.** to rob; pillage; fleece —**flay′er** *n.*

F layer the highest regular layer of the ionosphere, reflecting high-frequency radio waves

fl. dr. fluid dram; fluid drams

flea (flē) *n.* [< OE. *fleah*] a small, wingless jumping insect that bites animals to suck their blood

flea·bag (flē′bag′) *n.* ☆[Slang] a very cheap hotel

flea-bit·ten (-bit′'n) *adj.* **1.** bitten by or infested with fleas **2.** wretched; shabby; decrepit

flea market an outdoor market dealing mainly in cheap, secondhand goods

fleck (flek) *n.* [ON. *flekkr*: for IE. base see FLESH] **1.** a spot or small patch of color, etc.; speck **2.** a particle; flake —*vt.* to cover or sprinkle with flecks; speckle

FLEA
(to ⅛ in. long)

flec·tion (flek′shən) *n.* [< L. pp. of *flectere*, to bend] **1.** a bending; flexing **2.** a bent part **3.** *Anat. same as* FLEXION —**flec′tion·al** *adj.*

fled (fled) *pt. & pp. of* FLEE

fledge (flej) *vi.* **fledged, fledg′ing** [< OE. (*un*)*flycge*, (un)-fledged] to grow the feathers needed for flying —*vt.* **1.** to rear (a young bird) until it can fly **2.** to supply with feathers [to *fledge* an arrow]

fledg·ling (flej′liŋ) *n.* **1.** a young bird just fledged **2.** a young, inexperienced person Also, chiefly Brit., **fledge′ling**

flee (flē) *vi.* **fled, flee′ing** [OE. *fleon*] **1.** to run away or escape from danger, pursuers, etc. **2.** to pass away swiftly; vanish [night had *fled*] **3.** to go swiftly —*vt.* to run away from; shun —**fle′er** *n.*

fleece (flēs) *n.* [OE. *fleos*] **1.** the wool covering a sheep or similar animal **2.** the amount of wool cut from a sheep in one shearing **3.** a covering like a sheep's **4.** a soft, warm, napped fabric —*vt.* **fleeced, fleec′ing 1.** to shear fleece from **2.** to steal from by fraud; swindle —**fleec′er** *n.*

fleec·y (flēs′ē) *adj.* **fleec′i·er, fleec′i·est 1.** made of or covered with fleece **2.** like fleece; soft and light —**fleec′i·ly** *adv.* —**fleec′i·ness** *n.*

fleer (flir) *vi., vt.* [prob. < Scand.] to laugh derisively (at); sneer or jeer (at) —*n.* a derisive grimace, laugh, etc. —**fleer′ing·ly** *adv.*

fleet[1] (flēt) *n.* [OE. *fleot* < *fleotan*, to float: for IE. base see FLOW] **1.** *a)* a number of warships under one command *b)* the entire navy of a country **2.** any group of ships, trucks, buses, airplanes, etc. under one control

fleet[2] (flēt) *vi.* [OE. *fleotan:* see prec.] to move swiftly; fly — *adj.* swift; rapid [*fleet* of foot] —see SYN. at FAST[1] —**fleet′ly** *adv.* —**fleet′ness** *n.*

☆**fleet admiral** *U.S. Navy* an admiral of the highest rank, having the insignia of five stars

fleet·ing (flēt′iŋ) *adj.* passing swiftly; not lasting [a *fleeting* glimpse] —see SYN. at TRANSIENT —**fleet′ing·ly** *adv.* —**fleet′ing·ness** *n.*

Flem·ing (flem′iŋ) *n.* [< MDu. *Vlaming*] 1. a native of Flanders 2. a Flemish-speaking Belgian

Flem·ing (flem′iŋ), Sir **Alexander** 1881–1955; Brit. bacteriologist: co-discoverer of penicillin

Flem·ish (flem′ish) *adj.* of Flanders, the Flemings, or their language —*n.* the West Germanic language of the Flemings —**the Flemish** the people of Flanders

flense (flens) *vt.* **flensed, flens′ing** [< Du. *vlensen* or Dan. *flense*] to cut blubber or skin from (a whale, seal, etc.): also **flench** (flench)

flesh (flesh) *n.* [OE. *flæsc* < IE. base *plek-*, to tear off] 1. *a)* the soft substance of the body (of a person or animal); esp., the muscular tissue *b)* the skin of the body [to make one's *flesh* crawl] 2. meat; esp., meat other than fish or fowl 3. the pulpy or edible part of fruits and vegetables 4. the human body, as distinguished from the soul [more than *flesh* can bear] 5. human nature, esp. in its sensual aspect 6. all living beings, esp. all mankind [the way of all *flesh*] 7. kindred: now mainly in **one's (own) flesh and blood,** one's close relatives 8. the typical color of a white person's skin; yellowish pink —*vt.* 1. to incite to bloodshed, etc. by a foretaste 2. to fatten 3. to fill out by adding details, etc. (usually with *out*) —*vi.* to grow fat (usually with *out* or *up*) —**flesh and blood** the human body —**in the flesh** 1. alive 2. in person

flesh-col·ored (flesh′kul′ərd) *adj.* yellowish-pink

flesh·ly (-lē) *adj.* **-li·er, -li·est** 1. of the body; corporeal 2. fond of bodily pleasures; sensual 3. *same as* FLESHY —**flesh′li·ness** *n.*

flesh·pot (-pät′) *n.* 1. a pot for cooking meat 2. [*pl.*] *a)* bodily comfort and pleasures; luxuries *b)* a place where such pleasures are provided

flesh·y (-ē) *adj.* **flesh′i·er, flesh′i·est** 1. having much flesh; plump 2. of or like flesh 3. having a firm pulp: said of some fruits —**flesh′i·ness** *n.*

fleur-de-lis (flur′də lē′, -lēs′) *n., pl.* **fleurs-de-lis** (flur′də-lēz′) [< OFr. *flor de lis*, lit., flower of the lily] 1. *same as* IRIS (senses 3 & 4) 2. the coat of arms of the former French royal family 3. *Heraldry* a lilylike emblem Also sp. **fleur-de-lys**

flew (flōō) *pt.* of FLY[1]

flex[1] (fleks) *vt., vi.* [< L. *flexus*, pp. of *flectere*, to bend] 1. to bend (an arm, knee, etc.) 2. to contract (a muscle)

flex[2] (fleks) *n.* [< FLEXIBLE] [Brit.] flexible, insulated electric cord

FLEUR-DE-LIS

flex·i·ble (flek′sə b'l) *adj.* [< OFr. < L. *flexus:* see FLEX[1]] 1. able to bend without breaking 2. easily changed or managed; adaptable; adjustable [*flexible* office hours; a *flexible* personality] —**flex′i·bil′i·ty** *n.* —**flex′i·bly** *adv.*

flex·ion (flek′shən) *n.* 1. *same as* FLECTION 2. *Anat.* the bending of a joint or limb by means of the flexor muscles —**flex′ion·al** *adj.*

flex·or (flek′sər) *n.* [ModL. < L.: see FLEX[1]] a muscle that bends a limb or other part of the body

flex·u·ous (flek′shōō wəs) *adj.* winding or wavering —**flex′u·os′i·ty** (-wäs′ə tē) *n., pl.* **-ties**

flex·ure (flek′shər) *n.* 1. a bending, curving, or flexing, as of a heavy body under its own weight 2. a bend, curve, or fold —**flex′ur·al** *adj.*

flib·ber·ti·gib·bet (flib′ər tē jib′it) *n.* [< ?] an irresponsible, flighty person

flick[1] (flik) *n.* [echoic, but infl. by FLICKER[1]] 1. a light, quick stroke, jerk, or snap 2. a light, snapping sound 3. a fleck; speck —*vt.* 1. to strike, remove, etc. with a light, quick stroke [he *flicked* the ant off the table] 2. to make such a stroke with (a whip, etc.) —*vi.* to flutter

flick[2] (flik) *n.* [< FLICKER[1]] [Slang] *same as* MOVIE —**the flicks** [Slang] the movies (see MOVIE)

flick·er[1] (flik′ər) *vi.* [OE. *flicorian*] 1. to move with a quick, light, wavering motion [*flickering* shadows] 2. to burn or shine unsteadily, as a candle flame —*vt.* to make flicker —*n.* 1. a flickering 2. a flame or light that flickers 3. a quick, passing look or feeling [a *flicker* of pleasure crossed his face] —**flick′er·y** *adj.*

☆**flick·er**[2] (flik′ər) *n.* [echoic of its cry] any of several N. American woodpeckers, esp. one with a red mark on the back of the head and wings colored golden on the underside

flied (flīd) *pt. & pp.* of FLY[1] (*vi.* 8)

fli·er (flī′ər) *n.* 1. a thing that flies 2. an aviator ☆3. a bus, train, etc. on a fast schedule ☆4. a small handbill ☆5. [Colloq.] a reckless gamble or speculation Also, esp. for 2, 3, & 5, **fly′er**

flight[1] (flīt) *n.* [OE. *flyht*] 1. the act, manner, or power of flying or moving through space 2. the distance flown at one time, as by an airplane, bird, etc. 3. a group of birds, arrows, etc. flying together 4. *a)* a formation of military airplanes in flight ☆*b)* U.S. *Air Force* the smallest tactical unit, a subdivision of a squadron 5. an airplane scheduled to fly a certain trip 6. a trip by airplane 7. a soaring above the ordinary [a *flight* of fancy] 8. a set of stairs, as between floors 9. *Sports* a division of contestants grouped together according to ability —see SYN. at GROUP

flight[2] (flīt) *n.* [< OE. < base of *fleon*, to flee] a fleeing, as from danger —**put to flight** to force to flee —**take (to) flight** to run away; flee

flight control 1. the control from the ground, as by radio, of aircraft in flight 2. a station exercising such control

☆**flight deck** the upper deck of an aircraft carrier, that serves as a runway

flight feather any of the large feathers of the wings or tail that support a bird in flight

flight·less (flīt′lis) *adj.* not able to fly

flight·y (flīt′ē) *adj.* **flight′i·er, flight′i·est** not properly serious; frivolous or irresponsible —**flight′i·ly** *adv.* —**flight′i·ness** *n.*

flim-flam (flim′flam′) *n.* [< ?] 1. nonsense 2. a sly trick or deception —*vt.* **-flammed′, -flam′ming** [Colloq.] to trick or cheat —**flim′flam′mer·y** *n.*

flim·sy (flim′zē) *adj.* **-si·er, -si·est** [< ?] 1. thin and easily broken or damaged; fragile [a *flimsy* cardboard box] 2. weak or inadequate [a *flimsy* excuse] —*n.* 1. a sheet of thin paper 2. copy written on such paper, as by a reporter —**flim′si·ly** *adv.* —**flim′si·ness** *n.*

flinch (flinch) *vi.* [< OFr. *flenchir:* for IE. base see LANK] 1. to draw back, as from a blow, difficulty, etc. 2. to wince, as because of pain —*n.* a flinching

flin·ders (flin′dərz) *n.pl.* [< Scand., as in Norw. *flindra*, SPLINTER] splinters or fragments: chiefly in **break** (or **fly**) **into flinders**

fling (fliŋ) *vt.* **flung, fling′ing** [ME. *flingen*, to rush < ON. *flengja*, to whip] 1. to throw, esp. with force; hurl 2. to put abruptly or violently [the crowd was *flung* into confusion] 3. to move (one's limbs, head, etc.) suddenly or impulsively 4. to throw (oneself) energetically (*into* a task, etc.) 5. to cast aside [to *fling* caution to the winds] —*vi.* to move suddenly and with force; rush; dash [she *flung* out of the room in a rage] —*n.* 1. an act of flinging 2. a brief time of freely indulging oneself in pleasures 3. a lively dance [the Highland *fling*] 4. [Colloq.] a trial effort; try [have a *fling* at it] —see SYN. at THROW —**fling′er** *n.*

Flint (flint) [after nearby *Flint* River, so called from the flint stones in it] city in SE Mich.: pop. 193,000

flint (flint) *n.* [OE. < IE. base (*s*)*plei-*, to split] 1. a fine-grained, very hard quartz that makes sparks when struck with steel 2. a piece of this stone, used to start a fire, for primitive tools, etc. 3. anything like flint in hardness, use, etc. [a heart of *flint*, a lighter *flint* of iron-cerium alloy]

flint glass a hard, bright lead-oxide glass, used for lenses, crystal, etc.

FLICKER
(to 1 ft. long)

flint·lock (flint′läk′) *n.* **1.** a gunlock in which a flint in the hammer strikes sparks that ignite the powder **2.** an old-fashioned gun with such a lock

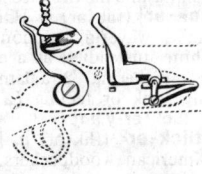

FLINTLOCK

flint·y (flin′tē) *adj.* **flint′i·er, flint′i·est** **1.** of or containing flint **2.** like flint; very hard or firm —**flint′i·ly** *adv.* —**flint′i·ness** *n.*

flip[1] (flip) *vt.* **flipped, flip′ping** [echoic] **1.** to move with a quick jerk **2.** to snap (a coin) into the air with the thumb, as in betting on which side will land uppermost **3.** to turn (a card, etc.) over quickly —*vi.* **1.** to make a quick, light stroke or move; snap **2.** to flip a coin **3.** to do a flip ☆**4.** [Slang] to lose self-control as a result of excitement, anger, etc.; go crazy: also **flip out, flip one's lid** —*n.* **1.** a flipping; snap, toss, etc. **2.** a somersault in the air **3.** *Phonet.* same as FLAP (*n.* 5)

flip[2] (flip) *n.* [prob. < prec.] a sweetened drink of wine or liquor mixed with egg, spices, etc.

flip[3] (flip) *adj.* **flip′per, flip′pest** [contr. < FLIPPANT] [Colloq.] flippant; saucy; impertinent

flip-flop (flip′fläp′) *n.* ☆**1.** a backward handspring **2.** an abrupt change, as to the opposite opinion **3.** a flapping noise **4.** *Electronics* a circuit with two stable states, that switches from one to the other on signal —*vi.* **-flopped′, -flop′ping** to do a flip-flop

flip·pan·cy (flip′ən sē) *n.* **1.** a being flippant **2.** *pl.* **-cies** a flippant act or remark

flip·pant (flip′ənt) *adj.* [Early ModE., nimble, prob. < FLIP[1]] joking or trying to be funny when one should be more serious or show more respect —**flip′pant·ly** *adv.*

flip·per (flip′ər) *n.* [< FLIP[1]] **1.** a broad, flat limb, as of a seal, adapted for swimming ☆**2.** a paddlelike rubber piece worn on each foot as a help in swimming **3.** [Slang] a hand

FLIPPERS

☆**flip side** [Colloq.] the reverse side (of a phonograph recording), esp. the less important or less popular side

flirt (flurt) *vt.* [< ? OFr. *fleureter*, lit., move from flower to flower < *fleur*, FLOWER] to move quickly back and forth [the bird *flirted* its tail] —*vi.* **1.** to move jerkily **2.** to behave in a playful, bold or coy way in trying to attract someone romantically **3.** to deal lightly (*with* something); play; toy [to *flirt* with an idea] —*n.* **1.** a flirting movement **2.** a person who flirts with others —see SYN. at TRIFLE —**flirt′y** *adj.*

flir·ta·tion (flər tā′shən) *n.* **1.** a flirting, or playing at love **2.** a passing interest or relationship of a flirting kind

flir·ta·tious (-shəs) *adj.* flirting or inclined to flirt —**flir·ta′tious·ly** *adv.* —**flir·ta′tious·ness** *n.*

flit (flit) *vi.* **flit′ted, flit′ting** [< ON. *flytja*] to pass or fly lightly and rapidly; dart; flutter [*flitting* from flower to flower] —*n.* a flitting —**flit′ter** *n.*

flitch (flich) *n.* [OE. *flicce*] the cured and salted side of a hog; side of bacon —*vt.* to cut into flitches

flit·ter (flit′ər) *vi., vt.* [< FLIT + -ER (sense 4)] [Chiefly Dial.] *same as* FLUTTER

☆**fliv·ver** (fliv′ər) *n.* [< ?] [Old Slang] a small, cheap automobile, esp. an old one

float (flōt) *n.* [OE. *flota* < *fleotan*: see FLEET[1]] **1.** anything staying, or making something else stay, on or at a liquid's surface; specif., *a)* a cork on a fishing line *b)* a floating ball, etc. that regulates the valve controlling the liquid level, as in a tank *c)* a raftlike platform anchored near a shore, as for use by swimmers *d)* a buoyant device on an aircraft to allow it to land on water **2.** a platform on wheels that carries a display or exhibit in a parade ☆**3.** a cold beverage with ice cream floating in it [a root beer *float*] **4.** a specified way of floating [to teach beginning swimmers the back *float*] —*vi.* **1.** to stay on or at a liquid's surface **2.** to drift gently on water, in air, etc. [leaves *floated* down from the trees] ☆**3.** to move about vaguely and without purpose —*vt.* **1.** to make float **2.** *a)* to put into circulation [*float* a bond issue] *b)* to establish or start (a business, etc.) **3.** to arrange for (a loan)

float·a·tion (flō tā′shən) *n. same as* FLOTATION

float·er (flōt′ər) *n.* **1.** one that floats ☆**2.** a person who illegally votes at several polling places ☆**3.** a person who changes his place of residence or work often **4.** an insurance policy covering movable property wherever it is at the time of loss

float·ing (-iŋ) *adj.* **1.** that floats **2.** not remaining in one place; moving about **3.** *Finance a)* designating an unfunded, short-time debt *b)* not permanently invested [*floating* capital] **4.** *Mech.* designating or of suspension that reduces vibration **5.** *Med.* displaced from the normal position and moving more freely [a *floating* kidney]

floating ribs the eleventh and twelfth pairs of ribs, not attached to the breastbone or to other ribs but only to the vertebrae

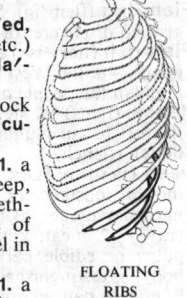

FLOATING RIBS

floc·cu·late (fläk′yoo lāt′) *vt., vi.* **-lat′ed, -lat′ing** to collect (clouds, precipitates, etc.) into small, flocculent masses —**floc′cu·la′tion** *n.*

floc·cu·lent (-lənt) *adj.* [< L. *floccus*, flock of wool + -ULENT] woolly; fluffy —**floc′cu·lence** *n.*

flock[1] (fläk) *n.* [OE. *flocc*, a troop] **1.** a group of certain animals, as goats or sheep, or of birds, living, feeding, or moving together **2.** any group, esp. a large one, as of church members —*vi.* to assemble or travel in a flock —see SYN. at GROUP

flock[2] (fläk) *n.* [< OFr. < L. *floccus*] **1.** a small tuft of wool, cotton, etc. **2.** wool or cotton waste used to stuff furniture, etc. **3.** tiny fibers of wool, rayon, etc. put on wallpaper, etc. to form a velvety surface or design Also sp. **floc** —*vt.* **flock′y** *adj.* **flock′i·er, flock′i·est**

flock·ing (fläk′iŋ) *n.* **1.** *same as* FLOCK[2] (sense 3) **2.** a material or surface with flock on it

floe (flō) *n.* [prob. < Norw. *flo*, layer] *same as* ICE FLOE

flog (fläg, flôg) *vt.* **flogged, flog′ging** [? cant abbrev. of L. *flagellare*, to whip] **1.** to beat with a stick, whip, etc. **2.** [Brit. Slang] to sell, esp. illegally —**flog′ger** *n.*

flood (flud) *n.* [OE. *flod*: for IE. base see FLOW] **1.** an overflowing of water on an area normally dry; deluge **2.** the flowing in of water from the sea as the tide rises **3.** a great flow or outpouring, as of words **4.** [Archaic] a large body of water —*vt.* **1.** to cover or fill with or as with a flood; inundate [rain *flooded* the earth; music *flooded* the room] **2.** to put much or too much liquid on or in [to *flood* a carburetor] —*vi.* **1.** to rise, flow, or gush out in or as in a flood **2.** to become flooded —**the Flood** *Bible* the great flood in Noah's time: Gen. 7

☆**flood control** the protection of land from floods by building dams and levees, planting trees, etc.

flood·gate (flud′gāt′) *n.* **1.** a gate in a stream or canal, to control water height and flow **2.** anything like this in controlling an outburst

flood·light (-līt′) *n.* **1.** a lamp that casts a broad beam of bright light **2.** such a beam of light —*vt.* **-light′ed** or **-lit′, -light′ing** to light with floodlights

flood tide the incoming or rising tide

floor (flôr) *n.* [OE. *flor*: for IE. base see FIELD] **1.** the inside bottom surface of a room **2.** any bottom surface [the ocean *floor*] **3.** the platform of a bridge, pier, etc. **4.** a level or story in a building [an office on the fifth *floor*] **5.** *a)* the part of a legislative chamber, stock exchange, etc. occupied by members *b)* the members as a group ☆**6.** the right to speak in an assembly [to ask the chairman for the *floor*] **7.** a lower limit set on anything —*vt.* **1.** to cover or furnish with a floor **2.** to knock down **3.** [Colloq.] *a)* to defeat *b)* to make unable to act, as by shocking or confusing

floor·age (flôr′ij) *n.* the area of a floor: also **floor space**

floor·board (flôr′bôrd′) *n.* **1.** a board in a floor **2.** the floor of an automobile, etc.

floor·ing (-iŋ) *n.* **1.** a floor **2.** floors collectively **3.** material for making a floor

☆**floor leader** a member of a legislature chosen by his political party to direct its actions on the floor

floor plan a scale drawing of the arrangement of rooms, halls, etc. on one floor of a building

floor show a show presenting singers, dancers, etc. in a restaurant, nightclub, etc.

☆**floor·walk·er** (-wôk′ər) *n.* formerly, a person employed by a department store to direct customers, supervise sales, etc.: now usually **floor manager**

☆**floo·zy, floo·zie** (floo′zē) *n., pl.* **-zies** [Slang] a loose, disreputable woman: also sp. **floo′sy, floo′sie**

flop (fläp) *vt.* **flopped, flop′ping** [var. of FLAP] to flap or throw noisily and clumsily [to *flop* one's arms about] —*vi.* **1.** *a)* to move or flap around loosely or clumsily [the fish *flopped* about in the boat] b) to fall or drop thus [to *flop* into a chair] **2.** [Colloq.] to be a failure —*n.* **1.** the act or sound of flopping ☆**2.** [Colloq.] a failure —*adv.* with a flop —**flop′per** *n.*

☆**flop·house** (fläp′hous′) *n.* [colloq.] a very cheap hotel used chiefly by vagrants

flop·py (-ē) *adj.* **-pi·er, -pi·est** [Colloq.] tending to flop — **flop′pi·ly** *adv.* —**flop′pi·ness** *n.*

Flo·ra (flôr′ə) [L. < *flos*, a flower (see BLOOM)] **1.** a feminine name **2.** *Rom. Myth.* the goddess of flowers —*n.* [**f-**] *pl.* **-ras, -rae** (-ē) the plants of a specified region or time [the *flora* of Africa]

flo·ral (flôr′əl) *adj.* of, made of, or like flowers

Flor·ence (flôr′əns, flär′-) [Fr. < L. *Florentia*, lit., a blooming < *flos*, a FLOWER] **1.** a feminine name **2.** city in Tuscany, C Italy: pop. 455,000

Flor·en·tine (flôr′ən tēn′) *adj.* of Florence, Italy, or its people, culture, or art —*n.* a native or inhabitant of Florence

Flo·res (flô′rĕs) island of Indonesia, west of Timor & south of Celebes: 5,500 sq. mi.

flo·res·cence (flô res′ns, flə-) *n.* [< L. prp. of *florescere* < *florere*, to bloom < *flos*, FLOWER] a blooming or flowering — **flo·res′cent** *adj.*

flo·ret (flôr′it) *n.* [< OFr. dim. of *flor* < L. *flos*, FLOWER] **1.** a small flower **2.** any of the small flowers making up the head of a composite plant

flo·ri·cul·ture (flôr′ə kul′chər) *n.* the cultivation of flowers — **flo′ri·cul′tur·al** *adj.* —**flo′ri·cul′tur·ist** *n.*

flor·id (flôr′id, flär′-) *adj.* [L. *floridus* < *flos*, FLOWER] **1.** flushed with red; ruddy: said of the complexion **2.** highly decorated; showy; ornate [a *florid* musical passage] —see SYN. at ROSY —**flo·rid·i·ty** (flô rid′ə tē, flə-), **flor′id·ness** *n.* —**flor′id·ly** *adv.*

Flor·i·da (flôr′ə də, flär′-) [Sp. < L. < *flos*, FLOWER] **1.** SE State of the U.S., mostly on a peninsula between the Atlantic & the Gulf of Mexico: 58,560 sq. mi.; pop. 6,789,000; cap. Tallahassee: abbrev. **Fla., FL 2. Straits of,** strait between the S tip of Fla. & Cuba —**Flo·rid·i·an** (flô rid′ē ən) *adj., n.*

Florida Keys chain of small islands extending southwest from the S tip of Fla.: see map at EVERGLADES

flor·in (flôr′in, flär′-) *n.* [< OFr. < It. < L. *flos*, FLOWER: the figure of a lily was stamped on the original coins] **1.** a gold coin of medieval Florence **2.** any of various European or South African silver or gold coins

Flo·ris·sant (flôr′ə sənt) [Fr., flourishing] city in E Mo.: suburb of St. Louis: pop. 66,000

flo·rist (flôr′ist, flär′-) *n.* [< L. *flos*, FLOWER] a person in the business of selling flowers, house plants, etc.

flo·ris·tic (flô ris′tik) *adj.* of flowers or flora

floss (flôs, fläs) *n.* [prob. < Fr. < L. *floccus*, FLOCK²] **1.** the rough silk covering a silkworm's cocoon **2.** short, downy waste fibers of silk **3.** a soft thread or yarn, as of silk (**floss silk**) or linen (**linen floss**), used in embroidery **4.** a soft, silky, flosslike substance, as in milkweed pods **5.** *same as* DENTAL FLOSS —*vt., vi.* to clean (the teeth) with dental floss

floss·y (flôs′ē, fläs′ē) *adj.* **floss′i·er, floss′i·est** of or like floss; downy; fluffy

flo·ta·tion (flō tā′shən) *n.* a floating; specif., the starting or financing of a business, etc., as by selling an entire issue of bonds

flo·til·la (flō til′ə) *n.* [Sp., dim. of *flota*, a fleet] **1.** a small fleet, or a fleet of small ships ☆**2.** *U.S. Navy* a unit consisting of two or more squadrons

flot·sam (flät′səm) *n.* [< OFr. < MDu. *vloten* (or OE. *flotian*), to float] **1.** the wreckage of a ship or its cargo floating at sea **2.** odds and ends **3.** unemployed people who drift from place to place The term **flotsam and jetsam,** which combines the marine senses of the two words, is also used for senses 2 & 3 of **flotsam**

flounce¹ (flouns) *vi.* **flounced, flounc′ing** [prob. < Scand.] to move with quick, flinging motions of the body, as in anger [she *flounced* out of the room] —*n.* the act of flouncing

flounce² (flouns) *n.* [earlier *frounce* < OFr. < *froncir*, to wrinkle] a wide, ornamental ruffle, as on a skirt or sleeve —*vt.* **flounced, flounc′ing** to trim with a flounce or flounces — **flounc′y** *adj.*

floun·der¹ (floun′dər) *vi.* [? var. of FOUNDER¹] **1.** to struggle or plunge about awkwardly, as in deep mud **2.** to speak or act in an awkward, confused way with many mistakes —*n.* a floundering

floun·der² (floun′dər) *n., pl.* **-ders, -der:** see PLURAL, II, D, 1 [< Scand.] any of a large group of flatfishes caught for food, as the halibut

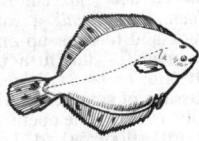

FLOUNDER
(to 30 in. long)

flour (flour) *n.* [var. of FLOWER, after Fr. *fleur de farine*, lit., flower (i.e., best) of meal] **1.** a fine, powdery substance produced by grinding and sifting grain, esp. wheat, or certain roots, etc. **2.** any finely powdered substance —*vt.* to put flour on or in — **flour′y** *adj.*

flour·ish (flur′ish) *vi.* [< OFr. *florir*, to blossom, ult. < L. *flos*, FLOWER] **1.** to grow vigorously; thrive; prosper [our house plants are *flourishing*; art *flourished* in ancient Greece] **2.** to be at the peak of development, activity, etc. **3.** to make showy, wavy motions —*vt.* to wave (a sword, hat, etc.) in the air —*n.* **1.** a sweeping movement [he entered the room with a *flourish*] **2.** a waving in the air **3.** a decorative or curved line or lines in writing **4.** an ornate musical passage; fanfare —**flour′ish·er** *n.* —**flour′ish·ing** *adj.* —**flour′ish·ing·ly** *adv.*

flout (flout) *vt.* [prob. < ME. *flouten*, to play the flute, hence, whistle at, as in scorn] to show scorn or contempt for [to *flout* a rule] —*n.* a flouting —**flout′er** *n.* —**flout′ing·ly** *adv.*

flow (flō) *vi.* [OE. *flowan* < IE. base *pleu-*, to run] **1.** to move as a liquid does **2.** to move like a stream [crowds *flowing* past] **3.** to move gently and smoothly; glide [the conversation *flowed* on for hours] **4.** to pour out **5.** to come (*from* or *out of* as a source); spring ["Praise God from Whom all blessings *flow*"] **6.** to hang loose or in waves [hair *flowing* down her back] **7.** to rise, as the tide **8.** to be plentiful —*n.* **1.** a flowing, or the manner or rate of flowing **2.** anything that flows; stream or current **3.** a continuous production [a *flow* of ideas] **4.** the rising of the tide

☆**flow chart** a diagram showing the progress of work through a sequence of operations, as in manufacturing

flow·er (flou′ər, flour) *n.* [< OFr. < L. *floris*, genitive of *flos*, a flower: for IE. base see BLOOM] **1.** *a)* the structure of many plants that produces seeds, typically with brightly colored petals and leaflike sepals; blossom; bloom *b)* the reproductive part of any plant **2.** a plant cultivated for its blossoms **3.** the best or finest part or example [the *flower* of a nation's youth] **4.** the best period of a person or thing [in the *flower* of his life] **5.** [*pl.*] *Chem.* a powder made from condensed vapors [*flowers* of sulfur] — *vi.* **1.** to produce flowers or blossoms; bloom **2.** to reach the best period [her musical talent *flowered* early] —*vt.* to decorate with flowers or floral patterns —**in flower** in a state of flowering —**flow′er·less** *adj.* —**flow′er·like′** *adj.*

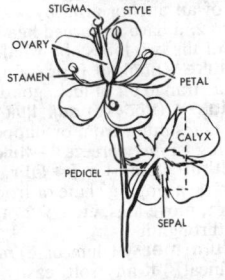

STIGMA　STYLE
OVARY
STAMEN　PETAL
CALYX
PEDICEL
SEPAL

FLOWER

flow·ered (flou′ərd) *adj.* **1.** bearing or containing flowers **2.** decorated with a design like flowers

flow·er·et (flou′ər it) *n. same as* FLORET

flow·er·ing (-ər iŋ) *adj.* **1.** having flowers; in bloom **2.** bearing showy flowers [a *flowering* shrub]

flow·er·pot (-pät′) *n.* a container, usually made of porous clay, in which to grow plants

flow·er·y (-ē) *adj.* **-er·i·er, -er·i·est 1.** covered or decorated with flowers **2.** of or like flowers **3.** full of fancy expressions and showy words [a *flowery* speech] —see SYN. at BOMBASTIC — **flow′er·i·ly** *adv.* —**flow′er·i·ness** *n.*

flown (flōn) *pp.* of FLY¹

Floyd (floid) [var. of LLOYD] a masculine name

fl. oz. fluid ounce; fluid ounces

flt. flight

flu (floo) *n.* **1.** *a shortened form for* INFLUENZA **2.** popularly,

---

fat, āpe, cär, ten, ēven, is, bīte; gō, hôrn, tōōl, look; oil, out; up, fur; get; joy; yet; chin; she; thin, then; zh, leisure; ŋ, ring; ə for a in ago, e in agent, i in sanity, o in comply, u in focus; ʼ as in able (ā′b'l); Fr. bál; ë, Fr. coeur; ö, Fr. feu; Fr. mon; ɔ, Fr. coq; ü, Fr. duc; r, Fr. cri; H, G. ich; kh, G. doch; ‡foreign; ☆ Americanism; < derived from. See inside front cover.

any of various respiratory or intestinal infections caused by a virus

☆**flub** (flub) *vt., vi.* **flubbed, flub′bing** [? < FL(OP) + (D)UB¹] [Colloq.] to botch (a job, chance, etc.); bungle —*n.* [Colloq.] a mistake or blunder

fluc·tu·ate (fluk′chŏŏ wāt′) *vi.* **-at′ed, -at′ing** [< L. pp. of *fluctuare* < *fluctus*, a wave: for IE. base see BALL¹] **1.** to move back and forth or up and down **2.** to vary irregularly [prices *fluctuated*] —**fluc′tu·a′tion** *n.*

flue (flŏŏ) *n.* [< ? OFr. *fluie*, a flowing] **1.** a tube or shaft for the passage of smoke, hot air, etc., as in a chimney **2.** *a) same as* FLUE PIPE *b)* the opening for air in a flue pipe

flu·ent (flŏŏ′ənt) *adj.* [< L. prp. of *fluere*, to flow] **1.** flowing smoothly and easily [*fluent* verse] **2.** able to write or speak easily, smoothly, and expressively [he is *fluent* in three languages] —**flu′en·cy** *n.* —**flu′ent·ly** *adv.*

flue pipe an organ pipe whose tone is produced by an air current striking a narrow side opening

fluff (fluf) *n.* [? blend of *flue*, downy mass + PUFF] **1.** soft, light down **2.** a loose, soft, downy mass, as of dust **3.** any light or trivial matter or talk **4.** *Theater, Radio, TV* an error in speaking a line —*vt.* **1.** to shake or pat until soft and fluffy [to *fluff* a pillow] **2.** *Theater, Radio, TV* to make an error in speaking (one's lines, etc.) **3.** to botch; bungle —*vi.* **1.** to become fluffy **2.** to make an error

fluff·y (fluf′ē) *adj.* **fluff′i·er, fluff′i·est** **1.** soft and light like fluff; feathery **2.** covered with fluff —**fluff′i·ness** *n.*

flu·id (flŏŏ′id) *adj.* [L. *fluidus* < *fluere*, to flow] **1.** that can flow; not solid **2.** of a fluid **3.** not settled or fixed [*fluid* plans] **4.** graceful in movement; flowing [the athlete's *fluid* stride] **5.** available for investment or as cash [*fluid* assets] —*n.* any substance that can flow; liquid or gas —see SYN. at LIQUID —**flu·id·ic** (flŏŏ wid′ik) *adj.* —**flu·id′i·ty, flu′id·ness** *n.* —**flu′id·ly** *adv.*

fluid dram (or **drachm**) a liquid measure equal to 1/8 fluid ounce

fluid ounce a liquid measure equal to 1/16 pint, or 29.57 ml.: also **flu′id·ounce′** *n.*

fluke¹ (flŏŏk) *n.* [OE. *floc*] **1.** any of several flatfishes, esp. flounders **2.** a parasitic flatworm found in the internal organs of vertebrates

fluke² (flŏŏk) *n.* [prob. < prec.] **1.** the triangular, pointed end of an anchor arm, by which the anchor catches in the ground ☆**2.** a barb or barbed head of an arrow, harpoon, etc. **3.** either of the two lobes of a whale's tail

fluke³ (flŏŏk) *n.* [orig., a lucky stroke in billiards < ?] [Colloq.] a strange bit of luck, good or bad

fluk·y (flŏŏ′kē) *adj.* **fluk′i·er, fluk′i·est** [< prec.] [Colloq.] **1.** resulting from or happening by chance **2.** uncertain; shifting [a *fluky* breeze] —**fluk′i·ness** *n.*

flume (flŏŏm) *n.* [< OFr. < L. *flumen*, river < *fluere*, to flow] ☆**1.** a sloping chute or trough for carrying water to furnish power, move logs, etc. ☆**2.** a narrow ravine with a stream running through it

flum·mer·y (flum′ər ē) *n., pl.* **-mer·ies** [W. *llymru*, soured oatmeal] **1.** any soft, easily eaten food, as custard **2.** meaningless flattery or silly talk

flung (fluŋ) *pt. & pp. of* FLING

☆**flunk** (fluŋk) *vt.* [19th-c. college slang < ?] [Colloq.] **1.** to fail in (schoolwork) [to *flunk* a science test] **2.** to give a grade of *failure* to (a student) —*vi.* [Colloq.] to fail, esp. in schoolwork —*n.* [Colloq.] a grade of *failure* —**flunk out** [Colloq.] to send or be sent away from school or college because of unsatisfactory work

flun·ky (fluŋ′kē) *n., pl.* **-kies** [orig. Scot. < ? Fr. *flanquer*, to flank, be at the side of] **1.** one who obeys superiors as if he were a servant ☆**2.** one having very minor or menial tasks Also sp. **flun′key** —**flun′ky·ism** *n.*

flu·or (flŏŏ′ər, -ôr) *n.* [ModL. < L. *flux* < *fluere*, to flow] *same as* FLUORITE

flu·o·resce (flŏŏ′ə res′; flŏŏ res′, flô-) *vi.* **-resced′, -resc′ing** to show or undergo fluorescence

flu·o·res·cence (-res′'ns) *n.* [< FLUOR (SPAR) + -ESCENCE] **1.** the property of a substance, such as fluorite, of producing light when acted upon by radiant energy, such as ultraviolet rays or X-rays **2.** the production of such light **3.** light so produced —**flu′o·res′cent** *adj.*

fluorescent lamp (or **tube**) a glass tube coated inside with a fluorescent substance giving off light (**fluorescent light**) when mercury vapor in the tube is acted upon by electrons from the cathode

☆**fluor·i·date** (flôr′ə dāt′, floor′-) *vt.* **-dat′ed, -dat′ing** to add fluorides to (a supply of drinking water) in an effort to reduce tooth decay —**fluor·i·da′tion** *n.*

flu·o·ride (floor′īd, flôr′-; flŏŏ′ə rīd′) *n.* a compound of fluorine and another element or radical

fluor·i·nate (flôr′ə nāt′, floor′-) *vt.* **-nat′ed, -nat′ing** **1.** to treat, or cause to combine, with fluorine ☆**2.** *same as* FLUORIDATE —**fluor′i·na′tion** *n.*

flu·o·rine (floor′ēn, flôr′-; flŏŏ′ə rēn′, -rin) *n.* [< FLUOR + -INE⁴] a poisonous, greenish-yellow gas that is a highly active chemical element, forming fluorides with almost all elements: symbol, F; at. wt., 18.9984; at. no., 9

flu·o·rite (floor′īt, flôr′-; flŏŏ′ə rīt′) *n.* [< FLUOR(O)- + -ITE] calcium fluoride, CaF₂, a transparent, crystalline mineral of various colors: it is the principal source of fluorine and is used as a flux, in glassmaking, etc.

flu·o·ro- *a combining form meaning:* **1.** fluorine **2.** fluorescence Also, before a vowel, **flu·or-**

flu·o·ro·car·bon (floor′ə kär′bən, flôr′-; flŏŏ′ər ə-, -ə rō′-) *n.* any of a class of inert organic compounds containing carbon, fluorine, and, sometimes, hydrogen: used as lubricants, plastics, etc.

☆**flu·o·rom·e·ter** (flŏŏ räm′ə tər, flŏŏ′ə-) *n.* an instrument for measuring the wavelength and intensity of fluorescence —**flu·o·ro·met·ric** (floor′ə met′rik, flŏŏ′ər ə-) *adj.* —**flu·o·rom′e·try** *n.*

☆**fluor·o·scope** (floor′ə skōp′, flôr′-) *n.* [FLUORO- + -SCOPE] a machine for examining internal structures by viewing the shadows cast on a fluorescent screen by objects through which X-rays are directed —*vt.* **-scoped′, -scop′ing** to examine with a fluoroscope —**fluor′o·scop′ic** (-skäp′ik) *adj.* —**fluor′o·scop′i·cal·ly** *adv.*

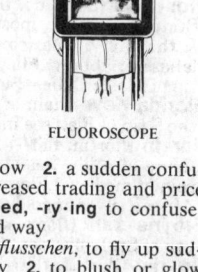

FLUOROSCOPE

☆**flu·o·ros·co·py** (flŏŏ räs′kə pē, flŏŏ′ə-) *n.* examination by fluoroscope —**flu·o·ros′co·pist** *n.*

fluor spar *same as* FLUORITE: also **fluor′·spar′** *n.*

flur·ry (flur′ē) *n., pl.* **-ries** [< ?] ☆**1.** a sudden, brief rush of wind or fall of snow **2.** a sudden confusion or commotion ☆**3.** a spurt of increased trading and price fluctuation in the stock market —*vt.* **-ried, -ry·ing** to confuse; agitate —*vi.* to move in a quick, flustered way

flush¹ (flush) *vi.* [blend of FLASH & ME. *flusschen*, to fly up suddenly] **1.** to flow and spread suddenly **2.** to blush or glow [she *flushed* with anger] **3.** to start up from cover: said of birds —*vt.* **1.** to make flow **2.** to clean or empty with a sudden flow of water, etc. **3.** to make blush or glow [excitement *flushed* her cheeks] **4.** to excite; exhilarate [*flushed* with victory] **5.** to drive (game birds) from cover **6.** to make level or even —*n.* **1.** a sudden, rapid flow, as of water **2.** a sudden, vigorous growth [the first *flush* of youth] **3.** sudden excitement or exhilaration **4.** a blush or glow **5.** a sudden feeling of heat, as in a fever —*adj.* **1.** well supplied, esp. with money **2.** abundant **3.** *a)* making an even line or plane [a door *flush* with the wall] *b)* even with a margin or edge **4.** direct; full [a blow *flush* in the face] —*adv.* **1.** so as to be level or in alignment **2.** directly; squarely

flush² (flush) *n.* [Fr. *flux*: see FLUX] a hand of cards all in the same suit: in poker it ranks above a straight

flus·ter (flus′tər) *vt., vi.* [prob. < Scand.] to make or become confused or nervous —*n.* a flustered state

flute (flŏŏt) *n.* [< OFr. < Pr. *flaüt* < ?] **1.** *a)* a high-pitched wind instrument consisting of a long, slender tube with finger holes and keys, played by blowing across a hole near one end *b)* any similar instrument, as the recorder **2.** a long, rounded groove, as in a column —*vt., vi.* **flut′ed, flut′ing** **1.** to sing, speak, etc. in a flutelike tone **2.** to play on the flute **3.** to make ornamental grooves (in)

flut·ing (flŏŏt′iŋ) *n.* **1.** a series of ornamental grooves, as in a column **2.** the act of one that flutes

flut·ist (-ist) *n.* a flute player; flautist

FLUTE

flut·ter (flut′ər) *vi.* [OE. *flotorian* < *flotian* < base of *fleotan* (see FLEET¹): see -ER (sense 4)] **1.** to flap the wings rapidly without flying or in a short flight **2.** to wave or vibrate rapidly and irregularly [a flag *fluttering* in the wind] **3.** to tremble; quiver **4.** to move about in a restless, fussy way —*vt.* **1.** to make flutter **2.** to excite or confuse —*n.* **1.** a fluttering movement; vibration **2.** a state of excitement or confusion —**flut′ter·er** *n.* —**flut′ter·y** *adj*

flutter kick a swimming kick in which the legs are moved up and down in short, rapid, steady strokes

flut·y (flo̅o̅t′ē) *adj.* **flut′i·er, flut′i·est** flutelike in tone; soft, clear, and high-pitched

flu·vi·al (flo̅o̅′vē əl) *adj.* [< L. < *fluvius*, a river < *fluere*, to flow] of, found in, or produced by a river

flux (fluks) *n.* [OFr. < L. *fluxus* < pp. of *fluere*, to flow] **1.** a flowing or flow **2.** a coming in of the tide **3.** continual change [fashion is always in a state of *flux*] **4.** any abnormal discharge of fluid matter from the body **5.** *a)* a substance used to help fuse metals together, as in soldering *b)* a substance used, as in smelting, to fuse with undesired matter in forming a more fluid slag **6.** *Physics* the rate of flow of energy, fluids, etc. over a surface —*vt.* **1.** to make fluid **2.** to fuse (metals)

fly¹ (flī) *vi.* **flew, flown, fly′ing** [OE. *fleogan:* for IE. base see FLOW] **1.** to move through the air by using wings, as a bird **2.** to travel through the air in an aircraft **3.** to be propelled through the air or through space, as a missile **4.** to operate an aircraft **5.** to wave or float in the air, as a flag or kite **6.** to move or go swiftly [the door *flew* open; time *flies*] **7.** to run away from danger or evil; flee ☆**8. flied, fly′ing** *Baseball* to hit a fly —*vt.* **1.** *a)* to cause to float in the air [to *fly* a kite] *b)* to display (a flag) as from a pole **2.** to operate (an aircraft) **3.** to travel over in an aircraft **4.** to carry in an aircraft **5.** to flee from or avoid —*n., pl.* **flies 1.** a flap concealing the zipper, buttons, etc. in a garment, esp. such a flap in the front of a pair of trousers **2.** a flap serving as a tent door **3.** the length of a flag from the staff outward **4.** *same as: a)* FLYWHEEL *b)* FLYLEAF ☆**5.** *Baseball* a ball batted high in the air, esp. within the foul lines **6.** [*pl.*] *Theater* the space behind and above the proscenium arch —**fly at** to attack by or as by springing toward —**fly out** *Baseball* to be put out by hitting a fly that is caught —**let fly (at) 1.** to shoot or throw (at) **2.** to direct a verbal attack (at) —**on the fly 1.** while in flight **2.** [Colloq.] while in a hurry

fly² (flī) *n., pl.* **flies** [OE. *fleoge:* see FLY¹] **1.** *a) same as* HOUSEFLY *b)* any of a large group of insects with two transparent wings, as the housefly and gnat *c)* any of several four-winged insects, as the mayfly **2.** a hooked lure for fishing, made to resemble an insect

fly agaric [orig. used as a fly poison] a poisonous mushroom, usually having an orange or russet cap

fly ash airborne bits of unburnable ash

fly·blown (-blōn′) *adj.* **1.** full of flies' eggs or larvae **2.** spoiled; tainted **3.** [Colloq.] shabby; dingy

☆**fly·by, fly-by** (-bī′) *n., pl.* **-bys′** a flight past a given point by an aircraft or spacecraft

fly-by-night (-bī nīt′) *adj.* not trustworthy; esp., financially unreliable —*n.* a fly-by-night person; esp., a debtor who runs away from his debts

fly·cast (-kast′) *vi.* **-cast′, -cast′ing** to fish by casting artificial flies, using a lightweight, flexible rod (**fly rod**)

fly·catch·er (-kach′ər) *n.* any of various small birds, as the pewee, that catch insects in flight

fly·er (-ər) *n. same as* FLIER

fly·ing (-iŋ) *adj.* **1.** that flies or can fly **2.** moving as if flying; moving swiftly; fast **3.** hasty and brief [a *flying* trip to the store] **4.** of or for aircraft or aviators **5.** organized to act quickly, as in an emergency [a *flying* squad] —*n.* the action of one that flies

flying boat an airplane with a hull that permits it to land on and take off from water

flying bridge a small structure over the main bridge of a ship, for use in navigating

flying buttress a buttress connected with a wall by an arch, serving to resist outward pressure

flying colors 1. flags flying in the air **2.** notable victory or success [he passed the test with *flying* colors]

flying fish any of a number of chiefly warm-water sea fishes with winglike pectoral fins by means of which the fish glide through the air

flying gurnard a marine fish with winglike pectoral fins for gliding short distances in the air

flying jib a small, triangular sail in front of the jib

☆**flying saucer** *same as* UFO

☆**flying squirrel** any of a number of squirrels with winglike folds of skin attached to the legs and body that enable them to make gliding leaps

fly·leaf (flī′lēf′) *n., pl.* **-leaves′** (-lēvz′) a blank leaf at the beginning or end of a book

fly·pa·per (-pā′pər) *n.* a sticky or poisonous paper set out to catch or kill flies

fly·speck (-spek′) *n.* **1.** a speck of fly excrement **2.** any tiny spot —*vt.* to make flyspecks on

fly·trap (-trap′) *n.* **1.** any device for catching flies **2.** a plant that catches insects

☆**fly·way** (-wā′) *n.* a flying route taken regularly by migratory birds

fly·weight (-wāt′) *n.* a boxer who weighs 112 pounds or less —*adj.* of flyweights

fly·wheel (-hwēl′) *n.* a heavy wheel attached to a machine so as to regulate its speed and motion

Fm *Chem.* fermium

FM frequency modulation

fm. **1.** fathom **2.** from

f-num·ber (ef′num′bər) *n. Photog.* the ratio of a lens diameter to its focal length: the lower the f-number, the shorter the exposure required

FLYING
BUTTRESS

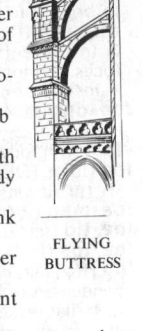

FLYING SQUIRREL
(head & body to 23 in.;
tail to 25 in.)

foal (fōl) *n.* [OE. *fola:* for IE. base see FEW] a young horse, mule, donkey, etc.; colt or filly —*vt., vi.* to give birth to (a foal)

foam (fōm) *n.* [OE. *fam*] **1.** the whitish mass of bubbles formed on or in liquids by agitation, fermentation, etc. **2.** something like foam, as frothy saliva **3.** a spongy cellular mass made by spreading gas bubbles in liquid rubber, plastic, etc. —*vi.* to produce foam; froth —*vt.* to cause to foam —**foam at the mouth** to be very angry; rage —**foam′less** *adj.*

foam rubber rubber made in the form of firm sponge, used in seats, mattresses, etc.

foam·y (fōm′ē) *adj.* **foam′i·er, foam′i·est 1.** foaming or covered with foam **2.** of or like foam —**foam′i·ly** *adv.* —**foam′i·ness** *n.*

fob¹ (fäb) *n.* [prob. < dial. G. *fuppe*, a pocket] **1.** a watch pocket in the front of a man's trousers ☆**2.** a short ribbon or chain hanging from a watch in such a pocket, often with an ornament at the end ☆**3.** such an ornament

fob² (fäb) *vt.* **fobbed, fob′bing** [< ME. *fobben*, to cheat] [Obs.] to cheat or deceive —**fob off 1.** to trick or put off (a person) with lies, excuses, something inferior, etc. **2.** to get rid of (something worthless or inferior) by deceit or trickery

F.O.B., f.o.b. free on board

fo·cal (fō′k'l) *adj.* of or at a focus —**fo′cal·ly** *adv.*

fo·cal·ize (fō′kə līz′) *vt., vi.* **-ized′, -iz′ing** to adjust or come to a focus —**fo′cal·i·za′tion** *n.*

focal length the distance from the optical center of a lens to the point where the light rays converge; length of the focus: also **focal distance**

Foch (fôsh), **Fer·di·nand** (fer dē nän′) 1851–1929; Fr. marshal; commander in chief of Allied forces (1918)

fo·c's·le (fōk′s'l) *n. phonetic spelling of* FORECASTLE

fo·cus (fō′kəs) *n., pl.* **fo′cus·es, fo·ci** (-sī) [ModL. < L., hearth] **1.** the point where rays of light, heat, etc. or waves of sound come together, or from which they spread or seem to spread; specif., the point where rays of light reflected by a mirror or refracted by a lens meet **2.** *same as* FOCAL LENGTH **3.** an adjustment of the focal length to make a clear image [to bring a

FISHING FLIES

camera into *focus*] **4.** any center of activity, attention, etc. **5.** a part of the body where an infection is most active **6.** *Math. a)* either of the two fixed points used in determining an ellipse: see illustration at ELLIPSE *b)* any similar point for a parabola or hyperbola —*vt.* **-cused** or **-cussed, -cus·ing** or **-cus·sing** **1.** to bring into focus [*to focus* light rays] **2.** to adjust the focal length of (the eye, a lens, etc.) so as to make a clear image **3.** to concentrate [*to focus* one's attention] —*vi.* to come to a focus —**in focus** clear; distinct —**out of focus** indistinct; blurred —**fo′cus·er** *n.*

fod·der (fäd′ər) *n.* [OE. *fodor* < *foda*, FOOD] coarse food for cattle, horses, etc., such as cornstalks, hay, and straw —*vt.* to feed with fodder

foe (fō) *n.* [OE. *fah*, hostile: for IE. base see FEUD[1]] *same as* ENEMY (in all senses) —see SYN. at OPPONENT

foe·man (fō′mən) *n., pl.* **-men** [Archaic] a foe

foe·tid (fet′id, fēt′-) *adj. same as* FETID

foe·tus (fēt′əs) *n. same as* FETUS —**foe′tal** *adj.*

fog (fôg, fäg) *n.* [prob. < Scand.] **1.** a large mass of water vapor condensed to fine particles, just above the earth's surface; thick mist that makes it hard to see **2.** a similar mass of smoke, dust, etc. in the air **3.** a vaporized liquid, as insecticide, widely spread **4.** a state of mental confusion **5.** a blur on a photograph or film —*vi.* **fogged, fog′ging** **1.** to become covered by fog **2.** to be or become blurred or dimmed —*vt.* **1.** to cover with fog **2.** to blur or dim **3.** to confuse

fog bank a dense mass of fog

fog·gy (fôg′ē, fäg′ē) *adj.* **-gi·er, -gi·est** **1.** full of fog; misty [a *foggy* night] **2.** dim; blurred **3.** confused; perplexed [a *foggy* idea] —**fog′gi·ly** *adv.* —**fog′gi·ness** *n.*

fog·horn (-hôrn′) *n.* a horn blown to give warning to ships in a fog

fo·gy (fō′gē) *n., pl.* **-gies** [< ?] a person who is old-fashioned or highly conservative: also **fo′gey,** *pl.* **-geys** —**fo′gy·ish** *adj.* —**fo′gy·ism** *n.*

foi·ble (foi′b'l) *n.* [obs. form of Fr. *faible*, FEEBLE] a small weakness in a person's character; frailty —see SYN. at FAULT

foil[1] (foil) *vt.* [< OFr. *fuler*, to trample on] to keep from being successful; thwart; frustrate [his evil plans were *foiled* again]

foil[2] (foil) *n.* [< OFr. < VL. < L. *folium:* see FOLIATE] **1.** a leaf-like, rounded space or design, as in windows, etc. in Gothic architecture **2.** a very thin sheet, leaf, or coating of metal **3.** a thin leaf of polished metal put under an inferior or artificial gem to give it brilliance **4.** a person or thing that makes another seem better by contrast [his dull answers served as a *foil* for her wit] **5.** [etym. unc.] *a)* a long, thin fencing sword with a button on the point to prevent injury *b)* [*pl.*] the art or sport of fencing with foils

FENCING FOIL

foist (foist) *vt.* [prob. < dial. Du. *vuisten*, to hide in the hand < *vuist*, a fist] to get (a thing) accepted by fraud, deception, etc.; palm off (with *on* or *upon*) [to *foist* a faulty product on the public]

Fo·kine (fô kēn′), **Mi·chel** (mē shel′) 1880–1942; U.S. choreographer, born in Russia

fol. **1.** folio **2.** following

fold[1] (fōld) *vt.* [OE. *faldan* < IE. base *pel-*, to fold] **1.** to bend or press (something) so that one part is over another [to *fold* the letter before mailing] **2.** to draw together and intertwine [to *fold* the arms] **3.** to draw (wings) close to the body **4.** to clasp in the arms; embrace [she *folded* the baby in her arms] **5.** to wrap up; envelop [he brought his lunch *folded* in a newspaper] —*vi.* **1.** to be or become folded ☆**2.** [Colloq.] *a)* to be forced to close, as a business *b)* to give up; fail suddenly [the team *folded* under pressure] —*n.* **1.** a folded part or layer **2.** a mark, hollow, or crease made by folding **3.** *Geol.* a rock layer folded by pressure —**fold in** *Cooking* to blend (an ingredient) into a mixture, using gentle, cutting strokes

fold[2] (fōld) *n.* [OE. *fald*] **1.** a pen in which to keep sheep **2.** a flock of sheep **3.** a group or organization with common aims, faith, etc., as a church —*vt.* to keep or confine in a pen

-fold (fōld) [OE. *-feald:* see FOLD[1]] *a suffix meaning:* **1.** having (a specified number of) parts [a *tenfold* division] **2.** (a specified number of) times as many or as much [to be repaid *fivefold*]

☆**fold·a·way** (fōld′ə wā′) *adj.* that can be folded for easy storage [a *foldaway* cot]

fold·boat (fōld′bōt′) *n.* a lightweight, collapsible, folding kayak

fold·er (fōl′dər) *n.* **1.** a person or thing that folds **2.** a sheet of heavy paper folded as a holder for papers ☆**3.** an unstitched, folded booklet

fol·de·rol (fäl′də räl′, fôl′də rôl′) *n. same as* FALDERAL

folding door a door with hinged leaves or accordion pleats that can be folded back

☆**folding money** [Colloq.] *same as* PAPER MONEY

fo·li·a·ceous (fō′lē ā′shəs) *adj.* [< L. < *folium:* see FOLIATE] **1.** of or like the leaf of a plant **2.** having leaves **3.** consisting of thin layers

fo·li·age (fō′lē ij) *n.* [< OFr. < VL. *folia* < L. *folium:* see FOLIATE] **1.** leaves, as of a plant or tree **2.** a decoration consisting of a representation of leaves, branches, flowers, etc.

fo·li·ate (fō′lē āt′; *for adj., usually* -it) *vt.* **-at′ed, -at′ing** [L. *foliatus*, leafy < *folium*, a leaf: for IE. base see BLOOM] to divide into thin layers **1.** to separate into layers **2.** to send out leaves —*adj.* having or covered with leaves

fo·li·a·tion (fō′lē ā′shən) *n.* **1.** a growing of or developing into a leaf or leaves **2.** the state of being in leaf **3.** the way leaves are arranged in the bud **4.** the act of beating metal into layers **5.** a leaflike decoration

fo·lic acid (fō′lik) [< L. *folium*, a leaf + -IC] a crystalline substance, $C_{19}H_{19}N_7O_6$, one of the vitamin B group, found in green leaves, etc. and used esp. in treating certain anemias

fo·li·o (fō′lē ō′) *n., pl.* **-li·os′** [L., abl. of *folium:* see FOLIATE] **1.** a large sheet of paper folded once, so that it forms two leaves, or four pages, of a book, etc. **2.** a book (the largest regular size), now often 12 by 15 inches, made of sheets so folded **3.** a leaf of a book, etc. numbered on only one side **4.** the number of a page in a book, etc. —*adj.* of the size of a folio —**in folio** in the form of a folio

folk (fōk) *n., pl.* **folk, folks** [OE. *folc:* for IE. base see FULL[1]] **1.** *a)* a people; nation; ethnic group *b)* the common people of such a group: with *the* **2.** [*pl.*] people or persons [the farmer disliked city *folk; folks* differ in their taste] —*adj.* of or having to do with the common people [*folk* music] —(one's) **folks** [Colloq.] (one's) family, esp. one's parents

folk dance **1.** a traditional dance of the common people of a country **2.** music for this

folk etymology the change that occurs in the form of a word that makes it seem as though the word has a connection with some other well-known word, as *cold slaw* used for *coleslaw*

folk·lore (fōk′lôr′) *n.* **1.** the traditional beliefs, legends, sayings, customs, etc. of a people **2.** the study of these —**folk′lor′ic** *adj.* —**folk′lor′ist** *n.*

folk medicine the treatment of disease, including the use of herbs, as practiced by the common people over many years

folk music music made and handed down among the common people

☆**folk-rock** (-räk′) *n.* music with a rock-and-roll beat combined with words in a folk-song style

folk song **1.** a song made and handed down among the common people **2.** a song composed in imitation of such a song —**folk singer**

☆**folk·sy** (-sē) *adj.* **-si·er, -si·est** [Colloq.] friendly or sociable in a simple and direct manner; now sometimes used to suggest that this manner is not genuine —**folk′si·ly** *adv.* —**folk′si·ness** *n.*

folk tale (or **story**) a story or legend made and handed down orally among the common people

☆**folk·way** (-wā′) *n.* any way of thinking, behaving, etc. characteristic of a certain social group

fol·li·cle (fäl′i k'l) *n.* [ModL. *folliculus* < L., a small bag, dim. of *follis*, bellows: for IE. base see BALL[1]] **1.** *Anat.* any small sac or cavity, as the pit from which a hair grows or the sac formed by certain glands **2.** *Bot.* a dry, one-celled seed capsule, opening along one side, as a milkweed pod —**fol·li·cu·lar** (fə lik′yoo lər) *adj.* —**fol·lic′u·late** (-lit, -lāt′), **fol·lic′u·lat′ed** *adj.*

fol·low (fäl′ō) *vt.* [< OE. *folgian*] **1.** to come or go after [we *followed* the usher] **2.** to chase; pursue [*follow* that car!] **3.** to go along [*follow* the road] **4.** to come after in time, in a series, etc. [spring *follows* winter] **5.** to take the place of in rank, position, etc. [Monroe *followed* Madison as President] **6.** to take up; engage in (a trade, etc.) **7.** to result from [famine *followed* the droughts] **8.** to take as a model; imitate [these dresses *follow* the Paris fashions] **9.** to accept the authority of; obey [*follow* the rules] **10.** to listen to, watch, or observe closely [he *follows* sports on TV] **11.** to understand the sense or logic of [I can't *follow* your reasoning] —*vi.* **1.** to come, go, or happen after something else in place, sequence, or time **2.** to result —**as follows** as will next be told or explained —**follow out**

to carry out fully —**follow through** to continue and complete a stroke or action —**follow up** 1. to follow closely and persistently 2. to carry out fully 3. to make more effective by doing something more

SYN·—**follow** is the general word meaning to come or happen after, but it does not necessarily imply that what goes before is a cause [sunshine *followed* by rain]; **ensue** implies that what follows comes logically from what preceded [dark clouds appeared and rain *ensued*]; **result** stresses a definite relationship of cause and effect between what follows and what preceded [superstition *results* from ignorance]—**ANT. precede**

fol·low·er (fäl′ə wər) *n.* one that follows; specif., a) a person who follows another's belief or teachings; disciple b) a servant or attendant

SYN·—**follower** is the general term for one who follows or believes in the teachings or theories of someone [a *follower* of Freud]; **supporter** applies to one who upholds or defends opinions or theories that are disputed or under attack [a *supporter* of socialized medicine]; **adherent** refers to a close, active follower of some cause or leader [the *adherents* of a political party]; **disciple** implies a personal, devoted relationship to the teacher of some doctrine or leader of some movement [Plato was a *disciple* of Socrates]

fol·low·ing (fäl′ə wiŋ) *adj.* 1. that follows; next after 2. moving in the same direction that a ship is moving, as the wind —*n.* a group of followers or adherents —*prep.* after [*following* dinner she went home] —**the following** 1. the one or ones to be mentioned immediately 2. what follows

fol·low-through (fäl′ō thrōō′) *n.* 1. the act or manner of continuing the swing or stroke of a club, racket, etc. after striking or releasing the ball, etc. 2. the completing of an undertaking

fol·low-up (-up′) *adj.* following as a review, addition, etc. [a *follow-up* letter] —*n.* 1. a follow-up thing or event 2. a following up, as with follow-up letters, visits, etc.

fol·ly (fäl′ē) *n.,* pl. **-lies** [< OFr. < *fol:* see FOOL] 1. a lack of sense or sensible conduct; foolishness 2. any foolish action or belief 3. any foolish and expensive undertaking

☆**Fol·som man** (fäl′səm, fōl′-) [< *Folsom,* village in NE N.Mex.] a member of a people believed to have lived in N. America at the time of the last glacial age

fo·ment (fō ment′) *vt.* [< OFr. < LL. *fomentare* < L. < *fovere,* to keep warm] 1. to treat with warm water, medicated lotions, etc. 2. to stir up; incite [to *foment* a riot] —see **SYN.** at INCITE — **fo′men·ta′tion** *n.*

fond (fänd) *adj.* [< ME. *fonned,* pp. of *fonnen,* to be foolish] 1. [Now Rare] foolishly naive or hopeful 2. tender and affectionate; loving or doting [*fond* parents; *fond* words] 3. greatly cherished [a *fond* hope] —**fond of** having a liking for —**fond′ly** *adv.* —**fond′ness** *n.*

fon·dant (fän′dənt) *n.* [Fr. < prp. of *fondre,* to melt] a soft, creamy candy made of sugar, used esp. as a filling for other candies

fon·dle (fän′d'l) *vt.* **-dled, -dling** [< obs. verb *fond* (< FOND) + -LE²] to stroke lovingly; caress —**fon′dler** *n.*

fon·due, fon·du (fän dōō′, fän′dōō) *n.* [Fr. < pp. of *fondre,* to melt] 1. cheese melted in wine, used as a dip for cubes of bread 2. any of various similar dishes, as one in which cubes of meat are dipped in hot oil for cooking 3. cheese soufflé with bread crumbs

font¹ (fänt) *n.* [OE. < L. *fons,* FOUNTAIN] 1. a bowl to hold the water used in baptismal services 2. a basin for holy water; stoup 3. [Poet.] a fountain or spring 4. any source; origin — **font′al** *adj.*

font² (fänt) *n.* [Fr. *fonte* < OFr. *fondre:* see FOUND³] *Printing* a complete assortment of type in one size and style

fon·ta·nel, fon·ta·nelle (fän′tə nel′) *n.* [ME. *fontinel,* a hollow < OFr. dim. of *fontaine,* FOUNTAIN] any of the soft, boneless areas in the skull of a baby, later closed over when bone forms

FONTANELS

food (fōōd) *n.* [OE. *foda* < IE. base *pa-,* to feed] 1. any substance taken into and assimilated by a plant or animal to keep up its life and growth; nourishment 2. solid substances of this sort: distinguished from *drink* 3. a specified kind of food 4. anything that nourishes or stimulates [*food* for thought] —*adj.* 1. of or having to do with food 2. used as food [a *food* fish]

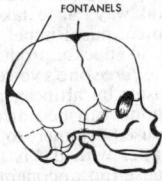

food chain a sequence of organisms in an ecological community in which each member feeds on the one below, as rabbits feed on grass, foxes on rabbits, etc.

food cycle all the individual food chains in an ecological community: also **food web**

food poisoning 1. sickness from eating food contaminated by bacteria 2. poisoning from naturally poisonous foods, as certain mushrooms, or from chemical contaminants in food

☆**food stamp** any of the Federal stamps used in place of cash by unemployed or low-income persons for buying food

food·stuff (-stuf′) *n.* any material made into or used as food

fool (fōōl) *n.* [< OFr. *fol* < LL. < L. *follis,* windbag: see FOLLICLE] 1. a silly person; simpleton 2. a man formerly kept by a nobleman or king to entertain as a clown; jester 3. a victim of a trick; dupe —*adj.* [Colloq.] foolish —*vi.* 1. to act like a fool; be silly 2. to joke 3. [Colloq.] to meddle or toy (*with*) —*vt.* to trick; deceive; dupe —**be no** (or **nobody's) fool** to be shrewd and capable —☆**fool around** [Colloq.] to trifle —**fool away** [Colloq.] to squander —**play the fool** to clown

fool·er·y (fōōl′ər ē) *n.,* pl. **-er·ies** foolish action

fool·har·dy (-här′dē) *adj.* **-di·er, -di·est** foolishly daring; rash —**fool′har′di·ly** *adv.* —**fool′har′di·ness** *n.*

fool·ish (-ish) *adj.* 1. without good sense; silly; unwise 2. a) absurd b) abashed; embarrassed —see **SYN.** at ABSURD —**fool′ish·ly** *adv.* —**fool′ish·ness** *n.*

☆**fool·proof** (-prōōf′) *adj.* so harmless, simple, or indestructible as not to be damaged, misunderstood, etc. even by a fool

fools·cap (fōōlz′kap′) *n.* 1. [from former watermark] a size of writing paper: in the U.S., 13 by 16 inches 2. *same as* FOOL'S CAP

fool's cap a jester's cap with bells

☆**fool's gold** iron pyrites or copper pyrites, like gold in color

fool's paradise a state of happiness or feeling of security that is not justified by the actual conditions

foot (foot) *n.,* pl. **feet:** see also sense 6 [OE. *fot* < IE. base *ped-, pod-,* foot] 1. the end part of the leg, on which a person or animal stands or moves 2. the base or bottom [the *foot* of a page] 3. the last of a series 4. the end, as of a bed, toward which the feet are directed 5. the part of a stocking, etc. covering the foot 6. a measure of length, equal to 12 inches (an average length of the human foot): symbol, ′ (e.g., 10′): abbrev. **ft.** (sing. & pl.): pl. often **foot** following a number [a six-*foot* man] 7. [Brit.] infantry 8. a group of syllables serving as a unit of meter in verse —*vi.* 1. to dance 2. to walk —*vt.* 1. to walk, dance, or run on, over, or through 2. to make the foot of (a stocking, etc.) 3. to add (a column of figures) and set down a total ☆4. [Colloq.] to pay (costs, etc.) [to *foot* the bill] —**foot it** [Colloq.] to dance, walk, or run —**of foot** in walking or running [swift *of foot*] —**on foot** 1. walking or running 2. in process —**put one's best foot forward** [Colloq.] 1. to do one's best 2. to try to appear at one's best —**put one's foot down** [Colloq.] to be firm; act decisively —**put one's foot in it** (or **in one's mouth**) [Colloq.] to make an embarrassing blunder —**under foot** 1. on the floor, etc. 2. in the way

foot·age (foot′ij) *n.* ☆length expressed in feet, as of motion-picture film [square *footage* gives the number of square feet of an area]

foot-and-mouth disease (foot′′n mouth′) an acute, contagious disease of cattle, deer, etc. causing fever and also blisters in the mouth and around the hoofs

foot·ball (foot′bôl′) *n.* [ME. *foteballe*] 1. any of several field games played with an inflated leather ball by two teams, the object being to get the ball across the opponents' goal: in U.S. & Canadian football, the players may kick, throw, or run with the ball, and may run ahead of it for interference, forward passes, etc.: see also SOCCER, RUGBY 2. the oval or (for soccer) round ball used in playing these games

foot·board (-bôrd′) *n.* 1. a board for supporting the feet or for standing on 2. a vertical piece across the foot of a bed

foot brake a brake worked by pressure of the foot

foot·bridge (-brij′) *n.* a narrow bridge for pedestrians

foot·can·dle (-kan′d'l) *n.* a unit for measuring illumination: it is equal to the amount of direct light thrown by one candle (*n.* 3) on a square foot of surface one foot away

foot·ed (-id) *adj.* having a foot or feet, esp. of a specified number or kind [four-*footed*]

-foot·er (-ər) *a combining form meaning* a person or thing (a specified number of) feet tall, high, long, etc. [six-*footer*]

foot·fall (-fôl´) *n.* the sound of a footstep

foot·gear (-gir´) *n.* covering for the feet; shoes, boots, etc.

☆**foot·hill** (-hil´) *n.* a low hill at or near the foot of a mountain or mountain range

foot·hold (-hōld´) *n.* **1.** a place to put a foot down securely, as in climbing **2.** a secure position from which one cannot easily be moved

foot·ie, foot·y (-ē) *n., pl.* **foot´ies** same as FOOTSIE

foot·ing (-iŋ) *n.* **1.** a secure placing of the feet [to lose one's *footing*] **2.** *a)* the condition of a surface for walking, running, etc. [poor *footing* after the rain] *b)* a secure place to put the feet [there's no *footing* on that ice] **3.** a secure position or basis [to put business on a sound *footing*] **4.** a basis for relationship [a friendly *footing*] **5.** *a)* the adding of a column of figures *b)* the sum obtained **6.** a projecting base under a column, wall, etc.: also **foot´er**

foot·less (-lis) *adj.* **1.** without a foot or feet **2.** without basis or substance **3.** [Colloq.] clumsy; inept

foot·lights (-līts´) *n.pl.* a row of lights along the front of a stage at the actors' foot level —**the footlights** the theater, or acting as a profession

☆**foot·lock·er** (-läk´ər) *n.* a small trunk for the belongings of a soldier, camper, etc. usually kept at the foot of one's bed

foot·loose (-lōōs´) *adj.* ☆free to go wherever one likes or do as one likes

foot·man (-mən) *n., pl.* **-men** a male servant who assists the butler in a household

foot·note (-nōt´) *n.* a note of comment or reference at the bottom of a page —*vt.* **-not´ed, -not´ing** to add such a note or notes to

foot·pad (-pad´) *n.* [see PAD³] a highway robber or holdup man who travels on foot

foot·path (-path´) *n.* a narrow path for pedestrians

foot-pound (-pound´) *n.* a unit of energy, equal to the amount of energy required to raise a weight of one pound a distance of one foot

foot-pound-sec·ond (-pound´sek´ənd) *adj.* designating or of a system of measurement using the foot, pound, and second as the units of length, mass, and time, respectively

foot·print (foot´print´) *n.* a mark left by a foot: also **foot´mark´** (-märk´)

foot·race (-rās´) *n.* a race run on foot

foot·rest (-rest´) *n.* a support to rest the feet on

☆**foot·sie, foot·sy** (-sē) *n., pl.* **-sies** the foot: a child's term —**play footsie (with)** [Colloq.] **1.** to touch feet or legs (with) in a caressing way, as under the table **2.** to flirt (with) or have secret dealings (with)

foot soldier a soldier on foot; infantryman

foot·sore (-sôr´) *adj.* having sore or tender feet, as from much walking

foot·step (-step´) *n.* **1.** the distance covered in a step **2.** the sound of a step; footfall **3.** a footprint **4.** a step on which to go up or down —**follow in (someone's) footsteps** to follow (someone's) example, vocation, etc.

foot·stool (-stōōl´) *n.* a low stool for supporting the feet of a seated person

☆**foot·wear** (-wer´) *n.* shoes, boots, slippers, etc.

foot·work (-wurk´) *n.* the act or manner of moving the feet, as in walking, boxing, dancing, etc.

fop (fäp) *n.* [ME. *foppe*, a fool, prob. < MDu. or MLowG.] a vain, affected man who pays too much attention to his clothes, appearance, etc.; dandy —**fop´per·y** *n., pl.* **-per·ies** —**fop´pish** *adj.* —**fop´pish·ly** *adv.* —**fop´pish·ness** *n.*

for (fôr; *unstressed* fər) *prep.* [OE.: for IE. base see FAR] **1.** in place of [to use coats *for* blankets] **2.** in the interest of [his agent acted *for* him] **3.** in defense of; in favor of [to fight *for* a cause; to vote *for* a levy] **4.** in honor of [to give a banquet *for* a notable] **5.** with the aim or purpose of [to carry a gun *for* protection] **6.** with the purpose of going to [to leave *for* home] **7.** in order to be, become, get, have, keep, etc. [to walk *for* exercise] **8.** in search of [looking *for* berries] **9.** meant to be received by a specified person or thing, or to be used in a specified way [flowers *for* a girl, money *for* paying bills] **10.** suitable to [a room *for* sleeping] **11.** with regard to [need *for* improvement, an ear *for* music] **12.** as being [to know *for* a fact] **13.** considering the nature of [cool *for* July] **14.** because of [to cry *for* pain] **15.** in spite of [stupid *for* all her learning] **16.** in proportion to [a dollar tax *for* every four earned] **17.** to the amount of [a bill *for* $50] **18.** at the price of [sold *for* $10]

19. to the length, duration, etc. of; throughout [to work *for* an hour] **20.** at (a specified time) [a date *for* two o'clock] —*conj.* because; seeing that [comfort him, *for* he is sad] —**for (one) to** that (one) will, should, must, etc. [a book *for* you *to* read] —**O!** **for** I wish that I had

for- [OE., replacing *fer-*] *an Old English and Middle English prefix meaning:* **1.** away, apart, off, etc. [forbid, forget, forgo] **2.** very much [forlorn]

for·age (fôr´ij, fär´-) *n.* [< OFr. < Frank. *fodr*, FOOD] **1.** food for domestic animals; fodder **2.** a search for food or provisions —*vi.* **-aged, -ag·ing** **1.** to search for food or provisions **2.** to search for what one needs or wants —*vt.* **1.** to get or take food or provisions from **2.** to provide with forage; feed **3.** to get by foraging —**for´ag·er** *n.*

fo·ra·men (fô rā´mən, fə-) *n., pl.* **-ram·i·na** (-ram´ə nə), **-ra´mens** [L. < *forare*, to bore] a small opening, esp. in a bone or in a plant ovule —**fo·ram´i·nal** (-ram´ə n´l), **fo·ram´i·nate** (-nit) *adj.*

foramen mag·num (mag´nəm) [ModL., large opening] the opening at the base of the skull through which the spinal cord passes to become the medulla oblongata

for·a·min·i·fer (fôr´ə min´ə fər, fär´-) *n., pl.* **fo·ram·i·nif·er·a** (fə ram´ə nif´ər ə) [< L. *foramen*: see prec. & -FER] any of a group of small, one-celled sea animals with calcareous shells full of tiny holes through which slender filaments project —**fo·ram´i·nif´er·al, fo·ram´i·nif´er·ous** *adj.*

for·as·much (fôr´əz much´) *conj.* inasmuch (as)

for·ay (fôr´ā) *vt., vi.* [< OFr. < *forrer*, to FORAGE] to raid for spoils; plunder —*n.* a sudden attack or raid, as for spoils

☆**forb** (fôrb) *n.* [Gr. *phorbē*, fodder < *pherbein*, to feed] any broad-leaved plant in a field, etc., as distinguished from the grasses

for·bade, for·bad (fər bad´, fôr-) *pt. of* FORBID

for·bear¹ (fôr ber´, fər-) *vt.* **-bore´** or archaic **-bare´, -borne´, -bear´ing** [< OE.: see FOR- & BEAR¹] to refrain from; avoid (doing, saying, etc.) —*vi.* **1.** to refrain or abstain **2.** to control oneself —see SYN. at REFRAIN¹ —**for·bear´er** *n.* —**for·bear´ing·ly** *adv.*

for·bear² (fôr´ber´) *n.* same as FOREBEAR

for·bear·ance (fôr ber´əns, fər-) *n.* **1.** the act of forbearing **2.** self-control; patience

for·bid (fər bid´, fôr-) *vt.* **-bade´** or **-bad´, -bid´den** or archaic **-bid´, -bid´ding** [< OE.: see FOR- & BID] **1.** to rule against; prohibit **2.** to command to stay away from; bar from **3.** to make impossible; prevent —**for·bid´dance** *n.* —**for·bid´den** *adj.*

for·bid·ding (-iŋ) *adj.* looking dangerous, threatening, or disagreeable; repellent —**for·bid´ding·ly** *adv.*

for·bore (fôr bôr´, fər-) *pt. of* FORBEAR¹

for·borne (-bôrn´) *pp. of* FORBEAR¹

force (fôrs) *n.* [OFr. < LL. < L. *fortis*: see FORT] **1.** strength; energy; power **2.** the intensity of power; impetus [the *force* of a blow] **3.** physical power or strength used against a person or thing **4.** *a)* the power to control, persuade, etc.; effectiveness [the *force* of logic; the *force* of threats] *b)* a person or thing having influence, power, etc. [a *force* for good] **5.** *a)* military, naval, or air power *b)* [pl.] the collective armed strength, as of a nation *c)* any organized group of soldiers, sailors, etc. **6.** any group of people organized for some activity [a sales *force*] **7.** *Law* binding power; validity **8.** *Physics* the cause, or agent, that puts an object at rest into motion or changes the motion of a moving object —*vt.* **forced, forc´ing** **1.** to cause to do something by force; compel **2.** to rape (a woman) **3.** *a)* to break open, into, or through by force *b)* to overpower or capture in this way **4.** to take by force; wrest; extort **5.** to drive as by force; push; impel **6.** to impose as by force (with *on* or *upon*) **7.** to effect or produce as by force [to *force* a smile] **8.** to strain [to *force* one's voice] **9.** to cause (plants, fruit, etc.) to develop faster by artificial means ☆**10.** *Baseball* *a)* to cause (a base runner) to be put out by a force-out: said of a batter *b)* to cause (a runner) to score or (a run) to be scored by walking the batter with the bases full (often with *in*) **11.** *Card Games* to cause (an opponent) to play (a particular card) or (one's partner) to make (a particular bid) —**in force** **1.** in full strength **2.** in effect; valid —**force´a·ble** *adj.* —**force´less** *adj.* —**forc´er** *n.*

SYN.—**force** implies the use of power in causing a person or thing to act, move, or give in and may refer to physical strength or to anything that causes something to happen [circumstances *forced* him to lie]; **compel** implies a driving, in a way that cannot be resisted, to some action, condition, etc. [*compelled* by his conscience]; **to coerce** is to compel someone to submit or obey by using or threatening to use one's power; **constrain** implies a force that restricts and therefore suggests a strained or unnatural quality in that which results *[constrained* to agree; a *constrained* laugh*]*

forced (fôrst) *adj.* **1.** done or brought about by force; compulsory *[forced* labor*]* **2.** produced by unusual effort; strained *[a forced* smile*]* **3.** due to an emergency *[a forced* landing*]* **4.** at a pace faster than usual *[a forced* march*]* —**forc·ed·ly** (fôr′sid lē) *adv.*

force-feed (fôrs′fēd′) *vt.* **-fed′, -feed′ing** to feed as by a tube through the throat to the stomach

force·ful (-fəl) *adj.* full of force; powerful, vigorous, effective, etc. —**force′ful·ly** *adv.* —**force′ful·ness** *n.*

force·meat (-mēt′) *n.* *[< farce meat < farce* (obs.), to stuff*]* meat chopped up and seasoned, usually for stuffing

☆**force-out** (-out′) *n. Baseball* an out that results when a base runner is forced from a base by a teammate's hit and fails to reach the next base before the ball does

for·ceps (fôr′səps) *n., pl.* **for′ceps** *[L., orig., smith's tongs < formus,* hot *+ capere,* to take*]* small tongs or pincers for grasping and pulling, used esp. by surgeons and dentists

force pump a pump with a valveless plunger for forcing a liquid through a pipe under pressure

for·ci·ble (fôr′sə b'l) *adj.* **1.** done or effected by force *[a forcible* entry*]* **2.** having force; forceful *[forcible* arguments*]* —**for′ci·ble·ness** *n.* —**for′ci·bly** *adv.*

FORCEPS
(A, fine bent;
B, scissors)

ford (fôrd) *n.* *[OE.]* a shallow place in a stream, river, etc., that can be crossed by wading, on horseback, in a car, etc. —*vt.* to cross (a stream) in this way —**ford′a·ble** *adj.*

Ford (fôrd), **1. Gerald R(udolph)**, 1913– ; 38th president of the U.S. (1974–77) **2. Henry** 1863–1947; U.S. automobile manufacturer

for·do (fôr dōō′) *vt.* **-did′, -done′, -do′ing** *[see* FOR- & DO[1]*]* [Archaic] **1.** to destroy, kill, or ruin **2.** to tire out; exhaust: only in the past participle Also sp. **fore·do′**

fore (fôr) *adv.* *[OE.:* see FAR*]* at, in, or toward the front: now only of a ship —*adj.* situated in front —*n.* the front thing or part —*interj. Golf* a shout warning those ahead that one is about to hit the ball —**to the fore 1.** to the front; into view **2.** available **3.** still active

'fore (fôr) *prep.* [Poet.] before

fore- *[OE.:* see FORE*]* a prefix meaning: **1.** before in time, place, order, or rank *[forenoon, foreman]* **2.** the front part of *[forearm]*

fore-and-aft (fôr′n aft′) *adj. Naut.* from the bow to the stern of a ship; lengthwise or set lengthwise, as sails

fore and aft 1. from the bow to the stern of a ship; lengthwise *[sails* rigged *fore and aft]* **2.** at, in, or toward both the bow and the stern

fore·arm[1] (fôr′ärm′) *n.* the part of the arm between the elbow and the wrist

fore·arm[2] (fôr ärm′) *vt.* to arm in advance; get ready for trouble before it comes

fore·bear (fôr′ber′) *n.* *[< FORE + BE + -ER]* an ancestor

fore·bode (fôr bōd′) *vt., vi.* **-bod′ed, -bod′ing** *[< OE.:* see FORE- & BODE[1]*]* **1.** to be an omen or warning of; portend (esp. something bad or harmful *[the heavy spring rains *forebode* floods*]* **2.** to have a premonition of (something bad about to happen) —see SYN. at FORETELL —**fore·bod′er** *n.*

fore·bod·ing (-bōd′iŋ) *n.* *[see* FOREBODE*]* a warning or a feeling that something bad is about to happen —*adj.* characterized by foreboding —see SYN. at OMINOUS —**fore·bod′ing·ly** *adv.*

fore·brain (fôr′brān′) *n.* the front part of the brain of a vertebrate embryo, or the parts developed from this, including the cerebrum

fore·cast (fôr′kast′; *for v., also occas.* fôr kast′) *vt.* **-cast′** or **-cast′ed, -cast′ing 1.** to estimate in advance; predict (weather, etc.) **2.** to serve as a prediction or prophecy of —*vi.* to make a forecast —*n.* a prediction —see SYN. at FORETELL — **fore′cast′er** *n.*

fore·cas·tle (fōk′s'l; fôr′kas′l *is a sp. pronun.*) *n.* *[FORE + CASTLE:* from the foremost of the two raised structures called

"castles" on early sailing ships*]* **1.** the upper deck of a ship in front of the foremast **2.** the front part of a merchant ship, where the sailors' quarters are located

fore·close (fôr klōz′) *vt.* **-closed′, -clos′ing** *[< OFr. pp. of forclore,* to exclude *< fors,* outside *+ clore,* CLOSE[2]*]* **1.** to shut out; exclude; bar **2.** to take away the right to redeem (a mortgage, etc.) when regular payments have not been kept up —*vi.* to foreclose a mortgage, etc. —**fore·clos′a·ble** *adj.* —**fore·clo′sure** (-klō′zhər) *n.*

fore·court (fôr′kôrt′) *n.* ☆**1.** *Basketball* the half of the court which contains the basket a given team is attempting to score in **2.** *Tennis* the part of the court nearest the net

fore·doom (fôr dōōm′) *vt.* to doom in advance; condemn beforehand

fore·fa·ther (fôr′fä′thər) *n.* an ancestor

fore·fin·ger (-fiŋ′gər) *n.* the finger nearest the thumb; index finger; first finger

fore·foot (-fŏŏt′) *n., pl.* **-feet** either of the front feet of an animal with four or more feet

fore·front (-frunt′) *n.* **1.** the part at the very front **2.** the position of most activity, importance, etc.

fore·gath·er (fôr gath′ər) *vi.* same as FORGATHER

fore·go[1] (fôr gō′) *vt., vi.* **-went′, -gone′, -go′ing** *[OE. foregan]* to go before in place, time, or degree; precede

fore·go[2] (fôr gō′) *vt.* same as FORGO

fore·go·ing (fôr′gō′iŋ) *adj.* previously said, written, etc. —see SYN. at PREVIOUS —**the foregoing 1.** the one or ones just mentioned **2.** what has already been said or written

fore·gone (fôr gôn′) *adj.* **1.** that has gone before; previous **2.** that is inevitable or not to be avoided *[it is a *foregone* conclusion thats he will win*]*

fore·ground (fôr′ground′) *n.* **1.** the part of a scene, picture, etc. nearest the viewer **2.** the most noticeable or conspicuous position

fore·hand (-hand′) *n.* a kind of stroke, as in tennis, made with the arm extended and the palm of the hand turned forward —*adj.* done as or with a forehand —*adv.* with a forehand

fore·hand·ed (fôr han′did) *adj.* **1.** providing for the future; thrifty; prudent **2.** same as FOREHAND —**fore·hand′ed·ly** *adv.* —**fore·hand′ed·ness** *n.*

fore·head (fôr′id, fär′-; fôr′hed, fär′-) *n.* **1.** the part of the face between the eyebrows and the hairline **2.** the front part of anything

FOREHAND
STROKE

for·eign (fôr′in, fär′-) *adj.* *[< OFr. forain < LL. < L. foras,* out-of-doors: for IE. base see DOOR*]* **1.** situated outside one's own country, locality, etc. **2.** of, from, or characteristic of another country *[a foreign* language*]* **3.** concerning the relations of one country to another *[foreign* affairs*]* **4.** *a)* not a natural or usual part *[a trait *foreign* to one's nature*] b)* not pertinent *[facts *foreign* to the subject under discussion*]* **5.** not normally belonging *[foreign* matter in the eye*]* —see SYN. at EXTRINSIC

for·eign-born (-bôrn′) *adj.* born in some other country —**the foreign-born** immigrants of a country

foreign correspondent a journalist who reports events from a foreign country

for·eign·er (-ər) *n.* a person from another country, thought of as an outsider; alien

foreign exchange 1. the settling of accounts or debts between residents of different countries **2.** foreign currency, bills, etc., used to settle such accounts

foreign legion a military force made up mainly of volunteers from foreign countries; esp., [F- L-] such a French force, orig. based in North Africa

foreign minister a member of a governmental cabinet in charge of foreign affairs for his country

foreign office in some countries, the office of government in charge of foreign affairs

fore·know (fôr nō′) *vt.* **-knew′, -known′, -know′ing** to know beforehand —**fore·know′a·ble** *adj.* —**fore·knowl·edge** (fôr′näl′ij) *n.*

☆**fore·la·dy** (fôr′lā′dē) *n., pl.* **-dies** *same as* FOREWOMAN

fore·land (fôr′land) *n.* a headland; promontory

fore·leg (-leg′) *n.* either of the front legs of an animal with four or more legs

fore·limb (-lim′) *n.* a front limb, as an arm, foreleg, wing, or flipper

fore·lock (-läk′) *n.* a lock of hair growing just above the forehead

fore·man (-mən) *n., pl.* **-men** [orig., foremost man, leader] **1.** the chairman of a jury **2.** a man in charge of a department or group of workers in a factory, etc. —**fore′man·ship′** *n.*

fore·mast (fôr′mast′, -məst) *n.* the mast nearest the bow of a ship

fore·most (-mōst′) *adj.* [< OE. superl. of *forma*, superl. of *fore*, FORE] **1.** first in place or time **2.** first in rank or importance —*adv.* first

fore·named (-nāmd′) *adj.* named or mentioned before

fore·noon (fôr′nōōn′) *n.* the time from sunrise to noon; morning —*adj.* of or in the forenoon

fo·ren·sic (fə ren′sik) *adj.* [< L. *forensis*, public < *forum*, marketplace] of, characteristic of, or suitable for a law court, public debate, or formal argument —*n.* [*pl.*] debate or formal argumentation —**fo·ren′si·cal·ly** *adv.*

forensic medicine *same as* MEDICAL JURISPRUDENCE

fore·or·dain (fôr′ôr dān′) *vt.* to ordain or determine beforehand; predestine —**fore′or·di·na′tion** (-d′n ā′shən) *n.*

fore·part (fôr′pärt′) *n.* **1.** the first or early part **2.** the part in front

fore·paw (fôr′pô′) *n.* an animal's front paw

fore·play (-plā′) *n.* sexual stimulation that leads to sexual intercourse

fore·quar·ter (-kwôr′tər) *n.* **1.** the front half of a side of beef or the like **2.** [*pl.*] the front quarters of a horse, etc., including the forelegs

fore·run·ner (fôr′run′ər, fôr run′ər) *n.* **1.** a messenger sent before or going before; herald **2.** a sign that tells or warns of something to follow **3.** *a)* a predecessor *b)* an ancestor

fore·sail (fôr′sāl′, -səl) *n.* **1.** the lowest sail on the foremast of a square-rigged ship **2.** the main triangular sail on the foremast of a fore-and-aft-rigged ship, as a schooner

fore·see (fôr sē′) *vt.* **-saw′, -seen′, -see′ing** to see or know beforehand [to *foresee* the future] —**fore·see′a·ble** *adj.* —**fore·se′er** *n.*

fore·shad·ow (-shad′ō) *vt.* to be a sign of (something to come) —**fore·shad′ow·er** *n.*

fore·shank (fôr′shaŋk′) *n.* **1.** the upper part of the front legs of cattle **2.** meat from this part

fore·sheet (-shēt′) *n.* **1.** one of the ropes used to trim a foresail **2.** [*pl.*] the space forward in an open boat

fore·shock (-shäk′) *n.* a minor earthquake preceding a greater one at or near the same place

fore·shore (-shôr′) *n.* the part of a shore between high-water mark and low-water mark

fore·short·en (fôr shôr′t′n) *vt.* to shorten some of the lines in (something drawn, painted, etc.) so as to lend perspective and make some parts seem farther from the eye than others

fore·show (-shō′) *vt.* **-showed′, -shown′** or **-showed′, -show′ing** to show or indicate beforehand

fore·sight (fôr′sīt′) *n.* **1.** *a)* a foreseeing *b)* the power to foresee **2.** a looking forward **3.** a looking ahead and planning for the future —**fore′sight′ed** *adj.* —**fore′sight′ed·ly** *adv.* —**fore′sight′ed·ness** *n.*

fore·skin (fôr′skin′) *n.* the fold of skin that covers the end of the penis and is removed in circumcision; prepuce

FORESHORTENED ARM

for·est (fôr′ist, fär′-) *n.* [OFr. < ML. (*silva*) *forestis*, as if (wood) unenclosed (< L. *foris*, out-of-doors), but prob. (wood) under court control (< L. *forum*, court)] a thick growth of trees and underbrush covering a large area of land; large woods —*adj.* of or in a forest —*vt.* to cover with trees or woods —**for′est·ed** *adj.*

fore·stall (fôr stôl′) *vt.* [OE. *foresteall*, ambush: see FORE & STALL[2]] **1.** to prevent by doing something ahead of time [to *forestall* an argument by changing the subject] **2.** to act in advance of; anticipate —see SYN. at PREVENT —**fore·stall′er** *n.* —**fore·stall′ment** *n.*

☆**for·est·a·tion** (fôr′is tā′shən, fär′-) *n.* the planting or care of forests

fore·stay (fôr′stā′) *n.* a rope or cable reaching from the head of a ship's foremast to the bowsprit, for supporting the foremast

for·est·er (fôr′is tər, fär′-) *n.* **1.** a person whose work is taking care of forests, fighting forest fires, etc. **2.** a person or animal that lives in a forest

for·est·ry (-trē) *n.* **1.** [Rare] forest land **2.** the science of planting and taking care of forests **3.** systematic forest management for the production of timber, conservation, etc.

fore·taste (fôr′tāst′; *for v.* fôr tāst′) *n.* a taste or sample of what can be expected [difficult courses in school gave Dick a *foretaste* of college] —*vt.* **-tast′ed, -tast′ing** [Rare] to taste beforehand

fore·tell (fôr tel′) *vt.* **-told′, -tell′ing** to tell or show beforehand; predict —**fore·tell′er** *n.*

SYN.—**foretell** is the general term for a telling or showing what will take place in the future; **predict** suggests a reasoning out of a future event from facts or data already known [the Chaldeans could *predict* eclipses]; **forecast** implies an estimating of the probable course or future condition of something [to *forecast* the weather, economic trends, etc.]; **prophesy** suggests prediction by one who claims to be inspired by God or to have mystic power [to *prophesy* the end of the world]; to **prognosticate** is to foretell by the study of signs or symptoms [to *prognosticate* a depression]; **presage** and **forebode** are more often used of things than of persons, **presage** referring to either favorable or unfavorable events [the red sky *presages* a fair day], and **forebode** to unfavorable events [his grim face *forebodes* refusal]

fore·thought (fôr′thôt′) *n.* **1.** a thinking or planning ahead of time **2.** prudent thought for the future; foresight —**fore′-thought′ful** *adj.* —**fore′thought′ful·ly** *adv.*

fore·to·ken (fôr′tō′kən; *for v.* fôr tō′kən) *n.* a prophetic sign; omen —*vt.* to foreshadow

fore·top (fôr′täp′, -təp) *n.* the platform at the top of a ship's foremast

fore-top·gal·lant (fôr′täp gal′ənt, fôr′tə-) *adj.* designating or of the mast, sail, yard, etc. just above the fore-topmast

fore-top·mast (fôr täp′mast′, -məst) *n.* the section of mast extending above the foremast

fore-top·sail (-sāl′, -s′l) *n.* a sail set on the fore-topmast, above the foresail

for·ev·er (fər ev′ər, fôr-) *adv.* **1.** for eternity; for always; endlessly **2.** at all times; always Also **for·ev′er·more′** (-môr′)

fore·warn (fôr wôrn′) *vt.* to warn ahead of time ["forewarned is forearmed"]

fore·went (-went′) *pt. of* FOREGO[1]

fore·wing (fôr′wiŋ′) *n.* either of the front pair of wings in most insects

fore·wom·an (-woom′ən) *n., pl.* **-wom′en** a woman serving as a foreman

fore·word (-wurd′, -wərd) *n.* a piece of writing at the beginning of a book that tells something about it; introduction or preface —see SYN. at INTRODUCTION

for·feit (fôr′fit) *n.* [< OFr. < *forfaire*, to transgress, ult. < L. *foris*, beyond + *facere*, to do] **1.** something that one has to give up because of some crime, fault, or neglect of duty; specif., a fine or penalty **2.** *a)* a thing taken away as a penalty for making some mistake in a game, and redeemable by a specified action *b)* [*pl.*] any game in which such forfeits are taken **3.** the act of forfeiting —*adj.* lost or taken away as a forfeit —*vt.* to lose or give up as a forfeit [to *forfeit* bail for not appearing at a trial] —**for′feit·a·ble** *adj.* —**for′feit·er** *n.*

for·fei·ture (fôr′fə chər) *n.* **1.** a forfeiting **2.** anything forfeited; penalty or fine

for·gath·er (fôr gath′ər) *vi.* **1.** to come together; meet; assemble **2.** to meet by chance

for·gave (fər gāv′, fôr-) *pt. of* FORGIVE

forge[1] (fôrj) *n.* [< OFr. < L. *fabrica*, workshop < *faber*, workman] **1.** a furnace for heating metal to be wrought **2.** a place where metal is heated and hammered or wrought into shape; smithy **3.** a place where wrought iron is made, as from iron ore —*vt.* **forged, forg′ing** **1.** to shape (metal) on a forge by heating and pounding **2.** to make (something) by or as by this method; form; shape; produce [to *forge* an alliance] **3.** to imitate for purposes of deception or fraud; esp., to imitate (another's signature) in signing (a check, etc.) —*vi.* **1.** to work at a forge **2.** to commit forgery —**forg′er** *n.*

forge[2] (fôrj) *vi.* **forged, forg′ing** [prob. altered < FORCE] **1.** to move forward steadily, as if against difficulties [to *forge* ahead through the snow] **2.** to move in a sudden spurt [to *forge* into the lead]

for·ger·y (fôr′jər ē) *n., pl.* **-ger·ies** **1.** the act or legal offense of forging documents, signatures, works of art, etc. to deceive **2.** anything forged

for·get (fər get′, fôr-) *vt.* **-got′** or archaic **-gat′** (-gat′), **-got′ten** or **-got′**, **-get′ting** [OE. *forgietan:* see FOR- & GET] **1.** to lose (facts, etc.) from the mind; be unable to remember **2.** to fail to do, bring, etc. without meaning to; neglect [*to forget* to lock the door; *to forget* one's keys] **3.** to overlook or ignore [*let's forget* our differences] *—vi.* to forget things **—forget it** don't trouble to think about it **—forget oneself 1.** to think only of others **2.** to behave in an improper or unseemly manner **—for·get′ta·ble** *adj.* **—for·get′ter** *n.*

for·get·ful (-f'l) *adj.* **1.** apt to forget; having a poor memory **2.** heedless or negligent **3.** [Poet.] causing to forget [a *forgetful* sleep] **—for·get′ful·ly** *adv.* **—for·get′ful·ness** *n.*

for·get-me-not (-mē nät′) *n.* a low-growing plant with clusters of small blue, white, or pink flowers

for·give (fər giv′, fôr-) *vt.* **-gave′**, **-giv′en**, **-giv′ing** [OE. *forgiefan:* see FOR- & GIVE] **1.** to give up being angry with or wanting to punish; pardon [she *forgave* him for his rudeness] **2.** to excuse or overlook (an offense) **3.** to cancel (a debt) *—vi.* to show forgiveness —see SYN. at ABSOLVE **—for·giv′a·ble** *adj.* **—for·giv′er** *n.*

for·give·ness (-nis) *n.* **1.** a forgiving; pardon **2.** a being ready to forgive

for·giv·ing (-iŋ) *adj.* that forgives; willing or ready to forgive **—for·giv′ing·ly** *adv.* **—for·giv′ing·ness** *n.*

for·go (fôr gō′) *vt.* **-went′**, **-gone′**, **-go′ing** [OE. *forgan*] to do without; abstain from **—for·go′er** *n.*

for·got (fər gät′, fôr-) *pt. & alt. pp.* of FORGET

for·got·ten (-'n) *pp.* of FORGET

for·int (fôr′int) *n.* [Hung.] *see* MONETARY UNITS, table (Hungary)

fork (fôrk) *n.* [OE. *forca* & Anglo-Fr. *forque,* both < L. *furca,* hayfork] **1.** an instrument with a handle and two or more prongs, used as an eating utensil or, in much larger form, for pitching hay, etc. **2.** something resembling a fork in shape: see TUNING FORK **3.** a division into branches; bifurcation ☆**4.** the point where a river, road, etc. is divided into branches **5.** any of these branches *—vi.* to divide into branches *—vt.* **1.** to make into the form of a fork **2.** to pick up, spear, or pitch with a fork **—☆fork over** (or **out, up**) [Colloq.] to pay out; hand over **— fork′ful′** *n., pl.* **-fuls′**

forked (fôrkt) *adj.* **1.** having a fork or forks; divided into branches [*forked* lightning] **2.** having prongs [*five-forked*]

☆**forked tongue** [prob. transl. of AmInd. expression] lying or deceitful talk [to speak with a *forked tongue*]

☆**fork·lift** (fôrk′lift′) *n.* a device, often on a truck (**forklift truck**), for lifting, stacking, etc. heavy objects: its projecting prongs are slid under the load and raised or lowered

for·lorn (fər lôrn′, fôr-) *adj.* [< OE. pp. of *forleosan,* to lose utterly: see FOR- & LOSE] **1.** abandoned or deserted **2.** wretched; miserable; pitiful **3.** without hope; desperate **4.** bereft (*of*) **—for·lorn′ly** *adv.* **—for·lorn′ness** *n.*

form (fôrm) *n.* [< OFr. < L. *forma*] **1.** the shape, outline, or configuration of anything; structure **2.** *a)* the body or figure of a person or animal *b)* a model of a human figure used as a clothes dummy **3.**

FORKLIFT TRUCK

anything used to give shape to something else; mold, as for poured concrete **4.** the mode of existence a thing has or takes [water in the *form* of vapor] **5.** arrangement; esp., orderly arrangement, often of a specified kind **6.** a way of doing something [one's golf *form*] **7.** a customary way of acting or behaving; ceremony; formality **8.** a fixed order of words; formula **9.** a printed document with blank spaces to be filled in [an application *form*] **10.** a particular kind, type, species, or variety [a *form* of plant life] **11.** a condition of mind or body [a boxer in good *form*] **12.** *a)* a chart giving information about horses in a race *b)* what can be expected, based on past performances [to react according to *form*] **13.** a long, wooden bench, as formerly in a schoolroom **14.** a grade or class in some private schools and in British secondary schools **15.** *Gram.* any of the different appearances of a word in changes of inflection, spelling, etc. [''am'' is a *form* of ''be''] **16.** *same as* LINGUISTIC FORM **17.** *Printing* the type, plates, etc. locked in a frame for printing *—vt.* **1.** to shape; fashion; make, as in some particular way **2.** to train [to *form* a child's character] **3.** to develop (habits) **4.** to think of; conceive **5.** to organize into [to *form* a club] **6.** to make up out of separate parts [the U.S. is *formed* of 50 States] *—vi.* **1.** to be formed **2.** to come into being; take form **3.** to take a specific form —see SYN. at MAKE **—good** (or **bad**) **form** conduct that is in (or not in) accord with social custom

-form (fôrm) [< OFr. < L. *-formis < forma,* form] a suffix meaning: **1.** having the form of [*cuneiform*] **2.** having (a specified number of) forms [*multiform*]

for·mal (fôr′məl) *adj.* [L. *formalis*] **1.** of external form or structure, rather than nature or content **2.** according to fixed customs, rules, etc. **3.** *a)* appearing to be suitable, correct, etc. but not really so *b)* stiff in manner **4.** *a)* designed for wear at ceremonies, etc. [*formal* dress] *b)* requiring such clothes [a *formal* dance] **5.** done or made in orderly, regular fashion; methodical **6.** rigidly symmetrical [a *formal* garden] **7.** done or made according to the forms that make explicit, definite, etc. [a *formal* contract] **8.** designating education in schools, colleges, etc. **9.** designating or of that form of English usage, chiefly in writing, in which the rules of traditional grammar are observed, complex sentences and vocabulary are used, etc.: distinguished from COLLOQUIAL *—n.* **1.** a formal dance or ball **2.** a woman's evening dress **—go formal** [Colloq.] to go dressed in evening clothes **—for′mal·ly** *adv.*

form·al·de·hyde (fôr mal′də hīd′, fər-) *n.* [FORM(IC) + ALDEHYDE] a colorless, pungent gas, HCHO, used in solution as a disinfectant and preservative

for·mal·ism (fôr′məl iz'm) *n.* strict attention to outward forms and customs, as in art or religion **—for′mal·ist** *n., adj.* **—for′mal·is′tic** *adj.*

for·mal·i·ty (fôr mal′ə tē) *n., pl.* **-ties 1.** a being formal; specif., *a)* the following of established customs, rules, ceremonies, etc.; propriety *b)* careful or too careful attention to order, regularity, or convention; stiffness **2.** a formal or conventional act or requirement; ceremony or form

for·mal·ize (fôr′mə līz′) *vt.* **-ized′**, **-iz′ing 1.** to give definite form to **2.** to make formal **3.** to make official, valid, etc. **—for′mal·i·za′tion** *n.*

for·mat (fôr′mat) *n.* [G. < L. pp. of *formare,* to form] **1.** the shape, size, and general makeup of a book, magazine, etc. **2.** general arrangement, as of a television program

for·ma·tion (fôr mā′shən) *n.* **1.** a forming or being formed **2.** a thing formed **3.** the way in which something is formed or arranged; structure **4.** an arrangement or positioning, as of troops, ships, airplanes, a football team, etc. **5.** *Geol.* a large body of rocks having some common character, as origin, composition, etc.

form·a·tive (fôr′mə tiv) *adj.* **1.** helping to shape, develop, or mold [a *formative* influence] **2.** of formation or development [one's *formative* years] **3.** *Linguis.* serving to form words, as an affix

form class *Linguis.* a class made up of words having a distinctive position in constructions and certain formal features in common, as the form class *noun* in English, made up of all words to which both the plural and possessive suffixes may be added

for·mer¹ (fôr′mər) *adj.* [ME. *formere,* compar. of *forme,* first < OE. *forma:* see FOREMOST] **1.** preceding in time; earlier; past [in *former* times; a *former* mayor] **2.** first mentioned of two: opposed to LATTER: often used as a noun (with *the*) —see SYN. at PREVIOUS

form·er² (fôr′mər) *n.* a person or thing that forms

for·mer·ly (fôr′mər lē) *adv.* at or in a former or earlier time; in the past [Iran, *formerly* called Persia]

for·mic (fôr′mik) *adj.* [< L. *formica,* an ant] **1.** of ants **2.** designating or of a colorless acid, HCOOH, found in ants, spiders, nettles, etc.

☆**For·mi·ca** (fôr mīk′ə) [arbitrary coinage] *a trademark for* a laminated, heat-resistant plastic used for table tops, etc.

for·mi·da·ble (fôr′mi də b'l) *adj.* [OFr. < L. < *formidare,* to dread] **1.** causing fear or dread **2.** hard to handle or overcome [a *formidable* task] **3.** awe-inspiring in size, excellence, etc. [a *formidable* vocabulary] **—for′mi·da·bil′i·ty, for′mi·da·ble·ness** *n.* **—for′mi·da·bly** *adv.*

---

fat, āpe, cär; ten, ēven; is, bīte; gō, hôrn, tōōl, look; oil, out; up, fur; get; joy; yet; chin; she; thin, *th*en; zh, leisure; ŋ, ring; ə for *a* in *ago, e* in *agent, i* in *sanity, o* in *comply, u* in *focus*; ' as in *able* (ā′b'l); Fr. bal; ë, Fr. coeur; ö, Fr. feu; Fr. mon; ô, Fr. coq; ü, Fr. duc; r, Fr. cri; H, G. ich; kh, G. doch; ‡foreign; ☆ Americanism; < derived from. See inside front cover.

form·less (fôrm′lis) *adj.* having no regular form or plan —**form′less·ly** *adv.* —**form′less·ness** *n.*

☆**form letter** one of a number of duplicated letters, with the date, address, etc. filled in separately

For·mo·sa (fôr mō′sə, -zə) *former (Portuguese)* name of TAIWAN —**For·mo′san** *adj., n.*

for·mu·la (fôr′myə lə) *n., pl.* **-las, -lae′** (-lē′) [L., dim. of *forma*, form] **1.** a fixed form of words, esp. one that is used only as a conventional expression, with its real meaning or force nearly lost [*"Very truly yours" is a formula used in letters*] **2.** a rule or method for doing something, esp. when conventional and used or repeated without thought [*a formula for crime novels*] **3.** an exact statement of religious faith or doctrine **4.** *a*) a prescription for a medicine, a baby's food, etc. *b*) something prepared from a prescription; often specif., a milk preparation for feeding a baby **5.** a set of symbols and figures expressing a mathematical fact, rule, etc. [*A = πr² is the formula for finding the area of a circle*] **6.** *Chem.* an expression of the composition of a compound by a group of symbols and figures [*H₂SO₄ is the formula for sulfuric acid*]

for·mu·lar·ize (-lə rīz′) *vt.* **-ized′, -iz′ing** *same as* FORMULATE (sense 1)

for·mu·lar·y (fôr′myə ler′ē) *n., pl.* **-lar′ies 1.** a collection of formulas or prescribed forms, as of prayers **2.** a formula **3.** *Pharmacy* a list of medicines with their formulas —*adj.* of formulas

for·mu·late (-lāt′) *vt.* **-lat′ed, -lat′ing 1.** to express in or reduce to a formula **2.** to express (a theory, plan, etc.) in a systematic way —**for′mu·la′tion** *n.* —**for′mu·la′tor** *n.*

for·mu·lize (-līz′) *vt.* **-lized′, -liz′ing** *same as* FORMULATE (sense 1)

for·ni·cate (fôr′nə kāt′) *vi.* **-cat′ed, -cat′ing** [< LL. pp. of *fornicari* < L. *fornix* (gen. *fornicis*), a brothel] to commit fornication —**for′ni·ca′tor** *n.*

for·ni·ca·tion (fôr′nə kā′shən) *n.* **1.** voluntary sexual intercourse between an unmarried woman and a man, esp. an unmarried man **2.** *Bible* any unlawful sexual intercourse

for·sake (fər sāk′, fôr-) *vt.* **-sook′** (-sook′), **-sak′en, -sak′ing** [< OE. < *for-*, FOR- + *sacan*, to strive < *sacu*: see SAKE¹] **1.** to give up or renounce (a habit, idea, etc.) **2.** to leave; abandon —see SYN. at ABANDON

for·sak·en (-sā′kən) *adj.* abandoned; desolate

for·sooth (fər sooth′, fôr-) *adv.* [OE. *forsoth*] [Archaic] in truth; no doubt; indeed

For·ster (fôr′stər), **E(dward) M(organ)** 1879–1970; Eng. novelist

for·swear (fôr swer′) *vt.* **-swore′** (-swôr′), **-sworn′, -swear′ing 1.** to swear or promise earnestly to give up **2.** to deny earnestly or on oath —*vi.* to swear falsely; commit perjury —**forswear oneself** to perjure oneself

for·syth·i·a (fər sith′ē ə, fôr-) *n.* [ModL., after W. *Forsyth*, 18th-c. Eng. botanist] a shrub of the olive family with yellow, bell-shaped flowers, which appear in early spring before the leaves

fort (fôrt) *n.* [OFr. < L. *fortis*, strong: for IE. base see BOROUGH] **1.** a fortified place or building for military defense ☆**2.** a permanent army post —☆**hold the fort 1.** to make a defensive stand **2.** [Colloq.] to keep things in operation; stay on duty, etc.

For·ta·le·za (fôr′tə lā′zə) seaport in NE Brazil, on the Atlantic: pop. 515,000

Fort-de-France (fôr də fräns′) seaport & capital of Martinique, in the West Indies: pop. 99,000

forte¹ (fôrt) *n.* [< OFr.: see FORT.] that which one does particularly well; one's strong point

for·te² (fôr′tā, -tē) *adj., adv.* [It. < L. *fortis*, strong] *Music* loud: a direction to the performer —*n.* a forte note or passage

Forth (fôrth) river in SE Scotland, flowing through a long estuary (**Firth of Forth**) into the North Sea

forth (fôrth) *adv.* [OE.] **1.** forward; onward [*from that day forth*] **2.** out into view, notice, etc. [*to come forth from dwelling places; to put forth shoots*] —**and so forth** and so on: equivalent to *etc.*

forth·com·ing (fôrth′kum′iŋ) *adj.* **1.** about to appear; approaching [*the author's forthcoming novel*] **2.** ready when needed [*help was not forthcoming*] —*n.* a coming forth; approach

forth·right (-rīt′) *adj.* frank and direct; not just hinted at [*forthright criticism*] —**forth′right·ly** *adv.* —**forth′right·ness** *n.*

forth·with (fôrth′with′, -with′) *adv.* immediately

for·ti·eth (fôr′tē ith) *adj.* **1.** coming after thirty-nine others in

a series; 40th **2.** designating any of the forty equal parts of something —*n.* **1.** the one following the thirty-ninth **2.** any of the forty equal parts of something; 1/40

for·ti·fi·ca·tion (fôr′tə fi kā′shən) *n.* **1.** the act or science of fortifying **2.** a fort or defensive earthwork, wall, etc. **3.** a fortified place

for·ti·fy (fôr′tə fī′) *vt.* **-fied′, -fy′ing** [< OFr. < LL. *fortificare* < L. *fortis*, strong (see FORT) + *facere*, to make, DO¹] **1.** to make strong or stronger; strengthen [*to fortify concrete with steel wire*] **2.** to strengthen against attack, as by building forts, walls, etc. **3.** *a*) to give support to [*to fortify an argument with many facts*] *b*) to give moral support to; encourage **4.** to strengthen (wine, etc.) by adding alcohol **5.** to add vitamins, minerals, etc. to (milk, etc.) so as to increase the food value —*vi.* to build military defenses —**for′ti·fi′a·ble** *adj.* —**for′ti·fi′er** *n.*

for·tis·si·mo (fôr tis′ə mō′) *adj., adv.* [It., superl. of *forte*, FORTE²] *Music* very loud: a direction to the performer —*n., pl.* **-mos′, -mi′** (-mē′) a fortissimo note or passage

for·ti·tude (fôr′tə tood′, -tyood′) *n.* [< L. < *fortis*: see FORT] the strength to bear misfortune, pain, etc. calmly and patiently; firm courage

Fort Knox [see KNOXVILLE] military reservation in N Ky., near Louisville: site of U.S. gold bullion depository

Fort La·my (fôr lä mē′) capital of Chad, in the SW part: pop. 86,000: also **Fort-Lamy**

Fort Lau·der·dale (lô′dər dāl′) [after Maj. Wm. *Lauderdale*] city on the SE coast of Fla.: pop. 140,000

Fort Mc·Hen·ry (mək hen′rē) [after J. *McHenry*, U.S. Secretary of War, 1796–1800] fort in Baltimore harbor, Md., where the British were repulsed in 1814

fort·night (fôrt′nīt′) *n.* [< OE., lit., fourteen nights] [Chiefly Brit.] two weeks

fort·night·ly (-lē) *adv., adj.* [Chiefly Brit.] (happening or appearing) once every fortnight, or at two-week intervals —*n., pl.* **-lies** a periodical issued at two-week intervals

☆**FORTRAN** (fôr′tran) *n.* [*for(mula) tran(slation)*] a digital computer language similar to algebra

for·tress (fôr′trəs) *n.* [< OFr., ult. < L. *fortis*: see FORT] a fortified place; fort: often used figuratively —*vt.* to protect by a fortress

Fort Smith [after Gen. T. *Smith*, d. 1865] city in W Ark., on the Arkansas River: pop. 63,000

for·tu·i·tous (fôr too′ə təs, -tyoo′-) *adj.* [< L. < *fortis*, genitive of *fors*, luck: for IE. base see BEAR¹] **1.** happening by chance; accidental [*a fortuitous meeting*] **2.** bringing, or happening by, good luck; fortunate —see SYN. at ACCIDENTAL —**for·tu′i·tous·ly** *adv.* —**for·tu′i·tous·ness** *n.*

for·tu·i·ty (-tē) *n., pl.* **-ties 1.** the fact of being fortuitous **2.** chance or an occurrence by chance

for·tu·nate (fôr′chə nit) *adj.* [< L. pp. of *fortunare* < *fortuna*, FORTUNE] **1.** having good luck; lucky **2.** bringing, or coming by, good luck; favorable —see SYN. at LUCKY —**for′tu·nate·ly** *adv.* —**for′tu·nate·ness** *n.*

for·tune (fôr′chən) *n.* [OFr. < L. *fortuna* < *fors*: see FORTUITOUS] **1.** the supposed power that brings good or bad to people; luck; chance; fate: often personified **2.** what happens to one; one's lot, esp. future lot, good or bad [*to tell one's fortune*] **3.** good luck; success **4.** wealth; riches

☆**fortune cookie** a hollow Chinese cookie with a slip of paper inside predicting the future

fortune hunter a person who tries to become rich, esp. by marrying a rich person

for·tune·tell·er (-tel′ər) *n.* a person who professes to foretell events in other people's lives —**for′tune·tell′ing** *n., adj.*

Fort Wayne [after Anthony WAYNE] city in NE Ind.: pop. 178,000

Fort Worth [after Wm. *Worth* (1794–1849)] city in N Tex.: pop. 393,000 (met. area 762,000)

for·ty (fôr′tē) *adj.* [OE. *feowertig*: see FOUR & -TY²] four times ten —*n., pl.* **-ties** the cardinal number between thirty-nine and forty-one; 40; XL —**the forties** the numbers or years, as of a century, from forty through forty-nine

☆**for·ty-nin·er** (fôr′tē nī′nər) *n.* [*also* F- N-] [Colloq.] one who went to California in the 1849 gold rush

forty winks [Colloq.] a short sleep; nap

fo·rum (fôr′əm) *n., pl.* **-rums, -ra** (-ə) [L., area out-of-doors: for IE. base see DOOR] **1.** the public square or marketplace of an

FORTUNE
COOKIE

ancient Roman city, where people met for legal and political business 2. a law court; tribunal 3. *a)* an assembly or program for the discussion of public matters *b)* an opportunity for open discussion *[the letters-to-the-editor section serves as a public forum]* —**the Forum** the forum of ancient Rome

for·ward (fôr′wərd) *adj.* [OE. *foreweard]* 1. at, toward, or of the front 2. advanced socially, politically, etc. 3. moving toward a point in front; onward; advancing *[the forward rush of the crowd]* 4. ready or eager; prompt *[he was forward in helping]* 5. too bold in manners; presumptuous *[her children are too forward with adults]* 6. of or for the future *[forward buying]* —*adv.* 1. toward the front; ahead *[move forward]* 2. toward the future *[to look forward]* 3. into view or prominence *[to bring forward an opinion]* —*n.* Basketball, Hockey, etc. any of the players in a front position —*vt.* 1. to help advance; promote *[she always tried to forward his interests]* 2. to send on, as to another address *[to forward mail]* —**for′ward·er** *n.* —**for′ward·ly** *adv.* —**for′ward·ness** *n.*

☆**forward pass** *Football* a pass from behind the line of scrimmage to a teammate in a forward position

for·wards (-wərdz) *adv.* same as FORWARD

for·went (fôr went′) *pt.* of FORGO

fos·sa (fäs′ə) *n.,* pl. **-sae** (-ē) [ModL. < L., a ditch: see BED] a cavity, pit, or small hollow in some part of the body —**fos′sate** (-āt) *adj.*

fosse, foss (fôs, fäs) *n.* [< OFr. < L. *fossa:* see FOSSA] a ditch or moat, esp. in fortifications

fos·sil (fäs′'l, fôs′-) *n.* [< Fr. < L. *fossilis,* dug up < pp. of *fodere,* to dig up: see BED] 1. any hardened remains or traces of plant or animal life of some previous geological age, preserved in the earth's crust 2. anything like a fossil 3. a person who has old-fashioned, fixed ideas —*adj.* 1. of, like, or forming a fossil 2. dug from the earth *[coal is a fossil fuel]* 3. belonging to the past; antiquated —**fos′sil·like′** *adj.*

fos·sil·if·er·ous (fäs′ə if′ər əs, fôs′-) *adj.* [< FOSSIL + -FEROUS] containing fossils

fos·sil·ize (fäs′ə līz′, fôs′-) *vt.* **-ized′, -iz′ing** 1. to change into a fossil; petrify 2. to make out of date, rigid, or incapable of change *[as time went on, his ideas became more and more fossilized]* —*vi.* to become fossilized —**fos′sil·i·za′tion** *n.*

fos·ter (fôs′tər, fäs′-) *vt.* [OE. *fostrian,* to nourish < base of *foda,* FOOD] 1. to bring up with care; rear 2. to help to develop; promote *[to foster discontent]* 3. to cling to in one's mind; cherish *[to foster a hope]* —*adj.* having the standing of a specified member of the family but not by birth or adoption *[a foster child; a foster sister]* —**fos′ter·er** *n.*

Fos·ter (fôs′tər, fäs′-), **Stephen Collins** 1826–64; U.S. composer of songs

foster home a home in which a child is raised by people other than the natural or adoptive parents

fought (fôt) *pt.* & *pp.* of FIGHT

foul (foul) *adj.* [OE. *ful* < IE. base *pu-,* to stink] 1. stinking; loathsome *[a foul odor]* 2. extremely dirty; disgustingly filthy *[a foul kitchen]* 3. full of dirt or foreign objects; clogged up *[a foul pipe]* 4. rotten: said of food 5. not decent; obscene *[foul language]* 6. wicked; abominable *[a foul crime]* 7. stormy; unfavorable *[foul weather]* 8. tangled; caught *[a foul rope]* 9. not according to the rules of a game; unfair *[a rabbit punch is a foul blow]* 10. treacherous; dishonest *[he gained success by foul means]* 11. [Colloq.] unpleasant, disagreeable, etc. *[we had a foul time at the party]* ☆12. *Baseball* not fair: see FOUL BALL, FOUL LINE 13. *Printing* marked to show errors or changes *[foul copy]* —*adv.* in a foul way —*n.* anything foul; specif., *a)* a collision of boats, contestants, etc. *b)* a breaking of rules, as of a game ☆*c) Baseball* same as FOUL BALL —*vt.* 1. to make foul; dirty; soil *[smoke that fouled the air]* 2. to dishonor or disgrace *[to foul a reputation]* 3. to block up; fill up *[grease fouls sink drains]* 4. to cover (a ship's bottom) with hindering growths, as barnacles 5. to entangle; catch *[a rope fouled in the shrouds]* 6. to collide with 7. to make a foul against, as in a game ☆8. *Baseball* to bat (the ball) so that it falls outside the foul lines —*vi.* 1. to be or become fouled (in various senses) 2. to break the rules of a game ☆3. *Baseball* to hit a foul ball — ☆**foul out** 1. *Baseball* to be put out by the catch of a foul ball 2. *Basketball* to be disqualified for a certain number of personal fouls —☆**foul up** [Colloq.] to make a mess of —**run** (or **fall** or **go**) **foul of** 1. to collide with and become tangled in 2. to get into trouble with —**foul′ly** *adv.* —**foul′ness** *n.*

fou·lard (foo lärd′) *n.* [Fr.] 1. a lightweight material of silk, rayon, or sometimes cotton, usually printed with a small design 2. a necktie, scarf, etc. of this material

☆**foul ball** *Baseball* a batted ball that is not a fair ball: see FAIR BALL

☆**foul line** 1. *Baseball* either of the lines extending from home plate through the outside corners of first base or third base and onward along the outfield 2. *Basketball* same as FREE-THROW LINE 3. *Tennis, Bowling,* etc. any of various lines bounding the playing area, beyond which the ball must not be hit, the player must not go, etc.

foul·mouthed (foul′mouthd′, -moutht′) *adj.* using obscene, indecent, or coarsely insulting language

foul play 1. unfair play; action that breaks the rules of the game 2. treacherous action or violence

found[1] (found) *pt.* & *pp.* of FIND

found[2] (found) *vt.* [< OFr. < L. < *fundus,* bottom: for IE. base see BOTTOM] 1. to set for support; base *[a statement founded on facts]* 2. to begin to organize; establish *[to found a college]*

found[3] (found) *vt.* [< OFr. < L. *fundere,* to pour < IE. base *gheu-]* 1. to melt and pour (metal) into a mold 2. to make by pouring molten metal into a mold; cast

foun·da·tion (foun dā′shən) *n.* 1. a founding or being founded; establishment 2. *a)* a fund or endowment to support a hospital, charity, research, etc. *b)* the organization that manages such a fund 3. the base on which something rests; specif., the supporting part of a wall, house, etc. 4. the basis on which an idea, belief, etc. rests *[he has no foundation for his accusation]* 5. a woman's corset or girdle: also ☆**foundation garment** —see SYN. at BASE[1] —**foun·da′tion·al** *adj.*

foun·der[1] (foun′dər) *vi.* [< OFr. < L. *fundus:* see FOUND[2]] 1. to stumble, fall, or go lame *[his horse foundered on the rocky slope]* 2. to become stuck as in soft ground 3. to fill with water and sink: said of a ship 4. to break down; collapse; fail —*vt.* to cause to founder

found·er[2] (foun′dər) *n.* a person who founds, or establishes

found·er[3] (foun′dər) *n.* a person who founds metals

found·ling (found′liŋ) *n.* a baby found abandoned by its parents, whose identity is not known

found·ry (foun′drē) *n.,* pl. **-ries** 1. the act or work of founding, or melting and molding, metals; casting 2. metal castings 3. a place where metal is cast

fount (fount) *n.* [< OFr. < L. *fons,* FOUNTAIN] 1. [Poet.] a fountain or spring 2. a source

foun·tain (foun′t'n) *n.* [< OFr. < LL. *fontana* < L. *fontis,* genitive of *fons,* spring] 1. a natural spring of water 2. a source or origin of anything *[a library is a fountain of knowledge]* 3. *a)* an artificial spring, jet, or flow of water *b)* the basin, pipes, etc. where this flows *c)* same as DRINKING FOUNTAIN *d)* same as SODA FOUNTAIN 4. a container or reservoir, as for ink, oil, etc.

foun·tain·head (-hed′) *n.* 1. a spring that is the source of a stream 2. the original or main source of anything

fountain pen a pen which is fed ink from a supply in a reservoir or cartridge

four (fôr) *adj.* [OE. *feower* < IE. base *kwetwer-]* totaling one more than three —*n.* 1. the cardinal number between three and five; 4; IV 2. anything having four units or members, or numbered four —**on all fours** 1. on all four feet 2. on hands and knees (or feet)

☆**four-bag·ger** (fôr′bag′ər) *n.* [Slang] same as HOME RUN

☆**four-flush** (fôr′flush′) *vi.* 1. *Stud Poker* to bluff when one holds four cards of the same suit (**four flush**) instead of the five in a true flush 2. [Colloq.] to pretend to be, have, or intend something in a way meant to deceive; bluff —**four′-flush′er** *n.*

four·fold (-fōld′) *adj.* [see -FOLD] 1. having four parts 2. having four times as much or as many —*adv.* four times as much or as many

four-foot·ed (-foot′id) *adj.* having four feet

☆**Four-H club, 4-H club** (fôr′āch′) [< its aim to improve the *head, hands, heart,* and *health]* a rural youth organization, sponsored by the U.S. Department of Agriculture, offering instruction in scientific agriculture and home economics

☆**four hundred** [also F- H-] the exclusive social set of a particular place (preceded by *the*)

Fou·rier (fōō ryā′) **1. Fran·çois Ma·rie Charles** (frän swä′má rē′ shärl) 1772–1837; Fr. socialist & reformer **2.** Baron **Jean Bap·tiste Jo·seph** (zhän bá tēst′ zhō zef′), 1768–1830; Fr. mathematician & physicist

four-in-hand (fôr′in hand′) **n. 1.** *a*) a team of four horses driven by one man *b*) a coach drawn by such a team ☆**2.** a necktie tied in the usual way, that is, in a slipknot with the ends left hanging —**adj.** of a four-in-hand

☆**four-letter word** (fôr′let′ər) any of several short words having to do with sex or body waste matter, generally thought of, esp. formerly, as objectionable or taboo

four-o'clock (-ə kläk′) **n.** a garden plant with tube-shaped flowers of various colors, that open in the late afternoon

four-post·er (-pōs′tər) **n.** a bedstead with tall corner posts often supporting a canopy or curtains

four·score (-skôr′) **adj., n.** four times twenty; eighty

four·some (-səm) **n.** a group of four people, as four people playing a round of golf together

four·square (-skwer′) **adj. 1.** perfectly square **2.** unyielding; firm **3.** frank; forthright [a *foursquare* answer] —**adv. 1.** in a square form **2.** forthrightly

four·teen (-tēn′) **adj.** [OE. *feowertyne*] four more than ten —**n.** the cardinal number between thirteen and fifteen; 14; XIV

four·teenth (-tēnth′) **adj. 1.** coming after thirteen others in a series; 14th **2.** designating any of the fourteen equal parts of something —**n. 1.** the one following the thirteenth **2.** any of the fourteen equal parts of something; 1/14

fourth (fôrth) **adj.** [OE. *feortha*] **1.** coming after three others in a series; 4th **2.** designating any of the four equal parts of something —**n. 1.** the one following the third **2.** any of the four equal parts of something; 1/4 **3.** the fourth forward gear ratio of a motor vehicle **4.** *Music a*) the fourth tone of an ascending diatonic scale, or a tone three degrees above or below a given tone *b*) the interval between two such tones, or a combination of them —**fourth′ly adv.**

fourth dimension a dimension in addition to those of length, width, and depth: in the theory of relativity, time is regarded as this dimension —**fourth′-di·men′sion·al adj.**

fourth estate *see* ESTATE

☆**Fourth of July** *see* INDEPENDENCE DAY

fourth world [*often* F- W-] the poorest, most underdeveloped countries of the third world

fo·ve·a (fō′vē ə) **n.** [L., pit] **1.** *Biol.* a small hollow or depression **2.** a pit without rods in the center of the retina, the point where vision is sharpest: in full, called **fovea cen·tra·lis** (sen trā′lis)

fowl (foul) **n.**, *pl.* **fowls, fowl:** see PLURAL, II, D, 1 [OE. *fugol*, related to G. *vogel*, bird] **1.** any bird: used in combination [*wildfowl*] **2.** any of the larger domestic birds used as food, as the chicken, duck, turkey, etc. **3.** the flesh of any of these birds used for food —**vi.** to hunt wild birds for food or sport —**fowl′er n.** —**fowl′ing n., adj.**

fowling piece a shotgun for hunting wild fowl

fox (fäks) **n.**, *pl.* **fox′es, fox:** see PLURAL, II, D, 1 [OE., related to G. *fuchs*] **1.** a small, wild, flesheating mammal of the dog family, with a bushy tail: thought of as sly and crafty **2.** its fur, commonly reddish-brown or gray **3.** a sly, crafty person —**vt. 1.** to cause (book leaves, prints, etc.) to develop brownish stains [an old family Bible, with *foxed* pages] **2.** to trick by slyness or craftiness **3.** to bewilder or baffle —**foxed adj.**

Fox (fäks), **George** 1624–91; Eng. religious leader, who founded the Society of Friends

FOX (average length 42 in., including tail)

fox fire a glowing light, as of decaying wood, caused by various fungi

fox·glove (fäks′gluv′) **n.** [OE. *foxes glofa*] same as DIGITALIS (sense 1)

fox·hole (-hōl′) **n.** a hole dug in the ground as a temporary protection for one or two soldiers against enemy gunfire or tanks

fox·hound (-hound′) **n.** a strong, swift hound with a keen scent, bred and trained to hunt foxes

fox·tail (-tāl′) **n. 1.** the tail of a fox **2.** a grass having cylindrical spikes bearing spikelets scattered at intervals among stiff bristles

fox terrier a small, active terrier with a smooth or wire-haired coat, usually white with dark patches: formerly trained to drive foxes out of hiding

☆**fox trot 1.** a dance for couples in 4/4 time with a variety of steps, some fast and some slow **2.** the music for such a dance —**fox′-trot′ vi. -trot′ted, -trot′ting**

fox·y (fäk′sē) **adj. fox′i·er, fox′i·est 1.** foxlike; crafty; sly **2.** covered with brownish stains —see SYN. at SLY —**fox′i·ly adv.** —**fox′i·ness n.**

foy·er (foi′ər, foi′ā, foi yā′) **n.** [Fr. < ML. < L. *focus,* hearth] an entrance hall or a lobby, as in a theater or hotel

F.P., f.p., fp foot-pound(s)

f.p., fp, fp freezing point

FPO *U.S. Navy* Fleet Post Office

fps, f.p.s. 1. feet per second **2.** foot-pound-second

Fr *Chem.* francium

Fr. 1. Father **2.** France **3.** French **4.** Friday

fr. franc; francs

Fra (frä) **n.** [It., abbrev. of *frate* < L. *frater*] brother: title given to an Italian friar or monk

fra·cas (frā′kəs, frak′əs) **n.** [Fr. < It. < *fracassare,* to smash] a noisy fight or loud quarrel; brawl

frac·tion (frak′shən) **n.** [< L. < pp. of *frangere,* BREAK] **1.** a small part, amount, etc.; portion; fragment [he saves only a *fraction* of his earnings] **2.** *Chem.* a part separated, as by distillation, from a mixture, at its particular boiling point, etc. **3.** *Math. a*) an indicated quotient of two whole numbers, as 1/2, 13/4, .24 *b*) any quantity expressed in terms of a numerator and denominator, as 2x/xy —see SYN. at PART

frac·tion·al (-əl) **adj. 1.** of or being a fraction or fractions **2.** very small or unimportant **3.** describing a process for separating the parts of a mixture by taking advantage of their differences, as of boiling points, solubility, etc. [the *fractional* distillation of petroleum] —**frac′tion·al·ly adv.**

frac·tion·ate (-āt′) **vt. -at′ed, -at′ing 1.** to separate into fractions, or parts **2.** *Chem.* to separate into fractions by distillation, etc. —**frac′tion·a′tion n.**

frac·tious (frak′shəs) **adj.** [prob. < *fraction* (in its obs. sense of "discord") + -OUS] **1.** hard to manage; unruly; rebellious **2.** hard to please; fretful; irritable; cross —**frac′tious·ly adv.** —**frac′tious·ness n.**

frac·ture (frak′chər) **n.** [< L. < L. *fractura* < pp. of *frangere,* BREAK] **1.** a breaking or being broken **2.** a break, crack, or split **3.** a break in a bone or, occasionally, a tear in a cartilage **4.** the texture of the broken surface of a mineral —**vt., vi. -tured, -tur·ing 1.** to break, crack, or split **2.** to break up; disrupt —see SYN. at BREAK —**frac′tur·al adj.**

frae (frā) **prep.** [Scot.] from

frag·ile (fraj′'l; *chiefly Brit. & Canad.,* -īl) **adj.** [< OFr. < L. *fragilis* < *frangere,* BREAK] easily broken, damaged, or destroyed; delicate [*fragile* china] —**fra·gil·i·ty** (frə jil′ə tē) **n.**

frag·ment (frag′mənt; *for v. also* frag ment′) **n.** [< L. < *frangere,* BREAK] **1.** a part broken away; broken piece **2.** a detached or incomplete part [a *fragment* of a song, novel, etc.] —**vt., vi.** to break into fragments —**frag′ment·ed adj.**

frag·men·tar·y (frag′mən ter′ē) **adj.** consisting of fragments or bits; not complete; disconnected [*fragmentary* talk; a *fragmentary* report] : also **frag·men′tal** (-men′təl) —**frag′men·tar′i·ly adv.** —**frag′men·tar′i·ness n.**

frag·men·tate (-tāt′) **vt., vi. -tat′ed, -tat′ing** to break into fragments —**frag′men·ta′tion n.**

Fra·go·nard (frà gô nàr′), **Jean Ho·no·ré** (zhän ô nô rā′) 1732–1806; Fr. painter

fra·grance (frā′grəns) **n.** a fragrant smell; pleasant odor: also [Now Rare] **fra′gran·cy,** *pl.* **-cies**

fra·grant (frā′grənt) **adj.** [L. prp. of *fragrare,* to emit a (sweet) smell] having a pleasant odor; sweet-smelling —**fra′grant·ly adv.**

frail (frāl) **adj.** [< OFr. < L. *fragilis,* FRAGILE] **1.** easily broken, damaged, or destroyed; fragile [a *frail* railing] **2.** slender and delicate; weak [a *frail* child] **3.** easily tempted; morally weak —see SYN. at WEAK —**frail′ly adv.** —**frail′ness n.**

frail·ty (frāl′tē) **n. 1.** the condition of being frail; weakness; esp., moral weakness **2.** *pl.* **-ties** any fault or wrongdoing resulting from such weakness

frame (frām) **vt. framed, fram′ing** [prob. < ON. *frami,* profit, benefit; some senses < OE. *framian,* to be helpful] **1.** to shape or form according to a pattern; design [to *frame* a constitution] **2.** to put together the parts of; construct **3.** to put into words; compose; devise [to *frame* an excuse] **4.** to adjust; adapt [a law *framed* to benefit a few] **5.** to enclose (a picture, mirror, etc.) in a border ☆**6.** [Colloq.] to set up false evidence, testimony, etc. beforehand so as to make (an innocent person) appear guilty —**n. 1.** *a*) formerly, anything made of parts fitted together according to a design *b*) body structure in general; build [*a man with a broad frame*] **2.** the basic structure or skeleton around which something is built [*the frame of a house*] **3.** the framework supporting the chassis of a motor vehicle **4.** the supporting case or border into which a window, door, etc. is set **5.** a border, often ornamental, in which a picture, mirror, etc. is enclosed **6.** [*pl.*] the framework for a pair of eyeglasses **7.** any of certain machines built in or on a framework **8.** the way that anything is constructed or put together; form [*the frame of a charter*] **9.** setting or background circumstances **10.** mood; temper [*a bad frame of mind*] **11.** an established order or system [*the frame of government*] ☆**12.** [Colloq.] the act of framing (sense 6) ☆**13.** [Colloq.] *Baseball* an inning **14.** *Bowling*, etc. any of the divisions of a game, in which all ten pins are set up anew ☆**15.** *Motion Pictures* each of the small exposures composing a strip of film **16.** *Pool* same as RACK¹ (n. 2) ☆**17.** *TV* a single scanning by the electron beam of the scene being transmitted —*adj.* having a wooden framework, usually covered with boards [*a frame house*] —**fram′er** *n.*

frame of reference 1. *Math.* the fixed points, lines, or planes from which coordinates are measured **2.** the set of ideas, facts, or circumstances within which something exists

☆**frame-up** (frām′up′) *n.* [Colloq.] a setting up of false evidence, testimony, etc. to make an innocent person seem guilty

frame·work (-wurk′) *n.* **1.** a structure to hold together or to support something built or stretched over or around it [*the framework of a house*] **2.** a basic structure, arrangement, or system [*the framework of society*] **3.** same as FRAME OF REFERENCE

franc (fraŋk) *n.* [Fr. < L. *Francorum rex*, king of the French, device on the coin in 1360] **1.** the monetary unit and a coin of France, Belgium, Switzerland, and Luxembourg **2.** the monetary unit of various other countries **3.** a unit of money in Morocco See MONETARY UNITS, table

France (frans, fräns) country in W Europe, on the Atlantic & the Mediterranean: 212,821 sq. mi.; pop. 50,620,000; cap. Paris

France (frans, fräns), **A·na·tole** (an′ə tōl′) (pseud. of *Jacques Anatole François Thibault*) 1844–1924; Fr. novelist & literary critic

Fran·ces (fran′sis) [< OFr. fem. of FRANCIS] a feminine name: dim. *Fran*

fran·chise (fran′chīz) *n.* [< OFr. < *franc*, free: see FRANK] **1.** any special right or privilege granted by a government, as to operate a public utility, etc. [*the city granted a franchise to the baseball club to operate the stadium*] **2.** the right to vote; suffrage **3.** *a*) the right to sell a product or provide a service in an area, as granted by a manufacturer or company *b*) the area over which such a right extends —*vt.* **-chised, -chis·ing** to grant a franchise to

Fran·cis (fran′sis) [< OFr. < ML. *Franciscus* < LL. *Francus:* see FRANK] **1.** a masculine name **2. Francis I** 1494–1547; king of France (1515–47) **3. Francis II** 1768–1835; last emperor of the Holy Roman Empire (1792–1806)

Fran·cis·can (fran sis′kən) *adj.* of Saint Francis of Assisi or the religious order founded by him in 1209 —*n.* any member of this order

Francis Ferdinand 1863–1914; archduke of Austria: his assassination led to the outbreak of World War I

Francis Joseph I 1830–1916; emperor of Austria (1848–1916) and king of Hungary (1867–1916)

Francis of As·si·si (ə sēs′ē), Saint (born *Giovanni Bernardone*) 1181?–1226; It. preacher: founder of the Franciscan Order

fran·ci·um (fran′sē əm) *n.* [ModL. < FRANCE] a radioactive, metallic chemical element of the alkali group: symbol, Fr; at. wt., 223(?); at. no., 87

Franck (fräŋk), **Cé·sar** (**Auguste**) (sā zàr′) 1822–90; Fr. composer, born in Belgium

Fran·co (fraŋ′kō; *Sp.* fräŋ′kô), **Fran·cis·co** (fran sis′kō; *Sp.* fräṅ thēs′kô) 1892–1975; dictator of Spain (1939–75)

Franco- [ML. < LL. *Francus*, a Frank] *a combining form meaning:* **1.** Frankish **2.** of France or the French **3.** France and; the French and [*Franco-German*]

Fran·co·ni·a (fraŋ kō′nē ə) region in SC Germany, a duchy in the Middle Ages —**Fran′co′ni·an** *adj., n.*

fran·gi·ble (fran′jə b'l) *adj.* [< OFr. < ML. < L. *frangere*, BREAK] breakable; fragile —**fran′gi·bil′i·ty** *n.*

fran·gi·pan·i (fran′jə pan′ē, -pän′ē) *n., pl.* **-pan′i, -pan′is** [It. < Marquis *Frangipani* (16th-c. It. nobleman), who is said to have first made the perfume] **1.** any of several tropical American shrubs and trees with large, fragrant flowers **2.** a perfume obtained from this flower **3.** a pastry made with ground almonds Also **fran′gi·pane′** (-pān′)

FRANGIPANI

‡**Fran·glais** (frän glä′) *n.* [Fr. < *Fran(çois)*, French + (*An*)*glais*, English] English words and phrases used in French

Frank (fraŋk) [dim. of FRANCIS] a masculine name —*n.* [< OE. & OFr. < LL. *Francus:* see next entry] **1.** a member of the Germanic tribes that established the Frankish Empire, which in the 9th cent. A.D. extended over what is now France, Germany, and Italy **2.** any western European: term used in the Near East

frank (fraŋk) *adj.* [< OFr. *franc*, free < ML. < LL. *Francus*, a Frank (hence a "free man," not one ruled by the Franks)] **1.** open and honest in expressing what one thinks or feels; candid [*a frank critic*] **2.** not hidden or disguised; open; clearly evident [*a frank discussion about sex*] —*vt.* **1.** to send (mail) free of postage, as because of one's official position **2.** to mark (mail) so that it can be sent free —*n.* **1.** the privilege of sending mail free **2.** a mark or signature on mail indicating this privilege **3.** any letter, etc. sent free in this way —**frank′ness** *n.*

SYN.—**frank** applies to a person, remark, etc. that is free or blunt in expressing the truth or an opinion and is not held back by the usual restraints [*a frank criticism*]; **candid** implies a basic honesty that makes it impossible for one to deceive or be sly, sometimes to the point where the listener could be embarrassed [*a candid opinion*]; **open** implies a lack of secrecy and often suggests a genuine and innocent quality [*her open admiration for him*]; **outspoken** suggests a lack of restraint in offering opinions, esp. when it might be better to keep quiet

Frank. Frankish

Frank·en·stein (fraŋ′kən stīn′) **1.** the title character in a novel (1818) by Mary SHELLEY: he is a young medical student who creates a monster that destroys him **2.** popularly, the monster —*n.* anything that becomes dangerous to its creator

Frank·fort (fraŋk′fərt) [orig. *Frank's Ford*, after S. *Frank*, a pioneer killed there] capital of Ky.: pop. 21,000

Frank·furt (fraŋk′fərt; *G.* fräŋk′foort) city in C West Germany, on the Main River: pop. 662,000: also **Frankfurt am Main**

☆**frank·furt·er, frank·fort·er** (fraŋk′fər tər) *n.* [G., after FRANKFURT] a smoked sausage of beef or of beef and pork, etc.: wiener: also **frank′furt, frank′fort,** [Colloq.] **frank**

frank·in·cense (fraŋ′kən sens′) *n.* [< OFr.: see FRANK & INCENSE¹] a gum resin from various Arabian and African trees: it is burned as incense

Frank·ish (fraŋ′kish) *adj.* of the Franks, their language, or culture —*n.* the West Germanic language of the Franks

Frank·lin¹ (fraŋk′lin) [< Anglo-Fr. < ML. < LL. *Francus:* see FRANK] **1.** a masculine name **2. Benjamin,** 1706–90; Am. statesman, scientist, & writer

Frank·lin² (fraŋk′lin) N district of the Northwest Territories, Canada, including the arctic islands

frank·lin (fraŋk′lin) *n.* [< Anglo-Fr. < ML. < *francus:* see FRANK] in England in the 14th and 15th cent., a landowner of free but not noble birth, ranking just below the gentry

☆**Franklin stove** a cast-iron heating stove like an open fireplace, invented by Benjamin Franklin

frank·ly (fraŋk′lē) *adv.* **1.** in a frank way **2.** to be frank; in truth [*frankly*, I'd rather not go]

fran·tic (fran′tik) *adj.* [see PHRENETIC] **1.** wild with anger, pain, worry, etc.; frenzied **2.** marked by frenzy [*frantic efforts*] —**fran′ti·cal·ly** or [Rare] **fran′tic·ly** *adv.*

☆**frap·pé** (fra pā′) *adj.* [Fr., pp. of *frapper*, to strike] partly frozen; iced; cooled —*n.* **1.** a dessert made of partly frozen beverages, as of fruit juices, etc. **2.** a drink made of some beverage poured over shaved ice **3.** [Eastern] a milkshake Also, esp. for *n.* 3, **frappe** (frap)

FRANKLIN STOVE

Fra·ser (frā′zər) river in British Columbia, Canada, flowing from the Rocky Mountains into the Pacific

☆**frat** (frat) *n.* [Colloq.] a fraternity, as at a college

fra·ter·nal (frə tur′n'l) *adj.* [< ML. < L. *fraternus* < *frater,* a brother: for IE. base see BROTHER] **1.** of or characteristic of brothers; brotherly **2.** of or like a fraternal order or a fraternity **3.** designating twins, of the same or different sex, developed from separately fertilized ova and so not identical —**fra·ter′-nal·ism** *n.* —**fra·ter′nal·ly** *adv.*

☆**fraternal order** (or **society, association**) a society, often secret, organized for fellowship or for work toward a common goal

fra·ter·ni·ty (frə tur′nə tē) *n., pl.* -**ties 1.** the relationship or feeling between brothers; brotherliness **2.** a group of men joined together by common interests, for fellowship, etc.; specif., a Greek-letter college organization **3.** a group of people with the same beliefs, interests, etc. [the medical *fraternity*]

frat·er·nize (frat′ər nīz′) *vi.* -**nized**′, -**niz**′**ing** to associate in a brotherly manner; be friendly; often, specif., to be intimate or friendly with members of an enemy nation in wartime —**frat′-er·ni·za′tion** *n.* —**frat′er·niz′er** *n.*

frat·ri·cide (frat′rə sīd′) *n.* [Fr. < LL. *fratricidium* < L. < *frater,* brother + *caedere,* to kill] **1.** *a)* the act of killing one's own brother or sister *b)* the act of killing relatives or fellow-countrymen, as in a civil war **2.** a person who kills his brother or sister —**frat′ri·ci′dal** (-sīd′'l) *adj.*

‡**Frau** (frou) *n., pl.* **Frau′en** (-ən) [G.] a married woman; wife: German title used like *Mrs.*

fraud (frôd) *n.* [< OFr. < L. *fraus*] **1.** deceit; trickery; cheating **2.** something said or done to cheat or trick **3.** a person who cheats or is not what he pretends to be

fraud·u·lent (frô′jə lənt) *adj.* **1.** acting with fraud; deceitful **2.** based on or characterized by fraud [a *fraudulent* scheme] **3.** done or obtained by fraud [his *fraudulent* wealth] —**fraud′u-lence, fraud′u·len·cy** *n.* —**fraud′u·lent·ly** *adv.*

fraught (frôt) *adj.* [< MDu. < *vracht,* a load] filled, charged, or loaded (*with*) [a life *fraught* with hardship]

‡**Fräu·lein** (froi′līn; *E.* froi′-, frou′-) *n., pl.* -**lein**, *E.* -**leins** [G.] an unmarried woman: German title used like *Miss*

fray[1] (frā) *n.* [< AFFRAY] a noisy quarrel or fight; brawl

fray[2] (frā) *vt., vi.* [< OFr. < L. *fricare,* to rub] **1.** to make or become worn, ragged, etc. by rubbing [a coat *frayed* at the elbows] **2.** to make or become weakened or strained [nerves *frayed* by the tension]

fraz·zle (fraz′'l) *vt., vi.* -**zled**, -**zling** [Brit. dial. & U.S., prob. < dial. *fazle*] [Colloq.] **1.** to wear out until in shreds; fray **2.** to make or become physically or emotionally exhausted —☆*n.* [Colloq.] the state of being frazzled

freak (frēk) *n.* [< ? OE. *frician,* to dance] **1.** *a)* a sudden fancy; odd notion; whim [by some *freak,* she decided to stay home that morning] *b)* an unusual happening **2.** any abnormal animal, person, or plant; monstrosity [a two-headed calf is a *freak*] ☆**3.** [Slang] *a)* a user of a certain drug [an acid *freak*] *b)* a person very fond of or enthusiastic about something [a rock *freak*] *c) same as* HIPPIE —*adj.* oddly different from what is normal; queer [*freak* weather] —**freak (out)** [Slang] **1.** to have the strange mental reactions, hallucinations, etc. brought on by certain drugs **2.** to make or become very excited, distressed, disorganized, etc. —**freak′ish, freak′y** *adj.* —**freak′ish·ly** *adv.* —**freak′ish·ness** *n.*

freck·le (frek′'l) *n.* [< Scand.] a small, brownish spot on the skin, esp. as a result of exposure to the sun —*vt.* -**led**, -**ling** to cause freckles to appear on —*vi.* to become spotted with freckles —**freck′led, freck′ly** *adj.*

Fre·da (frē′də) [var. of FRIEDA] a feminine name

Fred·er·i·ca (fred′ə rē′kə, fred rē′kə) [fem. of FREDERICK] a feminine name

Fred·er·ick (fred′rik, -ər ik) [< Fr. < G. < OHG. *Fridurih,* "peaceful ruler"] **1.** a masculine name: dim. *Fred;* var. *Frederic, Fredrick, Fredric* **2. Frederick I** 1123?-90; king of Germany (1152–90) & emperor of the Holy Roman Empire (1155–90): called *Frederick Barbarossa* **3. Frederick II** *same as* FREDERICK THE GREAT **4. Frederick III** 1463–1525; elector of Saxony (1486–1525)

Fred·er·icks·burg (fred′riks burg′) [after *Frederick* Louis (1707–51), father of GEORGE III] city in NE Va.: scene of Civil War battle (Dec., 1862) won by the Confederate forces

Frederick the Great 1712–86; king of Prussia (1740–86): also **Frederick II**

Fred·er·ic·ton (fred′ə rik tən) capital of New Brunswick, Canada: pop. 45,000

free (frē) *adj.* **fre′er, fre′est** [OE. *freo* < IE. base *prei-,* to love, from which also comes FRIEND] **1.** *a)* not under the control or power of another; able to act or think as one pleases; having liberty; independent *b)* characterized by or resulting from liberty [*free* speech] **2.** having, or existing under, a government that does not restrict the right to speak, assemble, petition, vote, etc. [a *free* people] **3.** able to move in any direction; not held; loose [grab the *free* end of the rope] **4.** not held or confined by a court, the police, etc. [*free* on bail] **5.** not held down or bothered by obligations, debts, discomforts, etc.; unhindered [*free* from pain] **6.** at liberty; allowed [*free* to leave] **7.** not following the usual rules or patterns [*free* verse] **8.** not literal; not exact [a *free* translation] **9.** not busy or not in use [the phone booth is *free* now] **10.** easy and graceful [a *free* gait] **11.** *a)* generous; lavish [a *free* spender] *b)* profuse; copious [a *free* flow of ideas] **12.** frank; straightforward [she was *free* in her criticism] **13.** too frank or familiar in speech, action, etc.; forward [don't be so *free* with me!] **14.** with no charge or cost [a *free* ticket] **15.** not requiring the usual payment of taxes or duties [a *free* port] **16.** with no blocking; clear or open [a *free* road ahead] **17.** open to all [a *free* market] **18.** not united; not combined [*free* oxygen] **19.** designating a linguistic form, or morpheme, that can exist alone as a word (Example: *boy* is a *free* form, but *-s* in *boys* is a bound form) —*adv.* **1.** without cost or payment [he let us in *free*] **2.** in a free manner [the wind blows *free*] —*vt.* **freed, free′ing** to make free; specif., *a)* to release from bondage or someone else's power, obligation, etc. [to *free* slaves] *b)* to clear of blocking, entanglement, etc.; disengage [use chemicals to *free* the drain] —**free and easy** informal; without ceremony —**free from** (or **of**) **1.** lacking; without (something unpleasant or painful) **2.** beyond —**make free with 1.** to use freely **2.** to take liberties with —**set free** to release; liberate —**with a free hand** with generosity; lavishly — **free′ly** *adv.* —**free′ness** *n.*

free agent ☆a professional athlete who is free to sign a contract with any team

free·board (frē′bôrd′) *n.* the height of a ship's side from the main deck or gunwale to the waterline

free·boot·er (-bōōt′ər) *n.* [< Du. < *vrij,* free + *buit,* plunder] a pirate; buccaneer —**free′boot′** *vi.*

free·born (-bôrn′) *adj.* **1.** born free, not in slavery **2.** of or fit for a person so born

free city a city that is an independent state

freed·man (frēd′mən) *n., pl.* -**men** a man legally freed from slavery or bondage —**freed′wom′an** *n.fem., pl.* -**wom′en**

free·dom (frē′dəm) *n.* **1.** the state or quality of being free; esp., *a)* the state of not being under the control of some other person or group; liberty; independence *b)* the state of not being restricted in a civil right; civil or political liberty [*freedom* of speech] *c)* the state of not being subject to a specified obligation, discomfort, etc. [*freedom* from want] *d)* a being able to act, move, use, etc. as one wishes [to have the *freedom* of the house] *e)* easiness, as of action [the tight coat hindered her *freedom* of movement] *f)* a being free from the usual rules, patterns, etc. *g)* frankness or easiness of manner; sometimes, too much frankness **2.** a right or privilege

free enterprise the economic theory or system of letting private industry operate freely with a minimum of regulation by the government

free fall the unchecked fall of a body through the air; specif., the part of a parachutist's jump before the parachute is opened

free flight the flight of a rocket after the fuel supply has been used up or shut off —**free′-flight′** *adj.*

☆**free-for-all** (frē′fər ôl′) *n.* a disorganized, general fight; brawl —*adj.* open to anyone

free-form (-fôrm′) *adj.* having an irregular, usually curved form or outline [a *free-form* swimming pool]

free·hand (-hand′) *adj.* drawn by hand without the use of instruments, measurements, etc.

free·hand·ed (-han′did) *adj.* generous; liberal

free·hold (-hōld′) *n.* **1.** an estate in land held for life or with the right to pass it on to heirs **2.** the holding of an estate in this way —*adj.* of or held by freehold —**free′hold′er** *n.*

free-lance (-lans′) *adj.* of or acting as a free lance —*vi.* -**lanced**′, -**lanc**′**ing** to work as a free lance

free lance 1. a medieval soldier who sold his services to any state or army **2.** one who acts according to his principles and is not influenced by any group **3.** a writer, artist, etc. who is not under contract to one employer but sells his services to individual buyers: also **free′-lanc′er** *n.*

free·liv·ing (frē′liv′iŋ) *adj.* **1.** freely satisfying one's appetites, desires, etc. **2.** *Biol.* not parasitic or symbiotic —**free liver**

☆**free·load·er** (-lō′dər) *n.* [Colloq.] a person who always manages to get others to supply him with free food, lodging, etc. —**free′load′** *vi.*

☆**free love** the belief or practice of freedom in sexual relations without marriage or other legal controls

free·man (-mən) *n., pl.* **-men** **1.** a person not in slavery or bondage **2.** a person with full civil and political rights; citizen

free market any market where trade can be carried on without restrictions as to price, etc.

Free·ma·son (frē′mās′'n) *n.* a member of an international secret society having brotherliness and mutual aid as its goals; Mason

Free·ma·son·ry (-rē) *n.* **1.** the principles, rituals, etc. of Freemasons **2.** the Freemasons **3.** [f-] a natural sympathy and understanding among persons with similar experiences

free on board delivered (by the seller) aboard the train, ship, etc. at the point of shipment, without charge

free·si·a (frē′zhē ə, -zhə, -zē ə) *n.* [ModL., after F. *Freese,* 19th-c. Ger. physician] a South African bulbous plant with fragrant, funnel-shaped flowers

☆**free silver** the free coinage of silver, esp. at a fixed ratio to the gold coined in the same period

☆**Free-Soil** (frē′soil′) *adj.* designating a political party (from 1848 to 1854), that was against allowing slavery to spread into U.S. Territories before the Civil War —**Free′-Soil′er** *n.*

free-spo·ken (-spō′k'n) *adj.* frank; outspoken

free-stand·ing (-stan′diŋ) *adj.* resting on its own foundation, with no extra support [a *free-standing* tower]

Free State ☆any State of the U.S. in which slavery was forbidden before the Civil War

free·stone (-stōn′) *n.* **1.** a stone, esp. sandstone or limestone, that can be cut easily without splitting **2.** *a)* a peach, plum, etc. in which the pit does not cling to the pulp of the ripened fruit *b)* such a pit —*adj.* having such a pit

free·think·er (-thiŋ′kər) *n.* a person who forms his opinions about God and religion using his own reason rather than the tradition or authority of established teachings —see SYN. at ATHEIST —**free′think′ing** *n., adj.* —**free thought**

Free·town (frē′toun′) seaport & capital of Sierra Leone, on the Atlantic: pop. 128,000

free throw *Basketball* an unhindered throw at the basket from a set line (**free-throw line**) allowed to a player as a penalty for a foul committed by an opponent: if successful, it counts for one point

free trade trade carried on without quotas on imports or exports, without protective tariffs, etc.

free verse poetry not following regular patterns of meter, rhyme, or forms of stanza

☆**free·way** (-wā′) *n.* **1.** an expressway with interchanges for getting on and off easily **2.** a highway without toll charges

free·will (-wil′) *adj.* freely given or done; voluntary

free will **1.** freedom of the will to act as one chooses without outside force; freedom of choice **2.** the doctrine that people have such freedom

freeze (frēz) *vi.* **froze, fro′zen, freez′ing** [OE. *freosan*] **1.** to be formed into ice; be hardened by cold **2.** to become covered or clogged with ice [the river *froze* overnight] **3.** to be or become very cold [we *froze* in the drafty hall] **4.** to become attached by freezing [the wheels *froze* to the ground] **5.** to die or be damaged by frost [our tomato plants *froze* last fall] ☆**6.** to become motionless or fixed [the fox *froze* in its tracks] **7.** to be made momentarily unable to move, act, or speak through fright, etc. **8.** to become formal or unfriendly [he *froze* at the critical remarks] **9.** *Mech.* to stick or become tight as a result of expansion of parts from overheating or not enough lubrication —*vt.* **1.** to cause to form into ice; harden or solidify by cold **2.** to cover or clog with ice **3.** to make very cold **4.** to remove feeling from, as with a local anesthetic [to *freeze* a jaw with Novocain] **5.** to preserve (food) by rapid refrigeration [cook some of the peas and *freeze* the rest] **6.** to make fixed or attached by freezing **7.** to kill or damage by exposure to cold **8.** to make or keep motionless or stiff ☆**9.** to discourage as by cool behavior [she *froze* me with her look] **10.** to make formal or unfriendly ☆**11.** *a)* to fix (prices, wages, an employee, etc.)

at a given level or place, as by government regulation *b)* to make (funds, assets, etc.) not available to the owners —*n.* **1.** a freezing or being frozen **2.** a period of cold, freezing weather —☆**freeze (on) to** [Colloq.] to hold fast to —**freeze out** ☆**1.** to die out through freezing, as plants ☆**2.** [Colloq.] to force out by a cold manner, competition, etc. —**freeze over** to become covered with ice —**freez′a·ble** *adj.*

freeze-dry (frēz′drī′) *vt.* **-dried′, -dry′ing** to preserve (food, vaccines, etc.) by quick-freezing, followed by drying under high vacuum at a low temperature —**freeze′-dry′er** *n.*

freez·er (-ər) *n.* ☆**1.** a refrigerator, compartment, or room for freezing and storing frozen foods at very low temperatures **2.** a hand-cranked or electrically operated device for making ice cream

freez·ing point the temperature at which a liquid freezes: for water, it is 32°F or 0°C

Frei·burg (frī′boork) city in SW West Germany: pop. 166,000: also **Freiburg im Bres·gau** (im brīs′gou)

freight (frāt) *n.* [< MDu. *vracht,* a load] **1.** a method or service for transporting goods by water, land, or air: freight is usually cheaper but slower than express **2.** the cost for such transportation **3.** the goods transported; cargo ☆**4.** *same as* FREIGHT TRAIN **5.** any load or burden —*vt.* **1.** to load with freight **2.** to load; burden **3.** to transport as by freight

freight·age (frāt′ij) *n.* **1.** the charge for transporting goods **2.** freight; cargo **3.** the transportation of goods

☆**freight car** a railroad car for transporting freight

freight·er (-ər) *n.* a ship or aircraft for carrying freight

☆**freight train** a railroad train of freight cars

Fre·mont (frē′mänt) [after J. C. Frémont (1813-90), U.S. politician, general, & explorer] city in W Calif.: suburb of Oakland: pop. 101,000

French (french) *adj.* of France, its people, their language, or culture —*n.* the Romance language of the French —**the French** the people of France —**French′man** (-mən) *n., pl.* **-men** —**French′wom′an** *n.fem., pl.* **-wom′en**

French (french), **Daniel Chester** 1850-1931; U.S. sculptor

☆**French and Indian War** a war fought in N. America from 1754 to 1763, in which the British defeated the French and their Indian allies and got control of Canada

French Canadian ☆a Canadian of French ancestry

French chalk a very soft chalk used for marking lines on cloth or removing grease spots

French Community political union of France, its overseas departments & territories, & six fully independent countries that are former French colonies

French cuff a double cuff turned back on itself and fastened with a link

French doors a pair of doors with glass panes from top to bottom, turning on hinges at opposite sides of a doorway and opening in the middle

☆**French dressing** a salad dressing made of vinegar, oil, and various seasonings

☆**French fry** [*often* f- f-] to fry in very hot, deep fat until crisp: French fried potatoes (colloquially, **French fries**) are first cut lengthwise into strips

French Guiana French overseas department in NE S.America: 35,135 sq. mi.; pop. 51,000

French horn a brass-wind instrument with a long, coiled tube ending in a wide, flaring bell: it has a soft, mellow tone

French·i·fy (french′ə fī′) *vt., vi.* **-fied′, -fy′ing** to make or become French or like the French in customs, ideas, manners, etc.

French leave the act of leaving secretly or in haste, esp. without permission

French Polynesia French territory in the South Pacific, consisting chiefly of five groups of islands: 1,545 sq. mi.; pop. 119,000; cap. Papeete

French Revolution the revolution of the people against the monarchy in France: it

FRENCH CUFFS

FRENCH HORN

began in 1789, resulted in the establishment of a republic, and ended in 1799 with the Consulate

☆**French toast** sliced bread dipped in a batter of egg and milk and then fried

French windows a pair of casement windows designed like French doors and usually reaching to the floor

fre·net·ic (frə net′ik) *adj.* [see PHRENETIC] frantic; frenzied: also **fre·net′i·cal** —**fre·net′i·cal·ly** *adv.*

fre·num (frē′nəm) *n., pl.* **-nums, -na** (-nə) [L., lit., a bridle] a fold of skin or mucous membrane that checks the movements of an organ, as the fold under the tongue

fren·zy (fren′zē) *n., pl.* **-zies** [< OFr. < ML. < L. *phrenesis*, ult. < Gr. *phrenitis*, madness < *phrēn*, mind] a wild outburst of feeling or action; brief period of strong emotion that is almost like madness [a *frenzy* of fear, joy, work, etc.] —*vt.* **-zied, -zy·ing** to make frantic; drive mad —**fren′zied·ly** *adv.*

freq. 1. frequent 2. frequentative

fre·quen·cy (frē′kwən sē) *n., pl.* **-cies** 1. frequent occurrence [the *frequency* of his tardiness] 2. the number of times any event, value, characteristic, etc. is repeated in a given period or group 3. *Physics* the number of repeated oscillations, vibrations, or waves per unit of time: now usually expressed in hertz

frequency modulation 1. the changing of the frequency of a radio carrier wave in accordance with the signal to be transmitted 2. the system of broadcasting that uses this

fre·quent (frē′kwənt; *for v., usually* frē kwent′) *adj.* [< OFr. < L. *frequens*, crowded] 1. happening often, time after time [his *frequent* requests for help] 2. constant; habitual [she is a *frequent* visitor to our school] —*vt.* to go to constantly; be at or in habitually [a man who *frequents* bars] —**fre·quen′ta·tion** *n.* —**fre·quent′er** *n.* —**fre·quent′ly** *adv.*

fre·quen·ta·tive (frē kwen′tə tiv) *adj. Gram.* expressing frequent and repeated action —*n. Gram.* a frequentative verb: *sparkle* is a frequentative of *spark*

‡**frère** (rer) *n.* [Fr.] 1. a brother 2. a friar

fres·co (fres′kō) *n., pl.* **-coes, -cos** [It., fresh < OHG. *frisc*] 1. the art of painting with watercolors on wet plaster 2. a painting or design so made —*vt.* to paint in fresco

fresh[1] (fresh) *adj.* [< OE. *fersc*, but altered after OFr. *fres, fresche*] 1. recently made, obtained, or grown [*fresh* coffee] 2. not salted, preserved, etc. [*fresh* meat] 3. not spoiled or stale [*fresh* eggs] 4. not tired; vigorous; lively [he felt *fresh* after a nap] 5. not worn, soiled, etc.; bright; clean [a *fresh* handkerchief] 6. youthful or healthy in appearance [a *fresh* complexion] 7. not known before; new; recent [*fresh* information] 8. additional; further [a *fresh* start] 9. inexperienced; unaccustomed [*fresh* on the job] 10. having just arrived [a youth *fresh* from a farm] 11. original and stimulating [*fresh* ideas] 12. cool and refreshing [a *fresh* spring day] 13. brisk; strong: said of the wind 14. not salt: said of water 15. giving milk because having borne a calf: said of a cow —see SYN. at NEW —**fresh out of** [Slang] having just sold or used up —**fresh′ly** *adv.* —**fresh′ness** *n.*

☆**fresh**[2] (fresh) *adj.* [< G. *frech*, bold] [Colloq.] too bold; rude or impudent —*adv.* [Colloq.] in a fresh way [don't talk *fresh* to your mother] —**fresh′ly** *adv.* —**fresh′ness** *n.*

fresh·en (fresh′ən) *vt., vi.* to make or become fresh —**freshen up** to bathe oneself, change clothes, etc. —**fresh′en·er** *n.*

fresh·et (-it) *n.* 1. a rush of fresh water flowing into the sea ☆2. a flooding of a stream because of melting snow or heavy rain

fresh·man (-mən) *n., pl.* **-men** 1. a beginner; novice 2. a student in the ninth grade in high school, or one in the first year of college

fresh·wa·ter (-wôt′ər, -wät′ər) *adj.* 1. of or living in water that is not salty [*freshwater* trout] 2. *a)* sailing only on inland waters, not on the sea [a *freshwater* sailor] *b)* unskilled

Fres·no (frez′nō) [< Sp. *fresno*, ash tree] city in C Calif.: pop. 166,000

fret[1] (fret) *vt.* **fret′ted, fret′ting** [OE. *fretan*, to eat up: for IE. base see EAT] 1. to wear away by gnawing, rubbing, corroding, etc. 2. to make by wearing away [the river had *fretted* grooves in the banks] 3. to make rough; disturb [wind *fretting* the water] 4. to irritate; vex; worry —*vi.* 1. to gnaw (*into, on,* or *upon*) 2. to become corroded, worn, etc. 3. to become rough or disturbed 4. to be irritated, vexed, etc.; worry [it *fretted* him to see her unhappy] —*n.* irritation; worry —**fret′ter** *n.*

fret[2] (fret) *n.* [prob. a mixing of OFr. *frete,* interlaced work & OE. *frætwa,* ornament] an ornamental pattern of straight bars joining one another at right angles to form a design —*vt.* **fret′ted, fret′ting** to ornament with a fret

fret[3] (fret) *n.* [OFr. *frette,* a band] any of the ridges across the fingerboard of a banjo, guitar, etc. to regulate the fingering —*vt.* **fret′ted, fret′ting** to furnish with frets

fret·ful (fret′fəl) *adj.* tending to fret; annoyed or worried —**fret′ful·ly** *adv.* —**fret′ful·ness** *n.*

fret·work (fret′wurk′) *n.* decorative openwork, as of frets

Freud (froid), **Sigmund** 1856–1939; Austrian physician & neurologist who founded psychoanalysis

FRETS

Freud·i·an (froi′dē ən) *adj.* of or according to Freud or his theories —*n.* a follower of Freud or his theories of psychoanalysis —**Freud′i·an·ism** *n.*

Fri. Friday

fri·a·ble (frī′ə b'l) *adj.* [Fr. < L. *friabilis* < *friare,* to rub] easily crumbled into powder [*friable* soil] —**fri′a·bil′i·ty, fri′a·ble·ness** *n.*

fri·ar (frī′ər) *n.* [< OFr. *frere* < L. *frater,* BROTHER] *R.C.Ch.* a member of any of several mendicant orders; esp., an Augustinian, Carmelite, Dominican, or Franciscan —**fri′ar·ly** *adj.*

fri·ar·y (-ē) *n., pl.* **-ar·ies** 1. a monastery where friars live 2. a brotherhood of friars

fric·as·see (frik′ə sē′, frik′ə sē′) *n.* [< Fr. < *fricasser,* to cut up and fry] meat cut into pieces, stewed or fried, and served in its own gravy —*vt.* **-seed′, -see′ing** to prepare as a fricassee

fric·a·tive (frik′ə tiv) *adj.* [< L. pp. of *fricare* (see FRICTION) + -IVE] pronounced by forcing the breath through a narrow slit formed at some point in the mouth, as *f, v, z* —*n.* a fricative consonant

fric·tion (frik′shən) *n.* [Fr. < L. < pp. of *fricare,* to rub] 1. a rubbing of one object or substance against another [the *friction* of air upon the plane had worn some paint away] 2. conflict because of differences of opinion, temperament, etc. [he agreed, but only to prevent *friction*] 3. the resistance to motion of moving surfaces that touch [ball bearings reduce *friction* in machines]

fric·tion·al (frik′shən əl) *adj.* of or caused by friction —**fric′tion·al·ly** *adv.*

Fri·day (frī′dē, -dā) *n.* [OE. *frigedæg,* lit., day of the goddess Frigg: see FRIGG] 1. the sixth day of the week 2. [after the devoted servant of ROBINSON CRUSOE] a faithful follower or efficient helper: usually **man** (or **girl**) **Friday**

Fri·days (-dēz, -dāz) *adv.* on or during every Friday [*Fridays* she bakes]

fried (frid) *pt. & pp. of* FRY[1]

Frie·da (frē′də) [G. < OHG. *fridu,* peace] a feminine name

☆**fried·cake** (frīd′kāk′) *n.* a small cake fried in deep fat; doughnut or cruller

friend (frend) *n.* [OE. *freond:* for IE. base see FREE] 1. a person whom one knows well and is fond of; close acquaintance 2. a person on the same side in a struggle; ally 3. a supporter or sympathizer [a *friend* of labor] 4. something thought of as like a friend ["a dog is a man's best *friend*"] 5. [F-] a member of the Society of Friends; Quaker —**make** (or **be**) **friends with** to become (or be) a friend of —**friend′less** *adj.* —**friend′less·ness** *n.*

friend·ly (frend′lē) *adj.* **-li·er, -li·est** 1. like, characteristic of, or suitable for a friend or friendship; kindly [let me give you some *friendly* advice] 2. not hostile; showing good and peaceful feelings [*friendly* nations] 3. supporting; favorable [a *friendly* wind] —*adv.* in a friendly manner [to act *friendly*] —**friend′li·ly** *adv.* —**friend′li·ness** *n.*

friend·ship (-ship′) *n.* 1. the state of being friends 2. friendly feeling or attitude

fri·er (frī′ər) *n. same as* FRYER

Fries·land (frēz′lənd) province of the N Netherlands: 1,310 sq. mi.; pop. 522,000

frieze[1] (frēz) *n.* [< Fr. < ML. *frisium* < ? Frank.] 1. a decoration forming an ornamental band around a room, mantel, etc. 2. a horizontal band, often decorated with sculpture, between the architrave and cornice of a building: see illustration at ENTABLATURE

frieze[2] (frēz) *n.* [< OFr. < MDu.] a heavy wool cloth with a shaggy, uncut nap on one side

PART OF A FRIEZE

frig·ate (frig′it) *n.* [< Fr. < It. *fregata*] **1.** a fast, medium-sized sailing warship of the 18th and early 19th cent. ☆**2.** a U.S. warship larger than a destroyer and smaller than a light cruiser

frigate bird a large, long-winged, tropical sea bird that robs other birds of their prey

Frigg (frig) [ON.] *Norse Myth.* the wife of Odin

fright (frīt) *n.* [OE. *fyrhto, fryhto*] **1.** sudden fear or terror; alarm **2.** an ugly, ridiculous, or startling person or thing [her new red wig is a *fright*] —*vt.* [Rare] to frighten

fright·en (frīt′'n) *vt.* **1.** to cause to feel fright; make suddenly afraid; scare **2.** to force (*away, out,* or *off*) or bring (*into* a specified condition) by frightening [they *frightened* him into confessing] —*vi.* to become suddenly afraid —see SYN. at AFRAID —**fright′en·ing·ly** *adv.*

fright·ful (-fəl) *adj.* **1.** causing fright; alarming [a *frightful* groan] **2.** shocking; terrible [won at a *frightful* cost] **3.** [Colloq.] *a)* unpleasant; annoying [a *frightful* bore] *b)* great [in a *frightful* hurry] —**fright′ful·ly** *adv.* —**fright′ful·ness** *n.*

frig·id (frij′id) *adj.* [< L. < *frigus*, coldness] **1.** extremely cold [a *frigid* day] **2.** without warmth of feeling or manner; stiff and formal [a *frigid* welcome] —**fri·gid·i·ty** (frə jid′ə tē), **frig′id·ness** *n.* —**frig′id·ly** *adv.*

Frigid Zone either of two zones of the earth (**North Frigid Zone** & **South Frigid Zone**) between the polar circles and the poles

☆**fri·jol** (frē′hōl) *n., pl.* **fri·jo·les** (frē′hōlz, frē hō′lēz) [Sp. *fríjol, fréjol*] a bean, esp. the kidney bean, used for food in Mexico and the southwestern U.S.: also **fri·jo·le** (frē hō′lē)

frill (fril) *n.* [< ?] **1.** a fringe of hair or feathers around the neck of a bird or animal **2.** any unnecessary ornament; thing added only for show [a simple office, furnished without *frills*] **3.** a ruffle —*vt.* to decorate with a frill —**frill′y** *adj.*

fringe (frinj) *n.* [< OFr. < L. *fimbria*] **1.** a border or trimming of cords or threads, hanging loose or tied in bunches **2.** anything like this [a *fringe* of hair] **3.** an outer edge; border; margin [at the *fringes* of the crowd] **4.** a part considered to be on the outer edge, extreme, or minor [the lunatic *fringe* of a political party] ☆**5.** same as FRINGE BENEFIT —*vt.* **fringed, fring′ing** **1.** to decorate with or as with fringe **2.** to be a fringe for; line [trees *fringed* the lawn] —*adj.* **1.** at the outer edge [a *fringe* area] ☆**2.** additional [*fringe* costs] ☆**3.** less important [*fringe* industries] —**fring′y** *adj.* **fring′i·er, fring′i·est**

☆**fringe benefit** an employee's benefit other than wages or salary, such as a pension or insurance

frip·per·y (frip′ər ē) *n., pl.* **-per·ies** [< Fr. < OFr. < *frepe*, a rag] **1.** cheap, gaudy clothes **2.** showy display in dress, manners, speech, etc.

☆**Fris·bee** (friz′bē) [< "Mother *Frisbie's*" cookie jar lids, orig. used in this way] *a trademark for* a plastic disk tossed back and forth in a game —*n.* [f-] such a disk

Fris·co (fris′kō) [Colloq.] *nickname for* SAN FRANCISCO

fri·sé (fri zā′) *n.* [Fr. < *friser*, to curl] a type of upholstery fabric with a thick pile of loops, some of which are sometimes cut to form a design

Fri·sian (frizh′ən, frē′zhən) *adj.* of the Frisian Islands or Friesland, their people, or their language —*n.* **1.** a native or inhabitant of the Frisian Islands or Friesland **2.** the West Germanic language of the Frisians

Frisian Islands island chain in the North Sea, extending along the coast of the N Netherlands, N West Germany, & SW Denmark

frisk (frisk) *n.* [OFr. *frisque* < OHG. *frisc*] **1.** a playful jumping about; frolic; gambol **2.** [Slang] the act of frisking a person —*vt.* [Slang] to search (a person) for concealed weapons, etc. by passing the hands quickly over his clothing —*vi.* to frolic

frisk·y (fris′kē) *adj.* **frisk′i·er, frisk′i·est** lively; frolicsome —**frisk′i·ly** *adv.* —**frisk′i·ness** *n.*

frith (frith) *n. var. of* FIRTH

frit·il·lar·y (frit′'l er′ē) *n., pl.* **-lar·ies** [ModL. < L. *fritillus*, dice box: from markings on the petals or wings] **1.** a plant of the lily family, with nodding, bell-shaped flowers **2.** any of a group of butterflies with spotted wings

FRISBEE

frit·ter[1] (frit′ər) *n.* [< ? OFr. < L. *fractura*: see FRACTURE] [Rare] a small piece —*vt.* **1.** [Rare] to break into small pieces **2.** to waste (money, time, etc.) bit by bit on petty things —**frit′-ter·er** *n.*

frit·ter[2] (frit′ər) *n.* [< OFr., ult. < L. pp. of *frigere*, to fry] a small cake of fried batter, usually containing corn, fruit, etc.

fri·vol·i·ty (fri väl′ə tē) *n.* **1.** a frivolous quality **2.** *pl.* **-ties** a frivolous act or thing

friv·o·lous (friv′ə ləs) *adj.* [L. *frivolus*] **1.** trifling; trivial [a *frivolous* objection] **2.** not properly serious or sensible; silly; giddy [a *frivolous* reply to an important question] —**friv′o·lous·ly** *adv.* —**friv′o·lous·ness** *n.*

frizz, friz (friz) *vt., vi.* **frizzed, friz′zing** [Fr. *friser*] to form into small, tight curls —*n.* hair, etc. that is frizzed

friz·zle[1] (friz′'l) *vt., vi.* **-zled, -zling** [echoic alteration of FRY[1]] **1.** to make or cause to make a sputtering, hissing noise, as in frying; sizzle **2.** to make or become crisp by broiling or frying

friz·zle[2] (friz′'l) *vt., vi.* **-zled, -zling** [FRIZZ + -LE[2]] to frizz; crimp —*n.* a small, tight curl

friz·zly (-lē) *adj.* **-zli·er, -zli·est** full of or covered with small, tight curls: also **friz′zy**, **-zi·er, -zi·est**

fro (frō) *adv.* [< ON. *frā*] backward; back: now only in *to and fro*: see under TO —*prep.* [Scot.] from

frock (fräk) *n.* [OFr. *froc* (or ML. *froccus*) < OFrank.] **1.** a robe worn by friars, monks, etc. **2.** any of various other garments; specif., *a)* a smock *b)* a dress *c)* same as FROCK COAT —*vt.* **1.** to clothe in a frock **2.** to ordain as a priest

frock coat a man's double-breasted dress coat with a full skirt reaching to the knees, worn chiefly in the 19th cent.

frog (frôg, fräg) *n.* [OE. *frogga*] **1.** a small, coldblooded animal with a smooth skin, webbed feet, and no tail: it has strong hind legs with which it leaps, and most species, when grown, can live either in water or on land **2.** a horny pad in the sole of a horse's foot **3.** a corded or braided loop used as a fastener or decoration on clothing ☆**4.** a device on railroad tracks for keeping cars on the proper rails at intersections or switches **5.** a device placed in a bowl, vase, etc. to hold the stems of flowers —**frog in the throat** a hoarseness due to throat irritation

frog·gy (-ē) *adj.* **-gi·er, -gi·est** **1.** of or like a frog **2.** full of frogs

frog·hop·per (-häp′ər) *n.* a small, leaping insect, whose nymphs produce white froth on plants

frog kick a swimming kick in which the legs are drawn up and spread outward at the knees and then straightened out and brought together with a snap

METAMORPHOSIS
OF FROG

frog·man (-man′) *n., pl.* **-men** (-mən) a person trained and equipped, as with scuba gear, for underwater demolition, exploration, etc.

Frois·sart (frwä sàr′; E. froi′särt), **Jean** (zhän) 1337?–1410?; Fr. chronicler & poet

frol·ic (fräl′ik) *adj.* [< Du. < MDu. *vrō*, merry] [Archaic] full of fun and pranks; merry —*n.* **1.** a playful trick; prank **2.** a lively party or game **3.** merriment; fun —*vi.* **-icked, -ick·ing** **1.** to make merry; have fun **2.** to play or romp about in a happy, carefree way —**frol′ick·er** *n.*

frol·ic·some (-səm) *adj.* full of fun or high spirits; playful; merry: also **frol′ick·y**

from (frum, främ; *unstressed* frəm) *prep.* [OE. *from, fram*: for IE. base see FAR] **1.** beginning at [to walk *from* the door] **2.** starting with [*from* noon to midnight] **3.** out of [he took a comb *from* his pocket] **4.** with (a person or thing) as the maker, speaker, source, etc. [facts learned *from* reading] **5.** at a place not near to [keep away *from* me] **6.** out of the whole of [take two *from* four] **7.** out of the possibility or use of [kept *from* going] **8.** out of the possession or control of [released *from* jail] **9.** as not being like [I can't tell one *from* another] **10.** by reason of; because of [to tremble *from* fear]

frond (fränd) *n.* [< L. *frondis*, genitive of *frons*, leafy branch] **1.** a leaf; specif., *a)* the leaf of a fern *b)* the leaf of a palm **2.** the leaflike part of a lichen, seaweed, etc. —**frond′ed** *adj.*

front (frunt) *n.* [< OFr. < L. *frontis,* genitive of *frons,* forehead] **1.** outward behavior or appearance, esp. when merely pretended [to put on a bold *front*] **2.** the part of something that faces forward; most important side **3.** the first part; beginning [toward the *front* of the book] **4.** the place or position directly before a person or thing **5.** a forward or leading position or situation ☆**6.** the first available bellhop, as in a hotel **7.** the land bordering a lake, ocean, street, etc. **8.** the most forward area, where actual fighting is going on in a war **9.** a specified area of activity [the home *front*] ☆**11.** a broad movement in which different groups are united in order to achieve certain political or social aims ☆**11.** a person who serves as a public representative of a business, group, etc., as because of his prestige ☆**12.** a person, group, etc. used to cover up some activity, esp. an illegal one [the barber shop was a *front* for the numbers racket] **13.** a stiff shirt bosom, worn with formal clothes **14.** a face of a building; esp., the face with the principal entrance **15.** *Meteorol.* the boundary between two masses of air that are different, as in density —*adj.* **1.** at, to, in, on, or of the front **2.** *Phonet.* sounded toward the front of the mouth [*i* in *bid* and *e* in *met* are *front* vowels] —*vt.* **1.** to face; be opposite to [our cottage *fronts* the ocean] **2.** to be before in place **3.** to meet; confront **4.** to defy; oppose **5.** to supply or be a front to [white stone *fronts* the building] —*vi.* **1.** to face in a certain direction ☆**2.** to be a front (senses 11 & 12) (with *for*) —**in front of** before; ahead of

front·age (-ij) *n.* **1.** the front part of a building **2.** the direction toward which this faces **3.** the land between the front edge of a building and the street **4.** *a)* the front boundary line of a lot facing the street *b)* the length of this line **5.** land bordering a street, river, lake, etc.

fron·tal (-'l) *adj.* **1.** of, in, on, at, or against the front [there is a *frontal* lobe of each half of the brain] **2.** of or for the forehead —*n.* the bone forming the forehead: in full, **frontal bone** —**fron′tal·ly** *adv.*

fron·tier (frun tir′) *n.* [< OFr. < *front:* see FRONT] **1.** the border between two countries ☆**2.** that part of a settled country which lies next to an unexplored region **3.** any new or not fully investigated field or area of learning, etc. [the *frontiers* of medicine] —*adj.* of, on, or near a frontier

☆**fron·tiers·man** (-tirz′mən) *n., pl.* **-men** a man who lives on the frontier

fron·tis·piece (frun′tis pēs′) *n.* [OFr. < LL. *frontispicium,* front view < L. *frons,* FRONT + *specere,* to SPY] **1.** an illustration facing the first page or title page of a book or division of a book **2.** *Archit. a)* the main façade *b)* a pediment over a door, window, etc.

front·let (frunt′lit) *n.* [< OFr., ult. < L. *frons,* FRONT] **1.** a decorative band, or specif., a phylactery worn on the forehead **2.** the forehead of an animal, esp. of a bird, when it has distinctive color or markings

☆**front office** the management or administration, as of a company

fron·ton (frän′tän; Sp. frôn tôn′) *n.* [Sp. *frontón,* orig., wall of a handball court < *fronte,* forehead: see FRONT] **1.** a building containing a jai alai court or courts **2.** the Mexican name of JAI ALAI

☆**front-page** (frunt′pāj′) *adj.* fit to be printed on the front page of a newspaper; important [*front-page* news]

front-run·ner (-run′ər) *n.* **1.** one who is leading in a race or competition **2.** one that runs best when in the lead

frost (frôst, fräst) *n.* [OE. < *freosan,* to freeze] **1.** a freezing or being frozen **2.** a temperature low enough to cause freezing **3.** frozen dew or vapor in the form of white crystals; hoarfrost **4.** coolness of action, feeling, manner, etc. —*vt.* **1.** to cover with frost **2.** to damage or kill by freezing **3.** to cover with frosting, or icing **4.** to give a frostlike surface to (glass) **5.** to bleach strands of (hair on the head) so that it looks streaked

Frost (frôst, fräst), **Robert** (**Lee**) 1874–1963; U.S. poet

frost·bite (-bīt′) *vt.* **-bit′, -bit′ten, -bit′ing** to injure the tissues of (a part of the body) by exposure to intense cold —*n.* tissue damage caused by such exposure

frost·ing (-iŋ) *n.* **1.** a mixture of sugar, butter, eggs, etc. for covering a cake; icing **2.** a dull, frostlike finish on glass, metal, etc.

☆**frost line** the level to which frost can penetrate the soil in any given area

frost·y (-ē) *adj.* **frost′i·er, frost′i·est 1.** cold enough to produce frost; freezing [a *frosty* day] **2.** covered as with frost **3.** cold in manner or feeling; unfriendly [a *frosty* greeting] — **frost′i·ly** *adv.* —**frost′i·ness** *n.*

froth (frôth, fräth) *n.* [ON. *frotha*] **1.** a whitish mass of bubbles; foam **2.** foaming saliva caused by disease or great excitement **3.** light, trifling, or worthless talk, ideas, etc. —*vt.* **1.** to cause to foam **2.** to cover with foam **3.** to spill forth as foam —*vi.* to produce froth; foam [animals with rabies sometimes *froth* at the mouth]

froth·y (frôth′ē, fräth′ē) *adj.* **froth′i·er, froth′i·est 1.** foamy [*frothy* beer] **2.** light; trifling; worthless [*frothy* talk] — **froth′i·ly** *adv.* —**froth′i·ness** *n.*

frou-frou (frōō′frōō′) *n.* [Fr.; echoic] **1.** a rustling or swishing, as of a skirt ☆**2.** [Colloq.] too much decoration, esp. on clothes; fancy elegance

fro·ward (frō′ərd, -wərd) *adj.* [ME., unruly: see FRO & -WARD] not easily controlled; stubborn in having one's own way —**fro′ward·ly** *adv.* —**fro′ward·ness** *n.*

frown (froun) *vi.* [< OFr. < *froigne,* sullen face < Gaul.] **1.** to wrinkle the forehead and draw the eyebrows together, as in anger or deep thought **2.** to show displeasure or disapproval (with *on* or *upon*) [he *frowns* on tardiness] —*vt.* to express (disapproval, etc.) by frowning —*n.* **1.** the act or look of frowning **2.** any expression of displeasure or disapproval —**frown′er** *n.* —**frown′ing·ly** *adv.*

frow·zy (frou′zē) *adj.* **-zi·er, -zi·est** [< ?] **1.** [Rare] bad-smelling **2.** dirty and untidy; slovenly Also sp. **frow′sy** — **frow′zi·ly** *adv.* —**frow′zi·ness** *n.*

froze (frōz) *pt. of* FREEZE

fro·zen (frō′z'n) *pp. of* FREEZE —*adj.* **1.** turned into or covered with ice [a *frozen* milkshake; a *frozen* river] **2.** damaged or killed by freezing **3.** having heavy frosts and extreme cold [the *frozen* north] **4.** preserved by freezing, as food **5.** stiff and not moving, as if turned into ice [*frozen* with terror] **6.** without warmth or affection [a *frozen* smile] **7.** arbitrarily kept at a fixed level or in a fixed position [prices were *frozen*] **8.** not readily converted into cash [*frozen* assets]

☆**frozen custard** a food like ice cream, but with less butterfat content and softer

FRS Federal Reserve System

F.R.S. Fellow of the Royal Society

frt. freight

fruc·ti·fy (fruk′tə fī′) *vi., vt.* **-fied′, -fy′ing** [< OFr. < L. *fructificare:* see FRUIT & -FY] to bear or cause to bear fruit —**fruc′ti·fi·ca′tion** *n.*

fruc·tose (fruk′tōs, frook′-) *n.* [< L. *fructus,* FRUIT + -OSE¹] a crystalline sugar, $C_6H_{12}O_6$, found in sweet fruits and in honey; fruit sugar; levulose

fru·gal (frōō′g'l) *adj.* [L. *frugalis* < *frugi,* fit for food < *frux,* fruits] **1.** not wasteful; thrifty [a *frugal* manager] **2.** not costly; inexpensive or meager [a *frugal* meal] —see SYN. at THRIFTY —**fru·gal′i·ty** (-gal′ə tē) *n., pl.* **-ties** —**fru′gal·ly** *adv.*

fruit (frōōt) *n.* see PLURAL, II, D, 3 [OFr. < L. *fructus* < pp. of *frui,* to enjoy < IE. base *bhrug-,* to enjoy] **1.** any plant product, as grain, flax, vegetables, etc.: *usually used in pl.* [the *fruits* of the field] **2.** a sweet part of a plant, consisting of a fruit (sense 5), usually eaten raw or as a dessert: many true fruits which are not sweet, as tomatoes, green peppers, etc., are popularly called *vegetables* **3.** the result or product of any action [the *fruit* of labor] **4.** [Archaic] offspring **5.** *Bot.* the mature ovary of a flowering plant, along with its contents, as the whole peach, pea pod, cucumber, etc. —*vi., vt.* to bear or cause to bear fruit

fruit·age (frōōt′ij) *n.* **1.** the bearing of fruit **2.** a crop of fruit **3.** a result; product; consequence

fruit bat any of a large group of bats that feed almost entirely on fruit

fruit·cake (-kāk′) *n.* a rich cake containing nuts, preserved fruit, citron, spices, etc.

fruit cup ☆mixed diced fruits served in a cup as an appetizer or dessert: also **fruit cocktail**

fruit fly 1. a small fly whose larvae feed on fruits and vegetables **2.** *same as* DROSOPHILA

fruit·ful (-fəl) *adj.* **1.** bearing much fruit **2.** producing much; productive; prolific [Mozart was a *fruitful* composer] **3.** producing results; profitable [a *fruitful* plan] —see SYN. at FERTILE — **fruit′ful·ly** *adv.* —**fruit′ful·ness** *n.*

fruit·ing body (frōōt′iŋ) the part of a fungus that bears the spores

fru·i·tion (frōō ish′ən) *n.* [OFr. < LL.

FRUIT BAT
(head & body
to 18 in.;
wingspread
to 5 ft.)

< *frui:* see FRUIT] **1.** the pleasure of using or possessing something; enjoyment **2.** the bearing of fruit **3.** a reaching or getting what was planned or worked for; fulfillment [his book is the *fruition* of years of research]

fruit·less (frōōt′lis) *adj.* **1.** without results; unsuccessful; vain [*fruitless* efforts] **2.** bearing no fruit; sterile; barren —see SYN. at FUTILE —**fruit′less·ly** *adv.* —**fruit′less·ness** *n.*

fruit sugar *same as* FRUCTOSE

fruit tree a tree that bears edible fruit

fruit·wood (-wood′) *n.* the wood of any of various fruit trees, used in furniture, paneling, etc.

fruit·y (frōōt′ē) *adj.* **fruit′i·er, fruit′i·est** **1.** like fruit in taste or smell **2.** rich or mellow in tone [a *fruity* voice] **3.** [Slang] crazy —**fruit′i·ly** *adv.* —**fruit′i·ness** *n.*

frump (frump) *n.* [< Du. *frompelen* < *rompelen*, to rumple] an unattractive woman who is not neat or stylish —**frump′ish** *adj.* —**frump′y** *adj.* **frump′i·er, frump′i·est**

Frun·ze (frōōn′ze) capital of the Kirghiz S.S.R., in the SC part: pop. 416,000

frus·trate (frus′trāt) *vt.* **-trat·ed, -trat·ing** [< L. pp. of *frustrare*, in vain] **1.** to keep from being carried out; nullify [to *frustrate* plans] **2.** to keep from a goal; thwart; foil [to *frustrate* a foe] **3.** to cause to feel discouraged, uneasy, etc. by thwarting [he's *frustrated* by his inability to win at chess] —*vi.* to become frustrated —**frus·tra′tion** *n.*

frus·tum (frus′təm) *n., pl.* **-tums, -ta** (-tə) [L., a piece, bit] the solid figure formed when the top of a cone or pyramid is cut off by a plane parallel to the base

fry[1] (frī) *vt., vi.* **fried, fry′ing** [< OFr. < L. *frigere*, to fry] **1.** to cook or be cooked, usually in hot fat or oil, over direct heat **2.** [Slang] to electrocute or be electrocuted —*n., pl.* **fries 1.** a fried food; esp., [*pl.*] fried potatoes ☆**2.** a social gathering where food is fried and eaten [a fish *fry*]

fry[2] (frī) *n., pl.* **fry** [prob. a merging of ON. *frjo*, seed, with Anglo-Fr. *frei*, spawn] **1.** young fish **2.** small adult fish, esp. in large groups **3.** offspring; children —**small fry 1.** children or a child **2.** unimportant people or things

fry·er (frī′ər) *n.* **1.** one that fries; specif., a deep pan for frying foods **2.** food to be cooked by frying, esp. a young, tender chicken

frying pan a shallow pan with a handle, for frying food: also **fry′pan′** *n.* —**out of the frying pan into the fire** from a bad situation into a worse one

f-stop (ef′stäp′) *n.* any of the settings for the f-number of a camera

ft. 1. foot; feet **2.** fort

FTC Federal Trade Commission

fth., fthm. fathom

fuch·sia (fyōō′shə) *n.* [ModL., after L. *Fuchs*, 16th-c. G. botanist] **1.** a shrubby plant with drooping pink, red, or purple flowers **2.** purplish red —*adj.* purplish-red

FRUSTUM

fu·cus (fyōō′kəs) *n., pl.* **fu′ci** (-sī), **fu′cus·es** [L. < Gr. *phykos*, kind of lichen] any of a group of brown algae with a flattened body bearing swollen bladders

fud·dle (fud′'l) *vt.* **-dled, -dling** [akin ? to G. dial. *fuddeln*, to swindle] to confuse or daze as with alcoholic liquor —*n.* a fuddled condition

fud·dy-dud·dy (fud′ē dud′ē) *n., pl.* **-dies** [prob. based on dial. *fud*, buttocks] [Slang] **1.** a fussy, critical person **2.** an old-fashioned person

FUCHSIA

fudge (fuj) *n.* [? echoic] **1.** empty talk; nonsense ☆**2.** [< ?] a soft candy made of butter, milk, sugar, flavoring, etc. —*vt.* **fudged, fudg′ing** to make dishonestly or carelessly; fake [to *fudge* a report] —*vi.* ☆**1.** to refuse to commit oneself; hedge [to *fudge* on an issue] ☆**2.** to cheat

fu·el (fyōō′əl, fyōōl) *n.* [< OFr. *fouaille*, ult. < L. *focus*, fireplace] **1.** coal, oil, gas, wood, etc. burned to supply heat or power **2.** fissionable material from which atomic energy can be obtained, as in a nuclear reactor **3.** anything that makes a strong feeling even stronger [his silence only added *fuel* to her anger] —*vt.* **-eled** or **-elled, -el·ing** or **-el·ling** to supply with fuel —*vi.* to get fuel —**fu′el·er, fu′el·ler** *n.*

fuel cell any of various devices that convert chemical energy directly into electrical energy

fuel injection the spraying of fuel directly into the combustion chambers of an internal-combustion engine, where it burns readily due to the heat of the compressed air in the chambers

☆**fuel oil** any oil used for fuel; esp., a product obtained in distilling petroleum and used in diesel engines

-fuge (fyōōj) [Fr. < L. *fugere*, to flee] a suffix meaning something that drives away [*vermifuge*]

fu·gi·tive (fyōō′jə tiv) *adj.* [< OFr. < L. pp. of *fugere*, to flee] **1.** fleeing or having fled, as from danger, justice, etc. **2.** passing quickly away; fleeting; evanescent [*fugitive* pleasures] **3.** on matters of temporary interest [*fugitive* essays] **4.** roaming; shifting —*n.* **1.** a person who flees or has fled from danger, justice, etc. **2.** a fleeting or elusive thing —**fu′gi·tive·ly** *adv.*

fugue (fyōōg) *n.* [Fr. < It. < L. < *fugere*, to flee] a musical composition in which a short theme is played or sung by one instrument or voice and then developed in counterpoint, one after another, by two or three others —**fu′gal** *adj.* —**fugu′ist** *n.*

‡**Füh·rer, Fueh·rer** (fü′rər; E. fyōor′ər) *n.* [G. < *führen*, to lead] leader: title used by A. Hitler

Fu·ji (fōō′jē) extinct volcano on Honshu island, Japan, near Tokyo: also **Fu′ji·ya′ma** (-yä′mə)

Fu·ku·o·ka (fōō′kōō ō′kə) seaport on the N coast of Kyushu island, Japan: pop. 750,000

-ful (fəl, f'l; *for 4, usually* fool) [OE. < *full*, FULL[1]] a suffix meaning: **1.** full of, characterized by, having [*joyful*] **2.** having the qualities of [*masterful*] **3.** able or tending to [*helpful*] **4.** *pl.* **-fuls** the quantity that fills [*handful*]: a colloquial plural is sometimes formed by adding -s- to the noun stem [*cupsful*]

ful·crum (fool′krəm, ful′-) *n., pl.* **-crums, -cra** (-krə) [L., akin to *fulcire*, to prop: see BALK] the support or point of support on which a lever turns in raising or moving something

ful·fill, ful·fil (fool fil′) *vt.* **-filled′, -fill′ing** [OE. *fullfyllan*] **1.** to carry out (something promised, predicted, etc.); cause to be or happen [to *fulfill* an oath] **2.** to do (something required); obey [to *fulfill* a duty] **3.** to satisfy (a condition) or answer (a purpose) **4.** to bring to an end; complete —see SYN. at PERFORM —**fulfill oneself** to achieve fully what one hoped to do or was capable of doing —**ful·fill′er** *n.* —**ful·fill′ment, ful·fil′ment** *n.*

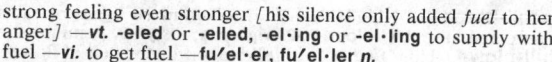
FULCRUM

ful·gent (ful′jənt, fool′-) *adj.* [< L. prp. of *fulgere*, to flash] [Now Rare] very bright; radiant

full[1] (fool) *adj.* [OE. < IE. base *pel-*, to fill] **1.** having in it all there is space for; filled [a *full* jar] **2.** *a)* having eaten all that one wants *b)* having had more than one can stand (*of*) [I'm *full* of his complaints] **3.** occupying all of a given space [a *full* load] **4.** well supplied or provided (with *of*) [a tank *full* of gas] **5.** filling the required number, measure, etc.; complete [a *full* dozen] **6.** thorough; absolute [come to a *full* stop] **7.** having reached the greatest development, size, etc. [a *full* moon] **8.** having the same parents [*full* brothers] **9.** having clearness, volume, and depth [a *full* tone] ☆**10.** of the highest rank [a *full* professor] **11.** plump; round [a *full* face] **12.** with loose, wide folds; ample [a *full* skirt] **13.** deeply affected, engrossed, etc. [*full* of plans for the future] ☆**14.** *Baseball a)* designating a count of three balls and two strikes on the batter *b)* with a runner at each of the three bases —*n.* the greatest amount, extent, number, etc. [she enjoyed life to the *full*] —*adv.* **1.** completely [a *full*-grown boy] **2.** directly [struck *full* in the face] **3.** very [he knows *full* well] —*vt.* to make (a skirt, etc.) with loose folds —*vi.* to become full: said of the moon —**in full 1.** to, for, or with the full amount, value, etc. [paid *in full*] **2.** not abbreviated or condensed [he quoted the letter *in full*]

full[2] (fool) *vt., vi.* [< OFr., ult. < L. *fullo*, cloth fuller] to shrink and thicken (cloth, esp. of wool) with moisture, heat, and pressure

full·back (fool′bak′) *n. Football* a member of the backfield on offense, traditionally the back farthest behind the line, who specializes in line plunges and power plays

---

fat, āpe, cär; ten, ēven; is, bīte; gō, hôrn, tōol, look; oil, out; up, fur; get; joy; yet; chin; she; thin, then; zh, leisure; ŋ, ring; ə for a in ago, e in agent, i in sanity, o in comply, u in focus; ′ as in able (ā′b'l); Fr. bal; ë, Fr. coeur; ö, Fr. feu; Fr. mon; ô, Fr. coq; ü, Fr. duc; r, Fr. cri; H, G. ich; kh, G. doch; ‡foreign; ☆ Americanism; < derived from. See inside front cover.

☆**full-blood·ed** (-blud'id) *adj.* **1.** of unmixed breed or race; purebred: also **full'-blood'** **2.** vigorous; lusty **3.** genuine

full-blown (-blōn') *adj.* **1.** in full bloom; open: said of flowers **2.** fully developed; mature

full-bod·ied (-bäd'ēd) *adj.* having much strength, flavor, substance, etc. [a *full-bodied* coffee]

full dress formal clothes for important occasions; esp., formal evening clothes —**full'-dress'** *adj.*

full·er (fool'ər) *n.* one whose work is to full cloth

full·er's earth (fool'ərz) a highly absorbent clay used to remove grease from cloth in fulling, to clarify oils, etc.

Ful·ler·ton (fool'ər tən) [after G. *Fullerton*, a founder] city in SW Calif.: suburb of Los Angeles: pop. 86,000

full-fash·ioned (fool'fash'’nd) *adj.* knitted to conform to the shape of body parts, as hosiery or sweaters

full-fledged (-flejd') *adj.* **1.** having a complete set of feathers; mature: said of a bird **2.** completely developed or trained; of full rank or status [a *full-fledged* pilot]

☆**full house** a poker hand containing three of a kind and a pair, as three jacks and two fives: it ranks higher than a flush

full moon the phase of the moon when it is seen as a full, lighted disk

full nelson *see* NELSON

full·ness, ful·ness (-nis) *n.* the quality or state of being full

full sail **1.** with every sail set **2.** with maximum speed and energy

full-scale (-skāl') *adj.* **1.** exactly the same as the original in size and proportions [a *full-scale* drawing] **2.** to the utmost limit, degree, etc. [*full-scale* war]

full-time (-tīm') *adj.* working, studying, etc. for periods regarded as one's full regular working hours [a *full-time* college student]

full time as a full-time employee, student, etc. [to work *full time*]

full·y (-ē) *adv.* **1.** to the full; completely [he understood *fully*] **2.** abundantly; amply [they were *fully* rewarded] **3.** at least [*fully* two hours later]

ful·mi·nate (ful'mə nāt') *vi.* -nat'ed, -nat'ing [< L. pp. of *fulminare* < *fulmen*, lightning: for IE. base see BLACK] **1.** to explode with violence; detonate **2.** to shout forth protests, criticism, censure, etc. —*vt.* **1.** to cause to explode **2.** to shout forth (protests, etc.) —*n.* any of certain highly explosive compounds used in detonators and percussion caps —**ful'mi·nant** *adj.* —**ful'mi·na'tion** *n.* —**ful'mi·na'tor** *n.*

ful·some (fool'səm, ful'-) *adj.* [ME. < *ful*, FULL[1] + -*som*, -SOME[1], but infl. by *ful*, foul] disgusting or sickening, esp. because too much or insincere [*fulsome* praise] —**ful'some·ly** *adv.* —**ful'some·ness** *n.*

Ful·ton (fool't’n), **Robert** 1765-1815; U.S. inventor & engineer, who designed the first commercially successful U.S. steamboat, the *Clermont* (1807)

fum·ble (fum'b'l) *vi.*, *vt.* -bled, -bling [prob. < ON. *famla*, to grope] **1.** to grope clumsily [she *fumbled* for a dime in her purse] **2.** to handle (a thing) clumsily; bungle **3.** to lose one's grasp on (a football, etc.) while trying to catch or hold it **4.** to make (one's way) as by groping —*n.* **1.** the act or fact of fumbling **2.** a ball that has been fumbled —**fum'bler** *n.* —**fum'bling·ly** *adv.*

fume (fyoom) *n.* [< OFr. < L. *fumus*: for IE. base see DOWN[2]] [often pl.] a gas, smoke, or vapor, esp. if sickening or suffocating —*vi.* fumed, fum'ing **1.** to give off fumes **2.** to rise up or pass off in fumes **3.** to show that one is angry, annoyed, etc. [he *fumed* at the long delay] —*vt.* **1.** to expose to fumes **2.** to give off as fumes

fu·mi·gant (fyoo'mə gənt) *n.* any substance used in fumigating

fu·mi·gate (-gāt') *vt.* -gat'ed, -gat'ing [< L. pp. of *fumigare* < *fumus* (see FUME), smoke + *agere*, to make] to expose to the action of fumes, esp. in order to disinfect or to kill the vermin in [the exterminator *fumigated* the garage to get rid of the hornets] —**fu'mi·ga'tion** *n.* —☆**fu'mi·ga'tor** *n.*

fum·y (fyoo'mē) *adj.* **fum'i·er, fum'i·est** full of or producing fumes; vaporous

fun (fun) *n.* [< ME. *fonne*, a fool, or *fonnen*, to be foolish < ?] **1.** *a)* lively, gay play or playfulness; amusement, sport, recreation, etc. *b)* enjoyment or pleasure [do you get any *fun* out of gardening?] **2.** a source of amusement; amusing person or thing [he's great *fun* at a party] —☆*adj.* [Colloq.] intended for pleasure and amusement [a *fun* gift] —*vi.* funned, fun'ning [Colloq.] to make fun; play or joke —**for** (or **in**) **fun** playfully; not seriously —**like fun** [Slang] by no means; not at all —**make fun of** (or **poke fun at**) to mock laughingly; ridicule

func·tion (funk'shən) *n.* [OFr. < L. *functio* < pp. of *fungi*, to perform < IE. base *bheug-*, to enjoy] **1.** the normal or characteristic action of anything; esp., any of the specialized actions of an organ or part of an animal or plant [one *function* of the liver is to secrete bile] **2.** a special duty or performance required in the course of work or activity [the *function* of a treasurer] **3.** a formal ceremony or social occasion **4.** a thing that depends on and varies with something else [the color of the enamel is partly a *function* of the heat in the kiln] **5.** *Math.* a quantity whose value depends on that of another quantity or quantities —*vi.* **1.** to act in a required manner; work [his brakes don't *function* properly] **2.** to have a function; be used (*as*) [that table can *function* as a desk]

SYN.—**function** is the broad, general term for the usual or expected activity of a person or thing [the *function* of a teacher, a carburetor, etc.]; **office**, in this connection, refers to the function of a person, as determined by his position or employment [the *office* of president]; **duty** is applied to a task that must be carried out because of one's occupation, rank, etc. [the *duties* of a priest]; **capacity** refers to a function or status that is not necessarily the usual one [the judge spoke to him in the *capacity* of a friend]

func·tion·al (-’l) *adj.* **1.** of a function or functions **2.** *a)* performing a function *b)* intended to be more useful than decorative [*functional* furniture] **3.** *Med.* affecting a function of some organ, but with no organic changes [a *functional* disorder of the liver] —**func'tion·al·ly** *adv.*

func·tion·al·ism (-ə liz'm) *n.* the practice of allowing the function of a thing to determine how it should be designed —**func'tion·al·ist** *n.*, *adj.* —**func'tion·al·is'tic** *adj.*

func·tion·ar·y (-er'ē) *n.*, *pl.* -ar'ies a person who performs a certain function; esp., an official

function word a word that has little or no meaning in itself but is used to show the grammatical relationship between other words [articles and conjunctions are *function words*]

fund (fund) *n.* [L. *fundus*, BOTTOM, land] **1.** a supply that can be drawn on; stock; store [a *fund* of good humor] **2.** *a)* a sum of money set aside for a particular purpose [a scholarship *fund*] *b)* an organization that manages such a fund *c)* [*pl.*] ready money [she lacks *funds* for the trip] —*vt.* **1.** to provide money to pay the interest on (a debt) **2.** to put or convert into a long-term debt that bears interest **3.** to put in a fund; accumulate **4.** to provide for with a fund [to *fund* a project]

fun·da·ment (fun'də mənt) *n.* [< OFr. < L. < *fundus*: see prec.] **1.** the buttocks **2.** the anus

fun·da·men·tal (fun'də men't'l) *adj.* [< ML. < L. *fundamentum*: see prec.] **1.** of or forming a foundation or basis; basic; essential [freedom of the press is *fundamental* to democracy] **2.** on which others are based; primary [a *fundamental* type] **3.** most important; chief [his *fundamental* needs] **4.** *Music a)* designating or of the lowest, or root, tone of a chord *b)* designating or of the prime or main tone of a harmonic series —*n.* **1.** a principle, law, etc. serving as a basis; essential part **2.** *Music* the fundamental tone of a chord or harmonic series —**fun'da·men'tal·ly** *adv.*

☆**fun·da·men·tal·ism** (-iz'm) *n.* [sometimes F-] **1.** the religious belief that the Bible must be read and interpreted in a literal way **2.** among some American Protestants, the movement based on these beliefs —**fun'da·men'tal·ist** *n.*, *adj.*

fundamental particle *same as* ELEMENTARY PARTICLE

Fun·dy (fun'dē), **Bay of** arm of the Atlantic, between New Brunswick & Nova Scotia, Canada: c. 140 mi. long: noted for its high tides of 60-70 ft.

fu·ner·al (fyoo'nər əl) *adj.* [< LL. < L. *funeris*, genitive of *funus*, a funeral] of or for a funeral —*n.* **1.** the ceremonies connected with burial or cremation of the dead **2.** the procession accompanying the body to the place of burial or cremation

☆**funeral director** the manager of a funeral home

☆**funeral home** (or **parlor**) a business establishment where the bodies of the dead are prepared for burial or cremation and where funeral services can be held

fu·ne·re·al (fyoo nir'ē əl) *adj.* suitable for a funeral; sad and solemn; gloomy —**fu·ne're·al·ly** *adv.*

fun·gi (fun'jī, fuŋ'gī) *n.* *pl. of* FUNGUS

BAY OF FUNDY

fun·gi·cide (fun′jə sīd′, fuŋ′gə-) *n.* [< FUNGUS & -CIDE] any substance that kills fungi —**fun′gi·cid′al** *adj.*

☆**fun·go** (fuŋ′gō) *n., pl.* **-goes** [< ?] a fly ball hit, esp. for fielding practice, by tossing the ball into the air oneself and batting it

fun·goid (fuŋ′goid) *adj.* like or characteristic of a fungus —*n.* a fungus

fun·gous (-gəs) *adj.* of, like, or caused by fungi [a *fungous* disease]

fun·gus (fuŋ′gəs) *n., pl.* **fun·gi** (fun′jī, fuŋ′gī), **fun′gus·es** [L., prob. < Gr. *spongos*, a sponge] **1.** any of a group of lower plants, including molds, mildews, mushrooms, rusts, and smut, that lack chlorophyll and leaves and reproduce by means of spores **2.** something that grows rapidly like a fungus —*adj.* of, like, or caused by a fungus

FUNGI

fu·nic·u·lar (fyoo nik′yoo lər) *adj.* [< L. *funiculus*, dim. of *funis*, a rope] of or worked by a rope or cable —*n.* a mountain railway on which a car being pulled up by a cable is counterbalanced by one being pulled down: also **funicular railway**

funk[1] (fuŋk) *n.* [< ? Fl. *fonck*, dismay] [Colloq.] **1.** the condition of being greatly afraid or in a panic **2.** a low, depressed mood: also **blue funk** —*vi.* [Colloq.] to be in a funk or panic —*vt.* [Colloq.] **1.** to be afraid of **2.** to shrink from in fear **3.** to frighten

funk[2] (fuŋk) *n.* [see FUNKY[2]] **1.** a musty odor, as of moldy tobacco ☆**2.** funky jazz

fun·ky[1] (fuŋ′kē) *adj.* **-ki·er, -ki·est** in a funk, or panic

fun·ky[2] (fuŋ′kē) *adj.* **-ki·er, -ki·est** [orig. Negro dialect, meaning earthy < obs. *funk*, smell, smoke] ☆*Jazz* having an earthy quality or style derived from early blues —**fun′ki·ness** *n.*

fun·nel (fun′'l) *n.* [< Pr. < L. (*in*)*fundibulum* < *in-*, in + *fundere*, to pour: see FOUND[3]] **1.** a slender tube with a wide, cone-shaped mouth, for pouring liquids and powders into containers with small openings **2.** anything shaped like a funnel **3.** *a)* a cylindrical smokestack, as of a steamship *b)* a chimney or flue —*vi., vt.* **-neled** or **-nelled, -nel·ing** or **-nel·ling 1.** to move or pour through a funnel **2.** to move into a central channel or place [traffic was *funneled* into a single lane]

fun·ny (fun′ē) *adj.* **-ni·er, -ni·est 1.** causing laughter; amusing; humorous **2.** [Colloq.] *a)* strange; queer [*it's funny* that he's late] ☆*b)* deceptive or tricky [no *funny* tricks, now!] —☆*n., pl.* **-nies** [Colloq.] *same as* COMIC STRIP: *usually in pl.* —☆**get funny with** [Colloq.] to be impudent to —**fun′ni·ly** *adv.* —**fun′ni·ness** *n.*

SYN.—**funny** is the simple, general term for anything that appeals to one's sense of humor or causes laughter; **laughable** is a usually scornful term for that which is fit to be laughed at [what a *laughable* excuse!]; something that is **amusing** brings laughter or smiles by its pleasant, entertaining quality; that which is **droll** amuses one because it is quaint or strange or because of its twisted humor; **comic** is applied to that which is like a comedy in amusing one in a thoughtful way; **comical** is used of that which brings on uncontrolled laughter; **farcical** suggests a comical quality that is based on nonsense, broad humor, etc.

funny bone [prob. a pun on HUMERUS (hence "humorous")] a place on the elbow where the ulnar nerve passes close to the surface: a sharp blow at this place causes a strange, tingling sensation in the arm

fur (fur) *n.* [< OFr. < *fuerre*, a sheath < Frank. *fodr*] **1.** the soft, thick hair covering the body of many mammals **2.** a skin bearing such hair, processed for making garments **3.** any garment made of such skins **4.** any fuzzy coating, as on the tongue in illness —*adj.* of fur —*vt.* **furred, fur′ring 1.** to line, cover, or trim with fur **2.** to coat with a furry deposit **3.** to make level with furring strips —*vi.* to become coated with a furry deposit —☆**make the fur fly 1.** to cause argument or fighting **2.** to work busily

fur·be·low (fur′bə lō′) *n.* [var. of Fr. *falbala*] **1.** a flounce or ruffle **2.** [*usually pl.*] showy trimming —*vt.* to decorate as with furbelows

fur·bish (fur′bish) *vt.* [< OFr. *forbir* < WGmc.] **1.** to brighten by rubbing or scouring; burnish **2.** to make usable again; renovate —**fur′bish·er** *n.*

fur·cate (fur′kāt; *for adj., also* -kit) *adj.* [< ML. < L. *furca*, a fork] forked —*vi.* **-cat·ed, -cat·ing** to branch; fork —**fur′cate·ly** *adv.* —**fur·ca′tion** *n.*

Fu·ries (fyoor′ēz) *Gr. & Rom. Myth.* three female spirits who punished wrongdoers

fu·ri·ous (fyoor′ē əs) *adj.* [< OFr. < L. *furiosus*] **1.** full of fury or wild rage **2.** violently overpowering [a *furious* attack] **3.** very great; intense [*furious* speed] —**fu′ri·ous·ly** *adv.* —**fu′ri·ous·ness** *n.*

furl (furl) *vt.* [< OFr. *ferlier* < *fermlier*, to tie up < *ferm*, FIRM[1] + *lier*, to tie] to roll up tightly and make secure, as a flag to a staff or a sail to a spar —*vi.* to become curled or rolled up —*n.* **1.** a roll or coil of something furled **2.** a furling or being furled

fur·long (fur′lôŋ) *n.* [< OE. < *furh*, a furrow + *lang*, LONG[1]] a measure of distance equal to 1/8 of a mile, or 220 yards

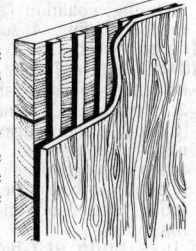

FURLED SAIL

fur·lough (fur′lō) *n.* [< Du. *verlof*] a leave of absence; esp., a leave granted to a soldier —☆*vt.* **1.** to grant a furlough to **2.** to lay off (employees), esp. temporarily

fur·nace (fur′nəs) *n.* [< OFr. < L. *fornax* < *fornus*, oven: for IE. base see WARM] **1.** an enclosed structure in which heat is produced for warming a building, reducing ores, melting metals, etc. **2.** any extremely hot place

fur·nish (fur′nish) *vt.* [< OFr. < *furnir* < OFrank.] **1.** to supply with whatever is necessary; esp., to put furniture into (a room, apartment, etc.) **2.** to give or provide [he *furnished* the information] —**fur′nish·er** *n.*

SYN.—**furnish** implies the giving or getting of all the things needed for a particular purpose [to *furnish* a home]; to **equip** is to provide with what is needed for efficient operation [a truck *equipped* with air brakes]; to **outfit** is to supply completely with the articles needed for an undertaking, occupation, etc. [that store *outfits* hunting parties]

fur·nish·ings (-iŋz) *n.pl.* **1.** the furniture, carpets, etc. for a room, apartment, etc. **2.** articles of dress; things to wear [men's *furnishings*]

fur·ni·ture (fur′ni chər) *n.* [Fr. *fourniture* < *fournir*, FURNISH] **1.** the movable things in a room, etc. which equip it for living, as chairs, tables, beds, etc. **2.** the necessary equipment of a ship, trade, etc.

fu·ror (fyoor′ôr) *n.* [< OFr. *fureur* < L. *furor*] **1.** fury; rage **2.** *a)* widespread enthusiasm; craze *b)* a commotion or uproar Also for 2, **fu′rore** (-ôr)

furred (furd) *adj.* **1.** made, trimmed, or lined with fur **2.** having fur **3.** wearing fur **4.** having a furry coating, as the tongue **5.** made level with furring strips

fur·ri·er (fur′ē ər) *n.* **1.** a dealer in furs **2.** one who processes furs or makes and repairs fur garments —**fur′ri·er·y** *n., pl.* **-er·ies**

fur·ring (fur′iŋ) *n.* **1.** the act of trimming, lining, etc. with fur **2.** fur so used **3.** a furry coating, as on the tongue **4.** *a)* the leveling of a floor, wall, etc., or the making of air spaces with thin strips of wood or metal before adding boards or plaster *b)* the strips (in full, **furring strips**) so used

fur·row (fur′ō) *n.* [OE. *furh*] **1.** a narrow groove made in the ground by a plow **2.** anything like this, as a wrinkle on the face —*vt.* to make furrows in [trouble had *furrowed* his brow] —*vi.* **1.** to make furrows **2.** to become wrinkled

fur·ry (fur′ē) *adj.* **-ri·er, -ri·est 1.** of, like, or made of fur **2.** covered with or wearing fur **3.** having a furlike coating [a *furry* tongue] —**fur′ri·ness** *n.*

FURRING STRIPS

fur·ther (fur′thər) *adj. a compar. of* FAR [OE. *furthra*] **1.** additional; more [can I be of *further* aid?] **2.** more distant; farther —*adv. a compar. of* FAR **1.** to a greater degree or extent [I'll study it *further*] **2.** in addition; moreover **3.** at or to a greater distance in space or time In sense 2 of the *adj.* and sense 3 of the *adv.*, FARTHER is more commonly used

—*vt.* [< OE. *fyrthrian* < *furthra*] to give aid to; promote [she *furthered* his education] —**fur'ther·er** *n.*

fur·ther·ance (-əns) *n.* a furthering, or helping forward; advancement; promotion [in *furtherance* of our goals]

fur·ther·more (-môr') *adv.* besides; moreover; in addition

fur·ther·most (-mōst') *adj.* most distant; furthest

fur·thest (fur'thist) *adj. a superl. of* FAR [ME.] most distant; farthest —*adv. a superl. of* FAR 1. at or to the greatest distance in space or time 2. to the greatest degree; most

fur·tive (fur'tiv) *adj.* [< Fr. < L. *furtivus*, stolen < *fur*, thief] done or acting in a sly, sneaky way [he took a *furtive* glance at the letter] —see SYN. at SECRET —**fur'tive·ly** *adv.* —**fur'tive·ness** *n.*

fu·ry (fyoor'ē) *n., pl.* -ries [< OFr. < L. *furia* < *furere*, to rage] 1. *a)* violent anger; wild rage *b)* a fit of this [in a *fury* over the loss] 2. violence; vehemence; fierceness [the *fury* of a storm] 3. a violent, vengeful person 4. [F-] any of the Furies —see SYN. at ANGER —**like fury** [Colloq.] violently, swiftly, etc.

furze (furz) *n.* [OE. *fyrs*] a prickly evergreen shrub with yellow flowers, growing esp. on wastelands

fuse[1] (fyooz) *vt., vi.* **fused, fus'ing** [< L. pp. of *fundere*: see FOUND[3]] 1. to melt or to join by melting, as metals 2. to unite or blend together

fuse[2] (fyooz) *n.* [< It. < L. *fusus*, hollow spindle] 1. a tube or wick filled with highly burnable material for setting off an explosive charge 2. *same as* FUZE[2] (*n.* 2) 3. *Elec.* a strip of easily melted metal placed in a circuit as a safeguard: if the current becomes too strong, the metal melts, thus breaking the circuit —*vt.* **fused, fus'ing** to connect a fuse to —**blow a fuse** 1. to cause an electrical fuse to melt 2. [Colloq.] to become very angry

fu·see (fyoo zē') *n.* [Fr. *fusée*, rocket < ML. < L. *fusus*: see prec.] 1. formerly, a friction match with a large head ☆2. a colored flare used as a signal by railroaders, truck drivers, etc.

fu·se·lage (fyoo'sə läzh', -läj', -lij; -zə-) *n.* [Fr. < *fuselé*, tapering] the body of an airplane, not including the wings, tail, and engines

fu·sel oil (fyoo'z'l, -s'l) [G. *fusel*, inferior liquor] an oily, sharp-smelling, poisonous liquid occurring in alcoholic products that have not been fully distilled: used as a solvent for oils, varnish, etc.

Fu·shun (foo'shoon') city in NE China: pop. 1,019,000

fu·si·ble (fyoo'zə b'l) *adj.* that can be fused or easily melted —**fu'si·bil'i·ty** *n.* —**fu'si·bly** *adv.*

fu·si·form (fyoo'zə fôrm') *adj.* [< L. *fusus*, a spindle + -FORM] shaped like a spindle

fu·sil (fyoo'z'l) *n.* [Fr., orig., steel for striking sparks < ML. < L. *focus*, hearth] a light flintlock musket

fu·sil·ier, fu·sil·eer (fyoo'zə lir') *n.* formerly, a soldier armed with a fusil: the term *Fusiliers* is still applied to certain British regiments

fu·sil·lade (fyoo'sə läd', -läd'; -zə-) *n.* [Fr. < *fusiller*, to shoot: see FUSIL] 1. a discharge of many firearms at the same time 2. something like this [a *fusillade* of questions] —*vt.* **-lad'ed, -lad'ing** to shoot down or attack with a fusillade

fu·sion (fyoo'zhən) *n.* 1. a fusing or melting together 2. a blending; coalition [a *fusion* of political parties] 3. anything made by fusing 4. *same as* NUCLEAR FUSION

fusion bomb *same as* HYDROGEN BOMB

fuss (fus) *n.* [prob. echoic] 1. a flurry of nervous, excited activity; bustle [she was in a *fuss* over the spilled water] 2. nervousness, agitation, etc. ☆3. [Colloq.] a quarrel 4. [Colloq.] a showy display of delight, etc. [they made a great *fuss* over the baby] —*vi.* 1. to cause or make a fuss 2. to bustle about or worry over trifles 3. to whine or fret, as a baby —*vt.* [Colloq.] to bother or worry unnecessarily —**fuss around** [Colloq.] 1. to spend time in an idle, aimless way 2. to do annoying things

☆**fuss·budg·et** (-buj'it) *n.* [FUSS + BUDGET, prob. in sense "bag"] [Colloq.] a fussy person

fuss·y (fus'ē) *adj.* **fuss'i·er, fuss'i·est** 1. bustling about or worrying over trifles 2. hard to please [he's *fussy* about his meals] 3. whining or fretting, as a baby 4. showing or needing careful attention [a very *fussy* job] 5. full of unnecessary details [a *fussy* painting] —**fuss'i·ly** *adv.* —**fuss'i·ness** *n.*

fus·tian (fus'chən) *n.* [< OFr. < ML. < L. *fustis*, wooden stick] 1. orig., a coarse cloth of cotton and linen 2. now, cotton corduroy or velveteen 3. talk or writing that sounds more important than it really is —*adj.* 1. made of fustian 2. pompous; pretentious

fus·ty (fus'tē) *adj.* **fus'ti·er, fus'ti·est** [< *fust*, a musty smell < OFr., wine cask, orig. tree trunk < L. *fustis* (see FUSTIAN)] 1. smelling stale or stuffy; musty; moldy 2. old-fashioned or conservative —**fus'ti·ly** *adv.* —**fus'ti·ness** *n.*

fut. future

fu·tile (fyoot''l; *chiefly Brit. & Canad.*, fyoo'tīl) *adj.* [Fr. < L. *futilis*, lit., that easily pours out, hence worthless < *fundere*: see FOUND[3]] 1. *a)* useless; vain; hopeless *b)* ineffective 2. trifling or unimportant [a lot of *futile* talk] —**fu'tile·ly** *adv.* —**fu·til·i·ty** (fyoo til'ə tē), *pl.* -ties, **fu'tile·ness** *n.*

SYN.—**futile** is applied to that which fails completely to do what was expected or hoped for [a *futile* attempt to reach an agreement]; **vain** also refers to failure but without so strong a suggestion of ineffectiveness [a *vain* but valiant effort to scale the wall]; **fruitless** stresses the idea of great effort over a long time that fails to yield results [a *fruitless* hunt for clues]; **useless** refers to that which has shown no results either in practice or in theory [those are *useless* suggestions] —**ANT.** effective, fruitful, effectual

fut·tock (fut'ək) *n.* [< ? pronun. of *foot hook*] any of the curved timbers forming the ribs of a wooden ship

fu·ture (fyoo'chər) *adj.* [< OFr. < L. *futurus*, about to be (used as the future participle of *esse*, to be)] 1. that is to be or come [his *future* bride] 2. indicating time to come [the *future* tense of a verb] —*n.* 1. the time that is to come [in the *future*] 2. what will happen; what is going to be [she tries to foretell the *future*] 3. prospective condition; chance to be successful [he has a great *future* in law] 4. [*usually pl.*] a contract for a commodity bought or sold for delivery at a later date 5. *Gram.* *a)* the future tense *b)* a verb form in this tense —**fu'ture·less** *adj.*

future perfect 1. a tense indicating an action or state as completed before a specified time in the future 2. a verb form in this tense (Ex.: by next week he *will have left*)

fu·tur·ism (fyoo'chər iz'm) *n.* a movement in the arts shortly before World War I which was opposed to traditional forms and methods and tried to express the energy and violence of the machine age —**fu'tur·ist** *n., adj.*

fu·tur·is·tic (fyoo'chər is'tik) *adj.* of or having to do with the future or futurism —**fu'tur·is'ti·cal·ly** *adv.*

fu·tu·ri·ty (fyoo toor'ə tē, -tyoor'-, -choor'-) *n., pl.* -ties 1. *a)* the future *b)* a future condition or event 2. the quality of being future ☆3. a horse race in which horses are entered far ahead of time: in full, **futurity race**

fuze[1] (fyooz) *vt., vi.* **fuzed, fuz'ing** *same as* FUSE[1]

fuze[2] (fyooz) *n.* 1. *same as* FUSE[2] (*n.* 1) 2. any of various devices for detonating a bomb, projectile, etc. —*vt.* **fuzed, fuz'ing** to connect a fuze to

fu·zee (fyoo zē') *n. same as* FUSEE

fuzz (fuz) *n.* [< ? Du. *voos*, or back-formation < FUZZY] very loose, light particles of down, wool, etc.; fine hairs or fibers [the *fuzz* on a peach] —*vi., vt.* 1. to cover or become covered with fuzz 2. to make or become fuzzy —☆**the fuzz** [< ? FUSSY (sense 2)] [Slang] a policeman or the police

fuzz·y (fuz'ē) *adj.* **fuzz'i·er, fuzz'i·est** [prob. < LowG. *fussig*, spongy] 1. of, like, or covered with fuzz 2. not clear, distinct, or precise; blurred [a *fuzzy* picture] —**fuzz'i·ly** *adv.* —**fuzz'i·ness** *n.*

fwd. forward

-fy (fī) [< OFr. *-fier* < L. *-ficare* < *facere*, to make, DO[1]] *a suffix meaning:* 1. to make; cause to be [*liquefy*] 2. to cause to have; fill or cover with [*glorify*] 3. to become [*putrefy*]

FYI for your information

G

G, g (jē) *n., pl.* **G's, g's** **1.** the seventh letter of the English alphabet **2.** a sound of *G* or *g* **3.** *Physics a)* gravitation *b)* acceleration of gravity or a unit of force equal to it, used to measure the force on a body undergoing acceleration

G (jē) *n.* **1.** [< G(RAND), *n.* 2] [Slang] one thousand dollars **2.** *Educ.* a grade meaning *good* **3.** *Music a)* the fifth tone in the ascending scale of C major *b)* the scale having this tone as the keynote

G. German

G., g. **1.** gauge **2.** gram(s) **3.** guilder(s) **4.** guinea(s) **5.** gulf

Ga *Chem.* gallium

Ga., GA Georgia

gab (gab) *vi.* **gabbed, gab′bing** [< ON. *gabba*, to mock: see GAPE] [Colloq.] to talk much or idly; chatter —*n.* [Colloq.] idle talk; chatter —**gift of (the) gab** [Colloq.] the ability to speak glibly —**gab′ber** *n.*

gab·ar·dine (gab′ər dēn′, gab′ər dēn′) *n.* [var. of GABERDINE] **1.** a twilled cloth of wool, cotton, rayon, etc., with fine, diagonal ribs, used for suits, coats, dresses, etc. **2.** a garment made of this cloth **3.** *same as* GABERDINE

gab·ble (gab′'l) *vi.* **-bled, -bling** [< GAB + -LE²] **1.** to talk rapidly without making any sense; jabber **2.** to utter rapid sounds, as a goose —*vt.* to utter rapidly and incoherently —*n.* rapid talk that is meaningless or hard to understand —**gab′bler** *n.*

gab·by (-ē) *adj.* **-bi·er, -bi·est** [Colloq.] fond of talking a lot; talkative —**gab′bi·ness** *n.*

gab·er·dine (gab′ər dēn′, gab′ər dēn′) *n.* [< OFr. *gaverdine*, kind of cloak < ? MHG. *walvart*, pilgrimage] **1.** a loose coat of coarse cloth worn by men in the Middle Ages **2.** *chiefly Brit. sp. of* GABARDINE

☆**gab·fest** (gab′fest′) *n.* [GAB + -FEST] [Colloq.] **1.** an informal gathering of people to talk with one another **2.** their talk

ga·bi·on (gā′bē ən) *n.* [Fr. < It. < *gabbia*, cage < L. *cavea*: see CAGE] **1.** a cylinder of wicker filled with earth or stones, formerly used in building fortifications **2.** a similar cylinder of metal, used in building dams, dikes, etc.

ga·ble (gā′b'l) *n.* [< OFr. < Gmc., as in ON. *gafl*, gable: < IE. base *ghebhel-*, head, from which also comes CEPHALIC] **1.** the triangular part of a wall between the sloping ends of a ridged roof **2.** an end wall having a gable at the top **3.** a triangular decoration, as over a door or window —*vt.* **-bled, -bling** to put a gable or gables on

gable roof a roof forming a gable at each end

Ga·bon (gà bōn′) country on the W coast of Africa: 103,089 sq. mi.; pop. 480,000; cap. Libreville —**Gab·on·ese** (gab′ə nēz′) *adj., n., pl.* **-ese′**

Ga·bo·ro·ne (gä′bə rō′nä) capital of Botswana, in the SE part: pop. c.20,000

Ga·bri·el (gā′brē əl) [Heb. *gabhrī′ēl*, lit., God is (my) strength] **1.** a masculine name: dim. *Gabe* **2.** *Bible* an archangel, the herald of good news

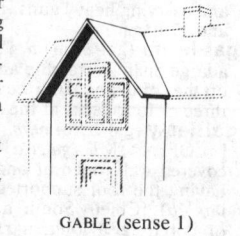

GABLE (sense 1)

Gad (gad) *interj.* [euphemism for GOD] [*also* g-] a mild oath or expression of surprise, etc.

gad¹ (gad) *vi.* **gad′ded, gad′ding** [? < OE. *gædeling*, companion] to wander about in a restless way, as in seeking amusement —*n.* a gadding: chiefly in **on the gad** —**gad′der** *n.*

gad² (gad) *n.* [ON. *gaddr*] *same as* GOAD

gad·a·bout (gad′ə bout′) *n.* a person who gads about, seeking fun, excitement, etc. —*adj.* fond of gadding

gad·fly (gad′flī′) *n., pl.* **-flies′** [GAD² + FLY²] **1.** a large fly that bites livestock, as the horsefly **2.** a person who annoys others, esp. by trying to stir them to action

gadg·et (gaj′it) *n.* [< ?] any small mechanical device, sometimes one that is merely clever and not too useful

☆**gadg·e·teer** (gaj′ə tir′) *n.* a person who likes to make or collect gadgets

gadg·et·ry (gaj′ət rē) *n.* **1.** gadgets as a group **2.** the paying of too much attention to gadgets

gad·o·lin·i·um (gad′'l in′ē əm) *n.* [ModL., after J. *Gadolin* (1760–1852), Finn. chemist] a metallic chemical element of the rare-earth group: symbol, Gd; at. wt., 157.25; at. no., 64

Gads·den (gadz′dən) [after J. *Gadsden* (1788–1858), U.S. diplomat] city in NE Ala.: pop. 54,000

gad·wall (gad′wôl) *n., pl.* **-walls, -wall**: see PLURAL, II, D, 1 [< ?] a grayish-brown wild duck of freshwater regions of N.America

Gae·a (jē′ə) [Gr. *Gaia* < *gē*, earth] *Gr. Myth.* the earth thought of as a goddess

Gael (gāl) *n.* [contr. < Gael. *Gaidheal*] a Celt of Scotland, Ireland, or the Isle of Man; esp., a Celt of the Scottish Highlands

Gael·ic (gāl′ik) *adj.* **1.** of the Gaels **2.** of any of their Celtic languages; of Scottish or Irish Gaelic —*n.* one of the Goidelic languages; esp., Scottish or Irish Gaelic Abbrev. **Gael.**

gaff (gaf) *n.* [< OFr. < Pr. *gaf* or Sp. *gafa* < ?] **1.** a large, strong hook on a pole, or a barbed spear, for lifting large fish out of the water **2.** a sharp metal spur fastened to the leg of a gamecock **3.** a spar or pole supporting a fore-and-aft sail **4.** [Slang] any secret device for cheating —*vt.* to strike or land (a fish) with a gaff —☆**stand the gaff** [Slang] to bear up well under difficulties, punishment, etc.

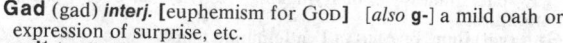

GAFF

gaffe (gaf) *n.* [Fr.] a blunder; faux pas

gaf·fer (gaf′ər) *n.* [altered < GODFATHER] an old man: now usually humorous

gag (gag) *vt.* **gagged, gag′ging** [echoic] **1.** to cause to retch or choke, as if about to vomit **2.** to cover or stuff the mouth of, so as to keep from talking, crying out, etc. **3.** to keep from speaking or expressing oneself freely, as by frightening **4.** to prevent or limit speech in (a legislative body) —*vi.* to retch or choke —*n.* **1.** something put into or over the mouth to prevent talking, etc. ☆**2.** anything that prevents free speech [threats to cancel a broadcaster's license can serve as a *gag*] **3.** *a)* a comical remark or act, as on the stage; joke *b)* a practical joke —**gag′ger** *n.*

Ga·ga·rin (gä gä′rin), **Yu·ri** (yōō′rē) 1934–68; Soviet cosmonaut; first man to orbit the earth in a space flight

---

gage[1] (gāj) *n.* [< OFr., a pledge, pawn < Gmc.] **1.** something given as a pledge that an obligation will be fulfilled; security **2.** a pledge to appear and fight, as a glove thrown down by a challenging knight **3.** a challenge —*vt.* **gaged, gag′ing** [Archaic] to offer as or bind by a pledge

gage[2] (gāj) *n., vt. same as* GAUGE

Gage (gāj), **Thomas** 1721-87; Brit. general in the American Revolution

gag·gle (gag′'l) *n.* [< ME. *gagelen,* to cackle] **1.** a flock of geese **2.** any group or cluster of persons or things

☆**gag·man** (gag′man′) *n., pl.* **-men** (-men′) a man who thinks up jokes, bits of comic business, etc. for entertainers

☆**gag rule** (or **law**) a rule that limits or prevents discussion, esp. in a legislature

gai·e·ty (gā′ə tē) *n., pl.* **-ties 1.** the state or quality of being gay; cheerfulness **2.** merrymaking; festivity **3.** finery; showy brightness

Gail (gāl) [dim. of ABIGAIL] a feminine name

gai·ly (gā′lē) *adv.* in a gay manner; specif., *a)* happily; merrily *b)* brightly [a *gaily* decorated hall]

gain (gān) *n.* [< OFr. < *gaaignier,* to earn] **1.** an increase; addition; specif., *a)* [*often pl.*] an increase in wealth, earnings, etc.; profit *b)* an increase in advantage; improvement **2.** the act of getting something; acquisition [his love of *gain* made him greedy] **3.** *Electronics a)* an increase in signal strength *b)* the ratio of output to input —*vt.* **1.** to get by labor; earn [to *gain* a livelihood] **2.** to get by effort or merit; win [he *gained* first prize] **3.** to attract [to *gain* one's interest] **4.** to get as an addition, profit, or advantage [he *gained* ten pounds] **5.** to make an increase in [to *gain* speed] **6.** to go faster by [my watch *gained* two minutes] **7.** to get to; reach [he *gained* his destination] —*vi.* **1.** to make progress; improve or advance, as in health **2.** to acquire profit **3.** to become heavier **4.** to be fast: said of a clock, etc. —see SYN. at GET and REACH —**gain on 1.** to draw nearer to (an opponent in a race, etc.) **2.** to make more progress than (a competitor) —**gain over** to win over to one's side

gain·er (gā′nər) *n.* **1.** a person or thing that gains **2.** a fancy dive in which the diver faces forward and does a backward somersault in the air

Gaines·ville (gānz′vil) [after Gen. E. *Gaines* (1777-1849)] city in NC Fla.: pop. 65,000

gain·ful (gān′f'l) *adj.* producing gain; profitable —**gain′ful·ly** *adv.* —**gain′ful·ness** *n.*

gain·ly (gān′lē) *adj.* **-li·er, -li·est** [< ON. *gegn,* straight, fit] shapely and graceful —**gain′li·ness** *n.*

gain·say (gān′sā′) *vt.* **-said′** (-sed′, -sād′), **-say′ing** [< OE. *gegn,* against + *secgan,* SAY] to deny or contradict [who could *gainsay* the truth of his statement?] —**gain′say′er** *n.*

Gains·bor·ough (gānz′bur′ō, -bər ə), **Thomas** 1727-88; Eng. painter

'gainst, gainst (genst, gānst) *prep. poet.* shortening of AGAINST

gait (gāt) *n.* [< ON. *gata,* path] **1.** manner of walking or running **2.** any of various foot movements of a horse, as a trot, canter, etc. —*vt.* to train (a horse) to certain gaits —**gait′ed** *adj.*

gai·ter (gāt′ər) *n.* [altered (after prec.) < Fr. *guêtre*] **1.** a cloth or leather covering for the instep and ankle and, sometimes, the calf of the leg; spat or legging ☆**2.** a shoe with elastic sides and no lacing ☆**3.** a high overshoe with a cloth upper

gal (gal) *n.* [Colloq.] a girl

Gal. Galatians

gal. gallon; gallons

ga·la (gā′lə, gal′ə) *n.* [It. < OFr. *gale,* enjoyment] a festive occasion; festival; celebration —*adj.* festive, or suitable for a festive occasion

GAITERS

ga·lac·tic (gə lak′tik) *adj.* [Gr. *galaktikos,* milky < *gala,* milk] **1.** of or obtained from milk **2.** *Astron.* of the Milky Way or some other galaxy

galactic noise radio waves reaching the earth from within the Milky Way

ga·lac·tose (gə lak′tōs) *n.* [< Gr. *galaktos,* genitive of *gala,* milk + -OSE[1]] a sugar, $C_6H_{12}O_6$, derived from lactose

Gal·a·had (gal′ə had′) in Arthurian legend, a knight who was successful in finding the Holy Grail because of his purity and noble spirit

gal·an·tine (gal′ən tēn′) *n.* [< OFr. < ML. *galatina,* jelly < L. pp. of *gelare,* CONGEAL] a mold of boned, seasoned, boiled white meat, as chicken or veal, chilled and served in its own jelly

Ga·lá·pa·gos Islands (gə lä′pə gōs′) group of islands in the Pacific on the equator, belonging to Ecuador: 3,028 sq. mi.

Gal·a·te·a (gal′ə tē′ə) *see* PYGMALION

Ga·la·tia (gə lā′shə) ancient kingdom in C Asia Minor, made a Roman province c.25 B.C. —**Ga·la′tian** *adj., n.*

Ga·la·tians (-shənz) a book of the New Testament: an epistle from the Apostle Paul to the Christians of Galatia

gal·ax·y (gal′ək sē) [< LL. *galaxias* < Gr. < *gala,* milk] [*often* G-] *same as* MILKY WAY —*n., pl.* **-ax·ies 1.** any of very many vast groupings of stars **2.** an assembly of famous people

gale (gāl) *n.* [< ?] **1.** a strong wind; specif., *Meteorol.* one ranging in speed from 32 to 63 miles an hour ☆**2.** an outburst [a *gale* of laughter]

Ga·len (gā′lən) (L. name *Claudius Galenus*) 130?-200? A.D.; Gr. physician & writer on philosophy

ga·le·na (gə lē′nə) *n.* [L., lead ore] lead sulfide, PbS, as found in nature, a shiny, lead-gray mineral: it is the principal ore of lead: also **ga·le′nite** (-nīt)

Ga·li·cia (gə lish′ə) **1.** region of SE Poland & NW Ukrainian S.S.R. **2.** region & former kingdom in NW Spain —**Ga·li′cian** *adj., n.*

Gal·i·le·an[1] (gal′ə lē′ən) *adj.* of Galilee or its people —*n.* a native or inhabitant of Galilee —**the Galilean** Jesus

Gal·i·le·an[2] (gal′ə lē′ən) *adj.* of Galileo

Gal·i·lee (gal′ə lē′) **1.** region of N Israel **2. Sea of,** lake of NE Israel, on the Syria border

Gal·i·le·o (gal′ə lē′ō, -lā′-) (born *Galileo Galilei*) 1564-1642; It. astronomer & physicist

gall[1] (gôl) *n.* [OE. *galla:* for IE. base see GOLD] **1.** bile, the bitter, greenish fluid secreted by the liver and stored in the gallbladder **2.** something bitter or distasteful **3.** bitter feeling ☆**4.** [Colloq.] rude boldness; impudence —see SYN. at TEMERITY

gall[2] (gôl) *n.* [OE. *gealla* < L. *galla:* see GALL[3]] **1.** a sore on the skin, esp. of a horse's back, caused by rubbing **2.** irritation or annoyance, or a cause of this —*vt.* **1.** to make sore by rubbing; chafe **2.** to irritate; annoy; vex

gall[3] (gôl) *n.* [< OFr. < L. *galla,* gallnut: for IE. base see CLAW] a tumor on plant tissue caused by fungi, insects, or bacteria: galls formed on oak trees have a high tannic acid content

gal·lant (gal′ənt; *for adj.* 4 & *n., usually* gə lant′) *adj.* [< OFr. prp. of *galer,* to rejoice < *gale:* see GALA] **1.** showy and gay in dress or appearance [knights in *gallant* attire] **2.** stately; imposing; dignified [a *gallant* ship] **3.** brave and noble **4.** polite and attentive to women —*n.* [Now Rare] **1.** a high-spirited, stylish man **2.** a man attentive and polite to women **3.** a lover —see SYN. at CIVIL —**gal′lant·ly** *adv.*

gal·lant·ry (gal′ən trē) *n., pl.* **-ries 1.** nobility of behavior or spirit; heroic courage **2.** the courtly manner of a gallant **3.** a polite act or remark **4.** the carrying on of secret love affairs

Gal·la·tin (gal′ə tin), (**Abraham Alfonse**) **Albert** 1761-1849; U.S. statesman & financier, born in Switzerland

gall·blad·der (gôl′blad′ər) *n.* a membranous sac attached to the liver, in which excess gall, or bile, is stored

gal·le·ass (gal′ē as′, -əs) *n.* [< Fr. < OFr. < It. < ML. *galea:* see GALLEY] a large, three-masted vessel having sails and oars and carrying heavy guns: used on the Mediterranean in the 16th and 17th cent.

gal·le·on (gal′ē ən) *n.* [Sp. *galeón* < ML. *galea:* see GALLEY] a large Spanish warship and trader of the 15th and 16th cent., with three or four decks at the stern

GALLEON

gal·ler·y (gal′ə rē) *n., pl.* **-ler·ies** [< OFr. < ML. *galeria*] **1.** *a)* a covered walk open at one side or having the roof supported by pillars *b)* [Chiefly South] a veranda or porch **2.** a long, narrow balcony on the outside of a building **3.** a platform at the stern of an early sailing ship **4.** *a)* a platform or projecting upper floor in a church, theater, etc.; esp., the highest of a series of such platforms in a theater, with the cheapest seats *b)* the people occupying these seats *c)* a group of spectators, as at a sporting event **5.** a long, narrow corridor or room **6.** a room, building, or establishment for showing or selling art works ☆**7.** a room or establishment used as a photographer's studio, or for practice shooting at targets, etc. **8.** an underground passage, as one used in mining —*vt.* **-ler·ied, -ler·y·ing** to furnish with a gallery —**play to the gallery** to try to win the approval of the public, esp. in a showy way

gal·ley (gal′ē) *n., pl.* **-leys** [< OFr. < ML. *galea* < MGr. *galaia*, a kind of ship] **1.** a long, low, usually single-decked ship moved along by oars and sails, used in ancient and medieval times **2.** a ship's kitchen **3.** *Printing a)* a shallow, narrow tray for holding composed type to be put into a form *b)* same as GALLEY PROOF

GALLEY

galley proof printer's proof taken from type in a galley to permit correction of errors before the type is made up in pages

galley slave **1.** a slave or convict sentenced or forced to pull an oar on a galley **2.** a drudge

gall·fly (gôl′flī) *n., pl.* **-flies**′ a fly whose eggs cause galls when deposited in plant stems

gal·liard (gal′yərd) *n.* [<OFr. *gaillard*, brave] **1.** a lively French dance in triple time, of the 16th and 17th cent. **2.** music for this

Gal·lic (gal′ik) *adj.* **1.** of ancient Gaul or its people **2.** French

gal·lic acid (gal′ik) [< Fr. < *galle*, GALL³] an acid, C₇H₆O₅·H₂O, prepared from nutgalls, tannin, etc. and used in photography and the manufacture of inks, dyes, etc.

Gal·li·cism, gal·li·cism (gal′ə siz′m) *n.* a French idiom, expression, custom, trait, etc.

Gal·li·cize, gal·li·cize (-sīz′) *vt., vi.* **-cized**′, **-ciz**′**ing** to make or become French or like the French in thought, language, etc.

gal·li·na·cean (gal′ə nā′shən) *adj. same as* GALLINACEOUS —*n.* any gallinaceous bird

gal·li·na·ceous (-shəs) *adj.* [< L. < *gallina*, hen < *gallus*, a cock] of, or having the nature of, an order of birds that nest on the ground, including poultry, pheasants, grouse, etc.

gall·ing (gôl′iŋ) *adj.* that galls; very annoying; irritating — **gall′ing·ly** *adv.*

gal·li·nule (gal′ə nyōol′, -nōol′) *n.* [ModL. < L. dim. of *gallina*: see GALLINACEOUS] any of various marsh birds that both swim and wade

Gal·lip·o·li Peninsula (gə lip′ə lē) peninsula in S European Turkey, forming the NW shore of the Dardanelles

gal·li·pot (gal′ə pät′) *n.* [see GALLEY & POT] a small pot or jar of glazed earthenware, esp. one used by druggists as a container for medicine

gal·li·um (gal′ē əm) *n.* [ModL. < L. *Gallia*, Gaul; also a pun on L. *gallus*, a cock, transl. of *Lecoq* (de Boisbaudran), its 19th-c. Fr. discoverer] a soft, bluish-white, metallic chemical element with a low melting point, used as a substitute for mercury: symbol, Ga; at. wt., 69.72; at. no., 31

gal·li·vant (gal′ə vant′) *vi.* [arbitrary elaboration of GALLANT] **1.** orig., to gad about with members of the opposite sex **2.** to go about in search of amusement or excitement —**gal′li·vant′er** *n.*

☆**gall·nut** (gôl′nut′) *n.* a nutlike gall, esp. on oaks

Gal·lo- (gal′ō) [L. < *Gallus*, a Gaul] *a combining form meaning:* **1.** French **2.** French and

gal·lon (gal′ən) *n.* [< ONormFr. *galon* < ML. *galo*, gallon, jug] **1.** a liquid measure, equal to 4 quarts (231 cubic inches): the British imperial gallon equals 277.42 cubic inches **2.** a dry measure, equal to 1/8 bushel **3.** a container that holds one gallon Abbrev. **gal.**

gal·lon·age (-ij) *n.* amount or capacity in gallons

gal·loon (gə lōon′) *n.* [< Fr. < *galonner*, to braid] a braid, as of cotton, silk, or metal thread, used for trimming or binding

gal·lop (gal′əp) *vi.* [< OFr. *galoper* < Frank.] **1.** to go at a gallop **2.** to move or act very fast; hurry —*vt.* **1.** to cause to gallop —*n.* **1.** the fastest gait of a horse, etc., consisting of a series of leaping strides with all the feet off the ground at one time **2.** a ride on a galloping animal **3.** any fast pace, speedy action, etc. —**gal′lop·er** *n.*

gal·lows (gal′ōz) *n., pl.* **-lows·es**, **-lows** [OE. *galga*] **1.** an upright frame with a crossbeam and a rope, for hanging condemned persons **2.** any structure like this **3.** the death sentence by hanging

☆**gallows humor** gruesome or cynical humor, as by one facing disaster

gall·stone (gôl′stōn′) *n.* a small, solid mass sometimes formed in the gallbladder or bile duct: it can block the flow of bile, causing pain

gal·lus·es (gal′əs iz) *n.pl.* [< *gallus*, dial. var. of GALLOWS] [Colloq.] suspenders; braces

gall wasp any of various small insects whose larvae produce galls in plants

gal·op (gal′əp) *n.* [Fr.: see GALLOP] **1.** a lively round dance in 2/4 time **2.** music for this —*vi.* to dance a galop

ga·lore (gə lôr′) *adv.* [Ir. *go leór*, enough] in abundance; plentifully [to attract crowds *galore*]

ga·losh, ga·loshe (gə läsh′) *n.* [< OFr. *galoche*, prob. < LL. *gallicula*, small shoe] an overshoe, esp. a high overshoe of rubber and fabric, worn in wet weather or snow

Gals·wor·thy (gôlz′wur′thē, galz′-), **John** 1867–1933; Eng. novelist & playwright

Gal·ton (gôl′t'n), **Sir Francis** 1822–1911; Eng. scientist & writer: pioneer in eugenics

Gal·va·ni (gal vä′nē), **Lu·i·gi** (lōo wē′jē) 1737–98; It. physiologist & physicist

gal·van·ic (gal van′ik) *adj.* [< GALVANISM] **1.** of, caused by, or producing an electric current, esp. from a battery **2.** stimulating or stimulated as if by electric shock; startling —**gal·van′i·cal·ly** *adv.*

gal·va·nism (gal′və niz′m) *n.* [< Fr. < It. after L. GALVANI] **1.** electricity produced by chemical action **2.** electrical current used in therapy

gal·va·nize (gal′və nīz′) *vt.* **-nized**′, **-niz**′**ing** **1.** to apply an electric current to **2.** to make (someone) do something as if by giving an electric shock; excite **3.** to coat (metal) with a layer of zinc —**gal′va·ni·za′tion** *n.*

gal·va·no- *a combining form meaning* galvanic, galvanism

gal·va·nom·e·ter (gal′və näm′ə tər) *n.* an instrument for detecting and measuring a small electric current —**gal′va·no·met′ric** (-nō met′rik) *adj.* —**gal′va·nom′e·try** (-trē) *n.*

Gal·ves·ton (gal′vis tən) [after B. de *Gálvez*, 18th-c. gov. of La.] seaport in SE Tex.: pop. 62,000

gam (gam) *n.* [< dial. Fr. *gambe* < ML. *gamba* < Gr. *kampē*, a joint] [Slang] a leg; often, specif., a woman's shapely leg

Gama, Vasco da *see* DA GAMA

Gam·bi·a (gam′bē ə) country on the W coast of Africa, surrounded on three sides by Senegal: a member of the Commonwealth: c.4,000 sq. mi.; pop. 375,000; cap. Banjul

gam·bit (gam′bit) *n.* [Fr. < OFr. < Sp. *gambito*, a tripping < It. < ML. *gamba*: see GAM] **1.** *Chess* an opening in which a pawn or other piece is sacrificed to get an advantage in position **2.** a maneuver or action intended to gain an advantage

gam·ble (gam′b'l) *vi.* **-bled**, **-bling** [OE. *gamenian*, to play] **1.** to play games of chance for money, etc. **2.** to take a risk in order to gain some advantage —*vt.* to bet; wager —*n.* an act or undertaking involving risk of a loss —**gamble away** to squander or lose in gambling —**gam′bler** *n.*

gam·boge (gam bōj′, -bōozh′) *n.* [ModL. *gambogium* < CAMBODIA] a gum resin obtained from a tropical Asian tree, used as a yellow pigment and as a cathartic

gam·bol (gam′b'l) *n.* [< Fr. < Pr. < It. *gambata*, a kick < *gamba*: see GAM & GAMBIT] a jumping and skipping about in play; frolic —*vi.* **-boled** or **-bolled**, **-bol·ing** or **-bol·ling** to jump and skip about in play; frolic

gam·brel (gam′brəl) *n.* [ONormFr. < OFr. *gambe*: see GAM] **1.** the hock of a horse or similar animal ☆**2.** same as GAMBREL ROOF

☆**gambrel roof** a roof with two slopes on each side, the lower steeper than the upper

game¹ (gām) *n.* [OE. *gamen*] **1.** any form of play; amusement; recreation; sport **2.** *a)* any specific amusement or sport involving persons or teams who compete against each other according to specific rules [baseball and chess are *games*] *b)* a single contest in such a competition [to win two out of three *games*] *c)* a subdivision of a contest, as in a set of tennis **3.** the number of points required for winning [the *game* is 25] **4.** a victory; win [the series is tied at 10 *games* each] **5.** a set of equipment used in playing a game like pachisi, checkers, etc.

GAMBREL ROOF

6. a way or quality of playing [to play a good *game*] **7.** any test of skill, endurance, etc. [the *game* of life] **8.** a project; scheme; plan [to see through another's *game*] **9.** *a)* wild birds or animals hunted for sport or food *b)* their flesh used as food **10.** any object of pursuit or attack: usually in **fair game 11.** [Colloq.] a business or occupation, esp. a risky one [the stockmarket *game*] —*vi.* **gamed, gam′ing** to play cards, etc. for stakes; gamble —*adj.* **1.** designating or of wild birds or animals hunted for sport or food **2. gam′er, gam′est** *a)* plucky; courageous *b)* having enough spirit; ready (*for* something) —☆**ahead of the game** [Colloq.] in the position of winning —**make game of** to make fun of; ridicule —**off one's game** performing poorly —**play the game** [Colloq.] to follow the rules; behave as fairness or custom requires —**the game is up** failure is certain —**game′-ly** *adv.* —**game′ness** *n.*

game² (gām) *adj.* [< ?] [Colloq.] lame or injured: said esp. of a leg

game·cock (gām′käk′) *n.* a specially bred rooster trained for cockfighting

game fish any fish regularly caught for sport

game·keep·er (-kēp′ər) *n.* a person employed to breed and take care of game birds and animals on State farms or private estates

game laws laws regulating hunting and fishing in order to preserve game

games·man·ship (gāmz′mən ship′) *n.* [< GAME¹ & (SPORT)SMANSHIP] skill in maneuvering in order to gain a victory or advantage over another person

game·some (gām′səm) *adj.* playful; full of fun —**game′some·ly** *adv.* —**game′some·ness** *n.*

game·ster (-stər) *n.* a gambler

gam·ete (gam′ēt, gə mēt′) *n.* [ModL. < Gr. *gametē*, a wife < *gamein*, to marry < *gamos:* see GAMO-] a reproductive cell that can unite with another gamete to form the cell (*zygote*) that develops into a new individual —**ga·met·ic** (gə met′ik) *adj.*

game theory a method of using mathematical analysis to select the best strategy so as to lessen one's maximum losses or increase one's minimum winnings in a game, war, business competition, etc.

ga·me·to- *a combining form meaning* gamete

ga·me·to·phyte (gə mēt′ə fīt′) *n.* in plants that have alternation of generations, the individual or generation that reproduces by eggs and sperms —**ga·me′to·phyt′ic** (-fit′ik) *adj.*

gam·in (gam′ən) *n.* [Fr.] **1.** a neglected child left to roam the streets **2.** a girl with a mischievous charm

gam·ing (gā′miŋ) *n.* the practice of gambling

gam·ma (gam′ə) *n.* [Gr.] **1.** the third letter of the Greek alphabet (Γ, γ) **2.** the third of a group or series

gamma globulin that fraction of blood serum which contains most antibodies: used in the temporary prevention of measles, hepatitis, etc.

gamma ray 1. an electromagnetic radiation given off by the nucleus of a radioactive substance: similar to an X-ray, but shorter in wavelength **2.** a stream of such radiation

gam·mon¹ (gam′ən) *n.* [< ONormFr. < *gambe:* see GAM] **1.** the bottom end of a side of bacon **2.** a smoked or cured ham or side of bacon

gam·mon² (gam′ən) *n.* [< ME. var. of *gamen:* see GAME¹] *Backgammon* a victory in which the winner gets rid of all his men before his opponent gets rid of any —*vt.* to defeat by scoring a gammon

gam·mon³ (gam′ən) *n., interj.* [< ?] [Brit. Colloq.] nonsense intended to deceive; humbug —*vt., vi.* [Brit. Colloq.] **1.** to talk nonsense (to) **2.** to deceive or mislead

gam·o- [< Gr. *gamos*, marriage] *a combining form meaning:* **1.** sexually united **2.** joined or united

gam·o·pet·al·ous (gam′ə pet′'l əs) *adj.* having the petals united so as to form a tubelike corolla

gam·o·sep·al·ous (-sep′'l əs) *adj.* having the sepals united

-ga·mous (gə məs) [< Gr. *gamos* (see GAMO-) + -OUS] *a combining form meaning* marrying, uniting sexually [*polygamous*]

gam·ut (gam′ət) *n.* [ML. *gamma ut* < *gamma*, the lowest note of the medieval scale < Gr. *gamma*, GAMMA + *ut* < L. *ut*, that, in a medieval song whose phrases began on successive ascending major tones: *Ut* queant laxis *Resonare fibris*, Mira gestorum *Famuli tuorum*, Solve polluti *Labii reatum*, Sancte *Iohannes*] **1.** *a)* the entire series of recog-

GAMOPETALOUS
FLOWER
(morning
glory)

nized notes in modern music *b)* any complete musical scale, esp. the major scale **2.** the entire range or extent, as of emotions —see SYN. at RANGE

gam·y (gā′mē) *adj.* **gam′i·er, gam′i·est 1.** having a strong, tangy flavor like that of cooked game **2.** strong in smell or taste **3.** high-spirited; plucky **4.** somewhat improper or indecent [a *gamy* story] —**gam′i·ly** *adv.* —**gam′i·ness** *n.*

-ga·my (gə mē) [< Gr. *gamos:* see GAMO-] *a combining form meaning* marriage, sexual union [*polygamy*]

gan·der (gan′dər) *n.* [OE. *gan(d)ra*] **1.** a male goose **2.** a stupid or silly fellow **3.** [Slang] a look: chiefly in the phrase **take a gander**

Gan·dhi (gän′dē, gan′-), **Mo·han·das K(aramchand)** (mō-hän′dəs) 1869–1948; Hindu nationalist leader & social reformer: called *Mahatma Gandhi* —**Gan′dhi·an** *adj.*

gang¹ (gaŋ) *n.* [OE. < base of *gangan* (see GANG²)] **1.** a group of people associated together in some way; specif., *a)* a group of workers directed by a foreman *b)* an organized group of criminals *c)* a group of youths from one neighborhood banded together; often, specif., a band of juvenile delinquents **2.** a set of tools, machines, parts, etc. designed to work together: often used as an adjective [a *gang* plow] —*vi.* ☆to form, or be associated in, a gang (with *up*) —*vt.* ☆[Colloq.] to attack as a gang —☆**gang up on** [Colloq.] to attack as a group

gang² (gaŋ) *vi.* [OE. *gangan*, to go < IE. base *ghengh-*] [Scot.] to go or walk

Gan·ges (gan′jēz) river in N India & Bangladesh, flowing from the Himalayas into the Bay of Bengal

gan·gling (gaŋ′gliŋ) *adj.* [? < dial. *gangrel*, "lanky person"] tall, thin, and awkward; of loose, lanky build: also **gan′gly**

gan·gli·on (gaŋ′glē ən) *n., pl.* **-gli·a** (-ə), **-gli·ons** [LL. < Gr. *ganglion*, tumor] **1.** a mass of nerve cells serving as a center from which nerve impulses are transmitted **2.** a center of force, energy, etc. —**gan′gli·on′ic** (-än′ik) *adj.*

☆**gang·plank** (gaŋ′plaŋk′) *n.* a narrow, movable platform by which to board or leave a ship

☆**gang plow** a plow with a number of shares fastened side by side for making several furrows at a time

gan·grene (gaŋ′grēn, gaŋ grēn′) *n.* [< Fr. < L. *gangraena* < Gr. < *gran*, to gnaw] decay of tissue in a part of the body when the blood supply is blocked by injury, disease, etc. —**gan′gre·nous** (-grə nəs) *adj.*

GANGPLANK

☆**gang·ster** (gaŋ′stər) *n.* a member of a gang of criminals —**gang′ster·ism** *n.*

Gang·tok (guŋ′täk′) capital of Sikkim: pop. 12,000

gang·way (gaŋ′wā′) *n.* [OE. *gangweg*] a passageway; specif., *a)* an opening in a ship's side for freight or passengers *b)* same as GANGPLANK —*interj.* make room! clear the way!

gan·net (gan′it) *n., pl.* **-nets, -net:** see PLURAL, II, D, 1 [OE. *ganot*] any of several large sea birds; esp., a white, gooselike bird with web-feet, that breeds on cliffs along the N Atlantic coast

gan·oid (gan′oid) *adj.* [< Fr. < Gr. *ganos*, brightness + *-eidēs*, -OID] of a group of fishes covered by rows of hard, glossy scales or plates, including the sturgeons and gars —*n.* a ganoid fish

GANNET
(to 35 in. long)

gant·let¹ (gônt′lit, gant′-) *n.* [< Sw. *gatlopp*, a run down a lane < *gata*, lane + *lopp*, a run] **1.** a former military punishment in which the offender ran between two rows of men who struck him with clubs, etc. as he passed **2.** a series of troubles or difficulties Now spelled equally **gauntlet** —**run the gantlet 1.** to be punished by means of the gantlet **2.** to proceed while under attack from both sides, as by criticism or gossip

gant·let² (gônt′lit, gänt′-) *n.* same as GAUNTLET¹

gan·try (gan′trē) *n., pl.* **-tries** [< OFr. < L. *canterius*, beast of burden < Gr. < *kanthōn*] **1.** a frame for holding barrels horizontally **2.** a framework that extends over a distance, as one on wheels that carries a traveling crane ☆**3.** a wheeled framework with a crane, platforms at different levels, etc. used to position and service a rocket at its launching site

Gan·y·mede (gan′ə mēd) *Gr. Myth.* a beautiful youth who was cupbearer to the gods

gaol (jāl) *n. Brit. sp. of* JAIL —**gaol′er** *n.*

gap (gap) *n.* [ON. < *gapa,* to yawn, GAPE] **1.** a hole or opening made by breaking, tearing, etc.; breach **2.** a mountain pass or ravine **3.** an empty space or time; blank **4.** a difference in ideas, natures, etc. **5.** *same as* SPARK GAP —*vi.* **gapped, gap′ping** to come apart; open

gape (gāp) *vi.* **gaped, gap′ing** [< ON. *gapa,* to yawn < IE. base *ghe-*] **1.** to open the mouth wide, as in yawning **2.** to stare with the mouth open, as in wonder **3.** to open wide, as a chasm —*n.* **1.** an open-mouthed stare **2.** a yawn **3.** a wide opening **4.** *Zool.* the measure of the widest possible opening of a mouth or beak —**the gapes 1.** a disease of poultry and birds, causing them to gape **2.** a fit of yawning —**gap′er** *n.* —**gap′ing·ly** *adv.*

☆**gar** (gär) *n., pl.* **gar, gars:** see PLURAL, II, D, 2 [contr. < GARFISH] any of a group of freshwater ganoid fishes with long, narrow bodies, long, beaklike snouts, and many sharp teeth

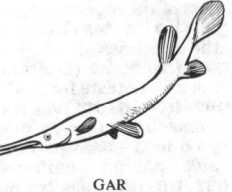

GAR
(to 10 ft. long)

G.A.R. Grand Army of the Republic

ga·rage (gə räzh′, -räj′; *Brit.* gar′äzh) *n.* [Fr. < *garer,* to GUARD] **1.** a closed shelter for automobiles **2.** a business establishment where automobiles are repaired, stored, etc. —*vt.* **-raged′, -rag′ing** to put or keep in a garage

☆**Gar·and rifle** (gar′ənd, gə rand′) [after J. C. *Garand,* U.S. inventor of it, c. 1930] a semiautomatic, rapid-firing, .30-caliber rifle

garb (gärb) *n.* [< OFr. < It. *garbo,* elegance, prob. ult. < Gr. < *kalos,* beautiful + *poiein,* to make] **1.** clothing; manner or style of dress **2.** external form, covering, or appearance —*vt.* to clothe

gar·bage (gär′bij) *n.* [ME., entrails of fowls] **1.** spoiled or waste food, as from a kitchen, that is thrown away **2.** worthless or offensive matter

gar·ble (gär′b'l) *vt.* **-bled, -bling** [< It. < *garbello,* a sieve < Ar. < *ghirbāl* < L. dim. *cribellum,* a small sieve] **1.** to select, leave out, exaggerate, etc. parts of (a story, etc.) in telling, so as to mislead or misrepresent **2.** to confuse or mix up (a story, etc.) without intending to —*n.* the act or result of garbling —**gar′bler** *n.*

‡**gar·çon** (gȧr sôn′) *n., pl.* **-çons** (-sôn′) [Fr.] **1.** a boy or young man **2.** a waiter or servant

gar·den (gär′d'n) *n.* [< ONormFr. *gardin* < Frank.: for IE. base see GIRD] **1.** a piece of ground, usually close to a house, for the growing of fruits, flowers, or vegetables **2.** an area of fertile, well-cultivated land: also **garden spot 3.** [*often pl.*] a parklike place for public enjoyment, sometimes having special displays of animals or plants —*vi.* to work in or take care of a garden, lawn, etc. —*vt.* to make a garden of —*adj.* **1.** of, for, or grown in a garden **2.** ordinary; commonplace [a *garden* variety of poet] —**lead (someone) down the garden path** to mislead or deceive (someone) —**gar′den·er** *n.*

☆**garden apartments** a group of low apartment buildings surrounded by lawn or landscaped areas

Garden Grove city in SW Calif.: suburb of Los Angeles: pop. 123,000

☆**gar·de·ni·a** (gär dēn′yə, -dē′nē ə) *n.* [ModL., after A. *Garden,* 18th-c. Am. botanist] any of a genus of chiefly subtropical plants with glossy leaves and fragrant, white or yellow, waxy flowers

Gar·field (gär′fēld), **James A(bram)** 1831–81; 20th president of the U.S. (1881): assassinated

gar·fish (gär′fish′) *n., pl.* **-fish′, -fish′es:** see FISH [< ME. *gare,* spear (OE. *gar:* see GORE³) + *fish,* fish] *same as* GAR

Gar·gan·tu·a (gär gan′choo wə) a giant king with an enormous appetite in Rabelais' *Gargantua and Pantagruel* —**Gargan′tu·an, gar·gan′tu·an** *adj.*

gar·gle (gär′g'l) *vt., vi.* **-gled, -gling** [< Fr. < *gargouille,* throat, spout] to rinse (the throat) with a liquid kept in motion by slowly forcing out air from the lungs —*n.* **1.** a liquid used for gargling **2.** a gargling sound

gar·goyle (gär′goil) *n.* [< OFr. *gargouille:* see GARGLE] **1.** a waterspout, usually in the form of a carved fantastic creature, sticking out from the gutter of a building **2.** a person with very strange or grotesque features

GARGOYLE

Gar·i·bal·di (gar′ə bôl′dē; *It.* gä rē bäl′dē), **Giu·sep·pe** (joo zep′pe) 1807–82; It. patriot & general: leader in movement to unify Italy

gar·ish (ger′ish) *adj.* [prob. < ME. *gauren,* to stare] too bright or gaudy; showy —see SYN. at GAUDY —**gar′ish·ly** *adv.* —**gar′ish·ness** *n.*

gar·land (gär′lənd) *n.* [< OFr. *garlande*] a wreath of flowers, leaves, etc. —*vt.* to form into or decorate with a garland or garlands

Gar·land (gär′lənd) [after A. *Garland,* U.S. attorney general (1885–89)] city in NE Tex.: suburb of Dallas: pop. 81,000

gar·lic (gär′lik) *n.* [< OE. < *gar,* a spear (see GORE³) + *leac,* a leek] **1.** a bulbous plant of the lily family **2.** its strong-smelling bulb, made up of small sections called cloves, used as a seasoning —**gar′lick·y** *adj.*

gar·ment (gär′mənt) *n.* [< OFr. *garnement* < *garnir:* see GARNISH] **1.** any article of clothing **2.** a covering —*vt.* to clothe

gar·ner (gär′nər) *n.* [< OFr. < L. *granarium* < *granum,* GRAIN] **1.** a place for storing grain; granary **2.** a store of something —*vt.* **1.** to gather up and store in or as in a granary **2.** to get or earn [to *garner* praise] **3.** to collect or gather [to *garner* data]

gar·net (gär′nit) *n.* [< OFr. < ML. *granatus* < *granatum,* garnet, lit., POMEGRANATE] **1.** any of a group of hard silicate minerals, chiefly crystalline: red varieties are used as gems **2.** a deep red

gar·nish (gär′nish) *vt.* [< OFr. *garnir,* to furnish, protect < Gmc.: for IE. base see GUARD] **1.** to decorate; adorn; trim **2.** to decorate (food) with something that adds color or flavor [to *garnish* potatoes with parsley] **3.** *Law* to bring garnishment proceedings against —*n.* **1.** a decoration; ornament **2.** something used to garnish food, as parsley —**gar′nish·er** *n.*

gar·nish·ee (gär′nə shē′) *n. Law* a person served with a garnishment —*vt.* **-eed′, -ee′ing** *Law* **1.** to take (a debtor's property, wages, etc.) by the authority of a court, so that it can be used to pay the debt **2.** to serve with a garnishment

gar·nish·ment (gär′nish mənt) *n.* **1.** a decoration; embellishment **2.** *Law* a notice ordering a person not to do anything with a defendant's property or money in his possession until the lawsuit has been settled

gar·ni·ture (gär′ni chər) *n.* garnish; decoration

Ga·ronne (gȧ rôn′) river in SW France, flowing from the Pyrenees northwest in the Gironde

☆**gar·pike** (gär′pīk′) *n. same as* GAR

gar·ret (gar′it) *n.* [ME. *garite,* a watchtower, loft < OFr. < *garir,* to watch < Frank.] the space or rooms just below the sloping roof of a house; attic

Gar·rick (gar′ik), **David** 1717–79; Eng. actor

gar·ri·son (gar′ə s'n) *n.* [< OFr. < *garir* (see GARRET)] **1.** troops stationed in a fort **2.** a military post or station —*vt.* **1.** to station troops in (a fortified place) for its defense **2.** to place (troops) on duty in a garrison

Gar·ri·son (gar′ə s'n), **William Lloyd** 1805–79; U.S. editor, lecturer, & abolitionist leader

gar·rote (gə rät′, -rōt′) *n.* [Sp., orig., a stick used to wind a cord < OFr. < Frank.] **1.** *a)* a method of execution, as formerly in Spain, by strangling with an iron collar *b)* the iron collar so used **2.** *a)* a cord, length of wire, etc. for strangling a person in a surprise attack *b)* a disabling by strangling in this way —*vt.* **-rot′ed** or **-rot′ted, -rot′ing** or **-rot′ting 1.** to execute or attack with a garrote or by strangling **2.** to disable by strangling, as in an attack for robbery Also sp. **ga·rotte′, garrotte′** —**gar·rot′er** *n.*

gar·ru·lous (gar′ə ləs, gar′yoo-) *adj.* [< L. < *garrire,* to chatter: for IE. base see CARE] talking much or too much, esp. about unimportant things; loquacious —see SYN. at TALKATIVE —**gar·ru·li·ty** (gə roo′lə tē), **gar′ru·lous·ness** *n.* —**gar′ru·lous·ly** *adv.*

gar·ter (gär′tər) *n.* [< ONormFr. *gartier* < OFr. *garet,* the back of the knee < Celt.] **1.** an elastic band for holding a stocking or sock in position, or such a band with a fastener for attaching it to the stocking or sock **2.** [G-] *a)* the badge of the Order of the Garter, the highest order of British knighthood *b)* the order itself —*vt.* to fasten with a garter

☆**garter belt** a wide belt, usually of elastic fabric, with garters hanging from it, worn by women

☆**garter snake** any of various small, harmless, striped snakes common in N. America

Gar·vey (gär′vē), **Mar·cus** (mär′kəs) 1880–1940; West Indian Negro leader in the U.S.

Gar·y (ger′ē, gar′ē) **1.** [< OE. word thought to be *Garwig,* lit., spear (of) battle < *gar,* spear + *wig,* battle] a masculine name **2.** [after E. *Gary* (1846–1927), U.S. industrialist] city in NW Ind., on Lake Michigan: pop. 175,000

gas (gas) *n.* [ModL., coined by the Belgian chemist, Van Helmont (1577–1644), after Paracelsus' use of Gr. *chaos,* CHAOS, to mean "air"] **1.** the fluid form of a substance in which it can expand to take up all the space open to it; form that is neither liquid nor solid; vapor [oxygen and carbon dioxide are *gases*] **2.** any mixture of gases that will burn easily, used for lighting, heating, or cooking **3.** any gas, as nitrous oxide, used as an anesthetic **4.** any substance spread through the air, as in war, that is poisonous, suffocating, or irritating **5.** gaseous matter formed in the stomach, bowels, etc. ☆**6.** [Colloq.] *a) short for* GASOLINE *b)* the accelerator in an automobile, etc. ☆**7.** [Slang] *a)* idle or boastful talk *b)* a person or thing that is very pleasing, exciting, etc. **8.** *Mining* a mixture of firedamp with air, that explodes if ignited —*vt.* **gassed, gas′sing 1.** to supply with gas **2.** to subject to the action of gas **3.** to injure or kill by gas, as in war ☆**4.** [Slang] to thrill, delight, etc. —*vi.* ☆[Slang] to talk idly or boastfully —*adj.* of or using gas

gas chamber a room in which people are put to be killed with poison gas

Gas·con (gas′kən) *adj.* **1.** of Gascony or its people, who are thought to be boastful **2.** [g-] boastful —*n.* **1.** a native of Gascony **2.** [g-] a boaster

gas·con·ade (gas′kə nād′) *n.* [see prec. & -ADE] boastful or noisy talk —*vi.* **-ad′ed, -ad′ing** to boast or talk noisily

Gas·co·ny (gas′kə nē) region on the SW coast of France: Fr. name, **Gas·cogne** (gȧs kôn′y′)

gas·e·ous (gas′ē əs, gas′yəs) *adj.* **1.** of, like, or in the form of gas **2.** [Colloq.] *same as* GASSY (sense 1) —**gas′e·ous·ness** *n.*

gas fitter a person whose work is installing and repairing gas pipes and fixtures

gash (gash) *vt.* [< OFr. *garser,* ult. < Gr. *charassein,* to sharpen, cut] to make a long, deep cut in; slash —*n.* a long, deep cut

gas·i·fy (gas′ə fī′) *vt., vi.* **-fied′, -fy′ing** to change into gas

gas jet 1. a flame of illuminating gas **2.** a nozzle or burner at the end of a gas fixture

gas·ket (gas′kit) *n.* [prob. < OFr. *garcette,* small cord] **1.** a piece or ring of rubber, metal, etc. placed tightly around a piston or joint to keep it from leaking **2.** a rope or cord used by sailors in tying a furled sail to the yard

gas·light (gas′līt′) *n.* **1.** the light produced by burning illuminating gas **2.** a gas jet or burner —*adj.* of or suggesting the period when gaslight was used for lighting [*gaslight* melodrama]

GASKET

gas mantle a mantle (*n.* 3) for a gas burner

gas mask a mask with a filter, worn over the face to protect against breathing in poisonous gases

☆**gas·o·hol** (gas′ə hôl′) *n.* [blend of GASOLINE & ALCOHOL] a mixture of gasoline and alcohol, usually 90 percent unleaded gasoline and 10 percent ethyl alcohol, used as a motor fuel

☆**gas·o·line, gas·o·lene** (gas′ə lēn′, gas′ə lēn′) *n.* [GAS + -OL(E) + -INE′, -ENE] a volatile, colorless liquid that burns very easily, is produced by the distillation of petroleum, and is used chiefly as a fuel in internal-combustion engines

gas·om·e·ter (gas äm′ə tər) *n.* **1.** a container for holding and measuring gas **2.** a tank for gas

gasp (gasp) *vi.* [< ON. *geispa,* to YAWN] to inhale suddenly, as when surprised, or breathe with effort, as when choking —*vt.* to say with gasps [he *gasped* out his story] —*n.* a gasping; catching of the breath with difficulty

Gas·pé Peninsula (gas pā′) peninsula in S Quebec, Canada, extending into the Gulf of St. Lawrence

☆**gas station** *same as* SERVICE STATION (sense 2)

gas·sy (gas′ē) *adj.* **-si·er, -si·est 1.** full of, containing, or pro-

ducing gas; esp., flatulent **2.** like gas **3.** [Colloq.] full of talk or fond of talking —**gas′si·ness** *n.*

gas·tric (gas′trik) *adj.* [GASTR(O)- + -IC] of, in, or near the stomach [*gastric* pains]

gastric juice the acid digestive fluid produced by glands in the mucous membrane lining the stomach: it contains enzymes and hydrochloric acid

gastric ulcer an ulcer of the stomach lining

gas·tri·tis (gas trīt′is) *n.* [GASTR(O)- + -ITIS] a condition in which the stomach or the stomach lining becomes inflamed

gas·tro- [< Gr. *gastēr,* the stomach] *a combining form meaning* the stomach (and): also, before a vowel, **gastr-**

gas·tro·en·ter·i·tis (gas′trō en′tə rīt′is) *n.* [< GASTRO- + ENTER(O)- + -ITIS] a condition in which the stomach and the intestines become irritated and inflamed

gas·tro·en·ter·ol·o·gy (-en′tə räl′ə jē) *n.* [GASTRO- + ENTERO- + -LOGY] the branch of medicine dealing with disorders of the digestive system —**gas′tro·en′ter·ol′o·gist** *n.*

gas·tro·in·tes·ti·nal (-in tes′tə n'l) *adj.* of the stomach and the intestines

gas·tro·nome (gas′trə nōm′) *n.* a person who enjoys and has a sensitive taste for foods

gas·tron·o·my (gas trän′ə mē) *n.* [< Fr. < Gr. < *gastēr,* the stomach + *nomos,* a rule] the art of good eating or of enjoying good food —**gas′tro·nom′ic** (-trə näm′ik), **gas′tro·nom′i·cal** *adj.* —**gas′tro·nom′i·cal·ly** *adv.*

gas·tro·pod (gas′trə päd′) *n.* [< ModL. < GASTRO- + -POD] any of a large group of mollusks having a single, straight or spiral shell, as snails, limpets, etc., or no shell, as certain slugs: most gastropods move by means of a broad, muscular foot

gas·tru·la (gas′troo lə) *n., pl.* **-lae′** (-lē′), **-las** [ModL. dim. < Gr. *gastēr,* the stomach] an embryo in an early stage of development, consisting of a sac with two layers, the ectoderm and endoderm

gat (gat) *archaic pt. of* GET

gate (gāt) *n.* [< OE. *geat*] **1.** a movable structure, esp. one that swings on hinges, controlling entrance or exit through an opening in a fence or wall **2.** an opening for passage through a fence or wall, with or without such a structure; gateway **3.** any means of entrance or exit, as any of the numbered exits at an airport terminal **4.** a movable barrier, as at a railroad crossing **5.** a structure controlling the flow of water, as in a pipe, canal, etc. **6.** *a)* the total amount of money paid by spectators to be admitted to a performance or exhibition *b)* the total number of such spectators **7.** *Electronics* a circuit that allows signals to pass only when certain input conditions are satisfied —☆**get the gate** [Slang] to be dismissed or rejected —☆**give (someone) the gate** to dismiss or reject (someone); get rid of

☆**gate·fold** (gāt′fōld′) *n.* a page larger than the others in a magazine or book, bound so that it can be folded out

gate·house (-hous′) *n.* a house beside or over a gateway, used as a porter's lodge, etc.

gate·keep·er (-kē′pər) *n.* a person in charge of a gate to control passage through it: also **gate′man,** *pl.* **-men**

gate·leg table (-leg′) a table with drop leaves supported by gatelike legs that swing back to let the leaves drop: also **gate′legged′ table**

gate·post (-pōst′) *n.* a post at the side of a gate, either the post on which a gate is hung or the one to which it is fastened when closed

Gates (gāts), **Horatio** 1728?-1806; Am. general in the Revolutionary War

gate·way (-wā′) *n.* **1.** an entrance in a fence, wall, etc. fitted with a gate **2.** a way of getting in or out or at [the *gateway* to progress]

GATELEG TABLE

gath·er (gath′ər) *vt.* [< OE. *gad(e)rian:* for IE. base see GOOD] **1.** to bring together in one place or group [the child *gathered* her toys] **2.** to get gradually from various places, sources, etc.; accumulate [to *gather* information] **3.** to bring close [to *gather* a blanket about one's legs] **4.** to pick or collect by picking; harvest [to *gather* crops] **5.** to get as an idea; infer; conclude [I *gather* that you disagree] **6.** to prepare (oneself, one's energies, etc.) to meet a situation **7.** to gain or acquire gradually [to *gather* speed] **8.** to draw (cloth) into fixed folds or pleats **9.** to wrinkle (one's brow) —*vi.* **1.** to come together; assemble [the families *gathered* for a reunion] **2.** to form pus; come to a head: said of a boil **3.** to increase **4.** to become wrinkled: said of the brow —*n.* a pleat —**gath′er·er** *n.*

SYN. —**gather** is the general term for a bringing or coming together [to *gather* scattered objects; people *gathered* at the shopping center*]*; **collect** usually implies careful choice in gathering from various sources, a bringing into proper order, etc. *[she collects coins]*; **assemble** applies especially to the gathering of persons or the putting together of things for some special purpose *[to assemble the parts of an automobile]* —see also **SYN.** at INFER

gath·er·ing (-iŋ) *n.* **1.** the act of one that gathers **2.** what is gathered; specif., *a)* a meeting; crowd *b)* a series of pleats **3.** a boil or abscess

☆**Gat·ling gun** (gat′liŋ) [after R. J. *Gatling*, 19th-c. U.S. inventor] an early kind of machine gun having a number of barrels arranged to rotate around an axis so that each barrel is shot one after the other

gauche (gōsh) *adj.* [Fr. < MFr. *gauchir*, to become warped, ult. < Frank.] lacking social grace; tending to commit social blunders; awkward; tactless —**gauche′ly** *adv.* —**gauche′ness** *n.*

gau·che·rie (gō′shə rē′) *n.* [see prec.] **1.** awkwardness; tactlessness **2.** a gauche act or expression

gau·cho (gou′chō) *n., pl.* **-chos** [AmSp.] a cowboy of Indian and Spanish ancestry, living on the S. American pampas

gaud (gôd) *n.* [ME. *gaude*, a trinket, prob. ult. < L. *gaudium*, joy] a cheap, showy ornament

gaud·y (gôd′ē) *adj.* **gaud′i·er, gaud′i·est** [GAUD + -Y[2]] bright and showy, but in bad taste; cheaply ornate —**gaud′i·ly** *adv.* —**gaud′i·ness** *n.*

SYN. —**gaudy** applies to that which is brightly colored and highly decorated but which is regarded as being in bad taste *[gaudy furniture]*; **tawdry** is used of something cheap and poorly made that is also gaudy *[a tawdry sofa]*; **garish** implies a glaring brightness of color and too much decoration *[garish wallpaper]*; **flashy** and **showy** imply a brightness that attracts attention but **flashy** implies that it is offensive to those with more conservative tastes *[a flashy sport coat]*, while **showy** does not always imply this *[showy blossoms]* —**ANT. subdued, quiet**

gauge (gāj) *n.* [< ONormFr. *gaugier*, to gauge] **1.** a standard measure or scale of measurement **2.** dimensions, capacity, thickness, etc. **3.** any device for measuring something, as the thickness of wire, steam pressure, etc. **4.** any means of estimating or judging **5.** the distance between the rails of a railway: see also STANDARD GAUGE, BROAD GAUGE, NARROW GAUGE **6.** the distance between parallel wheels at opposite ends of an axle **7.** the size of the bore of a shotgun expressed in terms of the number per pound of round lead balls of a diameter equal to that of the bore **8.** the thickness of sheet metal, diameter of wire, etc. **9.** the fineness of a machine-knitted fabric expressed in terms of the number of loops per 1½ inches —*vt.* **gauged, gaug′ing 1.** to measure accurately by means of a gauge **2.** to measure the size, amount, or capacity of **3.** to estimate; judge *[to gauge a person's honesty]* —see SYN. at STANDARD —**gauge′a·ble** *adj.* —**gaug′er** *n.*

Gau·guin (gō gan′), (**Eugène Henri**) **Paul** (pôl) 1848-1903; Fr. painter, in Tahiti after 1891

Gaul (gôl) ancient division of the Roman Empire, including what is now mainly France & Belgium (**Transalpine Gaul**) and N Italy (**Cisalpine Gaul**): see map at ROMAN EMPIRE —*n.* **1.** any of the Celtic-speaking people of Gaul **2.** a Frenchman

Gaul·ish (gôl′ish) *adj.* of Gaul or the Gauls —*n.* the Celtic language spoken in ancient Gaul

gaunt (gônt) *adj.* [ME. *gawnte, gant* < ?] **1.** thin and bony; hollow-eyed and haggard, as from hunger or illness **2.** looking grim, forbidding, or deserted *[the gaunt, rocky coast]* —see SYN. at LEAN[2] —**gaunt′ly** *adv.* —**gaunt′ness** *n.*

gaunt·let[1] (gônt′lit, gänt′-) *n.* [< OFr. dim. of *gant*, a glove < Frank.] **1.** a glove, usually of leather covered with metal plates, worn by knights in armor to protect the hand in combat: see illustration at ARMOR **2.** *a)* a long glove with a flaring cuff covering the lower part of the arm *b)* the cuff by itself — **take up the gauntlet** to accept a challenge —**throw down the gauntlet** to challenge, as to combat —**gaunt′let·ed** *adj.*

gaunt·let[2] (gônt′lit, gänt′-) *n. same as* GANTLET[1]

gauss (gous) *n.* [after K. *Gauss* (1777-1855), Ger. scientist] *Elec.* a cgs unit used in measuring magnetic induction or magnetic flux density

Gau·ta·ma (gout′ə mə, gôt′-) *see* BUDDHA

gauze (gôz) *n.* [Fr. *gaze*, prob. < Sp. < Ar. *kazz*, raw silk < Per.] **1.** any very thin, transparent, loosely woven material, as of cotton or silk **2.** a thin mist

gauz·y (gôz′ē) *adj.* **gauz′i·er, gauz′i·est** thin, light, and transparent, like gauze; diaphanous —**gauz′i·ly** *adv.* —**gauz′i·ness** *n.*

gave (gāv) *pt. of* GIVE

☆**gav·el** (gav′'l) *n.* [< Scot. *gable*, a tool < OE. *gafol*] a small mallet rapped on the table by a chairman, judge, etc. to call for attention or silence

ga·vi·al (gā′vē əl) *n.* [Fr. < Hindi *ghariyāl*] a large crocodile of India, with a very long snout

ga·votte (gə vät′) *n.* [Fr. < Pr. *gavoto*, dance of the *Gavots*, an Alpine people] **1.** a 17th-cent. dance like the minuet, but livelier **2.** the music for this, in 4/4 time Also sp. **gavot′**

Ga·wain (gä′win, -wān) [Fr.] in Arthurian legend, a knight of the Round Table, nephew of King Arthur

GAVEL

gawk (gôk) *n.* [prob. dial. var. of *gowk*, a simpleton] a clumsy, stupid fellow; simpleton —*vi.* to stare in a stupid way —**gawk′ish** *adj.*

gawk·y (gô′kē) *adj.* **gawk′i·er, gawk′i·est** [prob. < GAWK] awkward; clumsy; ungainly —**gawk′i·ly** *adv.* —**gawk′i·ness** *n.*

gay (gā) *adj.* [< OFr.] **1.** joyous and lively; merry **2.** bright; brilliant *[gay colors]* **3.** devoted to social pleasures and to having a good time *[a gay life]* ☆**4.** homosexual —*n.* a homosexual, esp. a male homosexual —**gay′ness** *n.*

Gay (gā), **John** 1685-1732; Eng. poet & playwright

gay·e·ty (gā′ə tē) *n., pl.* **-ties** *same as* GAIETY

Gay-Lus·sac's law (gā lü saks′) [first stated by J. *Gay-Lussac* (1778-1850), Fr. physicist] **1.** the statement that the volumes of two or more gases that combine to give a gaseous product are in the proportion of small whole numbers to each other and to the volume of the product **2.** *same as* CHARLES'S LAW

gay·ly (gā′lē) *adv. same as* GAILY

Ga·za (gä′zə; *for 2* gäz′ə, gaz′ə) **1.** ancient city in SW Palestine **2.** city on this site, surrounded by a strip of land (**Gaza Strip**) along the Mediterranean, administered (since 1967) by Israel, 100 sq. mi., pop. 365,000

gaze (gāz) *vi.* **gazed, gaz′ing** [< Scand.] to look intently and steadily; stare, as in wonder —*n.* a steady look —**gaz′er** *n.*

ga·ze·bo (gə zē′bō, -zā′-) *n., pl.* **-bos, -boes** [< ?] a turret, balcony, or summerhouse from which one can gaze at the scenery around it

ga·zelle (gə zel′) *n., pl.* **-zelles′, -zelle′**: see PLURAL, II, D, 1 [Fr. < Ar. *ghazāl*] any of various small, swift, graceful antelopes of africa, the near east, and Asia, with horns that twist back in a spiral and large, shining eyes

ga·zette (gə zet′) *n.* [Fr. < It. *gazzetta* < dial. *gazeta*, a small coin, price of a newspaper] **1.** a newspaper **2.** in England, any of various official publications containing announcements and bulletins —*vt.* **-zet′ted, -zet′ting** [Chiefly Brit.] to announce or list in a gazette

gaz·et·teer (gaz′ə tir′) *n.* **1.** [Archaic] a person who writes for a gazette **2.** a dictionary or index of geographical names

Ga·zi·an·tep (gä′zē än tep′) city in S Turkey, near the Syrian border: pop. 256,000

gaz·pa·cho (gäz pä′chō) *n.* [Sp.] a Spanish soup made with tomatoes, chopped cucumbers, onions, oil, vinegar, etc. and served cold

GRANT'S GAZELLE
(to 34 in. high at shoulder)

G.B. Great Britain

G.C.D., g.c.d. greatest common divisor

G clef *same as* TREBLE CLEF

GCT, G.C.T. Greenwich civil time

Gd *Chem.* gadolinium

Gdańsk (g'dänsk′) seaport in N Poland, on the Baltic Sea: pop. 370,000: Ger. name, DANZIG

Ge *Chem.* germanium

---

fat, āpe, cär, ten, ēven, is, bīte; gō, hôrn, tōōl, look; oil, out; up, fur; get; joy; yet; chin; she; thin, then; zh, leisure; ŋ, ring; ə for *a* in *ago, e* in *agent, i* in *sanity, o* in *comply, u* in *focus;* ' as in *able* (ā′b'l); Fr. bal; ë, Fr. coeur; ö, Fr. feu; Fr. mon; ð, Fr. coq; ü, Fr. duc; r, Fr. cri; H, G. ich; kh, G. doch; ‡foreign; ☆ Americanism; < derived from. See inside front cover.

gear (gir) *n.* [prob. < ON. *gervi*, preparation] **1.** clothing; apparel **2.** equipment for some particular purpose, as a workman's tools, a harness, etc. **3.** *a)* a wheel, disk, etc. with teeth designed to fit together with the teeth on another such wheel, disk, etc.: see also WORM GEAR *b)* [*often pl.*] a system of two or more such gears fitting together so that the motion of one is passed on to the others *c)* a certain arrangement of such a system: in motor-vehicle transmissions, *high gear* provides greatest speed and *low gear* greatest power *d)* any part of a mechanism performing a specific function [the steering *gear*] —*vt.* **1.** to furnish with gear; harness **2.** to adapt (one thing) so as to fit in with another [to *gear* production to demand] **3.** *a)* to connect by gears [the pedals of the bicycle are *geared* to the wheels] *b)* to furnish with gears —*vi.* to be in, or come into, proper adjustment or working order —**in gear 1.** connected to the motor **2.** in proper adjustment or working order —**out of gear** not in gear —☆**shift gears 1.** to change from one gear arrangement to another **2.** to change one's method or approach in handling a problem

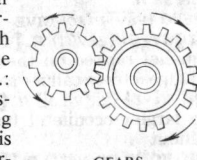
GEARS

gear·ing (gir′iŋ) *n.* **1.** the act or manner of fitting a machine with gears **2.** a system of gears or other parts for passing motion on from part to part

☆**gear·shift** (-shift′) *n.* a device used for connecting any of a number of sets of transmission gears to a motor, etc., or for disconnecting them

gear·wheel (-hwēl′, -wēl′) *n.* a toothed wheel in a system of gears; cogwheel

geck·o (gek′ō) *n., pl.* **-os, -oes** [Malay *gekok*, echoic of its cry] a soft-skinned, insect-eating, tropical lizard with suction pads on its feet

gee[1] (jē) *interj., n.* [Early ModE. < ?] a word of command to a horse, ox, etc., meaning "turn to the right!" —*vt., vi.* **geed, gee′ing** to turn to the right Opposed to HAW[2]

☆**gee**[2] (jē) *interj.* [contr. < JE(SUS)] [Slang] an exclamation of surprise, wonder, etc.

geese (gēs) *n. pl. of* GOOSE

gee·zer (gē′zər) *n.* [< dial. *guiser*, a mummer < GUISE] [Slang] an eccentric old man

GECKO
(to 15 in. long, including tail)

☆**ge·fil·te fish** (gə fil′tə) [Yid. < G. < pp. of *füllen*, to FILL, FISH] chopped fish mixed with chopped onion, egg, etc. and boiled: it is usually served cold in the form of cakes or balls

Ge·hen·na (gi hen′ə) [< Heb. *gēhinnōm*] *Bible* the valley of Hinnom, near Jerusalem, where refuse was burned: translated in the New Testament as "hell" —*n.* any place of torment

Gei·ger counter (gī′gər) [after H. *Geiger* (1882–1945), Ger. physicist] an instrument for detecting and counting ionizing particles: a refined version (**Geiger-Müller counter**) with an amplifying system is used for detecting and measuring radioactivity

gei·sha (gā′shə) *n., pl.* **-sha, -shas** [Jpn.] a Japanese girl trained in singing, dancing, etc., to serve as a hired companion to men

gel (jel) *n.* [< GELATIN] a jellylike substance formed by the coagulation of a colloidal solution into a solid phase —*vi.* **gelled, gel′ling** to form a gel

gel·a·tin, gel·a·tine (jel′ət 'n) *n.* [< Fr. < It. < *gelata*, a jelly < pp. of L. *gelare*, to freeze: for IE. base see COOL] **1.** the tasteless, odorless, brittle substance obtained by boiling bones, hoofs, etc.; also, a similar vegetable substance: gelatin dissolves in hot water, forming a jellylike substance when cool, and is used in various foods, photographic film, etc. **2.** something, as a jelly, made with gelatin

ge·lat·i·nize (jə lat′'n īz′, jel′ət 'n īz′) *vt.* **-nized′, -niz′ing 1.** to change into gelatin or gelatinous matter **2.** *Photog.* to coat with gelatin —*vi.* to be changed into gelatin or gelatinous matter —**ge·lat′i·ni·za′tion** *n.*

ge·lat·i·nous (jə lat′'n əs) *adj.* **1.** of or containing gelatin **2.** like gelatin or jelly; viscous —**ge·lat′i·nous·ly** *adv.* —**ge·lat′i·nous·ness** *n.*

geld (geld) *vt.* **geld′ed** or **gelt, geld′ing** [< ON. *gelda* < *geldr*, barren] **1.** to castrate (esp. a horse) **2.** to deprive of essential strength; weaken

geld·ing (gel′diŋ) *n.* a gelded animal; esp., a castrated horse

gel·id (jel′id) *adj.* [L. *gelidus* < *gelu*, frost] extremely cold; icy —**ge·lid·i·ty** (jə lid′ə tē) *n.*

Gel·sen·kir·chen (gel′zən kir′Hən) city in W West Germany, in the Ruhr valley: pop. 349,000

gem (jem) *n.* [< OFr. < L. *gemma*, a bud, gem] **1.** a precious stone or, occasionally, semiprecious stone, cut and polished for use as a jewel **2.** a highly valued person or thing ☆**3.** a kind of muffin —*vt.* **gemmed, gem′ming** to adorn or set with or as with gems

Ge·ma·ra (gə mä rä′, gə môr′ə) *n.* [Aram. *gemāra*, completion] **1.** the second part of the Talmud, which is a commentary on the first part (the MISHNA) **2.** loosely, the Talmud

gem·i·nate (jem′ə nāt′) *adj.* [< L. pp. of *geminare*, to double < *geminus*, a twin] growing or combined in pairs; coupled —*vt.* **-nat′ed, -nat′ing** to arrange in pairs; double —*vi.* to become doubled or paired —**gem′i·na′tion** *n.*

Gem·i·ni (jem′ə nī′, -nē′) [L., twins] **1.** a N constellation containing the stars Castor and Pollux, represented as twins seated **2.** the third sign of the zodiac: see illustration at ZODIAC

gem·ma (jem′ə) *n., pl.* **-mae** (-ē) [L.: see GEM] *Biol.* a budlike outgrowth which becomes detached and develops into a new organism

gem·mate (jem′āt) *adj.* [< L. pp. of *gemmare* < *gemma*, a bud] having gemmae or reproducing by gemmae —*vi.* **-mat·ed, -mat·ing** to have gemmae or reproduce by gemmae; bud —**gem·ma′tion** *n.*

gem·mule (jem′yool) *n. Biol.* a small gemma

gems·bok (gemz′bäk′) *n., pl.* **-bok′, -boks′:** see PLURAL, II, D, 2 [Afrik. < G. < *gemse* < VL. *camox*, CHAMOIS + *bock*, a buck] a large antelope of southern Africa, with long, straight horns and a tufted tail

gem·stone (jem′stōn′) *n.* any mineral that can be used as a gem when cut and polished

-gen (jən, jen) [< Fr. < Gr. < base of *gignesthai*, to be born: for IE. base see GENUS] *a suffix meaning:* **1.** something that produces [*oxygen, estrogen*] **2.** something produced (in a specified way) [*zymogen*]

Gen. 1. General **2.** Genesis

gen. 1. gender **2.** general **3.** genitive

GEMSBOK
(to 6 ft. high at shoulder)

gen·darme (zhän′därm; *Fr.* zhän-därm′) *n., pl.* **-darmes** (-därmz; *Fr.* -därm′) [Fr., ult. < L. *gens*, people + *de*, of + *arma*, arms] **1.** in France, Belgium, etc., a soldier serving as an armed policeman **2.** any policeman: used humorously

gen·dar·me·rie (zhän där′mə rē; *Fr.* zhän dàr mə rē′) *n.* [Fr.] gendarmes as a group: also **gen·dar′mer·y**

gen·der (jen′dər) *n.* [< OFr. *gendre* < L. *genus,* GENUS] **1.** *Gram. a)* the classifying of nouns, pronouns, adjectives, etc. into groups regarded as masculine, feminine, or neuter: in English, only some nouns (as *actor* and *actress*) and all pronouns in the third person singular (as *he, she,* and *it*) are classified into these groups *b)* any one of these groups **2.** [Colloq.] sex

☆**gene** (jēn) *n.* [< G. *gen* < *pangen* (< Gr. *pan-*, PAN- + *-gen*, -GEN)] *Genetics* any of the units occurring at specific points on the chromosomes, by which specific hereditary characters are passed on to the next generation: see DEOXYRIBONUCLEIC ACID (DNA)

ge·ne·al·o·gy (jē′nē äl′ə jē, -al′ə jē) *n., pl.* **-gies** [< OFr. < LL. < Gr. *genea*, race, stock (see GENUS) + *-logia*, -LOGY] **1.** a chart or recorded history of the ancestry or descent of a person or family **2.** the study of family descent **3.** descent from an ancestor; pedigree; lineage —**ge′ne·a·log′i·cal** (-ə läj′i k'l, jen′ē-) *adj.* —**ge′ne·a·log′i·cal·ly** *adv.* —**ge′ne·al′o·gist** *n.*

gen·er·a (jen′ər ə) *n. pl. of* GENUS

gen·er·al (jen′ər əl, jen′rəl) *adj.* [< OFr. < L. *generalis* < *generis,* genitive of *genus,* kind, GENUS] **1.** of, for, or from the whole or all; not particular or specialized [a *general* anesthetic] **2.** of, for, or applying to a whole genus, kind, class, order, or race [the *general* classifications of matter are those of animal, vegetable, and mineral] **3.** existing or occurring widely; common; widespread [there is *general* unrest among the people] **4.** most common; usual [the *general* spelling of a word] **5.** concerned with the main or overall features; lacking in details [a *general* survey of the situation] **6.** not exact; vague [to speak in *general* terms] **7.** highest in rank [an attorney *general*] —*n.* **1.** the main or overall fact, idea, etc. **2.** the head of a religious order **3.** any of various military officers ranking above a colonel; specif., *a*) *U.S. Army & U.S. Air Force* an officer ranking below a GENERAL OF THE ARMY (or AIR FORCE) and above a LIEUTENANT GENERAL *b*) *U.S. Marine Corps* an officer of the highest rank —see SYN. at UNIVERSAL —**in general 1.** in the main; usually **2.** without specific details

general assembly ☆**1.** in some States of the U.S., the legislative assembly **2.** [G- A-] the legislative assembly of the United Nations

☆**General Court** the legislature of New Hampshire or Massachusetts

☆**general election 1.** an election to choose from among candidates previously nominated, as in a primary election **2.** a nationwide or Statewide election

gen·er·al·is·si·mo (jen′ər ə lis′ə mō′, jen′rə-) *n., pl.* **-mos′** [It., superl. of *generale*, GENERAL] in certain countries, **1.** the commander in chief of all the armed forces **2.** the commanding officer of several armies in the field

gen·er·al·i·ty (jen′ə ral′ə tē) *n., pl.* **-ties 1.** the condition or quality of being general **2.** a statement, expression, etc. that is general or vague rather than definite or with details **3.** the greater number or part; main body [the *generality* of people are friendly]

gen·er·al·i·za·tion (jen′ər ə li zā′shən, jen′rəl i-) *n.* **1.** the act or process of generalizing **2.** a general idea, statement, etc. resulting from this

gen·er·al·ize (jen′ər ə līz′, jen′rə-) *vt.* **-ized′, -iz′ing** to make general; esp., *a*) to state in terms of a general law *b*) to infer or derive (a general law or rule) from (particular instances) *c*) to emphasize the general character rather than specific details of *d*) to cause to be widely known or used [the doctors hope to *generalize* the use of the vaccine] —*vi.* **1.** to form general principles from particulars **2.** to talk in generalities **3.** to become general or spread throughout an area

gen·er·al·ly (jen′ər əl ē; *also* jen′ər lē) *adv.* **1.** to or by most people; widely [is that fact *generally* known?] **2.** in most instances; usually [I *generally* go straight home] **3.** in a general way; without going into details [speaking *generally*, I'd agree]

general officer *Mil.* any officer above a colonel in rank

☆**general of the army** (or **air force**) the highest rank in the U.S. Army (or U.S. Air Force), having the insignia of five stars

general practitioner a practicing physician who does not specialize in any particular field of medicine

gen·er·al-pur·pose (-pur′pəs) *adj.* having a variety of uses; suitable for general use

gen·er·al·ship (-ship′) *n.* **1.** *a*) the rank, period of service, or authority of a general *b*) the military skill of a general **2.** highly skillful leadership

general staff *Mil.* a group of officers who assist the commander in planning and supervising operations

gen·er·ate (jen′ə rāt′) *vt.* **-at·ed, -at·ing** [< L. pp. of *generare* < *genus*, race, GENUS] **1.** to produce (offspring); beget **2.** to bring into being; cause to be [to *generate* hope] **3.** to originate or produce by a physical or chemical process [a dynamo *generates* electricity] **4.** *Math.* to trace out or form (a line, plane, figure, or solid) by the motion of a point, line, or plane

gen·er·a·tion (jen′ə rā′shən) *n.* **1.** the act or process of producing offspring **2.** a bringing into being; production **3.** a single stage in the history of a family [father and son are two *generations*] **4.** the average period (about thirty years) between the birth of one generation and the birth of the next **5.** *a*) all the people born at about the same time *b*) a group of such people having something in common **6.** *Math.* the generating of a line, figure, etc. —**gen′er·a′tion·al** *adj.*

gen·er·a·tive (jen′ər ə tiv, -ə rāt′iv) *adj.* of, or having the power of, generation or production

☆**generative grammar** a grammatical system consisting of a limited and unchanging set of rules using a list of symbols and words to generate or describe every possible structure in a language

gen·er·a·tor (jen′ə rāt′ər) *n.* a person or thing that generates; specif., *a*) a machine for producing gas or steam *b*) a machine for changing mechanical energy into electrical energy; dynamo

gen·er·a·trix (jen′ə rā′triks) *n., pl.* **-er·a·tri′ces** (-ər ə-trī′sēz, -ə rā′trə sēz′) *Math.* a point, line, or plane whose motion generates a line, plane, figure, or solid

ge·ner·ic (jə ner′ik) *adj.* [< ML.: see GENUS & -IC] **1.** of, applied to, or referring to a whole kind, class, or group; inclusive or general [the word "ship" is a *generic* term for many kinds of large watercraft] **2.** that is not a trademark **3.** *Biol.* of or having to do with a genus —see SYN. at UNIVERSAL —**ge·ner′i·cal·ly** *adv.*

gen·er·os·i·ty (jen′ə räs′ə tē) *n.* **1.** the quality of being generous; specif., *a*) nobility of mind; magnanimity; graciousness *b*) unselfishness **2.** *pl.* **-ties** a generous or unselfish act

gen·er·ous (jen′ər əs) *adj.* [L. *generosus*, of noble birth, excellent < *genus*: see GENUS] **1.** noble-minded; gracious; magnanimous [to forgive your enemy is a *generous* act] **2.** willing to give or share; unselfish **3.** large; ample [*generous* portions] **4.** full-flavored and strong: said of wine —**gen′er·ous·ly** *adv.* —**gen′er·ous·ness** *n.*

gen·e·sis (jen′ə sis) *n., pl.* **-ses′** (-sēz′) [< OE. & LL. < L. < Gr. < *gignesthai*, to be born] a beginning; origin —[G-] the first book of the Bible, telling the story of the Creation

-gen·e·sis (jen′ə sis) a combining form meaning origination, creation, evolution (of something specified)

gen·et¹ (jen′ət, jə net′) *n.* [< OFr. < Sp. < Ar. *jarnayt*] a small, spotted African animal related to the civet **2.** the fur of this animal Also **ge·nette** (jə-net′)

gen·et² (jen′ət) *n. same as* JENNET

ge·net·ic (jə net′ik) *adj.* [< GENESIS] **1.** of the genesis, or origin, of something **2.** of genetics Also **ge·net′i·cal** —**ge·net′i·cal·ly** *adv.*

genetic code the order in which four chemical parts are arranged in DNA molecules for passing on genetic information to the cells

GENET
(to 42 in. long,
including tail)

ge·net·ics (-iks) *n.pl.* [with sing. v.] [< GENETIC] the branch of biology that deals with heredity and the way that animals and plants pass on to their offspring such characteristics as size, color, etc. —**ge·net′i·cist** (-ə sist) *n.*

Ge·ne·va (jə nē′və) **1.** city in Switzerland, on Lake Geneva: pop. 171,000 **2. Lake (of)**, lake in SW Switzerland, on the border of France

Geneva Convention an international agreement signed at Geneva in 1864, establishing a code, later revised, for the care and protection in wartime of the sick, wounded, and prisoners of war

Gen·e·vieve (jen′ə vēv′) [Fr. < LL. *Genovefa* < ? Celt.] a feminine name

Gen·ghis Khan (geŋ′gis kän′, jeŋ′-) (born *Temuchin*) 1162?–1227; Mongol conqueror of central Asia

ge·nial (jēn′yəl, jē′nē əl) *adj.* [L. *genialis*, of birth < *genius*, GENIUS] **1.** promoting life and growth; warm and mild [a *genial* climate] **2.** cheerful, friendly, and sympathetic; amiable —see SYN. at AMIABLE —**ge·ni·al·i·ty** (jē′nē al′ə tē, jēn yal′-) *n.* —**ge′nial·ly** *adv.*

-gen·ic (jen′ik) a combining form: **1.** used to form adjectives from nouns ending in -GEN or -GENY [phylogenic] **2.** meaning suitable to [photogenic]

ge·nie (jē′nē) *n.* [Fr. *génie*] same as JINNI

gen·i·tal (jen′ə t'l) *adj.* [< OFr. < L. *genitalis* < pp. of *genere*, *gignere*, to beget: see GENUS] **1.** of reproduction or the sexual organs **2.** *Psychoanalysis* of an early stage of psychosexual development in which interest centers around the genital organs

gen·i·tals (-t'lz) *n.pl.* [< prec.] the reproductive organs; esp., the external sex organs: also **gen′i·ta′li·a** (-tāl′yə, -tā′lē ə)

gen·i·tive (jen′ə tiv) *adj.* [< OFr. < L. (*casus*) *genitivus*, lit., case of origin] of or in a grammatical case, as in Latin, in which certain endings on words express possession, origin, etc. —*n.* **1.** the genitive case **2.** a word or construction in the genitive case —**gen′i·ti′val** (-tī′v'l) *adj.* —**gen′i·ti′val·ly** *adv.*

gen·i·to·u·ri·nar·y (jen′ə tō yoor′ə ner′ē) *adj.* designating or of the genital and urinary organs together

---

Geologic Time Chart

MAIN DIVISIONS OF GEOLOGIC TIME

ERAS	PERIODS or SYSTEMS	Epochs or Series	PRINCIPAL PHYSICAL & BIOLOGICAL FEATURES
CENOZOIC	QUATERNARY	Recent 12,000*	Antarctica and Greenland are the only land masses still largely covered by glaciers; modern human culture develops and spreads.
CENOZOIC	QUATERNARY	Pleistocene 600,000	Great glaciers covered much of N North America & NW Europe; modern human beings appeared late in Pleistocene.
CENOZOIC	TERTIARY	Pliocene 10,000,000	W North America became highest part of continent; mammals continued to develop; first possible apelike human beings appeared in Africa.
CENOZOIC	TERTIARY	Miocene 25,000,000	Rockies and other mountains were raised higher; mammals began to take on present-day characteristics; dogs, solid-hoofed horses, and manlike apes appeared.
CENOZOIC	TERTIARY	Oligocene 35,000,000	Many earlier types of mammals died out completely; mastodons, first monkeys, and apes appeared.
CENOZOIC	TERTIARY	Eocene 55,000,000	Mountains were raised up in Rockies, Andes, Alps, & Himalayas; early mammals developed and increased; primitive horses appeared.
CENOZOIC	TERTIARY	Paleocene 65,000,000	Primitive mammals showed great development.
MESOZOIC	CRETACEOUS 135,000,000		Rocky Mountains began to rise; dinosaurs reached their largest size & then died out completely; mammals were small & very primitive.
MESOZOIC	JURASSIC 180,000,000		Sierra Nevada Mountains were raised up; conifers & cycads were the principal and most numerous plants; primitive birds appeared.
MESOZOIC	TRIASSIC 230,000,000		Modern corals appeared & some insects of types found today; reptiles including earliest dinosaurs increased greatly.
PALEOZOIC	PERMIAN 280,000,000		Trees of coal-forming forests declined; ferns became abundant; conifers were present; trilobites died out completely; reptiles became more abundant than amphibians.
PALEOZOIC	CARBONIFEROUS — PENNSYLVANIAN 310,000,000		Mountains formed along E coast of North America & in C Europe; great coal-forming swamp forests flourished in N Hemisphere; seed-bearing ferns were abundant; cockroaches & first reptiles appeared.
PALEOZOIC	CARBONIFEROUS — MISSISSIPPIAN 345,000,000		Many different kinds of land plants developed; crinoids reached greatest development; sharks related to modern types appeared; very few land animals existed.
PALEOZOIC	DEVONIAN 405,000,000		Land plants evolved rapidly, large trees appeared; brachiopods reached greatest development; many kinds of primitive fishes existed; first sharks, insects, & amphibians appeared.
PALEOZOIC	SILURIAN 425,000,000		Great mountains formed in NW Europe; first small land plants appeared; cephalopods with shells were abundant; trilobites began to disappear; first fish with jaws appeared.
PALEOZOIC	ORDOVICIAN 500,000,000		Large deposits of limestone formed in shallow seas; many kinds of invertebrate ocean animals developed; first jawless fish appeared.
PALEOZOIC	CAMBRIAN 600,000,000		Shallow seas covered parts of continents; various sea animals, esp. trilobites & brachiopods, appeared.
	LATE PRECAMBRIAN** 2,000,000,000		Sedimentary rocks and granite were formed; first living organisms appeared, as calcareous algae & invertebrates.
	EARLY PRECAMBRIAN** 4,500,000,000		Crust formed on molten earth; crystalline rocks underwent much disturbance; history unknown.

*Figures indicate approximate number of years since the beginning of each division. **Regarded as separate eras.

ge·nius (jēn′yəs, jē′nē əs) *n., pl.* **ge′nius·es** for 3, 4, 5; **ge·ni·i** (jē′nē ī′) for 1 & 2 [L., guardian spirit < base of *genere*, *gignere*, to produce: see GENUS] **1.** *a)* [*often* **G-**] the guardian spirit of a person, place, etc. *b)* either of two spirits, one good and one evil, supposed to influence one's destiny *c)* a person considered as having strong influence over another **2.** *same as* JINNI **3.** particular character or spirit of a nation, place, age, etc. **4.** a great natural ability (*for*) [a *genius* for making friends] **5.** *a)* great mental and inventive ability *b)* a person having this *c)* popularly, any person with a very high intelligence quotient —see SYN. at TALENT

Gen·o·a (jen′ə wə) seaport in NW Italy, on the Ligurian Sea: pop. 842,000: It. name, **Ge·no·va** (je′nô vä′) —**Gen′o·ese′** (-wēz′) *adj., n., pl.* **-ese′**

gen·o·cide (jen′ə sīd′) *n.* [< Gr. *genos*, race, GENUS + -CIDE] the deliberate killing or destroying of a whole national or ethnic group —**gen′o·ci′dal** (-sī′d′l) *adj.*

-gen·ous (jə nəs) [-GEN + -OUS] *a suffix meaning:* **1.** producing, generating [*nitrogenous*] **2.** produced by, generated in [*autogenous*]

gen·re (zhän′rə; *Fr.* zhän′r′) *n.* [Fr. < L. *genus*: see GENUS] **1.** a kind, or type: said of works of literature, art, etc. **2.** *same as* GENRE PAINTING

genre painting painting in which subjects from everyday life are treated realistically

gens (jenz) *n., pl.* **gen·tes** (jen′tēz) [L. < *gignere*, to beget: see GENUS] **1.** in ancient Rome, a clan united by descent through the male line from a common ancestor **2.** any tribe or clan

Gen·ser·ic (jen′sər ik, gen′-) 400?–477 A.D.; king of the Vandals (427–477): conqueror of Rome

gent (jent) *n.* [Colloq.] a gentleman; man

gen·teel (jen tēl′) *adj.* [< Fr. *gentil* < L. *gentilis*: see GENTLE] **1.** formerly, elegant or fashionable **2.** trying very hard to seem refined, polite, etc. —**gen·teel′ly** *adv.* —**gen·teel′ness** *n.*

gen·tian (jen′shən) *n.* [< OFr. < L. *gentiana*] **1.** any of a group of plants with blue, white, red, or yellow flowers **2.** the bitter root of the yellow gentian

gentian violet a violet dye used as an antiseptic and as a stain in microscopy

gen·tile (jen′tīl) *n.* [< Fr. *gentil* & L. *gentilis*: see GENTLE] [*also* **G-**] **1.** any person not a Jew; specif., a Christian **2.** formerly, among Christians, a heathen or pagan ☆**3.** among Mormons, any person not a Mormon —*adj.* [*also* **G-**] **1.** not Jewish **2.** heathen; pagan ☆**3.** not Mormon

gen·til·i·ty (jen til′ə tē) *n., pl.* **-ties** [< OFr. < L. < *gentilis*: see GENTLE] **1.** the condition of belonging by birth to the upper classes **2.** the quality of being genteel

gen·tle (jent′l) *adj.* **-tler, -tlest** [< OFr. < L. *gentilis*, of the same clan < *gens*, GENS] **1.** of the upper classes or polite society **2.** like or suitable to polite society; refined, courteous, etc. **3.** [Archaic] noble; chivalrous [a *gentle* knight] **4.** generous; kind [*gentle* reader] **5.** easily handled; tame [a *gentle* dog] **6.** kindly; patient [a *gentle* nature] **7.** not violent or harsh [a *gentle* tap] **8.** gradual [a *gentle* slope] —*vt.* **-tled, -tling 1.** to tame or train (a horse) **2.** to calm as by stroking —see SYN. at SOFT —**gen′tle·ness** *n.* —**gen′tly** *adv.*

gen·tle·folk (-fōk′) *n.pl.* people of high social standing: also **gen′tle·folks**

gen·tle·man (-mən) *n., pl.* **-men 1.** *a)* orig., a man born into a family of high social standing *b)* any man who has a large income and does not need to work for a living **2.** a courteous, gracious, honorable man **3.** a valet: chiefly in **gentleman's gentleman 4.** any man: a polite term

gen·tle·man-farm·er (-fär′mər) *n., pl.* **gen′tle·men-farm′ers** a wealthy man who owns and manages a farm as a hobby

gen·tle·man·ly (-lē) *adj.* of, characteristic of, or fit for a gentleman; well-mannered: also **gen′tle·man·like′** —**gen′tle·man·li·ness** *n.*

☆**gentlemen's** (or **gentleman's**) **agreement** an unwritten agreement guaranteed only by the parties' pledge of honor and not legally binding

gen·tle·wom·an (jent′′l wŏŏm′ən) *n., pl.* **-wom′en 1.** orig., a woman born into a family of high social standing; lady **2.** a courteous, gracious, considerate woman **3.** formerly, a woman in attendance on a lady of rank

gen·try (jen′trē) *n.* [< OFr. *genterise*, ult. < L. *gentilis*: see GENTLE] **1.** people of high social standing; esp., in Great Britain, the class of landowning people ranking just below the nobility **2.** people of a particular class or group [the newspaper *gentry*]

gen·u·flect (jen′yə flekt′) *vi.* [< ML. < L. *genu*, the knee + *flectere*, to bend] **1.** to bend the knee, as in reverence or worship **2.** to act in a humble way —**gen′u·flec′tion**, chiefly Brit. **gen′u·flex′ion** (-flek′shən) *n.* —**gen′u·flec′tor** *n.*

gen·u·ine (jen′yŏŏ wən) *adj.* [L. *genuinus* < base of *gignere*: see GENUS] **1.** of the original stock; purebred **2.** really being what it is said to be; true; authentic [a *genuine* diamond] **3.** sincere and frank; honest [*genuine* praise] —**gen′u·ine·ly** *adv.* —**gen′u·ine·ness** *n.*

ALTAR BOY GENUFLECTING

ge·nus (jē′nəs) *n., pl.* **gen·er·a** (jen′ər ə), sometimes **ge′nus·es** [L., birth, origin, race, kind < IE. base *gen-*, to beget, from which also come L. *gignere*, to beget & NATURE] **1.** a class; kind; sort **2.** *Biol.* a category that is used in classifying plants or animals that are similar in structure, etc.: a genus is the main subdivision of a family and includes one or more species; the genus name is capitalized, the species name is not (Ex.: *Homo sapiens*, modern man) **3.** *Logic* a class of things made up of subordinate classes, or species

-gen·y (jə nē) [< Gr.: see -GEN] *a suffix meaning* origin, production, development [*phylogeny*]

ge·o- [Gr. *geō-* < *gaia*, *gē*, the earth] *a combining form meaning:* **1.** earth, of the earth [*geocentric*] **2.** geographical [*geopolitics*]

ge·o·cen·tric (jē′ō sen′trik) *adj.* [GEO- + CENTRIC] **1.** measured or viewed as from the center of the earth **2.** having or thinking of the earth as a center Also **ge′o·cen′tri·cal** —**ge′o·cen′tri·cal·ly** *adv.*

ge·o·des·ic (jē′ə des′ik, -dē′sik) *adj.* **1.** *same as* GEODETIC (sense 1) **2.** *a)* designating the shortest line between two points on a surface, esp. a curved surface *b)* of or relating to the geometry of such lines —*n.* a geodesic line

☆**geodesic structure** a structure made of short, straight bars that form a grid of polygons, esp. one in the shape of a sphere or dome (**geodesic dome**)

ge·od·e·sy (jē äd′ə sē) *n.* [< Gr. *gē*, the earth + *daiein*, to divide] the branch of applied mathematics concerned with finding the size and shape of the earth or a large part of its surface, or with locating exactly points on its surface —**ge·od′e·sist** *n.*

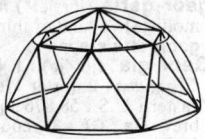

GEODESIC DOME

ge·o·det·ic (jē′ə det′ik) *adj.* **1.** of or arrived at by geodesy **2.** *same as* GEODESIC (sense 2) —**ge′o·det′i·cal·ly** *adv.*

Geof·frey (jef′rē) [< OFr. *Geoffroi* < Gmc.: 2d element < Gmc. word thought to be *frithu*, peace] a masculine name

geog. 1. geographic(al) **2.** geography

ge·o·graph·i·cal (jē′ə graf′i k'l) *adj.* **1.** of or according to geography **2.** having to do with the geography of a particular region Also **ge′o·graph′ic** —**ge′o·graph′i·cal·ly** *adv.*

ge·og·ra·phy (jē äg′rə fē) *n., pl.* **-phies** [< L. < Gr. < *geō-*, GEO- + *graphein*, to write: see GRAPHIC] **1.** the science dealing with the surface of the earth, its division into continents and countries, and the climate, plants, animals, natural resources, people, and industries of the various divisions **2.** the physical features of a region or place **3.** a book about geography —**ge·og′ra·pher** *n.*

geol. 1. geologic(al) **2.** geologist **3.** geology

ge·o·log·ic (jē′ə läj′ik) *adj.* of or according to geology: also **ge′o·log′i·cal** —**ge′o·log′i·cal·ly** *adv.*

ge·ol·o·gy (jē äl′ə jē) *n., pl.* **-gies** [< ML.: see GEO- & -LOGY] **1.** the science dealing with the physical nature of the earth, including the structure and development of its crust and interior, types of rocks, fossil forms, etc. **2.** the structure of the earth's crust in a given region or place **3.** a book about geology —**ge·ol′o·gist** *n.*

geom. 1. geometric(al) **2.** geometry

ge·o·met·ric (jē′ə met′rik) *adj.* **1.** of or according to geometry **2.** formed of straight lines, triangles, circles, etc., as a pattern Also **ge′o·met′ri·cal** —**ge′o·met′ri·cal·ly** *adv.*

geometric progression a series of terms in which the ratio of each term to the one just before it is the same throughout (Ex.: 1, 2, 4, 8, etc.)

ge·om·e·trid (jē äm′ə trid) *n.* [< ModL. < L. < Gr. < *geōmetrein*: see GEOMETRY] any of a group of moths whose larvae move by looping the body

ge·om·e·try (jē äm′ə trē) *n., pl.* **-tries** [< OFr. < L. < Gr. *geōmetrein* < *gē,* earth + *metrein,* to MEASURE] **1.** the branch of mathematics that deals with points, lines, surfaces, and solids, and examines their properties, measurement, and relations to one another in space **2.** a book about geometry —**ge·om′e·tri′cian** (-trish′ən) *n.* —**ge·om′e·ter** *n.*

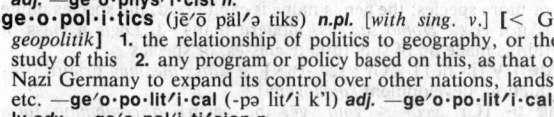

GEOMETRID
(moth & larva;
larvae to 2½ in.
long)

ge·o·phys·ics (jē′ō fiz′iks) *n.pl.* [*with sing. v.*] the science that deals with weather, winds, tides, etc. and their effect on the earth —**ge′o·phys′i·cal** *adj.* —**ge′o·phys′i·cist** *n.*

ge·o·pol·i·tics (jē′ō päl′ə tiks) *n.pl.* [*with sing. v.*] [< G. *geopolitik*] **1.** the relationship of politics to geography, or the study of this **2.** any program or policy based on this, as that of Nazi Germany to expand its control over other nations, lands, etc. —**ge′o·po·lit′i·cal** (-pə lit′i k'l) *adj.* —**ge′o·po·lit′i·cal·ly** *adv.* —**ge′o·pol′i·ti′cian** *n.*

George (jôrj) [< Fr. < LL. < Gr. < *geōrgos,* husbandman, lit., earthworker] **1.** a masculine name **2.** name of several kings of Great Britain & Ireland; specif., *a)* **George II** 1683–1760; king (1727–60) *b)* **George III** 1738–1820; king (1760–1820) *c)* **George V** 1865–1936; king (1910–36) **3.** **George VI** 1895–1952; king of Great Britain & Northern Ireland (1936–52) **4.** Saint, d. 303? A.D.; patron saint of England **5.** **Henry,** 1839–97; U.S. political economist; advocate of single tax —**by George!** an exclamation of mild surprise, determination, etc.

George·town (jôrj′toun′) seaport & capital of Guyana, on the Atlantic: pop. 195,000

geor·gette (jôr jet′) *n.* [after *Georgette* de la Plante, Parisian modiste] a kind of thin crepe fabric, used for dresses, etc.: also **georgette crepe**

Geor·gia (jôr′jə) **1.** [< GEORGE] a feminine name: var. *Georgiana* **2.** [after GEORGE II] Southern State of the southeastern U.S.: 58,876 sq. mi.; pop. 4,590,000; cap. Atlanta: abbrev. **Ga., GA 3.** republic of the U.S.S.R., on the Black Sea: 26,900 sq. mi.; pop. 4,700,000; cap. Tbilisi: in full, **Georgian Soviet Socialist Republic**

Geor·gian (jôr′jən) *adj.* **1.** of the reigns of George I, II, III, and IV of England (1714–1830) **2.** of the Georgian S.S.R., its people, language, or culture **3.** of the State of Georgia —*n.* **1.** *a)* a native or inhabitant of the Georgian S.S.R. *b)* the South Caucasian language of the Georgians ☆**2.** a native or inhabitant of the State of Georgia

ge·o·stat·ics (jē′ō stat′iks, jē′ə-) *n.pl.* [*with sing. v.*] [< GEO- + STATIC] the branch of physics dealing with the mechanics of the equilibrium of forces in rigid bodies

ge·ot·ro·pism (jē ät′rə piz′m) *n.* [GEO- + -TROPISM] movement or growth in response to the force of gravity, either downward, as of plant roots (**positive geotropism**), or upward, as of stems (**negative geotropism**) —**ge·o·trop·ic** (jē′ə träp′ik) *adj.*

Ger. 1. German **2.** Germany

ger. 1. gerund **2.** gerundive

Ger·ald (jer′əld) [< OFr. < OHG. < *ger,* spear + base of *waldan,* to rule] a masculine name: feminine **Ger′al·dine′** (-əl dēn′, -din)

ge·ra·ni·um (jə rā′nē əm, -rān′yəm) *n.* [L. < Gr. *geranion,* cranesbill: its seed capsule is beaked] **1.** a plant with showy pink or purple flowers and leaves with many lobes **2.** a pelargonium

Ger·ard (jə rärd′) [< OFr. < OHG. < *ger,* spear + *hart,* hard] a masculine name

ger·bil, ger·bille (jur′b'l) *n.* [Fr. *gerbille* < ModL. < *gerbo,* jerboa] an animal related to the mouse, with long hind legs and tail, native to Africa and Asia

ger·fal·con (jur′fal′k'n, -fôl′-, -fô′-) *n.* same as GYRFALCON

☆**ger·i·at·rics** (jer′ē at′riks) *n.pl.* [*with sing. v.*] [< Gr. *gēras,* old age + -IATRICS] the branch of medicine that deals with the diseases and hygiene of old age —**ger′i·at′ric** *adj.* —**ger′i·a·tri′cian** (-ə trish′ən), **ger′i·at′rist** *n.*

germ (jurm) *n.* [< OFr. < L. *germen,* a sprout, bud: for IE. base see GENUS] **1.** the seed, bud, etc. from which a new organism is developed **2.** any microscopic organism that can cause disease: esp., one of the bacteria **3.** that from which something can develop [the *germ* of an idea] —**germ′less** *adj.*

Ger·man (jur′mən) *adj.* [< L. *Germanus,* prob. < Celt.] of Germany, its people, language, or culture —*n.* **1.** a native or inhabitant of Germany **2.** the German language now spoken chiefly in Germany, Austria, and Switzerland, technically called *New High German* **3.** [g-] *a)* a cotillion (sense 1) *b)* a party at which the german is danced

ger·man (jur′mən) *adj.* [< OFr. < L. *germanus,* akin to *germen,* GERM] closely related: now chiefly in compounds, meaning: *a)* having the same parents [a brother-*german*] *b)* being a first cousin [a cousin-*german*]

ger·man·der (jer man′dər) *n.* [< OFr. < ML. *germandra,* < Gr. < *chamai,* on the ground + *drys,* tree] a plant of the mint family, with spikes of flowers that lack an upper lip

ger·mane (jər mān′) *adj.* [var. of GERMAN] truly relevant; pertinent; to the point —**SYN.** at RELEVANT

Ger·man·ic (jər man′ik) *adj.* **1.** of Germany or the Germans; German **2.** designating or of the original language of the German peoples or the languages descended from it; Teutonic —*n.* **1.** the original language of the Germanic peoples: now called **Proto-Germanic 2.** a principal branch of the Indo-European family of languages, consisting of this language and the languages descended from it, including Norwegian, Icelandic, Swedish, Danish (all *North Germanic*), German, Dutch, Flemish, Frisian, English (all *West Germanic*), the extinct Gothic (*East Germanic*), etc.

ger·ma·ni·um (jər mā′nē əm) *n.* [ModL. < L. *Germania,* Germany] a rare, grayish-white, metallic chemical element that can be a semiconductor: symbol, Ge; at. wt., 72.59; at. no., 32

Ger·man·ize (jur′mə nīz′) *vt., vi.* **-ized′, -iz′ing** to make or become German in character, thought, language, etc. —**Ger′man·i·za′tion** *n.*

German measles same as RUBELLA

Ger·man·o- *a combining form meaning* German, of Germany, or of the Germans

German shepherd dog a breed of dog wolflike in form and size, used in police work, as a guide for the blind, etc.: also (**German**) **police dog**

German silver same as NICKEL SILVER

Ger·ma·ny (jur′mə nē) former country in NC Europe, on the North & Baltic seas: divided (1945) into EAST GERMANY and WEST GERMANY

germ cell a cell from which a new organism can develop; egg or sperm cell

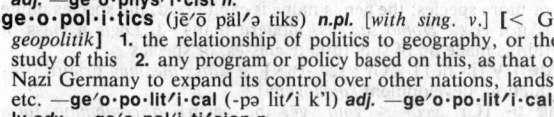

GERMAN SHEPHERD DOG
(to 2 ft. high at
shoulder)

ger·mi·cide (jur′mə sīd′) *n.* [< GERM + -CIDE] anything used to destroy germs —**ger′mi·ci′dal** *adj.*

ger·mi·nal (jur′mə n'l) *adj.* **1.** of, like, or characteristic of germs or germ cells **2.** in the first stage of growth or development —**ger′mi·nal·ly** *adv.*

ger·mi·nate (-nāt′) *vi., vt.* **-nat′ed, -nat′ing** [< L. pp. of *germinare* < *germen,* GERM] **1.** to sprout or cause to sprout, as from a seed **2.** to start developing or growing —**ger′mi·na′tion** *n.* —**ger′mi·na′tive** *adj.* —**ger′mi·na′tor** *n.*

Ger·mis·ton (jur′mis tən) city in S Transvaal, South Africa: pop. 197,000

germ plasm that part of the reproductive cells of an organism which is involved in heredity

germ warfare the deliberate spreading of disease germs in enemy territory in warfare

ger·on·tol·o·gy (jer′ən täl′ə jē) *n.* [< Gr., old man + -LOGY] the scientific study of the process of aging and of the problems of aged people —**ge·ron·to·log·i·cal** (jə rän′tə läj′i k'l) *adj.* —**ger′on·tol′o·gist** *n.*

-ger·ous (jər əs) [L. *-ger* < *gerere,* to bear + -OUS] *a suffix meaning* producing or bearing

☆**ger·ry·man·der** (jer′i man′dər, ger′-) *vt.* [< E. *Gerry,* governor of Mass. when the method was employed (1812) + SALA-

MANDER (the shape of the redistricted Essex County)] **1.** to divide (a voting area) so as to give one political party a majority in as many districts as possible **2.** to control unfairly so as to gain advantage —*vi.* to engage in gerrymandering —*n.* the act or result of gerrymandering

Ger·trude (gur′trōōd) [Fr. < G. < OHG. < *ger*, spear + *trut*, dear] a feminine name: dim. *Gert, Gertie*

ger·und (jer′ənd) *n.* [< LL. < L. *gerundus* < *gerere*, to do or carry out] *Gram.* a verbal noun ending in -*ing*, that is used like a noun but is able, like a verb, to take an object or an adverbial modifier (Ex.: *playing* in "Playing golf is his only exercise") —**ge·run·di·al** (jə run′dē əl) *adj.*

ge·run·dive (jə run′div) *n.* [< LL. < prec.] a Latin verbal adjective with an ending like a Latin verbal noun, used to express duty, necessity, fitness, etc.

ges·so (jes′ō) *n.* [It., gypsum < L. *gypsum*] plaster of Paris as used in sculpture or as a surface for painting

gest, geste (jest) *n.* [< OFr. < L. *gesta*, deeds, pl. pp. of *gerere*, to do, act] **1.** [Archaic] an adventure; exploit **2.** a romantic story of adventure, esp. a medieval tale in verse

Ge·stalt psychology (gə shtält′, -stält′, -stôlt′) [G., lit., shape, form] a school of psychology, orig. German, based on the idea that the response of an individual in a given situation is a response to the whole situation, not to its parts

☆**Ge·sta·po** (gə stä′pō; *G.* gə shtä′-) *n.* [< G. *Ge*(*heime*) *Sta*(*ats*)*po*(*lizei*), secret state police] the secret police force of the German Nazi state

ges·tate (jes′tāt) *vt.* -**tat·ed**, -**tat·ing** [< L. pp. of *gestare* < *gerere*, to bear] to carry in the uterus during pregnancy —**ges·ta′tion** *n.*

ges·tic·u·late (jes tik′yə lāt′) *vi.* -**lat·ed**, -**lat·ing** [< L. pp. of *gesticulari*, to gesture, ult. < pp. of *gerere*, to bear, do] to make or use gestures, esp. with the hands or arms, as in adding force to one's speech —*vt.* to express by gesticulating —**ges·tic′u·la′tive** *adj.* —**ges·tic′u·la′tor** *n.*

ges·tic·u·la·tion (jes tik′yə lā′shən) *n.* **1.** a gesticulating **2.** a gesture, esp. an energetic one —**ges·tic′u·la·to′ry** (-lə tôr′ē) *adj.*

ges·ture (jes′chər) *n.* [< ML. < L. pp. of *gerere*, to bear, do] **1.** a movement made with some part of the body, esp. with the hands or arms, to express or add force to ideas, emotions, etc. **2.** anything said or done to make known one's feelings or wishes, sometimes something said or done only for effect [his gift was a *gesture* of friendship] —*vi.* -**tured**, -**tur·ing** to make or use gestures —*vt.* to express with gestures —**ges′tur·al** *adj.*

get (get) *vt.* **got** or archaic & dial. **gat, got** or **got′ten, get′ting** [< ON. *geta*: for IE. base see PREHENSILE] **1.** to come into the state of having; receive, win, gain, obtain, acquire, etc. [he *got* a new car] **2.** to reach; arrive at [to *get* home early] **3.** to reach or receive by telephone, radio, television, etc. [dial "0" to *get* the operator; we can *get* four channels on TV] **4.** to go and bring [*get* your books] **5.** to catch; capture; gain hold of [*get* his attention] **6.** to have as the result [add 2 and 2 to *get* 4] **7.** to persuade (a person) to do something [*get* him to leave] **8.** to cause to act in a certain way [*get* the door to shut properly] **9.** to cause to be or arrive [he *got* his hands dirty; he *got* it there on time] **10.** to be sentenced to [he *got* ten years] **11.** to prepare [to *get* lunch] **12.** to give birth to; beget: usually said of animals **13.** [Colloq.] to be obliged to; feel a necessity to (with *have* or *has*) [he's *got* to pass] **14.** [Colloq.] to own; possess (with *have* or *has*) [he's *got* red hair] **15.** [Colloq.] to be or become the master of; esp., *a*) to overpower [his illness finally *got* him] *b*) to puzzle; baffle [this problem *gets* me] *c*) to take into custody, wound, or kill *d*) *Baseball*, etc. to put (an opponent) out **16.** [Colloq.] to strike; hit [the blow *got* him in the eye] ☆**17.** [Colloq.] to catch the meaning of; understand [did you *get* the joke?] ☆**18.** [Slang] to cause an emotional response in; irritate, please, thrill, etc. [her singing *gets* me] ☆**19.** [Slang] to notice [*get* the look on his face] —*vi.* **1.** to come or arrive [to *get* to work on time] **2.** to come to be (doing something); come to be (in a situation, condition, etc.) [he *got* caught in the rain] **3.** to manage or contrive [to *get* to do something] **4.** [Colloq.] to leave at once *Get* is used as an auxiliary for emphasis in passive construction [we *got* beaten] —*n.* **1.** the young of an animal; offspring **2.** a begetting —**get about 1.** to move from place to place **2.** to go to many social events,

places, etc. **3.** to circulate widely, as news —**get across** [Colloq.] **1.** to explain so as to be believed **2.** to succeed, as in making oneself understood —**get after** [Colloq.] **1.** to pursue or attack **2.** to urge on continually —**get along** *see phrase under* ALONG —**get around 1.** to get about (in all senses) ☆**2.** to avoid or overcome (a difficulty, etc.) **3.** to influence or gain favor with by cajoling, flattery, etc. —**get around to 1.** to find time for **2.** to get started on after a delay —**get at 1.** to approach or reach **2.** to find out **3.** to imply or suggest **4.** [Colloq.] to influence, as by bribery —**get away 1.** to go away; leave **2.** to escape **3.** to start —☆**get away with** [Slang] to succeed in doing or taking without being discovered or punished —**get back 1.** to return **2.** to recover ☆**3.** [Slang] to get revenge (usually with *at*) —**get by 1.** to be fairly acceptable ☆**2.** [Colloq.] to succeed without being discovered or punished **3.** [Colloq.] to survive; manage —**get down to** to begin to think about or act on —**get in 1.** to enter; join **2.** to arrive **3.** to put in **4.** to become closely associated (*with*) —**get it** [Colloq.] ☆**1.** to understand **2.** to be punished —**get off 1.** to come off, down, or out of **2.** to leave; go away **3.** to take off **4.** to escape **5.** to help to escape punishment **6.** to start, as in a race ☆**7.** to utter (a joke, witty reply, etc.) **8.** to have time off —**get on 1.** to go on or into **2.** to put on **3.** to proceed **4.** to grow older **5.** to succeed **6.** to agree —**get out 1.** to go out **2.** to go away **3.** to take out ☆**4.** to become no longer a secret **5.** to publish —**get out of 1.** to go out from **2.** to avoid or help to avoid **3.** to go beyond (sight, etc.) **4.** to find out from —**get over 1.** to recover from (an illness, etc.) **2.** to forget or overlook **3.** [Colloq.] to get across (in all senses) —**get somewhere** to succeed —**get through 1.** to finish **2.** to manage to survive **3.** to make oneself clear (*to*) —**get to** [Colloq.] **1.** to succeed in reaching ☆**2.** to influence, as by bribery —**get together 1.** to bring or come together; assemble ☆**2.** [Colloq.] to reach an agreement —**get up 1.** to rise (from a chair, from sleep, etc.) **2.** to plan; organize **3.** to dress elaborately **4.** to advance; make progress —**get′ta·ble, get′a·ble** *adj.* —**get′ter** *n.*

SYN.—**get** has the broad meaning to come into possession of, with or without effort [to *get* a job, an idea, a headache, etc.]; **obtain** implies that there is effort or desire in the getting [he has *obtained* aid]; **procure** suggests active effort or planning in getting something or bringing it to pass [to *procure* a settlement of the dispute]; **secure**, in narrow use, implies difficulty in obtaining something and in holding on to it [to *secure* a lasting peace]; **acquire** implies a lengthy process in the getting and connotes collecting or accumulating [he *acquired* a fine education]; **gain** always implies effort in the getting of something advantageous or profitable [to *gain* fame] —**ANT.** lose, forgo

get·a·way (get′ə wā′) *n.* **1.** the act of starting, as in a race **2.** the act of escaping, as from police

Geth·sem·a·ne (geth sem′ə nē) *Bible* a garden outside of Jerusalem, scene of the agony, betrayal, and arrest of Jesus: Matt. 26:36

☆**get-to·geth·er** (get′tə geth′ər) *n.* an informal social gathering or meeting

Get·tys·burg (get′iz burg′) [after J. *Gettys*, its 18th-c. founder] town in S Pa.: site of a crucial battle (July, 1863) of the Civil War: pop. 7,000

get-up (get′up′) *n.* [Colloq.] **1.** general arrangement or composition **2.** costume; outfit; dress **3.** driving ambition; energy: also **get′-up′-and-go′**

gew·gaw (gyōō′gô, gōō′-) *n.* [ME. *giuegoue, gugaw* < ?] something showy but useless; trinket

gey·ser (gī′zər, -sər; *Brit.* gā′-) *n.* [Ice. *Geysir*, a hot spring in Iceland, lit., gusher < ON. *gjosa*, to gush] a spring from which columns of boiling water and steam gush into the air from time to time

Gha·na (gä′nə) country in W Africa, on the Atlantic: a member of the Commonwealth: 91,843 sq. mi.; pop. 8,600,000; cap. Accra —**Gha·na·ian** (gä′nē ən, -nā-) *adj., n.*

ghast·ly (gast′lē) *adj.* -**li·er**, -**li·est** [< OE. < *gast*, spirit, GHOST] **1.** horrible; frightful [a *ghastly* sight] **2.** ghostlike; pale [the prisoner looked *ghastly*] **3.** [Colloq.] very unpleasant [a *ghastly* mistake] —*adv.* in a ghastly way —**ghast′li·ness** *n.*

SYN.—**ghastly** suggests the horror caused by the sight or suggestion of death [a *ghastly* smile on the dead man's face]; **grim** implies extremely disagreeable or even terrifying aspects [the *grim* life of the very poor]; **grisly** suggests an appearance or nature that causes one to be horrified [the *grisly* sights of the concentration camp*]*; **gruesome** suggests the fear and disgust caused by something horrible and evil *[the gruesome details of a murder]*; **macabre** implies a being concerned or fascinated with the gruesome aspects of death *[a macabre tale]*

ghat, ghaut (gôt, gät) *n.* [Hindi *ghāṭ*] in India, **1.** a mountain pass **2.** a flight of steps leading down to a river landing

Ghats (gôts, gäts) two mountain ranges (**Eastern Ghats** and **Western Ghats**) forming the east and the west edges of the Deccan Plateau, India

ghee (gē) *n.* [Hindi *ghī*] in India, a liquid butter specially made from cow's milk or buffalo milk

Ghent (gent) city in NW Belgium: pop. 156,000

gher·kin (gur'kin) *n.* [< Du. or LowG. *gurken,* ult. < Per. *angārah*] **1.** a variety of cucumber bearing small, prickly fruit, used for pickles **2.** the immature fruit of the cucumber when pickled

ghet·to (get'ō) *n., pl.* **-tos, -toes** [It., lit., foundry, ult. < L. *jactare,* to cast: the former Jewish quarter on a foundry site in Venice] **1.** in certain European cities, a section in which Jews were formerly forced to live **2.** any section of a city in which many members of some minority group live, or are forced to live by discrimination

Ghib·el·line (gib'ə lin, -lēn') *n.* any member of a political party in medieval Italy that supported the authority of the German emperors in Italy

Ghi·ber·ti (gē ber'tē), **Lo·ren·zo** (lô ren'tsô) (born *Lorenzo di Cione di Ser Buonaccorso*) 1378-1455; Florentine sculptor, painter, & worker in metals

ghost (gōst) *n.* [OE. *gast* < IE. base *gheizd-,* frightened] **1.** orig., the spirit or soul: now only in **give up the ghost** (to die) and in HOLY GHOST **2.** the spirit of a dead person, supposedly seen by the living as a pale, shadowy form **3.** a faint semblance; slight trace *[not a ghost of a chance]* ☆**4.** [Colloq.] *same as* GHOSTWRITER **5.** *Optics & TV* an unwanted secondary image or bright spot —*vi.* ☆[Colloq.] to work as a ghostwriter —*vt.* ☆[Colloq.] to be the ghostwriter of —**ghost'like'** *adj.*

ghost·ly (gōst'lē) *adj.* **-li·er, -li·est** of or like a ghost *[a ghostly visitor]* —**ghost'li·ness** *n.*

☆**ghost town** the remains of a town that has been permanently abandoned, esp. for economic reasons

☆**ghost·writ·er** (-rīt'ər) *n.* a person who writes speeches, articles, etc. for another who claims to be the author —**ghost'write' vt., vi.** **-wrote', -writ'ten, -writ'ing**

ghoul (gōōl) *n.* [Ar. *ghūl,* demon < *ghāla,* to seize] **1.** *Oriental Folklore* an evil spirit that robs graves and feeds on the dead **2.** a robber of graves **3.** one who enjoys things that disgust or trouble most people —**ghoul'ish** *adj.* —**ghoul'ish·ly** *adv.* —**ghoul'ish·ness** *n.*

GHQ, G.H.Q. General Headquarters

☆**GI** (jē'ī') *adj.* **1.** *Mil.* government issue: designating clothing, equipment, etc. issued to military personnel **2.** [Colloq.] *a)* of or characteristic of the U.S. armed forces *[a GI haircut] b)* strict in following or enforcing military regulations *c)* of or for veterans of the U.S. armed forces —*n., pl.* **GI's, GIs** [Colloq.] any member of the U.S. armed forces; esp., an enlisted soldier

GI, G.I., g.i. gastrointestinal

gi. gill (unit of measure); gills

gi·ant (jī'ənt) *n.* [< ONormFr. < VL. < L. *gigas* < Gr.] **1.** any imaginary being of human form but of superhuman size and strength **2.** a person or thing of great size, intellect, etc. —*adj.* of great size, strength, etc. —**gi'ant·ess** *n.fem.*

gi·ant·ism (-iz'm) *n.* abnormally great growth of the body, due to excessive production of growth hormone by the pituitary gland

giant panda a large, black-and-white, bearlike mammal of China and Tibet

giaour (jour) *n.* [< Turk. < Per. *gabr* < Ar. *kāfir,* infidel] in Moslem usage, a non-Moslem; esp., a Christian

gib·ber (jib'ər) *vi., vt.* [echoic] to talk or chatter in a confused or meaningless way —*n.* gibberish

gib·ber·ish (jib'ər ish; *Brit.* gib'-) *n.* confused or meaningless talk or chatter

gib·bet (jib'it) *n.* [< OFr. dim. < Frank. *gibb,* forked stick] **1.** a gallows **2.** a structure like a gallows, from which bodies of criminals already executed were hung and exposed to public scorn —*vt.* **1.** to execute by hanging **2.** to hang on a gibbet **3.** to expose to public scorn

gib·bon (gib'ən) *n.* [Fr.] a small, slender, long-armed ape of India, S China, and the East Indies, that lives in trees

Gib·bon (gib'ən), **Edward** 1737-94; Eng. historian

gib·bous (gib'əs) *adj.* [< L. *gibbosus* < *gibba,* a hump] **1.** rounded and bulging **2.** designating the moon or a planet when more than half, but not all, of the disk is illuminated **3.** humpbacked —**gib·bos·i·ty** (gi bäs'ə tē) *n.* —**gib'bous·ly** *adv.*

gibe (jīb) *vi., vt.* **gibed, gib'ing** [< ? OFr. *giber,* to handle roughly] to jeer, or taunt; scoff (at) —*n.* a jeering remark; taunt; scoff —see SYN. at SCOFF —**gib'er** *n.*

gib·let (jib'lit) *n.* [< OFr. *gibelet,* stew made of game] any of the parts of a fowl, as the heart, gizzard, neck, etc., usually cooked separately

Gi·bral·tar (ji brôl'tər) **1.** Brit. territory on a small peninsula at the S tip of Spain, including a port & naval base: it consists mostly of a rocky hill (**Rock of Gibraltar**) **2. Strait of,** strait between Spain & Morocco, joining the Mediterranean & the Atlantic —*n.* any strong fortress

gid·dy (gid'ē) *adj.* **-di·er, -di·est** [OE. *gydig,* insane, prob. < base of *god,* GOD (i.e., "possessed by a god")] **1.** having a whirling, dazed sensation; dizzy **2.** causing such a sensation *[a giddy height]* **3.** whirling **4.** not serious or steady in purpose; fickle; frivolous —**gid'di·ly** *adv.* —**gid'di·ness** *n.*

Gide (zhēd), **An·dré** (**Paul Guillaume**) (än drā') 1869-1951; Fr. novelist, critic, etc.

Gid·e·on (gid'ē ən) [Heb. *gidh'ōn,* lit., hewer] **1.** a masculine name **2.** *Bible* a judge of Israel: led a victory over the Midianites

gie (gē) *vt., vi.* **gied** or **gae, gi·en** (gē'ən), **gie'ing** [Scot. & Brit. Dial.] to give

gift (gift) *n.* [OE., wedding gift (< *giefan,* to GIVE) & < ON. *gipt,* gift] **1.** something given to show friendship, affection, support, etc.; present **2.** the act, power, or right of giving **3.** a natural ability; talent —see SYN. at PRESENT and TALENT

gift·ed (gift'id) *adj.* **1.** having a natural ability; talented *[a gifted pianist]* **2.** having superior intelligence *[a gifted child]*

gift of tongues *same as* GLOSSOLALIA

gig[1] (gig) *n.* [prob. < Scand.] **1.** a light, two-wheeled, open carriage drawn by one horse **2.** a long, light ship's boat

gig[2] (gig) *n.* [contr. < *fizgig* < Sp. *fisga,* kind of harpoon] a fish spear —*vt., vi.* **gigged, gig'ging** to spear or jab as with a gig

gig[3] (gig) *n.* [< ?] [Slang] a demerit —*vi.* **gigged, gig'ging** [Slang] to give a gig to

☆**gig**[4] (gig) *n.* [< ?] [Slang] **1.** a job to play or sing jazz, rock, etc. **2.** any stint of work

gi·ga- (jig'ə) [< Gr. *gigas,* giant] *a combining form meaning* one billion; the factor 10^9 *[gigahertz]*

gi·gan·tic (jī gan'tik) *adj.* [see GIANT] **1.** of, like, or fit for a giant **2.** huge; enormous; immense —see SYN. at ENORMOUS —**gi·gan'ti·cal·ly** *adv.*

gi·gan·tism (jī gan'tiz'm, jī'gan-) *n.* [see GIANT] **1.** the state of being gigantic **2.** *same as* GIANTISM

gig·gle (gig'l) *vi.* **-gled, -gling** [prob. < Du. *giggelen*] to laugh with rapid, high-pitched sounds in a silly or nervous way, as if trying to hold back; titter —*n.* the act or sound of giggling —see SYN. at LAUGH —**gig'gler** *n.* —**gig'gly** *adj.* **-gli·er, -gli·est**

gig·o·lo (jig'ə lō) *n., pl.* **-los** [Fr.] a man paid by a woman to be her escort or lover

gig·ot (jig'ət, zhē gō') *n.* [Fr. < OFr., dim. < MHG. *giga,* a fiddle] **1.** a leg of mutton, lamb, veal, etc. **2.** a leg-of-mutton sleeve

☆**Gi·la monster** (hē'lə) [< the *Gila* River, Arizona] a poisonous lizard having a thick body covered with beadlike scales of black and orange: found in deserts of the southwestern U.S. and in Mexico

Gil·bert (gil'bərt) [< OFr. < OHG. < *willo,* will + *beraht,* bright] **1.** a masculine name: dim. **Gil 2.** Sir **Humphrey,** 1539?-83; Eng. navigator & colonizer in N. America **3.** Sir **William Schwenck** (shweŋk), 1836-1911; Eng. librettist: collaborated with A. SULLIVAN in writing comic operas

Gilbert and Ellice Islands Brit. colo-

GIANT PANDA
(4 ft. high at shoulder)

GIBBON (18½-25 in. long, head & body)

GILA MONSTER
(to 24 in. long)

ny (1916–75): *see* GILBERT ISLANDS & ELLICE ISLANDS

Gilbert Islands Brit. territory in the WC Pacific, consisting mainly of three groups of atolls near the equator

gild[1] (gild) *vt.* **gild′ed** or **gilt, gild′ing** [OE. *gyldan* < base of *gold,* GOLD] **1.** *a)* to cover with a thin layer of gold *b)* to coat with a gold color **2.** to make appear bright and attractive **3.** to make (something) seem more attractive or valuable than it is

gild[2] (gild) *n.* same as GUILD

gild·ing (gil′diŋ) *n.* **1.** the art or process of applying gold leaf or a substance like gold to a surface **2.** the substance so applied

Gil·e·ad (gil′ē əd) mountainous region of ancient Palestine, east of the Jordan

gill[1] (gil) *n.* [prob. < Anglo-N.] **1.** the organ for breathing of most animals that live in water, as fish, lobsters, clams, etc. **2.** [*pl.*] *a)* the wattle of a fowl *b)* the fleshy jowl of a person **3.** any of the thin, leaflike, radiating parts on the undersurface of a mushroom —**gilled** *adj.*

gill[2] (jil) *n.* [< OFr. < LL. *gillo,* cooling vessel] a liquid measure, equal to 1/4 pint

gil·lie, gil·ly (gil′ē) *n., pl.* **-lies** [Scot. < Gael. *gille,* boy, page] **1.** in the Scottish Highlands, a sportsman's attendant **2.** a male servant

gil·li·flow·er (jil′ē flou′ər) *n.* [OFr. *gilofre* < LL. < Gr. < *karyon,* nut + *phyllon,* leaf] any of several plants with clove-scented flowers, as the clove pink: also sp. **gil′ly·flow′er**

gilt (gilt) *alt. pt. & pp. of* GILD[1] —*adj.* covered with gilding —*n.* same as GILDING

gilt-edged (gilt′ejd′) *adj.* **1.** having gilded edges **2.** of the highest quality or value [*gilt-edged* securities] Also **gilt′-edge′**

gim·bals (gim′b'lz, jim′-) *n.pl.* [with sing. v.] [< L. *gemellus,* dim. of *geminus,* twin] a pair of rings pivoted in axes at right angles to each other so that one is free to swing within the other: a ship's compass will keep a horizontal position when suspended in gimbals —**gim′baled** *adj.*

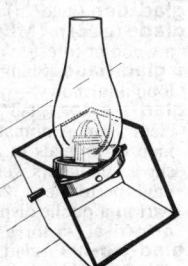

GIMBALS

gim·crack (jim′krak′) *adj.* [altered < ME. *gibbecrak,* an ornament] showy but cheap and useless —*n.* a cheap, showy, useless thing; knick-knack —**gim′crack′er·y** *n.*

gim·let (gim′lit) *n.* [< OFr. < MDu. dim. of *wimmel,* wimble] a small boring tool with a handle at right angles to a shaft with a spiral, pointed cutting edge —*vt.* to make a hole in as with a gimlet

GIMLET

gim·let-eyed (-ī′d′) *adj.* having a piercing glance

☆**gim·mick** (gim′ik) *n.* [< ? GIMCRACK] **1.** [Colloq.] *a)* a secret device for controlling a game of chance at a carnival, etc. *b)* anything used to trick or deceive **2.** [Slang] *a)* an attention-getting feature of no great worth, used for promoting a product, etc. *b)* any clever little gadget or ruse —*vt.* [Colloq.] to add gimmicks to (often with *up*) —☆**gim′mick·ry, gim′mick·er·y** *n.* —**gim′mick·y** *adj.*

gimp[1] (gimp) *n.* [< ? Du.] a ribbonlike braided fabric, used to trim garments, furniture, etc.

☆**gimp**[2] (gimp) *n.* [< ?] [Colloq.] **1.** a lame person **2.** a limp —*vi.* [Colloq.] to limp —**gimp′y** *adj.*

gin[1] (jin) *n.* [< *geneva* < Du. *genever* < OFr. < L. *juniperus,* juniper] a strong alcoholic liquor distilled from grain and usually flavored with juniper berries

gin[2] (jin) *n.* [< OFr., contr. < *engin,* ENGINE] **1.** a trap, as for game ☆**2.** same as COTTON GIN —*vt.* **ginned, gin′ning 1.** to catch in a trap **2.** to remove seeds from (cotton) with a gin

gin[3] (gin) *vt., vi.* **gan, gin′ning** [ME. *ginnen* < OE. *beginnan,* to begin] [Archaic] to begin

gin[4] (gin) *n.* ☆same as GIN RUMMY —*vi.* **ginned, gin′ning** ☆to win in gin rummy with no unmatched cards left in one's hand

gin·ger (jin′jər) *n.* [< OE. & OFr., both < ML. < L. *zingiber* < Gr. < Pali] **1.** an Asiatic plant grown for its spicy rhizome **2.** the rhizome, or the spice made from it **3.** a reddish-brown color ☆**4.** [Colloq.] vigor; spirit —**gin′ger·y** *adj.*

ginger ale a carbonated, sweet soft drink flavored with ginger

ginger beer a drink like ginger ale but with a stronger flavor

gin·ger·bread (-bred′) *n.* [ME. *ginge bred* < *gingebras,* preserved ginger < OFr.] **1.** a cake flavored with ginger and molasses **2.** showy decoration, as fancy carvings on gables, furniture, etc. —*adj.* cheap and showy; gaudy: also **gin′ger-bread′y**

gin·ger·ly (-lē) *adv.* very carefully or cautiously —*adj.* very careful; cautious —**gin′ger·li·ness** *n.*

gin·ger·snap (-snap′) *n.* a crisp, spicy cookie flavored with ginger and molasses

ging·ham (giŋ′əm) *n.* [< Du. or Fr., ult. < Malay *ginggang,* striped (cloth)] a cotton cloth, usually woven in stripes, checks, or plaids

gin·gi·vi·tis (jin′jə vīt′əs) *n.* [ModL. < L. *gingiva,* the gum + -ITIS] inflammation of the gums

gink·go (giŋ′kō) *n., pl.* **gink′goes** [Jpn. *ginkyo* < Chin.] an Asiatic tree with fan-shaped leaves and yellow seeds enclosing an edible kernel: also **ging′ko,** *pl.* **ging′koes**

☆**gin rummy** a variety of the card game rummy: a hand which totals no more than ten points in unmatched cards and has been exposed wins unless the opponent has fewer points or an equal number

gin·seng (jin′seŋ) *n.* [Chin. *jen shen*] **1.** a perennial plant with a thick, forked, aromatic root: some species are found in China and N. America **2.** the root of this plant, used as a medicine

Gior·gio·ne (jôr jô′ne), **Il** (ēl) (born *Giorgio Barbarelli*) 1478?–1510; Venetian painter

Giot·to (di Bondone) (jôt′tō; *E.* jät′ō) 1266?–1337; Florentine painter & architect

gip (jip) *n., vt., vi.* same as GYP

gip·sy (jip′sē) *n.* same as GYPSY

gi·raffe (jə raf′) *n., pl.* **-raffes′, -raffe′:** see PLURAL, II, D, 1 [Fr. < It. *giraffa* < Ar. *zarāfa*] a large, cud-chewing animal of Africa, with a very long neck and legs: the tallest of existing animals

gird (gurd) *vt.* **gird′ed** or **girt, gird′ing** [OE. *gyrdan* < IE. base *gherdh-,* to enclose] **1.** to encircle or fasten with a belt or band **2.** to encircle; enclose [farmlands *girded* the castle] **3.** to equip or endow [*girded* with strength] **4.** to prepare (oneself) for action

gird·er (gur′dər) *n.* [GIRD + -ER] a large beam of timber or steel, for supporting the joists of a floor, a framework, etc.

gir·dle (gur′d'l) *n.* [OE. *gyrdel:* for IE. base see GIRD] **1.** a belt or sash for the waist **2.** anything that surrounds or encircles ☆**3.** a woman's elasticized undergarment for supporting the waist and hips **4.** the rim of a cut gem ☆**5.** a ring made by removing the bark around the trunk of a tree —*vt.* **-dled, -dling 1.** to surround or bind, as with a girdle **2.** to encircle ☆**3.** to cut a ring of bark from around (a tree) —**gir′dler** *n.*

girl (gurl) *n.* [ME. *girle, gurle,* youngster] **1.** a female child **2.** a young, unmarried woman **3.** a female servant **4.** [Colloq.] a woman of any age **5.** [Colloq.] a sweetheart —**girl′ish** *adj.* —**girl′ish·ly** *adv.* —**girl′ish·ness** *n.*

☆**girl friend** (gurl′frend′) *n.* [Colloq.] **1.** a sweetheart of a boy or man **2.** a girl who is one's friend

girl·hood (-hood′) *n.* **1.** the state or time of being a girl **2.** girls as a group

girl·ie, girl·y (gur′lē) *n., pl.* **girl′ies** [Slang] a girl or woman

☆**girl scout** a member of the **Girl Scouts,** a U.S. organization founded in 1912 to provide character-building activities for girls

Gi·ronde (jə ränd′; *Fr.* zhē rônd′) estuary in SW France, formed by the juncture of the Garonne & Dordogne rivers and flowing into the Bay of Biscay

Gi·ron·dist (jə rän′dist) *n.* [orig. led by deputies from the department of Gironde, in SW France] a member of a moderate republican party in France from 1791 to 1793

girt[1] (gurt) *alt. pt. & pp. of* GIRD

girt[2] (gurt) *vt.* [var. of GIRD] **1.** to gird; girdle **2.** to fasten with a girth

GINKGO
(tree & leaves)

girth (gʉrth) *n.* [< ON. *gjörth*: for IE. base see GIRD] **1.** a band put around the belly of a horse, etc. to hold a saddle or pack **2.** the circumference, as of a tree trunk or person's waist —*vt.* to bind with a girth

☆**gis·mo** (giz′mō) *n., pl.* **-mos** [Slang] same as GIZMO

gist (jist) *n.* [< OFr. *giste*, point at issue < *gesir*, to lie < L. *jacere*] the main point or idea, as of an article or argument

git·tern (git′ərn) *n.* [< OFr. *guiterne*, altered < OSp. *guittarra*: see GUITAR] an obsolete, guitarlike musical instrument with wire strings

give (giv) *vt.* **gave, giv′en, giv′ing** [OE. *giefan*: for IE. base see HABIT] **1.** to turn over the control of without cost or exchange; make a gift of **2.** to hand or pass over to be cared for [he *gave* the porter his bag] **3.** to sell (goods, services, etc.) for a price or pay (a price) for goods, services, etc. **4.** to relay [*give* my regards] **5.** to cause to have; impart [music *gives* me pleasure] **6.** to confer (a title, position, etc.) **7.** to act as host of (a party, etc.) ☆**8.** to put in communication with by telephone **9.** to produce; supply [cows *give* milk] **10.** *a)* to sacrifice [he *gave* his life for his country] *b)* to devote fully [he *gives* all his time to his work] **11.** to show; exhibit [he *gave* few signs of intelligence] **12.** to offer; proffer [to *give* advice] **13.** to perform [to *give* a concert] **14.** to make (a gesture, movement, etc.) [*give* a leap] **15.** to utter (words, etc.); state [*give* a reply] **16.** to inflict (punishment, etc.) —*vi.* **1.** to make gifts; contribute **2.** to bend, sink, move, etc. from force or pressure [the board *gave* under his weight] **3.** to be resilient **4.** to provide a view of or access to [the window *gives* on the park] ☆**5.** [Colloq.] to happen: chiefly in **what gives?** —*n.* **1.** a bending, sinking, moving, etc. under pressure **2.** resiliency —**give away 1.** to make a gift of **2.** in a marriage ceremony, to present (the bride) to the bridegroom ☆**3.** [Colloq.] to reveal, as a secret; expose —**give back** to return —**give forth** (or **off**) to send forth; emit —**give in 1.** to hand in **2.** to surrender; yield —**give it to** [Colloq.] to beat or scold —**give or take** plus or minus [costing a dollar, *give or take* a few cents] —**give out 1.** to send forth; emit **2.** to make public **3.** to distribute **4.** to become worn out or used up —**give to understand** (or **believe**, etc.) to cause to understand (or believe, etc.) —**give up 1.** to hand over; relinquish **2.** to stop; cease [to *give up* smoking] **3.** to admit failure and stop trying **4.** to lose hope for **5.** to devote wholly —**giv′er** *n.*

SYN.—**give** is the general word meaning to transfer from one's own possession to that of another; **grant** implies that another has asked for the thing given [to *grant* a favor]; **present** implies a certain formality in the giving and often suggests that the gift has considerable value [to *present* a rare manuscript to the library]; **bestow** stresses that the giver acts only if and when he wishes to and often suggests that he looks upon those who receive the gift as being beneath him in worth, importance, etc. [to *bestow* charity upon the poor]; **confer** implies that the giver is a superior and that the thing given is an honor, privilege, etc. [to *confer* a college degree]

give-and-take (giv′'n tāk′) *n.* **1.** a yielding and conceding on both sides; compromise **2.** a fair and equal exchange of remarks or retorts

give·a·way (-ə wā′) *n.* [Colloq.] ☆**1.** a revealing of something without meaning to do so **2.** something given free or sold cheap to attract customers, etc. ☆**3.** the appropriation of public lands, resources, etc. for private profit ☆**4.** *Radio & TV* a program in which prizes are given to contestants

giv·en (giv′'n) *pp. of* GIVE —*adj.* **1.** bestowed; presented **2.** accustomed; inclined [*given* to lying] **3.** stated; specified [within a *given* period] **4.** assumed; granted [*given* that ABC is a right triangle] **5.** issued; executed [*given* under his seal as mayor]

given name the first name of a person [John Smith's *given name* is John]

Gi·za (gē′zə) city in N Egypt, near Cairo, on the Nile: pop. 250,000

☆**giz·mo** (giz′mō) *n., pl.* **-mos** [< ?] [Slang] **1.** any gadget or contrivance **2.** a gimmick

giz·zard (giz′ərd) *n.* [< OFr. *gisier* < L. *gigeria*, pl., cooked entrails of poultry] **1.** the second stomach of a bird: it has thick, muscular walls and a tough lining for grinding food **2.** [Colloq.] the stomach: humorous usage

Gk. Greek

gla·brous (glā′brəs) *adj.* [< L. *glaber*, bald] without hair, down, or fuzz; bald —**gla′brous·ness** *n.*

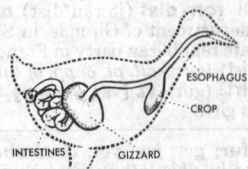
GIZZARD OF CHICKEN

[diagram labels: ESOPHAGUS, CROP, INTESTINES, GIZZARD]

gla·cé (gla sā′) *adj.* [Fr., pp. of *glacer*, to freeze < L. < *glacies*, ice] **1.** having a smooth, glossy surface **2.** candied or glazed, as fruits —*vt.* **-céed′, -cé′ing** to glaze (fruits, etc.)

gla·cial (glā′shəl) *adj.* [< L. < *glacies*, ice] **1.** of ice or glaciers **2.** of or produced by a glacier or a glacial epoch **3.** freezing; frigid [*glacial* weather] **4.** cold and unfriendly [a *glacial* stare] **5.** as slow as the movement of a glacier [*glacial* progress] **6.** *Chem.* having an icelike appearance —**gla′cial·ly** *adv.*

glacial epoch any extent of geologic time when large parts of the earth were covered with glaciers; specif., the Pleistocene Epoch, when a large part of the Northern Hemisphere was covered several times with glaciers; ice age

gla·ci·ate (glā′shē āt′, -sē-) *vt.* **-at′ed, -at′ing 1.** *a)* to cover over with ice or a glacier *b)* to form into ice; freeze **2.** to expose to or change by glacial action —**gla′ci·a′tion** *n.*

gla·cier (glā′shər) *n.* [Fr. < VL. < L. *glacies*, ice] a large mass of ice and snow that forms in areas where the rate of snowfall exceeds the melting rate: it moves slowly down a mountain, along a valley, etc. until it melts or breaks away

Glacier National Park national park in NW Mont., on the Canadian border: it contains many small glaciers

gla·cis (glā′sis, glas′is) *n., pl.* **-cis** (-sēz), **-cis·es** (-sis əz) [Fr. < OFr. *glacier*, to slip < *glace*, ice] **1.** a gradual slope **2.** an embankment sloping down from a fortification

glad[1] (glad) *adj.* **glad′der, glad′dest** [OE. *glæd*: for IE. base see GOLD] **1.** happy; pleased [I'm *glad* I wasn't there] **2.** causing pleasure or joy; making happy [*glad* tidings] **3.** very willing [I'm *glad* to help] **4.** bright or beautiful [a *glad* summer day] —*vt., vi.* **glad′ded, glad′ding** [Archaic] to gladden —see SYN. at HAPPY —**glad′ly** *adv.* —**glad′ness** *n.*

glad[2] (glad) *n.* [Colloq.] same as GLADIOLUS

glad·den (glad′'n) *vt., vi.* to make or become glad

glade (glād) *n.* [ME., prob. < *glad*, GLAD[1]] **1.** an open space in a wood or forest ☆**2.** an everglade

☆**glad hand** [Slang] a cordial welcome, esp. one that is overly loud and showy —**glad′-hand′ vt., vi.** —**glad′-hand′er** *n.*

glad·i·a·tor (glad′ē āt′ər) *n.* [L. < *gladius*, sword] **1.** in ancient Rome, a man who fought other men or animals in an arena as a public show: gladiators were slaves, captives, or paid performers **2.** any person taking part in a public dispute or fight —**glad′i·a·to′ri·al** (-ə tôr′ē əl) *adj.*

glad·i·o·lus (glad′ē ō′ləs; *occas.* glə-dī′ə ləs) *n., pl.* **-lus·es, -li** (-lī), **-lus** (-ləs, -loz) [ModL. < L. dim. of *gladius*, sword] a plant with swordlike leaves and tall spikes of funnel-shaped flowers in various colors: also **glad′i·o′la** (-lə)

glad·some (glad′səm) *adj.* joyful or cheerful —**glad′some·ly** *adv.* —**glad′some·ness** *n.*

GLADIATORS

Glad·stone (glad′stōn; *Brit.* -stən), **Wil·liam Ew·art** (yōō′ərt) 1809–98; English prime minister

Glad·stone (bag) (glad′stōn; *Brit.* -stən) [after prec.] a traveling bag hinged so that it can open flat into two compartments of equal size

Glad·ys (glad′is) [W. *Gwladys*, prob. < L. *Claudia*: see CLAUDIA] a feminine name

glair (gler) *n.* [< OFr. < L. *clarus*, CLEAR] **1.** raw white of egg, used in sizing or glazing **2.** a size or glaze made from this **3.** any sticky matter resembling raw egg white —*vt.* to cover with glair —**glair′y** *adj.*

glaive (glāv) *n.* [< OFr. < L. *gladius*, sword] [Archaic] a sword; esp., a broadsword

glam·or·ize (glam′ə rīz′) *vt.* **-ized′, -iz′ing** to make glamorous —**glam′or·i·za′tion** *n.*

glam·or·ous, glam·our·ous (glam′ər əs) *adj.* full of glamour; fascinating; alluring —**glam′or·ous·ly** *adv.*

glam·our, glam·or (glam′ər) *n.* [Scot. var. of *grammar* in sense of *gramarye*, magic] **1.** orig., a magic spell or charm ☆**2.** mysterious and alluring charm; attractive quality that excites one [the *glamour* of faraway lands]

glance (glans) *vi.* **glanced, glanc′ing** [prob. a blend < OFr. *glacier*, to slip + *guenchir*, to elude] **1.** to strike at a slant and go off at an angle [hail *glanced* off the roof] **2.** to make an indirect or passing reference **3.** to flash or gleam [sunlight *glanced* off the metal] **4.** to take a quick look [just *glance* at this] —*n.* **1.** a glancing off **2.** a flash or gleam **3.** a quick look

gland (gland) *n.* [< Fr. < OFr. < L. *glandula*, tonsil, dim. of

glans (gen. **glandis**), acorn] **1.** any organ that separates certain elements from the blood and secretes them in a form for the body to use (as an adrenal, which is a ductless gland, secretes epinephrine) or throw off (as a kidney, which is a gland with ducts, secretes urine) **2.** loosely, any structure like a gland in appearance, etc. [lymph *glands*]

glan·ders (glan'dərz) **n.pl.** [*with sing. v.*] [OFr. *glandres*, lit., glands] a contagious disease of horses, mules, etc. characterized by fever, swelling of glands beneath the jaw, nasal inflammation, etc.

glan·du·lar (glan'jə lər) *adj.* **1.** of, like, or having a gland or glands **2.** derived from or affected by glands —**glan'du·lar·ly** *adv.*

glandular fever *same as* INFECTIOUS MONONUCLEOSIS

glan·dule (glan'jool) *n.* [Fr.] a small gland

glans (glanz) *n., pl.* **glan·des** (glan'dēz) [L., lit., acorn] the head, or end, of the penis: in full, **glans penis**

glare[1] (gler) *vi.* **glared, glar'ing** [ME. *glaren* < or akin to MDu. *glaren*, to gleam & OE. *glær*, amber: for IE. base see GOLD] **1.** to shine with a steady, dazzling light **2.** to be too bright or showy **3.** to stare fiercely or angrily —*vt.* to express with a glare —*n.* **1.** a steady, dazzling light **2.** a too bright or dazzling display **3.** a fierce or angry stare

glare[2] (gler) *n.* [prob. < prec.] a smooth, bright, glassy surface, as of ice —*adj.* smooth, bright, and glassy

glar·ing (gler'iŋ) *adj.* **1.** dazzlingly bright **2.** too bright and showy [*glaring* colors] **3.** staring fiercely and angrily **4.** too obvious to be overlooked; flagrant [a *glaring* mistake] —see SYN. at FLAGRANT —**glar'ing·ly** *adv.*

glar·y (-ē) *adj.* **glar'i·er, glar'i·est** dazzlingly bright; glaring —**glar'i·ness** *n.*

Glas·gow (glas'kō, glaz'gō) seaport in SC Scotland: pop. 961,000 —**Glas·we·gi·an** (glas wē'jən, -jē ən) *adj., n.*

Glas·gow (glas'kō, glaz'gō), **Ellen (Anderson Gholson)** 1874-1945; U.S. novelist

glass (glas) *n.* [OE. *glæs*: for IE. base see GOLD] **1.** a hard, brittle substance, usually transparent, made by fusing silicates with soda or potash, lime, and, sometimes, metallic oxides **2.** *same as* GLASSWARE **3.** *a*) an article made of glass, as a drinking container, mirror, telescope, barometer, etc. *b*) [*pl.*] eyeglasses *c*) [*pl.*] binoculars **4.** the quantity contained in a drinking glass —*vt.* **1.** to put in glass jars for preserving **2.** to mirror; reflect **3.** to equip with glass; glaze **4.** to make glassy —*adj.* of, made of, or like glass —**glass in** to enclose with glass panes

glass blowing the art or process of shaping molten glass by blowing air into a mass of it at the end of a tube —**glass blower**

glass·ful (glas'fool') *n., pl.* **glass'fuls'** the amount that will fill a glass

glass·house (-hous') *n. Brit. var. of* GREENHOUSE

☆**glass·ine** (gla sēn') *n.* [GLASS + -INE[1]] a thin, tough paper used for the windows on envelopes, etc.

☆**glass snake** a legless lizard found in the southern U.S.: so called because its tail breaks off easily

glass·ware (-wer') *n.* articles made of glass

glass wool fine fibers of glass intertwined in a woolly mass, used in filters and as insulation

glass·wort (-wurt') *n.* a fleshy plant of the goosefoot family, found in saltwater marshes: its ash is rich in soda and formerly was used in making glass

glass·y (-ē) *adj.* **glass'i·er, glass'i·est** **1.** like glass, as in smoothness or transparency **2.** expressionless or lifeless [a *glassy* stare] —**glass'i·ly** *adv.* —**glass'i·ness** *n.*

glau·co·ma (glô kō'mə, glou-) *n.* [L. < Gr. < *glaukos*: see GLAUCOUS & -OMA] a disease of the eye marked by increased pressure in the eyeball: it leads to a gradual loss of sight —**glau·co'ma·tous** *adj.*

glau·cous (glô'kəs) *adj.* [< L. < Gr. *glaukos*, orig., gleaming] **1.** bluish-green or yellowish-green **2.** *Bot.* covered with a whitish bloom that can be rubbed off, as grapes, plums, etc.

glaze (glāz) *vt.* **glazed, glaz'ing** [ME. *glasen* < *glas*, GLASS] **1.** to fit (windows, etc.) with glass **2.** to give a hard, glossy finish or coating to; specif., *a*) to overlay (pottery, etc.) with a substance that gives a glassy finish when fused *b*) to cover (foods) with a glossy coating of sugar syrup, etc. **3.** to cover with a thin layer of ice —*vi.* **1.** to become glassy or glossy **2.** to form a glaze —*n.* **1.** *a*) a glassy finish, as on pottery *b*) any substance used to form this **2.** a film or coating [a thin *glaze* of ice on the pond] —**glaz'er** *n.*

gla·zier (glā'zhər) *n.* a person whose work is fitting glass in windows, etc. —**gla'zier·y** *n.*

glaz·ing (glā'ziŋ) *n.* **1.** the work of a glazier **2.** a glass set or to be set in frames **3.** a glaze or the application of a glaze

Gla·zu·nov (glä zōō nôf'), **A·lek·san·dr (Konstantinovich)** (ä lyek sän'dr') 1865-1936; Russ. composer

gleam (glēm) *n.* [OE. *glæm*: for IE. base see GOLD] **1.** a flash or beam of light **2.** a faint light [the *gleam* of dying embers] **3.** a reflected brightness, as from a polished surface **4.** a brief, faint show or sign [a *gleam* of hope] —*vi.* **1.** to shine with a gleam **2.** to appear briefly or suddenly —see SYN. at FLASH —**gleam'y** *adj.*

glean (glēn) *vt., vi.* [< OFr. < VL. *glennare* < Celt.] **1.** to collect (grain left by reapers) from a field **2.** to collect the remaining grain, etc. from (a reaped field) **3.** to collect (facts, etc.) bit by bit from (a source) —**glean'er** *n.*

glean·ings (glēn'iŋz) *n.pl.* that which is gleaned

glebe (glēb) *n.* [< L. *gleba*, clod] **1.** a piece of church land, often forming part or all of a benefice **2.** [Archaic] soil; earth; esp., a cultivated field

glee (glē) *n.* [OE. *gleo*] **1.** lively joy or merriment felt, often in gloating **2.** a song for a group (**glee club**) of three or more voices, usually without accompaniment —see SYN. at MIRTH

glee·ful (glē'fəl) *adj.* full of glee; merry: also **glee'some** —**glee'ful·ly** *adv.* —**glee'ful·ness** *n.*

glen (glen) *n.* [< ScotGael. word thought to be *glenn* (now *gleann*)] a narrow, secluded valley

Glen·dale (glen'dāl') [GLEN + DALE] city in SW Calif.: suburb of Los Angeles: pop. 133,000

Glen·gar·ry (glen gar'ē) *n., pl.* **-ries** [< *Glengarry*, valley in Scotland] [*sometimes* g-] a Scottish cap for men, creased lengthwise across the top and often having short ribbons at the back: also **Glengarry bonnet** (or **cap**)

Glenn, Glen (glen) [Celt.: see GLEN] a masculine name

glib (glib) *adj.* **glib'ber, glib'best** [orig., slippery < or akin to Du. *glibberig*, slippery] **1.** done in a smooth, offhand way **2.** speaking or spoken in a smooth, fluent manner, often in a way too smooth and easy to be convincing [a *glib* lawyer; *glib* flattery] —**glib'ly** *adv.* —**glib'ness** *n.*

glide (glīd) *vi.* **glid'ed, glid'ing** [OE. *glidan*: for IE. base see GOLD] **1.** to flow or move smoothly and easily, as in skating **2.** to pass gradually and unnoticed, as time **3.** *Aeron. a*) to fly in a glider *b*) to descend at a normal angle without engine power **4.** *Music, Phonet.* to make a glide —*vt.* to cause to glide —*n.* **1.** the act of gliding ☆**2.** a small disk or ball attached under furniture legs, etc. to allow easy sliding **3.** *Music* loosely, a slur **4.** *Phonet.* an intermediate sound made when the speech organs change from the position for one sound to that for another —see SYN. at SLIDE

glid·er (glīd'ər) *n.* **1.** a person or thing that glides **2.** an aircraft like an airplane except that it has no engine and is carried along by air currents ☆**3.** a porch seat suspended in an upright frame so that it can glide or swing back and forth

glim·mer (glim'ər) *vi.* [< base of OE. *glæm*, GLEAM] **1.** to give a faint, flickering light **2.** to appear or be seen faintly or dimly —*n.* **1.** a faint, flickering light **2.** a faint show or sign [a *glimmer* of hope]

glim·mer·ing (-iŋ) *n. same as* GLIMMER

GLIDER

glimpse (glimps) *vt.* **glimpsed, glimps'ing** [see GLIMMER] to catch a brief, quick view of, as in passing —*vi.* to look quickly; glance (*at*) —*n.* **1.** a faint, fleeting appearance; slight trace [a dull book containing only a few *glimpses* of wit] **2.** a brief, quick view

glint (glint) *vi.* [prob. < Scand.: for IE. base see GOLD] to gleam; flash —*n.* a gleam, flash, or glitter [a *glint* of mischief in his eyes]

glis·sade (gli säd', -sād') *n.* [Fr. < *glisser*, to slide] **1.** an intentional slide by a mountain climber down a steep, snow-covered slope **2.** *Ballet* a gliding step —*vi.* **-sad′ed, -sad′ing** to make a glissade

glis·san·do (gli sän′dō) *n., pl.* **-di** (-dē), **-dos** [formed as if It. < Fr. *glissant*, prp. of *glisser*, to slide] *Music* a sliding rapidly up or down scales by running a finger over the white keys of a piano, the strings of a harp, etc. —*adj., adv.* (performed) with such an effect

glis·ten (glis′'n) *vi.* [OE. *glisnian*: for IE. base see GOLD] to shine or sparkle with reflected light, as a wet or polished surface —*n.* a glistening —see SYN.at FLASH

glis·ter (glis′tər) *n. archaic var. of* GLISTEN

glitch (glich) *n.* [< G. colloq. *glitsche*, a slip] [Slang] a failure to function in a normal or expected way; malfunction

glit·ter (glit′ər) *vi.* [prob. < ON. *glitra*: for IE. base see GOLD] **1.** to shine with a sparkling light [all that *glitters* is not gold] **2.** to be brilliant, showy, or attractive [her speech *glittered* with wit] —*n.* **1.** a bright, sparkling light **2.** showy brilliance or attractiveness **3.** bits of glittering decorative material —see SYN.at FLASH —glit′ter·y *adj.*

glitz·y (glit′sē) *adj.* **glitz′i·er, glitz′i·est** [prob. via Yid. < G. *glitzern*, to glitter] [Slang] **1.** having glitter; sparkling; glittery **2.** attracting attention in a showy way

gloam·ing (glō′miŋ) *n.* [OE. *glomung* < *glom*, twilight] evening dusk; twilight

gloat (glōt) *vi.* [prob. < ON. *glotta*, to grin scornfully] to gaze or think with malicious pleasure [he *gloated* over his enemy's misfortunes] —*n.* the act of gloating —gloat′er *n.*

glob (gläb) *n.* [prob. contr. < GLOBULE, after BLOB] a rounded mass or lump, as of jelly or grease

glob·al (glō′b'l) *adj.* **1.** globe-shaped **2.** worldwide [global war] **3.** complete or comprehensive —glob′al·ly *adv.*

☆**glob·al·ism** (-iz'm) *n.* a policy, outlook, etc. that is worldwide in scope —glob′al·ist *n., adj.*

globe (glōb) *n.* [< L. *globus*, a ball: for IE. base see CLAW] **1.** any round, ball-shaped thing; sphere; specif., *a)* the earth *b)* a spherical model of the earth **2.** anything shaped like a globe, as a rounded glass cover for a lamp —*vt., vi.* **globed, glob′ing** to form into a globe —glo·bate (glō′bāt) *adj.*

globe·fish (glōb′fish′) *n., pl.* **-fish′, -fish′es**: see FISH any of several tropical fishes that can puff up into a globular form

globe-trot·ter (-trät′ər) *n.* a person who travels widely about the world, esp. for pleasure —globe′-trot′ting *n., adj.*

glo·bin (glō′bin) *n.* [< (HEMO)GLOBIN] the protein component of hemoglobin

glo·boid (glō′boid) *adj.* shaped somewhat like a globe or ball —*n.* anything globoid

glo·bose (-bōs) *adj.* [L. *globosus*] same as GLOBOID: also glo′bous (-bəs) —glo′bose·ly *adv.*

glob·u·lar (gläb′yə lər) *adj.* **1.** shaped like a globe or ball; spherical **2.** made up of globules [caviar is a *globular* mass of fish eggs] —see SYN.at ROUND

glob·ule (gläb′yool) *n.* [Fr. < L. dim. of *globus*, GLOBE] a tiny ball or globe; esp., a drop of liquid

glob·u·lin (-yə lin) *n.* [GLOBUL(E) + -IN[1]] any of a group of proteins in animal and vegetable tissue

glock·en·spiel (gläk′ən spēl′, -shpēl′) *n.* [G. < *glocke*, a bell + *spiel*, play] a percussion instrument with flat metal bars set in a frame, that produce bell-like tones of the scale when struck with small hammers

☆**glom** (gläm) *vt.* **glommed, glom′ming** [< Scot. dial.] [Slang] **1.** to seize **2.** to steal **3.** to look over —glom onto [Slang] to take and hold; get

GLOCKENSPIEL

glom·er·ate (gläm′ər it) *adj.* [< L. pp. of *glomerare* < *glomus*, a ball: for IE. base see CLAW] formed into a rounded mass; clustered —glom′er·a′tion *n.*

gloom (gloom) *vi.* [prob. < Scand.: for IE. base see GOLD] **1.** to be or look morose or dejected **2.** to be or become dark, dim, or dismal —*vt.* to make dark, dismal, dejected, etc. —*n.* **1.** darkness; dimness; obscurity [the dank *gloom* of the cave] **2.** deep sadness or hopelessness; dejection

gloom·y (gloom′ē) *adj.* **gloom′i·er, gloom′i·est 1.** overspread with or enveloped in darkness or dimness [a *gloomy* dungeon] **2.** melancholy or sullen [a *gloomy* mood] **3.** causing gloom; depressing [a *gloomy* story] —see SYN.at DARK — gloom′i·ly *adv.* —gloom′i·ness *n.*

☆**glop** (gläp) *n.* [< ? GL(UE) + (SL)OP] [Slang] any soft, gluey substance, thick liquid, etc.

Glo·ri·a (glôr′ē ə, glō′rē ə) [L., glory] a feminine name —*n.* **1.**

either of the Latin hymns beginning *Gloria in Excelsis Deo* (glory be to God on high) or *Gloria Patri* (glory be to the Father) **2.** the music for either of these

glo·ri·fy (glôr′ə fī′) *vt.* **-fied′, -fy′ing** [< OFr. < LL. < L. *gloria*, glory + *facere*, to make] **1.** to make glorious; give glory to [the famous names which *glorify* the Victorian Age] **2.** to exalt in worship [to *glorify* God] **3.** to praise highly; extol **4.** to make seem better, larger, finer, etc. than is actually the case [some old soldiers *glorify* war] —glo′ri·fi·ca′tion *n.* —glo′ri·fi′er *n.*

glo·ri·ous (glôr′ē əs) *adj.* **1.** having, giving, or deserving glory [glorious deeds] **2.** splendid; magnificent [a glorious symphony] **3.** [Colloq.] very delightful or enjoyable —see SYN.at SPLENDID —glo′ri·ous·ly *adv.* —glo′ri·ous·ness *n.*

glo·ry (glôr′ē) *n., pl.* **-ries** [< OFr. < L. *gloria*] **1.** *a)* great honor and admiration; fame; renown [he won *glory* as a statesman] *b)* anything bringing this **2.** worshipful adoration [glory to God] **3.** the condition of highest achievement, prosperity, etc. [ancient Athens in its *glory*] **4.** splendor; magnificence [the *glory* of the woods in autumn] **5.** heaven or the bliss of heaven **6.** same as HALO (*n.* 1 & 2) —*vi.* **-ried, -ry·ing** to be very proud; exult (with *in*) [she *gloried* in her victory] — gone to glory dead —in one's glory at one's best, happiest, etc.

gloss[1] (glôs, gläs) *n.* [prob. < Scand.: for IE. base see GOLD] **1.** the luster of a smooth, polished surface; sheen **2.** a deceptively pleasant outward appearance, as in manners or speech —*vt.* **1.** to give a polished, shiny surface to **2.** to cover up (an error, fault, etc.) by making little of (often with *over*) [to *gloss* over a mistake with a joke] —*vi.* to become shiny —gloss′er *n.*

gloss[2] (glôs, gläs) *n.* [< OFr. or < ML. < L. < Gr. *glōssa*, the tongue] **1.** a translation inserted between the lines of a text **2.** a note of comment or explanation, as in a footnote **3.** a glossary —*vt.* **1.** to furnish (a text) with glosses **2.** to interpret falsely —*vi.* to write explanatory notes for a text; annotate — gloss′er *n.*

gloss. glossary

glos·sa·ry (gläs′ə rē, glôs′-) *n., pl.* **-ries** [< L. < *glossa* < Gr. *glōssa*, the tongue] a list of difficult, technical, or foreign terms with definitions or translations, as for a particular author, subject, book, etc. —glos·sar·i·al (glä ser′ē əl) *adj.* —glos′sar·ist *n.*

glos·so·la·li·a (gläs′ə lā′lē ə, glôs′-) *n.* [ModL., ult. < Gr. *glōssa*, tongue + *lalein*, to speak] the sudden voicing of sounds that cannot be understood, esp. when thought of as happening in a religious trance

gloss·y (glôs′ē, gläs′-) *adj.* **gloss′i·er, gloss′i·est** having a smooth, shiny appearance or finish —*n., pl.* **gloss′ies** ☆**1.** a photographic print with a glossy surface **2.** [Colloq.] a magazine printed on glossy paper; slick —gloss′i·ly *adv.* —gloss′i·ness *n.*

glot·tal (glät′'l) *adj.* of or produced in or at the glottis: also glot′tic (-ik)

glot·tis (glät′is) *n., pl.* **-tis·es, -ti·des′** (-ə dēz′) [ModL. < Gr. < *glōtta*, var. of *glōssa*, the tongue] the opening between the vocal cords in the larynx

glove (gluv) *n.* [< OE. *glof* & ON. *glofi*] **1.** a covering for the hand, with a separate sheath for each finger and the thumb **2.** *Sports a)* a similar covering of padded leather worn by baseball players in the field *b)* a padded mitten worn by boxers: usually boxing glove —*vt.* **gloved, glov′ing 1.** to supply with gloves **2.** to cover as with a glove ☆**3.** *Baseball* to catch (a ball) with a glove —put on the gloves [Colloq.] to engage in boxing

glove box a sealed enclosure with a window and with openings covered by gloves that extend inside for handling toxic, sterile, etc. materials

glove compartment a compartment built into the dashboard of an automobile, for miscellaneous articles

glov·er (gluv′ər) *n.* one who makes or sells gloves

glow (glō) *vi.* [OE. *glowan*: for IE. base see GOLD] **1.** to give off a bright light as a result of great heat; be white-hot or red-hot **2.** to give out a steady, even light without flame [the lights of the city *glowed* in the distance] **3.** to be or feel hot **4.** to radiate health **5.** to feel or show great happiness, excitement, etc. [her compliments made him *glow*] **6.** to be bright with color [the autumn leaves *glowed* in the sunlight] —*n.* **1.** a light given off as the result of great heat **2.** steady, even light without flame or blaze **3.** warmth or brightness of color **4.** brightness of skin color; flush **5.** a sensation of warmth and well-being [a pleasant *glow* after a bath] **6.** warmth of emotion —glow′ing *adj.* —glow′ing·ly *adv.*

glow·er (glou′ər) *vi.* [prob. < ON.] to stare with sullen anger; scowl —*n.* a sullen, angry stare; scowl —**glow′er·ing** *adj.* —**glow′er·ing·ly** *adv.*

glow·worm (glō′wurm′) *n.* a wingless insect or insect larva that gives off a luminescent light; esp., the wingless female or the larva of the firefly

glox·in·i·a (gläk sin′ē ə) *n.* [ModL., after B. P. *Gloxin*, 18th-c. Ger. botanist] a cultivated tropical plant with bell-shaped flowers of various colors

gloze (glōz) *vt.* **glozed, gloz′ing** [< OFr. < *glose:* see GLOSS²] to explain away; gloss (often with *over*)

glu·cose (glōō′kōs) *n.* [Fr. < Gr. *gleúkos*, sweet wine, sweetness] a crystalline sugar, $C_6H_{12}O_6$, occurring naturally in fruits, honey, etc.: the commercial form, also containing dextrin and maltose, is prepared as a sweet syrup by hydrolyzing starch in the presence of dilute acids

glu·co·side (glōō′kə sīd′) *n.* [GLUCOS(E) + -IDE] any glycoside having glucose as its sugar constituent —**glu′co·sid′ic** (-sid′ik) *adj.*

glue (glōō) *n.* [< OFr. *glu*, birdlime < LL. *glus*, glue: for IE. base see CLAW] **1.** a thick, sticky liquid made by boiling animal skins, bones, hoofs, etc. and used to stick things together **2.** any similar adhesive made from casein, resin, etc. —*vt.* **glued, glu′ing** to make stick as with glue —**glu′er** *n.*

glue·y (glōō′ē) *adj.* **glu′i·er, glu′i·est 1.** like glue; sticky **2.** covered with or full of glue

glum (glum) *adj.* **glum′mer, glum′mest** [prob. < ME. var. of *gloum(b)en*, to look morose] feeling or looking gloomy, sullen, or morose —**glum′ly** *adv.* —**glum′ness** *n.*

glume (glōōm) *n.* [ModL. *gluma* < L., husk] either of the two empty bracts at the base of a grass spikelet, etc.

glut (glut) *vi.* **glut′ted, glut′ting** [< OFr. *gloter*, to swallow < L. *gluttire*] to eat like a glutton —*vt.* **1.** to feed, fill, etc. to excess; surfeit **2.** to flood (the market) with certain goods so that the supply is greater than the demand —*n.* **1.** a glutting or being glutted **2.** a supply of certain goods that is greater than the demand —see SYN. at SATIATE

glu·ten (glōōt′'n) *n.* [L., glue] a gray, sticky substance found in wheat and other grain: it is the protein part of flour and bread —**glu′ten·ous** *adj.*

glu·te·us (glōō tē′əs, glōōt′ē-) *n., pl.* **-te′i** (-ī) [ModL. < Gr. *gloutos*, rump] any of the three muscles forming each of the buttocks —**glu·te′al** *adj.*

glu·ti·nous (glōōt′'n əs) *adj.* [< L. < *gluten*, glue] gluey; sticky —**glu′ti·nous·ly** *adv.*

glut·ton (glut′'n) *n.* [< OFr. < L. *gluto* < *glutire*, to devour] **1.** a person who greedily eats too much **2.** a person with a great capacity for something [he is a *glutton* for hard work] **3.** a furry, northern animal related to the marten and weasel: the American variety is the WOLVERINE —**glut′ton·ize′** *vt., vi.* **-ized′, -iz′ing**

glut·ton·ous (-əs) *adj.* inclined to eat too much and greedily —**glut′ton·ous·ly** *adv.*

glut·ton·y (-ē) *n., pl.* **-ton·ies** the habit or act of eating too much

glyc·er·ide (glis′ər īd′) *n.* an ester of glycerol

glyc·er·in (glis′ər in, glis′rin) *n.* [< Fr. < Gr. *glykeros*, sweet] popular and commercial term for GLYCEROL: also sp. **glyc′er·ine**

glyc·er·ol (glis′ər ōl′, -ôl′) *n.* [< prec. + -OL¹] an odorless, colorless, syrupy liquid, $C_3H_8O_3$, produced by the hydrolysis of fats and oils: used as a solvent, skin lotion, etc., and in explosives, etc.

gly·co- [< Gr. < *glykys*, sweet] a combining form meaning glycerol, sugar, glycogen: also, before a vowel, **glyc-**

gly·co·gen (glī′kə jən) *n.* [GLYCO- + -GEN] a partially soluble, starchlike substance, $(C_6H_{10}O_5)^x$, produced in animal tissues, esp. in the liver and muscles, and changed into a simple sugar as the body needs it —**gly′co·gen′ic** (-jen′ik) *adj.*

gly·col (glī′kôl, -kōl) *n.* [GLYC(ERIN) + -OL¹] **1.** *same as* ETHYLENE GLYCOL **2.** any of a group of alcohols of which ethylene glycol is the type

gly·co·pro·tein (glī′kō prō′tēn, -tē in) *n.* a compound in which a protein is combined with a carbohydrate group

gly·co·side (glī′kə sīd′) *n.* [Fr. < *glycose* (for GLUCOSE) + -ide, -IDE] any of a group of sugar derivatives, widely distributed in plants, which on hydrolysis yield a sugar and one or more other substances —**gly′co·sid′ic** (-sid′ik) *adj.*

gm. gram; grams

G.M. 1. General Manager **2.** Grand Master

G-man (jē′man′) *n., pl.* **G′-men′** (-men′) [associated with g(*overnment*) *man*, but prob. < *G* division of the Dublin Police] [Colloq.] ☆ an agent of the Federal Bureau of Investigation

Gmc. Germanic

gnarl (närl) *n.* [< GNARLED] a knot on the trunk or branch of a tree —*vt., vi.* to make or become knotted or twisted

gnarled (närld) *adj.* [ult.< ME. *knur*, a knot] knotty and twisted [a *gnarled* tree, *gnarled* hands]: also **gnarl′y**

gnash (nash) *vt., vi.* [ME. *gnasten*, prob. < ON.: for IE. base see GNAW] to grind or strike (the teeth) together, as in anger or pain —*n.* the act of gnashing

gnat (nat) *n.* [OE. *gnæt*: for IE. base see GNAW] **1.** any of a number of small, two-winged insects some of which can bite or sting **2.** [Brit.] a mosquito —**gnat′ty** *adj.*

gnath·ic (nath′ik) *adj.* [Gr. *gnathos*, the jaw] of the jaw

gnaw (nô) *vt.* **gnawed, gnawed** or, rarely, **gnawn, gnaw′ing** [OE. *gnagen* < IE. base *ghen*-] **1.** to bite and wear away bit by bit [to *gnaw* a bone] **2.** to make by gnawing [to *gnaw* a hole] **3.** to consume; corrode **4.** to torment, as by constant pain, fear, etc. [worry *gnawed* him] —*vi.* **1.** to bite repeatedly (*on, at,* etc.) **2.** to have a gnawing effect (with *on, at,* etc.); torment

gnaw·ing (nô′iŋ) *n.* **1.** a sensation of dull, constant pain or suffering **2.** [*pl.*] pangs, as of hunger

gneiss (nīs) *n.* [< G. < OHG. *gneisto*, a spark] a coarse-grained, granitelike rock formed of layers of feldspar, quartz, mica, etc. —**gneiss′ic** *adj.*

gnome (nōm) *n.* [Fr., ult. < Gr. *gnōmē*, thought] *Folklore* a dwarf supposed to dwell in the earth and guard its treasures —**gnom′ish** *adj.*

gno·mic (nō′mik) *adj.* [< Gr. *gnōmikos* < *gnōmē*, thought] wise and pithy; full of aphorisms

gno·mon (nō′män) *n.* [L. < Gr. < base of *gignōskein*, to know] a column, pin on a sundial, etc. that casts a shadow indicating the time of day

gnos·tic (näs′tik) *adj.* [< Gr. *gnōstikos* < *gnōsis*, knowledge] **1.** of or having knowledge **2.** [G-] of the Gnostics or Gnosticism —*n.* [G-] a believer in Gnosticism

Gnos·ti·cism (näs′tə siz'm) *n.* a system of mystical belief, as among some early Christians, using ideas from Greek philosophy and Oriental mysticism

GNP gross national product

gnu (nōō, nyōō) *n., pl.* **gnus, gnu:** see PLURAL, II, D, 1 [< the native (Bushman) name] a large African antelope with an oxlike head and horns and a horselike mane and tail; wildebeest

go (gō) *vi.* **went, gone, go′ing** [OE. *gan* < IE. base *ghe*-, let go] **1.** to move along; travel; proceed [to *go* 90 miles an hour] **2.** to be in operation; work [the clock won't *go*] **3.** to gesture, act, or make sounds as specified or shown [the gun *went* bang] **4.** to take a particular course, line of action, etc.; proceed [to *go* south] **5.** to result; turn out [the war *went* badly] **6.** to pass: said of time **7.** to pass from person to person [the rumor *went* all over town] **8.** to be in a certain state [he *goes* in rags] **9.** to become; turn [to *go* mad] **10.** to be expressed, sung, etc. [as the saying *goes*] **11.** to be in harmony; fit in [that tie won't *go* with his shirt] **12.** to put oneself [to *go* to some trouble] **13.** to tend; help [facts that *go* to prove a case] ☆ **14.** to have force, acceptance, etc. [that rule still *goes*] **15.** to leave; depart **16.** to pass away [the pain is gone] **17.** to die **18.** to be removed or eliminated [this dead tree must *go*] **19.** to break away [the mast *went* in the storm] **20.** to fail; give way [his eyesight is *going*] **21.** to be given [the prize *goes* to you] **22.** to be sold [it *went* for $10] **23.** to extend to or along a specified place or time; reach [a road that *goes* to Rome] **24.** to turn to, enter, or participate in a certain activity, occupation, etc. [to *go* to college] **25.** to pass (*through*), fit (*into*), etc. **26.** to be a divisor (*into*) [5 *goes* into 10 twice]

GNU (40–50 in. high at shoulder)

27. to endure; last **28.** to continue (unpunished, unrewarded, etc.) [how long will his genius *go* unrecognized?] **29.** to have a regular place [pencils *go* on the desk] —*vt.* **1.** to travel or proceed along [he's *going* my way] **2.** to bet ☆**3.** [Colloq.] to tolerate [I can't *go* him] **4.** [Colloq.] to furnish (bail) **5.** [Colloq.] to be willing to pay, bid, etc. (a specified sum) —*n., pl.* **goes 1.** the act of going **2.** a success [to make a *go* of a marriage] **3.** [Colloq.] animation; energy [she has lots of *go*] **4.** [Colloq.] a state of affairs ☆**5.** [Colloq.] an agreement, or bargain [is it a *go?*] **6.** [Colloq.] a try; attempt [let me have a *go* at it] —☆*adj.* [Slang: orig. astronaut's jargon] functioning properly or ready to go —**as people** (or **things**) **go** in comparison with how other people (or things) are —**go about 1.** to be busy at; do **2.** to move from place to place; circulate **3.** to tack; change direction in a sailboat —**go after** [Colloq.] to try to catch or get —**go against** to be or act in opposition to —**go along 1.** to continue **2.** to agree **3.** to accompany —**go around 1.** to surround **2.** to be enough to provide a share for each **3.** to move from place to place; circulate —**go at** to attack or work at —☆**go back on** [Colloq.] **1.** to betray **2.** to break (a promise, etc.) —**go beyond** to exceed —**go by 1.** to pass **2.** to be guided by **3.** to be known or referred to by (the name of) —**go down 1.** to sink; set **2.** to suffer defeat **3.** to be recorded, as in history —**go for 1.** to be taken as **2.** to try to get ☆**3.** to support ☆**4.** [Colloq.] to attack **5.** [Colloq.] to be attracted by; like very much —**go hard with** to cause trouble to —☆**go in for** [Colloq.] to engage or indulge in —**go into 1.** to inquire into **2.** to take up as a study or occupation —**go in with** to share obligations with; join —**go it** [Colloq.] to carry on; proceed [to *go it* alone] —**go off 1.** to leave, esp. suddenly **2.** to explode **3.** to happen —**go on 1.** to continue **2.** to behave **3.** to happen [what's *going on* outside?] **4.** [Colloq.] to talk rapidly and foolishly, without stopping —**go out 1.** to be extinguished, become outdated, etc. **2.** to attend social affairs, the theater, etc. **3.** to go on strike **4.** to try out (*for* an athletic team, etc.) —**go over 1.** to examine thoroughly **2.** to do again **3.** to review **4.** [Colloq.] to be successful —☆**go some** [Colloq.] to do or achieve quite a lot —**go through 1.** to perform thoroughly **2.** to endure; experience ☆**3.** to search ☆**4.** to get approval or acceptance **5.** to spend [to *go through* $200 in one evening] —**go through with** to complete —**go together 1.** to harmonize ☆**2.** [Colloq.] to be sweethearts —**go under** ☆to fail, as in business —**go up** to rise in price, etc.; increase —**go with** [Colloq.] to be a sweetheart of —**go without** to do without —**let go 1.** to let escape **2.** to release one's hold **3.** to give up; abandon, as one's interest in something **4.** to dismiss from a job; fire —**let oneself go** to be unrestrained in emotion, action, etc. —**no go** [Colloq.] not possible; no use —**on the go** [Colloq.] in constant motion or action —**to go** [Colloq.] ☆**1.** to be taken out: said of food in a restaurant **2.** still to be completed, etc. [one finished, two *to go*] —☆**what goes?** [Slang] what's happening?

SYN.—**go** is the general word indicating motion away from the place where one is; **depart** is a somewhat more formal word and usually suggests a setting out on a journey [he *departed* for France]; **leave** stresses separation from a person, place, or thing [I can't *leave* while she's ill]; **withdraw** suggests a leaving for a definite, necessary, and sometimes unfortunate reason [he *withdrew* from the race because of a strained muscle] —ANT. **come, arrive**

Go·a (gō′ə) small region on the SW coast of India: before 1962, a territory of Portugal

goad (gōd) *n.* [OE. *gad*] **1.** a sharp-pointed stick for driving oxen **2.** anything that drives a person to do something; spur —*vt.* to drive as with a goad; urge on [*goaded* into a rage]

☆**go·a·head** (gō′ə hed′) *n.* permission or a signal to proceed [waiting for the *go-ahead* on the project from his boss]

goal (gōl) *n.* [ME. *gol*, boundary] **1.** the place where a race, trip, etc. is ended **2.** an end that one tries to reach; aim or purpose **3.** in certain games, *a)* the line, net, etc. over or into which the ball or puck must go to score *b)* the act of so scoring *c)* the score made

goal·keep·er (gōl′kēp′ər) *n.* in certain games, a player stationed at a goal to prevent the ball or puck from crossing or entering it: also **goal′ie** (-ē), **goal′tend′er**

goal post either of a pair of posts with a crossbar, used as a goal in football, soccer, etc.

goat (gōt) *n.* [OE. *gat*] **1.** *pl.* **goats, goat**: see PLURAL, II, D, 1 *a)* a cud-chewing mammal with hollow horns, related to the sheep ☆*b) same as* ROCKY MOUNTAIN GOAT ☆**2.** [Colloq.] a person forced to take the blame for others; scapegoat —[G-] the constellation Capricorn —☆**get one's goat** [Colloq.] to annoy

or anger one —**goat′ish** *adj.* —**goat′ish·ly** *adv.* —**goat′ish·ness** *n.*

☆**goat·ee** (gō tē′) *n.* a pointed beard on a man's chin

goat·herd (gōt′hurd′) *n.* one who herds goats

goat·skin (-skin′) *n.* **1.** the skin of a goat **2.** leather made from this **3.** a container for wine, water, etc., made of this leather

goat·suck·er (-suk′ər) *n.* a bird that is active at night and feeds on insects, as the whippoorwill

GOATEE

gob[1] (gäb) *n.* [< OFr. *gobe*, prob. < *gobet*: see GOBBET] **1.** a lump or mass, as of something soft **2.** [*pl.*] [Colloq.] a large quantity or amount [*gobs* of money]

☆**gob**[2] (gäb) *n.* [< ?] [Slang] a sailor in the U.S. Navy

gob·bet (gäb′it) *n.* [OFr. *gobet*, mouthful, prob. < Gaul.] [Archaic] **1.** a fragment or bit, esp. of raw flesh **2.** a lump; chunk **3.** a mouthful

gob·ble[1] (gäb′'l) *n.* [echoic, var. of GABBLE] the characteristic throaty sound made by a male turkey —*vi.* **-bled, -bling** to make this sound

gob·ble[2] (gäb′'l) *vt., vi.* **-bled, -bling** [prob. < OFr. *gober*, to swallow < *gobe*, mouthful, GOB[1]] **1.** to eat quickly and greedily **2.** to snatch (*up*)

☆**gob·ble·dy·gook** (gäb′'l dē gook′) *n.* [Slang] wordy and unclear talk or writing, esp. by public officials: also sp. **gob′-ble·de·gook′**

gob·bler (gäb′lər) *n.* a male turkey

Gob·e·lin (gäb′ə lin, gō′bə-; *Fr.* gô blan′) *adj.* of or like a kind of tapestry made at the Gobelin works in Paris —*n.* Gobelin tapestry

go·be·tween (gō′bi twēn′) *n.* one who deals with each of two sides in making arrangements between them; intermediary

Go·bi (gō′bē) large desert plateau in E Asia, chiefly in Mongolia

gob·let (gäb′lit) *n.* [< OFr. < *gobel* < ? Bret. *gob*] **1.** orig., a cup without handles **2.** a drinking glass with a base and stem

gob·lin (gäb′lin) *n.* [< OFr. < ML. *gobelinus*, ult. < ? Gr. *kobalos*, sprite] Folklore an ugly elf that is full of evil or mischief

go·by (gō′bē) *n., pl.* **-bies, -by**: see PLURAL, II, D, 1 [L. *gobio*, gudgeon < Gr. *kōbios*] any of a group of small, spiny-finned fishes: the ventral fins sometimes grow together into a suction disk

go-by (gō′bī′) *n.* [Colloq.] a passing by; esp., the act of ignoring or avoiding: chiefly in **give** (or **get**) **the go-by**, to snub or ignore (or be snubbed or ignored)

go-cart (-kärt′) *n.* **1.** a framework on casters, to support a child learning to walk ☆**2.** a small carriage in which a young child can sit and be pushed about **3.** *same as* KART (sense 2)

god (gäd, gôd) *n.* [OE. < IE. base *ghau-*, to invoke] **1.** any of various beings thought of as living forever and having power over people and nature; deity, esp. a male one **2.** an image that is worshiped; idol **3.** a person or thing that one thinks of as being most important [money is his *god*] —[G-] in monotheistic religions, the creator and ruler of the universe, thought of as being all-powerful, all-knowing, and perfectly good

god·child (gäd′chīld′) *n., pl.* **-chil′dren** the person for whom a godparent is sponsor

god·daugh·ter (gäd′dôt′ər) *n.* a female godchild

god·dess (gäd′is) *n.* **1.** a female god **2.** a woman greatly admired, as for her beauty

god·fa·ther (gäd′fä′thər) *n.* a male godparent

God-fear·ing (-fir′iŋ) *adj.* [*occas.* g-] **1.** fearing God **2.** very religious; devout; pious

God-for·sak·en (-fər sā′kən) *adj.* [*occas.* g-] **1.** very bad; wicked **2.** lonely, dreary, miserable, etc. [a *Godforsaken* wasteland]

God·frey (gäd′frē) [< OFr. < OHG. < *god*, GOD + *fridu*, peace, lit., peace (of) God] a masculine name

God-giv·en (gäd′giv′ən) *adj.* [*occas.* g-] **1.** given by God **2.** very welcome; just right for the purpose [a *God-given* opportunity to travel]

god·head (-hed′) *n.* **1.** godhood **2.** [G-] God

god·hood (-hood′) *n.* the state or quality of being a god; divinity

Go·di·va (gə dī′və) a legendary 11th-cent. noblewoman of Coventry who, on the dare of her husband, rode naked through the streets on horseback so that he would abolish a heavy tax

god·less (gäd′lis) *adj.* **1.** not believing in God or a god; irreligious **2.** evil; wicked —**god′less·ly** *adv.* —**god′less·ness** *n.*

god·like (-līk′) *adj.* like or fit for God or a god; divine

god·ly (-lē) *adj.* **-li·er, -li·est 1.** divine **2.** pious; devout; religious —**god'li·ness** *n.*

god·moth·er (-muth'ər) *n.* a female godparent

god·par·ent (-per'ənt, -par'-) *n.* a person who sponsors a child, as at baptism, and promises to be responsible for its religious upbringing; godmother or godfather

god·send (gäd'send') *n.* anything unexpected and needed or desired that comes at just the right time, as if sent by God

god·son (-sun') *n.* a male godchild

God·speed (-spēd') *n.* [contr. of *God speed you*] success; good fortune: a wish for a person starting on a trip, etc.

God·win Austen (gäd'win) mountain in N Jammu & Kashmir, near the Chinese border: second highest mountain in the world: 28,250 ft.

god·wit (gäd'wit) *n.* [? echoic] a brownish wading bird, with a long bill that curves up

go·er (gō'ər) *n.* one that goes

Goe·the (gö'tə; *also Anglicized to* gur'tə, gāt'ə), **Jo·hann Wolf·gang von** (yō'hän vôlf'gäŋ fôn) 1749–1832; Ger. poet & dramatist

☆**go·fer, go-fer** (gō'fər) *n.* [from being asked to *go for* whatever is needed] [Slang] an employee who has minor tasks, such as running errands

☆**go-get·ter** (gō'get'ər) *n.* [Colloq.] a person who is full of energy and new ideas

gog·gle (gäg'l) *vi.* **-gled, -gling** [ME. *gogelen*] **1.** to stare with bulging or wide-open eyes **2.** to bulge or open wide in a stare —*n.* **1.** a staring with bulging eyes **2.** [*pl.*] large spectacles, esp. those fitted with side guards to protect the eyes against dust, wind, etc. —*adj.* bulging, staring, or rolling [*goggle* eyes] —**gog'gle-eyed'** (-īd') *adj.*

Gogh, Vincent van *see* VAN GOGH

go-go (gō'gō') *adj.* [short for *à gogo* < Fr., at (one's) pleasure] **1.** of rock-and-roll dancing or dancers or the cafés, etc. featuring such dancing **2.** [Slang] lively, up-to-date, etc.

Go·gol (gô'gôl; *E.* gō'gəl), **Ni·ko·lai Va·sil·ie·vich** (nē'kô lī' vä sēl'yə vich) 1809–52; Russ. novelist & dramatist

Goi·del·ic (goi del'ik) *adj.* [< OIr. *Góidel*] **1.** of the Gaels **2.** designating or of their languages —*n.* the subbranch of Celtic languages that includes Irish Gaelic, Scottish Gaelic, and Manx

go·ing (gō'iŋ) *n.* **1.** the act of one who goes: usually used in compounds [opera-*going*] **2.** a departure [the comings and go-*ings* of the trains] **3.** the condition of the ground or land for traveling [the *going* was difficult through the mud] **4.** conditions as they affect progress [the *going* is rough for a person in a new job] —*adj.* **1.** moving; running; working **2.** operating successfully [a *going* concern] **3.** in existence or available [the best floor wax *going*] **4.** current [the *going* rate for plumbers] —**be going to** to be intending to; will or shall [I *am going to* see her] —☆**get going** [Colloq.] to start —☆**get one going** [Slang] to make one excited, angry, etc. —**going on** [Colloq.] nearing or nearly (a specified age or time)

go·ing-o·ver (-ō'vər) *n.* [Colloq.] ☆**1.** an inspection, esp. a thorough one ☆**2.** a severe scolding or beating

go·ings-on (gō'iŋz än') *n.pl.* [Colloq.] actions or events, esp. when they are disapproved of [such *goings-on!*]

goi·ter, goi·tre (goit'ər) *n.* [< Fr., ult. < L. *guttur*, throat] an enlarged thyroid gland, often visible as a swelling in the front of the neck —**goi·trous** (goi'trəs) *adj.*

gold (gōld) *n.* [OE. < IE. base *ghel-*, shining, yellow, from which also come GLOW & YELLOW] **1.** a heavy, yellow, metallic chemical element that is easily beaten and stretched into different shapes: it is a precious metal and is used in coins, jewelry, alloys, etc.: symbol, Au; at. wt., 196.967; at. no., 79 **2.** *a)* gold coins *b)* riches **3.** the bright yellow color of gold **4.** a thing regarded as having the value, brilliance, etc. of gold —*adj.* **1.** of, made of, or like gold **2.** having the color of gold

☆**gold·brick** (gōld'brik') *n.* **1.** [Colloq.] anything worthless passed off as genuine or valuable **2.** [Mil. Slang] one who avoids work; shirker: also **gold'brick'er** —*vi.* [Mil. Slang] to avoid work; loaf

☆**gold digger** [Old Slang] a woman who tries to get money and gifts from her men friends

gold dust gold in very small bits or as a powder

gold·en (gōl'd'n) *adj.* **1.** of, containing, or yielding gold **2.** bright-yellow, like gold **3.** very valuable; excellent **4.** prosperous and happy [the *Golden* Age of Greece] **5.** favorable; auspicious [a *golden* opportunity] **6.** rich and mellow [a *golden* singing voice] **7.** marking the 50th anniversary [a *golden* jubilee] —**gold'en·ly** *adv.* —**gold'en·ness** *n.*

golden ag·er (āj'ər) [Colloq.] [*also* G- A-] an elderly person, esp. one 65 or older and retired

gold·en·eye (gōl'd'n ī') *n., pl.* **-eyes', -eye':** see PLURAL, II, D, 1 a swift, diving wild duck of N. America and the Old World, with yellow eyes and a dark-green back

Golden Fleece *Gr. Myth.* the fleece of gold guarded by a dragon until captured by Jason

Golden Gate strait between San Francisco Bay & the Pacific

Golden Horn arm of the Bosporus in European Turkey, forming the harbor of Istanbul

golden mean the safe, sensible way between extremes; moderation

gold·en·rod (-räd') *n.* a N. American plant of the composite family, with small, yellow flowers in clusters on long stalks

golden rule the rule that one should behave toward others as he would want others to behave toward him, as in Matt. 7:12

golden wedding a 50th wedding anniversary

gold-filled (gōld'fild') *adj.* covered with a thin layer of gold [a *gold-filled* ring]

gold·finch (-finch') *n.* [OE. *goldfinc*] **1.** a European songbird with yellow-streaked wings ☆**2.** a small American finch: the male has a yellow body with black on the head and wings

gold·fish (-fish') *n., pl.* **-fish', -fish'es:** see FISH a small, golden-yellow or orange fish of the carp family, often kept in fishbowls

gold foil gold beaten into thin sheets slightly thicker than gold leaf —**gold'-foil'** *adj.*

gold leaf gold beaten into very thin sheets, used for gilding —**gold'-leaf'** *adj.*

☆**gold rush** a rush of people to territory where gold has recently been discovered

gold·smith (-smith') *n.* a skilled worker who makes articles of gold

Gold·smith (gōld'smith'), **Oliver** 1728–74; Brit. poet, playwright, & novelist, born in Ireland

☆**gold standard** a monetary standard in which the basic currency unit is made equal to and redeemable by a specified quantity of gold

golf (gôlf, gälf) *n.* [< ? Scot. *gowf*, to strike] an outdoor game played on a golf course with a small, hard ball and a set of clubs, the object being to hit the ball into each of 9 or 18 holes in turn, with the fewest possible strokes —*vi.* to play golf —**golf'er** *n.*

golf club any of a set of clubs used in golf: each has a wooden or metal head and a long, slender shaft

golf course (or **links**) a large piece of land for playing golf, with tees, fairways, greens, etc.

Gol·go·tha (gäl'gə thə) [see CALVARY] the place where Jesus was crucified; Calvary

Go·li·ath (gə lī'əth) *Bible* the Philistine giant killed by David with a stone from a sling

gol·ly (gäl'ē) *interj.* an exclamation of surprise, pleasure, etc.: a word used in place of God

go·losh, go·loshe (gə läsh') *n. Brit. var. of* GALOSH

Go·mor·rah, Go·mor·rha (gə môr'ə) *see* SODOM

Gom·pers (gäm'pərz), **Samuel** 1850–1924; U.S. labor leader, born in England

-gon (gän, gən) [< Gr. < *gōnia*, an angle] *a combining form meaning* a figure having (a specified number of) angles [pentagon]

go·nad (gō'nad; *occas.* gän'ad) *n.* [< ModL. < Gr. *gonē*, a seed: for IE. base see GENUS] an animal organ producing reproductive cells; ovary or testis —**go·nad'al** *adj.*

go·na·do·trop·in (gō nad'ə trō'pin) *n.* a hormone which stimulates the function of the gonads —**go'na·do·trop'ic** (-träp'ik), **go'na·do·troph'ic** (-träf'ik) *adj.*

GOLF CLUBS
(A, wood; B, iron; C, putter)

gon·do·la (gän′də lə, gän dō′lə) *n.* [It. (Venetian) < ?] **1.** a long, narrow boat with a high, pointed prow and stern, used on the canals of Venice: it is propelled by a pole or one oar ☆**2.** a flat-bottomed river barge ☆**3.** a railroad freight car with low sides and no top: also **gondola car 4.** a cabin fastened to the underside of an airship or balloon ☆**5.** a car suspended from and moved along a cable, for holding passengers

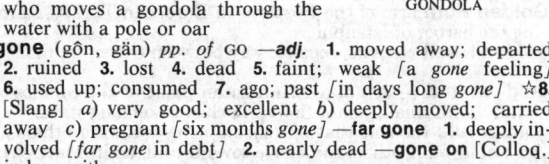

GONDOLA

gon·do·lier (gän′də lir′) *n.* a man who moves a gondola through the water with a pole or oar

gone (gôn, gän) *pp.* of GO —*adj.* **1.** moved away; departed **2.** ruined **3.** lost **4.** dead **5.** faint; weak [a *gone* feeling] **6.** used up; consumed **7.** ago; past [in days long *gone*] ☆**8.** [Slang] *a*) very good; excellent *b*) deeply moved; carried away *c*) pregnant [six months *gone*] —**far gone 1.** deeply involved [*far gone* in debt] **2.** nearly dead —**gone on** [Colloq.] in love with

gon·er (gôn′ər, gän′-) *n.* [Colloq.] one that is beyond help or that seems sure to die soon, be ruined, etc.

gon·fa·lon (gän′fə lən, -län′) *n.* [Fr. < OFr. < Frank. < *gund*, a battle + *fano*, banner] a flag hanging from a crosspiece instead of on an upright staff

gong (gôŋ, gäŋ) *n.* [Malay *guṅ*: echoic] **1.** a slightly convex metallic disk that gives a loud booming sound when struck **2.** a saucer-shaped bell with such a tone

go·nid·i·um (gō nid′ē əm) *n., pl.* **-nid′i·a** (-ə) [ModL., dim. < Gr. *gonos*: see GONAD] **1.** a reproductive cell produced asexually in certain algae **2.** an algal cell in the thallus of a lichen —**go·nid′i·al** *adj.*

-go·ni·um (gō′nē əm) [ModL. < Gr. *gonos*, seed] *a combining form meaning* a cell or structure in which reproductive cells are formed [*sporogonium*]

gon·o·coc·cus (gän′ə käk′əs) *n., pl.* **-coc′ci** (-käk′sī) [ModL. < Gr. *gonos*, a seed + COCCUS] the microorganism that causes gonorrhea

gon·or·rhe·a, gon·or·rhoe·a (gän′ə rē′ə) *n.* [< LL. < Gr. < *gonos*, a seed, semen + *rhein*, to flow] a venereal disease marked by inflammation of the mucous membrane of the genitourinary tract and a discharge of mucus and pus —**gon′or·rhe′al, gon′or·rhoe′al** *adj.*

-go·ny (gə nē) [< L. < Gr. < base of *gignesthai*, to be born] *a combining form meaning* something generated, produced, descended, etc. [*cosmogony*]

☆**goo** (gōō) *n.* [Slang] **1.** anything sticky, as glue **2.** anything sticky and sweet **3.** sentimentality

☆**goo·ber** (gōō′bər) *n.* [< native Afr. name *nguba*] [Chiefly South] a peanut

good (gōōd) *adj.* **bet′ter, best** [OE. *god* < IE. base *ghedh-*, to unite] **1.** *a*) right for the purpose; efficient [a lamp *good* to read by] *b*) helpful; beneficial [*good* exercise] **2.** fresh; unspoiled [*good* eggs] **3.** valid; genuine; real [*good* money] **4.** healthy; strong [*good* eyesight] **5.** financially sound [a *good* investment] **6.** honorable; respected [one's *good* name] **7.** enjoyable, happy, etc. [a *good* life] **8.** dependable; reliable [*good* advice] **9.** thorough; complete [do a *good* job] **10.** *a*) above average [a *good* novel] *b*) not for everyday use; best [her *good* china] **11.** adequate; satisfying [a *good* meal] **12.** morally sound or excellent; specif., *a*) virtuous; honest *b*) very religious; pious *c*) kind, friendly, etc. *d*) well-behaved [a *good* child] **13.** proper; correct [*good* manners] **14.** skillful; expert [a *good* swimmer] **15.** loyal or conforming [a *good* Democrat] **16.** to a large number, extent, etc. [a *good* many] **17.** at least; full [a *good* six hours] —*n.* something good; specif., *a*) worth; virtue; merit [the *good* in a man] *b*) benefit; advantage [for the *good* of all] *c*) something desirable or desired See also GOODS —*interj.* an exclamation of satisfaction, pleasure, etc. —*adv.* well, fully, etc.: regarded as nonstandard, dialectal, or colloquial [he did *good* on the test] —**as good as** nearly; practically —**for good (and all)** forever; permanently —☆**good and** [Colloq.] very [*good and* angry] —**good for 1.** able to last or be used for (a period of time) **2.** worth **3.** able to pay or give **4.** sure to result in [*good for* a laugh] ☆Also used to show approval [*good for* you!] —☆**make good 1.** to repay or replace **2.** to carry out (a promise, boast, etc.) **3.** to succeed in doing; accomplish **4.** to be successful **5.** to prove —**no good** useless or worthless —**the good 1.** those who are good **2.** what is morally good —**to the good** as a profit or advantage

good afternoon hello or goodbye: term used in the afternoon

Good Book the Bible (usually *with the*)

good·bye, good-bye (gōōd bī′) *interj., n., pl.* **-byes′** [contr. of God be with ye] farewell: term used when leaving someone: also **good′by′, good′-by′**

good day hello or goodbye

good evening hello or goodbye: term used in the evening

good-for-noth·ing (gōōd′fər nuth′iŋ) *adj.* useless or worthless —*n.* a useless or worthless person

Good Friday the Friday before Easter Sunday, observed as the anniversary of the crucifixion of Jesus

good-heart·ed (-här′tid) *adj.* kind and generous —**good′-heart′ed·ly** *adv.* —**good′-heart′ed·ness** *n.*

Good Hope, Cape of 1. cape at the SW tip of Africa **2.** province of South Africa, in the southernmost part

good humor a cheerful, agreeable, or pleasant mood —**good′-hu′mored** *adj.* —**good′-hu′mored·ly** *adv.*

good·ish (-ish) *adj.* fairly good or fairly large

good-look·ing (-lōōk′iŋ) *adj.* pleasing in appearance; beautiful or handsome —see SYN. at BEAUTIFUL

good·ly (-lē) *adj.* **-li·er, -li·est 1.** handsome; attractive [a *goodly* lad] **2.** of good quality; fine [a *goodly* land] **3.** rather large; ample [a *goodly* sum] —**good′li·ness** *n.*

good·man (-mən) *n., pl.* **-men** [Archaic] **1.** a husband or master of a household **2.** a title like *Mr.*, for a man ranking below a gentleman

good morning hello or goodbye: term used in the morning

good nature a pleasant, agreeable, or kindly disposition

good-na·tured (-nā′chərd) *adj.* having or showing good nature; pleasant and friendly —see SYN. at AMIABLE —**good′-na′tured·ly** *adv.*

good·ness (-nis) *n.* **1.** the state or quality of being good; specif., *a*) virtue; excellence *b*) kindness; generosity **2.** the best part —*interj.* an exclamation of surprise

good night goodbye: term used at night when leaving someone or going to bed

goods (gōōdz) *n.pl.* **1.** movable personal property [household *goods*] **2.** things made to be sold; wares **3.** fabric; cloth [dress *goods*] —☆**deliver the goods** [Colloq.] to do or produce the thing required —☆**get** (or **have**) **the goods on** [Slang] to discover (or know) something that proves a person has done wrong

good Samaritan one who pities and helps another or others in an unselfish way: Luke 10:30–37

Good Shepherd *a name given to* Jesus: John 10:11

good-sized (gōōd′sīzd′) *adj.* big or fairly big

good-tem·pered (-tem′pərd) *adj.* not easily angered or annoyed —**good′-tem′pered·ly** *adv.*

good turn a good deed; friendly, helpful act

good·wife (-wīf′) *n., pl.* **-wives′** (-wīvz′) [Archaic] **1.** a wife or mistress of a household **2.** a title like *Mrs.*, for a woman ranking below a lady

good will 1. a friendly or kindly attitude **2.** willingness to work or help **3.** the value of a business in terms of its regular customers, reputation, etc., over and beyond its merchandise, equipment, etc. Also **good′will′** *n.*

good·y¹ (-ē) *n., pl.* **good·ies** [Colloq.] **1.** something good to eat, as a piece of candy ☆**2.** *same as* GOODY-GOODY —*adj.* [Colloq.] *same as* GOODY-GOODY —*interj.* a child's exclamation of delight

good·y² (-ē) *n., pl.* **good·ies** [< GOODWIFE] [Archaic] an old woman or a housewife of lowly social status

Good·year (gōōd′yir′), **Charles** 1800–60; U.S. inventor of the process for vulcanizing rubber

good·y-good·y (gōōd′ē gōōd′ē) *adj.* [Colloq.] moral or religious in a self-satisfied, showy way —☆*n.* [Colloq.] a goody-goody person

☆**goo·ey** (gōō′ē) *adj.* **goo′i·er, goo′i·est** [Slang] **1.** sticky **2.** sticky and sweet **3.** sentimental

goof (gōōf) *n.* [prob. ult. < It. *goffo*, clumsy] [Slang] **1.** a stupid or silly person **2.** a mistake; blunder —*vi.* [Slang] **1.** to make a mistake; blunder, fail, etc. **2.** to waste time, avoid work, etc. (usually with *off* or *around*)

goof·y (gōōf′ē) *adj.* **goof′i·er, goof′i·est** [Slang] like or characteristic of a goof; stupid or silly —**goof′i·ly** *adv.* —**goof′i·ness** *n.*

☆**gook** (gōōk, gōōk) *n.* [GOO + (GUN)K] [Slang] any sticky, greasy, or slimy substance

☆**goon** (gōōn) *n.* [Slang] **1.** [< ? GUN] a ruffian or thug **2.** [after a comic-strip character of E.C. Segar, 20th-c. U.S. cartoonist] a person who is awkward, grotesque, stupid, etc.

goo·ney bird (g$\overline{oo}$′nē) [< *gooney*, sailors' name for the albatross] an albatross with black feet: also **goo′ny bird**

☆**goop** (g$\overline{oo}$p) *n.* [GOO + (SOU)P] [Slang] any thick, sticky substance —**goop′y** *adj.*

goose (g$\overline{oo}$s) *n., pl.* **geese;** for 4 & 5 **goos′es** [OE. *gos*] 1. a wild or domestic bird with a long neck and webbed feet, that is like a duck but larger, esp. the female 2. its flesh, used for food 3. a silly person 4. a tailor's pressing iron, with a long, curved handle 5. [Slang] a sudden, playful prod in the backside —*vt.* **goosed, goos′ing** [Slang] ☆1. to prod suddenly and playfully in the backside so as to startle ☆2. to stir into action —**cook one's goose** [Colloq.] to spoil one's chances, hopes, etc.

goose·ber·ry (g$\overline{oo}$s′ber′ē, g$\overline{oo}$s′bə rē; g$\overline{oo}$z′-) *n., pl.* **-ries** 1. a small, round, sour berry used in making pies, jam, etc. 2. the shrub it grows on

CANADA GOOSE
(to 45 in. long)

goose egg [Slang] ☆1. a zero 2. a large swelling or lump, esp. one caused by a blow

goose flesh a bumpy condition of the skin caused by cold, fear, etc.: also **goose bumps** (or **pimples** or **skin**)

goose·foot (g$\overline{oo}$s′foot′) *adj.* designating a family of plants including spinach and beets —*n., pl.* **-foots′** any of a group of plants of this family, with small, green flowers

goose·neck (-nek′) *n.* any of various mechanical devices shaped like a goose's neck, as a flexible rod for supporting a desk lamp

goose step a step, used as by troops marching in review, in which the legs are raised high and kept stiff —**goose′-step′** *vi.* **-stepped′, -step′ping**

GOP, G.O.P. Grand Old Party (Republican Party)

☆**go·pher** (gō′fər) *n.* [< ? Fr. *gaufre*, honeycomb: from its burrowing] 1. a burrowing rodent, about the size of a large rat, with wide cheek pouches: also **pocket gopher** 2. a striped ground squirrel of N. American prairies, related to the chipmunk

GOPHER
(7½–25 in. long, including tail)

Gor·di·an knot (gôr′dē ən) *Gr. Legend* a knot tied by King Gordius of Phrygia, to be undone only by the future master of Asia: Alexander the Great, failing to untie it, cut it with his sword —**cut the Gordian knot** to find a quick, bold solution for a problem

Gor·don (gôr′d'n) [Scot. < surname *Gordon*] a masculine name

gore[1] (gôr) *n.* [OE. *gor*, dung, filth: for IE. base see WARM] blood shed from a wound; esp., clotted blood

gore[2] (gôr) *vt.* **gored, gor′ing** [< OE. *gar:* see GORE[3]] to pierce as with a horn or tusk

gore[3] (gôr) *n.* [OE. *gara*, corner < base of *gar*, a spear < IE. base *ghaiso-*, a stake] a tapering piece of cloth in a skirt, sail, etc. to give it fullness —*vt.* **gored, gor′ing** to make or insert a gore or gores in

gorge (gôrj) *n.* [< OFr., throat, ult. < L. *gurges*, whirlpool] 1. the throat or gullet 2. the maw or stomach, or food filling it 3. a deep, narrow pass between steep heights ☆4. a mass, as of ice, blocking a passage —*vi., vt.* **gorged, gorg′ing** to stuff (oneself) with food; glut —**make one's gorge rise** to make one disgusted, angry, etc.

gor·geous (gôr′jəs) *adj.* [< OFr. *gorgias*, beautiful] 1. brilliantly colored; resplendent 2. [Slang] beautiful, wonderful, delightful, etc. —**gor′geous·ly** *adv.* —**gor′geous·ness** *n.*

gor·get (gôr′jit) *n.* [< OFr. < *gorge:* see GORGE] 1. a piece of armor to protect the throat: see illustration at ARMOR 2. a collar 3. a patch of color on a bird's throat

Gor·gon (gôr′gən) *n.* 1. *Gr. Myth.* any of three sisters with snakes for hair, so horrible that anyone who looked at them was turned to stone 2. [g-] any ugly, terrifying, or repulsive woman

Gor·gon·zo·la (gôr′gən zō′lə) *n.* [< *Gorgonzola*, town in Italy] a white Italian cheese with veins of blue-green mold and a strong flavor

☆**go·ril·la** (gə ril′ə) *n.* [< Gr. *gorillai* < an ancient W African name] 1. the largest and most powerful manlike ape, living in the jungles of tropical Africa 2. [Slang] *a)* a person regarded as like a gorilla in appearance, strength, etc. *b)* a gangster; thug

GORILLA
(50–70 in. high)

Gor·ki, Gor·kiy, Gor·ky (gôr′kē) city in E European R.S.F.S.R., on the Volga: pop. 1,139,000

Gor·ki (gôr′kē), **Max·im** (mak′sim) (pseud. of *Aleksei Maximovich Peshkov*) 1868–1936; Russ. novelist & playwright: also sp. **Gorky**

gor·mand (gôr′mənd) *n. same as* GOURMAND

gor·mand·ize (gôr′mən dīz′) *vi., vt.* **-ized′, -iz′ing** [< Fr. *gourmandise*, gluttony] to eat or devour like a glutton —**gor′mand·iz′er** *n.*

gorse (gôrs) *n.* [OE. *gorst*] furze —**gors′y** *adj.*

gor·y (gôr′ē) *adj.* **gor′i·er, gor′i·est** 1. covered with gore; bloody 2. full of bloodshed or killing [a *gory* movie] —**gor′i·ly** *adv.* —**gor′i·ness** *n.*

☆**gosh** (gäsh) *interj.* an exclamation of surprise, wonder, etc.: a word used in place of *God*

gos·hawk (gäs′hôk′) *n.* [< OE.: see GOOSE & HAWK[1]] a large, swift hawk with short wings

Go·shen (gō′shən) *Bible* the fertile land assigned to the Israelites in Egypt: Gen. 45:10 —*n.* a land of plenty

gos·ling (gäz′liŋ) *n.* [< ON.] a young goose

gos·pel (gäs′p'l) *n.* [OE. *gōdspel*, lit., good news] 1. [*often* **G-**] *a)* the teachings of Jesus and the Apostles *b)* the history of the life and teachings of Jesus 2. [**G-**] *a)* any of the first four books of the New Testament (*Matthew, Mark, Luke,* or *John*) *b)* an excerpt from any of these, read in a religious service 3. anything believed to be absolutely true [for us his word is *gospel*]: also **gospel truth** 4. any doctrine or rule widely or sincerely believed in [a new social *gospel*] 5. a style of folk singing originally associated with evangelistic revival meetings —*adj.* of (the) gospel or evangelism

gos·sa·mer (gäs′ə mər) *n.* [ME. *gosesomer*, lit., goose summer: the period in fall when geese are in season] 1. a filmy cobweb in the air or on bushes or grass 2. a very thin, soft, filmy cloth 3. anything like gossamer —*adj.* light, thin, and filmy [*gossamer* wings]: also **gos′sa·mer·y** (-mər ē)

gos·sip (gäs′əp) *n.* [< Late OE. *godsibbe*, godparent: see GOD & SIB] 1. [Obs. or Dial.] *a)* a godparent *b)* a close friend 2. one who chatters or repeats idle talk and rumors, esp. about others' private affairs 3. *a)* such talk or rumors *b)* chatter —*vi.* to be a gossip; indulge in idle talk or rumors about others —**gos′sip·er** *n.* —**gos′sip·y** *adj.*

got (gät) *pt. & alt. pp. of* GET

Gö·te·borg (yö′tə bôr′y′) seaport in SW Sweden, on the Kattegat: pop. 445,000

Goth (gäth, gôth) *n.* [< LL. < Gr. *Gothoi*, pl.] 1. a member of a Germanic people that invaded and conquered most of the Roman Empire in the 3d, 4th, and 5th centuries A.D. 2. a crude, uncivilized person

Goth., goth. Gothic

Goth·am (gäth′əm, gō′thəm; *for 1, Brit.* gät′-) 1. a village near Nottingham, England, whose inhabitants were, according to legend, very foolish 2. *nickname for* NEW YORK CITY —**Goth′am·ite′** (-īt′) *n.*

Goth·ic (gäth′ik) *adj.* 1. of the Goths or their language 2. designating or of a style of architecture developed in western Europe from the 12th to 16th cent., characterized by flying buttresses, pointed arches, etc. 3. [*sometimes* **g-**] *a)* medieval *b)* uncivilized; barbarous 4. of a style of literature using a medieval or gloomy, sinister setting, atmosphere, etc., to suggest horror and mystery —*n.* 1. the East Germanic language of the Goths 2. Gothic style, esp. in architecture ☆3. *Printing* [*often* **g-**] a plain style of type with straight lines of uniform width and no serifs —**Goth′i·cal·ly** *adv.*

Gothic arch a pointed arch

Got·land (gät′lənd; *Sw.* gôt′-) Swed. island in the Baltic, off the SE coast of Sweden

got·ten (gät′'n) *alt. pp. of* GET

gouache (gwäsh) *n.* [Fr. < It. *guazzo*, watercolor < L. < *aqua*, water] **1.** a way of painting with opaque watercolors mixed with a preparation of gum **2.** a pigment of this sort **3.** a painting made with such pigments

Gou·da (cheese) (gou′də, gōō′-) [< *Gouda*, city in Netherlands] a mild, semisoft to hard cheese made from curds and usually coated with red wax

gouge (gouj) *n.* [< OFr. < VL. *gubia*, for LL. *gulbia* < Celt.] **1.** a chisel with a curved, hollowed blade, for cutting grooves or holes in wood **2.** *a)* a gouging *b)* the groove or hole made by gouging ☆**3.** [Colloq.] an act of overcharging or cheating out of money; swindle —*vt.* **gouged, goug′ing 1.** to make grooves or holes in as with a gouge **2.** to scoop out [to *gouge* out dirt] ☆**3.** in fighting, to push one's thumb into the eye of ☆**4.** [Colloq.] to cheat out of money, etc.; also, to overcharge —☆**goug′er** *n.*

gou·lash (gōō′läsh, -lash) *n.* [< G. < Hung. *gulyás*, herdsman, hence herdsman's food] a stew of beef or veal and vegetables, seasoned with paprika, etc.: also **Hungarian goulash**

Gould (gōōld), **Jay** 1836–92; U.S. financier

Gou·nod (gōō nō′; *E.* gōō′nō), **Charles (François)** (shȧr′l) 1818–93; Fr. composer

gou·ra·mi (goor′ə mē, goo rä′mē) *n., pl.* **-mis, -mi:** see PLURAL, II, D, 1 [Malay *gurami*] **1.** a food fish of southeastern Asia, that builds a nest **2.** any of a number of related fishes, mostly brightly colored, that are often kept in aquariums, as the **kissing gourami**

gourd (gôrd, goord) *adj.* [< OFr. < L. *cucurbita*] designating a family of plants that includes the squash, melon, pumpkin, etc. —*n.* **1.** any trailing or climbing plant of this family **2.** *a)* same as CALABASH (sense 2*a*) *b)* the fruit of certain related plants, not fit for eating but often used as ornaments ☆**3.** the dried, hollowed-out shell of such a fruit, used as a drinking cup, dipper, etc.

GOURDS

gourde (goord) *n.* [Fr. < L. *gurdus*, dull, heavy] *see* MONETARY UNITS, table (Haiti)

gour·mand (goor′mənd, goor mänd′) *n.* [< OFr.] **1.** a person who likes good food and drink, sometimes one who eats and drinks too much **2.** same as GOURMET —see SYN. at EPICURE

gour·met (goor′mā; *Fr.* gōōr me′) *n.* [Fr. < OFr. *gourmet*, wine taster] a person who likes and is an excellent judge of fine foods and drinks; epicure —see SYN. at EPICURE

gout (gout) *n.* [< OFr. < L. *gutta*, a drop] **1.** a disease marked by deposits of uric acid salts in tissues and joints, esp. of the feet and hands, with swelling and great pain, esp. in the big toe **2.** a drop, splash, etc. [*gouts* of blood] —**gout′i·ly** *adv.* —**gout′i·ness** *n.* —**gout′y** *adj.* **gout′i·er, gout′i·est**

gov., Gov. 1. government **2.** governor

gov·ern (guv′ərn) *vt.* [< OFr. < L. *gubernare* < Gr. *kybernan*, to steer] **1.** to have control over; rule, direct, manage, etc. **2.** to influence the action or conduct of; guide [newspapers help *govern* public opinion] **3.** to hold in check; curb [he *governed* his temper] **4.** to regulate the speed of (an automobile, etc.) by means of a governor **5.** to be a rule or law for; determine [he thinks a few basic factors *govern* the history of all nations] **6.** *Gram. a)* to require (a word) to be in a particular case or mood *b)* to require (a particular case or mood) —*vi.* to govern someone or something; rule —**gov′ern·a·ble** *adj.*

SYN.—govern implies the use of power or authority to control the activities of the citizens of a political unit and to carry out public business, and suggests that this is done in a planned, orderly way for the good of all; **rule** now usually suggests the use of power in a way that is dictatorial and does not follow the rules and laws

gov·ern·ance (-ər nəns) *n.* control or rule

gov·ern·ess (-ər nəs) *n.* a woman employed in a private home to train and teach the children

gov·ern·ment (guv′ər mənt, -ərn mənt) *n.* **1.** *a)* control over a state, district, group, etc.; direction; rule *b)* the right, function, or power of governing **2.** *a)* a system of ruling, controlling, etc. [a centralized *government*] *b)* an established system of political administration by which a nation, state, etc. is governed *c)* the study of such systems; political science **3.** all the people that administer the affairs of a nation, state, institution, etc.; administration **4.** [*often* G-] the executive or administrative branch of government of a particular nation —☆**gov′ern·men′tal** *adj.* —☆**gov′ern·men′tal·ly** *adv.*

gov·er·nor (guv′ə nər, -ər nər) *n.* **1.** a person who governs; esp., *a)* one appointed to govern a dependency, province, etc.

☆*b)* the elected head of any State of the U.S. *c)* any of those who direct an organization or institution [the board of *governors* of a hospital] **2.** a device in an engine, etc. that automatically controls its speed **3.** [Brit. Colloq.] a person with authority; esp., one's father or employer —**gov′er·nor·ship′** *n.*

governor general *pl.* **governors general, governor generals** a governor with deputy governors under him, as in the Commonwealth: also, Brit., **gov′er·nor-gen′er·al** *n., pl.* **gov′-er·nors-gen′er·al**

Governors Island [set aside (1698) as the home for Eng. governors] island in New York Bay at the mouth of the East River, now occupied by a U.S. Coast Guard station

govt., Govt. government

gown (goun) *n.* [< OFr. < LL. *gunna*, loose robe] **1.** a woman's long dress, esp. one for formal wear **2.** *same as* DRESSING GOWN **3.** a nightgown **4.** a surgeon's smock **5.** a long, flowing, official robe worn by certain judges, clergymen, professors, etc. **6.** the members of a college or university as distinct from the other residents of the community in which it is located [conflicts between town and *gown*] —*vt.* to dress in a gown

Go·ya (y Lucientes) (gô′yä), **Fran·cis·co Jo·sé de** (frän-thēs′kō hô se′ *the*) 1746–1828; Sp. painter

G.P., g.p. general practitioner

GPO, G.P.O. Government Printing Office

Gr. 1. Grecian **2.** Greece **3.** Greek

gr. 1. grade **2.** grain(s) **3.** gram(s) **4.** gravity **5.** great **6.** gross

Graaf·i·an follicle (gräf′ē ən, graf′-) [after R. de *Graaf* (1641–73), Du. anatomist] any of the small sacs in the ovary of higher mammals, each of which contains a maturing egg

grab (grab) *vt.* **grabbed, grab′bing** [prob. < MDu., MLowG. *grabben*] **1.** to seize or snatch suddenly **2.** to take by force or in any way that is not right ☆**3.** [Slang] to impress (one) greatly —*vi.* to grab or try to grab something (often with *for, at,* etc.) —*n.* **1.** the act of grabbing [he made a *grab* for the handle] **2.** something grabbed **3.** a device for clutching something to be hoisted —☆**up for grabs** [Slang] available to the highest bidder, the most aggressive person, etc. —**grab′ber** *n.*

☆**grab bag** a container holding various articles that are wrapped or in bags: a buyer pays a fixed price and picks one at random without knowing what is in it

grab·by (grab′ē) *adj.* **-bi·er, -bi·est** grasping; greedy

Grac·chus (grak′əs), **Ga·ius Sem·pro·ni·us** (gā′əs sem prō′-nē əs) 153?–121 B.C., & **Ti·ber·i·us Sempronius** (tī bir′ē əs) 163?–133 B.C.; Roman statesmen & social reformers: brothers, called **the Grac·chi** (grak′ī)

Grace (grās) [see the next entry] a feminine name

grace (grās) *n.* [< OFr. < L. *gratia*, pleasing quality < *gratus*, pleasing < IE. base *giver-*, to praise] **1.** beauty or charm of form or movement [to dance with *grace*] **2.** an attractive quality, feature, manner, etc. [she has all the social *graces*] **3.** *a)* a sense of what is right and proper; decency [he at least had the *grace* to be embarrassed] *b)* thoughtfulness toward others **4.** good will; favor **5.** [Archaic] mercy **6.** a delay granted beyond the date set for doing or paying something [we have a week of *grace* to pay the rent] **7.** a short prayer of blessing or thanks for a meal **8.** [G-] a title of respect used in speaking to or of an archbishop, duke, or duchess, preceded by *His, Her,* or *Your* **9.** *Music* [*pl.*] all ornamental notes or effects, as appoggiaturas, trills, etc. **10.** *Theol. a)* the love and favor God shows toward man without his having earned or deserved them *b)* divine influence acting in man to make him pure and good *c)* the condition of a person thus influenced *d)* a special virtue given to a person by God —*vt.* **graced, grac′ing 1.** to give or add grace or graces to; adorn [paintings *graced* the walls] **2.** to honor; dignify [the mayor *graced* our meeting with his presence] —**in the good (or bad) graces of** in favor (or disfavor) with —**with good (or bad) grace** in a willing (or unwilling) way

grace·ful (grās′f'l) *adj.* having grace, or beauty of form or movement —**grace′ful·ly** *adv.* —**grace′ful·ness** *n.*

grace·less (-lis) *adj.* **1.** not showing any sense of what is right or proper [a *graceless* remark] **2.** without grace; clumsy; not elegant —**grace′less·ly** *adv.* —**grace′less·ness** *n.*

grace note *Music* a note not necessary to the melody, added only for ornamentation

Grac·es (grā′siz) *Gr. Myth.* three sister goddesses who controlled pleasure, charm, elegance, and beauty in human life and in nature

gra·cious (grā′shəs) *adj.* **1.** having or showing kindness, courtesy, charm, etc. [a *gracious* host] **2.** merciful; compassionate ["be *gracious* unto us"] **3.** marked by the taste, ease, etc. associated with prosperity, education, etc. [*gracious* living] —*interj.* an expression of surprise —**gra'cious·ly** *adv.* —**gra'·cious·ness** *n.*

grack·le (grak''l) *n.* [L. *graculus,* jackdaw: for IE. base see CRANE] ☆any of several American blackbirds smaller than a crow

☆**grad** (grad) *n.* [Colloq.] a graduate

grad. **1.** graduate **2.** graduated

gra·date (grā'dāt) *vt., vi.* -**dat·ed,** -**dat·ing** [back-formation < GRADATION] to change by degrees; shade into one another, as colors

gra·da·tion (grā dā'shən) *n.* [Fr. < L. *gradatio* < *gradus:* see GRADE] **1.** a forming or arranging in grades, stages, or steps **2.** a gradual change by steps or stages **3.** a shading of one tone or color into another **4.** a step, stage, or degree in a graded series [the many *gradations* between good and bad] **5.** *same as* ABLAUT —**gra·da'tion·al** *adj.*

GRACKLE
(to 12 in. long)

grade (grād) *n.* [Fr. < L. *gradus,* a step < *gradi,* to step < IE. base *ghredh-,* to stride] **1.** any of the stages in a series; step; degree [civil service jobs arranged in *grades*] **2.** *a)* a degree in a scale of quality, rank, etc. [*grade* A eggs] *b)* any of the official ranks or ratings of officers or enlisted men [an army colonel and a navy captain are in *grade* 0–6] *c)* an accepted standard or level [up to *grade*] *d)* a group of the same rank, merit, etc. ☆**3.** *a)* the degree of rise or descent of a slope, as of a road *b)* the slope itself [climbing a steep *grade*] **4.** the ground level around a building ☆**5.** a division in a school curriculum, usually equal to one year ☆**6.** a mark or rating on an examination, in a school course, etc. —*vt.* **grad'ed, grad'ing 1.** to arrange in grades; sort [to *grade* apples] ☆**2.** to give a grade (sense 6) to **3.** to gradate ☆**4.** to level or slope (ground) evenly for a road, etc. —*vi.* **1.** to be of a certain grade **2.** to change gradually [green *grading* into blue] —☆**make the grade 1.** to get to the top of a steep incline **2.** to overcome obstacles and succeed

-**grade** (grād) [< L. *gradi:* see GRADE] *a combining form meaning* walking or moving [plantigrade]

☆**grade crossing** a place where two railroads or a railroad and road intersect on the same level

☆**grad·er** (grā'dər) *n.* **1.** a person or thing that grades **2.** a pupil in a specified grade at school [a fifth *grader*]

☆**grade school** *same as* ELEMENTARY SCHOOL

gra·di·ent (grā'dē ənt, -dyənt) *adj.* [< L. prp. of *gradi,* to step: see GRADE] ascending or descending with a uniform slope —*n.* **1.** *a)* a slope, as of a road *b)* the degree of such slope **2.** *Physics* the rate of change of temperature, pressure, etc.

grad·u·al (graj'oo wəl) *adj.* [< ML. < L. *gradus:* see GRADE] taking place little by little, not sharply or suddenly —*n. Eccles.* **1.** a set of verses, esp. from the Psalms, following the Epistle at Mass **2.** a book containing these and other sung parts of the Mass —**grad'u·al·ly** *adv.* —**grad'u·al·ness** *n.*

☆**grad·u·al·ism** (-iz'm) *n.* the policy of trying to bring about social or political change in a gradual way —**grad'u·al·ist** *n., adj.* —**grad'u·al·is'tic** *adj.*

grad·u·ate (graj'oo wit; *for v., and occas. for n.,* -wāt') *n.* [< ML. pp. of *graduare,* to graduate < L. *gradus:* see GRADE] **1.** a person who has completed a course of study at a school or college and has received a degree or diploma **2.** a container marked off for measuring the contents —*vt.* -**at'ed,** -**at'ing 1.** to give a degree or diploma to upon completion of a course of study **2.** to mark (a flask, tube, etc.) with degrees for measuring **3.** to arrange in grades, steps, or stages [an income tax *graduated* so that the rich and poor are not taxed at the same rate] —*vi.* **1.** to become a graduate of a school, etc. **2.** to change, esp. to advance, by degrees —*adj.* **1.** graduated from a school, college, etc. ☆**2.** of or for studies leading to degrees above the bachelor's degree —**grad'u·a'tor** *n.*

grad·u·a·tion (graj'oo wā'shən) *n.* **1.** *a)* a graduating or being graduated from a school or college *b)* the ceremony connected with this; commencement **2.** *a)* a marking of a flask, tube, etc. with degrees for measuring *b)* a degree or the degrees marked **3.** a grading by size, quality, etc.

Grae·co- *same as* GRECO-

graf·fi·to (grə fēt'ō) *n., pl.* -**ti** (-ē) [It., a scribbling] an inscription, slogan, drawing, etc. scratched or scribbled on a wall, etc. in a public place

graft (graft) *n.* [< OFr. *graffe* < L. < Gr. *grapheion,* stylus: from resemblance of the scion to a pointed pencil] **1.** *a)* a shoot or bud of a plant or tree inserted into the stem or trunk of another so that it will grow there *b)* the inserting of such a shoot, etc. or the place of insertion *c)* a tree or plant with such an insertion **2.** a joining of one thing to another as if by grafting ☆**3.** *a)* a dishonest use of one's position to get money, property, etc., as by a public official *b)* anything gotten in this way **4.** *surgery a)* a piece of skin, bone, etc. transplanted from one body, or place on a body, to another, where it grows permanently *b)* such a transplanting —*vt.* **1.** *a)* to insert (a shoot or bud) as a graft *b)* to insert a graft of (one plant) in another *c)* to produce (a fruit, flower, etc.) by a graft **2.** to join as if by grafting **3.** *surgery* to transplant (a graft) —*vi.* **1.** to be grafted **2.** to make a graft on a plant ☆**3.** to obtain money, etc. by graft —**graft'age** *n.* —**graft'er** *n.*

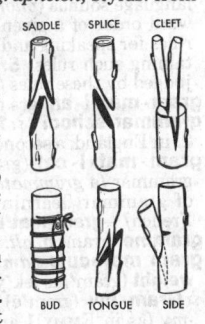

SADDLE   SPLICE   CLEFT

BUD   TONGUE   SIDE

TYPES OF GRAFT

☆**gra·ham** (grā'əm) *adj.* [after S. *Graham* (1794–1851), U.S. dietary reformer] designating or made of finely ground whole-wheat flour [*graham* crackers]

Grail (grāl) *n.* [< OFr. *graal* < ML. *gradalis,* cup < ?] *Medieval Legend* the cup or platter used by Jesus at the Last Supper and used to collect drops of blood from Jesus' body at the Crucifixion: also called **Holy Grail**

grain (grān) *n.* [< OFr. < L. *granum:* for IE. base see CORN[1]] **1.** a small, hard seed or seedlike fruit, esp. of a cereal plant, as wheat, rice, corn, etc. **2.** cereal seeds or cereal plants **3.** a tiny, solid particle, as of salt or sand **4.** a tiny bit [not a *grain* of sense] **5.** the smallest unit in the system of weights of the U.S. and Great Britain, equal to 0.0648 gram: one pound avoirdupois equals 7,000 grains **6.** *a)* the arrangement of fibers, layers, or particles of wood, leather, etc. *b)* the markings or texture due to this *c)* a granular surface appearance **7.** the side of leather from which the hair has been removed **8.** disposition; nature —*vt.* **1.** to form into grains; granulate **2.** to paint or finish (a surface) in imitation of the grain of wood, marble, etc. —*vi.* to form grains —**against the** (or **one's**) **grain** contrary to one's feelings, nature, etc.

grain alcohol ethyl alcohol, esp. when made from grain

☆**grain elevator** a tall structure for storing grain

grain·field (grān'fēld') *n.* a field where grain is grown

grain sorghum any of the kinds of sorghum grown chiefly for grain

grain·y (-ē) *adj.* **grain'i·er, grain'i·est 1.** having a well-defined grain [a *grainy* pine board] **2.** coarsely textured; granular [the *grainy* texture of sandpaper] —**grain'i·ness** *n.*

gram (gram) *n.* [< Fr. < LL. < Gr. *gramma,* a small weight, lit., what is written < *graphein:* see GRAPHITE] the basic unit of weight in the metric system, about 1/28 of an ounce

-**gram** (gram) [< Gr.: see prec.] *a combining form meaning:* **1.** something written or recorded [telegram] **2.** grams or part of a gram [kilogram, milligram]

gram. **1.** grammar **2.** grammatical

☆**gra·ma** (grā'mə, gram'ə) *n.* [Sp. < L. *gramen,* GRASS] any of a group of grasses growing wild on the plains of the western U.S.: also **grama grass**

gram atom *Chem.* the amount of an element having a weight in grams equal to the element's atomic weight [a *gram atom* of copper, which has an atomic weight of 63.54, is a quantity of copper weighing 63.54 grams] : also **gram·a·tom·ic weight** (gram'ə täm'ik)

gra·mer·cy (grə mur'sē, gram'ər sē) *interj.* [< OFr. < *grant,* great + *merci,* thanks] [Archaic] **1.** thank you very much **2.** an exclamation of surprise

☆**gram·i·ci·din** (gram'ə sīd''n) *n.* [GRAM(-POSITIVE) + -*i*- + -CID(E) + -IN[1]] any of a group of related antibiotics used in treating bacterial infections, esp. of the skin and eyes

gram·mar (gram′ər) *n.* [< OFr. < L. < Gr. *grammatikē* (*technē*), (art) of grammar, learning < *gramma*, something written: see GRAM] **1.** language study dealing with word forms (*morphology*), word order in sentences (*syntax*), and now often language sounds (*phonology*). **2.** the system of word forms and word order of a given language at a given time **3.** a body of rules for speaking and writing a given language **4.** a book containing such rules **5.** one's manner of speaking or writing as judged by these rules [her *grammar* was poor]

gram·mar·i·an (grə mer′ē ən) *n.* an expert in grammar

grammar school ☆**1.** *earlier name for* ELEMENTARY SCHOOL **2.** in England, a secondary school

gram·mat·i·cal (grə mat′i k'l) *adj.* **1.** of or according to grammar [a *grammatical* mistake] **2.** conforming to the rules of grammar [learning to write a *grammatical* sentence in French] —**gram·mat′i·cal·ly** *adv.* —**gram·mat′i·cal·ness** *n.*

gramme (gram) *n. alt. sp. of* GRAM

gram molecule *same as* MOLE[1]: also **gram-mo·lec·u·lar weight** (gram′mə lek′yoo lər)

☆**Gram·my** (gram′ē) *n., pl.* **-mys, -mies** [GRAM(OPHONE) + *-my* (as in EMMY)] any of the annual awards in the U.S. for special achievement in the recording industry

Gram-neg·a·tive (gram′neg′ə tiv) *adj.* [*also* g-] designating bacteria that lose the stain: see GRAM'S METHOD

☆**gram·o·phone** (gram′ə fōn′) *n.* [a rearrangement of the word PHONOGRAM] [Chiefly Brit.] a phonograph

Gram·pi·an Mountains (gram′pē ən) mountain range extending across C & N Scotland, dividing the Highlands from the Lowlands: also **Grampian Hills, Grampians**

Gram-pos·i·tive (gram′päz′ə tiv) *adj.* [*also* g-] designating bacteria that retain the stain: see GRAM'S METHOD

gram·pus (gram′pəs) *n., pl.* **-pus·es** [< OFr. *graspeis* < L. *crassus*, fat + *piscis*, fish] a small, black, fierce whale related to the dolphins

Gram's method (gramz) [after H. C. J. *Gram* (1853–1938), Dan. physician] a method of staining bacteria with gentian violet in order to classify them: some bacteria lose the stain when treated with alcohol, others do not

Gra·na·da (grə nä′də; *Sp.* grä nä′thä) **1.** former Moorish kingdom in S Spain **2.** city in S Spain: pop. 164,000

gran·a·dil·la (gran′ə dil′ə) *n.* [Sp. < dim. of *granada*, pomegranate, ult. < L. *granum*, GRAIN] the edible fruit of certain passionflowers

gran·a·ry (gran′ər ē, grā′nər ē) *n., pl.* **-ries** [< L. < *granum*, GRAIN] **1.** a building for storing threshed grain **2.** a region producing much grain

grand (grand) *adj.* [OFr. < L. *grandis*, large] **1.** higher in rank or status than others with the same title [a *grand* duke] **2.** most important; main [the *grand* ballroom] **3.** standing out because of great size and beauty; magnificent [*grand* scenery] **4.** splendid and costly; luxurious [a *grand* banquet] **5.** distinguished; illustrious [the *grand* old statesman] **6.** acting too important; pretentious [he spoke with *grand* gestures and fancy talk] **7.** lofty and dignified, as in style **8.** complete; overall [the *grand* total] **9.** [Colloq.] excellent, delightful, etc. [what a *grand* day!] —*n.* **1.** *same as* GRAND PIANO ☆**2.** [Slang] a thousand dollars —**grand′ly** *adv.* —**grand′ness** *n.*

grand- *a combining form meaning* of the generation older (or younger) than [grandmother, grandson]

gran·dam (gran′dam, -dəm) *n.* [< Anglo-Fr.: see GRAND & DAME] [Archaic] **1.** a grandmother **2.** an old woman Also sp. **gran′dame**

☆**Grand Army of the Republic** an association (1866–1949) of Union veterans of the Civil War

grand-aunt (grand′ant′) *n. same as* GREAT-AUNT

Grand Banks (or **Bank**) large shoal in the Atlantic, southeast of Newfoundland: noted fishing grounds See map at GULF STREAM

Grand Canal 1. canal in NE China, from Tientsin to Hangchow **2.** main canal in Venice, Italy

Grand Canyon 1. deep gorge of the Colorado River, in NW Ariz.: over 200 mi. long; 1 mi. deep **2.** national park (**Grand Canyon National Park**) including 105 mi. of this gorge

grand·child (gran′chīld′) *n., pl.* **-chil′dren** a child of one's son or daughter

Grand Cou·lee (koo′lē) dam on the Columbia River, NE Wash.: 500 ft. high

grand·dad, grand-dad (gran′dad′) *n.* [Colloq.] grandfather

grand·daugh·ter (-dôt′ər) *n.* a daughter of one's son or daughter

grand duchess 1. the wife or widow of a grand duke **2.** a woman who has the rank of a grand duke and rules a grand duchy **3.** in czarist Russia, a princess of the royal family

grand duchy the territory or a country ruled by a grand duke or a grand duchess

grand duke 1. the sovereign ruler of a grand duchy, ranking just below a king **2.** in czarist Russia, a royal prince

grande dame (gränd däm) [Fr., great lady] a woman, esp. an older one, of great dignity or prestige

gran·dee (gran dē′) *n.* [Sp. & Port. *grande:* see GRAND] **1.** a Spanish or Portuguese nobleman of the highest rank **2.** a man of high rank

gran·deur (gran′jər, -joor) *n.* [Fr. < *grand:* see GRAND] **1.** great size, beauty, dignity, etc.; splendor; magnificence [the *grandeur* of the Swiss Alps] **2.** moral and intellectual greatness; nobility [the *grandeur* of her sacrifice]

grand·fa·ther (gran′fä′thər, grand′-) *n.* **1.** the father of one's father or mother **2.** a forefather

grand·fa·ther·ly (-lē) *adj.* of or like a grandfather; kindly, not strict, etc.

gran·dil·o·quent (gran dil′ə kwənt) *adj.* [< L. < *grandis*, grand + *loqui*, to speak] using fancy language that sounds more important than it is —see SYN.at BOMBASTIC —**gran·dil′o·quence** *n.* —**gran·dil′o·quent·ly** *adv.*

gran·di·ose (gran′dē ōs′) *adj.* [Fr. < It. < L. *grandis*, great] **1.** having grandeur; imposing; impressive **2.** seeming or trying to seem very important; pompous and showy —**gran·di·ose′ly** *adv.* —**gran·di·os′i·ty** (-äs′ə tē) *n.*

grand jury a jury that investigates criminal charges against persons and indicts them for trial if there is sufficient evidence

Grand Lama *same as* DALAI LAMA

grand larceny *see* LARCENY

grand·ma (gran′mä, grä′mä) *n.* [Colloq.] grandmother

grand mal (gran′ mäl′) [Fr., lit., great ailment] a type of epilepsy in which there are convulsions and a loss of consciousness

grand·moth·er (gran′muth′ər, grand′-, grä′-) *n.* **1.** the mother of one's father or mother **2.** a female ancestor

grand·moth·er·ly (-lē) *adj.* of or like a grandmother; kindly, not strict, etc.

grand·neph·ew (gran′nef′yoo, grand′-; *chiefly Brit.* -nev′yoo) *n.* the grandson of one's brother or sister

grand·niece (-nēs′) *n.* the granddaughter of one's brother or sister

grand opera opera, generally on a serious theme, in which the whole text is set to music

grand·pa (gran′pä, grand′-, gram′-) *n.* [Colloq.] grandfather

grand·par·ent (-per′ənt) *n.* a grandfather or grandmother

grand piano a large piano with strings set horizontally in a harp-shaped case

Grand Prairie city in NE Tex.: suburb of Dallas: pop. 51,000

‡**grand prix** (grän prē′) [Fr., lit., great prize] first prize; highest award in a competition

Grand Rapids [after the *rapids* on the *Grand* River] city in SW Mich.: pop. 198,000 (met. area 539,000)

grand·sire (gran′sīr′, grand′-) *n.* [Archaic] **1.** a grandfather **2.** a male ancestor **3.** an old man

grand slam ☆**1.** *Baseball* (designating) a home run hit when the bases are loaded: also **grand′-slam′mer n. 2.** *Bridge* the winning of all the tricks in a deal

grand·son (gran′sun′, grand′-) *n.* a son of one's son or daughter

grand·stand (-stand′) *n.* the main seating structure for spectators at a sporting event, etc. —*vi.* [Colloq.] to make an unnecessarily showy play (**grandstand play**), as in baseball, to get applause —**grand′stand′er** *n.*

Grand Te·ton National Park (tē′tän) [Fr., lit., big breast: from the outline of the mountains] national park in NW Wyo., including a section of the Rockies

grand tour a tour of continental Europe, formerly part of the education of young men of the British upper class

grand·un·cle (grand′un′k'l) *n. same as* GREAT-UNCLE

grange (grānj) *n.* [< Anglo-Fr. < ML. *granica* < L. *granum*, GRAIN] **1.** a farm with its dwelling house, barns, etc. ☆**2.** [G-] *a)* the Patrons of Husbandry, an association of farmers organized in the U.S. in 1867 for mutual welfare and advancement *b)* any of its local lodges

GRAND PIANO

grang·er (grān′jər) n. ☆1. a farmer ☆2. [G-] a member of the Grange —**grang′er·ism** n.

gran·ite (gran′it) n. [< It. *granito*, grained, ult. < L. *granum*, GRAIN] a very hard, crystalline, plutonic rock consisting chiefly of feldspar and quartz —**gra·nit·ic** (grə nit′ik, gra-) adj.

gran·ite·ware (-wer′) n. a variety of ironware coated with a hard, grained enamel

gra·niv·o·rous (grə niv′ər əs) adj. [< L. *granum*, grain + -VOROUS] feeding on grain and seeds

gran·ny, gran·nie (gran′ē) n., pl. **-nies** [Colloq.] 1. a grandmother 2. an old woman 3. a fussy person 4. same as GRANNY KNOT

granny knot a knot like a square knot but with the ends crossed the wrong way, forming an awkward, insecure knot: also **granny's knot**: see illustration at KNOT

☆**gran·o·la** (grə nō′lə) n. [? < L. *granum*, grain] a packaged breakfast cereal of oats, wheat germ, sesame seeds, brown sugar or honey, bits of dried fruit or nuts, etc.

grant (grant) vt. [< OFr. *craanter*, to promise, ult. < L. prp. of *credere*: see CREED] 1. to give (what is asked or wanted); agree to [he *granted* permission for us to go] 2. a) to give formally or according to legal procedure [the 19th Amendment *granted* women the right to vote] b) to transfer (property) by a deed 3. to admit as true without proof; concede [I *grant* that you have reason to be angry] —n. 1. a granting 2. something granted, as property, a right, money, etc. [a *grant* of $5,000 for study] —see SYN. at GIVE —**take for granted** to accept as a matter of course —**grant′a·ble** adj. —**grant′er**, *Law* **grant′or** n.

Grant (grant), **Ulysses Simp·son** (simp′sən) (born *Hiram Ulysses Grant*) 1822–85; 18th president of the U.S. (1869–77); commander of Union forces in the Civil War

grant·ee (grant ē′) n. *Law* a person to whom a grant is made

grant-in-aid (grant′in ād′) n., pl. **grants′-in-aid′** a grant of funds, as by a foundation, to support a specific program

gran·u·lar (gran′yə lər) adj. 1. containing or consisting of grains or granules 2. like grains or granules 3. having a grainy surface —**gran′u·lar′i·ty** (-ler′ə tē) n. —**gran′u·lar·ly** adv.

gran·u·late (-lāt′) vt., vi. **-lat′ed**, **-lat′ing** 1. to form into grains or granules 2. to make or become rough on the surface by the development of granules —**gran′u·la′tion** n. —**gran′u·la′tive** adj. —**gran′u·la′tor, gran′u·lat′er** n.

gran·ule (gran′yool) n. [< LL. *granulum*, dim. of L. *granum*, GRAIN] 1. a small grain 2. a small, grainlike particle or spot

grape (grāp) n. [< OFr. *grape*, bunch of grapes < *graper*, to gather with a hook < Frank. *krappo*, hook: for IE. base see CRAM] 1. a small, round, smooth-skinned, juicy berry, growing in clusters on woody vines and eaten raw, used to make wine, etc. 2. a grapevine 3. a dark purplish red 4. same as GRAPESHOT

grape·fruit (grāp′frōōt′) n. 1. a large, round, edible citrus fruit with a pale-yellow rind and a somewhat sour, juicy pulp 2. the tree it grows on

grape·shot (-shät′) n. a cluster of small iron balls formerly fired as a cannon charge

grape sugar same as DEXTROSE

grape·vine (-vīn′) n. 1. a woody vine bearing grapes ☆2. a secret means of spreading information: in full, **grapevine telegraph** 3. a rumor

graph (graf) n. [short for *graphic formula*] 1. a diagram or chart that shows, as by the use of connected lines, how one thing changes in relation to another 2. *Math.* a drawing that shows the relationship between two variables as a set of points in a coordinate system —vt. to represent by a graph

-graph (graf) [Gr. *-graphos* < *graphein*: see GRAPHIC] a combining form meaning: 1. something that writes or records [telegraph] 2. something written [monograph]

-gra·pher (grə fər) a combining form meaning a person who writes, records, makes copies, etc. [telegrapher, stenographer]

GRAPH

graph·ic (graf′ik) adj. [< L. < Gr. *graphikos* < *graphein*, to write: for IE. base see CARVE] 1. described in realistic detail; vivid [a *graphic* account of the fire] 2. of the GRAPHIC ARTS 3. a) of or expressed in handwriting b) written or inscribed 4. shown by graphs or diagrams Also **graph′i·cal** —**graph′i·cal·ly** adv. —**graph′ic·ness** n.

-graph·ic (graf′ik) a combining form used to form adjectives from nouns ending in -GRAPH: also **-graph′i·cal**

graphic arts 1. the arts of painting, drawing, photography, etc. 2. those arts in which impressions are printed from various kinds of blocks, plates, etc., as etching, lithography, printing, etc.

graph·ics (graf′iks) n.pl. [with sing. v.] [< GRAPHIC] 1. the art of making drawings according to mathematical rules 2. same as GRAPHIC ARTS (sense 2)

graph·ite (graf′īt) n. [G. *graphit* < Gr. *graphein*: see GRAPHIC] a soft, black, shiny form of carbon found in nature and used for lead in pencils, for lubricants, electrodes, etc. —**gra·phit·ic** (grə fit′ik) adj.

graph·ol·o·gy (gra fäl′ə jē) n. [< Fr. < Gr. *graphein*, to write + -LOGY] the study of handwriting, esp. as a clue to character, aptitudes, etc. —**graph·ol′o·gist** n.

graph paper paper with small ruled squares on which to make graphs, diagrams, etc.

-gra·phy (grə fē) [< L. < Gr. < *graphein*: see GRAPHIC] a combining form meaning: 1. a process or method of writing, recording, or representing in a specified way [telegraphy, lithography] 2. a descriptive science [geography]

grap·nel (grap′n'l) n. [< OFr. *grapil* < Pr. < *grapa* < Frank. *krappo*: see GRAPE] 1. a small anchor with several flukes 2. an iron bar with claws at one end for grasping and holding things

grap·ple (grap′'l) n. [OFr. *grapil*: see prec.] 1. same as GRAPNEL (sense 2) 2. a device consisting of two or more hinged, movable iron prongs for grasping and moving heavy objects 3. a coming to grips; hand-to-hand fight; struggle —vt. **grap′pled**, **grap′pling** to grip and hold; seize —vi. 1. to use a grapnel (sense 2) 2. to struggle in hand-to-hand combat 3. to struggle or try to cope (*with*) [to *grapple* with a problem] —**grap′pler** n.

GRAPNEL

grappling iron (or **hook**) same as GRAPNEL (sense 2)

grap·y (grā′pē) adj. of or like grapes

grasp (grasp) vt. [ME. *graspen*, prob. < MLowG.] 1. to take hold of firmly as with the hand; grip 2. to take hold of eagerly; seize 3. to understand; comprehend [I could *grasp* what he meant] —vi. 1. to try to seize (with *at*) 2. to accept eagerly (with *at*) [to *grasp* at a chance to go] —n. 1. the act of grasping 2. control; possession [land in the *grasp* of the enemy] 3. the power to hold or seize [it's high, beyond my *grasp*] 4. understanding; comprehension [a good *grasp* of the subject] —**grasp′a·ble** adj. —**grasp′er** n.

grasp·ing (grasp′in) adj. 1. that grasps 2. eager for gain; greedy —see SYN. at GREEDY —**grasp′ing·ly** adv.

grass (gras) n. [OE. *gærs*, *græs* < IE. base *ghro-*, to become green] 1. any of a family of plants with long, narrow leaves, jointed stems, and seedlike fruit, as wheat, rye, oats, sugar cane, etc. 2. any of various green plants with long, narrow leaves that cover lawns and meadows [grazing animals feed on *grass*] 3. ground covered with grass; pasture land or lawn ☆4. [Slang] marijuana —vt. 1. to put (animals) out to pasture or graze 2. to grow grass over 3. to lay (textiles, etc.) on the grass for bleaching —vi. to become covered with grass —**grass′like′** adj.

grass·hop·per (gras′häp′ər) n. 1. any of a group of plant-eating insects with two pairs of wings and powerful hind legs adapted for jumping ☆2. *Mil. Slang* a small, light airplane for scouting, etc.

grass·land (-land′) n. 1. land with grass growing on it, used for grazing; pasture land 2. a region of grassy land, as a prairie

grass roots [Colloq.] ☆1. the common people, thought of in relation to their at-

GRASSHOPPER (1¼ in. long)

titudes on political issues ☆2. the basic source or support, as of a movement —**grass'-roots'** *adj.*

grass snake ☆any of various harmless, N. American snakes living in meadows, gardens, etc., including garter snakes and green snakes

grass widow a woman divorced or otherwise separated from her husband —**grass widower**

grass·y (-ē) *adj.* **grass'i·er, grass'i·est** **1.** of or consisting of grass **2.** covered with grass **3.** green like growing grass — **grass'i·ness** *n.*

grate[1] (grāt) *vt.* **grat'ed, grat'ing** [< OFr. *grater* < Frank.] **1.** to grind into particles by scraping [to *grate* onions] **2.** to rub against (an object) with a harsh, scraping sound **3.** to grind (the teeth) together with a rasping sound **4.** to irritate; annoy —*vi.* **1.** to grind or rub with a rasping sound [the wheel *grated* on the rusty axle] **2.** to make a harsh or rasping sound [his voice *grated*] **3.** to cause irritation or annoyance [his boasting *grated* on us all]

grate[2] (grāt) *n.* [< ML. < L. *cratis*, CRATE] **1.** *same as* GRATING[1] **2.** a frame of metal bars for holding fuel in a fireplace, etc. **3.** a fireplace —*vt.* **grat'ed, grat'ing** to provide with a grate or grates

grate·ful (grāt'fəl) *adj.* [obs. *grate* (< L. *gratus:* see GRACE), pleasing + -FUL] **1.** feeling or expressing gratitude; thankful **2.** causing gratitude; welcome [a *grateful* blessing] —**grate'ful·ly** *adv.* —**grate'ful·ness** *n.*

grat·er (grāt'ər) *n.* a kitchen utensil for grating vegetables, cheese, etc.

grat·i·fi·ca·tion (grat'ə fi kā'shən) *n.* **1.** a gratifying or being gratified **2.** a cause for satisfaction

grat·i·fy (grat'ə fī') *vt.* **-fied', -fy'ing** [< Fr. < L. *gratificare* < *gratus* (see GRACE) + -*ficare*, -FY] **1.** to give pleasure or satisfaction to [actors are *gratified* by applause] **2.** to give in to; indulge; humor [the child's every wish was *gratified*] —see SYN. at PLEASANT —**grat'i·fi·ca'tion** *n.* —**grat'i·fi'er** *n.*

grat·ing[1] (grāt'iŋ) *n.* a framework of parallel or latticed bars set in a window, door, etc.

grat·ing[2] (grāt'iŋ) *adj.* **1.** harsh and rasping **2.** irritating or annoying —**grat'ing·ly** *adv.*

gra·tis (grat'is, grāt'-) *adv., adj.* [L. < *gratia*, a favor: see GRACE] without charge or payment; free

grat·i·tude (grat'ə tōod', -tyōod') *n.* [Fr. < ML. < L. *gratus:* see GRACE] a feeling of thankful appreciation for favors received; thankfulness

gra·tu·i·tous (grə tōo'ə təs, -tyōo'-) *adj.* [< L. < *gratus:* see GRACE] **1.** *a)* given or received without charge; free [*gratuitous* lessons] *b)* granted without obligation **2.** without cause or reason; uncalled-for [a *gratuitous* lie] —**gra·tu'i·tous·ly** *adv.* —**gra·tu'i·tous·ness** *n.*

gra·tu·i·ty (grə tōo'ə tē, -tyōo'-) *n., pl.* **-ties** [see prec.] a gift of money, etc., esp. one given for a service rendered; tip

gra·va·men (grə vā'mən) *n., pl.* **-mens, gra·vam'i·na** (-vam'ə nə) [LL. < L. < *gravis:* see GRAVE[1]] **1.** a grievance **2.** *Law* the essential part of an accusation

grave[1] (grāv) *adj.* [Fr. < L. *gravis*, heavy < IE. base *giver-*, heavy] **1.** important; weighty [*grave* doubts] **2.** serious; threatening; ominous [a *grave* illness] **3.** dignified and solemn or sedate **4.** somber; dull [*grave* colors] **5.** low or deep in pitch —*n. same as* GRAVE ACCENT —see SYN. at SERIOUS —**grave'ly** *adv.* —**grave'ness** *n.*

grave[2] (grāv) *n.* [OE. *græf* < *grafan*, to dig < IE. base *ghrebh-*, to scratch] **1.** *a)* a hole in the ground in which to bury a dead body *b)* any place of burial; tomb **2.** final end or death —*vt.* **graved, grav'en** or **graved, grav'ing 1.** to carve out; sculpture **2.** [Archaic] to engrave; incise **3.** to impress or fix sharply and clearly —**grav'er** *n.*

grave accent a mark (`) used to indicate: **1.** in French, the quality of an open *e* (è), as in *chère* **2.** full pronunciation of a syllable normally cut short, as in *lovèd* (luv'id, *not* luvd) **3.** secondary stress, as in *typewriter*

grave·clothes (grāv'klōz', -klōthz') *n.pl.* the clothes in which a dead body is buried

grave·dig·ger (-dig'ər) *n.* a person whose work is digging graves

grav·el (grav''l) *n.* [< OFr. dim. of *grave*, coarse sand: for IE. base see CHROMATIC] **1.** a loose mixture of pebbles and rock fragments coarser than sand **2.** *Med.* a deposit of small bits like gravel in the kidneys, gallbladder, or urinary bladder —*vt.* **-eled** or **-elled, -el·ing** or **-el·ling 1.** to cover (a walk, etc.) with gravel **2.** to embarrass, confuse, or perplex **3.** [Colloq.] to irritate or annoy

grav·el·ly (-ē) *adj.* **1.** full of, like, or consisting of gravel **2.** sounding harsh or rasping [a *gravelly* voice]

grav·en (grāv''n) *alt. pp. of* GRAVE[2]

graven image an idol made from stone, wood, etc.

Graves (grāvz), **Robert (Ranke)** 1895– ; Eng. poet, novelist, & critic

☆**grave·side** (grāv'sīd') *n.* the area alongside a grave —*adj.* being, or taking place, beside a grave

grave·stone (-stōn') *n.* an engraved stone marking a grave; tombstone

grave·yard (-yärd') *n.* a burial ground; cemetery

☆**graveyard shift** [Colloq.] a work shift that starts during the night, usually at midnight

grav·i·tate (grav'ə tāt') *vi.* **-tat'ed, -tat'ing 1.** to move or be pulled by the force of gravity **2.** to be attracted or tend to move (*toward*) [the crowd *gravitated* toward the amusement area] — **grav'i·ta'tive** *adj.*

grav·i·ta·tion (grav'ə tā'shən) *n.* **1.** the act, process, or fact of gravitating **2.** *Physics a)* the force by which every mass or particle of matter attracts and is attracted by every other mass or particle of matter *b)* the tendency of these masses or particles to move toward each other —**grav'i·ta'tion·al** *adj.* —**grav'i·ta'tion·al·ly** *adv.*

grav·i·ty (grav'ə tē) *n., pl.* **-ties** [< L. < *gravis:* see GRAVE[1]] **1.** the state or condition of being grave; esp., *a)* a being solemn or calm; seriousness *b)* danger or threat [the *gravity* of his illness] *c)* seriousness, as of a situation **2.** weight; heaviness [specific *gravity*] **3.** lowness of musical pitch **4.** gravitation; esp., the force that tends to draw all bodies in the earth's sphere toward the center of the earth

gra·vure (grə vyoor', grā'vyoor) *n.* [Fr. < *graver*, to carve < Frank.] **1.** *a)* any process that makes or uses intaglio printing plates *b)* a plate or print so made **2.** *shortened form of: a)* PHOTOGRAVURE *b)* ROTOGRAVURE

gra·vy (grā'vē) *n., pl.* **-vies** [? a misreading of OFr. *grané* < ? *grain*, cooking ingredients] **1.** the juice given off by meat in cooking **2.** a sauce made with this juice and flour, seasoning, etc. ☆**3.** [Slang] *a)* money easily obtained *b)* any extra benefit

gravy boat a boat-shaped dish for serving gravy

☆**gravy train** [Slang] any means of easy profit or gain

gray (grā) *adj.* [< OE. *græg*] **1.** of the color gray **2.** *a)* darkish; dull *b)* dreary; dismal **3.** *a)* having hair that is gray *b)* old **4.** dressed in gray **5.** designating a vague area in the middle, as between morality and immorality —*n.* **1.** a color made by mixing black and white **2.** a gray animal or thing **3.** [often G-] a person dressed in a gray uniform —*vt., vi.* to make or become gray —**gray'ly** *adv.* —**gray'ness** *n.*

Gray (grā) **1. A·sa** (ās'ə), 1810–88; U.S. botanist **2. Thomas,** 1716–71; Eng. poet

gray·beard (grā'bird') *n.* an old man

gray·hound (-hound') *n. same as* GREYHOUND

gray·ish (-ish) *adj.* somewhat gray

gray·lag (-lag') *n.* [short for *gray lag goose:* from its color and its late migration] the European wild gray goose

gray·ling (-liŋ) *n., pl.* **-ling, -lings:** see PLURAL, II, D, 2 [GRAY + -LING[1]: from the color] **1.** a freshwater game fish related to the salmon **2.** any of several varieties of gray or brown butterfly

gray matter 1. grayish nerve tissue of the brain and spinal cord, consisting of nerve cells and some nerve fibers **2.** [Colloq.] intelligence

☆**gray squirrel** a large, gray squirrel with a bushy tail, native to eastern N. America

☆**gray wolf** a large, gray wolf that hunts in packs and was formerly common throughout the northern part of the Northern Hemisphere

Graz (gräts) city in SE Austria: pop. 237,000

graze[1] (grāz) *vt.* **grazed, graz'ing** [OE. *grasian* < *græs*, GRASS] **1.** to feed on (growing grass, herbage, etc.) **2.** to put livestock to feed on (a pasture, etc.) **3.** to cause (livestock) to graze **4.** to be pasture for —*vi.* to feed on growing grass, etc. —**graz'er** *n.*

graze[2] (grāz) *vt.* **grazed, graz'ing** [prob. < prec. in sense "to come close to the grass"] **1.** to touch or rub lightly in passing **2.** to scrape or scratch in passing [the shot *grazed* him] —*vi.* to scrape, touch, or rub lightly against something in passing —*n.* a grazing, or a scratch or scrape caused by it

gra·zier (grā'zhər; *Brit.* -zyər) *n.* [Chiefly Brit.] a person who grazes beef cattle for sale

graz·ing (grā'ziŋ) *n.* land to graze on; pasture

Gr. Brit., Gr. Br. Great Britain

grease (grēs; *for v. also* grēz) *n.* [< OFr., ult. < L. *crassus*, fat]
1. melted animal fat 2. any thick, oily substance or lubricant
—*vt.* **greased, greas'ing** 1. to smear or lubricate with grease
2. to bribe or tip: chiefly in **grease the palm** (or **hand**) **of** —
greas'er *n.*

grease·paint (grēs'pānt') *n.* a mixture of grease and coloring
matter used by performers in making up

☆**grease·wood** (-wood') *n.* a thorny plant of desert regions in
the western U.S., with fleshy leaves

greas·y (grē'sē, -zē) *adj.* **greas'i·er, greas'i·est** 1. smeared
or soiled with grease [*greasy* hands] 2. containing grease, esp.
much grease [*greasy* food] 3. like grease; oily; slippery —
greas'i·ly *adv.* —**greas'i·ness** *n.*

great (grāt) *adj.* [OE. *great:* see CHROMATIC] 1. of much more
than ordinary size, extent, number, etc. [the *Great* Lakes, a
great company] 2. much above the ordinary or average in
some quality or degree; esp., *a*) existing in a high degree; intense [*great* pain] *b*) very much of a [a *great* reader] *c*) eminent; distinguished; superior [a *great* playwright] *d*) very
impressive or imposing [*great* ceremony] *e*) having or showing nobility of mind, purpose, etc. [a *great* man] 3. of most
importance; main; chief [the *great* seal] 4. that is further
removed by one generation [*great*-grandmother] 5. [Colloq.]
clever; skillful [*great* at tennis] ☆6. [Colloq.] excellent, splendid, fine, etc. —*adv.* [Colloq.] very well —*n.* a great or distinguished person: *usually used in pl.* —see SYN. at LARGE —**great
on** [Colloq.] enthusiastic about —**great'ly** *adv.* —**great'ness** *n.*

great-aunt (grāt'ant') *n.* a sister of any of one's grandparents;
grandaunt

Great Australian Bight wide bay of the Indian Ocean, on the
southern coast of Australia

Great Barrier Reef coral reef off the NE coast of Queensland,
Australia

Great Basin vast inland region of the western U.S., between
the Sierra Nevadas & the Rockies: the rivers flowing into this
region form lakes which have no outlet to the sea

Great Bear the constellation URSA MAJOR

Great Bear Lake lake in Northwest Territories, NW Canada

Great Britain 1. principal island of the United Kingdom, including England, Scotland, & Wales 2. popularly, the United
Kingdom

great circle any circle traced on the surface of the earth or other
sphere by a plane which passes through the center of the sphere:
the shortest course between any two points on the earth's surface lies along a great circle passing through these points

great·coat (grāt'kōt') *n.* a heavy overcoat

Great Dane any of a breed of large, powerful dog with short,
smooth hair

☆**Great Divide** a principal mountain
watershed; specif., the main ridge of
the Rocky Mountains

great·en (grāt''n) *vt., vi.* to make or
become great or greater

Greater Antilles group of islands in
the West Indies, made up of the N &
W Antilles, including Cuba, Jamaica,
Hispaniola, & Puerto Rico

Great Falls city in WC Mont., on the
Missouri River: pop. 60,000

great-grand·child (-gran'child') *n.*,
pl. **great'-grand'chil'dren** a child of
any of one's grandchildren —**great'-
grand'daugh'ter** *n.* —**great'-
grand'son'** *n.*

GREAT DANE
(to 36 in. high
at shoulder)

great-grand·par·ent (-gran'per'ənt) *n.* a parent of any
of one's grandparents —**great'-grand'fa'ther** *n.* —**great'-
grand'moth'er** *n.*

great-great- *a combining form used with nouns of relationship to
indicate two degrees of removal* [great-great-grandparent]

great gross twelve gross

great-heart·ed (-här'tid) *adj.* 1. brave; fearless; courageous
2. generous; unselfish

great horned owl a large, pale gray and brownish owl of N.
America, with two hornlike tufts of black feathers on its head

Great Lakes chain of freshwater lakes in east central N. America; Lakes Superior, Michigan, Huron, Erie & Ontario

Great Mogul 1. the title of the ruler of the Mongol empire in
India in the 16th cent. 2. [**g- m-**] a person of importance

great-neph·ew (-nef'yoo; *chiefly Brit.* -nev'-) *n.* a grandson
of one's brother or sister; grandnephew —**great'-niece'** (-nēs')
n.fem.

Great Plains sloping region of valleys & plains in west central
N. America, east of the base of the Rockies

Great Rift Valley depression of SW Asia & E Africa, extending
from the Jordan River valley southwestward to the lakes region
of E Africa

Great Salt Lake shallow saltwater lake in NW Utah

great seal the chief seal of a nation, state, etc., with which official papers are stamped

Great Slave Lake lake in Northwest
Territories, NW Canada

Great Smoky Mountains mountain
range of the Appalachians, along the
Tenn.–N.C. border: site of a national
park (**Great Smoky Mountains National
Park**)

great-un·cle (-uŋ'k'l) *n.* a brother of
any of one's grandparents; granduncle

Great Wall of China stone & earth wall
extending across N China, built as a defense against invaders in the 3d cent.
B.C.

GREAT SEAL OF
UNITED STATES

greave (grēv) *n.* [< OFr. pl. of *greve*, shin] armor for the leg
from the ankle to the knee: see illustration at ARMOR

grebe (grēb) *n., pl.* **grebes, grebe:** see PLURAL, II, D, 1 [Fr. *grèbe*]
any of a family of diving and swimming birds related to the
loons, with partially webbed feet, and legs set far back on the
body

Gre·cian (grē'shən) *adj. same as* GREEK (sense 1) —*n.* a Greek

Greco, El *see* EL GRECO

Gre·co- *a combining form meaning:* 1. Greek or Greeks 2.
Greek and or Greece and

Gre·co-Ro·man (grē'kō rō'mən) *adj.* of or influenced by both
Greece and Rome

Greece (grēs) country in the S Balkan Peninsula, including islands in the Aegean, Ionian,
& Mediterranean seas:
50,534 sq. miles; pop.
8,835,000; cap. Athens: in
ancient times, the region
consisted of many small
monarchies & republics

greed (grēd) *n.* [back-forma-
tion < GREEDY] excessive
desire for getting or having,
esp. wealth; avarice

greed·y (grēd'ē) *adj.* **-i·er,
-i·est** [OE. *grædig* < IE. base
gher-, to crave] 1. wanting
or taking all that one can get;
desiring more than one needs
or deserves; avaricious 2.
having too strong a desire for
food and drink; gluttonous 3. intensely eager [he listened with
greedy interest] —**greed'i·ly** *adv.* —**greed'i·ness** *n.*

ANCIENT GREECE

SYN.—**greedy** implies a desire to get or have much more of something
than is one's share or than one needs; **avaricious** stresses greed for money
or riches and often suggests a being miserly; **grasping** suggests a strong
eagerness for gain that shows itself in a seizing of every opportunity to get
what one wants; **acquisitive** stresses the drive to keep gathering more and
more wealth or possessions; **covetous** implies a strong desire for something that belongs to another person

Greek (grēk) *n.* 1. a native or inhabitant of ancient or modern
Greece 2. the branch of the Indo-European language family
consisting of the dialects of Greece, ancient or modern —*adj.*
1. of ancient or modern Greece, its people, language, or culture
2. designating, of, or using the rite of the Orthodox Eastern
Church —**be Greek to one** to be meaningless to one

Greek cross a cross with four equal arms at right angles: see
illustration at CROSS

Greek fire a material that causes fires, used in ancient warfare
and described as able to burn in water

---

fat, āpe, cär; ten, ēven; is, bīte; gō, hôrn, tool, look; oil, out; up, fur; get; joy; yet; chin; she; thin, *th*en; zh, leisure; ŋ, ring;
ə for a in ago, e in agent, i in sanity, o in comply, u in focus; ' as in able (ā'b'l); Fr. bâl; ë, Fr. coeur; ö, Fr. feu; Fr. mon;
ô, Fr. coq; ü, Fr. duc; r, Fr. cri; H, G. ich; kh, G. doch; ‡ foreign; ☆ Americanism; < derived from. See inside front cover.

Greek (Orthodox) Church 1. the established church of Greece, a self-governing part of the Orthodox Eastern Church **2.** *popular name for* ORTHODOX EASTERN CHURCH

Gree·ley (grē′lē), **Horace** 1811–72; U.S. journalist & political leader

green (grēn) *adj.* [OE. *grene:* for IE. base see GRASS] **1.** having the color of growing grass **2.** overspread with green plants, etc. *[a green* field*]* **3.** keeping the green grass of summer; snowless *[a green* December*]* **4.** pale and sickly in complexion, as from illness, fear, etc. **5.** not ripe or mature *[green* bananas*]* **6.** not trained or experienced *[a green* camper*]* **7.** easily led or deceived; naive **8.** not dried, seasoned, or cured *[green* lumber*]* **9.** fresh; new **10.** flourishing, vigorous *[*to keep someone's memory *green]* **11.** [Colloq.] jealous —*n.* **1.** the color of growing grass; color between blue and yellow in the spectrum **2.** any green pigment or dye **3.** anything colored green, as clothing **4.** [*pl.*] green leaves, branches, etc., used for decoration **5.** [*pl.*] green leafy vegetables, as spinach, lettuce, turnip leaves, etc. **6.** an area of smooth, grassy ground set aside for special purposes *[a village green]* **7.** *Golf* a putting green —*vt., vi.* to make or become green —**the Green** Ireland's national color —**green′ish** *adj.* —**green′ly** *adv.* —**green′ness** *n.*

green algae any algae whose color is green because the chlorophyll is not hidden by other pigments

☆**green·back** (grēn′bak′) *n.* any piece of U.S. paper money printed in green ink on the back

Green Bay [transl. of Fr. *Baie Verte*, Green Bay, arm of Lake Michigan on which city is located] city in NE Wis.: pop. 88,000

☆**green bean** the immature green pod of any of several varieties of kidney bean, that is cooked and eaten as a vegetable

☆**green·bri·er** (-brī′ər) *n. same as* CAT BRIER

☆**green corn** young ears of sweet corn, in the milky stage, roasted or boiled for eating

green·er·y (grēn′ər ē) *n., pl.* **-er·ies 1.** green plants, shrubs, etc.; verdure **2.** greens: see GREEN (*n.* 4) **3.** a greenhouse

green-eyed (-īd′) *adj.* **1.** having green eyes **2.** very jealous

green·gage (-gāj′) *n.* [after Sir William *Gage*, who introduced it into England, c. 1725] a large plum with golden-green skin and flesh

green·gro·cer (-grō′sər) *n.* [Brit.] a retail dealer in fresh vegetables and fruit —**green′gro′cer·y** *n.*

green·horn (-hôrn′) *n.* [orig. with reference to a young animal with immature horns] an inexperienced person; beginner; novice

green·house (-hous′) *n.* a building made mainly of glass, with heat and humidity regulated for growing plants; hothouse

green·ing (-iŋ) *n.* ☆**1.** a becoming more mature and less naive, esp. in one's understanding of social and political forces **2.** any of various apples having greenish-yellow skins when ripe

Green·land (grēn′lənd) [< ON.: orig. so called to attract settlers] island of Denmark, northeast of N. America: the world's largest island: 840,000 sq. mi.

GREENHOUSE

☆**green light** [after the green ("go") signal of a traffic light] [Colloq.] permission or authorization to proceed with some undertaking: usually in **give** (or **get**) **the green light**

green manure 1. a crop of growing plants, as clover, plowed under while still green to fertilize the soil **2.** fresh manure

Green Mountains range of the Appalachians, extending the length of Vermont

green onion an immature onion with a long stalk and green leaves, eaten raw; scallion

☆**green pepper** the green, immature fruit of the sweet red pepper, eaten as a vegetable

☆**green revolution** the development of both new varieties of food plants and better agricultural methods, resulting in greatly increased crop yields, esp. in underdeveloped areas

Green River river flowing from W Wyo. south into the Colorado River in SE Utah

green·room (-rōōm′, -room′) *n.* a waiting room in some theaters, for use by performers when they are offstage

Greens·bor·o (grēnz′bʉr′ō) [after N. *Greene*, Am. general in Revolutionary War] city in north central N.C.: pop. 144,000

greens fee a fee paid to play golf on a golf course

☆**green snake** a small, harmless, greenish snake of N. America

green soap a soft soap made from potassium hydroxide and vegetable oils, with the glycerin left in: used in cleansing skin, treating skin diseases, etc.

green-stick fracture (grēn′stik′) a partial fracture in which the bone is broken on only one side

green·sward (-swôrd′) *n.* green, grassy ground

green tea tea prepared from leaves not fermented before drying

☆**green thumb** a special skill or talent for growing plants easily

green turtle a large, edible sea turtle with an olive-colored shell marked with yellow

Green·ville (grēn′vil) [see GREENSBORO] city in northwestern S.C.: pop. 61,000

Green·wich (mean) time (gren′ich; *chiefly Brit.* grin′ij) mean solar time of the prime meridian, which passes through Greenwich, a borough of London: used as the basis for standard time: see STANDARD TIME

Green·wich Village (gren′ich) section of New York City: noted as a center for artists, writers, etc.

green·wood (grēn′wood′) *n.* a forest in leaf

greet (grēt) *vt.* [OE. *gretan*] **1.** to address with polite or friendly words, as in meeting or by letter; hail; welcome **2.** to meet, receive, or acknowledge (a person, event, etc.) in a specified way *[she greeted* him with a kiss; the speech was *greeted* with boos*]* **3.** to come or appear to; meet *[a roaring sound greeted* his ears*]* —**greet′er** *n.*

greet·ing (grēt′iŋ) *n.* **1.** the act or words of a person who greets; salutation; welcome **2.** [*often pl.*] a message of regards from someone absent

greeting card a decorated card bearing a greeting for some occasion, as a birthday

gre·gar·i·ous (grə ger′ē əs) *adj.* [< L. < *grex* (gen. *gregis*), a flock: for IE. base see CRAM] **1.** living in herds or flocks **2.** fond of the company of others; sociable **3.** having to do with a herd, flock, or crowd **4.** *Bot.* growing in clusters —**gre·gar′i·ous·ly** *adv.* —**gre·gar′i·ous·ness** *n.*

Gre·go·ri·an (grə gôr′ē ən) *adj.* of or relating to Pope Gregory I or Pope Gregory XIII

Gregorian calendar a corrected form of the Julian calendar, introduced by Pope Gregory XIII in 1582 and now used in most countries of the world: it provides for an ordinary year of 365 days and a leap year of 366 days

Gregorian chant the kind of chant used in the Roman Catholic Church, introduced under Pope Gregory I: it is not accompanied by instruments

Greg·o·ry (greg′ər ē) [< LL. < Gr. *Grēgorios*, lit., vigilant, hence, watchman] **1.** a masculine name: dim. *Greg* **2. Gregory I,** Saint 540?–604 A.D.; Pope (590–604): called *the Great* **3. Gregory XIII** 1502–85; Pope (1572–85): see GREGORIAN CALENDAR

greige (grāzh) *n.* [Fr. *grège*, raw (silk)] a color blending gray and beige —*adj.* grayish-beige

grem·lin (grem′lən) *n.* [prob. < Dan. *græmling*, imp < obs. *gram*, a devil] an imaginary small creature humorously blamed for the faulty operation of airplanes or other disruptions

Gre·na·da (grə nā′də) **1.** southernmost island of the Windward group of the West Indies: 120 sq. mi. **2.** country consisting of this island and a nearby group: formerly a Brit. territory: 133 sq. mi.; pop. 95,000

gre·nade (grə nād′) *n.* [Fr. < OFr., pomegranate, ult. < L. *granatus*, having seeds < *granum*, GRAIN] **1.** a small bomb set off by a fuse and thrown by hand or fired from a rifle **2.** a glass container thrown to break when it hits something so that the chemicals inside it spread smoke, tear gas, etc.

gren·a·dier (gren′ə dir′) *n.* [Fr. < *grenade*] **1.** orig., an infantry soldier who threw grenades **2.** a member of a special regiment or corps, as the British Grenadier Guards

gren·a·dine¹ (gren′ə dēn′, gren′ə dēn′) *n.* [Fr. < *grenade*, pomegranate] a syrup made from pomegranate juice, used for flavoring drinks, etc.

gren·a·dine² (gren′ə dēn′, gren′ə dēn′) *n.* [Fr.] a thin, loosely woven cloth, used for dresses, etc.

Gre·no·ble (grə nō′b'l; *Fr.* grə nô′bl′) city in SE France, in the Alps: pop. 162,000

Gresh·am's law (gresh′əmz) [T. *Gresham*, 16th-c. Eng. financier, was once thought to have stated it] the principle that bad money will drive good money out of circulation because the good money tends to be hoarded

Gret·a (gret′ə, grēt′ə) [Sw. or G. *Grete*] a feminine name

Gretch·en (grech′n) [G.] a feminine name

Gret·na Green (gret′nə) **1.** border village in S Scotland, where, formerly, many eloping English couples went to be married **2.** any similar village

grew (grōō) *pt. of* GROW

grew·some (grōō′səm) *adj. same as* GRUESOME

grey (grā) *adj., n., vt., vi. Brit. sp. of* GRAY

Grey (grā) **1. Charles,** 2d Earl Grey, 1764-1845; Eng. statesman; prime minister (1830-34) **2. Sir Edward,** Viscount Grey of Fallodon, 1862-1933; Eng. statesman; foreign secretary (1905-16) **3. Lady Jane,** Lady Jane Dudley, 1537-54; queen of England (July 10-19, 1553): beheaded

grey·hound (grā′hound′) *n.* [OE. *grighund*] any of a breed of tall, slender, swift hound with a narrow, pointed head and a smooth coat

GREYHOUND (28 in. high at shoulder)

grid (grid) *n.* [short for GRIDIRON] **1.** a framework of parallel bars; gridiron; grating **2.** a network of crossing parallel lines, as on graph paper **3.** a metallic plate in a storage cell for conducting the electric current **4.** an electrode, usually a wire spiral or mesh, for controlling the passage of electrons or ions in an electron tube —☆*adj.* [Slang] of football

☆**grid·der** (grid′ər) *n.* [< GRID, *adj.* & GRIDIRON] [Slang] a football player

grid·dle (grid′'l) *n.* [< Anglo-Fr. *gridil* < OFr. *graïl* < L. < *craticula,* gridiron < *cratis:* see CRATE] a flat, metal plate or pan for cooking pancakes, etc. —*vt.* **-dled, -dling** to cook on a griddle

grid·dle·cake (-kāk′) *n. same as* PANCAKE (sense 1)

grid·i·ron (grid′ī′ərn) *n.* [ME. *gredirne,* folk etym. on *irne* (see IRON) < *gredire,* var. of *gredil:* see GRIDDLE] **1.** a framework of metal bars or wires on which to broil meat or fish; grill **2.** any framework resembling a gridiron ☆**3.** a football field

grief (grēf) *n.* [< OFr. < *grever:* see GRIEVE] **1.** deep and painful sorrow, as that caused by someone's death; great sadness **2.** a cause of such sorrow —see SYN. at SORROW —**come to grief** to fail or be ruined

grief-strick·en (grēf′strik′'n) *adj.* stricken with grief; keenly distressed; sorrowful

Grieg (grēg; *Norw.* grig), **Ed·vard (Hagerup)** (ed′värd; *Norw.* ed′värt) 1843-1907; Norw. composer

griev·ance (grē′vəns) *n.* **1.** a circumstance thought to be unjust or harmful and a basis for complaint or resentment **2.** complaint or resentment, or a statement expressing this, against a real or imagined wrong

grieve (grēv) *vt.* **grieved, griev′ing** [OFr. *grever* < L. *gravare,* to burden < *gravis:* see GRAVE[1]] to cause to feel grief; sadden or distress deeply —*vi.* to feel deep sorrow or distress; mourn; lament —**griev′er** *n.*

griev·ous (grē′vəs) *adj.* **1.** causing grief or deep sorrow [a *grievous* loss] **2.** showing or full of grief [a *grievous* cry] **3.** causing suffering; severe [*grievous* pain] **4.** very cruel or very bad; deplorable; atrocious [a *grievous* crime] —**griev′ous·ly** *adv.* —**griev′ous·ness** *n.*

grif·fin (grif′ən) *n.* [< OFr. < OHG. or It. *grifo,* both < L. *gryphus* < Gr. < *grypos,* hooked] a mythical animal, part eagle and part lion: also sp. **griffon**

Grif·fith (grif′ith) [W. *Gruffydd*] **1.** a masculine name **2. D(avid) (Lewelyn) W(ark)** 1875-1948; U.S. motion-picture director

☆**grift·er** (grif′tər) *n.* [prob. altered < *grafter*] [Slang] a petty swindler, as an operator of a dishonest gambling device at a carnival —**grift** *vi., vt., n.*

grill[1] (gril) *n.* [Fr. *gril* < OFr. *graïl:* see GRIDDLE] **1.** a gridiron (sense 1) **2.** a large griddle **3.** grilled food **4.** *short for* GRILLROOM —*vt.* **1.** to cook on a grill **2.** to torture by applying heat ☆**3.** to keep on questioning without stopping [the police *grilled* the suspect] —*vi.* to be subjected to grilling —**grilled** *adj.* —**grill′er** *n.*

grill[2] (gril) *n. same as* GRILLE

grille (gril) *n.* [Fr. < OFr. *graïlle:* see GRIDDLE] an open grating of wrought iron, wood, etc., forming a screen to a door, window, or other opening, or used as a divider —**grilled** *adj.*

GRIFFIN

grill·room (gril′rōōm′) *n.* a restaurant that makes a specialty of grilled foods

grill·work (-wurk′) *n.* a grille, or something worked into the form of a grille

grilse (grils) *n., pl.* **grilse, grils′es:** see PLURAL, II, D, 2 [<? OFr. dim. of *gris,* gray] a young salmon on its first return from the sea to fresh water

grim (grim) *adj.* **grim′mer, grim′mest** [OE. *grimm* < IE. base *ghrem-,* angry] **1.** fierce; cruel; savage [war is *grim*] **2.** hard and unyielding; relentless; stern [*grim* courage] **3.** appearing stern, forbidding, harsh, etc. [a *grim* face] **4.** frightful or shocking; ghastly [*grim* jokes about death] —see SYN. at GHASTLY —**grim′ly** *adv.* —**grim′ness** *n.*

gri·mace (gri mās′, grim′əs) *n.* [Fr. < OFr. *grimuche,* prob. < Frank.: for IE. base see CHRIST] a twisting of the face in fun or in a look of pain, disgust, etc. —*vi.* **-maced′, -mac′ing** to make grimaces —**gri·mac′er** *n.*

gri·mal·kin (gri mal′kin, -môl′-) *n.* [earlier *gray malkin* (cat)] **1.** a cat; esp., an old female cat **2.** a spiteful or harmful old woman

grime (grīm) *n.* [prob. < Fl. *grijm:* for IE. base see CHRIST] sooty dirt rubbed into or covering a surface, as of the skin —*vt.* **grimed, grim′ing** to make very dirty or grimy

Grimm (grim), **Ja·kob (Ludwig Karl)** (yä′kôp), 1785-1863 & **Wil·helm (Karl)** (vil′helm), 1786-1859; Ger. brothers who worked in language studies and together made a collection of fairy tales

grim·y (grī′mē) *adj.* **grim′i·er, grim′i·est** covered with grime; very dirty —**grim′i·ly** *adv.* —**grim′i·ness** *n.*

grin (grin) *vi.* **grinned, grin′ning** [OE. *grennian*] **1.** to smile broadly, as in amusement or embarrassment **2.** to draw back the lips and show the teeth in pain, scorn, etc. —*vt.* to express by grinning —*n.* the act or look of one who grins —**grin′ner** *n.*

grind (grīnd) *vt.* **ground, grind′ing** [OE. *grindan* < IE. base *ghren-*] **1.** to crush into bits or fine particles between two hard surfaces; pulverize **2.** to treat cruelly, harshly, etc.; oppress [a people *ground* by tyranny] **3.** to sharpen, shape, or smooth by friction [to *grind* a knife] **4.** to press down or rub together harshly or gratingly [to *grind* one's teeth] **5.** to work by turning the crank of [to *grind* a coffee mill] **6.** to produce as by grinding —*vi.* **1.** to perform the act of grinding something **2.** to undergo grinding **3.** to grate **4.** [Colloq.] to work or study hard and steadily —*n.* **1.** the act of grinding **2.** the degree of fineness of something ground into particles [we sell three *grinds* of coffee] **3.** long, difficult work or study ☆**4.** [Colloq.] a student who studies very hard —**grind out** to produce by steady effort in a way that seems mechanical or uninspired [to *grind out* a novel] —**grind′ing·ly** *adv.*

grind·er (grīn′dər) *n.* **1.** a person or thing that grinds; specif., *a)* any of various machines for crushing or sharpening *b)* a molar tooth *c)* [*pl.*] [Colloq.] the teeth ☆**2.** *same as* HERO SANDWICH

grind·stone (grīnd′stōn′) *n.* a revolving stone disk for sharpening tools or shaping and polishing things —**keep (or have or put) one's nose to the grindstone** to work hard and steadily

☆**grin·go** (griŋ′gō) *n., pl.* **-gos** [MexSp. < Sp., gibberish] among Spanish-Americans, a foreigner, esp. an American or Englishman: an unfriendly term

grip (grip) *n.* [< OE. *gripa,* handful < *gripan:* see GRIPE] **1.** a secure grasp; firm hold, as with the hand, teeth, etc. **2.** any special manner of clasping hands, as between members of a secret society **3.** the power of grasping firmly [to lose one's *grip*] **4.** the power of understanding; mental grasp [to have a good *grip* on a matter] **5.** firm control; mastery [in the *grip* of a disease; to get a *grip* on oneself] **6.** a mechanical contrivance for clutching or grasping **7.** the part by which something is grasped; handle ☆**8.** a small traveling bag or satchel **9.** *Sports* the manner of holding a bat, golf club, etc. —*vt.* **gripped** or **gript, grip′ping 1.** to take firmly and hold fast with the hand, teeth, etc. **2.** to give a grip (*n.* 2) to **3.** to fasten or join firmly (*to*) **4.** to get and hold the attention of, or to have a strong emotional effect on [the tale of terror *gripped* them] —*vi.* to get a grip —**come to grips** to struggle or try to deal (*with*) —**grip′per** *n.*

gripe (grīp) *vt.* **griped, grip′ing** [OE. *gripan,* to seize < IE. base *ghreib-,* to seize] **1.** formerly, *a)* to grasp; clutch *b)* to distress; afflict **2.** to cause sudden, sharp pain in the bowels of ☆**3.** [Slang] to annoy; irritate —*vi.* **1.** to feel sharp pains in the bowels ☆**2.** [Slang] to complain —*n.* **1.** distress; affliction **2.** a sudden, sharp pain in the bowels: *usually used in pl.* ☆**3.** [Slang] a complaint **4.** [Archaic] *a)* a grasping *b)* control — **grip′er** *n.*

grippe (grip) *n.* [Fr., lit., a seizure < *gripper* < Frank.] *earlier term for* INFLUENZA

☆**grip·sack** (grip′sak′) *n. earlier term for* GRIP (*n.* 8)

gript (gript) *alt. pt. & pp. of* GRIP

Gri·sel·da (gri zel′də, -sel′-) a heroine in old tales, famous for her patience

gri·sette (gri zet′) *n.* [Fr., orig., gray woolen dress cloth < *gris*, gray] a French working girl

gris·ly (griz′lē) *adj.* **-li·er, -li·est** [OE. *grislic:* for IE. base see CHRIST] very frightening; horrible; ghastly —see SYN. at GHASTLY —**gris′li·ness** *n.*

grist (grist) *n.* [OE.] grain that is to be or has been ground; esp., a batch of such grain —**grist to** (or **for**) **one's mill** anything one can use profitably

gris·tle (gris′'l) *n.* [OE.] cartilage, now esp. as found in meat —**gris′tli·ness** *n.* —**gris·tly** (gris′lē) *adj.*

grist·mill (grist′mil′) *n.* a mill for grinding grain, esp. for individual customers

grit (grit) *n.* [OE. *greot:* see CHROMATIC] **1.** rough, hard particles of sand, stone, etc. **2.** a sandstone with sharp grains ☆**3.** stubborn courage; pluck —*vt.* **grit′ted, grit′ting** to grind (the teeth) in anger or determination —*vi.* to make a grating sound

☆**grits** (grits) *n.pl.* [< OE. *grytte*] wheat or corn coarsely ground; esp., [South] fine hominy

grit·ty (grit′ē) *adj.* **-ti·er, -ti·est** **1.** of, like, or containing grit; sandy **2.** brave; plucky —**grit′ti·ly** *adv.* —**grit′ti·ness** *n.*

griz·zle (griz′'l) *n.* [< OFr. < *gris*, gray] **1.** [Archaic] gray hair **2.** gray —*vt., vi.* **-zled, -zling** to make or become gray —*adj.* [Archaic] gray

griz·zled (griz′'ld) *adj.* **1.** gray or streaked with gray [a *grizzled* beard] **2.** having gray hair [a *grizzled* head]

griz·zly (-lē) *adj.* **-zli·er, -zli·est** grayish; grizzled —*n., pl.* **-zlies** *short for* GRIZZLY BEAR

grizzly bear a large, fierce bear of western N. America, with brown, gray, or yellow fur

groan (grōn) *vi.* [OE. *granian*] **1.** to utter a deep sound expressing pain, distress, or disapproval [we *groaned* when our team lost] **2.** to make a creaking sound, as from great strain [the heavy gate *groaned* on its hinges] **3.** to be so weighed down as to groan [the table *groaned* with food] —*vt.* to utter with a groan or groans —*n.* a sound made in groaning —**groan′er** *n.* —**groan′ing·ly** *adv.*

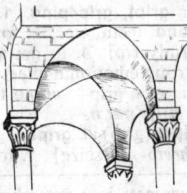

GRIZZLY BEAR
(to 3½ ft. high
at shoulder)

groat (grōt) *n.* [< MDu. or < MLowG. *grote*] **1.** an obsolete English silver coin worth fourpence **2.** a trifling sum

groats (grōts) *n.pl.* [< OE. *grotan*, pl.: for IE. base see CHROMATIC] any grain that is hulled, or hulled and coarsely cracked, esp. wheat, buckwheat, oats, or barley

gro·cer (grō′sər) *n.* [< OFr. *grossier* < *gros*, GROSS] a storekeeper who sells food and various household supplies

gro·cer·y (grō′sər ē) *n., pl.* **-cer·ies** ☆**1.** a grocer's store **2.** [*pl.*] the food and supplies sold by a grocer

grog (gräg) *n.* [after *Old Grog*, nickname of E. Vernon (1684–1757), Brit. admiral] any alcoholic liquor, as rum, esp. when diluted with water

grog·gy (gräg′ē) *adj.* **-gi·er, -gi·est** [< GROG + -Y²] **1.** orig., drunk; intoxicated **2.** shaky or dizzy, as from a blow, lack of sleep, etc. —**grog′gi·ly** *adv.* —**grog′gi·ness** *n.*

groin (groin) *n.* [prob. < OE. *grynde*, abyss] **1.** the hollow or fold where the leg joins the body in front **2.** *Archit.* the sharp, curved edge where two intersecting vaults meet, or the rib covering it —*vt.* to build with a groin

☆**grok** (gräk) *vt., vi.* **grokked, grok′·king** [coined 1961 by R. A. Heinlein] [Slang] to understand thoroughly because of being able to share in another's feelings (with *with*)

grom·met (gräm′it, grum′-) *n.* [< obs. Fr. *gromette*, a curb] **1.** a ring of rope or metal used to fasten

GROIN

edge of a sail to its stay, hold an oar in place, etc. **2.** an eyelet of metal, plastic, etc.

Gro·ning·en (grō′niŋ ən; *Du.* khrō′niŋ ən) city in the N Netherlands: pop. 157,000

groom (grōōm, grŏŏm) *n.* [ME. *grom*, boy < ?] **1.** a man or boy whose work is taking care of horses **2.** any of various officials of the British royal household **3.** *same as* BRIDEGROOM **4.** [Archaic] a manservant —*vt.* **1.** to clean and curry (a horse, dog, etc.) **2.** to make neat and tidy [to *groom* one's hair] ☆**3.** to train or develop for a particular purpose [to *groom* a man for political office]

grooms·man (grōōmz′mən, grŏŏmz′-) *n., pl.* **-men** a man who attends a bridegroom at the wedding

groove (grōōv) *n.* [< ON. *grof*, a pit: for IE. base see GRAVE²] **1.** a long, narrow hollow or furrow cut in a surface with a tool **2.** any channel or rut cut or worn in a surface **3.** a regular way of doing something, as by habit; settled routine ☆**4.** [Slang] an exciting or stimulating person, place, experience, etc. —*vt.* **grooved, groov′ing** to make a groove or grooves in —*vi.* ☆[Slang] to have understanding, appreciation, enjoyment, etc. in a relaxed, unthinking way (usually with *on* or *with*) —**in the groove** [Old Slang] performing or performed with smooth, effortless skill: orig. of jazz

☆**groov·y** (grōōv′ē) *adj.* **groov′i·er, groov′i·est** [< phrase *in the groove:* see prec.] [Slang] very pleasing or attractive

grope (grōp) *vi.* **groped, grop′ing** [OE. *grapian*, to seize: for IE. base see GRIPE] to feel or search about blindly or uncertainly [to *grope* for the keys in one's pocket; to *grope* for knowledge] —*vt.* to seek or find (one's way) by groping —*n.* an act or instance of groping —**grop′er** *n.* —**grop′ing·ly** *adv.*

Gro·pi·us (grō′pē əs), **Walter** 1883–1969; Ger. architect, in the U.S. after 1937

gros·beak (grōs′bēk′) *n.* [< Fr.: see GROSS & BEAK] any of various finchlike birds, with a thick, strong, cone-shaped bill

gro·schen (grō′shən) *n., pl.* **-schen** [G., ult. < ML. (*denarius*) *grossus*, lit., thick (denarius)] *see* MONETARY UNITS, table (Austria)

gros·grain (grō′grān′) *n.* [Fr. < OFr. *gros*, coarse + *grain*, GRAIN] a closely woven silk or rayon fabric with crosswise ribbing, used for ribbons, etc.

gross (grōs) *adj.* [< OFr. < LL. *grossus*, thick] **1.** big or fat and coarse-looking; corpulent [*gross* features] **2.** very bad; glaring [a *gross* error; a *gross* lie] **3.** dense; thick [*gross* underbrush] **4.** *a)* lacking fineness, as in texture *b)* lacking specific details [*gross* anatomy] **5.** insensitive or unrefined [too *gross* to appreciate art] **6.** vulgar; obscene [*gross* language] **7.** total; entire; with no deductions: opposed to NET² [*gross* income] —*n.* **1.** *pl.* **gross′es** overall total, as of income, before deductions **2.** *pl.* **gross** twelve dozen —*vt., vi.* [Colloq.] to earn (a specified total amount) before expenses are deducted —see SYN. at COARSE and FLAGRANT —**in the gross 1.** in bulk; as a whole **2.** wholesale: also **by the gross** —**gross′ly** *adv.* —**gross′ness** *n.*

gross national product the total value of a nation's annual output of goods and services

gross ton a unit of weight, equal to 2,240 pounds

gross weight the total weight of something sold, including the packaging or container

grosz (grōsh) *n., pl.* **grosz′y** (-ē) [Pol.] *see* MONETARY UNITS, table (Poland)

gro·tesque (grō tesk′) *adj.* [Fr. < It. < *grotta*, a grotto: from designs in Roman caves] **1.** in or of a style of painting, sculpture, etc. in which forms of persons and animals are mixed with leaves, flowers, etc. in a fantastic or bizarre design **2.** having a twisted, strange, unreal appearance, shape, etc.; bizarre [his injured face had *grotesque* features] **3.** so strange, twisted, different, etc. as to be funny; absurd [people often have *grotesque* adventures in their dreams] —*n.* **1.** a grotesque painting, sculpture, design, etc. **2.** a grotesque thing or quality —see SYN. at FANTASTIC —**gro·tesque′ly** *adv.* —**gro·tesque′ness** *n.*

Gro·ti·us (grō′shē əs), **Hugo** (born *Huig de Groot*) 1583–1645; Du. scholar, statesman, & writer on international law

grot·to (grät′ō) *n., pl.* **-toes, -tos** [< It. < ML. *grupta* < VL. *L. crypta*, crypt] **1.** a cave **2.** any shaded or sheltered summerhouse, shrine, etc. that is like a cave

☆**grouch** (grouch) *vi.* [< ME. *grucchen:* see GRUDGE] to grumble or complain in a sulky way —*n.* **1.** a person who grouches continually **2.** a grumbling or sulky mood **3.** a complaint

☆**grouch·y** (grou′chē) *adj.* **grouch′i·er, grouch′i·est** in a grouch; grumbling —**grouch′i·ly** *adv.* —**grouch′i·ness** *n.*

ground¹ (ground) *n.* [OE. *grund*, bottom: for IE. base see GRIND] **1.** *a)* orig., the lowest part or bottom of anything *b)* the bottom of a body of water **2.** the solid surface of the earth **3.** the soil of the earth; earth; land **4.** *a)* a particular piece of land [a hunting *ground*] *b)* [pl.] land surrounding or attached to a building; esp., the lawns, gardens, etc. of an estate **5.** any subject or topic of discussion, etc. [arguments covering the same *ground*] **6.** [often pl.] basis; foundation **7.** [often pl.] the logical basis of a conclusion, action, etc.; valid reason or cause [he hasn't much *ground* for complaint; on what *grounds* are you refusing?] **8.** the underlying surface or background of a painting, colored pattern, etc. **9.** [pl.] the particles that settle to the bottom of a liquid; dregs [coffee *grounds*] **10.** *Elec.* the connection of an electrical conductor with the ground —*adj.* **1.** of, on, or near the ground; growing or living in or on the ground —*vt.* **1.** to set on the ground or cause to touch the ground **2.** to cause (a ship, etc.) to run aground **3.** to found on a firm basis; establish **4.** to base (a claim, argument, etc.) on something specified **5.** to give good, sound training to (a person) in a subject [to *ground* students in science] **6.** to provide with a background **7.** to keep (an aircraft or pilot) from flying **8.** *Elec.* to connect (a conductor) with the ground —*vi.* **1.** to strike the bottom or run ashore: said of a ship ☆**2.** *Baseball a)* to hit a grounder *b)* to be put out on a grounder (usually with *out*) —**break ground 1.** to dig; excavate **2.** to plow **3.** to start any undertaking —**cover ground 1.** to move or go over a certain distance **2.** to make a certain amount of progress —**cut the ground from under one** (or **one's feet**) to deprive one of effective defense or argument —☆**from the ground up** completely; thoroughly —**gain ground 1.** to move forward **2.** to make progress **3.** to gain in strength, popularity, etc. —☆**get off the ground** to get (something) started; begin to make progress —**give ground** to withdraw under attack; yield —**hold** (or **stand**) **one's ground** to keep one's position against attack or opposition; not withdraw or retreat —**lose ground 1.** to drop back; fall behind **2.** to lose in strength, popularity, etc. —☆**run into the ground** [Colloq.] to do too long or too often; overdo —**shift one's ground** to change one's argument or defense

ground² (ground) *pt. & pp.* of GRIND

ground ball *same as* GROUNDER

ground control personnel, electronic equipment, etc. on the ground for guiding aircraft or spacecraft in takeoff, flight, and landing operations

ground cover any of various low, dense-growing plants, as ivy, myrtle, etc., used instead of grass for covering the ground

ground crew a group of people in charge of the maintenance and repair of aircraft

ground·er (groun′dər) *n. Baseball*, etc. a batted ball that strikes the ground almost immediately and rolls or bounces along

ground floor that floor of a building which is on or near the ground level; first floor —☆**in on the ground floor** [Colloq.] in at the beginning of an enterprise and thus having an advantage over those who come in later

ground glass 1. glass whose surface has been ground so that it spreads out light and is not transparent **2.** glass ground into fine particles

☆**ground·hog** (ground′hôg′, -häg′) *n.* [prob. transl. of Du. *aardvark*, AARDVARK] *same as* WOODCHUCK: also **ground hog**

☆**Groundhog Day** February 2, when, according to legend, if the groundhog sees his shadow, he returns to his hole for six more weeks of winter weather

ground·less (ground′lis) *adj.* without reason or cause — **ground′less·ly** *adv.* —**ground′less·ness** *n.*

ground·ling (-liŋ) *n.* **1.** *a)* a fish that lives close to the bottom of the water *b)* an animal that lives on or in the ground *c)* a plant that grows close to the ground **2.** [orig. of spectators in a theater pit] a person lacking careful judgment or good taste

ground·nut (-nut′) *n.* **1.** any of various plants with edible tubers or tuberlike parts, as the peanut **2.** the edible tuber or tuberlike part

ground plan 1. *same as* FLOOR PLAN **2.** a first or basic plan

☆**ground rule 1.** *Baseball* any of a set of rules made up to suit the playing conditions in a specific ballpark **2.** any of a set of rules governing a specific activity

ground·sel (ground′s'l, groun′-) *n.* [< OE., ? < *gund*, pus + *swelgan*, to swallow: from use in poultices] any of a group of plants of the composite family, with flowers that are usually yellow

ground·sill (ground′sil) *n.* the bottom horizontal timber in a framework: also **ground′sel** (-s'l)

grounds·keep·er (groundz′kē′pər) *n.* a person who tends the grounds of a playing field, estate, cemetery, etc.: also **ground′keep′er**

ground·speed (ground′spēd′) *n.* the speed of an aircraft in flight in relation to the ground it passes over

☆**ground squirrel** any of various small, burrowing animals related to tree squirrels and chipmunks

ground·swell (ground′swel′) *n.* **1.** a violent swelling or rolling of the ocean, caused by a distant storm or earthquake **2.** a rapidly growing wave of public opinion, etc.

ground water water found underground in porous rock strata and soils, as in a spring

☆**ground wire** a wire acting as a conductor from an electric circuit, antenna, etc. to the ground

ground·work (-wurk′) *n.* a foundation; basis —see SYN. at BASE¹

☆**ground zero** the surface area directly below or above the point where a nuclear bomb is set off

group (grōōp) *n.* [< Fr. < It. *gruppo*] **1.** a number of persons or things gathered together and forming a unit; cluster; band [a *group* of houses] **2.** a collection of objects or figures forming a design, as in a work of art **3.** a number of persons or things classified together because they are alike in certain ways or have common interests, etc. [the woodwind *group* of instruments] **4.** *Chem. a) same as* RADICAL *b)* a number of elements with similar properties, forming one of the vertical columns of the periodic table ☆**5.** *Math.* a collection of elements with an associative rule for combination of elements in which the product of any two elements is in the set, every element in the set has an inverse, and a unit (or identity) element is contained in the set ☆**6.** *U.S. Air Force* a unit under the command of a colonel ☆**7.** *U.S. Mil.* a unit made up of two or more battalions or squadrons —*vt., vi.* to form into a group or groups —*adj.* of or involving a group

SYN.—**group** is the basic, general word expressing the simple idea of an assembly of persons, animals, or things without any added meaning; **herd** is applied to a group of cattle, sheep, or similar large animals feeding, living, or moving together; **flock**, to goats, sheep, or birds; **drove**, to cattle, hogs, or sheep; **pack**, to hounds or wolves; **pride**, to lions; **swarm**, to insects; **school**, to fish, porpoises, whales, etc.; **bevy**, to quails; **covey**, to partridges or quails; **flight**, to birds flying together In extended use, **flock** connotes guidance and care, **herd**, **drove**, and **pack** are used as terms of contempt for people, **swarm** suggests a large mass or throng moving together, and **bevy** and **covey** are used of girls or women

group·er (grōōp′ər) *n., pl.* **-ers, -er:** see PLURAL, II, D, 1 [Port. *garoupa*] any of several large fishes found in warm seas

☆**group insurance** life or health insurance available to employees or members of an organization as a group at special, low rates

☆**group medicine 1.** the practice of medicine by a group of specialists working together **2.** medical care provided by such a group of specialists to a group of people who pay a fixed, yearly fee for such care

group therapy (or **psychotherapy**) a form of treatment for a group of patients with similar emotional problems or disorders, as by mutual criticism, usually under a therapist's supervision

group work social work in which the worker helps individuals develop and grow through cultural and recreational group activities —**group worker**

grouse¹ (grous) *n., pl.* **grouse** [Early ModE. < ?] any of a number of game birds with a round, plump body, as the ruffed grouse, sage hen, etc.

grouse² (grous) *vi.* **groused, grous′-ing** [orig. Brit. army slang < ?] [Colloq.] to complain; grumble —*n.* [Colloq.] a complaint —**grous′er** *n.*

grout (grout) *n.* [OE. *grut*] **1.** a thin mortar used to fill chinks or cracks, as between tiles **2.** a fine plaster for finishing surfaces —*vt.* to fill or finish with or as with grout —**grout′er** *n.*

grove (grōv) *n.* [< OE. *graf*] **1.** a small wood or group of trees without undergrowth **2.** a group of trees planted to bear fruit, nuts, etc.

RUFFED GROUSE
(wingspread to 25 in.)

grov·el (gruv''l, gräv'-) *vi.* **-eled** or **-elled**, **-el·ing** or **-el·ling** [< earlier *grovelling, adv.*, face downward < ON.] **1.** to lie or crawl on the ground with the face down, esp. as a way of humbling oneself before someone one fears **2.** to behave in a very humble or cringing way **3.** to wallow in what is low, worthless, or filthy —**grov'el·er**, **grov'el·ler** *n.*

grow (grō) *vi.* **grew**, **grown**, **grow'ing** [OE. *growan*: for IE. base see GRASS] **1.** to come into being or be produced naturally; spring up [oaks *grow* from acorns] **2.** to exist as living vegetation; thrive [cactus *grows* in sand] **3.** to increase in size and develop toward maturity, as a plant or animal does by taking in and using food [the boy has *grown* two inches taller] **4.** to increase in size, quantity, or degree [to *grow* in wisdom] **5.** to come to be; become [to *grow* weary] **6.** to become attached or united by growth —*vt.* **1.** to cause to grow; raise; cultivate [he *grew* corn on his land] **2.** to cover with a growth: used in the passive [the yard was *grown* over with weeds] **3.** to allow to grow [to *grow* a beard] **4.** to cause to be or to exist; develop — **grow into 1.** to develop so as to be [a boy *grows into* a man] **2.** to grow or develop so as to be fit or suited [he *grew into* his job] —**grow on** to become gradually more acceptable, likable, etc. to [she's a person that *grows on* one] —**grow out of 1.** to develop from **2.** to outgrow —**grow up** to reach maturity; become adult —**grow'er** *n.*

growing pains 1. pains that occur from time to time in the joints and muscles of growing children: a loose term without exact medical meaning **2.** difficulties in the early development of something, as a business

growl (groul) *vi.* [< ? OFr. < MDu. *grollen*, to be noisy] **1.** to make a low, rumbling, menacing sound in the throat, as a dog does **2.** to complain angrily —*vt.* to express by growling —*n.* the act or sound of growling —**growl'er** *n.* —**growl'ing·ly** *adv.*

grown (grōn) *pp.* of GROW —*adj.* **1.** having completed its growth; mature [a *grown* man] **2.** covered with a growth **3.** cultivated as specified [home-*grown*]

grown-up (grōn'up'; *for n.* -up') *adj.* **1.** adult **2.** of or for adults —*n.* an adult: also **grown'up'**

growth (grōth) *n.* **1.** a growing or developing **2.** degree or extent of increase in size, weight, power, etc. [a *growth* of two inches] **3.** something that grows or has grown [a thick *growth* of grass] **4.** an outgrowth or offshoot **5.** a tumor or other abnormal mass of tissue in or on the body

grub (grub) *vi.* **grubbed**, **grub'bing** [ME. *grubben*] **1.** to dig in the ground **2.** to work hard, esp. at boring jobs; drudge —*vt.* **1.** to clear (ground) of roots and stumps by digging them up **2.** to dig up as by the roots; uproot —*n.* **1.** the short, fat, wormlike larva of an insect, esp. of a beetle **2.** a person who works hard at some boring work; drudge **3.** [Slang] food — **grub'ber** *n.*

grub·by (grub'ē) *adj.* **-bi·er**, **-bi·est 1.** infested with grubs **2.** dirty; messy; untidy **3.** inferior, mean, etc. —**grub'bi·ly** *adv.* —**grub'bi·ness** *n.*

☆**grub·stake** (-stāk') *n.* [GRUB, *n.* 3 + STAKE] [Colloq.] **1.** money or supplies loaned to a prospector in return for a share in his findings **2.** money provided for any undertaking —*vt.* [Colloq.] **-staked'**, **-stak'ing** to provide with a grubstake —**grub'stak'er** *n.*

grudge (gruj) *vt.* **grudged**, **grudg'ing** [OFr. *grouchier*] **1.** to envy (someone) because of something he has; begrudge [to *grudge* a person his success] **2.** to give unwillingly [the miser *grudged* his dog its food] —*n.* a strong feeling of hostility or ill will against someone because of something he has done — **grudg'er** *n.* —**grudg'ing·ly** *adv.*

gru·el (grōō'əl, grōōl) *n.* [OFr., coarse meal] thin, easily digested broth made by cooking meal in water or milk

gru·el·ing, **gru·el·ling** (-iŋ) *adj.* [prp. of obs. v. *gruel*, to punish] very tiring; exhausting

grue·some (grōō'səm) *adj.* [< dial. *grue*, to shudder + -SOME] causing horror or disgust; grisly —see SYN. at GHASTLY —**grue'some·ly** *adv.* —**grue'some·ness** *n.*

gruff (gruf) *adj.* [< Early ModDu. *grof*] **1.** rough or unfriendly in manner or speech; rude [a *gruff* reply] **2.** harsh and throaty; hoarse [*gruff* voices] —see SYN. at BLUNT —**gruff'ly** *adv.* —**gruff'ness** *n.*

grum·ble (grum'b'l) *vi.* **-bled**, **-bling** [prob. < Du. *grommelen*: for IE. base see GRIM] **1.** to make low sounds in the throat that cannot be understood **2.** to mutter or complain in an angry way [the soldiers *grumbled* about the food] **3.** to rumble, as thunder —*vt.* to express by grumbling —*n.* **1.** a grumbling, esp. in complaint **2.** a rumble —**grum'bler** *n.* —**grum'bling·ly** *adv.* —**grum'bly** *adj.*

grump (grump) *n.* [prob. echoic] **1.** [*often pl.*] a fit of bad humor **2.** a grumpy person —*vi.* to complain and grumble

grump·y (grum'pē) *adj.* **grump'i·er**, **grump'i·est** [GRUMP + -Y²] grouchy; peevish; bad-tempered: also **grump'ish** — **grump'i·ly** *adv.* —**grump'i·ness** *n.*

Grun·dy, Mrs. (grun'dē) [a prudish busybody referred to in an 18th-c. play] an imaginary person thought of as being prudish, narrow-minded, faultfinding, etc. —**Grun'dy·ism** *n.*

☆**grun·ion** (grun'yən) *n., pl.* **-ion**, **-ions**: see PLURAL, II, D, 2 [prob. < Sp.] a sardine-shaped fish of the California coast

grunt (grunt) *vi.* [OE. *grunnettan* < *grunian*, to grunt] **1.** to make the short, deep, hoarse sound of a hog **2.** to make a sound like this, as in annoyance —*vt.* to express by grunting —*n.* **1.** the sound of grunting **2.** a saltwater fish that grunts when removed from water ☆**3.** [Slang] a U.S. infantryman in Vietnam —**grunt'er** *n.*

Gru·yère (cheese) (grōō yer', grē-) [< *Gruyère*, Switzerland] a light-yellow Swiss cheese, rich in butterfat, or an American cheese like this

gr. wt. gross weight

gryph·on (grif'ən) *n. same as* GRIFFIN

G.S., g.s. 1. general secretary **2.** ground speed

GSA, G.S.A. 1. General Services Administration **2.** Girl Scouts of America

☆**G-string** (jē'striŋ') *n.* **1.** a narrow loincloth **2.** a similar band, worn by striptease dancers

☆**G-suit** (-sōōt') *n.* [G for *gravity*] a garment for pilots or astronauts, pressurized to counteract the effects of rapid acceleration or deceleration

GT gross ton

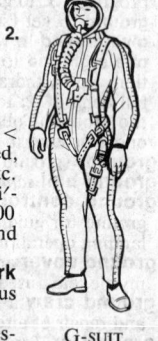

gt. 1. [L. *gutta*] *pl.* **gtt.** Pharmacy a drop **2.** great

Gt. Brit., Gt. Br. Great Britain

gtd. guaranteed

GU, g.u. genitourinary

☆**gua·ca·mo·le** (gwä'kə mō'lä) *n.* [AmSp. < Nahuatl] a thick sauce or paste of seasoned, puréed avocados, served as a dip, in salads, etc.

Gua·da·la·ja·ra (gwä'd'l ə här'ə; *Sp.* gwä'thä lä hä'rä) city in W Mexico: pop. 1,196,000

Gua·dal·ca·nal (gwä'd'l kə nal') Brit. island in the Solomon Islands, SW Pacific

Gua·da·lupe Mountains National Park (gwä'də lōōp') national park in a mountainous region of W Tex.

Gua·de·loupe (gwä'də lōōp') French possession consisting of two large islands and five smaller ones in the Leeward group of the West Indies

G-SUIT

guai·a·cum (gwī'ə kəm) *n.* [ModL. < genus name] **1.** *a)* any of several tropical American trees with purplish flowers and hard, strong wood *b)* this wood **2.** a greenish-brown resin from certain of these trees, used in medicine, in varnishes, etc.

Guam (gwäm) largest of the Mariana Islands, in the W Pacific: a possession of the U.S.: 209 sq. mi.; pop. 87,000; cap. Agaña

gua·na·co (gwə nä'kō) *n., pl.* **-cos**, **-co**: see PLURAL, II, D, 1 [Sp. < Quechua *huanacu*] a woolly, reddish-brown, wild animal of the Andes, related to the camel and llama

gua·nine (gwä'nēn) *n.* [< GUANO + -INE⁴] an organic base, $C_5H_5N_5O$, that is in deoxyribonucleic acid and is found in all plant and animal tissues

gua·no (gwä'nō) *n., pl.* **-nos** [Sp. < Quechua *huanu*, dung] **1.** the manure of sea birds, found especially on islands off the coast of Peru: it is used as a fertilizer **2.** any fertilizer resembling this

GUANACO
(4 ft. high at shoulder)

guar. guaranteed

Gua·ra·ní (gwä'rä nē') *n.* [*Guaraní*, lit., warrior] **1.** *pl.* **-nís'**, **-ní'** a member of a tribe of S. American Indians who lived east of the Paraguay River **2.** their language **3.** [g-] *pl.* **-nís'** *see* MONETARY UNITS, table (Paraguay)

guar·an·tee (gar'ən tē', gär'-) *n.* [altered < GUARANTY] **1.** *same as* GUARANTY (*n.* 1 & 3) **2.** *a)* a pledge that something will be replaced if it is not as represented [a thirty-day *guarantee* on the clock] *b)* a promise or assurance that something will be done in the manner specified [the landlord's *guarantee* to make repairs] **3.** a person who gives a guarantee; guarantor **4.** a person who receives a guaranty **5.** something that promises the happening of some event [the dark clouds were a *guarantee* of rain] —*vt.* **-teed'**, **-tee'ing** **1.** to give a guarantee or guaranty for **2.** to promise [I *guarantee* to be there]

guar·an·tor (gar'ən tôr', -tər; gär'-) *n.* one who makes or gives a guaranty or guarantee

guar·an·ty (-tē) *n., pl.* **-ties** [< OFr. < *garant*, a warrant < Frank.] **1.** a pledge by which a person promises to pay another's debt or fulfill another's obligation if the other fails to do so **2.** an agreement that makes the existence or maintenance of something sure or certain **3.** something given or held as security **4.** a guarantor —*vt.* **-tied**, **-ty·ing** same as GUARANTEE

guard (gärd) *vt.* [< the *n.*] **1.** to watch over and protect; defend; shield [*shepherds guard* their flocks by night] **2.** *a)* to keep from escape or trouble [two sentries *guarded* the prisoners] *b)* to hold in check; control; restrain [*guard* your talk in front of children] *Sports* to keep (an opponent) from making a gain or scoring; also, to cover (a goal or area) in defensive play —*vi.* **1.** to keep watch (*against*) [lock the door to *guard* against prowlers] **2.** to act as a guard —*n.* [< OFr. < *garder*, to protect < Gmc. < IE. base *wer-*, to take heed] **1.** the act or duty of guarding; defense; protection [keep a *guard* against strangers] **2.** a posture of defense, as in boxing, fencing, etc. **3.** any device that protects against injury or loss [the *guard* on a bracelet keeps it from falling off] **4.** a person or group that guards; specif., *a)* a sentinel or sentry *b)* a railway brakeman or gateman *c)* a person who guards prisoners *d)* [*pl.*] a special unit of troops assigned to the British royal household *e)* a military unit with a ceremonial function [a color *guard*] ☆**5.** *Basketball* either of the two players whose function is to set up offensive plays ☆**6.** *Football* either of two players on offense, left and right of the center —see SYN. at DEFEND —**mount guard** to go on sentry duty —**off (one's) guard** not alert for protection or defense —**on (one's) guard** alert for protection or defense —**stand guard** to do sentry duty —**guard'er** *n.*

guard·ed (-id) *adj.* **1.** kept safe; watched over and protected; defended **2.** kept from escape or trouble; held in check; supervised **3.** cautious; careful [a *guarded* reply] —**guard'ed·ly** *adv.* —**guard'ed·ness** *n.*

guard·house (-hous') *n. Mil.* **1.** a building used by the members of a guard when not on duty **2.** a building where personnel are confined for minor offenses or while awaiting court-martial

guard·i·an (-ē ən) *n.* **1.** a person who guards or takes care of another person, property, etc. **2.** a person legally placed in charge of the affairs of a minor or of someone incapable of managing his own affairs —*adj.* protecting —**guard'i·an·ship'** *n.*

guard·rail (-rāl') *n.* a protective railing, as along a highway

guard·room (-rōōm') *n. Mil.* a room used by the members of a guard when not on duty

guards·man (gärdz'mən) *n., pl.* **-men** a member of any military body called a "guard"; specif., ☆a member of a National Guard

Gua·te·ma·la (gwä'tə mä'lə) **1.** country in Central America, south & east of Mexico: 42,042 sq. mi.; pop. 5,014,000 **2.** its capital: pop. 769,000: also **Guatemala City** —**Gua'te·ma'lan** *adj., n.*

gua·va (gwä'və) *n.* [Sp. *guayaba* < native name in Brazil] **1.** any of several tropical American plants of the myrtle family, esp. a tree bearing a yellowish, pear-shaped fruit **2.** the fruit, used for jelly, preserves, etc.

Guay·a·quil (gwī'ä kēl') seaport in W Ecuador: pop. 680,000

Guay·na·bo (gwī nä'bō, -vō) city in NE Puerto Rico, near San Juan: pop. 54,000

☆**gua·yu·le** (gwä yōō'lē) *n.* [AmSp. < Nahuatl *quauhitl*, plant + *olli*, gum] **1.** a small shrub of the composite family, grown in northern Mexico, Texas, etc. **2.** rubber (**guayule rubber**) obtained from it

gu·ber·na·to·ri·al (gōō'bər nə tôr'ē əl) *adj.* [L. *gubernator*, governor < *gubernare*, to steer] of a governor or his office

☆**guck** (guk) *n.* [< ? G(OO) + (M)UCK] [Slang] any thick, viscous, sticky or slimy substance

gudg·eon (guj'ən) *n.* [< OFr. < L. *gobio* < Gr. *kōbios*] **1.** a small, European freshwater fish, easily caught, and used for bait **2.** a goby or killifish **3.** a person easily cheated or tricked; dupe —*vt.* to cheat; trick; dupe

Guelph¹, Guelf (gwelf) *n.* any member of a political party in medieval Italy supporting the Pope

Guelph² (gwelf) city in SE Ontario, Canada: pop. 51,000

guer·don (gur'd'n) *n., vt.* [< OFr., ult. < OHG. *widar*, back + *lōn*, reward] [Archaic] reward

Guern·sey (gurn'zē) one of the Channel Islands —*n., pl.* **-seys** **1.** any of a breed of dairy cattle, originally from this island, usually fawn-colored with white markings **2.** [orig. made on the island] [g-] a closefitting, knitted woolen shirt or sweater, worn by seamen

guer·ril·la, gue·ril·la (gə ril'ə) *n.* [Sp. dim. of *guerra*, war < OHG.] any member of a small defensive force of soldiers who are not part of a regular army and are usually volunteers, making surprise raids, esp. behind the lines of an invading enemy army —*adj.* of or by guerrillas

guess (ges) *vt., vi.* [prob. < MDu. *gessen*: for IE. base see GET] **1.** to form a judgment or estimate of (something) without actual knowledge or enough facts to be certain; conjecture; surmise [can you *guess* how old she is?] **2.** to judge correctly by doing this [he *guessed* her exact weight] **3.** to think or suppose [I *guess* I can do it] —*n.* **1.** the act of guessing **2.** something guessed; conjecture; surmise [your *guess* is as good as mine] —**guess'er** *n.*

SYN.—**guess** implies the forming of a judgment or estimate (often a correct one) haphazardly or according to chance [he **guessed** the number of beans in the jar]; to **conjecture** is to draw a conclusion or make a prediction based on incomplete or uncertain evidence [he *conjectured* who would win the election]; to **surmise** is to conjecture by using one's imagination or intuition [from the looks on their faces, she *surmised* the truth]

☆**guess·ti·mate** (ges'tə mit; for *vt.* -māt') *n.* [GUESS + (ES)TIMATE] [Slang] an estimate based on a guess or conjecture —*vt.* **-mat'ed**, **-mat'ing** [Slang] to form a guesstimate of Also sp. **gues'ti·mate**

guess·work (-wurk') *n.* **1.** the act of guessing **2.** a judgment, result, etc. arrived at by guessing

guest (gest) *n.* [ON. *gestr* < IE. base *ghostis*, stranger] **1.** *a)* a person entertained at the home of another; visitor *b)* a person entertained by another acting as host at a restaurant, theater, etc. **2.** any paying customer of a hotel, restaurant, etc. **3.** a person receiving the hospitality of a club, institution, etc. of which he is not a member **4.** a person who appears on a program by special invitation **5.** an organism, as an insect, that lives in the place where another organism lives —*adj.* **1.** for guests **2.** performing by special invitation [a *guest* artist] —*vt.* to entertain as a guest —*vi.* to be a guest or perform as a guest

☆**guff** (guf) *n.* [echoic] [Slang] **1.** foolish talk; nonsense **2.** bold or disrespectful talk

guf·faw (gə fô') *n.* [echoic] a loud, coarse burst of laughter —*vi.* to laugh in this way —see SYN. at LAUGH

Gui·a·na (gē an'ə, -än'ə) region in northern S. America, including Guyana, Surinam, & French Guiana

guid·ance (gīd''ns) *n.* **1.** the act of guiding; direction; leadership **2.** something that guides **3.** advice or assistance, as that given to students by school counselors **4.** the process of directing the course of a spacecraft, missile, etc.

guide (gīd) *vt.* **guid'ed**, **guid'ing** [OFr. *guider*, var. of *guier* < Frank.: for IE. base see WISE¹] **1.** to point out the way for; conduct; lead [he *guided* us through the museum] **2.** to direct the course of (a vehicle, implement, etc.) **3.** to direct in (policies, actions, work, etc.); manage; regulate [to *guide* the affairs of state] —*vi.* to act as a guide —*n.* a person or thing that guides; specif., *a)* one who leads others on a trip or tour *b)* one who directs, or serves as the model for, another in his conduct, career, etc. *c)* a part that controls the motion of other parts [the *guide* on a typewriter keeps the paper straight] *d)* a guidebook *e)* a book giving instruction in the elements of some subject; handbook [a *guide* to mathematics] —**guid'a·ble** *adj.*

SYN.—**guide** implies the showing of the way by one who is completely familiar with the course, and suggests that he is always present and giving directions and information [to *guide* a tourist, a mule, one's hand]; **lead** implies a going ahead in order to show the way and may also suggest the giving of orders [he *led* them to victory]; **steer** suggests a handling of the controls in order to keep on the correct course [to *steer* a ship]; **pilot** suggests a guiding over a difficult course, esp. one filled with obstacles or difficult turns [he *piloted* us through the maze of tunnels] —**ANT. follow**

guide·book (gīd′book′) *n.* a book containing directions and information for tourists

guided missile a military missile whose course is controlled by radio signals, radar devices, etc.

guide dog a dog trained to lead a blind person

guide·line (-līn′) *n.* ☆a standard or principle by which to make a judgment or determine a policy or course of action: also **guide line**

guide·post (-pōst′) *n.* **1.** a post, as at a roadside, with a sign and directions for travelers **2.** anything that serves as a guide, standard, etc.; guideline

guide word *same as* CATCHWORD (sense 1)

gui·don (gīd′'n, gī′dän) *n.* [Fr. < It. *guidone*] **1.** the identification flag of a military unit **2.** the soldier carrying it

guild (gild) *n.* [< OE. *gyld* and ON. *gildi*, both < base seen in OE. *gieldan*, to pay: see YIELD] **1.** in medieval times, a union of men in the same craft or trade to uphold standards and protect the members **2.** any group of people joined together to help one another and promote their common interests

guil·der (gil′dər) *n.* [< ME. < MDu.: see GULDEN] **1.** the monetary unit and a coin of the Netherlands: see MONETARY UNITS, table **2.** a former coin of the Netherlands, Germany, or Austria

guild·hall (gild′hôl′) *n.* **1.** a hall where a guild meets **2.** a town hall

guilds·man (gildz′mən) *n., pl.* **-men** (-mən) a member of a guild

guile (gīl) *n.* [OFr. *guile*, prob. < Frank. *wigila*, guile] slyness and cunning in dealing with others; craftiness

guile·ful (gīl′fəl) *adj.* full of guile; deceitful; tricky —**guile′ful·ly** *adv.* —**guile′ful·ness** *n.*

guile·less (-lis) *adj.* without guile; candid; frank —**guile′less·ly** *adv.* —**guile′less·ness** *n.*

guil·le·mot (gil′ə mät′) *n.* [Fr., dim. of *Guillaume*, William] any of various narrow-billed, northern diving birds

guil·lo·tine (gil′ə tēn′; *for v.* gil′ə tēn′) *n.* [Fr., after J. I. *Guillotin* (1738–1814), who advocated its use] an instrument for beheading by means of a heavy blade dropped between two grooved uprights —*vt.* **-tined′**, **-tin′ing** to behead with a guillotine

guilt (gilt) *n.* [OE. *gylt*, a sin] **1.** *a)* the act or state of having done a wrong or committed an offense *b)* a feeling of blaming oneself resulting from a belief that one has done something wrong or immoral **2.** conduct involving guilt; crime; sin

guilt·less (gilt′lis) *adj.* **1.** free from guilt; innocent **2.** having no knowledge or experience (with *of*) —**guilt′less·ly** *adv.* —**guilt′less·ness** *n.*

guilt·y (gil′tē) *adj.* **guilt′i·er**, **guilt′i·est 1.** having guilt; deserving blame or punishment [he is often *guilty* of losing his temper] **2.** having one's guilt proved; legally judged an offender [the jury found him *guilty* of robbery] **3.** showing or conscious of guilt [a *guilty* look] **4.** of or involving guilt or a sense of guilt [a *guilty* conscience] —**guilt′i·ly** *adv.* —**guilt′i·ness** *n.*

Guin·ea (gin′ē) country on the W coast of Africa, south of Senegal: 94,925 sq. mi.; pop. 3,702,000; cap. Conakry —**Guin′e·an** *adj., n.*

guin·ea (gin′ē) *n.* **1.** [first coined of gold from *Guinea*] a former English gold coin, last minted in 1813, equal to 21 shillings **2.** the sum of 21 English shillings **3.** *same as* GUINEA FOWL

Guin·ea-Bis·sau (-bi sou′) country in W Africa, between Senegal & Guinea: 15,505 sq. mi.; pop. 486,000

guinea fowl [orig. imported from *Guinea*] a domestic fowl with a featherless head, rounded body, and dark feathers spotted with white

guinea hen 1. a female guinea fowl **2.** any guinea fowl

guinea pig [prob. orig. brought to England by ships plying between England, *Guinea*, and S. America] **1.** a small, fat mammal of the rat family, with short ears and no external tail, used in biological experiments ☆**2.** any person or thing used in an experiment or test

Guin·e·vere (gwin′ə vir′) *Arthurian Legend* the wife of King Arthur and mistress of Sir Lancelot Also **Guin′e·ver′** (-vir′, -vər)

guise (gīz) *n.* [OFr. < OHG. *wisa*, manner] **1.** manner of dress; garb **2.** outward appearance **3.** a false appearance; pretense [under the *guise* of friendship] —*vt.* **guised**, **guis′ing** [Brit. Dial.] to disguise *same as* SYN. at APPEARANCE

gui·tar (gi tär′) *n.* [< Fr. < Sp. *guitarra* < Ar. < Gr. *kithara*, lyre] a musical instrument related to the lute but having a flat back and usually six strings that are plucked or strummed with the fingers or a plectrum —**gui·tar′ist** *n.*

GUITAR

☆**gulch** (gulch) *n.* [prob. < dial. *gulch*, to swallow greedily] a steep-walled valley cut by a swift stream; deep, narrow ravine

gul·den (gool′dən) *n., pl.* **-dens**, **-den** [MDu. *gulden* (*florijn*), golden (florin)] *same as* GUILDER

gulf (gulf) *n.* [< OFr. < It. *golfo*: ult. < Gr. *kolpos*, bosom] **1.** a large area of ocean, larger than a bay, reaching into land **2.** a wide, deep cut in the earth; large chasm or abyss **3.** a wide gap or separation that cannot be crossed or passed [there is a *gulf* between our beliefs] —*vt.* to swallow up; engulf

Gulf States States on the Gulf of Mexico; Fla., Ala., Miss., La., & Tex.

Gulf Stream warm ocean current flowing from the Gulf of Mexico along the E coast of the U.S., turning east at the Grand Banks toward Europe

gull[1] (gul) *n., pl.* **gulls**, **gull:** see PLURAL, II, D, 1 [< Celt.] a water bird with large wings, webbed feet, and white and gray feathers

gull[2] (gul) *n.* [prob. < ME. *golle*, silly fellow, lit., unfledged bird < ?] a person easily tricked; dupe —*vt.* to cheat; trick

☆**Gul·lah** (gul′ə) *n.* [< ? *Gola* (*Gula*) or < ? *Ngola*, tribal groups in Africa] **1.** any of a group of Negroes living in coastal S. Carolina and Georgia and esp. on the nearby sea islands **2.** their English dialect

GULF STREAM

gul·let (gul′ət) *n.* [OFr. *goulet* < L. *gula*, throat] **1.** the tube leading from the mouth to the stomach; esophagus **2.** the throat or neck

gul·li·ble (gul′ə b'l) *adj.* easily cheated or tricked; credulous —**gul′li·bil′i·ty** *n.* —**gul′li·bly** *adv.*

gul·ly (gul′ē) *n., pl.* **-lies** [altered < ME. *golet*, water channel, orig., gullet: see GULLET] a channel or hollow worn by running water; small, narrow ravine —*vt.* **-lied**, **-ly·ing** to make a gully or gullies in

gulp (gulp) *vt.* [prob. < Du. *gulpen*, to gulp] **1.** to swallow hastily, greedily, or in large amounts [he *gulped* his breakfast] **2.** to choke back as if swallowing [she *gulped* down her sobs] —*vi.* to catch the breath as in swallowing [the swimmer came up *gulping* for air] —*n.* **1.** the act of gulping **2.** the amount swallowed at one time [he took two *gulps* of milk] —**gulp′er** *n.* —**gulp′ing·ly** *adv.*

gum[1] (gum) *n.* [< OFr. < L. *gumma* < Egypt. *kemai*] **1.** a sticky, colloidal substance found in certain trees and plants, which dries into a brittle mass that dissolves or swells in water **2.** any similar plant secretion, as resin **3.** any plant gum processed for use in industry, art, etc. **4.** *a)* an adhesive, as on the back of a postage stamp *b)* any of various sticky or viscous substances or deposits **5.** *same as:* *a)* GUM TREE *b)* GUM-WOOD ☆**6.** *same as* CHEWING GUM —*vt.* **gummed**, **gum′ming** to coat, stick together, or stiffen with gum —*vi.* **1.** to secrete or form gum **2.** to become sticky or clogged —☆**gum up** [Slang] to put out of working order

gum² (gum) *n.* [OE. *goma*] [*often pl.*] the firm flesh surrounding the base of the teeth —☆*vt.* **gummed, gum′ming** to chew with toothless gums

gum ammoniac *same as* AMMONIAC

gum arabic a gum obtained from several African acacias, used in medicine and candy, for stabilizing emulsions, etc.

☆**gum·bo** (gum′bō) *n.* [< Bantu name for okra] **1.** *same as* OKRA **2.** a soup thickened with unripe okra pods **3.** a fine, silty soil of the Western prairies, which becomes sticky and non-porous when wet: also **gumbo soil**

gum·boil (gum′boil′) *n.* an abscess on the gum

☆**gum·drop** (gum′dräp′) *n.* a small, firm piece of jellylike candy, made of sweetened gum arabic or gelatin, usually colored and flavored

gum·my (gum′ē) *adj.* **-mi·er, -mi·est 1.** having the nature of gum; sticky **2.** covered with or containing gum **3.** giving off gum —**gum′mi·ness** *n.*

gump·tion (gump′shən) *n.* [< Scot. dial.] [Colloq.] **1.** orig., common sense **2.** courage and boldness

gum resin a mixture of gum and resin, given off by certain trees and plants

☆**gum·shoe** (gum′shōō′) *n.* **1.** orig., *a*) a rubber overshoe *b*) [*pl.*] sneakers **2.** [Slang] a detective

☆**gum tree** any of various trees that give off gum, as the sour gum, sweet gum, eucalyptus, etc.

gum·wood (gum′wood′) *n.* the wood of a gum tree

gun (gun) *n.* [< ON. *Gunnhildr*, fem. name (< *gunnr*, war + *hildr*, battle)] **1.** a weapon consisting of a metal tube from which a projectile is shot by the force of an explosive; specif., *a*) technically, a heavy weapon with a relatively long barrel fixed in a mount, as a cannon, etc. *b*) a rifle ☆*c*) popularly, a pistol or revolver **2.** any similar device that shoots or squirts something [an air *gun*, a spray *gun*] **3.** the shooting of a gun in signaling or saluting **4.** anything like a gun in shape or use ☆**5.** [Slang] *same as* GUNMAN (sense 1) —*vi.* **gunned, gun′ning** to shoot or hunt with a gun —*vt.* ☆**1.** [Colloq.] to shoot (a person) **2.** [Slang] to cause (an engine, automobile, etc.) to operate at high speed by opening the throttle —**give it the gun** [Slang] to cause something to start or gain speed —**go great guns** [Slang] to act with speed and efficiency —☆**gun for 1.** to hunt for with a gun **2.** [Slang] to try to get; seek —**jump the gun** [Slang] to begin before the signal has been given to start, or before the proper time —**stick to one's guns** to hold one's position under attack; be firm

gun·boat (gun′bōt′) *n.* a small armed ship that can move in shallow water, used to patrol rivers, etc.

gun·cot·ton (-kät′'n) *n.* nitrocellulose used as an explosive, made by treating cotton or other cellulose with nitric acid

gun·fight (-fīt′) *n.* ☆a fight between persons using pistols or revolvers —☆**gun′fight′er** *n.*

gun·fire (-fīr′) *n.* the firing of a gun or guns

☆**gung-ho** (guŋ′hō′) *adj.* [Chin., lit., work together] overly enthusiastic, cooperative, etc., often in a naive way

☆**gunk** (guŋk) *n.* [< ? G(OO) + (J)UNK¹] [Slang] any oily or thick, messy substance —**gunk′y** *adj.*

gun·lock (gun′läk′) *n.* in some guns, the mechanism by which the charge is set off

gun·man (-mən) *n., pl.* **-men** ☆**1.** a man armed with a gun, esp. an armed gangster or hired killer **2.** a man skilled in the use of a gun

gun·met·al (-met′'l) *n.* **1.** a kind of bronze formerly used for making cannons; also, any metal or alloy treated to resemble tarnished gunmetal **2.** the dark gray color (**gunmetal gray**) of tarnished gunmetal —*adj.* dark gray

gun·nel¹ (gun′'l) *n.* [< ?] a small, slimy fish resembling the blenny, found in the N Atlantic

gun·nel² (gun′'l) *n. same as* GUNWALE

gun·ner (gun′ər) *n.* **1.** a soldier, sailor, etc. who helps fire artillery **2.** a naval warrant officer in charge of a ship's guns **3.** a hunter with a gun

gun·ner·y (-ē) *n.* **1.** heavy guns **2.** the science of making and using heavy guns and projectiles

☆**gunnery sergeant** a noncommissioned Marine Corps officer ranking above a staff sergeant and below a master sergeant or first sergeant

gun·ny (gun′ē) *n., pl.* **-nies** [< Hindi < Sans. *gōnī*, a sack] a coarse, heavy fabric of jute or hemp, used for sacks

gun·ny·sack (-sak′) *n.* a sack made of gunny

☆**gun·play** (gun′plā′) *n.* an exchange of gunshots, as between gunmen and police

☆**gun·point** (-point′) *n.* the muzzle of a gun —**at gunpoint** under threat of being shot with a gun

gun·pow·der (-pou′dər) *n.* an explosive powder, esp. a mixture of sulfur, saltpeter, and charcoal, used in cartridges, shells, etc., for blasting, etc.

gun·run·ning (-run′iŋ) *n.* the smuggling of guns and ammunition into a country —**gun′run′ner** *n.*

gun·shot (-shät′) *n.* **1.** shot fired from a gun **2.** the distance a gun can be fired; range of a gun [a duck within *gunshot*] —*adj.* caused by a shot from a gun [a *gunshot* wound]

gun·shy (-shī′) *adj.* easily frightened at the firing of a gun [a *gun-shy* dog] —**gun′·shy′ness** *n.*

gun·smith (-smith′) *n.* a person who makes or repairs small guns

gun·stock (-stäk′) *n.* the wooden handle or butt to which the barrel of a gun is attached

gun·wale (gun′'l) *n.* [first applied to bulwarks supporting a ship's guns] the upper edge of the side of a ship or boat

gup·py (gup′ē) *n., pl.* **-pies** [after R. *Guppy*, of Trinidad] a tiny freshwater fish found in Barbados, Trinidad, and Venezuela, often kept in aquariums because of its bright coloring

GUPPY
(to 1½ in. long)

gur·gle (gur′g'l) *vi.* **-gled, -gling** [prob. echoic] **1.** to flow with a bubbling or rippling sound, as water from a narrow-necked bottle **2.** to make such a sound in the throat, as a contented baby does— *vt.* to say with a gurgle —*n.* the act or sound of gurgling

gur·nard (gur′nərd) *n., pl.* **-nards, -nard:** see PLURAL, II, D, 1 [< OFr. < *grogner*, to grunt] *same as* FLYING GURNARD

gu·ru (goor′ōō, goo roo′) *n.* [Hindi < Sans. *guru-ḥ*, venerable] **1.** in Hinduism, one's spiritual adviser or teacher **2.** a leader with devoted followers

gush (gush) *vi.* [prob. akin to ON. *gjosa*, to gush: see GUST] **1.** to flow out suddenly and plentifully; pour out; spout [water *gushed* from the broken pipe] **2.** to have a sudden, plentiful flow of blood, tears, etc. **3.** to express too much enthusiasm or feeling in a silly way —*vt.* to cause to flow out suddenly and plentifully —*n.* **1.** a sudden, plentiful outflow **2.** gushing talk or writing —**gush′ing** *adj.* —**gush′ing·ly** *adv.*

gush·er (gush′ər) *n.* **1.** a person who gushes ☆**2.** an oil well from which oil spouts without being pumped

gush·y (-ē) *adj.* **gush′i·er, gush′i·est** full of gush (*n.* 2) — **gush′i·ly** *adv.* —**gush′i·ness** *n.*

gus·set (gus′it) *n.* [< OFr. *gousset*] **1.** a triangular or diamond-shaped piece inserted in a garment, glove, etc. to make it stronger or roomier **2.** a triangular metal brace for reinforcing a corner or angle —*vt.* to furnish with a gusset

☆**gus·sie, gus·sy** (gus′ē) *vt., vi.* **-sied, -sy·ing** [< *Gussie*, nickname for AUGUSTA] [Slang] to dress (*up*) or decorate in a fine or showy way

gust (gust) *n.* [< ON. *gustr* < *gjosa*, to gush: for IE. base see FOUND³] **1.** a sudden, strong rush of air or wind **2.** a sudden outburst of rain, laughter, rage, etc. —*vi.* to blow in gusts

GUSSET

gus·ta·to·ry (gus′tə tôr′ē) *adj.* of or having to do with tasting or the sense of taste: also **gus′ta·tive** (-tiv), **gus′ta·to′ri·al** (-tôr′ē əl)

Gus·ta·vus (gəs tā′vəs, -tä′-) [ModL. < G. *Gustav* or Sw. *Gustaf*, lit., prob. staff of the Goths] **1.** a masculine name: dim. *Gus* **2. Gustavus I** 1496–1560; king of Sweden (1523–60) **3. Gustavus II** 1594–1632; king of Sweden (1611–32): grandson of *prec.* **4. Gustavus V** 1858–1950; king of Sweden (1907–50): officially, **Gus·taf V** (goos′täf) **5. Gustavus VI** 1882–1973; king of Sweden (1950–73): son of *prec.*: officially, **Gustaf VI Adolf**

---

fat, āpe, cär; ten, ēven; is, bīte; gō, hôrn, tōōl, look; oil, out; up, fur; get; joy; yet; chin; she; thin, then; zh, leisure; ŋ, ring; ə for a in ago, e in agent, i in sanity, o in comply, u in focus; ' as in able (ā′b'l); Fr. bâl; ë, Fr. coeur; ö, Fr. feu; Fr. mon; ô, Fr. coq; ü, Fr. duc; r, Fr. cri; H, G. ich; kh, G. doch; ‡foreign; ☆ Americanism; < derived from. See inside front cover.

gus·to (gus'tō) *n.* [It. & Sp. < L. *gustus*, taste: for IE. base see CHOOSE] **1.** taste; liking **2.** keen enjoyment; zest; relish **3.** great vigor or liveliness

gust·y (gus'tē) *adj.* **gust'i·er, gust'i·est** full of gusts of air or wind, or of sudden outbursts —**gust'i·ly** *adv.* —**gust'i·ness** *n.*

gut (gut) *n.* [OE. *guttas*, pl. < base of *geotan*, to pour: for IE. base see CHOOSE] **1.** *a*) [*pl.*] the bowels; entrails *b*) the stomach or belly Now sometimes thought to be not a polite use **2.** all or part of the alimentary canal, esp. the intestine **3.** tough cord made from animal intestines, used for violin strings, surgical sutures, etc. **4.** a narrow passage or gully **5.** [*pl.*] [Colloq.] the basic or inner parts **6.** [*pl.*] [Slang] *a*) daring, courage, etc. *b*) unashamed boldness; impudence *c*) power or force —*vt.* **gut'ted, gut'ting 1.** to remove the intestines from; eviscerate **2.** to destroy the interior of, as by fire —*adj.* [Slang] **1.** urgent and basic or fundamental [*gut* issues in politics] **2.** easy; simple [a *gut* course in college]

Gu·ten·berg (gōōt''n burg'), **Jo·hann** (yō'hän) (born *Johannes Gensfleisch*) 1400?–68; Ger. printer: thought to be the first European to print with movable type

gut·less (gut'lis) *adj.* [Slang] lacking courage, daring, etc. —**gut'less·ness** *n.*

guts·y (gut'sē) *adj.* **guts'i·er, guts'i·est** [Slang] full of guts; daring, courageous, forceful, etc.

gut·ta-per·cha (gut'ə pur'chə) *n.* [< Malay < *gĕtah*, gum + *pĕrchah*, tree from which it is obtained] a rubberlike gum produced from the latex of various southeastern Asian trees, used in electric insulation, dentistry, etc.

gut·ter (gut'ər) *n.* [< OFr. < L. *gutta*, a drop] **1.** a trough or channel along or under the eaves of a roof, to carry off rain water **2.** a narrow channel along the side of a road or street, to carry off water, as to a sewer **3.** a place or condition of living marked by filth, poverty, etc. **4.** a channel or groove like a gutter, as the groove on either side of a bowling alley **5.** the adjoining inner margins of two facing pages in a book, etc. —*vt.* to furnish with gutters —*vi.* **1.** to flow in a stream **2.** to melt rapidly so that the wax runs down the side in channels: said of a candle

gut·ter·snipe (gut'ər snīp') *n.* a child living in the slums, for the most part in the streets: a term of contempt

gut·tur·al (gut'ər əl) *adj.* [< L. *guttur*, throat: for IE. base see COVE] **1.** of the throat **2.** *a*) loosely, produced in the throat; harsh, rasping, etc.: said of sounds *b*) using such sounds [a *guttural* language] **3.** formed with the back of the tongue close to or against the soft palate, as the *k* in *keen* —*n.* a guttural sound —**gut'tur·al·ly** *adv.* —**gut'tur·al·ness** *n.*

Guy (gī) [Fr., lit., leader] a masculine name

guy¹ (gī) *n.* [< OFr. < *guier*, to GUIDE] a rope, chain, etc. attached to something to steady or guide it —*vt.* to guide or steady with a guy

guy² (gī) *n.* [after Guy FAWKES] **1.** a person who looks odd ☆**2.** [Slang] *a*) a man or boy; fellow *b*) any person —*vt.* to make fun of; ridicule

Guy·a·na (gī an'ə, -än'ə) country in northeastern S. America, on the Atlantic: a member of the Commonwealth: 83,000 sq. mi.; pop. 763,000; cap. Georgetown —**Guy'a·nese'** (-ə nēz') *adj., n., pl.* **-nese'**

guz·zle (guz'l) *vi., vt.* **-zled, -zling** [< ? OFr. < *gosier*, throat] to drink too much or in a greedy way —**guz'zler** *n.*

Gwa·li·or (gwä'lē ôr') city in NC India: pop. 301,000

Gwen·do·len, Gwen·do·line, Gwen·do·lyn (gwen'd'l-ən) [< Celt.; first element prob. W. *gwen*, white] a feminine name: dim. *Gwen*

gybe (jīb) *n., vi., vt.* **gybed, gyb'ing** *same as* JIBE¹

gym (jim) *n.* [Colloq.] *same as:* **1.** GYMNASIUM ☆**2.** PHYSICAL EDUCATION

gym·na·si·um (jim nā'zē əm) *n., pl.* **-si·ums, -si·a** (-ə) [L. < Gr. *gymnasion*, ult. < *gymnos*, naked: for IE. base see NAKED] **1.** a room or building equipped for physical training and athletic sports **2.** [G-] (gim nä'zē ōōm) in Germany and some other European countries, a secondary school for students preparing to enter a university

gym·nast (jim'nast) *n.* an expert in gymnastics

gym·nas·tic (jim nas'tik) *adj.* [< L. < Gr.: see GYMNASIUM] of or having to do with gymnastics —**gym·nas'ti·cal·ly** *adv.*

gym·nas·tics (-tiks) *n.pl.* exercises that develop and train the body and the muscles, esp. those exercises that can be done in a gymnasium

gym·no- [< Gr. *gymnos*, naked] a combining form meaning naked, stripped, bare [*gymnosperm*]: also, before a vowel, **gymn-**

gym·no·sperm (jim'nə spurm') *n.* [< ModL. < Gr.: see GYMNO- & -SPERM] any of a large group of seed plants having the ovules borne on open scales, usually in cones, as pines and cedars —**gym'no·sper'mous** (-spur'məs) *adj.* —**gym'no·sper'my** (-spur'mē) *n.*

☆**gym shoe** *same as* SNEAKER (sense 2)

gyn·e·co- [< Gr. < *gynē*, a woman] a combining form meaning woman, female: also, before a vowel, **gynec-**

gyn·e·col·o·gy (gī'nə käl'ə jē, jin'ə-, jī'nə-) *n.* [GYNECO- + -LOGY] the branch of medicine dealing with the specific functions, diseases, etc. of women —**gyn'e·co·log'ic** (-kə läj'ik), **gyn'e·co·log'i·cal** *adj.* —**gyn'e·col'o·gist** *n.*

gy·noe·ci·um (ji nē'sē əm, jī-, gī-) *n., pl.* **-ci·a** (-ə) [ModL. < L., ult. < Gr. *gynē*, a woman + *oikos*, house] the female organ or organs of a flower; pistil or pistils; the carpels, as a unit: also sp. **gy·nae·ce·um** (jī'nə sē'əm), *pl.* **-ce'a** (-ə) or **gy·ne'ci·um**, *pl.* **-ci·a** (-ə)

gyn·o·phore (jin'ə fôr', jī'nə-, gī'nə-) *n.* [< Gr. *gynē*, woman + -PHORE] a stalk bearing the gynoecium above the petals and stamens

-gy·nous (ji nəs) [< ModL. < Gr. < *gynē*, a woman] a combining form meaning: **1.** woman or female [*polygynous*] **2.** having female organs or pistils as specified [*androgynous*]

-gy·ny (ji nē) a combining form used to form nouns from adjectives ending in -GYNOUS

☆**gyp** (jip) *n.* [prob. < GYPSY] [Colloq.] **1.** an act of cheating; swindle **2.** a swindler: also **gyp'per, gyp'ster** —*vt., vi.* **gypped, gyp'ping** [Colloq.] to swindle; cheat

gyp·soph·i·la (jip säf'ə lə) *n.* [ModL.: see GYPSUM & -PHIL(E)] any of a group of plants of the pink family, bearing clusters of small white or pink flowers with a delicate fragrance, as baby's breath

gyp·sum (jip'səm) *n.* [L. < Gr. *gypsos*, chalk < Sem.] a hydrated sulfate of calcium, $CaSO_4·2H_2O$, occurring naturally in sedimentary rocks and used for making plaster of Paris, in treating soil, etc.

Gyp·sy (jip'sē) *n., pl.* **-sies** [< *Egipcien*, Egyptian: orig. thought to have come from Egypt] **1.** [*also* g-] a member of a wandering Caucasoid people with dark skin and black hair, believed to have originated in India: they are known throughout the world as musicians, fortunetellers, etc. **2.** *same as* ROMANY (sense 2) **3.** [g-] a person whose appearance or habits are like those of a Gypsy —*adj.* of or like a Gypsy or Gypsies

gypsy moth a European moth, brownish or white, now common in the eastern U.S.: its larvae feed on leaves, damaging trees and plants

gy·rate (jī'rāt) *vi.* **-rat·ed, -rat·ing** [< L. pp. of *gyrare*, to turn, ult. < Gr. *gyros*, a circle: for IE. base see COVE] to move in a circular or spiral path; rotate or revolve on an axis; whirl —*adj.* spiral, coiled, or circular —see SYN. at TURN —**gy·ra'tion** *n.* —**gy'ra·tor** *n.* —**gy'ra·to·ry** (-rə tôr'ē) *adj.*

gyr·fal·con (jur'fal'kən, -fôl'-, -fô'-) *n.* [< OFr. *girfaucon* < Frank.] a large, fierce, strong falcon of the Arctic

gy·ro (jī'rō) *n., pl.* **-ros** short for: **1.** GYROSCOPE **2.** GYROCOMPASS

gy·ro- [< Gr. *gyros*: see GYRATE] a combining form meaning: **1.** gyrating [*gyroscope*] **2.** gyroscope [*gyrocompass*] Also, before a vowel, **gyr-**

gy·ro·com·pass (jī'rō kum'pəs) *n.* a compass consisting of a motor-operated gyroscope whose rotating axis points to the geographic north pole instead of to the magnetic pole

gy·ro·scope (-skōp') *n.* [GYRO- + -SCOPE] a wheel mounted in a ring so that the shaft on which it spins is free to turn in any direction: when the wheel is spun rapidly, the shaft will stay any way it is tilted: gyroscopes are used to help moving ships, airplanes, etc. stay level —**gy'ro·scop'ic** (-skäp'ik) *adj.* —**gy'ro·scop'i·cal·ly** *adv.*

gy·ro·sta·bi·liz·er (jī'rō stā'bə lī'zər) *n.* a device consisting of a gyroscope spinning in a vertical plane, used to stabilize the side-to-side rolling of a ship

gyve (jīv) *n., vt.* **gyved, gyv'ing** [< Anglo-Fr. *gyves*, pl.] [Archaic or Poet.] fetter; shackle

GYPSY MOTH
(wingspread to 2 in.)

GYROSCOPE

H

H, h (āch) *n., pl.* **H's, h's** **1.** the eighth letter of the English alphabet **2.** the sound of *H* or *h*

H (āch) *n.* **1.** *Chem.* the symbol for hydrogen **2.** *Elec.* the symbol for henry **3.** [Slang] heroin —*adj.* shaped like *H*

H., h. **1.** harbor **2.** hard(ness) **3.** height **4.** high **5.** *Baseball* hits **6.** hour(s) **7.** husband

ha (hä) *interj.* [echoic] an exclamation variously expressing surprise, anger, triumph, etc.: repeated (**ha-ha**) it may express laughter, contempt, etc. —*n.* the sound of this exclamation or of a laugh

ha. hectare; hectares

Haar·lem (här'ləm) city in NW Netherlands: pop. 173,000

Ha·bak·kuk (hab'ə kuk, hə bak'ək) *Bible* **1.** a Hebrew prophet of the 7th cent. B.C. **2.** the book containing his prophecies: abbrev. **Hab.** Also, in the Douay Bible, **Ha'ba·cuc**

Ha·ba·na (ä bä'nä), (**La**) *Spanish name of* HAVANA

ha·be·as cor·pus (hā'bē əs kôr'pəs) [L., (that) you have the body] *Law* a writ requiring that a person being held be brought before a court to decide whether it is legal for him to be held or imprisoned

hab·er·dash·er (hab'ər dash'ər, hab'ə-) *n.* [prob. < Anglo-Fr. *hapertas*, kind of cloth] **1.** a person who sells men's furnishings, such as hats, shirts, gloves, etc. **2.** [Brit.] a dealer in various small articles, such as ribbons, thread, etc.

hab·er·dash·er·y (-ē) *n., pl.* **-er·ies** **1.** things sold by a haberdasher **2.** a haberdasher's shop

hab·er·geon (hab'ər jən) *n.* [OFr. *haubergeon*, dim. of *hauberc*, hauberk] **1.** a short, high-necked jacket of mail **2.** *same as* HAUBERK

ha·bil·i·ment (hə bil'ə mənt) *n.* [< MFr. < *habiller*, to clothe] **1.** [*usually pl.*] clothing; dress **2.** [*pl.*] furnishings or equipment; trappings

hab·it (hab'it) *n.* [OFr. < L. *habitus* < pp. of *habere*, to have < IE. base *ghabh-*, to grasp] **1.** a distinctive religious costume [a nun's *habit*] **2.** a costume for certain occasions [a riding *habit*] **3.** typical or usual way of being, doing, growing, etc.; character, tendency, disposition, etc. [it is the *habit* of bears to sleep through the winter] **4.** *a*) a thing done often and, hence, easily; practice; custom [it is her *habit* to go bowling on Thursdays] *b*) an acquired pattern of action that one follows without thinking and is thus difficult to break [the *habit* of biting one's fingernails] **5.** an addiction, esp. to narcotics **6.** *Biol.* the tendency of a plant or animal to grow in a certain way [a twining *habit*] —*vt.* to dress

SYN. —**habit** refers to an act repeated so often by someone that he does it without thinking about it [his *habit* of tugging at his ear when nervous]; **practice** also implies the regular repetition of an act but suggests that it is done willingly [the *practice* of reading in bed]; **custom** applies to any act or procedure that has become the accepted thing to do among a group of people [the *custom* of shaking

NUNS' HABITS
(left, traditional; right, modern)

hands]; **wont** is a literary or somewhat archaic substitute for **practice** [it is his *wont* to rise early]

hab·it·a·ble (hab'it ə b'l) *adj.* fit to be lived in —**hab'it·a·bil'i·ty** *n.* —**hab'it·a·bly** *adv.*

hab·it·ant (hab'it ənt) *n.* [Fr. < L. prp. of *habitare*, to inhabit: for IE. base see HABIT] an inhabitant; resident

hab·i·tat (hab'ə tat') *n.* [L., it inhabits] **1.** the region where a plant or animal naturally grows or lives; native environment **2.** the place where a person or thing is ordinarily found

hab·i·ta·tion (hab'ə tā'shən) *n.* **1.** an inhabiting; occupancy **2.** a place in which to live; dwelling; home **3.** a colony or settlement

hab·it-form·ing (hab'it fôr'miŋ) *adj.* resulting in the forming of a habit or in becoming addicted

ha·bit·u·al (hə bich'oo wəl) *adj.* **1.** done by habit or fixed as a habit; customary [*habitual* kindness] **2.** being or doing a certain thing by habit; steady [a *habitual* smoker] **3.** much seen, done, or used; usual [that chair is her *habitual* seat] —see SYN. at USUAL —**ha·bit'u·al·ly** *adv.* —**ha·bit'u·al·ness** *n.*

ha·bit·u·ate (hə bich'oo wāt') *vt.* **-at'ed, -at'ing** [< LL., ult. < L. *habitus*: see HABIT] to make used (*to*); accustom [she *habituated* herself to the cold climate] —**ha·bit'u·a'tion** *n.*

hab·i·tude (hab'ə tood', -tyood') *n.* **1.** habitual condition of mind or body; disposition **2.** usual way of doing something

ha·bit·u·é (hə bich'oo wā') *n.* [Fr.] a person who goes again and again to a certain place or places

Habs·burg (häps'bōōrkh) *same as* HAPSBURG

ha·chure (hə shoor'; *also, for n.,* hash'oor) *n.* [Fr. < OFr. *hacher*, to chop < *hache*, ax] any of a series of short parallel lines used to shade an area on a map, drawing, etc. —*vt.* **-chured', -chur'ing** to shade with hachures

☆ha·ci·en·da (hä'sē en'də, has'ē-) *n.* [Sp. < L. *facienda*, things to be done < *facere*, to do] in Spanish America, **1.** a large estate, ranch, etc. **2.** the main dwelling on any of these

hack[1] (hak) *vt.* [OE. *haccian* < IE. base *keg-*, a hook] **1.** *a*) to chop or cut roughly or irregularly *b*) to shape, trim, etc. thus **2.** to break up (land) with a hoe, etc. ☆**3.** [Slang] to deal with successfully ☆**4.** *Basketball* to foul by striking the arm of (an opponent who has the ball) with the hand or arm —*vi.* **1.** to make rough or irregular cuts **2.** to give harsh, dry coughs ☆**3.** *Basketball* to hack an opponent —*n.* **1.** a tool for hacking; ax, hoe, etc. **2.** a slash, gash, or notch **3.** a harsh, dry cough —☆**hack it** [Slang] to be successful in doing something, dealing with a situation, etc. — **hack'er** *n.*

hack[2] (hak) *n.* [contr. < HACKNEY] **1.** a horse for hire **2.** a saddle horse **3.** an old, worn-out horse **4.** a person hired to do routine writing ☆**5.** a devoted, unquestioning worker for a political party **6.** a carriage or coach for hire **7.** [Colloq.] *a*) a taxicab *b*) a cabdriver —*vt.* **1.** to employ as a hack **2.** to hire out (a horse, etc.) **3.** to wear out by constant, use

HACHURES

---

fat, āpe, cär; ten, ēven; is, bīte; gō, hôrn, tōol, lŏok; oil, out; up, fur; get; joy; yet; chin; she; thin, then; zh, leisure; ŋ, ring; ə for *a* in *ago*, *e* in *agent*, *i* in *sanity*, *o* in *comply*, *u* in *focus*; ' as in *able* (ā'b'l); Fr. bäl; ë, Fr. coeur; ö, Fr. feu; Fr. mon; ô, Fr. coq; ü, Fr. duc; r, Fr. cri; H, G. ich; kh, G. doch; ‡foreign; ☆ Americanism; < derived from. See inside front cover.

—vi. ☆[Colloq.] to drive a taxicab **—adj.** **1.** employed as a hack [a *hack* writer] **2.** done by a hack [a *hack* job] **3.** stale; trite; hackneyed

☆**hack·a·more** (hak′ə môr′) **n.** [altered < Sp. *jaquima*, halter < Ar. *shakīma*] [Western] a rope or rawhide halter, used in breaking horses

hack·ber·ry (hak′ber′ē) **n.**, pl. **-ries** [< Scand.] ☆**1.** an American tree with a small fruit resembling a cherry ☆**2.** its fruit or its wood

☆**hack·ie** (hak′ē) **n.** [Colloq.] a taxicab driver

hack·le¹ (hak′'l) **n.** [ME. *hechele*, prob. infl. by dial. *hackle*, bird's plumage < OE. *hacele*] **1.** a comb for separating the fibers of flax, hemp, etc. **2.** any of the long, slender feathers at the neck of a rooster, pigeon, etc. **3.** *Fishing* a) a tuft of feathers from a rooster's neck, used in making artificial flies b) a fly made with a hackle **4.** [pl.] the hairs on a dog's neck and back that bristle, as when the dog is ready to fight **—vt.** **-led, -ling** to separate the fibers of (flax, hemp, etc.) with a hackle **—get one's hackles up** to become tense with anger; bristle

hack·le² (hak′'l) **vt., vi.** **-led, -ling** [HACK¹ + -LE²] to cut rough-ly; hack; mangle

☆**hack·ma·tack** (hak′mə tak′) **n.** [AmInd. (Algonquian)] *same as* TAMARACK

hack·ney (hak′nē) **n.**, pl. **-neys** [< ME. < *Hackeney* (now *Hackney*), an English village] **1.** a horse for ordinary driving or riding **2.** a carriage for hire

hack·neyed (-nēd′) **adj.** made trite and commonplace by being used too much —see SYN. at TRITE

hack·saw (hak′sô′) **n.** a saw for cutting metal, consisting of a narrow, fine-toothed blade held in a frame: also **hack saw**

had (had; *unstressed* həd, əd) *pt. & pp. of* HAVE: also used with certain words and phrases, such as *rather*, *better*, *as well*, in showing what is preferred or necessary (Ex.: I *had* better go)

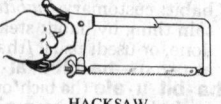

HACKSAW

had·dock (had′ək) **n.**, pl. **-dock, -docks:** see PLURAL, II, D, 2 [< ? OFr. *hadot*] a food fish related to the cod, found off the coasts of Europe and N. America

Ha·des (hā′dēz) **1.** *Gr. Myth.* a) the home of the dead, beneath the earth b) the ruler of the underworld **2.** the rest-ing place of the dead: used in some New Testament translations **—n.** [*often* h-] [Colloq.] hell

hadj (haj) **n.** *same as* HAJJ

hadj·i (-ē) **n.** *same as* HAJJI

had·n't (had′'nt) had not

Ha·dri·an (hā′drē ən) (L. name *Publius Aelius Hadrianus*) 76–138 A.D.; Roman emperor (117–138)

hadst (hadst) *the archaic second person singular in the past tense of* HAVE: *used with* thou

Haeck·el (hek′əl), **Ernst Hein·rich** (ernst hīn′riH) 1834–1919; Ger. biologist & philosopher

haemat-, haemato-, haemo- see HEMATO-, HEMO-

haf·ni·um (haf′nē əm) **n.** [ModL. < L. *Hafnia*, Roman name of Copenhagen] a metallic chemical element found with zir-conium and somewhat resembling it: symbol, Hf; at. wt., 178.49; at. no., 72

haft (haft) **n.** [OE. *hæft*: for IE. base see HAVE] a handle or hilt of a knife, ax, etc. **—vt.** to fit with a haft

hag (hag) **n.** [< OE. *hægtes* < *haga*, a hedge] **1.** a witch **2.** an ugly old woman, esp. one who is mean **—hag′gish adj.**

Hag. Haggai

Ha·gar (hā′gər) *Bible* a concubine of Abraham and slave of his wife Sarah

Ha·gen (hä′gən) city in W West Germany, in the Ruhr valley: pop. 200,000

hag·fish (hag′fish′) **n.**, pl. **-fish′, -fish′es:** see FISH [HAG + FISH] a small, eellike saltwater fish with a round, sucking mouth and horny teeth, with which it bores into other fish and devours them

Hag·ga·da, Hag·ga·dah (hä gä dä′; *E.* hə gä′də) **n.**, pl. **-ga·dot′** (-dôt′) [Heb. *haggādāh* < *higgid*, to tell] **1.** a) [*often* h-] in the *Talmud*, a story used to explain some point of law b) the part of the Talmud containing such stories **2.** the story of the Exodus read at the Seder during Passover, or a book con-taining this **—hag·gad′ic** (hə gad′ik, -gä′dik) *adj.*

Hag·ga·i (hag′ē ī′, hag′ī) *Bible* **1.** a Hebrew prophet who lived c. 500 B.C. **2.** the book he is thought to have written

hag·gard (hag′ərd) **adj.** [MFr. *hagard*, untamed] having a wild, wasted, worn look, as from grief, illness, hunger, etc.; gaunt; drawn **—hag′gard·ly adv.** **—hag′gard·ness n.**

Hag·gard (hag′ərd), **Sir H(enry) Rid·er** (rīd′ər) 1856–1925; Eng. novelist

hag·gis (hag′is) **n.** [ME. *hagas*, kind of pudding] a Scottish dish made of the lungs, heart, etc. of a sheep or calf, mixed with suet, seasoning, and oatmeal and boiled in the animal's stomach

hag·gle (hag′'l) **vt.** **-gled, -gling** [< Scot. *hag*, to chop, cut + -LE²] to hack; mangle **—vi.** to argue about terms, price, etc.; bargain; wrangle **—n.** the act of haggling **—hag′gler n.**

hag·i·o- [< Gr. *hagios*, holy] *a prefix meaning* saintly, sacred: also, before a vowel, **hag·i-**

hag·i·og·ra·phy (hag′ē äg′rə fē, hā′jē-) **n.**, pl. **-phies** [HAGIO- + -GRAPHY] **1.** the writing or study of lives of the saints **2.** a book or books containing such lives **—hag′i·og′ra·pher n.**

hag·i·ol·o·gy (-äl′ə jē) **n.**, pl. **-gies** [HAGIO- + -LOGY] **1.** lit-erature about saints' lives and legends, sacred writings, etc. **2.** a list of saints **—hag′i·o·log′ic** (-ə läj′ik), **hag′i·o·log′i-cal adj.** **—hag′i·ol′o·gist n.**

hag·rid·den (hag′rid′'n) **adj.** obsessed or harassed, as by fears

Hague (hāg), **The** city in W Netherlands; seat of the government (see AMSTERDAM): pop. 551,000

hah (hä) **interj., n.** *same as* HA

Hahn (hän), **Otto** 1879–1968; Ger. nuclear physicist

Hah·ne·mann (hä′nə mən), **(Christian Friedrich) Samuel** 1755–1843; Ger. physician: founder of homeopathy

Hai·fa (hī′fə) seaport in NW Israel: pop. 210,000

hai·ku (hī′koo) **n.** [Jap.] **1.** a Japanese verse form of three un-rhymed lines of 5, 7, and 5 syllables respectively, usually on some subject in nature **2.** pl. **-ku** a poem in this form

hail¹ (hāl) **vt.** [< ON. < *heill*, whole, HALE¹] **1.** to welcome, greet, etc. as with cheers; acclaim **2.** to salute as [they *hailed* him their leader] **3.** to call out to, as in summoning [to *hail* a taxi] **—vi.** to call out or signal to a ship: a sailor's term **—n.** **1.** a hailing or greeting **2.** the distance that a shout will carry [within *hail*] **—interj.** an exclamation of tribute, greeting, etc. **—hail fellow well met** very friendly to everyone, but not in a serious way: also **hail fellow, hail-fellow** **—hail from** to come from or be from [he *hails from* Detroit] **—hail′er n.**

hail² (hāl) **n.** [OE. *hægel*] **1.** small, rounded pieces of ice that sometimes fall during thunderstorms; hailstones **2.** a falling, showering, etc. of or like hail [a *hail* of bullets] **—vi.** to pour down hail [it is *hailing*] **—vt.** to shower, hurl, etc. violently like hail (often with *on* or *upon*) [to *hail* curses on someone]

Hai·le Se·las·sie (hī′lē sə las′ē, -läs′ē) (born *Tafari Makon-nen*) 1891–1975; emperor of Ethiopia (1930–74); deposed

Hail Mary pl. **Hail Marys** *same as* AVE MARIA (sense 2)

hail·stone (hāl′stōn′) **n.** a piece of hail

hail·storm (-stôrm′) **n.** a storm in which hail falls

Hai·nan (hī′nän′) island of China off its S coast, in the South China Sea: c.13,000 sq. mi.

Hai·phong (hī′fäŋ′) seaport in N North Vietnam: pop. 369,000

hair (her) **n.** [OE. *hær*] **1.** any of the fine, threadlike outgrowths from the skin of an animal or human being **2.** a growth of these; esp., the growth covering the human head or the skin of most mammals **3.** an extremely small space, margin, degree, etc. [you missed the bull's-eye by a *hair*] **4.** a threadlike growth on the leaves or stems of some plants **—adj.** **1.** made of or with hair **2.** for the care of the hair [*hair* tonic] **—☆get in one's hair** [Slang] to annoy one **—let one's hair down** [Slang] to be very informal, relaxed, and free in behavior **—make one's hair stand on end** to horrify one **—split hairs** to make small differences seem more important than they are; quibble **—to a hair** exactly; perfectly **—hair′less adj.** **—hair′like′ adj.**

hair·breadth (her′bredth′) **n.** an extremely small space or amount [our team won by a *hairbreadth*] **—adj.** very narrow; very close [a *hairbreadth* escape] Also **hairs′breadth′, hairs′-breadth′**

hair·brush (-brush′) **n.** a brush for grooming the hair

hair·cloth (-klôth′) **n.** cloth woven from horsehair, camel's hair, etc.: used esp. for covering furniture

hair·cut (-kut′) **n.** **1.** a cutting of the hair of the head **2.** the style in which the hair is cut **—hair′cut′ter n.**

☆**hair·do** (-doo′) **n.**, pl. **-dos′** the style in which a woman's hair is arranged; coiffure

hair·dress·er (-dres′ər) **n.** a person whose work is dressing women's hair **—hair′dress′ing n., adj.**

haired (herd) **adj.** having hair of a specified kind [fair-*haired*, short-*haired*]

hair·line (-līn′) **n.** **1.** a very thin line or stripe **2.** the outline of the hair on the head, esp. above the forehead

hair·net (-net′) **n.** a net or fine-meshed cap for keeping the hair in place

hair·piece (-pēs′) *n.* **1.** a toupee or wig **2.** a switch of hair, often styled, for a woman's hairdo

hair·pin (-pin′) *n.* a small, usually U-shaped, piece of wire, shell, etc., for keeping the hair in place —*adj.* shaped like a hairpin [*a hairpin* turn]

hair-rais·ing (-rā′ziŋ) *adj.* [Colloq.] causing the hair to stand on end; terrifying or shocking —**hair′-rais′er** *n.*

hair shirt a shirt or girdle of haircloth, worn by religious persons with the idea of punishing or purifying themselves

hair·split·ting (-split′iŋ) *adj., n.* treating small differences as if they were important; quibbling —**hair′split′ter** *n.*

hair·spring (-spriŋ′) *n.* a very slender, hairlike coil that controls the regular movement of the balance wheel in a watch or clock

hair trigger a trigger so delicately adjusted that slight pressure on it makes the firearm go off

hair·y (-ē) *adj.* **hair′i·er, hair′i·est** **1.** covered with hair **2.** of or like hair ☆**3.** [Slang] difficult, upsetting, etc. —**hair′i·ness** *n.*

Hai·ti (hāt′ē) country occupying the W portion of the island of Hispaniola, West Indies: 10,714 sq. mi.; pop. 4,206,000; cap. Port-au-Prince —**Hai·tian** (hā′shən, hāt′ē ən) *adj., n.*

hajj (haj) *n.* [Ar. *ḥajj* < *ḥajji*, to go on a pilgrimage] the pilgrimage to Mecca that every Moslem is expected to make at least once

haj·ji, haj·i (haj′ē) *n.* [< Ar., pilgrim: see prec.] a Moslem who has made a pilgrimage to Mecca

hake (hāk) *n., pl.* **hake, hakes:** see PLURAL, II, D, 2 [prob. < ON. *haki*, a hook (from shape of the jaw)] any of various sea fishes related to the cod and caught for food, as the **silver hake**

ha·kim[1] (hä kēm′) *n.* [Ar. *ḥakīm*, wise, learned] in Moslem regions, a doctor; physician

ha·kim[2] (hä′kēm, -kim) *n.* [Ar. *ḥakim*, governor] in Moslem regions, a ruler, judge, or governor

Hak·luyt (hak′lōōt), **Richard** 1552?-1616; Eng. geographer who wrote about explorations & discoveries

hal·berd (hal′bərd) *n.* [ult. < MHG. *helmbarte* < *helm*, handle + *barte*, an ax] a combination spear and battle-ax used in the 15th and 16th cent.: also **hal′bert** (-bərt) —**hal′berd·ier′** (-bər dir′) *n.*

hal·cy·on (hal′sē ən) *n.* [< L. < Gr. *alkyōn*, kingfisher] a bird somewhat like the kingfisher, spoken of in legend as having a peaceful, calming influence on the sea at the time when winter begins —*adj.* **1.** of the halcyon **2.** peaceful, happy, idyllic, etc.: esp. in phrase **halcyon days**

hale[1] (hāl) *adj.* **hal′er, hal′est** [OE. *hal* < IE. base *kailo-*, whole] sound in body; vigorous and healthy [grandfather is still *hale* and hearty] —see SYN. at HEALTHY —**hale′ness** *n.*

hale[2] (hāl) *vt.* **haled, hal′ing** [< OFr. *haler*, prob. < ODu. *halen:* see HAUL] to force (one) to go [*haled* him into court]

Hale (hāl), **Nathan** 1755-76; Am. soldier in the Revolutionary War: hanged by the British as a spy

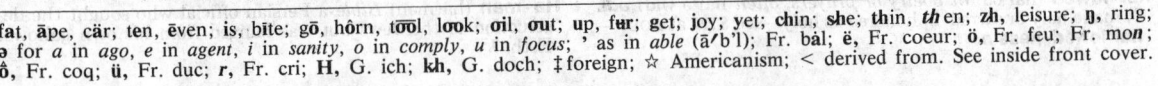

HALBERD

Ha·le·a·ka·la National Park (hä′lä ä′kä lä′) national park on the island of Maui, Hawaii, including a dormant volcano (**Haleakala**) with a crater of 19 sq. mi.

hal·er (häl′ər) *n., pl.* **-er·u′** (-ə rōō′), **-ers** [Czech, ult. < MHG. *Haller (pfenninc)*, (penny of) Hall, a Ger. coin made at Hall, Swabia] see MONETARY UNITS, table (Czechoslovakia)

half (haf) *n., pl.* **halves** [OE. *healf:* for IE. base see CUTLASS] **1.** *a)* either of the two equal parts of something [five is *half* of ten] *b)* either of two almost equal parts [he took the smaller *half* of the pie] **2.** *a)* a half hour [*half* past one] ☆*b)* a half dollar **3.** ☆*a)* Baseball either of the two parts of an inning ☆*b)* Basketball, Football, etc. either of the two equal periods of the game, between which the players rest —*adj.* **1.** *a)* being either of the two equal parts [a *half* gallon] *b)* being about a half of the amount, length, etc. [a *half* mask covered his eyes] **2.** incomplete; partial [I could barely see him in the *half* light] —*adv.* **1.** to an extent that is just about or exactly fifty percent of the whole [*half* full; *half* baked] **2.** [Colloq.] to some extent [I was *half* convinced] **3.** [Colloq.] by any means; at all: used with *not* [not *half* bad] —**by half** considerably; very much —**in half** into halves —**not the half of** only a small part of

half-and-half (haf′'n haf′) *n.* something that is half one thing

and half another; esp., ☆*a)* a mixture of equal parts of milk and cream *b)* [Chiefly Brit.] a mixture of equal parts of porter and ale, beer and stout, etc. —*adj.* combining two things equally —*adv.* in two equal parts

half·back (haf′bak′) *n. Football* either of two players whose position is behind the line of scrimmage together with the fullback and the quarterback

half·baked (-bākt′) *adj.* **1.** only partly baked **2.** not completely planned or thought out [a *half-baked* idea] **3.** having or showing little intelligence and experience

half·blood (-blud′) *n.* **1.** a person related to another through one parent only ☆**2.** *same as* HALF-BREED —*adj. same as* HALF-BLOODED

half blood **1.** kinship through one parent only [sisters of the *half blood*] **2.** *same as* HALF-BLOODED

half-blood·ed (-blud′id) *adj.* **1.** related through one parent only **2.** born of parents of different races

half boot a boot reaching halfway up the lower leg

☆**half-breed** (-brēd′) *n.* a person whose parents are of different races; esp., an offspring of an American Indian and a white person —*adj. same as* HALF-BLOODED Sometimes regarded as a term of contempt

half brother a brother through one parent only

half-caste (-kast′) *n.* a half-breed; esp., an offspring of one European parent and one Asiatic parent —*adj.* of a half-caste

half cock the halfway position of the hammer of a firearm, when the trigger is locked —**go off half-cocked** **1.** to go off too soon: said of a firearm **2.** to speak or act thoughtlessly or too hastily: also **go off at half cock** —**half′-cocked′** *adj.*

☆**half dollar** a coin of the U.S. and Canada, worth 50 cents

half gainer a fancy dive in which the diver, facing forward, does a back flip in the air so as to enter the water headfirst, facing the board

half-heart·ed (-här′tid) *adj.* with little enthusiasm, determination, interest, etc. [a *halfhearted* attempt] —**half′heart′ed·ly** *adv.* —**half′heart′ed·ness** *n.*

half hitch a knot made by passing the end of the rope around the rope and then through the loop thus made: it is the simplest kind of hitch: see illustration at KNOT

HALF GAINER

half-hour (-our′) *n.* **1.** half of an hour; thirty minutes **2.** the point thirty minutes after any given hour [take your medicine on the *half-hour*] —*adj.* **1.** lasting for thirty minutes **2.** occurring every thirty minutes —**half′-hour′ly** *adj., adv.*

half-life (-līf′) *n.* the period required for the disintegration of half of the atoms in a sample of some radioactive substance: also **half life**

half-mast (-mast′) *n.* the position of a flag lowered about halfway down its staff, as in public mourning for an important person who has died —*vt.* to hang (a flag) at half-mast

half-moon (-mōōn′) *n.* **1.** the moon between new moon and full moon, at either the first quarter or last quarter, when only half its disk is clearly seen **2.** anything shaped like a half-moon or crescent

half nelson *see* NELSON

half note *Music* a note held one half as long as a whole note: see illustration at NOTE

half-pen·ny (hā′pə nē, hāp′nē) *n., pl.* **-pence** (-pens), **-pennies** a former British coin equal to half a penny —*adj.* worth a halfpenny, or very little

half pint **1.** a liquid or dry measure equal to 1/4 quart ☆**2.** [Slang] a small person

half sister a sister through one parent only

half size any of a series of sizes in women's garments for short-waisted, mature figures

half slip a woman's slip without a top

half-sole (haf′sōl′) *vt.* **-soled′, -sol′ing** to repair (shoes or boots) by attaching new half soles

half sole a sole (of a shoe or boot) from the arch to the toe

☆**half-staff** (-staf′) *n. same as* HALF-MAST

---

fat, āpe, cär; ten, ēven; is, bīte; gō, hôrn, tōōl, look; oil, out; up, fur; get; joy; yet; chin; she; thin, *th*en; zh, leisure; ŋ, ring; ə for *a* in *ago, e* in *agent, i* in *sanity, o* in *comply, u* in *focus*; ′ as in *able* (ā′b'l); Fr. bâl; ë, Fr. coeur; ö, Fr. feu; Fr. mon; ô, Fr. coq; ü, Fr. duc; *r*, Fr. cri; H, G. ich; kh, G. doch; ‡foreign; ☆ Americanism; < derived from. See inside front cover.

half step 1. *Mil.* a short marching step of fifteen inches (in double time, eighteen inches) **2.** *Music same as* SEMITONE

half·tim·bered (-tim′bərd) *adj.* made with a wooden framework that can be seen and with the spaces in between filled with plaster, brick, etc. *[a half-timbered house]*

☆**half time** the rest period between halves of a football game, basketball game, etc.

half·tone (-tōn′) *n.* **1.** *Art* a tone or shading between light and dark **2.** *Music same as* SEMITONE **3.** *Photoengraving a)* a technique of shading by means of dots produced by photographing the object from behind a fine screen *b)* a photoengraving so made

☆**half·track** (-trak′) *n.* an army truck, armored vehicle, etc. with tractor treads instead of rear wheels, but with a pair of wheels in front

half-truth (-trōōth′) *n.* a statement or account containing only some of the facts, the rest often being left out with the intention of deceiving

half·way (-wā′) *adj.* **1.** equally distant between two points, states, etc.; midway *[they reached the halfway mark]* **2.** incomplete; partial *[to take halfway measures]* —*adv.* **1.** half the distance; to the midway point *[he had gone halfway home]* **2.** incompletely; partially *[the house is halfway built]* —**meet halfway** to try to reach an agreement by having each side give up something

halfway house ☆a place where persons are aided in adjusting to society again after having been in a prison, hospital, etc. for a time

half-wit (-wit′) *n.* a stupid, silly, or feeble-minded person; fool; dolt —**half′-wit′ted** *adj.*

hal·i·but (hal′ə bət) *n., pl.* **-but, -buts:** see PLURAL, II, D, 2 *[< ME. < hali,* holy + *butt,* a flounder: because eaten on holidays] a large flatfish found in northern seas and caught for food, esp. the **Atlantic halibut:** they sometimes weigh hundreds of pounds

Hal·i·car·nas·sus (hal′ə kär nas′əs) ancient city in SW Asia Minor, on the Aegean

hal·ide (hal′īd, hā′līd) *n.* [HAL(OGEN) + -IDE] *Chem.* a compound of a halogen with another element or a radical — *adj. same as* HALOID

Hal·i·fax (hal′ə faks′) capital of Nova Scotia; seaport on the Atlantic: pop. 118,000

hal·ite (hal′īt, hā′līt) *n.* [< Gr. *hals,* salt + -ITE] native sodium chloride; rock salt

☆**hal·i·to·sis** (hal′ə tō′sis) *n.* [ModL. < L. *halitus,* breath + -OSIS] bad-smelling breath

hall (hôl) *n.* [OE. *heall* < base of *helan,* to cover: see CELL] **1.** the large country house of a baron, squire, etc. **2.** [*sometimes* H-] a building containing public offices or the headquarters of an organization *[the city hall]* **3.** a large room or auditorium used for gatherings, entertainments, etc. **4.** [*sometimes* H-] a college dormitory, classroom building, etc. **5.** a passageway or room between the entrance and the interior of a building; vestibule, foyer, or lobby **6.** a passageway or corridor onto which rooms open

Hal·le (häl′ə; *E.* hal′ē) city in SC East Germany: pop. 266,000

hal·le·lu·jah, hal·le·lu·iah (hal′ə lōō′yə) *interj.* [< LL. < Gr. < Heb. < *hallelū,* praise + *yāh,* Jehovah] praise (ye) the Lord! —*n.* an exclamation, hymn, or song of praise to God

Hal·ley's comet (hal′ēz) a comet, last seen in 1910: it was predicted that the comet would reappear just about every 75 years by Edmund Halley (1656-1742), Eng. astronomer, that the comet would reappear just about every 75 years

hal·liard (hal′yərd) *n. same as* HALYARD

hall·mark (hôl′märk′) *n.* **1.** an official mark stamped on British gold and silver articles orig. at Goldsmiths' Hall in London, as a guarantee of genuineness **2.** any mark or symbol of genuineness or high quality —*vt.* to put a hallmark on

hal·lo, hal·loa (hə lō′) *interj., n., vi., vt. same as* HALLOO

hal·loo (hə lōō′) *vi., vt.* **-looed′, -loo′ing 1.** to call out in order to attract the attention of (a person) **2.** to urge on (hounds) by shouting **3.** to shout —*interj., n.* a shout or call

hal·low (hal′ō) *vt.* [OE. *halgian < halig,* HOLY] **1.** to make holy or sacred; consecrate **2.** to regard as holy; honor as sacred

hal·lowed (hal′ōd; *in poetry or prayers, often* hal′ə wid) *adj.* **1.** made holy or sacred **2.** honored as holy —see SYN. at HOLY — **hal′lowed·ness** *n.*

Hal·low·een, Hal·low·e'en (hal′ə wēn′, häl′-) *n.* [contr. < *all hallow even*] the evening of October 31, which is followed by All Saints' Day: Halloween is now generally celebrated with fun-making and masquerading: see TRICK OR TREAT

hal·lu·ci·nate (hə lōō′sə nāt′) *vi., vt.* **-nat′ed, -nat′ing** [< L. pp. of *hallucinari,* to wander mentally] to have or cause to have hallucinations

hal·lu·ci·na·tion (hə lōō′sə nā′shən) *n.* **1.** the seeing or hearing of things around one that are not really there at all *[people who are mentally ill sometimes have hallucinations]* **2.** the thing seen or heard in this way —see SYN. at DELUSION — **hal·lu′ci·na′tive, hal·lu′ci·na·to′ry** (-ə tôr′ē) *adj.*

hal·lu·ci·no·gen (hə lōō′sə nə jen, hal′yoo sin′ə jen) *n.* a drug or other substance that produces hallucinations —**hal·lu′ci·no·gen′ic** *adj.*

☆**hall·way** (hôl′wā′) *n.* **1.** a passageway or room between the entrance and the interior of a building **2.** a passageway; corridor; hall

Hal·ma·he·ra (häl′mə her′ə) island of Indonesia, east of Celebes: 6,870 sq. mi.

ha·lo (hā′lō) *n., pl.* **-los, -loes** [< L. < Gr. *halōs,* circular threshing floor, halo around the sun < *halein,* to grind] **1.** a ring of light that seems to encircle the sun, moon, etc. **2.** a symbolic ring or disk of light shown around the head of a saint, angel, etc., as in pictures; nimbus: often used as a symbol of holiness or innocence **3.** the glory that people give to a famed, revered, or idealized person or thing —*vt.* **-loed, -lo·ing** to encircle with a halo

hal·o·gen (hal′ə jən) *n.* [< Gr. *hals,* salt + -GEN] any of the five very active, nonmetallic chemical elements, fluorine, chlorine, bromine, astatine, and iodine —**ha·log·e·nous** (ha läj′ə nəs) *adj.*

hal·o·gen·ate (-jə nāt′) *vt.* **-at′ed, -at′ing** to treat or combine with a halogen —**hal′o·gen·a′tion** *n.*

hal·oid (hal′oid, hā′loid) *adj.* [< Gr. *hals,* salt + -OID] of or like a halide —*n. same as* HALIDE

Hals (häls), **Frans** (fräns) 1580?-1666; Du. painter

halt¹ (hôlt) *n.* [< Fr. < G. < *halten,* to hold] a stop, esp. a temporary one, as in marching; pause —*vi., vt.* to come or bring to a halt —☆**call a halt** to order a stop

halt² (hôlt) *vi.* [< OE. *healtian < healt,* adj.] **1.** [Archaic] to limp **2.** to be uncertain; hesitate *[to halt in one's speech]* **3.** to have defects in flow, as of rhythm or logic —*adj.* limping; lame —*n.* [Archaic] a lameness —**the halt** those who are lame —**halt′ing·ly** *adv.*

hal·ter (hôl′tər) *n.* [OE. *hælftre*] **1.** a rope, strap, etc. for tying or leading an animal **2.** a rope for hanging a person; noose **3.** a woman's garment for covering the breast, held up by a loop around the neck —*vt.* to put a halter on (an animal)

hal·vah, hal·va (häl vä′) *n.* [< Turk. < Ar. *halwa*] a Turkish confection made of ground sesame seeds and nuts mixed with honey, etc.

halve (hav) *vt.* **halved, halv′ing 1.** to divide into two equal parts **2.** to share equally (*with* someone) **3.** to reduce to half *[this new process will halve our costs]* **4.** *Golf* to play (a hole, match, etc.) in the same number of strokes as one's opponent

halves (havz) *n. pl. of* HALF —**by halves 1.** halfway; imperfectly **2.** halfheartedly —**go halves** to share expenses, etc. equally

hal·yard (hal′yərd) *n.* [< ME. *halier < halien* (see HALE²)] a rope or tackle for raising or lowering a flag, sail, etc.

Ham (ham) *Bible* Noah's second son: Gen. 6:10

ham (ham) *n.* [OE. *hamm*] **1.** the part of the leg behind the knee **2.** *a)* the back of the thigh *b)* the thigh and the buttock together **3.** the hock or hind leg of a four-legged animal **4.** the upper part of a hog's hind leg, or meat from this, salted, smoked, etc. for eating ☆**5.** [Colloq.] an amateur radio operator ☆**6.** [Slang] an incompetent actor or performer, esp. one who overacts

ham·a·dry·ad (ham′ə drī′əd, -ad) *n.* [< L. < Gr. < *hama,* together with + *dryas,* DRYAD] [*also* H-] *Gr. Myth.* a dryad; wood nymph whose life ended with the death of the tree she lived in

Ha·man (hā′mən) *Bible* a Persian official who sought the destruction of the Jews but was hanged from his own gallows: Esth. 7

HALIBUT
(to 12 ft. long)

HALTER

Ham·burg (ham′bərg; *G.* häm′boorkh) seaport in N West Germany, on the Elbe: pop. 1,833,000

☆**ham·burg·er** (ham′bʉr′gər) *n.* [after HAMBURG] **1.** ground beef **2.** a fried, broiled, or baked patty of such meat, often eaten as a sandwich in a round bun Also **ham′burg**

hame (hām) *n.* [< MDu., horse collar] either of the two rigid pieces along the sides of a horse's collar, to which the traces are attached

Ha·mil·car Bar·ca (hə mil′kär bär′kə; ham′l kär′) 270?-228? B.C.; Carthaginian general: father of HANNIBAL

Ham·il·ton (ham′əl t'n) **1.** city & port in SE Ontario, Canada, on Lake Ontario: pop. 298,000 **2.** [after A. HAMILTON] city in SW Ohio: pop. 68,000 **3.** capital of Bermuda: pop. 3,000

Ham·il·ton (ham′əl t'n), **Alexander** 1757-1804; Am. statesman; 1st secretary of the U.S. treasury (1789-95) —**Ham′il·to′ni·an** (-tō′nē ən) *adj., n.*

Ham·ite (ham′īt) *n.* **1.** a person regarded as descended from Ham **2.** a member of any of several usually dark-skinned peoples of N and E Africa, including the Egyptians, Berbers, etc.

Ham·it·ic (ha mit′ik, hə-) *adj.* **1.** of Ham or the Hamites **2.** designating or of a group of African languages, including ancient Egyptian, Berber, and Cushitic

Ham·let (ham′lit) **1.** a famous tragedy by Shakespeare (c. 1602) **2.** the hero of this play, a Danish prince who avenges the murder of his father, the king, by killing his uncle Claudius, the murderer

ham·let (ham′lit) *n.* [< OFr. dim. of *hamel,* itself dim. of LowG. *hamm,* enclosed area] a very small village

ham·mer (ham′ər) *n.* [OE. *hamor;* for IE. base see ACID] **1.** a tool for pounding, usually consisting of a metal head and a handle **2.** a thing like this tool in shape or use; specif., *a)* the mechanism that strikes the firing pin or cap in a firearm *b)* any of the felt-covered mallets that strike against the strings of a piano *c)* a power tool for pounding metal into shape, breaking up paved surfaces, etc. **3.** the malleus, one of the bones of the middle ear: see illustration at EAR **4.** an auctioneer's gavel **5.** *Sports* a heavy metal ball attached to a wire and thrown for distance in a field event (**hammer throw**) —*vt.* **1.** to strike again and again as with a hammer [he *hammered* on the door] **2.** to make or fasten with a hammer and, often, nails [he *hammered* together a box] **3.** to drive, force, or shape as with hammer blows [to *hammer* an idea into someone's head] —*vi.* to strike many blows as with a hammer —**hammer (away) at 1.** to work energetically at **2.** to keep emphasizing —**hammer out 1.** to shape or flatten by hammering **2.** to take out by hammering [to *hammer out* dents] **3.** to develop or work out by careful thought or repeated effort [to *hammer out* a plan] —**ham′mer·er** *n.* —**ham′mer·like′** *adj.*

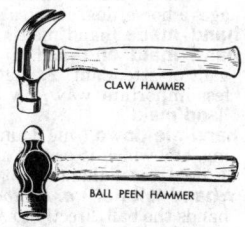

CLAW HAMMER

BALL PEEN HAMMER

TYPES OF HAMMER

hammer and sickle the emblem of Communist parties in some countries, consisting of a sickle (symbolizing peasants) placed across a hammer (symbolizing workers)

ham·mered (ham′ərd) *adj.* shaped or marked by hammer blows: said of metalwork

ham·mer·head (-hed′) *n.* **1.** the head of a hammer **2.** a medium-sized shark that has a mallet-shaped head with an eye near the center of each end

ham·mer·lock (-läk′) *n.* a wrestling hold in which one arm of the opponent is twisted upward behind his back

ham·mer·toe (-tō′) *n.* **1.** a condition in which the first joint of a toe is permanently bent downward, resulting in a clawlike deformity **2.** such a toe

ham·mock (ham′ək) *n.* [Sp. *hamaca* < native WInd. name] a length of netting, canvas, etc. swung from ropes at both ends and used as a bed or couch

HAMMERHEAD
SHARK
(to 15 ft. long)

Ham·mond (ham′ənd) [after G. *Hammond,* local meatpacker] city in NW Ind., near Chicago: pop. 108,000

Ham·mu·ra·bi (hä′moo rä′bē, ham′ə-) fl. 18th cent. B.C.; king of Babylon: a famous code of laws is named for him

ham·my (ham′ē) *adj.* **-mi·er, -mi·est** ☆[Slang] like or typical of a ham (actor); overacting

ham·per¹ (ham′pər) *vt.* [ME. *hampren*] to keep from moving or acting freely; hinder; impede; encumber [he was *hampered* by a heavy load]

ham·per² (ham′pər) *n.* [< OFr. < *hanap,* a cup < Frank.] a large basket, usually with a cover

Hamp·ton (hamp′tən) [after a town in England] seaport in SE Va., on Hampton Roads: pop. 121,000

Hamp·ton (hamp′tən, ham′-), **Wade** (wād) 1818-1902; U.S. politician & Confederate general

Hampton Roads [see HAMPTON & ROAD (sense 4)] channel in SE Va., linking the James River estuary with Chesapeake Bay

ham·ster (ham′stər) *n.* [G.] a ratlike animal with large cheek pouches: it is often used in scientific experiments or kept as a pet

ham·string (ham′striŋ′) *n.* **1.** one of the tendons at the back of the human knee **2.** the great tendon at the back of the hock in a four-legged animal —*vt.* **-strung′, -string′ing 1.** to disable by cutting a hamstring **2.** to take away the power of or make less effective

Han¹ (hän) river in C China, flowing southeastward into the Yangtze

Han² (hän) a Chinese dynasty (202 B.C.–220 A.D.) during which Buddhism was brought in and the arts were renewed

Han·cock (han′käk), **John** 1737-93; Am. statesman; 1st signer of the Declaration of Independence

hand (hand) *n.* [OE.] **1.** the part of the human arm below the wrist, used for grasping **2.** the part that is like this in apes, monkeys, etc. **3.** a side, direction, or position indicated by a hand [at one's right *hand*] **4.** possession or care [the papers are in my *hands*] **5.** control; power [to strengthen one's *hand*] **6.** an active part; share [take a *hand* in this work] **7.** *a)* a handshake, as a pledge *b)* a promise to marry **8.** skill; ability [a master's *hand*] **9.** *a)* handwriting *b)* a signature **10.** a clapping of hands; applause [they gave the singer a *hand*] **11.** assistance; help [to lend a *hand*] **12.** a person whose chief work is with his hands, as a sailor, farm laborer, etc. **13.** a person regarded as having some special skill [quite a *hand* at sewing] **14.** a person (or, sometimes, thing) from or through which something comes; source [to get a story at second *hand*] **15.** anything like a hand, as the pointer on a clock **16.** the breadth of a hand, about 4 inches [4 *hands*] **17.** a cluster of bananas **18.** *Card Games a)* the cards held by a player at one time *b)* a player *c)* a round of play —*adj.* of, for, made by, or controlled by the hand —*vt.* **1.** to give as with the hand; transfer **2.** to help, conduct, steady, etc. with the hand [to *hand* a lady into her car] —(at) **first hand** from the original source —**at hand 1.** near; close by **2.** immediately available —(at) **second hand 1.** not from the original source **2.** previously used —**at the hand** (or **hands**) **of** through the action of —**by hand** not by machines but with the hands —**change hands** to pass from one owner to another —**from hand to mouth** with just enough for present needs and nothing left over for the future —**hand and foot 1.** so that the hands and feet cannot move [bound *hand and foot*] **2.** constantly and diligently [he waited on her *hand and foot*] —**hand down 1.** to pass along, as from generation to generation ☆**2.** to announce (a verdict, etc.) —**hand in** to give; submit —**hand in hand 1.** holding one another's hand **2.** together; in cooperation —☆**hand it to** [Slang] to give deserved credit to —**hand on** to pass along; transmit —**hand out** to distribute —**hand over** to give up; deliver —**hand over fist** [Colloq.] easily and in large amounts —**hands down** without effort; easily —**hands off!** don't touch! don't interfere! —**hand to hand** at close quarters: said of fighting —**have one's hands full** to be extremely busy —**in hand 1.** in order or control **2.** in possession **3.** in process —**join hands 1.** to become associates or partners **2.** to become husband and wife —**lay hands on 1.** to attack physically **2.** to seize; take **3.** to touch with the hands in blessing, etc. —**not lift a hand** to do nothing; not even try —**off one's hands** no longer in one's care —**on every hand** on all sides —**on hand 1.** near ☆**2.** available ☆**3.** present —**on one's hands** in one's care —**on the one hand** from one point of view —**on the other hand** from the opposed point of view —**out of hand 1.** out of control **2.** immediately **3.** over and done with —**show** (or **tip**) **one's hand** to disclose one's intentions —**take in hand 1.** to take control of **2.** to handle; treat **3.** to try; attempt —**throw up one's hands** to give up in despair —**to hand 1.** near; accessible **2.** in one's possession —**turn** (or **put**) **one's hand to** to undertake; work at —**wash one's hands of** to refuse to go on with or take responsibility for —**with a heavy hand 1.** in a heavy manner; without delicacy or grace **2.** in a stern way —**with a high hand** with arrogance —**with clean hands** without guilt —**hand′less** *adj.*

hand- *a combining form meaning* of, with, by, or for a hand or hands *[handclasp, handcuff]*

hand·bag (hand′bag′) *n.* **1.** a small container for money, toilet articles, keys, etc., carried by women; purse **2.** a small suitcase or valise

hand·ball (-bôl′) *n.* **1.** a game in which players bat a small ball against a wall or walls with the hand **2.** the small rubber ball used in this game

hand·bar·row (-bar′ō) *n.* a frame carried by two people, each holding a pair of handles attached at either end

hand·bill (-bil′) *n.* a small printed notice, advertisement, etc. to be passed out by hand

hand·blown (-blōn′) *adj.* shaped individually by a glass-blower: said of objects made of glass

hand·book (-book′) *n.* **1.** a compact reference book on some subject; manual **2.** a guidebook

hand·breadth (-bredth′, -bretth′) *n.* the breadth of the human palm, about 4 inches

☆**hand·car** (-kär′) *n.* a small, open car, orig. hand-powered, used on railroads to transport workers, etc.

hand·cart (-kärt′) *n.* a small cart, often with only two wheels, pulled or pushed by hand

hand·clasp (-klasp′) *n.* a clasping of each other's hand in greeting, farewell, etc.

hand·craft (-kraft′) *n. same as* HANDICRAFT —*vt.* to make by hand with skill —**hand′craft′ed** *adj.*

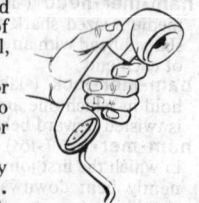

HANDCAR

hand·cuff (-kuf′) *n.* either of a pair of connected metal rings that can be locked about the wrists, as in fastening a prisoner to a policeman: *usually used in pl.* —*vt.* **1.** to put handcuffs on; manacle **2.** to check or hinder the activities of

hand·ed (han′did) *adj.* **1.** having a specified handedness, or for use by one having a specified handedness *[right-handed]* **2.** having or using a specified number of hands *[two-handed]* **3.** involving (a specified number of) players *[three-handed pinochle]*

hand·ed·ness (-nis) *n.* ability in using one hand more skillfully than the other

Han·del (han′d'l), **George Frederick** (born *Georg Friedrich Händel*) 1685-1759; Eng. composer, born in Germany

hand·feed (hand′fēd′) *vt.* **-fed′, -feed′ing** to feed by hand

hand·ful (hand′fool′) *n., pl.* **-fuls′ 1.** as much or as many as the hand will hold **2.** a relatively small number or amount *[a mere handful of people]* **3.** [Colloq.] someone or something hard to manage

hand grenade a small grenade thrown by hand and exploded by a timed fuse or when it hits something

hand·grip (hand′grip′) *n.* **1.** a handclasp or handshake **2.** a handle, as on a bicycle handlebar

hand·gun (-gun′) *n.* any firearm that is held and fired with one hand, as a pistol

hand·hold (-hōld′) *n.* **1.** a secure grip or hold with the hand or hands **2.** a part or thing to take hold of

hand·i·cap (han′dē kap′) *n.* [orig. a game in which forfeits were drawn from a cap < *hand in cap*] **1.** *a)* a race or other competition in which disadvantages are given to the expert contestants, or advantages given to the less expert, to make their chances of winning equal *b)* such a disadvantage or advantage *[a handicap of counting ten fewer strokes in a golf match]* **2.** something that holds a person back or makes things harder; disadvantage; hindrance *[the famous lawyer overcame the handicap of stuttering]* —*vt.* **-capped′, -cap′ping 1.** to give a handicap or handicaps to (contestants) **2.** to cause to be at a disadvantage; hinder —**the handicapped** those who are physically disabled or mentally retarded —**hand′i·cap′per** *n.*

hand·i·craft (han′dē kraft′) *n.* [OE. *handcræft*] **1.** skill in

working with the hands **2.** work or art calling for this kind of skill, as weaving —**hand′i·crafts′man** *n., pl.* **-men**

hand·i·ly (han′d'l ē) *adv.* **1.** in a handy manner; deftly or conveniently **2.** with no trouble; easily *[to win handily]*

hand·i·ness (han′dē nis) *n.* the quality of being handy; skill in working with the hands

hand·i·work (han′dē wurk′) *n.* **1.** *same as* HANDWORK **2.** anything made or done by a particular person *[is this poem your handiwork?]*

hand·ker·chief (haŋ′kər chif, -chēf′) *n., pl.* **-chiefs** (-chifs, -chēfs′, -chivz, -chēvz′) **1.** a small, square piece of cloth for wiping the nose or face, or worn for ornament **2.** a kerchief

hand-knit (hand′nit′) *adj.* knit by hand instead of by machine: also **hand′-knit′ted**

han·dle (han′d'l) *n.* [OE. < *hand*, HAND] **1.** that part of a utensil, tool, etc. which is to be held, turned, etc. with the hand **2.** a thing like a handle **3.** [Colloq.] a person's name, nickname, or title —*vt.* **-dled, -dling 1.** to touch, lift, etc. with the hand or hands **2.** to operate or use with the hands *[to handle a saw]* **3.** to manage, control, etc. *[police handled the traffic]* **4.** to deal with *[to handle a problem tactfully]* ☆**5.** to sell or deal in *[the drugstore handles many items]* **6.** to behave toward; treat —*vi.* to respond to control *[the car handles well]* —**fly off the handle** [Colloq.] to become violently angry or excited —**get a handle on** [Colloq.] to find a means of dealing with, understanding, etc. —**han′dle·less** *adj.*

han·dle·bar (-bär′) *n.* **1.** [often pl.] a curved metal bar with handles on the ends, for steering a bicycle, motorcycle, etc. ☆**2.** [Colloq.] a mustache with long curved ends: in full, **handlebar mustache**

han·dler (han′dlər) *n.* a person or thing that handles; specif., *a)* a boxer's trainer and second *b)* a person who trains and manages a horse, dog, etc. in a show or contest

hand·made (hand′mād′) *adj.* made by hand, not by machine

hand·maid·en (-mād′'n) *n.* **1.** [Archaic] a woman or girl servant or attendant **2.** that which accompanies in a useful but less important way *[law is the handmaiden of justice]* Also **hand′maid′**

hand-me-down (-mē doun′, *n.* [Colloq.] a used article of clothing, etc. which is passed along to someone else —*adj.* [Colloq.] **1.** used; secondhand **2.** ready-made and cheap

☆**hand-off** (-ôf′) *n. Football* an offensive play in which a back hands the ball directly to another back

☆**hand organ** a barrel organ played by turning a crank

☆**hand·out** (hand′out′) *n.* **1.** a gift of food, clothing, etc., as to a beggar or tramp **2.** a pamphlet or leaflet handed out as for publicity **3.** a statement or story prepared for release to the news media, as by a government

hand·pick (-pik′) *vt.* **1.** to pick (fruit or vegetables) by hand **2.** to choose with care or for a special purpose —**hand′picked′** *adj.*

hand·rail (-rāl′) *n.* a rail serving as a guard or hand support, as along a stairway

hand·saw (-sô′) *n.* a saw used with one hand: see illustration at SAW

hand's-breadth (handz′bredth′, -bretth′) *n. same as* HAND-BREADTH

hand·sel (han′s'l, hant′-) *n.* [< ON. *handsal*, sealing of a bargain by a handclasp] a present for good luck, as at the new year or on the launching of a new business —*vt.* **-seled** or **-selled, -sel·ing** or **-sel·ling** to give a handsel to

☆**hand·set** (hand′set′) *n.* a telephone mouthpiece and receiver in a single unit, held in one hand

hand·shake (-shāk′) *n.* a gripping of each other's hand in greeting, farewell, agreement, etc.

hands-off (handz′ôf′) *adj.* designating or of a policy, attitude, etc. of not trying to manage, control, or influence someone or something

hand·some (han′səm) *adj.* [orig., easily handled < ME.: see HAND & -SOME[1]] **1.** large; considerable *[a handsome sum]* **2.** generous; gracious *[a handsome gesture]* **3.** good-looking; of pleasing appearance, esp. in a manly or dignified way —see SYN. at BEAUTIFUL —**hand′some·ly** *adv.* —**hand′some·ness** *n.*

HANDSET

hand·spring (hand′spriŋ′) *n.* a stunt in tumbling in which the performer turns over in midair with one or both hands touching the ground

hand·stand (-stand′) *n.* a gymnastic stunt of supporting one-self upright on the hands with the legs in the air

hand-to-hand (han′tə hand′) *adj.* in close contact; at close quarters: said of fighting

hand-to-mouth (-mouth′) *adj.* with just enough to live on and with nothing left over [a *hand-to-mouth* existence]

hand·work (hand′wurk′) *n.* work done or made by hand, not by machine —**hand′worked** *adj.*

hand-wo·ven (-wō′vən) *adj.* woven on a loom operated by hand, not by machine power

hand·writ·ing (-rīt′iŋ) *n.* **1.** writing done by hand, with pen, pencil, etc. **2.** a person's way of forming letters and words in writing [her *handwriting* slants to the left] —**see the handwriting on the wall** to foresee a disaster, misfortune, etc. that seems about to happen —**hand′writ′ten** (-rit′'n) *adj.*

hand·y (han′dē) *adj.* **hand′i·er, hand′i·est 1.** close at hand; easily reached [the bus stop is *handy*] **2.** easily used; saving time or work [a *handy* device] **3.** easily managed or handled: said of a ship, etc. **4.** clever in using one's hands; deft —see SYN. at DEXTEROUS —**hand′i·ly** *adv.* —**hand′i·ness** *n.*

Han·dy (han′dē), **W**(illiam) **C**(hristopher) 1873–1958; U.S. jazz musician & composer

han·dy·man (-man′) *n., pl.* **-men′** a man employed at various small tasks; one who does odd jobs

hang (haŋ) *vt.* **hung, hang′ing;** for *vt.* 3 & *vi.* 4 **hanged** is preferred pt. & pp. [OE. *hangian* < IE. base *kenk*-] **1.** to attach to something above with no support from below; suspend [to *hang* curtains on a rod] **2.** to attach so as to permit free motion at the point of attachment [to *hang* a door on its hinges] **3.** to put to death by suspending from a rope about the neck **4.** to fasten (pictures, etc.) to a wall **5.** to ornament or cover (*with* things suspended) [to *hang* a room with pictures] **6.** to paste (wallpaper) to walls **7.** to let (one's head) droop downward ☆**8.** to deadlock (a jury) by one's vote **9.** to fix (something) *on* a person or thing —*vi.* **1.** to be suspended with no support from below **2.** to swing, as on a hinge **3.** to fall, flow, or drape, as cloth, a coat, etc. **4.** to die by hanging **5.** to droop; bend **6.** to be doubtful or undecided; hesitate **7.** to have one's pictures exhibited at a museum, etc. —*n.* the way that a thing hangs —☆**get** (or **have**) **the hang of 1.** to learn (or have) the knack of **2.** to understand the meaning or idea of —☆**hang around** (or **about**) **1.** to cluster around **2.** [Colloq.] to loiter around —**hang back** (or **off**) to be reluctant to advance, as because one is timid or shy —**hang fire** to be unsettled or undecided —**hang on 1.** to keep hold **2.** to go on doing; persevere **3.** to depend on **4.** to lean on **5.** to listen attentively to [she *hangs on* his every word] —**hang out 1.** to lean out **2.** to display, as by suspending **3.** [Slang] to spend much of one's time; frequent —**hang over** to project, hover, or loom over —**hang together 1.** to stick together **2.** to make sense, as a story —**hang up 1.** to put on a hanger, hook, etc. **2.** to end a telephone conversation by replacing the receiver **3.** to delay or stop for a time the progress of [we were *hung up* in traffic] —**not care** (or **give**) **a hang about** to not care the least bit about

hang·ar (haŋ′ər) *n.* [Fr., a shed ss a repair shed or shelter for aircraft] —*vt.* to put or keep in a hangar

Hang·chow (haŋ′chou′; *Chin.* hän′jō′) river & canal port in E China: pop. 784,000

hang·dog (haŋ′dôg′) *n.* a sneaking person regarded with contempt —*adj.* **1.** sneaking or regarded with contempt **2.** ashamed and cringing [a *hangdog* expression]

hang·er (haŋ′ər) *n.* **1.** a person who hangs things [a *paperhanger*] **2.** a thing on which garments, etc. are hung

hang·er-on (-än′) *n., pl.* **hang′ers-on′** a follower or dependent; specif., a follower who is not wanted or who wants to gain something for himself

☆**hang gliding** the sport of gliding through the air while hanging by a harness from a large type of kite (**hang glider**)

hang·ing (haŋ′iŋ) *adj.* **1.** suspended with no support from below **2.** leaning over; overhanging **3.** located on a steep slope [*hanging* gardens] **4.** deserving or giving the death penalty **5.** designating or of indention in which the first line of a paragraph touches the left margin, the other lines being indented beneath it **6.** not yet decided; unsettled —*n.* **1.** a suspending or being suspended **2.** a putting to death by hanging **3.** something hung, as a drapery or tapestry

hang·man (-mən) *n., pl.* **-men** an executioner who hangs convicted criminals

hang·nail (-nāl′) *n.* [altered < ME. *angnail* < OE. *angnægl*, a corn] a bit of torn skin hanging next to a fingernail

☆**hang·out** (-out′) *n.* [Slang] a place where some person or group spends much time

☆**hang·o·ver** (-ō′vər) *n.* **1.** something remaining from a previous time or state; a survival **2.** headache, nausea, etc. occurring as an aftereffect of drinking much alcoholic liquor

☆**hang-up** (-up′) *n.* [Slang] a problem or difficulty a person seems unable to deal with [to have a *hang-up* about being tall]

hank (haŋk) *n.* [prob. < Scand.] **1.** a loop or coil of something loose **2.** a standard length of coiled thread or yarn

hank·er (haŋ′kər) *vi.* [prob. < Du. or LowG.] to have a strong wish or longing; crave (followed by *after, for,* or an infinitive) —**hank′er·er** *n.* —**hank′er·ing** *n.*

han·kie, han·ky (haŋ′kē) *n., pl.* **-kies** [Colloq.] a handkerchief

han·ky-pan·ky (haŋ′kē paŋ′kē) *n.* [altered < HOCUS-POCUS] [Colloq.] trickery or deception

Han·nah, Han·na (han′ə) [var. of ANNA] a feminine name

Han·ni·bal (han′ə b'l) 247?–183? B.C.; Carthaginian general: crossed the Alps to invade Italy in 218 B.C.

Ha·noi (hä noi′, ha-) capital of Vietnam, in the N part: pop. 644,000

Han·o·ver[1] (han′ō vər) ruling family of England (1714–1901): founded by George I, orig. Elector of a territory which included the city of Hanover —**Han′o·ve′ri·an** (-vir′ē ən) *adj., n.*

Han·o·ver[2] (han′ō vər) city in N West Germany: pop. 527,000: Ger. name **Han·no·ver** (hä nō′vər, -fər)

Hans (hans, hanz; *G.* häns) [G. abbrev. of *Johannes,* JOHN] a masculine name

hanse (hans) *n.* [ult. < OHG. *hansa,* band of men] a medieval guild of merchants: also **han·sa** (han′sə) —**the Hanse** a medieval league of free towns in N Germany and nearby countries, joined to help one another in trade: also **Hanseatic League**

Han·se·at·ic (han′sē at′ik) *adj.* of the Hanse

han·sel (han′s'l) *n. same as* HANDSEL

Han·sen's disease (han′s'nz, hän′-) [after A. *Hansen* (1841–1912), Norw. physician] *same as* LEPROSY

han·som (**cab**) (han′səm) [after J. A. *Hansom* (1803–1882), Eng. inventor] a two-wheeled covered carriage for two passengers, pulled by one horse: the driver's seat is above and behind the cab

Han·son (han′s'n), **Howard** 1896– ; U.S. composer

Ha·nu·ka (khä′noo kä′, -kə; hä′-) *n.* [Heb. *hanûkkâh,* dedication] a Jewish festival in early winter commemorating the rededication of the Temple by the Maccabees in 165 B.C.: also **Ha′nuk·kah′, Ha′nuk·ka′**

HANSOM

hap (hap) *n.* [< ON. *happ*] chance; luck —*vi.* **happed, hap′ping** to occur by chance; happen

hap·haz·ard (hap′haz′ərd) *n.* [HAP + HAZARD] mere chance; accident —*adj.* not planned; casual —*adv.* by chance; casually [toys scattered *haphazard* on the floor] —see SYN. at RANDOM —**hap′haz′ard·ly** *adv.* —**hap′haz′ard·ness** *n.*

hap·less (hap′lis) *adj.* unfortunate; unlucky —**hap′less·ly** *adv.* —**hap′less·ness** *n.*

hap·loid (hap′loid) *adj.* [< Gr. *haploos,* single + -OID] *Biol.* having the full number of chromosomes normally occurring in the mature germ cell, equal to half the number of the normal somatic cell: see DIPLOID —**hap′loi′dy** (-loi′dē) *n.*

hap·ly (hap′lē) *adv.* [Archaic] by chance or accident; perhaps

hap·pen (hap′'n) *vi.* [ME. *happenen:* see HAP & -EN] **1.** to take place; occur [what *happened* at the party?] **2.** to be or occur by chance or without plan [it *happened* to rain that day] **3.** to have the luck or occasion; chance [I *happened* to see it] **4.** to come by chance (*along, by, in,* etc.) —**happen on** (or **upon**) to meet or find by chance —**happen to** to be done to or be the fate of; befall

SYN. —**happen** is the general word meaning to take place or come to pass and may suggest a direct cause or a seeming accident; **occur** is somewhat more formal and usually suggests a specific event at a specific time [what *happened?* the accident *occurred* at four o'clock]; **transpire** is now frequently used with the meaning of **happen** or **occur** in what some people regard as a loose usage [what *transpired* at the conference?]

hap·pen·ing (-iŋ) *n.* something that happens; occurrence; incident; event [the day's *happenings*]

☆**hap·pen·stance** (-stans′) *n.* [HAPPEN + (CIRCUM)STANCE] [Colloq.] chance occurrence; accidental happening

hap·py (hap′ē) *adj.* **-pi·er, -pi·est** [ME. *happi* < HAP] **1.** favored by circumstances; lucky; fortunate [the story has a *happy* ending] **2.** having, showing, or causing a feeling of pleasure, joy, etc. [a *happy* man; a *happy* song] **3.** suitable and clever; apt; felicitous [a *happy* suggestion] —**hap′pi·ly** *adv.* —**hap′pi·ness** *n.*

SYN.—**happy** generally suggests a feeling of great pleasure, contentment, etc. [a *happy* marriage]; **glad** more strongly implies a feeling of joy [your letter made her so *glad!*], but both **glad** and **happy** are commonly used in merely polite phrases expressing pleasure [I'm *glad,* or *happy,* to have met you]; **cheerful** implies a steady display of bright spirits, optimism, etc. [she is always *cheerful* in the morning]; **joyful** and **joyous** both imply very high spirits and rejoicing, the former generally because of a particular event [the good news made them *joyful*], and the latter usually because of a continuing situation [they were a *joyous* family] See also **SYN.** at LUCKY —**ANT.** sad

hap·py-go-luck·y (-gō luk′ē) *adj.* easygoing; trusting to luck; lighthearted and carefree

Haps·burg (haps′bʉrg′; *G.* häps′bōōrkh) ruling family of Austria, Austria-Hungary, Spain, & the Holy Roman Empire at various times from 1278 to 1918

ha·ra-ki·ri (hä′rə kir′ē, har′ə-; *popularly* her′ē ker′ē) *n.* [Jap. *hara,* belly + *kiri,* a cutting] suicide done as a ritual by cutting one's bowels open: it was practiced by high-ranking Japanese to avoid facing disgrace

ha·rangue (hə raŋ′) *n.* [< OFr. *arenge* < OIt. < *aringo,* site for public assemblies < Goth.] a long, blustering or scolding speech; tirade —*vi., vt.* **-rangued′, -rangu′ing** to give a harangue or speak to in a harangue —**ha·rangu′er** *n.*

har·ass (hə ras′, har′əs) *vt.* [Fr. *harasser* < OFr. *harer,* to set a dog on < Frank.] **1.** to trouble, worry, or torment, as with cares, debts, etc. **2.** to trouble by repeated raids or attacks, etc.; harry —**har·ass′er** *n.* —**har·ass′ment** *n.*

Har·bin (här′bin) city in NE China: pop. 1,552,000

har·bin·ger (här′bin jər) *n.* [OFr. *herbergeor,* provider of lodging < *herberge,* a shelter < Frank.] a person or thing that comes before to announce or indicate what will follow; herald [the first frost is a *harbinger* of winter] —*vt.* to serve as harbinger of; announce; foretell

har·bor (här′bər) *n.* [< OE. < *here,* army + *beorg,* a shelter] **1.** a place where one is safe or protected; shelter **2.** a protected inlet of a sea, lake, etc., where ships may anchor; port —*vt.* **1.** to provide a place of protection to; be a shelter or house for; conceal or hide [to *harbor* an outlaw] **2.** to hold in the mind; cling to [to *harbor* a grudge] —*vi.* to take shelter, as in a harbor —**har′bor·er** *n.* —**har′bor·less** *adj.*

har·bor·age (-ij) *n.* **1.** a shelter for ships **2.** shelter or lodgings

harbor master the official in charge of enforcing the regulations that should be followed by ships, boats, etc. using a harbor

har·bour (här′bər) *n., vt., vi. Brit. sp. of* HARBOR

hard (härd) *adj.* [OE. *heard:* for IE. base see CANCER] **1.** not easily pierced or crushed; firm to the touch; solid and compact [a *hard* shell] **2.** having firm muscles; vigorous and robust [his *hard,* lean body] **3.** powerful; violent [a *hard* blow] **4.** demanding great effort or labor; difficult; specif., *a*) difficult to do [*hard* work] *b*) difficult to understand or explain [a *hard* question] *c*) firmly fastened or tied [a *hard* knot] **5.** not easily moved; unfeeling [a *hard* heart] **6.** practical and shrewd [a *hard* customer] **7.** *a*) firm or definite, esp. in an aggressive way [a *hard* line in foreign policy] *b*) true or actual [*hard* facts] **8.** causing pain or discomfort; specif., *a*) difficult to endure [a *hard* life] *b*) harsh; severe; stern [a *hard* master] **9.** sharp or too sharp [*hard* outlines, a *hard* red] **10.** having in solution mineral salts that keep soap from making a lather: said of water **11.** energetic and persistent [a *hard* worker] **12.** *a*) containing alcohol [*hard* cider] *b*) strongly alcoholic [*hard* liquor] **13.** [Colloq.] designating any drug, as heroin, to which one can become addicted and which can be very damaging to the body or mind **14.** popularly, designating the letter *c* sounded as in *can* or the letter *g* sounded as in *gun* **15.** high and stable: said of a market, prices, etc. —*adv.* **1.** energetically and persistently [work *hard*] **2.** with strength, violence, or severity [hit *hard*] **3.** with difficulty [*hard*-earned] **4.** so as to withstand much

wear, use, etc. [*hard*-wearing clothes] **5.** firmly; tightly [hold on *hard*] **6.** close; near [we live *hard* by] **7.** so as to be or make firm or solid [to freeze *hard*] **8.** with vigor and to the fullest extent [turn *hard* right] —**be hard on 1.** to treat severely **2.** to be difficult or unpleasant for —**hard and fast** not to be changed; strict: said of rules, etc. —**hard of hearing** partially deaf —**hard put to it** having a great deal of difficulty —**hard up** [Colloq.] in great need of something, esp. money —**hard′ness** *n.*

SYN.—**hard** refers in a simple and direct way to whatever demands great physical or mental effort [*hard* work; a *hard* problem]; **difficult** applies especially to that which requires great skill, intelligence, tact, etc., rather than physical labor [a *difficult* situation]; **arduous** implies the need for diligent, prolonged effort [the *arduous* fight ahead of us]; **laborious** suggests long, wearisome toil [the *laborious* task of picking fruit] See also **SYN.** at FIRM[1] —**ANT. easy, simple**

hard·back (härd′bak′) *n.* a hard-cover book

☆**hard·ball** (-bôl′) *n. same as* BASEBALL

hard-bit·ten (-bit′'n) *adj.* stubborn; tough; enduring; dogged [*hard-bitten* soldiers]

☆**hard·board** (-bôrd′) *n.* a boardlike material made in sheets from wood-chip fibers, by pressing them together at high heats

hard-boiled (-boild′) *adj.* **1.** cooked in boiling water until both the white and the yolk become solid: said of an egg **2.** [Colloq.] not moved or touched by sentiment, pity, etc.; tough; callous

hard coal *same as* ANTHRACITE

hard-core (-kôr′) *adj.* **1.** that is or has to do with a hard core **2.** absolute; complete; thorough [*hard-core* pornography; a *hard-core* radical]

hard core the firm, unyielding, or unchanging central part or group

hard-cov·er (-kuv′ər) *adj.* designating any book bound in a relatively stiff cover, as of cloth-covered cardboard: also **hard′-bound′** (-bound′) See also PAPERBACK

hard·en (här′d'n) *vt., vi.* to make or become hard (in various senses) —**hard′en·er** *n.*

hard·ened (-d'nd) *adj.* **1.** made hard or harder **2.** set in one's ways, esp. ways that are wrong or immoral; habitual [a *hardened* criminal] —see **SYN.** at CHRONIC

hard-fist·ed (härd′fis′tid) *adj.* stingy; miserly

hard·goods (-goodz′) *n.pl.* goods lasting a relatively long time, such as automobiles, furniture, etc.: also **hard goods**

hard hat ☆**1.** a protective helmet worn by construction workers, miners, etc. ☆**2.** [Slang] such a worker

hard·head·ed (-hed′id) *adj.* **1.** having only practical thoughts and not moved by feeling [a *hardheaded* businessman] **2.** stubborn —**hard′head′ed·ly** *adv.* —**hard′head′ed·ness** *n.*

hard·heart·ed (-härt′id) *adj.* without pity or sympathy; cruel or unfeeling —**hard′-heart′ed·ly** *adv.* —**hard′heart′ed·ness** *n.*

har·di·hood (här′dē hood′) *n.* boldness, daring, fortitude, vigor, etc.

Har·ding (här′diŋ), **Warren Ga·ma·li·el** (gə mā′lē əl) 1865–1923; 29th president of the U.S. (1921–23)

HARD HAT

hard labor forced physical labor used, together with imprisonment, as a punishment for some crimes

☆**hard landing** a landing, as of a rocket on the moon, made at such a high speed as to destroy the equipment —**hard′-land′** *vi., vt.*

☆**hard-line** (härd′līn′) *adj.* having an aggressive, inflexible position in politics, foreign policy, etc.

hard·ly (härd′lē) *adv.* **1.** [Now Rare] *a*) with difficulty *b*) severely; harshly **2.** only just; scarcely [I can *hardly* tell them apart]: often used ironically to mean "not at all" [*hardly* the person to ask] **3.** probably not; not likely [that can *hardly* be the case]

☆**hard maple** *same as* SUGAR MAPLE

☆**hard-nosed** (-nōzd′) *adj.* [Slang] **1.** tough; stubborn **2.** shrewd and practical —**hard′nose′** *n.*

hard palate the bony part of the roof of the mouth, behind the upper front teeth

hard·pan (-pan′) *n.* **1.** a layer of hard, clayey soil through which it is difficult for roots and water to pass ☆**2.** the hard, underlying part of anything; solid foundation

☆**hard sauce** a creamy mixture of butter, sugar, and flavoring, served with plum pudding, etc.

☆**hard sell** high-pressure salesmanship —**hard′-sell′** *adj.*

hard-shell (-shel′) *adj.* **1.** having a hard shell: also **hard′-shelled′ 2.** [Colloq.] strict; strait-laced; firm or inflexible, esp. in religious matters

☆**hard-shelled** (or **hard-shell**) **crab** a crab before it has shed its hard shell, esp. an edible sea crab

hard·ship (-ship′) *n.* **1.** hard circumstances of life **2.** a thing hard to bear, as trouble, pain, suffering, etc. —see SYN. at DIFFICULTY

hard·tack (-tak′) *n.* [HARD + *tack* (food)] unleavened bread made in the form of very hard, large biscuits: traditionally a part of army and navy rations

☆**hard·top** (-täp′) *n.* an automobile like a convertible in having no post between the front and rear windows, but with a metal top that cannot fold back

hard·ware (-wer′) *n.* **1.** articles made of metal, as tools, nails, fittings, utensils, etc. ☆**2.** heavy military equipment or its parts ☆**3.** *a)* apparatus used for controlling spacecraft, etc. *b)* the mechanical, magnetic, and electronic design, structure, and devices of a computer: see also SOFTWARE

hard·wood (-wood′) *n.* **1.** any tough, heavy timber with a close grain **2.** *Forestry* wood other than that from a needle-bearing conifer **3.** a tree yielding hardwood

har·dy (här′dē) *adj.* **-di·er, -di·est** [< OFr. pp. of *hardir*, to make bold < Frank.] **1.** bold and determined; daring [a *hardy* adventurer] **2.** able to withstand fatigue, discomfort, etc.; strong and sturdy [he has a *hardy* constitution] **3.** able to survive the winter without special care: said of plants —**har′di·ly** *adv.* —**har′di·ness** *n.*

Har·dy (här′dē), **Thomas** 1840–1928; Eng. novelist & poet

hare (her) *n.*, *pl.* **hares, hare**: see PLURAL, II, D, 1 [OE. *hara*] a swift mammal related to the rabbit, with long ears, soft fur, a split upper lip, a short tail, and long, powerful hind legs; specif., one that does not burrow and whose young are furry at birth

hare·bell (her′bel′) *n.* a slender, delicate plant with clusters of blue, bell-shaped flowers

hare·brained (-brānd′) *adj.* having or showing little sense; reckless, flighty, giddy, rash, etc.

hare·lip (-lip′) *n.* **1.** a deformity that some people are born with, consisting of a harelike split of the lip **2.** a lip with such a deformity —**hare′lipped′** *adj.*

ha·rem (her′əm, har′-) *n.* [Ar. *ḥarīm*, lit., prohibited (place)] **1.** that part of a Moslem's household in which the women live **2.** the wives, concubines, women servants, etc. in a harem **3.** a number of female animals, as of fur seals, who mate and live together with one male Also **ha·reem** (hä rēm′)

Har·greaves (här′grēvz, -grāvz), **James** ?–1778; Eng. inventor of the spinning jenny

har·i·cot (har′ə kō′) *n.* [Fr., ult. < ? Nahuatl *ayecotli*, bean] [Chiefly Brit.] **1.** *same as* KIDNEY BEAN **2.** the pod or seed of other edible beans

ha·ri·ka·ri (her′ē ker′ē, hä′rē kä′rē) *n. same as* HARA-KIRI

hark (härk) *vi.* [< ? OE. *heorcnian*, to hearken] to listen carefully [*"Hark!* the herald angels sing"] —**hark back** to go back, as in thought [to *hark* back to one's childhood]

hark·en (här′k'n) *vi. same as* HEARKEN

Har·lem (här′ləm) [var. of HAARLEM] section of New York City, in N Manhattan

Har·le·quin (här′lə kwin, -kin) [< Fr. < OFr. *hierlekin*, demon] a traditional comic character in pantomime, who wears a mask and spangled, diamond-patterned tights of many colors —*n.* [h-] a clown; buffoon —*adj.* [h-] **1.** comic; laughably absurd **2.** of many colors; colorful

☆**harlequin bug** a black-and-red bug that feeds on cabbages, broccoli, and related plants

har·lot (här′lət) *n.* [OFr., rogue] a prostitute

har·lot·ry (-rē) *n.* prostitution

harm (härm) *n.* [OE. *hearm*] **1.** hurt; injury; damage [too much rain can do *harm* to the crops] **2.** moral wrong; evil [he meant no *harm* by his remark] —*vt.* to do harm to; hurt, damage, etc. —see SYN. at INJURE —**harm′er** *n.*

HARLEQUIN

harm·ful (härm′fəl) *adj.* causing or able to cause harm; hurtful —**harm′ful·ly** *adv.* —**harm′ful·ness** *n.*

harm·less (-lis) *adj.* causing or seeking to cause no harm; not harmful; inoffensive —**harm′less·ly** *adv.* —**harm′less·ness** *n.*

har·mon·ic (här män′ik) *adj.* **1.** harmonious in feeling or effect; agreeing **2.** *Music a)* of or in harmony *b)* pertaining to an overtone —*n.* **1.** *same as* OVERTONE (sense 1) **2.** *Elec.* an alternating-current voltage or current or a component of this, whose frequency is some integral multiple of a fundamental frequency —**har·mon′i·cal·ly** *adv.*

☆**har·mon·i·ca** (här män′i kə) *n.* [L.: see HARMONY] a small wind instrument played with the mouth; mouth organ: it has a series of metal reeds of different lengths, that vibrate and produce tones when air is blown or sucked across them

harmonic motion a periodic motion, or vibration, back and forth over a restricted path that is usually a straight line: it may be simple with only one frequency and amplitude, or it may have two or more simple components

har·mon·ics (här män′iks) *n.pl.* [with *sing. v.*] the physical science dealing with musical sounds

har·mo·ni·ous (här mō′nē əs) *adj.* [< Fr.: see HARMONY] **1.** having parts combined in an orderly or pleasing arrangement [a *harmonious* group of statues] **2.** having similar feelings, ideas, interests, etc. [a *harmonious* team] **3.** having musical tones combined to give a pleasing effect —**har·mo′ni·ous·ly** *adv.* —**har·mo′ni·ous·ness** *n.*

har·mo·ni·um (här mō′nē əm) *n.* [< Fr.: see HARMONY] a small kind of reed organ

har·mo·nize (här′mə nīz′) *vi.* **-nized′, -niz′ing 1.** to be in harmony; accord; agree [brown *harmonizes* with green] **2.** to sing in harmony [the bass and tenor *harmonize* nicely] —*vt.* **1.** to make harmonious; bring into agreement [to *harmonize* the colors in a room] **2.** to add chords to (a melody) so as to form a harmony —see SYN. at AGREE —**har′mo·ni·za′tion** *n.* —**har′mo·niz′er** *n.*

har·mo·ny (här′mə nē) *n.*, *pl.* **-nies** [< OFr. < L. < Gr. *harmonia* < *harmos*, a fitting: for IE. base see ART[1]] **1.** a combination of parts into a pleasing or orderly whole **2.** agreement in feeling, action, ideas, etc.; peaceable or friendly relations [we work in perfect *harmony*] **3.** a state of agreement or orderly arrangement according to color, size, shape, etc. **4.** agreeable sounds; music **5.** *Music a)* the sounding together of two or more tones, esp. when satisfying to the ear *b)* structure in terms of the arrangement, modulation, etc. of chords *c)* the study of this structure —see SYN. at SYMMETRY

har·ness (här′nis) *n.* [< OFr. *harneis*, armor < ON.] **1.** orig., armor for a man or horse **2.** the leather straps and metal pieces by which a horse, mule, etc. is fastened to a wagon, plow, etc. **3.** any arrangement of straps similar to this [the *harness* for fastening a parachute to a person] —*vt.* **1.** to put harness on (a horse, etc.) **2.** to control so as to use the power of [to *harness* one's energy] —**in harness** in or at one's routine work —**in harness with** in cooperation with

☆**harness race** a horse race between either trotters or pacers, each pulling a sulky and driver

Har·old (har′əld) [OE. *Hereweald* & *Harald* < ON. *Haraldr*, lit., leader of the army] **1.** a masculine name **2. Harold I** ?–1040; king of England (1035–40): son of CANUTE **3. Harold II** 1022?–66; last Saxon king of England (1066): killed in the Battle of Hastings

harp (härp) *n.* [OE. *hearpe*] **1.** a musical instrument with strings stretched across an open, triangular frame, held upright and played by plucking with the fingers **2.** a harp-shaped object or device —*vi.* **1.** to play a harp **2.** to talk or write about something so much or so often that it becomes boring [he's always *harping* on his illness] —**harp′er** *n.*

Har·pers Ferry (här′pərz) [the site of a ferry owned (c. 1747) by R. *Harper*] town in W.Va., at the juncture of the Potomac & Shenandoah rivers: site of the U.S. arsenal captured by John BROWN in 1859

harp·ist (här′pist) *n.* a harp player

har·poon (här poon′) *n.* [< MDu. < MFr. < *harper*, to claw < ON. *harpa*, to squeeze] a barbed spear with a line attached to it, used for spearing whales or other large sea animals —*vt.* to strike or catch with a harpoon —**har·poon′er** *n.*

harp·si·chord (härp′si kôrd′) *n.* [< obs. Fr. or < It.: see HARP
& CORD] a stringed musical instru-
ment with a keyboard, that came
before the piano: the strings are
plucked by leather or quill points
when the keys are pressed —**harp′-
si·chord′ist** *n.*

HARPSICHORD

Har·py (här′pē) *n., pl.* **-pies** [<
MFr. < L. < Gr. < *harpazein*, to
seize] **1.** *Gr. Myth.* any of several
hideous monsters with the head and
body of a woman and the wings,
tail, and claws of a bird **2.** [h-] a
greedy or grasping person
har·que·bus (här′kwi bəs) *n.* [<
Fr., ult. < Du. *haak*, hook + *bus*, a
gun] an early type of portable gun
har·ri·dan (har′i d′n) *n.* [prob. < Fr. *haridelle*, worn-out
horse] a nasty, bad-tempered old woman
har·ri·er¹ (har′ē ər) *n.* [< HARE + -IER] **1.** a dog like the
English foxhound, used for hunting hares and rabbits **2.** a
cross-country runner
har·ri·er² (har′ē ər) *n.* **1.** one who harries **2.** a hawk that
preys on small mammals, reptiles, etc.
Har·ri·et (har′ē it) [fem. dim. of HARRY] a feminine name:
var. *Harriot*
Har·ris (har′is), **Joel Chan·dler** (chan′dlər) 1848–1908; U.S.
writer, esp. of the *Uncle Remus* stories
Har·ris·burg (har′is burg′) [after John *Harris*, Jr., the
founder] capital of Pa., on the Susquehanna: pop. 68,000
Har·ri·son (har′ə s′n) **1. Benjamin**, 1833–1901; 23d president
of the U.S. (1889–93) **2. William Henry**, 1773–1841; 9th president of the U.S. (1841): grandfather of *Benjamin*
har·row (har′ō) *n.* [prob. < ON. *harfr*] a heavy frame with
spikes or sharp-edged disks, pulled by a horse or tractor and
used for breaking up and leveling plowed ground, covering
seeds, etc. —*vt.* **1.** to pull a harrow over (land) **2.** to cause pain,
fear, or discomfort in; torment; vex [she *harrowed* us with tales
of her miserable life] —*vi.* to take harrowing [ground that *har-
rows* well] —**har′row·er** *n.* —**har′row·ing** *adj.* —**har′row-
ing·ly** *adv.*
har·rumph (hə rumpf′) *vi.* [echoic] to clear one's throat, esp. in
a deliberate, pompous way —*n.* a harrumphing
Har·ry (har′ē) [< HENRY] a masculine name
har·ry (har′ē) *vt.* **-ried, -ry·ing** [< OE. *hergian* < base of *here*,
army < IE. base *koros*, war] **1.** to raid again and again and destroy or rob; plunder [the invaders *harried* the defeated tribes]
2. to worry or trouble; harass [*harried* by debts]
harsh (härsh) *adj.* [ME. *harsk*] **1.** unpleasantly sharp or rough
to the ear, eye, taste, or touch; grating, glaring, bitter, coarse,
etc. [*harsh* music; a *harsh* light; *harsh* medicine; *harsh* woolen
cloth] **2.** painful to the mind or feelings [the *harsh* realities of
death] **3.** rough, crude, or disagreeable in appearance [beneath
his *harsh* exterior] **4.** too severe; cruel or unfeeling [a *harsh*
punishment] —**harsh′ly** *adv.* —**harsh′ness** *n.*
hart (härt) *n., pl.* **harts, hart**: see PLURAL, II, D, 1 [OE. *heorot*:
for IE. base see HORN] a male European red deer, esp. after its
fifth year; stag
Harte (härt), **Bret** (bret) (born *Francis Brett Hart*) 1836–1902;
U.S. writer, esp. of short stories
har·te·beest (här′tə bēst′, härt′bēst′) *n., pl.* **-beests′,
-beest**: see PLURAL, II, D, 1 [obs. Afrik.
< *harte*, hart + *beest*, beast] a large,
swift South African antelope having
long horns curved backward at the tips
Hart·ford (härt′fərd) [after *Hert-
fordshire*, county in England] capital of
Conn., in the C part: pop. 158,000 (met.
area 664,000)
harts·horn (härts′hôrn′) *n.* **1.** a hart's
horn **2.** [Now Rare] ammonium carbonate, used in smelling salts: orig. obtained from deer's antlers
har·um-scar·um (her′əm sker′əm)
adj. [< ? HARE + SCARE + 'EM] acting
or done in a reckless or rash way —*adv.*
in a harum-scarum manner —*n.* a
harum-scarum person or action

HARTEBEEST
(4–5 ft. high
at shoulder)

Ha·run al-Ra·shid (hä rōōn′ äl rä
shēd′) 764?–809 A.D.; caliph of Baghdad (786–809): made famous by tales told of him in *The Arabian Nights*

ha·rus·pex (hə rus′peks, har′əs peks) *n., pl.* **-rus′pi·ces′** (-pə
sēz′) [L.] a fortuneteller in ancient Rome who claimed to be
able to foretell the future by interpreting the entrails of sacrificial animals —**ha·rus′pi·cal** (-pi k'l) *adj.*
har·vest (här′vist) *n.* [OE. *hærfest*: for IE. base see CARNAGE]
1. the time of the year when grain, fruit, vegetables, etc. are
reaped and gathered in **2.** all the grain, fruit, etc. gathered in
one season; crop [a large *harvest*] **3.** the gathering in of a crop
4. the outcome of any effort or series of events [the tyrant's
harvest of hate] —*vt., vi.* **1.** to gather in (a crop, etc.) **2.** to
gather the crop from (a field) **3.** to get (something) as the result of an action or effort —**har′vest·a·ble** *adj.*
har·vest·er (-ər) *n.* **1.** a person who gathers in a crop of grain,
fruit, etc. ☆**2.** a farm machine for harvesting crops
☆**harvest fly** *same as* CICADA
har·vest·man (-mən) *n., pl.* **-men 1.** a man who harvests **2.** a
spiderlike animal with long, thin legs and a short, broad, segmented abdomen; daddy-longlegs
harvest moon the full moon at or about the time of the autumnal equinox, September 22 or 23
Har·vey (här′vē) [< Fr. < OHG. *Herewig*, lit., army battle] **1.**
a masculine name **2. William**, 1578–1657; Eng. physician: discovered the circulation of the blood
Harz (Mountains) (härts) mountain range in C Germany:
highest peak, 3,747 ft.
has (haz; *unstressed* həz, əz) *third person singular in the present tense of* HAVE
has-been (haz′bin′) *n.* [Colloq.] a person or thing that was
once popular or effective but is not any longer
Has·dru·bal (haz′drōō bəl) ?-207 B.C.; Carthaginian general;
crossed the Alps in 207 to aid Hannibal, his brother: son of
HAMILCAR BARCA
ha·sen·pfef·fer (häs′n fef′ər) *n.* [G. < *hase*, rabbit + *pfeffer*,
pepper] a German dish of rabbit meat soaked in seasoned vinegar and then stewed in the vinegar mixture
hash¹ (hash) *vt.* [Fr. *hacher*, to chop] **1.** to chop (meat or
vegetables) into small pieces for cooking **2.** [Colloq.] to make a
mess of; bungle —*n.* **1.** a chopped mixture of cooked meat and
vegetables, usually baked or browned **2.** a mixture, as of things
used before in different forms; rehash **3.** a careless or jumbled
mixture; muddle —☆**hash out** [Colloq.] to settle by lengthy
discussion —☆**hash over** [Colloq.] to discuss at length —**make
(a) hash of** [Colloq.] **1.** to make a mess of; bungle **2.** to destroy or defeat (an opponent, argument, etc.) —**settle one's
hash** [Colloq.] to overcome or subdue one
hash² (hash) *n.* [Slang] hashish
☆**hash house** [Slang] a cheap restaurant
hash·ish (hash′ēsh, -ish) *n.* [Ar. *hashīsh*, dried hemp] a drug
made from the flowering tops of Indian hemp, chewed or
smoked for its intoxicating effects: also **hash′eesh** (-ēsh)
☆**hash mark** [Mil. Slang] *same as* SERVICE STRIPE
Has·i·dim (has′ə dim; *Heb.* khä sē′dim) *n.pl., sing.* **Has·id**
(has′id; *Heb.* khä′sid) [< Heb. *hāsid*, a pious person] a sect of
Jewish mystics, orig. in 18th-cent. Poland, that emphasizes joyful worship —**Ha·sid·ic** (ha sid′ik) *adj.*
has·n't (haz′′nt) has not
hasp (hasp) *n.* [OE. *hæpse*: for IE. base see HAVE] a hinged
metal fastening for a door, window, lid, etc.;
esp., a metal piece that fits over a staple and
is held in place by a pin or padlock
☆**has·sle** (has′′l) *n.* [< ?] [Colloq.] **1.** a
heated argument; squabble **2.** a troublesome situation —*vi.* **-sled, -sling** [Colloq.]
to have a heated argument —*vt.* [Colloq.] to
cause trouble or difficulty for; harass
has·sock (has′ək) *n.* [OE. *hassuc*] **1.** [Now
Rare] a thick clump or tuft of grass **2.** a
firmly stuffed cushion used as a footstool or
seat

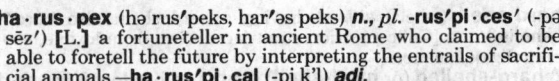

HASP

hast (hast; *unstressed* həst, əst) *the archaic
second person singular in the present tense of* HAVE: *used with*
thou
‡**has·ta la vis·ta** (äs′tä lä vēs′tä) [Sp., lit., until the meeting]
goodbye
has·tate (has′tāt) *adj.* [< L. < *hasta*, a spear] having a triangular shape like a spearhead, as some leaves
haste (hāst) *n.* [OFr. *haste* < Frank.] **1.** the act of hurrying;
quickness of motion [his *haste* in leaving] **2.** careless or reckless hurrying [*haste* makes waste] **3.** necessity for hurrying;
urgency [the air of *haste* which marks the undertaking] —*vt.,
vi.* **hast′ed, hast′ing** [Rare] *same as* HASTEN —**in haste 1.** in a

hurry **2.** in too great a hurry; without enough care —**make haste to hasten;** hurry

SYN.—**haste** implies quick or rash movement or action such as might result from the pressure of an emergency or from great eagerness; **hurry** can be used in place of **haste,** but also suggests excitement, bustle, or confusion [the *hurry* of city life]; **speed** implies rapid movement, operation, etc. that is also orderly and effective [to increase the *speed* of an assembly line]; **expedition** adds to **speed** the idea of quickness and skill of performance; **dispatch** comes close to **expedition** in meaning but more strongly stresses promptness in finishing a task —**ANT. slowness, delay**

has·ten (hās′'n) *vt.* to cause to be or come faster; speed up [to *hasten* one's departure] —*vi.* to move swiftly, hurry [*hasten* to call the doctor]

Has·tings (hās′tiŋz) city in SE England, on the English Channel: nearby is the site of the decisive battle of the Norman Conquest

Has·tings (hās′tiŋz), **Warren** 1732–1818; Eng. statesman; 1st governor general of India (1773–84)

hast·y (hās′tē) *adj.* **hast′i·er, hast′i·est 1.** done or made with haste; quick; hurried [a *hasty* lunch] **2.** done or made too quickly and with too little thought; rash [a *hasty* decision] **3.** short-tempered or likely to act with too little thought **4.** showing irritation or impatience [*hasty* words] —see **SYN.** at FAST[1] —**hast′i·ly** *adv.* —**hast′i·ness** *n.*

hasty pudding ☆**1.** mush made of cornmeal **2.** [Brit.] mush made of flour or oatmeal

hat (hat) *n.* [OE. *hætt* < IE. base *kadh-*, to cover] a covering for the head, usually with a brim and crown —*vt.* **hat′ted, hat′ting** to cover or provide with a hat —☆**pass the hat** to take up a collection, as at a meeting —**take one's hat off to** congratulate —☆**talk through one's hat** [Colloq.] to talk nonsense —☆**under one's hat** [Colloq.] secret —**hat′less** *adj.*

hat·band (hat′band′) *n.* a band of cloth around the crown of a hat, just above the brim

hat·box (-bäks′) *n.* a box or case for carrying or storing a hat or hats

hatch[1] (hach) *vt.* [ME. *hacchen*] **1.** *a)* to bring forth (young) from an egg or eggs by applying warmth *b)* to bring forth young from (an egg or eggs) **2.** to bring (a plan, idea, etc.) into existence; esp., to plan in secret; plot —*vi.* **1.** to produce young [how long does it take for hen eggs to *hatch?*] **2.** to come forth from the egg [our chicks *hatched* this morning] —*n.* **1.** the process of hatching **2.** the brood hatched —**hatch′er** *n.*

hatch[2] (hach) *n.* [OE. *hæcc,* a grating] **1.** the lower half of a door, gate, etc. that has two separate parts **2.** *same as* HATCHWAY **3.** a covering for a ship's hatchway, or a lid or trapdoor for a hatchway in a building

hatch[3] (hach) *vt.* [< OFr. < *hache,* an ax] to mark or engrave with fine, crossed or parallel lines so as to indicate shading —*n.* any of these lines

☆**hatch·back** (hach′bak′) *n.* [HATCH[2] + BACK] an automobile body with a rear that swings up, providing a wide opening into a storage area

hatch·el (hach′əl) *n., vt.* **-eled** or **-elled, -el·ing** or **-el·ling** *same as* HACKLE[1]

hatch·er·y (hach′ər ē) *n., pl.* **-er·ies** a place for hatching eggs, esp. those of fish or poultry

hatch·et (hach′it) *n.* [< OFr. dim. of *hache,* an ax] **1.** a small ax with a short handle, for use with one hand ☆**2.** *same as* TOMAHAWK —☆**bury the hatchet** to stop fighting; make peace

hatchet face a lean, narrow face, suggesting the cutting edge of a hatchet —**hatch′et-faced′** (-fāst′) *adj.*

☆**hatchet man** [Colloq.] **1.** a man hired to commit murder **2.** any person assigned by another to carry out disagreeable or unethical tasks

hatch·ing (hach′iŋ) *n.* [HATCH[3] + -ING] **1.** the drawing or engraving of fine, parallel or crossed lines to show shading **2.** such lines

hatch·way (hach′wā′) *n.* **1.** an opening in a ship's deck **2.** a similar opening in the floor or roof of a building

hate (hāt) *vt.* **hat′ed, hat′ing** [OE. *hatian* < IE. base *kad-*] **1.** to have strong dislike or ill will for; despise [to *hate* an enemy] **2.** to dislike or wish to avoid; shrink from [to *hate* ar-

SHINGLING HATCHET

CLAW HATCHET

TYPES OF HATCHET

guments] —*vi.* to feel hatred —*n.* **1.** a strong feeling of dislike or ill will; hatred **2.** a person or thing hated —**hate′a·ble, hat′a·ble** *adj.* —**hat′er** *n.*

SYN.—**hate** implies a feeling of great dislike or a strong wish to avoid, and, with persons as the object, suggests a wish to harm them; **detest** implies extreme dislike; **despise** suggests a looking down with great contempt upon the person or thing one hates; **loathe** implies intense dislike together with extreme disgust; **abhor** implies great dislike or disgust joined with feelings of moral disapproval —**ANT. love, like**

hate·ful (hāt′fəl) *adj.* **1.** [Now Rare] feeling or showing hate; malevolent **2.** causing or deserving hate; odious [a *hateful* lie] —**hate′ful·ly** *adv.* —**hate′ful·ness** *n.*

☆**hate·mon·ger** (-muŋ′gər, -mäŋ′-) *n.* a person who seeks to stir up hatred and prejudice, esp. against a minority group or groups

hath (hath) *the archaic third person singular in the present tense of* HAVE

hat·pin (hat′pin′) *n.* a long, fancy pin for fastening a woman's hat to her hair

hat·rack (hat′rak′) *n.* a rack, set of pegs or hooks, etc. to hold hats

ha·tred (hā′trid) *n.* [ME. < *hate,* HATE + *-red* < OE. *ræden,* state] strong dislike or ill will; hate

hat·ter (hat′ər) *n.* one who makes or sells hats, esp. men's hats

Hat·ter·as (hat′ər əs), **Cape** [< AmInd. tribal name] cape on an island of N.C., in the Atlantic

hau·ber·geon (hô′bər jən) *n. obs. var. of* HABERGEON

hau·berk (hô′bərk) *n.* [< OFr., ult. < Frank. *hals,* the neck + *bergan,* to protect] a medieval coat of armor, usually of chain mail

haugh·ty (hôt′ē) *adj.* **-ti·er, -ti·est** [< OFr. *haut,* high < L. *altus* + -Y[2]] **1.** having or showing great pride in oneself and contempt or scorn for others; arrogant **2.** [Archaic] noble —see **SYN.** at PROUD —**haugh′ti·ly** *adv.* —**haugh′ti·ness** *n.*

haul (hôl) *vt.* [< OFr. *haler,* to draw < ODu. *halen,* to fetch: for IE. base see CLAMOR] **1.** to move by pulling or drawing; tug; drag [we *hauled* the boat up on the beach] **2.** to transport by wagon, truck, etc. [to *haul* coal] **3.** *same as* HALE[2] **4.** *Naut.* to change the course of (a ship) by setting the sails —*vi.* **1.** to pull; tug **2.** to shift direction: said of the wind **3.** *Naut.* to change the course of a ship by trimming sail —*n.* **1.** the act of hauling; pull; tug [give a *haul* on the rope] **2.** *a)* the amount of fish taken in a single pull of a net *b)* [Colloq.] the amount gained, won, earned, etc. at one time [a good *haul* for one month of selling] **3.** the distance or route covered in transporting or traveling [it's a long *haul* to town] **4.** a load transported —see **SYN.** at PULL —**haul off** ☆[Colloq.] to draw the arm back before hitting —**in** (or **over**) **the long haul** over a long period of time —**haul′er** *n.*

haul·age (hôl′ij) *n.* **1.** the act or process of hauling **2.** the charge made for hauling, as by a railroad

haulm (hôm) *n.* [OE. *healm,* straw] **1.** the stalks or stems of cereal plants, peas, beans, etc., esp. after the crop has been gathered **2.** a stem of grass or grain

haunch (hônch, hänch) *n.* [< OFr. *hanche* < Gmc.] **1.** the part of the body including the hip, buttock, and thickest part of the thigh; hindquarter **2.** an animal's loin and leg together [a *haunch* of mutton]

haunt (hônt, hänt; *for n. 2, usually* hant) *vt.* [< OFr. *hanter,* to frequent] **1.** to visit (a place) often or continually [they *haunted* the drugstore] **2.** to seek the company or companionship of; run after **3.** to return or occur repeatedly to [memories *haunted* her] **4.** to fill the atmosphere of; pervade [a house *haunted* by sorrow] *Haunt* is often used with a ghost, spirit, etc. as its stated or implied subject —*n.* **1.** a place often visited [to make the library one's *haunt*] **2.** [Dial.] a ghost

haunt·ed (hônt′id, hänt′-) *adj.* supposedly lived in or visited by ghosts

haunt·ing (-iŋ) *adj.* often returning to the mind; not easily forgotten [a *haunting* melody] —**haunt′ing·ly** *adv.*

haus·to·ri·um (hô stôr′ē əm) *n., pl.* **-ri·a** (ə) [ModL. < L. pp. of *haurire,* to drink] a rootlike outgrowth in certain parasitic plants, through which food is absorbed from the host —**haus·to′ri·al** (-əl) *adj.*

haut·boy (hō′boi′, ō′-) *n.* [< Fr. < *haut,* high + *bois,* wood] *earlier name for* OBOE

‡**haute cou·ture** (ōt kōō tür′) [Fr., lit., high sewing] the leading designers and creators of new fashions in women's clothing, or their creations

hau·teur (hō tur′; *Fr.* ō tër′) *n.* [Fr. < *haut*, high, proud] scornful pride; haughty manner; snobbery

Ha·van·a (hə van′ə) capital of Cuba, on the Gulf of Mexico: pop. 788,000 —*n.* **1.** a cigar made in Cuba or of Cuban tobacco **2.** Cuban tobacco

have (hav; həv, əv; *before "to"* haf) *vt.* **had, hav′ing** [OE. *habban* < IE. base *kap*-, to grasp] **1.** to hold; own; possess [to *have* wealth] **2.** to possess as a part, characteristic, etc. [the week *has* seven days] **3.** to be affected by or afflicted with [to *have* a cold] **4.** to experience; undergo [to *have* a good time] **5.** to understand or know [to *have* a little Spanish] **6.** to hold or keep in the mind [to *have* an idea] **7.** to claim or say [so gossip *has* it] **8.** *a*) to get, take, or obtain [*have* a look at it] *b*) to eat or drink [*have* some tea] **9.** to bear or beget [to *have* twins] **10.** to perform; take part in [to *have* an argument] **11.** *a*) to cause to [*have* him sing] *b*) to cause to be [*have* it fixed] **12.** to be in a certain relation to [to *have* a wife] **13.** to feel and show [*have* pity on her] **14.** to permit; tolerate [I won't *have* this noise] **15.** [Colloq.] *a*) to hold at a disadvantage [I *had* my opponent now] *b*) to deceive; cheat [they were *had* in that business deal] *Have* is used as an auxiliary to form phrases expressing completed action, as in the perfect tenses (Ex.: I *had* left), and with infinitives to express obligation or necessity (Ex.: we *have* to go) *Have got* often replaces *have* *Have* is conjugated in the present indicative: (I) *have*, (he, she, it) *has*, (we, you, they) *have;* in the past indicative: (I, he, she, it, we, you, they) *had;* archaic forms are: (thou) *hast, hadst*, (he, she, it) *hath* —*n.* a person or nation with much wealth or rich resources [the *haves* and the have-nots] —**have at** to attack; strike —**have done** to stop; finish —**have had it** [Slang] **1.** to be defeated, disgusted, etc. **2.** to be no longer popular, useful, etc. —**have it good** [Colloq.] to be well-off —**have it out** to settle a disagreement by a fight or discussion —**have on** to be wearing —**have to be** ☆[Colloq.] to be without a doubt [this *has to be* the best movie of the year]

ha·ven (hā′vən) *n.* [OE. *hæfen:* for IE. base see HAVE] **1.** a port; harbor **2.** any sheltered, safe place; refuge

have-not (hav′nät′) *n.* a person or nation with little wealth or poor resources

have·n't (hav′′nt) have not

hav·er·sack (hav′ər sak′) *n.* [< Fr. < G. *habersack*, lit., sack of oats] a canvas bag for carrying food, etc., worn over one shoulder, as by soldiers and hikers

Ha·ver·sian (hə vur′shən) *adj.* [after C. *Havers*, Eng. physician (1650?-1702)] designating or of the canals through which blood vessels pass in bone

hav·oc (hav′ək) *n.* [< Anglo-Fr. < OFr. *havot*, plunder] great damage and destruction, as that resulting from hurricanes, wars, etc. —**cry havoc 1.** orig., to give (an army) the signal for pillaging **2.** to warn of great danger —**play havoc with** to devastate; destroy; ruin

Havre, Le *see* LE HAVRE

haw[1] (hô) *n.* [OE. *haga*] **1.** the berry of the hawthorn **2.** *same as* HAWTHORN

haw[2] (hô) *interj., n.* [< ?] a word of command to a horse, ox, etc., meaning "turn to the left!" —*vt., vi.* to turn to the left Opposed to GEE[1]

haw[3] (hô) *vi.* [echoic] to hesitate in speaking; falter: usually in HEM AND HAW (see HEM[2]) —*n.* a sound made by a speaker when hesitating briefly

Haw. Hawaiian

Ha·wai·i (hə wä′ē, -yē, -yə) [Haw. < ?] **1.** a State of the U.S., consisting of a group of islands (**Hawaiian Islands**) in the North Pacific: 6,424 sq. mi.; pop. 769,000; cap. Honolulu: abbrev. **HI 2.** largest of the islands of Hawaii

Ha·wai·ian (-yən) *adj.* of Hawaii, its people, language, etc. —*n.* **1.** a native or inhabitant of Hawaii; specif., a native of Polynesian descent **2.** the Polynesian language of the Hawaiians

Hawaii Volcanoes National Park national park on the island of Hawaii, including Mauna Loa

hawk[1] (hôk) *n.* [OE. *hafoc*] **1.** any of a group of birds of prey having short, rounded wings, a long tail and legs, and a hooked beak and claws: hawks include the falcons, buzzards, harriers, kites, and caracaras, but not vultures and eagles **2.** a person

HAVERSACK

who is in favor of war as a way of solving disputes between nations —*vi.* to hunt birds with the help of hawks —*vt.* to prey on as a hawk does —**hawk′ish** *adj.* —**hawk′like′** *adj.*

hawk[2] (hôk) *vt., vi.* [< HAWKER[1]] to advertise or peddle (goods) in the street by shouting

hawk[3] (hôk) *vi.* [echoic] to clear the throat noisily —*vt.* to bring up (phlegm) by coughing —*n.* a noisy clearing of the throat

hawk·er[1] (hôk′ər) *n.* [ult. < MLowG. *hoken*, to peddle] a person who hawks goods in the street; peddler

hawk·er[2] (-ər) *n.* a person who uses hawks for hunting

hawk-eyed (-īd′) *adj.* keen-sighted like a hawk

hawk·ing (-iŋ) *n.* hunting with hawks; falconry

Haw·kins (hô′kinz), Sir John 1532–95; Eng. naval officer

hawk·moth (hôk′môth′) *n.* a moth with a thick, tapering body and a long feeding tube used for sucking the nectar of flowers

hawks·bill (turtle) (hôks′bil′) a medium-sized turtle of warm seas, having a hawklike beak and a shell from which tortoise shell is obtained

hawk·weed (hôk′wēd′) *n.* a plant of the composite family, with yellow or scarlet ray flowers

hawse (hôz) *n.* [< ON. *hals*, the neck] **1.** that part of the bow of a ship containing the hawseholes **2.** *same as* HAWSEHOLE **3.** the space between the bow of a ship and the anchors

hawse·hole (hôz′hōl′) *n.* any of the holes in a ship's bow through which a hawser or cable is passed

haw·ser (hô′zər) *n.* [< Anglo-Fr. < OFr. *haucier*, ult. < L. *altus*, high] a large rope or small cable, by which a ship is anchored, moored, or towed

haw·thorn (hô′thôrn′) *n.* [< OE. < *haga*, hedge + *thorn*] a thorny shrub or small tree of the rose family, with flowers of white, pink, or red, and small, red fruits (*haws*)

Haw·thorne (hô′thôrn′) [after Nathaniel HAWTHORNE] city in SW Calif.: suburb of Los Angeles: pop. 53,000

Haw·thorne (hô′thôrn′), **Nathaniel** 1804–64; U.S. novelist & short-story writer

hay (hā) *n.* [OE. *hieg:* for IE. base see HEW] grass, alfalfa, clover, etc. cut and dried for use as food for cattle, horses, etc. —*vi.* to mow grass, alfalfa, etc. and spread it out to dry —☆**hit the hay** [Slang] to go to bed to sleep

hay·cock (hā′käk′) *n.* a small, cone-shaped heap of hay drying in a field

Hay·dn (hīd′'n), **Franz Jo·seph** (fränts yō′zef) 1732–1809; Austrian composer

Hayes (hāz), **Ruth·er·ford B(irchard)** (ruth′ər fərd) 1822–93; 19th president of the U.S. (1877–81)

hay fever an illness like a cold that makes the eyes water and causes sneezing and coughing: it is an allergic reaction, caused by the pollen of some grasses and trees

hay·field (hā′fēld′) *n.* a field of grass, alfalfa, etc. grown to make hay

hay·fork (-fôrk′) *n.* **1.** a pitchfork ☆**2.** a mechanically operated device for lifting or moving hay

hay·loft (-lôft′) *n.* a loft, or upper story, in a barn or stable, for storing hay

hay·mak·er (-mā′kər) *n.* **1.** a person who cuts hay and spreads it out to dry ☆**2.** [Slang] a powerful blow with the fist

hay·mow (-mou′) *n.* **1.** a pile of hay in a barn **2.** *same as* HAYLOFT

hay·rack (-rak′) *n.* **1.** a rack or frame from which cattle, horses, etc. eat hay ☆**2.** *a*) a framework extending up from a wagon, that allows larger amounts of hay to be carried *b*) a wagon having this

☆**hay·ride** (-rīd′) *n.* a pleasure ride taken by a group in a wagon partly filled with hay

hay·seed (-sēd′) *n.* **1.** grass seed shaken from mown hay ☆**2.** [Old Slang] an awkward, unsophisticated person thought of as typical of rural areas; yokel

hay·stack (-stak′) *n.* a large heap of hay piled up outdoors: also **hay′rick′** (-rik′)

Hay·ward (hā′wərd) [after W. *Hayward*, local postmaster] city in W Calif.: suburb of Oakland: pop. 93,000

☆**hay·wire** (hā′wīr′) *n.* wire for tying up bales of hay or straw —*adj.* [Slang] **1.** out of order; confused **2.** crazy: usually in **go haywire**, to become crazy

haz·ard (haz′ərd) *n.* [OFr. *hasard*, game of dice < Ar. *az-zahr*] **1.** an early game of chance played with dice **2.** chance **3.** risk; peril; danger [the *hazards* of icy streets] **4.** an obstacle on a golf course, as a pond or sand trap —*vt.* to take a chance on; risk [to *hazard* a try] —see SYN. at DANGER

haz·ard·ous (-əs) *adj.* risky; dangerous —**haz′ard·ous·ly** *adv.* —**haz′ard·ous·ness** *n.*

haze[1] (hāz) *n.* [prob. < HAZY] **1.** a thin vapor of fog, smoke, dust, etc. in the air, that makes it harder to see **2.** slight confusion or vagueness of mind —*vi., vt.* **hazed, haz′ing** to make or become hazy (often with *over*)

haze[2] (hāz) *vt.* **hazed, haz′ing** [< ? OFr. *haser*, to irritate] ☆to initiate or discipline by forcing to do humiliating or painful things [seniors are forbidden to *haze* freshmen at our school]

Ha·zel (hā′z'l) [Heb. *ḥazā'ēl*, lit., God sees] a feminine name

ha·zel (hā′z'l) *n.* [OE. *hæsel*] **1.** a shrub or tree related to the birch, bearing edible nuts **2.** *same as* HAZELNUT **3.** a light brown —*adj.* **1.** of the hazel tree **2.** light-brown: hazel eyes are usually flecked with green or gray —**ha′zel·ly** *adj.*

ha·zel·nut (-nut′) *n.* the small, edible, roundish nut of the hazel; filbert

Haz·litt (haz′lit), **William** 1778–1830; Eng. essayist

ha·zy (hā′zē) *adj.* **-zi·er, -zi·est** [prob. < OE. *hasu*, dusky] **1.** covered by or full of haze; somewhat foggy or smoky **2.** vague, obscure, confused, or indefinite [*hazy* thinking] —**ha′zi·ly** *adv.* —**ha′zi·ness** *n.*

Hb the symbol for hemoglobin

☆**H-bomb** (āch′bäm′) *n. same as* HYDRO-GEN BOMB

H.C. House of Commons

H.C.F., h.c.f. highest common factor

h.c.l., HCL [Colloq.] high cost of living

HD heavy duty

hd. head

hdbk. handbook

hdqrs. headquarters

he (hē; *unstressed* hi, ē, i) *pron. for pl. see* THEY [OE.: see HERE] **1.** the man, boy, or male animal being talked about **2.** the person; the one; anyone [*he* who laughs last laughs best] The case forms of the masculine third personal pronoun are: *he*, nominative; *him*, objective; *his*, possessive; *himself*, intensive and reflexive —*n., pl.* **hes** a man, boy, or male animal

he- *a combining form meaning* male: used in hyphenated compounds [he-dog]

He *Chem.* helium

head (hed) *n.* [OE. *heafod* < IE. base *kaput*-] **1.** the top part of the body in man, the apes, etc., or the front part in most other animals: in higher animals it is a bony structure containing the brain, eyes, ears, nose, and mouth **2.** mind; intelligence [use your *head*] **3.** a person [dinner at five dollars a *head*] **4.** *pl.* **head** the head as a unit of counting [fifty *head* of cattle] **5.** the main side of a coin, usually showing a head: often **heads** **6.** the highest or uppermost part or thing; top; specif., *a*) the top of a page, column, etc. *b*) a topic of a section, chapter, etc. in a speech or written work *c*) a headline *d*) froth floating on newly poured bubbling beverages, esp. on beer *e*) the upper edge of a sail **7.** the foremost part of a thing; front; specif., *a*) a part associated with the head of a human being [the *head* of a bed] *b*) the front part of a ship; bow *c*) *Naut.* a toilet, or lavatory *d*) the front position, as of a column of marching men *e*) either end of something **8.** the projecting part of something; specif., *a*) the part designed for holding, striking, etc. [the *head* of a pin] *b*) a point of land; headland *c*) a projecting place, as in a boil, where pus is about to break through *d*) the part of a tape recorder that records or plays back the magnetic signals on the tape **9.** the membrane stretched across the end of a drum, tambourine, etc. **10.** the source of a river, stream, etc. **11.** a source of water kept at some height to supply a mill, etc. **12.** the pressure in an enclosed fluid, as steam **13.** a position of leadership or honor [at the *head* of the class] **14.** the person in charge; leader, ruler, director, etc. [he is *head* of the committee] **15.** a headmaster **16.** *Bot. a*) a dense, flattened cluster of flowers, as in the dandelion *b*) a large, compact bud [a *head* of cabbage] **17.** *Music* the rounded part of a note, at the end of the stem **18.** [Slang] a habitual user of marijuana, LSD, etc. —*adj.* **1.** of or having to do with the head **2.** most important; principal; first [the *head* coach] **3.** to be found at the top or front **4.** striking against the front [*head* winds] —*vt.* **1.** to be chief of or in charge of [a colonel *heads* a regiment] **2.** to be at the top or beginning of; lead; precede [to *head* a list]

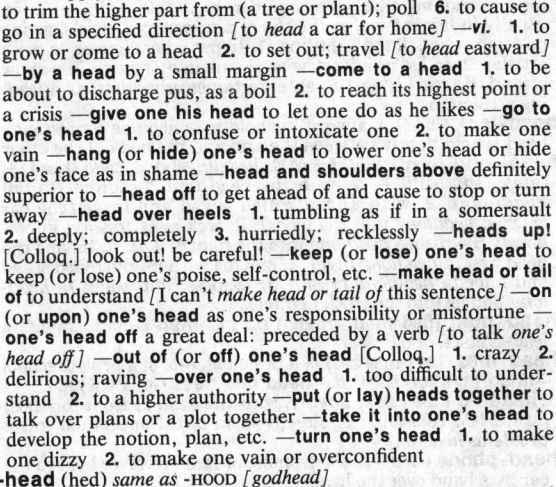

HAZELNUTS

3. to supply (a pin, etc.) with a head **4.** [Rare] to behead **5.** to trim the higher part from (a tree or plant); poll **6.** to cause to go in a specified direction [to *head* a car for home] —*vi.* **1.** to grow or come to a head **2.** to set out; travel [to *head* eastward] —**by a head** by a small margin —**come to a head 1.** to be about to discharge pus, as a boil **2.** to reach its highest point or a crisis —**give one his head** to let one do as one likes —**go to one's head 1.** to confuse or intoxicate one **2.** to make one vain —**hang** (or **hide**) **one's head** to lower one's head or hide one's face as in shame —**head and shoulders above** definitely superior to —**head off** to get ahead of and cause to stop or turn away —**head over heels 1.** tumbling as if in a somersault **2.** deeply; completely **3.** hurriedly; recklessly —**heads up!** [Colloq.] look out! be careful! —**keep** (or **lose**) **one's head** to keep (or lose) one's poise, self-control, etc. —**make head or tail of** to understand [I can't *make head or tail* of this sentence] —**on** (or **upon**) **one's head** as one's responsibility or misfortune —**one's head off** a great deal: preceded by a verb [to talk *one's head off*] —**out of** (or **off**) **one's head** [Colloq.] **1.** crazy **2.** delirious; raving —**over one's head 1.** too difficult to understand **2.** to a higher authority —**put** (or **lay**) **heads together** to talk over plans or a plot together —**take it into one's head** to develop the notion, plan, etc. —**turn one's head 1.** to make one dizzy **2.** to make one vain or overconfident

-head (hed) *same as* -HOOD [godhead]

head·ache (hed′āk′) *n.* **1.** a continuous pain in the head ☆**2.** [Colloq.] a cause of worry, trouble, etc. [that old car has been nothing but a *headache*]

head·band (-band′) *n.* a band worn around the head

head·board (-bôrd′) *n.* a board or frame that forms the head of a bed, etc.

☆**head·cheese** (-chēz′) *n.* a loaf of jellied, seasoned meat from the head and feet of hogs

head cold a common cold in which the nasal passages are stopped up

head·dress (-dres′) *n.* **1.** a covering or decoration for the head **2.** a style of arranging the hair

head·ed (-id) *adj.* **1.** formed into a head, as cabbage **2.** having a heading

-head·ed (-id) *a combining form meaning:* **1.** having a (specified kind of) head [clearheaded] **2.** having (a specified number of) heads [two-headed]

head·er (-ər) *n.* **1.** a person or device that puts heads on pins, nails, rivets, etc. ☆**2.** a machine that takes off the heads of grain and loads them into a truck **3.** [Colloq.] a fall or dive with the head first **4.** a wooden beam, as in flooring, placed between two long beams with the ends of short beams resting against it **5.** a brick or stone laid across the thickness of a wall so that a short end is exposed in the wall face

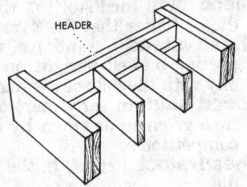

HEADER

head·first (-furst′) *adv.* **1.** with the head in front; headlong **2.** in a reckless, unthinking way; rashly; impetuously Also **head′fore′most′** (-fôr′mōst′)

☆**head gate** a gate that controls the flow of water into a canal lock, sluice, etc.

head·gear (-gir′) *n.* **1.** a covering for the head; hat, cap, headdress, etc. **2.** the harness for the head of a horse, mule, etc.

head·hunt·er (-hun′tər) *n.* a member of any of certain primitive tribes who remove the heads of slain enemies and preserve them as trophies —**head′hunt′ing** *n.*

head·ing (-iŋ) *n.* **1.** something forming or used to form the head, top, edge, or front; specif., an inscription at the top of a chapter, page, etc., giving the title, topic, etc. **2.** a topic or category **3.** the direction in which a ship, plane, etc. is moving: usually expressed as a compass reading

head·land (-lənd) *n.* a point of land reaching out into the water; esp., a promontory

head·less (-lis) *adj.* **1.** without a head **2.** without a leader **3.** stupid; foolish

☆**head·light** (-līt′) *n.* a light with a reflector and lens, at the front of an automobile, locomotive, etc.: also **head′lamp′** (-lamp′)

head·line (-līn′) *n.* **1.** a line at the top of a page in a book, giving the running title, page number, etc. ☆**2.** a line or lines, usually in larger type, at the top of a newspaper article, giving its topic —☆ *vt.* **-lined′, -lin′ing 1.** to put a headline on (a news article) **2.** to list or advertise as the main attraction in a show ☆**head·lin·er** (-lī′nər) *n.* an entertainer advertised as a leading attraction

head·lock (-läk′) *n.* a wrestling hold in which one contestant's head is held tightly between the arm and the body of the other

head·long (-lôŋ′) *adv.* [< ME. *hedelinge(s)* < *hede,* head + *-linge,* adv. suffix] **1.** with the head first; headfirst *[to fall headlong]* **2.** with uncontrolled speed and force *[the car crashed headlong into the fence]* **3.** recklessly; rashly; impetuously *[he rushed headlong into the fight]* —*adj.* **1.** having the head first *[a headlong dive]* **2.** moving with uncontrolled speed and force *[a headlong crash]* **3.** reckless; impetuous *[a headlong plunge into the stock market]*

head·man (hed′mən, -man′) *n., pl.* **-men** (-mən, -men′) a leader, chief, or overseer

head·mas·ter (-mas′tər) *n.* a principal, esp. of a private school —**head′mas′ter·ship′** *n.* —**head′mis′tress** (-mis′tris) *n.*

☆**head-on** (-än′) *adj., adv.* **1.** with the head or front foremost *[a head-on collision]* **2.** directly or in direct opposition *[meet problems head-on]*

head·phone (-fōn′) *n.* a telephone or radio receiver held to the ear by a band over the head

head·piece (-pēs′) *n.* a protective head covering, as a helmet

head·pin (-pin′) *n.* the pin at the front of a triangle of bowling pins

head·quar·ters (-kwôr′tərz) *n.pl.* [*often with sing. v.*] **1.** the main office, or center of operations, of one in command, as in an army or police force **2.** the main office in any organization —**head′quar′ter** *vt.*

head·rest (-rest′) *n.* a support for the head, as on a dentist's chair

head·room (-rōōm′) *n.* space or clearance overhead, as in a doorway or tunnel

head·set (-set′) *n.* an earphone or earphones, often with a mouthpiece transmitter attached

head·ship (-ship′) *n.* the position or authority of a chief or leader; leadership; command

heads·man (hedz′mən) *n., pl.* **-men** an executioner who beheads persons sentenced to die

head·stall (hed′stôl′) *n.* the part of a bridle or halter that fits over a horse's head

head·stand (-stand′) *n.* the act of supporting oneself upright on the head, usually with the help of the hands

head start an early start or other advantage given to or taken by a contestant or competitor

head·stock (-stäk′) *n.* the part of a lathe supporting the spindle

head·stone (-stōn′) *n.* **1.** [Rare] a cornerstone **2.** a stone marker placed at the head of a grave

head·stream (-strēm′) *n.* a stream that is the source of another and larger stream

head·strong (-strôŋ′) *adj.* **1.** determined not to follow orders, advice, etc. but to do as one pleases; willful; stubborn **2.** showing such determination *[headstrong behavior]*

head·wait·er (-wāt′ər) *n.* a supervisor of waiters, often in charge of table reservations

head·wa·ters (-wôt′ərz, -wät′-) *n.pl.* the small streams that are the sources of a river

head·way (-wā′) *n.* **1.** forward motion *[the boat made slow headway against the wind]* **2.** progress in work, etc. *[the club made little headway in raising funds]* **3.** *same as* HEADROOM ☆**4.** the difference in time or miles between two trains, ships, etc. traveling the same route in the same direction

head wind a wind blowing in the direction directly opposite the course of a ship or aircraft

head·work (hed′wʉrk′) *n.* mental effort; thought

head·y (-ē) *adj.* **head′i·er, head′i·est 1.** reckless or headstrong; rash **2.** tending to affect the senses; intoxicating *[a heady wine]* —**head′i·ly** *adv.* —**head′i·ness** *n.*

heal (hēl) *vt.* [OE. *hǣlan* < *hal,* sound, HALE[1]] **1.** to make well or healthy again *[heal the sick]* **2.** *a)* to cure (a disease) *b)* to cause (a wound, sore, etc.) to become closed or scarred **3.** to free from grief, troubles, evil, etc. **4.** to remedy or get rid of

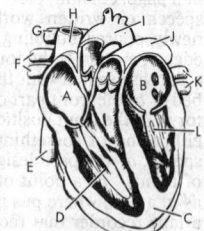

HEADSET

(grief, troubles, etc.) —*vi.* **1.** to become well or healthy again; be cured **2.** to become closed or scarred *[the wound healed slowly]* —see SYN. at CURE —**heal′er** *n.*

health (helth) *n.* [OE. *hǣlth* < *hal,* HALE[1] + -TH[1]] **1.** physical and mental well-being; freedom from disease or pain **2.** condition of body or mind *[good health]* **3.** a wish for a person's health and happiness, as in drinking a toast **4.** soundness or strength, as of a society or culture

☆**health food** food that is considered to be especially healthful, esp. if it has been grown and processed without the use of chemical fertilizers, preservatives, etc.

health·ful (helth′fəl) *adj.* **1.** helping to produce or maintain health; wholesome *[a healthful diet]* **2.** [Rare] *same as* HEALTHY —**health′ful·ly** *adv.* —**health′ful·ness** *n.*

health·y (hel′thē) *adj.* **health′i·er, health′i·est 1.** having good health *[a healthy child]* **2.** showing or resulting from good health *[a healthy appetite]* **3.** *same as* HEALTHFUL **4.** [Colloq.] large, energetic, powerful, etc. *[she took a healthy swing at the ball]* —**health′i·ly** *adv.* —**health′i·ness** *n.*

SYN.—**healthy** implies normal physical and mental strength and freedom from disease, weakness, disorder, etc.; **sound** suggests a condition of perfect health in which there is no sign of disease or weakness; **hale** is close to **sound** in meaning and is used esp. of elderly people who are lively and free from the weaknesses of old age; **robust** implies great bodily health and strength that can be seen in firm muscles, good color, large reserves of energy, etc.; **well** implies simply freedom from illness —**ANT.** ill, diseased, infirm, frail

heap (hēp) *n.* [OE. *heap,* a troop: for IE. base see COOP] **1.** a pile or mass of things jumbled together **2.** [Colloq.] a large amount; great deal *[to earn a heap of money]* —*vt.* **1.** to make a heap of *[toys heaped in the corner]* **2.** to give in large amounts *[to heap gifts on one]* **3.** to fill (a plate, etc.) full or to overflowing —*vi.* to pile up in a heap

hear (hir) *vt.* **heard** (hʉrd), **hear′ing** [OE. *hieran* < IE. base *kew-,* to notice] **1.** to perceive or sense (sounds) by the ear **2.** to listen to and consider; specif., *a)* to pay attention to *[hear what I tell you]* *b)* to listen to carefully or officially *[to hear a child's lesson]* *c)* to hold a hearing of (a law case, etc.); try *d)* to consent to; grant *[hear my prayer]* **3.** to be informed of; be told; learn *[to hear a rumor]* —*vi.* **1.** to be able to hear sounds **2.** to listen **3.** to be told (*of* or *about*) —**hear from 1.** to get a letter, telegram, etc. from **2.** to get a criticism or scolding from —**hear! hear!** well said!; that's right! —**not hear of** to refuse to think about or allow —**hear′er** *n.*

hear·ing (hir′iŋ) *n.* **1.** the act or process of perceiving sounds **2.** the sense by which sounds are perceived *[her hearing is poor]* **3.** opportunity to speak, sing, etc.; audience or audition **4.** a court appearance before a judge, other than a formal trial **5.** a formal meeting of an official body at which evidence is presented and testimony is given **6.** the distance a sound will carry *[within hearing]*

hearing aid a small electronic device that amplifies sounds, worn by a person with poor hearing

heark·en (här′kən) *vi.* [OE. *heorcnian* < *hieran,* to HEAR] to pay careful attention; listen carefully

Hearn (hʉrn), **Laf·cad·i·o** (laf kad′ē ō) (born *Patricio Lafcadio Tessima Carlos Hearn*) 1850–1904; U.S. writer, born in Greece: became a citizen of Japan

hear·say (hir′sā′) *n.* something one has heard but does not know to be true; rumor; gossip —*adj.* based on hearsay

hearse (hʉrs) *n.* [< OFr. < L. *hirpex,* a harrow] **1.** a vehicle used in a funeral for carrying the corpse **2.** [Archaic] a bier or coffin

Hearst (hʉrst), **William Randolph** 1863–1951; U.S. newspaper & magazine publisher

heart (härt) *n.* [OE. *heorte* < IE. base *kerd-*] **1.** the hollow, muscular organ that circulates the blood by expanding and then contracting over and over again **2.** any part or place centrally located like the heart *[hearts of celery, the heart of the city]* **3.** the central, vital, or main part; essence; core *[the heart of the matter]* **4.** the human heart considered as the center of emotions, personality traits, etc.; specif., *a)* inmost feeling *[to know in one's heart]* *b)* one's emo-

HUMAN HEART

(A, right atrium; B, left atrium; C, myocardium; D, right ventricle; E, inferior vena cava; F, pulmonary veins; G, pulmonary artery; H, superior vena cava; I, aorta; J, pulmonary artery; K, pulmonary veins; L, left ventricle)

tional nature; disposition [to have a kind *heart*] c) any of various humane feelings; love, sympathy, etc. [she was able to win his *heart*] d) mood; feeling [to have a heavy *heart*] e) spirit or courage [to lose *heart*] **5.** a person loved or admired [he's a brave *heart*] **6.** a figure or design (♡) shaped somewhat like the heart **7.** a) a playing card of a suit marked with this figure in red b) [pl.] this suit of cards ☆c) [pl.] a card game in which the object is to avoid getting hearts in the tricks taken —**after one's own heart** that suits or pleases one perfectly —**at heart** in one's innermost or hidden nature —**break one's heart** to overwhelm one with grief or disappointment —**by heart** by memorizing or from memory —☆**change of heart** a change of mind or feeling —**do one's heart good** to make one happy; please one —**eat one's heart out** to brood or feel unhappy over some disappointment or mistake —**have one's heart in one's mouth** (or **boots**) to be full of fear or nervousness —**have one's heart in the right place** to be well-meaning —**heart and soul** with all one's effort, enthusiasm, etc. —**in one's heart of hearts** in one's innermost nature or deepest feelings —**lose one's heart (to)** to fall in love (with) —**near one's heart** dear or important to one —**set one's heart on** to want very much —**take heart** to have more courage or confidence; cheer up —**take to heart 1.** to think about seriously **2.** to be troubled by —**to one's heart's content** as much as one wishes —**wear one's heart on one's sleeve** to show one's feelings plainly —**with all one's heart 1.** very sincerely **2.** very willingly; with pleasure

heart·ache (härt′āk′) **n.** sorrow or grief

heart·beat (-bēt′) **n.** one pulsation, or full contraction and expansion, of the heart

heart block a disorder of the heart that results from faulty timing of the impulses which control the heartbeat

heart·break (-brāk′) **n.** overwhelming sorrow, grief, or disappointment —**heart′break′ing adj.**

heart·bro·ken (-brō′k'n) **adj.** very disappointed or unhappy; filled with grief

heart·burn (-burn′) **n.** a burning feeling in or near the stomach caused by stomach acid flowing back into the esophagus

heart·ed (-id) **adj.** having a (specified kind of) heart: used in compounds [stouthearted]

heart·en (-'n) **vt.** to cheer up; encourage [I was greatly heartened by her kind letter]

heart failure the inability of the heart to pump enough blood through the body

heart·felt (-felt′) **adj.** with deep feeling; sincere [heartfelt gratitude] —see **SYN.** at SINCERE

hearth (härth) **n.** [OE. *heorth*: see CREMATE] **1.** the stone or brick floor of a fireplace, often extending out into the room **2.** a) the fireside b) family life; home **3.** the lowest part of a blast furnace, where the molten metal settles, or the floor of a furnace on which the ore or metal rests for exposure to the flame

hearth·stone (härth′stōn′) **n. 1.** the stone forming a hearth **2.** the home, or home life

heart·i·ly (härt′'l ē) **adv. 1.** in a sincere, cordial way [welcoming her heartily] **2.** with enthusiasm or vigor [to work heartily] **3.** with zestful appetite [to eat heartily] **4.** completely; fully; very [heartily sorry]

heart·i·ness (-ē nis) **n.** a hearty quality or state

heart·less (-lis) **adj. 1.** [Now Rare] lacking spirit or courage **2.** lacking kindness; hard and pitiless —**heart′less·ly adv.** —**heart′less·ness n.**

heart-rend·ing (-ren′diŋ) **adj.** causing much grief or pity [a heart-rending story] —**heart′-rend′ing·ly adv.**

hearts·ease, heart's-ease (härts′ēz′) **n. 1.** peace of mind **2.** same as WILD PANSY

heart·sick (härt′sik′) **adj.** sick at heart; very unhappy or upset about something unfortunate: also **heart′sore′** (-sôr′)

heart-strick·en (-strik′'n) **adj.** deeply grieved or greatly dismayed: also **heart′-struck′** (-struk′)

heart·strings (-striŋz′) **n.pl.** [orig. tendons or nerves formerly believed to brace and sustain the heart] deepest feelings or affections [a sad tale that tugged at her heartstrings]

heart·throb (-thräb′) **n. 1.** same as HEARTBEAT **2.** [Old Slang] one's sweetheart

heart-to-heart (-tə härt′) **adj.** intimate and frank [to have a heart-to-heart talk]

heart·warm·ing (-wôr′miŋ) **adj.** arousing warm, friendly,

cheerful feelings [a *heartwarming* story of love and devotion]

heart·wood (-wood′) **n.** the hard wood at the core of a tree trunk: see SAPWOOD

heart·y (härt′ē) **adj. heart′i·er, heart′i·est** [see HEART & -Y²] **1.** extremely warm and friendly; most cordial [a hearty welcome] **2.** enthusiastic; wholehearted [hearty support] **3.** strongly felt or expressed [a hearty dislike] **4.** strong and healthy [a hearty young farmer] **5.** a) nourishing and plentiful [a hearty meal] b) liking plenty of food [a hearty eater] —**n., pl.** **heart′ies** [Archaic] a friend; comrade; esp., a fellow sailor (usually preceded by my)

heat (hēt) **n.** [OE. *hætu* < IE. base *kai-*, heat] **1.** the quality of being hot; hotness: in physics, heat is considered a form of energy whose effect is produced by the accelerated vibration of molecules **2.** a) much hotness; great warmth b) same as FEVER **3.** degree of hotness or warmth [cook at low heat] **4.** a feeling of hotness or warmth **5.** hot weather or climate [the heat of the tropics] **6.** the warming of a room, house, etc., as by a furnace **7.** appearance as an indication of hotness [blue heat in metals] **8.** a) strong feeling; excitement, ardor, anger, etc. [arguing about the matter with great heat] b) the period or condition of such feeling; most violent stage [in the heat of battle] **9.** a single trial in a series; esp., any of the preliminary rounds of a race, etc., the winners of which compete in the final round **10.** a) sexual excitement b) the period of this in animals; esp., the estrus of females **11.** *Metallurgy* a single heating, as of metal, in a furnace or forge ☆**12.** [Slang] a) pressure to make someone do something b) great pressure or intensified activity, as in criminal investigation or law enforcement —**vt., vi. 1.** to make or become warm or hot **2.** to make or become excited

heat barrier same as THERMAL BARRIER

heat·ed (hēt′id) **adj. 1.** hot **2.** excited, highly emotional, or angry [a heated argument] —**heat′ed·ly adv.**

heat·er (-ər) **n.** a stove, furnace, radiator, etc. for heating a room, car, water, etc.

heat exchanger any device for transferring heat to a cooler medium from a warmer one

heat exhaustion a mild form of heatstroke, characterized by faintness, dizziness, sweating, etc.: also **heat prostration**

heath (hēth) **n.** [OE. *hæth*] **1.** a tract of open wasteland, esp. in the British Isles, covered with heather, low shrubs, etc.; moor **2.** any of various shrubs and plants that grow on heaths, as heather —**adj.** designating a family of woody plants, including the blueberry, cranberry, azalea, etc. —**one's native heath** the place of one's birth or childhood

heath·bird (hēth′burd′) **n.** same as BLACK GROUSE

hea·then (hē′thən) **n., pl.** **-thens, -then** [OE. *hæthen*] **1.** orig., a member of any people not worshiping the God of Israel **2.** anyone not a Jew, Christian, or Moslem; esp., a member of a tribe, nation, etc. worshiping many gods **3.** a person regarded as uncivilized, irreligious, etc. —**adj. 1.** of heathens; pagan **2.** irreligious, uncivilized, etc. —see **SYN.** at PAGAN —**hea′then·ish adj.** —**hea′then·ism n.**

hea·then·ize (-īz′) **vt., vi.** **-ized′, -iz′ing** to make or become heathen

heath·er (heth′ər) **n.** [altered (after HEATH) < ME. *haddyr*] a low-growing plant of the heath family, common in the British Isles, with stalks of small, bell-shaped, purplish-pink flowers —**adj.** like heather in color or appearance

heating pad a pad consisting of an electric heating element covered with fabric, for applying heat to parts of the body

☆**heat lightning** lightning without thunder, seen near the horizon, esp. on hot summer evenings

heat pump a device for cooling an enclosed space by pumping hot air out, and for warming it by taking heat from another source, as outdoor air, and pumping it in

heat rash same as PRICKLY HEAT

heat·stroke (hēt′strōk′) **n.** a condition of high fever and collapse, resulting from overexposure to intense heat

☆**heat wave 1.** unusually hot weather,

HEATHER

resulting from a slowly moving air mass of relatively high temperature **2.** a period of such weather

heaume (hōm) *n.* [Fr. < OFr. *helme:* see HELMET] a heavy helmet worn in the Middle Ages

heave (hēv) *vt.* **heaved** or (esp. by sailors) **hove, heav′ing** [< OE. *hebban:* for IE. base see HAVE] **1.** to raise or lift, esp. with effort **2.** to lift in this way and throw **3.** to make rise or swell, as one's chest **4.** to utter (a sigh, groan, etc.) with great effort **5.** *a)* to raise or haul (an anchor, etc.) by pulling with a rope or cable *b)* to cause (a ship) to move in a specified manner or direction —*vi.* **1.** to swell up; bulge out [heat caused the pavement to *heave* and crack] **2.** to rise and fall rhythmically [his chest *heaved* with sobs] **3.** *a)* to retch or vomit *b)* to pant; breathe hard; gasp **4.** *a)* to tug or haul (*on* or *at* a ship's cable, rope, etc.) *b)* to proceed; move [a ship *hove* into sight] —*n.* the act or effort of heaving —**heave ho!** pull hard!: a cry of sailors hauling in the anchor, etc. —**heave to 1.** to stop forward movement by hauling in or shortening sail and heading into the wind **2.** to stop —**heav′er** *n.*

heave-ho (hēv′hō′) *n.* ☆[Colloq.] dismissal, as from a job: chiefly in the phrase **give** (or **get**) **the** (**old**) **heave-ho**

heav·en (hev′'n) *n.* [OE. *heofon*] **1.** [*usually pl.*] the space surrounding the earth; the sky (in pl. used with *the*) **2.** *Theol. a)* [*often* H-] the place where God and his angels are and where the blessed go after death *b)* [H-] God; Providence **3.** *a)* any place of great beauty and pleasure *b)* a state of great happiness [it's *heaven* to be home again] Often used in exclamations of surprise, protest, etc. [for *heaven's* sake] —**move heaven and earth** to do all that can be done

heav·en·ly (-lē) *adj.* **1.** of or in the heavens [the sun is a *heavenly* body] **2.** *a)* causing or marked by great happiness, beauty, etc. *b)* [Colloq.] very pleasing, attractive, etc. **3.** *Theol.* of or in heaven; holy; divine [God is called our *heavenly* Father] —**heav′en·li·ness** *n.*

heav·en·ward (-wərd) *adv., adj.* toward heaven [a *heavenward* glance]: also **heav′en·wards** *adv.*

heaves (hēvz) *n.pl.* [*with sing. v.*] ☆a respiratory disease of horses, marked by forced breathing, coughing, heaving of the flanks, etc.

heav·i·ly (hev′ə lē) *adv.* in a heavy manner; specif., *a)* with a heavy weight [*heavily* burdened] *b)* slowly; clumsily; laboriously [to rise *heavily* from one's chair] *c)* severely; oppressively [*heavily* taxed] *d)* abundantly [*heavily* populated]

heav·i·ness (-ē nis) *n.* a heavy state or quality

Heav·i·side layer (hev′ē sīd′) [after O. *Heaviside* (1850–1925), Eng. physicist] *same as* E LAYER

heav·y (hev′ē) *adj.* **heav′i·er, heav′i·est** [OE. *hefig* < base of *hebban,* to HEAVE + *-ig, -Y²*] **1.** hard to lift or move because of great weight; weighty **2.** of great weight for the size [lead is a *heavy* metal] **3.** above the usual or a defined weight **4.** larger, greater, rougher, more intense, etc. than usual [a *heavy* blow, a *heavy* vote, a *heavy* sea, *heavy* thunder, *heavy* features] **5.** going beyond the average; to a greater than usual extent [a *heavy* drinker] **6.** serious; grave [a *heavy* responsibility] **7.** oppressive; burdensome [*heavy* demands] **8.** hard to do or manage; difficult [*heavy* work] **9.** hard to bear [*heavy* sorrow] **10.** burdened with grief; sorrowful [a *heavy* heart] **11.** burdened with sleep or fatigue [*heavy* eyelids] **12.** hard to digest [a *heavy* meal] **13.** not leavened properly [a *heavy* cake] **14.** clinging; penetrating [a *heavy* odor] **15.** cloudy; gloomy [a *heavy* sky] **16.** tedious; dull [*heavy* humor] **17.** clumsy; awkward [a *heavy* gait] ☆**18.** steeply inclined [a *heavy* grade] **19.** designating any large, basic industry that uses massive machinery **20.** designating, of, or equipped with heavy weapons, armor, etc. ☆**21.** [Slang] very good or pleasing: a general term of approval ☆**22.** [Slang] important, significant, profound, etc. **23.** *Chem.* designating an isotope of greater atomic weight than the normal or most abundant isotope **24.** *Theater* serious, tragic, or villainous —*adv.* heavily [*heavy*-laden] —*n., pl.* **heav′ies 1.** something heavy **2.** *Theater a)* a serious, tragic, or villainous role *b)* an actor who plays such roles —**hang heavy** to pass in a slow, boring way; drag: said of time —**heavy with child** pregnant

SYN.—**heavy** implies greater weight than is usual for its size [a tiny box which was surprisingly *heavy*] and is used to suggest a pressing down on the mind or spirits [*heavy* sorrow]; **weighty** implies absolute rather than relative heaviness and is used to suggest great importance [*weighty* matters of state]; **ponderous** applies to something that is very heavy because of its bulk and is used to suggest dullness and a lack of grace [a *ponderous* lecture, full of complicated sentences]; **massive** stresses great size and solidness but not necessarily great weight and suggests an impressiveness due to

great scope [a *massive* study of pollution control]; **cumbersome** applies to something that is difficult to handle because it is heavy and bulky, and suggests clumsiness [*cumbersome* rules that hinder change] —**ANT.** light

heav·y-du·ty (-dōōt′ē, -dyōōt′ē) *adj.* made to withstand great strain, bad weather, etc.

heav·y-hand·ed (-han′did) *adj.* **1.** clumsy or tactless **2.** cruel; tyrannical —**heav′y-hand′ed·ly** *adv.* —**heav′y-hand′ed·ness** *n.*

heav·y-heart·ed (-här′tid) *adj.* sad; depressed —**heav′y-heart′ed·ly** *adv.* —**heav′y-heart′ed·ness** *n.*

heavy hydrogen *same as* DEUTERIUM

heav·y-set (-set′) *adj.* stout or stocky in build

heavy spar *same as* BARITE

heavy water water composed of isotopes of hydrogen of atomic weight greater than one or of oxygen greater than 16, or of both; esp., deuterium oxide

heav·y-weight (-wāt′) *n.* **1.** a person or animal weighing much more than average **2.** a boxer or wrestler who weighs over 175 pounds ☆**3.** [Colloq.] a very intelligent or important person

Heb. **1.** Hebrew **2.** Hebrews

heb·dom·a·dal (heb däm′ə dəl) *adj.* [< L. < Gr. *hebdomas,* seven (days) < *hepta,* SEVEN] weekly —**heb·dom′a·dal·ly** *adv.*

He·be (hē′bē) *Gr. Myth.* the goddess of youth: she was a cupbearer to the gods

He·bra·ic (hi brā′ik) *adj.* of or characteristic of the Hebrews, their language, culture, etc.; Hebrew —**He·bra′i·cal·ly** *adv.*

He·bra·ism (hē′brī iz'm, -brā-) *n.* **1.** a Hebrew idiom, custom, etc. **2.** the ethical system, moral attitude, etc. of the Hebrews —**He′bra·ist** *n.* —**He′bra·is′tic** *adj.*

He·brew (hē′brōō) *n.* [< OFr., ult. < Heb. *'ibhri,* lit., one from across (the river)] **1.** any member of a group of Semitic peoples tracing descent from Abraham, Isaac, and Jacob; specif., an Israelite: in modern, but not recent, usage interchangeable with *Jew* **2.** *a)* the ancient Semitic language of the Israelites, in which most of the Old Testament was written *b)* its modern form, the official language of Israel —*adj.* **1.** of Hebrew or the Hebrews **2.** *same as* JEWISH

Hebrew calendar *same as* JEWISH CALENDAR

He·brews (hē′brōōz) *Bible* the Epistle to the Hebrews, a book of the New Testament

Heb·ri·des (heb′rə dēz′) a group of Scottish islands off the western coast of Scotland —**Heb′ri·de′an** (-dē′ən) *adj., n.*

Hec·a·te (hek′ə tē; *occas.* hek′it) *Gr. Myth.* a goddess of the moon, earth, and underworld, later regarded as the goddess of sorcery and witchcraft

hec·a·tomb (hek′ə tōm′, -tōōm′) *n.* [< L. < Gr. < *hekaton,* a hundred + *bous,* ox] **1.** in ancient Greece, the slaughter of 100 cattle at one time as an offering to the gods **2.** any large-scale slaughter

heck (hek) *interj., n.* [Colloq.] *a euphemism for* HELL

heck·le (hek′'l) *vt.* **-led, -ling** [ME. < *hechele:* see HACKLE¹] to annoy by interrupting with questions, shouting insults, etc. [members of the other party *heckled* the speaker] —see SYN. at BAIT —**heck′ler** *n.*

hec·tare (hek′ter) *n.* [Fr.: see HECTO- & ARE²] a unit of surface measure in the metric system, equal to 10,000 square meters (100 ares or 2.471 acres)

hec·tic (hek′tik) *adj.* [< OFr. < LL. < Gr. *hektikos,* habitual] **1.** of or characteristic of a wasting disease, as tuberculosis, or the fever accompanying this **2.** red or flushed, as with fever **3.** full of confusion, rush, excitement, etc. [the *hectic* life of a circus troupe] —**hec′ti·cal·ly** *adv.*

hec·to- [Fr. < Gr. *hekaton,* a hundred] *a combining form meaning* a hundred, the factor 10² [*hectogram*]: also, before a vowel, **hect-**

hec·to·gram (hek′tə gram′) *n.* [< Fr.: see HECTO- & GRAM] a metric measure of weight, equal to 100 grams (3.527 ounces)

hec·to·graph (-graf′) *n.* [< G. < *hekto-,* HECTO- + *-graph,* -GRAPH] a duplicating device by which written or typed matter is transferred to a sheet of gelatin, from which many copies can be taken —*vt.* to duplicate by means of a hectograph

hec·to·li·ter (-lēt′ər) *n.* [< Fr.: see HECTO- & LITER] a metric measure of capacity, equal to 100 liters (26.418 gallons or 2.8378 bushels)

hec·to·me·ter (-mēt′ər) *n.* [< Fr.: see HECTO- & METER¹] a metric measure of length, equal to 100 meters (109.36 yards)

Hec·tor (hek′tər) *Gr. Myth.* a Trojan hero killed by Achilles: he was Priam's oldest son

hec·tor (hek′tər) *vt., vi.* [after HECTOR: see prec.] to browbeat; bully —see SYN. at BAIT

Hec·u·ba (hek′yoo bə) *Gr. Myth.* wife of Priam and mother of Hector, Paris, and Cassandra

he'd (hēd) **1.** he had **2.** he would

hedge (hej) *n.* [OE. *hecg*] **1.** a row of shrubs, bushes, etc. planted close together to form a boundary or fence **2.** any fence or barrier; protection or defense of some kind [the bank account was a *hedge* against sudden expense] **3.** the act of hedging —*adj.* of, in, or near a hedge —*vt.* **hedged, hedg′ing 1.** to place a hedge around or along **2.** to hinder or guard as with a barrier; hem in [a country *hedged* in by mountains] **3.** to try to avoid loss in (a bet, risk, etc.) by making counterbalancing bets, investments, etc. —*vi.* to refuse to commit oneself; avoid direct answers [she *hedged* when asked which candidate she supported] —**hedg′er** *n.*

hedge·hog (hej′hôg′, -häg′) *n.* **1.** a small, insect-eating, old-world mammal, with sharp spines on the back, which bristle and form a defense when the animal curls up ☆**2.** the American porcupine

☆**hedge·hop** (-häp′) *vi.* **-hopped′, -hop′ping** [Colloq.] to fly an airplane very close to the ground, as for spraying insecticide —**hedge′hop′per** *n.*

HEDGEHOG
(5–10 in. long)

hedge·row (-rō′) *n.* a row of shrubs, bushes, etc., forming a hedge

he·do·nism (hēd′'n iz'm) *n.* [< Gr. *hēdonē*, pleasure] **1.** the philosophical doctrine that pleasure or happiness is the principal good in life and the proper aim of action **2.** pleasure-seeking as a way of life —**he′do·nist** *n.* —**he′do·nis′tic** *adj.* —**he′do·nis′ti·cal·ly** *adv.*

-he·dral (hē′drəl) *a combining form used to form adjectives from nouns ending in* -HEDRON

-he·dron (hē′drən) [< Gr. < *hedra*, a side, base] *a combining form meaning* a geometric figure or crystal with (a specified number of) surfaces [hexahedron]

heed (hēd) *vt., vi.* [OE. *hedan:* for IE. base see HAT] to pay close attention (to); take careful notice (of) [*heed* my advice] —*n.* close attention; careful notice [to pay no *heed* to a warning] —**heed′ful** *adj.* —**heed′ful·ly** *adv.*

heed·less (hēd′lis) *adj.* not taking heed; careless; unmindful —**heed′less·ly** *adv.* —**heed′less·ness** *n.*

hee·haw (hē′hô′) *n., vi.* [echoic] *same as* BRAY

heel[1] (hēl) *n.* [OE. *hela*] **1.** the back part of the human foot, under the ankle **2.** the corresponding part of the hind foot of an animal **3.** that part of a stocking, sock, etc. which covers the heel **4.** the built-up part of a shoe, supporting the heel **5.** anything like the human heel in location, shape, or function, as the end of a loaf of bread, the part of the palm of the hand nearest the wrist, the lower end of a ship's mast, etc. ☆**6.** [Colloq.] a person who behaves in a mean, dishonorable way —*vt.* **1.** to furnish with a heel [to *heel* shoes] **2.** to touch or drive forward as with the heel ☆**3.** [Colloq.] to provide (a person) with money —*vi.* to follow along at the heels of someone [to teach a dog to *heel*] —**at heel** just behind —**cool one's heels** [Colloq.] to be kept waiting for some time —**down at the heel(s) 1.** with the heels of one's shoes worn down **2.** shabby; seedy —**kick up one's heels** to be lively or merry —**on** (or **upon**) **the heels of** close behind —**out at the heel(s) 1.** having holes in the heels of one's shoes or socks **2.** shabby; seedy —**take to one's heels** to run away: also **show one's heels** —**to heel 1.** just behind **2.** under control [the rebels must be brought *to heel*] —**turn on one's heel** to turn around abruptly —**heel′less** *adj.*

heel[2] (hēl) *vi.* [OE. *hieldan*] to lean to one side; list: said esp. of a ship —*vt.* to make (a ship) list —*n.* the act or extent of heeling

heeled (hēld) *adj.* **1.** having a heel or heels ☆**2.** [Colloq.] *a)* having money *b)* armed, esp. with a gun

heel·er (hēl′lər) *n.* **1.** one that heels ☆**2.** [Colloq.] *same as* WARD HEELER

heel·tap (hēl′tap′) *n.* **1.** a layer of leather, etc. used as a lift in the heel of a shoe **2.** a bit of liquor left in a glass after drinking

heft (heft) *n.* [< base of HEAVE] [Colloq.] **1.** weight; heaviness **2.** importance; influence —*vt.* [Colloq.] **1.** to lift or heave **2.** to estimate the weight of by lifting —*vi.* [Colloq.] to weigh

heft·y (hef′tē) *adj.* **heft′i·er, heft′i·est** [Colloq.] **1.** weighty;

heavy [a *hefty* load] **2.** large and powerful [a *hefty* wrestler] **3.** big or fairly big [they won by a *hefty* margin] —**heft′i·ly** *adv.*

He·gel (hā′gəl), **Ge·org Wil·helm Frie·drich** (gā ôrkh′ vil′-helm frē′driH) 1770–1831; Ger. philosopher —**He·ge·li·an** (hā gā′lē ən, hi jēl′-) *adj., n.* —**He·ge′li·an·ism** *n.*

he·gem·o·ny (hi jem′ə nē; hej′ə mō′nē) *n., pl.* **-nies** [< Gr. < *hēgemōn*, leader] leadership or dominance, esp. that of one nation over others

he·gi·ra (hi jī′rə, hej′ər ə) *n.* [ML. < Ar. *hijrah*, lit., flight] **1.** [often **H**-] the forced journey of Mohammed from Mecca to Medina in 622 A.D.: the Moslem era dates from this event **2.** any journey made for the sake of safety or as an escape; flight

Hei·deg·ger (hī′di gər), **Martin** 1889–1976; Ger. philosopher

Hei·del·berg (hīd′'l bɑrg′; *G.* hī′dəl berkh′) city in SW West Germany: site of a famous university (founded 1386): pop. 122,000

heif·er (hef′ər) *n.* [OE. *heahfore*] a young cow that has not borne a calf

Hei·fetz (hī′fits), **Ja·scha** (yä′shə) 1901– ; U.S. violinist, born in Russia

heigh (hī, hā) *interj.* an exclamation to attract notice, show pleasure, express surprise, etc.

heigh-ho (hī′hō′, hā′hō′) *interj.* an exclamation of mild surprise, boredom, fatigue, greeting, etc.

height (hīt, *occas. colloq.* hītth) *n.* [OE. *heihthu* < *heah* (see HIGH & -TH[1])] **1.** the topmost point of anything **2.** the highest limit or degree; extreme [at the *height* of the storm] **3.** the distance from the bottom to the top [a man six feet in *height*] **4.** elevation or distance above a given level, as above the surface of the earth or sea; altitude [flying at a *height* of 20,000 feet] **5.** a relatively great distance above a given level or from bottom to top [lifted to a considerable *height* above the stage] **6.** [often *pl.*] a high place; eminence [castles built on the *heights*]

height·en (hīt′'n) *vt., vi.* **1.** to bring or come to a higher position **2.** to make or become larger, greater, stronger, etc.; increase [lessons to *heighten* one's appreciation of art]

Hei·ne (hī′nə), **Hein·rich** (hīn′riH) 1797–1856; Ger. poet & essayist

hei·nous (hā′nəs) *adj.* [< OFr. < *haine*, hatred: for IE. base see HATE] outrageously evil or wicked; abominable [a *heinous* crime] —see SYN. at OUTRAGEOUS —**hei′nous·ly** *adv.* —**hei′nous·ness** *n.*

heir (er) *n.* [< OFr. < L. *heres:* see HEREDITY] **1.** a person who inherits or is entitled to inherit another's property or title upon the other's death **2.** a person who appears to get some trait from a predecessor or to carry on in his tradition —**heir′dom, heir′ship′** *n.*

heir apparent *pl.* **heirs apparent** the heir whose right to a certain property or title cannot be denied if he outlives the ancestor

heir·ess (er′is) *n.* a woman or girl who is an heir, esp. to great wealth

heir·loom (-lōōm′) *n.* [HEIR + LOOM[1]] **1.** a piece of personal property that goes to an heir **2.** any treasured possession handed down from generation to generation

heir presumptive *pl.* **heirs presumptive** an heir whose right to a certain property or title will be lost if someone more closely related is born before the ancestor dies

Hei·sen·berg (hī′zən berkh), **Wer·ner (Karl)** (ver′nər) 1901–76; Ger. theoretical & nuclear physicist

☆**heist** (hīst) *n.* [< HOIST] [Slang] a robbery or holdup —*vt.* **1.** [Slang] to rob or steal **2.** *dial. var. of* HOIST —**heist′er** *n.*

He·jaz (he jaz′, hē-; -jäz′) district of NW Saudi Arabia: formerly a kingdom: c. 150,000 sq. mi.

he·ji·ra (hi jī′rə, hej′ər ə) *n. same as* HEGIRA

Hek·a·te (hek′ə tē) *same as* HECATE

hek·to- *same as* HECTO-

held (held) *pt. & pp. of* HOLD[1]

‡**hel·den·ten·or** (hel′dən tā nôr′) *n.* [G., heroic tenor] a robust tenor voice specially suited to roles in Wagner's operas

Hel·en (hel′ən) [< OFr. < L. < Gr. *Helenē*, lit., torch] a feminine name

Hel·e·na (hel′i nə; *also, for 1*, hə lē′nə) **1.** [var. of prec.] a feminine name **2.** [prob. ult. after *Helena* (?–338 A.D.), mother of CONSTANTINE I] capital of Mont.: pop. 23,000

Helen of Troy *Gr. Legend* the beautiful wife of Menelaus, king of Sparta: the Trojan War was started because Paris abducted her and took her to Troy

hel·i·cal (hel′i kəl, hē′lə-) *adj.* of, or having the form of, a helix; spiral —**hel′i·cal·ly** *adv.*

hel·i·ces (hel′ə sēz′, hē′lə-) *n. alt. pl. of* HELIX

hel·i·coid (hel′ə koid′, hē′lə-) *adj.* [< Gr. < *helix*, a spiral + *eidos*, form] shaped like a spiral; coiled: also **hel′i·coi′dal** —*n. Geom.* a spiral or screw-shaped surface

Hel·i·con (hel′ə kän′, -kən) mountain group in SC Greece: in Greek mythology, the home of the Muses —*n.* [prob. < Gr. *helix*, a spiral: from the shape] [h-] a brass-wind instrument, similar to a bass tuba

hel·i·cop·ter (hel′ə käp′tər, hē′lə-) *n.* [< Fr. < Gr. *helix*, a spiral + *pteron*, wing] a kind of aircraft moved in any direction, or kept hovering, by large, rotary blades (*rotors*) mounted horizontally —*vi., vt.* to fly by helicopter

HELICON

he·li·o- [L. < Gr. < *hēlios*, the sun] *a combining form meaning* the sun, bright, radiant: also **heli-**

he·li·o·cen·tric (hē′lē ō sen′trik) *adj.* [HELIO- + -CENTRIC] 1. calculated from, or viewed as from, the center of the sun 2. having or regarding the sun as the center

he·li·o·graph (hē′lē ə graf′) *n.* [HELIO- + -GRAPH] a device for sending a message (**heliogram**) or signaling by flashing the sun's rays from a mirror —*vt., vi.* to signal or communicate by heliograph —**he′li·og′ra·pher** (-äg′rə fər) *n.* —**he·li·o·graph′ic** *adj.* —**he·li·og′ra·phy** *n.*

He·li·op·o·lis (hē′lē äp′ə lis) ancient city in the Nile delta, just north of where Cairo now stands

He·li·os (hē′lē äs′) *Gr. Myth.* the sun god

he·li·o·trope (hē′lē ə trōp′, hēl′yə-) *n.* [< Fr. < L. < Gr. < *hēlios*, the sun + *trepein*, to turn] 1. formerly, a sunflower or other plant whose flowers turn to face the sun 2. a plant with fragrant clusters of small, white or reddish-purple flowers 3. reddish purple 4. *same as* BLOODSTONE —*adj.* reddish-purple

he·li·ot·ro·pism (hē′lē ät′rə piz′m) *n.* the tendency of certain plants or other organisms to turn toward or from light, esp. sunlight —**he·li·o·trop′ic** (-ə träp′ik) *adj.*

hel·i·port (hel′ə pôrt′) *n.* [HELI(COPTER) + (AIR)PORT] a flat place where helicopters land and take off

he·li·um (hē′lē əm) *n.* [ModL. < Gr. *hēlios*, the sun] one of the chemical elements, a very light, inert, colorless gas: it is used for inflating balloons, etc.: symbol, He; at. wt., 4.0026; at. no., 2

he·lix (hē′liks) *n., pl.* **-lix·es, -li·ces′** (hel′ə sēz′, hē′lə-) [L. < Gr., a spiral < *helissein*, to turn around] 1. any spiral, either lying in a single plane or, esp., moving around a cone, cylinder, etc. as a screw thread does 2. the folded rim of cartilage around the outer ear 3. *Archit.* an ornamental spiral

hell (hel) *n.* [OE. *hel* < base of *helan*, to hide: see CELL] 1. *Bible* the place where the spirits of the dead are 2. [often H-] *a*) *Christianity* the place where devils live and to which sinners and unbelievers go after death for punishment *b*) those in hell *c*) the powers of evil or darkness 3. any place or condition of evil, pain, cruelty, etc. [*the concentration camp was a hell*] 4. [Colloq.] *a*) any very disagreeable experience [*losing game after game can be hell*] *b*) devilishness [*full of hell*] —*vi.* [Slang] to live or act in a wild or reckless way (often with *around*) —*interj.* an exclamation of irritation, anger, surprise, disgust, etc.: regarded as profanity —☆**be hell on** [Slang] 1. to be very difficult or painful for 2. to be very strict with 3. to be very damaging to —**catch** (or **get**) **hell** [Slang] to receive a severe scolding, punishment, etc. —**for the hell of it** [Slang] for no serious reason —☆**hell of a** [Slang] very much of a: sometimes written **helluva**

he'll (hēl; *unstressed* hil, il) 1. he will 2. he shall

Hel·las (hel′əs) ancient name of GREECE: see map at GREECE

☆**hell·bend·er** (hel′ben′dər) *n.* a large, edible salamander, found esp. in the Ohio valley

☆**hell·bent** (-bent′) *adj.* [Slang] 1. firmly or recklessly determined [he was *hellbent* on having his way] 2. moving fast or recklessly

hell·cat (-kat′) *n.* 1. a witch 2. an evil, spiteful, bad-tempered woman

☆**hell·div·er** (-dī′vər) *n.* the American dabchick

hel·le·bore (hel′ə bôr′) *n.* [< OFr. < L. < Gr. *helleboros*, orig. prob. "plant eaten by fawns"] 1. any of a group of winter-blooming plants of the buttercup family, with flowers shaped like buttercups but of various colors 2. any of a group of plants of the lily family 3. the poisonous rhizomes of certain of these plants that have been used in medicine

Hel·lene (hel′ēn) *n.* [< Gr.] a Greek

Hel·len·ic (hə len′ik, he-) *adj.* 1. of the Hellenes; Greek 2. of the history, language, or culture of the ancient Greeks from the late 8th century B.C. to the death of Alexander the Great (323 B.C.) —*n.* the language of ancient Greece

Hel·len·ism (hel′ən iz′m) *n.* 1. a Greek phrase, idiom, or custom 2. the character, thought, culture, or ethics of ancient Greece 3. adoption of the Greek language, customs, etc.

Hel·len·ist (-ist) *n.* 1. a non-Greek, esp. a Jew of the Diaspora, who adopted the language, customs, etc. of the Greeks 2. a specialist or expert in the language and culture of the Greeks

Hel·len·is·tic (hel′ə nis′tik) *adj.* 1. of or characteristic of Hellenism 2. of Greek history, culture, etc. after the death of Alexander the Great (323 B.C.) —**Hel′len·is′ti·cal·ly** *adv.*

Hel·len·ize (hel′ə nīz′) *vt., vi.* **-ized′, -iz′ing** to make or become Greek, as in customs, ideals, etc. —**Hel′len·i·za′tion** *n.* —**Hel′len·iz′er** *n.*

☆**hell·er** (hel′ər) *n.* [Slang] a person who is noisy, wild, reckless, etc.

Hel·les·pont (hel′əs pänt′) ancient name of the DARDANELLES

hell·fire (hel′fīr′) *n.* the fire or torment of hell

☆**hell·gram·mite, hell·gra·mite** (hel′grə mīt′) *n.* [< ?] the larva of the dobsonfly, often used as fish bait

hell·hole (hel′hōl′) *n.* [Colloq.] any very unpleasant place

hell·ion (hel′yən) *n.* [Colloq.] a wild, mischievous, or troublesome person

hell·ish (hel′ish) *adj.* 1. of, from, or like hell 2. devilish; fiendish 3. [Colloq.] very unpleasant; detestable —**hell′ish·ly** *adv.* —**hell′ish·ness** *n.*

hel·lo (he lō′, hə lō′, hel′ō) *interj.* [var. of HOLLO] an exclamation *a*) of greeting or of response, as in telephoning *b*) to attract attention *c*) of surprise —*n., pl.* **-los** a saying of "hello" —*vi.* **-loed′, -lo′ing** to say "hello" (to)

helm[1] (helm) *n., vt.* [OE.] *archaic var. of* HELMET

helm[2] (helm) *n.* [OE. *helma*: for IE. base see CUTLASS] 1. *a*) the wheel or tiller by which a ship is steered *b*) the complete steering gear, including the wheel or tiller, rudder, etc. 2. the control or leadership, as of an organization [a new president has taken the *helm*]

hel·met (hel′mət) *n.* [OFr., dim. of *helme*, helmet < Frank.: for IE. base see CELL] 1. a hard, protective head covering, designed for use in combat, certain sports, diving, etc. 2. something like such a head covering in appearance or function —*vt.* to equip with a helmet —**hel′met·ed** *adj.*

Helm·holtz (helm′hōlts′), **Her·mann** (**Ludwig Ferdinand**) **von** (her′män fôn) 1821-94; Ger. physiologist & physicist

hel·minth (hel′minth) *n.* [Gr. *helmins* (gen. *helminthos*)] a worm or wormlike animal; esp., a worm parasite of the intestine, as the tapeworm, hookworm, or roundworm —**hel·min·thic** (hel min′thik) *adj.*

helms·man (helmz′mən) *n., pl.* **-men** the man at the helm; person who steers a ship

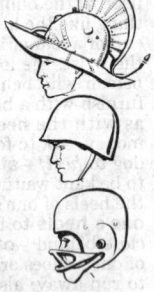

HELMETS

Hé·lo·ïse (ā lō ēz′; *E.* hel′ə wēz′) 1101?-64?; mistress &, later, wife of her teacher, Pierre ABÉLARD

Hel·ot (hel′ət, hē′lət) *n.* [< L. < Gr. *Heilōtes*, serfs] 1. a member of the lowest class of serfs in ancient Sparta 2. [h-] any serf or slave —**hel′ot·ism** *n.* —**hel′ot·ry** *n.*

help (help) *vt.* [OE. *helpan*] 1. to make things easier or better for (a person); aid; assist; specif., *a*) to give (one in need) relief, money, etc. [to *help* the poor] *b*) to share the labor of [*help* us lift this] *c*) to aid in getting (*up, down, in, to, into, out of*, etc.) [*help* her out of the canoe] 2. to make it easier for (something) to exist, happen, improve, etc.; promote [a tax to *help* the schools] 3. to remedy; relieve [this will *help* your cough] 4. *a*) to keep from; avoid [she can't *help* crying] *b*) to stop, prevent, change, etc. [faults that can't be *helped*] 5. to serve or wait on (a customer, client, etc.) —*vi.* 1. to give assistance; be useful or beneficial 2. to act as a waiter, clerk, etc. —*n.* 1. the act of helping or a thing that helps; aid; assistance [your advice was a great *help*] 2. relief; remedy [his condition is beyond *help*] ☆3. *a*) a hired helper, as a servant, farmhand, etc. *b*) hired helpers; employees —**cannot help**

but cannot fail to; be obliged to [one *cannot help but* like such a kind, warm person] —**cannot help oneself** to be the victim of circumstances, a habit, etc. —**help oneself to 1.** to serve oneself with (food, etc.) **2.** to steal —**help out** to help in getting or doing something —**so help me (God)** as God is my witness: used in oaths —**help′er** n.

SYN.—**help** is the simplest and most forceful of these words meaning to give or do something for others to take care of their needs, make things easier for them, etc.; **aid** and **assist** are somewhat more formal, **assist** especially implying that what is done by the helper is of less importance than what is done by the person helped [his son *assisted* him in his experiments]; **succor** suggests timely help to one in trouble or danger [to *succor* the snowbound mountain climbers] —**ANT.** hinder

help·ful (help′fəl) *adj.* giving help; useful —**help′ful·ly** adv. —**help′ful·ness** n.

help·ing (-iŋ) *n.* **1.** a giving of aid; assisting **2.** a portion of food served to one person

help·less (-lis) *adj.* **1.** not able to help oneself or take care of one's own needs; weak [a *helpless* infant] **2.** lacking help or protection [their guide having died, they were left *helpless* in the wilderness] **3.** incompetent; ineffective —**help′less·ly** adv. —**help′less·ness** n.

help·mate (-māt′) *n.* [altered < HELPMEET] a helpful companion; specif., a wife or husband

help·meet (-mēt′) *n.* [misreading of "an *help meet* (see MEET²) for him" (Gen. 2:18)] *same as* HELPMATE

Hel·sin·ki (hel′siŋ kē) capital of Finland; seaport on the Gulf of Finland: pop. 527,000

hel·ter-skel·ter (hel′tər skel′tər) *adv.* [coined to imitate the sound of running feet] in haste and confusion; in a disorderly, hurried manner [books tossed *helter-skelter* onto the desk] —*adj.* hurried and confused; disorderly [working in a *helter-skelter* way] —*n.* anything helter-skelter

helve (helv) *n.* [OE. *helfe*] the handle of a tool, esp. of an ax or hatchet —*vt.* **helved, helv′ing** to put a helve on

Hel·ve·tia (hel vē′shə) *Latin name of* SWITZERLAND —**Hel·ve′tian** adj., n.

hem¹ (hem) *n.* [OE.] **1.** the border on a garment or piece of cloth, usually made by folding the edge and sewing it down **2.** any border or edge —*vt.* **hemmed, hem′ming** to fold back the edge of and sew down [to *hem* a skirt] —**hem in** (or **around** or **about**) **1.** to encircle; surround [a lake *hemmed in* by mountains] **2.** to shut in; confine or restrain [farmers often feel *hemmed in* if they move to a city] —**hem′mer** n.

hem² (hem) *interj., n.* the sound made in or as if in clearing the throat —*vi.* **hemmed, hem′ming** **1.** to make this sound, as to get attention or show doubt **2.** to make this sound, or grope about in speech, while searching for the right words: usually in **hem and haw**

he·ma- *same as* HEMO-

he·ma·cy·tom·e·ter (hē′mə sī täm′ə tər, hem′ə-) *n.* [HEMA- + CYTO- + -METER] a device used to count the red and white cells in a blood sample

he·mag·glu·ti·nate (hē′mə glōōt′'n āt′, hem′ə-) *vt.* **-nat′ed, -nat′ing** [(HEM(O)- + AGGLUTINATE] to cause the clumping of red blood cells in —**he′mag·glu·ti·na′tion** n.

he·mal (hē′məl) *adj.* [HEM(O)- + -AL] having to do with the blood or blood vessels

☆**he-man** (hē′man′) *n.* [Colloq.] a strong, virile man

hem·a·tite (hem′ə tīt′, hē′mə-) *n.* [< L. < Gr. *haimatitēs*, bloodlike < *haima*, blood] native ferric oxide, Fe₂O₃, an important iron ore: it is brownish-red or black —**hem′a·tit′ic** (-tit′ik) adj.

hem·a·to- [< Gr. *haima* (gen. *haimatos*), blood] *a combining form meaning* blood: also, before a vowel, **hemat-**

hem·a·to·crit (hi mat′ə krit′) *n.* [< HEMATO- + Gr. *kritēs*, a judge] **1.** a centrifuge for measuring the relative volumes of blood cells and fluid in blood **2.** the proportion of blood cells to a volume of blood so measured: also **hematocrit reading**

hem·a·tog·e·nous (hem′ə täj′ə nəs) *adj.* **1.** forming blood **2.** spread by the bloodstream, as bacteria

he·ma·tol·o·gy (hē′mə täl′ə jē) *n.* the study of blood and its diseases —**he′ma·to·log′ic** (-tə läj′ik), **he′ma·to·log′i·cal** adj. —**he′ma·tol′o·gist** n.

he·ma·to·ma (-tō′mə) *n., pl.* **-mas, -ma·ta** (-tə) [ModL.: see HEMAT(O)- & -OMA] a local swelling or tumor filled with bloody fluid

hem·a·to·poi·e·sis (hem′ə tō poi ē′sis, hē′mə-) *n.* [< HEMATO- + Gr. *poiēsis*, a making: see POESY] the production of red blood cells by the blood-forming organs —**hem′a·to·poi·et′ic** (-et′ik) adj.

he·ma·tox·y·lin (hē′mə täk′sə lin, hem′ə-) *n.* a colorless, crystalline compound obtained from logwood and used as a biological stain

heme (hēm) *n.* the part of the hemoglobin molecule that is not protein and contains the iron

hem·er·a·lo·pi·a (hem′ər ə lō′pē ə) *n.* [ModL. < Gr. < *hēmera*, day + *alaos*, blind + *ōps*, eye + -IA] an eye defect in which vision is reduced in bright light —**hem′er·a·lop′ic** (-läp′ik) adj.

hem·i- [Gr. *hēmi-*] *a prefix meaning* half

hem·i·chor·date (hem′i kôr′dāt) *adj.* [HEMI- + CHORDATE] of or pertaining to a group of wormlike marine animals with gill slits and flimsy nervous and circulatory systems —*n.* any hemichordate animal

hem·i·dem·i·sem·i·qua·ver (hem′ē dem′ē sem′ē kwā′vər) *n.* [Brit.] *same as* SIXTY-FOURTH NOTE

Hem·ing·way (hem′iŋ wā′), **Ernest (Miller)** 1899–1961; U.S. novelist & short-story writer

he·mip·ter·an (hi mip′tər ən) *n.* [< ModL.: see HEMI- & PTERO-] any of a group of insects, including bedbugs, lice, aphids, etc., with piercing and sucking mouthparts —**he·mip′ter·ous** adj.

hem·i·sphere (hem′ə sfir′) *n.* [< L. < Gr.: see HEMI- & SPHERE] **1.** half of a sphere or globe **2.** *a)* any of the halves of the earth: the Northern, Southern, Eastern, or Western Hemisphere *b)* a model or map of any of these halves **3.** either lateral half of the cerebrum or cerebellum —**hem′i·spher′i·cal** (-sfer′i kəl), **hem′i·spher′ic** (-sfer′ik) adj.

hem·i·stich (hem′i stik′) *n.* [< L. < Gr. < *hēmi-*, half + *stichos*, a line] **1.** half a line of verse, esp. as divided by a caesura, or rhythmic pause, in the middle of a line **2.** a metrically short line of verse

hem·line (hem′līn′) *n.* **1.** the bottom edge of a dress, coat, etc. **2.** the height of this edge above the ground

hem·lock (hem′läk) *n.* [OE. *hymlic*] **1.** *a)* a poisonous European plant of the parsley family, with small, white flowers: also **poison hemlock** *b)* a poison made from this plant **2.** *a)* an evergreen tree of the pine family, with drooping branches and short, flat needles: the bark is used in tanning *b)* its wood

he·mo- [< Gr. < *haima*, blood] *a combining form meaning* blood [*hemoglobin*]: also, before a vowel, **hem-**

he·mo·cy·a·nin (hē′mə sī′ə nin) *n.* [HEMO- + *cyan-* (< Gr. *kyanos*, blue) + -IN¹] a blue, oxygen-carrying blood pigment containing copper, found in many crustaceans and mollusks

he·mo·cy·tom·e·ter (hē′mō sī täm′ə tər, hem′ō-) *n.* [HEMO- + CYTO- + -METER] a device for counting the number of cells in a sample of blood

he·mo·glo·bin (hē′mə glō′bin, hem′ə-; hē′mə glō′bin, hem′ə-) *n.* [shortened from earlier *haematoglobulin*: see HEMATO- & GLOBULIN] the red coloring matter of the red blood corpuscles: it carries oxygen from the lungs to the tissues, and carbon dioxide from the tissues to the lungs —**he′mo·glo′bin·ous** adj.

he·mo·ly·sin (hē′mə līs′'n, hem′ə-; hi mäl′ə sin) *n.* [< HEMO- + Gr. *lysis*, a dissolving + -IN¹] a substance that destroys red blood cells

he·mol·y·sis (hi mäl′ə sis) *n.* [HEMO- + -LYSIS] the destruction of red corpuscles with the freeing of hemoglobin into the surrounding fluid —**he·mo·lyt′ic** (hē′mə lit′ik, hem′ə-) adj.

he·mo·phil·i·a (hē′mə fil′ē ə, hem′ə-; -fil′yə) *n.* [ModL.: see HEMO-, -PHILE, & -IA] a hereditary condition in which one of the normal blood-clotting factors is absent, causing prolonged bleeding from even minor cuts —**he′mo·phil′i·ac** (-fil′ē ak, -fil′yak) n.

hem·or·rhage (hem′ər ij, hem′rij) *n.* [< Fr. < L. < Gr. < *haima*, blood + *rhēgnynai*, to break] the escape of large quantities of blood from a blood vessel; heavy bleeding —*vi.* **-rhaged, -rhag·ing** to have a hemorrhage —**hem′or·rhag′ic** (-ə raj′ik) adj.

hem·or·rhoid (hem′ə roid′, hem′roid) *n.* [< L. < Gr. < *haima*, blood + *rhein*, to flow] a painful swelling of a vein in the region of the anus, often with bleeding: *usually used in pl.* —**hem′or·rhoid′al** adj.

---

fat, āpe, cär; ten, ēven; is, bīte; gō, hôrn, tōōl, look; oil, out; up, fur; get; joy; yet; chin, she; thin, then; zh, leisure; ŋ, ring; ə for a in ago, e in agent, i in sanity, o in comply, u in focus; ' as in able (ā′b'l); Fr. bal; ë, Fr. coeur; ö, Fr. feu; Fr. mon; ô, Fr. coq; ü, Fr. duc; r, Fr. cri; H, G. ich; kh, G. doch; ‡foreign; ☆ Americanism; < derived from. See inside front cover.

he·mo·stat (hē′mə stat′, hem′ə-) *n.* [HEMO- + -STAT] anything used to stop bleeding; specif., a clamplike instrument used in surgery —**he′mo·stat′ic** *adj.*

hemp (hemp) *n.* [OE. *hænep*] **1.** *a)* a tall Asiatic plant having tough fiber in its stem *b)* the fiber, used to make rope, sailcloth, etc. *c)* a substance, such as marijuana, hashish, etc., made from the leaves and flowers of this plant **2.** *a)* any of various plants yielding a hemplike fiber, as sisal *b)* this fiber —**hemp′en** *adj.*

hem·stitch (hem′stich′) *n.* **1.** an ornamental stitch, used esp. at a hem, made by pulling out several parallel threads and tying the cross threads into small bunches **2.** decorative needlework done with this type of stitch —*vt.* to put hemstitches on —**hem′stitch′ing** *n.*

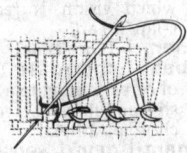

HEMSTITCH

hen (hen) *n.* [< OE. *henn*, fem. of *hana*, rooster: for IE. base see CHANT] **1.** the female of the chicken (the domestic fowl) **2.** the female of various other birds and of certain other animals, as the lobster **3.** [Slang] a woman, esp. an older woman

hen·bane (hen′bān′) *n.* a coarse, hairy, foul-smelling, poisonous plant of the nightshade family, used in medicine

hence (hens) *adv.* [< OE. *heonan*, from here + -(*e*)*s*, genitive suffix: for IE. base see HERE] **1.** from this place; away [go *hence*] **2.** from this time; after now [a year *hence*] **3.** from this life **4.** for this reason; therefore [he overeats and *hence* is overweight] —*interj.* [Archaic] go away! —**hence with** [Archaic] away with!

hence·forth (hens′fôrth′) *adv.* from this time on; after this: also **hence′for′ward**

hench·man (hench′mən) *n., pl.* **-men** [OE. *hengest*, male horse + -*man*: orig. sense prob. "groom"] **1.** a trusted helper or follower ☆**2.** a political underling who seeks to advance himself ☆**3.** any of the followers of a criminal gang leader

hen·e·quen (hen′ə kin) *n.* [< Sp. < native Yucatan name] **1.** a tropical American agave, cultivated for the hard fiber of the leaves **2.** the fiber, similar to the related sisal, used for making rope, twine, rugs, etc.

hen·house (hen′hous′) *n.* a shelter for poultry

hen·na (hen′ə) *n.* [Ar. *ḥinna′*] **1.** *a)* an old-world plant with white or red flowers *b)* a dye extracted from its leaves, often used to tint the hair auburn **2.** reddish brown —*adj.* reddish-brown —*vt.* **-naed, -na·ing** to tint with henna

hen·ner·y (hen′ər ē) *n., pl.* **-ner·ies** a place where poultry is kept or raised

hen party [Colloq.] a party for women only

hen·peck (hen′pek′) *vt.* to nag and domineer over (one's husband) —**hen′pecked′** *adj.*

Hen·ri·et·ta (hen′rē et′ə) [< Fr. fem. dim. of *Henri*, HENRY] a feminine name

Hen·ry (hen′rē) [< Fr. < G. < OHG. *Haganrih*, lit., ruler of an enclosure & *Heimerich*, lit., home ruler] **1.** a masculine name **2.** 1394-1460; prince of Portugal: called *Henry the Navigator* **3. Henry I** 1068-1135; king of England (1100-35): son of WILLIAM THE CONQUEROR **4. Henry II** 1133-89; king of England (1154-89); 1st Plantagenet king **5. Henry III** 1207-72; king of England (1216-72) **6. Henry IV** *a)* 1367-1413; king of England (1399-1413); 1st Lancastrian king *b)* 1553-1610; king of France (1589-1610); 1st Bourbon king **7. Henry V** 1387-1422; king of England (1413-22) **8. Henry VI** 1421-71; king of England (1422-61; 1470-71) **9. Henry VII** 1457-1509; king of England (1485-1509); 1st Tudor king **10. Henry VIII** 1491-1547; king of England (1509-47): established the Church of England **11. O.,** (pseud. of *William Sydney Porter*) 1862-1910; U.S. short-story writer **12. Patrick,** 1736-99; Am. patriot, statesman, & orator

☆**hen·ry** (hen′rē) *n., pl.* **-rys, -ries** [after J. *Henry* (1797-1878), U.S. physicist] *Elec.* the unit of inductance, equal to the inductance of a circuit in which the variation of current at the rate of one ampere per second induces an electromotive force of one volt

Hen·ry (hen′rē), **Cape** [after Prince *Henry*, son of JAMES I] cape in SE Va., at the entrance of Chesapeake Bay

☆**hep** (hep) *adj.* [< ?] [Slang] earlier form of HIP[4]

☆**hep·a·rin** (hep′ər in) *n.* [Gr. *hēpar*, the liver + -IN[1]] a substance found in the liver that prevents the clotting of blood: it is used in surgery and medicine

he·pat·ic (hi pat′ik) *adj.* [< L. < Gr. < *hēpar*, the liver] **1.** of or affecting the liver **2.** like the liver in color or shape

he·pat·i·ca (hi pat′i kə) *n.* [ModL. (see prec.): it has liver-shaped leaves] a small plant of the buttercup family, with white, pink, blue, or purple flowers that bloom in early spring

hep·a·ti·tis (hep′ə tīt′is) *n.* [ModL. < Gr. *hēpatos*, genitive of *hēpar*, liver + -ITIS] inflammation of the liver

He·phaes·tus (hi fes′təs) *Gr. Myth.* the god of fire and forge: identified with the Roman god Vulcan

Hep·ple·white (hep′'l hwīt′) *adj.* [after G. *Hepplewhite* (?-1786), Eng. cabinetmaker] designating or of a style of furniture with graceful curves

hep·ta- [< Gr. *hepta*, seven: for IE. base see SEVEN] *a combining form meaning* seven: also, before a vowel, **hept-**

☆**hep·ta·chlor** (hep′tə klôr′) *n.* an insecticide, $C_{10}H_7Cl_7$, similar to chlordane

hep·ta·gon (hep′tə gän′) *n.* [< Gr.: see HEPTA- & -GON] a plane figure with seven angles and seven sides —**hep·tag′o·nal** (-tag′ə n'l) *adj.*

hep·tam·e·ter (hep tam′ə tər) *n.* [HEPTA- + -METER] a line of verse with seven metrical feet

HEPPLEWHITE
CHAIR

hep·tane (hep′tān) *n.* [HEPT(A)- + -ANE] a flammable, colorless liquid, C_7H_{16}, used as a standard in octane rating, etc.

hep·tar·chy (hep′tär kē) *n., pl.* **-chies 1.** government by seven rulers **2.** a group of seven allied kingdoms, specif. [the H-] such a group supposed to have existed in Anglo-Saxon England before the 9th century

her (hur; *unstressed* ər) *pron.* [OE. *hire*: see HERE] *objective case of* SHE (Ex.: tell *her* to go): also used colloquially after a linking verb (Ex.: that's *her*) —*adj.* of, belonging to, made by, or done by her [*her* book; the pleasure of *her* company]

her. heraldry

He·ra (hir′ə) *Gr. Myth.* the wife of Zeus, queen of the gods, and goddess of marriage: identified with the Roman goddess Juno

Her·a·cli·tus (her′ə klīt′əs) fl. about 500 B.C.; Gr. philosopher

Her·a·kles, Her·a·cles (her′ə klēz′) *same as* HERCULES

her·ald (her′əld) *n.* [< OFr. *heralt* < Frank.] **1.** formerly, an official who made proclamations, carried state messages, took charge of tournaments, etc. **2.** in England, an official in charge of genealogies, heraldic arms, etc. **3.** a person who announces significant news: often used as the name of a newspaper **4.** a forerunner or harbinger [the crocus is a *herald* of spring] —*vt.* **1.** to announce, foretell, etc. **2.** to publicize

he·ral·dic (hə ral′dik) *adj.* of heraldry or heralds

her·ald·ry (her′əl drē) *n., pl.* **-ries 1.** the art or science having to do with coats of arms, genealogies, etc. **2.** heraldic devices **3.** heraldic ceremony or pomp

herb (urb, hurb) *n.* [< OFr. < L. *herba*] **1.** any seed plant whose stem withers away to the ground after each season's growth, as distinguished from a tree or shrub whose woody stem lives from year to year **2.** any plant used as a medicine, seasoning, or flavoring, as mint, thyme, basil, or sage —**herb′like′** *adj.* —**herb′y** *adj.*

her·ba·ceous (hər bā′shəs, ər-) *adj.* **1.** of or like an herb or herbs **2.** like a green leaf in texture, color, etc.

herb·age (ur′bij, hur′-) *n.* **1.** herbs collectively, esp. those used as pasturage; grass **2.** the green leaves and juicy stems of plants

herb·al (hur′b'l, ur′-) *adj.* of herbs —*n.* formerly, a book about herbs or plants

herb·al·ist (-ist) *n.* **1.** orig., a botanist **2.** a person who grows, collects, or deals in herbs, esp. medicinal herbs

her·bar·i·um (hər ber′ē əm, ər-) *n., pl.* **-i·ums, -i·a** (-ə) [LL. < L. *herba*, herb] **1.** a collection of dried plants used for botanical study **2.** a room, building, etc. for keeping such a collection

Her·bert (hur′bərt) [OE. *Herebeorht*, lit., bright army] **1.** a masculine name: dim. *Herb* **2. George,** 1593-1633; Eng. poet **3. Victor,** 1859-1924; U.S. composer, born in Ireland

her·bi·cide (hur′bə sīd′, ur′-) *n.* [< L. *herba*, herb + -CIDE] any chemical substance used to destroy plants, esp. weeds, or to check their growth —**her′bi·ci′dal** *adj.*

her·bi·vore (hur′bə vôr′) *n.* [Fr.] a herbivorous animal

her·biv·o·rous (hər biv′ər əs) *adj.* [< L. *herba*, herb + -VOROUS] feeding chiefly on grass or other plants

Her·ce·go·vi·na (hert′sə gō vē′nə) former independent duchy: now, with Bosnia, a republic of Yugoslavia: see BOSNIA AND HERCEGOVINA

Her·cu·la·ne·um (hur'kyə lā'nē əm) ancient city in S Italy, at the foot of Mt. Vesuvius: destroyed, together with Pompeii, in a volcanic eruption (79 A.D.)

Her·cu·le·an (hur'kyə lē'ən, hər kyoō'lē ən) adj. 1. of Hercules 2. [usually h-] a) having the great size and strength of Hercules b) calling for great strength, size, or courage; very difficult to do [a herculean task]

Her·cu·les (hur'kyə lēz') 1. Gr. & Rom. Myth. a son of Zeus, renowned for his strength and courage, esp. as shown in his performance of twelve labors imposed on him 2. a large N constellation —n. [h-] any very large, strong man

☆**Her·cu·les'-club** (-klub') n. [after the club carried by Hercules] 1. a small, very spiny tree with clusters of small, white flowers, found in the eastern U.S. 2. a spiny tree or shrub found in the southern U.S.

herd[1] (hurd) n. [OE. heord] 1. a number of cattle or other large animals feeding, living, or being driven together 2. a crowd 3. the common people; masses: a term showing contempt —vt., vi. to form into or move as a herd, group, crowd, etc. —see SYN. at GROUP

herd[2] (hurd) n. [OE. hierde] a herdsman: now chiefly in combination [cowherd] —vt. to tend or drive as a herdsman —☆**ride herd on** 1. to control a moving herd of (cattle) from horseback 2. to keep a close watch or control over —**herd'er** n.

herds·man (hurdz'mən) n., pl. **-men** a person who keeps or tends a herd

here (hir) adv. [OE. her < IE. base ko-, ke-, this one, from which also come HE & HER] 1. at or in this place: often used to add emphasis [John here is a good player] 2. toward, to, or into this place [come here] 3. at this point in action, speech, etc.; now [here everyone applauded] 4. in earthly life —interj. an exclamation used to call attention, answer a roll call, etc. —n. this place or point [they live near here] —**here and there** in, at, or to various places —**here goes!** an exclamation used when the speaker is about to do something daring, disagreeable, etc. —**neither here nor there** beside the point; irrelevant

here·a·bout (hir'ə bout') adv. in this general vicinity; about or near here: also **here'a·bouts'**

here·af·ter (hir af'tər) adv. 1. from now on; in the future [I'll be more careful hereafter] 2. following this, as in a book, essay, etc. 3. in the state or life after death —n. 1. the future 2. the state or life after death

here·at (hir at') adv. 1. at this time; when this occurred 2. at this; for this reason

here·by (hir'bī') adv. by this means [you are hereby ordered to appear in court]

he·red·i·ta·ble (hə red'i tə b'l) adj. same as HERITABLE —**he·red'i·ta·bil'i·ty** n.

he·red·i·tar·y (hə red'ə ter'ē) adj. [< L. hereditas: see HEREDITY] 1. a) of, or passed down by, inheritance from an ancestor [his hereditary home] b) having title, etc. by inheritance [a hereditary king] 2. of, or passed down by, heredity [a hereditary trait] 3. being such because of attitudes, beliefs, etc. passed down through generations [hereditary allies] —**he·red'i·tar'i·ly** adv. —**he·red'i·tar'i·ness** n.

he·red·i·ty (hə red'ə tē) n., pl. **-ties** [< Fr. < L. hereditas, heirship < heres, heir: for IE. base see GO] 1. the transmission of characteristics from parents to offspring by means of genes in the chromosomes 2. all the characteristics that one inherits genetically

Her·e·ford (hur'fərd, her'ə-) n. [orig. bred in Herefordshire, England] any of a breed of beef cattle having a white face and a red body with white markings

here·in (hir in') adv. 1. in here; in or into this place 2. in this writing [her name is listed herein] 3. in this matter, detail, etc. [you don't speak clearly and herein you are at fault]

here·in·a·bove (hir'in ə buv') adv. in the preceding part (of this document, speech, etc.): also **here'in·be·fore'** (-bi fôr')

here·in·af·ter (-af'tər) adv. in the following part (of this document, speech, etc.): also **here'in·be·low'** (-bi lō')

HEREFORD COW

here·in·to (hir in'toō) adv. 1. into this place 2. into this matter, condition, etc.

here·of (-uv') adv. 1. of this 2. concerning this

here·on (-än') adv. same as HEREUPON

here's (hirz) here is

here's to! here's a toast to! I wish success, joy, etc. to!

her·e·sy (her'ə sē) n., pl. **-sies** [< OFr. < L. < Gr. hairesis, a selection, sect < hairein, to take] 1. a) a religious belief opposed to the orthodox doctrines of a church; esp., such a belief that has been denounced by the church b) rejection of a belief that is part of church dogma 2. any opinion (in politics, science, etc.) opposed to established views or doctrines 3. the holding of any such belief or opinion [guilty of heresy]

her·e·tic (her'ə tik) n. a person who believes in a heresy; esp., a church member who holds beliefs opposed to church dogma —adj. same as HERETICAL

he·ret·i·cal (hə ret'i k'l) adj. 1. of heresy or heretics 2. characterized by, or having the nature of, heresy —**he·ret'i·cal·ly** adv.

here·to (hir toō') adv. to this (document, etc.) [attached hereto]: also **here·un·to** (-un'toō, -ən toō')

here·to·fore (hir'tə fôr', hir'tə fôr') adv. up to now; until the present; before this

here·un·der (hir un'dər) adv. 1. under or below this (in a document, etc.) 2. under the terms stated here

here·up·on (hir'ə pän', hir'ə pän') adv. 1. immediately following this; at once 2. concerning this

here·with (hir with', -with') adv. 1. along with this [payment is enclosed herewith] 2. by this method or means

her·it·a·ble (her'it ə b'l) adj. 1. that can be inherited 2. that can inherit —**her'it·a·bil'i·ty** n.

her·it·age (her'ət ij) n. [OFr. < LL. < L. hereditas: see HEREDITY] 1. property that is or can be inherited 2. a) something handed down from one's ancestors or the past, as a characteristic, a culture, tradition, etc. [our heritage of freedom] b) birthright

Her·man (hur'mən) [< G. < OHG. Hariman < heri, army + man, man] a masculine name

her·maph·ro·dite (hər maf'rə dīt') n. [< L. < Gr. < Hermaphroditos, son of Hermes and Aphrodite, united in a single body with a nymph] 1. a person or animal with the sexual organs of both the male and the female 2. a plant having stamens and pistils in the same flower 3. short for HERMAPHRODITE BRIG —**her·maph'ro·dit'ism, her·maph'ro·dism** n.

hermaphrodite brig a ship with a square-rigged foremast and a fore-and-aft-rigged mainmast

her·maph·ro·dit·ic (-dit'ik) adj. of or like a hermaphrodite: also **her·maph'ro·dit'i·cal** —**her·maph'ro·dit'i·cal·ly** adv.

Her·mes (hur'mēz) Gr. Myth. a god who served as messenger of the other gods: identified with the Roman god Mercury and pictured with winged shoes and hat, carrying a caduceus

her·met·ic (hər met'ik) adj. [< ModL. < L. < Gr. Hermēs (reputed founder of alchemy)] 1. hard to understand; obscure 2. [from use in alchemy] airtight: also **her·met'i·cal** —**her·met'i·cal·ly** adv.

her·mit (hur'mit) n. [< OFr. < LL. < LGr. < Gr. erēmitēs < eremos, solitary] a person who lives by himself away from others, often for religious reasons; recluse —**her·mit'ic, her·mit'i·cal** adj. —**her'mit·like'** adj.

her·mit·age (-ij) n. 1. the place where a hermit lives 2. a place where a person can live away from other people; retreat

hermit crab any of various soft-bellied crabs that live in the empty shells of certain mollusks, as snails

☆**hermit thrush** a N. American thrush with a brown body, spotted breast, and reddish-brown tail

Her·mon (hur'mən), **Mount** mountain on the border between Syria & Lebanon

Her·mo·sil·lo (er'mō sē'yō) city in NW Mexico: pop. 197,000

her·ni·a (hur'nē ə) n., pl. **-ni·as, -ni·ae'** (-ē') [L.: for IE. base see CORD] the sticking out of all or part of an organ, esp. a part of the intestine, through a tear in the wall of the surrounding structure; rupture —**her'ni·al** adj.

HERMIT CRAB
(to 18 in. long)

He·ro (hir′ō) *Gr. Legend* a priestess of Aphrodite: her lover, Leander, swam the Hellespont every night to be with her

he·ro (hir′ō, hē′rō) *n., pl.* **-roes** [< L. < Gr. *hērōs:* for IE. base see OBSERVE] **1.** *Myth. & Legend* a man of great strength and courage, favored by the gods and in part descended from them **2.** any man admired for his courage, nobility, or bold deeds **3.** any man thought of as an ideal or model **4.** the central male character in a novel, play, etc.: see also ANTIHERO **5.** a central figure who played an admirable role in any important event or period ☆**6.** *same as* HERO SANDWICH

Her·od (her′əd) Edomite family of ancient Palestine, including, esp., **1.** Herod (the Great) 73?–4 B.C.; king of Judea (37–4) **2.** Herod A·grip·pa (I) (ə grip′ə) 10? B.C.–44 A.D.; king of Judea (37–44): grandson of *Herod the Great* **3.** Herod Agrippa (II) 27?–100? A.D.; king of Judea (53–100): son of *prec.* **4.** Herod An·ti·pas (an′ti pas′) ?–40? A.D.; ruler of Galilee (4? B.C.–39 A.D.): son of *Herod the Great*

He·rod·o·tus (hə räd′ə təs) 485?–425? B.C.; Gr. historian: called the *Father of History*

he·ro·ic (hi rō′ik) *adj.* **1.** like or characteristic of a hero or his deeds; brave, noble, powerful, etc. [*heroic* conduct] **2.** of, about, or characterized by heroes and their deeds; epic [a *heroic* poem] **3.** grand; exalted [*heroic* words] **4.** exceptionally daring and risky [*heroic* measures] **5.** *Art* somewhat larger than life-size [a *heroic* statue] Also **he·ro′i·cal** —*n.* **1.** a) a heroic poem b) [*pl.*] *same as* HEROIC VERSE **2.** [*pl.*] extravagant or melodramatic talk or action, meant to seem heroic —**he·ro′i·cal·ly** *adv.*

heroic couplet a pair of rhymed lines in iambic pentameter

heroic verse the verse form in which epic poetry is traditionally written, as iambic pentameter in English

her·o·in (her′ə win) *n.* [G., orig. a trademark] a very powerful, habit-forming narcotic made from morphine

her·o·ine (her′ə win) *n.* a girl or woman hero in life or literature

her·o·ism (-wiz′m) *n.* the qualities and actions of a hero or heroine; great bravery, nobility, etc.

her·on (her′ən) *n., pl.* **-ons, -on:** see PLURAL, II, D, 1 [< OFr. *hairon* < Frank.] any of a group of wading birds with a long neck, long legs, and a long, tapered bill

her·on·ry (-rē) *n., pl.* **-ries** a place where many herons gather to breed

☆**hero sandwich** a large roll sliced lengthwise and filled with cold meats, cheese, vegetables, etc.

hero worship great or exaggerated admiration for persons regarded as heroes —**he′ro·wor′ship** *vt.* —**he′ro·wor′ship·er** *n.*

her·pes (hur′pēz) *n.* [L. < Gr. < *herpein,* to creep] a virus disease characterized by the eruption of small blisters on the skin and mucous membranes —**her·pet·ic** (hər pet′ik) *adj.*

GREAT BLUE HERON
(to 56 in. long, including bill)

herpes simplex a form of herpes mainly involving the mouth, lips, and face

herpes zos·ter (zäs′tər) [Gr. *zōstēr,* a girdle] an infection of a nerve by a virus, causing pain and blisters along the course of the nerve; shingles

her·pe·tol·o·gy (hur′pə täl′ə jē) *n.* [< Gr. *herpeton,* reptile + -LOGY] the branch of zoology having to do with the study of reptiles and amphibians —**her′pe·to·log′ic** (-tə läj′ik), **her′pe·to·log′i·cal** *adj.* —**her′pe·tol′o·gist** *n.*

‡**Herr** (her) *n., pl.* **Her′ren** (-ən) in Germany, a man; gentleman: German title used like *Mr.* or *sir*

Her·rick (her′ik), Robert 1591–1674; Eng. poet

her·ring (her′iŋ) *n., pl.* **-rings, -ring:** see PLURAL, II, D, 1 [OE. *hæring*] **1.** a small food fish of the N Atlantic: eaten cooked, dried, salted, or smoked: the young are canned as sardines **2.** loosely, the sprat, pilchard, etc.

her·ring·bone (-bōn′) *n.* **1.** the spine of a herring, with the ribs extending from opposite sides in rows of parallel, slanting lines **2.** a pattern with such a design or anything having such a pattern, as a twill weave **3.** a method of climbing a slope on skis with the ski tips turned outward —*adj.* having the pattern of a herringbone —*vi., vt.* **-boned′, -bon′ing 1.** to stitch, weave, arrange, etc. in a herringbone pattern **2.** to climb (a slope) on skis, using the herringbone method

hers (hurz) *pron.* that or those belonging to her: used without a following noun [that book is *hers; hers* are better]: also used after *of* to indicate possession [a friend of *hers*]

Her·schel (hur′shəl) **1.** Sir John Frederick William, 1792–1871; Eng. astronomer & physicist **2.** Sir William, (born *Friedrich Wilhelm Herschel*) 1738–1822; Eng. astronomer, born in Germany: father of *prec.*

her·self (hər self′) *pron.* a form of the 3d person singular, feminine pronoun, used: *a)* as an intensive [she went *herself*] *b)* as a reflexive [she hurt *herself*] *c)* as a kind of noun meaning "her real or true self" [she is not *herself* today]

hertz (hurts) *n., pl.* **hertz** [see HERTZIAN WAVES] the international unit of frequency, equal to one cycle per second

Hertz·i·an waves (hurt′sē ən, hert′-) [after H. R. *Hertz* (1857–1894), Ger. physicist] [*sometimes* h-] radio waves or other electromagnetic radiation resulting from the oscillations of electricity in a conductor

Herzegovina *same as* HERCEGOVINA

Herzl (her′ts′l), The·o·dore (tā′ô dôr′) 1860–1904; Austrian-Jewish writer, born in Hungary: founder of Zionism

he's (hēz) **1.** he is **2.** he has

Hesh·van (khesh vän′; *E.* hesh′vən) *n.* [Heb.] *see* JEWISH CALENDAR

He·si·od (hē′sē əd, hes′ē-) fl. 8th cent. B.C.; Gr. poet —**He′si·od′ic** (-äd′ik) *adj.*

hes·i·tan·cy (hez′ə tən sē) *n., pl.* **-cies** hesitation or indecision; doubt: also **hes′i·tance**

hes·i·tant (-tənt) *adj.* hesitating or undecided; doubtful —see SYN. at RELUCTANT —**hes′i·tant·ly** *adv.*

hes·i·tate (-tāt′) *vi.* **-tat′ed, -tat′ing** [< L. pp. of *haesitare* < *haerere,* to stick] **1.** to stop in indecision; pause or delay in acting or deciding because of feeling unsure [he never *hesitated* to speak the truth] **2.** to pause; stop momentarily [she *hesitated* at the door before knocking] **3.** to be reluctant; not be sure that one should [I *hesitate* to ask] **4.** to pause continually in speaking; stammer —**hes′i·tat′er, hes′i·ta′tor** *n.* —**hes′i·tat′ing·ly** *adv.*

SYN.—**hesitate** implies a temporary stopping because of feeling uncertain, unwilling, or confused [he *hesitated* before entering]; **vacillate** implies a shifting back and forth in a decision, opinion, etc. [she *vacillates* in her affection]; **waver** is often applied to a holding back or hesitating after a decision has been made [do not *waver* in your determination]; **falter** suggests a pausing or slowing down, as in fear or indecision [they never *faltered* in the counterattack]

hes·i·ta·tion (hez′ə tā′shən) *n.* **1.** a hesitating, or feeling of doubt, fear, etc.; unsure or unwilling feeling **2.** a halting or pausing for a moment [talk filled with *hesitations*] —**hes′i·ta′tive** *adj.* —**hes′i·ta′tive·ly** *adv.*

Hes·pe·ri·an (hes pir′ē ən) *adj.* [< L. < Gr. *Hesperios,* western, evening < *Hesperos,* the evening star] western

Hes·per·i·des (hes per′ə dēz′) *n.pl.* **1.** *sing.* **Hes·per·id** (hes′pər id) *Gr. Myth.* the nymphs who guarded the golden apples given as a wedding gift by Gaea to Hera **2.** the garden where the apples grew

Hes·per·us (hes′pər əs) *n.* [L.] the evening star, esp. Venus: also **Hes′per**

Hesse (hes, hes′i) former region in WC Germany, now a state of West Germany

Hes·se (hes′ə), **Her·mann** (her′män) 1877–1962; Ger. novelist in Switzerland

Hes·sian (hesh′ən) *adj.* of Hesse or its people —*n.* **1.** a native or inhabitant of Hesse **2.** any of the Hessian mercenaries who fought for the British in the Revolutionary War

☆**Hessian fly** a small, two-winged fly whose larvae destroy wheat crops

hest (hest) *n.* [< OE. *hæs,* command < *hatan,* to call] [Archaic] behest; order

Hes·ter, Hes·ther (hes′tər) [var. of ESTHER] a feminine name

Hes·ti·a (hes′tē ə) [Gr.] the Greek goddess of the hearth

he·tae·ra (hi tir′ə) *n., pl.* **-rae** (-ē), **-ras** [< Gr. < *hetairos,* companion] in ancient Greece, a woman, usually an educated slave, who served as a companion and prostitute to upper-class men: also **he·tai′ra** (-tī′rə), *pl.* **-rai** (-rī)

het·er·o- [< Gr. < *heteros,* the other (of two)] *a combining form* meaning other, another, different [*heterosexual*]: opposed to HOMO-: also, before a vowel, **heter-**

het·er·o·dox (het′ər ə däks′) *adj.* [< Gr. < *hetero-,* HETERO- + *doxa,* opinion] departing from or opposed to the usual beliefs or established doctrines, esp. in religion; unorthodox

het·er·o·dox·y (-däk′sē) *n., pl.* **-dox′ies 1.** the quality or fact of being heterodox **2.** a heterodox belief or doctrine

het·er·o·dyne (-dīn′) *adj.* [HETERO- + DYNE] designating or of the combination of two different radio frequencies to produce beats with new frequencies —*vi.* **-dyned′, -dyn′ing** to combine two different frequencies so as to produce such beats

het·er·oe·cious (het'ər ē'shəs) *adj.* [< HETERO- + Gr. *oikia*, a house + -OUS] *Biol.* living as a parasite on first one species of host and then another —**het'er·oe'cism** (-siz'm) *n.*

het·er·o·ge·ne·ous (het'ər ə jē'nē əs, het'rə-; -jēn'yəs) *adj.* [< ML. < Gr. < *hetero-*, HETERO- + *genos*, a kind] 1. differing or opposite in structure, quality, etc.; dissimilar 2. made up of parts that are unrelated or unlike; varied —**het'er·o·ge·ne'i·ty** (-jə nē'ə tē) *n., pl.* -ties —**het'er·o·ge·ne·ous·ly** *adv.*

het·er·o·mor·phism (het'ər ō môr'fiz'm) *n.* [HETERO- + -MORPH + -ISM] difference in form, structure, etc.: also **het'er·o·mor'phy** —**het'er·o·mor'phic, het'er·o·mor'phous** *adj.*

het·er·o·nym (het'ər ə nim') *n.* [< Gr. < *hetero-*, HETERO- + *onyma*, NAME] a word with the same spelling as another but with a different meaning and pronunciation (Ex.: *tear*, a drop from the eye, *tear*, to rip) —**het'er·on'y·mous** (-än'ə məs) *adj.*

het·er·o·sex·u·al (het'ər ə sek'shoo wəl) *adj.* of or having sexual desire for those of the opposite sex —*n.* a heterosexual person —**het'er·o·sex'u·al'i·ty** (-wal'ə tē) *n.*

het·er·o·sis (het'ər ō'sis) *n.* [HETER(O)- + -OSIS] a quality resulting from hybridization, in which offspring have greater strength, size, resistance, etc. than the parents —**het'er·ot'ic** (-ät'ik) *adj.*

het·man (het'mən) *n., pl.* -mans [Pol. < G. < *haupt*, head + *mann*, man] a Cossack chief

☆**het up** (het) [*het*, dial. pt. & pp. of *heat*] [Slang] excited or angry

heu·ris·tic (hyoo ris'tik) *adj.* [< G. < Gr. *heuriskein*, to invent, discover] helping to discover or learn; specif., designating a method of education or of computer programming in which the pupil or machine uses a trial-and-error approach to find solutions or better answers —**heu·ris'ti·cal·ly** *adv.*

hew (hyoo) *vt.* **hewed, hewed** or **hewn, hew'ing** [OE. *heawan* < IE. base *kau*-] 1. to chop or cut with an ax, knife, etc.; hack [*to hew* wood for a fire] 2. to make or shape by or as by cutting or chopping with an ax, etc. [a statue *hewn* from wood] 3. to chop (a tree) with an ax so as to cause it to fall (usually with *down*) —*vi.* 1. to make cutting or chopping blows with an ax, knife, etc. ☆2. to keep close or give one's support [*to hew* to a line; to *hew* to a principle] —**hew'er** *n.*

HEW (Dept. of) Health, Education, and Welfare

☆**hex** (heks) *n.* [< G. *hexe* < OHG.] 1. [Dial.] a witch or sorcerer 2. *a)* a sign, spell, etc. supposed to bring bad luck *b)* a jinx —*vt.* to cause to have bad luck; jinx

hex·a- [< Gr. *hex*, six: for IE. base see SIX] *a combining form meaning six* [*hexagram*]: also, before a vowel, **hex-**

hex·a·chlo·ro·phene (hek'sə klôr'ə fēn') *n.* [< HEXA- + CHLORO- + PHENOL] a white powder, $C_{13}Cl_6H_6O_2$, used, esp. formerly, to kill bacteria

hex·a·gon (hek'sə gän') *n.* [< L. < Gr.: see HEXA- & -GON] a plane figure with six angles and six sides

hex·ag·o·nal (hek sag'ə n'l) *adj.* 1. of, or having the form of, a hexagon 2. having a six-sided base or section: said of a solid figure 3. designating a crystal form having parallel sides perpendicular to two hexagonal faces —**hex·ag'o·nal·ly** *adv.*

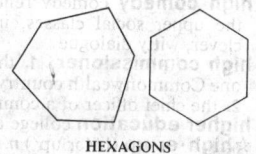
HEXAGONS

hex·a·gram (hek'sə gram') *n.* [HEXA- + -GRAM] a six-pointed star formed of two equilateral triangles that intersect: see illustration at STAR OF DAVID

hex·a·he·dron (hek'sə hē'drən) *n., pl.* -drons, -dra (-drə) [ModL. < Gr.: see HEXA- & -HEDRON] a solid figure with six plane surfaces —**hex'a·he'dral** *adj.*

hex·am·e·ter (hek sam'ə tər) *n.* [< L. < Gr.: see HEXA- & METER[1]] 1. a line of verse containing six metrical feet 2. verse consisting of hexameters —*adj.* having six metrical feet

hex·a·pod (hek'sə päd') *n.* [< Gr.: see HEXA- & -POD] an insect (sense 1) —*adj.* having six legs, as a true insect: also **hex·ap·o·dous** (hek sap'ə dəs)

hex·ose (hek'sōs) *n.* [HEX(A)- + -OSE[1]] any of a group of simple sugars with six carbon atoms, as dextrose or fructose

hey (hā) *interj.* [ME. *hei*, echoic formation] an exclamation used to attract attention, express surprise, etc., or in asking a question

hey·day (hā'dā') *n.* the time of greatest health, vigor, success, etc.; prime

Hez·e·ki·ah (hez'ə kī'ə) *Bible* a king of Judah: II Kings 18–20

Hf *Chem.* hafnium

HF, H.F., hf, h.f. high frequency

hf. half

Hg [L. *hydrargyrum*] *Chem.* mercury

HG., H.G. High German

hg. hectogram; hectograms

hgt. height

H.H. 1. His (or Her) Highness 2. His Holiness

hhd. hogshead

☆**H-hour** (āch'our') *n.* the hour at which an important operation, esp. a military operation, is to begin

☆**hi** (hī) *interj.* [ME. *hy*, var. of *hei*, HEY] an exclamation of greeting

HI Hawaii

Hi·a·le·ah (hī'ə lē'ə) [< ? Seminole-Creek *haiyakpo hili*, lit., pretty prairie] city in SE Fla.: suburb of Miami: pop. 102,000

hi·a·tus (hī āt'əs) *n., pl.* -tus·es, -tus [L., pp. of *hiare*, to gape: for IE. base see GAPE] 1. a break or gap where a part is missing or lost, as in a manuscript 2. any gap or opening 3. a slight pause in pronunciation between two successive vowel sounds, as between the *e*'s in *reentry*

Hi·a·wa·tha (hī'ə wô'thə, hē'-; -wä'-) the Indian hero of *The Song of Hiawatha*, a long narrative poem (1855) by Longfellow

hi·ba·chi (hi bä'chē) *n., pl.* -chis [Jpn. < *hi*, fire + *bachi*, bowl] a small, charcoal-burning grill of Japanese design

hi·ber·nal (hī bur'nəl) *adj.* [< L. < *hibernus*, wintry] of winter; wintry

hi·ber·nate (hī'bər nāt') *vi.* -nat'ed, -nat'ing [< L. pp. of *hibernare* < *hibernus*, wintry] to spend the winter in a dormant or inactive state: compare ESTIVATE —**hi'ber·na'tion** *n.* —**hi'ber·na'tor** *n.*

HIBACHI

Hi·ber·ni·a (hī bur'nē ə) [L.] *poet.* name of IRELAND —**Hi·ber'ni·an** *adj., n.*

hi·bis·cus (hī bis'kəs, hi-) *n.* [< L. *hibiscus*] a plant, shrub, or small tree related to the mallow, with large, colorful flowers

hic·cough (hik'əp) *n., vi.* [< HICCUP: spelling influenced by association with COUGH] *same as* HICCUP

hic·cup (hik'əp) *n.* [altered < Early ModE. *hikop*, *hicket*, of echoic origin] a sudden stopping of the breath with a sharp, gulping sound: hiccups usually occur in a series and are not easily controlled —*vi.* **-cuped** or **-cupped**, **-cup·ing** or **-cup·ping** to have hiccups

‡**hic ja·cet** (hik' jā'sit) [L.] 1. here lies: inscribed on tombstones 2. an epitaph

hick (hik) *n.* [altered < RICHARD] [Colloq.] an awkward, unsophisticated person, esp. one from a farming area or small town: a mild term of contempt —*adj.* [Colloq.] of or like a hick

☆**hick·ey** (hik'ē) *n., pl.* -eys, -ies [orig. U.S. dial.] [Colloq.] 1. a gadget 2. a pimple 3. a mark made on the skin, as by biting or sucking

☆**hick·o·ry** (hik'ər ē, hik'rē) *n., pl.* -ries [< AmInd. *pawcohiccora*, product made from the nuts] 1. a N. American tree related to the walnut, with smooth-shelled, edible nuts 2. its hard, tough wood 3. its nut: also **hickory nut**

hid (hid) *pt. & alt. pp.* of HIDE[1]

hi·dal·go (hi dal'gō) *n., pl.* -gos [Sp., contr. of *hijo de algo*, son of something] a Spanish nobleman of secondary rank, below that of a grandee

hid·den (hid'n) *alt. pp.* of HIDE[1] —*adj.* concealed; secret

HICKORY (leaf, nut & tree)

hide[1] (hīd) *vt.* **hid, hid'den** or **hid, hid'ing** [OE. *hydan* < IE. base *skew*-, to cover] 1. to put or keep out of sight; secrete; conceal [he *hid* the present in his pocket] 2. to keep others from knowing about; keep secret [to *hide* one's identity] **3.** to keep from being seen by covering up, obscuring, etc. [fog *hid* the road] **4.** to turn away [to *hide* one's head in shame] —*vi.* **1.** to be or lie out of sight or concealed **2.** to keep oneself out of sight; conceal oneself [I *hid* in the closet] —**hid′er** *n.*

SYN.—**hide**, the general word, refers to the putting of something in a place where it is not easily seen or found [the toy was *hidden* deep in the chest]; **conceal**, a more formal word, more often suggests a purpose or aim [to *conceal* one's face, motive, etc.]; **secrete** and **cache** suggest a careful hiding in a secret place [they *secreted*, or *cached*, the loot in the cellar], but **cache** now often refers only to a storing for later use [let's *cache* our supplies in the cave] —**ANT. reveal, expose**

hide² (hīd) *n.* [OE. *hid:* for IE. base see HIDE¹] **1.** an animal skin or pelt, either raw or tanned **2.** [Colloq.] the skin of a person —*vt.* **hid′ed, hid′ing** [Colloq.] to beat; flog —**neither hide nor hair** nothing whatsoever

hide-and-seek (hīd′'n sēk′) *n.* a children's game in which one player tries to find the other players, who have hidden: also **hide′-and-go-seek′**

hide·a·way (hīd′ə wā′) *n.* [Colloq.] a place where one can hide, be away from others, etc.

hide·bound (-bound′) *adj.* **1.** having the hide tight over the body structure, as an emaciated cow **2.** stubbornly conservative and narrow-minded

hid·e·ous (hid′ē əs) *adj.* [< Anglo-Fr. < OFr. < *hide*, fright] horrible; very ugly or disgusting; dreadful —**hid′e·ous·ly** *adv.* —**hid′e·ous·ness** *n.*

☆**hide-out** (hīd′out′) *n.* [Colloq.] a hiding place

hid·ing¹ (hīd′iŋ) *n.* **1.** *a*) the act of one that hides *b*) the condition of being hidden: usually in the phrase **in hiding 2.** a place to hide

hid·ing² (hīd′iŋ) *n.* [Colloq.] a severe beating

hie (hī) *vi., vt.* **hied, hie′ing** or **hy′ing** [OE. *higian*] to hurry or hasten: usually reflexive [you'd better *hie* yourself to school]

hi·er·arch (hī′ə rärk′) *n.* [< ML. < Gr. < *hieros*, sacred + *archos*, ruler] a chief priest

hi·er·ar·chy (hī′ə rär′kē) *n., pl.* **-chies** [< OFr. < ML.: see HI-ERARCH] **1.** a system of church government by priests or other clergy in different ranks or grades **2.** the group of officials in such a system **3.** a group of persons or things arranged in order of rank, grade, etc. —**hi′er·ar′chi·cal, hi′er·ar′chic, hi′er·ar′chal** *adj.* —**hi′er·ar′chi·cal·ly** *adv.*

hi·er·at·ic (hī′ə rat′ik) *adj.* [< L. < Gr. *hieratikos* < *hieros*, sacred] **1.** of or used by priests; priestly **2.** designating or of the shorter form of cursive hieroglyphic writing once used by Egyptian priests Also **hi′er·at′i·cal** —**hi′er·at′i·cal·ly** *adv.*

hi·er·o·glyph (hī′ər ə glif′, hī′rə-) *n. same as* HIEROGLYPHIC

hi·er·o·glyph·ic (hī′ər ə glif′ik, hī′rə-) *adj.* [< Fr. < LL. < Gr. < *hieros*, sacred + *glyphein*, to carve] **1.** of, like, or written in hieroglyphics **2.** hard to read or understand Also **hi′er·o·glyph′i·cal** —*n.* **1.** a picture or symbol representing a word, syllable, or sound, used by the ancient Egyptians and others **2.** [*usually pl.*] a method of writing using hieroglyphics **3.** a symbol, sign, etc. hard to understand **4.** [*pl.*] writing hard to decipher —**hi′er·o·glyph′i·cal·ly** *adv.*

hi·er·o·phant (hī′ər ə fant, hī′rə-) *n.* [< L. < Gr. < *hieros*, sacred + *phainein*, to show] a person who explains sacred mysteries or secret knowledge

HIEROGLYPHICS
(Translation: "No limit may be set to art, neither is there any craftsman that is fully master of his craft.")

☆**hi-fi** (hī′fī′) *n.* **1.** *same as* HIGH FIDELITY **2.** a radio, phonograph, etc. having high fidelity —*adj.* of or having high fidelity of sound reproduction

hig·gle (hig′'l) *vi.* **-gled, -gling** to argue about terms, price, etc.; haggle —**hig′gler** *n.*

hig·gle·dy-pig·gle·dy (hig′'l dē pig′'l dē) *adv.* [repetition of sounds, prob. based on PIG] in disorder; in jumbled confusion —*adj.* disorderly; jumbled; confused

high (hī) *adj.* [OE. *heah:* for IE. base see COOP] **1.** of more than normal height; lofty; tall [a *high* wall] **2.** extending upward a (specified) distance [a fence four feet *high*] **3.** situated far above the ground or other level [the plane was *high* in the

clouds] **4.** reaching to or done from a height [a *high* jump, a *high* dive] **5.** above others in rank, position, quality, character, etc.; superior; exalted [a *high* official; *high* ideals] **6.** grave; very serious [*high* treason] **7.** greatly developed; complex: usually in the comparative [*higher* mathematics] **8.** main; principal; chief [a *high* priest] **9.** greater in size, amount, degree, power, etc. than usual [*high* prices, *high* winds] **10.** advanced to its acme or fullness [*high* noon] **11.** expensive; costly [land is *high* now] **12.** luxurious and extravagant [*high* living] **13.** haughty; overbearing [acting *high* and mighty] **14.** raised in pitch [a *high* note] **15.** slightly tainted; strong-smelling: said of meat, esp. game **16.** extremely formal in matters of ceremony, doctrine, etc. [*High* Church] **17.** excited; elated; joyful or merry [*high* spirits] **18.** far from the equator [a *high* latitude] ☆**19.** designating or of that gear ratio of a motor vehicle transmission which produces the highest speed **20.** [Slang] *a*) drunk; intoxicated *b*) under the influence of a drug **21.** *Phonet.* produced with the tongue held in a relatively elevated position: said of a vowel, as (ē) —*adv.* **1.** in a high manner **2.** in or to a high level, degree, rank, etc. [throw the ball *high*] —*n.* **1.** a high level, place, etc. ☆**2.** an area of high barometric pressure ☆**3.** high gear (see *adj.* 19) **4.** [Slang] a condition of euphoria caused as by drugs —**high and dry** alone and helpless; stranded —**high and low** everywhere —**high on** [Colloq.] enthusiastic about; very interested in or impressed by —**on high 1.** high above **2.** in heaven

SYN.—**high** and **tall** both refer to something which extends farther upward than is normal for its kind, and **high** also refers to something in a place far above a given level [a *high* mountain; *high* clouds], but **tall** is usually applied to people, animals, and other growing things [a *tall* woman; a *tall* tree]; **lofty** and **towering** suggest great, imposing, or very noticeable height [*lofty* peaks; a *towering* castle] —**ANT. low, short**

☆**high·ball** (hī′bôl′) *n.* **1.** liquor, usually whiskey, served with water, soda water, ginger ale, etc. and ice in a glass **2.** a railroad signal meaning "go ahead" —*vi.* [from a railroad signal, orig. a hanging ball, meaning "go ahead"] [Slang] to go very fast

high·born (-bôrn′) *adj.* of noble birth

☆**high·boy** (-boi′) *n.* a high chest of drawers mounted on legs

high·bred (-bred′) *adj.* showing good breeding; cultivated

☆**high·brow** (-brou′) *n.* [Colloq.] a person who is or pretends to be intellectual —*adj.* [Colloq.] of or for a highbrow

High Church that group in the Anglican Church which emphasizes the importance of the priesthood and of traditional rituals and doctrines —**High′-Church′** *adj.* —**High′-Church′man** *n., pl.* **-men**

high-class (-klas′) *adj.* of a superior class, rank, quality, etc.

high comedy comedy reflecting the life of the upper social classes, in which there is clever, witty dialogue

HIGHBOY

high commissioner 1. the chief diplomatic representative of one Commonwealth country to another Commonwealth country **2.** the chief officer of a commission

higher education college or university education

☆**high·er-up** (hī′ər up′) *n.* [Colloq.] a person of higher rank or position

☆**high·fa·lu·tin, high·fa·lu·ting** (hī′fə loot′'n) *adj.* [Colloq.] ridiculously pretentious or pompous

high fidelity in radio, sound recording, etc., a nearly exact reproduction of a wide range of sound frequencies, from about 20 to 20,000 hertz

high-flown (-flōn′) *adj.* **1.** extravagantly ambitious **2.** high-sounding but meaningless; bombastic

high frequency any radio frequency between 3 and 30 megahertz

High German 1. the West Germanic dialects spoken in C and S Germany: distinguished from LOW GERMAN **2.** the official and literary form of the German language, technically called *New High German:* see also OLD HIGH GERMAN, MIDDLE HIGH GERMAN

high-grade (-grād′) *adj.* of superior quality

high-hand·ed (-han′did) *adj.* acting or done without thought for what others want or think; arrogant and arbitrary —**high′hand′ed·ly** *adv.* —**high′hand′ed·ness** *n.*

☆**high-hat** (-hat′) *adj.* [Slang] snobbish and aloof —*n.* [Slang] a snob —*vt.* **-hat′ted, -hat′ting** [Slang] to treat snobbishly; snub

☆**high hat** *same as* TOP HAT

High Holidays the period including Rosh Hashana and Yom Kippur in the Jewish calendar: also **High Holy Days**

☆**high·jack** (-jak′) *vt. same as* HIJACK —**high′jack′er** *n.*

high jump a contest in track and field in which the contestants jump for height over a horizontal bar set between two upright poles: after each successful jump the bar is raised

high-keyed (-kēd′) *adj.* emotionally tense; high-strung

high·land (-lənd) *n.* a region higher than adjacent land and containing many hills or mountains —*adj.* of, in, or from such a region —**the Highlands** mountainous region occupying nearly all of N Scotland —**high′land·er, High′land·er** *n.*

Highland fling a lively dance of the Highlands

high life the luxurious way of life of fashionable society

high·light (-līt′) *n.* **1.** *a)* a part on which light is brightest *[the highlights on the cheeks] b)* a part of a painting, etc. on which light is represented as brightest *c)* the representation or effect of such light in a painting, etc. Also **high light 2.** the most important or interesting part, scene, etc. —*vt.* **1.** to give a highlight or highlights to **2.** to give an important place to *[highlight these books in your display]* **3.** to be the most outstanding in *[that idea highlighted her speech]*

HIGHLIGHT

high·ly (-lē) *adv.* **1.** in a high office or rank *[a highly placed official]* **2.** very much; extremely *[highly pleased]* **3.** with high approval; favorably *[she speaks highly of you]* **4.** at a high wage, salary, etc. *[highly paid]*

High Mass *R.C.Ch.* a sung Mass, usually celebrated with the complete ritual, at which the celebrant is assisted by a deacon and subdeacon: also **Solemn High Mass, Solemn Mass**

high-mind·ed (-mīn′did) *adj.* **1.** [Obs.] haughty; proud **2.** having or showing high ideals, principles, etc. *[a high-minded attitude]* —**high′-mind′ed·ly** *adv.* —**high′-mind′ed·ness** *n.*

high·ness (-nis) *n.* **1.** the quality or state of being high; height **2.** [H-] a title used in speaking to or of a member of a royal family (with *His, Her,* or *Your)*

high-pitched (-picht′) *adj.* **1.** high in pitch; shrill *[a high-pitched siren]* **2.** lofty; exalted *[high-pitched thought]* **3.** showing intense feeling; agitated *[high-pitched emotions]* **4.** steep in slope *[a high-pitched roof]*

High Point [after its location, the highest point on the N.C. Railroad] city in central N.C.: pop. 63,000

high-pow·ered (-pou′ərd) *adj.* very powerful

high-pres·sure (-presh′ər) *adj.* **1.** *a)* having, using, or withstanding relatively high pressure *b)* having a high barometric pressure **2.** using strong methods or arguments in order to persuade or convince *[a high-pressure salesman]* —☆ *vt.* **-sured, -sur·ing** [Colloq.] to urge with strong methods or arguments

high priest a chief priest; specif., the chief priest of the ancient Jewish priesthood

high-proof (-proof′) *adj.* high in alcohol content

☆**high-rise** (-rīz′) *adj.* designating or of a tall apartment house, office building, etc. of many stories —*n.* a high-rise building

high·road (-rōd′) *n.* **1.** [Chiefly Brit.] a main road; highway **2.** an easy or direct way

☆**high roller** [from rolling the dice in gambling] [Slang] **1.** a person who gambles for very large sums of money **2.** a person who spends or invests money freely or recklessly

high school ☆a secondary school that usually includes grades 10, 11, and 12, and sometimes grade 9 —**high′-school′** *adj.*

high seas open ocean waters outside the territorial limits of any single nation

high-sound·ing (-soun′diŋ) *adj.* sounding pretentious or impressive

high-spir·it·ed (-spir′i tid) *adj.* **1.** having or showing a courageous or noble spirit **2.** spirited; fiery *[a high-spirited speech]* **3.** full of energy; lively *[a high-spirited horse]*

high-strung (-struŋ′) *adj.* very nervous and tense; excitable

☆**high-tail, high·tail** (hī′tāl′) *vi., vt.* [Colloq.] to leave or go in a hurry; scurry off: chiefly in **high-tail it**

high tea [Brit.] a tea served somewhat later and with more food than the usual tea

high-ten·sion (hī′ten′shən) *adj.* having, carrying, or operating under a high voltage

high-test (-test′) *adj.* **1.** passing difficult tests **2.** vaporizing at a relatively low temperature: said of gasoline

high tide 1. the highest level to which the tide rises **2.** the time when the tide is at this level **3.** any highest point or time

high time 1. time after the proper time, but before it is too late; none too soon ☆**2.** [Slang] a lively, exciting, enjoyable time: also **high old time**

high-toned (-tōnd′) *adj.* **1.** [Now Rare] high in tone or pitch **2.** characterized by dignity, high principles, etc.: often used in an ironic or humorous way ☆**3.** [Colloq.] of or imitating the manners, attitudes, etc. of the upper classes

high treason treason against the ruler or government

high water 1. *same as* HIGH TIDE **2.** the highest level reached by a body of water

high-wa·ter mark (hī′wôt′ər, -wät′ər) **1.** the highest level reached by a body of water **2.** the mark left after high water has gone down **3.** a culminating point; highest point

high·way (-wā′) *n.* **1.** a public road **2.** a main road; thoroughfare **3.** a direct way

high·way·man (-wā mən) *n., pl.* **-men** formerly, a man who robbed travelers on a highway

☆**high wire** a cable or wire stretched high above the ground, on which acrobats perform; tightrope

☆**hi·jack** (hī′jak′) *vt.* [prob. *hi* (for HIGH) + JACK, *v.*] **1.** to steal (a truck and its contents, other goods being transported, etc.), usually by force **2.** to force the pilot of (an aircraft) to fly to some place other than the destination —**hi′jack′er** *n.*

hike (hīk) *vi.* **hiked, hik′ing** [< dial. *heik*] **1.** to take a long, vigorous walk; tramp or march, esp. through the country, woods, etc. ☆**2.** to move up out of place *[her dress hiked up when she sat down]* —*vt.* [Colloq.] **1.** to pull up; hoist *[to hike up one's socks]* ☆**2.** to raise (prices, etc.) —☆ *n.* **1.** a long, vigorous walk **2.** [Colloq.] a moving upward; rise *[a hike in prices]* —**hik′er** *n.*

hi·lar·i·ous (hi ler′ē əs, hī-; -lar′-) *adj.* [< L. < Gr. *hilaros,* cheerful] **1.** noisily merry; boisterous and lively **2.** causing laughter; funny —**hi·lar′i·ous·ly** *adv.* —**hi·lar′i·ous·ness** *n.*

hi·lar·i·ty (-ə tē) *n.* the state or quality of being hilarious; noisy merriment —see SYN. at MIRTH

Hil·da (hil′də) [G. < Gmc. *hild-,* war] a feminine name

hill (hil) *n.* [OE. *hyll* < IE. base *kel-,* to project] **1.** a natural raised part of the earth's surface, often rounded, smaller than a mountain **2.** a small pile, heap, or mound *[an anthill]* **3.** *a)* a small mound of soil heaped over and around plant roots *[a hill of potatoes] b)* the plant or plants rooted in such a mound —*vt.* **1.** to shape into or like a hill **2.** to cover with a hill (sense *3a)* —**over the hill** [Colloq.] **1.** absent without permission; AWOL **2.** in one's decline; past the most creative or productive time in one's life, career, etc. —**hill′like′** *adj.*

☆**hill·bil·ly** (hil′bil′ē) *n., pl.* **-lies** [HILL + *Billy,* dim. of WILLIAM] [Colloq.] a person who lives in or comes from the mountains or backwoods, esp. of the South: sometimes a term of contempt —*adj.* [Colloq.] of or characteristic of hillbillies *[hillbilly music]*

Hil·lel (hil′el, -əl) 60? B.C.–10? A.D.; Jewish rabbi & scholar in Jerusalem

hill·ock (hil′ək) *n.* a small hill; mound —**hill′ock·y** *adj.*

☆**hill of beans** [Colloq.] a very small amount or value; trifle: used with a negative *[not worth a hill of beans]*

hill·side (hil′sīd′) *n.* the side or slope of a hill

hill·top (-täp′) *n.* the top of a hill

hill·y (-ē) *adj.* **hill′i·er, hill′i·est 1.** full of hills; uneven and rolling *[hilly country]* **2.** like a hill; steep —**hill′i·ness** *n.*

hilt (hilt) *n.* [OE.: for IE. base see GLADIATOR] the handle of a sword, dagger, tool, etc. **(up) to the hilt** thoroughly; entirely

hi·lum (hī′ləm) *n., pl.* **hi′la** (-lə) [ModL. < L., little thing] *Bot.* a scar on a seed, marking the place where it was attached to the seed stalk

HILUM

him (him; *unstressed* im, əm) *pron.* [OE.] objective case of HE (Ex.: tell *him* to go): also used colloquially afte a linking verb (Ex.: that's *him)*

Hi·ma·la·yas (him′ə lā′əz, hi mäl′yəz) mountains in SC Asia, along the India-Tibet border: highest peak, Mt. Everest: also **Himalaya Mountains** See map on next page —**Hi′mi·la′yan** *adj., n.*

---

fat, āpe, cär, ten, ēven, is, bīte; gō, hôrn, tōōl, look; oil, out; up, fur; get; joy; yet; chin; she; thin, then; zh, leisure; ŋ, ring; ə for *a* in *ago, e* in *agent, i* in *sanity, o* in *comply, u* in *focus;* ′ as in *able* (ā′b'l); Fr. bal; ë, Fr. coeur; ö, Fr. feu; Fr. mon; δ, Fr. coq; ü, Fr. duc; *r,* Fr. cri; H, G. ich; kh, G. doch; ‡foreign; ☆ Americanism; < derived from. See inside front cover.

him·self (him self′) **pron.** a form of the 3d person singular, masculine pronoun, used: *a)* as an intensive [he went *himself]* *b)* as a reflexive [he hurt *himself]* *c)* as a kind of noun meaning "his real or true self" [he is not *himself* today]

hind¹ (hīnd) **adj.** **hind′er, hind′most′** or **hind′er·most′** [prob. < HINDER²] back; rear; posterior [the *hind* legs of a dog]

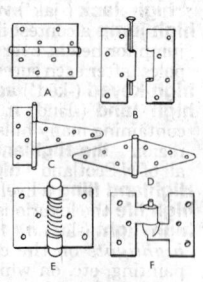

HIMALAYAS

hind² (hīnd) **n., pl. hinds, hind:** see PLURAL, II, D, 1 [OE.] the female of the deer, esp. the red deer, in and after its third year

hind³ (hīnd) **n.** [OE. *hina, higna*] **1.** in N England and Scotland, a skilled farm worker or servant **2.** [Archaic] a simple peasant; rustic

Hind. 1. Hindi **2.** Hindu **3.** Hindustani

hind·brain (hīnd′brān′) **n.** the hindmost part of the brain of a vertebrate embryo, or the parts developed from this, including the cerebellum, pons, and medulla oblongata

Hin·de·mith (hin′də məth; *G.* -mit), **Paul** 1895-1963; U.S. composer, born in Germany

Hin·den·burg (hin′dən burg′; *Gr.* -boorkh′), **Paul (Ludwig Hans Anton von Beneckendorf und) von** 1847-1934; Ger. field marshal; president of Germany (1925-34)

hin·der¹ (hin′dər) **vt.** [OE. *hindrian*] **1.** to keep back; restrain; get in the way of; prevent; stop [heavy snows *hindered* travel] **2.** to make difficult for; slow down; hamper [poor eyesight *hindered* him in his schoolwork] —**vi.** to delay action; be a hindrance

SYN.—**hinder** implies a holding back of something about to begin or a making progress difficult [*hindered* by a lack of education]; **obstruct** implies a slowing down or stopping of something by placing obstacles in the way [to *obstruct* the passage of a bill by a filibuster]; **block** implies the complete, but not necessarily permanent, stopping of a passage or progress [the road was *blocked* by a landslide]; **impede** suggests a slowing up or retarding of movement or progress by interfering with the normal action [a tight collar *impedes* the circulation of the blood]; **bar** implies an obstructing as if by means of a barrier [he was *barred* from the restaurant] —**ANT.** advance, further

hind·er² (hin′dər) **adj.** [OE. *hinder, adv.*, behind: now felt as compar. of HIND¹] hind; rear; posterior

Hin·di (hin′dē) **adj.** [Hindi *hindī* < *Hind:* see HINDU] of or associated with northern India —**n.** an Indo-Iranian language, the main, now official, language of India

hind·most (hīnd′mōst′) **adj. superl.** *of* HIND¹ [ME. *henmast:* see HIND¹ + -MOST] farthest back; last: also **hind′er·most′** (hin′dər-)

Hin·doo (hin′dōō) **adj., n., pl.** -**doos** same as HINDU

hind·quar·ter (hīnd′kwôr′tər) **n.** **1.** a hind leg and loin of a carcass of veal, beef, lamb, etc. **2.** [*pl.*] the hind part of a four-legged animal

hin·drance (hin′drəns) **n.** **1.** the act of hindering **2.** any person or thing that hinders; obstacle

hind·shank (hīnd′shaŋk′) **n.** **1.** the upper part of the hind legs of cattle **2.** meat from this part

☆**hind·sight** (hīnd′sīt′) **n.** an understanding, after the event, of what should have been done

Hin·du (hin′dōō) **n.** [< Per. < *Hind*, India, ult. < Sans. *sindhu*, river, the Indus] **1.** any of the peoples of India that speak an Indic language **2.** a follower of Hinduism **3.** popularly, any native of India —**adj.** **1.** of the Hindus, their language, etc. **2.** of Hinduism

Hin·du-Ar·a·bic numerals (-ar′ə bik) *same as* ARABIC NUMERALS

Hin·du·ism (hin′dōō wiz′m) **n.** the religion and social system of the Hindus

Hindu Kush (kōōsh) mountain range in SW Asia, mostly in Afghanistan, extending eastward to the Himalayas: highest peak, 25,230 ft. See map at KHYBER PASS

Hin·du·stan (hin′dōō stan′, -stän′) **1.** region in N India, where Hindi is spoken **2.** the entire Indian peninsula **3.** the country of India

Hin·du·sta·ni (-stan′ē, -stä′nē) **n.** [< Hindi < Per. (see HINDU) + *stān*, a place] the most important dialect of Western Hindi, used as a trade language in N India —**adj.** **1.** of Hindustan or its people **2.** of Hindustani

hinge (hinj) **n.** [< ME. *hengen*, to HANG] **1.** a joint, etc. on which a door, gate, lid, etc. swings **2.** a natural joint, as of the bivalve shell of a clam or oyster **3.** anything on which matters turn or depend —**vt. hinged, hing′ing** to equip with or attach by a hinge —**vi.** to be contingent; depend (*on*) [plans *hinging* on his success]

hin·ny (hin′ē) **n., pl.** -**nies** [L. *hinnus* < Gr. *innos*] the offspring of a male horse and a female donkey: see MULE¹

hint (hint) **n.** [< OE. *henten*, to seize] **1.** a slight suggestion that is not made in an open or direct way; inkling [when he looked bored, we took the *hint* and left] **2.** a very small amount or degree; trace [a *hint* of spice] —**vt., vi.** to suggest in an indirect way; give a hint [I *hinted* that I wanted to go; he *hinted* at future benefits] —see SYN. at SUGGEST —**take a hint** to act on a hint —**hint′er n.**

hin·ter·land (hin′tər land′) **n.** [G. < *hinter*, back + *land*, land] **1.** the land or district behind that bordering on a coast or river **2.** an area far from big cities and towns; back country

hip¹ (hip) **n.** [OE. *hype:* for IE. base see COOP] **1.** *a)* the part of the body surrounding and including the joint formed by each thighbone and pelvis; esp., the fleshy part between the waist and the thigh *b) same as* HIP JOINT **2.** the angle formed by the meeting of two sloping sides of a roof —**vt. hipped, hip′ping** to make (a roof) with such an angle

hip² (hip) **n.** [OE. *heope*] the fleshy fruit of the rose: it is rich in vitamin C

hip³ (hip) **interj.** an exclamation used in cheers [*hip, hip, hurray!*]

☆**hip⁴** (hip) **adj. hip′per, hip′pest** [< ? *hep*] [Slang] **1.** *a)* sophisticated; knowing; aware *b)* fashionable; stylish **2.** of or associated with hipsters or hippies —**get** (or **be**) **hip to** [Slang] to become (or be) informed or knowledgeable about —**hip′ness n.**

hip·bone (hip′bōn′) **n.** **1.** *same as: a)* INNOMINATE BONE *b)* ILIUM **2.** the neck of the femur

hip joint the place where the thighbone and its socket are joined in the pelvis

Hip·par·chus (hi pär′kəs) 2d cent. B.C.; Gr. astronomer

hipped¹ (hipt) **adj.** **1.** having hips of a specified kind [broad-*hipped*] **2.** *Archit.* having a hip or hips [a *hipped* roof]

hipped² (hipt) **adj.** [< HYP(OCHONDRIA)] ☆[Colloq.] having a great, often too great, interest; obsessed (*with on*)

☆**hip·pie** (hip′ē) **n.** [< HIP⁴ + -IE] [Slang] a young person who has turned away from conventional society to mysticism, drugs, communal living, etc.

hip·po (hip′ō) **n., pl.** -**pos** [Colloq.] a hippopotamus

Hip·poc·ra·tes (hi päk′rə tēz′) 460?-370? B.C.; Gr. physician: called the *Father of Medicine* —**Hip·po·crat·ic** (hip′ə-krat′ik) **adj.**

Hippocratic oath the oath, thought of as coming from Hippocrates, generally taken by medical graduates: it sets forth an ethical code for the medical profession

hip·po·drome (hip′ə drōm′) **n.** [< Fr. < L. < Gr. < *hippos*, a horse + *dromos*, a course] **1.** in ancient Greece and Rome, an oval course for horse races and chariot races, surrounded by sloping rows of seats **2.** an arena or building for a circus, etc.

hip·po·pot·a·mus (hip′ə pät′ə məs) **n., pl.** -**mus·es, -mi** (-mī′), -**mus:** see PLURAL, II, D, 1 [L. < Gr. < *hippos*, a horse + *potamos*, river] a large, plant-eating mammal with a heavy, thick-skinned, almost hairless body and short legs: it lives chiefly in or near rivers in Africa

☆**hip·py¹** (hip′ē) **n., pl.** -**pies** [Slang] *same as* HIPPIE

hip·py² (hip′ē) **adj.** [Colloq.] having large hips [she has a tendency to be *hippy*]

hip roof a roof with sloping ends and sides

☆**hip·ster** (hip′stər) **n.** [Slang] **1.** a hip person **2.** a beatnik: term of the 1950's and early 1960's

Hi·ram (hī′rəm) [Heb. *hīrām*, prob. < *'ahīrām*, exalted brother] a masculine name: dim. *Hi*

hir·cine (hur′sīn, -sin) **adj.** [< L. < *hircus*, goat] of or like a goat, esp. in odor

HIP ROOF

TYPES OF HINGE
(A, fast butt; B, loose pin butt; C, T hinge; D, strap, E, spring; F, shutter)

hire (hīr) *n.* [OE. *hyr*] **1.** the amount paid for the services of a person or the use of a thing **2.** a hiring or being hired —*vt.* **hired, hir′ing 1.** to get the services of (a person) or the use of (a thing) in return for payment; employ or engage **2.** to give the use of (a thing) or the services of (oneself or another) in return for payment (often with *out*) —**for hire** available for work or use, for payment: also **on hire** —☆**hire out** to work, esp. as a laborer, for payment —**hir′a·ble, hire′a·ble** *adj.* —**hir′er** *n.*
SYN.—to **hire**, in narrow usage, means to get, and **let** means to give, the use of something in return for payment, although **hire**, which is also applied to persons or their services, may be used in either sense [to *hire* a hall, a worker, etc.; rooms to *let*]; **lease** implies the letting or often the hiring of property (usually real property) by written contract; **rent** implies payment of a specific amount, usually at fixed periods of time, for hiring or letting a house, land, or other property; **charter** implies the hiring or leasing of an airplane, bus, etc.

hire·ling (hīr′liŋ) *n.* [see HIRE & -LING[1]] a person who will follow anyone's orders for pay; mercenary

Hi·ro·hi·to (hir′ō hē′tō) 1901– ; emperor of Japan (1926–)

Hi·ro·shi·ma (hir′ə shē′mə) seaport in SW Honshu, Japan: largely destroyed (Aug. 6, 1945) by a U.S. atomic bomb, the first ever used in warfare: pop. 504,000

hir·sute (hur′sōōt, hir′-; hər sōōt′) *adj.* [L. *hirsutus*] hairy; shaggy; bristly —**hir′sute·ness** *n.*

his (hiz) *pron.* [OE.] that or those belonging to him: used without a following noun [that book is *his; his* are better]: also used after *of* to indicate possession [a friend of *his*] —*adj.* of, belonging to, made by, or done by him [*his* book; the pleasure of *his* company]

His·pa·ni·a (his pā′nē ə, -pā′-) **1.** *Latin name of* IBERIA **2.** *poet. name of* SPAIN

His·pan·ic (his pan′ik) *adj.* Spanish or Spanish and Portuguese —**His·pan′i·cism** (-ə siz′m) *n.*

His·pan·io·la (his′pən yō′lə) island in the West Indies, between Cuba & Puerto Rico, divided between Haiti & the Dominican Republic

hiss (his) *vi.* [echoic] **1.** to make a sound like that of an *s* held for a time, as of a goose, snake, escaping steam, etc. **2.** to show dislike or disapproval by hissing —*vt.* **1.** to say or indicate by hissing **2.** to show dislike or disapproval of by hissing **3.** to force or drive by hissing [to *hiss* a performer off the stage] —*n.* the act or sound of hissing —**hiss′er** *n.*

hist (st; hist) *interj.* be quiet! listen!

hist. 1. historian **2.** historical **3.** history

his·ta·mine (his′tə mēn′, -mən) *n.* [see HISTO- & AMINE] an amine, $C_5H_9N_3$, released by the tissues in allergic reactions: it dilates blood vessels, stimulates gastric secretion, etc. —**his′ta·min′ic** (-min′ik) *adj.*

his·to- [< Gr. *histos*, a loom, web] *a combining form meaning* tissue [*histology*]: also, before a vowel, **hist-**

his·tol·o·gy (his täl′ə jē) *n.* [HISTO- + -LOGY] the branch of biology concerned with the microscopic study of the structure of tissues —**his·to·log′i·cal** (his′tə läj′i·k'l) *adj.* —**his′to·log′i·cal·ly** *adv.* —**his·tol′o·gist** *n.*

his·to·ri·an (his tôr′ē ən) *n.* **1.** a writer of history **2.** an authority on or specialist in history

his·tor·ic (his tôr′ik, -tär′-) *adj.* historical; esp., famous in history [a *historic* site]

his·tor·i·cal (-i k'l) *adj.* **1.** of or concerned with history as a science [the *historical* method] **2.** providing evidence for a fact of history [a *historical* document] **3.** based on people or events of the past [a *historical* novel] **4.** that really existed or happened in history; factual [*historical* persons and events] **5.** showing developments in chronological order [a *historical* account] **6.** famous in history: now usually HISTORIC —**his·tor′i·cal·ly** *adv.* —**his·tor′i·cal·ness** *n.*

historical materialism an interpretation of history, esp. in Marxian dialectic, that holds that economic factors chiefly determine the conditions of society and social institutions

historical present the present tense used in telling about past events: also **historic present**

his·to·ric·i·ty (his′tə ris′ə tē) *n.* the condition of having actually occurred in history

his·to·ri·og·ra·pher (his tôr′ē äg′rə fər) *n.* [< LL. < Gr. < *historia*, history + *graphein*, to write] **1.** a historian; esp., one appointed to write the history of some institution, country, etc. **2.** a person who studies the various ways in which history is

researched and written —**his·to·ri·o·graph′ic** (-ə graf′ik), **his·to·ri·o·graph′i·cal** *adj.* —**his·to·ri·o·graph′i·cal·ly** *adv.* —**his·to·ri·og′ra·phy** *n.*

his·to·ry (his′tə rē, his′trē) *n., pl.* **-ries** [< L. < Gr. *historia* < *histōr*, learned: for IE. base see WISE[1]] **1.** an account of what has happened; narrative **2.** *a)* what has happened in the life of a people, country, institution, etc. *b)* a systematic account of this **3.** all recorded events of the past **4.** the branch of knowledge that deals systematically with the recording, analyzing, and explaining of past events **5.** a known or recorded past [this coat has a *history*] —**make history** to be or do something important enough to be recorded

his·tri·on·ic (his′trē än′ik) *adj.* [< LL. < L. *histrio*, actor] **1.** of, or having the nature of, acting or actors **2.** overacted or overacting; theatrical; artificial —**his′tri·on′i·cal·ly** *adv.*

his·tri·on·ics (-iks) *n.pl.* [*sometimes with sing. v.*] **1.** theatricals; dramatics **2.** an artificial or affected manner, display of emotion, etc.

hit (hit) *vt.* **hit, hit′ting** [OE. *hittan* < ON. *hitta*, to meet with] **1.** to come against with force; strike [the car *hit* the tree] **2.** to give a blow to; strike [he was *hit* on the jaw] **3.** to strike by throwing or shooting a missile [to *hit* the target] **4.** to cause to bump or strike, as in falling, moving, etc. (often with *on* or *against*) [to *hit* one's head on a door] **5.** to affect strongly or harmfully [a town *hit* hard by floods] **6.** to come upon by accident or after search [to *hit* the right answer] ☆**7.** to reach; attain [stocks *hit* a new high] **8.** *same as* STRIKE, *vt.* 8, 9, 10, 11 ☆**9.** [Slang] to apply oneself to steadily or frequently [to *hit* the books] **10.** [Slang] to demand or require of [he *hit* me for a loan] ☆**11.** *Baseball* to get (a specified base hit) —*vi.* **1.** to give a blow or blows; strike **2.** to attack suddenly **3.** to knock, bump, or strike (usually with *against*) **4.** to come by accident or after search (with *on* or *upon*) ☆**5.** to ignite the combustible mixture in its cylinders: said of an internal-combustion engine ☆**6.** *Baseball* to get a base hit —*n.* **1.** a blow that strikes its mark **2.** a collision of one thing with another **3.** an effectively witty or sarcastic remark **4.** a stroke of good fortune **5.** a successful and popular song, book, play, etc. ☆**6.** *Baseball same as* BASE HIT —**see** SYN. at STRIKE —**hit it off** to get along well together; be congenial —**hit off** to imitate or describe briefly or well —**hit or miss** in a haphazard or aimless way —**hit (out) at 1.** to aim a blow at **2.** to attack in words; criticize strongly —☆**hit the road** [Slang] to leave; go away —**hit′ter** *n.*

☆**hit-and-run** (-′run′) *adj.* **1.** hitting someone in an accident and then fleeing [a *hit-and-run* driver] **2.** *Baseball* designating a play arranged beforehand in which a runner on base starts running with the pitch and the batter must strike at the ball to protect the runner

hitch (hich) *vi.* [ME. *hicchen*, to move jerkily < ?] **1.** to move jerkily; limp; hobble **2.** to become fastened or caught ☆**3.** [Slang] to hitchhike —*vt.* **1.** to move, pull, or shift with jerks [he *hitched* his chair forward] **2.** to fasten with a hook, knot, strap, etc. [to *hitch* a horse to a fence] **3.** [Colloq.] to marry: usually in the passive ☆**4.** [Slang] to hitchhike —*n.* **1.** a short, sudden movement or pull; tug; jerk [he gave a *hitch* to his pants] **2.** a hobble; limp **3.** a hindrance; obstacle [there was a *hitch* in their plans] **4.** a fastening or catch; part that connects two things together, as a trailer to an automobile ☆**5.** [Slang] a period of time served, as in military service **6.** *Naut.* a kind of knot that can be easily undone —**without a hitch** smoothly and successfully —**hitch′er** *n.*

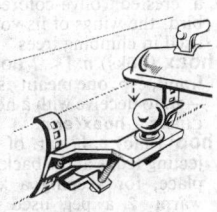
HITCH ON
CAR BUMPER

☆**hitch·hike** (hich′hīk′) *vi.* **-hiked′, -hik′ing** to travel by asking for rides from motorists along the way —*vt.* to get (a ride) or make (one's way) by hitchhiking —**hitch′hik′er** *n.*

hith·er (hith′ər) *adv.* [OE. *hider*] to this place; here —*adj.* on or toward this side; nearer

hith·er·most (-mōst′) *adv.* nearest

hith·er·to (-tōō′, hith′ər tōō′) *adv.* until this time; to now

Hit·ler (hit′lər), **Adolf** 1889–1945; Nazi dictator of Germany (1933–45), born in Austria

Hit·ler·ism (-iz'm) *n.* the fascist program, ideas, and methods of Hitler and the Nazis —**Hit'ler·ite'** (-īt') *n., adj.*

hit-or-miss (hit'ər mis') *adj.* haphazard; random

☆**hit-skip** (hit'skip') *adj. same as* HIT-AND-RUN (sense 1)

Hit·tite (hit'īt) *n.* **1.** any of an ancient people of Asia Minor and Syria (fl. 1700–700 B.C.) **2.** the language of the Hittites —*adj.* of the Hittites, their language, or culture

hive (hīv) *n.* [OE. *hyf*: for IE. base see COOP] **1.** a box or other shelter for a colony of domestic bees; beehive **2.** a colony of bees living in a hive **3.** a crowd of busy, active people **4.** a place with many busy people —*vt.* **hived, hiv'ing 1.** to gather (bees) into a hive **2.** to store up (honey) in a hive —*vi.* **1.** to enter a hive **2.** to live together as in a hive —**hive'less** *adj.* —**hive'like** *adj.*

hives (hīvz) *n.* [orig. Scot. dial.] an allergic skin condition characterized by the appearance of intensely itching, raised patches

hl. hectoliter; hectoliters

h'm (həm) *interj. same as* HEM[2] *or* HUM[2]

hm. hectometer; hectometers

H.M. **1.** Her Majesty **2.** His Majesty

H.M.S. **1.** His (or Her) Majesty's Service **2.** His (or Her) Majesty's Ship or Steamer

ho (hō) *interj.* an exclamation of surprise, scorn, etc.: also used to get attention [land *ho!*]

Ho *Chem.* holmium

☆**hoa·gy, hoa·gie** (hō'gē) *n., pl.* **-gies** [< ?] *same as* HERO SANDWICH

hoar (hôr) *adj.* [OE. *har*: for IE. base see HUE[1]] *same as* HOARY —*n. same as* HOARFROST

hoard (hôrd) *n.* [OE. *hord*: for IE. base see HIDE[1]] a supply stored up and hidden or kept in reserve —*vi.* to store away money, goods, etc. —*vt.* to accumulate and hide or store away [to *hoard* food before prices go up] —**hoard'er** *n.* —**hoard'ing** *n.*

hoard·ing (hôr'diŋ) *n.* [< OFr. < Frank. *hurda*, a pen, fold] [Brit.] **1.** a temporary wooden fence around a site of building construction or repair **2.** a billboard

hoar·frost (hôr'frôst') *n.* white, frozen dew on the ground, leaves, etc.; rime

hoar·hound (hôr'hound') *n. same as* HOREHOUND

hoarse (hôrs) *adj.* **hoars'er, hoars'est** [OE. *has*: for IE. base see HEAT] **1.** sounding harsh and grating, rough and husky, etc. **2.** having a rough, husky voice —**hoarse'ly** *adv.* —**hoarse'ness** *n.*

hoars·en (hôr's'n) *vt., vi.* to make or become hoarse

hoar·y (hôr'ē) *adj.* **hoar'i·er, hoar'i·est 1.** white, gray, or grayish-white [ground *hoary* with frost] **2.** having white or gray hair because very old [a *hoary* head] **3.** very old; ancient [*hoary* laws] —**hoar'i·ly** *adv.* —**hoar'i·ness** *n.*

ho·at·zin (hō at'sin, -wät'-) *n.* [AmSp. < Nahuatl *uatzin*] a crested, olive-colored S. American bird: the wings of its young have claws, used in climbing trees

hoax (hōks) *n.* [< ? HOCUS] a trick or fraud, esp. one meant as a practical joke —*vt.* to deceive with a hoax —see SYN. at CHEAT —**hoax'er** *n.*

hob[1] (häb) *n.* [? var. of HUB] **1.** a projecting ledge at the back or side of a fireplace, for keeping a kettle, pan, etc. warm **2.** a peg used as a target in quoits, etc.

hob[2] (häb) *n.* [old form of *Rob*, for *Robin* Goodfellow, elf of English folklore] an elf; goblin —**play** (or **raise**) **hob with** to make trouble for

Ho·bart (hō'bərt, -bärt) capital of Tasmania, on the SE coast: pop. (with suburbs) 124,000

Hobbes (häbz), **Thomas** 1588–1679; Eng. social philosopher —**Hobbes'i·an** *adj., n.* —**Hob'bism** *n.*

hob·bit (häb'it) *n.* [coined by J.R.R. Tolkien, 20th-cent. Eng. novelist] an imaginary being having a very small human form with some rabbitlike qualities, and characterized by friendliness, devotion to home and family, and a peace-loving nature

hob·ble (häb''l) *vi.* **-bled, -bling** [ME. *hobelen* < base of *hoppen*, HOP[1] + -LE[2]] **1.** to go unsteadily, haltingly, etc. **2.** to walk lamely; limp —*vt.* **1.** to cause to limp **2.** to hamper the movement of (a horse, etc.) by tying two legs together **3.** to hinder —*n.* **1.** a halting walk; limp **2.** a rope, strap, etc. used to hobble a horse —**hob'bler** *n.*

HOATZIN
(to 3 ft. long, including tail)

hobble skirt a woman's long skirt so narrow at the ankles that the wearer must take small steps

hob·by (häb'ē) *n., pl.* **-bies** [ME. *hoby* < ? Du. *hobben*, to move back and forth] **1.** a hobbyhorse **2.** something that a person likes to work at, collect, etc. in his spare time —**ride a hobby** to give too much time or thought to one's favorite pastime or subject —**hob'by·ist** *n.*

hob·by·horse (-hôrs') *n.* **1.** a toy consisting of a horse's head on a stick that one pretends to ride **2.** *same as* ROCKING HORSE

hob·gob·lin (häb'gäb'lin) *n.* [HOB[2] + GOBLIN] **1.** an elf; goblin **2.** an imaginary being that scares one; bogy; bugbear

hob·nail (häb'nāl') *n.* [HOB[1], sense 2 + NAIL] a short nail with a broad head, put on the soles of heavy shoes to prevent wear or slipping —*vt.* to put hobnails on —**hob'nailed'** *adj.*

hob·nob (häb'näb') *vi.* **-nobbed', -nob'-bing** [< ME. *habben*, to have + *nabben*, not to have, esp. with reference to alternation in drinking] to be on close terms (*with*); associate in a familiar way

☆**ho·bo** (hō'bō) *n., pl.* **-bos, -boes 1.** esp. formerly, a migratory worker **2.** a vagrant; tramp —see SYN. at VAGRANT

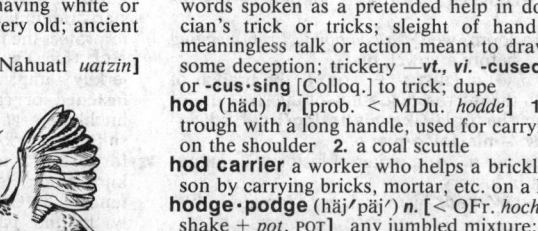

HOBNAILS

Hob·son's choice (häb'sənz) [after T. *Hobson* (1544?–1631), Eng. liveryman, who rented horses in strict order according to their position near the door] a choice of taking what is offered or nothing

Ho Chi Minh (hō' chē' min') 1890?–1969; president of North Vietnam (1954–69)

hock[1] (häk) *n.* [OE. *hoh*, the heel] the joint bending backward in the hind leg of a horse, ox, etc., but corresponding to the human ankle —*vt.* to disable by cutting the tendons of the hock

hock[2] (häk) *n.* [< *Hochheimer* < *Hochheim*, Germany] [Chiefly Brit.] a white Rhine wine

☆**hock**[3] (häk) *vt., n.* [< Du. *hok*, prison, (slang) debt] [Slang] *same as* PAWN[1]

hock·ey (häk'ē) *n.* [prob. < OFr. *hoquet*, bent stick] ☆**1.** a team game played on ice, in which the players, using curved sticks (**hockey sticks**) and wearing skates, try to drive a rubber disk (*puck*) into their opponents' goal **2.** a similar game played on foot on a field with a small ball instead of a puck

☆**hock·shop** (häk'shäp') *n.* [Slang] a pawnshop

ho·cus (hō'kəs) *vt.* **-cused** or **-cussed, -cus·ing** or **-cus·sing** [see the next entry] **1.** to play a trick on; dupe **2.** to drug **3.** to put drugs in (a drink)

ho·cus-po·cus (-pō'kəs) *n.* [imitation L.] **1.** meaningless words spoken as a pretended help in doing tricks **2.** a magician's trick or tricks; sleight of hand; legerdemain **3.** any meaningless talk or action meant to draw attention away from some deception; trickery —*vt., vi.* **-cused** or **-cussed, -cus·ing** or **-cus·sing** [Colloq.] to trick; dupe

hod (häd) *n.* [prob. < MDu. *hodde*] **1.** a V-shaped wooden trough with a long handle, used for carrying bricks, mortar, etc. on the shoulder **2.** a coal scuttle

hod carrier a worker who helps a bricklayer, plasterer, or mason by carrying bricks, mortar, etc. on a hod

hodge·podge (häj'päj') *n.* [< OFr. *hochepot*, stew < *hocher*, to shake + *pot*, POT] any jumbled mixture; mess

Hodg·kin's disease (häj'kinz) [after Dr. T. *Hodgkin* (1798–1866)] a disease in which the lymph nodes become enlarged and other lymphoid tissues, esp. of the spleen, are inflamed

hoe (hō) *n.* [< OFr. *houe* < OHG. < *houwan*, to HEW] a tool with a thin, flat blade set across the end of a long handle, used for weeding, loosening soil, etc. —*vt., vi.* **hoed, hoe'ing** to dig, cultivate, weed, etc. with a hoe —**ho'er** *n.*

☆**hoe·cake** (hō'kāk') *n.* a thin bread made of cornmeal, orig. baked on a hoe at the fire

☆**hoe·down** (-doun') *n.* [HOE + (BREAK)-DOWN, sense 2] **1.** a lively dance, often a square dance **2.** music for this **3.** a party at which hoedowns are danced

hog (hôg, häg) *n., pl.* **hogs, hog:** see PLURAL, II, D, 1 [OE. *hogg*] **1.** a pig; esp., a full-grown pig of more than 120 lbs. raised for its meat **2.** [Colloq.] a selfish, greedy, or filthy person —*vt.* **hogged, hog'ging** ☆[Slang] to take all of or an unfair share of —**go (the) whole hog** [Slang] to go

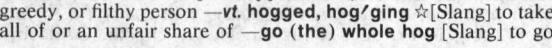

TYPES OF HOE
(A, nursery; B, weeding; C, garden; D, serrated)

all the way; do or accept something fully —☆**high on** (or **off**) **the hog** [Colloq.] in a luxurious or costly way —☆**hog wild** [Colloq.] highly excited; not restrained

☆**ho·gan** (hō′gôn, -gän) *n.* [Navaho *qoghan*, house] the typical dwelling of the Navaho Indians, built of earth walls supported by timbers

Ho·garth (hō′gärth), **William** 1697-1764; Eng. painter & engraver

hog·back (hôg′bak, häg′-) *n.* a ridge with a sharp crest and sides that slope sharply

☆**hog cholera** a highly contagious virus disease of hogs that is often fatal

hog·gish (hôg′ish, häg′-) *adj.* like a hog; very selfish, greedy, coarse, or filthy —**hog′gish·ly** *adv.* —**hog′gish·ness** *n.*

☆**hog·nose snake** (hôg′nōz′, häg′-) any of several small, harmless N. American snakes with a flat snout: also **hog′nosed′ snake**

hogs·head (hôgz′hed′, hägz′-) *n.* [ME. *hoggeshede*, lit., hog's head] **1.** a large barrel or cask holding from 63 to 140 gallons **2.** any of various liquid measures, esp. one equal to 63 gallons

☆**hog·tie** (hôg′tī′, häg′-) *vt.* **-tied′, -ty′ing** or **-tie′ing 1.** to tie the four feet or the hands and feet of [the robbers *hogtied* and gagged their victims] **2.** [Colloq.] to make unable to act effectively [*hogtied* by petty rules]

hog·wash (-wôsh′, -wäsh′) *n.* **1.** watery garbage fed to hogs; swill **2.** useless or insincere talk, writing, etc.

Hoh·en·zol·lern (hō′ən tsôl′ərn) ruling family of Prussia (1701-1918) & of Germany (1871-1918)

ho-hum (hō′hum′) *interj.* an exclamation of boredom, lack of interest, weariness, etc.

hoi pol·loi (hoi′ pə loi′) [Gr., the many] the common people; the masses: commonly but not properly used with the article *the*

hoist (hoist) *vt.* [< earlier *hyce* < Du. *hijschen* & LowG. *hissen*] to raise aloft; lift, esp. by means of a pulley, crane, etc. [*hoist* the statue into place] —*n.* **1.** the act of hoisting [give Bill a *hoist* over the fence] **2.** an apparatus for raising heavy things; elevator, block and tackle, etc.

hoi·ty-toi·ty (hoit′ē toit′ē) *adj.* [< obs. *hoit*, to romp noisily] **1.** haughty; arrogant **2.** peevish; touchy; huffy

☆**hoke** (hōk) *vt.* **hoked, hok′ing** [< HOKUM] [Slang] to treat in an overly sentimental, crudely comic, or artificial way: usually with *up* —*n.* [Slang] *same as* HOKUM —**hok′ey** *adj.*

Hok·kai·do (hō kī′dō) one of the four main islands of Japan, north of Honshu: 30,364 sq. mi.

☆**ho·kum** (hō′kəm) *n.* [altered < HOCUS(-POCUS)] [Slang] **1.** crude comedy or tearful sentiment brought into a play, story, etc., just to get a quick response of laughter or tears **2.** nonsense; humbug

Hol·bein (hōl′bīn), **Hans** (häns) **1.** 1460?-1524; Ger. painter: called *the Elder* **2.** 1497?-1543; Ger. painter in England: son of *prec.*: called *the Younger*

hold¹ (hōld) *vt.* **held, hold′ing;** archaic pp. **hold′en** [OE. *haldan*] **1.** to take and keep with the hands, arms, or other means; grasp; clutch [*hold* the baby for a while] ☆**2.** to keep from going away; not let escape [to *hold* a prisoner] **3.** to keep in a certain position or condition [*hold* your head up] **4.** to restrain or control; specif., *a*) to keep from falling; bear the weight of; support *b*) to keep from acting [*hold* your tongue] *c*) to get and keep control of [he could *hold* our attention] *d*) to maintain [to *hold* a course] *e*) to keep or reserve (a room, etc.) for use later *f*) to resist the effects of (alcoholic liquor) **5.** to have and keep as one's own; own; occupy [he *holds* the office of mayor] **6.** to have or conduct together; specif., to carry on (a meeting, conversation, etc.) **7.** to have room for; contain [this can *holds* a pint] **8.** to have or keep in the mind **9.** to regard; consider [to *hold* a statement to be untrue] **10.** *Law a*) to decide; decree *b*) to possess by legal title [to *hold* a mortgage] **11.** *Music* to prolong (a tone or rest) —*vi.* **1.** to retain a hold, firm contact, etc. [*hold* tight] **2.** to go on being firm, loyal, etc. [he *held* to his resolve] **3.** to remain unbroken or unyielding [the rope *held*] **4.** to be true or valid [a rule which still *holds*] **5.** to keep up; continue [the wind *held* steady] **6.** to stop oneself; halt: usually in the imperative —*n.* **1.** a grasping or seizing; grip; specif., a way of gripping an opponent in wrestling **2.** a thing to hold on by [he looked for a *hold* along the cliff] **3.** a controlling force or strong influence [to have a *hold* over

someone] **4.** an order to make a temporary halt or delay **5.** an order reserving something or putting something aside **6.** *a*) a prison, as in a castle *b*) [Archaic] a stronghold **7.** *Music same as* FERMATA —see **SYN.** at CONTAIN —**catch hold of** to seize; grasp —**get hold of 1.** to seize; grasp **2.** to acquire —**hold back 1.** to keep from acting; restrain **2.** to refrain **3.** to retain —**hold down 1.** to restrain ☆**2.** [Colloq.] to have and keep (a job) —**hold forth 1.** to speak for a long time; preach; lecture **2.** to offer; propose, as a plan —**hold in 1.** to keep in or back **2.** to control (oneself or one's feelings) —**hold off 1.** to keep away; keep at a distance **2.** to keep from attacking or doing something —**hold on 1.** to retain one's hold **2.** to persist **3.** [Colloq.] stop! wait! —**hold one's own** to keep one's place or condition in spite of obstacles —**hold out 1.** to last; endure **2.** to stand firm **3.** to offer ☆**4.** [Colloq.] to refuse to give (what should be given) —**hold out for** [Colloq.] to stand firm in demanding —**hold over 1.** to postpone consideration of or action on **2.** to keep or stay for an additional period ☆**3.** to keep as a threat or advantage over —**hold up 1.** to prop up **2.** to show; exhibit **3.** to last; endure **4.** to stop; delay; impede ☆**5.** to stop by force and rob —**hold with 1.** to agree with **2.** to approve of —**lay** (or **take**) **hold of 1.** to seize; grasp **2.** to get control of —**no holds barred** [Colloq.] with no set rules or limits

hold² (hōld) *n.* [altered < HOLE or < MDu. < *hol*, a ship's hold] **1.** the interior of a ship below the deck, in which the cargo is carried **2.** the compartment for cargo in an aircraft

hold·er (hōld′ər) *n.* **1.** a person who holds something; specif., one who holds a bill, note, or check and has the legal right to receive payment on it **2.** a device for holding something [a cigarette *holder*]

hold·fast (-fast′) *n.* a specialized organ or part by which certain animals and plants attach themselves to an object

hold·ing (-iŋ) *n.* **1.** land, esp. a farm, rented from another **2.** [*usually pl.*] property owned, esp. stocks or bonds

☆**holding company** a corporation organized to hold bonds or stocks of other corporations, which it usually controls

hold·out (-out′) *n.* ☆a player in a professional sport who delays signing his contract because he wants better terms

hold·o·ver (-ō′vər) *n.* ☆[Colloq.] a person or thing staying on from an earlier period

☆**hold·up** (-up′) *n.* **1.** a stoppage; delay **2.** the act of stopping by force and robbing

hole (hōl) *n.* [OE. *hol*] **1.** a hollow place; cavity [a *hole* in the ground, a swimming *hole*] **2.** an animal's burrow or lair; den **3.** *a*) a small, dim, dirty place *b*) a prison cell **4.** *a*) an opening in or through anything; gap [*holes* in the roof] *b*) a tear or rent, as in a garment **5.** a flaw; fault; defect [*holes* in an argument] **6.** [Colloq.] an embarrassing situation; predicament [his thoughtless remark put us all in a *hole*] **7.** *Golf a*) any of the small cups sunk into the greens, into which the ball is to be hit *b*) any of the separate sections of a course, from the tee through the green [a standard course has 18 *holes*] —*vt.* **holed, hol′ing 1.** to put or drive into a hole **2.** to create by making a hole [to *hole* a tunnel through a mountain] —**hole in one** *Golf* the act of getting the ball into the hole on one drive from the tee —**hole out** *Golf* to hit the ball into the hole —**hole up** [Colloq.] **1.** to hibernate, usually in a hole **2.** to shut oneself in **3.** to hide out —☆**in the hole** [Colloq.] owing or needing money —**pick holes in** to pick out errors or flaws in —**hole′y** *adj.*

☆**hole in the wall** a small, dirty or shabby room, shop, etc., esp. one in an out-of-the-way or rarely visited place

Hol·guin (ôl gwēn′) city in E Cuba: pop. 227,000

hol·i·day (häl′ə dā′) *n.* **1.** a religious festival: see HOLY DAY **2.** a day on which one does not have to work; day for leisure and recreation **3.** [*often pl.*] [Chiefly Brit.] a vacation **4.** a day set aside, as by law, when work and business are not carried on, to commemorate some event [Thanksgiving is a *holiday* in all States] —*adj.* of or suited to a holiday; joyous; gay

☆**ho·li·er-than-thou** (hō′lē ər than thou′) *adj.* acting as though one were more moral or righteous than others

ho·li·ly (hō′lə lē) *adv.* in a holy manner

ho·li·ness (-lē nis) *n.* **1.** a being holy **2.** [H-] a title of the Pope (with *His* or *Your*)

Hol·ins·hed (häl′inz hed′, -in shed′), **Raphael** ?-1580?; Eng. writer of history

Hol·land (häl′ənd) *same as the* NETHERLANDS —**Hol′land·er**

hol·land (häl′ənd) *n.* [< prec., where first made] a linen or cotton cloth used for clothing, window shades, etc.

hol·lan·daise sauce (häl′ən dāz′) [Fr., of Holland] a creamy sauce, as for vegetables, made of butter, egg yolks, lemon juice, etc.

Hol·lands (häl′əndz) *n.* gin made in the Netherlands

hol·ler (häl′ər) *vi., vt., n.* [altered < HOLLO] [Colloq.] shout or yell

hol·lo (häl′ō, hə lō′) *interj., n., pl.* **-los** 1. a shout or call, as to attract a person's attention or to urge on hounds in hunting 2. a shout of greeting or surprise —*vi., vt.* **-loed, -lo·ing** 1. to shout (at) so as to attract attention 2. to urge on (hounds) by calling out "hollo" 3. to shout, in greeting or surprise

hol·low (häl′ō) *adj.* [OE. *holh*] 1. having a cavity within it; not solid [a *hollow* log] 2. shaped like a cup or bowl; concave 3. deeply set; sunken [*hollow* cheeks] 4. empty or worthless [*hollow* praise] 5. hungry [a *hollow* feeling in the pit of her stomach] 6. deep-toned and muffled, as though resounding from something hollow [a *hollow* voice] —*adv.* in a hollow manner —*n.* 1. a hollow place; cavity; hole 2. a valley —*vt., vi.* to make or become hollow —see SYN. at VAIN —**beat all hollow** [Colloq.] to outdo or surpass by far —**hollow out** to make by hollowing —**hol′low·ly** *adv.* —**hol′low·ness** *n.*

hol·lo·ware (häl′ō wer′) *n.* bowls, dishes, etc., esp. of silver, that are more or less hollow or concave: also **hol′low-ware′**

hol·low-eyed (häl′ō īd′) *adj.* having deep-set eyes or dark areas under the eyes, as from being sick or weary

hol·ly (häl′ē) *n., pl.* **-lies** [OE. *holegn*] 1. a small tree or shrub with glossy, sharp-pointed leaves and bright-red berries 2. the leaves and berries, used as Christmas ornaments

hol·ly·hock (häl′ē häk′) *n.* [< OE. *halig,* holy + *hoc,* mallow] 1. a tall, biennial plant of the mallow family, with a hairy stem and large, showy flowers of various colors 2. its flower

Hol·ly·wood (häl′ē wood′) [HOLLY + WOOD] 1. section of Los Angeles, once the site of many U.S. motion-picture studios; hence, the U.S. motion-picture industry or its life, etc. 2. city on the SE coast of Fla., near Miami: pop. 107,000

HOLLYHOCK

☆**Hollywood bed** a bed consisting of a mattress on a box spring that rests on a metal frame or has attached legs: it sometimes has a headboard

holm (hōm) *n. same as* HOLM OAK

Holmes (hōmz, hōlmz) 1. **Oliver Wen·dell** (wen′d'l), *a)* 1809–94; U.S. writer & physician *b)* 1841–1935; associate justice, U.S. Supreme Court (1902–32): son of *prec.* 2. **Sherlock,** *see* SHERLOCK HOLMES

hol·mi·um (hōl′mē əm) *n.* [ModL. < *Holmia,* Latinized form of *Stockholm*] a metallic chemical element of the rare-earth group: symbol, Ho; at. wt., 164.930; at. no., 67

holm oak [< OE. *holegn,* holly] 1. a south European evergreen oak with hollylike leaves 2. its wood

hol·o- [Fr. < L. < Gr. *holos,* whole] *a combining form meaning* whole, entire [*holography*]

hol·o·caust (häl′ə kôst′, hō′lə-) *n.* [< OFr. < LL. < Gr. < *holos,* whole + *kaustos,* burnt: see CAUSTIC] great destruction of life, esp. by fire —**the Holocaust** the destruction of millions of Jews by Nazi Germany

hol·o·gram (häl′ə gram′, hō′lə-) *n.* a picture made by holography

hol·o·graph (-graf′) *adj.* [< Fr. < LL. < LGr. < Gr. *holos,* whole + *graphein,* to write] written entirely in the handwriting of the person under whose name it appears —*n.* a holograph document, letter, etc. —**hol′o·graph′ic** *adj.*

ho·log·ra·phy (hə läg′rə fē) *n.* [HOLO- + -GRAPHY] a photographic method that uses no lens but records on film tiny interference patterns made by splitting a laser beam into two parts: when laser light or white light is shone through the developed film, a three-dimensional picture can be seen —**hol·o·graph·ic** (häl′ə graf′ik, hō′lə-) *adj.*

hol·o·thu·ri·an (häl′ə thoor′ē ən, hō′lə-) *n.* [< L. < Gr. pl. of *holothourion,* kind of water polyp] any of various echinoderms with a long, wormlike body and a mouth surrounded by tentacles; sea cucumber

holp (hōlp) *archaic pt. & obs. pp. of* HELP

hol·pen (hōl′p'n) *archaic pp. of* HELP

Hol·stein (hōl′stēn, -stīn) *n.* [after SCHLESWIG-HOLSTEIN, where orig. bred] ☆any of a breed of large, black-and-white dairy cattle, that produce low-fat milk: also **Hol·stein-Frie·sian** (-frē′zhən)

HOLSTEIN COW

hol·ster (hōl′stər) *n.* [Du.] a pistol case, usually of leather and attached to a belt or saddle

ho·ly (hō′lē) *adj.* **-li·er, -li·est** [OE. *halig* < base of *hal,* sound, whole, HALE¹] [*often* H-] 1. set apart for religious use; consecrated; sacred 2. spiritually pure; sinless; saintly 3. regarded with deep respect or reverence, or worthy of such respect [the fight for civil rights was a *holy* cause to him] ☆4. [Slang] very much of a [a *holy* terror] Often used in compounds to form interjections of astonishment, emphasis, etc. [*holy* cow! *holy* smoke!] —*n., pl.* **-lies** a holy thing or place

SYN.—**holy** is a general word for that which is associated with a religion and has a spiritual quality [the *Holy* Ghost, *holy* love]; **sacred** refers to that which is set apart as holy or is dedicated to some high purpose [Parnassus was *sacred* to Apollo; a *sacred* trust]; **consecrated** and **hallowed** describe that which has been made sacred or holy [the priest *consecrated* the water; her *hallowed* memory], **consecrated** also suggesting serious dedication [a life *consecrated* to art], and **hallowed,** something that is revered [*hallowed* ground]; **divine** is used of that which is thought to come from God or is like God or a god [the *divine* right of kings] and is also used to suggest supreme greatness [the *divine* music of Mozart] —ANT. profane, unholy

Holy Communion any of various Christian rites in which bread and wine are consecrated and received as the body and blood of Jesus or as symbols of them; sacrament of the Eucharist

holy day a day set apart for religious observances

Holy Father a title of the Pope

Holy Ghost the third person of the Trinity

Holy Grail *see* GRAIL

Holy Land *same as* PALESTINE (sense 1)

holy of holies 1. the innermost part of the Jewish tabernacle and Temple, where the ark of the covenant was kept 2. any most sacred place

Hol·yoke (hōl′yōk) [after E. *Holyoke,* 18th-c. president of Harvard U.] city in SW Mass.: pop. 50,000

holy orders 1. the sacrament or rite of ordination 2. ranks or grades of the Christian ministry; specif., *a)* R.C.Ch. *same as* MAJOR ORDERS or, sometimes, MINOR ORDERS *b)* Anglican Ch. bishops, priests, and deacons —**take holy orders** to be ordained as a Christian minister

Holy Roman Empire empire of WC Europe, that was begun in 800 A.D. with Charlemagne or, according to some, in 962 with Otto I: it lasted until 1806

Holy Scripture (or **Scriptures**) *same as* BIBLE (senses 1 & 2)

Holy See the position, authority, or court of the Pope

Holy Spirit the spirit of God; specif., the third person of the Trinity

hol·y·stone (hō′lē stōn′) *n.* [< ?] a flat piece of sandstone for scouring a ship's wooden decks —*vt.* **-stoned′, -ston′ing** to scour with a holystone

HOLY ROMAN EMPIRE
(12th cent.)

Holy Synod the administrative council of any branch of the Orthodox Eastern Church

holy water water blessed by a priest

Holy Week the week before Easter

Holy Writ the Bible

hom·age (häm′ij, äm′-) *n.* [< OFr. < ML. *hominaticum* < L. *homo,* a man < IE. base *ghthem-,* earth, ground] 1. orig., *a)* a pledge of allegiance by a vassal to his lord in the Middle Ages *b)* an act done or thing given to show the relationship between lord and vassal 2. anything given or done to show respect, honor, etc.: usually with *do* or *pay* [to pay *homage* to a hero] —see SYN. at HONOR

☆**hom·bre** (äm′brā, -brē) *n.* [Sp. < L. *homo,* a man] [Colloq.] a man; fellow

hom·burg (häm′bərg) *n.* [< *Homburg,* Prussia] a man's felt hat with a dent in the crown from front to back and a stiff, slightly curved brim

home (hōm) *n.* [OE. *ham:* for IE. base see CITY] **1.** the place where a person (or family) lives; one's dwelling place **2.** the city, state, or country where one was born or reared **3.** a place where one likes to be; restful or congenial place *[the library is home to her]* **4.** the members of a family as a unit; a household and its affairs *[he came from a broken home]* **5.** an institution for the care of orphans, the aged, etc. **6.** the natural environment of an animal, plant, etc. *[India is the home of the tiger]* **7.** the place of origin, development, etc. *[Paris is the home of fashion]* **8.** in many games, the base or goal; esp., ☆the home plate in baseball —*adj.* **1.** of one's home or country; domestic **2.** that is the headquarters; main or central *[the home office of a company]* **3.** played in the city, at the school, etc. where the team originates *[a home game]* —*adv.* **1.** at, to, or in the direction of home *[we're heading home]* **2.** to the point aimed at *[he drove the nail home]* **3.** to the heart of a matter; closely; directly *[her argument hit home]* —*vi.* **homed, hom′ing 1.** to go to one's home **2.** to have a home *[where does the eagle home?]* —*vt.* to send to, or provide with, a home —**at home 1.** in one's own house, city, or country **2.** as if in one's own home; comfortable; at ease **3.** willing to receive visitors —**bring (something) home** to impress upon or make clear to — ☆**home free** [Slang] no longer in doubt about the success or victory one will shortly have —**home (in) on** to be directed as by radar to (a destination) —**home′less** *adj.* —**home′like** *adj.*

☆**home·bod·y** (hōm′bäd′ē) *n., pl.* **-bod′ies** a person who likes to stay home and whose interests mainly have to do with affairs of the home

home-brew (-brōō′) *n.* beer, ale, etc. brewed at home

home·com·ing (-kum′iŋ) *n.* **1.** a coming or returning to one's home ☆**2.** in many colleges, an annual celebration for alumni

☆**home economics** the science and art of homemaking, including nutrition, budgeting, etc.

home-grown (hōm′grōn′) *adj.* grown or produced at home or locally *[home-grown tomatoes]*

home·land (-land′) *n.* the country in which one was born or makes one's home

home·ly (-lē) *adj.* **-li·er, -li·est 1.** characteristic of or suitable for home or home life; plain or simple *[homely virtues]* **2.** not elegant or sophisticated *[he spoke the blunt truth in homely language]* **3.** not good-looking; unattractive —**home′li·ness** *n.*

home·made (-mād′) *adj.* **1.** made at home **2.** as if made at home; esp., plain, simple, or crude

home·mak·er (-mā′ kər) *n.* a person who manages a home; esp., a housewife —**home′mak′ing** *n.*

ho·me·o- [Gr. *homoio-* < *homos,* same] *a combining form meaning* like, the same, similar

ho·me·op·a·thy (hō′mē äp′ə thē) *n.* [< G.: see HOMEO- & -PATHY] a system of medical treatment based on the theory that certain diseases can be cured with small doses of drugs which in a healthy person and in large doses would produce symptoms like those of the disease: opposed to ALLOPATHY — **ho′me·o·path′** (-ə path′), **ho′me·op′a·thist** *n.* —**ho′me·o·path′ic** (-ə path′ik) *adj.*

☆**ho·me·o·sta·sis** (hō′mē ō stā′sis) *n.* [ModL.: see HOMEO- & STASIS] the tendency within an organism, social group, etc. to keep a balance or equilibrium of all the interrelated elements; also, such a state of equilibrium —**ho′me·o·stat′ic** (-stat′ik) *adj.*

home·own·er (hōm′ō′nər) *n.* a person who owns the house he lives in

☆**home plate** *Baseball* the slab that the batter stands beside, across which the pitcher must throw the ball for a strike: it is the last base that must be touched in scoring a run

Ho·mer (hō′mər) **1.** Gr. epic poet thought to have lived about the 8th cent. B.C. and to have written the *Iliad* & the *Odyssey* **2. Wins·low** (winz′lō), 1836–1910; U.S. painter

hom·er (hō′mər) *n.* ☆[Colloq.] *same as* HOME RUN —☆*vi.* [Colloq.] to hit a home run

Ho·mer·ic (hō mer′ik) *adj.* of, like, or characteristic of the poet Homer, his poems, or the Greek civilization that they describe (c. 1200–800 B.C.)

☆**home·room** (hōm′rōōm′) *n.* the room where a class in school meets daily to be checked for attendance, receive school bulletins, etc.: also **home room**

home rule self-government of a country, colony, city, etc. granted to the citizens who live in it by the larger political unit that controls it

☆**home run** *Baseball* a safe hit that allows the batter to touch all bases and score a run

home·sick (-sik′) *adj.* unhappy or depressed at being away from home and family; longing for home —**home′sick′ness** *n.*

home·spun (-spun′) *n.* **1.** cloth made of yarn spun at home **2.** coarse, loosely woven cloth like this —*adj.* **1.** spun at home **2.** made of homespun **3.** plain or simple *[homespun humor]*

home·stead (-sted′) *n.* ☆**1.** a place where a family makes its home, including the land, house, and outbuildings ☆**2.** a 160-acre tract of public land granted by the U.S. government to a settler to develop as a farm —☆*vi.* to become a settler on a homestead —☆**home′stead′er** *n.*

☆**homestead law** any law granting tracts of public land to settlers for development as farms

☆**home·stretch** (hōm′strech′) *n.* **1.** the part of a race track between the last turn and the finish line **2.** the final part of any undertaking

home·ward (hōm′wərd) *adv., adj.* toward home: also **home′wards** *adv.*

home·work (-wurk′) *n.* **1.** work done at home **2.** lessons to be studied or schoolwork to be done outside the classroom ☆**3.** study or research done before undertaking some project or activity: usually in **do one's homework**

home·y (-ē) *adj.* **hom′i·er, hom′i·est** like home; comfortable, familiar, cozy, etc. —**home′y·ness** *n.*

hom·i·cide (häm′ə sīd′, hō′mə-) *n.* [< OFr. < LL. < L. < *homo,* a man + *caedere,* to cut, kill] **1.** any killing of one human being by another **2.** a person who kills another —**hom′i·ci′dal** *adj.*

hom·i·let·ics (häm′ə let′iks) *n.pl.* [*with sing. v.*] [< LL. < Gr. < *homilein,* to converse < *homilos:* see HOMILY] the art of writing and preaching sermons —**hom′i·let′ic** *adj.*

hom·i·ly (häm′ə lē) *n., pl.* **-lies** [< OFr. < LL. *homilia* < Gr. < *homilos,* assembly, prob. < *homou,* together + *ilē,* a crowd] **1.** a sermon, esp. one about something in the Bible **2.** a serious talk or writing on morals, esp. a long, dull one —**hom′i·list** *n.*

homing pigeon a pigeon trained to find its way home from distant places: see CARRIER PIGEON

hom·i·nid (häm′ə nid) *n.* [< ModL. *Hominidae,* scientific name of the family] any form of man, extinct or living

hom·i·noid (häm′ə noid′) *n.* [< ModL. *Hominoidea,* scientific name of the superfamily] any form of man or the great apes, extinct or living —*adj.* manlike

☆**hom·i·ny** (häm′ə nē) *n.* [contr. < *rockahominy* < Algonquian] dry corn with the hull and germ removed and often coarsely ground (**hominy grits**): it is boiled for food

ho·mo (hō′mō) *n., pl.* **hom·in·es** (häm′ə nēz′) [L., a man] any of a genus of primates including modern man (*Homo sapiens*) and extinct species of man

ho·mo- [< Gr. < *homos,* SAME] *a combining form meaning* same, equal, like *[homograph]*

ho·mo·ge·ne·ous (hō′mə jē′nē əs, häm′ə-) *adj.* [< ML. < Gr. < *homos,* same + *genos,* a race, kind] **1.** the same in structure, quality, etc.; similar or identical **2.** made up of similar or identical parts; uniform *[a homogeneous group of people]* — **ho′mo·ge·ne′i·ty** (-jə nē′ə tē) *n.* —**ho′mo·ge′ne·ous·ly** *adv.*

ho·mog·e·nize (hə mäj′ə nīz′) *vt.* **-nized′, -niz′ing 1.** to make homogeneous **2.** to make more uniform throughout; specif., ☆to process (milk) so that the fat particles are so finely divided and emulsified that the cream does not separate and rise to the top —**ho·mog′e·ni·za′tion** *n.*

hom·o·graph (häm′ə graf′, hō′mə-) *n.* [HOMO- + -GRAPH] a word with the same spelling as another but with a different meaning and origin (Ex.: *bow,* the front part of a ship, *bow,* to bend) —**hom′o·graph′ic** *adj.*

ho·mol·o·gize (hō mäl′ə gīz′, hə-) *vt.* **-gized′, -giz′ing** to make, or show to be, homologous —*vi.* to be homologous

ho·mol·o·gous (hō mäl′ə gəs, hə-) *adj.* [< Gr. < *homos,* same + *legein,* to say] **1.** corresponding in structure, position, character, etc. **2.** *Biol.* corresponding in structure and origin, as the wing of a bat and the foreleg of a mouse 3. *Chem.* of a series of compounds of which each member differs in a regular way from the one before, as by the addition of a CH₂ group

ho·mol·o·gy (hō mäl′ə jē, hə-) *n., pl.* **-gies** 1. the quality or state of being homologous 2. a homologous correspondence or relationship, as of animal organs, chemical compounds, etc.

ho·mol·o·sine projection (hə mäl′ə sin, hō-; -sīn′) [< Gr. *homalos*, even, level + SINE] a map of the earth's surface with the land areas shown in their proper relative size and form, so that there is little distortion

HOMOLOSINE PROJECTION

ho·mo·mor·phism (hō′-mə môr′fiz'm, häm′ə-) *n.* [HOMO- + -MORPH + -ISM] similarity in form, structure, etc.: also **ho′mo·mor′phy** —**ho′mo·mor′phic, ho′mo·mor′phous** *adj.*

hom·o·nym (häm′ə nim, hō′mə-) *n.* [< Fr. < L. < Gr. < *homos*, same + *onyma*, name] a word with the same pronunciation as another but with a different meaning, origin, and, usually, spelling (Ex.: *bore* and *boar*) —**ho·mon·y·mous** (hō män′ə məs), **hom′o·nym′ic** *adj.*

ho·mo·phile (hō′mō fīl′, häm′ə-) *n., adj.* [HOMO- + -PHILE] *same as* HOMOSEXUAL

hom·o·phone (häm′ə fōn′) *n.* [< Gr. < *homos*, same + *phōnē*, a sound] 1. any of two or more letters or groups of letters having the same pronunciation [the *c* in *civil* and *s* in *song* are *homophones*] 2. *same as* HOMONYM

hom·o·phon·ic (häm′ə fän′ik, hō′mə-) *adj.* [< Gr.: see prec.] 1. *Music* having a single part, or voice, carrying the melody 2. of, or having the nature of, a homonym —**ho·moph·o·ny** (hō mäf′ə nē) *n., pl.* **-nies**

ho·mop·ter·ous (hō mäp′tər əs) *adj.* [HOMO- + -PTEROUS] belonging to a group of insects with sucking mouthparts and two pairs of membranous wings of the same thickness throughout, as aphids, cicadas, etc.

Ho·mo sa·pi·ens (hō′mō sā′pē enz′, hō′mō sap′ē ənz) [ModL.: see HOMO & SAPIENT] modern man; mankind; human being: scientific name of the only living species of the genus *Homo*

ho·mo·sex·u·al (hō′mə sek′shoo wəl) *adj.* of or having sexual desire for those of the same sex as oneself —*n.* a homosexual person —**ho′mo·sex′u·al′i·ty** (-wal′ə tē) *n.* —**ho′mo·sex′u·al·ly** *adv.*

ho·mun·cu·lus (hō muŋ′kyoo ləs) *n., pl.* **-li** (-lī′) [L., dim. of *homo*, man] a little man; dwarf

hom·y (hō′mē) *adj.* **hom′i·er, hom′i·est** *same as* HOMEY —**hom′i·ness** *n.*

Hon., hon. 1. honorable 2. honorary

Hon·du·ras (hän door′əs, -dyoor′-) country in Central America, between Guatemala and Nicaragua: 43,227 sq. mi.; pop. 2,495,000; cap. Tegucigalpa —**Hon·du′ran** *adj., n.*

hone (hōn) *n.* [< OE. *han*, a stone] a whetstone used to sharpen cutting tools, esp. razors —*vt.* **honed, hon′ing** to sharpen as with a hone

Ho·neg·ger (hän′ə gər; *Fr.* ô ne ger′), **Arthur** 1892–1955; Swiss composer in France

hon·est (än′əst) *adj.* [< OFr. < L. *honestus < honor*, honor] 1. that will not lie, cheat, or steal; trustworthy; truthful 2. *a)* showing fairness and sincerity; without any deceit [an *honest* effort] *b)* gained by fair methods [an *honest* living] 3. being what it seems; genuine [to give *honest* measure; he made an *honest* error] 4. frank and open [an *honest* face] 5. [Archaic] chaste —*adv.* [Colloq.] honestly; truly: used for emphasis —see SYN. at UPRIGHT

hon·est·ly (-lē) *adv.* 1. in an honest manner 2. truly; really: used for emphasis [*honestly*, it is so]

hon·es·ty (än′əs tē) *n.* the state or quality of being honest; specif., *a)* a being truthful, trustworthy, or upright *b)* sincerity; straightforwardness [in all *honesty*, I cannot recommend him]

SYN.—**honesty** is the general term for uprightness and trustworthiness, with an absence of lying, stealing, and cheating [*honesty* is the best policy]; **honor** implies faithfulness to the morals or ethics that are expected of one in his social class, profession, position, etc. [*honor* among thieves]; **integrity** implies a soundness of moral character that cannot be corrupted [elect men of *integrity*]; **probity** suggests honesty or uprightness that has been proved in past behavior; **veracity** specifically emphasizes truthfulness [a witness of unquestioned *veracity*] —ANT. **dishonesty, deceitfulness**

hon·ey (hun′ē) *n., pl.* **-eys** [OE. *hunig*] 1. a thick, sweet, yellow syrup that bees make as food from the nectar of flowers and store in honeycombs: used as a food and sweetener by man 2. sweet quality; sweetness 3. sweet one; darling 4. [Colloq.] something pleasing or excellent of its kind [a *honey* of an idea] —*adj.* 1. of or like honey 2. sweet; dear —*vt.* **-eyed** or **-ied, -ey·ing** 1. to make sweet or pleasant as with honey 2. to speak in a sweet or flattering way to

hon·ey·bee (-bē′) *n.* a bee that makes honey

hon·ey·comb (-kōm′) *n.* 1. the structure of six-sided wax cells made by bees to hold their honey, eggs, etc. 2. anything like this —*vt.* 1. to fill with holes like a honeycomb; riddle [the hill is *honeycombed* with caves] 2. to spread through so as to weaken [*honeycombed* with intrigue] —*adj.* of, like, or patterned after a honeycomb: also **hon′ey·combed′**

hon·ey·dew (-doo′, -dyoo′) *n.* 1. a sweet fluid that comes from the leaves of some plants in summer 2. a sweet substance made by aphids and other insects that suck juice from plants ☆3. *short for* HONEYDEW MELON

☆**honeydew melon** a variety of melon with a smooth, whitish rind and sweet, greenish flesh

hon·eyed (hun′ēd) *adj.* 1. sweetened, covered, or filled with honey 2. sweet as honey; flattering or affectionate [*honeyed* words]

☆**honey locust** a N. American tree with strong, thorny branches, featherlike foliage, and large, twisted pods

hon·ey·moon (hun′ē moon′) *n.* [as if < HONEY + MOON, but ? folk etym. for ON. *hjānōttsmanathr*, lit., wedding-night month] 1. formerly, the first month of marriage 2. the vacation spent together by a newly married couple 3. a brief period of agreement, happiness, etc. —*vi.* to have or spend a honeymoon —**hon′ey·moon′er** *n.*

hon·ey·suck·le (-suk′'l) *n.* 1. any of a group of largely woody plants with small, fragrant flowers of red, yellow, or white 2. any of several similar plants, as columbine and several types of rhododendron

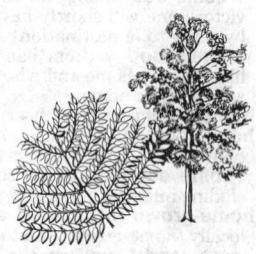

HONEY LOCUST
(tree & leaves)

Hong Kong (häŋ′ käŋ′, hôŋ′ kôŋ′) Brit. crown colony consisting of a small area on the SE coast of China & several offshore islands: also **Hong′kong′**

hon·ied (hun′ēd) *adj. same as* HONEYED

☆**honk** (hôŋk, häŋk) *n.* [echoic] 1. the call of a wild goose 2. any similar sound, as of an automobile horn —*vi., vt.* to make or cause to make such a sound —**honk′er** *n.*

☆**hon·ky-tonk** (hôŋ′kē tôŋk′, häŋ′kē täŋk′) *n.* [< ?] [Slang] a cheap, noisy cabaret or nightclub

Hon·o·lu·lu (hän′ə loo′loo, hō′nə-) [Haw., lit., sheltered bay] capital of Hawaii; seaport on Oahu: pop. 325,000 (met. area 631,000)

hon·or (än′ər) *n.* [< OFr. < L. *honor, honos*] 1. high regard or great respect given or received; esp., *a)* glory; fame; renown [the *honor* of winning a Nobel prize] *b)* good reputation; credit [uphold the *honor* of the family] 2. a keen sense of right and wrong; a being true to principles considered right [her sense of *honor* kept her from cheating] 3. chastity or virginity: an old-fashioned usage 4. high rank or position; distinction [the great *honor* of the presidency] 5. [H-] a title given to certain officials, as judges (preceded by *His, Her,* or *Your*) 6. something done or given as a token of respect; specif., *a)* a social courtesy [may I have the *honor* of this dance?] *b)* [pl.] public ceremonies of respect [buried with full military *honors*] *c)* [pl.] special distinction given to students for high academic achievement [to graduate with *honors*]; also, an advanced course of study for exceptional students 7. one that brings respect and fame to a school, country, etc. [he is an *honor* to his profession] 8. *Bridge* *a)* any of the five highest cards in a suit *b)* [pl.] the four or five highest cards of the trump suit *c)* [pl.] in a no-trump hand, the aces 9. *Golf* the privilege of driving first from the tee —*vt.* 1. to respect greatly; regard highly [*honor* your father and your mother] 2. to treat with deference and courtesy 3. to worship (a deity) 4. to do something in honor of [we *honored* our track team with a banquet] 5. to accept and pay when due [to *honor* a check] —*adj.* of or showing honor [*honor* roll] —**do honor to** 1. to show great respect for 2. to bring honor

to —**do the honors** to act as host or hostess, esp. by making introductions, serving at table, etc. —**on** (or **upon**) **one's honor** staking one's good name on one's truthfulness or reliability
SYN.—honor, as compared here, implies public recognition of one's right to great respect *[a plaque in honor of the martyred dead]*; **homage** suggests highest respect shown by giving praise and tributes *[to pay homage to the genius of Mozart]*; **reverence** implies deep respect mixed with love *[he held her memory in reverence]*; **deference** suggests a showing of polite regard, as for an older person or one of higher position, by giving in to his wishes or opinions *[in deference to her age, he decided not to argue the point]* See also **SYN.** at HONESTY

hon·or·a·ble (än⁄ər ə b'l) *adj.* **1.** worthy of being honored; specif., *a)* of, or having a position of, high rank or worth: used [H-] as a title of courtesy before the name of a judge, governor, congressman, etc. *[our mayor, the Honorable Paul Burns]* *b)* noble; illustrious *c)* of good reputation; respectable *[an honorable trade; an honorable name]* **2.** having or showing a sense of right and wrong; upright *[honorable intentions]* **3.** bringing honor *[honorable mention]* **4.** accompanied with marks of respect *[an honorable burial]* —see **SYN.** at UPRIGHT —**hon⁄or·a·bly** *adv.*

hon·o·rar·i·um (än⁄ə rer⁄ē əm) *n., pl.* **-ri·ums, -ri·a** (-ə) [L. *honorarium* (*donum*), honorary (gift)] a payment as to a professional person for services on which no fee is set

hon·or·ar·y (än⁄ə rer⁄ē) *adj.* [L. *honorarius,* of or conferring honor] **1.** given as an honor only, without the usual requirements or privileges *[an honorary degree]* **2.** *a)* designating an office held as an honor only, without service or pay *b)* holding such an office *[an honorary chairman of a fund drive]* —**hon⁄or·ar⁄i·ly** *adv.*

hon·or·if·ic (än⁄ə rif⁄ik) *adj.* [< L. < *honor* + *facere,* to make] conferring honor; showing respect *[an honorific title]* —**hon⁄or·if⁄i·cal·ly** *adv.*

☆**honor system** in some schools, prisons, etc., a system whereby individuals are trusted to obey rules, do their work, take tests, etc. without being supervised

hon·our (än⁄ər) *n., vt., adj.* Brit. var. of HONOR

Hon·shu (hän⁄shōō) largest of the islands forming Japan: 88,946 sq. mi.

☆**hooch** (hōōch) *n.* [< Alaskan Ind. *hoochinoo,* crude alcoholic liquor] [Slang] alcoholic liquor, esp. when made or obtained illegally

hood¹ (hood) *n.* [OE. *hod:* for IE. base see HAT] **1.** a covering for the head and neck, worn separately or as part of a robe or cloak **2.** anything like a hood in shape or use; specif., ☆*a)* the metal cover over the engine of an automobile *b)* Falconry the covering for a falcon's head when it is not chasing game *c)* the expanded fold of skin near an excited cobra's head —*vt.* to cover as with a hood —**hood⁄ed** *adj.* —**hood⁄less** *adj.*

☆**hood**² (hood, hōōd) *n.* [Slang] short for HOODLUM

-hood (hood) [< OE. *had,* order, condition, rank] a suffix meaning: **1.** state, quality, condition *[childhood]* **2.** the whole group of (a specified class, profession, etc.) *[priesthood]*

Hood (hood), **Mount** mountain of the Cascade Range, in N Oreg.

Hood, Robin see ROBIN HOOD

hood·ed (hood⁄id) *adj.* **1.** having or covered with a hood **2.** shaped like a hood

☆**hood·lum** (hōōd⁄ləm) *n.* [prob. < G. dial. *hudilump,* wretch] a wild, lawless person, often a member of a gang of criminals —**hood⁄lum·ism** *n.*

☆**hoo·doo** (hōō⁄dōō) *n., pl.* **-doos** [var. of VOODOO] **1.** same as VOODOO **2.** [Colloq.] *a)* a person or thing that causes bad luck *b)* bad luck —*vt.* [Colloq.] to bring bad luck to

hood·wink (hood⁄wiŋk⁄) *vt.* [HOOD¹ + WINK] **1.** orig., to blindfold **2.** to deceive; trick; dupe

☆**hoo·ey** (hōō⁄ē) *interj., n.* [echoic] [Slang] nonsense; bunk

hoof (hoof, hōōf) *n., pl.* **hoofs, hooves** (hoovz, hōōvz) [OE. *hof*] **1.** the horny covering on the feet of cattle, deer, horses, etc. **2.** the entire foot of such an animal —*vt., vi.* [Colloq.] to walk (often with *it*) —**on the hoof** not butchered; alive —**hoofed** *adj.* —**hoof⁄less** *adj.*

hoof-and-mouth disease (-'n mouth⁄) same as FOOT-AND-MOUTH DISEASE

hoof·beat (-bēt⁄) *n.* the sound made by the hoof of an animal when it runs, walks, etc.

☆**hoof·er** (hoof⁄ər, hōōf⁄-) *n.* [Slang] a professional dancer, esp. a tap dancer, soft-shoe dancer, etc.

Hoogh·ly (hōōg⁄lē) river in NE India, flowing into the Bay of Bengal: a channel of the Ganges delta

hook (hook) *n.* [< OE. *hoc:* for IE. base see HACK¹] **1.** a curved or bent piece of metal, wood, etc. used to catch, hold, or pull something; specif., *a)* a curved piece of wire with a barbed end, for catching fish *b)* a curved piece of metal, wood, etc. fastened as to a wall and used to hang things on, etc. *[a coat hook]* *c)* a small metal catch inserted in a loop, or eye, to fasten clothes together **2.** a curved metal implement for cutting grain, etc. **3.** something shaped like a hook; specif., *a)* a curving point of land: used in place names *[Sandy Hook]* *b)* a bend in a stream **4.** *a)* the path of a hit or thrown ball that curves away to the left from a right-handed player or to the right from a left-handed player *b)* a ball that follows such a path **5.** *Boxing* a short blow delivered with the arm bent at the elbow **6.** *Music same as* FLAG¹ (sense 4) —*vt.* **1.** to fasten as with a hook **2.** to take hold of or catch as with a hook *[to hook a fish]* **3.** to shape into a hook *[he hooked his arm around the pole]* ☆**4.** to make (a rug) by drawing strips of cloth or yarn back and forth with a hook through a canvas or burlap backing **5.** to hit or throw (a ball) in a hook (*n.* 4a) **6.** [Colloq.] to steal; snatch **7.** *Boxing* to hit with a hook —*vi.* **1.** to curve as a hook does **2.** to be fastened with a hook or hooks *[the skirt hooks at the side]* —**by hook or by crook** by any means, honest or dishonest —☆**hook, line, and sinker** [Colloq.] completely; altogether —**hook up** to arrange and connect the parts of (a radio, etc.) —**off the hook** [Colloq.] out of trouble, freed from an obligation, etc. —☆**on one's own hook** [Colloq.] by oneself, without help from others

hook·ah, hook·a (hook⁄ə) *n.* [Ar. *huqqah*] an Oriental tobacco pipe with a long, flexible tube by means of which the smoke is drawn through water in a vase or bowl and cooled

hook and eye a device for fastening clothes, etc., consisting of a small loop and a hook that catches on it

☆**hook and ladder** a fire engine that carries long ladders, hooks for tearing down ceilings, and other equipment

hooked (hookt) *adj.* **1.** curved like a hook **2.** having a hook or hooks ☆**3.** made with a hook *[a hooked rug]* ☆**4.** *a)* [Slang] addicted to the use of a drug (often with *on*) *[hooked on heroin]* *b)* having one's attention or thoughts taken up with some person, fad, etc. (often with *on*) **5.** [Slang] married

HOOKAH

hook·er (hook⁄ər) *n.* **1.** one that hooks ☆**2.** [Slang] a drink of whiskey ☆**3.** [Slang] a prostitute

☆**hook shot** *Basketball* a one-handed shot in which the arm is brought sideways over the head in tossing the ball toward the basket

☆**hook·up** (hook⁄up⁄) *n.* **1.** the arrangement and connection of parts, circuits, etc. in a radio, telephone system, network of radio stations, etc. **2.** [Colloq.] a connection or alliance, as between two countries

☆**hook·worm** (-wurm⁄) *n.* a small roundworm with hooks around the mouth, that may infest the small intestine and cause a disorder (**hookworm disease**) that results in anemia, weakness, and pain in the abdomen

☆**hook·y** (hook⁄ē) *n.* see PLAY HOOKY

hoo·li·gan (hōō⁄li gən) *n.* [< ? an Irish family name] [Slang] a hoodlum, esp. a young one —**hoo⁄li·gan·ism** *n.*

hoop (hōōp) *n.* [OE. *hop:* for IE. base see COOP] **1.** a circular band or ring for holding together the staves of a barrel, cask, etc. **2.** anything like a hoop; specif., *a)* any of the rings forming the framework of a hoop skirt ☆*b)* *Basketball* the metal rim of the basket *c)* *Croquet same as* WICKET

☆**hoop·la** (hōōp⁄lä) *n.* [Colloq.] **1.** great excitement; bustle **2.** loud, exaggerated advertising or publicity

hoo·poe (hōō⁄pōō) *n.* [< Fr. < L. *upupa,* prob. echoic] a European bird with a long, curved bill and a high crest

☆**hoop skirt** a skirt worn over a framework of hoops, or rings, to make it spread out

hoo·ray (hoo rā⁄, hə-, hōō-) *interj., n., vi., vt. same as* HURRAH

fat, āpe, cär; ten, ēven; is, bīte; gō, hôrn, tōōl, look; oil, out; up, fur; get; joy; yet; chin; she; thin, then; zh, leisure; ŋ, ring; ə for *a* in *ago, e* in *agent, i* in *sanity, o* in *comply, u* in *focus;* ' as in *able* (ā⁄b'l); Fr. bal; ë, Fr. coeur; ö, Fr. feu; Fr. mon; ô, Fr. coq; ü, Fr. duc; r, Fr. cri; H, G. ich; kh, G. doch; ‡foreign; ☆ Americanism; < derived from. See inside front cover.

☆**hoose·gow, hoos·gow** (hoos'gou) *n.* [< Sp. *juzgado*, court of justice, ult. < L. *judex*, JUDGE] [Slang] a jail

☆**Hoo·sier** (hoo'zhər) *n.* [prob. < dial. *hoozer*, something big] [Colloq.] a native or inhabitant of Indiana

hoot (hoot) *vi.* [echoic] **1.** to make its characteristic hollow sound: said of an owl **2.** to make a sound like this **3.** to shout, esp. in scorn or disapproval —*vt.* **1.** to express (scorn, disapproval, etc.) by hooting **2.** to express scorn or disapproval of by hooting **3.** to chase away by hooting [to *hoot* an actor off the stage] —*n.* **1.** the sound that an owl makes **2.** any sound like this **3.** a shout of scorn or disapproval ☆**4.** the least bit; whit [not worth a *hoot*] —**hoot'er** *n.*

☆**hoot·en·an·ny** (hoot''n an'ē) *n., pl.* **-nies** [coined < ?] a gathering of people for singing folk songs

Hoo·ver (hoo'vər) **1. Herbert Clark,** 1874-1964; 31st president of the U.S. (1929-33) **2. J(ohn) Edgar,** 1895-1972; director of the FBI (1924-72)

Hoover Dam [after Pres. HOOVER] dam on the Colorado River, between Ariz. & Nev.: formerly **Boulder Dam**

hooves (hoovz, hoovz) *n.* alt. *pl.* of HOOF

hop[1] (häp) *vi.* **hopped, hop'ping** [OE. *hoppian*: for IE. base see COOP] **1.** to make a short leap or leaps on one foot **2.** to move by leaping or springing on both (or all) feet at once, as a bird, frog, etc. **3.** [Colloq.] *a)* to go or move briskly [he *hopped* to attention] *b)* to take a short, quick trip (with *up, down,* or *over*) [let's *hop* up to Boston for the weekend] —*vt.* **1.** to jump over [to *hop* a fence] ☆**2.** to get aboard [to *hop* a train] —*n.* **1.** a hopping ☆**2.** a bounce, as of a baseball **3.** [Colloq.] a dance, esp. an informal one **4.** [Colloq.] a short flight in an airplane —see SYN. at SKIP[2] —**hop on** (or **all over**) [Slang] to scold; reprimand

hop[2] (häp) *n.* [< MDu. *hoppe*] **1.** a twining vine with the female flowers borne in small catkins like cones **2.** [*pl.*] the dried ripe catkins, used for flavoring beer, ale, etc. —*vt.* **hopped, hop'ping** to flavor with hops —☆**hop up** [Slang] **1.** to stimulate by or as by a drug **2.** to supercharge (an automobile engine, etc.)

HOP
(leaves & cones)

Hope (hōp) [see the next entry] a feminine name

hope (hōp) *n.* [OE. *hopa*: ? < same IE. base as HOP[1]] **1.** a feeling that what is wanted will happen [we never gave up our *hope* for peace] **2.** the thing that one has a hope for [it is her *hope* to go to college] **3.** a reason for hope **4.** a person or thing on which one may base some hope [he is our last *hope* for a victory in the series] **5.** [Archaic] trust; reliance —*vt.* **hoped, hop'ing** **1.** to want and expect [we *hope* that you'll visit us] **2.** to want to believe [I hope you don't think we meant you] —*vi.* **1.** to have hope (*for*) [to *hope* for rain] **2.** [Archaic] to trust or rely —see SYN. at EXPECT —**hope against hope** to continue having hope though it seems in vain —**hop'er** *n.*

☆**hope chest** a chest in which a young woman hoping to get married collects linen, clothing, etc.

hope·ful (hōp'fəl) *adj.* **1.** feeling or showing hope **2.** inspiring or giving hope [a *hopeful* sign] —*n.* a person who hopes, or seems likely, to succeed —**hope'ful·ness** *n.*

hope·ful·ly (-ē) *adv.* **1.** in a hopeful manner **2.** it is to be hoped (that) [*hopefully* we will win]: regarded by some as a loose usage

hope·less (-lis) *adj.* **1.** without hope [a *hopeless* prisoner] **2.** allowing no hope; causing despair; discouraging [a hopeless situation] **3.** impossible to solve, deal with, etc. [he's *hopeless* when he loses his temper] —**hope'less·ly** *adv.* —**hope'less·ness** *n.*

SYN.—**hopeless** means not expecting a favorable outcome [he grew *hopeless* as the trial dragged on]; **despondent** implies a being in very low spirits due to a loss of hope and a feeling that it is useless to continue trying [he was *despondent* over the loss of his job]; **despairing** implies a total loss of hope and the extreme discouragement it causes [the *despairing* lover spoke of suicide]; **desperate** implies such a loss of hope as to make one turn to extreme action [hunger makes men *desperate*] —**ANT.** hopeful, optimistic

Ho·pi (hō'pē) *n.* [Hopi *Hópitu*, lit., good, peaceful] **1.** *pl.* **-pis, -pi** a member of a Pueblo tribe of Indians in NE Arizona **2.** their language

Hop·kins (häp'kinz) **1. Gerard Man·ley** (man'lē), 1844-89; Eng. poet & Jesuit priest **2. Mark,** 1802-87; U.S. educator

hop·lite (häp'līt) *n.* [< Gr. < *hoplon*, a tool] a heavily armed foot soldier of ancient Greece

hop·per (häp'ər) *n.* **1.** a person or thing that hops **2.** any hopping insect **3.** a container like a large funnel, from which the contents can be emptied slowly and evenly [the *hopper* of an automatic coal stoker]

☆**hop·sack·ing** (häp'sak'iŋ) *n.* [lit., sacking for hops] **1.** a coarse material for bags, made of jute or hemp **2.** a fabric of cotton, wool, synthetics, etc. somewhat like this, used for suits, etc. Also **hop'sack'**

hop·scotch (häp'skäch') *n.* [HOP[1] + SCOTCH, a scratch, or line] a children's game in which a player tosses a pebble, etc. into one section after another of a figure drawn on the ground, hopping from section to section after each toss to pick up the object

ho·ra (hôr'ə, hō'rə) *n.* [< ModHeb. < Romanian < Turk. *hora*] **1.** a lively Romanian and Israeli folk dance performed in a circle **2.** music for this dance

Hor·ace (hôr'is, här'-) [< L. *Horatius*] **1.** a masculine name **2.** (L. name *Quintus Horatius Flaccus*) 65-8 B.C.; Roman poet: known for his odes —**Ho·ra·tian** (hə rā'shən, hô-) *adj.*

Ho·ra·ti·o (hə rā'shō, -shē ō; hô-) [< L. *Horatius*, name of a Roman gens] a masculine name

Ho·ra·ti·us (-shəs, -shē əs) a hero in Roman legend who defended a bridge over the Tiber against the Etruscans

horde (hôrd) *n.* [< Fr. < G. < Pol. *horda* < Turk. *ordū*, a camp] **1.** a wandering tribe, as of early Mongols **2.** a large, moving crowd; swarm [a *horde* of picnickers] —*vi.* **hord'ed, hord'ing** to form or gather in a horde —see SYN. at CROWD[1]

Ho·reb (hôr'eb) *Bible* the mountain where Moses saw the burning bush: usually identified with Mt. SINAI

hore·hound (hôr'hound') *n.* [< OE. < *har*, white + *hune*, horehound] **1.** a bitter plant of the mint family, with white, downy leaves **2.** a bitter juice extracted from its leaves **3.** cough medicine or candy made with this juice

ho·ri·zon (hə rī'z'n) *n.* [< OFr. < L. < Gr. *horizōn* (*kyklos*), the bounding (circle)] **1.** the line where the sky seems to meet the earth: called **visible** or **apparent horizon** **2.** [usually *pl.*] the limit of one's experience, interest, knowledge, etc. [travel widens one's *horizons*] **3.** *Geol.* a layer of soil or rock with distinct characteristics, particular fossils, etc.

hor·i·zon·tal (hôr'ə zän't'l, här'-) *adj.* **1.** *a)* parallel to the plane of the horizon; not vertical *b)* placed or acting in a horizontal direction **2.** flat and even; level **3.** at, or made up of elements at, the same level or status [a *horizontal* union] —*n.* a horizontal line, plane, etc. —**hor'i·zon·tal'i·ty** (-tal'ə tē) *n.* —**hor'i·zon'tal·ly** *adv.*

horizontal union same as CRAFT UNION

hor·mone (hôr'mōn) *n.* [< Gr. < *horman*, to excite < *hormē*, impulse] **1.** a substance formed in some organ of the body, as the adrenal glands, pituitary, etc., and carried to another organ or tissue, where it has a specific effect: certain hormones control growth, sexual activity, etc. and are often prepared synthetically **2.** a similar substance in plants —**hor·mo·nal** (-mō'n'l), **hor·mon·ic** (-män'ik) *adj.*

horn (hôrn) *n.* [OE. < IE. base *ker-*, highest part of the body, horn, peak] **1.** *a)* a hard, permanent outgrowth on the head of cattle, sheep, etc., usually growing in pairs *b)* the antler of a deer, shed annually **2.** anything that sticks out from the head of an animal, as a tentacle of a snail **3.** the substance that horns are made of, mostly keratin, or a synthetic substance like this **4.** a container made by hollowing out a horn [a powder *horn*] **5.** a cornucopia **6.** anything shaped like a horn; specif., *a)* a peninsula or cape *b)* either end of a crescent ☆*c)* a projection above the pommel of a cowboy's saddle **7.** *a)* an instrument made of horn and sounded by blowing, as the shofar *b)* any brass-wind instrument; specif., the French horn; also, ☆*Jazz* any wind instrument *c)* a device sounded to give a warning [a *foghorn*] *d)* a horn-shaped loudspeaker —*vt.* **1.** to strike or gore with the horns **2.** to furnish with horns —*adj.* made of horn [*horn*-rimmed glasses] —**blow one's own horn** [Colloq.] to boast —☆**horn in (on)** [Colloq.] to meddle (in); butt in [to *horn in on* a conversation] —**lock horns** ☆to have a disagreement or conflict —**on the horns of a dilemma** having to make a choice between two, usually unpleasant things —**pull (or draw or haul) in one's horns 1.** to hold oneself back **2.** to withdraw; recant —**horned** *adj.* —**horn'less** *adj.* —**horn'like'** *adj.*

Horn, Cape southernmost point of S. America, on an island (**Horn Island**) in Tierra del Fuego, Chile

horn·beam (hôrn'bēm') *n.* **1.** a small, hardy tree with smooth, gray bark and large clusters of light-green nuts **2.** the very hard, white wood of this tree, which takes a hornlike polish

horn·bill (hôrn'bil') *n.* any of a family of large, tropical, old-world birds with a huge, curved bill

horn·blende (-blend') *n.* [G.: see HORN & BLENDE] a black, rock-forming mineral, a type of amphibole common in some types of granite and other rocks

horn·book (-book') *n.* **1.** a parchment sheet with the alphabet, numbers, etc. on it, mounted on a small board under a clear plate of horn: formerly used as a child's primer **2.** any elementary text

horned (hôrnd) *adj.* **1.** having a horn or horns [two-*horned*] **2.** having a hornlike projection [*horned* toad]

☆**horned pout** *same as* BULLHEAD: also **horn'pout'** *n.*

☆**horned toad** any of several small, scaly new-world lizards that eat insects and have short tails and hornlike spines

horned viper a poisonous N African snake with a hornlike spine above each eye

hor·net (hôr'nit) *n.* [OE. *hyrnet:* for IE. base see HORN] any of several large, yellow-and-black social wasps

horn of plenty *same as* CORNUCOPIA

horn·pipe (hôrn'pīp') *n.* **1.** an obsolete wind instrument with a bell and mouthpiece made of horn **2.** a lively dance formerly popular with sailors, accompanied by the hornpipe

horn·y (hôr'nē) *adj.* **horn'i·er, horn'i·est 1.** of, like, or made of horn **2.** having horns **3.** toughened and calloused [the carpenter's *horny* hands] —**horn'i·ness** *n.*

ho·ro·loge (hôr'ə lōj', här'-) *n.* [< OFr. < L. < Gr. < *hōra,* hour + *legein,* to tell] a timepiece; clock, hourglass, sundial, etc.

ho·rol·o·gist (hô räl'ə jist) *n.* an expert in horology; esp., one who makes timepieces: also **ho·rol'o·ger**

ho·rol·o·gy (hô räl'ə jē) *n.* [< Gr. *hōra,* hour + -LOGY] the science or art of measuring time or making timepieces —**hor·o·log·ic** (hôr'ə läj'ik, här'-), **hor'o·log'i·cal** *adj.*

hor·o·scope (hôr'ə skōp', här'-) *n.* [Fr. < L. < Gr. < *hōra,* hour + *skopos,* watcher] **1.** the position of the planets and stars with relation to one another at a given time, esp. at a person's birth, regarded in astrology as having an influence on his life **2.** a chart of the signs of the zodiac and the positions of the planets, etc., by which astrologers claim to predict a person's future **3.** such a prediction, as for a particular day —**hor'o·scop'ic** *adj.*

hor·ren·dous (hô ren'dəs, hə-) *adj.* [L. *horrendus* < prp. of *horrere:* see HORROR] horrible; frightful —**hor·ren'dous·ly** *adv.*

hor·ri·ble (hôr'ə b'l, här'-) *adj.* [< OFr. < L. < *horrere:* see HORROR] **1.** causing a feeling of horror; terrible; dreadful [a *horrible* accident] **2.** [Colloq.] very bad, ugly, unpleasant, etc. [what a *horrible* color!] —**hor'ri·bly** *adv.*

hor·rid (hôr'id, här'-) *adj.* **1.** causing a feeling of horror; terrible; revolting [the *horrid* face of the monster] **2.** very bad, ugly, unpleasant, etc. [what a *horrid* thing to say!] —**hor'rid·ly** *adv.* —**hor'rid·ness** *n.*

hor·ri·fy (hôr'ə fī', här'-) *vt.* **-fied', -fy'ing 1.** to cause to feel horror **2.** [Colloq.] to shock or disgust [his bad manners *horrified* us] —*see* SYN. at DISMAY —**hor'ri·fi·ca'tion** *n.*

hor·ror (hôr'ər, här'-) *n.* [< OFr. < L. *horror* < *horrere,* to bristle, be afraid < IE. base *ghers-,* to bristle] **1.** the strong feeling caused by something frightful or shocking; terror and disgust **2.** strong dislike or a wish to avoid [she has a *horror* of being photographed] **3.** the quality of causing horror [the *horror* of starvation] **4.** something that causes horror [the *horrors* of war] **5.** [Colloq.] something very bad, ugly, disagreeable, etc. —*adj.* intended to cause horror [*horror* movies] —**the horrors** [Colloq.] a fit of extreme nervousness, panic, etc.

‡**hors de com·bat** (ôr' də kôn bä') [Fr., out of combat] put out of action; disabled

hors d'oeu·vre (ôr'durv', -duv') *pl.* **hors' d'oeuvres'** (durvz', duvz') [Fr., lit., outside of work, that is, not part of the meal itself] an appetizer, as olives, anchovies, canapés, etc., served usually before a meal

CRESTED HORNBILL
(to 4½ ft. long, including tail)

horse (hôrs) *n., pl.* **hors'es, horse:** see PLURAL, II, D, 1 [OE. *hors*] **1.** a large, strong animal with four legs, solid hoofs, and flowing mane and tail, used since ancient times for drawing loads, carrying riders, etc. **2.** the full-grown male of the horse **3.** a frame on legs to support something [a *sawhorse*] **4.** *slang for: a)* HORSE-POWER ☆*b)* HEROIN **5.** *Gym.* a padded block on legs, used for exercises in jumping or vaulting **6.** *Mil.* [*with pl. v.*] mounted troops; cavalry —*vt.* **horsed, hors'ing** to supply with a horse or horses; put on horseback —*vi.* to mount or go on horseback —*adj.* **1.** of a horse or horses **2.** mounted on horses [*horse* troops] —**from the horse's mouth** [Colloq.] from the original or authoritative source of information —☆**hold one's horses** [Slang] to control one's impatience —☆**horse around** [Slang] to engage in horse-play —**horse of another** (or **a different**) **color** an entirely different matter —**on one's high horse** [Colloq.] acting in a too proud or scornful manner —**to horse!** mount your horse!

HORSE (sense 5)

horse·back (hôrs'bak') *n.* the back of a horse —*adv.* on horse-back

☆**horse·car** (-kär') *n.* a streetcar drawn by horses

horse chestnut 1. *a)* a tree with large, hand-shaped leaves, clusters of white flowers, and glossy brown seeds growing in burs *b)* its seed **2.** any of various related shrubs or trees, including the buckeyes

horse·flesh (-flesh') *n.* **1.** the flesh of the horse, esp. as food **2.** horses as a group

horse·fly (-flī') *n., pl.* **-flies'** any of various large flies, the female of which sucks the blood of horses, cattle, etc.

horse·hair (-her') *n.* **1.** hair from the mane or tail of a horse **2.** a stiff fabric made from this hair; haircloth —*adj.* **1.** of horsehair **2.** covered or stuffed with horsehair

horse·hide (-hīd') *n.* **1.** the hide of a horse **2.** leather made from this

horse latitudes either of two belts of mainly calm weather and high barometric pressure, at about 30° N. latitude and 30° S. latitude

horse·laugh (-laf') *n.* a loud, boisterous laugh, usually showing scorn; guffaw

horse·less (-lis) *adj.* **1.** without a horse **2.** not pulled by a horse; self-propelled [the automobile was at first called a *horseless* carriage]

horse·man (-mən) *n., pl.* **-men 1.** a man who rides on horse-back **2.** a man skilled in the riding or care of horses —**horse'man·ship'** *n.*

☆**horse opera** [Slang] a motion picture or play about cowboys, rustlers, etc., esp. in the western U.S.

horse pistol a large pistol formerly carried by horsemen

horse·play (-plā') *n.* rough, boisterous fun

horse·pow·er (-pou'ər) *n.* a unit for measuring the power of motors or engines, equal to 746 watts or to the force needed to raise 550 lbs. at the rate of one foot per second

horse·rad·ish (-rad'ish) *n.* **1.** a plant of the mustard family, grown for its white root, which is grated to make a relish with a burning taste **2.** this relish

☆**horse sense** [Colloq.] ordinary common sense

horse·shoe (hôr'shoo', hôrs'-) *n.* **1.** a flat, U-shaped metal plate nailed to a horse's hoof to protect it **2.** anything shaped like this **3.** [*pl.*] a game in which the players toss horseshoes in an attempt to encircle a stake or come as close to it as possible —*vt.* **-shoed', -shoe'ing** to fit with a horseshoe or horseshoes —**horse'sho'er** *n.*

☆**horseshoe crab** a sea animal, like a crab, shaped like the base of a horse's foot and having a long, spinelike tail

HORSESHOE CRAB
(to 2 ft. long, including spine)

horse·tail (hôrs′tāl′) *n.* **1.** a horse's tail **2.** a rushlike plant with hollow, jointed stems and scalelike leaves

☆**horse trade** bargaining in which there is shrewd, careful thought by both parties —**horse′-trade′** *vi.* **-trad′ed, -trad′ing** —**horse′-trad′er** *n.*

horse·whip (-hwip′, -wip′) *n.* a whip for driving or managing horses —*vt.* **-whipped′, -whip′ping** to lash with a horsewhip

horse·wom·an (-woom′ən) *n., pl.* **-wom′en 1.** a woman who rides on horseback **2.** a woman skilled in the riding or care of horses

hors·y (hôr′sē) *adj.* **hors′i·er, hors′i·est 1.** of, like, or suggesting a horse; esp., having large features and a big body that looks strong but awkward **2.** of, like, or characteristic of people who are fond of horses, fox hunting, or horse racing Also **hors′ey** —**hors′i·ly** *adv.* —**hors′i·ness** *n.*

hort. 1. horticultural **2.** horticulture

hor·ta·to·ry (hôr′tə tôr′ē) *adj.* [< LL. < L. pp. of *hortari*, to urge: for IE. base see GREEDY] encouraging or urging, esp. to do good deeds: also **hor′ta·tive** (-tiv)

Hor·tense (hôr tens′, hôr′tens) [Fr. < L. < *hortensius*, of a garden] a feminine name

hor·ti·cul·ture (hôr′tə kul′chər) *n.* [< L. *hortus*, a garden + *cultura*, culture] the art or science of growing flowers, fruits, vegetables, etc. —**hor′ti·cul′tur·al** *adj.* —**hor′ti·cul′tur·ist** *n.*

Hos. Hosea

ho·san·na (hō zan′ə) *n., interj.* [< OE. < LL. < Gr. *hōsanna* < Heb. *hōshi‘āh nnā*, lit., save, we pray] an exclamation of praise to God

hose (hōz) *n., pl.* **hose** or, for 3, usually **hos′es** [OE. *hosa:* for IE. base see HIDE¹] **1.** orig., a man's tightfitting outer garment covering the hips, legs, and feet **2.** [*pl.*] *a)* stockings *b)* socks **3.** [prob. infl. by Du. *hoos*, water pipe] a flexible pipe or tube, used to carry fluids, esp. water from a hydrant —*vt.* **hosed**, **hos′ing 1.** to wet or wash with water from a hose ☆**2.** [Slang] to beat as with a hose

Ho·se·a (hō zā′ə, -zē′ə) *Bible* **1.** a Hebrew prophet of the 8th cent. B.C. **2.** the book containing his writings

ho·sen (hō′z'n) *n. archaic pl. of* HOSE (*n.* 1 & 2)

ho·sier (hō′zhər) *n.* [Chiefly Brit.] a person who makes or sells hosiery

ho·sier·y (-ē) *n.* **1.** hose; stockings and socks **2.** [Chiefly Brit.] *a)* similar knitted or woven goods *b)* the business or shop of a hosier

hos·pice (häs′pis) *n.* [Fr. < L. < *hospes*, host: for IE. base see GUEST] a place of shelter for travelers, esp. such a shelter kept by monks

hos·pi·ta·ble (häs′pi tə b'l, häs pit′ə-) *adj.* [MFr. < ML. < L. < *hospes*: see prec.] **1.** showing or characterized by friendliness, kindness, and generosity toward guests **2.** favoring health, growth, etc. [a *hospitable* climate] **3.** having an open mind, as to new ideas —**hos′pi·ta·bly** *adv.*

hos·pi·tal (häs′pi t'l) *n.* [< OFr. < LL. *hospitale*, inn < L. < *hospes:* see HOSPICE] an institution where the sick or injured receive medical or surgical treatment, nursing care, etc.

hos·pi·tal·i·ty (häs′pə tal′ə tē) *n., pl.* **-ties** the act, practice, or quality of being hospitable

hos·pi·tal·i·za·tion (häs′pi t'l i zā′shən) *n.* **1.** a hospitalizing or being hospitalized ☆**2.** [Colloq.] *same as* HOSPITALIZATION INSURANCE

☆**hospitalization insurance** insurance that pays all or part of the hospital expenses of those who subscribe to it

hos·pi·tal·ize (häs′pi t'l īz′) *vt.* **-ized′, -iz′ing** to put in or admit to a hospital

host¹ (hōst) *n.* [< OFr. < ML. < L. *hostia*, animal sacrificed] a wafer of the Eucharist; esp., [H-] a consecrated wafer

host² (hōst) *n.* [< OFr. < L. *hospes:* see HOSPICE] **1.** a man who entertains guests in his own home or at his own expense **2.** a man who keeps an inn or hotel **3.** any organism on or in which another (called a *parasite*) lives —*vi., vt.* to act as host or hostess (to)

host³ (hōst) *n.* [< OFr. < ML. < L. *hostis*, army] **1.** an army **2.** a multitude; great number [a *host* of tourists in Europe] —see SYN. at CROWD¹

hos·tage (häs′tij) *n.* [< OFr. < *hoste:* see HOST²] a person given as a pledge, or taken prisoner as by an enemy, until certain conditions are met

hos·tel (häs′t'l) *n.* [see HOSPITAL] a lodging place; inn; hostelry; specif., *same as* YOUTH HOSTEL

hos·tel·er (-ər) *n.* **1.** [Archaic] an innkeeper **2.** a traveler who stops at youth hostels

hos·tel·ry (-rē) *n., pl.* **-ries** a lodging place; inn; hotel

host·ess (hōs′tis) *n.* **1.** a woman who entertains guests in her own home or at her own expense **2.** *a)* a stewardess, as on an airplane *b)* a woman employed in a restaurant to seat patrons, be in charge of waitresses, etc. *c)* a woman who is paid to dance with patrons at a public dance hall

hos·tile (häs′t'l; *chiefly Brit.* -tīl) *adj.* [< L. < *hostis*, enemy] **1.** of or characteristic of an enemy; warlike [*hostile* nations] **2.** having or showing dislike or ill will; unfriendly; antagonistic [a *hostile* gesture] —*n.* a hostile person —**hos′tile·ly** *adv.*

hos·til·i·ty (häs til′ə tē) *n., pl.* **-ties 1.** a feeling of dislike, ill will, unfriendliness, opposition, etc. **2.** *a)* an expression of dislike and ill will; hostile act *b)* [*pl.*] acts of war; warfare —see SYN. at ENMITY

hos·tler (häs′lər, äs′-) *n.* [contr. of HOSTELER] one who takes care of horses at an inn, stable, etc.

hot (hät) *adj.* **hot′ter, hot′test** [OE. *hat*] **1.** *a)* having a high temperature, esp. one that is higher than that of the human body [her forehead felt *hot* to his touch] *b)* having an unusually high temperature; very warm [a *hot* day] **2.** producing a burning feeling in the mouth, throat, etc. [*hot* pepper] **3.** full of or characterized by any strong feeling or great activity, as *a)* fiery excitable [a *hot* temper] *b)* violent; angry [*hot* words] *c)* full of enthusiasm; eagerly intent [a *hot* interest in folk music] *d)* having strong sexual desire; lustful *e)* very controversial [the subject was too *hot* to handle for television] *f)* very lucky or effective [a *hot* winning streak] **4.** *a)* following closely [*hot* pursuit] *b)* close to what is being sought [you're getting *hot*] ☆**5.** as if heated by friction; specif., *a)* electrically charged [a *hot* wire] *b)* highly radioactive **6.** designating or of a color that suggests heat, as intense red **7.** [Colloq.] that has not yet lost heat, freshness, etc.; specif., *a)* recent; new [*hot* news] *b)* clear; strong [a *hot* scent] ☆*c)* recent and from an inside source [a *hot* tip] *d)* currently very popular [a *hot* recording] ☆**8.** [Slang] *a)* recently stolen [a *hot* car] *b)* sought by the police **9.** [Slang] excellent, good, etc. [that's *hot!*]: sometimes used sarcastically **10.** *Jazz* designating or of music or a style of playing that has exciting rhythms and tones, a fast tempo, improvisation, etc. —*adv.* in a hot manner —**hot under the collar** [Slang] very angry —**hot up** [Slang] to heat or warm up —**make it hot for** [Colloq.] to make things difficult or uncomfortable for —**hot′ly** *adv.* —**hot′ness** *n.*

hot air ☆[Slang] empty or high-sounding talk

hot·bed (hät′bed′) *n.* **1.** a bed of earth covered with glass and heated by manure, for forcing plants **2.** any place that causes something to grow or develop rapidly [a *hotbed* of crime]

hot-blood·ed (-blud′id) *adj.* easily excited; excitable, ardent, passionate, reckless, etc.

☆**hot·box** (-bäks′) *n.* an overheated bearing on an axle or shaft

☆**hot cake** *same as* GRIDDLECAKE —**sell like hot cakes** [Colloq.] to be sold rapidly in large quantities

hot cross bun a bun marked with a cross of frosting, eaten esp. during Lent

☆**hot dog** [Colloq.] a frankfurter or wiener, esp. one served in a soft roll

ho·tel (hō tel′) *n.* [< Fr. < OFr. *hostel*, HOSTEL] an establishment providing lodging, and often meals, esp. for travelers

‡**hô·tel de ville** (ō tel′ də vēl′) [Fr.] a town hall

ho·tel·ier (hō′tel yā′, -tə lir′) *n.* [Fr.] an owner or manager of a hotel

hot·foot (hät′foot′) *adv.* [Colloq.] in great haste —☆*vi.* [Colloq.] to hurry; hasten: with *it* —*n., pl.* **-foots′** the prank of secretly inserting and then lighting a match between the sole and upper of a victim's shoe

hot·head (-hed′) *n.* a hotheaded person

hot·head·ed (-hed′id) *adj.* **1.** quick-tempered; easily made angry **2.** hasty; rash —**hot′head′ed·ly** *adv.* —**hot′head′ed·ness** *n.*

hot·house (-hous′) *n.* a heated building for growing plants; greenhouse —*adj.* **1.** grown in a hothouse [*hothouse* tomatoes] **2.** needing careful treatment; delicate

☆**hot line** a telephone or telegraph line by which heads of state can communicate quickly and directly in an emergency or crisis

hot pepper any of various sharp-tasting peppers

hot plate a small gas or electric stove or burner for cooking

hot potato ☆[Colloq.] a difficult or risky problem that no one wants to handle

☆**hot rod** [Slang] an automobile, esp. an old one, modified or rebuilt for quick acceleration and high speed

☆**hot seat** [Slang] **1.** *same as* ELECTRIC CHAIR **2.** any difficult position in which a person is likely to get criticism, etc.

☆**hot·shot** (hät′shät′) *n.* [Slang] a person who behaves like an expert in something or acts in a very important or showy way: also **hot shot, hot-shot**

☆**hot spot** [Slang] 1. a place where there is or may be trouble or violence 2. a lively nightclub, resort area, etc.

hot spring a spring whose water is above 98°F. (36.7°C)

Hot Springs National Park national park in central Ark., containing 47 hot mineral springs

hot-tem·pered (-tem′pərd) *adj.* having a fiery temper; easily made angry

Hot·ten·tot (hät′'n tät′) *n.* [Afrik.: echoic origin] 1. a member of a Negro people of SW Africa 2. their language —*adj.* of the Hottentots or their language

hot war actual warfare: opposed to COLD WAR

hot water [Colloq.] trouble: preceded by *in* or *into*

Hou·din·i (hōō dē′nē), **Harry** (born *Ehrich Weiss*) 1874–1926; U.S. stage magician

hound (hound) *n.* [OE. *hund*, a dog: for IE. base see CANINE] 1. any of several breeds of hunting dogs with long, drooping ears and short hair 2. any dog 3. a mean, dislikable person ☆4. [Slang] a person who gets great pleasure from something; devotee or fan [an autograph *hound*] —*vt.* 1. to hunt or chase with or as with hounds; keep after; nag [to *hound* a debtor] 2. to urge on —see SYN. at BAIT —**follow the** (or **ride to**) **hounds** to hunt (a fox, etc.) on horseback with hounds

hounds·tooth check (houndz′tōōth′) a pattern of irregular broken checks, used in woven material

hour (our) *n.* [< OFr. < L. < Gr. *hōra*, hour, time] 1. a division of time, one of the twenty-four parts of a day; sixty minutes 2. a point or period of time; specif., *a)* a fixed point or period of time for a particular activity, etc. [the dinner *hour*] *b)* [pl.] a period fixed for work, etc. [office *hours*] *c)* [pl.] the usual times for getting up or going to bed [to keep late *hours*] 3. the time of day as indicated by a timepiece [the *hour* is 4:30 P.M.] 4. a measure of distance set by the time it takes to travel it [three *hours* from Cleveland to Detroit by car] 5. *Astron.* 1/24 of a SIDEREAL DAY 6. *Eccles. a)* same as CANONICAL HOUR *b)* the prayers said at a canonical hour ☆7. *Educ.* a class session of about an hour: each hour of a course per week is a unit of academic credit —**after hours** after the regular hours for business, school, etc. —**hour after hour** every hour —**hour by hour** each hour —**of the hour** prominent at this time [the man of the *hour*] —**the small** (or **wee**) **hours** the hours just after midnight

hour·glass (our′glas′) *n.* an instrument for measuring time by the trickling of sand, mercury, etc. from one glass bulb to another below it: it takes one hour to empty the top bulb

hou·ri (hoor′ē, hou′rē) *n., pl.* **-ris** [Fr. < Per. *ḥuri* < Ar., ult. < *ḥawira*, to be dark-eyed] any of the beautiful young women who give pleasure in the Moslem Paradise

hour·ly (our′lē) *adj.* 1. done or happening every hour or during an hour [the *hourly* output] 2. reckoned by the hour [*hourly* wage] 3. continual [to live in *hourly* dread] —*adv.* 1. at or during every hour [bells ring *hourly*] 2. at any hour; soon [we expect him *hourly*] 3. continually

HOURGLASS

house (hous; *for v.* houz) *n., pl.* **hous·es** (hou′ziz) [OE. *hus*: for IE. base see HIDE[1]] 1. a building for human beings to live in; specif., *a)* the building or part of a building occupied by one family *b)* a building where a group of people live as a unit [a fraternity *house*] 2. the people who live in a house; family; household 3. a family as including kin, ancestors, and descendants, esp. a royal family [the *House* of Tudor] 4. something thought of as a house, in providing shelter; specif., *a)* the place where an animal lives, as the shell of a mollusk *b)* a building where things are kept or stored [the elephant *house* at the zoo; a *warehouse*; a *courthouse*] 5. *a)* a theater *b)* the audience in a theater [we played to a large *house* last night] 6. *a)* a place of business *b)* a business firm ☆7. the management of a gambling establishment [the *house* has the odds in its favor] 8. [often H-] *a)* the building or rooms where a legislative assembly meets *b)* a legislative assembly [the *House* of Representatives] 9. *Astrol.* any of the twelve parts into which the heavens are divided —*vt.* **housed** (houzd), **hous′ing** 1. to provide a house or lodgings for [the cottage *housed* a small family] 2. to store in a house [we *housed* their furniture in our attic] 3. to cover, shelter, etc. as if by putting in a house [the phonograph is *housed* in a strong cabinet] —*vi.* 1. to take shelter 2. to reside; live —**bring down the house** [Colloq.] to get enthusiastic applause —**clean house** 1. to put a home in order ☆2. to get rid of unwanted things, conditions, etc. —**keep house** to take care of the affairs of a home —☆**on the house** given free, at the expense of the owner of the business —**set** (or **put**) **one's house in order** to put one's affairs in order

house·boat (hous′bōt′) *n.* a large, flat-bottomed boat designed for use as a dwelling place

house·break (-brāk′) *vt.* **-broke′, -bro′ken, -break′ing** to make housebroken

house·break·ing (-brāk′iŋ) *n.* the act of breaking into another's house in order to steal or commit some other felony —**house′break′er** *n.*

house·bro·ken (-brōk′ən) *adj.* trained to live in a house (that is, to empty the bladder and bowels outdoors or in a special place): said of a dog, cat, etc.

☆**house·clean·ing** (-klēn′iŋ) *n.* 1. the cleaning of the furniture, floors, etc. of a house 2. a getting rid of unwanted things —**house′clean′** *vi., vt.*

☆**house·coat** (-kōt′) *n.* a woman's long, loose garment for casual wear at home

house·dress (-dres′) *n.* any fairly cheap dress, as of printed cotton, worn at home for housework

house·fly (-flī′) *n., pl.* **-flies′** a two-winged fly found in and around houses: it feeds on garbage, manure, and food and can carry typhoid and other diseases

house·ful (-fool′) *n.* as much as a house will hold or provide room for [a *houseful* of guests]

house·hold (-hōld′) *n.* 1. all those living in one house; family, or family and servants 2. the home and its affairs [to manage a *household*] —*adj.* 1. of a household [*household* duties] 2. common; ordinary [a *household* expression]

house·hold·er (-hōl′dər) *n.* 1. one who owns or maintains a house 2. the head of a household

household word a very familiar word, saying, or name that nearly everyone knows

house·keep·er (-kēp′ər) *n.* a woman who manages a home, esp. one hired to do so —**house′keep′ing** *n.*

house·lights (-līts′) *n.pl.* lights that illuminate the part of a theater where the audience sits

house·maid (-mād′) *n.* a woman servant who does housework

housemaid's knee an inflammation of the sac over the kneecap, caused by much kneeling

house·moth·er (-muth′ər) *n.* a woman in charge of a dormitory, sorority house, etc., often as housekeeper

☆**House of Burgesses** the lower branch of the colonial legislature of Virginia

house of cards any flimsy structure, plan, etc. that is easily destroyed

House of Commons the lower branch of the legislature of Great Britain or Canada

house of correction a place where persons convicted of minor offenses are confined for a short period supposedly to be rehabilitated

House of Delegates ☆the lower branch of the legislature of Maryland, Virginia, or West Virginia

House of Lords the upper branch of the legislature of Great Britain, made up of the nobility and high-ranking clergy

☆**House of Representatives** the lower branch of the legislature of the U.S., certain other countries, and most of the States of the U.S.

☆**house organ** a magazine or newspaper published by a business firm for its employees, customers, etc.

house party the entertainment of guests overnight or over a period of a few days, as in a home or a fraternity house

house physician a resident physician of a hospital, hotel, etc.: also **house doctor**

☆**house-rais·ing** (-rā′ziŋ) *n.* a gathering of neighbors, esp. in a farm community, to help one of them build his house or its framework

house·top (-täp′) *n.* the top of a house; roof —**from the housetops** publicly and widely

house·wares (-werz´) *n.pl.* articles for household use, esp. in the kitchen, such as dishes, glassware, etc.

house·warm·ing (-wôr´miŋ) *n.* a party given by or for someone moving into a new home

house·wife (-wīf´; *for 2, usually* huz´if) *n., pl.* **-wives´** (-wīvz´; *for 2, usually* huz´ivz) **1.** a woman, esp. a married woman, who manages a household **2.** a small sewing kit —**house´wife´ly** *adj., adv.* —**house´wif´er·y** *n.*

house·work (-wurk´) *n.* the work done in housekeeping, such as cleaning, cooking, and laundering

hous·ing[1] (hou´ziŋ) *n.* **1.** the act of providing shelter or lodging [the problem of *housing* for the elderly] **2.** shelter or lodging; houses, apartments, etc. [new *housing* in the area] **3.** a shelter; covering **4.** *Mech.* a frame, box, etc. for containing some part [the *housing* of an engine]

hous·ing[2] (hou´ziŋ) *n.* [< OFr. *houce* < Frank.] an ornamental covering draped over a horse

Hous·man (hous´mən), **A(lfred) E(dward)** 1859-1936; Eng. poet & classical scholar

Hous·ton (hyōōs´tən) [after Samuel Houston] city in SE Tex.: pop. 1,233,000 (met. area 1,985,000)

Hous·ton (hyōōs´tən), **Samuel** 1793-1863; U.S. general & statesman; president of the Republic of Texas (1836-38; 1841-44)

Hou·yhn·hnm (hōō in´əm, hwin´əm) *n.* in Swift's *Gulliver's Travels*, any of a race of horses who are able to reason and have human qualities

hove (hōv) *alt. pt. & pp. of* HEAVE

hov·el (huv´'l, häv´-) *n.* [ME. < ?] **1.** a low, open shed for sheltering animals, storing equipment, etc. **2.** any small, miserable dwelling; hut —*vt.* **-eled** or **-elled, -el·ing** or **-el·ling** to shelter in a hovel

hov·er (huv´ər, häv´-) *vi.* [< ME. *hoven*, to stay] **1.** to stay fluttering in the air near one place [the butterfly *hovered* over the flower] **2.** to linger or wait close by, esp. in a protective way [the courtiers *hovered* about the queen] **3.** to be in an uncertain condition; waver [to *hover* between hope and despair] —*n.* the act of hovering —**hov´er·er** *n.*

how (hou) *adv.* [OE. *hu:* for IE. base *see* WHO] **1.** in what manner or way [*how* do you start the motor?] **2.** in what state or condition [*how* is she today?] **3.** for what reason; why [*how* is it that you don't know?] **4.** by what name [*how* is he known?] **5.** with what meaning [*how* was that statement to be taken?] **6.** to what extent, degree, amount, etc. [*how* high will it fly?] ☆**7.** [Colloq.] what: usually a request to repeat something said *How* is also used in exclamations and to add force to adjectives [*how* lovely!] —*n.* the way of doing; manner; method [the *how* and why of a scheme] —**how about** what is your thought concerning? —**how much** at what price? —**how now?** what is the meaning of this? —**how so?** how is it so?

How·ard (hou´ərd) [< the surname *Howard*] a masculine name

how·be·it (hou bē´it) *adv.* [Archaic] however it may be; nevertheless

how·dah (hou´də) *n.* [Anglo-Ind. < Hindi < Ar. *haudaj*] a seat for riding on the back of an elephant or camel, often with a canopy

how·dy (hou´dē) *interj.* [contr. < *how do you (do)?*] [Dial. or Colloq.] hello: a greeting

Howe (hou) **1.** **E·li·as** (i lī´əs), 1819-67; U.S. inventor of a sewing machine **2.** Sir **William**, 1729-1814; commander in chief of Brit. forces in American Revolution (1775-78)

How·ells (hou´əlz), **William Dean** (dēn) 1837-1920; U.S. novelist, critic, & editor

HOWDAH

how·ev·er (hou ev´ər) *adv.* **1.** no matter how; to whatever degree or extent [*however* hard the task, he always completes it] **2.** by what means; in whatever way [*however* did he escape?] **3.** nevertheless; yet: often used as a conjunctive adverb [you're right; *however*, say nothing about it] Also [Poet.] **how·e'er´** (-er´)

how·itz·er (hou´it sər) *n.* [< Du. < Early ModG. < Czech *haufnice*, orig., a sling] a short cannon, firing shells in a relatively high curve

howl (houl) *vi.* [ME. *houlen* < echoic base] **1.** to make the long, wailing cry of wolves, dogs, etc. **2.** to make a similar cry of pain, anger, etc. **3.** to make a sound like this [the wind *howls*]

4. to shout or laugh in scorn, mirth, etc. —*vt.* **1.** to express, announce, etc. in a loud, howling way **2.** to drive by howling [the audience *howled* the actor off the stage] —*n.* **1.** the long, wailing cry of a wolf, dog, etc. **2.** any similar sound **3.** [Colloq.] something hilarious [his imitation was a *howl*] —**howl down** to drown out with shouts of scorn, etc.

howl·er (houl´ər) *n.* **1.** a person or thing that howls **2.** [Colloq.] a ridiculous blunder

howl·ing (-iŋ) *adj.* **1.** that howls **2.** mournful; dreary **3.** [Slang] great [a *howling* success] —**howl´ing·ly** *adv.*

How·rah (hou´rə) city in NE India, in the Ganges delta, near Calcutta: pop. 513,000

how·so·ev·er (hou´sō ev´ər) *adv.* **1.** to whatever degree or extent **2.** by whatever means

hoy·den (hoid´'n) *n.* [< ? Du. *heiden*, heathen] a bold, boisterous girl; tomboy —*adj.* bold and boisterous; tomboyish —*vi.* to behave like a hoyden —**hoy´den·ish** *adj.*

Hoyle (hoil) *n.* a book of rules and instructions for card games, orig. compiled by Edmond Hoyle (1672-1769) —**according to Hoyle** according to the rules and regulations; in a fair way

HP, H.P., hp, h.p. **1.** high pressure **2.** horsepower

HQ, HQ., hq, h.q. headquarters

hr. *pl.* **hrs.** hour; hours

H.R. House of Representatives

h.r., hr, HR home run

H.R.H. His (or Her) Royal Highness

H.S., h.s. high school

HT high tension

ht. **1.** heat **2.** *pl.* **hts.** height

☆**hua·ra·ches** (hə rä´chēz) *n.pl.* [MexSp.] flat sandals with straps or woven strips for uppers

Huas·ca·rán (wäs´kä rän´) mountain of the Andes, in WC Peru

hub (hub) *n.* [? akin to HOB[1]] **1.** the center part of a wheel, etc., into which the axle goes or is fastened **2.** a center of interest, importance, or activity [Detroit is the *hub* of the auto industry] —☆**the Hub** Boston

hub·bub (hub´ub´) *n.* [prob. < Celt.] a confused sound of many voices; tumult —see SYN. at NOISE

hub·by (hub´ē) *n., pl.* **-bies** [Old Colloq.] a husband

hub·cap (hub´kap´) *n.* a tightfitting metal cap for the hub of a wheel, esp. of a car

Hu·bert (hyōō´bərt) [Fr. < OHG. < *hugu*, mind, spirit + *beraht*, bright] a masculine name

hu·bris (hyōō´bris) *n.* [Gr. *hybris*] a haughty or overbearing manner that comes from too great pride —**hu·bris´tic** *adj.*

huck·a·back (huk´ə bak´) *n.* [< ?] a coarse linen or cotton cloth with a rough surface, used for towels: also **huck**

☆**huck·le·ber·ry** (huk´'l ber´ē) *n., pl.* **-ries** [prob. < *hurtleberry*, WHORTLEBERRY] **1.** a shrub of the heath family having dark-blue berries with ten large seeds **2.** the fruit of this shrub

huck·ster (huk´stər) *n.* [< MDu. *hoekster* < *hoeken*, to peddle: related to HAWKER] **1.** a peddler, esp. of fruits, vegetables, etc. **2.** a merchant who haggles or uses unfair methods ☆**3.** [Colloq.] a person engaged in advertising or promotion —*vt.* to sell or advertise, esp. in an unfair or misleading way —**huck´ster·ism** *n.*

HUD (Dept. of) Housing and Urban Development

hud·dle (hud´'l) *vi.* **-dled, -dling** [? var. of ME. *hoderen*, to cover up] **1.** to crowd close together, as cows do in a storm **2.** to draw or hunch oneself up, as from cold [they *huddled* under the blanket] ☆**3.** [Colloq.] to hold a private, informal conference ☆**4.** *Football* to gather in a huddle —*vt.* **1.** to crowd close together **2.** to hunch or draw (oneself) up —*n.* **1.** a confused crowd or heap [his clothes lay in a *huddle* on the floor] **2.** confusion; jumble ☆**3.** [Colloq.] a private, informal conference ☆**4.** *Football* a grouping of a team behind the line of scrimmage to receive signals before a play

Hud·son (hud´s'n) [after Henry HUDSON] river in eastern N.Y., flowing southward into the Atlantic at New York City

Hud·son (hud´s'n) **1.** **Henry**, ?-1611; Eng. explorer, esp. of the waters about northeastern N. America **2.** **W(illiam) H(enry)**, 1841-1922; Eng. naturalist & writer

Hudson Bay inland sea in NE Canada; arm of the Atlantic

☆**Hudson seal** muskrat fur treated to resemble seal

Hue (hwā, wā) city in N South Vietnam, on the South China Sea: pop. 104,000

hue[1] (hyōō) *n.* [OE. *heow* < IE. base *kei-*, dark-colored] **1.** color; esp., the characteristics of a given color that determine its place in the spectrum **2.** a particular shade or tint of a given color [orange of a reddish *hue*] —**hued** *adj.*

hue² (hyōō) *n.* [< OFr. *hu,* a warning cry] a shouting; outcry: now only in **hue and cry,** meaning: *a)* orig., a loud shout or cry by those chasing a criminal *b)* any loud outcry, as of alarm or anger

huff (huf) *vt.* [prob. echoic] to make angry; offend —*vi.* **1.** to blow; puff **2.** to become angry —*n.* a fit of anger or resentment

huff·y (huf'ē) *adj.* **huff'i·er, huff'i·est 1.** easily offended; touchy **2.** angered or offended —**huff'i·ly** *adv.* —**huff'i·ness** *n.*

hug (hug) *vt.* **hugged, hug'ging** [prob. < ON. *hugga,* to comfort] **1.** to put the arms around and hold closely, esp. affectionately **2.** to squeeze tightly with the forelegs, as a bear does **3.** to cling to (a belief, opinion, etc.) **4.** to keep close to [the bus *hugged* the curb] —*vi.* to embrace one another closely —*n.* **1.** a close, fond embrace **2.** a tight hold with the arms, as in wrestling **3.** a bear's squeeze

huge (hyōōj, yōōj) *adj.* [OFr. *ahuge*] very large; gigantic; immense —see SYN. at ENORMOUS —**huge'ly** *adv.* —**huge'ness** *n.*

hug·ger·mug·ger (hug'ər mug'ər) *n.* [prob. based on ME. *mokeren,* to conceal] a confusion; muddle; jumble —*adj.* confused; muddled —*adv.* in a confused or jumbled manner

Hugh (hyōō) [< OFr. < OHG. *Hugo,* prob. < *hugu,* heart, mind] a masculine name

Hughes (hyōōz), **Charles Ev·ans** (ev'ənz) 1862–1948; U.S. jurist; chief justice of the U.S. (1930–41)

Hu·go (hyōō'gō) **1.** [var. of HUGH] a masculine name **2.** (*also* Fr. ü gō') **Vic·tor Ma·rie** (vēk tōr' mà rē') 1802–85; Fr. poet, novelist, & playwright

Hu·gue·not (hyōō'gə nät') *n.* [MFr. < G. *eidgenosse,* confederate] any French Protestant of the 16th or 17th century

huh (hu, hun) *interj.* an exclamation used in showing contempt, surprise, etc., or in asking a question

Hu·he·hot (hōō'hā'hōt') city in Inner Mongolia, N China: pop. 860,000

☆**hu·la** (hōō'lə) *n.* [Haw.] a native Hawaiian dance, with flowing gestures of the arms and hands: also **hu'la-hu'la**

hulk (hulk) *n.* [OE. *hulc*] **1.** a big ship that is hard to handle **2.** the body of a ship, esp. if old and taken apart **3.** a deserted wreck or ruins **4.** a big, clumsy person or thing —*vi.* to appear in a large, bulky form

hulk·ing (hul'kiŋ) *adj.* big and clumsy: also **hulk'y** (-kē)

Hull (hul) **1.** seaport in NE England: pop. 295,000: officially *Kingston upon Hull* **2.** city in SW Quebec, Canada, near Ottawa: pop. 60,000

hull¹ (hul) *n.* [OE. *hulu:* see CELL] **1.** the outer covering of a seed or fruit, as the husk of grain, shell of nuts, etc. **2.** the calyx of some fruits, as the strawberry **3.** any outer covering —*vt.* to take the hull or hulls off [to *hull* peas] —**hull'er** *n.*

hull² (hul) *n.* [special use of HULL¹, but influenced by Du. *hol,* ship's hold] **1.** the frame or body of a ship, excluding the masts, sails, rigging, superstructure, etc. **2.** *a)* the main body of an airship *b)* the frame or main body of a flying boat, amphibian, hydrofoil, etc. —*vt.* to pierce the hull of (a ship) with a torpedo, etc.

hul·la·ba·loo (hul'ə bə lōō') *n.* [echoic] loud noise and confusion; hubbub

hul·lo (hə lō') *interj., n., vt., vi.* same as: **1.** HOLLO **2.** HELLO

hum¹ (hum) *vi.* **hummed, hum'ming** [echoic] **1.** to make the low, murmuring sound of a bee, a motor, etc. **2.** to sing with the lips closed, not producing words **3.** to give forth a confused, droning sound [the room *hummed* with voices] **4.** [Colloq.] to be busy or full of activity [business is *humming*] —*vt.* **1.** to sing (a tune, etc.) with the lips closed **2.** to produce an effect on by humming [to *hum* a child to sleep] —*n.* the act or sound of humming —**hum'mer** *n.*

hum² (həm) *interj., n.* same as: **1.** HEM² **2.** HUMPH —*vi.* **hummed, hum'ming** same as HEM²

hu·man (hyōō'mən, yōō'-) *adj.* [< OFr. < L. *humanus,* related to *homo,* man: see HOMAGE] **1.** that is a person or has to do with people or mankind in general [a *human* being; the *human* race] **2.** consisting of or produced by men [*human* society] **3.** having or showing qualities that are typical of people in general ["to err is *human*"] —*n.* a person: the full phrase **human being** is still preferred by some —**hu'man·ness** *n.*

hu·mane (hyōō mān', hyoo-, yōō-) *adj.* [earlier form of HUMAN] **1.** kind, tender, merciful, etc. **2.** that makes people more civilized [*humane* learning] —**hu·mane'ly** *adv.* —**hu·mane'ness** *n.*

hu·man·ism (hyōō'mə niz'm, yōō'-) *n.* **1.** the quality of being human; human nature **2.** any system of thought or action based on the interests and ideals of man; specif., a philosophical movement that holds that man can be moral and find meaning in his life through reason, without the aid of supernatural religion **3.** the study of the humanities **4.** [H-] the intellectual and cultural movement that arose from the study of classical Greek and Roman culture in the Middle Ages and helped give rise to the Renaissance

hu·man·ist (-nist) *n.* **1.** a student of human nature and human affairs **2.** a student of the humanities or [H-] a follower of Humanism **3.** a follower of any system of humanism —*adj.* of humanism or the humanities —**hu'man·is'tic** *adj.* —**hu'man·is'ti·cal·ly** *adv.*

hu·man·i·tar·i·an (hyōō man'ə ter'ē ən, hyoo-, yōō-) *n.* a person who spends much time on the welfare of mankind, esp. by seeking to relieve pain and suffering; philanthropist —*adj.* helping humanity —**hu·man'i·tar'i·an·ism** *n.*

hu·man·i·ty (hyōō man'ə tē, hyoo-, yōō-) *n., pl.* **-ties 1.** the fact or quality of being human; human nature [it is our common *humanity* to be both greedy and unselfish] **2.** the human race; mankind; people [atomic warfare threatens *humanity*] **3.** the fact or quality of being humane; kindness, mercy, sympathy, etc. [she showed her *humanity* by helping the sick] —**the humanities 1.** languages and literature, esp. classical Greek and Latin **2.** studies that deal with human thought and relations; esp., literature, philosophy, the fine arts, history, etc.

hu·man·ize (hyōō'mə nīz', yōō'-) *vt.* **-ized', -iz'ing 1.** to give a human nature or qualities to **2.** to make humane; make kind, merciful, sympathetic, etc. —**hu'man·i·za'tion** *n.* —**hu'man·iz'er** *n.*

hu·man·kind (hyōō'mən kīnd', yōō'-) *n.* the human race; mankind; people

hu·man·ly (-lē) *adv.* **1.** in a human manner **2.** by human means [all that is *humanly* possible] **3.** from a human viewpoint [*humanly* speaking]

hu·man·oid (-oid') *adj.* nearly human, as in appearance or behavior —*n.* a nearly human creature; specif., *a)* any of the earliest ancestors of modern man *b)* in science fiction, a creature of another planet that is able to reason

Hum·ber (hum'bər) estuary in NE England, flowing into the North Sea

hum·ble (hum'b'l, um'-) *adj.* **-bler, -blest** [OFr. < L. *humilis,* low, akin to *humus,* HUMUS] **1.** having or showing an awareness of one's weaknesses and faults; not proud; modest [his failure did not make him *humble*] **2.** low in condition or rank; lowly; simple [a *humble* home] —*vt.* **-bled, -bling 1.** to lower in condition or rank; take away the power or fame of [they *humbled* the powerful invader] **2.** to make modest or humble in mind [he was *humbled* by the great man's speech] —**hum'ble·ness** *n.* —**hum'bler** *n.* —**hum'bly** *adv.*

SYN.—**humble,** in its good sense, suggests a modest nature in which there is no boastful pride or haughtiness [a *humble* genius], but in a less favorable sense implies a belittling of oneself or a lack of self-respect; **lowly** is an older substitute for **humble** and is now often used with a humorous tone ["and I, a *lowly* sailor"]; **meek** suggests a mild and patient nature which is not easily made angry or resentful and, in a less favorable sense, implies weakness in giving in readily See also SYN. at DEGRADE —**ANT. proud, conceited**

humble pie [< *umbles,* entrails of a deer < OFr. *nombles* < L. < *lumbus,* loin] formerly, a pie made of the inner parts of a deer, served to the servants after a hunt —**eat humble pie** to let oneself be humiliated, as by admitting a mistake and apologizing

hum·bug (hum'bug') *n.* [< ?] **1.** *a)* something said or done to cheat or trick; fraud; sham *b)* misleading or empty talk; nonsense **2.** a person who is not what he claims to be; imposter —*vt.* **-bugged', -bug'ging** to cheat or trick; deceive; hoax —*interj.* nonsense! —**hum'bug'ger** *n.* —**hum'bug'ger·y** *n.*

☆**hum·ding·er** (hum'diŋ'ər) *n.* [Slang] a person or thing that is especially fine or excellent

hum·drum (hum'drum') *adj.* lacking variety; dull; monotonous —*n.* humdrum talk, routine, etc.

Hume (hyōōm), **David** 1711–76; Scot. philosopher & historian

hu·mec·tant (hyōō mek'tənt) *n.* [< L. prp. of *humectare,* ult.

< *umere,* to be moist] a substance, as glycerol, added or applied to another to help it keep moisture in

hu·mer·al (hyōō′mər əl) *adj.* **1.** of or near the humerus **2.** of or near the shoulder or shoulders

hu·mer·us (hyōō′mər əs) *n., pl.* **-mer·i′** (-ī′) [L. *humerus, umerus,* the upper arm] the bone of the upper arm or forelimb, extending from shoulder to elbow: see illustration at ULNA

hu·mid (hyōō′mid, yōō′-) *adj.* [< Fr. < L. *humidus,* ult. < *umere,* to be moist] full of water vapor; damp; moist [*humid* air, a *humid* day] —see SYN. at WET —**hu′mid·ly** *adv.*

hu·mid·i·fy (hyōō mid′ə fī′, yōō-) *vt.* **-fied′, -fy′ing** to make humid; moisten —**hu·mid′i·fi·ca′tion** *n.* —**hu·mid′i·fi′er** *n.*

hu·mid·i·ty (-tē) *n., pl.* **-ties** **1.** moistness; dampness **2.** the amount of moisture in the air —**relative humidity** the ratio of the amount of moisture in the air to the maximum amount that the air could contain at the same temperature: it is stated as a percentage

☆**hu·mi·dor** (hyōō′mə dôr′, yōō′-) *n.* a jar, case, etc. for storing tobacco, with a device for keeping the air moist

hu·mil·i·ate (hyōō mil′ē āt′, hyoo-, yōō-) *vt.* **-at′ed, -at′ing** [< L. pp. of *humiliare* < L. *humilis,* HUMBLE] to hurt the pride or dignity of by causing to seem foolish, etc.; mortify [it *humiliated* her to be ignored] —see SYN. at DEGRADE —**hu·mil′i·a′tion** *n.*

hu·mil·i·ty (hyōō mil′ə tē) *n.* [< OFr. < L. *humilitas*] the state or quality of being humble; absence of boastful pride

☆**hum·ming·bird** (hum′iŋ burd′) *n.* any of a group of very small, brightly colored birds with a long, slender bill, used to suck nectar from flowers, and narrow wings that beat rapidly, with a humming sound

hum·mock (hum′ək) *n.* [orig. naut. < ?] **1.** a low, rounded hill; knoll **2.** a ridge or raised mound in an ice field ☆**3.** a tract of wooded land, higher than a surrounding marshy area —**hum′mock·y** *adj.*

HUMMINGBIRD
4¹/₄–4³/₄ in. long)

☆**hu·mon·gous** (hyōō mäŋ′gəs, -muŋ′-) *adj.* [prob. a blend of HUGE, MONSTROUS, & TREMENDOUS] [Slang] of enormous size or extent; very large or great

hu·mor (hyōō′mər, yōō′-) *n.* [< OFr. < L. *humor, umor,* moisture, fluid] **1.** formerly, any of the four fluids (**cardinal humors**) considered responsible for one's health and nature; blood, phlegm, choler (yellow bile), or melancholy (black bile) **2.** *a)* a person's temperament or nature *b)* a mood; state of mind [she was in a bad *humor* and wouldn't answer] **3.** whim; fancy; caprice [he ate when it pleased his *humor*] **4.** comic or amusing quality [a play full of *humor*] **5.** *a)* the ability to appreciate or express what is funny, amusing, or ludicrous [he has no sense of *humor* and rarely laughs] *b)* the expression of this in speech, writing, or action **6.** any fluid or fluidlike substance of the body [the aqueous *humor*] —*vt.* to give in to the mood or whim of (another); indulge [everyone tried to *humor* the sick child] —see SYN. at INDULGE and MOOD¹ and WIT¹ —**out of humor** not in a good mood; cross; disagreeable —**hu′mor·less** *adj.*

hu·mor·esque (hyōō′mə resk′) *n.* [G. *humoreske*] a light, fanciful or playful musical composition

hu·mor·ist (hyōō′mər ist, yōō′-) *n.* **1.** a person with a good sense of humor **2.** a professional writer or teller of amusing stories, jokes, etc.

hu·mor·ous (-əs) *adj.* having or expressing humor; funny; amusing; comical —see SYN. at WITTY —**hu′mor·ous·ly** *adv.*

hu·mour (hyōō′mər, yōō′-) *n., vt. Brit. sp. of* HUMOR

hump (hump) *n.* [< or akin to LowG. *humpe,* thick piece: for IE. base see COOP] **1.** a rounded lump that sticks out, as the fleshy mass on the back of a camel: in man, a hump is caused by a deformity of the spine **2.** a hummock; mound —*vt.* to hunch; arch [the cat *humped* its back] —*vi.* ☆[Slang] **1.** to try hard; exert oneself **2.** to hurry —☆**over the hump** [Colloq.] over the worst or most difficult part —**humpy′** *adj.*

hump·back (hump′bak′) **1.** a humped back **2.** a person having a humped back; hunchback ☆**3.** a large whale having a dorsal fin resembling a humpback —**hump′backed′** *adj.*

humped (humpt) *adj.* having a hump

Hum·per·dinck (hoom′pər diŋk′; *E.* hum′pər diŋk′), **Eng·el·bert** (eŋ′gəl bert′) 1854–1921; Ger. composer

humph (humf) *interj., n.* a snorting or grunting sound expressing doubt, surprise, scorn, disgust, etc.

Hump·ty Dump·ty (hump′tē dump′tē) an egg in an old nursery rhyme, represented as a short, squat person, who fell from a wall and broke into pieces

hu·mus (hyōō′məs, yōō′-) *n.* [L., earth: for IE. base see HOMAGE] the brown or black organic part of the soil, resulting from the partial decay of plant and animal matter

Hun (hun) *n.* **1.** a member of a warlike Asian people who invaded eastern and central Europe in the 4th and 5th centuries A.D. **2.** [*often* h-] any savage or destructive person; vandal

hunch (hunch) *vt.* [< ?] to draw (one's body, etc.) up so as to form a hump —*vi.* **1.** to push oneself forward jerkily [he *hunched* slowly through the crowd] **2.** to sit or stand with the back arched [he *hunched* forward nervously] —*n.* **1.** a hump **2.** a chunk; hunk **3.** [Colloq.] a guess or feeling not based on known facts; premonition or suspicion [I have a *hunch* he's in]

hunch·back (hunch′bak′) *n. same as* HUMPBACK (senses 1, 2) —**hunch′backed′** *adj.*

hun·dred (hun′drid, -dərd) *n.* [OE.: for IE. base see CENT] **1.** the cardinal number next above ninety-nine; ten times ten; 100; C **2.** a division of an English county **3.** a similar U.S. division, now only in Delaware —*adj.* ten times ten

hun·dred·fold (-fōld′) *adj.* [see -FOLD] having a hundred times as much or as many —*adv.* a hundred times as much or as many

hun·dredth (hun′dridth) *adj.* **1.** coming after ninety-nine others in a series; 100th **2.** designating any of the hundred equal parts of something —*n.* **1.** the one following the ninety-ninth **2.** any of the hundred equal parts of something; 1/100

hun·dred·weight (hun′drid wāt′, -dərd-) *n.* a unit of weight equal to 100 pounds in the U.S. and 112 pounds in England: abbrev. **cwt.**

Hundred Years' War a series of wars between England and France in the years from 1337 to 1453

hung (huŋ) *pt. & pp. of* HANG —☆**hung up (on)** [Slang] **1.** made nervous or disturbed (by) **2.** addicted (to) or obsessed (by)

Hung. **1.** Hungarian **2.** Hungary

Hun·gar·i·an (huŋ ger′ē ən) *adj.* of Hungary, its people, their language, or culture —*n.* **1.** a native or inhabitant of Hungary **2.** the Finno-Ugric language of the Hungarians; Magyar

Hun·ga·ry (huŋ′gər ē) country in SC Europe: 35,919 sq. mi.; pop. 10,331,000; cap. Budapest

hun·ger (huŋ′gər) *n.* [OE. *hungor*] **1.** *a)* the discomfort, pain, or weakness caused by a need for food *b)* famine; starvation **2.** a need or appetite for food [the meal satisfied their *hunger*] **3.** any strong desire; craving [a *hunger* for knowledge] —*vi.* **1.** to be hungry **2.** to crave; long (with *for* or *after*) [to *hunger* for love]

hunger strike a refusal, as of a prisoner, to eat until certain demands are granted

hun·gry (huŋ′grē) *adj.* **-gri·er, -gri·est** **1.** feeling or showing hunger; specif., *a)* wanting or needing food *b)* craving; eager [*hungry* for praise] **2.** not fertile; barren: said of soil —**hun′gri·ly** *adv.* —**hun′gri·ness** *n.*

hunk (huŋk) *n.* [Fl. *hunke,* hunk] [Colloq.] a large piece, lump, or slice of bread, meat, etc.

hun·ker (huŋ′kər) *vi.* [prob. < or akin to ON. *hokra,* to creep] to settle down on one's haunches; squat or crouch: often with *down* —*n.* [*pl.*] haunches

☆**hun·ky-do·ry** (huŋ′kē dôr′ē) *adj.* [Slang] all right; satisfactory; fine

hunt (hunt) *vt.* [OE. *huntian*] **1.** to go out to kill or catch (game) for food or as a sport **2.** to search carefully for; try to find [to *hunt* a job] **3.** *a)* to chase; drive [the mob *hunted* him out of town] *b)* to hound; harry; persecute [a *hunted* man] **4.** *a)* to go through (a woods, etc.) in seeking or chasing game *b)* to search (a place) carefully **5.** to use (dogs or horses) in chasing game —*vi.* **1.** to go out after game **2.** to search; seek —*n.* **1.** a hunting **2.** a group of people who hunt together **3.** a district covered in hunting **4.** a search [a treasure *hunt*] —**hunt down 1.** to chase until successful in catching or killing **2.** to search for until successful in finding —**hunt up 1.** to hunt or search for **2.** to find by searching

Hunt (hunt) **1.** (**James Henry**) **Leigh** (lē), 1784–1859; Eng. poet, critic, & essayist **2.** (**William**) **Hol·man** (hōl′mən), 1827–1910; Eng. painter

hunt·er (-ər) *n.* **1.** a person who hunts **2.** a horse or dog trained for hunting

hunt·ing (-iŋ) *n.* the act of a person or animal that hunts —*adj.* of or for hunting

hunting horn a horn used to sound signals during a hunt

☆**hunting knife** a large, sharp knife used by hunters to skin and cut up game

Hun·ting·ton (hun′tiŋ tən) [after C. P. *Huntington* (1821-1900), its founder] city in western W.Va., on the Ohio: pop. 74,000

Huntington Beach [after H. *Huntington*, U.S. railroad executive] city in SW Calif.: suburb of Los Angeles: pop. 116,000

hunt·ress (hun′tris) *n.* a woman who hunts

hunts·man (hunts′mən) *n., pl.* **-men 1.** a hunter **2.** the manager of a hunt

Hunts·ville (hunts′vil′) [after J. *Hunt*, its 1st settler (1805)] city in N Ala.: pop. 138,000

hur·dle (hur′d'l) *n.* [OE. *hyrdel:* for IE. base see CRATE] **1.** [Brit.] a frame, as of twigs woven together, used as a movable fence **2.** any of a series of barriers over which horses or runners must leap in a race (the **hurdles**) **3.** a difficulty to be overcome; obstacle [passing the final exams is our last *hurdle*] —*vt.* **-dled, -dling 1.** to fence off with hurdles **2.** to jump over (a barrier), as in a race **3.** to overcome (an obstacle, difficulty, etc.) —**hur′dler** *n.*

hur·dy-gur·dy (hur′dē gur′dē) *n., pl.* **-gur′dies** [prob. echoic] **1.** an early instrument like a lute, played by turning a crank so as to cause a wheel to revolve against the strings **2.** *same as* BARREL OR-GAN

HURDLES

hurl (hurl) *vt.* [prob. < ON.] **1.** to throw with force or violence [to *hurl* a javelin] **2.** to say in a strong or angry way [to *hurl* insults] —*vi.* **1.** to throw or fling something **2.** to move with force or violence; rush [he *hurled* into the room] ☆**3.** to be a baseball pitcher [he *hurled* for the Tigers in 1952] —*n.* a violent throw —see SYN. at THROW —**hurl′er** *n.*

hurl·y-burl·y (hur′lē bur′lē) *n., pl.* **-burl′ies** a turmoil; uproar —*adj.* disorderly and confused

Hu·ron (hyoor′ən, -än) *n.* [Fr., ruffian] **1.** *pl.* **-rons, -ron** a member of a confederation of Indian tribes that lived east of Lake Huron and now live in Oklahoma and Quebec **2.** their Iroquoian language

Huron, Lake second largest of the Great Lakes, between Mich. & Ontario, Canada: 24,328 sq. mi.; 247 mi. long

hur·rah (hə rô′, -rä′) *interj.* a shout of joy, approval, etc. —*n.* **1.** a shouting of "hurrah" **2.** excitement, commotion, etc. —*vi., vt.* to cheer; shout "hurrah" (for) Also **hur·ray′** (-rā′)

hur·ri·cane (hur′ə kān′, -kən) *n.* [< Sp. < WInd. *huracan*] a violent tropical cyclone with winds of 73 or more miles per hour, often with very heavy rains, and originating usually in the West Indies

☆**hurricane deck** the upper deck of a passenger ship, esp. of a river steamer

hurricane lamp an oil lamp or candlestick with a tall glass chimney to keep the flame from being blown out

hur·ried (hur′ēd) *adj.* in a hurry; done or acting quickly or too quickly; rushed or rushing [his *hurried* throw went into the stands] —**hur′ried·ly** *adv.* —**hur′ried·ness** *n.*

hur·ry (hur′ē) *vt.* **-ried, -ry·ing** [prob. akin to HURL] **1.** to move, send, or carry with haste [a taxi *hurried* us home] **2.** to cause to occur or be done more rapidly or too rapidly [please try to *hurry* dinner; he makes errors when he *hurries* his typing] **3.** to urge or cause to act soon or too soon [don't *hurry* me when I'm eating] —*vi.* to move or act with haste [you fell because you *hurried*] —*n.* **1.** a rush; urgency [there's no *hurry* about repaying me] **2.** eagerness to do, act, go, etc. quickly [he left the door open in his *hurry*] —see SYN. at HASTE —**hur′ri·er** *n.*

hur·ry-scur·ry, hur·ry-skur·ry (-skur′ē) *n.* an excited, confused rushing about —*vi.* **-ried, -ry·ing** to hurry and scurry about; move or act in a hurried, confused way —*adj.* hurried and 'used —*adv.* in a hurried, confused manner

(hurt) *vt.* **hurt, hurt′ing** [OFr. *hurter*, to push, hit, prob. < nk.] **1.** to cause pain or injury to; wound [the fall *hurt* my leg] **2.** to harm or damage in any way [water won't *hurt* this table top] **3.** to offend or make unhappy [she was *hurt* by his insults] —*vi.* **1.** to cause injury, damage, or pain [the alcohol on the open sore really *hurt*] **2.** to give or have the sensation of pain; be sore [my head *hurts*] —*n.* **1.** a pain or injury **2.** harm or damage **3.** something that wounds the feelings —*adj.* damaged [*hurt* books] —see SYN. at INJURE —**hurt′er** *n.*

hurt·ful (hurt′fəl) *adj.* causing hurt; harmful —**hurt′ful·ly** *adv.* —**hurt′ful·ness** *n.*

hur·tle (hurt′'l) *vi.* **-tled, -tling** [< ME. *hurten*, HURT] **1.** orig., to crash; collide **2.** to move swiftly and with great force [the racing cars *hurtled* through the town] —*vt.* to throw, shoot, or fling with great force; hurl [the horse *hurtled* its rider to the ground]

hus·band (huz′bənd) *n.* [Late OE. *husbonda* < ON. < *hūs*, house + *bondi*, freeholder (for IE. base see BONDAGE)] a married man; specif., the man to whom a certain woman is married —*vt.* to manage in an economical way [to *husband* one's money]

hus·band·man (-mən) *n., pl.* **-men** [Archaic] a farmer

hus·band·ry (huz′bən drē) *n.* **1.** orig., management of one's home affairs, resources, etc. **2.** careful, thrifty management **3.** the business of running a farm; farming

hush (hush) *vt.* [< ME. < *huscht*, quiet] **1.** to make quiet or silent [he could *hush* a class with just a look] **2.** to soothe; lull —*vi.* to be or become quiet or silent —*n.* quiet; silence —*interj.* an exclamation calling for silence —see SYN. at STILL[1] —**hush up 1.** to keep quiet **2.** to keep secret; suppress [they *hushed* up the scandal] —**hushed** *adj.*

hush-hush (hush′hush′) *adj.* [Colloq.] very secret; most confidential

hush money money paid to a person to keep him from telling something

☆**hush puppy** [< ?] in the southern U.S., a small, fried ball of cornmeal dough

husk (husk) *n.* [prob. < MDu. *huuskijn*, dim. of *huus*, a house] **1.** the dry outer covering of various fruits or seeds, as of an ear of corn **2.** the dry, rough, or useless outside covering of anything —*vt.* to remove the husk from —**husk′er** *n.*

☆**husk·ing (bee)** (hus′kiŋ) *same as* CORNHUSKING

☆**husk·y**[1] (hus′kē) *n., pl.* **-kies** [altered < ? ESKIMO] [*sometimes* H-] a hardy dog used for pulling sleds in the Arctic

husk·y[2] (hus′kē) *adj.* **husk′i·er, husk′i·est 1.** *a)* full of or consisting of husks *b)* like a husk **2.** sounding deep and hoarse; rough [a *husky* voice] ☆**3.** big and strong; robust; burly —*n., pl.* **husk′ies** a husky person —**husk′i·ly** *adv.* —**husk′i·ness** *n.*

Huss (hus), **John** 1369?-1415; Bohemian religious reformer & martyr, burned as a heretic: Czech name **Jan Hus** (yän hoos) —**Huss′ite** (-īt) *n., adj.*

hus·sar (hoo zär′, hə-) *n.* [< Hung. < Serb. *husar* < L. *cursus*: see CORSAIR] a member of any European regiment of light-armed cavalry, usually with brilliant dress uniforms

hus·sy (huz′ē, hus′-) *n., pl.* **-sies** [contr. < ME. *huswife*, housewife] **1.** a woman, esp. one of low morals **2.** a bold, saucy girl; minx

hus·tings (hus′tiŋz) *n.pl.* [*usually with sing. v.*] [OE. < ON. < *hūs*, a house + *thing*, assembly] **1.** the proceedings at an election **2.** the campaign route followed by a person running for political office

hus·tle (hus′'l) *vt.* **-tled, -tling** [Du. *hutseln*, to shake up] **1.** to push about; jostle in a rude, rough manner **2.** to force in a rough, hurried manner [to *hustle* a rowdy customer out the door] ☆**3.** [Colloq.] to hurry (a person, a job, etc.) ☆**4.** [Slang] to get, sell, victimize, etc. by aggressive tactics —*vi.* **1.** to move hurriedly [he *hustled* along the corridor] **2.** [Colloq.] to work or act rapidly or energetically ☆**3.** [Slang] *a)* to obtain money by aggressive or dishonest means *b)* to work as a prostitute —*n.* **1.** the act of hustling ☆**2.** [Colloq.] energetic action or effort; drive [the *hustle* and bustle of city life; an athlete with lots of *hustle*] ☆**3.** [Slang] a way of making money, often a dishonest or fraudulent way —**hus′tler** *n.*

hut (hut) *n.* [< Fr. < MHG. < OHG. *hutta:* for IE. base see HIDE[1]] a little house or cabin of the plainest or crudest kind —*vt., vi.* **hut′ted, hut′ting** to shelter or be sheltered in or as in a hut

hutch (huch) *n.* [OFr. *huche*, bin < ML. *hutica*, a chest] **1.** a bin, chest, or box for storage ☆**2.** a china cabinet with open shelves on top **3.** a pen or coop for small animals **4.** a hut

Hux·ley (huks′lē) **1. Al·dous (Leonard)** (ôl′dəs), 1894-1963; Eng. novelist. **2.** Sir **Julian (Sorrell)**, 1887-1975; Eng. biologist & writer: brother of *Aldous* **3. Thomas Henry,** 1825–95; Eng. biologist & writer: grandfather of *Aldous & Julian*

Huy·gens, Huy·ghens (hī′gənz; *Du.* hoi′gəns), **Christian** 1629–95; Du. physicist, mathematician, & astronomer

huz·zah, huz·za (hə zä′) *interj., n., vi., vt.* [echoic] *former var. of* HURRAH

H.V., HV, h.v., hv high voltage

Hwang Ho (hwäng′ hō′) river in N China, flowing from Tibet into the Yellow Sea: c. 2,900 mi.

hwy. highway

hy·a·cinth (hī′ə sinth′) *n.* [< L. < Gr. *hyakinthos*] **1.** *a)* among the ancients, a blue gem *b)* a reddish-orange or brownish gem **2.** a plant of the lily family, with spikes of fragrant, bell-shaped flowers **3.** a bluish purple —**hy′a·cin′thine** (-sin′thin, -thīn) *adj.*

hy·ae·na (hī ē′nə) *n. same as* HYENA

hy·a·line (hī′ə lin, -līn′) *adj.* [< LL. < Gr. < *hyalos*, glass] transparent as glass; glassy: also **hy′a·loid′** (-loid′) —*n.* anything transparent or glassy, as a clear sky

hy·a·lite (hī′ə līt′) *n.* [< Gr. *hyalos*, glass + -ITE] a colorless variety of opal

hy·brid (hī′brid) *n.* [L. *hybrida*, offspring of mixed parentage] **1.** the offspring of two animals or plants of different varieties, species, etc. *[the mule is a* hybrid, *being the offspring of a donkey and a horse]* **2.** anything of mixed origin, unlike parts, etc. **3.** *Linguis.* a word made up of elements from different languages —*adj.* of, or having the nature of, a hybrid —**hy′brid·ism, hy·brid′i·ty** *n.*

hy·brid·ize (hī′brə dīz′) *vi., vt.* **-ized′, -iz′ing** to produce or cause to produce hybrids; crossbreed —**hy′brid·i·za′tion** *n.* —**hy′brid·iz′er** *n.*

hybrid vigor *same as* HETEROSIS

hy·da·tid (hī′də tid) *n.* [Gr. *hydatis*, watery vesicle] a cyst containing watery fluid and the larvae of a tapeworm, found in the body of many animals, esp. canines

Hyde Park (hīd) **1.** public park in London **2.** village in southeastern N.Y.: site of the estate & burial place of Franklin D. Roosevelt

Hy·der·a·bad (hī′dər ə bad′, -bäd′; hī′drə-) city in SC India: pop. 1,119,000

hydr- *same as* HYDRO-: used before vowels

Hy·dra (hī′drə) [< OFr. *ydre* < L. < Gr. *hydra*, water serpent] *Gr. Myth.* the nine-headed serpent slain by Hercules: when any of its heads was cut off, it was replaced by two others —*n., pl.* **-dras, -drae** (-drē) [h-] **1.** any continuing or ever-increasing evil **2.** a small, freshwater polyp with a soft, tubelike body and a mouth surrounded by tentacles

hy·dran·ge·a (hī drān′jə, -dran′-; -jē ə) *n.* [ModL. < HYDR- + Gr. *angeion*, vessel] a shrubby plant, with opposite leaves and large, showy clusters of white, blue, or pink flowers

☆**hy·drant** (hī′drənt) *n.* [< Gr. *hydōr*, water] **1.** a large discharge pipe with a valve for drawing water from a water main; fireplug **2.** [Dial.] a faucet

hi·dranth (hī′dranth) *n.* [< HYDR- + Gr. *anthos*, a flower] any of the feeding members of a colony of hydroids

hy·drate (hī′drāt) *n.* [HYDR- + -ATE¹] a compound formed by the chemical combination of water and some other substance *[plaster of Paris, 2CaSO₄·H₂O, is a* hydrate*]* —*vi., vt.* **-drat·ed, -drat·ing** **1.** to become or cause to become a hydrate **2.** to combine with water —**hy·dra′tion** *n.* —**hy′dra·tor** *n.*

hy·drau·lic (hī drô′lik, -drô′-) *adj.* [< Fr. < L. < Gr. *hy·draulikos*; ult. < *hydōr*, water + *aulos*, tube] **1.** of hydraulics **2.** operated by the movement and pressure of liquid, esp. of a liquid forced through an aperture, tube, etc. *[hydraulic brakes]* **3.** setting or hardening under water *[hydraulic mortar]* —**hy·drau′li·cal·ly** *adv.*

hydraulic ram a device to move a portion of a flowing liquid to a higher level by using the momentum of the flowing liquid

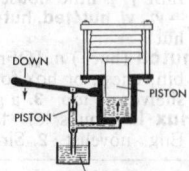

HYDRAULIC PRESS

HYACINTH

HYDRA (¼–½ in. long)

hy·drau·lics (-liks) *n.pl.* [with sing. v.] the branch of physics having to do with the mechanical properties of water and other liquids in motion and with the application of these properties in engineering

hy·dra·zine (hī′drə zēn′, -zin) *n.* [HYDR- + AZ(O) + -INE⁴] a colorless liquid base, NH₂NH₂, used as a jet and rocket fuel

hy·dric (hī′drik) *adj.* [HYDR- + -IC] of or containing hydrogen

hy·dride (hī′drīd) *n.* [HYDR- + -IDE] a compound of hydrogen with another element or a radical

hy·dro- [< Gr. *hydōr*, water: for IE. base see WATER] *a combining form meaning:* **1.** water *[hydrometer]* **2.** containing hydrogen *[hydrocyanic]*

hy·dro·car·bon (hī′drə kär′bən) *n.* any compound, as benzene, containing only hydrogen and carbon

hy·dro·ceph·a·lus (hī′drə sef′ə ləs) *n.* [ModL. < Gr. < *hydōr*, water + *kephalē*, head] a condition characterized by an abnormal amount of fluid in the cranium, causing enlargement of the head and destruction of the brain: also **hy′dro·ceph′a·ly** (-lē) —**hy′dro·ce·phal′ic** (-sə fal′ik) *adj., n.* —**hy′dro·ceph′a·lous** (-ləs) *adj.*

hy·dro·chlo·ric acid (hī′drə klôr′ik) [HYDRO- + CHLORIC] a strong, corrosive acid, HCl, that is a solution of the gas hydrogen chloride in water

hy·dro·chlo·ride (-klôr′īd) *n.* a compound of hydrochloric acid and an organic base

☆**hy·dro·cor·ti·sone** (-kôrt′ə sōn′, -zōn′) *n.* same as COR-TISOL

hy·dro·cy·an·ic acid (-sī an′ik) [HYDRO- + CYANIC] a weak, highly poisonous acid, HCN, a colorless liquid with the odor of bitter almonds

hy·dro·dy·nam·ics (-dī nam′iks) *n.pl.* [with sing. v.] the branch of physics dealing with the motion and action of water and other liquids —**hy′dro·dy·nam′ic** *adj.* —**hy′dro·dy·nam′i·cal·ly** *adv.*

hy·dro·e·lec·tric (-i lek′trik) *adj.* producing electricity by water power, or of electricity so produced —**hy′dro·e·lec·tric′i·ty** *n.*

hy·dro·fluor·ic acid (hī′drə flôr′ik, -floor′-) [HYDRO- + FLUOR(INE) + -IC] an acid, HF, existing as a colorless, fuming, corrosive liquid: it is used in etching glass

hy·dro·foil (hī′drə foil′) *n.* [HYDRO- + (AIR)FOIL] **1.** a winglike structure on the hull of some watercraft: at high speeds the craft skims along on the hydrofoils **2.** a craft with hydrofoils

HYDROFOIL

hy·dro·gen (hī′drə jən) *n.* [< Fr.: see HYDRO- + -GEN] a flammable, colorless, odorless, gaseous chemical element, the lightest of all known substances: symbol, H; at. wt., 1.00797; at. no., 1 —**hy·drog·e·nous** (hī dräj′ə nəs) *adj.*

hy·dro·gen·ate (hī′drə jə nāt′, hī dräj′ə-) *vt.* **-at·ed, -at·ing** to combine or treat with hydrogen *[oil is* hydrogenated *to produce a solid fat]* —**hy′dro·gen·a′tion** *n.*

☆**hydrogen bomb** a highly destructive nuclear bomb, in which the atoms of heavy hydrogen are fused by explosion of a nuclear-fission unit in the bomb

hydrogen ion the positively charged ion in all acids: symbol, H⁺

hy·dro·gen·ize (hī′drə jə nīz′, hī dräj′ə-) *vt.* **-ized′, -iz′ing** *same as* HYDROGENATE

hydrogen peroxide an unstable liquid, H₂O₂, often used, diluted, as a bleach or disinfectant, and in more concentrated form as a rocket fuel

hydrogen sulfide a poisonous gas, H₂S, that has the odor of rotten eggs

hy·drog·ra·phy (hī dräg′rə fē) *n.* [< Fr.: see HYDRO- & -GRA-PHY] the study, description, and mapping of oceans, lakes, and rivers, esp. so as to show their uses in navigation and commerce —**hy·drog′ra·pher** *n.* —**hy·dro·graph·ic** (hī′drə graf′ik), **hy′dro·graph′i·cal** *adj.*

hy·droid (hī′droid) *adj.* [HYDR(A) + -OID] **1.** like a hydra or polyp **2.** of or related to the group of hydrozoans of which the hydra is a member —*n.* any member of a group of hydrozoans, mostly sea animals and consisting of polyps, with one kind specialized for feeding a colony and the other for reproduction

hy·drol·o·gy (hī dräl′ə jē) *n.* [< ModL.: see HYDRO- & -LOGY] the science dealing with the waters of the earth, their distribution on the surface and underground, and the cycle involving evaporation and precipitation —**hy·dro·log·ic** (hī′drə läj′ik), **hy′dro·log′i·cal** adj. —**hy·drol′o·gist** n.

hy·drol·y·sis (hī dräl′ə sis) n., pl. **-ses** (′-sēz′) [HYDRO- + -LYSIS] the breaking up of a substance, often in the presence of a catalyst, into other substances by reaction with water, as a starch into glucose, natural fats into glycerol and fatty acids, etc. —**hy·dro·lyt·ic** (hī′drə lit′ik) adj.

hy·dro·lyte (hī′drə līt′) n. any substance undergoing hydrolysis

hy·dro·lyze (hī′drə līz′) vt., vi. **-lyzed′, -lyz′ing** to undergo or cause to undergo hydrolysis —**hy′dro·lyz′a·ble** adj.

hy·drom·e·ter (hī dräm′ə tər) n. [HYDRO- + -METER] an instrument for measuring the specific gravity of liquids: it is a graduated tube that sinks in a liquid up to the point determined by the density of the liquid —**hy·dro·met·ric** (hī′drə met′rik), **hy′dro·met′ri·cal** adj. —**hy·drom′e·try** (-trē) n.

hy·dro·ni·um (hī drō′nē əm) n. a hydrogen ion to which a water molecule is attached, H_3O^+: also **hydronium ion**

hy·dro·phil·ic (hī′drə fil′ik) adj. [HYDRO- + -PHIL(IA) + -IC] capable of uniting with or absorbing water: also **hy′dro·phile′** (-fīl′)

hy·dro·pho·bi·a (hī′drə fō′bē ə) n. [LL. < Gr.: see HYDRO- & -PHOBIA] **1.** an abnormal fear of water **2.** [from the symptomatic inability to swallow liquids] same as RABIES

hy·dro·pho·bic (-fō′bik, -fäb′ik) adj. **1.** of or having hydrophobia **2.** not capable of uniting with or absorbing water: also **hy′dro·phobe′** (-fōb′) —**hy′dro·pho·bic′i·ty** (-fō bis′ə tē) n.

hy·dro·phone (hī′drə fōn′) n. [HYDRO- + -PHONE] an instrument for detecting sound transmitted through water and showing the direction it is coming from

hy·dro·phyte (hī′drə fīt′) n. [HYDRO- + -PHYTE] any plant growing only in water or very wet earth —**hy′dro·phyt′ic** (-fit′ik) adj.

hy·dro·plane (-plān′) n. [HYDRO- + PLANE⁴] **1.** a small, light motorboat with hydrofoils or with a flat bottom rising in steps to the stern so that it can skim along the water at high speeds **2.** same as SEAPLANE —vi. **-planed′, -plan′ing 1.** to drive or ride in a hydroplane **2.** to skim along like a hydroplane

☆**hy·dro·pon·ics** (hī′drə pän′iks) n.pl. [with sing. v.] [< HYDRO- + Gr. ponos, labor + -ICS] the cultivation of plants in solutions, or moist inert material, containing minerals, instead of in soil —**hy′dro·pon′ic** adj. —**hy′dro·pon′i·cal·ly** adv.

hy·dro·pow·er (hī′drə pou′ər) n. hydroelectric power

hy·dro·qui·none (hī′drō kwi nōn′, -kwin′ōn) n. [HYDRO- + QUIN(INE) + -ONE] a white, crystalline substance used in medicine and in photography as a developer: also **hy′dro·quin′ol** (-kwin′ol, -ôl)

hy·dro·space (hī′drə spās′) n. the ocean waters and ocean depths of the earth, esp. as an area for scientific investigation

hy·dro·sphere (-sfir′) n. [HYDRO- + -SPHERE] **1.** all the water on the surface of the earth **2.** the moisture in the atmosphere surrounding the earth

hy·dro·stat·ics (hī′drə stat′iks) n.pl. [with sing. v.] [< Fr.: see HYDRO- & STATIC] the branch of physics having to do with the pressure and equilibrium of water and other liquids —**hy′dro·stat′ic, hy′dro·stat′i·cal** adj. —**hy′dro·stat′i·cal·ly** adv.

hy·dro·ther·a·peu·tics (hī′drō ther′ə pyōōt′iks) n.pl. [with sing. v.] same as HYDROTHERAPY —**hy′dro·ther′a·peu′tic** adj.

hy·dro·ther·a·py (-ther′ə pē) n. [HYDRO- + THERAPY] the treatment of disease, esp. in physical therapy, by the use of baths, compresses, etc.

hy·drot·ro·pism (hī drät′rə piz′m) n. [HYDRO- + -TROPISM] movement or growth, as of a plant root, in response to the stimulus of moisture —**hy·dro·trop·ic** (hī′drə träp′ik) adj.

hy·drous (hī′drəs) adj. [HYDR- + -OUS] containing water, as certain chemical compounds

hy·drox·ide (hī dräk′sīd) n. [HYDR- + OXIDE] a compound consisting of an element or radical combined with the hydroxyl radical (OH)

hy·drox·yl (hī dräk′sil) n. the monovalent radical OH, present in all hydroxides

hy·dro·zo·an (hī′drə zō′ən) adj. [< HYDRA + ZO(O)- + -AN] of a class of coelenterate animals having a saclike body and a mouth that opens directly into the body cavity —n. any animal of this class, as a hydra, hydroid, etc.

hy·e·na (hī ē′nə) n. [< L. < Gr. hyaina < hys, a hog] a wolflike animal of Africa and Asia, that makes a shrill cry: hyenas feed on carrion and are thought of as cowardly

Hy·ge·ia (hī jē′ə) Gr. Myth. the goddess of health

hy·giene (hī′jēn) n. [< Fr. < Gr. hygieinē < hygiēs, healthy] **1.** the science of health and its maintenance; system of principles for preserving health and preventing disease **2.** sanitary practices; cleanliness [personal hygiene]

HYENA
(2½–3 ft. high at shoulder)

hy·gi·en·ic (hī′jē en′ik, -jē′nik, -jen′ik) adj. **1.** of hygiene or health **2.** promoting health; sanitary —**hy′gi·en′i·cal·ly** adv.

hy·gi·en·ics (-iks) n.pl. [with sing. v.] same as HYGIENE (sense 1)

hy·gi·en·ist (hī′jē ə nist, -jē nist; hī jē′nist) n. an expert in hygiene

hy·gro- [< Gr. hygros, wet] a combining form meaning wet, moisture: also, before a vowel, **hygr-**

hy·grom·e·ter (hī gräm′ə tər) n. [< Fr.: see HYGRO- & -METER] any of various instruments for measuring moisture in the air —**hy·gro·met·ric** (hī′grə met′rik) adj. —**hy·grom′e·try** (-trē) n.

hy·gro·scope (hī′grə skōp′) n. [HYGRO- + -SCOPE] an instrument that indicates changes in atmospheric humidity without actually measuring such changes

hy·gro·scop·ic (hī′grə skäp′ik) adj. **1.** a) absorbing moisture from the air b) changed by the absorption of moisture **2.** of or according to a hygroscope —**hy′gro·scop′i·cal·ly** adv.

hy·ing (hī′iŋ) alt. prp. of HIE

hy·la (hī′lə) n. [< Gr. hylē, wood] same as TREE FROG

Hy·men (hī′mən) Gr. Myth. the god of marriage

hy·men (hī′mən) n. [Gr. hymēn, membrane] the thin membrane that usually closes part of the opening of the vagina in a virgin —**hy′men·al** adj.

hy·me·ne·al (hī′mə nē′əl) adj. [see HYMEN] of marriage —n. [Poet.] a wedding song

hy·me·nop·ter·an (hī′mə näp′tər ən) n. [< Gr. < hymēn, membrane + pteron, a wing + -AN] any of a large group of insects, including wasps, bees, ants, etc., which have a biting or sucking mouth and, when winged, four membranous wings —**hy′me·nop′ter·ous** adj.

hymn (him) n. [< OE. & OFr. < LL. < Gr. hymnos] **1.** a song in praise or honor of God, a god, or gods **2.** any song of praise —vt. to praise in a hymn —vi. to sing a hymn

hym·nal (him′nəl) n. a collection of religious hymns: also **hymn′book′** —adj. of hymns

hym·no·dy (him′nə dē) n. [< ML. < Gr.: see HYMN & ODE] **1.** the singing of hymns **2.** hymns as a group **3.** same as HYMNOLOGY —**hym′no·dist** n.

hym·nol·o·gy (him näl′ə jē) n. [< ML. < Gr.: see HYMN & -LOGY] **1.** the study of hymns, their history, use, etc. **2.** the composition of hymns **3.** same as HYMNODY (sense 2) —**hym·nol′o·gist** n.

hy·oid (hī′oid) adj. [< Fr. < ModL. < Gr. hyoeidēs, shaped like the letter v (upsilon) < hy, upsilon + eidos, form] designating or of a U-shaped bone at the base of the tongue —n. a hyoid bone

hyp- same as HYPO-: used before a vowel

hyp. 1. hypotenuse **2.** hypothesis **3.** hypothetical

☆**hype** (hīp) vt. **hyped, hyp′ing** [< HYPODERMIC] [Slang] **1.** to stimulate, excite, artificially by or as by the injection of a drug: usually with up **2.** to try to arouse interest in (a product, idea, etc.) as by exaggerated advertising or praise —n. [Slang] the act of hyping a product, idea, etc.

hy·per- [Gr. < hyper, over, above] a prefix meaning over, above, more than normal, excessive [hypercritical]

hy·per·a·cid·i·ty (hī′pər ə sid′ə tē) n. excessive acidity, as of the gastric juice —**hy′per·ac′id** (-as′id) adj.

hy·per·ac·tive (-ak′tiv) adj. extremely or abnormally active —**hy′per·ac·tiv′i·ty** (-tiv′ə tē) n.

hy·per·bar·ic (hī′pər bar′ik) adj. [< HYPER- + Gr. barys, weighty + -IC] **1.** of or having a pressure or specific gravity greater than that within the body tissues or fluids **2.** designating or of a chamber in which pressure and oxygen content are regulated, used in treating various diseases and conditions

hy·per·bo·la (hī pʉr′bə lə) *n., pl.* **-las,** occas. **-lae′** (-lē′) [ModL. < Gr. *hyperbolē* < *hyper-,* over + *ballein,* to throw] a curve formed by the section of a cone cut by a plane more steeply inclined to the base than to the side of the cone

hy·per·bo·le (hī pʉr′bə lē) *n.* [L. < Gr.: see prec.] exaggeration used in speaking or writing to create an effect, and not meant to be taken literally (Ex.: He's as strong as an ox)

hy·per·bol·ic (hī′pər bäl′ik) *adj.* **1.** of, having the nature of, or using hyperbole; exaggerating or exaggerating **2.** of a hyperbola, or having the form of a hyperbola Also **hy′per·bol′i·cal** —**hy′per·bol′i·cal·ly** *adv.*

hy·per·bo·lize (hī pʉr′bə līz′) *vt., vi.* **-lized′, -liz′ing** to express with or use hyperbole

hy·per·bo·re·an (hī′pər bôr′ē ən, -bə rē′ən) *adj.* [< LL. < L. < Gr. *hyperboreos,* beyond the north wind] **1.** of the far north **2.** very cold —*n.* [H-] *Gr. Myth.* an inhabitant of a region of sunshine and eternal spring, beyond the north wind

hy·per·crit·i·cal (hī′pər krit′i k'l) *adj.* too critical; hard to please—see SYN. at CRITICAL —**hy′per·crit′i·cal·ly** *adv.* —**hy′per·crit′i·cism** *n.*

hy·per·e·mi·a (hī′pər ē′mē ə) *n.* [ModL.: see HYPER- & -EMIA] an increased blood flow or congestion of blood anywhere in the body —**hy′per·e′mic** (-mik) *adj.*

hy·per·gly·ce·mi·a (hī′pər glī sē′mē ə) *n.* [ModL. < HYPER- + Gr. *glykys,* sweet + -EMIA] an abnormally high amount of sugar in the blood —**hy′per·gly·ce′mic** (-mik) *adj.*

hy·per·gol·ic (hī′pər gäl′ik, -gôl′ik) *adj.* [< G. *hypergol,* a rocket fuel] igniting with a sudden flash when mixed together, as a rocket fuel mixed with an oxidizer

Hy·pe·ri·on (hī pir′ē ən) *Gr. Myth.* **1.** a Titan, father of the sun god Helios **2.** Helios himself

hy·per·me·tro·pi·a (hī′pər mi trō′pē ə) *n.* [ModL. < Gr. *hypermetros,* excessive + *-ōpia,* -OPIA] farsightedness; abnormal vision in which the rays of light are focused behind the retina so that distant objects are seen more clearly than near ones —**hy′per·me·trop′ic** (-träp′ik) *adj.*

hy·per·on (hī′pər än′) *n.* [HYPER- + (BARY)ON] a baryon which is heavier than a nucleon

hy·per·o·pi·a (hī′pər ō′pē ə) *n. same as* HYPERMETROPIA —**hy′per·op′ic** (-äp′ik) *adj.*

hy·per·pne·a (hī′pər nē′ə, -pərp nē′ə) *n.* [ModL. < HYPER- + Gr. *pnoe,* breathing] abnormally rapid breathing; panting —**hy′per·pne′ic** *adj.*

hy·per·sen·si·tive (-sen′sə tiv) *adj.* abnormally or excessively sensitive —**hy′per·sen′si·tiv′i·ty** *n.*

hy·per·son·ic (-sän′ik) *adj.* designating, of, or moving at a speed equal to about five times the speed of sound or greater: see SONIC

hy·per·ten·sion (-ten′shən) *n.* abnormally high blood pressure, or a disease of which this is the chief sign —**hy′per·ten′sive** *adj., n.*

hy·per·thy·roid·ism (-thī′roid iz′m) *n.* **1.** above-normal activity of the thyroid gland **2.** the disorder caused by this and resulting in loss of weight, nervousness, a rapid pulse, etc. —**hy′per·thy′roid** *adj., n.*

hy·per·ton·ic (-tän′ik) *adj.* **1.** having abnormally high tension or tone, esp. of the muscles **2.** having an osmotic pressure higher than that of an isotonic solution —**hy′per·to·nic′i·ty** (-tə nis′ə tē) *n.*

hy·per·tro·phy (hī pʉr′trə fē) *n.* [ModL.: see HYPER- & -TRO-PHY] an abnormal increase in the size of an organ or tissue —*vi., vt.* **-phied, -phy·ing** to undergo or cause to undergo hypertrophy —**hy′per·troph′ic** (-träf′ik) *adj.*

hy·per·ven·ti·la·tion (hī′pər ven′t'l ā′shən) *n.* very rapid or deep breathing that supplies to the blood more oxygen than needed, causing dizziness, fainting, etc. —**hy′per·ven′ti·late′** *vi., vt.* **-lat′ed, -lat′ing**

hy·pha (hī′fə) *n., pl.* **-phae** (-fē) [ModL. < Gr. *hyphē,* a web] any of the threadlike parts making up the mycelium of a fungus —**hy′phal** *adj.*

hy·phen (hī′f'n) *n.* [LL. < Gr. < *hypo-,* under + *hen* < *heis,* one] a mark (-) used between the parts of a compound word (as *court-martial*) or the syllables of a divided word, as at the end of a line —*vt. same as* HYPHENATE

hy·phen·ate (-āt′) *vt.* **-at′ed, -at′ing** **1.** to connect by a hyphen **2.** to write or print with a hyphen —*adj.* hyphenated —**hy′phen·a′tion** *n.*

hyp·no- [< Gr. *hypnos,* sleep] *a combining form meaning:* **1.** sleep **2.** hypnotism

hyp·noid (hip′noid) *adj.* resembling sleep or hypnosis

hyp·nol·o·gy (hip näl′ə jē) *n.* [HYPNO- + -LOGY] the science dealing with sleep and hypnotism

hyp·no·sis (hip nō′sis) *n., pl.* **-ses** (-sēz) [ModL.: see HYPNO- & -OSIS] **1.** a sleeplike condition in which a person will do or say many of the things suggested to him by the one who has put him into this condition **2.** *same as* HYPNOTISM

hyp·not·ic (hip nät′ik) *adj.* [< Fr. < LL. < Gr. *hypnotikos,* tending to sleep < *hypnos,* sleep] **1.** causing sleep; soporific [*hypnotic* drugs] **2.** of, like, or causing hypnosis [a *hypnotic* trance] **3.** easily hypnotized —*n.* **1.** any drug or substance causing sleep **2.** a hypnotized person or one easily hypnotized —**hyp·not′i·cal·ly** *adv.*

hyp·no·tism (hip′nə tiz'm) *n.* **1.** the act or practice of causing hypnosis **2.** the science of hypnosis —**hyp′no·tist** (-tist) *n.*

hyp·no·tize (-tīz′) *vt.* **-tized′, -tiz′ing** **1.** to put into a state of hypnosis **2.** to spellbind by or as if by hypnotism —**hyp′no·tiz′a·ble** *adj.*

hy·po¹ (hī′pō) *n., pl.* **-pos** (-pōz) *short for:* ☆**1.** HYPODERMIC **2.** HYPOCHONDRIAC —☆*vt.* **-poed, -po·ing** [Slang] to boost, stimulate, etc. by or as if by a hypodermic injection

hy·po² (hī′pō) *n.* [contr. < HYPOSULFITE] *same as* SODIUM THIO-SULFITE

hy·po- [Gr. < *hypo,* less than] *a prefix meaning:* **1.** under, beneath [*hypodermic*] **2.** less than, deficient in [*hypothyroid*] **3.** *Chem.* having a lower state of oxidation

hy·po·chlo·rite (hī′pə klôr′īt) *n.* any salt of hypochlorous acid

hy·po·chlo·rous acid (-klôr′əs) [HYPO- + CHLOROUS] an unstable acid, HClO, known only in solution and used as a bleach and oxidizer

hy·po·chon·dri·a (hī′pə kän′drē ə) *n.* [ModL. < LL., pl., abdomen (where the condition was thought to start) < Gr. < *hypo-,* under + *chondros,* cartilage of the sternum] worry or anxiety over one's health so great that one may become very depressed or imagine oneself to have some illness

hy·po·chon·dri·ac (-ak′) *adj.* of or having hypochondria: also **hy′po·chon·dri′a·cal** (-kən drī′ə k'l) —*n.* a person who has hypochondria —**hy′po·chon·dri′a·cal·ly** *adv.*

hy·po·chon·dri·a·sis (hī′pə kən drī′ə sis) *n. same as* HYPO-CHONDRIA: *hypochondriasis* is the term preferred in medicine

hy·po·cot·yl (hī′pə kät′'l) *n.* [HYPO- + COTYL(EDON)] the part of the axis, or stem, below the cotyledons in the embryo of a plant —**hy′po·cot′y·lous** *adj.*

hy·poc·ri·sy (hi päk′rə sē) *n., pl.* **-sies** [< OFr. < L. < Gr. *hypokrisis,* acting a part, ult. < *hypo-,* under + *krinesthai,* to dispute] a pretending to be what one is not, or to feel what one does not feel; esp., a pretending to be virtuous, pious, etc. without really being so

hyp·o·crite (hip′ə krit) *n.* [< OFr. < L. *hypocrita,* an actor: see prec.] a person who pretends to be better than he really is, or to be pious, virtuous, etc. without really being so —**hyp′o·crit′i·cal** (-krit′i k'l) *adj.* —**hyp′o·crit′i·cal·ly** *adv.*

hy·po·der·mic (hī′pə dʉr′mik) *adj.* [HYPO- + DERM(A)¹ + -IC] **1.** of the parts under the skin **2.** injected under the skin —*n. same as:* **1.** HYPODERMIC INJECTION **2.** HYPODERMIC SYRINGE —**hy′po·der′mi·cal·ly** *adv.*

hypodermic injection the injection of a medicine or drug under the skin

hypodermic syringe a syringe of glass or plastic made like a piston and attached to a hollow metal needle (**hypodermic needle**), used for giving hypodermic injections

hy·po·der·mis (hī′pə dʉr′mis) *n.* [ModL.: see HYPO- & DERMIS] **1.** *Bot.* a specialized layer of cells, as for support or water storage, just beneath the epidermis of a plant **2.** *Zool.* an epidermis secreting an overlying cuticle, as in arthropods and annelids

hy·po·ge·al (hī′pə jē′əl) *adj.* [< LL. < Gr. < *hypo-,* under + *gē,* earth] growing, living, or occurring beneath the surface of the earth: also **hy′po·ge′ous**

hy·po·glos·sal (hī′pə gläs′'l, -glôs′-) *adj.* [< HYPO- + Gr. *glōssa,* the tongue] under the tongue; esp., designating or of the motor nerves of the tongue —*n.* a hypoglossal nerve

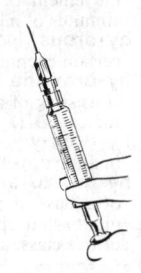

HYPODERMIC SYRINGE

hy·po·gly·ce·mi·a (hī′pə glī sē′mē ə) *n.* [ModL. < HYPO- + Gr. *glykys*, sweet + -EMIA] an abnormally low amount of sugar in the blood —**hy′po·gly·ce′mic** (-mik) *adj.*

hy·pog·y·nous (hī päj′ə nəs) *adj.* [HYPO- + -GYNOUS] **1.** growing attached to the receptacle, below and free from the pistil: said of the parts of some flowers **2.** having the parts so arranged [*hypogynous* flowers] —**hy·pog′y·ny** (-nē) *n.*

hy·po·phos·phate (hī′pə fäs′fāt) *n.* a salt or ester of hypophosphoric acid

hy·po·phos·phite (-fäs′fīt) *n.* a salt or ester of hypophosphorous acid

hy·po·phos·phor·ic acid (-fäs fôr′ik) an acid, $H_4P_2O_6$, obtained when phosphorus is slowly oxidized in moist air

hy·po·phos·pho·rous acid (-fäs′fər əs, -fäs fôr′əs) a monobasic acid of phosphorus, H_3PO_2: it is a strong reducing agent

hy·poph·y·sis (hī päf′ə sis) *n.*, *pl.* **-ses** (-sēz′) [Gr., undergrowth] *same as* PITUITARY GLAND

hy·po·sul·fite (hī′pə sul′fīt) *n.* **1.** any salt of hyposulfurous acid **2.** *a popular but erroneous var. of* SODIUM THIOSULFATE

hy·po·sul·fu·rous acid (-səl fyoor′əs) an unstable acid, $H_2S_2O_4$: it is a strong reducing agent

hy·po·ten·sion (-ten′shən) *n.* abnormally low blood pressure —**hy′po·ten′sive** *adj.*

hy·pot·e·nuse (hī pät′'n oos′, -yoos′) *n.* [< L. < Gr. *hypoteinousa*, lit., subtending < *hypo-*, under + *teinein*, to stretch] the side of a right-angled triangle opposite the right angle: also **hy·poth′e·nuse′** (hī päth′-)

hy·po·thal·a·mus (hī′pə thal′ə məs) *n.*, *pl.* **-mi′** (-mī′) [ModL.: see HYPO- & THALAMUS] the part of the brain that forms the floor of the third ventricle and regulates many body functions, such as temperature —**hy′po·tha·lam′ic** (-thə lam′ik) *adj.*

hy·poth·e·cate (hī päth′ə kāt′) *vt.* **-cat′ed, -cat′ing** [< ML. pp. of *hypothecare*, ult. < Gr. *hypotithenai*, to pledge] **1.** to pledge (property) to another as security; mortgage **2.** *same as* HYPOTHESIZE —**hy·poth′e·ca′tion** *n.* —**hy·poth′e·ca′tor** *n.*

hy·poth·e·sis (hī päth′ə sis, hi-) *n.*, *pl.* **-ses** (-sēz′) [Gr. < *hypo-*, under + *tithenai*, to place] an unproved theory, proposition, etc. that is accepted for the time being, only in order to explain certain facts: a **working hypothesis** is one that is used as a basis for further study, argument, etc. —see SYN. at THEORY

hy·poth·e·size (-sīz′) *vi.* **-sized′, -siz′ing** to make a hypothesis —*vt.* to assume; suppose

hy·po·thet·i·cal (hī′pə thet′i k'l) *adj.* **1.** based on or involving a hypothesis; assumed; supposed [a *hypothetical* case, not an actual one] **2.** given to the use of hypotheses [a *hypothetical* mind] **3.** *Logic* conditional ["If x equals 3, then 2x equals 6" is a *hypothetical* proposition] Also **hy′po·thet′ic** —**hy′po·thet′i·cal·ly** *adv.*

hy·po·thy·roid·ism (hī′pō thī′roid iz'm) *n.* **1.** below-normal activity of the thyroid gland **2.** the disorder caused by this and resulting in a low metabolism, sluggishness, puffiness, etc. —**hy′po·thy′roid** *adj.*, *n.*

hy·po·ton·ic (hī′pō tän′ik) *adj.* **1.** having abnormally low tension or tone, esp. of the muscles **2.** having an osmotic pressure lower than that of an isotonic solution —**hy′po·to·nic′i·ty** (-tə nis′ə tē) *n.*

hy·pox·i·a (hī päk′sē ə, hi-) *n.* [ModL.: see HYPO- & OXY-[1] & -IA] an abnormal condition resulting from a decrease in the oxygen needed by body tissue

hy·rax (hī′raks) *n.*, *pl.* **-rax·es, -ra·ces′** (-rə sēz′) [Gr., shrew mouse] a small, hoofed mammal of Africa and SW Asia, that feeds on plants

hys·sop (his′əp) *n.* [< OFr. < L. < Gr. *hyssōpos* < Heb. *ēzōbh*] **1.** *a)* a fragrant, blue-flowered plant of the mint family, used in folk medicine as a tonic, stimulant, etc. *b)* its flower **2.** *Bible* a plant whose twigs were used for sprinkling in certain ancient Jewish rites

hys·ter·ec·to·my (his′tə rek′tə mē) *n.*, *pl.* **-mies** [< Gr. *hystera*, uterus + -ECTOMY] surgical removal of all or part of the uterus

hys·ter·e·sis (his′tə rē′sis) *n.* [Gr., a deficiency] *Physics* a lag of effect, as in magnetization, when the forces acting on a body are changed

hys·te·ri·a (his tir′ē ə, -ter′-) *n.* [ModL.: see HYSTERIC & -IA] **1.** a mental illness in which a person may become highly excited or extremely anxious, and seem to be blind, deaf, paralyzed, etc. without anything being physically wrong in the body **2.** any outbreak of wild, uncontrolled excitement, such as fits of laughing and crying

hys·ter·ic (his ter′ik) *adj.* [< L. < Gr. *hysterikos*, suffering in the womb < *hystera*, uterus: the ancients thought of hysteria as a woman's disorder caused by disturbances of the uterus] *same as* HYSTERICAL —*n.* **1.** [usually *pl.*, occas. with sing. *v.*] a fit of uncontrolled laughing, crying, etc. **2.** a person subject to hysteria

hys·ter·i·cal (-i k'l) *adj.* **1.** of, like, or characteristic of hysteria **2.** extremely comical **3.** having or subject to hysteria

Hz, hz hertz

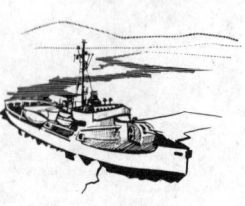

I

I, i (ī) *n., pl.* **I's, i's** **1.** the ninth letter of the English alphabet **2.** a sound of *I* or *i*

I¹ (ī) *n.* **1.** a Roman numeral for 1: it adds one unit when placed after another numeral (for example, VI = 6) and it subtracts one when placed before a larger numeral (for example, IV = 4) **2.** *Chem.* iodine —*adj.* shaped like *I*

I² (ī) *pron. for pl. see* WE [OE. *ic*] the person speaking or writing: the case forms of the first personal singular pronoun are: *I,* nominative; *me,* objective; *my* and *mine,* possessive; *myself,* intensive and reflexive —*n., pl.* **I's** the ego; the self

i (ī) *n.* **1.** a Roman numeral for 1 [page *iii*] **2.** *Math.* the symbol for $\sqrt{-1}$, the square root of −1

I., i. **1.** island(s) **2.** isle(s)

-i·a (ē ə, yə) [L. & Gr.] *a suffix used in:* **1.** names of certain diseases [*pneumonia*] **2.** names of some plants and animals [*zinnia*]

Ia., IA Iowa

I·a·go (ē ä′gō) the villain in Shakespeare's *Othello*

-i·al (ē əl, yəl, əl) [L. *-ialis, -iale*] *same as* -AL (senses 1, 2) [*racial, centennial*]

i·amb (ī′amb, -am) *n.* [< Fr. < L. < Gr. *iambos*] a metrical foot of two syllables, the first unaccented and the other accented, as in English verse (Example: "Tŏ bé,|ŏr nót|tŏ bé")

i·am·bic (ī am′bik) *adj.* of or made up of iambs —*n.* **1.** an iamb **2.** a poem or line of poetry written in iambs

-i·an (ē ən, yən, ən) [< L. *-ianus*] *same as* -AN [*Indian, reptilian, Grecian*]

-i·an·a (ē an′ə) *same as* -ANA

-i·a·sis (ī′ə sis) [< Gr. *-iasis*] *a combining form meaning* diseased condition [*psoriasis*]

-i·at·rics (ē at′riks) [< Gr. < *iatros,* physician] *a combining form meaning* treatment of disease [*pediatrics*]

i·at·ro·gen·ic (ī at′rə jen′ik) *adj.* [< Gr. *iatros,* physician + -GENIC] caused by a physician's words or actions: said esp. of imagined symptoms

-i·a·try (ī′ə trē) [< Gr. *iatreia,* healing] *a combining form meaning* medical treatment [*psychiatry*]

I·ba·dan (ē bä′dän) city in SW Nigeria: pop. 800,000

I·be·ri·a (ī bir′ē ə) large peninsula in SW Europe, comprising Spain & Portugal: often called **Iberian Peninsula** —**I·be′ri·an** *adj., n.*

i·bex (ī′beks) *n., pl.* **i′bex·es, i·bi·ces** (ib′ə sēz′, ī′bə-), **i′bex:** see PLURAL, II, D, 1 [L.] any of certain wild goats of Europe, Asia, or Africa: the male has large, backward-curved horns

ibid. [L. *ibidem*] in the same place: used in citing again the book, page, etc. cited just before

-i·bil·i·ty (ə bil′ə tē) *pl.* **-ties** [< L. *-ibilitas*] *a suffix used to form nouns from adjectives ending in* -IBLE [*sensibility*]

i·bis (ī′bis) *n., pl.* **i′bis·es, i′bis:** see PLURAL, II, D, 1 [L. < Gr. < Egypt. *hib*] a large wading bird related to the herons, with long legs and a long, curved bill, as the sacred ibis of the Nile

-i·ble (i b'l, ə b'l) [L. *-ibilis*] *same as* -ABLE [*legible*]

NUBIAN IBEX
(3 ft. high at shoulder)

Ib·sen (ib′s'n), **Hen·rik** (hen′rik) 1828–1906; Norw. playwright & poet

-ic (ik) [< Fr. *-ique* or L. *-icus* or Gr. *-ikos*] **1.** *a suffix meaning:* *a)* of, having to do with [*volcanic*] *b)* like, having the nature of [*angelic*] *c)* produced by, caused by [*photographic*] *d)* producing, causing [*psychedelic*] *e)* consisting of, containing [*dactylic*] *f)* having, affected by [*lethargic*] *g) Chem.* of or derived from [*citric*]; also, of a higher valence than the compound ending in *-ous* [*nitric*] **2.** *a suffix forming nouns, meaning* a person or thing having the nature of, affected by, belonging to, producing, etc. [*paraplegic, cynic, hypnotic*]

IC integrated circuit

-i·cal (i k'l, ə k'l) [< LL. < *-icus,* -IC + *-alis,* -AL] *same as* -IC: adjectives formed with *-ical* sometimes have special meanings (as for *historical, economical*) beyond those of the corresponding *-ic* forms

Ic·a·rus (ik′ə rəs) *Gr. Myth.* the son of Daedalus: using wings made by Daedalus, Icarus flew so high that the sun's heat melted the wax by which his wings were fastened, and he fell to his death in the sea —**I·car·i·an** (i ker′ē ən, ī-) *adj.*

ICBM intercontinental ballistic missile

ICC, I.C.C. Interstate Commerce Commission

ice (īs) *n.* [OE. *is*] **1.** water frozen solid by cold **2.** a piece, layer, or sheet of this **3.** anything like frozen water in appearance, etc. **4.** coldness in manner or attitude **5.** *a)* a frozen dessert, usually of water, fruit juice, and sugar *b)* [Brit.] ice cream ☆**6.** [Slang] diamonds —*vt.* **iced, ic′ing** **1.** to change into ice; freeze **2.** to cover with ice **3.** to cool by putting ice on, in, or around [*to ice a drink*] **4.** to cover with icing [*to ice a cake*] **5.** *Ice Hockey* to shoot (the puck) from defensive to offensive territory —*vi.* to freeze (often with *up* or *over*) —**break the ice** **1.** to make a start by getting over the first problems **2.** to make a start toward getting better acquainted —☆**cut no ice** [Colloq.] to have no effect —☆**on ice** [Slang] **1.** in readiness or reserve **2.** sure to result in victory or success [*this game is on ice*] —**on thin ice** [Colloq.] in a risky situation

-ice (is, əs) [< OFr. *-ice* < L. *-itius*] *a suffix meaning* condition or quality of [*justice*]

Ice. **1.** Iceland **2.** Icelandic

ice age *same as* GLACIAL EPOCH

ice bag a bag, as of rubber, for holding ice, applied to the body to reduce a swelling, ease pain, etc.

ice·berg (īs′burg) *n.* [prob. via Du. *ijsberg,* lit., ice mountain < Scand.] a great mass of ice broken off from a glacier and floating in the sea

☆**iceberg lettuce** a variety of lettuce with crisp leaves tightly folded into a round, compact head

ice·boat (-bōt′) *n.* **1.** a light, boatlike frame, often triangular, equipped with runners and driven over ice by a sail, propeller, or jet engine **2.** *same as* ICEBREAKER (sense 1)

ice·bound (-bound′) *adj.* **1.** held·fast by ice, as a boat **2.** blocked up by ice, as a port

☆**ice·box** (-bäks′) *n.* a cabinet with ice in it for keeping foods, etc. cold; also, any refrigerator

☆**ice·break·er** (-brā′kər) *n.* **1.** a sturdy ship for breaking a

ICEBREAKER

channel through ice   **2.** anything encouraging informality, ease of conversation, etc., as at a party

ice·cap (-kap′) *n.* a mass of glacial ice that spreads slowly out from a center

ice-cold (īs′kōld′) *adj.* very cold

☆**ice cream** [orig., *iced cream*] a sweet, creamy frozen food made from variously flavored cream and milk products and often containing gelatin, eggs, fruits, etc. —**ice′-cream′** *adj.*

ice field   1. *same as* ICECAP   **2.** a very large area of floating sea ice

ice floe   1. *same as* ICE FIELD (sense 2)   **2.** a single piece, large or small, of floating sea ice

ice hockey *same as* HOCKEY (sense 1)

Ice·land (īs′lənd) island country in the North Atlantic, southeast of Greenland: 39,768 sq. mi.; pop. 204,000; cap. Reykjavik —**Ice′land·er** *n.*

Ice·lan·dic (īs lan′dik) *adj.* of Iceland, its people, their language, or culture —*n.* the N. Germanic language of the Icelanders

Iceland moss a lichen found in the Arctic and sometimes used as a food and in folk medicine

Iceland spar a transparent, colorless calcite, found esp. in Iceland: it is used by opticians

ice·man (īs′man′, -mən) *n., pl.* -**men** (-men′, -mən) a person who sells or delivers ice

☆**ice milk** a frozen dessert like ice cream, but with a lower butterfat content

ice pack   1. a large, floating expanse of ice masses frozen together   **2.** an ice bag, folded cloth, etc. filled with crushed ice and applied to the body, as to reduce a swelling or ease pain

☆**ice pick** a sharply pointed metal tool used to chop ice into small pieces

ice sheet a thick layer of ice covering a very large area for a long period, as in the ice age

ice shelf a thick mass of glacial ice along a shore in a polar region, often extending hundreds of miles out to sea

ice skate a skate designed for skating on ice: see SKATE[1] (sense 1) —**ice′-skate′** *vi.* -**skat′ed**, -**skat′ing** —**ice skater**

ice water   1. melted ice   **2.** water chilled as with ice

ich·neu·mon (ik nyōō′mən, -nōō′-) *n.* [L. < Gr. *ichneumōn*, lit., tracker < *ichnos*, a track]   **1.** the Egyptian species of mongoose   **2.** *same as* ICHNEUMON FLY

ichneumon fly a hymenopteran insect whose larvae live as parasites in or on other insect larvae: also **ichneumon wasp**

i·chor (ī′kôr, -kər) *n.* [Gr. *ichōr*]   **1.** *Gr. Myth.* the fluid flowing instead of blood in the veins of the gods   **2.** a watery discharge from a wound or sore —**i′chor·ous** (-kər əs) *adj.*

ich·thy·o- [< Gr. < *ichthys*, a fish] *a combining form meaning* fish, like a fish: also, before a vowel, **ichthy-**

ich·thy·ol·o·gy (ik′thē äl′ə jē) *n.* [< ModL.: see ICHTHYO- & -LOGY] the branch of zoology dealing with fishes —**ich′thy·o·log′i·cal** (-ə läj′i k'l), **ich′thy·o·log′ic** *adj.* —**ich′thy·ol′o·gist** *n.*

ich·thy·o·saur (ik′thē ə sôr′) *n.* [< ModL. < ICHTHYO- + Gr. *sauros*, lizard] a prehistoric marine reptile, now extinct, which had a fishlike body, four paddle-shaped flippers, and a dolphinlike head —**ich′thy·o·sau′ri·an** (-sôr′ē ən) *adj.*

-i·cian (ish′ən) [< Fr.: see -IC & -IAN] *a suffix meaning* a person engaged in, practicing, or specializing in [*mortician*]

i·ci·cle (ī′si k'l) *n.* [< OE. < *is*, ice + *gicel*, piece of ice] a hanging piece of ice, formed by the freezing of dripping water

ic·ing (ī′siŋ) *n.* a mixture, as of sugar, butter, flavoring, etc., for covering a cake or pastries; frosting

☆**ick·y** (ik′ē) *adj.* **ick′i·er**, **ick′i·est** [baby talk for STICKY] [Slang]   **1.** unpleasantly sticky   **2.** sentimental in a sickening way   **3.** very distasteful; disgusting —**ick′i·ness** *n.*

i·con (ī′kän) *n.* [L. < Gr. *eikōn*, an image]   **1.** an image   **2.** *Orthodox Eastern Ch.* an image or picture of Jesus, Mary, a saint, etc., regarded as sacred —**i·con·ic** (ī kän′ik) *adj.*

i·con·o- [< Gr. *eikōn*, an image] *a combining form meaning* image, likeness, figure: also, before a vowel, **icon-**

i·con·o·clast (ī kän′ə klast′) *n.* [< ML. < MGr. < Gr. *eikōn*, an image + *klaein*, to break]   **1.** anyone opposed to the religious use of images   **2.** a person who attacks or ridicules traditional or highly respected institutions or ideas —**i·con′o·clasm** *n.* —**i·con′o·clas′tic** *adj.* —**i·con′o·clas′ti·cal·ly** *adv.*

☆**i·con·o·scope** (ī kän′ə skōp′) *n.* [ICONO- + -SCOPE] an early form of television camera tube

-ics (iks) [-IC + -s (pl.)] *a pl. suffix meaning:*   **1.** [*usually with sing. v.*] *a)* art, science, study [*economics*] *b)* arrangement, system [*statistics*]   **2.** [*usually with pl. v.*] *a)* activities, practices [*histrionics*] *b)* qualities, properties [*atmospherics*]

ic·tus (ik′təs) *n., pl.* -**tus·es**, -**tus** [< L. < pp. of *icere*, to hit]   **1.** rhythmical or metrical stress, or accent   **2.** *Med.* a stroke or sudden attack

i·cy (ī′sē) *adj.* **i′ci·er**, **i′ci·est**   **1.** having much ice; full of or covered with ice [*icy* streets]   **2.** like ice; slippery or very cold [*icy* fingers]   **3.** cold in manner; unfriendly [an *icy* look] — **i′ci·ly** *adv.* —**i′ci·ness** *n.*

id (id) *n.* [ModL. < L., it] *Psychoanalysis* the part of the psyche which is thought of as being made up of unconscious desires, instincts, drives, etc.

-id (id, əd) [ult. < L. or Gr.] *a suffix meaning:*   **1.** a thing belonging to or connected with [*Aeneid, arachnid*]   **2.** *Chem.* *same as* -IDE

ID, I.D. identification —*n.* (ī′dē′), *pl.* **ID's, I.D.'s** ☆a card (**ID card**) or document that identifies a person, proves his age, etc.

id. [L. *idem*] the same

I'd (īd)   **1.** I had   **2.** I would   **3.** I should

I·da (ī′də) [ML. < OHG.: akin ? to ON. *Ithunn*, goddess of youth]   **1.** a feminine name   **2.** **Mount**, *a)* highest mountain in Crete, in the C part: 8,058 ft.   *b)* mountain in NW Asia Minor, near the site of Troy

Ida. Idaho

-i·dae (i dē′) [ModL.] *a suffix used to form the name of* a zoological family [*Canidae* (the dog family)]

I·da·ho (ī′də hō′) [< AmInd. tribal name] Mountain State of the northwestern U.S.: 83,557 sq. mi.; pop. 713,000; cap. Boise: abbrev. **Ida., ID** —**I′da·ho′an** *adj., n.*

-ide (īd; *occas.* id) [< (OX)IDE] *a suffix added to part of the name of* the nonmetallic or electronegative element or radical in a binary compound [sodium *chloride*] or used in forming the name of a class of compounds [*glycoside*]

i·de·a (ī dē′ə) *n.* [L. < Gr. *idea*, appearance of a thing: for IE. base see WISE[1]]   **1.** a thought; mental conception or image; notion [a clear *idea* of what his duties are]   **2.** an opinion or belief [political *ideas* based on Jefferson's writings]   **3.** a plan; scheme; intention [an *idea* for making money]   **4.** a hazy perception; vague impression; inkling [I have an *idea* he may come]   **5.** meaning or significance [he read the message, but couldn't get the *idea* of it]   **6.** *Philos.* according to Plato, an unchanging, eternal model of which material things in the world are only imperfect imitations

SYN.—**idea** may be applied to anything existing in the mind as a result of thinking, imagining, or perceiving; **concept** refers to any abstract idea or to a generalized idea of a class of objects, based on knowledge of individual members of that class [his *concept* of a republic]; **conception**, often used to mean the same thing as **concept**, refers specifically to something conceived in the mind, or imagined [her *conception* of how the role should be played]; **thought** refers to any idea, whether or not expressed, that occurs to the mind in reasoning or meditating [she rarely speaks her *thoughts*]; **notion** suggests a vague idea or concept or a sudden whim [he has a *notion* he would like to change jobs]; **impression** refers to a vague or uncertain idea formed in response to something external [her first *impression* was that he was handsome]

i·de·al (ī dē′əl; *also, esp. for adj. 2 & 3 and for n.*, ī dēl′) *adj.* [< Fr. < LL. < L. *idea*: see prec.]   **1.** existing as an idea or model in philosophy   **2.** thought of as perfect; exactly as one would wish [an *ideal* day for a walk]   **3.** existing only in the mind as an image or concept; imaginary [a utopia is an *ideal* society]   **4.** *Philos.* of idealism —*n.*   **1.** a conception of something in its most excellent form [their house is for them the *ideal* of comfort]   **2.** a perfect model or standard [his father was the boy's *ideal*]   **3.** a goal or principle [laws based on *ideals* of justice]

i·de·al·ism (ī dē′əl iz'm) *n.*   **1.** behavior or thought based on a conception of things as one thinks they should be   **2.** the representation of idealized persons or things in art or literature   **3.** a striving to achieve one's ideals   **4.** *Philos.* any theory which holds that things exist only as ideas in the mind or that things are really imperfect imitations of unchanging models or forms having independent existence apart from the material world: see MATERIALISM

i·de·al·ist (-ist) *n.* **1.** *a*) a person who tries to live according to his ideals *b*) an impractical dreamer **2.** a person who believes in philosophic idealism **3.** a person who believes in or practices idealism in art or literature —*adj.* same as IDEALISTIC

i·de·al·is·tic (ī'dē ə lis'tik, ī dē'ə-) *adj.* **1.** of or characteristic of an idealist **2.** of, characterized by, or based on idealism —i'de·al·is'ti·cal·ly *adv.*

i·de·al·ize (ī dē'ə līz') *vt.* **-ized′, -iz′ing** to make ideal; think of or show as perfect or more nearly perfect than is true —*vi.* to represent things in the manner of an idealist —i·de'al·i·za'tion *n.* —i·de'al·iz'er *n.*

i·de·al·ly (ī dē'əl ē) *adv.* **1.** in an ideal manner; perfectly [*ideally* suited to her needs] **2.** in theory [*ideally*, everyone has the same chance to win]

i·de·ate (ī'dē āt', ī dē'āt) *vt., vi.* **-at′ed, -at′ing** to form an idea (of) —i'de·a'tion *n.* —i'de·a'tion·al *adj.* —i'de·a'tion·al·ly *adv.*

‡i·dée fixe (ē dā fēks') [Fr.] a fixed idea; obsession

‡i·dem (ī'dem, ē'-) *pron.* [L.] the same as that previously mentioned

i·den·ti·cal (ī den'ti k'l) *adj.* [< ML. < LL. *identitas* (see IDENTITY) + -AL] **1.** the very same [he is the *identical* man I saw yesterday] **2.** exactly alike [the handwriting on both letters is *identical*] **3.** designating twins, always of the same sex, developed from a single fertilized ovum and very much alike in appearance —see SYN. at SAME —i·den'ti·cal·ly *adv.*

i·den·ti·fi·ca·tion (ī den'tə fi kā'shən, i-) *n.* **1.** an identifying or being identified **2.** anything by which a person or thing can be identified [fingerprints are used as *identification*] **3.** *Psychoanalysis* a mainly unconscious process by which a person thinks, feels, and acts in a way which seems close to the way that another person who is important to him would

i·den·ti·fy (ī den'tə fī', i-) *vt.* **-fied′, -fy′ing** **1.** to make identical; treat as the same [to *identify* his interests with those of his friend] **2.** to recognize as being or show to be the very person or thing known, described, or claimed [to *identify* a biological specimen] **3.** to connect or associate closely [she is *identified* with the new political party] **4.** *Psychoanalysis* to make identification of (oneself) with someone else —*vi.* to understand and share another's feelings; sympathize (*with*) —i·den'ti·fi'a·ble *adj.* —i·den'ti·fi'er *n.*

i·den·ti·ty (ī den'tə tē, i-) *n., pl.* **-ties** [< Fr. < LL. *identitas* < L. *idem*, the same] **1.** the condition or fact of being the same or exactly alike; sameness [groups united by an *identity* of interests] **2.** *a*) the condition or fact of being a specific person or thing; individuality [to mask one's *identity*] *b*) the condition of being the same as a person or thing described or claimed **3.** *Math.* an equation which is true for all permissible sets of values of the variables which appear in it: example: $x^2 - y^2 = (x + y)(x - y)$

id·e·o- [< Fr. *idéo-* or < Gr. *idea*] a combining form meaning idea [*ideology*]

id·e·o·gram (id'ē ə gram', ī'dē-) *n.* [IDEO- + -GRAM] **1.** a graphic symbol representing an object or idea without expressing the sounds that form its name **2.** a symbol representing an idea rather than a word (Ex.: 5, +, ÷) Also **id′e·o·graph′**

id·e·o·graph·ic (id'ē ə graf'ik) *adj.* of, or having the nature of, an ideogram: also **id′e·o·graph′i·cal** —id'e·o·graph'i·cal·ly *adv.*

id·e·o·log·i·cal (ī'dē ə läj'i k'l, id'ē ə-) *adj.* of or concerned with ideology: also **i′de·o·log′ic** —i'de·o·log'i·cal·ly *adv.*

id·e·ol·o·gy (ī'dē äl'ə jē, id'ē-) *n., pl.* **-gies** [< Fr.: see IDEO- & -LOGY] **1.** the study of ideas, their nature and source **2.** thinking that is idealistic, abstract, or impractical **3.** the doctrines, opinions, or way of thinking of an individual, class, etc.; specif., the ideas on which a political, economic, or social system is based —i'de·ol'o·gist *n.*

ides (īdz) *n.pl.* [often with sing. v.] [Fr. < L. *idus*] in the ancient Roman calendar, the 15th day of March, May, July, or October, or the 13th of the other months

‡id est (id est) [L.] that is (to say)

id·i·o·cy (id'ē ə sē) *n., pl.* **-cies** **1.** the state of being an idiot **2.** great foolishness or stupidity

id·i·om (id'ē əm) *n.* [< Fr. & LL. < Gr. *idios*, one's own] **1.** the language or dialect of a people, region, etc. **2.** the usual way in which the words of a particular language are joined together to express thought **3.** an accepted phrase or expression having a meaning different from the literal ["to catch one's eye," meaning "to attract one's attention," is an *idiom*] **4.** the style of expression typical of a certain individual **5.** a style followed in a certain period or by a certain group, as in art or music

id·i·o·mat·ic (id'ē ō mat'ik) *adj.* **1.** using the typical idioms of a particular language [he speaks an *idiomatic* French] **2.** using or having many idioms **3.** of, or having the nature of, an idiom or idioms —id'i·o·mat'i·cal·ly *adv.*

id·i·o·path·ic (id'ē ə path'ik) *adj.* [< Gr. *idiopatheia*, feeling for oneself alone] designating or of a disease whose cause is unknown or uncertain

id·i·o·syn·cra·sy (id'ē ə siŋ'krə sē, -sin'-) *n., pl.* **-sies** [< Gr. < *idio-*, one's own + *synkrasis*, mixture < *syn-*, together + *kerannynai*, to mix] **1.** the special temperament that a certain person or group has **2.** any personal peculiarity, mannerism, reaction, etc. —id'i·o·syn·crat'ic (-sin krat'ik) *adj.* —id'i·o·syn·crat'i·cal·ly *adv.*

SYN.—*idiosyncrasy* refers to any personal mannerism or peculiarity and suggests strong individuality [the *idiosyncrasies* of a writer's style]; *eccentricity* implies a mannerism or peculiarity that differs widely from what is usual or customary and suggests behavior that is odd but amusing [his *eccentricity* of wearing earmuffs in the summer]

id·i·ot (id'ē ət) *n.* [OFr. < L. < Gr. *idiōtēs*, ignorant person < *idios*, one's own] **1.** a person having severe mental retardation: term now rarely used: see MENTAL RETARDATION **2.** a very foolish or stupid person

id·i·ot·ic (id'ē ät'ik) *adj.* of or like an idiot; very foolish or stupid —id'i·ot'i·cal·ly *adv.*

i·dle (ī'd'l) *adj.* **i′dler, i′dlest** [OE. *idel*, empty] **1.** *a*) worthless; useless [*idle* talk] *b*) futile; pointless [an *idle* wish] **2.** not based on fact; unfounded [*idle* rumors] **3.** *a*) unemployed; not busy [*idle* men] *b*) not in use [*idle* machines] **4.** not wanting to work; lazy —*vi.* **i′dled, i′dling** **1.** to move slowly or aimlessly **2.** to be unemployed or inactive **3.** to operate without transmitting any power; esp., to run slowly while out of gear [let the engine *idle* to warm it up] —*vt.* **1.** to waste; squander (usually with *away*) [*idling* away one's youth] **2.** to make (a motor, etc.) idle **3.** to make inactive or unemployed [the strike *idled* hundreds] —see SYN. at LOITER and VAIN —i'dle·ness *n.* —i'dly *adv.*

i·dler (īd'lər) *n.* **1.** one who loafs; lazy person **2.** *a*) a gearwheel placed between two others to transfer motion from one to the other without changing their direction or speed: also **idler gear** (or **wheel**), **idle wheel** *b*) a pulley guiding a belt or taking up slack: also **idler pulley**

IDLE WHEEL

i·dol (ī'd'l) *n.* [< OFr. < L. < Gr. *eidōlon*, an image < *eidos*, form] **1.** an image of a god, used as an object of worship **2.** an object of excessive devotion or admiration [money is his *idol*]

i·dol·a·ter (ī däl'ə tər) *n.* [< OFr. < LL. < LGr. < *eidōlon* (see prec.) + *latris*, servant] **1.** a worshiper of idols **2.** a devoted admirer; adorer —i·dol'a·tress (-tris) *n.fem.*

i·dol·a·trize (-trīz') *vt., vi.* **-trized′, -triz′ing** to worship as an idolater

i·dol·a·trous (-trəs) *adj.* **1.** of, or having the nature of, idolatry **2.** worshiping idols **3.** having or showing excessive admiration or devotion [the singer's *idolatrous* fans] —i·dol'a·trous·ly *adv.* —i·dol'a·trous·ness *n.*

i·dol·a·try (-trē) *n., pl.* **-tries** **1.** worship of idols **2.** excessive devotion or reverence

i·dol·ize (ī'd'l īz') *vt.* **-ized′, -iz′ing** **1.** to make an idol of **2.** to love or admire excessively —*vi.* to worship idols —i'dol·i·za'tion *n.* —i'dol·iz'er *n.*

Id·u·mae·a, Id·u·me·a (id'yoo mē'ə, īd'-) *Gr. name of* EDOM —Id'u·mae'an, Id'u·me'an *adj., n.*

i·dyll, i·dyl (ī'd'l; *Brit. often* id'l) *n.* [< L. < Gr. dim. of *eidos*, a form, image] **1.** a short poem or story describing a simple, pleasant, peaceful scene of rural or pastoral life **2.** a scene or happening about which such a poem or story could be written **3.** a long narrative poem ["The *Idylls* of the King"] —i'dyll·ist *n.*

i·dyl·lic (ī dil'ik) *adj.* **1.** of, or having the nature of, an idyll **2.** pleasing and simple; pastoral or picturesque [an *idyllic* vacation] —i·dyl'li·cal·ly *adv.*

-ie (ē) [earlier form of -Y¹] *a suffix meaning:* **1.** small, little [*doggie*]: often used to express affection **2.** one that is as specified [*softie*]

IE, I.E. Indo-European

i.e. [L. *id est*] that is (to say)

-i·er (ir, ər, ē'ər, yər) [< OFr. < L. *-arius*] *a suffix meaning* a person concerned with (a specified action or thing) [*bombardier*, *furrier*]

if (if) *conj.* [OE. *gif*] **1.** on condition that; in case that [*if* I come, I'll see him] **2.** granting that [*if* he was there, I didn't see him] **3.** whether [ask him *if* he knows her] *If* is also used in exclamations expressing: *a)* a wish [*if* I had only known!] *b)* surprise, annoyance, etc. [*if* that isn't the limit!] —*n.* **1.** a supposition; assumption [an explanation based on a number of *ifs*] **2.** a condition or restriction [a straightforward acceptance with no *ifs*] —**as if** as the situation would be if; as though

if·fy (if′ē) *adj.* [Colloq.] full of uncertainty; not definite [an *iffy* situation]

IFR Instrument Flight Rules

ig·loo (ig′lōō) *n., pl.* **-loos** [Esk. *igdlu*, snow house] an Eskimo house or hut, usually dome-shaped and built of blocks of packed snow

IGLOO

Ig·na·tius (of) **Loy·o·la** (ig-nā′shəs loi ō′lə), Saint (born *Iñigo López de Recalde*) 1491-1556; Sp. priest: founder of the Society of Jesus (Jesuit order)

ig·ne·ous (ig′nē əs) *adj.* [< L. < *ignis*, a fire] **1.** of, like, or containing fire **2.** formed by great heat, esp. by the action of volcanoes [granite is an *igneous* rock]

ig·nis fat·u·us (ig′nis fach′ōō wəs) *pl.* **ig·nes fat·u·i** (ig′nēz fach′ōō wī′) [ML. < L. *ignis*, a fire + *fatuus*, foolish] **1.** a light seen at night moving over swamps, etc., probably caused by the burning of gases rising from decaying plants: popularly called *will-o′-the-wisp* or *jack-o′-lantern* **2.** a deceptive hope or goal; delusion

ig·nite (ig nīt′) *vt., vi.* **-nit′ed, -nit′ing** [< L. pp. of *ignire* < *ignis*, a fire] **1.** to start burning [a spark *ignited* the leaves] **2.** to get excited [his speech *ignited* the crowd] —**ig·nit′a·ble, ig·nit′i·ble** *adj.* —**ig·nit′er, ig·ni′tor** *n.*

ig·ni·tion (ig nish′ən) *n.* **1.** an igniting or means of igniting **2.** in an internal-combustion engine, *a)* the igniting of the explosive mixture in the cylinder *b)* the device or system for doing this

ig·no·ble (ig nō′b′l) *adj.* [MFr. < L. < *in-*, not + *nobilis*, known] not noble in character or quality; dishonorable; base; shameful [the traitor's *ignoble* act] —see SYN. at BASE[2] —**ig·no′ble·ness** *n.* —**ig·no′bly** *adv.*

ig·no·min·i·ous (ig′nə min′ē əs) *adj.* **1.** causing or deserving shame or disgrace; dishonorable, contemptible, etc. [*ignominious* conduct] **2.** degrading; humiliating [an *ignominious* defeat] —**ig′no·min′i·ous·ly** *adv.* —**ig′no·min′i·ous·ness** *n.*

ig·no·min·y (ig′nə min′ē) *n., pl.* **-min′ies** [< Fr. < L. *ignominia* < *in-*, without + *nomen*, NAME] **1.** loss of one's reputation; shame and dishonor **2.** disgraceful or shameful quality or action —see SYN. at DISGRACE

ig·no·ra·mus (ig′nə rā′məs, -ram′əs) *n., pl.* **-mus·es** [< the name of a lawyer in a 17th-c. play; L., lit., we ignore (a legal term)] an ignorant person

ig·no·rance (ig′nər əns) *n.* the condition or quality of being ignorant; lack of knowledge

ig·no·rant (-ənt) *adj.* [< OFr. < L. prp. of *ignorare*: see IGNORE] **1.** having little knowledge, education, or experience **2.** caused by or showing lack of knowledge or education [an *ignorant* suggestion] **3.** unaware (of) [*ignorant* of the rules] —**ig′no·rant·ly** *adv.*

SYN.—**ignorant** implies a lack of knowledge, either in general [an *ignorant* man] or on some particular matter [*ignorant* of the reason for their quarrel]; **illiterate** implies an inability to read or write; **unlettered** is sometimes used as a milder substitute for **illiterate**, but often implies unfamiliarity with fine literature [although a graduate engineer, he is relatively *unlettered*]; **uneducated** and **untutored** imply a lack of formal schooling [he had a brilliant, though *uneducated*, mind] —ANT. educated, erudite, learned

ig·nore (ig nôr′) *vt.* **-nored′, -nor′ing** [< Fr. < L. *ignorare* < *in-*, not + base of *gnarus*, knowing: for IE. base see KNOW] to disregard deliberately; pay no attention to; refuse to consider —**ig·nor′er** *n.*

I·go·rot (ig′ə rōt′, ē′gə-) *n.* **1.** *pl.* **-rots′, -rot′** a member of a Malayan people of Luzon, in the Philippines **2.** their Indonesian language

i·gua·na (i gwä′nə) *n.* [Sp. < S. AmInd. *iuana*] a large, harmless, tropical American lizard with a row of spines from neck to tail: it feeds on insects and vegetation

IHP, I.H.P., ihp., i.h.p. indicated horsepower

IHS a monogram for *Jesus* that results from a misreading of his name in Greek

IJs·sel·meer (ī′səl mer′) freshwater lake in N & C Netherlands: formerly part of the Zuider Zee

i·kon (ī′kän) *n. var. of* ICON

il- *see* IN-[1], IN-[2]

IL Illinois

LAND IGUANA
(to 5 ft. long)

-ile (il, əl, 'l; *also, chiefly Brit.* īl) [< Fr. *-il, -ile* < L. *-ilis*] *a suffix meaning* of, having to do with, that can be, like, suitable for [*docile, missile*]: sometimes **-il** [*civil*]

il·e·i·tis (il′ē īt′is) *n.* inflammation of the ileum

il·e·um (il′ē əm) *n., pl.* **il′e·a** (-ə) [ModL. < L., flank, groin (var. of *ilium*)] the lowest part of the small intestine, opening into the large intestine: see illustration at INTESTINE —**il′e·ac′** (-ak′), **il′e·al** (-əl) *adj.*

i·lex (ī′leks) *n.* [L.] *same as:* **1.** HOLLY **2.** HOLM OAK

Il·i·ad (il′ē əd) [< L. < Gr. < *Ilios*, Troy] a long Greek epic poem that Homer is thought to have written: it deals with events near the end of the Trojan War

-il·i·ty (il′ə tē) *pl.* **-ties** *a suffix used to form nouns from adjectives ending in -ILE, -IL* [*imbecility, civility*]

Il·i·um (il′ē əm) *Latin name for* TROY (sense 1)

il·i·um (il′ē əm) *n., pl.* **il′i·a** (-ə) [ModL.: see ILEUM] the flat, uppermost section of the innominate bone —**il′i·ac′** (-ak′) *adj.*

ilk (ilk) *adj.* [Scot. dial. < OE. *ilca*, same] [Obs.] same; like —*n.* kind; sort: only in **of that** (or **his, her,** etc.) **ilk,** of the same sort or class: from a misunderstanding of the orig. Scottish phrase meaning "of the same name"

ill (il) *adj.* **worse, worst** [< ON. *illr*] **1.** *a)* morally bad [*ill* repute] *b)* causing pain, hardship, etc.; adverse [*ill* fortune] *c)* not kind or friendly [*ill* will] *d)* promising trouble; unfavorable [an *ill* omen] **2.** not healthy, normal, or well; sick **3.** not according to rule, custom, etc.; faulty; improper [*ill* breeding] —*n.* anything causing harm, trouble, pain, etc. —*adv.* **worse, worst 1.** in an ill way; specif., *a)* in a bad way; improperly [*ill*-gotten gains] *b)* unkindly; harshly [to speak *ill* of someone] **2.** with difficulty; hardly [he can *ill* afford to refuse] —see SYN. at SICK[1] —**ill at ease** uneasy; uncomfortable

I'll (īl) **1.** I shall **2.** I will

Ill. Illinois

ill. 1. illustrated **2.** illustration

ill·ad·vised (il′əd vīzd′) *adj.* showing or resulting from a lack of sound advice or careful thought; unwise —**ill′-ad·vis′ed·ly** (-vī′zid lē) *adv.*

ill-bred (-bred′) *adj.* badly brought up; rude; impolite

ill·con·sid·ered (-kən sid′ərd) *adj.* not properly considered; not suitable or wise

ill·dis·posed (-dis pōzd′) *adj.* **1.** having a bad disposition; likely to behave in a cruel or unkind way **2.** unfriendly or unfavorable (*toward*)

il·le·gal (i lē′gəl) *adj.* not lawful; against the law or against the rules —**il·le·gal·i·ty** (il′ē gal′ə tē) *n., pl.* **-ties** —**il·le′gal·ly** *adv.*

il·leg·i·ble (i lej′ə b'l) *adj.* difficult or impossible to read because badly written or printed, faded, etc. —**il·leg′i·bil′i·ty** *n.* —**il·leg′i·bly** *adv.*

il·le·git·i·mate (il′ə jit′ə mit) *adj.* **1.** born of parents not married to each other **2.** incorrectly deduced; not logical [an *illegitimate* conclusion] **3.** not lawful [the dictator's *illegitimate* seizure of power] —**il′le·git′i·ma·cy** (-mə sē) *n., pl.* **-cies** —**il′le·git′i·mate·ly** *adv.*

ill-fat·ed (il′fāt′id) *adj.* **1.** having or sure to have an evil fate or unhappy end [the *ill-fated* ship struck a reef] **2.** causing bad luck; unlucky [on that *ill-fated* day when we met]

ill-fa·vored (-fā′vərd) *adj.* **1.** not pleasant to look at; ugly [an *ill-favored* man] **2.** offensive

ill-found·ed (-foun′did) *adj.* not supported by facts or sound reasons

fat, āpe, cär; ten, ēven; is, bīte; gō, hôrn, tōōl, lcok; oil, out; up, fur; get; joy; yet; chin; she; thin, then; zh, leisure; ŋ, ring; ə for *a* in *ago*, *e* in *agent*, *i* in *sanity*, *o* in *comply*, *u* in *focus*; ' as in *able* (ā′b'l); Fr. bal; ë, Fr. coeur; ö, Fr. feu; Fr. mon; ô, Fr. coq; ü, Fr. duc; r, Fr. cri; H, G. ich; kh, G. doch; ‡foreign; ☆ Americanism; < derived from. See inside front cover.

ill·got·ten (-gät′'n) *adj.* gotten in an evil, unlawful, or dishonest way [*ill-gotten* gains]

ill humor a disagreeable, cross, or sullen mood or state of mind —ill′-hu′mored *adj.* —ill′-hu′mored·ly *adv.*

il·lib·er·al (i lib′ər əl) *adj.* **1.** not liberal; intolerant; narrow-minded **2.** not generous; stingy —il·lib′er·al′i·ty (-ə ral′ə tē) *n.* —il·lib′er·al·ly *adv.*

il·lic·it (i lis′it) *adj.* not allowed by law, custom, etc.; unlawful or improper —il·lic′it·ly *adv.* —il·lic′it·ness *n.*

il·lim·it·a·ble (i lim′it ə b'l) *adj.* without limit or bounds —il·lim′it·a·bil′i·ty, il·lim′it·a·ble·ness *n.* —il·lim′it·a·bly *adv.*

Il·li·nois[1] (il′ə noi′; *occas.* -noiz′) *n.* [Fr. < Illinois *ileniwe*, man] **1.** *pl.* **-nois′** a member of a tribe or confederacy of Indians who lived in northern Illinois, southern Wisconsin, and parts of Iowa and Missouri **2.** their Algonquian dialect

Il·li·nois[2] (il′ə noi′; *occas.* -noiz′) [after the Indian tribe: see prec.] Middle Western State of the U.S.: 56,400 sq. mi.; pop. 11,114,000; cap. Springfield: abbrev. **Ill., IL** —**Il′li·nois′an** (-noi′ən, -noiz′ən) *adj., n.*

il·lit·er·a·cy (i lit′ər ə sē) *n.* **1.** the state of being illiterate; esp., an inability to read or write **2.** *pl.* **-cies** a mistake (in writing or speaking) suggesting poor education

il·lit·er·ate (-it) *adj.* **1.** ignorant; uneducated; esp., not knowing how to read or write **2.** having or showing limited knowledge, experience, or culture, esp. in a particular field [musically *illiterate*] **3.** violating accepted usage in language [an *illiterate* sentence] —*n.* an illiterate person; esp., one not knowing how to read or write —see SYN. at IGNORANT —il·lit′er·ate·ly *adv.*

ill-man·nered (il′man′ərd) *adj.* having or showing bad manners; rude; impolite—see SYN. at RUDE

ill nature an unpleasant, disagreeable, or mean disposition —ill′-na′tured *adj.* —ill′-na′tured·ly *adv.*

ill·ness (il′nis) *n.* the condition of being ill, or in poor health; sickness; disease

il·log·i·cal (i läj′i k'l) *adj.* not logical; using or based on faulty reasoning —il·log′i·cal′i·ty (-i kal′ə tē), il·log′i·cal·ness *n.* —il·log′i·cal·ly *adv.*

ill-spent (il′spent′) *adj.* misspent; wasted

ill-starred (-stärd′) *adj.* [< astrological notion of being born or conceived under an evil star] unlucky; doomed

ill-tem·pered (-tem′pərd) *adj.* having or showing a bad temper; quarrelsome; sullen; irritable

ill-timed (-tīmd′) *adj.* coming or done at the wrong time; inopportune [an *ill-timed* remark]

ill-treat (il′trēt′) *vt.* to treat unkindly, cruelly, or unfairly; abuse —ill′-treat′ment *n.*

il·lu·mi·nant (i lōō′mə nənt) *adj.* giving light; illuminating —*n.* something that illuminates, or gives light

il·lu·mi·nate (-nāt′) *vt.* **-nat′ed, -nat′ing** [< L. pp. of *illuminare* < *in-*, in + *luminare*, to light < *lumen*, a light: for IE. base see LIGHT[1]] **1.** *a)* to give light to; light up [candles *illuminated* the room] *b)* to brighten; animate [a face *illuminated* with joy] **2.** *a)* to make clear; explain [an essay that *illuminates* the difficult poem] *b)* to inform; enlighten [trying to *illuminate* voters on the issues] **3.** to decorate with lights **4.** to decorate (an initial letter, a page border, etc.) with designs of gold, bright colors, etc. —il·lu′mi·na′tive *adj.* —il·lu′mi·na′tor *n.*

il·lu·mi·na·tion (i lōō′mə nā′shən) *n.* **1.** an illuminating or being illuminated **2.** the intensity of light per unit of area **3.** the designs used in illuminating manuscripts

il·lu·mine (i lōō′min) *vt.* **-mined, -min·ing** to illuminate; light up —il·lu′mi·na·ble *adj.*

illus., illust. 1. illustrated **2.** illustration

ill-us·age (il′yōō′sij, -zij) *n.* unfair, unkind, or cruel treatment; abuse: also **ill us·age**

ill-use (-yōōz′; *for n.* -yōōs′) *vt.* **-used′, -us′ing** to treat in an unfair, unkind, or cruel way; abuse —*n.* same as ILL-USAGE

il·lu·sion (i lōō′zhən) *n.* [< OFr. < L. < pp. of *illudere*, to mock] **1.** a false idea or mistaken belief [his harsh words destroyed any *illusion* she had about his sweet nature]

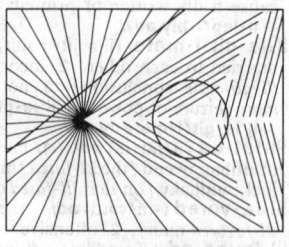

OPTICAL ILLUSION
(heavy line is perfectly straight and circle is perfectly round)

2. an unreal or misleading appearance [a large mirror gives the *illusion* of space in a small room] **3.** *a)* a false impression of what one sees *b)* a misleading image that causes one to have such a false impression [a mirage is an optical *illusion*]: see illustration in preceding column —see SYN. at DELUSION —il·lu′sion·al, il·lu′sion·ar′y *adj.*

il·lu·sion·ist (-ist) *n.* an entertainer who performs sleight-of-hand tricks

il·lu·sive (i lōō′siv) *adj.* illusory; unreal —il·lu′sive·ly *adv.* —il·lu′sive·ness *n.*

il·lu·so·ry (-sər ē) *adj.* causing or caused by illusion; deceptive; unreal —il·lu′so·ri·ly *adv.* —il·lu′so·ri·ness *n.*

il·lus·trate (il′ə strāt′, i lus′trāt) *vt.* **-trat′ed, -trat′ing** [< L. pp. of *illustrare* < *in-*, in + *lustrare*, to illuminate: for IE. base see LIGHT[1]] **1.** to make clear or plain, as by examples or comparisons [the census figures *illustrate* how the nation is growing] **2.** *a)* to provide (books, etc.) with drawings, pictures, etc. that explain or decorate *b)* to explain or decorate: said of pictures, etc. [a diagram *illustrating* the operation of a pump] —*vi.* to illustrate something —il′lus·tra′tor *n.*

il·lus·tra·tion (il′ə strā′shən) *n.* **1.** an illustrating or being illustrated **2.** an explanatory example, story, etc. [he gave many *illustrations* of the way the law works] **3.** an explanatory or decorative picture, diagram, etc. —see SYN. at INSTANCE —il′lus·tra′tion·al *adj.*

il·lus·tra·tive (i lus′trə tiv, il′ə strāt′iv) *adj.* serving as an illustration or example [the speaker used *illustrative* slides in his talk] —il·lus′tra·tive·ly *adv.*

il·lus·tri·ous (i lus′trē əs) *adj.* [< L. *illustris*, bright] very distinguished; famous; outstanding [an *illustrious* scientist] —see SYN. at FAMOUS —il·lus′tri·ous·ly *adv.* —il·lus′tri·ous·ness *n.*

ill will unfriendly feeling; hostility; hate —see SYN. at MALICE

il·ly (il′lē) *adv.* [Now Dial.] badly; ill

Il·lyr·i·a (i lir′ē ə) ancient region along the E coast of the Adriatic: see map at GREECE —**Il·lyr′i·an** *adj., n.*

ILS instrument landing system

I'm (īm) I am

im- see IN-[1], IN-[2]

im·age (im′ij) *n.* [OFr. < L. < *imago* < base of *imitari*, to imitate] **1.** a representation of a person or thing, drawn, painted, etc.; esp., a statue **2.** the visual impression of something produced by a mirror, lens, etc. **3.** a person or thing much like another; copy [she is the *image* of her mother] **4.** *a)* a mental picture of something; idea; impression ☆*b)* the public conception of a person, product, etc., often created by publicity **5.** a typical example; symbol [he is the *image* of laziness] **6.** a figure of speech; a metaphor or simile [Homer often uses the *image* of "rosy-fingered dawn"] —*vt.* **-aged, -ag·ing 1.** to portray; delineate **2.** to reflect; mirror **3.** to picture in the mind **4.** to be a symbol of **5.** to describe vividly

im·age·ry (im′ij rē, -ər ē) *n., pl.* **-ries 1.** mental images, as produced by memory or imagination **2.** descriptions and figures of speech [the *imagery* in a poem]

i·mag·i·na·ble (i maj′ə nə b'l) *adj.* that can be imagined [the worst crime *imaginable*] —i·mag′i·na·bly *adv.*

i·mag·i·nar·y (i maj′ə ner′ē) *adj.* existing only in the imagination; unreal —i·mag′i·nar′i·ly *adv.* —i·mag′i·nar′i·ness *n.* SYN.—**imaginary** is applied to that which exists in the imagination only and which is, therefore, unreal [unicorns and other *imaginary* beasts]; **fanciful** refers to that which has been pictured in the fancy and usually suggests playfulness and an odd kind of humor [Lewis Carroll's *fanciful* tales]; **visionary** refers to something unreal that is seen or thought of as in a vision and usually suggests that the thing is impractical or impossible [the airplane was once a *visionary* dream]; **fantastic** applies to something which seems so strange and unreal as to be beyond belief [the *fantastic* strides made in exploring outer space] —ANT. real, actual

imaginary number 1. an even root of a negative quantity **2.** a complex number in the form $a + bi$, where b is not zero: when a is zero, it is a **pure imaginary number**

i·mag·i·na·tion (i maj′ə nā′shən) *n.* **1.** *a)* the act or power of forming mental images of what is not actually present *b)* the act or power of creating mental images of what has never been actually experienced, or of creating new images or ideas by combining previous experiences **2.** anything imagined **3.** the ability to understand and appreciate the imaginative creations of others, esp. works of art and literature **4.** the ability to deal with new or unusual experiences; resourcefulness

i·mag·i·na·tive (i maj′ə nə tiv, -nāt′iv) *adj.* **1.** having, using, or showing imagination **2.** given to imagining **3.** of or resulting from imagination [*imaginative* literature] —i·mag′i·na·tive·ly *adv.* —i·mag′i·na·tive·ness *n.*

i·mag·ine (i maj′in) *vt., vi.* **-ined, -in·ing** [< OFr. < L. *imaginari* < *imago*, an IMAGE] **1.** to make a mental image (of); form an idea (of) [*imagine* that you are on Mars] **2.** to suppose; guess; think [I *imagine* he'll be there] —*interj.* an exclamation of surprise

im·ag·ism (im′ə jiz′m) *n.* a movement in poetry (c. 1909–1917) which stressed the use of brief, clear, exact images and free verse —**im′ag·ist** *n., adj.* —**im′ag·is′tic** *adj.*

i·ma·go (i mā′gō) *n., pl.* **-goes, -gos, i·mag·i·nes** (i maj′ə nēz′) [ModL. < L., an IMAGE] an insect in its final, adult, reproductive stage, generally having wings

i·mam (i mäm′) *n.* [Ar. *imām*] **1.** the prayer leader in a Moslem mosque **2.** [*often* I-] title for a Moslem ruler

im·bal·ance (im bal′əns) *n.* lack of balance, as in proportion, force, functioning, etc.

im·be·cile (im′bə s′l) *n.* [< Fr. < L. *imbecilis*, feeble] **1.** a person having moderate mental retardation: term now rarely used: see MENTAL RETARDATION **2.** a very foolish or stupid person —*adj.* very foolish or stupid: also **im′be·cil′ic** (-sil′ik)

im·be·cil·i·ty (im′bə sil′ə tē) *n., pl.* **-ties 1.** the state of being an imbecile **2.** great foolishness or stupidity **3.** a foolish or stupid act or remark

im·bed (im bed′) *vt. same as* EMBED

im·bibe (im bīb′) *vt.* **-bibed′, -bib′ing** [< L. *imbibere* < *in-*, in + *bibere*, to drink < IE. base *poi-*, to drink] **1.** *a*) to drink (esp. alcoholic liquor) *b*) to take in with the senses or mind; drink in **2.** to absorb (moisture) —*vi.* to drink, esp. alcoholic liquor —**im·bib′er** *n.*

im·bri·cate (im′brə kit; *also, and for v. always,* -kāt′) *adj.* [< LL. pp. of *imbricare*, to cover with tiles < L. *imbrex*, gutter tile < *imber*, rain] **1.** overlapping evenly, as tiles or fish scales **2.** ornamented as with overlapping scales —*vt., vi.* **-cat·ed, -cat·ing** to make or be imbricate —**im′bri·cate·ly** *adv.* —**im′bri·ca′tion** *n.*

im·bro·glio (im brōl′yō) *n., pl.* **-glios** [It. < *imbrogliare*, to embroil] **1.** a complicated and confusing situation **2.** a confused misunderstanding or disagreement [a hopeless *imbroglio* over national boundaries]

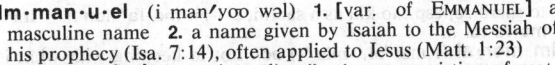

IMBRICATIONS

im·brue (im brōō′) *vt.* **-brued′, -bru′ing** [< OFr., ult. < L. *imbibere*: see IMBIBE] to wet, soak, or stain, esp. with blood —**im·brue′ment** *n.*

im·bue (im byōō′) *vt.* **-bued′, -bu′ing** [< L. *imbuere*] **1.** [Rare] to saturate **2.** to fill with color; dye **3.** to fill or inspire (*with* principles, ideas, emotions, etc.) [*imbued* with a feeling of patriotism]

imit. 1. imitation **2.** imitative

im·i·tate (im′ə tāt′) *vt.* **-tat·ed, -tat·ing** [< L. pp. of *imitari*, to imitate] **1.** to follow the example of; take as one's model [children learn by *imitating* adults] **2.** to act the same as; mimic [the comedian *imitated* famous movie stars] **3.** to make a copy of **4.** to look like; resemble [glass cut to *imitate* diamonds] —**im′i·ta·ble** (-tə b′l) *adj.* —**im′i·ta·tor** *n.*

im·i·ta·tion (im′ə tā′shən) *n.* **1.** an imitating **2.** the result or product of imitating; copy or likeness —*adj.* made to resemble something that is usually superior or genuine; not real [*imitation* leather]

im·i·ta·tive (im′ə tāt′iv) *adj.* **1.** formed from a model [the *imitative* sounds of a parrot] **2.** given to imitating **3.** not genuine **4.** sounding like the thing signified: said of such words as *hiss, ripple, clang* —**im′i·ta′tive·ly** *adv.* —**im′i·ta′tive·ness** *n.*

im·mac·u·late (i mak′yə lit) *adj.* [< L. < *in-*, not + pp. of *maculare*, to soil < *macula*, a spot] **1.** perfectly clean; spotless **2.** perfectly correct; without a flaw or error **3.** pure; innocent; without sin —**im·mac′u·late·ly** *adv.* —**im·mac′u·late·ness, im·mac′u·la·cy** (-lə sē) *n.*

Immaculate Conception *R.C.Ch.* the doctrine that the Virgin Mary was from the moment of conception free from original sin

im·ma·nent (im′ə nənt) *adj.* [< LL. prp. of *immanere* < *in-*, in + *manere*, to remain] **1.** living, remaining, or operating within; inherent **2.** present throughout the universe: said of God — **im′ma·nence, im′ma·nen·cy** *n.* —**im′ma·nent·ly** *adv.*

Im·man·u·el (i man′yoo wəl) *n.* **1.** [var. of EMMANUEL] a masculine name **2.** a name given by Isaiah to the Messiah of his prophecy (Isa. 7:14), often applied to Jesus (Matt. 1:23)

im·ma·te·ri·al (im′ə tir′ē əl) *adj.* **1.** not consisting of matter; spiritual **2.** that does not matter; of little or no importance [cost is *immaterial* to him] —**im′ma·te′ri·al′i·ty** (-al′ə tē) *n., pl.* **-ties** —**im′ma·te′ri·al·ly** *adv.*

im·ma·ture (im′ə toor′, -choor′, -tyoor′) *adj.* **1.** not mature or ripe; not completely grown or developed **2.** not finished; incomplete [plans are still *immature*] —**im′ma·ture′ly** *adv.* —**im′ma·tu′ri·ty, im′ma·ture′ness** *n.*

im·meas·ur·a·ble (i mezh′ər ə b′l) *adj.* too large or too much to be measured; boundless; vast [the *immeasurable* space of the universe] —**im·meas′ur·a·bil′i·ty, im·meas′ur·a·ble·ness** *n.* —**im·meas′ur·a·bly** *adv.*

im·me·di·a·cy (i mē′dē ə sē) *n.* the quality or condition of being immediate

im·me·di·ate (i mē′dē it) *adj.* [< LL.: see IN-² & MEDIATE] having nothing coming between; specif., *a*) not separated in space; in direct contact; closest; also, close by [our *immediate* neighbors] *b*) not separated in time; without delay; instant [the medicine had an *immediate* effect] *c*) of the present *d*) next in order, succession, etc.; also, directly or closely related [one's *immediate* family] *e*) acting in a direct way; direct [an *immediate* cause]

im·me·di·ate·ly (-lē) *adv.* in an immediate manner; specif., *a*) with nothing coming between; directly [*immediately* adjacent] *b*) without delay; at once [go home *immediately*] — *conj.* [Chiefly Brit.] as soon as [go *immediately* he comes]

im·me·mo·ri·al (im′ə môr′ē əl) *adj.* back beyond memory or record [customs handed down from time *immemorial*] —**im′me·mo′ri·al·ly** *adv.*

im·mense (i mens′) *adj.* [Fr. < L. < *in-*, not + pp. of *metiri*, to measure] **1.** very large; vast; huge **2.** [Slang] very good; excellent —see SYN. at ENORMOUS —**im·mense′ly** *adv.* —**im·mense′ness** *n.*

im·men·si·ty (i men′sə tē) *n., pl.* **-ties 1.** great size or extent; vastness **2.** infinite space or being

im·merge (i murj′) *vi.* **-merged′, -merg′ing** [see IMMERSE] to plunge, as into a liquid

im·merse (i murs′) *vt.* **-mersed′, -mers′ing** [< L. pp. of *immergere*, to plunge: see IN-¹ & MERGE] **1.** to plunge or dip into or as if into a liquid **2.** to baptize by dipping under water **3.** to absorb deeply; engross [*immersed* in study] —**im·mers′i·ble** *adj.* —**im·mer′sion** (i mur′shən, -zhən) *n.*

immersion heater an electric coil or rod that heats water while directly immersed in it

☆ **im·mi·grant** (im′ə grənt) *n.* one that immigrates —*adj.* immigrating

im·mi·grate (im′ə grāt′) *vi.* **-grat·ed, -grat·ing** [< L. pp. of *immigrare*: see IN-¹ & MIGRATE] to come into a new country or region, esp. in order to settle there [*immigrating* to the U.S. from Europe]: opposed to EMIGRATE —**im′mi·gra′tion** *n.*

im·mi·nence (im′ə nəns) *n.* a being imminent [the *imminence* of danger]: also **im′mi·nen·cy**

im·mi·nent (-nənt) *adj.* [< L. prp. of *imminere* < *in-*, in + *minere*, to project: for IE. base see MOUNT¹] likely to happen soon; about to take place; threatening [war seemed to be *imminent*] —**im′mi·nent·ly** *adv.*

im·mis·ci·ble (i mis′ə b′l) *adj.* [< IN-² + MISCIBLE] that cannot be mixed, as oil and water —**im·mis′ci·bil′i·ty** *n.*

im·mo·bile (i mō′b′l, -bēl, -bīl) *adj.* not movable or moving; stable; motionless —**im′mo·bil′i·ty** *n.*

im·mo·bi·lize (i mō′bə līz′) *vt.* **-lized′, -liz′ing 1.** to make immobile **2.** to prevent the movement of (a limb or joint) with splints or a cast —**im·mo′bi·li·za′tion** *n.*

im·mod·er·ate (i mäd′ər it) *adj.* not moderate; not kept under control; excessive [an *immoderate* appetite] —see SYN. at EXCESSIVE —**im·mod′er·ate·ly** *adv.* —**im·mod′er·a′tion, im·mod′er·ate·ness, im·mod′er·a·cy** (-ə sē) *n.*

im·mod·est (i mäd′ist) *adj.* not modest; specif., *a*) indecent; improper [*immodest* dress] *b*) not shy or humble; bold; forward [an *immodest* boast] —**im·mod′est·ly** *adv.* —**im·mod′es·ty** *n.*

im·mo·late (im′ə lāt′) *vt.* **-lat·ed, -lat·ing** [< L. pp. of *immolare*, to sprinkle with sacrificial meal < *in-*, on + *mola*, meal] to sacrifice; esp., to kill as a sacrifice —**im′mo·la′tion** n. —**im′·mo·la′tor** n.

im·mor·al (i môr′əl, -mär′-) adj. not in keeping with what is generally thought of as moral or right; not good, decent, chaste, etc. —**im·mor′al·ly** adv.

im·mo·ral·i·ty (im′ə ral′ə tē, im′ô-) n. 1. the state or quality of being immoral 2. immoral behavior 3. pl. **-ties** an immoral act or practice

im·mor·tal (i môr′t'l) adj. 1. not mortal; living or lasting forever [the immortal gods] 2. of immortal beings or immortality 3. lasting a long time; enduring [immortal fame] 4. having lasting fame [an immortal poet] —n. an immortal being; specif., a) [pl.] the ancient Greek or Roman gods b) a person of lasting fame —**im′mor·tal·i·ty** (-tal′ə tē) n. —**im·mor′tal·ly** adv.

im·mor·tal·ize (i môr′tə līz′) vt. **-ized′, -iz′ing** to make immortal; esp., to give lasting fame to [Whistler immortalized his mother in a painting] —**im·mor′tal·i·za′tion** n. —**im·mor′tal·iz′er** n.

im·mor·telle (im′ôr tel′) n. [Fr. fem. of immortel, undying] same as EVERLASTING (n. 2)

im·mov·a·ble (i mōō′və b'l) adj. 1. that cannot be moved; firmly fixed 2. motionless; stationary 3. not changing; steadfast [an immovable purpose] 4. not easily moved emotionally; unemotional —n. [pl.] Law immovable objects or property, as land, buildings, etc. —**im·mov′a·bil′i·ty, im·mov′a·ble·ness** n. —**im·mov′a·bly** adv.

im·mune (i myōōn′) adj. [< L. immunis, exempt < in-, without + munia, duties: for IE. base see MIGRATE] having immunity; specif., a) exempt from or protected against something disagreeable or harmful [immune from punishment] b) not susceptible to a specified disease because of the presence of specific antibodies [immune to smallpox]

immune body same as ANTIBODY

im·mu·ni·ty (i myōōn′ə tē) n., pl. **-ties** 1. exemption or freedom from something burdensome or otherwise unpleasant [immunity from taxation] 2. resistance to or protection against a specified disease

im·mu·nize (im′yə nīz′) vt. **-nized′, -niz′ing** to make immune, as by inoculation —**im′mu·ni·za′tion** n.

im·mu·no·gen·ic (im′yoo nō jen′ik) adj. producing immunity —**im′mu·no·gen′i·cal·ly** adv.

☆**im·mu·nol·o·gy** (im′yoo näl′ə jē) n. the branch of medicine dealing with immunity to disease or with allergic reactions, etc. —**im′mu·no·log′i·cal** (-nə läj′i k'l), **im′mu·no·log′ic** adj. —**im′mu·no·log′i·cal·ly** adv. —**im′mu·nol′o·gist** n.

im·mure (i myoor′) vt. **-mured′, -mur′ing** [< OFr. < ML. immurare < L. im-, in + murus, a wall] to shut up as within walls; confine —**im·mure′ment** n.

im·mu·ta·ble (i myōōt′ə b'l) adj. never changing or varying; unchangeable [certain immutable laws of nature] —**im·mu′ta·bil′i·ty, im·mu′ta·ble·ness** n. —**im·mu′ta·bly** adv.

imp (imp) n. [< OE., ult. < Gr. emphyta, scion < em-, in + phyton, a plant] 1. a child of a devil; young demon 2. a mischievous child

imp. 1. imperative 2. imperfect 3. imperial 4. impersonal 5. import 6. importer 7. imprimatur

im·pact (im pakt′; for n. im′pakt) vt. [< L. pp. of impingere, to press firmly together: see IMPINGE] to force tightly together; wedge —n. 1. a striking together; collision 2. the force of a collision; shock 3. the power of an event, idea, etc. to produce changes, move feelings, etc. [the impact of Freud's theories on 20th-century thought] —**im·pac′tion** n.

im·pact·ed (im pak′tid) adj. 1. firmly lodged in the jaw: said of a tooth unable to erupt because of its abnormal position ☆2. densely populated; overcrowded [an impacted area]

im·pair (im per′) vt. [< OFr., ult. < L. in-, intens. + pejor, worse] to make worse, less, weaker, etc.; damage; reduce [disease impaired his hearing] —see SYN. at INJURE —**im·pair′ment** n.

im·pa·la (im pä′lə, -pal′ə) n., pl. **-la, -las**: see PLURAL, II, D, 2 [Zulu] a medium-sized, reddish antelope of central and southern Africa

im·pale (im pāl′) vt. **-paled′, -pal′ing** [< Fr. < ML. impalare < L. in-, on + palus, a pole] 1. to pierce through with something pointed [to impale a dead moth on a pin] 2. to torture by fixing on a stake 3. to make helpless, as if fixed on a stake [impaled by her glance] —**im·pale′ment** n.

IMPACTED
TOOTH

im·pal·pa·ble (im pal′pə b'l) adj. 1. that cannot be felt by touching [an impalpable shadow] 2. not plain and clear to the mind [an impalpable change] —**im·pal′pa·bil′i·ty** n. —**im·pal′pa·bly** adv.

im·pan·el (im pan′'l) vt. **-eled or -elled, -el·ing or -el·ling** 1. to enter the name or names of on a jury list 2. to choose (a jury) from such a list —**im·pan′el·ment** n.

im·part (im pärt′) vt. [< OFr. < L. impartire: see IN-¹ & PART] 1. to give a share or portion of; give [the onion imparted its smell to the soup] 2. to tell; reveal [to impart news] —**im·part′a·ble** adj. —**im·part′er** n.

im·par·tial (im pär′shəl) adj. not favoring one side or party more than another; fair —see SYN. at FAIR¹ —**im·par′ti·al′i·ty** (-shē al′ə tē) n. —**im·par′tial·ly** adv.

im·pass·a·ble (im pas′ə b'l) adj. that cannot be passed, crossed, or traveled over [ice made the roads impassable] —**im·pass′a·bil′i·ty** n. —**im·pass′a·bly** adv.

im·passe (im′pas, im pas′) n. [Fr.] 1. a passage open only at one end; blind alley 2. a difficulty that cannot be solved or an argument where no agreement is possible; deadlock

im·pas·si·ble (im pas′ə b'l) adj. [< OFr. < LL. < L. im-, not + passibilis < pati, to suffer] 1. that cannot feel pain 2. that cannot be injured 3. that cannot be moved emotionally —**im·pas′si·bil′i·ty** n. —**im·pas′si·bly** adv.

im·pas·sioned (im pash′ənd) adj. filled with passion; having or showing strong feeling; passionate; fiery; ardent —see SYN. at PASSIONATE —**im·pas′sioned·ly** adv.

im·pas·sive (im pas′iv) adj. 1. not feeling pain; insensible 2. not feeling or showing emotion; placid; calm —**im·pas′sive·ly** adv. —**im·pas·siv′i·ty** (im′pə siv′ə tē) n.

SYN.—impassive means not having or showing any feeling or emotion, but it does not necessarily suggest that one cannot be moved emotionally [John's impassive face hid his anger]; **apathetic** suggests a bored or listless lack of interest or involvement [an apathetic voting public]; **stoic** implies a firm control over one's emotions and specifically suggests the ability to endure suffering without flinching [he received the bad news with stoic calm]; **stolid** suggests dullness or stupidity in one who is not easily moved or excited; **phlegmatic** is applied to one who is rather dull and sluggish by nature and thus not easily stirred up emotionally

im·pas·to (im päs′tō) n. [< It. impastare, to paste over] painting in which the paint is laid thickly on the canvas

im·pa·tience (im pā′shəns) n. lack of patience; specif., a) annoyance because of delay, opposition, etc. b) restless eagerness to do something, go somewhere, etc.

im·pa·ti·ens (im pā′shē enz′, -shənz) n. [ModL. < L., IMPATIENT] a plant with slender, tubelike flowers and pods that burst and scatter their seeds when ripe

im·pa·tient (im pā′shənt) adj. [< OFr. < L.: see IN-² & TIENT] feeling or showing impatience —**im·pa′tient·ly** adv.

im·peach (im pēch′) vt. [< OFr. < LL. impedicare, to entangle < L. in-, in + pedica, a fetter < pes, FOOT] 1. to raise questions or doubts about (a person's honor, etc.) 2. to challenge the practices or honesty of; esp., to bring (a public official) before the proper tribunal on a charge of wrongdoing —**im·peach′a·bil′i·ty** n. —**im·peach′a·ble** adj. —**im·peach′ment** n.

im·pec·ca·ble (im pek′ə b'l) adj. [< L. < in-, not + peccare, to sin] 1. incapable of sin or wrongdoing 2. without defect or error; flawless; perfect [impeccable manners] —**im·pec′ca·bil′i·ty** n. —**im·pec′ca·bly** adv.

im·pe·cu·ni·ous (im′pi kyōō′nē əs) adj. [< IN-² + obs. pecunious, wealthy < OFr. < L. < pecunia, money] having no money; penniless —see SYN. at POOR —**im′pe·cu′ni·os′i·ty** (-äs′ə tē), **im′pe·cu′ni·ous·ness** n. —**im′pe·cu′ni·ous·ly** adv.

im·ped·ance (im pēd′'ns) n. [IMPED(E) + -ANCE] the total opposition offered by an electric circuit to the flow of an alternating current of a single frequency: it is a combination of resistance and reactance and is measured in ohms

im·pede (im pēd′) vt. **-ped′ed, -ped′ing** [< L. impedire < in-, in + pes (gen. pedis), FOOT] to bar or hinder the progress of; obstruct or delay [the accident impeded traffic] —see SYN. at HINDER¹ —**im·ped′er** n.

im·ped·i·ment (im ped′ə mənt) n. [< L. impedimentum, hindrance] anything that impedes; specif., a speech defect; lisp, stammer, etc.

im·ped·i·men·ta (im ped′ə men′tə) n.pl. [L., pl.: see prec.] things hindering progress, as on a trip; esp., baggage, supplies, etc.

im·pel (im pel′) vt. **-pelled′, -pel′ling** [L. impellere < in-, on + pellere, to drive: for IE. base see FELT¹] 1. to push, drive, or move forward; propel 2. to force, compel, or urge [what impels him to lie?] —**im·pel′lent** adj., n. —**im·pel′ler** n.

im·pend (im pend´) *vi.* [L. *impendere* < *in-*, in + *pendere*, to hang] to be about to happen; threaten [an *impending* storm]

im·pen·e·tra·ble (im pen´i trə b'l) *adj.* 1. that cannot be penetrated or passed through [an *impenetrable* jungle] 2. that cannot be solved or understood; unfathomable [the *impenetrable* mystery of death] 3. not open to ideas, influences, etc. [an *impenetrable* mind] —**im·pen·e·tra·bil·i·ty** *n.* —**im·pen·e·tra·bly** *adv.*

im·pen·i·tent (im pen´ə tənt) *adj.* not feeling shame, regret, or remorse; not sorry for what one has done —*n.* an impenitent person —**im·pen´i·tence, im·pen´i·ten·cy** *n.* —**im·pen´i·tent·ly** *adv.*

imper. imperative

im·per·a·tive (im per´ə tiv) *adj.* [< LL. < pp. of L. *imperare*, to order] 1. of or indicating power or authority; commanding [an *imperative* gesture] 2. absolutely necessary; urgent [quick action is *imperative*] 3. *Gram.* designating or of the mood of a verb that expresses a command or strong request —*n.* 1. a rule that must be obeyed, duty that must be done, etc. 2. a command 3. *Gram. a)* the imperative mood *b)* a verb in this mood —**im·per´a·tive·ly** *adv.* —**im·per´a·tive·ness** *n.*

im·per·a·tor (im´pə rāt´ər, -rät´-; -ôr) *n.* [L. < pp. of *imperare*, to command] in ancient Rome, a title of honor for generals and, later, emperors —**im·per·a·to·ri·al** (im pir´ə tôr´ē əl) *adj.*

im·per·cep·ti·ble (im´pər sep´tə b'l) *adj.* so small or slight that it is not easily noticed [an *imperceptible* scar] —**im´per·cep·ti·bil·i·ty** *n.* —**im´per·cep´ti·bly** *adv.*

im·per·cep·tive (-tiv) *adj.* not quick and alert in perceiving or noticing things: also **im´per·cip´i·ent** (-sip´ē ənt) —**im´per·cep´tive·ness** *n.*

imperf. 1. imperfect 2. imperforate

im·per·fect (im pur´fikt) *adj.* 1. not finished or complete; lacking in something [an *imperfect* knowledge of French] 2. not perfect; having a defect or error 3. *Gram.* in certain languages with many inflected forms, designating or of a verb tense indicating an incomplete or continuous past action or state: in English, "was writing" is a form like the imperfect tense —*n. Gram.* 1. the imperfect tense 2. a verb in this tense —**im·per´fect·ly** *adv.* —**im·per´fect·ness** *n.*

imperfect flower a diclinous flower

imperfect fungus any of a large group of fungi for which no sexual stage of reproduction is known

im·per·fec·tion (im´pər fek´shən) *n.* 1. a being imperfect 2. a shortcoming; defect —see SYN. at DEFECT

im·per·fo·rate (im pur´fər it, -fə rāt´) *adj.* 1. having no holes or openings 2. having a straight edge without perforations: said of a postage stamp Also **im·per´fo·rat´ed** —*n.* an imperforate stamp —**im·per´fo·ra´tion** *n.*

im·pe·ri·al (im pir´ē əl) *adj.* [< OFr. < L. < *imperium*, empire] 1. of an empire 2. of a country having control over other countries or colonies 3. of, or having the rank of, an emperor or empress 4. having supreme authority 5. majestic; imposing 6. of great size or superior quality 7. *a)* of the British Commonwealth *b)* of a system of weights and measures fixed by British law [the *imperial* gallon is equal to about 1⅕ U.S. gallons] —*n.* 1. a size of writing paper (23 × 31 in.) ☆2. a pointed tuft of beard on the lower lip and chin —**im·pe´ri·al·ly** *adv.*

IMPERIAL
(beard)

im·pe·ri·al·ism (-iz'm) *n.* 1. imperial state, authority, or government 2. the policy and practice of forming and maintaining an empire by conquest, colonization, economic or political domination, etc. —**im·pe´ri·al·ist** *n., adj.* —**im·pe´ri·al·is´tic** *adj.* —**im·pe´ri·al·is´ti·cal·ly** *adv.*

Imperial Valley irrigated agricultural region in S Calif. & NW Mexico, reclaimed from the desert

im·per·il (im per´əl) *vt.* -**iled** or -**illed**, -**il·ing** or -**il·ling** to put in peril; endanger [their lives were *imperiled* by the fire] —**im·per´il·ment** *n.*

im·pe·ri·ous (im pir´ē əs) *adj.* [< L. < *imperium*, empire] 1. arrogant; domineering [he ordered us away in an *imperious* voice] 2. urgent; necessary; imperative [an *imperious* duty] —see SYN. at MASTERFUL —**im·pe´ri·ous·ly** *adv.* —**im·pe´ri·ous·ness** *n.*

im·per·ish·a·ble (im per´ish ə b'l) *adj.* that will not die or decay; indestructible [an *imperishable* ideal] —**im·per´ish·a·bil´i·ty** *n.* —**im·per´ish·a·bly** *adv.*

im·pe·ri·um (im pir´ē əm) *n.* [L.: see EMPIRE] supreme power; absolute authority

im·per·ma·nent (im pur´mə nənt) *adj.* not permanent; not lasting; temporary —**im·per´ma·nence, im·per´ma·nen·cy** *n.* —**im·per´ma·nent·ly** *adv.*

im·per·me·a·ble (im pur´mē ə b'l) *adj.* not permeable; not permitting fluids to pass through it; impenetrable —**im·per´me·a·bil´i·ty** *n.* —**im·per´me·a·bly** *adv.*

im·per·son·al (im pur´s'n əl) *adj.* 1. not personal; specif., *a)* without reference to any particular person [an *impersonal* comment] *b)* not existing as a person [an *impersonal* force] *c)* revealing nothing about one's nature, feelings, etc. [his cool, *impersonal* manner] 2. *Gram. a)* designating or of a verb occurring only in the third person singular, usually with *it* as the subject (Example: "it is snowing") *b)* indefinite: said of a pronoun —*n.* an impersonal verb or pronoun —**im·per´son·al´i·ty** (-al´ə tē) *n.* —**im·per´son·al·ly** *adv.*

im·per·son·al·ize (-ə līz´) *vt.* -**ized´**, -**iz´ing** to make impersonal

im·per·son·ate (im pur´sə nāt´) *vt.* -**at·ed**, -**at´ing** to act the part of; specif., *a)* to mimic (a person) for purposes of entertainment *b)* to pretend to be (an officer, etc.) with the purpose of cheating or deceiving others —**im·per´son·a´tion** *n.* —**im·per´son·a´tor** *n.*

im·per·ti·nence (im pur´t'n əns) *n.* 1. the quality or fact of being impertinent 2. an impertinent act, remark, etc. Also **im·per´ti·nen·cy**, *pl.* -**cies**

im·per·ti·nent (-ənt) *adj.* 1. not pertinent; having no connection with a given matter; irrelevant 2. not showing proper respect; insolent —**im·per´ti·nent·ly** *adv.*

SYN.—**impertinent** is used of speech or behavior that shows a lack of respect by not following the usual rules of politeness and good manners; **impudent** suggests bold, open, deliberate rudeness or impertinence; **insolent** implies extreme disrespect shown in speech or behavior that is deliberately insulting or filled with contempt; **saucy** suggests a light, flippant manner and improper informality in dealing with someone to whom respect should be shown

im·per·turb·a·ble (im´pər tur´bə b'l) *adj.* not easily perturbed or excited; impassive; calm —**im´per·turb·a·bil´i·ty** *n.* —**im´per·turb´a·bly** *adv.*

im·per·vi·ous (im pur´vē əs) *adj.* 1. not allowing something to pass through or penetrate [a fabric *impervious* to moisture] 2. not affected by (with *to*) [*impervious* to criticism] —**im·per´vi·ous·ly** *adv.* —**im·per´vi·ous·ness** *n.*

im·pe·ti·go (im´pə tī´gō) *n.* [L. < *impetere*: see IMPETUS] a contagious skin disease characterized by many small swellings that look like pimples and are filled with a yellowish liquid

im·pet·u·os·i·ty (im pech´oo wäs´ə tē, im´pech-) *n.* 1. the quality of being impetuous 2. *pl.* -**ties** an impetuous action or feeling

im·pet·u·ous (im pech´oo wəs) *adj.* [< OFr. < LL. < L. *impetus*: see IMPETUS] 1. moving with great force or violence; rushing 2. acting or done suddenly with little thought; rash; impulsive —**im·pet´u·ous·ly** *adv.* —**im·pet´u·ous·ness** *n.*

im·pe·tus (im´pə təs) *n., pl.* -**tus·es** [L. < *impetere*, to attack < *in-*, in + *petere*, to rush at: for IE. base see FEATHER] 1. the force with which a body moves, resulting from its mass and velocity; momentum 2. a stimulus to action; incentive [new loans gave fresh *impetus* to the building program]

im·pi·e·ty (im pī´ə tē) *n.* 1. lack of piety, esp. toward God 2. *pl.* -**ties** an impious act or remark

im·pinge (im pinj´) *vi.* -**pinged´**, -**ping´ing** [L. *impingere* < *in-*, in + *pangere*, to strike: for IE. base see PEACE] 1. *a)* to strike or hit (*on*, *upon*, or *against* something) [the sound of trumpets *impinged* on their eardrums] *b)* to touch (*on* or *upon*); have an effect [an idea that *impinges* on one's mind] 2. to make inroads or encroach (*on* or *upon* the property or rights of another) [censorship *impinges* on our freedoms] —**im·pinge´ment** *n.* —**im·ping´er** *n.*

im·pi·ous (im´pē əs) *adj.* not pious; specif., lacking reverence for God —**im´pi·ous·ly** *adv.* —**im´pi·ous·ness** *n.*

imp·ish (im′pish) *adj.* of or like an imp; mischievous —**imp′ish·ly** *adv.* —**imp′ish·ness** *n.*

im·plac·a·ble (im plak′ə b'l, -plā′kə-) *adj.* not placable; that cannot be made calm or peaceful; relentless [*implacable* enemies] —**im·plac′a·bil′i·ty** *n.* —**im·plac′a·bly** *adv.*

im·plant (im plant′; *for n.* im′plant) *vt.* **1.** to plant firmly; embed **2.** to fix firmly in the mind; instill [*respect for the law was implanted in them*] **3.** *Med.* to insert (an organ, piece of living tissue, etc.) within the body —*n. Med.* an implanted organ, etc. —**im′plan·ta′tion** (-plan tā′shən) *n.*

im·plau·si·ble (im plô′zə b'l) *adj.* not plausible; not seeming to be true; unlikely —**im·plau′si·bil′i·ty** *n., pl.* **-ties** —**im·plau′si·bly** *adv.*

im·ple·ment (im′plə mənt; *for v.* -ment′) *n.* [< LL. *implementum*, a filling up < L. *implere* < *in-*, in + *plere*, to fill: for IE. base see FULL[1]] **1.** any tool, instrument, utensil, etc. used or needed in a given activity **2.** any person or thing used as a means to some end —*vt.* **1.** to carry out; put into effect [to *implement* a plan] **2.** to provide with implements —**im′ple·men′tal** *adj.* —**im′ple·men·ta′tion** (-mən tā′shən) *n.*

im·pli·cate (im′plə kāt′) *vt.* **-cat′ed, -cat′ing** [< L. pp. of *implicare*: see IMPLY] **1.** to show to have a connection with a crime, fault, etc.; involve [*his reply implicated Jones in the crime*] **2.** [Rare] to imply —**im′pli·ca′tive** *adj.* —**im′pli·ca′tive·ly** *adv.*

im·pli·ca·tion (im′plə kā′shən) *n.* **1.** an implicating or being implicated **2.** an implying, or suggesting **3.** something implied [do you understand all the *implications* of his offer?]

im·plic·it (im plis′it) *adj.* [< L. pp. of *implicare*: see IMPLY] **1.** suggested or to be understood though not plainly expressed; implied [he gave *implicit* approval by his silence]: distinguished from EXPLICIT **2.** without reservation or doubt; unquestioning; absolute [to have *implicit* faith in another] —**im·plic′it·ly** *adv.* —**im·plic′it·ness** *n.*

im·plied (im plīd′) *adj.* involved, suggested, or understood without being directly expressed

im·plode (im plōd′) *vt., vi.* **-plod′ed, -plod′ing** [< IN-[1] + (EX)-PLODE] to burst inward —**im·plo′sion** (-plō′zhən) *n.*

im·plore (im plôr′) *vt.* **-plored′, -plor′ing** [< L. *implorare* < *in-*, intens. + *plorare*, to cry out] **1.** to ask for with much feeling; beseech [he *implored* my help] **2.** to beg (a person) to do something —see SYN. at BEG —**im·plor′ing·ly** *adv.*

im·ply (im plī′) *vt.* **-plied′, -ply′ing** [< OFr. < L. *implicare*, to involve < *in-*, in + *plicare*, to fold: for IE. base see FOLD[1]] **1.** to have as a necessary part, condition, or effect [war *implies* killing] **2.** to indicate indirectly; hint; suggest [his frown *implied* disapproval] —see SYN. at SUGGEST

im·po·lite (im′pə līt′) *adj.* not polite; discourteous —see SYN. at RUDE —**im′po·lite′ly** *adv.* —**im′po·lite′ness** *n.*

im·pol·i·tic (im päl′ə tik) *adj.* not politic; not wise or careful; showing poor judgment [it was *impolitic* of him to insult his superior] —**im·pol′i·tic·ly** *adv.*

im·pon·der·a·ble (im pän′dər ə b'l) *adj.* [< LL.: see IN-[2] & PONDER] **1.** that cannot be weighed or measured **2.** that cannot be clearly determined or explained [the effects of such an act are *imponderable*] —*n.* anything imponderable —**im·pon′der·a·bil′i·ty** *n.* —**im·pon′der·a·bly** *adv.*

im·port (im pôrt′; *also, and for n. always,* im′pôrt) *vt.* [< L. *importare* < *in-*, in + *portare*, to carry] **1.** *a)* to bring in from the outside [the school *imports* girls for the dances] *b)* to bring (goods) from another country, esp. for selling **2.** to mean; signify [some say a red sunset *imports* a fair day to follow] —*vi.* to be of importance; matter [what he wants *imports* very little] —*n.* **1.** the importing of goods **2.** something imported **3.** meaning [the *import* of a remark] **4.** importance [a matter of no *import*] —see SYN. at MEANING —**im·port′a·ble** *adj.* —**im·port′er** *n.*

im·por·tance (im pôr′t'ns) *n.* the state or quality of being important; significance; consequence

SYN.—**importance**, the broadest of these terms, implies greatness of worth, meaning, influence, etc. [news of *importance*]; **consequence** often specifically suggests importance with regard to results or effects [a disagreement of no *consequence*]; **moment** expresses the same idea as **consequence** but more strongly [matters of great *moment*]; **weight** implies an estimation of the relative importance of something [his word carries little *weight* with us]; **significance** implies importance because of a special meaning that may or may not be understood [we missed the *significance* of the seemingly minor event]

im·por·tant (-t'nt) *adj.* [Fr. < OIt. < ML. prp. of *importare*: see IMPORT] **1.** meaning a great deal; having much significance or value **2.** having, or acting as if one had, power or authority —**im·por′tant·ly** *adv.*

im·por·ta·tion (im′pôr tā′shən) *n.* **1.** an importing or being imported **2.** something imported

im·por·tu·nate (im pôr′chə nit) *adj.* urgent and demanding; asking again and again in a pestering way [an *importunate* job seeker] —**im·por′tu·nate·ly** *adv.* —**im·por′tu·nate·ness** *n.*

im·por·tune (im′pôr tōon′, -tyōon′; im pôr′chən) *vt.* **-tuned′, -tun′ing** [< Fr. < OFr. < L. *importunus*, troublesome < *in-*, not + (*op*)*portunus*: see OPPORTUNE] to trouble with requests or demands; urge repeatedly [Tim kept *importuning* his father to take him to the circus] —*vi.* to be importunate —see SYN. at BEG and URGE —**im′por·tun′er** *n.*

im·por·tu·ni·ty (-tōon′ə tē, -tyōon′-) *n., pl.* **-ties** an importuning or being importunate

im·pose (im pōz′) *vt.* **-posed′, -pos′ing** [< Fr. < L. *imponere* < *in-*, on + *ponere*, to place] **1.** to place (a burden, tax, etc. *on* or *upon*) **2.** to force (oneself) on another **3.** to pass off by deception [to *impose* false cures on unsuspecting patients] **4.** to arrange (pages of type) in a frame for printing —**impose on** (or **upon**) **1.** to put to some trouble or use unfairly for one's own benefit **2.** to cheat or trick —**im·pos′er** *n.*

im·pos·ing (im pō′ziŋ) *adj.* impressive in size, manner, looks, etc. [an *imposing* statue] —**im·pos′ing·ly** *adv.*

im·po·si·tion (im′pə zish′ən) *n.* **1.** an imposing or imposing on; specif., a taking advantage of friendship, courtesy, etc. [staying for a meal when you are not invited is an *imposition*] **2.** something imposed, as a tax or unjust burden

im·pos·si·bil·i·ty (im päs′ə bil′ə tē) *n.* **1.** the fact or quality of being impossible **2.** *pl.* **-ties** something that is impossible

im·pos·si·ble (im päs′ə b'l) *adj.* not possible; specif., *a)* not capable of being, being done, or happening [an *impossible* task] *b)* very unpleasant or hard to put up with [an *impossible* child] —**im·pos′si·bly** *adv.*

im·post[1] (im′pōst) *n.* [OFr. < ML. < L. *impositus*, pp. of *imponere*: see IMPOSE] **1.** a tax; esp., a duty on imported goods **2.** the weight that must be carried by a horse in a handicap race

im·post[2] (im′pōst) *n.* [< Fr. < It. *imposta*: ult. < L. and related to IMPOST[1]] the top part of a pillar, pier, etc. supporting an arch

im·pos·tor (im päs′tər) *n.* [see IMPOSE] a person who deceives or cheats others, esp. by pretending to be someone or something that he is not

im·pos·ture (-chər) *n.* the act or practice of an impostor; fraud; deception

im·po·tence (im′pə təns) *n.* the quality or condition of being impotent: also **im′po·ten·cy** (-tən sē)

im·po·tent (-tənt) *adj.* [see IN-[2] & POTENT] **1.** lacking physical strength; weak **2.** ineffective, powerless, or helpless [impotent rage] **3.** physically unable to engage in sexual intercourse: said of a male —**im′po·tent·ly** *adv.*

im·pound (im pound′) *vt.* **1.** to shut up (an animal) in a pound **2.** to take and hold (evidence, etc.) in legal custody **3.** to gather and enclose (water) for irrigation, etc. —**im·pound′ment** *n.*

im·pov·er·ish (im päv′ər ish, -päv′rish) *vt.* [< OFr. < *em-* (< L. *in-*, in) + *povre* (< L. *pauper*, poor)] **1.** to make poor **2.** to make lose strength, resources, etc. [strip mining can *impoverish* the land] —see SYN. at POOR —**im·pov′er·ished** *adj.* —**im·pov′er·ish·ment** *n.*

im·prac·ti·ca·ble (im prak′ti kə b'l) *adj.* that cannot be put into practice or used [an *impracticable* plan] —**im·prac′ti·ca·bil′i·ty, im·prac′ti·ca·ble·ness** *n.* —**im·prac′ti·ca·bly** *adv.*

im·prac·ti·cal (im prak′ti k'l) *adj.* not practical; specif., *a)* not workable or useful [an *impractical* invention] *b)* not handling practical matters well [an *impractical* manager] *c)* idealistic [an *impractical* dreamer] —**im·prac′ti·cal·i·ty, im·prac′ti·cal·ness** *n.*

im·pre·cate (im′prə kāt′) *vt.* **-cat′ed, -cat′ing** [< L. pp. of *imprecari* < *in-*, on + *precari*, to PRAY] to pray for or invoke (evil, a curse, etc.) —**im′pre·ca′tion** *n.* —**im′pre·ca′tor** *n.* —**im′pre·ca·to·ry** (-kə tôr′ē) *adj.*

im·pre·cise (im′pri sīs′) *adj.* not precise, exact, or definite —**im′pre·cise′ly** *adv.* —**im′pre·ci′sion** *n.*

im·preg·na·ble[1] (im preg′nə b'l) *adj.* [< OFr.: see IN-[2] & PREGNABLE] **1.** not capable of being captured or entered by force [an *impregnable* fortress] **2.** unshakable; firm [an *impregnable* belief] —**im·preg′na·bil′i·ty** *n.* —**im·preg′na·bly** *adv.*

im·preg·na·ble[2] (im preg′nə b'l) *adj.* [IMPREGN(ATE) + -ABLE] that can be impregnated

im·preg·nate (im preg′nāt; *for adj.* -nit) *vt.* **-nat·ed, -nat·ing** [< LL. pp. of *impraegnare*, to make pregnant < L. *in-*, in + *praegnans*, PREGNANT] **1.** to fertilize (an ovum, land, etc.) **2.**

to make pregnant **3.** to fill or saturate [*clothing impregnated with smoke*] **4.** to fill or inspire (*with* ideas, feelings, etc.) — *adj.* impregnated —see **SYN.** at SOAK —im′**preg**·**na**′**tion** *n.* —im·**preg**′**na**·**tor** *n.*

im·pre·sa·ri·o (im′prə sär′ē ō, -ser′-) *n., pl.* -**ri·os** [It. < *impresa,* enterprise, ult. < L. *in-,* in + *prehendere:* see PREHENSILE] the organizer or manager of an opera company, concert series, etc.

im·pre·scrip·ti·ble (im′pri skrip′tə b'l) *adj.* that cannot rightfully be taken away, lost, or revoked; inviolable —im′pre·**scrip**′**ti·bly** *adv.*

im·press¹ (im pres′) *vt.* [< IN-¹ + PRESS²] **1.** to force (men) into public service, esp. into a navy **2.** to levy or seize (money, property, etc.) for public use —im·**press**′**ment** *n.*

im·press² (im pres′; *for n.* im′pres) *vt.* [< L. pp. of *imprimere:* see IN-¹ & PRESS¹] **1.** to use pressure on so as to leave a mark [*to impress clay with a die*] **2.** to mark by using pressure; stamp; imprint [*her name was impressed on the envelopes*] **3.** *a)* to affect strongly the mind or emotions of [*he impressed me as a clever actor*] *b)* to arouse the interest or approval of [*his quick answers impressed us all greatly*] **4.** to fix in the memory or mind [*let me impress on you the importance of the fire drills*] —*n.* **1.** an impressing **2.** any mark, imprint, etc.; stamp **3.** a quality or effect produced by some strong influence

im·press·i·ble (-ə b'l) *adj.* that can be impressed; impressionable —im·**press**′**i·bil**′**i·ty** *n.* —im·**press**′**i·bly** *adv.*

im·pres·sion (im presh′ən) *n.* **1.** an impressing **2.** *a)* a mark, imprint, etc. made by physical pressure [*a fingerprint impression*] *b)* an effect produced on the mind or senses [*the play made a great impression on her*] *c)* the effect produced by any effort or activity [*cleaning made no impression on the stain*] **3.** a vague notion or feeling [*I have the impression that he was here*] **4.** an amusing impersonation **5.** *Printing a)* a printed copy *b)* all the copies printed at one time from a set of type or plates —see **SYN.** at IDEA —im·**pres**′**sion·al** *adj.*

im·pres·sion·a·ble (-ə b'l) *adj.* easily affected by impressions; capable of being influenced; sensitive —im·**pres**′**sion·a·bil**′**i·ty** *n.* —im·**pres**′**sion·a·bly** *adv.*

im·pres·sion·ism (-iz′m) *n.* a theory and school of art whose chief aim is to capture an impression of a subject, esp. to reproduce the play of light on surfaces: the term has been extended to literature and music which seeks to suggest moods and impressions —im·**pres**′**sion·ist** *n., adj.* —im·**pres**′**sion·is**′**tic** *adj.* —im·**pres**′**sion·is**′**ti·cal·ly** *adv.*

im·pres·sive (im pres′iv) *adj.* impressing or tending to have a strong effect on the mind or emotions; striking, imposing, etc. —im·**pres**′**sive·ly** *adv.*

im·pri·ma·tur (im′pri mät′ər, -māt′-) *n.* [ModL., let it be printed (see IMPRINT)] **1.** license or permission to publish or print a book, article, etc.; specif., *R.C.Ch.* such permission granted by an ecclesiastical censor **2.** any official approval

im·print (im print′; *for n.* im′print) *vt.* [< OFr. < L. *imprimere* < *in-,* on + *premere,* to PRESS¹] **1.** to mark by pressing or stamping; impress [*a diploma imprinted with the college seal*] **2.** to press or apply [*to imprint a kiss on the cheek*] **3.** to fix in the memory —*n.* **1.** a mark made by imprinting [*the imprint of a dirty hand on the wall*] **2.** a lasting effect or characteristic result [*the imprint of starvation on his body*] **3.** a publisher's note, as on the title page of a book, giving his name, the time and place of publication, etc.

im·print·ing (im print′iŋ) *n. Psychol.* a way of learning by very young animals in which a stimulus early in life sets up a pattern of behavior that continues every time the same stimulus occurs [*by imprinting,* young birds follow after and imitate their parents]

im·pris·on (im priz′'n) *vt.* **1.** to put or keep in prison; jail **2.** to restrict, limit, or confine in any way —im·**pris**′**on·ment** *n.*

im·prob·a·ble (im präb′ə b'l) *adj.* not probable; unlikely to happen or be true [*it is improbable that he will win again*] —im′**prob·a·bil**′**i·ty** *n., pl.* -**ties** —im·**prob**′**a·bly** *adv.*

im·promp·tu (im prämp′tōō, -tyōō) *adj., adv.* [Fr. < L. *in promptu,* in readiness: see PROMPT] without preparation or advance thought; offhand —*n.* an impromptu speech, performance, etc.

im·prop·er (im präp′ər) *adj.* **1.** not proper or suitable; poorly adapted; unfit [*sandals are improper shoes for tennis*] **2.** not true; wrong; incorrect [*an improper street address*] **3.** not in good taste; indecent; indecorous [*improper jokes*] **4.** not normal or regular [*an improper diet*] —im·**prop**′**er·ly** *adv.* —im·**prop**′**er·ness** *n.*

SYN.—**improper** refers to anything that is not proper or suitable, esp. to that which is not in line with conventional standards; **unseemly** applies to that which is not the proper or right thing for a particular situation [*her unseemly laughter at the funeral*]; **unbecoming** applies to that which is not what one expects of a certain kind of person, his character, etc. [*cowardly behavior, unbecoming* to an officer] —**ANT.** proper, decorous

improper fraction a fraction in which the denominator is less than the numerator (Ex.: 5/3)

im·pro·pri·e·ty (im′prə prī′ə tē) *n., pl.* -**ties** **1.** the quality of being improper **2.** improper action or behavior **3.** an improper use of a word [*the use of "its" instead of "it's" in "its ready" is an impropriety*]

im·prove (im prōōv′) *vt.* -**proved**′, -**prov**′**ing** [< Anglo-Fr. < *en-,* in + *prou,* gain < LL. < L. *prodesse,* to be of advantage] **1.** to make good use of [*to improve one's spare time by reading*] **2.** to make better [*exercise improved his health*] ☆**3.** to make (land or structures) more valuable by cultivation, construction, etc. —*vi.* to become better [*business has improved*] —**improve on** (or **upon**) to do or make better than, as by additions or changes —im·**prov**′**a·bil**′**i·ty** *n.* —im·**prov**′**a·ble** *adj.* —im·**prov**′**er** *n.*

SYN.—**improve** and **better** both imply correction or progress in something that is not in itself necessarily bad, the former by taking care of a lack or want [*to improve* a method] and the latter by seeking something more desirable [*he has bettered himself in his new job*]; **ameliorate** implies a situation that was bad, unpleasant, or unbearable to begin with [*to ameliorate* the living conditions of the poor] —**ANT.** worsen, impair

im·prove·ment (-mənt) *n.* **1.** an improving or being improved; esp., *a)* a making or becoming better [*your playing shows improvement*] *b)* an increase in value *c)* profitable use **2.** *a)* an addition or change that improves something or adds to its value [*they had the house air-conditioned and made other improvements*] *b)* a person or thing that is better than another [*the new choir is an improvement over the old one*]

im·prov·i·dent (im präv′ə dənt) *adj.* failing to provide for the future; lacking foresight or thrift —im·**prov**′**i·dence** *n.* —im·**prov**′**i·dent·ly** *adv.*

im·prov·i·sa·tion (im präv′ə zā′shən, im′prə vi-) *n.* **1.** an improvising **2.** something improvised —im·**prov**′**i·sa**′**tion·al** *adj.*

im·pro·vise (im′prə vīz′) *vt., vi.* -**vised**′, -**vis**′**ing** [< Fr. < It. < *improvviso,* unprepared < L. < *in-,* not + pp. of *providere,* to foresee, PROVIDE] **1.** to compose and perform at the same time without any preparation; extemporize [*musicians may improvise* variations on popular songs] **2.** to make, provide, or do with whatever is at hand [*to improvise* a bed by putting chairs together] —im′**pro·vis**′**er**, im′**pro·vi**′**sor**, im·**prov**′**i·sa·tor** (im präv′ə zāt′ər) *n.*

im·pru·dent (im prōōd′'nt) *adj.* not prudent; without thought of the consequences; rash; indiscreet —im·**pru**′**dence** *n.* —im·**pru**′**dent·ly** *adv.*

im·pu·dence (im′pyōō dəns) *n.* **1.** the quality of being impudent **2.** impudent speech or behavior: also im′**pu·den·cy**, *pl.* -**cies**

im·pu·dent (-dənt) *adj.* [< Fr. < L. < *in-,* not + prp. of *pudere,* to feel shame] **1.** orig., immodest; shameless **2.** shamelessly bold; disrespectful; insolent [*an impudent sneer*] —see **SYN.** at IMPERTINENT —im·**pu**′**dent·ly** *adv.*

im·pugn (im pyōōn′) *vt.* [< OFr. < L. < *in-,* against + *pugnare,* to fight: for IE. base see POINT] to attack by argument or criticism; oppose or challenge as false; question [*do you impugn my sincerity?*] —im·**pugn**′**a·ble** *adj.* —im·**pug·na·tion** (im′pəg nā′shən) *n.* —im·**pugn**′**er** *n.*

im·pulse (im′puls) *n.* [< L. pp. of *impellere,* IMPEL] **1.** *a)* an impelling, or driving forward with sudden force *b)* the force that drives something forward; push [*the impulse of a bat hitting a ball*] *c)* the motion or impetus caused by such a force [*the impulse of the batted ball*] **2.** *a)* a stirring up to action arising from a state of mind or an outside stimulus *b)* a sudden feeling that makes one want to act, without conscious thought [*she had an impulse to scream*] **3.** *Elec.* a momentary surge in one direction of voltage or current **4.** *Physiol.* a stimulus passed on by a muscle or nerve, which causes or prevents activity

im·pul·sion (im pul'shən) *n.* **1.** an impelling or being impelled **2.** an impelling force **3.** movement resulting from this force; impetus **4.** *same as* IMPULSE (sense 2)

im·pul·sive (-siv) *adj.* **1.** impelling; driving forward **2.** *a)* acting or likely to act on impulse [an *impulsive* person] *b)* resulting from impulse [an *impulsive* remark] —see SYN. at SPONTANEOUS —**im·pul'sive·ly** *adv.* —**im·pul'sive·ness** *n.*

im·pu·ni·ty (im pyoo'nə tē) *n.* [< Fr. < L. < *impunis* < *in-*, without + *poena*, punishment] freedom from the danger of being punished or harmed

im·pure (im pyoor') *adj.* not pure; specif., *a)* unclean; dirty [smoke made the air *impure*] *b)* unclean according to religious ritual *c)* not decent; immoral [impure thoughts] *d)* mixed with things that do not belong; adulterated [impure gold] *e)* mixed so as to lack purity in color, style, etc. *f)* not idiomatic or grammatical —**im·pure'ly** *adv.* —**im·pure'ness** *n.*

im·pu·ri·ty (-pyoor'ə tē) *n.* **1.** a being impure **2.** *pl.* **-ties** something mixed in that makes another thing impure

im·pute (im pyoot') *vt.* **-put'ed, -put'ing** [< OFr. < L. < *in-*, to + *putare*, to estimate, think] to consider to be guilty of; blame or charge with [to *impute* a crime to someone] —**im·put'a·bil'i·ty** *n.* —**im·put'a·ble** *adj.* —**im·put'a·bly** *adv.* —**im'pu·ta'tion** *n.* —**im·put'a·tive** *adj.*

in (in, ən, 'n) *prep.* [OE.: for IE. base see ENTER] **1.** contained or enclosed by; inside [in the room] **2.** wearing [a lady in red] **3.** during the course of [done in a day] **4.** at or near the end of [return in an hour] **5.** perceptible to (one of the senses) [in sight] **6.** out of a group of [one in ten] **7.** amidst; surrounded by [in a storm] **8.** affected by; having [in trouble] **9.** employed at or occupied by [in business, in a search for truth] **10.** with regard to; as concerns [weak in faith, in my opinion] **11.** with; by; using [to paint in oil, speak in French] **12.** made of [done in wood] **13.** because of; for [to cry in pain] **14.** by way of [do this in my defense] **15.** belonging to [not in his nature] **16.** into [come in the house] *In* expresses a being enclosed, contained, or involved with relation to space, place, time, state, circumstances, manner, quality, a class, etc. —*adv.* **1.** from a point outside to one inside [to invite visitors in] **2.** to or toward a certain place or direction [he flew in today] **3.** at or inside one's home, office, etc. [forced to stay in for a day] **4.** *a)* so as to be contained by a certain space or condition [how much did you put in?] *b)* so as to be in office or in power [a new mayor was voted in] **5.** so as to be agreeing or involved [he fell in with our plans] **6.** so as to form a part [mix in the cream] —*adj.* **1.** that is successful or in power [the in group] **2.** inner; inside **3.** for incoming messages [the in basket] **4.** gathered, counted, etc. [the votes are in] **5.** [Colloq.] currently fashionable, popular, etc. [an in place to dine] —*n.* **1.** a person, group, etc. in power, office, etc.: *usually used in pl.* ☆**2.** [Colloq.] special influence, favor, etc. —**have it in for** [Colloq.] to hold a grudge against —**in for** certain to have or get (usually an unpleasant experience) —**in on** having a share or part of —**ins and outs** all the parts, details, and intricacies —**in that** because; since —**in with** associated with as a friend, partner, etc.

in-¹ [< the prep. IN; also < OE. & MFr. *in-* or OFr. *en-* < L. *in-* < *in*] a prefix meaning: **1.** in, into, within, on, toward [inbreed, induct] **2.** thoroughly: used to add emphasis in some words of Latin origin [inflame] and changed to *il-* before *l* [illuminate], *ir-* before *r* [irrigate], and *im-* before *m, p,* and *b* [immigrate, impeach, imbibe]

in-² [< OFr. & ML. < L. *in-*] a prefix meaning no, not, without, non- [inhumane]: changed to *il-* before *l* [illegal], *ir-* before *r* [irregular], and *im-* before *m, p,* and *b* [immaterial, impossible, imbecile]

-in¹ (in) [see -INE⁴] a suffix used in forming the names of various compounds [albumin, streptomycin]

-in² (in) a combining form used in terms patterned after SIT-IN to describe other similar group actions [teach-in]

In *Chem.* indium

IN Indiana

in. inch; inches

-i·na (ē'nə) [L.] a suffix used to form feminine names, titles, etc. [Christina, czarina]

in·a·bil·i·ty (in'ə bil'ə tē) *n.* a being unable; lack of ability, capacity, means, or power

in ab·sen·ti·a (in əb sen'shə, ab sen'shē ə) [L., lit., in absence] although not present [to receive a college degree in absentia]

in·ac·ces·si·ble (in'ək ses'ə b'l) *adj.* not accessible; specif., *a)* impossible to reach or enter [their cottage is *inaccessible* except by boat] *b)* that cannot be seen, talked to, etc. [an in-

accessible public official] *c)* not obtainable [inaccessible information] —**in'ac·ces'si·bil'i·ty** *n.* —**in'ac·ces'si·bly** *adv.*

in·ac·cu·ra·cy (in ak'yər ə sē) *n.* **1.** lack of accuracy **2.** *pl.* **-cies** an error; mistake

in·ac·cu·rate (-yər it) *adj.* not accurate; not correct; not exact; in error —**in·ac'cu·rate·ly** *adv.*

in·ac·tion (in ak'shən) *n.* absence of action or motion; inertness or idleness

in·ac·ti·vate (in ak'tə vāt') *vt.* **-vat'ed, -vat'ing** **1.** to make inactive **2.** *Chem.* to destroy the activity of (a substance), as by heat —**in·ac'ti·va'tion** *n.*

in·ac·tive (in ak'tiv) *adj.* **1.** not active or moving; inert **2.** idle; sluggish **3.** not in use or force; not functioning **4.** not in active service in the armed forces —**in·ac'tive·ly** *adv.* —**in'ac·tiv'i·ty** *n.*

in·ad·e·quate (in ad'ə kwət) *adj.* not adequate; not sufficient —**in·ad'e·qua·cy** *pl.* **-cies**, **in·ad'e·quate·ness** *n.* —**in·ad'e·quate·ly** *adv.*

in·ad·mis·si·ble (in'əd mis'ə b'l) *adj.* not admissible; not to be allowed, granted, etc. —**in'ad·mis'si·bil'i·ty** *n.* —**in'ad·mis'si·bly** *adv.*

in·ad·vert·ence (in'əd vur'təns) *n.* **1.** a being inadvertent **2.** an instance of this; oversight; mistake Also **in'ad·vert'en·cy**, *pl.* **-cies**

in·ad·vert·ent (-tənt) *adj.* due to oversight; not intended [inadvertent humor] —**in'ad·vert'ent·ly** *adv.*

in·ad·vis·a·ble (in'əd vī'zə b'l) *adj.* not advisable; not wise or prudent —**in'ad·vis·a·bil'i·ty** *n.*

in·al·ien·a·ble (in āl'yən ə b'l) *adj.* that may not be taken away or transferred [inalienable rights] —**in·al'ien·a·bil'i·ty** *n.* —**in·al'ien·a·bly** *adv.*

in·am·o·ra·ta (in am'ə rät'ə, in'am-) *n.* [It. < *innamorare*, to fall in love] a man's sweetheart or mistress

in·ane (in ān') *adj.* [L. *inanis*] **1.** empty **2.** lacking sense; silly; foolish [an *inane* smile] —**in·ane'ly** *adv.*

in·an·i·mate (in an'ə mit) *adj.* **1.** not animate; without life [a rock is an *inanimate* object] **2.** not animated; dull [an *inanimate* style of writing] —**in·an'i·mate·ly** *adv.* —**in·an'i·mate·ness** *n.*

in·a·ni·tion (in'ə nish'ən) *n.* [< OFr., ult. < pp. of L. *inanire*, to empty < *inanis,* inane] emptiness; specif., *a)* exhaustion from lack of food *b)* lack of strength or spirit

in·an·i·ty (in an'ə tē) *n.* **1.** a being inane; specif., *a)* emptiness *b)* silliness **2.** *pl.* **-ties** something inane; senseless or silly act, remark, etc.

in·ap·pli·ca·ble (in ap'li kə b'l) *adj.* not applicable; not suitable; inappropriate —**in'ap·pli·ca·bil'i·ty** *n.* —**in·ap'pli·ca·bly** *adv.*

in·ap·po·site (in ap'ə zit) *adj.* not apposite; irrelevant —**in·ap'po·site·ly** *adv.*

in·ap·pre·ci·a·ble (in'ə prē'shə b'l, -shē ə-) *adj.* too small to be observed or have any value; negligible —**in'ap·pre'ci·a·bly** *adv.*

in·ap·pro·pri·ate (in'ə prō'prē it) *adj.* not appropriate; not suitable, fitting, or proper —**in'ap·pro'pri·ate·ly** *adv.* —**in'ap·pro'pri·ate·ness** *n.*

in·apt (in apt') *adj.* **1.** not apt; not suitable; inappropriate [an *inapt* remark] **2.** lacking skill or aptitude; inept —**in·apt'i·tude'** (-ap'tə tood', -tyood') *n.* —**in·apt'ly** *adv.* —**in·apt'ness** *n.*

in·ar·tic·u·late (in'är tik'yə lit) *adj.* **1.** produced without the articulation or clearness of normal speech [an *inarticulate* cry] **2.** *a)* unable to speak; mute *b)* not able to speak clearly or effectively [inarticulate with rage] **3.** *Zool.* without joints, hinges, etc. —**in'ar·tic'u·late·ly** *adv.* —**in'ar·tic'u·late·ness** *n.*

in·ar·tis·tic (in'är tis'tik) *adj.* not artistic; lacking artistic taste —**in'ar·tis'ti·cal·ly** *adv.*

in·as·much as (in'əz much'əz) **1.** seeing that; since; because **2.** to the extent that

in·at·ten·tion (in'ə ten'shən) *n.* failure to pay attention; carelessness; negligence

in·at·ten·tive (-tiv) *adj.* not attentive; careless —see SYN. at ABSENT-MINDED —**in'at·ten'tive·ly** *adv.* —**in'at·ten'tive·ness** *n.*

in·au·di·ble (in ô'də b'l) *adj.* not audible; that cannot be heard —**in'au·di·bil'i·ty** *n.* —**in·au'di·bly** *adv.*

in·au·gu·ral (in ô'gyə rəl, -gə rəl) *adj.* [Fr.] **1.** of an inauguration, or ceremony at which a person is inaugurated **2.** that begins a series —*n.* ☆**1.** an inaugural ceremony or speech ☆**2.** an inauguration

in·au·gu·rate (-rāt′) *vt.* **-rat′ed, -rat′ing** [< L. pp. of *inaugurare*, to practice augury] **1.** to place in a public office with a formal ceremony **2.** to make a formal beginning of [*to inaugurate a new policy*] **3.** to celebrate formally the first public use of [*to inaugurate a new bridge*] —**in·au′gu·ra′tion** *n.* —**in·au′gu·ra′tor** *n.*

in·aus·pi·cious (in′ô spish′əs) *adj.* not auspicious; unfavorable; unlucky; ill-omened —**in′aus·pi′cious·ly** *adv.* —**in′aus·pi′cious·ness** *n.*

in·board (in′bôrd′) *adv., adj.* [< *in board:* see BOARD] **1.** inside the hull or bulwarks of a ship or boat **2.** close or closer to the fuselage or hull of an aircraft —*n.* **1.** an inboard motor for a boat **2.** a boat with such a motor

☆**in·board-out·board** (-out′bôrd′) *adj.* designating or of a power unit for small watercraft that has an inboard motor connected by a drive shaft to a propeller at the stern —*n.* a boat thus powered

in·born (in′bôrn′) *adj.* that is or seems to have been born in one; innate; natural —see SYN. at INNATE

in·bound (-bound′) *adj.* traveling or going inward

in·bred (in′bred′) *adj.* **1.** innate or deeply instilled **2.** bred from closely related parents; resulting from inbreeding —see SYN. at INNATE

in·breed (in′brēd′) *vt.* **-bred′, -breed′ing** to breed by continual mating of individuals of the same or closely related stocks —*vi.* **1.** to engage in such breeding **2.** to become limited in outlook because of associating with only certain kinds of people

inc. **1.** inclosure **2.** including **3.** inclusive **4.** incorporated **5.** increase

In·ca (iŋ′kə) *n.* any member of a group of Indian tribes that ruled ancient Peru until the Spanish conquest: the Incas had a highly developed civilization —**In′can** *adj.*

in·cal·cu·la·ble (in kal′kyə lə b'l) *adj.* **1.** that cannot be calculated; too great or too many to be counted [*incalculable damage*] **2.** too uncertain to be counted on; unpredictable [*the incalculable future*] —**in·cal′cu·la·bil′i·ty** *n.* —**in·cal′cu·la·bly** *adv.*

in cam·er·a (in kam′ər ə) [L., in chamber] **1.** in a judge's private office rather than in open court **2.** in closed session, as a committee meeting or hearing not open to the public

in·can·desce (in′kən des′) *vi., vt.* **-desced′, -desc′ing** to become or make incandescent

in·can·des·cent (-des′'nt) *adj.* [< L.: see IN-¹ & CANDESCENT] **1.** glowing with intense heat; red-hot or, esp., white-hot **2.** very bright; shining brilliantly —**in′can·des′cence** *n.* —**in′can·des′cent·ly** *adv.*

incandescent lamp a lamp in which the light is produced by a filament contained in a vacuum and heated by an electric current until it glows

in·can·ta·tion (in′kan tā′shən) *n.* [OFr. < LL. < L. pp. of *incantare*, enchant < *in-*, IN-¹ + *cantare*, to chant] **1.** the chanting of special words or a formula in magic spells or rites **2.** words or a formula so chanted —**in′can·ta′tion·al** *adj.* —**in·can′ta·to′ry** (-kan′tə tôr′ē) *adj.*

in·ca·pa·ble (in kā′pə b'l) *adj.* not capable; lacking the necessary ability, competence, qualifications, etc. —**incapable of** **1.** not allowing or admitting; not able to accept or experience [*incapable of change*] **2.** lacking the ability or fitness for [*incapable of* lifting heavy loads*] **3.** not legally qualified for —**in′ca·pa·bil′i·ty, in·ca′pa·ble·ness** *n.* —**in·ca′pa·bly** *adv.*

in·ca·pac·i·tate (in′kə pas′ə tāt′) *vt.* **-tat′ed, -tat′ing** **1.** to make unable or unfit; esp., to disable [*incapacitated* by a broken leg] **2.** *Law* to disqualify —**in′ca·pac′i·ta′tion** *n.*

in·ca·pac·i·ty (in′kə pas′ə tē) *n., pl.* **-ties** **1.** lack of capacity, power, or fitness; disability **2.** legal ineligibility

in·car·cer·ate (in kär′sə rāt′) *vt.* **-at′ed, -at′ing** [< ML. pp. of *incarcerare* < L. *in*, in + *carcer*, prison] **1.** to put in prison; jail **2.** to shut up; confine —**in·car′cer·a′tion** *n.* —**in·car′cer·a′tor** *n.*

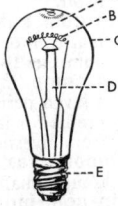

INCANDESCENT LAMP
(A, inert gas filling; B, coiled tungsten wire filament; C, glass envelope; D, glass support; E, metal base)

in·car·na·dine (in kär′nə dīn′, -din, -dēn′) *adj.* [< Fr. < It. *incarnatino* < LL. *incarnatus:* see INCARNATE] **1.** flesh-colored; pink **2.** red; esp., blood-red —*n.* the color of either flesh or blood —*vt.* **-dined′, -din′ing** to make incarnadine

in·car·nate (in kär′nit; *also, and for v. always,* -nāt) *adj.* [< LL. *incarnatus*, pp. of *incarnari*, to become flesh < L. *in-*, in + *caro,* flesh] in human form; being a living example of [*evil incarnate*] —*vt.* **-nat·ed, -nat·ing** **1.** to give bodily form to; embody **2.** to give actual form to; make real **3.** to be the type or living example of [*he incarnates* the courage of the nation]

in·car·na·tion (in′kär nā′shən) *n.* [see prec.] **1.** a taking on of human form **2.** [I-] the taking on of human form and nature by Jesus as the Son of God **3.** any person or animal serving as the bodily form of a god or spirit **4.** any person or thing serving as the living example or symbol of a quality or concept [*the incarnation* of evil]

in·case (in kās′) *vt.* **-cased′, -cas′ing** *same as* ENCASE —**in·case′ment** *n.*

in·cau·tion (in kô′shən) *n.* lack of caution

in·cau·tious (-shəs) *adj.* not cautious; not careful or prudent; reckless; rash —**in·cau′tious·ly** *adv.* —**in·cau′tious·ness** *n.*

in·cen·di·ar·y (in sen′dē er′ē) *adj.* [< L. < *incendium*, a fire < *incendere:* see INCENSE¹] **1.** relating to the willful destruction of property by fire **2.** designed to cause fires, as certain bombs **3.** willfully stirring up strife, riot, etc. —*n., pl.* **-ar′ies** **1.** a person who willfully destroys property by fire **2.** a person who willfully stirs up strife, riot, etc. **3.** an incendiary bomb, substance, etc. —**in·cen′di·a·rism** (-ə riz′m) *n.*

in·cense¹ (in′sens) *n.* [< OFr. < LL. < L. pp. of *incendere*, to inflame < *in-*, in + *candere:* see CANDESCENT] **1.** *a)* any substance burned for its pleasant odor *b)* the odor or smoke so produced **2.** any pleasant odor **3.** pleasing attention or praise —*vt.* **-censed, -cens·ing** **1.** to make fragrant with incense **2.** to burn or offer incense to —*vi.* to burn incense

in·cense² (in sens′) *vt.* **-censed′, -cens′ing** [< OFr. < L. pp. of *incendere:* see prec.] to make very angry; enrage —**in·cense′ment** *n.*

in·cen·tive (in sen′tiv) *adj.* [< LL. *incentivum* < L. < *in-*, on + *canere:* see CHANT] stimulating one to take action; encouraging; motivating —*n.* something that makes one want to take action, work harder, etc.; stimulus; motive —see SYN. at MOTIVE

in·cep·tion (in sep′shən) *n.* [< L. < pp. of *incipere:* see INCIPIENT] a beginning; start; commencement —see SYN. at ORIGIN

in·cep·tive (-tiv) *adj.* [< OFr. < LL. < L. pp. of *incipere:* see INCIPIENT] **1.** beginning; introductory **2.** *Gram.* expressing the beginning of an action —*n.* an inceptive verb —**in·cep′tive·ly** *adv.*

in·cer·ti·tude (in sur′tə tood′, -tyood′) *n.* [Fr. < ML.: IN-² + CERTITUDE] **1.** an uncertain state of mind; doubt **2.** insecurity

in·ces·sant (in ses′'nt) *adj.* [< LL. < L. *in-*, not + prp. of *cessare*, to CEASE] never ceasing; continuing or repeated endlessly; constant [*incessant* chatter] —see SYN. at CONTINUAL —**in·ces′san·cy, in·ces′sant·ness** *n.* —**in·ces′sant·ly** *adv.*

in·cest (in′sest) *n.* [< L. < *in-*, not + *castus*, chaste] sexual intercourse between persons too closely related to marry legally

in·ces·tu·ous (in ses′choo wəs) *adj.* **1.** guilty of incest **2.** of, or having the nature of, incest —**in·ces′tu·ous·ly** *adv.* —**in·ces′tu·ous·ness** *n.*

inch (inch) *n.* [OE. *ynce* < L. *uncia*, a twelfth, OUNCE¹] **1.** a measure of length equal to 1/12 foot: symbol, ″ (Ex.: 10″): abbrev. **in.** (sing. & pl.) **2.** a fall (of rain, snow, etc.) that would cover a surface to the depth of one inch **3.** a very small amount, degree, or distance —*vt., vi.* to move by degrees; move very slowly [he *inched* along the ledge] —**every inch** in all respects; thoroughly —**inch by inch** gradually; slowly: also **by inches** —**within an inch of** very close to; almost to —**within an inch of one's life** almost to one's death

inch·meal (inch′mēl′) *adv.* [INCH + MEAL¹] gradually; inch by inch: also **by inchmeal**

in·cho·ate (in kō′it) *adj.* [< L. pp. of *inchoare, incohare*, to begin, orig. "hitch up" < *in-*, in + *cohum*, a strap from plow to yoke] **1.** just begun; in the early stages **2.** not yet clearly formed —**in·cho′ate·ly** *adv.* —**in·cho′ate·ness** *n.* —**in·cho·a′tion** (-ā′shən) *n.*

in·cho·a·tive (-ə tiv) *adj., n. Gram. same as* INCEPTIVE

☆**inch·worm** (inch′wʉrm′) *n. same as* MEASURING WORM

in·ci·dence (in′si dəns) *n.* **1.** the act, fact, or manner of falling upon or influencing **2.** the degree or range of occurrence or effect; extent of influence [the *incidence* of flu was widespread that year] See also ANGLE OF INCIDENCE

in·ci·dent (-dənt) *adj.* [< OFr. < ML. < prp. of L. *incidere* < *in-,* on + *cadere,* to fall: see CASE¹] **1.** likely to happen in connection with; incidental (*to*) [the cares *incident* to parenthood] **2.** falling upon or affecting [*incident* rays] —*n.* **1.** something that happens; occurrence **2.** a minor event or episode, esp. one in a novel, play, etc. **3.** an apparently minor conflict, etc. that may have serious results

in·ci·den·tal (in′si den′t'l) *adj.* **1.** happening or likely to happen in connection with something more important; casual [*incidental* benefits] **2.** secondary or minor, but usually associated [*incidental* expenses] —*n.* **1.** something incidental **2.** [*pl.*] miscellaneous or minor items —see SYN. at ACCIDENTAL

in·ci·den·tal·ly (-dent′lē, den′t'l ē) *adv.* **1.** in an incidental way; along with something else **2.** by the way [*incidentally*, what time is it?]

in·cin·er·ate (in sin′ə rāt′) *vt., vi.* -at′ed, -at′ing [< ML. pp. of *incinerare* < L. *in,* to + *cinis,* ashes] to burn to ashes; burn up —**in·cin′er·a′tion** *n.*

in·cin·er·a·tor (-rāt′ər) *n.* a furnace or other device for incinerating trash

in·cip·i·ent (in sip′ē ənt) *adj.* [< L. prp. of *incipere,* to begin < *in-,* on + *capere,* to take] just beginning to exist or to come to notice [an *incipient* illness] —**in·cip′i·ence, in·cip′i·en·cy** *n.* —**in·cip′i·ent·ly** *adv.*

in·cise (in sīz′) *vt.* -cised′, -cis′ing [< Fr. < L. pp. of *incidere* < *in-,* into + *caedere,* to cut] to cut into with a sharp tool; specif., to engrave or carve —**in·cised′** *adj.*

in·ci·sion (-sizh′ən) *n.* **1.** the act or result of incising; cut **2.** incisive quality **3.** *Surgery* a cut made into a tissue or organ

in·ci·sive (in sī′siv) *adj.* **1.** cutting into **2.** sharp; keen; penetrating; acute [an *incisive* mind] —**in·ci′sive·ly** *adv.* —**in·ci′sive·ness** *n.*

SYN.—**incisive** is applied to speech or writing that seems to get directly to the heart of the matter, resulting in clear statements free from any doubt as to meaning [an *incisive* criticism]; **trenchant** implies clear and clean-cut expression that results in sharply defined categories, differences, etc. [a *trenchant* analysis]

in·ci·sor (in sī′zər) *n.* any of the front cutting teeth between the canines in either jaw

in·cite (in sīt′) *vt.* -cit′ed, -cit′ing [< OFr. < L. < *in-,* in, on + *citare,* to arouse: see CITE] to urge to action; stir up; rouse —**in·cite′ment, in·ci·ta·tion** (in′sī tā′shən, -si-) *n.* —**in·cit′er** *n.*

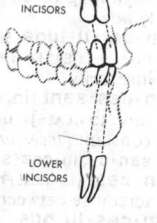

UPPER INCISORS

LOWER INCISORS

SYN.—**incite** implies an urging or stimulating to action of either a worthy or unworthy sort [*incited* to achievement by competition]; **instigate** always implies responsibility for planning or plotting the action, usually for a purpose that is bad or evil [who *instigated* the assassination?]; **arouse** means little more than a bringing into being or action [it *aroused* my suspicions]; **foment** suggests continued urging to action over a long period of time [the ambitious generals *fomented* rebellion] —ANT. restrain, inhibit

in·ci·vil·i·ty (in′sə vil′ə tē) *n.* [see IN-² & CIVIL] **1.** a lack of courtesy or politeness; rudeness **2.** *pl.* -ties a rude or discourteous act

incl. **1.** inclosure **2.** including **3.** inclusive

in·clem·ent (in klem′ənt) *adj.* [< L.: see IN-² & CLEMENT] **1.** rough; severe; stormy [*inclement* weather] **2.** lacking mercy or leniency; harsh [an *inclement* judge] —**in·clem′en·cy** *n., pl.* -cies —**in·clem′ent·ly** *adv.*

in·cli·na·tion (in′klə nā′shən) *n.* **1.** an inclining, leaning, bowing, etc. [the *inclination* of the head in prayer] **2.** a slope; slant [the *inclination* of a roof] **3.** the extent or degree of incline from the horizontal or vertical **4.** the angle made by two lines or planes **5.** a natural liking for something; tendency [an *inclination* to talk] —**in′cli·na′tion·al** *adj.*

in·cline (in klīn′; *for n., usually* in′klīn) *vi.* -clined′, -clin′ing [< OFr. < L. < *in-,* on + *clinare,* to lean: for IE. base see CLIENT] **1.** to lean; slope; slant [the chimney *inclines* toward the left] **2.** to bow the body or head **3.** to have a tendency or liking [he *inclines* to be lazy] —*vt.* **1.** to cause to lean, slope, etc. **2.** to bend or bow (the body or head) **3.** to make willing; influence —*n.* an inclined plane or surface; slope; grade [a road

with a steep *incline*] —**incline one's ear** to listen willingly —**in·clin′a·ble** *adj.* —**in·clin′er** *n.*

inclined plane a plane surface set at any angle other than a right angle against a horizontal surface

in·cli·nom·e·ter (in′klə näm′ə-tər) *n.* [< INCLINE + -METER] **1.** *same as* CLINOMETER **2.** an instrument that measures the inclination of an axis of an aircraft or ship in relation to the horizontal

INCLINED PLANE

in·close (in klōz′) *vt.* -closed′, -clos′ing *same as* ENCLOSE —**in·clo′sure** (-klō′zhər) *n.*

in·clude (in klōod′) *vt.* -clud′ed, -clud′ing [< L. < *in-,* in + *claudere,* CLOSE²] **1.** to shut up or in; enclose **2.** to have as part of a whole; contain; comprise [the cost *includes* taxes] **3.** to take into account; put in a total, category, etc. [to be *included* as a candidate] —**in·clud′a·ble, in·clud′i·ble** *adj.*

SYN.—**include** implies a containing as part of a whole; **comprise**, in careful use, means to consist of and takes as its object the various parts that make up the whole [his library *comprises* 2000 volumes and *includes* many first editions]; **comprehend** suggests that the object is contained within the total scope or range of the subject, sometimes by being implied [the word "beauty" *comprehends* various qualities]; **embrace** emphasizes the variety of objects comprehended [he had *embraced* a number of hobbies]; **involve** implies that an object is included because of its connection with the subject as a cause or result [acceptance of high office *involves* responsibilities] —ANT. exclude

in·clu·sion (in klōo′zhən) *n.* **1.** an including or being included **2.** something included

in·clu·sive (in klōo′siv) *adj.* **1.** including or tending to include; esp., taking everything into account **2.** including the terms, limits, or extremes mentioned [the first to the tenth *inclusive*] —**inclusive of** including —**in·clu′sive·ly** *adv.* —**in·clu′sive·ness** *n.*

incog. incognito

in·cog·ni·to (in′käg nēt′ō, in käg′ni tō) *adv., adj.* [It. < L. < *in-,* not + pp. of *cognoscere,* to know: see COGNITION] with true identity unrevealed or disguised; hidden under a false name, rank, etc. [the king toured the country *incognito*] —*n., pl.* -tos **1.** a person who is incognito **2.** *a)* the state of being incognito *b)* the disguise taken on —**in·cog·ni·ta** (-ə, -tə) *adj., n.fem., pl.* -tas

in·co·her·ence (in′kō hir′əns) *n.* **1.** a being incoherent; lack of coherence **2.** incoherent speech, thought, etc. Also **in′co·her′en·cy,** *pl.* -cies

in·co·her·ent (-ənt) *adj.* not coherent; specif., *a)* lacking cohesion; not sticking together *b)* not logically connected; disjointed [the play has an *incoherent* plot made up of unrelated episodes] *c)* not showing or using coherent speech, thought, etc. [he mumbled an *incoherent* sentence] —**in′co·her′ent·ly** *adv.*

in·com·bus·ti·ble (in′kəm bus′tə b'l) *adj.* not combustible; that cannot be burned —*n.* an incombustible substance —**in′·com·bus′ti·bil′i·ty** *n.*

in·come (in′kum′) *n.* the money or other gain received, esp. in a given period, by an individual, corporation, etc. as wages or profits for labor or services, or rent from property, or interest from investments, etc.

income tax a tax on net income or on that part of income which is more than a certain amount

in·com·ing (in′kum′iŋ) *adj.* coming in or about to come in [the *incoming* tide; the *incoming* mayor] —*n.* a coming in [the *incoming* of the flood waters]

in·com·men·su·ra·ble (in′kə men′shər ə b'l, -sər-) *adj.* **1.** that cannot be measured or compared by the same standard or measure [the value of his work and its cost are *incommensurable*] **2.** not worthy of comparison [his achievement is *incommensurable* with his father's] **3.** having no common divisor: said of two or more numbers or quantities —*n.* an incommensurable thing, quantity, etc. —**in′com·men′su·ra·bil′i·ty** *n.* —**in′com·men′su·ra·bly** *adv.*

in·com·men·su·rate (-it) *adj.* not commensurate; specif., *a)* not in proper proportion; not adequate [a supply *incommensurate* to the demand] *b)* same as INCOMMENSURABLE (sense 1) —**in′com·men′su·rate·ly** *adv.*

in·com·mode (in′kə mōd′) *vt.* -mod′ed, -mod′ing [< Fr. < L. < *in-,* not + *commodus,* convenient] to inconvenience; put to some trouble; bother [the delay *incommoded* us]

in·com·mo·di·ous (-mō′dē əs) *adj.* **1.** causing inconvenience; uncomfortable **2.** inconveniently small, narrow, etc. —**in′com·mo′di·ous·ly** *adv.* —**in′com·mo′di·ous·ness** *n.*

in·com·mu·ni·ca·ble (in′kə myoo′ni kə b′l) *adj.* that cannot be communicated or told —**in′com·mu′ni·ca·bil′i·ty** *n.* —**in′com·mu′ni·ca·bly** *adv.*

☆**in·com·mu·ni·ca·do** (in′kə myoo′nə kä′dō) *adj.* [Sp.] unable or not allowed to communicate with others [prisoners held *incommunicado*]

in·com·pa·ra·ble (in käm′pər ə b′l; *occas.* in′kəm par′-ə b′l) *adj.* that cannot be compared; *specif.,* *a)* having no common basis for being compared [economic systems so different as to be *incomparable*] *b)* beyond comparison; unequaled; matchless [*incomparable* skill] —**in·com′pa·ra·bil′i·ty** *n.* —**in·com′pa·ra·bly** *adv.*

in·com·pat·i·ble (in′kəm pat′ə b′l) *adj.* **1.** not compatible; not able to exist in harmony; not going, or getting along, well together (often followed by *with*) [*incompatible* partners; *incompatible* colors] **2.** logically contradictory **3.** not suitable for being used together: said of certain drugs or medicines —*n.* an incompatible person or thing —**in′com·pat′i·bil′i·ty** *n.,* pl. **-ties** —**in′com·pat′i·bly** *adv.*

in·com·pe·tent (in käm′pə tənt) *adj.* **1.** without adequate ability, knowledge, fitness, etc. [an *incompetent* typist] **2.** not fit according to the law [he was judged *incompetent* and given a guardian] —*n.* an incompetent person; esp., one who is mentally retarded —**in·com′pe·tence, in·com′pe·ten·cy** *n.* —**in·com′pe·tent·ly** *adv.*

in·com·plete (in′kəm plēt′) *adj.* **1.** lacking a part or parts **2.** unfinished; not concluded **3.** not perfect; not thorough —**in′com·plete′ly** *adv.* —**in′com·plete′ness, in′com·ple′tion** *n.*

in·com·pre·hen·si·ble (in′käm pri hen′sə b′l, in käm′-) *adj.* not comprehensible; that cannot be understood —**in′com·pre·hen′si·bil′i·ty** *n.* —**in′com·pre·hen′si·bly** *adv.*

in·com·pre·hen·sion (-shən) *n.* lack of comprehension; inability to understand

in·com·press·i·ble (in′kəm pres′ə b′l) *adj.* that cannot be compressed —**in′com·press′i·bil′i·ty** *n.*

in·con·ceiv·a·ble (in′kən sē′və b′l) *adj.* that cannot be conceived; that cannot be thought of, imagined, or believed [it is *inconceivable* that he would lie] —**in′con·ceiv′a·bil′i·ty, in′con·ceiv′a·ble·ness** *n.* —**in′con·ceiv′a·bly** *adv.*

in·con·clu·sive (in′kən kloo′siv) *adj.* not conclusive or final; not leading to a definite result [the experiments were *inconclusive*] —**in′con·clu′sive·ly** *adv.* —**in′con·clu′sive·ness** *n.*

in·con·gru·ent (in kän′groo wənt, in′kən groo′ənt) *adj.* not congruent —**in·con′gru·ence** *n.*

in·con·gru·i·ty (in′kən groo′ə tē) *n.* **1.** a being incongruous; *specif.,* *a)* lack of harmony or agreement *b)* lack of fitness or appropriateness **2.** pl. **-ties** something incongruous

in·con·gru·ous (in kän′groo wəs) *adj.* not congruous; *specif.,* *a)* lacking harmony or agreement *b)* having parts, elements, etc. that are not consistent or in harmony *c)* not fitting or proper; unsuitable; inappropriate —**in·con′gru·ous·ly** *adv.*

in·con·se·quent (in kän′sə kwent, -kwənt) *adj.* not consequent; *specif.,* *a)* not following as a result *b)* not following as a logical conclusion; irrelevant *c)* not proceeding in logical sequence; showing a lack of logic —**in·con′se·quence′** *n.* —**in·con′se·quent′ly** *adv.*

in·con·se·quen·tial (in kän′sə kwen′shəl) *adj.* **1.** inconsequent; illogical **2.** of no consequence; unimportant [it cost an *inconsequential* sum] —*n.* something inconsequential —**in′con·se·quen′ti·al′i·ty** (-shē al′ə tē) *n.* —**in·con·se·quen′tial·ly** *adv.*

in·con·sid·er·a·ble (in′kən sid′ər ə b′l) *adj.* not worth consideration; trivial; small —**in′con·sid′er·a·ble·ness** *n.* —**in′con·sid′er·a·bly** *adv.*

in·con·sid·er·ate (-it) *adj.* without thought or consideration for others; thoughtless —**in′con·sid′er·ate·ly** *adv.* —**in′con·sid′er·ate·ness, in′con·sid′er·a′tion** (-ə rā′shən) *n.*

in·con·sis·ten·cy (in′kən sis′tən sē) *n.* **1.** a being inconsistent **2.** pl. **-cies** an inconsistent act, remark, etc. Also **in′con·sis′tence**

in·con·sis·tent (-tənt) *adj.* not consistent; *specif.,* *a)* not in agreement or harmony; incompatible [the excuse he gave you is *inconsistent* with the one he gave me] *b)* not uniform; self-contradictory [*inconsistent* testimony] *c)* not holding to the same principles or practice; changeable [she is so *inconsistent* that you can't depend on her] —**in′con·sis′tent·ly** *adv.*

in·con·sol·a·ble (in′kən sōl′ə b′l) *adj.* that cannot be consoled; very sad or unhappy —**in′con·sol′a·bil′i·ty, in′con·sol′a·ble·ness** *n.* —**in′con·sol′a·bly** *adv.*

in·con·so·nant (in kän′sə nənt) *adj.* not consonant; not in harmony or agreement —**in·con′so·nance** *n.* —**in·con′so·nant·ly** *adv.*

in·con·spic·u·ous (in′kən spik′yoo wəs) *adj.* not conspicuous; attracting little attention —**in′con·spic′u·ous·ly** *adv.* —**in′con·spic′u·ous·ness** *n.*

in·con·stant (in kän′stənt) *adj.* not constant; changeable; *specif.,* *a)* not remaining firm in mind or purpose [an *inconstant* supporter] *b)* fickle [an *inconstant* friend] *c)* not uniform; irregular [an *inconstant* speed] —**in·con′stan·cy** *n.* —**in·con′stant·ly** *adv.*

in·con·test·a·ble (in′kən tes′tə b′l) *adj.* not to be contested or disputed; unquestionable —**in′con·test′a·bil′i·ty** *n.* —**in′con·test′a·bly** *adv.*

in·con·ti·nent (in känt′'n ənt) *adj.* [< OFr. < L.: see IN-² & CONTINENT] **1.** *a)* without self-restraint, in regard to sexual activity *b)* unrestrained **2.** incapable of containing, holding, etc. **3.** unable to restrain a natural discharge, as of urine —**in·con′ti·nence** *n.* —**in·con′ti·nent·ly** *adv.*

in·con·tro·vert·i·ble (in′kän trə vur′tə b′l, in kän′-) *adj.* that cannot be controverted; not disputable or debatable; undeniable —**in′con·tro·vert′i·bil′i·ty** *n.* —**in′con·tro·vert′i·bly** *adv.*

in·con·ven·ience (in′kən vēn′yəns) *n.* **1.** a being inconvenient; lack of comfort, ease, etc. **2.** anything inconvenient Also **in′con·ven′ien·cy,** pl. **-cies** —*vt.* **-ienced, -ienc·ing** to cause inconvenience to; trouble; bother

in·con·ven·ient (-yənt) *adj.* not convenient; not favorable to one's comfort; causing trouble, bother, etc. —**in′con·ven′ient·ly** *adv.*

in·con·vert·i·ble (in′kən vur′tə b′l) *adj.* that cannot be converted; that cannot be changed or exchanged [paper money that is *inconvertible* into silver] —**in′con·vert′i·bil′i·ty** *n.*

in·cor·po·rate (in kôr′pər it; *for v.* -pə rāt′) *adj.* [< LL.: see IN-¹ & CORPORATE] combined, merged, or incorporated —*vt.* **-rat′ed, -rat′ing** **1.** to make part of another thing; combine with something already formed; embody [*incorporate* these new facts into your report] **2.** to bring together into a single whole; merge [the two novels were *incorporated* into one volume] **3.** to admit into association as a member **4.** to form into a corporation [the owner of a store may *incorporate* his business] **5.** to give material form to —*vi.* **1.** to unite or combine into a single whole **2.** to form a corporation —**in·cor′po·ra′tion** *n.* —**in·cor′po·ra′tive** *adj.* —**in·cor′po·ra′tor** *n.*

in·cor·po·re·al (in′kôr pôr′ē əl) *adj.* not corporeal; without material body or substance —**in′cor·po′re·al·ly** *adv.*

in·cor·rect (in′kə rekt′) *adj.* not correct; *specif.,* *a)* improper [*incorrect* conduct] *b)* untrue; inaccurate; wrong; faulty [an *incorrect* answer] —**in′cor·rect′ly** *adv.* —**in′cor·rect′ness** *n.*

in·cor·ri·gi·ble (in kôr′i jə b′l, -kär′-) *adj.* not corrigible; that cannot be corrected, improved, or reformed, esp. because firmly set, as a habit, or because set in bad habits, as a child —*n.* an incorrigible person —**in·cor′ri·gi·bil′i·ty, in·cor′ri·gi·ble·ness** *n.* —**in·cor′ri·gi·bly** *adv.*

in·cor·rupt (in′kə rupt′) *adj.* not corrupt; sound, pure, upright, honest, etc. —**in′cor·rupt′ly** *adv.* —**in′cor·rupt′ness** *n.*

in·cor·rupt·i·ble (-rup′tə b′l) *adj.* that cannot be corrupted, esp. morally —**in′cor·rupt′i·bil′i·ty** *n.* —**in′cor·rupt′i·bly** *adv.*

incr. **1.** increase **2.** increased **3.** increasing

in·crease (in krēs′; *also, and for n. always,* in′krēs) *vi.* **-creased′, -creas′ing** [< OFr. < L. < in- + *crescere:* see CRESCENT] **1.** to become greater in size, amount, etc.; grow [his power *increased* as he became wealthy] **2.** to become greater in numbers by producing offspring; multiply —*vt.* to cause to become greater in size, amount, etc. —*n.* **1.** an increasing or becoming increased **2.** the result or amount of an increasing [a population *increase* of 10%] —**on the increase** increasing —**in·creas′a·ble** *adj.* —**in·creas′er** *n.*

SYN.—**increase** means, generally, to make or become greater in size, amount, degree, etc. [to *increase* one's weight, one's power, debts, etc.]; **enlarge** specifically implies a making or becoming greater in size, volume, extent, etc. [to *enlarge* a house, a business, etc.]; **augment,** a more formal word, generally implies increase by addition, often of something that is

---

fat, āpe, cär; ten, ēven; is, bīte; gō, hôrn, tool, look; oil, out; up, fur; get; joy; yet; chin; she; thin, then; zh, leisure; ŋ, ring; ə for a in ago, e in agent, i in sanity, o in comply, u in focus; ′ as in able (ā′b′l); Fr. bal; ë, Fr. coeur; ö, Fr. feu; Fr. mon; ô, Fr. coq; ü, Fr. duc; r, Fr. cri; H, G. ich; kh, G. doch; ‡foreign; ☆ Americanism; < derived from. See inside front cover.

already somewhat large in size, amount, etc. [to *augment* one's income] **multiply** suggests increase in number [sales *multiplied* under the new management] —**ANT. decrease, diminish, lessen**

in·creas·ing·ly (in krēs′iŋ lē) *adv.* more and more; to an ever-increasing degree

in·cred·i·ble (in kred′ə b'l) *adj.* **1.** not credible; unbelievable [an *incredible* story] **2.** so great, unusual, etc. as to seem impossible [*incredible* speed] —**in·cred′i·bil′i·ty** *n.* —**in·cred′i·bly** *adv.*

in·cre·du·li·ty (in′krə dōō′lə tē, -dyōō′-) *n.* unwillingness or inability to believe; doubt

in·cred·u·lous (in krej′oo ləs) *adj.* **1.** unwilling or unable to believe; doubting **2.** showing doubt or disbelief [an *incredulous* look] —**in·cred′u·lous·ly** *adv.*

in·cre·ment (in′krə mənt, iŋ′-) *n.* **1.** a becoming greater or larger; increase; gain **2.** amount of increase [an annual *increment* of $300 in salary] **3.** *Math.* the quantity, usually small, by which a variable increases or is increased: a negative increment results in a decrease —**in′cre·men′tal** (-men′t'l) *adj.*

in·crim·i·nate (in krim′ə nāt′) *vt.* **-nat′ed, -nat′ing** [< ML.: see IN-[1] & CRIMINATE] **1.** to charge with a crime; accuse **2.** to involve in, or make appear guilty of, a crime or fault [his fingerprints on the murder weapon tend to *incriminate* him] —**in·crim′i·na′tion** *n.* —**in·crim′i·na·to′ry** *adj.*

in·crust (in krust′) *vt.* **1.** to cover as with a crust or hard coating [shoes *incrusted* with mud] **2.** to decorate, as with gems [a bracelet *incrusted* with rubies] —*vi.* to form a crust

in·crus·ta·tion (in′krus tā′shən, in krus′-) *n.* **1.** an incrusting or being incrusted **2.** a crust; hard layer or coating **3.** an elaborate decorative coating, inlay, etc.

in·cu·bate (in′kyə bāt′, in-) *vt.* **-bat′ed, -bat′ing** [< L. pp. of *incubare* < *in-*, on + *cubare*, to lie] **1.** to sit on and hatch (eggs) **2.** to keep (eggs, embryos, etc.) in a favorable environment for hatching or developing **3.** to cause to develop, as by thought or planning —*vi.* **1.** to undergo incubation **2.** to develop or take form, esp. little by little [an idea was *incubating* in my mind]

in·cu·ba·tion (in′kyə bā′shən, in′-) *n.* **1.** an incubating or being incubated **2.** the phase in the development of a disease between the infection and the first appearance of symptoms —**in′cu·ba′tion·al** *adj.* —**in′cu·ba′tive** *adj.*

in·cu·ba·tor (in′kyə bāt′ər, in′-) *n.* a person or thing that incubates; specif., *a)* an artificially heated container for hatching eggs *b)* a similar apparatus in which premature babies are kept for a period *c)* an apparatus for developing bacterial cultures

in·cu·bus (in′kyə bəs, in′-) *n., pl.* **-bus·es, -bi′** (-bī′) [< LL., nightmare (in ML., a demon) < L. *incubare*: see INCUBATE] **1.** a spirit or demon thought in medieval times to lie on sleeping women **2.** a nightmare **3.** anything that weighs one down; burden

in·cul·cate (in kul′kāt, in′kul-kāt′) *vt.* **-cat·ed, -cat·ing** [< L. pp. of *inculcare* < *in-*, in + *calcare*, to trample underfoot < *calx*, a heel] to fix firmly in the mind by repetition or continued urging —**in′cul·ca′tion** *n.* —**in·cul′ca·tor** *n.*

in·cul·pate (in kul′pāt, in′kul pāt′) *vt.* **-pat·ed, -pat·ing** [< ML. pp. of *inculpare* < L. *in, in* + *culpa*, a fault, blame] same as INCRIMINATE —**in′cul·pa′tion** *n.* —**in·cul′pa·to′ry** *adj.*

in·cum·ben·cy (in kum′bən sē) *n., pl.* **-cies 1.** a duty or obligation **2.** *a)* the holding and administering of a position *b)* the time during which a person is in office

in·cum·bent (-bənt) *adj.* [< L. prp. of *incumbere* < *in-*, on + *cubare*, to lie down] **1.** lying, resting, or pressing with its weight on something else **2.** currently in office —*n.* the person holding an office, position, or benefice —**incumbent on** (or **upon**) resting upon as a duty or obligation

in·cum·ber (in kum′bər) *vt.* same as ENCUMBER

in·cum·brance (-brəns) *n.* **1.** *Law* a lien, claim, mortgage, etc. on property **2.** same as ENCUMBRANCE

in·cu·nab·u·la (in′kyoo nab′yə lə) *n.pl., sing.* **-u·lum** (-ləm) [< L. *in-*, in + *cunabula*, neut. pl., a cradle] **1.** the very first stages of anything; beginnings **2.** early printed books; esp., books printed before 1500 —**in′cu·nab′u·lar** *adj.*

in·cur (in kur′) *vt.* **-curred′, -cur′ring** [< L. *in-*, in + *currere*, to run] **1.** to acquire (something undesirable) [to *incur* a debt]

INCUBATOR

2. to bring upon oneself through one's own actions [to *incur* someone's anger]

in·cur·a·ble (in kyoor′ə b'l) *adj.* not curable; that cannot be remedied or corrected —*n.* a person having an incurable disease —**in·cur′a·bil′i·ty** *n.* —**in·cur′a·bly** *adv.*

in·cu·ri·ous (in kyoor′ē əs) *adj.* not curious; not eager to find out; uninterested; indifferent —**in·cu·ri·os·i·ty** (in′kyoor ē-äs′ə tē), **in·cu′ri·ous·ness** *n.* —**in·cu′ri·ous·ly** *adv.*

in·cur·sion (in kur′zhən; *chiefly Brit.* -shən) *n.* [< L. *incursio* < *incurrere:* see INCUR] **1.** a running in or coming in, esp. when undesired; inroad **2.** a sudden, brief invasion or raid [the *incursions* of armed bands at a border] —**in·cur′sive** *adj.*

in·curve (in kurv′; *for n.* in′kurv′) *vt., vi.* **-curved′, -curv′ing** to curve inward —*n.* ☆*Baseball* same as SCREWBALL

in·cus (iŋ′kəs) *n., pl.* **in·cu·des** (in kyōō′dēz) [ModL. < L., anvil] the central one of the three small bones in the middle ear: also called *anvil*

Ind. 1. India **2.** Indian **3.** Indiana **4.** Indies

ind. 1. independent **2.** index **3.** industrial

in·debt·ed (in det′id) *adj.* **1.** in debt **2.** obliged; owing thanks [I am *indebted* to him for saving my life]

in·debt·ed·ness (-nis) *n.* **1.** a being indebted **2.** the amount owed; all one's debts

in·de·cen·cy (in dē′s'n sē) *n.* **1.** a being indecent **2.** *pl.* **-cies** an indecent act, statement, etc.

in·de·cent (-s'nt) *adj.* not decent; specif., *a)* not proper and fitting; unseemly [*indecent* vanity] *b)* morally offensive; obscene [to call someone an *indecent* name] —**in·de′cent·ly** *adv.*

in·de·ci·pher·a·ble (in′di sī′fər ə b'l) *adj.* that cannot be deciphered; illegible —**in′de·ci′pher·a·bil′i·ty** *n.*

in·de·ci·sion (in′di sizh′ən) *n.* inability to decide or a tendency to change the mind frequently

in·de·ci·sive (-sī′siv) *adj.* **1.** not decisive; not deciding or settling anything [an *indecisive* reply] **2.** showing indecision; hesitating or vacillating —**in′de·ci′sive·ly** *adv.* —**in′de·ci′sive·ness** *n.*

in·de·clin·a·ble (in′di klīn′ə b'l) *adj. Gram.* having no case inflections; not declinable

in·dec·o·rous (in dek′ər əs; *occas.* in′di kôr′əs) *adj.* lacking decorum, good taste, etc.; not proper or fitting —**in·dec′o·rous·ly** *adv.* —**in·dec′o·rous·ness** *n.*

in·de·co·rum (in′di kôr′əm) *n.* **1.** lack of decorum; lack of good manners or good taste **2.** indecorous conduct, speech, etc.

in·deed (in dēd′) *adv.* [see IN, *prep.* & DEED] certainly; truly; admittedly [it is *indeed* beautiful; did he *indeed* tell you that?] —*interj.* an exclamation of surprise, doubt, sarcasm, etc.

indef. indefinite

in·de·fat·i·ga·ble (in′di fat′i gə b'l) *adj.* [< MFr. < L. < *in-*, not + *defatigare*, to tire out: see DE- & FATIGUE] that cannot be tired out; untiring —**in′de·fat′i·ga·bil′i·ty** *n.* —**in′de·fat′i·ga·bly** *adv.*

in·de·fea·si·ble (in′di fē′zə b'l) *adj.* that cannot be undone or made void —**in′de·fea′si·bil′i·ty** *n.* —**in′de·fea′si·bly** *adv.*

in·de·fen·si·ble (in′di fen′sə b'l) *adj.* **1.** that cannot be defended or protected [an *indefensible* bridge] **2.** that cannot be justified or excused [an *indefensible* act] —**in′de·fen′si·bil′i·ty** *n.* —**in′de·fen′si·bly** *adv.*

in·de·fin·a·ble (in′di fīn′ə b'l) *adj.* that cannot be defined [an *indefinable* feeling] —**in′de·fin′a·bly** *adv.*

in·def·i·nite (in def′ə nit) *adj.* not definite; specif., *a)* having no exact limits [an *indefinite* area] *b)* not clear or exact in meaning; vague [*indefinite* instructions] *c)* not clear in outline; blurred [an *indefinite* image] *d)* not sure; uncertain [*indefinite* plans] *e) Gram.* not limiting or specifying [*a* and *an* are *indefinite* articles; *any* is an *indefinite* pronoun] —**in·def′i·nite·ly** *adv.* —**in·def′i·nite·ness** *n.*

indefinite integral *Math.* any function whose derivative is the given function

in·de·his·cent (in′di his′'nt) *adj.* not dehiscent; not opening to release its seeds when it is fully developed [the apple is an *indehiscent* fruit] —**in′de·his′cence** *n.*

in·del·i·ble (in del′ə b'l) *adj.* [< L., ult. < *in-*, not + *delere*, to destroy] **1.** that cannot be erased, blotted out, eliminated, etc.; permanent [an *indelible* impression] **2.** leaving an indelible mark [*indelible* ink] —**in·del′i·bil′i·ty** *n.* —**in·del′i·bly** *adv.*

in·del·i·ca·cy (in del′i kə sē) *n.* **1.** the quality of being indelicate **2.** *pl.* **-cies** an indelicate act, remark, etc.

in·del·i·cate (-kit) *adj.* not delicate; coarse; esp., not proper, refined, or tactful [*indelicate* jokes] —see SYN. at COARSE —**in·del′i·cate·ly** *adv.* —**in·del′i·cate·ness** *n.*

in·dem·ni·fy (in dem′nə fī′) *vt.* **-fied′, -fy′ing** [< L. *indemnis*, unhurt < *in-*, not + *damnum*, hurt + -FY] **1.** to protect against future loss, damage, etc.; insure **2.** *a)* to repay (someone) for loss or damage *b)* to make good (a loss) —**in·dem′ni·fi·ca′tion** *n.* —**in·dem′ni·fi′er** *n.*

in·dem·ni·ty (-tē) *n., pl.* **-ties 1.** protection or insurance against loss, damage, etc. **2.** legal exemption from penalties incurred by one's actions **3.** repayment for loss, damage, etc.; compensation

in·dent[1] (in dent′; *for n., usually* in′dent) *vt.* [< OFr. < ML. < L. *in*, in + *dens*, TOOTH] **1.** *a)* to cut toothlike points into (an edge or border); notch; also, to join by mating notches *b)* to make jagged or uneven in outline [a coast *indented* with bays] **2.** to space (the first line of a paragraph, an entire paragraph, a column of figures, etc.) in from the regular margin —*vi.* **1.** to form or be marked by notches, points, or a jagged border **2.** to space in from the margin —*n.* **1.** a notch or cut in an edge **2.** an indenture, or written contract **3.** an indented line, paragraph, etc.

in·dent[2] (in dent′; *for n., usually* in′dent) *vt.* [IN-[1] + DENT] **1.** to make a dent in **2.** to press (a mark, etc.) in —*n.* a dent, or slight hollow

in·den·ta·tion (in′den tā′shən) *n.* **1.** an indenting or being indented **2.** a notch, cut, or inlet on a coastline, etc. **3.** a dent, or slight hollow **4.** an indention; space in from a margin

in·den·tion (in den′shən) *n.* **1.** a spacing in from the margin **2.** an empty or blank space left by this **3.** *a)* a dent *b)* the making of a dent

in·den·ture (in den′chər) *n.* [< INDENT[1]: orig., duplicates of a contract had correspondingly jagged edges for identification] **1.** a written contract or agreement **2.** [*often pl.*] a contract binding a person to work for another, as an apprentice to a master —*vt.* **-tured, -tur·ing** to bind by indenture [an *indentured* servant]

In·de·pend·ence (in′di pen′dəns) [after A. JACKSON, alluding to his *independence* of character] city in W Mo.: suburb of Kansas City: pop. 112,000

in·de·pend·ence (in′di pen′dəns) *n.* the condition of being independent; freedom from the control of another

☆**Independence Day** the Fourth of July, the anniversary of the adoption of the Declaration of Independence on July 4, 1776: a legal holiday in the U.S.

in·de·pend·en·cy (-dən sē) *n.* [Rare] *same as* INDEPENDENCE

in·de·pend·ent (in′di pen′dənt) *adj.* **1.** free from the influence or control of others; specif., *a)* free from the rule of another; self-governing *b)* free from persuasion or bias; objective [an *independent* observer] *c)* relying on one's own abilities, judgment, etc.; self-confident; self-reliant [*independent* in his thinking] *d)* not supporting any single political party [an *independent* voter] *e)* not connected with others; separate [an *independent* grocer] **2.** *a)* not depending on another, esp. for financial support *b)* designating, of, or having an income large enough to enable one to live without working —*n.* a person who is independent in thinking, action, etc.; ☆specif., [*often* I-] a voter not supporting any single political party —**independent of** apart from; regardless of —**in′de·pend′ent·ly** *adv.*

independent clause *Gram. same as* MAIN CLAUSE

independent variable *Math.* a quantity whose value may be determined freely without reference to other variables

in-depth (in′depth′) *adj.* carefully worked out, detailed, thorough, etc. [an *in-depth* study]

in·de·scrib·a·ble (in′di skrī′bə b'l) *adj.* that cannot be described; beyond the power of description —**in′de·scrib′a·bil′i·ty** *n.* —**in′de·scrib′a·bly** *adv.*

in·de·struct·i·ble (in′di struk′tə b'l) *adj.* that cannot be destroyed —**in′de·struct′i·bil′i·ty** *n.* —**in′de·struct′i·bly** *adv.*

in·de·ter·mi·na·ble (in′di tur′mi nə b'l) *adj.* not determinable; specif., *a)* that cannot be decided *b)* that cannot be found out —**in′de·ter′mi·na·ble·ness** *n.* —**in′de·ter′mi·na·bly** *adv.*

in·de·ter·mi·nate (-nit) *adj.* not determinate; specif., *a)* inexact in its limits, nature, etc.; indefinite; vague *b)* not yet settled; inconclusive —**in′de·ter′mi·na·cy, in′de·ter′mi·nate·ness** *n.* —**in′de·ter′mi·nate·ly** *adv.*

in·de·ter·mi·na·tion (in′di tur′mə nā′shən) *n.* **1.** lack of determination **2.** the state or quality of being indeterminate

in·dex (in′deks) *n., pl.* **-dex·es, -di·ces′** (-də sēz′) [L. < *indicare*, INDICATE] **1.** *short for* INDEX FINGER **2.** a pointer, as the needle on a dial **3.** an indication or sign [performance is an *index* of ability] **4.** *a)* an alphabetical list of names, subjects, etc. together with the page numbers where they appear in the text, usually placed at the end of a publication *b) short for* THUMB INDEX *c)* a catalog [a library *index*] **5.** *a)* the relation or ratio of one amount or dimension to another, or the formula expressing this relation *b)* a number used to measure changes in prices, wages, etc.: it shows percentage variation from an arbitrary standard, usually 100, representing the status at some earlier time: in full, **index number 6.** [I-] *R.C.Ch.* formerly, a list of books forbidden to be read without special permission **7.** *Math. a)* an exponent (sense 3) *b)* a subscript *c)* a number or symbol placed above and to the left of a radical (Examples: $\sqrt[3]{8}$, $\sqrt[n]{x}$) **8.** *Printing* a sign (☞) calling special attention to certain information —*vt.* **1.** *a)* to make an index of or for *b)* to include in an index *c)* to supply with a thumb index **2.** to be an index or sign of; indicate —**in′dex·er** *n.*

index finger the finger next to the thumb; forefinger

index of refraction the ratio of the speed of light in a vacuum or a particular medium to its speed in a second medium

In·di·a (in′dē ə) **1.** region in S Asia, south of the Himalayas, including a large peninsula between the Arabian Sea & the Bay of Bengal **2.** republic in C & S India: member of the Commonwealth: 1,177,000 sq. mi.; pop. 536,984,000; cap. New Delhi

India ink 1. a black pigment of lampblack mixed with a gelatinous substance and dried into cakes or sticks **2.** a liquid ink made from this

In·di·an (in′dē ən) *adj.* **1.** of India or the East Indies, their people, or culture **2.** of any of the aboriginal peoples (**American Indians**) of N. America, S. America, or the West Indies, or of their cultures **3.** of a type used or made by Indians —*n.* **1.** a native of India or the East Indies **2.** a member of any of the aboriginal peoples of N. America, S. America, or the West Indies: originally so named from the belief, held by early explorers, that these regions were part of Asia **3.** popularly, any of the languages spoken by American Indians

In·di·an·a (in′dē an′ə) [ModL., "land of the Indians"] Middle Western State of the U.S.: 36,291 sq. mi.; pop. 5,194,000; cap. Indianapolis: abbrev. **Ind., IN** —**In′di·an/i·an** *adj., n.*

☆**Indian agent** a U.S. or Canadian official representing the government in dealings with American Indians, as on reservations

In·di·an·ap·o·lis (in′dē ə nap′ə lis) [INDIANA + Gr. *polis*, city] capital of Indiana, in the C part: pop. 745,000 (met. area 1,110,000)

☆**Indian club** a club of wood, metal, etc. shaped like a tenpin and swung in the hand for exercise

☆**Indian corn** *same as* CORN[1] (sense 2)

☆**Indian file** *same as* SINGLE FILE: it was the American Indians' way of walking a trail

☆**Indian meal** *same as* CORNMEAL

Indian Ocean ocean south of Asia, between Africa & Australia

☆**Indian paintbrush** any of various plants of the figwort family, with red or orange flowers and brilliant red or yellow upper leaves

☆**Indian pipe** a leafless, fleshy, white plant native to the forests of the Northern Hemisphere, bearing a single, nodding, white flower

INDIAN CLUBS

☆**Indian pudding** a cornmeal pudding made with milk, molasses, etc.

☆**Indian summer** a period of mild, warm, hazy weather following the first frosts of late autumn

Indian Territory former territory (1834-90) of the U.S., reserved for the settlement of Indians: now a part of Oklahoma

☆**Indian tobacco** a poisonous annual plant, common in the eastern U.S., with light blue flowers in spikes

India paper a thin, strong, opaque printing paper, used for some Bibles, dictionaries, etc.

India (or **india**) **rubber** crude, natural rubber obtained from latex —**In′di·a-rub′ber** *adj.*

In·dic (in′dik) *adj.* **1.** of India **2.** designating or of a subgroup of the Indo-Iranian branch of the Indo-European language family, including many of the languages of India, Pakistan, etc.

indic. indicative

in·di·cate (in′də kāt′) *vt.* **-cat′ed, -cat′ing** [< L. pp. of *indicare* < *in-*, in + *dicare*, to declare: for IE. base see DICTION] **1.** to direct attention to; point out; show [to *indicate* a route on a road map] **2.** to be or give a sign of; signify [fever *indicates* illness] **3.** to show the need for; call for; make necessary [a fabric for which dry cleaning is *indicated*] **4.** to point to as the required treatment [bed rest is *indicated*] **5.** to state briefly or generally [to *indicate* guidelines for action]

in·di·ca·tion (in′də kā′shən) *n.* **1.** an indicating **2.** something that indicates, or shows; sign **3.** something that is indicated as necessary **4.** the amount or degree registered by an indicator

in·dic·a·tive (in dik′ə tiv) *adj.* **1.** giving an indication or intimation; signifying; showing [a look *indicative* of joy]: also **indic·a·to·ry** (in dik′ə tôr′ē, in′dik-) **2.** designating or of that mood of a verb used to express an actual fact, state, etc. or to ask a question of fact: see SUBJUNCTIVE, IMPERATIVE —*n.* **1.** the indicative mood **2.** a verb in this mood —**in·dic′a·tive·ly** *adv.*

in·di·ca·tor (in′də kāt′ər) *n.* **1.** a person or thing that indicates; specif., any device, as a gauge, dial, register, or pointer, that measures something **2.** any substance used to indicate the acidity or alkalinity of a solution, the beginning or end of a chemical reaction, etc., by changes in color

in·di·ces (in′də sēz′) *n. alt. pl. of* INDEX

in·di·ci·a (in dish′ē ə, -dish′ə) *n.pl.* [L., ult. < *index:* see INDEX] marks or tokens; ☆esp., printed markings on mail in place of stamps or cancellations

in·dict (in dīt′) *vt.* [< Anglo-L. *indictare*, ult. < L. *in*, against + *dictare;* see DICTATE] to charge with having committed a crime; esp., to bring a formal indictment against —**in·dict′a·ble** *adj.* —**in·dict′er, in·dict′or** *n.*

INDICIA

in·dict·ment (in dīt′mənt) *n.* **1.** an indicting or being indicted **2.** a charge; specif., a formal accusation charging someone with a crime, presented by a grand jury to the court when the jury has found, after examining the evidence presented, that there is a valid case

In·dies (in′dēz) **1.** *same as:* a) EAST INDIES (sense 1) b) WEST INDIES **2.** formerly, *same as* EAST INDIES (sense 2)

in·dif·fer·ence (in dif′ər əns, -dif′rəns) *n.* a being indifferent; specif., a) lack of concern or interest b) lack of importance or meaning

in·dif·fer·ent (in dif′ər ənt, -dif′rənt) *adj.* **1.** having or showing no preference; neutral; impartial **2.** having or showing no interest, concern, etc.; uninterested or unmoved **3.** of no importance **4.** not particularly good or bad; average or mediocre [an *indifferent* singer] —**in·dif′fer·ent·ly** *adv.*
SYN.—indifferent implies a remaining uninvolved or neutral, esp. when one has a choice [to remain *indifferent* in a dispute]; **unconcerned** implies a lack of concern, care, or worry, as because one is callous, unaware, etc. [to remain *unconcerned* in a time of danger]; **detached** implies a being impartial or aloof in the way one can be when one's feelings are not affected [he viewed the struggle with *detached* interest]; **disinterested** strictly implies a being impartial in an honest way as when one has no selfish motive or desire to benefit oneself [a *disinterested* opinion].

in·di·gence (in′di jəns) *n.* the condition of being indigent: also **in′di·gen·cy** —see SYN. at POVERTY

in·dig·e·nous (in dij′ə nəs) *adj.* [< LL. < L. *indigena* < OL. *indu*, in + *gignere*, to be born] **1.** existing, growing, or produced naturally in a region or country; native (*to*) [the kangaroo is *indigenous* to Australia] **2.** innate; inborn —see SYN. at NATIVE —**in·dig′e·nous·ly** *adv.* —**in·dig′e·nous·ness** *n.*

in·di·gent (in′di jənt) *adj.* [OFr. < L. prp. of *indigere*, to be in need < OL. *indu*, in + *egere*, to need] poor; needy —*n.* an indigent person —see SYN. at POOR —**in′di·gent·ly** *adv.*

in·di·gest·i·ble (in′di jes′tə b'l, -dī-) *adj.* that cannot be digested or is hard to digest —**in′di·gest′i·bil′i·ty** *n.*

in·di·ges·tion (in′di jes′chən, -jesh′-) *n.* **1.** inability to digest, or difficulty in digesting, food **2.** the discomfort caused by this

in·dig·nant (in dig′nənt) *adj.* [< L. prp. of *indignari*, to consider unworthy, ult. < *in-*, not + *dignus*, worthy: see DIGNITY] angry about something that seems unjust, unfair, mean, etc. [he

was *indignant* when she suggested that he had lied] —**in·dig′-nant·ly** *adv.*

in·dig·na·tion (in′dig nā′shən) *n.* anger at something that seems unjust, unfair, mean, etc. —see SYN. at ANGER

in·dig·ni·ty (in dig′nə tē) *n., pl.* **-ties** something that insults, or hurts one's dignity or pride; affront [to suffer the *indignity* of being called a fool]

in·di·go (in′di gō′) *n., pl.* **-gos′, -goes′** [Sp. < L. *indicum* < Gr. < *Indikos*, Indian < *India*, India] **1.** a blue dye obtained from certain plants or made synthetically **2.** a plant of the legume family that yields indigo **3.** a deep violet blue: also **indigo blue** —*adj.* of a deep violet-blue: also **in′di·go′-blue′**

☆**indigo bunting** (or **bird**) a small finch of the eastern U.S.: the male is indigo, the female brown

in·di·rect (in′di rekt′, -dī-) *adj.* not direct; specif., a) not straight; roundabout [an *indirect* route] b) not straight to the point or object [an *indirect* reply] c) not straightforward; dishonest [*indirect* dealing] d) not immediate; secondary [an *indirect* result] —**in′di·rect′ly** *adv.* —**in′di·rect′ness** *n.*

indirect discourse statement of what a person said, without quoting his exact words (Ex.: she said that she would go)

in·di·rec·tion (-rek′shən) *n.* **1.** roundabout act, procedure, or means **2.** deceit; dishonesty **3.** lack of direction or purpose

indirect lighting lighting reflected, as from a ceiling, or diffused so as to avoid glare

indirect object the word or words naming the person or thing that something (the *direct object*) is given to or done for (Ex.: *him* in "give *him* the ball," "do *him* a favor")

indirect tax a tax on manufactured goods, imports, etc. that is paid indirectly by the consumer because it is included in the price

in·dis·cern·i·ble (in′di sur′nə b'l, -zur′-) *adj.* that cannot be discerned; not distinct to the mind or senses —**in′dis·cern′i·bly** *adv.*

in·dis·creet (in′dis krēt′) *adj.* not discreet; not careful about what one says or does; unwise —**in′dis·creet′ly** *adv.* —**in′dis·creet′ness** *n.*

in·dis·cre·tion (in′dis kresh′ən) *n.* **1.** lack of good judgment or care in what one says or does; imprudence **2.** an indiscreet act or remark

in·dis·crim·i·nate (in′dis krim′ə nit) *adj.* **1.** not based on careful selection or a discerning taste; confused or random [an *indiscriminate* buyer of books] **2.** not discriminating; not making careful choices or distinctions [*indiscriminate* praise for everyone] —**in′dis·crim′i·nate·ly** *adv.* —**in′dis·crim′i·nate·ness, in′dis·crim′i·na′tion** *n.*

in·dis·pen·sa·ble (in′dis pen′sə b'l) *adj.* that cannot be dispensed with or done without; absolutely necessary or required [good brakes are *indispensable* in a car] —*n.* an indispensable person or thing —see SYN. at ESSENTIAL —**in′dis·pen′sa·bil′i·ty** *n.* —**in′dis·pen′sa·bly** *adv.*

in·dis·pose (in′dis pōz′) *vt.* **-posed′, -pos′ing** **1.** to make unfit or unable **2.** to make unwilling or disinclined **3.** to make slightly ill

in·dis·posed (-pōzd′) *adj.* **1.** slightly ill **2.** unwilling; disinclined —see SYN. at SICK[1]

in·dis·po·si·tion (in′dis pə zish′ən) *n.* **1.** a slight illness **2.** unwillingness; disinclination

in·dis·pu·ta·ble (in′dis pyōōt′ə b'l, in dis′pyōō tə-) *adj.* that cannot be disputed or doubted; certain [an *indisputable* truth] —**in′dis·pu·ta·bil′i·ty** *n.* —**in′dis·pu·ta·bly** *adv.*

in·dis·sol·u·ble (in′di säl′yoo b'l) *adj.* that cannot be dissolved, broken up, or destroyed; firm; lasting [an *indissoluble* bond of friendship] —**in′dis·sol′u·bil′i·ty** *n.* —**in′dis·sol′u·bly** *adv.*

in·dis·tinct (in′dis tiŋkt′) *adj.* not distinct; not clearly seen, heard, or understood; vague, confused, etc. [an *indistinct* murmur of voices] —**in′dis·tinct′ly** *adv.* —**in′dis·tinct′ness** *n.*

in·dis·tin·guish·a·ble (in′dis tiŋ′gwish ə b'l) *adj.* that cannot be distinguished or recognized as different or separate [the twins are *indistinguishable*] —**in′dis·tin′guish·a·bly** *adv.*

in·dite (in dīt′) *vt.* **-dit′ed, -dit′ing** [< OFr., ult. < L.: see INDICT] to put in writing; compose and write [to *indite* a poem] —**in·dite′ment** *n.* —**in·dit′er** *n.*

in·di·um (in′dē əm) *n.* [ModL. < L. *indicum*, indigo: from its spectrum] a rare metallic chemical element, soft, ductile, and silver-white: symbol, In; at. wt., 114.82; at. no., 49

in·di·vid·u·al (in′di vij′ōō wəl, -vij′əl) *adj.* [< ML. < L. *individuus*, not divisible] **1.** existing as a separate thing or being; single; particular [presents for each *individual* child] **2.** of, for, or by each single person or thing [*individual* reports from the staff] **3.** of or relating to a particular person or thing; personal, unusual, or unique [an *individual* style] —*n.* **1.** a single thing, being, or organism, esp. as a member of a class, species, group, etc. **2.** a person —see SYN. at CHARACTERISTIC

in·di·vid·u·al·ism (-iz'm) *n.* **1.** individual character; individuality **2.** the doctrine that individual freedom in economic enterprise should not be restricted by the government **3.** the doctrine that the state exists to serve the individual **4.** the doctrine that self-interest is the proper goal of all human actions; egoism **5.** *a)* action based on any of these doctrines *b)* the leading of one's life in one's own way without conforming to conventions —**in'di·vid'u·al·ist** *n., adj.* —**in'di·vid'u·al·is'tic** *adj.*

in·di·vid·u·al·i·ty (in'di vij'oo wal'ə tē) *n., pl.* **-ties 1.** the qualities that set one person or thing apart from others; individual character **2.** the condition of being individual, or different from others [houses in the suburbs often have no *individuality*] **3.** an individual person or thing

in·di·vid·u·al·ize (-vij'oo wə līz', -vij'oo līz') *vt.* **-ized', -iz'ing 1.** to make individual; mark as different from others **2.** to make suitable for a particular individual **3.** to consider individually —**in'di·vid'u·al·i·za'tion** *n.*

in·di·vid·u·al·ly (-vij'oo wəl ē, -vij'əl ē) *adv.* **1.** one at a time; separately [the items are sold in sets or *individually*] **2.** as individuals or in an individual way [each child reacted *individually*; he handled all requests *individually*]

in·di·vis·i·ble (in'di viz'ə b'l) *adj.* **1.** that cannot be divided **2.** *Math.* that cannot be divided without leaving a remainder —*n.* anything indivisible —**in'di·vis'i·bil'i·ty** *n.* —**in'di·vis'i·bly** *adv.*

In·do·chi·na (in'dō chī'nə) **1.** large peninsula south of China, including Burma, Thailand, Indochina (sense 2), & the Malay Peninsula **2.** E part of this peninsula, consisting of Laos, Cambodia, & Vietnam Also sp. **Indo-China, Indo China**

In·do·chi·nese (-chī nēz') *adj.* of Indochina, its Mongoloid people, their languages, or their culture —*n., pl.* **-nese'** a native or inhabitant of Indochina Also sp. **Indo-Chinese**

INDOCHINA

in·doc·tri·nate (in däk'trə nāt') *vt.* **-nat'ed, -nat'ing** [prob. < OFr. *endoctriner*: see IN-[1] & DOCTRINE] **1.** to instruct in particular doctrines, theories, or beliefs **2.** to instruct; teach —**in·doc'tri·na'tion** *n.* —**in·doc'tri·na'tor** *n.*

In·do-Eu·ro·pe·an (in'dō yoor'ə pē'ən) *adj.* designating or of a family of languages that includes most of those spoken in Europe and many of those spoken in southwestern Asia and India —*n.* **1.** this family of languages, including the Indo-Iranian, Greek, Italic, Germanic, and Slavic languages **2.** the hypothetical language from which these languages are thought to have descended

In·do-I·ra·ni·an (-i rā'nē ən) *adj.* designating or of a subfamily of the Indo-European language family that includes the Indic and Iranian branches

in·do·lent (in'də lənt) *adj.* [< LL. < L. *in-*, not + prp. of *dolere*, to feel pain] disliking or avoiding work; idle; lazy —**in'do·lence** *n.* —**in'do·lent·ly** *adv.*

in·dom·i·ta·ble (in däm'it ə b'l) *adj.* [< LL. < L. < *in-*, not + pp. of *domitare*, < *domare*, to tame] not easily discouraged or defeated; unyielding [*indomitable* courage] —**in·dom'i·ta·bil'i·ty, in·dom'i·ta·ble·ness** *n.* —**in·dom'i·ta·bly** *adv.*

In·do·ne·sia (in'də nē'zhə, -shə) republic in the Malay Archipelago, consisting of Java, Sumatra, most of Borneo, Celebes, West Irian, & many smaller islands: 736,510 sq. mi.; pop. 113,721,000; cap. Djakarta

In·do·ne·sian (-zhən, -shən) *adj.* **1.** of Indonesia, its people, etc. **2.** designating or of a large group of Malayo-Polynesian languages spoken in Indonesia, the Philippines, Java, etc. —*n.* **1.** a member of a light-brown people of Indonesia, the Philippines, Java, etc., apparently of mixed Polynesian and Mongoloid stock **2.** an inhabitant of Indonesia **3.** the Indonesian languages **4.** the official Malay language of Indonesia

in·door (in'dôr') *adj.* **1.** of the inside of a house or building [*indoor* lighting] **2.** living, belonging, or carried on within a house or building [*indoor* games]

in·doors (in'dôrz') *adv.* in or into a house or other building

In·dore (in dôr') city in C India: pop. 395,000

in·dorse (in dôrs') *vt.* **-dorsed', -dors'ing** *same as* ENDORSE

In·dra (in'drə) [Sans.] the chief god of the early Hindu religion, a god associated with rain and thunder

in·du·bi·ta·ble (in doo'bi tə b'l, -dyoo'-) *adj.* that cannot be doubted; unquestionable [*indubitable* evidence] —**in·du'bi·ta·bly** *adv.*

in·duce (in doos', -dyoos') *vt.* **-duced', -duc'ing** [< L. *inducere* < *in-*, in + *ducere*, to lead: see DUKE] **1.** to lead on to some action, condition, etc.; persuade [can't we *induce* you to stay another week?] **2.** to bring on; cause [to *induce* vomiting with an emetic] **3.** to draw (a general rule or conclusion) from particular facts **4.** *Physics* to bring about (an electric or magnetic effect) in a body by exposing it to the influence of a field of force —see SYN. at PERSUADE —**in·duc'er** *n.* —**in·duc'i·ble** *adj.*

in·duce·ment (-mənt) *n.* **1.** an inducing or being induced **2.** anything that induces; motive; incentive —see SYN. at MOTIVE

in·duct (in dukt') *vt.* [< L. pp. of *inducere*: see INDUCE] **1.** formerly, to bring or lead in **2.** to place formally in an official position **3.** *a)* to initiate into a society *b)* to provide with knowledge of something not open to all [*inducting* him into the secrets of the trade] ☆*c)* to enroll (esp. a draftee) in the armed forces

in·duct·ance (in duk'təns) *n.* the property of an electric circuit by which a varying current in it produces a varying magnetic field that induces voltages in the same circuit or in a nearby circuit: it is measured in henrys

☆**in·duct·ee** (in duk'tē') *n.* a person inducted or being inducted, esp. into the armed forces

in·duc·tile (in duk't'l) *adj.* not ductile, malleable, or pliant

in·duc·tion (in duk'shən) *n.* **1.** an inducting or being inducted; installation or initiation **2.** a bringing forward of separate facts or instances, esp. so as to prove a general statement **3.** *Logic* reasoning from particular facts to a general conclusion; also, a conclusion so reached: opposed to DEDUCTION **4.** *Physics* the act or process by which an electric or magnetic effect is produced in an electrical conductor or magnetizable body when it is exposed to the influence of a field of force

induction coil an apparatus made up of two magnetically coupled coils in a circuit in which interruptions of the direct-current supply to one coil produce an alternating current of high potential in the other

induction heating the heating of a conducting material by means of electric current induced by an alternating magnetic field

in·duc·tive (in duk'tiv) *adj.* **1.** of or using logical induction [*inductive* reasoning] **2.** produced by induction **3.** of inductance or electrical or magnetic induction —**in·duc'tive·ly** *adv.*

in·duc·tor (-tər) *n.* a person or thing that inducts; specif., a coil used to introduce inductance into an electric circuit

in·due (in doo', -dyoo') *vt.* **-dued', -du'ing** *same as* ENDUE

in·dulge (in dulj') *vt.* **-dulged', -dulg'ing** [L. *indulgere*, to be kind to] **1.** to yield to or satisfy (a desire); give oneself up to [to *indulge* a craving for sweets] **2.** to gratify the wishes of; humor —*vi.* to indulge oneself; take pleasure (*in* something) [to *indulge* in sports] —**in·dulg'er** *n.*

SYN.—**indulge** implies a yielding to the wishes or desires of oneself or another, as because of a weak will or an agreeable nature [to *indulge* in self-pity; he *indulges* his son too much]; **humor** suggests a giving in to the whims of another [they *humored* him by laughing at all his jokes]; **pamper** implies constant, tender treatment, often to the point of overindulgence [to *pamper* a patient; to *pamper* a willful child]; **spoil** emphasizes the harm done to the personality by overindulgence or too much attention [grandparents often *spoil* children]; **baby** implies the sort of pampering infants get and suggests a possible loss of self-reliance [because he was sickly, his mother continued to *baby* him] —**ANT.** discipline, restrain

in·dul·gence (in dul'jəns) *n.* **1.** an indulging or being indulgent **2.** a thing indulged in [golf is his one *indulgence*] **3.** a giving way to one's desires **4.** a favor or right granted; permission **5.** *R.C.Ch.* freeing from all or part of the punishment due in purgatory for a sin

in·dul·gent (-jənt) *adj.* indulging or inclined to indulge; kind or too kind; not strict *[indulgent parents]* —**in·dul′gent·ly** *adv.*

in·du·rate (in′doo rāt′, -dyoo-) *vt.* **-rat′ed, -rat′ing** [< L. pp. of *indurare* < *in-*, in + *durare*, to harden] **1.** to make hard; harden **2.** to make callous or unfeeling **3.** to cause to be firmly established —*vi.* to become indurated —*adj.* **1.** hardened **2.** callous or unfeeling —**in′du·ra′tion** *n.* —**in′du·ra′tive** *adj.*

In·dus (in′dəs) river in S Asia, flowing from SW Tibet into the Arabian Sea: c.1,900 mi.

in·dus·tri·al (in dus′trē əl) *adj.* **1.** characterized by industries *[our industrial society]* **2.** of, connected with, or resulting from industries *[industrial design; industrial workers; industrial wastes]* **3.** of, or concerned with people working in industries *[industrial unions]* **4.** for use by industries: said of products *[industrial diamonds]* —**in·dus′tri·al·ly** *adv.*

industrial arts the mechanical and technical skills used in industry, ☆esp. as taught in schools

in·dus·tri·al·ism (in dus′trē əl iz′m) *n.* social and economic organization characterized by large industries, machine production, concentration of workers in cities, etc.

in·dus·tri·al·ist (-əl ist) *n.* a person who owns or manages an industrial enterprise

in·dus·tri·al·ize (-ə līz′) *vt.* **-ized′, -iz′ing** **1.** to develop industrialism in *[to industrialize a country]* **2.** to organize as an industry —*vi.* to become industrial —**in·dus′tri·al·i·za′tion** *n.*

☆**industrial park** an area zoned for industrial and business use, usually located on the outskirts of a city and having coordinated plant design

industrial relations relations between industrial employers and their employees

Industrial Revolution *[often* i- r-*]* the great social and economic changes coming with the introduction of machine and power tools and large-scale industrial production: it began in England about 1760

industrial union a labor union to which all workers in a given industry may belong, regardless of occupation or trade: see CRAFT UNION

in·dus·tri·ous (in dus′trē əs) *adj.* characterized by earnest, steady effort; hard-working —see SYN. at BUSY —**in·dus′tri·ous·ly** *adv.* —**in·dus′tri·ous·ness** *n.*

in·dus·try (in′dəs trē) *n., pl.* **-tries** [< MFr. < L. *industria* < *industrius*, active] **1.** earnest, steady effort; diligence in work **2.** *a)* any branch of manufacturing *[the garment industry]* *b)* any large-scale business activity *[the motion-picture industry; the tourist industry]* **3.** *a)* all industry as a group *b)* the owners and managers of industry

in·dwell (in dwel′) *vi., vt.* **-dwelt′, -dwell′ing** to dwell (in) as an inner force or spirit —**in′dwell′er** *n.*

-ine[1] (īn, in, ēn, ən) [< Fr. < L. *-inus*] *a suffix meaning* of, having the nature of, like *[divine, marine, crystalline]*

-ine[2] (in, ən, īn, ēn) [< L. < Gr. *-inē*] *a suffix used to form feminine nouns [heroine]*

-ine[3] (in, ən) [Fr. < L. *-ina*] *a suffix used to form certain abstract nouns [medicine, doctrine]*

-ine[4] (ēn, in, ən) [arbitrary use of L. *-inus*] *a suffix used to form certain commercial names [Vaseline]* or *the chemical names of a)* halogens *[iodine]* *b)* alkaloids or nitrogen bases *[morphine]*

in·e·bri·ate (in ē′brē āt′; *for adj. & n., usually* -it) *vt.* **-at′ed, -at′ing** [< L. pp. of *inebriare*, ult. < *in-*, thoroughly + *ebrius*, drunk] **1.** to make drunk; intoxicate **2.** to excite; exhilarate —*adj.* drunk; intoxicated —*n.* a drunken person, esp. a drunkard —**in·e′bri·at′ed** *adj.* —**in·e′bri·a′tion** *n.*

in·e·bri·e·ty (in′ē brī′ə tē) *n.* drunkenness

in·ed·i·ble (in ed′ə b'l) *adj.* not edible; not fit to be eaten —**in′ed·i·bil′i·ty** *n.*

in·ed·u·ca·ble (in ej′ə kə b'l) *adj.* thought to be incapable of being educated

in·ef·fa·ble (in ef′ə b'l) *adj.* [< MFr. < L. < *in-*, not + *effabilis*, utterable < *ex-*, out + *fari*, to speak] **1.** too overwhelming to be expressed in words; inexpressible *[ineffable beauty]* **2.** too sacred to be spoken *[the ineffable name of God]* —**in′ef·fa·bil′i·ty, in·ef′fa·ble·ness** *n.* —**in·ef′fa·bly** *adv.*

in·ef·face·a·ble (in′i fās′ə b'l) *adj.* that cannot be effaced; impossible to wipe out —**in′ef·face′a·bil′i·ty** *n.* —**in′ef·face′a·bly** *adv.*

in·ef·fec·tive (in′i fek′tiv) *adj.* **1.** not effective; not producing the desired effect *[an ineffective medicine]* **2.** not capable

of performing satisfactorily; incompetent; inefficient *[an ineffective mayor]* —**in′ef·fec′tive·ly** *adv.* —**in′ef·fec′tive·ness** *n.*

in·ef·fec·tu·al (in′i fek′choo wəl) *adj.* not effectual; not producing or not able to produce the desired effect *[ineffectual efforts]* —**in′ef·fec′tu·al′i·ty** (-wal′ə tē), **in′ef·fec′tu·al·ness** *n.* —**in′ef·fec′tu·al·ly** *adv.*

in·ef·fi·ca·cious (in′ef ə kā′shəs) *adj.* not efficacious; unable to produce the desired effect *[an inefficacious medicine]* —**in′ef·fi·ca′cious·ly** *adv.* —**in′ef·fi·ca′cious·ness** *n.*

in·ef·fi·ca·cy (in ef′i kə sē) *n.* lack of efficacy; inability to produce the desired effect

in·ef·fi·cient (in′ə fish′ənt) *adj.* not efficient; specif., *a)* not producing the desired effect with the least effort or waste *[an inefficient motor]* *b)* lacking the necessary ability or skill; incapable *[an inefficient worker]* —**in′ef·fi′cien·cy** *n.* —**in′ef·fi′cient·ly** *adv.*

in·e·las·tic (in′i las′tik) *adj.* not elastic; inflexible, rigid, unyielding, unadaptable, etc. —**in′e·las·tic′i·ty** (-las tis′ə tē) *n.*

in·el·e·gance (in el′ə gəns) *n.* **1.** lack of elegance **2.** something inelegant Also **in·el′e·gan·cy,** *pl.* **-cies**

in·el·e·gant (-gənt) *adj.* not elegant; lacking refinement, good taste, grace, etc.; coarse; crude *[inelegant manners]* —**in·el′e·gant·ly** *adv.*

in·el·i·gi·ble (in el′i jə b'l) *adj.* not eligible; not qualified under the rules *[ineligible to vote]* —*n.* an ineligible person —**in·el′i·gi·bil′i·ty** *n.* —**in·el′i·gi·bly** *adv.*

in·e·luc·ta·ble (in′i luk′tə b'l) *adj.* [< L. < *in-*, not + *eluctabilis*, resistible < *eluctari*, to struggle] not to be avoided or escaped; inevitable *[ineluctable fate]* —**in′e·luc′ta·bil′i·ty** *n.* —**in′e·luc′ta·bly** *adv.*

in·ept (in ept′) *adj.* [< Fr. < L. < *in-*, not + *aptus*, fit] **1.** unsuitable; unfit **2.** wrong in a foolish and awkward way *[inept praise]* **3.** clumsy or bungling; inefficient *[inept at cooking]* —**in·ept′ly** *adv.* —**in·ept′ness** *n.*

in·ept·i·tude (in ep′tə tood′, -tyood′) *n.* **1.** the quality or condition of being inept **2.** an inept act, remark, etc.

in·e·qual·i·ty (in′i kwäl′ə tē, -kwôl′-) *n., pl.* **-ties** **1.** a being unequal; lack of equality **2.** an instance of this; specif., *a)* a difference in size, amount, quality, rank, etc. *b)* an unevenness in surface *c)* a lack of proper proportion; unequal distribution **3.** *Math. a)* the relation between two unequal quantities *b)* an expression of this

in·eq·ui·ta·ble (in ek′wit ə b'l) *adj.* not equitable; unfair; unjust —**in·eq′ui·ta·bly** *adv.*

in·eq·ui·ty (in ek′wət ē) *n.* **1.** lack of justice; unfairness **2.** *pl.* **-ties** an instance of this

in·e·rad·i·ca·ble (in′i rad′ə kə b'l) *adj.* that cannot be eradicated or wiped out —**in′e·rad′i·ca·bly** *adv.*

in·ert (in urt′) *adj.* [< L. < *in-*, not + *ars*, ART[1]] **1.** without power to move or act **2.** inactive; dull; slow **3.** having few or no active properties *[an inert gas]* —**in·ert′ly** *adv.* —**in·ert′ness** *n.*

in·er·tia (in ur′shə) *n.* [L.: see prec.] **1.** *Physics* the tendency of matter to stay at rest, or to keep on moving in the same direction, unless acted on by an outside force **2.** a feeling that keeps one from wanting to do things, make changes, etc. *[inertia kept him from looking for a new job]* —**in·er′tial** *adj.*

inertial guidance (or **navigation**) the guidance (or navigation) of an aircraft, spacecraft, etc. along a set course by means of self-contained, automatic instruments that adjust for inertial effects

in·es·cap·a·ble (in′ə skāp′ə b'l) *adj.* that cannot be escaped or avoided; inevitable *[an inescapable conclusion]* —**in′es·cap′a·bly** *adv.*

in·es·sen·tial (in′ə sen′shəl) *adj.* not essential —*n.* something inessential

in·es·ti·ma·ble (in es′tə mə b'l) *adj.* too great or valuable to be properly measured or appreciated *[treasure of inestimable value]* —**in·es′ti·ma·bly** *adv.*

in·ev·i·ta·ble (in ev′ə tə b'l) *adj.* [< L. < *in-*, not + *evitabilis*, avoidable] that cannot be avoided; certain to happen *[his downfall is inevitable]* —**in·ev′i·ta·bil′i·ty** *n.* —**in·ev′i·ta·bly** *adv.*

in·ex·act (in′ig zakt′) *adj.* not exact or accurate; not strictly correct —**in′ex·act′ly** *adv.* —**in′ex·act′ness** *n.*

in·ex·cus·a·ble (in′ik skyoo′zə b'l) *adj.* that cannot or should not be excused or forgiven; unpardonable; unjustifiable *[his conduct was inexcusable]* —**in′ex·cus′a·bil′i·ty** *n.* —**in′ex·cus′a·bly** *adv.*

in·ex·haust·i·ble (in'ig zôs'tə b'l) *adj.* that cannot be exhausted; specif., *a)* that cannot be used up or emptied *[an inexhaustible water supply] b)* tireless —**in'ex·haust'i·bil'i·ty** *n.* —**in'ex·haust'i·bly** *adv.*

in·ex·o·ra·ble (in ek'sər ə b'l) *adj.* [< L. < *in*-, not + *exorare*, to move by entreaty] **1.** that cannot be influenced by entreaty; unrelenting *[inexorable determination]* **2.** that cannot be altered, checked, etc. *[inexorable fate]* —**in'ex·o·ra·bil'i·ty** *n.* —**in·ex'o·ra·bly** *adv.*

in·ex·pe·di·ent (in'ik spē'dē ənt) *adj.* not expedient; not suitable or practicable; unwise —**in'ex·pe'di·en·cy, in'ex·pe'di·ence** *n.* —**in'ex·pe'di·ent·ly** *adv.*

in·ex·pen·sive (in'ik spen'siv) *adj.* not expensive; costing relatively little; cheap —see SYN. at CHEAP —**in'ex·pen'sive·ly** *adv.* —**in'ex·pen'sive·ness** *n.*

in·ex·pe·ri·ence (in'ik spir'ē əns) *n.* lack of experience or of the knowledge or skill resulting from experience —**in'ex·pe'ri·enced** *adj.*

in·ex·pert (in ek'spərt, in'ik spurt') *adj.* not expert; unskillful; amateurish —**in·ex'pert·ly** *adv.* —**in·ex'pert·ness** *n.*

in·ex·pi·a·ble (in ek'spē ə b'l) *adj.* that cannot be expiated or atoned for *[an inexpiable sin]*

in·ex·pli·ca·ble (in eks'pli kə b'l, in'iks plik'ə b'l) *adj.* not explicable; that cannot be explained or understood —**in·ex'pli·ca·bil'i·ty** *n.* —**in·ex'pli·ca·bly** *adv.*

in·ex·press·i·ble (in'ik spres'ə b'l) *adj.* that cannot be expressed or described *[inexpressible sorrow]* —**in'ex·press'i·bil'i·ty** *n.* —**in'ex·press'i·bly** *adv.*

in·ex·pres·sive (in'ik spres'iv) *adj.* not expressive; lacking meaning or expression —**in'ex·pres'sive·ly** *adv.*

‡**in ex·ten·so** (in ik sten'sō) [L.] at full length

in·ex·tin·guish·a·ble (in'ik stiŋ'gwish ə b'l) *adj.* not extinguishable; that cannot be put out or stopped *[an inextinguishable fire; inextinguishable hope]* —**in'ex·tin'guish·a·bly** *adv.*

‡**in ex·tre·mis** (in' ik strē'mis) [L., in extremity] at the point of death

in·ex·tri·ca·ble (in eks'tri kə b'l, in'ik strik'ə b'l) *adj.* **1.** that one cannot extricate or free himself from *[an inextricable difficulty]* **2.** that cannot be disentangled or untied **3.** too complicated or involved to solve or clear up *[inextricable confusion]* —**in·ex'tri·ca·bil'i·ty** *n.* —**in·ex'tri·ca·bly** *adv.*

I·nez (ī'niz, ī'nez', ī nez') [Sp. *Iñez*] a feminine name

inf. 1. [L. *infra*] below **2.** infantry: also **Inf. 3.** infinitive **4.** information

in·fal·li·ble (in fal'ə b'l) *adj.* [< ML.: see IN-2 & FALLIBLE] **1.** incapable of error; never wrong **2.** not liable to fail, go wrong, etc.; reliable *[infallible proof]* **3.** *R.C.Ch.* incapable of error in setting forth doctrine on faith and morals: said esp. of the Pope when speaking in his official capacity —**in·fal'li·bil'i·ty** *n.* —**in·fal'li·bly** *adv.*

in·fa·mous (in'fə məs) *adj.* **1.** having a very bad reputation; notorious *[an infamous thief]* **2.** very bad or wicked *[an infamous crime]* —see SYN. at VICIOUS —**in'fa·mous·ly** *adv.*

in·fa·my (in'fə mē) *n., pl.* **-mies** [< OFr. < L.: see IN-2 & FAMOUS] **1.** very bad reputation; disgrace; dishonor *[he brought infamy upon himself by his crime]* **2.** the quality of being infamous; great wickedness **3.** an infamous act —see SYN. at DISGRACE

in·fan·cy (in'fən sē) *n., pl.* **-cies 1.** the state or period of being an infant; babyhood **2.** the beginning or earliest stage of anything *[in 1900 the automobile industry was in its infancy]* **3.** *Law* the state of being a minor; period before the age of legal majority, usually twenty-one

in·fant (in'fənt) *n.* [< OFr. < L., ult. < *in*-, not + prp. of *fari*, to speak: see BAN1] **1.** a very young child; baby **2.** *Law* a minor —*adj.* **1.** of or for infants or infancy *[a book on infant care]* **2.** in a very early stage *[an infant nation]*

in·fan·ta (in fan'tə, -fän'-) *n.* [Sp. & Port., fem. of INFANTE] **1.** any daughter of a king of Spain or Portugal **2.** the wife of an infante

in·fan·te (in fan'tā, -fän'-) *n.* [Sp. & Port. < L.: see INFANT] any son of a king of Spain or Portugal, except the heir to the throne

in·fan·ti·cide (in fan'tə sīd') *n.* [Fr. < LL.: see INFANT & -CIDE] **1.** the murder of a baby **2.** a person guilty of this

in·fan·tile (in'fən tīl', -til) *adj.* **1.** of infants or infancy *[infantile diseases]* **2.** like or characteristic of an infant; babyish *[infantile behavior]* **3.** in the earliest stage of development

infantile paralysis *same as* POLIOMYELITIS

in·fan·ti·lism (in'fən t'l iz'm, in fan'-) *n.* immature or childish behavior or characteristics; specif., an abnormal state in which such characteristics continue into later life

in·fan·try (in'fən trē) *n., pl.* **-tries** [< Fr. < It. < *infante*, child, knight's page, foot soldier] **1.** foot soldiers as a group; esp., that branch of an army consisting of soldiers trained and equipped to fight chiefly on foot **2.** [I-] a (designated) infantry regiment

in·fan·try·man (-mən) *n., pl.* **-men** (-mən) a soldier in the infantry

in·farct (in färkt', in'färkt) *n.* [< L. pp. of *infarcire* < L. *in*-, + *farcire*, to stuff] an area of dying or dead tissue, as in heart muscle, resulting from the blocking of a blood vessel to the part —**in·farc'tion** *n.*

in·fat·u·ate (in fach'oo wāt') *vt.* **-at·ed, -at'ing** [< L. pp. of *infatuare* < *in*-, entirely + *fatuus*, foolish: for IE. base see BAT1] **1.** to make foolish **2.** to inspire with foolish or shallow love —*adj.* infatuated

in·fat·u·at·ed (-id) *adj.* completely carried away by foolish or shallow love or attraction

in·fat·u·a·tion (in fach'oo wā'shən) *n.* the condition or an instance of being infatuated —see SYN. at LOVE

in·fect (in fekt') *vt.* [< MFr. < L. pp. of *inficere*, to stain < *in*-, in + *facere*, to make, DO1] **1.** to contaminate with a germ, virus, etc. that can cause disease *[to infect a water supply]* **2.** to make diseased by bringing into contact with such a germ, virus, etc. **3.** to invade (an individual, organ, tissue, etc.) as germs, etc. do **4.** to spread feelings, ideas, etc. of a good or bad kind to (others) —**in·fec'tor** *n.*

in·fec·tion (in fek'shən) *n.* **1.** an infecting; specif., *a)* a causing to become diseased *b)* an affecting with one's feelings or beliefs **2.** a being infected, esp. by bacteria, viruses, etc. **3.** something that results from infecting or being infected; specif., a disease resulting from infection (sense 2) **4.** anything that infects

in·fec·tious (-shəs) *adj.* **1.** likely to cause infection **2.** caused by infection (sense 2) *[shingles is an infectious disease, but not contagious]* **3.** tending to spread to others *[an infectious laugh]* —**in·fec'tious·ly** *adv.* —**in·fec'tious·ness** *n.*

infectious hepatitis a virus disease causing inflammation of the liver

infectious mononucleosis an acute disease, esp. of young people, characterized by fever, swollen lymph nodes, sore throat, etc.: it is thought to be caused by a virus

in·fec·tive (in fek'tiv) *adj.* likely to cause infection

in·fe·lic·i·tous (in'fə lis'ə təs) *adj.* not felicitous; unfortunate or unsuitable *[an infelicitous remark]* —**in'fe·lic'i·tous·ly** *adv.*

in·fe·lic·i·ty (-tē) *n.* **1.** a being infelicitous **2.** *pl.* **-ties** something infelicitous; unsuitable or inapt remark, action, etc.

in·fer (in fur') *vt.* **-ferred', -fer'ring** [< L. *inferre* < *in*-, in + *ferre*, BEAR1] **1.** to conclude by reasoning from something known or assumed **2.** to lead to as a conclusion; imply: regarded by some as a loose usage *[his questions inferred that he disapproved]* —*vi.* to draw inferences —**in·fer'a·ble** *adj.* —**in·fer'a·bly** *adv.* —**in·fer'rer** *n.*

SYN.—**infer** suggests the arriving at a decision or opinion by reasoning from known facts or evidence *[from your smile, I infer that you are pleased]*; **deduce** stresses the use of logical and systematic reasoning in inferring something *[the existence of the planet Neptune was deduced before its actual discovery]*; **conclude** strictly implies an inference that is the final logical result in a process of reasoning *[I must, therefore, conclude that you are right]*; **judge** stresses the careful checking and weighing of statements, arguments, etc. in reaching a conclusion; **gather** is an informal substitute for infer and conclude *[I gather that you don't care]*

in·fer·ence (in'fər əns) *n.* **1.** the act or process of inferring **2.** a conclusion or opinion arrived at by inferring

in·fer·en·tial (in'fə ren'shəl) *adj.* of or based on inference —**in'fer·en'tial·ly** *adv.*

in·fe·ri·or (in fir'ē ər) *adj.* [L., compar. of *inferus*, low] **1.** lower in position than another thing, part, organ, etc. **2.** lower in order, status, rank, etc. *[a captain is inferior to a major]* **3.** lower in quality or value *[a copy inferior to the original]* **4.** poor in quality; below average *[inferior merchandise]* —*n.* an inferior person or thing —**in·fe'ri·or'i·ty** (-ôr'ə tē, -är'-) *n.*

---

fat, āpe, cär; ten, ēven; is, bīte; gō, hôrn, tōōl, lōōk; oil, out; up, fur; get; joy; yet; chin; she; thin, then; zh, leisure; ŋ, ring; ə for *a* in *ago, e* in *agent, i* in *sanity, o* in *comply, u* in *focus;* ' as in *able* (ā'b'l); Fr. bâl; ë, Fr. coeur; ö, Fr. feu; Fr. mon; ô, Fr. coq; ü, Fr. duc; r, Fr. cri; H, G. ich; kh, G. doch; ‡foreign; ☆ Americanism; < derived from. See inside front cover.

inferiority complex a feeling of being inferior or inadequate that may express itself in a show of boldness, bossiness, etc.

in·fer·nal (in fur'n'l) *adj.* [< OFr. < LL. *infernalis*, ult. < L. *inferus*: see INFERIOR] **1.** *a)* of the ancient mythological world of the dead *b)* of hell **2.** hellish; fiendish [*infernal* torture] **3.** [Colloq.] hateful; annoying [stop that *infernal* noise!] —**in·fer'nal·ly** *adv.*

in·fer·no (in fur'nō) *n., pl.* **-nos** [It. < L.: see INFERNAL] hell or any place suggesting hell

in·fer·tile (in fur't'l) *adj.* **1.** not fertile; barren; sterile **2.** not fertilized, as an egg —**in·fer·til·i·ty** (in'fər til'ə tē) *n.*

in·fest (in fest') *vt.* [< Fr. < L. < *infestus*, hostile] **1.** to overrun or swarm about in large numbers, usually so as to be harmful or bothersome [a barn *infested* with bats] **2.** to be parasitic in or on —**in'fes·ta'tion** *n.*

in·fi·del (in'fə d'l) *n.* [< MFr. < L. < *in-*, not + *fidelis*, faithful: for IE. base see FAITH] **1.** a person who does not believe in a particular religion, esp. in the main religion of the area [among Moslems, an *infidel* is one who does not accept Islam] **2.** a person who holds no religious belief —*adj.* **1.** that is an infidel; unbelieving **2.** of infidels —see SYN. at ATHEIST

in·fi·del·i·ty (in'fə del'ə tē) *n., pl.* **-ties** **1.** the fact or state of being an infidel **2.** unfaithfulness or disloyalty to another; esp., sexual unfaithfulness of a husband or wife; adultery **3.** an unfaithful or disloyal act

in·field (in'fēld') *n.* ☆**1.** *a)* the area enclosed by the four base lines on a baseball field *b)* the infielders as a group, or the area they cover ☆**2.** the area inside a race track or running track: field events of a track meet are often held on it

☆**in·field·er** (-ər) *n. Baseball* a player whose position is in the infield; shortstop, first baseman, second baseman, or third baseman

in·fight·ing (in'fīt'iŋ) *n.* **1.** fighting, esp. boxing, at close range **2.** sharp or bitter struggle, as within an organization or group [political *infighting*] —**in'fight'er** *n.*

in·fil·trate (in fil'trāt, in'fil trāt') *vi., vt.* **-trat·ed, -trat·ing** **1.** to pass into or through (a substance), as in filtering **2.** to pass, or cause (individual troops) to pass, through weak places in the enemy's lines **3.** to enter, or cause to enter, (a region or organization) for the secret purpose of gaining influence or control or for spying —*n.* something that infiltrates —**in'fil·tra'tion** *n.* —**in'fil·tra'tive** *adj.* —**in'fil·tra'tor** *n.*

infin. infinitive

in·fi·nite (in'fə nit) *adj.* [< L.: see IN-² & FINITE] **1.** lacking limits or bounds; extending beyond measure or comprehension; without beginning or end [is the universe *infinite?*] **2.** very great; vast [*infinite* mercy] **3.** *Math.* indefinitely large; greater than any finite number —**the Infinite** (**Being**) God —**in'fi·nite·ly** *adv.* —**in'fi·nite·ness** *n.*

in·fin·i·tes·i·mal (in'fin ə tes'ə məl, in fin'-) *adj.* [< ModL. < L. *infinitus*, infinite (patterned after *centesimus*, hundredth)] too small to be measured; infinitely small —*n.* an infinitesimal quantity —**in'fin·i·tes'i·mal·ly** *adv.*

in·fin·i·tive (in fin'ə tiv) *adj.* [< LL. < L. *infinitus (modus)*, lit., unlimited (mood)] *Gram.* of or connected with an infinitive —*n. Gram.* the form of the verb which expresses existence or action without reference to person, number, or tense: usually following the marker *to* (*to go*) or another verb form (*let him try*)

in·fin·i·tude (in fin'ə tood', -tyood') *n.* **1.** a being infinite **2.** an infinite quantity or extent

in·fin·i·ty (in fin'ə tē) *n., pl.* **-ties** **1.** the quality of being infinite **2.** endless or unlimited space, time, distance, amount, etc. **3.** an indefinitely large number or amount **4.** *Photog.* a distance so far from a camera that rays of light reflected from a subject at that distance may be regarded as parallel: the setting for this on the focusing scale is marked with the symbol ∞

in·firm (in furm') *adj.* **1.** not firm or strong physically; weak; feeble, as from old age **2.** not firm in mind or will; vacillating [*infirm* of purpose] **3.** not stable; frail; shaky, as a structure **4.** not secure or valid [an *infirm* title to property] —see SYN. at WEAK —**in·firm'ly** *adv.* —**in·firm'ness** *n.*

in·fir·ma·ry (in fur'mə rē) *n., pl.* **-ries** a place for the care of the sick, injured, or infirm; esp., a building or room, as in a school, that serves as a hospital or dispensary

in·fir·mi·ty (in fur'mə tē) *n.* **1.** a being infirm; feebleness; weakness **2.** *pl.* **-ties** *a)* a physical weakness or defect *b)* a moral weakness

in·fix (in fiks', in'fiks) *vt.* **1.** to fasten or set firmly in or on **2.** to fix firmly in the mind; instill

‡**in fla·gran·te de·lic·to** (in flə gran'tē di lik'tō) [L.] in the very act of committing the offense

in·flame (in flām') *vt.* **-flamed', -flam'ing** [< OFr. < L.: see IN-¹ & FLAME] **1.** to set on fire **2.** to arouse strong feeling or violence in; excite greatly **3.** to make (anger, desire, etc.) greater or stronger **4.** to cause inflammation in (some organ or tissue) —*vi.* **1.** to become roused, excited, etc. **2.** to catch fire **3.** to become hot, feverish, sore, etc. —**in·flam'er** *n.*

in·flam·ma·ble (in flam'ə b'l) *adj.* **1.** *same as* FLAMMABLE **2.** easily angered or excited —*n.* anything flammable —**in·flam'·ma·bil'i·ty** *n.* —**in·flam'ma·bly** *adv.*

in·flam·ma·tion (in'flə mā'shən) *n.* **1.** an inflaming or being inflamed **2.** a condition of some part of the body in reaction to injury, infection, etc., characterized by redness, pain, heat, and swelling

in·flam·ma·to·ry (in flam'ə tôr'ē) *adj.* **1.** rousing or likely to rouse excitement, anger, violence, etc. [an *inflammatory* speech] **2.** *Med.* of or characterized by inflammation

in·flate (in flāt') *vt.* **-flat'ed, -flat'ing** [< L. pp. of *inflare* < *in-*, in + *flare*, to blow] **1.** to blow full or swell out as with air or gas [to *inflate* a balloon] **2.** to puff up, esp. in a way that is vain, pompous etc. [*inflated* with pride; a speech *inflated* with bombast] **3.** to increase or raise beyond what is normal; specif., to cause inflation of (money, prices, etc.) —*vi.* to become inflated —**in·flat'a·ble** *adj.* —**in·flat'er, in·fla'tor** *n.*

in·fla·tion (in flā'shən) *n.* **1.** an inflating or being inflated ☆**2.** an increase in the amount of money in circulation that causes a fall in its value and a rise in prices —**in·fla'tion·ar'y** *adj.*

in·fla·tion·ist (-ist) *adj.* favoring or promoting monetary inflation —*n.* a person who is inflationist

in·flect (in flekt') *vt.* [< L. *inflectere* < *in-*, in + *flectere*, to bend] **1.** to turn, bend, or curve **2.** to vary the tone or pitch of (the voice) **3.** *Gram.* to change the form of (a word) by inflection, as in conjugating or declining —*vi.* to be changed by inflection —**in·flec'tive** *adj.*

in·flec·tion (in flek'shən) *n.* **1.** a turn, bend, or curve **2.** a change in tone or pitch of the voice [a rising *inflection* at the end of a sentence often means a question] **3.** *Gram. a)* the change of form by which some words show number, case, gender, tense, comparison, etc. *b)* an inflected form *c)* an inflectional element

in·flec·tion·al (-'l) *adj.* of, having, or showing grammatical inflection —**in·flec'tion·al·ly** *adv.*

in·flex·i·ble (in flek'sə b'l) *adj.* not flexible; specif., *a)* that cannot be bent or curved; rigid [an *inflexible* steel rod] *b)* firm in mind or purpose; stubborn [an *inflexible* will] *c)* that cannot be changed; unalterable [*inflexible* rules] —**in·flex'i·bil'i·ty, in·flex'i·ble·ness** *n.* —**in·flex'i·bly** *adv.*

in·flict (in flikt') *vt.* [< L. pp. of *infligere* < *in-*, against + *fligere*, to strike] **1.** to cause (pain, wounds, etc.) as by striking **2.** to impose (a punishment, disagreeable task, etc. *on* or *upon*) —**in·flict'er, in·flic'tor** *n.* —**in·flic'tive** *adj.*

in·flic·tion (in flik'shən) *n.* **1.** an inflicting **2.** something inflicted, as punishment

in-flight (in'flīt') *adj.* done, occurring, shown, etc. while an aircraft is in flight [*in-flight* movies]

in·flo·res·cence (in'flô res''ns, -flə-) *n.* [< ModL. < LL.: see IN-¹ & FLORESCENCE] *Bot.* **1.** the producing of blossoms; flowering **2.** the arrangement of flowers on a stem or axis **3.** a flower cluster on a common axis —**in'flo·res'cent** *adj.*

in·flow (in'flō') *n.* **1.** a flowing in or into **2.** anything that flows in

in·flu·ence (in'floo-wəns) *n.* [< OFr. < ML. < L. prp. of *influere* < *in-*, in + *fluere*, to flow: for IE. base see BALL¹] **1.** *a)* the power of persons or things to affect others *b)* the effect of such power **2.** power based on wealth, high position, success, etc. [a man of *influence*] **3.** one that has influence [she's a good *influence* on the children] —*vt.* **-enced, -enc·ing** to have influence

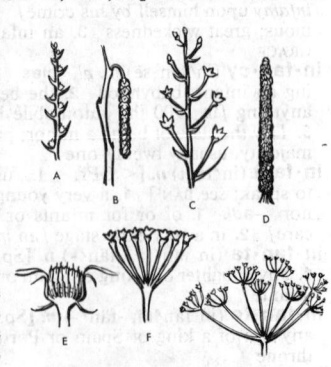

TYPES OF INFLORESCENCE
(A, spike; B, catkin; C, raceme; D, spadix; E, head with disk flowers and ray flowers; F, umbel; G, compound umbel)

on; affect the nature, behavior, or thought of [her advice *influenced* my decision]

in·flu·en·tial (in′floo wen′shəl) *adj.* having or exerting influence, esp. great influence; powerful —**in′flu·en′tial·ly** *adv.*

in·flu·en·za (in′floo wen′zə) *n.* [It., lit., an influence (of the stars)] an acute, contagious virus disease, like a bad cold but more serious, with fever, muscular pain, etc. —**in′flu·en′zal** *adj.*

in·flux (in′fluks′) *n.* [Fr. < LL. pp. of *influere*: see INFLUENCE] 1. a flowing in or continual coming in; inflow [an *influx* of tourists] 2. the point where a river joins another body of water

in·fold (in fōld′) *vt. same as* ENFOLD

in·form (in fôrm′) *vt.* [< OFr. < L.: see IN-¹ & FORM] 1. to inspire with or give a particular quality or character 2. to give knowledge of something to; tell [*inform* us of your plans] —*vi.* 1. to give information 2. to give information laying blame or accusation upon another [the spy *informed* against his friends] —see SYN. at NOTIFY

in·for·mal (in fôr′məl) *adj.* not formal; specif., *a)* not according to fixed customs, rules, etc. [an *informal* agreement on trade] *b)* casual, easy, or relaxed [an *informal* manner] *c)* for everyday use or casual wear [*informal* clothes] *d)* not requiring formal dress [an *informal* dinner] *e)* of or used in the ordinary, everyday talk and writing of most people: see COLLOQUIAL —**in·for′mal·ly** *adv.*

in·for·mal·i·ty (in′fôr mal′ə tē) *n.* 1. the quality or condition of being informal 2. *pl.* **-ties** an informal act

in·form·ant (in fôr′mənt) *n.* a person who gives information or facts about something

in·for·ma·tion (in′fər mā′shən) *n.* 1. an informing or being informed; esp., a telling or being told of something [this is for your *information* only] 2. news; word [the latest *information* on the kidnapping] 3. knowledge acquired in any manner; facts; data [an encyclopedia gives *information* about many things] 4. a person or agency answering questions as a service to others [call *information* for that phone number] 5. any data stored in a computer 6. *Law* an accusation of a criminal offense made by a public officer, rather than by a grand jury indictment —**in′for·ma′tion·al** *adj.*

SYN.—**information** applies to facts that are gathered in any way, as by reading, observation, hearsay, etc. and does not necessarily imply that these are accurate [misleading *information*]; **knowledge** applies to any body of facts gathered by study, observation, etc. and to the ideas inferred from these facts, and suggests an understanding of what is known [man's *knowledge* of the universe]; **learning** is knowledge gained by study, esp. in languages, literature, philosophy, etc.; **erudition** implies learning that is too deep or difficult for most people to understand; **wisdom** implies superior judgment and understanding based on wide knowledge and experience

in·form·a·tive (in fôr′mə tiv) *adj.* giving information; instructive —**in·form′a·tive·ly** *adv.*

in·formed (in fôrmd′) *adj.* having much information, knowledge, or education

in·form·er (in fôr′mər) *n.* a person who informs; esp., one who secretly accuses, or gives evidence against, another, often for a reward

in·fra- [< L. *infra*, below] *a prefix meaning* below, beneath [*infrared*]

in·frac·tion (in frak′shən) *n.* [< L. < pp. of *infringere*: see INFRINGE] a breaking of a law, pact, etc.; violation

in·fra·red (in′frə red′) *adj.* designating or of those invisible rays just beyond the red of the visible spectrum: their waves are longer than those of the spectrum colors and they can go deep inside an object to produce heat: used in cooking, photography, etc.

in·fra·son·ic (in′frə sän′ik) *adj.* designating or of a frequency of sound below the range audible to the human ear

in·fra·struc·ture (in′frə struk′chər) *n.* the basic facilities on which a city, state, etc. depends, as roads, power plants, transportation systems, or schools —**in′fra·struc′tur·al** *adj.*

in·fre·quent (in frē′kwənt) *adj.* not frequent; happening seldom; rare —see SYN. at RARE¹ —**in·fre′quen·cy, in·fre′quence** *n.* —**in·fre′quent·ly** *adv.*

in·fringe (in frinj′) *vt.* **-fringed′, -fring′ing** [L. *infringere* < *in-*, in + *frangere*, to break] to break (a law or agreement); violate —**infringe on** (or **upon**) to break in on; encroach or trespass on (the rights, patents, etc. of others) —**in·fringe′ment** *n.* —**in·fring′er** *n.*

in·fu·ri·ate (in fyoor′ē āt′) *vt.* **-at′ed, -at′ing** [< ML. pp. of *infuriare* < L. *in-*, in + *furia*, rage] to cause to become very angry; enrage —**in·fu′ri·at′ing·ly** *adv.* —**in·fu′ri·a′tion** *n.*

in·fuse (in fyooz′) *vt.* **-fused′, -fus′ing** [< L. pp. of *infundere* < *in-*, in + *fundere*, to pour] 1. to put (qualities, ideas, etc.) into, as if by pouring; instill; impart [the teacher *infused* a desire to learn into the students] 2. to fill (*with* a quality, feeling, etc.); imbue; inspire [he *infused* us with hope] 3. to steep or soak (tea leaves, etc.) so as to draw out the flavor or other qualities —**in·fus′er** *n.*

in·fu·si·ble (in fyoo′zə b'l) *adj.* that cannot be fused or melted —**in·fu′si·bil′i·ty, in·fu′si·ble·ness** *n.*

in·fu·sion (in fyoo′zhən) *n.* 1. an infusing 2. something infused 3. the liquid extract that results from steeping a substance in water

in·fu·so·ri·an (in′fyoo sôr′ē ən) *n.* [< ModL.: from their occurrence in infusions] any of certain protozoans having cilia that permit free movement —*adj.* of these protozoans: also **in′·fu·so′ri·al**

-ing (iŋ) 1. [< OE. *-ende*] *a suffix used to form the present participle* [hearing] 2. [< OE. *-ung*] *a suffix used to form verbal nouns meaning*: *a)* the act or an instance of [talking] *b)* something produced by the action of [painting] *c)* something that does the action of [a head *covering*] *d)* material used for [carpeting]

in·gen·ious (in jēn′yəs) *adj.* [< MFr. < L. < *ingenium*, ability < *in-*, in + *gignere*, to produce: see GENUS] 1. clever, resourceful, and inventive [an *ingenious* designer] 2. cleverly or originally made or done [an *ingenious* plan] —see SYN. at CLEVER —**in·gen′ious·ly** *adv.* —**in·gen′ious·ness** *n.*

in·gé·nue (an′zhə noo′, -jə-; Fr. an zhā nü′) *n., pl.* **-nues′** (-nooz′; Fr. -nü′) [< Fr. < L. *ingenuus*, INGENUOUS] 1. an innocent, inexperienced young woman 2. *Theater a)* the role of such a character *b)* an actress playing such a role

in·ge·nu·i·ty (in′jə noo′ə tē, -nyoo′-) *n.* [< L. < *ingenuus* (see INGENIOUS): associated with INGENIOUS] a being ingenious; cleverness, originality, etc.

in·gen·u·ous (in jen′yoo wəs) *adj.* [< L. *ingenuus* < *in-*, in + *gignere*, to produce: see GENUS] 1. frank; open; candid 2. innocent in an open or natural way; simple; naive [the *ingenuous* girl believed that everyone loved her] —see SYN. at NAIVE —**in·gen′u·ous·ly** *adv.* —**in·gen′u·ous·ness** *n.*

in·gest (in jest′) *vt.* [< L. pp. of *ingerere* < *in-*, into + *gerere*, to carry] to take (food, drugs, etc.) into the body, as by swallowing or absorbing —**in·ges′tion** *n.* —**in·ges′tive** *adj.*

in·gle (iŋ′g'l) *n.* [Scot. < Gael. *aingeal*, fire] [Brit. Dial.] 1. a fire or blaze 2. a fireplace

in·gle·nook (-nook′) *n.* [Chiefly Brit.] a corner by a fireplace: also **ingle nook**

in·gle·wood (iŋ′g'l wood′) [after the home town in Canada of the owner of the site] city in SW Calif.: suburb of Los Angeles: pop. 90,000

in·glo·ri·ous (in glôr′ē əs) *adj.* 1. not giving or deserving glory; shameful; disgraceful [an *inglorious* defeat] 2. [Now Rare] without glory; not famous —**in·glo′ri·ous·ly** *adv.* —**in·glo′ri·ous·ness** *n.*

in·go·ing (in′gō′iŋ) *adj.* going in; entering

in·got (iŋ′gət) *n.* [< MFr. *lingot* (with faulty separation of *l-*) < OPr.] a mass of metal cast into a bar or other convenient shape

in·graft (in graft′) *vt. same as* ENGRAFT

in·grained (in grānd′, in′grānd) *adj.* 1. worked into the fiber; firmly fixed or established [*ingrained* principles] 2. firmly settled in a habit, practice, etc.; inveterate; thoroughgoing [an *ingrained* liar]

in·grate (in′grāt) *n.* [< OFr. < L. < *in-*, not + *gratus*, grateful: see GRACE] an ungrateful person

in·gra·ti·ate (in grā′shē āt′) *vt.* **-at′ed, -at′ing** [< L. < *in*, in + *gratia*, favor: see GRACE] to bring (oneself) into another's favor or good graces by doing things that please [he *ingratiated* himself by flattering her] —**in·gra′ti·at′ing·ly** *adv.* —**in·gra′ti·a′tion** *n.*

in·grat·i·tude (in grat′ə tood′, -tyood′) *n.* lack of gratitude; ungratefulness

in·gre·di·ent (in grē′dē ənt) *n.* [< L. prp. of *ingredi*: see INGRESS] 1. any of the things that a mixture is made of [sugar is a basic *ingredient* of candy] 2. a component part of anything

In·gres (an′gr′), Jean Au·guste Do·mi·nique (zhän ô güst′ dô mē nēk′) 1780–1867; Fr. painter

in·gress (in′gres) *n.* [< L. pp. of *ingredi*, to enter < *in-*, into + *gradi*: see GRADE] **1.** the act of entering: also **in·gres′sion** (-gresh′ən) **2.** the right to enter [the guard refused us *ingress*] **3.** an entrance —**in·gres′sive** *adj.*

Ing·rid (iŋ′grid) [< Scand.; ult. < ON. *Ingvi*, name of a Gmc. god + *rida*, ride] a feminine name

in·grow·ing (in′grō′iŋ) *adj.* growing within, inward, or into; esp., growing into the flesh [an *ingrowing* hair]

in·grown (-grōn′) *adj.* grown within, inward, or into; esp., grown into the flesh, as a toenail

in·gui·nal (iŋ′gwə n′l) *adj.* [< L. < *inguen*, the groin] of or near the groin [an *inguinal* hernia]

in·gulf (in gulf′) *vt.* same as ENGULF

in·hab·it (in hab′it) *vt.* [< OFr. < L. *inhabitare* < *in-*, in + *habitare*, to dwell] to live in (a region, house, etc.); occupy —**in·hab′i·ta′tion** *n.* —**in·hab′it·er** *n.*

in·hab·it·a·ble (-ə b′l) *adj.* that can be inhabited; fit to live in; habitable —**in·hab′it·a·bil′i·ty** *n.*

in·hab·it·ant (in hab′i tənt) *n.* a person or animal that inhabits some specified region, house, etc.

in·hal·ant (in hāl′ənt) *adj.* used in breathing in —*n.* a medicine to be breathed in as a vapor

in·ha·la·tion (in′hə lā′shən) *n.* **1.** the act of inhaling **2.** same as INHALANT

☆**in·ha·la·tor** (in′hə lāt′ər) *n.* **1.** an apparatus for giving medicinal vapors that are to be breathed in **2.** same as RESPIRATOR (sense 2)

in·hale (in hāl′) *vt., vi.* **-haled′, -hal′ing** [L. *inhalare* < *in-*, in + *halare*, to breathe] to breathe in; draw (air, vapor, smoke, etc.) into the lungs

in·hal·er (-ər) *n.* **1.** a person who inhales **2.** same as: *a)* RESPIRATOR (sense 1) *b)* INHALATOR (sense 1)

in·har·mon·ic (in′här män′ik) *adj.* not harmonic; discordant

in·har·mo·ni·ous (-mō′nē əs) *adj.* not harmonious; not blending well or getting along well together [*inharmonious* relations] —**in′har·mo′ni·ous·ly** *adv.* —**in′har·mo′ni·ous·ness** *n.*

in·here (in hir′) *vi.* **-hered′, -her′ing** [< L. < *in-*, in + *haerere*, to stick] to be inherent; exist as a quality, characteristic, or right (*in*)

in·her·ence (in hir′əns, -her′-) *n.* the fact or state of inhering or being inherent

in·her·en·cy (-ən sē) *n., pl.* **-cies 1.** same as INHERENCE **2.** something inherent

in·her·ent (in hir′ənt, -her′-) *adj.* [see INHERE] existing in someone or something as a natural or inseparable quality or right; inborn [his *inherent* shyness kept him from speaking] —**in·her′ent·ly** *adv.*

in·her·it (in her′it) *vt.* [< OFr. < LL., ult. < L. *in*, in + *heres*, HEIR] **1.** to receive (something, esp. property) as the heir of someone; get from another when he dies [he *inherited* his uncle's fortune] **2.** to have (certain characteristics) by heredity [she *inherited* her mother's intelligence] —*vi.* to receive an inheritance —**in·her′i·tor** *n.* —**in·her′i·tress** (-i tris) *n.fem.*

in·her·it·a·ble (-ə b′l) *adj.* **1.** capable of inheriting; having the rights of an heir. **2.** that can be inherited —**in·her′it·a·bil′i·ty, in·her′it·a·ble·ness** *n.*

in·her·it·ance (-əns) *n.* **1.** the action of inheriting **2.** something inherited or to be inherited; legacy; bequest **3.** right to inherit **4.** anything received as if by inheritance **5.** any characteristic passed on by heredity

inheritance tax a tax on inherited property

in·hib·it (in hib′it) *vt.* [< L. pp. of *inhibere*, to curb < *in-*, in + *habere*: see HABIT] to hold back or keep from some action, feeling, etc. [a person *inhibited* by fear; drugs that *inhibit* sweating] —see SYN. at RESTRAIN —**in·hib′i·tive, in·hib′i·to′ry** (-i tôr′ē) *adj.*

in·hi·bi·tion (in′hi bish′ən, in′ə-) *n.* **1.** an inhibiting or being inhibited **2.** a mental or psychological process that holds one back from some action, emotion, or thought [his *inhibitions* kept him from laughing]

in·hib·i·tor (in hib′it ər) *n.* a person or thing that inhibits; esp., any substance that slows or prevents a chemical or organic reaction: also **in·hib′it·er**

in·hos·pi·ta·ble (in häs′pi tə b′l, in′häs pit′ə b′l) *adj.* **1.** not hospitable **2.** not offering protection, shelter, etc.; barren; forbidding [an *inhospitable* climate] —**in·hos′pi·ta·bly** *adv.*

in·hos·pi·tal·i·ty (in′häs pi tal′ə tē, in häs′-) *n.* lack of hospitality; inhospitable treatment

in-house (in′hous′) *adj.* originating within an organization, company, etc., rather than brought in from outside

in·hu·man (in hyōō′mən, -yōō′-) *adj.* not human; esp., not having normal human characteristics; unfeeling, heartless, etc. —see SYN. at CRUEL —**in·hu′man·ly** *adv.*

in·hu·mane (in′hyōō mān′, -yoo-) *adj.* not humane; unmoved by the suffering of others; cruel, brutal, unkind, etc. —**in′hu·mane′ly** *adv.*

in·hu·man·i·ty (-man′ə tē) *n.* **1.** a being inhuman or inhumane **2.** *pl.* **-ties** an inhuman or inhumane act or remark

in·im·i·cal (in im′i k′l) *adj.* [< LL. < L. *inimicus*, ENEMY] **1.** hostile; unfriendly [*inimical* acts led to war] **2.** in opposition; adverse; harmful [laws *inimical* to freedom; a climate *inimical* to health] —**in·im′i·cal·ly** *adv.*

in·im·i·ta·ble (in im′ə tə b′l) *adj.* that cannot be imitated or matched; too good to be equaled or copied [Mark Twain's *inimitable* humor] —**in·im′i·ta·bil′i·ty, in·im′i·ta·ble·ness** *n.* —**in·im′i·ta·bly** *adv.*

in·iq·ui·tous (in ik′wə təs) *adj.* showing iniquity; wicked; unjust —see SYN. at VICIOUS —**in·iq′ui·tous·ly** *adv.* —**in·iq′ui·tous·ness** *n.*

in·iq·ui·ty (-wə tē) *n.* [< OFr. < L. < *iniquus*, unequal < *in-*, not + *aequus*, equal] **1.** lack of righteousness or justice; wickedness **2.** *pl.* **-ties** a wicked, unjust, or unrighteous act

in·i·tial (i nish′əl) *adj.* [< Fr. < L. *initialis*, ult. < *in-*, in + *ire*, to go: see YEAR] having to do with or occurring at the beginning [the *initial* stage of a disease; the *initial* letter of a word] —*n.* a capital, or upper-case, letter; specif., the first letter of a name —*vt.* **-tialed** or **-tialled, -tial·ing** or **-tial·ling** to mark or sign with one's initials [he *initialed* the letter after he read it]

in·i·tial·ly (-ē) *adv.* at the beginning; at first

in·i·ti·ate (i nish′ē āt′; for adj. & n., usually -it) *vt.* **-at′ed, -at′ing** [< L. pp. of *initiare*: see INITIAL] **1.** to bring into practice or use [to *initiate* a new course of studies] **2.** to give the first knowledge or experience of some subject to [he *initiated* me into the game of chess] **3.** to admit as a member into a fraternity, club, etc., esp. with a special or secret ceremony —*adj.* initiated —*n.* a person who has recently been, or is about to be, initiated —see SYN. at BEGIN —**in·i′ti·a′tor** *n.*

in·i·ti·a·tion (i nish′ē ā′shən) *n.* **1.** an initiating or being initiated **2.** the ceremony by which one is initiated into a fraternity, etc.

in·i·ti·a·tive (i nish′ē ə tiv, -nish′ə-) *adj.* of, or having the nature of, initiation —*n.* **1.** the action of taking the first step or move [he took the *initiative* in forming our club] **2.** the characteristic of originating new ideas or methods; ability to think and act without needing to be told what to do **3.** *a)* the right of a legislature to introduce new legislation *b)* the right of a group of citizens to introduce a matter for legislation to the legislature or directly to the voters *c)* the procedure for this

in·i·ti·a·to·ry (-tôr′ē) *adj.* **1.** beginning; introductory **2.** of or used in an initiation

in·ject (in jekt′) *vt.* [< L. pp. of *injicere* < *in-*, in + *jacere*, to throw] **1.** to force or drive (a fluid) into something; esp., to force (a liquid) into some part of the body by means of a hypodermic syringe, etc. **2.** to fill by injection **3.** to introduce (a missing quality, etc.) [to *inject* a note of humor into a story] **4.** to throw in (a remark, etc.), as into a discussion —**in·ject′a·ble** *adj.* —**in·jec′tor** *n.*

in·jec·tion (in jek′shən) *n.* **1.** an injecting **2.** something injected; esp., a liquid injected into the body

in·ju·di·cious (in′jōō dish′əs) *adj.* not judicious; showing poor judgment; not discreet or wise —**in′ju·di′cious·ly** *adv.* —**in′ju·di′cious·ness** *n.*

in·junc·tion (in juŋk′shən) *n.* [< LL. < pp. of *injungere*, ENJOIN] **1.** an enjoining; command **2.** an order **3.** a writ or order from a court prohibiting a person or group from carrying out a given action, or ordering a given action to be done —**in·junc′tive** *adj.*

in·jure (in′jər) *vt.* **-jured, -jur·ing** [see INJURY] **1.** to do physical harm to; hurt or damage **2.** to offend (one's feelings, etc.) **3.** to weaken (a reputation, etc.) **4.** to be unjust to

SYN.—**injure** implies that the appearance, health, soundness, etc. of a person or thing has been made less than perfect [apples *injured* by bruising]; **damage** stresses the loss, as in value, usefulness, etc., resulting from an injury [*damaged* goods]; **harm** and **hurt** both imply a causing of any kind of injury or damage [the rumors did not *harm* (or *hurt*) his business], **hurt** often suggesting resulting pain or suffering [to *hurt* one's leg; to *hurt* someone's feelings]; to **impair** something is to cause it to lessen in quality, value, strength, etc. [*impaired* hearing]; **spoil** implies such serious impairment of a thing as to destroy its value, usefulness, etc. [the canned food was *spoiled*]

in·ju·ri·ous (in joor′ē əs) *adj.* **1.** injuring or likely to injure; harmful or damaging **2.** offensive or abusive; slanderous or libelous —**in·ju′ri·ous·ly** *adv.* —**in·ju′ri·ous·ness** *n.*

in·ju·ry (in′jər ē) *n.*, *pl.* **-ries** [< L. *injuria*, ult. < *in-*, not + *jus*, right: see JURY¹] **1.** harm or damage done to a person or thing **2.** an injurious act; injustice, as in injuring a person's feelings or rights, a reputation, etc. —see SYN. at INJUSTICE

in·jus·tice (in jus′tis) *n.* **1.** the quality of being unjust or unfair **2.** an unjust act; injury [the *injustice* of imprisonment without a trial]

SYN.—**injustice** implies unjust treatment of another or a violation of his rights; **injury** and **wrong** are specially applied when legal action can be taken to correct the injustices, both applying to a violation of the private rights of an individual, and **wrong** alone, to crimes and misdemeanors which affect the whole community —ANT. justice

ink (iŋk) *n.* [OFr. *enque* < LL. < Gr. *enkauston*, red ink < *enkaiein*, to burn in] **1.** a colored liquid used for writing, etc. **2.** a sticky, colored paste used in printing **3.** a dark, liquid secretion squirted out by cuttlefish, etc. for protection —*vt.* **1.** to cover with ink **2.** to mark or color with ink (often with *in*) —**ink′er** *n.* —**ink′like′** *adj.*

ink·blot (iŋk′blät′) *n.* any of a group of irregular blots of ink, used as in the Rorschach test

ink·horn (-hôrn′) *n.* a small container of horn, etc., formerly used to hold ink

ink·ling (iŋk′liŋ) *n.* **1.** a slight suggestion; hint **2.** a vague idea or notion

ink·stand (iŋk′stand′) *n.* **1.** a small stand holding an inkwell, pens, etc. **2.** *same as* INKWELL

ink·well (iŋk′wel′) *n.* a container for holding ink, usually set in a desk, inkstand, etc.

ink·y (iŋ′kē) *adj.* **ink′i·er**, **ink′i·est** **1.** like ink in color; dark; black **2.** colored, marked, or covered with ink —**ink′i·ness** *n.*

in·laid (in′lād′, in lād′) *adj.* **1.** set in pieces into a surface of another material so as to form a smooth surface [an *inlaid* design in a table top] **2.** decorated with such a surface [an *inlaid* floor]

in·land (in′lənd; *for n. & adv.*, *usually* -land′) *adj.* **1.** of, located in, or confined to the interior of a country or region; away from the coast or border **2.** [Brit.] within a country; domestic —*n.* inland areas —*adv.* into or toward the interior —**in·land·er** (in′lən dər) *n.*

Inland Sea arm of the Pacific surrounded by the Japanese islands of Honshu, Shikoku, & Kyushu

in·law (in′lô′) *n.* [< (MOTHER-)IN-LAW, etc.] [Colloq.] a relative by marriage

in·lay (in′lā′; *for v.*, *also* in lā′) *vt.* **-laid′**, **-lay′ing** **1.** *a)* to set (pieces of wood, metal, etc.) into a surface to make a design that is usually level with the surface *b)* to decorate with such pieces **2.** to add extra silverplating to —*n.*, *pl.* **-lays** **1.** inlaid decoration or material **2.** a filling for a tooth made from a mold and cemented into the cavity —**in′lay′er** *n.*

in·let (in′let, -lit) *n.* **1.** *a)* a narrow strip of water extending into a body of land from a river, lake, ocean, etc. *b)* a narrow strip of water between islands **2.** an opening or entrance, as to a culvert

‡**in loc. cit.** [L. *in loco citato*] in the place cited

‡**in lo·co pa·ren·tis** (in lō′kō pə ren′tis) [L.] in the place of a parent, or of a parent's authority

in·ly (in′lē) *adv.* [Poet.] **1.** inwardly **2.** intimately

in·mate (in′māt′) *n.* [IN-¹ + MATE¹] a person living with others in the same building, now esp. one confined with others in a prison, etc.

‡**in me·di·as res** (in mā′dē äs rās′) [L., lit., into the midst of things] in the middle of the action

in me·mo·ri·am (in mə môr′ē əm) [L.] in memory (of)

in-mi·grant (in′mī′grənt) *adj.* coming in from another region of the same country [*in-migrant* workers] —*n.* an in-migrant person —**in′-mi′grate** (-grāt) *vi.* **-grat·ed**, **-grat·ing** —**in′-mi·gra′tion** *n.*

in·most (in′mōst′) *adj.* **1.** located farthest within **2.** most intimate or secret; innermost [*inmost* thoughts]

INLAID WOOD

inn (in) *n.* [OE.] **1.** an establishment providing food and lodging for travelers; hotel **2.** a restaurant or tavern Now chiefly in the names of such places

in·nards (in′ərdz) *n.pl.* [< INWARD(S)] [Dial. or Colloq.] **1.** the internal organs of the body; viscera **2.** the inner parts of anything

in·nate (i nāt′, in′āt) *adj.* [< L. pp. of *innasci* < *in-*, in + *nasci*, to be born] **1.** existing naturally rather than acquired [*innate* talent] **2.** existing as a natural quality [the *innate* humor of a situation] —**in·nate′ly** *adv.* —**in·nate′ness** *n.*

SYN.—**innate** and **inborn** can often be used in place of one another, but **innate** has a broader meaning, describing that which belongs to something as part of its nature or makeup, and **inborn**, the simpler term, more specifically suggesting qualities so much a part of one's nature as to seem to have been born in or with one [*inborn* modesty]; **inbred** refers to qualities that are deeply instilled by breeding or early training [an *inbred* love of learning]

in·ner (in′ər) *adj.* **1.** located farther within; interior [*inner* rooms] **2.** of the mind or spirit [*inner* peace] **3.** more intimate or secret [the *inner* emotions]

inner circle a small, exclusive group of people who control or influence customs, thought, etc.

☆**inner city** the sections of a large city in or near its center, esp. when crowded or in bad condition

inner ear a cavity next to the middle ear, consisting of the cochlea, the vestibule, and the semicircular canals

Inner Mongolia region in NE China, south & southeast of the Mongolian People's Republic

in·ner·most (in′ər mōst′) *adj.* **1.** located farthest within [the *innermost* chamber] **2.** most intimate or secret [one's *innermost* thoughts]

In·ness (in′is), George 1825–94; U.S. painter

in·ning (in′iŋ) *n.* [OE. *innung*, a getting in] **1.** *Baseball & (pl.) Cricket a)* the period of play in which a team has a turn at bat *b)* a numbered round of play in which both teams have a turn at bat **2.** [often pl.] the period of, or opportunity for, action, exercise of authority, etc. [the reform party now had its *innings*]

inn·keep·er (in′kē′pər) *n.* the proprietor of an inn

in·no·cence (in′ə səns) *n.* **1.** the being innocent; specif., *a)* freedom from sin or guilt *b)* guilelessness; simplicity *c)* naiveté *d)* harmlessness *e)* ignorance Also **in′no·cen·cy** ☆**2.** *same as* BLUET

In·no·cent (in′ə sənt) any of 13 popes, including **1.** Innocent I, Saint ?–417 A.D.; Pope (401–417) **2.** Innocent III 1161?–1216; Pope (1198–1216) **3.** Innocent IV ?–1254; Pope (1243–54) **4.** Innocent XI 1611–89; Pope (1676–89)

in·no·cent (in′ə sənt) *adj.* [< OFr. < L. < *in-*, not + prp. of *nocere*, to do wrong to] **1.** free from sin, evil, or guilt; specif., *a)* doing or thinking nothing morally wrong; pure *b)* not guilty of a specific crime or offense [another's confession proved him *innocent* of the robbery] *c)* free from harmful effect or cause [*innocent* entertainment] **2.** *a)* knowing no evil [an *innocent* child] *b)* without guile or cunning; artless *c)* naive *d)* ignorant **3.** totally lacking (with *of*) [*innocent* of decoration] —*n.* **1.** a person knowing no evil or sin, as a child **2.** a very naive person —**in′no·cent·ly** *adv.*

in·noc·u·ous (i näk′yoo wəs) *adj.* [< L. < *in-*, not + *nocuus*, harmful < *nocere*, to harm] **1.** that does not injure or harm; harmless [an *innocuous* insect] **2.** not controversial or offensive; dull and uninspiring [an *innocuous* speech] —**in·noc′u·ous·ly** *adv.*

in·nom·i·nate bone (i näm′ə nit) [< LL. *innominatus*, unnamed + BONE] either of two large, irregular bones of the pelvis, each formed of the ilium, ischium, and pubis; hipbone

in·no·vate (in′ə vāt′) *vi.* **-vat′ed**, **-vat′ing** [< L. pp. of *innovare* < *in-*, in + *novare*, to alter < *novus*, new] to introduce new methods, devices, etc. —*vt.* to bring in as an innovation —**in′no·va′tive** *adj.* —**in′no·va′tor** *n.*

in·no·va·tion (in′ə vā′shən) *n.* **1.** an innovating **2.** something

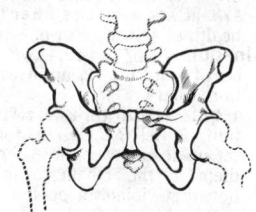

INNOMINATE BONE

fat, āpe, cär; ten, ēven; is, bīte; gō, hôrn, tōōl, look; oil, out; up, fur; get; joy; yet; chin; she; thin, then; zh, leisure; ŋ, ring; ə for *a* in *ago*, *e* in *agent*, *i* in *sanity*, *o* in *comply*, *u* in *focus*; ′ as in *able* (ā′b'l); Fr. bal; ë, Fr. coeur; ö, Fr. feu; Fr. mon; ô, Fr. coq; ü, Fr. duc; r, Fr. cri; H, G. ich; kh, G. doch; ‡ foreign; ☆ Americanism; < derived from. See inside front cover.

newly introduced; new method, practice, device, etc. —**in′no·va′tion·al** *adj.*

Inns·bruck (inz′brook′; *G.* ins′brook) city in the Tirol, W Austria; pop. 101,000

in·nu·en·do (in′yoo wen′dō) *n.*, *pl.* **-does, -dos** [L., abl. of gerund of *innuere*, to nod to, hint] a hint or sly remark, esp. one that suggests something bad about someone; insinuation

in·nu·mer·a·ble (i noo′mər ə b′l, -nyoo′-) *adj.* too numerous to be counted; countless —see SYN. at MANY —**in·nu′mer·a·bil′i·ty** *n.* —**in·nu′mer·a·ble·ness** *n.* —**in·nu′mer·a·bly** *adv.*

in·oc·u·late (i näk′yoo lāt) *vt.* **-lat′ed, -lat′ing** [< L. pp. of *inoculare*, to engraft a bud < *in-*, in + *oculus*, an eye, bud] **1.** to inject a serum, vaccine, etc. into a (living organism), esp. in order to create immunity **2.** to implant microorganisms into (soil, a culture medium, etc.) to develop a culture, fix nitrogen, etc. **3.** to introduce ideas, etc. into the mind of; imbue —**in·oc′u·la·bil′i·ty** *n.* —**in·oc′u·la·ble** *adj.* —**in·oc′u·la′tive** *adj.* —**in·oc′u·la′tor** *n.*

in·oc·u·la·tion (i näk′yoo lā′shən) *n.* the injection of a disease agent into an animal or plant, usually to cause a mild form of the disease and build up immunity to it

in·of·fen·sive (in′ə fen′siv) *adj.* not offensive; unobjectionable; causing no harm or annoyance —**in′of·fen′sive·ly** *adv.* —**in′of·fen′sive·ness** *n.*

in·op·er·a·ble (in äp′ər ə b′l) *adj.* not operable; specif., *a)* that cannot be done or used; not practicable *b)* that cannot be dealt with by surgery [*an inoperable cancer*]

in·op·er·a·tive (-ər ə tiv, -ə rāt′iv) *adj.* not operative; not working; without effect [*an inoperative law*]

in·op·por·tune (in äp′ər toon′, -tyoon′) *adj.* not opportune; coming or happening at a poor time; not appropriate [*the dinner hour was an inopportune time to call*] —**in·op′por·tune′ly** *adv.* —**in·op′por·tune′ness** *n.*

in·or·di·nate (in ôr′d′n it) *adj.* [< L.: see IN-[2] & ORDINATE] too great; excessive; immoderate [*an inordinate appetite*] —see SYN. at EXCESSIVE —**in·or′di·nate·ly** *adv.*

in·or·gan·ic (in′ôr gan′ik) *adj.* not organic; specif., *a)* designating or composed of matter that is not animal or vegetable; not living *b)* not like an organism in structure *c)* designating or of any chemical compound not classified as organic *d)* designating or of the branch of chemistry dealing with these compounds —**in′or·gan′i·cal·ly** *adv.*

in·o·si·tol (i nō′sə tōl′, -tôl′) *n.* [< Gr. *inos*, genitive of *is*, muscle + -IT(E) + -OL[1]] a sweet crystalline alcohol, $C_6H_6(OH)_6$, esp. the form found in the vitamin B complex that may have some effect on cholesterol metabolism

in·pa·tient (in′pā′shənt) *n.* a patient who is lodged and fed in a hospital, clinic, etc. while receiving treatment

‡in per·pe·tu·um (in′ pər pech′oo wəm) [L.] forever

in·put (in′poot) *n.* what is put in; specif., *a)* the amount of money, material, effort, etc. put into a project or process *b)* electric current or power put into a circuit, machine, etc. *c)* information fed into a computer, etc.

in·quest (in′kwest) *n.* [< OFr. < VL. pp.: see INQUIRE] **1.** a judicial inquiry, as a coroner's investigation of a death **2.** the jury or group holding such an inquiry **3.** the verdict of such an inquiry

in·qui·e·tude (in kwī′ə tood′, -tyood′) *n.* restlessness; uneasiness

in·quire (in kwīr′) *vi.* **-quired′, -quir′ing** [< OFr. < VL. word no longer known, for L. *inquirere* < *in-*, into + *quaerere*, to seek] **1.** to ask a question or questions [*the student inquired about his grades*] **2.** to carry out an examination or investigation (usually with *into*) [*he inquired into the health conditions of the prison*] —*vt.* to seek information about [*to inquire the way*] —see SYN. at ASK —**inquire after** to pay respects by asking about the health of —**in·quir′er** *n.* —**in·quir′ing·ly** *adv.*

in·quir·y (in′kwə rē, -kwī′-; in kwīr′ē) *n.*, *pl.* **-quir·ies 1.** the act of inquiring **2.** an investigation or examination **3.** a question; query

in·qui·si·tion (in′kwə zish′ən) *n.* **1.** an inquiring; investigation **2.** [I-] *R.C.Ch. a)* formerly, the general court that was set up to uncover those thought of as heretics and to punish them *b)* the activities of this court **3.** *a)* an official investigation that violates a person's civil liberties and seeks to punish him for his beliefs *b)* any relentless questioning **4.** *Law* an inquest or any judicial inquiry —**in′qui·si′tion·al** *adj.*

in·quis·i·tive (in kwiz′ə tiv) *adj.* **1.** inclined to ask many questions or seek information **2.** asking more questions than is necessary or proper; unnecessarily curious; prying —see SYN. at CURIOUS —**in·quis′i·tive·ly** *adv.* —**in·quis′i·tive·ness** *n.*

in·quis·i·tor (-tər) *n.* **1.** an official whose work is making an inquisition **2.** any harsh or prying questioner **3.** [I-] an official of the Inquisition

in·quis·i·to·ri·al (in kwiz′ə tôr′ē əl) *adj.* **1.** of, or having the nature of, an inquisitor or an inquisition **2.** inquisitive (sense 2) —**in·quis′i·to′ri·al·ly** *adv.*

in re (in rē, rā) [L.] in the matter (of); concerning

I.N.R.I. [L. *Iesus Nazarenus, Rex Iudaeorum*] Jesus of Nazareth, King of the Jews

in·road (in′rōd′) *n.* **1.** a sudden invasion or raid **2.** [*usually pl.*] any harmful or damaging advance or encroachment [*inroads on one's health*]

in·rush (-rush′) *n.* a rushing in; inflow; influx

ins. 1. inches **2.** insulated **3.** insurance

in·sane (in sān′) *adj.* **1.** not sane; mentally ill; mad: see INSANITY ☆**2.** of or for insane people [*mental hospitals were once called insane asylums*] **3.** very foolish; senseless —**in·sane′ly** *adv.*

in·san·i·tar·y (in san′ə ter′ē) *adj.* not sanitary; unhealthful

in·san·i·ty (in san′ə tē) *n.*, *pl.* **-ties 1.** the state of being insane; mental illness **2.** great folly; extreme senselessness
SYN.—**insanity,** current in popular and legal language but not used as a term in psychiatry, implies the mental illness of one who is regarded as not being rational or capable of handling his own affairs; **lunacy** is now most commonly used in its extended sense of extreme folly; **dementia** is the general term for an acquired mental disorder, now generally one of organic origin, as distinguished from *amentia* (mental deficiency existing at birth); **psychosis** is the psychiatric term for any of various special mental disorders, functional or organic, in which the personality is seriously disorganized —ANT. sanity

in·sa·ti·a·ble (in sā′shə b′l, -shē ə-) *adj.* constantly wanting more; that cannot be satisfied; very greedy [*insatiable hunger*] —**in·sa′ti·a·bil′i·ty** *n.* —**in·sa′ti·a·bly** *adv.*

in·sa·ti·ate (-shē it) *adj.* not satiated; insatiable —**in·sa′ti·ate·ly** *adv.* —**in·sa′ti·ate·ness** *n.*

in·scribe (in skrīb′) *vt.* **-scribed′, -scrib′ing** [< L.: see IN-[1] & SCRIBE] **1.** *a)* to mark or engrave (words, symbols, etc.) on some surface *b)* to write on, mark, or engrave (a surface) **2.** to add the name of (someone) to a list; enroll **3.** *a)* to dedicate (a book, etc.) informally *b)* to write a short, signed message in (a book, etc. one is presenting as a gift) **4.** to fix or impress deeply in the mind, memory, etc. **5.** *Geom.* to draw (a figure) inside another figure so that their boundaries touch at as many points as possible —**in·scrib′a·ble** *adj.* —**in·scrib′er** *n.*

in·scrip·tion (in skrip′shən) *n.* **1.** an inscribing **2.** something inscribed or engraved, as on a coin or monument **3.** *a)* an informal dedication in a book, etc. *b)* a short, signed message written in a book, etc. one is presenting as a gift —**in·scrip′tive, in·scrip′tion·al** *adj.*

in·scru·ta·ble (in skroot′ə b′l) *adj.* [< LL. < L. *in-*, not + *scrutari*, to examine] that cannot be easily understood; completely obscure or mysterious; enigmatic [*an inscrutable look*] —**in·scru′ta·bil′i·ty** *n.* —**in·scru′ta·bly** *adv.*

in·seam (in′sēm′) *n.* the inner seam from the crotch to the bottom of a trouser leg

in·sect (in′sekt) *n.* [< L. *insectum* (*animale*), lit., notched (animal): from the segmented bodies] **1.** any of a large group of small arthropod animals, including beetles, bees, flies, wasps, etc., having, in the adult state, a head, thorax, and abdomen, three pairs of legs, and, usually, two pairs of membranous wings **2.** popularly, any of a group of small animals, usually wingless, including spiders, centipedes, ticks, mites, etc.

in·sec·ti·cide (in sek′tə sīd′) *n.* any substance used to kill insects —**in·sec′ti·ci′dal** *adj.*

in·sec·ti·vore (in sek′tə vôr′) *n.* [< ModL.: see INSECT & -VOROUS] **1.** any of a group of insect-eating mammals, including moles, shrews, hedgehogs, etc. **2.** any animal or plant that feeds on insects

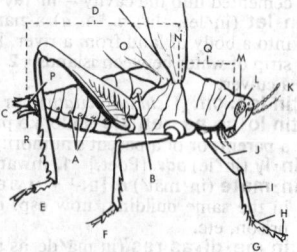

INSECT (locust)
(A, spiracles; B, tympanum;
C, ovipositor; D, abdomen; E,
hind leg; F, middle leg; G, foreleg; H, tarsus; I, tibia; J, femur;
K, antennae; L, compound eye;
M, head; N, forewing; O, hind
wing; P, cercus; Q, thorax;
R, anus)

in·sec·tiv·o·rous (in′sek tiv′ər əs) *adj.* feeding chiefly on insects

in·se·cure (in′si kyoor′) *adj.* not secure; specif., *a)* not safe; dangerous [an *insecure* mountain ledge] *b)* not confident; filled with anxieties [she was *insecure* in her new job] *c)* not firm or dependable [an *insecure* partnership] —**in′se·cure′ly** *adv.* —**in′se·cu′ri·ty** *n., pl.* **-ties**

in·sem·i·nate (in sem′ə nāt′) *vt.* **-nat′ed, -nat′ing** [< L. pp. of *inseminare* < *in-*, in + *seminare*, to sow < *semen*, seed] **1.** to introduce semen into the vagina of; impregnate **2.** to implant (ideas, etc.) in (the mind, etc.) —**in·sem′i·na′tion** *n.*

in·sen·sate (in sen′sāt, -sit) *adj.* **1.** not having any of the senses, because not living; inanimate [*insensate* rocks] **2.** without sense or reason; stupid [*insensate* fury] **3.** without feeling for others; insensitive [an *insensate* judge] —**in·sen′sate·ly** *adv.*

in·sen·si·ble (in sen′sə b'l) *adj.* **1.** lacking sensation; not able to notice or feel [his frozen fingers were *insensible* to pain] **2.** having lost sensation; unconscious [she fainted and lay *insensible*] **3.** not recognizing or realizing; unaware; indifferent [factory workers become *insensible* to noise] **4.** so small or slight that it is not easily seen or felt [the *insensible* movement of the hour hand] —**in·sen′si·bil′i·ty** *n.* —**in·sen′si·bly** *adv.*

in·sen·si·tive (-tiv) *adj.* not sensitive; having little or no reaction (to) [*insensitive* to music] —**in·sen′si·tive·ly** *adv.* —**in·sen′si·tiv′i·ty, in·sen′si·tive·ness** *n.*

in·sen·ti·ent (in sen′shē ənt, -shənt) *adj.* not sentient; without life, consciousness, or feeling —**in·sen′ti·ence** *n.*

in·sep·a·ra·ble (in sep′ər ə b'l) *adj.* that cannot be separated or parted [*inseparable* friends] —*n.* [pl.] inseparable persons or things —**in·sep′a·ra·bil′i·ty, in·sep′a·ra·ble·ness** *n.* —**in·sep′a·ra·bly** *adv.*

in·sert (in surt′; *for n.* in′sərt) *vt.* [< L. pp. of *inserere* < *in-*, in + *serere*, to join] to put or fit (something) into something else; set in [to *insert* a hand in the pocket] —*n.* anything inserted or to be inserted; esp., an extra leaf or section inserted in a newspaper, etc. —**in·sert′er** *n.*

in·ser·tion (in sur′shən) *n.* **1.** an inserting or being inserted **2.** something inserted; specif., *a)* a piece of lace or embroidery that can be set into a piece of cloth for ornamentation *b)* a single placement of an advertisement, as in a newspaper

☆**in·ser·vice** (in′sur′vis) *adj.* designating or of training given to employees in connection with their work to help them develop skills, etc.

in·ses·so·ri·al (in′se sôr′ē əl) *adj.* [< ModL., ult. < L. *in-*, in + *sedere*, to SIT] perching or adapted for perching

in·set (in set′; *also, and for n. always,* in′set) *vt.* **-set′, -set′ting** to set into something; insert —*n.* something inserted or set in, as a small map set inside the border of a larger one

in·shore (in′shôr′, in shôr′) *adv., adj.* **1.** in toward the shore **2.** near the shore —**inshore of** nearer than (something else) to the shore

in·side (in′sīd′, -sīd′; *for prep. & adv., usually* in′sīd′) *n.* **1.** the part within; inner side, surface, or part [wash the windows on the *inside*] **2.** the part closest to something implied, as the part of a sidewalk closest to the buildings [walk on the *inside*] **3.** [pl.] [Colloq.] the internal organs of the body; viscera —*adj.* **1.** on or in the inside; internal [an *inside* page] **2.** working or used indoors [an *inside* switch for the porch light] ☆**3.** known only to insiders; secret or private [the *inside* story] —*adv.* **1.** on or to the inside; within **2.** indoors [the children play *inside* when it rains] —*prep.* inside of; in; within [*inside* the box] —☆**inside of** within the space or time of —**inside out 1.** with the inside where the outside should be; reversed **2.** [Colloq.] thoroughly; completely —**on the inside** ☆**1.** in a position to receive special information, advantage, or favor, etc. **2.** in one's inner thoughts or feelings

inside job [Colloq.] a crime committed by, or with the aid of, a person employed or trusted by the victim

☆**Inside Passage** sea route along the W coast of N.America, from Seattle, Wash., to the N Alaska panhandle

INSESSORIAL FEET

in·sid·er (in sī′dər) *n.* **1.** a person inside a given place or group **2.** a person having or likely to have secret or confidential information

☆**inside track 1.** the inner, shorter way around a curved race track **2.** a favorable position in any competition

in·sid·i·ous (in sid′ē əs) *adj.* [< L. < *insidiae*, an ambush < *in-*, in + *sedere*, SIT] **1.** treacherous in a sly, tricky way [an *insidious* plot] **2.** working in a slow, subtle way; more dangerous than it seems to be [an *insidious* disease] —**in·sid′i·ous·ly** *adv.* —**in·sid′i·ous·ness** *n.*

in·sight (in′sīt′) *n.* **1.** the ability to see and understand clearly the inner nature of things, esp. by intuition **2.** a clear understanding of the inner nature of some specific thing —**in′sight′ful** *adj.*

in·sig·ni·a (in sig′nē ə) *n.pl.* (*in sense 1*), *n.sing.* (*in sense 2*) [< L., pl. of *insigne*, ult. < *in-*, in + *signum*, a mark] **1.** *sing.* **in·sig′ne** (-nē) badges, emblems, etc., as of rank or membership **2.** *pl.* **in·sig′ni·as** such a badge, emblem, etc.

in·sig·nif·i·cant (in′sig nif′ə kənt) *adj.* **1.** having little or no importance or meaning; trivial [*insignificant* details] **2.** small in size, amount, scope, etc. [to add an *insignificant* amount of salt] **3.** low or unimpressive in position, character, etc. [an *insignificant* public official] —**in′sig·nif′i·cance, in′sig·nif′i·can·cy** *n.* —**in′sig·nif′i·cant·ly** *adv.*

in·sin·cere (in′sin sir′) *adj.* not sincere; not meaning what one says or does; deceptive or hypocritical —**in′sin·cere′ly** *adv.*

in·sin·cer·i·ty (-ser′ə tē) *n.* **1.** a being insincere **2.** *pl.* **-ties** an insincere act, remark, etc.

in·sin·u·ate (in sin′yoo wāt′) *vt.* **-at′ed, -at′ing** [< L. pp. of *insinuare* < *in-*, in + *sinus*, curved surface] **1.** to introduce or work into gradually, indirectly, and skillfully [to *insinuate* oneself into another's favor] **2.** to hint indirectly; imply in a sly way [are you *insinuating* that I lied?] —*vi.* to make insinuations —see SYN. at SUGGEST —**in·sin′u·at′ing·ly** *adv.* —**in·sin′u·a′tive** *adj.* —**in·sin′u·a′tor** *n.*

in·sin·u·a·tion (in sin′yoo wā′shən) *n.* **1.** an insinuating **2.** something insinuated; specif., *a)* a sly hint or suggestion, esp. against someone *b)* an act or remark intended to win favor

in·sip·id (in sip′id) *adj.* [< Fr. < LL. < L. *in-*, not + *sapidus*, savory < *sapere*, to taste] **1.** without flavor; tasteless **2.** not exciting; dull; lifeless [*insipid* talk] —**in′si·pid′i·ty, in·sip′id·ness** *n.* —**in·sip′id·ly** *adv.*

SYN.—**insipid** implies a lack of taste or flavor and is used of anything that is lifeless, dull, etc. [*insipid* sermons]; **vapid** and **flat** suggest that which has lost freshness, sharpness, tang, zest, etc. and become stale, dull, etc. [the *vapid*, or *flat*, comedy skits that had once so delighted him]; **banal** is used of that which is so overused or common as to seem very vapid or flat [the *banal* plots of western movies] —**ANT.** zesty, spicy, pungent

in·sist (in sist′) *vi.* [< MFr. < L. *insistere* < *in-*, in + *sistere*, to STAND] to take a stand or make a firm demand and stick strongly to it (often with *on* or *upon*) [he *insisted* on getting his full share] —*vt.* **1.** to demand strongly [I *insist* that you come] **2.** to declare firmly [I *insist* that I saw her there] —**in·sist′er** *n.* —**in·sist′ing·ly** *adv.*

in·sist·ence (in sis′təns) *n.* **1.** a being insistent **2.** an act or instance of insisting Also **in·sist′en·cy,** *pl.* **-cies**

in·sist·ent (in sis′tənt) *adj.* **1.** insisting or demanding; persistent in demands or assertions [*insistent* pleas] **2.** that forces or keeps one's attention [an *insistent* rhythm] —**in·sist′ent·ly** *adv.*

‡**in si·tu** (in sī′too) [L.] in position

in·snare (in sner′) *vt.* **-snared′, -snar′ing** *same as* ENSNARE

in·so·bri·e·ty (in′sə brī′ə tē, -sō-) *n.* lack of sobriety; esp., drunkenness or intemperance

in·so·far (in′sə fär′, -sō-) *adv.* to such a degree or extent (usually with *as*) [*insofar* as one can tell]

in·sole (in′sōl′) *n.* **1.** the inside sole of a shoe **2.** an extra, removable inside sole for comfort

in·so·lent (in′sə lənt) *adj.* [< L. < *in-*, not + prp. of *solere*, to be accustomed] **1.** boldly disrespectful in speech or behavior; impertinent; impudent; rude **2.** [Now Rare] overbearing —see SYN. at IMPERTINENT —**in′so·lence** *n.* —**in′so·lent·ly** *adv.*

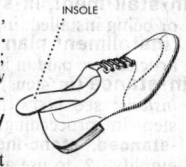
INSOLE

in·sol·u·ble (in säl′yoo b'l) *adj.* **1.** that

cannot be solved; unsolvable [an *insoluble* problem] **2.** that cannot be dissolved; not soluble [an *insoluble* powder] —**in·sol′u·bil′i·ty, in·sol′u·ble·ness** *n.* —**in·sol′u·bly** *adv.*

in·solv·a·ble (in säl′və b'l) *adj.* that cannot be solved

in·sol·vent (in säl′vənt) *adj.* **1.** not solvent; unable to pay debts; bankrupt **2.** not enough to pay all debts [an *insolvent* estate] **3.** of insolvents —*n.* an insolvent person —**in·sol′ven·cy** *n., pl.* **-cies**

in·som·ni·a (in säm′nē ə) *n.* [< L. < *in*-, without + *somnus*, sleep] a condition in which it is difficult for one to fall asleep or stay asleep —**in·som′ni·ac′** (-ak′) *n., adj.*

in·so·much (in′sō much′, -sə-) *adv.* **1.** to such a degree or extent; so (with *that*) [he worked fast, *insomuch* that he finished first] **2.** inasmuch (*as*)

in·sou·ci·ant (in sōō′sē ənt) *adj.* [Fr.] calm and unbothered; indifferent in a casual or carefree way —**in·sou′ci·ance** (-əns) *n.* —**in·sou′ci·ant·ly** *adv.*

in·spect (in spekt′) *vt.* [< L. pp. of *inspicere* < *in*-, at + *specere*, to look: see SPY] **1.** to look at carefully; examine critically [*inspect* the house before buying it] **2.** to examine or review (troops, etc.) officially —**in·spec′tive** *adj.*

in·spec·tion (in spek′shən) *n.* **1.** careful examination **2.** official examination, as of troops

in·spec·tor (in spek′tər) *n.* **1.** one who inspects; official examiner **2.** an officer on a police force, ranking next below a superintendent or police chief —**in·spec′to·ral, in·spec′to·ri·al** (-tôr′ē əl) *adj.* —**in·spec′tor·ship′** *n.*

in·spi·ra·tion (in′spə rā′shən) *n.* **1.** a breathing in; inhaling **2.** an inspiring or being inspired [our cheers gave *inspiration* to the team] **3.** *a)* something that inspires creative thought or action [the view was an *inspiration* to the artist] *b)* an inspired idea, action, etc. [your bringing the camera was an *inspiration*] **4.** a prompting of something written or said **5.** *Theol.* a divine influence upon human beings, as in the writing of the Scriptures —**in′spi·ra′tion·al** *adj.* —**in′spi·ra′tion·al·ly** *adv.*

in·spire (in spīr′) *vt.* **-spired′, -spir′ing** [< OFr. < L. *inspirare* < *in*-, in + *spirare*, to breathe] **1.** to draw (air) into the lungs; inhale **2.** to influence, stimulate, or urge, as to some creative or effective effort [the sunset *inspired* her to write a poem] **3.** to guide or motivate by divine influence [the Bible is an *inspired* book] **4.** to arouse or bring about (a thought or feeling) [kindness *inspires* love] **5.** to affect (a person) with a specified feeling [praise *inspires* us with confidence] **6.** to cause to be written or said [to *inspire* a rumor] —*vi.* **1.** to inhale **2.** to give inspiration —**in·spir′a·ble** *adj.* —**in·spir′er** *n.* —**in·spir′ing·ly** *adv.*

in·spir·it (in spir′it) *vt.* to put spirit into; cheer; hearten

in·spis·sate (in spis′āt, in′spə sāt′) *vt., vi.* **-sat·ed, -sat·ing** [< LL., ult. < L. *in*-, in + *spissus*, thick] to thicken by evaporation; condense —**in′spis·sa′tion** *n.* —**in′spis·sa′tor** *n.*

Inst. 1. Institute **2.** Institution

inst. 1. instant (*adj.* 2) **2.** instrumental

in·sta·bil·i·ty (in′stə bil′ə tē) *n.* unstable condition; lack of firmness, steadiness, etc.

in·sta·ble (in stā′b'l) *adj.* same as UNSTABLE

in·stall, in·stal (in stôl′) *vt.* **-stalled′, -stall′ing** [< ML. < *in*-, in + *stallum* < OHG. *stal*, a place, STALL[1]] **1.** to place in an office, rank, etc. with formality **2.** to establish in a place or condition [to *install* oneself in a seat] **3.** to fix in position for use [to *install* new fixtures] —**in·stall′er** *n.*

in·stal·la·tion (in′stə lā′shən) *n.* **1.** an installing or being installed **2.** apparatus, etc. installed [a heating *installation*] **3.** any military post, camp, base, etc.

in·stall·ment, in·stal·ment[1] (in stôl′mənt) *n.* [< earlier *estall*, to arrange payments for < OFr. < OHG. *stal*: see INSTALL] **1.** any of the parts of a debt or other sum of money to be paid at regular times over a specified period **2.** any of several parts, as of a serial story, appearing at intervals

in·stall·ment, in·stal·ment[2] (in stôl′mənt) *n.* an installing or being installed; installation

☆**installment plan** a system by which debts, as for purchased articles, are paid in installments

in·stance (in′stəns) *n.* [OFr. < L. *instantia*, a being present < *instans*: see INSTANT] **1.** an example; case; illustration **2.** a step in proceeding; occasion [in the first *instance*] —*vt.* **-stanced, -stanc·ing 1.** to show by means of an instance; exemplify **2.** to use as an example; cite —**at the instance of** at the suggestion of —**for instance** as an example

SYN.—**instance** refers to a person, thing, or event that is given as proof or support of something [the gift is an *instance* of his generosity]; **case** is applied to a happening or situation of a specified kind [a *case* of mistaken

identity]; **example** is applied to something that is mentioned as typical of the members of its group [his novel is an *example* of science fiction]; **illustration** is used of an instance or example that helps to explain or make something clear [this sentence is an *illustration* of the use of a word]

in·stant (in′stənt) *adj.* [< MFr. < L. *instans*, prp. of *instare* < *in*-, upon + *stare*, to STAND] **1.** calling for fast action; urgent [an *instant* need for reform] **2.** of the current month [your letter of the 13th *instant*] **3.** without delay; immediate [an *instant* response] **4.** designating a food or beverage in concentrated or precooked form, that can be prepared quickly, as by adding water [*instant* coffee] —*adv.* [Poet.] at once —*n.* **1.** a very short time; moment [wait just an *instant*] **2.** a particular moment [at that *instant* the bell rang] —**the instant** as soon as

in·stan·ta·ne·ous (in′stən tā′nē əs, -tān′yəs) *adj.* **1.** done, made, or happening in an instant [an *instantaneous* effect] **2.** done or made without delay; immediate [an *instantaneous* reply] —**in′stan·ta·ne·ous·ly** *adv.* —**in′stan·ta·ne·ous·ness** *n.*

in·stan·ter (in stan′tər) *adv.* [L., pressingly] immediately

in·stant·ly (in′stənt lē) *adv.* **1.** in an instant; without delay; immediately **2.** [Archaic] urgently; pressingly —*conj.* as soon as; the instant that [I came *instantly* I saw the need]

in·state (in stāt′) *vt.* **-stat′ed, -stat′ing** to put in a particular status, position, or rank; install —**in·state′ment** *n.*

in·stead (in sted′) *adv.* [IN + STEAD] in place of the person or thing mentioned [to feel like crying and laugh *instead*] —**instead of** in place of

in·step (in′step′) *n.* **1.** the upper part of the arch of the foot, between the ankle and the toes **2.** the part of a shoe or stocking covering this

in·sti·gate (in′stə gāt′) *vt.* **-gat′ed, -gat′ing** [< L. pp. of *instigare*, to incite: for IE. base see STICK] **1.** to urge on or incite to some action [to *instigate* others to argue] **2.** to cause by inciting; foment [to *instigate* a rebellion] —see SYN. at INCITE —**in′sti·ga′tion** *n.* —**in′sti·ga′tive** *adj.* —**in′sti·ga′tor** *n.*

in·still, in·stil (in stil′) *vt.* **-stilled′, -still′ing** [< MFr. < L. *instillare*, ult. < *in*-, in + *stilla*, a drop] **1.** to put in drop by drop **2.** to put (an idea, principle, etc.) *in* or *into* gradually [he *instilled* honesty in his children] —**in·stil·la′tion** *n.* —**in·still′er** *n.* —**in·still′ment, in·stil′ment** *n.*

in·stinct (in′stiŋkt; *for adj.* in stiŋkt′) *n.* [< L. pp. of *instinguere*, to impel: for IE. base see STICK] **1.** (an) inborn tendency to behave in a way characteristic of a species; natural, unacquired response to stimuli [suckling is an *instinct* in mammals] **2.** a natural ability; talent; knack; gift [an *instinct* for doing the right thing] —*adj.* filled or charged (*with*) [a look *instinct* with pity] —**in·stinc·tu·al** (in stiŋk′chōō wəl) *adj.*

in·stinc·tive (in stiŋk′tiv) *adj.* **1.** of, or having the nature of, instinct **2.** caused or done by instinct [an *instinctive* fear of the dark] —see SYN. at SPONTANEOUS —**in·stinc′tive·ly** *adv.*

in·sti·tute (in′stə tōōt′, -tyōōt′) *vt.* **-tut′ed, -tut′ing** [< L. pp. of *instituere* < *in*-, in + *statuere*, to set up: for IE. base see STAND] **1.** to set up; establish; found [the modern Olympic games were *instituted* in 1896] **2.** to start; initiate [to *institute* a search] **3.** to install in office —*n.* something instituted; specif., *a)* an established principle, law, or custom *b)* an organization for the promotion or teaching of art, science, research, etc. *c)* a school specializing in art, music, technical subjects, etc. ☆*d)* a short course or workshop for those in a special field of work [a bankers' *institute*] *e)* same as INSTITUTION (sense 3) —**in′sti·tut′er, in′sti·tu′tor** *n.*

in·sti·tu·tion (in′stə tōō′shən, -tyōō′-) *n.* **1.** an instituting or being instituted; establishment **2.** an established law, custom, practice, etc. [the *institution* of marriage] **3.** *a)* an organization having a social, educational, or religious purpose, as a school, church, reformatory, etc. *b)* the building housing such an organization **4.** [Colloq.] a person or thing long established in a place

in·sti·tu·tion·al (-'l) *adj.* **1.** of, or having the nature of, an institution **2.** of or to institutions, rather than individuals [*institutional* sales] **3.** of advertising intended primarily to gain prestige rather than immediate sales —**in′sti·tu′tion·al·ly** *adv.*

in·sti·tu·tion·al·ism (-'l iz'm) *n.* **1.** a belief in the value of established institutions **2.** the care of the needy, homeless, etc. by or in public institutions **3.** the nature of such care, thought of as impersonal, standardized, etc.

in·sti·tu·tion·al·ize (-'l īz′) *vt.* **-ized′, -iz′ing 1.** to make into an institution **2.** to make institutional **3.** to place in an institution, as for treatment —**in′sti·tu′tion·al·i·za′tion** *n.*

instr. 1. instructor **2.** instrument

in·struct (in strukt′) *vt.* [< L. pp. of *instruere*, to erect < *in*-, in + *struere*, to pile up: for IE. base see STREW] **1.** to give lessons to; teach [she *instructed* me in algebra] **2.** to give certain facts, rules, etc. to; inform or guide [the judge *instructs* the jury] **3.** to order or direct [to *instruct* a sentry to shoot] —see SYN. at COMMAND and TEACH

in·struc·tion (in struk′shən) *n.* **1.** an instructing; education **2.** *a)* knowledge, information, etc. given or taught *b)* a lesson or rule **3.** *a)* a command or order *b)* [*pl.*] directions [*instructions* for a test] —**in·struc′tion·al** *adj.*

in·struc·tive (-tiv) *adj.* serving to instruct; giving knowledge or information [an *instructive* book] —**in·struc′tive·ly** *adv.* —**in·struc′tive·ness** *n.*

in·struc·tor (-tər) *n.* **1.** a teacher ☆**2.** a college teacher ranking below an assistant professor —**in·struc′tor·ship′** *n.* —**in·struc′tress** [Now Rare] *n.fem.*

in·stru·ment (in′strə mənt) *n.* [< OFr. < L. *instrumentum* < *instruere:* see INSTRUCT] **1.** *a)* a thing by means of which something is done; means *b)* a person used by another to bring something about [people once believed in witches as *instruments* of the devil] **2.** a tool or implement [surgical *instruments*] **3.** a device for indicating or measuring conditions, performance, etc., or, sometimes, for controlling operations, esp. in aircraft **4.** any of various devices producing musical sound, as a flute, violin, etc. **5.** *Law* a document, as a deed, contract, etc. —*vt.* to provide with instruments

in·stru·men·tal (in′strə men′t'l) *adj.* **1.** serving as a means; helpful (*in* bringing something about) [she was *instrumental* in finding me a job] **2.** of or performed with an instrument or tool **3.** of, performed on, or written for a musical instrument or instruments [Bach wrote both *instrumental* and vocal music] —**in′stru·men′tal·ly** *adv.*

in·stru·men·tal·ist (-men′t'l ist) *n.* a person who performs on a musical instrument

in·stru·men·tal·i·ty (in′strə men tal′ə tē) *n., pl.* **-ties 1.** a being instrumental, or serving as a means **2.** a thing by which something is done; means or agency

in·stru·men·ta·tion (-tā′shən) *n.* **1.** the arrangement of music for instruments **2.** a using or equipping with instruments, esp. scientific instruments **3.** the instruments used, as in a mechanical apparatus or in a particular musical score, band, etc. **4.** same as INSTRUMENTALITY

instrument flying the method of flying an aircraft by the use of instruments only, without being able to observe points or objects on the ground

instrument landing a landing made by using only the instruments of an aircraft and electronic or radio signals from the ground

instrument panel (or **board**) a panel or board with instruments, gauges, etc. mounted on it, as in an automobile or airplane

in·sub·or·di·nate (in′sə bôr′d'n it) *adj.* not giving in to authority; disobedient —*n.* an insubordinate person —**in′sub·or′di·nate·ly** *adv.* —**in′sub·or′di·na′tion** *n.*

in·sub·stan·tial (in′səb stan′shəl) *adj.* not substantial; specif., *a)* not real; imaginary [the *insubstantial* dream world] *b)* not solid or firm [the statue rests on an *insubstantial* base] —**in′sub·stan′ti·al′i·ty** (-shē al′ə tē) *n.*

in·suf·fer·a·ble (in suf′ər ə b'l) *adj.* not sufferable; hard to put up with; unbearable [an *insufferable* bore] —**in·suf′fer·a·bly** *adv.*

in·suf·fi·cien·cy (in′sə fish′ən sē) *n., pl.* **-cies 1.** lack of sufficiency; deficiency; inadequacy **2.** inability of an organ, etc. to function normally

in·suf·fi·cient (-ənt) *adj.* not sufficient; not enough; inadequate —**in·suf·fi′cient·ly** *adv.*

in·su·lar (in′sə lər, -syoo-) *adj.* [< L. < *insula,* island] **1.** of, or in the form of, an island **2.** living or situated on an island **3.** like an island **4.** of or like islanders, esp. when regarded as limited in outlook —**in′su·lar′i·ty** (-lar′ə tē), **in′su·lar·ism** *n.* —**in′su·lar·ly** *adv.*

in·su·late (in′sə lāt′, -syoo-) *vt.* **-lat′ed, -lat′ing** [< L. *insulatus,* made like an island < *insula,* island] **1.** to set apart; detach from the rest; isolate **2.** to separate or cover with a nonconducting material in order to prevent the passage or leakage of electricity, heat, sound, etc.

in·su·la·tion (in′sə lā′shən, -syoo-) *n.* **1.** an insulating or being insulated **2.** any material used to insulate

in·su·la·tor (in′sə lāt′ər, -syoo-) *n.* anything that insulates; esp., a device of glass or porcelain for insulating and supporting electric wires

in·su·lin (in′sə lin, -syoo-) *n.* [< L. *insula,* island + -IN[1]: referring to ISLETS OF LANGERHANS in the pancreas] **1.** a secretion of the pancreas, which helps the body use sugar and other carbohydrates **2.** an extract from the pancreas of sheep, oxen, etc., given by hypodermic injection in the treatment of diabetes mellitus

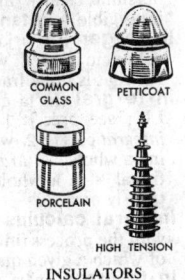

COMMON GLASS   PETTICOAT

PORCELAIN

HIGH TENSION

INSULATORS

in·sult (in sult′; *for n.* in′sult) *vt.* [< MFr. < L. *insultare* < *in-,* in, on + *saltare* < *salire,* to leap: see SALIENT] to treat or speak to with scorn, rudeness, or disrespect [he *insulted* me by ignoring my question] —*n.* **1.** an insulting act, remark, etc. **2.** *Med.* damage or injury to tissues or organs —see SYN. at OFFEND —**in·sult′er** *n.* —**in·sult′ing** *adj.* —**in·sult′ing·ly** *adv.*

in·su·per·a·ble (in soo′pər ə b'l, -syoo′-) *adj.* not superable; that cannot be overcome or passed over; insurmountable [*insuperable* difficulties] —**in·su′per·a·bil′i·ty** *n.* —**in·su′per·a·bly** *adv.*

in·sup·port·a·ble (in′sə pôrt′ə b'l) *adj.* not supportable; specif., *a)* intolerable; not bearable; unendurable *b)* incapable of being upheld, proved, etc. —**in′sup·port′a·bly** *adv.*

in·sur·ance (in shoor′əns) *n.* **1.** an insuring or being insured against loss by fire, accident, death, etc. **2.** *a)* a contract (**insurance policy**) whereby the insurer guarantees the insured that a certain sum will be paid for a specified loss *b)* the premium specified for such a contract **3.** the amount for which life, property, etc. is insured [how much *insurance* does he have on his car?] **4.** the business of insuring against loss

in·sure (in shoor′) *vt.* **-sured′, -sur′ing** [see ENSURE] **1.** to take out or issue insurance on (something or someone) [she *insured* her jewels against theft; will your company *insure* my house against storm damage?] **2.** same as ENSURE —*vi.* to give or take out insurance —**in·sur′a·bil′i·ty** *n.* —**in·sur′a·ble** *adj.*

in·sured (in shoord′) *n.* a person whose life, property, etc. is insured against loss

in·sur·er (in shoor′ər) *n.* a person or company that insures others against loss or damage

in·sur·gence (in sur′jəns) *n.* a rising in revolt; insurrection: also **in·sur′gen·cy**

in·sur·gent (-jənt) *adj.* [< L. prp. of *insurgere* < *in-,* upon + *surgere,* to rise: see SURGE] rising up against established authority; rebellious —*n.* one engaged in insurgent activity —**in·sur′gent·ly** *adv.*

in·sur·mount·a·ble (in′sər moun′tə b'l) *adj.* not surmountable; that cannot be overcome [*insurmountable* obstacles] —**in′sur·mount′a·bil′i·ty** *n.* —**in′sur·mount′a·bly** *adv.*

in·sur·rec·tion (in′sə rek′shən) *n.* [< MFr. < LL. < pp. of L. *insurgere:* see INSURGENT] a rising up against established authority; rebellion; revolt —see SYN. at REBELLION —**in′sur·rec′tion·al** *adj.* —**in′sur·rec′tion·ar′y** *adj., n., pl.* **-ar′ies** —**in′sur·rec′tion·ist** *n.*

in·sus·cep·ti·ble (in′sə sep′tə b'l) *adj.* not susceptible (*to* or *of*); not easily affected or influenced —**in′sus·cep·ti·bil′i·ty** *n.* —**in′sus·cep′ti·bly** *adv.*

int. 1. interest **2.** interior **3.** internal **4.** international **5.** intransitive

in·tact (in takt′) *adj.* [< L. < *in-,* not + *tactus,* pp. of *tangere,* to touch: see CONTACT] with nothing missing or injured; kept or left whole —**in·tact′ness** *n.*

in·tagl·io (in tal′yō, -tāl′-) *n., pl.* **-ios** [It. < *in-,* in + *tagliare,* to cut < LL. *taliare:* see TAILOR] **1.** a design or figure carved or engraved into a hard material so that it is below the surface **2.** a gem or stone ornamented in this way **3.** the art of making such designs or figures —*vt.* **-ioed, -io·ing** to carve, etc. in intaglio

in·take (in′tāk′) *n.* **1.** a taking in [a gasp is a sharp *intake* of breath] **2.** the amount or thing taken in [cash *intake;* a small *intake* of food] **3.** the place in a pipe, channel, etc. where water, air, or gas is taken in [a sewer *intake*]

in·tan·gi·ble (in tan′jə b'l) *adj.* not tangible; specif., *a)* that cannot be touched *b)* not material or physical; abstract [good will is an *intangible* asset in a business] *c)* hard to define or understand clearly [an *intangible* feeling of dread] —*n.* something intangible —**in·tan'gi·bil/i·ty** *n., pl.* **-ties** —**in·tan'gi·bly** *adv.*

in·te·ger (in'tə jər) *n.* [L., untouched, whole] **1.** anything complete in itself; whole **2.** any whole number or zero; a number that is not a fraction

in·te·gral (in'tə grəl; *also, exc. for adj.* **4,** in teg'rəl) *adj.* [< LL.: see prec.] **1.** necessary for completeness; essential [an *integral* part] **2.** whole or complete **3.** made up of parts forming a whole **4.** *Math.* of or having to do with integers; not fractional —*n.* a whole —**in'te·gral/i·ty** (-gral/ə tē) *n.* —**in'te·gral·ly** *adv.*

integral calculus the branch of higher mathematics dealing with the process (**integration**) of finding the quantity or function of which a given quantity or function is the differential

in·te·grate (in'tə grāt') *vt.* **-grat'ed, -grat'ing** [< L. pp. of *integrare* < *integer,* whole] **1.** to make whole or complete **2.** to bring (parts) together into a whole; unify [to *integrate* the study of history with the study of English] **3.** to indicate the sum or total of ☆**4.** *a)* to do away with the segregation of (racial groups) *b)* to abolish segregation in; desegregate (a school, etc.) —*vi.* to become integrated —**in'te·gra'tion** *n.* —**in·te·gra'tive** *adj.* —**in'te·gra'tor** *n.*

integrated circuit an electronic circuit containing interconnected amplifying devices and circuit elements formed on a single body, or chip, of semiconductor material

☆**in·te·gra·tion·ist** (-grā'shən ist) *n.* one who advocates integration, esp. of racial groups —*adj.* believing in or advocating integration

in·teg·ri·ty (in teg'rə tē) *n.* [see INTEGER] **1.** the condition of being complete; wholeness; entirety [wars destroyed Germany's territorial *integrity*] **2.** strong, stable condition; soundness [the *integrity* of a nation's currency] **3.** uprightness, honesty, and sincerity [a man of *integrity* never takes a bribe] —see SYN. at HONESTY

in·teg·u·ment (in teg'yoo mənt) *n.* [< L. < *in-,* upon + *tegere,* to cover] an outer covering, as of the body or of a plant; skin, shell, hide, husk, rind, etc. —**in·teg'u·men'ta·ry** *adj.*

in·tel·lect (in't'l ekt') *n.* [< L. < pp. of *intellegere,* to understand < *inter-,* between + *legere,* to choose: for IE. base see LOGIC] **1.** the ability to reason or understand **2.** great mental ability; high intelligence **3.** *a)* a mind or intelligence *b)* a person of high intelligence

in·tel·lec·tu·al (in't'l ek/choo wəl) *adj.* **1.** of, pertaining to, or appealing to the intellect **2.** *a)* requiring intelligence and clear thinking [chess is an *intellectual* game] *b)* tending to take part in and enjoy intellectual activities **3.** having or showing high intelligence —*n.* a person having intellectual tastes or doing intellectual work —see SYN. at INTELLIGENT —**in'tel·lec'tu·al·i·ty** (-choo wal/ə tē) *n.* —**in'tel·lec'tu·al·ly** *adv.*

in·tel·lec·tu·al·ism (-iz'm) *n.* a being intellectual; devotion to intellectual pursuits —**in'tel·lec'tu·al·is'tic** *adj.*

in·tel·lec·tu·al·ize (-īz') *vt.* **-ized', -iz'ing** to make intellectual; give an intellectual quality to —*vi.* to reason; think —**in'tel·lec·tu·al·i·za'tion** *n.*

in·tel·li·gence (in tel'ə jəns) *n.* [< OFr. < L. *intelligentia* < prp. of *intelligere:* see INTELLECT] **1.** *a)* the ability to learn or understand from experience; mental ability *b)* the ability to respond successfully to a new situation *c)* cleverness, shrewdness, etc. **2.** news or information [secret *intelligence* about the enemy's plans] **3.** *a)* the gathering of secret information, as for military purposes *b)* the persons or agency employed at this **4.** an intelligent being

☆**intelligence quotient** a number indicating a person's level of intelligence: it is the mental age (as shown by intelligence tests) multiplied by 100 and divided by the chronological age

intelligence test a series of problems intended to test the relative intelligence of an individual

in·tel·li·gent (-jənt) *adj.* **1.** having or using intelligence **2.** having or showing an alert mind or high intelligence; bright, clever, wise, etc. **3.** [Archaic] aware (*of* something) —**in·tel'li·gent·ly** *adv.*

SYN.—**intelligent** implies the ability to learn or understand from experience or to deal successfully with new or puzzling situations; **clever** implies quickness in thinking or learning, but may suggest a lack of thoroughness or depth; **alert** emphasizes quickness in sizing up a situation; **bright** and **smart** are somewhat informal, less precise equivalents for any of the preceding; **brilliant** implies an unusually high degree of intelligence; **intellectual** suggests keen intelligence together with interest and ability in subjects and activities which require much thought —ANT. stupid, dull

in·tel·li·gent·si·a (in tel'ə jent'sē ə, -gent'-) *n.pl.* [also with *sing. v.*] [< Russ. < L.: see INTELLIGENCE] the people regarded as, or regarding themselves as, the educated class; intellectuals as a group

in·tel·li·gi·ble (in tel'i jə b'l) *adj.* [< L. < *intelligere:* see INTELLECT] that can be understood; clear; comprehensible —**in·tel'li·gi·bil/i·ty** *n.* —**in·tel'li·gi·bly** *adv.*

in·tem·per·ance (in tem'pər əns) *n.* **1.** a lack of control or self-control; immoderation **2.** the drinking of too much alcoholic liquor

in·tem·per·ate (-it) *adj.* **1.** not temperate; specif., *a)* having or showing a lack of self-control; not moderate; excessive [*intemperate* language] *b)* severe or violent [an *intemperate* climate] **2.** drinking too much alcoholic liquor —**in·tem'per·ate·ly** *adv.*

in·tend (in tend') *vt.* [< OFr. < L. *intendere,* to aim at < *in-,* at + *tendere,* to stretch: see TEND[2]] **1.** to have in mind as a purpose; plan [I *intend* to leave tomorrow] **2.** to mean (something) to be or be used (*for*); design; destine [the cake is *intended* for the party] **3.** to mean or signify [what did he *intend* by that remark?] —*vi.* to have a purpose or intention —**in·tend'er** *n.*

SYN.—**intend** implies having in mind something to be done, said, etc. [I *intended* to write to you]; **mean** does not suggest so clearly a definite purpose [he always *means* well]; **design** suggests careful planning in order to bring about a certain result [their delay was *designed* to put off suspicion]; **propose** implies a clear statement of one's intention, either to others or to oneself [I *propose* to speak for an hour]

in·tend·ed (in ten'did) *adj.* **1.** meant or planned [we set off on our *intended* trip] **2.** prospective; future [his *intended* bride] —*n.* [Colloq.] the person whom one has agreed to marry

intens. 1. intensified **2.** intensifier **3.** intensive

in·tense (in tens') *adj.* [< MFr. < L. pp. of *intendere:* see INTEND] **1.** occurring or existing in a high degree; very strong [an *intense* light; *intense* joy] **2.** strained to the utmost; earnest [*intense* thought] **3.** having or showing strong emotion and deep seriousness [an *intense* person] —**in·tense'ly** *adv.* —**in·tense'ness** *n.*

in·ten·si·fy (in ten'sə fī') *vt., vi.* **-fied', -fy'ing** to make or become intense or more intense; increase; strengthen [we must *intensify* our efforts] —**in·ten'si·fi·ca'tion** *n.* —**in·ten'si·fi'er** *n.*

in·ten·si·ty (in ten'sə tē) *n., pl.* **-ties 1.** a being intense; specif., *a)* extreme degree of anything *b)* great energy or force of emotion, thought, or activity **2.** relative strength, magnitude, etc. **3.** the degree of purity of color; saturation **4.** *Physics* the amount of force or energy of heat, light, sound, etc. per unit of area, volume, etc.

in·ten·sive (-siv) *adj.* **1.** of or characterized by intensity; thorough; exhaustive [an *intensive* search] **2.** designating very attentive hospital care given to patients, as after surgery **3.** giving force or emphasis ["very" in "the very same man" is an *intensive* adverb] —*n.* anything that intensifies **2.** an intensive word, prefix, etc. —**in·ten'sive·ly** *adv.* —**in·ten'sive·ness** *n.*

in·tent (in tent') *adj.* [< L. pp. of *intendere:* see INTEND] **1.** firmly directed; earnest; intense [an *intent* look] **2.** *a)* having the mind or attention firmly fixed; engrossed [*intent* on his studies] *b)* strongly resolved [*intent* on going] —*n.* **1.** an intending **2.** something intended; specif., *a)* a purpose; aim [it was not my *intent* to harm you] *b)* meaning or import [what was the *intent* of the speech?] **3.** *Law* one's mental attitude at the time of doing an act [shooting with *intent* to kill] —to all intents and purposes in almost every respect; practically —**in·tent'ly** *adv.* —**in·tent'ness** *n.*

in·ten·tion (in ten'shən) *n.* **1.** an intending; determination to do a specified thing or act in a specified way **2.** *a)* anything intended; aim or purpose *b)* [*pl.*] purpose in regard to marriage

in·ten·tion·al (-shən 'l) *adj.* **1.** having to do with intention **2.** done purposely; intended —see SYN. at VOLUNTARY —**in·ten'tion·al·ly** *adv.*

in·ter (in tur') *vt.* **-terred', -ter'ring** [< OFr. < L. *in,* in + *terra,* earth] to put (a dead body) into a grave or tomb; bury

in·ter- [L. < *inter,* between, among] *a combining form meaning:* **1.** between or among [*interstate*] **2.** with or on each other (or one another), together, mutual, reciprocal, mutually, or reciprocally [*interact*]

in·ter·act (in'tər akt') *vi.* to act on one another —**in'ter·ac'tion** *n.* —**in'ter·ac'tive** *adj.*

†**in·ter a·li·a** (in'tər ā'lē ə) [L.] among other things

in·ter·breed (in'tər brēd') *vt., vi.* **-bred', -breed'ing** same as HYBRIDIZE

in·ter·ca·lar·y (in tur'kə ler'ē) *adj.* [< L.: see INTERCALATE] added to the calendar: said of an extra day or month inserted in a calendar year so it will correspond to the solar year

in·ter·ca·late (-lāt') *vt.* -lat'ed, -lat'ing [< L. pp. of *intercalare*, to insert < *inter-*, between + *calare*, to call] **1.** to insert (a day, month, etc.) in the calendar **2.** to interpolate or insert —**in·ter'ca·la'tion** *n.*

in·ter·cede (in'tər sēd') *vi.* -ced'ed, -ced'ing [< L. < *inter-*, between + *cedere*, to go] **1.** to plead or make a request in behalf of another or others [to *intercede* with the authorities for the prisoner] **2.** to intervene for the purpose of producing agreement; mediate [to *intercede* in another's quarrel] —**in'ter·ced'er** *n.*

in·ter·cel·lu·lar (-sel'yoo lər) *adj.* located between or among cells

in·ter·cept (in'tər sept'; *for n.* in'tər sept') *vt.* [< L. pp. of *intercipere* < *inter-*, between + *capere*, to take] **1.** to seize, stop, or interrupt on the way; cut off [to *intercept* a message] **2.** *Math.* to mark off between two points, lines, or planes —*n.* **1.** *Math.* the part of a line, plane, etc. intercepted **2.** *Mil.* the intercepting of enemy aircraft, missiles, etc. —**in'ter·cep'tion** *n.* —**in'ter·cep'tive** *adj.*

in·ter·cep·tor (-sep'tər) *n.* a person or thing that intercepts; esp., a fast-climbing military airplane used in fighting off enemy air attacks: also **in'ter·cept'er**

in·ter·ces·sion (in'tər sesh'ən) *n.* an interceding; mediation; pleading, or prayer in behalf of another or others —**in'ter·ces'sion·al** *adj.*

in·ter·ces·sor (in'tər ses'ər, in'tər ses'ər) *n.* a person who intercedes —**in'ter·ces'so·ry** *adj.*

in·ter·change (in'tər chānj'; *for n.* in'tər chānj') *vt.* -changed', -chang'ing **1.** to give and take mutually; exchange [to *interchange* ideas] **2.** to put (each of two things) in the other's place [to *interchange* the middle letters of "clam" and get "calm"] **3.** to alternate [to *interchange* work with play] —*vi.* to change places with each other —*n.* **1.** an interchanging **2.** any of the places on a freeway where traffic can enter or depart, usually by means of a cloverleaf

in·ter·change·a·ble (in'tər chān'jə b'l) *adj.* that can be interchanged, esp. in position or use [the tires on an automobile are *interchangeable*] —**in'ter·change'a·bil'i·ty** *n.* —**in'ter·change'a·bly** *adv.*

in·ter·col·le·gi·ate (-kə lē'jət, -jē ət) *adj.* between or among colleges and universities [*intercollegiate* sports]

in·ter·com (in'tər käm') *n.* a radio or telephone intercommunication system, as between rooms of a building

in·ter·com·mu·ni·cate (in'tər kə myōo'nə kāt') *vt., vi.* -cat'ed, -cat'ing to communicate with or to each other or one another —**in'ter·com·mu'ni·ca'tion** *n.*

in·ter·con·nect (-kə nekt') *vt., vi.* to connect with one another —**in'ter·con·nec'tion** *n.*

in·ter·con·ti·nen·tal (-kän'tə nen't'l) *adj.* **1.** between or among continents **2.** able to travel from one continent to another, as a plane, rocket-launched missile, etc.

in·ter·cos·tal (-käs't'l) *adj.* [see INTER- & COSTAL] between the ribs —**in'ter·cos'tal·ly** *adv.*

in·ter·course (in'tər kôrs') *n.* [< OFr. < L.: see INTER- & COURSE] **1.** communication or dealings between or among people, countries, etc.; exchange of products, services, ideas, etc. **2.** the sexual joining of two individuals; copulation: in full, **sexual intercourse**

in·ter·cross (in'tər krôs'; *for n.* in'tər krôs') *vt., vi.* same as HYBRIDIZE —*n.* same as HYBRID (sense 1)

in·ter·de·nom·i·na·tion·al (in'tər di näm'ə nā'shən 'l) *adj.* between, among, shared by, or involving different religious denominations

in·ter·de·part·men·tal (-di pärt'men't'l) *adj.* between or among departments

in·ter·de·pend·ence (-di pen'dəns) *n.* dependence on each other; mutual dependence: also **in'ter·de·pend'en·cy** —**in'ter·de·pend'ent** *adj.* —**in'ter·de·pend'ent·ly** *adv.*

in·ter·dict (in'tər dikt'; *for n.* in'tər dikt') *vt.* [< OFr. < L. pp. of *interdicere*, to forbid < *inter-*, between + *dicere*, to speak: see DICTION] **1.** to prohibit (an action); forbid with authority **2.** to restrain from doing or using something **3.** to hinder (the enemy) or isolate (an area, etc.) by bombing, etc. **4.** *R.C.Ch.* to exclude (a person, parish, etc.) from certain acts or privileges —*n.* an official prohibition or restraint; specif., *R.C.Ch.* an interdicting of a person, parish, etc. —**in'ter·dic'tion** *n.* —**in'ter·dic'to·ry, in'ter·dic'tive** *adj.*

in·ter·dis·ci·pli·nar·y (-dis'ə pli ner'ē) *adj.* involving two or more disciplines, or branches of learning [an *interdisciplinary* approach to cultural history]

in·ter·est (in'trist, in'tər ist; *for v. also* -tə rest') *n.* [< ML. *interesse*, compensation < L. < *inter-*, between + *esse*, to be: altered after OFr. *interest* < L., it interests] **1.** a right or claim to something [an *interest* in an estate] **2.** *a)* a share or participation in something [to buy an *interest* in a business] *b)* anything in which one participates or has a share **3.** [*often pl.*] advantage; welfare; benefit [she has our best *interests* at heart] **4.** [*usually pl.*] a group of people having a common concern or dominant power in some industry, occupation, cause, etc. [the steel *interests*] **5.** *a)* a feeling of concern or curiosity about something [an *interest* in politics] *b)* the power of causing this feeling [books of *interest* to children] *c)* something causing this feeling [golf is his main *interest*] **6.** importance; consequence [a matter of little *interest*] **7.** *a)* money paid for the use of money *b)* the rate of such payment, expressed as a percentage per unit of time **8.** an increase over what is owed [to repay kindness with *interest*] —*vt.* **1.** to cause to have an interest (*in*) or take part (*in*) [can I *interest* you in a game of cards?] **2.** to excite the attention or curiosity of [her new movie *interests* me] —**in the interest** (or **interests**) **of** for the sake of; in order to promote

in·ter·est·ed (-id) *adj.* **1.** having an interest or share; concerned [stockholders and other *interested* parties] **2.** influenced by personal interest; biased or prejudiced [disregard the testimony of *interested* witnesses] **3.** feeling or showing interest, or curiosity [bored, but pretending to be *interested*] —**in'ter·est·ed·ly** *adv.* —**in'ter·est·ed·ness** *n.*

in·ter·est·ing (-iŋ) *adj.* exciting interest, curiosity, or attention —**in'ter·est·ing·ly** *adv.*

in·ter·face (in'tər fās') *n.* **1.** a surface forming the common boundary between two parts of matter or space **2.** a point at which two different systems, groups, etc. interact —*vi., vt.* -faced', -fac'ing to interact or cause to interact with another system, group, etc.

in·ter·faith (in'tər fāth') *adj.* between or involving persons of different religions

in·ter·fere (in'tər fir') *vi.* -fered', -fer'ing [< OFr. < *entre-*, INTER- + *férir* < L. *ferire*, to strike: for IE. base see BORE[1]] **1.** to come into collision or opposition; clash; conflict [noise *interferes* with his work] **2.** *a)* to come between for some purpose; intervene [the teacher *interfered* in the boys' fight] *b)* to meddle in another's affairs [her parents seldom *interfere* in her plans] **3.** *Sports* to be guilty of interference **4.** *Physics* to affect each other by interference: said of vibrating waves —**interfere with** to hinder; prevent —**in'ter·fer'er** *n.*

in·ter·fer·ence (-fir'əns) **1.** an interfering **2.** something that interferes ☆ **3.** *a) Football* the legal blocking of opposing players in order to clear the way for the ball carrier; also, the player or players who do such blocking *b) Sports* the illegal hindering of an opposing player, as one who is receiving a pass in football **4.** *Physics* the mutual action of two waves of vibration, as of sound, light, etc., in reinforcing or neutralizing each other **5.** *Radio & TV* static, unwanted signals, etc., producing a distortion of sounds or images

in·ter·fer·om·e·ter (in'tər fi räm'ə tər) *n.* [< INTERFERE + -METER] an instrument for measuring wavelengths of light and very small distances and thicknesses, for analyzing parts of a spectrum by means of the interference phenomena of light, etc.

in·ter·fer·on (-fir'än) *n.* [INTERFER(E) + -on, suffix with no definite meaning] a cellular protein produced by the body to check the growth of an infecting virus

in·ter·fold (-fōld') *vt., vi.* to fold together or inside one another

in·ter·fuse (-fyōoz') *vt.* -fused', -fus'ing **1.** to combine by mixing, blending, or fusing together **2.** to spread itself through; pervade —*vi.* to fuse; blend —**in'ter·fu'sion** *n.*

in·ter·ga·lac·tic (-gə lak'tik) *adj.* existing or occurring between or among galaxies

in·ter·gla·cial (-glā'shəl) *adj.* formed or occurring between two glacial epochs

in·ter·group (in'tər groop') *adj.* between or involving different social, ethnic, or racial groups

in·ter·im (in'tər im) *n.* [L., meanwhile < *inter*, between] the period of time between; meantime [in the *interim*] —*adj.* temporary; provisional [an *interim* mayor]

in·te·ri·or (in tir'ē ər) *adj.* [< MFr. < L., compar. of *inter*, between] 1. situated within; inner 2. away from the coast, border, etc.; inland 3. of the domestic affairs of a country 4. private —*n.* 1. the inside or inner part [an old house with a modern *interior*] 2. the inland part of a country or region 3. the inner nature of a person or thing 4. the domestic affairs of a country [the U.S. Department of the *Interior*] —**in·te'ri·or'i·ty** (-ôr'ə tē) *n.* —**in·te'ri·or·ly** *adv.*

interior angle any of the four angles formed on the inside of two straight lines by a straight line cutting across them

interior decoration the decorating and furnishing of the interior of a room, house, etc..

in·te·ri·or·ize (-īz') *vt.* **-ized', -iz'ing** to make (a concept, value, etc.) part of one's inner nature

interj. interjection

in·ter·ject (in'tər jekt') *vt.* [< L. pp. of *interjicere* < *inter*-, between + *jacere*, to throw: see JET[1]] to throw in between; insert; interpose [to *interject* a question] —**in'ter·jec'tor** *n.*

INTERIOR ANGLES

in·ter·jec·tion (-jek'shən) *n.* 1. an interjecting 2. something interjected, as a word or phrase 3. *Gram.* an exclamatory word or phrase, such as *ah! good grief!* —**in'ter·jec'tion·al, in'ter·jec'to·ry** *adj.* —**in'ter·jec'tion·al·ly** *adv.*

in·ter·lace (-lās') *vt., vi.* **-laced', -lac'ing** [< OFr.: see INTER- & LACE] 1. to unite by passing over and under each other; weave together 2. to connect closely; intermingle —**in'ter·lace'ment** *n.*

in·ter·lard (-lärd') *vt.* [< Fr.: see INTER- & LARD] 1. to intersperse; diversify [to *interlard* a lecture with quotations] 2. to be intermixed in

in·ter·lay (-lā') *vt.* **-laid'** (-lād'), **-lay'ing** to lay or put between or among —**in'ter·lay'er** *n.*

in·ter·leaf (in'tər lēf') *n., pl.* **-leaves'** (-lēvz') a leaf, usually blank, bound between the other leaves of a book, for notes, etc.

in·ter·leave (in'tər lēv') *vt.* **-leaved', -leav'ing** to put an interleaf or interleaves in

in·ter·line[1] (in'tər līn') *vt.* **-lined', -lin'ing** to write or print (something) between the lines of (a text, document, etc.) —**in'ter·lin'e·a'tion** (-lin'ē ā'shən) *n.*

in·ter·line[2] (in'tər līn') *vt.* **-lined', -lin'ing** to put a lining between the outer material and the ordinary lining of (a garment)

in·ter·lin·e·ar (in'tər lin'ē ər) *adj.* 1. written or printed between the lines [interlinear notes] ☆2. having the same text in different languages printed in alternate lines [an *interlinear* Bible] Also **in'ter·lin'e·al**

in·ter·lin·ing (in'tər lī'niŋ) *n.* a lining between the outer material and the ordinary lining of a garment

in·ter·link (in'tər liŋk') *vt.* to link together

in·ter·lock (-läk') *vt., vi.* to lock or fit tightly together; join with one another —*n.* a being interlocked

interlocking directorates boards of directors having some members in common, so that their corporations are more or less under the same control

in·ter·loc·u·tor (-läk'yə tər; *for 2, often* -läk'ə tər) *n.* [< L. pp. < *inter*, between + *loqui*, to talk] 1. a person taking part in a conversation ☆2. the master of ceremonies in a minstrel show

in·ter·loc·u·to·ry (-läk'yə tôr'ē) *adj.* 1. of or in dialogue; conversational 2. *Law* made during the course of a suit; not final [an *interlocutory* divorce decree]

in·ter·lop·er (in'tər lō'pər) *n.* [prob. < INTER- + LOPE] a person who meddles in others' affairs; intruder

in·ter·lude (in'tər lood') *n.* [< OFr. < ML. < L. *inter*, between + *ludus*, play: see LUDICROUS] 1. a short, humorous play formerly presented between the parts of a miracle play or morality play 2. any performance between the acts of a play 3. music played between the parts of a song, play, etc. 4. anything that fills time between two events

in·ter·mar·riage (in'tər mar'ij) *n.* marriage between persons of different races, religions, castes, etc. —**in'ter·mar'ry** *vi.* **-ried, -ry·ing**

in·ter·med·dle (-med''l) *vi.* **-dled, -dling** to meddle in the affairs of others —**in'ter·med'dler** *n.*

in·ter·me·di·ar·y (-mē'dē er'ē) *adj.* 1. acting between two persons; acting as a mediator 2. being or happening between; intermediate —*n., pl.* **-ar'ies** a go-between; mediator

in·ter·me·di·ate (-mē'dē it; *for v.* -āt') *adj.* [< ML. < L. *inter*-, between + *medius*, middle] coming between two other things or events; in the middle [an *intermediate* stage of development] —*n.* 1. anything intermediate 2. *same as* INTERMEDIARY —*vi.* **-at'ed, -at'ing** to act as an intermediary; mediate —**in'ter·me'di·ate·ly** *adv.* —**in'ter·me'di·ate·ness, in'ter·me'di·a·cy** (-ə sē) *n.* —**in'ter·me'di·a'tion** *n.*

intermediate frequency a radio frequency resulting from combining the incoming signal with a locally generated signal

in·ter·ment (in tur'mənt) *n.* an interring; burial

in·ter·mez·zo (in'tər met'sō, -med'zō) *n., pl.* **-zos, -zi** (-sē, -zē) [It.] 1. a short, light musical entertainment between the acts of a play or opera 2. *Music a)* a short movement connecting the main parts of a composition *b)* any of certain short works similar to this

in·ter·mi·na·ble (in tur'mi nə b'l) *adj.* not terminable; lasting, or seeming to last, forever; endless [an *interminable* lecture] —**in'ter'mi·na·bly** *adv.*

in·ter·min·gle (in'tər miŋ'g'l) *vt., vi.* **-gled, -gling** to mix together; mingle; blend

in·ter·mis·sion (-mish'ən) *n.* 1. an intermitting or being intermitted; interruption [he worked all day without *intermission*] 2. an interval of time between periods of activity; pause, as between acts of a play

in·ter·mit (-mit') *vt., vi.* **-mit'ted, -mit'ting** [< L. < *inter*-, between + *mittere*, to send] to stop for a time; cease at intervals

in·ter·mit·tent (-mit''nt) *adj.* stopping and starting again at intervals; pausing from time to time; periodic —**in'ter·mit'tence** *n.* —**in'ter·mit'tent·ly** *adv.*

SYN.—**intermittent** and **recurrent** both refer to something that stops and starts, or disappears and reappears, from time to time, but **intermittent** usually stresses the breaks or pauses, while **recurrent** usually stresses the repetition or return [an *intermittent* fever; *recurrent* attacks of the hives]; **periodic** refers to something that happens or comes, again at more or less regular intervals [*periodic* economic crises] —**ANT.** continued, continuous

in·ter·mix (-miks') *vt., vi.* to mix together; blend —**in'ter·mix'ture** *n.*

in·ter·mo·lec·u·lar (-mə lek'yoo lər) *adj.* between or among molecules

☆**in·tern** (in'tərn; *for vt. usually* in turn') *n.* [< Fr. < L. *internus*, internal] 1. a doctor receiving additional training by assisting other doctors in a hospital, generally just after graduation from medical school 2. an apprentice teacher, journalist, etc. —*vi.* to serve as an intern —*vt.* to detain and confine within a country or a definite area [to *intern* aliens in time of war] —**tern'ment** *n.*

in·ter·nal (in tur'n'l) *adj.* [< ML. < L. *internus*] 1. of or on the inside; inner 2. to be taken inside the body [*internal* remedies] 3. of or belonging to the inner nature of a thing; intrinsic [*internal* evidence] 4. of or belonging to a person's inner nature or mind; subjective 5. having to do with the domestic affairs of a country [*internal* revenue] —**in·ter·nal'i·ty** (-nal'ə tē) *n.* —**in·ter'nal·ly** *adv.*

in·ter·nal-com·bus·tion engine (-kəm bus'chən) an engine, as in an automobile, in which the power is produced by the combustion of a fuel-and-air mixture within the cylinders

in·ter·nal·ize (in tur'n'l īz') *vt.* **-ized', -iz'ing** to make internal; specif., to make (others' ideas, values, etc.) a part of one's own patterns of thinking —**in·ter'nal·i·za'tion** *n.*

internal medicine the branch of medicine dealing with the diagnosis and nonsurgical treatment of diseases

☆**internal revenue** governmental income from taxes on income, profits, luxuries, etc.

internal rhyme a rhyming of words within the same line of verse

internal secretion *same as* HORMONE

in·ter·na·tion·al (in'tər nash'ən 'l) *adj.* 1. between or among nations [an *international* treaty] 2. concerned with the relations between nations [an *international* court] 3. for the use of all nations [*international* waters] 4. of, for, or by people in various nations [an *international* organization] —*n.* an international organization; esp., [I-] any of several international socialist organizations in existence at various times from 1864 on —**in'ter·na'tion·al'i·ty** *n.* —**in'ter·na'tion·al·ly** *adv.*

international date line *same as* DATE LINE

in·ter·na·tion·al·ism (in'tər nash'ən 'l iz'm) *n.* the principle or policy of international cooperation for the common good —**in'ter·na'tion·al·ist** *n.*

in·ter·na·tion·al·ize (-īz′) *vt.* **-ized′, -iz′ing** to make international; bring under international control —**in′ter·na′tion·al·i·za′tion** *n.*

International Phonetic Alphabet a set of phonetic symbols for international use: each symbol represents a single sound

☆**in·terne** (in′tərn) *n. same as* INTERN

in·ter·ne·cine (in′tər nē′sin, -sīn; -nes′′n) *adj.* [< L. < *inter-*, between + *necare*, to kill] deadly or harmful to both sides in a conflict; mutually destructive [*internecine* warfare]

in·tern·ee (in′tər nē′) *n.* a person interned as a prisoner of war or enemy alien

in·ter·neu·ron (in′tər noor′än, -nyoor′-) *n. same as* INTERNUNCIAL NEURON

☆**in·ter·nist** (in′tər nist, in tur′nist) *n.* a doctor who specializes in internal medicine

☆**in·tern·ship** (in′tərn ship′) *n.* **1.** the position of an intern **2.** the period of service as an intern

in·ter·nun·ci·al neuron (in′tər nun′sē əl) [< It. < L. < *inter-*, between + *nuntius*, messenger] any of various nerve cells connecting neurons that receive stimuli with neurons that produce reactions to these stimuli

in·ter·o·cep·tor (in′tər ō sep′tər) *n.* [ModL.: see INTERNAL & RECEPTOR] a specialized cell that receives and transmits stimuli arising within the body, as in the stomach, muscles, etc.

in·ter·of·fice (in′tər ôf′is, -äf′-) *adj.* between or among the offices within an organization [an *interoffice* memo]

in·ter·pen·e·trate (-pen′ə trāt′) *vt., vi.* **-trat′ed, -trat′ing** **1.** to penetrate thoroughly; permeate **2.** to penetrate (each other) —**in′ter·pen′e·tra′tion** *n.*

in·ter·per·son·al (-pur′sə n′l) *adj.* **1.** between persons [*interpersonal* relationships] **2.** of or involving relations between persons —**in′ter·per′son·al·ly** *adv.*

☆**in·ter·phone** (in′tər fōn′) *n.* an intercom telephone system, as between departments of an office

in·ter·plan·e·tar·y (in′tər plan′ə ter′ē) *adj.* **1.** between planets [*interplanetary* travel] **2.** within the solar system but outside the atmosphere of any planet or the sun

in·ter·play (in′tər plā′) *n.* action or influence on each other or one another; interaction [the *interplay* of ideas]

in·ter·po·late (in tur′pə lāt′) *vt.* **-lat′ed, -lat′ing** [< L. < *inter-*, between + *polire*, to polish] **1.** *a)* to change (a book, text, etc.) by putting in new words, subject matter, etc. *b)* to insert (words) in a book, text, etc. **2.** to insert between or among others [to *interpolate* a remark] **3.** *Math.* to estimate (a missing value) by taking an average of known values at neighboring points —*vi.* to make interpolations —**in′ter·po·lat′er, in′ter·po·la′tor** *n.* —**in′ter·po·la′tion** *n.* —**in′ter·po·la′tive** *adj.*

in·ter·pose (in′tər pōz′) *vt.* **-posed′, -pos′ing** [< Fr. < L. < *inter-*, between + *ponere*, to put] **1.** to place between; insert [to *interpose* a barrier between the properties] **2.** to put forward as interference [to *interpose* an objection] **3.** to break into a conversation, debate, etc. with (a remark, opinion, etc.) —*vi.* **1.** to be or come between [our view is cut off by an *interposing* wall] **2.** to come between opponents; intervene **3.** to interrupt —**in′ter·pos′al** *n.* —**in′ter·pos′er** *n.* —**in′ter·po·si′tion** (-pə zish′ən) *n.*

in·ter·pret (in tur′prit) *vt.* [< MFr. < L. *interpretari* < *interpres*, negotiator] **1.** to explain the meaning of; make clear [to *interpret* a poem] **2.** to translate (oral remarks) **3.** to have one's own understanding of; construe [to *interpret* her silence as contempt] **4.** to show one's own understanding of (a piece of music, a role in a play, etc.) by the way one performs it —*vi.* to act as an interpreter; translate —see SYN. at EXPLAIN —**in′ter′pret·a·ble** *adj.* —**in·ter′pre·tive** (-prə tiv), **in·ter′pre·ta′tive** (-tāt′iv) *adj.*

in·ter·pre·ta·tion (in tur′prə tā′shən) *n.* **1.** the act or result of interpreting; explanation, meaning, etc. [the *interpretation* of dreams] **2.** the expression of a person's understanding of a work of art, subject, etc. through acting, writing, etc. [a pianist's *interpretation* of a sonata] —**in′ter′pre·ta′tion·al** *adj.*

in·ter·pret·er (in tur′prə tər) *n.* a person who interprets; specif., a person whose work is translating things said in another language

in·ter·ra·cial (in′tər rā′shəl) *adj.* between, among, or for persons of different races

in·ter·reg·num (-reg′nəm) *n., pl.* **-reg′nums, -reg′na** (-nə)

[L. < *inter-*, between + *regnum*, a REIGN] **1.** an interval between two successive reigns, when the country has no sovereign **2.** any period without the usual ruler, governor, etc. **3.** any break or pause; interval

in·ter·re·late (-ri lāt′) *vt., vi.* **-lat′ed, -lat′ing** to make, be, or become related to each other or one another —**in′ter·re·la′tion** *n.* —**in′ter·re·la′tion·ship′** *n.*

interrog. interrogative

in·ter·ro·gate (in ter′ə gāt′) *vt.* **-gat′ed, -gat′ing** [< L. pp. of *interrogare* < *inter-*, between + *rogare*, to ask] to ask questions of formally in examining [to *interrogate* a witness] —see SYN. at ASK —**in′ter′ro·ga′tor** *n.*

in·ter·ro·ga·tion (in ter′ə gā′shən) *n.* **1.** an interrogating or being interrogated; examination **2.** a question —**in·ter′ro·ga′tion·al** *adj.*

interrogation mark (or **point**) *same as* QUESTION MARK

in·ter·rog·a·tive (in′tə räg′ə tiv) *adj.* asking, or having the form of, a question [an *interrogative* sentence] —*n.* an interrogative word, element, etc., such as *what? where?* —**in′ter·rog′a·tive·ly** *adv.*

in·ter·rog·a·to·ry (-ə tôr′ē) *adj.* expressing a question [an *interrogatory* glance] —*n., pl.* **-ries** a formal set of questions —**in′ter·rog′a·to′ri·ly** *adv.*

in·ter·rupt (in′tə rupt′) *vt.* [< L. pp. of *interrumpere* < *inter-*, between + *rumpere*, to break: see RUPTURE] **1.** *a)* to break into (a discussion, etc.) *b)* to break in upon (a person) while he is speaking, working, etc. **2.** to make a break in; obstruct; cut off [to *interrupt* the smooth flow of goods] —*vi.* to make an interruption, esp. in another's speech, action, etc.—**in′ter·rupt′er** *n.* —**in′ter·rup′tive** *adj.*

in·ter·rup·tion (in′tə rup′shən) *n.* **1.** an interrupting or being interrupted **2.** anything that interrupts **3.** a break, pause, or halt

in·ter·scho·las·tic (in′tər skə las′tik) *adj.* between or among schools [an *interscholastic* debate]

in·ter·sect (in′tər sekt′) *vt.* [< L. pp. of *intersecare* < *inter-*, between + *secare*, to cut: see SAW¹] to divide into two parts by passing through or across [a river *intersects* the plain] —*vi.* to cross each other [the lines *intersect* to form right angles]

in·ter·sec·tion (-sek′shən) *n.* **1.** an intersecting **2.** a place of intersecting; specif., *a)* the point or line where two lines or surfaces meet or cross *b)* the place where two streets cross **3.** *Math.* the set containing all the points common to two or more given sets

in·ter·sec·tion·al (-′l) *adj.* **1.** of or forming an intersection **2.** between sections or regions [*intersectional* football games]

in·ter·sperse (in′tər spurs′) *vt.* **-spersed′, -spers′ing** [< L. pp. of *interspergere* < *inter-*, among + *spargere*, to scatter] **1.** to scatter among other things; put here and there [sprigs of mistletoe were *interspersed* in the wreath] **2.** to vary with things scattered here and there [black hair *interspersed* with gray] —**in′ter·sper′sion** (-spur′zhən, -shən) *n.*

☆**in·ter·state** (in′tər stāt′) *adj.* between or among states of a federal government [*interstate* commerce]

in·ter·stel·lar (in′tər stel′ər) *adj.* [INTER- + STELLAR] between or among the stars [*interstellar* space]

in·ter·stice (in tur′stis) *n., pl.* **-stic·es** (-stis iz, -stə sēz′) [Fr. < LL. < *inter-*, between + *sistere*, to set < *stare*, to STAND] a small space between things or parts; crevice; crack —**in·ter·sti·tial** (in′tər stish′əl) *adj.* —**in′ter·sti′tial·ly** *adv.*

in·ter·tid·al (in′tər tīd′′l) *adj.* of or having to do with the part of a shore between the levels of low and high tide

in·ter·twine (in′tər twīn′) *vt., vi.* **-twined′, -twin′ing** to twine together; intertwist [strands of hemp are *intertwined* to make rope]

in·ter·twist (-twist′) *vt., vi.* to twist together

☆**in·ter·ur·ban** (-ur′bən) *adj.* [INTER- + URBAN] between cities or towns [an *interurban* bus]

in·ter·val (in′tər v′l) *n.* [< OFr. < L. < *inter-*, between + *vallum*, a WALL] **1.** a space between two things; distance [an *interval* of three feet between desks] **2.** a period of time between two events [an *interval* of a year] **3.** the extent of difference between two qualities, conditions, etc. [the *interval* between talent and genius] **4.** *Music* the difference in pitch between two tones —**at intervals** **1.** now and then **2.** here and there —**in′ter·val′lic** (-val′ik) *adj.*

in·ter·vene (in'tər vēn') *vi.* **-vened', -ven'ing** [< L. < *inter-*, between + *venire*, to come] **1.** to come or be between [an *intervening* lake] **2.** to occur between two events, etc. [two days *intervened* between semesters] **3.** to come in so as to help settle, stop, etc. [to *intervene* in a dispute] **4.** to get in the way; interfere [if nothing *intervenes*, I'll see you Friday] —**in'ter·ven'er,** *Law* **in'ter·ve'nor** *n.*

in·ter·ven·tion (in'tər ven'shən) *n.* **1.** an intervening **2.** any interference in the affairs of others, esp. of one country in the affairs of another —**in'ter·ven'tion·ist** *n., adj.*

in·ter·view (in'tər vyōō') *n.* [< Fr.: see INTER- & VIEW] **1.** a meeting of people face to face to talk about something [an *interview* with an employer about a job] ☆**2.** *a*) a meeting in which a person is asked about his opinions, activities, etc., as by a reporter *b*) a published account of this —☆*vt.* to have an interview with —**in'ter·view·ee'** *n.* —**in'ter·view'er** *n.*

in·ter·weave (in'tər wēv') *vt., vi.* **-wove', -wo'ven, -weav'ing 1.** to weave together; interlace **2.** to connect closely; intermingle

in·tes·tate (in tes'tāt, -tit) *adj.* [< L. < *in-*, not + pp. of *testari*, to make a will] **1.** having made no will [he died *intestate*] **2.** not disposed of by a will —*n.* a person who has died intestate —**in·tes'ta·cy** (-tə sē) *n.*

in·tes·tin·al (in tes'ti n'l) *adj.* of or in the intestines —**in·tes'tin·al·ly** *adv.*

☆**intestinal fortitude** stubborn courage; grit: a humorously dignified substitute for GUTS (see GUT, sense 6 *a*)

in·tes·tine (in tes'tin) *adj.* [< L. *intestinus* < *intus*, within: for IE. base see ENTER] of or having to do with the internal affairs of a country or community; domestic —*n.* [*usually pl.*] the lower part of the alimentary canal, extending from the stomach to the anus and consisting of an upper part with many coils (**small intestine**) and a lower part of greater diameter (**large intestine**); bowel(s): food passes from the stomach into the intestines for further digestion

INTESTINES

(A, stomach; B, pancreas; C, descending colon; D, rectum; E, appendix; F, ileum; G, jejunum; H, ascending colon; I, transverse colon; J, duodenum; K, liver)

in·thrall, in·thral (in thrôl') *vt.* **-thralled', -thrall'ing** same as ENTHRALL

in·ti·ma·cy (in'tə mə sē) *n., pl.* **-cies 1.** a being intimate; closeness, as in friendship **2.** an intimate act, often one of a sexual nature

in·ti·mate[1] (in'tə mit) *adj.* [< Fr. < L. *intimus*, superlative of *intus*: see INTESTINE] **1.** fundamental; essential [the *intimate* structure of the atom] **2.** most private or personal [one's *intimate* feelings] **3.** closely associated; very familiar [an *intimate* friend] **4.** suggesting privacy, romance, etc. [an *intimate* restaurant] **5.** *a*) resulting from careful study [an *intimate* knowledge of physics] *b*) very close [*intimate* kinship] **6.** having sexual relations —*n.* an intimate friend or companion —**in'ti·mate·ly** *adv.* —**in'ti·mate·ness** *n.*

in·ti·mate[2] (in'tə māt') *vt.* **-mat'ed, -mat'ing** [< L. pp. of *intimare*, to announce < *intimus*: see prec.] to hint or imply —see SYN. at SUGGEST —**in'ti·ma'tion** *n.*

in·tim·i·date (in tim'ə dāt') *vt.* **-dat'ed, -dat'ing** [< ML. pp. of *intimidare* < L. *in-*, + *timidus*, afraid] **1.** to make timid; make afraid **2.** to make do something or keep from doing something by means of threats; cow —**in·tim'i·da'tion** *n.* —**in·tim'i·da'tor** *n.*

in·ti·tle (in tīt''l) *vt.* **-tled, -tling** same as ENTITLE

intl. international

in·to (in'tōō, -too, -tə) *prep.* [OE.: see IN & TO] **1.** to the inside of; toward and within [*into* a house] **2.** advancing to the midst of (a period of time) [dancing far *into* the night] **3.** to the form, substance, or condition of [turned *into* a swan; divided *into* parts] **4.** so as to strike [to bump *into* a door] **5.** to the work, activity, etc. of [to go *into* teaching] **6.** in the direction of [to head *into* a storm] ☆**7.** [Colloq.] involved in or concerned with [she's very much *into* opera now] **8.** *Math. used to indicate division* [3 *into* 21 is 7]

in·tol·er·a·ble (in täl'ər ə b'l) *adj.* not tolerable; unbearable; too severe, painful, etc. to be endured —**in·tol'er·a·bil'i·ty, in·tol'er·a·ble·ness** *n.* —**in·tol'er·a·bly** *adv.*

in·tol·er·ance (in täl'ər əns) *n.* **1.** lack of tolerance, esp. of others' opinions, beliefs, etc.; bigotry **2.** an allergy or sensitivity to some food, medicine, etc.

in·tol·er·ant (-ənt) *adj.* not tolerant; unwilling to put up with others' opinions, beliefs, etc. or with persons of other races, background, etc.; bigoted —**intolerant** of not able or willing to tolerate —**in·tol'er·ant·ly** *adv.* —**in·tol'er·ant·ness** *n.*

in·to·na·tion (in'tə nā'shən) *n.* **1.** an intoning **2.** the manner of singing or playing tones with regard to accuracy of pitch **3.** the way the voice rises and falls in pitch in speaking **4.** the manner of applying final pitch to a spoken sentence or phrase [to ask a question with a rising *intonation*] —**in'to·na'tion·al** *adj.*

in·tone (in tōn') *vt.* **-toned', -ton'ing** [< OFr. < ML.: see IN-[1] & TONE] **1.** to utter or recite in a singing tone or chant [to *intone* a prayer] **2.** to give a particular intonation to —*vi.* to speak or recite in a singing tone or chant —**in·ton'er** *n.*

in to·to (in tō'tō) [L.] as a whole; entirely

in·tox·i·cant (in täk'sə kənt) *n.* something that intoxicates; esp., alcoholic liquor —*adj.* intoxicating

in·tox·i·cate (-kāt') *vt.* **-cat'ed, -cat'ing** [< ML. pp. of *intoxicare*, to poison, ult. < L. *in-*, in + *toxicum*, a poison: see TOXIC] **1.** to have an effect on the nervous system of, so as to cause a loss of control; make drunk: said of alcoholic liquor or a drug **2.** to make wild with excitement or happiness [he was *intoxicated* by his new wealth] **3.** *Med.* to poison or have a poisonous effect on

in·tox·i·ca·tion (in täk'sə kā'shən) *n.* **1.** a making or becoming drunk **2.** a feeling of wild excitement; frenzy **3.** *Med.* a poisoning or becoming poisoned

intr. intransitive

in·tra- [L. < *intra*, within] *a combining form meaning* within, inside of [*intramural*]

in·tra·cel·lu·lar (in'trə sel'yoo lər) *adj.* of or taking place within individual cells

in·trac·ta·ble (in trak'tə b'l) *adj.* not tractable; specif., *a*) hard to manage; unruly or stubborn [an *intractable* prisoner] *b*) hard to manipulate, cure, etc. [an *intractable* material, disease, etc.] —**in·trac'ta·bil'i·ty, in·trac'ta·ble·ness** *n.* —**in·trac'ta·bly** *adv.*

in·tra·dos (in'trə däs', -dōs'; in trā'dōs) *n.* [Fr. < L. *intra*, within + Fr. *dos* < L. *dorsum*, the back] the inside curve or surface of an arch or vault

in·tra·mo·lec·u·lar (in'trə mə lek'yə lər) *adj.* acting, existing, or taking place within a molecule or molecules

in·tra·mu·ral (in'trə myoor'əl) *adj.* [INTRA- + MURAL] **1.** within the walls or limits of a city, college, etc. **2.** between or among members of the same school, college, etc. [*intramural* athletics] —**in'tra·mu'ral·ly** *adv.*

intrans. intransitive

in·tran·si·gent (in tran'sə jənt) *adj.* [< Fr. < Sp. < L. *in-*, IN-[2] + prp. of *transigere*, to settle] refusing to compromise, change one's mind, come to an agreement, etc. —*n.* one who is intransigent, esp. in politics —**in·tran'si·gence, in·tran'si·gen·cy** *n.* —**in·tran'si·gent·ly** *adv.*

in·tran·si·tive (in tran'sə tiv) *adj.* not transitive; designating a verb that does not require a direct object to complete its meaning —*n.* an intransitive verb —**in·tran'si·tive·ly** *adv.*

☆**in·tra·state** (in'trə stāt') *adj.* within a state; esp., within a State of the U.S.

in·tra·u·ter·ine (-yōōt'ər in, -yōō'tə rīn') *adj.* within the uterus

☆**intrauterine (contraceptive) device** any of various devices, as a coil or loop of plastic, inserted in the uterus as a contraceptive

in·tra·ve·nous (-vē'nəs) *adj.* [INTRA- + VENOUS] in, or directly into, a vein or veins [an *intravenous* injection] —**in'tra·ve'nous·ly** *adv.*

in·trench (in trench') *vt., vi.* same as ENTRENCH

in·trep·id (in trep'id) *adj.* [< L. < *in-*, not + *trepidus*, alarmed] unafraid; bold; fearless; very brave —see SYN. at BRAVE —**in'tre·pid'i·ty** (-trə pid'ə tē), **in·trep'id·ness** *n.* —**in·trep'id·ly** *adv.*

Int. Rev. internal revenue

in·tri·ca·cy (in'tri kə sē) *n.* **1.** an intricate quality or state; complexity [the *intricacy* of a design] **2.** *pl.* **-cies** something intricate; involved matter, proceeding, etc. [a plot full of *intricacies*]

in·tri·cate (in'tri kit) *adj.* [< L. pp. of *intricare*, to entangle < *in-*, in + *tricae*, perplexities] **1.** hard to follow or understand because full of puzzling parts, details, or relationships [an *intricate* problem] **2.** full of elaborate detail [an *intricate* pattern] —see SYN. at COMPLEX —**in'tri·cate·ly** *adv.* —**in'tri·cate·ness** *n.*

in·trigue (in trēg'; *for n., also* in'trēg) *vi.* **-trigued', -trigu'ing** [< Fr. < It. < L. *intricare*: see prec.] **1.** to carry on a secret love affair **2.** to plot or scheme secretly, slyly, or dishonestly —*vt.* to stir up the interest or curiosity of; fascinate [movies *intrigue* her] —*n.* **1.** secret or underhanded plotting **2.** a secret or underhanded plot or scheme **3.** a secret love affair —see SYN. at PLOT —**in·trigu′er** *n.* —**in·trigu′ing·ly** *adv.*

in·trin·sic (in trin′sik, -zik) *adj.* [< MFr. < LL. *intrinsecus*, inward < L. < *intra-*, within + *secus*, close] belonging to the real nature of a thing; essential [a man's *intrinsic* worth cannot be measured by his wealth]: also **in·trin′si·cal** —**in·trin′si·cal·ly** *adv.* —**in·trin′si·cal·ness** *n.*

in·tro- [L. < *intro*, on the inside] *a combining form meaning* into, within, inward [introvert]

introd., intro. 1. introduction **2.** introductory

in·tro·duce (in′trə dōōs′, -dyōōs′) *vt.* **-duced′, -duc′ing** [< L. < *intro-*, within + *ducere*, to lead: see DUKE] **1.** to lead or bring in **2.** to put in; insert [to *introduce* a drain into a wound] **3.** to add as a new feature [*introduce* some humor into the play] **4.** to bring into use; make popular or common [space science has *introduced* many new words] **5.** *a)* to make acquainted; present (*to*) [*introduce* me to her] *b)* to present (a person) to society *c)* to give knowledge or experience of [they *introduced* him to music] **6.** to bring forward; bring to notice formally [*introduce* a bill into Congress] **7.** to start; begin [to *introduce* a talk with a joke] —**in′tro·duc′er** *n.*

in·tro·duc·tion (-duk′shən) *n.* **1.** an introducing or being introduced **2.** anything brought into use, knowledge, or fashion [transistors are a fairly recent *introduction*] **3.** anything that introduces, or prepares the way for; specif., *a)* the preliminary section of a book, speech, etc. *b)* a guide or text for beginning students *c)* an opening section of a musical composition **4.** the formal presentation of one person to another; to an audience, etc.

SYN.—**introduction**, in strict use, refers to the opening section of a book, etc. that leads into what follows and gives a general explanation of the subject; **preface** refers to a separate section at the beginning of a book, etc. written by the author or someone else to explain the purpose or plan of the work or how it was prepared; **foreword** usually refers to a very brief or simple preface —ANT. **conclusion, epilogue**

in·tro·duc·to·ry (-duk′tər ē) *adj.* used as an introduction; preliminary [an *introductory* course in science]: also **in′tro·duc′tive** —**in′tro·duc′to·ri·ly** *adv.*

in·tro·it (in trō′it; in′trō it, -troit) *n.* [< MFr. < L. *introitus*, an entrance, ult. < *intro-*, within + *ire*, to go] **1.** a psalm or hymn at the opening of a Christian worship service **2.** [I-] *R.C.Ch.* the first variable part of the Mass, consisting of a few psalm verses followed by the *Gloria Patri* and then repeated

in·tro·mit (in′trə mit′) *vt.* **-mit′ted, -mit′ting** [< L. < *intro-*, within + *mittere*, to send] to cause to enter; put in; insert —**in′tro·mis′sion** (-mish′ən) *n.* —**in′tro·mit′tent** *adj.*

in·trorse (in trôrs′) *adj.* [< L. contr. of *introversus*, turned inward] *Bot.* facing inward, or toward the center —**in·trorse′ly** *adv.*

in·tro·spec·tion (in′trə spek′shən) *n.* [< L. < pp. of *introspicere*, ult. < *intro-*, within + *specere*, to look] a looking into one's own mind, feelings, etc.; observation and analysis of oneself —**in′tro·spec′tive** *adj.* —**in′tro·spec′tive·ly** *adv.* —**in′tro·spec′tive·ness** *n.*

in·tro·ver·sion (-vur′zhən) *n.* [see INTROVERT] *Psychol.* an attitude in which a person directs his interest to his own experiences and feelings rather than to things outside himself and to other people: opposed to EXTROVERSION —**in′tro·ver′sive** *adj.* —**in′tro·ver′sive·ly** *adv.*

in·tro·vert (in′trə vurt′; for v., also in′trə vurt′) *vt.* [< L. *intro-*, within + *vertere*, to turn] **1.** to direct (one's interest, mind, etc.) upon oneself **2.** to bend (something) inward —*vi.* to become introverted —*n. Psychol.* a person who is more interested in his own thoughts and feelings than in the people and things around him: opposed to EXTROVERT —*adj.* showing introversion: usually **in′tro·vert′ed**

in·trude (in trōōd′) *vt.* **-trud′ed, -trud′ing** [< L. < *in-*, in + *trudere*, to THRUST] **1.** to push or force (something *in* or *upon*) **2.** to force (oneself or one's thoughts) upon others without being asked or wanted **3.** *Geol.* to force (liquid magma, etc.) into or between solid rocks —*vi.* to intrude oneself upon others [I hope I'm not *intruding*] —**in·trud′er** *n.*

SYN.—**intrude** implies the forcing of oneself or something upon another without being asked or wanted or without having the right to do so [to

intrude upon another's privacy]; **obtrude** suggests even more strongly that the intrusion causes an unwanted distraction or great unpleasantness [side issues keep *obtruding*]

in·tru·sion (in trōō′zhən) *n.* **1.** the act of intruding **2.** *Geol. a)* the movement of liquid magma, etc. into or between solid rock *b)* the body of rock resulting from this

in·tru·sive (-siv) *adj.* **1.** intruding; coming in without being asked or wanted **2.** *Geol.* formed by intruding —**in·tru′sive·ly** *adv.* —**in·tru′sive·ness** *n.*

in·trust (in trust′) *vt. same as* ENTRUST

in·tu·it (in tōō′it, -tyōō′-) *vt., vi.* to know or learn by intuition —**in·tu′it·a·ble** *adj.*

in·tu·i·tion (in′tōō wish′ən, -tyōō-) *n.* [LL. < L. pp. of *intueri* < *in-*, in + *tueri*, to look at] **1.** *a)* the direct knowing or learning of something without the conscious use of reasoning; instant understanding [to sense danger by a flash of *intuition*] *b)* the ability to know or learn things in this way **2.** something known or learned in this way —**in′tu·i′tion·al** *adj.* —**in′tu·i′tion·al·ly** *adv.*

in·tu·i·tive (in tōō′i tiv, -tyōō′-) *adj.* **1.** having to do with, having, or knowing by, intuition [an *intuitive* person] **2.** perceived by intuition [an *intuitive* truth] —**in·tu′i·tive·ly** *adv.* —**in·tu′i·tive·ness** *n.*

in·tu·mes·cence (in′tōō mes′′ns, -tyōō-) *n.* [< L. < *in-*, thoroughly + *tumescere*, to swell up] a swollen or enlarged mass, as a tumor; swelling —**in′tu·mesce′** (-mes′) *vi.* **-mesced′, -mesc′ing** —**in′tu·mes′cent** *adj.*

in·u·lin (in′yōō lin) *n.* [< ModL. *Inula*, genus of plants + -IN[1]] a white, starchlike polysaccharide which yields fructose: found in the roots and tubers of many composite plants

in·un·date (in′ən dāt′) *vt.* **-dat′ed, -dat′ing** [< L. pp. of *inundare* < *in-*, in + *undare*, to flood < *unda*, a wave: for IE. base see WATER] to cover as with a flood; deluge; flood [creek water *inundated* the road; he was *inundated* with mail] —**in·un·dant** (in un′dənt) *adj.* —**in′un·da′tion** *n.* —**in′un·da′tor** *n.* —**in·un·da·to·ry** (-də tôr′ē) *adj.*

in·ure (in yoor′) *vt.* **-ured′, -ur′ing** [< ME. *in*, in + *ure*, practice, work < OFr. *ovre* < L. *opera*, a work] to make accustomed to something difficult, painful, etc. [his term as mayor has *inured* him to criticism] —*vi.* to come into use or take effect [sick pay *inures* from the first day of illness] —**in·ure′ment** *n.*

inv. 1. invented **2.** inventor **3.** invoice

‡**in va·cu·o** (in vak′yōō ō′) [L.] in a vacuum

in·vade (in vād′) *vt.* **-vad′ed, -vad′ing** [< L. < *in-*, in + *vadere*, to go] **1.** to enter forcibly, as with an army in order to conquer **2.** to crowd into; throng [tourists *invading* the beaches] **3.** to break into; intrude upon [he *invaded* my privacy] **4.** to spread through with harmful effects [disease *invades* tissue] —*vi.* to make an invasion —**in·vad′er** *n.*

in·vag·i·nate (in vaj′ə nāt′) *vt.* **-nat′ed, -nat′ing** [< ML. pp. of *invaginare* < L. *in-*, in + *vagina*, a sheath] to place or receive into a sheath —*vi.* to become invaginated —**in·vag′i·na′tion** *n.*

in·va·lid[1] (in′və lid) *adj.* [< Fr. < L.: see IN-[2] + VALID] **1.** not well; weak and sickly **2.** of or for invalids [an *invalid* home] —*n.* a weak, sickly person; esp., one who is likely to be ill or disabled for some time —*vt.* **1.** to disable or weaken **2.** [Chiefly Brit.] to remove (a soldier, sailor, etc.) from active duty because of injury or illness —**in′va·lid·ism** *n.*

in·val·id[2] (in val′id) *adj.* not valid; having no force [an unsigned check is *invalid*] —**in·va·lid·i·ty** (in′və lid′ə tē) *n.* —**in·val′id·ly** *adv.*

in·val·i·date (in val′ə dāt′) *vt.* **-dat′ed, -dat′ing** to make invalid; deprive of legal force —see SYN. at NULLIFY —**in·val′i·da′tion** *n.* —**in·val′i·da′tor** *n.*

in·val·u·a·ble (in val′yōō wə b'l, -yə b'l) *adj.* too valuable to be measured; priceless —**in·val′u·a·ble·ness** *n.* —**in·val′u·a·bly** *adv.*

in·var·i·a·ble (in ver′ē ə b'l) *adj.* not variable; unchanging; constant; uniform [an *invariable* rule] —**in·var′i·a·bil′i·ty**, **in·var′i·a·ble·ness** *n.* —**in·var′i·a·bly** *adv.*

in·va·sion (in vā′zhən) *n.* an invading; specif., *a)* an entering or being entered by an attacking military force *b)* an intruding upon others —**in·va′sive** *adj.*

in·vec·tive (in vek′tiv) *n.* [< MFr. < LL. < L. pp. of *invehere*: see INVEIGH] a violent verbal attack; strong criticism, insults, curses, etc.

fat, āpe, cär; ten, ēven; is, bīte; gō, hôrn, tōōl, look; oil, out; up, fur; get; joy; yet; chin; she; thin, then; zh, leisure; ŋ, ring; ə for a in ago, e in agent, i in sanity, o in comply, u in focus; ′ as in able (ā′b'l); Fr. bal; ë, Fr. coeur; ö, Fr. feu; Fr. mon; ô, Fr. coq; ü, Fr. duc; r, Fr. cri; H, G. ich; кh, G. doch; ‡foreign; ☆ Americanism; < derived from. See inside front cover.

in·veigh (in vā′) *vi.* [< L. *invehi*, to attack < *invehere* < *in-*, + *vehere*, to carry: for IE. base see WAY] to make a violent verbal attack; talk or write bitterly (*against*); rail —**in·veigh′er** *n.*

in·vei·gle (in vē′g'l, -vā′-) *vt.* **-gled, -gling** [< MFr. *aveugler*, to blind < L. *ab*, from + *oculus*, an eye] to lead on with deception; lure or trick into doing something, going somewhere, etc. [Tom Sawyer *inveigled* his friends into painting his fence] —**in·vei′gle·ment** *n.* —**in·vei′gler** *n.*

in·vent (in vent′) *vt.* [< L. pp. of *invenire* < *in-*, on + *venire*, to come: see BASIS] **1.** to think up; create in the mind [to *invent* excuses] **2.** to think out or produce (a new device, process, etc.); devise for the first time [Alexander Graham Bell *invented* the telephone]

in·ven·tion (in ven′shən) *n.* **1.** an inventing or being invented **2.** the ability to invent; inventiveness, imagination, etc. [a novelist who shows much *invention* in telling his story] **3.** something invented; specif., *a)* something thought up; esp., a falsehood *b)* a new device, plan, etc. [the many *inventions* of Edison] **4.** *Music* a short composition developing a motif in counterpoint

in·ven·tive (-tiv) *adj.* **1.** of or characterized by invention [*inventive* powers] **2.** skilled in inventing; creative [an *inventive* person] —**in·ven′tive·ly** *adv.* —**in·ven′tive·ness** *n.*

in·ven·tor (-tər) *n.* a person who invents; esp., one who thinks out or produces (something) for the first time

in·ven·to·ry (in′vən tôr′ē) *n., pl.* **-ries** [< ML. < LL. < L. pp. of *invenire*: see INVENT] **1.** a complete list of goods, property, etc., as of a business [we prepare an *inventory* of our stock every year] **2.** the stock of goods on hand [because of fewer sales, dealers have high *inventories*] **3.** any detailed list [an *inventory* of one's record collection] **4.** the act of making such a list [all employees are asked to help with *inventory* next week] —*vt.* **-ried, -ry·ing 1.** to make an inventory of **2.** to place on an inventory —**take inventory 1.** to make an inventory of stock on hand **2.** to make an appraisal, as of one's situation —**in′ven·to′ri·al** *adj.* —**in′ven·to′ri·al·ly** *adv.*

In·ver·ness (in′vər nes′) *n.* [after county in Scotland] [*often* i-] **1.** an overcoat with a long, removable cape **2.** the cape: also **Inverness cape**

in·verse (in vurs′, in′vurs′) *adj.* **1.** inverted; reversed in order or relation; directly opposite [237 in *inverse* order is 732] **2.** *Math.* designating or of an operation which, when applied after a specific operation, cancels it [subtraction is the *inverse* operation of addition] —*n.* **1.** any inverse thing; direct opposite **2.** *Math. a)* the result of an inversion *b)* the result obtained after dividing 1 by the given number [the *inverse* of x is 1/x] —**in·verse′ly** *adv.*

in·ver·sion (in vur′zhən, -shən) *n.* **1.** an inverting or being inverted **2.** something inverted; reversal **3.** a reversal of the normal order of words in a sentence (Ex.: "said he" for "he said") **4.** *Math. a)* the process of using an opposite rule or method *b)* an interchange of the terms of a ratio **5.** *Meteorol.* an atmospheric condition in which a layer of warm air traps cooler air near the surface of the earth, preventing the normal rising of surface air **6.** *Music* the reversal of the position of the tones in an interval or chord, as by raising the lower tone by an octave **7.** *same as* HOMOSEXUALITY —**in·ver′sive** *adj.*

in·vert (in vurt′; *for n.* in′vurt′) *vt.* [< L. < *in-*, to + *vertere*, to turn: see VERSE] **1.** to turn upside down **2.** to change to the direct opposite; reverse the order, position, direction, etc. of **3.** to subject to inversion **4.** *Math.* to divide 1 by (a given quantity) —*n.* an inverted person or thing —**in·vert′i·ble** *adj.*

in·ver·te·brate (in vur′tə brit, -brāt′) *adj.* **1.** not vertebrate; having no backbone, or spinal column **2.** of invertebrates —*n.* any animal without a backbone; any animal other than a fish, amphibian, reptile, bird, or mammal

in·vert·er (in vur′tər) *n. Elec.* a device for changing direct current into alternating current

in·vert sugar (in′vurt′) a mixture of dextrose and levulose found in fruits and also produced artificially

in·vest (in vest′) *vt.* [< L. < *in-*, in + *vestire*, to clothe < *vestis*, clothing] **1.** to clothe; array **2.** *a)* to cover or surround as if with a garment [fog *invests* the city] *b)* to provide with certain qualities, attributes, etc. [a woman *invested* with an air of mystery] **3.** to install in office with ceremony **4.** to furnish with power, privilege, or authority [to *invest* the governor with emergency powers] **5.** to put (money) into business, stocks, bonds, etc. for the purpose of obtaining a profit **6.** to spend (time,

effort, etc.) in order to get something in return [he *invested* ten years in his search for a cure] **7.** *Mil.* to besiege (a town, port, etc.) —*vi.* to invest money —**in·ves′tor** *n.*

in·ves·ti·gate (in ves′tə gāt′) *vt.* **-gat·ed, -gat·ing** [< L. pp. of *investigare*, to trace out < *vestigium*, a track] to search into so as to learn the facts; examine in detail [to *investigate* a claim] —*vi.* to make an investigation —**in·ves′ti·ga·ble** (-gə b'l) *adj.* —**in·ves′ti·ga′tive** (-gāt′iv), **in·ves′ti·ga·to′ry** (-gə tôr′ē) *adj.* —**in·ves′ti·ga′tor** *n.*

in·ves·ti·ga·tion (in ves′tə gā′shən) *n.* **1.** an investigating or being investigated **2.** a careful examination or inquiry —**in·ves′ti·ga′tion·al** *adj.*

in·ves·ti·ture (in ves′tə chər) *n.* **1.** the act or ceremony of investing with an office, power, authority, etc. **2.** anything that clothes or covers

in·vest·ment (in vest′mənt) *n.* **1.** an investing or being invested **2.** an outer covering **3.** *same as* INVESTITURE (sense 1) **4.** *a)* the investing of money *b)* the amount of money invested *c)* anything in which money is or may be invested [he found real estate to be a good *investment*]

in·vet·er·ate (in vet′ər it) *adj.* [< L. pp. of *inveterare*, to age < *in-*, in + *vetus*, old] **1.** firmly established over a long period; deep-rooted [an *inveterate* custom] **2.** settled in a habit, practice, prejudice, etc.; habitual [an *inveterate* liar] —see SYN. at CHRONIC —**in·vet′er·a·cy** *n.* —**in·vet′er·ate·ly** *adv.*

in·vid·i·ous (in vid′ē əs) *adj.* [< L. < *invidia*, ENVY] **1.** likely to cause bad feeling or envy; giving offense [an *invidious* remark] **2.** unfair because dealing with things that are not really equal —**in·vid′i·ous·ly** *adv.* —**in·vid′i·ous·ness** *n.*

in·vig·or·ate (in vig′ə rāt′) *vt.* **-at·ed, -at·ing** [IN-¹ + VIGOR + -ATE¹] to give vigor to; fill with energy; enliven —**in·vig′or·a′tion** *n.* —**in·vig′or·a′tive** *adj.* —**in·vig′or·a′tor** *n.*

in·vin·ci·ble (in vin′sə b'l) *adj.* [< MFr. < L.: see IN-² & VINCIBLE] that cannot be defeated or overcome; unconquerable —**in·vin′ci·bil′i·ty, in·vin′ci·ble·ness** *n.* —**in·vin′ci·bly** *adv.*

in·vi·o·la·ble (in vī′ə lə b'l) *adj.* **1.** that should not be violated or broken; sacred [an *inviolable* promise] **2.** that cannot be violated; indestructible [their *inviolable* morality] —**in·vi′o·la·bil′i·ty, in·vi′o·la·ble·ness** *n.* —**in·vi′o·la·bly** *adv.*

in·vi·o·late (in vī′ə lit, -lāt′) *adj.* not violated; kept sacred or unbroken —**in·vi′o·la·cy** (-lə sē), **in·vi′o·late·ness** *n.* —**in·vi′o·late·ly** *adv.*

in·vis·i·ble (in viz′ə b'l) *adj.* **1.** not visible; that cannot be seen [oxygen is *invisible*] **2.** out of sight [the moon was *invisible* behind the clouds] **3.** too small or too faint to be seen; imperceptible [most body cells are *invisible* except under a microscope] **4.** kept hidden [*invisible* assets] —*n.* an invisible thing or being —**the Invisible 1.** God **2.** the unseen world —**in·vis′i·bil′i·ty, in·vis′i·ble·ness** *n.* —**in·vis′i·bly** *adv.*

in·vi·ta·tion (in′və tā′shən) *n.* **1.** an inviting to come somewhere or do something **2.** the message or note used in inviting

in·vi·ta·tion·al (-'l) *adj.* participated in only by those invited [an *invitational* art exhibit]

in·vite (in vīt′; *for n.* in′vīt) *vt.* **-vit·ed, -vit·ing** [< Fr. < L. *invitare*] **1.** to ask courteously to come somewhere or do something **2.** to make a request for [to *invite* questions] **3.** to tend to bring on; give the chance for [action that *invites* scandal] **4.** to tempt; entice —*n.* [Colloq.] an invitation —see SYN. at CALL

in·vit·ing (in vīt′iŋ) *adj.* tempting or attractive [an *inviting* display of foods]

in vi·tro (in vē′trō) [L., lit., in glass] outside the living organism and maintained artificially, as in a test tube

in vi·vo (in vē′vō) [L., lit., in one that is living] occurring within the living organism

in·vo·ca·tion (in′və kā′shən) *n.* **1.** the act of invoking, or calling on, God, the Muses, etc. for blessing, help, etc. **2.** a formal prayer used in invoking, as at the beginning of a church service **3.** *a)* the act of calling up evil spirits *b)* an incantation —**in′vo·ca′tion·al** *adj.* —**in·voc′a·to′ry** (-väk′ə tôr′ē) *adj.*

in·voice (in′vois) *n.* [prob. < pl. of ME. *envoie*, a message: see ENVOY¹] **1.** an itemized list of goods shipped to a buyer, stating quantities, prices, shipping charges, etc., often with a request for payment **2.** a shipment of invoiced goods —*vt.* **-voiced, -voic·ing** to present an invoice for or to

in·voke (in vōk′) *vt.* **-voked′, -vok′ing** [< MFr. < L. < *in-*, on + *vocare*, to call: see VOCATIVE] **1.** to call on (God, the Muses, etc.) for blessing, help, etc. **2.** to put into use (a law, penalty, etc.) as properly applying [to *invoke* an article of the U.N. Charter] **3.** to call forth; cause **4.** to summon (evil spirits) by incantation; conjure **5.** to ask solemnly for; implore [to *invoke* aid] —**in·vok′er** *n.*

INVERNESS

in·vo·lu·cre (in'və loo'kər) *n.* [Fr. < L. *involucrum*, wrapper < *involvere*, INVOLVE] *Bot.* a ring of bracts at the base of a flower, flower cluster, or fruit —**in'vo·lu'cral** (-krəl) *adj.*

in·vol·un·tar·y (in väl'ən ter'ē) *adj.* not voluntary; specif., *a)* not done of one's own free will [the *involuntary* labor of prisoners] *b)* unintentional; accidental *c)* not consciously controlled [sneezing is *involuntary*] —see SYN. at SPONTANEOUS —**in·vol'un·tar'i·ly** *adv.* —**in·vol'un·tar'i·ness** *n.*

in·vo·lute (in'və loot') *adj.* [L. *involutus*, pp. of *involvere*, INVOLVE] **1.** intricate; involved **2.** rolled up or curled in a spiral; having the whorls wound closely around the axis [*involute* shells] **3.** *Bot.* rolled inward at the edges [*involute* leaves] —*n. Math.* the curve traced by a point on a taut string when it is unwound from a fixed curve on the same plane —*vi.* **-lut'ed, -lut'ing** to become involute or undergo involution

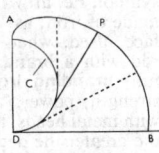

INVOLUTE
(AB, involute
made by point P
of string unrolled
from curve C)

in·vo·lu·tion (in'və loo'shən) *n.* **1.** an involving or being involved; entanglement **2.** anything that is complex or involved; complication; intricacy **3.** *Math.* the raising of a quantity to any given power —**in'vo·lu'tion·al** *adj.* —**in'vo·lu'tion·ar'y** *adj.*

in·volve (in välv') *vt.* **-volved', -volv'ing** [< L. < *in-*, in + *volvere*, to roll: see WALK] **1.** orig., to enfold or envelop **2.** to make difficult or complicated [an *involved* set of instructions] **3.** to entangle in difficulty, trouble, etc.; implicate [repairs on his house *involved* him in debt] **4.** to draw or hold within itself; include [a riot that *involved* thousands] **5.** to include as a necessary part; entail; require [saving money *involves* thrift] **6.** to relate to or affect [his honor is *involved*] **7.** to make busy; occupy [*involved* in research] —see SYN. at INCLUDE —**in·volve'ment** *n.*

in·volved (in välvd') *adj.* **1.** not easily understood; complicated; intricate [an *involved* sentence] **2.** brought in as having had a part in the matter; implicated [each of the men *involved* was arrested] —see SYN. at COMPLEX

in·vul·ner·a·ble (in vul'nər ə b'l) *adj.* **1.** that cannot be wounded or injured **2.** able to resist attack without being damaged [an *invulnerable* reputation] —**in·vul'ner·a·bil'i·ty** *n.* —**in·vul'ner·a·bly** *adv.*

in·ward (in'wərd) *adj.* **1.** situated within; internal **2.** of the mind or feelings [she felt an *inward* calm] **3.** directed toward the inside [the *inward* pull of a centrifuge] —*n.* **1.** the inside **2.** [*pl.*] the entrails —*adv.* **1.** toward the inside or center **2.** into the mind or spirit Also **in'wards** *adv.*

in·ward·ly (-lē) *adv.* **1.** in or on the inside; internally **2.** in the mind or spirit [*inwardly* contented] **3.** toward the inside or center

in·ward·ness (-nis) *n.* **1.** the inner nature or meaning **2.** spirituality **3.** depth of thought or feeling

in·weave (in wēv') *vt.* **-wove', -wo'ven** or **-wove', -weav'ing** to weave in

in·wrought (in rôt') *adj.* **1.** worked or woven into a fabric; said of a pattern, etc. **2.** closely blended with other things

I·o (ī'ō) *Gr. Myth.* a maiden loved by Zeus and changed by him into a heifer to hide her from his jealous wife, Hera

Io *Chem.* ionium

i·o·dide (ī'ə dīd') *n.* a compound of iodine with another element or with a radical

i·o·dine (ī'ə dīn', -din; *Brit. & among chemists,* -dēn') *n.* [Fr. *iode* (< Gr. *iōdēs*, violetlike < *ion*, a violet + *eidos*, a form) + -INE[4]] **1.** a nonmetallic chemical element of the halogen family, consisting of grayish-black crystals that give off a violet-colored vapor: used as an antiseptic, in photography, etc.: symbol, I; at. wt., 126.9044; at. no., 53: a radioactive isotope (**iodine 131**) is used in medicine **2.** tincture of iodine, used as an antiseptic

i·o·dize (ī'ə dīz') *vt.* **-dized', -diz'ing** to treat (a wound, photographic plate, etc.) with iodine or an iodide

iodized salt common table salt to which a small amount of sodium iodide or potassium iodide has been added

i·o·do- [< Fr. *iode*, iodine] *a combining form meaning* iodine or a compound of iodine: also, before a vowel, **iod-**

i·o·do·form (ī ō'də fôrm') *n.* [IODO- + FORM(IC)] a yellowish,

crystalline compound of iodine, CHI₃, used as an antiseptic in surgical dressings

i·o·dop·sin (ī'ə däp'sin) *n.* [< IOD(O)- + Gr. *opsis*, sight + -IN[1]] a violet pigment in the cones of the retina, thought to be responsible for changing light stimuli to nerve impulses

☆**I·o moth** (ī'ō) a large, yellowish N. American moth with an eyelike spot on each hind wing

i·on (ī'ən, -än) *n.* [< Gr. *iōn*, prp. of *ienai*, to go] an atom or group of atoms that has become electrically charged by the loss or gain of one or more electrons: such loss (resulting in a positive ion, or CATION), or gain (resulting in a negative ion, or ANION), occurs during electrolysis, by the action of certain forms of radiant energy, etc. —**i·on·ic** (ī-än'ik) *adj.*

IO MOTH
(wingspread to 3 in.)

-ion [< Fr. < L. *-io* (gen. *-ionis*)] *a suffix meaning* the act, condition, or result of [*translation, correction*]

Io·nes·co (yə nes'kō, ē'ə-), **Eugene** 1912– ; Fr. playwright, born in Romania

I·o·ni·a (ī ō'nē ə) ancient region along the W coast of Asia Minor, colonized by the Greeks in the 11th cent. B.C. —**I·o'ni·an** *adj., n.*

Ionian Sea section of the Mediterranean, between Greece, Sicily, & the southern part of the Italian peninsula

I·on·ic (ī än'ik) *adj.* **1.** of Ionia or its people **2.** designating or of that one of the three orders of Greek architecture having ornamental scrolls on the capitals: see also CORINTHIAN and DORIC

i·on·ic (ī än'ik) *adj.* of or being an ion or ions

i·o·ni·um (ī ō'nē əm) *n.* [ION + ModL. ending *-ium*] a radioactive isotope of thorium

IONIC CAPITAL

i·on·ize (ī'ə nīz') *vt., vi.* **-ized', -iz'ing** to change or be changed into ions; dissociate into ions, as a salt dissolved in water, or become electrically charged, as a gas under radiation —**i'on·i·za'tion** *n.* —**i'on·iz'er** *n.*

i·on·o·sphere (ī än'ə sfir') *n.* the outer part of the earth's atmosphere, beginning at an altitude of about 25 miles and extending to the highest parts of the atmosphere: it consists of changing layers of ionized gases —**i·on'o·spher'ic** *adj.*

i·o·ta (ī ōt'ə) *n.* **1.** the ninth letter of the Greek alphabet (I, ι) **2.** a very small quantity; jot [he hasn't an *iota* of envy in him]

IOU, I.O.U. (ī'ō'yoo') **1.** I owe you **2.** a signed note with these letters on it, given to acknowledge a debt

-ious (ē əs, yəs, əs) [see -OUS] *a suffix used to form adjectives corresponding to nouns that end in* -ION [*rebellious*] *or meaning* having, characterized by [*furious*]

I·o·wa (ī'ə wə; *occas.* -wä') [after a tribe of Indians who lived in the area, prob. < AmInd. *Ayuba*, lit., sleepy ones] Middle Western State of the U.S.: 56,290 sq. mi.; pop. 2,825,000; cap. Des Moines: abbrev. **Ia., IA** —**I'o·wan** *adj., n.*

IPA International Phonetic Alphabet

☆**ip·e·cac** (ip'ə kak') *n.* [< Port. < Tupi] **1.** a tropical S. American plant of the madder family **2.** the dried roots of this plant **3.** a medicine made from the dried roots, used to cause vomiting Also **ip·e·cac·u·an·ha** (ip'ə kak'yoo wan'ə)

Iph·i·ge·ni·a (if'ə jə nī'ə) *Gr. Myth.* a daughter of Agamemnon, offered by him as a sacrifice to Artemis

Ip·po·li·tov-I·va·nov (ē'pō lü'tôf ē vä'nôf), **Mi·kha·il** (**Mikhailovich**) (mi khä ēl') 1859–1935; Russ. composer

‡**ip·se dix·it** (ip'sē dik'sit) [L., he himself has said (it)] a statement made with authority but without proof

ip·so fac·to (ip'sō fak'tō) [L.] by that very fact

IQ, I.Q. intelligence quotient

ir- *see* IN-[1] & IN-[2]

Ir *Chem.* iridium

IR, ir, i·r infrared

Ir. 1. Ireland **2.** Irish

I·ra (ī'rə) [Heb. 'īrā, lit., watchful] a masculine name

IRA, I.R.A. Irish Republican Army

I·ran (i ran′, ĭ-; ē rän′) country in SW Asia, between the Caspian Sea & the Persian Gulf: 636,000 sq. mi.; pop. 30,218,000; cap. Tehran

Iran. Iranian

I·ra·ni·an (i rā′nē ən, ĭ-) *adj.* of Iran, its people, their language, or culture —*n.* **1.** one of the people of Iran; Persian **2.** a branch of the Indo-European family of languages, including Persian

I·raq (i räk′, -rak′; ē-) country in SW Asia, at the head of the Persian Gulf: 171,599 sq. mi.; pop. 9,431,000; cap. Baghdad: also sp. **Irak**

I·ra·qi (i rä′kē, -rak′ē) *n.* **1.** *pl.* **-qis** a native or inhabitant of Iraq **2.** the Arabic dialect spoken in Iraq —*adj.* of Iraq, its people, their language, or culture

i·ras·ci·ble (i ras′ə b'l, ī-) *adj.* [< MFr. < LL. < L. *irasci:* see IRATE] **1.** easily made angry; quick-tempered **2.** full of anger [an *irascible* comment] —see SYN. at IRRITABLE —**i·ras′ci·bil′i·ty, i·ras′ci·ble·ness** *n.* —**i·ras′ci·bly** *adv.*

i·rate (ī rāt′, ī′rāt) *adj.* [L. *iratus* < *irasci,* to be angry < *ira,* IRE] angry; wrathful; incensed —**i·rate′ly** *adv.* —**i·rate′ness** *n.*

IRBM intermediate range ballistic missile

ire (īr) *n.* [< OFr. < L. *ira* < IE. base *eis-,* to move violently] anger; wrath —**ire′ful** *adj.* —**ire′ful·ly** *adv.* —**ire′ful·ness** *n.*

Ire. Ireland

Ire·land (īr′lənd) **1.** island of the British Isles, west of Great Britain **2.** republic consisting of the southern portion and part of the northern portion of this island: 27,136 sq. mi.; pop. 2,921,000; cap. Dublin See NORTHERN IRELAND

I·rene (ī rēn′) [< Fr. < L. < Gr. *Eirēnē,* lit., peace] a feminine name

i·ren·ic (ī ren′ik, ī rē′nik) *adj.* [< Gr. < *eirēnē,* peace] bringing peace; pacific: also **i·ren′i·cal** —**i·ren′i·cal·ly** *adv.*

ir·i·des·cent (ir′ə des′'nt) *adj.* [< L. *iris* (< Gr. *iris*), rainbow + -ESCENT] having or showing shifting changes in color or a play of rainbowlike colors [soap bubbles are often *iridescent*] —**ir′i·des′cence** *n.* —**ir′i·des′cent·ly** *adv.*

i·rid·i·um (i rid′ē əm, ī-) *n.* [ModL. < L. *iris* (< Gr. *iris*), rainbow: from the changing color of some of its salts] a white, heavy, brittle, metallic chemical element found in platinum ores: alloys of iridium are used for pen points and bearings of watches: symbol, Ir; at. wt., 192.2; at. no., 77 —**i·rid′ik** (-ik) *adj.*

I·ris (ī′ris) [L. < Gr. *iris,* rainbow] **1.** a feminine name **2.** *Gr. Myth.* the goddess of the rainbow and a messenger of the gods

i·ris (ī′ris) *n., pl.* **i′ris·es,** also, for 1 & 2, **ir·i·des** (ir′ə dēz′, ī′rə-) [L. < Gr. *iris,* rainbow] **1.** a rainbow **2.** the round, colored membrane surrounding the pupil of the eye: it adjusts the size of the pupil to regulate the amount of light entering the eye: see illustration at EYE **3.** a plant with sword-shaped leaves and showy flowers composed of three petals and three drooping sepals **4.** the flower of this plant

iris diaphragm a device made up of thin, overlapping metal plates that can be adjusted to form an opening of varying size for letting light through a camera lens, etc.

I·rish (ī′rish) *adj.* of Ireland, its people, their language, or culture —*n.* **1.** *same as* IRISH GAELIC **2.** the English dialect of Ireland —**the Irish** the people of Ireland

IRIS

Irish Gaelic the Celtic language of Ireland

I·rish·man (ī′rish mən) *n., pl.* **-men 1.** a native or inhabitant of Ireland, esp. a man **2.** a person, esp. a man, whose ancestors were Irish —**I′rish·wom′an** *n.fem., pl.* **-wom′en**

Irish moss *same as* CARRAGEEN

Irish potato the common white potato

Irish Republican Army an underground organization founded to work for Irish independence from England

Irish Sea arm of the Atlantic between Ireland & Great Britain

Irish setter any of a breed of setter with a coat of long, silky, reddish-brown hair

Irish stew a stew of meat, potatoes, onions, and other vegetables

Irish terrier any of a breed of small, lean dog with a wiry, reddish coat

Irish wolfhound any of a breed of very large, heavy, powerful dog with a rough coat

irk (urk) *vt.* [ME. *irken,* to be weary of] to annoy, disgust, irritate, etc. [his continual laughter *irked* her] —see SYN. at ANNOY

irk·some (urk′səm) *adj.* that tends to irk; tiresome or annoying [*irksome* duties] —**irk′some·ly** *adv.* —**irk′some·ness** *n.*

Ir·kutsk (ir kootsk′) city in S Asiatic R.S.F.S.R.: pop. 453,000

Ir·ma (ur′mə) [G.< OHG. *Irmin,* name of a Gmc. god of war] a feminine name

i·ron (ī′ərn) *n.* see PLURAL, II, D, 3 [< OE. *iren, isern, isen* < Gmc.: for IE. base see IRE] **1.** a white, malleable, ductile, metallic chemical element that rusts rapidly in moist or salty air and is vital to plant and animal life: it is the most common and important of all metals, and its alloys, as steel, are widely used: symbol, Fe; at. wt., 55.847; at. no., 26 **2.** any tool, device, etc. made of iron, as *a)* a device with a handle and flat undersurface, used, when heated, for pressing clothes or cloth *b)* a rod with a brand at one end, heated for branding cattle: in full, **branding iron 3.** [*pl.*] iron shackles or chains **4.** firm strength; power [a will of *iron*] **5.** any of a set of golf clubs with metal heads, numbered 1 through 9: the higher the number, the greater the degree of loft **6.** a medicine containing iron —*adj.* **1.** of or consisting of iron [*iron* bars] **2.** like iron, as *a)* firm; unyielding [*iron* determination] *b)* strong [an *iron* constitution] **3.** cruel; merciless [the *iron* rule of a dictator] —*vt.* **1.** to furnish or cover with iron **2.** to press (clothes or cloth) with a hot iron —*vi.* to iron clothes or cloth —**have many** (or **several,** etc.) **irons in the fire** to be engaged in many (or several, etc.) activities —☆**iron out** to smooth out; eliminate [trying to *iron out* their problems] —**strike while the iron is hot** to act while there is a good opportunity to do so

Iron Age the period of human culture when iron tools and weapons were introduced: in Europe, c. 1000 B.C. to c. 100 A.D.

i·ron·bound (ī′ərn bound′) *adj.* **1.** bound with iron **2.** hard; rigid; unyielding; inflexible **3.** with rocks or cliffs at the edge [an *ironbound* coast]

i·ron·clad (-klad′) *adj.* **1.** covered or protected with iron **2.** difficult to change or break [an *ironclad* lease] —*n.* formerly, a warship armored with thick iron plates

iron curtain 1. secrecy and censorship thought of as a wall cutting off the Soviet Union and other countries in its sphere from the rest of the world **2.** any similar barrier

iron hand harsh, strict, severe control [a king who ruled with an *iron hand*] —**i′ron·hand′ed** *adj.*

☆**iron horse** [Old Colloq.] a locomotive

i·ron·i·cal (ī rän′i k'l) *adj.* [< L. < Gr. < *eirōneia* (see IRONY) + -AL] **1.** meaning the opposite of what is expressed ["our humble home" was his *ironical* description of their mansion] **2.** using or tending to use irony **3.** directly opposite to what might be expected [it was *ironical* that the lifeguard drowned] Also **i·ron′ic** —see SYN. at SARCASTIC —**i·ron′i·cal·ly** *adv.*

ironing board (or **table**) a cloth-covered board or stand on which clothes are ironed

☆**iron lung** a large machine enclosing all of the body but the head, used for forcing air into and out of the lungs of a person who cannot breathe by himself

i·ron·mon·ger (ī′ərn muŋ′gər, -mäŋ′-) *n.* [Brit.] a dealer in hardware —**i′ron·mon′ger·y** *n.*

iron pyrites *same as* PYRITE

I·ron·sides (ī′ərn sīdz′) **1.** *nickname of* Oliver CROMWELL **2.** *a)* his regiment *b)* his whole army —*n.pl.* [i-] [*with sing. v.*] *same as* IRONCLAD

i·ron·stone (-stōn′) *n.* a hard variety of white ceramic ware

i·ron·ware (-wer′) *n.* things made of iron; hardware

i·ron·weed (-wēd′) *n.* a plant of the composite family, with clusters of small, tube-shaped, purple flowers

i·ron·wood (-wood′) *n.* **1.** any of various trees with extremely hard wood **2.** the wood

i·ron·work (-wurk′) *n.* articles or parts made of iron

i·ron·work·er (-wur′kər) *n.* **1.** a person who makes iron or articles of iron **2.** a worker who helps build the framework of steel bridges, etc.

i·ron·works (-wurks′) *n.pl.* [*often with sing. v.*] a place where iron is smelted or heavy iron goods are made

i·ro·ny (ī′rən ē, ī′ər nē) *n., pl.* **-nies** [< Fr. < L. < Gr. *eirōneia* < *eirōn,* dissembler in speech < *eirein,* to speak: for IE. base see WORD] **1.** a method of humorous or sarcastic expression in which the intended meaning of the words is the direct opposite of their usual sense [she used *irony* when she called the stupid plan "clever"] **2.** an event or result that is the opposite of what might be expected [that the fire station burned down was an *irony*] —see SYN. at WIT[1]

☆**Ir·o·quoi·an** (ir′ə kwoi′ən) *adj.* of an important language family of N. American Indians, including speakers of Huron,

Cherokee, Mohawk, etc. —*n.* **1.** a member of an Iroquoian tribe **2.** the family of Iroquoian languages

Ir·o·quois (ir'ə kwoi') *n.* [Fr. < Algonquian *Irinakoiw*, lit., real adders] **1.** *pl.* **-quois'** (-kwoi', -kwoiz') a member of a confederation of Iroquoian Indian tribes that lived in W and N New York and in nearby Canada: see FIVE NATIONS **2.** the Iroquoian language family —*adj.* of the Iroquois

ir·ra·di·ate (i rā'dē āt'; *for adj., usually* -it) *vt.* **-at'ed, -at'ing** [< L. pp. of *irradiare*: see IN-[1] & RADIATE] **1.** to shine upon; light up; make bright **2.** to make clear; enlighten **3.** to radiate; spread; give out **4.** to expose to or treat by exposing to X-rays, ultraviolet rays, or some other form of radiant energy —*vi.* to emit rays; shine —*adj.* lighted up; irradiated —**ir·ra'di·ance** (-əns), **ir·ra'di·an·cy** *n.* —**ir·ra'di·ant** (-ənt) *adj.* —**ir·ra'di·a'tion** *n.* —**ir·ra'di·a'tive** *adj.* —**ir·ra'di·a'tor** *n.*

ir·ra·tion·al (i rash'ən 'l) *adj.* **1.** lacking the power to reason [he was *irrational* with rage] **2.** not making sense; unreasonable; absurd [an *irrational* fear of cats] **3.** *Math.* designating a real number not capable of being expressed as an integer or as a quotient of two integers —**ir·ra'tion·al·i·ty** (-ə nal'ə tē) *n., pl.* **-ties** —**ir·ra'tion·al·ly** *adv.*

SYN.—**irrational** implies a loss of mental balance or of control over one's emotions, or it may be used of that which goes directly against reason [his *irrational* belief that everyone was his enemy]; **unreasonable** suggests that bad judgment, stubbornness, prejudice, etc. are responsible for something that goes against reason [it would be *unreasonable* to raise their rent now] —ANT. rational, reasonable

Ir·ra·wad·dy (ir'ə wä'dē, -wô'-) river flowing from N Burma south into the Indian Ocean

ir·re·claim·a·ble (ir'i klā'mə b'l) *adj.* that cannot be reclaimed —**ir're·claim'a·bil'i·ty** *n.* —**ir're·claim'a·bly** *adv.*

ir·rec·on·cil·a·ble (i rek'ən sīl'ə b'l, i rek'ən sil'-) *adj.* that cannot be reconciled; that cannot be brought into agreement; incompatible [*irreconcilable* enemies; *irreconcilable* theories] —*n.* **1.** a person who is irreconcilable and refuses to compromise **2.** [*pl.*] ideas, beliefs, etc. that cannot be brought into agreement —**ir·rec'on·cil'a·bil'i·ty** *n.* —**ir·rec'on·cil'a·bly** *adv.*

ir·re·cov·er·a·ble (ir'i kuv'ər ə b'l) *adj.* that cannot be recovered, regained, or got back; irretrievable [an *irrecoverable* loss] —**ir're·cov'er·a·bly** *adv.*

ir·re·deem·a·ble (ir'i dēm'ə b'l) *adj.* **1.** that cannot be bought back ☆**2.** that cannot be exchanged for coin, as certain kinds of paper money **3.** that cannot be changed or reformed —**ir're·deem'a·bly** *adv.*

ir·re·den·tist (ir'i den'tist) *n.* [< It. < (*Italia*) *irredenta*, unredeemed (Italy)] a person who is in favor of trying to recover territory formerly a part of his country; specif., [*usually* I-] a member of an Italian political party, after 1878, with such a policy —**ir're·den'tism** *n.*

ir·re·duc·i·ble (ir'i d̅oo̅s'ə b'l, -dy̅oo̅s'-) *adj.* that cannot be reduced —**ir're·duc'i·bil'i·ty** *n.* —**ir're·duc'i·bly** *adv.*

ir·re·fra·ga·ble (i ref'rə gə b'l) *adj.* [< LL. < L. *in-*, IN-[2] + *refragari*, to oppose] that cannot be refuted; indisputable —**ir·ref'ra·ga·bil'i·ty** *n.* —**ir·ref'ra·ga·bly** *adv.*

ir·re·fu·ta·ble (i ref'yoo tə b'l, ir'i fyoot'ə b'l) *adj.* that cannot be refuted or disproved —**ir·ref'u·ta·bil'i·ty** *n.* —**ir·ref'u·ta·bly** *adv.*

irreg. **1.** irregular **2.** irregularly

☆**ir·re·gard·less** (ir'i gärd'lis) *adj., adv.* a nonstandard or humorous variant of REGARDLESS

ir·reg·u·lar (i reg'yə lər) *adj.* **1.** not according to an established rule, method, usage, standard, etc.; out of the ordinary [an *irregular* diet] **2.** immoral; lawless; dishonest **3.** not straight or even; not symmetrical; not uniform in shape, design, etc. [an *irregular* outline] **4.** uneven in occurrence; variable [appearing at *irregular* intervals] ☆**5.** having minor flaws: said of merchandise **6.** *Gram.* not inflected in the usual way [*go* is an *irregular* verb] **7.** *Mil.* not belonging to the regularly established army —*n.* a person or thing that is irregular —**ir·reg'u·lar'i·ty** *n., pl.* **-ties** —**ir·reg'u·lar·ly** *adv.*

SYN.—**irregular** is used of that which differs a great deal from the customary rule, standard, etc. [*irregular* courtroom procedure]; **abnormal** and **anomalous** apply to that which differs sharply from the normal condition or type, with **abnormal** stressing form or character that is not typical [*abnormal* strength; *abnormal* weakness], and **anomalous** suggesting a condition or circumstance that is the exception [in the *anomalous* position of a

leader without followers]; **unnatural** applies to that which seems to be against nature or natural law [an *unnatural* appetite for chalk] —ANT. regular, normal, natural

ir·rel·e·vant (i rel'ə vənt) *adj.* not relevant; having nothing to do with the subject; not to the point —**ir·rel'e·vance, ir·rel'e·van·cy** *n., pl.* **-cies** —**ir·rel'e·vant·ly** *adv.*

ir·re·li·gious (ir'i lij'əs) *adj.* **1.** not religious; not interested in religion **2.** opposed to religion —**ir're·li'gion** *n.* —**ir·re·li'gion·ist** *n.* —**ir're·li'gious·ly** *adv.*

ir·re·me·di·a·ble (ir'i mē'dē ə b'l) *adj.* that cannot be remedied, cured, or corrected —**ir're·me'di·a·ble·ness** *n.* —**ir're·me'di·a·bly** *adv.*

ir·re·mis·si·ble (-mis'ə b'l) *adj.* not remissible; specif., *a)* that cannot be excused or pardoned *b)* that cannot be shirked —**ir're·mis'si·bly** *adv.*

ir·re·mov·a·ble (-m̅oo̅v'ə b'l) *adj.* not removable —**ir're·mov·a·bil'i·ty** *n.* —**ir're·mov'a·bly** *adv.*

ir·rep·a·ra·ble (i rep'ər ə b'l) *adj.* not reparable; that cannot be repaired, mended, remedied, etc. [*irreparable* damage] —**ir·rep'a·ra·bil'i·ty** *n.* —**ir·rep'a·ra·bly** *adv.*

ir·re·place·a·ble (ir'i plās'ə b'l) *adj.* not replaceable

ir·re·press·i·ble (-pres'ə b'l) *adj.* that cannot be repressed or held back [his *irrepressible* good humor] —**ir're·press'i·bil'i·ty** *n.* —**ir're·press'i·bly** *adv.*

ir·re·proach·a·ble (-prō'chə b'l) *adj.* not reproachable; that cannot be blamed or criticized; faultless —**ir're·proach'a·bil'i·ty**, —**ir're·proach'a·ble·ness** *n.* —**ir're·proach'a·bly** *adv.*

ir·re·sist·i·ble (-zis'tə b'l) *adj.* that cannot be resisted; too strong, fascinating, etc. to be withstood [an *irresistible* force] —**ir're·sist'i·bil'i·ty, ir're·sist'i·ble·ness** *n.* —**ir're·sist'i·bly** *adv.*

ir·res·o·lute (i rez'ə l̅oo̅t') *adj.* not resolute; not able to decide or make up one's mind; hesitating —**ir·res'o·lute'ly** *adv.* —**ir·res'o·lute'ness** *n.* —**ir·res'o·lu'tion** (-l̅oo̅'shən) *n.*

ir·re·spec·tive (ir'i spek'tiv) *adj.* regardless [vote for the best candidate, *irrespective* of religion, race, or sex] —**ir're·spec'tive·ly** *adv.*

ir·re·spon·si·ble (ir'i spän'sə b'l) *adj.* not responsible; specif., *a)* not likely to be held accountable for actions [an *irresponsible* tyrant] *b)* lacking a sense of responsibility; unreliable, lazy, etc. *c)* said or done as by an irresponsible person [an *irresponsible* accusation] —*n.* an irresponsible person —**ir're·spon'si·bil'i·ty, ir're·spon'si·ble·ness** *n.* —**ir're·spon'si·bly** *adv.*

ir·re·spon·sive (ir'i spän'siv) *adj.* not responsive —**ir're·spon'sive·ness** *n.*

ir·re·triev·a·ble (-trēv'ə b'l) *adj.* that cannot be retrieved, recovered, restored, or recalled —**ir're·triev'a·bil'i·ty** *n.* —**ir're·triev'a·bly** *adv.*

ir·rev·er·ence (i rev'ər əns) *n.* **1.** lack of reverence **2.** an act or statement showing this —**ir·rev'er·ent** *adj.* —**ir·rev'er·ent·ly** *adv.*

ir·re·vers·i·ble (ir'i vur'sə b'l) *adj.* not reversible; specif., *a)* that cannot be annulled or undone [an *irreversible* decision] *b)* that cannot be run backward, turned inside out, etc. —**ir're·vers'i·bil'i·ty** *n.* —**ir're·vers'i·bly** *adv.*

ir·rev·o·ca·ble (i rev'ə kə b'l) *adj.* that cannot be revoked or undone [an *irrevocable* choice] —**ir·rev'o·ca·bil'i·ty, ir·rev'o·ca·ble·ness** *n.* —**ir·rev'o·ca·bly** *adv.*

ir·ri·ga·ble (ir'i gə b'l) *adj.* that can be irrigated

ir·ri·gate (ir'ə gāt') *vt.* **-gat'ed, -gat'ing** [< L. pp. of *irrigare* < *in-*, in + *rigare*, to water, moisten] **1.** to supply (land) with water by means of artificial ditches or channels or by sprinklers **2.** *Med.* to wash out (a cavity, wound, etc.) with water or other fluid —**ir'ri·ga'tion** *n.* —**ir'ri·ga'tive** *adj.* —**ir'ri·ga'tor** *n.*

ir·ri·ta·ble (ir'i tə b'l) *adj.* **1.** easily annoyed or made angry **2.** *Med.* too highly sensitive to a stimulus, esp. in a way that is unhealthy **3.** *Physiol.* able to respond to a stimulus —**ir'ri·ta·bil'i·ty, ir'ri·ta·ble·ness** *n.* —**ir'ri·ta·bly** *adv.*

SYN.—**irritable** implies a being excitable or restless because of tension, a slight illness, etc., so that one becomes easily angered or annoyed; **irascible** and **choleric** are used of people who are hot-tempered and who can quickly be made angry over the slightest annoyance; **splenetic** suggests a moody person who is quick to show his displeasure in a mean, spiteful way; **cranky** and **cross** suggest moods in which one cannot be easily pleased or satisfied, **cranky** because of odd notions that one holds on to stubbornly, **cross** because of ill humor

---

fat, āpe, cär; ten, ēven; is, bīte; gō, hôrn, to̅o̅l, look; oil, out; up, fur; get; joy; yet; chin; she; thin, then; zh, leisure; ŋ, ring; ə for *a* in *ago*, *e* in *agent*, *i* in *sanity*, *o* in *comply*, *u* in *focus*; ' as in *able* (ā'b'l); Fr. bal; ë, Fr. coeur; ö, Fr. feu. Fr. mon; ô, Fr. coq; ü, Fr. duc; r, Fr. cri; H, G. ich; kh, G. doch; ‡foreign; ☆ Americanism; < derived from. See inside front cover.

ir·ri·tant (ir′ə tənt) *adj.* causing irritation —*n.* something causing irritation —**ir′ri·tan·cy** *n.*

ir·ri·tate (ir′ə tāt′) *vt.* **-tat′ed, -tat′ing** [< L. pp. of *irritare*, to excite] **1.** to make feel impatient or angry; annoy **2.** to make (a part of the body) inflamed or sore [harsh soap *irritates* her skin] **3.** *Physiol.* to excite (an organ, muscle, etc.) by a stimulus to react in a characteristic way —**ir′ri·ta′tive** *adj.*

SYN.—*irritate* is the most general of the words here and may suggest mild impatience, continued annoyance, or a flare-up of anger [their smugness *irritates* her]; **provoke** suggests the causing of strong feelings of annoyance, resentment, or anger, often with a wish to get even [*provoked* by the insult]; **nettle** implies irritation caused as by petty, nagging remarks or actions that hurt one's pride [subtle taunts that *nettled* him]; **exasperate** implies great irritation caused by something that makes one lose one's patience or self-control [*exasperated* by the clerk's many careless mistakes]

ir·ri·ta·tion (ir′ə tā′shən) *n.* **1.** the act or process of irritating **2.** the fact or condition of being irritated **3.** something that irritates **4.** *Med.* a sore or inflamed condition

ir·rupt (i rupt′) *vi.* [< L. pp. of *irrumpere* < *in-*, in + *rumpere*, to break] **1.** to burst suddenly or violently (*into*) **2.** *Ecol.* to increase suddenly in size of population —**ir·rup′tion** *n.* —**ir·rup′-tive** *adj.*

IRS, I.R.S. Internal Revenue Service

Ir·tysh (ir tish′) river in C Asia, flowing from NW China northwestward into the Ob River

Ir·ving[1] (ʉr′viŋ) [< a surname, prob. orig. a place name] **1.** a masculine name **2. Washington,** 1783–1859; U.S. writer

Ir·ving[2] (ʉr′viŋ) [prob. a name chosen for no special reason] city in NE Tex.: suburb of Dallas: pop. 97,000

Ir·win (ʉr′win) [var. of ERWIN] a masculine name

is (iz) [OE. < IE. base *es-*, to be] *third person singular in the present tense of* BE

is- *same as* ISO-: used before a vowel

is. **1.** island(s) **2.** isle(s)

Isa., Is. Isaiah

I·saac (ī′zək) [< LL. < Gr. < Heb. *yitshāq*, lit., laughter] **1.** a masculine name **2.** *Bible* one of the patriarchs, son of Abraham and Sarah, and father of Jacob and Esau: Gen. 21:3

Is·a·bel (iz′ə bel′) [Sp., prob. altered < *Elizabeth*] a feminine name: var. *Isabelle, Isabella*

Is·a·bel·la (iz′ə bel′ə) [It.] **1.** a feminine name **2. Isabella I** 1451–1504; wife of Ferdinand V & queen of Castile (1474–1504): gave help to Columbus in his expedition

Is·a·dor·a (iz′ə dôr′ə) [fem. of ISIDORE] a feminine name

i·sa·go·ge (ī′sə gō′jē) *n.* [L. < Gr., ult. < *eis-*, into + *agein*, to lead] an introduction, as to a branch of study —**i′sa·gog′ic** (-gäj′ik) *adj.*

I·sa·iah (ī zā′ə; *chiefly Brit.* -zī′-) [< LL. < Gr. < Heb. *yĕsha ′yah*, lit., God is salvation] a masculine name **2.** *Bible a)* a Hebrew prophet of the 8th cent. B.C. *b)* the book containing his teachings Also, in the Douay Bible, **I·sa·ias** (-əs)

Is·car·i·ot (is ker′ē ət) *see* JUDAS

is·che·mi·a (is kē′mē ə) *n.* [ModL. < Gr. < *ischein*, to hold + *haima*, blood] a lack of blood supply in an organ or tissue

is·chi·um (is′kē əm) *n., pl.* **-chi·a** (-ə) [L. < Gr. *ischion*, hip] the lowermost of the three sections of the hipbone

-ise (īz) *chiefly Brit.* var. of -IZE

I·seult (i sōōlt′) [Fr.] *same as* ISOLDE

-ish (ish) **1.** [OE. *-isc*] *a suffix meaning: a)* of or belonging to (a specified people) [*Spanish*] *b)* like or characteristic of [*devilish*] *c)* tending or inclined to be [*knavish*] *d)* somewhat; rather [*tallish*] *e)* [Colloq.] approximately; about [*thirtyish*] **2.** [< OFr.] *a suffix found in verbs of French origin or in verbs formed like these* [*finish*]

Ish·ma·el (ish′mē əl, -mā-) [< LL. < Heb. *yishmā′ē′l*, lit., God hears] *Bible* the son of Abraham and Hagar: he and his mother were made outcasts: Gen. 21:9–21 —*n.* an outcast

Ish·ma·el·ite (-ə līt′) *n.* **1.** a descendant of Ishmael **2.** an outcast —**Ish′ma·el·it′ish** *adj.*

Ish·tar (ish′tär) the Babylonian and Assyrian goddess of love and fertility

Is·i·dore, Is·i·dor (iz′ə dôr′) [ult. < Gr. *Isidōros*, lit., gift of Isis] a masculine name: var. *Isadore, Isador*

i·sin·glass (ī′z′n glas′, -ziŋ-) *n.* [prob. < MDu. < *huizen*, sturgeon + *blas*, bladder] **1.** a form of gelatin prepared from fish bladders, used for making glue, clarifying wine, etc. **2.** mica, esp. in thin sheets

I·sis (ī′sis) the Egyptian goddess of fertility, sister and wife of Osiris

isl. *pl.* **isls.** **1.** island **2.** isle

Is·lam (is′läm, iz′-; -ləm, -lam; is läm′) *n.* [Ar. *islām*, lit., submission (to God's will)] **1.** the Moslem religion, a monotheistic religion in which God is called Allah and the founder and chief prophet is Mohammed **2.** all Moslems **3.** all the lands in which mostly Moslems live —**Is·lam·ic** (-lam′-, -läm′-), **Is′-lam·it′ic** (-lə mit′ik) *adj.* —**Is′lam·ism** *n.* —**Is′lam·ite′** (-lə mīt′) *n.*

Is·lam·a·bad (is läm′ə bäd′) capital of Pakistan, in the NE part, near Rawalpindi: pop. 50,000

Is·lam·ize (is′lə mīz′, iz′-) *vt., vi.* **-ized′, -iz′ing** to make or become Islamic —**Is′lam·i·za′tion** *n.*

is·land (ī′lənd) *n.* [< ME. *iland* (respelled after unrelated ISLE) < OE. *igland*, lit., island land & *ealand*, lit., water land] **1.** a land mass not as large as a continent, surrounded by water **2.** anything like an island in position or in being isolated, as ☆the superstructure above the flight deck of an aircraft carrier: see also TRAFFIC ISLAND —*vt.* **1.** to make into or like an island **2.** to intersperse as with islands [a prairie *islanded* with wooded tracts]

is·land·er (-ər) *n.* a native or inhabitant of an island

isle (īl) *n.* [< OFr. < ML. < L. *insula*] an island, esp. a small one —*vt.* **isled, isl′ing** *same as* ISLAND

Isle Roy·ale (roi′əl) [Fr., royal island] island in N Lake Superior, in the State of Michigan: it and nearby islets make up a national park (**Isle Royale National Park**)

is·let (ī′lit) *n.* a very small island

islets (or **islands**) **of Lang·er·hans** (läŋ′ər häns′) [after P. *Langerhans* (1847–88), G. histologist] irregular groups of endocrine cells in the pancreas: they produce insulin

ism (iz′m) *n.* a doctrine, theory, system, etc., esp. one whose name ends in *-ism*

-ism (iz′m) [< OFr. & < L. *-isma* (< Gr. *-isma*) & *-ismus* (< Gr. *-ismos*)] *a suffix meaning:* **1.** the act, practice, or result of [*terrorism*] **2.** the condition of being [*pauperism*] **3.** conduct or qualities characteristic of [*patriotism*] **4.** the doctrine, school, or theory of [*socialism*] **5.** devotion to [*nationalism*] **6.** an instance or example of [*witticism*] **7.** an abnormal condition caused by [*alcoholism*]

is·n't (iz′′nt) is not

i·so- [< Gr. *isos*, equal] *a combining form meaning:* **1.** equal, similar, alike, identical [*isomorphic*] **2.** isomeric [*isopropyl*]

i·so·bar (ī′sə bär′) *n.* [< ISO- + Gr. *baros*, weight] **1.** a line on a map connecting points on the earth's surface having equal barometric pressure **2.** any of two or more forms of an atom having the same atomic weight but different atomic numbers —**i′so·bar′ic** (-bar′ik) *adj.*

ISOBARS

i·soch·ro·nal (ī säk′rə n′l) *adj.* [< ModL. < *isos*, equal + *chronos*, time + -AL] **1.** equal in length of time **2.** occurring at equal intervals of time Also **i·soch′ro·nous** —**i·soch′ro·nism** *n.*

i·so·ga·mete (ī′sō gam′ēt, -gə mēt′) *n.* a gamete having the same size, structure, and function as another with which it unites —**i′so·ga·met′ic** (-gə met′ik) *adj.*

i·sog·a·my (ī säg′ə mē) *n.* [ISO- + -GAMY] reproduction by the uniting of isogametes —**i·sog′a·mous** (-məs) *adj.*

i·so·gon·ic (ī′sə gän′ik) *adj.* [ISO- + -GON + -IC] **1.** of or having equal angles **2.** connecting or showing points on the earth's surface having the same magnetic declination [*isogonic* lines on a map] —*n.* an isogonic line

i·so·late (ī′sə lāt′, is′ə-; *for n., usually* -lit) *vt.* **-lat′ed, -lat′ing** [back-formation < *isolated* < It. < *isola* (< L. *insula*), island] **1.** to set apart from others; place alone [the infected mice were *isolated* in the laboratory] **2.** *Chem.* to separate (an element or compound) in pure form from another compound or mixture —*n.* a person or group set apart —**i′so·la·ble** (-lə b′l) *adj.* —**i′so·la′tor** *n.*

i·so·la·tion (ī′sə lā′shən, is′ə-) *n.* an isolating or being isolated —see SYN. at SOLITUDE

☆**i·so·la·tion·ist** (-ist) *n.* a person who advocates isolation; specif., one who is against having his country become involved in international agreements, alliances, etc. —*adj.* of isolationists or their policy —**i′so·la′tion·ism** *n.*

I·sol·de (i sōl′də, i sōld′) *see* TRISTRAM

i·so·mer (ī′sə mər) *n.* [< Gr. < *isos*, equal + *meros*, a part] **1.** any of two or more chemical compounds having the same elements in the same proportion by weight but having different properties because the atoms in the molecules are arranged differently 2. *Physics* any of two or more nuclei having the same number of neutrons and protons, but having different radioactive properties —i′so·mer′ic (-mer′ik) *adj.* —i·som·er·ism (ī säm′ər iz'm) *n.*

i·som·er·ous (ī säm′ər əs) *adj.* [see ISOMER] *Bot.* having the same number of parts in each whorl

i·so·met·ric (ī′sə met′rik) *adj.* [< Gr. < *isos*, equal + *metron*, a measure + -IC] 1. of or having measurements equal to one another: also **i′so·met′ri·cal** 2. *same as* CUBIC (sense 3) 3. of isometrics —*n.* [*pl.*] a method of physical exercise in which one set of muscles is briefly pitted against another set of muscles or against the resistance offered by an immovable object —i′so·met′ri·cal·ly *adv.*

i·so·mor·phic (-môr′fik) *adj.* [ISO- + -MORPHIC] having similar or identical structure or form: also **i′so·mor′phous** (-fəs) — **i′so·mor′phism** *n.*

i·so·pod (ī′sə päd′) *n.* [ISO- + -POD] any of a large group of crustaceans with a flat, oval body and seven pairs of similar legs, each pair attached to a segment of the thorax —*adj.* of an isopod or the isopods Also **i·sop·o·dan** (ī säp′ə dən)

i·so·prene (ī′sə prēn′) *n.* [< ISO- + PR(OPYL) + -ENE] a colorless, volatile liquid, C_5H_8, used in making synthetic rubber

i·so·pro·pyl (ī′sə prō′pil) *n.* the radical $(CH_3)_2CH$, an isomer of the propyl radical, C_3H_7

i·sos·ce·les (ī säs′ə lēz′) *adj.* [LL. < Gr. *isoskelēs* < *isos*, equal + *skelos*, a leg] designating a triangle with two equal sides, or a trapezoid having its two nonparallel sides equal

i·so·therm (ī′sə thurm′) *n.* [< Fr. < *iso-*, ISO- + Gr. *thermē*, heat] a line on a map connecting points on the earth's surface having the same mean temperature or the same temperature at a given time

ISOSCELES TRIANGLES

i·so·ther·mal (ī′sə thur′m'l) *adj.* 1. of or indicating equal or steady temperatures 2. of isotherms —*n. same as* ISOTHERM —i′so·ther′mal·ly *adv.*

i·so·ton·ic (-tän′ik) *adj.* [< Gr. < *isos*, equal + *tonos*, a stretching + -IC] 1. having equal tension 2. designating or of a salt solution having the same osmotic pressure as blood, so that when used in the body it will leave the red blood cells unchanged —i′so·ton′i·cal·ly *adv.* —i′so·to·nic′i·ty (-tō nis′ə-tē) *n.*

i·so·tope (ī′sə tōp′) *n.* [< ISO- + Gr. *topos*, place] any of two or more forms of an element having the same or very closely related chemical properties and the same atomic number but different atomic weights [uranium *isotopes* U 235, U 238, U 239] —i′so·top′ic (-täp′ik, -tō′pik) *adj.*

i·so·trop·ic (ī′sə träp′ik, -trō′pik) *adj.* [ISO- + -TROPIC] having physical properties, as conductivity, elasticity, etc., that are the same regardless of the direction of measurement: also **i·sot·ro·pous** (ī sät′rə pəs) —i·sot′ro·py (-pē) *n.*

Is·ra·el (iz′rē əl, -rā-) *n.* [< OFr. < LL. < Gr. < Heb. *yisrā'ēl*, lit., contender with God] 1. a masculine name 2. *Bible* Jacob: so named after wrestling with the angel: Gen. 32:28 3. the Jewish people, as descendants of Jacob 4. ancient land of the Hebrews, at the SE end of the Mediterranean 5. ancient kingdom in the N part of this region 6. country between the Mediterranean Sea & the country of Jordan: established (1948) by the UN as a Jewish state: 7,992 sq. mi.; pop. 3,068,000; cap. Jerusalem

Is·rae·li (iz rā′lē) *adj.* of modern Israel or its people —*n., pl.* **-lis, -li** a native or inhabitant of modern Israel

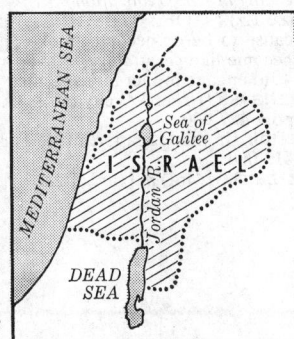

ISRAEL (8th cent. B.C.)

Is·ra·el·ite (iz′rē ə līt′, -rā-) *n.* any of the people of ancient Israel or their descendants; Jew; Hebrew —*adj.* of ancient Israel or the Israelites; Jewish: also **Is′ra·el·it·ish** (-līt′ish), **Is′ra·el·it′ic** (-lit′ik)

☆**is·sei** (ē′sā) *n., pl.* **-sei, -seis** [Jpn., lit., 1st generation] [*also* I-] a Japanese who emigrated to the U.S. between 1907 and 1952

☆**is·su·ance** (ish′ōō wəns) *n.* the act of issuing

is·sue (ish′ōō; *chiefly Brit.* is′yōō) *n.* [< OFr. pp. of *isser*, to go out < L. *exire* < *ex-*, out + *ire*, to go: see YEAR] 1. an outgoing; outflow [the *issue* of water from a pipe] 2. a place or means of going out; exit; outlet 3. a result; consequence [the *issue* of the battle was in doubt] 4. offspring; a child or children [Elizabeth I died without *issue*] 5. profits, as from property; proceeds 6. a point or matter under dispute [the candidates will debate the *issues*] 7. a sending or giving out [the *issue* of uniforms to the troops] 8. the thing or set of things put forth and circulated at one time [the May *issue* of a magazine, an *issue* of bonds] 9. *Med.* a discharge of blood, pus, etc. —*vi.* **-sued, -su·ing** 1. to go, pass, or flow out; emerge [a stream *issued* from the cave] 2. to be descended; be born 3. to be derived or result (*from* a cause) [will any practical results *issue* from their research?] 4. to end or result (*in* an effect) [their efforts *issued* in victory] 5. to come as revenue 6. to be published; be put forth and circulated —*vt.* 1. to let out; discharge 2. to give or deal out [to *issue* supplies] 3. to publish; put forth publicly or officially [to *issue* bonds, periodicals, an edict, etc.] —*at* (or *in*) **issue** in dispute; still to be decided —**join issue** to meet in conflict, argument, etc. —**take issue** to disagree —is′su·a·ble *adj.* —is′su·er *n.*

-ist (ist, əst) [< OFr. < L. < Gr. *-istēs*] *a suffix meaning:* 1. a person who does, makes, or practices [*moralist, satirist*] 2. a person who works at, esp. one skilled in [*druggist, violinist*] 3. one who believes in or supports; adherent of [*anarchist*]

Is·tan·bul (is′tan bool′, -tän-; -bool′; *Turk.* is täm′bool) seaport in NW Turkey, on the Bosporus: pop. 2,248,000

isth·mi·an (is′mē ən) *adj.* 1. of an isthmus 2. [I-] *a)* of the Isthmus of Panama *b)* of the Isthmus of Corinth or the games held there in ancient times —*n.* a native or inhabitant of an isthmus

isth·mus (is′məs) *n., pl.* **-mus·es, -mi** (-mī) [L. < Gr. *isthmos*, a neck] 1. a narrow strip of land having water at each side and connecting two larger bodies of land 2. *Anat.* a narrow strip of tissue connecting two larger parts of an organ

-is·tic (is′tik) [< MFr. < L. < Gr. *istikos*, or in Eng. < -IST + -IC] *a suffix used to form adjectives from nouns ending in* -ISM *and* -IST [*realistic, artistic*]: also **-is′ti·cal**

is·tle (ist′lē) *n.* [< AmSp. < Nahuatl *ichtli*] a fiber obtained from certain tropical American plants, used for ropes, baskets, etc.

Is·tri·a (is′trē ə) peninsula in NW Yugoslavia, reaching into the N Adriatic: also **Is′tri·an Peninsula**

it (it) *pron. for pl. see* THEY [OE. *hit*] the animal or thing mentioned before [I read that book and liked *it*] It is also used as: *a)* the subject of an impersonal verb [*it* is snowing] *b)* the grammatical subject of a clause of which the actual subject is a following clause, etc. [*it* is settled that he will go] *c)* an object with no definite meaning [to lord *it* over someone] *d)* the antecedent to a relative pronoun from which it is separated by a predicate [*it* is your car that I want] *e)* a reference to something indefinite but understood [*it's* all right, no harm was done] ☆*f)* [Colloq.] a pronoun used in the predicate to refer to the final or ultimate person, thing, etc. [zero hour is here; this is *it*] —*n.* the player, as in the game of tag, who must do some specific thing —☆**with it** [Slang] alert, informed, or aware

It., Ital. 1. Italian 2. Italic 3. Italy

i/t·a, I.T.A. Initial Teaching Alphabet

ital. italic (type)

‡**I·tal·ia** (ē täl′yä) *It.* name of ITALY

I·tal·ian (i tal′yən) *adj.* of Italy, its people, their language, etc. —*n.* 1. a native or inhabitant of Italy 2. the Romance language of the Italians

Italian sonnet *same as* PETRARCHAN SONNET

I·tal·ic (i tal′ik) *adj.* 1. of ancient Italy, its people, etc. 2. designating or of the group of Indo-European languages that includes Latin and the Romance languages —*n.* the Italic group of languages

i·tal·ic (i tal′ik, ī-) *adj.* [< its first use in an *Italian* edition of Virgil] designating or of a printing type in which the characters slant upward to the right, used esp. to call attention to words [*this is italic type*] —*n.* [*usually pl., sometimes with sing. v.*] italic type or print

i·tal·i·cize (i tal′ə sīz′, ī-) *vt.* -cized′, -ciz′ing 1. to print in italics 2. to underline (something written or typed) to indicate that it is to be printed in italics —**i·tal′i·ci·za′tion** *n.*

It·a·ly (it′'l ē) country in S Europe, mostly on a peninsula & including Sicily & Sardinia: 116,304 sq. mi.; pop. 54,388,000; cap. Rome

itch (ich) *vi.* [OE. *giccan*] 1. to feel an irritating or tickling sensation on the skin, that makes one want to scratch 2. to have a restless desire [*he's itching to leave*] —*vt.* 1. to make itch [*the wool shirt itches his skin*] 2. to irritate or annoy —*n.* 1. an itching on the skin 2. a restless desire; hankering [*an itch to travel*] —**the itch** any of various skin disorders in which there is irritation of the skin; specif., *same as* SCABIES

itch·y (ich′ē) *adj.* **itch′·i·er, itch′·i·est** like, feeling, or causing an itch —**itch′·i·ly** *adv.* —**itch′·i·ness** *n.*

-ite (īt) [< OFr. or L. *-ītēs*] *a suffix meaning:* 1. a native or inhabitant of [*Brooklynite*] 2. a descendant from [*Israelite*] 3. one who believes in or supports [*laborite*] 4. a commercially manufactured product [*dynamite*] 5. a fossil [*trilobite*] 6. a salt or ester of an acid whose name ends in *-ous* [*nitrite*] 7. a (specified) mineral or rock [*anthracite*]

i·tem (īt′əm) *adv.* [< L. < *ita*, so, thus] also: used before each article in a series being enumerated —*n.* 1. an article; unit; separate thing [*check each item on this list*] 2. a bit of news or information

☆**i·tem·ize** (-īz′) *vt.* -ized′, -iz′ing to list the items of; set down item by item [*itemize the bill*] —**i′·tem·i·za′tion** *n.*

it·er·ate (it′ə rāt′) *vt.* -at′ed, -at′ing [< L. pp. of *iterare* < *iterum*, again] to say or do again or repeatedly —**it′er·ant** (-ər·ənt) *adj.* —**it′er·a′tion** *n.* —**it′er·a′tive** *adj.*

Ith·a·ca (ith′ə kə) Gr. island off the W coast of Greece: legendary home of Odysseus

i·tin·er·an·cy (ī tin′ər ən sē, i-) *n.* 1. a traveling from place to place 2. official work that requires one to travel from place to place, as in order to preside over courts in a circuit Also **i·tin·er·a·cy** (-ə sē)

i·tin·er·ant (ī tin′ər ənt, i-) *adj.* [< LL. prp. of *itinerari*, to travel < L. *iter*, a walk] traveling from place to place or on a circuit [*itinerant laborers*] —*n.* a person who travels from place to place —**i·tin′er·ant·ly** *adv.*

i·tin·er·ar·y (ī tin′ə rer′ē, i-) *adj.* [see prec.] of traveling, journeys, routes, or roads —*n., pl.* -**ar′ies** 1. a route 2. a record of a journey 3. a guidebook for travelers 4. a detailed plan or outline for a proposed journey

i·tin·er·ate (ī tin′ə rāt′, i-) *vi.* -at′ed, -at′ing [< LL. pp. of *itinerari*: see ITINERANT] to travel from place to place or on a circuit —**i·tin′er·a′tion** *n.*

-i·tion (ish′ən) [< Fr. *-ition* or L. *-itio*] *var. of* -ATION [*nutrition*]

·i·tious (ish′əs) [L. *-icius, -itius*] *a suffix that is used to form adjectives from nouns ending in* -ITION *and that means* of, having the nature of, characterized by [*nutritious*]

-i·tis (īt′əs, -is) [ModL. < L. < Gr. *-itis*] *a suffix meaning:* 1. inflammatory disease or inflammation of (a specified part or organ) [*sinusitis*] 2. such great interest in or concern with as to cause weariness or distress: used freely in making up words [*footballitis, homeworkitis*]

it'll (it′'l) 1. it will 2. it shall

its (its) *pron.* that or those belonging to it —*adj.* of, belonging to, or done by it [*give the cat its dinner; the frost had done its work*]

it's (its) 1. it is 2. it has

it·self (it self′) *pron.* a form of the third person singular, neuter pronoun, used: *a*) as an intensive [*the work itself is easy*] *b*) as a reflexive [*the dog bit itself*] *c*) as a kind of noun meaning "its real, true, or actual self" [*the bird is not itself today*]

it·ty-bit·ty (it′ē bit′ē) *adj.* [baby talk for *little bit*] [Colloq.] very small; tiny Also **it·sy-bit·sy** (it′sē bit′sē)

-i·ty (ə tē, i-) [< OFr. *-ité* < L. *-itas*] *a suffix meaning* state, condition [*chastity, possibility*]

IU, I.U. international unit(s)

IUD intrauterine (contraceptive) device: also **IUCD**

i.v. 1. initial velocity 2. intravenous(ly)

I·van (ī′vən; *Russ.* i vän′) [Russ. < Gr.: see JOHN] 1. a masculine name 2. **Ivan III** 1440–1505; grand duke of Muscovy (1462–1505): called *the Great* 3. **Ivan IV** 1530–84; grand duke of Muscovy (1533–84) & 1st czar of Russia (1547–84): called *the Terrible*

I·va·no·vo (ē vä′nô vô′) city in C European R.S.F.S.R.: pop. 415,000

I've (īv) I have

-ive (iv) [< Fr. *-if*, fem. *-ive* < L. *-ivus*] *a suffix meaning:* 1. of, relating to, having the nature of [*instinctive*] 2. tending to [*creative*]

Ives (īvz), **Charles Edward** 1874–1954; U.S. composer

i·vied (ī′vēd) *adj.* covered or overgrown with ivy

i·vo·ry (ī′vər ē, īv′rē) *n., pl.* -**ries** [< OFr. < L. < *ebur* < Egypt. *āb, ābu*, elephant] 1. the hard, white substance forming the tusks of elephants, walruses, etc. 2. any substance like ivory 3. the color of ivory; creamy white 4. a tusk of an elephant, etc. 5. [*pl.*] things made of or suggesting ivory; specif., [Slang] *a*) piano keys *b*) teeth *c*) dice —*adj.* 1. of or like ivory 2. creamy-white

Ivory Coast country on the WC coast of Africa: 124,500 sq. mi.; pop. 3,750,000; cap. Abidjan

ivory nut *same as* VEGETABLE IVORY

☆**ivory tower** a place or condition into which one withdraws to get away from the world of action or reality

I·vy (ī′vē) [< the next entry] a feminine name

i·vy (ī′vē) *n., pl.* **i′vies** [OE. *ifig*] 1. a climbing vine with a woody stem and evergreen leaves, grown as an ornament on buildings, walls, etc.; English ivy 2. any of various similar plants, as Boston ivy, poison ivy, etc.

☆**Ivy League** [< the ivy-covered buildings often found there] a group of colleges in the northeastern U.S. forming a league for intercollegiate sports: often used to describe the traditional fashions, attitudes, etc. associated with their students —**Ivy Leaguer**

ENGLISH IVY

I.W.W., IWW Industrial Workers of the World

Ix·i·on (ik sī′ən) Gr. *Myth.* a Thessalian king who was bound to a revolving wheel in Tartarus because he made love to Hera

ix·tle (iks′tlē, is′-) *n. same as* ISTLE

I·yar (ē yär′, ē′yär) *n.* [Heb.] *see* JEWISH CALENDAR

-i·za·tion (ə zā′shən, ī-) *a suffix used to form nouns from verbs ending in* -IZE [*realization*]

-ize (īz) [< OFr. < LL. < Gr. *-izein*] *a suffix meaning:* 1. to cause to be or become; make [*democratize*] 2. to become or become like [*crystallize*] 3. to treat or combine with [*oxidize*] 4. to engage in; act in a specified way [*soliloquize, theorize*]

I·zhevsk (i zhefsk′) city in the U.S.S.R., in E European Russia: pop. 422,000

Iz·mir (iz mir′) seaport in W Turkey, on the Aegean Sea: pop. 412,000

iz·zard (iz′ərd) *n.* [var. of ZED] [Archaic or Dial.] the letter Z

J

J, j (jā) *n., pl.* **J's, j's** **1.** the tenth letter of the English alphabet **2.** the sound of *J* or *j*

j *Physics a symbol for* joule

J. **1.** Journal **2.** Judge **3.** Justice

Ja. January

J.A. Judge Advocate

jab (jab) *vt., vi.* **jabbed, jab'bing** [< ME. *jobben,* to peck] **1.** to poke or thrust, as with a sharp instrument **2.** to punch with short, straight blows —*n.* a quick thrust, blow, or punch

jab·ber (jab'ər) *vi., vt.* [prob. echoic] to speak or say quickly, in a silly, rambling way, without making sense; chatter —*n.* talk of this kind —**jab'ber·er** *n.*

jab·ber·wock·y (jab'ər wäk'ē) *n.* [< *Jabberwocky,* nonsense poem by Lewis Carroll] meaningless syllables that seem to make sense; gibberish

ja·bot (zha bō', ja-) *n.* [Fr., bird's crop] a trimming or frill, as of lace, attached to the neck or front of a blouse, bodice, or shirt

jac·a·ran·da (jak'ə ran'də) *n.* [ModL. < Port. < Tupi] a tropical American tree with large clusters of lavender flowers, often grown in the southern U.S.

ja·cinth (jā'sinth, jas'inth) *n.* [< OFr. < L. *hyacinthus:* see HYA-CINTH] **1.** *same as* HYACINTH (sense 1 *b*) **2.** a reddish-orange color

jack (jak) [< OFr. < LL. *Jacobus,* JACOB] [J-] *a nickname for* JOHN —*n., pl.* for 5, 6, 7 **jacks, jack:** see PLURAL, II, D, 1 **1.** [*often* J-] *a)* a man or boy; fellow *b)* a sailor **2.** a jack-of-all-trades **3.** a fruit-flavored alcoholic drink, as applejack **4.** *a)* any of various devices used to lift or hoist something heavy a short distance [*hy-draulic* jack, *automobile* jack] *b)* a device for turning a spit in roasting **5.** a male donkey ☆**6.** *short for* JACK RAB-BIT **7.** any of various fishes, as the pickerel, pike, etc. ☆**8.** [Old Slang] money **9.** *Elec.* a device into which a plug is inserted to make electric contact **10.** *Games a)* a playing card with a page boy's picture on it; knave *b)* any of the small pebbles or six-pronged metal pieces used in playing jacks: see JACKS *c)* in the game of bowls, the target ball **11.** *Naut.* a small flag flown on a ship's bow as a signal or to show nationality —*vt.* to raise by means of a jack —*adj.* male: of some animals —**every man jack** everyone —**jack up 1.** to raise by means of a jack ☆**2.** [Colloq.] to raise (prices, salaries, etc.) ☆**3.** [Colloq.] to encourage to perform one's duty

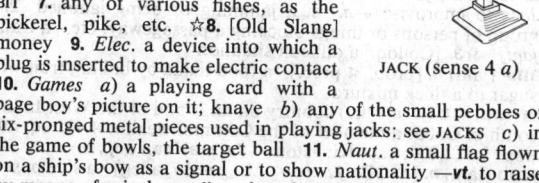

JACK (sense 4 *a*)

jack- [see prec.] *a combining form meaning:* **1.** male [*jackass*] **2.** large or strong [*jackboot*] **3.** boy; fellow: used in hyphenated compounds [*jack-in-the-box*]

jack·al (jak'əl, -ôl) *n., pl.* **-als, -al:** see PLURAL, II, D, 1 [< Turk. < Per. *shagāl* < Sans.] **1.** a yellowish-gray wild dog of Asia and N Africa, smaller than the wolf: jackals hunt in packs, also feeding on carrion left by other animals **2.** one who does low, often dishonest tasks for another: from the legend that the jackal finds game for the lion and eats the leavings

jack·a·napes (jak'ə nāps') *n.* [< nickname of a 15th-c. Duke of Suffolk] **1.** formerly, a monkey **2.** a conceited, impudent young person; saucy rascal

jack·ass (jak'as') *n.* [JACK- + ASS¹] **1.** a male donkey **2.** a stupid or foolish person; nitwit

jack·boot (-boot') *n.* [JACK- + BOOT¹] a heavy, sturdy military boot that reaches above the knee

jack·daw (-dô') *n.* [JACK- + DAW] **1.** a European black bird related to the crow, but smaller **2.** *same as* GRACKLE

jack·et (jak'it) *n.* [< OFr. dim. of *jaque* < Sp. *jaco,* coat < Ar. *shakk*] **1.** a short coat **2.** an outer covering; specif., *a) same as* DUST JACKET ☆*b)* a cardboard holder for a phonograph record *c)* the casing that serves as insulation on a boiler, etc. *d)* the skin of a potato, etc. —*vt.* **1.** to put a jacket, or coat, on **2.** to cover with a casing, wrapper, etc.

Jack Frost frost or cold weather represented as a person

☆**jack·ham·mer** (-ham'ər) *n.* [JACK- + HAMMER] a large kind of hammer worked by compressed air and used for breaking up rock, brick, concrete, etc.

jack-in-the-box (jak'in *th*ə bäks') *n., pl.* **-box'es** a toy consisting of a box from which a little figure on a spring jumps up when the lid is lifted: also **jack'-in-a-box'**

☆**jack-in-the-pul·pit** (-pool'pit) *n., pl.* **-pits** an American wildflower that grows in the woods and has an upright flower spike with a hoodlike covering arching over it

☆**jack·knife** (jak'nīf') *n., pl.* **-knives'** (-nīvz') [JACK- + KNIFE] **1.** a large pocketknife **2.** a dive in which the diver keeps his knees unbent, touches his feet with his hands while in the air, and then straightens out just before plunging into the water hands first —*vi.* **-knifed', -knif'ing 1.** to bend at the middle as in a jackknife dive **2.** to turn on the hitch so as to form a sharp angle with each other: said of a vehicle and its trailer

JACKHAMMER

☆**jack·leg** (-leg') *adj.* not properly trained or qualified [a *jack-leg* plumber] —*n.* a jackleg person

jack-of-all-trades (jak'əv ôl'trādz') *n., pl.* **jacks'-** [see JACK-, 3] [*often* J-] a person who can do many kinds of work acceptably; handyman

jack-o'-lan·tern (jak'ə lan'tərn) *n., pl.* **-terns 1.** a shifting light seen over marshes at night; will-o'-the-wisp **2.** a hollow pumpkin, real or artificial, cut to look like a face and used as a lantern or esp. as a decoration at Halloween

☆**jack pine** a pine of Canada and the northern U.S., having short needles in pairs and many wooden cones

☆**jack·pot** (jak'pät') *n.* [JACK, *n.* 10 *a* + POT] **1.** a pot in a poker game made up of accumulated stakes, played for only when some player has a pair of jacks or better to open **2.** any cumulative stakes or highest prize, as in a slot machine —**hit the jackpot** [Slang] **1.** to win the jackpot **2.** to attain the highest success or reward

☆**jack rabbit** [JACK(ASS) + RABBIT: from its long ears] a large hare of W N. America, with long ears and strong hind legs

---

fat, āpe, cär; ten, ēven; is, bīte; gō, hôrn, tool, look; oil, out; up, fur; get; joy; yet; chin; she; thin, *th*en; zh, leisure; ŋ, ring; ə for *a* in *ago, e* in *agent, i* in *sanity, o* in *comply, u* in *focus;* ' as in *able* (ā'b'l); Fr. bal; ë, Fr. coeur; ö, Fr. feu; Fr. mon; ô, Fr. coq; ü, Fr. duc; r, Fr. cri; H, G. ich; kh, G. doch; ‡foreign; ☆ Americanism; < derived from. See inside front cover.

jacks (jaks) *n.pl.* [< JACKSTONE] [*with sing. v.*] a children's game in which pebbles or small, six-pronged metal pieces are tossed and picked up in various ways, esp. while bouncing a small ball

jack·screw (jak′skrōō′) *n.* [JACK- + SCREW] a machine for raising heavy things a short distance, operated by turning a screw

Jack·son (jak′s'n) [after A. JACKSON] capital of Miss., in the SW part: pop. 154,000

Jack·son (jak′s'n) **1. Andrew,** 1767–1845; 7th president of the U.S. (1829–37) **2. Thomas Jonathan,** (nickname *Stonewall Jackson*) 1824–63; Confederate general in the Civil War

Jack·son·ville (jak′s'n vil′) [after A. JACKSON] port in NE Fla.: pop. 529,000

jack·stone (jak′stōn′) *n.* [orig. *checkstone* < *check*, pebble] **1.** same as JACK (*n.* 10 b) **2.** [*pl., with sing. v.*] same as JACKS

jack·straw (-strô′) *n.* [JACK- + STRAW] a narrow strip of wood, plastic, etc. used in a game (**jackstraws**) played by tossing a number of such strips into a jumbled heap and trying to remove them one at a time without moving any of the others

Ja·cob (jā′kəb) [< LL. < Gr. < Heb. *ja'aqob,* lit., seizing by the heel] **1.** a masculine name: dim. *Jake* **2.** *Bible* a son of Isaac and father of the founders of the twelve tribes of Israel: Gen. 25–50

Jac·o·be·an (jak′ə bē′ən) *adj.* [< *Jacobus,* Latinized form of *James*] **1.** of James I of England **2.** of the period in England when he was king (1603–1625) —*n.* a poet, diplomat, etc. of this period

Jac·o·bin (jak′ə bin) *n.* [< the Church of St. *Jacques* in Paris, the society's meeting place] **1.** any member of a society of radical democrats in France during the Revolution of 1789 **2.** a political radical —*adj.* of the Jacobins: also **Jac′o·bin′ic, Jac′o·bin′i·cal —Jac′o·bin·ism** *n.*

Jac·o·bite (jak′ə bīt′) *n.* [see JACOBEAN] a supporter of James II of England after he was deposed, or a supporter of his descendants' claims to the throne —**Jac′o·bit′ic** (-bit′ik), **Jac′o·bit′i·cal** *adj.*

Jacob's ladder 1. *Bible* the ladder to heaven that Jacob saw in a dream: see Gen. 28:12 **2.** a ladder made of rope, wire, etc., used on ships

Jac·quard (jə kärd′) *n.* [after the Fr. inventor, J. M. *Jacquard* (1752–1834)] a figured weave produced on a loom (**Jacquard loom**) having an endless belt of cards punched with holes arranged to produce the desired pattern

Jac·que·line (jak′wə lin, jak′ə-) [Fr., fem. of *Jacques,* JACK] a feminine name: dim. *Jacky*

Jacques-Car·tier (zhàk kàr tyā′; *E.* zhak′kär tyā′) city in S Quebec, near Montreal: pop. 53,000

jade¹ (jād) *n.* [Fr. < Sp. < *piedra de ijada,* stone of the side: from the notion that it cured pains in the side] **1.** a hard stone, usually green or white, used in jewelry, artistic carvings, etc. **2.** a green color of medium hue —*adj.* **1.** made of jade **2.** green like jade

jade² (jād) *n.* [< ON. *jalda,* a mare < Finn.] **1.** a horse, esp. a worn-out, worthless one **2.** a woman of low morals **3.** [Now Rare] a saucy young woman —*vt., vi.* **jad′ed, jad′ing** to make or become tired, weary, or worn-out —**jad′ish** *adj.*

jad·ed (jā′did) *adj.* **1.** tired; worn-out; wearied **2.** having the senses dulled from too much indulgence; satiated —**jad′ed·ly** *adv.* —**jad′ed·ness** *n.*

jae·ger (yā′gər) *n.* [< G. *jäger,* huntsman] any of several sea birds which force other, weaker birds to leave or give up their prey

Jaf·fa (yä′fə, jaf′ə) see TEL AVIV-JAFFA

jag¹ (jag) *n.* [ME. *jagge*] **1.** a sharp, toothlike projection **2.** [Archaic] a notch or pointed tear, as in cloth —*vt.* **jagged, jag′ging 1.** to notch or pink (cloth, etc.) **2.** to tear or cut unevenly, or raggedly

jag² (jag) *n.* [< ?] [Slang] **1.** an intoxicated condition due to liquor or drugs **2.** a drunken spree **3.** a period of some activity that gets out of control [*a crying jag*]

jag·ged (jag′id) *adj.* having sharp projecting points or notches —**jag′ged·ly** *adv.* —**jag′ged·ness** *n.*

jag·uar (jag′wär, -yoo wär′) *n., pl.* **-uars, -uar:** see PLURAL, II, D, 1 [Port. < Tupi] a large cat, yellowish with black spots, found from the southwestern U.S. to Argentina: it is similar to the leopard, but larger

jag·ua·run·di (jag′wə run′dē) *n.* [AmSp. & Port. < Tupi] a small wildcat of tropical and subtropical America, with a slender body and a long tail: also sp. **jag′ua·ron′di**

Jah·veh, Jah·ve, Jah·weh, Jah·we (yä′ve) *same as* JEHO-VAH

jai a·lai (hī′lī′, hī′ə lī′) [Sp. < Basque *jai,* celebration + *alai,* merry] a Latin American game like handball, but played with a curved basket fastened to the arm, for catching the ball and hurling it against the wall

jail (jāl) *n.* [< OFr. *gaole* < LL. *caveola,* dim. of L. *cavea,* a CAGE] **1.** a building for locking up people who are awaiting trial or who have been convicted of minor offenses **2.** imprisonment —*vt.* to put or keep in jail

jail·bird (-bʉrd′) *n.* [Colloq.] **1.** a prisoner in a jail **2.** a person often put in jail; habitual lawbreaker

☆**jail·break** (-brāk′) *n.* a breaking out of jail

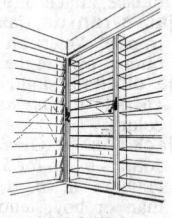

JAI ALAI PLAYER

jail·er, jail·or (-ər) *n.* a person in charge of a jail or of prisoners

Jain (jīn) *n.* [< Hindi < Sans. *jina,* saint] a believer in Jainism —*adj.* of the Jains or their religion Also **Jai·na** (jī′nə), **Jain′ist**

Jain·ism (jīn′iz'm) *n.* a Hindu religion founded in the 6th cent. B.C.: it teaches that all life is sacred and that one can gain salvation by knowledge, faith, and right living

Jai·pur (jī′poor) city in NW India: pop. 403,000

Ja·kar·ta (jə kär′tə) *same as* DJAKARTA

jal·ap (jal′əp) *n.* [Fr. < Sp. < *Jalapa,* city in Mexico] **1.** the dried root of a Mexican plant, formerly used as a powerful cathartic **2.** the plant

☆**ja·lop·y** (jə läp′ē) *n., pl.* **-lop′ies** [< ?] [Slang] an old, shabby automobile

jal·ou·sie (jal′ə sē′) *n.* [Fr. < OFr. *gelosie,* jealousy (see JEALOUS)] a window, shade, or door formed of horizontal slats of wood, metal, or glass, that can be adjusted to regulate the air or light entering

jam¹ (jam) *vt.* **jammed, jam′ming** [< ?] **1.** to squeeze into or through a tight space [he *jammed* the book into his pocket] **2.** to bruise or crush [he *jammed* his thumb in the car door] **3.** to push or crowd **4.** to pack full or tight [to *jam* a drawer with clothes] **5.** to fill or block (a passageway, etc.) by crowding in [cars *jammed* the drive] **6.** to wedge or make stick so that it cannot move or work [the bolt on his rifle is *jammed*] **7.** to make (radio or radar signals) unintelligible, as by sending out others on the same wavelength ☆**8.** to push or shove hard [she *jammed* her foot on the brakes] —*vi.* **1.** to become wedged or stuck fast, esp. so as to become unworkable **2.** to push against one another in a confined space ☆**3.** [Slang] *Jazz* to improvise —*n.* **1.** a jamming or being jammed **2.** a group of persons or things blocking a passageway, etc. [a traffic *jam*] ☆**3.** [Colloq.] a difficult situation

jam² (jam) *n.* [prob. < prec.] a food made by boiling fruit with sugar to a thick mixture

JALOUSIES

Ja·mai·ca (jə mā′kə) country on an island of the West Indies, south of Cuba: a member of the Commonwealth: 4,411 sq. mi.; pop. 1,972,000; cap. Kingston —**Ja·mai′can** *adj., n.*

jamb (jam) *n.* [< OFr. *jambe* < LL. *gamba,* a leg] a side post of an opening for a door, window, etc.

☆**jam·ba·lay·a** (jum′bə lī′ə) *n.* [AmFr. < ModPr. *jambalaia*] a Creole stew made of rice and shrimp, oysters, crabs, ham, chicken, etc.

☆**jam·bo·ree** (jam′bə rē′) *n.* [< ?] **1.** [Colloq.] *a)* a lively, noisy party or celebration *b)* a gathering with planned entertainment **2.** a national or international assembly of boy scouts

James¹ (jāmz) *n.* [< OFr. < LL. *Jacomus,* later form of *Jacobus,* JACOB] **1.** a masculine name *2. Bible a)* either of two Christian apostles *b)* a brother of Jesus; also, a book of the New Testament sometimes attributed to him **3. James I** 1566–1625; king of England (1603–25) & (as **James VI**) king of Scotland (1567–1625): son of MARY, QUEEN OF SCOTS **4. James II** 1633–1701; king of England & (as **James VII**) king of Scotland (1685–88): deposed: son of CHARLES I **5. Henry,** 1843–1916; U.S. novelist, in England **6. Jesse** (Woodson), 1847–82; U.S. outlaw **7. William,** 1842–1910; U.S. psychologist & philosopher: brother of *Henry*

James² (jāmz) river in Va., flowing from the W part southeast into Chesapeake Bay

James·town (jāmz′toun′) [after JAMES I] first successful

English colony in America, set up in 1607 at the mouth of the James River, in Va.

Jam·mu and Kashmir (jum′ōō) state of N India: control of it is claimed by both India and Pakistan

☆**jam·packed** (jam′pakt′) *adj.* tightly packed; crammed

☆**jam session** an informal gathering of jazz musicians to play together, esp. by improvising on popular themes

Jan. January

Jane (jān) [var. of JOANNA] a feminine name —*n.* [j-] [Slang] a girl or woman

Jan·et (jan′it) [dim. of JANE] a feminine name

jan·gle (jaŋ′g'l) *vi.* -gled, -gling [< OFr. *jangler*] 1. to make a harsh, jarring sound, as of a bell out of tune 2. to quarrel noisily —*vt.* 1. to cause to make a harsh sound 2. to irritate very much [to *jangle* one's nerves] —*n.* 1. noisy talk or arguing 2. a harsh sound —**jan′gler** *n.*

Jan·ice (jan′is) [< JANE, JANET] a feminine name

jan·i·tor (jan′i tər) *n.* [L., doorkeeper < *janua*, door] the custodian of a building, who takes care of cleaning and general repairs —**jan′i·to′ri·al** (-ə tôr′ē əl) *adj.*

jan·i·zar·y (jan′ə zer′ē) *n., pl.* -zar′ies [< Fr. < It. < Turk. < *yeni*, new + *cheri*, soldiery] [often J-] 1. a Turkish soldier, orig. one in the sultan's guard that was created in the 14th cent. and ended in 1826 2. any very loyal supporter Also **jan′is·sar′y** (-ser′ē)

Jan·u·ar·y (jan′yoo wer′ē) *n., pl.* -ar′ies [< L. *Januarius* (*mensis*), (the month) of Janus] the first month of the year, having 31 days: abbrev. **Jan., Ja.**

Ja·nus (jā′nəs) *Rom. Myth.* the god who was guardian of gates and doors and who kept special watch over beginnings and endings: his head is shown with two faces, one in front, the other at the back of his head

Jap. 1. Japan 2. Japanese

Ja·pan (jə pan′) island country off the E coast of Asia, including Hokkaido, Honshu, Kyushu, Shikoku, & many smaller islands: 142,726 sq. mi.; pop. 104,650,000; cap. Tokyo

ja·pan (jə pan′) *n.* [orig. from Japan] 1. a lacquer or varnish giving a hard, glossy finish 2. a liquid used as a paint drier 3. objects decorated and varnished in the Japanese style —*vt.* -panned′, -pan′ning to lacquer or varnish with japan

Japan Current warm ocean current of the Pacific, flowing from east of the Philippines northeast past Japan

Jap·a·nese (jap′ə nēz′) *adj.* of Japan, its people, language, culture, etc. —*n.* 1. *pl.* -nese′ a native of Japan 2. the language of Japan

☆**Japanese beetle** a shiny, green-and-brown beetle, orig. from Japan, which eats leaves, fruits, and grasses, and is damaging to crops

Japanese lantern same as CHINESE LANTERN

Japanese quince a spiny plant of the rose family, with pink or red flowers and green fruit

jape (jāp) *vi.* japed, jap′ing [ME. *japen*] 1. to joke; jest 2. to play tricks —*vt.* [Now Rare] to make fun of —*n.* 1. a joke or jest 2. a trick —**jap′er·y** *n., pl.* -er·ies

Ja·pheth (jā′fith) *Bible* the youngest of Noah's three sons: Gen. 5:32

ja·pon·i·ca (jə pän′i kə) *n.* [ModL., fem. of *Japonicus*, of Japan < *Japonia*, Japan < Fr. *Japon*] *a popular name for* JAPANESE QUINCE, CAMELLIA, etc.

jar[1] (jär) *vi.* jarred, jar′ring [echoic] 1. to make a harsh sound; grate 2. to have a harsh, irritating effect (*on* one) [an uproar that *jarred* on her nerves] 3. to vibrate from a sudden impact 4. to clash, disagree, or quarrel [a rude remark that *jarred* with his refined manners] —*vt.* 1. to make vibrate by sudden impact 2. to cause to give a harsh or discordant sound 3. to jolt or shock [the news of his death *jarred* us] —*n.* 1. a harsh, grating sound 2. a vibration due to a sudden impact 3. a jolt or shock 4. a sharp clash or quarrel

jar[2] (jär) *n.* [Fr. *jarre* < OPr. or Sp. < Ar. *jarrah*, earthen water container] 1. a container made of glass, stone, or earthenware, with a large opening and no spout 2. as much as a jar will hold: also **jar′ful′**

jar·di·niere (jär′d'n ir′; *Fr.* zhàr dē nyer′) *n.* [< Fr. < *jardin*, a garden] 1. an ornamental bowl, pot, or stand for flowers or plants 2. a garnish for meats, of several vegetables cooked separately

jar·gon (jär′gən) *n.* [MFr., a chattering] 1. speech that makes no sense because it is confused or meaningless; gibberish 2. a language or dialect unknown to one so that it seems impossible to understand 3. a language or dialect that is a mixture of others; esp., pidgin 4. the specialized vocabulary and idioms of those in the same work, profession, etc., as of sportswriters: see SLANG —see SYN. at DIALECT —**jar′gon·is′tic** *adj.*

Jas. James

jas·mine, jas·min (jaz′min; *chiefly Brit.* jas′-) *n.* [< Fr. < Ar. < Per. *yāsamīn*] 1. a tropical and subtropical plant of the olive family, with fragrant flowers of yellow, red, or white 2. any of several other similar plants with fragrant flowers 3. pale yellow

Ja·son (jās′'n) [< L. *Iason* < Gr., lit., healer] 1. a masculine name 2. *Gr. Myth.* a prince who led the Argonauts and got the Golden Fleece

jas·per (jas′pər) *n.* [< MFr. < L. < Gr. *iaspis*] 1. an opaque variety of colored quartz, usually reddish, yellow, or brown 2. *Bible* a precious stone, probably an opaque green quartz

ja·to, JA·TO (jā′tō) *n.* [*j(et)-a(ssisted) t(ake)o(ff)*] an airplane takeoff assisted by small rockets or jet engines

jaun·dice (jôn′dis, jän′-) *n.* [< OFr. *jaunisse*, ult. < L. *galbinus*, greenish yellow < *galbus*, yellow] 1. *a*) a condition in which the eyeballs, skin, and urine become abnormally yellow as a result of bile pigments in the blood *b*) popularly, a disease causing this, as hepatitis 2. bitterness, prejudice, or warped outlook caused by jealousy, hate, etc. —*vt.* -diced, -dic·ing 1. to cause to have jaundice 2. to make bitter or prejudiced through jealousy, hate, etc.

jaunt (jônt, jänt) *vi.* [< ?] to take a short trip for pleasure —*n.* such a trip; excursion —see SYN. at TRIP

jaunting car a light, open, two-wheeled cart used in Ireland, with seats on both sides

jaun·ty (jôn′tē, jän′-) *adj.* -ti·er, -ti·est [< Fr. *gentil*, genteel] 1. in fashion; stylish; chic 2. gay and carefree; sprightly; perky [with a *jaunty* wave of his hand] —**jaun′ti·ly** *adv.* —**jaun′ti·ness** *n.*

Jav. Javanese

Ja·va (jä′və, jav′ə) large island of Indonesia, southeast of Sumatra: 48,842 sq. mi. —*n.* ☆1. a coffee grown on Java and nearby islands ☆2. [often j-] [Slang] any coffee

Java man a type of primitive man known from fossil remains found in Java

JAUNTING CAR

Jav·a·nese (jav′ə nēz′) *adj.* of Java, its people, etc. —*n.* 1. *pl.* -nese′ a native or inhabitant of Java 2. the Indonesian language of Java

jav·e·lin (jav′lin, jav′ə lin) *n.* [MFr. *javeline*, fem. dim. < *javelot*, a spear] 1. a light spear for throwing 2. a pointed wooden or metal shaft, about 8½ ft. long, thrown for distance as a field event (**javelin throw**) in track and field meets

jaw (jô) *n.* [< ? OFr. *joue*, cheek] 1. either of the two bony parts that hold the teeth and form the frame of the mouth 2. either of two parts that open and close to grip or crush something, as in a monkey wrench or vise 3. [*pl.*] *a*) the mouth *b*) the entrance of a canyon, valley, etc. 4. something that seems about to grasp like a pair of jaws [snatched from the *jaws* of death] —*vi.* [Slang] to talk, esp. in a boring or insulting way

jaw·bone (jô′bōn′) *n.* a bone of a jaw, esp. of the lower jaw —☆*vt., vi.* -boned′, -bon′ing to try to persuade by using the influence of one's high office [the President had been *jawboning* for wage and price controls]

jaw·break·er (-brā′kər) *n.* 1. a machine with jaws for crushing rocks, ore, etc. ☆2. a hard, usually round candy 3. [Slang] a word that is hard to pronounce

jay (jā) *n.* [< OFr. *gai* < LL. *gaius*, a jay] **1.** any of several birds of the crow family **2.** *same as* BLUE JAY **3.** [Colloq.] a stupid or foolish person

Jay (jā), **John** 1745–1829; Am. statesman & jurist: 1st chief justice of the U.S. (1789–95)

☆**Jay·hawk·er** (jā′hô′kər) *n.* [Colloq.] *a nickname for* a Kansan: also **Jay′hawk′**

☆**jay·walk** (jā′wôk′) *vi.* [JAY, 3 + WALK] to walk in or across a street carelessly without obeying traffic rules and signals —**jay′walk′er** *n.* —**jay′walk′ing** *n.*

☆**jazz** (jaz) *n.* [< ? Creole patois *jass*, sexual term] **1.** a kind of music that originated with Southern blacks in the late 19th cent.: it is characterized by free improvising, strong rhythms, and unusual tonal effects on the saxophone, clarinet, trumpet, trombone, etc. **2.** loosely, any popular dance music **3.** [Slang] *a)* remarks, acts, etc. regarded as insincere, tiresome, trite, or the like [don't give me that *jazz* about when you were a boy] *b)* related things, activities, etc. [she likes golf, tennis, and all that *jazz*] —*adj.* of, in, or like jazz —*vt.* **1.** to play or arrange as jazz **2.** [Slang] to make more exciting or lively; enliven (usually with *up*) —**jazz′i·ly** *adv.* —**jazz′i·ness** *n.* —**jazz′y** *adj.* **-i·er, -i·est**

☆**jazz·man** (jaz′man′) *n., pl.* **-men** (-men′) a jazz musician

jct. junction

JD juvenile delinquency (or delinquent)

Je. June

jeal·ous (jel′əs) *adj.* [< OFr. *gelos* < ML. *zelosus:* see ZEAL] **1.** very watchful or careful in guarding or keeping [jealous of one's rights] **2.** *a)* suspicious or worried that someone is taking the love or attention one has or wants [a *jealous* husband] *b)* unhappy because another has something one would like; resentfully envious [he was *jealous* of her good fortune] *c)* resulting from such feelings [a *jealous* rage] **3.** [Now Rare] requiring complete loyalty and devotion [a *jealous* God] — **jeal′ous·ly** *adv.* —**jeal′ous·ness** *n.*

jeal·ous·y (-ē) *n., pl.* **-ous·ies 1.** the quality or condition of being jealous **2.** an instance of this; jealous feeling

Jean (jēn) **1.** [Fr., equiv. of JOHN] a masculine name **2.** [var. of JOANNA] a feminine name

jean (jēn) *n.* [< OFr. *Janne* < ML. < L. *Genua*, Genoa] **1.** a durable, twilled cotton cloth, used for work clothes and casual wear **2.** [*pl.*] trousers of this material, often blue, or of denim

Jeanne (jēn) [var. of JOANNA] a feminine name

Jeanne d'Arc (zhän därk) *see* JOAN OF ARC

Jean·nette (jə net′) [dim. of JEANNE] a feminine name

jee (jē) *interj., n., vt., vi. same as* GEE¹

☆**jeep** (jēp) *n.* [after a creature in a comic strip by E. C. Segar (1894–1938): later associated with *G.P.* (for *General Purpose* car)] a small, rugged, military automotive vehicle with a 1/4-ton capacity and four-wheel drive —[**J-**] *a trademark for* a similar vehicle for civilian use

☆**jee·pers** (jē′pərz) *interj.* [altered < JESUS] a mild exclamation of surprise, etc.

jeer (jir) *vt., vi.* [< ? CHEER] to make fun of (a person or thing) in a rude, sarcastic manner; mock; scoff (at) —*n.* a jeering remark; sarcastic or derisive comment —see SYN. at SCOFF —**jeer′er** *n.* —**jeer′ing·ly** *adv.*

Jef·fer·son (jef′ər s'n), **Thomas** 1743–1826; Am. statesman; 3d president of the U.S. (1801–09): drew up the Declaration of Independence —**Jef′fer·so′ni·an** (-sō′nē ən) *adj., n.*

Jefferson City [after T. JEFFERSON] capital of Mo., on the Missouri River: pop. 32,000

Jeff·rey (jef′rē) [var. of GEOFFREY] a masculine name: dim. *Jeff*

Je·hosh·a·phat (ji häs′ə fat′, -häsh′-) *Bible* a king of Judah in the 9th cent. B.C.: II Chr. 17–21

Je·ho·vah (ji hō′və) [transliteration of the consonants of the Heb. sacred name for God (YHWH or JHVH), with vowels added later] God; (the) Lord

Jehovah's Witnesses a Christian sect founded by Charles T. Russell (1852–1916): it believes the world will soon come to an end and actively seeks to convert others

je·hu (jē′hōō, -hyōō) *n.* [< *Jehu* in the Bible: II Kings 9] [Colloq.] a fast, reckless driver

je·june (ji jōōn′) *adj.* [L. *jejunus*, empty] **1.** not nourishing **2.** not interesting or satisfying; dull [a *jejune* philosophy] **3.** [? by confusion with JUVENILE] not mature; childish —**je·june′ly** *adv.* —**je·june′ness** *n.*

je·ju·num (ji jōō′nəm) *n., pl.* **-na** (-nə) [< L. *jejunus*, empty: it was formerly thought to lie empty after death] the middle part of the small intestine, between the duodenum and the ileum: see illustration at INTESTINE —**je·ju′nal** *adj.*

Je·kyll (jē′k'l, jek′'l), **Dr.** a kind, good doctor in R. L. Stevenson's story *The Strange Case of Dr. Jekyll and Mr. Hyde*, who discovers drugs that enable him to change himself into a vicious, brutal creature named Mr. Hyde and back again

☆**jell** (jel) *vi., vt.* [back-formation < JELLY] **1.** to become or make into jelly **2.** [Colloq.] to take or give definite form; crystallize [the plans didn't *jell*] —*n.* [Dial.] *same as* JELLY

jel·li·fy (jel′ə fī′) *vt., vi.* **-fied′, -fy′ing** to change into jelly — **jel′li·fi·ca′tion** *n.*

☆**Jell-O** (jel′ō) *a trademark for* a flavored gelatin eaten as a dessert or used in molded salads —**jell′o** *n.* such a gelatin

jel·ly (jel′ē) *n., pl.* **-lies** [< OFr. pp. of *geler* < L. *gelare*, to freeze: see GELATIN] **1.** a soft, partially transparent, gelatinous food resulting from the cooling of fruit juice boiled with sugar, or of meat juice cooked down **2.** any substance like this —*vt.* **-lied, -ly·ing 1.** to make into jelly **2.** to coat, fill, or serve with jelly —*vi.* to become jelly —**jel′ly·like′** *adj.*

☆**jel·ly·bean** (-bēn′) *n.* a small, bean-shaped, gummy candy with a colored sugar coating

jel·ly·fish (-fish′) *n., pl.* **-fish′, -fish′es:** see FISH **1.** an invertebrate sea animal with a body made up largely of jellylike substance and shaped like an umbrella: it has long, hanging tentacles with stinging cells on them **2.** [Colloq.] a weak-willed person

jel·ly·roll (-rōl′) *n.* a thin sheet of spongecake spread with jelly and rolled so as to form layers

Jen·ghiz Khan (jen′gis) *same as* GENGHIS KHAN

Jen·ner (jen′ər) **1. Edward,** 1749–1823; Eng. physician: introduced vaccination **2. Sir William,** 1815–98; Eng. physician

jen·net (jen′it) *n.* [< MFr. < Sp. *jinete*, horseman < Ar. *Zenāta*, a tribe of Barbary] **1.** any of a breed of small Spanish horses **2.** a female donkey

Jen·ni·fer (jen′i fər) [altered < GUINEVERE] a feminine name

Jen·ny (jen′ē) [dim. of JANE] a feminine name

jen·ny (jen′ē) *n., pl.* **-nies** [< prec.] **1.** *short for* SPINNING JENNY **2.** *a)* the female of some birds [a *jenny* wren] *b)* a female donkey or key

jeop·ard·ize (jep′ər dīz′) *vt.* **-ized′, -iz′ing** to put in jeopardy; risk loss, failure, etc. of; endanger [she *jeopardized* her career by supporting her friend]

jeop·ard·y (-dē) *n., pl.* **-ard·ies** [< OFr. *jeu parti*, lit., a game with even chances < L. *jocus*, a game + pp. of *partire*, to divide] **1.** great danger; peril [a miner's life is often in *jeopardy*] **2.** *Law* the danger of being convicted and punished; the situation of an accused person on trial for a crime —see SYN. at DANGER

Jer. Jeremiah

jer·bo·a (jər bō′ə) *n.* [Ar. *yarbū'*] any of various small, leaping rodents of N Africa and Asia, with very long hind legs: it is active at night

jer·e·mi·ad (jer′ə mī′əd) *n.* [< JEREMIAH, believed to be the author of the book of *Lamentations*] a lamentation or tale of woe

Jer·e·mi·ah (jer′ə mī′ə) [< LL. < Gr. < Heb. *yirmeyāh*, lit., the Lord loosens (i.e., from the womb)] **1.** a masculine name: var. *Jeremy* **2.** *Bible a)* a Hebrew prophet of the 7th and 6th cent. B.C. *b)* the book containing his warnings and prophecies Also, in the Douay Bible, **Jer′e·mi′as** (-əs)

Jer·i·cho (jer′ə kō′) city in W Jordan: site of an ancient city whose walls, according to the Bible, were miraculously destroyed when trumpets were sounded: see Josh. 6

jerk¹ (jurk) *vt.* [< ?] **1.** to pull, twist, push, or throw with a sudden, sharp movement ☆**2.** [Colloq.] to make and serve (ice cream sodas) *vi.* **1.** to move with a jerk or in jerks **2.** to twitch —*n.* **1.** a sharp, abrupt pull, twist, push, etc. **2.** a sudden contraction of a muscle, caused by a reflex action ☆**3.** [Slang] a person regarded as stupid, foolish, etc.

jerk² (jurk) *vt.* [< JERKY²] to preserve (meat) by slicing into strips and drying, orig. in the sun —*n. same as* JERKY²

Captions (right column, by illustrations):

JELLYFISH (to 16 in. long)

JERBOA (4½–16 in. long, including tail)

jer·kin (jur′kin) *n.* [< ?] a closefitting, sleeveless jacket of a kind worn in the 16th and 17th cent.

☆**jerk·wa·ter** (jurk′wôt′ər, -wät′-) *n.* [JERK¹ + WATER] water for such trains often had to be got by bucket brigades from nearby creeks] a train on an early branch railroad —*adj.* [Colloq.] small, unimportant, etc. [*a jerkwater* town]

jerk·y¹ (jur′kē) *adj.* **jerk′i·er, jerk′i·est** **1.** characterized by jerks; making sudden starts and stops; spasmodic ☆**2.** [Slang] stupid, dull, foolish, etc. —**jerk′i·ly** *adv.* —**jerk′i·ness** *n.*

☆**jer·ky**² (jur′kē) *n.* [< Sp. *charqui* < Quechua] meat, esp. beef, that has been preserved by being sliced into strips and dried, orig. in the sun

Je·rome (jə rōm′) [Fr. < L. < Gr. < *hieros*, holy + *onyma*, name] **1.** a masculine name: dim. *Jerry* **2.** Saint, (born *Eusebius Hieronymus Sophronius*) 340?–420 A.D.; monk & church scholar: translator of the Bible in a Latin version (*Vulgate*)

jer·ry-built (jer′ē bilt′) *adj.* [prob. < name *Jerry*, infl. by JURY²] built poorly, of cheap materials

Jer·sey (jur′zē) largest of the Channel Islands —*n., pl.* **-seys** **1.** any of a breed of small, reddish-brown dairy cattle, originally from Jersey: its milk has a high butterfat content **2.** [J-] *a*) a soft, elastic, knitted cloth of wool, cotton, rayon, etc. *b*) any closefitting, knitted upper garment

Jersey City city in northeastern N.J., across the Hudson from New York City: pop. 261,000 (met. area 609,000)

Je·ru·sa·lem (jə rōō′sə ləm) capital of modern Israel, in the C part: pop. 283,000

Jerusalem artichoke [altered < It. *girasole*, sunflower] **1.** a tall N. American sunflower with potatolike tubers that are eaten **2.** such a tuber

Jes·per·sen (yes′pər sən), (**Jens**) **Otto** (**Harry**) 1860–1943; Dan. linguist who specialized in studies of English

jess (jes) *n.* [< OFr. *gets*, pl. < L. *jactus*, a casting] a strap for a falcon's leg, with a ring for attaching a leash —*vt.* to fasten jesses on

jes·sa·mine (jes′ə min) *n. same as* JASMINE

Jes·se (jes′ē) [Heb. *yĭshai*] **1.** a masculine name: dim. *Jess* **2.** *Bible* the father of David: see I Sam. 16

Jes·si·ca (jes′i kə) a feminine name: var. *Jessie*

jest (jest) *n.* [OFr. *geste*, an exploit < L. pp. of *gerere*, to perform] **1.** a mocking remark; gibe; taunt **2.** a joke or humorous remark **3.** mere fun; joking; playfulness [it was said in *jest*, but it hurt her feelings] **4.** something to be laughed at or joked about; laughingstock —*vi.* **1.** to make fun; jeer; mock **2.** to be playful in speech and actions; joke

jest·er (jes′tər) *n.* one who jests; esp., a clown hired by a medieval ruler to amuse him with jokes and tricks

Je·su (jē′zōō, -sōō; jā′-) *archaic var. of* JESUS

Jes·u·it (jezh′ōō wit, jez′-; -yōō-) *n.* a member of the Society of Jesus, a Roman Catholic religious order for men founded by Ignatius Loyola in 1534

Je·sus (jē′zəs) [LL. *Iesus* < Gr. *Iēsous* < Heb. *yēshū‘a*, contr. of *yĕhōshu‘a*, help of Jehovah] c. 8–4 B.C.–29? A.D. (see CHRISTIAN ERA): founder of the Christian religion: also called **Jesus Christ, Jesus of Nazareth**: see also CHRIST

jet¹ (jet) *vt., vi.* **jet′ted, jet′ting** [< MFr. *jeter*, ult. < L. *jactare*, < *jacere*, to throw < IE. base *ye-*, to throw] **1.** to spout, gush, or shoot out in a stream **2.** to travel or carry by jet airplane [they *jetted* us over to Paris] —*n.* **1.** a stream of liquid or gas forced out, as from a spout or nozzle **2.** a spout or nozzle for emitting a jet **3.** a jet-propelled airplane: in full, **jet** (**air**)**plane** **4.** *short for* JET ENGINE —*adj.* **1.** jet-propelled **2.** of jet propulsion or jet-propelled aircraft [the *jet* age]

jet² (jet) *n.* [< OFr. < L. < Gr. *gagatēs*, jet < *Gagas*, town in Asia Minor] **1.** a hard, black variety of lignite: sometimes polished and used in jewelry **2.** a deep, lustrous black —*adj.* **1.** made of jet **2.** black like jet [her *jet* hair]

jet-black (-blak′) *adj.* glossy black, like jet

jet engine an engine for aircraft, ships, etc. that operates by jet propulsion when gases are formed, as by burning a mixture of fuel and oxygen from the atmosphere

jet·lin·er (-lī′nər) *n.* a commercial jet aircraft for passengers

jet·port (-pôrt′) *n.* an airport with long runways, for use by jet airplanes

jet-pro·pelled (-prə peld′) *adj.* driven by jet propulsion

jet propulsion a method of moving airplanes, boats, etc. forward by the reaction caused when gases are forced backward under pressure through a rear vent or vents

jet·sam (jet′səm) *n.* [var. of JETTISON] **1.** that part of the cargo thrown overboard to lighten a ship in danger: see also FLOTSAM **2.** such discarded cargo washed ashore **3.** discarded things

jet stream **1.** any of several bands of high-velocity winds moving from west to east around the earth at altitudes of from 8 to 10 mi. **2.** the stream of exhaust from a rocket engine

jet·ti·son (jet′ə s'n, -z'n) *n.* [< Anglo-Fr. < OFr. *getaison* < L. < *jactare*: see JET¹] **1.** a throwing overboard of goods to lighten a ship, airplane, etc. in an emergency **2.** *same as* JETSAM —*vt.* **1.** to throw (goods) overboard **2.** to discard; get rid of

jet·ty (jet′ē) *n., pl.* **-ties** [< OFr. *jetée*, orig. pp. of *jeter*: see JET¹] **1.** a kind of wall built out into the water to control currents, protect a harbor, etc. **2.** a landing pier —*vi.* **-tied, -ty·ing** to project, or jut out

Jew (jōō) *n.* [< OFr. < L. *Judaeus* < Gr. < Heb. *yehūdī*, member of the tribe of Judah] **1.** a person descended, or regarded as descended, from the ancient Hebrews **2.** a person whose religion is Judaism

jew·el (jōō′əl) *n.* [< OFr. *joel* < *jeu*, a trifle < L. *jocus*, a JOKE] **1.** a valuable ring, necklace, etc., esp. one set with gems **2.** a precious stone; gem **3.** any person or thing that is very precious or valuable **4.** a small gem or gemlike bit used as one of the bearings in a watch —*vt.* **-eled** or **-elled, -el·ing** or **-el·ling** to decorate or set with jewels

jew·el·er, jew·el·ler (-ər) *n.* a person who makes, deals in, or repairs jewelry, watches, etc.

jew·el·ry (jōō′əl rē) *n.* jewels or ornaments made with jewels: Brit. sp. **jew′el·ler·y**

☆**jew·el·weed** (-wēd′) *n.* any of a group of plants bearing yellow or orange-yellow flowers and seedpods that split open when ripe if they are touched

Jew·ess (jōō′is) *n.* a Jewish woman or girl: term not used by those who regard the *-ess* suffix as patronizing or discriminatory

jew·fish (-fish′) *n., pl.* **-fish′, -fish′es**: see FISH any of several large fish found in warm seas, as a grouper found off Florida

Jew·ish (-ish) *adj.* of or having to do with Jews or Judaism —*n.* [Colloq.] *same as* YIDDISH —**Jew′ish·ness** *n.*

Jewish calendar a calendar used by the Jews in calculating holidays, etc., based on the lunar month and reckoned from 3761 B.C., the traditional date of the Creation

Months of the Jewish Calendar

1. **Tishri** (30 days)	7. **Nisan** (30 days)
2. **Heshvan** (29 or 30 days)	8. **Iyar** (29 days)
3. **Kislev** (29 or 30 days)	9. **Sivan** (30 days)
4. **Tebet** (29 days)	10. **Tammuz** (29 days)
5. **Shebat** (30 days)	11. **Ab** (30 days)
6. **Adar** (29 or 30 days)	12. **Elul** (29 days)

N.B. About once every three years an extra month, **Veadar** or **Adar Sheni** (29 days), falls between *Adar* and *Nisan. Tishri* begins in late September or early October

Jew·ry (jōō′rē) *n., pl.* **-ries** **1.** formerly, a district of a city in which Jews lived; ghetto **2.** Jewish people as a group [American *Jewry*]

jew's-harp, jews'-harp (jōōz′härp′) *n.* a small musical instrument consisting of a lyre-shaped metal frame held between the teeth and played by plucking a flexible bent piece with the finger: it makes a twanging sound

Jez·e·bel (jez′ə bel′, -b'l) [Heb.] *Bible* the wicked woman who married Ahab, king of Israel —*n.* [also **j-**] any shameless, wicked woman

JEW'S-HARP

jg, j.g. junior grade: designation of the lower rank of lieutenant in the U.S. Navy

jib¹ (jib) *n.* [prob. < GIBBET] **1.** the projecting arm of a crane **2.** the boom of a derrick

jib² (jib) *vi., vt.* **jibbed, jib′bing** [< Dan. *gibbe*, to jibe] *Naut.* to jibe; shift —*n.* a triangular sail projecting ahead of the foremast: see illustration at MAINSAIL —**cut of one's jib** [Colloq.] one's appearance or way of dressing

jib³ (jib) *vi.* **jibbed, jib′bing** [prob. < prec.] **1.** to stop and refuse to go forward; balk **2.** to start or shy (*at* something) —*n.* an animal that jibs, as a horse —**jib′ber** *n.*

---

jib boom a spar reaching out from the bowsprit of a ship: the jib is attached to it

jibe[1] (jīb) *vi.* **jibed, jib′ing** [< Du. *gijpen*] **1.** to shift from one side of a ship to the other, as a fore-and-aft sail when the course is changed in a following wind **2.** to change the course of a ship so that the sails shift thus **3.** [Colloq.] to be in harmony, agreement, or accord [*their stories don't jibe*] —*vt. Naut.* to cause to jibe —*n.* a shift of sail or boom from one side of a ship to another

jibe[2] (jīb) *vi., vt., n.* same as GIBE —**jib′er** *n.*

Jid·da, Jid·dah (jid′ə) seaport in Saudi Arabia, on the Red Sea: pop. c.300,000

jif·fy (jif′ē) *n., pl.* **-fies** [< ?] [Colloq.] a very short time; instant [*done in a jiffy*]: also **jiff**

jig (jig) *n.* [prob. < MFr. *giguer*, to dance < *gigue*, a fiddle] **1.** *a)* a fast, gay, bouncy dance, usually in triple time *b)* the music for such a dance **2.** any of various fishing lures that are jiggled up and down in the water **3.** any of several mechanical devices operated in a jerky manner, as a sieve for separating ores, a drill, etc. **4.** a device used as a guide for a tool or as a template —*vi., vt.* **jigged, jig′ging 1.** to dance (a jig) **2.** to move jerkily up and down or to and fro —☆**in jig time** [Old Slang] very quickly —☆**the jig is up** [Slang] all chances for success are gone: said of a risky or improper activity

jig·ger[1] (jig′ər) *n.* [prob. < Afr. origin] ☆same as CHIGGER

jig·ger[2] (jig′ər) *n.* **1.** one who jigs ☆**2.** *a)* a small glass used to measure liquor, containing usually 1½ fluid ounces *b)* the quantity of liquor in a jigger **3.** any device or contraption whose name one does not know or cannot recall; thingamajig; gadget **4.** same as JIG (*n.* 2) **5.** *Mech.* any of several devices that operate with a jerky, up-and-down motion **6.** *Naut. a)* a small tackle *b)* a small sail *c)* same as JIGGER MAST

jigger mast a mast in the stern of a ship

jig·gle (jig′'l) *vt., vi.* **-gled, -gling** [< JIG, *vi.* + -LE[2]] to move with a series of quick, slight jerks; rock lightly [*he jiggled the loose tooth until it came out*] —*n.* a jiggling movement

jig·gly (jig′lē) *adj.* moving or tending to move with a jiggle; unsteady

☆**jig·saw** (jig′sô′) *n.* a saw with a narrow blade set in a frame, that moves with an up-and-down motion for cutting along curved or irregular lines, as in scrollwork: also **jig saw** —*vt.* to cut or form with a jigsaw

☆**jigsaw puzzle** a puzzle made by cutting up a picture into pieces of irregular shape, which must be put together again

JIGSAW

ji·had (ji häd′) *n.* [Ar., a contest, war] **1.** a war by Moslems against unbelievers, carried out as a religious duty **2.** any fanatic campaign for or against an idea; crusade

Jill (jil) [< proper name *Gillian* < L. *Juliana*] a feminine name —*n.* [*often* **j-**] [Now Rare] a girl or woman; esp., a sweetheart

jilt (jilt) *n.* [< *jillet*, dim. of JILL] a woman who rejects a lover after accepting or encouraging him —*vt.* to reject or have nothing more to do with (a lover or sweetheart)

Jim (jim) *a nickname for* JAMES[1]

☆**Jim Crow** [name of an early Negro minstrel song] [*also* **j- c-**] [Colloq.] the practice of discriminating against blacks or segregating them —**Jim′-Crow′** *vt., adj.* —**Jim Crow′ism**

jim·my (jim′ē) *n., pl.* **-mies** [< dim. of JAMES[1]] a short crowbar, used by burglars to pry open windows, etc. —☆*vt.* **-mied, -my·ing** to pry open with a jimmy or similar tool

☆**jim·son weed** (jim′s'n) [< JAMESTOWN, Va.] a poisonous annual weed of the nightshade family, with foul-smelling leaves, prickly fruit, and trumpet-shaped flowers

jin·gle (jiŋ′g'l) *vi.* **-gled, -gling** [ME. *gingelen*, prob. echoic] **1.** to make light, ringing sounds, as small bells or bits of metal striking together; tinkle **2.** to have obvious, easy rhythm, simple rhymes, etc., as some poetry and music —*vt.* **1.** to cause to jingle —*n.* **1.** a jingling sound **2.** a verse or tune that jingles [*advertising on radio is often in jingles*] —**jin′gly** (-glē) *adj.*

jin·go (jiŋ′gō) *n., pl.* **-goes** [< phr. *by jingo* in a patriotic Brit. music-hall song (1878)] one who boasts of his patriotism and favors an aggressive foreign policy that could lead to war; chauvinist —*adj.* of jingoes —**jin′go·ism** *n.* —**jin′go·ist** *n.* —**jin′go·is′tic** *adj.* —**jin′go·is′ti·cal·ly** *adv.*

jinn (jin) *n. pl.* of JINNI: in popular use, thought to be a singular, with the pl. **jinns**

jin·ni (ji nē′, jin′ē) *n., pl.* **jinn** [< Ar.] *Moslem Legend* a supernatural being that can take human or animal form and either help or harm people

jin·rik·i·sha (jin rik′shô, -shä) *n.* [< Jap. < *jin*, a man + *riki*, power + *sha*, carriage] a small, two-wheeled carriage with a hood, pulled by one or two men, esp. formerly in the Orient: also sp. **jin·rick′sha, jin·rik′sha**

☆**jinx** (jiŋks) *n.* [< L. *iynx* < Gr. *iynx*, the wryneck (bird used in black magic)] [Colloq.] **1.** a person or thing supposed to bring bad luck **2.** a spell of bad luck —*vt.* [Colloq.] to bring bad luck to

☆**jit·ney** (jit′nē) *n., pl.* **-neys** [< ? Fr. *jeton*, a token] **1.** [Old Slang] a five-cent coin; nickel **2.** a small bus or car that carries passengers for a low fare, originally five cents

☆**jit·ter** (jit′ər) *vi.* [? echoic] [Colloq.] to be nervous; have the jitters; fidget —**the jitters** [Colloq.] a very uneasy, nervous feeling; the fidgets —**jit′ter·y** *adj.*

☆**jit·ter·bug** (-bug′) *n.* [JITTER + BUG] **1.** a dance for couples, esp. in the early 1940's, involving fast, acrobatic movements to swing music **2.** a dancer of the jitterbug —*vi.* **-bugged′, -bug′ging** to dance the jitterbug

jiu·jit·su, jiu·jut·su (jōō jit′sōō) *n. var. of* JUJUTSU

☆**jive** (jīv) *vt.* **jived, jiv′ing** [altered < JIBE[2]] [Slang] to speak in a way that is exaggerated, insincere, flippant, etc., esp. in trying to fool or mislead —*n.* **1.** [Slang] talk used in jiving someone **2.** *former term* (c. 1930–45) *for* JAZZ *or* SWING

Jl. July

jo (jō) *n., pl.* **joes** [var. of JOY] [Scot.] a sweetheart

Joan (jōn, jō′ən) [var. of JOANNA] a feminine name

Jo·an·na (jō an′ə) [ML., fem. of *Johannes*: see JOHN] a feminine name: var. *Joanne, Johanna*

Joan of Arc (ärk) Saint (Fr. name *Jeanne d'Arc*) 1412–31; Fr. heroine who led the troops that defeated the English at Orléans (1429): burned at the stake for witchcraft: called the *Maid of Orléans*

Job (jōb) *Bible* **1.** a man who endured much suffering but did not lose his faith in God **2.** the book telling of him

job (jäb) *n.* [< ?] **1.** a specific piece of work, as in one's trade, or done by agreement for pay [we let Brown have the *job* of painting the house] **2.** something that one must do; task; chore; duty [it is my *job* to do the shopping] **3.** the thing or material being worked on or the resulting product [the lamp Sue made is a fine *job*] ☆**4.** a position of employment; work [to look for a new *job*] **5.** [Colloq.] a criminal act or deed, as a theft, etc. **6.** [Colloq.] any happening, affair, matter, object, etc. —*adj.* hired or done by the job or piece [*job* work] —*vi.* **jobbed, job′bing 1.** to do odd jobs **2.** to act as a jobber or broker **3.** [Chiefly Brit.] to engage in jobbery —*vt.* **1.** to buy and sell (goods) as a wholesaler; handle as middleman **2.** to let or sublet (work, contracts, etc.) —see SYN. at POSITION —**odd jobs** miscellaneous pieces of work —**on the job 1.** while working at one's job [learning *on the job*] **2.** [Slang] attentive to one's task or duty —**job′less** *adj.*

job·ber (jäb′ər) *n.* **1.** a person who buys goods wholesale and sells to dealers; middleman **2.** a person who works by the job or who does piecework

job·ber·y (jäb′ər ē, -rē) *n.* [Chiefly Brit.] the carrying on of public business dishonestly for private gain

Job Corps a U.S. government program for training underprivileged youth so that they may be employed

☆**job·hold·er** (jäb′hōl′dər) *n.* a person who has a steady job; specif., a government employee

job·less (-lis) *adj.* **1.** without a job; unemployed **2.** having to do with the unemployed —**the jobless** those who are unemployed —**job′less·ness** *n.*

job lot 1. a group of different sorts of goods for sale as one quantity **2.** any collection of things, esp. when of little worth

Jo·cas·ta (jō kas′tə) *Gr. Myth.* the queen who unknowingly married her own son, Oedipus

jock (jäk) *n. shortened form of:* **1.** JOCKEY **2.** JOCKSTRAP; esp., an athlete

jock·ey (jäk′ē) *n., pl.* **-eys** [< Scot. dim. of JACK] **1.** a person whose work is riding horses in races ☆**2.** [Slang] the operator of a specified vehicle, machine, etc. —*vt., vi.* **-eyed, -ey·ing 1.** to ride (a horse) in a race **2.** to cheat; swindle **3.** to move or maneuver in a skillful way so as to get some advantage [to *jockey* for a promotion] ☆**4.** [Slang] to be the operator, pilot, etc. (of)

jock·strap (jäk′strap′) *n.* [*jock*, penis + STRAP] **1.** an elastic belt with a pouch to support the genitals, worn by men **2.** [Slang] an athlete

jo·cose (jō kōs', jə-) *adj.* [< L. < *jocus,* a JOKE] joking or playful; humorous —see SYN. at WITTY —**jo·cose'ly** *adv.* —**jo·cos'i·ty** (-käs'ə tē) *pl.* -**ties, jo·cose'ness** *n.*

joc·u·lar (jäk'yə lər) *adj.* [< L. dim. of *jocus,* a JOKE] **1.** joking; full of fun **2.** said as a joke —see SYN. at WITTY —**joc'u·lar'i·ty** (-lar'ə tē) *n., pl.* -**ties** —**joc'u·lar·ly** *adv.*

joc·und (jäk'ənd, jō'kənd) *adj.* [< OFr. < LL. < L. *jucundus,* pleasant < *juvare,* to help] friendly and happy; cheerful —**jo·cun·di·ty** (jō kun'də tē) *n., pl.* -**ties** —**joc'und·ly** *adv.*

jodh·pur (jäd'pər) *n.* [after *Jodhpur,* former state in India] **1.** [*pl.*] riding breeches made loose and full above the knees and tight from knees to ankles **2.** an ankle-high boot

Joe (jō) *a nickname for* JOSEPH —☆*n.* [Slang] **1.** [*often* **j-**] fellow; guy **2.** [**j-**] coffee

Jo·el (jō'əl) [< LL. < Gr. < Heb. *yō'ēl,* lit., the Lord is God] **1.** a masculine name **2.** *Bible a)* a Hebrew prophet, probably of the 5th cent. B.C. *b)* the book of his preachings

jog¹ (jäg) *vt.* **jogged, jog'ging** [ME. *joggen,* to spur] **1.** *a)* to give a little shake, shove, or jerk to [*jog* her to see if she's awake] *b)* to nudge **2.** to shake up or revive (a person's memory) **3.** to cause to jog —*vi.* to move along at a slow, steady, jolting pace or trot —*n.* **1.** a little shake or nudge **2.** a slow, steady, jolting motion or trot —**jog'ger** *n.*

jog² (jäg) *n.* [var. of JAG¹] **1.** a projecting or notched part, esp. one at right angles, in a surface or line **2.** a sharp, temporary change of direction, as in a road —*vi.* **jogged, jog'ging** to form or make a jog [*turn left where the road *jogs*]

jog·gle¹ (jäg''l) *vt., vi.* -**gled, -gling** [< JOG¹ + -LE²] to shake or jolt slightly —*n.* a slight jolt

jog·gle² (jäg''l) *n.* [< JOG²] **1.** a joint made between two surfaces by putting a notch in one surface and a projection in the other to fit into it **2.** the notch or projection —*vt.* -**gled, -gling** to join by joggles

Jo·han·nes·burg (jō han'is burg', yō hän'-) city in the Transvaal, South Africa: pop. 1,295,000

John (jän) [< OFr. < ML. *Johannes* < LL. < Gr. < Heb. contr. of *yehōhānān,* lit., Yahweh is gracious] **1.** a masculine name: dim. *Johnnie, Johnny* **2.** 1167?-1216; king of England (1199-1216): forced to sign the Magna Charta (1215) **3.** *Bible a)* a Christian apostle, credited with having written the fourth Gospel, the three Epistles of John, and Revelation: called *the Evangelist & the Divine b)* the fourth book of the New Testament *c) same as* JOHN THE BAPTIST **4. John XXIII** 1881–1963; Pope (1958–63)

john (jän) *n.* [Slang] a toilet

John Barleycorn *a name used for* corn liquor, malt liquor, etc.

John Bull *a name used for* England or an Englishman

John Doe *see* DOE

John Do·ry (dôr'ē) *pl.* **John Do'rys** [JOHN + *dory,* gilded, ult. < L. *de-,* thoroughly + *aurum,* gold] a saltwater fish with long spines on its back and a yellow-ringed black spot on each side of its flat body: it is caught for food

John Hancock ☆[Colloq.] one's signature: John Hancock's signature on the Declaration of Independence is bold and easy to read

John Henry the black hero in an American legend, who dies while proving that, with a sledgehammer, he can work faster than a steam drill

☆**john·ny·cake** (jän'ē kāk') *n.* [< Eng. dial. *jannock,* bread of oatmeal] corn bread baked on a griddle

☆**John·ny-jump-up** (-jump'up') *n.* **1.** *same as: a)* WILD PANSY *b*) DAFFODIL **2.** any of various American violets

John Paul I 1912–1978; Pope (1978)

John Paul II 1920– ; Pope (1978–)

John·son (jän's'n) **1. Andrew,** 1808–75; 17th president of the U.S. (1865–69) **2. Lyn·don Baines** (lin'dən bānz), 1908–73; 36th president of the U.S. (1963–69) **3. Samuel,** 1709–84; Eng. lexicographer & writer: known as *Dr. Johnson*

Johns·ton (jän'stən), **Joseph Eg·gles·ton** (eg''l stən) 1807–91; Confederate general

Johns·town (jänz'toun') [after *J. Johns,* local landowner] city in SW Pa.: site of a disastrous flood (1889): pop. 42,000

John the Baptist *Bible* the forerunner and baptizer of Jesus: Matt. 3

‡**joie de vi·vre** (zhwȧd vē'vr') [Fr.] joy of living

join (join) *vt.* [< OFr. *joindre* < L. *jungere:* for IE. base see YOKE] **1.** to bring together; connect; combine [we *joined* hands] **2.** to make into one; unite [*join* forces, *joined* in wedlock] **3.** to become a part or member of (a club, etc.) **4.** to go to and combine with [the path *joins* the highway] **5.** to enter into the company of; accompany [*join* us soon] **6.** [Colloq.] to adjoin —*vi.* **1.** to come together; meet **2.** to enter into association or become a member: often with *up* **3.** to participate (*in* a conversation, singing, etc.) —*n.* a place of joining, as a seam in a coat —**join battle** to start fighting

SYN. —**join** is the general term meaning a bringing or coming together of two or more things and may suggest direct contact, becoming a member of a group, etc.; **combine** implies a mingling together of things or a complete merging of distinct elements [to *combine* milk and water]; **unite** implies a joining or combining of things to form a single whole [the *United* States]; **connect** implies attachment by some fastening or relationship [roads *connected* by a bridge; the duties *connected* with a job]; **link** stresses firmness of a connection [*linked* together in a common cause]; **consolidate** implies a merger of distinct and separate units into a single whole for making something compact, strong, efficient, etc. [to *consolidate* one's debts] —ANT· **separate, part**

join·er (join'ər) *n.* **1.** a person or thing that joins **2.** a workman who finishes interior woodwork, as doors, molding, etc. ☆**3.** [Colloq.] a person who likes to join various organizations

join·er·y (-ər ē) *n.* **1.** the work or skill of a joiner **2.** any of various joints made in woodworking

joint (joint) *n.* [< OFr. < L. pp. of *jungere,* to JOIN] **1.** a place where, or way in which, two things or parts are joined [water leaked from the *joint* in the pipe] **2.** any of the parts that are connected by joints **3.** a large cut of meat with the bones still in it, as for a roast ☆**4.** [Slang] *a)* a cheap bar, restaurant, etc. *b)* any building, etc. ☆**5.** [Slang] a marijuana cigarette **6.** *Anat.* a place or part where two bones, etc. are joined, usually so that they can move [the elbow *joint*] **7.** *Bot.* a point where a branch or leaf grows out of the stem —*adj.* **1.** done or owned by two or more [a *joint* effort; *joint* property] **2.** sharing with someone else [a *joint* owner] —*vt.* **1.** to fasten together by a joint or joints [bamboo is *jointed*] **2.** to give a joint or joints to **3.** to cut (meat) into joints —**out of joint 1.** not in place at the joint; dislocated **2.** disordered or disorganized —**joint'ed** *adj.*

joint account a bank account in the name of two or more persons, each of whom may withdraw funds

joint·ly (joint'lē) *adv.* in common; together

☆**joint resolution** a resolution passed by a legislature with two houses: it becomes a law if signed by the chief executive or passed over his veto

joint return a single income tax return filed by a married couple, combining their incomes

joint-stock company (-stäk') a business firm owned by the stockholders in shares which each may sell or transfer independently

join·ture (join'chər) *n.* [< OFr. < L. < *jungere,* to JOIN] *Law* **1.** an arrangement by which a husband grants real property to his wife for her use after his death **2.** the property thus settled

joist (joist) *n.* [< OFr. *giste,* a bed; ult. < L. *jacere,* to lie] any of the parallel beams that hold up the planks of a floor or the laths of a ceiling —*vt.* to provide with joists

joke (jōk) *n.* [L. *jocus* < IE. base *jek-,* to speak] **1.** anything said or done to arouse laughter; a funny anecdote or amusing trick **2.** a thing done or said merely in fun **3.** a person or thing to be laughed at —*vi.* **joked, jok'ing 1.** to tell or play jokes **2.** to say or do something as a joke; jest —*vt.* to bring to a specified condition by joking —**no joke** a serious matter —**jok'ing·ly** *adv.*

jok·er (jō'kər) **1.** a person who jokes ☆**2.** a hidden provision put into a law, legal document, etc. to make it different from what it seems to be ☆**3.** any hidden, unsuspected difficulty ☆**4.** an extra playing card used in some games

Jo·li·et (jō'lē et', jō'lē et') [after L. *Joliet,* 17th-c. Fr.-Canad. explorer] city in NE Ill.: pop. 80,000

Jo·liot-Cu·rie (zhô' lyō kü rē') **1. (Jean) Fré·dé·ric** (frā dā rēk'), (born *Jean Frédéric Joliot*) 1900–58; Fr. nuclear physicist **2. I·rène** (ē ren'), (born *Irène Curie*) 1897–1956; Fr. nuclear physicist: wife of *Frédéric* & daughter of *Pierre & Marie CURIE*

JOISTS

---

fat, āpe, cär, ten, ēven, is, bīte; gō, hôrn, tōōl, look; oil, out; up, fur; get; joy; yet; chin; she; thin, then; zh, leisure; ŋ, ring; ə for *a* in *ago, e* in *agent, i* in *sanity, o* in *comply, u* in *focus*; ' as in *able* (ā'b'l); Fr. bâl; ë, Fr. coeur; ö, Fr. feu; Fr. mon; ô, Fr. coq; ü, Fr. duc; r, Fr. cri; H, G. ich; kh, G. doch; ‡foreign; ☆ Americanism; < derived from. See inside front cover.

jol·li·fy (jäl′ə fī′) *vt.*, *vi.* **-fied′**, **-fy′ing** [Colloq.] to make or be jolly or merry —**jol′li·fi·ca′tion** *n.*

jol·li·ty (-ə tē) *n.* a being jolly; fun; gaiety —see SYN. at MIRTH

jol·ly (jäl′ē) *adj.* **-li·er**, **-li·est** [< OFr. *joli*, joyful; prob. < ON. *jol*, YULE] **1.** full of high spirits and good humor **2.** [Colloq.] enjoyable; pleasant [*a jolly party*] —*adv.* [Brit. Colloq.] very; altogether —*vt.*, *vi.* **-lied**, **-ly·ing** [Colloq.] ☆**1.** to try to make (a person) feel good or agreeable by coaxing, flattering, etc. (often with *along*) **2.** to make fun of (someone) —**get one's jollies** [Slang] to have fun or pleasure —**jol′li·ly** *adv.* —**jol′li·ness** *n.*

jolly (boat) [< MDu. *jolle*, yawl] a ship's small boat

Jolly Roger a black flag of pirates, with white skull and crossbones

jolt (jōlt) *vt.* [earlier *jot*, to jog, orig. echoic: ? infl. by obs. *jowl*, to strike] **1.** to shake up or jar, as with a bumpy ride or sharp blow **2.** to shock or surprise —*vi.* to move along in a bumpy, jerky manner [the car *jolted* over the ruts in the road] —*n.* **1.** a sudden jerk, bump, etc., as from a blow **2.** a shock or surprise [the news gave us a *jolt*] —**jolt′er** *n.* —**jolt′ing·ly** *adv.* —**jolt′y** *adj.*

Jo·nah (jō′nə) [< LL. < Gr. < Heb. *yōnāh*, lit., a dove] **1.** a masculine name: var. *Jonas* **2.** *Bible a)* a Hebrew prophet: thrown overboard in a storm, he was swallowed by a big fish, but later was cast up on the shore unharmed *b)* the book telling Jonah's story Also, esp. in the Douay Bible, **Jo′nas** (-nəs) —*n.* any person said to bring bad luck by his presence

Jon·a·than (jän′ə thən) [< Heb. < *yehōnāthān*, lit., Yahweh has given] **1.** a masculine name: dim. *Jon* **2.** *Bible* Saul's oldest son, a close friend of David: I Sam. 18–20 —*n.* ☆a late fall variety of apple

Jones (jōnz) **1.** In·i·go (in′i gō′), 1573–1652; Eng. architect & stage designer **2.** John Paul, (born *John Paul*) 1747–92; Am. naval officer in the Revolutionary War, born in Scotland

jon·gleur (jäŋ′glər; *Fr.* zhōn glër′) *n.* [Fr. < OFr. *jogleor*, juggler: see JUGGLE] a wandering minstrel in medieval France and England

jon·quil (jäŋ′kwəl, jän′-) *n.* [< Fr. < Sp. dim. *junquillo* < L. *juncus*, a rush] **1.** a narcissus having relatively small yellow flowers and long, slender leaves **2.** its bulb or flower

Jon·son (jän′s'n), **Ben** 1572?–1637; Eng. dramatist & poet —**Jon·so′ni·an** (-sō′nē ən) *adj.*

Jor·dan (jôr′d'n) **1.** river in the Near East, flowing into the Dead Sea **2.** country in the Near East, east of Israel: 37,300 sq. mi.; pop. 2,418,000; cap. Amman —**Jor·da′ni·an** (-dā′nē ən) *adj.*, *n.*

Jordan almond [prob. < OFr. *jardin*, garden] a variety of large Spanish almond used in candies

Jo·seph (jō′zəf, -səf) [LL. < Gr. < Heb. *yōseph*, lit., may he add] **1.** a masculine name **2.** *Bible a)* Jacob's eleventh son, who was sold into slavery in Egypt by his jealous brothers but became a high official there: Gen. 37, 39–41 *b)* the husband of Mary, mother of Jesus: Matt. 1:18–25

Jo·se·phine (jō′zə fēn′, -sə-) [< Fr. fem. of JOSEPH] **1.** a feminine name: dim. *Jo, Josie* **2.** 1763–1814; wife of Napoleon (1796–1809) & empress of France (1804–09)

Jo·se·phus (jō sē′fəs), **(Flavius)** 37–95? A.D.; Jewish historian

☆**josh** (jäsh) *vt.*, *vi.* [< ?] [Colloq.] to make fun of in a good-humored way; tease jokingly; banter —**josh′er** *n.* —**josh′ing·ly** *adv.*

Josh·u·a (jäsh′ōō wə) [Heb. *yehōshū′a*, lit., help of Jehovah] **1.** a masculine name **2.** *Bible a)* Moses' successor, and leader of the Israelites into the Promised Land *b)* the book telling about him: also, in the Douay Bible, **Jos·u·e** (jäs′yōō wē′) Abbrev. **Josh**

☆**Joshua tree** [< ?] a tree of the southwestern U.S., related to the agave and having dagger-shaped leaves

joss (jäs) *n.* [PidE. < Port. *deos* < L. *deus*, a god] a figure of a Chinese god

joss house a Chinese temple

joss stick a thin stick of dried, fragrant wood dust, burned by the Chinese as incense

jos·tle (jäs′'l) *vt.*, *vi.* **-tled**, **-tling** [earlier *justle* < see JOUST & -LE²] **1.** to bump or push, as in a crowd; shove roughly **2.** to contend (*with* someone *for* something) —*n.* a jostling; rough bump or shove

JOSHUA TREE

jot (jät) *n.* [< L. < Gr. *iōta*, the letter *i*, the smallest letter] a trifling amount; the smallest bit [don't change it a *jot*] —*vt.* **jot′ted**, **jot′ting** to make a brief note of (usually with *down*) [he *jotted* down the address] —**jot′ter** *n.*

jo·ta (hō′tə) *n.* [Sp. < OSp. < *sotar*, to dance] a Spanish dance in 3/4 time performed by a man and woman to the rhythm of castanets

jot·ting (jät′iŋ) *n.* a short note jotted down

joule (jōōl, joul) *n.* [after J. P. *Joule*, 19th-c. Eng. physicist] *Physics* a unit of work or energy equal to 10,000,000 ergs

jounce (jouns) *n.*, *vt.*, *vi.* **jounced**, **jounc′ing** [< ?] shake, jolt, or bounce, as in riding —**jounc′y** *adj.*

jour·nal (jur′n'l) *n.* [< OFr., lit., daily < L. *diurnalis* < *dies*, day: see DEITY] **1.** a daily record of happenings, as a diary **2.** a written record of what happens at the meetings of a legislature, club, etc. **3.** a ship's logbook **4.** a newspaper, magazine, etc. **5.** *Bookkeeping* a book for recording every sale, purchase, payment, etc. as it occurs **6.** *Mech.* the part of a rotatory axle or shaft that turns in a bearing

journal box *Mech.* a housing for a journal

jour·nal·ese (jur′n'l ēz′) *n.* a style of writing typical of many newspapers, magazines, etc.; smooth and superficial style, with many clichés

jour·nal·ism (jur′n'l iz'm) *n.* **1.** the work of gathering, writing, and publishing or spreading news, as through newspapers, etc. or by radio and TV **2.** all newspapers and magazines as a group

jour·nal·ist (-ist) *n.* a person whose occupation is journalism; reporter, news editor, etc. —**jour′nal·is′tic** *adj.* —**jour′nal·is′ti·cal·ly** *adv.*

jour·ney (jur′nē) *n.*, *pl.* **-neys** [< OFr. *journee* < LL. < L. *diurnus*, daily: see JOURNAL] a traveling from one place to another; trip —*vi.* **-neyed**, **-ney·ing** to go on a trip; travel —see SYN. at TRIP

jour·ney·man (-mən) *n.*, *pl.* **-men** [ME. < *journee*, day's work + *man*] **1.** formerly, a worker qualified to work at his trade, after serving his apprenticeship **2.** now, a worker who has learned his trade **3.** an experienced craftsman who is competent but not exceptional

joust (joust, just, jōōst) *n.* [< OFr. < *juster* < L. *juxta*, beside] **1.** a combat with lances between two knights on horseback **2.** [*pl.*] a tournament —*vi.* to engage in a joust —**joust′er** *n.*

Jove (jōv) *same as* JUPITER —**by Jove!** an exclamation of surprise, emphasis, etc. —**Jo·vi·an** (jō′vē ən) *adj.*

jo·vi·al (jō′vē əl, -vyəl) *adj.* [Fr. < LL. *Jovialis*, of Jupiter < L. *Jovis*, Jove] full of hearty, playful good humor; genial and jolly —**jo′vi·al′i·ty** (-al′ə tē) *n.* —**jo′vi·al·ly** *adv.*

jowl¹ (joul, jōl) *n.* [< OE. *ceafl*, jaw] **1.** a jaw; esp., the lower jaw with the chin and cheeks **2.** the cheek **3.** the meat of a hog's cheek

jowl² (joul, jōl) *n.* [< OE. *ceole*, throat] [*often pl.*] the fleshy, hanging part under the lower jaw —**jowl′y** *adj.*

joy (joi) *n.* [< OFr. *joie* < LL. < L. *gaudium*, joy < L. base *gau-*, to rejoice] **1.** a very glad feeling; happiness; delight **2.** anything causing such feeling [this book is a *joy* to read] —*vi.* to be full of joy; rejoice —see SYN. at PLEASURE

Joyce (jois) [< L. fem. of *jocosus*, merry] **1.** a feminine name **2.** James (Augustine Aloysius), 1882–1941; Ir. novelist & poet —**Joyc·e·an** (jois′ē ən) *adj.*

joy·ful (joi′fəl) *adj.* feeling, expressing, or causing joy; glad —see SYN. at HAPPY —**joy′ful·ly** *adv.* —**joy′ful·ness** *n.*

joy·less (-lis) *adj.* without joy; unhappy; sad —**joy′less·ly** *adv.* —**joy′less·ness** *n.*

joy·ous (-əs) *adj.* full of joy; happy; gay; glad —see SYN. at HAPPY —**joy′ous·ly** *adv.* —**joy′ous·ness** *n.*

☆**joy ride** [Colloq.] an automobile ride merely for pleasure, often with reckless speed and, sometimes, in a stolen car —**joy rider** —**joy riding**

J.P. justice of the peace

Jr., jr. junior

Ju. June

Ju·an de Fu·ca Strait (hwän də fyōō′kə) strait between Vancouver Island and NW Washington

ju·bi·lant (jōō′b'l ənt) *adj.* [L. *jubilans*, prp. of *jubilare*: see JUBILATE] joyful and triumphant; elated —**ju′bi·lance** *n.* —**ju′bi·lant·ly** *adv.*

ju·bi·late (jōō′bə lāt′) *vi.* **-lat′ed**, **-lat′ing** [< L. pp. of *jubilare*, to shout for joy < *jubilum*, wild shout] to rejoice, as in triumph; exult

ju·bi·la·tion (jōō′bə lā′shən) *n.* **1.** a jubilating **2.** a happy celebration, as of victory

ju·bi·lee (jōō′bə lē′, jōō′bə lē′) *n.* [< OFr. < LL. < Gr. < Heb. *yōbēl*, a ram's horn (trumpet): infl. by L. *jubilum*, wild shout] **1.** *Jewish History* a celebration held every fifty years in which all bondmen were freed, mortgaged lands restored to the owners, etc.: Lev. 25:8–17 **2.** a 50th or 25th anniversary **3.** a time or occasion of rejoicing **4.** jubilation; rejoicing **5.** *R.C.Ch.* a year proclaimed as a solemn time for gaining a plenary indulgence

Ju·dah (jōō′də) [Heb. *yehūdhāh* < ?] **1.** a masculine name **2.** *Bible a)* the fourth son of Jacob *b)* the tribe descended from him **3.** the kingdom in the S part of ancient Palestine formed by the tribes of Judah and Benjamin

Ju·da·ic (jōō dā′ik) *adj.* of the Jews or Judaism; Jewish —**Ju·da′i·cal·ly** *adv.*

Ju·da·ism (jōō′də iz′m, -dē-) *n.* **1.** the Jewish religion, a religion based on a belief in one God and on the laws and teachings of the Holy Scripture and the Talmud **2.** observance of Jewish morality, traditions, etc. —**Ju′da·ist** *n.* —**Ju′da·is′tic** *adj.*

Ju·da·ize (-īz′) *vi., vt.* -ized′, -iz′ing to become or make Jewish in culture, traditions, etc. —**Ju′da·i·za′tion** *n.*

Ju·das (jōō′dəs) [var. of JUDAH] *Bible* **1.** Judas Iscariot, the disciple who betrayed Jesus **2.** *same as* JUDE (sense 1) —*n.* a traitor or betrayer

Judas tree a tree of the legume family, with clusters of rose-pink flowers

Jude (jōōd) *Bible* **1.** a Christian apostle: also called *Judas* (not Iscariot) **2.** *a)* a book of the New Testament, the Epistle of Jude *b)* its author

Ju·de·a (jōō dē′ə) ancient region of S Palestine: it corresponded roughly to the Biblical Judah: also sp. **Ju·dae′a** —**Ju·de′an** *adj., n.*

Ju·de·o- (jōō dē′ō, -dā′-) *a* combining form meaning: **1.** Judaic; Jewish **2.** Jewish and [*Judeo*-Christian]

Judg. Judges

judge (juj) *n.* [< OFr. < L. *judex* < *jus*, law + *dicere*, to say (see JURY[1] & DICTION)] **1.** a public official with authority to hear and decide cases in a court of law **2.** a person designated to determine the winner in a contest, settle a controversy, etc. **3.** a person qualified to decide on the relative worth of anything [a good *judge* of music] **4.** any of the governing leaders of the ancient Israelites before the time of the kings —*vt., vi.* **judged, judg′ing 1.** to hear and pass judgment (*on*) in a court of law **2.** to determine the winner of (a contest) or settle (a controversy) **3.** to form an opinion about (something) [don't *judge* by first impressions] **4.** to criticize or blame [I ask you not to *judge* me too harshly] **5.** to think or suppose [how tall do you *judge* him to be?] **6.** *Jewish History* to govern —see SYN. at INFER —**judg′er** *n.* —**judge′ship′** *n.*

judge advocate *pl.* **judge advocates** a military legal officer; esp., an officer acting as prosecutor at a court-martial

Judg·es (juj′iz) a book of the Bible telling the history of the Jews from the death of Joshua to the birth of Samuel

judg·ment (juj′mənt) *n.* **1.** a judging; deciding **2.** a legal decision; order or sentence given by a judge or law court [the *judgment* was in favor of the defendant] **3.** a debt resulting from a court order **4.** an opinion or estimate [in my *judgment*, he is a good doctor] **5.** criticism or blame [to pass *judgment* on someone] **6.** power of comparing and deciding; understanding; good sense [a man of clear *judgment*] **7.** [J-] *short for* LAST JUDGMENT Also sp. **judge′ment** —**judg·men′tal** (-men′t'l) *adj.*

Judgment Day *Theol.* the time of God's final judgment of all people; end of the world

ju·di·ca·ble (jōō′di kə b'l) *adj.* [< L. *judicare*: see JUDICATORY] **1.** that can be judged **2.** liable to be judged

ju·di·ca·to·ry (jōō′di kə tôr′ē) *adj.* [< LL. < L. pp. of *judicare*, to judge < *judex*, a JUDGE] having to do with giving out

justice; judging —*n., pl.* -ries **1.** a court of law; tribunal **2.** law courts as a group

ju·di·ca·ture (-chər) *n.* **1.** the giving out of justice **2.** the position, duties, or legal power of a judge **3.** the extent of legal power of a judge or court of law **4.** a court of law **5.** judges or courts of law as a group

ju·di·cial (jōō dish′əl) *adj.* [< OFr. < L. *judicialis* < *judex*, a JUDGE] **1.** of judges, law courts, or their duties **2.** allowed, enforced, or set by order of a judge or law court **3.** like or befitting a judge **4.** careful in forming opinions or making decisions; fair; unbiased [a *judicial* mind] —**ju·di′cial·ly** *adv.*

ju·di·ci·ar·y (jōō dish′ē er′ē, -dish′ər ē) *adj.* of judges, law courts, or their duties —*n., pl.* -ar′ies **1.** the part of government that gives out justice **2.** a system of law courts **3.** judges as a group

ju·di·cious (-dish′əs) *adj.* [< Fr. < L. *judicium*, judgment < *judex*, a JUDGE] having, applying, or showing sound judgment; wise and careful —see SYN. at WISE[1] —**ju·di′cious·ly** *adv.* —**ju·di′cious·ness** *n.*

Ju·dith (jōō′dith) [LL. < Gr. < Heb. *yehūdhīth*, woman of Judah] **1.** a feminine name: dim. *Judy* **2.** *a)* a book of the Apocrypha and the Douay Bible *b)* the Jewish heroine told about in this book

ju·do (jōō′dō) *n.* [Jap. < *jū*, soft + *dō*, art] a form of jujitsu, esp. as a means of self-defense

jug (jug) *n.* [a pet form of JUDITH or JOAN] **1.** *a)* a container for liquids, with a small opening and a handle *b)* the contents of a jug **2.** [Slang] a jail —*vt.* **jugged, jug′ging 1.** to put into a jug **2.** to stew in a covered earthen-ware container **3.** [Slang] to jail

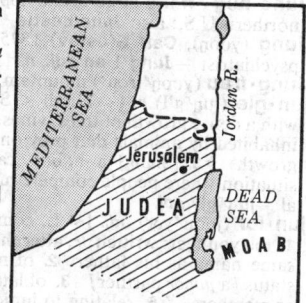

JUDO

ju·gate (jōō′gāt, -git) *adj.* [< L. pp. of *jugare*, to yoke < *jugum*, a YOKE] *Biol.* paired or connected

Jug·ger·naut (jug′ər nôt′) *n.* [< Hindi < Sans. < *jagat*, world + *nātha*, lord] **1.** an image of the Hindu god Vishnu: his worshipers supposedly threw themselves to be crushed under the wheels of a large car carrying his idol **2.** [*usually* j-] *a)* anything that demands and gets blind devotion *b)* any terrible force that cannot be resisted

jug·gle (jug′'l) *vt.* -gled, -gling [< OFr. *jogler* < L. *joculari*, to joke < *jocus*, a JOKE] **1.** to perform skillful tricks of sleight of hand with (balls, knives, etc.) **2.** to make awkward attempts to catch or hold (a ball, etc.) **3.** to use trickery on to deceive or cheat [to *juggle* figures to show a profit] —*vi.* to toss up a number of balls, knives, etc. and keep them continuously in the air —*n.* **1.** a juggling **2.** a clever trick or deception —**jug·gler** (jug′lər) *n.* —**jug′gler·y** *n., pl.* -gler·ies

Ju·go·sla·vi·a (yōō′gō slä′vē ə) *same as* YUGOSLAVIA —**Ju′go·slav′** *adj., n.* —**Ju′go·sla′vi·an** *adj., n.* —**Ju′go·slav′ic** *adj.*

jug·u·lar (jug′yoo lər, jōō′g′-) *adj.* [< LL. < L. *jugulum*, collarbone < *jugum*, a YOKE] **1.** of the neck or throat **2.** of a jugular vein —*n.* either of two large veins in the neck carrying blood back from the head to the heart: in full, **jugular vein**

juice (jōōs) *n.* [< OFr. < L. *jus*] **1.** the liquid part of a plant, fruit, or vegetable **2.** a liquid in or from animal tissue [gastric *juice*] **3.** [Colloq.] energy; vitality ☆**4.** [Slang] *a)* electricity *b)* gasoline, oil, or any liquid fuel ☆**5.** [Slang] alcoholic liquor —*vt.* **juiced, juic′ing** ☆to squeeze juice from —☆**juice up** to add power, vigor, excitement, etc. to —**juice′less** *adj.* —☆**juic′er** *n.*

juic·y (jōō′sē) *adj.* **juic′i·er, juic′i·est 1.** full of juice; succulent [a *juicy* plum] **2.** [Colloq.] full of interest; exciting [a *juicy* story] **3.** [Colloq.] highly profitable [a *juicy* investment] —**juic′i·ly** *adv.* —**juic′i·ness** *n.*

ju·jit·su (jōō jit′sōō) *n.* [< Jap. < *jū*, soft + *jutsu*, art] a Japanese system of wrestling in which the strength and weight of an opponent are used against him: also **ju·jut·su** (-jit′sōō, -jut′-)

ju·jube (jōō′jōōb; for 3, often jōō′jōō bē′) *n.* [Fr. < ML. < L. *zizyphum* < Gr. *zizyphon*] **1.** the edible, datelike fruit of a tree or shrub growing in warm climates **2.** this tree or shrub **3.** a piece of gelatinous, fruit-flavored candy

☆**juke·box** (jōōk′bäks′) *n.* [Gullah *juke*, wicked (as in *jukehouse*, house of prostitution), WAfr. orig.] a coin-operated electric phonograph: a record is chosen by pushing a button: also **juke box**

---

fat, āpe, cär; ten, ēven; is, bīte; gō, hôrn, tōōl, look; oil, out; up, fur; get; joy; yet; chin; she; thin, then; zh, leisure; ŋ, ring; ə for a in ago, e in agent, i in sanity, o in comply, u in focus; ′ as in able (ā′b'l); Fr. bal; ë, Fr. coeur; ö, Fr. feu; Fr. mon; ō̇, Fr. coq; ü, Fr. duc; r, Fr. cri; H, G. ich; kh, G. doch; ‡foreign; ☆ Americanism; < derived from. See inside front cover.

ju·lep (jōō′ləp) *n.* [< MFr. < Ar. < Per. < *gul,* rose + *āb,* water] ☆*same as* MINT JULEP

Jul·ia (jōōl′yə) [L., fem. of JULIUS] a feminine name: var. *Julie*

Jul·ian (jōōl′yən) [< L. < *Julius:* see JULIUS] 1. a masculine name 2. (L. name *Flavius Claudius Julianus*) 331-363 A.D.; Rom. general; emperor of Rome (361-363): called *Julian the Apostate* —*adj.* of Julius Caesar

Julian calendar the calendar introduced by Julius Caesar in 46 B.C., in which the ordinary year had 365 days and every fourth year was a leap year, with 366 days: replaced by the Gregorian calendar

ju·li·enne (jōō′lē en′; *Fr.* zhü lyen′) *n.* [Fr., origin obscure] a clear soup containing vegetables cut into strips or bits —*adj.* *Cooking* cut into strips: said of vegetables

Ju·li·et (jōōl′yət, -ē ət, jōō′lē et′) [< Fr. < L. *Julia*] 1. a feminine name 2. the heroine of Shakespeare's tragedy *Romeo and Juliet*

Jul·ius (jōōl′yəs) [L., name of a Roman gens] a masculine name

Julius Caesar *see* Julius CAESAR

Ju·ly (jōō lī′, jōō-, jə-) *n., pl.* **-lies′** [< Anglo-Fr. < L. < *mensis Julius,* the month of Julius (Caesar)] the seventh month of the year, having 31 days: abbrev. **Jul., Jl., Jy.**

jum·ble (jum′b'l) *vt.* **-bled, -bling** [? blend of JUMP + TUMBLE] 1. to mix in a confused, disorderly heap 2. to confuse mentally —*vi.* to be jumbled —*n.* 1. a confused mixture or heap 2. a muddle —see SYN. at CONFUSION

☆**jum·bo** (jum′bō) *n., pl.* **-bos** [< Gullah *jamba,* elephant; orig. Afr.; infl. by P. T. BARNUM's use of it for his elephant, *Jumbo*] a very large person, animal, or thing —*adj.* very large; larger than usual of its kind

Jum·na (jum′nə) river in N India, flowing from the Himalayas southwest into the Ganges

jump (jump) *vi.* [< ?] 1. to move oneself suddenly from the ground, etc. by using the leg muscles; leap; spring [to *jump* up and touch a branch] 2. to jerk; bob; bounce [the line *jumped* when the fish took the bait] 3. to leap from an aircraft, using a parachute 4. to act or react eagerly (often with *at*) [she *jumped* at the chance to go] 5. to pass suddenly from one thing or topic to another 6. to rise suddenly [prices have *jumped*] 7. [Slang] to be lively and animated [the party was *jumping*] 8. *Bridge* to make an unnecessarily high bid (**jump bid**) to increase the previous bid ☆9. *Checkers* to move a piece over an opponent's piece, thus capturing it —*vt.* 1. *a)* to leap over [he *jumped* the creek] *b)* to skip over 2. to cause to leap [to *jump* a horse over a fence] ☆3. to advance (a person) by bypassing others ☆4. to leap upon; spring aboard [to *jump* a moving train] 5. to cause (prices, etc.) to rise suddenly 6. [Colloq.] to attack suddenly 7. [Colloq.] to react to before the proper time, in anticipation [to *jump* a traffic light] ☆8. [Slang] to leave suddenly or without permission [to *jump* town] ☆9. *Checkers* to capture (an opponent's piece) —*n.* 1. a jumping; leap 2. a distance jumped [a *jump* of ten feet] 3. a descent from an aircraft by parachute 4. a thing to be jumped over 5. a sudden shift, as to another topic 6. a sudden rise, as in prices 7. a sudden, nervous start or jerk; twitch 8. *Athletics* a contest in jumping [the high *jump;* the long *jump*] ☆9. *Checkers* a move by which an opponent's piece is captured —☆**get** (or **have**) **the jump on** [Slang] to get (or have) an advantage over —☆**jump a claim** to seize mining rights or land claimed by someone else —☆**jump bail** to forfeit one's bail by running away —**jump on** (or **all over**) [Slang] to scold; criticize —☆**jump the track** to go suddenly off the rails —**on the jump** [Colloq.] very busy

jump·er¹ (jum′pər) *n.* 1. a person, animal, or thing that jumps 2. a short wire used to make a temporary electrical connection

jump·er² (jum′pər) *n.* [< dial. *jump,* short coat, prob. < Fr. *jupe* < Sp. < Ar. *jubbah,* undergarment] 1. a loose jacket or blouse, worn as to protect clothing or as part of a sailor's outfit 2. a sleeveless dress worn over a blouse or sweater ☆3. [*pl.*] rompers: see ROMPER (sense 2)

☆**jumping bean** the seed of a Mexican plant, which is made to jump or roll about by the movements of a moth larva inside it

jumping jack a child's toy consisting of a little jointed figure made to jump about by pulling a string

☆**jump·ing-off place** (jum′piŋ ôf′) 1. an inhabited place, as at the edge of a wilderness, beyond which few or no people live 2. starting point for a trip, venture, etc.

JUMPER

☆**jump shot** *Basketball* a shot made by a player while in the air during a jump

☆**jump suit** 1. a coverall worn by paratroops, garage mechanics, etc. 2. any one-piece garment like this

jump·y (jum′pē) *adj.* **jump′i·er, jump′i·est** 1. moving in jumps, jerks, etc. 2. easily startled; apprehensive —**jump′i·ly** *adv.* —**jump′i·ness** *n.*

Jun., jun. junior

Junc., junc. junction

jun·co (juŋ′kō) *n., pl.* **-cos** [< ModL. < Sp. < L. *juncus,* a rush] ☆a sparrowlike bird of North and Central America, with a gray or black head

junc·tion (juŋk′shən) *n.* [< L. < *jungere,* to YOKE] 1. a joining or being joined 2. a place or point of joining or crossing, as of highways or railroads 3. the region separating two kinds of semiconductor material —**junc′tion·al** *adj.*

junc·ture (-chər) *n.* [< L.: see prec.] 1. a joining or being joined 2. a point or line of joining or connection; joint 3. a point of time or a critical moment [at this *juncture,* we changed our plans] 4. *Linguis.* the transition marking the boundary between one speech sound and the next

June (jōōn) [< L. *Junius,* name of a Roman gens] a feminine name —*n.* [< OFr. < L. < *mensis Junius,* the month of JUNO] the sixth month of the year, having 30 days: abbrev. **Je., Ju., Jun.**

Ju·neau (jōō′nō) [after J. *Juneau,* a prospector] capital of Alas., on the SE coast: pop. 6,000

☆**June·ber·ry** (jōōn′ber′ē, -bər ē) *n., pl.* **-ries** 1. any of various N. American shrubs and trees of the rose family, with white flowers and purple-black fruits 2. the fruit

June bug ☆1. a large beetle appearing in May or June in the northern U.S.: also **June beetle** ☆2. *same as* FIGEATER

Jung (yoong), **Carl G(ustav)** 1875-1961; Swiss psychologist & psychiatrist —**Jung′i·an** *adj., n.*

Jung·frau (yoong′frou′) mountain in the Alps of S Switzerland

jun·gle (juŋ′g'l) *n.* [< Hindi < Sans. *jañgala,* desert] 1. land with a dense growth of trees, vines, etc., as in the tropics, usually inhabited by animals that prey on one another 2. any tangled growth ☆3. [Slang] a hobos' camp ☆4. [Slang] a place or situation where people compete ruthlessly or struggle for survival —**jun′gly** *adj.*

jun·ior (jōōn′yər) *adj.* [< L. compar. of *juvenis:* see JUVENILE] 1. the younger: written *Jr.* after the name of a son who bears the same name as his father 2. of more recent position or lower status [a *junior* partner] 3. of later date 4. made up of younger members ☆5. relating to juniors in a high school or college —*n.* 1. a younger person 2. a person of lower standing or rank ☆3. a student in the next-to-last year of a high school or college ☆4. a size of clothing for slight women and girls with high waistlines —**one's junior** a person younger than oneself

☆**junior college** a school offering courses two years beyond the high school level

☆**junior high school** a school intermediate between elementary school and senior high school: it usually includes the 7th, 8th, and 9th grades

☆**Junior League** any of the branches of an organization of young society women with leisure to do volunteer welfare work

☆**junior varsity** a team that represents a school, college, etc. on a level just below the varsity team in games or contests

ju·ni·per (jōō′nə pər) *n.* [L. *juniperus*] a small evergreen shrub or tree with scalelike leaves and berrylike cones

junk¹ (juŋk) *n.* [< ? Port. *junco,* a reed < L. *juncus*] 1. orig., rope used for making oakum, mats, etc. 2. old metal, paper, rags, etc. 3. [Colloq.] useless stuff; trash; rubbish ☆4. [Slang] a narcotic drug; esp., heroin —*vt.* ☆[Colloq.] to throw away or sell as junk; discard —**junk′y** *adj.*

junk² (juŋk) *n.* [Sp. & Port. *junco* < Jav. *joñ*] a Chinese flat-bottomed ship

Jun·ker (yoong′kər) *n.* [G. < MHG. < OHG. *jung,* young + *herro,* lord] a German of the militaristic, landowning class; Prussian aristocrat

☆**junk·er** (juŋ′kər) *n.* [< JUNK¹, *vt.*] [Slang] an old, shabby car or truck

junk·et (juŋ′kit) *n.* [ult. < L. *juncus,* a rush: orig. sold in reed baskets] 1. formerly, curds with cream 2. milk sweetened, flavored, and thickened into curd with rennet 3. a feast or picnic 4. a trip for pleasure ☆5. a trip by an official, paid for out of public funds —*vi.* to go on a jun-

JUNK

ket —**vt.** to entertain at a feast —☆**jun′ket·eer′** (-kə tir′),
☆**jun′ket·er** n.

☆**junk food** any snack food that is high in sugar and fats but low in other food values, such as protein

☆**junk·ie, junk·y** (juŋ′kē) n., pl. **junk′ies** [Slang] a narcotics addict, esp. one addicted to heroin

☆**junk mail** advertisements, requests for aid, etc. mailed to a large number of people on mailing lists

☆**junk·man** (juŋk′man′) n., pl. **-men′** (-men′) a dealer in old metal, paper, rags, etc.

☆**junk·yard** (-yärd′) n. a place where old metal, paper, etc. is kept and sold or old cars are junked

Ju·no (jōō′nō) [L.] Rom. Myth. wife of Jupiter; queen of the gods and goddess of marriage: identified with the Greek goddess Hera

Ju·no·esque (jōō′nō esk′) adj. dignified and majestic like Juno

jun·ta (hoon′tə, jun′-) n. [Sp. < L. pp. of jungere, JOIN] 1. a Spanish or Latin American legislature or council 2. a group of political plotters; also, a group of military men in power after a coup d'état: also **jun·to** (jun′tō), pl. **-tos**

Ju·pi·ter (jōō′pə tər) [L.] 1. the chief Roman god: identified with the Greek god Zeus 2. the largest planet of the solar system and the fifth in distance from the sun: diameter, c.88,000 mi.

Ju·ra Mountains (joor′ə) mountain range along the border of France & Switzerland

Ju·ras·sic (joo ras′ik) adj. [Fr. jurassique < Jura (Mountains)] designating or of the second period of the Mesozoic Era, immediately following the Triassic —**the Jurassic** the Jurassic Period or its rocks: see GEOLOGIC TIME CHART

ju·rid·i·cal (joo rid′i k'l) adj. [< L. < jus, law + dicere, to declare + -AL: see JUDGE] of judicial proceedings, or of law: also **ju·rid′ic** —**ju·rid′i·cal·ly** adv.

ju·ris·dic·tion (joor′is dik′shən) n. [< OFr. < L. < jus, law + dictio < dicere, to declare: see JUDGE] 1. the giving out of justice; authority to hear and decide cases [the juvenile court has jurisdiction over children] 2. authority or power in general 3. the limits or territory over which one's authority reaches [this area is outside the jurisdiction of the city police] —see SYN. at POWER —**ju′ris·dic′tion·al** adj. —**ju′ris·dic′tion·al·ly** adv.

ju·ris·pru·dence (-prōō′d'ns) n. [< L. < jus, law + prudentia, a foreseeing] 1. the science or philosophy of law 2. a certain branch of law [medical jurisprudence] —**ju′ris·pru·den′tial** (-den′shəl) adj. —**ju′ris·pru·den′tial·ly** adv.

ju·rist (joor′ist) n. [< MFr. < ML. < L. jus, law: see JURY¹] 1. an expert in law; writer on law 2. a judge

ju·ris·tic (joo ris′tik) adj. of jurists or jurisprudence; relating to law —**ju·ris′ti·cal·ly** adv.

ju·ror (joor′ər) n. 1. a member of a jury; juryman 2. a person taking an oath, as of allegiance

ju·ry¹ (joor′ē) n., pl. **-ries** [< OFr. < ML. < L. jurare, to swear < juris, genitive of jus, law < IE. base yewos, fixed rule]— 1. a group of people sworn to hear evidence in a law case, and to give a decision in accordance with their findings 2. a group selected to decide the winners in a contest

ju·ry² (joor′ē) adj. [< ?] for temporary use on a ship; makeshift [a jury mast]

ju·ry·man (joor′ē mən) n., pl. **-men** same as JUROR (sense 1)

ju·ry-rigged (joor′ē rigd′) adj. [see JURY²] rigged for temporary use on a ship

just¹ (just) adj. [< OFr. < L. justus, lawful < jus, law: see JURY¹] 1. right or fair [a just decision] 2. righteous; upright [a just man] 3. deserved; merited [just praise] 4. lawful 5. proper, fitting, etc. [a just balance of colors] 6. well-founded; reasonable [a just suspicion] 7. correct or true [a just account] 8. accurate; exact [a just measurement] —adv. 1. neither more nor less than; precisely; exactly [just one o'clock] 2. almost at the point of [just leaving] 3. no more than; only [just a taste] 4. by a very small amount; barely [just missed the train] 5. a very short time ago [just left the room] 6. immediately [just to my right] 7. [Colloq.] quite; really [feeling just fine] —see SYN. at FAIR and UPRIGHT —**just now** a moment ago —☆**just the same** [Colloq.] nevertheless —**just′ness** n.

just² (just) n., vi. same as JOUST

jus·tice (jus′tis) n. 1. a being righteous 2. fairness; impartiality [there is justice in her demand] 3. a being correct 4. sound reason; rightfulness [he valued the justice of my comments] 5. reward or penalty as deserved [the prisoner asked only for justice] 6. the use of authority to uphold what is right, just, or lawful 7. the giving out of law [a court of justice] 8. same as: a) JUDGE b) JUSTICE OF THE PEACE —**bring to justice** to cause (a wrongdoer) to be tried in court and duly punished —**do justice to** 1. to treat fitly or fairly 2. to enjoy properly [to do justice to a meal] —**do oneself justice** to do something in a manner worthy of one's abilities

jus·tice·ship (-ship′) n. the position, duties, or term of office of a justice

justice of the peace a local magistrate, authorized to decide law cases for minor offenses, and to commit persons to trial in a higher court, perform marriages, etc.

jus·ti·fi·a·ble (jus′tə fī′ə b'l, jus′tə fī′ə b'l) adj. that can be justified or defended as correct —**jus′ti·fi·a·bil′i·ty** n. —**jus′ti·fi′a·bly** adv.

jus·ti·fi·ca·tion (jus′tə fi kā′shən) n. 1. a justifying or being justified 2. a fact that justifies [can there be any justification for such behavior?]

justification by faith Theol. the act by which a sinner is freed through faith from the penalty of his sin and is accepted by God as righteous

jus·ti·fy (jus′tə fī′) vt. **-fied′, -fy′ing** [< OFr. < LL., ult. < L. justus, just + facere, to make] 1. to show to be just, right, or reasonable [her higher pay is justified by the extra work she does] 2. to free from blame or guilt 3. to supply good or lawful grounds or reasons for; warrant [can one justify such a decision?] 4. to space (type) to make the lines correct in length —vi. Law to show an adequate reason for something done —**jus′ti·fi′er** n.

Jus·tin·i·an I (jəs tin′ē ən) (L. name Flavius Ancius Justinianus) 483–565 A.D.; Byzantine emperor (527–565): known for the codification of Roman law (**Justinian code**): called **the Great**

jus·tle (jus′'l) vt., vi., n. same as JOSTLE

just·ly (just′lē) adv. 1. in a just manner [treating us all justly] 2. rightly [justly called our finest poet] 3. in a way that is deserved [justly rewarded]

jut (jut) vi., vt. **jut′ted, jut′ting** [prob. var. of JET¹] to stick out; project [a jutting cliff] —n. a part that juts

Jute (jōōt) n. a member of any of several early Germanic tribes in Jutland: Jutes settled in SE England in the 5th cent. A.D. —**Jut′ish** adj.

jute (jōōt) n. [Hindi jhuto < Sans. jūṭa, matted hair] 1. a strong fiber used for making burlap, sacks, rope, etc. 2. either of two East Indian plants yielding this fiber

Jut·land (jut′lənd) peninsula of N Europe, forming the mainland of Denmark

Ju·ve·nal (jōō′və n'l) (L. name Decimus Junius Juvenalis) 60?–140? A.D.; Rom. satirical poet

ju·ve·nes·cent (jōō′və nes′'nt) adj. [< L. prp. of juvenescere, to become young < juvenis: see JUVENILE] becoming young; growing youthful —**ju′ve·nes′cence** n.

ju·ve·nile (jōō′və n'l, -nīl′) adj. [< L. < juvenis, young: for IE. base see YOUNG] 1. a) young; youthful b) immature; childish 2. of, characteristic of, or suitable for children or young persons —n. 1. a young person; child or youth 2. an actor who plays youthful roles ☆3. a book for children 4. Biol. an immature animal or plant —see SYN. at YOUNG —**ju′ve·nil′i·ty** (-nil′ə tē) n.

☆**juvenile court** a law court for cases involving young persons under a specified age, usually 18 years

juvenile delinquency unlawful or antisocial behavior by minors of not more than a specified age, usually 18 —**juvenile delinquent**

ju·ve·nil·i·a (jou′və nil′ē ə, -nil′yə) n.pl. [L. < juvenilis, juvenile < juvenis: see JUVENILE] writings, paintings, etc. done in childhood or youth

jux·ta·pose (juk′stə pōz′) vt. **-posed′, -pos′ing** [< Fr. < juxta- (< L. juxta, near) + poser, POSE¹] to put side by side or close together —**jux′ta·po·si′tion** n.

Jy. July

Jyl·land (yül′län) Dan. name of JUTLAND

K

K, k (kā) *n., pl.* **K's, k's** **1.** the eleventh letter of the English alphabet **2.** the sound of *K* or *k*

K **1.** karat (carat) **2.** *Physics* Kelvin **3.** *Chess* king **4.** knit **5.** [ModL. *kalium*] *Chem.* potassium

K., k. **1.** *Elec.* capacity **2.** karat (carat) **3.** *Physics* Kelvin **4.** kilo **5.** knight

K2 (kā′tōō′) *same as* GODWIN AUSTEN

Kaa·ba (kä′bə, kä′ə bə) [Ar. *ka'bah,* lit., square building < *ka'b,* a cube] the sacred Moslem shrine at Mecca, toward which believers turn when praying: it contains a black stone supposedly given to Abraham by the angel Gabriel

kab·a·la, kab·ba·la (kab′ə lə, kə bä′lə) *n. same as* CABALA

ka·bob (kə bäb′) *n. same as* KEBAB

Ka·bu·ki (kä bōō′kē, kə-) [Jpn. < *kabu,* music and dancing + *ki,* spirit] [*also* k-] a formal kind of Japanese drama with pantomime, dance, and song, and with male actors in all roles

Ka·bul (kä′bool) capital of Afghanistan, in the NE part: pop. 456,000

kad·dish (käd′ish) *n.* [Aram. *qaddish,* holy] *Judaism* a hymn in praise of God, recited as part of the daily service or, in one form, as a prayer during mourning for someone who has died

ka·di (kä′dē, kä′-) *n. same as* CADI

☆**kaf·fee·klatsch** (kä′fä kläch′, kô′fē klach′) *n.* [G.] [*also* K-] an informal gathering, as of housewives during the day, to drink coffee and chat: also **kaffee klatsch**

Kaf·fir (kaf′ər) *n.* [Ar. *kāfir,* infidel < prp. of *kafara,* to be skeptical] **1.** a member of any of several Bantu-speaking tribes in South Africa **2.** [k-] *same as* KAFIR

kaf·fi·yeh (kä fē′yə) *n.* [< Ar.] a headdress of draped cotton cloth worn by Arabs

kaf·ir (kaf′ər) *n.* [Ar. *kāfir:* see KAFFIR] **1.** a grain sorghum grown in dry regions for grain and fodder: also **kafir corn** **2.** [K-] *same as* KAFFIR

Kaf·ka (käf′kə), **Franz** (fränts) 1883–1924; Austrian writer, born in Prague

kaf·tan (kaf′tən, käf tän′) *n. same as* CAFTAN

Ka·hoo·la·we (kä′hōō lä′wē) [Haw.] island of Hawaii, southwest of Maui

kai·ak (kī′ak) *n. same as* KAYAK

kai·ser (kī′zər) *n.* [Gmc. borrowing < L. *Caesar*] emperor: the title [K-] of the rulers of the Holy Roman Empire (962–1806), of Austria (1804–1918), and of Germany (1871–1918)

Ka·la·ha·ri (kä′lä hä′rē) desert plateau in S Africa, mostly in Botswana

Kal·a·ma·zoo (kal′ə mə zōō′) [< Fr. < Ojibwa < ?] city in SW Mich.: pop. 86,000

kale (kāl) *n.* [Scot. var. of COLE] a hardy cabbage with loose, spreading, curled leaves instead of the usual head

ka·lei·do·scope (kə lī′də skōp′) *n.* [< Gr. *kalos,* beautiful + *eidos,* form + -SCOPE] **1.** a small tube containing loose bits of colored glass, plastic, etc. reflected by mirrors so that patterns appear one after the other when the tube is rotated **2.** anything that constantly changes **—ka·lei·do·scop'ic** (-skäp′ik) *adj.* **—ka·lei·do·scop'i·cal·ly** *adv.*

kal·ends (kal′əndz) *n.pl. same as* CALENDS

Ka·le·va·la (kä′lə vä′lä) [Finn., lit., land of heroes] a Finnish epic poem

Ka·li (kä′lē) a Hindu goddess viewed both as destroying life and giving it

Ka·li·man·tan (kä′lē män′tän) S part of the island of Borneo, belonging to Indonesia

Ka·li·nin (kä lē′nin) city in W European R.S.F.S.R., on the Volga: pop. 345,000

☆**kal·mi·a** (kal′mē ə) [ModL., after P. *Kalm,* 18th-cent. Swed. botanist] any of various evergreen shrubs, as the mountain laurel, with flowers of white or rose

Kal·muck, Kal·muk (kal′muk) *n.* **1.** a member of a group of Mongol peoples living chiefly in the NE Caucasus and N Sinkiang **2.** their Altaic, western Mongolic language Also **Kal'myk** (-mik)

kal·so·mine (kal′sə mīn′, -min) *n., vt.* **-mined′, -min'ing** *same as* CALCIMINE

Ka·ma (kä′mə) river in European R.S.F.S.R., flowing from the Urals southwest into the Volga

Ka·ma·su·tra (kä′mə sōō′trə) [Sans. < *kāma,* love + *sūtra,* manual] an 8th-cent. Hindu love manual: also **Kama Sutra**

Kam·chat·ka (käm chät′kä; *E.* kam chat′kə) peninsula in NE Siberia, between the Sea of Okhotsk & the Bering Sea

ka·mi·ka·ze (kä′mi kä′zē) *n.* [Jap., lit., divine wind] an air attack in World War II in which a Japanese pilot dived his airplane loaded with explosives into a target; also, the airplane or pilot

Kam·pa·la (käm pä′lä) capital of Uganda: pop. 80,000

kam·pong (käm′pôŋ′) *n.* [Malay] a small Malay village

Kam·pu·che·a (kam′pōō chē′ə) country in the S Indochinese peninsula: 69,884 sq. mi.; pop. 6,701,000; cap. Phnom Penh

Ka·nak·a (kə nak′ə, kan′ə kə) *n.* [Haw., man] **1.** a Hawaiian **2.** a native of the South Sea Islands

Kan·din·sky (kan din′skē), **Was·si·ly** (vas′ə lē) 1866–1944; Russ. painter in Germany & France

kan·ga·roo (kaŋ′gə rōō′) *n., pl.* **-roos′, -roo′:** see PLURAL, II, D, 1 [said (by James COOK) to be native name] a leaping, plant-eating mammal native to Australia and neighboring islands, with short forelegs, strong, large hind legs, and a long, thick tail: the female has a pouch in front, in which she carries her young

☆**kangaroo court** [Colloq.] a court set up without legal authority that holds trials and punishes people in an unlawful way, as among frontiersmen or prison inmates

kangaroo rat ☆a small, jumping, mouselike rodent of desert regions in the southwestern U.S. and Mexico

KANGAROO
(to 5 ft. high)

Kan·pur (kän′poor) city in N India, on the Ganges: pop. 895,000

Kan·sas (kan′zəs) [Fr. < Siouan tribal name] **1.** Middle Western State of the U.S.: 82,264 sq. mi.; pop. 2,249,000; cap. Topeka: abbrev. **Kans., KS** **2.** river in NE Kans., flowing east into the Missouri **—Kan'san** *adj., n.*

Kansas City **1.** city in W Mo., on the Missouri River: pop. 507,000 **2.** city next to it in Kans., on the Missouri & Kansas rivers: pop. 168,000 (Both are in a single met. area, pop. 1,257,000)

Kant (kant; *G.* känt), **Immanuel** 1724–1804; Ger. philosopher **—Kant'i·an** *adj., n.*

ka·o·lin (kā′ə lin) *n.* [Fr. < Chin. *kao-ling,* name of hill where found] a fine white clay used in making porcelain and in medicine in the treatment of diarrhea

ka·on (kā′än) *n.* [*ka* (the letter K) + (MES)ON] any of four mesons having a mass about 970 times that of an electron

ka·pok (kā′päk) *n.* [Malay *kapoq*] the silky fibers around the seeds of a tropical tree: used for stuffing mattresses, sleeping bags, etc.

kap·pa (kap′ə) *n.* [Gr.] the tenth letter of the Greek alphabet (K, κ)

ka·put (kə pŏŏt′, -pŏŏt′) *adj.* [G. *kaputt*, ruined < Fr. *capot*, having lost all tricks at cards] [Slang] ruined, destroyed, etc.

Ka·ra·chi (kə rä′chē) seaport in Pakistan, on the Arabian Sea: pop. 3,060,000

Ka·ra·gan·da (kä′rə gän′də) city in EC Kazakh S.S.R.: pop. 505,000

Ka·ra·ko·ram (kä′rä kôr′əm, kar′ə-) NW range of the Himalayas, in India, near the Chinese border

kar·a·kul (kar′ə kəl) *n.* [< *Kara Kul*, lake in the south central U.S.S.R.] 1. a broad-tailed sheep of C Asia 2. *same as* BROADTAIL (sense 2)

kar·at (kar′ət) *n.* [var. of CARAT] one 24th part (of pure gold) [14-*karat* gold is 14 parts pure gold and 10 parts alloy]

ka·ra·te (kə rä′tē) *n.* [Jpn. < *kara*, empty + *te*, hand] a Japanese system of self-defense in which sharp, quick blows are delivered with the hands and feet

Ka·re·li·a (kə rēl′yə; *Russ.* kä rē′lē ä) division of the R.S.F.S.R., east of Finland —**Ka·re′li·an** *adj.*, *n.*

Kar·en (kar′ən) [Scand. var. of CATHERINE] a feminine name

Karl (kärl) [var. of CARL] a masculine name

Karl-Marx-Stadt (kärl′märks′-shtät′) city in S East Germany: pop. 295,000

Karls·ruh·e (kärls′rŏŏ ə; *E.* kärlz′rŏŏ ə) city in SW West Germany, on the Rhine: pop. 253,000

KARATE

kar·ma (kär′mə, kur′-) *n.* [Sans., a deed, fate] *Buddhism & Hinduism* all of a person's actions in one lifetime thought of as determining his fate in his next lifetime

Kar·nak (kär′nak) village in S Egypt, on the Nile: site of ancient Thebes

kart (kärt) *n.* [altered < CART] ☆1. any of various small vehicles ☆2. a small, flat, 4-wheeled, motorized vehicle for one person, used in racing (**karting**)

kar·y·o- [ModL. < Gr. *karyon*, a nut, kernel] *a combining form meaning:* 1. nut, kernel 2. *Biol.* the nucleus of a cell

kas·bah (käz′bä) *n. same as* CASBAH

Kash·mir (kash′mir) region in SE Asia, between Afghanistan & Tibet: part of Jammu & Kashmir: see JAMMU AND KASHMIR —**Kash·mir′i·an** *adj.*, *n.*

kash·rut, kash·ruth (käsh rŏŏt′, käsh′rŏŏt) *n.* the dietary regulations of Judaism: see KOSHER

Kas·sel (käs′əl) city in C West Germany: pop. 212,000

kat·a- *same as* CATA-: also, before a vowel, **kat-**

Kath·ar·ine, Kath·er·ine (kath′ər in, kath′rin) [see CATHERINE] a feminine name: dim. **Kate, Kay**

Kath·leen (kath′lēn, kath lēn′) [Ir. var. of CATHERINE] a feminine name

Kat·man·du (kät′män dŏŏ′) capital of Nepal, in the C part: pop. 195,000: also sp. **Kath′man·du′**

Ka·to·wi·ce (kä′tô vē′tse) city in S Poland: pop. 290,000

Kat·te·gat (kat′i gat′) strait between SW Sweden & E Jutland, Denmark

☆**ka·ty·did** (kāt′ē did′) *n.* [echoic of shrill sound made by the males] a large, green insect that lives in trees and looks like the grasshopper

Ka·u·a·i (kä′ŏŏ ä′ē, kou′ī′) [Haw.] island of Hawaii, northwest of Oahu

Kau·nas (kou′näs) city in SC Lithuanian S.S.R.: pop. 306,000

kau·ri (kou′rē) *n.* [Maori] 1. a tall pine tree of New Zealand 2. its wood 3. a resin (**kauri resin, kauri gum**) from this tree, used in varnishes, linoleum, etc.

Ka·wa·sa·ki (kä′wä sä′kē) city in C Honshu, Japan, between Tokyo & Yokohama: pop. 855,000

kay·ak (kī′ak) *n.* [Esk.] an Eskimo canoe made of skins completely covering a wooden frame except for an opening in the middle for the paddler

KAYAK

☆**kay·o** (kā′ō′) *vt.* **-oed′, -o′ing** [< KO] [Slang] *Boxing* to knock out —*n.* [Slang] *Boxing* a knockout

Ka·zakh Soviet Socialist Republic (kä zäk′) republic of the U.S.S.R., in W Asia: 1,048,000 sq. mi.; pop. 12,700,000: also **Ka·zakh·stan** (kä′zäk stän′)

Ka·zan (kä zän′; *Russ.* kå zän′y′) city in the western R.S.F.S.R., on the Volga: pop. 837,000

ka·zat·sky, ka·zat·ski (kə zät′skē) *n., pl.* **-skies** (-skēz) [Russ.] a vigorous Russian folk dance performed by a man who does a step in which, from a squatting position, he kicks out first one leg and then the other: also **ka·zat′ska** (-skä)

☆**ka·zoo** (kə zŏŏ′) *n.* [echoic] a toy musical instrument consisting of a small, open tube with a top hole covered by a membrane, as of paper, that vibrates to give a buzzing quality to tones hummed through the tube

kc, kc. kilocycle; kilocycles

K.C. 1. King's Counsel 2. Knight(s) of Columbus

kcal. kilocalorie; kilocalories

Kčs koruna; korunas

ke·a (kā′ə, kē′ə) *n.* [Maori] a large, green parrot of New Zealand, that sometimes kills sheep by tearing at their backs to eat the kidney fat

Keats (kēts), **John** 1795–1821; Eng. poet

ke·bab (kə bäb′) *n.* [Ar. *kabāb*] 1. [*often pl.*] a dish consisting of small pieces of marinated meat broiled or roasted on a skewer, often with alternating pieces of onion, tomato, etc. 2. a piece of such meat

Kech·ua (kech′wä) *n. same as* QUECHUA —**Kech′uan** *adj.*, *n.*

kedge (kej) *n., vi.* **kedged, kedg′ing** [ME. *caggen*, to fasten < ?] to move (a ship) by hauling on a rope fastened to an anchor dropped at some distance —*n.* a light anchor, esp. for such use: also **kedge anchor**

keel (kēl) *n.* [< ON. *kjolr*] 1. the chief timber or steel piece along the entire length of the bottom of a ship or boat 2. anything like a ship's keel in position, appearance, etc. —*vt., vi.* to turn over on its side so as to turn up the keel —☆**keel over** 1. to turn over; upset 2. to fall in a faint, etc. —**on an even keel** upright and level, steady, stable, etc.

keel·haul (kēl′hôl′) *vt.* 1. to haul (a person) under the keel of a ship as a punishment 2. to scold harshly

keel·son (kel′s'n, kēl′-) *n.* [prob. via Du. *kolsem* < Dan. < *kjøl*, KEEL + *sville*, sill] a set of timbers or metal plates fastened inside a ship's hull along the keel for added strength

keen¹ (kēn) *adj.* [OE. *cene*, wise: for IE. base see KNOW] 1. having a sharp edge or point [a *keen* knife] 2. sharp in force; piercing [a *keen* wind] 3. sharp and quick in seeing, hearing, thinking, etc.; acute [*keen* eyesight; a *keen* mind] 4. eager; enthusiastic [is he *keen* about going?] 5. strong or intense [*keen* desire; *keen* competition] ☆6. [Slang] good, fine, excellent, etc. —see SYN. at SHARP —**keen′ly** *adv.* —**keen′ness** *n.*

keen² (kēn) *n.* [< Ir. < *caoinim*, I wail] [Irish] a wailing for the dead; dirge —*vt., vi.* [Irish] to lament or wail for (the dead)

keep (kēp) *vt.* **kept, keep′ing** [< OE. *cepan*, to behold, lay hold of] 1. to observe with due ceremony; celebrate [*keep* the Sabbath] 2. to fulfill (a promise, etc.) 3. to follow (a routine, diet, etc.) 4. to go on maintaining [*keep* pace] 5. to protect; guard; defend [*keep* him from harm] 6. to watch over; take care of; tend [to *keep* house for someone] 7. to raise (livestock) 8. to maintain in good order or condition; preserve [to *keep* one's health] 9. to provide for; support [to *keep* a family] 10. to supply with food or lodging for pay [to *keep* boarders] 11. to have in one's service or for one's use [to *keep* servants] 12. to make regular entries in, detailing transactions, happenings, etc. [to *keep* books, a diary, etc.] 13. to carry on; conduct; manage [to *keep* a business] 14. to make stay in a specified condition, position, etc. [to *keep* an engine running] 15. to hold for future use or a long time [to *keep* extra cash in the house] 16. to have regularly in stock for sale 17. to hold in custody [he was *kept* a prisoner] 18. to prevent from leaving; detain **19.** to hold back; restrain [to *keep* someone from talking] **20.** to withhold [*keep* the news from her] **21.** to conceal (a secret) **22.** to continue to have or hold; not lose or give up [to *keep* one's self-respect] **23.** to stay in or at (a path, course, or place) —**vi. 1.** to stay in a specified condition, position, etc. **2.** to continue; go on; persevere (often with *on*) [to *keep* on talking] **3.** to hold oneself back; refrain [to *keep* from telling someone] **4.** to stay fresh; not spoil; last [how long will the milk *keep*?] **5.** to require no immediate attention [a task that will *keep*] —**n. 1.** orig., care, charge, or custody **2.** *a)* a donjon *b)* a fort; castle **3.** food and shelter; support; livelihood [to earn one's *keep*] —see **SYN.** at CELEBRATE —☆**for keeps** [Colloq.] **1.** with the winner keeping what he wins **2.** forever — **keep at** to continue doing; persist in —**keep to 1.** to stick to or abide by [he *kept* to the rules] **2.** to remain in [to *keep* to one's room] —**keep to oneself 1.** to avoid others **2.** to refrain from telling —**keep up 1.** to maintain in good condition **2.** to continue; go on **3.** to maintain the pace **4.** to remain informed about (with *on* or *with*)

keep·er (kēp'ər) *n.* a person or thing that keeps; specif., *a)* a guard, as of prisoners, animals, etc. *b)* a guardian or protector *c)* a caretaker ☆*d)* *Football* a play in which the quarterback takes the ball from the center and runs with it

keep·ing (-iŋ) *n.* **1.** observance (of a rule, holiday, etc.) **2.** care; charge **3.** maintenance or means of this; keep **4.** reservation for future use; preservation —**in keeping with** in agreement or accord with

keep·sake (-sāk') *n.* something kept, or to be kept, in memory of the giver; memento

Kee·wa·tin (kē wä'tin) district of Northwest Territories, Canada, on Hudson Bay

keg (keg) *n.* [< or akin to ON. *kaggi,* keg] **1.** a small barrel, usually one holding less than ten gallons **2.** a unit of weight for nails, equal to 100 lbs.

☆**keg·ler** (keg'lər) *n.* [G. < *kegel,* pin, as in ninepins] [Colloq.] a person who bowls; bowler

Kel·ler (kel'ər), **Helen Adams** 1880–1968; U.S. writer & lecturer: blind & deaf from infancy, she was taught to speak & read

Kel·ly (green) (kel'ē) [*also* **k-**] a bright, yellowish green

ke·loid (kē'loid) *n.* [< Fr. < Gr. *chēlē,* claw + *-oeidēs,* -OID] an excessive growth of scar tissue on the skin —**ke·loi'dal** *adj.*

kelp (kelp) *n.* [ME. *culp*] **1.** any of various large, coarse, brown seaweeds **2.** ashes of seaweed, from which iodine is obtained

kel·pie, kel·py (kel'pē) *n., pl.* **-pies** [Scot. < ? Gael. *calpa,* colt] *Gaelic Folklore* a water spirit, supposed to take the form of a horse and drown people

Kelt (kelt) *n.* same as CELT —**Kelt'ic** *adj., n.*

kel·ter (kel'tər) *n.* [Colloq.] same as KIL-TER

Kel·vin (kel'vin) *adj.* designating, of, or according to the Kelvin scale

Kelvin scale [after Baron *Kelvin,* 19th-c. Brit. physicist] *Physics* a scale of temperature measured in degrees Celsius from absolute zero (−273.15°C)

KELP

Ke·mal A·ta·turk (ke mäl' ät ə turk') 1881–1938; 1st president of Turkey (1923–38): also called **Mus·ta·fa Kemal** (mōōs'tä fä) & **Kemal Pasha**

Ke·me·ro·vo (kem'e rô vô) city in south central R.S.F.S.R.: pop. 385,000

Kem·pis (kem'pis), **Thomas à** (born *Thomas Hamerken* or *Hammerlein*) 1380?–1471; Ger. monk & scholar

ken (ken) *vt., vi.* **kenned, ken'ning** [OE. *cennan,* lit., to cause to know] [Scot.] to know (*of* or *about*) —*n.* range of knowledge; understanding [beyond one's *ken*]

ke·naf (kə naf') *n.* [Per.] **1.** a tropical Asiatic plant, widely grown for its jutelike fiber **2.** this fiber

Ken·ne·dy (ken'ə dē), **Cape** [after J. F. KENNEDY] *former name* (1963–73) *of* Cape CANAVERAL

Ken·ne·dy (ken'ə dē), **John Fitzgerald** 1917–63; 35th president of the U.S. (1961–63): assassinated

ken·nel (ken''l) *n.* [< OFr. *chenil* < L. *canis,* a DOG] **1.** a doghouse **2.** [*often pl.*] a place where dogs are bred or kept **3.** a pack of dogs —*vt.* **-neled** *or* **-nelled, -nel·ing** *or* **-nel·ling** to place or keep in a kennel —*vi.* to live or take shelter in a kennel

Ken·neth (ken'ith) [Scot. < Gael. *Caioneach,* lit., handsome] a masculine name: dim. *Ken*

☆**ke·no** (kē'nō) *n.* [< Fr. *quine,* five winning numbers < L.] a gambling game resembling lotto

Ke·no·sha (ki nō'shə) [< Fr. < Algonquian *kinōzhan,* lit., pickerel] city in SW Wis., on Lake Michigan: pop. 79,000

Kent (kent) county of SE England, on the English Channel: formerly an Anglo-Saxon kingdom

Ken·tuck·y (kən tuk'ē, ken-) [< Iroquoian, level land] eastern central State of the U.S.: 40,395 sq. mi.: pop. 3,219,000; cap. Frankfort: abbrev. **Ky., KY** —**Ken·tuck'i·an** *adj., n.*

☆**Kentucky Derby** an annual horse race run at Churchill Downs in Louisville, Kentucky

Ken·ya (ken'yə, kēn'-) country in EC Africa, on the Indian Ocean: a member of the Commonwealth: 224,960 sq. mi.; pop. 10,890,000; cap. Nairobi —**Ken'yan** *adj., n.*

kep·i (kep'ē, kā'pē) *n., pl.* **kep'is** [Fr. *képi* < G. dial. *käppi,* dim. of *kappe,* a CAP] a visored cap with a flat, round top, worn by French soldiers

Kep·ler (kep'lər), **Jo·hann** (yō'hän) 1571–1630; Ger. astronomer & mathematician

KEPI

kept (kept) *pt. & pp. of* KEEP —*adj.* maintained as a mistress [a *kept* woman]

ker·a·tin (ker'ət 'n) *n.* [< Gr. *keratos,* genitive of *keras,* horn + -IN¹] a tough, fibrous, insoluble protein forming the principal matter of hair, nails, horns, etc.

kerb (kurb) *n. Brit. sp. of* CURB (*n.* 4)

ker·chief (kur'chif) *n.* [< OFr. *covrechef* < *covrir,* to cover + *chef,* the head] **1.** a piece of cloth worn over the head or around the neck **2.** a handkerchief —**ker'chiefed** (-chift) *adj.*

kerf (kurf) *n.* [OE. *cyrf* < *ceorfan,* to CARVE] the cut made by a saw —*vt.* to make a kerf in

ker·mes (kur'mēz) *n.* [< Fr. < Ar. & Per. *qirmiz,* crimson] **1.** the dried bodies of certain Mediterranean insects, used to make a purple-red dye **2.** the dye

ker·mis, ker·mess (kur'mis) *n.* [< Du. < *kerk,* a church + *mis,* MASS] **1.** in the Netherlands, Belgium, etc., an outdoor fair or carnival ☆**2.** any similar fair or entertainment, usually for charity

kern (kurn) *n.* [Fr. *carne,* a hinge < OFr. < L. *cardo*] that part of the face of a letter of type which sticks out beyond the body

ker·nel (kur'n'l) *n.* [OE. *cyrnel,* dim. of *corn,* seed: see CORN¹] **1.** a grain or seed, as of corn, wheat, etc. **2.** the inner, softer part of a nut, fruit pit, etc. **3.** the central, most important part of something; essence —*vt.* **-neled** *or* **-nelled, -nel·ing** *or* **-nel·ling** to enclose as a kernel

☆**ker·o·sene** (ker'ə sēn', ker'ə sēn') *n.* [Gr. *kēros,* wax + -ENE] a thin oil distilled from petroleum or shale oil, used in lamps, stoves, etc.; coal oil: also, esp. in science and industry, sp. **kerosine**

ker·ri·a (ker'ē ə) *n.* [ModL., after Wm. *Kerr,* Brit. botanist (d. 1814)] a Chinese plant of the rose family, with bright yellow flowers

ker·sey (kur'zē) *n., pl.* **-seys** [< *Kersey,* village in England] a coarse, lightweight woolen cloth, usually ribbed and with a cotton warp

kes·trel (kes'trəl) *n.* [OFr. *cresserelle:* origin echoic] a small, brown-and-gray European falcon that can hover in the air against the wind

ketch (kech) *n.* [< ME. *cacchen,* to catch: orig. used of fishing vessels] a fore-and-aft rigged sailing vessel with a mainmast toward the bow and a relatively tall mizzenmast, forward of the rudderpost, toward the stern: distinguished from YAWL

ketch·up (kech'əp) *n.* [Malay *kēchap,* a fish sauce < Chin. *ketsiap*] a sauce for meat, fish, etc.; esp., a thick sauce (**tomato ketchup**) made of tomatoes flavored with onion, salt, sugar, and spice

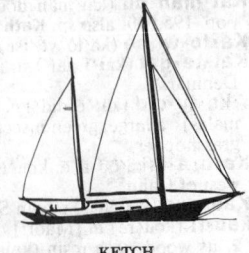

KETCH

ke·tone (kē'tōn) *n.* [G. *keton,* var. of Fr. *acétone:* see ACETONE] an organic chemical compound containing the bivalent radical CO in combination with two hydrocarbon radicals

ketone body any of three related compounds including acetone, found as waste products in the blood and urine of those suffering from starvation, diabetes mellitus, etc.

Ket·ter·ing (ket′ər iŋ) [after C. *Kettering*, 1876–1958, U.S. inventor] city in SW Ohio: suburb of Dayton: pop. 70,000

ket·tle (ket′'l) *n.* [ON. *ketill* < L. dim. of *catinus*, bowl] **1.** a metal container as for cooking things; pot **2.** a teakettle

ket·tle·drum (-drum′) *n.* a percussion instrument consisting of a hollow hemisphere of copper or brass and a parchment top that can be tightened or loosened to change the pitch; timpano

kettle of fish 1. a difficult situation **2.** a matter to be dealt with

kev, Kev (kev) *n., pl.* **kev, Kev** [K(ILO-)E(LECTRON-)V(OLTS)] a unit of energy equal to one thousand (10³) electron-volts

key[1] (kē) *n., pl.* **keys** [OE. *cæge*] **1.** an instrument, usually of metal, for moving the bolt of a lock and thus locking or unlocking something **2.** anything like this; specif., *a*) a device to turn a bolt, etc. [a skate *key*] *b*) a pin, bolt, etc. put into a

KETTLEDRUMS

hole or space to hold parts together *c*) any of the levers, or the disks, etc. connected to them, pressed down to operate a piano, clarinet, typewriter, etc. *d*) a device for opening or closing an electric circuit **3.** a place so located as to give control of a region [the mountain pass is the *key* to the whole valley] **4.** a thing that explains or solves something else, as a book of answers or a set of symbols for pronouncing words **5.** a controlling or essential person or thing [the steel industry is the *key* to our nation's economy] **6.** tone of voice; pitch **7.** tone of thought or expression [in a cheerful *key*] **8.** *Music* a system of notes forming a given scale whose lowest note is the keynote; tonality —*adj.* controlling; essential; important [a *key* person on the team] —*vt.* **keyed, key′ing 1.** to fasten or lock with a key **2.** to furnish with a key **3.** to set the tone or pitch of **4.** to bring into harmony —**key up** to make tense or excited

key[2] (kē) *n., pl.* **keys** [Sp. *cayo*] a reef or low island

Key (kē), **Francis Scott** 1779–1843; U.S. lawyer: wrote "The Star-Spangled Banner"

key·board (kē′bôrd′) *n.* **1.** the row or rows of keys of a piano, typewriter, linotype, etc. **2.** a musical instrument with a keyboard; esp., an electronic piano as used in rock or jazz —☆ *vt., vi.* to set (type) using a keyboard typesetting machine

keyed (kēd) *adj.* **1.** having keys, as some musical instruments **2.** reinforced with a key or keystone **3.** pitched in a specified key **4.** adjusted so as to be suitable

key·hole (kē′hōl′) *n.* **1.** an opening (in a lock) into which a key is inserted ☆ **2.** *Basketball* the free-throw lane, shaped like a keyhole

Keynes (kānz), **John May·nard** (mā′nərd), 1st Baron Keynes, 1883–1946; Eng. economist & writer —**Keynes′i·an** *adj.*

key·note (kē′nōt′) *n.* **1.** the lowest, basic note or tone of a musical scale, or key; tonic **2.** the basic idea or ruling principle, as of a speech, policy, etc. —☆ *vt.* **-not′ed, -not′ing 1.** to give the keynote of **2.** to give the keynote speech at —☆**key′not′er** *n.*

KEYHOLE

☆**keynote speech** (or **address**) a speech, as at a convention, setting forth the main line of policy

key punch a keyboard machine that records data by punching holes in cards that can then be fed into machines for sorting, accounting, etc.

key ring a metal ring for holding keys

key signature *Music* one or more sharps or flats placed after the clef on the staff to show what the key is

key·stone (-stōn′) *n.* **1.** the central, topmost stone of an arch **2.** a main or supporting part or principle

Key West westernmost island of a chain of small islands (**Florida Keys**) off the S tip of Fla.

kg, kg. 1. keg(s) **2.** kilogram(s)

Kha·cha·tu·ri·an (kach′ə toor′ē ən;

Russ. khä′chä too ryän′), **A·ram** (ar′əm; *Russ.* ä räm′) 1903?–1978; Russ. composer

kha·ki (kak′ē, kä′kē) *adj.* [< Hindi < Per. *khāk*, dust] **1.** dull yellowish-brown **2.** made of khaki (cloth) —*n., pl.* **-kis 1.** a dull yellowish brown **2.** strong, twilled cloth of this color, used esp. for uniforms **3.** [often *pl.*] a khaki uniform or pants

khan[1] (kän, kan) *n.* [< Turki *khān*, lord < Tatar] **1.** a title for the Turkish, Tatar, and Mongol rulers of Asia in the Middle Ages **2.** a title of honor in Iran, Afghanistan, etc. —**khan′ate** (-āt) *n.*

khan[2] (kän, kan) *n.* [Ar. *khān*] in Turkey and other Eastern countries, an inn or caravansary

Khar·kov (kär′kôf; *Russ.* khär′kôf) city in NE Ukrainian S.S.R.: pop. 1,223,000

Khar·toum (kär toom′) capital of Sudan, on the Nile: pop. 185,000 (met. area 490,000)

Khayyám, Omar *see* OMAR KHAYYÁM

khe·dive (kə dēv′) *n.* [< Fr. < Turk. < Per. *khidīw*, prince] the title of the Turkish viceroys of Egypt, from 1867 to 1914

Khí·os (khē′ôs) Gr. island in the Aegean, off the W coast of Turkey

Khrush·chev (kroos′chev, -chôf′; *Russ.* khroosh′chyôf), **Ni·ki·ta (Sergeyevich)** (ni kē′tä) 1894–1971; premier of the U.S.S.R. (1958–64)

Khu·fu (koo′foo) fl. c. 2650 B.C.; king of Egypt: builder of the Great Pyramid near Gîza

Khy·ber Pass (kī′bər) mountain pass in the Hindu Kush, between Afghanistan & Pakistan

kHz kilohertz

Ki. Kings

kib·ble (kib′'l) *vt.* **-bled, -bling** [< ?] to grind into coarse bits —*n.* kibbled food for dogs, etc.

kib·butz (ki boots′, -boots′) *n., pl.* **kib·but·zim** (kē′boo tsēm′) [ModHeb.] an Israeli collective settlement, esp. a collective farm

☆**kib·itz** (kib′its) *vi.* [Colloq.] to act as a kibitzer

☆**kib·itz·er** (-ər) *n.* [Yid. < colloq. G. *kiebitzen*, to look on < *kiebitz*, meddlesome onlooker] [Colloq.] **1.** an onlooker at a card game, etc., esp. one who volunteers advice **2.** a person who gives unwanted advice or meddles in others' affairs

ki·bosh (kī′bäsh) *n.* [< ? Yid.] [Slang] orig., nonsense —**put the kibosh on** [Slang] to squelch; veto

kick (kik) *vi.* [ME. *kiken* < ?] **1.** to strike out with the foot or feet **2.** to spring back suddenly, as a gun when fired; recoil **3.** [Colloq.] to object; complain **4.** *Football* to kick the ball —*vt.* **1.** to strike suddenly with the foot or feet **2.** to drive (a ball, etc.) in this way **3.** to make (one's way) by kicking **4.** to score (a goal or point in football) by kicking ☆ **5.** [Slang] *a*) to stop taking (a narcotic drug) *b*) to get rid of (a habit) —*n.* **1.** a blow with the foot **2.** a kicking ☆ **3.** [Colloq.] an objection; complaint **4.** [Colloq.] a stimulating effect, as of alcoholic liquor ☆ **5.** [Colloq.] [often *pl.*] pleasure; thrill **6.** *Football a*) a kicking of the ball *b*) the kicked ball *c*) the distance that a kicked ball travels —☆**kick around** (or **about**) [Colloq.] **1.** to treat roughly **2.** to move from place to place **3.** to lie about unnoticed **4.** to think about or discuss in an informal way —**kick back 1.** [Colloq.] to recoil suddenly and unexpectedly ☆ **2.** [Slang] to give back (part of one's pay, etc.) —☆**kick in** [Slang] to pay (one's share) —**kick off 1.** to put a football into play with a place kick ☆ **2.** to start (a campaign, etc.) ☆ **3.** [Slang] to die —**kick on** [Colloq.] **1.** to turn on (a switch, etc.) **2.** to begin operating —**kick out** [Colloq.] to get rid of; expel; dismiss —**kick over** to begin, or make begin, to operate, as an automobile engine —**kick up** [Colloq.] to cause (trouble, etc.) —☆**on a kick** [Slang] enthusiastic about a specified activity

☆**kick·back** (kik′bak′) *n.* **1.** [Colloq.] a sharp reaction **2.** [Slang] *a*) a giving back of part of one's pay, commission, etc., often because one is forced to or has agreed to b) the money returned

kick·ball (-bôl′) *n.* a children's game similar to baseball, but using a large ball that is kicked rather than batted

kick·er (-ər) *n.* **1.** one that kicks **2.** [Slang] *a)* a surprise ending *b)* a hidden difficulty

kick·off (-ôf′) *n.* ☆**1.** *Football* a place kick from the forty-yard line of the kicking team, that puts the ball into play at the beginning of each half or after a touchdown or field goal ☆**2.** a beginning of a campaign, drive, etc.

kick·shaw (kik′shô′) *n.* [< Fr. *quelque chose*, something] **1.** a fancy food or dish; delicacy **2.** a trinket; trifle; gewgaw Also **kick′shaws′** (-shôz′)

☆**kick·stand** (kik′stand′) *n.* a short metal bar fastened to a bicycle or motorcycle: when kicked down it holds the stationary cycle upright

kid (kid) *n.* [prob. < Anglo-N.] **1.** a young goat **2.** its flesh, used as food **3.** leather from the skin of young goats, used for gloves, shoes, etc. —*adj.* **1.** made of kidskin ☆**2.** [Colloq.] younger [my *kid* sister] —*vt.*, *vi.* **kid′ded, kid′ding** [Colloq.] to deceive, fool, or tease playfully —☆**no kidding!** [Colloq.] I can hardly believe it!: an exclamation of doubt or surprise —**kid′der** *n.* —**kid′like′, kid′dish** *adj.*

Kidd (kid), Captain (**William**) 1645?–1701; Brit. privateer & pirate, born in Scotland: hanged

kid·dy, kid·die (kid′ē) *n., pl.* **-dies** [dim. of KID] [Colloq.] a child

kid gloves soft, smooth gloves made of kidskin —☆**handle with kid gloves** [Colloq.] to treat with care, tact, etc.

kid·nap (-nap′) *vt.* **-naped′** or **-napped′, -nap′ing** or **-nap′ing** [KID + dial. *nap*, NAB] **1.** to steal (a child) **2.** to seize and hold (a person) against his will, by force or trickery, often in order to get a ransom —**kid′nap′er, kid′nap′per** *n.*

kid·ney (kid′nē) *n., pl.* **-neys** [ME. *kidenei* < ?] **1.** either of a pair of glandular organs in the body that take out water and waste products from the blood and pass them out as urine **2.** an animal kidney, used as food **3.** kind; sort [a man of the right *kidney* for the deed]

kidney bean **1.** the kidney-shaped seed of the common garden bean of the legume family, used as a vegetable **2.** the common garden bean plant

kidney stone a small stone of hard mineral formed in the kidney from phosphates, urates, etc.

kid·skin (kid′skin′) *n.* leather from the skin of young goats, used for gloves, shoes, etc.

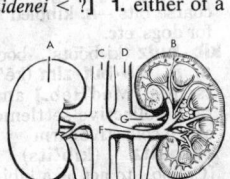

KIDNEYS
(A, right kidney; B, left kidney; C, vena cava; D, aorta; E, ureter; F, renal vein; G, renal artery; left kidney shown in cross section)

Kiel (kēl) seaport in N West Germany, on a canal (**Kiel Canal**) connecting the North Sea & the Baltic Sea: pop. 270,000

kiel·ba·sa (kēl bä′sə) *n., pl.* **-si** (-sē), **-sas** [Pol.] a smoked Polish sausage spiced with garlic

Kier·ke·gaard (kir′kə gärd′; *Dan.* kir′kə gôr), **Sø·ren** (**Aabye**) (sö′rən) 1813–55; Dan. philosopher & theologian

Ki·ev (kē′ef; *E.* kē ev′, kē′ev) capital of the Ukrainian S.S.R., on the Dnepr: pop. 1,632,000

Ki·ga·li (ki gä′lē) capital of Rwanda: pop. 7,000

kil. kilometer; kilometers

Kil·i·man·ja·ro (kil′ə män jä′rō) mountain in NE Tanzania, near the Kenya border: highest mountain in Africa: 19,340 ft.

kill[1] (kil) *vt.* [ME. *killen* < ? OE. *cwellan*] **1.** to cause the death of; make die **2.** *a)* to destroy the vital or active qualities of [spices *killed* its natural flavor] *b)* to destroy; put an end to [to *kill* one's hopes] **3.** to defeat or veto (legislation) **4.** to spend (time) on trivial matters ☆**5.** to stop (an engine, etc.), turn off (a light, etc.), or muffle (sound) ☆**6.** to prevent publication of (a newspaper story) **7.** to spoil the effect of: said of colors, etc. **8.** [Colloq.] to overcome with laughter, dismay, etc. **9.** [Colloq.] to make feel great pain or exhaustion **10.** [Slang] to drink

the last of or all of (a bottle of liquor, etc.) —*vi.* **1.** to destroy life **2.** to be killed [plants that *kill* easily] —*n.* **1.** an act of killing **2.** an animal or animals killed **3.** an enemy plane, ship, etc. destroyed —**in at the kill 1.** present when the hunted animal is killed **2.** present at the end of some action

☆**kill**[2] (kil) *n.* [< Du. < MDu. *kille*] a stream; channel; creek: used esp. in place names

☆**kill·deer** (kil′dir′) *n., pl.* **-deers′, -deer′:** see PLURAL, II, D, 1 [echoic of its cry] a small, N. American bird of the plover family, with a high, piercing cry: also **kill′dee′** (-dē′)

kill·er (kil′ər) *n.* **1.** a person, animal, or thing that kills, esp. habitually **2.** same as KILLER WHALE

killer whale any of several fierce, grayish to black, small whales that hunt in large packs and prey on large fish, seals, and other whales

KILLER WHALE
(to 25 ft. long)

☆**kil·li·fish** (kil′ē fish′) *n., pl.* **-fish′, -fish′es:** see FISH [< KILL² + -IE + FISH] any of several minnowlike freshwater fishes used in mosquito control and as bait: also **kil′lie** (-ē), *pl.* **-lies**

kill·ing (kil′iŋ) *adj.* **1.** causing death; deadly **2.** exhausting; fatiguing [to work at a *killing* pace] **3.** [Colloq.] very funny or comical —*n.* **1.** slaughter; murder **2.** [Colloq.] a sudden, great profit or success —**kill′ing·ly** *adv.*

kill·joy (-joi′) *n.* a person who destroys or lessens other people's enjoyment: also **kill′joy′**

kiln (kil, kiln) *n.* [< OE. *cylne* < L. *culina*, cookstove] a furnace or oven for drying, burning, or baking something, as bricks, pottery, or grain —*vt.* to dry, burn, or bake in a kiln

kiln-dry (kil′drī′, kiln′-) *vt.* **-dried′, -dry′ing** to dry in a kiln

ki·lo (kē′lō, kil′ō) *n., pl.* **-los** [Fr.] *short for:* **1.** KILOGRAM **2.** KILOMETER

kil·o- [Fr. < Gr. *chilioi*, thousand] *a combining form meaning* a thousand; the factor 10³ [*kilogram*]

kilo. 1. kilogram **2.** kilometer

kil·o·bar (kil′ə bär′) *n.* [see KILO- & BAR²] a metric unit of pressure equal to 1,000 bars

kil·o·cal·o·rie (kil′ə kal′ər ē) *n.* same as CALORIE (sense 2)

kil·o·cy·cle (-sī′k'l) *n.* former name for KILOHERTZ

kil·o·gram (-gram′) *n.* a unit of weight and mass, equal to 1,000 grams (2.2046 lb.): also, chiefly Brit., **kil′o·gramme′**

kil·o·gram-me·ter (-gram′mēt′ər) *n.* a unit of energy or work, being the amount needed to raise one kilogram one meter: it is equal to 7.2334 foot-pounds: also, chiefly Brit., **kil′o·gram′-me′tre**

kil·o·hertz (-hurts′) *n., pl.* **-hertz′** 1,000 hertz

kil·o·li·ter (-lēt′ər) *n.* a unit of capacity, equal to 1,000 liters, or one cubic meter (264.18 gal., or 1.308 cu. yd.): also, chiefly Brit., **kil′o·li′tre**

kil·o·me·ter (ki läm′ə tər, kil′ə mēt′ər) *n.* a unit of length or distance, equal to 1,000 meters (3,280.8 ft., or about 5/8 mi.): also, chiefly Brit., **kil′o·me′tre** —**kil·o·met·ric** (kil′ə met′rik) *adj.*

kil·o·ton (kil′ə tun′) *n.* the explosive force of 1,000 tons of TNT

kil·o·volt (-vōlt′) *n.* 1,000 volts

kil·o·watt (-wät′) *n.* a unit of electrical power, equal to 1,000 watts

kil·o·watt-hour (-our′) *n.* a unit of electrical energy or work, equal to that done by one kilowatt acting for one hour

kilt (kilt) *vt.* [ME. *kilten*, prob. < Scand.] **1.** [Scot.] to tuck up (a skirt, etc.) **2.** to pleat **3.** to provide a kilt for —*n.* a pleated skirt reaching to the knees; esp., the tartan skirt worn sometimes by men of the Scottish Highlands

kil·ter (kil′tər) *n.* [< ?] [Colloq.] good condition; working order: now chiefly in **out of kilter** [our TV is *out of kilter*]

Kim·ber·ley (kim′bər lē) city in N Cape of Good Hope province, South Africa: diamond-mining center: pop. 95,000

ki·mo·no (kə mō′nə, -nō) *n., pl.* **-nos** [Jpn.] **1.** a loose outer garment with short, wide sleeves and a sash, a traditional costume of Japanese men and women: see the illustration on the next page **2.** a woman's dressing gown like this

KILT

kin (kin) *n.* [< OE. *cynn:* for IE. base see GENUS] relatives; family; kindred —*adj.* related, as by blood — (near) of kin (closely) related

-kin (kin) [< MDu. *-ken, -kijn,* dim. suffix] a suffix meaning little [*lambkin*]

kind (kīnd) *n.* [< OE. *cynd:* for IE. base see GE-NUS] **1.** [Archaic] *a)* origin *b)* nature *c)* manner **2.** a natural group or division [a bird of the parrot *kind*] **3.** sort; class; variety [a choice of two *kinds* of soup] —*adj.* **1.** sympathetic, friendly, gentle, generous, etc. **2.** cordial [*kind* regards] —in kind **1.** in goods, services, etc. instead of money **2.** with something like that received; in the same way — kind of somewhat; rather [it's *kind* of cold here] —of a kind **1.** of the same kind; alike [the twins are two *of a kind*] **2.** mediocre or inferior [entertainment *of a kind*]

KIMONO

SYN.—kind implies the possession of sympathetic or generous qualities, either as a matter of habit or in a specific instance, or is applied to actions which show these qualities [he is *kind* only to his parents; your *kind* remarks]; kindly implies a nature or disposition usually marked by such qualities [his *kindly* old uncle]; benign suggests a mild or kindly nature and is applied especially to a gracious superior [a *benign* employer]; benevolent implies a charitable or unselfish concern for the welfare of others [his *benevolent* interest in orphans] See also SYN. at TYPE —ANT. un-kind, unfeeling, cruel

kin·der·gar·ten (kin'dər gär't'n) *n.* [G., lit., garden of children] a school or class of children, usually four to six years old, preparing them for first grade by games, music, simple handi-craft, etc. —kin'der·gart'ner, kin'der·gar'ten·er *n.*

kind·heart·ed (kīnd'här'tid) *adj.* having or resulting from a kind heart; sympathetic; kindly —kind'heart'ed·ly *adv.* — kind'heart'ed·ness *n.*

kin·dle (kin'd'l) *vt.* **-dled, -dling** [ME. *kindlen,* freq. < ON. *kynda*] **1.** to set on fire; ignite [to *kindle* logs in a fireplace] **2.** to start (a fire) **3.** to arouse or excite (interest, feelings, etc.) [insults *kindled* her anger] **4.** to make bright —*vi.* **1.** to catch fire **2.** to become excited **3.** to become bright [her eyes *kindled* with joy] —kin'dler *n.*

kin·dling (kin'dlin) *n.* bits of dry wood or other easily lighted material for starting a fire

kind·ly (kīnd'lē) *adj.* **-li·er, -li·est** **1.** kind; gracious; benign **2.** agreeable; pleasant [a *kindly* climate] —*adv.* **1.** in a kind, gracious, or pleasant way [please treat my cousins *kindly*] **2.** please [*kindly* reply] —see SYN. at KIND —take kindly to **1.** to be naturally attracted to **2.** to accept willingly —thank kindly to thank heartily —kind'li·ness *n.*

kind·ness (-nis) *n.* **1.** the state, quality, or habit of being kind **2.** a kind act or treatment

kin·dred (kin'drid) *n.* [< OE. *cynn,* KIN + *ræden,* condition] **1.** formerly, family relationship **2.** relatives or family; kin — *adj.* of like nature; similar [they are *kindred* spirits]

kine (kīn) *n.pl.* [ME. *kin* < *cou* (< OE. *cy,* pl. of *cu,* COW[1]) + *-(e)n*] [Archaic] cows; cattle

kin·e·mat·ics (kin'ə mat'iks) *n.pl.* [with sing. v.] [< Fr. < Gr. *kinēma,* motion < *kinein,* to move + -ICS] the branch of mechanics dealing with abstract motion, without reference to force or mass —kin'e·mat'ic, kin'e·mat'i·cal *adj.*

☆**kin·e·scope** (kin'ə skōp') *n.* [< Gr. < *kinein,* to move + -SCOPE] **1.** a cathode-ray tube used in television receivers, etc. for picture display **2.** a motion-picture record of a television program from a kinescope

ki·ne·sics (ki nē'siks, kī-) *n.pl.* [with sing. v.] [< Gr. *kinēsis,* motion + -ICS] the study of bodily movements, facial expressions, etc. as ways of making oneself understood without speaking, or along with speech —ki·ne'sic *adj.*

ki·ne·si·ol·o·gy (ki nē'sē äl'ə jē) *n.* [< Gr. *kinēsis,* motion + -LOGY] the study of human muscles and muscular movements, esp. as applied in physical education

kin·es·the·si·a (kin'is thē'zhə, -zhē ə) *n.* [ModL. < Gr. *ki-nein,* to move + *aisthēsis,* perception] the sensation of position, movement, or tension of parts of the body, as felt through nerve end organs in muscles, tendons, and joints —kin'es·thet'ic (-thet'ik) *adj.*

ki·net·ic (ki net'ik) *adj.* [Gr. *kinētikos < kinein,* to move] **1.** of or resulting from motion [*kinetic* energy] **2.** energetic or dynamic

kinetic art sculpture or assemblage involving the use of moving parts, sounds, shifting lights, etc.

ki·net·ics (-iks) *n.pl.* [with sing. v.] same as DYNAMICS (sense 1)

kin·folk (kin'fōk') *n.pl.* family; relatives; kin: also kin'folks'

king (kiŋ) *n.* [OE. *cyning*] **1.** the male ruler of a monarchy; male monarch: kings today usually have little power to rule **2.** *a)* an important or powerful man in some field [an oil *king*] *b)* something supreme in its class **3.** a playing card with a picture of a king on it **4.** *Checkers* a piece crowned upon reaching the opponent's base and hence movable backward and forward **5.** *Chess* the chief piece, movable one square in any direction: see CHECKMATE —*adj.* chief (in size, importance, etc.)

King (kiŋ), **Martin Luther, Jr.** 1929–68; U.S. clergyman & civil rights leader

king·bird (kiŋ'bʉrd') *n.* ☆any of several American flycatchers

king·bolt (-bōlt') *n.* a vertical bolt connecting the front axle of a wagon, etc., or the truck of a railroad car, with the body, to allow pivoting

☆**king crab** **1.** same as HORSESHOE CRAB **2.** any of various very large crabs

king·dom (-dəm) *n.* [OE. *cyningdom:* see KING & -DOM] **1.** a government or country headed by a king or queen; monarchy **2.** a realm; domain [the *kingdom* of poetry] **3.** any of the three great divisions of things in nature (the animal, vegetable, and mineral kingdoms)

king·fish (-fish') *n.* **1.** *pl.* **-fish', -fish'es:** see FISH any of various large food fishes of the Atlantic or Pacific coast ☆**2.** [Colloq.] a person holding absolute power in some group or place

king·fish·er (-fish'ər) *n.* a bright-colored bird with a large, crested head, a large, strong beak, and a short tail

King James Version same as AUTHOR-IZED VERSION

King Lear (lir) **1.** a tragedy by Shake-speare **2.** its main character, a legendary British king

king·let (kiŋ'lit) *n.* **1.** an unimportant king **2.** any of several small songbirds with a bright-colored crown

king·ly (kiŋ'lē) *adj.* **-li·er, -li·est** of, like, or fit for a king; royal; regal; noble — *adv.* [Archaic] in the manner of a king — king'li·ness *n.*

king·pin (-pin') *n.* **1.** same as KINGBOLT **2.** the headpin or center pin in bowling, etc. ☆**3.** [Colloq.] the main or essential person or thing

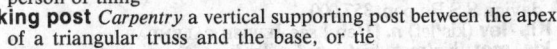
KINGFISHER
(to 18 in. long)

king post *Carpentry* a vertical supporting post between the apex of a triangular truss and the base, or tie beam

Kings (kiŋz) **1.** either of two books of the Bible (I Kings, II Kings) about the reigns of the Jewish kings after David **2.** any of four books of the Douay Bible including I & II Samuel and I & II Kings

☆**king salmon** same as CHINOOK SALMON

Kings Canyon National Park national park in EC Calif., in the Sierra Nevada mountains

KING POST

king's (or **queen's**) **English,** the standard English usage in speech and writing, esp. in England

king·ship (kiŋ'ship') *n.* **1.** the position, rank, or dignity of a king **2.** the rule of a king

☆**king-size** (-sīz') *adj.* [Colloq.] larger than the regular kind [a *king-size* bed]: also king'-sized'

☆**king snake** any of several large, harmless snakes of C and S North America: they eat mice, rats, lizards, and other snakes

Kings·ton (kiŋz'tən, kiŋz'stən) **1.** seaport & capital of Jamai-ca: pop. 123,000 (met. area 422,000) **2.** port in SE Ontario, Canada: pop. 59,000

kink (kiŋk) *n.* [< Scand.] **1.** a short twist, curl, or bend in a rope, hair, etc. **2.** a painful cramp, as in the neck ☆**3.** a queer notion; eccentricity; quirk **4.** a difficulty or defect, as in a plan —*vi., vt.* to form or cause to form a kink

kin·ka·jou (kiŋ'kə jōō') *n.* [Fr., *quincajou,* a misapplication of AmInd. name, whence CARCAJOU] a raccoonlike mammal of

Central and South America, with yellowish-brown fur, large eyes, and a long tail: it lives in trees and moves about at night

kink·y (kiŋ′kē) *adj.* **kink′i·er, kink′i·est** ☆**1.** full of kinks; tightly curled [*kinky* hair] **2.** [Slang] weird, bizarre, eccentric, etc. —**kink′i·ness** *n.*

kins·folk (kinz′fōk′) *n.pl. var. of* KINFOLK

Kin·sha·sa (kēn shä′sä) capital of Zaire, in the W part: pop. 1,226,000

kin·ship (kin′ship′) *n.* **1.** family relationship **2.** relationship; close connection

kins·man (kinz′mən) *n., pl.* **-men** a relative; esp., a male relative —**kins′wom′an** (-woom′ən) *n.fem., pl.* **-wom′en** (-wim′ən)

ki·osk (kē′äsk, kē äsk′) *n.* [< Fr. < Turk. < Per. *kushk,* palace] **1.** in Turkey and Persia, a summerhouse or pavilion open on all or most sides **2.** a somewhat similar small structure open at one or more sides, used as a newsstand, bandstand, etc.

kip[1] (kip) *n.* [prob. < Du.] the untanned hide of a calf, lamb, or other young or small animal

kip[2] (kip) *n., pl.* **kips, kip** [Thai] *see* MONETARY UNITS, table (Laos)

kip[3] (kip) *n.* [KI(LO) + P(OUND)[1]] a unit of weight equal to 1,000 pounds

Kip·ling (kip′liŋ), **(Joseph) Rud·yard** (rud′yərd) 1865–1936; Eng. writer, born in India

kip·per (kip′ər) *vt.* [< ? the *n.*] to cure (herring, salmon, etc.) by cleaning, salting, and drying or smoking —*n.* [OE. cypera] **1.** a male salmon or sea trout during or shortly after the spawning season **2.** a kippered herring, salmon, etc.

Kir·ghiz (kir gēz′) *n.* **1.** *pl.* **-ghiz′, -ghiz′es** a member of a Mongolian people of SC Asia **2.** their Turkic language

Kirghiz Soviet Socialist Republic republic of the U.S.S.R., in SC Asia: 76,460 sq. mi.; pop. 2,800,000; cap. Frunze: also **Kir·ghi′zia** (-gē′zhə, -zhē ə) —**Kir·ghi′zian** *adj., n.*

Kir·i·bati (kir′ə bas′) country on three groups of atolls in the WC Pacific: a member of the Commonwealth: 264 sq. mi.; pop. 52,000

kirk (kurk; *Scot.* kirk) *n.* [ME. *kirke* < OE. *cirice,* CHURCH] [Scot. & North Eng.] a church

kir·mess (kur′mis) *n. var. of* KERMIS

kir·tle (kur′t'l) *n.* [OE. *cyrtel,* ult. < L. *curtus,* short + *-el,* dim. suffix] [Archaic] **1.** a man's tunic or coat **2.** a woman's dress or skirt

Ki·shi·nev (ki shi nyôf′; E. kish′i nef′) capital of the Moldavian S.S.R.; pop. 357,000

Kis·lev (kis′lef) *n.* [Heb.] *see* JEWISH CALENDAR

kis·met (kiz′met, kis′-) *n.* [< Turk. < Ar. *qismah,* a portion, fate] fate; destiny

kiss (kis) *vt.* [OE. *cyssan*] **1.** to touch or caress with the lips in affection, greeting, etc. **2.** to touch lightly —*vi.* to kiss each other —*n.* **1.** a kissing **2.** any of various candies —**kiss good-bye 1.** to kiss in leaving ☆**2.** [Colloq.] to give up all hope of gaining or regaining —**kiss′a·ble** *adj.*

kiss·er (kis′ər) *n.* **1.** a person who kisses **2.** [Slang] *a)* the mouth or lips *b)* the face

☆**kiss of death** an action or quality, often one that seems helpful, which turns out to be harmful, destructive, or defeating

kit (kit) *n.* [prob. < MDu. *kitte,* a wooden tub] **1.** personal equipment, esp. as packed for travel **2.** *a)* a set of tools or implements *b)* equipment for some particular activity, sport, etc. [a first-aid *kit*] *c)* a set containing a number of parts to be put together [a model airplane *kit*] **3.** a container for such equipment, tools, etc. **4.** [Colloq.] lot; collection: now chiefly in ☆**the whole kit and caboodle,** everybody or everything

Ki·ta·kyu·shu (kē′tä kyoō′shoō) seaport on the N coast of Kyushu, Japan: pop. 1,042,000

kitch·en (kich′ən) *n.* [< OE. *cycene* < VL. < LL. *coquina* < L. *coquere,* to COOK] **1.** a room or place for preparing and cooking food; also, the equipment used **2.** the staff of a kitchen

Kitch·e·ner (kich′ə nər) city in SE Ontario, Canada: pop. 132,000

Kitch·e·ner (kich′ə nər), **Horatio Herbert,** 1st Earl, Kitchener of Khartoum, 1850–1916; Brit. military officer & statesman, born in Ireland

☆**kitch·en·ette, kitch·en·et** (kich′ə net′) *n.* a small, compact kitchen, as in some apartments

KIOSK

kitchen midden [transl. of Dan. *kökkenmödding*] a mound of shells, animal bones, etc. marking a prehistoric settlement

☆**kitchen police 1.** soldiers detailed to assist the cooks in an army kitchen **2.** this duty

kitch·en·ware (kich′ən wer′) *n.* utensils used in the kitchen

kite (kīt) *n.* [OE. *cyta*] **1.** a bird of the hawk family, with long, pointed wings and, usually, a forked tail **2.** a light wooden frame covered with paper or cloth, to be flown in the wind at the end of a string **3.** [*pl.*] the highest sails of a ship **4.** a bad check or the like used to raise money or maintain credit temporarily —*vi.* **kit′ed, kit′ing 1.** [Colloq.] *a)* to fly like a kite *b)* to move lightly and rapidly **2.** to get money or credit by using bad checks, etc. —*vt.* to issue (a bad check, etc.) as a kite

kith (kith) *n.* [OE. *cyth* < base of *cuth,* known: see UNCOUTH] friends or neighbors: now only in **kith and kin,** friends, acquaintances, and relatives; also, often, relatives, or kin

kitsch (kich) *n.* [G., gaudy trash < dial. *kitschen,* to smear] art, writing, etc. designed to appeal to popular tastes and pretending to have artistic value —**kitsch′y** *adj.*

kit·ten (kit′'n) *n.* [< OFr. var. of *chaton,* dim. of *chat,* cat] a young cat

kit·ten·ish (-ish) *adj.* like a kitten; playful; frisky; often, playfully coy —**kit′ten·ish·ly** *adv.* —**kit′ten·ish·ness** *n.*

kit·ti·wake (kit′i wāk′) *n., pl.* **-wakes′, -wake′:** see PLURAL, II, D, 1 [echoic of its cry] any of several sea gulls of the Arctic and North Atlantic

Kit·ty (kit′ē) [dim. of CATHERINE] a feminine name

kit·ty[1] (kit′ē) *n., pl.* **-ties 1.** a kitten **2.** *a pet name for* a cat

kit·ty[2] (kit′ē) *n., pl.* **-ties** [prob. < KIT] **1.** in poker, etc., *a)* the stakes or pot *b)* a pool from the winnings, to pay for refreshments, etc. **2.** any money pooled for some special use

kit·ty-cor·nered (kit′ē kôr′nərd) *adj., adv. same as* CATER-CORNERED: also **kit′ty-cor′ner**

Kitty Hawk [< AmInd.] village on an offshore island of N.C., near where the first controlled & sustained airplane flight was made by Orville & Wilbur Wright in 1903

☆**Ki·wa·nis** (kə wä′nis) *n.* [said to be < AmInd. *keewanis,* to make (oneself) known] an international service club of business and professional men —**Ki·wa′ni·an** (-nē ən) *adj., n.*

ki·wi (kē′wē) *n., pl.* **-wis** [Maori: echoic of its cry] a tailless New Zealand bird with undeveloped wings, hairlike feathers, and a long, slender bill

KJV, K.J.V. King James Version (of the Bible)

K.K.K., KKK Ku Klux Klan

kl, kl. kiloliter; kiloliters

Klan (klan) *n. short for* KU KLUX KLAN —**Klans′man** *n., pl.* **-men**

klatch, klatsch (kläch, klach) *n.* [G. *klatsch,* gossip] [Colloq.] an informal gathering, as to chat

☆**Klax·on** (klak′s'n) *a trademark for* a kind of electric horn with a loud, shrill sound —*n.* [**k**-] such a horn

Klee (klā), **Paul** 1879–1940; Swiss abstract painter

☆**Klee·nex** (klē′neks) *a trademark for* soft tissue paper used as a handkerchief, etc. [*occas.* **k**-] a piece of such paper

klep·to·ma·ni·a (klep′tə mā′nē ə) *n.* [ModL. < Gr. *kleptes,* thief + -MANIA] an abnormal, continuing impulse to steal, not caused by need —**klep′to·ma′ni·ac′** (-ak′) *n.*

☆**klieg light** (klēg) [after A. & J. *Kliegl,* 20th-c. U.S. inventors] a very bright, hot arc light used to light motion-picture sets: also sp. **kleig**

Klon·dike (klän′dīk) gold-mining region along a tributary **(Klondike River)** of the Yukon River, in W Yukon Territory, Canada

klys·tron (klīs′trən, klis′-; -trän) *n.* [< Gr. < *klyzein,* to wash + (ELEC)TRON] an electron tube used as an oscillator, amplifier, etc. in ultrahigh frequency circuits to modify the velocity of an electron stream

km, km. kilometer; kilometers

knack (nak) *n.* [ME. *knak,* sharp blow: prob. echoic] **1.** a clever way of doing something **2.** a special ability or skill [she has the *knack* of making friends] — see SYN. at TALENT

KLONDIKE

knack·wurst (näk′wurst′; *G.* knäk′voorsht′) *n.* [G.] a thick, highly seasoned sausage

knap·sack (nap′sak′) *n.* [Du. *knapzak* < *knappen*, to eat + *zak*, a sack] a leather or canvas bag or case worn on the back, as by soldiers or hikers, for carrying equipment or supplies

knave (nāv) *n.* [OE. *cnafa*, boy] **1.** [Archaic] *a)* a male servant *b)* a man of humble status **2.** a dishonest, deceitful person; rogue **3.** a jack (the playing card)

knav·er·y (nāv′ər ē) *n., pl.* **-er·ies** behavior or an act typical of a knave; rascality; dishonesty

knav·ish (-ish) *adj.* like a knave; esp., dishonest; tricky — **knav′ish·ly** *adv.* —**knav′ish·ness** *n.*

knead (nēd) *vt.* [OE. *cnedan* < IE. base *gen-*, to press together, from which also come KNOT & KNOB] **1.** to keep pressing and squeezing (dough, clay, etc.), usually with the hands, until it is easy to shape **2.** to massage with similar movements [to *knead* a sore muscle] **3.** to make or form as by kneading

knee (nē) *n.* [OE. *cneow* < IE. base *geneu-*] **1.** the joint between the thigh and the lower part of the human leg **2.** any similar or corresponding joint, as in an animal's forelimb **3.** anything like a knee, esp. like a bent knee **4.** the part of a stocking, trouser leg, etc. covering the knee —*vt.* **kneed, knee′-ing** to hit or touch with the knee —**bring to one's knees** to force to submit or give in

knee·cap (nē′kap′) *n.* a movable bone at the front of the human knee; patella: also **knee′pan′** (-pan′)

knee-deep (-dēp′) *adj.* **1.** sunk to the knees [standing *knee-deep* in water] **2.** so deep as to reach the knees [the snow is *knee-deep*] **3.** very much involved [*knee-deep* in politics]

knee-high (-hī′) *adj.* so high or tall as to reach to the knees [the corn had grown *knee-high*]

knee·hole (-hōl′) *n.* a space for the knees, as under a desk top

☆**knee-jerk** (-jurk′) *adj.* [< the reflex jerk of the leg when the kneecap is tapped] [Colloq.] responding in an automatic way that shows a lack of thought [a *knee-jerk* bigot]

kneel (nēl) *vi.* **knelt** or **kneeled, kneel′ing** [OE. *cneowlian* < *cneow*, KNEE] to rest on a knee or the knees —**kneel′er** *n.*

knee·pad (nē′pad′) *n.* a pad worn to protect the knee, as by a basketball player

knell (nel) *vi.* [OE. *cnyllan*] **1.** to ring in a slow, solemn way; toll **2.** to sound ominously or mournfully —*vt.* to announce or warn as by a knell [the judge's sentence *knelled* his death] —*n.* **1.** the sound of a bell rung slowly, as at a funeral **2.** a warning that something will end or pass away [the invention of the automobile sounded the *knell* of the horse and buggy]

knelt (nelt) *alt. pt. and pp. of* KNEEL

knew (nōō, nyōō) *pt. of* KNOW

☆**Knick·er·bock·er** (nik′ər bäk′ər) *n.* [< Diedrich *Knickerbocker*, fictitious Du. author of Washington Irving's *History of New York*] ☆**1.** a descendant of the early Dutch settlers of New York ☆**2.** any New Yorker **3.** [k-] [*pl.*] short, loose trousers gathered in at or just below the knees, as those worn by Dutch settlers of New York; knickers

knick·ers (nik′ərz) *n.pl.* **1.** knickerbockers **2.** [Chiefly Brit.] a woman's underpants

knick·knack (nik′nak′) *n.* [redupl. of KNACK] a small ornamental article or contrivance [her shelves were loaded with china figures and other *knickknacks*]

knife (nīf) *n., pl.* **knives** [OE. *cnif:* for IE. base see KNEAD] **1.** a cutting or stabbing instrument with a sharp blade, single-edged or double-edged, set in a handle **2.** a cutting blade, as in a machine —*vt.* **knifed, knif′ing 1.** to cut or stab with a knife ☆**2.** [Colloq.] to use underhanded methods in order to hurt, defeat, or betray —*vi.* to pass into or through something quickly, like a sharp knife —☆**under the knife** [Colloq.] undergoing surgery —**knife′like′** *adj.*

knife-edge (nīf′ej′) *n.* **1.** the edge of a knife **2.** any very sharp edge

knight (nīt) *n.* [OE. *cniht*, boy: for IE. base see KNEAD] **1.** in the Middle Ages, *a)* a military attendant of the king or other feudal superior, typically holding land in fief *b)* later, a man of high birth who after serving as page and squire was formally raised to honorable military rank and promised to be chivalrous **2.** in Great Britain, a man who for some achievement is given honorary nonhereditary rank next below a baronet and has the right to use *Sir* before his given name **3.** [*usually* K-] a

member of any society that officially calls its members *knights* **4.** [Poet.] a lady's devoted champion **5.** *Chess* a piece shaped like a horse's head —*vt.* to give the rank of knight to

knight-er·rant (nīt′er′ənt) *n., pl.* **knights′-er′rant 1.** a medieval knight wandering in search of adventures in which he can be brave and chivalrous **2.** a person who is chivalrous or idealistic but impractical —**knight′-er′rant·ry** (-er′ən trē) *n., pl.* **-ries**

knight·hood (-hood′) *n.* **1.** the rank or vocation of a knight **2.** knightly conduct; chivalry **3.** knights as a group

knight·ly (-lē) *adj.* **1.** of or like a knight; chivalrous, brave, etc. **2.** consisting of knights —**knight′li·ness** *n.*

☆**Knights of Columbus** an international fraternal society of Roman Catholic men

Knight Templar *pl.* **Knights Templars** for 1, **Knights Templar** for 2 **1.** a member of a military and religious order established among the Crusaders c. 1118 **2.** a member of a certain order of Masons

knish (kə nish′) *n.* [Yid. < Russ., a kind of cake] a piece of thin rolled dough folded over a filling, as of mashed potatoes, chopped meat, etc., and baked

knit (nit) *vt., vi.* **knit′ted** or **knit, knit′ting** [OE. *cnyttan* < base of *cnotta*, a KNOT] **1.** to make (cloth or clothing) by looping yarn or thread together with special needles **2.** to form into cloth in this way instead of by weaving **3.** to join or grow together in a close and firm way [my broken leg *knit* slowly; our family is close *knit*] **4.** to draw (the brows) together —*n.* cloth or a garment made by knitting —**knit′ter** *n.*

knit·ting (nit′iŋ) *n.* **1.** the action of a person or thing that knits **2.** knitted work

knitting needle an eyeless, usually long, needle of metal, bone, plastic, etc., with a blunt point at one or both ends, used in pairs, etc. in knitting by hand

knit·wear (-wer′) *n.* knitted clothing

knives (nīvz) *n. pl. of* KNIFE

knob (näb) *n.* [< or akin to MLowG. *knobbe*, a knot, bud: see KNEAD] **1.** a rounded lump or part that sticks out **2.** a handle, usually round, of a door, drawer, etc. **3.** a hill or mountain with a round top —**knobbed** *adj.*

knob·by (näb′ē) *adj.* **-bi·er, -bi·est 1.** covered with knobs **2.** like a knob —**knob′bi·ness** *n.*

knock (näk) *vi.* [OE. *cnocian*] **1.** to strike a blow, as with the fist; esp., to rap on a door **2.** to bump; collide **3.** to make a thumping or tapping noise [an engine *knocks* when the combustion is faulty] ☆**4.** [Colloq.] to find fault; criticize —*vt.* **1.** to hit; strike **2.** to make by hitting or striking [to *knock* a hole in the wall] ☆**3.** [Colloq.] to find fault with —*n.* **1.** a knocking **2.** a sharp blow; rap, as on a door **3.** a thumping or tapping noise, as in an engine ☆**4.** [Colloq.] any faultfinding; criticism **5.** [Colloq.] a misfortune or trouble [the school of hard *knocks*] —see SYN. at STRIKE —**knock about (or around)** [Colloq.] **1.** to wander about; roam **2.** to treat roughly —**knock down; 1.** to hit so as to cause to fall ☆**2.** to take apart for convenience in shipping **3.** to indicate the sale of (an article) at an auction **4.** [Slang] to earn as pay —☆**knock it off!** [Slang] quit it! specif., stop talking! —**knock off 1.** [Colloq.] to stop working **2.** [Colloq.] to deduct **3.** [Colloq.] to do; accomplish ☆**4.** [Slang] to kill, overcome, etc. —☆**knock (oneself) out** to exert oneself until one is exhausted —**knock out 1.** *Boxing* to score a knockout over **2.** to make unconscious or exhausted **3.** to defeat, destroy, etc. **4.** [Colloq.] to do; make; specif., to compose, write, etc., esp. casually or hastily —**knock together** to make or compose hastily or crudely —**knock up** [Brit. Colloq.] **1.** to exhaust **2.** to wake (someone) as by knocking at the door

knock·a·bout (näk′ə bout′) *n.* ☆**1.** a small, one-masted yacht with a mainsail, jib, and centerboard or keel, but no bowsprit **2.** something for knockabout use —*adj.* **1.** rough; noisy; boisterous **2.** made or suitable for rough use

knock·down (-doun′) *adj.* **1.** that knocks down; overwhelming ☆**2.** made so as to be easily taken apart [a *knockdown* table] —*n.* **1.** a knocking down; felling **2.** a blow that knocks one down

knock·er (-ər) *n.* one that knocks; specif., a small metal ring, knob, etc. on a door, for knocking

knock-knee (-nē′) *n.* **1.** a condition in which the legs bend inward at the knees **2.** [*pl.*] such knees —**knock′-kneed′** *adj.*

knock·out (-out′) *adj.* that knocks out, as a blow —*n.* **1.** a knocking out or being knocked out **2.** *a)* a blow that knocks out *b) Boxing* a victory won when the opponent is knocked down and cannot rise before an official count of ten ☆**3.** [Slang] a very attractive or striking person or thing

knock·wurst (näk′wurst′) *n. same as* KNACKWURST

knoll (nōl) *n.* [OE. *cnoll*: for IE. base see KNEAD] a small, rounded hill; mound

Knos·sos (näs′əs) *same as* CNOSSUS

knot (nät) *n.* [OE. *cnotta*: see KNEAD] **1.** a lump or knob in a thread, cord, etc., formed as by a tangle drawn tight **2.** a fastening made by intertwining or tying together pieces of string, rope, etc. **3.** an ornamental bow of ribbon or twist of braid **4.** a small group or cluster *[a knot of people]* **5.** something that joins closely; esp., the bond of marriage **6.** a problem; difficulty **7.** a knotlike part, as in a tense muscle; specif., *a)* a hard lump on a tree where a branch grows out *b)* a cross section of such a lump, appearing cross-grained in a board· *c)* a joint on a plant stem where leaves grow out **8.** *Naut.* a unit of speed of one nautical mile (6,076.12 feet) an hour *[a speed of 10 knots]* —*vt.* **knot′ted, knot′ting 1.** to tie or intertwine in or with a knot **2.** to tie closely or intricately; entangle —*vi.* to form a knot or knots —**tie the knot** [Colloq.] to get married —**knot′ter** *n.*

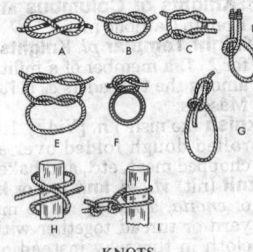

KNOTS
(A, figure-of-eight knot; B, overhand knot; C, thief knot; D, half hitch; E, square knot; F, granny knot; G, bowline knot; H, clove hitch; I, round turn and two half hitches)

knot·grass (nät′gras′) *n.* a common weed with slender stems and narrow leaves: also **knot′weed**′ (-wēd′)

knot·hole (-hōl′) *n.* a hole in a board, etc. where a knot has fallen out

knot·ted (-id) *adj.* **1.** tied or fastened in or with a knot or knots **2.** having or full of knots

knot·ty (-ē) *adj.* **-ti·er, -ti·est 1.** full of knots *[a knotty board]* **2.** hard to solve; puzzling *[a knotty problem]* —**knot′ti·ness** *n.*

knout (nout) *n.* [Russ. *knut* < Sw., a KNOT] a leather whip formerly used in Russia to flog criminals —*vt.* to flog with a knout

know (nō) *vt.* **knew, known, know′ing** [OE. *cnawan* < IE. base *gen*-, *gno*-, from which also comes L. *gnoscere*, *know*] **1.** to be sure of or well informed about *[to know the facts]* **2.** to be aware of; have perceived or learned *[to know that one is loved]* **3.** to have firmly in the memory *[the actor knows his lines]* **4.** to be acquainted or familiar with *[I know your brother well]* **5.** to have understanding of or skill in as a result of study or experience *[to know music]* **6.** to recognize *[I'd know that face anywhere]* **7.** to be able to tell the difference in; distinguish *[to know right from wrong]* —*vi.* **1.** to have knowledge **2.** to be sure, informed, or aware —**in the know** [Colloq.] having confidential information —**know best** to be the best guide, authority, etc. —**know′a·ble** *adj.* —**know′er** *n.*

☆**know-how** (nō′hou′) *n.* [Colloq.] knowledge of how to do something well; technical skill

know·ing (-iŋ) *adj.* **1.** having knowledge or information **2.** shrewd; clever **3.** implying shrewd understanding or secret knowledge *[a knowing look]* —**know′ing·ness** *n.*

know·ing·ly (-lē) *adv.* **1.** in a knowing way **2.** on purpose; deliberately *[he would not knowingly lie]*

knowl·edge (näl′ij) *n.* **1.** the act, fact, or state of knowing *[knowledge of the murder spread through the town]* **2.** acquaintance with facts; range of information, awareness, or understanding *[his knowledge of movies is enormous]* **3.** what is known; learning; enlightenment *[a man of great knowledge]* **4.** all the facts, principles, etc. known by mankind —see SYN. at INFORMATION —**to (the best of) one's knowledge** as far as one knows

knowl·edge·a·ble (-ə b'l) *adj.* having or showing knowledge or intelligence —**knowl′edge·a·bil′i·ty, knowl′edge·a·ble·ness** *n.* —**knowl′edge·a·bly** *adv.*

known (nōn) *pp. of* KNOW

know-noth·ing (nō′nuth′iŋ) *n.* **1.** an ignorant person; ignoramus **2.** [K- N-] a member of a U.S. secret political party in the 1850's with a program of keeping out of public office anyone not a native-born American

Knox (näks), **John** 1505?–72; Scot. Protestant clergyman & religious reformer

Knox·ville (näks′vil) [after Gen. H. *Knox* (1750–1806), 1st secretary of war] city in E Tenn., on the Tennessee River: pop. 175,000

knuck·le (nuk′'l) *n.* [< or akin to MDu. & MLowG. *knokel*, little bone: for IE. base see KNEAD] **1.** a joint of the finger; esp., the joint connecting a finger to the rest of the hand **2.** the knee or hock joint of a pig or other animal, used as food **3.** [*pl.*] *same as* BRASS KNUCKLES —*vt.* **-led, -ling** to strike or press with the knuckles —☆**knuckle down 1.** to rest the knuckles on the ground in shooting a marble **2.** to work hard —**knuckle under** to yield; give in

☆**knuckle ball** *Baseball* a slow pitch without spin thrown with the first knuckles, or the nails, of the middle fingers pressed against the ball: also **knuck·ler** (nuk′lər) *n.*

☆**knuck·le·head** (-hed′) *n.* [Colloq.] a stupid person

knurl (nurl) *n.* [prob. blend of *knur*, a knot + GNARL] **1.** a knot, knob, nodule, etc. **2.** any of a series of small beads or ridges, as along the edge of a coin —*vt.* to make knurls on —**knurled** *adj.*

knurl·y (nur′lē) *adj.* **knurl′i·er, knurl′i·est** full of knurls, as wood; gnarled

Knut (k'nōōt)′ *same as* CANUTE

☆**KO** (kā′ō′) *vt.* **KO'd, KO'ing** [Slang] *Boxing* to knock out —*n.*, *pl.* **KO's** [Slang] *Boxing* a knockout Also **K.O., k.o.**

ko·a·la (kō ä′lə) *n.* [< the native name] an Australian mammal that lives in trees: the female has a pouch in front, in which she carries her young

KOALA
(27–35 in. long)

Ko·be (kō′bā′; *E.* kō′bē) seaport on the S coast of Honshu, Japan: pop. 1,217,000

Kø·ben·havn (kö′b'n houn′) *Dan. name of* COPENHAGEN

kob·o (käb′ō) *n., pl.* **kob′o** [native name for an ancient coin] *see* MONETARY UNITS, table (Nigeria)

Koch (kōk; *G.* kôkh), **Robert** 1843–1910; Ger. bacteriologist & physician

Ko·dá·ly (kô′dä y′), **Zol·tán** (zôl′tän) 1882–1967; Hung. composer

ko·di·ak bear (kō′dē ak′) a very large, brown bear found on Kodiak Island and in nearby areas

Ko·di·ak Island (kō′dē ak′) [< Russ. < ? native name meaning "island"] island off the SW coast of Alas., in the State of Alas.

K. of C. Knight (or Knights) of Columbus

Koh·i·noor, Koh-i-noor (kō′ə noor′) [< Per.] a famous large Indian diamond, now one of the British crown jewels

kohl (kōl) *n.* [Ar. *kuḥl*] a cosmetic preparation used, esp. in Eastern countries, for eye makeup

kohl·ra·bi (kōl′rä′bē, kōl′rä′bē) *n., pl.* **-bies** [G. < It., pl. of *cavolo rapa*, cole rape: see COLE & RAPE²] a garden vegetable related to the cabbage, with an edible, rounded stem

ko·la (kō′lə) *n. same as* COLA

kola nut the seed of the cola

ko·lin·sky (kō lin′skē) *n., pl.* **-skies** [< Russ. < *Kola*, Russian district] **1.** any of several weasels of Asia **2.** the golden-brown fur of such a weasel

Köln (köln) *Ger. name of* COLOGNE

Kol Nid·re (kōl nē′drä, nid′rə) [Aram. *kōl nidhrē*, lit., all our vows] **1.** the prayer of atonement recited in synagogues at the opening of Yom Kippur eve services **2.** the music for this

koo·doo (kōō′dōō) *n., pl.* **-doos, -doo** see PLURAL, II, D, 1 *same as* KUDU

☆**kook** (kōōk) *n.* [< ? *cuckoo*] [Slang] a person thought of as silly, eccentric, crazy, etc. —**kook′y, kook′ie** *adj.* **kook′i·er, kook′i·est**

kook·a·bur·ra (kōōk′ə bur′ə, -bur′ə) *n.* [<native name] an Australian kingfisher with a cry like loud laughter

ko·peck, ko·pek (kō′pek) *n.* [< Russ. < *kopye*, a lance] a monetary unit, and a coin, equal to 1/100 of a ruble

Ko·ran (kō rän′, -rän′; kô-, kə-) *n.* [Ar. *qur'ān*, lit., book, reading < *qara'a*, to read] the sacred book of the Moslems, believed by them to contain things revealed to Mohammed by Allah —**Ko·ran′ic** *adj.*

Ko·re·a (kô rē′ə, kō-) peninsula in E Asia, extending south from NE China: divided (1948) into two countries: *a)* **North Korea**, occupying the N half of the peninsula, 47,255 sq. mi., pop. 11,568,000, cap. Pyongyang, and *b)* **South Korea**, occupying the S half, 38,030 sq. mi., pop. 33,153,000, cap. Seoul

Ko·re·an (-ən) *adj.* of Korea, its people, etc. —*n.* **1.** a native of Korea **2.** the language of the Koreans

ko·ru·na (kô rōō'nä) *n., pl.* **ko·ru'nas, ko·run'** (-rōōn') [Czech < L. *corona*, a crown] *see* MONETARY UNITS, table (Czechoslovakia)

Kos·ci·us·ko (käs'ē us'kō; *Pol.* kôsh chōōsh'kô), **Thad·de·us** (thad'ē əs) (born *Tadeusz Kościuszko*) 1746–1817; Pol. patriot & general: served in the Am. Revolutionary army

ko·sher (kō'shər; *for v., usually* käsh'ər) *adj.* [Heb. *kāshēr*, fit, proper] **1.** *Judaism a*) clean or fit to eat according to the dietary laws: Lev. 11 *b*) serving or dealing in such food [a *kosher* kitchen] ☆**2.** [Slang] all right, proper, etc. —*n.* kosher food — *vt.* to make kosher

Kos·suth (käs'ōōth; *Hung.* kô'shoot), **Louis** (Hung. name *Lajos Kossuth*) 1802–94; Hung. patriot & statesman

Ko·sy·gin (kô sē'gyin; *E.* kä sē'gin), **A·lek·sei** (**Nikolaevich**) (ä lyik sä') 1904– ; premier of the U.S.S.R. (1964–)

ko·to (kōt'ō) *n.* [Jpn.] a Japanese musical instrument consisting of a long box with thirteen silk strings stretched over it

Kow·loon (kou'lōōn') city in the mainland section of the colony of Hong Kong, SE China: pop. 1,350,000

kow·tow (kou'tou', kō'-) *n.* [Chin. *k'o-t'ou*, lit., knock head] the act of kneeling and touching the ground with the forehead to show great humbleness, respect, obedience, etc. —*vi.* **1.** to make a kowtow **2.** to show obedience or respect (*to*)

KOTO

KP, K.P. kitchen police

Kr *Chem.* krypton

kraal (kräl, krôl) *n.* [Afrik. < Port. *curral*, pen for cattle] **1.** a village of South African natives, usually surrounded by a barrier **2.** an enclosure for cattle or sheep in South Africa; pen

krait (krīt) *n.* [Hindi *karait*] a very poisonous, yellow-banded snake, found in south-central and southeastern Asia

Kra·ków (kra'kou'; *Pol.* krä'koof) city in S Poland, on the Vistula: pop. 577,000

Kras·no·dar (kräs'nô där') city in southwestern R.S.F.S.R., in the N Caucasus: pop. 465,000

Kras·no·yarsk (kräs'nô yärsk') city in central R.S.F.S.R., in NC Asia: pop. 648,000

Kre·feld (krā'felt) city in W West Germany, on the Rhine: pop. 224,000

Kreis·ler (krīs'lər), **Fritz** (frits) 1875–1962; U.S. violinist & composer, born in Austria

krem·lin (krem'lin) *n.* [Fr. < Russ. *kreml'*] in Russia, the fortress of a city —**the Kremlin 1.** a large fortress in Moscow, formerly housing government offices of the Soviet Union **2.** the government of the Soviet Union

krim·mer (krim'ər) *n.* [G. < *Krim*, Crimea] a grayish, tightly curled fur made from the pelts of Crimean lambs

kris (krēs) *n.* [Malay *kerīs*] a Malay dagger with a wavy blade

Krish·na (krish'nə) the Hindu god Vishnu in one of the human forms taken by him

☆**Kriss Krin·gle** (kris' kriŋ'g'l) [< G. < *Christ*, Christ + *kindl*, dim. of *kind*, child] *same as* SANTA CLAUS

Kri·voi Rog (kri voi' rôk') city in SC Ukrainian S.S.R.: pop. 573,000

kro·na (krō'nə; *Sw.* krōō'na) *n., pl.* **-nor** (-nôr) [Sw. < L. *corona*, crown] *see* MONETARY UNITS, table (Sweden)

kró·na (krō'nə) *n., pl.* **-nur** (-nər) [Ice. < ML. *corona*, a crown] *see* MONETARY UNITS, table (Iceland)

kro·ne (krō'nə) *n., pl.* **-ner** (-nər) [Dan. < L. *corona*, crown] *see* MONETARY UNITS, table (Denmark, Norway)

Kru·ger (krōō'gər), **Paul** (born *Stephanus Johannes Paulus Kruger*) 1825–1904; South African statesman

☆**krul·ler** (krul'ər) *n. same as* CRULLER

kryp·ton (krip'tän) *n.* [< Gr. neut. of *kryptos*, hidden < *kryptein*, to hide] an inert, gaseous chemical element present in very small quantities in air: symbol, Kr; at. wt., 83.80; at. no., 36

KS Kansas

Kt *Chess* knight

kt. 1. karat **2.** kiloton(s)

Kua·la Lum·pur (kwä'lə loom poor') city in the SW Malay Peninsula; capital of Malaysia: pop. c.400,000

Ku·blai Khan (kōō'blī kän', -blə) 1216?–94; Mongol emperor of China (1260?–94): founder of the Mongol dynasty: grandson of GENGHIS KHAN

☆**ku·chen** (kōō'kən, -khən) *n.* [G., cake] a coffeecake made of yeast dough, covered with sugar and spices and often filled with raisins, nuts, etc.

ku·dos (kōō'däs, -dōs; kyōō'-) *n.* [Gr. *kydos*, glory] [Colloq.] praise for an achievement; glory; fame: sometimes wrongly taken to be the plural (*pron.* -dōz) of an assumed word "kudo"

ku·du (kōō'dōō) *n., pl.* **-dus, -du**: see PLURAL, II, D, 1 [Hottentot] a large, grayish-brown African antelope with long, twisted horns

Kui·by·shev (kwē'bi shef') city in southwestern R.S.F.S.R., on the Volga: pop. 1,014,000

☆**Ku Klux** (kōō' kluks', kyōō') [< Gr. *kyklos*, a circle] **1.** *short for* KU KLUX KLAN **2.** a member of the Ku Klux Klan: also **Ku Klux'er**

☆**Ku Klux Klan** (klan) [prec. + *klan*, made-up sp. for CLAN] **1.** a secret society of white men founded in the Southern States after the Civil War to reestablish and maintain white supremacy **2.** a U.S. secret society organized in 1915: it is anti-black, anti-Semitic, anti-Catholic, etc. and uses terrorist methods

KUDU
(to 4 ft. high at shoulder)

ku·lak (kōō läk') *n.* [Russ., lit., fist < Estonian] a well-to-do farmer in Russia who profited from the labor of poorer peasants and opposed the Soviet land policies

ku·miss (kōō'mis) *n.* [G. < Russ. < Tatar *kumiz*] **1.** mare's or camel's milk fermented and used as a drink by Tatar nomads of Asia **2.** a similar drink made from cow's milk

küm·mel (kim'l; *G.* küm'əl) *n.* [G., caraway < OHG. *kumil* < L. *cuminum*: see CUMIN] a colorless liqueur flavored with caraway seeds, anise, cumin, etc.

kum·quat (kum'kwät, -kwôt) *n.* [< Chin. *chin-chü*, golden orange] **1.** a small, orange-colored, oval fruit, with a sour pulp and a sweet rind **2.** a tree that bears this fruit

kung fu (kooŋ' fōō', gōōŋ') [< Chin.] a Chinese system of self-defense, like karate but with an emphasis on circular rather than sharp, straight movements

Kuo·min·tang (kwō'min taŋ'; *Chin.* gwō'min'däŋ') [Chin.] nationalist political party of China, organized chiefly by Sun Yat-sen in 1911 and afterward led by Chiang Kai-shek

Kurd (kurd, koord) *n.* [Turk. & Ar.] any of a nomadic Moslem people living chiefly in Kurdistan —**Kurd'ish** *adj., n.*

Kur·di·stan (kur'di stan', koor'-; -stän') region occupying SE Turkey, N Iraq, & NW Iran

Ku·ril (or **Ku·rile**) **Islands** (kōō'ril, koo rēl') chain of islands belonging to the U.S.S.R., between N Hokkaido, Japan, and Kamchatka Peninsula

Kush·it·ic (kush it'ik) *adj., n. same as* CUSHITIC

Ku·wait (kōō wāt', -wīt') independent Arab state in E Arabia, on the NW coast of the Persian Gulf: 6,000 sq. mi.; pop. 914,000

kw. kilowatt; kilowatts

kwa·cha (kwä'chä) *n., pl.* **-cha** [native term, lit., dawn] *see* MONETARY UNITS, table (Malawi, Zambia)

Kwang·chow (kwäŋ'chô; *Chin.* gwäŋ'jô') port in SE China: pop. 2,200,000: also sp. **Kwangchou**

kwa·shi·or·kor (kwä'shē ôr'kôr) *n.* [< name in Ghana] a severe disease of young children, caused by a poor diet and characterized by stunted growth, edema, etc.

kwh, K.W.H., kw.-hr., kw-hr kilowatt-hour

Ky., KY Kentucky

kyat (kyät) *n.* [Burmese] *see* MONETARY UNITS, table (Burma)

Kym·ric (kim'rik) *adj., n. same as* CYMRIC

Kym·ry, Kym·ri (-rē) *n.pl. same as* CYMRY

Kyo·to (kyô'tô'; *E.* kē ôt'ō) city in S Honshu, Japan: pop. 1,365,000

Kyu·shu (kyōō'shōō') one of the four main islands of Japan, south of Honshu: 16,223 sq. mi.

---

fat, āpe, cär, ten, ēven, is, bīte; gō, hôrn, tōōl, look; oil, out; up, fur; get; joy; yet; chin; she; thin, *th*en; zh, leisure; ŋ, ring; ə for *a* in *ago*, *e* in *agent*, *i* in *sanity*, *o* in *comply*, *u* in *focus*; ' as in *able* (ā'b'l); Fr. bál; ë, Fr. coeur; ö, Fr. feu; ô, Fr. mon; ô, Fr. coq; ü, Fr. duc; r, Fr. cri; H, G. ich; kh, G. doch; ‡foreign; ☆ Americanism; < derived from. See inside front cover.

L

L, l (el) *n., pl.* **L's, l's** **1.** the twelfth letter of the English alphabet **2.** the sound of *L* or *l*

L (el) *n., pl.* **L's** **1.** an object shaped like L; ☆esp., an extension of a building that gives the whole a shape resembling L **2.** a Roman numeral for 50 —*adj.* shaped like L

L. **1.** Latin **2.** Licentiate

L., l. **1.** lake **2.** latitude **3.** law **4.** leaf **5.** league **6.** left **7.** length **8.** *pl.* **LL., ll.** line **9.** link **10.** lira; lire **11.** liter **12.** low **13.** [L. *libra,* pl. *librae*] pound(s)

la¹ (lä, lô) *interj.* [Dial. or Archaic] an exclamation of surprise or emphasis

la² (lä) *n.* [see GAMUT] *Music* a syllable representing the sixth tone of the diatonic scale

La *Chem.* lanthanum

La., LA Louisiana

L.A. [Colloq.] Los Angeles

lab (lab) *n.* [Colloq.] a laboratory

la·bel (lā′b'l) *n.* [OFr., a rag, strip < Gmc.: for IE. base see LAP¹] **1.** a card, strip of paper, etc. marked and attached to an object to show what it is, what it contains, who owns it, etc. **2.** a descriptive word or phrase applied to a person, group, etc. [*"liberal" and "conservative" are useful* labels *but not very precise*] ☆**3.** an identifying brand of a company, as of a phonograph recording company —*vt.* **-beled** or **-belled, -bel·ing** or **-bel·ling** **1.** to attach a label to [*to* label *a package*] **2.** to classify as; call; describe [*no one wants to be* labeled *a "coward"*] —**la′bel·er, la′bel·ler** *n.*

la·bel·lum (lə bel′əm) *n., pl.* **-bel′la** (-ə) [ModL. < L., dim. of *labrum,* a lip] the lowest of the three petals of an orchid, usually the largest of the petals and often spurred

la·bi·a (lā′bē ə) *n.* *pl.* of LABIUM

la·bi·al (lā′bē əl) *adj.* [< ML. < L. *labium,* a lip] **1.** of the labia, or lips **2.** *Phonet.* formed mainly with the lips: said esp. of *b, m,* and *p* —*n.* a labial sound —**la′bi·al·ly** *adv.*

la·bi·ate (lā′bē āt′, -it) *adj.* [< L. *labium,* a lip] **1.** formed or functioning like a lip **2.** having a lip or lips **3.** *Bot.* having the calyx or corolla so divided that one part overlaps the other like a lip

LABELLUM

la·bile (lā′b'l, -bīl) *adj.* [< L. < *labi,* to slip] liable to change; unstable [*labile* chemical compounds]

la·bi·o·den·tal (lā′bē ō den′t'l) *adj.* [< L. *labium,* a lip + DENTAL] *Phonet.* formed with the lower lip against the upper teeth, as the sounds of *f* and *v* —*n.* a labiodental sound

la·bi·um (lā′bē əm) *n., pl.* **-bi·a** (-ə) [L., a lip] *Anat., Bot.,* etc. a lip or liplike organ; specif., [*pl.*] the outer folds of skin (**labia majora**) or the inner folds of mucous membrane (**labia minora**) of the vulva

la·bor (lā′bər) *n.* [< OFr. < L. *labor*] **1.** physical or mental exertion; work; toil **2.** a piece of work; task [*the twelve* labors *of Hercules*] **3.** *a)* all wage-earning workers as a group: distinguished from CAPITAL¹ or MANAGEMENT *b)* all manual workers whose work is characterized largely by physical exertion **4.** labor unions as a group **5.** [L-] *same as* LABOR PARTY **6.** the work accomplished by workers as a group **7.** *Med.* the process

of giving birth to a child —*vi.* [< OFr. < L. *laborare* < the *n.*] **1.** to work; toil [*coal miners* labor *underground*] **2.** to exert oneself to get or do something; strive [*he was* laboring *to understand the speech*] **3.** to move slowly and with difficulty [*the car* labored *up the hill*] **4.** to be burdened (with *under*) [*to* labor *under a delusion*] **5.** to undergo, and suffer the pains of, childbirth —*vt.* to work out in too great detail [*to* labor *a point*] —see SYN. at WORK

lab·o·ra·to·ry (lab′rə tôr′ē, -ər ə tôr′ē; *Brit.* lə bär′ə tər ē) *n., pl.* **-ries** [< ML. < L.: see LABOR, *vi.*] **1.** a room or building for scientific experimentation or research **2.** a place for preparing chemicals, drugs, etc. ☆**3.** a place where theories and methods, as in education, are tested, demonstrated, etc. [*a reading* laboratory] —*adj.* of or performed in, or as in, a laboratory [*laboratory* tests were conducted]

☆**Labor Day** in the U.S. & Canada, the first Monday in September, a legal holiday in honor of labor

la·bored (lā′bərd) *adj.* made or done with great effort; not easy and natural; strained [*a* labored *joke;* labored *breathing*]

la·bor·er (lā′bər ər) *n.* one who labors; esp., a wage-earning worker whose work calls for hard physical effort but little skill

la·bo·ri·ous (lə bôr′ē əs) *adj.* **1.** involving or calling for much hard work; difficult [*laborious* tasks] **2.** industrious; hard-working —see SYN. at HARD —**la·bo′ri·ous·ly** *adv.* —**la·bo′ri·ous·ness** *n.*

☆**la·bor·ite** (lā′bə rīt′) *n.* **1.** a member or supporter of a labor party **2.** [L-] a member or supporter of the British Labor Party: *Brit.* sp. **La′bour·ite′**

labor party **1.** a political party organized to protect and further the rights of workers, or one dominated by organized labor **2.** [L- P-] such a party in Great Britain: *Brit.* sp. **Labour Party**

la·bor-sav·ing (lā′bər sā′viŋ) *adj.* eliminating or lessening physical labor [*labor-saving* appliances]

☆**labor union** an association of workers to protect and further the welfare, interests, and rights of its members

la·bour (lā′bər) *n., vi., vt. Brit. sp. of* LABOR

Lab·ra·dor (lab′rə dôr′) **1.** region along the E coast of Canada, making up the mainland part of the province of Newfoundland **2.** large peninsula occupied by this region & most of Quebec

Labrador Current icy arctic current flowing south from Baffin Bay past Labrador into the Gulf Stream

Labrador retriever any of a breed of medium-sized hunting dog used in retrieving game, having a black, brown, or yellow coat of short, thick hair

la·bur·num (lə bur′nəm) *n.* [L.] a small, poisonous tree or shrub of the legume family, with drooping racemes of yellow flowers

lab·y·rinth (lab′ə rinth′) *n.* [< L. < Gr. *labyrinthos*] **1.** a structure containing an intricate network of winding passages hard to follow without losing one's way; maze; specif., [L-] *Gr. Myth.* such a structure built for King Minos, to house the Minotaur **2.** a complicated, puzzling arrangement, condition, etc. **3.** *Anat.* the inner ear

lab·y·rin·thine (lab′ə rin′thin, -thēn) *adj.* of or like a labyrinth; intricate; complicated

lac (lak) *n.* [< Hindi < Sans. *lākṣa*] **1.** a resinous substance secreted on various

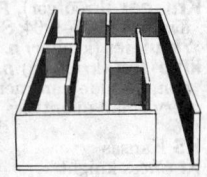

LABYRINTH

532

trees in southern Asia by certain scale insects: when melted, strained, and rehardened, it forms shellac **2.** *same as* LAKH

lace (lās) *n.* [OFr. *laz* < L. *laqueus*, a noose] **1.** a string, ribbon, etc. used to draw together and fasten the parts of a shoe, corset, etc. **2.** braid of gold or silver, as for trimming uniforms **3.** a fine netting or openwork fabric of linen, silk, etc., woven in ornamental designs —*vt.* **laced, lac'ing 1.** to draw the ends of (a garment, shoe, etc.) together and fasten with a lace **2.** to pass (a cord, etc.) in and out *through* eyelets, fabric, etc. **3.** to weave together; intertwine *[lacing* boughs together into a wreath*]* **4.** to trim with lace **5.** to streak, as with color; intersperse **6.** to thrash; beat **7.** to add a dash of alcoholic liquor to *[coffee laced* with rum*]* —*vi.* **1.** to be fastened with a lace *[these shoes lace]* **2.** [Colloq.] to attack physically or verbally (with *into*)

Lac·e·dae·mon (las'ə dē'mən) *same as* SPARTA —**Lac'e·dae·mo'ni·an** (-di mō'nē ən) *adj., n.*

lac·er·ate (las'ə rāt'; *also for adj.* -ər it) *vt.* **-at'ed, -at'ing** [< L. pp. of *lacerare* < *lacer*, mangled] **1.** to tear jaggedly; mangle *[he lacerated* his arm on the barbed wire*]* **2.** to hurt (someone's feelings, etc.) deeply —*adj.* **1.** torn; mangled **2.** *Bot.* having jagged edges *[lacerate* leaves*]*

lac·er·a·tion (las'ə rā'shən) *n.* **1.** a lacerating **2.** the result of lacerating; a jagged tear or wound

lace·wing (lās'wiŋ') *n.* any of a large group of insects with four delicate, transparent wings

lach·es (lach'iz) *n.* [OFr. *laschesse*, ult. < L. *laxus*, lax] *Law* failure to do the required thing at the proper time

Lach·e·sis (lak'ə sis) *Gr. & Rom. Myth.* that one of the three Fates who determines the length of life

lach·ry·mal (lak'rə məl) *adj.* [< ML. < L. *lacrima*, TEAR²] **1.** of, characterized by, or producing tears **2.** *same as* LACRIMAL (sense 1)

lach·ry·ma·to·ry (-mə tôr'ē) *adj.* of, causing, or producing tears

lach·ry·mose (-mōs') *adj.* [< L. < *lacrima*, TEAR²] **1.** inclined to shed many tears; tearful **2.** causing tears; sad *[a lachrymose* poem*]* —**lach'ry·mose'ly** *adv.*

lac·ing (lās'iŋ) *n.* **1.** the act of a person who laces **2.** a thrashing; beating **3.** a cord or lace, as a shoelace

lack (lak) *n.* [< or akin to MLowG., MDu. *lak:* for IE. base see LEAK] **1.** the fact or condition of not having enough; shortage; deficiency *[lack* of intelligence*]* **2.** the fact or condition of not having any; complete absence *[lack* of a car kept him from taking the job*]* **3.** the thing that is lacking or needed *[our most serious lack* was fresh water*]* —*vi.* **1.** to be wanting or missing *[money* is *lacking* to buy a new car*]* **2.** to be short (with *in* or *for*) *[he* is *lacking* in bravery*]* —*vt.* **1.** to be deficient in or entirely without *[the soil lacks* nitrogen*]* **2.** to fall short by *[lacking* one ounce of being a pound*]*

SYN.—**lack** implies an absence or shortage of something necessary, important, or desired *[she lacks* experience*]*; **want** (in this sense, chiefly British) and **need** stress the importance of supplying what is lacking as soon as possible *[this matter needs,* or *wants,* attention*]*; **require** suggests that what is needed cannot be done without *[his work requires* great powers of concentration*]* —**ANT.** have, possess

lack·a·dai·si·cal (lak'ə dā'zi k'l) *adj.* [ult. < *alack the day]* showing lack of interest or spirit; listless; languid —**lack'a·dai'si·cal·ly** *adv.*

lack·ey (lak'ē) *n., pl.* **-eys** [< Fr. < Sp. *lacayo]* **1.** a male servant of low rank **2.** a follower who carries out another's orders like a servant; toady

lack·lus·ter (lak'lus'tər) *adj.* **1.** lacking brightness; dull *[lackluster* eyes*]* **2.** lacking energy or vitality; boring, unimaginative, etc. *[a lackluster* performance*]* Also, chiefly Brit. sp., **lack'lus'tre**

La·co·ni·a (lə kō'nē ə) ancient region on the S coast of the Peloponnesus, dominated by the city of Sparta: see map at GREECE —**La·co'ni·an** *adj., n.*

la·con·ic (lə kän'ik) *adj.* [< L. < Gr. *Lakōn*, a Laconian, Spartan] brief or concise in speaking or writing; using few words —see SYN. at CONCISE —**la·con'i·cal·ly** *adv.*

lac·quer (lak'ər) *n.* [< Fr. < Port. < *laca*, gum lac] **1.** a coating substance of natural or synthetic resins, nitrocellulose, etc. dissolved in a solvent that evaporates rapidly leaving a tough film that sticks fast: pigments are often added to form **lacquer enamels 2.** a natural resin varnish obtained from certain trees

in China and Japan, used to give a hard, smooth, highly polished finish to wood **3.** articles of wood (in full, **lac'quer·ware', lac'quer·work')** coated with this lacquer —*vt.* to coat with or as with lacquer —**lac'quer·er** *n.*

lac·ri·mal (lak'rə məl) *adj.* **1.** *Anat.* designating, of, or near the glands that secrete tears **2.** *same as* LACHRYMAL (sense 1)

lac·ri·ma·tion (lak'rə mā'shən) *n.* [< L. < pp. of *lacrimare*, to weep < *lacrima*, TEAR²] normal or excessive secretion or shedding of tears

☆**la·crosse** (lə krôs', -kräs') *n.* [CanadFr. < Fr. *la*, the + *crosse*, a crutch] a ball game in which two teams of ten men each, using webbed rackets with long handles, try to advance a small rubber ball across the field into the opponents' goal

La Crosse (lə krôs', kräs') [so called because once a favorite place of Indians for playing LACROSSE] city in W Wis., on the Mississippi: pop. 51,000

lac·tase (lak'tās) *n.* [LACT(O)- + (DIAST)ASE] an enzyme, present in certain yeasts and in the intestines of animals, which splits lactose into glucose and galactose

LACROSSE

lac·tate (lak'tāt) *vi.* **-tat·ed, -tat·ing** [< L. pp. of *lactare* < *lac* (see LACTO-)] to secrete milk —*n.* any salt or ester of lactic acid

lac·ta·tion (lak tā'shən) *n.* **1.** the secretion of milk by a mammary gland **2.** the period during which milk is secreted

lac·te·al (lak'tē əl) *adj.* [< L. *lacteus* < *lac* (see LACTO-) + -AL] **1.** of or like milk; milky **2.** containing or carrying chyle, the milky fluid that is a product of digestion —*n.* any of the lymphatic vessels that carry chyle from the small intestine to the blood

lac·tic (lak'tik) *adj.* [< Fr.: see LACTO- & -IC] of or obtained from milk

lactic acid a yellowish or clear, syrupy organic acid, $C_3H_6O_3$, produced as by the fermentation of lactose when milk sours and used in tanning leather, as a preservative, etc.

lac·tif·er·ous (lak tif'ər əs) *adj.* [< LL. < L. *lac* (see LACTO-) + *ferre*, to BEAR¹ + -OUS] **1.** giving or carrying milk **2.** forming a milky fluid

lac·to- [< L. *lactis*, genitive of *lac*, milk] *a combining form meaning:* **1.** milk **2.** *Chem.* lactic acid or lactate Also, before a vowel, **lact-**

lac·tose (lak'tōs) *n.* [LACT(O)- + -OSE¹] a white, crystalline sugar, $C_{12}H_{22}O_{11}$, found in milk and used in infant foods, medicine, etc.

la·cu·na (lə kyōō'nə) *n., pl.* **-nas, -nae** (-nē) [L., a ditch < *lacus*, lake] **1.** a space where something has been omitted or has come out; missing part; gap; hiatus **2.** *Anat., Biol.* any of the very small cavities in bone that are filled with bone cells —**la·cu'nar** (-nər), **la·cu'nal** *adj.*

la·cus·trine (lə kus'trin) *adj.* [< Fr. < L. *lacus*, lake] **1.** of or having to do with lakes **2.** found or formed in lakes

lac·y (lā'sē) *adj.* **lac'i·er, lac'i·est 1.** of lace **2.** like lace; having a delicate open pattern —**lac'i·ly** *adv.* —**lac'i·ness** *n.*

lad (lad) *n.* [ME. *ladde]* **1.** a boy or youth **2.** [Colloq.] any man; fellow

lad·der (lad'ər) *n.* [OE. *hlæder:* for IE. base see CLIENT] **1.** a framework of two parallel sidepieces connected by rungs or crosspieces on which a person steps in climbing up or down **2.** anything by means of which a person climbs or rises *[the ladder* of success*]*

lad·die (lad'ē) *n.* [Chiefly Scot.] a young lad

lade (lād) *vt., vi.* **lad'ed, lad'ed** or **lad'en, lad'ing** [OE. *hladan]* **1.** to load **2.** to dip (water, etc.) with a ladle

lad·en (lād''n) *alt. pp. of* LADE —*adj.* **1.** loaded **2.** burdened; afflicted *[laden* with sorrow*]*

la-di-da, la-de-da (lä'dē dä') *adj.* [Colloq.] affected in speech, manners, etc.; refined or in a showy way

☆**Ladies' Day** a special day on which women may attend a particular event, as a baseball game, free or at reduced cost

lad·ing (lā'diŋ) *n.* **1.** the act of one that lades **2.** a load; cargo; freight

la·dle (lā'd'l) *n.* [OE. *hlædel* < *hladan*, to draw water] a cuplike spoon with a long handle, for dipping out liquids —*vt.* **-dled, -dling 1.** to dip out with or as with a ladle **2.** to carry in a ladle —**la'dle·ful'** *n., pl.* **-fuls'** —**la'dler** *n.*

---

fat, āpe, cär; ten, ēven; is, bīte; gō, hôrn, tōōl, lŏŏk; oil, out; up, fur; get; joy; yet; chin; she; thin, then; zh, leisure; ŋ, ring; ə for *a* in *ago*, *e* in *agent*, *i* in *sanity*, *o* in *comply*, *u* in *focus*; ' as in *able* (ā'b'l); Fr. bàl; ë, Fr. coeur; ö, Fr. feu; Fr. mon; ô, Fr. coq; ü, Fr. duc; r, Fr. crl; H, G. ich; kh, G. doch; ‡foreign; ☆ Americanism; < derived from. See inside front cover.

La·do·ga (lä′dô gä), **Lake** lake in the northwestern R.S.F.S.R., near the border of Finland: c.7,000 sq. mi.

la·dy (lä′dē) *n., pl.* **-dies** [OE. *hlæfdige < hlaf,* loaf + base of *dæge,* kneader (see DOUGH)] **1.** a woman with the rights, rule, or authority of a lord **2.** *a)* a woman of high social position *b)* a woman who is polite, refined, and well-mannered **3.** any woman **4.** [L-] the Virgin Mary (usually with *Our*) **5.** [L-] in Great Britain, the title given to women of certain ranks —*adj.* female *[a lady barber]* —see **SYN**· at WOMAN

la·dy·bug (-bug′) *n.* a small, roundish beetle with a spotted back, that feeds chiefly on insect pests and their eggs: also **la′dy·bird′ (beetle)**

Lady Day *Brit. name for* ANNUNCIATION (sense 2 *b*)

la·dy·fin·ger (-fin′gər) *n.* a small spongecake shaped a little like a finger

la·dy-in-wait·ing (-in wāt′iŋ) *n., pl.* **la′-dies-in-wait′ing** a woman attending, or waiting upon, a queen or princess

la·dy·like (-līk′) *adj.* like or suitable for a lady; refined; well-bred

la·dy·love (-luv′) *n.* a sweetheart

la·dy·ship (-ship′) *n.* the rank or position of a lady: used in speaking to or of a woman having the title of *Lady,* preceded by *your* or *her*

la·dy-slip·per (-slip′ər) *n.* any of certain wild or cultivated orchids whose flowers somewhat resemble a slipper: also **la′dy's-slip′per**

la·e·trile (lä′ə tril) *n. [lae(vo-rotatory glycosidic ni)trile]* a compound obtained from various plant substances, esp. from apricot kernels, that is claimed to be helpful in treating cancers

La·fa·yette (laf′i yet′, lä′fi-, lə fā′it) [after the marquis de LAFAYETTE] city in SC La.: pop. 69,000

La·fa·yette (lä′fi yet′, laf′i-; *Fr.* là fà yet′), marquis **de** 1757–1834; Fr. general & statesman: served in Am. army in the American Revolution

La Fol·lette (lə fäl′it), **Robert Marion** 1855–1925; U.S. legislator & Progressive Party leader

La Fon·taine (lä fōn ten′; *E.* lə fän tān′), **Jean de** (zhän də) 1621–95; Fr. poet & writer of fables

lag (lag) *vi.* **lagged, lag′ging** [? akin to MDan. *lakke,* to go slowly] **1.** *a)* to fall, move, or stay behind; loiter *[the tired hikers lagged behind] b)* to move or develop more slowly than expected, hoped for, etc. *[the assembly line was lagging in production]* **2.** to become gradually less strong, energetic, etc.; wane; flag *[her interest in sports was lagging]* —*n.* **1.** a falling behind or being slowed or delayed in motion, development, etc. **2.** the amount of such falling behind *[a great lag between social behavior and scientific knowledge]* —**lag′ger** *n.*

lag bolt *same as* LAG SCREW

☆**la·ger (beer)** (lä′gər) [G. *lagerbier,* lit., storehouse beer] a beer which is stored for several months for aging after it has been brewed

lag·gard (lag′ərd) *n.* [< LAG + -ARD] a slow person, esp. one who is always falling behind —*adj.* slow or backward *[a laggard pupil]* —**lag′gard·ly** *adv., adj.* —**lag′gard·ness** *n.*

☆**la·gniappe, la·gnappe** (lan yap′, lan′yap) *n.* [Creole < Fr. *la,* the + Sp. *ñapa,* lagniappe < Quechua *yapa*] **1.** [Chiefly South] a small gift given to a customer with a purchase **2.** a gratuity or tip

la·goon (lə gōōn′) *n.* [< Fr. *lagune* & It. *laguna* < L. *lacuna,* lake] **1.** a shallow lake or pond, esp. one connected with a larger body of water **2.** the water enclosed by a circular coral reef **3.** shallow salt water separated from the sea by dunes

La·gos (lä′gäs, -gəs) capital of Nigeria; seaport on the Atlantic: pop. 665,000

La·grange (lä gränzh′), comte **Jo·seph Louis** (zhô zef′ lwē′) 1736–1814; Fr. mathematician & astronomer

lag screw a wood screw with a head like that of a bolt

lah-di-dah, lah-de-dah (lä′dē dä′) *adj. same as* LA-DI-DA

La·hore (lə hôr′, lä-) city in NE Pakistan: pop. 1,296,000

la·ic (lä′ik) *adj.* [< LL. *laicus* < Gr. < *laos,* the people] of the laity; secular; lay: also **la′i·cal** —**la′i·cal·ly** *adv.*

la·i·cize (lä′ə sīz′) *vt.* **-cized′, -ciz′ing** [LAIC + -IZE] to turn over to laymen; secularize

laid (lād) *pt. & pp. of* LAY[1]

lain (lān) *pp. of* LIE[1]

lair (ler) *n.* [OE. *leger:* for IE. base see LIE[1]] the resting place of a wild animal; den

laird (lerd; *Scot.* lärd) *n.* [Scot. form of LORD] in Scotland, a landowner, esp. a wealthy one

lais·sez faire (les′ā fer′, lez′-) [Fr., let (people) do (as they please)] the policy or practice of letting people act without interference; specif., the policy of letting the owners of industries and businesses operate without governmental regulation or control: also sp. **lais′ser faire′** —**lais′sez-faire′** *adj.*

la·i·ty (lä′ət ē) *n., pl.* **-ties** [< LAY[3]] **1.** all the people not included among the clergy; laymen as a group **2.** all the people not belonging to a particular profession

lake[1] (lāk) *n.* [OE. *lacu* & OFr. *lac,* both < L. *lacus,* lake] **1.** a large inland body of water, usually fresh water **2.** a pool of oil or other liquid

lake[2] (lāk) *n.* [see LAC] **1.** *a)* a dark-red pigment prepared from cochineal *b)* its color **2.** an insoluble coloring compound separated from a solution of a dye by adding a metallic salt

Lake Charles [after *Charles* Sallier, an early settler] city in SW La.: pop. 78,000

Lake District (or **Country**) lake & mountain region in NW England: home of Wordsworth, Coleridge, & Southey (the **Lake poets**)

lake dwelling a dwelling built on wooden piles rising above the surface of a lake, esp. a dwelling of this kind in prehistoric times

Lake of the Woods lake in N Minn. & in Ontario & Manitoba, Canada

☆**lak·er** (lā′kər) *n.* **1.** a fish, esp. a trout, found in lakes **2.** a lake ship, esp. one on the Great Lakes

lake trout ☆a large, gray game fish of deep, cold lakes of the northern U.S. and Canada

Lake·wood (lāk′wood) **1.** city in NC Colo.: suburb of Denver: pop. 93,000 **2.** city in SW Calif.: suburb of Los Angeles: pop. 83,000 **3.** city in NE Ohio: suburb of Cleveland: pop. 70,000

lakh (lak) *n.* [< Hindi (see LAC): prob. in reference to the abundance of the insects] in India and Pakistan, **1.** the sum of 100,000: used esp. of rupees **2.** any indefinitely large number

☆**lal·ly·gag** (läl′ē gag′) *vi.* **-gagged′, -gag′ging** [Colloq.] *same as* LOLLYGAG

lam[1] (lam) *vt., vi.* **lammed, lam′ming** [< Scand., as in ON. *lemja*] [Slang] to beat; strike; thrash

☆**lam**[2] (lam) *n.* [< ?] [Slang] headlong flight, usually to escape punishment for a crime —*vi.* **lammed, lam′ming** [Slang] to run away; escape —**on the lam** [Slang] in flight, as from the police —**take it on the lam** [Slang] to run away; escape

Lam. Lamentations

la·ma (lä′mə) *n.* [Tibetan *blama*] a priest or monk in Lamaism: see DALAI LAMA

La·ma·ism (lä′mə iz′m) *n.* a form of Buddhism practiced in Tibet and Mongolia: it has a complex ritual and ranks of priests —**La′ma·ist** *adj., n.* —**La′ma·is′tic** *adj.*

La·marck (lä märk′; *E.* lə märk′), chevalier **de** 1744–1829; Fr. naturalist who advanced the evolutionary theory that acquired characters can be inherited (see ACQUIRED CHARACTER) —**La·marck′i·an** *adj., n.* —**La·marck′ism** *n.*

la·ma·ser·y (lä′mə ser′ē) *n., pl.* **-ser′ies** [< Fr.] a monastery of lamas

lamb (lam) *n.* [OE.] **1.** a young sheep **2.** its flesh, used as food **3.** lambskin **4.** a gentle or innocent person, esp. a child **5.** a loved person; dear —*vi.* to give birth: said of a ewe —**the Lamb** Jesus —**lamb′like′** *adj.*

Lamb (lam), **Charles** 1775–1834; Eng. essayist & critic

lam·baste (lam bāst′, -bast′) *vt.* **-bast′ed, -bast′ing** [LAM[1] + BASTE[3]] [Colloq.] **1.** to beat or thrash **2.** to scold or criticize harshly Also sp. **lam·bast′**

lamb·da (lam′də) *n.* the eleventh letter of the Greek alphabet (Λ, λ)

lam·bent (lam′bənt) *adj.* [< L. prp. of *lambere,* to lick] **1.** moving about lightly over a surface; flickering: said of a flame, etc. **2.** softly glowing *[a lambent sky]* **3.** light and graceful *[lambent wit]* —**lam′ben·cy** *n.* —**lam′bent·ly** *adv.*

lamb·kin (lam′kin) *n.* a little lamb

Lamb of God Jesus: John 1:29, 36

lamb·skin (lam′skin′) *n.* **1.** the skin of a lamb, esp. with the fleece left on it **2.** leather or parchment made from the skin of a lamb

lamb's-quar·ters (lamz′kwôr′tərz) *n.* an annual weed of the goosefoot family, with mealy leaves sometimes used for greens

lame (lām) *adj.* [OE. *lama*] **1.** crippled; esp., having an injured leg or foot that makes one limp **2.** stiff and painful *[a lame* back*]* **3.** poor, weak, unconvincing, etc. *[a lame* excuse*]* —*vt.* **lamed, lam′ing** to make lame —**lame′ly** *adv.* —**lame′ness** *n.*

la·mé (la mā′) *n.* [Fr., laminated < *lame,* metal plate] a fabric interwoven with metal threads

☆**lame·brain** (lām′brān′) *n.* [Colloq.] a slow-witted or stupid person —**lame′brained′** *adj.*

lame duck ☆an elected official whose term extends beyond the time of the election at which he was not reelected

la·mel·la (lə mel′ə) *n., pl.* **-lae** (-ē), **-las** [L., dim. of LAMINA] *Biol.* a thin, flat part, layer, organ, or structure —**la·mel′lar, la·mel·late** (lam′ə lāt′, lə mel′āt) *adj.* —**la·mel′li·ly** *adv.*

la·mel·li·branch (lə mel′i braŋk′) *n.* [see prec. & BRANCHIAE] any of a class of mollusks, including the clams, oysters, etc., having thin, flat gills and bivalve shells

la·ment (lə ment′) *vi.* [< Fr. < L. < *lamentum,* a wailing] to feel or express deep sorrow; mourn; grieve —*vt.* **1.** to mourn or grieve for *[to lament* a person's death*]* **2.** to regret deeply *[you will lament* that choice*]* —*n.* **1.** an outward expression of sorrow; lamentation; wail **2.** a song, poem, etc. mourning a loss, death, etc.; elegy or dirge —**la·ment′er** *n.* —**la·ment′ing·ly** *adv.*

lam·en·ta·ble (lam′ən tə b'l, lə men′tə b'l) *adj.* to be lamented; regrettable; distressing *[a lamentable* accident*]* —**lam′-en·ta·bly** *adv.*

lam·en·ta·tion (lam′ən tā′shən) *n.* a lamenting; wailing because of grief

Lam·en·ta·tions (lam′ən tā′shənz) a book of the Bible said to have been written by Jeremiah

la·ment·ed (lə men′tid) *adj.* mourned for: usually said of someone dead —**la·ment′ed·ly** *adv.*

lam·i·na (lam′ə nə) *n., pl.* **-nae** (-nē′), **-nas** [L.] **1.** a thin flake, scale, or layer, as of metal, animal tissue, etc. **2.** the broad, flat part of a leaf —**lam′i·nar** (-nər), **lam′i·nal** *adj.*

lam·i·nate (lam′ə nāt′; *for adj. & n. usually* -nit) *vt.* **-nat′ed, -nat′ing** **1.** to form or press into a thin sheet or layer **2.** to separate into thin layers **3.** to cover with or bond to thin layers, as of clear plastic **4.** to make (plywood, etc.) by building up in layers —*vi.* to split into thin layers —*adj. same as* LAMINATED —*n.* something made by laminating —**lam′i·na′tor** *n.*

lam·i·nat·ed (lam′ə nā′tid) *adj.* made up of or built in thin sheets or layers, as of fabric, wood, plastic, etc., that have been bonded or pressed together

lam·i·na·tion (lam′ə nā′shən) *n.* **1.** a laminating **2.** a laminated structure; something built up in layers **3.** a thin layer

lam·mer·gei·er, lam·mer·gey·er (lam′ər gī′ər) *n.* [< G. < *pl.* of *lamm,* lamb + *geier,* vulture] a large European and Asiatic bird of prey of the vulture family

lamp (lamp) *n.* [< OFr. < VL. *lampade,* ult. < Gr. *lampein,* to shine] **1.** a container with a wick for burning oil, alcohol, etc. to produce light or heat **2.** any device for producing light or healthful rays, as a gas jet with a mantle, an electric light bulb, or an ultraviolet bulb **3.** a holder, stand, or base for such a device

lamp·black (lamp′blak′) *n.* fine soot produced by the incomplete burning of oils and other forms of carbon: used as a pigment in paint, ink, etc.

lamp·light (-līt′) *n.* light given off by a lamp

lamp·light·er (-līt′ər) *n.* a person whose work is lighting and putting out gas street lamps

lam·poon (lam pōōn′) *n.* [< Fr. < *lampons,* let us drink (refrain in a drinking song)] a piece of satirical writing, usually attacking or making fun of someone —*vt.* to attack or make fun of in a lampoon —**lam·poon′er, lam·poon′ist** *n.*

lamp·post (lamp′pōst′, lamp′-) *n.* a post supporting a street lamp

lam·prey (lam′prē) *n., pl.* **-preys** [< OFr. < ML. *lampreda*] a fish like an eel, with a funnel-shaped, sucking mouth: it preys on other fish

lamp shell [from its resemblance to an ancient Roman oil lamp] a brachiopod

La·na·i (lä nä′ē) [Haw., var. of *nanai,* a swelling: so called because of its shape] island of Hawaii, west of Maui

LAMPREY
(to 3 ft. long)

☆**la·nai** (lä nī′, la-) *n.* [Haw.] a veranda or open-sided living room of a kind found in Hawaii

Lan·cas·ter[1] (laŋ′kəs tər) ruling family of England (1399–1461) —**Lan·cas′tri·an** (-kas′trē ən) *adj., n.*

Lan·cas·ter[2] (laŋ′kəs tər) [after a city in England] city in SE Pa.: pop. 58,000

lance (lans) *n.* [OFr. < L. *lancea*] **1.** a weapon consisting of a long wooden shaft with a sharp metal head **2.** a lancer **3.** any sharp instrument like a lance, as a fish spear **4.** a surgical lancet —*vt.* **lanced, lanc′ing** **1.** to attack or pierce with a lance **2.** to cut open as with a lancet *[to lance* a boil*]*

lance corporal **1.** *Brit. Army* a private acting temporarily as a corporal ☆**2.** *U.S. Marine Corps* an enlisted man ranking below a corporal and above a private first class

lance·let (lans′lit) *n.* [LANCE + -LET] a small, invertebrate, fishlike sea animal closely related to the vertebrates; amphioxus

Lan·ce·lot (lan′sə lät′, -lət) *Arthurian Legend* the bravest and most famous of the Knights of the Round Table: he was Guinevere's lover

lan·ce·o·late (lan′sē ə lāt′, -lit) *adj.* [< LL. < *lanceola,* little lance] narrow and tapering like the head of a lance, as certain leaves

lanc·er (lan′sər) *n.* a cavalry soldier armed with a lance, or a member of a cavalry regiment originally armed with lances

lanc·ers (lan′sərz) *n.pl.* [*with sing. v.*] [< prec.] **1.** a 19th-cent. quadrille **2.** music for this

lance sergeant *Brit. Army* a corporal acting temporarily as a sergeant

lan·cet (lan′sit) *n.* [< OFr. dim. of *lance,* LANCE] **1.** a small, pointed surgical knife, usually two-edged, used for making small incisions, skin punctures, etc. **2.** *same as: a)* LANCET ARCH *b)* LANCET WINDOW

lancet arch a narrow, sharply pointed arch

lancet window a narrow, sharply pointed window set in a lancet arch

lance·wood (lans′wood′) *n.* **1.** a tough, elastic wood used for fishing rods, billiard cues, etc. **2.** a tropical tree yielding such wood

land (land) *n.* [OE. < IE. base *lendh-,* heath] **1.** the solid part of the earth's surface not covered by water **2.** *a)* a country, region, etc. *[a distant land,* one's native *land] b)* a country's people **3.** ground or soil *[rich land,* high *land]* **4.** ground thought of as property *[to invest in land]* **5.** rural or farming regions *[to return to the land]* **6.** *Econ.* natural resources —*vt.* **1.** to put on shore from a ship *[the ship landed* its cargo*]* **2.** to cause to end up in a particular place or condition *[a fight landed* him in jail*]* **3.** to set (an aircraft) down on land or water **4.** to catch *[to land* a fish*]* **5.** [Colloq.] to get or win *[to land* a job*]* **6.** [Colloq.] to deliver (a blow) —*vi.* **1.** to leave a ship and go on shore *[the tourists landed]* **2.** to come to a port or to shore: said of a ship **3.** to arrive at a specified place *[he landed* in Phoenix after a long bus ride*]* **4.** to alight or come to rest, as after a flight, jump, or fall *[the cat landed* on its feet*]* —**land on** ☆[Colloq.] to scold or criticize harshly

lan·dau (lan′dou, -dô) *n.* [< *Landau,* German town where orig. made] **1.** a four-wheeled carriage with the top in two sections, which can be lowered independently **2.** a former style of automobile with a top whose back could be folded down

land breeze a breeze blowing from the land out to sea

land contract a contract in which a purchaser of real estate, upon making an initial payment, agrees to pay set amounts at specified intervals until the total purchase price is paid, at which time the seller transfers his interest in the property

LANDAU

land·ed (lan′did) *adj.* **1.** owning land *[landed* gentry*]* **2.** consisting of land or real estate *[a landed* estate*]*

land·fall (land′fôl′) *n.* **1.** a sighting of land from a ship at sea **2.** the land sighted **3.** a landing by ship or airplane

land·fill (-fil′) *n.* **1.** the disposal of garbage, rubbish, etc. by burying it under a shallow layer of ground **2.** a place used for this purpose **3.** garbage, rubbish, etc. so disposed of

---

land·form (-fôrm′) *n.* a feature on the earth's surface, as a hill or valley, caused by erosion, volcanic action, etc.

☆**land-grab·ber** (-grab′ər) *n.* a person who gets to own a piece of land unfairly or dishonestly

☆**land grant** a grant of public land by the government for a railroad, State college, etc.

land·grave (land′grāv′) *n.* [< G. < *land,* LAND + *graf,* a count] **1.** in medieval Germany, a count having jurisdiction over a specified territory **2.** later, the title of certain German princes

land·hold·er (-hōl′dər) *n.* an owner or occupant of land — **land′hold′ing** *adj., n.*

land·ing (lan′diŋ) *n.* **1.** the act of coming to shore or putting ashore **2.** the place where a ship can land; pier, dock, etc. **3.** a platform at the end of a flight of stairs **4.** the act of coming to the ground, as after a flight, jump, or fall

landing craft naval craft designed to bring troops and equipment close to shore

landing field a field with a smooth surface to enable airplanes to land and take off easily

landing gear the undercarriage of an aircraft, including wheels, pontoons, etc.

landing net a baglike net attached to a long handle, for taking a hooked fish from the water

landing strip *same as* AIRSTRIP

land·la·dy (land′lā′dē) *n., pl.* **-dies** a woman landlord

land·less (-lis) *adj.* not owning land

land·locked (-läkt′) *adj.* **1.** entirely or almost entirely surrounded by land, as a bay or a country **2.** living in fresh water, cut off from the sea *[landlocked salmon]*

land·lord (-lôrd′) *n.* **1.** a person, esp. a man, who rents or leases land, houses, etc. to others **2.** a man who keeps a rooming house, inn, etc.

land·lub·ber (-lub′ər) *n.* a person who has had little experience at sea, and is therefore awkward aboard a ship: a sailor's term of contempt

land·mark (-märk′) *n.* **1.** any fixed object used to mark the boundary of a piece of land **2.** a tree, building, etc. that is easily seen and thus helps one to find or recognize a place **3.** an event, discovery, etc. considered as a high point or turning point in the development of something *[a landmark in the history of science]*

land·mass (-mas′) *n.* a very large area of land; esp., a continent

land mine an explosive charge hidden under the surface of the ground and set off by pressure upon it

☆**land office** a government office that handles and records the sales and transfers of public lands

☆**land-of·fice business** (land′ôf′is) [with reference to Western U.S. land offices in the 19th c.] a booming business *[the store does a land-office business before Christmas]*

Land of Promise *same as* PROMISED LAND

land·own·er (land′ō′nər) *n.* one who owns land —**land′own′er·ship′** *n.* —**land′own′ing** *adj., n.*

☆**land-poor** (land′poor′) *adj.* owning land, often much land, but poor, or lacking ready money, because of high taxes on the land, its low yield, etc.

land reform the redistribution of agricultural land by breaking up large landholdings and giving out shares to small farmers, peasants, etc.

land·scape (land′skāp′) *n.* [< Du. < *land,* land + *-schap,* -SHIP] **1.** a picture representing natural, inland scenery *[to paint a mountain landscape]* **2.** an expanse of natural scenery seen in one view —*vt.* **-scaped′, -scap′ing** to change the natural features of (a piece of land) so as to make it more attractive, as by adding lawns, bushes, trees, etc. —*vi.* to work as a landscape architect or gardener —**land′scap′er** *n.*

☆**landscape architecture** the art or profession of planning or changing the natural scenery of a place for a desired purpose or effect —**landscape architect**

landscape gardening the art or work of arranging lawns, trees, etc. on a plot of ground to make it more attractive —**landscape gardener**

land·scap·ist (land′skāp′ist) *n.* a painter of landscapes

Land·seer (land′sir), Sir **Edwin Harry** 1802–73; Eng. painter

Land's End cape in Cornwall at the southwesternmost point of England: also **Lands End**

☆**land·slide** (land′slīd′) *n.* **1.** the sliding of a mass of loosened rocks or earth down a hillside or slope **2.** the mass sliding down **3.** an overwhelming majority of votes for a candidate, party, etc. in an election

land·slip (-slip′) *n.* [Chiefly Brit.] *same as* LANDSLIDE (senses 1 & 2)

lands·man (landz′mən) *n., pl.* **-men 1.** a person who lives on land: distinguished from SEAMAN **2.** [partly via Yid. < MHG.] a fellow countryman

Land·stei·ner (land′stī′nər; *G* länt′shtī′nər), **Karl** 1868–1943; U.S. pathologist & immunologist, born in Austria

land·ward (land′wərd) *adv.* toward the land: also **land′wards** —*adj.* situated or facing toward the land

lane (lān) *n.* [OE. *lanu*] **1.** a narrow way between hedges, walls, etc.; narrow country road or city street **2.** any narrow way, as an opening in a crowd **3.** *same as: a)* AIR LANE *b)* SEA LANE ☆**4.** a marked strip of road wide enough for a single line of cars, trucks, etc. **5.** any of the parallel courses marked off for contestants in a race **6.** *Bowling* a long, narrow strip of highly polished wood, along which the balls are rolled; alley

lang. language

Lang·er (laŋ′ər), **Susanne K(atherina)** (born *Susanne Katherina Knauth*) 1895– ; U.S. philosopher

Lang·land (laŋ′lənd), **William** 1332?–1400?; Eng. poet

Lang·ley (laŋ′lē), **Samuel Pier·pont** (pir′pänt) 1834–1906; U.S. astronomer & pioneer in airplane construction

‡**lan·gouste** (län gōōst′) *n.* [Fr.] *same as* SPINY LOBSTER

lang·syne (laŋ′sīn′, -zīn′) *adv.* [Scot. < *lang,* LONG[1] + *syne,* since] [Scot.] long ago —*n.* [Scot.] the long ago; bygone days Also **lang syne**

lan·guage (laŋ′gwij) *n.* [< OFr. < *langue,* tongue < L. *lingua:* see TONGUE] **1.** *a)* human speech *b)* the ability to communicate by human speech *c)* the vocal sounds used in speech, or the written symbols for them **2.** *a)* any means of communicating, as gestures, animal sounds, etc. *b)* a special set of symbols, rules, etc. used for handling information, as in a computer **3.** all the vocal sounds, spoken or written words, and ways of combining them common to a particular nation, tribe, etc. *[the French language]* **4.** the special words, phrases, and style of expression of a particular group, writer, profession, etc. *[the language of teen-agers]* **5.** the study of language or languages; linguistics —**speak one's** (or **the same**) **language** to have the same beliefs, attitudes, etc. as another

‡**langue d'oc** (läng dôk′) [Fr., lit., language of *oc:* from the characteristic use of Pr. *oc* for "yes": see next entry] a group of French dialects spoken in southern France in the Middle Ages and surviving in Provençal

‡**langue d'o·ïl** (läng dô ēl′) [Fr., lit., language of *oïl:* from the characteristic use of OFr. *oïl* for "yes": see prec.] a group of French dialects spoken in most of central and northern France in the Middle Ages: it is the Old French from which modern French is derived

lan·guid (laŋ′gwid) *adj.* [< Fr. < L. < *languere,* to be faint: for IE. base see LAX] **1.** without vigor or vitality; drooping; weak **2.** without interest or spirit; listless **3.** sluggish; slow —**lan′guid·ly** *adv.* —**lan′guid·ness** *n.*

lan·guish (laŋ′gwish) *vi.* [< OFr. < L. < *languere:* see prec.] **1.** to lose vigor or vitality; become weak; droop **2.** to live under distressing conditions *[to languish in poverty]* **3.** to become slack or dull *[his interest languished]* **4.** to suffer with longing; pine **5.** to pretend to have tender or sad feelings —**lan′guish·er** *n.* —**lan′guish·ing** *adj.* —**lan′guish·ing·ly** *adv.* —**lan′guish·ment** *n.*

lan·guor (laŋ′gər) *n.* [< OFr. < L. < *languere:* see LANGUID] **1.** a feeling of being weak or tired *[the hot sun filled her with languor]* **2.** a lack of interest or spirit; listlessness **3.** tenderness of mood or feeling **4.** the condition of being still, sluggish, or dull —see SYN. at LETHARGY —**lan′guor·ous** *adj.* —**lan′guor·ous·ly** *adv.* —**lan′guor·ous·ness** *n.*

lan·gur (luŋ′goor′) *n.* [< Hindi < Sans. *laṅgūlin,* lit., having a tail] any of certain monkeys of SE Asia, with a long tail and a chin tuft

lan·iard (lan′yərd) *n. same as* LANYARD

La·nier (lə nir′), **Sidney** 1842–81; U.S. poet

lank (laŋk) *adj.* [OE. *hlanc* < IE. base *kleng-,* to bend] **1.** long and slender; lean **2.** straight and limp; not curly: said of hair —**lank′ly** *adv.* —**lank′ness** *n.*

lank·y (laŋ′kē) *adj.* **lank′i·er, lank′i·est** [LANK + -Y[2]] awkwardly tall and lean or long and slender —see SYN. at LEAN[2] —**lank′i·ly** *adv.* —**lank′i·ness** *n.*

lan·o·lin (lan′'l in) *n.* [< L. *lana,* wool + *oleum,* oil + -IN[1]] a fatty substance obtained from sheep wool and used in ointments, cosmetics, etc.: also **lan′o·line** (-in, -ēn)

Lan·sing (lan′siŋ) [after J. *Lansing* (1751–1829), U.S. jurist] capital of Mich.: pop. 132,000

lan·ta·na (lan tä′nə, -tä′-) *n.* [ModL. < It. dial., viburnum] any of a group of shrubby plants growing in tropical America

lan·tern (lan'tərn) *n.* [< OFr. < L. *lanterna* < Gr. *lamptēr* < *lampein*, to shine] **1.** a transparent case for holding a light and protecting it from wind and weather **2.** the room containing the lamp at the top of a lighthouse **3.** an open or windowed structure on a roof or dome, for letting in light and air

lantern jaw 1. a lower jaw that juts out **2.** [*pl.*] long, thin jaws, with sunken cheeks, that give the face a gaunt look —**lan'tern-jawed'** *adj.*

lantern slide a photographic slide for projection, as, originally, by a magic lantern

lan·tha·nide series (lan'thə nīd') [< LANTHANUM] the rare-earth group of chemical elements from element 58 (cerium) through element 71 (lutetium)

lan·tha·num (lan'thə nəm) *n.* [ModL. < Gr. *lanthanein*, to be concealed] a silvery, metallic chemical element of the rare-earth group: symbol, La; at. wt., 138.91; at. no., 57

lan·yard (lan'yərd) *n.* [< MFr. *laniere* < OFr. < *lasne*, noose: altered after YARD[1]] **1.** a short rope used on board ship for holding or fastening something **2.** a cord used by sailors, etc. to hang a knife, whistle, etc. around the neck **3.** a cord for firing certain types of cannon

La·oc·o·ön (lā äk'ə wän') *Gr. Legend* a Trojan priest who, with his two sons, was destroyed by two huge sea serpents after he had warned the Trojans against the wooden horse

La·os (lä'ōs, lous) kingdom in the NW part of the Indochinese peninsula; 91,429 sq. mi.; pop. 2,893,000; caps. Vientiane & Luang Prabang —**La·o·tian** (lā ō'shən) *adj., n.*

Lao-tse (lou'dzu') 604? B.C.–?; Chin. philosopher: reputed founder of Taoism: also sp. **Lao-tzu, Lao-tsze**

lap[1] (lap) *n.* [OE. *læppa* < IE. base *leb-*, to hang down] **1.** [Now Rare] the skirt of a coat or gown **2.** *a)* the front part from the waist to the knees of a person in a sitting position *b)* the part of the clothing covering this **3.** that in which one is cared for, sheltered, etc. [raised in the *lap* of luxury] **4.** *a)* an overlapping part *b)* the overlapping of one part by another *c)* amount or place of this **5.** a turn or loop, as of a rope around a post **6.** a revolving disk for cutting and polishing glass, gems, etc. **7.** *a)* one complete circuit around a race track, in a race consisting of more than one *b)* one part or stage of a lengthy task, trip, etc. **8.** the act or condition of lapping —*vt.* **lapped, lap'ping 1.** to fold (*over* or *on*) **2.** to wrap; enfold **3.** to hold as in the lap; envelop **4.** to place partly upon something else [to *lap* one board over another] **5.** to lie partly upon; overlap [one board *laps* the other] **6.** to cut or polish (glass, gems, etc.) with a lap **7.** to get a lap ahead of (an opponent) in a race —*vi.* **1.** to lie partly on something or on one another; overlap **2.** to extend beyond something in space or time (with *over*) [the English class *lapped* over into the next period] —**drop** (or **dump**, etc.) **into someone's lap** to cause to be someone's responsibility —**in the lap of the gods** beyond human control

lap[2] (lap) *vi., vt.* **lapped, lap'ping** [OE. *lapian*] **1.** to drink (a liquid) by dipping it up with the tongue as a dog does **2.** to move or strike gently with a light splashing sound: said of waves, etc. —*n.* **1.** the act of lapping **2.** the sound of lapping —**lap up 1.** to take up (liquid) by lapping **2.** [Colloq.] to take in eagerly —**lap'per** *n.*

La Paz (lä päs'; *E.* lə päz') city in W Bolivia: seat of government (see SUCRE): pop. 482,000

lap·board (lap'bôrd') *n.* a flat board placed on or over the lap and used as a table or desk

lap dissolve *Motion Pictures & TV* a dissolving view in which a new scene is blended in with a scene being faded out, as by lapping two exposures on one film

lap dog a pet dog small enough to hold in the lap

la·pel (lə pel') *n.* [dim. of LAP[1]] either of the front parts of a coat folded back and forming a continuation of the collar

lap·ful (lap'fool') *n., pl.* -**fuls'** as much as a lap can hold

lap·i·dar·y (lap'ə der'ē) *n., pl.* -**dar'ies** [< LL. *lapidarius* < L.

< *lapis*, a stone] a workman who cuts, polishes, and engraves precious stones —*adj.* **1.** of or connected with the art of cutting and engraving precious stones **2.** like an inscription on a monument; short, precise, and elegant

lap·in (lap'in) *n.* [Fr., rabbit] rabbit fur, generally dyed in imitation of more valuable skins

lap·is laz·u·li (lap'is laz'yoo lī', lazh'-; -lē') [ModL. < L. *lapis*, a stone + ML. genitive of *lazulus*, azure < Ar.: see AZURE] an azure-blue, opaque, semiprecious stone

lap joint a joint made by overlapping parts and fastening them together: also **lapped joint** —**lap'-joint'** *vt.*

La·place (lä pläs'), marquis **Pierre Si·mon de** (pyer sē môn' də) 1749–1827; Fr. mathematician & astronomer

Lap·land (lap'land') region of N Europe, including the N parts of Scandinavia & Finland & a NW section of the U.S.S.R., inhabited by the Lapps

La Pla·ta (lä plä'tä) seaport in E Argentina, on the Río de la Plata: pop. 337,000

Lapp (lap) *n.* **1.** a member of a Mongoloid people living in Lapland and partly nomadic there: also **Lap'land·er 2.** their Finno-Ugric language: also **Lap'pish**

lap·pet (lap'it) *n.* [dim. of LAP[1]] a small fold or flap, as of a garment or as of flesh

☆**lap robe** a heavy blanket, fur wrap, etc. laid over the lap and legs for warmth, as when watching outdoor sports

lapse (laps) *n.* [L. *lapsus*, a fall < pp. of *labi*, to slip: for IE. base see LAP[1]] **1.** a slip or small error [a *lapse* of memory] **2.** *a)* a falling away from a moral standard; moral slip *b)* a falling or slipping into a lower or worse condition, esp. for a short time **3.** a falling away from one's belief or faith **4.** a passing away, as of time **5.** *Law* the termination of a right or privilege through disuse or failure to meet stated obligations —*vi.* **lapsed, laps'ing 1.** to slip into a specified state [to *lapse* into a coma] **2.** to slip from a higher standard or fall back into former ways; backslide **3.** to pass away: said of time **4.** to come to an end; stop [his subscription *lapsed*] **5.** to become void because of failure to pay the premium at the stipulated time: said of an insurance policy —**laps'a·ble, laps'i·ble** *adj.*

lap·wing (lap'win') *n.* [altered by folk etym. < OE. *hleapewince* < *hleapan*, to leap + *wince* < *wincian*, WINK] an old-world crested plover noted for its irregular, wavering flight

lar·board (lär'bərd, -bôrd') *n.* [< OE. *hladan*, to lade + *bord*, side] the left-hand side of a ship as one faces forward; port —*adj.* on or of this side Now largely replaced by PORT[4]

lar·ce·ny (lär'sə nē) *n., pl.* -**nies** [< Anglo-Fr. < OFr. < L. < *latrocinari*, to rob < *latro*, robber] *Law* the unlawful taking away of another's property with the intention of depriving him of it; theft: sometimes separated into **grand larceny** (more than a stated amount varying from State to State, usually between $25 and $60) and **petit,** or **petty, larceny** (less than this amount) —**lar'ce·nist** *n.* —**lar'ce·nous** *adj.*

larch (lärch) *n.* [< G. < L. *larix*] **1.** a tree of the pine family, found throughout the N Hemisphere, bearing cones and needle-like leaves that are shed annually **2.** the tough wood of this tree

lard (lärd) *n.* [< OFr. < L. *lardum*] the fat of hogs, melted down and prepared as a soft, white solid —*vt.* **1.** to smear with lard or other fat; grease **2.** to put strips of fat pork, bacon, etc. on or into (meat or poultry) before cooking **3.** to add to here and there; embellish [a talk *larded* with jokes] —**lard'y** *adj.* **lard'i·er, lard'i·est**

lard·er (lär'dər) *n.* [< OFr. *lardier* < ML. < L. *lardum*, lard] **1.** a place where the food supplies of a household are kept; pantry **2.** a supply of food

Lard·ner (lärd'nər) **Ring(gold Wilmer)** 1885–1933; U.S. sports reporter & humorist

LANTERNS
(A, gasoline; B, garden; C, Chinese; D, electric)

LAP JOINT

ARCTIC OCEAN
NORWAY SWEDEN FINLAND LAPLAND U.S.S.R.
LAPLAND

La·re·do (lə rā′dō) [after *Laredo*, town in Spain] city in S Tex., on the Rio Grande: pop. 69,000

lar·es (ler′ēz, lā′rēz) *n.pl., sing.* **lar** (lär) [L.] in ancient Rome, the deified spirits of ancestors, who watched over the households of their descendants

lares and penates 1. the household gods of the ancient Romans **2.** the treasured belongings of a family or household

large (lärj) *adj.* **larg′er, larg′est** [OFr. < L. *largus*] **1.** big; great; specif., *a*) taking up much space; bulky *b*) enclosing much space; spacious [a *large* office] *c*) of great extent or amount [a *large* sum] **2.** big as compared with others of its kind [a *large* mouth] **3.** operating on a big scale [a *large* manufacturer] —*adv.* in a large way [to write *large*] —**at large 1.** free; not confined [the runaway bull was still *at large*] **2.** in general; taken altogether [in the interests of the community *at large*] ☆**3.** representing an entire State or area rather than only a subdivision [a congressman *at large*] —**large′ness** *n.*

SYN.—**large, big,** and **great** are often used interchangeably in referring to something of more than usual size, extent, etc. [a *large, big,* or *great* oak], but **large** is usually used with special reference to dimensions or quantity [a *large* studio, amount, etc.], **big** with special reference to bulk, weight, or extent [a *big* baby, a *big* difference], and **great** with special reference to size or extent that is impressive, imposing, surprising, etc. [the *Great* Lakes, a *great* success, etc.] —**ANT. small, little**

large·heart·ed (lärj′här′tid) *adj.* generous; kindly

large intestine the broader part of the intestines, between the small intestine and the anus, including the cecum, colon, and rectum

large·ly (lärj′lē) *adv.* **1.** much; in great amounts **2.** for the most part; mainly [he is *largely* to blame]

large-mind·ed (lärj′mīn′did) *adj.* liberal in one's views; tolerant; broad-minded

large-scale (lärj′skāl′) *adj.* **1.** drawn to a large scale [a *large-scale* map] **2.** of wide scope; extensive [*large-scale* business operations]

lar·gess, lar·gesse (lär jes′, lär′jis) *n.* [OFr. < *large*, LARGE] **1.** generous giving **2.** a generous gift or gifts

lar·ghet·to (lär get′ō) *adj., adv.* [It. < *largo*: see LARGO] *Music* relatively slow, but faster than largo —*n., pl.* **-tos** a larghetto movement or passage

larg·ish (lär′jish) *adj.* rather large

lar·go (lär′gō) *adj., adv.* [It., large, slow < L. *largus*, large] *Music* slow and stately in tempo —*n., pl.* **-gos** a largo movement or passage

☆**lar·i·at** (lar′ē it) *n.* [Sp. *la reata*, the rope] **1.** a rope used for tying grazing horses, etc. **2.** *same as* LASSO —*vt.* to tie or catch with a lariat

lark[1] (lärk) *n.* [OE. *læwerce*] **1.** any of a large family of chiefly old-world songbirds; esp., the skylark **2.** any of various similar birds, as the meadowlark

lark[2] (lärk) *vi.* [? altered after prec. < dial. *lake* < ME. *laike*, to play] to play or frolic —*n.* a frolic or spree; happy time — **lark′ish, lark′y** *adj.*

lark·spur (lärk′spur′) *n. a common name for* DELPHINIUM

La Roche·fou·cauld (là rôsh fōō kō′), duc **Fran·çois de** (frän swä′ də) 1613–80; Fr. moralist & writer of maxims

lar·rup (lar′əp) *vt.* [akin to or < Du. *larpen*] [Colloq.] to whip; flog; beat

lar·va (lär′və) *n., pl.* **-vae** (-vē), **-vas** [L., ghost] the early, free-living, immature form of an insect or of any animal that changes in structure when it becomes an adult [the caterpillar is the *larva* of the butterfly; the tadpole is the *larva* of the frog): see also PUPA —**lar′val** *adj.*

la·ryn·ge·al (lə rin′jē əl) *adj.* **1.** of, in, or near the larynx **2.** used for treating the larynx

lar·yn·gi·tis (lar′ən jīt′əs) *n.* [see -ITIS] inflammation of the larynx, often with a temporary loss of voice —**lar′yn·git′ic** (-jit/ik) *adj.*

la·ryn·go- [< Gr.] *a combining form meaning:* **1.** the larynx **2.** laryngeal and Also, before a vowel, **laryng-**

la·ryn·go·scope (lə rin′gə skōp′) *n.* [see -SCOPE] an instrument for examining the larynx —**lar·yn·gos·co·py** (lar′in·gäs′kə pē) *n.*

lar·ynx (lar′inks) *n., pl.* **lar′ynx·es, la·ryn·ges** (lə rin′jēz) [< Gr. *larynx*] **1.** the structure of muscle and cartilage at the upper end of the human trachea, containing the vocal cords and serving as the organ of voice: see illustration at EPIGLOTTIS **2.** a similar structure in other animals

la·sa·gna (lə zän′yə) *n.* [It., the noodle < L. *lasanum* (< Gr. *lasanon*), a pot] a dish of wide, flat noodles baked in layers with cheese, tomato sauce, and ground meat

La Salle (là sàl′; *E.* lə sal′), sieur **Ro·bert Cave·lier de** (rô·ber′ kàv lyä′ də) 1643–87; Fr. explorer in N. America

las·car (las′kər) *n.* [< Hindi < Per. *lashkar* < Ar. *al-'askar*, army] an Oriental sailor, esp. one who is a native of India

las·civ·i·ous (lə siv′ē əs) *adj.* [< ML. < L. *lascivus*, wanton: for IE. base see LUST] **1.** characterized by or expressing lust or lewdness; wanton **2.** tending to excite lustful feelings —**las·civ′i·ous·ly** *adv.* —**las·civ′i·ous·ness** *n.*

lase (lāz) *vi.* **lased, las′ing** to emit laser light

☆**la·ser** (lā′zər) *n.* [*l*(*ight*) *a*(*mplification by*) *s*(*timulated*) *e*(*mission of*) *r*(*adiation*)] a device that amplifies focused light waves and concentrates them in a narrow, very intense beam

lash[1] (lash) *n.* [ME. *lassche* < ?] **1.** a whip, esp. the flexible striking part **2.** a stroke as with a whip **3.** an eyelash —*vt.* **1.** to strike or drive as with a lash; flog **2.** to swing quickly or angrily; switch [the cat *lashed* her tail] **3.** to strike with great force [waves *lashed* the cliffs] **4.** to attack violently in words; censure or rebuke **5.** to stir up by appealing to the emotions [to *lash* the crowd into a frenzy] —*vi.* **1.** to move quickly or violently; switch **2.** to make strokes as with a whip —**lash out 1.** to strike out violently **2.** to speak angrily —**lash′er** *n.*

lash[2] (lash) *vt.* [< OFr. *lachier*: see LACE] to fasten or tie with a rope, etc.

lash·ing[1] (lash′iŋ) *n.* **1.** a whipping **2.** a strong rebuke

lash·ing[2] (lash′iŋ) *n.* **1.** the act of fastening or tying with a rope, etc. **2.** a rope, etc. so used

Las Pal·mas (läs päl′məs) seaport, & largest city, in the Canary Islands: pop. 244,000

La Spe·zia (lä spät′syä) seaport in NW Italy, on the Ligurian Sea: pop. 129,000

lass (las) *n.* [ME. *lasse*, prob. < ON.] **1.** a young woman; girl **2.** a sweetheart

Las·sen Volcanic National Park (las′'n) [after P. *Lassen*, Danish immigrant to Calif. in 1840] national park in N Calif., with an active volcano (**Lassen Peak**)

las·sie (las′ē) *n.* [dim. of LASS] [Scot.] **1.** a young girl **2.** a sweetheart

las·si·tude (las′ə tōōd′, -tyōōd′) *n.* [Fr. < L. < *lassus*, faint: for IE. base see LET[1]] a state or feeling of being tired and listless; weariness; languor —see **SYN.** at LETHARGY

☆**las·so** (las′ō, -ōō) *n., pl.* **-sos, -soes** [Sp. *lazo* < L. *laqueus*, noose] a long rope with a sliding noose at one end, used to catch cattle or horses —*vt.* **-soed, -so·ing** to catch with a lasso —**las′so·er** *n.*

LASSO

last[1] (last) *alt. superl. of* LATE *adj.* [< OE. *latost*, superl. of *læt*: see LATE] **1.** being or coming after all others in place or time; furthest from the first; final [the *last* day of the year] **2.** only remaining [the *last* cookie in the jar] **3.** most recent [*last* month] **4.** least likely [the *last* person to suspect] **5.** utmost; greatest **6.** lowest in rank, as a prize **7.** newest [the *last* thing in hats] **8.** conclusive [the *last* word in scientific research] **9.** individual; single: used for added force [eat every *last* bite] —*adv.* **1.** after all others; at the end [to come in *last*] **2.** most recently [I saw her *last* in June] **3.** finally [*last*, I will discuss foreign affairs] —*n.* **1.** someone or something which comes last [the *last* of the kings] **2.** end [friends to the *last*] —**at (long) last** after a long time —**see the last of** to see for the last time

SYN.—**last** applies to that which comes after all others in a series or sequence and suggests that nothing else follows [he was the *last* one to enter]; **final** applies to that which comes at the end and implies that it is so conclusive or decisive that no further change will take place [that's my *final* offer]; **terminal** applies to that which marks an end, limit, or extremity [the *terminal* outpost of a settlement]; **ultimate** applies to a concluding point or result beyond which it is impossible to go [the *ultimate* goal of a campaign] —**ANT. first**

last[2] (last) *vi.* [< OE. *læstan*: for IE. base see LEARN] **1.** to remain in existence or operation; continue; go on [it seemed the play *lasted* forever] **2.** to remain in good condition; wear well [stone *lasts* longer than wood] **3.** to continue unconsumed, unspent, etc.; be enough (for) [food to *last* (for) a month] —*vt.* to continue or endure throughout: often with *out* [doubtful whether he can *last* (out) the year] —see **SYN.** at CONTINUE —**last′er** *n.*

last[3] (last) *n.* [OE. *læste* < *last*, footstep < same base as prec.] a form shaped like a foot, on which shoes are made or repaired

—*vt.* to form with a last —**stick to one's last** **1.** to keep to one's own work **2.** to mind one's own business —**last′er** *n.*

last-ditch (last′dich′) *adj.* made, done, etc. in a final, often desperate effort to resist or oppose

Las·tex (las′teks) [< (E)LAS(TIC) + TEX(TILE)] *a trademark for* a fine, round rubber thread wound with cotton, silk, etc. and woven or knitted into fabric

last·ing (las′tiŋ) *adj.* that lasts a long time; enduring; durable [a *lasting* peace] —**last′ing·ly** *adv.* —**last′ing·ness** *n.*

Last Judgment *Theol.* the final judgment of mankind at the end of the world

last·ly (last′lē) *adv.* in conclusion; finally

last rites **1.** final rites for a dead person **2.** sacraments administered to a dying person

last straw [from the last straw that broke the camel's back in the fable] the last of a sequence of troubles or annoyances that results in a breakdown, loss of patience, etc.

Last Supper the last supper eaten by Jesus with his disciples before the Crucifixion

last word **1.** *a*) the final word or speech, regarded as settling the argument *b*) final authority [the president has the *last word* in such matters] **2.** something regarded as perfect **3.** [Colloq.] the very latest style

Las Ve·gas (läs vā′gəs) [Sp., the plains or meadows] city in SE Nev.: pop. 126,000

Lat. Latin

lat. latitude

La·ta·ki·a (lat′ə kē′ə) *n.* [< *Latakia*, a seaport in Syria] a fine grade of Turkish smoking tobacco

latch (lach) *n.* [OE. *læccan*, to catch] **1.** a fastening for a door or gate consisting of a bar that falls into a notch on the doorjamb or gatepost: now often used of a spring lock on a door **2.** a fastening for a window, etc. —*vt., vi.* to fasten with a latch ☆**latch onto** [Colloq.] to get or obtain —**on the latch** fastened by the latch but not bolted

latch·key (lach′kē′) *n.* a key for drawing back or unfastening the latch of a door from the outside

latch·string (-striŋ′) *n.* a cord fastened to a latch so that it can be raised from the outside

late (lāt) *adj.* **lat′er** or **lat′ter, lat′est** or **last** [OE. *læt:* for IE. base see LET[1]] **1.** happening, coming, etc. after the usual or expected time; tardy [the train was *late*] **2.** *a*) happening, continuing, etc. far on in the day, night, year, etc. [a *late* party] *b*) far advanced in a period, development, etc. [the *late* Middle Ages] **3.** recent [a *late* news bulletin] **4.** having been so recently but not now [our *late* allies] **5.** having recently died [her *late* father] —*adv.* **lat′er, lat′est** or **last 1.** after the usual or expected time [the roses bloomed *late*] **2.** at or until an advanced time of the day, night, year, etc. [we stayed up *late*] **3.** toward the end of a period, development, etc. [she arrived *late* in the day] **4.** recently [as *late* as yesterday] —see SYN. at DEAD —**of late** lately; recently —**late′ness** *n.*

LATCH

la·teen (la tēn′, lə-) *adj.* [< Fr. < (*voile*) *latine*, Latin (sail)] **1.** designating or of a triangular sail attached to a long yard suspended from a short mast: used chiefly on Mediterranean vessels **2.** having such a sail —*n.* a vessel with such a sail: also **la·teen′er**

Late Greek the Greek language of the period after classical Greek, seen chiefly in writings from c.200 to c.600 A.D.

Late Latin the Latin language of the period after classical Latin, seen chiefly in writings from c.200 to c.600 A.D.

LATEEN SAIL

late·ly (lāt′lē) *adv.* recently; a short while ago

la·tent (lāt′'nt) *adj.* [< L. prp. of *latere*, to lurk] lying hidden and undeveloped within a person or thing; concealed, dormant, etc. [a *latent* talent] —**la′ten·cy** *n.* —**la′tent·ly** *adv.*

latent heat additional heat needed to change a substance from a solid to a liquid at its melting point, or from a liquid to a gas at its boiling point, after the temperature of the substance has reached either of these points

latent period the time in the course of a disease between infection and the first appearance of the symptoms; incubation period

lat·er (lāt′ər) *alt. compar. of* LATE (adj.) —*adv. compar. of* LATE at a later time; subsequently —**later on** subsequently

lat·er·al (lat′ər əl) *adj.* [< L. < *lateris*, genitive of *latus*, a side] of, at, from, or toward the side; sideways [*lateral* movement] —*n.* **1.** any lateral part, growth, etc. ☆**2.** *Football short for* LATERAL PASS —**lat′er·al·ly** *adv.*

☆**lateral pass** *Football* a short pass parallel to the goal line or in a slightly backward direction

lat·er·ite (lat′ə rīt′) *n.* [L. *later*, brick + -ITE] *Geol.* a red, residual soil containing large amounts of aluminum and ferric hydroxides, formed by the decomposition of rocks —**lat′er·it′ic** (-rit′ik) *adj.*

lat·est (lāt′ist) *alt. superl. of* LATE —**at the latest** no later than (the time specified) —**the latest** the most recent thing, development, etc.

la·tex (lā′teks) *n., pl.* **lat·i·ces** (lat′ə sēz′), **la′tex·es** [L., a fluid] **1.** a milky liquid in certain plants and trees, as the rubber tree, milkweed, etc.: used esp. as the basis of rubber **2.** an emulsion in water of particles of synthetic rubber or plastic: used in rubber goods, adhesives, paints, etc.

lath (lath) *n., pl.* **laths** (lathz, laths) [OE. *lætt*] **1.** any of the thin, narrow strips of wood used in building lattices or nailed to two-by-fours, rafters, etc. as a groundwork for plastering, tiling, etc. **2.** any framework for plaster, as wire screening **3.** laths, esp. when used as a base for plaster —*vt.* to cover with laths

lathe (lāth) *n.* [prob. < MDu. *lade*] a machine for shaping an article of wood, metal, etc. by holding and turning it rapidly against the edge of a cutting tool —*vt.* **lathed, lath′ing** to shape on a lathe

lath·er (lath′ər) *n.* [OE. *leathor*, washing soda or soap < IE. base *lou-*, to wash, from which also comes L. *lavare*, to wash] **1.** the foam formed by soap or other detergent in water **2.** foamy sweat, as on a race horse ☆**3.** [Slang] an excited or agitated state —*vt.* to cover with lather [he *lathered* his face and shaved] —*vi.* to form, or become covered with, lather [few soaps *lather* in salt water] —**lath′er·y** *adj.*

lath·ing (lath′iŋ) *n.* **1.** laths, esp. when used as a base for plaster **2.** the putting up of laths on walls, etc. Also **lath′work′** (-wurk′)

lat·i·mer·i·a (lat′ə mir′ē ə) *n.* [ModL., after M. Courtenay-*Latimer* (1907–)] a deep-sea coelacanth fish with large, circular scales and six of its seven fins paddlelike: believed to be extinct until the recent discovery of specimens

Lat·in (lat′'n) *adj.* **1.** of ancient Latium or its people **2.** of ancient Rome or its people **3.** of or in the language of ancient Latium and ancient Rome **4.** designating or of the languages derived from Latin, the peoples who speak them, their countries, etc. **5.** of the Roman Catholic Church —*n.* **1.** a native or inhabitant of ancient Latium or ancient Rome **2.** the Italic language of ancient Latium and ancient Rome **3.** a person, as a Spaniard or Italian, whose language is derived from Latin

Latin America that part of the Western Hemisphere, south of the U.S., where Spanish, Portuguese, & French are official languages —**Latin American**

Lat·in·ate (-āt′) *adj.* of, derived from, or similar to Latin: also **La·tin·ic** (la tin′ik)

Latin Church *same as* ROMAN CATHOLIC CHURCH

Latin cross a plain, right-angle cross having the lowest arm the longest: see illustration at CROSS

Lat·in·ism (-iz′m) *n.* a Latin idiom or expression, used in another language

Lat·in·ist (-ist) *n.* a scholar in Latin

Lat·in·ize (-īz′) *vt.* **-ized′, -iz′ing 1.** to translate into Latin **2.** to give Latin form or characteristics to —*vi.* to use Latin expressions, forms, etc. —**Lat′in·i·za′tion** *n.* —**Lat′in·iz′er** *n.*

Latin Quarter [transl. of Fr. *Quartier Latin*] a section of Paris, south of the Seine, where many artists and students live

Latin Rite the liturgy used in the Roman Catholic Church

lat·ish (lāt′ish) *adj., adv.* somewhat late

lat·i·tude (lat′ə tōōd′, -tyōōd′) *n.* [OFr. < L. *latitudo* < *latus*, wide] **1.** freedom from narrow restrictions; freedom of opinion or action [a school that allows some *latitude* in choosing courses] **2.** *Geog. a*) angular distance, measured in degrees,

---

north or south from the equator [*a ship at forty degrees north latitude*] *b*) a place or region in relation to its latitude [*in this latitude it rarely snows*] —**lat′i·tu′di·nal** *adj.* —**lat′i·tu′di·nal·ly** *adv.*

lat·i·tu·di·nar·i·an (lat′ə tōōd′'n er′ē ən, -tyōōd′-) *adj.* [see prec. & -ARIAN] liberal in one's views; permitting free thought, esp. in religious matters —*n.* one who is very liberal in his views and, in religion, cares little about particular creeds and forms —**lat′i·tu′di·nar′i·an·ism** *n.*

La·ti·um (lā′shē əm) ancient country on the central coast of Italy, southeast of Rome

la·trine (lə trēn′) *n.* [Fr. < L. *latrina* < *lavare:* see LATHER] a toilet, privy, etc. for the use of many people, as in an army camp

-la·try (lə trē) [< Gr. < *latreia,* service] *a combining form meaning* worship of or too great devotion to [*idolatry*]

lat·ter (lat′ər) *adj. alt. compar. of* LATE [OE. *lættra,* compar. of *læt,* LATE] **1.** *a)* later; more recent *b)* nearer the end or close [*the latter part of May*] **2.** last mentioned or tioned of two: opposed to FORMER[1]: often used as a noun (with *the*) [*Jack and Bill are twins, but the latter is shorter than the former*]

LATIUM (4th cent. B.C.)

lat·ter-day (lat′ər dā′) *adj.* of recent or present time; modern

☆**Lat·ter-day Saint** *see* MORMON

lat·ter·ly (lat′ər lē) *adv.* lately; recently

lat·tice (lat′is) *n.* [OFr. *lattis* < MHG. *latte,* a lath] **1.** an openwork structure of crossed strips of wood, metal, etc. used as a screen, support, etc. **2.** a door, shutter, trellis, etc. formed of such a structure **3.** *Physics* a three-dimensional pattern of points in space, as of atoms in a solid or crystal —*vt.* **-ticed, -tic·ing 1.** to arrange like a lattice **2.** to furnish with a lattice

lat·tice·work (lat′is wurk′) *n.* **1.** a lattice **2.** lattices as a group Also **lat′tic·ing**

Lat·vi·a (lat′vē ə) republic of the U.S.S.R., in NE Europe, on the Baltic Sea: 24,594 sq. mi.; pop. 2,300,000; cap. Riga: in full, **Latvian Soviet Socialist Republic**

LATTICE

Lat·vi·an (lat′vē ən) *adj.* **1.** of Latvia or its people **2.** of the group of Baltic dialects spoken in Latvia —*n.* **1.** a native or inhabitant of Latvia **2.** the Baltic language of the Latvians

laud (lôd) *n.* [< OFr. < ML. *laudes,* pl. < L. *laus,* praise] **1.** praise **2.** any song of praise **3.** [*pl.*] *Eccles.* [*often* L-] the service which constitutes the second (or, together with matins, the first) of the canonical hours and includes psalms of praise to God —*vt.* to praise; extol—see SYN. at PRAISE

laud·a·ble (lôd′ə b'l) *adj.* worthy of being lauded; praiseworthy —**laud′a·bil′i·ty, laud′a·ble·ness** *n.* —**laud′a·bly** *adv.*

laud·a·num (lôd′'n əm) *n.* [ModL., altered use of ML. var. of L. *ladanum,* mastic] **1.** formerly, any of various opium preparations **2.** a solution of opium in alcohol

lau·da·tion (lô dā′shən) *n.* a lauding or being lauded; praise; commendation

laud·a·to·ry (lôd′ə tôr′ē) *adj.* expressing praise; eulogistic: also **laud′a·tive**

laugh (laf) *vi.* [OE. *hleahhan*] **1.** to make a series of quick sounds with the voice that show one is amused or happy or, sometimes, that show scorn **2.** to feel or suggest joyousness; appear bright and gay [*laughing eyes*] —*vt.* **1.** to express with laughter **2.** to cause to be, get rid of, etc. by means of laughter [*to laugh oneself hoarse*] —*n.* **1.** the act or sound of laughing **2.** anything that calls forth or is fit to call forth laughter **3.** [*pl.*] [Colloq.] mere fun or pleasure [*to do something for laughs*] — **have the last laugh** to win after seeming to have lost —**laugh at 1.** to be amused by **2.** to make fun of **3.** to be indifferent to or contemptuous of —**laugh off** to scorn, avoid, or reject by laughter or ridicule —**laugh on** (or **out of**) **the other** (or **wrong**) **side of the mouth** to change from joy to sorrow, from amusement to

annoyance, etc. —**no laughing matter** a serious matter — **laugh′er** *n.*

SYN.—**laugh** is the general word for the sounds made in expressing happiness, amusement, ridicule, etc.; **chuckle** implies the soft laughter in low tones that expresses mild amusement or inner satisfaction; **giggle** and **titter**, both often associated with children or girls, refer to a half-suppressed laugh consisting of a series of rapid, high-pitched sounds, suggesting embarrassment, silliness, etc.; **snicker** is used of a sly, half-suppressed laugh, as at another's embarrassment, confusion, etc.; **guffaw** refers to loud, hearty, coarse laughter

laugh·a·ble (laf′ə b'l) *adj.* of such a nature as to cause laughter; amusing or ridiculous —see SYN. at FUNNY —**laugh′a·ble·ness** *n.* —**laugh′a·bly** *adv.*

laugh·ing (-iŋ) *adj.* **1.** that laughs or seems to laugh [*a laughing brook*] **2.** uttered with laughter [*a laughing remark*] —*n.* laughter —**laugh′ing·ly** *adv.*

laughing gas nitrous oxide used as an anesthetic: it may cause laughter and exhilaration

laugh·ing·stock (laf′iŋ stäk′) *n.* a person or thing made the object of ridicule

laugh·ter (laf′tər) *n.* **1.** the action or sound of laughing **2.** an expression of amusement [*with laughter in her eyes*]

launch[1] (lônch, länch) *vt.* [< OFr. *lanchier* < LL. < L. *lancea,* LANCE] **1.** to hurl, discharge, or send off (a weapon, blow, rocket, etc.) **2.** to cause (a newly built vessel) to slide into the water; set afloat **3.** to set in operation; start [*to launch an attack*] **4.** to start (a person) on some course or career —*vi.* **1.** to put to sea (often with *out* or *forth*) **2.** to start on some new course or enterprise (often with *out* or *forth*) **3.** to throw oneself (*into*) with vigor; plunge [*to launch into a tirade*] —*n.* the act or process of launching a ship, spacecraft, etc. —*adj.* designating or of facilities, sites, etc. used in launching spacecraft or missiles —**launch′er** *n.*

launch[2] (lônch, länch) *n.* [Sp. or Port. *lancha* < ?] **1.** formerly, the largest boat carried by a warship **2.** an open, or partly enclosed, motorboat

launch pad the platform from which a rocket, guided missile, etc. is launched: also **launching pad**

launch window the period of time during which a spacecraft or missile must be launched if it is to reach its target

laun·der (lôn′dər, län′-) *vt.* [< ME. < ML. < LL. *lavandaria,* things to be washed < L. < *lavare:* see LATHER] to wash, or wash and iron, (clothes, etc.) —*vi.* **1.** to withstand washing [*this fabric launders well*] **2.** to do laundry —**laun′der·er** *n.*

☆**Laun·der·ette** (lôn′də ret′, län′-) *a service mark for* a self-service laundry —*n.* [l-] such a laundry

laun·dress (lôn′dris, län′-) *n.* a woman whose work is washing clothes, ironing, etc.

☆**Laun·dro·mat** (lôn′drə mat′, län′-) [< a trademark for an automatic washing machine] *a service mark for* a self-service laundry —*n.* [l-] such a laundry

laun·dry (lôn′drē, län′-) *n., pl.* **-dries 1.** the act or process of laundering **2.** a place where laundering is done **3.** clothes, linens, etc. that have been, or are about to be, laundered

laun·dry·man (-mən) *n., pl.* **-men** a man who works for a laundry, esp. one who collects and delivers laundry

laun·dry·wom·an (-woom′ən) *n., pl.* **-wom′en** *same as* LAUNDRESS

Lau·ra (lôr′ə) [fem. of LAURENCE] a feminine name

lau·re·ate (lôr′ē it) *adj.* [< L. < *laurea* (*corona*), laurel (wreath) < *laurus,* laurel] **1.** crowned with a laurel wreath as a mark of honor **2.** famous and honored —*n.* **1.** a scientist, writer, etc. who has been given a special honor **2.** *same as* POET LAUREATE —**lau′re·ate·ship′** *n.*

lau·rel (lôr′əl, lär′-) *n.* [< OFr. < L. *laurus*] **1.** an evergreen tree or shrub, native to southern Europe, with large, glossy leaves **2.** the leaves of this tree, esp. as woven into wreaths such as those used by the ancient Greeks to crown victors in contests **3.** [*pl.*] *a)* fame; honor *b)* victory ☆**4.** a tree or shrub resembling the true laurel, as the mountain laurel —*vt.* **-reled** or **-relled, -rel·ing** or **-rel·ling 1.** to crown with laurel **2.** to honor —**look to one's laurels** to beware of having one's achievements surpassed —**rest on one's laurels** to be satisfied with what one has already achieved

LAUREL WREATH

Lau·rence (lôr′əns, lär′-) [L. *Laurentius,* prob. < *laurus,* laurel] a masculine name

Lau·ren·tian Mountains (lô ren′shən) mountain range in S Quebec, Canada, extending along the St. Lawrence River valley

Lau·sanne (lō zan′) city in W Switzerland, on Lake Geneva: pop. 139,000

la·va (lä′və, lav′ə) *n.* [It. < dial. *lave* < L. *labes*, a fall < *labi*, to slide: for IE. base see LAP¹] **1.** melted rock flowing from a volcano **2.** such rock when cool and solid

la·vage (lə väzh′, lav′ij) *n.* [Fr. < L. *lavare*: see LAVE] *Med.* a washing out of an organ, as the stomach or sinuses

La·val (lə val′) city in SW Quebec, near Montreal: pop. 220,000: also **Ville de La·val** (vēl də lä väl′)

lav·a·liere, lav·a·lier (lav′ə lir′, lä′və-) *n.* [Fr. *lavallière*, kind of tie < Duchesse de *La Vallière*, mistress of Louis XIV] an ornament hanging from a chain, worn around the neck

lav·a·to·ry (lav′ə tôr′ē) *n., pl.* **-ries** [LL. *lavatorium* < L. *lavare*: see LAVE] **1.** a washbowl **2.** a room equipped with a washbowl, flush toilet, etc.

lave (lāv) *vt., vi.* **laved, lav′ing** [< OE. *lafian* & OFr. *laver*, both < L. *lavare*, to wash: see LATHER] [Poet.] to wash or bathe

lav·en·der (lav′ən dər) *n.* [< Anglo-Fr. < ML. *lavandria* < L. *lavare*: see prec.] **1.** a fragrant European plant of the mint family, having spikes of pale-purplish flowers and yielding a sweet-smelling oil (**oil of lavender**) **2.** the dried flowers, leaves, and stalks of this plant, used in sachets to perfume clothes, linens, etc. **3.** a pale purple —*adj.* pale-purple

la·ver¹ (lā′vər) *n.* [< OFr. < L. *lavare*: see LAVE] [Archaic] a large basin to wash in

la·ver² (lā′vər) *n.* [L., water plant] any of various large, edible, ribbonlike seaweeds

lav·ish (lav′ish) *adj.* [< MFr. < OFr. *lavasse*, torrent of rain, prob. < *laver* < L. *lavare*: see LAVE] **1.** very generous or liberal in giving or spending, often extravagantly so **2.** more than enough; very great or costly [*lavish* entertainment; a *lavish* allowance] —*vt.* to give or spend freely or too freely [to *lavish* time and money on pets] —**lav′ish·ly** *adv.* —**lav′ish·ness** *n.*

La·voi·sier (là vwà zyā′; *E.* lə vwä′zē ā′), **An·toine Lau·rent** (än twän′ lō rän′) 1743–94; Fr. pioneer in chemistry

law (lô) *n.* [OE. *lagu* < Anglo-N.: for IE. base see LIE¹] **1.** *a)* all the rules of conduct established and enforced by the authority, legislation, or custom of a given community, state, or other group *b)* any one of such rules; a statute, ordinance, etc. [a *law* against jaywalking] **2.** the condition existing when people in general obey such rules [to establish *law* and order] **3.** the branch of knowledge dealing with such rules; jurisprudence **4.** the system of courts intended to bring justice by following such rules [to resort to *law*] **5.** all such rules dealing with a particular activity [business *law*] **6.** common law, as distinguished from equity **7.** the profession of lawyers, judges, etc. (often with *the*) **8.** a sequence of events in nature or in human activities always occurring in the same way under the same conditions; also, the principle involved in this [the *law* of gravitation; the *law* of supply and demand] **9.** any rule or principle expected to be followed [the *laws* of health] **10.** *Eccles.* a divine commandment **11.** *Math., Logic,* etc. a general principle to which all applicable cases must conform [the *laws* of exponents] —**go to law** to take a dispute to a law court for settlement —**lay down the law 1.** to give orders in an authoritative manner **2.** to give a scolding (*to*) —**read law** to study to become a lawyer —**the Law 1.** the Mosaic law, or the part of the Hebrew Scriptures containing it; specif., the Pentateuch ☆**2.** [l-] [Colloq.] a policeman or the police

SYN.—**law** refers to statutes, ordinances, etc. set down and enforced by a ruling authority [the *law* of the land]; a **rule** may or may not be enforced in a formal, authoritative way, but it is generally followed for the sake of order, uniformity, etc. [the *rules* of golf]; **regulation** refers to any of the rules for managing a group or organization, enforced by authority [military *regulations*] —see also SYN. at THEORY

law-a·bid·ing (lô′ə bīd′iŋ) *adj.* obeying the law [*law-abiding* citizens]

law·break·er (-brā′kər) *n.* a person who does something that is against the law —**law′break′ing** *adj., n.*

law court a court for administering justice under the law

law·ful (-fəl) *adj.* **1.** in keeping with the law; permitted by law [a *lawful* act] **2.** recognized by law; just [*lawful* debts] —**law′-ful·ly** *adv.* —**law′ful·ness** *n.*

law·giv·er (-giv′ər) *n.* one who draws up a code of laws for a nation or people

law·less (-lis) *adj.* **1.** without law; not regulated by the au-thority of law [a *lawless* city] **2.** not in keeping with the law; illegal [*lawless* practices] **3.** not obeying the law; unruly —**law′less·ly** *adv.* —**law′less·ness** *n.*

law·mak·er (-mā′kər) *n.* one who makes or helps to make laws; esp., a member of a legislature; legislator —**law′mak′ing** *adj., n.*

law·man (-mən) *n., pl.* **-men′** (-men′) a law officer; esp., a marshal, sheriff, etc.

lawn¹ (lôn) *n.* [< OFr. < Bret. *lann*, country: for IE. base see LAND] land covered with grass kept closely mowed, esp. around a house —**lawn′y** *adj.*

lawn² (lôn) *n.* [< *Laon*, city in France, where made] a fine, sheer cloth of linen or cotton, used for blouses, curtains, etc. —**lawn′y** *adj.*

lawn mower a hand-propelled or power-driven machine for cutting the grass of a lawn

lawn tennis *see* TENNIS

Law·rence¹ (lôr′əns, lär′-) **1.** a masculine name: see LAU-RENCE **2.** **D(avid) H(erbert),** 1885–1930; Eng. novelist & poet **3.** **Sir Thomas,** 1769–1830; Eng. portrait painter **4.** **T(homas) E(dward),** (changed name, 1927, to *Thomas Edward Shaw*) 1888–1935; Brit. adventurer & writer: called **Lawrence of Arabia**

Law·rence² (lôr′əns, lär′-) [after A. *Lawrence* (1814–86) of Boston] city in NE Mass.: pop. 67,000

☆**law·ren·ci·um** (lô ren′sē əm, lä-) *n.* [after E. O. *Lawrence,* 20th-c. U.S. physicist] a radioactive chemical element produced by nuclear bombardment of californium: symbol, Lr; at. wt., 256(?); at. no., 103

law·suit (lô′sōōt′) *n.* a suit at law between private parties; case before a civil court

Law·ton (lôt′'n) [after Gen. H. W. *Lawton* (1843–99)] city in SW Okla.: pop. 74,000

law·yer (lô′yər) *n.* a person whose profession is advising others in matters of law or representing them in lawsuits

SYN.—**lawyer** is the general term for a person trained in the law, who advises or represents others in legal matters; **counselor** and **attorney** are now general synonyms for lawyer, but in earlier use **counselor** referred to a lawyer who conducts cases in court, as does the British **barrister,** and **attorney** referred to one who prepares briefs, draws up contracts and wills, etc., as does the British **solicitor; counsel,** often equivalent to counselor, is frequently used for a group of lawyers working together to advise a client or conduct a case in court

lax (laks) *adj.* [L. *laxus* < IE. base (*s*)*leg-*, to be loose] **1.** loose; slack; not rigid or tight [a *lax* rope] **2.** not strict or exact; careless [*lax* morals] **3.** *Bot.* loose; open: said of a flower cluster **4.** *Phonet.* pronounced with the jaw and tongue relatively relaxed: said of certain vowels, as *e* in *met, i* in *hill:* opposed to TENSE¹ —see SYN. at REMISS —**lax′ly** *adv.* —**lax′ness** *n.*

lax·a·tive (lak′sə tiv) *adj.* [< OFr. < ML. *laxativus* < LL. < pp. of L. *laxare* < *laxus:* see LAX] tending to make lax; specif., making the bowels loose and relieving constipation —*n.* any laxative medicine; mild cathartic

lax·i·ty (lak′sə tē) *n.* the quality or condition of being lax; looseness

lay¹ (lā) *vt.* **laid, lay′ing** [OE. *lecgan* < pt. base of OE. *licgan,* to LIE¹] **1.** to cause to fall with force; knock down [one punch *laid* him low] **2.** to place or put so as to rest, lie, etc.; deposit (with *on, in,* etc.) [*lay* the pen on the desk] **3.** *a)* to put down (bricks, carpeting, etc.) in the correct way for a specific purpose *b)* to situate in a particular place [the scene is *laid* in France] *c)* to prepare as a basis or for use [to *lay* the groundwork] **4.** to place; put; set [to *lay* emphasis on accuracy] **5.** to produce and deposit (an egg or eggs) **6.** *a)* to cause to settle [to *lay* the dust] *b)* to allay, overcome, or quiet [to *lay* one's fears] **7.** to smooth down [to *lay* the nap of cloth] **8.** to stake as a bet; wager [to *lay* ten dollars that the bay horse wins] **9.** to impose (a tax, penalty, etc. *on* or *upon*) **10.** to work out; devise [to *lay* plans] **11.** to set (a table) with silverware, plates, etc. **12.** to present or put forth [to *lay* claim to property; to *lay* a matter before the voters] **13.** to attribute; charge; impute [to *lay* the blame on Tom] —*vi.* **1.** to lay an egg or eggs **2.** to lie; recline: in this sense not considered a standard usage **3.** *Naut.* to go; proceed [all hands *lay* aft to the fantail] —*n.* the way in which something is situated or arranged [the *lay* of the land] —**lay aside** to set aside for the future; save: also **lay away, lay by** —**lay down 1.** to sacrifice (one's life) **2.** to declare emphatically **3.** to store away, as wine in a cellar —**lay for** [Colloq.] to be waiting to attack —**lay in** to get and store away —**lay into** [Slang] to attack with blows or words —**lay it on** (**thick**) [Colloq.] **1.** to exaggerate **2.** to flatter in an exaggerated way —**lay off** ☆**1.** to discharge (an employee), esp. temporarily **2.** to mark off the boundaries of ☆**3.** [Slang] *a*) to cease *b*) to stop criticizing, teasing, etc. —**lay on 1.** to spread on **2.** to attack with force —**lay open 1.** to cut open **2.** to expose; uncover [to *lay* oneself *open* to criticism] —**lay out 1.** to spend **2.** to arrange according to a plan **3.** to spread out (clothes, equipment, etc.) **4.** to make (a dead body) ready for burial **5.** [Slang] to knock down or make unconscious **6.** [Slang] to scold (someone) —**lay over** ☆to stop a while in a place before going on —**lay to 1.** to attribute to **2.** to apply oneself with vigor **3.** *Naut. a*) to check the motion of a ship and cause it to become stationary *b*) to lie stationary with the bow to the wind —**lay up 1.** to store for future use **2.** to disable; confine to bed or the sickroom

lay² (lā) *pt. of* LIE¹

lay³ (lā) *adj.* [< OFr. < LL. *laicus* < Gr. < *lāos*, the people] **1.** of the laity, or ordinary people, as distinguished from the clergy **2.** not belonging to or connected with a given profession [a legal handbook for *lay* readers]

lay⁴ (lā) *n.* [OFr. *lai*] **1.** a short poem, esp. a narrative poem, for singing **2.** [Archaic or Poet.] a song or melody

lay·a·bout (lā′ə bout′) *n.* [Chiefly Brit. Colloq.] a loafer; bum

lay analyst a psychoanalyst who is not a medical doctor

lay·a·way (plan) (lā′ə wā′) a method of buying by making a deposit on something which is delivered only after it is paid for in full

lay·er (lā′ər) *n.* **1.** a person or thing that lays [these hens are poor *layers*] **2.** a single thickness, coat, fold, or stratum **3.** a shoot (of a living plant) bent down and partly covered with earth so that it may take root —*vt., vi.* to grow (a plant) by means of a layer

☆**layer cake** a cake of two or more layers, with icing, preserves, etc. between them

lay·ette (lā et′) *n.* [Fr., dim. of *laie*, drawer < Fl. < MDu. *lade*, a chest] a complete outfit for a newborn baby, including clothes, bedding, etc.

lay figure [earlier *layman* < Du. < MDu. *led*, limb + *man*, man] **1.** an artist's jointed model of the human form, on which drapery is arranged **2.** a person who is a mere puppet or a nonentity

lay·man (lā′mən) *n., pl.* -**men** [LAY³ + MAN] **1.** a member of the laity; person not a clergyman **2.** a person not belonging to or skilled in a given profession [a medical textbook not for the *layman*]

☆**lay·off** (lā′ôf′) *n.* the act of laying off; esp., temporary unemployment, or the period of this

lay of the land 1. the arrangement of the natural features of an area **2.** the existing state of affairs Also **lie of the land**

☆**lay·out** (lā′out′) *n.* **1.** the act of laying something out **2.** the way in which something is laid out; arrangement; specif., the plan or makeup of a newspaper, page, advertisement, etc. **3.** the thing laid out **4.** an outfit or set, as of tools **5.** [Colloq.] a residence, factory, etc., esp. when large

☆**lay·o·ver** (-ō′vər) *n.* a stopping for a while in some place during a journey

lay·up (-up′) *n.* ☆*Basketball* a leaping, one-handed shot made from a position close to the basket, usually off the backboard

la·zar (laz′ər, lā′zər) *n.* [< ML. *lazarus*, leper < LL. < Gr. *Lazaros*, LAZARUS] [Rare] a poor, diseased, esp. leprous person

laz·a·ret·to (laz′ə ret′ō) *n., pl.* -**tos** [It. < Santa Madonna di *Nazaret*, Venetian church used as a plague hospital; *l-* after *lazzaro*, leper] **1.** formerly, a public hospital for poor people having contagious diseases, esp. for lepers **2.** a building or ship used as a quarantine station **3.** on some ships, a storage space Also, and for 3 usually, **laz′a·ret′, laz′a·rette** (-ret′)

Laz·a·rus (laz′ə rəs) *Bible* **1.** the brother of Mary and Martha, raised from the dead by Jesus: John 11 **2.** the diseased beggar in Jesus' parable: Luke 16:19–31

laze (lāz) *vi.* **lazed, laz′ing** to be lazy or idle; loaf —*vt.* to spend (time, etc.) in idleness (often with *away*)

la·zy (lā′zē) *adj.* -**zi·er, -zi·est** [prob. < MLowG. or MDu.] **1.** not eager or willing to work or exert oneself; indolent **2.** slow and heavy; sluggish [a *lazy* river] **3.** tending to cause laziness [a *lazy* day] —*vi., vt.* -**zied, -zy·ing** same as LAZE —**la′zi·ly** *adv.* —**la′zi·ness** *n.*

la·zy·bones (-bōnz′) *n.* [Colloq.] a lazy person

☆**Lazy Susan** a revolving tray placed on a dining table, with sections for relishes, condiments, etc.

lb. [L. *libra*, pl. *librae*] pound; pounds

lbs. pounds

L/C, l/c letter of credit

l.c. 1. [L. *loco citato*] in the place cited **2.** *Printing* lower case

☆**LCD** [*l*(*iquid*)-*c*(*rystal*) *d*(*isplay*)] a device for displaying information, as a unit for showing the time on a digital watch: it uses a liquid that has some properties of a crystal and that is sealed between specially treated pieces of glass and is activated by a light from any source

L.C.D., l.c.d. least (or lowest) common denominator

L.C.M., l.c.m. least (or lowest) common multiple

-le¹ (′l) [ME. *-el, -le* < OE. *-ol*] a suffix meaning small [thimble]

-le² (′l) [ME. *-len* < OE. *-lian*] a suffix meaning over and over again; frequently and repeatedly [sparkle, suckle]

lea (lē) *n.* [OE. *leah*] [Chiefly Poet.] a meadow, grassy field, or pasture; grassland

leach (lēch) *vt.* [prob. < OE. *leccan*, to water: for IE. base see LEAK] **1.** to cause (a liquid) to filter down through some material **2.** to subject to the washing action of a filtering liquid [wood ashes are *leached* to extract lye] **3.** to extract (a soluble substance) from some material by causing water to filter down through the material [lye is *leached* from wood ashes] —*vi.* **1.** to lose soluble matter as a result of the filtering through of water [soil that has *leached* badly] **2.** to dissolve and be washed away —*n.* **1.** the action of leaching **2.** a sievelike container used in leaching —**leach′a·ble** *adj.* —**leach′er** *n.*

lead¹ (lēd) *vt.* **led, lead′ing** [OE. *lædan* < IE. base *leit*(h)-, to go] **1.** *a*) to direct the course of by going before or along with; conduct; guide *b*) to mark the way for [lights to *lead* you there] **2.** to guide by physical contact, pulling a rope, etc. [to *lead* a horse] **3.** to conduct (water, steam, rope, etc.) in a certain direction, channel, etc. [drainpipes *lead* the water away] **4.** to guide or direct by influence, persuasion, etc. to a course of action or thought; cause; prompt [her advice *led* me to change jobs] **5.** to be the head or leader of (an expedition, orchestra, etc.) **6.** *a*) to be at the head of [to *lead* one's class] *b*) to be ahead of by a specified margin **7.** to live; spend [to *lead* a hard life] **8.** to aim a rifle, throw a ball, etc. just ahead of (a moving target or receiver) **9.** *Card Games* to begin the play with (a card or suit) —*vi.* **1.** to show the way by going before or along; act as guide **2.** to submit to being led: said esp. of a horse **3.** to be or form a way (to, from, under, etc.); go [this path *leads* to the lake] **4.** to come, or bring one, as a result (with *to*) [a cold can *lead* to pneumonia] **5.** to be or go first ☆**6.** *Boxing* to aim a first blow **7.** *Card Games* to play the first card —*n.* **1.** leadership [to take the *lead* in a project] **2.** example [follow his *lead*] **3.** *a*) first or front place; precedence [the horse in the *lead*] *b*) the amount or distance ahead [a *lead* of six points in the game] **4.** same as LEASH **5.** anything that serves as a guide or clue [the police followed up every *lead*] ☆**6.** *Baseball* a position taken by a base runner away from his base in the direction of the next ☆**7.** *Boxing* a blow used in leading **8.** *Card Games* the right of playing first, or the card or suit played **9.** *Elec.* a wire carrying current from one point to another in a circuit **10.** *Journalism* the opening paragraph of a news story ☆**11.** *Mining* a stratum of ore **12.** *Music* the main melody in a harmonic composition **13.** *Theater a*) a main role in a play *b*) an actor or actress playing such a role —*adj.* acting as leader [the *lead* horse] —**see SYN.** at GUIDE —**lead off 1.** to begin ☆**2.** *Baseball* to be a team's first batter in the lineup or of an inning —**lead on 1.** to conduct further **2.** to lure or tempt —**lead up to** to prepare the way for —**lead with one's chin** [Colloq.] to act so rashly or hastily as to tend to bring on disaster

lead² (led) *n.* [OE.] **1.** a heavy, soft, malleable, bluish-gray metallic chemical element used for piping and in numerous alloys: symbol, Pb; at. wt., 207.19; at. no., 82 **2.** anything made of this metal; specif., *a*) a weight attached to a line (**lead line**) for measuring depths at sea, etc. *b*) *Printing* a thin strip of type metal inserted to increase the space between lines of type **3.** bullets **4.** a thin stick of graphite, used in pencils —*adj.* made of or containing lead —*vt.* **1.** to cover, line, or weight with lead **2.** *Printing* to increase the space between (lines of type) by inserting leads

lead acetate a poisonous, colorless, crystalline compound used as a mordant in dyeing, and in making varnishes and paints

lead arsenate a very poisonous, colorless, crystalline compound used as an insecticide and, sometimes, as a herbicide

lead·en (led′'n) *adj.* **1.** made of lead **2.** heavy; hard to move [a *leaden* weight] **3.** heavy in action, feeling, etc.; sluggish; dull **4.** depressed; gloomy [*leaden* spirits] **5.** of a dull gray [a *leaden* sky] —**lead′en·ly** *adv.* —**lead′en·ness** *n.*

lead·er (lē′dər) *n.* **1.** a person or thing that leads; guiding head, as of a group or activity **2.** a horse harnessed in front of the other horses in a team **3.** a pipe for carrying fluid **4.** a tendon **5.** a section of blank film or recording tape at the beginning of a reel, for use in threading, etc. ☆**6.** a featured, low-priced article of trade: see LOSS LEADER **7.** *Bot.* the central stem of a plant ☆**8.** *Fishing* a short piece of catgut, etc. often used to attach the hook, lure, etc. to the fish line **9.** *Journalism a)* the leading news article in a newspaper *b)* [Brit.] an important editorial **10.** *Music a)* a conductor, esp. of a dance band *b)* the main performer, as in a vocal section **11.** [*pl.*] *Printing* dots, dashes, etc. in a line, used to direct the eye across the page —**lead′er·less** *adj.*

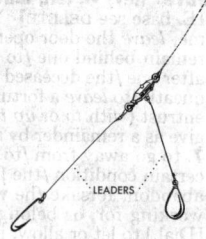
LEADERS

lead·er·ship (-ship′) *n.* **1.** the position or guidance of a leader **2.** the ability to lead **3.** the leaders of a group

lead glass (led) glass that contains lead oxide

lead-in (lēd′in′) *n.* **1.** the wire leading from an aerial or antenna to a receiver or transmitter **2.** an introduction —*adj.* that is a lead-in

lead·ing[1] (led′iŋ) *n.* **1.** a covering or being covered with lead **2.** strips or sheets of lead

lead·ing[2] (lē′diŋ) *n.* guidance; direction —*adj.* **1.** that leads; guiding [a *leading* question] **2.** principal; chief [he played a *leading* part in our campaign] **3.** playing the lead in a play, motion picture, etc. [a *leading* lady]

lead·ing edge (lē′diŋ) *Aeron.* the front edge of a propeller blade or airfoil

lead·ing light (lē′diŋ) an important or influential member of a club, community, etc.

lead·ing question (lē′diŋ) a question put in such a way as to suggest the answer sought

lead·off (lēd′ôf′) *n.* the first in a series of actions, moves, etc. —*adj.* ☆ *Baseball* designating a team's first batter in the lineup or of an inning

lead pencil (led) a pencil consisting of a slender stick of graphite encased in wood, etc.

lead poisoning (led) an acute or chronic poisoning caused by lead being absorbed into the body

lead tetraethyl *same as* TETRAETHYL LEAD

leaf (lēf) *n., pl.* **leaves** [OE. *leaf* < IE. base *leugh-*, to peel off] **1.** any of the flat, thin parts, usually green, growing from the stem of a plant: leaves manufacture food for the plant by means of photosynthesis **2.** a petal [a rose *leaf*] **3.** leaves; foliage [made of choice tobacco *leaf*] **4.** a sheet of paper, as in a book, with a page on each side **5.** metal in very thin sheets [gold *leaf*] **6.** *a)* a hinged section of a table top *b)* a board inserted into a table top to increase its surface **7.** a flat, hinged or movable part of a folding door, shutter, etc. ☆**8.** any of the metal strips in a leaf spring —*vi.* **1.** to put forth or bear leaves (often with *out*) **2.** to turn the pages of a book, etc., esp. so as to glance quickly (with *through*) —*vt.* to turn the pages of —**in leaf** having the leaves grown; with foliage —**take a leaf from someone's book** to follow someone's example —**turn over a new leaf** to make a new start —**leaf′less** *adj.* —**leaf′like′** *adj.*

leaf·age (lēf′ij) *n.* leaves; foliage

☆**leaf hopper** an insect that leaps from one plant to another, sucking the juices and often passing on plant diseases

leaf insect a sluggish, winged insect that looks like a leaf

leaf·let (-lit) *n.* **1.** one of the divisions of a compound leaf **2.** a small or young leaf **3.** a separate sheet of printed matter, often folded but not stitched [an advertising *leaflet*]

leaf miner any of a large number of unrelated small moths and flies that in the larval stage burrow into and eat the soft tissues of leaves and green stems

☆**leaf spring** a spring made up of layers of curved metal strips: see illustration at SPRING

leaf·stalk (-stôk′) *n.* the slender, usually cylindrical portion of a leaf, which supports the blade and is attached to the stem

leaf·y (lēf′ē) *adj.* **leaf′i·er, leaf′i·est 1.** of, consisting of, or like a leaf or leaves **2.** having many leaves **3.** having broad leaves, as spinach —**leaf′i·ness** *n.*

league[1] (lēg) *n.* [< OFr. < It. *liga* < *legare* < L. *ligare*, to bind < IE. base *leig-*, to bind] **1.** an agreement made by nations, groups, or individuals for promoting common interests, etc. **2.** an association or alliance formed by such an agreement **3.** *Sports* a group of teams organized to compete against one another ☆**4.** [Colloq.] a division according to grade or quality [not in the same *league* with the top writers] —*vt., vi.* **leagued, leagu′ing** to form into a league —see SYN. at ALLIANCE —**in league** united for a common purpose; allied —**leagu′er** *n.*

league[2] (lēg) *n.* [< OFr. < LL. *leuga,* Gallic mile < Celt.] an old measure of distance, usually about 3 miles

League of Nations an association of nations (1920–46), established to promote international cooperation and peace: it was replaced by the United Nations in 1946

Le·ah (lē′ə) [? Heb. *le'ah,* gazelle, or ? *la'āh,* to tire, weary] **1.** a feminine name **2.** *Bible* the elder of the sisters who were wives of Jacob: Gen. 29:13–30

leak (lēk) *vi.* [< ON. *leka,* to drip < IE. base *leg-*, to drip] **1.** to let a fluid substance out or in by accident [the boat *leaks*] **2.** to enter or escape in this way, as a fluid (often with *in* or *out*) [the air in the tire *leaked* out through the valve] **3.** to become known little by little [the truth *leaked* out] —*vt.* **1.** to allow (water, air, light, radiation, etc.) to leak **2.** to allow (seemingly secret or private information) to become known —*n.* **1.** an accidental hole or crack that lets something out or in [sand spilled from the *leak* in the bag] **2.** any means of escape for something that ought not to be let out, lost, etc. **3.** a leaking in or out; leakage [a slow *leak* in the tire] ☆**4.** a disclosure, supposedly accidental but actually intentional: in full, **news leak 5.** *a)* a loss of electrical charge through faulty insulation *b)* the point where this occurs

leak·age (lēk′ij) *n.* **1.** an act or instance of leaking; leak **2.** something that leaks in or out **3.** the amount that leaks

leak·y (lēk′ē) *adj.* **leak′i·er, leak′i·est** having a leak or leaks —**leak′i·ness** *n.*

leal (lēl) *adj.* [< OFr. < L. *legalis:* see LEGAL] [Archaic or Scot.] loyal; true —**leal′ly** *adv.*

lean[1] (lēn) *vi.* **leaned** or **leant, lean′ing** [OE. *hlinian:* for IE. base see CLIENT] **1.** to bend from an upright position; stand at a slant; incline [the old tree *leans* toward the barn] **2.** to bend the body so as to rest part of one's weight upon something [he *leaned* on the desk] **3.** to depend for advice, aid, etc.; rely (*on* or *upon*) [he still *leans* on his parents] **4.** to have a preference; tend (*toward* or *to* a certain opinion, attitude, etc.) —*vt.* to cause to lean [to *lean* a ladder against the house; to *lean* one's head back] —*n.* a leaning; inclination; slant —**lean′er** *n.*

lean[2] (lēn) *adj.* [OE. *hlæne*] **1.** with little flesh or fat; thin; spare [a *lean* athlete] **2.** containing little or no fat: said of meat **3.** *a)* lacking in richness, profit, etc.; meager [a *lean* year for business] *b)* characterized by being brief, direct, etc. [a *lean* style] —*n.* meat containing little or no fat —**lean′ly** *adv.* —**lean′ness** *n.*

SYN.—**lean** implies a healthy, natural absence of fat or fleshiness; **spare** suggests a muscular frame without any unnecessary flesh; **lanky** implies an awkward tallness and leanness, and, often, loose-jointedness; **skinny** and **scrawny** imply extreme thinness that is unattractive and that indicates a lack of strength and energy; **gaunt** implies a bony thinness such as that caused by a wasting away of the flesh from hunger or suffering —see also **SYN.** at THIN —**ANT.** fleshy, fat, stout

Le·an·der (lē an′dər) *Gr. Legend* see HERO

lean·ing (lēn′iŋ) *n.* **1.** the act of a person or thing that leans **2.** tendency; inclination

leant (lent) *alt. pt. & pp. of* LEAN[1]

lean-to (lēn′tōō′) *n., pl.* **lean′-tos′ 1.** a shelter with a sloping roof resting against trees or posts **2.** a shed whose sloping roof (**lean-to roof**) rests against a wall or building

leap (lēp) *vi.* **leaped** or **leapt** (lept, lēpt), **leap′ing** [OE. *hleapan*] **1.** to jump; spring [the cat *leaped* into my lap] **2.** to move suddenly or swiftly, as if by jumping; bound [the deer were *leaping* across the meadow] **3.** to accept eagerly something offered (with *at*) [to *leap* at a chance] —*vt.* **1.** to pass over by a jump [to *leap* a brook] **2.** to cause to leap [to *leap* a

LEAN-TO

horse over a wall/ —*n.* **1.** a jump; spring /over the fence in one *leap*/ **2.** the distance covered in a jump **3.** a place that is, or is to be, leaped over or from —**by leaps and bounds** very rapidly —**leap in the dark** a risky act whose results cannot be foreseen —**leap'er** *n.*

leap·frog (lēp'frôg', -fräg') *n.* a game in which each player in turn jumps over the bent back of each of the other players —*vi.* **-frogged', -frog'ging 1.** to skip (*over*) **2.** to move or progress in jumps or stages —*vt.* to jump or skip over

leap year a year of 366 days, occurring every fourth year: the additional day is February 29: a leap year is a year whose number can be divided exactly by four, or, in the case of century years, by 400

Lear (lir) **1.** *see* KING LEAR **2.** Edward, 1812–88; Eng. humorist

learn (lurn) *vt.* **learned** or **learnt** (lurnt), **learn'ing** [OE. *leornian* < IE. base *leis-*, a track, furrow] **1.** to get knowledge of (a subject) or skill in (an art, trade, etc.) by study, training, experience, etc. **2.** to come to know /to *learn* what happened/ **3.** to come to know how /to *learn* to save/ **4.** to fix in the mind; memorize /*learn* this poem by tomorrow/ **5.** to acquire as a habit or attitude /to *learn* humility/ **6.** [Dial.] to teach —*vi.* **1.** to gain knowledge or skill /he never *learns* from experience/ **2.** to be informed; hear (*of* or *about*) /when did you *learn* of her illness?/ —**learn'a·ble** *adj.* —**learn'er** *n.*

SYN. —**learn,** as considered here, implies a finding out of something without conscious effort /I *learned* of his marriage from a friend/; **ascertain** implies a finding out with certainty by careful inquiry, experimentation, research, etc. /he *ascertained* the firm's credit rating/; **determine** stresses intention to establish the facts exactly, often so as to settle something in doubt /to *determine* the exact meaning of a word/; **discover** implies a finding out, by chance, exploration, etc., of something already existing or known to others /to *discover* a plot, a star, etc./

learn·ed (lur'nid; *for 3* lurnd) *adj.* **1.** having or showing much learning; erudite /a *learned* professor/ **2.** of or characterized by scholarship, study, and learning /a *learned* society/ **3.** acquired by study, experience, etc. /a *learned* response/ —**learn'ed·ly** *adv.* —**learn'ed·ness** *n.*

learn·ing (lur'niŋ) *n.* **1.** the acquiring of knowledge or skill /a few tumbles are part of a baby's *learning* to walk/ **2.** acquired knowledge or skill /a woman of great *learning*/ —see SYN. at INFORMATION

lear·y (lir'ē) *adj.* **lear'i·er, lear'i·est** *same as* LEERY

lease (lēs) *n.* [< Anglo-Fr. *les* < OFr. < L. *laxare*, to loosen < *laxus*, LAX] a contract by which a landlord gives to a tenant the use of lands, buildings, etc. for a specified time and for fixed payments; also, the period of time specified /a three-year *lease*/ —*vt.* **leased, leas'ing 1.** to give by a lease; let /the landlord will not *lease* the apartment to noisy tenants/ **2.** to get by a lease /I *leased* this car for a week/ —see SYN. at HIRE —**new lease on life** another chance to lead a happy life, be successful, etc. because of a new situation —**leas'a·ble** *adj.* —**leas'er** *n.*

leash (lēsh) *n.* [< OFr. < L. *laxa*, fem. of *laxus*, LAX] a cord, strap, etc. by which a dog or other animal is held in check —*vt.* **1.** to put a leash on **2.** to control as by a leash /to *leash* the energy of a river with a dam/ —**hold in leash** to control —**strain at the leash** to be impatient to be free

least (lēst) *adj. alt. superl. of* LITTLE [< OE. *læsest, læst,* superl. of *læssa,* LESS] smallest in size, degree, importance, etc. /the *least* movement/ —*adv. superl. of* LITTLE in the smallest degree /I was *least* impressed by the music/ —*n.* the smallest in size, amount, importance, degree, etc. /the *least* you can do is apologize/ —**at (the) least 1.** at the very lowest figure, amount, etc.; with no less **2.** at any rate; in any event /at *least* I tried/ —**not in the least** not at all

least common denominator the least common multiple of the denominators of two or more fractions

least common multiple the smallest positive whole number that can be divided exactly by two or more given whole numbers /the *least common multiple* of 4, 5, and 10 is 20/

least·wise (lēst'wīz') *adv.* [Colloq.] at least; anyway Also [Chiefly Dial.] **least'ways'** (-wāz')

leath·er (leth'ər) *n.* [OE. *lether-*] **1.** a material made from animal skin by cleaning and tanning it **2.** any article made of this —*adj.* of or made of leather —*vt.* **1.** to cover with leather **2.** [Colloq.] to whip with a leather strap

Leath·er·ette (leth'ə ret') *a trademark for* imitation leather made of paper or cloth —*n.* [l-] imitation leather similar to this

leath·ern (leth'ərn) *adj.* **1.** made of leather **2.** like leather

leath·er·neck (leth'ər nek') *n.* [from the leather-lined collar, formerly part of the Marine uniform] ☆[Slang] a U.S. Marine

leath·er·y (-ē) *adj.* like leather; tough and flexible /a *leathery* skin/ —**leath'er·i·ness** *n.*

leave[1] (lēv) *vt.* **left, leav'ing** [OE. *læfan,* lit., to let remain: for IE. base see DELETE] **1.** to let stay or be /leave some cake for me; *leave* the door open/ **2.** to make, place, etc., and cause to remain behind one /to *leave* footprints/ **3.** to have remaining after one /the deceased *leaves* a widow/ **4.** to give by a will; bequeath /to *leave* a fortune to charity/ **5.** to let be in the care of; entrust (with *to* or *up to*) /to *leave* a decision to another/ **6.** to give as a remainder by subtraction /ten minus two *leaves* eight/ **7.** to go away from /to *leave* the house/ **8.** to cause to be in a certain condition /the flood *left* them homeless/ **9.** to give up; abandon; forsake /he was *left* for dead/ **10.** to stop living in, working for, or belonging to /he *left* the city last year/ **11.** [Dial.] to let or allow: in this sense not a standard usage /*leave* us go now/ —*vi.* to go away or set out /Jo *left* early/ —see SYN. at GO —**leave off 1.** to stop; cease **2.** to stop doing or using —**leave out 1.** to omit **2.** to fail to consider —**leave (someone) alone** to stop bothering (someone) —**leav'er** *n.*

leave[2] (lēv) *n.* [OE. *leaf:* for IE. base see BELIEVE] **1.** permission **2.** *a)* permission to be absent from duty or work, esp. such permission given to persons in the armed services *b)* the period for which this is granted /a three-day *leave*/ —**beg leave** to ask permission —**by your leave** with your permission —**on leave** absent from duty with permission —**take leave of** to say goodbye to —**take one's leave** to depart

leave[3] (lēv) *vi.* **leaved, leav'ing** [see LEAF] to put forth, or bear, leaves; leaf

leaved (lēvd) *adj.* having leaves /narrow-*leaved*/

leav·en (lev'n) *n.* [< OFr. < L. *levamen,* alleviation < *levare,* to raise: see LEVER] **1.** a small piece of fermenting dough used for producing fermentation in a fresh batch of dough **2.** *same as* LEAVENING —*vt.* **1.** to make (batter or dough) rise with a leavening agent **2.** to spread through, causing a gradual change /reforms intended to *leaven* social ills/

leav·en·ing (-iŋ) *n.* **1.** a substance, such as yeast, used to make batter or dough rise by the formation of gas: also **leavening agent 2.** any influence working to bring about a gradual change /humor is a welcome *leavening* to conversation/

Leav·en·worth (lev''n wurth') [after U.S. Army Col. H. *Leavenworth* (1783–1834)] city in NE Kans.: site of a Federal prison: pop. 25,000

leave of absence a leave from work or duty, esp. for a long time; also, the period of time

leaves (lēvz) *n. pl. of* LEAF

leave-tak·ing (lēv'tāk'iŋ) *n.* the act of taking leave, or saying goodbye

leav·ings (-iŋz) *n.pl.* things left over; leftovers, refuse, etc.

Leb·a·non (leb'ə nən) **1.** country in SW Asia, on the Mediterranean: c.4,000 sq. mi.; pop. 2,367,000; cap. Beirut **2.** mountain range extending nearly the entire length of Lebanon —**Leb'a·nese'** (-nēz') *adj., n., pl.* **-nese'**

lech·er (lech'ər) *n.* [< OFr. < *lechier,* to be a debauchee, lit., lick] a man who engages in lechery; lewd or lustful man

lech·er·ous (-əs) *adj.* engaging in or characterized by lechery; lustful; lewd —**lech'er·ous·ly** *adv.* —**lech'er·ous·ness** *n.*

lech·er·y (-ē) *n., pl.* **-er·ies** a constant thinking about sexual matters or an indulging in sexual activity without restraint; lewdness

lec·i·thin (les'ə thin) *n.* [< Gr. *lekithos,* yolk of an egg + -IN[1]] a fatty compound found in nerve tissue, blood, egg yolk, and some vegetables: used in medicines, foods, etc.

Le Cor·bu·sier (lə kôr bü zyā') (pseud. of *Charles-Édouard Jeanneret-Gris*) 1887–1965; Swiss architect in France

lec·tern (lek'tərn) *n.* [< OFr. < ML. *lectrum* < L. pp. of *legere:* see LOGIC] **1.** a reading desk in a church; esp., such a desk from which a part of the Scriptures is read during the service **2.** a stand for holding the notes, speech, etc., as of a lecturer

lec·ture (lek'chər) *n.* [< ML. *lectura* < pp. of L. *legere,* to read: see LOGIC] **1.** an informative talk given before an audience, class, etc., and usually prepared beforehand **2.** a lengthy scolding —*vi.* **-tured, -tur·ing 1.** to give a lecture —*vt.* **1.** to give a lecture to **2.** to scold at length —see SYN. at SPEECH —**lec'tur·er** *n.* —**lec'ture·ship'** *n.*

led (led) *pt. & pp. of* LEAD[1]

☆**LED** [*l*(*ight-*)*e*(*mitting*) *d*(*iode*)] a semiconductor diode that gives out light when voltage is applied: used as for displaying the time on digital watches

Le·da (lē'də) *Gr. Myth.* mother of Clytemnestra and Castor

LECTERN

and Pollux and (by Zeus, who visited her in the form of a swan) of Helen of Troy

ledge (lej) *n.* [prob. < ME. *leggen*: see LEDGER] **1.** a shelf or shelflike projection [a window *ledge*] **2.** a projecting ridge of rocks **3.** *Mining* a vein or layer of ore-bearing rock —**ledg′y** *adj.*

ledg·er (lej′ər) *n.* [prob. < ME. *leggen*, to lay, or *liggen*, to lie: for IE. base see LIE[1]] *Bookkeeping* the book of final entry, in which a record of debits, credits, and all money transactions is kept

ledger line *same as* LEGER LINE

Lee (lē) **1.** [var. of LEIGH] a masculine or feminine name **2. Henry**, 1756–1818; Am. general in the Revolutionary War: called *Light-Horse Harry Lee* **3. Robert E(dward)**, 1807–70; commander in chief of the Confederate army: son of *Henry*

lee (lē) *n.* [OE. *hleo*, shelter: for IE. base see CALDRON] **1.** shelter; protection **2.** a sheltered place, esp. one on the side away from the wind **3.** *Naut.* the side or part away from the wind —*adj.* of or on the side away from the wind

leech[1] (lēch) *n.* [OE. *læce*] **1.** formerly, a physician **2.** any of a number of annelid worms with suckers, living in water or wet earth: one bloodsucking species was formerly used to bleed patients **3.** a person who stays close to another to get what he can from him; parasite —*vt.* **1.** to bleed with leeches; to drain dry —*vi.* to act as a parasite (often with *onto*)

leech[2] (lēch) *n.* [LME. *lyche*] the free or outside edge of a sail

LEECH
(to 3 in. long)

Leeds (lēdz) city in Yorkshire, N England: pop. 506,000

leek (lēk) *n.* [OE. *leac*] an onionlike vegetable having a bulb with a cylindrical stem, and broad leaves

leer (lir) *n.* [OE. *hleor*] a sly, sidelong look together with a suggestive or wicked smile —*vi.* to look with a leer —**leer′ing·ly** *adv.*

leer·y (lir′ē) *adj.* **leer′i·er, leer′i·est** on one's guard; wary; suspicious [I am *leery* of anyone who promises me something for nothing]

lees (lēz) *n.pl.* [< OFr. < ML. *lia*: for IE. base see LIE[1]] dregs or sediment, as of wine

lee shore the shore on the lee side of a ship; shore toward which the wind is blowing and driving a ship

Leeu·wen·hoek (lā′vən hook′), **An·ton van** (än′tôn vän) 1632–1723; Du. naturalist & pioneer in microscopy

lee·ward (lē′wərd, loo′ərd) *adj.* in the direction toward which the wind blows; of the lee side: opposed to WINDWARD —*n.* the lee part or side —*adv.* toward the lee

Lee·ward Islands (lē′wərd) N group of islands in the Lesser Antilles of the West Indies

lee·way (lē′wā′) *n.* **1.** the leeward drift of a ship or aircraft from the true course **2.** [Colloq.] *a)* more time, money, etc. than might be needed [he gives himself a ten-minute *leeway* when he goes to school in bad weather] *b)* room for freedom of action [she was given much *leeway* in planning the program]

left[1] (left) *adj.* [OE. *lyft*, weak] **1.** *a)* designating or of that side of one's body which is toward the west when one faces north, the side of the less-used hand in most people *b)* designating or of the corresponding side of anything *c)* closer to the left side of a person directly facing the thing mentioned [the top *left* drawer of a desk] **2.** of the bank of a river on the left of a person facing downstream **3.** of the political left; radical or liberal —*n.* **1.** *a)* the left side [forks are placed at the *left* of the plate] *b)* a turn toward the left side [take a *left* at the intersection] **2.** *Boxing a)* the left hand *b)* a blow delivered with the left hand **3.** [often L-] *Politics* a radical or liberal position, party, etc. (often with *the*): from the seating on the left of radicals and liberals in some European legislatures —*adv.* on or toward the left hand or left side —see SYN. at LIBERAL —**have two left feet** to be very clumsy

left[2] (left) *pt. & pp.* of LEAVE[1]

☆**left field** *Baseball* the left-hand part of the outfield (as viewed from home plate) —**out in left field** [Slang] not reasonable, sensible, or probable

left-hand (left′hand′) *adj.* **1.** on or directed toward the left **2.** of, for, or with the left hand

left-hand·ed (-han′did) *adj.* **1.** using the left hand more skillfully than the right **2.** done with the left hand [a *left-handed* throw] **3.** clumsy; awkward **4.** designating an insincere or ambiguous compliment **5.** made for use with the left hand [*left-handed* scissors] **6.** turning from right to left; worked by counterclockwise motion —*adv.* with the left hand [to write *left-handed*] —**left′-hand′ed·ly** *adv.* —**left′-hand′ed·ness** *n.* —**left′-hand′er** *n.*

left·ist (left′ist) *n.* a person whose political position is radical or liberal; member of the left —*adj.* radical or liberal —**left′ism** *n.*

☆**left·o·ver** (-ō′vər) *n.* something left over, as from a meal —*adj.* remaining unused, etc.

left·ward (-wərd) *adv., adj.* on or toward the left: also **left′-wards** *adv.*

left wing [see LEFT[1], *n.* 3] the more radical or liberal section of a political party, group, etc. —**left′-wing′** *adj.* —**left′-wing′er** *n.*

☆**left·y** (lef′tē) *n., pl.* **left′ies** [Slang] a left-handed person: often used as a nickname

leg (leg) *n.* [< ON. *leggr*] **1.** one of the parts of the body by means of which animals stand and walk: in human beings, either of the two lower limbs **2.** a cut of meat consisting of the leg **3.** the part of a garment covering the leg **4.** anything resembling a leg in shape or use, as one of the supports of a piece of furniture **5.** any of the stages of a course or journey **6.** *Math.* either of the sides of a triangle other than its base or, in a right-angled triangle, its hypotenuse —*vi.* **legged, leg′ging** [Colloq.] to walk or run: used chiefly in the phr. **leg it** —**get up on one's hind legs** [Colloq.] to become forceful, aggressive, etc. —**not have a leg to stand on** [Colloq.] to have absolutely no defense, excuse, etc. —**on one's** (or *its*) **last legs** [Colloq.] not far from death, breakdown, etc. —**pull someone's leg** [Colloq.] to make fun of or fool someone —**shake a leg** [Slang] to hurry —**stretch one's legs** to walk, esp. after sitting a long time —**leg′less** *adj.*

leg. **1.** legal **2.** legislative **3.** legislature

leg·a·cy (leg′ə sē) *n., pl.* **-cies** [< OFr. *legacie* < ML. < L. *legatus*: see LEGATE] **1.** money or property left to someone by a will **2.** anything handed down from, or as from, an ancestor [the *legacy* of freedom]

le·gal (lē′gəl) *adj.* [< MFr. < L. *legalis* < *legis*, genitive of *lex*, law: for IE. base see LOGIC] **1.** of, based on, or authorized by law [*legal* studies] **2.** permitted by law [a *legal* act] **3.** that can be enforced in a court of law [*legal* rights] **4.** of or applicable to lawyers [*legal* ethics] **5.** in terms of the law [a *legal* offense] —**le′gal·ly** *adv.*

legal age the age at which a person is able by law to marry without consent, sign contracts, vote, etc.

☆**legal cap** writing paper for use by lawyers, 8½ by 13 or 14 inches, with a ruled margin

le·gal·ese (lē′gə lēz′) *n.* the special vocabulary of legal forms, documents, etc., often thought of by the layman as impossible to understand

☆**legal holiday** a holiday set by law, during which government and, usually, business affairs are suspended

le·gal·ism (lē′gəl iz′m) *n.* strict following of the law, often a sticking too closely to the letter rather than the spirit of the law —**le′gal·ist** *n.* —**le′gal·is′tic** *adj.*

le·gal·i·ty (li gal′ə tē) *n., pl.* **-ties** quality, condition, or instance of being legal or lawful

le·gal·ize (lē′gə līz′) *vt.* **-ized′, -iz′ing** to make legal or lawful —**le′gal·i·za′tion** *n.*

☆**legal separation** an agreement by which a man and wife live apart but are not divorced

legal tender money that may be legally offered in payment of an obligation and that a creditor must accept

leg·ate (leg′it) *n.* [< OFr. < L. pp. of *legare*, to send as ambassador < *lex*: see LEGAL] an envoy or ambassador, esp. one officially representing the Pope —**leg′ate·ship′** *n.*

leg·a·tee (leg′ə tē′) *n.* one to whom a legacy is left by a will

le·ga·tion (li gā′shən) *n.* **1.** a diplomatic minister and his staff, representing their government in a foreign country and ranking just below an embassy **2.** their headquarters

le·ga·to (li gät′ō) *adj., adv.* [It., pp. of *legare* < L. *ligare*, to tie] *Music* in a smooth, even style, with no noticeable interruption between the notes

leg·end (lej′ənd) *n.* [< OFr. < ML. *legenda*, things to be read <

L. neut. pl. gerundive of *legere*, to read: see LOGIC] **1.** *a*) a story handed down for generations and popularly believed to have a historical basis *b*) all such stories belonging to a particular group of people *[famous in Irish* legend*]* **2.** *a*) a notable person much talked about in his own time *b*) the stories of his exploits **3.** an inscription on a coin, medal, etc. **4.** a descriptive title, key, etc., as under an illustration

leg·end·ar·y (lej′ən der′ē) *adj.* of, based on, or presented in legends; traditional

leg·end·ry (-drē) *n.* legends as a group

leg·er·de·main (lej′ər di mān′) *n.* [< MFr. *leger de main*, lit., light of hand] **1.** sleight of hand; tricks of a stage magician **2.** trickery; deceit

leg·er line (lej′ər) [altered < *ledger line*] *Music* a short line written above or below the staff, for notes beyond the range of the staff

leg·ged (leg′id, legd) *adj.* having (a specified number or kind of) legs *[long-*legged*]*

leg·ging (leg′iŋ, -ən) *n.* a covering of canvas, leather, etc. for protecting the leg below the knee

leg·gy (leg′ē) *adj.* **-gi·er, -gi·est 1.** having long and awkward legs *[a* leggy *colt]* **2.** [Colloq.] having long, well-shaped legs — **leg′gi·ness** *n.*

Leg·horn (leg′hôrn, leg′ərn) city in Tuscany, W Italy: pop. 172,000 —*n.* [after prec.] **1.** [*sometimes* l-] any of a breed of small chicken, orig. developed in the Mediterranean region **2.** [l-] *a*) braided Italian wheat straw *b*) a broad-brimmed hat of this straw

leg·i·ble (lej′ə b'l) *adj.* [< LL. *legibilis* < *legere*, to read: see LOGIC] that can be read or read easily *[*legible *handwriting]* — **leg′i·bil′i·ty** *n.* —**leg′i·bly** *adv.*

le·gion (lē′jən) *n.* [< OFr. < L. *legio* < *legere*, to select: see LOGIC] **1.** *Rom. History* a military division varying at times from 3,000 to 6,000 foot soldiers, with additional cavalrymen **2.** a large group of soldiers; army **3.** a large number; multitude *[a* legion *of followers]*

le·gion·ar·y (-er′ē) *adj.* of or making up a legion or legions —*n., pl.* **-ar′ies** a member of a legion

le·gion·naire (lē′jə ner′) *n.* [< Fr. < L.] a member of a legion

Legion of Honor a French honorary society founded in 1802 by Napoleon for recognition of distinguished military or civil service

leg·is·late (lej′is lāt′) *vi.* **-lat′ed, -lat′ing** [< LEGISLATOR] to make or pass a law or laws —*vt.* to cause to be, become, go, etc. by making laws *[to* legislate *better working conditions]*

leg·is·la·tion (lej′is lā′shən) *n.* [< LL. < L. *lex*, law (see LEGAL) + *latio*, a proposing < *ferre*, to BEAR¹] **1.** the making of a law or laws **2.** the law or laws made

leg·is·la·tive (lej′is lāt′iv) *adj.* **1.** of legislation *[*legislative *powers]* ☆**2.** of a legislature or its members *[*legislative *party whip]* **3.** having the power to make laws *[a* legislative *assembly]* **4.** brought about or enforced by legislation —*n.* the lawmaking branch of a government —**leg′is·la′tive·ly** *adv.*

leg·is·la·tor (-lāt′ər) *n.* [L.: see LEGISLATION] a member of a legislative assembly; lawmaker

leg·is·la·ture (-lā′chər) *n.* a body of persons given the responsibility and power to make laws for a country, State, etc.

le·git (lə jit′) *n.* [Slang] the legitimate theater, drama, etc. —*adj.* [Slang] legitimate

le·git·i·ma·cy (lə jit′ə mə sē) *n.* a being legitimate

le·git·i·mate (lə jit′ə mit; *for v.* -māt′) *adj.* [< ML. pp. of *legitimare*, to make lawful, ult. < L. *lex*: see LEGAL] **1.** born of parents legally married to each other **2.** *a*) allowed by law or custom; lawful *[a* legitimate *claim]* *b*) staying or being within the law *[a* legitimate *business]* **3.** ruling by the rights of heredity *[a* legitimate *king]* **4.** *a*) logically correct; reasonable *[a* legitimate *conclusion]* *b*) justifiable or justified *[a* legitimate *complaint]* **5.** following established rules, standards, etc. *[a* legitimate *contest entry]* **6.** *Theater* designating or of stage plays, as distinguished from motion pictures, vaudeville, etc. —*vt.* **-mat′ed, -mat′ing** *same as* LEGITIMIZE —**le·git′i·mate·ly** *adv.* —**le·git′i·ma′tion** *n.*

le·git·i·ma·tize (lə jit′ə mə tīz′) *vt.* **-tized′, -tiz′ing** *same as* LEGITIMIZE

le·git·i·mist (-mist) *n.* a supporter of legitimate authority or, esp., of claims to monarchy based on the rights of heredity —**le·git′i·mism** *n.*

le·git·i·mize (-mīz′) *vt.* **-mized′, -miz′ing 1.** to make or declare legitimate **2.** to make seem just, right, or reasonable —**le·git′i·mi·za′tion** *n.*

☆**leg-man** (leg′man′) *n., pl.* **-men′** a newspaperman who gathers information at the scene of events or at various sources

leg-of-mut·ton (leg′ə mut′'n, -əv-) *adj.* shaped like a leg of mutton, as a sleeve that puffs out toward the shoulder

leg·room (leg′rōōm′) *n.* adequate space for the legs while seated, as in a car

leg·ume (leg′yōōm, li gyōōm′) *n.* [< Fr. < L. *legumen* < *legere*, to gather: see LOGIC] **1.** any of a large family of plants, including the peas, beans, clovers, etc., with fruit that is a pod splitting along two sutures: many legumes are nitrogen-fixing **2.** the pod or seed of some members of this family, used for food

le·gu·mi·nous (li gyōō′min əs) *adj.* **1.** of, having the nature of, or bearing legumes **2.** of the family of plants to which peas and beans belong

☆**leg·work** (leg′wurk′) *n.* [Colloq.] travel away from the center of work as a necessary, but routine, part of a job, as of a newspaper reporter

Le·hár (lā′här), **Franz** (fränts) 1870–1948; Hung. composer of operettas

Le Ha·vre (lə häv′rə; *Fr.* lə à′vr′) seaport in NW France, on the English Channel: pop. 200,000

le·hu·a (lā hōō′ə) *n.* [Haw.] **1.** a hardwood tree of Hawaii and other Pacific islands, with clusters of bright-red flowers **2.** its flower

lei (lā, lā′ē) *n., pl.* **leis** [Haw.] in Hawaii, a wreath of flowers and leaves, generally worn about the neck

Leib·niz (līp′nits), Baron **Gott·fried Wil·helm von** (gôt′frēt vil′helm fôn) 1646–1716; Ger. philosopher & mathematician: also sp. **Leibnitz**

Leices·ter (les′tər) city in C England: pop. 280,000

Leicester, Earl of (*Robert Dudley*) 1532–88; Eng. courtier & general: favorite of Elizabeth I

Lei·den (līd′'n) city in W Netherlands: pop. 103,000

Leigh (lē) [< surname *Leigh* < OE. *leah*, LEA] a masculine or feminine name

Leip·zig (līp′sig, -sik; *G.* līp′tsiH) city in SC East Germany: pop. 592,000

lei·sure (lē′zhər, lezh′ər) *n.* [< OFr. < L. *licere*, to be permitted] free, unoccupied time that can be used for rest, recreation, etc. —*adj.* **1.** free and unoccupied; spare *[*leisure *time]* **2.** having much leisure *[the* leisure *class]* —**at leisure 1.** having free time **2.** with no hurry **3.** not occupied or engaged —**at one's leisure** when one has the time or opportunity —**lei′sured** *adj.*

lei·sure·ly (-lē) *adj.* without haste; slow *[we made a* leisurely *inspection of the place]* —*adv.* in an unhurried manner *[we talked* leisurely*]* —**lei′sure·li·ness** *n.*

leit·mo·tif, leit·mo·tiv (līt′mō tēf′) *n.* [< G. < *leiten*, to lead + *motiv*, MOTIVE] **1.** a recurring musical phrase connected with a given character, situation, etc. as in Wagner's operas **2.** a dominant theme or underlying pattern

lek (lek) *n. see* MONETARY UNITS, table (Albania)

lem·an (lem′ən, lē′mən) *n.* [ME. *lemman* < *lef*, dear (see LIEF) + *man*] [Archaic] a sweetheart or lover (man or woman); esp., a mistress

Le·man (lē′mən), **Lake** *same as* Lake GENEVA: Fr. name **Lac Lé·man** (làk lā män′)

Le Mans (lə män′) city in W France: pop. 143,000

lem·ming (lem′iŋ) *n., pl.* **-mings, -ming:** *see* PLURAL, II, D, 1 [Dan. < ON.] a small arctic rodent resembling the mouse but having a short tail and fur-covered feet

lem·on (lem′ən) *n.* [< MFr. < Ar. *laimūn* < Per. *līmūn*] **1.** a small citrus fruit with a pale-yellow rind and a juicy, sour pulp, used to make drinks and flavor foods **2.** the small, spiny, semitropical tree bearing this fruit **3.** pale yellow ☆**4.** [Slang] *a*) something, esp. a manufactured article, that is defective or imperfect *b*) a person who is disliked —*adj.* **1.** pale-yellow **2.** made with or flavored like lemon —**lem′on·y** *adj.*

lem·on·ade (lem′ə nād′) *n.* a drink made of lemon juice and water, usually sweetened

☆**lemon butter 1.** a spread made of butter flavored with lemon **2.** a sauce of melted butter, lemon juice, and seasoning, used on fish, vegetables, etc.

☆**lemon drop** a small, hard, lemon-flavored candy

lem·pi·ra (lem pir′ə) *n., pl.* **-ras** [AmSp., after *Lempira*, native chief] *see* MONETARY UNITS, table (Honduras)

le·mur (lē′mər) *n.* [< L. *lemures*, ghosts] a small animal related to the monkeys, with large eyes and soft, woolly fur: found mainly in the old-world tropics and active mostly at night

LEMUR
(27–37 in. long, including tail)

Le·na (lē′nə; *also, for 2, Russ.* lye′nä) **1.** [dim. of HELEN] a feminine name **2.** river in east central R.S.F.S.R., flowing northeast into the Arctic Ocean

lend (lend) *vt.* **lent, lend′ing** [OE. *lænan* < *læn,* a LOAN] **1.** to let another use or have (a thing) for a while [will you *lend* me your umbrella until tomorrow?] **2.** to let out (money) at interest **3.** to give; impart [to *lend* an air of mystery] —*vi.* to make a loan or loans —**lend itself** (or **oneself**) **to** to be useful for or open to —**lend′er** *n.*

lending library a library from which books may be borrowed, usually for a daily fee

☆**lend-lease** (lend′lēs′) *n.* in World War II, material aid in the form of munitions, tools, food, etc. granted to foreign countries whose defense was thought vital to the defense of the U.S. — **lend′-lease′** *vt.* **-leased′, -leas′ing**

L'En·fant (län fän′), **Pierre Charles** (pyer shàrl) 1754–1825; Fr. engineer & architect who drew plans for Washington, D.C.

length (leŋkth, leŋth) *n.* [OE. *lengthu* < base of *lang,* LONG¹ + -TH¹] **1.** the measure of how long a thing is from end to end; the greatest of the two or three dimensions of anything [*length,* width, and breadth] **2.** extent in space or time [a movie two hours in *length*] **3.** a long stretch or extent [a *length* of dirt road into town] **4.** the state or fact of being long [wearied by the *length* of the lecture] **5.** a piece of a certain length [a *length* of pipe] **6.** a unit of measure consisting of the length of an object or animal, as in a race [the boat won by two *lengths*] **7.** the duration of a vowel sound —**at full length** stretched out; completely extended —**at length 1.** after a long time; finally **2.** in full —**go to any length** (or **great lengths**) to do whatever is necessary

-length (leŋkth, leŋth) *a combining form meaning* of a length that reaches [knee-*length*]

length·en (leŋkth′'n, leŋth′-) *vt., vi.* to make or become longer —see SYN. at EXTEND —**length′en·er** *n.*

length·wise (-wīz′) *adv., adj.* in the direction of the length: also **length′ways′** (-wāz′)

☆**length·y** (-ē) *adj.* **length′i·er, length′i·est** long; esp., too long, or so long as to be tiresome [a *lengthy* voyage; a *lengthy* sermon] —**length′i·ly** *adv.* —**length′i·ness** *n.*

le·ni·ent (lē′ni ənt, lēn′yənt) *adj.* [< L. prp. of *lenire,* to soften < *lenis,* soft: for IE. base see LET¹] not harsh or severe in disciplining, punishing, judging, etc.; mild; merciful —**le′ni·en·cy,** *pl.* **-cies, le′ni·ence** *n.* —**le′ni·ent·ly** *adv.*

Len·in (len′in; *Russ.* lye′nyin), **V(ladimir) I(lyich)** (orig. surname *Ulyanov:* also called *Nikolai Lenin*) 1870–1924; Russ. Communist revolutionary leader; premier of the U.S.S.R. (1917–24)

Len·in·grad (len′in grad′; *Russ.* lye′nin grät′) seaport in northwestern R.S.F.S.R., on the Gulf of Finland: pop. 3,752,000

Len·in·ism (len′in iz'm) *n.* the communist theories and policies of Lenin —**Len′in·ist** *n., adj.*

len·i·tive (len′ə tiv) *adj.* [< ML. < L. pp. of *lenire:* see LENIENT] soothing or easing; lessening pain or distress —*n.* a lenitive medicine, etc.

len·i·ty (-tē) *n.* [< OFr. < L. < *lenis,* mild: see LENIENT] **1.** a being lenient; mildness; gentleness **2.** *pl.* **-ties** a lenient act

Le·nore (lə nôr′) [var. of ELEANOR] a feminine name

lens (lenz) *n.* [L., lentil: a double-convex lens is shaped like the seed] **1.** *a)* a piece of glass, or other transparent substance, with two curved surfaces, or one plane and one curved, bringing together or spreading rays of light passing through it: lenses are used in optical instruments *b)* a combination of two or more lenses **2.** any of various devices used to focus microwaves, electrons, sound waves, etc. **3.** a transparent part in the eye, that focuses light rays upon the retina: see illustration at EYE

LIGHT RAYS

A

LIGHT RAYS

B

LENSES
(A, double-convex;
B, double-concave)

Lent (lent) *n.* [OE. *lengten,* the spring < *lang,* LONG¹: because the spring days lengthen] the period of forty weekdays from Ash Wednesday to Easter, observed in Christian churches, as by fasting and repenting for sins

lent (lent) *pt. & pp.* of LEND

-lent (lənt) [L. *-lentus,* -ful] *a suffix meaning* full of, characterized by [*virulent, fraudulent*]

Lent·en (lent′'n) *adj.* [*also* l-] of, connected with, or suitable for Lent

len·tic·u·lar (len tik′yoo lər) *adj.* [< L. < dim. of *lens:* see LENS] **1.** shaped like a lentil or biconvex lens **2.** of a lens **3.** of the lens of the eye

len·til (lent′'l) *n.* [< OFr. < L. *lenticula,* dim. of *lens,* lentil] **1.** an old-world plant with small seeds, shaped like double-convex lenses, that grow in pods and are used as food **2.** the seed of this plant

len·to (len′tō) *adv., adj.* [It. < L. *lentus,* slow] *Music* slow —*n., pl.* **-tos** a lento passage or movement

Le·o (lē′ō) [L.: see LION] **1.** a masculine name: var. *Leon* **2.** a N constellation between Cancer and Virgo **3.** the fifth sign of the zodiac: see ZODIAC **4.** **Leo I,** Saint 400?–461 A.D.; Pope (440–461): called *the Great* **5.** **Leo III,** Saint ?–816 A.D.; Pope (795–816) **6.** **Leo XIII** 1810–1903; Pope (1878–1903)

Le·ón (le ôn′) region in NW Spain: formerly a kingdom See map at CASTILE

Le·o·na (lē ō′nə) [< LEO] a feminine name

Leon·ard (len′ərd) [< Fr. < OFr. < OHG. < *lewo,* lion + *hart,* strong] a masculine name

Le·on·ca·val·lo (le ôn′kä väl′lō), **Rug·gie·ro** (rōōd je′rô) 1858–1919; It. operatic composer

le·one (lē ōn′) *n. see* MONETARY UNITS, table (Sierra Leone)

Le·on·i·das (lē än′ə dəs) ?–480 B.C.; king of Sparta (491?–480): defeated & killed by the Persians at Thermopylae

Le·o·nids (lē′ə nidz) *n.pl.* a shower of meteors visible yearly about November 15, appearing to radiate from the constellation Leo: also **Le·on·i·des** (lē än′ə dēz′)

le·o·nine (lē′ə nīn′) *adj.* [< OFr. < L. < *leo,* LION] of, characteristic of, or like a lion

leop·ard (lep′ərd) *n., pl.* **-ards, -ard:** see PLURAL, II, D, 1 [< OFr. < LL. < Gr. *leopardos* < *leōn,* lion + *pardos,* panther] **1.** a large, ferocious animal of the cat family, with a black-spotted tan coat, found in Africa and Asia **2.** *same as* JAGUAR —**leop′ard·ess** *n.fem.*

Le·o·pold (lē′ə pōld′) [G. < OHG. < *liut,* people + *balt,* strong] **1.** a masculine name **2. Leopold I** *a)* 1640–1705; emperor of the Holy Roman Empire (1658–1705) *b)* 1790–1865; king of Belgium (1831–65) **3. Leopold II** *a)* 1747–92; emperor of the Holy Roman Empire (1790–92) *b)* 1835–1909; king of Belgium (1865–1909): son of *Leopold I*

Lé·o·pold·ville (lē′ə pōld vil′, lā′-) *former name of* KINSHASA

le·o·tard (lē′ə tärd′) *n.* [after J. *Léotard,* 19th-c. Fr. aerialist] a one-piece, tightfitting garment, with or without sleeves, worn by acrobats, dancers, etc.

lep·er (lep′ər) *n.* [< OFr. < L. < Gr. < *lepros,* rough, scaly < *lepein,* to peel] **1.** a person having leprosy **2.** a person to be shunned

lep·i·dop·ter·an (lep′ə däp′tər ən) *n.* [< ModL. < Gr. *lepis,* a scale + -PTER(OUS) + -AN] any of a large group of insects, including the butterflies and moths, characterized by two pairs of broad, membranous wings covered with very fine scales, often brightly colored: the larvae are caterpillars —**lep′i·dop′ter·ous** *adj.*

LEOTARDS

lep·re·chaun (lep′rə kôn′, -kän′) *n.* [Ir. *lupracán* < OIr. < *lu,* little + dim. of *corp* (< L. *corpus,* body) *Irish Folklore* a fairy in the form of a little old man who can reveal a buried crock of gold to anyone who catches him

lep·ro·sy (lep′rə sē) *n.* [see LEPER] a chronic, infectious disease caused by a bacterium that attacks the skin, flesh, nerves, etc.: it is characterized by ulcers, white scaly scabs, deformities, and wasting of body parts

lep·rous (-rəs) *adj.* **1.** of or like leprosy **2.** having leprosy

-lep·sy (lep′sē) [< Gr. *-lēpsia* < *lēpsis*, an attack] *a combining form meaning* a fit, attack, seizure [*catalepsy*]: also **-lep′si·a** (-ə)

lep·ton[1] (lep′tän) *n., pl.* **-ta** (-tə) [Gr. < *leptos*, thin, small < *lepein*, to peel] *see* MONETARY UNITS, table (Greece)

lep·ton[2] (lep′tän) *n.* [< Gr. *leptos*, thin] any of a class of fundamental particles that do not interact strongly with other particles or nuclei, including the electrons, muons, etc.

Le·roy (lə roi′, lē′roi) [< Fr. *le roi*, the king] a masculine name

les·bi·an (lez′bē ən) *adj.* [referring to Sappho and her followers, in Lesbos] [*sometimes* L-] of homosexuality between women —*n.* [*sometimes* L-] a homosexual woman —**les′bi·an·ism** *n.*

Les·bos (lez′bäs, -bəs) Gr. island in the Aegean, off the coast of Asia Minor

lese maj·es·ty (lēz′ maj′is tē) [< Fr. < L. fem. of *laesus*, pp. of *laedere*, to hurt + *majestas*, majesty] **1.** a crime against the ruler; treason **2.** the insulting of someone to whom respect is due

le·sion (lē′zhən) *n.* [< MFr. < L. *laesio* < pp. of *laedere*, to harm] **1.** an injury; hurt **2.** an injury, sore, etc. in an organ or tissue of the body resulting in a weakening or loss of function

Les·lie (les′lē, lez′-) [ult. < *less lee* (*lea*), i.e., smaller meadow] a masculine or feminine name

Le·so·tho (le sut′hō, -sō′thō) country in SE Africa, surrounded by South Africa: a member of the Commonwealth: 11,716 sq. mi.; pop. 997,000; cap. Maseru

☆**les·pe·de·za** (les′pə dē′zə) *n.* [after V. M. de *Zespedes*, 18th-c. Sp. governor of E Florida] a plant of the legume family, cultivated for forage, hay, soil improvement, etc.

less (les) *adj. alt. compar. of* LITTLE [OE. *læs, læssa*] not so much, so many, so great, etc.; smaller; fewer [6 is *less* than 8] —*adv. compar. of* LITTLE not so much; to a smaller extent [talk *less* and work more] —*n.* a smaller amount [she ate *less* than I did] —*prep.* minus [$5,000 *less* taxes] —**less and less** decreasingly —**no less a person than** a person of no lower importance, rank, etc. than

-less (lis, ləs) [OE. *-leas* < *leas*, free] *a suffix meaning:* **1.** without, lacking [*valueless*] **2.** that does not [*tireless*] **3.** that cannot be [*dauntless*]

les·see (les ē′) *n.* [see LEASE] a person to whom property is leased; tenant

less·en (les′'n) *vt.* **1.** to make less; decrease [your help *lessens* my work] **2.** [Archaic] to make little of; disparage —*vi.* to become less [the rain *lessened*] —see SYN. at DECREASE

Les·seps (les′əps; *Fr.* le seps′), vicomte **Fer·di·nand Ma·rie de** (fer dē nän′ mà rē′ də) 1805-94; Fr. engineer & diplomat: promoter & planner of the Suez Canal

less·er (les′ər) *adj. alt. compar. of* LITTLE [LESS + -ER] smaller, less, or less important —*adv.* less [the *lesser* known twin]

Lesser Antilles group of islands in the West Indies, southeast of Puerto Rico, including the Leeward Islands & the Windward Islands

lesser panda a reddish, raccoonlike mammal of the Himalayan region

les·son (les′'n) *n.* [< OFr. *leçon* < L. < pp. of *legere*, to read: see LOGIC] **1.** something to be learned; specif., *a)* an exercise that a student is to prepare or learn *b)* the instruction given during one class period *c)* something that needs to be learned for one's safety, etc. [my narrow escape taught me a *lesson*] *d)* [*pl.*] course of instruction [music *lessons*] **2.** a selection from the Bible, read as part of a church service **3.** a rebuke; reproof

les·sor (les′ôr, les ôr′) *n.* [Anglo-Fr. < *lesser*: see LEASE] one who gives a lease; landlord

lest (lest) *conj.* [< OE. < *thy læs the*, lit., by the less that] **1.** for fear that; in case [speak low *lest* you be overheard] **2.** that: used after words showing fear [afraid *lest* he should fall]

Les·ter (les′tər) [< LEICESTER] a masculine name

let[1] (let) *vt., vi.* or *obs.* **let′ted, let′ting** [OE. *lætan*, to leave behind < IE. base *lei-*, to let go] **1.** to leave; abandon: now only in **let alone** (or **let be**), to keep from bothering, disturbing, etc. **2.** to rent; hire out [we *let* our spare room] *b)* to give out (work); assign (a contract) **3.** to allow or cause to escape or flow out [to *let* blood] **4.** to allow to pass, come, or go [*let* me in] **5.** to allow; permit [*let* me help] **6.** to cause to: usually with *know* or *hear* [*let* me hear from you] **7.** to suppose; as-

sume [*let x* be equal to 7 in this equation] When used in commands, suggestions, or dares, *let* serves as an auxiliary [*let* us go; just *let* him try to stop us] —*vi.* to be rented or leased [house to *let*] —**let down 1.** to lower **2.** to slow up **3.** to disappoint —**let off 1.** to give forth (steam, etc.) **2.** to deal lightly or leniently with —**let on** [Colloq.] **1.** to indicate one's awareness of a fact **2.** to pretend —**let out 1.** to release **2.** to rent out **3.** to reveal (a secret, etc.) **4.** to make a garment larger by reducing (the seams, hem, etc.) ☆**5.** to dismiss or be dismissed, as school —**let up 1.** to relax **2.** to stop; cease —☆**let up on** [Colloq.] to stop dealing harshly or severely with

SYN.—let is the informal word implying a giving of permission, but often simply suggests a doing nothing to keep something from happening [*let* him have his say; how did we *let* this happen?]; **allow** and **permit** both imply power to give or deny consent, **permit** stressing a formal consenting or authorizing [he was *permitted* to talk to the prisoner], and **allow** suggesting a setting aside of the usual requirements [honor students were *allowed* to miss the examinations]—see also **SYN.** at HIRE

let[2] (let) *vt.* **let′ted** or **let, let′ting** [OE. *lettan*, lit., to make late: from same base as prec.] [Archaic] to hinder; obstruct —*n.* **1.** an obstacle or impediment: used in the legal phrase **without let or hindrance 2.** in tennis, etc., an interference with the course of the ball in some specific way, making it necessary to play the point over again

-let (lit, lət) [< MFr. *-el* (< L. *-ellus*) + *-et*, both dim. suffixes] *a suffix meaning:* **1.** small [*booklet, ringlet*] **2.** a small object worn as a band on [*anklet*]

let·down (let′doun′) *n.* **1.** a slowing up or feeling of low spirits, as after great excitement, effort, etc. **2.** a disappointment or disillusionment

le·thal (lē′thəl) *adj.* [L. *let(h)alis* < *letum*, death: for IE. base see LET[1]] **1.** causing or capable of causing death; fatal or deadly [a *lethal* blow] **2.** of or suggestive of death —see **SYN.** at FATAL —**le·thal′i·ty** (-thal′ə tē) *n.* —**le′thal·ly** *adv.*

lethal gene a gene that causes death during some immature stage in the development of an organism: also **lethal factor**

le·thar·gic (li thär′jik) *adj.* **1.** of or producing lethargy **2.** abnormally drowsy or dull, sluggish, etc. —**le·thar′gi·cal·ly** *adv.*

leth·ar·gize (leth′ər jīz′) *vt.* **-gized′, -giz′ing** to make lethargic

leth·ar·gy (leth′ər jē) *n., pl.* **-gies** [< OFr. < LL. < Gr. < *lēthargos*, forgetful < *lēthē*, oblivion + *argos*, idle < *a-*, not + *ergon*, work] **1.** a condition of abnormal drowsiness or inactivity **2.** a great lack of energy; sluggishness, apathy, etc.

SYN.—lethargy implies a dull, sluggish state brought on by illness, great fatigue, overeating, etc.; **languor** suggests a lazy or limp feeling that results from weather that weakens one physically, a dreamy, tender mood, etc.; **lassitude** suggests a tired or listless feeling resulting from overwork, depression, etc.; **stupor** suggests a state in which the senses are deadened, as by shock, alcohol, or narcotics; **torpor** implies a temporary loss of all or part of the power of feeling or motion

Le·the (lē′thē) [L. < Gr. *lēthē*, oblivion] *Gr. & Rom. Myth.* the river of forgetfulness, in Hades, whose water produced loss of memory in those who drank of it —*n.* oblivion; forgetfulness —**Le·the·an** (lē thē′ən) *adj.*

let's (lets) let us

Lett (let) *n.* **1.** a member of a people living in Latvia and nearby Baltic regions **2.** *same as* LETTISH

let·ter (let′ər) *n.* [< OFr. < L. *littera*] **1.** any of the characters of the alphabet, used in writing or printing to stand for speech sounds **2.** a written or printed message, usually sent by mail **3.** [*usually pl.*] an official document authorizing someone to do something **4.** [*pl.*] *a)* literature generally *b)* learning; knowledge **5.** literal meaning, as different from the purpose or spirit; exact wording [the judge enforced the *letter* of the law] ☆**6.** the first letter of the name of a school or college, awarded and worn for superior performance in sports, etc. —*vt.* **1.** to mark with letters [to *letter* a poster] **2.** to set down in hand-printed letters [to *letter* one's name] —*vi.* **1.** to make hand-printed letters ☆**2.** [Colloq.] to earn a school letter —**to the letter** just as written or directed —**let′ter·er** *n.*

letter box *same as* MAILBOX

letter carrier *same as* MAIL CARRIER

let·tered (let′ərd) *adj.* **1.** able to read and write **2.** very well educated **3.** inscribed or marked with letters

let·ter·head (let′ər hed′) *n.* **1.** the name, address, etc. of a person or firm printed as a heading on sheets of letter paper **2.** such a sheet

let·ter·ing (-iŋ) *n.* **1.** the process of putting letters on something by stamping, carving, printing, etc. **2.** the letters so made

☆**let·ter·man** (-man′) *n., pl.* **-men** (-men′) a student who has won a school letter

letter of credit a letter from a bank asking that the holder of the letter be allowed to draw specified sums of money from other banks or agencies

let·ter-per·fect (-pur′fikt) *adj.* **1.** correct in every detail **2.** knowing one's lesson, theatrical role, etc. perfectly

let·ter·press (-pres′) *n.* **1.** *a)* the method of printing from raised surfaces, as set type *b)* matter printed by this method **2.** [Chiefly Brit.] reading matter, as distinguished from illustrations

letters (or **letter**) **of marque** formerly, a government document authorizing an individual to arm a ship and capture enemy merchant ships: also **letters** (or **letter**) **of marque and reprisal**

letters patent a document granting a patent

Let·tish (let′ish) *adj.* of the Letts or their language —*n.* the Baltic language of the Letts; Latvian

let·tuce (let′is) *n.* [< OFr. < L. *lactuca* < *lac*, milk: from its milky juice] **1.** a hardy, annual composite plant, grown for its crisp, green leaves **2.** the leaves, much used for salads **3.** [Slang] paper money

☆**let·up** (let′up′) *n.* [< phr. *let up*] [Colloq.] **1.** a slackening or lessening, as of effort **2.** a stop or pause

le·u (le′oo) *n., pl.* **lei** (lā) [Romanian < L. *leo*, lion] *see* MONETARY UNITS, table (Romania)

leu·co·plast (loo′kə plast′) *n.* [< LEUKO- + -*plast*, a combining form meaning "a unit of protoplasm"] any of the colorless particles found in the protoplasm of vegetable cells, in which starch forms in the absence of light

leu·ke·mi·a (loo kē′mē ə) *n.* [ModL.: see LEUKO- & -EMIA] any of a group of diseases of the blood-forming organs, resulting in an abnormal increase in the production of leukocytes: also sp. **leu·kae′mi·a** —**leu·ke′mic** (-mik) *adj.* —**leu·ke′moid** (-moid) *adj.*

leu·ko- [< Gr. *leukos*, white] *a combining form meaning* white or colorless: also, before a vowel, **leuk-** and, esp. in former usage, **leuco-, leuc-**

leu·ko·cyte (loo′kə sīt′) *n.* [see LEUKO- & -CYTE] any of the small, colorless cells in the blood, lymph, and tissues, which are important in the body's defenses against infection; white blood corpuscle —**leu′ko·cyt′ic** (-sit′ik) *adj.*

lev (lef) *n., pl.* **le·va** (le′və) [Bulg., lit., lion < Gr. *leōn*] *see* MONETARY UNITS, table (Bulgaria)

Lev. Leviticus

Le·vant (lə vant′) [< Fr. < It. *levante* (< L. prp. of *levare*, to raise], applied to the East, where the sun "rises"] region on the E Mediterranean, including all countries bordering the sea between Greece & Egypt —**Lev·an·tine** (lev′ən tīn′, -tēn′; lə van′tin) *adj., n.*

le·va·tor (lə vāt′ər) *n., pl.* **lev·a·to·res** (lev′ə tôr′ēz), **le·va′tors** [ModL. < pp. of L. *levare*, to raise] a muscle that raises a limb or other part of the body

☆**lev·ee** (lev′ē) *n.* [< Fr. pp. of *lever*, to raise: see LEVER] **1.** a bank built alongside a river to prevent high water from flooding bordering land **2.** a landing place for ships along the bank of a river; quay **3.** a low ridge of earth around a field to be irrigated —*vt.* **lev′eed, lev′ee·ing** to build a levee along

lev·ee (lev′ē; lə vē′, -vā′) *n.* [< Fr. < *se lever*, to rise, reflexive of *lever*: see prec.] formerly, a reception held by a sovereign or person of high rank, usually upon arising in the morning

lev·el (lev′'l) *n.* [< OFr. < L. *libella*, dim. of *libra*, a balance] **1.** an instrument for determining whether a surface is evenly horizontal: it has a glass tube partly filled with liquid so as to leave an air bubble that moves to the center of the tube when the instrument is on an even horizontal plane **2.** *a)* a horizontal plane or line; esp., such a plane as a basis for measur-

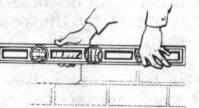

LEVEL (n. 1)

ing elevation [sea *level*] *b)* the height of such a plane [the water in the tank rose to a *level* of five feet] **3.** a relatively flat and even area of land or other surface; horizontal area **4.** the same horizontal plane [the seats are on a *level*] **5.** usual or normal position or height [water seeks its *level*] **6.** position, rank, degree of concentration, etc. in a scale of values [*levels* of income] —*adj.* **1.** perfectly flat and even [a *level* plain] **2.** not sloping **3.** even in height (*with*) [this pile is *level* with the other] **4.** even with the top of the container [a *level* teaspoonful] **5.** *a)*

equal in importance, rank, degree, etc. *b)* conforming to a specified level [high-*level* talks] *c)* equally advanced in development *d)* uniform in tone, color, pitch, volume, rate, etc. **6.** *a)* well-balanced; equable *b)* calm or steady [keep a *level* head] ☆**7.** [Slang] honest —*vt.* **-eled** or **-elled**, **-el·ing** or **-el·ling** **1.** to make level, even, flat, equal (as in rank), etc. [to *level* ground with a bulldozer] **2.** to knock to the ground; demolish [the storm *leveled* the tree] **3.** to raise (a gun, etc.) to a level position for firing **4.** to aim or direct [he *leveled* a great deal of criticism at me] —*vi.* **1.** to aim a gun, etc. (*at*) **2.** to bring people or things to an equal rank, condition, etc. (usually with *down* or *up*) ☆**3.** [Slang] to be frank and honest (*with* someone) —**find one's** (or **its**) **level** to reach one's proper or natural place —**level off 1.** to give a flat, horizontal surface to **2.** *Aeron.* to come or bring to a horizontal line of flight: also **level out 3.** to become stable or constant —**one's level best** [Colloq.] the best one can do —☆**on the level** [Slang] honest(ly) and fair(ly) —**lev′el·er, lev′el·ler** *n.* —**lev′el·ly** *adv.* —**lev′el·ness** *n.*

☆**lev·el·head·ed** (-hed′id) *adj.* having or showing an even temper and sound judgment; sensible —**lev′el·head′ed·ly** *adv.* —**lev′el·head′ed·ness** *n.*

lev·er (lev′ər, lē′vər) *n.* [< OFr. < *lever*, to raise < L. *levare* < *levis*, LIGHT²] **1.** a bar used as a pry to lift or move something **2.** a means to an end **3.** *Mech.* a device consisting of a bar turning about a fixed point, the fulcrum, using power or force applied at a second point to lift or hold up a weight at a third point; hence, any handle, etc. used to operate something [a gearshift *lever*] —*vt.* to move, lift, etc. with a lever —*vi.* to use a lever

lev·er·age (-ij) *n.* **1.** the action of a lever **2.** the mechanical power that comes from using a lever **3.** increased means of accomplishing some purpose [his wealth gave him *leverage* in winning votes]

LEVERS

lev·er·et (lev′ər it) *n.* [< MFr. dim. of *levre* < L. *lepus*, hare] a hare during its first year

Le·vi (lē′vī) *Bible* the third son of Jacob and Leah: see also LEVITE

le·vi·a·than (lə vī′ə thən) *n.* [LL. < Heb. *liwyāthān*] **1.** *Bible* a sea monster, thought of as a reptile or a whale **2.** anything huge or very powerful

lev·i·er (lev′ē ər) *n.* one who levies taxes, etc.

☆**Le·vi's** (lē′vīz) [after *Levi* Strauss, the U.S. maker] *a trademark for* closefitting trousers of heavy denim, reinforced at the seams, etc. with small copper rivets —*n.pl.* such trousers: usually written **le′vis**

lev·i·tate (lev′ə tāt′) *vt.* **-tat′ed, -tat′ing** [< L. *levis*, LIGHT², patterned after GRAVITATE] to cause to rise and float in the air —*vi.* to rise and float in the air —**lev′i·ta′tor** *n.*

lev·i·ta·tion (lev′ə tā′shən) *n.* **1.** a levitating or being levitated **2.** the illusion of raising and keeping a heavy body in the air with little or no support

Le·vite (lē′vīt) *n. Bible* any member of the tribe of Levi, chosen to assist the priests in the Temple

Le·vit·i·cal (lə vit′i k'l) *adj.* **1.** of the Levites **2.** of Leviticus or its laws

Le·vit·i·cus (lə vit′i kəs) the third book of the Bible, containing the laws relating to priests and Levites

lev·i·ty (lev′ə tē) *n., pl.* **-ties** [< OFr. < L. *levitas* < *levis*, LIGHT²] **1.** [Rare] buoyancy **2.** lightness of disposition, conduct, etc.; esp., gaiety and joking when it is out of place **3.** fickleness; instability

le·vo- [< L. *laevus*, left] *a combining form meaning:* **1.** toward the left; counterclockwise [*levorotatory*] **2.** levorotatory [*levulose*] Also, before a vowel, **lev-**

le·vo·ro·ta·to·ry (lē′və rōt′ə tôr′ē) *adj.* **1.** turning to the left, in a counterclockwise direction **2.** turning the plane of polarized light counterclockwise: said of certain crystals, solutions, etc.

lev·u·lose (lev′yoo lōs′) *n.* [LEV(O)- + -UL(E) + -OSE¹: so called because levorotatory] *same as* FRUCTOSE

lev·y (lev′ē) *n., pl.* **lev′ies** [< MFr. fem. pp. of *lever:* see LEVER] **1.** an order that a tax, fine, etc. is to be paid **2.** the amount levied **3.** *a*) the enforced enrolling of persons for military service *b*) a group so enlisted —*vt.* **lev′ied, lev′y·ing 1.** to order the payment of (a tax, fine, etc.) **2.** to force (troops) to be enrolled for military service **3.** to wage (war) —*vi.* **1.** to make a levy **2.** *Law* to seize property in order to pay off a debt

lewd (lōōd) *adj.* [OE. *læwede*, lay, unlearned] showing, or intended to excite, lust or sexual desire, esp. in a way that offends one's sense of morality —**lewd′ly** *adv.* —**lewd′ness** *n.*

Lew·is (lōō′is) **1.** [see LOUIS] a masculine name **2.** John L(lewellyn), 1880–1969; U.S. labor leader **3.** Mer·i·weth·er (mer′ē weth′ər), 1774–1809; Am. explorer, with William Clark, of the Northwest **4.** Sinclair, 1885–1951; U.S. novelist

☆**lew·is·ite** (lōō′ə sīt′) *n.* [after W.L. *Lewis* (1878–1943), U.S. chemist] a pale-yellow, odorless compound, $ClCH:CHAsCl_2$, used as a blistering poison gas

†**lex** (leks) *n., pl.* **le·ges** (lē′jēz, lā′gās) [L.] law

lex·i·cal (lek′si k'l) *adj.* **1.** of a lexicon or lexicography **2.** of the vocabulary of a language

lex·i·cog·ra·pher (lek′sə käg′rə fər) *n.* [< LGr. < Gr. *lexikon*, LEXICON + *graphein*, to write] a person who writes or compiles a dictionary

lex·i·cog·ra·phy (-fē) *n.* [see prec.] the act, art, or work of writing or compiling a dictionary —**lex·i·co·graph·ic** (lek′si kə graf′ik), **lex′i·co·graph′i·cal** *adj.*

lex·i·con (lek′si kən, -kän′) *n.* [Gr. *lexikon* < *lexis*, a word < *legein*: see LOGIC] **1.** a dictionary, esp. of an ancient language **2.** the special vocabulary of a particular author, subject, etc.

Lex·ing·ton (lek′siŋ tən) **1.** [after the city in Mass.] city in NC Ky.: pop. 108,000 **2.** [after the 2d Baron of *Lexington* (1661–1723)] suburb of Boston, in E Mass.: with Concord, site of one of the 1st battles of the Revolutionary War: pop. 32,000

Ley·den jar (or **vial**) (līd′'n) [< LEIDEN, where invented] a condenser for static electricity, consisting of a glass jar with a coat of tinfoil outside and inside and a metallic rod connecting with the inner lining and passing through the lid

Ley·te (lāt′ē) island of the EC Philippines, between Luzon & Mindanao

LF, L.F., lf, l.f. low frequency

lf., lf 1. *Baseball* left field (or fielder) **2.** lightface

LG., L.G. Low German

LGr., L.Gr. Late Greek

l.h., L.H., LH left hand

Lha·sa (lä′sə) capital of Tibet: pop. 70,000

Lhasa ap·so (ap′sō) *pl.* **-sos** [LHASA + Tibetan *apso*, sentinel] a small Tibetan dog with very long hair and a tail that curls over the back

Li *Chem.* lithium

L.I. Long Island

li·a·bil·i·ty (lī′ə bil′ə tē) *n., pl.* **-ties 1.** the state of being liable *[liability* to error; *liability* for damages] **2.** anything for which a person is liable **3.** [*pl.*] *Accounting* all the entries on a balance sheet showing the debts of a person or business, as accounts and notes payable **4.** something that works against one; disadvantage

li·a·ble (lī′ə b'l; *also, esp. for 3,* lī′b'l) *adj.* [prob. via Anglo-Fr. < L. *ligare*, to bind: see LEAGUE¹] **1.** legally bound, as to make good a loss; responsible **2.** likely to have, suffer from, etc. *[liable* to heart attacks] **3.** likely (*to* do, have, get, etc. something unpleasant or unwanted) *[liable* to cause hard feelings; *liable* to fall] —see SYN. at LIKELY

li·ai·son (lē′ə zän′, -zōn′; lē ā′zän; *occas.* lā′ə zän′; *for 3,* lē′ə zōn′) *n.* [Fr. < OFr. < L. < *ligare*: see LIABLE] **1.** a connecting of the parts of a whole, as of military units, so that they can work together effectively **2.** a love affair between unmarried persons **3.** in spoken French, the linking of words by pronouncing the final consonant of one word as though it were the first consonant of the following word, as in the phrase *chez elle* (pronounced shā zel′)

li·a·na (lē än′ə, -an′ə) *n.* [NormFr. *liane*, ult. < L. *viburnum*, wayfaring tree] any luxuriantly growing, woody, tropical vine that roots in the ground and climbs, as around tree trunks: also **li·ane′** (-än′, -an′)

li·ar (lī′ər) *n.* a person who tells lies

lib (lib) *n. clipped form of* LIBERATION

lib. 1. [L. *liber*] book **2.** librarian **3.** library

li·ba·tion (lī bā′shən) *n.* [< L. *libatio* < *libare*, to pour out] **1.** the ritual of pouring out wine or oil upon the ground as a sacrifice to a god **2.** the liquid so poured **3.** an alcoholic drink: used humorously —**li·ba′tion·al** *adj.*

li·bel (lī′b'l) *n.* [OFr. < L. *libellus*, dim. of *liber*, a book: see LIBRARY] **1.** any false and malicious written or printed statement, or any sign, picture, etc., tending to injure a person's reputation unjustly **2.** the act of publishing such a thing **3.** anything that gives an unflattering or damaging picture of the subject it is dealing with —*vt.* **-beled** or **-belled, -bel·ing** or **-bel·ling 1.** to publish or make a libel against **2.** to give an unflattering or damaging picture of —**li′bel·er, li′bel·ler** *n.*

li·bel·ous, li·bel·lous (-əs) *adj.* **1.** of or involving a libel **2.** given to writing and publishing libels; defamatory —**li′bel·ous·ly, li′bel·lous·ly** *adv.*

lib·er·al (lib′ər əl, lib′rəl) *adj.* [OFr. < L. *liberalis* < *liber*, free < IE. base *leudh-*, to grow up] **1.** orig., suitable for a freeman; not restricted: now only in LIBERAL ARTS, LIBERAL EDUCATION, etc. **2.** giving freely; generous *[a liberal* contributor to charity] **3.** ample; abundant *[a liberal* reward] ☆**4.** not restricted to the literal meaning *[a liberal* interpretation of the Bible] **5.** broad-minded; tolerant; specif., not orthodox or conventional **6.** favoring reform or progress, as in religion, education, etc.; specif., favoring political reforms tending toward democracy and personal freedom for the individual; progressive **7.** [L-] designating or of a political party upholding liberal principles, as in England or Canada —*n.* **1.** a person favoring liberalism **2.** [L-] a member of a liberal political party —**lib′er·al·ly** *adv.*

SYN.—**liberal** implies tolerance of others' views as well as openmindedness to ideas that challenge tradition, established institutions, etc.; **progressive** is the opposite of *reactionary* or *conservative* and is applied to persons who favor progress and reform in politics, education, etc. and are inclined to take direct action; **radical** is applied to those who favor fundamental or extreme change, specifically of the social structure; **left** is applied to those who are liberal or radical in their political views

liberal arts the subjects of an academic college course, including literature, philosophy, languages, history, etc., as distinguished from professional or technical subjects

liberal education an education mainly in the liberal arts, providing a broad cultural background

lib·er·al·ism (-iz'm) *n.* the quality or state of being liberal, esp. in politics or religion

lib·er·al·i·ty (lib′ə ral′ə tē) *n., pl.* **-ties** the quality or state of being liberal; specif., *a*) generosity *b*) tolerance; broadmindedness

lib·er·al·ize (lib′ər ə līz′, lib′rə-) *vt., vi.* **-ized′, -iz′ing** to make or become liberal —**lib′er·al·i·za′tion** *n.*

lib·er·ate (lib′ə rāt′) *vt.* **-at′ed, -at′ing** [< L. pp. of *liberare*, to free < *liber*: see LIBERAL] **1.** to release from slavery, enemy occupation, etc. **2.** [Slang] to steal or loot, esp. from a defeated enemy in wartime **3.** *Chem.* to free from combination in a compound —**lib′er·a′tor** *n.*

lib·er·a·tion (lib′ə rā′shən) *n.* **1.** a liberating or being liberated ☆**2.** the securing of equal social and economic rights *[the movement for women's liberation]*

Li·ber·i·a (lī bir′ē ə) country on the W coast of Africa: founded by freed slaves from the U.S.: 43,000 sq. mi.; pop. 1,571,000; cap. Monrovia —**Li·ber′i·an** *adj., n.*

lib·er·tar·i·an (lib′ər ter′ē ən) *n.* a person who advocates full civil liberties —*adj.* of or upholding such liberties —**lib′er·tar′i·an·ism** *n.*

lib·er·tine (lib′ər tēn′, -tin) *n.* [< L. < *libertus*, freedman < *liber*: see LIBERAL] a man who leads an unrestrained, immoral life and has many sexual relations; rake —*adj.* typical of a libertine —**lib′er·tin·ism, lib′er·tin·age** *n.*

lib·er·ty (lib′ər tē) *n., pl.* **-ties** [< OFr. < L. *libertas* < *liber*, free: see LIBERAL] **1.** freedom from slavery, captivity, or any other form of control by others **2.** all the rights possessed in common by the people of a community, state, etc.: see also CIVIL LIBERTIES **3.** a particular right, franchise, freedom, etc. **4.** a too free, too friendly, or bold action or attitude **5.** the area in which one is free to move or go *[we had the liberty* of the whole house] **6.** *U.S. Navy* permission given to an enlisted person to be absent from duty for a period of 72 hours or less **7.** *Philos.* freedom to choose —**at liberty 1.** not shut up; free **2.** allowed (to do or say something) **3.** not busy or in use —**take liberties 1.** to be too friendly or bold in action or speech **2.** to deal (*with* facts, etc.) so as to make them seem different from what they are

☆**Liberty Bell** the bell of Independence Hall in Philadelphia, rung on July 8, 1776, to proclaim the independence of the U.S.

li·bid·i·nous (li bid′'n əs) *adj.* [see LIBIDO] full of or characterized by strong sexual desire —**li·bid′i·nous·ly** *adv.*

li·bi·do (li bē′dō, -bī′-) *n.* [L., desire, wantonness < *libet*, it pleases: see BELIEVE] **1.** the sexual urge or instinct **2.** *Psychoanalysis* energy of the psyche associated with the positive, loving instincts —**li·bid′i·nal** (-bid′'n əl) *adj.* —**li·bid′i·nal·ly** *adv.*

Li·bra (lī′brə, lē′-) [L., a balance] **1.** a S constellation between Virgo and Scorpio **2.** the seventh sign of the zodiac: see ZODIAC

li·bra (lī′brə) *n., pl.* **-brae** (-brē) [L.] pound

li·brar·i·an (lī brer′ē ən) *n.* **1.** a person in charge of a library **2.** a person trained in library science —**li·brar′i·an·ship′** *n.*

li·brar·y (lī′brer′ē, -brə rē) *n., pl.* **-brar′ies** [< OFr. *libraire*, copyist < L. < *liber*, a book: for IE. base see LEAF] **1.** a room or building where a collection of books, periodicals, etc. is kept for reading or reference **2.** a public or private institution in charge of the care and circulation of such a collection **3.** a collection of books, periodicals, etc.

Library of Congress the public national library in Washington, D.C., established in 1800 by the U.S. Congress

☆**library science** the study of library organization and management

li·bret·tist (li bret′ist) *n.* a writer of librettos

li·bret·to (li bret′ō) *n., pl.* **-tos, -ti** (-ē) [It., dim. of *libro*, a book < L. *liber*] **1.** the words, or text, of an opera, oratorio, etc. **2.** a book containing these words

Li·bre·ville (lē br′ vēl′) capital of Gabon; seaport on the Gulf of Guinea; pop. 73,000

Lib·y·a (lib′ē ə) **1.** ancient Greek & Roman name of N Africa, west of Egypt **2.** country in N Africa, on the Mediterranean: 679,359 sq. mi.; pop. 2,016,000; caps. Benghazi & Tripoli —**Lib′y·an** *adj., n.*

lice (līs) *n. pl. of* LOUSE

li·cense (līs′'ns) *n.* [< OFr. < L. *licentia* < prp. of *licere*, to be permitted] **1.** formal or legal permission to do something specified [a *license* to marry, hunt, etc.] **2.** a document, tag, etc. that shows that such permission has been granted **3.** *a)* freedom to ignore strict rules or customs [poetic *license*] *b)* an instance of this **4.** excessive freedom, that goes beyond what is right or proper Also, Brit. sp., **licence** —*vt.* **-censed, -cens·ing** to give license or a license to or for; permit formally —**li′cens·a·ble** *adj.*

li·cen·see (līs′'n sē′) *n.* a person to whom a license is granted

li·cens·er (līs′'n sər) *n.* a person with authority to grant licenses: also sp., *Law,* **li′cen·sor**

li·cen·ti·ate (lī sen′shē it, -āt′) *n.* **1.** a person licensed to practice a specified profession **2.** in certain European and Canadian universities, an academic degree between that of bachelor and that of doctor —**li·cen′ti·ate·ship′** *n.*

li·cen·tious (lī sen′shəs) *adj.* [< L. < *licentia:* see LICENSE] **1.** [Rare] disregarding accepted rules and standards **2.** morally unrestrained, esp. in sexual activity; lascivious —**li·cen′tious·ly** *adv.* —**li·cen′tious·ness** *n.*

li·chee (lē′chē′) *n. same as* LITCHI

li·chen (lī′kən) *n.* [L. < Gr., prob. < *leichein,* to lick] any of a large group of small plants composed of a fungus and an alga growing in close association to form a dual plant, commonly adhering in colored patches to rock, wood, soil, etc. — **li′chen·ous, li′chen·ose′** (-ōs′) *adj.*

licht (likht) *adj., adv., n., vi., vt. Scot. var. of* LIGHT

lic·it (lis′it) *adj.* [< L. pp. of *licere,* to be permitted] permitted; lawful — **lic′it·ly** *adv.* —**lic′it·ness** *n.*

lick (lik) *vt.* [OE. *liccian*] **1.** to pass the tongue over [to *lick* one's lips] **2.** to bring into a certain condition by passing the tongue over [to *lick* one's fingers clean] **3.** to pass lightly over like a tongue [flames *licking* the logs] **4.** [Colloq.] *a)* to whip; thrash *b)* to overcome or vanquish —*vi.* to move lightly and quickly, as a flame —*n.* **1.** the act of licking with the tongue **2.** a small quantity; bit [he didn't do a *lick* of work] ☆**3.** *short for* SALT LICK **4.** [Colloq.] *a)* a sharp blow *b)* a short, rapid burst of activity *c)* a fast pace; clip ☆**5.** [Slang] a phrase of jazz music, esp. an interpolated improvisation **6.** [often pl.] [Slang] chance; turn [to get one's *licks* in] —**lick and a promise** a hasty, superficial effort in cleaning, etc. —**lick into shape** [Colloq.] to bring into proper condition —**lick one's chops** to anticipate eagerly —**lick up** to consume as by licking

LICHENS

lick·er·ish (lik′ər ish) *adj.* [< Anglo-Fr. form of OFr. *lecheros*] [Archaic] **1.** lecherous; lustful; lewd **2.** greedy or eager, esp. to eat or taste

☆**lick·e·ty-split** (lik′ə tē split′) *adv.* [fanciful formation based on LICK, *n.* 4 *c*] [Colloq.] at great speed

lick·ing (lik′iŋ) *n.* **1.** the act of a person or thing that licks **2.** [Colloq.] *a)* a whipping *b)* a defeat

lick·spit·tle (lik′spit′'l) *n.* a person who flatters and fawns on another; toady: also **lick′spit′**

lic·o·rice (lik′ər ish, -is; lik′rish) *n.* [< OFr. < LL. *liquiritia,* ult. < Gr. *glykys,* sweet + *rhiza,* root] **1.** a European plant of the legume family **2.** its dried root or the black flavoring extract made from this **3.** candy flavored with or as with this extract

lic·tor (lik′tər) *n.* [L.] a minor Roman official who carried the fasces and cleared the way for the chief magistrates

lid (lid) *n.* [OE. *hlid:* for IE. base see CLIENT] **1.** a movable cover, as for a box, pot, etc. **2.** *short for* EYELID ☆**3.** [Colloq.] a curb or restraint [to put a *lid* on gambling] **4.** [Slang] a cap, hat, etc. —**lid′ded** *adj.* —**lid′less** *adj.*

lie¹ (lī) *vi.* **lay, lain, ly′ing** [OE. *licgan* < IE. base *legh-,* to lie, lay] **1.** to be or put oneself in a reclining position along a relatively horizontal surface (often with *down*) **2.** to rest on a support in a more or less horizontal position: said of inanimate things **3.** to be or remain in a specified condition [motives that *lie* hidden] **4.** to be situated [Canada *lies* to the north] **5.** to extend [the road that *lies* before us] **6.** to be; exist [the love that *lies* in her eyes] **7.** to be buried or entombed **8.** [Archaic] to stay overnight or for a short while **9.** [Archaic] to have sexual intercourse (*with*) —*n.* **1.** the way in which something is situated or arranged; lay **2.** an animal's lair —☆**lie down on the job** [Colloq.] to put forth less than one's best efforts —**lie in** to be in confinement for childbirth —**lie off** to stay at a distance from shore or another ship —☆**lie over** to stay and wait until some future time —**lie to** to be stationary with the head to the wind: said of a ship —**take lying down** to accept (anything that punishes or wrongs one) without protesting or resisting —**li′er** *n.*

lie² (lī) *vi.* **lied, ly′ing** [OE. *leogan*] **1.** to make a statement or statements that one knows to be false, esp. with intent to deceive **2.** to give a false impression; deceive one [statistics can *lie*] —*vt.* to bring, put, accomplish, etc. by lying [to *lie* oneself into office] —*n.* **1.** a thing said or done in lying; falsehood **2.** anything that gives or is meant to give a false impression —**give the lie to 1.** to charge with telling a lie **2.** to prove to be false

SYN.—**lie** is the simple, direct word meaning to make a deliberately false statement; **prevaricate** strictly means to quibble or confuse the issue in order to avoid telling the truth, but it is loosely used as a substitute for **lie**; **equivocate** means to say things that have more than one meaning, in order to deceive or mislead; **fib** implies the telling of a falsehood about something unimportant and is sometimes used as a polite substitute for **lie**

Lie·big (lē′biH), Baron **Jus·tus von** (yōōs′tōōs fôn) 1803-73; Ger. chemist

Liech·ten·stein (lēH′tən shtīn′) country in WC Europe, on the Rhine: 61 sq. mi.; pop. 21,000; cap. Vaduz

lied (lēd; *G.* lēt) *n., pl.* **lied′er** (lē′dər; *G.* -dər) [G.] a German song, esp. one of a lyrical, often popular, character

☆**Lie·der·kranz** (lē′dər krants′) [G., lit., garland of songs] *a trademark for* a soft cheese having a strong odor and flavor

☆**lie detector** a polygraph used on persons suspected of lying, to record certain changes in body functions that are thought to occur when the subject tells lies in answering questions

lief (lēf) *adj.* [OE. *leof:* see BELIEVE] [Archaic or Obs.] **1.** dear; beloved **2.** willing —*adv.* willingly; gladly: only in **would** (or **had) as lief**

Li·ège (lē āzh′; *Fr.* lyezh) city in E Belgium, on the Meuse: pop. 152,000

liege (lēj) *adj.* [< OFr., prob. < Frank. base but infl. by L. *ligare:* see LEAGUE¹] **1.** *Feudal Law a)* entitled to the service and allegiance of his vassals [a *liege* lord] *b)* bound to give service and allegiance to the lord [*liege* subjects] **2.** loyal; faithful —*n. Feudal Law* **1.** a lord or sovereign **2.** a subject or vassal

liege·man (lēj′mən) *n., pl.* **-men 1.** a vassal **2.** a loyal follower Also **liege man**

li·en (lēn, lē′ən) *n.* [Fr. < L. *ligamen,* a band < *ligare:* see LEAGUE¹] *Law* a claim on the property of another as security for the payment of a debt

lieu (lōō) *n.* [OFr. < L. *locus*, place] place: now chiefly in **in lieu of,** in place of; instead of

lieu·ten·ant (lōō ten′ənt; *Brit. & Canad. army* lef ten′-) *n.* [< MFr. < *lieu*, place + *tenant*, holding < L. *tenere*, to hold] **1.** one who acts for a superior, as during the latter's absence **2.** an officer ranking below a captain, as in a police department **3.** *U.S. Mil.* an officer ranking below a captain: see also FIRST LIEUTENANT, SECOND LIEUTENANT **4.** *U.S. Navy* an officer ranking just above a lieutenant junior grade Abbrev. **Lieut., Lt.** — **lieu·ten·an·cy** (-ən sē) *n., pl.* **-cies**

lieutenant colonel *U.S. Mil.* an officer ranking above a major

lieutenant commander *U.S. Navy* an officer ranking above a lieutenant

lieutenant general *U.S. Mil.* an officer ranking above a major general

lieutenant governor **1.** an elected official of a State who ranks below and substitutes for the governor in case of the latter's absence or death **2.** the official head of government of a Canadian province, appointed by the governor general: also **lieu·ten′ant-gov′er·nor** *n.*

lieutenant junior grade *U.S. Navy* an officer ranking above an ensign

life (līf) *n., pl.* **lives** [OE. *lif* < IE. base *leibh-*, to live] **1.** that quality of plants and animals which makes it possible for them to take in food, get energy from it, grow, adapt themselves to their surroundings, and reproduce their kind: it makes a living animal or plant different from inorganic matter or a dead organism **2.** the state of possessing this quality [brought back to *life*] **3.** a living being, esp. a human being [the *lives* lost in wars] **4.** living things as a group [plant *life*] **5.** the time a person or thing is alive, or a specific portion of such time [his early *life*] **6.** a sentence of imprisonment for the rest of one's life **7.** one's manner of living [a *life* of ease] **8.** the people and activities of a given time, or in a given setting or class [military *life*, low *life*] **9.** human existence and activity [to learn from *life*] **10.** *a)* an individual's lifetime experiences *b)* an account of this **11.** the existence of the soul [eternal *life*] **12.** something essential to the continued existence of something else [freedom of speech is the *life* of democracy] **13.** the source of vigor or liveliness [the *life* of the party] **14.** vigor; liveliness **15.** the period of flourishing, usefulness, functioning, etc. [fads have a short *life*] **16.** representation in art from living models [a class in *life*] **17.** [Colloq.] another chance [to get a *life*] —*adj.* of, in, or for life [*life* processes; a *life* sentence] —**a matter of life and death 1.** something whose outcome determines whether a person lives or dies **2.** any extremely important matter —**as large (or big) as life 1.** life-size **2.** in actual fact; truly —**bring to life 1.** to bring back to consciousness **2.** to make lively; animate —**come to life 1.** to recover consciousness **2.** to become lively or animated —**for dear life** with a desperate intensity —**for life 1.** for the duration of one's life **2.** in order to save one's life —**from life** from a living model —☆**not on your life** [Colloq.] by no means; certainly not —**see life** to have a wide variety of experiences —**take life** to kill —**take one's (own) life** to commit suicide —☆**the life of Riley** [Colloq.] a very pleasant or luxurious way of living —**to the life** like the living original; exactly —**true to life** true to reality

life belt a life preserver in the form of a belt

life·blood (līf′blud′) *n.* **1.** the blood necessary to life **2.** the vital part of anything [oil is the *lifeblood* of the economy]

life·boat (-bōt′) *n.* any of the small boats carried by a ship for use if the ship must be abandoned

life buoy same as LIFE PRESERVER

life cycle the series of changes in form from the earliest stage in one generation to the earliest stage in the next of an organism

life expectancy the number of years that an individual of a given age may expect on the average to live, as shown in statistical tables

life-giv·ing (-giv′iŋ) *adj.* **1.** that gives or can give life **2.** strengthening; inspiring; refreshing —**life′-giv′er** *n.*

life·guard (-gärd′) *n.* ☆an expert swimmer employed at a beach, a pool, etc. to prevent drownings

life history **1.** the history of the changes that an organism goes through in its development from the egg, spore, etc. to its death as an adult **2.** one series of such changes **3.** the story of a person's life

life insurance insurance in which a specified sum of money is paid to the beneficiary or beneficiaries at the death of the insured, or to the insured when he reaches a specified age

life jacket (or **vest**) a life preserver in the form of a sleeveless jacket or vest

life·less (-lis) *adj.* **1.** without life; specif., *a)* that never had life [a *lifeless* statue] *b)* no longer living; dead [the *lifeless* body of the accident victim] *c)* having no living beings [a *lifeless* planet] **2.** not lively or active; dull [a *lifeless* speech] — **life′less·ly** *adv.* —**life′less·ness** *n.*

life·like (-līk′) *adj.* **1.** resembling actual life [lifelike dialogue in the movie] **2.** closely resembling a real person or thing [a *lifelike* portrait]

life·line (-līn′) *n.* **1.** a rope for saving life, as one thrown to a person in the water **2.** the rope used to raise or lower a diver **3.** a commercial route or transport line of vital importance

life·long (-lôŋ′) *adj.* lasting or not changing during one's whole life [a *lifelong* love]

☆**life net** a strong net used by firemen, etc. as to catch people jumping from a burning building

life preserver a floating device for saving a person from drowning by keeping his body afloat, as a ring or sleeveless jacket of canvas-covered cork

lif·er (līf′ər) *n.* [Slang] a person sentenced to imprisonment for life

life raft a small raft or boat that can be filled with air and used as an emergency craft at sea

☆**life·sav·er** (-sā′vər) *n.* **1.** a person or thing that saves people from drowning, as a lifeguard **2.** [Colloq.] a person or thing that gives aid in time of stress or need —**life′sav′ing** *adj.*

life-size (-sīz′) *adj.* of the same size as the person or thing represented: said of a picture, sculpture, etc.: also **life′-sized′**

LIFE PRESERVER

life span **1.** same as LIFETIME **2.** the longest period of time that a typical individual can be expected to live

☆**life style** one's way of life as typified by one's activities, attitudes, possessions, etc.

life·time (-tīm′) *n.* the length of time that someone lives, or that something lasts, functions, etc. —*adj.* lasting for such a period [a *lifetime* job]

life·work (-wʉrk′) *n.* the work or task to which a person devotes his life; chief work in life

life zone any of the zones of a continent, region, etc. divided according to the kinds of plant and animal life in the zone

lift (lift) *vt.* [< ON. *lypta* < *lopt*, air] **1.** to bring up to a higher position; raise [he *lifted* the child to his shoulder] **2.** to pick up and move or set [*lift* the box down from the shelf] **3.** to hold up **4.** to raise in rank, condition, spirits, etc.; elevate; exalt [to *lift* oneself from poverty] **5.** to pay off (a mortgage, debt, etc.) **6.** to end (a blockade, siege, etc.) by withdrawing forces **7.** to revoke or take back (a ban or order) **8.** to subject to FACE LIFTING **9.** [Colloq.] to plagiarize [to *lift* a passage from another writer] **10.** [Slang] to steal —*vi.* **1.** to use strength in raising or trying to raise something **2.** to rise and vanish; be dispelled [the fog *lifted*] **3.** to become raised; go up —*n.* **1.** a lifting, raising, or rising **2.** the amount lifted **3.** the distance through which something is lifted **4.** lifting force, power, or influence **5.** a raising of one's spirits [his praise gave her a *lift*] **6.** position, as of the neck, head, etc., in being held or carried high **7.** a ride in the direction one is going **8.** help of any kind **9.** a rise in the ground **10.** the means by which something is lifted; specif., *a)* any layer of leather in the heel of a shoe *b)* [Brit.] an elevator *c)* a device used to transport people up or down a slope *d)* a device for lifting an automobile for repairs **11.** *Aeron.* the total force of air supporting an aircraft in flight against the pull of gravity —**lift′er** *n.*

SYN.—**lift** implies the use of some effort in bringing something up to a higher position [help me *lift* the table]; **raise,** often used in place of **lift,** specifically implies that something is brought into an upright position by lifting it at one end [to *raise* a flagpole]; **elevate** is usually used when a specific or relative height is mentioned [the balloon had been *elevated* 500 feet; the platform is slightly *elevated*]; **rear** is a literary word used in place of **raise** or **lift** [the giant trees *reared* their branches to the sky] All these terms are used like figures of speech to imply a bringing into a higher or better state [to *lift* one's spirits; to *raise* one's hopes; to *elevate* one's mind; to *rear* children] —**ANT.** lower

☆**lift·off** (lift′ôf′) *n.* the thrust and rise of a spacecraft, missile, etc. straight up into the air as it is launched

lig·a·ment (lig′ə mənt) *n.* [< L. < *ligare*: see LIGATURE] **1.** a bond or tie connecting one thing with another **2.** a band of tough body tissue connecting bones or holding organs in place

li·gate (lī′gāt) *vt.* **-gat·ed, -gat·ing** to tie with a ligature, as a bleeding artery —**li·ga′tion** *n.*

lig·a·ture (lig′ə chər) *n.* [< MFr. < LL. < pp. of L. *ligare*, to bind: for IE. base see LEAGUE[1]] **1.** a tying or binding together **2.** a thing used for this; tie, bond, etc. **3.** a written or printed character containing two or more letters united, as **æ**, **fl**, **th** **4.** *Music a)* a curved line indicating a slur *b)* the notes slurred **5.** *Surgery* a thread or wire used to tie up an artery, etc. —*vt.* **-tured, -tur·ing** to tie or bind together with a ligature

li·ger (lī′gər) *n.* [LI(ON) + (TI)GER] the offspring of a male lion and a female tiger

light[1] (līt) *n.* [OE. *leoht* < IE. base *leuk-*, to shine, from which also come L. *lux* & *lumen*, light] **1.** *a)* the form of radiation that acts upon the retina of the eye, optic nerve, etc., making it possible to see: the speed of light is 186,000 miles per second *b)* a similar form of radiant energy not acting on the normal retina of the eye, as ultraviolet and infrared radiation **2.** the sensation that light stimulates in the organs of sight **3.** brightness; illumination, often of a specified kind [the dim *light* of a candle] **4.** a source of light, as the sun, a lamp, etc. [turn off the *light*] **5.** *same as* TRAFFIC LIGHT **6.** the light from the sun; daylight or dawn [window shutters to keep out the *light*] **7.** a thing by means of which something can be started burning [a *light* for a cigar] **8.** the means by which light is let in; window or windowpane **9.** knowledge or information; enlightenment [to shed *light* on the past] **10.** spiritual inspiration [the *light* of the Scriptures] **11.** public knowledge or view [to bring new facts to *light*] **12.** the way in which something is seen; aspect [presented in a favorable *light*] **13.** facial expression [a *light* of recognition in his eyes] **14.** an outstanding person [one of the shining *lights* of the school] —*adj.* **1.** having light; bright [a *light*, airy room] **2.** pale in color; whitish; fair [a *light* yellow] —*adv.* palely [a *light* blue color] —*vt.* **light′ed** or **lit, light′ing** **1.** to set on fire; ignite [to *light* a bonfire] **2.** to cause to give off light [to *light* a lamp] **3.** to cast light on or in; illuminate [lamps *light* the streets] **4.** to brighten; animate [the good news *lighted* her face with joy] **5.** to show the way to by giving light [a beacon *lights* the ships to harbor] —*vi.* **1.** to catch fire [the fuel *lighted* at once] **2.** to become bright (usually with *up*) —**according to one's lights** as one's opinions, information, or standards may guide one —**in the light of** considering —**see the light (of day) 1.** to come into existence **2.** to come into public view ☆**3.** to understand

light[2] (līt) *adj.* [OE. *leoht* < IE. base *legwh-*, from which also comes L. *levis*] **1.** having little weight; not heavy [a *light* load] **2.** having little weight for its size **3.** below the usual or defined weight [a *light* coin] **4.** less than usual or normal in amount, extent, force, intensity, etc.; specif., *a)* striking with little force [a *light* blow] *b)* of less than the usual quantity or density [a *light* rain] *c)* not coarse, massive, etc.; graceful [*light* tracery] *d)* soft, muted, or muffled [a *light* sound] *e)* not prolonged or intense [*light* applause] **5.** of little importance; not serious [*light* conversation] **6.** easy to bear; not burdensome [a *light* tax] **7.** easy to do; not difficult [*light* work] **8.** gay; happy; buoyant [*light* spirits] **9.** flighty; frivolous; capricious **10.** loose in morals; wanton **11.** dizzy; giddy **12.** of an amusing or nonserious nature [*light* reading] **13.** containing little alcohol [*light* wine] **14.** *a)* not as full as usual [a *light* meal] *b)* easy to digest **15.** well leavened; soft and spongy [a *light* cake] **16.** easily crumbled; porous [*light* sand] **17.** moving with ease and nimbleness [*light* on one's feet] **18.** carrying little weight [a *light* truck] **19.** unstressed or slightly stressed: said of syllables **20.** designating or of industry equipped with relatively light machinery and producing small products **21.** designating, of, or equipped with light weapons, armor, etc. —*adv.* lightly —*vi.* **light′ed** or **lit, light′ing** **1.** [Now Dial.] to get down, as from a horse; alight **2.** to come to rest after traveling through the air [ducks *lighting* on the pond] **3.** to come or happen (on or *upon*) by chance [he *lighted* on the right answer] **4.** to strike suddenly, as a blow —**light in the head 1.** dizzy **2.** simple; foolish —☆**light into** [Colloq.] **1.** to attack **2.** to scold —☆**light out** [Colloq.] to depart suddenly —**make light of** to treat as unimportant; pay little or no attention to —**light′ish** *adj.*

light air a wind speed of 1 to 3 miles per hour

light breeze a wind speed of 4 to 7 miles per hour

light·en[1] (līt′'n) *vt.* **1.** to make light; illuminate **2.** to make light or pale —*vi.* **1.** to become light; grow brighter **2.** to shine brightly; flash **3.** to give off flashes of lightning —**light′en·er** *n.*

light·en[2] (līt′'n) *vt.* **1.** *a)* to make lighter in weight *b)* to reduce the load of **2.** to make less severe, harsh, etc. [to *lighten*

a punishment] **3.** to make more cheerful [his jokes *lightened* our spirits] —*vi.* **1.** to become lighter in weight **2.** to become more cheerful —see SYN. at RELIEVE —**light′en·er** *n.*

light·er[1] (līt′ər) *n.* a person or thing that lights something or starts it burning [a cigarette *lighter*]

light·er[2] (līt′ər) *n.* [< MDu. < *lichten*, to make light < *licht*, LIGHT[2]] a large, open barge used chiefly in loading or unloading larger ships lying offshore —*vt., vi.* to transport (goods) in a lighter

light·er·age (-ər ij) *n.* **1.** the loading or unloading of a ship, or transportation of goods, by means of a lighter **2.** the charge for this

light·er-than-air (līt′ər thən er′) *adj.* designating or of an aircraft that is a balloon filled with a gas lighter than air

light·face (līt′fās′) *n. Printing* type having thin, light lines — *adj.* having thin, light lines: also **light′faced′**

light-fin·gered (-fiŋ′gərd) *adj.* skillful at stealing, esp. by picking pockets

light-foot·ed (-foot′id) *adj.* stepping lightly and gracefully: also [Poet.] **light′-foot′** —**light′-foot′ed·ly** *adv.*

light-hand·ed (-han′did) *adj.* **1.** having a light, delicate touch **2.** having little to carry

light-head·ed (-hed′id) *adj.* **1.** mentally confused or feeling giddy; dizzy **2.** not sensible; flighty; frivolous —**light′-head′ed·ly** *adv.* —**light′head′ed·ness** *n.*

light-heart·ed (-här′tid) *adj.* free from care; gay or cheerful —**light′heart′ed·ly** *adv.* —**light′heart′ed·ness** *n.*

☆**light heavyweight** a boxer or wrestler between a middleweight and heavyweight (in boxing, 161–175 pounds)

light·house (-hous′) *n.* a tower located at some place important or dangerous to navigation; it has a very bright light at the top, and often foghorns, sirens, etc., by which ships are guided and warned

LIGHTHOUSE

light·ing (-iŋ) *n.* **1.** a giving light or being lighted; illumination; ignition **2.** the distribution of light and shade, as in a painting **3.** the art or manner of arranging stage lights

light·ly (-lē) *adv.* **1.** with little weight or pressure; gently **2.** to a small degree or amount [to spend *lightly*] **3.** with grace and skill; nimbly; deftly [skipping *lightly* along] **4.** cheerfully; merrily **5.** with indifference or neglect; in a careless way [taking his responsibility *lightly*] **6.** with little or no reason **7.** with little or no punishment [to let someone off *lightly*]

light-mind·ed (-mīn′did) *adj.* not serious; frivolous —**light′-mind′ed·ly** *adv.* —**light′-mind′ed·ness** *n.*

light·ness[1] (-nis) *n.* **1.** the quality or intensity of lighting; brightness **2.** *a)* paleness *b)* the relative amount of light reflected by an object

light·ness[2] (-nis) *n.* **1.** the state of being light, not heavy **2.** mildness, nimbleness, delicacy, cheerfulness, lack of seriousness, etc.

light·ning (-niŋ) *n.* [< ME. *lightnen*, to LIGHTEN[1]] **1.** a flash of light in the sky caused by the discharge of atmospheric electricity from one cloud to another or between a cloud and the earth **2.** such a discharge of electricity —*vi.* to give off such a discharge —*adj.* like lightning

☆**lightning arrester** a device that protects radio or electrical equipment from lightning by causing the discharge to be carried to the ground

☆**lightning bug** (or **beetle**) *same as* FIREFLY

☆**lightning rod** a pointed metal rod placed high on a building, etc. and grounded to carry off lightning from the structure

light opera a short, amusing musical play

☆**light pen** a penlike electronic device housing a photoelectric cell that can be pointed at the screen of a cathode-ray tube controlled by a computer: the pen signals the computer to add to, change, erase, etc. information shown on the screen

lights (līts) *n.pl.* [from their light weight] [Dial.] the lungs of animals, as sheep, hogs, cattle, etc., used as food

light·ship (līt′ship′) *n.* a ship moored in a place dangerous to navigation and bearing lights, foghorns, sirens, etc. to warn or guide pilots

light·some (-səm) *adj.* **1.** nimble, graceful, or lively **2.** light-hearted; gay **3.** not serious; frivolous

light·weight (-wāt') *n.* **1.** one below normal weight **2.** a boxer or wrestler between a featherweight and a welterweight (in boxing, 127–135 pounds) ☆**3.** [Colloq.] a person having little influence, intelligence, etc. —*adj.* **1.** light in weight **2.** not important or serious

light-year (-yir') *n. Astron.* a unit of distance equal to the distance that light travels in a vacuum in one year, approximately 6 trillion miles

lig·ne·ous (lig'nē əs) *adj.* [< L. *ligneus* < *lignum*, wood] of, or having the nature of, wood; woody

lig·nite (lig'nīt) *n.* [< Fr.: see LIGNEOUS & -ITE] a soft, brownish-black coal in which the texture of the original wood can still be seen —**lig·nit·ic** (-nit'ik) *adj.*

lig·num vi·tae (lig'nəm vīt'ē) [ModL. < L., wood of life] **1.** same as GUAIACUM (sense 1) **2.** commercial name for the very hard wood of the guaiacum, used in bearings, casters, etc.

lig·ro·in (lig'rō in) *n.* [prob. < Gr. *liguros*, clear + -IN¹] chemists' term for BENZINE

Li·gu·ri·a (li gyoor'ē ə) region of NW Italy, on an arm (**Ligurian Sea**) of the Mediterranean: chief city, Genoa —**Li·gu'ri·an** *adj., n.*

lik·a·ble (līk'ə b'l) *adj.* having qualities that make one liked; attractive, genial, etc. —**lik'a·ble·ness, lik'-a·bil'i·ty** *n.*

like¹ (līk) *adj.* [OE. *gelic*] **1.** having almost or exactly the same characteristics; similar; equal [a cup of sugar and a *like* amount of flour] **2.** [Dial.] likely —*adv.* [Colloq.] likely [*like* as not, he is already there] —*prep.* **1.** similar to; resembling [she is *like* a bird] **2.** similarly to [she sings *like* a bird] **3.** characteristic of [not *like* her to cry] **4.** in the mood for; desirous of [to feel *like* sleeping] **5.** indicative of [it looks *like* a clear day tomorrow] **6.** as for example [fruit, *like* pears, for dessert] **NOTE:** *like* was originally an adjective in senses 1, 3, 4, 5, and an adverb in sense 2, and is still considered so by some grammarians —*conj.* [Colloq.] **1.** as [it was just *like* you said] **2.** as if [it looks *like* he is late] —*n.* a person or thing regarded as the equal or counterpart of another or of the person or thing being discussed [did you ever see the *like* of it?] —*vt.* **liked, lik'ing** [Obs.] to liken —*vi.* [Dial.] to be about (*to* have done something) **NOTE:** *like* is also used without meaning or grammatical function, as in hip talk [it's *like* hot] —**and the like** and others of the same kind —**like anything** [Colloq.] very much —**like blazes** (or **crazy, the devil, mad,** etc.) [Colloq.] with furious energy, speed, etc. —**nothing like** not at all like —**something like** almost like; about —**the like** (or **likes**) **of** [Colloq.] any person or thing like

like² (līk) *vi.* **liked, lik'ing** [OE. *lician*] to be so inclined; choose [leave whenever you *like*] —*vt.* **1.** to be pleased with; have a preference for; enjoy **2.** to want or wish [I would *like* to go] —*n.* [*pl.*] the things one enjoys or prefers —**lik'er** *n.*

-like (līk) [see LIKE¹] a suffix meaning like, characteristic of, suitable for [doglike, homelike]

like·a·ble (līk'ə b'l) *adj.* same as LIKABLE

like·li·hood (līk'lē hood') *n.* the fact of being likely to happen or something that is likely to happen [some *likelihood* of rain]

like·ly (līk'lē) *adj.* **-li·er, -li·est** [prob. < OE. *geliclic* or < cognate ON. *likligr*] **1.** credible; probable [a *likely* cause] **2.** reasonably to be expected [it is *likely* to rain] **3.** suitable; well-suited, etc. [a *likely* woman for the job] **4.** having good prospects; promising [a *likely* lad] —*adv.* probably [she will very *likely* go]

SYN.—**likely** suggests probability or a possible happening that can reasonably be expected [he's not *likely* to win]; **liable** and **apt** are loosely or informally used in place of **likely**, but in strict usage, **liable** implies being exposed or open to something undesirable [he's *liable* to be killed if he plays with firearms] and **apt** suggests a natural or habitual tendency [young children are *apt* to be shy of strangers]; **prone** suggests a strong tendency to do something that cannot be avoided [he's *prone* to have accidents] See also SYN. at PROBABLE —**ANT.** unlikely, indisposed

LIGURIA

like-mind·ed (līk'mīn'did) *adj.* having the same ideas, tastes, etc. —**like'-mind'ed·ly** *adv.* —**like'-mind'ed·ness** *n.*

lik·en (-'n) *vt.* to represent or describe as being like, or similar; compare [the poet *likened* her lips to rubies]

like·ness (-nis) *n.* **1.** the state or quality of being like; similarity **2.** (the same) form or shape [Zeus took on the *likeness* of a bull] **3.** something that is like; copy, facsimile, etc.

SYN.—**likeness** implies being closely alike in appearance, qualities, nature, etc. [her remarkable *likeness* to her brother]; **similarity** suggests a being alike only in a certain way or to some extent [your problem bears a certain *similarity* to mine]; **resemblance** usually implies being alike in a superficial way or only seeming alike, as in looks [the *resemblance* between a diamond and a zircon] —**ANT.** unlikeness, difference

like·wise (-wīz') *adv.* [short for *in like wise*] **1.** in the same manner [she gave generously and we must do *likewise*] **2.** also; too; moreover [Jim will sing and Mary *likewise*]

lik·ing (līk'iŋ) *n.* **1.** fondness; affection **2.** preference; taste; pleasure [not to my *liking*]

li·ku·ta (lē koo'tä) *n., pl.* **ma·ku·ta** (mä-) see MONETARY UNITS, table (Zaire)

li·lac (lī'lək, -läk, -lak) *n.* [Fr. < Ar. < Per. *nīlak*, bluish < *nīl*, indigo] **1.** a shrub or tree of the olive family, with large clusters of tiny, fragrant flowers ranging from white to lavender or crimson **2.** the flower cluster of this plant **3.** a pale-purple color —*adj.* pale-purple

Lil·i·an, Lil·li·an (lil'ē ən) [prob. < L. *lilium*, lily] a feminine name: dim. *Lil, Lily, Lilly*

Lille (lēl) city in N France: pop. 191,000

Lil·li·put (lil'ə put', -pət) in Swift's *Gulliver's Travels*, a land inhabited by tiny people about six inches tall

Lil·li·pu·tian (lil'ə pyoo'shən) *adj.* **1.** of Lilliput or its people **2.** very small; tiny **3.** narrow-minded —*n.* **1.** an inhabitant of Lilliput **2.** a very small person **3.** a narrow-minded person

Li·long·we (li lôn'wā) capital of Malawi, in the W part: pop. 103,000

lilt (lilt) *vt., vi.* [ME. *lilten*] to sing, speak, or play with a light, graceful rhythm —*n.* **1.** a gay song or tune with a swingy rhythm **2.** a light, swingy, and graceful rhythm or movement —**lilt'ing** *adj.* —**lilt'ing·ly** *adv.*

lil·y (lil'ē) *n., pl.* **lil'ies** [< OE. < L. *lilium*] **1.** any of a large group of plants of the lily family, grown from a bulb and having typically trumpet-shaped flowers, white or colored **2.** the flower or the bulb of any of these **3.** any of several similar plants, as the waterlily **4.** the fleur-de-lis, as in the royal arms of France —*adj.* **1.** designating a family of plants including the lilies, tulips, onions, etc. **2.** like a lily, as in whiteness, delicacy, purity, etc. —**gild the lily** to try to make something better that is already perfect

lil·y-liv·ered (lil'ē liv'ərd) *adj.* cowardly; timid

lily of the valley *pl.* **lilies of the valley** a plant of the lily family which has a single pair of oblong leaves and a single stem with small, white, bell-shaped flowers having a sweet smell

lil·y-white (-hwīt', -wīt') *adj.* **1.** white as a lily **2.** innocent and pure: often used with ironical meaning ☆**3.** practicing discrimination against nonwhites, esp. blacks, as by keeping them out [a *lily-white* suburb]

Li·ma (lē'mə; *for 2,* lī'-) **1.** capital of Peru, in the WC part: pop. 1,795,000 **2.** [after the city in Peru] city in W Ohio: pop. 54,000

li·ma bean (lī'mə) [after LIMA, Peru] [also L-b-] **1.** a bean plant with creamy flowers and broad pods **2.** its broad, flat seed, used as a vegetable

limb¹ (lim) *n.* [OE. *lim*] **1.** an arm, leg, or wing **2.** a large branch of a tree **3.** a part that projects like an arm or leg **4.** a person or thing regarded as a part or agent —☆**out on a limb** [Colloq.] in a dangerous position or situation —**limb'less** *adj.*

limb² (lim) *n.* [< Fr. < ML. < L. *limbus*, edge] a border or edge; specif., *a) Astron.* the apparent outer edge of a heavenly body *b) Bot.* the spreading outer part of the corolla of certain flowers

limbed (limd) *adj.* having (a specified number or kind of) limbs [four-*limbed*, straight-*limbed*]

lim·ber¹ (lim'bər) *adj.* [< ? LIMB¹] easily bent or able to bend easily; lithe; flexible [*limber* pine branches; a *limber* body]

LILAC
(flowers & leaves)

LILY OF THE VALLEY

—*vt.* to make limber [*exercise* limbers *the fingers*] —*vi.* to make oneself limber, as by exercises (usually with *up*) —**lim′ber·ness** *n.*

lim·ber[2] (lim′bər) *n.* [< ?] the two-wheeled front part of a gun carriage: it formerly carried an ammunition chest

lim·bo[1] (lim′bō) *n., pl.* **-bos** [< L. (*in*) *limbo*, (in or on) the border] **1.** [*often* L-] in some Christian theologies, a region bordering on hell, a place of the dead for unbaptized children and righteous people who lived before Jesus **2.** a place or condition in which forgotten or neglected persons, things, causes, etc. end up **3.** a condition midway between two others

lim·bo[2] (lim′bō) *n., pl.* **-bos** [prob. altered < LIMBER[1]] a dance, originally done in the West Indies, in which the dancers bend from the knees as far back as possible to pass beneath a bar that is put lower and lower

Lim·bur·ger (cheese) (lim′bər-gər) [< *Limburg*, a Belgian province] a semisoft cheese of whole milk, with a strong odor: also **Lim′burg (cheese)**

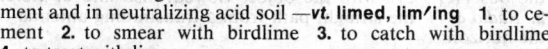

LIMBO DANCER

lime[1] (līm) *n.* [OE. *lim*: for IE. base see DELETE] **1.** *short for* BIRDLIME **2.** a white substance, calcium oxide, CaO, obtained by the action of heat on limestone, shells, etc. and used in making mortar and cement and in neutralizing acid soil —*vt.* **limed, lim′ing** **1.** to cement **2.** to smear with birdlime **3.** to catch with birdlime **4.** to treat with lime

lime[2] (līm) *n.* [Fr. < Pr. < Ar. *līma*] **1.** a small, greenish-yellow citrus fruit with a juicy, sour pulp used to make drinks and flavor foods **2.** the small, semitropical tree that it grows on **3.** greenish yellow —*adj.* **1.** made with or flavored like lime **2.** greenish-yellow

lime[3] (līm) *n.* [< earlier *line* < ME. *lind*: see LINDEN] *same as* LINDEN

☆**lime·ade** (līm′ād′) *n.* a drink of lime juice and water, usually sweetened

lime·kiln (līm′kil′, -kiln′) *n.* a furnace in which limestone, shells, etc. are burned to make lime

lime·light (-līt′) *n.* **1.** a brilliant light made by heating lime till it glows, formerly used in theaters to throw an intense beam of light upon a particular part of the stage, an actor, etc. **2.** a prominent position before the public [*in the limelight*]

lim·er·ick (lim′ər ik, lim′rik) *n.* [prob. < Ir. refrain containing the name *Limerick*, a county of Ireland] a rhymed, nonsense poem of five lines, usually in the following form: A flea and a fly / in a flue/ Were imprisoned so what could they do?/ Said the flea, "Let us fly!"/ Said the fly, "Let us flee!"/ So they flew through a flaw in the flue

lime·stone (līm′stōn′) *n.* rock consisting mainly of calcium carbonate, often composed of the organic remains of sea animals and used as building stone, a source of lime, etc.: see also MARBLE

lime·wa·ter (-wôt′ər, -wät′ər) *n.* a solution of calcium hydroxide in water, used to neutralize acids

☆**lim·ey** (lim′ē) *n.* [from the LIME[2] juice formerly served to British sailors to prevent scurvy] [Slang] **1.** an English sailor or, sometimes, soldier **2.** an Englishman —*adj.* [Slang] British

lim·it (lim′it) *n.* [< OFr. < L. *limitis*, genitive of *limes*, boundary] **1.** the point, line, or edge where something ends or must end [*beyond the limit of his strength*] **2.** [*pl.*] bounds or boundaries [*city limits*] **3.** the greatest amount allowed [*a catch of ten trout is the limit*] —*vt.* to set a limit to; restrict; curb —**the limit** [Colloq.] ☆any person or thing regarded as absolutely unbearable, remarkable, etc. —**lim′it·a·ble** *adj.*

SYN.—**limit** implies the setting of a point in space, time, extent, etc. beyond which it is impossible or forbidden to go [*limit your talk to ten minutes*]; **bound** implies an enclosing within boundaries or borders [a field *bounded* by hills]; **circumscribe** suggests something that is definitely cut off and exists only within strict limits or rules [he leads the *circumscribed* life of a monk] —ANT. widen, expand

lim·i·ta·tion (lim′ə tā′shən) *n.* **1.** a limiting or being limited **2.** something that limits, as some factor in a person's makeup

which holds him back **3.** *Law* a period of time, fixed by statute, during which legal action can be brought, as for settling a claim —**lim′i·ta′tive** *adj.*

lim·it·ed (lim′it id) *adj.* **1.** *a*) confined within bounds; restricted *b*) narrow in scope ☆**2.** making a restricted number of stops, and often charging extra fare: said of a train, bus, etc. **3.** exercising governmental powers under constitutional restrictions [a *limited* monarch] **4.** [Chiefly Brit.] restricting the liability of each partner or shareholder to the amount of his actual investment [a *limited* company] —*n.* a limited train, bus, etc. —**lim′it·ed·ly** *adv.* —**lim′it·ed·ness** *n.*

lim·it·ing (-iŋ) *adj. Gram.* designating or of any of a class of adjectives that limit or restrict the words modified (Ex.: *several, four*, etc.)

lim·it·less (-lis) *adj.* without limits; unbounded; vast —**lim′it·less·ly** *adv.* —**lim′it·less·ness** *n.*

limn (lim) *vt.* **limned, limn·ing** (lim′iŋ, -niŋ) [< OFr. *enluminer* < L. *illuminare*, to make light] **1.** to paint or draw **2.** to portray in words; describe —**limn·er** (lim′ər, -nər) *n.*

Li·moges (lē mōzh′; *Fr.* lē mồzh′) city in WC France: pop. 133,000 —*n.* fine porcelain made there: also **Limoges ware**

li·mo·nite (lī′mə nīt′) *n.* [< Gr. *leimōn*, meadow + -ITE] a brownish, hydrous ferric oxide: an important ore of iron

lim·ou·sine (lim′ə zēn′, lim′ə zēn′) *n.* [Fr., lit., a hood] **1.** any large, luxurious sedan, esp. one driven by a chauffeur ☆**2.** a buslike sedan used to carry passengers to or from an airport, etc.

limp[1] (limp) *vi.* [< a sense of OE. *limpan*, to befall: for IE. base see LAP[1]] **1.** to walk with or as with a lame leg **2.** to move jerkily, laboriously, etc. —*n.* a halt or lameness in walking —**limp′er** *n.* —**limp′ing·ly** *adv.*

limp[2] (limp) *adj.* [< base of prec.] **1.** lacking stiffness; drooping, wilted, etc. [as *limp* as a wet rag] **2.** lacking firmness or vigor —**limp′ly** *adv.* —**limp′ness** *n.*

limp·et (lim′pit) *n.* [< OE. < ML. *lempreda*] a mollusk which clings to rocks, timbers, etc. by means of a thick, fleshy foot

lim·pid (lim′pid) *adj.* [< Fr. < L. *limpidus* < OL. *limpa*, water] **1.** perfectly clear; transparent [*limpid* waters] **2.** clear and simple [*limpid* prose] —**lim·pid′i·ty, lim′pid·ness** *n.* —**lim′pid·ly** *adv.*

Lim·po·po River (lim pō′pō) river in SE Africa, flowing from South Africa into the Indian Ocean

lim·y (lī′mē) *adj.* **lim′i·er, lim′i·est** **1.** covered with, consisting of, or like birdlime; sticky **2.** of, like, or containing lime —**lim′i·ness** *n.*

lin·age (lī′nij) *n.* **1.** the number of written or printed lines on a page **2.** payment based on the number of lines produced by a writer

linch·pin (linch′pin′) *n.* [< OE. *lynis*, linchpin] a pin that goes through the end of an axle outside the wheel to keep the wheel from coming off

Lin·coln (liŋ′kən) [after Pres. LINCOLN] capital of Nebr., in the SE part: pop. 150,000

Lin·coln (liŋ′kən), **Abraham** 1809-65; 16th president of the U.S. (1861-65): assassinated —☆**Lin·coln·i·an** (liŋ kō′nē ən) *adj.*

Lincoln Park city in SE Mich.: suburb of Detroit: pop. 53,000

Lind (lind), **Jenny** (born *Johanna Maria Lind*) 1820-87; Swed. soprano

Lin·da (lin′də) [dim. of BELINDA] a feminine name

Lind·bergh (lind′bərg, lin′-), **Charles Augustus** 1902-74; U.S. aviator

lin·den (lin′dən) *n.* [ME., *adj.*, < OE. *lind*, linden] a tree with dense, heart-shaped leaves

Lind·say (lin′zē, lind′-), (**Nicholas**) **Va·chel** (vā′chəl) 1879-1931; U.S. poet

line[1] (līn) *n.* [merging of OE. *line*, a cord, with OFr. *ligne* (both < L. *linea*, lit., linen thread < *linum*, flax)] **1.** *a*) a cord, rope, wire, or string *b*) a fine, strong cord with a hook, used in fishing *c*) a cord, steel tape, etc. used in measuring or leveling ☆**2.** *a*) a wire or system of wires connecting stations in a telephone or telegraph system *b*) open contact between stations [hold the *line*, please] **3.** any wire, pipe, etc., or system of these, for conducting gas, water, electricity, etc. **4.** a thin, threadlike mark; specif., *a*) a long, thin mark made by a pencil, pen, chalk, knife, etc. *b*) a mark made on the ground in certain sports *c)* a thin crease in the palm or on the face ☆**5.** a border or boundary [the State *line*] **6.** a limit or division between conditions, classes, etc. [below the poverty *line*] **7.** outline; contour **8.** [*usually pl.*] a plan of making or doing [built on modern *lines*] **9.** a row or series of persons or things; specif., *a)* a row of written or printed characters across a page or column ☆*b)* a row of persons waiting in turn, as to buy something *c) same as* ASSEMBLY LINE **10.** *same as* LINEAGE¹ **11.** the descendants of a common ancestor or of a particular breed **12.** ☆*a)* a transportation system consisting of regular trips by buses, ships, etc. between points ☆*b)* a company operating such a system *c)* one branch of such a system *d)* a single track of a railroad **13.** the course or direction anything moving takes [the *line* of fire] **14.** course of conduct, action, explanation, etc. [a new *line* in foreign policy] **15.** a person's trade or occupation, or the things he deals in [what's his *line?*] ☆**16.** a stock of goods of a particular quality, quantity, variety, etc. **17.** *a)* the field of one's special knowledge or interest *b)* a source or piece of information [a *line* on a bargain] **18.** a short letter, note, or card [drop me a *line*] **19.** a verse of poetry in a single metrical unit **20.** [*pl.*] all the speeches of any one character in a play **21.** [Colloq.] flattering talk that is insincere ☆**22.** *Football* the players arranged in a row even with the ball at the start of each play, or those directly opposite them **23.** *Geog.* an imaginary circle of the earth or of the celestial sphere, as the equator **24.** *Math. a)* the path of a moving point *b)* such a path when considered perfectly straight **25.** *Mil. a)* a formation of ships, troops, etc. abreast of each other *b)* the area or position in closest contact with the enemy during combat *c)* the troops in this area ☆*d)* the branches of the army that take part in combat, considered as separate from the supporting branches and the staff **26.** *Music* any of the long parallel marks forming the staff —*vt.* **lined, lin'ing 1.** to mark with lines [a face *lined* by age] **2.** to trace with or as with lines **3.** to bring into alignment or into a straight row (often with *up*) **4.** to form a line along [elms *line* the street] **5.** to place objects along the edge of ☆**6.** *Baseball* to hit as a line drive —*vi.* **1.** to form a line (usually with *up*) ☆**2.** *Baseball* to hit a line drive —**all along the line 1.** everywhere **2.** at every turn of events —**bring** (or **come, get**) **into line** to bring (or come) into alignment or into a straight row —**down the line** completely; entirely —**draw the** (or **a**) **line** to set a limit —☆**get a line on** [Colloq.] to find out about —**hold the line** to stand firm —**in** (or **out of**) **line** (in or not in) alignment, agreement, or conformity —**in line for** being considered for —**lay** (or **put**) **it on the line 1.** to pay up **2.** to speak frankly and in detail —**line out** ☆*Baseball* to be put out by hitting a line drive that is caught by a fielder —**line up** to bring into or take a specified position —**on a line** in the same plane; level —**read between the lines** to discover a hidden meaning or purpose in something written, said, or done —**lin'a·ble, line'a·ble** *adj.*

line² (līn) *vt.* **lined, lin'ing** [< OE. *lin*, ult. < or akin to L. *linum*, flax] **1.** to put a layer or lining of a different material on the inside of [the coat is *lined* with fur] **2.** to be used as a lining in [cloth *lined* the trunk] **3.** to fill; stuff: now chiefly in **line one's pockets**, to make money, esp. in a greedy or dishonest way

lin·e·age¹ (lin'ē ij) *n.* [< OFr. *lignage* < *ligne*: see LINE¹] **1.** direct descent from an ancestor **2.** ancestry; family; stock **3.** *same as* LINE¹ (*n.* 11)

line·age² (lī'nij) *n. same as* LINAGE

lin·e·al (lin'ē əl) *adj.* **1.** in the direct line of descent from an ancestor, as from father to son to grandson **2.** hereditary **3.** of or made up of lines; linear —**lin'e·al·ly** *adv.*

lin·e·a·ment (lin'ē ə mənt) *n.* [< L. *lineamentum* < *linea*, LINE¹] **1.** any of the features of the body, usually of the face, esp. with regard to its outline **2.** a distinctive feature or characteristic *Usually used in pl.*

lin·e·ar (lin'ē ər) *adj.* **1.** of or relating to a line or lines **2.** made of or using lines [*linear* design] **3.** in relation to length only; extended in a line [*linear* measure] **4.** designating or of a style of art in which line is emphasized **5.** having an effect directly proportional to its cause: used esp. of electronic devices **6.** *Algebra* involving terms of the first degree [a *linear* function] —**lin'e·ar'i·ty** (-ē ar'ə tē) *n.* —**lin'e·ar·ly** *adv.*

linear equation an algebraic equation whose variable quantity or quantities are in the first power only and whose graph is a straight line (Example: $2x + 3y - 5 = 0$)

linear measure 1. measurement of length **2.** a system of measuring length, esp. the system in which 12 inches = 1 foot or that in which 100 centimeters = 1 meter: see TABLE OF WEIGHTS AND MEASURES in Supplements

☆**line·back·er** (līn'bak'ər) *n. Football* any player on defense placed directly behind the line

line drawing a drawing done entirely in lines, from which a cut (**line cut**) can be photoengraved for printing

☆**line drive** *Baseball* a hard-hit ball that travels close to the ground and nearly parallel with the ground

line·man (līn'mən) *n., pl.* **-men 1.** a person who carries a surveying line, tape, etc. **2.** a person whose work is setting up and repairing telephone, telegraph, or electric power lines ☆**3.** *Football* one of the players in the line

☆**linemen's climber** a device with sharp spikes, fastened to the shoe or strapped to the leg to aid in climbing telephone poles, etc.

lin·en (lin'ən) *n.* see PLURAL, II, D, 3 [OE. < *lin*, flax] **1.** thread or cloth made of flax **2.** [*often pl.*] things made of linen, or of cotton, etc., as tablecloths, sheets, etc. —*adj.* **1.** spun from flax [*linen* thread] **2.** made of linen

line officer 1. *Mil.* a commissioned officer in charge of combat troops **2.** *U.S. Navy* a commissioned officer with the training required to command a ship at sea

line of fire 1. the course of a bullet, shell, etc. **2.** a position open to attack of any kind

line of force a line in a field of electrical or magnetic force that indicates the direction taken by the force at any point

☆**line of scrimmage** *Football* an imaginary line, parallel to the goal lines, on which the ball rests at the start of each play and on either side of which the teams line up

line of sight 1. an imaginary straight line joining the center of the observer's eye with the object viewed: also **line of vision 2.** *Radio & TV* the straight path from a transmitting antenna to the horizon

lin·er¹ (lī'nər) *n.* **1.** a person or thing that traces lines ☆**2.** a steamship, passenger airplane, etc. in regular service for a specific line ☆**3.** *same as* LINE DRIVE **4.** a cosmetic applied in a fine line, as along the eyelid

lin·er² (lī'nər) *n.* **1.** a person who makes or attaches linings **2.** a lining or something that suggests a lining by fitting inside something else [a helmet *liner*] ☆**3.** the jacket of a long-playing record, usually containing information (**liner notes**) on the back about the music, performers, etc.

lines·man (līnz'mən) *n., pl.* **-men 1.** *same as* LINEMAN **2.** *Football* an official who measures and marks the gains or losses in ground **3.** *Tennis* an official who reports whether the ball is inside or outside the lines he is assigned to watch

☆**line·up** (līn'up') *n.* an arrangement of persons or things in or as in a line; specif., *a)* a group of suspected criminals lined up by the police for identification *b)* *Football, Baseball,* etc. the list of a team's players arranged according to playing position, order at bat, etc.

ling¹ (liŋ) *n., pl.* **ling, lings:** see PLURAL, II, D, 2 [akin to MDu. *lange,* ON. *langa*] a food fish related to the cod, found in the North Atlantic

ling² (liŋ) *n.* [ON. *lyng*] *same as* HEATHER

-ling¹ (liŋ) [OE.] *a suffix added to nouns, meaning:* **1.** small [*duckling*] **2.** having a connection, esp. of an unimportant or worthless kind, with the specified thing [*hireling*]

-ling² (liŋ) [OE.] [Archaic or Dial.] *a suffix meaning* extent or condition [*darkling*]

ling. linguistics

lin·ger (liŋ'gər) *vi.* [< North ME. *lengen*, to delay < OE. < base of *lang,* LONG¹] **1.** to continue to stay, esp. because unwilling to leave [the last guest *lingered*] **2.** to continue to live although very close to death **3.** to be unnecessarily slow in doing something; loiter —see SYN. at STAY³ —**lin'ger·er** *n.* —**lin'ger·ing** *adj.* —**lin'ger·ing·ly** *adv.*

lin·ge·rie (län'zhə rā', -rē'; lan'-; -jə-) *n.* [Fr.] women's underwear and night clothes of silk, nylon, lace, etc.

lin·go (liŋ'gō) *n., pl.* **-goes** [Pr. < L. *lingua,* TONGUE] language; esp., a dialect, jargon, or special vocabulary that one is not familiar with: used in a joking or mocking way

☆**ling·on·ber·ry** (liŋ'ən ber'ē) *n., pl.* **-ries** [< Sw. *lingon,* lingonberry + BERRY] *same as* COWBERRY

lin·gua fran·ca (liŋ'gwə fraŋ'kə) *pl.* **lin'gua fran'cas, lin'guae fran'cae** (liŋ'gwē fran'sē) [It., lit., Frankish language] **1.** a hybrid language made up of Italian, Spanish, French, Greek, Arabic, and Turkish elements, spoken in certain Mediterranean ports **2.** any language like this, as pidgin English, used as a common language by people who speak different languages

lin·gual (liŋ'gwəl) *adj.* [< ML. < L. *lingua,* the tongue: see LANGUAGE] **1.** of the tongue **2.** of language or languages **3.** produced by using the tongue —*n. Phonet.* a lingual sound, as *l* or *t* —**lin′gual·ly** *adv.*

lin·gui·ne (lin gwē′nē) *n.* [< It. pl. of *linguina*, dim. of *lingua*, TONGUE] a kind of pasta like spaghetti but flat, often served with seafood

lin·guist (liŋ′gwist) *n.* [< L. *lingua*, the tongue + -IST] **1.** a specialist in linguistics **2.** same as POLYGLOT (sense 1)

lin·guis·tic (liŋ gwis′tik) *adj.* **1.** of language **2.** of linguistics —**lin·guis′ti·cal·ly** *adv.*

linguistic atlas an atlas showing by charts the spread of linguistic forms and usages in various geographical areas

linguistic form a unit of speech, as a morpheme, word, phrase, sentence, etc. that has meaning

lin·guis·tics (liŋ gwis′tiks) *n.pl.* [*with sing. v.*] **1.** the science of language, including phonology, morphology, syntax, and semantics: often **general linguistics 2.** the study of the structure, development, etc. of a particular language

lin·i·ment (lin′ə mənt) *n.* [< LL. < L. *linere*, to smear: see DELETE] a medicated liquid to be rubbed on the skin to soothe sore, sprained, or inflamed areas

lin·ing (līn′iŋ) *n.* [see LINE²] the material covering an inner surface [the *lining* of a hat]

link¹ (liŋk) *n.* [< Scand.: for IE. base see LANK] **1.** any of the series of rings or loops making up a chain **2.** *a)* a section of something resembling a chain [a *link* of sausage] *b)* an element in a series of circumstances [a weak *link* in the evidence] **3.** anything serving to connect or tie [a *link* with the past] **4.** one division (1/100) of a surveyor's chain, equal to 7.92 in. **5.** *Chem.* same as BOND¹ —*vt., vi.* to join together with a link or links —see SYN. at JOIN —**link′er** *n.*

link² (liŋk) *n.* [prob. < ML. < L. *lychnus*, a light] a torch made of tow and pitch

link·age (liŋ′kij) *n.* **1.** a linking or being linked **2.** a series or system of links; esp., a series of connecting rods for passing along power or motion **3.** *Biol.* The tendency of some genes to remain together and act as a unit (**linkage group**) in inheritance **4.** *Chem. a)* same as BOND¹ *b)* the type of bonding between various atoms or groups in a molecule

linking verb a verb that functions chiefly as a connection between a subject and the word or words in the predicate that tell about the subject (Ex.: *be, seem, become,* etc.); copula

links (liŋks) *n.pl.* [OE. *hlinc,* a slope] same as GOLF COURSE

link·up (liŋk′up′) *n.* a joining together of two objects, groups, interests, etc.

Lin·nae·an, Lin·ne·an (li nē′ən) *adj.* [after C. *Linnaeus,* 18th-c. Swed. botanist] designating or of a system of classifying plants and animals by using a double name, the first word naming the genus, and the second the species

lin·net (lin′it) *n.* [OFr. *linette < lin* (< L. *linum*), flax: the bird feeds on flaxseed] a small finch found in Europe, Asia, and Africa

li·no·cut (lī′nə kut′) *n.* [LINO(LEUM) + CUT] **1.** a design cut into the surface of a linoleum block **2.** a print made from this

lin·o·le·ic acid (lin′ə lē′ik, li nō′lē ik) [< L. *linum,* flax + OLEIC] an unsaturated fatty acid, $C_{18}H_{32}O_2$, found in linseed oil and other fats and oils: used in soaps, foods, etc.

lin·o·le·nic acid (lin′ə lē′nik) [< LINOL(EIC) + -EN(E) + -IC] an unsaturated fatty acid, $C_{18}H_{30}O_2$, found in fats and oils: used in varnishes, paints, foods, etc.

li·no·le·um (li nō′lē əm) *n.* [coined < L. *linum,* flax + *oleum,* oil] a hard, washable floor covering made of a mixture of ground cork, ground wood, and oxidized linseed oil with a canvas backing

☆**Lin·o·type** (līn′ə tīp′) [< *line of type*] *a trademark for* a typesetting machine that casts an entire line of type in one bar, or slug: it is operated from a keyboard —*n.* [*often* l-] **1.** a machine of this kind **2.** matter set in this way —*vt., vi.* [l-] -**typed′,** -**typ′ing** to set (matter) with this machine —**lin′o·typ′ist, lin′o·typ′er** *n.*

lin·seed (lin′sēd′) *n.* [OE. *linsæd*] the seed of flax

linseed oil a yellowish oil pressed from flaxseed, used in oil paints, printer's ink, etc.

lin·sey-wool·sey (lin′zē wool′zē) *n., pl.* -**wool′seys** [ME. < *lin,* flax + *wolle,* wool] a coarse cloth made of linen (or cotton) and wool: also **lin′sey**

lint (lint) *n.* [prob. < *lin,* linen] **1.** scraped and softened linen

formerly used as a dressing for wounds **2.** bits of thread, ravelings, or fluff from cloth or yarn —*vi.* to give off lint —**lint′less** *adj.* —**lint′y** *adj.* **lint′i·er, lint′i·est**

lin·tel (lin′t'l) *n.* [OFr., ult. < L. *limen,* threshold] the horizontal crosspiece over a door, window, etc., carrying the weight of the structure above it

☆**lin·ters** (lin′tərz) *n.pl.* the short, fuzzy fibers clinging to cotton seeds after ginning, used in making cotton batting, etc.

lin·y (līn′ē) *adj.* **lin′i·er, lin′i·est 1.** like a line; thin **2.** marked with lines

Linz (lints) city in N Austria: pop. 196,000

li·on (lī′ən) *n., pl.* **li′ons, li′on:** see PLURAL, II, D, 1 [OFr. < L. *leonis,* genitive of *leo* < Gr. *leōn*] **1.** a large, powerful mammal of the cat family, found in Africa and southwestern Asia, with a tan coat and a tufted tail: the adult male has a shaggy mane **2.** a person of great courage or strength **3.** a famous person; celebrity —**li′on·ess** *n.fem.*

li·on·heart·ed (lī′ən här′tid) *adj.* very brave

li·on·ize (lī′ə nīz′) *vt.* -**ized′,** -**iz′ing** to treat as a famous person —**li′on·i·za′tion** *n.* —**li′on·iz′er** *n.*

lion's share the biggest and best portion

lip (lip) *n.* [OE. *lippa:* for IE. base see LAP¹] **1.** either of the two fleshy folds forming the edges of the mouth **2.** anything like a lip, as in structure or in being an edge or rim; specif., *a)* the projecting rim of a pitcher, cup, etc. *b)* the mouthpiece of a wind instrument *c)* same as LABIUM **3.** [Slang] boldly disrespectful talk —*vt.* **lipped, lip′ping 1.** to touch with the lips; specif., to place the lips in the proper position for playing (a wind instrument) **2.** to utter softly —*adj.* **1.** formed with a lip or the lips; labial [a *lip* consonant] **2.** from the lips only; spoken, but insincere [to pay *lip* service to an idea one does not really believe] —**bite one's lip** to keep back one's anger, annoyance, etc. —**hang on the lips of** to listen to with close attention —☆**keep a stiff upper lip** [Colloq.] to avoid becoming frightened or discouraged —**lip′less** *adj.*

li·pase (lī′pās, lip′ās) *n.* [LIP(O)- + -ASE] an enzyme that aids digestion by hydrolizing fats into fatty acids and glycerol

lip·id (lip′id, lī′pid) *n.* [LIP(O)- + -ID] any of a group of organic compounds consisting of the fats and other similar substances: they are insoluble in water, soluble in fat solvents and alcohol, and are important parts of living cells: also **lip·ide** (lip′īd, -id; lī′pīd, -pid)

lip·o- [< Gr. *lipos,* fat] *a combining form meaning* of or like fat, fatty: also, before a vowel, **lip-**

li·poid (lip′oid, lī′poid) *adj.* [LIP(O)- + -OID] *Biochem., Chem.* resembling fat: also **li·poi′dal** —*n.* a fat or fatlike substance; lipid

li·pol·y·sis (li päl′ə sis) *n.* [ModL.: see LIPO- & -LYSIS] the breaking up of fat, as during digestion —**lip·o·lyt·ic** (lip′ə lit′ik) *adj.*

li·po·ma (li pō′mə, lī-) *n., pl.* -**po′ma·ta** (-tə), -**po′mas** [ModL.: see LIPO- & -OMA] a tumor made up of fat tissue —**li·pom′a·tous** (-päm′ə təs) *adj.*

lip·o·pro·tein (lip′ə prō′tēn, -prō′tē in) *n.* any of a group of proteins combined with a lipid, found in blood plasma, egg yolk, brain tissue, etc.

lipped (lipt) *adj.* having a lip or lips: often in compounds [tight-lipped]

Lip·pi (lēp′pē; *E.* lip′ē), **Fra Fi·lip·po** (fi lēp′pô) 1406?-69; Florentine painter: also called **Fra Lip·po Lippi** (lēp′pô)

lip·py (lip′ē) *adj.* -**pi·er, -pi·est** [Slang] impudent, disrespectful, or insolent —**lip′pi·ness** *n.*

lip-read (lip′rēd′) *vt., vi.* -**read′** (-red′), -**read′ing** to recognize (a speaker's words) by lip reading —**lip reader**

lip reading the act or skill of recognizing a speaker's words by watching his lips move: it is taught esp. to the deaf

☆**lip·stick** (-stik′) *n.* a small stick of cosmetic paste, set in a case, for coloring the lips

lip-sync, lip-synch (lip′siŋk′) *vt., vi.* [< *lip sync(hronization)*] to move the lips silently so as to seem to be speaking or singing (something recorded) —*n.* the act or process of lip-syncing

liq. 1. liquid **2.** liquor

liq·ue·fa·cient (lik′wə fā′shənt) *n.* [< L.: see LIQUEFY] something that causes liquefaction

liq·ue·fac·tion (-fak′shən) *n.* a liquefying or being liquefied

liquefied petroleum gas a compressed or liquefied gas, generally a mixture of propane and butane, made during the refining of petroleum: used as a fuel

liq·ue·fy (lik′wə fī′) *vt., vi.* **-fied′, -fy′ing** [< Fr. < L. < *liquere*, to be liquid + *facere*, to make] to change into a liquid —**liq′ue·fi′a·ble** *adj.*

li·ques·cent (li kwes′′nt) *adj.* [< L. prp. of *liquescere* < *liquere*, to be liquid] becoming liquid; melting —**li·ques′cence** *n.*

li·queur (li kʉr′) *n.* [Fr.] any of certain sweet, syrupy alcoholic liquors, variously flavored

liq·uid (lik′wid) *adj.* [< OFr. < L. *liquidus* < *liquere*, to be liquid] **1.** readily flowing; fluid; specif., that can move freely, unlike a solid, but does not expand indefinitely like a gas **2.** clear; limpid *[liquid eyes]* **3.** flowing smoothly and gracefully *[liquid verse]* **4.** readily convertible into cash *[liquid assets]* **5.** without friction and like a vowel, as the consonants *l* and *r* —*n.* **1.** a liquid substance **2.** a liquid consonant —**liq·uid′i·ty, liq′uid·ness** *n.* —**liq′uid·ly** *adv.*

SYN.—**liquid** refers to a substance that flows readily and takes on the form of its container but stays the same in volume *[water that is neither ice nor steam is a liquid]*; **fluid** applies to any substance that flows *[all liquids, gases, and viscous substances are fluids]* —**ANT. solid**

liquid air air brought to a liquid state by being subjected to great pressure and then cooled by its own expansion: it is used in refrigeration

liq·ui·date (lik′wə dāt′) *vt.* **-dat′ed, -dat′ing** [< ML. pp. of *liquidare*, to make clear < L. *liquidus*, liquid] **1.** to settle the amount of (debts, damages, etc.) **2.** to settle the accounts of (a bankrupt business, etc.) by deciding which debts are to be paid out of any remaining assets **3.** to pay or settle (a debt) **4.** to sell (one's stocks, bonds, or other assets) for cash **5.** to dispose of or get rid of, as by killing —*vi.* to liquidate debts, accounts, etc. —**liq′ui·da′tion** *n.* —**liq′ui·da′tor** *n.*

liq·uid·ize (lik′wə dīz′) *vt.* **-ized′, -iz′ing** to cause to have a liquid quality

liquid measure 1. the measurement of liquids **2.** a system of measuring liquids; esp., the system in which 2 pints = 1 quart, 4 quarts = 1 gallon, etc.: see TABLE OF WEIGHTS AND MEASURES in Supplements

liquid oxygen a light-bluish liquid boiling at −183°C, produced by fractionation of liquid air

liq·uor (lik′ər) *n.* [< OFr. *licor* < L. *liquor*] **1.** any liquid or juice, as sap from trees or juice from meat **2.** an alcoholic drink, esp. one made by distillation, as whiskey or rum —*vt., vi.* [Colloq.] to drink or cause to drink alcoholic liquor, esp. so as to make one intoxicated

liq·uo·rice (lik′ər ish, -is; lik′rish) *n. chiefly Brit. sp.* of LICORICE

li·ra (lir′ə) *n., pl.* **-re** (-ā), for 2 **-ras** [It. < L. *libra*, a balance] the monetary unit of: **1.** Italy **2.** Turkey See MONETARY UNITS, table

Lis·bon (liz′bən) capital, & a seaport, of Portugal: pop. 826,000 (met. area 1,450,000): Port. name **Lis·bo·a** (lēzh bô′ə)

lisle (līl) *n.* [< *Lisle*, earlier sp. of LILLE, France] **1.** a fine, hard, extra-strong cotton thread: in full, **lisle thread 2.** a fabric, or stockings, gloves, etc., knit or woven of lisle —*adj.* made of lisle

lisp (lisp) *vi.* [< OE. < *wlisp*, a lisping] **1.** to substitute the sounds (th) and (*th*) for the sounds of *s* and *z*, as in pronouncing *sing* as though it were *thing* **2.** to speak imperfectly or like a child —*vt.* to utter with a lisp or in an imperfect or childish way —*n.* **1.** the act or speech defect of lisping **2.** the sound of lisping —**lisp′er** *n.* —**lisp′ing·ly** *adv.*

lis·some, lis·som (lis′əm) *adj.* [altered < *lithesome*] moving gracefully or with ease and lightness; lithe, limber, agile, etc. —**lis′some·ly, lis′som·ly** *adv.* —**lis′some·ness, lis′som·ness** *n.*

list¹ (list) *n.* [merging of OE. *liste* & Anglo-Fr. *liste* < OFr. < Gmc.] **1.** formerly, *a)* a narrow strip or border; specif., *a)* a strip of cloth *b)* a stripe of color *c)* a boundary **2.** the selvage of cloth **3.** a series of names, words, numbers, etc. set forth in order; catalog, roll, etc. **4.** *same as* LIST PRICE See also LISTS —*vt.* **1.** formerly, to edge with, or arrange in, stripes or bands **2.** *a)* to set forth (a series of names, items, etc.) in order *b)* to enter in a list, directory, catalog, etc. —*vi.* to be listed for sale, in a catalog (at the price specified) —**list′er** *n.* —**list′ing** *n.*

list² (list) *vt.* [OE. *lystan* < base of *lust:* see LUST] [Archaic] to be pleasing to; suit —*vi.* [Archaic] to wish; like; choose

list³ (list) *vt., vi.* [prob. specialized use of prec.] to tilt to one side, as a ship —*n.* a tilting or inclining to one side

list⁴ (list) *vt., vi.* [IE. *hlystan* < base of *hlyst*, hearing < IE. base *kleu-*, to hear] [Archaic] to listen (to)

lis·ten (lis′′n) *vi.* [OE. *hlysnan*: for base see prec.] **1.** to make a conscious effort to hear; attend closely, so as to hear *[listen to the music]* **2.** to give heed; take advice *[if you had listened, you wouldn't be in trouble]* —*n.* the act of listening —☆**listen in 1.** to listen to others' conversation; esp., to eavesdrop **2.** to listen to a broadcast —**lis′ten·er** *n.*

list·er (lis′tər) *n.* [< LIST¹ + -ER] ☆a plow with a double moldboard, which heaps the earth on both sides of the furrow: it is sometimes combined with a drill that plants seed

Lis·ter (lis′tər), **Joseph** 1827–1912; Eng. surgeon: introduced antiseptic surgery

list·less (list′lis) *adj.* [LIST² + -LESS] having or showing no interest in what is going on, as because of illness, weariness, sadness, etc.; spiritless —**list′less·ly** *adv.* —**list′less·ness** *n.*

list price retail price as given in a list or catalog, discounted in sales to dealers, etc.

lists (lists) *n.pl.* [ME. *listes*, specialized use of *liste*, strip, border] **1.** *a)* the high fence enclosing an area where knights held tournaments *b)* this area itself or the tournament held there **2.** any place or area of combat, conflict, etc. —**enter the lists** to enter a contest or struggle

Liszt (list), **Franz** (fränts) 1811–86; Hung. composer & pianist

lit (lit) *alt. pt. & pp. of* LIGHT

lit. 1. liter(s) **2.** literal **3.** literally **4.** literary **5.** literature

lit·a·ny (lit′′n ē) *n., pl.* **-nies** [< OFr. < LL. < Gr. *litaneia* < *litē*, a request] **1.** a form of prayer in which the clergy and the congregation take turns in the reading of prayers and fixed responses **2.** any dreary telling of facts or details

li·tchi (lē′chē′) *n.* [Chin. *li-chih*] **1.** a Chinese evergreen tree **2.** its dried or preserved fruit (**litchi nut**), with a single seed, a sweet pulp, and a rough, papery shell

-lite (līt) [Fr., for -*lithe:* see -LITH] *a combining form meaning* stone: used in the names of minerals, rocks, and fossils *[chrysolite]*

li·ter (lēt′ər) *n.* [Fr. *litre* < ML. < Gr. *litra*, a pound] the basic unit of capacity in the metric system, equal to 1 cubic decimeter (1.0567 liquid quarts or .908 dry quart)

lit·er·a·cy (lit′ər ə sē) *n.* the state or quality of being literate; ability to read and write

lit·er·al (lit′ər əl) *adj.* [< MFr. < LL. *litteralis* < L. *littera*, a letter] **1.** following the exact words of the original *[a literal translation]* **2.** based on the actual words in their ordinary meaning; in a basic or strict sense *[the literal meaning of a passage]* **3.** habitually interpreting statements or words according to their actual or strict meaning; matter-of-fact *[a literal mind]* **4.** real; not going beyond the actual facts *[the literal truth]* **5.** being so in fact but not in name; virtual *[the chairman is a literal dictator]* —**lit′er·al′i·ty** (-ə ral′ə tē) *n., pl.* **-ties** —**lit′er·al·ness** *n.*

lit·er·al·ism (-iz′m) *n.* **1.** the tendency to take words, statements, etc. in their literal sense **2.** thoroughgoing realism in art —**lit′er·al·ist** *n.* —**lit′er·al·is′tic** *adj.*

lit·er·al·ize (-ə līz′) *vt.* **-ized′, -iz′ing** to interpret in a literal sense —**lit′er·al·i·za′tion** *n.*

lit·er·al·ly (lit′ər əl ē) *adv.* in a literal manner or sense; specif., *a)* word for word; not freely; so as to avoid fanciful or figurative language *[to translate a passage literally]* *b)* actually; in fact *[the house literally burned to the ground]* *c)* seemingly, but not really: a loose usage *[he literally flew from the room]*

lit·er·ar·y (lit′ə rer′ē) *adj.* **1.** *a)* of or dealing with literature *b)* of or having to do with books *[literary agents]* **2.** using the more formal language of literature rather than the informal language of speech **3.** *a)* familiar with or versed in literature *b)* making literature a profession —**lit′er·ar′i·ness** *n.*

lit·er·ate (lit′ər it) *adj.* [< L. < *littera*, a letter] **1.** able to read and write **2.** having or showing extensive learning or culture —*n.* a literate person —**lit′er·ate·ly** *adv.*

lit·e·ra·ti (lit′ə rät′ē, -rä′tī) *n.pl.* [It. < L.] men of letters; scholarly or learned people

‡**lit·e·ra·tim** (-rät′im, -rät′-) *adv.* [ML. < L. *littera*, a letter] letter for letter; literally

lit·er·a·ture (lit′ər ə chər, lit′rə choor′) *n.* [< OFr. < L. *litteratura* < *littera*, a letter] **1.** the profession of an author **2.** *a)* all the writings of a particular time, country, etc., esp. those that have lasting value because of their beauty, imagination, etc., as fine poems, plays, and novels *[American literature]* *b)* all the writings on a particular subject *[the medical literature]* **3.** [Colloq.] printed matter of any kind, as advertising, political leaflets, etc.

-lith (lith) [Fr. *-lithe* < Gr. *lithos*, stone] *a combining form meaning* stone [*monolith*]

Lith. **1.** Lithuania **2.** Lithuanian

lith., litho., lithog. **1.** lithograph **2.** lithography

lith·arge (lith′ärj, li thärj′) *n.* [< OFr. < L. < Gr. *lithargyros* < *lithos*, a stone + *argyros*, silver] an oxide of lead, PbO, used in storage batteries, paints, etc.

lithe (līth) *adj.* **lith′er, lith′est** [OE. *lithe,* soft, mild] bending easily; supple; limber: also **lithe′some** (-səm) —**lithe′ly** *adv.* —**lithe′ness** *n.*

lith·i·a (lith′ē ə) *n.* [ModL. < Gr. *lithos*, stone] lithium oxide, Li₂O, a white, crystalline compound
(note: use Li_2O)

-lith·ic (lith′ik) *a combining form meaning* of a (specified) stage in the use of stone [*neolithic*]

lith·i·um (lith′ē əm) *n.* [ModL. < LITHIA] a soft, silver-white, metallic chemical element, the lightest known metal: symbol, Li; at. wt., 6.939; at. no., 3

lithium carbonate a white, powdery salt, Li_2CO_3, used in making glass, dyes, etc. and as a drug in treating certain mental illnesses

lith·o (lith′ō) *n., pl.* **-os;** *vt., vi.* **-oed, -o·ing** *clipped form of* LITHOGRAPH

lith·o- [< Gr. *lithos*, a stone] *a combining form meaning* stone, rock: also, before a vowel, **lith-**

lith·o·graph (lith′ə graf′) *n.* a print made by lithography —*vi., vt.* to make (prints or copies) by lithography —**li·thog·ra·pher** (li thäg′rə fər) *n.*

li·thog·ra·phy (li thäg′rə fē) *n.* [LITHO- + -GRAPHY] the art or process of printing from a flat stone or metal plate: the design is put on the surface with a greasy material, and first water and then printing ink are applied; the greasy parts, which repel water, absorb the ink, but the wet parts do not —**lith·o·graph·ic** (lith′ə graf′ik) *adj.* —**lith′o·graph′i·cal·ly** *adv.*

lith·o·sphere (lith′ə sfir′) *n.* [LITHO- + SPHERE] the solid, rocky part of the earth; earth's crust

Lith·u·a·ni·a (lith′oo wā′nē ə) republic of the U.S.S.R., in NE Europe, on the Baltic Sea: 25,170 sq. mi.; pop. 3,100,000; cap. Vilnius: in full, **Lithuanian Soviet Socialist Republic**

Lith·u·a·ni·an (-ən) *adj.* of Lithuania, its people, or their language —*n.* **1.** a native or inhabitant of Lithuania **2.** the Baltic language of the Lithuanians

lit·i·ga·ble (lit′i gə b'l) *adj.* that gives cause for litigation, or a lawsuit; actionable

lit·i·gant (lit′ə gənt) *n.* a person taking part in a lawsuit

lit·i·gate (-gāt′) *vt.* **-gat′ed, -gat′ing** [< L. pp. of *litigare* < *litis,* genitive of *lis,* dispute + *agere,* to do] to contest in a lawsuit —*vi.* to carry on a lawsuit —**lit′i·ga′tor** *n.*

lit·i·ga·tion (lit′ə gā′shən) *n.* **1.** the carrying on of a lawsuit **2.** a lawsuit

li·ti·gious (li tij′əs) *adj.* **1.** *a)* given to carrying on litigations *b)* quarrelsome **2.** disputable at law **3.** of lawsuits —**li·ti′gious·ly** *adv.* —**li·ti′gious·ness** *n.*

lit·mus (lit′məs) *n.* [ON. *litmose,* lichen used in dyeing < *litr,* color + *mosi,* moss] a purple coloring matter obtained from various lichens: it turns blue in bases and red in acids

litmus paper absorbent paper treated with litmus and used to test whether a solution is an acid or a base

li·tre (lēt′ər) *n. chiefly Brit. sp. of* LITER

Litt.D. [L. *Lit(t)erarum Doctor*] Doctor of Letters; Doctor of Literature

lit·ter (lit′ər) *n.* [< OFr. *litiere* < ML. < L. *lectus,* a couch] **1.** a framework having long horizontal shafts near the bottom and enclosing a couch on which a person can be carried **2.** a stretcher for carrying the sick or wounded **3.** straw, hay, etc. used as bedding for animals, as a covering for plants, etc. **4.** the young borne at one time by a dog, cat, etc. **5.** things lying about in disorder; esp., bits of scattered rubbish [pick up your *litter* after a picnic] —*vt.* **1.** to bring forth (a number of young) at one

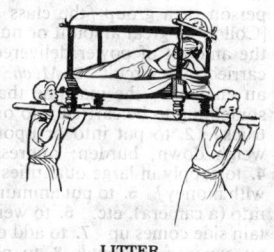

LITTER

time: said of certain animals **2.** to make messy with things scattered about [her desk is *littered* with papers] **3.** to scatter about carelessly [he *littered* peanut shells on the rug] —*vi.* to bear a litter of young

lit·té·ra·teur (lit′ər ə tur′) *n.* [Fr.] a literary man; man of letters: also written **litterateur**

☆**lit·ter·bug** (lit′ər bug′) *n.* a person who litters a public place with trash, garbage, etc.

lit·tle (lit′'l) *adj.* **lit′tler** or **less** or **less′er, lit′tlest** or **least** [OE. *lytel* < IE. base *leud-,* to stoop] **1.** small in size; not big, large, or great [a *little* house] **2.** small in amount, number, or degree; not much [*little* sugar, *little* danger] **3.** short in time or distance; brief [wait a *little* while; go a *little* way with me] **4.** small in importance or power [the rights of the *little* man] **5.** small in force, intensity, etc.; weak [she gave it a *little* push] **6.** not important; trivial; trifling [just a *little* error] **7.** lacking in breadth of vision; narrow-minded [a *little* mind] **8.** young: said of children or animals *Little* is sometimes used to express endearment [bless your *little* heart] —*adv.* **less, least 1.** in a small degree; only slightly; not much [he is a *little* better] **2.** not in the least [he *little* suspects the plot] —*n.* **1.** *a)* a small amount, degree, etc. [a *little* goes a long way] *b)* not much [*little* was done] **2.** a short time or distance [sit a *little* with me] —**see** SYN· at SMALL —**little by little** by slow degrees or small amounts; gradually —**make little of** to treat as unimportant —**not a little** very much; very —**lit′tle·ness** *n.*

Little Bear the constellation URSA MINOR

☆**Little Dipper** a dipper-shaped group of stars in the constellation Ursa Minor

☆**Little League** a league of baseball teams for youngsters —**Little Leaguer**

☆**lit·tle·neck** (lit′'l nek′) *n.* [< *Little Neck,* Long Island] the young of the quahog, a round, thick-shelled clam, usually eaten raw: also **littleneck clam**

Little Rock [after a rocky cape in the river] capital of Ark., on the Arkansas River: pop. 132,000

little slam *Bridge* the winning of all but one trick

☆**little theater 1.** a small theater, as of a college, art group, etc., usually noncommercial and amateur **2.** drama produced by such theaters

lit·to·ral (lit′ər əl) *adj.* [L. *litoralis* < *litoris,* genitive of *litus,* seashore] of, on, or along the shore —*n.* the region along the shore

li·tur·gi·cal (li tur′jə k'l) *adj.* **1.** of or relating to a liturgy **2.** used in or using a liturgy —**li·tur′gi·cal·ly** *adv.*

lit·ur·gy (lit′ər jē) *n., pl.* **-gies** [< Fr. < ML. < Gr. *leitourgia,* public service, ult. < *leōs,* people + *ergon,* work] **1.** certain forms or ritual planned for public worship in any of various religions or churches **2.** the Eucharistic service

liv·a·ble (liv′ə b'l) *adj.* **1.** fit or pleasant to live in, as a house **2.** that can be lived through; endurable [she found life on the island quite *livable*] **3.** agreeable to live with: said of a person Also sp. **liveable** —**liv′a·bil′i·ty, liv′a·ble·ness** *n.*

live¹ (liv) *vi.* **lived, liv′ing** [OE. *libban:* for IE. base see LIFE] **1.** to be alive; have life [no one *lives* forever] **2.** *a)* to remain alive [he *lived* to be 100 years old] *b)* to last; endure [the Iliad has *lived* through the centuries] **3.** *a)* to pass one's life in a specified manner [to *live* happily] *b)* to conduct one's life [to *live* by a strict moral code] **4.** to enjoy a full and varied life [that man has *lived*] **5.** *a)* to maintain life [to *live* on a pension] *b)* to be dependent for a living (with *off*) **6.** to feed; subsist [to *live* on fruits and nuts] **7.** to make one's dwelling; reside [we *live* on a farm] —*vt.* **1.** to carry out in one's life [to *live* one's faith] **2.** to spend; pass [to *live* a useful life] —**live down** to live in such a way as to wipe out the shame of (some fault, misdeed, etc.) —**live high** (or **well**) to live in luxury —**live in** to sleep at the place where one is a domestic servant —**live it up** [Slang] to enjoy pleasures, extravagances, etc. that one usually does without —**live out** to live until the end of; last through —**live up to** to act in accordance with (ideals, promises, etc.) —**live with** to tolerate; endure

live² (līv) *adj.* [< ALIVE] **1.** having life; not dead **2.** of the living state or living beings **3.** having positive qualities, as of warmth, vigor, vitality, brilliance, etc. [a *live* organization] ☆**4.** of immediate or present interest [a *live* issue] **5.** *a)* still burning or glowing [a *live* spark] *b)* not extinct [a *live* volcano] **6.** unexploded [a *live* shell] **7.** unused; unexpended [*live* steam] **8.** carrying electrical current [a *live* wire] **9.** *a)* involving a performance in person, not one on film, tape, etc.; transmitted during the actual performance [a *live* broadcast] *b)* recorded at a public performance **10.** *Mech.* giving motion or power

-lived (līvd; *occas.* livd) [see LIFE & -ED] *a combining form meaning* having (a specified kind or length of) life [short-*lived*]

live·li·hood (līv'lē hood') *n.* [OE. liflad < lif, LIFE + -lad, course] means of supporting life; subsistence [he earns his livelihood by repairing radios]

live·long (liv'lôŋ') *adj.* [ME. lefe longe, lit., lief long (see LIEF), here meaning "very long"] long or long and boring; whole; entire [the livelong day]

live·ly (līv'lē) *adj.* **-li·er, -li·est** [OE. liflic] **1.** full of life; active; vigorous [a *lively* puppy] **2.** full of spirit; exciting; animated [a *lively* debate] **3.** gay; cheerful [a *lively* voice] **4.** moving quickly and lightly, as a dance **5.** vivid; keen; intense [*lively* colors] ☆**6.** having plenty of bounce [a *lively* ball] — *adv.* in a lively manner —**live'li·ness** *n.*

liv·en (lī'vən) *vt., vi.* to make or become lively or gay; cheer (*up*)

☆**live oak 1.** *a)* an evergreen oak of the southeastern U.S. *b)* an oak of California **2.** the hard wood of these trees

liv·er[1] (liv'ər) *n.* [OE. lifer] **1.** the largest glandular organ in animals with a backbone: it secretes bile, plays an important part in metabolism, and helps in building red blood cells **2.** the liver of cattle, fowl, etc. used as food **3.** the reddish-brown color of liver

liv·er[2] (liv'ər) *n.* a person who lives (in a specified way or place) [a clean *liver*]

liv·er·ied (liv'ər ēd, liv'rēd) *adj.* wearing a livery

liv·er·ish (liv'ər ish) *adj.* [Colloq.] **1.** having liver trouble; bilious **2.** having a sour disposition; peevish; cross —**liv'er·ish·ness** *n.*

Liv·er·pool (liv'ər pool') seaport in NW England: pop. 688,000 —**Liv'er·pud'li·an** (-pud'lē ən) *adj., n.*

liver spot a brownish spot on the skin, formerly thought to be caused by faulty functioning of the liver

liv·er·wort (liv'ər wurt') *n.* any of a group of plants, often forming dense, green mosslike mats on rocks, soil, etc. in moist places

☆**liv·er·wurst** (liv'ər wurst') *n.* [LIVER[1] + G. wurst, sausage] a sausage containing ground liver: also **liver sausage**

liv·er·y (liv'ər ē, liv'rē) *n., pl.* **-er·ies** [< OFr. livree, gift of clothes to a servant < livrer, to deliver < L. liberare, to LIBERATE] **1.** an identifying uniform such as is worn by servants or those in some particular group, trade, etc. **2.** the people wearing such uniforms **3.** characteristic dress or appearance **4.** *a)* the keeping and feeding of horses for a fixed charge *b)* the keeping of horses, vehicles, or both, for hire ☆*c)* a stable providing these services: also **livery stable**

liv·er·y·man (-mən) *n., pl.* **-men** a person who owns or works in a livery stable

lives (līvz) *n. pl. of* LIFE

live·stock (līv'stäk') *n.* domestic animals kept for use on a farm or raised for sale and profit

live wire 1. a wire carrying an electric current ☆**2.** [Colloq.] a person full of energy and willing to take on new projects

liv·id (liv'id) *adj.* [< Fr. < L. lividus] **1.** discolored by a bruise; black-and-blue **2.** grayish-blue; lead-colored [*livid* with rage]: sometimes taken to mean pale, white, or red —see SYN. at PALE[1] —**li·vid·i·ty** (li vid'ə tē), **liv'id·ness** *n.*

liv·ing (liv'iŋ) *adj.* **1.** alive; having life **2.** in active operation or use [a *living* institution] **3.** of persons alive [within *living* memory] **4.** in its natural state or place, or having its natural force, etc. [hewn from the *living* rock] **5.** still spoken and undergoing changes [a *living* language] **6.** true to reality; lifelike [the *living* image] **7.** of life or the continuing of life [*living* conditions] **8.** suited for social and recreational activities in a house [the *living* area] **9.** presented in person before a live audience [*living* theater] **10.** very [the *living* daylights] —*n.* **1.** the state of being alive **2.** the means of supporting oneself; livelihood [to work for a *living*] **3.** manner of existence [the standard of *living*] **4.** in England, a church benefice —**the living** those that are still alive

SYN.—**living** and **alive** are the simple, basic terms for organisms having life or existence, **living** in general suggesting continued existence or activity [a

living faith] and **alive**, full force or strength [prejudices kept *alive* by ignorance]; **animate**, opposed to *inanimate*, is applied to living organisms as distinguished from lifeless ones or inorganic objects; **animated** is applied to inanimate things which are made to seem alive or moving [*animated* cartoons]; **vital** is applied to that which is necessary to organic life [*vital* functions] or to the energy, force, etc. shown by living things [a *vital* young school teacher]

living death a life of nothing but misery

living room ☆a room in a home, with sofas, chairs, etc., used for social activities, entertaining, etc.

Liv·ing·stone (liv'iŋ stən), **David** 1813-73; Scot. missionary & explorer in Africa

living wage a wage that is high enough for a person to keep himself and his family in some comfort beyond food and shelter

Li·vo·ni·a (li vō'nē ə) former Baltic province of Russia city in SE Mich.: suburb of Detroit: pop. 110,000

Li·vor·no (lē vôr'nō) *It. name of* LEGHORN

Liv·y (liv'ē) (L. name *Titus Livius*) 59 B.C.-17 A.D.; Rom. historian

liz·ard (liz'ərd) *n.* [< OFr. lesard < L. lacerta] **1.** any of a group of reptiles with a long slender body and tail, a scaly skin, and four legs, as the gecko, chameleon, and iguana **2.** loosely, any of various similar animals, as alligators or salamanders

LIZARD

Lju·blja·na (lyoo'blyä nä) city in Slovenia, NW Yugoslavia: pop. 157,000

'll *contraction of* will or shall [I'll go]

LL., L.L. Late Latin

ll., ll lines

lla·ma (lä'mə) *n., pl.* **-mas, -ma:** see PLURAL, II, D, 1 [Sp. < Quechua] a S. American animal related to the camel but smaller and without humps: it is used as a beast of burden and for its wool, flesh, and milk

lla·no (lä'nō; *Sp.* lyä'nō) *n., pl.* **-nos** (-nōz; *Sp.* -nôs) [Sp. < L. *planus*, plain] a grassy plain in the Southwest and in Spanish America

LL.B. [L. *Legum Baccalaureus*] Bachelor of Laws

LL.D. [L. *Legum Doctor*] Doctor of Laws

Llew·el·lyn (loo wel'ən) [W. *Llewelyn*, lit., prob., lionlike] a masculine name

Lloyd (loid) [W. *Llwyd*, lit., gray] a masculine name

Lloyd George, **David** 1863-1945; Brit. statesman; prime minister (1916-22)

LLAMA
(to 4 ft. high at shoulder)

lo (lō) *interj.* [OE. la] look! see!

loach (lōch) *n.* [< OFr. loche] a small, old-world, freshwater fish with barbels around the mouth

load (lōd) *n.* [OE. lad, a course, way: for IE. base see LEAD[1]] **1.** something carried or to be carried at one time; burden [a heavy *load* on his back] **2.** the amount that can be carried: a measure of weight or quantity varying with the type of carrier [a carload of coal] **3.** something carried with difficulty; specif., *a)* a heavy burden or weight *b)* a great mental burden [a *load* off one's mind] **4.** the weight that a structure bears or the stresses that are put upon it **5.** a single charge, as of powder and bullets, for a firearm ☆**6.** the amount of work carried by a person or a group [the class *load* of a teacher] **7.** [often pl.] [Colloq.] a great amount or number [*loads* of friends] **8.** *Elec.* the amount of power delivered by a generator, motor, etc. or carried by a circuit **9.** *Mech.* the external resistance offered to an engine by the machine that it is operating —*vt.* **1.** to put something to be carried into or upon; fill with a load [to *load* a truck] **2.** to put into or upon a carrier [to *load* coal] **3.** to weigh down; burden; oppress [she is *loaded* with troubles] **4.** to supply in large quantities [to *load* one with honors, *loaded* with money] **5.** to put ammunition into (a gun or firearm), film into (a camera), etc. **6.** to weight (dice) unevenly so that a certain side comes up **7.** to add extra costs, a filler, etc. to [to *load* an expense account] **8.** to phrase (a question, etc.) so as to draw out a desired response ☆**9.** *Baseball* to have or cause to have runners on (all bases) —*vi.* **1.** to put in or receive a charge of ammunition **2.** to put on or take on passengers, goods, etc. [the bus is *loading*] —☆**get a load of** [Slang] **1.** to listen to or hear **2.** to look at or see —**have a load on** [Slang] to be intoxicated —**load'er** *n.* —**load'ing** *n.*

LIVER
(A, liver; B, stomach; C, small intestine; D, large intestine)

load·ed (lōd′id) *adj.* **1.** carrying a load **2.** filled, charged, weighted, etc. [a *loaded* gun; a *loaded* camera] **3.** [Slang] under the influence of liquor or drugs ☆**4.** [Slang] well supplied with money

load·star (lōd′stär′) *n.* same as LODESTAR

load·stone (lōd′stōn′) *n.* same as LODESTONE

loaf[1] (lōf) *n., pl.* **loaves** (lōvz) [OE. *hlaf*] **1.** a portion of bread baked in one piece, usually having a shape longer than it is wide **2.** any mass of food shaped somewhat like a loaf of bread and baked [a salmon *loaf*]

☆**loaf**[2] (lōf) *vi.* [prob. < LOAFER] to spend time doing little or nothing; loiter or lounge about; idle, dawdle, etc. [to *loaf* on the job] —*vt.* to spend (time) idly (often with *away*)

☆**loaf·er** (lōf′ər) *n.* [prob. < G. *landläufer*, a vagabond] a person who loafs; idler —[L-] *a trademark for* a moccasinlike sport shoe; also, [l-] a shoe like this

loam (lōm) *n.* [OE. *lam:* for IE. base see DELETE] **1.** a rich soil of clay, sand, and organic matter **2.** popularly, any rich, dark soil —*vt.* to fill or top with loam —**loam′y** *adj.*

loan (lōn) *n.* [< ON. *lān* < IE. base *leikw-,* to leave behind] **1.** the act of lending **2.** something lent; esp., a sum of money lent, often at interest —*vt., vi.* to lend —**on loan** lent for temporary use or service

loan·er (lōn′ər) *n.* **1.** one who loans **2.** a car, radio, etc. lent in place of one left for repair

☆**loan shark** [Colloq.] a person who lends money at unreasonably high or illegal rates of interest

loan·word (-wurd′) *n.* [after G. *lehnwort*] a word of one language taken into another and made part of the second language (Ex.: KINDERGARTEN < G.)

loath (lōth) *adj.* [OE. *lath*, hostile] unwilling; reluctant [to be *loath* to depart] —**nothing loath** willing(ly) —see SYN. at RELUCTANT

loathe (lōth) *vt.* **loathed, loath′ing** [OE. *lathian*, to be hateful] to feel intense dislike or disgust for; detest —see SYN. at HATE

loath·ing (lōth′iŋ) *n.* intense dislike, disgust, or hatred; abhorrence —see SYN. at AVERSION

loath·ly[1] (lōth′lē) *adv.* [Rare] unwillingly

loath·ly[2] (lōth′lē) *adj.* rare var. of LOATHSOME

loath·some (lōth′səm, lōth′-) *adj.* causing loathing; disgusting —**loath′some·ly** *adv.* —**loath′some·ness** *n.*

loaves (lōvz) *n. pl. of* LOAF[1]

lob (läb) *n.* [ME. *lobbe-*, lit., "heavy, thick"] *Tennis* a stroke in which the ball is sent high into the air, dropping into the back of the opponent's court —*vt.* **lobbed, lob′bing** to send (a ball) in a lob —*vi.* **1.** to move heavily and clumsily (often with *along*) **2.** to lob a ball —**lob′ber** *n.*

Lo·ba·chev·ski (lō′bä chyef′skē), **Ni·ko·lai I·va·no·vich** (nē kō lī′ ē vä′nō vich) 1793–1856; Russ. mathematician

lo·bar (lō′bər, -bär) *adj.* of a lobe or lobes

lo·bate (-bāt) *adj.* having or formed into a lobe or lobes

lo·ba·tion (lō bā′shən) *n.* **1.** the condition of having lobes **2.** the process of forming lobes **3.** a lobe

lob·by (läb′ē) *n., pl.* **-bies** [LL. *lobia:* see LODGE] **1.** an entrance hall or waiting room, as of a hotel, theater, etc. ☆**2.** a group of lobbyists for the same special interest [the oil *lobby*] —*vi.* **-bied, -by·ing** to act as a lobbyist —☆*vt.* to get or try to get legislators to vote for or against a (measure) by lobbying

☆**lob·by·ist** (-ist) *n.* a person, acting for a special interest group, who tries to influence the voting on legislation or the decisions of government administrators —**lob′by·ism** *n.*

lobe (lōb) *n.* [Fr. < LL. < Gr. *lobos:* for IE. base see LAP[1]] a rounded part that sticks out; specif., *a)* the fleshy lower end of the human ear *b)* any of the main divisions of an organ [a *lobe* of the brain, lung, or liver] *c)* any of the rounded divisions of the leaves of certain trees —**lobed** *adj.*

lo·be·li·a (lō bēl′yə, -bē′lē ə) *n.* [ModL., after Matthias de *L'Obel* (1538–1616), Fl. botanist] any of a group of plants with white, blue, or red flowers of irregular shape

lob·lol·ly (läb′läl′ē) *n., pl.* **-lies** [prob. < dial. *lob*, to boil + dial. *lolly*, broth] ☆**1.** a common pine of the southeastern U.S., having long needles ☆**2.** the wood of this tree: also **loblolly pine**

☆**lo·bo** (lō′bō) *n.* [Sp. < L. *lupus*] same as GRAY WOLF

lo·bot·o·my (lō bät′ə mē) *n., pl.* **-mies** [< LOBE + -TOMY] a surgical operation in which a lobe of the brain is cut into or across

lob·ster (läb′stər) *n., pl.* **-sters, -ster:** see PLURAL, II, D, 1 [OE. *lopustre* < *loppe*, spider (from external resemblance) + *-estre:* see -STER] **1.** a large sea crustacean with compound eyes, long antennae, and five pairs of legs, the first pair of which are modified into large pincers **2.** any similar crustacean, as the spiny lobster **3.** the flesh of these animals used as food

LOBSTER
(to 24 in. long)

lobster pot a basketlike trap for catching lobsters

lobster tail a tail of a lobster (sense 2), or its flesh used as food, often broiled in the shell

lob·ule (läb′yool) *n.* **1.** a small lobe **2.** a subdivision of a lobe —**lob′u·lar** (-yoo lər) *adj.* —**lob′u·late** (-lāt′) *adj.*

lo·cal (lō′k'l) *adj.* [OFr. < LL. *localis* < L. *locus,* a place: for IE. base see STALL[1]] **1.** relating to place **2.** of, characteristic of, or confined to a particular place or district [items of *local* interest] **3.** not broad; narrow [*local* outlook] **4.** of or for a particular part of the body [a *local* anesthetic] ☆**5.** making all stops along its run [a *local* bus] —*n.* ☆**1.** a local train, bus, etc. ☆**2.** a newspaper item of local interest only ☆**3.** a chapter or branch, as of a labor union **4.** a resident of the local town or district [he tried to convince the *locals*]

local color behavior, speech, etc. characteristic of a certain region or time, introduced into a novel, play, etc. to supply realism

lo·cale (lō kal′) *n.* [Fr. *local*] a place or locality, esp. as regards events, etc. connected with it, often as a setting for a story, etc.

local government **1.** government of the affairs of a town, district, etc. by the people living there **2.** the people chosen to administer this government

lo·cal·ism (lō′k'l iz'm) *n.* **1.** a local custom or way of speaking **2.** a word, meaning, expression, pronunciation, etc. used only in a certain region **3.** narrow outlook; provincialism

lo·cal·i·ty (lō kal′ə tē) *n., pl.* **-ties** **1.** position in relation to surrounding objects, landmarks, etc. [a sense of *locality*] **2.** a place; district

lo·cal·ize (lō′kə līz′) *vt.* **-ized′, -iz′ing** to make local; limit, confine, or trace to a particular place, area, or locality [the pain is *localized* in his hand] —**lo′cal·i·za′tion** *n.*

lo·cal·ly (lō′k'l ē) *adv.* **1.** in a local way **2.** within a given area or areas [the damage done by a tornado *locally*]

local option the right to decide by a vote of the residents whether something, esp. the sale of liquor, shall be permitted in their locality

lo·cate (lō′kāt, lō kāt′) *vt.* **-cat·ed, -cat·ing** [< L. pp. of *locare* < *locus:* see LOCAL] **1.** to mark off or designate the site of (a mining claim, etc.) **2.** to establish in a certain place [offices *located* downtown] **3.** to discover the position of after a search [to *locate* a lost object] **4.** to show the position of [to *locate* Guam on a map] **5.** to assign to a particular place, etc. —*vi.* ☆[Colloq.] to settle [to *locate* in Boston] —**lo′cat·er, lo·ca′tor** *n.*

lo·ca·tion (lō kā′shən) *n.* **1.** a locating or being located **2.** position; place; situation [a fine *location* for a restaurant] **3.** an area marked off for a specific purpose ☆**4.** *Motion Pictures* an outdoor set or setting, away from the studio, where scenes are photographed: chiefly in **on location** —**lo·ca′tion·al** *adj.*

loc·a·tive (läk′ə tiv) *adj.* [< L. pp. of *locare:* see LOCATE] *Linguis.* expressing place at which or in which —*n.* **1.** the locative case (in Latin, Greek, etc.) **2.** a word in this case

loc. cit. [L. *loco citato*] in the place cited

loch (läk, läkh) *n.* [< Gael. & OIr.] [Scot.] **1.** a lake **2.** an arm of the sea, esp. when narrow and nearly surrounded by land

lo·ci (lō′sī) *n. pl. of* LOCUS

lock[1] (läk) *n.* [OE. *loc,* a bolt, enclosure < IE. base *leug-,* to bend] **1.** a mechanical device for fastening a door, strongbox, etc. by means of a key or combination **2.** anything that fastens something else and prevents it from operating **3.** a locking together; jam **4.** an enclosed part of a canal, waterway, etc.

LOCK IN CANAL

fat, āpe, cär; ten, ēven; is, bīte; gō, hôrn, tōol, look; oil, out; up, fur; get; joy; yet; chin; she; thin, then; zh, leisure; ŋ, ring; ə for a in ago, e in agent, i in sanity, o in comply, u in focus; ' as in able (ā′b'l); Fr. bal; ë, Fr. coeur; ö, Fr. feu; Fr. mon; ô, Fr. coq; ü, Fr. duc; r, Fr. cri; H, G. ich; kh, G. doch; ‡foreign; ☆ Americanism; < derived from. See inside front cover.

equipped with gates so that the level of the water can be changed to raise or lower boats from one level to another **5.** the mechanism of a firearm used to explode the ammunition charge **6.** *same as* AIR LOCK **7.** *Wrestling* a hold in which a part of the opponent's body is firmly gripped —*vt.* **1.** to fasten (a door, trunk, etc.) by means of a lock **2.** to shut (*up, in,* or *out*); confine [*locked* in jail] **3.** to fit closely; link [we *locked* arms] **4.** to embrace tightly **5.** to jam together so as to make immovable [*locked* gears] **6.** to put in a fixed position [a throttle *locked* in the idle position] **7.** to move (a ship) through a lock —*vi.* **1.** to become locked **2.** to intertwine or interlock [the two elks *locked* horns while fighting] —**lock out** to keep (workers) from a place of employment in seeking to force terms upon them — **lock, stock, and barrel** [Colloq.] completely —**lock up 1.** to fasten the doors of (a house, etc.) by means of locks **2.** to put in a jail **3.** to make certain to have the result one wants [to have an election *locked up*]

lock² (läk) *n.* [OE. *loc* < same base as prec.] **1.** a curl, tress, or ringlet of hair **2.** [*pl.*] [Poet.] the hair of the head **3.** a tuft of wool, cotton, etc.

Locke (läk), **John** 1632–1704; Eng. philosopher

lock·er (läk′ər) *n.* **1.** a person or thing that locks **2.** a chest, closet, drawer, etc. which can be locked, esp. one for individual use ☆**3.** a large freezer compartment, as one rented in a cold-storage plant

☆**locker room** a room equipped with lockers, as at a gymnasium, swimming pool, factory, etc., for storing one's clothes and equipment

lock·et (läk′it) *n.* [< OFr. *locquet,* dim. of *loc,* a latch < Frank.] a small, hinged, ornamental case of gold, silver, etc., for holding a picture, lock of hair, etc.: it is usually worn on a necklace

lock·jaw (läk′jô′) *n.* [short for earlier *locked jaw*] *same as* TETANUS

lock·out (-out′) *n.* the refusal by an employer to allow his employees to come in to work until they agree to his terms

lock·smith (-smith′) *n.* a person whose work is making or repairing locks and keys

lock step a way of marching in very close file

lock·up (-up′) *n.* a jail

☆**lo·co** (lō′kō) *n.* [MexSp. < Sp., mad < L. *ulucus,* owl] [Western] *same as:* **1.** LOCOWEED **2.** LOCO DISEASE —*vt.* **-coed, -co·ing** to poison with locoweed —*adj.* [Slang] crazy; demented

lo·co- [< L. *locus,* a place] *a combining form meaning* from place to place [*locomotion*]

‡**lo·co ci·ta·to** (lō′kō sī tät′ō) [L.] in the place cited or quoted

☆**loco disease** a nervous disease of horses, sheep, and cattle, caused by locoweed poisoning: also **lo′co·ism** *n.*

lo·co·mo·tion (lō′kə mō′shən) *n.* [LOCO- + MOTION] motion, or the power of moving, from one place to another

lo·co·mo·tive (-mōt′iv) *adj.* **1.** of locomotion **2.** moving or capable of moving from one place to another **3.** designating or of engines that move under their own power [*locomotive* design] —*n.* an engine that can move about by its own power; esp., an electric, steam, or diesel engine on wheels, designed to push or pull a railroad train

lo·co·mo·tor (lō′kə mōt′ər) *adj.* of locomotion

locomotor ataxia *same as* TABES DORSALIS

☆**lo·co·weed** (lō′kō wēd′) *n.* any of several plants of the legume family, which are common in western N. America and cause loco disease

loc·u·lus (läk′yə ləs) *n., pl.* **-li** (-lī′) [< L., dim. of *locus,* place] any small cavity or empty space in plant or animal tissue: also **loc′ule** (-yool) —**loc′u·lar** *adj.*

lo·cus (lō′kəs) *n., pl.* **lo·ci** (-sī) [L.: see LOCAL] **1.** a place **2.** *Genetics* the position on a chromosome occupied by a particular gene **3.** *Math.* a line, plane, etc. every point of which satisfies a given condition

lo·cust (lō′kəst) *n.* [< L. *locusta*] **1.** any of various large grasshoppers; specif., a migratory grasshopper often traveling in great swarms destroying vegetation **2.** *same as* SEVENTEEN-YEAR LOCUST ☆**3.** *a)* a spiny tree of the legume family, native to eastern and central U.S. and having racemes of fragrant white flowers *b)* the yellowish, hard wood of this tree ☆**4.** *same as* HONEY LOCUST

LOCUST
(to 2 in. long)

lo·cu·tion (lō kyōō′shən) *n.* [< L. *locutio* < pp. of *loqui,* to speak] **1.** a word, phrase, or expression **2.** a particular style of speech

lode (lōd) *n.* [var. of LOAD (< OE. *lad,* course)] *Mining* **1.** a vein containing metallic ore and filling a fissure in rock **2.** any deposit of ore separated from the adjoining rock **3.** any rich source

lo·den (lō′d'n) *adj.* [G. < MHG. < OHG. *lodo,* coarse cloth] **1.** designating or of a waterproof wool cloth, used for coats **2.** of a dark olive green often used for this cloth

lode·star (lōd′stär′) *n.* [see LODE & STAR] a star by which one directs his course; esp., the North Star

lode·stone (-stōn′) *n.* **1.** a strongly magnetic variety of the mineral magnetite **2.** anything that attracts strongly

lodge (läj) *n.* [< OFr. *loge,* arbor < LL. *lobia* < Gmc.: for IE. base see LEAF] **1.** *a)* a small house for some special use [a hunting *lodge*] *b)* a resort hotel or motel **2.** *a)* the meeting place of a local chapter, as of a fraternal organization *b)* such a local chapter *b)* the den of certain animals, esp. beavers ☆**4.** *a)* the hut or tent of an American Indian *b)* those who live in it —*vt.* **lodged, lodg′ing 1.** to provide with a place to live or sleep in, esp. temporarily **2.** to rent rooms to **3.** to deposit for safekeeping **4.** to put or send into a place or position by shooting, thrusting, etc. (with *in*) [to *lodge* an arrow in a target] **5.** to bring (a complaint, etc.) before legal authorities **6.** to confer (powers) upon (with *in*) —*vi.* **1.** to live in a certain place for a time **2.** to live (*with* another or *in* his home) as a paying guest **3.** to come to rest and remain firmly fixed (*in*) [a bone *lodged* in her throat]

lodg·er (läj′ər) *n.* a person or thing that lodges; esp., one who rents a room in another's home

lodg·ing (-iŋ) *n.* **1.** a place to live in, esp. temporarily **2.** [*pl.*] a room or rooms rented in a private home

lodging house *same as* ROOMING HOUSE

lodg·ment (-mənt) *n.* **1.** a lodging or being lodged **2.** a lodging place **3.** a pile of material that has become lodged in a place Also sp. **lodge′ment**

Łódz (looj) city in C Poland: pop. 749,000

lo·ess (les, lō′es) *n.* [G. *löss* < *lösch,* loose] a fine-grained, yellowish-brown, extremely fertile loam deposited by the wind —**lo·ess′i·al** *adj.*

loft (lôft, läft) *n.* [OE. < ON. *lopt,* upper room, sky: for IE. base see LEAF] **1.** *a)* an attic or atticlike space just below the roof of a house, barn, etc. *b)* an upper story of a warehouse or factory **2.** a gallery [the choir *loft* in a church] **3.** *a)* the slope given to the face of a golf club to aid in hitting the ball in a high curve *b)* the height of a ball hit or thrown in a high curve —*vt.* **1.** to store in a loft **2.** *a)* to hit or throw (a golf ball, baseball, etc.) into the air in a high curve *b)* to throw (a bowling ball) so that it strikes the alley sharply some distance past the foul line —**loft′er** *n.*

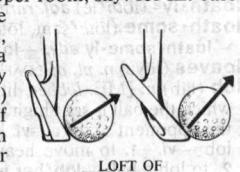

LOFT OF
GOLF CLUBS

loft·y (lôf′tē) *adj.* **loft′i·er, loft′i·est 1.** very high [a *lofty* mountain] **2.** elevated; noble; grand [*lofty* sentiments] **3.** haughty; too proud [the king's *lofty* manner] —see SYN. at HIGH —**loft′i·ly** *adv.* —**loft′i·ness** *n.*

log¹ (lôg, läg) *n.* [ME. *logge,* prob. < or akin to ON. *lag,* felled tree: for IE. base see LIE¹] **1.** a section of the trunk or of a large branch of a felled tree **2.** a device (orig. a quadrant of wood) for measuring the speed of a ship **3.** a daily record of a ship's speed, progress, etc. and of the events in its voyage; logbook **4.** *a)* a similar record of an aircraft's flight *b)* a record of a pilot's flying time, experience, etc. **5.** any record of progress or occurrences —*adj.* made of a log or logs —*vt.* **logged, log′ging 1.** to saw (trees) into logs ☆**2.** to cut down the trees of (a region) **3.** to enter or record in a log **4.** to sail or fly (a specified distance) —☆*vi.* to cut down trees and transport the logs to a sawmill

log² (lôg, läg) *n. shortened form of* LOGARITHM

-log *same as* -LOGUE

Lo·gan (lō′gən), **Mount** mountain in SW Yukon, Canada: highest mountain in Canada: 19,850 ft.

☆**lo·gan·ber·ry** (lō′gən ber′ē) *n., pl.* **-ries** [after J. H. *Logan* (1841–1928), U.S. horticulturist] **1.** a hybrid bramble developed from the blackberry and the red raspberry **2.** its purplish-red fruit

log·a·rithm (lôg′ə rith′m, läg′-) *n.* [ModL. < Gr. *logos,* a ratio + *arithmos,* number] *Math.* the exponent of the power to which a fixed number (the *base*) must be raised in order to produce a given number (the *antilogarithm*): logarithms are normally computed to the base of 10 and are used for shortening mathematical calculations [the *logarithm* of 100 is 2, when 10 is taken as the base ($10^2 = 100$)] **—log′a·rith′mic** *adj.* **—log′a·rith′mi·cal·ly** *adv.*

log·book (lôg′book′, läg′-) *n.* *same as* LOG[1] (senses 3, 4, & 5)

loge (lōzh) *n.* [Fr.: see LODGE] **1.** a box in a theater **2.** the forward section of a mezzanine or balcony in a theater

☆**log·ger** (lôg′ər, läg′-) *n.* a person whose work is logging; lumberjack

log·ger·head (lôg′ər hed′, läg′-) *n.* [dial. *logger*, block of wood (< LOG[1]) + HEAD] **1.** a sea turtle of the Atlantic with a large head: also **loggerhead turtle 2.** [Dial.] a stupid person — **at loggerheads** in disagreement; quarreling

log·gi·a (lä′jē ə, lä′jə; lô′-; *It.* lôd′jä) *n., pl.* **-gi·as;** *It.* **log′gie** (-je) [It.: see LODGE] an arcaded or roofed gallery built into or projecting from the side of a building, often one overlooking an open court

LOGGIA

☆**log·ging** (lôg′iŋ, läg′-) *n.* the occupation of cutting down trees, cutting them into logs, and transporting the logs to a sawmill

log·ic (läj′ik) *n.* [< OFr. < L. < Gr. *logikē* (*technē*), logical (art) < *logos*, word, thought < *legein*, to speak, collect < IE. base *leg-*, to gather, from which also comes L. *legere*, to speak, collect] **1.** the science that deals with the rules of correct reasoning and with proof by reasoning **2.** a book on this science **3.** correct reasoning; valid induction or deduction [the lack of *logic* in his scheme] **4.** way of reasoning [poor *logic*] **5.** necessary connection or outcome, as through the working of cause and effect [the *logic* of events]

log·i·cal (läj′i k'l) *adj.* **1.** of or used in the science of logic **2.** according to the principles of logic, or correct reasoning [a *logical* explanation] **3.** necessary or expected because of what has gone before [the *logical* result of one's acts] **4.** using or accustomed to use correct reasoning [a *logical* thinker] **—log′i·cal·i·ty** (-kal′ə tē), **log′i·cal·ness** *n.* **—log′i·cal·ly** *adv.*

-log·i·cal (läj′i k'l) *a suffix used to form adjectives from nouns ending in* -LOGY [biological] : also **-log·ic**

lo·gi·cian (lō jish′ən) *n.* an expert in logic

lo·gis·tics (lō jis′tiks) *n.pl.* [with sing. *v.*] [< Fr. < *logis*, lodgings < *loger*, to quarter] the branch of military science having to do with transporting, and supplying the needs of, armed forces **—lo·gis′tic, lo·gis′ti·cal** *adj.* **—lo·gis′ti·cal·ly** *adv.*

☆**log·jam** (lôg′jam′, läg′-) *n.* **1.** logs jammed together in a river, etc. **2.** an accumulation of many items to deal with [a *logjam* of orders to be filled]

log·o (lôg′ō, läg′ō; lôg′ō) *n.* shortened form of LOGOTYPE

log·o·type (lôg′ō tīp′, läg′-) *n.* [< Gr. *logos*, (see LOGIC) + -TYPE] a piece of type used for printing a company trademark, colophon, emblem, etc.

☆**log·roll** (lôg′rōl′, läg′-) *vi.* to take part in logrolling **—vt.** to get passage of (a bill) by logrolling **—log′roll′er** *n.*

☆**log·roll·ing** (-rōl′iŋ) *n.* **1.** the act of rolling logs away, as by a group clearing land **2.** mutual aid, esp. among politicians, as by voting for each other's bills **3.** *same as* BIRLING

-logue (lôg, läg) [Fr. < L. < Gr. < *logos*: see LOGIC] *a combining form meaning:* **1.** a (specified kind of) speaking or writing [monologue] **2.** a student or scholar

log·wood (lôg′wood′, läg′-) *n.* [from being imported in logs] **1.** the brownish-red wood of a Central American and West Indian tree: it yields a dye used as a stain **2.** this tree or dye

lo·gy (lō′gē) *adj.* **-gi·er, -gi·est** [< ? Du. *log*, heavy, dull] [Colloq.] dull or sluggish, as from overeating **—lo′gi·ness** *n.*

-lo·gy (lə jē) [ult. < Gr. < *logos*: see LOGIC] *a combining form meaning:* **1.** a (specified kind of) speaking [eulogy] **2.** science, doctrine, or theory of [biology, theology]

Lo·hen·grin (lō′ən grin′) *Ger. Legend* a knight of the Holy Grail, son of Parsifal

loin (loin) *n.* [< OFr. *loigne*, ult. < L. *lumbus*] **1.** [usually *pl.*] the lower part of the back on either side of the backbone between the hipbones and the ribs **2.** the front part of the hindquarters of beef, lamb, pork, etc. with the flank removed: see illustrations at BEEF and PORK **3.** [*pl.*] the hips and the lower abdomen thought of as the part of the body having to do with

physical strength and with reproduction **—gird (up) one's loins** to prepare to do something difficult

loin·cloth (loin′klôth′, -kläth′) *n.* a cloth worn about the loins, as by some tribes in warm climates

Loire (lwär) river flowing from S France north & west into the Bay of Biscay

Lo·is (lō′is) [LL. < Gr. *Lōis*] a feminine name

loi·ter (loit′ər) *vi.* [< MDu. *loteren*] **1.** to spend time idly; linger [don't *loiter* in the halls] **2.** to move slowly and lazily, with frequent pauses **—vt.** to spend (time) idly **—loi′ter·er** *n.*

SYN. **—loiter** implies either staying around a place without having anything to do there or moving along in a slow, rambling way [to *loiter* on street corners]; **dawdle** implies wasting time over trifles or taking more time to do something than is necessary [to *dawdle* over dinner]; **dally** suggests spending time in silly or pointless activity; **idle** suggests laziness or avoidance of work [to *idle* away the hours]

Lo·ki (lō′kē) *Norse Myth.* the god who constantly created discord and mischief

loll (läl) *vi.* [< MDu. *lollen*] **1.** to lean or move about in a lazy manner **2.** to hang down; droop [the dog's tongue *lolled* out] **—vt.** to let droop or hang loosely **—loll′er** *n.*

☆**lol·la·pa·loo·za, lol·la·pa·loo·sa** (läl′ə pə lōō′zə) *n.* [< ?] [Slang] something very striking or unusual

Lol·lard (läl′ərd) *n.* [< MDu. *lollaerd*, lit., a mutterer (of prayers)] any of the followers of John Wycliffe in 14th- and 15th-cent. England

lol·li·pop, lol·ly·pop (läl′ē päp′) *n.* [prob. < dial. *lolly*, the tongue + *pop*] a piece of hard candy fixed to the end of a small stick; sucker

☆**lol·ly·gag** (läl′ē gag′) *vi.* **-gagged′, -gag′ging** [< ?] [Colloq.] to waste time in silly or pointless activity

Lom·bard (läm′bärd, lum′-; -bärd) *n.* **1.** a native or inhabitant of Lombardy **2.** a member of a Germanic tribe that settled in the Po Valley **—adj.** of Lombardy or the Lombards: also **Lom·bar′dic**

Lom·bar·dy (läm′bər dē, lum′-) region of N Italy, on the border of Switzerland: chief city, Milan: see map at LIGURIA

Lombardy poplar a tall, slender poplar with branches that grow sharply upward

Lo·mé (lô mā′) capital of Togo; seaport on the Gulf of Guinea: pop. 135,000

Lo·mond (lō′mənd), **Loch** lake in WC Scotland

Lon·don (lun′dən) **1.** an administrative county in SE England, consisting of the City of London & 28 metropolitan boroughs; capital of England, the United Kingdom, & the Commonwealth **2.** this county with its suburbs: pop. 11,025,000: called *Greater London* **3.** city in SE Ontario, Canada: pop. 240,000 **4.** City of, historic center of the county of London: pop. 4,800 **—Lon′don·er** *n.*

LOMBARDY POPLAR (tree & leaves)

Lon·don (lun′dən), **Jack** 1876–1916; U.S. writer

London broil a boneless cut of beef, as of the flank, that is marinated, broiled, and served in thin slices

Lon·don·der·ry (lun′dən der′ē) seaport in NW Northern Ireland: pop. 56,000

lone (lōn) *adj.* [< ALONE] **1.** by oneself; solitary **2.** unmarried or widowed **3.** standing apart from others of its kind; isolated [a *lone* pine tree] **—see** SYN. **at** ALONE **—lone′ness** *n.*

lone·ly (lōn′lē) *adj.* **-li·er, -li·est 1.** alone; solitary [a *lonely* cottage] **2.** with few or no people [a *lonely* island] **3.** unhappy at being alone **4.** causing such a feeling [a *lonely* town] **—see** SYN. **at** ALONE **—lone′li·ly** *adv.* **—lone′li·ness** *n.*

☆**lon·er** (lō′nər) *n.* [Colloq.] one who prefers to be alone

lone·some (lōn′səm) *adj.* **1.** having or causing a lonely feeling [a *lonesome* sentry; a *lonesome* whistle] **2.** seldom used, remote, uninhabited, etc. [a *lonesome* country road] **—n.** [Colloq.] self [all by my *lonesome*] **—see** SYN. **at** ALONE **—lone′some·ly** *adv.* **—lone′some·ness** *n.*

☆**lone wolf** *same as* LONER

long[1] (lôŋ) *adj.* [OE. < IE. base *del-*, from which also comes L. *longus*] **1.** measuring much from one end or point to the other in space or time; not short or brief [a *long* trip; a *long* wait] **2.** of a specified extent in length [a foot *long*] **3.** of greater than usual or standard length, quantity, etc. [a *long* game; a *long* ton] **4.** overextended in length [the curtain is *long* for the window] **5.** taking too much time; tedious; slow **6.** extending to what is distant in space or time; far-reaching [a *long* view of the matter] **7.** large; big [*long* odds, a *long* chance] **8.** well supplied [*long* on excuses] ☆**9.** holding a supply of a commodity or security in anticipation of a rise in price **10.** requiring a relatively long time to pronounce: said of a speech sound —*adv.* **1.** for a long time [don't be gone *long*] **2.** from the beginning to the end [all day *long*] **3.** at a much earlier or a much later time than the time indicated [to stay *long* after midnight] —*n.* **1.** a variation of a clothing size longer than average for that size **2.** a long signal, syllable, etc. **3.** a long time [it won't take *long*] —**as** (or **so**) **long as 1.** during the time that **2.** seeing that; since **3.** provided that —**before long** soon —**the long and** (**the**) **short of** the whole story of in a few words; gist or point of

long² (lôŋ) *vi.* [OE. *langian* < same base as prec.] to feel a strong yearning; wish very much [to *long* to go home]

long. longitude

Long Beach seaport in SW Calif., on the Pacific: pop. 359,000

long·boat (lôŋ′bōt′) *n.* the largest boat carried on a merchant sailing ship

long·bow (-bō′) *n.* a large bow drawn by hand and shooting a long, feathered arrow: see CROSSBOW

☆**long distance** a telephone service or system for calls to distant places —**long′-dis′tance** *adj., adv.*

long division the process of dividing one number by another and putting the steps down in full

long-drawn (-drôn′) *adj.* continuing for a long time; prolonged: also **long′-drawn′-out′**

lon·gev·i·ty (län jev′ə tē, lôn-) *n.* [< L. < *longus*, LONG¹ + *aevum*, age] **1.** *a*) long life; great span of life *b*) length of life **2.** length of service

long face a glum or sad look —**long′-faced′** *adj.*

Long·fel·low (lôŋ′fel′ō), **Henry Wads·worth** (wädz′wərth′) 1807–82; U.S. poet

☆**long·hair** (lôŋ′her′) *adj.* [Colloq.] designating or of intellectuals or their tastes; specif., preferring classical music to jazz or popular tunes: also **long′haired′** —*n.* [Colloq.] **1.** an intellectual **2.** *same as* HIPPIE

long·hand (-hand′) *n.* ordinary handwriting, with the words written out in full

long-head·ed, long·head·ed (-hed′id) *adj.* **1.** having a long head **2.** shrewd or sensible —**long′-head′ed·ness** *n.*

long·horn (-hôrn′) *n.* ☆any of a breed of long-horned cattle formerly raised in great numbers in the Southwest

long·ing (-iŋ) *n.* strong desire; yearning —*adj.* feeling or showing a yearning —**long′ing·ly** *adv.*

long·ish (-ish) *adj.* somewhat long

Long Island island in southeast N.Y., between Long Island Sound & the Atlantic: pop. 7,115,000

Long Island Sound arm of the Atlantic, between N Long Island & S Conn.

LONGHORN
(to 5 ft. high at shoulder)

lon·gi·tude (län′jə tōōd′, -tyōōd′) *n.* [< L. *longitudo* < *longus*, LONG¹] distance east or west on the earth's surface, measured as an arc of the equator (in degrees up to 180° or by the difference in time) between the meridian passing through a particular place and a standard or prime meridian, usually the one passing through Greenwich, England [Chicago is at 87° west *longitude*]

lon·gi·tu·di·nal (län′jə tōōd′'n əl, -tyōōd′-) *adj.* **1.** of or in length **2.** running or placed lengthwise **3.** of longitude —**lon′gi·tu′di·nal·ly** *adv.*

☆**long johns** [Colloq.] long underwear: also **long′ies, n.pl.**

long jump a contest in track and field that is a jump for distance rather than height

☆**long·leaf pine** (lôŋ′lēf′) a pine native to the southern U.S., having very long needles and valued for its hard wood

long-lived (lôŋ′līvd′, -livd′) *adj.* living or lasting for a long time

long-play·ing (lôŋ′plā′iŋ) *adj.* designating or of a phonograph

record with very narrow grooves, for playing at 33⅓ revolutions per minute

long-range (-rānj′) *adj.* **1.** having a range of great distance [*long-range* guns] **2.** taking the future into consideration [*long-range* plans]

long·shore·man (-shôr′mən) *n., pl.* -**men** [(*a*)*longshore* + *man*] a person who works on the waterfront loading and unloading ships

long shot 1. [Colloq.] *a*) a betting choice that has little chance of winning and, hence, carries great odds *b*) any venture that is not likely to succeed, but that will be very rewarding if it should **2.** *Motion Pictures, TV* a scene shot with the camera at some distance from the action —☆**not by a long shot** [Colloq.] not at all

long-sight·ed (-sīt′id) *adj. same as* FARSIGHTED —**long′-sight′ed·ly** *adv.* —**long′sight′ed·ness** *n.*

long-stand·ing (-stan′diŋ) *adj.* having continued for a long time

long-suf·fer·ing (-suf′ər iŋ) *adj.* bearing injuries, insults, trouble, etc. patiently for a long time —*n.* long and patient endurance of injuries, insults, trouble, etc. —**long′-suf′fer·ing·ly** *adv.*

long suit 1. the suit in which a card player holds the most cards **2.** something at which one excels

long-term (-turm′) *adj.* **1.** for or extending over a long time **2.** designating or of a loan, capital gain, etc. taking place over a relatively long period

long-time (-tīm′) *adj.* over a long period of time [a *longtime* friend]

long ton the British ton, equal to 2,240 pounds

long-waist·ed (lôŋ′wās′tid) *adj.* having a low waistline

long·ways (-wāz′) *adv. same as* LENGTHWISE: also **long′wise′** (-wīz′)

long-wind·ed (-win′did) *adj.* **1.** not getting out of breath easily **2.** *a*) speaking or writing at great, often boring length *b*) so long as to be boring: said of a speech, book, etc. —**long′-wind′ed·ly** *adv.* —**long′-wind′ed·ness** *n.*

loo¹ (lōō) *n.* [< Fr. *lanturelu*] a card game played for a pool into which forfeits are paid

loo² (lōō) *n.* [< Fr. *lieux*, short for *les lieux d'aisances*, lit., places of conveniences] [Brit. Slang] a toilet

look (look) *vi.* [OE. *locian*] **1.** to see **2.** *a*) to direct one's eyes in order to see *b*) to direct one's attention [just *look* at the trouble you've caused] **3.** to search [*look* through your pockets] **4.** to appear; seem [he *looks* sick] **5.** to be facing in a specified direction [the hotel *looks* to the west] —*vt.* **1.** to direct one's eyes on [*look* him in the face] **2.** to express by one's looks [to *look* one's disgust] **3.** to have the appearance of; seem to be [he *looks* his age; she *looks* the part] **4.** to expect (followed by an infinitive) [I *look* to arrive by noon] —*n.* **1.** the act of looking; glance **2.** outward appearance; aspect [the *look* of a beggar] **3.** [Colloq.] *a*) [*usually pl.*] appearance; the way something seems to be [from the *looks* of things] *b*) [*pl.*] personal appearance, esp. of a pleasing nature [to have *looks* and youth] —*interj.* **1.** see! **2.** pay attention! —see SYN. at APPEARANCE —**look after** to take care of —**look alive** (or **sharp**)! [Colloq.] be alert! —**look down on** (or **upon**) to regard with contempt; despise —**look for 1.** to search for **2.** to expect —**look forward to** to anticipate, esp. eagerly —**look in** (**on**) to pay a brief visit (to) —**look into** to examine carefully; investigate —**look on 1.** to be an observer or spectator **2.** to consider; regard —**look** (**like**) **oneself** to seem in normal health, spirits, etc. —**look out** to be on the watch; be careful —**look out for 1.** to be cautious about **2.** to take care of —**look over** to examine; inspect —**look to 1.** to take care of **2.** to rely upon —**look up 1.** to search for in a reference book, etc. **2.** [Colloq.] to pay a visit to **3.** [Colloq.] to get better; improve —**look up and down 1.** to search everywhere **2.** to look at very carefully; examine closely —**look up to** to admire —**look′er** *n.*

look·er-on (look′ər än′) *n., pl.* **look′ers-on′** an observer or spectator; onlooker

look-in (look′in′) *n.* **1.** a quick glance **2.** a brief visit

looking glass a (glass) mirror

look·out (look′out′) *n.* **1.** a careful watching for someone or something [she's on the *lookout* for a new job] **2.** a place for keeping watch, esp. a high place **3.** a person who keeps watch; guard **4.** [Colloq.] concern; worry [that's your *lookout*]

Lookout Mountain mountain ridge in Tenn., Ga., & Ala.: the section near Chattanooga was the site of a Civil War battle (1863) in which Union forces were victorious

look-see (-sē′) *n.* [Slang] a quick look or inspection

loom¹ (lōōm) *n.* [OE. (*ge*)*loma*, tool, utensil] a machine for weaving thread or yarn into cloth —*vt.* to weave on a loom

loom² (lōōm) *vi.* [< ?] to appear, take shape, or come in sight indistinctly, esp. in a large or threatening form [the peak *loomed* up before us, disaster *loomed* ahead]

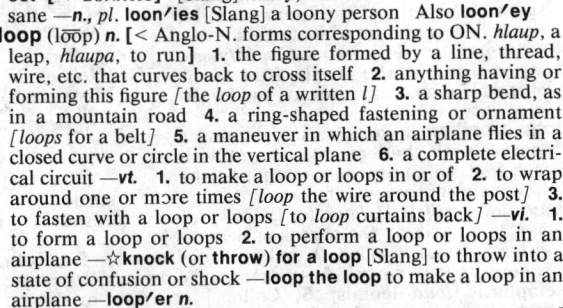

LOOM

loon¹ (lōōn) *n.* [earlier *loom* < ON. *lomr*] a diving bird that eats fish and has a sharp bill and webbed feet: noted for its weird cry

loon² (lōōn) *n.* [Scot. *loun* < ?] 1. a clumsy, stupid person 2. a crazy person

loon·y (lōō'nē) *adj.* **loon'i·er, loon'i·est** [< LUNATIC] [Slang] crazy; insane —*n., pl.* **loon'ies** [Slang] a loony person Also **loon'ey**

loop (lōōp) *n.* [< Anglo-N. forms corresponding to ON. *hlaup*, a leap, *hlaupa*, to run] 1. the figure formed by a line, thread, wire, etc. that curves back to cross itself 2. anything having or forming this figure [the *loop* of a written *l*] 3. a sharp bend, as in a mountain road 4. a ring-shaped fastening or ornament [*loops* for a belt] 5. a maneuver in which an airplane flies in a closed curve or circle in the vertical plane 6. a complete electrical circuit —*vt.* 1. to make a loop or loops in or of 2. to wrap around one or more times [*loop* the wire around the post] 3. to fasten with a loop or loops [to *loop* curtains back] —*vi.* 1. to form a loop or loops 2. to perform a loop or loops in an airplane —☆**knock (or throw) for a loop** [Slang] to throw into a state of confusion or shock —**loop the loop** to make a loop in an airplane —**loop'er** *n.*

loop·hole (lōōp'hōl') *n.* [prob. < MDu. *lupen*, to peer + HOLE] 1. a hole or narrow slit in the wall of a fort, etc. for looking or shooting through 2. a way of getting around something required or forbidden as by law or rule

loose (lōōs) *adj.* [< ON. *lauss*: for IE. base see LOSE] 1. not confined or tied up; free [the dog is *loose*] 2. not put up in a special package or box [*loose* salt] 3. readily available [*loose* cash] 4. not firmly fastened down or in [a *loose* tooth; a *loose* wheel] 5. not taut; slack 6. not tight [*loose* clothing] 7. not packed down or compactly constructed [*loose* soil, a *loose* frame] 8. not restrained; irresponsible [*loose* talk] 9. not precise; inexact [a *loose* translation] 10. sexually immoral; lewd [to lead a *loose* life] 11. *a)* not strained or hard [a *loose* cough] *b)* moving freely or too freely [*loose* bowels] 12. [Colloq.] relaxed; easy —*adv.* loosely; in a loose manner [the coat hung *loose*] —*vt.* **loosed, loos'ing** 1. to make loose; specif., *a)* to set free; unbind [we *loosed* the wild horse] *b)* to make less rigid; relax 2. to let fly; release [he *loosed* the arrow] —*vi.* to loose something or become loose —**break loose** to free oneself; escape —**cast loose** to untie or unfasten —**let loose (with)** to release; let go —**on the loose** 1. not confined or bound; free 2. [Colloq.] having fun in a free, uncontrolled manner —**set (or turn) loose** to make free; release —**loose'ly** *adv.* —**loose'ness** *n.*

loose ends minor bits of unfinished business —**at loose ends** disorganized, uncertain, unemployed, etc.

loose-joint·ed (lōōs'join'tid) *adj.* 1. having loose joints 2. moving freely; limber —**loose'-joint'ed·ly** *adv.* —**loose'-joint'ed·ness** *n.*

loose-leaf (-lēf') *adj.* having or designed to have leaves, or sheets, that can easily be removed or replaced [a *loose-leaf* notebook]

loos·en (lōōs''n) *vt., vi.* to make or become loose or looser —☆**loosen up** [Colloq.] 1. to talk freely 2. to give money generously 3. to relax —**loos'en·er** *n.*

loose-strife (-strīf') *n.* [transl. of L. *lysimachia* < Gr. < *lyein*, to slacken + *machē*, battle] 1. a plant with leafy stems and loose spikes of white, rose, or yellow flowers 2. a plant (**purple loosestrife**) with spikes of purple flowers

loose-tongued (-tuŋd') *adj.* talking too much; careless or thoughtless about what one says

loot (lōōt) *n.* [Hindi *lūt* < Sans. *luṇṭ*, to rob] 1. goods stolen or taken by force; plunder; spoils 2. [Slang] money, gifts, etc. —*vt., vi.* to rob or plunder —**loot'er** *n.*

lop¹ (läp) *vt.* **lopped, lop'ping** [OE. *loppian*, prob. < Scand.] 1. to trim (a tree, etc.) by cutting off branches or twigs 2. to remove by or as by cutting off (usually with *off*) [to *lop* off the dead branches] —**lop'per** *n.*

lop² (läp) *vi.* **lopped, lop'ping** [prob. akin to LOB] 1. to hang down loosely 2. to move in a halting way —*adj.* hanging down loosely [*lop* ears]

lope (lōp) *vi.* **loped, lop'ing** [< ON. *hlaupa*, to leap] to move with a long, swinging stride or in an easy canter —*vt.* to cause to lope —*n.* a long, easy, swinging stride —**lop'er** *n.*

lop-eared (läp'ird') *adj.* having ears that droop or hang down

lo·pho·phore (lō'fə fôr') *n.* [< Gr. *lophos*, crest + -PHORE] a usually horseshoe-shaped ring of threadlike tentacles around the mouth of certain water animals, as in brachiopods

lop·sid·ed (läp'sīd'id) *adj.* 1. heavier, bigger, or lower on one side than on the other 2. not balanced; uneven —**lop'sid'ed·ly** *adv.* —**lop'sid'ed·ness** *n.*

lo·qua·cious (lō kwā'shəs) *adj.* [< L. *loquax* < *loqui*, to speak] very talkative; fond of talking —see SYN. at TALKATIVE —**lo·qua'cious·ly** *adv.* —**lo·qua'cious·ness** *n.*

lo·quac·i·ty (lō kwas'ə tē) *n.* a being loquacious; tendency to talk too much

Lo·rain (lô rān') [ult. after LORRAINE (France)] city in N Ohio, on Lake Erie: pop. 78,000

Lor·an (lôr'an) *n.* [< *Lo*(ng) *Ra*(nge) *N*(avigation)] [*also* l-] a system by which a ship or aircraft can determine its position by the difference in time between radio signals sent from two or more known stations

lord (lôrd) *n.* [OE. *hlaford* < *hlaf*, loaf + *weard*, keeper] 1. a person having great power and authority; ruler; master 2. the head of a feudal estate 3. [L-] *a)* God *b)* Jesus Christ 4. in Great Britain, *a)* a nobleman holding the rank of baron, viscount, earl, or marquess; member of the House of Lords *b)* a man who by courtesy or because of his office is given the title of Lord, as a bishop or the son of a duke *c)* [L-] the title of a lord 5. [L-] [*pl.*] the House of Lords in the British Parliament —*interj.* [*often* L-] an exclamation of surprise or irritation —**lord it (over)** to act in a haughty, scornful way (toward)

lord·ly (lôrd'lē) *adj.* **-li·er, -li·est** of, like, characteristic of, or suitable to a lord; specif., *a)* noble; grand *b)* overly proud; scornful —*adv.* in a lordly way —**lord'li·ness** *n.*

lor·do·sis (lôr dō'sis) *n.* [ModL. < Gr. < *lordos*, bent backward] forward curvature of the spine, producing a hollow in the back

Lord's day Sunday

lord·ship (lôrd'ship') *n.* 1. the rank or authority of a lord 2. rule; dominion 3. [*also* L-] a title used in speaking of or to a lord: with *his* or *your*

Lord's Prayer the prayer beginning *Our Father*, which Jesus taught his disciples: Matt. 6:9–13

lords spiritual the archbishops and bishops who are members of the British House of Lords

Lord's Supper 1. *same as* LAST SUPPER 2. Holy Communion; Eucharist

lords temporal those members of the British House of Lords who are not clergymen

lore (lôr) *n.* [OE. *lar*: for IE. base see LEARN] knowledge or learning; specif., all the knowledge of a particular group or having to do with a particular subject, esp. that of a traditional nature [Indian *lore*; bird *lore*]

Lor·e·lei (lôr'ə lī') [G.] *German Legend* a siren whose singing lured sailors to shipwreck on rocks in the Rhine

Lo·ret·ta (lô ret'ə, lə-) [dim. of LAURA] a feminine name

lor·gnette (lôr nyet') *n.* [Fr. < *lorgner*, to spy, peep < OFr. *lorgne*, squinting] a pair of eyeglasses, or opera glasses, attached to a handle

lo·ris (lôr'is) *n., pl.* **lo'ris** [ModL. < Fr. < Du. *loer*, a clown] a small, slow-moving, large-eyed Asiatic lemur that lives in trees and is active at night

LORGNETTE

lorn (lôrn) *adj.* [ME., pp. of *losen*, to LOSE] 1. [Obs.] lost; ruined 2. [Archaic] forsaken, forlorn, or desolate

Lor·raine (lô rān'; *Fr.* lô ren') [Fr.] 1. a feminine name 2. former province of NE France: see ALSACE-LORRAINE

lor·ry (lôr′ē, lär′-) *n., pl.* **-ries** [prob. < dial. *lurry, lorry,* to tug] **1.** a low, flat wagon without sides **2.** [Brit.] a motor truck

lo·ry (lôr′ē) *n., pl.* **-ries** [Malay *lūrī*] a small, brightly colored parrot native to Australia and nearby islands

Los Al·a·mos (lôs al′ə mōs′, läs) [Sp., the poplars] town in north central N. Mex.: center for atomic research

Los An·gel·es (lôs an′jə ləs, läs; aŋ′gə ləs, -lēz′) [Sp., lit., the angels] city & seaport on the SW coast of Calif.: pop. 2,816,000 (met. area 7,032,000)

lose (lo͞oz) *vt.* **lost, los′ing** [< OE. *losian,* to be lost + *leosan,* to lose < IE. base *leu-,* to cut off] **1.** to bring to ruin or destruction [the ship was lost in a storm] **2.** to become unable to find; mislay [I lost my key] **3.** to have taken from one by accident, death, etc. [she lost a brother in the war] **4.** to get rid of [dieting to lose weight] **5.** to fail to keep or maintain [to lose one's temper, to lose one's job] **6.** *a)* to fail to see, hear, or understand [she did not lose a word of the lecture] *b)* to fail to keep in sight, mind, etc. **7.** to fail to have, get, take, etc.; miss [I lost my chance] **8.** to fail to win [to lose a game] **9.** to cause the loss of [it lost him his job] **10.** to wander from and not be able to find [she lost her way in the woods] **11.** to confuse, bewilder, or alienate [his explanation lost me completely] **12.** to waste [to lose time] **13.** to leave behind; outdistance [the rabbit ran through brambles and lost the dogs] **14.** to absorb or preoccupy [to lose in reverie] **15.** to go slower by [my watch lost a minute] —*vi.* **1.** to suffer loss **2.** to be defeated in a contest, etc. —**lose oneself 1.** to lose one's way; become confused **2.** to become so absorbed in something as to notice nothing else —☆**lose out** [Colloq.] to fail; be unsuccessful —☆**lose out on** [Colloq.] to fail to win, gain, or take advantage of —**los′·a·ble** *adj.*

los·er (lo͞o′zər) *n.* **1.** one that loses; esp., [Colloq.] one that seems doomed to lose or be unsuccessful **2.** a person who reacts to defeat in a specified way [a poor loser] **3.** [Slang] a person who has been imprisoned for crime a (specified) number of times [a three-time loser]

los·ing (-ziŋ) *n.* [pl.] losses by gambling —*adj.* **1.** that loses [a losing team] **2.** resulting in loss [a losing proposition]

loss (lôs, läs) *n.* [< ? OE. *los,* ruin] **1.** a losing or being lost **2.** the damage, disadvantage, etc. caused by losing something [the death of the president was a great loss to the country] **3.** the person, thing, or amount lost [the company's losses last year were great] **4.** *a)* [pl.] military personnel lost in combat by death, injury, or capture *b)* [pl.] ships, aircraft, etc. lost in battle —**at a loss 1.** puzzled or uncertain **2.** so as to lose money [to operate a business at a loss] —**at a loss to** not able to; uncertain how to

☆**loss leader** any article that a store sells cheaply or below cost in order to attract customers

lost (lôst, läst) *pt. & pp. of* LOSE —*adj.* **1.** destroyed; ruined [a ship lost at sea] **2.** not to be found; missing **3.** no longer held, possessed, seen, heard, or known [a lost love; a person lost in a crowd] **4.** not gained or won **5.** having wandered from the way **6.** bewildered; ill at ease [she feels lost in such company] **7.** not used well; wasted [lost time] —**lost in** absorbed in —**lost on** without effect on —**lost to 1.** no longer in the possession of **2.** no longer available to **3.** having no sense of (shame, right, etc.)

☆**lost cause** an undertaking that has failed or is sure to fail

lot (lät) *n.* [OE. *hlot:* for IE. base see CLOSE[2]] **1.** any of a number of slips of paper, counters, etc. drawn from at random to decide a matter by chance [the use of such a method [to choose men by lot] **3.** the decision arrived at by this means **4.** what one receives as the result of such a decision; share **5.** one's fate in life; fortune [her unhappy lot] **6.** a plot of ground [a lot to build a house on] **7.** *a)* a number of persons or things regarded as a group [the best of the lot] *b)* a quantity of material processed or manufactured at the same time **8.** [often pl.] [Colloq.] a great number or amount [a lot of cars; lots of money] **9.** [Colloq.] sort (of person) [he's a bad lot] ☆**10.** a motion-picture studio —*adv.* very much [a lot richer]: also **lots** —*vt.* **lot′ted, lot′ting** to divide into lots —*vi.* to draw or cast lots —see SYN. at FATE —**cast (or throw) in one's lot with** to take one's chances along with —**draw (or cast) lots** to decide an issue by using lots —**the lot** [Colloq.] the entire amount or number

Lot (lät) *Bible* Abraham's nephew, who, warned by angels, fled from Sodom: his wife looked back to see it destroyed and was turned into a pillar of salt: Gen. 19:1–26

loth (lōth) *adj. alt. sp. of* LOATH

Lo·thar·i·o (lō ther′ē ō′) *n., pl.* **-i·os′** [after the young rake in a play by Nicholas Rowe (1674–1718)] [*often* l-] a lighthearted young man who goes about seducing women; roué; rake

lo·tion (lō′shən) *n.* [< L. < pp. of *lavare,* to wash: see LATHER] a liquid preparation used, as on the skin, for washing, soothing, healing, etc.

lot·ter·y (lät′ər ē) *n., pl.* **-ter·ies** [< MFr. < MDu. < *lot,* LOT] **1.** a form of gambling in which people buy numbered chances on prizes, the winning numbers being drawn by lot **2.** anything in which the result is decided by chance

lot·to (lät′ō) *n.* [It. < Fr. < MDu. *lot,* LOT] a game of chance played with cards having squares numbered in rows: counters are placed on the numbered squares corresponding to numbers that are drawn by lot

lo·tus, lo·tos (lōt′əs) *n.* [L. < Gr. *lōtos* < Heb. *lōt*] **1.** *Gr. Legend* a plant whose fruit was supposed to make those who ate it dreamy and forgetful **2.** any of several tropical African and Asiatic waterlilies, as the **white lotus** of Egypt **3.** a plant of the legume family, with yellow, purple, or white flowers

lo·tus-eat·er (-ēt′ər) *n.* in the *Odyssey,* one of a people who ate the fruit of the lotus and became lazy, dreamy, and forgetful of duty

lotus position in yoga, an upright sitting posture with the legs crossed and with each foot, sole upturned, resting on the upper thigh of the opposite leg

LOTUS (sense 2)

loud (loud) *adj.* [OE. *hlud:* for IE. base see LIST[1]] **1.** striking the organs of hearing with force: said of sound **2.** making a loud sound [a loud bell] **3.** noisy [a loud party] **4.** so strong as to demand attention; emphatic [loud denials] **5.** [Colloq.] too bright or showy; flashy [a loud pattern] —*adv.* in a loud manner —**loud′ish** *adj.* —**loud′ly** *adv.* —**loud′ness** *n.*

loud·mouthed (loud′moutht′, -mouthd′) *adj.* talking in a loud, irritating voice —**loud′mouth′** *n.*

loud·speak·er (-spē′kər) *n.* a device that changes electric current into sound waves and amplifies this sound

Lou·is (lo͞o′ē; *for 1, usually* lo͞o′is; *Fr.* lwē) [Fr., ult. < OHG. *Hluodowig* < Gmc. bases meaning "famous in war"] **1.** a masculine name: dim. *Lou, Louie* **2.** **Louis XIV** 1638–1715; king of France (1643–1715) **3.** **Louis XV** 1710–74; king of France (1715–74): great-grandson of *prec.* **4.** **Louis XVI** 1754–93; king of France (1774–92): guillotined: grandson of *prec.*

lou·is d'or (lo͞o′ē dôr′) [Fr., gold louis: after *Louis* XIII (1601–43), king of France] **1.** an old French gold coin of varying value **2.** a later French gold coin worth 20 francs

Lou·ise (lo͞o wēz′) [Fr., fem. of LOUIS] **1.** a feminine name: dim. *Lou;* var. *Louisa* **2.** **Lake,** small lake in SW Alberta, Canada

Lou·i·si·an·a (lo͞o wē′zē an′ə, lo͞o′ə zē-) [< Fr., ult. after LOUIS XIV] Southern State of the U.S., on the Gulf of Mexico: 48,523 sq. mi.; pop. 3,643,000; cap. Baton Rouge: abbrev. **La.,** **LA** —**Lou·i′si·an′i·an, Lou·i′si·an′an** *adj., n.*

☆**Louisiana Purchase** land bought by the U.S. from France in 1803: it extended from the Mississippi to the Rocky Mountains & from the Gulf of Mexico to Canada

Louis Napoleon (surname *Bonaparte*) 1808–73; president of France (1848–52) &, as Napoleon III, emperor (1852–70): deposed: nephew of NAPOLEON I

Lou·is·ville (lo͞o′ē vil; *locally* lo͞o′ə vəl) [after LOUIS XVI] city in N Ky., on the Ohio River: pop. 361,000 (met. area 827,000)

LOUISIANA PURCHASE

lounge (lounj) *vi.* **lounged, loung′ing** [Scot. dial. < ? *lungis,* laggard] **1.** to stand, move, sit, etc. in a relaxed or lazy way **2.** to spend time in idleness —*vt.* to spend (time) by lounging [to lounge the summer away] —*n.* **1.** an act or time of lounging **2.** a room, as in a hotel, with comfortable furniture and, often, an adjoining restroom **3.** a couch or sofa, esp. one without a back but with a headrest at one end —**loung′er** *n.*

lour (lour) *vi., n. same as* LOWER[2]

Lourdes (loord, loordz; *Fr.* lo͞ord) town in SW France: site of a famous Catholic shrine

louse (lous; *also, for v.,* louz) *n., pl.* **lice** [OE. *lus* (pl. *lys*)] **1.** *a)* a small, wingless insect that lives in the hair or on the skin of man and some other mammals and sucks their blood *b)* any of various arthropods that suck blood or juice from other animals or plants **2.** any of various other insects, arachnids, etc. that are not parasitic, as the wood louse **3.** *pl.* **lous′es** [Slang] a person thought of as mean, disgusting, etc. —*vt.* **loused, lous′ing** [Rare] to delouse —☆**louse up** [Slang] to botch; spoil; ruin

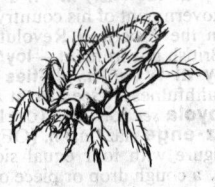

LOUSE
(to ¹/₄ in. long)

lous·y (lou′zē) *adj.* **lous′i·er, lous′i·est 1.** infested with lice **2.** [Slang] dirty, disgusting, or contemptible [a *lousy* trick to play on a person] ☆**3.** [Slang] poor; inferior [a *lousy* golfer] ☆**4.** [Slang] oversupplied (*with*) [*lousy* with money] —**lous′i·ly** *adv.* —**lous′i·ness** *n.*

lout (lout) *n.* [prob. < ME. *lutien,* to lurk < OE. *lutian:* for IE. base see LITTLE] a clumsy, stupid fellow; boor —**lout′ish** *adj.* — **lout′ish·ly** *adv.* —**lout′ish·ness** *n.*

lou·ver (lo͞o′vər) *n.* [MFr. *lover* < MDu. *love,* theater gallery: for IE. base see LEAF] **1.** an opening fitted with sloping slats that let in light and air but keep out rain **2.** any of these slats: also **louver board 3.** any set of slats or fins used to control the amount of air or light that enters Also **lou′vre** —**lou′vered** *adj.*

Lou·vre (lo͞o′vrə, lo͞ov′; *Fr.* lo͞o′vr′) ancient royal palace in Paris, now an art museum

lov·a·ble (luv′ə b'l) *adj.* that deserves to be loved; easily loved; endearing: also sp. **love′a·ble** —**lov′a·bil′i·ty, lov′a·ble·ness** *n.* —**lov′a·bly** *adv.*

love (luv) *n.* [OE. *lufu:* see BELIEVE] **1.** a deep and tender affection for or attachment or devotion to someone [a father's *love* for his child] **2.** good will toward others [her *love* for all mankind] **3.** *a)* a strong liking for or interest in something [a *love* of music] *b)* the object of such liking **4.** *a)* a strong, usually passionate, affection of one person for another *b)* the object of this; sweetheart **5.** sexual passion or sexual intercourse **6.** [L-] Cupid **7.** *Tennis* a score of zero —*vt.* **loved, lov′ing 1.** to feel love for **2.** to show love for by hugging, kissing, etc. **3.** to take great pleasure in [to *love* books] **4.** to benefit from [plants *love* light] —*vi.* to feel the emotion of love —**fall in love (with)** to begin to feel love (for) —**for the love of** for the sake of —**in love** feeling love —**make love 1.** to hug, kiss, etc. as lovers do **2.** to have sexual intercourse

SYN. —**love** implies intense fondness or deep devotion and may apply to various relationships or objects [sexual *love,* brotherly *love,* *love* of one's work, etc.]; **affection** suggests warm, tender feelings, usually not as powerful or as deep as those implied by **love** [he has no *affection* for children]; **attachment** implies connection by ties of affection, loyalty, devotion, etc. and may be felt for nonliving things as well as for people [an *attachment* to an old hat]; **infatuation** implies a passion or affection that is foolish or shows poor judgment, often one that lasts only a short time [an elderly man's *infatuation* with a young girl]

love affair a romantic relationship between two people who are not married to each other

love apple [Archaic] the tomato

love·bird (luv′burd′) *n.* any of various small parrots, often kept as cage birds: the mates seem to show fondness for each other

Love·lace (luv′lās′), **Richard** 1618–58; Eng. poet

love·less (-lis) *adj.* without love; specif., *a)* feeling no love *b)* not loved —**love′less·ly** *adv.* —**love′less·ness** *n.*

love-lies-bleed·ing (luv′lĭz′blēd′iŋ) *n.* a cultivated amaranth with drooping spikes of small, red flowers

love·lorn (-lôrn′) *adj.* deserted by one's sweetheart; sad because one is not loved in return

love·ly (-lē) *adj.* **-li·er, -li·est** having qualities that inspire love, admiration, etc.; specif., *a)* beautiful *b)* very pleasing in character; good, noble, gracious, etc. *c)* [Colloq.] highly enjoyable [a *lovely* party] —*n., pl.* **-lies** [Colloq.] a beautiful young woman —**see SYN·** at BEAUTIFUL —**love′li·ly** *adv.* —**love′li·ness** *n.*

love·mak·ing (-mā′kiŋ) *n.* the act of making love

love potion a magic drink supposed to make the drinker feel love for a certain person

lov·er (luv′ər) *n.* a person who loves; specif., *a)* a sweetheart *b)* [*pl.*] a couple in love with each other *c)* a partner, esp. the male partner, in a love affair *d)* a person who greatly enjoys some (specified) thing [a *lover* of jazz] —**lov′er·ly** *adj., adv.*

love seat a small sofa seating two persons

love·sick (-sik′) *adj.* **1.** so much in love as to be unable to act normally **2.** expressive of such a condition [a *lovesick* song] — **love′sick′ness** *n.*

lov·ing (luv′iŋ) *adj.* feeling or showing love [a *loving* parent] — **lov′ing·ly** *adv.* —**lov′ing·ness** *n.*

loving cup a large drinking cup with two handles, formerly used at banquets: now often given as a trophy in sports

lov·ing-kind·ness (-kīnd′nis) *n.* kindness resulting from or expressing love

low¹ (lō) *adj.* [ME. *lah* < ON. *lagr:* for IE. base see LIE¹] **1.** *a)* not high or tall [a *low* building] *b)* not far above the ground [*low* clouds] **2.** below the surrounding surface or normal elevation [*low* land] **3.** of little depth; shallow [the river is *low*] **4.** of little quantity, degree, value, etc. [a *low* cost] **5.** of less than normal height, quantity, degree, etc. [*low* voltage] **6.** below others in order, position, rating, etc. [*low* marks in school] **7.** near the horizon [the sun is *low*] **8.** near the equator [*low* latitudes] **9.** exposing the neck and shoulders [a dress with a *low* neckline] **10.** in hiding [stay *low*] **11.** deep [a *low* bow] **12.** lacking energy; weak [the patient is very *low* today] **13.** sad or gloomy; melancholy [in *low* spirits] **14.** not of high rank; humble [a man of *low* birth] **15.** vulgar; undignified [*low* jokes] **16.** mean; contemptible [a *low* trick] **17.** unfavorable [to have a *low* opinion of someone] **18.** having less than a normal amount of some usual element [*low* in calories] **19.** not advanced in evolution, development, etc. [a *low* form of plant life] **20.** relatively recent [a manuscript of a *low* date] ☆**21.** designating or of the gear ratio of a motor vehicle transmission which produces the lowest speed and greatest power **22.** *a)* not well supplied with; short (*on*) [*low* on fuel] *b)* [Colloq.] short of ready cash **23.** *a)* not loud [speak in a *low* voice] *b)* deep in pitch [the *low* tones of a bass] **24.** *Phonet.* produced with the tongue held low in the mouth: said of some vowels, as (ä) —*adv.* **1.** in, to, or toward a low position, level, etc. [throw the ball *low*] **2.** in a low manner **3.** quietly; softly [speak *low*] **4.** with a deep pitch —*n.* something low; specif., ☆*a)* low gear (see *adj.* 21), or a similar arrangement in an automatic transmission *b)* a low level, point, degree, etc. [the stock market *low* for the day] ☆*c) Meteorol.* an area of low barometric pressure —**see SYN·** at BASE² —**lay low 1.** to cause to fall by hitting **2.** to overcome or kill —**lie low** ☆**1.** to keep oneself hidden ☆**2.** to wait patiently for an opportunity —**low′ness** *n.*

low² (lō) *vi.* [OE. *hlowan:* for IE. base see CLAMOR] to make the characteristic sound of a cow; moo —*vt.* to express by lowing — *n.* the characteristic sound of a cow

low·born (lō′bôrn′) *adj.* of humble birth

low·boy (-boi′) *n.* ☆a chest of drawers mounted on short legs to about the height of a table

low·bred (-bred′) *adj.* having bad manners; vulgar; rude

☆**low·brow** (-brou′) *n.* [Colloq.] a person with little interest in intellectual matters —*adj.* [Colloq.] of or for a lowbrow

☆**low-cal** (-kal′) *adj.* producing few calories in the body [a *low-cal* dessert]

Low Church that group in the Anglican Church which attaches little importance to the priesthood and to traditional rituals, doctrines, etc. —**Low′-Church′** *adj.*

low comedy comedy, such as burlesque and slapstick, that gets its effect mainly from action and situation rather than from witty dialogue and characterization

Low Countries the Netherlands, Belgium, & Luxembourg

☆**low-down** (lō′doun′; *for adj.* -doun′) *n.* [Slang] the important facts; esp., secret information (with *the*) —*adj.* [Colloq.] mean; contemptible; nasty

Low·ell (lō′əl) [after F.C. *Lowell* (1775–1817), industrialist] city in NE Mass.: pop. 94,000

Low·ell (lō′əl) **1. Amy,** 1874–1925; U.S. poet **2. James Russell,** 1819–91; U.S. poet, essayist, & editor **3. Robert,** 1917–77; U.S. poet

low·er¹ (lō′ər) *compar. of* LOW¹ —*adj.* **1.** below or farther down in place, rank, dignity, etc. [a *lower* berth; the *lower* baseball leagues] **2.** less in quantity, value, intensity, etc. [a light of lower wattage] **3.** farther south, closer to the mouth of a river, etc. [the lower Mississippi] **4.** [L-] *Geol.* earlier: used of a division of a period —*vt.* **1.** to let or put down [lower the window] **2.** to reduce in height, amount, value, etc. [to lower prices] **3.** to weaken or lessen [to lower one's resistance] **4.** to bring down in respect, dignity, etc.; demean; degrade [he lowered himself by accepting a bribe] **5.** to reduce (a sound) in volume or in pitch —*vi.* to become lower; sink; fall

low·er² (lou′ər) *vi.* [ME. *louren*] **1.** to scowl or frown **2.** to appear dark and threatening —*n.* a frowning or threatening look

Lower California *same as* BAJA CALIFORNIA

lower case [see CASE², *n.* 6] small-letter type used in printing, as distinguished from capital letters (upper case) —**low′er-case′** *adj.* —**low′er-case′** *vt.* **-cased′, -cas′ing**

lower class the social class below the middle class; working class, or proletariat

☆**low·er·class·man** (lō′ər klas′mən) *n., pl.* **-men** a student who is a freshman or sophomore

Lower House [often l- h-] in a legislature having two branches, the branch that is larger and over which the voters have more control, as the U.S. House of Representatives

low·er·ing (lou′ər iŋ) *adj.* **1.** scowling; frowning darkly **2.** dark, as if about to rain or snow —**low′er·ing·ly** *adv.*

low·er·most (lō′ər mōst′) *adj.* lowest

lower world *same as* NETHER WORLD

lowest common denominator *same as* LEAST COMMON DENOMINATOR

lowest common multiple *same as* LEAST COMMON MULTIPLE

low frequency any radio frequency between 30 and 300 kilohertz

Low German 1. *same as* PLATTDEUTSCH **2.** the West Germanic languages other than High German, including Plattdeutsch, English, Dutch, Frisian, etc.

low-grade (lō′grād′) *adj.* **1.** of inferior quality **2.** of low degree [a low-grade infection]

low-key (-kē′) *adj.* of low intensity, tone, etc.; subdued or restrained [a low-key advertising campaign]: also **low′-keyed′**

low·land (lō′lənd; *also, for n.,* -land′) *n.* land that is below the level of the surrounding land —*adj.* of, in, or from such a region —**the Lowlands** lowland region in SC Scotland —**low′land·er, Low′land·er** *n.*

Low Latin nonclassical, esp. medieval, Latin

low·ly (-lē) *adj.* **-li·er, -li·est 1.** of or suited to a low position or rank [a lowly job] **2.** humble; meek [the lowly manner of the slave] —*adv.* **1.** humbly; meekly **2.** in a low manner, position, etc. **3.** softly; gently —see SYN. at HUMBLE —**low′li·ness** *n.*

Low Mass a Mass said, not sung, less ceremonial than High Mass, and offered by one priest

low-mind·ed (-mīn′did) *adj.* having or showing a coarse, vulgar mind —**low′-mind′ed·ly** *adv.* —**low′-mind′ed·ness** *n.*

low-necked (-nekt′) *adj.* having a low neckline; décolleté

low-pitched (-picht′) *adj.* **1.** having a low tone or a low range of tone [a low-pitched voice] **2.** having little slope, as a roof **3.** of low intensity; restrained [a low-pitched appeal for funds]

low-pres·sure (-presh′ər) *adj.* **1.** *a)* having or using a relatively low pressure *b)* having a low barometric pressure **2.** not energetic or forceful

low profile ☆a condition of being barely noticed that results from avoiding attention, publicity, etc.

low-proof (-prōōf′) *adj.* low in alcohol content

low relief *same as* BAS-RELIEF

low-spir·it·ed (-spir′i tid) *adj.* in low spirits; sad; depressed —**low′-spir′it·ed·ly** *adv.*

low-test (-test′) *adj.* vaporizing at a relatively high temperature: said of gasoline

low tide 1. the lowest level reached by the ebbing tide **2.** the time when the tide is at this level **3.** the lowest point reached by anything

low water 1. *same as* LOW TIDE **2.** water at its lowest level, as in a stream

low-wa·ter mark (-wôt′ər, -wät′-) **1.** a mark showing the lowest level reached by a body of water **2.** the lowest point reached by anything

lox¹ (läks) *n.* [via Yid. < G. *lachs*, salmon] a variety of salty smoked salmon

lox² (läks) *n.* [l(iquid) ox(ygen)] oxygen in a liquid state, used in a fuel mixture for rockets

loy·al (loi′əl) *adj.* [Fr. < OFr. < L. *legalis*: see LEGAL] **1.** faithful to one's country **2.** faithful to those persons, ideals, etc. that one has a duty to defend or support [a loyal son; a loyal

party member] **3.** having to do with or showing loyalty [a loyal remark] —see SYN. at FAITHFUL —**loy′al·ly** *adv.*

loy·al·ist (-ist) *n.* **1.** a person who supports the established government of his country during times of revolt ☆**2.** [often L-] in the American Revolution, a colonist who was loyal to the British government —**loy′al·ism** *n.*

loy·al·ty (-tē) *n., pl.* **-ties** the quality or condition of being loyal; faithfulness —see SYN. at ALLEGIANCE

Loyola see IGNATIUS (OF) LOYOLA

loz·enge (läz′′nj) *n.* [OFr. *losenge*, prob. < Gaul.] **1.** a plane figure with four equal sides and two obtuse angles; diamond **2.** a cough drop or piece of hard candy, at one time made in this shape

☆**LP** [L(ong) P(laying)] *a trademark for* a long-playing record —*n.* a long-playing record

LPG liquefied petroleum gas: also **LP-gas**

LPN, L.P.N. Licensed Practical Nurse

Lr *Chem.* lawrencium

LSD [l(y)s(ergic acid) d(iethylamide)] a psychedelic drug that produces hallucinations, delusions, etc.

Lt. Lieutenant

Ltd., ltd. limited

Lu *Chem.* lutetium

Lu·an·da (lōō än′də, -an′-) capital of Angola, on the Atlantic: pop. 347,000

Lu·ang Pra·bang (lōō äŋ′ prə bäŋ′) royal capital of Laos, on the Mekong River: pop. 22,000

lu·au (lōō ou′, lōō′ou′) *n.* [Haw.] a Hawaiian feast, usually with entertainment

lub·ber (lub′ər) *n.* [< ME. < *lobbe-* (see LOB)] **1.** a big, slow, clumsy person **2.** an inexperienced, clumsy sailor; landlubber —**lub′ber·li·ness** *n.* —**lub′ber·ly** *adj., adv.*

Lub·bock (lub′ək) [after T.S. *Lubbock*, Confederate officer] city in NW Tex.: pop. 149,000

☆**lube** (lōōb) *n.* **1.** a lubricating oil for machinery: also **lube oil** **2.** [Colloq.] a lubrication

Lü·beck (lü′bek; *E.* lōō′-) city & port in N West Germany: pop. 243,000

lu·bri·cant (lōō′brə kənt) *adj.* reducing friction by providing a smooth film as a covering over parts that move against each other —*n.* a substance for reducing friction in this way, as oil or grease

lu·bri·cate (-kāt′) *vt.* **-cat·ed, -cat·ing** [< L. pp. of *lubricare* < *lubricus*, smooth] **1.** to make slippery or smooth **2.** to apply a lubricant to —*vi.* to serve as a lubricant —**lu′bri·ca′tion** *n.* —**lu′bri·ca′tive** *adj.* —**lu′bri·ca′tor** *n.*

lu·bric·i·ty (lōō bris′ə tē) *n., pl.* **-ties** [< Fr. < LL. *lubricitas*] **1.** slipperiness; smoothness **2.** trickiness **3.** lewdness —**lu·bri′cious** (-brish′əs), **lu′bri·cous** (-bri kəs) *adj.*

lu·cent (lōō′s′nt) *adj.* [< L. prp. of *lucere*, to shine] **1.** giving off light; shining [a lucent sky] **2.** translucent or clear [a lucent stream] —**lu′cen·cy** *n.* —**lu′cent·ly** *adv.*

Lu·cerne (lōō sʉrn′; *Fr.* lü sern′), **Lake (of)** lake in C Switzerland

lu·cerne, lu·cern (lōō sʉrn′) *n.* [< Fr. < ModPr., ult. < L. *lucerna*, a lamp < *lucere*, to shine] [Chiefly Brit.] *same as* ALFALFA

Lu·cia (lōō′shə) [It. < L., fem. of LUCIUS] a feminine name

Lu·cian (lōō′shən) **1.** [< L.: see LUCIUS] a masculine name **2.** 2d cent. A.D.; Gr. writer of satires

lu·cid (lōō′sid) *adj.* [< L. < *lucere*, to shine: for IE. base see LIGHT¹] **1.** [Poet.] bright; shining **2.** that can be seen through; clear [lucid water] **3.** clearheaded; rational [he had a few lucid moments during his delirium] **4.** easily understood; not vague or confused [a lucid explanation] —**lu·cid′i·ty, lu′cid·ness** *n.* —**lu′cid·ly** *adv.*

Lu·ci·fer (lōō′sə fər) [OE. < L. < *lucis*, genitive of *lux*, LIGHT¹ + *ferre*, to BEAR¹] **1.** [Poet.] the planet Venus when it is the morning star **2.** *Theol.* Satan, esp. as leader of the revolt of the angels before his fall —*n.* [l-] an early type of friction match

lu·cif·er·in (lōō sif′ər in) *n.* [L. *lucifer* (see LUCIFER) + -IN¹] a substance in certain organisms, as fireflies, that produces light with almost no heat when it combines with oxygen

Lu·cille, Lu·cile (lōō sēl′) [var. of LUCY] a feminine name

☆**Lu·cite** (lōō′sīt) [< L. *lux*, light + -ITE²] *a trademark for* a transparent or translucent acrylic resin or plastic

Lu·cius (lōō′shəs) [L. < *lux*, LIGHT¹] a masculine name

luck (luk) *n.* [prob. < MDu. *luk* < *gelucke*] **1.** the seemingly chance happening of events, either good or bad; fortune; fate **2.** good fortune, success, etc. [I had the luck to get there first] —*vi.* [Colloq.] to be lucky enough to come (into, on, through, etc.) —☆**crowd** (or **push**) **one's luck** [Slang] to take unnecessary risks in a situation that is already favorable —**down on one's luck** in misfortune; unlucky —**in luck** lucky —☆**luck out** [Colloq.] to have things turn out favorably for one —**out of luck** unlucky —**try one's luck** to try to do something without being sure of the outcome —**worse luck** unfortunately

luck·less (luk′lis) *adj.* having no good luck; unlucky —**luck′·less·ly** *adv.* —**luck′·less·ness** *n.*

Luck·now (luk′nou) city in NC India: pop. 595,000

luck·y (luk′ē) *adj.* **luck′i·er, luck′i·est** **1.** having good luck; fortunate **2.** having a good result by chance [a *lucky* accident led to the discovery] **3.** believed to bring good luck [a *lucky* rabbit's foot] —**luck′i·ly** *adv.* —**luck′i·ness** *n.*

SYN.—**lucky** implies something favorable that happens by mere chance, often unexpectedly [a *lucky* find, guess, etc.]; **fortunate**, a more formal word, emphasizes that the benefits have not strictly been earned [a *fortunate* throw of the dice]; **providential** implies the influence of God or some higher force in bringing about the favorable event [a *providential* escape from death]; **happy** emphasizes the pleasure felt by the person affected by the lucky event [marriage resulted from that *happy* encounter] —**ANT.** unlucky, disastrous

lu·cra·tive (loo′krə tiv) *adj.* [< L. pp. of *lucrari*, to gain < *lucrum*: see LUCRE] producing wealth or profit; profitable [a *lucrative* investment] —**lu′cra·tive·ly** *adv.* —**lu′cra·tive·ness** *n.*

lu·cre (loo′kər) *n.* [< L. *lucrum*, gain, riches] riches; money: chiefly a scornful word, as in **filthy lucre**

Lu·cre·tius (loo krē′shəs) (born *Titus Lucretius Carus*) 96?–55? B.C.; Rom. poet & philosopher

lu·cu·brate (loo′kyoo brāt′) *vi.* **-brat′ed, -brat′ing** [< L. pp. of *lucubrare*, to work by candlelight < *lux*, light: for IE. base see LIGHT[1]] **1.** to work, study, or write with much effort, esp. late at night **2.** to write in a scholarly manner —**lu′cu·bra′tor** *n.*

lu·cu·bra·tion (loo′kyoo brā′shən) *n.* **1.** a lucubrating; hard work, study, etc., esp. when done late at night **2.** a learned or carefully developed work resulting from this **3.** [*often pl.*] any piece of writing that is dull and labored

Lu·cul·lus (loo kul′əs), (**Lucius Lucinius**) 110?–57? B.C.; Rom. general: famous for his wealth and luxurious life —**Lu·cul′lan** (-ən), **Lu·cul′li·an** (-ē ən) *adj.*

Lu·cy (loo′sē) [prob. via Fr. < L. *Lucia*, fem. of LUCIUS] a feminine name

lu·di·crous (loo′di krəs) *adj.* [L. *ludicrus* < *ludus*, a game < IE. base *leid-*, to play] causing laughter because absurd or ridiculous —see SYN. at ABSURD —**lu′di·crous·ly** *adv.* —**lu′di·crous·ness** *n.*

luff (luf) *n.* [< ODu. *loef*, weather side (of a ship)] **1.** a sailing close to the wind **2.** the forward edge of a fore-and-aft sail —*vi.* to turn the bow of a ship toward the wind

lug[1] (lug) *vt.* **lugged, lug′ging** [ME. *luggen*, prob. < Scand.] to carry or drag with effort [they *lugged* the crate upstairs] —*n.* **1.** an earlike projection by which a thing is held or supported **2.** a heavy nut used with a bolt to secure a wheel to an axle ☆**3.** a shallow box in which fruit is shipped **4.** [Slang] a clumsy, stupid fellow

lug[2] (lug) *n.* clipped form of LUGSAIL

lug[3] (lug) *n.* clipped form of LUGWORM

luge (loozh) *n.* [Fr.] a racing sled for one or two persons —*vi.* **luged, lug′ing** to race with luges

Lu·ger (loo′gər) [G.] *a trademark for* a German semiautomatic pistol —*n.* [*often* l-] this pistol

lug·gage (lug′ij) *n.* [LUG[1] + -AGE] suitcases, valises, trunks, etc.; baggage

lug·ger (lug′ər) *n.* a small vessel equipped with a lugsail or lugsails

lug·sail (lug′s'l, -sāl′) *n.* [< ? LUG[1]] a four-sided sail attached to an upper yard that hangs at a slant across the mast

lu·gu·bri·ous (loo goo′brē əs, -gyoo′-) *adj.* [L. *lugubris* < *lugere*, to mourn + -OUS] very sad or mournful, esp. in a way that seems exaggerated or ridiculous —**lu·gu′bri·ous·ly** *adv.* —**lu·gu′bri·ous·ness** *n.*

lug·worm (lug′wurm) *n.* [< ? + WORM] a bristly worm that burrows in muddy sand along the shore and is used for bait

LUGSAIL

Luke (look) [< LL. < Gr.] **1.** a masculine name **2.** *Bible a)* one of the four Evangelists, a physician said to be the author of the third Gospel *b)* this book

luke·warm (look′wôrm′) *adj.* [ME. *luke*, tepid (for IE. base see CALDRON) + *warm*, WARM] **1.** barely or moderately warm: said of liquids **2.** not very eager or enthusiastic [*lukewarm* praise] —**luke′warm′ly** *adv.* —**luke′warm′ness** *n.*

lull (lul) *vt.* [ME. *lullen*, origin echoic] **1.** to calm by gentle sound or motion: chiefly in **lull to sleep 2.** to bring into a specified condition by soothing and reassuring [to *lull* people into a false sense of security] **3.** to make less intense; quiet; allay [to *lull* one's fears] —*vi.* to become calm [the storm *lulled*] —*n.* a short period of quiet or of less activity [a *lull* in business]

lull·a·by (lul′ə bī′) *n., pl.* **-bies** a song for lulling a baby to sleep —*vt.* **-bied, -by′ing** to lull as with a lullaby

Lul·ly (lü lē′), **Jean Bap·tiste** (zhän bà tēst′) 1632–87; Fr. composer, born in Italy

lum·ba·go (lum bā′gō) *n.* [< L. *lumbus*, loin] backache, esp. in the lower back

lum·bar (lum′bər, -bär) *adj.* [< L. *lumbus*, loin] of or near the loins; specif., designating or of the vertebrae, nerves, etc. in that part of the body

lum·ber[1] (lum′bər) *n.* [< ? LOMBARD: orig., pawnshop, hence pawned or stored articles] **1.** household articles, furniture, etc. no longer used and so stored away or taking up room ☆**2.** timber sawed into beams, boards, etc. of convenient sizes —*vt.* **1.** to clutter with useless articles or rubbish ☆**2.** to remove (timber) from (an area) —☆*vi.* to cut down timber and saw it into lumber —☆**lum′ber·er** *n.*

lum·ber[2] (lum′bər) *vi.* [ME. *lomeren* < ? Scand.] **1.** to move heavily, clumsily, and, often, noisily [the truck *lumbered* up the hill] **2.** to rumble —**lum′ber·ing** *adj.* —**lum′ber·ing·ly** *adv.*

lum·ber·ing (lum′bər iŋ) *n.* ☆the work or business of cutting down trees and preparing lumber

lum·ber·jack (lum′bər jak′) *n.* same as LOGGER

☆**lum·ber·man** (-mən) *n., pl.* **-men 1.** same as LOGGER **2.** one who deals in lumber

☆**lum·ber·yard** (-yärd′) *n.* a place where lumber is kept for sale

lu·men (loo′mən) *n., pl.* **-mi·na** (-mi nə), **-mens** [ModL. < L., LIGHT[1]] **1.** a unit of measure for the flow of light, equal to the amount of flow from a uniform point source of one candle **2.** the bore of a hollow needle, catheter, etc.

lu·mi·nar·y (loo′mə ner′ē) *n., pl.* **-nar′ies** [< OFr. < LL. < L. *luminare* < *lumen*, LIGHT[1]] **1.** a body that gives off light, such as the sun or moon **2.** a famous or well-known person

lu·mi·nesce (loo′mə nes′) *vi.* **-nesced′, -nesc′ing** [back-formation < LUMINESCENCE] to be or become luminescent

lu·mi·nes·cence (-'ns) *n.* [< L. *lumen*, LIGHT[1] + -ESCENCE] any giving off of light, such as fluorescence, caused by the absorption of radiant energy, etc. and not by incandescence; any cold light —**lu′mi·nes′cent** *adj.*

lu·mi·nif·er·ous (loo′mə nif′ər əs) *adj.* [< L. *lumen*, LIGHT[1] + -FEROUS] giving off or transmitting light

lu·mi·nos·i·ty (loo′mə näs′ə tē) *n., pl.* **-ties 1.** the fact or condition of being luminous; brightness **2.** something luminous

lu·mi·nous (loo′mə nəs) *adj.* [L. *luminosus* < *lumen*, LIGHT[1]] **1.** giving off light; bright [the *luminous* rays of the sun] **2.** filled with light; illuminated [a *luminous* room] **3.** glowing in the dark, as paint with a phosphor in it **4.** very clear; easily understood [a *luminous* explanation] **5.** intellectually brilliant —see SYN. at BRIGHT —**lu′mi·nous·ly** *adv.* —**lu′mi·nous·ness** *n.*

luminous flux the rate of flow of light radiation

lum·mox (lum′əks) *n.* [< ?] [Colloq.] a clumsy, stupid person

lump[1] (lump) *n.* [ME. *lumpe*] **1.** a solid mass of no special shape; hunk [a *lump* of clay] **2.** a small cube, etc., specif. of sugar **3.** a swelling; bulge [the bee sting made a *lump* on his neck] **4.** a large amount; mass **5.** a dull, insensitive person ☆**6.** [*pl.*] [Colloq.] hard blows, criticism, or the like: in **get** (or **take**) **one's lumps** or **give someone his lumps** —*adj.* **1.** in lumps [*lump* sugar] **2.** in a single total; not in parts [he was paid in a *lump* sum] —*vt.* **1.** to put together in a lump or lumps **2.** to treat or deal with in a mass, or as a group [they *lumped* all their expenses together] **3.** to make lumps in —*vi.* to become lumpy —**in the lump** all together —**lump in one's throat** a tight feeling in the throat, as from trying to keep from crying

lump² (lump) *vt.* [Early ModE., to look sour] ☆[Colloq.] to put up with (something disagreeable) anyhow [if you don't like it, you can *lump* it]

lump·ish (lump'ish) *adj.* 1. like a lump 2. clumsy, dull, etc. —**lump'ish·ly** *adv.* —**lump'ish·ness** *n.*

lump·y (lum'pē) *adj.* **lump'i·er, lump'i·est** 1. full of lumps [*lumpy* pudding] 2. covered with lumps 3. rough: said of water 4. like a lump; heavy; clumsy —**lump'i·ly** *adv.* —**lump'i·ness** *n.*

Lu·na (lōō'nə) [L., moon] 1. *Rom. Myth.* the goddess of the moon 2. the moon represented as a person

lu·na·cy (lōō'nə sē) *n., pl.* **-cies** [LUNA(TIC) + -CY] 1. [Now Rare] insanity 2. great foolishness —see SYN. at INSANITY

☆**luna moth** a large N. American moth with light-green wings having crescent marks: the hind pair of wings end in long tails

lu·nar (lōō'nər) *adj.* [< L. < *luna*, the moon] 1. of, on, or like the moon 2. measured by the moon's revolutions [a *lunar* year]

lunar eclipse see ECLIPSE (sense 1)

lunar month see MONTH (sense 3)

lunar year a period of twelve lunar months

lu·nate (lōō'nāt) *adj.* [< L. < *luna*, the moon] crescent-shaped: also **lu'nat·ed** —**lu'nate·ly** *adv.*

lu·na·tic (lōō'nə tik) *adj.* [< OFr. < LL. *lunaticus*, moonstruck, crazy < L. *luna*, the moon] 1. [Now Rare] *a)* insane *b)* of lunacy *c)* of or for insane persons 2. extremely foolish —*n.* [Now Rare] an insane person

☆**lunatic fringe** the minority considered foolishly fanatical in any political, social, or other movement

lunch (lunch) *n.* [earlier, a piece: ? < Sp. *lonja*, slice of ham] 1. any light meal; esp., the midday meal between breakfast and dinner 2. the food prepared for such a meal —*vi.* to eat lunch —*vt.* to provide lunch for —**lunch'er** *n.*

lunch·eon (lun'chən) *n.* [< prec., prob. after dial. *nuncheon*, a snack] a lunch; esp., a formal lunch with others

☆**lunch·eon·ette** (lun'chə net') *n.* [see -ETTE] a small restaurant where light lunches can be had

luncheon meat meat prepared in loaves, sausages, etc. and ready to eat

☆**lunch·room** (lunch'rōōm') *n.* a restaurant where light, quick meals, as lunches, are served or, as in schools, where lunches brought from home can be eaten

lung (luŋ) *n.* [OE. *lungen:* for IE. base see LIGHT²] either of two spongelike organs of breathing in the thorax of vertebrates, that put oxygen into the blood and remove carbon dioxide from it —**at the top of one's lungs** in one's loudest voice

lunge (lunj) *n.* [< Fr. < *allonger*, to lengthen < *a-* (< L. *ad*), to + *long* (< L. *longus*), long] 1. a sudden thrust, as with a sword 2. a sudden plunge forward —*vi., vt.* **lunged, lung'ing** to move, or cause to move, with a lunge —**lung'er** *n.*

lung·fish (luŋ'fish') *n., pl.* **-fish', -fish'es:** see FISH any of various fishes having lungs as well as gills

lung·wort (-wurt') *n.* [OE. *lungenwyrt*] a plant with large, spotted leaves and clusters of blue or purple flowers

lu·nu·la (lōō'nyōō lə) *n., pl.* **-lae'** (-lē') [ModL. < L., dim. of *luna*, the moon] any part or marking in the shape of a crescent, as the whitish half-moon at the base of a fingernail: also **lu·nule** (lōō'nyool) —**lu'nu·lar** *adj.*

lu·nu·late (-lit, -lāt') *adj.* [see LUNULA & -ATE¹] 1. crescent-shaped 2. having crescent-shaped markings Also **lu'nu·lat'ed**

Lu·per·ca·li·a (lōō'pər kā'lē ə, -kal'yə) *n.pl.* an ancient Roman fertility festival, held in February: also **Lu'per·cal'** (-kal') *n.sing.* —**Lu'per·ca'li·an** *adj.*

lu·pine¹ (lōō'pin) *n.* [< L. < *lupus*, a wolf: reason for name uncertain] 1. a plant of the legume family, with spikes of white,

LUNA MOTH
(wingspread to 5 in.)

rose, yellow, or blue flowers and pods containing beanlike seeds 2. the seed of this plant, used in some parts of Europe as food

lu·pine² (lōō'pin) *adj.* [< L. < *lupus*, a wolf] 1. of a wolf or wolves 2. wolflike; fierce

lu·pus (lōō'pəs) *n.* [ModL. < L., a wolf] any of various diseases causing skin sores, esp. tuberculosis of the skin

lurch¹ (lurch) *vi.* [< ?] 1. to roll, pitch, or sway suddenly forward or to one side 2. to stagger —*n.* a lurching movement [the bus started with a *lurch*]

lurch² (lurch) *vi.* [var. of LURK] [Obs.] to lurk —*vt.* [Archaic] to cheat; steal; rob

lurch³ (lurch) *n.* [Fr. *lourche*, name of a 16th-c. game, prob. < OFr. *lourche*, duped] a situation in certain card games, in which the loser has less than half the score of the winner —**leave in the lurch** to leave (a person) in trouble and needing help

lure (loor) *n.* [< MFr. < OFr. *loirre*, prob. < Gmc.] 1. a bunch of feathers on the end of a long cord, used in falconry as bait to recall the hawk 2. *a)* the power of attracting or enticing [the *lure* of the South Sea Islands] *b)* anything having this power 3. an artificial bait used in fishing —*vt.* **lured, lur'ing** to attract; entice [the sunny day *lured* him from his studies] —**lur'er** *n.*

SYN.—**lure** suggests a strong force, as desire, greed, curiosity, etc., that attracts someone, often to something harmful or evil [*lured* into the plot by their false promises]; **entice** implies a clever or skillful luring [he *enticed* the squirrel to eat from his hand]; **decoy** implies the use of false appearances in luring into a trap [artificial birds are used to *decoy* wild ducks]; **beguile** suggests the use of subtle tricks in leading someone on [*beguiled* by her sweet words]; **tempt** suggests a powerful attraction that tends to overcome doubts or judgment [*tempted* by a chance for profit to invest his savings] —ANT. repel

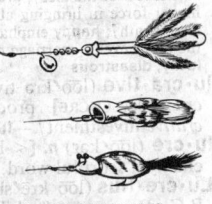

FISHING LURES

lu·rid (loor'id) *adj.* [L. *luridus*, pale yellow, ghastly] 1. [Rare] deathly pale 2. glowing through a haze, as flames enveloped by smoke 3. *a)* so terrible as to shock or startle; startling; sensational [the *lurid* details of the murder] *b)* full of violent passion or crime [a *lurid* novel] —**lu'rid·ly** *adv.* —**lu'rid·ness** *n.*

lurk (lurk) *vi.* [ME. *lurken*, akin to *louren*, LOWER²] 1. to stay hidden, ready to attack, etc. 2. to be present as a hidden or inactive threat, thought, etc. [notions of revenge *lurking* in the back of her mind] 3. to move secretly —**lurk'er** *n.*

Lu·sa·ka (lōō sä'kä) capital of Zambia: pop. 238,000

lus·cious (lush'əs) *adj.* [ME. *lucius*, prob. var. of *licious*, DELICIOUS, infl. by LUSH¹] 1. very pleasing to taste or smell; delicious [a *luscious* aroma] 2. *a)* delighting any of the senses [the *luscious* sound of the violins] *b)* attractive in a voluptuous way [a *luscious* starlet] —**lus'cious·ly** *adv.* —**lus'cious·ness** *n.*

lush¹ (lush) *adj.* [< OFr. *lasche*, lax, loose, ult. < L. *laxus*, LAX] 1. tender and full of juice [a *lush* peach] 2. of or characterized by rich growth [*lush* vegetation, *lush* fields] 3. characterized by richness, fullness, etc., often too much so [*lush* writing] —**lush'ly** *adv.* —**lush'ness** *n.*

lush² (lush) *n.* [< ? *Lushington*, former actors' club in London] [Slang] 1. alcoholic liquor 2. an alcoholic —*vi., vt.* [Slang] to drink (liquor)

Lu·si·ta·ni·a (lōō'sə tā'nē ə) ancient Roman province corresponding largely to modern Portugal

lust (lust) *n.* [OE., pleasure, appetite < IE. base *las*-, to be eager] 1. a desire to satisfy one's sexual needs; esp., strong sexual desire 2. *a)* excessive desire [a *lust* for power] *b)* great zest; strong enthusiasm [a *lust* for living] —*vi.* to feel an intense desire, esp. sexual desire (often with *after* or *for*) —**lust'ful** *adj.* —**lust'ful·ly** *adv.* —**lust'ful·ness** *n.*

lus·ter (lus'tər) *n.* [< Fr. < It. < L. *lustrare*, to illumine < *lustrum*, LUSTRUM] 1. a shining by reflected light; gloss; sheen [the *luster* of polished brass] 2. brightness; radiance [the *luster* of his eyes] 3. *a)* radiant beauty *b)* fame; glory [bravery gave new *luster* to his name] 4. a glossy fabric of cotton and wool 5. the reflecting quality and brilliance of the surface of a mineral 6. the metallic appearance of glazed pottery —*vt.* 1. to give a lustrous finish to 2. to add glory to —*vi.* to be or become lustrous

lus·ter·ware (-wer') *n.* earthenware decorated by applying a glaze that contains metallic oxides, that give a glossy appearance: also, chiefly Brit. adj., **lustreware**

lus·tral (lus'trəl) *adj.* [< L. < *lustrum*, LUSTRUM] of, used in, or connected with purification as performed by means of certain religious ceremonies

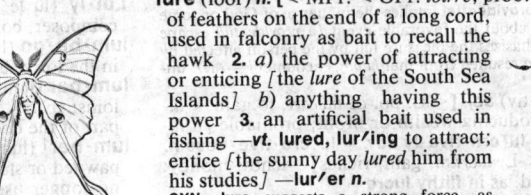

LUNGS
(A, trachea; B, bronchus; C, visceral pleura; D, parietal pleura; E, bronchiole; F, diaphragm; G, upper lobe; H, middle lobe; I, lower lobe)

lus·trate (lus′trāt) *vt.* **-trat·ed, -trat·ing** [< L. pp. of *lustrare:* see LUSTRUM] to purify by means of certain ceremonies —**lus·tra′tion** *n.*

lus·tre (lus′tər) *n., vt., vi.* **-tred, -tring** *chiefly Brit. sp.* of LUSTER

lus·trous (-trəs) *adj.* having luster; shining; bright —see SYN. at BRIGHT —**lus′trous·ly** *adv.* —**lus′trous·ness** *n.*

lus·trum (lus′trəm) *n., pl.* **-trums, -tra** (-trə) [L., orig., prob. illumination: for IE. base see LIGHT[1]] **1.** in ancient Rome, a purification of all the people by means of ceremonies held every five years **2.** a five-year period

lust·y (lus′tē) *adj.* **lust′i·er, lust′i·est** full of vigor; strong, robust, hearty, etc. [the baby gave a *lusty* cry] —**lust′i·ly** *adv.* —**lust′i·ness** *n.*

Lü·ta (lōō′dä′) city in NE China, formed by merging two seaports on the Yellow Sea: pop. 3,600,000

lu·ta·nist, lu·te·nist (lōōt′'n ist) *n.* a lute player

lute[1] (lōōt) *n.* [< MFr. < OFr. < Ar. *al-ūd*, lit., the wood] an early stringed instrument related to the guitar, with a rounded back and a long, fretted neck often bent in a sharp angle

lute[2] (lōōt) *n.* [< OFr. < L. *lutum*, mud, clay] a clay or cement used to seal the joints of pipes, etc. —*vt.* **lut′ed, lut′ing** to seal with lute

LUTE

lu·te·in·ize (lōōt′ē ə nīz′) *vt.* **-ized′, -iz′ing** to produce corpus luteum in —*vi.* to become part of the corpus luteum —**lu′te·in·i·za′tion** *n.*

lu·te·ti·um (lōō tē′shē əm) *n.* [ModL. < L. *Lutetia*, ancient Rom. name of Paris] a metallic chemical element of the rare-earth group: symbol, Lu; at. wt., 174.97; at. no., 71

Lu·ther (lōō′thər) [G. < OHG. *Chlothar* < Gmc. bases meaning "famous fighter"] **1.** a masculine name **2. Martin,** 1483–1546; Ger. theologian: leader of the Protestant Reformation in Germany

Lu·ther·an (-ən) *adj.* **1.** of Martin Luther **2.** of the Protestant denomination founded by Luther, or of its doctrines, etc. —*n.* a member of a Lutheran church —**Lu′ther·an·ism** *n.*

lut·ist (lōōt′ist) *n.* a lute player

lux (luks) *n., pl.* **lux, lux′es** [L., LIGHT[1]] *Physics* a unit of light equal to one lumen per square meter

Lux·em·bourg (luk′səm burg′; *Fr.* lük sän bōōr′) **1.** grand duchy in W Europe, bounded by Belgium, West Germany, & France: 998 sq. mi.; pop. 337,000 **2.** its capital: pop. 79,000 Also sp. **Luxemburg**

Lux·or (luk′sôr, lōōk′-) city in S Egypt, on the Nile, near the ruins of ancient Thebes

lux·u·ri·ant (lug zhoor′ē ənt, luk shoor′-) *adj.* [< L. prp. of *luxuriare:* see LUXURIATE] **1.** growing thick, strong, and in abundance; lush; teeming [*luxuriant* vines] **2.** richly or too richly full, varied, elaborate, etc. [a *luxuriant* imagination] **3.** *same as* LUXURIOUS —**lux·u′ri·ance, lux·u′ri·an·cy** *n.* —**lux·u′ri·ant·ly** *adv.*

lux·u·ri·ate (-āt′) *vi.* **-at′ed, -at′ing** [< L. pp. of *luxuriare*, to be too fruitful < *luxuria*, LUXURY] **1.** to grow thick, strong, and in great abundance **2.** to live in great luxury **3.** to take great pleasure; revel (*in*) [he *luxuriated* in the hot bath] —**lux·u′ri·a′tion** *n.*

lux·u·ri·ous (-əs) *adj.* **1.** fond of or marked by luxury [*luxurious* tastes] **2.** filled with or providing luxury; splendid, rich, comfortable, etc. [a big, soft, *luxurious* chair] —**lux·u′ri·ous·ly** *adv.* —**lux·u′ri·ous·ness** *n.*

lux·u·ry (luk′shə rē, lug′zhə-) *n., pl.* **-ries** [< OFr. < L. *luxuria* < *luxus*, luxury: for IE. base see LOCK[1]] **1.** the enjoyment of the best and most costly things that offer the greatest comfort and satisfaction [a life of *luxury*] **2.** anything giving such enjoyment, usually something considered unnecessary to life and health **3.** any unusual pleasure or comfort [the *luxury* of a day with no tasks or chores] —*adj.* characterized by luxury [*luxury* apartments]

Lu·zon (lōō zän′) main island of the Philippines: 40,420 sq. mi.; chief city, Manila

Lvov (lvôf) city in W Ukrainian S.S.R.: pop. 524,000

LXX Septuagint

-ly[1] (lē) [OE. *-lic*] *a suffix used to form adjectives and meaning:* **1.** like, characteristic of, suitable to [*manly*] **2.** happening (once) every (specified period of time) [*monthly*]

-ly[2] (lē) [OE. *-lice* < *-lic*] *a suffix used to form adverbs and meaning:* **1.** in a (specified) manner, to a (specified) extent or direction, in or at a (specified) time or place [*harshly, outwardly, hourly*] **2.** in the (specified) order [*secondly*]

ly·can·thrope (lī′kən thrōp′) *n.* [< ModL. < Gr. < *lykos*, wolf + *anthrōpos*, man] *same as* WEREWOLF

‡ly·cée (lē sā′) *n.* [Fr. < L.: see LYCEUM] in France, a public secondary school that prepares students for a university

Ly·ce·um (lī sē′əm, lī sē-) [L. < Gr. *Lykeion*, the Lyceum: from the temple of *Apollōn Lykeios* near it] the grove at Athens where Aristotle taught —*n.* [l-] **1.** a lecture hall **2.** an organization presenting public lectures, concerts, etc.

Ly·ci·a (lish′ē ə) ancient country in SW Asia Minor, on the Mediterranean —**Ly′ci·an** *adj., n.*

ly·co·pod (lī′kə päd′) *n. same as:* **1.** LYCOPODIUM (sense 1) **2.** CLUB MOSS

ly·co·po·di·um (lī′kə pō′dē əm) *n.* [ModL. < Gr. *lykos*, wolf + *podion*, dim. of *pous*, foot] **1.** a creeping or erect club moss, often evergreen, used as a Christmas decoration **2.** the flammable yellow powder found in the spore cases of these plants, used in fireworks and medicine

Ly·cur·gus (lī kur′gəs) real or legendary Spartan lawgiver of about the 9th cent. B.C.

lydd·ite (lid′īt) *n.* [< *Lydd*, village in England, where first made + -ITE] a powerful explosive containing picric acid

Lyd·i·a (lid′ē ə) [LL. < Gr. fem. of *Lydios*, Lydian] **1.** a feminine name **2.** ancient kingdom in W Asia Minor —**Lyd′i·an** *adj., n.*

lye (lī) *n.* [OE. *leag:* for IE. base see LATHER] **1.** orig., a strong alkaline solution obtained by leaching wood ashes **2.** any strongly alkaline substance, usually sodium or potassium hydroxide Lye is used in cleaning and in making soap

ly·ing[1] (lī′iŋ) *prp.* of LIE[1]

ly·ing[2] (lī′iŋ) *prp.* of LIE[2] —*adj.* false; not truthful —*n.* the telling of a lie or lies

ly·ing-in (-in′) *n.* the condition of a woman just before and during childbirth —*adj.* of or for childbirth [a *lying-in* hospital] An old-fashioned term

LYDIA (c. 7th cent. B.C.)

Lyl·y (lil′ē), **John** 1554?–1606; Eng. writer

lymph (limf) *n.* [L. *lympha*, spring water (infl. by Gr. *nymphē*, NYMPH)] a clear, yellowish fluid resembling blood plasma, that circulates through the body in a system of tubes

lym·phat·ic (lim fat′ik) *adj.* **1.** of, containing, or circulating lymph [*lymphatic* vessels] **2.** sluggish; without energy —*n.* a lymphatic vessel

lymph node any of many small masses of tissue lying in groups along the course of the lymphatic vessels and producing lymphocytes: also, esp. formerly, **lymph gland**

lym·pho- *a combining form meaning* of lymph or the lymphatics: also, before a vowel, **lymph-**

lym·pho·cyte (lim′fə sīt′) *n.* [LYMPHO- + -CYTE] any of the colorless cells formed in lymphatic tissue and important in the forming of antibodies —**lym′pho·cyt′ic** (-sit′ik) *adj.*

lymph·oid (lim′foid) *adj.* of or like lymph or the tissue of the lymph nodes

☆lynch (linch) *vt.* [< LYNCH LAW] to murder (an accused person) by the action of a mob and without lawful trial —**lynch′er** *n.* —**lynch′ing** *n.*

Lynch·burg (linch′burg) [after J. *Lynch*, reputed founder] city in C Va.: pop. 54,000

☆lynch law [after Capt. William *Lynch* (1742–1820), a vigilante in Pittsylvania, Virginia, in 1780] the lawless practice of killing by lynching

Lynn (lin) [prob. < Brit. place name *Lynn* < Celt.] **1.** a masculine or feminine name **2.** city in NE Mass.: suburb of Boston: pop. 90,000

lynx (liŋks) *n., pl.* **lynx′es, lynx:** see PLURAL, II, D, 1 [L. < Gr. *lynx*] any of a group of wildcats found throughout the Northern Hemisphere and characterized by a short tail, long, tufted ears, and keen vision

lynx-eyed (liŋks′īd′) *adj.* having very keen sight

Lyon (lyōn) city in EC France, on the Rhone: pop. 528,000: Eng. name **Lyons** (lī′ənz)

ly·on·naise (lī′ə nāz′; *Fr.* lyô-nez′) *adj.* [Fr., fem. of *Lyonnais*, of Lyon] prepared with finely sliced onions [*lyonnaise* potatoes are prepared with fried onions]

Ly·ra (lī′rə) a N constellation: it contains Vega

ly·rate (lī′rāt) *adj.* shaped like a lyre

lyre (līr) *n.* [< L. < Gr. *lyra*] a small stringed instrument of the harp family, used by the ancient Greeks to accompany singing and reciting

lyre·bird (līr′burd′) *n.* an Australian songbird: the long tail feathers of the male resemble a lyre when spread

lyr·ic (lir′ik) *adj.* [< Fr. or L.: both < Gr. *lyrikos*] 1. suitable for singing, as to the accompaniment of a lyre; songlike; specif., designating poetry expressing the poet's emotions and thoughts: sonnets, odes, etc. are lyric poems 2. writing lyric poetry [a *lyric* poet] 3. *same as* LYRICAL

CANADA LYNX
(to 3½ ft. long)

LYRE

4. having a relatively high voice with a light, flexible quality [a *lyric* tenor] —*n.* 1. a lyric poem 2. [*usually pl.*] the words of a song

lyr·i·cal (-i k'l) *adj.* 1. *same as* LYRIC 2. expressing great excitement or enthusiasm [he gave a *lyrical* account of his trip] — **lyr′i·cal·ly** *adv.*

lyr·i·cism (lir′ə siz′m) *n.* lyric quality, style, expression, etc.

lyr·i·cist (-sist) *n.* a writer of lyrics, esp. lyrics for popular songs

ly·ser·gic acid (lī sur′jik) [< Gr. *lysis* (see LYSIS) + ERG(OT) + -IC] an acid extracted from ergot alkaloids or made in a chemical laboratory: see LSD

ly·sin (lī′s'n) *n.* [< Gr. *lysis* (see LYSIS) + -IN[1]] any antibody capable of dissolving bacteria, blood corpuscles, etc.

ly·sine (lī′sēn) *n.* [< Gr. < *lysis* (see LYSIS) + -INE[4]] an important amino acid formed by the hydrolysis of certain proteins in digestion or prepared synthetically

ly·sis (lī′sis) *n.* [ModL. < Gr. *lysis*, a loosening < *lyein*, to loose: for IE. base see LOSE] 1. cell destruction by lysins 2. the gradual ending of disease symptoms

-ly·sis (lə sis) [see LYSIS] *a combining form meaning* a loosing, dissolution, dissolving, destruction [*catalysis, paralysis*]

ly·so·zyme (lī′sə zīm′) *n.* [< Gr. *lysis* (see LYSIS) + ZYME] an enzyme present in egg white, tears, saliva, etc., that can kill certain bacteria by dissolving the cell walls

-lyte (līt) [< Gr. *lytos* < *lyein*: see LYSIS] *a combining form meaning* a substance that can be decomposed [*hydrolyte*]

-lyt·ic (lit′ik) 1. *a combining form used to form adjectives from nouns ending in* -LYSIS [*catalytic*] 2. *Biochem. a combining form meaning* hydrolysis by enzymes

-lyze (līz) *a combining form used to form verbs from nouns ending in* -LYSIS [*electrolyze*]

M

M, m (em) *n., pl.* **M's, m's** **1.** the thirteenth letter of the English alphabet **2.** the sound of *M* or *m*

M (em) *n.* a Roman numeral for 1,000

M'- *same as* MAC- [M'Coy]

M. **1.** Manitoba **2.** Medieval **3.** *Music* mezzo **4.** Monday **5.** *pl.* **MM.** Monsieur

M., m. **1.** majesty **2.** male **3.** married **4.** masculine **5.** *Physics* mass **6.** meridian **7.** mile(s) **8.** mill(s) **9.** minim **10.** minute(s) **11.** month **12.** [L. *meridies*] noon [A.M., P.M.]

m, m. meter; meters

ma (mä; *dial.* mô) *n.* [Colloq.] mamma; mother

MA Massachusetts

MA, M.A. *Psychol.* mental age

M.A. [L. *Magister Artium*] Master of Arts

ma'am (mam, mäm; *unstressed* məm, 'm) *n.* [Colloq.] madam: used in direct address

Ma·bel (mā′b'l) [< *Amabel* < L. *amabilis,* lovable] a feminine name

Mac- [< Ir. & Gael. *mac,* son < OCelt.] *a prefix meaning* son of: used in Scottish and Irish family names

ma·ca·bre (mə käb′rə, mə käb′, -kä′bər) *adj.* [Fr. < OFr. (*danse*) *Macabré,* (dance) of death] gruesome; grim and horrible: also **ma·ca′ber** (-kä′bər) [a *macabre* sight greeted those who entered the camp] —**see SYN** at GHASTLY

mac·ad·am (mə kad′əm) *n.* [after J. L. *McAdam* (1756–1836), Scot. engineer] **1.** small broken stones used in making roads, usually combined with tar or asphalt **2.** a macadamized road

mac·a·dam·i·a nut (mak′ə dā′mē ə) [after J. *Macadam* (d. 1865), Scot. chemist in Australia] a hard-shelled, edible nut from an Australian tree cultivated in Hawaii, etc.

mac·ad·am·ize (mə kad′ə mīz′) *vt.* **-ized′, -iz′ing** to make, repair, or cover (a road) by rolling layers of macadam on it

Ma·cao (mə kou′) Port. territory consisting of a peninsula on the SE coast of China & two small nearby islands: 6 sq. mi.; pop. 280,000: also, Port. sp., **Macau**

ma·caque (mə käk′) *n.* [Fr. < Port. *macaco*] any of a group of monkeys of Asia, Africa, and the East Indies, with a tail that is usually short

mac·a·ro·ni (mak′ə rō′nē) *n.* [It. *maccaroni,* pl. < LGr. *makaria,* broth of barley, ult. < Gr. *makar,* blessed] **1.** pasta in the form of tubes, etc., often baked with cheese, ground meat, etc. **2.** *pl.* **-nies** an 18th-cent. English dandy

mac·a·roon (mak′ə rōōn′) *n.* [< Fr. < It. *maccaroni,* MACARONI] a small cookie made chiefly of egg white, crushed almonds or coconut, and sugar

Ma·cau·lay (mə kô′lē), **Thomas Bab·ing·ton** (bab′iŋ tən), 1st Baron Macaulay, 1800–59; Eng. historian, writer, & statesman

ma·caw (mə kô′) *n.* [Port. *macao,* prob. < Braz. (Tupi) native name] a large, bright-colored parrot of Central and South America, that has a harsh voice

PIG-TAILED MACAQUE
(to 2½ ft. long)

Mac·beth (mək beth′, mak-) **1.** a tragedy (c. 1606) by Shakespeare **2.** its title character: urged on by his wife, he murders the king so that he may become king

Mac·ca·bae·us (mak′ə bē′əs), **Judas** *see* MACCABEES

Mac·ca·bees (mak′ə bēz′) **1.** family of Jewish patriots who, under Judas Maccabaeus, headed a successful revolt against Syria (175–164 B.C.) and ruled Palestine until 37 B.C. **2.** *Bible* two books of the Roman Catholic canon that tell of this revolt —**Mac′ca·be′an** *adj.*

Mac·Dow·ell (mək dou′əl), **Edward Alexander** 1861–1908; U.S. composer & pianist

mace[1] (mās) *n.* [< OFr. *masse*] **1.** a heavy, spiked club, used in the Middle Ages as a weapon to smash armor **2.** *a*) a staff used as a symbol of authority by certain officials *b*) a person who carries a mace: also **mace′bear′er** —☆[M-] *a trademark* (in full, **Chemical Mace**) *for* a chemical compound used as a tear gas and a nerve gas

mace[2] (mās) *n.* [< OFr. *macis* < ML. < L. < Gr. *makir,* a fragrant resin] a spice, usually ground, made from the dried outer covering of the nutmeg

Mac·e·do·ni·a (mas′ə dō′nē ə, -dōn′yə) **1.** ancient kingdom in SE Europe, now divided among Greece, Yugoslavia, & Bulgaria **2.** republic of Yugoslavia, in the SE part: 9,928 sq. mi.; cap. Skopje —**Mac′e·do′ni·an** *adj., n.*

mac·er·ate (mas′ə rāt′) *vt.* **-at′ed, -at′ing** [< L. pp. of *macerare,* to soften] **1.** to soften and break down the parts of by soaking in liquid for some time [flax is *macerated* to get the fibers for making linen] **2.** loosely, to break, tear, chop, etc. into bits **3.** to cause to waste away or grow thin [fasting *macerated* his body] —*vi.* to waste away; grow thin —**mac′er·a′tion** *n.*

Mach (mäk) *n. clipped form of* MACH NUMBER

mach. **1.** machine **2.** machinery **3.** machinist

ma·che·te (mə shet′ē, -chet′ē) *n.* [Sp., dim. of *macho,* ult. < L. *marcus,* a hammer] a large, heavy-bladed knife used for cutting down sugar cane or underbrush in Central and South America

Mach·i·a·vel·li (mä′kyä vel′lē; *E.* mak′ē ə vel′ē), **Nic·co·lò (di Bernardo)** (nē′kō lô′) 1469–1527; Italian statesman & writer on government

Mach·i·a·vel·li·an (mak′ē ə vel′ē ən, -vel′yən) *adj.* of or like Machiavelli or the political principles of slyness and trickery that he said might be used in order to gain and hold power —*n.* a follower of such principles —**Mach′i·a·vel′li·an·ism** *n.*

ma·chic·o·late (mə chik′ə lāt′) *vt.* **-lat′ed, -lat′ing** [< ML. pp. of *machicolare* < MFr., prob. < *macher,* to crush + *col,* the neck: from use of machicolations to drop stones, etc.] to put machicolations in (a parapet, etc.)

MACES
(weapon
& staff)

MACHETE

fat, āpe, cär, ten, ēven, is, bīte; gō, hôrn, tōol, look; oil, out; up, fur; get; joy; yet; chin; she; thin, then; zh, leisure; ŋ, ring; ə for *a* in *ago, e* in *agent, i* in *sanity, o* in *comply, u* in *focus;* ' as in *able* (ā′b'l); Fr. bal; ë, Fr. coeur; ö, Fr. feu; Fr. mon; ô, Fr. coq; ü, Fr. duc; r, Fr. cri; H, G. ich; kh, G. doch; ‡foreign; ☆ Americanism; < derived from. See inside front cover.

573

ma·chic·o·la·tion (mə chik'ə lā'shən) *n.* an opening, as in the floor of a gallery or parapet, through which hot liquids, rocks, etc. could be dropped by the defenders of a fortress

mach·i·nate (mak'ə nāt'; *sometimes* mash'-) *vi.*, *vt.* **-nat'ed, -nat'ing** [< L. pp. of *machinari,* to plot < *machina,* a MACHINE] to plan in a sly or secret way, esp. to do something wrong

mach·i·na·tion (mak'ə nā'shən; *sometimes* mash'-) *n.* a sly or secret plot or scheme, esp. an evil one: *usually used in pl.* — see SYN. at PLOT

ma·chine (mə shēn') *n.* [Fr. < L. *machina* < Gr. < *mēchos,* contrivance: for IE. base see MAY] **1.** a vehicle, as an automobile: old-fashioned term **2.** a structure consisting of a framework and various fixed and moving parts, for doing some kind of work; mechanism [a sewing *machine*] **3.** a person or organization regarded as acting like a machine; esp., *a)* one who acts mechanically, without thought or will *b)* a smoothly functioning complex organization [the military *machine*] ☆**4.** the members of a political party who control policy and give patronage **5.** *Mech.* a device, as a lever or pulley, that transmits, or changes the application of, energy —*adj.* **1.** of a machine or machines **2.** made or done by machinery [a *machine* product] —*vt.* **-chined', -chin'ing** to make, shape, etc. by machinery

☆**machine gun** an automatic gun, usually with a cooling apparatus, firing a rapid stream of bullets fed into it by a belt — **ma·chine'-gun'** (-gun') *vt.* **-gunned', -gun'ning**

ma·chin·er·y (mə shēn'ər ē, -shēn'rē) *n., pl.* **-er·ies 1.** machines as a group [the *machinery* of a factory] **2.** the working parts of a machine [the *machinery* of a printing press] **3.** any means by which something is kept in action or a desired result is obtained [the *machinery* of government]

☆**machine shop** a factory for making or repairing machines or machine parts

machine tool a power-driven tool, as an electric lathe or drill — **ma·chine'-tool'** *adj., vt.*

ma·chin·ist (-ist) *n.* a person who makes, repairs, or operates machinery or is skilled in using machine tools

‡**ma·chis·mo** (mä chēz'mō) *n.* [Sp. < *macho* (see MACHO)] the fact of being masculine in a strong or aggressive way

Mach number (mäk) [after Ernst *Mach* (1838–1916), Austrian physicist] [*also* m-] a number representing the ratio of the speed of an object to the speed of sound through the same medium, as air [*Mach* (*number*) three means a speed three times that of sound]

‡**ma·cho** (mä'chō) *adj.* [Sp. < Port., ult. < L. *masculus,* MASCULINE] masculine, virile, courageous, etc.

Mac·ken·zie (mə ken'zē) **1.** river in NW Canada, flowing from the Great Slave Lake into the Arctic Ocean **2.** district of Northwest Territories, Canada, in the W part

mack·er·el (mak'ər əl, mak'rəl) *n., pl.* **-el, -els:** see PLURAL, II, D, 2 [< OFr. *makerel* < ?] a food fish of the North Atlantic, with a greenish, blue-striped back and a silvery belly

mackerel sky a sky with rows of small, fleecy clouds, like the streaks on a mackerel's back

Mack·i·nac (mak'ə nô'), **Straits of** strait connecting Lake Huron & Lake Michigan

Mackinac Island [CanadFr. < AmInd. *mitchimakinak,* large turtle: ? from its shape] small island in the Straits of Mackinac

Mack·i·naw (coat) (mak'ə nô') [< MACKINAC ISLAND] a short, double-breasted coat of heavy woolen cloth, usually plaid

mack·in·tosh, mac·in·tosh (mak'in täsh') *n.* [after C. *Macintosh* (1766–1843), the Scot. inventor] a waterproof raincoat, or the fabric for it, made of rubberized cloth

Mac·Leish (mə klēsh'), **Archibald** 1892– ; U.S. poet

Ma·con (mā'kən) [after N. *Macon* (1758–1837), N.C. patriot] city in C Ga.: pop. 122,000

mac·ra·mé (mak'rə mā') *n.* [Fr. < It. < Turk. *makrama,* napkin < Ar. *miqramah,* a veil] a coarse fringe or lace of thread or cord knotted in designs

mac·ro- [< Gr. *makros:* see MACRON] *a combining form meaning* long (in space or time), large, enlarged, or longer: also, before a vowel, **macr-**

mac·ro·bi·ot·ics (mak'rō bī ät'iks) *n.pl.* [*with sing. v.*] [< MACRO- + Gr. *biōtikos* < *bios,* life] the art of extending life, as by a special diet —**mac'ro·bi·ot'ic** *adj.*

mac·ro·ceph·a·ly (mak'rə sef'ə lē) *n.* [MACRO- + CEPHAL(O)- + -Y³] a condition in which the head or cranium is ab-

MACRAMÉ

normally large —**mac'ro·ceph'a·lous, mac'ro·ce·phal'ic** (-si fal'ik) *adj.*

mac·ro·cosm (mak'rə käz'm) *n.* [< Fr. < ML.: see MACRO- & COSMOS] **1.** the universe **2.** any large, complex system —**mac'ro·cos'mic** *adj.*

mac·ro·mol·e·cule (mak'rə mäl'ə kyōōl') *n.* a very large molecule, as a polymer molecule, made up of hundreds or thousands of atoms: also **mac'ro·mole'** (-mōl')

ma·cron (mā'krən, -krän) *n.* [< Gr. neut. of *makros,* long: for IE. base see MEAGER] a short, straight mark (¯) placed over a vowel to show that it is long or is to be pronounced in a certain way

mac·ro·nu·tri·ent (mak'rə nōō'trē ənt) *n.* [MACRO- + NUTRIENT] any of the chemical elements, such as carbon, needed in relatively large quantities for plant growth

mac·ro·scop·ic (mak'rə skäp'ik) *adj.* [MACRO- + -SCOP(E) + -IC] large enough to be seen without the aid of a microscope

mac·u·la (mak'yoo lə) *n., pl.* **-lae** (-lē'), **-las** [L.] a spot, blotch, etc.; esp., *a)* a discolored spot on the skin *b)* a sunspot — **mac'u·lar** *adj.*

mad (mad) *adj.* **mad'der, mad'dest** [< OE. pp. of (ge)*mædan,* to drive mad < IE. base *mai-,* to cut] **1.** mentally ill; insane **2.** wildly excited; frenzied; frantic [*mad* with fear] **3.** foolish and rash; unwise [a *mad* scheme] **4.** foolishly enthusiastic or fond [*mad* about clothes] **5.** wildly amusing; hilarious [a *mad* comedy] **6.** having rabies [a *mad* dog] **7.** *a)* angry (often with *at*) [she's *mad* at us for leaving] *b)* showing anger [a *mad* scowl] —**have a mad on** [Colloq.] to be angry —**mad as a hatter** (or **March hare**) completely crazy

Mad·a·gas·car (mad'ə gas'kər) country that is an island off the SE coast of Africa: 228,000 sq. mi.; pop. 6,750,000; cap. Antananarivo

mad·am (mad'əm) *n., pl.* **mad'ams;** *for 1, usually* **mesdames** (mā däm') [< Fr., orig. *ma dame* < L. *mea domina,* my lady] **1.** a woman; lady: a polite term of address **2.** the mistress of a household ☆**3.** a woman in charge of a group of prostitutes

mad·ame (mad'əm, mə dam'; *Fr.* má dám') *n., pl.* **mesdames** (mā däm'; *Fr.* mā dám') [Fr.: see prec.] a married woman: French title used like *Mrs.:* also used in English as a title of respect for any distinguished woman: abbrev. **Mme., Mdme.**

mad·cap (mad'kap') *n.* [MAD + CAP, used for "head"] a reckless, impulsive person, esp. a girl —*adj.* reckless and impulsive

mad·den (mad''n) *vt., vi.* to make or become mad; make or become insane, angry, or wildly excited —**mad'den·ing** *adj.* — **mad'den·ing·ly** *adv.*

mad·der (mad'ər) *n.* [OE. *mædere*] **1.** any of various related plants, chiefly tropical; esp., a perennial vine with small, yellow flowers **2.** *a)* the red root of this vine *b)* a red dye made from this **3.** crimson

mad·ding (mad'iŋ) *adj.* [Rare] **1.** driven mad; raving; frenzied ["the *madding* crowd"] **2.** making mad; maddening

made (mād) *pt. & pp. of* MAKE —*adj.* **1.** constructed; formed [a well-*made* house] **2.** produced artificially [*made* flowers] **3.** invented; contrived [a *made* word] **4.** prepared from various ingredients [a *made* dish] **5.** sure of success [a *made* man] — ☆**have (got) it made** [Slang] to be assured of success

Ma·dei·ra (mə dir'ə) **1.** group of Portuguese islands in the Atlantic, off the W coast of Morocco **2.** largest island of this group **3.** river in NW Brazil, flowing northeast into the Amazon —*n.* [*also* m-] a strong white wine made on this island

mad·e·leine (mad''l in) *n.* [Fr., after *Madeleine* Paulnier, 19th-c. Fr. cook] a small, rich cupcake

Mad·e·line (mad''l in, -ēn') [< MAGDALENE] a feminine name

ma·de·moi·selle (mad'ə mə zel', mam zel'; *Fr.* mád mwá zel') *n., Fr. pl.* **mesde·moi·selles** (mād mwä zel') [Fr. < *ma,* my + *demoiselle,* young lady] an unmarried woman or girl: French title used like *Miss:* abbrev. **Mlle., Mdlle.**

made-to-or·der (mād'tə ôr'dər) *adj.* **1.** made just as the customer ordered; custom-made [a *made-to-order* bed] **2.** perfectly suited [a play *made-to-order* for her talents]

made-up (-up') *adj.* **1.** put together; arranged [a *made-up* page of type] **2.** invented; false [a *made-up* story] **3.** with cosmetics applied [a *made-up* face]

Madge (maj) [dim. of MARGARET] a feminine name

mad·house (mad'hous') *n.* **1.** a place where the mentally ill were at one time confined **2.** any place of turmoil, noise, and confusion

Mad·i·son (mad'i s'n) [after J. MADISON] capital of Wis., in the SC part: pop. 173,000

Mad·i·son (mad′i s'n), **James** 1751–1836; 4th president of the U.S. (1809–1817)

mad·ly (mad′lē) *adv.* **1.** insanely **2.** wildly; furiously *[they applauded madly]* **3.** foolishly **4.** extremely *[madly in love]*

mad·man (mad′man′, -mən) *n., pl.* **-men′** (-men′, -mən) an insane person; lunatic —**mad′wom′an** *n.fem., pl.* **-wom′en**

mad·ness (-nis) *n.* **1.** insanity **2.** great anger **3.** great folly **4.** wild excitement **5.** rabies

Ma·don·na (mə dän′ə) *n.* [It. < *ma*, my (< L. *mea*) + *donna*, lady (< L. *domina*)] **1.** Mary, mother of Jesus **2.** a picture or statue of Mary

Ma·dras (mə dras′, -dräs′) seaport on the SE coast of India: pop. c. 2,000,000

ma·dras (mad′rəs, mäd′-; mə dras′, -dräs′) *n.* [< prec.] a fine, firm cotton cloth, usually striped or plaid, used for shirts, dresses, etc.

‡**ma·dre** (mä′dre) *n.* [Sp.] mother

mad·re·pore (mad′rə pôr′) *n.* [< Fr. < It. < *madre*, mother + *poro*, a pore] any of various branching corals that form reefs and islands in tropical seas —**mad′re·por′ic**, **mad′re·por′i·an** *adj.*

Ma·drid (mə drid′; *Sp.* mä thrēth′) capital of Spain, in the C part: pop. 3,080,000

mad·ri·gal (mad′ri gəl) *n.* [< It. *madrigale* < ?] **1.** a short poem, usually of love, that can be set to music **2.** a song with parts for several voices, sung with counterpoint and without accompaniment: popular in the 15th to 17th cent. **3.** loosely, any song —**mad′ri·gal·ist** *n.*

☆**ma·dro·ño** (mə drō′nyō) *n., pl.* **-nos** [Sp. < *maduro* < L. *maturus*, mature] an evergreen tree of western N. America, having red bark, leathery leaves, and red berries that can be eaten: also **ma·dro′ne** (-nə), **ma·dro′ña** (-nyə)

Ma·du·ra (mä door′ä) island of Indonesia, northeast of Java: 1,770 sq. mi.

Ma·du·rai (mä də rī′) city in S India: pop. 425,000

Mae (mā) [dim. of MARY] a feminine name

Mae·ce·nas (mi sē′nəs), (**Gaius Cilnius**) 70?–8 B.C.; Rom. statesman & patron of Horace & Virgil —*n.* any wealthy, generous patron, esp. of literature or art

Mael·strom (māl′strəm) [Early ModDu. < *malen*, to grind + *stroom*, a stream] a dangerous whirlpool off the W coast of Norway —*n.* [m-] **1.** any large or violent whirlpool **2.** a violently excited or confused state of mind, emotions, affairs, etc.

mae·nad (mē′nad) *n.* [< L. < Gr. < *mainesthai*, to rave] **1.** a female worshiper of Dionysus; bacchante **2.** a woman who is greatly excited or in a rage —**mae·nad·ic** (mi nad′ik) *adj.*

ma·es·to·so (mīs tō′sō; *It.* mä′e stô′sô) *adj., adv.* [It.] *Music* with majesty or dignity

ma·es·tro (mīs′trō; mä es′-) *n., pl.* **-tros**, **-tri** (-trē) [It. < L. *magister*, a MASTER] a master in any art; esp., a great composer, conductor, or teacher of music

Mae·ter·linck (māt′ər liŋk, met′-), Count **Maurice** 1862–1949; Belgian playwright & poet

Mae West (mā′ west′) [< *Mae West* (1892–), shapely U.S. actress] an inflatable vest worn as a life preserver, as by aviators shot down at sea

Ma·fi·a, Maf·fi·a (mä′fē ə) *n.* [It. *maffia*, hostility to law] a secret society of criminals thought to exist in the U.S. and other countries

Ma·fi·o·si (mä′fē ō′sē) *n.pl., sing.* **-so′** (-sō′) [It.] members of the Mafia

mag. **1.** magazine **2.** magnetism **3.** magnitude

mag·a·zine (mag′ə zēn′, mag′ə zēn′) *n.* [< Fr. < OFr. < It. < Ar. < *makhzan*, a granary < *khazana*, to store up] **1.** a place of storage, as a warehouse or military supply depot **2.** a space in which explosives are stored, as in a fort or warship **3.** a supply chamber, as the space in a rifle from which the cartridges are fed, the space in a camera from which the film is fed, etc. **4.** things kept in a magazine, as munitions or supplies **5.** a publication, usually with a paper back, that comes out regularly, often weekly or monthly, and contains stories, articles, etc. and, usually, advertisements

Mag·da·lene (mag′də lēn, -lin) [LL. < Gr. < *Magdala*, town in Galilee] *same as* MARY MAGDALENE —*n.* [m-] a former prostitute who repents her earlier life

Mag·de·burg (mäg′də boorkh; *E.* mag′də burg′) city & port in W East Germany, on the Elbe: pop. 268,000

Ma·gel·lan (mə jel′ən), **Ferdinand** 1480?–1521; Port. navigator in the service of Spain

Magellan, Strait of channel between the S. American mainland & Tierra del Fuego

Mag·el·lan·ic cloud (maj′ə lan′ik) [after F. MAGELLAN] *Astron.* either of two cloudlike galaxies that are nearest to the Milky Way and can be seen in the southern heavens

ma·gen·ta (mə jen′tə) *n.* [< *Magenta*, town in Italy: the dye was discovered at the time (1859) of a battle fought there] **1.** a purplish-red dye **2.** purplish red —*adj.* purplish-red

STRAIT OF MAGELLAN

mag·got (mag′ət) *n.* [ME. *magotte*] **1.** a wormlike insect larva, as the legless larva of the housefly **2.** an odd notion; whim —**mag′got·y** *adj.*

Ma·gi (mā′jī) *n.pl., sing.* **Ma′gus** (-gəs) [L., pl. of *magus* < Gr. < OPer. *magus*: for IE. base see MAY] **1.** priests of ancient Media and Persia **2.** *Douay Bible* the wise men from the East who brought gifts to the infant Jesus: Matt. 2:1–13 —**Ma′gi·an** (-jē ən) *adj., n.*

mag·ic (maj′ik) *n.* [< OFr. < L. < Gr. < *magikos*, of the MAGI] **1.** the use of charms, spells, etc. in seeking or pretending to make things happen in an unnatural way **2.** any power or influence that seems mysterious or hard to explain *[the magic of love]* **3.** the art of producing illusions as an entertainment by sleight of hand, trick devices, etc. —*adj.* **1.** of, produced by, or using magic **2.** producing extraordinary results, as if by magic *[his magic playing of the violin]*

mag·i·cal (maj′i k'l) *adj.* magic (esp. in sense 2) NOTE *magical* is used in the predicate *[the effect was magical]* as well as before a noun, but *magic* is usually used before a noun *[their magic rites]* —**mag′i·cal·ly** *adv.*

ma·gi·cian (mə jish′ən) *n.* [< OFr. *magicien*] an expert in magic; specif., *a)* a sorcerer; wizard *b)* a performer skilled in magic (sense 3)

magic lantern *old-fashioned term for* a slide projector

mag·is·te·ri·al (maj′is tir′ē əl) *adj.* [< ML. < LL. < L. *magister*, a MASTER] **1.** of or suitable for a magistrate or master *[magisterial robes]* **2.** that shows authority; authoritative *[a magisterial manner]* **3.** domineering; pompous —see SYN. at MASTERFUL —**mag′is·te′ri·al·ly** *adv.*

mag·is·tra·cy (maj′is trə sē) *n., pl.* **-cies** **1.** the position, office, or district of a magistrate **2.** magistrates as a group

mag·is·trate (maj′is trāt′, -trit) *n.* [< L. < *magister*, MASTER] **1.** a civil officer empowered to administer the law: the President of the U.S. may be called the *chief magistrate* **2.** a minor official with some powers to judge, as a justice of the peace

mag·ma (mag′mə) *n.* [L. < Gr. < *massein*, to knead] molten rock deep in the earth, from which igneous rock is formed

Mag·na Char·ta (or **Car·ta**) (mag′nə kar′tə) [ML., lit., great charter] **1.** the charter that King John was forced by the English barons to grant at Runnymede, June 15, 1215, interpreted as guaranteeing certain civil and political liberties **2.** any constitution guaranteeing certain liberties

‡**mag·na cum lau·de** (mäg′nä koom lou′de, mag′nə kum lô′dē) [L.] with great praise: phrase used to signify graduation with high honors from a university or college

mag·na·nim·i·ty (mag′nə nim′ə tē) *n.* **1.** a magnanimous quality or state **2.** *pl.* **-ties** a magnanimous act

mag·nan·i·mous (mag nan′ə məs) *adj.* [< L. < *magnus*, great + *animus*, soul] generous in overlooking injury or insult; rising above pettiness or meanness —**mag·nan′i·mous·ly** *adv.*

mag·nate (mag′nāt) *n.* [< LL. < L. *magnus*, great] a very important or powerful person, esp. in business

mag·ne·sia (mag nē′zhə, -shə) *n.* [ModL., ult. a blend of Gr. *Magnēsia*, area in Thessaly & ModL. *magnes carneus*, lit., flesh magnet (so called because it clings to the lips)] magnesium oxide, MgO, a white, tasteless powder used as a mild laxative and antacid, and as an insulating substance —**mag·ne′sian, mag·ne′sic** (-sik) *adj.*

mag·ne·si·um (mag nē′zē əm, -zhē əm, -zhəm) *n.* [ModL. < MAGNESIA] a light, silver-white, metallic chemical element: it burns with a hot, white light, and is used in photographic flashbulbs, etc.: symbol, Mg; at. wt., 24.312; at. no., 12

mag·net (mag′nit) *n.* [< OFr. < L. *magnes* < Gr. *Magnētis* (*lithos*), (stone) of Magnesia: see MAGNESIA] **1.** any piece of iron, steel, or lodestone that has the property of attracting iron, steel, etc. naturally or that has been given this property as an electromagnet **2.** a person or thing that attracts

mag·net·ic (mag net′ik) *adj.* **1.** having the properties of a magnet [a *magnetic* needle] **2.** of, producing, or caused by magnetism **3.** of the earth's magnetism [the *magnetic* poles] **4.** that can be magnetized **5.** powerfully attractive [a *magnetic* personality] —**mag·net′i·cal·ly** *adv.*

magnetic compass an instrument for showing directions magnetically, as by the action of the earth's magnetic field on a magnetic needle

magnetic field a region of space in which there is a measurable magnetic force

magnetic flux the sum of all the lines of force in a magnetic field

magnetic force the attracting or repelling force as between a magnet and a magnetic material

magnetic mine a naval mine exploded when the metal hull of a ship passing near it moves a magnetic needle, thus setting off the charge

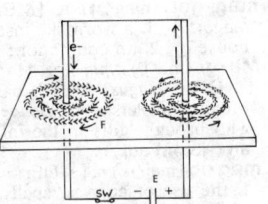

MAGNETIC FIELD
(F, direction of the magnetic flow; E, electromotive force; e-, current flow; SW, switch)

magnetic needle a slender bar of magnetized steel which, when swinging freely on a pivot, as in a compass, points toward the magnetic poles

magnetic north the direction toward which a magnetic needle points, usually not true north

magnetic pickup a phonograph pickup in which a part of the stylus assembly vibrates in a magnetic field between two coils so as to induce a current

magnetic pole **1.** either pole of a magnet **2.** either point on the earth's surface toward which a magnetic needle points: the north and south magnetic poles are not exactly the same as the geographical poles

magnetic recording the recording of electrical signals, as of sound, video, or computer data, by means of changes in areas of magnetization on a tape (**magnetic tape**) or disc

magnetic storm a disturbance of the earth's magnetic field, believed to be caused by sunspot activity

magnetic tape a thin plastic ribbon coated with magnetic particles, as of iron oxide, used for magnetic recording

mag·net·ism (mag′nə tiz'm) *n.* **1.** the property or quality of being magnetic **2.** the force to which this is due **3.** the branch of physics dealing with magnets, their properties, etc. **4.** the power to attract or charm; personal charm

mag·net·ite (-tīt′) *n.* a black iron oxide, Fe_3O_4, an important iron ore: called *lodestone* when magnetic

mag·net·ize (mag′nə tīz′) *vt.* **-ized′, -iz′ing** **1.** to give magnetic properties to (steel, iron, etc.); make into a magnet **2.** to attract or charm (a person) —*vi.* to become magnetic —**mag′net·iz′a·ble** *adj.* —**mag′net·i·za′tion** *n.* —**mag′net·iz′er** *n.*

mag·ne·to (mag nēt′ō) *n., pl.* **-tos** a dynamo in which one or more permanent magnets produce the magnetic field; esp., a small machine of this sort connected with and run by some internal-combustion engines to generate the current providing a spark for the ignition

mag·ne·to- [see MAGNET] *a combining form meaning* magnetism, magnetic force [*magnetoelectric*]

mag·ne·to·e·lec·tric (mag nēt′ō i lek′trik) *adj.* of electricity produced by changing magnetic fields affecting electric conductors —**mag·ne′to·e·lec′tri·cal·ly** (-tris′ə tē) *n.*

mag·ne·tom·e·ter (mag′nə täm′ə tər) *n.* **1.** an instrument for measuring magnetic forces, esp. the earth's magnetic field **2.** an instrument for magnetically detecting concealed metallic weapons on the person or in the luggage of airline passengers

mag·ne·to·sphere (mag nēt′ə sfir′) *n.* [MAGNETO- + -SPHERE] that region surrounding a planet, as the earth, containing that planet's magnetic field

mag·ne·tron (mag′nə trän′) *n.* [MAGNE(T) + (ELEC)TRON] an electron tube in which the flow of electrons is acted upon by a magnetic field to produce microwave frequencies

☆**magnet school** a public school that offers special courses and training in order to attract students from many parts of a city and thus help to bring about desegregation

mag·ni- [< L. *magnus,* great: for IE. base see MASTER] *a combining form meaning* great, big, large [*magnificent*]

Mag·nif·i·cat (mag nif′i kat′, män yif′i kät′) *n.* [L.] **1.** the hymn of the Virgin Mary in Luke 1:46–55 **2.** any musical setting for this

mag·ni·fi·ca·tion (mag′nə fi kā′shən) *n.* **1.** a magnifying or being magnified **2.** the power of magnifying **3.** a magnified image or copy

mag·nif·i·cence (mag nif′ə s'ns) *n.* [OFr. < L. < *magnificus,* noble < *magnus* (see MAGNI-) + *facere,* DO[1]] richness and splendor, as of furnishings, color, dress, etc.; grandeur

mag·nif·i·cent (mag nif′ə s'nt) *adj.* [OFr. < LL. *magnificens:* see prec.] **1.** beautiful in a grand or stately way; rich or splendid, as in construction, decoration, etc. **2.** exalted; lofty: said of ideas, etc. [a *magnificent* work of literature] **3.** [Colloq.] very good; excellent —**mag·nif′i·cent·ly** *adv.*

mag·ni·fi·co (mag nif′ə kō′) *n., pl.* **-coes′, -cos′** [It. < L. *magnificus:* see MAGNIFICENCE] a person of high rank

mag·ni·fy (mag′nə fī′) *vt.* **-fied′, -fy′ing** [< OFr. < L. *magnificare:* see MAGNIFICENCE] **1.** [Rare] to make greater **2.** to make seem greater, more important, etc. than is really so; exaggerate [to *magnify* one's sufferings] **3.** to make look larger than the actual size, esp. by means of a lens [using a microscope to *magnify* bacteria] **4.** [Archaic] to praise; extol —*vi.* to have the power of making things look larger —**mag′ni·fi′er** *n.*

magnifying glass a lens that makes an object seen through it look larger than it really is

mag·nil·o·quent (mag nil′ə kwənt) *adj.* [< L. < *magnus,* great + prp. of *loqui,* to speak] **1.** pompous or too grand in speaking or writing **2.** boastful or bombastic —**mag·nil′o·quence** *n.* —**mag·nil′o·quent·ly** *adv.*

mag·ni·tude (mag′nə tood′, -tyood′) *n.* [< L. < *magnus,* great: see MAGNI-] **1.** greatness, as of size, extent, or influence [the *magnitude* of Newton's achievements] **2.** *a)* size [an empire of relatively small *magnitude*] *b)* loudness (of sound) *c)* importance [a poet of minor *magnitude*] **3.** *Astron.* the degree of brightness of a fixed star: the brightest stars are of the first magnitude, and those barely seen without a telescope are of the sixth magnitude **4.** *Math.* a number given to a member of a set for purposes of comparison with other members of the same set —**of the first magnitude** of the greatest importance

☆**mag·no·li·a** (mag nō′lē ə, -nōl′yə) *n.* [ModL., after P. *Magnol* (1638–1715), Fr. botanist] **1.** any of a group of trees or shrubs with large, fragrant flowers of white, pink, or purple **2.** the flower

mag·num (mag′nəm) *n.* [L., neut. sing. of *magnus:* see MAGNI-] a wine bottle holding twice as much as the usual bottle, or about 2/5 of a gallon

‡**mag·num o·pus** (mag′nəm ō′pəs) [L.] **1.** a great work, esp. of art or literature; masterpiece **2.** a person's greatest work or undertaking

MAGNOLIA(tree, leaves & flower)

mag·pie (mag′pī′) *n.* [< *Mag,* dim. of MARGARET + PIE[3]] **1.** a noisy bird related to the crows and jays, with black-and-white coloring and a long tail **2.** a person who chatters **3.** a person who collects odds and ends

mag·uey (mag′wā; *Sp.* mä ge′ē) *n.* [Sp.] **1.** an agave of the southwestern U.S., Mexico, and Central America, with fleshy leaves from which tough fibers are got; esp., the century plant **2.** the fiber from this plant

Mag·yar (mag′yär; *Hung.* môd′yär) *n.* [Hung.] **1.** a member of the people who form the main ethnic group in Hungary **2.** their Finno-Ugric language; Hungarian —*adj.* of the Magyars, their language, etc.

Ma·ha·bha·ra·ta (mə hä′bä′rə tə) [Sans.] one of the two great epics of India, written in Sanskrit about 200 B.C.

ma·ha·ra·jah, ma·ha·ra·ja (mä′hə rä′jə) *n.* [< Sans. < *mahā,* great + *rājā,* king] formerly in India, a prince, specif. one who ruled any of the chief native states

ma·ha·ra·ni, ma·ha·ra·nee (mä'hə rä'nē) *n.* [< Hindi < *mahā*, great + *rānī*, queen] in India, the wife of any of the former maharajahs

ma·hat·ma (mə hat'mə, -hät'-) *n.* [< Sans. < *mahā*, great + *ātman*, soul] any of a class of wise and holy persons in India: used as a Hindu title of respect

Mah·di (mä'dē) *n.* [Ar. *mahdīy*, lit., one properly guided] **1.** a prophet expected by Moslems to appear on earth as the Messiah **2.** a Moslem claiming to be the Messiah

Ma·hi·can (mə hē'kən) *n.* [< Algonquian, lit., a wolf] **1.** a confederacy or tribe of Algonquian Indians who lived chiefly in the upper Hudson Valley **2.** an Indian of this confederacy **3.** *same as* MOHEGAN —*adj.* of this confederacy

mah-jongg, mah·jong (mä'jôŋ', -jäŋ', -zhôŋ', -zhäŋ') *n.* [< Chin. *ma-ch'iao*, lit., house sparrow (a figure on one of the tiles)] a game of Chinese origin, played with 136 or 144 small tiles: the object is to get winning sets of these tiles

Mah·ler (mä'lər), **Gus·tav** (gōōs'täf) 1860–1911; Austrian composer & conductor, born in Bohemia

ma·hog·a·ny (mə häg'ə nē, -hôg'-) *n., pl.* **-nies** [< ?] **1.** any of various tropical trees, esp. one of tropical America, with hard, reddish-brown wood valued for furniture **2.** the wood of any of these trees **3.** reddish brown —*adj.* **1.** made of mahogany **2.** reddish-brown

Ma·hom·et (mə häm'it) *same as* MOHAMMED —**Ma·hom'·et·an** *adj.*

☆**ma·ho·ni·a** (mə hō'nē ə) *n.* [ModL., after B. *McMahon* (c. 1775–1816), U.S. botanist] a low evergreen shrub with yellow flowers and blue berries

ma·hout (mə hout') *n.* [< Hindi < Sans. *mahāmātra*, lit., great in measure] in India and the East Indies, an elephant driver or elephant keeper

maid (mād) *n.* [< ME. contr. < *maiden*] **1.** *a)* a girl or young unmarried woman *b)* a virgin **2.** a girl or woman servant

maid·en (mād''n) *n.* [OE. *mægden*] **1.** *a)* a girl or young unmarried woman *b)* a virgin **2.** a race horse that has never won a race —*adj.* **1.** of, characteristic of, or suitable for a maiden or maidens **2.** unmarried [a *maiden* aunt] **3.** untried; unused; new **4.** first or earliest [a *maiden* voyage]

maid·en·hair (-her') *n.* any of various ferns with delicate brown to black fronds and slender stalks: also **maidenhair fern**

maid·en·head (-hed') *n.* **1.** [Archaic] maidenhood; virginity **2.** the hymen

maid·en·hood (-hood') *n.* the state or time of being a maiden

maid·en·ly (-lē) *adj.* **1.** of a maiden **2.** like or suitable for a maiden; modest, gentle, etc. —**maid'en·li·ness** *n.*

maiden name the family name that a woman had before she was married

maid of honor ☆**1.** an unmarried woman acting as chief attendant to the bride at a wedding **2.** an unmarried woman, usually of noble birth, attending a queen or princess

Maid of Orléans *name for* JOAN OF ARC

maid·ser·vant (mād'sur'vənt) *n.* a woman servant

mail¹ (māl) *n.* [OFr. *male*, ult. < OHG. *malaha*, wallet] **1.** *a)* letters, papers, packages, etc. carried and delivered by a postal system *b)* their collection or delivery at a certain time [late for the morning *mail*] **2.** [*also pl.*] the postal system [send it by *mail*] —*vt.* having to do with mail [a *mail* truck] —*vt.* to send by mail, as by putting into a mailbox —**mail'a·ble** *adj.*

mail² (māl) *n.* [OFr. *maille* < L. *macula*, mesh of a net] **1.** a flexible body armor made of small, linked metal rings, loops of chain, or scales **2.** the hard protective covering of some animals, as turtles —*vt.* to cover or protect as with mail [a *mailed* fist] —**mailed** *adj.*

☆**mail·bag** (māl'bag') *n.* **1.** a bag, as of leather, in which a mailman carries the mail he delivers: also **mail pouch 2.** a heavy canvas bag in which mail is transported: also **mail sack**

mail·box (-bäks') *n.* ☆**1.** a box into which mail is put when delivered, as at one's home ☆**2.** a box, as on a street, into which mail is put for collection Also **mail box**

☆**mail carrier** one whose work is carrying and delivering mail; mailman; postman

MAIL

mailed fist the use or threat of force, as between nations

☆**mail·er** (māl'ər) *n.* **1.** a container in which something is to be mailed **2.** an advertising leaflet for mailing out

Mail·gram (māl'gram') *a trademark for* a telegram delivered with the regular mail —*n.* [*also* m-] such a telegram

☆**mail·ing list** (māl'iŋ) a special list of names and addresses used by an organization, business, etc. in mailing out its literature, advertising matter, etc.

mail·man (māl'man', -mən) *n., pl.* **-men** (-men', -mən) *same as* MAIL CARRIER

☆**mail order** an order for goods to be sent through the mail —**mail'-or'der** *adj.*

☆**mail-order house** a business that takes mail orders and sends goods by mail

maim (mām) *vt.* [OFr. *mahaigner*] to injure so as to cause to lose the use of a necessary part of the body; cripple; mutilate

Mai·mon·i·des (mī män'ə dēz') (born *Moses ben Maimon*) 1135–1204; Sp. rabbi, physician, & philosopher, in Egypt

Main (mīn; *E.* mān) river in S West Germany, flowing west into the Rhine

main (mān) *n.* [OE. *mægen*: for IE. base see MAY] **1.** physical strength; force: now only in **with might and main**, with all one's strength **2.** the principal part or point: usually in **in the main**, mostly, chiefly **3.** any of the larger pipes or lines in a system from which smaller pipes carry water, gas, etc. to buildings **4.** [Poet.] the ocean —*adj.* **1.** orig., strong; powerful **2.** chief in size, importance, etc.; principal [their *main* office] —**by main force** (or **strength**) by sheer force (or strength)

main clause a clause that is a part of a sentence but that could stand alone as a complete sentence; independent clause

☆**main drag** [Slang] the main street of a city or town

Maine (mān) [prob. from its being the *main* part of New England] New England State of the U.S.: 33,215 sq. mi.; pop. 994,000; cap. Augusta: abbrev. **Me.**, **ME**

main·frame (mān'frām') *n.* the central unit of a large computer, that does the processing

main·land (mān'land', -lənd) *n.* the main land mass of a continent, as apart from nearby islands, etc. —**main'land'er** *n.*

main·line (-līn') *n.* the principal road, course, etc. —☆ *vt.* **-lined'**, **-lin'ing** [Slang] to inject (a narcotic drug) directly into a large vein —**main'lin'er** *n.*

main·ly (-lē) *adv.* chiefly; principally; in the main

main·mast (-məst, -mast') *n.* the principal mast of a vessel

main·sail (-s'l, -sāl') *n.* **1.** in a square-rigged vessel, the sail set from the main yard: also **main course 2.** in a fore-and-aft-rigged vessel, the large sail set from the mainmast

main·sheet (-shēt') *n.* the line controlling the angle at which a mainsail is set

main·spring (-spriŋ') *n.* **1.** the principal spring in a clock, watch, etc. **2.** the chief motive or cause

main·stay (-stā') *n.* **1.** the supporting line run forward from the mainmast **2.** a chief support [she is the *mainstay* of her family]

☆**main stem** [Slang] *same as* MAIN DRAG

main·stream (-strēm') *n.* the main current or the general trend of thought, action, etc. [in the *mainstream* of politics]

☆**Main Street 1.** the principal street of any small town **2.** the typical inhabitants of a small town, regarded as unsophisticated and conservative

main·tain (mān tān') *vt.* [< OFr. *maintenir*, ult. < L. *manu tenere*, to hold in the hand] **1.** to keep or keep up; carry on [*maintain* this speed] **2.** *a)* to keep in existence or continuance [food *maintains* life] *b)* to keep in a certain condition, as of repair [to *maintain* roads] **3.** to hold (a place, etc.) against attack **4.** *a)* to uphold or defend, as by argument [to *maintain* the position that capital punishment is wrong] *b)* to declare positively; assert [he still *maintains* that he's innocent] **5.** to provide the means of existence for [to *maintain* a family] —see SYN. at SUPPORT —**main·tain'a·ble** *adj.* —**main·tain'er** *n.*

---

main·te·nance (mān't'n əns) *n.* **1.** a maintaining or being maintained; upkeep, continuance, support, defense, etc. [taxes pay for the *maintenance* of schools] **2.** means of support or sustenance; livelihood [his job barely provides a *maintenance*]

main·top (mān'täp') *n.* a platform at the head of the lower section of the mainmast

main·top·mast (mān'täp'məst) *n.* the section of the mainmast above the maintop

main·top·sail (-s'l, -sāl) *n.* the sail above the mainsail on the mainmast

main yard the lower yard on the mainmast

Mainz (mīnts) city in West Germany, on the Rhine: pop. 177,000

mai·tre d' (māt'ər dē') [< next entry] [Colloq.] a headwaiter

‡**mai·tre d'hô·tel** (me'tr' dô tel') [Fr., lit., master of the house] **1.** a butler or steward **2.** a headwaiter

maize (māz) *n.* [Sp. *maíz* < WInd. *mahiz*] **1.** *chiefly Brit.* name for CORN[1] (sense 2) **2.** the color of ripe corn; yellow —*adj.* yellow

Maj. Major

ma·jes·tic (mə jes'tik) *adj.* having majesty; grand, stately, dignified, etc. [he walks with a *majestic* stride]: also **ma·jes'ti·cal** —**ma·jes'ti·cal·ly** *adv.*

maj·es·ty (maj'is tē) *n., pl.* **-ties** [< OFr. < L. *majestas* < base of *major*: see MAJOR] **1.** sovereign power or dignity [the *majesty* of the law] **2.** [M-] a title used in speaking to or of a sovereign, preceded by *His*, *Her*, or *Your* **3.** grandeur or stateliness [the *majesty* of the Alps]

ma·jol·i·ca (mə jäl'i kə, -yäl'-) *n.* [It. *maiolica* < *Maiolica*, MAJORCA] a variety of Italian pottery, enameled, glazed, and richly colored and decorated

ma·jor (mā'jər) *adj.* [L., compar. of *magnus*, great: see MASTER] **1.** *a)* greater in size, amount, or extent [electing him will require a *major* effort] *b)* greater in importance or rank [a *major* poet] **2.** of full legal age **3.** constituting the majority [the *major* part of our group agrees] ☆**4.** *Educ.* designating a field of study in which a student specializes **5.** *Music a)* designating an interval greater than the corresponding minor by a semitone *b)* characterized by major intervals, scales, etc. [a *major* key] *c)* based on the scale pattern of the major mode: see MAJOR SCALE —*vi.* ☆*Educ.* to make some subject one's major field of study; specialize [to *major* in physics] —*n.* **1.** a superior in some class or group **2.** *U.S. Mil.* an officer ranking above a captain ☆**3.** *Educ. a)* a major field of study [her *major* is history] *b)* a student specializing in a (specified) subject [he is an English *major*] **4.** *Law* a person of full legal age **5.** *Music* a major interval, key, etc. —**the Majors** ☆*Baseball* the Major Leagues

Ma·jor·ca (mə jôr'kə, -yôr'-) largest of the Balearic Islands

ma·jor·do·mo (mā'jər dō'mō) *n., pl.* **-mos** [< Sp. or It. < LL. < L. *major*, greater, an elder + *domus*, house] **1.** a man in charge of a great or royal household; chief steward **2.** any steward or butler: humorous usage

☆**ma·jor·ette** (mā'jər et') *n.* short for DRUM MAJORETTE

major general *pl.* **major generals** *U.S. Mil.* an officer ranking above a brigadier general

ma·jor·i·ty (mə jôr'ə tē, -jär'-) *n., pl.* **-ties** [< Fr. < ML. < L. *major*: see MAJOR] **1.** the greater part or larger number; more than half [the *majority* voted to adjourn] ☆**2.** the excess of the larger number of votes cast for one candidate, bill, etc. over all the rest of the votes [if candidate A gets 100 votes, candidate B, 200, and candidate C, 350, C has a *majority* of 50] **3.** the group or party with the majority of votes **4.** the state or time of being legally an adult **5.** *Mil.* the rank or position of a major

☆**major league** a principal league in a professional sport; specif., [M- L-] [pl.] the two main leagues of professional baseball clubs in the U.S., the National League and the American League —**ma'jor-league'** *adj.* —**ma'jor-leagu'er** *n.*

major orders 1. *R.C.Ch.* the orders of priest, deacon, and subdeacon **2.** in certain other Christian churches, the orders of bishop, priest, and deacon

major scale one of the two standard diatonic musical scales, with half steps instead of whole steps after the third and seventh tones

major suit *Bridge* hearts or spades

make (māk) *vt.* **made, mak'ing** [OE. *macian* < IE. base *mag-*, to knead] **1.** to bring into being; specif., *a)* to form by shaping or putting parts, ideas, etc. together; build, create, devise, etc. [to *make* a dinner, a fire, a contract, etc.] *b)* to cause; bring about [to *make* corrections] *c)* to cause to be available; provide [to *make* room] **2.** to cause to be, become, or seem [make him chairman]: sometimes used reflexively [make yourself comfortable] **3.** to prepare for use [make the beds] **4.** to amount to; equal [two pints *make* a quart] **5.** to have, or prove to have, the qualities of or for [to *make* a fine leader] **6.** to set up; establish [to *make* rules] **7.** *a)* to acquire, as by one's behavior [to *make* friends] *b)* to get by earning, investing, etc. [to *make* a fortune] **8.** to cause the success of [good pitching can *make* a baseball team] **9.** to understand as the meaning (of) [what do you *make* of his strange behavior?] **10.** to estimate to be [I *make* the distance about 500 miles] **11.** *a)* to do, execute, accomplish, etc. [to *make* a quick turn] *b)* to engage in [to *make* war] **12.** to deliver (a speech) or utter (remarks, etc.) **13.** to cause or force [*make* him behave] **14.** *a)* to arrive at; reach [the ship *made* port] *b)* to arrive at in time [to *make* the train] **15.** to go or travel; traverse [to *make* 500 miles the first day] **16.** [Colloq.] to succeed in getting a position on, being mentioned in, etc. [to *make* the team; to *make* the news] ☆**17.** [Slang] to seduce sexually **18.** *Card Playing a)* to win (tricks) or fulfill (one's bid) *b)* to shuffle (the cards) **19.** *Elec.* to close (a circuit); effect (a contact) **20.** *Games* to score —*vi.* **1.** to start (to do something) [she *made* as if to go] **2.** to tend, extend, or point (*to, toward*, etc.) **3.** to behave in a specified manner [*make* bold, *make* merry] **4.** to cause something to be in a specified condition [*make* ready] —*n.* **1.** the way in which something is made; style; build **2.** type, sort, or brand [a foreign *make* of car] **3.** character; nature [a man of this *make*] **4.** *Elec.* the closing of a circuit —**make after** to chase or follow —**make away with 1.** to steal **2.** to get rid of **3.** to eat all of **4.** to kill —**make believe** to pretend —**make for 1.** to head for **2.** to attack **3.** to help bring about [honesty and affection *make for* a happy home] —**make it** [Colloq.] to do or achieve a certain thing —☆**make like** [Slang] to imitate —**make off with** to steal —**make or break** to cause the success or failure of —**make out 1.** to see with some difficulty **2.** to understand **3.** to write out **4.** to fill out (a blank form, etc.) **5.** to (try to) show or prove to be **6.** to succeed; get along ☆**7.** [Slang] to kiss, caress, etc. —**make over 1.** to change; cause to be different **2.** to transfer the ownership of, as by signing a legal document **3.** [Colloq.] to be demonstrative toward or about —**make up 1.** to put together; compose **2.** to form; be the parts of **3.** to invent **4.** to complete by providing what is lacking **5.** to compensate (*for*) **6.** to become friendly again after a quarrel **7.** to put cosmetics on **8.** to decide (one's mind) **9.** to select and arrange type, illustrations, etc. for (a book, page, etc.) ☆**10.** *Educ.* to take again (a test one has failed) or take (a test one has missed) —**make up to** to try to make oneself liked, as by flattering, being friendly to, etc. —☆**on the make** [Colloq.] trying to succeed financially, socially, etc., esp. in an aggressive way

SYN.—**make** is the general term meaning to bring into being or produce, either physically or mentally [make a dress; make a decision]; **form** suggests a definite contour, figure, etc. in the thing made [form the wet sand into a mound]; **shape** suggests the giving of a specific form as by molding, cutting, hammering, etc. [blowing air into the heated glass to shape it]; **fashion** implies inventiveness, cleverness, skill, etc. [he fashioned a birdhouse from an old hatbox]; **construct** implies a putting of parts together according to a design [construct a garage]; **manufacture** implies a producing from raw materials, now especially by machinery and on a large scale [manufacture trucks]; **fabricate** implies building or manufacturing, as by putting together standardized parts

make-be·lieve (māk'bə lēv') *n.* a pretending or imagining, as in play —*adj.* pretended; imagined [a *make-believe* friend]

mak·er (māk'ər) *n.* **1.** a person or thing that makes **2.** [M-] God **3.** *Law* the signer of a promissory note —**meet one's Maker** to die

make·shift (māk'shift') *n.* a thing that will do for a while as a substitute; temporary expedient —*adj.* that will do for a while as a substitute —see **SYN.** at RESOURCE

make-up, make-up (-up') *n.* **1.** the way in which something is put together; composition [the *makeup* of the atom] **2.** nature; disposition [to have a cheerful *makeup*] **3.** the cosmetics, wigs, costumes, etc. put on for theatrical roles **4.** cosmetics generally **5.** the arrangement of type, illustrations, etc. in a book, newspaper, etc. ☆**6.** [Colloq.] a special test taken by a student to make up a test he has missed or failed to pass —*adj.* of or for making up

Ma·key·ev·ka (mä kā'yif kä') city in SE Ukrainian S.S.R., in the Donets river valley: pop. 415,000

mak·ing (māk'kiŋ) *n.* **1.** the act of one that makes or the process of being made **2.** the cause of success or advancement [an experience that will be the *making* of him] **3.** *a)* something made *b)* the quantity made at a single time **4.** [*often pl.*] the material or potential qualities needed [to have the *makings* of a good doctor]

mal- [Fr. < L. < *male,* badly < *malus,* bad] *a prefix meaning* bad or badly, wrong, ill [*maladjustment*]

Mal. 1. Malachi 2. Malay 3. Malayan

Mal·a·bar Coast (mal′ə bär′) coastal region of SW India

Ma·lac·ca (mə lak′ə) 1. state of W Malaya, on the Strait of Malacca 2. **Strait of,** strait between Sumatra & the Malay Peninsula

Malacca cane [< MALACCA] a lightweight walking stick of rattan, often with brown mottling

Mal·a·chi (mal′ə kī′) *Bible* 1. a Hebrew prophet of the 5th cent. B.C. 2. the book containing prophecies said to have been written by him

mal·a·chite (mal′ə kīt′) *n.* [< L. < Gr. *malachē,* mallow: from its color] native copper carbonate, $CuCO_3fCu(OH)_2$, a green mineral used for table tops, vases, etc.

mal·a·col·o·gy (mal′ə käl′ə jē) *n.* [< Fr. < Gr. *malakos,* soft + -LOGY] the branch of zoology dealing with mollusks

mal·a·dap·tive (mal′ə dap′tiv) *n.* not well adapted to a situation, function, etc. [*maladaptive* behavior] —**mal′ad·ap·ta′tion** (-ad əp tā′shən) *n.*

mal·ad·just·ed (mal′ə jus′tid) *adj.* poorly adjusted, esp. to the conditions of one's life —**mal′ad·just′ment** *n.*

mal·ad·min·is·ter (-əd min′ə stər) *vt.* to administer badly or dishonestly —**mal′ad·min′is·tra′tion** (-ə strā′shən) *n.*

mal·a·droit (mal′ə droit′) *adj.* [Fr.: see MAL- & ADROIT] awkward; clumsy; bungling —**mal′a·droit′ly** *adv.* —**mal′a·droit′ness** *n.*

mal·a·dy (mal′ə dē) *n., pl.* **-dies** [< OFr. *malade,* sick < VL. *male habitus,* out of condition: see MAL- & HABIT] a disease; illness; sickness

Má·la·ga (mä′lä gä′; *E.* mal′ə gə) seaport in S Spain, on the Mediterranean: pop. 351,000

Mal·a·ga (mal′ə gə) *n.* 1. a large, white, oval grape 2. a white, sweet wine, orig. from Málaga

Mal·a·gas·y (mal′ə gas′ē) *n.* 1. *pl.* **-gas′y, -gas′ies** a native or inhabitant of Madagascar 2. the Indonesian language of the Malagasy —*adj.* of the Malagasy or their language

Malagasy Republic *former name of* MADAGASCAR

mal·a·gue·na (mal′ə gān′yə, -gwä′nə) *n.* [< Sp. < MÁLAGA] a Spanish folk tune or dance, esp. one like the fandango

ma·laise (ma lāz′) *n.* [Fr. < *mal,* bad (see MAL-) + *aise,* EASE] a vague feeling of discomfort or uneasiness, such as one feels early in an illness

☆**mal·a·mute** (mal′ə myōōt′) *n.* [< *Malemute,* name of an Eskimo tribe] *same as* ALASKAN MALAMUTE

mal·a·pert (mal′ə purt′) *adj.* [< OFr. < *mal,* badly + *appert,* expert, clever] [Archaic] impudent in a lively, bold way; pert —**mal′a·pert′ly** *adv.* —**mal′a·pert′ness** *n.*

mal·a·prop (mal′ə präp′) *adj.* [< MALAPROPISM] using or characterized by malapropisms: also **mal·a·prop′i·an** (-ē ən) —*n. same as* MALAPROPISM

mal·a·prop·ism (mal′ə präp iz′m) *n.* [after Mrs. *Malaprop,* a character in Sheridan's *The Rivals*] 1. a laughable or ridiculous misuse of words, esp. by confusing words that sound somewhat alike 2. an instance of this, as the use of "cinnamon" for "synonym"

mal·ap·ro·pos (mal′ap rə pō′, mal ap′-) *adj., adv.* [Fr.: see MAL- & APROPOS] not at the right time or place; inappropriate or inappropriately

ma·lar·i·a (mə ler′ē ə) *n.* [It. < *mala aria,* bad air] an infectious disease caused by protozoans that are carried to man by the bite of an infected mosquito, esp. the anopheles: it is characterized by severe chills and fever that keep coming back from time to time —**ma·lar′i·al, ma·lar′i·an** *adj.*

☆**ma·lar·key, ma·lar·ky** (mə lär′kē) *n.* [< ? Irish surname] [Slang] insincere or meaningless talk; nonsense

☆**mal·a·thi·on** (mal′ə thī′än) *n.* an organic phosphate, $C_{10}H_{19}O_6S_2P$, used as an insecticide

Ma·la·wi (mä′lä wē) country in SE Africa: a member of the Commonwealth: 46,066 sq. mi.; pop. 4,530,000; cap. Lilongwe

Ma·lay (mä′lā, mə lā′) *n.* 1. a member of a large group of brown-skinned peoples living in the Malay Peninsula, the Malay Archipelago, and nearby islands 2. their Indonesian language —*adj.* of the Malays, their country, language, etc.

Ma·lay·a (mə lā′ə) 1. *same as* MALAY PENINSULA 2. group of eleven states at the S end of the Malay Peninsula: it is a part of Malaysia and is called *Peninsular Malaysia* (formerly *Federation of Malaya*)

Mal·a·ya·lam (mal′ə yä′ləm) *n.* a Dravidian language spoken on the SW coast of India

Ma·lay·an (mə lā′ən) *adj. same as* INDONESIAN (sense 2) —*n.* 1. *same as* MALAY (sense 1) 2. *same as* INDONESIAN (sense 3)

Malay Archipelago large group of islands between the mainland of SE Asia & Australia

Ma·lay·o-Pol·y·ne·sian (mə lā′ō pä′ē nē′zhən, -shən) *adj.* designating or of a family of languages spoken over a large area in the central and western Pacific, including Polynesian, Indonesian, etc. —*n.* these languages

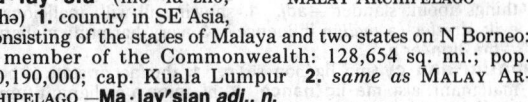

Malay Peninsula peninsula in SE Asia, including the S part of Thailand & the states of Malaya

Ma·lay·sia (mə lā′zhə, -shə) 1. country in SE Asia, consisting of the states of Malaya and two states on N Borneo: a member of the Commonwealth: 128,654 sq. mi.; pop. 10,190,000; cap. Kuala Lumpur 2. *same as* MALAY ARCHIPELAGO —**Ma·lay′sian** *adj., n.*

MALAY ARCHIPELAGO

Mal·colm (mal′kəm) [Celt. *Maolcolm,* lit., servant of (St.) Columba] a masculine name

mal·con·tent (mal′kən tent′) *adj.* [OFr.: see MAL- & CONTENT[1]] not satisfied with the way things are and ready to rebel —*n.* a dissatisfied or rebellious person

‡**mal de mer** (mál də mer′) [Fr.] seasickness

Mal·den (môl′dən) [after *Maldon,* town in England] city in E Mass.: suburb of Boston: pop. 56,000

Mal·dive Islands (mal′dīv) country on a group of islands in the Indian Ocean, southwest of Ceylon: 115 sq. mi.; pop. 104,000; also **Mal′dives**

male (māl) *adj.* [< OFr. < L. *masculus,* dim. of *mas,* a male] 1. designating or of the sex that fertilizes the ovum of the female and begets offspring 2. of, like, or suitable to members of this sex; masculine 3. of men or boys [a *male* chorus] 4. having a part shaped to fit into a corresponding hollow part (called *female*): said of electric plugs, etc. 5. *Bot.* having only stamens or antheridia —*n.* a male person, animal, or plant —**male′ness** *n.*

SYN. —**male** is the basic term used to distinguish by sex from females: it is used of animals and plants as well as of human beings; **masculine** is applied to qualities, such as strength, boldness, etc., usually thought of as characteristic of men, or to things or activities traditionally considered suitable for men; **manly** suggests the noble qualities, such as courage, independence, etc., associated with a man of mature character; **mannish** is used of women who have traits, manners, etc. usually considered more characteristic of men; **virile** refers to such qualities as strength, force, and esp. sexual vigor, that are associated with a mature man in his prime

mal·e·dic·tion (mal′ə dik′shən) *n.* [OFr. < LL. *maledictio* < L., abuse: see MAL- & DICTION] a calling down of evil on someone; curse

mal·e·fac·tion (mal′ə fak′shən) *n.* wrongdoing; crime

mal·e·fac·tor (mal′ə fak′tər) *n.* [L. < pp. of *malefacere* < *male,* evil + *facere,* to do] an evildoer or criminal

ma·lef·i·cent (mə lef′ə s'nt) *adj.* [see prec.] harmful; hurtful; evil —**ma·lef′i·cence** *n.*

ma·lev·o·lent (mə lev′ə lənt) *adj.* [< OFr. < L. < *male,* evil + prp. of *velle,* to wish] wishing evil or harm to others; having or showing ill will; malicious —**ma·lev′o·lent·ly** *adv.*

ma·lev·o·lence (mə lev′ə ləns) *n.* the quality or state of being malevolent; malice; ill will —**see SYN·** at MALICE

mal·fea·sance (mal fē′z'ns) *n.* [obs. Fr. *malfaisance* < *mal,* evil + prp. of *faire,* to do] wrongdoing or misconduct, esp. by a public official; doing of an act that is unlawful, as the taking of graft: distinguished from MISFEASANCE, NONFEASANCE —**mal·fea′sant** *adj.*

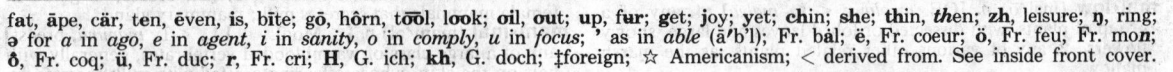

mal·for·ma·tion (mal'fôr mā'shən) *n.* faulty, irregular, or abnormal formation of a body or part —**mal·formed'** (-fôrmd') *adj.*

mal·func·tion (mal funk'shən) *vi.* to fail to function as it should —*n.* the act or an instance of malfunctioning [the launch was delayed by the *malfunction* of a rocket]

Ma·li (mä'lē) country in W Africa, south & east of Mauritania: 464,873 sq. mi.; pop. 5,143,000

mal·ic acid (mal'ik, mā'lik) [< Fr. < L. < Gr. *mēlon*, apple] a colorless acid, $C_4H_6O_5$, occurring in apples and other fruits

mal·ice (mal'is) *n.* [OFr. < L. < *malus*, bad] 1. ill will; desire to harm another; spite 2. *Law* the state of mind shown by the doing of something unlawful on purpose —**malice aforethought** an intention and plan to do something unlawful on purpose
SYN.—**malice** implies a deep hatred or dislike causing one to get pleasure from hurting others or seeing them suffer; **ill will** implies unfriendly feelings that lead one to wish harm, unhappiness, etc. to others; **malevolence**, a formal term for **ill will**, may also suggest that the unfriendly feelings are stronger and more evil; **spite** suggests a mean desire to get back at others by hurting or annoying them, esp. in nasty, petty ways; **rancor** implies bitter, long-lasting ill will; **malignity** suggests great malevolence that shows itself in acts of cruelty without pity

ma·li·cious (mə lish'əs) *adj.* having, showing, or caused by malice; spiteful [out of jealousy, he started *malicious* rumors] —**ma·li'cious·ly** *adv.* —**ma·li'cious·ness** *n.*

ma·lign (mə līn') *vt.* [< OFr. < LL. < L. *malignus*, wicked < *male*, ill + base of *genus*, born] to say damaging or unfair things about —*adj.* 1. showing ill will; malicious 2. evil; sinister [a *malign* influence] 3. very harmful; malignant —**ma·lign'er** *n.*

ma·lig·nan·cy (mə lig'nən sē) *n.* 1. the fact or state of being malignant: also **ma·lig'nance** 2. *pl.* -**cies** a malignant tumor

ma·lig·nant (mə lig'nənt) *adj.* [< LL. < L. *malignus*: see MALIGN] 1. having an evil influence; malign 2. wishing evil; malevolent 3. very harmful 4. causing or likely to cause death, esp. by spreading unchecked through the body [a cancer is a *malignant* growth] —**ma·lig'nant·ly** *adv.*

ma·lig·ni·ty (mə lig'nə tē) *n.* 1. very strong ill will or desire to harm others; great malice 2. the quality of being very harmful or dangerous 3. *pl.* -**ties** a malignant act, event, or feeling —see **SYN.** at MALICE

ma·lines (mə lēn') *n.* [< *Malines*, Belgian city] a thin, somewhat stiff, silk net, like tulle: also **ma·line'**

ma·lin·ger (mə liŋ'gər) *vi.* [< Fr. *malingre*, sickly < *mal-*, bad + OFr. *heingre*, haggard] to pretend to be ill in order to escape duty or work; shirk —**ma·lin'ger·er** *n.*

mall (môl, mal) *n.* [var. of MAUL: orig. a mallet used in a game (*pall-mall*), later the lane or alley where it was played] 1. a shaded walk or public promenade ☆2. *a*) a street for pedestrians only, with shops on each of the sides *b*) a completely enclosed, air-conditioned shopping center like this 3. a median strip: see MEDIAN (*n.* 2)

mal·lard (mal'ərd) *n.,* *pl.* -**lards**, -**lard**: see PLURAL, II, D, 1 [OFr. *malart*] the common wild duck from which the domestic duck is descended: the male has a green head and a band of white around the neck

Mal·lar·mé (mà làr mā'), **Sté·phane** (stā fàn') 1842–98; Fr. poet

mal·le·a·ble (mal'ē ə b'l) *adj.* [< ML. < L. *malleare*, to hammer < *malleus*, a hammer] 1. that can be hammered, pounded, or pressed into various shapes without breaking [silver is a *malleable* metal] 2. that can be changed, trained, etc.; pliable; adaptable [a *malleable* mind] —see **SYN.** at PLIABLE —**mal'le·a·bil'i·ty**, **mal'le·a·ble·ness** *n.*

mal·let (mal'it) *n.* [< MFr. dim. of *mail* < OFr. *maile*: see MAUL] 1. a kind of hammer, usually with a wooden head and a short handle, for driving a chisel, etc. 2. *a*) a long-handled hammer used in playing croquet *b*) a similar instrument used in playing polo 3. a small, light hammer used for playing a vibraphone, xylophone, etc.

mal·le·us (mal'ē əs) *n.,* *pl.* **mal·le·i** (-ī') [L., a hammer] the outermost of the three small bones in the middle ear of mammals, shaped somewhat like a hammer

MALLET

Mal·lor·ca (mäl yôr'kä, mä-) *Sp. name of* MAJORCA

mal·low (mal'ō) *n.* [OE. *mealuwe* < L. *malva*] 1. any of a group of plants, with dissected or lobed leaves and large, showy flowers 2. any of various other related plants, as the marsh mallow

Malm·ö (mälm'ö; *E.* mal'mō) seaport in S Sweden: pop. 254,000

malm·sey (mäm'zē) *n.* [< ML. < Gr. *Monembasia*, Greek town] 1. a strong, full-flavored, sweet white wine 2. the grape from which this is made

mal·nour·ished (mal nur'isht) *adj.* improperly nourished

mal·nu·tri·tion (mal'nōō trish'ən) *n.* faulty nutrition; poor nourishment caused by not getting enough food, esp. not enough of the right kind

mal·oc·clu·sion (mal'ə klōō'zhən) *n.* a condition in which the upper and lower teeth do not meet properly in biting: see OCCLUSION

mal·o·dor·ous (mal ō'dər əs) *adj.* having a bad odor; stinking —see **SYN.** at STINKING —**mal·o'dor·ous·ly** *adv.*

Mal·o·ry (mal'ər ē), **Sir Thomas** ?–1471?; Eng. writer who collected and translated from French tales about King Arthur

mal·prac·tice (mal prak'tis) *n.* 1. harmful or improper treatment of a patient by a physician or surgeon, as because of carelessness or lack of skill 2. improper conduct by any professional or official person —**mal'prac·ti'tion·er** (-tish'ən ər) *n.*

malt (môlt) *n.* [OE. *mealt*: for IE. base see MILL[1]] 1. barley or other grain softened by soaking in water until it sprouts and then kiln-dried: used in brewing and distilling 2. a drink brewed from malt, esp. beer, ale, etc. ☆3. [Colloq.] same as MALTED MILK —*adj.* made with malt —*vt.* 1. to change (barley, etc.) into malt 2. to prepare (milk, etc.) with malt or malt extract —*vi.* 1. to be changed into malt 2. to change barley, etc. into malt —**malt'y** *adj.* **malt'i·er**, **malt'i·est**

TYPES OF MALOCCLUSION

Mal·ta (môl'tə) 1. country on a group of islands in the Mediterranean, south of Sicily: a member of the Commonwealth: 122 sq. mi.; pop. 328,000; cap. Valletta 2. main island of this group

☆**malted milk** a drink made by mixing a powdered preparation of dried milk and malted cereals with milk and, usually, ice cream and a flavoring

Mal·tese (môl tēz') *adj.* of Malta, its inhabitants, etc. —*n.* 1. *pl.* **Mal·tese'** a native or inhabitant of Malta 2. the Arabic language of Malta 3. a variety of domestic cat with bluish-gray fur: in full, **Maltese cat**

MALTA

Maltese cross a cross whose arms look like arrowheads pointing inward: see illustration at CROSS

malt extract a sticky, sugary substance obtained from malt soaked in water

Mal·thu·sian (mal thōō'zhən, -zē ən) *adj.* [after T. *Malthus* (1766–1834), Eng. economist] designating or of a theory that the population of the world increases faster than the food supply, but that it is naturally held down by war, famine, and disease —*n.* a supporter of this theory

malt liquor beer, ale, etc. made from malt by fermentation

malt·ose (môl'tōs) *n.* a white, crystalline sugar, $C_{12}H_{22}O_{11}\cdot H_2O$, obtained by the action of the diastase of malt on starch: also called **malt sugar**

mal·treat (mal trēt') *vt.* [< Fr.: see MAL- & TREAT] to treat roughly, unkindly, or brutally; abuse —**mal·treat'ment** *n.*

mam·ba (mäm'bə) *n.* [Zulu *imamba*] any of several very poisonous, African tree snakes related to the cobras but not having a hood

☆**mam·bo** (mäm'bō) *n.* [AmSp.] a ballroom dance to music of Cuban origin in 4/4 time with a heavy accent on the second and fourth beats —*vi.* to dance the mambo

mam·ma[1] (mä'mə; *occas.* mə mä') *n.* [like L. *mamma*, mother, Sans. *mā*, Gr. *mammē* < baby talk] mother: a child's word: also **ma'ma**

mam·ma[2] (mam'ə) *n.,* *pl.* -**mae** (-ē) [L., breast] a gland in female mammals that secretes milk; mammary gland

mam·mal (mam'əl) *n.* [< ModL. < LL. < L. *mamma*, breast] any of a large class of warmblooded vertebrates, generally with hair on the skin, whose offspring are fed with milk secreted by the female mammary glands —**mam·ma·li·an** (mə māʹlē ən, ma-) *adj., n.*

mam·mal·o·gy (mə malʹə jē, ma-) *n.* the branch of zoology dealing with mammals —**mam·malʹo·gist** *n.*

mam·ma·ry (mamʹər ē) *adj.* designating or of the milk-secreting glands; of the mammae

mam·mil·la (ma milʹə, mə-) *n., pl.* **-lae** (-ē) [< L. dim of *mamma*, breast] 1. a nipple 2. any thing or part that swells out like a nipple —**mam·milʹlar·y** (mamʹə lerʹē) *adj.*

mam·mon (mamʹən) *n.* [< LL. < Gr. < Aram. *māmōnā*, riches] [*often* M-] riches or wealth thought of as an evil that some people worship —**mamʹmon·ism** *n.*

mam·moth (mamʹəth) *n.* [Russ. *mamont*] an extinct elephant with a hairy skin and long tusks curving upward —☆*adj.* very big; huge; enormous —see SYN. at ENORMOUS

Mammoth Cave National Park national park in southwestern Ky., containing enormous caverns

mam·my (mamʹē) *n., pl.* **-mies** [var. of MAMMA¹] 1. mamma; mother: a child's word ☆2. a black woman who takes care of white children, esp. as formerly in the Southern States

HAIRY MAMMOTH
(to 13 ft. high
at shoulder)

man (man) *n., pl.* **men** (men) [OE. *mann* < IE. base *manu-*] 1. a human being; person; specif., any member of a species (see HOMO SAPIENS) of primates having the most highly developed brain and communicating by speech [*"that all men are created equal"*] 2. the human race; mankind: used without *the* or *a* [*man's conquest of space*] 3. an adult male human being 4. *a*) an adult male servant, follower, subordinate, etc. *b*) a male employee *c*) [Archaic] a vassal 5. a husband or a lover 6. a person with qualities generally thought of as manly, such as strength, forcefulness, etc. [*they hoped the experience would make a man of their son*] 7. any of the pieces used in chess, checkers, etc. 8. [Slang] fellow; chap: used as a general term of address —*vt.* **manned, manʹning** 1. to furnish with men for work, defense, etc. [*to man a ship*] 2. to take assigned places in, on, or at [*man the guns!*] 3. to strengthen; brace [*to man oneself for an ordeal*] —*interj.* [Slang] an exclamation used for emphasis [*man! am I ever tired!*]: also used, as in hip talk, merely to fill a pause in speech —*adj.* male [*man talk*] —**as a** (or **one**) **man** all together; in unison; unanimously —**be one's own man** 1. to be free and independent 2. to be in full control of oneself —**man and boy** first as a boy and then as a man —☆**the Man** [Slang] the person having authority over one, as a policeman or boss —**to a man** with everyone taking part

-man (mən, man) *a combining form meaning* man or person of a certain country, work, activity, etc. [*Frenchman, sportsman*]

Man. 1. Manila (paper) 2. Manitoba

man. manual

Man (man), **Isle of** one of the Brit. Isles, between Northern Ireland & England: 227 sq. mi.; pop. 48,000

man about town a worldly man who spends much time in fashionable restaurants, clubs, etc.

man·a·cle (manʹə k'l) *n.* [< OFr. < L. *manicula*, dim. of *manus*, hand: see MANUAL] 1. a handcuff; fetter or shackle for the hand 2. any restraint *Usually used in pl.* —*vt.* **-cled, -cling** 1. to put handcuffs on; fetter 2. to restrain; hamper

man·age (manʹij) *vt.* **-aged, -ag·ing** [It. *maneggiare* < *mano*, hand < L. *manus*: see MANUAL] 1. orig., to train (a horse) in his paces 2. to control the movement or behavior of [*she can't manage her children*] 3. to have charge of; direct [*to manage a household*] 4. to get (a person) to do what one wishes, esp. by tact, flattery, etc. 5. to succeed in doing or getting; contrive [*we managed to find shelter*] —*vi.* 1. to carry on business or direct affairs 2. to get along somehow [*don't worry, we'll manage*] —see SYN. at CONDUCT

man·age·a·ble (manʹij ə b'l) *adj.* that can be managed —**manʹage·a·bilʹi·ty, manʹage·a·ble·ness** *n.* —**manʹage·a·bly** *adv.*

managed currency a currency regulated by a government which controls the amount of money in circulation so as to control credit, prices, etc.

man·age·ment (manʹij mənt) *n.* 1. the act, art, or manner of managing, controlling, etc. [*the business succeeded because of skillful management*] 2. the persons managing a business, institution, etc. 3. all such persons as a group [*the problems of labor and management*]

man·ag·er (manʹij ər) *n.* a person who manages the affairs of a business, institution, client, team, etc. —**manʹag·erʹship** *n.*

man·a·ge·ri·al (manʹə jirʹē əl) *adj.* of a manager or management —**manʹa·ge·riʹal·ism** *n.* —**manʹa·ge·riʹal·ly** *adv.*

Ma·na·gua (mä näʹgwä) 1. lake in W Nicaragua 2. capital of Nicaragua, on this lake: pop. 300,000 (1967): devastated by an earthquake, 1972

‡**ma·ña·na** (mä nyäʹnä) *n.* [Sp.] tomorrow —*adv.* 1. tomorrow 2. at some indefinite future time

Ma·nas·sas (mə nasʹəs) [< ?] town in NE Va., near Bull Run, where the Union army was defeated in two battles of the Civil War

Ma·nas·seh (mə nasʹə) *Bible* 1. the elder son of Joseph 2. the tribe of Israel descended from him

man-at-arms (manʹət ärmzʹ) *n., pl.* **men′-at-arms′** (menʹ-) formerly, a soldier; esp., a heavily armed medieval soldier on horseback

man·a·tee (manʹə tēʹ, manʹə tēʹ) *n.* [Sp. *manatí* < native (Carib) name] a large, plant-eating sea mammal living in shallow tropical waters, having flippers and a broad, flat, rounded tail; sea cow

MANATEE
(8–13 ft. long)

Man·ches·ter (manʹchesʹtər, -chi stər) 1. city & port in NW England: pop. 603,000 2. [after the city in England] city in southern N.H.: pop. 88,000

Man·chu (man chōōʹ, manʹchōō) *n.* 1. *pl.* **-chus′, -chu′** a member of a Mongolian people of Manchuria: the Manchus conquered China in 1643-44 and ruled until 1912 2. the language of the Manchus —*adj.* of Manchuria, the Manchus, their language, etc.

Man·chu·ri·a (man chōorʹē ə) region of NE China, north of Korea —**Man·chuʹri·an** *adj., n.*

man·ci·ple (manʹsi p'l) *n.* [< OFr. < ML., ult. < L. *manus*, a hand + base of *capere*, to take] a person responsible for buying provisions, as for an English college, a monastery, etc.

-man·cy (manʹsē) [< OFr. < LL. < Gr. *manteia*, divination] *a combining form meaning* divination [*chiromancy*]

man·da·la (munʹdə lə) *n.* [Sans. *maṇḍala*] a circular design with various geometric forms, that is a symbol of the universe in Hinduism and Buddhism

Man·da·lay (manʹdə lāʹ, manʹdə-lāʹ) city in C Burma, on the Irrawaddy River: pop. 360,000

man·da·mus (man dāʹməs) *n.* [L., we command] *Law* a writ commanding that a specified thing be done, issued by a higher court to a lower one, or to a corporation, agency, official, etc.

MANDALA

man·da·rin (manʹdə rin) *n.* [< Port. < Hindi *mantrī*, minister of state < Sans. < *mantra*, counsel: for IE. base see MIND] 1. a high official of China under the Empire, before 1911 2. a member of any elite group, esp. of conservative intellectuals or politicians who have great power 3. [M-] the official or main dialect of Chinese 4. a small, sweet orange with a loose rind: in full, **mandarin orange** —**manʹda·rin·ism** *n.*

man·date (manʹdāt) *n.* [< L. neut. pp. of *mandare*, to command < *manus*, a hand + pp. of *dare*, to give] 1. an order or command by someone in authority 2. *a*) formerly, a commission from the League of Nations to a country to administer some region, colony, etc. *b*) the area so administered 3. the wishes of the members of a country, organization, etc. expressed to a representative, legislature, etc. as by their votes, and regarded as an order 4. *Law* an order from a higher court or official to a lower one —*vt.* **-dat·ed, -dat·ing** to assign (a region, etc.) as a mandate —**manʹda·torʹ** *n.*

man·da·to·ry (manʹdə tôrʹē) *adj.* 1. of, like, or containing a mandate 2. commanded or required by those in authority;

obligatory [the company has a *mandatory* retirement age of 65]
3. holding a mandate (sense 2) —**man'da·to'ri·ly** *adv.*

man·di·ble (man'də b'l) *n.* [OFr. < LL. < *mandibulum* < L. *mandere*, to chew: for IE. base see MOUTH] the jaw; specif., *a)* the lower jaw of a vertebrate *b)* either of the most forward pair of biting jaws of an insect or other arthropod *c)* either jaw of a beaked animal, as of a squid —**man·dib'u·lar** (-dib'yoo-lər) *adj.*

man·do·lin (man'd'l in', man'də lin') *n.* [< Fr. < It. dim. of *mandola* < LL. < LGr. *pandoura*, kind of lute] a musical instrument with four or five pairs of strings and a deep, rounded sound box: it is played with a plectrum —**man'do·lin'ist** *n.*

MANDOLIN

man·drake (man'drāk) *n.* [< OE. *mandragora* < LL. < Gr. *mandragoras*, but confused by folk etym. with MAN + obs. *drake*, dragon] **1.** *a)* a poisonous plant of the nightshade family, with a short stem and a thick, often forked root *b)* the root, formerly used in medicine as a narcotic Also **man·drag·o·ra** (man drag'-ər ə) ☆**2.** *same as* MAY APPLE

man·drel, man·dril (man'drəl) *n.* [prob. < Fr. *mandrin*] **1.** a spindle or bar inserted into something to hold it while it is being machined **2.** a metal bar used as a core around which metal, glass, etc. is cast, molded, or shaped

man·drill (man'dril) *n.* [MAN + DRILL[4]] a large, fierce, strong baboon of W Africa: the male has blue and red patches on the face and rump

mane (mān) *n.* [OE. *manu*] **1.** the long hair growing from the top or sides of the neck of certain animals, as the horse, lion, etc. **2.** long, thick hair on a person's head —**maned** *adj.*

man-eat·er (man'ēt'ər) *n.* a shark, tiger, etc. that eats, or is thought to eat, human flesh —**man'-eat'ing** *adj.*

ma·nège, ma·nege (ma nezh', -nāzh') *n.* [Fr. < It. *maneggio*: see MANAGE] **1.** the art of riding and training horses **2.** a school teaching this art **3.** the paces of a trained horse

ma·nes (mā'nēz) *n.pl.* [L.] [*often* M-] Ancient Rom. Religion the souls of the dead, esp. of dead ancestors, regarded as gods

Ma·net (má nā'), **É·douard** (ā dwàr') 1832–83; Fr. impressionist painter

ma·neu·ver (mə nōō'vər, -nyōō'-) *n.* [Fr. *manœuvre* < VL. < L. *manu operare*, to work by hand] **1.** a planned and controlled movement of troops, warships, aircraft, etc. **2.** [*pl.*] exercises in tactics carried out on a large scale by troops, warships, aircraft, etc. **3.** any skillful change of movement or direction in driving a vehicle, controlling an aircraft, etc. **4.** any move or action meant as a skillful or shrewd step toward some goal; stratagem [a *maneuver* to get control of a business] —*vi., vt.* **1.** to perform or cause to perform maneuvers **2.** to manage or plan skillfully; scheme **3.** to move, get, put, make, etc. by some stratagem [I *maneuvered* him into asking the question for me] —see SYN. at TRICK —**ma·neu'ver·a·bil'i·ty** *n.* —**ma·neu'ver·a·ble** *adj.*

man Friday see FRIDAY

man·ful (man'fəl) *adj.* manly; brave, resolute, strong, etc. —**man'ful·ly** *adv.* —**man'ful·ness** *n.*

man·ga·nese (maŋ'gə nēs', -nēz') *n.* [< Fr. < It. < ML. *magnesia*: see MAGNESIA] a grayish-white, metallic chemical element, usually hard and brittle, which rusts like iron but is not magnetic: used in various alloys: symbol, Mn; at. wt., 54.9380; at. no., 25

man·gan·ic (man gan'ik) *adj.* designating or of chemical compounds in which manganese has a valence of three

man·gan·ous (maŋ'gə nəs, man gan'əs) *adj.* designating or of chemical compounds in which manganese has a valence of two

mange (mānj) *n.* [< OFr. *mangeue*, an itch, ult. < L. *manducare*: see MANGER] a skin disease of mammals caused by parasitic mites, with itching, loss of hair, etc.

man·gel-wur·zel (maŋ'g'l wur'z'l, -wurt'-) *n.* [G., ult. < *mangold*, beet + *wurzel*, a root] a variety of large beet, used as food for cattle, esp. in Europe: also **mangel**

man·ger (mān'jər) *n.* [OFr. *mangeure*, ult. < L. *manducare*, to eat < *mandere*, to chew: for IE. base see MOUTH] a box or trough to hold hay, etc. for horses or cattle to eat

man·gle[1] (maŋ'g'l) *vt.* **-gled, -gling** [Anglo-Fr. *mangler* < OFr. *mehaigner*, to maim] **1.** to mutilate by repeatedly and roughly cutting, hacking, tearing, etc. **2.** to spoil; botch; mar [to *mangle* a piano solo]

man·gle[2] (maŋ'g'l) *n.* [Du. *mangel* < G. < MHG. < L. < Gr. *manganon*, war machine] a machine for pressing and smooth-

ing cloth, esp. sheets and other flat pieces, between heated rollers —*vt.* **-gled, -gling** to press in a mangle —**man'gler** *n.*

man·go (maŋ'gō) *n., pl.* **-goes, -gos** [Port. *manga* < Malay < Tamil *mān-kāy*] **1.** a yellow-red, somewhat acid tropical fruit with a thick rind and juicy pulp: it is eaten fresh when ripe or pickled while still green **2.** the tree on which it grows

man·grove (maŋ'grōv) *n.* [altered (by the influence of GROVE) < Port. *mangue* < Sp. *mangle* < the WInd. name] a tropical tree growing in swampy ground along river banks, with branches that spread and send down roots, thus forming more trunks

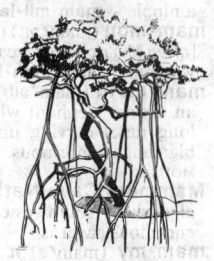

MANGROVE

man·gy (mān'jē) *adj.* **-gi·er, -gi·est** **1.** having or caused by the mange [a *mangy* dog] **2.** shabby and filthy; squalid [he lived in a *mangy* hut] **3.** mean and low; despicable [that was a pretty *mangy* trick!] —**man'gi·ly** *adv.* —**man'gi·ness** *n.*

man·han·dle (man'han'd'l) *vt.* **-dled, -dling** **1.** [Rare] to move or do by human strength only, without mechanical aids **2.** to handle roughly

Man·hat·tan (man hat''n, mən-) [< Du. < AmInd. < ?] **1.** island in southeastern N.Y., between the Hudson & East rivers: also **Manhattan Island** **2.** borough of New York City consisting chiefly of this island: pop. 1,525,000 —*n.* ☆[*often* m-] a cocktail made of whiskey and vermouth, usually with a dash of bitters

man·hole (man'hōl') *n.* an opening, often with a cover, through which a man can get into a sewer, conduit, ship's tank, etc. for repair work or inspection

man·hood (man'hood') *n.* **1.** the state or time of being a man **2.** the qualities usually thought of as proper to a man, as virility, courage, etc. [a test of one's *manhood*] **3.** men as a group

man-hour (man'our') *n.* a time unit used in industry, equal to one hour of work done by one person

☆**man·hunt** (-hunt') *n.* a hunt for a man, esp. a fugitive: also **man hunt**

ma·ni·a (mā'nē ə, mān'yə) *n.* [LL. < Gr. *mania* < *mainesthai*, to rage: for IE. base see MIND] **1.** a mental disorder in which there is wild or violent talk or behavior **2.** an enthusiasm for something that seems unreasonably great; obsession; craze [he has a *mania* for sports cars]

-ma·ni·a (mā'nē ə, mān'yə) [see prec.] *a combining form meaning:* **1.** a (specified) type of mental disorder [*kleptomania*] **2.** a continuing, intense enthusiasm or craving for [*bibliomania*]

ma·ni·ac (mā'nē ak') *adj.* of, having, or showing mania; wildly insane —*n.* a violently insane person; madman

ma·ni·a·cal (mə nī'ə k'l) *adj.* of, having, or showing mania; wildly insane; raving —**ma·ni·a·cal·ly** *adv.*

man·ic (man'ik) *adj.* having, characterized by, or like mania

man·ic-de·pres·sive (-di pres'iv) *adj.* designating, of, or having severe mental illness in which there are periods of mania followed by periods of great depression —*n.* a person who has this illness

Man·i·chae·ism, Man·i·che·ism (man'ə kē'iz'm) *n.* [after *Manichaeus*, 3d-cent. Persian prophet] a religious philosophy of the 3d to 7th cent. A.D. that originated in Persia and stressed conflict through the universe between good and evil: also **Man'i·chae'an·ism** —**Man'i·chae'an** *n., adj.*

man·i·cot·ti (man'i kät'ē) *n.* [It., pl., lit., muffs] broad tubes of pasta, stuffed with cheese and baked with a tomato sauce

man·i·cure (man'ə kyoor') *n.* [Fr. < L. *manus*, a hand + *cura*, care] the care of the hands; esp., a trimming, polishing, etc. of the fingernails —*vt.* **-cured, -cur'ing** **1.** *a)* to trim, polish, etc. (the fingernails) *b)* to give a manicure to (a person) **2.** [Colloq.] to trim, clip, etc. neatly and carefully [to *manicure* a lawn] —**man'i·cur'ist** *n.*

man·i·fest (man'ə fest') *adj.* [< OFr. < L. *manifestus*, lit., struck by the hand; that can be felt] clear to the senses, esp. to sight, or to the mind; evident; obvious [he shuddered with *manifest* fear] —*vt.* **1.** to make clear or evident; reveal [to *manifest* impatience] **2.** to prove; be evidence of [her kindness to them *manifested* her love] —*vi.* to appear to the senses —*n.* **1.** an itemized list of a ship's cargo, to be shown to customs officials **2.** a list of passengers and cargo on an aircraft —see SYN. at EVIDENT —**man'i·fest'a·ble** *adj.* —**man'i·fest'ly** *adv.*

man·i·fes·ta·tion (man'ə fes tā'shən, -fəs-) *n.* **1.** a manifesting or being manifested **2.** something that manifests [his smile was a *manifestation* of joy] **3.** any of the forms in which a being is thought to manifest itself [the gods of mythology appear in various *manifestations*] **4.** a public demonstration

☆**Manifest Destiny** a 19th-century doctrine which held that it was the obvious destiny of the United States to go on expanding its territory

man·i·fes·to (man′ə fes′tō) *n., pl.* **-toes** [It. < *manifestare,* to MANIFEST] a public declaration by a government or by an important person or group, giving its policies, beliefs, plans, etc.

man·i·fold (man′ə fōld′) *adj.* [OE. *manigfeald:* see MANY & -FOLD] **1.** having many and various forms, parts, etc. [*manifold* wisdom] **2.** of many sorts; many and varied [*manifold* duties] **3.** being such in many ways [a *manifold* villain] **4.** made up of or operating several units or parts of one kind —*n.* **1.** something that is manifold **2.** a pipe with one inlet and several outlets or with one outlet and several inlets, for connecting with other pipes, as such a pipe in an automobile, for carrying away exhausts from the cylinders to the exhaust pipe —*vt.* **1.** to make manifold **2.** to make a number of copies of [to *manifold* a letter with carbon paper] —see SYN. at MANY —**man′i·fold′er** *n.* —**man′i·fold′ly** *adv.*

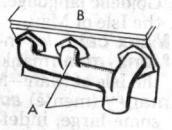

MANIFOLD (A, manifold; B, cylinder)

man·i·kin (man′ə k'n) *n.* [Du. *manneken* < *man,* man + dim. suffix *-ken*] **1.** a little man; dwarf **2.** a lifelike model of the human body, usually with movable and detachable parts, used in medical schools, art classes, etc. **3.** *same as* MANNEQUIN

Ma·nil·a (mə nil′ə) capital & seaport of the Philippines, in SW Luzon, on an inlet of the South China Sea: pop. 1,499,000 (met. area 3,100,000) —*n.* [*often* m-] *same as:* **1.** MANILA HEMP **2.** MANILA PAPER Also, for *n.,* **Ma·nil′la**

Manila hemp [*often* m-] a strong, tough fiber from the leafstalks of the abacá, used in making rope, paper, etc.

Manila paper [*often* m-] strong, buff or brownish paper orig. made of Manila hemp, now of various fibers

man in the street the average person

man·i·oc (man′ē äk′) *n.* [Fr. < Tupi *manioca*] *same as* CASSAVA

man·i·ple (man′ə p'l) *n.* [L. *manipulus,* a handful < *manus,* hand + base of *plere,* to fill: from use of bundles of hay as standards of the maniples] **1.** a subdivision of the ancient Roman legion, consisting of either 60 or 120 men **2.** [< MFr. < ML. *manipulus* < L.] a silk band worn hanging over the left forearm by some clergy as during Mass

ma·nip·u·late (mə nip′yə lāt′) *vt.* **-lat′ed, -lat′ing** [back-formation < MANIPULATION] **1.** to work, operate, or treat with or as with the hands, esp. with skill **2.** to manage or control cleverly, often in an unfair or fraudulent way [to *manipulate* an election by bribing the voters] **3.** to change or falsify (figures, accounts, etc.) for one's own purposes or profit; rig; specif., to cause (prices of stock, etc.) to fall or rise —**ma·nip′u·la·ble** *adj.* —**ma·nip′u·la′tive** *adj.* —**ma·nip′u·la′tor** *n.*

ma·nip·u·la·tion (mə nip′yə lā′shən) *n.* [Fr., ult. < L. *manipulus:* see MANIPLE] a manipulating or being manipulated; skillful handling or operation, clever or dishonest management or control, etc.

Man·i·to·ba (man′ə tō′bə) **1.** province of SC Canada: 251,000 sq. mi.; pop. 1,022,000; cap. Winnipeg: abbrev. **Man. 2.** Lake, lake in SW Manitoba —**Man′i·to′ban** *adj., n.*

☆**man·i·tou** (man′ə tōō′) *n.* [< Algonquian name] any of various nature spirits believed in by Algonquian Indians: also **man′i·tu′, man′i·to′** (-tō′)

man·kind (man′kīnd′; *also, & for 2 always,* man′kīnd′) *n.* **1.** all human beings; the human race **2.** all human males; the male sex

man·like (man′līk′) *adj.* **1.** like or characteristic of a man or men **2.** fit for a man; masculine

man·ly (-lē) *adj.* **-li·er, -li·est 1.** having qualities regarded as befitting a man; strong, brave, honorable, etc. **2.** fit for a man [*manly* sports] —*adv.* in a manly way —see SYN. at MALE —**man′li·ness** *n.*

man-made (-mād′) *adj.* made by man; synthetic

Mann (man; *for 2* män) **1.** Horace, 1796–1859; U.S. educator **2.** Thom·as (G. tō′mäs), 1875–1955; Ger. novelist in the U.S. & Switzerland

man·na (man′ə) *n.* [OE. < LL. < Gr. < Aram. *mannā* < Heb. *mān*] **1.** *Bible* food miraculously provided for the Israelites in the wilderness: Ex. 16:14–36 **2.** anything badly needed that comes unexpectedly

man·ne·quin (man′ə kin) *n.* [Fr. < Du.: see MANIKIN] **1.** a model of the human body, used by window dressers, artists, etc. **2.** a woman whose work is modeling clothes in stores, etc.

man·ner (man′ər) *n.* [< OFr., ult. < L. *manuarius,* of the hand < *manus:* see MANUAL] **1.** a way or method in which something is done or happens **2.** a way of acting; personal, esp. customary, behavior or bearing **3.** [*pl.*] *a)* ways of social life [a comedy of *manners*] *b)* ways of social behavior; deportment [good *manners*] *c)* polite ways of social behavior [the child lacks *manners*] **4.** characteristic style or method in art, etc. **5.** *a)* kind; sort [what *manner* of person is she?] *b)* [*with pl. v.*] kinds; sorts [all *manner* of things] —see SYN. at METHOD —**by all manner of means** of course; surely —**by any manner of means** in any way; at all —**by no manner of means** in no way; definitely not —**in a manner of speaking** in a certain sense or way —**to the manner born** accustomed from birth to the way or usage spoken of —**man′ner·less** *adj.*

man·nered (-ərd) *adj.* **1.** having manners or a manner of a specified sort [ill-*mannered,* soberly *mannered*] **2.** artificial, stylized, or affected [a *mannered* literary style]

man·ner·ism (man′ər iz'm) *n.* **1.** excessive use of some distinctive manner in art, literature, speech, or behavior **2.** a peculiarity of manner in behavior, speech, etc. that has become a habit [she had a *mannerism* of scratching her ear] —**man′ner·ist** *n.* —**man′ner·is′tic** *adj.*

man·ner·ly (-lē) *adj.* showing good manners; polite —*adv.* politely —**man′ner·li·ness** *n.*

Mann·heim (man′hīm; *G.* män′-) city in SW West Germany, on the Rhine: pop. 324,000

man·ni·kin (man′ə kin) *n. alt. sp. of* MANIKIN

man·nish (man′ish) *adj.* of, like, or fit for a man: used in referring to a woman with masculine characteristics [she walks with a *mannish* stride] —see SYN. at MALE —**man′nish·ly** *adv.* —**man′nish·ness** *n.*

ma·noeu·vre (mə nōō′vər, -nyōō′-) *n., vi., vt.* **-vred, -vring** *chiefly Brit. sp. of* MANEUVER

man of God **1.** a holy man; saint, hermit, etc. **2.** a clergyman; minister, priest, rabbi, etc.

man of letters a writer, scholar, etc., esp. one whose work is in the field of literature

man of the world a man familiar with and tolerant of various sorts of people and their ways

man-of-war (man′əv wôr′, -ə wôr′) *n., pl.* **men′-of-war′** an armed naval vessel; warship

man-of-war bird *same as* FRIGATE BIRD

ma·nom·e·ter (mə näm′ə tər) *n.* [< Fr. < Gr. *manos,* rare (in sense "thin, sparse") + Fr. *-mètre,* -METER] an instrument for measuring the pressure of gases or liquids —**man·o·met·ric** (man′ə met′rik), **man′o·met′ri·cal** *adj.*

man·or (man′ər) *n.* [< OFr. < *manoir,* to dwell < L. *manere,* to remain] **1.** in England, a landed estate, orig. of a feudal lord and subject to the jurisdiction of his court **2.** in colonial America, a district granted as a manor and leased to tenants **3.** a mansion, as on an estate —**ma·no·ri·al** (mə nôr′ē əl) *adj.*

manor house the house of the lord of a manor

man·pow·er (man′pou′ər) *n.* **1.** power furnished by human physical strength **2.** the collective strength or availability for work of the people in a given place Also **man power**

‡**man·qué** (män kā′) *adj.* [Fr. < *manquer,* to fail < It. < L. *mancus,* infirm] **1.** unsuccessful or defective **2.** that wants to be; would-be Placed after the noun [a poet *manqué*]

man·sard (roof) (man′särd) [after F. *Mansard,* 17th-c. Fr. architect] a roof with two slopes on each of the four sides, the lower steeper than the upper

manse (mans) *n.* [< ML. < pp. of L. *manere,* to dwell] **1.** the house that a church provides for its minister, esp. a Presbyterian minister; parsonage **2.** [Archaic] a mansion

MANSARD ROOF

man·ser·vant (man′sur′vənt) *n., pl.* **men′ser′vants** (men′-) a male servant

Mans·field (manz'fēld', mans'-) [after J. *Mansfield* (1759–1830), surveyor] city in NC Ohio: pop. 55,000

man·sion (man'shən) *n.* [OFr. < L. *mansio*, a dwelling < pp. of *manere*, to dwell] a large, stately house

man-sized (man'sīzd') *adj.* [Colloq.] of a size fit for a man; large; big: also **man'-size'**

man·slaugh·ter (-slôt'ər) *n.* the killing of a human being by another; esp., such killing when unlawful but without malice

man·ta (ray) (man'tə) [Sp. < LL. *mantum*, a cloak] *same as* DEVILFISH (sense 1)

man·tel (man't'l) *n.* [see MANTLE] **1.** the facing of stone, marble, etc. about a fireplace, including a shelf or slab above it **2.** the shelf or slab

man·tel·et (man't'l it, mant'lit) *n.* [OFr., dim. of MANTEL] **1.** a short mantle or cape **2.** a protective shelter or screen: also **mant'let**

man·tel·piece (man't'l pēs') *n.* a mantel shelf, or this shelf and the side elements framing the fireplace in front

man·til·la (man til'ə, -tē'ə) *n.* [Sp. < LL. < L. *mantellum*, a mantle] a woman's scarf, as of lace, worn over the hair and shoulders, as in Spain or Mexico

man·tis (man'tis) *n., pl.* **-tis·es, -tes** (-tēz) [ModL. < Gr. *mantis*, prophet, seer: for IE. base see MIND] a long, slender insect that feeds on other insects and grasps its prey with stout, spiny forelegs often held up together as if praying

MANTIS
(to 5 in. long)

man·tis·sa (man tis'ə) *n.* [L., (useless) addition] the decimal part of a logarithm: see also CHARACTERISTIC (sense 2)

man·tle (man't'l) *n.* [< OE. & OFr. < L. *mantellum*] **1.** a loose, sleeveless cloak or cape **2.** anything that cloaks or envelops **3.** a small, mesh hood which becomes white-hot over a flame and gives off light **4.** *same as* MANTEL **5.** *Geol. a)* the layer of the earth's interior between the crust and the core *b) same as* MANTLEROCK **6.** *Zool. a)* the glandular flap or folds of the body wall of a mollusk, etc., typically secreting a shell-forming fluid *b)* the plumage on the back and folded wings of certain birds when the color markings are distinct —*vt.* **-tled, -tling** to cover with or as with a mantle; cloak —*vi.* **1.** to be or become covered, as a surface with froth **2.** to blush or flush

man·tle·rock (-räk') *n.* the loose material, including rocks, sand, and soil, on the solid rock of the earth's crust

man·tra (mun'trə, man'-) *n.* [Sans., akin to *mantar*, thinker] *Hinduism* a hymn or text, esp. from the Veda, chanted as an incantation or prayer

man·u·al (man'yoo wəl) *adj.* [< OFr. < L. < *manus*, a hand < IE. base *man-*, a hand] **1.** of a hand or the hands [*manual skill*] **2.** made, done, worked, or used by the hands [*manual controls*] **3.** involving or doing hard physical work requiring use of the hands [*manual labor*] —*n.* **1.** a handy book of facts, instructions, etc. for use as a guide; handbook **2.** a keyboard of an organ console or harpsichord **3.** prescribed drill in the handling of a weapon, esp. a rifle: also **manual of arms** —**man'u·al·ly** *adv.*

☆**manual training** training in practical arts and crafts, as metalworking and woodworking

man·u·fac·ture (man'yə fak'chər) *n.* [Fr. < ML. < L. < *manus*, a hand + *factura*, a making < *facere*, to make] **1.** the making of goods by hand or, esp., by machinery, often on a large scale and with division of labor **2.** anything so made **3.** the making of something in a way regarded as mechanical —*vt.* **-tured, -tur·ing 1.** to make by hand or, esp., by machinery, often on a large scale, etc. **2.** to work (wool, steel, etc.) into usable form **3.** to produce (art, literature, etc.) in a way regarded as mechanical and uninspired **4.** to make up (excuses, evidence, etc.) —**see SYN** at MAKE

man·u·fac·tur·er (-chər ər) *n.* a person or company in the business of manufacturing; esp., a factory owner

man·u·mis·sion (man'yə mish'ən) *n.* [see next entry] a freeing or being freed from slavery; emancipation

man·u·mit (-mit') *vt.* **-mit'ted, -mit'ting** [< OFr. < L. < *manus*, a hand + *mittere*, to send] to free from slavery; liberate (a slave, serf, etc.) —**man'u·mit'ter** *n.*

ma·nure (mə noor', -nyoor') *vt.* **-nured', -nur'ing** [< Anglo-Fr. < OFr. *manouvrer*, to work with the hands, cultivate] to put manure on or into (soil) —*n.* animal excrement or other substance used to fertilize soil —**ma·nur'er** *n.*

man·u·script (man'yə skript') *adj.* [< L. < *manus*, a hand + pp. of *scribere*, to write] **1.** written by hand or with a typewriter **2.** designating writing that consists of unconnected letters resembling print; not cursive —*n.* **1.** a written or typewritten book, article, etc.; esp., an author's copy of his work, as sent to a publisher or printer **2.** writing as distinguished from print [*a novel still in manuscript*]

Manx (maŋks) *adj.* of the Isle of Man, its people, etc. —*n.* their Goidelic language, now nearly extinct —**the Manx** the people of the Isle of Man

Manx cat [*also* m-] a domestic cat of a breed that has no tail

Manx·man (maŋks'mən) *n., pl.* **-men** a native or inhabitant of the Isle of Man —**Manx'wom'an** *n.fem., pl.* **-wom'en**

man·y (men'ē) *adj.* **more, most** [OE. *manig*] **1.** consisting of some large, indefinite number; numerous **2.** relatively numerous (preceded by *as, too,* etc.) —*n.* a large number (of persons or things) —*pron.* many persons or things **Many a** (or **an, another**) with a singular noun or pronoun is equivalent to *many* with the plural (for example, "*many a* man has tried" means the same as "*many* men have tried") —**a good many** [*with pl. v.*] a relatively large number —**a great many** [*with pl. v.*] an extremely large number —**the many 1.** the majority of people **2.** the masses

SYN. —**many** is the simple, common word implying a relatively large number of units [*many* children, excuses, etc.]; **numerous**, a more formal word than **many**, sometimes suggests a crowding of one unit upon another [*numerous* complaints have come in]; **manifold** carries the idea of great variety [*manifold* problems] or, in modifying a singular noun, great complexity in the parts that make up the whole [*manifold* sorrow]; **multifarious** adds the idea of there being great differences, or even conflicting differences, in the variety [*multifarious* interests]; **innumerable** implies a number too great to count and is often used to give emphasis by exaggerating [*innumerable* instances of her kindness] —**ANT.** few

man·y·plies (men'ē plīz') *n. same as* OMASUM

man·y-sid·ed (-sīd'id) *adj.* **1.** having many sides or aspects **2.** having many possibilities, qualities, interests, etc.

☆**man·za·ni·ta** (man'zə nēt'ə) *n.* [AmSp. < Sp., dim. of *manzana*, apple] any of several shrubs or small trees of the heath family, found in the western U.S.

Mao·ism (mou'iz'm) *n.* the communist theories and policies of Mao Tse-tung —**Mao'ist** *adj., n.*

Ma·o·ri (mou'rē, mä'ō rē; mä ôr'ē) *n.* **1.** *pl.* **-ris, -ri** any of a brown-skinned people native to New Zealand, of Polynesian origin **2.** their Polynesian language —*adj.* of the Maoris, their language, etc.

mao-tai (mou'tī') *n.* [after *Mao-t'ai*, town in SW China] strong, colorless, Chinese liquor distilled from grain

Mao Tse-tung (mou' dzu'doōŋ') 1893–1976; Chin. statesman; chairman of the People's Republic of China (1949–59) & of the Chin. Communist Party (1949–1976)

map (map) *n.* [< ML. *mappa (mundi)*, map (of the world) < L. *mappa*, napkin] **1.** a representation, usually flat, of all or part of the earth's surface, ordinarily showing countries, bodies of water, cities, etc. **2.** a similar representation of the sky, showing stars, planets, etc. **3.** any maplike representation **4.** [Slang] the face —*vt.* **mapped, map'ping 1.** to make a map of; represent on a map **2.** to plan in detail [to *map* out a project] **3.** to survey for making a map —**put on the map** to make well known —☆**wipe off the map** to put out of existence

ma·ple (mā'p'l) *n.* [OE. *mapel(treo)*] **1.** any of a large group of trees with lobed leaves and two-winged fruits, grown for wood, sap, or shade **2.** the hard, fine-grained, light-colored wood of such a tree, used for furniture, flooring, etc. **3.** the flavor of maple syrup —*adj.* **1.** of maple **2.** flavored with maple

☆**maple sugar** sugar made by boiling down maple syrup

☆**maple syrup** syrup made by boiling down the sap of any of various maples, esp. the sugar maple

Ma·pu·to (mə pōōt'ō) capital of Mozambique; seaport on the Indian Ocean: pop. 799,000

ma·quis (mä kē') *n., pl.* **-quis'** (-kēz', -kē') [Fr. < It. *macchia*, a thicket (where guerrilla fighters might hide)] [*often* M-] a member of the French underground fighting against the Nazis

mar (mär) *vt.* **marred, mar'ring** [OE. *mierran*, to hinder] to hurt or spoil the looks, value, perfection, etc. of; damage

Mar. March

mar. 1. marine **2.** maritime **3.** married

mar·a·bou (mar'ə bōō') *n.* [Fr. < Port. < Ar. *murābit*, hermit] **1.** any of certain large storks; esp., *a)* a dark-green African species *b)* the Indian adjutant **2.** soft feathers from the wings and tail of the marabou Also **mar'a·bout'** (-bōōt')

ma·ra·ca (mə rä′kə) *n.* [Port. *maracá* < the Braz. native name] a percussion instrument consisting of a dried gourd or a gourd-shaped rattle with loose pebbles in it, shaken to beat out a rhythm

Mar·a·cai·bo (mar′ə kī′bō; *Sp.* mä′rä kī′bô) seaport in NW Venezuela: pop. 625,000

Ma·ra·ñón (mä′rä nyôn′) river in W & N Peru that joins the Ucayali to form the Amazon

mar·a·schi·no (mar′ə skē′nō, -shē′-) *n.* [It. < *marasca*, kind of cherry < *amaro*, bitter] a strong, sweet liqueur or cordial made from the fermented juice of a black wild cherry

MARACAS

maraschino cherries cherries in a syrup flavored with maraschino or, now usually, imitation maraschino

Ma·rat (mà rà′), **Jean Paul** (zhän pôl) 1743-93; Fr. Revolutionary leader, born in Switzerland

Mar·a·thon (mar′ə thän′) ancient Greek village in E Attica, or a plain nearby, where the Athenians defeated the Persians (490 B.C.)

mar·a·thon (mar′ə thän′) *n.* **1.** a footrace of 26 miles, 385 yards: so called in memory of the Greek runner who carried word of the victory at Marathon to Athens **2.** any long-distance contest or endurance contest

ma·raud (mə rôd′) *vi.* [< Fr. < *maraud*, vagabond, prob. < dial. *maraud*, tomcat, echoic of cry] to rove in search of plunder; make raids —*vt.* to raid; plunder —**ma·raud′er** *n.*

MARATHON (5th cent. B.C.)

mar·ble (mär′b′l) *n.* [< OFr. < L. < Gr. *marmaros*, white glistening stone] **1.** a hard, metamorphic limestone, white or colored and sometimes streaked or mottled, which can take a high polish: it is much used in building and sculpture **2.** *a*) a piece or slab of this stone, used as a monument, etc. *b*) a piece of sculpture in marble **3.** anything like marble in hardness, smoothness, coldness, coloration, etc. **4.** *a*) a little ball of stone, glass, or clay, used in games *b*) [*pl.*, *with sing. v.*] a children's game in which a marble is propelled with the thumb at other marbles in a marked circle **5.** [*pl.*] [Slang] brains; good sense [to lose one's *marbles*] —*adj.* of or like marble —*vt.* -bled, -bling **1.** to stain (book edges) to look mottled or streaked like marble **2.** to cause fat to be evenly distributed in narrow streaks through (meat) —**mar′bled, mar′bly** *adj.*

☆**marble cake** a cake made of light and dark batter mixed to give a streaked, marblelike appearance

☆**mar·ble·ize** (mär′b′l īz′) *vt.* -ized′, -iz′ing to make, color, grain, or streak in imitation of marble

mar·bling (-bliŋ) *n.* **1.** the art or process of staining or veining like marble, as in decorating book edges **2.** a streaked, veined, or mottled appearance like that of marble [the *marbling* of fat in prime meat]

Marc Antony see ANTONY

mar·ca·site (mär′kə sīt′) *n.* [< Fr. < ML. < Ar. *marqashīta*] **1.** a pale, crystallized pyrite (**white iron pyrite**) **2.** this mineral or polished steel cut and used like brilliants

mar·cel (mär sel′) *n.* [after *Marcel* Grateau, early 20th-c. Fr. hairdresser] a series of even waves put in the hair with a curling iron: also **marcel wave** —*vt.* -celled′, -cel′ling to put such waves in (hair)

March (märch) *n.* [< OFr. < L. *Martius* (*mensis*), (month) of *Mars*] the third month of the year, having 31 days: abbrev. **Mar.**

march¹ (märch) *vi.* [Fr. *marcher* < OFr., prob. < Frank.] **1.** to walk with regular, steady steps, as in a military formation **2.** to walk in a grave, stately way **3.** to advance or progress steadily [time *marches on*] —*vt.* **1.** to cause (troops, etc.) to march **2.** to cause or force to go [he *marched* the children off to bed] —*n.* **1.** a marching **2.** a steady advance; progress [the *march* of events] **3.** a regular, steady step or pace **4.** the distance covered in marching [a day's *march*] **5.** a long, tiring walk **6.** a piece of music with a steady, even beat, for marching **7.** an organized walk by people demonstrating on a public issue [a peace *march*] —**on the march** marching —**steal a march on** to get an advantage over secretly —**march′er** *n.*

march² (märch) *n.* [OFr. *marche* < Frank. word thought to be *marka*, boundary, border, or frontier

March hare a hare in breeding time, proverbially regarded as an example of madness

marching orders orders to march, go, or leave

mar·chion·ess (mär′shən is, mär′shə nes′) *n.* [< ML. fem. of *marchio*, prefect of the marches, or borderlands] **1.** the wife or widow of a marquess **2.** a lady whose own rank equals that of a marquess

march·pane (märch′pān′) *n.* same as MARZIPAN

Mar·cia (mär′shə) [< L. < *Mars*, MARS] a feminine name

Mar·co·ni (mär kō′nē; *It.* mär kô′nē), **Gu·gliel·mo** (gōō lyel′mô) 1874-1937; It. physicist: developed wireless telegraphy

Marco Polo see POLO

Mar·cus Aurelius (mär′kəs) see AURELIUS

☆**Mar·di gras** (mär′di grä′) [Fr., lit., fat Tuesday] Shrove Tuesday, the last day before Lent: a day of carnival, as in New Orleans

mare¹ (mer) *n.* [OE. *mere*, fem. of *mearh*, horse] a fully mature female horse, mule, donkey, etc.; specif., a female horse that has reached the age of five

ma·re² (mer′ē, mär′ē) *n.*, *pl.* **-ri·a** (-ē ə) [L., sea: for IE. base see MARSH] **1.** a sea **2.** a large, dark area on the surface of the moon or of Mars

mare's-nest (merz′nest′) *n.* **1.** a hoax; delusion **2.** a disorderly or confused condition; mess

mare's-tail (-tāl′) *n.* long, narrow formations of cirrus cloud, shaped somewhat like a horse's tail

Mar·ga·ret (mär′grit, -gər it) [< OFr. < L. *margarita*, a pearl] a feminine name: dim. *Marge*; var. *Margery*, *Margot*, *Marguerite*

mar·ga·rine (mär′jə rin) *n.* [Fr.] a spread or cooking fat made of refined vegetable oils processed so as to resemble butter, often churned with pasteurized skim milk, and generally fortified with vitamins A and D: also **mar′ga·rin**

marge (märj) *n.* [Fr. < L. *margo*, MARGIN] [Archaic or Poet.] a border; edge; margin

mar·gin (mär′jən) *n.* [L. *marginis*, genitive of *margo*: for IE. base see MARK] **1.** a border, edge, or brink **2.** the blank border of a printed or written page **3.** a limit to what is desirable or possible **4.** *a*) an amount of money, supplies, etc. beyond what is needed *b*) provision for increase, addition, or advance **5.** the amount by which something is higher or lower **6.** *Business, Finance a*) the difference between the cost and selling price of goods *b*) money or collateral deposited with a broker, etc. either to meet legal requirements or to insure him against loss on contracts which he undertakes for a buyer or seller of stocks, etc. **7.** *Econ.* the minimum return of profit needed to continue activities —*vt.* **1.** to provide with a margin **2.** *Business* ☆to deposit a margin upon

mar·gin·al (-'l) *adj.* **1.** written or printed in the margin **2.** of a margin **3.** at, on, or close to the margin **4.** close to a margin or a lower limit [a *marginal* standard of living] **5.** *Econ.* on the border between being profitable or nonprofitable [a *marginal* business] —**mar′gin·al′i·ty** (-al′ə tē) *n.* —**mar′gin·al·ly** *adv.*

mar·gin·ate (mär′jə nāt′; *also for adj.* -nit) *vt.* -at′ed, -at′ing to provide with a margin —*adj.* having a distinct margin: also **mar′gin·at′ed** —**mar′gin·a′tion** *n.*

mar·grave (mär′grāv) *n.* [< MDu. < MHG. < OHG. < *marc*, a border + *graf*, a count] **1.** orig., a military governor of a border province in Germany **2.** the title of certain princes of Germany

mar·gue·rite (mär′gə rēt′) *n.* [Fr., a pearl] **1.** *same as* DAISY (sense 1) **2.** a cultivated chrysanthemum with a single flower **3.** any of various daisylike plants of the composite family

Ma·ri·a (mə rī′ə, -rē′-) [see MARY] a feminine name

ma·ri·a (mer′ē ə, mär′-) *n. pl. of* MARE²

☆**ma·ri·a·chi** (mär′ē ä′chē) *n., pl.* **-chis** [MexSp. < ?] **1.** one of a strolling band of musicians in Mexico **2.** their music

Mar·i·an (mer′ē ən, mar′-) [var. of MARION] a feminine name: var. *Marianne —adj.* of the Virgin Mary

Ma·ri·an·a Islands (mer′ē an′ə, mar′-) group of islands in the W Pacific, consisting of Guam and a self-governing U.S. commonwealth (called **Northern Marianas**)

Ma·ria·na·o (mä′ryä nä′ð) city in NW Cuba: suburb of Havana: pop. 230,000

Maria Theresa 1717–80; queen of Bohemia & Hungary & archduchess of Austria (1740–80): mother of MARIE ANTOINETTE

Ma·rie (mə rē′) [var. of MARY] a feminine name

Marie An·toi·nette (an′twə net′, -tə-), (**Josèphe Jeanne**) 1755–93; wife of Louis XVI; queen of France (1774–92): guillotined

Marie Louise 1791–1847; 2d wife of Napoleon I & empress of France (1810–15)

mar·i·gold (mar′ə gōld′) *n.* [< *Marie* (prob. the Virgin Mary) + *gold,* GOLD] **1.** a plant of the composite family, with red, yellow, or orange flowers **2.** its flower **3.** any of several unrelated plants, as the pot marigold

☆**ma·ri·jua·na, ma·ri·hua·na** (mar′ə wä′nə, mär′-; -hwä′-) *n.* [AmSp. < ? native word] **1.** the hemp plant **2.** its dried leaves and flowers, smoked for the psychological effects

Mar·i·lyn (mar′ə lin) [var. of MARY] a feminine name

ma·rim·ba (mə rim′bə) *n.* [< Afr. (Bantu), a kind of percussive instrument] a kind of xylophone, usually with resonators under the wooden bars

ma·ri·na (mə rē′nə) *n.* [It. & Sp., seacoast < L. *marinus:* see MARINE] ☆a small harbor with dockage, supplies, and services for small pleasure craft

MARIMBA

mar·i·nade (mar′ə nād′) *n.* [Fr. < Sp. < *marinar,* to pickle, ult. < L. *marinus:* see MARINE] **1.** a spiced pickling solution, esp. with oil and wine or vinegar, in which meat, fish, or salad is steeped, often before cooking **2.** meat, etc. so steeped —*vt.* **-nad′ed, -nad′ing** *same as* MARINATE

mar·i·nate (mar′ə nāt′) *vt.* **-nat′ed, -nat′ing** [< It. < *marinare,* to pickle: see prec.] to steep (meat, etc.) in a marinade —**mar′i·na′tion** *n.*

ma·rine (mə rēn′) *adj.* [< L. *marinus < mare,* the sea: see MARE²] **1.** of, found in, or formed by the sea or ocean [seaweed is a *marine* plant] **2.** *a)* of navigation on, or shipping by, the sea; nautical; maritime [*marine* law] *b)* naval **3.** used, or to be used, at sea [a *marine* engine] **4.** *a)* trained for service at sea, etc., as certain troops *b)* of such troops —*n.* **1.** one of a marine military force; specif. ☆[*often* M-], a member of the MARINE CORPS **2.** naval or merchant ships as a group [the merchant *marine*] **3.** a picture of a ship or sea scene

☆**Marine Corps** a branch of the U.S. armed forces trained for land, sea, and aerial combat

mar·i·ner (mar′ə nər) *n.* [< Anglo-Fr. < ML. < L. *marinus,* MARINE] a sailor; seaman

Mar·i·on (mar′ē ən, mer′-) [Fr., orig. dim. of *Marie,* MARY] **1.** a masculine or feminine name **2.** **Francis,** 1732?–95; Am. general in the Revolutionary War: called the *Swamp Fox*

mar·i·o·nette (mar′ē ə net′) *n.* [Fr., dim. of MARION] a puppet or little jointed doll moved by strings or wires from above, often on a little stage

☆**Mar·i·po·sa lily** (or **tulip**) (mar′ə pō′zə, -sə) [AmSp. < Sp. *mariposa,* butterfly] **1.** a plant of the lily family, of W N. America, with tuliplike flowers **2.** its flower

Ma·ri·tain (má rē tan′), **Jacques** (zhàk) 1882–1973; Fr. philosopher

mar·i·tal (mar′ə t′l) *adj.* [< L. < *maritus,* a husband] of marriage —**mar′i·tal·ly** *adv.*

mar·i·time (mar′ə tīm′) *adj.* [L. *maritimus < mare,* the sea: see MARE²] **1.** on, near, or living near the sea [*maritime* provinces; a *maritime* people]

MARIONETTE

2. of sea navigation, shipping, etc. [*maritime* law] **3.** characteristic of sailors; nautical

Maritime Provinces Canad. provinces of Nova Scotia, New Brunswick, & Prince Edward Island

mar·jo·ram (mär′jər əm) *n.* [< OFr. < ML., prob. < L. *amaracus* < Gr. *amarakos*] any of various perennial plants of the mint family; esp., **sweet marjoram,** having fragrant leaves used in cooking

Mar·jo·rie, Mar·jo·ry (mär′jər ē) [var. of MARGARET] a feminine name

Mark (märk) **1.** [< L. *Marcus < Mars,* MARS] a masculine name **2.** *Bible a)* one of the four Evangelists, said to be the author of the second Gospel *b)* this book

mark¹ (märk) *n.* [OE. *mearc,* orig., boundary < IE. base *mereg-,* boundary] **1.** a line, spot, stain, scratch, mar, etc. on a surface **2.** a sign, symbol, or indication; specif., *a)* a printed or written sign or stroke [punctuation *marks*] *b)* a brand, label, etc. put on an article to show the owner, maker, etc. *c)* a sign of some quality, character, etc. [courtesy is the *mark* of a gentleman] *d)* a grade; rating [a *mark* of B in history] *e)* a cross, etc. made by a person unable to write his signature **3.** a standard of quality, etc. [up to the *mark*] **4.** importance; distinction [a man of *mark*] **5.** impression; influence [she left her *mark* in history] **6.** a visible object of known position, serving as a guide **7.** a line, dot, etc. used to indicate position, as on a graduated scale **8.** an object aimed at; target; end; goal **9.** the butt of an attack, criticism, etc. **10.** a taking notice; heed **11.** *Sports a)* the starting line of a race *b)* a spare or strike in bowling —*vt.* **1.** to put or make a mark or marks on **2.** to identify as by a mark [abilities that *mark* one for success] **3.** to draw, write, record, etc. **4.** to show by a mark **5.** to show plainly; make clear [a smile *marking* joy] **6.** to set off in a special way; distinguish; characterize [scientific discoveries that *marked* the 19th century] **7.** to take notice of; heed [*mark* my words] **8.** to grade; rate [to *mark* examination papers] **9.** to put price tags on **10.** to keep (score, etc.); record —*vi.* **1.** to make a mark or marks **2.** to observe; take note **3.** *Games* to keep score —**hit the mark 1.** to achieve one's aim **2.** to be right —**make one's mark** to win success or fame —**mark down 1.** to write down; record ☆**2.** to mark for sale at a reduced price —**mark off** (or **out**) to mark the limits of —**mark time 1.** to keep time while at a halt by lifting the feet as if marching **2.** to suspend progress for a time —**mark up 1.** to cover with marks ☆**2.** to mark for sale at an increased price —**miss the mark 1.** to fail in achieving one's aim **2.** to be inaccurate —**wide of** (or **beside**) **the mark 1.** not striking the point aimed at **2.** not to the point; irrelevant

mark² (märk) *n.* [< OE. < ON. *mǫrk,* a half pound of silver] a monetary unit of the old German Empire, superseded by the reichsmark, and of East Germany: see MONETARY UNITS, table

Mark Antony *see* ANTONY

☆**mark·down** (märk′doun′) *n.* **1.** a marking for sale at a reduced price **2.** the amount of reduction in price

marked (märkt) *adj.* **1.** having a mark or marks **2.** singled out as an object of suspicion, hostility, etc. [a *marked* man] **3.** noticeable [a *marked* change] —**mark·ed·ly** (mär′kid lē) *adv.*

mark·er (mär′kər) *n.* a person or thing that marks; specif., *a)* a scorekeeper *b)* a device for marking lines, as on a tennis court *c)* a bookmark *d)* a memorial tablet or gravestone ☆*e)* a milestone or similar sign

mar·ket (mär′kit) *n.* [< ONormFr. < L. *mercatus,* trade < pp. of *mercari,* to trade < *merx,* merchandise] **1.** *a)* a gathering of people for buying and selling things *b)* the people gathered **2.** an open space or a building where goods are shown for sale from stalls or booths **3.** a store selling provisions [a meat *market*] **4.** a region where goods can be bought and sold [the European *market*] **5.** *a)* trade in goods, stocks, etc. [an active *market*] *b)* trade in a specified commodity [the wheat *market*] *c)* the people associated in such trade **6.** *short for* STOCK MARKET **7.** opportunity to sell, or demand (for goods or services) [a good *market* for new products] **8.** opportunity to buy, or supply (of goods or services) [reduced labor *market*] **9.** *same as: a)* MARKET PRICE *b)* MARKET VALUE —*vt.* **1.** to send or take to market **2.** to offer for sale **3.** to sell —*vi.* **1.** to buy or sell **2.** to buy provisions or food for the home —**be in the market for** to be seeking to buy —**be on the market** to be offered for sale —**buyer's market** a state of trade favorable to the buyer (relatively heavy supply and low prices) —**put on the market** to offer for sale —**seller's market** a state of trade favorable to the seller (relatively heavy demand and high prices) —**mar′ket·er, mar′ket·eer′** (-kə tir′) *n.* —**mar′ket·ing** *n.*

mar·ket·a·ble (-ə b'l) *adj.* **1.** *a)* that can be sold; fit for sale *b)* that can be easily sold **2.** of buying or selling *[marketable* value*]* —**mar′ket·a·bil′i·ty** *n.*

mar·ket·place (-plās′) *n.* **1.** a place, esp. an open place, where goods are offered for sale **2.** the world of trade, business, economic affairs, etc.

market price the price that a commodity brings when sold in a given market; prevailing price

market research the study of the demands or needs of consumers in relation to particular goods or services

market value the price that a commodity can be expected to bring when sold in a given market

mark·ing (mär′kiŋ) *n.* **1.** the act of making a mark or marks **2.** a mark or marks **3.** the characteristic arrangement of marks, as on fur or feathers

mark·ka (märk′kä) *n., pl.* **-kaa** (-kä) [Finn. < Sw. *mark:* see MARK²] *see* MONETARY UNITS, table (Finland)

marks·man (märks′mən) *n., pl.* **-men** a person who shoots, esp. with skill —**marks′man·ship′** *n.*

☆**mark·up** (märk′up′) *n.* **1.** a marking for sale at an increased price **2.** the amount of increase **3.** the amount added to the cost to cover overhead and profit in arriving at a selling price

marl (märl) *n.* [< OFr. < ML. *marga,* marl < Gaul.] a crumbly mixture of clay, sand, and limestone, usually with shell fragments —*vt.* to cover or fertilize with marl —**marl′y** *adj.*

Marl·bor·ough (märl′bur′ō, -ə; *Brit.* môl′bər ə), 1st Duke of, (*John Churchill*) 1650–1722; Eng. general & statesman

mar·lin (mär′lin) *n., pl.* **-lin, -lins**: see PLURAL, II, D, 2 [< MARLINESPIKE] any of several large, slender deep-sea fishes related to the sailfish, esp. the **blue marlin** of the Atlantic

mar·line (mär′lin) *n.* [Du. *marlijn,* altered (after *lijn,* LINE¹)] a small cord of two loose strands for winding around the ends of ropes to prevent fraying: also **mar′lin, mar′ling** (-liŋ)

mar·line·spike, mar·lin·spike (-spīk′) *n.* a pointed iron instrument for separating rope strands, as in splicing: also **mar′-ling·spike′** (-liŋ-)

Mar·lowe (mär′lō), **Christopher** 1564–93; Eng. dramatist & poet

mar·ma·lade (mär′mə lād′) *n.* [< OFr. < Port. < *marmelo,* quince < L. *melimelum* < Gr. < *meli,* honey + *mēlon,* apple] a jamlike preserve made by boiling the pulp, and usually the sliced-up rinds, of oranges or some other fruits with sugar

Mar·ma·ra (mär′mə rə), **Sea of** sea between European & Asiatic Turkey, connected with the Black Sea by the Bosporus & with the Aegean Sea by the Dardanelles: also sp. **Marmora** See map at DARDANELLES

mar·mo·re·al (mär môr′ē əl) *adj.* [< L. < *marmor,* marble + -AL] of or like marble: also **mar′mo′re·an**

mar·mo·set (mär′mə zet′, -set′) *n.* [< OFr. *marmouset,* grotesque figure] a very small monkey of South and Central America, with thick, soft fur

mar·mot (mär′mət) *n.* [< Fr. < earlier *marmottaine,* prob. < L. *mus montanus,* mountain mouse] any of a group of thick-bodied, gnawing and burrowing rodents with coarse fur and a short, bushy tail, as the woodchuck

Marne (märn) river in NE France, flowing northwest into the Seine at Paris

ma·roon¹ (mə rōōn′) *n., adj.* [Fr. *marron,* chestnut < It. *marrone*] dark brownish red

ma·roon² (mə rōōn′) *n.* [< Fr. < AmSp. *cimarrón,* wild < OSp. *cimarra,* thicket] in the West Indies and Surinam, **1.** *orig.,* a fugitive Negro slave **2.** a descendant of such slaves —*vt.* **1.** to put (a person) ashore in some desolate place and abandon him there **2.** to leave abandoned, helpless, etc. *[the storm marooned us]*

Marq. 1. Marquess **2.** Marquis

marque¹ (märk) *n.* [MFr. < Pr. *marca*] reprisal: obsolete except in LETTERS OF MARQUE

marque² (märk) *n.* [Fr., ult. < OIt. *marca,* a mark] an identifying nameplate or emblem on an automobile

mar·quee (mär kē′) *n.* [< Fr. *marquise* (misunderstood as pl.), orig. a canopy over an officer's tent] **1.** [Chiefly Brit.] a large tent, as for an outdoor entertainment ☆**2.** a rooflike projection or awning over an entrance, as to a theater

mar·quess (mär′kwis) *n.* **1.** a British nobleman ranking above an earl and below a duke **2.** *same as* MARQUIS

mar·que·try, mar·que·terie (mär′kə trē) *n.* [< Fr. < *marque,* a mark] decorative inlaid work of wood, ivory, etc., as in furniture or flooring

Mar·quette (mär ket′), **Jacques** (zhàk) 1637–75; Fr. Jesuit missionary & explorer, in N. America: called *Père Marquette*

mar·quis (mär′kwis; *Fr.* mår kē′) *n., pl.* **-quis·es;** *Fr.* **-quis′** (-kē′) [< OFr. < ML. *marchisus,* prefect of a frontier town < *marca,* borderland] in some European countries, a nobleman ranking above an earl or count and below a duke: see MARQUESS —**mar′quis·ate** (-kwə zit) *n.*

mar·quise (mär kēz′; *Fr.* mår kēz′) *n.* **1.** the wife or widow of a marquis **2.** a lady whose rank in her own right equals that of a marquis **3.** a gem cut as a pointed oval

mar·qui·sette (mär′ki zet′, -kwi-) *n.* [dim. of Fr. *marquise,* awning: see MARQUEE] a thin, meshlike fabric used for curtains, dresses, etc.

Mar·ra·kech, Mar·ra·kesh (mə rä′kesh, mar′ə kesh′) city in C Morocco; traditional S capital: pop. 295,000

mar·riage (mar′ij) *n.* [OFr. < *marier:* see MARRY¹] **1.** the state of being married; relation between husband and wife; wedlock **2.** the act or rite of marrying; wedding **3.** any close union

SYN.—**marriage** refers to the relation between a man and a woman who have become husband and wife or to the ceremony at which they become married; **matrimony,** a formal word, applies specifically to the religious sacrament of marriage and stresses the rights and duties of married persons *[the bonds of holy matrimony];* **wedlock** now applies specifically to marriage as a legal relationship *[a child born out of wedlock];* **wedding** refers specifically to the marriage ceremony and also to any festivities that go with it; **nuptials** is a highly formal, somewhat pretentious term for a wedding ceremony and celebration

mar·riage·a·ble (mar′i jə b'l) *adj.* old enough to get married —**mar′riage·a·bil′i·ty** *n.*

marriage portion *same as* DOWRY

mar·ried (mar′ēd) *adj.* **1.** living together as husband and wife **2.** having a husband or wife **3.** of marriage or married people *[married life]* **4.** closely joined —*n.* a married person: chiefly in **young marrieds**

mar·row (mar′ō) *n.* [OE. *mearg*] **1.** the soft, vascular, fatty tissue that fills the cavities of most bones **2.** the innermost, essential, or choicest part; pith —**mar′row·y** *adj.*

marrow bean a variety of the common field bean, grown for its dry, plump seeds, used as a vegetable

mar·row·bone (-bōn′) *n.* a bone containing marrow, esp. one used in cooking

mar·row·fat (-fat′) *n.* a variety of large, rich pea: also **marrow-fat pea, marrow pea**

mar·ry¹ (mar′ē) *vt.* **-ried, -ry·ing** [< OFr. *marier* < L. < *maritus,* a husband] **1.** *a)* to join as husband and wife *b)* to join (a man) to a woman as her husband, or (a woman) to a man as his wife **2.** to take as husband or wife **3.** to join closely —*vi.* **1.** to get married **2.** to enter into a close relationship —**marry off** to give in marriage: said of a parent or guardian —**mar′ri·er** *n.*

mar·ry² (mar′ē) *interj.* [a respelling of (the Virgin) *Mary*] [Archaic or Dial.] an exclamation of surprise, anger, etc.

Mars (märz) **1.** *Rom. Myth.* the god of war: identified with the Greek god Ares **2.** *a name used for* war **3.** a planet of the solar system, fourth in distance from the sun: diameter, c.4,200 miles

Mar·sa·la (mär sä′lä) *n.* [< *Marsala,* seaport in W Sicily] a light, sweet white wine

Mar·seil·laise (mär′sə lāz′; *Fr.* mår se yez′) [Fr., lit., of Marseille] the French national anthem, composed (1792) during the French Revolution

Mar·seille (mår se′y′; *E.* mär sā′) seaport in SE France, on the Mediterranean: pop. 889,000

Mar·seilles (mär sā′; *chiefly Brit.* -sälz′; *for n.* -sälz′) Eng. *sp.* of MARSEILLE —*n.* a thick, strong cotton cloth with a raised weave

marsh (märsh) *n.* [OE. *merisc* < IE. base *mori,* sea] a tract of low, wet, soft land; swamp; bog; morass

mar·shal (mär′shəl) *n.* [< OFr. *mareschal* < OHG. < *marah,* horse + *scalh,* servant] **1.** a high official of a medieval royal household **2.** a military commander; specif., *a) same as* FIELD

MARSHAL *b)* in various foreign armies, a general officer of the highest rank **3.** an official in charge of ceremonies, processions, etc. ☆**4.** a U.S. officer of various kinds; specif., *a)* a Federal officer appointed to a judicial district to perform functions like those of a sheriff *b)* the head of a police or fire department in some cities —*vt.* **-shaled** or **-shalled, -shal·ing** or **-shal·ling 1.** to arrange (troops, things, ideas, etc.) in order; dispose **2.** *a)* to direct as a marshal; manage *b)* to lead or guide ceremoniously —**mar′shal·cy, mar′shal·ship′** *n.*

Mar·shall (mär′shəl) **1.** George C(atlett), 1880–1959; U.S. general & statesman **2.** John, 1755–1835; U.S. jurist; chief justice of the U.S. (1801–35)

Mar·shall Islands (mär′shəl) group of islands in the W Pacific: see Trust Territory of the PACIFIC ISLANDS

marsh gas a gaseous product, chiefly methane, formed from decomposing vegetable matter, as in marshes

marsh·mal·low (marsh′mel′ō, -mal′ō) *n.* **1.** orig., a confection made from the root of the marsh mallow **2.** a soft, spongy confection of sugar, starch, corn syrup, and gelatin

marsh mallow a pink-flowered, perennial, European plant with a root sometimes used in medicine

marsh marigold a marsh plant of the buttercup family, with bright-yellow flowers

marsh·y (mär′shē) *adj.* **marsh′i·er, marsh′i·est 1.** of, like, or containing a marsh or marshes; swampy **2.** growing in marshes —**marsh′i·ness** *n.*

mar·su·pi·al (mär soo′pē əl) *adj.* **1.** of or like a marsupium **2.** of an order of mammals whose young are carried by the female for several months after birth in an external pouch of the abdomen —*n.* an animal of this kind, as a kangaroo, opossum, etc.

mar·su·pi·um (-əm) *n., pl.* **-pi·a** (-ə) [ModL. < L. < Gr. dim. of *marsypos,* a pouch] the pouch on the abdomen of a female marsupial

mart (märt) *n.* [MDu., var. of *markt*] a market, or trading center

Mar·tel (mär tel′), **Charles** 688?–741 A.D.; ruler of the Franks (714–741): grandfather of CHARLEMAGNE

mar·ten (mär′t'n) *n., pl.* **-tens, -ten:** see PLURAL, II, D, 1 [< OFr. < *martre*] **1.** a small, flesh-eating mammal like a weasel but larger, with soft, thick, valuable fur **2.** the fur

Mar·tha (mär′thə) [LL. < Gr. < Aram. *Mārthā,* lit., lady] **1.** a feminine name **2.** *Bible* a woman rebuked by Jesus for fussing over chores while he talked with her sister Mary: Luke 10:40

Martha's Vineyard [after a *Martha* Gosnold and the wild grapes there] island off the SE coast of Mass.

mar·tial (mär′shəl) *adj.* [< L. *martialis,* of Mars] **1.** of or connected with war, soldiers, etc.; military [*martial* music] **2.** warlike; militaristic [*martial* spirit] —**mar′tial·ism** *n.* —**mar′tial·ist** *n.* —**mar′tial·ly** *adv.*

martial law temporary rule by the military authorities over the civilians, as in time of war

Mar·tian (mär′shən) *adj.* of Mars (god or planet) —*n.* an imagined inhabitant of the planet Mars

Mar·tin (mär′t'n) [Fr. < L. < *Martis,* genitive of *Mars,* Mars: hence, lit., warlike] **1.** a masculine name **2.** Saint, 315?–397? A.D.; bishop of Tours: see MARTINMAS

mar·tin (mär′t'n) *n.* [Fr.] **1.** a stout-billed bird of the swallow family, as the purple martin **2.** any of various swallowlike birds

mar·ti·net (mär′t'n et′) *n.* [after Gen. J. *Martinet,* 17th-c. Fr. drillmaster] a very strict disciplinarian or stickler for rigid regulations

mar·tin·gale (mär′t'n gāl′) *n.* [Fr., prob. < Sp. *almártaga,* check, rein < Ar.] **1.** the strap of a horse's harness passing from the noseband to the girth between the forelegs, to keep the horse from rearing or throwing back its head **2.** a lower stay for the jib boom of a sailing vessel Also **mar′tin·gal′** (-gal′)

☆**mar·ti·ni** (mär tē′nē) *n., pl.* **-nis** [altered < earlier *Martinez:* reason for name unc.] [*also* **M-**] a cocktail of gin (or vodka) and dry vermouth

Mar·ti·nique (mär′tə nēk′) French island possession in the Windward group of the West Indies: cap. Fort-de-France

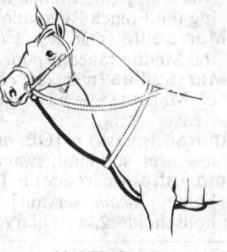

MARTINGALE

Mar·tin·mas (mär′t'n məs) *n.* [see -MAS] Saint Martin's Day, a church festival held on November 11

mar·tyr (mär′tər) *n.* [OE. < LL. < Gr. *martyr,* a witness: for IE. base see MEMORY] **1.** a person tortured or killed because of his faith or beliefs **2.** a person suffering great pain or misery a long time —*vt.* to make a martyr of —**mar′tyr·dom** *n.*

mar·tyr·ize (mär′tə rīz′) *vt.* **-ized′, -iz′ing** to make a martyr of —*vi.* to be or become a martyr —**mar′tyr·i·za′tion** *n.*

mar·tyr·ol·o·gy (mär′tə räl′ə jē) *n., pl.* **-gies 1.** a list of martyrs **2.** a historical account of religious martyrs **3.** such accounts as a group —**mar′tyr·ol′o·gist** *n.*

mar·vel (mär′v'l) *n.* [< OFr. *merveille* < VL. < L. neut. pl. of *mirabilis,* wonderful < *mirari,* to admire: for IE. base see SMILE] a wonderful or astonishing thing; prodigy or miracle —*vi.* **-veled** or **-velled, -vel·ing** or **-vel·ling** to be amazed; wonder —*vt.* to wonder at or about (followed by a clause)

Mar·vell (mär′v'l), **Andrew** 1621–78; Eng. poet

mar·vel·ous (mär′v'l əs) *adj.* **1.** causing wonder; astonishing, extraordinary, incredible, etc. **2.** [Colloq.] fine; splendid Also, chiefly Brit. sp., **mar′vel·lous** —**mar′vel·ous·ly** *adv.* —**mar′vel·ous·ness** *n.*

Mar·vin (mär′vin) [prob. ult. < Gmc. bases meaning "sea" & "friend"] a masculine name

Marx (märks), **Karl (Heinrich)** 1818–83; Ger. social philosopher & political economist whose doctrines are the basis of modern socialism

Marx·ism (märk′siz'm) *n.* the system of thought developed by Karl Marx, his co-worker Friedrich Engels, and their followers: also **Marx′i·an·ism** —**Marx′ist, Marx′i·an** *adj., n.*

Mar·y (mer′ē, mar′ē, mā′rē) [< OE. < LL. *Maria* < Gr. < Heb. *Miryam* or Aram. *Maryam,* lit., rebellion] **1.** a feminine name **2.** Mary I (*Mary Tudor*) 1516–58; queen of England (1553–58): daughter of HENRY VIII & wife of PHILIP II of Spain **3.** Mary II 1662–94; queen of England, Scotland, & Ireland, ruling jointly with her husband, WILLIAM III **4.** *Bible a)* mother of Jesus: Matt. 1:18–25 *b)* sister of Martha: Luke 10:38–42

Mary Janes ☆*a trademark for* low-heeled, patent-leather slippers with a strap, for little girls

Mar·y·land (mer′ə lənd) [after Queen Henrietta *Maria,* wife of CHARLES I of England] E State of the U.S., on the Atlantic: 10,577 sq. mi.; pop. 3,922,000; cap. Annapolis: abbrev. **Md., MD**

Mary Magdalene *Bible* woman out of whom Jesus cast seven devils: Luke 8:2: identified with the repentant woman in Luke 7:37–50

Mary, Queen of Scots (*Mary Stuart*) 1542–87; queen of Scotland (1542–67): beheaded

mar·zi·pan (mär′zi pan′) *n.* [G. < It. *marzapane,* confection < ML. < Ar.] a confection of various shapes and colors made of a paste of ground almonds, sugar, and egg white

-mas (məs) *a combining form for* MASS *meaning* a (specified) church festival [*Martinmas*]

Ma·sai (mä sī′) *n.* **1.** *pl.* **-sai′, -sais′** any member of a pastoral people of Kenya and Tanganyika **2.** their language

masc., mas. masculine

Mas·ca·gni (mäs kä′nyē), **Pie·tro** (pye′trô) 1863–1945; It. composer of operas

mas·ca·ra (mas kar′ə) *n.* [< Sp. < It. *maschera:* see MASK] a cosmetic for coloring the eyelashes —*vt.* **-ca′raed, -ca′ra·ing** to put mascara on

mas·cot (mas′kät, -kət) *n.* [< Fr. < Pr. dim. of *masco,* sorcerer] any person, animal, or thing supposed to bring good luck by being present

mas·cu·line (mas′kyə lin) *adj.* [< OFr. < L. *masculus,* male < *mas,* male] **1.** male; of men or boys **2.** having qualities thought of as those that men and boys have, as strength, vigor, etc. **3.** suitable to or for a man **4.** mannish: said of a woman **5.** *Gram.* designating or of the gender of words referring to males or things originally thought of as male **6.** *Poetry* designating or of a rhyme of stressed final syllables (Ex.: enjoy, destroy) —*n. Gram.* **1.** the masculine gender **2.** a word or form in this gender —see SYN. at MALE —**mas′cu·line·ly** *adv.* —**mas′cu·lin′i·ty** *n.*

mas·cu·lin·ize (-li nīz′) *vt.* **-ized′, -iz′ing** to make masculine; esp., to produce male characteristics in (a female)

Mase·field (mās′fēld, māz′-), **John** 1878–1967; Eng. writer, esp. of poetry

☆**ma·ser** (mā′zər) *n.* [*m*(icrowave) *a*(mplification by) *s*(timulated) *e*(mission of) *r*(adiation)] a device, operating at microwave, infrared, etc. frequencies, in which atoms in a crystal or gas are concentrated, raised to a higher energy level, then radiated in a very narrow beam

Ma·se·ru (maz′ə rōō′) capital of Lesotho: pop. 11,000

mash (mash) *n.* [< OE. *masc-*, in *mascwyrt*, infused malt] **1.** crushed or ground malt or meal soaked in hot water for making wort, used in brewing beer **2.** a mixture of bran, meal, etc. in warm water for feeding horses, etc. **3.** any soft mixture or mass —*vt.* **1.** to mix (crushed malt, etc.) in hot water for making wort **2.** to change into a soft mass by beating, crushing, etc. [to *mash* potatoes] **3.** to crush and injure or damage

mash·er (mash′ər) *n.* **1.** one that mashes; specif., a device for mashing vegetables, etc. ☆**2.** [Slang] a man who makes unwanted advances to women not acquainted with him, esp. in public places

Mash·had (mə shäd′) city in NE Iran: pop. 417,000

mask (mask) *n.* [Fr. *masque* < It. *maschera*, prob. < Ar. *mask-hara*, buffoon] **1.** a covering to conceal or disguise all or part of the face **2.** anything that conceals or disguises **3.** a masque or masquerade **4.** a person wearing a mask **5.** *a)* a sculptured or molded likeness of the face *b)* a grotesque or comic representation of a face, worn to amuse or frighten **6.** a protective covering for the face or head [a gas *mask*] **7.** a covering for the mouth and nose, as for giving someone an anesthetic, preventing infection, etc. **8.** the face or head of a dog, fox, etc. —*vt.* to conceal, cover, disguise, etc. with or as with a mask —*vi.* **1.** to put on a mask **2.** to hide or disguise one's true motives, character, etc. —**masked** *adj.* —**mask′er** *n.*

MASKS

masked ball a ball at which masks and fancy costumes are worn

mask·ing tape (mas′kiŋ) an adhesive tape for covering borders, etc., as during painting

mas·och·ism (mas′ə kiz′m, maz′-) *n.* [after L. von Sacher-*Masoch* (1835–1895), Austrian writer] the getting of pleasure, specif. sexual pleasure, from being dominated or hurt physically or psychologically —**mas′och·ist** *n.* —**mas′och·is′tic** *adj.* —**mas′och·is′ti·cal·ly** *adv.*

ma·son (mā′s'n) *n.* [< OFr. < ML. *matio*] **1.** a person whose work is building with stone, brick, etc. **2.** [M-] *same as* FREEMASON

Ma·son-Dix·on line (mā′s'n dik′s'n) [after C. *Mason* & J. *Dixon*, who surveyed it, 1763–67] boundary line between Pa. & Md., regarded as separating the North from the South: also **Mason and Dixon's line**

Ma·son·ic (mə sän′ik) *adj.* [also m-] of Masons (Freemasons) or Masonry (Freemasonry)

☆**Ma·son·ite** (mā′s'n it′) [after W. H. *Mason* (1877–1947?), U.S. engineer] *a trademark for* a kind of hardboard made from pressed wood fibers, used as building material, etc. —*n.* such hardboard

☆**Mason jar** [patented in 1858 by J. *Mason* of New York] [also m-] a wide-mouthed glass jar with a screw top, for preserving foods, esp. in home canning

ma·son·ry (mā′s'n rē) *n.*, *pl.* **-ries** **1.** the trade or art of a mason **2.** something built by a mason or masons; brickwork or stonework **3.** [usually M-] *same as* FREEMASONRY

masque (mask) *n.* [see MASK] **1.** a masquerade; masked ball **2.** a kind of play in verse put on for kings and nobles in the 16th and 17th centuries, using fancy costumes, music, dancing, etc.

mas·quer·ade (mas′kə rād′) *n.* [< Fr. < It. dial. var. of *mascherata* (< *maschera*): see MASK] **1.** a ball or party at which masks and fancy costumes are worn **2.** a costume for such a ball, etc. **3.** the act of hiding who one is, how one feels, etc.; disguise —*vi.* **-ad′ed, -ad′ing** **1.** to take part in a masquerade **2.** to hide who one is by pretending to be someone else —**mas′quer·ad′er** *n.*

Mass (mas) *n.* [OE. *mæsse* < LL. < *missa* in L. *ite, missa est* (*contio*), go, (the meeting) is dismissed] [also m-] **1.** the service of the Eucharist in the Roman Catholic Church and some other churches, consisting of a series of prayers and ceremonies **2.** a musical setting for certain parts of this service

mass (mas) *n.* [OFr. *masse* < L. < Gr. *maza*, barley cake: for IE. base see MAKE] **1.** a piece or amount of indefinite shape or size [a *mass* of clay, a *mass* of cold air] **2.** a large quantity or number [a *mass* of bruises] **3.** bulk; size [he can't move the piano because of its *mass*] **4.** the main part; majority [the *mass* of opinion favors the plan] **5.** *Physics* the quantity of matter in a body as measured in its relation to inertia —*adj.* **1.** *a)* of a large number of things [*mass* production] *b)* of a large number of persons [a *mass* demonstration] **2.** of, like, or for the masses [*mass* education] —*vt., vi.* to gather or form into a mass [crowds were *massing* in the streets] —see SYN. at BULK —**in the mass** as a whole; taken together —**the masses** the great mass of common people; specif., the working people

Mas·sa·chu·setts (mas′ə chōō′sits) [< Algonquian *Massaadchu-es-et*, lit., at the big hill] New England State of the U.S.: 8,257 sq. mi.; pop. 5,689,000; cap. Boston: abbrev. **Mass., MA**

Massachusetts Bay inlet of the Atlantic, on the E coast of Mass.

mas·sa·cre (mas′ə kər) *n.* [Fr. < OFr. *maçacre*, shambles] **1.** the merciless killing of a large number of human beings; wholesale slaughter **2.** a large-scale slaughter of animals —*vt.* **-cred, -cring** to kill mercilessly and in large numbers —see SYN. at SLAUGHTER —**mas′sa·crer** (-krər) *n.*

mas·sage (mə säzh′) *n.* [Fr. < *masser*, to massage < Ar. *massa*, to touch] a rubbing, kneading, etc. of part of the body, as to stimulate circulation and loosen up muscles or joints —*vt.* **-saged′, -sag′ing** to give a massage to —**mas·sag′er** *n.*

Mas·sa·soit (mas′ə soit′) 1580?–1661; chief of an American Indian tribe of Mass.; signed a treaty with the Pilgrims

☆**mass·cult** (mas′kult′) *n.* [MASS + CULT(URE)] [Colloq.] an artificial, commercialized culture popularized for the masses through the mass media

Mas·se·net (mas′ə nā′; *Fr.* màs ne′), **Jules** (**Émile Frédéric**) (zhül) 1842–1912; Fr. composer

mas·sé (**shot**) (ma sā′) [Fr. < *masse*, billiard cue] a stroke in billiards made by hitting the cue ball off center with the cue held straight up so as to make the ball move in a curve

mas·seur (ma sur′, mə-) *n.* [Fr.] a man whose work is giving massages —**mas·seuse′** (-sōōz′, -sōōz′) *n.fem.*

mas·sive (mas′iv) *adj.* **1.** *a)* forming or consisting of a large mass; big and solid; bulky [a *massive* statue] *b)* larger or greater than normal [a *massive* dose of drugs] **2.** large and imposing or impressive [a *massive* building] **3.** large-scale; of wide extent [a *massive* attack] **4.** *Geol.* *a)* of a single kind of structure, without strata [*massive* rock formations] *b)* occurring in thick beds: said of some stratified rocks —see SYN. at HEAVY —**mas′sive·ly** *adv.* —**mas′sive·ness** *n.*

mass media those means of communication that reach and influence large numbers of people, esp. newspapers, magazines, radio, and television

☆**mass meeting** a large public meeting to discuss public affairs, demonstrate public approval or disapproval, etc.

☆**mass noun** a noun used for something that is an abstraction or that is uncountable: it is not preceded by *a* or *an* (Examples: *love, girlhood, butter, news*)

mass number *Physics, Chem.* the number of neutrons and protons in the nucleus of an atom

mass production the production of goods in large quantities, esp. by machinery and division of labor —**mass′-pro·duce′** *vt.* **-duced′, -duc′ing**

mast¹ (mast) *n.* [OE. *mæst*] **1.** a tall spar or hollow metal structure rising vertically from the keel or deck of a vessel and used to support the sails, yards, radar and radio equipment, etc. **2.** any vertical pole, as in a crane —*vt.* to put masts on —**before the mast** [Now Rare] as a common sailor

mast² (mast) *n.* [OE. *mæst*: for IE. base see MEAT] beechnuts, acorns, chestnuts, etc., esp. as food for hogs

mas·ta·ba, mas·ta·bah (mas′tə bə) *n.* [< Ar.] a structure, longer than it is wide, with a flat roof and sloping sides, built over the opening of a mummy chamber or burial pit in ancient Egypt and used as a tomb

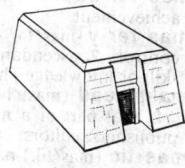

MASTABA

mas·tec·to·my (mas tek′tə mē) *n.*, *pl.* **-mies** [MAST(O)- + -ECTOMY] the removal of a breast by surgery

mas·ter (mas′tər) *n.* [< OE. *mægester* & OFr. *maistre*; both < L. *magister* < base of L. *magnus*, great < IE. base *meg-*, great, from which also comes Gr. *megas*, great] **1.** a man who rules others or has control, authority, or power over something; specif., *a)* a man who is head of a household or institution *b)* an employer *c)* an owner of an animal or slave *d)* the captain of a merchant ship *e)* one that excels in a contest, skill, etc.; victor *f)* [Chiefly Brit.] a male schoolteacher *g)* a person whose teachings in religion, philosophy, etc. one follows *h)* [**M-**] Jesus Christ (with *our, the,* etc.) **2.** a person very skilled in some work, profession, etc.; expert; specif., *a)* a highly skilled workman qualified to follow his trade independently *b)* an artist regarded as great **3.** [**M-**] a title variously applied to *a)* any man or youth: now replaced by the variant *Mister,* usually written *Mr.* *b)* a boy thought of as too young to be addressed as *Mr.* *c)* a man who heads some institution, group, etc. *d)* in Scotland, the heir apparent of a viscount or baron *e)* a person who is a MASTER OF ARTS (or SCIENCE, etc.) **4.** a metal mold made from the original recording and used to produce phonograph records in quantity **5.** *Law* any of several court officers appointed to assist the judge —*adj.* **1.** being a master [a *master* workman] **2.** of a master **3.** chief; main; controlling; specif., designating a mechanism or device that controls others, sets a standard or norm, etc. [a *master* switch; a *master* test sheet] —*vt.* **1.** to become master of; control, conquer, etc. [he *mastered* his fear] **2.** to become an expert in (an art, science, etc.)

mas·ter-at-arms (-ət ärmz′) *n., pl.* **mas′ters-at-arms′** any naval petty officer who is responsible for keeping order, taking charge of prisoners, etc. on a warship

master builder 1. a person skilled in building; esp., formerly, an architect **2.** a building contractor

mas·ter·ful (-fəl) *adj.* **1.** fond of acting the part of a master; imperious **2.** having or showing the ability of a master; expert; skillful [a *masterful* pianist] —**mas′ter·ful·ly** *adv.* —**mas′ter·ful·ness** *n.*

SYN.—**masterful** implies having such a strong personality that one is able to impose his will on others [a *masterful* orchestra conductor]; **domineering** implies the arrogant, tyrannical manner of one who openly tries to dominate another [a *domineering* mother]; **imperious** suggests the absolute power of an emperor, but implies less arrogance than **domineering** does [the *imperious* old dean of the college]; **magisterial**, while not suggesting the taking on of absolute power, implies too much use or display of such powers as a magistrate might have [he dismissed me with a *magisterial* air]

master key a key that will open every one of a set of locks

mas·ter·ly (-lē) *adj.* showing the ability or skill of a master; expert [a *masterly* job of repair work] —*adv.* in a masterly manner —**mas′ter·li·ness** *n.*

master mechanic a skilled mechanic, esp. one serving as foreman

mas·ter·mind (-mīnd′) *n.* a very intelligent person, esp. one with the ability to plan or direct a group project —*vt.* to be the mastermind of (a project)

Master of Arts (or ☆**Science**, etc.) **1.** a degree given by a college or university to a person who has completed a required program of graduate study in the humanities (or in science, etc.) **2.** a person who has this degree

master of ceremonies 1. a person who supervises a ceremony ☆**2.** a person in charge of an entertainment, introducing the participants, filling in the intervals with jokes, etc.

mas·ter·piece (-pēs′) *n.* **1.** a thing made or done with masterly skill **2.** the greatest work made or done by a person or group: also **mas′ter·work′**

Mas·ters (mas′tərz), **Edgar Lee** 1869–1950; U.S. poet

☆**master sergeant** *U.S. Mil.* a noncommissioned officer of high rank; in the Army, the rank just above sergeant first class; in the Air Force, just above technical sergeant; in the Marine Corps, just above gunnery sergeant

mas·ter·ship (mas′tər ship′) *n.* **1.** the state of being a master; rule; control **2.** the position, duties, or term of office of a master **3.** masterly ability; expert skill

mas·ter·stroke (-strōk′) *n.* a masterly action, move, or achievement

mas·ter·y (mas′tər ē, -trē) *n., pl.* **-ter·ies 1.** mastership; rule; control **2.** ascendancy or victory; the upper hand **3.** expert skill or knowledge [his *mastery* of chess]

mast·head (mast′hed′) *n.* **1.** the top part of a ship's mast ☆**2.** that part of a newspaper or magazine stating its address, publishers, editors, etc. —*vt.* to display at the masthead

mas·tic (mas′tik) *n.* [OFr. < LL. < L. < Gr. *mastichē*] **1.** a yellowish resin obtained from a Mediterranean evergreen tree, used as an astringent and in making varnish, adhesives, etc. **2.** the tree: in full, **mastic tree**

mas·ti·cate (mas′tə kāt′) *vt.* **-cat′ed, -cat′ing** [< LL. pp. of *masticare* < Gr. *mastichan*, to gnash < *mastax*, a mouth: for IE.

base see MOUTH] **1.** to chew up (food, etc.) **2.** to grind, cut, or knead (rubber, etc.) to a pulp —**mas′ti·ca′tion** *n.* —**mas′ti·ca′tor** *n.*

mas·ti·ca·to·ry (-kə tôr′ē) *adj.* of or for mastication; specif., adapted for chewing —*n., pl.* **-ries** any substance chewed but not swallowed, to increase saliva flow

mas·tiff (mas′tif) *n.* [< OFr. *mastin*, ult. < L. *mansuetus*, tame] a large, powerful, smooth-coated dog with hanging lips and drooping ears

mas·ti·tis (mas tīt′is) *n.* [MAST(O)- + -ITIS] inflammation of the breast or udder

mas·to- [< Gr. *mastos*, the breast: for IE. base see MEAT] a combining form meaning of or like a breast: also, before a vowel, **mast-**

mas·to·don (mas′tə dän′) *n.* [ModL. < Fr. < Gr. *mastos*, a breast + *odous*, a tooth: from the nipplelike ridges on its molars] a large animal, now extinct, that resembled the elephant but was larger

mas·toid (mas′toid) *adj.* [< Gr. < *mastos* (see MASTO-) + *eidos*, form] **1.** shaped like a breast or nipple **2.** that is or is near a part of the temporal bone that sticks out behind the ear —*n.* **1.** this part of the temporal bone **2.** [Colloq.] *same as* MASTOIDITIS

mas·toid·ec·to·my (mas′toi dek′tə mē) *n., pl.* **-mies** [see -ECTOMY] the surgical removal of part or all of a mastoid

mas·toid·i·tis (mas′toi dīt′is) *n.* inflammation of the mastoid

mas·tur·bate (mas′tər bāt′) *vi.* **-bat′ed, -bat′ing** [< L. pp. of *masturbari*, ult. < *manus*, hand + *stuprum*, defilement] to stimulate one's genitals so as to get sexual satisfaction, without sexual intercourse —**mas′tur·ba′tion** *n.* —**mas′tur·ba′tor** *n.*

mat¹ (mat) *n.* [< OE. *meatt* < LL. *matta* < Phoen.] **1.** a flat, coarse fabric of woven or plaited hemp, straw, etc. **2.** a piece of this or of corrugated rubber, etc., used as a doormat, etc. **3.** a flat piece of cloth, woven straw, etc. put under a vase, dish, etc. **4.** a thickly padded floor covering, as in a gymnasium for wrestling, etc. **5.** anything growing or interwoven in a thick tangle [a *mat* of hair] —*vt.* **mat′ted, mat′ting 1.** to cover as with a mat **2.** to form into a thick tangle —*vi.* to become felted or thickly tangled

mat² (mat) *adj.* [Fr. < OFr. *mat,* defeated, prob. < L. *mattus,* drunk < *madere,* to be drunk] *same as* MATTE —*n.* **1.** *same as* MATTE **2.** a border, as of cardboard or cloth, put around a picture, usually between the picture and the frame —*vt.* **mat′ted, mat′ting 1.** to produce a dull surface or finish on (metal, glass, etc.) **2.** to frame (a picture) with a mat

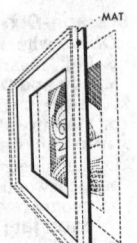

MAT

mat³ (mat) *n.* [Colloq.] a matrix; printing mold

mat·a·dor (mat′ə dôr′) *n.* [Sp. < *matar,* to kill < *mate,* checkmate] the bullfighter who kills the bull with a sword after performing a series of actions with a cape to anger and tire the animal

Ma·ta·mo·ros (mä′tä mô′rôs; *E.* mat′ə-môr′əs) city in NE Mexico, on the Rio Grande, opposite Brownsville, Tex.: pop. 175,000

match¹ (mach) *n.* [< OFr. *mesche,* prob. < L. *myxa,* lamp wick < Gr.] **1.** orig., a wick or cord prepared to burn at a uniform rate, used for firing guns or explosives **2.** a slender piece of wood, cardboard, etc. tipped with a composition that catches fire by friction, sometimes only on a specially prepared surface

match² (mach) *n.* [OE. *(ge)mæcca,* a mate < base of *macian,* MAKE] **1.** any person or thing equal or similar to another in some way; specif., *a)* a person, group, or thing able to cope with another as an equal [he met his *match* in chess when he played her] *b)* a counterpart or facsimile **2.** two or more persons or things that go together in appearance, size, etc. [a purse and shoes that are a good *match*] **3.** a contest or game; competition [a tennis *match*] **4.** a marriage or mating **5.** a person regarded as a suitable mate —*vt.* **1.** to join in marriage; mate **2.** to compete with successfully [he was able to *match* his opponent] **3.** to put in opposition (*with*); pit (*against*) [to *match* one's strength against an enemy] **4.** to be equal, similar, or suitable to [he could never *match* her in an argument] **5.** to make, show, or get a competitor, counterpart, or equivalent to [*match* this cloth] **6.** to suit or fit (one thing) to another **7.** to fit (things) together **8.** to compare ☆**9.** *a)* to flip or reveal (coins) to decide something contested, the winner being determined by the combination of faces thus exposed *b)* to match coins with (another person) —*vi.* to be equal, similar, suitable, etc. in some way —**match′a·ble** *adj.* —**match′er** *n.*

match·book (mach′book′) *n.* ☆a folder of book matches

match·box (mach′bäks′) *n.* a small box for holding matches

match·less (mach′lis) *adj.* having no equal; peerless — **match′less·ly** *adv.* —**match′less·ness** *n.*

match·lock (-läk′) *n.* **1.** an old type of gunlock in which the charge of powder was ignited by a slow-burning match (wick or cord) **2.** a musket with such a gunlock

match·mak·ing¹ (-mā′kiŋ) *n.* the work or business of making matches (for burning) —**match′mak′er** *n.*

match·mak·ing² (-mā′kiŋ) *n.* **1.** the arranging of marriages for others **2.** the arranging of wrestling or boxing matches, etc. —**match′mak′er** *n.*

match play *Golf* a form of play in which the score is calculated by counting holes won rather than strokes taken: see MEDAL PLAY

match point the final point needed to win the match, as in tennis

match·wood (-wood′) *n.* **1.** wood for making matches **2.** very small pieces; splinters

mate¹ (māt) *n.* [MDu. < *gemate* < Gmc.] **1.** a companion or fellow worker: often used in compounds [*classmate*] **2.** one of a matched pair **3.** *a)* a husband or wife *b)* the male or female of paired animals **4.** an officer of a merchant ship, ranking below the captain ☆**5.** *U.S. Navy* any of various petty officers [a carpenter's *mate*] —*vt., vi.* **mat′ed, mat′ing 1.** to join as a pair **2.** to couple in marriage or sexual union

mate² (māt) *n., interj., vt.* **mat′ed, mat′ing** *same as* CHECKMATE

ma·té (mä′tā, mat′ā) *n.* [AmSp. < Quechua *mati*, calabash (used to steep the brew)] **1.** a beverage made from the dried leaves of a S. American tree **2.** this tree or its leaves Also sp. **mate**

ma·ter (māt′ər, mät′-) *n.* [L.] [Chiefly Brit. Colloq.] mother

ma·te·ri·al (mə tir′ē əl) *adj.* [< LL. < L. *materia*, MATTER] **1.** of matter; relating to or consisting of what occupies space; physical [a *material* object] **2.** *a)* of the body or bodily needs, etc. [*material* pleasures] *b)* of or fond of comfort, wealth, etc.; worldly [*material* success] **3.** important, essential, etc. (*to* the matter under discussion) —*n.* **1.** what a thing is, or may be, made of; elements or parts **2.** ideas, notes, etc. that may be worked up; data [*material* for a story] **3.** cloth or other fabric **4.** [*pl.*] tools, articles, etc. for a specified use [*writing* materials] —**ma·te′ri·al′i·ty** (-al′ə tē) *n.*

SYN.—**material** is applied to anything that is formed of matter or substance [chairs are *material* objects]; **physical** applies either to material things known through the senses or to forces that can be measured scientifically [the *physical* world; the *physical* properties of sound]; **corporeal** applies only to material objects that have bodily form and can be touched [a house is *corporeal* property] —**ANT.** spiritual, mental

ma·te·ri·al·ism (-iz′m) *n.* **1.** the philosophical doctrine that everything in the world, including thought, will, and feeling, can be explained only in terms of matter **2.** the tendency to be more concerned with material than with spiritual values —**ma·te′ri·al·ist** *adj., n.* —**ma·te′ri·al·is′tic** *adj.* —**ma·te′ri·al·is′ti·cal·ly** *adv.*

ma·te·ri·al·ize (mə tir′ē ə līz′) *vt.* **-ized′, -iz′ing 1.** to give physical form to; represent in material form [to *materialize* an idea by drawing a sketch of it] **2.** to make (a spirit, etc.) appear in bodily form —*vi.* **1.** to become fact; be realized [a plan that never *materialized*] **2.** to take on, or appear in, bodily form: said of spirits, etc. **3.** to appear suddenly or unexpectedly —**ma·te′ri·al·i·za′tion** *n.*

ma·te·ri·al·ly (-lē) *adv.* **1.** with regard to the matter, content, etc. and not the form **2.** with regard to material objects, interests, etc.; physically **3.** to a great extent; considerably [he is *materially* improved]

ma·te·ri·a med·i·ca (mə tir′ē ə med′i kə) [ML. < L. *materia*, matter + fem. of *medicus*, medical] **1.** the drugs and other substances used as remedies in medicine **2.** the branch of medical science that deals with such substances, their uses, etc.

ma·te·ri·el, ma·té·ri·el (mə tir′ē el′) *n.* [Fr.: see MATERIAL] the necessary materials and tools; specif., weapons, supplies, etc. of armed forces

ma·ter·nal (mə tur′n'l) *adj.* [< MFr. < L. *mater*, MOTHER¹] **1.** of or like a mother; motherly **2.** derived or inherited from a mother **3.** related through the mother's side of the family [*maternal* grandparents] —**ma·ter′nal·ly** *adv.*

ma·ter·ni·ty (mə tur′nə tē) *n.* **1.** the state of being a mother; motherhood **2.** the qualities of a mother; motherliness —*adj.*

1. for pregnant women [a *maternity* dress] **2.** for the care of women giving birth and of newborn babies [a *maternity* ward]

math (math) *n. clipped form of* MATHEMATICS

math. 1. mathematical **2.** mathematician **3.** mathematics

math·e·mat·i·cal (math′ə mat′i k'l) *adj.* [< ML. < L. < Gr. < *mathēma*, what is learned < *manthanein*, to learn] **1.** of, like, or having to do with mathematics **2.** thoroughly precise, accurate, etc. —**math′e·mat′i·cal·ly** *adv.*

math·e·ma·ti·cian (math′ə mə tish′ən, math′mə-) *n.* an expert or specialist in mathematics

math·e·mat·ics (math′ə mat′iks) *n.pl.* [with *sing. v.*] [see MATHEMATICAL & -ICS] the group of sciences (arithmetic, geometry, algebra, calculus, etc.) dealing with quantities, magnitudes, and forms, and their relationships, qualities, etc., by the use of numbers and symbols

Math·er (math′ər) **1.** Cot·ton (kät′'n), 1663-1728; Am. clergyman & writer: son of *Increase* **2.** In·crease (in′krēs), 1639-1723; Am. clergyman & writer

Ma·til·da, Ma·thil·da (mə til′də) [< ML. < OHG. < *maht*, power + *hiltia*, battle] a feminine name

mat·in (mat′'n) *n.* [OFr. < L. *matutinus*, of the morning < *Matuta*, goddess of dawn: for IE. base see MATURE] **1.** [*pl.*] [often **M-**] *a)* R.C.Ch. the first of the canonical hours, usually joined with lauds *b)* Anglican Ch. the service of public morning prayer **2.** [Poet.] a morning song —*adj.* **1.** of matins **2.** of morning —**mat′in·al** *adj.*

mat·i·nee, mat·i·née (mat′'n ā′, mat′'n ā′) *n.* [< Fr.: see prec.] a daytime reception, etc.; esp., a performance, as of a play, in the afternoon

Ma·tisse (mà tēs′), Hen·ri (än rē′) 1869-1954; Fr. painter

ma·tri- [< L. *matris*, genitive of *mater*, a mother] *a combining form meaning* mother [*matriarch*]

ma·tri·arch (mā′trē ärk′) *n.* [MATRI- + -ARCH] a mother who rules her family or tribe; specif., a woman who is head of a matriarchy —**ma′tri·ar′chal** (-är′k'l) *adj.*

ma·tri·ar·chy (-trē är′kē) *n., pl.* **-chies 1.** a form of social organization in which the mother is head of the family or tribe, descent being traced through female ancestors **2.** rule or domination by women —**ma′tri·ar′chic** *adj.*

mat·ri·cide (mat′rə sīd′, mā′trə-) *n.* [< L. < *mater*, MOTHER¹ + *caedere*, to kill] **1.** the act of killing one's mother **2.** a person who kills his mother —**mat′ri·ci′dal** *adj.*

ma·tric·u·late (mə trik′yoo lāt′; *also, for n.*, -lit) *vt., vi.* **-lat′ed, -lat′ing** [< ML. pp. of *matriculare*, to register < LL. dim. of *matrix*, MATRIX] to enroll, esp. as a student in a college or university —*n.* a person so enrolled —**ma·tric′u·lant** *n.* —**ma·tric′u·la′tion** *n.*

mat·ri·mo·ny (mat′rə mō′nē) *n., pl.* **-nies** [< OFr. < L. *matrimonium* < *mater*, a mother] **1.** the act or rite of marriage **2.** the state of being husband and wife **3.** married life —see SYN. at MARRIAGE —**mat′ri·mo′ni·al** *adj.* —**mat′ri·mo′ni·al·ly** *adv.*

ma·trix (mā′triks) *n., pl.* **-tri·ces′** (mā′trə sēz′, mat′rə-), **-trix·es** [LL., womb, ult. < L. *mater*, MOTHER¹] **1.** orig., the womb; uterus **2.** that within which something originates, takes form, etc.; specif., a die or mold for casting or shaping **3.** *Geol.* the rock or earthy material in which a crystal, fossil, etc. is enclosed **4.** *Linguis.* an independent clause **5.** *Math.* a set of numbers or terms arranged in rows and columns between parentheses or double lines **6.** *Printing a)* a metal mold for casting the face of type *b)* an impression, as of papier-mâché, from which a plate can be made **7.** *Zool. a)* any nonliving substance by which living cells are surrounded, as in bone, cartilage, etc. *b)* the formative cells from which a nail, tooth, etc. grows

ma·tron (mā′trən) *n.* [< OFr. < L. *matrona* < *mater*, MOTHER¹] **1.** a wife or widow, esp. one who is mature and dignified **2.** a woman manager in charge of the living arrangements of a hospital, prison, or other institution **3.** a woman guard, as in a jail —**ma′tron·al** *adj.*

ma·tron·ly (-lē) *adj.* of, like, or suitable for a matron; mature and dignified —**ma′tron·li·ness** *n.*

☆**matron of honor** a married woman acting as principal attendant to the bride at a wedding

Matt. Matthew

matte (mat) *n.* [var. of MAT²] a dull surface or finish, often roughened —*adj.* not shiny or glossy; dull Also sp. **matt**

fat, āpe, cär; ten, ēven; is, bīte; gō, hôrn, tōol, look; oil, out; up, fur; get; joy; yet; chin; she; thin, then; zh, leisure; ŋ, ring; ə for *a* in *ago*, *e* in *agent*, *i* in *sanity*, *o* in *comply*, *u* in *focus*; ′ as in *able* (ā′b'l); Fr. bàl; ë, Fr. coeur; ö, Fr. feu; ö, Fr. mon; ô, Fr. coq; ü, Fr. duc; r, Fr. cri; H, G. ich; kh, G. doch; ‡foreign; ☆ Americanism; < derived from. See inside front cover.

mat·ted (mat′id) *adj.* **1.** closely tangled together in a dense mass *[matted* hair] **2.** covered with matting or mats

mat·ter (mat′ər) *n.* [< OFr. < L. *materia,* material: for IE. base see MOTHER¹] **1.** what a thing is made of; constituent material **2.** whatever occupies space and can be recognized by the senses in some way: in modern physics, it is known that matter can be converted into energy, and energy into matter **3.** any specified sort of substance *[coloring matter]* **4.** material or content of thought or expression, as distinguished from style or form **5.** an amount or quantity *[a matter* of a few days] **6.** *a)* something that is the subject of discussion, action, etc.; thing or affair *[business matters] b)* cause or occasion *[no laughing matter]* **7.** importance; significance *[it's of no matter]* **8.** trouble; difficulty (with *the*) *[what's the matter?]* **9.** things sent by mail; mail *[second-class matter]* **10.** a substance discharged by the body; specif., pus **11.** *Printing a)* copy *b)* type set up —*vi.* **1.** to be of importance; have significance *[the things that matter* to me] **2.** to form and discharge pus; suppurate —**as a matter of fact** in fact; really —**for that matter** as far as that is concerned: also **for the matter of that** —**no matter 1.** it is of no importance **2.** regardless of *[no matter* what you say]

Mat·ter·horn (mat′ər hôrn′) mountain of the Pennine Alps, on the border between Switzerland & Italy

mat·ter-of-course (mat′ər əv kôrs′) *adj.* **1.** coming naturally in the course of events; routine **2.** reacting to events in a calm and natural way

matter of course a thing to be expected as a natural or logical occurrence

mat·ter-of-fact (-əv fakt′, -ə fakt′) *adj.* sticking strictly to facts; literal, unimaginative, etc. —**mat′ter-of-fact′ly** *adv.* — **mat′ter-of-fact′ness n.**

Mat·thew (math′yōō) [< OFr. < LL. < Gr. < Heb. *mattīthyāh,* lit., gift of God] **1.** a masculine name: dim. *Mat(t);* var. *Matthias* **2.** *Bible a)* one of the four Evangelists, said to be the author of the first Gospel *b)* this book

mat·ting¹ (mat′iŋ) *n.* **1.** a fabric of fiber, as straw or hemp, for mats, floor covering, wrapping, etc. **2.** mats as a group **3.** the making of mats

mat·ting² (mat′iŋ) *n.* [see MATTE] **1.** the production of a dull finish **2.** such a finish on metal, glass, etc. **3.** a mat, or border

mat·tins (mat′nz) *n.pl. Brit. var. of* MATINS (see MATIN, *n.* 1)

mat·tock (mat′ək) *n.* [OE. *mattuc*] a tool like a pickax but with at least one flat blade, for loosening the soil, digging up roots, etc.

mat·tress (mat′ris) *n.* [< OFr. < It. *materasso* < Ar. *matrah,* cushion] **1.** a casing of strong cloth filled with cotton, hair, foam rubber, etc., and usually coiled springs, and used on or as a bed **2.** a pad that can be inflated and used in the same way: in full, **air mattress**

MATTOCK

mat·u·rate (mach′oo rāt′, mat′yoo-) *vi.* **-rat′ed, -rat′ing** [< L. pp. of *maturare,* to MATURE] **1.** to suppurate; discharge pus **2.** to ripen; mature —**ma·tur·a·tive** (mə tyoor′ə tiv, mach′oo rāt′iv, mat′yoo-) *adj.* —**mat′u·ra′tion n.**

ma·ture (mə toor′, -choor′, -tyoor′) *adj.* [< L. *maturus,* ripe < IE. base *ma-,* good, in good time] **1.** *a)* full-grown, as plants or animals *b)* ripe, as fruits *c)* fully developed, as a person **2.** fully developed, perfected, etc. *[a mature* scheme] **3.** of a state of full development *[of mature* age] **4.** due: said of a note, bond, etc. —*vt.* **-tured′, -tur′ing 1.** to bring to full growth, or to ripeness **2.** to develop fully —*vi.* **1.** to become fully grown or ripe **2.** to become due: said of a note, etc. —**ma·ture′ly** *adv.* —**ma·ture′ness n.**

ma·tu·ri·ty (-ə tē) *n.* **1.** *a)* a being full-grown, ripe, or fully developed *b)* a being perfect, complete, or ready **2.** *a)* a becoming due *b)* the time at which a note, etc. becomes due

ma·tu·ti·nal (mə tōōt′'n əl, -tyōōt′-; *chiefly Brit.* mach′oo tī′n'l) *adj.* [< L. < *matutinus:* see MATIN] of or in the morning

mat·zo (mät′sə, -sô) *n., pl.* **mat′zot, mat′zoth** (-sōt), **mat′zos** [< Heb. *matstsāh,* unleavened] flat, thin unleavened bread eaten by Jews during the Passover, or a piece of this

Maud, Maude (môd) [< MATILDA] a feminine name

maud·lin (môd′lin) *adj.* [< ME. *Maudeleyne,* (Mary) Magdalene (often represented as weeping)] **1.** foolishly and tearfully or weakly sentimental **2.** tearfully sentimental from drinking too much liquor —**see SYN·** at SENTIMENTAL

Maugham (môm), **(William) Som·er·set** (sum′ər set′) 1874-1965; Eng. novelist & playwright

mau·gre, mau·ger (mô′gər) *prep.* [< OFr. *maugré,* lit., with displeasure] [Archaic] in spite of

Mau·i (mou′ē) [Haw.] island of Hawaii, southeast of Oahu

maul (môl) *n.* [< OFr. < L. *malleus,* a hammer] a very heavy hammer or mallet for driving stakes, etc. —*vt.* **1.** to injure by beating or tearing; bruise or lacerate *[the lion mauled* its victim] **2.** to handle roughly or clumsily; manhandle —**see SYN·** at BEAT —**maul′er n.**

Mau·na Lo·a (mou′nə lō′ə) [Haw., lit., long mountain] active volcano on the island of Hawaii

maun·der (môn′dər) *vi.* [prob. < obs. *maund,* to beg + -ER (sense 4)] **1.** to move or act in a confused, aimless way **2.** to talk in a confused, rambling way —**maun′der·er n.**

Maun·dy Thursday (môn′dē) [OFr. *mandé* < LL. *mandatum,* commandment of God < L.: from use in a prayer on that day] the Thursday before Easter

Mau·pas·sant (mō′pə sänt′; *Fr.* mō pà sän′) **(Henri René Albert) Guy de** (gē də) 1850–93; Fr. writer

Mau·re·ta·ni·a (môr′ə tā′nē ə, -tān′yə) ancient country & Roman province in NW Africa: see map at ROMAN EMPIRE

Mau·rice (môr′is, mär′-; mô rēs′) [Fr. < LL. *Maurus,* a Moor] a masculine name

Mau·ri·ta·ni·a (môr′ə tā′nē ə, -tān′yə) country in W Africa, on the Atlantic: 419,230 sq. mi.; pop. 1,120,000; cap. Nouakchott —**Mau′ri·ta′ni·an adj., n.**

Mau·ri·ti·us (mô rish′ē əs, -rish′əs) island country in the Indian Ocean, east of Madagascar: a member of the Commonwealth: 809 sq. mi.; pop. 810,000; cap. Port Louis

Mau·so·le·um (mô′sə lē′əm, -zə-) the tomb of Mausolus, king of an ancient land in Asia Minor —*n.* **[m-]** *pl.* **-le′ums, -le′a** (-lē′ə) a large, impressive tomb —**mau′so·le′an** (-ən) *adj.*

mauve (mōv, môv) *n.* [Fr., mallow < L. *malva,* mallow] any of several shades of pale purple —*adj.* of such a color

☆**ma·ven, ma·vin** (mā′vən) *n.* [Yid. < LHeb. *mēvin*] a person who has or claims to have special knowledge in some subject; expert

☆**mav·er·ick** (mav′ər ik, mav′rik) *n.* [after S. *Maverick,* 19th-c. Texas rancher who did not brand his cattle] **1.** an unbranded animal, esp. a strayed calf, formerly the property of the first person who branded it **2.** [Colloq.] one who acts independently of one's political party or group

ma·vis (mā′vis) *n.* [< OFr.] *same as* SONG THRUSH

ma·vour·neen, ma·vour·nin (mə voor′nēn, -vôr′-) *n.* [Ir. *mo muirnin*] my darling

maw (mô) *n.* [OE. *maga*] **1.** orig., the stomach **2.** the throat, gullet, jaws, etc. of some animals **3.** anything thought of as consuming, devouring, etc. without end

mawk·ish (mô′kish) *adj.* [lit., maggoty < ON. *mathkr,* maggot] **1.** having a sweet, weak, sickening taste **2.** sentimental in a tearful way, so as to be sickening —**see SYN·** at SENTIMENTAL —**mawk′ish·ly** *adv.* —**mawk′ish·ness n.**

max. maximum

☆**max·i-** [< MAXI(MUM)] *a combining form meaning* maximum, very large, very long *[maxicoat]*

max·il·la (mak sil′ə) *n., pl.* **-lae** (-ē) [L.] **1.** in vertebrates, the upper jaw, or a major bone or cartilage of it **2.** in insects, crabs, etc., any of the outgrowths just behind the mandibles that serve as additional jaws

max·il·lar·y (mak sil′ə rē; *chiefly Brit.* mak sil′ə rē) *adj.* designating, of, or near the jaw or jawbone

max·im (mak′sim) *n.* [< MFr. < ML. < LL. *maxima (propositio),* the greatest (premise): see MAXIMUM] a rule of conduct or a statement of a general truth expressed in a few words; precept —**see SYN·** at SAYING

max·i·ma (mak′sə mə) *n. alt. pl. of* MAXIMUM

max·i·mal (mak′sə m'l) *adj.* highest or greatest possible; of or being a maximum —**max′i·mal·ly** *adv.*

Max·i·mil·ian (mak′sə mil′yən) [? a blend of the L. names *Maximus* & *Aemilianus*] **1.** a masculine name: dim. *Max* **2.** (Ferdinand Maximilian Joseph) 1832–67; archduke of Austria; emperor of Mexico (1864–67): executed

max·i·mize (mak′sə mīz′) *vt.* **-mized′, -miz′ing** to increase to the maximum —**max′i·mi·za′tion n.** —**max′i·miz′er n.**

max·i·mum (mak′sə məm) *n., pl.* **-mums, -ma** (-mə) [L., neut. of *maximus,* superl. of *magnus,* great: see MASTER] **1.** the greatest quantity, number, etc. possible or allowed *[forty pounds of luggage is the maximum* that you can take] **2.** the highest degree or point reached or recorded *[today's maximum* was 95°F] —*adj.* **1.** greatest possible, allowed, or reached *[maximum* speed] **2.** of, marking, or setting a maximum *[maximum* level of achievement]

Max·ine (mak sēn′) [fem. of *Max:* see MAXIMILIAN] a feminine name

Max·well (maks′wel, -wəl), **James Clerk** (klärk) 1831–79; Scot. physicist

May[1] (mā) *n.* [OFr. < L. < *Maia,* goddess of increase] **1.** the fifth month of the year, having 31 days **2.** the springtime of life; youth

May[2] (mā) [contr. of MARY, MARGARET] a feminine name

may (mā) *v.aux. pt.* **might** [OE. *mæg* < IE. base *magh-,* to be able] a helping verb followed by an infinitive (without *to*) and meaning: **1.** to be possible or likely to *[it may rain]* **2.** to be allowed or have permission to *[you may go]* **3.** to be able to as a result *[they died that we may be free]* **4.** it is to be wished or hoped that *[may she rest in peace]* —see SYN. at CAN[1]

Ma·ya (mä′yə) *n.* **1.** *pl.* **Ma′yas, Ma′ya** a member of a tribe of Indians in SE Mexico and Central America, who had a highly developed civilization **2.** their language —*adj.* of the Mayas — **Ma′yan** *adj., n.*

Ma·ya·güez (mä′yä gwes′) seaport in W Puerto Rico: pop. 69,000

☆**May apple 1.** a woodland plant with shield-shaped leaves and a single large, white flower, found in the eastern U.S. **2.** its yellow, oval fruit

may·be (mā′bē) *adv.* [ME. (for *it may be*)] perhaps

May·day (mā′dā′) *n.* [< Fr. (*venez*) *m'aider,* (come) help me] the international radiotelephone signal for help, used by ships and aircraft in distress

May Day May 1: as a traditional spring festival, often celebrated by dancing, crowning a May queen, etc.; as an international labor holiday, observed in many countries by parades, demonstrations, etc.

may·est (mā′ist) *archaic second person singular in the present tense of* MAY: *used with* thou

may·flow·er (-flou′ər) *n.* a plant that flowers in early spring; esp., ☆*a*) in the U.S., the trailing arbutus, etc. *b*) in England, the cowslip, marsh marigold, etc. —[M-] the ship on which the Pilgrims came to America (1620)

may·fly (-flī′) *n., pl.* **-flies′** a slender insect with gauzy wings that it holds straight up when at rest: the adult lives only a few hours or a few days

may·hap (mā′hap′, mā′hap′) *adv.* [< *it may hap(pen)*] [Archaic] perhaps; maybe: also **may′hap′pen**

may·hem (mā′hem, mā′əm) *n.* [see MAIM]
1. *Law* the offense of maiming a person; specif., *a*) orig., injury done to another so as to cause loss of a part or function necessary for self-defense *b*) any intentional damaging or crippling of another's body **2.** loosely, any destruction or violence done on purpose

May·ing (mā′iŋ) *n.* [*also* m-] the celebration of May Day, as by gathering flowers, dancing, etc.

may·n't (mā′nt, mānt) may not

may·o (mā′ō) *n.* [Colloq.] *clipped form of* MAYONNAISE

May·o (mā′ō), **Charles Horace,** 1865–1939, & his brother **William James,** 1861–1939; U.S. surgeons

may·on·naise (mā′ə nāz′) *n.* [Fr., prob. ult. < *Mahón,* Minorca] a creamy salad dressing made by beating together egg yolks, oil, lemon juice or vinegar, and seasoning

may·or (mā′ər, mer) *n.* [< OFr. *maire* < L. *major,* greater: for IE. base see MASTER] the chief official of a city, town, or other municipality: under a city-manager plan, a mayor is only a figurehead —**may′or·al** *adj.*

may·or·al·ty (-əl tē) *n., pl.* **-ties** the office or term of a mayor

May·pole (mā′pōl′) *n.* a high pole wreathed with streamers, around which merrymakers dance on May Day

May queen a girl chosen to be queen of the merrymakers on May Day

mayst (māst) *archaic second person singular in the present tense of* MAY: *used with* thou

May·time (mā′tīm′) *n.* the month of May: also **May′tide′**

Ma·za·rin (mä zà ran′; E. maz′ər in), **Jules** (zhül), Cardinal, (born *Giulio Mazarini*) 1602–61; Fr. statesman & prelate, born in Italy

maze (māz) *n.* [< OE. *amasian,* to amaze & pp. *amasod,* puzzled] **1.** a confusing, intricate network of winding pathways; labyrinth, specif. one used in psychological experiments and tests **2.** a state of confusion or bewilderment — **ma′zy** *adj.* **-zi·er, -zi·est** — **ma′zi·ly** *adv.* —**ma′zi·ness** *n.*

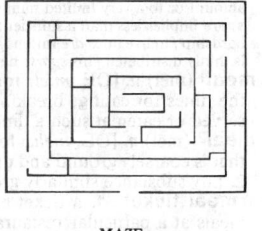

MAZE

ma·zur·ka, ma·zour·ka (mə zur′kə, -zoor′-) *n.* [Pol. *mazurka,* woman from Mazovia, region of C Poland] **1.** a lively Polish dance like the polka **2.** music for this, generally in 3/4 or 3/8 time

Maz·zi·ni (mät tsē′nē, mäd dzē′nē), **Giu·sep·pe** (jōō zep′pe) 1805–72; It. patriot & revolutionist

M.B.A. Master of Business Administration

M·ba·ba·ne ('m bä bä′nä) capital of Swaziland: pop. 14,000

Mc- *same as* MAC-

M.C. 1. Master of Ceremonies **2.** Member of Congress

☆**Mc·Car·thy·ism** (mə kär′thē iz'm) *n.* [after J. *McCarthy,* U.S. senator (1946–57)] the use of careless, often false, accusations and methods of investigating that violate civil liberties

Mc·Clel·lan (mə klel′ən), **George Brin·ton** (brin′t'n) 1826–85; Union general in the Civil War

Mc·Cor·mick (mə kôr′mik), **Cyrus Hall** (hôl) 1809–84, U.S. inventor of the reaping machine

Mc·Coy (mə koi′), **the** (**real**) [Slang] the real person or thing, not a substitute

Mc·In·tosh (mak′in täsh′) *n.* [after J. *McIntosh,* of Ontario, Can., who first cultivated it (1796)] a late-maturing variety of red apple: also **McIntosh Red**

Mc·Kin·ley (mə kin′lē), **Mount** [after President McKINLEY] mountain in SC Alas.: highest peak in N. America: 20,320 ft.: in a national park (**Mount McKinley National Park**)

Mc·Kin·ley (mə kin′lē), **William** 1843–1901; 25th president of the U.S. (1897–1901): assassinated

Md *Chem.* mendelevium

Md., MD Maryland

M.D. [L. *Medicinae Doctor*] Doctor of Medicine

Mdlle. *pl.* **Mdlles.** Mademoiselle

Mdm. *pl.* **Mdms.** Madam

Mdme. *pl.* **Mdmes.** Madame

mdse. merchandise

MDu. Middle Dutch

me (mē) *pron.* [OE.] *objective case of* I (Ex.: help *me* to win): also used colloquially after a linking verb (Ex.: it's *me*)

ME. Middle English

Me., ME Maine

M.E. 1. Master of Education **2.** Mechanical Engineer **3.** Methodist Episcopal **4.** Mining Engineer

‡**me·a cul·pa** (mē′ə kul′pə, mä′ä kool′pä) [L.] (by) my fault; I am to blame

mead[1] (mēd) *n.* [OE. *meodu*] an alcoholic drink made from fermented honey, often with spices, fruit, malt, etc. added

mead[2] (mēd) *n.* [OE. *mæd:* see MEADOW] [Poet.] a meadow

Mead (mēd), **Lake** [after E. *Mead* (1858–1936), U.S. engineer] lake in SE Nev. & NW Ariz., formed by the Hoover Dam

Mead (mēd), **Margaret** 1901–78; U.S. anthropologist

Meade (mēd), **George Gordon** 1815–72; Union general in the Civil War

mead·ow (med′ō) *n.* [< OE. *mædwe,* oblique case of *mæd* < IE. base *me-,* to mow] **1.** a piece of grassland, esp. one whose grass is grown for use as hay **2.** low, level grassland near a stream, etc. —**mead′ow·y** *adj.*

☆**mead·ow·lark** (-lärk′) *n., pl.* **-larks′, -lark′:** see PLURAL, II, D, 1 either of two N. American songbirds having brown-and-black upper parts and a yellow breast

mea·ger (mē′gər) *adj.* [< OFr. < L. *macer,* lean < IE. base *mak-,* thin] **1.** thin; lean; emaciated **2.** of poor quality or small amount; inadequate *[a meager lunch]* Also, Brit., **mea′gre** —**mea′ger·ly** *adv.* —**mea′ger·ness** *n.*

SYN. —meager implies thinness due to wasting away and suggests a lack of those qualities which make something rich, strong, etc. *[a meager edu-*

cation*]*; **scanty** implies that there is too little or not enough of something really needed *[a scanty income]*; **scant** is applied to a barely sufficient amount or to a very limited number *[the scant attendance at the concert]*; **spare** implies less than a sufficient amount but not so little as to cause great hardship *[to live on spare rations]*; **sparse** applies to a scanty quantity that is thinly distributed *[his sparse hair]* —**ANT. ample, abundant, plentiful**

meal[1] (mēl) *n.* [OE. *mæl:* for IE. base see MEASURE] **1.** any of the times for eating; breakfast, lunch, dinner, etc. **2.** the food served or eaten at such a time

meal[2] (mēl) *n.* [OE. *melu:* for IE. base see MILL[1]] **1.** any grain that is coarsely ground and unsifted and used as food *[cornmeal]* **2.** any substance similarly ground or powdered

☆**meal ticket** **1.** a ticket entitling one to a specified value in meals at a particular restaurant **2.** [Slang] a person, job, skill, etc. that one depends on as one's means of support

meal·time (mēl'tīm') *n.* the usual time for eating a meal

meal·y (mēl'ē) *adj.* **meal'i·er, meal'i·est** **1.** like meal; powdery, dry, etc. **2.** of or containing meal **3.** covered with meal **4.** floury in color; pale **5.** mealy-mouthed —**meal'i·ness** *n.*

meal·y-mouthed (-mouthd', -moutht') *adj.* not willing to speak frankly or plainly; insincere

mean[1] (mēn) *vt.* **meant** (ment), **mean'ing** [OE. *mænan* < IE. base *maino-*, opinion] **1.** to have in mind; intend; purpose *[he means to go]* **2.** to intend for a certain person or purpose *[a gift meant for you]* **3.** to intend to express or imply *[to say what one means]* **4.** to be a sign of; signify; denote *[the German word "ja" means "yes"]* —*vi.* **1.** to have a purpose in mind: chiefly in **mean well**, to have good intentions **2.** to have a (specified) degree of importance, effect, etc. *[she means little to him]* —see SYN. at INTEND —**mean well by** to have good intentions toward

mean[2] (mēn) *adj.* [OE. *(ge)mæne:* for IE. base see MIGRATE] **1.** low in quality, value, or importance; poor *[paid no mean sum]* **2.** poor in appearance; shabby *[a mean dwelling]* **3.** not honorable; base; petty **4.** stingy; miserly *[a miser is mean with his money]* ☆**5.** bad-tempered; unmanageable: said of a horse, etc. ☆**6.** bad-tempered, unkind, selfish, etc. in a shameful way ☆**7.** humiliated ☆**8.** [Colloq.] in poor health ☆**9.** [Slang] *a)* hard to cope with; difficult *[to throw a mean curve in baseball]* *b)* skillful; expert *[to play a mean game of chess]* —see SYN. at BASE[2] —**mean'ly** *adv.* —**mean'ness** *n.*

mean[3] (mēn) *adj.* [< OFr. < L. *medianus* < *medius*, middle: see MID[1]] **1.** halfway between extremes; intermediate as to quantity, quality, etc. *[the mean temperature was 70, between a high of 85 and a low of 55]* **2.** average; middling —*n.* **1.** what is between extremes; intermediate state, quality, course, etc. *[their house is a happy mean between a cottage and a mansion]* **2.** moderation **3.** *Math. a)* a number between the smallest and largest values of a set of quantities, obtained by some prescribed method: unless otherwise qualified, *same as* ARITHMETIC MEAN *b)* the second or third term of a four-term proportion See also MEANS

me·an·der (mē an'dər) *n.* [< L. < Gr. *maiandros* < the name of a winding river in Asia Minor] **1.** [*pl.*] windings or twistings, as of a stream **2.** an aimless wandering —*vi.* **1.** to take a winding course: said of a stream **2.** to wander aimlessly or idly —see SYN. at ROAM —**me·an'drous** (-drəs) *adj.*

mean·ie, mean·y (mē'nē) *n., pl.* **mean'ies** [Colloq.] a person who is mean, selfish, cruel, etc.

mean·ing (mē'niŋ) *n.* **1.** what is meant; what is intended to be understood, signified, indicated, etc.; import, sense, or significance *[the meaning of a word]* **2.** [Archaic] intention —*adj.* **1.** that has meaning; significant **2.** intending

SYN.—meaning is the general word for what is intended to be expressed or understood by something *[the meaning of a sentence]*; **sense** refers especially to any of the various meanings of a word or phrase *[this word has several slang senses]*; **import** refers to all of what is being implied by something said or done, including any subtle or hidden meanings *[the full import of his remark came to me later]*; **purport** refers to the general meaning, or main point, of something *[what was the purport of her letter?]*; **signification** is applied especially to the meaning that a certain sign, symbol, character, etc. commonly suggests to people *[the signification of the ace of spades in fortunetelling]*

mean·ing·ful (-fəl) *adj.* full of meaning; having significance or purpose —**mean'ing·ful·ly** *adv.* —**mean'ing·ful·ness** *n.*

mean·ing·less (-lis) *adj.* having no meaning; without significance or purpose —**mean'ing·less·ly** *adv.* —**mean'ing·less·ness** *n.*

means (mēnz) *n.pl.* [< MEAN[3], *n.*] **1.** [*with sing. or pl. v.*] that by which something is done or obtained; agency *[a fast means of travel]* **2.** resources or wealth *[a person of means]* —**by all means** **1.** without fail **2.** certainly —**by any means** in any

way possible; somehow —**by means of** by using; with the aid of —**by no (manner of) means** not at all; certainly not —**means to an end** a method of getting what one wants

mean (solar) time time having exactly equal divisions

means test an investigation of a person's means of support to see if he qualifies for welfare aid, public housing, etc.

meant (ment) *pt. & pp.* of MEAN[1]

mean·time (mēn'tīm') *adv.* **1.** in or during the time between **2.** at the same time —*n.* the time between Also, and for adv. now usually, **mean'while'** (-hwīl')

mea·sles (mē'z'lz) *n.pl.* [*with sing. v.*] [ME. *maseles,* ? influenced by ME. *mesel,* leper < OFr. < L. *misellus,* wretch] **1.** an acute, contagious virus disease, causing small red spots on the skin, high fever, etc., usually in childhood **2.** any of various similar but milder diseases; esp., rubella (called *German measles*)

mea·sly (mēz'lē) *adj.* **-sli·er, -sli·est** **1.** infected with measles **2.** [Colloq.] shamefully slight, worthless, or skimpy

meas·ur·a·ble (mezh'ər ə b'l) *adj.* that can be measured —**meas'ur·a·bil'i·ty, meas'ur·a·ble·ness** *n.* —**meas'ur·a·bly** *adv.*

meas·ure (mezh'ər, mā'zhər) *n.* [< OFr. *mesure* < L. *mensura* < pp. of *metiri,* to measure < IE. base *me-*] **1.** the extent, dimensions, capacity, etc. of anything, esp. as determined by a standard *[the measure of the bucket is four gallons]* **2.** a determining of extent, dimensions, etc.; measurement **3.** *a)* unit of measurement, as an inch, yard, or bushel *b)* any standard of valuation, comparison, judgment, etc.; criterion *[are grades a true measure of learning?]* **4.** a system of measurement *[dry measure]* **5.** an instrument or container for measuring *[a quart measure]* **6.** a definite quantity measured out *[ten buckets filled with different measures of sand]* **7.** an extent or degree not to be exceeded *[keep the cost within measure]* **8.** proportion, quantity, or degree *[in large measure]* **9.** course of action; step *[reform measures]* **10.** a statute; law *[Congress passed a measure for flood control]* **11.** *a)* rhythm in verse; meter *b)* a metrical unit; foot of verse **12.** a dance or dance movement **13.** [*pl.*] *Geol.* strata: now chiefly in **coal measures** **14.** *Music a)* the notes or rests, or both, contained between two bars on the staff *b)* musical time or rhythm —*vt.* **-ured, -ur·ing** **1.** to find out or estimate the extent, dimensions, etc. of, esp. by a standard *[measure his height]* **2.** to set apart or mark off by measuring (often with *off* or *out*) *[measure out three pounds of sugar]* **3.** to make a judgment of by comparing *[to measure one's foe]* **4.** to bring into comparison or rivalry (*against*) *[measure her score against the class average]* **5.** to be a device for measuring *[a clock measures time]* —*vi.* **1.** to get or take measurements **2.** to be of specified measurements *[the table measures five feet on each side]* **3.** to allow of measurement —**beyond (or above) measure** exceedingly; extremely —**for good measure** as a bonus or something extra —**in a measure** to some extent; somewhat —**made to measure** custom-made: said of clothes —☆**measure up** to prove to be qualified —☆**measure up to** to meet (expectations, a standard, etc.) —**take measures** to do things to accomplish a purpose —**take someone's measure** to estimate or judge someone's ability, character, etc. —**meas'ur·er** *n.*

MEASURES

meas·ured (-ərd, -zhərd) *adj.* **1.** set or marked off according to a standard *[a measured mile]* **2.** regular or uniform *[measured steps]* **3.** *a)* rhythmical *b)* metrical **4.** planned with care *[measured words]* —**meas'ured·ly** *adv.*

meas·ure·less (mezh'ər lis, mā'zhər-) *adj.* too large to be measurable; vast; immense —**meas'ure·less·ly** *adv.*

meas·ure·ment (-mənt) *n.* **1.** a measuring or being measured **2.** extent or quantity determined by measuring *[a waist measurement of 32 inches]* **3.** a system of measuring *[liquid measurement]*

☆**measuring worm** the caterpillar larva of any geometrid moth

meat (mēt) *n.* [OE. *mete* < IE. base *mad-*, to be moist] **1.** food: now dialectal except in **meat and drink** **2.** the flesh of animals used as food; esp., the flesh of mammals and, sometimes, of fowl **3.** the inner part that can be eaten *[the meat of a nut]* **4.** the main part or meaning *[the meat of a story]* **5.** [Archaic] a meal —

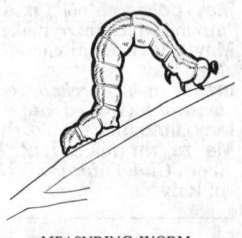

MEASURING WORM
(to 2 in. long)

☆**one's meat** [Slang] something that one especially enjoys or is skillful at [golf's my *meat*] —**meat′less** *adj.*

meat·ball (mēt′bôl′) *n.* a small ball of ground meat, seasoned and cooked, often with sauce, etc.

☆**meat·pack·ing** (-pak′iŋ) *n.* the process or industry of slaughtering animals and preparing their meat for market —**meat′-pack′er** *n.*

me·a·tus (mē āt′əs) *n., pl.* -**tus·es**, -**tus** [LL. < L., a passage, pp. of *meare*, to pass] a natural passage or duct in the body, or its opening

meat·y (mēt′ē) *adj.* **meat′i·er**, **meat′i·est** **1.** of, like, or having the flavor of, meat **2.** full of meat ☆**3.** full of substance; thought-provoking, pithy [a *meaty* speech] —**meat′i·ness** *n.*

Mec·ca (mek′ə) religious capital of Saudi Arabia: birthplace of Mohammed & hence a holy city of Islam, to which Moslems make pilgrimages: pop. c.250,000 —*n.* (**often m-**] any place that many people feel drawn to [a tourist *mecca*] —**Mec′can** *adj., n.*

mech. **1.** mechanical **2.** mechanics

me·chan·ic (mə kan′ik) *adj.* [< L. < Gr. < *mēchanē*, a MACHINE] *rare or archaic var. of* MECHANICAL —*n.* a worker skilled in using tools or in making, operating, and repairing machines

me·chan·i·cal (-i k'l) *adj.* **1.** having to do with machinery or tools, or having skill in their use **2.** produced or operated by machinery [a *mechanical* toy] **3.** of, or in accordance with, the science of mechanics **4.** automatic, as if from force of habit; machinelike [her acting is *mechanical*] —**me·chan′i·cal·ly** *adv.*

mechanical drawing drawing done, as by a draftsman, with T squares, scales, compasses, etc.

mech·a·ni·cian (mek′ə nish′ən) *n.* a person skilled in the design, operation, care, etc. of machinery

me·chan·ics (mə kan′iks) *n.pl.* [*with sing. v.*] **1.** the branch of physics that deals with the motion of material bodies and the action of forces on bodies: see STATICS, DYNAMICS, KINEMATICS **2.** knowledge of machinery **3.** the mechanical aspect; technical part [the *mechanics* of writing]

mech·a·nism (mek′ə niz'm) *n.* [< ModL. < Gr. *mēchanē*, a MACHINE] **1.** the working parts of a machine; works [the *mechanism* of a clock] **2.** *a)* a system whose parts work together as in a machine [the *mechanism* of the universe] *b)* any physical or mental process by which some result is produced **3.** the mechanical aspect; technical part **4.** the theory that all phenomena, particularly life, can ultimately be explained in terms of physics and chemistry

mech·a·nist (-nist) *n.* a person who believes in the theory of mechanism

mech·a·nis·tic (mek′ə nis′tik) *adj.* **1.** of or in accordance with the theory of mechanism **2.** of mechanics or mechanical concepts —**mech′a·nis′ti·cal·ly** *adv.*

mech·a·nize (mek′ə nīz′) *vt.* -**nized′**, -**niz′ing** **1.** to make mechanical **2.** to do or operate by machinery, not by hand [to *mechanize* the picking of cotton] **3.** to bring about the use of machinery in (an industry, etc.) **4.** to equip (an army, etc.) with motor vehicles, tanks, etc. —**mech′a·ni·za′tion** *n.* —**mech′a·niz′er** *n.*

mech·an·o·ther·a·py (mek′ə nō ther′ə pē) *n.* [< Gr. *mēchanē*, a machine + THERAPY] the treatment of disease by mechanical means, especially mechanical devices

med. **1.** medical **2.** medicine **3.** medieval **4.** medium

M.Ed. Master of Education

med·al (med′'l) *n.* [< Fr. < It. *medaglia*, ult. < LL. *medialis*, MEDIAL] **1.** a small, flat piece of metal with a design or inscription on it, made to commemorate some event, or awarded for some distinguished action, merit, etc. **2.** a disk bearing a religious symbol, blessed as by a priest and worn as a religious token

med·al·ist (-'l ist, -list) *n.* **1.** a person who designs or makes medals **2.** a person who has been awarded a medal **3.** *Golf* the low scorer in a qualifying round of medal play coming before a tournament Also, Brit. sp., **med′al·list**

me·dal·lion (mə dal′yən) *n.* [< Fr. < It.: see MEDAL] **1.** a large medal **2.** any of various designs, carvings, etc. like a medal in shape, used decoratively, as in architecture

☆**Medal of Honor** the highest U.S. military decoration, awarded by Congress for gallantry at the risk of life above and beyond the call of duty

medal play *Golf* a form of play in which the score is calculated by counting the total number of strokes taken to play the designated number of holes: see also MATCH PLAY

med·dle (med′'l) *vi.* -**dled**, -**dling** [< OFr. *medler* < VL. < L. *miscere*, to mix] **1.** to concern oneself with other people's affairs without being asked or needed; interfere (*in* or *with*) **2.** to tamper (*with*) —**med′dler** *n.*

med·dle·some (-səm) *adj.* meddling or inclined to meddle —**med′dle·some·ness** *n.*

Mede (mēd) *n.* a native or inhabitant of Media

Me·de·a (mi dē′ə) *Gr. Myth.* a sorceress who helped Jason get the Golden Fleece

Me·del·lín (me′de yēn′) city in northwestern Colombia: pop. 1,089,000

Med·ford (med′fərd) [? for the meadlike marshes once there] city in E Mass.: suburb of Boston: pop. 64,000

Me·di·a (mē′dē ə) ancient kingdom in the part of SW Asia that is now NW Iran: cap. Ecbatana See map at ELAM —**Me′di·an** *adj., n.*

me·di·a (mē′dē ə) *n. alt. pl.* of MEDIUM: see MEDIUM (*n.* 3)

me·di·ae·val (mē′dē ē′v'l, med′ē-, mid′ē-) *adj. same as* MEDIEVAL —**me′di·ae′val·ism** *n.*

me·di·al (mē′dē əl) *adj.* [< LL. < L. *medius*, middle: see MID[1]] **1.** of or in the middle; median **2.** average; mean —**me′di·al·ly** *adv.*

me·di·an (mē′dē ən) *adj.* [< L. < *medius*, middle: see MID[1]] **1.** middle; intermediate **2.** *a)* designating a line from a vertex of a triangle to the middle of the opposite side *b)* designating a line joining the midpoints of the nonparallel sides of a trapezoid **3.** lying in a plane that divides a body or part into symmetrical halves **4.** *Statistics* designating the middle number in a series arranged in order of size (as, 7 in the series 1, 4, 7, 16, 43) or, if there is no middle value, the average of the two middle numbers (as, 10 in the series 3, 4, 8, 12, 46, 72) —*n.* **1.** a median number, point, or line ☆**2.** a strip of land separating opposing traffic on a divided highway: in full, **median strip** —**me′di·an·ly** *adv.*

me·di·ate (mē′dē āt′; *for adj.* -it) *vi.* -**at′ed**, -**at′ing** [< LL. pp. of *mediare*, to divide in the middle < L. *medius*, middle: see MID[1]] **1.** to be in an intermediate position **2.** to act as a judge or go-between in trying to settle a dispute between persons or sides —*vt.* **1.** to settle (a dispute) or bring about (a settlement) by mediating **2.** to be the medium for bringing about or passing along (something specified) —*adj.* dependent on, acting by, or connected through some agency in between —**me′di·ate·ly** *adv.* —**me′di·a·tor** *n.*

me·di·a·tion (mē′dē ā′shən) *n.* a mediating; work done as a go-between in settling differences between persons, nations, etc. —**me′di·a′tive** *adj.* —**me′di·a·to·ry** (-ə tôr′ē) *adj.*

med·ic[1] (med′ik) *n.* [Colloq.] **1.** a physician or surgeon ☆**2.** a medical student or intern **3.** a member of a military medical corps, esp. one who gives first aid in combat

med·ic[2] (med′ik) *n.* [< L. < Gr. *mēdikē (poa)*, (grass) of Media] any of various leguminous plants, as alfalfa: also sp. **med′ick**

med·i·ca·ble (med′i kə b'l) *adj.* that can be cured, healed, or relieved by medical treatment

☆**Med·i·caid** (med′i kād′) *n.* [MEDIC(AL) + AID] [*also* **m-**] a State and Federal public health plan for persons with low income or no income

med·i·cal (med′i k'l) *adj.* [< Fr. < LL. < L. *medicus*, physician < IE. base *med-*, to measure, consider] of or connected with the practice or study of medicine —**med′i·cal·ly** *adv.*

medical jurisprudence the application of medical knowledge to questions of law, as in determining cause of death, proper medical practice, etc.

med·i·ca·ment (med′i kə mənt, mə dik′ə-) *n. same as* MEDICATION (sense 2)

Med·i·care (med′i ker′) *n.* [MEDI(CAL) + CARE] [*also* **m-**] a national health program for providing medical and hospital care for the aged from Federal, mostly social security, funds

med·i·cate (med′ə kāt′) *vt.* -**cat′ed**, -**cat′ing** [< L. pp. of *medicari*, to heal] **1.** to treat with medicine [it is often dangerous to *medicate* oneself without a doctor's advice] **2.** to add a medicinal substance to [these cough drops are *medicated*] —**med′i·ca′tive** *adj.*

med·i·ca·tion (med′ə kā′shən) *n.* **1.** a medicating or being medicated **2.** a medicine; substance for curing or healing, or for relieving pain

Med·i·ci (med′ə chē′; *It.* me′dē chē′) family of rich, powerful bankers, merchants, & rulers of Florence & Tuscany in the 14th to 16th cent., also known as patrons of the arts; specif., *a)* **Catherine de′**, 1519–89; queen of Henry II of France (1547–59) *b)* **Cos·i·mo de′** (kô′zē mô de), 1389–1464; head of the Florentine Republic *c)* **Lo·ren·zo de′** (lô ren′tsô de), 1449–92; ruler of Florence (1469–92) *d)* **Maria de′**, 1573–1642; queen of Henry IV of France (1600–10); queen regent (1610–17) — **Med′i·ce′an** (-sē′ən, -chē′ən) *adj.*

me·dic·i·nal (mə dis′′n ′l) *adj.* of, or having the properties of, medicine; curing, healing, or relieving —**me·dic′i·nal·ly** *adv.*

med·i·cine (med′ə s′n; *Brit.* med′sin) *n.* [< OFr. < L. < *medicus:* see MEDICAL] **1.** the science and art of diagnosing, treating, and preventing disease **2.** the branch of this science that makes use of drugs, diet, etc., as distinguished esp. from surgery **3.** any substance, as a drug, used in treating disease, healing, relieving pain, etc. ☆**4.** among North American Indians, *a)* any object, rite, etc. supposed to have supernatural powers to cure illness, ward off evil, etc. *b)* magical power —*vt.* **-cined, -cin·ing** to give medicine to —☆**take one's medicine** to endure just punishment or accept the results of one's action

☆**medicine ball** a large, heavy, leather-covered ball, tossed from one person to another for exercise

☆**medicine man** among North American Indians, etc., a man supposed to have supernatural powers of curing disease and controlling spirits; shaman

☆**medicine show** formerly, a show given by entertainers who traveled from town to town, in order to sell cure-alls, etc.

med·i·co (med′i kō′) *n., pl.* **-cos′** [It.] [Colloq.] **1.** a doctor **2.** a medical student

me·di·e·val (mē′dē ē′v′l, med′ē-, mid′ē-) *adj.* [< L. *medius* (see MID[1]) + *aevum*, AGE] of, like, characteristic of, or suggestive of the Middle Ages —**me′di·e′val·ly** *adv.*

MEDICINE BALL

Medieval Greek the Greek language as it was used in the Middle Ages, from c.600–c.1500 A.D.

me·di·e·val·ism (-iz′m) *n.* **1.** medieval spirit, beliefs, customs, etc. **2.** devotion to these **3.** a belief, custom, etc. of the Middle Ages

me·di·e·val·ist (-ist) *n.* **1.** a specialist in medieval history, literature, art, etc. **2.** a person devoted to medieval customs, beliefs, etc.

Medieval Latin the Latin language used in Europe in the Middle Ages, from c.600–c.1500 A.D.

Me·di·na (mə dē′nə) city in NW Saudi Arabia: site of Mohammed's tomb: pop. c.60,000

me·di·o·cre (mē′dē ō′kər, mē′dē ō′kər) *adj.* [< Fr. < L. *mediocris* < *medius*, middle + *ocris*, a peak] **1.** neither very good nor very bad; ordinary; average **2.** not good enough; inferior

me·di·oc·ri·ty (mē′dē äk′rə tē) *n., pl.* **-ties 1.** a being mediocre **2.** mediocre ability or accomplishment **3.** a person of mediocre abilities, etc.

Medit. Mediterranean

med·i·tate (med′ə tāt′) *vt.* **-tat′ed, -tat′ing** [< L. pp. of *meditari:* for IE. base see MEDICAL] **1.** [Rare] to study; ponder **2.** to plan or intend [to *meditate* making a change] —*vi.* to spend some time in meditation; reflect —see SYN. at PONDER — **med′i·ta′tor** *n.*

med·i·ta·tion (med′ə tā′shən) *n.* **1.** act of meditating; deep reflection or quiet thought, esp. of a mystical or religious nature **2.** [*often pl.*] oral or written material, as a sermon, based on meditation

med·i·ta·tive (med′ə tāt′iv) *adj.* **1.** meditating or liking to meditate **2.** showing meditation —see SYN. at PENSIVE —**med′i·ta′tive·ly** *adv.*

Med·i·ter·ra·ne·an (med′i tə rā′nē ən) *adj.* [< L. < *medius*, middle + *terra*, land] of the Mediterranean Sea or nearby regions —*n.* a person who lives near the Mediterranean Sea

Mediterranean Sea large sea surrounded by Europe, Africa, & Asia: c.2,300 mi. long

me·di·um (mē′dē əm) *n., pl.* **-di·ums**; also (except sense 7), and for sense 3 usually, **-di·a** (-ə) [L., neut. of *medius*, middle: see MID[1]] **1.** *a)* something in the middle *b)* a middle state or degree; mean [a temperature of 70° is a happy *medium*] **2.** a thing through which a force acts or an effect is made [copper is a good *medium* for conducting heat] **3.** any means, agency, etc.; specif., a means of communication, as television, that reaches the general public and carries advertising: in this sense, a singular form **media** (*pl.* **medias**) is now sometimes heard **4.** any surrounding substance in which bodies exist **5.** environment **6.** a nourishing substance, as agar, for cultivating bacteria, etc. ☆**7.** a person through whom messages are supposedly sent from the spirits of the dead **8.** any material or technique as used in art **9.** a liquid mixed with pigments to give smoothness —*adj.* **1.** intermediate in quality, amount, degree, size, etc. [a *medium* price] **2.** neither rare nor well-done: said of cooked meat

medium frequency any radio frequency between 300 kilohertz and 3 megahertz

medium of exchange anything used as a measure of value in exchange for goods or services; money, etc.

me·di·um-sized (-sīzd′) *adj.* of a medium size; neither large nor small

med·lar (med′lər) *n.* [< OFr. < L. < Gr. *mespilon*] **1.** a small tree of the rose family, growing in Europe and Asia **2.** its small, brown, applelike fruit, eaten when partly decayed

med·ley (med′lē) *n., pl.* **-leys** [< OFr. < pp. of *medler:* see MEDDLE] **1.** a mixture of things not usually placed together **2.** a musical piece made up of tunes or passages from various works

me·dul·la (mi dul′ə) *n., pl.* **-dul′las, -dul′lae** (-ē) [L., the marrow] **1.** *Anat. a)* same as MEDULLA OBLONGATA *b)* the inner substance of an organ, as of the kidney *c)* bone marrow **2.** *Bot.* same as PITH (*n.* 1) —**med·ul·lar·y** (med′ə ler′ē, mej′-; mi dul′ər ē) *adj.*

medulla ob·lon·ga·ta (äb′lôŋ gät′ə, -gät′-) [ModL., oblong medulla] the widening continuation of the spinal cord forming the lowest part of the brain: it controls breathing, circulation, etc.: see illustration at BRAIN

medullary ray *Bot.* a thin strand of cells extending from the pith to the bark in stems and serving to carry liquids

medullary sheath 1. *Anat.* a layer of myelin around some nerve fibers **2.** *Bot.* a layer of cells around the pith of some stems

Me·du·sa (mə doo′sə, -dyoo′-; -zə) *Gr. Myth.* one of the three Gorgons, slain by Perseus —**m-** [*pl.*] **-sas, -sae** (-sē, -zē) *Zool.* same as JELLYFISH —**me·du′san, me·du′soid** *adj., n.*

meed (mēd) *n.* [OE. *med*] [Archaic] a deserved compensation or reward

meek (mēk) *adj.* [< ON. *miukr*, gentle; for IE. base see MUCK] **1.** patient and mild; not showing anger or resentment **2.** very humble or too humble in one's feelings, actions, etc.; not showing spirit —see SYN. at HUMBLE —**meek′ly** *adv.* —**meek′ness** *n.*

meer·schaum (mir′shəm, -shôm) *n.* [G. < *meer*, sea + *schaum*, foam] **1.** a soft, white, claylike mineral used for tobacco pipes, etc. because heat-resistant **2.** a pipe made of this

meet[1] (mēt) *vt.* **met, meet′ing** [OE. *metan:* for IE. base see MOOT] **1.** to come upon; esp., to come face to face with [we *met* two friends walking down the street] **2.** to be present at the arrival of [to *meet* a bus] **3.** to come into contact, connection, etc. with [the ball *met* the bat] **4.** *a)* to come into the presence of *b)* to be introduced to; get acquainted with [I *met* her at your party] *c)* to keep an appointment with [I'll *meet* you at noon] **5.** *a)* to contend with *b)* to face [to *meet* angry words with a laugh] *c)* to deal with effectively [to *meet* an objection] **6.** to experience [to *meet* disaster] **7.** to come within the notice of (the eye, ear, etc.) **8.** *a)* to comply with; satisfy (requirements, a demand, etc.) *b)* to pay (a bill, etc.) —*vi.* **1.** to come together, as from different directions [go to where the two roads *meet*] **2.** to come into contact, connection, etc. [the cars *met* with a crash] **3.** to become acquainted; be introduced [have you two *met?*] **4.** to be opposed in or as in battle; fight **5.** to be united **6.** to assemble [the school board *meets* today] **7.** to come together for discussion, etc. (with) [I have *met* with their representative] —*n.* **1.** a meeting, gathering, etc. [a track *meet*] **2.** the people who meet or the place of meeting —**meet with 1.** to experience [to *meet* with an accident] **2.** to receive **3.** to encounter; come upon

meet[2] (mēt) *adj.* [< OE. (ge)*mæte*, fitting] [Now Rare] suitable; proper; fit —**meet′ly** *adv.*

meet·ing (mēt′iŋ) *n.* **1.** a coming together of persons or things **2.** an assembly; gathering of people **3.** an assembly or place of assembly for worship **4.** a series of horse or dog races **5.** a point of contact; junction

meet·ing·house (-hous′) *n.* a building used for public meetings, esp. for public worship

meg·a- [Gr. < *megas*, great: see MASTER] *a combining form meaning:* **1.** large, great, powerful [*megaphone*] **2.** a million; the factor 10^6 [*megaton*] Also, before a vowel, **meg-**

☆**meg·a·death** (meg′ə deth′) *n.* [see MEGA-] one million dead persons, as from a hypothetical nuclear explosion

meg·a·hertz (-hurts′) *n.*, *pl.* **-hertz** [see MEGA-] one million hertz: formerly **meg′a·cy·cle** (-sī′k'l)

meg·a·lith (-lith′) *n.* [MEGA- + -LITH] a huge stone, esp. one used in prehistoric monuments or in the construction work of ancient peoples —**meg′a·lith′ic** *adj.*

meg·a·lo- [ModL. < Gr. < *megas*: see MEGA-] *a combining form meaning:* **1.** large, great, powerful [*megalomania*] **2.** abnormal enlargement

meg·a·lo·ma·ni·a (meg′ə lō mā′nē ə, -mān′yə) *n.* [ModL.: see prec. & MANIA] **1.** a mental disorder characterized by delusions of grandeur, wealth, power, etc. **2.** a strong urge to have great power, importance, etc. —**meg′a·lo·ma′ni·ac′** (-ak′) *adj.*, *n.* —**meg′a·lo·ma·ni′a·cal** (-mə nī′ə k'l) *adj.* —**meg′a·lo·man′ic** (-man′ik) *adj.*

meg·a·lop·o·lis (meg′ə läp′ə ləs) *n.* [Gr., great city] a vast, heavily populated urban area, including many cities —**meg′a·lo·pol′i·tan** (-lə päl′ə t'n) *adj.*, *n.*

☆**meg·a·phone** (meg′ə fōn′) *n.* [see MEGA-] a large, funnel-shaped device for increasing the volume of the voice and directing it —*vt.*, *vi.* **-phoned′**, **-phon′ing** to magnify or direct (the voice) with a megaphone —**meg′a·phon′ic** (-fän′ik) *adj.*

meg·a·spore (meg′ə spôr′) *n.* [MEGA- + -SPORE] a haploid spore usually larger than a microspore of the same plant, which gives rise to a female gametophyte —**meg′a·spor′ic** *adj.*

MEGAPHONE

meg·a·ton (-tun′) *n.* [see MEGA-] the explosive force of a million tons of TNT: a unit for measuring the power of thermonuclear weapons —**meg′a·ton′nage** *n.*

Me·gid·do (mə gid′ō) ancient town in N Palestine, dating from c. 3500 B.C.: thought to be the Biblical Armageddon

me·grim (mē′grəm) *n.* [< OFr.: see MIGRAINE] **1.** [Archaic] a whim; fancy **2.** [*pl.*] [Rare] low spirits

mei·o·sis (mī ō′sis) *n.* [ModL. < Gr. < *meioun*, to make smaller] the process in the forming of germ cells in which the nucleus divides and reduces the number of chromosomes to one half the number present in the somatic cells of an animal or plant —**mei·ot′ic** (-ät′ik) *adj.*

Meis·ter·sing·er (mīs′tər siŋ′ər, -ziŋ′ər) *n.*, *pl.* **-sing′er** [G., lit., master singer] a member of one of the German guilds organized in the 14th-16th cent. for cultivating music and poetry

Mé·ji·co (mā′hē kô′) *Sp. name of* MEXICO

Mek·nès (mek′nes) city in NC Morocco: pop. 205,000

Me·kong (mā′käŋ′, -kôŋ′) river flowing from SW China through Indochina into the South China Sea

mel·a·mine (mel′ə mēn′) *n.* [G. *melamin*] a white, crystalline compound, $C_3H_6N_6$, used in making synthetic resins and plastics for dishes, utensils, etc.

mel·an·cho·li·a (mel′ən kō′lē ə, -kōl′yə) *n.* [ModL. < LL.: see MELANCHOLY] a mental disorder characterized by extreme depression, brooding, etc. —**mel′an·cho′li·ac′** (-kō′lē ak′) *adj.*, *n.*

mel·an·chol·y (mel′ən käl′ē) *n.*, *pl.* **-chol′ies** [< OFr. < LL. < Gr. *melancholia* < *melas*, black + *cholē*, bile: orig., referring to black bile as the humor causing this] **1.** *a)* sadness and depression of spirits *b)* a tendency to be sad or depressed **2.** sad thoughtfulness; pensiveness —*adj.* **1.** sad and depressed; gloomy **2.** causing sadness or depression [a *melancholy* rain] **3.** sadly or soberly thoughtful; pensive —see SYN. at SAD —**mel′an·chol′ic** *adj.* —**mel′an·chol′i·cal·ly** *adv.*

Me·lanch·thon (mə laŋk′thən), **Phi·lipp** 1497-1560; Ger. Protestant reformer

Mel·a·ne·sia (mel′ə nē′zhə, -shə) a major division of the Pacific islands, south of the equator, west of the international date line, & east of Australia & New Guinea

Mel·a·ne·sian (-zhən, -shən) *adj.* of Melanesia, its people, or their languages —*n.* **1.** a member of the dark-skinned native people of Melanesia **2.** the branch of Malayo-Polynesian languages of Melanesia

mé·lange (mā länzh′, -länj′) *n.* [Fr. < *mêler*, to mix] a mixture or medley; hodgepodge

mel·a·nin (mel′ə nin) *n.* [MELAN(O)- + -IN¹] a brownish-black pigment found in skin, hair, etc.

mel·a·nism (-niz′m) *n.* [MELAN(O)- + -ISM] abnormal development of dark coloring in the skin, hair, etc. —**mel′a·nis′-tic** *adj.*

mel·a·no- [< Gr. *melanos*, genitive of *melas*, black] *a combining form meaning* black, very dark: also, before a vowel, **melan-**

mel·a·no·ma (mel′ə nō′mə) *n.*, *pl.* **-mas**, **-ma·ta** (-mə tə) [ModL.: see MELANO- & -OMA] a tumor whose cells contain melanin: usually malignant

Mel·ba toast (mel′bə) [after Nellie *Melba* (1861-1931), Australian soprano] very thin, dry toast

Mel·bourne (mel′bərn) seaport in SE Australia: pop. 2,110,000

☆**meld** (meld) *vt.*, *vi.* [G. *melden*, to announce] *Card Games* to declare (a combination of cards in one's hand) for a score, esp. by putting (them) face up on the table —*n.* **1.** a melding **2.** the cards melded

me·lee, mê·lée (mā′lā, mā lā′) *n.* [Fr. *mêlée* < OFr.: see MEDLEY] a noisy, confused, hand-to-hand fight among a number of people

mel·io·rate (mēl′yə rāt′) *vt.*, *vi.* **-rat′ed**, **-rat′ing** [< LL. pp. of *meliorare* < L. *melior*, better] to make or become better; improve —**mel′io·ra·ble** (-yər ə b'l) *adj.* —**mel′io·ra′tion** *n.* —**mel′io·ra′tive** *adj.* —**mel′io·ra′tor** *n.*

mel·lif·lu·ous (mə lif′loo wəs) *adj.* [< L. < *mel*, honey + *fluere*, to flow] sounding sweet and smooth; honeyed [*mellifluous* tones]: also **mel·lif′lu·ent** (-wənt) —**mel·lif′lu·ous·ly** *adv.* —**mel·lif′lu·ous·ness** *n.*

mel·low (mel′ō) *adj.* [prob. < OE. *melu*, MEAL²] **1.** soft, sweet, and juicy because ripe: said of fruit **2.** full-flavored; matured: said of wine, etc. **3.** full, rich, soft, and pure: said of sound, light, etc. **4.** moist and rich: said of soil **5.** made soft, gentle, and understanding by experience [a *mellow* old man] —*vt.*, *vi.* to make or become mellow —**mel′low·ly** *adv.* —**mel′low·ness** *n.*

☆**me·lo·de·on** (mə lō′dē ən) *n.* [G. *melodion* < *melodie*, melody] a small keyboard organ in which air is drawn through metal reeds by means of a bellows

me·lod·ic (mə läd′ik) *adj.* **1.** of or like melody **2.** *same as* MELODIOUS —**me·lod′i·cal·ly** *adv.*

me·lo·di·ous (mə lō′dē əs) *adj.* **1.** containing or producing melody **2.** pleasing to hear; tuneful —**me·lo′di·ous·ly** *adv.* —**me·lo′di·ous·ness** *n.*

mel·o·dist (mel′ə dist) *n.* a singer or composer of melodies

mel·o·dra·ma (mel′ə drä′mə, -dram′ə) *n.* [< Fr., ult. < Gr. *melos*, a song + *drama*, drama] **1.** a play in which there is much suspense and strong feeling, and a great exaggeration of good and evil in the characters and situations **2.** any sensational, highly emotional action or talk —**mel′o·dram′a·tist** (-dram′ə tist) *n.*

mel·o·dra·mat·ic (mel′ə drə mat′ik) *adj.* of or like melodrama; sensational, violent, and extravagantly emotional —**mel′o·dra·mat′i·cal·ly** *adv.*

mel·o·dra·mat·ics (-iks) *n.pl.* melodramatic behavior

mel·o·dy (mel′ə dē) *n.*, *pl.* **-dies** [< OFr. < LL. < Gr. *melōidia* < *melos*, song + *aeidein*, to sing] **1.** any pleasing series of sounds [a *melody* sung by birds] **2.** *Music* *a)* a series of single tones forming a rhythmic whole; often, a tune, song, etc. *b)* the leading part in a harmonic composition

SYN.—**melody** refers to a pleasing series of tones in rhythm, arranged to express a musical idea; **air**, esp. formerly, refers to the main, or leading, melody of a composition in two or more parts, and **melody** also is now often so used; **tune** is the popular term, and **air** an earlier one, for any easily remembered melody of a song, dance, etc.

mel·on (mel′ən) *n.* [< OFr. < LL. *melo* for L. *melopepo* < Gr. < *mēlon*, apple + *pepon*, melon] the large, juicy, many-seeded fruit of certain trailing plants of the gourd family, as the watermelon, cantaloupe, etc. —☆**cut a melon** [Slang] to distribute profits, etc., as among stockholders

Mel·pom·e·ne (mel päm′ə nē′) *Gr. Myth.* the Muse of tragedy

melt (melt) *vt.*, *vi.* **melt′ed**, **melt′ing**, archaic pp. **molt′en** [OE. *meltan*, *vi.*; *mieltan*, *vt.*: for IE. base see MILL¹] **1.** to change from a solid to a liquid state, generally by heat [the butter *melted* in the sunlight] **2.** to dissolve; disintegrate [the candy *melted* in her mouth/ **3.** to disappear or cause to disappear gradually (often with *away*) /his fear *melted* away/ **4.** to merge gradually; blend /the sea seemed to *melt* into the sky/ **5.** to make or become gentle and tender; soften /a story to *melt* our hearts/ — *n.* a melting or being melted —**melt down** to melt (previously formed metal) so that it can be cast or molded again —**melt in one's mouth 1.** to require little chewing **2.** to taste especially delicious —**melt'a·ble** *adj.* —**melt'er** *n.* —**melt'ing·ly** *adv.*

melt·down (melt'doun') *n.* a situation in which a defect in the cooling system of a nuclear reactor can result in the melting of the fuel rods, the sinking of the core into the earth, and the release of dangerous radiation

melting point the temperature at which a specified solid becomes liquid: abbrev. **melt. pt.**

melting pot a country, etc. in which people of various nationalities and races are absorbed into the main cultural body

mel·ton (mel't'n) *n.* [< *Melton* Mowbray, England] a heavy woolen cloth with a short nap

Mel·ville (mel'vil), **Herman** 1819–91; U.S. novelist

Mel·vin (mel'vin) [< ? OE. *mæl*, council + *wine*, friend] a masculine name

mem. 1. member **2.** memorandum

mem·ber (mem'bər) *n.* [< OE. < L. *membrum*] **1.** a limb or other part or organ of a person, animal, or plant **2.** a distinct part of a whole, as of a series, an equation, a structure, etc. **3.** a person belonging to an organization or group

mem·ber·ship (-ship') *n.* **1.** the state of being a member **2.** all the members of a group **3.** the number of members

mem·brane (mem'brān) *n.* [L. *membrana* < *membrum*, member] a thin, soft layer of animal or plant tissue that covers or lines an organ or part —**mem'bra·nous** (-brə nəs) *adj.*

me·men·to (mi men'tō, mə-) *n., pl.* -**tos**, -**toes** [L., imperative of *meminisse*, to remember] anything serving as a reminder; esp., a souvenir /a toy kept as a *memento* of one's childhood/

‡**me·men·to mo·ri** (mi men'tō mō'rī, -rē) [L., remember you must die] any reminder of death

Mem·non (mem'nän) **1.** *Gr. Myth.* an Ethiopian king killed by Achilles in the Trojan War **2.** a huge statue of an Egyptian king at Thebes, said to have made a musical sound at sunrise

mem·o (mem'ō) *n., pl.* -**os** shortened *form of* MEMORANDUM

mem·oir (mem'wär) *n.* [< Fr. *mémoire* < L. *memoria*, MEMORY] **1.** a biography, usually one written by someone who knew the person well **2.** [*pl.*] an autobiography **3.** [*pl.*] a record of events based on the writer's personal observation or knowledge **4.** a report of a scientific or scholarly study

mem·o·ra·bil·i·a (mem'ər ə bil'ē ə, -bil'yə; -bēl'-) *n.pl., sing.* **mem'o·rab'i·le** (-ə rab'ə lē) [L.] things worth remembering or recording and collecting

mem·o·ra·ble (mem'ər ə b'l, mem'rə-) *adj.* worth remembering; notable —**mem'o·ra·bil'i·ty** *n.* —**mem'o·ra·bly** *adv.*

mem·o·ran·dum (mem'ə ran'dəm) *n., pl.* -**dums**, -**da** (-də) [L.] **1.** *a)* a short note written to help one remember something *b)* a record, as of events, for future use **2.** an informal written message, as in a business office **3.** a short written statement as of the terms of an agreement or contract

me·mo·ri·al (mə môr'ē əl) *adj.* [see MEMORY] serving to help people remember some person or event —*n.* **1.** anything meant to help people remember some person or event, as a statue, holiday, etc. **2.** a statement of facts, often with a petition for action, sent to a governing body, official, etc.

☆**Memorial Day** a U.S. holiday (the last Monday in May in most States) in memory of the dead servicemen of all wars

me·mo·ri·al·ize (-īz') *vt.* -**ized'**, -**iz'ing 1.** to honor the memory of **2.** to present a petition or memorial to

mem·o·rize (mem'ə rīz') *vt.* -**rized'**, -**riz'ing** ☆to fix in one's memory; learn word for word —**mem'o·ri·za'tion** *n.*

mem·o·ry (mem'ər ē, mem'rē) *n., pl.* -**ries** [< OFr. < L. *memoria* < *memor*, mindful < IE. base (*s*)*mer*-, to remember] **1.** the power, act, or process of recalling to mind facts or experiences **2.** the total of what one remembers **3.** a person, thing, etc. remembered /the music brought back *memories*/ **4.** the period over which remembering extends /within the *memory* of living men/ **5.** commemoration or remembrance /in *memory* of her son/ **6.** reputation after death **7.** the part of a computer, etc. that stores information

SYN. —**memory** refers to the ability or power of keeping in or bringing to mind past thoughts, images, ideas, etc. /to have a good *memory*/; **remembrance** applies to the act or process of having such events or things come to mind again /the *remembrance* of things in the past/; **recollection** implies a careful effort to remember the details of some event /his *recollection* of the campaign is not too clear/; **reminiscence** implies the thoughtful or nostalgic recollection of long-past events, usually pleasant

ones, or the telling of these /*reminiscences* of one's childhood/ —**ANT. forgetfulness, oblivion**

Mem·phis (mem'fis) **1.** capital of ancient Egypt, on the Nile just south of Cairo **2.** [after the Egyptian city] city in SW Tenn., on the Mississippi: pop. 624,000 (met. area 770,000)

mem·sa·hib (mem sä'ib, -säb') *n.* [Anglo-Ind.: *mem* for MA'AM + Hindi *ṣāḥib*, SAHIB] in India formerly, a term of address for a European married woman as used by servants, etc.

men (men) *n. pl. of* MAN

men·ace (men'is) *n.* [< OFr. < L. *minacia* < *minax*, threatening < *minari*, to threaten: for IE. base see MOUNT[1]] **1.** a threat or threatening **2.** anything threatening harm or evil **3.** [Colloq.] an annoying person —*vt., vi.* -**aced**, -**ac·ing** to threaten or be a danger (to) /rust fungus *menaced* the crops/ — see **SYN.** at THREATEN —**men'ac·ing·ly** *adv.*

me·nad (mē'nad) *n. alt. sp. of* MAENAD

mé·nage, me·nage (mā näzh', mə-) *n.* [< Fr. < OFr. *manage* < *manoir* (see MANOR)] **1.** a household **2.** the management of a household

me·nag·er·ie (mə naj'ər ē, -nazh'-) *n.* [< Fr. < *ménage*: see prec.] **1.** a collection of wild animals kept in cages for exhibition **2.** a place where such animals are kept

Men·ci·us (men'shē əs) (L. name of *Meng-tse*) 372?-289? B.C.; Chin. Confucian philosopher

Men·cken (meŋ'k'n), **H** (enry) **L** (ouis) 1880–1956; U.S. writer, editor, & critic

mend (mend) *vt.* [ME. *menden*, shortened from *amenden*, AMEND] **1.** to repair (something broken, torn, or worn); restore to good condition **2.** to make better; improve; reform /mend your manners/ **3.** to atone for: now only in **least said, soonest mended** —*vi.* **1.** to improve, esp. in health **2.** to grow together or heal, as a bone fracture —*n.* **1.** a mending; improvement **2.** a mended place, as on a garment —**on the mend** improving, esp. in health —**mend'a·ble** *adj.* —**mend'er** *n.*

SYN. —**mend** implies a making whole again something that has been broken, torn, etc. /to *mend* a toy, dress, etc./; **repair** is the word preferred when the object that needs to be fixed or put back into working order is one that is quite complicated /to *repair* an automobile, radio, etc./

men·da·cious (men dā'shəs) *adj.* [< L. *mendacis*, genitive of *mendax*, lying] not truthful; lying; false —**men·da'cious·ly** *adv.* —**men·da'cious·ness** *n.*

men·dac·i·ty (men das'ə tē) *n., pl.* -**ties 1.** the quality or state of being mendacious **2.** a lie; falsehood

Men·del (men'd'l), **Gre·gor Jo·hann** (grā'gôr yō'hän) 1822–84; Austrian monk & botanist: see MENDEL'S LAWS

☆**men·de·le·vi·um** (men'də lē'vē əm) *n.* [ModL., after D.I. *Mendeleev* (1834–1907), Russ. chemist] a radioactive chemical element of the actinide series: symbol, Md; at. wt., 258(?); at. no., 101

Men·de·li·an (men dē'lē ən, -dēl'yən) *adj.* **1.** of Gregor Mendel **2.** of, or inherited according to, Mendel's laws

Men·del·ism (men'd'l iz'm) *n.* the theory of heredity as described by Gregor Mendel —**Men'del·ist** *adj., n.*

Mendel's laws the principles of heredity discovered and described by Mendel, holding that characters, as height, color, etc., are inherited in definite combinations from each parent

Men·dels·sohn (men'd'l sən; *G.* -dəls zōn'), **Fe·lix** (fā'liks) 1809–47; Ger. composer

men·di·cant (men'di kənt) *adj.* [< L. prp. of *mendicare*, to beg] asking for alms; begging /mendicant friars/ —*n.* **1.** a beggar **2.** a mendicant friar —**men'di·can·cy** *n.*

mend·ing (men'diŋ) *n.* **1.** the act of one who mends **2.** things to be repaired by sewing, darning, patching, etc.

Men·e·la·us (men'ə lā'əs) *Gr. Myth.* a king of Sparta, brother of Agamemnon, and husband of Helen of Troy

men·folk (men'fōk') *n.pl.* [Dial. or Colloq.] men: also **men'folks'**

☆**men·ha·den** (men hād'n) *n., pl.* -**den**, -**dens**: see PLURAL, II, D, 2 [< Algonquian name] a sea fish related to the herring, common along the Atlantic coast: used for making oil and fertilizer

me·ni·al (mē'nē əl, mēn'yəl) *adj.* [< Anglo-Fr. < OFr. *meisniee*, household < L. *mansio*: see MANSION] **1.** of or fit for servants **2.** servile; low; mean —*n.* **1.** a domestic servant **2.** a servile, low person —**me'ni·al·ly** *adv.*

me·nin·ges (mə nin'jēz) *n.pl., sing.* **me·ninx** (mē'niŋks) [ModL., pl. of *meninx* < Gr. *mēninx*, a membrane] the three membranes that envelop the brain and spinal cord —**me·nin'ge·al** (-jē əl) *adj.*

men·in·gi·tis (men'in jīt'is) *n.* inflammation of the meninges, esp. as the result of infection by bacteria or viruses — **men'in·git'ic** (-jit'ik) *adj.*

me·nis·cus (mi nis′kəs) *n., pl.* **-nis′cus·es, -nis′ci** (-nis′ī, -kī) [ModL. < Gr. *mēniskos,* dim. of *mēnē,* the moon] **1.** a crescent-shaped thing **2.** a lens convex on one side and concave on the other **3.** the curved upper surface of a column of liquid

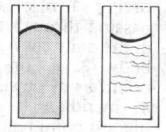

MENISCUS
(left, mercury;
right, water)

Men·non·ite (men′ə nīt′) *n.* [after *Menno Simons* (1496?–1561?), a leader] a member of an evangelical Christian sect: Mennonites oppose the taking of oaths and military service, and favor plain dress

men·o·pause (men′ə pôz′) *n.* [< Gr. *mēn,* month + *pauein,* to make cease] the final stopping of menstruation or the time when this takes place, usually between the ages of 40 and 50; change of life —**men′o·paus′al** *adj.*

men·o·rah (mə nō′rə, -nôr′ə) *n.* [Heb., lamp stand] a candelabrum with seven branches, a symbol of Judaism, or with nine branches, used during Hanuka

Me·nor·ca (me nôr′kä) *Sp. name of* MINORCA

Me·not·ti (mə nät′ē), **Gian Car·lo** (jän kär′lō) 1911– ; It. operatic composer, in U.S. since 1928

men·ses (men′sēz) *n.pl.* [L., pl. of *mensis,* month] the periodic flow of blood from the uterus, normally occurring in nonpregnant women about every four weeks, from puberty to menopause

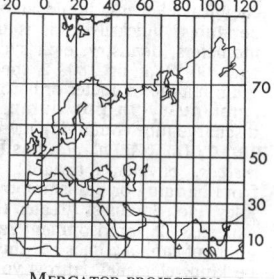

MENORAH

Men·she·vik (men′shə vik′) *n., pl.* **-viks′, -vik′i** (-vē′kē) [Russ. < *menshe,* the smaller] [*also* m-] a member of the minority faction of the Social Democratic Party of Russia, which opposed the more radical Bolsheviks from 1903 on —**Men′she·vism** *n.* —**Men′she·vist** *n., adj.*

men·stru·ate (men′stroo wāt′, -strāt) *vi.* -**at′ed, -at′ing** [< L. pp. of *menstruare* < *mensis,* month] to have a normal flow of blood from the uterus, about every four weeks: see MENSES —**men′stru·al** *adj.* —**men′stru·a′tion** *n.*

men·sur·a·ble (men′shər ə b′l, -sər-) *adj.* that can be measured; measurable —**men′sur·a·bil′i·ty** *n.*

men·su·ra·tion (men′shə rā′shən, -sə-) *n.* [< LL. < pp. of *mensurare* < L. *mensura,* MEASURE] **1.** a measuring **2.** the branch of mathematics dealing with the measuring of length, area, or volume —**men′su·ra·tive** (-rāt′iv) *adj.*

mens·wear (menz′wer′) *n.* clothing for men: also **men's wear**

-ment (mənt, mint) [< OFr. < L. *-mentum*] *a suffix meaning:* **1.** a result or product [*improvement*] **2.** a means or instrument [*adornment*] **3.** the act, process, or art [*movement*] **4.** the state, fact, or degree [*disappointment*]

men·tal (men′t′l) *adj.* [< MFr. < LL. < L. *mentis,* genitive of *mens,* the mind] **1.** of or for the mind [*mental* aids] **2.** done by or in the mind [*mental* arithmetic] **3.** mentally ill [a *mental* patient] **4.** for the mentally ill [a *mental* hospital] **5.** having to do with mind reading, telepathy, etc. —**men′tal·ly** *adv.*

☆**mental healing** the treatment of diseases by mental concentration or hypnotic suggestion

men·tal·i·ty (men tal′ə tē) *n., pl.* **-ties** mental capacity, power, or activity; mind

mental reservation a qualification (of a statement) that one thinks but does not express

mental retardation the condition of being below normal in intelligence: it ranges from *mild* (IQ of 70–85) to *moderate* (IQ of 50–70) and *severe* (IQ below 50): these terms have replaced *moron, imbecile,* and *idiot:* formerly called **mental deficiency**

men·thol (men′thōl, -thôl, -thäl) *n.* [G. < L. *mentha,* MINT² + *-ol,* -OL¹] a white, waxy, crystalline alcohol, $C_{10}H_{19}OH$, obtained from oil of peppermint and used in medicine, cosmetics, etc.

men·tho·lat·ed (men′thə lāt′id) *adj.* containing or filled with menthol

men·tion (men′shən) *n.* [OFr. < L. *mentio* < stem of *mens,* the MIND] a brief reference to or statement about someone or something —*vt.* to refer to or speak about briefly or incidentally —**make mention of** to mention —**not to mention** without even mentioning —**men′tion·a·ble** *adj.*

Men·tor (men′tər, -tôr) *Gr. Myth.* the loyal friend and adviser of Odysseus —*n.* [m-] **1.** a wise, loyal adviser **2.** a teacher or coach

men·u (men′yōo, mān′-) *n., pl.* **men′us** [Fr., small, detailed < L. *minutus:* see MINUTE²] **1.** a detailed list of the foods served at a meal or available at a restaurant **2.** the foods served

me·ow, me·ou (mē ou′, myou) *n.* [echoic] the characteristic vocal sound made by a cat —*vi.* to make such a sound

me·per·i·dine (mə per′ə dēn′) *n.* a synthetic narcotic, $C_{15}H_{21}O_2N$, used as a sedative and pain reliever

Meph·i·stoph·e·les (mef′ə stäf′ə lēz′) a devil in medieval legend to whom Faust sells his soul for knowledge and power —*n.* a crafty, evil person Also **Me·phis·to** (mə fis′tō) —**Me·phis·to·phe·le·an, Me·phis·to·phe·li·an** (mef′is tə fē′lē ən, mə fis′-) *adj.*

me·phit·ic (mə fit′ik) *adj.* [< L. *mephitis,* a stench] **1.** bad-smelling **2.** poisonous; noxious

☆**me·pro·ba·mate** (mə prō′bə māt′) *n.* a bitter, white powder, $C_9H_{18}N_2O_4$, used as a tranquilizer

mer·can·tile (mur′kən til, -tīl′, -tēl′) *adj.* [Fr. < It. < *mercante,* a merchant < L. prp. of *mercari:* see MERCHANT] **1.** of or characteristic of merchants or trade; commercial **2.** of mercantilism

mer·can·til·ism (-iz′m) *n.* the earlier doctrine that the economic interests of a nation could be strengthened by the government through protective tariffs, by a balance of exports over imports, etc. —**mer′can·til·ist** *n., adj.*

Mer·ca·tor projection (mər kāt′ər) [after G. *Mercator* (1512–94), Fl. cartographer] a method of making maps on which the meridians are equally spaced parallel straight lines and the parallels of latitude are parallel straight lines spaced farther apart as they get farther from the equator: areas are increasingly distorted toward the poles

MERCATOR PROJECTION

mer·ce·nar·y (mur′sə ner′ē) *adj.* [< L. < *merces,* wages] **1.** working or done for payment only; greedy for money or profit [the *mercenary* landlord raised rents steeply] **2.** designating a soldier serving for pay in a foreign army —*n., pl.* **-nar′ies 1.** a mercenary soldier **2.** any person who will do anything for money; hireling —**mer′ce·nar′i·ly** *adv.* —**mer′ce·nar′i·ness** *n.*

mer·cer (mur′sər) *n.* [< OFr. < *merz,* goods < L. *merx*] [Brit.] a dealer in textiles

mer·cer·ize (mur′sə rīz′) *vt.* **-ized′, -iz′ing** [after J. *Mercer* (1791–1866), Eng. calico dealer] to treat (cotton thread or fabric) with a caustic soda solution in order to strengthen it, give it a silky luster, and make it better able to absorb dyes

mer·chan·dise (mur′chən dīz′; *for n., also* -dis′) *n.* [< OFr. < *marchant,* MERCHANT] things bought and sold; goods; wares —*vt., vi.* **-dised′, -dis′ing 1.** to buy and sell; carry on trade in (some kind of goods) **2.** to promote and organize the sale of (a product) Also sp. **merchandize** —**mer′chan·dis′er** *n.*

mer·chant (mur′chənt) *n.* [OFr. *marchant,* ult. < L. *mercari,* to trade < *merx,* wares] **1.** a person whose business is buying and selling goods for profit [the munitions *merchants*] **2.** a person who sells goods at retail in a store; storekeeper —*adj.* **1.** of or used in trade; commercial **2.** of the merchant marine [a *merchant* ship] —*vt.* to deal in; trade

mer·chant·a·ble (mur′chən tə b′l) *adj.* that can be sold; marketable

mer·chant·man (-mən) *n., pl.* **-men** a ship used in commerce

merchant marine 1. all the ships of a nation that are used in commerce **2.** their personnel

‡**mer·ci** (mer sē′) *interj.* [Fr.] thank you

Mer·cia (mur′shə) former Anglo-Saxon kingdom in central and southern England

Mer·cian (mur′shən) *adj.* of Mercia, its people, etc. —*n.* **1.** a native or inhabitant of Mercia **2.** the Old English dialect of the Mercians

mer·ci·ful (mur'si fəl) *adj.* full of mercy; having, feeling, or showing mercy; lenient; clement —**mer'ci·ful·ly** *adv.* —**mer'ci·ful·ness** *n.*

mer·ci·less (-lis) *adj.* without mercy; having, feeling, or showing no mercy; pitiless; cruel —**mer'ci·less·ly** *adv.* —**mer'ci·less·ness** *n.*

mer·cu·ri·al (mər kyoor'ē əl) *adj.* **1.** [M-] of Mercury (the god or planet) **2.** of or containing mercury **3.** caused by the use of mercury **4.** having qualities suggestive of mercury; quick, quick-witted, changeable, fickle, etc. —*n.* a drug or preparation containing mercury —**mer·cu'ri·al·ly** *adv.* —**mer·cu'ri·al·ness** *n.*

mer·cu·ric (mər kyoor'ik) *adj.* of or containing mercury, esp. with a valence of two

mercuric chloride a very poisonous, white, crystalline compound, $HgCl_2$, used in photography and as an antiseptic, insecticide, etc.

☆**Mer·cu·ro·chrome** (mər kyoor'ə krōm') [see MERCURY, *n.* & -CHROME] *a trademark for* a compound used as an antiseptic in the form of a red solution —*n.* [m-] this solution

mer·cu·rous (mər kyoor'əs, mur'kyoo rəs) *adj.* of or containing mercury, esp. with a valence of one

Mer·cu·ry (mur'kyoo rē) [L. *Mercurius*] **1.** *Rom. Myth.* the messenger of the gods, god of commerce, manual skill, eloquence, and cleverness; identified with the Greek god Hermes **2.** the smallest planet in the solar system and the one nearest to the sun: diameter, c.3,000 mi. [< ML. < L., *Mercury*] [m-] **1.** a heavy, silver-white metallic chemical element, liquid at ordinary temperatures; quicksilver: it is used in thermometers, dentistry, etc.; symbol, Hg; at. wt., 200.59; at. no., 80 **2.** the mercury column in a thermometer or barometer

☆**mer·cu·ry-va·por lamp** (-vā'pər) a discharge tube containing mercury vapor

mer·cy (mur'sē) *n.*, *pl.* -**cies** [< OFr. < L. *merces*, payment, reward] **1.** a keeping from harming or punishing offenders, enemies, etc.; kindness greater than might be expected **2.** imprisonment rather than death for those found guilty of capital crimes **3.** the power or disposition to forgive or be kind; clemency [throw yourself on the *mercy* of the court] **4.** kind or compassionate treatment [acts of *mercy* were frequent during the flood] **5.** a fortunate thing; blessing [it's a *mercy* he wasn't killed] —*interj.* a mild exclamation showing surprise, annoyance, etc. —**at the mercy of** completely in the power of

mercy killing *same as* EUTHANASIA

mercy seat *Bible* the gold covering of the Ark of the Covenant, regarded as the resting place of God: Ex. 25:17

mere[1] (mir) *adj. superl.* **mer'est** [< L. *merus*, unmixed; pure: for IE. base see MORNING] nothing more or other than; only (as said to be) [a *mere* boy]

mere[2] (mir) *n.* [OE.: for IE. base see MARSH] **1.** [Poet.] a lake or pond **2.** [Obs.] the sea or an arm of the sea

-mere (mir) [< Gr. *meros*, a part] *a combining form meaning part* [metamere]

Mer·e·dith (mer'ə dith), **George** 1828–1909; Eng. novelist & poet

mere·ly (mir'lē) *adv.* no more than; and nothing else; only

mer·e·tri·cious (mer'ə trish'əs) *adj.* [< L. < *meretrix*, a prostitute < *mereri*, to serve for hire] attractive in a false, showy way; flashy or specious [*meretricious* advertising] —**mer'e·tri'cious·ly** *adv.* —**mer'e·tri'cious·ness** *n.*

mer·gan·ser (mər gan'sər) *n.*, *pl.* -**sers**, -**ser**: see PLURAL, II, D, 1 [ModL. < L. *mergus*, diver + *anser*, goose] a large, fish-eating, diving duck with a long, slender beak and, usually, a crested head

merge (murj) *vi.*, *vt.* **merged**, **merg'ing** [L. *mergere*, to dip] **1.** to lose or cause to lose identity by being absorbed, swallowed up, or combined [the two grocery stores were *merged* into one large supermarket] **2.** to unite; combine [the sea seemed to *merge* with the sky]

merg·er (mur'jər) *n.* a merging; specif., ☆the combination of several companies, corporations, etc. in one

Mé·ri·da (me'rē dä) city in SE Mexico, on the Yucatán Peninsula: pop. 254,000

Mer·i·den (mer'i dən) [MERRY + DEN (in obs. sense of "valley")] city in C Conn.: pop. 56,000

me·rid·i·an (mə rid'ē ən) *adj.* [< OFr. < L. < *meridies*, noon, ult. < *medius*, MID[1] + *dies*, day: see DEITY] **1.** of or at noon **2.** of or passing through the highest point in the daily course of any heavenly body **3.** of or at the highest point, as of power **4.** of or along a meridian —*n.* **1.** orig., the highest point reached by a heavenly body in its course **2.** the highest point of power, prosperity, etc.; zenith **3.** a great circle of the celestial sphere passing through the poles of the heavens and the zenith and nadir of any given point **4.** *a)* a great circle of the earth passing through the geographical poles and any given point on the earth's surface *b)* the half of such a circle between the poles *c)* any of the lines of longitude on a globe or map, representing such a half circle

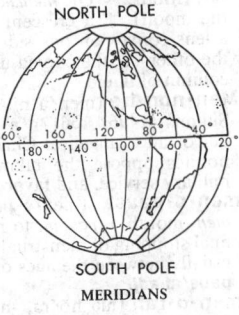

NORTH POLE

SOUTH POLE

MERIDIANS

me·rid·i·o·nal (mə rid'ē ə n'l) *adj.* [< OFr. < LL. < L. < *meridianus*: see MERIDIAN] **1.** southern; southerly **2.** of or characteristic of the south or people living in the south, esp. of France **3.** of or like a meridian —*n.* [*often* M-] an inhabitant of the south, esp. of France —**me·rid'i·o·nal·ly** *adv.*

me·ringue (mə raŋ') *n.* [Fr. < ?] **1.** egg whites mixed with sugar, beaten until stiff, spread over pies, cakes, etc., and often browned in the oven **2.** a baked shell made of this

me·ri·no (mə rē'nō) *n.*, *pl.* -**nos** [Sp., prob. < (Beni) *Merin*, name of a nomadic Berber tribe] **1.** one of a hardy breed of sheep with long, fine wool **2.** the wool **3.** a fine, soft yarn made from this wool **4.** a soft, thin cloth made of this yarn —*adj.* designating or of this sheep, wool, etc.

mer·i·stem (mer'ə stem') *n.* [< Gr. < *merizein*, to divide < *meros*, a part + *-ēm(a)*, *n.* suffix] plant tissue, as the growing tips of roots and stems, consisting of actively growing and dividing cells that give rise to various permanent tissues —**mer'i·ste·mat'ic** (-stə mat'ik) *adj.*

mer·it (mer'it) *n.* [< OFr. < L. *meritum* < pp. of *mereri*, to earn: for IE. base see MEMORY] **1.** [*sometimes pl.*] the state, fact, or quality of deserving well or ill; desert **2.** worth; value; excellence [a plan of great *merit*] **3.** something deserving reward, praise, etc. **4.** a mark, badge, etc. awarded for excellence **5.** [*pl.*] essential rightness or wrongness [to decide a case on its *merits*] —*vt.* to deserve [to *merit* praise] —**mer'it·less** *adj.*

mer·i·to·ri·ous (mer'ə tôr'ē əs) *adj.* having merit; deserving reward, praise, etc. —**mer'i·to'ri·ous·ly** *adv.* —**mer'i·to'ri·ous·ness** *n.*

☆**merit system** a system of hiring and promoting people to civil service positions on the basis of merit as determined by competitive examinations

merl, merle (murl) *n.* [< OFr. < L. *merula*] [Archaic or Poet.] the European blackbird

Mer·lin (mur'lin) *Arthurian Legend* a magician and seer, helper of King Arthur

mer·lin (mur'lin) *n.* [< OFr. < dim. of *esmeril*, merlin < OHG.] **1.** a small European falcon **2.** *same as* PIGEON HAWK

mer·lon (mur'lən) *n.* [Fr. < It. *merlo*, a battlement] the solid part of a battlement or parapet, between the openings

mer·maid (mur'mād') *n.* [see MERE[2] & MAID] **1.** an imaginary sea creature with the body of a beautiful woman and the tail of a fish **2.** a woman who swims well —**mer'man'** *n.masc.*, *pl.* -**men'**

MERMAID

-mer·ous (mər əs) [< Gr. *meros*, a part] *a suffix meaning* having (a specified number of) parts

Mer·o·vin·gi·an (mer'ə vin'jē ən, -jən) *adj.* designating or of the Frankish line of kings who reigned in Gaul (ancient France) from c. 500 to 751 A.D. —*n.* a king of this line

Mer·ri·mac, Mer·ri·mack (mer'ə mak') a U.S. frigate made into an ironclad warship by the Confederates and engaged in a battle against the Monitor in March, 1862

mer·ri·ment (mer'i mənt) *n.* merrymaking; gaiety and fun; mirth; hilarity —see SYN. at MIRTH

mer·ry (mer'ē) *adj.* -**ri·er**, -**ri·est** [OE. *myrge*] **1.** full of fun

MERCURY

and laughter; gay; mirthful **2.** festive [the *merry* month of May] —**make merry** to have fun —**mer′ri·ly** *adv.* —**mer′ri·ness** *n.*

mer·ry-an·drew (mer′ē an′drōō) *n.* [MERRY + ANDREW: orig. unc.] a buffoon; clown

mer·ry-go-round (-gō round′) *n.* **1.** a circular, revolving platform with wooden animals and seats on it, used as an amusement ride: it is turned by machinery, usually to music; carrousel **2.** a whirl or busy series of activities, as parties, dancing, etc.

mer·ry·mak·ing (-mā′kiŋ) *n.* **1.** a making merry and having fun; festivity **2.** a merry festival or entertainment —*adj.* taking part in merrymaking; gay and festive —**mer′ry·mak′er** *n.*

Mer·sey (mur′zē) river in NW England, flowing into the Irish Sea at Liverpool

Mer·thi·o·late (mər thī′ə lāt′) [(*sodium ethyl-*) *mer*(*curi-*) *thio*(*salicy*)*late*] *a trademark for* a compound used chiefly in solutions as an antiseptic for surface wounds

Mer·vin (mur′vin) [prob. var. of MARVIN] a masculine name: var. *Mervyn, Merwin, Merwyn*

Me·sa (mā′sə) [see next entry] city in SC Ariz., near Phoenix: pop. 63,000

☆**me·sa** (mā′sə) *n.* [Sp. < L. *mensa*, a table] a small, high plateau or flat tableland with steep sides, esp. in the southwestern U.S.

me·sal·li·ance (mā zal′ē əns, mā′zə lī′əns; *Fr.* mā zà lyäns′) *n.* [Fr.] a marriage with a person of lower social status

Me·sa Ver·de National Park (mā′sə ver′dā, vur′dē, vurd′) [Sp. *mesa verde*, green plateau] national park in SW Colo., containing ruins of early cliff dwellings

☆**mes·cal** (mes kal′) *n.* [Sp. *mezcal* < Nahuatl *mexcalli*] **1.** a colorless, alcoholic, Mexican liquor made from the fermented juice of various agaves **2.** any plant from which this liquor is made **3.** a small cactus whose buttonlike tops (**mescal buttons**) when chewed cause hallucinations

mes·ca·line (mes′kə lēn′, -lin) *n.* [MESCAL + -INE[4]] a white, crystalline alkaloid, $C_{11}H_{17}O_3N$, a psychedelic drug obtained from mescal buttons

mes·dames (mā däm′; *Fr.* mā dàm′) *n. pl. of* MADAME, MADAM (sense 1), or MRS.: abbrev. **Mmes.**

mes·de·moi·selles (mā′də mə zel′; *Fr.* mād mwà zel′) *n. pl. of* MADEMOISELLE: abbrev. **Mlles.**

me·seems (mē sēmz′) *v.impersonal pt.* **me·seemed′** [Archaic] (it) seems to me: also **me·seem′eth**

mes·en·ceph·a·lon (mez′en sef′ə län′, mes′-) *n.* [ModL.: see MESO- & ENCEPHALON] *same as* MIDBRAIN

mes·en·ter·y (mez′′n ter′ē, mes′-) *n., pl.* **-ter′ies** [< ML. < Gr. < *mesos*, middle + *enteron*, intestine] a supporting membrane or membranes enfolding some internal organ, as the intestine, and attaching it to the body wall or to another organ —**mes′en·ter′ic** *adj.*

mesh (mesh) *n.* [prob. < MDu. *maesche*] **1.** any of the open spaces of a net, screen, sieve, etc. **2.** [*pl.*] the threads, cords, etc. forming these openings **3.** a net or network **4.** a netlike, woven material, as that used for stockings **5.** a structure of interlocking metal links **6.** anything that entangles or snares — *vt., vi.* **1.** to entangle or become entangled as in a mesh ☆**2.** to engage or become engaged: said of gears or gear teeth **3.** to fit closely together; interlock —**in mesh** with the gears engaged; interlocked —**mesh′y** *adj.*

Mesh·ed (me shed′) *same as* MASHHAD

mesh·work (mesh′wurk′) *n.* meshes; network

mes·mer·ism (mez′mər iz′m, mes′-) *n.* [after F. A. *Mesmer* (1734–1815), G. physician] **1.** hypnotism **2.** hypnotic or irresistible attraction; fascination —**mes·mer′ic** (-mer′ik) *adj.* — **mes·mer′i·cal·ly** *adv.* —**mes′mer·ist** *n.*

mes·mer·ize (-īz′) *vt.* **-ized′, -iz′ing** to hypnotize; esp., to spellbind, or fascinate —**mes′mer·i·za′tion** *n.* —**mes′mer·iz′er** *n.*

mes·o- [< Gr. *mesos*, middle] *a combining form meaning* in the middle, intermediate: also, before a vowel, **mes-**

mes·o·blast (mes′ə blast′, mez′-) *n.* [MESO- + -BLAST] *same as* MESODERM —**mes′o·blas′tic** *adj.*

mes·o·carp (-kärp′) *n.* [MESO- + -CARP] the middle layer of the wall of a ripened ovary or fruit, as the flesh of a plum — **mes′o·car′pic** *adj.*

mes·o·ce·phal·ic (mes′ō sə fal′ik, mez′-; mē′sō-, -zō-) *adj.* [MESO- + CEPHALIC] having a head form intermediate between brachycephalic and dolichocephalic: also **mes′o·ceph′a·lous** (-sef′ə ləs) —**mes′o·ceph′a·ly** (-sef′ə lē) *n.*

mes·o·derm (mes′ə durm′, mez′-) *n.* [MESO- + -DERM] the middle layer of cells of an embryo, from which the skeleton, muscles, etc. develop —**mes′o·der′mal, mes′o·der′mic** *adj.*

mes·o·lith·ic (mes′ə lith′ik, mez′-) *adj.* [MESO- + -LITHIC] designating or of an old-world cultural period between the paleolithic and neolithic, during which certain animals and plants were domesticated

mes·o·mor·phic (mes′ə môr′fik, mez′-) *adj.* [MESO- + -MORPHIC] designating a muscular type of body build, in which the structures developed from the mesoderm are most prominent —**mes′o·morph′** *n.*

☆**mes·on** (mes′än, mez′-; mē′sän, -zän) *n.* [MES(O)- + (ELECTR)ON] an unstable particle between the electron and proton in mass, first observed in cosmic rays

Mes·o·po·ta·mi·a (mes′ə pə tā′mē ə) ancient country in SW Asia, between the Tigris & Euphrates rivers: part of modern Iraq —**Mes′o·po·ta′mi·an** *adj., n.*

mes·o·sphere (mes′ə sfir′, mez′-) *n.* [MESO- + SPHERE] a zone of the atmosphere, above the stratosphere, reaching from about 15 to 50 miles above the earth's surface

MESOPOTAMIA (c. 2100 B.C.)

Mes·o·zo·ic (mes′ə zō′ik, mez′-) *adj.* [MESO- + ZO- + -IC] designating or of a geologic era after the Paleozoic and before the Cenozoic; age of the reptiles, during which dinosaurs lived —**the Mesozoic** the Mesozoic Era or its rocks: see GEOLOGIC TIME CHART

Mes·quite (mes kēt′) [after the *mesquite* trees found there] city in NE Tex.: suburb of Dallas: pop. 55,000

☆**mes·quite, mes·quit** (mes kēt′, mes′kēt) *n.* [Sp. *mezquite* < Nahuatl *mizquitl*] a thorny tree or shrub common in the southwestern U.S. and in Mexico: its sugary, beanlike pods are used as fodder

mess (mes) *n.* [< OFr. < L. *missus*, a course (at a meal): for IE. base see MISSION] **1.** a quantity of food for a meal or dish **2.** a portion of soft food, as porridge **3.** unappetizing food **4.** *a)* a group of people who regularly have their meals together, as in the army *b)* the meal eaten by such a group **5.** a disorderly or confused mass of things; jumble; hodgepodge [clothes in a *mess* on the bed] **6.** *a)* a state of trouble or difficulty [he's in a *mess* because he lied] *b)* a state of being untidy or dirty [your room is in a *mess*] ☆*c)* [Colloq.] a person in either of these states —*vt.* **1.** to supply meals to **2.** to make dirty or untidy; also, to bungle; botch: often with *up* —*vi.* **1.** to eat as one of a mess (sense 4 *a*) **2.** to make a mess **3.** to putter or meddle [don't *mess* with my books] —**mess around** (or **about**) **1.** to putter around **2.** [Colloq.] to get involved (*with*)

mes·sage (mes′ij) *n.* [OFr. < ML. < pp. of L. *mittere*: see MISSION] **1.** a piece of news, a request, facts, etc. sent from one person to another, either by speaking or writing **2.** a formal, official report [the President's *message* to Congress] **3.** the chief idea that an artist, writer, etc. seeks to communicate in a work —*vt.* **-saged, -sag·ing** to send (as) a message —**get the message** [Colloq.] to understand what is being hinted at

mes·sen·ger (mes′′n jər) *n.* [< OFr. *messagier*: see MESSAGE] **1.** a person who carries a message or is sent on an errand **2.** [Archaic] a harbinger

☆**mess hall** a room or building where a group, as of soldiers, regularly have their meals

Mes·si·ah (mə sī′ə) [< LL. < Gr. *Messias* < Aram. < Heb. *māshīah*, lit., anointed] **1.** *Judaism* the promised and expected deliverer of the Jews **2.** *Christianity* Jesus —*n.* [m-] any expected savior —**Mes·si·an·ic** (mes′ē an′ik) *adj.*

mes·sieurs (mes′ərz; *Fr.* mā syö′) *n. pl. of* MONSIEUR: abbrev. **MM.**: see also MESSRS.

Mes·si·na (mə sē′nə, me-) seaport in NE Sicily, on a strait (**Strait of Messina**) between Sicily & Italy: pop. 269,000

mess jacket a man's short, closefitting jacket, as that worn by waiters or busboys

mess kit the compactly arranged metal or plastic plates and eating utensils carried by a soldier or camper for use in the field: also **mess gear**

mess·mate (mes′māt′) n. a person with whom one regularly has meals, as in the army

Messrs. (mes′ərz) Messieurs: now used chiefly as the pl. of Mr.

mess·y (mes′ē) adj. **mess′i·er, mess′i·est** in or like a mess; untidy, disordered, dirty, etc. —**mess′i·ly** adv. —**mess′i·ness** n.

mes·ti·zo (mes tē′zō) n., pl. **-zos, -zoes** [Sp. < LL. misticius, of mixed race < L. pp. of miscere, to mix] a person of mixed parentage; esp., the offspring of a Spaniard or Portuguese and an American Indian —**mes·ti·za** (-zə) n.fem.

met (met) pt. & pp. of MEET[1]

met. metropolitan

met·a- [< Gr. meta, along with, after, between] a prefix meaning: **1.** changed, transposed [metamorphosis, metathesis] **2.** after, beyond, higher [metaphysics] Also, before a vowel, **met-**

me·tab·o·lism (mə tab′ə liz′m) n. [< Gr. metabolē, change < meta, beyond + ballein, to throw] the continuous processes in living organisms and cells, consisting of those by which food is built up into protoplasm and those by which protoplasm is broken down into simpler substances or waste matter, with the release of energy for all vital functions —**met·a·bol·ic** (met′ə·bäl′ik) adj.

me·tab·o·lize (-līz′) vt., vi. **-lized′, -liz′ing** to change by or subject to metabolism —**me·tab′o·liz′a·ble** adj.

me·tab·o·lous (-ləs) adj. [< Gr. metabolos, changeable < -OUS] of or undergoing metamorphosis

met·a·car·pus (met′ə kär′pəs) n., pl. **-pi** (-pī) [ModL. < Gr. < meta, beyond + karpos, the wrist] **1.** the part of the hand consisting of the five bones between the wrist and the fingers **2.** the part of a land vertebrate's forelimb between the carpus and the phalanges —**met′a·car′pal** adj., n.

met·al (met′'l) n. [OFr. < L. metallum < Gr. metallon, mine] **1.** a) any of a class of chemical elements, as iron, gold, aluminum, etc., that are typically malleable, ductile, lustrous, able to conduct heat and electricity, and able to replace the hydrogen of an acid to form a salt b) an alloy of such elements, as brass, bronze, etc. **2.** any substance consisting of metal [trays made of either plastic or metal] **3.** material; substance; stuff [he is made of stronger metal than his brother] **4.** molten material for making glassware **5.** [Brit.] broken stones, cinders, etc. used as in making roads —adj. made of metal —vt. **-aled** or **-alled, -al·ing** or **-al·ling** to cover or supply with metal

metal., metall. **1.** metallurgical **2.** metallurgy

metal lath lath made of expanded metal or metal mesh

me·tal·lic (mə tal′ik) adj. **1.** of, or having the nature of, metal [a metallic chemical element] **2.** containing, yielding, or producing metal [metallic ores] **3.** like or suggestive of metal [a metallic sound] —**me·tal′li·cal·ly** adv.

met·al·lif·er·ous (met′'l if′ər əs) adj. [< L. metallum, metal + ferre, to BEAR[1] + -OUS] containing, yielding, or producing metal or ore

met·al·log·ra·phy (met′'l äg′rə fē) n. [< Fr.: see METAL & -GRAPHY] the study of the structure and physical properties of metals and alloys, esp. by the use of the microscope and X-rays —**met·al·lo·graph·ic** (mə tal′ə graf′ik) adj.

met·al·loid (met′'l oid′) n. an element having some of, but not all, the properties of metals, as arsenic or silicon —adj. **1.** like a metal in appearance **2.** of, or having the nature of, a metalloid

met·al·lur·gy (met′'l ʉr′jē) n. [ModL. < Gr. < metallon, metal, mine + ergon, work] the science of separating metals from their ores and preparing them for use, by smelting, refining, etc. —**met·al·lur′gi·cal, met·al·lur′gic** adj. —**met·al·lur′gi·cal·ly** adv. —**met·al·lur′gist** n.

met·al·ware (met′'l wer′) n. kitchenware, etc. of metal

met·al·work (-wʉrk′) n. **1.** things made of metal **2.** the making of such things: also **met′al·work′ing** —**met′al·work′er** n.

met·a·mere (met′ə mir′) n. [META- + -MERE] any of a series of similar body segments in a worm, crayfish, etc. —**met·a·**

mer·ic (met′ə mer′ik) adj. —**me·tam·er·ism** (mə tam′ər·iz′m) n.

met·a·mor·phic (met′ə môr′fik) adj. of, characterized by, causing, or formed by metamorphism or metamorphosis

met·a·mor·phism (-môr′fiz′m) n. **1.** same as METAMORPHOSIS **2.** change in the structure of rocks under pressure, heat, etc. which turns limestone into marble, granite into gneiss, etc.

met·a·mor·phose (-môr′fōz, -fōs) vt., vi. **-phosed, -phos·ing** to change in form or nature; transform; subject to or undergo metamorphosis or metamorphism —see SYN. at TRANSFORM

met·a·mor·pho·sis (-môr′fə sis, -môr fō′sis) n., pl. **-ses** (-sēz) [L. < Gr. < metamorphoun, to transform < meta, over + morphē, form] **1.** a) change of form or structure, as, in myths, by magic b) the form resulting from this **2.** a marked change of character, appearance, etc. **3.** Biol. a change in form or function as a result of development; specif., the series of changes undergone by various animals from embryo to adult, as by an insect or frog

EGG
LARVA
PUPA
ADULT

METAMORPHOSIS OF MONARCH BUTTERFLY

met·a·phor (met′ə fôr′, -fər) n. [< Fr. < L. < Gr., ult. < meta, over + pherein, to carry] a figure of speech that suggests a likeness by speaking of one thing as if it were another, different thing (Ex.: the curtain of night, "all the world's a stage"): see also SIMILE —**mix metaphors** to use two or more metaphors together that do not fit together at all (Ex.: the storm of protest was nipped in the bud) —**met·a·phor′i·cal, met·a·phor′ic** adj. —**met·a·phor′i·cal·ly** adv.

met·a·phys·i·cal (met′ə fiz′i k'l) adj. **1.** of, or having the nature of, metaphysics **2.** so subtle or abstract as to be hard to understand **3.** beyond the physical or material; supernatural **4.** designating or of the school of early 17th-cent. English poets, whose verse is characterized by subtle and fanciful images —**met′a·phys′i·cal·ly** adv.

met·a·phys·ics (met′ə fiz′iks) n.pl. [with sing. v.] [< ML. < Gr. (ta) meta (ta) physika, lit., (that) after (the) Physics (in Aristotle's works)] **1.** the branch of philosophy that deals with first principles and seeks to explain the nature of being or reality and of the origin and structure of the world **2.** speculative philosophy in general —**met·a·phy·si·cian** (-fə zish′ən) n.

☆**met·a·se·quoi·a** (met′ə si kwoi′ə) n. [ModL.: see META- & SEQUOIA] same as DAWN REDWOOD

me·tas·ta·sis (mə tas′tə sis) n., pl. **-ses** (-sēz′) [ModL. < LL. < Gr. < meta, after + histanai, to place] the spread of disease from one part of the body to another unrelated to it, as of cancer cells by way of the bloodstream —**met·a·stat·ic** (met′ə stat′ik) adj. —**met·a·stat′i·cal·ly** adv.

me·tas·ta·size (-sīz′) vi. **-sized′, -siz′ing** to spread to other parts of the body by metastasis

met·a·tar·sus (met′ə tär′səs) n., pl. **-tar′si** (-sī) [ModL. < Gr. meta-, after + tarsus, sole of the foot] **1.** the part of the human foot consisting of the five bones between the ankle and toes **2.** the part of a land vertebrate's hind limb, between the tarsus and phalanges —**met·a·tar′sal** adj., n.

me·tath·e·sis (mə tath′ə sis) n., pl. **-ses′** (-sēz′) [LL. < Gr. < meta, over + tithenai, to place] transposition or interchange; specif., the transposition of letters or sounds in a word, as in clasp (from Middle English clapse) —**met·a·thet·ic** (met′ə thet′ik), **met·a·thet′i·cal** adj. —**met·a·thet′i·cal·ly** adv.

met·a·zo·an (met′ə zō′ən) n. [ModL. metazoa (see META- & -ZOA) + -AN] any of the very large zoological division of animals whose bodies are composed of many cells arranged into definite organs —adj. of the metazoans

mete[1] (mēt) vt. **met′ed, met′ing** [OE. metan: for IE. base see MEDICAL] **1.** to allot; distribute; apportion (usually with out) **2.** [Archaic] to measure

mete[2] (mēt) n. [OFr. < L. meta] a boundary

me·tem·psy·cho·sis (mi temp′si kō′sis, -tem′-; met′əm sī-) n., pl. **-ses** (-sēz) [LL. < Gr. < meta, over + empsychoun, to put a soul into < en, in + psychē, soul] the supposed passing of the soul at death into another body, either human or animal; transmigration

me·te·or (mēt′ē ər) n. [< ML. < Gr. meteōra, things in the air < meta, beyond + eōra, a hovering in the air] **1.** the flash and streak of light, the ionized trail, etc. occurring when a meteoroid is heated by its entry into the earth's atmosphere:

popularly called *shooting* (or *falling*) *star* **2.** loosely, a meteoroid or meteorite

me·te·or·ic (mēt′ē ôr′ik, -är′-) *adj.* **1.** atmospheric or meteorological [*hail is a meteoric phenomenon*] **2.** of a meteor or meteors **3.** like a meteor; momentarily brilliant, flashing, or swift [*the singer's meteoric rise to fame*] —**me′te·or′i·cal·ly** *adv.*

me·te·or·ite (mēt′ē ə rīt′) *n.* that part of a relatively large meteoroid that survives passage through the atmosphere and falls to earth as a mass of metal or stone

me·te·or·oid (mēt′ē ə roid′) *n.* any of the many small, solid bodies traveling through outer space, which are seen as meteors when they enter the earth's atmosphere

meteorol., meteor. **1.** meteorological **2.** meteorology

me·te·or·o·log·i·cal (mēt′ē ər ə läj′i k'l) *adj.* **1.** of the atmosphere and weather **2.** of meteorology: also **me′te·or·o·log′ic** —**me′te·or·o·log′i·cal·ly** *adv.*

me·te·or·ol·o·gy (mēt′ē ə räl′ə jē) *n.* [< Gr.: see METEOR & -LOGY] the science of the atmosphere and its phenomena; study of weather, including weather forecasting —**me′te·or·ol′o·gist** *n.*

me·ter[1] (mēt′ər) *n.* [< OFr. < L. < Gr. *metron*, measure: for IE. base see MEASURE] **1.** rhythm in verse; regular arrangement of accented and unaccented syllables in each line **2.** rhythm in music; esp., the division into measures, or bars, having a uniform number of beats [*marches are often in 4/4 meter*, with four equal beats in each measure] **3.** the basic unit of length in the metric system, equal to 39.37 inches

me·ter[2] (mēt′ər) *n.* [< -METER] **1.** an instrument or apparatus for measuring and recording the quantity or rate of flow of gas, electricity, water, etc. passing through it ☆**2.** *same as:* a) PARKING METER b) POSTAGE METER —*vt.* to measure or record with a meter

-me·ter (mēt′ər, mi tər) [Fr. *-mètre* or ModL. *-metrum*, both < Gr. *metron*: see METER[1]] *a suffix meaning:* **1.** a device for measuring (a specified thing) [*thermometer, barometer*] **2.** meters or part of a meter [*kilometer, millimeter*] **3.** having (a specified number of) metrical feet [*pentameter*]

me·ter·age (mēt′ər ij) *n.* measurement as by a meter

me·ter-kil·o·gram-sec·ond (mēt′ər kil′ə gram sek′ənd) *adj.* designating or of a system of measurement in which the meter, kilogram, and second are used as the units of length, mass, and time, respectively

Meth. Methodist

meth·a·done (meth′ə dōn′) *n.* [an acronym of the chemical name] a synthetic narcotic drug, $C_{21}H_{27}ON$, sometimes used in treating persons addicted to heroin

meth·ane (meth′ān) *n.* [METH(YL) + -ANE] a colorless, odorless, flammable gas, CH_4, present in marsh gas, firedamp, and natural gas: it is used as a fuel, etc.

methane series a series of saturated hydrocarbons having the general formula C_nH_{2n+2}: methane is the first member

☆**meth·a·nol** (meth′ə nôl′, -nōl′) *n.* [METHAN(E) + -OL[1]] a colorless, flammable, poisonous liquid, CH_3OH, obtained by the destructive distillation of wood or made synthetically and used as a fuel, solvent, and antifreeze, and in the making of paints, etc.; methyl alcohol

☆**Meth·e·drine** (meth′ə drēn′) *a trademark for* a methyl derivative of amphetamine, used in medicine like amphetamine —*n.* [m-] this drug

me·thinks (mi thiŋks′) *v.impersonal pt.* **me·thought′** [< OE. < *me*, to me + *thyncth*, it seems < *thyncan*, to seem] [Archaic] it seems to me

meth·od (meth′əd) *n.* [< Fr. < L. < Gr. *methodos*, pursuit < *meta*, after + *hodos*, a way] **1.** a way of doing anything; mode; process; esp., a regular, orderly procedure or way of teaching, investigating, etc. **2.** a system in doing things or handling ideas **3.** regular, orderly arrangement

SYN.—method implies a regular, orderly, logical series of actions for getting something done [*a method* of vulcanizing rubber]; **manner** applies to a special, often personal, method [*her manner* of speech]; **mode** refers to a customary, established, or usual method or manner [*the Amish mode* of dress]; **way** is a simple, common, but more general synonym for any of the preceding words [*a way* of walking, preparing something, etc.]; **fashion**, also a general term, is often used specifically to refer to ways of dressing, living, etc. that are in style [*it is the fashion* to wear bright colors]; **system** implies a highly developed, complicated method [*a system* of government]

meth·od·i·cal (mə thäd′i k'l) *adj.* characterized by method; orderly; systematic: also **me·thod′ic** —see SYN. at ORDERLY —**me·thod′i·cal·ly** *adv.* —**me·thod′i·cal·ness** *n.*

Meth·od·ist (meth′ə dist) *n.* a member of a Protestant Christian denomination that developed from the evangelistic teachings of John and Charles Wesley —*adj.* of or characteristic of the Methodists —**Meth′od·ism** *n.*

meth·od·ize (meth′ə dīz′) *vt.* **-ized′, -iz′ing** to make methodical; systematize —**meth′od·iz′er** *n.*

meth·od·ol·o·gy (meth′ə däl′ə jē) *n., pl.* **-gies** [ModL.: see METHOD & -LOGY] **1.** the science of method, or orderly arrangement; specif., the branch of logic concerned with the application of the principles of reasoning to scientific and philosophical inquiry **2.** a system of methods, as in any particular science —**meth′od·o·log′i·cal** (-də läj′i k'l) *adj.* —**meth′od·o·log′i·cal·ly** *adv.* —**meth′od·ol′o·gist** *n.*

me·thought (mi thôt′) *pt. of* METHINKS

Me·thu·se·lah (mə thoo′zə lə, -thyoo′-) *Bible* one of the patriarchs, who lived 969 years: Gen. 5:27

meth·yl (meth′əl) *n.* [< Fr., ult. < Gr. *methy*, wine + *hylē*, wood] the monovalent hydrocarbon radical CH_3

methyl alcohol *same as* METHANOL

meth·yl·ene blue (meth′ə lēn′) a bluish-green aniline dye used as a bacteriological stain

me·tic·u·lous (mə tik′yoo ləs) *adj.* [L. *meticulosus*, fearful < *metus*, fear] very careful or too careful about details; scrupulous or finicky —**me·tic′u·lous·ly** *adv.* —**me·tic′u·lous·ness, me·tic′u·los′i·ty** (-läs′ə tē) *n.*

mé·tier (mā tyā′) *n.* [Fr. < OFr. *mestier* < L.: see MINISTRY] a trade, profession, or occupation; esp., the work that one is particularly suited for

me·ton·y·my (mə tän′ə mē) *n., pl.* **-mies** [< LL. < Gr. < *meta*, change + *onyma*, name] use of the name of one thing for that of another associated with it (Examples: "the press" for "journalists"; "the White House" for "the President") —**met·o·nym·ic** (met′ə nim′ik), **met′o·nym′i·cal** *adj.*

me·tre (mē′tər) *n. chiefly Brit. sp. of* METER[1]

met·ric (met′rik) *adj.* **1.** *same as* METRICAL **2.** a) of the meter (unit of length) b) designating or of the system of measurement based on the meter: see METRIC SYSTEM

met·ri·cal (-ri k'l) *adj.* **1.** of or composed in meter or verse **2.** of, involving, or used in measurement; metric —**met′ri·cal·ly** *adv.*

met·ri·ca·tion (met′rə kā′shən) *n.* the process of changing over to the metric system of weights and measures

met·ri·cize (met′rə sīz′) *vt.* **-cized′, -ciz′ing** to change over to the metric system of weights and measures

metric system a decimal system of weights and measures in which the gram (.0022046 pound), the meter (39.37 inches), and the liter (61.025 cubic inches) are the basic units of weight, length, and capacity, respectively: see TABLES OF WEIGHTS AND MEASURES in Supplements

metric ton a measure of weight equal to 1,000 kilograms or 2,204.62 pounds

met·ro (met′rō) *adj.* metropolitan —*n., pl.* **-ros** [often M-] a metropolitan government, subway, etc.

met·ro·nome (met′rə nōm′) *n.* [< Gr. *metron*, measure + *nomos*, law] a clockwork device that beats time, as in setting a musical tempo, at a rate determined by the position of a sliding weight on a stem that sweeps back and forth —**met′ro·nom′ic** (-näm′ik) *adj.*

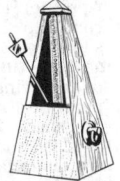
METRONOME

me·trop·o·lis (mə träp′'l is) *n., pl.* **-lis·es** [L. < Gr. < *mētēr*, a mother + *polis*, a city] **1.** the main city, often the capital, of a country, state, etc. **2.** any large city or center of population, culture, etc. **3.** the main diocese of a church province

met·ro·pol·i·tan (met′rə päl′ə t'n) *adj.* **1.** of or being a metropolis **2.** designating or of a metropolitan ☆**3.** designating or of a population area consisting of a central city and smaller surrounding communities —*n.* **1.** a person who lives in and is wise in the ways of a metropolis (senses 1 & 2) **2.** a) an archbishop having authority over the bishops of a church province b) a bishop just below a Patriarch in the Orthodox Eastern Church

-me·try (mə trē) [< Gr. < *metron*, MEASURE] *a terminal combining form meaning* the process, art, or science of measuring [geometry]

Met·ter·nich (met′ər nik; *G.* met′ər niH′), Prince (**Klemens Wenzel Nepomuk Lothar**) **von** 1773–1859; Austrian statesman & diplomat

met·tle (met′'l) *n.* [var. of METAL, used figuratively] quality of character; spirit; courage; ardor —**on one's mettle** prepared to do one's best

met·tle·some (-səm) *adj.* full of mettle; ardent, brave, etc.

Metz (mets) city in NE France, on the Moselle: pop. 108,000

Meuse (myōōz; *Fr.* möz) river flowing from NE France, through Belgium & the Netherlands into the North Sea

mev, Mev (mev) *n., pl.* **mev, Mev** [M(ILLION) E(LECTRON-)V(OLTS)] a unit of energy equal to one million electron-volts

mew[1] (myōō) *n.* [< OFr. < *muer* < L. *mutare*, to change] **1.** a cage, as for hawks while molting **2.** a secret place or den See also MEWS —*vt.* to confine in or as in a cage

mew[2] (myōō) *n.* [echoic] the characteristic vocal sound made by a cat —*vi.* to make this sound

mew[3] (myōō) *n.* [OE. *mæw*] a sea gull

mewl (myōōl) *vi.* [< MEW[2] + -LE[2]] to cry weakly, like a baby; whimper or whine —**mewl′er** *n.*

mews (myōōz) *n.pl.* [*usually with sing. v.*] [< MEW[1]] [Chiefly Brit.] **1.** stables or carriage houses, now often converted into dwellings, as along an alley **2.** such an alley

Mex. 1. Mexican **2.** Mexico

Mex·i·cal·i (mek′sə kal′ē) city in Baja California, NW Mexico, on the U.S. border: pop. 390,000

Mex·i·can (mek′si kən) *adj.* of Mexico, its people, their dialect of Spanish, or their culture —*n.* **1.** a native or inhabitant of Mexico **2.** Nahuatl

Mexican War a war between the U.S. and Mexico (1846–48)

Mex·i·co (mek′si kō′) **1.** country in N. America, south of the U.S.: 760,373 sq. mi.; pop. 48,313,000; cap. Mexico City **2. Gulf of,** arm of the Atlantic, east of Mexico Mexican name **Méx·i·co** (me′hē kô′), Spanish name, MÉJICO

Mexico City capital of Mexico, in a federal district, **México, D(istrito) F(ederal),** in the SC part of Mexico: pop., of district, 7,006,000

MexSp Mexican Spanish

Mey·er·beer (mī′ər bir′, -ber′), **Gia·co·mo** (jä′kə mō) (born *Jakob Liebmann Beer*) 1791–1864; Ger. composer

me·zu·za (mə zoo′zə) *n., pl.* **-zot** (-zōt), **-zas** [Heb. *mĕzūzāh*, doorpost] *Judaism* a small scroll inscribed with Biblical verses (Deuteronomy 6:4–9 & 11:13–21) and attached in a case to the doorpost of the home: also sp. **me·zu′zah**

mez·za·nine (mez′ə nēn′, mez′ə nēn′) *n.* [Fr. < It. < *mezzano*, middle, ult. < L. *medius*: see MID[1]] **1.** a low-ceilinged story between two main stories in a building, usually in the form of a balcony projecting partly over the main floor: also **mezzanine floor 2.** in some theaters, the first few rows of a theater balcony

mez·zo (met′sō, med′zō, mez′ō) *adj.* [It. < L. *medius*, middle] *Music* medium; moderate; half —*adv. Music* moderately; somewhat —*n., pl.* **-zos** shortened form of: **1.** MEZZO-SOPRANO **2.** MEZZOTINT

mez·zo-so·pra·no (-sə pran′ō, -prä′nō) *n., pl.* **-nos, -ni** (-prä′nē) [It.] **1.** a woman's voice or part between soprano and contralto **2.** a singer with such a voice —*adj.* of or for a mezzo-soprano

mez·zo·tint (-tint′) *n.* [< It.: see MEZZO & TINT] **1.** a method of engraving on a copper or steel plate by scraping or polishing parts of a roughened surface to produce impressions of light and shade **2.** an engraving so made —*vt.* to engrave in this way

mf *Music* mezzo forte

mfg. manufacturing

MFr. Middle French

mfr. *pl.* **mfrs.** manufacturer

Mg *Chem.* magnesium

mg, mg. milligram; milligrams

MGr. Medieval (or Middle) Greek

Mgr. 1. Manager **2.** Monseigneur **3.** Monsignor

MHG. Middle High German

mho (mō) *n.* [OHM spelled backward] a unit of electrical conductance, reciprocal of the ohm

MHz, Mhz megahertz

MI Michigan

mi (mē) *n.* [ML.: see GAMUT] *Music* a syllable representing the third tone of the diatonic scale

mi. 1. mile(s) **2.** mill(s)

Mi·am·i (mī am′ē, -ə) [< Fr.] city on the SE coast of Fla.: pop. 335,000 (met. area 1,268,000)

Miami Beach resort city in SE Fla., on an island opposite Miami: pop. 87,000

mi·aow, mi·aou (mē ou′, myou) *n., vi.* same as MEOW

mi·as·ma (mī az′mə, mē-) *n., pl.* **-mas, -ma·ta** (-mə tə) [ModL. < Gr. < *miainein*, to pollute] **1.** a vapor rising as from marshes or rotting animal or vegetable matter, formerly supposed to poison the air **2.** an unwholesome atmosphere, influence, etc. —**mi·as′mal, mi′as·mat′ic** (-mat′ik), **mi·as′mic** *adj.*

Mic. Micah

mi·ca (mī′kə) *n.* [ModL. < L., a crumb, infl. by *micare*, to shine] any of a group of minerals that crystallize in thin, somewhat flexible, easily separated layers, resistant to heat and electricity: a transparent form is often called ISINGLASS

Mi·cah (mī′kə) *Bible* **1.** a Hebrew prophet of the 8th cent. B.C. **2.** the book containing his prophecy

mice (mīs) *n. pl. of* MOUSE

Mich. 1. Michaelmas **2.** Michigan

Mi·chael (mī′k'l) [LL. < Gr. < Heb. *mīkhā'ēl*, lit., who is like God?] **1.** a masculine name: dim. *Mike, Mickey* **2.** *Bible* one of the archangels

Mich·ael·mas (-məs) *n.* [see -MAS] the feast of the archangel Michael, celebrated, chiefly in England, on September 29: also **Michaelmas Day**

Mi·chel·an·ge·lo (**Buonarroti**) (mī′k'l an′jə lō′, mik′′l-) 1475–1564; It. sculptor, painter, architect, & poet

Mi·chel·son (mī′k'l s'n), **Albert Abraham** 1852–1931; U.S. physicist, born in Germany

Mich·i·gan (mish′ə gən) [< Fr. < Algonquian, lit., great water] **1.** Middle Western State of the U.S.: 58,216 sq. mi.; pop. 8,875,000; cap. Lansing: abbrev. **Mich., MI 2. Lake,** one of the Great Lakes, between Mich. & Wis.: 22,178 sq. mi. —**Mich′i·gan′der** (-gan′dər) *n.* —**Mich′i·ga′ni·an** (-gä′nē ən), **Mich′i·gan·ite′** (-īt′) *adj., n.*

☆**Mick·ey Finn** (mik′ē fin′) [< ?] [*also* **m- f-**] [Slang] a drink of liquor to which a drug or strong laxative has been secretly added: often shortened to **Mick′ey, mick′ey** *n., pl.* **-eys**

☆**Mickey Mouse** [< DISNEY cartoon character] [Slang] childish, oversimplified, unrealistic, etc. [a *Mickey Mouse* college course]

mick·le (mik′'l) *adj., adv., n.* [OE. *micel*] [Archaic or Scot.] much

Mic·mac (mik′mak) *n., pl.* **-macs, -mac** [Algonquian, lit., allies] a member of a tribe of Indians in Newfoundland and the Maritime Provinces of Canada

mi·cra (mī′krə) *n. alt. pl. of* MICRON

mi·cro- [< Gr. < *mikros*, small] *a combining form meaning:* **1.** little; small; minute [*microfilm*] **2.** enlarging or amplifying [*microscope, microphone*] **3.** microscopic [*microchemistry*] **4.** one millionth part of (a specified unit); the factor 10⁻⁶ [*microgram*]

mi·cro·bar (mī′krə bär′) *n.* [< MICRO- + BAR[2]] a metric unit of pressure, including acoustical pressure, equal to one dyne per square centimeter

mi·crobe (mī′krōb) *n.* [Fr. < Gr. *mikros*, small + *bios*, life] any living thing too small to be seen without a microscope; esp., a disease germ —**mi·cro′bic, mi·cro′bi·al** *adj.*

mi·cro·bi·ol·o·gy (mī′krō bī äl′ə jē) *n.* the branch of biology that deals with microorganisms —**mi·cro·bi′o·log′i·cal** (-läj′ə k'l), **mi·cro·bi′o·log′ic** *adj.* —**mi′cro·bi·ol′o·gist** *n.*

mi·cro·ceph·a·ly (mī′krə sef′'l ē) *n.* [MICRO- + CEPHAL(O)- + -Y[3]] a condition in which the head is abnormally small —**mi′cro·ceph′a·lous, mi′cro·ce·phal′ic** (-sə fal′ik) *adj.*

mi·cro·chem·is·try (-kem′is trē) *n.* the chemistry of microscopic or submicroscopic quantities or objects

mi·cro·cir·cuit (mī′krə sur′kit) *n.* a highly miniaturized electronic circuit, used in computers, etc. —**mi′cro·cir′cuit·ry** *n.*

mi·cro·coc·cus (mī′krə käk′əs) *n., pl.* **-coc′ci** (-käk′sī) [ModL.: see MICRO- & -COCCUS] any of various spherical or egg-shaped bacteria

mi·cro·com·put·er (mī′krō kəm pyōōt′ər) *n.* a very small computer controlled by a tiny silicon chip that contains circuits for input, output, and memory

mi·cro·cop·y (mī′krə käp′ē) *n., pl.* **-cop′ies** a copy of printed matter, etc. produced in very greatly reduced size, as by microfilming

mi·cro·cosm (mī′krə käz′m) *n.* a little world; miniature universe; specif., man, a community, etc. regarded as a miniature of the world —**mi′cro·cos′mic** *adj.*

mi·cro·far·ad (mī′krə far′ad, -əd) *n.* one millionth of a farad

mi·cro·fiche (-fēsh′) *n.* [Fr. < *micro-*, MICRO- + *fiche*, a small card] a small sheet of microfilm, containing a number of greatly reduced pages of microcopy

mi·cro·film (-film′) *n.* film on which documents, printed pages, etc. are photographed in a reduced size for convenience in storage and use: enlarged prints can be made from such film, or the film can be viewed by projection —*vt., vi.* to photograph on microfilm

mi·cro·gram (-gram′) *n.* one millionth of a gram: also, chiefly Brit. sp., **mi′cro·gramme′**

mi·cro·graph (-graf′) *n.* [MICRO- + -GRAPH] a photograph or drawing of an object as seen through a microscope

☆**mi·cro·groove** (-grōōv′) *n.* a very narrow needle groove, as for a long-playing phonograph record

mi·crom·e·ter (mī kräm′ə tər) *n.* [< Fr.: see MICRO- & -METER] **1.** an instrument for measuring very small distances, angles, etc., used on a telescope or microscope **2.** *same as* MICROMETER CALIPER —**mi·crom′e·try** (-trē) *n.*

micrometer caliper (or **calipers**) calipers with a micrometer screw, for extremely accurate measurement

MICROMETER

micrometer screw a finely threaded screw of definite pitch, with a head graduated to show how much the screw has been moved in or out

mi·cro·min·i·a·tur·ize (mī′krə min′ē ə chə rīz′) *vt.* **-ized′, -iz′ing** to provide with electronic equipment of very small size —**mi′cro·min′i·a·tur·i·za′tion** *n.*

mi·cron (mī′krän) *n., pl.* **-crons, -cra** (-krə) [ModL. < Gr. *mikros*, small] one millionth of a meter, or one thousandth of a millimeter

Mi·cro·ne·sia (mī′krə nē′zhə, -shə) a major division of the Pacific islands, north of the equator, west of the international date line, & east of the Philippines

Mi·cro·ne·sian (-zhən, -shən) *adj.* of Micronesia, its people, their language, etc. —*n.* **1.** a native of Micronesia **2.** any of the Malayo-Polynesian languages of Micronesia

mi·cro·nu·tri·ent (mī′krō nōō′trē ənt) *n.* any of the chemical elements, such as zinc, needed in minute quantities for the growth of an organism; trace element

mi·cro·or·gan·ism (mī′krō ôr′gə niz′m) *n.* any microscopic or ultramicroscopic organism; esp., any of the bacteria, protozoans, viruses, etc.

mi·cro·phone (mī′krə fōn′) *n.* [MICRO- + -PHONE] an instrument containing a device that converts the mechanical energy of sound waves into an electric signal, as for radio —**mi′cro·phon′ic** (-fän′ik) *adj.*

mi·cro·print (-print′) *n.* a photographic copy so greatly reduced that it can be read only through a magnifying device

mi·cro·scope (mī′krə skōp′) *n.* [< ModL.: see MICRO- & -SCOPE] an instrument consisting essentially of a lens or combination of lenses, for making very small objects, as microorganisms, look larger: see also ELECTRON MICROSCOPE

mi·cro·scop·ic (mī′krə skäp′ik) *adj.* **1.** so small as not to be seen except through a microscope; minute **2.** of or with a microscope [a *microscopic* examination] **3.** like or suggestive of a microscope [*microscopic* detail] Also **mi′cro·scop′i·cal** —**mi′cro·scop′i·cal·ly** *adv.*

mi·cros·co·py (mī kräs′kə pē; *occas.* mī′krə skō′pē) *n.* the use of a microscope; investigation by means of a microscope —**mi·cros′co·pist** *n.*

mi·cro·spore (mī′krə spôr′) *n.* a haploid spore, usually smaller than a megaspore of the same plant, which gives rise to a male gametophyte —**mi′cro·spor′ic** *adj.*

mi·cro·wave (mī′krə wāv′) *adj.* designating of the electromagnetic spectrum lying between the far infrared and some lower frequency limit, usually between 300,000 and 300 megahertz —*n.* any electromagnetic wave of such frequency

mic·tu·rate (mik′chōō rāt′) *vi.* **-rat′ed, -rat′ing** [< L. pp. of *micturire* < *mingere*, to urinate] to urinate —**mic′tu·ri′tion** (-rish′ən) *n.*

mid¹ (mid) *adj.* [OE. *midd* < IE. base *medhjo-*, middle, from which also come L. *medius* & Gr. *mesos*] **1.** *same as* MIDDLE **2.** *Phonet.* produced with the tongue in a position midway between high and low: said of some vowels, as the *e* in *set* or the *o* in *sold* —*n.* [Archaic] the middle

mid² (mid) *prep.* [Poet.] amid: also **'mid**

mid- *a combining form meaning* middle or middle part of [*mid-brain, midday*]

mid·air (mid′er′) *n.* any point in space, not in contact with the ground or other surface

Mi·das (mī′dəs) Gr. Myth. a king of Phrygia able to turn everything that he touched into gold

mid·brain (mid′brān′) *n.* the middle part of the brain

☆**mid·cult** (mid′kult′) *n.* [Colloq.] a culture popularized for middlebrows through the mass media

mid·day (mid′dā′) *n.* [OE. *middæg*] the middle part of the day; noon —*adj.* of midday

mid·den (mid′'n) *n.* [prob. < Scand.] **1.** [Brit.] a dunghill or refuse heap **2.** *short for* KITCHEN MIDDEN

mid·dle (mid′'l) *adj.* [OE. *middel*: see MID¹] **1.** halfway between two given points, times, limits, etc.; also, equally distant from the ends, etc.; in the center **2.** in between; intermediate **3.** [M-] *Geol.* designating a division, as of a period, between *Upper* and *Lower* **4.** [M-] *Linguis.* designating a stage in language development intermediate between *Old* and *Modern* [*Middle English*] —*n.* **1.** a point or part halfway between extremes; middle point, part, time, etc. **2.** something intermediate **3.** the middle part of the body; waist

middle age the time of life between youth and old age: now usually the years from about 40 to about 65 —**mid′dle-aged′** *adj.*

Middle Ages the period of European history between ancient and modern times, 476 A.D.–c.1450 A.D.

Middle America 1. Mexico, Central America, and, sometimes, the West Indies ☆**2.** the American middle class, esp. of the Middle West

Middle Atlantic States New Jersey, New York, & Pennsylvania

☆**mid·dle·brow** (mid′'l brou′) *n.* [Colloq.] a person regarded as having the conventional tastes or opinions of the middle class —*adj.* [Colloq.] of or for a middlebrow

middle C the musical note of the first leger line below the treble staff and the first above the bass staff

middle class the social class between the aristocracy or very wealthy and the lower working class —**mid′dle-class′** *adj.*

middle distance the space between the foreground and the background in a picture

middle ear the eardrum and the adjacent cavity containing the hammer, the anvil, and the stirrup

Middle East 1. area from Afghanistan to Egypt, including Arabia, Cyprus, & Asiatic Turkey **2.** sometimes, the Near East, excluding the Balkans —**Middle Eastern**

Middle English the English language as written and spoken between c.1100 and c.1500

Middle French the French language as written and spoken between the 14th and 16th centuries

Middle Greek *same as* MEDIEVAL GREEK

Middle High German the High German language as written and spoken between c.1100 and c.1500

Middle Latin *same as* MEDIEVAL LATIN

Middle Low German the Low German language as written and spoken between c.1100 and c.1500

mid·dle·man (mid′'l man′) *n., pl.* **-men′** (-men′) **1.** a trader who buys commodities from the producer and sells them to the retailer or, sometimes, directly to the consumer **2.** a go-between

mid·dle·most (-mōst′) *adj. same as* MIDMOST

☆**mid·dle-of-the-road** (-əv thə rōd′) *adj.* avoiding extremes, esp. of the political left or right

middle school a school between elementary school and high school, variously between grades 5 and 9

mid·dle·weight (-wāt′) *n.* a boxer or wrestler between a welterweight and a light heavyweight (in boxing, 148–160 pounds)

Middle West region of the north central U.S. between the Rocky Mountains & the E border of Ohio, north of the Ohio River & the S borders of Kans. & Mo. —**Middle Western**

mid·dling (mid′liŋ) *adj.* of middle size, quality, grade, state, etc.; medium —*adv.* [Colloq.] moderately; somewhat —*n.* **1.** [*pl.*] products of medium quality, size, or price **2.** [*pl.*] particles of coarsely ground grain, often mixed with bran and used as feed —**fair to middling** [Colloq.] moderately good or well

mid·dy (mid′ē) *n., pl.* **-dies** 1. [Colloq.] a midshipman ☆2. a loose blouse with a sailor collar, worn by women and children: in full, **middy blouse**

Mid·east (mid′ēst′) *n.* same as MIDDLE EAST (sense 1)

Mid·gard (mid′gärd′) *Norse Myth.* the earth: also **Mid′garth′** (-gärth′)

midge (mij) *n.* [OE. *mycg* < IE. base *mu-*, fly, gnat] 1. a small, two-winged, gnatlike insect 2. a very small person

midg·et (mij′it) *n.* [dim. of MIDGE] 1. a very small person 2. anything very small of its kind —*adj.* very small of its kind; miniature —see SYN. at DWARF

Mi·di (mē dē′) [Fr.] southern France

mid·i·ron (mid′ī′ərn) *n.* a golf club with a metal head, used for fairway shots of medium distance: now usually *number 2 iron*

Mid·land (mid′lənd) [from being about midway between Fort Worth & El Paso] city in WC Tex.: pop. 59,000

mid·land (mid′lənd) *n.* 1. the middle region of a country; interior 2. [M-] *a)* an English dialect of the Midlands *b)* a dialect of American English spoken in an area that begins in parts of New Jersey, Pennsylvania, Delaware, etc. and broadens in the Middle West, spreading north and south from it to include most of the area to the west —*adj.* 1. of or in the midland; inland 2. [M-] of the Midlands —**the Midlands** region in WC England, around Birmingham

mid·most (mid′mōst′) *adj.* exactly in the middle, or nearest the middle —*adv.* in the middle or midst —*prep.* in the middle or midst of —*n.* the middle part

mid·night (-nīt′) *n.* the middle of the night; twelve o'clock at night —*adj.* 1. of or at midnight [a *midnight* ride] 2. like midnight; very dark [*midnight* blue] —**burn the midnight oil** to study or work very late at night

midnight sun the sun visible at midnight in the arctic or antarctic regions during the summer

mid·point (-point′) *n.* a point at or close to the middle or center, or equally distant from the ends

mid·rib (-rib′) *n.* the central vein of a leaf

mid·riff (mid′rif) *n.* [< OE. < *midd*, MID¹ + *hrif*, belly] 1. same as DIAPHRAGM (sense 1) 2. *a)* the middle part of the body, between the abdomen and the chest *b)* that part of a garment that covers this part, or that is cut away to expose it

mid·sec·tion (-sek′shən) *n.* the section in the middle

mid·ship (-ship′) *adj.* of the middle of a ship

mid·ship·man (-ship′mən) *n., pl.* **-men** 1. a student in training for the rank of ensign; specif., such a student at the U.S. Naval Academy at Annapolis 2. formerly, a junior British naval officer ranking just above a naval cadet

mid·ships (-ships′) *adv.* same as AMIDSHIPS

midst¹ (midst, mitst) *n.* the middle; central part: now mainly in phrases as below —**in our** (or **your, their**) **midst** among us (or you, them) —**in the midst of** 1. in the middle of; surrounded by 2. in the course of; during

midst² (midst, mitst) *prep.* [Poet.] in the midst of; amidst; amid: also **'midst**

mid·stream (mid′strēm′) *n.* the middle of a stream

mid·sum·mer (-sum′ər) *n.* 1. the middle of summer 2. popularly, the time of the summer solstice, about June 21 —*adj.* of, in, or like midsummer

mid·term (-turm′) ☆ *adj.* occurring in the middle of the term —*n.* ☆ [Colloq.] a midterm examination, as in a college course

mid·Vic·to·ri·an (mid′vik tôr′ē ən) *adj.* 1. of or characteristic of the middle part of Queen Victoria's reign in Great Britain (c.1850–1890) 2. old-fashioned, prudish, morally strict, etc. —*n.* 1. a person who lived during this period 2. a person of mid-Victorian ideas, manners, etc.

mid·way (mid′wā′; *also, for adj. & adv.,* -wā′) *n.* 1. orig., a middle way or course ☆2. that part of a fair or exposition where sideshows, rides, games, food stands, etc. are located —*adj., adv.* in the middle; halfway

Midway Islands U.S. territory in the North Pacific, northwest of Hawaii, consisting of an atoll & two islets

mid·week (-wēk′) *n.* the middle of the week —*adj.* in the middle of the week —**mid′week′ly** *adj., adv.*

Mid·west (mid′west′) *n.* same as MIDDLE WEST —*adj.* same as MIDWESTERN

Mid·west·ern (-ərn) *adj.* of, in, or characteristic of the Middle West —**Mid′west′ern·er** *n.*

mid·wife (mid′wīf′) *n., pl.* **-wives** (-wīvz′) [OE. *mid*, with + *wif*, woman] a woman whose work is helping women in childbirth

mid·wife·ry (mid′wī′fə rē, -wīf′rē) *n.* the work of a midwife

mid·win·ter (-win′tər) *n.* 1. the middle of the winter 2. popularly, the time of the winter solstice, about December 22 —*adj.* of, in, or like midwinter

mid·year (-yir′) *adj.* ☆occurring in the middle of the (calendar or academic) year —*n.* ☆[Colloq.] a midyear examination, as in a college course

mien (mēn) *n.* [< DEMEAN², but altered after Fr. *mine*, look, air] 1. a way of carrying and conducting oneself; manner 2. a way of looking; appearance

miff (mif) *n.* [prob. echoic of a sound of disgust] [Colloq.] a trivial quarrel or fit of the sulks; tiff or huff —*vt., vi.* [Colloq.] to offend or take offense

MIG (mig) *n.* [after A. *Mikoyan* & M. *Gurevich*, its Soviet designers] a small, fast jet military aircraft that is highly maneuverable: also written **MIG**

might¹ (mīt) *v.* [OE. *mihte*] 1. *pt.* of MAY 2. a helping verb used in the present or future tense and having about the same meaning as *may*, but often showing a bit more doubt [he *might* have said it] or some obligation [you *might* lend me a hand]

might² (mīt) *n.* [OE. *miht*: for IE. base see MAY] 1. physical strength, esp. great physical strength [a man of *might*] 2. strength, power, force, or influence of any kind [the *might* of the pen; the *might* of the Roman Empire]

might·y (mīt′ē) *adj.* [OE. *mihtig*] **might′i·er, might′i·est** 1. having might; powerful; strong [a *mighty* blow] 2. remarkably large, extensive, etc.; great [a *mighty* undertaking] —*adv.* [Colloq.] very; extremely [she's *mighty* tired] —**might′i·ly** *adv.* —**might′i·ness** *n.*

mi·gnon (min′yän; *Fr.* mē nyôn′) *adj.* [Fr.] small and pretty; dainty —**mi·gnonne** (min′yən; *Fr.* mē nyôn′) *adj.fem.*

mi·gnon·ette (min′yə net′) *n.* [< Fr. dim. of *mignon*: see prec.] a plant bearing spikes of small greenish, whitish, or reddish flowers

mi·graine (mī′grān) *n.* [Fr. < OFr. < LL. *hemicrania* < Gr. < *hēmi-*, half + *kranion*, skull] a very painful headache that keeps coming back and is usually limited to one side of the head —**mi·grain′ous** *adj.*

mi·grant (mī′grənt) *adj.* migrating; migratory —*n.* a person, bird, or animal that migrates; ☆specif., a farm laborer who moves from place to place to harvest seasonal crops

mi·grate (mī′grāt) *vi.* **-grat·ed, -grat·ing** [< L. pp. of *migrare*, to migrate < IE. base *mei-*, to change, move] 1. to move from one place to another, esp. to another country 2. to move from one region to another with the change in seasons, as many birds 3. to move from place to place to harvest seasonal crops —**mi′gra·tor** *n.*

MIGNON-ETTE

mi·gra·tion (mī grā′shən) *n.* 1. a migrating 2. a group of people, or of birds, fishes, etc., migrating together 3. *Chem. a)* the shifting of position of one or more atoms within a molecule *b)* the movement of ions toward an electrode during electrolysis —**mi·gra′tion·al** *adj.*

mi·gra·to·ry (mī′grə tôr′ē) *adj.* 1. migrating; characterized by migration 2. of migration 3. roving; wandering

mi·ka·do (mi kä′dō) *n., pl.* **-dos** [Jap. < *mi*, exalted + *kado*, gate] [often **M-**] the emperor of Japan: title no longer used

☆**mike** (mīk) *n.* [Colloq.] a microphone —*vt.* **miked, mik′ing** [Colloq.] to record, amplify, etc. by means of a microphone

mil (mil) *n.* [< L. *mille*, thousand] 1. a unit of length, equal to 1/1000 inch, used in measuring the diameter of wire 2. a unit of angular measurement for artillery fire, missile launching, etc., equal to 1/6400 of a circle 3. *see* MONETARY UNITS, table (Cyprus)

mil. 1. military 2. militia

mi·la·dy, mi·la·di (mi lā′dē) *n.* [Fr. < E. *my lady*] 1. an English noblewoman or gentlewoman ☆2. a woman of fashion: advertisers' term

mil·age (mīl′ij) *n. alt. sp.* of MILEAGE

Mi·lan (mi lan′) city in NW Italy: pop. 1,684,000: It. name **Mi·la·no** (mē lä′nô) —**Mil·a·nese** (mil′ə nēz′) *adj., n., pl.* **-nese**

milch (milch) *adj.* [OE. *-milce*] giving milk; kept for milking [*milch* cows]

mild (mīld) *adj.* [OE. *milde*: for IE. base see MILL¹] 1. *a)* gentle or kind in disposition, action, or effect; not severe, harsh, etc. [a *mild* manner] *b)* not extreme; moderate [a *mild* winter; *mild* reforms] 2. having a soft, pleasant flavor; not strong, bitter, etc.: said of tobacco, cheese, etc. —see SYN. at SOFT —**mild′ly** *adv.* —**mild′ness** *n.*

mil·dew (mil′doo′, -dyoo′) *n.* [OE. *meledeaw*, lit., honeydew] 1. a fungus that attacks various plants or appears on damp cloth, paper, etc. as a furry, whitish coating 2. any such coating or discoloration —*vt.*, *vi.* to affect or become affected with mildew —**mil′dew′y** *adj.*

Mil·dred (mil′drid) [< OE. < *milde*, mild + *thryth*, power] a feminine name: dim. *Millie*, *Milly*

mile (mīl) *n.*, *pl.* **miles**, dial. **mile** [< OE. < L. *milia* (*passuum*), thousand (paces)] a unit of linear measure, equal to 1,760 yards (5,280 feet or 1,609.35 meters), used in the U.S., Great Britain, etc.: in full, **statute mile**: see NAUTICAL MILE

☆**mile·age** (mīl′ij) *n.* 1. an allowance for traveling expenses at a specified amount per mile 2. total number of miles traveled, recorded, etc. 3. rate per mile, as in travel allowance or freight charges 4. the number of miles a motor vehicle will go on a gallon of fuel, a tire will run before it wears out, etc. 5. the amount of use, service, or benefit one can get from something

☆**mile·post** (-pōst′) *n.* a signpost showing the distance in miles from a specified place

mil·er (mīl′ər) *n.* one who competes in mile races

Miles (mīlz) [OFr. < OHG. *Milo*, lit., mild, peaceful] a masculine name

mile·stone (mīl′stōn′) *n.* 1. a stone or pillar set up to show the distance in miles from a specified place 2. a significant event in history, in one's career, etc.

Mi·le·tus (mī lēt′əs) city in ancient Ionia, SW Asia Minor

Mil·ford (mil′fərd) [? after *Milford*, town in England] city in SW Conn., near Bridgeport: pop. 51,000

Mil·haud (mē yō′), **Da·rius** (dà ryüs′) 1892–1974; Fr. composer

mi·lieu (mēl yoo′; *Fr.* mē lyö′) *n.*, *pl.* **-lieus**′; *Fr.* **-lieux**′ (-lyö′) [*Fr.* < OFr. *mi*, middle + *lieu*, a place] environment; esp., social or cultural setting

mil·i·tant (mil′i tənt) *adj.* [< L. prp. of *militare*, to serve as a soldier < *miles* (gen. *militis*), a soldier] 1. at war; fighting 2. ready and willing to fight; esp., vigorous in support of a cause [a *militant* defender of freedom] —*n.* a militant person —see SYN. at AGGRESSIVE —**mil′i·tan·cy** *n.* —**mil′i·tant·ly** *adv.*

mil·i·ta·rism (mil′ə tər iz′m) *n.* 1. military spirit or its dominance in a nation 2. the policy of maintaining a strong military organization in aggressive preparedness for war —**mil′i·ta·rist** *n.* —**mil′i·ta·ris′tic** *adj.* —**mil′i·ta·ris′ti·cal·ly** *adv.*

mil·i·ta·rize (mil′i tə rīz′) *vt.* **-rized**′, **-riz′ing** 1. to equip and prepare for war 2. to fill with warlike spirit —**mil′i·ta·ri·za′-tion** *n.*

mil·i·tar·y (mil′ə ter′ē) *adj.* [< Fr. < L. *militaris* < *miles*: see MILITANT] 1. of, characteristic of, for, fit for, or done by soldiers or the armed forces 2. of, for, or fit for war 3. of the army as distinguished from the navy —**the military** the army or the armed forces; esp., army officers as an influential force — **mil′i·tar′i·ly** (*also* mil′ə ter′ə lē) *adv.*

military attaché an army officer attached to his nation's embassy or legation in a foreign country

military police soldiers assigned to carry on police duties for the army

mil·i·tate (mil′ə tāt′) *vi.* **-tat′ed**, **-tat′ing** [< L. pp. of *militare*: see MILITANT] to be directed (*against*); operate or work (*against* or, rarely, *for*): said of facts, actions, etc. [careless habits *militate* against chances of success]

mi·li·tia (mə lish′ə) *n.* [L., soldiery < *miles*: see MILITANT] any army composed of citizens rather than professional soldiers, called up in time of emergency [members of the National Guard and of the Reserves make up the organized *militia* of the U.S.] —**mi·li′tia·man** (-mən) *n.*, *pl.* **-men**

milk (milk) *n.* [OE. *meolc*] 1. a white liquid secreted by the mammary glands of female mammals for suckling their young 2. cow's milk, etc. drunk by humans as a food or used to make butter, cheese, etc. 3. any liquid or juice like this [coconut *milk*, *milk* of magnesia] —*vt.* 1. to draw milk from the mammary glands of (a cow, etc.) 2. to extract (something) as if by milking [to *milk* venom from a snake] 3. to extract something from as if by milking [to *milk* a rich uncle for his money] —*vi.* 1. to give milk 2. to draw milk —**milk′er** *n.* —**milk′ing** *n.*

milk-and-wa·ter (milk′ən wôt′ər, -wät′-) *adj.* insipid; weak; wishy-washy; namby-pamby

milk glass glass of a milky-white color

milk·maid (-mād′) *n.* a girl or woman who milks cows or works in a dairy; dairymaid

milk·man (-man′) *n.*, *pl.* **-men** (-men′) a man who sells or delivers milk for a dairy

milk of magnesia a milky-white fluid, a suspension of magnesium hydroxide, $Mg(OH)_2$, in water, used as a laxative and antacid

milk run [Slang] a routine mission, as of a bomber aircraft, that is not expected to be dangerous

☆**milk·shake** (-shāk′) *n.* a drink made of milk, flavoring, and, usually, ice cream, mixed until frothy

☆**milk·shed** (-shed′) *n.* [MILK + (WATER)SHED] all the dairy farms supplying milk for a given city

☆**milk snake** a harmless snake, gray or reddish with black-rimmed markings: it feeds on rodents, etc.

milk·sop (-säp′) *n.* an unmanly man or boy; sissy

milk sugar *same as* LACTOSE

☆**milk toast** a dish consisting of toast in warm milk

milk tooth any of the temporary, first set of teeth in a child or the young of other mammals

milk·weed (-wēd′) *n.* any of a group of plants with a milky juice and pods which when ripe burst to release plumed seeds

milk·y (mil′kē) *adj.* **milk′i·er**, **milk′i·est** 1. like milk; esp., white as milk 2. of or containing milk 3. timid, meek, etc. — **milk′i·ness** *n.*

Milky Way a broad, faint band of light seen as an arch across the sky at night, formed by the system (or *Galaxy*) of billions of stars of which our sun is a part

MILKWEED PODS

mill[1] (mil) *n.* [OE. *mylen*, ult. < LL. *molina* < L. *mola*, millstone < IE. base *mel-*, to grind, crush] 1. a) a building with machinery for grinding grain into flour or meal b) a machine for grinding grain 2. a machine for grinding or crushing any solid material [a coffee *mill*] 3. a) any of various machines for cutting, stamping, shaping, etc. ☆b) [Colloq.] a place where things are done, produced, issued, etc. in a rapid, mechanical way [a diploma *mill*] 4. a factory [a textile *mill*] 5. a raised edge, ridged surface, etc. made by milling —*vt.* 1. to grind, work, form, etc. by, in, or as in a mill 2. to raise and ridge the edge of (a coin) —*vi.* ☆to move slowly in a circle, as cattle, or aimlessly, as a confused crowd (often with *around* or *about*) —**through the mill** [Colloq.] through a hard, painful, instructive experience, training, test, etc. —**milled** *adj.*

☆**mill**[2] (mil) *n.* [for L. *millesimus*, thousandth < *mille*, thousand] one tenth of a cent; $.001: a unit used in calculating but not as a coin [a 2-*mill* levy for schools]

Mill (mil), **John Stuart** 1806–73; Eng. philosopher & political economist

☆**mill·age** (mil′ij) *n.* [MILL[2] + -AGE] taxation in mills per dollar of valuation

Mil·lais (mi lā′), Sir **John Everett** 1829–96; Eng. painter

Mil·lay (mi lā′), **Edna St. Vincent** 1892–1950; U.S. poet

mill·dam (mil′dam′) *n.* a dam built across a stream to raise its level enough to provide water power for turning a mill wheel

mil·len·ni·um (mi len′ē əm) *n.*, *pl.* **-ni·ums**, **-ni·a** (-ə) [ModL. < L. *mille*, thousand + *annus*, year] 1. a period of 1,000 years 2. *Theol.* the period of a thousand years during which some believe Christ will reign on earth (with *the*): Rev. 20:1–5 3. a period of peace and happiness for everyone —**mil·len′ni·al** *adj.* —**mil·len′ni·al·ism** *n.*

mil·le·pede (mil′ə pēd′) *n. same as* MILLIPEDE

mil·le·pore (-pôr′) *n.* [< Fr. < *mille*, thousand + L. *porus*, PORE[2]] any of a genus of hydrozoans that form leaflike, porous masses of coral

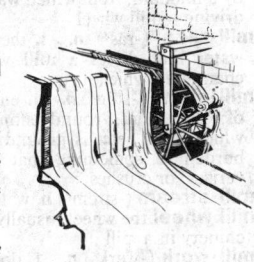

MILLDAM

mill·er (mil′ər) *n.* 1. a person who owns or operates a mill, esp. a flour mill **2.** a tool used for milling **3.** a moth with wings that look dusty or powdered, suggesting a miller's clothes

Mil·ler (mil′ər), **Arthur** 1915– ; U.S. playwright

mill·er's-thumb (mil′ərz thum′) *n.* any of several small freshwater fishes with spiny fins and a broad, flat head

mil·let (mil′it) *n.* see PLURAL, II, D, 3 [< MFr., dim. of *mil* < L. *milium*, millet] **1.** a cereal grass whose small grain is used for food in Europe and Asia **2.** the grain

Mil·let (mē le′; *E.* mi lā′), **Jean Fran·çois** (zhän frän swà′) 1814–75; Fr. painter

mil·li- [< L. *mille*, thousand] *a combining form meaning* a 1000th part of; the factor 10⁻³ [*millimeter*]

mil·li·am·pere (mil′ē am′pir) *n.* one thousandth of an ampere

mil·liard (mil′yərd, -yärd) *n.* [Fr. < *million* (see MILLION) + *-ard* (see -ARD), orig. "large million"] [Brit.] 1,000 millions; billion

mil·li·bar (mil′ə bär′) *n.* [< MILLI- + Gr. *baros*, weight] a unit of atmospheric pressure equal to 1/1000 bar, or 1,000 dynes per square centimeter

Mil·li·cent (mil′ə s'nt) [< OFr. < OHG. < *amal*, work + word thought to be *swind*, strong] a feminine name

mil·li·cu·rie (mil′ə kyoor′ē) *n.* one thousandth of a curie

mil·lieme (mēl yem′, mē-) *n.* [< Fr. < MFr. < *mille*, a thousand < L.] *see* MONETARY UNITS, table (Libya)

mil·li·gram (mil′ə gram′) *n.* one thousandth of a gram: also, chiefly Brit. sp., **mil′li·gramme**

Mil·li·kan (mil′ə kən), **Robert An·drews** (an′drooz) 1868–1953; U.S. physicist

mil·li·li·ter (mil′ə lēt′ər) *n.* one thousandth of a liter: also, chiefly Brit. sp., **mil′li·li′tre**

mil·lime (mil′ēm, -im) *n.* [Fr.: see MILLIEME] *see* MONETARY UNITS, table (Tunisia)

mil·li·me·ter (mil′ə mēt′ər) *n.* one thousandth of a meter: also, chiefly Brit. sp., **mil′li·me′tre**

mil·li·mi·cron (mil′ə mī′krän) *n., pl.* **-crons, -cra** one thousandth of a micron, or ten angstroms: a unit of length for measuring waves of light, etc.

mil·li·ner (mil′ə nər) *n.* [< *Milaner*, importer of dress wares from Milan] a person who designs, makes, trims, or sells women's hats

mil·li·ner·y (mil′ə ner′ē; *chiefly Brit.* -nər i) *n.* **1.** women's hats, headdresses, etc. **2.** the work or business of a milliner

mill·ing (mil′iŋ) *prp. of* MILL¹ —*n.* **1.** the process or business of grinding grain into flour or meal **2.** the grinding, cutting, or processing of metal, cloth, etc. in a mill

milling machine a machine with a table on which material rests as it is fed against a rotating cutter (**milling cutter**) for cutting, grinding, shaping, etc.

mil·lion (mil′yən) *n.* [OFr. < It. *milione* < *mille*, thousand < L.] **1.** a thousand thousands; 1,000,000 **2.** a very large, indefinite number [he knows *millions* of jokes] —*adj.* **1.** amounting to one million in number **2.** very many —**mil′lionth** *adj., n.*

mil·lion·aire (mil′yə ner′) *n.* [< Fr.] a person worth at least a million dollars, pounds, etc.

mil·li·pede (mil′ə pēd′) *n.* [< L. < *mille*, thousand + *pedis*, genitive of *pes*, a foot] a many-legged arthropod with two pairs of legs on most of its segments

mill·pond (mil′pänd′) *n.* a pond formed by a milldam, from which water flows for driving a mill wheel

mill·race (-rās′) *n.* **1.** the current of water that drives a mill wheel **2.** the channel in which it runs

mill·stone (-stōn′) *n.* **1.** either of a pair of large, flat, round stones between which grain, etc. is ground **2.** a heavy burden **3.** something that grinds, pulverizes, or crushes

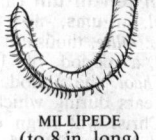

MILLIPEDE
(to 8 in. long)

mill·stream (-strēm′) *n.* water flowing in a millrace

mill wheel the wheel, usually a water wheel, that drives the machinery in a mill

mill·work (-wurk′) *n.* **1.** doors, windows, etc. made in a planing mill **2.** work done in a mill —**mill′work·er** *n.*

mill·wright (-rīt′) *n.* **1.** one who designs, builds, or installs mills or their machinery **2.** a worker who installs or repairs machinery in a plant

Milne (miln), **A(lan) A(lexander)** 1882–1956; Eng. playwright & writer of children's books

mi·lord (mi lôrd′) *n.* [Fr. < E. *my lord*] an English nobleman: used as a term of address

Mi·los (mē′lôs) Gr. island of the SW Cyclades, in the Aegean Sea: 61 sq. mi.: It. name **Mi·lo** (mē′lô)

☆**milque·toast** (milk′tōst′) *n.* [< Caspar *Milquetoast*, comic-strip character by H. T. Webster (1885–1952), U.S. cartoonist: prob. based on MILK TOAST] a timid, apologetic person

milt (milt) *n.* [prob. < Scand.] **1.** the reproductive glands of male fishes, esp. when filled with germ cells and the milky fluid containing them **2.** fish sperm —*adj.* breeding: said of male fishes —*vt.* to fertilize (fish roe) with milt —**milt′er** *n.*

Mil·ti·a·des (mil tī′ə dēz′) ?–489? B.C.; Athenian general: defeated the Persians at Marathon

Mil·ton (mil′t'n) [< OE. *Middel-tun*, Middletown, or *Mylen-tun*, Mill town] **1.** a masculine name: dim. *Milt* **2. John,** 1608–74; Eng. poet —**Mil·ton′ic** (-tän′ik), **Mil·to′ni·an** (-tō′nē ən) *adj.*

Mil·wau·kee (mil wô′kē) [< Fr. < Algonquian, lit., good land] city in SE Wis., on Lake Michigan: pop. 717,000 (met. area 1,404,000)

mime (mīm) *n.* [< L. < Gr. *mimos*] **1.** an ancient Greek or Roman farce, in which people and events were mimicked and burlesqued **2.** the representation of an action, character, mood, etc. by means of gestures and actions rather than words **3.** an actor who performs in mimes —*vt.* **mimed, mim′ing** to imitate, mimic, or act out as a mime —*vi.* to act as a mime; imitate, usually without speaking —**mim′er** *n.*

☆**mim·e·o·graph** (mim′ē ə graf′, mim′yə-) *n.* [a former trademark < Gr. *mimeomai*, I imitate + -GRAPH] a machine for making copies of written, drawn, or typewritten matter by means of a stencil —*vt.* **1.** to make copies of on such a machine **2.** to make (copies) on such a machine

mi·met·ic (mi met′ik, mī-) *adj.* [< Gr. < *mimeisthai*, to imitate] **1.** of or characterized by imitation; imitative **2.** of or characterized by mimicry —**mi·met′i·cal·ly** *adv.*

mim·ic (mim′ik) *adj.* [< L. < Gr. < *mimos*, a mime] **1.** imitative **2.** of, or having the nature of, mimicry or imitation **3.** make-believe; mock [*mimic* tears] —*n.* a person or thing that imitates; esp., an actor skilled in mimicry —*vt.* **mim′icked, mim′ick·ing 1.** to imitate in speech or action, as in making fun of [he cruelly *mimicked* the stutterer] **2.** to copy closely [parakeets *mimic* human voices] **3.** to have or take on the appearance of [the treated paper *mimicked* wood] —**mim′ick·er** *n.*

mim·ic·ry (-rē) *n., pl.* **-ries 1.** the practice or art, or an instance or way, of mimicking **2.** close resemblance of one organism to another or to some natural object, as of some insects to the leaves or twigs of plants

mi·mo·sa (mi mō′sə) *n.* [ModL. < L. *mimus:* see MIME: from seeming to mimic the behavior of animals when it is touched] a tree, shrub, or herb of the legume family, growing in warm regions and having heads or spikes of small, white, yellow, or pink flowers, as the SENSITIVE PLANT

min. 1. mineralogy **2.** minim(s) **3.** minimum **4.** mining **5.** minor **6.** minute(s)

mi·na (mī′nə) *n. same as* MYNA: also sp. **mi′nah**

min·a·ret (min′ə ret′, min′ə ret′) *n.* [Fr. < Turk. < Ar. *manārah*, lighthouse] a high, slender tower attached to a Moslem mosque, with balconies from which a muezzin, or crier, calls the people to prayer

min·a·to·ry (min′ə tôr′ē) *adj.* [< OFr. < LL. < pp. of L. *minari*, to threaten] menacing; threatening

mince (mins) *vt.* **minced, minc′ing** [OFr. *mincier*, ult. < L. *minutus*, MINUTE²] **1.** to cut up (meat, etc.) into very small pieces **2.** to say or do with a great show of being very careful or refined **3.** to lessen the force of; weaken [to *mince* no words] —*vi.* **1.** to speak or act in a way that is too careful or refined **2.** to walk with short steps or in an artificial, dainty manner —*n. same as* MINCE-MEAT —**not mince matters** to speak frankly —**minc′er** *n.*

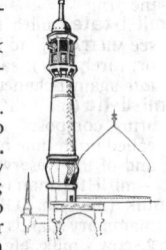

MINARET

mince·meat (mins′mēt′) *n.* a mixture of chopped apples, spices, suet, raisins, etc., and sometimes meat, used as a pie filling —**make mincemeat of** to defeat or prove completely wrong

mince pie a pie with a filling of mincemeat

minc·ing (min′siŋ) *adj.* elegant or dainty in an unnatural way; affected [a *mincing* smile] —**minc′ing·ly** *adv.*

mind (mīnd) *n.* [OE. (ge)*mynd* < IE. base *men-*, to think] **1.** memory or remembrance [that brings to *mind* a funny story] **2.** what one thinks; opinion [speak your *mind*] **3.** *a)* that which thinks, feels, is aware of things, etc.; the seat of consciousness *b)* the intellect or intelligence [a good *mind* for mathematics] *c)* attention [keep your *mind* on what you are doing] *d)* the psyche (sense 2) **4.** the intellect in its normal state; reason; sanity [to lose one's *mind*] **5.** a very intelligent person [the great *minds* of today] **6.** way, state, or direction of thinking and feeling [the reactionary *mind*] —*vt.* **1.** to direct one's mind to; specif., *a)* [Now Dial.] to become aware of; observe *b)* to pay attention to; heed [*mind* your manners] *c)* to obey [the dog *minds* its master] *d)* to take care of; look after [*mind* the baby] *e)* to be careful about [*mind* those rickety stairs] **2.** *a)* to•care about; feel concern about [don't *mind* what others may say] *b)* to object to; dislike [I don't *mind* the cold] **3.** [Dial.] to remember **4.** [Dial. or Archaic] to remind —*vi.* **1.** to pay attention; give heed **2.** to be obedient **3.** to be careful **4.** *a)* to care; feel concern *b)* to object —**bear (or keep) in mind** to remember —**be in one's right mind** to be sane —**be of one mind** to agree about something —☆**blow one's mind** [Slang] **1.** to have hallucinations, etc. as a result of taking drugs **2.** to be amazed, confused, delighted, etc. —**call to mind 1.** to remember **2.** to be a reminder of —**change one's mind** to change one's opinion or one's intention —**give (someone) a piece of one's mind** to criticize or scold (someone) sharply —**have a (good or great) mind to** to feel (strongly) inclined to —**have half a mind to** to be somewhat inclined to —**have in mind 1.** to remember **2.** to think of **3.** to intend —**know one's own mind** to know one's own real thoughts, desires, etc. —**make up one's mind** to form a definite opinion or decision —**meeting of (the) minds** an agreement —**never mind** don't be concerned; it doesn't matter —**on one's mind 1.** filling one's thoughts **2.** worrying one —**out of one's mind 1.** insane **2.** wildly excited (*with* worry, grief, etc.) —**put in mind** to remind —**take one's mind off** to stop one from thinking about —**to one's mind** in one's opinion —**mind′er** *n.*

Min·da·na·o (min′də nou′, -nä′ō) 2d largest island of the Philippines, at the S end of the group: 36,906 sq. mi.

mind·ed (mīn′did) *adj.* **1.** having a (specified kind of) mind [high-*minded*] **2.** inclined; disposed

mind·ful (mīnd′f'l) *adj.* having in mind; aware or careful (*of*) [to be *mindful* of the danger] —**mind′ful·ly** *adv.* —**mind′ful·ness** *n.*

mind·less (-lis) *adj.* **1.** showing little or no intelligence; stupid or foolish [a *mindless* remark] **2.** taking no thought; heedless or careless (*of*) —**mind′less·ly** *adv.* —**mind′less·ness** *n.*

Min·do·ro (min dôr′ō) island of the Philippines, south of Luzon: 3,759 sq. mi.

mind reader one who claims to be able to know another's thoughts —**mind reading**

mind's eye the imagination

mine[1] (mīn) *pron.* [OE. *min*] that or those belonging to me: used without a following noun [this is *mine*, *mine* are better]: also used after *of* to indicate possession [a friend of *mine*] —*adj.* [Mainly Archaic] my: formerly used before a vowel or *h* [*mine* eyes, *mine* honor], now used after a noun in direct address [daughter *mine*]

mine[2] (mīn) *n.* [< MFr. < ? Celt.] **1.** *a)* a large excavation made in the earth, from which to take out metallic ores, coal, etc. *b)* a deposit of ore, coal, etc. **2.** a large store or supply [a *mine* of information] **3.** *Mil. a)* a tunnel dug under an enemy's trench, fort, etc., esp. one in which an explosive is placed to destroy the enemy fortifications *b)* an explosive charge in a container, buried in the ground for destroying enemy troops on land, or placed in the sea for destroying enemy ships —*vi.* **mined, min′ing** to dig a mine; specif., *a)* to dig ores, coal, etc. from the earth *b)* to dig or place military mines —*vt.* **1.** *a)* to dig in (the earth) for ores, coal, etc. *b)* to dig (ores, coal, etc.) from the earth **2.** to take from (a source) **3.** to place explosive mines in or under [to *mine* a harbor] **4.** to make hollows under the surface of **5.** to undermine or ruin slowly by secret methods

mine detector an electromagnetic device for locating the position of hidden explosive mines

mine field an area on land or in water where explosive mines have been placed

mine·lay·er (mīn′lā′ər) *n.* a ship especially equipped to lay explosive mines in the water

min·er (mīn′ər) *n.* a person whose work is digging coal, ore, etc. in a mine

min·er·al (min′ər əl, min′rəl) *n.* [OFr. < ML. neut. of *mineralis* < *minera*, a mine] **1.** an inorganic substance, as iron or salt, occurring naturally in the earth and having distinctive physical properties and a composition that can be expressed by a chemical formula: sometimes applied to organic substances in the earth, such as coal **2.** an ore **3.** any substance that is neither vegetable nor animal **4.** any of certain elements, as iron, needed by animals and plants in order to stay alive —*adj.* of, like, or containing a mineral or minerals

mineral. 1. mineralogical **2.** mineralogy

min·er·al·ize (min′ər ə līz′, min′rə-) *vt.* **-ized′, -iz′ing 1.** to convert (organic matter) into a mineral **2.** to fill (water, etc.) with minerals **3.** to convert (a metal) into an ore —**min′er·al·i·za′tion** *n.* —**min′er·al·iz′er** *n.*

min·er·al·o·gy (min′ə räl′ə jē, -ral′-) *n.* the scientific study of minerals —**min′er·a·log′i·cal** (-ər ə läj′i k'l) *adj.* —**min′er·a·log′i·cal·ly** *adv.* —**min′er·al′o·gist** *n.*

mineral oil 1. any oil found in the rock strata of the earth; specif., petroleum **2.** a colorless, tasteless oil derived from petroleum and used as a laxative

mineral water water containing mineral salts or gases

☆**mineral wool** a fibrous material made from rock and melted slag and used to insulate buildings

Mi·ner·va (mi nur′və) [L.] **1.** a feminine name **2.** the ancient Roman goddess of wisdom, technical skill, and invention: identified with the Greek goddess Athena

mi·ne·stro·ne (min′ə strō′nē; *occas.* -strōn′) *n.* [It., ult. < L. *ministrare*, to serve] a thick vegetable soup containing vermicelli, barley, etc. in a meat broth

mine sweeper a ship especially equipped for destroying enemy mines at sea

Ming (miŋ) Chinese dynasty (1368–1644): period noted for scholarly achievements and artistic works

min·gle (miŋ′g'l) *vt.* **-gled, -gling** [< OE. *mengan*, to mix: for IE. base see MAKE] to mix together; combine; blend [a reaction that *mingled* joy and sorrow] —*vi.* **1.** to be or become mixed, blended, etc. **2.** to join or unite with others [we *mingled* with the crowd to watch the parade] —see SYN. at MIX —**min′gler** *n.*

min·i- [< MINI(ATURE)] *a combining form meaning:* **1.** miniature, very small, very short [*miniskirt*] **2.** of less scope, extent, etc. than usual [*mini-crisis*]

min·i·a·ture (min′ē ə chər, min′i chər) *n.* [< It. *miniatura* < ML. < L. *miniare*, to paint red < *minium*, red lead] **1.** *a)* a very small painting, esp. a portrait *b)* the art of making these **2.** a copy or model on a very small scale —*adj.* on or done on a very small scale; minute [a *miniature* golf course] —see SYN. at SMALL —**in miniature** on a small scale; greatly reduced —**min′i·a·tur·ist** *n.*

min·i·a·tur·ize (-chər īz′) *vt.* **-ized′, -iz′ing** to make in a small and compact form —**min′i·a·tur·i·za′tion** *n.*

min·im (min′im) *n.* [< L. *minimus*: see MINIMUM] **1.** the smallest liquid measure, 1/60 fluid dram, or about a drop **2.** a tiny portion **3.** [Brit.] *same as* HALF NOTE

min·i·mal (min′ə məl) *adj.* smallest or least possible; minimum [the storm did *minimal* damage] —**min′i·mal·ly** *adv.*

min·i·mize (min′ə mīz′) *vt.* **-mized′, -miz′ing 1.** to reduce to a minimum; make as small as possible [proper care will *minimize* the danger] **2.** to make seem small or unimportant [he *minimized* his act of bravery] —see SYN. at DISPARAGE —**min′i·mi·za′tion** *n.* —**min′i·miz′er** *n.*

min·i·mum (-məm) *n., pl.* **-mums, -ma** (-mə) [L., neut. of *minimus*, least < *minor*, MINOR] **1.** the smallest quantity, number, or degree possible or allowed [the patient must have a *minimum* of excitement] **2.** the lowest degree or point reached or recorded [the temperature dropped to a *minimum* of 14°] —*adj.* **1.** smallest possible, allowed, or reached **2.** of, marking, or setting a minimum or minimums

minimum wage a wage established by contract or by law as the lowest that may be paid to employees doing a specified type of work

min·ing (mī′niŋ) *n.* the act, process, or work of removing ores, coal, etc. from a mine

min·ion (min′yən) *n.* [Fr. *mignon*, darling] **1.** a person who follows or serves another in a slavish way: term of contempt **2.** a subordinate official

minion of the law *same as* POLICEMAN

---

fat, āpe, cär; ten, ēven; is, bīte; gō, hôrn, tōōl, lōōk; oil, out; up, fur; get; joy; yet; chin; she; thin, then; zh, leisure; ŋ, ring; ə for *a* in *ago*, *e* in *agent*, *i* in *sanity*, *o* in *comply*, *u* in *focus*; ′ as in *able* (ā′b'l); Fr. bál; ë, Fr. coeur; ö, Fr. feu; Fr. mon; ô, Fr. coq; ü, Fr. duc; r, Fr. cri; H, G. ich; kh, G. doch; ‡foreign; ☆ Americanism; < derived from. See inside front cover.

min·is·cule (min′ə skyōōl′) *adj.* mistaken sp. of MINUSCULE

min·i·skirt (min′ē skurt′) *n.* [MINI- + SKIRT] a very short skirt ending well above the knee

min·is·ter (min′is tər) *n.* [< OFr. < L. *minister*, a servant < *minor*, MINOR] **1.** a person appointed to take charge of some department of a government, as in Great Britain **2.** a diplomatic officer sent to a foreign nation to represent his government **3.** anyone authorized by a church to conduct worship, preach, baptize and marry people, etc.; pastor, esp. of a Protestant church **4.** any person or thing thought of as serving as the agent of some power, force, etc. [*a minister* of evil] —*vt.* [Archaic] to administer —*vi.* **1.** to serve as a minister in a church **2.** to give help (*to*) [to *minister* to the poor]

min·is·te·ri·al (min′is tir′ē əl) *adj.* **1.** of a minister or ministers as a group **2.** serving as an agent; subordinate **3.** administrative; executive —**min′is·te′ri·al·ly** *adv.*

minister plenipotentiary *pl.* **ministers plenipotentiary** a diplomatic representative with full authority to negotiate

min·is·trant (min′is trənt) *adj.* serving as a minister; ministering —*n.* a person who ministers, or serves

min·is·tra·tion (min′is trā′shən) *n.* **1.** the act of serving as a minister or clergyman **2.** the act or an instance of giving help or care; service —**min′is·tra′tive** *adj.*

min·is·try (min′is trē) *n., pl.* **-tries 1.** the act of ministering, or serving **2.** *a)* the office or duties of a minister of religion, or the period of time that he serves *b)* such ministers as a group; clergy **3.** *a)* the department under a minister of government *b)* his term of office *c)* his headquarters *d)* such ministers as a group

min·i·ver (min′ə vər) *n.* [< OFr. < *menu*, small + *vair*, kind of fur < L. *varius*, variegated] a white fur used for trimming garments, esp. robes used in official ceremonies, as by royalty

mink (miŋk) *n., pl.* **minks, mink:** see PLURAL, II, D, 1 [< Scand.] **1.** a slim, flesh-eating mammal with partly webbed feet; esp., a dark-brown weasel living in water part of the time **2.** its valuable fur, soft, thick, and white to brown in color

MINK
(17–28 in. long, including tail)

Min·ne·ap·o·lis (min′ē ap′′l is) [< nearby Minnehaha Falls (< Sioux *minne*, water, and *haha*, waterfall) + Gr. *polis*, city] city in E Minn., on the Mississippi: pop. 434,000 (met. area, with adjacent St. Paul, 1,814,000)

min·ne·sing·er (min′i siŋ′ər) *n.* [G. < MHG. *minne*, love + *senger*, singer] any of a number of German lyric poets and singers of the 12th to 14th cent.

Min·ne·so·ta (min′ə sōt′ə) [< Sioux, lit., milky blue water] Middle Western State of the U.S.: 84,068 sq. mi.; pop. 3,805,000; cap. St. Paul: abbrev. **Minn., MN** —**Min′ne·so′tan** *adj., n.*

min·now (min′ō) *n., pl.* **-nows, -now:** see PLURAL, II, D, 1 [< or akin to OE. *myne*] **1.** any of a large number of usually small freshwater fishes, used commonly as bait **2.** any very small fish Also [Dial. or Colloq.] **min′ny** (-ē), *pl.* **-nies**

Mi·no·an (mi nō′ən) *adj.* [< MINOS + -AN] designating or of an advanced prehistoric culture that flourished in Crete from c.2800–c.1100 B.C.

mi·nor (mī′nər) *adj.* [L. < IE. base *mei-*, to lessen] **1.** *a)* lesser in size, amount, or extent [*a minor* traffic accident; a *minor* part of one's time] *b)* lesser in importance or rank [*a minor* official] **2.** under full legal age ☆**3.** *Educ.* designating a field of study in which a student specializes, but to a lesser degree than in his major **4.** *Music a)* designating an interval smaller than the corresponding major by a semitone *b)* characterized by minor intervals, scales, etc. [*a minor* key] *c)* based on the scale pattern of the minor mode: see MINOR SCALE —*vi.* ☆*Educ.* to make some subject one's minor field of study [to *minor* in French] —*n.* **1.** a person under full legal age ☆**2.** *Educ.* a minor field of study **3.** *Music* a minor interval, key, etc. —**the minors** ☆the minor leagues, esp. in baseball

Mi·nor·ca (mi nôr′kə) 2d largest of the Balearic Islands

mi·nor·i·ty (mə nôr′ə tē, mī-; -när′-) *n., pl.* **-ties** [< ML. < L. *minor*, MINOR] **1.** the lesser part or smaller number; less than half [*a minority* of the Senate voted for the law] **2.** a racial, religious, or political group smaller than and differing from the larger, controlling group in a community, nation, etc. **3.** the period or condition of being under full legal age

☆**minor league** any league in a professional sport, as baseball, other than the major leagues —**mi′nor-league′** *adj.* —**mi′nor-leagu′er** *n.*

minor orders *R.C.Ch.* the four lower orders below that of subdeacon, which those who seek the major orders must pass through

minor scale one of the two standard diatonic scales, with half steps instead of whole steps after the second and seventh tones (**melodic minor scale**) or after the second, fifth, and seventh tones (**harmonic minor scale**)

minor suit *Bridge* diamonds or clubs

Mi·nos (mī′nəs, -näs) *Gr. Myth.* a king of Crete who after he died became a judge of the dead in the lower world

Min·o·taur (min′ə tôr′) *Gr. Myth.* a monster with the body of a man and the head of a bull, confined by Minos in a labyrinth and annually fed young Athenians, until killed by Theseus

Minsk (minsk; *Russ.* mēnsk) capital of the Byelorussian S.S.R.: pop. 916,000

MINOTAUR

min·ster (min′stər) *n.* [OE. *mynster* < LL. *monasterium*, MONASTERY] **1.** the church of a monastery **2.** any of various large churches or cathedrals

min·strel (min′strəl) *n.* [< OFr., servant, orig., official < LL. < L. *ministerium*, ministry] **1.** any of a class of lyric poets and singers of the Middle Ages, who traveled from place to place singing and reciting **2.** [Poet.] a poet, singer, or musician ☆**3.** a performer in a minstrel show

☆**minstrel show** a comic variety show presented by a company of performers in blackface, who sing, tell jokes, etc.

min·strel·sy (-sē) *n., pl.* **-sies 1.** the art or occupation of a minstrel **2.** a group of minstrels **3.** a collection of minstrels' ballads or songs

mint¹ (mint) *n.* [OE. *mynet*, coin < L. < *Moneta*, a name given to Juno, in whose temple money was coined] **1.** a place where money is coined by the government **2.** a large amount [he made a *mint* of money] **3.** a place where something is made — *adj.* new, as if freshly minted [in *mint* condition] —*vt.* **1.** to coin (money) **2.** to invent or create; fabricate [a newly *minted* phrase] —**mint′er** *n.*

mint² (mint) *n.* [OE. *minte*] **1.** a plant of the mint family with leaves used for flavoring and in medicine **2.** a candy flavored with mint —*adj.* designating a family of plants, as the spearmint, peppermint, and basil, with fragrant leaves and oil

mint·age (min′tij) *n.* **1.** the act or process of minting money **2.** money so produced **3.** the cost of minting money **4.** the impression made on a coin

☆**mint julep** a frosted drink consisting of whiskey or brandy, sugar, and mint leaves

min·u·end (min′yoo wend′) *n.* [< L. gerundive of *minuere*: see MINUTE²] *Arith.* the number or quantity from which another is to be subtracted

min·u·et (min′yoo wet′) *n.* [Fr. *menuet* (see MENU), orig., very small: from the small steps taken] **1.** a slow, graceful dance for groups of couples, popular in the 17th and 18th cent. **2.** the music for this, in 3/4 time

Min·u·it (min′yoo wit, min′ə-), Peter 1580?–1638; Du. colonial official; 1st chief administrator of New Netherland

mi·nus (mī′nəs) *prep.* [L., neut. sing. of *minor*, MINOR] **1.** reduced by the subtraction of; less [four *minus* two] **2.** [Colloq.] without [this cup is *minus* a handle] —*adj.* **1.** indicating subtraction [a *minus* sign] **2.** negative [a *minus* quantity] **3.** somewhat less than [a grade of A *minus*] ☆**4.** *Elec.* same as NEGATIVE [the *minus* terminal] —*n.* **1.** a minus sign **2.** a negative quantity

mi·nus·cule (mi nus′kyool, min′ə skyool′) *adj.* [Fr. < L. *minusculus*, rather small] very small

minus sign *Math.* a sign (−), indicating subtraction or a negative quantity

min·ute¹ (min′it) *n.* [< OFr. < ML. *minuta* < L. (*pars*) *minuta* (*prima*), (first) small (part): see MINUTE²] **1.** the sixtieth part of any of certain units; specif., *a)* 1/60 of an hour; sixty seconds *b)* 1/60 of a degree of an arc **2.** a short period of time; moment; instant [he'll be done in a *minute*] **3.** a specific point in time [come home this *minute*] **4.** a measure of the distance usually covered in a minute [ten *minutes* from downtown] **5.** a note or memorandum; specif., [*pl.*] an official record of what was said and done at a meeting, etc. —*vt.* **-ut·ed, -ut·ing** to make minutes of; record —**the minute (that)** just as soon as —☆**up to the minute** in the latest style, fashion, etc.

mi·nute[2] (mī nōōt′, mi-; -nyōōt′) *adj.* [< L. pp. of *minuere*, to lessen < *minor*, MINOR] **1.** very small; tiny **2.** of little importance; trifling **3.** of or paying attention to tiny details; exact; precise [she keeps a *minute* account of expenses] —see SYN. at SMALL —**mi·nute′ly** *adv.* —**mi·nute′ness** *n.*

minute hand the longer hand of a clock or watch, which indicates the minutes and moves around the dial once every hour

☆ **min·ute·man** (min′it man′) *n., pl.* **-men′** (-men′) [*also* M-] a member of the American citizen army during the American Revolution who volunteered to be ready for military service at a minute's notice

☆ **min·ute steak** (min′it) a small, thin steak that can be cooked quickly

mi·nu·ti·ae (mi nōō′shi ē′, -nyōō′-) *n.pl., sing.* **-ti·a** (-shē ə, -shə) [L. < *minutus*, MINUTE[2]] small or relatively unimportant details

minx (miŋks) *n.* [< ?] a bold, lively young woman

Mi·o·cene (mī′ə sēn′) *adj.* [< Gr. *meiōn*, less + *kainos*, recent] designating or of the fourth epoch of the Tertiary Period in the Cenozoic Era —**the Miocene** the Miocene Epoch or its rocks: see GEOLOGIC TIME CHART

Mi·ra·beau (mir′ə bō′; *Fr.* mē rà bō′), comte (**Honoré Gabriel Riqueti**) **de** 1749–91; Fr. revolutionist & statesman

mir·a·cle (mir′ə k'l) *n.* [OFr. < L. *miraculum* < *mirari*, to wonder at < *mirus*, wonderful: for IE. base see SMILE] **1.** an event or action that seems to be against known scientific laws and is thus thought of as caused by God or a god [the *miracles* in the Bible] **2.** a remarkable thing; marvel [it will be a *miracle* if we win] **3.** a wonderful example [a *miracle* of tact] **4.** *same as* MIRACLE PLAY

miracle play any of a class of medieval religious dramas dealing with events in the lives of the saints

mi·rac·u·lous (mi rak′yoo ləs) *adj.* **1.** having the nature of a miracle; supernatural **2.** like a miracle; amazing; marvelous **3.** able to work miracles —**mi·rac′u·lous·ly** *adv.* —**mi·rac′u·lous·ness** *n.*

mi·rage (mi räzh′) *n.* [Fr. < (*se*) *mirer*, to be reflected < VL. *mirare*, to look at, for L. *mirari*: see MIRACLE] **1.** an optical illusion in which the image of a distant object, as an oasis, is made to appear nearby: it is caused by the refraction of light rays from the object through layers of air of different temperatures and densities **2.** something that seems to be real but is not

mire (mīr) *n.* [< ON. *myrr*] **1.** an area of wet, soggy ground; bog **2.** deep mud or slush —*vt.* **mired, mir′ing 1.** to cause to get stuck in or as in mire **2.** to soil with mud or dirt —*vi.* to sink or stick in mud

Mir·i·am (mir′ē əm) [< Heb.: see MARY] **1.** a feminine name **2.** *Bible* the sister of Moses and Aaron: Ex. 15:20

mirk (murk) *n. alt. sp. of* MURK —**mirk′y** *adj.* **mirk′i·er, mirk′i·est**

Mi·ró (mē rō′), **Joan** (hwän) 1893– ; Sp. painter

mir·ror (mir′ər) *n.* [< OFr. < VL. *mirare*: see MIRAGE] **1.** a smooth surface that reflects images; esp., a piece of glass coated on the back as with silver; looking glass **2.** anything that truly pictures or describes [a play that is a *mirror* of life] —*vt.* to reflect as in a mirror [the moon was *mirrored* in the lake]

mirth (murth) *n.* [OE. *myrgth* < base of *myrig*, pleasant] joyfulness, gaiety, or merriment, esp. when shown by laughter

SYN.—**mirth** implies gaiety, gladness, or great amusement, esp. as expressed by laughter; **glee** implies a great, open display of joy, or it may suggest delight over another's suffering or unhappiness; **jollity** and **merriment** imply very great mirth or joy like that displayed at an especially lively and merry party or celebration; **hilarity** implies noisy and lively merriment and sometimes suggests an excessively loud display of high spirits —**ANT.** sadness, melancholy

mirth·ful (murth′fəl) *adj.* full of, showing, or causing mirth; merry —**mirth′ful·ly** *adv.* —**mirth′ful·ness** *n.*

mirth·less (-lis) *adj.* without mirth or joy; humorless; sad —**mirth′less·ly** *adv.* —**mirth′less·ness** *n.*

☆ **MIRV** (murv) *n., pl.* **MIRV's** [*m*(*ultiple*) *i*(*ndependently targeted*) *r*(*eentry*) *v*(*ehicle*)] **1.** an intercontinental ballistic missile with several warheads, each of which can be directed to a different target or to the same target at intervals **2.** any such warhead

mir·y (mīr′ē) *adj.* **mir′i·er, mir′i·est 1.** boggy; swampy **2.** muddy; dirty —**mir′i·ness** *n.*

mis- [OE. *mis-* or OFr. *mes-*] a prefix meaning: **1.** wrong or wrongly, bad or badly [*misplace, misrule*] **2.** no, not [*mistrust, misfire*]

mis·ad·ven·ture (mis′əd ven′chər) *n.* an unlucky accident; bad luck; mishap

mis·ad·vise (-əd vīz′) *vt.* **-vised′, -vis′ing** to advise badly

mis·al·li·ance (-ə lī′əns) *n.* an improper alliance; esp., an unsuitable marriage

mis·an·thrope (mis′ən thrōp′, miz′-) *n.* [< Gr. < *misein*, to hate + *anthrōpos*, a man] one who hates or distrusts all people: also **mis·an·thro·pist** (mis an′thrə pist) —**mis′an·throp′ic** (-thräp′ik), **mis′an·throp′i·cal** *adj.* —**mis′an·throp′i·cal·ly** *adv.*

mis·an·thro·py (mis an′thrə pē) *n.* hatred or distrust of all people

mis·ap·ply (mis′ə plī′) *vt.* **-plied′, -ply′ing 1.** to apply or use badly, incorrectly, or wastefully [to *misapply* one's energies] **2.** to handle dishonestly or illegally [to *misapply* a trust fund] —**mis′ap·pli·ca′tion** *n.*

mis·ap·pre·hend (-ap rə hend′) *vt.* to misunderstand —**mis·ap·pre·hen′sion** (-hen′shən) *n.*

mis·ap·pro·pri·ate (mis′ə prō′prē āt′) *vt.* **-at′ed, -at′ing** to use in a bad, incorrect, or dishonest way [the lawyer *misappropriated* his client's money] —**mis′ap·pro·pri·a′tion** *n.*

mis·be·come (-bi kum′) *vt.* **-came′, -come′, -com′ing** to be unbecoming to; be unsuitable for

mis·be·got·ten (-bi gät′'n) *adj.* wrongly or unlawfully begotten; specif., born to parents who are not married to each other

mis·be·have (-bi hāv′) *vi.* **-haved′, -hav′ing** to behave badly —*vt.* to conduct (oneself) improperly —**mis′be·hav′er** *n.* —**mis′be·hav′ior** (-yər) *n.*

mis·be·lief (-bə lēf′) *n.* wrong, false, or unorthodox belief

misc. 1. miscellaneous **2.** miscellany

mis·cal·cu·late (mis kal′kyə lāt′) *vt., vi.* **-lat′ed, -lat′ing** to calculate incorrectly; miscount or misjudge [to *miscalculate* the distance] —**mis·cal·cu·la′tion** *n.*

mis·call (-kôl′) *vt.* to call by a wrong name

mis·car·riage (-kar′ij) *n.* **1.** failure to carry out what was intended [a *miscarriage* of justice] **2.** failure of mail, freight, etc. to reach its destination **3.** the coming out of a fetus from the womb before it is developed enough to survive

mis·car·ry (-kar′ē) *vi.* **-ried, -ry·ing 1.** *a*) to go wrong; fail [our plans *miscarried*] *b*) to go astray; fail to arrive: said of mail, freight, etc. **2.** to have a miscarriage

mis·cast (-kast′) *vt.* **-cast′, -cast′ing** to cast (an actor or a play) unsuitably

☆ **mis·ce·ge·na·tion** (mis′i jə nā′shən, mi sej′ə-) *n.* [coined (c.1863) < L. *miscere*, to mix + *genus*, race + -ATION] marriage or sexual relations between a man and woman of different races, esp., in the U.S., between a white and a black

mis·cel·la·ne·ous (mis′ə lā′nē əs, -lān′yəs) *adj.* [< L. *miscellus*, mixed < *miscere*, to mix] **1.** consisting of many different kinds; varied; mixed [a *miscellaneous* collection of books] **2.** having various qualities, abilities, etc.; many-sided [a *miscellaneous* talent] —**mis′cel·la′ne·ous·ly** *adv.* —**mis′cel·la′ne·ous·ness** *n.*

mis·cel·la·ny (mis′ə lā′nē; *Brit.* mi sel′ə nē) *n., pl.* **-nies 1.** a miscellaneous collection **2.** [*often pl.*] such a collection of writings, as in a book

mis·chance (mis chans′) *n.* an unlucky accident; bad luck; misfortune

mis·chief (mis′chif) *n.* [< OFr. < *meschever*, to come to grief < *mes-*, MIS- + *chief*, end] **1.** harm or damage, esp. that done by a person [gossip can cause great *mischief*] **2.** *a*) action that causes harm or trouble *b*) a person causing damage or annoyance **3.** a tendency to annoy with playful tricks **4.** *a*) a prank; playful, annoying trick *b*) harmless teasing; playful spirits [a child full of *mischief*]

mis·chief-mak·er (-mā′kər) *n.* a person who causes mischief; esp., one who creates trouble by gossiping —**mis′chief-mak′ing** *n., adj.*

mis·chie·vous (mis′chi vəs) *adj.* **1.** causing mischief; specif., *a*) injurious; harmful [*mischievous* slander] *b*) prankish; teasing; full of tricks **2.** inclined to annoy with playful tricks; naughty: said esp. of a child —**mis′chie·vous·ly** *adv.* —**mis′chie·vous·ness** *n.*

---

fat, āpe, cär; ten, ēven; is, bīte; gō, hôrn; tōōl, lᴏᴏk; ᴏil, ᴏut; up, fᴜr; get; joy; yet; chin; she; thin, *th*en; zh, leisure; ŋ, ring; ə for *a* in *ago*, *e* in *agent*, *i* in *sanity*, *o* in *comply*, *u* in *focus*; ′ as in *able* (ā′b'l); Fr. bàl; ë, Fr. coeur; ö, Fr. feu; Fr. mon; ô, Fr. coq; ü, Fr. duc; r, Fr. cri; H, G. ich; kh, G. doch; ‡foreign; ☆ Americanism; < derived from. See inside front cover.

mis·ci·ble (mis'ə b'l) *adj.* [< ML. < L. *miscere*, to mix] that can be mixed —**mis'ci·bil'i·ty** *n.*

mis·con·ceive (mis'kən sēv') *vt., vi.* -ceived', -ceiv'ing to get a wrong idea about; misunderstand —**mis'con·cep'tion** (-sep'shən) *n.*

mis·con·duct (-kən dukt'; *for n.* mis kän'dukt) *vt.* 1. to manage badly or dishonestly 2. to behave (oneself) improperly —*n.* 1. bad or dishonest management [*misconduct* of diplomatic affairs] 2. bad or wrong behavior, esp. when deliberate

mis·con·struc·tion (mis'kən struk'shən) *n.* an incorrect explanation or interpretation; misunderstanding

mis·con·strue (-kən strōō') *vt.* -strued', -stru'ing to think of or explain wrongly; misunderstand; misinterpret [he *misconstrued* her silence as approval]

mis·count (mis kount'; *for n. usually* mis'kount) *vt., vi.* to count incorrectly —*n.* an incorrect count, as of votes in an election

mis·cre·ant (mis'krē ənt) *adj.* [OFr. *mescreant*, unbelieving < *mes-*, mis- + prp. of *croire*, to believe] 1. villainous; evil 2. [Archaic] unbelieving —*n.* 1. a criminal; villain 2. [Archaic] an unbeliever —**mis'cre·an·cy** *n.*

mis·cue (mis kyōō') *n.* 1. *Billiards* a faulty shot in which the tip of the cue slips off the ball 2. [Colloq.] a mistake; error —*vi.* -cued', -cu'ing 1. to make a miscue 2. *Theater* to miss one's cue or answer the wrong cue

mis·date (-dāt') *vt.* -dat'ed, -dat'ing to put a wrong date on (a document, letter, etc.) or assign a wrong date to (an event); date incorrectly —*n.* a wrong date

mis·deal (-dēl') *vt., vi.* -dealt', -deal'ing to deal (playing cards) wrongly —*n.* a wrong deal —**mis'deal'er** *n.*

mis·deed (-dēd') *n.* a wrong or wicked act; crime, sin, etc.

mis·de·mean·or (mis'di mēn'ər) *n.* 1. [Rare] a misbehaving 2. *Law* any minor offense, as the breaking of a municipal ordinance, which is less serious than a felony and brings a less severe punishment, usually a fine or a short term in jail Also, Brit. sp., **mis'de·mean'our**

mis·di·rect (mis'də rekt', -dī-) *vt.* to direct wrongly or badly [to *misdirect* a blow, letter, etc.] —**mis'di·rec'tion** *n.*

mis·do (mis dōō') *vt.* -did', -done', -do'ing to do wrongly — **mis·do'er** *n.*

mis·do·ing (-iŋ) *n.* wrongdoing

mis·doubt (-dout') *vt.* [Archaic] 1. to have doubts about; distrust 2. to fear —*vi.* [Archaic] to have doubts —*n.* [Archaic] suspicion; doubt

‡mise en scène (mē zän sen') [Fr.] 1. the staging of a play, motion picture, etc., including the setting, arrangement of the actors, etc. 2. general surroundings; environment

mis·em·ploy (mis'em ploi') *vt.* to employ wrongly or badly; misuse —**mis'em·ploy'ment** *n.*

mi·ser (mī'zər) *n.* [L., wretched] a greedy, stingy person who saves up money for its own sake, spending very little even for his own comfort

mis·er·a·ble (miz'ər ə b'l, miz'rə-) *adj.* [< Fr. < L. *miserabilis* < *miser*, wretched] 1. in a condition of misery; sad; wretched 2. causing misery, pain, discomfort, etc. [*miserable* weather] 3. bad; inferior; inadequate [a *miserable* performance] 4. causing feelings of pity; pitiable [his life was a *miserable* failure] 5. shameful; disgraceful [his *miserable* treatment of his friend] —**mis'er·a·ble·ness** *n.* —**mis'er·a·bly** *adv.*

Mis·e·re·re (miz'ə rer'ē, -rir'-) *n.* [LL., have mercy: first word of the psalm in the Vulgate] 1. the 51st Psalm (50th in the Douay Version) 2. a musical setting for this

mi·ser·ly (mī'zər lē) *adj.* like or characteristic of a miser; greedy and stingy —see SYN. at STINGY —**mi'ser·li·ness** *n.*

mis·er·y (miz'ər ē) *n., pl.* -er·ies [< OFr. < L. < *miser*, wretched] 1. a condition of great unhappiness or suffering, because of pain, sorrow, poverty, etc.; distress 2. a cause of such suffering; pain, sorrow, poverty, illness, etc.

mis·fea·sance (mis fē'z'ns) *n.* [< OFr. < *mes-*, mis- + *faire* (< L. *facere*, to do] *Law* wrongdoing; specif., the doing of a lawful act in an unlawful or improper manner that violates the rights of others: distinguished from MALFEASANCE, NONFEASANCE

mis·file (-fīl') *vt.* -filed', -fil'ing to file (papers, etc.) in the wrong place or order

mis·fire (-fīr') *vi.* -fired', -fir'ing 1. to fail to ignite properly: said of an internal-combustion engine 2. to fail to go off, or be discharged: said of a firearm, missile, etc. 3. to fail to produce the desired effect [his plan *misfired*] —*n.* an act or instance of misfiring

mis·fit (mis fit'; *for n. also, & for 3 always,* mis'fit') *vt., vi.* -fit'ted, -fit'ting to fit badly —*n.* 1. a misfitting 2. a garment, etc.

that does not fit right 3. a person who does not get along well in his job, with certain people, etc.

mis·for·tune (mis fôr'chən) *n.* 1. bad luck; ill fortune; trouble; adversity 2. an instance of this; unlucky accident; mishap

mis·give (-giv') *vt.* -gave', -giv'en, -giv'ing to cause fear, doubt, or suspicion in [his heart *misgave* him] —*vi.* to feel fear, doubt, etc.

mis·giv·ing (-giv'iŋ) *n.* [*often pl.*] a disturbed feeling of fear, doubt, worry, etc. [he had *misgivings* about whether he could do the job] —see SYN. at QUALM

mis·gov·ern (-guv'ərn) *vt.* to govern or administer badly — **mis·gov'ern·ment** *n.*

mis·guide (-gīd') *vt.* -guid'ed, -guid'ing to guide wrongly; lead into error or doing wrong; mislead [the *misguided* boy had run away from home] —**mis·guid'ance** *n.* —**mis·guid'ed·ly** *adv.* —**mis·guid'ed·ness** *n.* —**mis·guid'er** *n.*

mis·han·dle (mis han'd'l) *vt.* -dled, -dling to handle badly or roughly; abuse, mismanage, etc.

mis·hap (mis'hap') *n.* an unlucky accident

mish·mash (mish'mash') *n.* a confused mixture; hodgepodge; jumble: also **mish'mosh'** (-mäsh)

Mish·na, Mish·nah (mish nä', mish'nə) *n., pl.* **Mish·na·yot** (mish'nä yōt') [< ModHeb. < Heb. *shanah*, to repeat, learn] the first part of the Talmud, containing interpretations of materials in the Old Testament concerning religious practices, marriage, dietary laws, etc.: compiled about 200 A.D.

mis·in·form (mis'in fôrm') *vt.* to give false or misleading information to —**mis'in·form'ant, mis'in·form'er** *n.* — **mis'in·for·ma'tion** *n.*

mis·in·ter·pret (-in tur'prit) *vt.* to interpret wrongly; understand or explain incorrectly —**mis'in·ter·pre·ta'tion** *n.* — **mis'in·ter·pret·er** *n.*

mis·judge (mis juj') *vt., vi.* -judged', -judg'ing to judge wrongly or unfairly —**mis·judg'ment, mis·judge'ment** *n.*

mis·la·bel (-lā'b'l) *vt., vi.* -beled or -belled, -bel·ing or -bel·ling to label incorrectly

mis·lay (-lā') *vt.* -laid', -lay'ing 1. to put someplace and then forget where 2. to put down or install improperly [to *mislay* floor tiles]

mis·lead (-lēd') *vt.* -led', -lead'ing 1. to lead in a wrong direction [that old map will *mislead* you] 2. to lead into error; deceive or delude [he *misled* us into thinking he would help] 3. to lead into wrongdoing [he was *misled* by criminals] —see SYN. at DECEIVE —**mis·lead'ing** *adj.* —**mis·lead'ing·ly** *adv.*

mis·like (-līk') *vt.* -liked', -lik'ing 1. [Archaic] *same as* DISPLEASE 2. [Now Rare] to be displeased at; dislike

mis·man·age (-man'ij) *vt., vi.* -aged, -ag·ing to manage or administer badly —**mis·man'age·ment** *n.*

mis·match (-mach') *vt.* to match badly or unsuitably —*n.* a bad or unsuitable match

mis·mate (mis māt') *vt., vi.* -mat'ed, -mat'ing to mate badly or unsuitably

mis·name (-nām') *vt.* -named', -nam'ing to give or apply a wrong or unsuitable name to

mis·no·mer (mis nō'mər) *n.* [< OFr. < *mes-*, mis- + *nommer*, to name < L. *nominare:* see NOMINATE] 1. the use of a wrong name for some person or thing 2. a name wrongly used ["fish" is a *misnomer* for a whale]

mis·o- [< Gr. < *misein*, to hate] *a combining form meaning* hatred or hating [*misogyny*]: also, before a vowel, **mis-**

mi·sog·a·my (mi säg'ə mē) *n.* [MISO- + -GAMY] hatred of marriage —**mi·sog'a·mist** *n.*

mi·sog·y·ny (mi säj'ə nē) *n.* [< Gr.: see MISO- & -GYNY] hatred of women —**mi·sog'y·nist** *n.* —**mi·sog'y·nous, mi·sog'y·nic** *adj.*

mis·place (mis plās') *vt.* -placed', -plac'ing 1. to put in a wrong place [he *misplaced* the book of poems in the science section] 2. to give (one's trust, affection, etc.) unwisely 3. *same as* MISLAY (sense 1) —**mis·place'ment** *n.*

mis·play (-plā') *vt., vi.* to play wrongly or badly, as in a game —☆*n.* a wrong or bad play

mis·print (mis print'; *for n. usually* mis'print) —*vt.* to print incorrectly —*n.* an error in printing

mis·pri·sion (mis prizh'ən) *n.* [< OFr. < pp. of *mesprendre*, to take wrongly < *mes-*, mis- + *prendre* < L. *prehendere*, to take] *Law* misconduct or neglect of duty, esp. by a public official

mis·pri·sion of felony (or **treason**) *Law* the offense of concealing knowledge of another's felony (or treason)

mis·prize (mis prīz') *vt.* -prized', -priz'ing [< OFr. < *mes-*, mis- + LL. *pretiare*, to value < L. *pretium*, a price] to feel scorn or contempt for, or fail to recognize the true value of

mis·pro·nounce (mis′prə nouns′) *vt., vi.* **-nounced′, -nounc′ing** to give (a word) a pronunciation different from any of the accepted standard pronunciations —**mis′pro·nun′ci·a′tion** (-nun′sē ā′shən) *n.*

mis·quote (mis kwōt′) *vt., vi.* **-quot′ed, -quot′ing** to quote incorrectly —**mis′quo·ta′tion** *n.*

mis·read (-rēd′) *vt., vi.* **-read′** (-red′), **-read′ing** (-rēd′iŋ) to read wrongly, esp. so as to misinterpret or misunderstand [to *misread* a poem, instructions, etc.]

mis·rep·re·sent (mis′rep ri zent′) *vt.* **1.** to represent falsely; give an untrue idea of [he *misrepresented* the terms of the contract] **2.** to be a bad representative of —**mis′rep·re·sen·ta′tion** *n.*

mis·rule (mis rōōl′) *vt.* **-ruled′, -rul′ing** to rule badly or unjustly; misgovern —*n.* **1.** bad or unjust government **2.** disorder or riot —**mis·rul′er** *n.*

miss[1] (mis) *vt.* [OE. *missan:* for IE. base see MIGRATE] **1.** to fail to hit, meet, catch, do, see, hear, etc. [the arrow *missed* the target; I *missed* the last line of the joke] **2.** to let (an opportunity, etc.) go by [you *missed* your turn] **3.** to escape; avoid [he just *missed* being hit] **4.** to fail or forget to do, keep, attend, etc. [he *missed* a class] **5.** to notice, feel, or regret the absence or loss of [I suddenly *missed* my watch; he *missed* his friends back home] —*vi.* **1.** to fail to hit something aimed at **2.** to fail to be successful **3.** to misfire [the engine *misses* occasionally] —*n.* a failure to hit, obtain, etc.

miss[2] (mis) *n., pl.* **miss′es** [contr. of MISTRESS] **1.** [M-] a title used in speaking to or of an unmarried woman or girl, placed before the name [*Miss* Smith, the *Misses* Smith] **2.** a young unmarried woman or girl

Miss. Mississippi

mis·sal (mis′'l) *n.* [< ML. < LL. *missa,* MASS] R.C.Ch. a book containing all the prayers, rites, etc. for the Mass throughout the year

mis·shape (mis shāp′) *vt.* **-shaped′, -shaped′** or archaic **-shap′en, -shap′ing** to shape badly; deform

mis·shap·en (-'n) *adj.* badly shaped; deformed —**mis·shap′en·ly** *adv.* —**mis·shap′en·ness** *n.*

mis·sile (mis′'l) *adj.* [L. *missilis* < pp. of *mittere:* see MISSION] that can be, or is, thrown or shot —*n.* a weapon or other object, as a spear, bullet, rocket, etc., designed to be thrown or shot toward a target; often, specif., a guided missile

☆**mis·sile·man** (-mən) *n., pl.* **-men** one who builds or launches guided missiles: also **mis′sil·eer′** (-ir′)

mis·sile·ry, mis·sil·ry (-rē) *n.* **1.** the science of building and launching guided missiles **2.** guided missiles as a group

miss·ing (mis′iŋ) *adj.* absent; lost; lacking; specif., absent after combat, but not known to be dead or a prisoner

missing link something needed to complete a series; specif., a hypothetical animal believed to have existed between the anthropoid apes and man in the evolutionary process

mis·sion (mish′ən) *n.* [L. *missio* < pp. of *mittere,* to send < IE. base *smeit-,* to send off] **1.** a being sent out with authority to perform a special duty, as by a church, government, etc. **2.** *a)* a group of persons sent by a church to spread its religion, esp. in a foreign land *b)* its headquarters *c)* [*pl.*] organized missionary work, esp. for spreading Christianity **3.** a group of persons sent to a foreign government to carry on dealings; diplomatic delegation; embassy **4.** a group of technicians, specialists, etc. sent to a foreign country **5.** the special duty or work that a person or group is sent out to do [a *mission* to make a treaty] **6.** the special task for which a person is apparently destined in life; calling [Joan of Arc's *mission* was to set France free] **7.** any charitable or religious organization for doing welfare work for the needy **8.** *Mil.* an assigned combat operation; esp., a single combat flight by an airplane or group of airplanes —*adj.* or a mission or missions

mis·sion·ar·y (-er′ē) *adj.* of or characteristic of religious missions or missionaries —*n., pl.* **-ar′ies** a person sent out by a church to spread its religion, as in a foreign country

mis·sis (mis′əz) *n.* [altered < MRS.] [Colloq. or Dial.] one's wife: also used with *the:* also **mis′sus**

Mis·sis·sip·pi (mis′ə sip′ē) [< Fr. < Algonquian, lit., big river] **1.** river in the central U.S., flowing from N Minn. to the Gulf of Mexico: 2,348 mi. **2.** Southern State of the U.S.: 47,716 sq. mi.; pop. 2,217,000; cap. Jackson: abbrev. **Miss., MS**

Mis·sis·sip·pi·an (-ən) *adj.* **1.** of the Mississippi River **2.** of the State of Mississippi **3.** designating or of the first coal-forming period of the Paleozoic Era in N. America —*n.* a native or inhabitant of Mississippi —**the Mississippian** the Mississippian Period or its rocks: see GEOLOGIC TIME CHART

mis·sive (mis′iv) *n.* [Fr. < ML. < L. pp. of *mittere:* see MISSION] a letter or written message

Mis·sour·i (mi zoor′ē) [< Algonquian, lit., people of the big canoes] **1.** river in the west central U.S., flowing from NW Mont. to the Mississippi: 2,466 mi. **2.** Middle Western State of the central U.S.: 69,686 sq. mi.; pop. 4,677,000; cap. Jefferson City: abbrev. **Mo., MO** —**from Missouri** [Colloq.] not easily convinced —**Mis·sour′i·an** *adj., n.*

mis·spell (mis spel′) *vt., vi.* **-spelled′** or **-spelt′, -spell′ing** to spell incorrectly

mis·spell·ing (-spel′iŋ) *n.* (an) incorrect spelling

mis·spend (-spend′) *vt.* **-spent′, -spend′ing** to spend improperly or wastefully

mis·state (-stāt′) *vt.* **-stat′ed, -stat′ing** to state incorrectly or falsely —**mis·state′ment** *n.*

☆**mis·step** (mis step′) *n.* **1.** a wrong or awkward step **2.** a mistake in conduct; social blunder

miss·y (mis′ē) *n., pl.* **miss′ies** [Colloq.] miss: used in speaking to or about a young girl

mist (mist) *n.* [OE.] **1.** a large mass of water vapor like a light fog [the morning *mist* along the river] **2.** a cloud of dust, gas, etc. **3.** a fine spray, as of perfume **4.** a film before the eyes, blurring the vision [through a *mist* of tears] **5.** anything that dims or confuses the understanding, memory, etc. [lost in the *mists* of the past] —*vt., vi.* to cover, dim, or blur with or as with a mist [windows *misted* by steam]

mis·take (mi stāk′) *vt.* **-took′, -tak′en** or obs. **-took′, -tak′ing** [ON. *mistaka,* to take wrongly] **1.** to get a wrong idea of; interpret or judge incorrectly [to *mistake* someone's motives] **2.** to take to be another; identify incorrectly [she *mistook* me for my sister] —*vi.* to make a mistake —*n.* **1.** a fault in understanding, interpretation, etc. **2.** a blunder; error [a *mistake* in subtraction] —see SYN. at ERROR —**and no mistake** [Colloq.] certainly —**mis·tak′a·ble** *adj.*

mis·tak·en (-stāk′'n) *adj.* **1.** wrong in what one thinks; having an incorrect understanding, perception, etc. [he is *mistaken* about that] **2.** incorrect; misunderstood [a *mistaken* idea] —**mis·tak′en·ly** *adv.*

mis·ter (mis′tər) *n.* [weakened form of MASTER] **1.** [M-] *a)* a title used in speaking to or of a man, placed before his name or office and usually written *Mr.* [*Mr.* Green; *Mr.* Mayor] ☆*b)* a title before the name of a place, occupation, etc. to designate an outstanding man in it [*Mr.* Television] **2.** [Colloq.] sir: in direct address, not followed by a name [what time is it, *mister?*] **3.** [Colloq.] one's husband: also used with *the*

mis·time (mis tīm′) *vt.* **-timed′, -tim′ing** **1.** to do or say at an inappropriate time **2.** to misjudge the time of

mis·tle·toe (mis′'l tō′) *n.* [< OE. < *mistel,* mistletoe + *tan,* a twig] **1.** an evergreen plant with yellowish-green leaves and white, poisonous berries, that grows as a parasite on trees **2.** a sprig of this, hung as a Christmas decoration

mis·took (mi stook′) *pt. & obs. pp.* of MISTAKE

mis·tral (mis′trəl, mi sträl′) *n.* [Fr. < Pr., lit., master-wind < L. < *magister,* MASTER] a cold, dry north wind that blows over the Mediterranean coast of France and nearby regions

mis·trans·late (mis trans′lāt, -tranz′-) *vt.* **-lat′ed, -lat′ing** to translate incorrectly —**mis′trans·la′tion** *n.*

MISTLETOE

mis·treat (mis trēt′) *vt.* to treat wrongly or badly —**mis·treat′ment** *n.*

mis·tress (mis′tris) *n.* [< OFr. fem. of *maistre,* MASTER] **1.** a woman who rules others or has control over something; specif., *a)* a woman head of a household, school, etc. *b)* [Chiefly Brit.] a woman schoolteacher **2.** [*sometimes* M-] something that is thought of as feminine and that has control, power, etc. [England was *Mistress* of the seas] **3.** a woman who has sexual relations with, and may be supported by, a man for a period of time without being married to him **4.** [Archaic] a sweetheart **5.** [**M-**] formerly, a title placed before the name of a woman: now replaced by *Mrs., Miss,* or *Ms.*

mis·tri·al (mis trī′əl) *n. Law* a trial having no legal effect or result because of *a)* an error in the proceedings ☆*b)* the inability of the jury to reach a verdict

mis·trust (-trust′) *n.* lack of trust or confidence; suspicion —*vt., vi.* to have no trust or confidence in (someone or something); doubt —**mis·trust′ful** *adj.* —**mis·trust′ful·ly** *adv.*

mist·y (mis′tē) *adj.* **mist′i·er, mist′i·est 1.** of or like mist **2.** characterized by or covered with mist **3.** *a)* blurred or dimmed, as by mist *b)* confusing or vague *[a misty* idea*]* —**mist′i·ly** *adv.* —**mist′i·ness** *n.*

mis·un·der·stand (mis′un dər stand′, mis un′-) *vt.* **-stood′, -stand′ing** to fail to understand correctly; miscomprehend or misinterpret

mis·un·der·stand·ing (-stan′diŋ) *n.* **1.** a failure to understand correctly **2.** a quarrel or disagreement

mis·un·der·stood (-stood′) *adj.* **1.** not properly understood **2.** not properly appreciated

mis·us·age (mis yōō′sij, -zij) *n.* **1.** incorrect usage, as of words **2.** bad or harsh treatment

mis·use (mis yōōz′; *for n.* -yōōs′) *vt.* **-used′, -us′ing 1.** to use improperly; misapply *[to misuse* one's time*]* **2.** to treat badly or harshly; abuse *[no good farmer misuses* his livestock*]* —*n.* incorrect or improper use *[the misuse* of an adverb for an adjective*]* —**mis·us′er** *n.*

Mitch·ell (mich′əl), **Maria** 1818–89; U.S. astronomer

Mitch·ell (mich′əl), **Mount** [after E. *Mitchell* (1793–1857), who first determined its height] mountain of the Appalachians, in western N.C.: highest peak of the eastern U.S.: 6,684 ft.

mite[1] (mīt) *n.* [OE.: for IE. base see MAD] any of a large number of tiny arachnids, often living as a parasite upon animals, insects, or plants, or living in prepared foods

mite[2] (mīt) *n.* [< MDu., ult. same as prec.] **1.** *a)* a very small sum of money *b)* formerly, a coin of very small value **2.** a bit; a little *[a mite* slow*]* **3.** a very small creature

mi·ter[1] (mīt′ər) *n.* [< OFr. < L. < Gr. *mitra,* a headband] **1.** a tall cap with peaks in front and back, worn by bishops and abbots as a mark of office **2.** the office or rank of a bishop —*vt.* to place in the office of bishop

mi·ter[2] (mīt′ər) *n.* [prob. < prec.] *Carpentry* **1.** a corner joint formed by fitting together two pieces cut at an angle: also **mi·ter joint 2.** either of the facing surfaces of such a joint —*vt.* **1.** to fit together in a miter **2.** to cut the edges to form a miter

miter box a device used to guide the saw in cutting wood at an angle for a miter joint

Mith·ri·da·tes VI (mith′rə dāt′ēz) 132?-63 B.C.; king of Pontus (120–63): called *the Great*

mit·i·gate (mit′ə gāt′) *vt., vi.* **-gat·ed, -gat′ing** [< L. pp. of *mitigare,* to make mild < *mitis,* mild + *agere,* to drive] to make or become milder or less severe *[an aspirin helped to mitigate* the pain*]* —see SYN. at RELIEVE —**mit′i·ga·ble** (-i gə b'l) *adj.* —**mit′i·ga′tion** *n.* —**mit′i·ga′tive** *adj.* —**mit′i·ga′tor** *n.* —**mit′i·ga·to′ry** (-gə tôr′ē) *adj.*

Mit·i·lí·ni (mit′'l ē′nē) *same as* LESBOS

mi·to·chon·dri·on (mīt′ə kän′drē ən) *n., pl.* **-dri·a** (-ə) [ModL. < Gr. *mitos,* a thread + *chondrion,* a small cartilage] a very small, usually rodlike structure in the cytoplasm of most cells: it contains enzymes that serve in the conversion of food energy to a form the cell can use

mi·to·sis (mī tō′sis, mi-) *n., pl.* **-ses** (-sēz) [ModL. < Gr. *mitos,* thread + -OSIS] *Biol.* the usual process of cell division, during which each chromosome is duplicated and the duplicates are then separated so that when the nucleus divides into two, each of the daughter nuclei has the normal number of chromosomes —**mi·tot′ic** (-tät′ik) *adj.* —**mi·tot′i·cal·ly** *adv.*

mi·tral (mī′trəl) *adj.* of or like a miter or the mitral valve

mitral valve the valve between the left atrium and left ventricle of the heart

mi·tre (mīt′ər) *n., vt.* **-tred, -tring** *Brit. sp. of* MITER

mitt (mit) *n.* [contr. < MITTEN] **1.** a woman's glove covering part of the arm, the hand, and sometimes part of the fingers

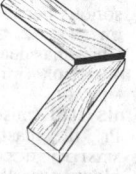

MITER

MITER JOINT

2. *same as* MITTEN ☆**3.** [Slang] a hand ☆**4.** *Baseball* a padded glove with a thumb but usually without separate fingers *[a catcher's mitt]*

mit·ten (mit′'n) *n.* [< OFr. *mitaine*] a glove with a thumb but no separately divided fingers

mitz·vah (mits vä′, mits′və) *n., pl.* **mitz′voth** (-vōt′) **mitz′vahs** [< Heb.] *Judaism* **1.** a commandment or moral rule, as one in the Bible **2.** an act in keeping with such a rule; good deed

mix (miks) *vt.* **mixed** or **mixt** (mikst), **mix′ing** [prob. < *mixt,* mixed < Fr. < L. pp. of *miscere,* to mix] **1.** to put or blend together in a single mass or compound *[mix* red and yellow paint to get orange*]* **2.** to make by blending ingredients *[to mix* a cake*]* **3.** to join; combine *[to mix* work and play*]* **4.** to cause to join or associate *[to mix* boys with girls in a school*]* —*vi.* **1.** to be mixed; be blended; mingle *[oil and water won't mix]* **2.** to associate or get along *[she mixes* well with all kinds of people*]* —*n.* **1.** a mixing or being mixed **2.** a state of confusion ☆**3.** a mixture, as of ingredients for making something *[a cake mix]* **4.** soda, ginger ale, etc. for mixing with alcoholic liquor —**mix up 1.** to mix thoroughly **2.** to confuse **3.** to involve (*in* some matter) *[mixed up* in a scandal*]* —**mix′a·ble** *adj.*

SYN.—**mix** implies a combining of things so that the resulting substance is the same throughout, whether or not the separate elements can be distinguished *[to mix* paints*]*; **mingle** usually implies that the separate elements can be distinguished *[mingled* feelings of joy and sorrow*]*; **blend** implies a mixing of different varieties to produce a desired quality *[a blended* tea, whiskey, etc.*]* or the mingling of different elements to form a pleasing whole *[a novel blending* fact and fiction*]*

mixed (mikst) *adj.* **1.** joined or blended in a single mass or compound **2.** made up of different parts, elements, races, etc. *[mixed* nuts; *mixed* neighborhoods*]* **3.** consisting of or involving both sexes *[mixed* company*]* **4.** confused; muddled *[he got his dates mixed]*

☆**mixed bag** a random gathering or mixture, esp. of very different sorts of things, people, etc.

mixed marriage marriage between persons of different religions or races

mixed media 1. the use of more than two media for an effect, as by combining acting, flashing lights, tape recordings, etc. **2.** *Painting* the use of different media, as oil and crayon, in the same composition

mixed number a number consisting of a whole number and a fraction, as 3 $^2/_3$

mix·er (mik′sər) *n.* **1.** one that mixes; specif., ☆*a)* a person as regards his ability to get along with others *[a good mixer] b)* a machine or an electric appliance for mixing *[concrete mixer]* ☆**2.** [Slang] a social gathering for getting people acquainted

mix·ture (miks′chər) *n.* **1.** a mixing or being mixed **2.** something mixed **3.** *Chem.* a substance containing two or more substances: distinguished from COMPOUND[1] in that the substances are not in fixed proportions, do not lose their individual characteristics, and can be separated by physical means

mix-up (miks′up′) *n.* **1.** a condition or instance of confusion **2.** [Colloq.] a fight

miz·zen, miz·en (miz′'n) *adj.* [< or akin to MFr. *misaine* < It. < L. *medianus:* see MEDIAN] of the mizzenmast —*n.* **1.** a fore-and-aft sail set on the mizzenmast: see illustration at MAINSAIL **2.** *clipped form of* MIZZENMAST

miz·zen·mast (-məst, -mast′) *n.* the mast nearest the stern in a ship with two or three masts: see illustration at MAINSAIL

mk. 1. *pl.* **mks.** mark (monetary unit) **2.** markka

mks, m.k.s., M.K.S. meter-kilogram-second

mkt. market

ML. Medieval (or Middle) Latin

ml. 1. mail **2.** milliliter(s): also **ml**

Mlle. *pl.* **Mlles.** Mademoiselle

MLowG. Middle Low German

mm, mm. 1. millimeter(s) **2.** [L. *millia*] thousands

MM. Messieurs

Mme. Madame

Mmes. Mesdames

MN Minnesota

Mn *Chem.* manganese

mne·mon·ic (nē män′ik) *adj.* [< Gr. < *mnēmōn,* mindful < *mnasthai,* to remember: for IE. base see MIND] **1.** helping, or meant to help, the memory **2.** of mnemonics or memory —**mne·mon′i·cal·ly** *adv.*

mne·mon·ics (-iks) *n.pl.* [*with sing. v.*] a technique for improving memory, as by the use of certain set phrases or rhymes

-mo (mō) [< a L. ending] *a suffix meaning* having (a specified number of) leaves as a result of folding a sheet of paper [*twelvemo*]

Mo *Chem.* molybdenum

Mo. 1. Missouri: also **MO** 2. Monday

mo. 1. money order 2. *pl.* **mos.** month

M.O., MO, m.o. money order

mo·a (mō′ə) *n.* [< native (Maori) name] any of a group of very large, flightless birds of New Zealand: they resembled the ostrich and are no longer living

Mo·ab (mō′ab) ancient kingdom east & south of the Dead Sea: see map at JUDEA —**Mo′ab·ite′** (-ə bīt′) *adj., n.*

moan (mōn) *n.* [prob. < base of OE. *mænan*, to complain: see MEAN¹] 1. formerly, a complaint; lamentation 2. a low, mournful sound of sorrow or pain 3. any similar sound, as of the wind —*vi.* 1. to make a moan 2. to complain, lament, etc. —*vt.* 1. to say with a moan 2. to complain about; bewail [to *moan* one's fate]

moat (mōt) *n.* [OFr. *mote*] a deep, broad ditch dug around a fortress or castle, and often filled with water, for protection against invasion —*vt.* to surround with or as with a moat

mob (mäb) *n.* [< L. *mobile* (*vulgus*), movable (crowd)] 1. a disorderly and lawless crowd; rabble 2. any crowd 3. the common people: a term of contempt 4. [Slang] a gang of criminals —*vt.* **mobbed, mob′bing** 1. to crowd around and attack, jostle, annoy, etc. 2. to fill with many people; throng [the theater was *mobbed*] —see SYN. at CROWD —**mob′bish** *adj.*

mob·cap (mäb′kap′) *n.* [< MDu. *mop*, woman's cap + CAP] formerly, a woman's cap, worn indoors, with a high, puffy crown, often tied under the chin

Mo·bile (mō bēl′, mō′bēl) [< Fr. < AmInd.] seaport in SW Ala., on an arm (**Mobile Bay**) of the Gulf of Mexico: pop. 190,000

mo·bile (mō′b'l, -bīl; *also, & for n. usually,* -bēl) *adj.* [OFr. < L. *mobilis* < *movere*, to MOVE] 1. *a*) moving, or able to move, from place to place *b*) movable by means of a motor vehicle [a *mobile* home] 2. that can change rapidly or easily, as to suit moods or needs; flexible, adaptable, fluid, etc. [she has *mobile* features] 3. designating or of a society in which one may move freely or advance from one class to another —*n.* an abstract sculpture with parts that can move, as an arrangement of thin forms, rings, etc. balanced and suspended in midair —**mo·bil·i·ty** (mō bil′ə tē) *n.*

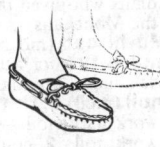

MOBILE

☆**mobile home** a large trailer outfitted as a home, to be parked somewhere more or less permanently

mo·bi·lize (mō′bə līz′) *vt.* **-lized′, -liz′ing** 1. *a*) to make movable *b*) to put into motion, circulation, or use [the body *mobilizes* its defenses against disease] 2. to make ready for immediate active service in war [to *mobilize* the armed forces] 3. to organize (people, resources, etc.) for any active service or use —*vi.* to become mobilized, as for war —**mo′bi·liz′a·ble** *adj.* —**mo·bi·li·za′tion** *n.* —**mo′bi·liz′er** *n.*

Mö·bi·us strip (mā′bē əs, mō′-) [after A. *Möbius* (1790-1868), G. mathematician] a surface with only one side, formed from a strip of paper given a half twist and then pasted together

mob·oc·ra·cy (mäb äk′rə sē) *n., pl.* **-cies** [MOB + (DEM)OCRACY] 1. rule by a mob 2. the mob as ruler

mob·ster (mäb′stər) *n.* [Slang] a gangster

Mo·çam·bi·que (mōō′səm bē′kə) *Port.* name of MOZAMBIQUE

☆**moc·ca·sin** (mäk′ə s'n) *n.* [< Algonquian] 1. a heelless slipper of soft, flexible leather, worn orig. by N. American Indians 2. a similar slipper, but with a hard sole and heel 3. *same as* WATER MOCCASIN

☆**moccasin flower** *same as* LADY-SLIPPER

mo·cha (mō′kə) *n.* [after *Mocha*, seaport in Yemen] 1. a choice grade of coffee grown orig. in Arabia 2. [Colloq.] any coffee 3. a flavoring made from coffee or coffee and chocolate 4. a type of soft,

MOCCASINS

velvety leather —*adj.* 1. flavored with coffee or coffee and chocolate 2. reddish-brown

mock (mäk) *vt.* [OFr. *mocquer*, to mock] 1. to make fun of; ridicule [many scientists *mocked* Darwin's theories] 2. to imitate or mimic, as in fun or contempt [it is cruel to *mock* a limping person] 3. to lead on and disappoint; deceive [the weather *mocked* them by changing suddenly] 4. to defeat or make useless [the high wall *mocked* his hopes of escaping] —*vi.* to express scorn, ridicule, etc. —*n.* 1. a mocking 2. an object of scorn 3. an imitation —*adj.* sham; false; imitation [a *mock* battle] —see SYN. at RIDICULE —**mock′er** *n.* —**mock′ing·ly** *adv.*

mock·er·y (mäk′ər ē) *n., pl.* **-er·ies** 1. a mocking 2. a person or thing deserving to be made fun of 3. a very poor imitation [a plastic rose is a *mockery* of the real flower] 4. useless or disappointing effort; futility [rain made a *mockery* of our picnic]

mock-he·ro·ic (-hi rō′ik) *adj.* that mocks or makes fun of any heroic manner, action, or character —**mock′-he·ro′i·cal·ly** *adv.*

☆**mock·ing·bird** (mäk′iŋ burd′) *n.* an American songbird able to imitate many birdcalls

mock orange ☆any of a group of shrubs with fragrant white flowers like those of the orange

mock turtle soup a soup made from calf's head, veal, etc., spiced to taste like turtle soup

mock-up (mäk′up′) *n.* a scale model or full-sized copy of a structure or apparatus, used for instructional or experimental purposes

mod (mäd) *adj.* [< MOD(ERN)] [*also* M-] designating a showy or very ornate style of clothing popular among young people, originating in England in the 1960's

mod. 1. moderate 2. modern

mod·al (mōd′'l) *adj.* of or indicating a mode or mood; specif., *Gram.* of or expressing mood [a *modal* verb] —**mo·dal·i·ty** (mō dal′ə tē) *n., pl.* **-ties** —**mod′al·ly** *adv.*

modal auxiliary an auxiliary verb used with another to indicate its mood: *can, may, might, must, should,* and *would* are *modal auxiliaries*

mode (mōd) *n.* [L. *modus*, measure, manner: for IE. base see MEDICAL] 1. a manner or way of acting, doing, or being [a new *mode* of transportation] 2. [Fr. < L. *modus*] customary usage, or current fashion or style [women dressed in the latest *mode*] 3. *Gram. same as* MOOD² 4. *Music* the arrangement, or any specific arrangement, of tones and semitones in a scale 5. *Statistics* the value, number, etc. occurring most frequently in a given series —see SYN. at FASHION and METHOD

mod·el (mäd′'l) *n.* [< Fr. < It. *modello*, dim. of *modo* < L. *modus*, MODE] 1. *a*) a small copy or representation of an existing or planned object, as a ship, building, etc. *b*) *same as* ARCHETYPE (sense 1) *c*) a representation of the supposed structure of something [a *model* of a uranium atom] *d*) a piece of sculpture in wax or clay from which a finished work in bronze, marble, etc. is to be made 2. a person or thing considered as a standard of excellence to be imitated [he is the very *model* of honesty] 3. a style or design [a 1972 *model*] 4. *a*) a person who poses for an artist or photographer *b*) any person or thing serving as a subject for an artist *c*) a person employed to display clothes by wearing them —*adj.* 1. serving as a model, or standard of excellence [a *model* student] 2. representative of others of the same kind, style, etc.; typical [a *model* home] —*vt.* **-eled** or **-elled, -el·ing** or **-el·ling** 1. *a*) to make a model of *b*) to plan or form after a model [a museum *modeled* after a Greek temple] *c*) to make conform to a standard of excellence [to *model* one's behavior on that of one's father] 2. to shape or form in or as in clay, wax, etc. 3. to display (a dress, etc.) by wearing —*vi.* 1. to make a model of models [to *model* in clay] ☆2. to serve as a model (sense 4) —**mod′el·er, mod′el·ler** *n.*

mod·er·ate (mäd′ər it; *for v.* -ə rāt′) *adj.* [< L. pp. of *moderare*, to restrain] 1. within reasonable limits; avoiding extremes; temperate [a *moderate* fee] 2. mild; not violent [*moderate* weather] 3. of average or medium quality, range, etc. [*moderate* skills] —*n.* a person holding moderate views, as in politics or religion —*vt., vi.* **-at′ed, -at′ing** 1. to make or become moderate 2. to serve as chairman at (a meeting, etc.) —**mod′er·ate·ly** *adv.* —**mod′er·ate·ness** *n.*

SYN.—moderate and **temperate** are often used in place of each other in the sense of keeping within reasonable limits, but in narrow usage, **moder-**

ate implies merely that excesses or extremes are absent [*moderate* demands], while **temperate** suggests that one is making a definite effort to control oneself [a *temperate* reply] —**ANT. excessive, extreme**

mod·er·a·tion (mäd/ə rā/shən) *n.* **1.** a moderating, or bringing within limits **2.** a keeping away from extremes **3.** absence of violence; calmness —**in moderation** to a moderate degree; without excess

mod·e·ra·to (-rät/ō) *adj., adv.* [It.] *Music* with moderation in tempo

mod·er·a·tor (mäd/ə rāt/ər) *n.* a person or thing that moderates; specif., a person who serves as chairman in conducting a meeting, debate, etc. —**mod/er·a/tor·ship/** *n.*

mod·ern (mäd/ərn) *adj.* [< Fr. < LL. *modernus* < L. *modo*, just now, orig. a form of *modus:* see MODE] **1.** of the present or recent times; specif., *a)* of the latest styles, methods, ideas, etc.; up-to-date [a *modern* home, with air conditioning] *b)* designating or of certain present-day trends in art, music, literature, dance, etc. **2.** of the period of history from c.1450 A.D. to now **3.** [*often* M-] designating the most recent stage of a language [*Modern* English] —*n.* **1.** a person living in modern times **2.** a person with modern ideas, standards, etc. —see SYN. at NEW —**mo·der/ni·ty** (mä dur/nə tē, mə-) *n., pl.* **-ties** —**mod/ern·ly** *adv.* —**mod/ern·ness** *n.*

☆**modern dance** a form of dance as a performing art which has body movements and rhythms less formal than in classical ballet and is less firmly related to any fixed musical form

Modern English the English language since about the mid-15th cent.: see also EARLY MODERN ENGLISH

Modern Hebrew Hebrew in post-Biblical times, esp. as the language of modern Israel

mod·ern·ism (-iz'm) *n. a)* modern practices, ideas, etc., or devotion to these *b)* a modern idiom, practice, or usage **2.** [M-] any movement to restate Christian doctrine in the light of modern science, etc. —**mod/ern·ist** *n., adj.*

mod·ern·is·tic (mäd/ər nis/tik) *adj.* **1.** of or related to modernism or modernists **2.** modern: used esp. in speaking of certain present-day trends and schools of art, music, etc., sometimes scornfully —see SYN. at NEW —**mod/ern·is/ti·cal·ly** *adv.*

mod·ern·ize (mäd/ər nīz/) *vt., vi.* **-ized/, -iz/ing** to make or become modern in style, design, methods, etc. —**mod/ern·i·za/tion** *n.* —**mod/ern·iz/er** *n.*

Modern Latin the Latin used since c.1500, chiefly in scientific literature

mod·est (mäd/ist) *adj.* [< Fr. < L. *modestus* < *modus:* see MODE] **1.** having or showing a moderate opinion of one's own value, abilities, etc.; not vain [a *modest* hero] **2.** not forward; shy or reserved [*modest* behavior] **3.** behaving, dressing, etc. properly or decently **4.** moderate or reasonable; not extreme [a *modest* request] **5.** quiet and humble in appearance, style, etc. [a *modest* home] —see SYN. at SHY[1] —**mod/est·ly** *adv.*

Mo·des·to (mə des/tō) [Sp., lit., modest] city in C Calif.: pop. 62,000

mod·es·ty (mäd/is tē) *n.* the quality or state of being modest; specif., *a)* shy or humble behavior *b)* lack of excesses; moderation *c)* proper behavior; decency

ModGr. Modern Greek

ModHeb. Modern Hebrew

mod·i·cum (mäd/i kəm) *n.* [L., neut. of *modicus*, moderate] a small amount; bit [a *modicum* of common sense]

mod·i·fi·ca·tion (mäd/ə fi kā/shən) *n.* a modifying or being modified; specif., *a)* a partial or slight change in form [the new model has a few *modifications*] *b)* a product of this *c)* a slight reduction [a *modification* in price] *d)* a qualification or limitation of meaning *e) Biol.* a change in an organism that is caused by its environment and that cannot be passed on through inheritance

mod·i·fi·er (mäd/ə fī/ər) *n.* a person or thing that modifies; esp., a word, phrase, or clause that limits the meaning of another word or phrase [adjectives and adverbs are *modifiers*]

mod·i·fy (mäd/ə fī/) *vt.* **-fied/, -fy/ing** [< MFr. < L. *modificare*, to limit < *modus* (see MODE) + *facere*, DO[1]] **1.** to change or alter, esp. slightly or partially [modern exploration has *modified* our maps of Antarctica] **2.** to limit or lessen slightly [to *modify* a penalty] **3.** *Gram.* to limit the meaning of; qualify ["old" *modifies* "man" in *old man*] **4.** *Linguis.* to change (a vowel) by umlaut —*vi.* to be modified —see SYN. at CHANGE —**mod/i·fi/a·ble** *adj.*

Mo·di·glia·ni (mō/dē lyä/nē), **A·me·de·o** (ä/me de/ō) 1884-1920; It. painter, in France

mod·ish (mōd/ish) *adj.* in the latest style; fashionable —**mod/ish·ly** *adv.* —**mod/ish·ness** *n.*

mo·diste (mō dēst/) *n.* [Fr. < *mode:* see MODE] a woman who makes or deals in fashionable clothes, hats, etc. for women: somewhat old-fashioned term

ModL. Modern Latin

mod·u·lar (mäj/ə lər) *adj.* **1.** of a module or modulus ☆**2.** designating or of units of standardized size, design, etc. that can be arranged or fitted together in various ways

mod·u·late (-lāt/) *vt.* **-lat/ed, -lat/ing** [< L. pp. of *modulari* < dim. of *modus:* see MODE] **1.** to regulate, adjust, or adapt [to *modulate* the light in a room] **2.** to vary the pitch, intensity, etc. of (the voice) **3.** *Radio* to vary the amplitude, frequency, or phase of (an oscillation, as a carrier wave) in accordance with some signal —*vi.* to shift from one key to another within a musical composition —**mod/u·la/tion** *n.* —**mod/u·la/tor** *n.* —**mod/u·la·to/ry** *adj.*

mod·ule (mäj/ōōl) *n.* [Fr. < L. dim. of *modus:* see MODE] **1.** a standard or unit of measurement, as in architecture ☆**2.** *a)* any of a set of units, as cabinets, designed to be arranged or joined in various ways *b)* a detachable section, compartment, or unit with a specific function, as in a spacecraft *c) Electronics* a compact assembly functioning as a component of a larger unit

mod·u·lus (mäj/ə ləs) *n., pl.* **-u·li/** (-lī/) [ModL. < L.: see prec.] **1.** *Math. a)* same as ABSOLUTE VALUE (sense 2) *b)* a number or quantity that gives the same remainder when it is the divisor of each of two quantities **2.** *Physics* a constant expressing the measure of some property, as elasticity

‡**mo·dus o·pe·ran·di** (mō/dəs äp/ə ran/dī, -dē) [L.] mode of operation; way of doing or making; procedure

‡**modus vi·ven·di** (vi ven/dī, -dē) [L.] **1.** manner of living or of getting along **2.** a compromise agreed on until a final agreement can be reached

Moe·si·a (mē/shē ə) ancient Roman province in SE Europe, south of the Danube

Mo·ga·di·shu (mō/gä dē/shōō) capital of Somalia; seaport on the Indian Ocean: pop. 100,000

Mo·gul (mō/gul, -g'l; mō gul/) *n.* [Per. *Mughul*] **1.** a Mongol, or Mongolian; esp., any of the Mongolian conquerors of India or their descendants **2.** [m-] a powerful or important person

mo·hair (mō/her) *n.* [< OIt. < Ar. *mukhayyar*] **1.** the hair of the Angora goat **2.** yarn or a fabric made from this hair —*adj.* of mohair

Mo·ham·med (mō ham/id) 570?-632 A.D.; Arabian prophet; founder of the Moslem religion

Mo·ham·med·an (mō ham/i d'n) *adj.* of Mohammed or the Moslem religion —*n. same as* MOSLEM: term used mainly by non-Moslems

Mo·ham·med·an·ism (-iz'm) *n. same as* ISLAM: term used mainly by non-Moslems

Mo·ha·ve (mō hä/vē) *n.* [< Mohave words for "three" & "mountain"] **1.** *pl.* **-ves, -ve** a member of an Indian tribe living along the Colorado River in Arizona **2.** their language —*adj.* of the Mohaves

Mo·hawk[1] (mō/hôk) *n.* [< Algonquian word meaning "man-eaters"] **1.** *pl.* **-hawks, -hawk** a member of an Iroquoian Indian tribe orig. of the Mohawk Valley, New York, now in Canada and New York **2.** their language —*adj.* of the Mohawks

Mo·hawk[2] (mō/hôk) [< prec.] river in central and eastern N.Y., flowing into the Hudson

Mo·he·gan (mō hē/gən) *n.* [< Algonquian, lit., a wolf] **1.** *pl.* **-gans, -gan** a member of a Mahican tribe of Algonquian Indians who lived in Connecticut **2.** *same as* MAHICAN —*adj.* of the Mohegans

Mo·hi·can (mō hē/kən) *n., adj. same as* MAHICAN

moi·e·ty (moi/ə tē) *n., pl.* **-ties** [< OFr. < L. < *medius*, middle] **1.** a half **2.** an indefinite part

moil (moil) *vi.* [< OFr. *moillier*, to moisten < L. *mollis*, soft] to work hard; toil —*vt.* [Archaic] to moisten or soil —*n.* **1.** hard work; toil **2.** confusion; turmoil —**moil/er** *n.*

moire (mwär, môr) *n.* [Fr., watered silk < E. MOHAIR] a fabric, as silk or rayon, having a watered, or wavy, pattern

moi·ré (mwä rā/, mô-; môr/ā) *adj.* [Fr.] having a watered, or wavy, pattern —*n.* **1.** a watered pattern pressed into cloth, etc. with engraved rollers **2.** *same as* MOIRE

MODULES
(sense 2a)

moist (moist) *adj.* [OFr. *moiste* < L. *mucidus*, moldy < *mucus*, MUCUS] **1.** slightly wet; damp **2.** tearful [*moist eyes*] —see SYN. at WET —**moist′ly** *adv.* —**moist′ness** *n.*

mois·ten (mois′'n) *vt., vi.* to make or become moist —**mois′-ten·er** *n.*

mois·ture (mois′chər) *n.* water, etc. causing a slight wetness or dampness —**mois′ture·less** *adj.*

mois·tur·ize (-īz′) *vt., vi.* **-ized′, -iz′ing** to add or restore moisture to (the skin, air, etc.) —**mois′tur·iz′er** *n.*

Mo·ja·ve (mō hä′vē) *n., adj. same as* MOHAVE

Mojave Desert desert in SE Calif.

mol (mōl) *n. same as* MOLE[4]

MOL manned orbiting laboratory

mol. **1.** molecular **2.** molecule

mo·lar[1] (mō′lər) *adj.* [< L. < *mola*, millstone] **1.** used for or capable of grinding **2.** designating or of a tooth or teeth adapted for grinding —*n.* a molar tooth: in man there are twelve molars

mo·lar[2] (mō′lər) *adj. Chem.* relating to the mole; specif., designating a solution containing one mole of solute per liter of solution

mo·las·ses (mə las′iz) *n.* [< Port. *melaco* < LL. *mellaceum*, must < L. < *mel*, honey] a thick, usually dark-brown syrup produced during the refining of sugar, or from sorghum, etc.

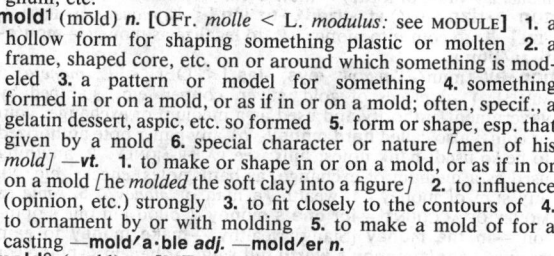

UPPER MOLARS

LOWER MOLARS

mold[1] (mōld) *n.* [OFr. *molle* < L. *modulus*: see MODULE] **1.** a hollow form for shaping something plastic or molten **2.** a frame, shaped core, etc. on or around which something is modeled **3.** a pattern or model for something **4.** something formed in or on a mold, or as if in or on a mold; often, specif., a gelatin dessert, aspic, etc. so formed **5.** form or shape, esp. that given by a mold **6.** special character or nature [men of his *mold*] —*vt.* **1.** to make or shape in or on a mold, or as if in or on a mold [he *molded* the soft clay into a figure] **2.** to influence (opinion, etc.) strongly **3.** to fit closely to the contours of **4.** to ornament by or with molding **5.** to make a mold of for a casting —**mold′a·ble** *adj.* —**mold′er** *n.*

mold[2] (mōld) *n.* [ME. *moul*: sp. prob. influenced by MOLD[3]] **1.** a fuzzy or furry fungous growth on organic matter, esp. when the matter is damp or decaying **2.** any fungus producing such a growth —*vt., vi.* to make or become moldy

mold[3] (mōld) *n.* [OE. *molde*, earth: for IE. base see MILL[1]] loose, soft soil, esp. when rich with decayed organic matter

Mol·da·vi·a (mäl dā′vē ə, -dāv′yə) **1.** region in E Romania **2.** republic of the U.S.S.R., near this region: 13,000 sq. mi.; pop. 3,500,000; cap. Kishinev: in full, **Moldavian Soviet Socialist Republic** —**Mol·da′vi·an** *adj., n.*

mold·board (mōld′bôrd′) *n.* **1.** a curved iron plate on a plowshare, for turning over the soil ☆**2.** a large plate like this at the front of a bulldozer or snowplow, bent at an angle to push material aside **3.** one of the boards used to form a mold for concrete

mold·er (mōl′dər) *vi., vt.* [see MOLD[3] & -ER] to crumble into dust; decay; waste away [iron in time *molders* away] —see SYN. at DECAY

mold·ing (mōl′diŋ) *n.* **1.** the act of one that molds **2.** something molded **3.** *a)* the ornamental outline of a cornice, jamb, etc. *b)* a cornice or similar ornamentation that sticks out *c)* a shaped strip of wood, etc., for finishing or decorating walls (esp. near the ceiling), furniture, etc.

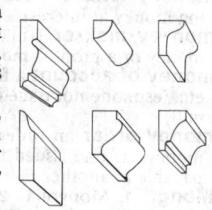

MOLDINGS

mold·y (mōl′dē) *adj.* **mold′i·er, mold′i·est 1.** covered with a growth of mold [*moldy* bread] **2.** musty or stale, as from age or decay [a *moldy* smell] —**mold′i·ness** *n.*

mole[1] (mōl) *n.* [OE. *mal*] a small, usually dark-colored spot on the human skin: it is there at birth, often slightly raised and hairy

mole[2] (mōl) *n.* [< or akin to MDu. *mol*] a small, burrowing, insect-eating mammal with small eyes and ears, shovellike forefeet, and soft fur: moles live mainly underground

mole[3] (mōl) *n.* [< Fr. < LGr. < L. *moles*, a mass < IE. base *molo-*, to strive] **1.** a breakwater **2.** a harbor formed by a breakwater

mole[4] (mōl) *n.* [< G. *mol*] *Chem.* the quantity of a substance having a weight in grams numerically equal to its molecular weight: one mole of a substance contains 6.02257×10^{23} molecules

Mo·lech (mō′lek) *Bible* an ancient god of the Phoenicians, etc., to whom children were sacrificed by burning —*n.* anything demanding terrible sacrifice

mo·lec·u·lar (mə lek′yə lər) *adj.* of, produced by, or existing between molecules —**mo·lec′u·lar′i·ty** (-lar′ə tē) *n.* —**mo·lec′u·lar·ly** *adv.*

molecular biology the branch of biology dealing with the chemical and physical structure and activities of the molecules in living matter

molecular weight the sum of the atomic weights of all atoms in a given molecule

mol·e·cule (mäl′ə kyōol′) *n.* [< Fr. < ModL. *molecula*, dim. of L. *moles*, a mass: see MOLE[3]] **1.** the smallest particle of an element or compound that can exist in the free state and still retain the characteristics of the element or compound: the molecules of elements consist of one atom or two or more similar atoms; those of compounds consist of two or more different atoms **2.** a small particle

mole·hill (mōl′hil′) *n.* a small ridge or mound of earth, formed by a burrowing mole —**make a mountain out of a molehill** to treat a small problem as a large, important one

mole·skin (-skin′) *n.* **1.** the soft, dark-gray skin of the mole, used as fur **2.** *a)* a strong cotton fabric with a soft nap, used for work clothes, etc. *b)* [*pl.*] trousers of this **3.** a soft fabric, often with an adhesive backing, used for foot pads

mo·lest (mə lest′, mō-) *vt.* [< OFr. < L. < *molestus*, troublesome < *moles*, a burden: see MOLE[3]] **1.** to annoy or meddle with so as to trouble or harm ☆**2.** to make improper sexual advances to —**mo·les·ta·tion** (mō′les tā′shən, mäl′əs-) *n.* —**mo·lest′er** *n.*

Mo·lière (mōl yer′; *Fr.* mô lyer′) (pseud. of *Jean Baptiste Poquelin*) 1622–73; Fr. dramatist

moll (mäl) *n.* [< var. of name MOLLY] [Slang] **1.** a gangster's mistress **2.** a prostitute

mol·lah (mäl′ə) *n. same as* MULLAH

mol·li·fy (mäl′ə fī′) *vt.* **-fied′, -fy′ing** [< MFr. < LL. < L. *mollis*, soft + *facere*, to make] **1.** to soothe, pacify, or appease [she *mollified* the crying child] **2.** to make less severe or violent [he *mollified* his criticism] —see SYN. at PACIFY —**mol′li·fi·ca′tion** *n.* —**mol′li·fi′er** *n.*

mol·lusk, mol·lusc (mäl′əsk) *n.* [< Fr. < ModL. < L. *molluscus*, soft < *mollis*, soft] any of a large group of animals, including clams, oysters, snails, squids, etc., having a soft body without a backbone, often enclosed in a hard shell and usually having gills and a foot —**mol·lus·kan, mol·lus·can** (mə lus′kən) *adj., n.*

Mol·ly (mäl′ē) [dim. of MARY] a feminine name: also **Mol′lie**

mol·ly (mäl′ē) *n., pl.* **-lies** [< ModL. < F. N. *Mollien* (1758–1850), Fr. statesman] any of certain brightly colored tropical and subtropical American fishes often kept in aquariums: also **mol′lie**

mol·ly·cod·dle (mäl′ē käd′'l) *n.* [MOLLY + CODDLE] a man or boy used to being coddled, or protected, pampered, etc. —*vt.* **-dled, -dling** to pamper; coddle —**mol′ly·cod′dler** *n.*

Mo·loch (mō′läk, mäl′ək) *same as* MOLECH

Mo·lo·kai (mō′lō kī′) [Haw.] island of Hawaii: site of a leper colony

Mo·lo·tov cocktail (mô′lə täf) [after V. M. *Molotov* (1890–), Russ. statesman] [Slang] a bottle of gasoline, etc., plugged with a rag, ignited, and hurled as a grenade against vehicles, etc.

molt (mōlt) *vi.* [OE. (*be*)*mutian*, to exchange < L. *mutare*, to MUTATE] to shed skin, feathers, etc., before replacement by a new growth: said of reptiles, birds, etc. —*vt.* to shed thus —*n.* **1.** a molting **2.** the parts shed —**molt′er** *n.*

mol·ten (mōl′t'n) *archaic pp. of* MELT —*adj.* **1.** melted or made liquid by heat [*molten* iron] **2.** made by being melted and cast in a mold [a *molten* statue]

mol·to (mōl′tō) *adv.* [It.] *Music* very; much

---

fat, āpe, cär; ten, ēven; is, bīte; gō, hôrn, tōōl, lŏŏk; oil, out; up, fur; get; joy; yet; chin; she; thin, *th*en; zh, leisure; ŋ, ring; ə for *a* in *ago*, *e* in *agent*, *i* in *sanity*, *o* in *comply*, *u* in *focus*; ′ as in *able* (ā′b'l); Fr. bâl; ë, Fr. coeur; ö, Fr. feu; Fr. mon; ô, Fr. coq; ü, Fr. duc; r, Fr. cri; H, G. ich; kh, G. doch; ‡foreign; ☆ Americanism; < derived from. See inside front cover.

Mo·luc·cas (mō luk′əz) group of islands in Indonesia, between Celebes & New Guinea: also **Molucca Islands**

mol. wt. molecular weight

mo·lyb·de·nite (mə lib′də nīt′) *n.* a scaly or layered, lead-gray ore of molybdenum, MoS₂

mo·lyb·de·num (-nəm) *n.* [ModL. < L. *molybdaena* < Gr. *molybdos*, lead] a soft, silver-white metallic chemical element, used in alloys, etc.: symbol, Mo; at. wt., 95.94; at. no., 42

mom (mäm) *n.* [Colloq.] MOTHER¹

Mom·ba·sa (mäm bä′sə, -bas′ə) seaport on the SE coast of Kenya: pop. 246,000

mo·ment (mō′mənt) *n.* [< L. *momentum*, movement < *movere*, to MOVE] **1.** an indefinitely brief period of time; instant [to pause for a *moment*] **2.** a definite point in time [at that *moment* the bell rang] **3.** a brief time of being important or outstanding [they had their *moment* in history] **4.** importance; consequence [news of great *moment*] **5.** *Mech. a)* the tendency to cause rotation about a point or axis *b)* a measure of this —see SYN. at IMPORTANCE —**the moment** the present time

mo·men·tar·i·ly (mō′mən ter′ə lē) *adv.* **1.** for a moment or short time [I saw him *momentarily* between classes] **2.** in an instant **3.** from moment to moment; at any moment [we expect him *momentarily*]

mo·men·tar·y (mō′mən ter′ē) *adj.* **1.** lasting for only a moment; passing [a *momentary* pain] **2.** [Now Rare] recurring every moment **3.** likely to occur at any moment —see SYN. at TRANSIENT —**mo′men·tar′i·ness** *n.*

mo·ment·ly (mō′mənt lē) *adv.* **1.** every moment **2.** at any moment **3.** for a single moment

mo·men·tous (mō men′təs) *adj.* of great moment; very important [a *momentous* decision] —**mo·men′tous·ly** *adv.* —**mo·men′tous·ness** *n.*

mo·men·tum (mō men′təm) *n., pl.* **-tums, -ta** (-tə) [ModL. < L.: see MOMENT] **1.** the force of a moving object **2.** strength or force that keeps growing [a campaign that gained *momentum*] **3.** *Physics & Mech.* the quantity of motion of a moving body, equal to the product of its mass and its velocity

Momm·sen (mōm′zən; *E.* mäm′s'n, -z'n), **The·o·dor** (tā′ō dōr) 1817–1903; Ger. historian

mom·my (mäm′ē) *n., pl.* **-mies** *child's term for* MOTHER¹

mon- *same as* MONO-: used before a vowel

Mon. **1.** Monastery **2.** Monday **3.** Monsignor

mon. **1.** monastery **2.** monetary

Mon·a·co (män′ə kō, mə nä′kō) a small country on the Mediterranean; enclave in SE France: 1/2 sq. mi.; pop. 23,000

mo·nad (mō′nad, män′ad) *n.* [LL. *monadis*, genitive of *monas*, a unit < Gr. < *monos*, alone] **1.** a unit; something simple, which cannot be divided **2.** *Biol.* any simple, single-celled organism **3.** *Chem.* an atom, element, or radical with a valence of one —*adj.* of a monad or monads —**mo·nad′ic, mo·nad′i·cal** *adj.*

mo·nan·drous (mə nan′drəs) *adj.* [Gr. *monandros*, having one husband] **1.** having only one husband at a time **2.** having only one stamen, as some flowers —**mo·nan′dry** (-drē) *n.*

mon·arch (män′ərk, -ärk) *n.* [< LL. < Gr. < *monos*, alone + *archein*, to rule] **1.** the hereditary head of a state; king, queen, etc. **2.** a person or thing superior to others of the same kind **3.** a large, migrating butterfly of N. America

mo·nar·chal (mə när′k'l) *adj.* of, like, or suitable for a monarch: also **mo·nar′chi·al** (-kē əl) —**mo·nar′chal·ly** *adv.*

mo·nar·chi·cal (-ki k'l) *adj.* **1.** of or like a monarch or monarchy **2.** favoring a monarchy Also **mo·nar′chic** —**mo·nar′chi·cal·ly** *adv.*

mon·ar·chism (män′ər kiz'm, -är-) *n.* monarchical principles or devotion to these principles —**mon′ar·chist** *n., adj.* —**mon′ar·chis′tic** *adj.*

mon·ar·chy (-kē) *n., pl.* **-ar·chies** a government or state headed by a monarch

mon·as·ter·y (män′ə ster′ē) *n., pl.* **-ter′ies** [< LL. < LGr. *monastērion < monazein*, to be alone < *monos*, alone] the residence of a group of people, esp. monks, retired from the world and living according to religious vows —**mon′as·te′ri·al** (-stir′ē əl) *adj.*

mo·nas·tic (mə nas′tik) *adj.* **1.** of or characteristic of monasteries **2.** of or characteristic of monks or nuns; ascetic;

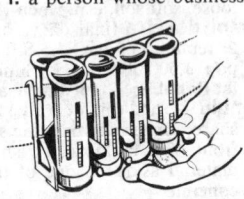

MONARCH BUTTERFLY

self-denying Also **mo·nas′ti·cal** —*n.* a monastic person —**mo·nas′ti·cal·ly** *adv.*

mo·nas·ti·cism (-tə siz'm) *n.* the monastic system, state, or way of life

mon·au·ral (män ôr′'l) *adj.* [MON(O)- + AURAL] designating or of sound reproduction that uses only one source of sound, giving a monophonic effect —**mon·au′ral·ly** *adv.*

mon·a·zite (män′ə zīt′) *n.* [G. *monazit* < Gr. *monazein*, to be alone] a native phosphate of the rare-earth metals, a major source of cerium, lanthanum, etc. and thorium

Mon·day (mun′dē, -dā) *n.* [OE. *monandæg*, moon's day] the second day of the week

Mon·days (-dēz, -dāz) *adv.* on or during every Monday [*Mondays* she does the laundry]

‡**mon Dieu** (môn dyö′) [Fr.] my God

Mon·dri·an (môn′drē än′), **Piet** (pēt) (born *Pieter Cornelis Mondriaan*) 1872–1944; Du. painter

mo·ne·cious (mə nē′shəs, mō-) *adj. same as* MONOECIOUS

☆**Mo·nel metal** (mō nel′) [after A. *Monell* (d. 1921), U.S. manufacturer] *a trademark for* an alloy mainly of nickel and copper, very resistant to rusting

Mo·net (mō nā′, mə-; *Fr.* mô ne′), **Claude** 1840–1926; Fr. painter

mon·e·tar·y (män′ə ter′ē, mun′-) *adj.* [< LL. < L. *moneta*, a MINT¹] **1.** of the coinage or currency of a country: see table of MONETARY UNITS on next page **2.** in money; pecuniary [the *monetary* value of a car] —**mon′e·tar′i·ly** *adv.*

mon·e·tize (-tīz′) *vt.* **-tized′, -tiz′ing** [< L. *moneta*, a MINT¹ + -IZE] **1.** to coin into money **2.** to legalize as money —**mon′e·ti·za′tion** *n.*

mon·ey (mun′ē) *n., pl.* **-eys, -ies** [< OFr. < L. *moneta*, a MINT¹] **1.** *a)* pieces of gold, silver, copper, etc., stamped by government authority and used as a medium of exchange; coin or coins: also called **hard money** *b)* any paper note authorized to be so used; bank notes; bills: see PAPER MONEY **2.** anything used as a medium of exchange, as bank notes, checks, etc. **3.** any sum of money **4.** wealth [a man of *money*] **5.** *same as* MONEY OF ACCOUNT —**for one's money** [Colloq.] in one's opinion —**in the money** [Slang] wealthy —**make money** to gain profits —**one's money's worth** full value or benefit —**place** (or **put**) **money on** to bet on —**put money into** to invest money in —**mon′ey·less** *adj.*

mon·ey·bag (-bag′) *n.* **1.** a bag for money **2.** [*pl., with sing. v.*] [Colloq.] a rich person

mon·ey·chang·er (-chān′jər) *n.* **1.** a person whose business is money-changing ☆**2.** a device holding stacked coins for making change quickly

mon·ey·chang·ing (-chān′jiŋ) *n.* the exchanging of currency, usually the currency of one country for that of another, esp. at an established or official rate

mon·eyed (mun′ēd) *adj.* **1.** wealthy; rich **2.** of, from, or representing money [*moneyed* interests]

mon·ey·grub·ber (-grub′ər) *n.* a person who is greedy to get or make money —**mon′ey·grub′bing** *adj., n.*

mon·ey·lend·er (-len′dər) *n.* a person whose business is lending money at interest

mon·ey·mak·er (-mā′kər) *n.* a person or thing that makes money or a profit —**mon′ey·mak′ing** *adj., n.*

money of account a form of money used in keeping accounts, etc., esp. one not issued in coin or in paper money (as, the U.S. mill)

money order an order for the payment of a specified sum of money, as one issued for a fee at one post office or bank and payable at another

Mong. **1.** Mongolia **2.** Mongolian

mon·ger (muŋ′gər, mäŋ′-) *n.* [OE. *mangere* < L. *mango*, dealer] a dealer or trader: usually in compounds, esp. in Brit. usage [*fishmonger*]: sometimes used in a figurative way [*scandalmonger*]

mon·go (mäŋ′gō) *n., pl.* **-gos** see MONETARY UNITS, table (Mongolia)

Mon·gol (mäŋ′g'l, -gōl) *adj. same as* MONGOLIAN —*n.* **1.** a native of Mongolia (sense 1) or of a nearby region in E Siberia **2.** *same as* MONGOLOID **3.** any Mongolic language, esp. that of the Mongolian People's Republic

Mongol. Mongolian

MONEY-CHANGER

Monetary Units of All Nations

(The exchange rates in this list are unofficial.)

Country	Basic Unit	Equiv. in U.S. Currency	Chief Fractional Unit	Country	Basic Unit	Equiv. in U.S. Currency	Chief Fractional Unit
Afghanistan	afghani	.028	pul	Lesotho	rand	1.24	cent
Albania	lek	.255	qintar	Liberia	dollar	1.00	cent
Algeria	dinar	.268	centime	Libya	dinar	3.42	millieme
Andorra	franc	.224	centime	Liechtenstein	franc	.54	rappen
	peseta	.014	centimo	Luxembourg	franc	.033	centime
Angola	kwanza	.038	lwei	Madagascar	franc	.005	centime
Argentina	peso	.001	centavo	Malawi	kwacha	1.22	tambala
Australia	dollar	1.11	cent	Malaysia	ringgit	.44	cent
Austria	schilling	.07	groschen	Maldive Is.	rupee	.25	cent
Bahamas	dollar	1.01	cent	Mali	franc	.002	centime
Bahrain	dinar	2.65	fils	Malta	pound	2.85	cent
Bangladesh	taka	.07	paisa	Mauritania	ougiya	.02	khoms
Barbados	dollar	.52	cent	Mauritius	rupee	.173	cent
Belgium	franc	.033	centime	Mexico	peso	.046	centavo
Benin	franc	.005	centime	Monaco	franc	.224	centime
Bhutan	ngultrum	.11	chhetrum	Mongolia	tugrik	.32	mongo
Bolivia	peso boliviano	.05	centavo	Morocco	dirham	.263	franc
Botswana	pula	1.32	thebe	Mozambique	escudo	.035	centavo
Brazil	cruzeiro	.021	centavo	Nauru	dollar	1.09	cent
Bulgaria	lev	1.17	stotinka	Nepal	rupee	.085	pice
Burma	kyat	.158	pya	Netherlands	guilder	.503	cent
Burundi	franc	.012	centime	New Zealand	dollar	.95	cent
Cameroun	franc	.005	centime	Nicaragua	cordoba	.143	centavo
Canada	dollar	.84	cent	Niger	franc	.005	centime
Cape Verde	escudo	.0275	centavo	Nigeria	naira	1.85	kobo
Central African Republic	franc	.005	centime	Norway	krone	.198	ore
				Oman	rial	2.90	paisa
Chad	franc	.005	centime	Pakistan	rupee	.103	paisa
Chile	peso	.0275	centavo	Panama	balboa	1.00	centesimo
China	yuan	.66	fen	Papua New Guinea	kina	1.45	toea
Colombia	peso	.021	centavo				
Comoros	franc	.005	centime	Paraguay	guarani	.008	centimo
Congo	franc	.005	centime	Peru	sol	.004	centavo
Costa Rica	colon	.12	centimo	Philippines	peso	.138	centavo
Cuba	peso	1.21	centavo	Poland	zloty	.04	grosz
Cyprus	pound	2.93	mil	Portugal	escudo	.023	centavo
Czechoslovakia	koruna	.198	haler	Qatar	riyal	.28	dirham
Denmark	krone	.177	ore	Romania	leu	.21	ban
Djibouti	franc	.006	centime	Rwanda	franc	.011	centime
Dominica	dollar	.37	cent	San Marino	lira	.0012	centesimo
Dominican Republic	peso	1.00	centavo	Sao Tomé and Príncipe	conto	.026	
Ecuador	sucre	.04	centavo	Saudi Arabia	riyal	.30	qursh
Egypt	pound	1.45	piaster	Senegal	franc	.005	centime
El Salvador	colon	.40	centavo	Seychelles	rupee	.185	cent
Equatorial Guinea	ekuele	.017	centimo	Sierra Leone	leone	1.00	cent
Ethiopia	birr	.49	santim	Singapore	dollar	.45	cent
Fiji	dollar	1.19	cent	Solomon Is.	dollar	1.09	cent
Finland	markka	.26	penni	Somalia	shilling	.16	cent
France	franc	.224	centime	South Africa	rand	1.24	cent
Gabon	franc	.005	centime	Spain	peseta	.015	centimo
Gambia	dalasi	.55	butut	Sri Lanka	rupee	.069	cent
Germany, East	mark	.29	pfennig	St. Lucia	dollar	.37	cent
Germany, West	deutsche mark	.56	pfennig	St. Vincent	dollar	.37	cent
Ghana	cedi	.37	pesewa	Sudan	pound	2.02	piaster
Greece	drachma	.026	lepton	Surinam	guilder	.57	cent
Grenada	dollar	.37	cent	Swaziland	lilangeni	1.24	cent
Guatemala	quetzal	1.00	centavo	Sweden	krona	.23	ore
Guinea	syli	.063	kori	Switzerland	franc	.602	rappen
Guinea-Bissau	peso	.03	centavo	Syria	pound	.26	piaster
Guyana	dollar	.42	cent	Taiwan	dollar	.029	cent
Haiti	gourde	.20	centime	Tanzania	shilling	.124	cent
Honduras	lempira	.50	centavo	Thailand	baht	.051	satang
Hungary	forint	.05	fillér	Togo	franc	.005	centime
Iceland	króna	.004	eyrir	Tonga	pa'anga	1.40	seniti
India	rupee	.13	paisa	Trinidad & Tobago	dollar	.43	cent
Indonesia	rupiah	.002	sen	Tunisia	dinar	2.54	millime
Iran	rial	.014	dinar	Turkey	lira	.014	piaster
Iraq	dinar	3.41	fils	Tuvalu	dollar	1.25	cent
Ireland	pound	2.04	penny	Uganda	shilling	.13	cent
Israel	shekel	.29	agora	United Arab Emirates	riyal	.26	dirham
Italy	lira	.0012	centesimo	United Kingdom	pound	2.28	penny
Ivory Coast	franc	.005	centime	United States	dollar	1.00	cent
Jamaica	dollar	.58	cent	Upper Volta	franc	.005	centime
Japan	yen	.004	sen	Uruguay	peso	.12	centesimo
Jordan	dinar	3.36	fils	U.S.S.R.	ruble	1.54	kopeck
Kampuchea	(no currency)			Vatican City	lira	.0012	centesimo
Kenya	shilling	.14	cent	Venezuela	bolivar	.233	centimo
Kiribati	dollar	1.25	cent	Vietnam	dong	.45	sau
Korea, North	won	.53	chon	Western Samoa	tala	1.35	sene
Korea, South	won	.002		Yemen, People's Democratic Rep. of	dinar	2.95	fils
Kuwait	dinar	3.63	fils	Yemen Arab Rep.	riyal	.22	bugshah
Laos	kip	.003	at	Yugoslavia	dinar	.06	para
Lebanon	pound	.30	piaster	Zaire	zaire	.35	likuta
				Zambia	kwacha	1.33	ngwee
				Zimbabwe	dollar	1.75	cent

Mon·go·li·a (mäŋ gō′lē ə, män-; -gōl′yə) **1.** region in EC Asia, consisting of Inner Mongolia & Mongolia (sense 2) **2.** country in EC Asia, north of China: 592,600 sq. mi.; pop. 1,283,000; cap. Ulan Bator: in full, **Mongolian People's Republic**

Mon·go·li·an (-ən, -yən) *adj.* **1.** of Mongolia, its people, or their culture **2.** *same as* MONGOLOID **3.** *same as* MONGOLIC (*adj.* 1) —*n.* **1.** a native of Mongolia **2.** *same as* MONGOLOID **3.** any Mongolic language

Mon·gol·ic (mäŋ gäl′ik, män-) *adj.* **1.** designating or of a subfamily of Altaic languages spoken by the Mongols and including Kalmuck **2.** *same as: a)* MONGOLIAN (*adj.* 1) *b)* MONGOLOID (*adj.* 1 & 2) —*n.* any Mongolic language

Mon·gol·ism (mäŋ′gə liz'm) *n.* [*often* m-] *earlier term for* DOWN'S SYNDROME

Mon·gol·oid (-loid′) *adj.* **1.** of or characteristic of the natives of Mongolia **2.** designating or of one of the major groups of mankind: it includes most of the peoples of Asia, the Eskimos, the N. American Indians, etc. **3.** [*often* m-] of or having Down's syndrome —*n.* **1.** a member of the Mongoloid group **2.** [*often* m-] a person having Down's syndrome

mon·goose (mäŋ′gōos) *n., pl.* **-goos·es** [< native name] an old-world, ferretlike, flesh-eating mammal, noted for its ability to kill rodents, snakes, etc.

MONGOOSE
(body 9–25 in. long; tail 9–20 in. long)

mon·grel (muŋ′grəl, mäŋ′-) *n.* [< base of OE. *mengan*, to mix] **1.** an animal or plant produced by crossing breeds or varieties; esp., a dog of this kind **2.** anything produced by careless or unplanned mixture —*adj.* of mixed breed, race, origin, or character Often used to show contempt —**mon′grel·i·za′tion** *n.* —**mon′grel·ize′** *vt.*

'mongst, mongst (muŋst) *prep. archaic var. of* AMONGST

mon·ied (mun′ēd) *adj. same as* MONEYED

mon·ies (mun′ēz) *n. alt. pl. of* MONEY

mon·i·ker, mon·ick·er (män′i kər) *n.* [< ?] [Slang] a person's name or nickname

mo·nism (mō′niz'm, män′iz'm) *n.* [ModL. *monismus* < Gr. *monos*, single] *Philos.* the doctrine that there is only one basic substance or principle, whether mind (*idealism*), matter (*materialism*), or something that is the basis of both —**mo′nist** *n.* —**mo·nis′tic, mo·nis′ti·cal** *adj.* —**mo·nis′ti·cal·ly** *adv.*

mo·ni·tion (mō nish′ən) *n.* [OFr. < L.: see MONITOR] **1.** admonition; warning; caution **2.** an official or legal notice

mon·i·tor (män′ə tər) *n.* [L. < pp. of *monere*, to warn: for IE. base see MIND] **1.** [Rare] one who advises or warns **2.** in some schools, a student chosen to help keep order, record attendance, etc. **3.** a reminder **4.** a large, flesh-eating lizard of Africa, S Asia, and Australia ☆**5.** [< the *Monitor*, first such ship, built in 1862] formerly, an armored warship with a low, flat deck and heavy guns in revolving turrets **6.** a person who monitors **7.** a device or instrument used for monitoring **8.** *Radio & TV* a receiver or speaker, as in a control room, for checking how well a broadcast is coming through —*vt., vi.* **1.** to watch or check on (a person or thing) for some reason **2.** to check on or regulate the performance of (a machine, airplane, etc.) **3.** to test for radioactive contamination with an instrument that measures the ionizing radiation being given off **4.** to listen in on (a broadcast, another's telephone conversation, etc.) to gather some specified type of information **5.** *Radio & TV* to check (a broadcast) with a monitor —**mon′i·to′ri·al** (-tôr′ē əl) *adj.* —**mon′i·tor·ship′** *n.*

mon·i·to·ry (män′ə tôr′ē) *adj.* giving monition; warning; admonishing —*n., pl.* **-ries** a monitory letter

monk (muŋk) *n.* [OE. *munuc* < LL. < LGr. < Gr. *monos*, alone] **1.** orig., a man living alone and denying himself any comforts because of religious reasons **2.** a man who has joined a religious order whose members usually live in a monastery, after taking vows to give up worldly goods, never to marry, and to obey their superiors in the order —**monk′ish** *adj.*

mon·key (muŋ′kē) *n., pl.* **-keys** [prob. < or akin to MLowG. *Moneke*, the son of Martin the Ape in the medieval beast epic *Reynard the Fox*] **1.** any of the primates except man and the lemurs; specif., any of the smaller, long-tailed primates **2.** a person thought of as like a monkey, as a mischievous child —*vi.* ☆[Colloq.] to play, trifle, or meddle (often followed by *around*, *with*, or *around with*)

☆**monkey business** [Colloq.] foolish, mischievous, or dishonest tricks or behavior

☆**mon·key·shine** (-shīn′) *n.* [Colloq.] a mischievous trick or prank: *usually used in pl.*

monkey wrench a wrench with one movable jaw, adjusted by a screw to fit various sizes of nut, etc.: see illustration at WRENCH —☆**throw a monkey wrench into** [Colloq.] to disturb (something) so that it cannot work properly or turn out as expected

monk's cloth a heavy cloth, as of cotton, with a basket weave, used for drapes, etc.

monks·hood (muŋks′hood′) *n. same as* ACONITE (sense 1)

Mon·mouth·shire (män′məth shir′) county between England & Wales, on the Severn estuary, usually thought of as part of Wales: also called **Mon′mouth**

mon·o (män′ō) *adj. clipped form of* MONOPHONIC —*n. clipped form of* MONONUCLEOSIS

mon·o- [Gr. < *monos*, single] *a prefix meaning* one, alone, single [*monograph*]

mon·o·bas·ic (män′ō bā′sik) *adj. Chem.* designating an acid whose molecule contains one hydrogen atom replaceable by a metal or positive radical

mon·o·chro·mat·ic (-krō mat′ik) *adj.* [< L. < Gr.: see MONOCHROME & -IC] of or having one color: also **mon′o·chro′ic** (-krō′ik) —**mon′o·chro·mat′i·cal·ly** *adv.*

mon·o·chrome (män′ə krōm′) *n.* [< ML. < Gr. < *monos*, single + *chrōma*, color] a painting, drawing, or photograph in one color or shades of one color —**mon′o·chro′mic** *adj.*

mon·o·cle (män′ə k'l) *n.* [Fr. < LL. *monoculus*, one-eyed < Gr. *monos*, single + L. *oculus*, eye] an eyeglass for one eye only —**mon′o·cled** *adj.*

mon·o·cli·nal (män′ə klī′n'l) *adj. Geol.* designating or of strata dipping in one direction —*n. same as* MONOCLINE

mon·o·cline (män′ə klīn′) *n.* [< MONO- + Gr. *klinein*, to incline] a monoclinal rock fold or structure

mon·o·clin·ic (män′ə klin′ik) *adj.* [see prec. & -IC] designating a crystal form that has three unequal axes, two of which intersect at right angles while the third is oblique to one of the others: see illustration at CRYSTAL

mon·o·cli·nous (män′ə klī′nəs) *adj.* [< ModL. < MONO- + Gr. *klinē*, a bed] having stamens and pistils in the same flower

MONOCLE

mon·o·cot·y·le·don (män′ə kät′'l ē′d'n) *n.* a flowering plant with one seed leaf (cotyledon): also **mon′o·cot′** —**mon′o·cot′y·le′don·ous** *adj.*

mo·noc·u·lar (mə näk′yə lər) *adj.* [< LL. *monoculus* (see MONOCLE) + -AR] **1.** having only one eye **2.** of, or for use by, only one eye —*n.* a field glass or telescopic device with a single eyepiece

mon·o·cyte (män′ə sīt′) *n.* [MONO- + -CYTE] a large white blood cell with a small, kidney-shaped nucleus

mon·o·dy (män′ə dē) *n., pl.* **-dies** [< LL. < Gr. *monōidia* < *monos*, alone + *aeidein*, to sing] **1.** a solo lament or dirge, as in ancient Greek tragedy **2.** a poem mourning someone's death **3.** *Music a)* a style of composition in which the melody is carried by one part, or voice *b)* a composition in this style —**mo·nod·ic** (mə näd′ik), **mo·nod′i·cal** *adj.* —**mo·nod′i·cal·ly** *adv.*

mo·noe·cious (mə nē′shəs, mō-) *adj.* [< MON(O)- + Gr. *oikos*, a house] *Bot.* having separate male flowers and female flowers on the same plant, as in maize —**mo·noe′cism** (-siz'm) *n.*

mon·o·fil·a·ment (män′ə fil′ə mənt) *n.* a single, untwisted strand of synthetic material: also **mon′o·fil′**

mo·nog·a·my (mə näg′ə mē) *n.* [< Fr. < LL. < Gr.: see MONO- & -GAMY] **1.** the practice or state of being married to only one person at a time **2.** *Zool.* the practice of having only one mate —**mo·nog′a·mist** *n.* —**mo·nog′a·mous, mon·o·gam·ic** (män′ə gam′ik) *adj.*

mon·o·gram (män′ə gram′) *n.* [< LL. < Gr. *mono-*, MONO- + *gramma*, letter] the initials of a name, combined in a single design: used on writing paper, ornaments, clothing, etc. —*vt.* **-grammed′, -gram′ming** to put a monogram on —**mon′o·gram·mat′ic** (-grə mat′ik) *adj.*

mon·o·graph (män′ə graf′) *n.* [MONO- + -GRAPH] a book or long article, esp. a scholarly one, on a single subject or aspect of a subject —**mon′o·graph′ic** *adj.*

mon·o·lith (män′ə lith′) *n.* [< Fr. < L. < Gr. < *monos*, single + *lithos*, stone] **1.** a single large block or piece of stone **2.** something made of this, as an obelisk **3.** something like a monolith in size, unity of structure or purpose, etc. —**mon′o·lith′ic** *adj.* —**mon′o·lith′ism** *n.*

mon·o·logue, mon·o·log (män'ə lôg', -läg') *n.* [Fr. < Gr. < *monos*, alone + *legein*, to speak] **1.** a long speech, esp. one that keeps anyone else from talking **2.** a poem or story in which a single character speaks or tells the story **3.** a part of a play in which one character speaks alone; soliloquy **4.** a play, skit, or recitation for one actor only —**mon'o·logu·ist, mo·nol·o·gist** (mə näl'ə jist) *n.*

mon·o·ma·ni·a (män'ə mā'nē ə) *n.* **1.** an excessive interest in or enthusiasm for some one thing; craze **2.** a mental disorder in which a person is not rational on a certain subject — **mon'o·ma'ni·ac'** (-mā'nē ak') *n.* —**mon'o·ma·ni'a·cal** (-mə nī'ə k'l) *adj.*

mon·o·mer (män'ə mər) *n.* [MONO- + Gr. *meros*, a part] a simple molecule that can form polymers by combining with identical or similar molecules —**mon'o·mer'ic** (-mer'ik) *adj.*

mon·o·met·al·lism (män'ə met''l iz'm) *n.* the use of only one metal, usually gold or silver, as the monetary standard — **mon'o·me·tal'lic** (-mə tal'ik) *adj.* —**mon'o·met'al·list** *n.*

mo·no·mi·al (mō nō'mē əl, mä-) *adj.* [MO(NO)- + (BI)NOMIAL] consisting of only one term, esp. in algebra —*n.* a monomial expression, quantity, etc.

mon·o·mo·lec·u·lar (män'ō mə lek'yə lər) *adj.* **1.** of a single molecule **2.** designating or of a layer one molecule thick

Mo·non·ga·he·la (mə näŋ'gə hē'lə) [< Algonquian] river in northern W.Va. & southwestern Pa., joining the Allegheny to form the Ohio: 128 mi.

mon·o·nu·cle·o·sis (män'ə no͞o'klē ō'sis, -nyo͞o'-) *n.* [MONO- + NUCLE(US) + -OSIS] **1.** same as INFECTIOUS MONONUCLEOSIS **2.** presence in the blood of too many cells with a single nucleus

mon·o·phon·ic (-fän'ik) *adj.* designating or of sound reproduction using a single channel to carry and reproduce sounds through one or more loudspeakers

mon·o·plane (män'ə plān') *n.* an airplane with only one pair of wings

mo·nop·o·list (mə näp'ə list) *n.* **1.** a person who has a monopoly **2.** a person who favors monopoly —**mo·nop'o·lis'tic** *adj.* —**mo·nop'o·lis'ti·cal·ly** *adv.*

mo·nop·o·lize (-līz') *vt.* **-lized', -liz'ing** **1.** to get or have a monopoly of **2.** to get full control of; dominate completely [to *monopolize* a conversation] —**mo·nop'o·li·za'tion** *n.* —**mo·nop'o·liz'er** *n.*

mo·nop·o·ly (mə näp'ə lē) *n., pl.* **-lies** [< L. < Gr. < *monopōlia*, exclusive sale < *monos*, single + *pōlein*, to sell] **1.** complete control of a commodity or service in a given market, or control that makes possible the fixing of prices **2.** such control granted and regulated by a government [the city gave the bus company a *monopoly* for ten years] **3.** any complete possession or control [no one has a *monopoly* on brains] **4.** something held or controlled as a monopoly **5.** a company, etc. that has a monopoly —☆[M-] *a trademark for* a game played on a special board by two or more players: they move according to the throw of the dice, pretending to buy and sell land and buildings with play money

SYN.—monopoly applies to the complete control of a commodity or service; a **trust** is a combination of corporations, organized for the purpose of gaining a monopoly, in which stock is turned over to trustees who issue stock certificates to the stockholders: **trusts** are now usually illegal in the U.S.; **cartel**, the European term for a trust, now usually implies an international trust; a **syndicate** is now usually a group of bankers, corporations, etc. organized to buy large blocks of securities, afterwards selling them in small quantities to the public at a profit

☆**mon·o·pro·pel·lant** (män'ō prə pel'ənt) *n.* [MONO- + PROPELLANT] a liquid or solid propellant that is a single substance, or a mixture of substances, and acts as both fuel and oxidizer

mon·o·rail (män'ə rāl') *n.* **1.** a single rail serving as a track for cars suspended from it or balanced on it **2.** a railway with such a track

mon·o·sac·cha·ride (män'ə sak'ə rīd') *n.* [MONO- + SACCHARIDE] a carbohydrate that cannot be separated by hydrolysis; simple sugar, as glucose

mon·o·so·di·um glu·ta·mate (män'ə sō'dē əm glo͞o'tə māt') a white, crystalline powder, $C_5H_8O_4NaN$, used in foods to make the flavor stronger

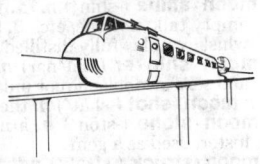
MONORAIL

mon·o·syl·lab·ic (män'ə si lab'ik) *adj.* **1.** having only one syllable [a *monosyllabic* word] **2.** consisting of, using, or speaking in monosyllables —**mon'o·syl·lab'i·cal·ly** *adv.*

mon·o·syl·la·ble (män'ə sil'ə b'l) *n.* a word of one syllable

mon·o·the·ism (män'ə thē iz'm) *n.* [MONO- + THEISM] the doctrine or belief that there is only one God —**mon'o·the·ist** *n.* —**mon'o·the·is'tic, mon'o·the·is'ti·cal** *adj.* —**mon'o·the·is'ti·cal·ly** *adv.*

mon·o·tone (-tōn') *n.* **1.** the saying of a series of words without change of pitch or key **2.** monotony of tone, style, color, etc. **3.** a single, unchanging musical tone **4.** recitation, singing, etc. in such a tone **5.** a person who sings in such a tone —*adj. same as* MONOTONOUS —**mon'o·ton'ic** (-tän'ik) *adj.*

mo·not·o·nous (mə nät''n əs) *adj.* [< LL. < Gr.: see MONO & TONE] **1.** going on in the same tone without variation [a *monotonous* voice] **2.** having little or no variety [a *monotonous* trip] **3.** tiresome because unvarying [*monotonous* work] —**mo·not'o·nous·ly** *adv.* —**mo·not'o·nous·ness** *n.*

mo·not·o·ny (-ē) *n.* **1.** sameness of tone or pitch **2.** lack of variety **3.** a being always the same and tiresome

mon·o·treme (män'ə trēm') *n.* [< ModL. < Gr. *monos*, single + *trēma*, hole] any of the lowest order of mammals (platypuses and echidnas), which lay eggs and have a single opening for the excretory and genital organs —**mon'o·trem'a·tous** (-trem'ə təs, -trē'mə-) *adj.*

mon·o·type (män'ə tīp') *n.* [MONO- + -TYPE] **1.** *Biol.* the only type of its group **2.** *Printing* type produced by Monotype — ☆[M-] *a trademark for* either of a pair of machines for casting and setting up type in separate characters: one, a casting machine, is controlled by a paper tape pierced with holes made by the other, a keyboard machine

mon·o·typ·ic (män'ə tip'ik) *adj.* **1.** having only one type **2.** having the nature of a monotype

mon·o·va·lent (män'ə vā'lənt) *adj. Chem. same as* UNIVALENT —**mon'o·va'lence, mon'o·va'len·cy** *n.*

mon·ox·ide (mə näk'sīd, män äk'-) *n.* an oxide with one atom of oxygen in each molecule

Mon·roe (mən rō') [after President MONROE] city in N La.: pop. 56,000

Mon·roe (mən rō'), **James** 1758–1831; 5th president of the U.S. (1817–25)

Monroe Doctrine the doctrine, stated by President Monroe, that the U.S. would regard as an unfriendly act any attempt by a European nation to interfere in the affairs of the American countries or increase its possessions on the American continents

Mon·ro·vi·a (mən rō'vē ə) capital of Liberia; seaport on the Atlantic: pop. c.100,000

Mon·sei·gneur (män'sen yur'; Fr. mōn se nyër') *n., pl.* **Messei·gneurs** (mes'en yurz'; Fr. mā se nyër') [Fr., lit., my lord] **1.** a French title of honor given to persons of high birth or rank, as princes, bishops, etc. **2.** [*often* m-] a person with this title

mon·sieur (mə syur'; Fr. mə syö') *n., pl.* **mes·sieurs** (mes'ərz; Fr. mā syö') [Fr., lit., my lord] a man; gentleman: French title used like *Mr.* or *sir*: abbrev. **M., Mons.**

Monsig. **1.** Monseigneur **2.** Monsignor

Mon·si·gnor (män sēn'yər; It. mōn'sē nyôr') *n., pl.* **-gnors** (-yərz) It. **-gno'ri** (-nyô'rē) [It., lit., my lord] **1.** a title of certain Roman Catholic prelates **2.** [*often* m-] a person with this title

mon·soon (män so͞on') *n.* [< MDu. < Port. < Ar. *mausim*, a season] **1.** a seasonal wind of the Indian Ocean and S Asia, blowing from the southwest from April to October, and from the northeast the rest of the year **2.** the rainy season, when this wind blows from the southwest —**mon·soon'al** *adj.*

mon·ster (män'stər) *n.* [< OFr. < L. *monstrum*, divine portent < *monere*: see MONITOR] **1.** any plant or animal that is not normal in shape or form **2.** any imaginary creature that is part human and part animal, as a centaur, or has parts from different animals, as a unicorn **3.** something monstrous **4.** any very cruel or wicked person **5.** any huge animal or thing [a *monster* of a house] —*adj.* huge; enormous; monstrous

mon·strance (män'strəns) *n.* [OFr. < ML. < L. *monstrare*, to show] *R.C.Ch.* a receptacle in which the consecrated Host is open to view for adoration

mon·stros·i·ty (män sträs'ə tē) *n.* **1.** the state or quality of being monstrous **2.** *pl.* **-ties** a monstrous thing or creature

fat, āpe, cär; ten, ēven; is, bīte; gō, hôrn, to͞ol, lo͝ok; oil, out; up, fur; get; joy; yet; chin; she; thin, *th*en; zh, leisure; ŋ, ring; ə for *a* in *ago*, *e* in *agent*, *i* in *sanity*, *o* in *comply*, *u* in *focus*; ' as in *able* (ā'b'l); Fr. bàl; ë, Fr. coeur; ö, Fr. feu; Fr. mon; ô, Fr. coq; ü, Fr. duc; r, Fr. cri; H, G. ich; kh, G. doch; ‡foreign; ☆ Americanism; < derived from. See inside front cover.

mon·strous (män′strəs) *adj.* **1.** abnormally large; enormous [a *monstrous* building] **2.** very unnatural in shape, type, or character [a *monstrous* face] **3.** having the character or appearance of a monster **4.** horrible; hideous; shocking [a *monstrous* crime] **5.** hideously wrong or evil [a *monstrous* mistake] —*adv.* [Chiefly Dial.] very; extremely —see **SYN.** at **OUTRAGEOUS** —**mon′strous·ly** *adv.* —**mon′strous·ness** *n.*

mon·tage (män täzh′, mōn-) *n.* [Fr. < *monter,* **MOUNT**[2]] **1.** *a)* the art or process of making one picture put together from a number of different pictures *b)* a picture so made **2.** *Motion Pictures a)* the art or process of producing a series of suddenly changing scenes or images, often with one on top of the other *b)* such a series **3.** any technique, as in literature, with a similar series of elements —*vt.* **-taged′, -tag′ing** to include or combine in a montage

Mon·ta·gnard (män′tən yärd′) *n.* [Fr., lit., mountaineer] a member of a people living in the hills of central Vietnam

Mon·taigne (män tän′; *Fr.* mōn ten′y′), **Mi·chel Ey·quem de** (mē shel′ e kem′ də) 1533-92; Fr. essayist

Mon·tan·a (män tan′ə) [L. *montana,* mountainous region] Mountain State of the northwestern U.S.: 147,138 sq. mi.; pop. 694,000; cap. Helena: abbrev. **Mont., MT** —**Mon·tan′an** *adj., n.*

Mont·calm (mōn kälm′; *E.* mänt käm′), marquis **Louis Joseph de** (zhō zef′ də) 1712-59; Fr. general defeated & killed by Brit. forces at Quebec

☆**mon·te** (män′tē) *n.* [Sp., lit., mountain, hence heap of cards] a game in which players bet on the color of cards to be turned up

Mon·te Car·lo (män′ti kär′lō) town in Monaco: gambling resort: pop. 9,500

Mon·te·ne·gro (män′tə nē′grō) republic of S Yugoslavia: 5,333 sq. mi. —**Mon′te·ne′grin** (-grin) *adj., n.*

Mon·ter·rey (män′tə rā′; *Sp.* mōn′ter rā′) city in NE Mexico: pop. 830,300

Mon·tes·quieu (mōn tes kyö′; *E.* män′təs kyōō′), (baron **de la Brède et de**) 1689-1755; Fr. philosophical writer on history

Mon·tes·so·ri method (or **system**) (män′tə sôr′ē) [after Maria *Montessori* (1870-1952), It. educator who devised it] a system of teaching young children which emphasizes training of the senses and guidance to encourage self-education

Mon·te·ver·di (mōn′te ver′dē), **Clau·dio** (**Giovanni Antonio**) (klou′dyō) 1567-1643; It. composer

Mon·te·vid·e·o (män′tə vid′ē ō′; *Sp.* mōn′te vē the′ō) capital of Uruguay, on the Río de la Plata: pop. 1,204,000

Mon·te·zu·ma II (män′tə zōō′mə) 1479?-1520; Aztec emperor of Mexico (1502-20)

Mont·gom·er·y (mənt gum′ər ē, mänt-, mən-; -gum′rē) [after Gen. R. *Montgomery* (1736?-75)] capital of Ala., in the SC part: pop. 133,000

month (munth) *n.* [OE. *monath:* for IE. base see **MEASURE**] **1.** any of the twelve parts into which the calendar year is divided: also **calendar month 2.** *a)* the time from any day of one month to the corresponding day of the next *b)* a period of four weeks or 30 days **3.** the period of a complete revolution of the moon (in full, **lunar month**): about 29 1/2 days **4.** one twelfth of the solar year (in full, **solar month**) —**month after month** every month —**month by month** each month —**month in, month out** every month

month·ly (munth′lē) *adj.* **1.** continuing or lasting for a month **2.** done, happening, payable, etc. once a month or every month [a *monthly* magazine] —*n., pl.* **-lies 1.** a periodical published once a month **2.** [Colloq.] [*also pl.*] the menses —*adv.* once a month; every month

Mon·ti·cel·lo (män′tə sel′ō, -chel′ō) [It., little mountain] home of Thomas Jefferson, in central Va.

Mont·mar·tre (mōn mar′t'r′) district in Paris, in N part: noted for its cafés and as an artists' quarter

Mont·pel·ier (mänt pēl′yər) [after **MONTPELLIER** (see next entry)] capital of Vt., in the NC part: pop. 9,000

Mont·pel·lier (mōn pel yā′) city in S France: pop. 162,000

Mont·re·al (män′trē ôl′, mun′-) seaport in SW Quebec, Canada, on an island in the St. Lawrence River: pop. 1,081,000 (met. area 2,802,000): Fr. name **Mont·ré·al** (mōn rä äl′)

Montreal North suburb of Montreal: pop. 97,000: Fr. name **Montréal Nord** (nôr)

Mont·ser·rat (mänt′sə rat′) island of the Leeward group of the West Indies: a self-governing territory under Brit. protection: 33 sq. mi.; pop. 12,000

Mont-St-Mi·chel (mōn san mē shel′) islet off the NW coast of France: noted for its fortified abbey: also **Mont Saint Michel**

mon·u·ment (män′yə mənt) *n.* [OFr. < L. *monumentum* <

monere: see **MONITOR**] **1.** something set up to keep alive the memory of a person or event, as a tablet, statue, building, etc. **2.** a writing, etc. serving as a memorial **3.** *a)* a work of enduring significance [*monuments* of learning] *b)* an outstanding example [a *monument* of bigotry] ☆**4.** a stone shaft or other object set in the earth to mark a boundary **5.** [Obs.] a tomb

mon·u·men·tal (män′yə men′t'l) *adj.* **1.** of, suitable for, or serving as a monument **2.** like a monument; massive, enduring, etc. **3.** of lasting importance or value [the *monumental* symphonies of Beethoven] **4.** very great; colossal [*monumental* pride] —**mon′u·men′tal·ly** *adv.*

-mo·ny (mō′nē) [L. *-monia, -monium*] a suffix meaning a resulting thing or state [*patrimony, sanctimony*]

moo (mōō) *n., pl.* **moos** [echoic] the vocal sound made by a cow; lowing sound —*vi.* **mooed, moo′ing** to make this sound

mooch (mōōch) *vi., vt.* [ult. < OFr. *muchier,* to hide] [Slang] to get (food, money, etc.) by begging or sponging —**mooch′er** *n.*

mood[1] (mōōd) *n.* [OE. *mod,* mind < IE. base *me-,* to strive] **1.** a particular state of mind or feeling; humor, or temper **2.** a prevailing feeling, spirit, or tone **3.** [*pl.*] fits of morose, sullen, or uncertain temper

SYN. —**mood** refers to a temporary state of mind and emphasizes a specified feeling [she's in a happy *mood*]; **humor** emphasizes an uncertain or changing quality in the mood [he wept and laughed as his *humor* moved him]; **temper** applies to a mood marked by a single, strong emotion, especially that of anger [my, he's in a nasty *temper!*]

mood[2] (mōōd) *n.* [< **MODE,** altered after prec.] *Gram.* that aspect of verbs which shows whether a verb is regarded as expressing a fact (*indicative mood*), a wish, desire, or possibility (*subjunctive mood*), or a command (*imperative mood*)

mood·y (mōō′dē) *adj.* **mood′i·er, mood′i·est 1.** having or inclined to have gloomy or changing moods **2.** resulting from or showing such a mood —**mood′i·ly** *adv.* —**mood′i·ness** *n.*

moon (mōōn) *n.* [OE. *mona:* for IE. base see **MEASURE**] **1.** the satellite of the earth, that revolves around it once in 29 1/2 days and shines at night by reflecting the sun's light: the moon's diameter is about 2,160 miles and its mean distance from the earth is about 238,857 miles

PHASES OF THE MOON

2. this body as it appears at a particular time of the month: see **NEW MOON, HALF-MOON, FULL MOON, OLD MOON 3.** a month; esp., a lunar month **4.** *same as* **MOONLIGHT 5.** anything shaped like the moon (as an orb or crescent) **6.** any satellite of a planet —*vi.* to behave in an idle, dreamy, or aimless way —*vt.* to pass (time) in mooning

moon·beam (mōōn′bēm′) *n.* a ray of moonlight

moon·calf (-kaf′) *n.* **1.** an idiot or fool **2.** a youth who spends time mooning about

moon-faced (-fāst′) *adj.* round-faced

moon·fish (-fish′) *n., pl.* **-fish′, -fish′es:** see **FISH** an oval-shaped sea fish found in the warmer coastal waters of North and South America

moon·let (-lit) *n.* a small moon or artificial satellite

moon·light (-līt′) *n.* the light of the moon —*adj.* **1.** of moonlight **2.** lighted by the moon **3.** done or occurring by moonlight, or at night —*vi.* to engage in moonlighting

moon·light·ing (-līt′iŋ) *n.* [from the usual night hours of such jobs] ☆the practice of holding a second regular job in addition to one's main job —**moon′light·er** *n.*

moon·lit (-lit′) *adj.* lighted by the moon

☆**moon·quake** (-kwāk′) *n.* a trembling of the surface of the moon, thought to be caused by rock slippage inside it or, possibly, by a meteorite hitting it

moon·scape (-skāp′) *n.* [**MOON** + (**LAND**)**SCAPE**] the surface of the moon or a representation of it

moon·shine (-shīn′) *n.* **1.** the light of the moon **2.** foolish or empty talk, notions, etc. **3.** [Colloq.] *a)* smuggled whiskey ☆*b)* whiskey unlawfully distilled

moon·shin·er (-shī′nər) *n.* [Colloq.] ☆a person who makes and sells alcoholic liquor unlawfully

☆**moon·shot** (-shät′) *n.* the launching of a rocket to the moon

moon·stone (-stōn′) *n.* a milky-white feldspar with a pearly luster, used as a gem

moon·struck (-struk′) *adj.* **1.** crazed; insane **2.** romantically dreamy **3.** dazed or confused Also **moon′strick′en** (-strik′'n)

☆**moon·walk** (-wôk′) *n.* a walking about by an astronaut on the surface of the moon

moon·y (-ē) *adj.* **moon′i·er, moon′i·est** mooning; dreamy

Moor (moor) *n.* [< OFr. < L. < Gr. *Mauros*] **1.** a member of a Moslem people of mixed Arab and Berber descent living in NW

Africa **2.** a member of a group of this people that invaded and occupied Spain in the 8th cent. A.D. —**Moor′ish** *adj.*

moor[1] (moor) *n.* [OE. *mor:* for IE. base see MARSH] [Brit.] a tract of open, rolling wasteland, usually covered with heather and often marshy; heath

moor[2] (moor) *vt.* [< or akin to MDu. *maren,* LowG. *moren,* to tie] **1.** to hold (a ship, etc.) in place by cables or chains as to a pier or buoy **2.** to cause to be held in place; secure *[a tent firmly* moored *by strong ropes]* —*vi.* **1.** to moor a ship, etc. **2.** to be secured as by cables —**moor′age** (-ij) *n.*

Moore (moor, môr) **1. George (Augustus),** 1852–1933; Ir. novelist & playwright **2. Henry,** 1898– ; Eng. sculptor **3. Marianne (Craig),** 1887–1972; U.S. poet **4. Thomas,** 1779–1852; Ir. poet

moor·hen (moor′hen′) *n.* a common gallinule of Europe and the eastern U.S.

moor·ing (-iŋ) *n.* **1.** [*often pl.*] the lines, cables, etc. by which a ship, etc. is moored **2.** [*pl.*] a place where a ship, etc. is moored **3.** [*often pl.*] beliefs, habits, ties, etc. that make one feel secure

moor·land (-land′) *n.* [Brit.] *same as* MOOR[1]

☆**moose** (moos) *n., pl.* **moose** [< Algonquian] **1.** the largest animal of the deer family, native to the northern U.S. and Canada; the male has huge antlers **2.** *same as* ELK (sense 1)

MOOSE
(4½–6 ft. high at shoulder)

moot (moot) *n.* [OE. *mot, gemot,* a meeting < IE. base *mod-,* to meet] **1.** an early English assembly of freemen to administer justice, etc. **2.** a discussion or argument, esp. of a case in a moot court: see MOOT COURT —*adj.* open for discussion or debate; debatable *[a* moot *point]* —*vt.* **1.** to debate or discuss **2.** to propose for discussion or debate

moot court a mock court for trying cases made up to give law students practice

mop (mäp) *n.* [ult. < ? L. *mappa,* napkin] **1.** a bundle of rags or yarn, or a sponge, etc., fastened to the end of a stick, as for washing floors **2.** anything suggestive of this, as a thick head of hair —*vt.* **mopped, mop′ping** to wash, wipe, or remove with or as with a mop —**mop up 1.** [Colloq.] *a)* to finish *b)* to defeat completely **2.** *Mil.* to clear out beaten enemy forces still in (a town, battle area, etc.) —**mop′per** *n.*

mope (mop) *vi.* **moped, mop′ing** [akin to MDu. *mopen* < IE. base *mu-,* echoic of sound made with closed lips] to be gloomy and without spirit —*n.* **1.** a person who mopes **2.** [*pl.*] low spirits —**mop′er** *n.* —**mop′ey, mop′y, mop′ish** *adj.* —**mop′ish·ly** *adv.*

☆**mo·per·y** (mo′pər ē) *n.* [MOP(E) + -ERY] [Slang] an unimportant or absurd violation of law

mop·pet (mäp′it) *n.* [dim. of ME. *moppe,* rag doll < ?] [Colloq.] a little child: a term of affection

mo·raine (mə rān′, mô-) *n.* [Fr. < *morre,* a muzzle] a mass of rocks, gravel, sand, etc. deposited by a glacier, along its side (**lateral moraine**), at its lower end (**terminal moraine**), or beneath the ice (**ground moraine**) —**mo·rain′al, mo·rain′ic** *adj.*

mor·al (môr′əl, mär′-) *adj.* [< L. < *mos,* pl. *mores,* manners: for IE. base see MOOD[1]] **1.** relating to, dealing with, or capable of distinguishing between, right and wrong in conduct *[a* moral *question]* **2.** of, teaching, or in accordance with, the principles of right and wrong *[a* moral *story]* **3.** good, right, or decent in conduct or character, esp. in sexual conduct **4.** that shows sympathy but gives no active help *[moral support]* **5.** regarded as such because of its effect on thoughts, attitudes, etc. *[a* moral *victory]* **6.** based on strong probability *[a* moral *certainty]* —*n.* **1.** a moral lesson taught by a fable, event, etc. **2.** [*pl.*] principles, standards, or habits having to do with right or wrong in conduct; ethics; sometimes, specif., standards of sexual behavior —**mor′al·ly** *adv.*

SYN.—**moral** implies living according to accepted standards of goodness or rightness in conduct or character, especially in sexual conduct *[a* moral *woman]*; **ethical** implies following a carefully planned ideal code of moral principles, often the code of a particular profession *[an* ethical *lawyer]*; **virtuous** implies a morally excellent character concerned about justice, integ-

rity, and, often, chastity; **righteous** implies taking a moral stand based on good or just reasons *[righteous* anger] —**ANT. immoral**

mo·rale (mə ral′, mô-) *n.* [Fr., fem. of *moral:* see prec.] moral or mental condition in relation to courage, discipline, confidence, enthusiasm, etc. *[the* morale *of the troops was low]*

mor·al·ist (môr′əl ist, mär′-) *n.* **1.** a person who moralizes **2.** a person who lives according to a system of moral teaching **3.** a person who tries to force his moral values on other people —**mor′al·is′tic** *adj.* —**mor′al·is′ti·cal·ly** *adv.*

mo·ral·i·ty (mə ral′ə tē, mô-) *n., pl.* **-ties 1.** moral quality or character; rightness or wrongness, as of an action **2.** a being in accord with the principles or standards of right conduct; virtue **3.** principles of right and wrong in conduct; ethics **4.** moral instruction or lesson **5.** a narrative with a moral lesson **6.** *same as* MORALITY PLAY

morality play any of certain dramas of the 15th and 16th cent. that were also allegories in which the characters had such names as Everyman, Vice, Virtue, etc.

mor·al·ize (môr′ə līz′, mär′-) *vi.* **-ized′, -iz′ing** to consider or discuss matters of right and wrong, often in a self-righteous way —*vt.* **1.** *a)* to explain in terms of right and wrong *b)* to draw a moral from **2.** to improve the morals of —**mor′al·i·za′tion** *n.* —**mor′al·iz′er** *n.*

moral philosophy *same as* ETHICS

mo·rass (mə ras′, mô-) *n.* [< Du. < OFr. < Frank. *marisk,* a swamp] a tract of low, soft, watery ground; bog; swamp: often used figuratively of a difficult or troublesome state of affairs

mor·a·to·ri·um (môr′ə tôr′ē əm, mär′-) *n., pl.* **-ri·ums, -ri·a** (-ə) [ModL. < LL. < L. < *mora,* a delay] **1.** a legal authorization, usually by an emergency law, to delay payment of money due, as by a bank or a debtor nation **2.** the period during which such an authorization is in effect **3.** any authorized delay or stopping of some specified activity

Mo·ra·vi·a (mô rā′vē ə, mə-) region in central Czechoslovakia: chief city, Brno

Mo·ra·vi·an (mô rā′vē ən, mə-) *adj.* **1.** of Moravia, its people, etc. **2.** of the religious sect of Moravians —*n.* **1.** a native or inhabitant of Moravia **2.** the Czech dialect of Moravia **3.** a member of a Protestant sect founded by people from Moravia (c.1722)

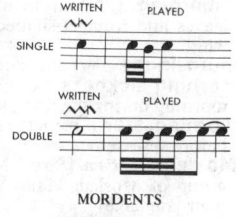
MORAVIA

☆**mo·ray** (môr′ā; mô rā′, mə-) *n.* [< Port. < L. *muraena,* kind of fish < Gr. *myraina*] a brilliantly colored eel that feeds on other fish, found esp. among coral reefs: in full, **moray eel**

mor·bid (môr′bid) *adj.* [L. *morbidus,* sickly < *morbus,* disease < IE. base *mer-,* to wear away] **1.** of, having, or caused by disease; diseased **2.** having or showing an unhealthy interest in gruesome or gloomy matters **3.** gruesome; horrible *[morbid* details of a crime] —**mor·bid′i·ty, mor′bid·ness** *n.* —**mor′bid·ly** *adv.*

mor·dant (môr′d'nt) *adj.* [< OFr. prp. of *mordre* < L. *mordere,* to bite: for IE. base see MORBID] **1.** biting, caustic, or sarcastic *[mordant* wit] **2.** corrosive **3.** acting as a mordant —*n.* **1.** a substance used in dyeing to fix the colors **2.** an acid, etc. used in etching to bite lines, areas, etc. into the surface —**mor′dan·cy** *n.* —**mor′dant·ly** *adv.*

mor·dent (môr′d'nt) *n.* [G. < It. prp. of *mordere* < L., to bite] *Music* the practice of changing rapidly from a principal tone to the tone a half step or whole step below and back, as a kind of decoration or flourish: in a **double mordent,** the quick change is repeated twice

more (môr) *adj. superl.* MOST [OE. *mara*] **1.** greater in amount, quantity, or degree: used as the comparative of MUCH *[to earn* more *money]* **2.** greater in number: used as the comparative of MANY

WRITTEN   PLAYED
SINGLE
WRITTEN   PLAYED
DOUBLE
MORDENTS

[to produce *more* cars] **3.** additional; further [take *more* tea] —**n. 1.** a greater amount, quantity, or degree [he spends *more* of his time at work] **2.** [*with pl. v.*] a greater number (*of*) [*more* of us are going] **3.** something additional or further [*more* can be said] —*adv. superl.* MOST **1.** in or to a greater degree or extent: used with many adjectives and adverbs (regularly with those of three or more syllables) to form comparatives [*more* beautiful; *more* intensely] **2.** in addition; further [try once *more*] —**more and more 1.** increasingly **2.** a constantly increasing amount, quantity, degree, or number (of persons or a specified thing) —**more or less 1.** somewhat **2.** approximately; about

More (môr), Sir **Thomas** 1478-1535; Eng. statesman & writer: executed: canonized in 1935

Mo·re·a (mô rē′ə) *former name of* PELOPONNESUS

mo·rel (mə rel′, mô-) *n.* [< Fr. < MDu. < OHG. *morhila*. dim. of *morha*, carrot] a mushroom that looks like a sponge on a stalk and can be eaten

more·o·ver (môr ō′vər) *adv.* in addition to what has been said; besides; further; also

☆**mo·res** (môr′ēz, -āz) *n.pl.* [L., pl. of *mos*, custom: see MORAL] folkways that develop the force of law because most people follow them

Mor·gan[1] (môr′gən) *n.* [after Justin *Morgan* (1747–98), New Englander who owned the sire of the breed] ☆any of a breed of strong, light harness or saddle horses

Mor·gan[2] (môr′gən) **1.** Sir **Henry,** 1635?–88; Welsh buccaneer in the Spanish Main **2.** **J(ohn) P(ierpont),** 1837–1913; U.S. financier **3.** Lewis Henry, 1818–81; U.S. anthropologist

MOREL

mor·ga·nat·ic (môr′gə nat′ik) *adj.* [< ML. < *morganaticum,* altered < OHG. *morgengeba, lit.,* morning gift, gift given to the wife on the day after marriage in place of any share in the husband's property] designating of a form of marriage in which a man of royalty or nobility marries a woman of inferior social status with the provision that neither she nor their offspring may lay claim to his rank or property —**mor′ga·nat′i·cal·ly** *adv.*

morgue (môrg) *n.* [Fr.] **1.** a place where the bodies of dead persons who are unknown or whose cause of death is unknown are kept to be examined, identified, etc. ☆**2.** a newspaper office's reference library of back numbers, clippings, photographs, etc.

mor·i·bund (môr′ə bund′) *adj.* [< L. *moribundus < mori,* to die] **1.** dying **2.** coming to an end **3.** having little or no vitality left —**mor′i·bund′i·ty** *n.*

mo·ri·on (môr′ē än′) *n.* [Fr. < Sp. < *morra,* crown of the head] a hatlike, crested helmet of the 16th and 17th cent., without a visor and with a curved brim coming to a peak in front and in back

Mo·ris·co (mə ris′kō, mô-) *adj.* [Sp. < *Moro,* Moor] Moorish —*n., pl.* **-cos, -coes** a Moor; esp., one of the Moors of Spain

Mor·i·son (môr′i sən), **Samuel Eliot** 1887– ; U.S. historian

☆**Mor·mon** (môr′mən) *n.* a member of the Church of Jesus Christ of Latter-day Saints (commonly called the *Mormon Church*), founded in the U.S. in 1830 by Joseph Smith —*adj.* of the Mormons or their religion —**Mor′mon·ism** *n.*

morn (môrn) *n.* [OE. *morne*] [Poet.] morning

morn·ing (môr′niŋ) *n.* [ME. *morweninge* (by analogy with EVE-NING) < OE. *morgen* < IE. base *mer-,* to glimmer] **1.** the first or early part of the day, from midnight, or esp. dawn, to noon **2.** the first or early part [the *morning* of life] **3.** dawn; daybreak —*adj.* of, suited to, or occurring, appearing, etc. in the morning

morning dress formal daytime dress for men, including a cutaway (**morning coat**)

☆**morning glory** a twining annual vine with heart-shaped leaves and trumpet-shaped flowers of lavender, blue, pink, or white

morn·ings (-niŋz) *adv.* during every morning or most mornings

morning sickness nausea and vomiting that take place in the morning during the first months of pregnancy

morning star a planet, esp. Venus, visible in the eastern sky before sunrise

Mo·ro (môr′ō) *n.* [Sp., a Moor] **1.** *pl.* **-ros, -ro** a member of a group of Moslem Malay tribes living in the S Philippines **2.** their language

Mo·roc·co (mə rä′kō) kingdom on the NW coast of Africa: c.171,300 sq. mi.; pop. 15,102,000; cap. Rabat —*n.* [m-] a fine, soft leather made, orig. in Morocco, from goatskins: also **morocco leather** —**Mo·roc′can** *adj., n.*

☆**mo·ron** (môr′än) *n.* [arbitrary use of Gr. neut. of *mōros,* foolish] **1.** a person having mild mental retardation: term now rarely used: see MENTAL RETARDATION **2.** a very foolish or stupid person —**mo·ron′ic** *adj.* —**mo·ron′i·cal·ly** *adv.* —**mo·ron′i·ty, mo′ron·ism** *n.*

mo·rose (mə rōs′, mô-) *adj.* [L. *morosus,* fretful < *mos:* see MORAL] **1.** ill-tempered; gloomy, sullen, etc. **2.** full of gloom —**mo·rose′ly** *adv.* —**mo·rose′ness** *n.*

-morph (môrf) [< Gr. *morphē,* form] *a combining form meaning* one having a (specified) form [*allomorph*]

mor·pheme (môr′fēm) *n.* [< Fr. < Gr. *morphē,* form] the smallest meaningful unit or form in a language: it may be an affix (*re-* in *refill*), a base (*do* in *undo*), or an inflectional form (*-s* in *girls*) —**mor·phe′mic·al·ly** *adv.*

Mor·pheus (môr′fē əs, -fyoos) *Gr. Myth.* the god of dreams

-mor·phic (môr′fik) [< Gr. *morphē,* form + -IC] *a combining form meaning* having a (specified) form or shape [*anthropomorphic*]

mor·phine (môr′fēn) *n.* [< G. or Fr. < ModL. *morphium* < L. *Morpheus,* MORPHEUS] a bitter, white or colorless, crystalline alkaloid derived from opium and used in medicine to relieve pain: also **mor′phi·a** (-fē ə)

mor·phin·ism (môr′fin iz'm) *n.* **1.** a being addicted to the use of morphine **2.** the diseased condition resulting from this

mor·pho·gen·e·sis (môr′fə jen′ə sis) *n.* [ModL.: see -MORPH & -GENESIS] *Zool.* the changes in structure that occur during the development of an organism, organ, or part

mor·phol·o·gy (môr fäl′ə jē) *n.* [< G. < Gr. *morphē,* form + -LOGY] **1.** the branch of biology dealing with the form and structure of animals and plants **2.** the branch of linguistics dealing with the forms and formation of words, as distinguished from their sounds, meanings, etc. **3.** any scientific study of form and structure, as in physical geography **4.** form and structure, of an organism, regarded as a whole —**mor′pho·log′i·cal** (-fə läj′i k'l), **mor′pho·log′ic** *adj.* —**mor′pho·log′i·cal·ly** *adv.* —**mor·phol′o·gist** *n.*

-mor·phous (môr′fəs) [< Gr. < *morphē,* form] *same as* -MORPHIC

Mor·ris (môr′is, mär′-) **1.** [var. of MAURICE] a masculine name **2.** **Gouv·er·neur** (guv′ər nir′), 1752–1816; Am. statesman & diplomat **3.** **William,** 1834–96; Eng. poet, artist, craftsman, & socialist

Morris chair [after Wm. MORRIS] an armchair with an adjustable back and removable cushions

mor·ris (**dance**) (môr′is, mär′-) [< ME. *morys,* Moorish] an old English folk dance, in which fancy costumes were worn, esp. on May Day

mor·ro (mär′ō) *n., pl.* **-ros** [Sp.] a rounded hill or point of land

mor·row (mär′ō, môr′ō) *n.* [< OE. *morgen,* MORNING] [Poet.] **1.** morning **2.** the next day **3.** the time just after some particular event

Morse (môrs) *adj.* [after S. F. B. MORSE] [*often* m-] designating or of a code, or alphabet, consisting of a system of dots and dashes, or short and long sounds, used in radiotelegraphy, etc. —*n.* the Morse code

Morse (môrs), **Samuel F(inley) B(reese)** 1791–1872; U.S. inventor of the telegraph

mor·sel (môr′s'l) *n.* [< OFr. dim. of *mors* < L. *morsum,* a bite < pp. of *mordere:* see MORDANT] **1.** a small bite or portion of food **2.** a small amount; bit

mor·tal (môr′t'l) *adj.* [< OFr. < L. *mortalis < mortis,* genitive of *mors,* death: for IE. base see MORBID] **1.** that must eventually die [all *mortal* beings] **2.** of man as a being who must eventually die [their *mortal* failings] **3.** of this world [every *mortal* comfort] **4.** of death [in *mortal* agony] **5.** causing death; fatal [a *mortal* wound] **6.** to the death [*mortal* combat] **7.** not to be pacified [a *mortal* enemy] **8.** very intense; grievous [*mortal* terror] **9.** [Colloq.] *a)* extreme; very great [it's a *mortal* pity] *b)* very long and tedious [waiting for three *mortal* hours] *c)* possible [of no *mortal* good to anyone] **10.** *R.C.Ch.* causing spiritual death: said of sins regarded as serious —*n.* a being who must eventually die; esp., a human being —*adv.* [Dial.] extremely —see SYN. at FATAL —**mor′tal·ly** *adv.*

mor·tal·i·ty (môr tal′ə tē) *n.* **1.** the condition of being mortal or sure to die **2.** death on a large scale, as from disease or war **3.** the proportion of deaths to the population of a region, nation, etc.; death rate **4.** the proportion that fail [the high *mortality* of college freshmen] **5.** all human beings; mankind

mortality table a statistical table, based on a sample group, stating the percentage of people who live to any given age and the life expectancy of any individual at a given age

mor·tar (môr′tər) *n.* [< OE. & OFr. < L. *mortarium:* for IE. base see MORBID] **1.** a very hard bowl in which substances are ground or pounded to a powder with a pestle **2.** a short-barreled cannon which hurls shells in a high curve **3.** a mixture of cement or lime with sand and water, used between bricks, etc., or as plaster —*vt.* **1.** to plaster together with mortar **2.** to attack with mortar shells

mor·tar·board (-bôrd′) *n.* **1.** a square board with a handle beneath, on which mortar is carried **2.** an academic cap with a square, flat top, worn at commencements, etc.

mort·gage (môr′gij) *n.* [< OFr. < *mort,* dead (see MORTAL) + *gage,* GAGE¹] *Law* **1.** an agreement in which a person borrowing money gives the lender a claim to a certain piece of property as a pledge that the debt will be paid **2.** the deed, or legal paper, by which this pledge is made —*vt.* **-gaged, -gag·ing** **1.** *Law* to pledge (property) by a mortgage in order to borrow money [they *mortgaged* their house to buy a new car] **2.** to put a claim on; make risky [he *mortgaged* his future by piling up debts]

mort·ga·gee (môr′gə jē′) *n.* the lender to whom property is mortgaged

mort·ga·gor, mort·gag·er (môr′gi jər) *n.* the borrower who mortgages his property

mor·tice (môr′tis) *n., vt.* alt. sp. of MORTISE

☆**mor·ti·cian** (môr tish′ən) *n.* [< L. *mors,* death (see MORTAL) + -ICIAN] *same as* FUNERAL DIRECTOR

mor·ti·fi·ca·tion (môr′tə fi kā′shən) *n.* **1.** a mortifying or being mortified; specif., *a)* the control of physical desires by self-denial, fasting, etc. *b)* shame, humiliation, etc. **2.** something causing shame, humiliation, etc. **3.** *old term for* GANGRENE

mor·ti·fy (môr′tə fī′) *vt.* **-fied′, -fy′ing** [< OFr. < LL. *mortificare,* to kill < L. *mors,* death (see MORTAL) + *facere,* to make] **1.** to punish (one's body) or control (one's physical desires) by self-denial, fasting, etc., as for religious reasons **2.** to shame, humiliate, etc. **3.** [Now Rare] to make gangrenous —*vi.* [Now Rare] to become gangrenous —**mor′ti·fi′er** *n.*

mor·tise (môr′tis) *n.* [MFr. *mortaise* < Ar. *murtazza,* joined] a notch or hole cut, as in a piece of wood, so that a part (*tenon*) sticking out from another piece will exactly fit into it to form a joint —*vt.* **-tised, -tis·ing** **1.** to join or fasten securely, esp. with a mortise and tenon **2.** to cut a mortise in

mort·main (môrt′mān′) *n.* [< OFr. < ML. < L. pp. of *mori,* to die + *manus,* hand] *Law* a transfer of lands or houses to a corporate body, as a church, for perpetual ownership

mor·tu·ar·y (môr′choo wer′ē) *n., pl.* **-ar′ies** [< L. < L. *mortuus,* dead] a place where dead bodies are kept before burial or cremation, as a morgue or funeral home —*adj.* **1.** of or having to do with the burial of the dead **2.** of death

mos. months

Mo·sa·ic (mō zā′ik) *adj.* of Moses or the writings, principles, etc. thought to be his

mo·sa·ic (mō zā′ik) *n.* [< OFr. < ML. *musaicum* < LL. < L. *musa,* MUSE] **1.** the process of making pictures or designs by inlaying small bits of colored stone, glass, etc. in mortar **2.** a picture or design so made **3.** anything resembling this **4.** the photosensitive plate in a television camera tube —*adj.* of or resembling mosaic or a mosaic —*vt.* **-icked, -ick·ing** to make by or as by mosaic —**mo·sa′i·cal·ly** *adv.* —**mo·sa′i·cist** (-ə sist) *n.*

Mosaic law the ancient Hebrew law, contained mainly in the Pentateuch and thought to have been set down by Moses

Mos·cow (mäs′kou, -kō) capital of the U.S.S.R. & of the R.S.F.S.R., in western R.S.F.S.R.: pop. 6,942,000 (met. area 7,061,000): Russ. name, **Mos·kva** (mōs kvä′)

Mo·selle (mō zel′) river in NE France & N West Germany, flowing into the Rhine

Mo·ses (mō′ziz) [LL. < Gr. < Heb. *mōsheh,* prob. < Egypt. *mes,* child] **1.** a masculine name **2.** *Bible* the leader who brought the Israelites out of slavery in Egypt and led them to the Promised Land, and who received the Ten Commandments

☆**mo·sey** (mō′zē) *vi.* [< *vamose,* var. of VAMOOSE] [Slang] **1.** to amble along **2.** to go away

Mos·lem (mäz′ləm, muz′-, mäs′-) *n.* [Ar. *muslim,* true believer < *aslama,* to resign oneself (to God)] a believer in the religion of Islam —*adj.* of Islam or the Moslems: also **Mos·lem′ic** (-lem′ik) —**Mos′lem·ism** *n.*

mosque (mäsk) *n.* [< MFr. < It. < Ar. *masjid* < *sajada,* to pray] a Moslem temple or place of worship

mos·qui·to (mə skēt′ō, -ə) *n., pl.* **-toes, -tos** [Sp. & Port., dim. of *mosca* < L. *musca,* a fly: for IE. base see MIDGE] a two-winged insect, the female of which has skin-piercing, bloodsucking mouthparts: some varieties transmit diseases, as malaria and yellow fever —**mos·qui′to·ey** (-ē) *adj.*

☆**mosquito net** (or **netting**) a fine mesh cloth or a curtain made of this for keeping out mosquitoes

moss (môs, mäs) *n.* [OE. *mos,* a swamp] **1.** a very small, green plant growing in velvety clusters on rocks, trees, moist ground, etc. **2.** any of various similar plants, as some lichens, algae, etc. —*vt.* to cover with a growth of moss —**moss′like′** *adj.*

moss agate agate with mosslike markings

☆**moss·back** (môs′bak′, mäs′-) *n.* [Colloq.] an old-fashioned or very conservative person

☆**moss pink** a hardy, perennial phlox forming sprawling mats with bristly, narrow leaves and white, pink, or lavender flowers

moss rose **1.** *same as* PORTULACA **2.** a variety of the cabbage rose with a roughened, mossy flower stalk and calyx

moss·y (-ē) *adj.* **moss′i·er, moss′i·est** **1.** full of or covered with moss or a mosslike growth **2.** like moss —**moss′i·ness** *n.*

most (mōst) *adj., compar.* MORE [OE. *mast*] **1.** greatest in amount, quantity, or degree: used as the superlative of MUCH [who won the *most* money?] **2.** greatest in number; almost all: used as the superlative of MANY [*most* children like candy] **3.** in the greatest number of instances [*most* fame is fleeting] —*n.* **1.** the greatest amount, quantity, or degree [he took *most* of the credit] **2.** [with pl. v.] the greatest number (of) [*most* of us are going] —*adv.* **1.** *compar.* MORE in or to the greatest degree or extent: used with many adjectives and adverbs (regularly with those of three or more syllables) to form superlatives [*most* horrible; *most* quickly] **2.** very [a *most* beautiful morning] **3.** [for ALMOST] [Colloq.] almost; nearly —**at (the) most** at the very limit; not more than —**make the most of** to make the greatest use of

-most (mōst) [OE. *-mest*] *a suffix used in forming superlatives* [foremost, hindmost]

most·ly (mōst′lē) *adv.* **1.** for the most part **2.** chiefly; principally **3.** usually; generally

Mo·sul (mō sool′) city in N Iraq, on the Tigris River: pop. 243,000

mot (mō) *n.* [Fr., a word < L. *muttum,* a grunt] a witty or clever remark expressed in few words

mote (mōt) *n.* [OE. *mot*] a speck, as of dust

☆**mo·tel** (mō tel′) *n.* [MO(TORIST) + (HO)TEL] a hotel for those traveling by car, usually with a parking area easily reached from each room

mo·tet (mō tet′) *n.* [< OFr. dim. of *mot,* a word] a song of a sacred nature having two or more melodies in harmony, usually sung by a chorus without instrumental accompaniment

moth (môth) *n., pl.* **moths** (môthz, môths) [OE. *moththe*] a four-winged insect that usually flies at night, related to the butterfly but generally smaller and less brightly colored; specif., a small moth (**clothes moth**) whose larvae eat holes in woolens, furs, etc.

moth·ball (môth′bôl′) *n.* a small ball of naphthalene or, sometimes, camphor, the fumes of which repel moths, as from woolens, furs, etc. —*vt.* to store with protective covering or set aside indefinitely for possible future use—*adj.* in storage or reserve [a *mothball* fleet] —**in** (or **out of**) **mothballs** put into (or taken from) storage

moth-eat·en (-ēt′'n) *adj.* **1.** gnawed away in patches by moths, as cloth **2.** looking shabby or worn-out **3.** outdated

moth·er¹ (muth′ər) *n.* [OE. *modor* < IE. base *mater-,* ult. < *ma-,* echoic of baby talk] **1.** a woman who has borne a child; esp., a woman as she is related to her child or children **2.** *a)* a stepmother *b)* a mother-in-law **3.** the female parent of a plant or animal **4.** that which is the origin, source, or nurturer of something /which State is the *mother* of Presidents?/ **5.** *a)* a woman having the responsibility and authority of a mother *b)* a woman who is the head (**mother superior**) of a religious establishment **6.** an elderly woman: used as a title of affectionate respect —*adj.* **1.** of, like, or like that of a mother **2.** native /*mother* tongue/ —*vt.* **1.** to be the mother of **2.** to care for as a mother does —**moth′er·less** *adj.*

moth·er[2] (mu*th*′ər) *n.* [altered (after prec.) < MDu. *moeder*] *same as* MOTHER OF VINEGAR

Mother Car·ey's chicken (ker′ēz) [< ?] any of various oceanic petrels; esp., *same as* STORMY PETREL (sense 1)

mother country *same as* MOTHERLAND

mother figure a person that one thinks of as if she were one's mother

Mother Goose the imaginary creator of a collection of English nursery rhymes

moth·er·hood (mu*th*′ər hood′) *n.* **1.** the state of being a mother **2.** the qualities or character of a mother **3.** mothers as a group

Mother Hub·bard (hub′ərd) **1.** a character in an old nursery rhyme **2.** [from the costume in old illustrations of the rhyme] a full, loose gown for women

moth·er-in-law (-ən lô′) *n., pl.* **moth′ers-in-law′** the mother of one's husband or wife

moth·er·land (-land′) *n.* a person's native land or, sometimes, the land of his ancestors

☆**mother lode** the main lode, or vein of ore, in a particular region or district

moth·er·ly (-lē) *adj.* of, like, or befitting a mother; maternal —**moth′er·li·ness** *n.*

moth·er-of-pearl (-əv purl′) *n.* the hard, pearly layer on the inside of certain seashells, as of the pearl oyster, used for making pearl buttons, etc.; nacre —*adj.* of mother-of-pearl

mother of vinegar [see MOTHER[2]] a stringy, gummy, slimy substance formed by bacteria in vinegar or on the surface of fermenting liquids: used as a starter to make vinegar

☆**Mother's Day** the second Sunday in May, a day set aside (in the U.S.) in honor of mothers

mother tongue 1. one's native language **2.** a language from which another has developed

mother wit native intelligence; common sense

moth·proof (môth′prōōf′) *adj.* treated with chemicals so as to repel moths —*vt.* to make mothproof

moth·y (môth′ē) *adj.* **moth′i·er, moth′i·est 1.** full of moths **2.** moth-eaten

mo·tif (mō tēf′) *n.* [Fr.: see MOTIVE] **1.** a main element, idea, etc.; specif., a theme or subject that is repeated with various changes, as in a piece of music, a book, etc. **2.** a repeated figure in a design

mo·tile (mōt′'l) *adj.* [< L. pp. of *movere*, to MOVE + -ILE] *Biol.* that is able to move about —**mo·til·i·ty** (mō til′ə tē) *n.*

mo·tion (mō′shən) *n.* [< L. *motio* < pp. of *movere*, to MOVE] **1.** a moving from one place to another; movement /the car's forward *motion*/ **2.** a moving of the body or any of its parts **3.** a meaningful movement of the hand, eyes, etc.; gesture **4.** a suggestion; esp., a proposal formally made in an assembly or meeting —*vi.* to make a meaningful movement of the hand, head, etc. —*vt.* to direct or command by a meaningful gesture /she *motioned* us to stop/ —**go through the motions** to do something in a mechanical or merely formal way —**in motion** moving or in operation —**mo′tion·less** *adj.* —**mo′tion·less·ly** *adv.* —**mo′tion·less·ness** *n.*

motion picture 1. a series of photographs or drawings flashed on a screen rapidly, one after the other, so that persons and objects in them seem to be moving **2.** a play, story, etc. photographed as a motion picture

motion sickness sickness in which one is nauseated, dizzy, etc., caused by the motion of an aircraft, boat, etc.

motion study *see* TIME STUDY

mo·ti·vate (mōt′ə vāt′) *vt.* **-vat′ed, -vat′ing** to give a motive to or be a motive for; incite or impel /love *motivated* his actions/ —**mo′ti·va′tion** *n.* —**mo′ti·va′tion·al** *adj.* —**mo′ti·va′tive** *adj.* —**mo′ti·va′tor** *n.*

mo·tive (mōt′iv) *n.* [< OFr. *motif* < ML. < L. pp. of *movere*, to MOVE] **1.** some inner drive, impulse, etc. that causes one to act in a certain way; incentive; goal **2.** *same as* MOTIF —*adj.* of, causing, or tending to cause motion —*vt.* **-tived, -tiv·ing** *same as* MOTIVATE —**mo′tive·less** *adj.*

SYN. —**motive** refers to any impulse, emotion, or desire that causes one to do something /greed was his only *motive* for stealing/; **incentive** applies to a stimulus, often a reward, that encourages or inspires one to do something /she needs no *incentive* other than the desire to be useful/; **inducement** always refers to an outer stimulus, rather than an inner urge, that tempts or entices one to do something /the money offered her was an added *inducement*/ See also **SYN.** at CAUSE

-mo·tive (mōt′iv) [< prec.] *a suffix meaning* moving, of motion /*automotive, locomotive*/

‡**mot juste** (mō zhüst′) *pl.* **mots justes** (mō zhüst′) [Fr.] the right word; exact, appropriate word or phrase

mot·ley (mät′lē) *adj.* [< ?] **1.** of many colors **2.** wearing many-colored garments /a *motley* fool/ **3.** of many different or clashing elements /a *motley* group/ —*n.* **1.** cloth of mixed colors **2.** a garment of various colors, worn by a jester **3.** a combination of many different or clashing elements

mo·to·cross (mō′tō krôs′) *n.* [Fr. < *motocyclette,* motorcycle + Eng. *cross-country*] a race for lightweight motorcycles on a course over rough, hilly ground

mo·tor (mōt′ər) *n.* [L., a mover < pp. of *movere,* to MOVE] **1.** anything that produces motion in something or gives motion to it **2.** an engine; esp., an internal-combustion engine for making a vehicle go **3.** *Elec.* a machine for converting electrical energy into mechanical energy —*adj.* **1.** producing motion **2.** of or powered by a motor /a *motor* bicycle/ **3.** of, by, or for motor vehicles /a *motor* trip/ **4.** for motorists /a *motor* inn/ **5.** designating or of a nerve carrying impulses from the central nervous system to a muscle producing motion **6.** of, having to do with, or involving muscular movements /*motor* skills/ —*vi.* to travel by automobile

☆**mo·tor·bike** (-bīk′) *n.* [Colloq.] **1.** a bicycle made to go by a motor **2.** a light motorcycle

mo·tor·boat (-bōt′) *n.* a boat made to go by a motor

mo·tor·bus (-bus′) *n.* a passenger bus made to go by a motor: also **motor coach**

☆**mo·tor·cade** (-kād′) *n.* [MOTOR + (CAVAL)CADE] a procession of automobiles, as an escort for an important person

mo·tor·car (-kär′) *n.* **1.** *same as* AUTOMOBILE ☆**2.** a small, open car made to go by a motor and used on a railroad by workmen: also **motor car**

mo·tor·cy·cle (-sī′k'l) *n.* a two-wheeled vehicle, like a bicycle, made to go by an internal-combustion engine —*vi.* **-cled, -cling** to ride a motorcycle —**mo′tor·cy′clist** *n.*

☆**motor hotel** *same as* MOTEL: also **motor court, motor inn, motor lodge**

mo·tor·ist (mōt′ər ist) *n.* a person who drives an automobile or travels by automobile

mo·tor·ize (mōt′ə rīz′) *vt.* **-ized′, -iz′ing 1.** to equip with motor-driven vehicles **2.** to make mobile by mounting on a motor vehicle **3.** to equip (a vehicle, etc.) with a motor —**mo′tor·i·za′tion** *n.*

☆**mo·tor·man** (mōt′ər mən) *n., pl.* **-men** a person who drives an electric streetcar or electric locomotive

☆**motor pool** a group of motor vehicles kept for use as needed, as by military personnel

motor scooter *see* SCOOTER

motor truck a motor-driven truck for hauling loads

motor vehicle a vehicle on wheels having its own motor and not running on rails, for use on streets or highways, as an automobile, truck, or bus

mot·tle (mät′'l) *vt.* **-tled, -tling** [back-formation < *mottled* < MOTLEY + -ED] to mark with blotches or streaks of different colors —*n.* a mottled pattern, as of marble —**mot′tled** *adj.*

mot·to (mät′ō) *n., pl.* **-toes, -tos** [It., a word: see MOT] **1.** a word, phrase, or sentence chosen because it expresses the goals or ideals of a nation, group, etc. and written or marked on a seal, banner, coin, etc. **2.** a maxim adopted as a rule to live by —**see SYN.** at SAYING

‡**moue** (mōō) *n., pl.* **moues** (mōō) [Fr. < OFr. *moue,* a grimace] a pouting grimace

mould (mōld) *n., vt., vi. chiefly Brit. sp.* of MOLD (all terms and senses) —**mould′y** *adj.* **mould′i·er, mould′i·est**

mould·board (mōld′bôrd′) *n. chiefly Brit. sp.* of MOLDBOARD

mould·er (mōl′dər) *vt., vi. chiefly Brit. sp.* of MOLDER

mould·ing (mōl′diŋ) *n. chiefly Brit. sp.* of MOLDING

moult (mōlt) *n., vt., vi. chiefly Brit. sp.* of MOLT

mound (mound) *n.* [< ? MDu. *mond,* protection, infl. by MOUNT[1]] **1.** a heap or bank of earth, sand, etc., whether built or natural; small hill **2.** any heap or pile ☆**3.** *Baseball* the slightly raised area on which the pitcher must stand when pitching —*vt.* to heap up in a mound

☆**Mound Builders** the early Indian peoples who built the burial mounds and other earthworks found in the Middle West and the Southeast

mount[1] (mount) *n.* [< OE. *munt* & OFr. *mont*, both < L. *mons* < IE. base *men-*, to project] a mountain or hill: now poetic or [M-] before a proper name [*Mount McKinley*]

mount[2] (mount) *vi.* [< OFr. *munter*, ult. < L. *mons*: see prec.] **1.** to climb; ascend (often with *up*) **2.** to climb up on something; esp., to get on a horse or bicycle, etc. for riding **3.** to increase in amount [*profits are mounting*] —*vt.* **1.** to go up; ascend; climb [*to mount stairs*] **2.** *a)* to get up on (a horse, bicycle, etc.) for riding *b)* to set on or provide with a horse *c)* to get up on (a platform, stool, etc.) **3.** to place on something raised (with *on*) [*mount the statue on a pedestal*] **4.** to place or fix on or in the proper support, backing, etc., as a gem in a setting, a specimen on a microscope slide, a picture on a mat, etc. **5.** to arrange (a skeleton, dead animal, etc.) for exhibition **6.** to furnish the costumes, settings, etc. for producing (a play) **7.** to prepare for and undertake (an expedition, campaign, etc.) **8.** *Mil. a)* to place (a gun) into position for use *b)* to be armed with (cannon) [*this ship mounts six cannon*] *c)* to post (a guard) on sentry duty *d)* to go on (guard) as a sentry —*n.* **1.** the act or manner of mounting (a horse, etc.) **2.** a horse, bicycle, etc. for riding **3.** the support, setting, etc. on or in which something is mounted —**mount′a·ble** *adj.* —**mount′er** *n.*

moun·tain (moun′t'n) *n.* [< OFr. *montaigne*, ult. < L. *mons*, MOUNT[1]] **1.** a natural raised part of the earth's surface, larger than a hill **2.** [*pl.*] a chain or group of such elevations: also **mountain chain, mountain range** **3.** a large pile, heap, or mound [*a mountain of trash*] **4.** a very large amount —*adj.* **1.** of mountains **2.** situated, living, or used in the mountains **3.** like a mountain; esp., very large

mountain ash a small tree with clusters of white flowers and red or orange berries

mountain cat any of various animals, as the cougar, bobcat, etc.

moun·tain·eer (moun′t'n·ir′) *n.* **1.** a person who lives in a mountainous region **2.** a mountain climber —*vi.* to climb mountains, as for sport

☆**mountain goat** same as ROCKY MOUNTAIN GOAT

☆**mountain laurel** an evergreen shrub of eastern N. America, with pink and white flowers and shiny leaves

☆**mountain lion** same as COUGAR

MOUNTAIN ASH
(tree, branch & berries)

moun·tain·ous (moun′t'n əs) *adj.* **1.** full of mountains [*a mountainous region*] **2.** like a mountain; esp., very large

☆**mountain sheep** any of various wild sheep found in mountain regions; esp., *same as* BIGHORN

moun·tain·side (-sīd′) *n.* the side of a mountain

☆**Mountain Standard Time** *see* STANDARD TIME

Mountain State any of the eight States of the western U.S. through which the Rocky Mountains pass; Montana, Idaho, Wyoming, Nevada, Utah, Colorado, Arizona, and New Mexico

moun·tain·top (-täp′) *n.* the top of a mountain

Mountain View city in W Calif., near San Jose: pop. 51,000

moun·te·bank (moun′tə baŋk′) *n.* [< It. < *montare*, to mount + *in*, on + *banco*, a bench] **1.** orig., a person who sold quack medicines in a public place, attracting an audience by tricks, stories, etc. **2.** any charlatan, or quack —*vi.* to act as a mountebank —**moun′te·bank′er·y** *n.*

mount·ed (moun′tid) *adj.* provided with a mount, or horse, vehicle, support, etc. [*mounted police*]

Mount·ie, Mount·y (moun′tē) *n.*, *pl.* **-ies** [Colloq.] a member of the Royal Canadian Mounted Police

mount·ing (moun′tiŋ) *n.* something serving as a backing, support, setting, etc.

Mount McKinley National Park *see* McKINLEY

Mount Rainier National Park *see* RAINIER

Mount Ver·non (vur′nən) **1.** [after E. *Vernon* (see GROG)] home of George Washington, in N Va., on the Potomac **2.** [after prec.] city in southeastern N.Y.: suburb of New York City: pop. 73,000

mourn (môrn) *vi., vt.* [OE. *murnan*: for IE. base see MEMORY] **1.** to feel or express sorrow for (something regrettable) **2.** to grieve for (someone who has died) —**mourn′er** *n.*

mourn·ful (môrn′fəl) *adj.* **1.** of mourning; feeling or expressing grief or sorrow **2.** causing sorrow; melancholy —**mourn′-ful·ly** *adv.* —**mourn′ful·ness** *n.*

mourn·ing (môr′niŋ) *n.* **1.** a sorrowing; specif., the expression of grief at someone's death **2.** black clothes, drapery, etc., worn or displayed as a conventional sign of grief for the dead **3.** the period during which one mourns the dead —*adj.* of or expressing mourning —**mourn′ing·ly** *adv.*

mourning cloak a common butterfly having purplish-brown wings with a wide yellow border, found throughout Europe and N. America

☆**mourning dove** a gray, wild dove of the U.S.: so called because of its cooing, regarded as mournful

mouse (mous; *for v.*, *usually* mouz) *n.*, *pl.* **mice** [OE. *mus* < IE. base *mus*] **1.** any of numerous small rodents found throughout the world; esp., the **house mouse**, which gets into human dwellings **2.** a timid or spiritless person **3.** [Slang] a dark, swollen bruise under the eye —*vi.* **moused, mous′ing** **1.** to hunt for mice **2.** to search for something busily and stealthily —*vt.* to hunt for

mous·er (mou′zər, -sər) *n.* a cat, dog, etc. as regards its ability to catch mice [*a poor mouser*]

mouse·trap (mous′trap′) *n.* a trap for catching mice

mous·ey (mou′sē, -zē) *adj.* same as MOUSY

mousse (moos) *n.* [Fr., foam, prob. < L. *mulsa*, kind of mead] a light chilled or frozen food made with egg white, gelatin, whipped cream, etc., often served with fruit or flavoring for dessert

mous·tache (mə stash′, mus′tash) *n. var. of* MUSTACHE

mous·y (mou′sē, -zē) *adj.* **mous′i·er, mous′i·est** **1.** of, characteristic of, or like a mouse; quiet, timid, etc. **2.** full of mice —**mous′i·ness** *n.*

mouth (mouth; *for v.* mouth) *n.*, *pl.* **mouths** (mouthz) [OE. *muth* < IE. base *menth-*, to chew, from which also comes L. *mandere*, to chew] **1.** the opening through which an animal takes in food; specif., the cavity in the head which contains the teeth and tongue and through which sounds are uttered **2.** the mouth regarded as the organ of eating and speaking **3.** a person or animal regarded as a being needing food [*six mouths to feed*] **4.** the lips, or the part of the face surrounding the lips **5.** a wry face; grimace **6.** any opening regarded as like the mouth [*the mouth of a river, of a jar, of a cavern, etc.*] —*vt.* **1.** to say, esp. in an affected or pompous manner **2.** to form (a word) with the mouth soundlessly **3.** to rub with the mouth or lips —*vi.* to speak in a pompous manner; declaim —**down in** (or **at**) **the mouth** [Colloq.] depressed; unhappy —**mouth′er** (mouth′-) *n.* —**mouth′like′** *adj.*

-mouthed (mouthd) *a combining form meaning* having a (specified kind of) mouth, voice, etc. [*loudmouthed*]

mouth·ful (mouth′fool′) *n.*, *pl.* **-fuls′** **1.** as much as the mouth can hold **2.** the usual amount taken into the mouth **3.** a small amount, esp. of food **4.** [Colloq.] a long word or group of words hard to say ☆**5.** [Slang] a pertinent, important, or correct remark: chiefly in **say a mouthful**

mouth organ ☆*same as* HARMONICA

mouth·part (-pärt′) *n.* any of various structures or organs around the mouth in arthropods, used for biting, grasping, etc.: *usually used in pl.*

mouth·piece (-pēs′) *n.* **1.** a part placed at, or forming, a mouth [*the mouthpiece of a telephone*] **2.** the part of a musical instrument held in or to the mouth **3.** a person, periodical, etc. used by others to express their views, ideas, etc. **4.** [Slang] a criminal's lawyer

☆**mouth-to-mouth** (mouth′tə mouth′) *adj.* designating a method of resuscitation in which the rescuer forces his breath directly into the mouth and lungs of a person who has stopped breathing

mouth·wash (-wôsh′, -wäsh′) *n.* a flavored liquid, often an antiseptic one, used for rinsing the mouth or gargling

---

fat, āpe, cär; ten, ēven; is, bīte; gō, hôrn, tōōl, lŏŏk; oil, out; up, fur; get; joy; yet; chin; she; thin, then; zh, leisure; ŋ, ring; ə for a in ago, e in agent, i in sanity, o in comply, u in focus; ' as in able (ā'b'l); Fr. bal; ë, Fr. coeur; ö, Fr. feu; ü, Fr. mon; ô, Fr. coq; ü, Fr. duc; r, Fr. cri; H, G. ich; kh, G. doch; ‡foreign; ☆ Americanism; < derived from. See inside front cover.

mouth·y (mou′*thē*, -thē) *adj.* **mouth′i·er, mouth′iest** overly talkative, esp. in a bombastic or rude way —**mouth′i·ly** *adv.* — **mouth′i·ness** *n.*

mou·ton (mōō′tän) *n.* [Fr., sheep: see MUTTON] lambskin, processed and dyed to resemble beaver, seal, etc.

mov·a·ble (mōō′və b'l) *adj.* **1.** that can be moved from one place to another **2.** changing in date from one year to the next [*movable* holidays] —*n.* **1.** something movable **2.** *Law* personal property, as furniture: *usually used in pl.* Also **move′a·ble** —**mov′a·bil′i·ty** *n.* —**mov′a·bly** *adv.*

move (mōōv) *vt.* **moved, mov′ing** [< Anglo-Fr. < OFr. < L. *movere* < IE. base *mew-*, to push away] **1.** to change the place or position of [*move* your chair closer] **2.** to set or keep in motion; impel, stir, etc. [the fan *moves* fresh air into the room] **3.** to cause (*to act, do, say,* etc.); prompt **4.** to arouse the emotions, passions, etc. of [her plea *moved* us deeply] **5.** to propose; esp., to propose formally, as in a meeting [he *moved* that we adjourn for lunch] **6.** to cause (the bowels) to evacuate **7.** *Commerce* to dispose of (goods) by selling —*vi.* **1.** to change place or position **2.** to change the place where one lives [they *moved* to another city] **3.** to be active [to *move* in artistic circles] **4.** to make progress; advance [the game *moved* slowly] **5.** to take action [the police are *moving* against crime] **6.** to be, or be set, in motion; turn, revolve, etc. [the wheels *moved* faster and faster] **7.** to make a formal application (*for*) [*move* for a new trial] **8.** to evacuate: said of the bowels **9.** [Colloq.] to depart [time to be *moving* on] **10.** *Chess, Checkers,* etc. to change the position of a piece **11.** *Commerce* to be disposed of by sale: said of goods —*n.* **1.** act of moving; movement **2.** one of a series of actions toward some goal [the city's latest *move* in its housing program] **3.** a change of where one lives **4.** *Chess, Checkers,* etc. the act of moving or one's turn to move —☆**get a move on** [Slang] **1.** to start moving **2.** to hurry —☆**move in on** [Slang] to draw near to and try to gain control of —**move up** to promote or be promoted —**on the move** [Colloq.] moving about from place to place; very busy

move·ment (mōōv′mənt) *n.* **1.** the act, process, or manner of moving; specif., *a*) an action or motion of a person or group [the graceful *movements* of a dancer] *b*) a shift in position *c*) an evacuation (of the bowels) *d*) *Mil.* a change in the location of troops, ships, etc., as part of a maneuver **2.** *a*) organized action by people working together toward some goal [the *movement* for world peace] *b*) those active in this way **3.** a tendency; trend [an upward *movement* in prices] **4.** the progress of events in a literary work; action **5.** the effect of motion in painting, sculpture, etc. **6.** *Mech.* the moving parts of a mechanism [the *movement* of a clock] **7.** *Music a*) any of the principal divisions of a symphony or other extended composition *b*) *same as* TEMPO OR RHYTHM **8.** in poetry, rhythmic flow

mov·er (-ər) *n.* a person or thing that moves; specif., ☆a person whose work or business is moving furniture, etc. for those changing from one living place to another

☆**mov·ie** (mōō′vē) *n.* [contr. < MOVING PICTURE] **1.** a motion picture **2.** a motion-picture theater —**the movies 1.** the motion-picture industry **2.** a showing of a motion picture [an evening at *the movies*]

☆**mov·ie·go·er** (-gō′ər) *n.* a person who goes to see motion pictures, esp. often or regularly

mov·ing (mōō′viŋ) *adj.* **1.** that moves; specif., *a*) changing, or causing to change, place or position [*moving* parts] *b*) causing motion or action [she's the *moving* spirit in our group] *c*) stirring the emotions [a *moving* drama] **2.** involving a moving motor vehicle [a *moving* violation (of a traffic law)] —**mov′ing·ly** *adv.*

SYN.—**moving** implies a general arousing or stirring of the emotions or feelings, sometimes of sympathy or pity [her *moving* pleas for help]; **poignant** is applied to that which is sharply painful to the feelings [the *poignant* cry of a lost child]; **affecting** applies to that which stirs one's emotions, often so that one weeps [the *affecting* scene of their reunion]; **touching** is used of that which arouses tender feelings, as of love, gratitude, etc. [her *touching* little gift to me]; **pathetic** applies to that which arouses pity or compassion, sometimes pity mingled with contempt [his *pathetic* attempt to be amusing]

moving picture *same as* MOTION PICTURE

☆**moving staircase** (or **stairway**) *same as* ESCALATOR

mow[1] (mō) *vt., vi.* **mowed, mowed** or **mown, mow′ing** [OE. *mawan*: for IE. base see MEADOW] **1.** to cut down (standing grass or grain) with a sickle, lawn mower, etc. **2.** to cut grass or grain from (a lawn, field, etc.) —**mow down 1.** to cause to fall like grass or grain being cut; knock down **2.** to kill or destroy as with swift, sudden strokes, gunfire, etc. —**mow′er** *n.*

mow[2] (mou) *n.* [OE. *muga*] **1.** a stack or heap of hay, grain,

etc., esp. in a barn **2.** the part of a barn where hay or grain is stored

mown (mōn) *alt. pp. of* MOW[1]

Mo·zam·bique (mō′zəm bēk′) country on the SE coast of Africa: c.302,300 sq. mi.; pop. 8,519,000; cap. Maputo

Mo·zart (mō′tsärt), **Wolf·gang A·ma·de·us** (vôlf′gäŋk′ ä′mä dā′oos) 1756–91; Austrian composer

moz·za·rel·la (mät′sə rel′ə) *n.* [It.] a soft, white, mild-flavored Italian cheese

MP, M.P. Military Police

mp [It. *mezzo piano*] *Music* moderately soft

M.P. 1. Member of Parliament **2.** Mounted Police

M.P., m.p. melting point

mpg, m.p.g. miles per gallon

mph, m.p.h. miles per hour

Mr. (mis′tər) *pl.* **Messrs.** (mes′ərz) mister: used before the name or title of a man

Mrs. (mis′iz) *pl.* **Mmes.** (mā däm′) mistress: now used as a title before the name of a married woman

MS 1. Mississippi **2.** multiple sclerosis

MS., ms., ms *pl.* **MSS., mss., mss** manuscript

☆**Ms.** (miz, em′es′) a title used before the name of a woman who may or may not be married in place of either *Miss* or *Mrs.*

M.S., M.Sc. Master of Science

MScand. Middle Scandinavian

MSG monosodium glutamate

Msgr. Monsignor

MSgt, M/Sgt Master Sergeant

m'sieur (mə syʉr′; *Fr.* mə syö′) *n.* monsieur

MST, M.S.T. Mountain Standard Time

MSW, M.S.W. Master of Social Work

MT Montana

Mt., mt. *pl.* **mts. 1.** mount **2.** mountain

M.T. metric ton

mtg. 1. meeting **2.** mortgage: also **mtge.**

mtn. mountain

mu (myōō, mōō) *n.* [< Gr.] the twelfth letter of the Greek alphabet (M, μ)

much (much) *adj.* **more, most** [OE. *mycel*: for IE. base see MASTER] great in quantity, amount, degree, etc. [*much* applause; *much* joy] —*adv.* **more, most 1.** to a great degree or extent [*much* happier] **2.** just about; nearly [*much* the same] **3.** at frequent intervals; often [do you dine out *much*?] —*n.* **1.** a great amount or quantity [*much* to be done] **2.** something great, outstanding, etc. [not *much* to look at] —**as much as 1.** to the degree that **2.** practically; virtually —**make much of** to treat or consider as of great importance —**much as 1.** almost as **2.** however; although —**not much of a** not particularly good as a —**much′ness** *n.*

mu·ci·lage (myōō′s'l ij) *n.* [< MFr. < LL. *mucilago,* musty juice < L. *mucere,* to be moldy: for IE. base see MUCK] **1.** any of various thick, sticky substances produced in certain plants ☆**2.** any watery solution of gum, glue, etc. used for making things stick together

mu·ci·lag·i·nous (myōō′sə laj′ə nəs) *adj.* **1.** of or like mucilage; sticky **2.** producing mucilage

mu·cin (myōō′sin) *n.* [< Fr.: see MUCUS & -IN[1]] any of various glycoproteins present in connective tissue, saliva, mucus, etc. —**mu′cin·oid′, mu′cin·ous** *adj.*

muck (muk) *n.* [< or akin to ON. *myki,* dung < IE. base *meuk-*, slippery] **1.** moist manure **2.** black earth containing decaying matter, used as a fertilizer **3.** *a*) mire; mud *b*) anything unclean or degrading; dirt; filth —*vt.* **1.** to fertilize with muck **2.** [Colloq.] to dirty as with muck (often with *up*) **3.** [Chiefly Brit. Colloq.] to spoil; bungle (often with *up*) —**muck′y** *adj.* **muck′i·er, muck′i·est**

muck·rake (muk′rāk′) *vi.* **-raked′, -rak′ing** [coined c.1906: see MUCK & RAKE[1]] ☆to search for and publicize corrupt dealings by public officials, businessmen, etc. —☆**muck′rak′er** *n.*

mu·co·sa (myōō kō′sə) *n., pl.* **-sae** (-sē), **-sas** [ModL. < fem. of L. *mucosus, mucous*] *same as* MUCOUS MEMBRANE —**mu·co′sal** *adj.*

mu·cous (myōō′kəs) *adj.* [L. *mucosus,* slimy < *mucus,* MUCUS] **1.** of, containing, or secreting mucus **2.** like mucus or covered with or as with mucus; slimy

mucous membrane a mucus-secreting membrane lining body cavities and canals that are open to the air, as the mouth, nose, etc.

mu·cus (myōō′kəs) *n.* [L.: for IE. base see MUCK] the slimy secretion that moistens and protects the mucous membranes

mud (mud) *n.* [prob. < a LowG. source] **1.** wet, soft, sticky earth **2.** libel or slander

☆**mud·der** (mud′ər) *n.* a race horse that performs especially well on a wet, muddy track

mud·dle (mud′'l) *vt.* **-died, -dling** [< MUD] **1.** to mix up; jumble; bungle **2.** to confuse; befuddle, as with liquor —*vi.* to act or think in a confused way —*n.* **1.** a mess, jumble, etc. **2.** a confused state of mind —see SYN. at CONFUSION —**muddle through** [Chiefly Brit.] to succeed in spite of confusion

mud·dle-head·ed (mud′'l hed′id) *adj.* stupid; blundering; confused —**mud′dle-head′ed·ness** *n.*

mud·dy (mud′ē) *adj.* **-di·er, -di·est 1.** full of or spattered with mud **2.** *a)* not clear; cloudy [*muddy* coffee] *b)* not light or bright; dull [a *muddy* complexion] **3.** confused, obscure, etc. [*muddy* thinking] —*vt., vi.* **-died, -dy·ing** to make or become muddy —**mud′di·ly** *adv.* —**mud′di·ness** *n.*

mud·fish (-fish′) *n., pl.* **-fish′, -fish′es:** see FISH ☆any of various fishes that live in mud or muddy water

mud·guard (-gärd′) *n. older name for* FENDER (sense *a*)

mud hen any of various birds that live in marshes, as the coot, gallinule, etc.

mud·pack (-pak′) *n.* a paste made up of fuller's earth, astringents, etc., used as a facial

☆**mud puppy** a N. American salamander that lives in mud under water

mud·sill (-sil′) *n.* the lowest sill in the foundation of a structure, placed in or on the ground

mud·sling·ing (-sliŋ′iŋ) *n.* mean, unfair attacks against an opponent, as in a political campaign — **mud′sling′er** *n.*

MUD PUPPY
(to 18 in. long)

☆**mud snake** a long, bluish-black snake with a sharp spine at the tip of the tail, found in the southeastern U.S.

☆**mud turtle** a small turtle of North and Central America that lives in muddy ponds, streams, etc.

Muen·ster (mun′stər, moon′-) *n.* [after *Munster*, in E France] a semisoft, light-yellow, mild cheese

mu·ez·zin (myoo ez′in) *n.* [< Ar. *mu'adhdhin* < *adhana*, to proclaim] a Moslem crier who calls the people to prayer at the proper hours

muff (muf) *n.* [Du. *mof* < Walloon < Fr. *moufle*, a mitten] **1.** a cylindrical covering of fur, etc. into which the hands are placed from either end for warmth **2.** *a) Baseball*, etc. a failure to hold the ball when catching it *b)* any bungling action —*vt., vi.* to do (something) badly or awkwardly; specif., to miss (a catch) or bungle (a play), as in baseball

muf·fin (muf′'n) *n.* [? akin to OFr. *moufflet*, soft] a quick bread made with eggs, baked in a small, cup-shaped mold and usually eaten hot

muf·fle (muf′'l) *vt.* **-fled, -fling** [prob. akin to OFr. *enmouflé*, muffled < *moufle*, a mitten] **1.** to wrap in a shawl, blanket, etc. so as to hide, keep warm, etc. [*muffled* up in a scarf against the cold] **2.** to wrap or cover in order to deaden or prevent sound **3.** to deaden (a sound) **4.** to stifle —*n.* a covering, etc. used for muffling

muf·fler (muf′lər) *n.* **1.** a scarf worn around the throat, as for warmth **2.** a device for deadening noises, as ☆a section in the exhaust pipe of an internal-combustion engine

muf·ti (muf′tē) *n., pl.* **-tis** [Ar. < *āfta*, to judge] **1.** in Moslem countries, an interpreter of religious law **2.** ordinary clothes, esp. when worn by one who usually wears a uniform

mug (mug) *n.* [prob. < Scand.] **1.** a heavy drinking cup of earthenware or metal with a handle **2.** as much as a mug will hold **3.** [Slang] *a)* the face *b)* the mouth *c)* a hoodlum, thug, etc. ☆*d)* a photograph of the face of a criminal or suspect: also **mug shot** —*vt.* **mugged, mug′ging 1.** to assault, esp. from behind and usually with intent to rob ☆**2.**

MUFFLER

[Slang] to photograph, as for police records —*vi.* **1.** to mug, or assault, someone **2.** [Slang] to grimace, esp. in overacting — **mug′ger** *n.*

mug·gy (mug′ē) *adj.* **-gi·er, -gi·est** [prob. < or akin to ON. *mugga*, a drizzle: for IE. base see MUCK] hot, damp, and close [*muggy* weather] —**mug′gi·ness** *n.*

☆**mug·wump** (mug′wump′) *n.* [< Algonquian *mugquomp*, chief] an independent, esp. in politics

Mu·ham·mad (moo ham′əd) *same as* MOHAMMED —**Mu·ham′mad·an** *adj., n.* —**Mu·ham′mad·an·ism** *n.*

‡**mu·jik** (moo zhēk′, moo′zhik) *n. same as* MUZHIK

Muk·den (mook′dən, mook den′) *former name of* SHENYANG

☆**muk·luk** (muk′luk′) *n.* [Esk. *muklok*, a large seal] **1.** an Eskimo boot made of sealskin or reindeer skin **2.** a canvas or rubber boot like this

mu·lat·to (mə lat′ō, myoo-) *n., pl.* **-toes** [Sp. & Port. *mulato*, of mixed breed < *mulo*, mule < L. *mulus*] **1.** a person who has one black parent and one white parent **2.** popularly, any person with mixed black and white ancestry An old-fashioned term

mul·ber·ry (mul′ber′ē, -bər ē) *n., pl.* **-ries** [OE. *morberie* < L. *morum*, mulberry + OE. *berie*, a berry] **1.** any of several trees that bear edible fruits resembling the raspberry **2.** this fruit **3.** purplish red —*adj.* designating a family of plants including the mulberry, fig, and breadfruit

MUKLUKS

mulch (mulch) *n.* [ME. *molsh*, soft] leaves, straw, etc. spread on the ground around plants to prevent evaporation of water from the soil, freezing of roots, etc. —*vt.* to apply mulch to

mulct (mulkt) *vt.* [L. *mulctare* < *multa*, fine] **1.** to punish by a fine or by depriving of something **2.** to take (money) away from (someone), as by fraud —*n.* a fine or similar penalty

mule[1] (myool) *n.* [< OFr. < L. *mulus*] **1.** the (usually sterile) offspring of a donkey and a horse, esp. of a jackass and a mare **2.** a machine that draws and spins cotton fibers into yarn and winds the yarn **3.** [Colloq.] a stubborn person

mule[2] (myool) *n.* [Fr., ult. < L. *mulleus*, red shoe] a lounging slipper that does not cover the heel

☆**mule deer** a long-eared deer of the western U.S., with a black tail

☆**mule skinner** [Colloq.] a driver of mules

mu·le·ta (moo lāt′ə, -let′ə) *n.* [Sp.] a red flannel cloth draped over a stick and manipulated by the matador in a bullfight

mu·le·teer (myoo′lə tir′) *n.* [< OFr.] a driver of mules

mul·ey (myoo′lē, mool′ē) *adj.* [Scot. *moiley* < Celt.] hornless: said of cattle

Mül·heim (mül′hīm′) city in W West Germany, on the Ruhr: pop. 189,000

mul·ish (myool′ish) *adj.* like a mule; stubborn; obstinate — **mul′ish·ly** *adv.* —**mul′ish·ness** *n.*

mull[1] (mul) *vt., vi.* [OE. *myl*, dust: for IE. base see MILL[1]] [Colloq.] to think or ponder (usually with *over*) [to *mull* over the plan]

mull[2] (mul) *vt.* [< ?] to heat, sweeten, and spice (ale, cider, wine, etc.]

mul·lah, mul·la (mul′ə, mool′-) *n.* [Turk., Per., & Hindi *mulla* < Ar. *mawlā*] a Moslem teacher or interpreter of the religious law: used as a general term of respect for a learned man

mul·lein (mul′in) *n.* [OFr. *moleine*, ult. < L. *mollis*, soft] a tall plant of the figwort family, with spikes of yellow, lavender, or white flowers: see illustration at SPIKE

Mül·ler (mül′ər; *E.* mul′ər, mil′-), (Friedrich) Max (mäks) 1823–1900; Eng. philologist & mythologist, born in Germany

mul·let (mul′it) *n., pl.* **-lets, -let:** see PLURAL, II, D, 1 [OFr. *mulet*, dim. < L. *mullus*, red mullet] any of certain spiny-rayed food fishes found in fresh and salt waters; specif., the **striped** (or **gray) mullet**, or the **red mullet** or **goatfish**

☆**mul·li·gan** (mul′i g'n) *n.* [prob. < personal name] **1.** [Slang] a stew made of odd bits of meat and vegetables, esp. as prepared by hobos: also **mulligan stew 2.** *Golf* in informal play, a free drive, esp. off the first tee after a poor shot

mul·li·ga·taw·ny (mul′i gə tô′nē) *n.* [Tamil *milagutaṇṇir*, pepper water] an East Indian soup of meat, etc., flavored with curry

mul·lion (mul′yən) *n.* [prob. < OFr. *moienel* < L. *medianus*, middle] a slender, vertical dividing bar between the lights of windows, panels, etc. —*vt.* to furnish with mullions —**mul′lioned** *adj.*

mul·tan·gu·lar (mul taŋ′gyoo lər) *adj.* having many angles: also **mul′ti·an·gu·lar** (mul′tē aŋ′-)

mul·ti- [L. < *multus*, much, many] *a combining form meaning:* **1.** having many [*multicolored*] **2.** more than two [*multilateral*] **3.** many times more than [*multimillionaire*] Also, before a vowel, **mult-** The meanings of the following words can be determined by combining the meanings of their component elements:

MULLIONS

mul′ti·cel′lu·lar	mul′ti·lin′gual	mul′ti·ra′cial
mul′ti·col′ored	mul′ti·lo′bate	mul′ti·speed′
mul′ti·di·men′sion·al	mul′ti·na′tion·al	mul′ti·spi′ral
mul′ti·di·rec′tion·al	mul′ti·nu′cle·ate	mul′ti·sto′ried
mul′ti·fold′	mul′ti·phase′	mul′ti·valve′
mul′ti·fo′li·ate	mul′ti·pin′nate	mul′ti·vi′ta·min
mul′ti·lev′el	mul′ti·po′lar	mul′ti·voiced′
mul′ti·lin′e·ar	mul′ti·pur′pose	mul′ti·vol′ume

mul·ti·dis·ci·pli·nar·y (mul′ti dis′ə pli ner′ē) *adj.* of or combining the disciplines of many different branches of learning

mul·ti·far·i·ous (mul′tə far′ē əs, -fer′-) *adj.* [L. *multifarius* < *multus*, many] having many kinds of parts or elements; of great variety; diverse —see SYN. at MANY —**mul′ti·far′i·ous·ly** *adv.* —**mul′ti·far′i·ous·ness** *n.*

mul·ti·fid (mul′tə fid) *adj.* [< L.: see MULTI- & -FID] cut into many divisions or lobes, as a leaf

mul·ti·flo·ra rose (mul′tə flôr′ə) a rose with thick clusters of small flowers, grown esp. for hedges

mul·ti·form (mul′tə fôrm′) *adj.* having many forms, shapes, etc. —**mul′ti·for′mi·ty** *n.*

mul·ti·lat·er·al (mul′ti lat′ər əl) *adj.* **1.** many-sided **2.** involving more than two nations, etc. [a *multilateral* treaty] —**mul′ti·lat′er·al·ly** *adv.*

mul·ti·me·di·a (-mē′dē ə) *n.* same as MIXED MEDIA

☆**mul·ti·mil·lion·aire** (-mil′yə ner′) *n.* a person whose wealth amounts to many millions of dollars, francs, etc.

mul·tip·a·rous (mul tip′ər əs) *adj.* [< ModL.: see MULTI- & -PAROUS] *Zool.* normally bearing more than one offspring at a delivery

mul·ti·par·tite (mul′ti pär′tīt) *adj.* **1.** divided into many parts **2.** *same as* MULTILATERAL (sense 2)

mul·ti·ple (mul′tə p'l) *adj.* [Fr. < L. *multiplex* < *multus*, many + *-plex*, -fold: see DUPLEX] **1.** having or consisting of many parts, elements, etc.; manifold **2.** *Elec.* designating or of a circuit with two or more conductors in parallel —*n.* a number that is a product of some specified number and another number [10 is a *multiple* of 5]

☆**mul·ti·ple-choice** (mul′tə p'l chois′) *adj.* designating a question for which one of several proposed answers is to be chosen as correct, or a test made up of such questions

multiple factors *Genetics* a series of two or more pairs of allelic genes that act as a single unit in passing along certain characters, such as size, pigmentation, etc.

multiple fruit a false fruit formed by a fused cluster of the ovaries of several flowers, as a pineapple or mulberry

multiple sclerosis a disease in which there is damage to the central nervous system: it is marked by speech defects, loss of muscular coordination, etc.

mul·ti·plex (mul′tə pleks′) *adj.* [L. *multiplex*, MULTIPLE] **1.** multiple **2.** designating or of a system for sending or receiving two or more messages or signals over a common circuit, carrier wave, etc. at the same time —*vt.* to send (messages or signals) by a multiplex system

mul·ti·pli·cand (mul′tə pli kand′) *n.* [< L. *multiplicandus*, to be multiplied] *Math.* the number that is, or is to be, multiplied by another (the *multiplier*)

mul·ti·pli·ca·tion (mul′tə pli kā′shən) *n.* a multiplying or being multiplied; specif., *Math.* a method used to find the result (*product*) of adding a specified quantity (*multiplicand*) repeated a specified number of times (*multiplier*)

mul·ti·plic·i·ty (mul′tə plis′ə tē) *n.* [< LL. < L. *multiplex*, MULTIPLE] **1.** the quality or condition of being manifold or various **2.** a great number [a *multiplicity* of plans]

mul·ti·pli·er (mul′tə plī′ər) *n.* **1.** a person or thing that multiplies or increases **2.** *Math.* the number by which another num-

ber (the *multiplicand*) is, or is to be, multiplied **3.** *Physics* any device for multiplying, or intensifying, some effect

mul·ti·ply[1] (mul′tə plī′) *vt.* **-plied′, -ply′ing** [< OFr. < L. *multiplicare* < *multiplex*, MULTIPLE] **1.** to cause to increase in number, amount, degree, etc. **2.** *Math.* to find the product of by multiplication —*vi.* **1.** to increase in number, amount, etc., specif. by having offspring [most rodents *multiply* rapidly] **2.** *Math.* to do multiplication —see SYN. at INCREASE

mul·ti·ply[2] (mul′tə plē) *adv.* in multiple ways

mul·ti·stage (mul′ti stāj′) *adj.* having several propulsion systems, used and discarded in sequence: said of a rocket or missile

mul·ti·tude (mul′tə tood′, -tyood′) *n.* [OFr. < L. *multitudo* < *multus*, many] **1.** a large number of persons or things, esp. when gathered together or thought of as a unit; host, myriad, etc. **2.** the masses (preceded by *the*)

mul·ti·tu·di·nous (mul′tə tood′'n əs, -tyood′-) *adj.* **1.** very numerous; many **2.** consisting of many parts, elements, etc. —**mul′ti·tu′di·nous·ly** *adv.*

mul·ti·va·lent (mul′ti vā′lənt, mul tiv′ə lənt) *adj. Chem.* same as POLYVALENT (sense 2) —**mul′ti·va′lence** *n.*

☆**mul·ti·ver·si·ty** (mul′tə vur′sə tē) *n., pl.* **-ties** the modern large and complex university with its many colleges, extensions, etc., regarded as being impersonal, bureaucratic, etc.

mum[1] (mum) *vi.* **mummed, mum′ming** [< OFr. *momer* < *momo*, echoic for grimace] to wear a mask or costume in fun; specif., to act as a mummer at Christmas time

☆**mum**[2] (mum) *n.* [Colloq.] a chrysanthemum

mum[3] (mum) *adj.* [ME. *momme*, echoic of sound made with closed lips] silent; not speaking [keep *mum*] —*interj.* do not speak! —**mum's the word** say nothing

mum·ble (mum′b'l) *vt., vi.* **-bled, -bling** [ME. *momelen*] **1.** to speak or say indistinctly, as with the mouth partly closed; mutter **2.** [Rare] to chew as one does with toothless gums —*n.* mumbled talk or sound —see SYN. at MURMUR —**mum′bler** *n.* —**mum′bling·ly** *adv.*

mum·ble·ty·peg (mum′b'l tē peg′) *n.* a game in which a jack-knife is tossed in various ways to make it land with the blade in the ground

mum·bo jum·bo (mum′bō jum′bō) [of Afr. origin: < ?] **1.** [M- J-] among certain West African tribes, an idol or fetish supposed to protect the people from evil **2.** any idol or fetish **3.** meaningless ritual, gibberish, etc.

Mum·ford (mum′fərd), **Lewis** 1895– ; U.S. social philosopher & architectural critic

mum·mer (mum′ər) *n.* [see MUM[1]] **1.** one who wears a mask or disguise for fun; specif., in England, any of the masked and costumed persons who act out pantomimes at Christmas time **2.** any actor

mum·mer·y (-ē) *n., pl.* **-mer·ies** **1.** performance by mummers **2.** any show or ceremony regarded as pretentious or hypocritical

mum·mi·fy (mum′ə fī′) *vt.* **-fied′, -fy′ing** to make into or like a mummy —*vi.* to shrivel or dry up —**mum′mi·fi·ca′tion** *n.*

mum·my (mum′ē) *n., pl.* **-mies** [< Fr. < ML. < Ar. *mūmiyā* < Per. *mum*, wax] **1.** a dead body preserved by the method of embalming the ancient Egyptians used **2.** any well-preserved dead body

mumps (mumps) *n.pl.* [with *sing. v.*] [pl. of obs. *mump*, a grimace] an acute contagious disease, caused by a virus and characterized by swelling of the salivary glands

mun. municipal

munch (munch) *vt., vi.* [ME. *monchen*, echoic] to chew steadily, often with a crunching sound

WRAPPED MUMMY IN AN OPENED CASE

Mun·chau·sen (mun′chou′zən, moon′-; -chô′-), **Baron** 1720–97; Ger. soldier & adventurer known for his exaggerated tales of his deeds

Mun·cie (mun′sē) [after the *Munsee* (Delaware) Indians] city in EC Ind.: pop. 69,000

mun·dane (mun dān′, mun′dān) *adj.* [< OFr. < L. < *mundus*, world] **1.** of the world; esp., worldly, as distinguished from heavenly, spiritual, etc. **2.** commonplace; everyday —see SYN. at EARTHLY

Mu·nich (myoo′nik) city in SE West Germany; capital of Bavaria: pop. 1,326,000: Ger. name **Mün·chen** (mün′Hən)

mu·nic·i·pal (myoo nis′ə p'l) *adj.* [< L. < *municeps*, citizen of a free town < *munia*, official duties + *capere*, to take] **1.** of or having to do with a city, town, etc. or its local government **2.** having local self-government —**mu·nic′i·pal·ly** *adv.*

mu·nic·i·pal·i·ty (myoo nis′ə pal′ə tē) *n., pl.* **-ties** [see prec.] a city, town, etc. having its own incorporated government for local affairs

mu·nic·i·pal·ize (myoo nis′ə pə līz′) *vt.* **-ized′, -iz′ing** **1.** to bring under the control or ownership of a municipality **2.** to make a municipality of —**mu·nic′i·pal·i·za′tion** *n.*

mu·nif·i·cent (myoo nif′ə s'nt) *adj.* [< L. < *munificus*, bountiful < *munus*, a gift + *facere*, to make] **1.** very generous in giving **2.** characterized by great generosity [a *munificent* reward] —**mu·nif′i·cence** *n.* —**mu·nif′i·cent·ly** *adv.*

mu·ni·tion (myoo nish′ən) *vt.* to provide with munitions

mu·ni·tions (myoo nish′ənz) *n.pl.* [< MFr. < L. < *munire*, to fortify] war supplies; esp., weapons and ammunition

Mün·ster (mün′stər) city in NW West Germany: pop. 203,000

mu·on (myoo′än) *n.* [MU + (MES)ON] a positively or negatively charged subatomic particle with a mass 207 times that of an electron

mu·ral (myoor′əl) *adj.* [Fr. < L. *muralis* < *murus*, a wall] **1.** of, on, in, or for a wall **2.** like a wall —*n.* a picture or photograph, esp. a large one, painted or applied directly on a wall —**mu′ral·ist** *n.*

Mur·ci·a (mur′shə, -shē ə; *Sp.* moōr′thyä) city in SE Spain: pop. 262,000

☆**Mur·cott** (mur′kät) *n.* [after C. *Murcott* Smith, Florida citrus grower, who developed it c. 1922] a kind of citrus fruit that is a cross between an orange and a tangerine: also **honey tangerine**

mur·der (mur′dər) *n.* [OE. *morthor* & OFr. *mordre*: for IE. base see MORBID] **1.** the unlawful killing of one person by another, esp. when done on purpose or while committing another crime ☆**2.** [Colloq.] something very hard or unsafe to do or deal with —*vt.* **1.** to kill (a person) unlawfully and on purpose **2.** to kill in a brutal way, as in war **3.** to spoil or botch, as in performance [she *murdered* that song] —*vi.* to commit murder —☆**get away with murder** [Slang] to escape being found out or punished for wrongdoing —**mur′der·er** *n.* —**mur′der·ess** *n.fem.*

mur·der·ous (-əs) *adj.* **1.** of, having the nature of, or characteristic of murder; brutal [a *murderous* act] **2.** capable or guilty of, or intending, murder ☆**3.** [Colloq.] very dangerous, trying, etc. [a *murderous* trip through ice and snow] —**mur′der·ous·ly** *adv.* —**mur′der·ous·ness** *n.*

Mu·res (moo resh′) river flowing west from the Carpathian Mountains through Romania into SE Hungary

mu·rex (myoor′eks) *n., pl.* **-ri·ces′** (-ə sēz′), **-rex·es** [ModL. < L., the purple fish] a flesh-eating snail found in warm salt waters: it has a rough, spiny shell and yields a purple substance once used as a dye

mu·ri·at·ic acid (myoor′ē at′ik) [< Fr. < L. < *muria*, brine] hydrochloric acid: a commercial term

Mu·ri·el (myoor′ē əl) [prob. < Celt. < *muir*, sea + *geal*, bright] a feminine name

Mu·ril·lo (moo rē′lyô; *E.* myoo ril′ō), **Bar·to·lo·mé Es·te·ban** (bär′tô lô me′ es·te′bän) 1617–82; Sp. painter

mu·rine (myoor′in, -in) *adj.* [< L. < *mus*, MOUSE] of the family of rodents including the rats and mice

MUREX

murk (murk) *n.* [< ON. *myrkr*, dark] darkness; gloom —*adj.* [Archaic] dark or dim

murk·y (mur′kē) *adj.* **murk′i·er, murk′i·est** **1.** dark or gloomy **2.** heavy and obscure with smoke, mist, etc. —see SYN. at DARK —**murk′i·ly** *adv.* —**murk′i·ness** *n.*

Mur·mansk (moor mänsk′) seaport on the NW coast of the U.S.S.R., on the Arctic Ocean: pop. 296,000

mur·mur (mur′mər) *n.* [< OFr. < L.: echoic word] **1.** a low, indistinct, continuous sound, as of a stream, far-off voices, etc. **2.** a mumbled complaint **3.** *Med.* any abnormal sound heard by auscultation, esp. such a sound in the region of the heart —*vi.* **1.** to make a murmur **2.** to mumble a complaint —*vt.* to say in a murmur —**mur′mur·er** *n.* —**mur′mur·ing** *adj.* —**mur′mur·ous** *adj.*

SYN.—**murmur** implies a steady flow of words or sounds in a low, indistinct voice and may suggest either a contented or complaining feeling [to *murmur* a prayer]; **mutter** usually suggests angry or complaining words or sounds of this kind [to *mutter* curses]; to **mumble** is to utter words or sounds in low tones and with the mouth almost closed so that they are very hard to hear or understand [an old woman *mumbling* to herself]

☆**Mur·phy bed** (mur′fē) [after W. L. *Murphy*, its U.S. inventor (c.1900)] a bed that swings up or folds into a closet or cabinet when not in use

mur·rain (mur′in) *n.* [< OFr. *morine* < L. *mori*, to die] **1.** any of various infectious diseases of cattle **2.** [Archaic] a pestilence; plague

Mur·ray[1] (mur′ē) [< the surname *Murray*] a masculine name

Mur·ray[2] (mur′ē) river in SE Australia, flowing into the Indian Ocean

murre (mur) *n., pl.* **murres, murre**: see PLURAL, II, D, 1 [< ?] any of several swimming and diving birds related to the guillemots and auks

Mur·rum·bidg·ee (mur′əm bij′ē) river in S New South Wales, Australia, flowing west into the Murray

mur·ther (mur′thər) *n., vt., vi. dial. var. of* MURDER

mus. **1.** museum **2.** music **3.** musical

mus·ca·dine (mus′kə din, -dīn′) *n.* [altered < MUSCATEL] a variety of grape grown in the southeastern U.S.

Mus·cat (mus kat′) capital of Oman; seaport on the Gulf of Oman: pop. 6,000

mus·cat (mus′kət, -kat) *n.* [Fr. < Pr. < It. *moscato*, musk, wine < LL. *muscus*, MUSK] **1.** a variety of sweet European grape from which muscatel and raisins are made **2.** same as MUSCATEL (sense 1)

mus·ca·tel (mus′kə tel′) *n.* [OFr. *muscadel*, ult. < It. *moscato*, MUSCAT] **1.** a rich, sweet wine made from the muscat **2.** same as MUSCAT (sense 1) Also **mus′ca·del′** (-del′)

mus·cle (mus′'l) *n.* [Fr. < L. *musculus*, dim. of *mus*, MOUSE] **1.** any of the fleshy parts of the body made up of bundles of cells or fibers that can be contracted and expanded to produce bodily movements **2.** the tissue making up such a fleshy part **3.** muscular strength; brawn ☆**4.** [Colloq.] power or influence based on force —*vi.* **-cled, -cling** ☆[Colloq.] to make one's way by sheer force (usually with *in*)

mus·cle-bound (-bound′) *adj.* having some of the muscles enlarged and less elastic, as from too much exercise

Mus·co·vite (mus′kə vīt′) *n.* a Russian, esp. of Moscow —*adj.* of Russia or of Moscow

Mus·co·vy (mus′kə vē) **1.** former grand duchy surrounding & including Moscow **2.** former name of RUSSIA

Muscovy duck [altered < *musk duck*] a common domesticated duck with a large crest and red wattles

mus·cu·lar (mus′kyə lər) *adj.* **1.** of, consisting of, or done by a muscle or muscles [*muscular* effort] **2.** having well-developed muscles; strong; brawny [*muscular* legs] —**mus′cu·lar′i·ty** (-lar′ə tē) *n.* —**mus′cu·lar·ly** *adv.*

muscular dystrophy a chronic disease characterized by a progressive wasting of the muscles

mus·cu·la·ture (mus′kyə lə chər) *n.* [Fr.] the arrangement of the muscles of a body or of some part of the body; muscular system

Muse (myooz) *n.* [< OFr. < L. < Gr. *mousa*] **1.** *Gr. Myth.* any of the nine goddesses who presided over literature and the arts and sciences **2.** [m-] the spirit regarded as inspiring a poet or artist

muse (myooz) *vi.* **mused, mus′ing** [< OFr. *muser*, to loiter] to think about various things in a quiet, unhurried way —*vt.* to think or say while musing —see SYN. at PONDER

mu·se·um (myoo zē′əm) *n.* [L. < Gr. *mouseion*, place for the Muses < *mousa*, a Muse] a building, room, etc. for keeping or showing a collection of things having to do with art, history, science, etc.

MUSCULATURE

mush[1] (mush) *n.* [prob. var. of MASH] **1.** a thick porridge of boiled cornmeal **2.** any thick, soft mass **3.** [Colloq.] sentimental feeling, talk, etc. that seems silly or overdone

mush[2] (mush) *interj.* [prob. < *mush on*, altered < Fr. *marchons*, let's go] in Canada and Alaska, a shout commanding sled dogs to start or to go faster —*vi.* to travel on foot over snow, usually with a dog sled —*n.* a journey by mushing

mush·room (mush′rōōm′, -room′) *n.* [OFr. *moisseron* < LL. *mussirio*] **1.** any of various rapid-growing, fleshy fungi having a stalk with an umbrellalike top; popularly, any edible variety, as distinguished from the poisonous ones (*toadstools*) **2.** anything like a mushroom in shape or rapid growth —*adj.* **1.** of or made with mushrooms **2.** like a mushroom in shape or rapid growth —*vi.* **1.** to grow or spread rapidly **2.** to flatten out at the end so as to resemble a mushroom

mush·y (mush′ē) *adj.* mush′i·er, mush′i·est **1.** like mush; thick and soft **2.** [Colloq.] affectionate or sentimental in a way that seems silly or overdone —**mush′i·ly** *adv.* —**mush′i·ness** *n.*

mu·sic (myōō′zik) *n.* [< OFr. < L. < Gr. *mousikē* (*technē*), musical (art) < *mousa*, a Muse] **1.** the art of putting tones together in various melodies, rhythms, and harmonies to form compositions for singing or for playing on instruments **2.** the tones so arranged, or their arrangement **3.** any rhythmic sequence of pleasing sounds [the *music* of the birds] **4.** *a)* a musical composition, esp. in the form of a written or printed score *b)* the musical compositions of a particular style, period, or composer **5.** ability to respond to or take pleasure in music —☆**face the music** [Colloq.] to accept the consequences, however unpleasant —**set to music** to compose music for (a poem, etc.)

mu·si·cal (myōō′zi k′l) *adj.* **1.** of or for the creation or performance of music **2.** melodious or harmonious **3.** fond of or skilled in music **4.** set to music —*n.* ☆a theatrical or film production with dialogue and a musical score with popular songs and dances: in full, **musical comedy** (or **play**, or **drama**) —**mu′si·cal′i·ty** (-kal′ə tē) *n.* —**mu′si·cal·ly** *adv.*

musical chairs a game in which the players march to music around empty chairs (always one fewer than the number of players) and rush to sit down each time the music stops: the player with no seat is eliminated in each round

☆**mu·si·cale** (myōō′zə kal′) *n.* [Fr.] a party or social affair featuring a musical program

music box a mechanical musical instrument containing a bar with tuned steel teeth that are struck by pins so arranged on a revolving cylinder as to produce a certain tune or tunes

music hall **1.** an auditorium for musical productions **2.** [Brit.] a vaudeville theater

mu·si·cian (myōō zish′ən) *n.* a person skilled in music; esp., a professional performer of music —**mu·si′cian·ly** *adv.* —**mu·si′cian·ship′** *n.*

mu·si·col·o·gy (myōō′zi käl′ə jē) *n.* [< It.: see MUSIC & -LOGY] the systematized study of the science, history, and methods of music —**mu′si·co·log′i·cal** (-kə läj′i k′l) *adj.* —**mu′si·col′o·gist** *n.*

mus·ing (myōō′ziŋ) *adj.* that muses; meditative —*n.* meditation; reflection —**mus′ing·ly** *adv.*

musk (musk) *n.* [< OFr. < LL. < Gr. < Per. *mušk*, musk < Sans. *muṣka*, testicle, dim. of *mus*, MOUSE] **1.** a substance with a strong, penetrating odor, obtained from a small sac (**musk bag**) under the skin of the abdomen in the male musk deer: used as the basis of numerous perfumes **2.** the odor of this substance, now often created synthetically —**musk′like′** *adj.*

musk deer a small, hornless deer of the uplands of C Asia: the male secretes musk

mus·keg (mus′keg) *n.* [< Ojibwa native name] a kind of bog or marsh containing thick layers of decaying vegetable matter, mosses, etc., found esp. in Canada and Alaska

☆**mus·kel·lunge** (mus′kə lunj′) *n.*, *pl.* -lunge′ [< Ojibwa *maskinoje*] a large pike of the Great Lakes and upper Mississippi: also called **mus′kie** (-kē)

mus·ket (mus′kit) *n.* [< MFr. < It. *moschetto*, orig. fledged arrow < L. *musca*, a fly: for IE. base see MIDGE] a smoothbore, long-barreled firearm, used, as by infantry soldiers, before the invention of the rifle

mus·ket·eer (mus′kə tir′) *n.* a soldier armed with a musket

mus·ket·ry (mus′kə trē) *n.* **1.** the skill of firing muskets or other small arms **2.** muskets or musketeers, collectively

musk·mel·on (musk′mel′ən) *n.* [MUSK + MELON] any of several roundish fruits growing on a vine of the gourd family, as the cantaloupe: they have a thick rind and sweet, juicy flesh

☆**Mus·ko·ge·an** (mus kō′gē ən, -jē-) *adj.* designating or of a N. American Indian language family of the southeastern U.S.: also **Mus·kho′ge·an**

musk ox a hardy ox of arctic America and Greenland, with a long, coarse, hairy coat, large, curved horns, and a musklike odor

☆**musk·rat** (musk′rat′) *n.*, *pl.* -rats′, -rat′: see PLURAL, II, D, 1 **1.** a N. American rodent living in water and having glossy brown fur, webbed hind feet, and a musklike odor **2.** its fur

musk·y (mus′kē) *adj.* musk′i·er, musk′i·est of, like, or smelling of musk —**musk′i·ness** *n.*

Mus·lim (muz′ləm, mooz′-) *n.*, *adj.* same as MOSLEM

mus·lin (muz′lin) *n.* [< Fr. < It. *mussolino* < *Mussolo*, Mosul, city in Iraq] a strong, often sheer cotton cloth of plain weave; esp., a heavy variety used for sheets, pillowcases, etc.

MUSKRAT
(body 9–13 in.
long; tail 7–11
in. long)

muss (mus) *n.* [prob. var. of MESS] **1.** [Now Rare] a mess **2.** [Old Slang or Dial.] a squabble —*vt.* to make messy or untidy; disarrange (often with *up*)

mus·sel (mus′'l) *n.* [< OE., ult. < L. *musculus*, mussel, MUSCLE] any of various bivalve mollusks; specif., *a)* an edible saltwater variety *b)* a large freshwater variety with a pearly shell formerly made into buttons

Mus·set (mü sě′), (**Louis Charles**) **Al·fred de** (al fred′ də) 1810–57; Fr. poet & writer

Mus·so·li·ni (mōōs′sō lē′nē; *E.* moos′ə lē′nē, mus′-), **Be·ni·to** (be nē′tō) 1883–1945; It. dictator; Fascist prime minister of Italy (1922–43): executed

Mus·sorg·sky (mōō sôrg′skē), **Mo·dest Pe·tro·vich** (mô′dyest′ pyi trô′vich) 1839–81; Russ. composer

Mus·sul·man (mus′'l mən) *n.*, *pl.* -mans [< Per. < Ar. *muslim*] [Now Rare] a Moslem

muss·y (mus′ē) *adj.* muss′i·er, muss′i·est [Colloq.] messy; disordered, rumpled, etc. —**muss′i·ness** *n.*

must[1] (must; *unstressed* məst) *v.aux., pt.* must [< OE. *moste*, pt. of *motan*, may: for IE. base see MEDICAL] a helping verb used with the infinitive of various verbs (without *to*) to express: **1.** compulsion, obligation, or necessity [I *must* pay her] **2.** probability [you *must* be my cousin] **3.** certainty [all men *must* die] *Must* is sometimes used with the verb understood [shoot if you *must*] —*n.* [Colloq.] something that must be done, had, read, seen, etc. [this book is a *must*] —*adj.* [Colloq.] that must be done, etc.; necessary; essential

must[2] (must) *n.* [OE. < L. *mustum*, new wine < *mustus*, fresh] the juice pressed from grapes or other fruit before fermentation

must[3] (must) *n.* a musty quality or state; mustiness

mus·tache (mə stash′, mus′tash) *n.* [< Fr. < It. *mostacchio* < MGr. < Gr. *mystax*, upper lip] **1.** the hair on the upper lip of men **2.** the hair or bristles growing about an animal's mouth

mus·ta·chio (məs tä′shō, -shē ō′) *n.*, *pl.* -chios [< Sp. or It.] a mustache, esp. a large, bushy one —**mus·ta′chioed** *adj.*

Mustafa Kemal same as KEMAL ATATURK

☆**mus·tang** (mus′taŋ) *n.* [< AmSp. < Sp. *mesteño*, belonging to the graziers, wild] a small wild or half-wild horse of the southwestern plains of the U.S.

mus·tard (mus′tərd) *n.* [< OFr. *moustarde* < L. *mustum*, MUST[2] (orig. added to the condiment)] **1.** any of several plants of the mustard family, with yellow flowers and slender pods **2.** the ground or powdered seeds from these pods, often prepared as a paste, used as a sharp seasoning **3.** a dark yellow —*adj.* designating or of a family of plants with cross-shaped flowers, including cabbage, turnip, radish, alyssum, etc. —☆**cut the mustard** [Colloq.] to do the work required of one

mustard gas [from its mustardlike odor] a vaporizing liquid, $(CH_2ClCH_2)_2S$, used in warfare as a poison gas: it is very irritating and has a blistering effect

mustard plaster a plaster made with powdered mustard, applied to the skin as a counterirritant

mus·ter (mus′tər) *vt.* [< OFr. < ML. < L. *monstrare*, to show < *monere*: see MONITOR] **1.** to assemble (troops, etc.), as for inspection or roll call **2.** to gather up; collect; summon (often with *up*) [to *muster* up strength] **3.** to total in number —*vi.* to assemble as for inspection or roll call —*n.* **1.** an assembling, as of troops for inspection **2.** *a)* the persons or things assembled *b)* the total of these **3.** the list of persons in a military or naval unit: also **muster roll** —☆**muster in** (or **out**) to enlist in (or discharge from) military service —**pass muster** to measure up to the required standards

must·n't (mus′'nt) must not

mus·ty (mus′tē) *adj.* -ti·er, -ti·est [ult. < ? MOIST] **1.** having a stale, moldy smell or taste [a *musty* attic; *musty* bread] **2.** stale, trite, or outdated [*musty* ideas] —**mus′ti·ly** *adv.* —**mus′ti·ness** *n.*

mu·ta·ble (myoōt'ə b'l) *adj.* [< L. < *mutare:* see MUTANT] **1.** that can be changed **2.** tending to frequent change; inconstant **3.** subject to mutation —**mu'ta·bil'i·ty, mu'ta·ble·ness** *n.* —**mu'ta·bly** *adv.*

mu·tant (myoot''nt) *adj.* [< L. prp. of *mutare*, to change: for IE. base see MIGRATE] having to do with or undergoing mutation —*n.* an animal or plant with inheritable characters that differ from those of the parents

mu·tate (myoo'tāt) *vi., vt.* **-tat·ed, -tat·ing** [< L.: see MUTANT] to change; specif., to undergo or cause to undergo mutation

mu·ta·tion (myoo tā'shən) *n.* [< OFr. < L. < *mutare:* see MUTANT] **1.** a changing or being changed **2.** a change, as in form, nature, etc. **3.** *Biol.* *a)* a sudden variation in some inheritable character in a germ cell of an animal or plant, as distinguished from a variation resulting from generations of gradual change *b)* an individual resulting from such variation; mutant —**mu'ta·tion·al** *adj.* —**mu'ta·tion·al·ly** *adv.*

mute (myoōt) *adj.* [< OFr. < L. *mutus:* for IE. base see MOPE] **1.** not speaking; keeping silent **2.** unable to speak; not spoken [a *mute* appeal] **4.** not pronounced; silent, as the *e* in *mouse* **5.** *Law* refusing to plead when arraigned: used in the phrase **stand mute** —*n.* **1.** a person who does not speak; specif., one who, deaf ever since infancy, has not learned to speak; deaf-mute **2.** a letter that is not pronounced **3.** *Music* a device used to soften the tone of an instrument —*vt.* **mut'ed, mut'ing 1.** to soften the sound of, as with a mute **2.** to tone down (a color) —see SYN. at VOICELESS —**mute'ly** *adv.* —**mute'ness** *n.*

mu·ti·late (myoōt''l āt') *vt.* **-lat'ed, -lat'ing** [< L. pp. of *mutilare* < *mutilus*, maimed] **1.** to cut off or damage a limb or other important part of (a person or animal) **2.** to damage or otherwise make imperfect, esp. by removing an essential part or parts [to *mutilate* a book by ripping out pages] —**mu'ti·la'tion** *n.* —**mu'ti·la'tor** *n.*

mu·ti·neer (myoōt''n ir') *n.* one guilty of mutiny

mu·ti·nous (myoōt''n əs) *adj.* **1.** taking part or likely to take part in a mutiny **2.** of or having to do with mutiny —**mu'ti·nous·ly** *adv.* —**mu'ti·nous·ness** *n.*

mu·ti·ny (myoōt''n ē) *n., pl.* **-nies** [< Fr. < OFr. *mutin*, riotous < *meute*, a revolt, ult. < L. *movere*, MOVE] forcible revolt against established authority; esp., rebellion of soldiers or sailors against their officers —*vi.* **-nied, -ny·ing** to take part in a mutiny; revolt —see SYN. at REBELLION

☆**mutt** (mut) *n.* [prob. < *muttonhead*, a dolt] [Slang] **1.** a stupid person; blockhead **2.** a mongrel dog; cur

mut·ter (mut'ər) *vi., vt.* [ME. *moteren:* for IE. base see MOPE] to speak or say in low tones with the lips almost closed, often in an angry or complaining way; grumble —*n.* **1.** a muttering **2.** something muttered —see SYN. at MURMUR —**mut'ter·er** *n.*

mut·ton (mut''n) *n.* [OFr. *moton*, a ram < ML. *multo*, sheep] the flesh of a sheep, esp. a grown sheep, used as food —**mut'ton·y** *adj.*

mutton chop 1. a piece cut from the rib of a sheep for broiling or frying **2.** [*pl.*] side whiskers shaped like mutton chops

mu·tu·al (myoō'choo wəl) *adj.* [< MFr. < L. *mutuus*, reciprocal < *mutare:* see MUTANT] **1.** *a)* done, felt, etc. by each of two or more for or toward the other or others; reciprocal [*mutual* admiration] *b)* of each other [*mutual* enemies] **2.** shared in common; joint [our *mutual* friend] —**mu'tu·al'i·ty** (-wal'ə tē) *n., pl.* **-ties** —**mu'tu·al·ly** *adv.*

mutual fund a trust or corporation that invests funds from its shareholders in various securities

mu·tu·al·ism (myoō'choo wəl-

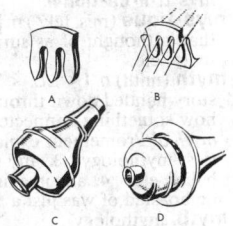

MUTES
(A, violin mute; B, on violin bridge; C, trumpet mute; D, in bell of trumpet)

MUTTON CHOPS

iz'm) *n. Biol.* symbiosis with mutual advantage to both or all organisms involved

☆**mu·tu·el** (myoō'choo wəl) *n. same as* PARIMUTUEL

☆**muu·muu** (moō'moō) *n.* [< Haw., lit., cut off] a full, long, loose garment for women, usually in a bright print as originally worn in Hawaii

☆**Mu·zak** (myoō'zak) *a trademark for* a system of transmitting recorded music to restaurants, factories, etc. —*n.* the music transmitted

‡**mu·zhik, mu·zjik** (moō zhēk', moō'zhik) *n.* [Russ.] in czarist Russia, a peasant

muz·zle (muz'l) *n.* [< OFr. *musel*, snout < ML. *musum* < ?] **1.** the part of the head of a dog, horse, etc. including the mouth, nose, and jaws; snout **2.** a device, as of straps, fastened over the mouth of an animal to prevent its biting or eating **3.** anything that prevents free speech **4.** the front end of the barrel of a firearm —*vt.* **-zled, -zling 1.** to put a muzzle on (an animal) **2.** to prevent from talking or expressing an opinion [laws that *muzzle* the press] —**muz'zler** *n.*

muz·zle·load·er (-lōd'ər) *n.* any firearm loaded through the muzzle —**muz'zle·load'ing** *adj.*

my (mī; *unstressed, often* mə) *adj.* [OE. *min*] of, belonging to, made by, or done by me [*my* book; *my* work] —*interj.* an exclamation of surprise, dismay, etc. [Oh, *my!*]

my·as·the·ni·a (mī'əs thē'nē ə) *n.* [ModL.: see MYO- & ASTHENIA] muscular weakness or fatigue —**my'as·then'ic** (-then'ik) *adj.*

my·ce·li·um (mī sē'lē əm) *n., pl.* **-li·a** (-ə) [ModL. < Gr. *mykēs*, a mushroom] the thallus, or vegetative part, of a fungus, made of a mass of threadlike tubes —**my·ce'li·al** *adj.*

My·ce·nae (mī sē'nē) ancient city in the NE Peloponnesus

My·ce·nae·an (mī'sə nē'ən) *adj.* **1.** of Mycenae **2.** designating or of a civilization that existed in Greece, Asia Minor, etc. from 1500 to 1100 B.C.

-my·cete (mī'sēt, mī sēt') [< ModL. < Gr. < *mykēs*, a mushroom] *a combining form meaning* one of a specified class of fungi

my·co- [< Gr. *mykēs*, fungus] *a combining form meaning* fungus: also, before a vowel, **myc-**

my·col·o·gy (mī käl'ə jē) *n.* [< ModL.: see MYCO- & -LOGY] the branch of botany dealing with fungi —**my·co·log·ic** (mī'kə läj'ik), **my'co·log'i·cal** *adj.* —**my·col'o·gist** *n.*

my·co·sis (mī kō'sis) *n., pl.* **-ses** (-sēz) [ModL.: see MYC(O)- & -OSIS] **1.** the growth of parasitic fungi in any part of the body **2.** a disease caused by such fungi —**my·cot'ic** (-kät'ik) *adj.*

my·e·lin (mī'ə lin) *n.* [G. < Gr. *myelos*, marrow] a white, fatty substance forming a sheath around certain nerve fibers —**my'e·lin'ic** *adj.*

my·e·li·tis (mī'ə līt'is) *n.* [ModL. < Gr. *myelos*, marrow + -ITIS] inflammation of the spinal cord or the bone marrow

my·e·lo·gram (mī'ə lō gram') *n.* [< Gr. *myelos*, marrow + -GRAM] an X-ray of the spinal cord, taken after the injection of a substance that will show contrast on the developed photograph —**my'e·log'ra·phy** (-läg'rə fē) *n.*

☆**My·lar** (mī'lär) *a trademark for* a polyester used for recording tapes, fabrics, etc. —*n.* [m-] this substance

my·na, my·nah (mī'nə) *n.* [Hindi *mainā*] any of a group of tropical birds of southeastern Asia related to the starling: some species can mimic speech

my·o- [< Gr. *mys* (gen. *myos*), a muscle] *a combining form meaning* muscle: also, before a vowel, **my-**

my·o·car·di·um (mī'ō kär'dē əm) *n.* [ModL.: see prec. + CARDIO-] the muscular substance of the heart: see illustration at HEART —**my'o·car'di·al** *adj.*

my·o·pi·a (mī ō'pē ə) *n.* [ModL. < Gr. *myein*, to close + *ōps*, an eye] **1.** abnormal vision in which light rays from distant objects focus in front of the retina instead of on it, so that the objects are not seen distinctly; nearsightedness **2.** lack of foresight —**my·op'ic** (-äp'ik) *adj.* —**my·op'i·cal·ly** *adv.*

My·ra (mī'rə) [< ? Ir. *Moira*] a feminine name

myr·i·a- [< Gr. *myrias:* see MYRIAD] *a combining form meaning:* **1.** many, numerous **2.** ten thousand; the factor 10^4

MYNA
(to 12 in. long)

myr·i·ad (mir′ē əd) *n.* [< Gr. *myriados*, genitive of *myrias*, ten thousand < *myrios*, countless] **1.** orig., ten thousand **2.** any indefinitely large number **3.** a great number of persons or things —*adj.* **1.** countless; innumerable **2.** of a highly varied nature

myr·i·a·pod (mir′ē ə päd′) *adj.* [see prec. & -POD] having many legs; specif., of a large group of arthropods having a long body of many segments, each with one or more pairs of jointed legs, as the centipedes —*n.* any animal of this group

Myr·mi·don (mur′mə dän′, -dən) *n., pl.* **-dons, Myr·mid·o·nes** (mər mid′ə nēz′) **1.** *Gr. Legend* any of a tribe of Thessalian warriors who fought under Achilles, their king, in the Trojan War **2.** [m-] an unquestioning follower or subordinate

myrrh (mur) *n.* [< OE. & OFr. < L. < Gr. *myrrha* < Ar. *murr*] **1.** a fragrant, bitter-tasting gum resin given off by any of several trees and shrubs of Arabia and eastern Africa, used in making incense, perfume, etc. **2.** any of these plants

Myr·tle (mur′t'l) [see next entry] a feminine name

myr·tle (mur′t'l) *n.* [< OFr. < ML. dim. of L. *myrtus* < Gr. *myrtos*] **1.** a shrub with evergreen leaves, white or pink flowers, and dark berries **2.** any of various other evergreen plants, as the periwinkle —*adj.* designating a family of evergreen trees and shrubs, including myrtle, eucalyptus, guava, clove, and blue gum

my·self (mī self′, mə-) *pron.* a form of the 1st person singular pronoun, used: *a)* as an intensive [I'll do it *myself*] *b)* as a reflexive [I hurt *myself*] *c)* as a kind of noun meaning "my real or true self" [I am not *myself* today]

My·sore (mī sôr′) city in S India: pop. 254,000

mys·te·ri·ous (mis tir′ē əs) *adj.* of, containing, suggesting, or characterized by mystery; hard to explain or solve —**mys·te′ri·ous·ly** *adv.* —**mys·te′ri·ous·ness** *n.*

mys·ter·y[1] (mis′tə rē, -trē) *n., pl.* **-ter·ies** [< L. < Gr. *mystērion*, ult. < *myein*, to initiate into the mysteries, orig., to close (eyes or mouth): for IE. base see MOPE] **1.** something unexplained, unknown, or kept secret **2.** *a)* anything that remains so secret or obscure as to arouse curiosity *b)* a novel, play, etc. involving an event of this kind, esp. one about a crime and its solution **3.** the quality of being secret or hard to explain; obscurity or secrecy [an air of *mystery* about her] **4.** [*pl.*] secret religious rites known only to the people who have taken part in them [the Eleusinian *mysteries*] **5.** same as MYSTERY PLAY **6.** *Theol.* any religious truth accepted on faith as having been revealed by or from God

SYN.—**mystery** may apply to something beyond human understanding or simply to anything the answer to which is not known [the *mystery* of life; the *mystery* of the missing gloves]; **enigma** specifically applies to a statement or question worded in such a puzzling or ambiguous way that its meaning is unclear, and generally, to anything hard to understand or explain; **riddle** specifically applies to a seemingly contradictory or absurd question asked in guessing games (Example: What has 18 legs and red spots and catches flies? A baseball team with the measles), and generally, to any difficult problem

mys·ter·y[2] (mis′tə rē) *n., pl.* **-ter·ies** [< ML. *misterium*, altered < L. *ministerium*, office, by confusion with *mysterium*, a secret rite] [Archaic] a craft or craft guild

mystery play any of a class of medieval dramatic representations of Biblical events

mys·tic (mis′tik) *adj.* [< L. < Gr. *mystikos* < *mystēs*, one initiated] **1.** same as MYSTICAL **2.** mysterious, secret, occult, awe-inspiring, etc. [*mystic* rites, *mystic* powers] —*n.* one who claims to have mystical experiences by which he learns truths not known by ordinary people

mys·ti·cal (mis′ti k'l) *adj.* **1.** of mystics or mysticism; esp., based on intuition, meditation, etc. of a spiritual nature **2.** spiritually symbolic [the *mystical* rose, a symbol of the Virgin Mary] **3.** same as MYSTIC (sense 2) —**mys′ti·cal·ly** *adv.*

mys·ti·cism (mis′tə siz'm) *n.* **1.** the beliefs or practices of mystics **2.** the doctrine that meditation can lead to a direct knowledge of God or of spiritual truths **3.** vague or obscure thinking or belief

mys·ti·fy (mis′tə fī′) *vt.* **-fied′, -fy′ing** [< Fr. < *mystère*, mystery + -*fier*, -FY] **1.** *a)* to puzzle or perplex [his abrupt departure *mystified* us] *b)* to bewilder deliberately [*mystified* by magic tricks] **2.** to make obscure or hard to understand —**mys′ti·fi·ca′tion** *n.*

mys·tique (mis tēk′) *n.* [Fr., mystic] a kind of mystical quality that is thought of as surrounding some person, institution, activity, etc.

myth (mith) *n.* [< LL. < Gr. *mythos*, a word, legend] **1.** an old story handed down through the years, serving usually to explain how something connected with man or nature came to be [the *myth* of Prometheus explains how man got fire] **2.** all such stories; mythology **3.** any fictitious story, or unscientific account, belief, etc. **4.** any imaginary person or thing [the wealthy uncle he boasted of was just a *myth*]

myth. mythology

myth·i·cal (mith′i k'l) *adj.* **1.** of, or having the nature of, a myth or myths [*mythical* tales] **2.** existing only in myth [*mythical* monsters] **3.** imaginary or fictitious; not based on fact [his *mythical* bank account] Also **myth′ic** —**myth′i·cal·ly** *adv.*

my·thol·o·gize (mi thäl′ə jīz′) *vi.* **-gized′, -giz′ing** to relate, compile, or explain myths —*vt.* to make into a myth: also **myth·i·cize** (mith′ə sīz′) **-cized′, -ciz′ing** —**my·thol′o·giz′er** *n.*

my·thol·o·gy (mi thäl′ə jē) *n., pl.* **-gies** [< LL. < Gr. < *mythos*, myth + -*logia*, -LOGY] **1.** the study of myths **2.** myths as a group; esp., all the myths of a specific people or about a specific being [Greek *mythology*] —**myth·o·log·i·cal** (mith′ə läj′i k'l) *adj.* —**myth′o·log′i·cal·ly** *adv.* —**my·thol′o·gist** *n.*

myth·os (mith′äs, mī′thäs) *n.* **1.** a myth or body of myths **2.** the attitudes, beliefs, etc. most characteristic of a particular group or society

Myt·i·le·ne (mit′'l ē′nē) same as LESBOS

myx·e·de·ma (mik′sə dē′mə) *n.* [ModL. < Gr. *myxa*, mucus + *oidēma*, a swelling] a disease caused by failure of the thyroid gland and marked by a drying and thickening of the skin and sluggishness of the mind and body —**myx′e·de′ma·tous** (-təs) *adj.*

myx·o·my·cete (mik′sō mī sēt′) *n.* [< Gr. *myxa*, mucus + -MYCETE] same as SLIME MOLD —**myx′o·my·ce′tous** (-sē′təs) *adj.*

N

N, n (en) *n., pl.* **N's, n's** **1.** the fourteenth letter of the English alphabet **2.** the sound of *N* or *n*

n (en) *n.* **1.** *Math. the symbol for* an indefinite number **2.** *Physics the symbol for* neutron

N *Chem.* nitrogen

N, N., n, n. **1.** north **2.** northern

N. **1.** National(ist) **2.** Navy **3.** Norse **4.** November

n. **1.** net **2.** neuter **3.** noon **4.** noun **5.** number

Na [L. *natrium*] *Chem.* sodium

N.A. North America

NAACP, N.A.A.C.P. National Association for the Advancement of Colored People

nab (nab) *vt.* **nabbed, nab′bing** [prob. var. of dial. *nap*, to snatch < Scand.] [Colloq.] **1.** to seize suddenly; snatch **2.** to arrest or catch (a criminal or wrongdoer) **—nab′ber** *n.*

na·bob (nā′bäb) *n.* [< Hindi < Ar. *nuwwāb*, pl. of *nā′ib*, deputy] **1.** a native provincial deputy or governor of the old Mogul Empire in India **2.** a very rich or important man

na·celle (nə sel′) *n.* [Fr. < LL. *navicella*, dim. of L. *navis*, a ship] a streamlined enclosure on an aircraft, esp. that which houses an engine

na·cre (nā′kər) *n.* [Fr. < It. < Ar. *naqqārah*, drum] *same as* MOTHER-OF-PEARL

na·cre·ous (nā′krē əs) *adj.* **1.** of or like nacre **2.** yielding nacre **3.** iridescent; lustrous

Na·dine (nə dēn′, nā-) [Fr. < Russ. *nadezhda*, hope] a feminine name

na·dir (nā′dər, -dir) *n.* [< MFr. < ML. < Ar. *nazīr* (*as-samt*), opposite (the zenith)] **1.** that point of the celestial sphere directly opposite to the zenith and directly below the observer **2.** the lowest point [at the *nadir* of his career]

nae (nā) *adv.* [Scot.] no; not **—adj.** no

nag[1] (nag) *vt.* **nagged, nag′ging** [< Scand. < ON. *gnaga*, to gnaw: for IE. base see GNAW] **1.** to annoy by continual scolding, faultfinding, urging, etc. **2.** to keep troubling, worrying, etc. [the unpaid debt *nagged* his conscience] **—vi.** **1.** to urge, scold, etc. constantly **2.** to cause continual discomfort, pain, etc. [a *nagging* toothache] **—n.** a person, esp. a woman, who nags: also **nag′ger** **—nag′ging·ly** *adv.* **—nag′gy** *adj.* **-gi·er, -gi·est**

nag[2] (nag) *n.* [ME. *nagge* < ?] **1.** a horse that is worn-out, old, etc. ☆**2.** [Slang] a racehorse, esp. an inferior one

Na·ga·sa·ki (nä′gə sä′kē) seaport on the W coast of Kyushu, Japan: partly destroyed (Aug. 9, 1945) by a U.S. atomic bomb: pop. 405,000

Na·go·ya (nä′gô yä′) seaport in S Honshu, Japan: pop. 1,935,000

Nag·pur (näg′poor) city in C India: pop. 690,000

Na·hua·tl (nä′wät ′l) *n.* [Nahuatl] **1.** *pl.* **Na′hua·tls, Na′hua·tl** a member of any of a number of Indian tribes of Mexico **2.** their Uto-Aztecan language **3.** a branch of the Uto-Aztecan language family, spoken in Mexico and Central America

Na·hum (nā′əm, -həm) *Bible* **1.** a Hebrew prophet of the 7th cent. B.C. **2.** the book containing his prophecies: abbrev. **Nah.**

nai·ad (nā′ad, nī′-; -əd) *n., pl.* **-ads, -a·des′** (-ə dēz′) [< Fr. < L. < Gr. *Naïas* < *naein*, to flow] **1.** [also N-] *Gr. & Rom. Myth.*

any of the nymphs living in and giving life to springs, fountains, rivers, etc. **2.** a girl or woman swimmer **3.** *Zool. a)* the aquatic nymph of certain insects, as the dragonfly and mayfly *b)* any of various freshwater mussels

na·if, na·ïf (nä ēf′) *adj.* [Fr.] *same as* NAIVE

nail (nāl) *n.* [OE. *nægl*] **1.** *a)* the thin, horny substance growing out at the ends of the fingers and toes *b)* a claw **2.** a tapered piece of metal, commonly pointed and with a head, driven with a hammer to hold pieces of wood together, serve as a peg, etc. **—vt.** **1.** to attach, fasten together, or fasten shut with nails **2.** to fix (the eyes, attention, etc.) steadily on an object **3.** to discover or expose (a lie, etc.) **4.** [Colloq.] to catch, capture, etc. **5.** [Colloq.] to hit squarely **—hit the nail on the head** to do or say whatever is exactly right **—nail down** to settle definitely; make sure **—nail′er** *n.*

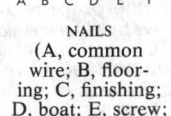

NAILS
(A, common wire; B, flooring; C, finishing; D, boat; E, screw; F, masonry)

nail·brush (nāl′brush′) *n.* a small, stiff brush for cleaning the fingernails

☆**nail file** a small, flat file for smoothing down and shaping the fingernails

nail polish a kind of lacquer, usually colored, applied to the fingernails or toenails as a cosmetic

nail set a tool for sinking the head of a nail so that it is below the surface of the wood

nain·sook (nān′sook) *n.* [< Hindi < *nain*, the eye + *sukh*, pleasure] a thin, lightweight cotton fabric

nai·ra (nī′rə) *n., pl.* **nai′ra** [dim. of NIGERIA] the monetary unit of Nigeria: see MONETARY UNITS, table

Nai·ro·bi (nī rō′bē) capital of Kenya: pop. 509,000

na·ive, na·ïve (nä ēv′) *adj.* [Fr., fem. of *naïf* < L. *nativus*, natural] **1.** simple in an unaffected, or sometimes foolish, way; childlike; unsophisticated **2.** not suspicious; credulous **—na·ive′ly, na·ïve′ly** *adv.*

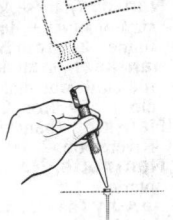

NAIL SET

SYN.—naive implies a being simple and innocent in a trusting way, but sometimes suggests an almost foolish lack of worldly wisdom [his *naive* belief that all advertising is honest]; **ingenuous** suggests a childlike frankness or straightforwardness [his *ingenuous* delight in any kind of flattery]; **artless** implies the appealing open and natural quality of one who is indifferent to the effect he has on others [a simple, *artless* style of folk singing]; **unsophisticated** implies a lack of poise, worldliness, subtlety, etc. resulting from a limited experience of life [an *unsophisticated* farm boy] **—ANT. sophisticated, artful**

na·ive·té, na·ïve·té (nä ēv tā′, -ēv′tä) *n.* [Fr.] **1.** the quality of being naive **2.** a naive action or remark Also **na·ive′ness, na·ïve′ness, na·ive′ty** (-tē), **na·ïve′ty**

na·ked (nā′kid) *adj.* [OE. *nacod* < IE. base *nogw-*] **1.** *a)* completely unclothed; nude *b)* uncovered; exposed: said of parts of the body **2.** destitute **3.** without protection or defense

4. without its usual covering; specif., *a)* out of its sheath *[a naked* sword*] b)* without vegetation, leaves, etc. *[the naked* earth; *naked* trees*] c)* without decoration, etc. *[a naked* wall*]* **5.** without additions, etc.; plain *[the naked* truth*]* **6.** not aided by a microscope, telescope, etc. *[the naked* eye*]* —see **SYN.** at **BARE**[1] —**na′ked·ly** *adv.* —**na′ked·ness** *n.*

NAM, N.A.M. National Association of Manufacturers

nam·by-pam·by (nam′bē pam′bē) *adj.* [orig. satirical nickname of *Ambrose Philips,* 18th-c. Eng. poet] weakly sentimental; insipidly pretty or nice; not strong, definite, etc. —*n., pl.* **-bies** **1.** namby-pamby talk or writing **2.** a namby-pamby person

name (nām) *n.* [OE. *nama* < IE. base *(o)nomn-,* from which also come L. *nomen* & Gr. *onoma*] **1.** a word or phrase by which a person, thing, or class of things is known; title **2.** a word or phrase expressing some quality considered descriptive; epithet **3.** *a)* reputation *b)* good reputation **4.** a family or clan *[the last of his name]* **5.** appearance only, not reality *[chief in name only]* **6.** a famous person *[a great name in science]* —*adj.* ☆**1.** well-known *[a name* brand*]* **2.** carrying a name *[a name* tag*]* —*vt.* **named, nam′ing** **1.** to give a name or title to **2.** to designate or refer to by name **3.** to identify by the right name *[name* the oceans*]* **4.** to nominate or appoint to a post or office **5.** to set or specify (a day, price, etc.) **6.** to speak about; mention —**call names** to swear at —**in the name of** **1.** in appeal to **2.** by the authority of **3.** as belonging to —**name names** to identify specific persons, esp. as doing wrong —**to one's name** belonging to one —**name′a·ble, nam′a·ble** *adj.* —**nam′er** *n.*

name-call·ing (nām′kôl′iŋ) *n.* the use of abusive names in attacking another —**name′-call′er** *n.*

name-drop·per (-dräp′ər) *n.* a person who tries to impress others by often mentioning famous or important persons in a familiar way —**name′-drop′ping** *n.*

name·less (-lis) *adj.* **1.** without a name **2.** left unnamed; anonymous *[a rogue who shall be nameless]* **3.** not publicly known; obscure **4.** illegitimate **5.** that cannot be described *[nameless* dread*]* **6.** too horrible to specify *[nameless* crimes*]* —**name′less·ly** *adv.* —**name′less·ness** *n.*

name·ly (-lē) *adv.* that is to say; to wit *[a choice of two desserts, namely,* cake or pie*]*

name·plate (-plāt′) *n.* a piece of metal, etc. on which a name is inscribed

name·sake (-sāk′) *n.* a person with the same name as another, esp. if named after the other

Na·mib·i·a (nä mib′ē ə) *official (UN) name for* SOUTH WEST AFRICA

Nan·cy (nan′sē; *also for* 2, Fr. nän sē′) [prob. by faulty division of MINE[1] + *Ancy,* dim. of ME. *Annis,* Agnes] **1.** a feminine name **2.** city in NE France: pop. 123,000

nan·keen, nan·kin (nan kēn′) *n.* [< NANKING, from which the cloth was first imported] **1.** a buff-colored, durable cotton cloth, orig. from China **2.** *[pl.]* trousers made of this

Nan·king (nan′kiŋ′, nän′-) city in E China, on the Yangtze River: pop. 2,700,000

Nan·nette, Na·nette (na net′) *[dim. of* ANNA*]* a feminine name

nan·ny (nan′ē) *n., pl.* **-nies** [< *Nan,* dim. of ANN(A)] [Brit.] a child's nurse

nanny goat [see prec.] [Colloq.] a female goat

na·no- (nan′ō) [< Gr. *nanos,* dwarf] *a combining form meaning* one billionth part of; the factor 10^{-9} *[nanosecond]*

Nan·sen (nan′sən), **Frid·tjof** (frit′yäf) 1861–1930; Norw. arctic explorer, naturalist, & statesman

Nantes (nänt; *E.* nants) **1.** city in W France, on the Loire: pop. 259,000 **2. Edict of,** a decree issued (1598) in France, giving political equality to the Huguenots: it was revoked in 1685

Nan·tuck·et (nan tuk′it) [AmInd., lit., faraway land] island of Mass., south of Cape Cod

Na·o·mi (nā ō′mē, na-; nā′ə mī′) [Heb. *na′omī,* lit., my delight] **1.** a feminine name **2.** *Bible* the mother-in-law of Ruth: Ruth 1

nap[1] (nap) *vi.* **napped, nap′ping** [OE. *hnappian*] **1.** to sleep lightly for a short time **2.** to be careless or unprepared —*n.* a brief, light sleep

nap[2] (nap) *n.* [< or akin to MDu. & MLowG. *noppe*] **1.** the downy or hairy surface of cloth formed by short hairs or fibers, raised by brushing, etc. **2.** any similar surface, as that raised on the flesh side of leather *[the nap of* suede*]* —*vt.* **napped, nap′ping** to raise a nap on by brushing, etc. —**nap′less** *adj.* —**napped** *adj.*

☆**na·palm** (nā′päm) *n.* *[na(phthene) + palm(itate)],* salt of pal-

mitic acid] a jellylike substance with gasoline or oil in it, used in flame throwers and bombs —*vt.* to attack or burn with napalm

nape (nāp, nap) *n.* [ME.] the back of the neck

na·per·y (nā′pər ē) *n.* [< MFr. < OFr. *nappe:* see NAPKIN] household linen; esp., table linen

naph·tha (naf′thə, nap′-) *n.* [L. < Gr. < Per. *neft,* pitch] **1.** a flammable liquid that vaporizes quickly, made by distilling petroleum, coal tar, wood, etc. and used as a fuel, solvent, etc. **2.** *same as* PETROLEUM

naph·tha·lene (-lēn′) *n.* [NAPHTHA + -*l*- + -ENE] a white, crystalline hydrocarbon, $C_{10}H_8$, with a strong smell, made by distilling coal tar and used in moth repellents and in certain dyes, etc.: also **naph′tha·lin′**

naph·thol (naf′thōl, -thôl; nap′-) *n.* [NAPHTH(ALENE) + -OL[1]] either of two white, crystalline compounds, $C_{10}H_7OH$, derived from naphthalene and used as antiseptics and in dyes, etc.

Na·pi·er (nā′pē ər, nə pir′), **John** 1550–1617; Scot. mathematician: inventor of logarithms

nap·kin (nap′kin) *n.* [< OFr. *nappe* < L. *mappa,* cloth] **1.** a small piece of cloth or paper, usually square, used while eating for protecting the clothes and wiping the fingers or lips **2.** any small cloth, towel, etc.

Na·ples (nā′p'lz) **1.** seaport in S Italy, on the Bay of Naples: pop. 1,263,000 **2. Bay of,** inlet of the Tyrrhenian Sea, on the S coast of Italy

na·po·le·on (nə pō′lē ən, -pōl′yən) *n.* [after NAPOLEON I] **1.** a former gold coin of France, equivalent to 20 francs **2.** a card game similar to euchre ☆**3.** a layered puff pastry with a custardlike filling

Na·po·le·on I (nə pō′lē ən, -pōl′yən) (full Fr. name *Napoléon Bonaparte*) 1769–1821; Fr. military leader & emperor of France (1804–15) —**Na·po′le·on′ic** (-pō′lē än′ik) *adj.*

Napoleon III *see* LOUIS NAPOLEON

Na·po·li (nä′pô lē′) *It. name of* NAPLES

nap·py (nap′ē) *adj.* **-pi·er, -pi·est** covered with nap; downy, shaggy, etc. —**nap′pi·ness** *n.*

Nar·ba·da (nur bud′ə) river in C India, flowing west into the Arabian Sea: c.800 mi.

☆**narc** (närk) *n.* an undercover police official who hunts down violators of the narcotics laws: also **nar·co** (när′kō)

nar·cis·sism (när′sə siz'm) *n.* [< G.: see NARCISSUS & -ISM] self-love; too great an interest in one's own appearance, comfort, importance, etc. —**nar′cis·sist** *n.,* —**nar′cis·sis′tic** *adj.*

Nar·cis·sus (när sis′əs) *Gr. Myth.* a beautiful youth who pined away for love of his own reflection in a spring and was changed into the narcissus —*n.* [n-] *pl.* **-cis′sus, -cis′sus·es, -cis′si** (-ī) [ModL. < L. < Gr. *narkissos,* ? akin to *narkē* (see NARCOTIC): in reference to the narcotic properties] any of a genus of bulb plants with smooth leaves and white, yellow, or orange flowers, including the daffodils and jonquils

nar·co- [< Gr. *narkē,* stupor] *a combining form meaning* narcosis, sleep, stupor: also, before a vowel, **narc-**

nar·co·sis (när kō′sis) *n.* a condition of deep stupor which passes into unconsciousness, caused by a narcotic or certain chemicals

nar·co·syn·the·sis (när′kō sin′thə sis) *n.* [NARCO- + SYN-THESIS] a method of treating a neurosis caused by shock by working with a patient while he is under the influence of a hypnotic drug

nar·cot·ic (när kät′ik) *n.* [< OFr. < ML. < Gr. *narkoun,* to benumb < *narkē,* numbness] **1.** a drug, as opium, morphine, heroin, etc., used to relieve pain and bring sleep: one can become addicted to narcotics, and when they are abused they can damage the body or bring death **2.** anything with a soothing, lulling, or dulling effect —*adj.* **1.** of, like, or producing narcosis **2.** of, by, or for narcotic addicts

nar·co·tism (när′kə tiz'm) *n.* **1.** *same as* NARCOSIS **2.** addiction to narcotics

nar·co·tize (när′kə tīz′) *vt.* **-tized′, -tiz′ing** **1.** to subject to a narcotic; stupefy **2.** to lull or dull the senses of —**nar′co·ti·za′tion** *n.*

nard (närd) *n.* [< OFr. < L. < Gr. *nardos,* ult. < Sans.] *same as* SPIKENARD (sense 2)

nar·es (ner′ēz) *n.pl., sing.* **nar′is** (-is) [L.] the nasal passages; esp., the nostrils —**nar′i·al** (-ē əl), **nar′ine** (-in, -īn) *adj.*

nar·ghi·le (när′gə lē′, -lä′) *n.* [< Turk. & Per. < Per. *nargīl,* coconut tree: orig. made of coconut shell] *same as* HOOKAH: also sp. **nar′gi·le′, nar′gi·leh′**

nark (närk) *n.* **1.** [< Romany *nāk,* a nose] [Brit. Slang] an informer; stool pigeon ☆**2.** [Slang] *same as* NARC

Nar·ra·gan·sett Bay (nar′ə gan′sit) [after an extinct tribe of Algonquian Indians who lived around the bay] inlet of the Atlantic, extending into R.I.

nar·rate (nar′āt, na rāt′) *vt., vi.* **-rat·ed, -rat·ing** [< L. pp. of *narrare*, to relate: for IE. base see KNOW] **1.** to tell (a story) in writing or speech **2.** to give an account of (events) —see SYN. at TELL

nar·ra·tion (na rā′shən) *n.* **1.** a narrating, or telling of a story or of happenings **2.** a story or account; narrative **3.** writing or speaking that narrates, as history, biography, or fiction — **nar·ra′tion·al** *adj.*

nar·ra·tive (nar′ə tiv) *adj.* **1.** in story form [a *narrative* history of England] **2.** concerned with narration [a *narrative* poet] —*n.* **1.** a story; account; tale **2.** the art or practice of telling stories or events; narration —see SYN. at STORY[1] —**nar′ra·tive·ly** *adv.*

nar·ra·tor (nar′āt ər, na rāt′ər) *n.* **1.** a person who relates a story, etc. **2.** a person who reads narrative passages, as between scenes of a play

nar·row (nar′ō, ner′ō) *adj.* [OE. *nearu*] **1.** small in width; not wide **2.** limited in meaning, size, amount, or extent [a *narrow* majority] **3.** limited in outlook; not liberal; prejudiced **4.** close; careful [a *narrow* inspection] **5.** with barely enough space, time, etc. [a *narrow* escape] **6.** limited in means [*narrow* circumstances] **7.** *Phonetics* tense: said of the tongue —*vi., vt.* to decrease or limit in width, extent, or scope —*n.* **1.** a narrow part or place, esp. in a valley, road, etc. **2.** [*usually pl.*] a narrow passage, as between two bodies of water; strait —**nar′row·ly** *adv.* —**nar′row·ness** *n.*

narrow gauge 1. a width (between railroad rails) less than standard (56½ in.) ☆**2.** a narrow-gauge railroad or car —**nar′row-gauge′, nar′row-gauged′** *adj.*

nar·row-mind·ed (-mīn′did) *adj.* not keeping one's mind open to the beliefs, ways of life, etc. of others; not liberal or tolerant; prejudiced; bigoted —**nar′row-mind′ed·ly** *adv.* —**nar′row-mind′ed·ness** *n.*

nar·thex (när′theks) *n.* [LGr., exterior portico] **1.** in early Christian churches, a porch or portico **2.** a church vestibule leading to the nave

nar·whal (när′wəl, -hwəl) *n.* [Norw. & Dan. *narhval* < ON. *nahvalr*, lit., corpse whale: so called from its coloring] an arctic sea mammal related to the whale and valued for its oil and ivory: the male has a long, spiral tusk extending from the upper jaw: also **nar′wal** (-wəl), **nar′-whale′** (-hwāl′)

nar·y (ner′ē) *adj.* [< *ne′er a*, never a] [Dial.] not any; no (with *a* or *an*) [*nary* a doubt]

NASA (nas′ə) National Aeronautics and Space Administration

na·sal (nā′z′l) *adj.* [< ModL. < L. *nasus*, a nose] **1.** of the nose [*nasal* passages] **2.** produced by making breath go through the nose, as the sounds of *m, n, ng* (ŋ) **3.** characterized by such sounds [a *nasal* voice] —*n.* a nasal sound —**na·sal·i·ty** (nā zal′ə tē) *n.* —**na′sal·ly** *adv.*

na·sal·ize (nā′zə līz′) *vt., vi.* **-ized′, -iz′ing** to pronounce or speak with a nasal sound or sounds —**na′sal·i·za′tion** *n.*

Nas·by (naz′bē), **Pe·tro·le·um V.** (pə trō′lē əm) (pseud. of *David Ross Locke*) 1833–88; U.S. humorist

nas·cent (nas′′nt, nā′s′nt) *adj.* [< L. prp. of *nasci*, to be born] **1.** coming into being; being born **2.** beginning to form, grow, or develop: said of ideas, cultures, etc. —**nas′cence, nas′cen·cy** *n.*

Nash (nash), **Og·den** (äg′dən, ôg′-) 1902–71; U.S. writer of humorous verse

Nash·u·a (nash′oo wə) [< Algonquian, lit., ? the land between] city in southern N.H.: pop. 56,000

Nash·ville (nash′vil) [after Gen. F. *Nash* (1720–77)] capital of Tenn., on the Cumberland River: together with the county of which it is a part, it constitutes a metropolitan government: pop. 448,000

na·so- [< L. *nasus*, nose] *a combining form meaning:* **1.** nose, nasal **2.** nasal and

Nas·sau (nas′ô) **1.** capital of the Bahamas: pop., with the island on which it is located, 81,000 **2.** region in C West Germany: formerly a duchy **3.** ruling family of this former duchy, which, as the House of Orange, has ruled the Netherlands since 1815

Nas·ser (nas′ər), **Ga·mal Ab·del** (gä mäl′ äb′dəl) 1918–70; Egypt. president of the United Arab Republic (1958–70)

na·stur·tium (nə stur′shəm, na-) *n.* [L. < *nasus*, nose + pp. of *torquere*, to twist: from its sharp odor] **1.** a plant with shield-shaped leaves and red, yellow, or orange flowers **2.** the flower

nas·ty (nas′tē) *adj.* **-ti·er, -ti·est** [< ? or akin to Du. *nestig*, dirty] **1.** very dirty; filthy [a *nasty*, smelly room] **2.** sickening or disgusting [a *nasty* taste] **3.** morally offensive; indecent **4.** very unpleasant, mean, or harmful [*nasty* weather; a *nasty* temper; a *nasty* fall] —**nas′ti·ly** *adv.* —**nas′ti·ness** *n.*

nat. 1. national **2.** native **3.** natural

Na·tal (nə tal′, -täl′) province of E South Africa, on the Indian Ocean

na·tal (nāt′′l) *adj.* [< L. *natalis* < pp. of *nasci*, to be born: see NATURE] **1.** of or connected with one's birth [one's *natal* day] **2.** dating from birth **3.** native [one's *natal* land]

Nat·a·lie (nat′′l ē) [Fr. < LL. < L. *natalis* (*dies*), natal (day), name given to children born on Christmas Day] a feminine name

na·tant (nāt′′nt) *adj.* [< L. prp. of *natare*, to swim] swimming or floating; esp., floating on the surface of water

na·ta·to·ri·al (nāt′ə tôr′ē əl) *adj.* [< LL. < L. *natator*, swimmer (see prec.) + -AL] of, characterized by, or adapted for swimming: also **na′ta·to′ry**

☆**na·ta·to·ri·um** (-əm) *n., pl.* **-ri·ums, -ri·a** (-ə) [LL.] a swimming pool, esp. one indoors

☆**natch** (nach) *adv.* [Slang] naturally; of course

na·tes (nā′tēz) *n.pl.* [L.] the buttocks

Na·than (nā′thən) [Heb. *nāthān*, lit., gift] a masculine name: dim. *Nat, Nate*

Na·than·a·el (nə than′yəl, -than′ē əl) [LL. < Gr. < Heb. *nĕthan′ēl*, lit., gift of God] a masculine name: dim. *Nat:* also sp. **Nathaniel**

nathe·less (nāth′lis, nath′-) *adv.* [< OE. < *na*, never + *the*, the + *læs*, less] [Archaic] nevertheless —*prep.* [Archaic] notwithstanding Also **nath′less** (nath′-)

na·tion (nā′shən) *n.* [< OFr. < L. *natio* < pp. of *nasci*, to be born: see NATURE] **1.** a community of people with a territory, history, economic life, culture, and language in common **2.** the people of a territory united under a single government; country **3.** *a*) a people or tribe; esp., ☆a tribe of N. American Indians, sometimes one belonging to a confederation ☆*b*) [N-] the territory of a particular Indian tribe or tribes —**na′tion·hood′** (-hood′) *n.*

Na·tion (nā′shən), **Car·ry** (kar′ē) (born *Carry Amelia Moore*) 1846–1911; U.S. temperance reformer

na·tion·al (nash′ə n′l) *adj.* **1.** of a nation or the nation [the *national* anthem] **2.** having to do with the nation as a whole [a *national* election; a *national* crisis] **3.** maintained by the Federal government [a *national* park] —*n.* a citizen of a nation —see SYN. at CITIZEN —**na′tion·al·ly** *adv.*

national bank 1. a bank or system of banks owned and operated by a government ☆**2.** in the U.S., a member bank of the Federal Reserve System, chartered by the Federal government

☆**National Guard** in the U.S., the organized militia forces of individual States, which can be called into active Federal service by the President in time of emergency

na·tion·al·ism (nash′ə n′l iz′m) *n.* **1.** devotion to one's nation or country; sometimes, specif., a concern for only one's own country that is so great as to seem selfish, aggressive, etc. **2.** the desire for or advocacy of national independence —**na′tion·al·ist** (-ist) *n., adj.* —**na′tion·al·is′tic** *adj.* —**na′tion·al·is′ti·cal·ly** *adv.*

na·tion·al·i·ty (nash′ə nal′ə tē) *n., pl.* **-ties 1.** national quality or character **2.** the status of belonging to a particular nation by birth or naturalization **3.** the condition or fact of being a nation **4.** a national group, esp. of immigrants from some other country: in full, **nationality group**

NASTURTIUM

NARWHAL
(body 11–16 ft.
long; tusk to
9 ft. long)

---

na·tion·al·ize (nash′ə nə līz′) *vt.* **-ized′, -iz′ing 1.** to make national **2.** to transfer ownership or control of (land, resources, industries, etc.) to the national government —**na′tion·al·i·za′tion** *n.* —**na′tion·al·iz′er** *n.*

☆**national monument** a natural geographic feature or historic site, as a mountain, canyon, old fort, etc., kept and protected by the Federal government for the public to visit

☆**national park** an area of scenic beauty, historical and scientific interest, etc. kept and protected by the Federal government for the public to visit

National Socialism *see* NAZI

☆**National Weather Service** the division of the U.S. Department of Commerce that gathers data on weather conditions, on the basis of which weather forecasts are made

na·tion-state (nā′shən stāt′) *n.* the modern nation thought of as a unit of political organization

na·tion·wide (nā′shən wīd′) *adj.* by or throughout the whole nation; national

na·tive (nāt′iv) *adj.* [< MFr. < L. *nativus* < pp. of *nasci*, to be born: see NATURE] **1.** inborn or innate rather than acquired [*native* intelligence, ability, etc.] **2.** belonging to a locality or country by birth, production, or growth; indigenous [a *native* Bostonian; *native* industry; *native* plants] **3.** *a*) being the place of one's birth [one's *native* land] *b*) belonging to one because of the place of one's birth [one's *native* language] **4.** as found in nature; unaltered by man; natural **5.** occurring in a pure state in nature [*native* gold] **6.** of or having to do with the natives of a place [a *native* custom; *native* dances] —*n.* **1.** a person born in a certain place or country **2.** an original inhabitant of a region, as distinguished from an explorer, invader, colonist, etc. **3.** a plant or animal indigenous to a place and growing or living there naturally **4.** a lifelong resident, not a mere visitor —**go native** to adopt a simple way of life —**na′tive·ly** *adv.* —**na′tive·ness** *n.*

SYN.—**native** applies to a person born, or thing originating, in a certain place or country [a *native* Italian; *native* fruits]; **indigenous**, which also suggests natural origin in a particular region, is applied to groups or species rather than to individuals [the potato is *indigenous* to South America]; **aboriginal** applies to the earliest known inhabitants (or, rarely, animals or plants) of a region [the Indians are the *aboriginal* Americans]; **endemic** is applied esp. to plants and diseases commonly found, or widespread, in a particular region [typhus is *endemic* in various countries] See also SYN. at CITIZEN.—ANT. **alien, foreign**

na·tive-born (-bôrn′) *adj.* born in a specified place or country

na·tiv·i·ty (nə tiv′ə tē, nā-) *n., pl.* **-ties** [see NATIVE] **1.** birth **2.** *Astrol.* the horoscope for one's birth —**the Nativity 1.** the birth of Jesus **2.** a representation of this **3.** Christmas Day

natl. national

NATO (nā′tō) North Atlantic Treaty Organization

nat·ty (nat′ē) *adj.* **-ti·er, -ti·est** [< ? NEAT¹] trim and smart in appearance or dress [a *natty* suit] —**nat′ti·ly** *adv.* —**nat′ti·ness** *n.*

nat·u·ral (nach′ər əl, nach′rəl) *adj.* [< OFr. < L. *naturalis*, by birth] **1.** of or arising from nature [*natural* wonders] **2.** produced or existing in nature; not artificial [*natural* gas] **3.** dealing with nature [a *natural* science] **4.** as found in nature; unaltered by man **5.** real or physical, rather than spiritual, intellectual, or imaginary **6.** *a*) innate; inborn [*natural* abilities] *b*) having been born with certain qualities [a *natural* comedian] **7.** based on moral feeling common to everyone [*natural* rights] **8.** true to nature; lifelike [a *natural* likeness] **9.** normal or usual [a *natural* outcome] **10.** customarily expected [a *natural* courtesy] **11.** free from affectation [a *natural* smile] **12.** *a*) illegitimate [a *natural* child] *b*) related biologically rather than by adoption [*natural* parents] **13.** *Music a*) without flats or sharps *b*) neither sharped nor flatted —*n.* **1.** [Colloq.] a person who has or seems to have a natural ability or talent for something [he's a *natural* for the job] ☆**2.** [Colloq.] a sure success **3.** *Music a*) the sign (♮) canceling a preceding sharp or flat: in full, **natural sign** *b*) the note affected *c*) a white key on the piano —**nat′u·ral·ness** *n.*

natural childbirth a method of childbirth in which the expectant mother helps in the delivery, for which she has been prepared by instruction, exercises, etc., and needs little or no anesthesia

natural gas a mixture of gaseous hydrocarbons, chiefly methane, occurring naturally in the earth and conveyed through pipes to be used as a fuel

natural history the study of the animal, vegetable, and mineral world, esp. in a popular way

nat·u·ral·ism (nach′ər əl iz'm) *n.* **1.** action or thought based on natural desires or instincts **2.** *Literature, Art*, etc. faithful

adherence to nature; realism: specif. applied to the realism of a group of 19th-cent. French writers **3.** *Philos.* the belief that the natural world is all that exists

nat·u·ral·ist (-ist) *n.* **1.** a person who studies animals and plants **2.** a person who believes in or practices naturalism —*adj. same as* NATURALISTIC

nat·u·ral·is·tic (nach′ər ə lis′tik) *adj.* **1.** of natural history or naturalists **2.** of or characterized by naturalism **3.** in accordance with, or in imitation of, nature —**nat′u·ral·is′ti·cal·ly** *adv.*

nat·u·ral·ize (nach′ər ə līz′, nach′rə-) *vt.* **-ized′, -iz′ing 1.** to confer citizenship upon (an alien) **2.** to adopt and make common (a custom, word, etc.) from another country or place **3.** to adapt (a plant or animal) to a new environment —*vi.* to become naturalized —**nat′u·ral·i·za′tion** *n.*

natural logarithm a logarithm to the base *e* (approximately 2.71828)

nat·u·ral·ly (nach′ər əl ē, nach′rə lē) *adv.* **1.** in a natural manner [to behave *naturally*] **2.** by nature; innately [he is *naturally* shy] **3.** as one might expect; of course [*naturally* he felt weak after his severe cold]

natural number any positive whole number, as 1, 2, 3, etc.

natural philosophy *earlier name for* NATURAL SCIENCE (specif., physics)

natural resources the forms of wealth supplied by nature, as coal, oil, water power, etc.

natural science the systematized knowledge of nature and the physical world, including biology, chemistry, physics, geology, etc.

natural selection the process in evolution by which those individuals (of a species) with characters that help them to become adapted to their specific environment tend to survive and transmit their characters, while those less able to become adapted tend to die out

na·ture (nā′chər) *n.* [< OFr. < L. *natura* < pp. of *nasci*, to be born: for IE. base see GENUS] **1.** the quality or qualities that make something what it is; essence [the *nature* of light] **2.** inborn character, disposition, or tendencies [a man of happy *nature*] **3.** kind; sort [books, magazines, and things of that *nature*] **4.** the basic biological functions, instincts, drives, etc. **5.** normal or acceptable behavior **6.** the sum total of all things in the physical universe **7.** [*sometimes* N-] the power, force, etc. that seems to regulate this [*nature* heals an animal's wounds] **8.** the primitive state of man **9.** a simple way of life close to or in the outdoors [a return to *nature*] **10.** natural scenery, and the plants and animals in it [the beauties of *nature*] —see SYN. at TYPE —**by nature** naturally; inherently —**of** (or **in**) **the nature of** having the essential character of; like

-na·tured (nā′chərd) *a combining form meaning* having or showing a (specified kind of) nature, disposition, or temperament [good-*natured*]

☆**Naug·a·hyde** (nôg′ə hīd′) [a made-up word] *a trademark for* a kind of imitation leather, used for upholstery —*n.* [n-] this material

naught (nôt) *n.* [< OE. < *na*, no + *wiht*, a person] **1.** nothing **2.** *Arith.* the figure zero (0) —**set at naught** to defy; scorn

naugh·ty (nôt′ē) *adj.* **-ti·er, -ti·est** [< obs. *naught*, wicked] **1.** not behaving properly; mischievous or disobedient: used esp. of children or their behavior **2.** improper or obscene —**naugh′ti·ly** *adv.* —**naugh′ti·ness** *n.*

Na·u·ru (nä ōō′rōō) country on an island in the W Pacific, near the equator: 8 sq. mi.; pop. 7,000

nau·se·a (nô′shə, -sē ə, -zē ə, -zhə) *n.* [L. < Gr. *nausia*, seasickness < *naus*: see NAUTICAL] **1.** a feeling of sickness at the stomach, with an urge to vomit **2.** great disgust; loathing

nau·se·ate (-shē āt′, -sē-, -zē-, -zhē-) *vt., vi.* **-at′ed, -at′ing** to feel or cause to feel nausea —**nau′se·at′ing·ly** *adv.* —**nau′se·a′tion** *n.*

nau·seous (nô′shəs, -zē əs, -sē-) *adj.* **1.** causing nausea; sickening **2.** [Colloq.] feeling nausea —**nau′seous·ly** *adv.* —**nau′seous·ness** *n.*

naut. nautical

nautch (nôch) *n.* [< Hindi < Prakrit < Sans. *nṛtya*, dancing < *nṛt*, to dance] in India, a performance by professional dancing girls (**nautch girls**)

nau·ti·cal (nôt′i k'l) *adj.* [< Fr. < L. < Gr. < *nautēs*, sailor < *naus*, a ship < IE. base *naus*, boat] of or relating to sailors, ships, or navigation —**nau′ti·cal·ly** *adv.*

nautical mile an international unit of distance for sea and air navigation, equal to 6,076.11549 ft. (1,852 meters), which is one minute of arc of a great circle of the earth

nau·ti·lus (nôt''l əs) *n., pl.* **-lus·es, -li'** (-ī') [ModL. < L. < Gr. *nautilos*, sailor < *naus:* see NAUTICAL] **1.** any of a genus of tropical, cephalopod mollusks with a many-chambered, spiral shell having a pearly interior **2.** *same as* PAPER NAUTILUS

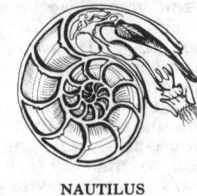

NAUTILUS
(shown in
cross section)

nav. 1. naval **2.** navigation **3.** navigator

Nav·a·ho (nav'ə hō') *n.* [< Sp. < AmInd. *Navahú*, lit., great fields] **1.** *pl.* **-hos', -ho', -hoes'** a member of an Indian tribe, the largest in the U.S., of Arizona, New Mexico, and Utah **2.** their Athapascan language Also sp. **Nav'a·jo'**

na·val (nā'v'l) *adj.* [< Fr. < L. *navalis* < *navis:* see NAVY] having, characteristic of, or for a navy, its ships, personnel, etc.

Na·varre (nə vär') region in NE Spain & SW France: formerly a kingdom See map at CASTILE

nave[1] (nāv) *n.* [ML. *navis* < L.: see NAVY] the main part of a church, extending between side aisles from the chancel to the principal entrance

nave[2] (nāv) *n.* [OE. *nafu*] the hub of a wheel

na·vel (nā'v'l) *n.* [OE. *nafela*] the small scar or hollow in the middle of the abdomen, where the umbilical cord was attached to the fetus

☆**navel orange** a seedless orange having a navellike hollow containing a small, undeveloped secondary fruit

navig. 1. navigation **2.** navigator

nav·i·ga·ble (nav'i gə b'l) *adj.* [see NAVIGATE] **1.** wide or deep enough, or free enough from obstructions, for ships, etc. to go through [a *navigable* river] **2.** that can be steered or directed [a *navigable* balloon] —**nav'i·ga·bil'i·ty** *n.* —**nav'i·ga·bly** *adv.*

nav·i·gate (nav'ə gāt') *vi.* **-gat·ed, -gat·ing** [< L. pp. of *navigare* < *navis*, a ship (see NAVY) + *agere*, to lead (see ACT)] **1.** to steer, or direct, a ship or aircraft ☆**2.** [Colloq.] to make one's way; walk —*vt.* **1.** to travel through or over (water, air, or land) in a ship or aircraft **2.** to steer, or direct the course of (a ship or aircraft) **3.** to plot the course for (a ship or aircraft) **4.** [Colloq.] to make one's way on or through

nav·i·ga·tion (nav'ə gā'shən) *n.* **1.** the act or practice of navigating; esp., the science of locating the position and plotting the course of ships and aircraft **2.** traffic by ship —**nav'i·ga'tion·al** *adj.* —**nav'i·ga'tion·al·ly** *adv.*

nav·i·ga·tor (nav'ə gāt'ər) *n.* **1.** a person who navigates; esp., one skilled in the navigation of a ship or aircraft **2.** an explorer by ship

nav·vy (nav'ē) *n., pl.* **-vies** [abbrev. of prec.] [Brit.] an unskilled laborer, as on canals, roads, etc.

na·vy (nā'vē) *n., pl.* **-vies** [< OFr. *navie*, ult. < L. *navis*, a ship: for IE. base see NAUTICAL] **1.** [Archaic] a fleet of ships **2.** all warships of a nation **3.** [*often* N-] *a*) the entire sea force of a nation, including vessels, personnel, yards, etc. *b*) the governmental department in charge of this **4.** *same as* NAVY BLUE

☆**navy bean** [from common use in the U.S. Navy] a small, white variety of kidney bean

navy blue [from the color of the Brit. naval uniform] very dark, purplish blue

navy yard a dockyard for building and repairing naval ships, storing naval supplies, etc.

na·wab (nə wäb', -wôb') *n.* [Hindi *navāb*] *same as* NABOB

nay (nā) *adv.* [< ON. < *ne*, not + *ei*, ever] **1.** no: now seldom used except in a voice vote **2.** not that only, but also [she is well-off, *nay*, rich] —*n.* **1.** a refusal or denial **2.** a negative vote or voter **3.** a negative answer

Naz·a·rene (naz'ə rēn', naz'ə rēn') *adj.* of Nazareth or the Nazarenes —*n.* **1.** a native or inhabitant of Nazareth **2.** a member of an early sect of Christians of Jewish origin who continued to observe much of the Mosaic law —**the Nazarene** Jesus

Naz·a·reth (naz'ər əth) town in Galilee, N Israel, where Jesus lived as a child

Naz·a·rite, Naz·i·rite (naz'ə rīt') *n.* [< LL. < Gr. < Heb. *nāzar*, to consecrate] among the ancient Hebrews, a person adhering to certain strict religious vows

Na·zi (nät'sē, nat'-) *adj.* [G., shortened from *Nationalsozialistische* in party name] designating or of the German fascist political party (*National Socialist German Workers' Party*), that ruled Germany under Hitler (1933–45) —*n.* **1.** a member of this party **2.** [*often* n-] a supporter of this party or its ideology; fascist —**Na'zi·fi·ca'tion** *n.* —**Na'zi·fy', na'zi·fy'** *vt.* **-fied', -fy'ing** —**Na'zism** (-siz'm), **Na'zi·ism** (-sē iz'm) *n.*

Nb *Chem.* niobium

N.B. New Brunswick

N.B., n.b. [L. *nota bene*] note well

NBA, N.B.A. 1. National Basketball Association **2.** National Boxing Association

NBC National Broadcasting Company

NBS, N.B.S. National Bureau of Standards

N.C., NC 1. no charge **2.** North Carolina **3.** nurse corps

NCAA, N.C.A.A. National Collegiate Athletic Association

NCO, N.C.O. noncommissioned officer

Nd *Chem.* neodymium

N.D., n.d. no date

N.Dak., ND North Dakota

né, ne (nā) *adj.* [Fr., born: see NEE] born: used before the original name of a man who uses another name [George Orwell, *né* Eric Blair]

ne- *same as* NEO-: used before a vowel

Ne *Chem.* neon

NE Nebraska

NE, N.E., n.e. 1. northeast **2.** northeastern

N.E. 1. Naval Engineer **2.** New England

NEA, N.E.A. National Education Association

Neal (nēl) [prob. < Ir. *Niul* < *niadh*, a champion] a masculine name

Ne·an·der·thal (nē an'dər thôl', -täl') *adj.* [name of German valley where remains were found] designating or of a form of primitive man of the paleolithic period

neap (nēp) *adj.* [OE. *nep-* in *nepflod*, neap tide] designating either of the two lowest monthly tides, occurring just after the first and third quarters of the lunar month: at these times the difference between high and low tides is smallest —*n.* neap tide

Ne·a·pol·i·tan (nē'ə päl'ə t'n) *adj.* of Naples —*n.* a native or inhabitant of Naples

☆**Neapolitan ice cream** brick ice cream made up of several flavors in layers, often chocolate, strawberry, and vanilla

near (nir) *adv.* [OE. *near*, nearer, compar. of *neah*, nigh] **1.** at a short distance in space or time [winter draws *near*] **2.** relatively close in degree; almost [*near* right] : now usually *nearly* **3.** closely; intimately —*adj.* **1.** close in distance or time; not far [a house *near* to the school; in the *near* past] **2.** close in relationship; akin **3.** close in friendship; intimate **4.** *a*) close in degree; narrow [a *near* escape] *b*) almost happening [a *near* accident] **5.** on the left side, facing forward: said of an animal in double harness, a wagon wheel, etc.: opposed to OFF **6.** short or direct [the *near* way] **7.** stingy **8.** somewhat resembling; approximating [a *near* likeness] —**prep.** close to in space, time, degree, etc. [they sat *near* us] —*vt., vi.* to draw near (to); approach [slow down as you *near* the curve] —**near at hand** very close in time or space —**near'ness** *n.*

near·by (nir'bī') *adj., adv.* near; close at hand

Near East 1. countries near the E end of the Mediterranean, including those of SW Asia, NE Africa, &, sometimes, the Balkans **2.** [Brit.] the Balkans

near·ly (-lē) *adv.* almost; not quite [*nearly* finished] —**not nearly** not at all; far from

near·sight·ed (-sīt'id) *adj.* having better vision for near things than for far ones; myopic —**near'sight'ed·ly** *adv.* —**near'sight'ed·ness** *n.*

neat[1] (nēt) *adj.* [< Fr. < L. *nitidus*, shining, trim < *nitere*, to shine] **1.** *a*) clean and orderly; trim; tidy *b*) tidy, skillful, and precise [a *neat* worker] *c*) free of superfluities; simple **2.** unmixed; straight [to drink whiskey *neat*] **3.** well-proportioned; shapely [a *neat* figure] **4.** cleverly phrased or done; adroit [a *neat* trick] **5.** [Slang] nice, pleasing, fine, etc. —**neat'ly** *adv.* —**neat'ness** *n.*

SYN. —**neat** implies a clean and orderly quality in the appearance of things [a *neat* house]; **tidy** stresses great care in keeping things in order so that nothing is out of place [a *tidy* closet]; **trim** implies a pleasing absence of anything unnecessary, and suggests smart, simple lines, good proportion, etc. [a *trim* ship] —ANT. **slovenly, sloppy**

neat2 (nēt) *n., pl.* **neat** [OE. *neat*] [Now Rare] a bovine animal; ox, cow, etc.

neat·en (nēt′'n) *vt.* to make neat

'neath, neath (nēth) *prep.* [Poet.] beneath

neat·herd (nēt′hurd′) *n.* [Now Rare] a cowherd

neat's-foot oil (nēts′foot′) a light-yellow oil obtained by boiling the feet and shinbones of cattle, used mainly as a dressing for leather

neb (neb) *n.* [OE. *nebb*] [Now Chiefly Brit. Dial.] **1.** a beak, nose, or snout **2.** a nib

Ne·bras·ka (nə bras′kə) [< Siouan name of Platte River, lit., flat water] Middle Western State of the U.S.: 77,227 sq. mi.; pop. 1,484,000; cap. Lincoln: abbrev. **Nebr., NE** —**Ne·bras′kan** *adj., n.*

Neb·u·chad·nez·zar (neb′yə kəd nez′ər, neb′ə-) ?–562 B.C.; king of Babylonia (605?–562), who conquered Jerusalem & deported many Jews into Babylonia: II Kings 24; Dan. 1–4 Also **Neb′u·chad·rez′zar** (-rez′ər)

neb·u·la (neb′yə lə) *n., pl.* **-lae** (-lē), **-las** [ModL. < L., fog] any of several vast cloudlike patches seen in the night sky, consisting of very distant groups of stars or of gaseous masses or of galaxies —**neb′u·lar** *adj.*

nebular hypothesis the theory that the solar system was once a nebula which condensed to form the sun and the planets

neb·u·los·i·ty (neb′yə läs′ə tē) *n.* **1.** a nebulous quality or condition **2.** *pl.* **-ties** a nebula

neb·u·lous (neb′yə ləs) *adj.* **1.** of or like a nebula **2.** unclear; vague; indefinite Also **neb′u·lose′** (-lōs′) —**neb′u·lous·ly** *adv.* —**neb′u·lous·ness** *n.*

nec·es·sar·i·ly (nes′ə ser′ə lē, nes′ə ser′-) *adv.* **1.** because of necessity [infants must *necessarily* be cared for] **2.** as a necessary result [cloudy skies do not *necessarily* mean rain]

nec·es·sar·y (nes′ə ser′ē) *adj.* [< L. < *necesse*, unavoidable < *ne-*, not + *cedere*, to give way: see CEDE] **1.** that cannot be done without; essential; indispensable [the food *necessary* to life] **2.** that must happen; inevitable [a *necessary* result] **3.** that must be done; required [*necessary* repairs] **4.** that follows logically; undeniable [a *necessary* conclusion] —*n., pl.* **-sar'ies** a thing necessary to life, to some purpose, etc.: *often used in pl.* —see SYN. at ESSENTIAL

ne·ces·si·tate (nə ses′ə tāt′) *vt.* **-tat′ed, -tat′ing** **1.** to make (something) necessary or unavoidable [the hard words in the article *necessitated* the use of a dictionary] **2.** [Now Rare] to compel —**ne·ces′si·ta′tion** *n.*

ne·ces·si·tous (-təs) *adj.* **1.** needy; destitute **2.** that calls for action at once; urgent —**ne·ces′si·tous·ly** *adv.*

ne·ces·si·ty (nə ses′ə tē) *n., pl.* **-ties** [< OFr. < L. < *necesse*: see NECESSARY] **1.** the demands that nature makes on one **2.** anything inevitable, unavoidable, etc. **3.** *a)* the demands that circumstances, custom, law, etc. make on one *b)* what is required by this **4.** great need [call me in case of *necessity*] **5.** something that cannot be done without; necessary thing: *often used in pl.* [food and shelter are *necessities*] **6.** the state or quality of being necessary **7.** poverty; want [to live in great *necessity*] —see SYN. at NEED —**of necessity** necessarily

neck (nek) *n.* [OE. *hnecca* < IE. base *ken-*, to squeeze] **1.** that part of man or animal joining the head to the body **2.** a narrow part between the head, or end, and the body, or base, of any object, as of a violin **3.** that part of a garment which covers or is nearest the neck **4.** a narrow, necklike part; specif., *a)* a narrow strip of land *b)* the narrowest part of a bottle, vase, etc. or of an organ of the body *c)* a strait —*vt., vi.* ☆[Slang] to hug, kiss, and caress in making love —☆**get it in the neck** [Slang] to be severely reprimanded or punished —**neck and neck** very close or even, as in a race —**neck of the woods** ☆a region or locality [not far from this *neck of the woods*] —**risk one's neck** to put one's life, career, etc. in danger —**stick one's neck out** to expose oneself to possible failure, ridicule, loss, etc. by taking a chance —**neck'er** *n.* —**neck'ing** *n.*

neck·band (nek′band′) *n.* **1.** a band worn around the neck **2.** the part of a garment that encircles the neck; esp., the part to which the collar is fastened

neck·er·chief (nek′ər chif, -chēf′) *n.* a kerchief worn around the neck

neck·lace (nek′lis) *n.* [NECK + LACE] a string of beads, jewels, etc. or a fine chain of gold, silver, etc. worn as an ornament around the neck

neck·line (-līn′) *n.* the line formed by the edge of a garment around or nearest the neck

neck·piece (-pēs′) *n.* **1.** a decorative scarf, esp. of fur **2.** a piece of armor for the neck

neck·tie (-tī′) *n.* a decorative band for the neck, tied in front in a slipknot or bow

neck·wear (-wer′) *n.* articles worn about the neck, as neckties, scarfs, etc.

nec·ro- [< Gr. *nekros*, dead body < IE. base *nek-*, death] *a combining form meaning* death, corpse: also **necr-**

ne·crol·o·gy (ne kräl′ə jē) *n., pl.* **-gies** [see prec. & -LOGY] **1.** a list of people who have died within a certain period **2.** an obituary —**nec·ro·log·i·cal** (nek′rə läj′i k'l) *adj.* —**nec′ro·log′i·cal·ly** *adv.* —**ne·crol′o·gist** *n.*

nec·ro·man·cy (nek′rə man′sē) *n.* [< OFr. < ML. *nigromantia* < L. < Gr. *nekros* (see NECRO-) + *manteia*, divination] **1.** the practice of pretending to foretell the future by supposedly getting messages from the dead **2.** black magic; sorcery —**nec′·ro·man′cer** *n.* —**nec′ro·man′tic** *adj.*

ne·crop·o·lis (nə kräp′ə lis) *n., pl.* **-lis·es** [< Gr. < *nekros* (see NECRO-) + *polis*, city] a cemetery, esp. one belonging to an ancient city

ne·cro·sis (ne krō′sis) *n., pl.* **-ses** (-sēz) [ModL. < LL. < Gr. < *nekroun*, to make dead < *nekros* (see NECRO-)] the death or decay of tissue in a part of a living body or plant, as from disease —**ne·crose** (ne krōs′, nek′rōs) *vt., vi.* **-crosed′, -cros′ing**, —**ne·crot′ic** (-krät′ik) *adj.*

nec·tar (nek′tər) *n.* [L. < Gr. *nektar*, lit., that overcomes death] **1.** *Gr. Myth.* the drink of the gods **2.** any very delicious beverage **3.** the sweet liquid in many flowers, used by bees for the making of honey —**nec′tar·ous** *adj.*

nec·tar·ine (nek′tə rēn′, nek′tə rēn′) *n.* [orig. adj. of *nectar*] a variety of peach having a smooth skin without down

nec·ta·ry (nek′tər ē) *n., pl.* **-ries** the part of a flower that secretes nectar —**nec·tar′i·al** (-ter′ē əl) *adj.*

Ne·der·land (nā′dər länt′) Du. name of NETHERLANDS

nee, née (nā; *now often* nē) *adj.* [Fr., fem. pp. of *naître* < L. *nasci*, to be born] born: used to indicate the maiden name of a married woman [Mrs. Helen Jones, *nee* Smith]

need (nēd) *n.* [OE. *nied*] **1.** necessity or obligation [no *need* to worry] **2.** lack of something necessary, useful, or wanted [he feels the *need* of companionship] **3.** something that one wants or must have; requirement [one's daily *needs*] **4.** *a)* a time or condition when help is wanted or required [a friend in *need*] *b)* poverty; extreme want [food and clothing for those in *need*] —*vt.* to have need of; lack; require *Need* is often used as an auxiliary followed by an infinitive with or without *to*, meaning "to be obliged, must" [he *need* not come, he *needs* to be careful] —*vi.* to be in need See also NEEDS —**have need to** to be required to; must —**if need be** if it is required —**need′er** *n.*

SYN. —**need** is the simple, direct word and **necessity** the more formal term referring to a lack of something that is wanted or must be had, or to the thing that is required [they are in *need* of food; food is a *necessity* for all living things]; **exigency** refers to a necessity brought about by some emergency or by specific events [the *exigencies* created by the flood]; **requisite** applies to something that cannot be done without in order to carry out some activity [a sense of rhythm is a *requisite* in a dancer] See also SYN. at LACK

need·ful (nēd′fəl) *adj.* **1.** necessary **2.** [Archaic] needy — **need′ful·ly** *adv.* —**need′ful·ness** *n.*

nee·dle (nēd′'l) *n.* [OE. *nædl*] **1.** a small, slender, sharp-pointed piece of steel with a hole for thread, used for sewing **2.** *a)* a slender, hooked rod of steel, bone, etc., for crocheting *b)* a similar but hookless rod, for knitting **3.** the short, pointed piece of metal, often tipped as with diamond, that moves in the grooves of a phonograph record to pick up the vibrations **4.** a pointed instrument for etching or engraving **5.** the pointer of a compass, gauge, meter, etc. **6.** the thin, short, pointed leaf of the pine, spruce, etc. **7.** a thin rod that opens or closes a passage in a valve (**needle valve**) **8.** the sharp, very slender metal tube at the end of a hypodermic syringe **9.** *same as* ELECTRIC NEEDLE **10.** a needlelike structure or part —*vt.* **-dled, -dling** **1.** to sew, puncture, etc. with a needle **2.** [Colloq.] *a)* to goad *b)* to tease or heckle —**nee′dle·like′** *adj.* —**nee′dler** *n.*

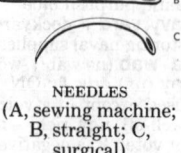

NEEDLES
(A, sewing machine; B, straight; C, surgical)

nee·dle·point (-point′) *n.* **1.** an embroidery of yarns on threads on canvas, as in tapestry **2.** lace made on a paper pattern with a needle, not a bobbin: in full, **needlepoint lace**

need·less (nēd′lis) *adj.* not needed; unnecessary —**need′·less·ly** *adv.* —**need′less·ness** *n.*

nee·dle·wom·an (nēd′'l woom′ən) *n., pl.* **-wom′en** a woman who does needlework; esp., a seamstress

nee·dle·work (-wʉrk') *n.* work done with a needle; sewing or fancywork —**nee'dle·work'er** *n.*

need·n't (nēd''nt) need not

needs (nēdz) *adv.* [OE. *nedes*] of necessity; necessarily (with *must*) [he must *needs* obey]

need·y (nēd'ē) *adj.* **need'i·er, need'i·est** in need; very poor; destitute —**need'i·ness** *n.*

ne'er (ner) *adv.* [Poet.] never

ne'er-do-well (ner'dŏŏ wel') *n.* a shiftless, irresponsible person —*adj.* lazy, worthless, etc.

ne·far·i·ous (ni fer'ē əs) *adj.* [< L. < *nefas*, crime < *ne-*, not + *fas*, lawful: for IE. base see BAN¹] very wicked; iniquitous; evil [a *nefarious* scheme] —see SYN. at VICIOUS —**ne·far'i·ous·ly** *adv.* —**ne·far'i·ous·ness** *n.*

Nef·er·ti·ti (nef'ər tē'tē) 14th cent. B.C.; queen of Egypt: also **Nef're·te'te** (-rə-)

neg. 1. negative 2. negatively

ne·gate (ni gāt') *vt.* **-gat'ed, -gat'ing** [see NEGATION] 1. to deny the existence or truth of [the pardon does not *negate* the fact that he committed the crime] 2. to make ineffective —see SYN. at NULLIFY —**ne·ga'tor, ne·gat'er** *n.*

ne·ga·tion (ni gā'shən) *n.* [< Fr. < L. < pp. of *negare*, to deny] 1. a denying; denial 2. the lack or opposite of something positive [death is the *negation* of life]

neg·a·tive (neg'ə tiv) *adj.* [see prec.] 1. expressing denial or refusal; saying "no" 2. opposite to or lacking what is positive, as, lacking confidence, agreement, optimism, cooperation, etc. [a *negative* personality; a *negative* approach]; specif., *a*) *Biol.* directed away from the source of a stimulus [*negative* tropism] *b*) *Math.* designating a quantity less than zero, or one to be subtracted; minus *c*) *Med.* not indicating the presence of a specific disease, condition, etc. *d*) *Photog.* with the relation of light and shade the opposite of that in the thing photographed ☆3. *Elec.* *a*) of, generating, or charged with NEGATIVE ELECTRICITY *b*) having an excess of electrons —*adv.* no; not so: so used in radio communication —*n.* 1. a word, phrase, statement, etc. expressing denial, rejection, or refusal ["no" and "not" are *negatives*] 2. the side that is opposed to the proposition being debated (with *the*) 3. an impression of a sculpture, etc. that shows it in reverse 4. the plate in a voltaic battery where the lower potential is 5. *Math.* a negative quantity 6. *Photog.* an exposed and developed negative film or plate, from which positive prints are made —*vt.* **-tived, -tiv·ing** 1. *a*) to refuse; reject ☆*b*) to veto 2. to deny; contradict 3. to disprove 4. to neutralize —**in the negative** 1. in refusal or denial of a plan, etc. 2. with a negative answer —**neg'a·tive·ly** *adv.* —**neg'a·tive·ness, neg'a·tiv'i·ty** *n.*

☆**negative electricity** the kind of electricity in a piece of resin rubbed with wool: it has an excess of electrons

neg·a·tiv·ism (neg'ə tiv iz'm) *n.* 1. the attitude of ignoring or resisting suggestions or orders from others 2. an attitude or system of thought that is doubting, skeptical, etc. —**neg'a·tiv·ist** *n., adj.* —**neg'a·tiv·is'tic** *adj.*

Ne·gev (neg'ev) region in S Israel of partially reclaimed desert: also **Ne'geb** (-eb)

neg·lect (ni glekt') *vt.* [< L. pp. of *neglegere* < *neg-*, not + *legere*, to gather (see LOGIC)] 1. to ignore or disregard [to *neglect* the advice of others] 2. to fail to take care of or attend to properly; give too little attention to [to *neglect* one's family] 3. to leave undone, as because of carelessness [he *neglected* to lock the door] —*n.* 1. a neglecting or being neglected 2. lack of proper care —**neg·lect'er, neg·lec'tor** *n.*

neg·lect·ful (-fəl) *adj.* neglecting; heedless; negligent (often with *of*) —see SYN. at REMISS —**neg·lect'ful·ly** *adv.* —**neg·lect'ful·ness** *n.*

neg·li·gee (neg'lə zhā', neg'lə zhā') *n.* [< Fr., fem. pp. of *négliger*, to neglect] 1. a woman's dressing gown with soft, flowing lines 2. any informal or careless attire

neg·li·gence (neg'li jəns) *n.* 1. the quality or condition of being negligent 2. an instance of this 3. *Law* failure to use a reasonable amount of care when such failure results in injury or damage to another

neg·li·gent (-jənt) *adj.* [< OFr. < L. prp. of *negligere:* see NEGLECT] 1. habitually failing to do the required thing 2. careless, lax, inattentive, etc. —see SYN. at REMISS —**neg'li·gent·ly** *adv.*

neg·li·gi·ble (neg'li jə b'l) *adj.* that can be neglected or disregarded because small, unimportant, etc. [a *negligible* error] —**neg'li·gi·bil'i·ty** *n.* —**neg'li·gi·bly** *adv.*

ne·go·ti·a·ble (ni gō'shē ə b'l, -shə b'l) *adj.* that can be negotiated; specif., *a*) legally transferable by endorsement, as a promissory note, check, etc. *b*) that can be passed, crossed, etc. [a *negotiable* hill] —**ne·go'ti·a·bil'i·ty** *n.*

ne·go·ti·ate (ni gō'shē āt') *vi.* **-at'ed, -at'ing** [< L. pp. of *negotiari* < *negotium*, business < *nec-*, not + *otium*, ease] to confer or discuss with a view to reaching agreement —*vt.* 1. to settle or conclude (a transaction, treaty, etc.) 2. to transfer or sell (negotiable paper) 3. to succeed in crossing, moving through, etc. [to *negotiate* a flooded river] —**ne·go'ti·a'tor** *n.*

ne·go·ti·a·tion (ni gō'shē ā'shən) *n.* a negotiating; specif., [often *pl.*] a conferring or bargaining to reach agreement —**ne·go'ti·a·to·ry** (-ə tôr'ē) *adj.*

Ne·gress (nē'gris) *n.* a Negro woman or girl: term not used by those who regard the *-ess* suffix as patronizing or discriminatory

Ne·gri·to (nə grēt'ō) *n., pl.* **-tos, -toes** [Sp., dim. of *negro*, NEGRO¹] a member of any of various groups of dwarfish Negroid peoples of the East Indies, the Philippines, and Africa —**Ne·grit'ic** (-grit'ik) *adj.*

ne·gri·tude (neg'rə tŏŏd', nē'grə-; -tyŏŏd') *n.* [Fr. *négritude*, coined < *nègre*, black + *-i-* + *-tude*, -TUDE] [also **N-**] awareness by blacks, esp. in Africa, of their own special culture, and a sense of pride in that culture

Ne·gro¹ (nē'grō) *n., pl.* **-groes** [Sp. & Port. *negro* < L. *niger*, black] 1. a member of the Negroid peoples of Africa, living chiefly south of the Sahara 2. *same as* NEGROID 3. any person with Negro ancestors See BLACK (*n.* 3) —*adj.* of Negroes

Ne·gro² (nä'grō; *Port.* -grŏŏ; *Sp.* -grô) river in N Brazil, flowing southeast into the Amazon: c.1,400 mi.

Ne·groid (nē'groid) *adj.* designating or of a major group of mankind that includes the dark-skinned peoples of Africa and of Melanesia, New Guinea, etc. —*n.* a Negroid person

Ne·gros (nä'grōs) island of the C Philippines, between Cebu & Panay: 4,905 sq. mi.

ne·gus (nē'gəs) *n.* [after Col. Francis *Negus* (d. 1732), who first made it] a beverage of hot water, wine, and lemon juice, sweetened and spiced

Ne·he·mi·ah (nē'ə mī'ə) *Bible* 1. a Hebrew leader of about the 5th cent. B.C. 2. the book that tells about his work: abbrev. **Neh.** Also, in the Douay Bible, **Ne'he·mi'as** (-əs)

Neh·ru (nā'rŏŏ), **Ja·wa·har·lal** (jə wä'hər läl') 1889-1964; prime minister of India (1947-64)

neigh (nā) *vi.* [OE. *hnægan*] to utter the characteristic cry of a horse; whinny —*n.* this cry

neigh·bor (nā'bər) *n.* [< OE. < *neah* (see NIGH) + word thought to be *gebur*, farmer] 1. a person who lives near another 2. a person or thing situated near another 3. a fellow man ["love thy *neighbor*"] —*adj.* nearby; adjacent —*vt., vi.* to live or be situated near or nearby Also, Brit. sp., **neighbour**

neigh·bor·hood (-hŏŏd') *n.* 1. a being neighbors 2. a district or area of a city, town, etc., esp. with regard to some characteristic [an old *neighborhood*] 3. people living near one another; community [the whole *neighborhood* helped] 4. *Math.* the set of all points which lie within a stated distance of a given point —☆**in the neighborhood of** [Colloq.] 1. near (a place) [in the *neighborhood of* the zoo] 2. approximately; nearly [in the *neighborhood of* $10]

neigh·bor·ly (nā'bər lē) *adj.* like or appropriate to neighbors; friendly —**neigh'bor·li·ness** *n.*

Neil (nēl) [var. of NEAL] a masculine name

Neis·se (nī'sə) river in N Europe, flowing from Czechoslovakia into the Oder on the Polish-German border

nei·ther (nē'thər, nī'-) *adj., pron.* [OE. *na-hwæther*, lit., not whether] not one or the other of two; not either [*neither* boy went, *neither* of them sings] —*conj.* 1. not either: used before the first of two words or phrases separated by *nor* [he can *neither* laugh *nor* cry about it] 2. nor yet; and not either [he doesn't smoke, *neither* does he drink] —*adv.* [Dial. or Colloq.] also (after negative expressions) [if she won't go, I won't *neither*]

Nejd (nezhd) district in C & E Saudi Arabia

Nell (nel) [dim. of HELEN] a feminine name

Nel·lie, Nel·ly (nel'ē) [dim. of HELEN] a feminine name

Nel·son (nel's'n) [< the surname *Nelson*, Neal's son] 1. a masculine name **2.** Horatio, Viscount Nelson, 1758–1805; Eng. admiral

nel·son (nel′s'n) *n.* [< personal name *Nelson*] a wrestling hold; specif., a hold (**half nelson**) in which one arm is placed under the opponent's arm from behind with the hand pressing the back of his neck, or a hold (**full nelson**) in which both arms are so placed under the opponent's arms

nem·a·to- [< Gr. *nēmatos,* genitive of *nēma,* thread] *a combining form meaning* thread, threadlike [*nematocyst*] : also, before a vowel, **nemat-**

nem·a·to·cyst (nem′ə tō sist′) *n.* [NEMATO- + -CYST] a stinging structure in coelenterates, as the jellyfish, that contains a coiled, threadlike sting —**nem′a·to·cys′tic** *adj.*

nem·a·tode (nem′ə tōd′) *n.* [< ModL. name of the phylum: see NEMATO-] any of a group of worms, often parasites of animals and plants, with long, cylindrical, unsegmented bodies, as the hookworm, pinworm, etc.

☆**Nem·bu·tal** (nem′byə tôl′) [N(A) + E(THYL) + M(ETHYL) + BU(TYL) + (BARBI)TAL] *a trademark for* PENTOBARBITAL SODIUM

Nem·e·sis (nem′ə sis) [L. < Gr. < *nemein,* to deal out] *Gr. Myth.* the goddess of retribution or vengeance —*n.* [*usually* n-] *pl.* **-ses′** (-sēz′) **1.** *a)* punishment that is deserved *b)* one who imposes it **2.** anyone or anything that it seems will surely defeat or thwart one

N.Eng. 1. New England **2.** North England

ne·o- [< Gr. *neos,* new] *a combining form meaning:* **1.** [*often* N-] new, recent [*neolithic*] **2.** in a new or different way [*neocolonialism*]

ne·o·clas·sic (nē′ō klas′ik) *adj.* designating or of a revival of classic style in art, literature, etc., as in England from c. 1660 to c. 1740: also **ne′o·clas′si·cal** —**ne′o·clas′si·cism** *n.* —**ne′o·clas′si·cist** *n.*

ne·o·co·lo·ni·al·ism (-kə lō′nē əl iz'm) *n.* the survival or revival of colonialism, as by the exploitation of a supposedly independent region by a foreign power —**ne′o·co·lo′ni·al** *adj.* —**ne′o·co·lo′ni·al·ist** *n., adj.*

ne·o·dym·i·um (nē′ə dim′ē əm) *n.* [< NEO- + (DI)DYMIUM] a metallic chemical element of the rare-earth group: symbol, Nd; at. wt., 144.24; at. no., 60

ne·o·lith·ic (nē′ə lith′ik) *adj.* [NEO- + -LITHIC] designating or of the later part of the Stone Age, during which man developed polished stone tools, metal tools, pottery, weaving, stock rearing, and agriculture

ne·ol·o·gism (nē äl′ə jiz'm) *n.* [< Fr.: see NEO-, -LOGY, & -ISM] **1.** a new word or a new meaning for an established word **2.** the use of these Also **ne·ol′o·gy,** *pl.* **-gies** —**ne·o·log′i·cal** (nē′ə läj′i k'l) *adj.* —**ne′o·log′i·cal·ly** *adv.* —**ne·ol′o·gis′tic,** —**ne·ol′o·gis′ti·cal** *adj.*

ne·ol·o·gize (-jīz′) *vi.* -**gized′, -giz′ing** to invent or use neologisms —**ne·ol′o·gist** *n.*

ne·o·my·cin (nē′ə mī′sin) *n.* [< NEO- + Gr. *mykēs,* fungus + -IN[1]] a broad-spectrum antibiotic used esp. in treating infections of the skin and eye

ne·on (nē′än) *n.* [ModL. < Gr. *neon,* neut. of *neos,* new] a rare, colorless, and inert gaseous chemical element: symbol, Ne; at. wt., 20.183; at. no., 10

neon lamp a tube containing neon, which glows red when an electric current is sent through it: used esp. in advertising signs

ne·o·phyte (nē′ə fīt′) *n.* [< LL. < Gr. < *neos,* new + *phytos* < *phyein,* to produce] **1.** a new convert **2.** any beginner; novice

ne·o·plasm (nē′ə plaz'm) *n.* [NEO- + -PLASM] an abnormal growth of tissue, as a tumor —**ne′o·plas′tic** *adj.*

☆**ne·o·prene** (nē′ə prēn′) *n.* [NEO- + (chloro)prene, an acetylene derivative] a synthetic rubber highly resistant to oil, heat, light, and oxidation

Ne·pal (ni pôl′, ne-; -päl′) country in the Himalayas, between India & Tibet: 54,362 sq. mi.; pop. 10,845,000; cap. Katmandu —**Nep·a·lese** (nep′ə lēz′) *adj., n., pl.* **-lese′**

ne·pen·the (ni pen′thē) *n.* [L. < Gr. < *nē-,* not + *penthos,* sorrow] **1.** a drug supposed by the ancient Greeks to cause forgetfulness of sorrow **2.** anything causing this Also **ne·pen′thes** (-thēz) —**ne·pen′the·an** (-thē an) *adj.*

neph·ew (nef′yōo; *chiefly Brit.* nev′-) *n.* [< OFr. < L. *nepos*] **1.** the son of one's brother or sister **2.** the son of one's brother-in-law or sister-in-law

ne·phrid·i·um (ne frid′ē əm) *n., pl.* **-i·a** (-ə) [ModL. < Gr. dim. of *nephros,* kidney] **1.** a passage for waste found in many invertebrates, as in worms **2.** a waste-discharging tube of a vertebrate embryo —**ne·phrid′i·al** *adj.*

ne·phrit·ic (ne frit′ik) *adj.* [< LL. < Gr. < *nephros,* kidney] **1.** of a kidney or the kidneys; renal **2.** of or having nephritis

ne·phri·tis (ne frīt′əs) *n.* [NEPHRO- + -ITIS] a disease of the kidneys, characterized by inflammation, fibrosis, etc.

neph·ro- [< Gr. *nephros,* kidney] *a combining form meaning* kidney: also, before a vowel, **nephr-**

neph·ro·gen·ic (nef′rə jen′ik) *adj.* [NEPHRO- + -GENIC] **1.** originating in the kidneys **2.** producing kidney tissue

ne plus ul·tra (nē plus ul′trə) [L., no more beyond] the highest point of perfection

nep·o·tism (nep′ə tiz'm) *n.* [< Fr. < It. < L. *nepos* (gen. *nepotis*), nephew] favoritism shown to relatives, esp. in appointing them to desirable positions —**nep′o·tist** *n.* —**nep′o·tis′tic** *adj.*

Nep·tune (nep′tōon, -tyōon) **1.** *Rom. Myth.* the god of the sea: identified with the Greek god Poseidon **2.** a planet of the solar system, eighth in distance from the sun: diameter, c.29,500 mi.

☆**nep·tu·ni·um** (nep tōo′nē əm, -tyōo′-) *n.* [ModL.: named after the planet Neptune] a radioactive chemical element produced by irradiating uranium atoms with neutrons: symbol, Np; at. wt., 237.00; at. no., 93

☆**nerd** (nurd) *n.* [< ?] [Slang] a person regarded as dull, stupid, unskillful, etc.

Ne·re·id (nir′ē id) *n. Gr. Myth.* any of the sea nymphs, the fifty daughters of Nereus

ne·re·is (nir′ē is) *n., pl.* **ne·re·i·des** (nə rē′ə dēz′) [ModL.: after NEREUS] any of a group of relatively large flesh-eating worms that live in the ocean

Ne·re·us (nir′ōos, -ē əs) *Gr. Myth.* a benevolent sea god, father of the fifty Nereids

ne·rit·ic (nə rit′ik) *adj.* [< Gr. *nēritēs,* a sea snail] designating or of that part of the sea next to the coast

Ne·ro (nir′ō) (*Nero Claudius Caesar Drusus Germanicus*) 37–68 A.D.; emperor of Rome (54–68): noted for his cruelty

Ne·ru·da (ne rōo′thä; *E.* nə rōo′də), **Pa·blo** (pä′blō) (pseud. of *Ricardo Neftali Reyes*) 1904–73; Chilean poet

ner·va·tion (nər vā′shən) *n. same as* VENATION

nerve (nurv) *n.* [< OFr. < L. *nervus*] **1.** a tendon: now chiefly in **strain every nerve,** to try as hard as possible **2.** any of the cordlike fibers carrying impulses between the body organs and the central nervous system **3.** emotional control; coolness in danger; courage [she tried to jump but lost her *nerve*] **4.** strength; vigor **5.** [*pl.*] the nervous system thought of as indicating health, emotional stability, etc. **6.** [*pl.*] nervousness [a bad case of *nerves*] **7.** [Colloq.] disrespectful boldness; audacity [he had a lot of *nerve,* going where he wasn't wanted] **8.** *Biol.* a vein in a leaf or insect's wing —*vt.* **nerved, nerv′ing** to give strength or courage to [she *nerved* herself for the ordeal] —**get on one's nerves** [Colloq.] to make one annoyed or angry —see SYN. at TEMERITY

nerve block a method of local anesthesia in which the passage of impulses through a particular nerve is stopped

nerve cell 1. *same as* NEURON **2.** occasionally, a nerve cell body without its processes

nerve center 1. any group of nerve cells that function together in controlling some specific sense or bodily activity, as breathing **2.** a control center; headquarters

nerve fiber any of the threadlike parts, either dendrites or axons, making up a nerve

nerve gas any of several liquids whose vapors can paralyze the respiratory and central nervous systems when absorbed through the eyes, lungs, or skin

nerve impulse an electrical wave transmitted along a nerve that has been stimulated

nerve·less (nurv′lis) *adj.* **1.** without strength, force, courage, etc.; weak; unnerved **2.** not nervous; calm; controlled **3.** *Biol.* without nerves —**nerve′less·ly** *adv.* —**nerve′less·ness** *n.*

nerve-rack·ing, nerve-wrack·ing (-rak′iŋ) *adj.* very trying to one's patience or even temper

nerv·ous (nur′vəs) *adj.* **1.** orig., strong; sinewy **2.** vigorous, forceful, lively, etc. [a fine, *nervous* style of writing] **3.** of the nerves [a *nervous* reaction] **4.** made up of or containing nerves [the *nervous* system] **5.** characterized by or having a disordered state of the nerves [a *nervous* condition] **6.** characterized by or showing emotional tension, restlessness, etc. [her *nervous* pacing back and forth] **7.** fearful; uneasy [thunder makes him *nervous*] —**nerv′ous·ly** *adv.* —**nerv′ous·ness** *n.*

☆**nervous breakdown** a severe emotional disorder that makes it difficult for a person to function in a normal way: a popular term, not a technical one

nervous system all the nerve cells and nervous tissues in an organism, including, in vertebrates, the brain, spinal cord, etc.

ner·vure (nur′vyoor) *n.* [Fr.: see NERVE & -URE] *Zool. same as* VEIN (*n.* 2)

nerv·y (nur′vē) *adj.* **nerv′i·er, nerv′i·est 1.** [Brit.] nervous; excitable **2.** full of courage; bold ☆**3.** [Colloq.] rudely bold; brazen; impudent —**nerv′i·ly** *adv.* —**nerv′i·ness** *n.*

nes·ci·ent (nesh′ənt, -ē ənt) *adj.* [< L. prp. of *nescire* < *ne-,* not + *scire,* to know] ignorant —**nes′ci·ence** *n.*

-ness (nis, nəs) [OE. *-nes(s)*] *a suffix meaning* state, quality, or instance of being *[greatness, sadness, weakness]*

nest (nest) *n.* [OE. < IE. base *nizdos* < base *ni-,* down + *sed-,* to SIT] **1.** the structure made or the place chosen by birds for laying their eggs and sheltering their young **2.** the place used by hornets, fish, etc. for spawning or breeding **3.** a cozy place to live or rest; retreat **4.** a resort, haunt, or den or those who go to such a place frequently *[a nest of thieves]* **5.** a swarm or colony of birds, insects, etc. **6.** a set of similar things, each fitting within the one next larger —*vi.* **1.** to build or live in a nest *[swallows often nest in chimneys]* **2.** to fit one into another —*vt.* **1.** to place in or as in a nest **2.** to fit (an object) closely within another —**nest′a·ble** *adj.*

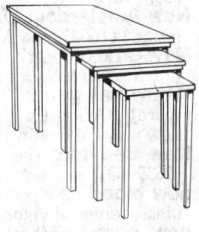

NEST OF TABLES

‡**n'est-ce pas?** (nes pä′) [Fr.] isn't that so?

nest egg 1. an artificial or real egg left in a nest to induce a hen to lay more eggs there **2.** money, etc. saved for the future

nes·tle (nes′'l) *vi.* **-tled, -tling** [OE. *nestlian:* see NEST & -LE[2]] **1.** to settle down comfortably and snugly *[the baby nestled in his mother's arms]* **2.** to press close for comfort or in affection *[she nestled the puppy in her lap]* **3.** to lie sheltered or partly hidden *[a house nestled in the hills]* —*vt.* **1.** to rest or press (a baby, one's head, etc.) in a snug, affectionate manner **2.** to house as in a nest; shelter —**nes′tler** *n.*

nest·ling (nest′liŋ, nes′-) *n.* **1.** a young bird not yet ready to leave the nest **2.** a young child

Nes·tor (nes′tər) *Gr. Myth.* a wise old counselor who fought with the Greeks at Troy

net[1] (net) *n.* [OE. *nett* < IE. base *ned-,* to tie] **1.** a fabric of string, cord, etc., loosely knotted in an openwork pattern and used to catch birds, fish, etc. **2.** any trap or snare *[caught in the net of his own lies]* **3.** a piece of meshed fabric used to hold, protect, or mark off something *[a hairnet, tennis net]* **4.** a fine, meshed cloth like lace, used to make curtains, trim garments, etc. **5.** *same as* NETWORK (sense 2) **6.** *Tennis,* etc. a ball that hits the net, whether or not it goes over: in full, **net ball** —*vt.* **net′ted, net′ting 1.** to make into a net **2.** to catch as with a net **3.** to enclose as with a net **4.** *Tennis,* etc. to hit (the ball) into the net —*vi.* to make nets or network —**net′like** *adj.*

net[2] (net) *adj.* [Fr.: see NEAT[1]] **1.** remaining after certain deductions have been made *[net profit is the profit left after expenses; net weight is the weight of an article without its container]* **2.** after all factors have been taken into consideration; final *[net result]* —*n.* a net amount, profit, weight, price, etc. —*vt.* **net′ted, net′ting** to gain as profit, etc. *[to net $10]*

Neth. Netherlands

neth·er (neth′ər) *adj.* [OE. *neothera* < IE. base *ni-* (see NEST) + compar. suffix] lower *[the nether world]*

Neth·er·lands (neth′ər ləndz) **1.** country in W Europe, on the North Sea: 12,978 sq. mi.; pop. 13,033,000; cap. Amsterdam; seat of govt. The Hague **2.** kingdom consisting of the independent states of the Netherlands & Netherlands Antilles Often with *the* —**Neth′er·land·er** (-lan′dər, -lən dər) *n.*

Netherlands Antilles three islands off the coast of Venezuela & two islands & part of another in the Leeward group of the West Indies, together making up a state of the Netherlands: 394 sq. mi.; pop. 224,000; cap. Willemstad

Netherlands (East) Indies former possessions of the Netherlands in the East Indies: now part of Indonesia

neth·er·most (neth′ər mōst′) *adj.* lowest

nether world *Theol. & Myth.* the world of the dead or of punishment after death; hell

Net·tie, Net·ty (net′ē) [dim. of ANTOINETTE, JEANETTE, etc.] a feminine name

net·ting (net′iŋ) *n.* **1.** the act or process of making nets or fishing with them **2.** netted material

net·tle (net′'l) *n.* [OE. *netele:* for IE. base see NET[1]] any of a number of related weeds with stinging hairs —*vt.* **-tled, -tling 1.** to sting with or as with nettles **2.** to irritate; annoy; vex — see SYN. at IRRITATE —**net′tler** *n.*

net·tle·some (-səm) *adj.* that nettles or irritates

net ton *same as* SHORT TON

net·work (net′wurk′) *n.* **1.** any arrangement or fabric of parallel wires, threads, etc. crossed at regular intervals by others so as to leave open spaces; netting; mesh **2.** a thing resembling this; specif., *a*) a system of connecting roads, canals, etc. *b*) *Radio & TV* a chain of transmitting stations operated as a unit *c*) a system, group, etc. of cooperating individuals —*adj.* broadcast over all or most of the stations of a network

Neuf·châ·tel (cheese) (nōō′shə tel′, nyōō′-) [after a town in N France] a soft, white cheese made from whole or skim milk

neu·ral (noor′əl, nyoor′-) *adj.* [NEUR(O)- + -AL] of a nerve, nerves, or the nervous system

neu·ral·gia (noo ral′jə, nyoo-) *n.* [ModL.: see NEURO- & -ALGIA] severe pain along the course of a nerve —**neu·ral′gic** (-jik) *adj.*

neu·ras·the·ni·a (noor′əs thē′nē ə, nyoor′-) *n.* [ModL. < NEUR(O)- + Gr. *astheneia,* weakness] a type of neurosis, usually the result of emotional conflicts, characterized by irritability, fatigue, worry, etc. —**neu·ras·then′ic** (-then′ik) *adj.*

neu·ri·lem·ma (noor′ə lem′ə, nyoor′-) *n.* [ModL. < Gr. < *neuron,* nerve + *eilēma,* a covering < *eilyein,* to wind, wrap] the thin outer covering of a nerve fiber

neu·ri·tis (noo rīt′əs, nyoo-) *n.* [ModL. < NEURO- + -ITIS] inflammation of a nerve or nerves, accompanied by pain —**neu·rit′ic** (-rit′ik) *adj.*

neu·ro- [< Gr. *neuron,* nerve] *a combining form meaning* of a nerve, nerves, or the nervous system *[neuropathy]* : also, before a vowel, **neur-**

neu·rog·li·a (noo räg′lē ə, nyoo-) *n.* [ModL. < NEURO- + MGr. *glia,* for Gr. *gloios,* glue] the special kind of tissue that binds together and supports the nerve tissue of the central nervous system —**neu·rog′li·al** *adj.*

neu·ro·lep·tic (noor′ō lep′tik, nyoor′-) *n.* [< Fr. < Gr. *neuron,* NERVE + *leptos,* seizing] a tranquilizer

neu·rol·o·gy (noo räl′ə jē, nyoo-) *n.* [ModL.: see NEURO- & -LOGY] the branch of medicine dealing with the nervous system and its diseases —**neu·ro·log·i·cal** (noor′ə läj′i k'l, nyoor′-) *adj.* —**neu·rol′o·gist** *n.*

neu·ro·mus·cu·lar (noor′ō mus′kyə lər, nyoor′-) *adj.* of or involving both nerves and muscles

neu·ron (noor′än, nyoor′-) *n.* [ModL. < Gr. *neuron,* nerve] the basic working unit of the nervous system, consisting of the nerve cell body and all its processes: also **neu′rone** (-ōn) —**neu′ro·nal** (-ə nəl), **neu·ron·ic** (noo rän′ik, nyoo-) *adj.*

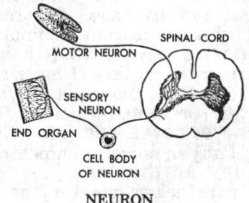

SPINAL CORD
MOTOR NEURON
SENSORY NEURON
END ORGAN
CELL BODY OF NEURON
NEURON

neu·rop·a·thy (noo räp′ə thē, nyoo-) *n.* [NEURO- + -PATHY] any disease of the nervous system —**neu·ro·path·ic** (noor′ə path′ik, nyoor′-) *adj.*

neu·rop·ter·an (noo räp′tər ən, nyoo-) *n.* [< ModL. < NEURO- + Gr. *pteron,* wing + -AN] any of a group of insects with four transparent wings and biting mouthparts

neu·ro·sis (noo rō′sis, nyoo-) *n., pl.* **-ses** (-sēz) [ModL.: see NEURO- & -OSIS] a mental disorder without known physical cause, in which there is great worry or fear for no apparent reason, an uncontrollable urge to do a certain thing, etc.

neu·ro·sur·ger·y (noor′ō sur′jər ē, nyoor′-) *n.* the branch of surgery involving some part of the nervous system, including the brain and the spinal cord

neu·rot·ic (noo rät′ik, nyoo-) *adj.* of or having a neurosis —*n.* a neurotic person —**neu·rot′i·cal·ly** *adv.* —**neu·rot′i·cism** (-ə siz′m) *n.*

neu·ro·tox·in (noor′ō täk′sin, nyoor′-) *n.* a toxin that destroys nerves or nervous tissue —**neu′ro·tox′ic** *adj.*

neut. neuter

---

neu·ter (nōōt′ər, nyōōt′-) *adj.* [< MFr. < L. < *ne-*, not + *uter*, either] **1.** [Archaic] neutral **2.** *Biol. a)* having no sexual organs; asexual *b)* having sexual organs that never develop fully, as the worker bee **3.** *Gram.* designating or of the gender that refers to things thought of as neither male nor female /"it" is a *neuter* pronoun/ —*n.* **1.** a castrated or spayed animal **2.** *Biol.* a neuter plant or animal **3.** *Gram. a)* the neuter gender *b)* a neuter word —*vt.* to castrate or spay (an animal)

neu·tral (nōō′trəl, nyōō′-) *adj.* [Fr. < ML. < L. < *neuter*, NEUTER] **1.** not taking part in either side of a quarrel or war /a *neutral* nation/ **2.** of or characteristic of a nation not taking part in a war or not taking sides in a power struggle /a *neutral* position/ **3.** not one thing or the other; indefinite, middling, etc. /a *neutral* state between joy and sadness/ **4.** having little or no decided color /gray is a *neutral* color/ **5.** *Biol.* same as NEUTER **6.** *Chem.* neither acid nor alkaline **7.** *Elec.* neither negative nor positive; uncharged **8.** *Phonet.* pronounced as the vowel is in most unstressed syllables, which tends to become (ə) —*n.* **1.** a nation not taking part in a war **2.** a neutral person **3.** a neutral color **4.** *Mech.* the position of gears when they are not meshed together and therefore cannot pass on power from the engine —**neu′tral·ly** *adv.*

neu·tral·ism (-iz′m) *n.* a policy of remaining neutral, esp. in international power conflicts —**neu′tral·ist** *adj., n.*

neu·tral·i·ty (nōō tral′ə tē, nyōō-) *n.* **1.** the quality, state, or character of being neutral **2.** the status or policy of a nation not participating in a war between other nations

neu·tral·ize (nōō′trə līz′, nyōō′-) *vt.* **-ized′, -iz′ing 1.** to declare (a nation, etc.) neutral in war **2.** to destroy or work against the effectiveness, force, etc. of /bad reviews of a movie can *neutralize* an expensive advertising campaign/ **3.** *Chem.* to destroy the active properties of /an alkali *neutralizes* an acid/ **4.** *Elec.* to make electrically neutral —**neu′tral·i·za′tion** *n.* —**neu′tral·iz′er** *n.*

neutral spirits ethyl alcohol of 190 proof or over, used in blended whiskeys, liqueurs, cordials, etc.

neu·tri·no (nōō trē′nō, nyōō-) *n., pl.* **-nos** [It., coined by E. FERMI < *neutrone* (< NEUTRON) + dim. suffix *-ino*] *Physics* a subatomic particle with no charge and almost no mass

neu·tron (nōō′trän, nyōō-) *n.* [NEUTR(AL) + (ELECTR)ON] a fundamental particle in the nucleus of an atom: neutrons are uncharged and have about the same mass as protons

☆**neutron bomb** a small nuclear bomb that would send out deadly radiation but cause little blast or burning, so as to kill people without destroying much property

Ne·vad·a (nə vad′ə, -vä′də) [< (SIERRA) NEVADA] Mountain State of the U.S.: 110,540 sq. mi.; pop. 489,000; cap. Carson City: abbrev. **Nev., NV** —**Ne·vad′an** *adj., n.*

né·vé (nā vā′) *n.* [Fr. (Swiss dial.), glacier, ult. < L. *nivis*, genitive of *nix*, snow] the area above or at the head of a glacier where more snow accumulates than melts during the summer

nev·er (nev′ər) *adv.* [OE. *næfre* < *ne*, not + *æfre*, ever] **1.** not ever; at no time /I *never* saw her again/ **2.** not at all; in no case; under no conditions /*never* mind what he says/

nev·er·more (nev′ər môr′) *adv.* never again

never-never land [after the fairyland in J. M. Barrie's *Peter Pan*] an unreal or unrealistic place or situation

nev·er·the·less (nev′ər thə les′) *adv.* in spite of that; nonetheless; however /they were losing the game; *nevertheless*, they kept on trying/

Nev·il, Nev·ille (nev′′l) [< *Neuville*, town in Normandy (lit., new city)] a masculine name

Ne·vis (nē′vis, nev′is) an island in the Leeward group of the West Indies: 50 sq. mi.; pop. 15,000: see ANGUILLA

Nevski, Alexander see ALEXANDER NEVSKI

ne·vus (nē′vəs) *n., pl.* **ne′vi** (-vī) [ModL. < L. *naevus*] a birthmark or mole —**ne′void** (-void) *adj.*

new (nōō, nyōō) *adj.* [OE. *niwe* < IE. base *newos*, new, from which also come L. *novus* & Gr. *nēos*] **1.** appearing, thought of, developed, discovered, made, etc. for the first time /a *new* song; a *new* plan; a *new* star/ **2.** *a)* different /her *new* hairdo/ *b)* strange; unfamiliar /languages *new* to one/ **3.** not yet familiar or accustomed /*new* to the job/ **4.** designating the more recent or most recent one /Sue is the *new* president of our club/ **5.** recently grown; fresh /*new* potatoes/ **6.** not previously used or worn /*new* and used cars/ **7.** modern; recent; fashionable /the *newest* style in shoes/ **8.** more; additional /two *new* inches of snow/ **9.** starting as a repetition of a cycle, series, etc. /the *new* year/ **10.** having just reached a position, rank, place, etc. /a *new* arrival/ **11.** refreshed in spirits, health, etc. /a *new* man/ **12.** [N-] same as MODERN (sense 3) —*n.* something new (with

the) —*adv.* **1.** again **2.** newly; recently /the *new*-fallen snow/ —**new′ish** *adj.* —**new′ness** *n.*

SYN. —**new** is applied to that which has never existed before or which has only just come into being, possession, use, etc. /a *new* coat, plan, etc./; **fresh** is used of something so new that it still has its original appearance, quality, strength, etc. /*fresh* eggs; a *fresh* start/; **novel** implies a newness that is very strange or unusual /a *novel* idea, combination, etc./; **modern** and **modernistic** refer to that which is associated with the present time rather than an earlier period and imply up-to-dateness, with **modernistic** sometimes being used to suggest contempt as well /*modern* dance; a *modernistic* painting/; **original** is used of that which not only is new but is also the first of its kind /an *original* plan, melody, etc./ —**ANT· old**

New Amsterdam Du. colonial town on Manhattan Island: renamed (1664) New York by the British

New·ark (nōō′ərk, nyōō′-) [after *Newark,* England] city in northeastern N.J.: pop. 382,000 (met. area 1,857,000)

☆**new ball game** [? from use in baseball when a team ties the score] [Colloq.] a situation which has changed so much that new ways of dealing with it are needed

New Bed·ford (bed′fərd) [after W. Russell, Duke of *Bedford* (1639–83)] seaport in SE Mass.: pop. 102,000

new blood new people, thought of as a possible source of fresh ideas, renewed vigor, etc.

new·born (nōō′bôrn′, nyōō′-) *adj.* **1.** recently born; just born /a *newborn* calf/ **2.** born again; revived /*newborn* hope/

New Britain city in C Conn.: pop. 83,000

New Brunswick province of SE Canada, on the Gulf of St. Lawrence: 28,354 sq. mi.; pop. 677,000; cap. Fredericton: abbrev. **N.B.**

New·burg (nōō′bərg, nyōō′-) *adj.* ☆served in a rich, creamy sauce made with butter, egg yolks, and wine

New Caledonia Fr. island in the SW Pacific, west of Australia

new candle see CANDLE (*n.* 3)

New·cas·tle (nōō′kas′′l, nyōō′-; -käs′-) seaport in N England: pop. 237,000: in full, **New′cas′tle-up·on-Tyne′** (-tīn′) —**carry coals to Newcastle 1.** to take things to a place where they are plentiful: Newcastle was a center for coal **2.** to do an unnecessary thing

new·com·er (nōō′kum′ər, nyōō′-) *n.* a recent arrival

☆**New Deal** the economic and political principles and policies adopted by President Franklin D. Roosevelt in the 1930's to improve economic and social conditions —**New Dealer**

New Delhi capital of India, next to old Delhi: pop. 261,000

new·el (nōō′əl, nyōō′-) *n.* [< OFr. < LL. *nucalis*, like a nut < L. *nux*, NUT] **1.** the upright pillar around which the steps of a winding staircase turn **2.** the post at the top or bottom of a flight of stairs, supporting the handrail: also **newel post**

New England [so named (1616) by Capt. John SMITH] ☆the six NE States of the U.S.: Me., Vt., N.H., Mass., R.I., and Conn. —**New Englander**

New English Bible a British translation of the Bible, published in 1970

new·fan·gled (nōō′faŋ′g′ld, nyōō′-) *adj.* [< ME. < *newe*, new + *-fangel* < base of OE. *fon*, to take] new; novel: a term showing mild contempt /*newfangled* gadgets/

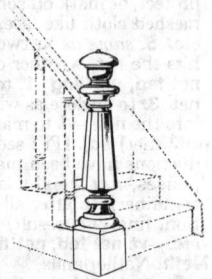

NEWEL POST

new-fash·ioned (-fash′ənd) *adj.* **1.** recently come into fashion **2.** new in form or style

New·found·land (nōō′fənd land′, -lənd; nyōō′-; nyōō foūnd′-land′) **1.** an island of Canada, off the E coast **2.** province of E Canada, including this island & Labrador: 156,185 sq. mi.; pop. 558,000; cap. St. John's: abbrev. **Nfld.** —**New′found·land′er** *n.*

Newfoundland dog any of a North American breed of large, powerful, shaggy-haired dogs

New France Fr. possessions in N. America, from the end of the 16th cent. to 1763, including E Canada, the Great Lakes region, & the Mississippi valley

New·gate (nōō′gāt, nyōō′-) former prison in London: torn down in 1902

New Granada 1. former Spanish possessions consisting of northwestern S. America and Panama **2.** former country made up of present-day Colombia and Panama

New Guinea 1. large island in the East Indies, north of Australia: divided between West Irian (in Indonesia) & the country of Papua New Guinea: c. 333,000 sq. mi. **2. Trust Territory of,** former Australian trust territory including the NE part of New

Guinea & many nearby islands in the SW Pacific: united (1973) with the Territory of PAPUA

New Hamp·shire (hamp′shir, ham′-) [after *Hampshire*, county in England] New England State of the U.S.: 9,304 sq. mi.; pop. 738,000; cap. Concord: abbrev. **N.H., NH**

New Ha·ven (hā′vən) city in S Conn., on Long Island Sound: pop. 138,000

New Hebrides group of islands in the SW Pacific, west of Fiji: under Brit. & Fr. joint rule: see map at FIJI

New High German *see* GERMAN, HIGH GERMAN

New Jersey [after the island of JERSEY] Eastern State of the U.S.: 7,836 sq. mi.; pop. 7,168,000; cap. Trenton: abbrev. **N.J., NJ** —**New Jer′sey·ite′** (-īt′)

New Jerusalem *Bible* heaven: Rev. 21:2

☆**New Left** a U.S. political movement that developed in the 1960's as a loose combination of various organizations, mainly of young people, seeking radical social and economic change

new·ly (nōō′lē, nyōō′-) *adv.* **1.** recently; lately [a *newly* paved road] **2.** anew; afresh [*newly* painted for the third time in a month] **3.** in a new way or style

new·ly·wed (-wed′) *n.* a recently married person

New·man (nōō′mən, nyōō′-), **John Henry,** Cardinal Newman, 1801–90; Eng. theologian & writer

☆**new math** a system for teaching basic mathematics based on the use of sets

New Mexico [translation of Sp. *Nuevo Méjico*] Mountain State of the U.S.: 121,666 sq. mi.; pop. 1,016,000; cap. Santa Fe: abbrev. **N.Mex., NM** —**New Mexican**

new moon the phase of the moon when it is between the earth and the sun, with its dark side toward the earth: after a few days it reappears as a thin crescent curving to the right

New Neth·er·land (neth′ər lənd) Du. colony (1613–64) in eastern N. America: taken by England & divided into the colonies of New York & New Jersey

New Or·le·ans (ôr′lē ənz, ôr lēnz′; *chiefly Southern* ôr′lənz) [after ORLÉANS, France] city in SE La., on the Mississippi: pop. 593,000 (met. area 1,046,000)

New·port (nōō′pôrt′, nyōō′-) seaport in SE Wales: pop. 112,000

Newport News [< ?] seaport in SE Va., at Hampton Roads: pop. 138,000

New Ro·chelle (rə shel′) [after *La Rochelle*, France] city in southeastern N.Y., on Long Island Sound: pop. 75,000

news (nōōz, nyōōz) *n.pl.* [*with sing. v.*] [after OFr. *noveles* or ML. *nova*, pl. of *novum*, what is new: see NEW] **1.** new information about anything; information previously unknown **2.** reports of recent happenings, esp. those broadcast, printed in a newspaper, etc. **3.** any person or thing featured in such reports —**make news** to do something reported as news

☆**news agency** an organization that supplies news to newspapers, radio and TV stations, etc. that subscribe to its services

news·boy (nōōz′boi′, nyōōz′-) *n.* a boy who sells or delivers newspapers

☆**news·cast** (-kast′) *n.* [NEWS + (BROAD)CAST] a program of news broadcast over radio or TV —**news′cast′er** *n.* —**news′cast′ing** *n.*

☆**news conference** *same as* PRESS CONFERENCE

☆**news·deal·er** (-dēl′ər) *n.* a person who sells newspapers, magazines, etc., esp. as a retailer

news·let·ter (-let′ər) *n.* a bulletin issued at regular intervals, containing news of interest to a special group [the congressman sends out a *newsletter* to voters in his district]

news·man (-man′, -mən) *n., pl.* -**men** (-men′, -mən) **1.** *same as* NEWSDEALER **2.** one who gathers and reports news for a newspaper, radio or TV station, etc.

news·mon·ger (-muŋ′gər, -mäŋ′gər) *n.* a gossip

New South Wales state of SE Australia, on the Pacific

New Spain former Sp. province (1535–1821) including Mexico, the southwestern U.S., most of Central America, the West Indies, and the Philippines

news·pa·per (-pā′pər) *n.* a regular publication, usually a daily or weekly, containing news, opinions, advertisements, etc.

news·pa·per·man (-man′) *n., pl.* -**men** (-men′) **1.** a person who works for a newspaper, esp. as a reporter, editor, etc. **2.** a person who owns or publishes a newspaper —**news′pa′per·wom′an** *n. fem., pl.* -**wom′en**

new·speak (nōō′spēk′, nyōō′-) *n.* [*sometimes* N-] the use of ambiguous and deceptive talk, as by government officials, in seeking to mold public opinion

news·print (nōōz′print′, nyōōz′-) *n.* a cheap paper made mainly from wood pulp and used chiefly for newspapers

☆**news·reel** (-rēl′) *n.* a short motion picture of news events

☆**news·stand** (-stand′) *n.* a stand at which newspapers, magazines, etc. are sold

New Style the method of reckoning time according to the Gregorian calendar

news·wor·thy (nōōz′wur′thē, nyōōz′-) *adj.* timely and important or interesting

news·y (-ē) *adj.* **news′i·er, news′i·est** [Colloq.] containing much news [a *newsy* letter]

newt (nōōt, nyōōt) *n.* [< ME. *an eute* (with the -*n* of the article shifting to *eute*) < OE. *efeta*, eft] any of various small salamanders that can live on land or in water

New Testament the part of the Bible containing the life and teachings of Jesus and his followers

New·ton [¹] (nōōt′'n, nyōōt′'n) [< *New Towne*, orig. name of Cambridge, Mass.] city in E Mass.: suburb of Boston: pop. 91,000

New·ton [²] (nōōt′'n, nyōōt′'n) [< surname *Newton* < Eng. place name < OE. *neowa tun,* new town] **1.** a masculine name **2.** Sir **Isaac,** 1642–1727; Eng. mathematician & scientist —**New·to′ni·an** (-tō′nē ən) *adj., n.*

new·ton (nōōt′'n, nyōōt′'n) *n.* [after Sir Isaac NEWTON] the unit of force in the mks system: the force which causes a mass of 1 kilogram to accelerate at a rate of 1 meter per second per second

New World the Western Hemisphere —**new′-world′** *adj.*

new year [*also* N- Y-] **1.** the year just about to begin or just begun (usually with *the*) **2.** the first day or days of the new year

New Year's (Day) January 1, the first day of a calendar year, usually a legal holiday

New Year's Eve the evening before New Year's Day

New York [after the Duke of *York*] **1.** State of the northeastern U.S.: 49,576 sq. mi.; pop. 18,191,000; cap. Albany: abbrev. **N.Y., NY 2.** city in southeastern N.Y., at the mouth of the Hudson: often called **New York City:** pop. 7,868,000 (met. area 11,529,000) —**New York′er**

New York State Barge Canal system of waterways, including the Erie Canal, connecting Lake Erie & the Hudson River

New Zea·land (zē′lənd) country made up of two large islands & several small islands in the S Pacific, southeast of Australia: a member of the Commonwealth: 103,736 sq. mi.; pop. 2,809,000; cap. Wellington —**New Zea′land·er**

next (nekst) *adj.* [OE. *neahst,* superl. of *neah,* nigh] nearest; coming just before or just after [the *next* boy in line; *next* Monday] —*adv.* **1.** in the time, place, degree, or rank coming just before or just after [he sits *next* to me in school] **2.** on the first occasion after this [when *next* we meet] —*prep.* beside; nearest to [sit *next* the tree] —*n.* the one immediately following —☆**get next to** [Slang] to become friendly with —**next door (to) 1.** in or at the house adjacent (to) **2.** almost

next-door (neks′dôr′) *adj.* in or at the next house, building, etc.

next of kin one's relative(s) most nearly related

nex·us (nek′səs) *n., pl.* -**us·es, nex′us** [L. < pp. of *nectere,* to bind] **1.** a connection, tie, or link between individuals of a group, members of a series, etc. **2.** a connected group or series

Nez Per·cé (nez′ pər sā′, purs′) *pl.* **Nez Per·cés′, Nez Per·cé′** [Fr., lit., pierced nose: from the false notion that they pierced the nose] a member of a N. American Indian tribe of the Northwest

Nfld., Nfd. Newfoundland

N.G. 1. National Guard: also **NG 2.** New Guinea

N.G., n.g. [Slang] no good

ngwee ('n gwē′) *n., pl.* **ngwee** [native term, lit., bright] *see* MONETARY UNITS, table (Zambia)

N.H., NH New Hampshire

Ni *Chem.* nickel

N.I. Northern Ireland

NEWT
(3–4 in. long)

☆**ni·a·cin** (nī'ə sin) *n.* [NI(COTINIC) AC(ID) + -IN¹] a white, odorless substance, $C_6H_5O_2N$, found in protein foods: it is a member of the vitamin B complex, used in treating pellagra

Ni·ag·a·ra (nī ag'rə, -ər ə) [< Iroquoian town name] river between western N.Y. & SE Ontario, Canada, flowing from Lake Erie into Lake Ontario

Niagara Falls 1. waterfall on the Niagara River: divided by an island into two falls, Horseshoe, or Canadian, Falls & American Falls 2. city in western N.Y., at Niagara Falls: pop. 86,000 3. city in SE Ontario, opposite Niagara Falls, N.Y.: pop. 57,000

Nia·mey (nyä mā') capital of Niger, in the SW part, on the Niger River: pop. 70,000

nib (nib) *n.* [var. of NEB] 1. the bill or beak of a bird 2. the point of a pen 3. the projecting end of anything; point

nib·ble (nib'l) *vt., vi.* **-bled, -bling** [prob. akin to MLowG. *nibbelen*] 1. to eat (food) with quick, small bites, as a mouse does 2. to bite at (something) with small, gentle bites —*n.* 1. a small bite or amount 2. a nibbling —**nib'bler** *n.*

Ni·be·lung (nē'bə loon') *n.* [G.] *Germanic Legend* any of a race of dwarfs who owned a magic ring and a hoard of gold, taken from them by Siegfried

Ni·be·lung·en·lied (nē'bə loon'ən lēt') a Middle High German epic poem by an unknown author of the 13th cent.

nibs (nibz) *n.* [< ?] [Colloq.] an important, or esp. self-important, person (with *his*)

Nic·a·ra·gua (nik'ə rä'gwə) 1. country in Central America, on the Caribbean & the Pacific: 54,342 sq. mi.; pop. 1,984,000; cap. Managua 2. Lake, lake in S Nicaragua —**Nic'a·ra'guan** *adj., n.*

Nice (nēs) seaport & resort in SE France: pop. 322,000

nice (nīs) *adj.* **nic'er, nic'est** [OFr., stupid < L. *nescius*, ignorant < *ne-*, not + *scire*, to know] 1. difficult to please; very particular [he shows *nice* taste in books] 2. delicate; precise; subtle [a *nice* distinction] 3. calling for accuracy, care, tact, etc. [a *nice* problem] 4. *a)* keenly aware of small differences [a *nice* ear for musical pitch] *b)* extremely accurate, as an instrument 5. having high standards of conduct; scrupulous 6. *a)* agreeable; pleasant [a *nice* time] *b)* attractive; pretty [a *nice* dress] *c)* kind; considerate [a *nice* neighbor] *d)* respectable [she dates only *nice* boys] *e)* good; excellent [a *nice* throw to first base] —*adv.* pleasingly, attractively, etc.: regarded as substandard, dialectal, or colloquial —**nice and** [Colloq.] altogether; very [my tea is *nice and* hot] —**nice'ly** *adv.* —**nice'ness** *n.*

Ni·cene Creed (nī'sēn, nī sēn') [< *Nicaea*, ancient city in Asia Minor where it was formulated] a confession of faith for Christians, adopted in 325 A.D.: now used in various forms by most denominations

ni·ce·ty (nī'sə tē) *n., pl.* **-ties** 1. a being nice; specif., *a)* careful attention to what is right or proper *b)* precision; accuracy [the *nicety* with which he estimated the distance] *c)* the quality of being very particular or hard to please [the *nicety* of her tastes in music] 2. the quality of calling for delicacy or precision in handling 3. a small detail, fine distinction, etc. [the *niceties* of grammar] 4. something choice or dainty [the *niceties* of life] —**to a nicety** exactly

niche (nich) *n.* [Fr. < OFr., ult. < L. *nidus*, a nest] 1. a recess in a wall for a statue, bust, or vase 2. a place or position for which a person or thing is especially well suited [he found his *niche* in teaching] 3. *Ecol.* the particular role of an organism in its total environment —*vt.* **niched, nich'ing** to place in a niche

Nich·o·las (nik'l əs) [< OFr. < L. < Gr. < *nikē*, victory + *laos*, the people] 1. a masculine name: dim. **Nick** 2. **Nicholas I** 1796–1855; czar of Russia (1825–55) 3. **Nicholas II** 1868–1918; last czar of Russia (1894–1917): forced to abdicate; executed 4. **Saint**, 4th cent. A.D.: patron saint of Russia, of Greece, & of young people: see SANTA CLAUS

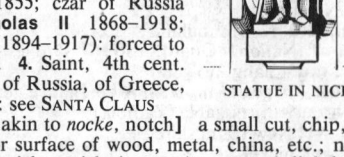

STATUE IN NICHE

nick (nik) *n.* [prob. akin to *nocke*, notch] a small cut, chip, etc. made in an edge or surface of wood, metal, china, etc.; notch —*vt.* 1. to make a nick or nicks in 2. *a)* to wound slightly *b)* to strike glancingly 3. [Slang] *a)* to fine *b)* to overcharge or cheat —**in the nick of time** just before it is too late

nick·el (nik'l) *n.* [Sw. < G. < *kupfer*, copper + *nickel*, demon: so called because of the deceptive appearance of the ore, which looks like copper but contains none] 1. a hard, silver-white, malleable metallic chemical element, used in alloys and for plating: symbol, Ni; at. wt., 58.71; at. no., 28 ☆2. a U.S. or Canadian coin made of an alloy of nickel and copper and equal to five cents —*vt.* **-eled** or **-elled, -el·ing** or **-el·ling** to plate with nickel

☆**nick·el·o·de·on** (nik'ə lō'dē ən) *n.* [< NICKEL + Fr. *odéon*, concert hall] 1. formerly, a motion-picture theater, etc. where admission was five cents 2. a player piano or early type of jukebox operated by putting a nickel in a slot

nickel plate a thin layer of nickel deposited by electrolysis on objects made of other metal, to prevent rust —**nick'el-plate'** *vt.* **-plat'ed, -plat'ing**

nickel silver a hard, tough, ductile, malleable alloy composed of nickel, copper, and zinc

nickel steel a steel alloy made harder, stronger, and more rust-resistant than ordinary steel by the addition of up to five percent of nickel

nick·er (nik'ər) *vi.* [prob. < NEIGH + -ER (sense 4)] to utter a low, whinnying sound: said of a horse —*n.* this sound

nick·nack (nik'nak') *n. same as* KNICKKNACK

nick·name (nik'nām') *n.* [< ME. *an ekename*, a surname (with the *-n* of the article shifting to *ekename*)] 1. a substitute name given to a person or thing in fun, affection, etc.: usually descriptive, as "Doc," "Shorty," etc. 2. a familiar, often shorter, form of a proper name, as "Dick" for "Richard" —*vt.* **-named', -nam'ing** to give a nickname to

Nic·o·si·a (nik'ə sē'ə) capital of Cyprus: pop. 109,000

nic·o·tine (nik'ə tēn', -tin) *n.* [Fr. < ModL., after J. *Nicot*, 16th-c. Fr. diplomat who introduced tobacco into France] a poisonous alkaloid, $C_{10}H_{14}N_2$, found in tobacco leaves and used as an insecticide —**nic'o·tin'ic** (-tin'ik, -tē'nik) *adj.*

nicotinic acid *same as* NIACIN

nic·tate (nik'tāt) *vi.* **-tat·ed, -tat·ing** *same as* NICTITATE —**nic·ta'tion** *n.*

nic·ti·tate (nik'tə tāt') *vi.* **-tat·ed, -tat·ing** [< ML. pp. of *nictitare* < L. *nictare*, to wink] to wink or blink rapidly, as birds and animals with a nictitating membrane —**nic'ti·ta'tion** *n.*

nictitating membrane a transparent third eyelid hinged at the inner side or lower lid of the eye of various animals

Nie·buhr (nē'boor), **Rein·hold** (rīn'hōld) 1892–1971; U.S. clergyman & Protestant theologian

niece (nēs) *n.* [< OFr. < LL. < L. *neptis*] 1. the daughter of one's brother or sister 2. the daughter of one's brother-in-law or sister-in-law

Nie·tzsche (nē'chə), **Frie·drich Wil·helm** (frē'driH vil'helm) 1844–1900; Ger. philosopher —**Nie'tzsche·an** (-chē ən) *adj., n.*

☆**nif·ty** (nif'tē) *adj.* **-ti·er, -ti·est** [prob. < MAGNIFICENT] [Slang] attractive, smart, stylish, enjoyable, etc. —*n., pl.* **-ties** a nifty thing; esp., a clever remark

Ni·ger (nī'jər) 1. river in W Africa, flowing from Guinea through Mali, Niger, & Nigeria into the Atlantic 2. country in WC Africa, north of Nigeria: c.458,500 sq. mi.; pop. 4,016,000; cap. Niamey

Ni·ger·i·a (nī jir'ē ə) country in WC Africa, on the Atlantic: a member of the Commonwealth: 327,186 sq. mi.; pop. 69,524,000; cap. Lagos —**Ni·ger'i·an** *adj., n.*

nig·gard (nig'ərd) *n.* [prob. < Scand.] a stingy person; miser —*adj.* stingy; miserly

nig·gard·ly (-lē) *adj.* 1. stingy; miserly 2. small, few, or scanty [a *niggardly* sum] —*adv.* in a stingy way —see SYN. at STINGY —**nig'gard·li·ness** *n.*

nig·gle (nig'l) *vi.* **-gled, -gling** [prob. akin to Norw. dial. *nigla*] to work fussily; pay too much attention to petty details —**nig'gler** *n.* —**nig'gling** *adj., n.*

nigh (nī) *adv.* [OE. *neah*] [Chiefly Archaic or Dial.] 1. near in time, place, etc. 2. almost —*adj.* nigh'er, nigh'est or, older, next [Chiefly Archaic or Dial.] 1. near; close 2. direct or short 3. on the left: said of animals, vehicles, etc. —*prep.* [Chiefly Archaic or Dial.] near —*vi., vt.* [Archaic] to approach

night (nīt) *n.* [OE. *niht* < IE. base *nekwt-*] 1. the period of darkness between sunset and sunrise 2. the evening at the end of a specified day [Christmas *night*] 3. the darkness of night 4. any period or condition of darkness or gloom, as a time of sorrow, death, etc. —*adj.* 1. of, for, or at night 2. active or working at night —**make a night of it** to celebrate all night —**night and day** continually

night blindness imperfect vision in the dark or in dim light: a symptom of vitamin A deficiency

night-bloom·ing cereus (nīt'blōō'miŋ) any of various cactuses that bloom at night

night·cap (-kap′) *n.* **1.** a cap worn in bed, esp. formerly, to protect the head from cold **2.** [Colloq.] an alcoholic drink taken at bedtime ☆**3.** *Baseball* the second game of a double-header

night clothes clothes to be worn in bed, as pajamas

night·club (-klub′) *n.* a place of entertainment open at night for eating, drinking, dancing, etc.

☆**night crawler** any large earthworm that comes to the surface at night, commonly used as fish bait

night·dress (-dres′) *n. same as:* **1.** NIGHTGOWN **2.** NIGHT CLOTHES

night·fall (-fôl′) *n.* the close of day; dusk

night·gown (-goun′) *n.* a loose gown worn in bed by women or small children

night·hawk (-hôk′) *n.* ☆**1.** any of a group of new-world night birds related to the goatsuckers and the whippoorwill **2.** *same as: a)* NIGHTJAR ☆*b)* NIGHT OWL

night·ie (nīt′ē) *n. colloq. dim. of* NIGHTGOWN

night·in·gale (nīt′'n gāl′, -iŋ-) *n.* [< OE. < *niht*, night + base of *galan*, to sing] a small European thrush with a reddish-brown back and yellowish-brown breast, known for the sweet singing of the male, esp. at night

Night·in·gale (nīt′'n gāl′, -iŋ-), **Florence** 1820–1910; Eng. nurse: pioneer in modern nursing

night·jar (nīt′jär′) *n.* [NIGHT + JAR¹] the European goatsucker

NIGHTHAWK (wingspread to 18 in.)

night latch a door latch with a bolt opened from the outside by a key and from the inside by a knob

☆**night letter** a telegram with a minimum charge for 100 words or fewer, sent at night at a cheaper rate than a regular telegram

night light a small, dim light kept on all night, as in a hallway, bathroom, sickroom, etc.

night·long (-lôŋ′) *adj.* lasting the entire night —*adv.* during the entire night

night·ly (-lē) *adj.* done or occurring every night [his *nightly* bath] —*adv.* every night [he reads a chapter *nightly*]

night·mare (-mer′) *n.* [< ME. < *niht*, night + *mare*, demon] **1.** a frightening dream, often accompanied by a feeling of being helpless and weighed down with worry **2.** any frightening experience —**night′mar′ish** *adj.*

night owl ☆a person who works at night or likes to stay up late

nights (nīts) *adv.* on every night or most nights [to work *nights*]

night school a school held in the evening, as one for adults unable to attend by day

night·shade (nīt′shād′) *n.* [OE. *nihtscada*] **1.** any of a large group of flowering plants of the nightshade family, including BLACK NIGHTSHADE **2.** *same as* BELLADONNA (sense 1) —*adj.* designating a large family of poisonous and nonpoisonous plants, including the tobacco, tomato, potato, petunia, and eggplant

night·shirt (-shurt′) *n.* a loose garment like a long shirt, worn in bed, esp. formerly, by men or boys

☆**night·spot** (-spät′) *n. colloq. var. of* NIGHTCLUB

☆**night stand** a small table at the bedside

☆**night stick** a club carried by a policeman

night·time (-tīm′) *n.* the period of darkness from sunset to sunrise

night watch **1.** a watching or guarding during the night **2.** the person or persons doing such guarding **3.** the time of their guarding

night·wear (-wer′) *n. same as* NIGHT CLOTHES

night·y (-ē) *n., pl.* **night′ies** *alt. sp. of* NIGHTIE

NIH, N.I.H. National Institutes of Health

ni·hil·ism (nī′ə liz'm, nē′-, nī′hi-) *n.* [< L. *nihil*, nothing + -ISM] **1.** *Philos. a)* the doctrine that there is no basis for knowledge or truth *b)* the rejection of all customary beliefs in morality, religion, etc. **2.** the belief that there is no meaning or purpose in existence **3.** *a)* the doctrine that existing social, political, and economic institutions must be completely destroyed

b) [N-] a movement in Russia (c.1860–1917) which advocated such revolutionary reform *c)* loosely, any revolutionary movement using force and threats —**ni′hil·ist** *n.* —**ni′hil·is′tic** *adj.*

Ni·i·ha·u (nē′ē hä′oo, nē′hou) [Haw.] an island of Hawaii, west of Kauai

Nij·me·gen (nī′mā′gən; *Du.* nī′mā′khən) city in the E Netherlands: pop. 149,000

-nik (nik) [< Russ. *-nik*, -ER] *a suffix used to form slang or colloquial words, meaning* one who is or has to do with

Ni·ke (nī′kē) *Gr. Myth.* the winged goddess of victory

nil (nil) *n.* [L., contr. of *nihil*] nothing

Nile (nīl) river in NE Africa, flowing through Egypt into the Mediterranean: with one of its main headstreams, over 4,000 mi.

nil·gai (nil′gī) *n., pl.* **-gais, -gai:** see PLURAL, II, D, 1 [Per. *nīlgāw*, blue cow] a large, gray antelope of India: also **nil′gau** (-gô)

nim·ble (nim′b'l) *adj.* **-bler, -blest** [< OE. *numol* < *niman*, to take] **1.** having or showing mental quickness; quick-witted; alert [a *nimble* mind] **2.** moving quickly and lightly [the *nimble* fingers of the pianist] —see SYN. at AGILE —**nim′ble·ness** *n.* —**nim′bly** *adv.*

nim·bo·stra·tus (nim′bō strāt′əs, -strat′əs) *n.* [ModL.: see NIMBUS & STRATUS] a large, dark, low-level cloud, commonly bringing rain or snow

nim·bus (nim′bəs) *n., pl.* **-bi** (-bī), **-bus·es** [L., rain cloud] **1.** orig., any rain-producing cloud **2.** a bright cloud supposedly surrounding gods or goddesses appearing on earth **3.** an atmosphere of splendor about any person or thing **4.** a halo surrounding the heads of saints, etc., as in pictures

Nîmes (nēm) city in S France: pop. 123,000

Nim·rod (nim′räd) *Bible* a mighty hunter: Gen. 10:8–9 —*n.* [often n-] a hunter

nin·com·poop (nin′kəm poop′, niŋ′-) *n.* [< ?] a stupid, silly person; fool; simpleton

nine (nīn) *adj.* [OE. *nigon*] totaling one more than eight —*n.* **1.** the cardinal number between eight and ten; 9; IX **2.** anything having nine units or members, or numbered nine; specif., a baseball team —**to the nines 1.** to perfection **2.** in the most elaborate or showy manner [dressed *to the nines*]

nine·fold (nīn′fōld′) *adj.* [see -FOLD] **1.** having nine parts **2.** having nine times as much or as many —*adv.* nine times as much or as many

nine·pins (-pinz′) *n.pl.* [with sing. v.] a British version of tenpins, in which nine pins are used

nine·teen (-tēn′) *adj.* [OE. *nigontyne*] nine more than ten —*n.* the cardinal number between eighteen and twenty; 19; XIX

nine·teenth (-tēnth′) *adj.* **1.** coming after eighteen others in a series; 19th **2.** designating any of the nineteen equal parts of something —*n.* **1.** the one following the eighteenth **2.** any of the nineteen equal parts of something; 1/19

nine·ti·eth (nīn′tē ith) *adj.* **1.** coming after eighty-nine others in a series; 90th **2.** designating any of the ninety equal parts of something —*n.* **1.** the one following the eighty-ninth **2.** any of the ninety equal parts of something; 1/90

nine·ty (nīn′tē) *adj.* [OE. *nigontig*] nine times ten —*n., pl.* **-ties** the cardinal number between eighty-nine and ninety-one; 90; XC (or LXXXX) —**the nineties** the numbers or years, as of a century, from ninety through ninety-nine

Nin·e·veh (nin′ə və) capital of ancient Assyria

nin·ny (nin′ē) *n., pl.* **-nies** [prob. < *an innocent* (with the *-n* of the article shifting to *innocent*)] a fool; dolt

ninth (nīnth) *adj.* [OE. *nigonthe*] **1.** coming after eight others in a series; 9th **2.** designating any of the nine equal parts of something —*n.* **1.** the one following the eighth **2.** any of the nine equal parts of something; 1/9 —**ninth′ly** *adv.*

Ni·o·be (nī′ə bē′) *Gr. Myth.* a queen of Thebes, daughter of Tantalus, who, weeping for her slain children, was turned into a stone from which tears continued to flow

ni·o·bi·um (nī ō′bē əm) *n.* [ModL. < L. *Niobe*, NIOBE: from association with tantalum: see TANTALUM] a gray or white metallic chemical element used in chromium steels, in jet engines and rockets, etc.: symbol, Nb; at. wt., 92.906; at. no., 41

nip¹ (nip) *vt.* **nipped, nip′ping** [prob. < MLowG. *nippen* or ON. *hnippa*] **1.** to pinch, squeeze, or bite [he *nipped* his finger in the door] **2.** to sever (shoots, buds, etc.) by pinching or clipping **3.** to stop the growth, spread, etc. of [we should *nip* those ru-mots immediately] **4.** to have a painful or harmful effect on because of cold [frost *nipped* the plants] —*vi.* to give a nip or nips —*n.* **1.** a nipping; pinch; bite **2.** a piece nipped off **3.** a stinging quality, as in cold air **4.** stinging cold; frost —☆**nip and tuck** so close or even that one cannot tell how it will turn out

nip² (nip) *n.* [prob. < Du. < base of *nippen*, to sip] a small drink of liquor; dram; sip —*vt., vi.* to drink (liquor) in nips

nip·per (nip′ər) *n.* **1.** anything that nips, or pinches **2.** [*pl.*] any of various tools for grasping or cutting wire, etc., as pliers, pincers, or forceps **3.** the pincerlike claw of a crab, lobster, etc. **4.** [Brit. Colloq.] a small boy

nip·ple (nip′'l) *n.* [prob. < dim. of NEB] **1.** the part of a breast or udder through which a baby or young animal sucks milk from its mother; teat **2.** a teatlike part, as of rubber, for a baby's bottle **3.** any projection or thing resembling a nipple in shape or use

NIPPERS

Nip·pon (nip′än, ni pän′) *a Japanese name for* JAPAN

Nip·pon·ese (nip′ə nēz′) *adj., n., pl.* -**ese′** [< NIPPON] *same as* JAPANESE

nip·py (nip′ē) *adj.* -**pi·er**, -**pi·est 1.** tending to nip **2.** cold in a stinging way —**nip′pi·ness** *n.*

nir·va·na (nir vä′nə, nər-; -van′ə) *n.* [< Sans.] [*also* N-] *Buddhism* the state of perfect contentment in which one no longer feels desire and passion and one's soul becomes part of the supreme spirit of the universe

Ni·san (nē sän′, nis′ən) *n.* [Heb.] *see* JEWISH CALENDAR

☆**ni·sei** (nē′sā) *n., pl.* **ni′sei, ni′seis** [Jap., lit., second generation] [*also* N-] a native U.S. or Canadian citizen born of immigrant Japanese parents and educated in America

nit (nit) *n.* [OE. *hnitu*] **1.** the egg of a louse or similar insect **2.** a young louse, etc.

ni·ter (nīt′ər) *n.* [< MFr. < L. < Gr. *nitron*] *same as:* **1.** POTASSIUM NITRATE **2.** SODIUM NITRATE Also, chiefly Brit., **ni′tre**

☆**nit-pick·ing** (nit′pik′iŋ) *adj., n.* paying too much attention to petty details —**nit′-pick′er** *n.*

ni·trate (nī′trāt) *n.* [Fr. < *nitre*, NITER] **1.** a salt or ester of nitric acid **2.** potassium nitrate or sodium nitrate, used as a fertilizer —*vt.* -**trat·ed**, -**trat·ing** to treat or combine with nitric acid or a nitrate; esp., to make into a nitrate —**ni·tra′tion** *n.*

ni·tric (nī′trik) *adj.* **1.** of or containing nitrogen **2.** designating or of compounds in which nitrogen has a higher valence than in the corresponding nitrous compounds

nitric acid a strong, colorless, corrosive acid, HNO_3, that eats into metal, cloth, etc.

nitric oxide a colorless gas, NO, prepared by the action of nitric acid on copper or directly from the air in various ways

ni·tride (nī′trīd) *n.* [NITR(O)- + -IDE] a compound of nitrogen with a more electropositive element

ni·tri·fy (nī′trə fī′) *vt.* -**fied′**, -**fy′ing** [< Fr.: see NITER & -FY] **1.** to cause (soil, etc.) to be full of nitrates **2.** to cause the oxidation of (ammonium salts, atmospheric nitrogen, etc.) to nitrites and nitrates, as by the action of soil bacteria, etc. —**ni′tri·fi·ca′tion** *n.* —**ni′tri·fi′er** *n.*

ni·trite (nī′trīt) *n.* a salt or ester of nitrous acid

ni·tro- [see NITER] *a combining form used to indicate:* **1.** the presence of nitrogen compounds made as by the action of nitric or nitrous acid [*nitrocellulose*] **2.** the presence of the NO_2 radical [*nitrobenzene*] Also, before a vowel, **nitr-**

ni·tro·bac·te·ri·a (nī′trō bak tir′ē ə) *n.pl., sing.* -**ri·um** (-əm) [ModL.: see NITRO- & BACTERIA] bacteria in the soil that oxidize ammonia compounds in nitrites, or nitrites into nitrates

ni·tro·ben·zene (-ben′zēn) *n.* a poisonous yellow liquid, $C_6H_5NO_2$, prepared by treating benzene with nitric acid, used in dyes, as a solvent, etc.

ni·tro·cel·lu·lose (-sel′yoo lōs′) *n.* a substance produced by the action of nitric acid upon wood, cotton, etc.: used in making explosives, plastics, etc. —**ni′tro·cel′lu·los′ic** *adj.*

ni·tro·gen (nī′trə jən) *n.* [< Fr.: see NITRO- & -GEN] a colorless, tasteless, odorless gaseous chemical element forming nearly four fifths of the atmosphere: it is found in all living things: symbol N; at. wt., 14.0067; at. no., 7 —**ni·trog·e·nous** (nī träj′ə-nəs) *adj.*

nitrogen cycle the cycle of natural processes through which nitrogen in the atmosphere is converted by nitrogen fixation and

nitrification into compounds used by plants and animals to form proteins and is eventually returned by decay and denitrification to its original state

nitrogen dioxide a poisonous, reddish-brown gas, NO_2, used in making nitric acid, as a rocket-fuel oxidizer, etc.

nitrogen fixation 1. the conversion of atmospheric nitrogen into nitrates by soil bacteria (**nitrogen fixers**) in the nodules of legumes **2.** the conversion of free nitrogen into useful nitrogenous compounds by any of various industrial processes —**ni′tro·gen-fix′ing** *adj.*

ni·trog·e·nize (nī träj′ə nīz′, nī′trə jə-) *vt.* -**nized′**, -**niz′ing** to combine with nitrogen or its compounds

nitrogen mustard any of a class of compounds similar to mustard gas, used in cancer research and treatment

ni·tro·glyc·er·in, ni·tro·glyc·er·ine (nī′trə glis′ər in, -trō-) *n.* a thick, explosive oil, $C_3H_5(ONO_2)_3$, prepared by treating glycerin with a mixture of nitric and sulfuric acids: used in medicine and in making dynamites and propellants

ni·trous (nī′trəs) *adj.* **1.** of, like, or containing niter **2.** designating or of compounds in which nitrogen has a lower valence than in the corresponding nitric compounds

nitrous acid an acid, HNO_2, known only in solution or in the form of its salts (*nitrites*)

nitrous oxide a colorless, nonflammable gas, N_2O, used as an anesthetic and in aerosols

☆**nit·ty-grit·ty** (nit′ē grit′ē) *n.* [formed as a rhyme of GRITTY] [Slang] the actual, basic facts, elements, issues, etc.

☆**nit-wit** (nit′wit′) *n.* [*nit* (< G. dial. for G. *nicht*, not) or ? NIT + WIT¹] a stupid person

nix¹ (niks) *n., pl.* **nix′es**, G. NIX′e, G. **nix′e** (nik′sə) [G.] *Germanic Myth.* a water sprite —**nix·ie** (nik′sē) *n.fem.*

☆**nix²** (niks) *adv.* [G. *nichts*] [Slang] **1.** no **2.** not at all —*interj.* [Slang] an exclamation meaning: **1.** stop! **2.** I forbid, refuse, disagree, etc. —*n.* [Slang] **1.** nothing **2.** refusal or rejection —*vt.* [Slang] to disapprove of or put a stop to

Nix·on (nik′s'n), **Richard M**(**ilhous**) 1913– ; 37th president of the U.S. (1969–74); resigned under threat of impeachment

N.J., NJ New Jersey

N.L. National League

NLRB, N.L.R.B. National Labor Relations Board

N.Mex. New Mexico: also **NM, N.M.**

NNE, N.N.E., n.n.e. north-northeast

NNW, N.N.W., n.n.w. north-northwest

no¹ (nō) *adv.* [OE. *na* < *ne a*, lit., not ever < IE. base *ne*, not] **1.** [Scot. or Rare] not [*whether or no*] **2.** not in any degree [*no worse*] **3.** nay; not so: the opposite of YES, used to deny, refuse, or disagree —*adj.* not any; not a [*no errors*] —*n., pl.* **noes, nos 1.** the act of saying no; refusal or denial **2.** a negative vote, or a person who casts such a vote

no² (nō) *n., pl.* **no** [Jap. *nō*] [*often* N-] a traditional form of Japanese drama with music and dancing, in which the actors wear masks

No *Chem.* nobelium

No. **1.** north **2.** northern **3.** number: also **no.**

NOAA National Oceanic and Atmospheric Administration

no-ac·count (nō′ə kount′) *adj.* [Colloq.] worthless; good-for-nothing —*n.* a lazy, worthless person

No·ah (nō′ə) *n.* [Heb. *nōaḥ*, lit., rest, comfort] **1.** a masculine name **2.** *Bible* the patriarch commanded by God to build the ark on which he, his family, and two of every kind of creature survived the Flood: Gen. 5:28–10:32

No·bel (nō bel′), **Al·fred Bern·hard** (äl′frned ber′närd) 1833–96; Swed. industrialist & inventor of dynamite: established the Nobel prizes

no·bel·i·um (nō bel′ē əm) *n.* [after *Nobel* Institute in Stockholm, where discovered] a radioactive chemical element produced by the nuclear bombardment of curium: symbol, No; at. wt., 255(?); at. no., 102

Nobel prizes annual international prizes given by the Nobel Foundation for outstanding work in physics, chemistry, medicine, economics, and literature, and for promoting peace

no·bil·i·ty (nō bil′ə tē) *n., pl.* -**ties 1.** the quality of being noble **2.** high station or rank in society **3.** the class of people of noble rank: in Great Britain, the peerage (with *the*)

no·ble (nō′b'l) *adj.* -**bler**, -**blest** [OFr. < L. *nobilis*, lit., well-known: for IE. base see KNOW] **1.** famous or renowned **2.** having or showing high moral qualities [*noble* ideals] **3.** having excellent qualities; superior [a *noble* brand of wines] **4.** grand; stately [a *noble* oak] **5.** of high rank or title which is inherited; aristocratic [a *noble* family] —*n.* a person having noble rank or title; nobleman; peer —**no′ble·ness** *n.* —**no′bly** *adv.*

no·ble·man (-mən) *n., pl.* **-men** a member of the nobility; peer —**no′ble·wom′an** *n.fem., pl.* **-wom′en**

no·blesse o·blige (nō bles′ ō blēzh′) [Fr., lit., nobility obliges] the responsibility of people of high rank or social position to be kind and generous to others

no·bod·y (nō′bud′ē, -bäd′ē, -bəd ē) *pron.* not anybody; no one —*n., pl.* **-bod′ies** a person of no importance

nock (näk) *n.* [< Scand.] **1.** a notch at either end of a bow for holding the string **2.** the notch in the end of an arrow, into which the bowstring is fitted —*vt.* **1.** to make a nock in **2.** to fit (an arrow) onto the bowstring

noc·tu·id (näk′chōō wid) *n.* [< ModL. < L. *noctua,* night owl < *nox,* NIGHT] any of a large group of moths which fly at night, including many of those flying into lighted houses

noc·tur·nal (näk tur′n'l) *adj.* [LL. *nocturnalis* < L. < *nox,* NIGHT] **1.** of, done, or happening in the night [a *nocturnal* adventure] **2.** active during the night [the bat is a *nocturnal* animal] —**noc·tur′nal·ly** *adv.*

noc·turne (näk′tərn) *n.* [Fr. < L.: see NOCTURNAL] **1.** a painting of a night scene **2.** a romantic, dreamy musical composition, that is thought to suggest the night

nod (näd) *vi.* **nod′ded, nod′ding** [ME. *nodden*] **1.** to bend the head forward quickly, as in agreement, greeting, command, etc. **2.** to have the head fall forward because of drowsiness **3.** to be careless; make a slip **4.** to sway back and forth or up and down, as flowers in the wind —*vt.* **1.** to bend (the head) forward quickly **2.** to show (agreement, approval, etc.) by doing this —*n.* **1.** a nodding, as of the head **2.** [N-] the imaginary realm of sleep and dreams: usually **land of Nod** —**nod′der** *n.*

nodding acquaintance a slight, not close, acquaintance with a person or thing

nod·dy (näd′ē) *n., pl.* **-dies** [< ? NOD] **1.** a fool; simpleton **2.** a tropical sea bird with dark feathers and a short tail

node (nōd) *n.* [L. *nodus,* knot: for IE. base see NET[1]] **1.** a knot; knob; swelling **2.** a central point **3.** *Astron.* either of the two points at which the orbit of a heavenly body intersects a fundamental plane, as that of the ecliptic **4.** *Bot.* that part of a stem from which a leaf starts to grow **5.** *Physics* the point, line, or surface of a vibrating object where there is little or no vibration —**nod·al** (nōd′'l) *adj.*

VIBRATING STRING

NODES
(N, nodes formed when vibrating string is stopped at intervals along its length; L, loops between nodes)

nod·ule (näj′ōōl) *n.* [L. *nodulus,* dim of *nodus:* see NODE] **1.** a small knot or rounded lump **2.** *Bot.* a small knot or joint on a stem or root, esp. one containing nitrogen-fixing bacteria —**nod·u·lar** (näj′ə lər), **nod′u·lose′** (-lōs′), **nod′u·lous** (-ləs) *adj.*

no·el, no·ël (nō el′) *n.* [Fr. *noël* < OFr. < L. *natalis,* NATAL] **1.** a Christmas carol **2.** [N-] *same as* CHRISTMAS

☆**no-fault** (nō′fôlt′) *adj.* **1.** designating or of a form of insurance in which the victim as of an automobile accident or medical mishap collects damages without an attempt to determine who caused the accident **2.** designating a form of divorce granted without trying to determine who is at fault in the matter

nog, nogg (näg) *n.* [< East Anglian dial.] **1.** [Brit.] a strong ale ☆**2.** *same as* EGGNOG

nog·gin (näg′in) *n.* [prob. < prec.] **1.** a small cup or mug **2.** one fourth of a pint: a measure for ale or liquor ☆**3.** [Colloq.] the head

no-good (nō′good′) *adj.* [Slang] good-for-nothing; worthless

No·gu·chi (nō gōō′chē), **Hi·de·yo** (hē′de yō′) 1876–1928; Japanese bacteriologist in the U.S.

☆**no-hit·ter** (nō′hit′ər) *n.* a baseball game in which the pitcher allows the opposing team no base hits

no·how (nō′hou′) *adv.* [Dial.] in no manner; not at all

noise (noiz) *n.* [OFr. < L. *nausea:* see NAUSEA] **1.** *a)* loud shouting; clamor *b)* any loud or disagreeable sound **2.** sound [the *noise* of rain] **3.** any unwanted electrical signal within a communication system —*vt.* **noised, nois′ing** to spread (a report, rumor, etc.): usually with *about, around, abroad,* etc.

SYN.—**noise** is the general word for any loud, unmusical, or disagreeable sound; **din** refers to a very loud sound that goes on and on and is painful to the ears [the *din* of the machinery in the factory]; **uproar** is applied to a loud, confused sound, as of shouting, laughing, etc., and suggests wild excitement or disturbance [his remarks threw the audience into an *uproar*]; **clamor** is used of loud, continued, excited shouting, as in protest or demand [the *clamor* of the angry demonstrators]; **hubbub** implies the sound of many voices talking at once [the *hubbub* of a subway station]; **racket** refers to a loud, clattering combination of noises that is very annoying [he couldn't work for the *racket* next door] —ANT. quiet

noise·less (noiz′lis) *adj.* with little or no noise; silent —see SYN. at STILL[1] —**noise′less·ly** *adv.* —**noise′less·ness** *n.*

noise·mak·er (-mā′kər) *n.* a person or thing that makes noise; specif., a horn, cowbell, etc. used in celebration, as on New Year's Eve

noi·some (noi′səm) *adj.* [see ANNOY & -SOME[1]] **1.** injurious to health; harmful **2.** having a bad odor; foul-smelling; offensive [a *noisome* swamp] —see SYN. at STINKING —**noi′some·ly** *adv.* —**noi′some·ness** *n.*

nois·y (noi′zē) *adj.* **nois′i·er, nois′i·est 1.** making noise [a *noisy* bell] **2.** making more sound than is expected or customary [a *noisy* car] **3.** full of noise; clamorous [a *noisy* theater] —**nois′i·ly** *adv.* —**nois′i·ness** *n.*

nol·le pros·e·qui (näl′ē präs′ə kwī′) [L., to be unwilling to prosecute] *Law* formal notice that prosecution in a criminal case or civil suit will be partly or entirely ended

no·lo con·ten·de·re (nō′lō kən ten′də rē) [L., I do not wish to contest (it)] *Law* a plea by the defendant in a criminal case declaring that he will not make a defense, but not admitting guilt

☆**nol-pros** (näl′präs′) *vt.* **-prossed′, -pros′sing** [< abbrev. of NOLLE PROSEQUI] to abandon (all or part of a suit) by entering a nolle prosequi on the court records

nom. nominative

no·mad (nō′mad) *n.* [< L. < Gr. < *nemein,* to pasture: for IE. base see -NOMY] **1.** a member of a tribe or people having no permanent home, but moving about constantly in search of food, pasture, etc. **2.** any wanderer who has no fixed home —*adj.* wandering: also **no·mad′ic** —**no·mad′i·cal·ly** *adv.* —**no′mad·ism** *n.*

no man's land 1. a piece of land which no one owns **2.** the area on a battlefield between the opposing forces **3.** an indefinite area of operation, involvement, etc. [a political *no man's land* which neither party controls]

nom de guerre (näm′ də ger′) *pl.* **noms′ de guerre** [Fr., lit., a war name] a pseudonym

nom de plume (näm′ də plōōm′) *pl.* **noms′ de plume** [Fr.] a pen name; pseudonym

Nome (nōm) [< nearby Cape *Nome,* prob. < ? *name,* query on an early map, misread as *C. Nome*] city in W Alas., on the Bering Sea: pop. 2,500

no·men·cla·ture (nō′mən klā′chər) *n.* [< L. < *nomen,* a NAME + pp. of *calare,* to call] **1.** the system of names used in a branch of learning, or for the parts of a mechanism [the *nomenclature* of botany] **2.** a system of naming

nom·i·nal (näm′i n'l) *adj.* [< L. < *nomen,* a NAME] **1.** of, or having the nature of, a name **2.** of or having to do with a noun **3.** in name only, not in fact [the queen is the *nominal* ruler of the country] **4.** very small; slight [a *nominal* fee] —*n.* a noun; also, any word or phrase, as an adjective, used like a noun —**nom′i·nal·ly** *adv.*

nom·i·nate (näm′ə nāt′) *vt.* **-nat′ed, -nat′ing** [< L., < pp. of *nominare* < *nomen,* a NAME] **1.** to name or appoint to an office or position **2.** *a)* to name as a candidate for election or appointment *b)* to propose as a candidate for an award or honor —**nom′i·na′tor** *n.*

nom·i·na·tion (näm′ə nā′shən) *n.* the act of nominating or the fact of being nominated

nom·i·na·tive (näm′ə nə tiv; *for adj. 1, also* -nāt′iv) *adj.* **1.** named or appointed, rather than elected, to a position or office **2.** *Gram.* designating or of the case of the subject of a verb and the words (appositives, predicate adjectives, etc.) that agree with it ["she," "we," and "who" are in the *nominative* case] —*n.* **1.** the nominative case **2.** a word in this case

nom·i·nee (näm′ə nē′) *n.* [NOMIN(ATE) + -EE] a person who is nominated, esp. as a candidate for election

-no·my [< Gr. < *nomos,* law < *nemein,* to distribute < IE. base *nem-,* to assign, take] a combining form meaning the systematized knowledge of [astronomy]

non- [< L. *non,* not: for IE. base see NO[1]] a prefix meaning not: used to give a negative force, esp. to nouns, adjectives, and ad-

fat, āpe, cär; ten, ēven; is, bīte; gō, hôrn, tōōl, lōōk; oil, out; up, fur; get; joy; yet; chin; she; thin, then; zh, leisure; ŋ, ring; ə for *a* in *ago, e* in *agent, i* in *sanity, o* in *comply, u* in *focus;* ' as in *able* (ā′b'l); Fr. bäl; ë, Fr. coeur; ö, Fr. feu; Fr. mon; ô, Fr. coq; ü, Fr. duc; r, Fr. cri; H, G. ich; kh, G. doch; ‡foreign; ☆ Americanism; < derived from. See inside front cover.

verbs: *non-* is less forceful than *in-* and *un-*, which often give a word an opposite meaning (Ex.: *nonhuman, inhuman*) The list at the bottom of this page and the following pages includes the more common compounds formed with *non-:* they will be understood if *not* is used before the meaning of the base word

non·age (nän′ij, nō′nij) *n.* [< Anglo-Fr. < OFr.: see NON- & AGE] **1.** *Law* the state of being under full legal age, usually under twenty-one **2.** the period of immaturity

non·a·ge·nar·i·an (nän′ə ji ner′ē ən, nō′nə-) *adj.* [< L. < *nonaginta,* ninety] ninety years old, or between the ages of ninety and one hundred —*n.* a person of this age

non·ag·gres·sion pact (nän′ə gresh′ən) an agreement between two nations not to attack each other, usually for a specified period of years

non·a·gon (nän′ə gän′) *n.* [< L. *nonus,* ninth + -GON] a polygon with nine angles and nine sides

non·a·ligned (nän′ə līnd′) *adj.* ☆not aligned with either side in a conflict —**non′a·lign′ment** *n.*

non·ap·pear·ance (-ə pir′əns) *n.* a failure to appear, esp. in court

non·be·ing (nän′bē′iŋ) *n. same as* NONEXISTENCE

nonce (näns) *n.* [ME. (*for the) nones < (for then) ones,* lit., for the once (with the *-n* of *then* shifting to *ones)*] the present use, occasion, or time; time being: chiefly in **for the nonce**

nonce word a word coined and used only once or for a particular occasion

non·cha·lance (nän′shə läns′, nän′shə ləns) *n.* the state or quality of being nonchalant —see SYN. at EQUANIMITY

non·cha·lant (nän′shə länt′, nän′shə lənt) *adj.* [Fr. < *non,* not + *chaloir,* to care for < L. *calere,* to be warm] showing cool lack of concern; not worried, excited, embarrassed, etc.; casually indifferent [he is *nonchalant* about his debts] —see SYN. at COOL —**non′cha·lant′ly** *adv.*

NONAGON

non·com (nän′käm′) *n.* [Colloq.] *clipped form of* NONCOMMISSIONED OFFICER

non·com·bat·ant (nän käm′bə tənt, nän′kəm bat′ənt) *n.* **1.** a member of the armed forces whose duties do not include actual combat, as a chaplain **2.** any civilian in wartime —*adj.* not fighting; of noncombatants

non·com·mis·sioned officer (nän′kə mish′ənd) an enlisted person of any of various grades in the armed forces, as, in the U.S. Army, from corporal to sergeant major: see also PETTY OFFICER

☆**non·com·mit·tal** (-kə mit′'l) *adj.* not committing one to any point of view or course of action; not revealing one's opinion or purpose [he answered with a *noncommittal* smile] —**non′com·mit′tal·ly** *adv.*

non·com·pli·ance (-kəm plī′əns) *n.* failure to comply; refusal to agree, obey, etc. —**non′com·pli′ant** *adj.*

non com·pos men·tis (nän′ käm′pəs men′tis) [L.] *Law* not of sound mind; mentally incapable of handling one's own affairs: often **non compos**

non·con·duc·tor (nän′kən duk′tər) *n.* a substance that does not readily conduct certain forms of energy, as electricity, sound, heat, etc. [glass is a *nonconductor* of electricity]

non·con·form·ist (-kən fôr′mist) *adj.* not following the customs, beliefs, etc. which most people accept —*n.* a person who is nonconformist; esp. [N-], a Protestant in England who is not a member of the Anglican Church —**non′con·form′ism** *n.*

non·con·form·i·ty (-kən fôr′mə tē) *n.* **1.** failure or refusal to follow generally accepted beliefs and practices; esp., [N-] refusal to accept the doctrines or practices of the Anglican Church **2.** lack of agreement or harmony

non·co·op·er·a·tion (-kō äp′ə rā′shən) *n.* **1.** failure to work together or in unison with a person or group **2.** refusal to cooperate with a government through various acts of civil disobedience, as by nonpayment of taxes: used as a form of protest —**non′co·op′er·a′tion·ist** *n.* —**non′co·op′er·a·tive** *adj.* —**non′co·op′er·a′tor** *n.*

non′a·bra′sive	non′as·sign′a·ble	non′clin′i·cal	non′con·sent′
non′ab·sorb′ent	non′as·sim′i·la·ble	non′co·ag′u·lat′ing	non′con·ser′va·tive
non′ac·a·dem′ic	non′as·sim′i·la′tion	non′co·a·lesc′ing	non′con·sti·tu′tion·al
non′ac·cept′ance	non′ath·let′ic	non′co·er′cive	non′con·struc′tive
non·ac′id	non′at·mos·pher′ic	non′co·he′sive	non′con·sul′ta·tive
non·ac′tin·ic	non′at·tend′ance	non′col·laps′i·ble	non′con·ta′gious
non·ac′tive	non′at·trib′u·tive	non′col·lect′a·ble	non′con·tem′po·rar′y
non′ad·dic′tive	non′au·thor′i·ta′tive	non′col·lect′i·ble	non′con·ten′tious
non′ad·ja′cent	non′au·to·mat′ic	non′col·le′giate	non′con·tig′u·ous
non′ad·jec·ti′val	non′bac·te′ri·al	non·com′bat	non′con·ti·nen′tal
non′ad·just′a·ble	non·bas′ic	non·com′bin′ing	non′con·tin′u·ance
non′ad·min′is·tra′tive	non·be·liev′er	non′com·bus′ti·ble	non′con·tin′u·ous
non′ad·van·ta′geous	non·be·liev′ing	non′com·mer′cial	non′con′tra·band′
non′ad·ver′bi·al	non·bel·lig′er·ent	non′com·mu′ni·ca·ble	non′con·tra·dic′to·ry
non′aes·thet′ic	non′-Bib′li·cal	non′com·mu′ni·cant	non′con·trib′u·to′ry
non′af·fil′i·at′ed	non·bloom′ing	non′com·mu′ni·cat′ing	non′con·trolled′
non′-Af′ri·can	non·break′a·ble	non′-Com′mu·nist	non′con·tro·ver′sial
non·ag·gres′sive	non′-Brit′ish	non′com·pen·sat′ing	non′con·ven′tion·al
non′a·gree′ment	non′-Bud′dhist	non·com′pe·tent	non′con·ver′gent
non′ag·ri·cul′tur·al	non·bud′ding	non′com·pet′ing	non′con·vert′i·ble
non′al·co·hol′ic	non′bu·reau·crat′ic	non′com·pet′i·tive	non′con·vic′tion
non′al·ge·bra′ic	non·burn′a·ble	non·com′pla·cent	non′co·or′di·nat′ing
non′al·ler·gen′ic	non·busi′ness	non·com·ple′tion	non′cor·rec′tive
non′al·ler′gic	non·cak′ing	non′com·ply′ing	non′cor·re·spond′ing
non′al·pha·bet′ic	non·ca·lor′ic	non′com·pres′si·ble	non′cor·rod′i·ble
non′a·mend′a·ble	non·can′cer·ous	non′com·pres′sion	non′cor·rod′ing
non′-A·mer′i·can	non′ca·non′i·cal	non′com·pul′so·ry	non′cor·ro′sive
non′an·a·lyt′ic	non′cap·i·tal·is′tic	non′con·cil′i·at′ing	non′cre·a′tive
non′-An′gli·can	non′car·bon·at′ed	non′con·clu′sive	non·crim′i·nal
non′an·tag′o·nis′tic	non′car·niv′o·rous	non′con·cur′rence	non·crit′i·cal
non′a·pol′o·get′ic	non′cat·e·gor′i·cal	non′con·dens′ing	non·cru′cial
non′ap·os·tol′ic	non′-Cath′o·lic	non′con·du′cive	non·crys′tal·line
non′ap·pear′ance	non′-Cau·ca·soid′	non′con·duct′ing	non·cul′pa·ble
non′ap·pear′ing	non·cel′lu·lar	non′con·fer′ra·ble	non·cu′mu·la′tive
non′ap·pli·ca·ble	non·ce′re·al	non′con·fi·den′tial	non·cur′rent
non′a·quat′ic	non·cer′ti·fied′	non′con·flict′ing	non·cy′clic
non′-Ar′ab	non·charge′a·ble	non′con·form′ance	non·dam′age·a·ble
non′-Ar′a·bic	non·chem′i·cal	non′con·form′ing	non′de·cay′ing
non′a·ris′to·crat′ic	non′-Chris′tian	non′con·geal′ing	non′de·cay′ing
non′ar·ith·met′i·cal	non·cit′i·zen	non′con·gen′i·tal	non′de·cid′u·ous
non′ar·tis′tic	non·civ′i·lized′	non′-Con·gres′sion·al	non′de·duct′i·ble
non′-Ar′y·an	non·clas′si·cal	non′con·nec′tive	non′de·fam′a·to′ry
non′-A·si·at′ic	non·clas′si·fi′a·ble	non′con·scious	non′de·fen′sive
non′as·sert′ive	non·cler′i·cal	non′con·sec′u·tive	non′de·fer′ra·ble

non·de·script (nän′di skript′, nän′di skript′) *adj.* [< L. *non*, not + pp. of *describere*, DESCRIBE] without distinctive features; hard to describe; colorless —*n.* a nondescript person or thing

non·du·ra·ble goods (-door′ə b′l, -dyoor′-) goods usable for a relatively short time, as food, clothing, or fabrics: also **non·du′ra·bles** *n.pl.*

none[1] (nun) *pron.* [OE. *nan* < *ne*, not (see NO[1]) + *an*, one] **1.** no one; not anyone *[none* but Jack can do it] **2.** [*usually with pl. v.*] no persons or things; not any [there are *none* on the table] —*n.* no part; nothing [I want *none* of it] —*adv.* in no way; not at all *[none* the worse for wear]

none[2] (nōn) *n.* [OE. *non*: see NOON] *Eccles.* [*often* **N-**] the fifth of the canonical hours

non·en·ti·ty (nän en′tə tē) *n., pl.* **-ties 1.** the state of not existing **2.** something that exists only in the mind **3.** a person of no importance

nones (nōnz) *n.pl.* [< L. < *nonus*, ninth < *novem*, nine] **1.** in the ancient Roman calendar, the ninth day before the ides of a month **2.** *same as* NONE[2]

non·es·sen·tial (nän′i sen′shəl) *adj.* **1.** not essential; of relatively no importance; unnecessary **2.** *Biochem.* designating or of those amino acids required by man that can be made in the body —*n.* a nonessential person or thing

none·such (nun′such′) *n.* a person or thing having no rival or equal; someone or something unique; nonpareil

none·the·less (nun′thə les′) *adv.* in spite of that; nevertheless: also **none the less**

non-Eu·clid·e·an (nän′yoo klid′ē ən) *adj.* designating or of a geometry that rejects any of Euclid's postulates, esp. his postulate that only one line parallel to another line can be drawn through a given point

non·ex·ist·ence (-ig zis′təns) *n.* **1.** the condition of not existing **2.** something that does not exist —**non′ex·ist′ent** *adj.*, *n.*

non·fea·sance (nän fē′z′ns) *n. Law* failure to do what duty requires to be done: distinguished from MALFEASANCE, MISFEASANCE

non·fer·rous (-fer′əs) *adj.* **1.** not made of or containing iron **2.** designating or of metals other than iron

no·nil·lion (nō nil′yən) *n.* [Fr. < L. *nonus*, ninth + Fr. *million*] ☆**1.** in the U.S. and France, the number represented by 1 followed by 30 zeros **2.** in Great Britain and Germany, the number represented by 1 followed by 54 zeros —*adj.* amounting to one nonillion in number

non·in·ter·ven·tion (nän′in tər ven′shən) *n.* the state or fact of not intervening; esp., a refusal by one nation to interfere in the affairs of another —**non′in·ter·ven′tion·ist** *adj.*, *n.*

non·ju·ror (nän joor′ər) *n.* a person who refuses to take an oath of allegiance, as to his ruler or government —**non·ju′ring** *adj.*

non′de·file′ment	non′e·co·nom′ic	non′fed′er·al	non′in·clu′sive
non′de·fin′ing	non′ed′i·ble	non′fed′er·at′ed	non′in·de·pend′ent
non′de·his′cent	non′ed·i·to′ri·al	non′fer′tile	non′-In′di·an
non′de·liv′er·y	non′ed′u·ca·ble	non′fes′tive	non′in·dict′a·ble
non′de·mand′	non′ed·u·ca′tion·al	non·fic′tion	non′in·di·vid′u·al·is′tic
non′dem·o·crat′ic	non′ef·fec′tive	non·fic′tion·al	non′in·dus′tri·al
non′de·nom′i·na′tion·al	non′ef·fer·ves′cent	non·fig′u·ra·tive	non′in·fect′ed
non′de·part·men′tal	non′ef·fi′cient	non′fil′ter·a·ble	non′in·fec′tious
non′de·par′ture	non′e·las′tic	non′fi·nan′cial	non′in·flam′ma·ble
non′de·pend′ence	non′e·lec′tive	non′fire′proof	non′in·flam′ma·to′ry
non′de·pos′i·tor	non′e·lec′tric	non·fis′cal	non′in·fla′tion·ar′y
non′de·pre′ci·at′ing	non′e·lec′tri·cal	non·fis′sion·a·ble	non′in·flec′tion·al
non′de·riv′a·tive	non′e·lec′tro·lyte′	non·flam′ma·ble	non′in·form′a·tive
non′de·struc′tive	non′e·mo′tion·al	non·flow′er·ing	non′in·her′it·a·ble
non′de·tach′a·ble	non′em·pir′i·cal	non·flow′ing	non′in·ju′ri·ous
non′det′o·nat′ing	non′en·dem′ic	non·fluc′tu·at′ing	non′in·struc′tion·al
non′de·vel′op·ment	non′en·force′a·ble	non·fly′ing	non′in·stru·men′tal
non′de·vo′tion·al	non′en·force′ment	non·fo′cal	non′in·te·grat′ed
non′di·a·lec′tal	non′-Eng′lish	non′for·fei′ture	non′in·tel·lec′tu·al
non′dic·ta·to′ri·al	non′en·tailed′	non·for′mal	non′in·tel′li·gent
non′di·dac′tic	non′e·pis′co·pal	non·freez′ing	non′in′ter·course′
non′dif·fer·en′ti·a′tion	non′e·qual′	non′-French′	non′in·ter·fer′ence
non′dif·frac′tive	non′e·quiv′a·lent	non′ful·fill′ment	non′in·ter·na′tion·al
non′dif·fus′i·ble	non′e·rot′ic	non′func′tion·al	non′in·ter·sect′ing
non′dif·fus′ing	non′e·ter′nal	non′fun·da·men′tal	non′in·tox′i·cant
non′dip·lo·mat′ic	non′e·th′i·cal	non′gas′e·ous	non′in·tox′i·cat′ing
non′di·rec′tion·al	non′eu·gen′ic	non′ge·net′ic	non′in·tu′i·tive
non′di·rec′tive	non′-Eu·ro·pe′an	non′-Ger·man′ic	non′in·volve′ment
non′dis·ap·pear′ing	non′e·van·gel′i·cal	non′gov·ern·men′tal	non·i′o·dized′
non′dis·charg′ing	non′ev·o·lu′tion·ar′y	non·gran′u·lar	non·i′on·ized′
non′dis·ci·pli·nar′y	non′ex·change′a·ble	non′-Greek′	non′ir·ra′di·at′ed
non′dis·crim′i·na′tion	non′ex·clu′sive	non′gre·gar′i·ous	non·ir′ri·tant
non′dis·crim′i·na·to′ry	non′ex·cus′a·ble	non′hab′it·a·ble	non′ir′ri·tat′ing
non′dis·par′ag·ing	non′ex·ec′u·tive	non′ha·bit′u·al	non′-Is·lam′ic
non′dis·pos′al	non′ex·empt′	non′ha·bit′u·at′ing	non′-Jew′ish
non′dis·tinc′tive	non′ex·pan′sive	non′haz′ard·ous	non′ju·di′cial
non′di·ver′gent	non′ex·pend′a·ble	non′-Hel·len′ic	non′-Lat′in
non′di·vis′i·ble	non′ex·pe′ri·enced	non′he·red′i·tar′y	non·le′gal
non′doc′tri·nal	non′ex·per′i·men′tal	non′her′it·a·ble	non·le′thal
non′doc·u·men′ta·ry	non′ex·pert′	non′his·tor′ic	non′li′censed
non′dog·mat′ic	non′ex·plo′sive	non·hu′man	non′lin′e·ar
non′dra·mat′ic	non′ex·port′a·ble	non′hu′mor·ous	non·liq′ue·fy′ing
non′drink′er	non′ex·ten′sion	non′i·den′ti·cal	non·liq′uid
non·driv′er	non′ex·tra·dit′a·ble	non′id·i·o·mat′ic	non′liq′ui·dat′ing
non·dry′ing	non·fac′tu·al	non′i·mag′i·nar′y	non′lit′er·ar′y
non′du′ti·a·ble	non·fad′ing	non′im·i·ta′tive	non·lit′er·ate
non′dy·nas′tic	non·fat′	non·im·mune′	non′li·tur′gi·cal
non′earn′ing	non·fa′tal	non′im·mu′nized′	non′liv′ing
non′ec·cle′si·as′ti·cal	non′fa·tal·is′tic	non′im·por·ta′tion	non·lo′cal
	non·fat′ten·ing	non′im·preg′nat·ed	non·lu′mi·nous

non·met·al (-met′'l) *n.* an element lacking the characteristics of a metal; specif., any of the elements (e.g., oxygen, carbon, nitrogen) whose oxides form acids —**non′me·tal′lic** *adj.*

non·mor·al (-môr′əl, -mär′-) *adj.* not connected in any way with morality; not moral and not immoral

non·nu·cle·ar (-nōō′klē ər) *adj.* not nuclear; specif., not operated by or using nuclear energy

non·ob·jec·tive (nän′əb jek′tiv) *adj. same as* NONREPRESENTATIONAL —**non′ob·jec′tiv·ism** *n.* —**non′ob·jec′tiv·ist** *n.*

non·pa·reil (nän′pə rel′) *adj.* [Fr. < *non,* not + *pareil,* equal, ult. < L. *par,* equal] having no equal; peerless —*n.* **1.** someone or something having no equal or rival **2.** a small wafer of chocolate covered with tiny sugar pellets

non·par·ti·san (nän pär′tə z'n) *adj.* not partisan; esp., not controlled by, or supporting, any single political party [*nonpartisan* candidates for the office of judge] : also **non·par′ti·zan** —**non·par′ti·san·ship′** *n.*

non·per·son (nän′pur′s'n) *n.* a person completely ignored, esp. by the government, as if not existing

non·plus (nän plus′, nän′plus′) *n.* [L. *non,* not + *plus,* more] a condition of being so confused that one is unable to speak or act —*vt.* **-plused′** or **-plussed′, -plus′ing** or **-plus′sing** to make so confused that one cannot speak or act; bewilder [the speaker was *nonplused* by the boos from a supposedly friendly audience]

non·pro·duc·tive (nän′prə duk′tiv) *adj.* **1.** not producing the goods or results wanted [*nonproductive* farms; a *nonproductive* plan] **2.** not directly related to the production of goods, as clerks, salesmen, etc. —**non′pro·duc′tive·ly** *adv.*

non·prof·it (nän präf′it) *adj.* not intending or intended to earn a profit [a *nonprofit* organization]

non·pro·lif·er·a·tion (nän′prō lif′ə rā′shən) *n.* a not proliferating; specif., the limitation of production of nuclear weapons

non-pros (nän′präs′) *vt.* **-prossed′, -pros′sing** to enter a judgment of non prosequitur against (a plaintiff or his suit)

non pro·se·qui·tur (nän′ prō sek′wi tər) [L., he does not prosecute] *Law* a judgment entered against a plaintiff who fails to appear at the court proceedings of his suit

non·rat·ed (nän rāt′id) *adj. U.S. Navy* designating an enlisted person who is not a petty officer

non·rep·re·sen·ta·tion·al (nän′rep ri zən tā′shən 'l) *adj.* designating or of art that does not attempt to represent in recognizable form any object in nature; abstract —**non′rep·re·sen·ta′tion·al·ism** *n.*

non·res·i·dent (nän rez′ə dənt) *adj.* not residing in a specified place; esp., not having one's home in the place or area where one works, attends school, etc. —*n.* a nonresident person —**non·res′i·dence, non·res′i·den·cy** *n.* —**non′res·i·den′tial** *adj.*

non·re·sist·ant (nän′ri zis′tənt) *adj.* not resistant; giving in to force or to authority, however unjust —*n.* a person who believes that force and violence should not be used to oppose authority, however unjust —**non′re·sist′ance** *n.*

non·re·stric·tive (-ri strik′tiv) *adj. Gram.* designating a clause, phrase, or word that is not absolutely necessary to the meaning of a sentence and is therefore set off by commas (Ex.: John, *who is six feet tall,* is younger than Bill)

☆**non·sched·uled** (nän skej′oold) *adj.* designating or of an airline, plane, etc. making commercial flights on demand, not on a regular schedule

non·sec·tar·i·an (nän′sek ter′ē ən) *adj.* not sectarian; not confined to or connected with any specific religion

---

non′mag·net′ic	non′ob·struc′tive	non′pref·er·en′tial	non′re·mov′a·ble
non·mail′a·ble	non′oc·cu·pa′tion·al	non′prej·u·di′cial	non′re·new′a·ble
non·main′te·nance	non′oc·cur′rence	non′pre·scrip′tive	non′re·pay′a·ble
non′ma·lig′nant	non·o′dor·ous	non′pres·i·den′tial	non′re·pent′ance
non·mal′le·a·ble	non′of·fi′cial	non′pro·duc′er	non′rep·re·sent′a·tive
non·mar′i·tal	non′op·er·at′ing	non′pro·fes′sion·al	non′re·pro·duc′tive
non·mar′i·time	non′op·er·a′tion·al	non·pro·fes·so′ri·al	non′re·sid′u·al
non·mar′ket·a·ble	non′op·er·a′tive	non·prof′it·a·ble	non·res′o·nant
non·mar′ry·ing	non′-O·ri·en′tal	non′pro·gres′sive	non′re·strict′ed
non·mar′tial	non·or′tho·dox′	non′pro·hib′i·tive	non′re·ten′tive
non·ma·te′ri·al	non·ox′i·diz′ing	non·pro·lif′ic	non′re·tir′ing
non′ma·te′ri·al·is′tic	non·ox′y·gen·at′ed	non·pro·phet′ic	non′re·trac′tile
non·ma·ter′nal	non·pal′a·tal	non′pro·por′tion·al	non′ret·ro·ac′tive
non′math·e·mat′i·cal	non·pa′pal	non′pro·pri′e·tar′y	non′re·turn′a·ble
non′me·chan′i·cal	non′par·al·lel′	non′pro·scrip′tive	non′re·vers′i·ble
non′mech·a·nis′tic	non′par·a·sit′ic	non′pro·tec′tive	non′re·vert′i·ble
non′me·dic′i·nal	non·pa·ren′tal	non·pro′tein	non′re·volv′ing
non·me·lo′di·ous	non′pa·rish′ion·er	non′-Prot′es·tant	non′rhe·tor′i·cal
non·mem′ber	non′par·lia·men′ta·ry	non·psy′chic	non·rhym′ing
non·mem′ber·ship′	non′pa·ro′chi·al	non·pub′lic	non·rhyth′mic
non·mer′can·tile	non′par·tic′i·pant	non′punc·tur·a·ble	non·rig′id
non′met·a·phys′i·cal	non′par·tic′i·pat′ing	non·pun′ish·a·ble	non′rit·u·al·is′tic
non′met·ro·pol′i·tan	non′par·tic′i·pa′tion	non·pu′ru·lent	non·ri′val
non′mi·gra·to′ry	non·pas′ser·ine	non·ra′cial	non′-Ro′man
non·mil′i·tant	non·pay′ing	non·ra′di·at′ing	non′ro·man′tic
non·mil′i·tar′y	non·pay′ment	non·rad′i·cal	non·ro′tat·ing
non·min′er·al	non′per·cep′tu·al	non′ra·di·o·ac′tive	non·roy′al
non·mor′tal	non′per·fo·rat′ed	non·rat′a·ble	non·ru′ral
non′-Mos′lem	non′per·form′ance	non·ra′tion·al	non·sa′cred
non·mo′tile	non′per·form′ing	non′re·ac′tive	non′sac·ri·fi′cial
non′mu·nic′i·pal	non′pe·ri·od′i·cal	non·read′er	non·sal′a·ble
non·mus′cu·lar	non′per·ish·a·ble	non′re·al·is′tic	non·sal′a·ried
non·mys′ti·cal	non′per·ma·nent	non′re·al′i·ty	non·sal′u·tar′y
non·myth′i·cal	non′per·me·a·ble	non′re·cip′ro·cal	non·sat′u·rat′ed
non′nar·cot′ic	non′per·mis′si·ble	non′re·cip′ro·cat′ing	non′-Scan·di·na′vi·an
non·na′tion·al	non′per·pen·dic′u·lar	non′rec·og·ni′tion	non′scho·las′tic
non·na′tive	non′per·se·cu′tion	non′re·cov′er·a·ble	non′sci·en·tif′ic
non·nat′u·ral	non′per·sist′ent	non′re·cur′rent	non·scor′ing
non·nav′i·ga·ble	non′phil·o·soph′i·cal	non′re·cur′ring	non·sea′son·al
non′ne·go′ti·a·ble	non′phys′i·cal	non′re·deem′a·ble	non·se′cret
non′-Ne′gro	non′phys·i·o·log′i·cal	non′re·fill′a·ble	non′se·cre′to·ry
non·neu′tral	non·plas′tic	non′re·gen′er·at′ing	non′sec·tion·al
non·nu′cle·at′ed	non′po·et′ic	non′reg·i·ment′ed	non·sec′u·lar
non′nu·tri′tious	non·poi′son·ous	non′reg·is·tered	non′sed·en·tar′y
non′nu·tri·tive	non′po·lit′i·cal	non′reg·is·tra·ble	non′se·di′tious
non′o·be′di·ence	non·po′rous	non′reg·u·la′tion	non′seg·re·gat′ed
non′ob·lig′a·to·ry	non′pos·ses′sion	non·reign′ing	non′seg·re·ga′tion
non′ob·serv′ance	non·pred′a·to·ry	non′rel′a·tive	non′se·lec′tive
non′ob·serv′ant	non′pre·dict′a·ble	non′re·li′gious	non′-Se·mit′ic

non·sense (nän′sens, -səns) *n.* [NON- + SENSE] **1.** words or actions that have an absurd meaning or no meaning at all **2.** things of relatively no importance or value **3.** disrespectful or foolish behavior [a teacher who would stand for no *nonsense* from his classes] —*adj.* designating or containing syllables or words constructed so as to have no meaning [Lewis Carroll's *nonsense* poetry] —*interj.* how foolish! how absurd!

non·sen·si·cal (nän sen′si k'l) *adj.* not making sense; foolish, absurd, etc. —**non·sen′si·cal·ly** *adv.* —**non·sen′si·cal·ness, non·sen′si·cal/i·ty** (-kal′ə tē) *n.*

non se·qui·tur (nän′ sek′wi tər) [L., lit., it does not follow] **1.** a conclusion or inference that does not follow from the premises **2.** a remark having no bearing on what has just been said

☆**non-sked** (nän′sked′) *adj.* [Colloq.] *same as* NONSCHEDULED —*n.* [Colloq.] a nonscheduled airline, plane, etc.

non·skid (nän′skid′) *adj.* having the tread so constructed as to reduce skidding: said of a tire, etc.

non·stand·ard (nän stan′dərd) *adj.* not standard; specif., designating or of words, phrases, pronunciations, etc. not considered to be standard speech, as dialectal differences, slang, obscenities, etc.

non·stop (nän′stäp′) *adj., adv.* without a stop [to fly *nonstop* from New York to Paris]

non·such (nun′such′) *n. same as* NONESUCH

non·suit (nän′sōot′) *n.* [< Anglo-Fr.: see NON- & SUIT] *Law* a judgment against a plaintiff because of his failure to proceed to trial, to show that he has a valid case, or to produce adequate evidence —*vt.* to bring a nonsuit against (a plaintiff or his case)

non·sup·port (nän′sə pôrt′) *n.* failure to provide for a legal dependent

non trop·po (nän trō′pō) [It.] *Music* not too much; moderately

non·un·ion (nän yoon′yən) *n.* failure to mend or unite: said of a broken bone —*adj.* **1.** not belonging to a labor union [a *nonunion* plumber] **2.** not made or serviced by union workers or under conditions required by a labor union [*nonunion* goods] **3.** refusing to recognize a labor union [a *nonunion* company] —**non·un′ion·ism** *n.* —**non·un′ion·ist** *n.*

non·vi·o·lence (-vī′ə ləns) *n.* the policy or practice of not using violence or physical force, as in opposing government policy —**non·vi′o·lent** *adj.*

non·vot·er (nän vōt′ər) *n.* a person who does not vote or is not permitted to vote —**non·vot′ing** *adj.*

noo·dle¹ (noo′d'l) *n.* [prob. < earlier *noddle*, the head] **1.** a simpleton; fool **2.** [Slang] the head

☆**noo·dle²** (noo′d'l) *n.* [G. *nudel*] a flat, narrow strip of dry dough, usually made with egg and served in soup, baked in casseroles, etc.

noo·dle³ (noo′d'l) *vi.* -**dled, -dling** [prob. var. of DOODLE] [Colloq.] to play idly or improvise on a musical instrument

nook (nook) *n.* [ME. *nok*] **1.** a corner, esp. of a room, or a part cut off from the main part [breakfast *nook*] **2.** a small, sheltered spot [a picnic in a shady *nook*]

noon (noon) *n.* [OE. *non* < L. *nona* (*hora*), ninth (hour), that is, the ninth hour after sunrise] **1.** twelve o'clock in the daytime; midday **2.** the highest point or culmination; time of greatest power, etc. —*adj.* of or occurring at noon, or midday

noon·day (noon′dā′) *n., adj.* noon

no one no person; not anybody; nobody

noon·time (-tīm′) *n., adj.* noon: also **noon′tide′**

noose (noos) *n.* [prob. via Pr. < L. *nodus*] **1.** a loop formed in a rope, cord, etc. by means of a slipknot so that the loop tightens as the rope is pulled **2.** anything that limits one's freedom; tie, bond, etc. —*vt.* **noosed, noos′ing 1.** to catch or hold as in a noose **2.** to form a noose in (a rope, etc.) —**the noose** death by hanging

no-par (nō′pär′) *adj.* having no stated par value [a *no-par* certificate of stock]

☆**nope** (nōp) *adv.* [Slang] no: a negative reply

nor (nôr; *unstressed* nər) *conj.* [ME., shortened form of *nother*, neither] and not; and not either: used as the second of the correlatives *neither* . . . *nor* or after some other negative words [I can *neither* go *nor* stay; they have no car, *nor* do they want one]

nor¹, nor (nôr) north: used especially in compounds [*nor′western*]

Nor. **1.** North **2.** Norway **3.** Norwegian

No·ra (nôr′ə) [Ir., dim. of ELEANOR] a feminine name

Nor·dic (nôr′dik) *adj.* [< ModL. < Fr. < *nord*, north < OE. *north*] designating or of a physical type with characteristics like those of the Scandinavians, such as blond hair, a long head, and above-average height

nor·ep·i·neph·rine (nôr′ep′ə nef′rin, -rēn) *n.* [< NOR(MAL) + EPINEPHRINE] a hormone, $C_8H_{11}NO_3$, secreted by the adrenal medulla: it constricts blood vessels, helps transmit nerve impulses, etc.

Nor·folk (nôr′fək) [after *Norfolk*, county in England] seaport in southeastern Va., on Hampton Roads & Chesapeake Bay: pop. 308,000

HANG-MAN'S NOOSE

non·sen′si·tive	non·spir′it·u·al	non′syn·tac′tic	non·us′a·ble
non·sen′si·tized	non·spir′it·u·ous	non′syn′the·sized′	non·use′
non·sen′so·ry	non·spot′ta·ble	non′sys·tem·at′ic	non·us′er
non·sen′su·ous	non·stain′ing	non·tar′nish·a·ble	non·u′ter·ine
non·se′ri·ous	non·stand′ard·ized′	non·tax′a·ble	non·u·til′i·tar′i·an
non·ser′vile	non·start′er	non·teach′a·ble	non·u′ti·lized′
non·sex′u·al	non·start′ing	non·tech′ni·cal	non·vas′cu·lar
non′-Shake·spear′e·an	non·stat′ic	non·ter·res′tri·al	non·veg′e·ta′tive
non·shar′ing	non·sta′tion·ar′y	non·ter·ri·to′ri·al	non·ve·ne′re·al
non·shat′ter·ing	non·sta·tis′ti·cal	non·tes·ta·men′ta·ry	non·ven′om·ous
non·shrink′a·ble	non·stat′u·to′ry	non·the·at′ri·cal	non·ve′nous
non·sink′a·ble	non·stra·te′gic	non·the·o·log′i·cal	non·ver′bal
non·slave′hold′ing	non·stretch′a·ble	non·ther·a·peu′tic	non·ver·nac′u·lar
non′-Slav′ic	non·stri′at·ed	non·think′ing	non·ver′ti·cal
non·smok′er	non·strik′er	non·tox′ic	non·vi′a·ble
non·smok′ing	non·strik′ing	non·tra·di′tion·al	non′vi·bra′to·ry
non·so′cial	non·struc′tur·al	non·trag′ic	non′vi·o·la′tion
non·so′cial·ist	non·sub·mis′sive	non·trans·fer′a·ble	non·vir′u·lent
non·sol′id	non·sub·scrib′er	non′tran·si′tion·al	non·vis′cous
non·sol′vent	non·suc·cess′ful	non·trans·par′ent	non·vis′u·al
non·sov′er·eign	non·suc·ces′sive	non·trea′son·a·ble	non·vit′re·ous
non′-Span′ish	non·sup·port′ing	non·trib′u·tar′y	non·vo′cal
non·spar′ing	non·sup·pu′ra·tive	non·trop′i·cal	non·vo·ca′tion·al
non·speak′ing	non·sus·tain′ing	non·tu·ber′cu·lous	non·vol′a·tile
non·spe′cial·ist	non′sym·bol′ic	non·typ′i·cal	non·vol·can′ic
non·spe′cial·ized′	non′sym·met′ri·cal	non′ty·ran′ni·cal	non·vol′un·tar′y
non·spe′cial·iz′ing	non′sym·pa·thiz′er	non·ul′cer·ous	non·white′
non·spe·cif′ic	non′sym·phon′ic	non′un·der·stand′a·ble	non·work′er
non·spec′u·la′tive	non′symp·to·mat′ic	non·u′ni·form′	non·wo′ven
non·spher′i·cal	non′syn·chro′nous	non′u·ni·ver′sal	non·yield′ing

Norfolk jacket (or **coat**) a loose-fitting, single-breasted jacket with a belt and box pleats

Nor·ge (nôr′gə) *Norw.* name of NORWAY

no·ri·a (nôr′ē ə) *n.* [Sp. < Ar. *nā'ūrah*] in Spain and the Orient, a water wheel with buckets at its circumference to raise and release water

norm (nôrm) *n.* [< L. *norma*, carpenter's square] a standard or model for a group; esp., *a)* a standard of achievement based on the average achievement of a large group *b)* an ideal standard of conduct or one typical of a certain group

Norm. Norman

Nor·ma (nôr′mə) [< L. *norma:* see NORM] a feminine name

nor·mal (nôr′m'l) *adj.* [< L. < *norma*, a rule] 1. agreeing with or used as an accepted standard or norm; esp., corresponding to the average of a large group; natural; usual; regular [it is *normal* to make a mistake sometimes] 2. occurring naturally [*normal* immunity] 3. *Chem. a)* designating or of a salt formed by replacing all the replaceable hydrogen of an acid with a metal or metals *b)* designating a solution of an acid or base containing 1.00797 grams of hydrogen ions per liter 4. *Math.* perpendicular; at right angles 5. *Med., Psychol. a)* free from disease, disorder, etc.; esp., average in intelligence or development *b)* mentally sound —*n.* 1. anything normal 2. the usual state, amount, degree, etc. [his blood pressure is above *normal*] 3. *Math.* a perpendicular —**nor′mal·cy** (-sē), **nor·mal′i·ty** (-măl′ə tē) *n.*

nor·mal·ize (nôr′mə līz′) *vt., vi.* **-ized′, -iz′ing** 1. to bring or come to the normal, or usual, state 2. to bring or come into agreement with a standard —**nor′mal·i·za′tion** *n.* —**nor′mal·iz′er** *n.*

nor·mal·ly (-lē) *adv.* 1. in a normal manner [to behave *normally*] 2. under normal circumstances; ordinarily [*normally* we eat at home]

normal school esp. formerly, a school for training high-school graduates to become teachers

Nor·man[1] (nôr′mən) *n.* [< OE. < OHG. *Nordemann*, lit., Northman] a masculine name; dim. *Norm* 2. [ult. after A. *Norman*, railroad surveyor] city in C Okla., near Oklahoma City: pop. 52,000

Nor·man[2] (nôr′mən) *n.* [< OFr. *Normant* or ML. *Normannus*, both < Frank.] 1. any of the Scandinavians who occupied Normandy in the 10th cent. A.D. 2. a descendant of the Normans and French who conquered England in 1066 3. same as NORMAN FRENCH 4. a native or inhabitant of Normandy —*adj.* of Normandy, the Normans, their language, or culture

Norman Conquest the conquest of England by the Normans under William the Conqueror in 1066

Nor·man·dy (nôr′mən dē) region & former province in NW France, on the English Channel

Norman French the French spoken in England by the Norman conquerors; Anglo-French —**Nor′man-French′** *adj.*

norm·a·tive (nôr′mə tiv) *adj.* of, having to do with, or establishing a norm, or standard

Nor·ris (nôr′is, när′-) 1. **Frank,** (born *Benjamin Franklin Norris, Jr.*) 1870–1902; U.S. novelist 2. **George William,** 1861–1944; U.S. senator (1913–43)

NORMANDY

Norse (nôrs) *adj.* [prob. < Du. *Noorsch*, a Norwegian < *noord*, north] Scandinavian, esp. West Scandinavian (Norwegian, Icelandic, and Faeroese) —*n.* 1. the Scandinavian, esp. the West Scandinavian, group of languages 2. same as NORWEGIAN —**the Norse** 1. the Scandinavians 2. the West Scandinavians

Norse·man (nôrs′mən) *n., pl.* **-men** a member of the ancient Scandinavian people; Northman

north (nôrth) *n.* [OE.] 1. the direction to the right of a person facing the sunset (0° or 360° on the compass, opposite south) 2. a region or district in or toward this direction 3. [*often* N-]

the northern part of the earth, esp. the arctic regions —*adj.* 1. in, of, to, or toward the north 2. from the north [a *north* wind] 3. [N-] designating the northern part of a continent, country, etc. [*North* Africa] —*adv.* in or toward the north —**the North** ☆that part of the U.S. bounded on the south by Maryland, the Ohio River, and Missouri

North, Frederick, 2d Earl of Guilford; 1732–92; Eng. statesman; prime minister of Great Britain (1770–82): called *Lord North*

North America N continent in the Western Hemisphere: including adjacent islands, c.9,330,000 sq. mi.; pop. 314,000,000 —**North American**

☆**north·bound** (nôrth′bound′) *adj.* going northward

North Carolina [see CAROLINA[1]] Southern State of the U.S.: 52,712 sq. mi.; pop. 5,082,000; cap. Raleigh: abbrev. **N.C., NC** —**North Carolinian**

North Cascades National Park national park in the N Cascade Range, N Wash.

North Channel strait between Northern Ireland & SW Scotland

North Dakota [see DAKOTA[1]] Middle Western State of the U.S.: 70,665 sq. mi.; pop. 618,000; cap. Bismarck: abbrev. **N.Dak., ND** —**North Dakotan**

north·east (nôrth′ēst′, nôr-) *n.* 1. the direction halfway between north and east; 45° east of due north 2. a region or district in or toward this direction —*adj.* 1. in, of, to, or toward the northeast 2. from the northeast [a *northeast* wind] —*adv.* in, toward, or from the northeast —**the Northeast** the northeastern part of the U.S., esp. New England

☆**north·east·er** (nôrth′ēs′tər, nôr-) *n.* a storm or strong wind from the northeast

north·east·er·ly (-tər lē) *adj., adv.* 1. in or toward the northeast 2. from the northeast [a *northeasterly* wind]

north·east·ern (-tərn) *adj.* 1. in, of, or toward the northeast 2. from the northeast [a *northeastern* wind] ☆3. [N-] of or characteristic of the Northeast or New England —**North′east′ern·er** *n.*

north·east·ward (nôrth′ēst′wərd, nôr-) *adv., adj.* toward the northeast: also **north′east′wards** (-wərdz) *adv.* —*n.* a northeastward direction, point, or region

north·east·ward·ly (-lē) *adj., adv.* 1. toward the northeast 2. from the northeast [a *northeastwardly* wind]

☆**north·er** (nôr′thər) *n.* a storm or strong wind from the north

north·er·ly (-lē) *adj., adv.* 1. toward the north 2. from the north [a *northerly* wind]

north·ern (nôr′thərn) *adj.* 1. in, of, or toward the north 2. from the north [a *northern* wind] 3. [N-] of or characteristic of the North

north·ern·er (nôr′thər nər, -thə nər) *n.* a native or inhabitant of the north, specif. ☆[N-] of the northern part of the U.S.

Northern Hemisphere that half of the earth north of the equator

Northern Ireland division of the United Kingdom, in the NE part of the island of Ireland: 5,462 sq. mi.; pop. 1,512,000; cap. Belfast

northern lights same as AURORA BOREALIS

north·ern·most (nôr′thərn mōst′) *adj.* farthest north

Northern Rhodesia former name of ZAMBIA

☆**Northern Spy** a yellowish-red winter apple

Northern Territory territory of N Australia, on the Pacific

North Island N island of the two main islands of New Zealand

north·land (nôrth′land′, -lənd) *n.* [*also* N-] the northern region of a country —**north′land·er** *n.*

North Little Rock city in C Ark., on the Arkansas River opposite Little Rock: pop. 60,000

North·man (-mən) *n., pl.* **-men** same as NORSEMAN

north-north·east (nôrth′nôrth′ēst′, nôr′nôr-) *n.* the direction halfway between due north and northeast; 22°30′ east of due north —*adj., adv.* 1. in or toward this direction 2. from this direction

north-north·west (-west′) *n.* the direction halfway between due north and northwest; 22°30′ west of due north —*adj., adv.* 1. in or toward this direction 2. from this direction

North Pole the northern end of the earth's axis

North Sea arm of the Atlantic, east of Great Britain & west of Norway & Denmark

North Star Polaris, the bright star almost directly above the North Pole; polestar

North·um·bri·a (nôr thum′brē ə) former Anglo-Saxon kingdom in Great Britain, south of the Firth of Forth

North·um·bri·an (-ən) *adj.* of Northumbria, its people, or their dialect —*n.* 1. a native or inhabitant of Northumbria 2. the Old English dialect of Northumbria

north·ward (nôrth'wərd, nôr'thərd) **adv., adj.** toward the north: also **north'wards** (-wərdz) **adv.** —**n.** a northward direction, point, etc.

north·ward·ly (-lē) **adj., adv.** 1. toward the north 2. from the north [a *northwardly* wind]

north·west (nôrth'west', nôr-) **n.** 1. the direction halfway between north and west; 45° west of due north 2. a district or region in or toward this direction —**adj.** 1. in, of, or toward the northwest 2. from the northwest [a *northwest* wind] —**adv.** in, toward, or from the northwest —☆**the Northwest** the northwestern part of the U.S., esp. Wash., Oreg., and Ida.

north·west·er (nôrth'wes'tər, nôr-) **n.** a storm or strong wind from the northwest

north·west·er·ly (-tər lē) **adj., adv.** 1. in or toward the northwest 2. from the northwest [a *northwesterly* wind]

north·west·ern (-tərn) **adj.** 1. in, of, or toward the northwest 2. from the northwest [a *northwestern* wind] ☆3. [N-] of or characteristic of the Northwest —**North'west'ern·er n.**

Northwest Passage a route for sailing from the Atlantic to the Pacific, through the arctic islands of Canada

Northwest Territories division of Canada, on the Arctic Ocean: 1,304,903 sq. mi.; pop. 43,000; cap. Yellowknife: abbrev. **N.W.T.**

☆**Northwest Territory** region north of the Ohio River, between Pa. & the Mississippi (established 1787): it now forms Ohio, Ind., Ill., Mich., Wis., & part of Minn.

north·west·ward (nôrth'west'wərd, nôr-) **adv., adj.** toward the northwest: also **north'west'wards adv.** —**n.** a northwestward direction, point or region

north·west·ward·ly (-lē) **adj., adv.** 1. toward the northwest 2. from the northwest, as a wind

Norw. 1. Norway 2. Norwegian

Nor·walk (nôr'wôk') [< AmInd.] 1. city in SW Calif.: suburb of Los Angeles: pop. 92,000 2. city in SW Conn.: pop. 79,000

Nor·way (nôr'wā') country in N Europe, in the W & N Scandinavian Peninsula: 125,064 sq. mi.; pop. 3,851,000; cap. Oslo

Nor·we·gian (nôr wē'jən) **adj.** of Norway, its people, their language, etc. —**n.** 1. a native or inhabitant of Norway 2. the North Germanic language of the Norwegians

Nor·wich (nôr'ij, -ich; när'-) city in E England: pop. 119,000

Nos., nos. numbers

nose (nōz) **n.** [OE. *nosu* < IE. base *nas-*, nostril] 1. the part of the human face between the mouth and the eyes, having two openings for breathing and smelling 2. a part like this in animals; snout, muzzle, etc. 3. the sense of smell 4. power to track or perceive as by scent [a *nose* for news] 5. anything resembling a nose in shape or position; part that sticks out, as a prow, front of an airplane, etc. 6. the nose, regarded as a symbol of prying or meddling [to poke one's *nose* into another's affairs] —**vt. nosed, nos'ing** 1. to discover or perceive as by smell 2. to rub with the nose 3. to push with the nose (with *aside*, etc.) 4. to push (a way, etc.) with the front forward [the ship *nosed* its way into the harbor] —**vi.** 1. to smell; sniff 2. to meddle in another's affairs 3. to advance; move forward —☆**by a nose** 1. by the length of the animal's nose in horse racing, etc. 2. by a very small margin —**cut off one's nose to spite one's face** to injure one's own interests, in a fit of anger, resentment, etc. —**lead by the nose** to dominate completely —**look down one's nose at** [Colloq.] to show dislike or scorn for —**nose out** 1. to defeat by a very small margin 2. to discover, as by smelling —**nose over** to turn over on its nose: said of an airplane moving on the ground —**on the nose** [Slang] 1. that (a specified horse, etc.) will finish first in a race 2. precisely; exactly —**pay through the nose** to pay an unreasonable price —**put someone's nose out of joint** to ruin someone's plans, hopes, etc. —**turn up one's nose at** to sneer at; scorn —**under one's (very) nose** in plain view

nose bag *same as* FEED BAG

nose·band (nōz'band') **n.** that part of a bridle or halter which passes over the animal's nose

nose·bleed (-blēd') **n.** a bleeding from the nose

nose cone the cone-shaped foremost part of a rocket or missile, resistant to intense heat

nose dive 1. a swift, steep, downward plunge of an airplane, nose first 2. any sudden, sharp drop, as in profits or prices — **nose'-dive' vi. -dived', -div'ing**

nose drops medication given by putting it into or through the nose with a dropper

nose·gay (nōz'gā') **n.** [NOSE + GAY (in obs. sense of "gay object")] a small bouquet, esp. for carrying in the hand

nose·piece (-pēs') **n.** 1. that part of a helmet which protects the nose 2. *same as* NOSEBAND 3. anything like a nose in form or position 4. the bridge of a pair of eyeglasses

nose ring a metal ring passed through the nose of an animal for leading it about

nos·ey (nō'zē) **adj. nos'i·er, nos'i·est** *same as* NOSY

nosh (näsh) **vt., vi.** [< Yid. < G. *naschen*, to nibble] [Slang] to eat (a snack) —**n.** [Slang] a snack — **nosh'er n.**

NOSE RING

☆**no-show** (nō'shō') **n.** [Colloq.] one who fails to claim or cancel a reservation, as for a flight

nos·tal·gia (näs tal'jə, nəs-, nôs-; -jē ə) **n.** [ModL. < Gr. *nostos*, a return + -ALGIA] 1. a longing for home; homesickness 2. a longing to return to, or a thinking fondly of, some past period or irrecoverable condition —**nos·tal'gic** (-jik) **adj.** —**nos·tal'gi·cal·ly adv.**

Nos·tra·da·mus (näs'trə dā'məs, nō'strə dä'məs) (born *Michel de Notredame*) 1503-66; Fr. astrologer

nos·tril (näs'trəl) **n.** [OE. *nosthyrl* < *nosu*, NOSE + *thyrel*, hole] 1. either of the openings into the nose 2. the fleshy wall on either side of the nose [with flaring *nostrils*]

nos·trum (näs'trəm) **n.** [L., ours] 1. *a)* a medicine made by the person selling it *b)* a quack medicine 2. a pet scheme for solving some problem: word used by those who dislike the plan

nos·y (nō'zē) **adj. nos'i·er, nos'i·est** [Colloq.] too curious about others' affairs; prying —**nos'i·ly adv.** —**nos'i·ness n.**

Nosy Par·ker (pär'kər) [NOSY + proper name *Parker*] [also **n-p-, n- P-**] [Colloq.] a nosy person

not (nät) **adv.** [ME., unstressed form of *nought*] in no manner; to no degree: a term of negation

‡**no·ta be·ne** (nō'tə be'nē, nō'tä be'nä) [L.] note well; take particular notice

no·ta·bil·i·ty (nōt'ə bil'ə tē) **n.** 1. *pl.* **-ties** a notable person 2. the quality of being notable

no·ta·ble (nōt'ə b'l) **adj.** [OFr. < L. *notabilis* < *notare*, to note] worthy of notice; remarkable; outstanding [a *notable* success] —**n.** a famous or well-known person —**no'ta·bly adv.**

no·tar·i·al (nō ter'ē əl) **adj.** of or done by a notary public

☆**no·ta·rize** (nōt'ə rīz') **vt. -rized', -riz'ing** to sign (a document) and stamp it with one's seal as a notary public — **no'ta·ri·za'tion n.**

no·ta·ry (nōt'ər ē) **n., pl. -ries** [< OFr. < L. *notare*, to note] *clipped form of* NOTARY PUBLIC

notary public *pl.* notaries public, notary publics an official authorized to witness the signing of a deed, will, etc. and to declare that a person has sworn to the truth of something

no·ta·tion (nō tā'shən) **n.** [< L. *notare*, to note] 1. the use of a system of signs or symbols for words, quantities, etc. 2. any such system used in algebra, music, etc. 3. a brief note jotted down 4. the noting of something in writing —**no·ta'tion·al adj.**

notch (näch) **n.** [by syllabic merging of ME. *an oche* < OFr. *oche*, a notch] 1. a V-shaped cut in an edge or surface ☆2. a narrow, deep pass; gap 3. [Colloq.] a step; degree [a *notch* below average] —**vt.** 1. to cut a notch or notches in 2. to record or tally, as by means of notches —**notched adj.**

note (nōt) **n.** [OFr. < L. *nota*, a mark, sign < pp. of *noscere*, to KNOW] 1. a special mark or feature [a *note* of joy] 2. importance or distinction [a man of *note*] 3. *a)* a brief, written statement of a fact, etc., as to help one remember, or to inform someone else; memorandum *b)* [*pl.*] a record of experiences, etc. [the *notes* of a journey] 4. a comment or an explanation, esp. one that is printed at the foot of a

NOTES
(A, whole; B, half; C, quarter; D, eighth; E, sixteenth; F, thirty-second; G, sixtyfourth)

page **5.** close attention; notice; heed [worthy of *note*] **6.** *a*) a short, informal letter *b*) a formal official letter from one government to another **7.** *a*) any of certain commercial papers relating to debts or payment of money [a promissory *note*] *b*) a piece of paper currency [a Federal Reserve *note*] **8.** a cry or call, as of a bird **9.** a signal or hint [a *note* of warning] **10.** [Archaic] a tune or song **11.** *Music a*) a tone of definite pitch *b*) a symbol for a tone, indicating pitch and duration *c*) a key of a piano, etc. —**vt. not′ed, not′ing 1.** to notice; observe **2.** to put in writing; make a note of **3.** to mention specially — **compare notes** to exchange opinions; discuss —**take notes** to write down notes, as of what is said during a lecture —**note′less adj.**

note·book (nōt′book′) *n.* a book in which notes are kept, as to help one remember things

not·ed (nōt′id) *adj.* well-known; distinguished; renowned; eminent —see SYN. at FAMOUS —**not′ed·ly adv.** —**not′ed·ness n.**

note paper paper for writing notes, or letters

note·wor·thy (-wur′thē) *adj.* worthy of note; worth noticing or paying attention to; outstanding —**note′wor′thi·ly adv.** — **note′wor′thi·ness n.**

noth·ing (nuth′iŋ) *n.* [OE. *na thing*] **1.** *a*) no thing; not anything *b*) no part, trace, etc. [*nothing* of kindness in him] **2.** nothingness **3.** a thing that does not exist **4.** *a*) something of little or no value, importance, etc. *b*) a person considered of no value or importance **5.** a nought; zero —*adv.* not at all [the adventure left him *nothing* wiser] —**for nothing 1.** at no cost; free **2.** in vain **3.** without reason —☆**in nothing flat** [Colloq.] in almost no time at all —**make nothing of 1.** to treat as of little importance **2.** to fail to understand —**nothing but** nothing other than —**nothing doing** [Colloq.] **1.** no: used in refusal **2.** no result, accomplishment, etc. —**nothing less than** no less than: also **nothing short of** —**think nothing of 1.** to attach no importance to **2.** to regard as easy to do

noth·ing·ness (-nis) *n.* **1.** the condition of not existing **2.** lack of value, meaning, etc. **3.** unconsciousness or death **4.** anything that does not exist or is useless, etc.

no·tice (nōt′is) *n.* [MFr. < L. *notitia* < *notus:* see NOTE] **1.** announcement or warning, esp. in a formal way, as in a newspaper [a legal *notice*] **2.** a brief mention or review of a book, play, etc. **3.** a written or printed sign giving some public information, warning, or rule [a *notice* of a change in bus schedules] **4.** *a*) attention; regard; heed [she paid him no *notice*] *b*) courteous attention **5.** a formal warning of intention to end an agreement or contract at a certain time [to give one's employer *notice* that one is quitting] —*vt.* **-ticed, -tic·ing 1.** to observe; pay attention to [he *noticed* her new dress] **2.** to be courteous or responsive to [to *notice* each guest personally] —see SYN. at DISCERN —**serve notice** to give formal warning, as of intentions; announce —**take notice** to pay attention; observe

no·tice·a·ble (-ə b'l) *adj.* **1.** readily noticed; easily seen; conspicuous **2.** worth noticing; significant —**no′tice·a·bly adv.**

SYN.—**noticeable** is applied to that which is likely to be noticed or worth noticing [a *noticeable* improvement]; **remarkable** applies to that which is noticeable because it is unusual or exceptional [*remarkable* beauty; *remarkable* strength]; **prominent** refers to that which stands out from or as from its background or setting [a *prominent* nose; a *prominent* author]; an **outstanding** person or thing is remarkable as compared with others of its kind [an *outstanding* sculptor; an *outstanding* feat]; **conspicuous** applies to that which is so obvious as to be immediately seen [a *conspicuous* stain; *conspicuous* bravery]; **striking** is used of something so out of the ordinary that it leaves a sharp impression on the mind [a *striking* contrast; a *striking* design]

no·ti·fi·ca·tion (nōt′ə fi kā′shən) *n.* **1.** a notifying or being notified **2.** the notice given or received, or the letter, form, etc. containing such a notice [a *notification* to appear in court]

no·ti·fy (nōt′ə fī′) *vt.* **-fied′, -fy′ing** [< MFr. < L. < *notus* (see NOTE) + *facere*, to make] **1.** to give notice to; inform **2.** [Chiefly Brit.] to give notice of; announce —**no′ti·fi′er n.**

SYN.—**notify** implies a sending of formal notice giving required or necessary information [*notify* me when the next meeting will be]; **inform** implies a making aware of something by giving knowledge of it [he *informed* me of your decision to join us]; **acquaint** suggests a making familiar with something that was unknown to one before [she *acquainted* me with her problem]; **apprise** implies a notifying someone of something that has particular interest for him [the officer arresting him *apprised* him of his rights]

no·tion (nō′shən) *n.* [Fr. < L. < *notus:* see NOTE] **1.** a general idea or vague thought [have you any *notion* of what he meant?] **2.** a belief; opinion; view [he has the *notion* no one likes him] **3.** a sudden fancy; inclination; whim [I had half a *notion* to call you] **4.** an intention [he has no *notion* of going] ☆**5.**

[*pl.*] small, useful articles, as needles, thread, etc., sold in a store —see SYN. at IDEA

no·tion·al (-'l) *adj.* **1.** of or expressing notions, or ideas **2.** imaginary; not actual [he lives in a *notional* world] ☆**3.** having visionary ideas; fanciful —**no′tion·al·ly adv.**

no·to·chord (nōt′ə kôrd′) *n.* [< Gr. *nōton*, the back + CHORD¹] a long, rod-shaped structure running along the back in the embryos or adults of all chordates

no·to·ri·e·ty (nōt′ə rī′ə tē) *n.* the quality or state of being notorious

no·to·ri·ous (nō tôr′ē əs) *adj.* [ML. *notorius* < LL. < L. *notus:* see NOTE] **1.** well-known **2.** widely known or talked about for something bad —see SYN. at FAMOUS —**no·to′ri·ous·ly adv.** —**no·to′ri·ous·ness n.**

no-trump (nō′trump′) *adj. Bridge* with no suit being trumps —*n. Bridge* a no-trump bid or hand

Not·ting·ham (nät′iŋ əm) city in C England: pop. 305,000

not·with·stand·ing (nät′with stan′diŋ, -with-) *prep.* in spite of [he flew on, *notwithstanding* the storm] —*adv.* all the same; nevertheless [he will go, *notwithstanding*] —*conj.* although

Nouak·chott (nwäk shät′) capital of Mauritania, in the W part: pop. 20,000

nou·gat (nōo′gət) *n.* [Fr. < Pr. < *noga* < L. *nux*, nut] a confection of sugar paste with almonds or other nuts, and, sometimes, fruit

nought (nôt) *n.* [OE. *nowiht* < *ne*, not + *awiht*, aught] **1.** nothing [all his dreams came to *nought*] **2.** *Arith.* the figure zero (0) —*adj.* [Archaic or Obs.] **1.** worthless **2.** evil —*adv.* [Archaic] in no way; not at all —**set at nought** to defy; scorn

noun (noun) *n.* [< OFr. < L. *nomen*, a NAME] *Gram.* **1.** any of a class of words naming or denoting a person, thing, action, quality, etc. [Ex.: *boy, water*, and *truth* are *nouns*] **2.** any word, phrase, or clause so used —**noun′al adj.**

nour·ish (nur′ish) *vt.* [< OFr. *norrir* < L. *nutrire:* see NURSE] **1.** to feed or provide with substances necessary to life and growth **2.** to foster; develop; promote (a feeling, attitude, habit, etc.) —**nour′ish·er n.** —**nour′ish·ing adj.** —**nour′ish·ing·ly adv.**

nour·ish·ment (-mənt) *n.* **1.** a nourishing or being nourished **2.** something that nourishes

nou·veau riche (nōo′vō rēsh′) *pl.* **nou·veaux riches** (nōo′vō rēsh′) [Fr., newly rich] a person who has only recently become rich: often connoting lack of taste, culture, etc.

Nov. November

no·va (nō′və) *n., pl.* **-vae** (-vē), **-vas** [ModL. < L. *nova* (*stella*), new (star)] *Astron.* a star that suddenly increases greatly in brightness and then decreases in brightness over a period of months to years

No·va Sco·tia (nō′və skō′shə) province of SE Canada, consisting of a peninsula & an island at the mouth of the Gulf of St. Lawrence: 21,425 sq. mi.; pop. 756,000; cap. Halifax: abbrev. **N.S.** —**No′va Sco′tian**

nov·el (näv′'l) *adj.* [< OFr. < L. *novellus*, dim. of *novus*, new: for IE. base see NEW] new and unusual —*n.* [< It. < L. *novella*, new things < *novellus*] **1.** a relatively long narrative in prose with a more or less complex plot about imaginary people and happenings **2.** the type of literature that includes all such narratives (with *the*) —see SYN. at NEW —**nov′el·is′tic adj.** — **nov′el·is′ti·cal·ly adv.**

nov·el·ette (näv′ə let′) *n.* a short novel

nov·el·ist (näv′'l ist) *n.* a person who writes novels

nov·el·ize (näv′ə līz′) *vt.* **-ized′, -iz′ing** to make into or like a novel —**nov′el·i·za′tion n.**

no·vel·la (nō vel′ə; *It.* nô vel′lä) *n., pl.* **-las, -le** (-ē; *It.* -le) [It.] **1.** a short prose narrative, often satiric, as a tale by Boccaccio **2.** a short novel; novelette

nov·el·ty (näv′'l tē) *n., pl.* **-ties 1.** the quality of being novel; newness [when the *novelty* of being alone had worn off, she was bored] **2.** something novel; innovation [it was a *novelty* for us to swim in the ocean] **3.** a small, often cheap, toy, decoration, souvenir, etc.: *usually used in pl.*

No·vem·ber (nō vem′bər) *n.* [< OFr. < L. < *novem*, nine: the ancient Roman year began with March] the eleventh month of the year, having 30 days: abbrev. **Nov., N.**

no·ve·na (nō vē′nə) *n.* [ML. < L. < *novem*, nine] *R.C.Ch.* the saying of prayers and devotions during a nine-day period, usually to seek some special favor

nov·ice (näv′is) *n.* [OFr. < L. *novicius* < *novus:* see NOVEL] **1.** a person who is going through a test period in a religious group or order before becoming a full member by taking vows **2.** a person new to a particular activity, etc.; beginner

no·vi·ti·ate (nō vish′ē it, -āt′; -vish′it) *n.* **1.** the period or state of being a novice **2.** a novice **3.** the quarters where religious novices live

☆**No·vo·cain** (nō′və kān′) [L. *nov(us)*, new + (C)OCAIN(E)] *a trademark for* PROCAINE: also sp. **Novocaine**

No·vo·kuz·netsk (nô′vô kōōz nyetsk′) city in south central R.S.F.S.R.: pop. 495,000

No·vo·si·birsk (nô′vô si birsk′) city in the south central R.S.F.S.R., on the Ob River: pop. 1,079,000

now (nou) *adv.* [OE. *nu*] **1.** *a)* at the present time [he's home *now*] *b)* at once [don't wait, come *now*] **2.** at the time referred to; then; next [*now* the war began] **3.** *a)* very recently [he left just *now*] *b)* very soon [he's leaving just *now*] **4.** with things as they are [*now* I'll never know] *Now* is often used to emphasize or introduce something said [*now* look here] —*conj.* since; seeing that [*now* that you're here, we can leave] —*n.* the present time [that's all for *now*] —*adj.* of the present time [the *now* generation] —*interj.* an exclamation of warning, reproach, etc. —**now and then** sometimes: also **now and again**

now·a·days (nou′ə dāz′) *adv.* in these days; at the present time —*n.* the present time

no·way (nō′wā′) *adv.* in no manner; by no means; not at all: now often written as two words (**no way**) and used for emphasis Also **no′ways′** (-wāz′)

no·where (nō′hwer′, -wer′) *adv.* not in, at, or to any place; not anywhere: also [Dial. or Colloq.] **no′wheres′** —*n.* **1.** a place that is nonexistent, remote, etc. [lost in the middle of *nowhere*] **2.** a place or state of obscurity —**nowhere near** not nearly

no·wise (-wīz′) *adv.* in no manner; noway [he's *nowise* at fault]

nox·ious (näk′shəs) *adj.* [< L. < *noxa*, injury < *nocere*: see NUISANCE] harmful to health or morals; injurious; unwholesome —see SYN. at PERNICIOUS —**nox′ious·ly** *adv.* —**nox′ious·ness** *n.*

noz·zle (näz′'l) *n.* [dim. of NOSE] **1.** a spout at the end of a hose, etc., for controlling a stream of liquid or gas **2.** [Slang] the nose

Np *Chem.* neptunium

N.P., n.p. Notary Public

N/S, n/s *Banking* not sufficient funds: also **N.S.F.**

N.S. 1. New Style **2.** not specified: also **n.s. 3.** Nova Scotia

N.S.W. New South Wales

-n't a contracted form of *not* [*aren't*]

NT., NT, N.T. New Testament

nth (enth) *adj.* **1.** expressing the ordinal equivalent to *n* **2.** of the indefinitely large or small quantity represented by *n* —**to the nth degree** (or **power**) **1.** to an indefinite degree or power **2.** to an extreme

nt. wt. net weight

NOZZLE

nu (nōō, nyōō) *n.* [Gr.] the thirteenth letter of the Greek alphabet (N, ν)

nu·ance (nōō′äns, nyōō′-; nōō äns′) *n.* [Fr. < *nuer*, to shade, ult. < L. *nubes*, a cloud] a slight or delicate variation in tone, color, meaning, etc.; shade of difference [his acting conveys every *nuance* of emotion in the role] —**nu′anced** *adj.*

nub (nub) *n.* [var. of *knub*, for KNOB] **1.** *a)* a knob or lump *b)* small piece ☆**2.** [Colloq.] the point of a story or gist of a matter

nub·bin (nub′in) *n.* [dim. of NUB] ☆**1.** a small or imperfect ear of Indian corn **2.** anything small or undeveloped [*nubbins* of coal]

nub·ble (nub′'l) *n.* [dim. of NUB] a small knob or lump — **nub′bly** *adj.* **-bli·er, -bli·est**

nub·by (-ē) *adj.* **-bi·er, -bi·est** covered with small nubs, or lumps; having a rough, knotted surface [a *nubby* fabric] — **nub′bi·ness** *n.*

Nu·bi·a (nōō′bē ə, nyōō′-) region & former kingdom in NE Africa, between the Red Sea & the Sahara, in Egypt & Sudan —**Nu′bi·an** *adj., n.*

nu·bile (nōō′b'l, nyōō′-; -bīl) *adj.* [Fr. < L. < *nubere*, to marry] old enough to get married: said of a young woman who seems fully developed sexually —**nu·bil′i·ty** *n.*

nu·cle·ar (nōō′klē ər, nyōō′-) *adj.* **1.** of, like, or forming a nucleus **2.** of or relating to atomic nuclei [*nuclear* energy]

3. of or operated by atomic energy [*nuclear* weapons] **4.** of, having, or involving nuclear weapons [*nuclear* war]

nuclear fission the splitting of the nuclei of atoms, with the release of great amounts of energy, as in an atomic bomb

nuclear fusion the combining of lightweight atomic nuclei, as of deuterium, into a nucleus of heavier mass, as of helium, with the release of great amounts of energy, as in a hydrogen bomb

nuclear physics the branch of physics dealing with the structure of atomic nuclei, nuclear forces, etc.

nuclear reactor a device that starts and maintains a controlled nuclear chain reaction in a material that can undergo nuclear fission, used for the production of energy or of more such material

nu·cle·ase (nōō′klē ās′, nyōō′-) *n.* [NUCLE(O)- + -ASE] any of various enzymes that speed up the hydrolysis of nucleic acids

nu·cle·ate (-it; *also, & for v. always,* -āt′) *adj.* having a nucleus —*vt.* **-at′ed, -at′ing** to form into or around a nucleus —*vi.* to form a nucleus —**nu′cle·a′tion** *n.* —**nu′cle·a′tor** *n.*

nu·cle·i (nōō′klē ī′, nyōō′-) *n. pl. of* NUCLEUS

nu·cle·ic acid (nōō klē′ik, nyōō-) any of a group of complex organic acids found esp. in the nucleus of all living cells and essential to life

nu·cle·o- *a combining form meaning:* **1.** nucleus **2.** nuclear **3.** nucleic acid Also, before a vowel, **nu·cle-**

nu·cle·o·lus (nōō klē′ə ləs, nyōō-) *n., pl.* **-li′** (-lī′) [ModL. < LL., dim. of L. *nucleus*, a nut] a small, usually globe-shaped body containing protein and RNA, found in the nucleus of most cells —**nu·cle′o·lar** *adj.*

nu·cle·on (nōō′klē än′, nyōō′-) *n.* [NUCLE(US) + (PROT)ON] a neutron or proton, either of the fundamental particles of the atomic nucleus —**nu′cle·on′ic** *adj.*

nu·cle·on·ics (nōō′klē än′iks, nyōō′-) *n.pl.* [with sing. v.] the branch of physics dealing with nucleons or with nuclear phenomena

nu·cle·o·pro·tein (nōō′klē ō prō′tēn, nyōō′-; -prōt′ē in) *n.* [NUCLEO- + PROTEIN] any of a group of proteins linked to a nucleic acid, found in all living cells

nu·cle·o·side (nōō′klē ə sīd′, nyōō′-) *n.* [NUCLE(O)- + -OS(E)[1] + -IDE] a compound consisting of a purine or pyrimidine base linked to a carbohydrate

nu·cle·o·tide (-tīd′) *n.* a nucleoside combined with phosphoric acid

nu·cle·us (nōō′klē əs, nyōō′-) *n., pl.* **-cle·i′** (-ī′), **-cle·us·es** [ModL. < L., a kernel: for IE. base see NECK] **1.** a central thing or part around which other things or parts are grouped **2.** any center of growth or development [his few books became the *nucleus* of a large library] **3.** *Astron.* the bright central part of the head of a comet **4.** *Biol.* the central, usually rounded mass of protoplasm in most plant and animal cells, controlling the cell's growth, reproduction, etc. **5.** *Chem., Physics* the central part of an atom, composed of protons and neutrons and making up almost all the mass of the atom: it carries a positive charge

nu·clide (nōō′klīd, nyōō′-) *n.* [NUCL(EUS) + -ide < Gr. *eidos*, form] a specific type of atom that exists for a measurable time and is characterized by the number of neutrons and protons in its nucleus —**nu·clid′ic** (-klid′ik) *adj.*

nude (nōōd, nyōōd) *adj.* [L. *nudus:* for IE. base see NAKED] completely unclothed or uncovered; naked; bare —*n.* **1.** a nude person **2.** a nude human figure in painting, sculpture, etc. **3.** the condition of being nude [in the *nude*] —see SYN. at BARE[1] —**nude′ly** *adv.* —**nude′ness** *n.*

nudge (nuj) *vt.* **nudged, nudg′ing** [prob. akin to Norw. dial. *nyggja*, to push] to push gently, esp. with the elbow, so as to get attention, etc. —*n.* a gentle push with the elbow, etc. — **nudg′er** *n.*

nud·ism (nōō′diz'm, nyōō′-) *n.* the practice or cult of going nude as for reasons of health —**nud′ist** *n., adj.*

nu·di·ty (nōō′də tē, nyōō′-) *n.* **1.** a being nude; nakedness **2.** *pl.* **-ties** a nude figure, as in art

☆**nud·nik** (nood′nik) *n.* [< Yid. < Russ.] [Slang] a dull, tiresome person

Nue·vo La·re·do (nwe′vô lä re′dô) city in N Mexico, on the Rio Grande, opposite Laredo, Tex.: pop. 151,000

nu·ga·to·ry (nōō′gə tôr′ē, nyōō′-) *adj.* [< L. < pp. of *nugari*, to trifle] **1.** trifling; worthless **2.** not operative; invalid

nug·get (nug′it) *n.* [prob. dim. of E. dial. *nug*, lump] a lump, esp. of gold ore

nui·sance (nōō′s′ns, nyōō′-) *n.* [< OFr. < *nuisir* < L. *nocere*, to annoy: for IE. base see NECRO-] an act, thing, person, etc. causing trouble, annoyance, or inconvenience

nuisance tax a tax considered a nuisance because it is paid in very small amounts by the consumer

null (nul) *adj.* [< MFr. < L. *nullus*, none < *ne-*, not + *ullus*, any] 1. without legal force; invalid: usually in **null and void** 2. amounting to nought; nil 3. of no value, effect, etc.; insignificant 4. *Math.* designating, of, or being zero

nul·li·fi·ca·tion (nul′ə fi kā′shən) *n.* 1. a nullifying or being nullified ☆2. the refusal of a State of the U.S. to recognize or enforce a Federal law, esp. such a refusal by a Southern State before the Civil War

nul·li·fy (nul′ə fī′) *vt.* **-fied′, -fy′ing** [< LL. < L. *nullus*, none + *facere*, to make] 1. to make legally null; make void 2. to make valueless or useless 3. to cancel out —☆nul′li·fi′er *n.*
SYN.—to **nullify** is literally to bring something to nothing, as by taking away its effectiveness, validity, etc. [the bad weather *nullified* whatever advantage we'd had; his losses *nullified* his profits]; **invalidate** and **void** specifically imply a taking away of legal force or authority from something [to *invalidate*, or *void*, a contract, will, etc.]; **negate** implies a putting of something out of existence, as by destroying or denying [good *negates* evil]

nul·li·ty (nul′ə tē) *n.* 1. a being null 2. *pl.* **-ties** anything that is null, as an act that has no legal force

Num. (the book of) Numbers

num. 1. number 2. numeral(s)

numb (num) *adj.* [< ME. *nomen*, pp. of *nimen*, to take: for IE. base see -NOMY] weakened in or deprived of the power of feeling or moving; deadened; insensible [*numb* with cold; *numb* with grief] —*vt.* to make numb —**numb′ly** *adv.* —**numb′ness** *n.*

num·ber (num′bər) *n.* [< OE. < L. *numerus*: for IE. base see -NOMY] 1. a symbol or word, or a group of either of these, showing how many or which one in a series: see CARDINAL NUMBER, ORDINAL NUMBER 2. [*pl.*] *same as* ARITHMETIC 3. the sum or total of persons or units 4. a collection of persons or things; assemblage [a small *number* of people] 5. *a*) [*often pl.*] a large group [to cut down *numbers* of trees] *b*) [*pl.*] the condition of being a very great number [there is safety in *numbers*] 6. quantity, as consisting of units [a *number* of errors] 7. *a*) a single issue of a periodical [the May *number*] *b*) a single song, skit, etc. in a program 8. [Colloq.] a person or thing singled out [this hat is a smart *number*] 9. *Gram. a*) the change in form used to show whether one or more than one is meant *b*) the form itself See SINGULAR, PLURAL 10. [*pl.*] *a*) metrical form; meter *b*) metrical lines; verses —*vt.* 1. to count; enumerate 2. to give a number to; designate by number 3. to include as one of a group (among) 4. to limit the number of [his days are *numbered*] 5. to comprise; total [the group *numbers* almost eighty] —*vi.* 1. to total; count 2. to be numbered; be included —**a number of** several or many —**beyond** (or **without**) **number** too many to be counted —☆**get** (or **have**) **one's number** [Slang] to discover (or know) one's true character or motives —**one's number is up** [Slang] one's time to die, suffer punishment, etc. has arrived —☆**the numbers** an illegal lottery involving small bets on the order of numbers in a tabulation, as of financial reports published in newspapers: also called **numbers pool** (or **racket**, etc.) —**num′ber·er** *n.*

num·ber·less (-lis) *adj.* 1. too many to be counted 2. without a number or numbers

number one [Colloq.] 1. oneself ☆2. the first quality or grade, usually the very best

Num·bers (num′bərz) [so named from containing the census of the Hebrews after the Exodus] the fourth book of the Pentateuch in the Bible

numb·skull (num′skul′) *n. same as* NUMSKULL

nu·mer·a·ble (nōō′mər ə b′l, nyōō′-) *adj.* that can be numbered or counted

nu·mer·al (nōō′mər əl, nyōō′-) *adj.* [< LL. < L. *numerus*, NUMBER] of, expressing, or standing for a number or numbers —*n.* 1. a figure, letter, or word, or a group of any of these, expressing a number: see ARABIC NUMERALS, ROMAN NUMERALS 2. [*pl.*] numbers that show the year one will graduate from a school or college, given as a prize in sports, etc. and worn on a sweater or the like

nu·mer·ate (-mə rāt′) *vt.* **-at′ed, -at′ing** 1. *same as* ENUMERATE 2. to read words (numbers expressed in figures)

nu·mer·a·tion (nōō′mə rā′shən, nyōō′-) *n.* 1. a numbering or counting; calculation 2. a system of numbering 3. a numerating (sense 2)

nu·mer·a·tor (nōō′mə rāt′ər, nyōō′-) *n.* 1. a person or thing that numbers 2. *Math.* the term above the line in a fraction, indicating how many parts of the denominator are taken [in the fraction 2/5, 2 is the numerator]

nu·mer·i·cal (nōō mer′i k′l, nyōō-) *adj.* 1. of or having to do with numbers [a navy with *numerical* superiority in ships] 2. in or by numbers [arranged in *numerical* order from one to a hundred] 3. denoting a number [a *numerical* symbol] 4. expressed by numbers, not letters [a *numerical* grading system] —**nu·mer′i·cal·ly** *adv.*

nu·mer·ol·o·gy (nōō′mə räl′ə jē, nyōō′-) *n.* [< L. *numerus*, a NUMBER + -LOGY] the practice of pretending to foretell the future by giving meanings to certain numbers, as those of birth dates

nu·mer·ous (nōō′mər əs, nyōō′-) *adj.* [< L. < *numerus*, a NUMBER] 1. made up of a large number [a *numerous* collection of animals] 2. very many [*numerous* friends] —see SYN. at MANY —**nu′mer·ous·ly** *adv.* —**nu′mer·ous·ness** *n.*

Nu·mid·i·a (nōō mid′ē ə, nyōō-) ancient country in N Africa, mainly in what is now E Algeria: see map at ROMAN EMPIRE —**Nu·mid′i·an** *adj., n.*

nu·mis·mat·ic (nōō′miz mat′ik, nyōō′-; -mis-) *adj.* [< Fr. < L. *numisma*, a coin < Gr. < *nomizein*, to sanction < *nomos*: see -NOMY] 1. of coins or medals 2. of or having to do with currency 3. of numismatics —**nu′mis·mat′i·cal·ly** *adv.*

nu·mis·mat·ics (-iks) *n.pl.* [with *sing. v.*] the study or collection of coins, medals, etc. —**nu·mis·ma·tist** (nōō miz′mə tist, nyōō-; -mis′-) *n.*

num·skull (num′skul′) *n.* [NUM(B) + SKULL] a stupid person; dolt; dunce

nun (nun) *n.* [< OE. < LL. *nonna*] a woman who has joined a religious order whose members usually live in a convent, after taking vows to give up wordly goods, never to marry, and to obey their superiors in the order

nun buoy [after its resemblance to the traditional headdress of a nun] a cone-shaped buoy, usually used to mark a channel

Nunc Di·mit·tis (nuŋk′ di mit′is, nooŋk′) [L., now thou lettest depart] 1. a hymn based on the words in Luke 2:29–32 2. [**n- d-**] *a*) departure or farewell, esp. from life *b*) permission to depart; dismissal

nun·ci·o (nun′shē ō′, -sē-) *n., pl.* **-ci·os′** [It. < L. *nuntius*, messenger] an ambassador of the Pope to a foreign government

nun·ner·y (nun′ər ē) *n., pl.* **-ner·ies** *a former name for* CONVENT

nup·tial (nup′shəl, -chəl) *adj.* [< L. < *nuptiae*, marriage < pp. of *nubere*, to marry] 1. of marriage or a wedding [a *nuptial* feast] 2. of mating —*n.* [*pl.*] a wedding; marriage ceremony —see SYN. at MARRIAGE

Nu·rem·berg (noor′əm burg′, nyoor′-) city in NC Bavaria, West Germany: pop. 472,000: Ger. name **Nürn·berg** (nürn′berkh′)

nurse (nurs) *n.* [< OFr. < LL. < L. < *nutrix* < *nutrire*, to nourish < IE. base *sna-*, to flow] 1. a woman hired to take full care of another's young child or children 2. a person trained to take care of the sick or aged, assist surgeons, etc.; specif., *same as: a*) REGISTERED NURSE *b*) PRACTICAL NURSE 3. a person or thing that fosters, protects, etc. —*vt.* **nursed, nurs′ing** 1. to give milk from the breast to (an infant) 2. to suck milk from the breast of 3. to take care of (a child or children) 4. to bring up; rear 5. to take care of (the sick or aged) 6. to nourish or foster [to *nurse* a grudge] 7. to treat, or try to cure [to *nurse* a cold] 8. *a*) to use, handle, etc. carefully, so as to avoid pain, etc. [to *nurse* an injured leg] *b*) to consume, spend, etc. slowly or carefully so as to make last longer [to *nurse* a drink] 9. to hold carefully —*vi.* 1. to suck milk from its mother; feed at the breast 2. to suckle a child 3. to take care of the sick, etc. as a nurse —**nurs′er** *n.*

nurse·maid (nurs′mād′) *n.* a woman hired to take care of a child or children: also **nurs′er·y·maid′**

nurs·er·y (nur′sə rē, nurs′rē) *n., pl.* **-er·ies** 1. a room in a home, set aside for the children 2. *same as: a*) NURSERY SCHOOL *b*) DAY NURSERY 3. a place where young trees or plants are raised for transplanting, for sale, etc. 4. anything that nourishes, fosters, etc.

nurs·er·y·man (-mən) *n., pl.* **-men** a person who owns, operates, or works for a nursery for growing trees, plants, etc.

nursery rhyme a short poem for children

nursery school a school for young children aged usually 3 to 5, before they go to kindergarten

nursing home a place to live that provides care for the infirm, chronically ill, disabled, etc.

nurs·ling (nʉrs′liŋ) *n.* **1.** a young baby still being nursed **2.** anything that is being carefully tended or cared for Also **nurse′ling**

nur·ture (nʉr′chər) *n.* [< OFr. < LL. pp. of L. *nutrire:* see NURSE] **1.** anything that nourishes; food **2.** training, upbringing, fostering, etc.: also **nur′tur·ance 3.** the influences on a person of his environment, thought of as separate from his nature, or heredity —*vt.* **-tured, -tur·ing 1.** to nourish **2.** to train, rear, foster, etc. —**nur′tur·ant, nur′tur·al** *adj.* —**nur′tur·er** *n.*

nut (nut) *n.* [OE. *hnutu:* for IE. base see NECK] **1.** a dry, one-seeded fruit, which has a kernel, often one that can be eaten, in a woody or leathery shell, as the walnut, chestnut, etc. **2.** the kernel itself **3.** loosely, any hard-shelled fruit keeping more or less indefinitely, as a peanut **4.** a small block, usually of metal, with a threaded hole through the center, for screwing onto a bolt, etc. **5.** [Colloq.] the cost of an undertaking that must be met by sales before a profit can be made **6.** [Slang] *a)* a foolish, crazy, or eccentric person *b)* a devotee; fan See also NUTS — *vi.* **nut′ted, nut′ting** to hunt for or gather nuts —**hard** (or **tough**) **nut to crack** a person or thing hard to understand or deal with —**off one's nut** [Slang] crazy

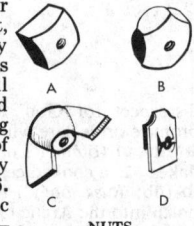

NUTS
(A, square neckline; B, hexagon machine; C, wing; D, snap-on)

nut·crack·er (nut′krak′ər) *n.* **1.** a device, usually hinged, for cracking the shells of nuts **2.** any of various birds of the crow family that feed on nuts

nut·gall (-gôl′) *n.* a small, nut-shaped gall on the oak and other trees

nut·hatch (-hach′) *n.* a small, nut-eating bird with a sharp beak and short tail

nut·meat (-mēt′) *n.* the kernel of a nut

nut·meg (nut′meg′) *n.* [ME. *note-mygge,* partial transl. of OFr. *noiz muscade,* lit., musky nut] the hard, aromatic seed of an East Indian tree: it is grated and used as a spice **2.** the tree

☆**nut·pick** (nut′pik′) *n.* a small, sharp instrument for digging out the kernels of cracked nuts

☆**nu·tri·a** (nōō′trē ə, nyōō′-) *n.* [Sp. < L. *lutra,* otter] **1.** a S. American rodent that lives in water and has webbed feet and a long, almost hairless tail **2.** its short-haired, soft, brown fur

nu·tri·ent (nōō′trē ənt, nyōō′-) *adj.* [< L. prp. of *nutrire:* see NURSE] nutritious; nourishing —*n.* anything nutritious

nu·tri·ment (-trə mənt) *n.* [< L. < *nutrire:* see NURSE] anything that nourishes; food

nu·tri·tion (nōō trish′ən, nyōō-) *n.* [< L. < *nutrire:* see NURSE]

NUTHATCH
(to 6 in. long)

1. a nourishing or being nourished; esp., the series of processes by which an organism takes in food and uses it in living and growing and in repairing tissues **2.** nourishment; food **3.** the science or study of proper diet —**nu·tri′tion·al** *adj.* —**nu·tri′tion·al·ly** *adv.* —**nu·tri′tion·ist** *n.*

nu·tri·tious (-əs) *adj.* nourishing; of value as food —**nu·tri′tious·ly** *adv.* —**nu·tri′tious·ness** *n.*

nu·tri·tive (nōō′trə tiv, nyōō′-) *adj.* **1.** having to do with nutrition **2.** nutritious —**nu′tri·tive·ly** *adv.*

nuts (nuts) *adj.* [see NUT, 6] ☆[Slang] crazy; foolish —☆*interj.* [Slang] an exclamation of disgust, scorn, refusal, etc.: often in the phrase **nuts to** (**someone** or **something**) —**be nuts about** [Slang] to love or like very much

nuts and bolts [Colloq.] the practical details of something, rather than the theory —**nuts′-and-bolts′** *adj.*

nut·shell (nut′shel′) *n.* the shell enclosing the kernel of a nut —**in a nutshell** in a few words; briefly; concisely

nut·ty (nut′ē) *adj.* **-ti·er, -ti·est 1.** containing or producing many nuts **2.** nutlike in flavor **3.** [Slang] *a)* very enthusiastic *b)* queer, foolish, crazy, mad, etc. —**nut′ti·ly** *adv.* —**nut′ti·ness** *n.*

nux vom·i·ca (nuks′ väm′i kə) [ML. < L. *nux,* nut + *vomere,* to vomit] **1.** the poisonous seed of an Asiatic tree, containing strychnine **2.** the tree

nuz·zle (nuz′'l) *vt.* **-zled, -zling** [< NOSE] to push against or rub with the nose, snout, etc. —*vi.* **1.** to push or rub with the nose, etc. against or into something **2.** to lie close; nestle; snuggle —**nuz′zler** *n.*

NV Nevada

NW, N.W., n.w. 1. northwest **2.** northwestern

N.W.T. Northwest Territories

N.Y., NY New York

Nya·sa (nyä′sə, nī as′ə), **Lake** lake in SE Africa, between Malawi & Mozambique

Nya·sa·land (-land′) *former name of* MALAWI

N.Y.C. New York City

nyc·ta·lo·pi·a (nik′tə lō′pē ə) *n.* [LL. < Gr. < *nyktos,* genitive of *nyx,* night + *alaos,* blind + *ōps,* eye] *same as* NIGHT BLINDNESS —**nyc′ta·lop′ic** (-läp′ik) *adj.*

nyl·ghai (nil′gī) *n. same as* NILGAI

☆**ny·lon** (nī′län) *n.* [a made-up word] **1.** a synthetic that is a polymeric amide made into fiber, bristles, etc. that are very strong and elastic **2.** any of the materials made from nylon; specif., [*pl.*] stockings of nylon yarn

nymph (nimf) *n.* [< OFr. < L. < Gr. *nymphē*] **1.** *Gr. & Rom. Myth.* any of a group of minor nature goddesses, thought of as beautiful maidens living in rivers, trees, etc. **2.** a lovely young woman **3.** the form of some insects before they become fully adult —**nymph′al, nymph′e·an** *adj.*

nym·pho·ma·ni·a (nim′fə mā′nē ə, -mān′yə) *n.* [ModL. < Gr. *nymphē,* bride, nymph + -MANIA] abnormal and uncontrollable desire by a woman for sexual intercourse —**nym′pho·ma′ni·ac′** (-ak′) *adj., n.*

Nyx (niks) [Gr.] *Gr. Myth.* the goddess of night

N.Z., N.Zeal. New Zealand

O, o (ō) *n., pl.* **O's, o's** **1.** the fifteenth letter of the English alphabet **2.** a sound of O or o **3.** the numeral zero **4.** an object shaped like O or o **5.** *Physics the symbol for* ohm —*adj.* circular or oval in shape

O (ō) *interj.* an exclamation variously used: **1.** before someone's name or title, in talking to him [*O* Lord, help us!] **2.** to express surprise, fear, wonder, pain, etc. —*vi* oh **3.** at the end of a line in some ballads —*n., pl.* **O's** a use of this exclamation

o' (ə, ō) *prep. an abbreviated form of:* **1.** of [*o'*clock] **2.** [Archaic or Dial.] on

O 1. *Linguis.* Old [*OFr.*] **2.** *Chem.* oxygen

O. 1. Ocean **2.** October **3.** Ohio **4.** Ontario

O., o. 1. octavo **2.** old **3.** [L. *octarius*] *Pharmacy* pint

oaf (ōf) *n.* [< ON. *alfr*, elf] a stupid, clumsy fellow; lout — **oaf'ish** *adj.* —**oaf'ish·ly** *adv.* —**oaf'ish·ness** *n.*

O·a·hu (ō ä'hoo) [Haw. < ?] chief island of Hawaii, on which Honolulu is located

oak (ōk) *n.* see PLURAL, II, D, 3 [OE. *ac*] **1.** a large hardwood tree or bush bearing nuts called *acorns* **2.** its wood **3.** any of various plants resembling an oak —*adj.* of oak: also **oak'en**

oak apple an applelike gall on oak trees

Oak·land (ōk'lənd) [after *oak* groves orig. there] seaport in W Calif., on San Francisco Bay, opposite San Francisco: pop. 362,000

Oak Ridge [after the many *oak* trees there] city in E Tenn.: center for atomic research: pop. 28,000

oa·kum (ō'kəm) *n.* [OE. *acumba* < *a-*, out + *camb*, a comb] loose, stringy, hemp fiber got by taking apart old ropes: used in filling seams in wooden boats

OAK (tree, leaf & acorn)

oar (ôr) *n.* [OE. *ar*] **1.** a long pole with a broad blade at one end, used in rowing **2.** a person who uses an oar; rower —*vt., vi.* to row —**put one's oar in** to meddle —**rest on one's oars** to stop to rest or relax —**oared** *adj.*

oar·fish (ôr'fish') *n., pl.* **-fish, -fish'es:** see FISH a narrow, serpentlike, deep-sea fish, up to 30 ft. long, with a fin along the length of the back and a crest like a mane behind the head

oar·lock (-läk') *n.* a device, often U-shaped, for holding the oar in place in rowing

oars·man (ôrz'mən) *n., pl.* **-men** a man who rows; esp., an expert at rowing —**oars'man·ship'** *n.*

OAS, O.A.S. Organization of American States

o·a·sis (ō ā'sis) *n., pl.* **-ses** (-sēz) [L. < Gr. *oasis:* orig. Coptic] **1.** a fertile place in a desert, due to the presence of water **2.** any place or thing offering welcome relief in the midst of difficulty, dullness, etc.

oat (ōt) *n.* [OE. *ate*] **1.** [*usually pl.*] *a)* a hardy cereal grass *b)* its grain used as food **2.** any related grass; esp., the wild oat **3.** [Obs. or Poet.] a musical pipe made of an oat stalk —☆**feel one's oats** [Slang] **1.** to be frisky **2.** to feel and act important —**oat'en** *adj.*

oat·cake (ōt'kāk') *n.* a thin, flat cake made of oatmeal

oath (ōth) *n., pl.* **oaths** (ōthz, ōths) [OE. *ath*] **1.** a serious promise or declaration in the name of God or of some revered person or thing that one will speak the truth, keep a promise, etc. **2.** the use of the name of God or some other religious word to express anger or add force to what one says: such use shows disrespect for God **3.** a swearword; curse —**take oath** to promise or declare with an oath

oat·meal (ōt'mēl') *n.* **1.** oats ground or rolled into meal or flakes **2.** a cooked cereal made from this

Ob (ōb; *Russ.* ôb'y') river in W Siberia, flowing northwest & north into the Arctic Ocean: 2,495 mi.

ob- [< L. *ob*] *a prefix meaning:* **1.** to, toward, before [*object*] **2.** opposed to, against [*obnoxious*] **3.** upon, over [*obfuscate*] **4.** completely, totally [*obsolete*] **5.** inversely, oppositely [*objurgate*] In words of Latin origin, *ob-* is changed to *o-* before *m* [*omit*]; *oc-* before *c* [*occur*]; *of-* before *f* [*offer*]; and *op-* before *p* [*oppress*]

OB, O.B. 1. obstetrician **2.** obstetrics

ob. [L. *obiit*] he (or she) died

O·ba·di·ah (ō'bə dī'ə) *Bible* **1.** a minor Hebrew prophet **2.** the book containing his prophecies: abbrev. **Ob., Obad.**

ob·bli·ga·to (äb'lə gät'ō) *adj.* [It., lit., obliged < L.] *Music* indispensable: said earlier of an accompaniment essential to the proper performance of a piece, but now usually of one that can be omitted —*n., pl.* **-tos, -ti** (-ē) such an accompaniment

ob·du·rate (äb'door ət, -dyoor-) *adj.* [< L. pp. of *obdurare* < *ob-*, very much + *durare*, to harden] **1.** not easily moved to pity or sympathy; hardhearted **2.** not feeling sorry for what one has done; hardened and unrepenting **3.** not giving in readily; obstinate; stubborn —**ob'du·ra·cy** (-ə sē) *n.* —**ob'du·rate·ly** *adv.*

o·be·di·ence (ō bē'dē əns, ə-) *n.* the state or fact of obeying, or a willingness to obey

o·be·di·ent (-ənt) *adj.* [< OFr. < L. prp. of *obedire*, OBEY] obeying or willing to obey; submissive —**o·be'di·ent·ly** *adv.*

SYN.—**obedient** suggests a giving in to the orders or instructions of someone in authority or control [an *obedient* child]; **docile** implies a disposition that is easily led or controlled or that does not resist being dominated [a *docile* student]; **submissive** suggests not only humbleness but often a slavelike following of those in authority; **tractable** implies a being easily managed or controlled but less so than **docile** does, and it applies to things as well as to people [silver is a *tractable* metal, one that is easily worked]; **compliant** suggests a weakness of character that allows one to yield meekly to another's request or demand [army life had made him *compliant*]; **amenable** suggests such a desire or willingness to be agreeable as would lead one to give in readily [he is *amenable* to suggestion] —**ANT.** disobedient, refractory

o·bei·sance (ō bā's'ns, -bē'-) *n.* [< OFr. < prp. of *obeir*, OBEY] **1.** a gesture of respect or reverence, as a bow **2.** deep respect shown; homage; deference —**o·bei'sant** *adj.*

ob·e·lisk (äb'ə lisk, ō'bə-) *n.* [< L. < Gr. *obeliskos*, dim. of *obelos*, a spit] a tall stone pillar with four sides that tapers to a pointed top

O·ber·am·mer·gau (ō'bər äm'ər gou') village in Bavaria, S West Germany: site of a Passion play performed usually every ten years

O·ber·hau·sen (ō'bər hou'z'n) city in W West Germany: pop. 260,000

O·ber·on (ō'bə rän', -bər ən) in early folklore, the king of fairyland and husband of Titania

o·bese (ō bēs') *adj.* [< L. pp. of *obedere* < *ob-* (see OB-) + *edere*, to eat] very fat —**o·be·si·ty** *n.*

o·bey (ō bā', ə-) *vt.* [< OFr. < L. *obedire* < *ob-* (see OB-) + *audire*, to hear: see AUDIENCE] **1.** to carry out the orders of **2.** to carry out (an order) **3.** to be guided by [to obey one's conscience] —*vi.* to be obedient —**o·bey'er** *n.* —**o·bey'ing·ly** *adv.*

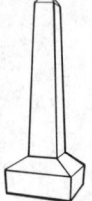

OBELISK

ob·fus·cate (äb′fəs kāt′, äb fus′kāt) *vt.* **-cat′ed, -cat′ing** [< L. pp. of *obfuscare* < *ob-* (see OB-) + *fuscare*, to obscure < *fuscus*, dark] **1.** to cloud over; make dark or unclear **2.** to muddle; confuse; bewilder —**ob′fus·ca′tion** *n.*

o·bi (ō′bē) *n.* [Jpn.] a broad sash with a bow in back, worn with a Japanese kimono

o·bit (ō′bit) *n. same as* OBITUARY

ob·i·ter dic·tum (äb′i tər dik′təm, ō′bi-), *pl.* **ob′i·ter dic′ta** (-tə) [L.] **1.** an opinion expressed by a judge that has no bearing upon the case in question and is not binding **2.** any casual remark

o·bit·u·ar·y (ō bich′ōō wer′ē, ə-) *n., pl.* **-ar′ies** [< ML. < L. *obitus*, death < pp. of *obire*, to die < *ob-* (see OB-) + *ire*, to go] a written or printed notice of someone's death, usually with a brief story of his life —*adj.* of or recording a death or deaths

obj. 1. object **2.** objection **3.** objective

ob·ject (äb′jikt; *for v.* əb jekt′, äb-) *n.* [< ML. *objectum*, something thrown in the way < L. pp. of *objicere* < *ob-* (see OB-) + *jacere*, to throw: see JET] **1.** a thing that can be seen or touched; material thing **2.** a person or thing to which action, thought, or feeling is directed [the *object* of her affection is her cat] **3.** aim; purpose; goal [his *object* in life] **4.** *Gram.* a noun or substantive receiving the action of a verb (see DIRECT OBJECT, INDIRECT OBJECT), or one governed by a preposition: in "Give me the book," *book* is the *direct object* and *me* is the *indirect object* **5.** *Philos.* anything that can be perceived by the mind —*vt.* to state in opposition or disapproval [it was *objected* that the new tax law was unfair] —*vi.* **1.** to make a protest; be opposed [he *objected* to our going] **2.** to feel or express disapproval [the public *objected* when the prices rose] —**ob′ject·less** *adj.* —**ob·jec′tor** *n.*

SYN.—**object** implies opposition to something because of strong dislike or disapproval [I *object* to her meddling]; **protest** implies the making of strong, formal, often written objection to something [they *protested* the new tax increases]; **remonstrate** implies protest and argument in demonstrating to another that he is wrong or at fault [she *remonstrated* against his hostile attitude]; **expostulate** suggests strong, earnest pleading or argument to change another's views or actions [she *expostulated* with the judge about his decision] —ANT. agree, consent, acquiesce

object glass *same as* OBJECTIVE (*n.* 4)

ob·jec·ti·fy (əb jek′tə fī′, äb-) *vt.* **-fied′, -fy′ing** to give objective form to; make concrete —**ob·jec′ti·fi·ca′tion** *n.*

ob·jec·tion (əb jek′shən, äb-) *n.* **1.** an objecting **2.** a feeling or expression of opposition, disapproval, or dislike **3.** a reason for opposing, disapproving, or disliking

ob·jec·tion·a·ble (-ə b'l) *adj.* likely to be objected to; disagreeable; offensive —**ob·jec′tion·a·bly** *adv.*

ob·jec·tive (əb jek′tiv, äb-) *adj.* **1.** of or having to do with a known or perceived object, not one that is imagined **2.** having existence independent of the mind; real; actual [*objective* reality] **3.** concerned with the actual features of the thing dealt with rather than the thoughts, feelings, etc. of the artist, writer, or speaker [an *objective* description] **4.** without bias or prejudice [a judge should be *objective*] **5.** being the aim or goal [an *objective* point] ☆**6.** designating a test that requires only simple answers or checking, as a multiple-choice or true-false test **7.** *Gram.* designating or of the case of an object (sense 4) —*n.* **1.** anything outside the mind or independent of the mind; reality **2.** aim; goal **3.** *Gram. a)* the objective case *b)* a word in this case **4.** *Optics* the lens or lenses nearest the object observed, as in a microscope or telescope —see SYN. at FAIR[1] —**ob·jec′tive·ly** *adv.* —**ob·jec′tive·ness** *n.*

ob·jec·tiv·i·ty (äb′jek tiv′ə tē) *n.* **1.** the state or quality of being objective **2.** objective reality

ob·jec·tiv·ize (əb jek′tə vīz′, äb-) *vt.* **-ized′, -iz′ing** to make objective; objectify —**ob·jec′ti·vi·za′tion** *n.*

object lesson an actual or practical demonstration or illustration of some principle

ob·jet d'art (äb′zhā där′, ub′-) *pl.* **ob·jets d'art** (äb′zhā-, ub′-) [Fr.] a relatively small object of artistic value, as a figurine, vase, etc.

ob·jur·gate (äb′jər gāt′, əb jur′gāt) *vt.* **-gat′ed, -gat′ing** [< L. pp. of *objurgare* < *ob-* (see OB-) + *jurgare*, to chide] to chide

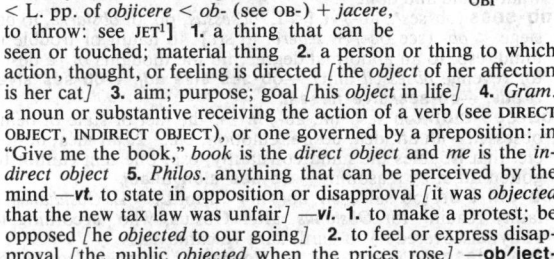

OBI

vehemently; upbraid sharply; berate —**ob′jur·ga′tion** *n.* —**ob·jur′ga·to·ry** (-gə tôr′ē) *adj.*

obl. 1. oblique **2.** oblong

ob·lan·ce·o·late (äb lan′sē ə lit, -lāt′) *adj.* [OB- + LANCEOLATE] lance-shaped, with the broad end at the tip, as some leaves

ob·late[1] (äb′lāt, äb lāt′) *adj.* [ModL. *oblatus* < OB- + *-latus* as in *prolatus:* see PROLATE] *Geom.* flattened at the poles [an *oblate* spheroid]

ob·late[2] (äb′lāt) *n.* [< ML. *oblatus* < L. pp. of *offerre* to OFFER] *R.C.Ch.* a person living in or associated with a religious community but not bound by vows

ob·la·tion (äb lā′shən) *n.* [OFr. < L. < *oblatus,* pp. of *offerre:* see OFFER] **1.** an offering made to God or a god **2.** the thing or things offered; esp., the bread and wine of the Eucharist —**ob·la′tion·al** *adj.*

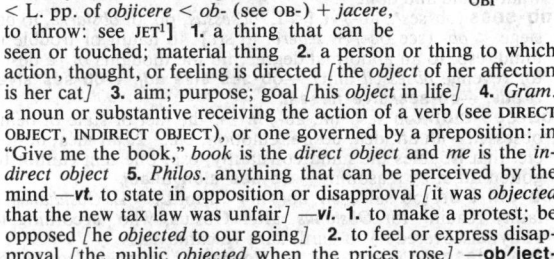

OBLANCEOLATE
LEAF

ob·li·gate (äb′lə gāt′) *vt.* **-gat′ed, -gat′ing** [< L. pp. of *obligare:* see OBLIGE] to bind by a contract, promise, feeling of duty, indebtedness, etc. [I am *obligated* to you for your help]

ob·li·ga·tion (äb′lə gā′shən) *n.* **1.** an obligating or being obligated **2.** *a)* a legal or moral responsibility *b)* the thing that such a responsibility binds one to do [his *obligations* as a parent] **3.** binding power of a contract, promise, etc. **4.** *a)* a feeling of indebtedness for a favor, service, etc. done for one *b)* such a favor, service, etc. —see SYN. at DUTY —**ob′li·ga′tion·al** *adj.*

ob·li·ga·to (äb′lə gät′ō) *adj., n., pl.* **-tos, -ti** (-ē) *same as* OBBLIGATO

ob·li·ga·to·ry (ə blig′ə tôr′ē, äb′lig ə-) *adj.* legally or morally binding; required by law or one's feeling of duty [paying taxes is *obligatory*] —**ob·lig′a·to·ri·ly** *adv.* —**ob·lig′a·to′ri·ness** *n.*

o·blige (ə blīj′, ō-) *vt.* **o·bliged′, o·blig′ing** [< OFr. < L. *obligare* < *ob-* (see OB-) + *ligare,* to bind: see LEAGUE[1]] **1.** to force to do something because the law, one's conscience, etc. demands it [his religion *obliges* him to fast on certain days] **2.** to make indebted for a kindness; do a favor for [I am much *obliged* for all your help] —*vi.* to do a favor or service —**o·blig′er** *n.*

o·blig·ing (ə blī′jiŋ) *adj.* ready to do favors; helpful; accommodating —see SYN. at AMIABLE —**o·blig′ing·ly** *adv.*

ob·lique (ə blēk′, ō-; *also, esp. in mil. use,* -blīk′) *adj.* [< L. *obliquus* < *ob-* (see OB-) + *liquis,* awry] **1.** neither perpendicular nor horizontal; slanting **2.** not straight to the point; indirect [an *oblique* glance; an *oblique* remark] **3.** evasive, underhanded, etc. **4.** indirectly aimed at or attained [*oblique* results] **5.** *Gram.* designating or of any case but the nominative and vocative —*n.* something oblique, as an oblique angle —*vi.* **-liqued′, -liqu′ing** to veer from the perpendicular; slant —**ob·lique′ly** *adv.* —**ob·liq·ui·ty** (ə blik′wə tē, ō-), **ob·lique′ness** *n.*

oblique angle any angle other than a right angle; acute or obtuse angle

ob·lit·er·ate (ə blit′ə rāt′, ō-) *vt.* **-at′ed, -at′ing** [< L. pp. of *obliterare,* to blot out < *ob-* (see OB-) + *litera,* a letter] **1.** to blot out or wear away, leaving no traces; efface [spilled ink *obliterated* her signature] **2.** to do away with; destroy [bombs *obliterated* the bridge] —see SYN. at ERASE —**ob·lit·er·a′tion** *n.* —**ob·lit′er·a′tive** *adj.* —**ob·lit′er·a′tor** *n.*

ob·liv·i·on (ə bliv′ē ən, ō-) *n.* [< OFr. < L. < *oblivisci,* to forget] **1.** a forgetting or having forgotten; forgetfulness **2.** a being forgotten

ob·liv·i·ous (-əs) *adj.* **1.** forgetful or not noticing (usually with *of* or *to*) [*oblivious* of the noise] **2.** causing forgetfulness [the carefree *oblivious* days of vacation] —**ob·liv′i·ous·ly** *adv.* —**ob·liv′i·ous·ness** *n.*

ob·long (äb′lôŋ) *adj.* [< L. < *ob-* (see OB-) + *longus,* LONG[1]] longer than broad; elongated; specif., rectangular and longer in one direction than in the other, esp. longer horizontally —*n.* an oblong figure

ob·lo·quy (äb′lə kwē) *n., pl.* **-quies** [< LL. < *obloqui,* to speak against < *ob-* (see OB-) + *loqui,* to speak] **1.** loud and angry criticism of a person or thing, especially by many people **2.** disgrace or dishonor resulting from this

ob·nox·ious (əb näk′shəs, äb-) *adj.* [< L. < *obnoxius*, in danger < *ob-* (see OB-) + *noxa*, a harm] very unpleasant; objectionable; offensive —**ob·nox′ious·ly** *adv.* —**ob·nox′ious·ness** *n.*

o·boe (ō′bō) *n.* [It. < Fr. *hautbois*: see HAUTBOY] a double-reed woodwind instrument having a high, penetrating, melancholy tone —**o′bo·ist** *n.*

Obs., obs. obsolete

ob·scene (äb sēn′, əb-) *adj.* [< Fr. < L. *obscenus*, filthy, repulsive] **1.** offensive to feelings of modesty or decency of an individual or of a community in general; lewd **2.** disgusting; repulsive —see SYN. at COARSE —**ob·scene′ly** *adv.*

ob·scen·i·ty (äb sen′ə tē, əb-) *n.* **1.** the state or quality of being obscene **2.** *pl.* **-ties** an obscene remark, act, etc.

ob·scu·rant·ism (äb skyoor′ənt-iz′m, əb-) *n.* [< L. *obscurans*, obscuring] **1.** opposition to human progress or enlightenment **2.** the practice of being deliberately obscure or vague —**ob·scu′rant·ist** *n., adj.*

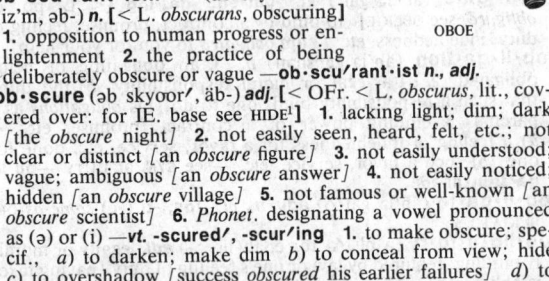

OBOE

ob·scure (əb skyoor′, äb-) *adj.* [< OFr. < L. *obscurus*, lit., covered over: for IE. base see HIDE[1]] **1.** lacking light; dim; dark [the *obscure* night] **2.** not easily seen, heard, felt, etc.; not clear or distinct [an *obscure* figure] **3.** not easily understood; vague; ambiguous [an *obscure* answer] **4.** not easily noticed; hidden [an *obscure* village] **5.** not famous or well-known [an *obscure* scientist] **6.** *Phonet.* designating a vowel pronounced as (ə) or (i) —*vt.* **-scured′, -scur′ing 1.** to make obscure; specif., *a)* to darken; make dim *b)* to conceal from view; hide *c)* to overshadow [success *obscured* his earlier failures] *d)* to confuse [his testimony *obscured* the issue] **2.** *Phonet.* to pronounce (a vowel) as (ə) or (i) —**ob·scure′ly** *adv.* —**ob·scure′-ness** *n.*

SYN.—**obscure** applies to that which is unclear to the senses or to the mind either because it is concealed, veiled, or imprecisely stated or because of dullness or lack of insight in the perceiver [his motives remain *obscure*]; **vague** applies to that which is so lacking in precision or exactness that it is indistinct or unclear [a *vague* notion]; **enigmatic** and **cryptic** are used of that which baffles or bewilders, the latter word implying a deliberate intention to puzzle [his *enigmatic* behavior; a *cryptic* warning]; **ambiguous** applies to that which puzzles because it can be understood in more than one way ["The Lead Horse" is an *ambiguous* title]; **equivocal** is used of something ambiguous that is used to mislead or confuse [the politician's *equivocal* answer] —**ANT.** clear, distinct, obvious

ob·scu·ri·ty (əb skyoor′ə tē, äb-) *n.* **1.** the quality or condition of being obscure **2.** *pl.* **-ties** an obscure person or thing

ob·se·quies (äb′sə kwēz) *n.pl.* [< OFr. < ML. *obsequiae* (< L. *obsequium*: see OBSEQUIOUS), substituted for L. *exsequiae*, funeral rites] funeral services

ob·se·qui·ous (əb sē′kwē əs, äb-) *adj.* [< L. < *obsequium*, compliance < *obsequi*, to comply with] showing too great a willingness to serve or obey; fawning —**ob·se′qui·ous·ly** *adv.* —**ob·se′qui·ous·ness** *n.*

ob·serv·a·ble (əb zurv′və b′l, äb-) *adj.* **1.** that can be observed; visible; noticeable **2.** deserving of attention **3.** that can or must be kept or celebrated [an *observable* holiday] —**ob·serv′a·bly** *adv.*

ob·serv·ance (əb zur′vəns, äb-) *n.* **1.** the act or practice of observing a law, duty, custom, etc. **2.** a customary act, rite, etc. **3.** the act of observing, or noting; observation **4.** *R.C.Ch.* the rule to be observed by a religious order

ob·serv·ant (-vənt) *adj.* **1.** strict in observing a rule, custom, etc. (often with *of*) [*observant* of the rules of etiquette] **2.** paying careful attention **3.** perceptive or alert —**ob·serv′ant·ly** *adv.*

ob·ser·va·tion (äb′zər vā′shən) *n.* **1.** *a)* the act, practice, or power of noticing *b)* something noticed **2.** a being seen or noticed [seeking to avoid *observation*] **3.** *a)* a noting and recording of facts, as for some scientific study *b)* a fact or event so noted and recorded **4.** a comment based on something observed **5.** the act of determining the altitude of the sun, a star, etc., in order to find a ship's position at sea —*adj.* for observing [an *observation* tower] —see SYN. at REMARK —**ob′ser·va′tion·al** *adj.*

☆**observation car** a railway car with extra-large windows or a transparent dome for providing a broad view of the scenery

ob·serv·a·to·ry (əb zur′və tôr′ē, äb-) *n., pl.* **-ries 1.** a building or institution equipped for scientific observation, esp. one with a large telescope for astronomical research **2.** any building or place providing an extensive view of the surrounding land

OBSERVATORY

ob·serve (əb zurv′, äb-) *vt.* **-served′, -serv′ing** [< OFr. < L. *observare*, to watch < *ob-* (see OB-) + *servare*, to keep < IE. base *ser-*, to watch over] **1.** to adhere to or keep (a law, custom, duty, etc.) **2.** to celebrate (a holiday, etc.) **3.** according to custom **3.** *a)* to notice or perceive (something) *b)* to pay special attention to **4.** to conclude after study **5.** to say casually; remark ["It may rain," he *observed*] **6.** to examine scientifically —*vi.* **1.** to take notice or make observations **2.** to comment (*on* or *upon*) —see SYN. at CELEBRATE and DISCERN —**ob·serv′ing·ly** *adv.*

ob·serv·er (əb zur′vər, äb-) *n.* a person who observes something; specif., a person who attends a convention, assembly, etc., not as an official delegate but only to observe and report what is said and done

ob·sess (əb ses′, äb-) *vt.* [< L. *obsessus*, pp. of *obsidere*, to besiege < *ob-* (see OB-) + *sedere*, to SIT] to haunt or trouble in mind, esp. to an abnormal degree; fill the thoughts of [a desire for revenge *obsessed* him] —**ob·ses′sive** *adj.* —**ob·ses′sive·ly** *adv.* —**ob·ses′sive·ness** *n.*

ob·ses·sion (əb sesh′ən, äb-) *n.* **1.** the fact or state of being obsessed with an idea, desire, emotion, etc. **2.** an idea, desire, etc. that troubles the mind constantly, esp. one that cannot be gotten rid of by reasoning —**ob·ses′sion·al** *adj.*

ob·sid·i·an (əb sid′ē ən, äb-) *n.* [< ModL. < L. *Obsidianus*, a faulty reading for *Obsianus*, after Obsius, who, according to Pliny, discovered it] a hard, dark volcanic glass

ob·so·lesce (äb′sə les′) *vi.* **-lesced′, -lesc′ing** to be or become obsolescent

ob·so·les·cent (äb′sə les′′nt) *adj.* in the process of becoming obsolete —**ob′so·les′cence** *n.* —**ob′so·les′cent·ly** *adv.*

ob·so·lete (äb′sə lēt′, äb′sə lēt′) *adj.* [< L. pp. of *obsolescere* < *ob-* (see OB-) + *solere*, to become accustomed] **1.** no longer in use or practice; discarded **2.** no longer in fashion; out-of-date; passé —*vt.* **-let′ed, -let′ing** to make obsolete, as by replacing with something newer —**ob′so·lete′ly** *adv.* —**ob′so·lete′ness** *n.*

ob·sta·cle (äb′sti k′l) *n.* [OFr. < L. *obstaculum* < *ob-* (see OB-) + *stare*, to STAND] anything that gets in the way or hinders; obstruction

ob·stet·ric (əb stet′rik, äb-) *adj.* [< ModL. < L. < *obstetrix*, midwife, lit., she who stands before] of or having to do with childbirth or obstetrics: also **ob·stet′ri·cal**

ob·ste·tri·cian (äb′stə trish′ən) *n.* a medical doctor who specializes in obstetrics

ob·stet·rics (əb stet′riks, äb-) *n.pl.* [with sing. v.] the branch of medicine concerned with the care and treatment of women in pregnancy, childbirth, and the period immediately following

ob·sti·na·cy (äb′stə nə sē) *n.* **1.** the state or quality of being obstinate **2.** *pl.* **-cies** an obstinate act, attitude, etc.

ob·sti·nate (äb′stə nit) *adj.* [< L. pp. of *obstinare*, to resolve on, ult. < *ob-* (see OB-) + *stare*, to STAND] **1.** unreasonably determined to have one's own way; stubborn; dogged **2.** resisting treatment [an *obstinate* fever] **3.** not easily subdued, ended, etc. —see SYN. at STUBBORN —**ob′sti·nate·ly** *adv.* —**ob′sti·nate·ness** *n.*

ob·strep·er·ous (əb strep′ər əs, äb-) *adj.* [< L., ult. < *ob-* (see OB-) + *strepere*, to roar] noisy, boisterous, or unruly, esp. in resisting or opposing [the *obstreperous* horse threw its rider] —see SYN. at VOCIFEROUS —**ob·strep′er·ous·ly** *adv.* —**ob·strep′er·ous·ness** *n.*

ob·struct (əb strukt′, äb-) *vt.* [< L. pp. of *obstruere* < *ob-* (see OB-) + *struere*, to pile up: for IE. base see STREW] **1.** to block (a passage) with obstacles; clog **2.** to hinder (progress, an activity, etc.); impede **3.** to block (the view) —see SYN. at HINDER[1] —**ob·struct′er, ob·struc′tor** *n.* —**ob·struc′tive** *adj.* —**ob·struc′tive·ly** *adv.* —**ob·struc′tive·ness** *n.*

ob·struc·tion (əb struk′shən, äb-) *n.* **1.** an obstructing or being obstructed [the *obstruction* of justice] **2.** anything that obstructs; hindrance [to remove an *obstruction* from a pipe]

ob·struc·tion·ist (-ist) *n.* anyone who obstructs progress; esp., a member of a legislature who hinders the passage of legislation by technical maneuvers —*adj.* of obstructionists: also **ob·struc′tion·is′tic** —**ob·struc′tion·ism** *n.*

ob·tain (əb tān′, äb-) *vt.* [< OFr. < L. *obtinere* < *ob-* (see OB-) + *tenere*, to hold: see TENANT] to get possession of by effort; procure —*vi.* to be in force or in effect; prevail [a law that no longer *obtains*]—see SYN. at GET —**ob·tain′a·ble** *adj.* —**ob·tain′er** *n.* —**ob·tain′ment** *n.*

ob·trude (əb trōōd′, äb-) *vt.* -trud′ed, -trud′ing [< L. *obtrudere* < *ob-* (see OB-) + *trudere*, to thrust] 1. to thrust forward; push out; eject 2. to force (oneself, one's opinions, etc.) upon others without being asked or wanted —*vi.* to obtrude oneself (*on* or *upon*) [to *obtrude* upon another's privacy]—see SYN. at INTRUDE —**ob·trud′er** *n.* —**ob·tru′sion** (-trōō′zhən) *n.*

ob·tru·sive (əb trōō′siv, äb-) *adj.* 1. inclined to obtrude 2. obtruding itself; esp., calling attention to itself in a displeasing way [an *obtrusive* billboard] —**ob·tru′sive·ly** *adv.* —**ob·tru′sive·ness** *n.*

ob·tuse (äb tōōs′, əb-; -tyōōs′) *adj.* [< L. pp. of *obtundere*, to blunt < *ob-* (see OB-) + *tundere*, to strike] 1. not sharp or pointed; blunt 2. greater than 90 degrees and less than 180 degrees [an *obtuse* angle] 3. slow to understand or perceive; dull or insensitive 4. not acute [an *obtuse* pain]—see SYN. at DULL —**ob·tuse′ly** *adv.* —**ob·tuse′ness** *n.*

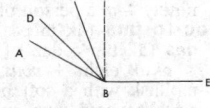
OBTUSE ANGLES
(ABE, DBE, CBE)

ob·verse (äb vurs′, əb-; *also*, & *for n. always*, äb′vərs) *adj.* [< L. pp. of *obvertere* < *ob-* (see OB-) + *vertere*, to turn: see VERSE] 1. turned toward the observer 2. narrower at the base than at the top [an *obverse* leaf] 3. forming a counterpart —*n.* 1. the side, as of a coin or medal, bearing the main design 2. the front or main surface of anything 3. a counterpart —**ob·verse′ly** *adv.*

ob·vi·ate (äb′vē āt′) *vt.* -at′ed, -at′ing [< L. pp. of *obviare* < *obvius:* see OBVIOUS] to do away with or prevent by effective measures; make unnecessary [proper care of one's car can *obviate* the need for costly emergency repairs]—see SYN. at PREVENT —**ob′vi·a′tion** *n.*

ob·vi·ous (äb′vē əs) *adj.* [L. *obvius*, in the way: see OB- & VIA] easy to see or understand; evident [the need for safety devices is *obvious*]—see SYN. at EVIDENT —**ob′vi·ous·ly** *adv.* —**ob′vi·ous·ness** *n.*

oc- *see* OB-

o/c overcharge

Oc., oc. ocean

oc·a·ri·na (äk′ə rē′nə) *n.* [It., dim. of *oca* < LL. *auca*, a goose: from its shape] a small, simple wind instrument with finger holes and a mouthpiece: it produces soft, hollow tones

O'Ca·sey (ō kā′sē), Sean (shôn) 1880–1964; Ir. playwright

occas. 1. occasion 2. occasional 3. occasionally

oc·ca·sion (ə kā′zhən) *n.* [< OFr. < L. < pp. of *occidere* < *ob-* (see OB-) + *cadere*, to fall] 1. a favorable time; opportunity [I found no *occasion* to mention it to her] 2. a fact or event that makes something else possible [a chance meeting was the *occasion* of the renewal of their friendship] 3. *a)* a happening; occurrence *b)* a particular time [on the *occasion* of his birth] 4. a special time or event, suitable for celebration 5. need arising from circumstances —*vt.* to be the occasion of; cause [a poor harvest *occasioned* a rise in grain prices] —see SYN. at CAUSE —**on occasion** once in a while; sometimes —**rise to the occasion** to meet an emergency —**take (the) occasion** to use the opportunity (to do something)

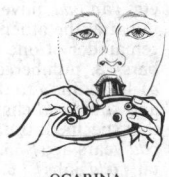
OCARINA

oc·ca·sion·al (-'l) *adj.* 1. occurring on a particular occasion 2. of or for a special occasion [an *occasional* poem is one written for a birthday, anniversary, etc.] 3. acting only on special occasions 4. happening now and then; infrequent [an *occasional* trip to town] 5. for use only now and then; extra [*occasional* chairs] —**oc·ca′sion·al·ly** *adv.*

oc·ci·dent (äk′sə dənt) *n.* [< OFr. < L. *occidens*, direction of the setting sun < *occidere:* see OCCASION] the west: now rare, except [O-] the part of the world west of Asia, esp. Europe and the Americas —**oc′ci·den′tal, Oc′ci·den′tal** *adj., n.*

oc·cip·i·tal (äk sip′ə t'l) *adj.* of the occiput or the occipital bone —*n.* same as OCCIPITAL BONE —**oc·cip′i·tal·ly** *adv.*

occipital bone the bone that forms the back part of the skull

oc·ci·put (äk′si put′) *n., pl.* **oc·cip·i·ta** (äk sip′ə tə), **-puts′** [< MFr. < L. < *ob-* (see OB-) + *caput*, head] the back part of the skull or head

oc·clude (ə klōōd′, ä-) *vt.* -clud′ed, -clud′ing [< L. *occludere* < *ob-* (see OB-) + *claudere*, to CLOSE[2]] 1. to close or block (a passage) 2. to prevent the passage of; shut in or out 3. *Chem.* to retain or absorb (a gas, liquid, or solid) —*vi. Dentistry* to meet with the cusps fitting closely: said of the upper and lower teeth —**oc·clud′ent** *adj.* —**oc·clu′sive** *adj.*

☆**occluded front** *Meteorol.* the front formed when a warm front is overtaken by a cold front and the original air mass is forced aloft up the warm-front or cold-front surface

oc·clu·sion (ə klōō′zhən, ä-) *n.* 1. an occluding or being occluded 2. *Dentistry* the fitting together of the upper and lower teeth, or the way in which these fit together when the jaws are closed 3. *Meteorol.* same as OCCLUDED FRONT

oc·cult (ə kult′, ä′kult) *adj.* [< L. pp. of *occulere*, to conceal < *ob-* (see OB-) + *celare*, to hide (see CONCEAL)] 1. hidden 2. secret or known only to certain chosen persons 3. beyond human understanding; mysterious 4. designating or of those arts regarded as mystic, such as alchemy, astrology, etc. —*vt., vi.* to hide or become hidden —**the occult** the occult arts —**oc·cult′ism** *n.* —**oc·cult′ist** *n.*

NORMAL
OCCLUSION

oc·cul·ta·tion (äk′ul tā′shən) *n.* 1. the state of becoming hidden or disappearing from view 2. *Astron.* an eclipse in which the eclipsed body seems much smaller than the eclipsing body

oc·cu·pan·cy (äk′yə pən sē) *n., pl.* -cies 1. *a)* an occupying; a taking or keeping in possession *b)* the period during which a house, etc. is occupied 2. the condition of being occupied 3. *Law* the taking possession of a previously unowned object

oc·cu·pant (äk′yə pənt) *n.* 1. one who occupies a house, position, etc. 2. one who acquires possession by occupancy

oc·cu·pa·tion (äk′yə pā′shən) *n.* 1. an occupying or being occupied; specif., the seizure and control of a country or area by military forces 2. (one's) trade, profession, or business —**oc′cu·pa′tion·al** *adj.* —**oc′cu·pa′tion·al·ly** *adv.*

☆**occupational disease** a disease commonly acquired by people in a particular occupation [silicosis is an *occupational disease* of miners]

☆**occupational therapy** therapy by means of work, as arts and crafts, designed to divert the mind or to correct a physical defect

oc·cu·py (äk′yə pī′) *vt.* -pied, -py′ing [< OFr. < L. *occupare*, to possess < *ob-* (see OB-) + *capere*, to seize] 1. to take possession of by settlement or seizure [pioneers *occupied* the western wilderness] 2. to hold possession of by tenure; specif., *a)* to dwell in *b)* to hold (an official position or office) 3. to take up or fill up (space, time, etc.) [the store *occupies* the entire building] 4. to employ or busy (oneself, one's mind, etc.) [many problems *occupied* his mind] —**oc′cu·pi′er** *n.*

oc·cur (ə kur′) *vi.* -curred′, -cur′ring [< L. *occurrere* < *ob-* (see OB-) + *currere*, to run: see CURRENT] 1. to be found; exist [fish *occur* in most waters] 2. to present itself; come to mind [an idea *occurred* to him] 3. to take place; happen [the accident *occurred* last week] —see SYN. at HAPPEN

oc·cur·rence (-əns) *n.* 1. the act or fact of occurring [the *occurrence* of minor errors in the textbook] 2. something that occurs; event; incident —**oc·cur′rent** *adj.*

SYN.—**occurrence** is the general word for anything that happens or takes place [an unforeseen *occurrence*]; an **event** is a relatively important occurrence, especially one growing out of earlier happenings or conditions [an account of *events* that followed the surrender]; an **incident** is a relatively unimportant occurrence, often one connected with a more important event [these *incidents* led to his running for mayor]; an **episode** is a clearly marked-off occurrence that is complete in itself but that forms a part of a larger event or of a series of related happenings [his service in the navy was an important *episode* in his career]; a **circumstance** is something that happens along with another, often more important event, and that may influence it [the *circumstances* surrounding my decision]

o·cean (ō′shən) *n.* [< OFr. < L. *oceanus* < Gr. *Ōkeanos*] 1. the great body of salt water that covers about 71% of the earth's surface **2.** any of its five principal divisions: the Atlantic, Pacific, Indian, Arctic, or Antarctic Ocean **3.** any great expanse or quantity —**o·ce·an·ic** (ō'shē an'ik) *adj.*

☆**o·cean·ar·i·um** (ō'shən er'ē əm) *n., pl.* **-i·ums, -i·a** (-ə) a large saltwater aquarium for ocean fish and animals

☆**o·cean·aut** (ō'shən ôt') *n.* [< OCEAN + Gr. *nautēs*, sailor] *same as* AQUANAUT

o·cean·go·ing (-gō'iŋ) *adj.* of, having to do with, or made for travel on, the ocean

O·ce·an·i·a (ō'shē an'ē ə) islands in the Pacific, including Melanesia, Micronesia, & Polynesia &, sometimes, Australia, New Zealand, & the Malay Archipelago: also **O'ce·an'i·ca** (-i kə) —**O'ce·an'i·an** *adj., n.*

o·ce·a·nog·ra·phy (ō'shə näg'rə fē, ō'shē ə-) *n.* the study of the environment in the oceans, including the waters, depths, beds, plants, etc. —**o'ce·a·nog'ra·pher** *n.* —**o'ce·a·no·graph'ic** (-nə graf'ik), **o'ce·a·no·graph'i·cal** *adj.*

☆**o·ce·an·ol·o·gy** (-näl'ə jē) *n.* **1.** the study of the sea in all its aspects, including oceanography, undersea exploration, economic uses, etc. **2.** *same as* OCEANOGRAPHY —**o'ce·an·ol'o·gist** *n.*

ocean sunfish a large, sluggish ocean fish, with a globelike body and stumpy tail

o·cel·lus (ō sel'əs) *n., pl.* **-li** (-ī) [L., dim. of *oculus*, an EYE] **1.** the simple eyespot of certain invertebrates **2.** an eyelike spot —**o·cel'lar** *adj.*

o·ce·lot (äs'ə lät', ō'sə-) *n., pl.* **-lots, -lot:** see PLURAL, II, D, 1 [Fr. < Nahuatl *ocelotl*, jaguar] a large cat of N. and S. America, with a yellow or gray coat marked with black spots

OCelt. Old Celtic

o·cher (ō'kər) *n.* [< L. < Gr. < *ōchros*, pale-yellow] **1.** a yellow or reddish-brown clay colored by iron oxide, used as a pigment **2.** the color of ocher; esp., dark yellow —*vt.* to color with ocher —**o'cher·ous** *adj.*

o·chre (ō'kər) *n., vt.* **o'chred, o'chring** *alt. sp. of* OCHER — **o'chre·ous** (-kər əs, -krē əs) *adj.*

Ock·ham (äk'əm), **William** of 1300?-49?; Eng. philosopher

o'clock (ə kläk', ō-) *adv.* **1.** of or according to the clock **2.** as if on a clock dial, with the number 12 straight ahead or directly overhead: used to indicate direction, esp. of an approaching aircraft

☆**o·co·til·lo** (ō'kə tēl'yō) *n., pl.* **-los** (-yōz) [AmSp. < Nahuatl *ocotl*] a spiny, low-growing plant with scarlet flowers, found in the deserts of the southwestern U.S. and Mexico

OCS, O.C.S. Officer Candidate School

oct- *same as:* **1.** OCTA- **2.** OCTO- Used before a vowel

Oct. October

oct. octavo

oc·ta- [Gr. *okta-* < *oktō*, eight] *a combining form meaning* eight [*octagon*]

oc·ta·gon (äk'tə gän') *n.* [< L. < Gr.: see OCTA- & -GON] a plane figure with eight angles and eight sides —**oc·tag·o·nal** (äk tag'ə n'l) *adj.* —**oc·tag'o·nal·ly** *adv.*

oc·ta·he·dron (äk'tə hē'drən) *n., pl.* **-drons, -dra** (-drə) [< Gr.: see OCTA- & -HEDRON] a solid figure with eight plane surfaces —**oc'ta·he'dral** *adj.*

oc·tane (äk'tān) *n.* [< OCT(O)- + -ANE] an oily paraffin hydrocarbon, C_8H_{18}, found in petroleum

☆**octane number** (or **rating**) a number representing the antiknock quality of a gasoline, etc.: the higher the number, the greater this quality

OCTAHEDRON

oc·tant (äk'tənt) *n.* [LL. *octans*, eighth part < L. *octo*, eight] **1.** an eighth of a circle **2.** an instrument like the sextant, for measuring angles

oc·tave (äk'tiv, -tāv) *n.* [< OFr. < L. *octavus*, eighth < *octo*, eight] **1.** *a)* the eighth day following a church festival, counting the festival day as the first *b)* the period between the festival and this day **2.** the first eight lines of a sonnet, esp. the Petrarchan sonnet **3.** any group of eight **4.** *Music a)* the eighth full tone above or below a given tone *b)* the interval of eight diatonic degrees between a tone and either of its octaves *c)* the series of tones (a full scale) within this interval, or the keys of an instrument producing such a series *d)* a tone and either of its octaves sounded together —*adj.* consisting of eight, or an octave —**oc·ta·val** (äk tā'v'l, äk'tə v'l) *adj.*

Oc·ta·vi·an (äk tā'vē ən) *see* AUGUSTUS (sense 2)

oc·ta·vo (äk tā'vō, -tā'-) *n., pl.* **-vos** [< L. (*in*) *octavo*, (in)

eight] **1.** the page size (about 6 by 9 inches) of a book made up of printer's sheets folded into eight leaves **2.** a book with pages of this size Also written **8vo** or **8°** —*adj.* with pages of this size

oc·tet, oc·tette (äk tet') *n.* [< OCT(O)- + (DU)ET] **1.** any group of eight; esp., an octave (sense 2) **2.** *Music a)* a composition for eight voices or eight instruments *b)* the eight performers of this

oc·til·lion (äk til'yən) *n.* [Fr. < L. *octo*, eight + Fr. (*m*)*illion*] ☆**1.** in the U.S. and France, the number represented by 1 followed by 27 zeros **2.** in Great Britain and Germany, the number represented by 1 followed by 48 zeros —*adj.* amounting to one octillion in number

oc·to- [< Gr. *oktō-* < *oktō*, eight] *a combining form meaning* eight

Oc·to·ber (äk tō'bər) *n.* [OE. < L. < *octo*, eight: it was the eighth month of the ancient Roman year] the tenth month of the year, having 31 days: abbrev. **Oct., O.**

oc·to·ge·nar·i·an (äk'tə ji ner'ē ən) *adj.* [< L. < *octoginta*, eighty] eighty years old, or between the ages of eighty and ninety —*n.* a person of this age

oc·to·pus (äk'tə pəs) *n., pl.* **-pus·es, -pi'** (-pī'), **oc·top·o·des** (äk täp'ə dēz') [ModL. < Gr. < *oktō*, eight + *pous*, a foot] **1.** a mollusk with a soft body and eight arms covered with suckers **2.** anything suggesting an octopus; esp., a powerful organization with widespread influence and many branches

oc·u·lar (äk'yə lər) *adj.* [< LL. < L. *oculus*, EYE] **1.** of, for, or like the eye **2.** that can be seen; visual [an *ocular* demonstration] —*n.* the eyepiece of an optical instrument

oc·u·list (äk'yə list) *n.* [< Fr. < L. *oculus*, EYE] *earlier term for* OPHTHALMOLOGIST

OD (ō'dē') *n., pl.* **ODs, OD's** [Slang] an overdose, esp. of a narcotic —*vi.*

OD'd, ODed, OD'ing, ODing [Slang] to take an overdose; specif., to die as a result of taking an overdose of a narcotic

OD, O.D. **1.** Officer of the Day **2.** olive drab **3.** outside diameter **4.** overdraft **5.** overdrawn

o·da·lisque, o·da·lisk (ōd'l isk) *n.* [Fr. < Turk. *ōdalik*, chambermaid] **1.** a female slave or concubine in an Oriental harem **2.** a painting of an odalisque lying down

odd (äd) *adj.* [< ON. *oddi*, triangle, hence (from the third angle) odd number] **1.** *a)* remaining or separated from a pair, a set, etc. [an *odd* glove, a few *odd* volumes of Dickens] *b)* remaining after the others are paired, grouped, taken, etc. **2.** having a remainder of one when divided by two; not even: said of numbers **3.** numbered with an odd number [the *odd* months] **4.** *a)* in addition to that mentioned in a round number [ten dollars and some *odd* change] *b)* with a relatively small number over that specified: usually joined to the number by a hyphen [thirty-*odd* years ago] **5.** not usual, regular, etc.; occasional [an *odd* sound!] *b)* queer; eccentric **7.** out-of-the-way [in *odd* corners] —see SYN. at STRANGE —**odd'ly** *adv.* —**odd'ness** *n.*

☆**odd·ball** (äd'bôl') *n.* [ODD + BALL[1]] [Slang] an eccentric, unconventional, or nonconforming person —*adj.* strange or unconventional

odd·i·ty (äd'ə tē) *n.* **1.** queerness; peculiarity **2.** *pl.* **-ties** an odd person or thing

odd·ment (äd'mənt) *n.* **1.** any of various kinds of items **2.** a scrap or remnant

odds (ädz) *n.pl.* **1.** [Now Rare] difference **2.** difference in favor of one side over the other; advantage [a struggle against great *odds*] **3.** an equalizing advantage given to a bettor or competitor in proportion to the assumed chances against him [If a bettor gets odds of 10 to 1, he will receive ten times as much as he has bet if he should win] —**at odds** in disagreement; quarreling —**by all odds** by far —**the odds are** it is likely

odds and ends scraps; remnants; oddments

odds-on (ädz'än', -ôn') *adj.* having better than an even chance of winning [an *odds-on* favorite]

ode (ōd) *n.* [Fr. < LL. < Gr. *ōidē*, song < *aeidein*, to sing] a lyric poem typically addressed to some person or thing and characterized by lofty feeling and dignified style —**od·ic** (ō'dik) *adj.*

-ode (ōd) [< Gr. *hodos*, way, path] *a suffix meaning* way, path [*cathode*]

O·der (ō'dər) river in C Europe, flowing northeast through Czechoslovakia & Poland into the Baltic

OCTOPUS
(diameter with outspread arms, from 1 in. to 25 ft.)

O·des·sa (ō des'ə; *Russ.* ô de'sä) **1.** seaport in S Ukrainian S.S.R., on the Black Sea: pop. 797,000 **2.** city in WC Tex.: pop. 78,000

O·dets (ō dets'), **Clifford** 1906-63; U.S. playwright

O·din (ō'din) *Norse Myth.* the chief god: identified with the Teutonic god Woden

o·di·ous (ō'dē əs) *adj.* [< OFr. < L. < *odium:* see ODIUM] arousing or deserving hatred or loathing; disgusting —**o'di·ous·ly** *adv.* —**o'di·ous·ness** *n.*

o·di·um (ō'dē əm) *n.* [L. *odium,* hatred < *odi,* I hate] **1.** *a)* hatred *b)* a being hated **2.** the disgrace brought on by hateful action; opprobrium [will he ever live down the *odium* of his crime?] —see SYN. at DISGRACE

O·do·a·cer (ō'dō ā'sər) 435?-493 A.D.; 1st barbarian ruler of Italy (476-493)

☆**o·dom·e·ter** (ō däm'ə tər) *n.* [< Fr. < Gr. < *hodos,* way + *metron,* a measure] an instrument for measuring the distance traveled by a vehicle

-o·dont (ə dänt') [< Gr. *odontos,* genitive of *odōn,* tooth] *a combining form meaning* tooth

o·dont·o- [see -ODONT] *a combining form meaning* tooth or teeth: also, before a vowel, **odont-**

o·don·tol·o·gy (ō'dän täl'ə jē) *n.* [< Fr.: see -ODONT & -LOGY] the science dealing with the structure, growth, and diseases of the teeth —**o·don'to·log'i·cal** (-tə läj'i k'l) *adj.* —**o'don·tol'o·gist** *n.*

o·dor (ō'dər) *n.* [< OFr. < L.] **1.** *a)* that characteristic of a substance which makes it possible to smell it *b)* a smell, whether pleasant or unpleasant; fragrance, stench, etc. **2.** [Archaic] a perfume —**be in bad** (or **ill**) **odor** to have a poor reputation —**o'dor·less** *adj.*

o·dor·if·er·ous (ō'də rif'ər əs) *adj.* giving off an odor, often, specif., a fragrant one —**o'dor·if'er·ous·ly** *adv.* —**o'dor·if'er·ous·ness** *n.*

o·dor·ous (ō'dər əs) *adj.* having an odor; esp., fragrant —**o'dor·ous·ly** *adv.* —**o'dor·ous·ness** *n.*

o·dour (ō'dər) *n. Brit. sp.* of ODOR

-o·dyn·i·a (ə din'ē ə, -dīn'-) [ModL. < Gr. < *odynē,* pain] *a combining form meaning* pain in (a specified organ or part)

O·dys·se·us (ō dis'yoos, -dis'ē əs) the hero of the *Odyssey,* a king of Ithaca and one of the Greek leaders in the Trojan War: Latin name, *Ulysses*

Od·ys·sey (äd'ə sē) an ancient Greek epic poem, thought to be by Homer, about the wanderings of Odysseus during the ten years after the fall of Troy —*n.* [sometimes **o-**] *pl.* **-seys** any long journey with many adventures

oe- an earlier variant spelling for many words of Gr. and L. origin now usually written with **e-**

OE., OE, O.E. Old English

Oed·i·pal (ed'ə pəl, ē'də-) *adj.* [also **o-**] of or relating to the Oedipus complex

Oed·i·pus (ed'ə pəs, ē'də-) *Gr. Myth.* a king of Thebes who killed his father and married his mother, not knowing they were his parents

Oedipus complex *Psychoanalysis* the unconscious tendency of a child, sometimes continuing into adulthood, to be attached to the parent of the opposite sex and hostile toward the other parent

o'er (ôr) *prep., adv. chiefly poet. contr. of* OVER

oer·sted (ur'stəd) *n.* [after H. C. *Oersted* (1777-1851), Dan. physicist] the cgs electromagnetic unit of magnetic intensity, or magnetizing force, equal to a force of one dyne acting upon a unit magnetic pole in a vacuum

oe·soph·a·gus (i säf'ə gəs) *n. chiefly Brit. sp.* of ESOPHAGUS

oes·trus (es'trəs, ēs'-) *adj. Brit. sp.* of ESTRUS

of (uv, äv; *unstressed* əv, ə) *prep.* [OE., unstressed var. of *af, æf,* away (from) < IE. base *apo-,* from] **1.** from; specif., *a)* derived or coming from [men of Ohio] *b)* as relates to [how wise *of* her] *c)* resulting from; through [to die *of* fever] *d)* at a distance from [east *of* the city] *e)* proceeding as a product from; by [the poems *of* Poe] *f)* separated from [robbed *of* his money] *g)* from the whole, or from the total number, constituting [part *of* the time] *h)* made from [a sheet *of* paper] **2.** belonging to [pages *of* a book] **3.** *a)* possessing [a man *of* property] *b)* containing [a bag *of* nuts] **4.** that is; specified as [a height *of* six feet] **5.** with (something specified) as object,

goal, etc. [a reader *of* books] **6.** characterized by [a man *of* honor] **7.** concerning; about [think well *of* me] **8.** set aside for [a day *of* rest] **9.** during [*of* late years] **10.** before: used in telling time [ten *of* nine] **11.** [Archaic] by [rejected *of* men] *Of* is also used in various idiomatic expressions, many of which are entered in this dictionary under the key words

of- *see* OB-

off (ôf) *adv.* [LME. variant of *of,* OF] **1.** so as to be or keep away or at a distance [to move *off,* to ward *off*] **2.** so as to be measured, divided, etc. [to mark *off*] **3.** so as to be no longer on, attached, etc. [take *off* your hat] **4.** (a specified distance) away in space or time [200 yards *off,* two weeks *off*] **5.** so as to be no longer working, going on, etc. [turn the motor *off*] **6.** so as to be less, smaller, etc. [5% *off* for cash] **7.** so as to lose consciousness [to doze *off*] **8.** away from one's work [take a day *off*] —*prep.* **1.** no longer (or not) on, attached, etc. [the car is *off* the road] **2.** away from [to live *off* the campus] **3.** *a)* from the substance of; on [to live *off* the land] *b)* at the expense of **4.** branching out from [an alley *off* Main Street] **5.** free or relieved from [*off* duty] **6.** not up to the usual level, standard, etc. of [*off* one's game] **7.** [Colloq.] no longer using, supporting, etc. [to be *off* liquor] **8.** [Colloq.] from [to buy it *off* him] —*adj.* **1.** not on, attached, etc. [his hat is *off*] **2.** not working, taking place, etc. [the motor is *off*] **3.** on the way [be *off* to bed] **4.** less, smaller, etc. [sales are *off*] **5.** away from work, etc. [the maid is *off* today] **6.** not up to what is usual, standard, etc. [an *off* day] **7.** more remote; further [on the *off* chance] **8.** on the right side, facing forward: said of an animal in double harness, a wagon wheel, etc.: opposed to NEAR **9.** taken care of, provided for, etc. [to be well *off*] **10.** not correct; in error [his figures are *off*] **11.** *Cricket* designating the side of the field facing the batsman **12.** *Naut.* toward the sea —*n.* the fact or condition of being off —*vt.* ☆[Slang] to kill; murder —*interj.* go away! stay away! —**off** and now and then —**off with!** take off! remove! —**off with you!** go away! depart!

off. **1.** office **2.** officer **3.** official

of·fal (ôf'l, äf-) *n.* [ME. *ofall,* lit., off-fall] **1.** [*with sing. or pl. v.*] the entrails, etc. of a butchered animal **2.** refuse; garbage

off·beat (ôf'bēt') *adj.* [< a rhythm in jazz] [Colloq.] not fitting the usual pattern or trend; unconventional, unusual, etc.

☆**off-Broad·way** (ôf'brôd'wā') *adj., adv.* outside the main commercial theatrical district in New York City —*n.* off-Broadway theaters and their productions Also written **Off Broadway**

off-col·or (ôf'kul'ər) *adj.* **1.** varying from the usual, standard, or required color ☆**2.** not quite proper; in poor taste; risqué [an off-color joke]

Of·fen·bach (ôf'n bäk'), **Jacques** (zhäk) (born *Jakob Eberscht*) 1819?-80; Fr. composer, born in Germany

of·fence (ə fens') *n. Brit. sp.* of OFFENSE

of·fend (ə fend') *vi.* [< OFr. < L. *offendere* < *ob-* (see OB-) + *fendere,* to hit: see DEFEND] **1.** to commit a sin or crime; do wrong **2.** to create resentment, anger, etc. —*vt.* **1.** to hurt the feelings of; make resentful, angry, etc. **2.** to be displeasing to (the taste, sense, etc.) —**of·fend'er** *n.*

SYN.—**offend** implies a causing displeasure or resentment in another, either on purpose or without meaning to, by hurting his feelings or by behaving in a way he considers improper [she will be *offended* if she is not invited]; **affront** implies an open and deliberate showing of disrespect or contempt [his uncalled-for criticism of their school *affronted* the graduates]; **insult** implies an affront so insolent or rude that it causes deep humiliation and resentment [to *insult* someone by calling him a liar]

of·fense (ə fens'; ôf'fens, ä'-) *n.* **1.** an offending; specif., *a)* a breaking of the law; sin or crime *b)* a creating of resentment, hurt feelings, etc. **2.** a being offended; esp., a feeling hurt, resentful, or angry **3.** [Rare] something that causes wrongdoing **4.** something that causes resentment, anger, etc. **5.** *a)* the act of attacking *b)* the action of seeking to score in any contest **6.** *a)* the person, army, etc. that is attacking ☆*b)* the side that is seeking to score in any contest —**give offense** to anger, insult, etc.; offend —**take offense** to become offended; feel hurt, angry, etc. —**of·fense'less** *adj.*

SYN.—**offense** implies feelings of being displeased or hurt because of a slight, insult, etc. [don't take *offense* at my criticism]; **resentment,** a stronger word than offense, implies brooding over a wrong or injury along with indignation and ill will toward the offender [his long-lasting *resentment* finally led him to seek revenge]; **umbrage** implies offense or resent-

---

fat, āpe, cär; ten, ēven; is, bīte; gō, hôrn, tool, look; oil, out; up, fur; get; joy; yet; chin; she; thin, then; zh, leisure; ŋ, ring; ə for *a* in *ago, e* in *agent, i* in *sanity, o* in *comply, u* in *focus;* ' as in *able* (ā'b'l); Fr. bàl; ë, Fr. coeur; ö, Fr. feu; ô, Fr. mon; ô, Fr. coq; ü, Fr. duc; r, Fr. cri; H, G. ich; kh, G. doch; ‡foreign; ☆ Americanism; < derived from. See inside front cover.

ment at being slighted or having one's pride hurt [he took *umbrage* at the haughty tone of her letter]; **pique** suggests a temporary feeling of wounded pride, usually over a trifle [her *pique* at not having been invited]; **displeasure** may indicate a feeling varying from dissatisfaction or disapproval to indignation or anger

of·fen·sive (ə fen′siv) *adj.* 1. attacking; aggressive 2. of or for attack ☆3. designating or of the side that is seeking to score in any contest 4. unpleasant; disgusting; repugnant [an *offensive* odor] 5. causing resentment, anger, etc.; insulting [*offensive* remarks] —*n.* 1. attitude or position of attack [to take the *offensive*] 2. an attack or hostile action, esp. by armed forces [to launch an *offensive*] —**of·fen′sive·ly** *adv.* —**of·fen′sive·ness** *n.*

of·fer (ôf′ər, äf′-) *vt.* [OE. *offrian* < LL. *offerre*, to sacrifice < *ob-* (see OB-) + *ferre*, to BEAR¹] 1. to present in an act of worship [to *offer* prayers] 2. to present for acceptance or consideration [to *offer* one's services, a suggestion, etc.] 3. to express willingness or intention (to do something) [to *offer* to go] 4. to show or give signs of [to *offer* resistance] 5. *a*) to present for sale *b*) to bid (a price, etc.) [to *offer* $3.00 for the book] 6. to make a presentation in worship 2. to occur; present itself [when the opportunity *offers*] —*n.* the act of offering or thing offered [will you accept a lower *offer?*] —**of′fer·er, of′fer·or** *n.*

SYN.—offer is the basic term meaning to make something available to another who may accept it or refuse it [to *offer* money, help, etc.]; **proffer**, a somewhat old-fashioned literary term, usually implies an offer to do something for someone, made in a dignified and courteous manner [she refused the gentleman's *proffered* assistance]; **tender** is a highly formal synonym for **offer** [to *tender* one's thanks, resignation, etc.] and is applied specifically to something offered in payment of an obligation; **present** often adds to **offer** the idea of outward show, formality, or ceremony [to *present* a petition to Congress; to *present* a new play]

of·fer·ing (-iŋ) *n.* 1. the act of making an offer 2. something offered; specif., *a*) a contribution *b*) a presentation made in an act of worship ☆*c*) something offered for sale *d*) a theatrical presentation

of·fer·to·ry (ôf′ər tôr′ē, äf′-) *n.*, *pl.* **-ries** [< ML. < LL. *offertorium*, place for offerings < *offerre*, OFFER] [*often* O-] 1. that part of Holy Communion during which the Eucharistic bread and wine are offered to God 2. any collection of money at a church service, or the part of the service for this 3. the prayers or music accompanying the offertory

off·hand (ôf′hand′) *adv.* without prior preparation; at once [can you tell us *offhand* how many will be needed?] —*adj.* 1. said or done offhand; extemporaneous 2. casual, curt, rude, etc. Also **off′hand′ed** —**off′hand′ed·ly** *adv.* —**off′hand′ed·ness** *n.*

of·fice (ôf′is, äf′-) *n.* [< OFr. < L. *officium* < *opus*, a work + *facere*, to DO¹] 1. something done for another; service [I got the job through his good *offices*] 2. an assigned duty, esp. one that is an essential part of one's work; function; task 3. a position of authority or trust, esp. in a government, business, etc. [appointed to high *office*] 4. ☆*a*) any of the branches of the U.S. Government ranking next below the departments [the Printing *Office*] *b*) [Chiefly Brit.] a governmental department [the Foreign *Office*] 5. a place where work or business that is clerical, administrative, professional, etc. is carried on [a lawyer's *office*; the main *office* of a company] 6. a religious ceremony or rite; specif., *a*) [O-] *shortened form of* DIVINE OFFICE *b*) [*often pl.*] any special rites —see SYN. at FUNCTION and POSITION

☆**office boy** a boy who works in an office, doing odd jobs and errands

of·fice·hold·er (-hōl′dər) *n.* a government official

of·fi·cer (ôf′ə sər, äf′-) *n.* 1. anyone holding an office or position of authority in a government, business, society, etc. 2. a policeman 3. a person holding a position of authority in the armed forces; specif., *same as* COMMISSIONED OFFICER 4. the captain or any of the mates of a nonnaval ship —*vt.* 1. to provide with officers 2. to command; direct

officer of the day the military officer in overall charge of the interior guard and security of his garrison for any given day

of·fi·cial (ə fish′əl) *adj.* 1. of or holding an office, or position of authority 2. by, from, or with the proper authority; authorized or authoritative [an *official* request] 3. formal or ceremonious and often involving persons of authority [an *official* welcome to the city] 4. formally set or prescribed [the *official* cial date of publication] —*n.* 1. a person holding office ☆2. *Sports* one who supervises an athletic contest —**of·fi′cial·ly** *adv.*

of·fi·cial·dom (ə fish′əl dəm) *n.* 1. officials as a group 2. the domain or position of officials

of·fi·cial·ese (ə fish′ə lēz′) *n.* the pompous, wordy, and involved language typical of official communications and reports

of·fi·cial·ism (ə fish′əl iz′m) *n.* the characteristic practices of officials, especially in being too much concerned with official routine and regulations

of·fi·ci·ate (ə fish′ē āt′) *vi.* **-at·ed, -at·ing** 1. to perform the duties of an office 2. to be in charge of a religious ceremony [a Lutheran minister *officiated* at the wedding] 3. *Sports* to act as referee, umpire, etc. —**of·fi′ci·a′tion** *n.* —**of·fi′ci·a′tor** *n.*

of·fi·cious (ə fish′əs) *adj.* [< L. < *officium*, OFFICE] offering unwanted advice or services; meddlesome —**of·fi′cious·ly** *adv.* —**of·fi′cious·ness** *n.*

off·ing (ôf′iŋ) *n.* [< OFF] 1. the distant part of the sea visible from the shore 2. distance, or position at a distance, from the shore —**in the offing** 1. at some distance but in sight 2. at some indefinite time in the future

off·ish (ôf′ish) *adj.* [Colloq.] *same as* STANDOFFISH

off-key (ôf′kē′) *adj.* 1. not on the right note; flat or sharp 2. not quite in accord with what is normal, fitting, etc.

off-lim·its (ôf′lim′its) *adj.* ruled to be a place that cannot be entered, visited, patronized, etc. by a specific group [*off*-limits to military personnel]

off·set (ôf′set′; *for v. usually* ôf set′) *n.* 1. an offshoot; extension; branch; spur 2. anything that balances or compensates for something else 3. a ledge formed in a wall by a reduction in its thickness above 4. *Mech.* a bend in a pipe, rod, etc. to permit it to pass an obstruction 5. *a*) *same as* OFFSET PRINTING *b*) an impression made by this process —*adj.* 1. of, relating to, or being an offset 2. that is offset —*vt.* **-set′, -set′ting** 1. to balance, compensate for, etc. [the farmer's profit on wheat *offset* his loss on corn] 2. to make an offset in 3. to make (an impression) by offset printing —*vi.* to project or develop as an offset

offset printing a lithographic printing process in which the inked impression of a plate is first made on a rubber-covered roller, from which it is transferred to paper

off·shoot (ôf′shoot′) *n.* 1. a shoot growing from the main stem of a plant 2. anything that branches off, or derives from, a main source

OFFSHOOT

off·shore (ôf′shôr′) *adj.* 1. moving away from the shore [an *offshore* breeze] 2. at some distance from shore [an *offshore* island] —*adv.* away or far from the shore

off·side (ôf′sīd′) *adj.* *Sports* not in the proper position for play, as a football player who is ahead of the ball before the play has begun —*n.* an offside play

off·spring (ôf′spriŋ′) *n.*, *pl.* **-spring′, -springs′** 1. a child or animal as related to its parent 2. descendants; progeny 3. a result

off·stage (ôf′stāj′) *n.* that part of a stage, as the wings, not seen by the audience —*adj.* 1. in or from the offstage —*adv.* 1. to the offstage [to go *offstage*] 2. when not actually appearing before the public

off-white (ôf′hwīt′, -wīt′) *adj.* of any of various shades of grayish-white or yellowish-white

☆**off year** 1. a year in which a major election does not take place 2. a year of little production, poor crops, not much activity, etc. —**off′-year′** *adj.*

OFr. Old French

oft (ôft) *adv.* [OE.] *chiefly poetic var. of* OFTEN

of·ten (ôf′'n, ôf′t'n) *adv.* [ME. var. of OFT] many times; frequently —*adj.* [Archaic] frequent

of·ten·times (-tīmz′) *adv. same as* OFTEN: also [Chiefly Poet.] **oft′times′**

Og·den (äg′dən, ôg′-) [after P. *Ogden*, local fur trader] city in N Utah: pop. 69,000

o·gee (ō′jē, ō jē′) *n.* [< OFr. *ogive*] 1. an S-shaped curve, line, molding, etc. 2. a pointed arch formed with the curve of an ogee on each side: also **ogee arch**

o·gle (ō′g'l, ä′-) *vi., vt.* **o′gled, o′gling** [prob. < LowG. *oegeln* < *oog*, the eye] to keep looking (at) boldly and with obvious desire; make eyes (at) —*n.* an ogling look —**o′gler** *n.*

O·gle·thorpe (ō′g'l thôrp′), **James Edward** 1696-1785; Eng. philanthropist: founder of the colony of Georgia (1733)

OGEE ARCH

o·gre (ō′gər) *n.* [Fr. < ? L. *Orcus*, Pluto, Hades] **1.** in fairy tales and folklore, a monster or giant who eats people **2.** a hideous or cruel man —**o′gre·ish, o′grish** (-grish) *adj.* — **o′gress** (-gris) *n.fem.*

oh (ō) *interj.* **1.** an exclamation of surprise, fear, wonder, pain, etc. **2.** a word used in speaking directly to someone, as to attract attention [*oh*, waiter!] —*n., pl.* **oh's, ohs** a use of this exclamation

OH Ohio

O. Henry *see* HENRY

OHG, OHG., O.H.G. Old High German

O·hi·o (ō hī′ō) **1.** [after the river] Middle Western State of the U.S.: 41,222 sq. mi.; pop. 10,652,000; cap. Columbus: abbrev. **O., OH 2.** [ult. < Iroquoian, lit., large river] river flowing from SW Pa. southwestward into the Mississippi —**O·hi′o·an** (-ə wən) *adj., n.*

ohm (ōm) *n.* [after G. S. *Ohm* (1789–1854), G. physicist] a unit of electrical resistance, equal to the resistance of a circuit in which an electromotive force of one volt maintains a current of one ampere —**ohm′ic** *adj.*

ohm·me·ter (ōm′mēt′ər) *n.* an instrument for measuring directly electrical resistance in ohms

-oid (oid) [< Gr. < *eidos*, a form, shape: for IE. base see VISION] *a suffix meaning* like, resembling [*crystalloid*]

oil (oil) *n.* [< OFr. < L. *oleum* < Gr. *elaion*, (olive) oil] **1.** any of various greasy substances that come from animal, vegetable, and mineral sources and that can be burned: oils are liquid at ordinary temperatures and soluble in certain organic solvents, as ether, but not in water **2.** *same as* PETROLEUM **3.** any of various substances that look and feel like oil **4.** *same as: a)* OIL COLOR *b)* OIL PAINTING —*vt.* to lubricate or supply with oil — *adj.* of, from, or like oil, or having to do with the production or use of oil —**oiled** *adj.* —**oil′er** *n.*

oil cake a mass of crushed linseed, cottonseed, etc. from which the oil has been pressed out, used as livestock feed and as a fertilizer

oil·can (oil′kan′) *n.* a can for holding oil, esp. one with a spout, used for lubricating machinery, etc.

oil·cloth (-klôth′, -kläth′) *n.* cloth made waterproof with oil or with heavy coats of paint: used to cover tables, shelves, etc.

oil color paint made by grinding a pigment in oil

☆**oil field** a place where valuable deposits of oil are found

oil of vitriol *same as* SULFURIC ACID

oil painting 1. a picture painted in oil colors **2.** the art of painting in oil colors

oil·pa·per (-pā′pər) *n.* paper made transparent and waterproof by treatment with oil

oil shale a kind of shale from which oil can be obtained by distillation

oil·skin (-skin′) *n.* **1.** cloth made waterproof by treatment with oil **2.** [*often pl.*] a garment or outfit made of this, as a suit of jacket and trousers

☆**oil slick** a film of oil on water, forming a smooth area

oil·stone (-stōn′) *n.* a whetstone treated with oil

☆**oil well** a well bored through layers of rock, etc. to a supply of petroleum

oil·y (-ē) *adj.* **oil′i·er, oil′i·est 1.** of, like, or containing oil **2.** covered with oil; greasy **3.** too polite or flattering —**oil′i·ly** *adv.* —**oil′i·ness** *n.*

☆**oink** (oiŋk) *n.* the grunt of a pig, or a sound imitating it —*vi.* to grunt as or like a pig

oint·ment (oint′mənt) *n.* [< OFr., ult. < L. *unguentum*: see UNGUENT] an oily substance rubbed on the skin to heal it or make it smooth and soft; unguent

Oise (wäz) river flowing from S Belgium southwest through N France into the Seine

O·jib·wa (ō jib′wä, -wä, -wə) *n.* [Algonquian *ojibway*, to pucker: from the puckered seam on their moccasins] **1.** *pl.* **-was, -wa** a member of a group of N. American tribes living in an area between Michigan and North Dakota **2.** their Algonquian language —*adj.* of these tribes Also **O·jib′way** (-wā)

☆**OK, O.K.** (ō′kā′; *also, & for v. & n. usually,* ō′kā′) *adj., adv., interj.* [abbrev. for "oll korrect," jocular misspelling of ALL CORRECT] all right; correct —*n., pl.* **OK's, O.K.'s** approval —*vt.* **OK'd** or **O.K.'d, OK'ing** or **O.K.'ing** to put an OK on; approve

OK Oklahoma

o·ka·pi (ō kä′pē) *n., pl.* **-pis, -pi:** see PLURAL, II, D, 1 [native Afr. name] an African animal related to the giraffe, but having a much shorter neck

☆**o·kay** (ō′kā′) *adj., adv., interj., n., vt.* *colloq. var. of* OK

O·kee·cho·bee (ō′kē chō′bē), **Lake** [< AmInd.] lake in SE Fla., at the N edge of the Everglades: see map at EVERGLADES

O·ke·fe·no·kee Swamp (ō′kə fə nō′kē) [< AmInd., lit., trembling earth] swamp in SE Ga. & NE Fla.

O·khotsk (ō kätsk′; *Russ.* ô khôtsk′), **Sea of** arm of the Pacific, off the E coast of Siberia

☆**O·kie** (ō′kē) *n.* [OK(LAHOMA) + -IE] a migratory farm worker, esp. one forced from Oklahoma by drought, loss of farms through foreclosed mortgages, etc., in the late 1930's

O·ki·na·wa (ō′kə nä′wə) largest island of the Ryukyus, northeast of Taiwan

O·kla·ho·ma (ō′klə hō′mə) [< Choctaw *okla*, people + *homma*, red] State of the south central U.S.: 69,919 sq. mi.; pop. 2,559,000; cap. Oklahoma City: abbrev. **Okla., OK** —**O′kla·ho′man** *adj., n.*

Oklahoma City capital of Okla., in the central part: pop. 366,000 (met. area 641,000)

o·kra (ō′krə) *n.* [< WAfr. name] **1.** a tall plant with slender, ribbed, sticky green pods **2.** the pods, used as a cooked vegetable, in soups, etc.

-ol¹ (ōl, ôl) [< (ALCOH)OL] *a suffix used in chemistry to mean* an alcohol or phenol [*menthol*]

-ol² (ōl, ôl) *var. of* -OLE

OL., O.L. Old Latin

O·laf (ō′ləf, -läf) **1. Olaf II, Saint,** (*Olaf Haraldsson*) 995?–1030; king of Norway (1015–28); patron saint of Norway **2. Olaf V** 1903– ; king of Norway (1957–) Also sp. **Olav**

old (ōld) *adj.* **old′er** or **eld′er, old′est** or **eld′est** [OE. *ald* < IE. base *al-*, to grow] **1.** having lived or existed for a long time; aged **2.** of or characteristic of aged people **3.** of a certain age [a boy ten years *old*] **4.** made some time ago; not new **5.** known from the past [up to his *old* tricks] **6.** [*often* O-] designating the earliest stage of a language [*Old* English] **7.** worn out by age or use; shabby **8.** former [he returned to his *old* neighborhood] **9.** having had long experience [an *old* hand at this work] **10.** having existed long ago; ancient [an *old* civilization] **11.** of long standing [an *old* tradition] **12.** designating the earlier or earliest of two or more [the *Old* World] **13.** [Colloq.] dear: a term of affection [*old* boy] Also used colloquially to add emphasis [a fine *old* time] —*n.* **1.** time long past; yore [days of *old*] **2.** a person of a specified age: used in hyphenated compounds [a six-year-*old*] **3.** something old (with *the*) —**old′ish** *adj.* —**old′ness** *n.*

old age the later years of a long life, when one becomes less strong and vigorous: see also MIDDLE AGE

☆**old country** the country from which an immigrant came, esp. a country in Europe

old·en (ōl′d'n) [Poet.] of former times; old; ancient

Old English the West Germanic, Low German language of the Anglo-Saxons, spoken in England from c. 400 to c. 1100 A.D.

old-fash·ioned (ōld′fash′ənd) *adj.* suited to or favoring the styles, ideas, etc. of past times; out-of-date —☆*n.* [*also* O- F-] a cocktail made with whiskey, soda water, bitters, sugar, and fruit

old fogy, old fogey *see* FOGY

Old French the French language from c. 800 to c. 1550 A.D., esp. French from the 9th to the 14th century

☆**Old Glory** the flag of the United States

Old Guard [after Napoleon's imperial guard (1804)] **1.** any group that has long defended a cause **2.** the most conservative element of a group, party, etc.

old hand a person having much skill or experience

old hat [Slang] **1.** old-fashioned **2.** well-known to the point of being trite or commonplace

Old High German the High German language from the 8th to the 12th century

OKAPI
(to 5 ft. high at shoulder)

☆**old·ie, old·y** (ōl'dē) *n., pl.* **old'ies** [Colloq.] an old joke, song, movie, etc.

Old Irish Irish Gaelic before the 11th century

old lady [Slang] **1.** one's mother **2.** one's wife

Old Latin the Latin language before c. 75 B.C.

old-line (ōld'līn') *adj.* **1.** old and well-established **2.** following tradition; conservative

Old Low German the Low German language from its earliest period to the 12th century A.D.

old maid 1. a woman, esp. an older woman, who has never been married; spinster **2.** a prim, prudish, fussy person — **old'-maid'ish** *adj.*

old man [Slang] **1.** one's father **2.** one's husband **3.** [*usually* O- M-] any man in authority, as the head of a company, captain of a ship, etc.

old master 1. any great European painter before the 18th cent. **2.** a painting by any of these

old moon the moon in its last quarter, when it appears as a crescent curving to the left

Old Nick [prob. contr. < NICHOLAS] the Devil; Satan: also **Old Harry**

Old Norman French *same as* NORMAN FRENCH

Old Norse the North Germanic language of the Scandinavian peoples before the 14th century

Old Prussian a Baltic language which became extinct in the 17th century

old rose grayish or purplish red —**old'-rose'** *adj.*

Old Saxon a West Germanic language known chiefly from manuscripts of the 9th and 10th centuries A.D.

old school a group of people who cling to traditional or conservative ideas, methods, etc.

☆**Old South** the South before the Civil War

☆**old squaw** a black-and-white sea duck of northern regions, with a long, pointed tail

old·ster (ōld'stər) *n.* [Colloq.] a person who is no longer a youngster; old or elderly person

old style 1. an old style of type with narrow, light letters **2.** [O- S-] the old method of reckoning time according to the Julian calendar, which was off one day every 128 years — **old'-style'** *adj.*

Old Testament *name given by Christians to* the Holy Scriptures of Judaism, the first of the two general divisions of the Christian Bible

old-time (ōld'tīm') *adj.* **1.** of or like past times **2.** of long standing or experience [an *old-time* member of the club]

old-tim·er (-tī'mər) *n.* [Colloq.] **1.** a longtime resident, employee, etc. **2.** an old-fashioned person

old wives' tale a silly story or superstition

Old World the Eastern Hemisphere, often specifically Europe —**old'-world'** *adj.*

‡**o·lé** (ō lā') *interj., n.* [Sp.] a shout of approval, triumph, joy, etc., as at bullfights

-ole (ōl) [< L. *oleum*, oil] *a suffix used in chemistry indicating:* **1.** a five-member, closed-chain compound **2.** a compound without hydroxyl

o·le·ag·i·nous (ō'lē aj'i nəs) *adj.* [< Fr. < L. < *olea*, olive tree] oily; greasy; unctuous —**o'le·ag'i·nous·ly** *adv.* —**o'le·ag'i·nous·ness** *n.*

o·le·an·der (ō'lē an'dər, ō'lē an'dər) *n.* [ML.] a poisonous evergreen shrub with fragrant white, pink, or red flowers

o·le·as·ter (ō'lē as'tər) *n.* [< L. < *olea*, olive tree] any of a group of plants often grown for ornament; esp., *same as* RUSSIAN OLIVE

o·le·ate (ō'lē āt') *n.* a salt or ester of oleic acid

o·le·fin (ō'lə fin) *n.* [< Fr. < L. *oleum*, oil + *facere*, to make] any unsaturated hydrocarbon with the general formula C_nH_{2n}, as ethylene: also **o'le·fine** (-fin, -fēn') —**o'le·fin'ic** *adj.*

o·le·ic (ō lē'ik, ō'lē-) *adj.* [< L. *oleum*, oil + -IC] **1.** of or from oil **2.** of oleic acid

oleic acid an oily acid, $C_{17}H_{33}COOH$, present in most fats and oils as an ester, used in soaps, etc.

o·le·in (ō'lē in) *n.* [< Fr. < L. *oleum*, an oil] **1.** a liquid glyceride, present in olive oil, etc. **2.** the liquid part of a fat

☆**o·le·o** (ō'lē ō') *n. clipped form of* OLEOMARGARINE

o·le·o- [< L. *oleum*, an oil] *a combining form meaning* oil, olein, or oleic [*oleomargarine*]

☆**o·le·o·mar·ga·rine, o·le·o·mar·ga·rin** (ō'lē ō mär'jə rin) *n.* [< Fr.: see prec. & MARGARINE] *full name of* MARGARINE

o·le·o·res·in (ō'lē ō rez'n) *n.* **1.** a mixture of a resin and an essential oil, as turpentine, occurring naturally in various plants **2.** a prepared solution of resin in an essential oil

ol·fac·tion (äl fak'shən, ōl-) *n.* [see OLFACTORY] **1.** the sense of smell **2.** the act of smelling

ol·fac·to·ry (-tər ē, -trē) *adj.* [< L. pp. of *olfacere*, to smell < *olere*, to have a smell + *facere*, to make] of the sense of smell: also **ol·fac'tive** —*n., pl.* **-ries** [*usually pl.*] an organ of smell

OLG, OLG., O.L.G. Old Low German

ol·i·garch (äl'ə gärk') *n.* any of the rulers of an oligarchy

ol·i·gar·chy (-gär'kē) *n., pl.* **-chies** [Gr. *oligarchia:* see OLIGO- & -ARCHY] **1.** a form of government in which a few persons hold the ruling power **2.** a state so governed **3.** those ruling such a state —**ol'i·gar'chic, ol'i·gar'chi·cal, ol'i·gar'chal** (-k'l) *adj.*

ol·i·go- [Gr. < *oligos*, small] *a combining form meaning* few, small, little: also **olig-**

Ol·i·go·cene (äl'ə gō sēn') *adj.* [< OLIGO- + Gr. *kainos*, new] designating of the third epoch of the Tertiary Period in the Cenozoic Era —**the Oligocene** the Oligocene Epoch or its rocks: see GEOLOGIC TIME CHART

ol·i·gop·o·ly (äl'ə gäp'ə lē) *n., pl.* **-lies** [OLIG(O)- + (MON)OPOLY] control of a certain market by a few companies or suppliers —**ol'i·gop'o·list** *n.* —**ol'i·gop'o·lis'tic** *adj.*

o·li·o (ō'lē ō') *n., pl.* **o'li·os'** [< Sp. *olla:* see OLLA] **1.** a spicy stew **2.** a medley, as of musical numbers

ol·ive (äl'iv) *n.* [OFr. < L. *oliva* < Gr. *elaia*] **1.** *a)* an evergreen tree of southern Europe and the Near East, with an edible fruit *b)* the small, oval fruit, having a single, hard pit: it is eaten green or ripe, or pressed to extract its oil *c)* the wood of this tree **2.** an olive branch or wreath **3.** the dull, yellowish-green color of the unripe fruit —*adj.* **1.** of the olive **2.** olive-colored **3.** designating a family of trees and shrubs with loose clusters of four-parted flowers, including the olives, ashes, lilacs, etc.

OLIVE (tree, leaves & fruit)

olive branch 1. the branch of the olive tree, a symbol of peace **2.** any peace offering

olive drab 1. a shade of greenish brown **2.** woolen cloth dyed this color and used for U.S. Army uniforms **3.** [*pl.*] such a uniform —**ol'ive-drab'** *adj.*

olive oil a light-yellow oil pressed from ripe olives, used in cooking, soap, etc.

Ol·i·ver (äl'ə vər) [Fr. *Olivier*, prob. < MLowG. < *alf*, elf + *hari*, an army] a masculine name

ol·i·vine (äl'ə vēn') *n.* [OLIV(E) + -INE⁴] a green silicate of magnesium and iron

ol·la (äl'ə; *Sp.* ôl'yä) *n.* [Sp. < L.] ☆**1.** a large-mouthed pot or jar **2.** a spicy stew

Ol·mec (äl'mek) *n., pl.* **-mecs, -mec** a member of an ancient Indian people in Mexico —*adj.* of the Olmecs

ol·o·gy (äl'ə jē) *n., pl.* **-gies** [< -LOGY] a branch of learning; science: humorous usage

O·lym·pi·a (ō lim'pē ə, ə-) **1.** plain in the W Peloponnesus: site of the ancient Olympic games: see map at GREECE **2.** [ult. < Mount OLYMPUS] capital of Wash., on Puget Sound: pop. 23,000

O·lym·pi·ad (ō lim'pē ad') *n.* [*often* o-] **1.** in ancient Greece, any of the four-year periods between Olympic games, used in reckoning time **2.** a celebration of the modern Olympic games

O·lym·pi·an (ō lim'pē ən) *n.* **1.** *Gr. Myth.* any of the gods on Mount Olympus **2.** a native of Olympia **3.** a participant in the Olympic games —*adj.* **1.** of Olympia or Mount Olympus **2.** powerful and majestic, like a god [*Olympian* dignity] **3.** of the ancient Olympic games

O·lym·pic (ō lim'pik, ə-) *adj. same as* OLYMPIAN —*n.* [*pl.*] the Olympic games (preceded by *the*)

Olympic games 1. an ancient Greek festival with contests in athletics, poetry, and music, held every four years at Olympia to honor Zeus **2.** a modern international athletic competition generally held every four years in a selected city

Olympic Mountains one of the Coast Ranges, in NW Wash.

Olympic National Park national park in NW Wash., in the Olympic Mountains

O·lym·pus (ō lim'pəs, ə-), **Mount** mountain in N Greece, between Thessaly & Macedonia: in Greek mythology, the home of the gods

-o·ma (ō'mə) [ModL. < Gr. *-ōma*] *a suffix meaning* tumor [*sarcoma*]

O·ma·ha (ō′mə hô, -hä) [< Fr. < name of a Sioux tribe, lit., ? upstream people] city in E Nebr., on the Missouri River: pop. 347,000 (met. area 541,000)

O·man (ō män′) **1.** country in SE Arabia, on the Arabian Sea: 82,000 sq. mi.; pop. c.750,000; cap. Muscat **2. Gulf of,** arm of the Arabian Sea, between Iran & Oman

O·mar Khay·yám (ō′mär kī yäm′, ō′mər kī yam′) ?–1123?; Persian poet & mathematician

o·ma·sum (ō mā′səm) **n.,** pl. **-sa** (-sə) [ModL. < L., bullock's tripe < Gaul.] the third division in the stomach of a cudchewing animal, as the cow: see illustration at RUMINANT

OMB, O.M.B. Office of Management and Budget

om·buds·man (äm′bədz mən) **n.,** pl. **-men** [Sw. < ombud, deputy + man, MAN] a public official appointed to investigate citizens' complaints against government agencies that may be violating the rights of individuals

Om·dur·man (äm′door män′) city in WC Sudan, on the Nile, opposite Khartoum: pop. 154,000

o·me·ga (ō mā′gə, -meg′ə, -mē′gə) **n.** [Gr. o mega, lit., great (i.e., long) o] **1.** the twenty-fourth and final letter of the Greek alphabet (Ω, ω) **2.** the last (of any series); end

om·e·let, om·e·lette (äm′lit, äm′ə let) **n.** [< Fr., ult. < L. lamella, small plate] eggs beaten up, often with milk or water, cooked as a pancake in a frying pan and served usually folded over and often with a filling, as of jelly

o·men (ō′mən) **n.** [L.] a thing or happening supposed to foretell a future event, either good or evil; augury [a red sunset is an omen of good weather] —**vt.** to be an omen of; augur

om·i·cron, om·i·kron (äm′ə krän′, ō′mə-; Brit. ō mī′krən) **n.** [Gr. o mikron, lit., small o] the fifteenth letter of the Greek alphabet (O, o)

om·i·nous (äm′ə nəs) **adj.** [L. ominosus] of or serving as an evil omen; threatening; sinister —**om′i·nous·ly adv.**

SYN- —**ominous** is used of something that seems to threaten but does not necessarily suggest that a disaster will result [her request was met by an ominous silence]; **portentous** is applied literally to a sign or warning, esp. of evil, but is now more often used of that which causes awe or amazement because of its wonderful or extraordinary character [the first landing on the moon was a portentous event]; **fateful** may imply control by or as if by fate, but is now usually applied to that which is of very important or crucial significance [a fateful truce conference]; **foreboding** implies a feeling that something evil or harmful will happen [a foreboding anxiety]

o·mis·si·ble (ō mis′ə b'l) **adj.** that can be omitted

o·mis·sion (ō mish′ən) **n.** [< LL. omissio] **1.** an omitting or being omitted **2.** anything omitted

o·mit (ō mit′) **vt.** **o·mit′ted, o·mit′ting** [< L. omittere < ob- (see OB-) + mittere, to send: see MISSION] **1.** to fail to include; leave out [to omit a name from a roster] **2.** to fail to do; neglect [don't omit to inform your sister] —**o·mit′ter n.**

om·ni- [L. < omnis, all] a combining form meaning all, everywhere [omniscient]

om·ni·bus (äm′nə bəs, -ni bus′) **n.,** pl. **-bus·es** [Fr. < L., lit., (carriage) for all] **1.** same as BUS (sense 1) **2.** a one-volume collection of works by one author, or on one theme, published separately earlier —**adj.** providing for many things at once [an omnibus clause in a contract]

☆**omnibus bill** a bill in a legislature covering various items, appropriations, etc.

om·ni·di·rec·tion·al (äm′ni də rek′shən 'l) **adj.** [OMNI- + DIRECTIONAL] for sending or receiving radio or sound waves in or from any direction [an omnidirectional antenna]

om·ni·far·i·ous (äm′nə fer′ē əs) **adj.** [< L. omnifarius < omnis, all + fari, to speak] of all kinds, varieties, or forms

om·nip·o·tence (äm nip′ə təns) **n.** **1.** the state or quality of being omnipotent **2.** [O-] God

om·nip·o·tent (äm nip′ə tənt) **adj.** [OFr. < L. < omnis, all + potens, able] having unlimited power or authority; all-powerful —**the Omnipotent** God —**om·nip′o·tent·ly adv.**

om·ni·pres·ent (äm′ni prez′'nt) **adj.** [< ML. < L. omnis, all + praesens, present] present in all places at the same time —**om′ni·pres′ence n.**

SYN- —**omnipresent** strictly applies only to God as being present in all places at the same time but is loosely used of anything that is always present in a particular situation [the omnipresent spirit of competition in business]; **ubiquitous** is used of that which seems to be present everywhere, but not always at the same time or place [the ubiquitous tourists]

☆**om·ni·range** (äm′nə ränj′) **n.** [< omni(directional radio)

range] a system of navigation by means of a radio transmitter on the ground that sends signals in all directions, from which an airplane pilot can receive his bearing

om·nis·cient (äm nish′ənt) **adj.** [< ML. < L. omnis, all + prp. of scire, to know] knowing all things —**the Omniscient** God —**om·nis′cience n.** —**om·nis′cient·ly adv.**

om·ni·um-gath·er·um (äm′nē əm gath′ər əm) **n.** [L. omnium, of all + imitation Latin form of GATHER] a miscellaneous collection of persons or things

om·niv·o·rous (äm niv′ər əs) **adj.** [< L.: see OMNI- & -VOROUS] **1.** eating any sort of food, whether animal or vegetable [bears are omnivorous] **2.** taking in everything, without choosing [an omnivorous reader] —**om·niv′o·rous·ly adv.** —**om·niv′o·rous·ness n.**

Omsk (ômsk) city in W Siberia, on the Irtysh: pop. 800,000

on (än, ôn) **prep.** [OE. on, an] **1.** above, but in contact with and supported by; upon [a pack on her back] **2.** in contact with; covering or attached to [a cloth on the table] **3.** so as to be supported by [to lean on one's elbow] **4.** in the surface of [a scratch on his arm] **5.** near to [a cottage on the lake] **6.** at the time of [on entering] **7.** with (something specified) as the basis [on purpose] **8.** connected with, as a part [on the faculty] **9.** engaged in [on a trip] **10.** in a state of [on parole] **11.** as a result of [a profit on the sale] **12.** in the direction of [a light shone on us] **13.** so as to affect [to put a curse on someone] **14.** through the use of; by means of [most cars run on gasoline] **15.** concerning [an essay on war] **16.** coming after [insult on insult] ☆**17.** [Colloq.] chargeable to; at the expense of [have a drink on me] ☆**18.** [Slang] using; addicted to [to be on drugs] **19.** [Slang] carried by; with [I have no money on me] —**adv.** **1.** in a situation of contacting, being supported by, or covering [put your shoes on] **2.** in a direction toward someone or something [looked on] **3.** forward; ahead [move on] **4.** continuously [she sang on] **5.** into operation or action [turn the light on] ☆**6.** Baseball on base **7.** Theater on stage —**adj.** **1.** in action or operation [the TV is on] **2.** arranged or planned for [tomorrow's game is still on] —**n.** the fact or state of being on —**and so on** and more like what comes before; and so forth —☆**have something** (or **nothing**) **on someone** [Colloq.] to have some (or no) harmful information about someone —**on and off** not continuously; from time to time; intermittently —**on and on** continuously; without stopping —☆**on to** [Slang] aware of, esp. aware of the real nature or meaning of

-on (än) a suffix designating: **1.** [< -on in argon] an inert gas [radon] **2.** [< -on in ion] a basic particle [electron]

ON., ON, O.N. Old Norse

on·a·ger (än′ə jər) **n.,** pl. **-gri′** (-grī′), **-gers** [< L. < Gr. < onos, ass + agrios, wild] **1.** a wild ass of central Asia **2.** a catapult used in ancient warfare for throwing stones

o·nan·ism (ō′nə niz′m) **n.** [< Onan in the Bible: Gen. 38:9] **1.** withdrawal in sexual intercourse before ejaculation takes place **2.** masturbation —**o′nan·ist n.** —**o′nan·is′tic adj.**

once (wuns) **adv.** [ME. ones, genitive of on, ONE] **1.** one time; one time only [she eats only once a day] **2.** at any time; ever [he'll succeed if once given a chance] **3.** at some time in the past; formerly [a once famous poet] **4.** by one degree [a cousin once removed] —**conj.** as soon as; if ever [once I find the book, I'll get it to you] —**adj.** former —**n.** one time [go this once] —**all at once 1.** all at the same time **2.** suddenly —**at once 1.** immediately **2.** at the same time —**for once** for at least one time —**once and again** time after time; repeatedly —**once (and) for all** finally; decisively —**once in a while** now and then; occasionally —**once or twice** not often; a few times —**once upon a time** long ago

☆**once-o·ver** (wuns′ō′vər) **n.** [Colloq.] **1.** a swift glance taking in the main details **2.** a quick cleaning or going-over

on·col·o·gy (äŋ käl′ə jē, än-) **n.** [< Gr. onkos, a mass + -LOGY] the branch of medicine dealing with tumors —**on′co·log′ic** (-kə läj′ik) **adj.** —**on·col′o·gist n.**

on·com·ing (än′kum′iŋ) **adj.** coming toward one; approaching [oncoming traffic] —**n.** approach [the oncoming of spring]

one (wun) **adj.** [OE. an] **1.** being a single thing [one man] **2.** forming a whole; united [with one accord] **3.** designating a person or thing as contrasted with another [from one day to another] **4.** being unique; only [the one answer to a problem] **5.** single in kind; the same [of one mind] **6.** a certain but unspecified [one day last week] : also used in place of "a" for emphasis [she's one beautiful girl] —n. 1. the first and lowest cardinal number; 1; I 2. a single person or thing [I'll take the blue one] 3. anything consisting of a single unit or having the number "one"; specif., ☆[Colloq.] a one-dollar bill —pron. 1. some, or a certain, person or thing [one of us must go] 2. any person or thing; anyone or anything [what else can one do?] 3. the person or thing previously mentioned [he rents a house, but I own one] —all one making no difference —at one of the same opinion; in accord —one and all everybody —one another each one the other; each other: see EACH OTHER, under EACH —one by one one following the other —one of those things something that cannot be avoided, changed, etc.

-one (ōn) [arbitrary use of Gr. -ōnē] a suffix used in chemistry, meaning a ketone [acetone]

☆**one-base hit** (wun′bās′) Baseball a hit by which the batter reaches first base safely: also [Slang] **one′-bag′ger** (-bag′ər) n.

one-horse (wun′hôrs′) adj. 1. drawn by or using one horse ☆2. [Colloq.] small, unimportant, etc. [a one-horse town]

O·nei·da (ō nī′də) n. [Iroquois Oneiute, lit., standing rock] 1. pl. **-das, -da** a member of a tribe of Indians orig. of New York State but now also of Wisconsin and Ontario 2. their Iroquoian language

O'Neill (ō nēl′), **Eugene** (**Gladstone**) 1888–1953; U.S. playwright

one·ness (wun′nis) n. 1. singleness; unity 2. unity of mind, feeling, etc. 3. sameness; identity

☆**one-night stand** (wun′nīt′) a single appearance in a town by a traveling show, lecturer, etc.

☆**one-on-one** (wun′än wun′, -ôn-) adj., adv. Basketball, Football, etc. concentrating one's play against a single player on the opposing team

on·er·ous (än′ər əs, ō′nər-) adj. [< MFr. < L. onerosus < onus, a load] hard to put up with; being a burden —**on′er·ous·ly** adv. —**on′er·ous·ness** n.

SYN. —**onerous** applies to that which is hard to put up with, often because it is boring or annoying [the onerous task of taking inventory]; **burdensome** applies to that which tires or troubles the mind or spirit as well as the body [burdensome responsibilities]; **oppressive** emphasizes the cruelty of the person or thing that causes hardship, or the harshness of the hardship itself [oppressive weather; an oppressive king]; **exacting** suggests the making of great demands on the attention, skill, care, etc. [an exacting supervisor; the exacting work of an accountant]

one·self (wun′self′, wunz′-) pron. a person's own self: also **one's self** —**be oneself** 1. to act normally 2. to be natural or sincere —**by oneself** alone; unaccompanied —**come to oneself** to recover one's senses or ability to judge

one·sid·ed (wun′sīd′id) adj. 1. on, having, or involving only one side 2. larger, heavier, etc. on one side; lopsided 3. favoring one side; unfair [a one-sided report in a newspaper] 4. uneven or unequal [a one-sided race] —**one′-sid′ed·ly** adv. —**one′-sid′ed·ness** n.

one-step (-step′) n. an old ballroom dance with quick walking steps in 2/4 time —vi. **-stepped′, -step′ping** to dance the one-step

one-time (-tīm′) adj. at a past time; former [our one-time mayor]

one-to-one (wun′tə wun′) adj. 1. permitting the pairing of an element of one group with a single corresponding element of another group 2. Math. with each member of one set having a partner in the other set

one-track (wun′trak′) adj. 1. having a single track ☆2. [Colloq.] limited in scope [a one-track mind]

one-up (-up′) adj. [Colloq.] having an advantage (over another): often in **be one-up on** —vt. **-upped′, -up′ping** [Colloq.] to seize an advantage over (another) —**one′-up′man·ship′** n.

one-way (-wā′) adj. 1. moving, or allowing movement, in one direction only [a one-way street] 2. without any action or obligation in return [a one-way contract]

on·go·ing (än′gō′iŋ) adj. going on; in process

on·ion (un′yən) n. [< OFr. < L. unio, oneness, unity, hence a kind of single onion] 1. a plant of the lily family, with an edible bulb having a strong, sharp smell and taste 2. the bulb

on·ion·skin (-skin′) n. ☆a tough, thin, translucent paper, often used for carbon copies

on·look·er (än′look′ər) n. one who watches without taking part; spectator —**on′look′ing** adj., n.

on·ly (ōn′lē) adj. [OE. anlic < an, one + -lic, -LY¹] 1. alone of its or their kind; sole [the only suit he owns; her only son] 2. alone in being the best; finest [the only one for the job] — adv. 1. and no other; and no (or nothing) more; solely [drink

water only] 2. (but) in what follows or in the end [to meet one crisis, only to face another] 3. as recently as [only last fall] — conj. [Colloq.] except that; but [I'd go, only it's late] —**if . . .** only would that; I wish that [if she would only leave!] —**only too** very [I'll be only too glad to do it]

on·o·mat·o·poe·ia (än′ə mat′ə pē′ə, -mät′-) n. [LL. < Gr. onoma, a NAME + poiein, to make: see POEM] 1. formation of a word (as chickadee or tinkle) by imitating the sound associated with the object or action 2. the use of such words, as in poetry —**on′o·mat′o·poe′ic, on′o·mat′o·po·et′ic** (-pō et′ik) adj.

On·on·da·ga (än′ən dô′gə, ōn′-; -dä′-) n. [Iroquois Ononta'ge', lit., on top of the hill] 1. pl. **-gas, -ga** a member of a tribe of Indians orig. of New York State but now also of Ontario 2. their Iroquoian language —**On′on·da′gan** adj.

ONormFr. Old Norman French

on·rush (än′rush′, ôn′-) n. a headlong dash forward; strong onward rush —**on′rush′ing** adj.

on·set (-set′) n. 1. an attack [the onset of enemy troops forced a retreat] 2. a beginning; start [the onset of winter]

on·shore (-shôr′) adj. 1. moving onto or toward the shore 2. on land [an onshore patrol] —adv. toward the shore

on·side (-sīd′) adj. 1. not offside ☆2. Football designating a kickoff that goes far enough to be legal: said esp. of such a kick kept short on purpose in the hope that the receiver will fumble

on·slaught (-slôt′) n. [< Du. annslag < slagen, to strike] a violent, intense attack

On·tar·i·o (än ter′ē ō) 1. [after the lake, below] province of SC Canada, between the Great Lakes & Hudson Bay: 412,582 sq. mi.; pop. 8,264,000; cap. Toronto: abbrev. **Ont.** 2. [after the province in Canada] city in S Calif.: pop. 64,000 3. **Lake,** [< Fr. < Iroquoian, lit., fine lake] smallest & easternmost of the Great Lakes, between N.Y. & Ontario, Canada: 7,313 sq. mi.

on·to (än′tōō, ôn′-; -tə) prep. 1. to a position on [she climbed onto the roof] ☆2. [Slang] aware of the real nature or meaning of [he's onto our schemes] Also **on to**

onto- [< Gr. prp. of einai, to be] a combining form meaning: 1. being; existence 2. organism

on·tog·e·ny (än täj′ə nē) n. [ONTO- + -GENY] the development or life cycle of an individual organism: distinguished from PHYLOGENY: also **on·to·gen·e·sis** (än′tə jen′ə sis) — **on′to·ge·net′ic** (-jə net′ik), **on′to·gen′ic** adj.

on·tol·o·gy (än täl′ə jē) n. [< ModL.: see ONTO- & -LOGY] the branch of philosophy dealing with the nature of being or reality —**on·to·log·i·cal** (än′tə läj′i k'l) adj. —**on′to·log′i·cal·ly** adv. —**on·tol′o·gist** n.

o·nus (ō′nəs) n. [L.] 1. a hard or unpleasant task, duty, etc.; burden [the onus of cleaning the garage fell to him] 2. responsibility for a wrong; blame [who bears the onus for the attack] 3. same as BURDEN OF PROOF

on·ward (än′wərd, ôn′-) adv. toward or at a position ahead; forward [they marched onward] : also **on′wards** —adj. moving or directed ahead; advancing [an onward course]

on·yx (än′iks) n. [< OFr. < L. < Gr. onyx, nail, claw: its color resembles that of the fingernail] a variety of agate with different colored layers

o·o- [< Gr. ōion] a combining form meaning egg or ovum: also written **oö-**

oo·dles (ōō′d'lz) n.pl. [< ? HUDDLE] [Colloq.] a great amount; very many [she has oodles of friends]

ONYX

o·o·gen·e·sis (ō′ə jen′ə sis) n. [OO- + -GENESIS] Biol. the process by which the ovum is formed and becomes mature —**o′o·ge·net′ic** (-jə net′ik) adj.

o·o·lite (ō′ə līt′) n. [< Fr.: see OO- & -LITE] 1. a tiny particle formed of layers of calcium carbonate in the sea: also **o′o·lith** (-lith) 2. a rock made up of many such particles —**o′o·lit′ic** (-lit′ik) adj.

o·ol·o·gy (ō äl′ə jē) n. [OO- + -LOGY] the study of birds' eggs —**o·o·log·i·cal** (ō′ə läj′i k'l) adj. —**o·ol′o·gist** n.

oo·long (ōō′lôn′) n. [< Chin. wulung, lit., black dragon] a dark Chinese tea, partly fermented before being dried

oo·mi·ac, oo·mi·ak (ōō′mē ak′) n. same as UMIAK

oops (ōōps, oops) interj. same as WHOOPS

ooze¹ (ōōz) n. [OE. wos, sap] an oozing or something that oozes —vi. **oozed, ooz′ing** 1. to flow or leak out slowly, as through tiny holes; seep [oil oozed through small cracks] 2. to give forth moisture, as through pores **3.** to escape or disappear gradually /hope *oozed* away/ —*vt.* to give forth, or exude /the tree *oozed* sap; a voice that *oozed* friendliness/

ooze² (o̅o̅z) *n.* [OE. *wase:* for IE. base see VIRUS] **1.** soft mud or slime; esp., the sediment at the bottom of a lake, ocean, etc. **2.** a muddy area; bog

oo·zy¹ (o̅o̅′zē) *adj.* **-zi·er, -zi·est** oozing moisture —**oo′zi·ly** *adv.* —**oo′zi·ness** *n.*

oo·zy² (o̅o̅′zē) *adj.* **-zi·er, -zi·est** full of or like ooze; slimy — **oo′zi·ly** *adv.* —**oo′zi·ness** *n.*

op- *see* OB-

op. 1. opera **2.** operation **3.** opposite **4.** opus

O.P. Order of Preachers (Dominicans)

O.P., OP, o.p., op 1. out of print **2.** *Philately* overprint

o·pac·i·ty (o̅ pas′ə tē) *n.* **1.** the state, quality, or degree of being opaque **2.** *pl.* **-ties** an opaque thing

o·pal (o̅′p'l) *n.* [< L. < Gr. *opallios* < Sans. *upala,* precious stone] a mineral that is an amorphous form of silica, of various colors that usually show shifting changes as light passes through: some varieties are used as semiprecious stones

o·pal·es·cent (o̅′pə les′'nt) *adj.* showing shifting changes of color, like opal —**o′pal·esce′** *vi.* **-esced′, -esc′ing** —**o′pal·es′cence** *n.*

o·pal·ine (o̅′p'l in, -ēn′, -īn′) *adj.* of or like opal —*n.* a translucent, milky glass

o·paque (o̅ pāk′) *adj.* [L. *opacus,* shady] **1.** not letting light through; not transparent /an *opaque* screen/ **2.** not reflecting light or not shining; dull /the desk had an *opaque* surface/ **3.** hard to understand; obscure **4.** slow in understanding; obtuse; stupid —*n.* anything opaque —*vt.* **o·paqued′, o·paqu′ing** to make opaque —**o·paque′ly** *adv.* —**o·paque′ness** *n.*

☆**op** (**art**) (äp) [< OP(TICAL)] a style of abstract painting using geometrical patterns to create various optical illusions

op. cit. [L. *opere citato*] in the work cited

ope (o̅p) *adj., vt., vi.* oped, op′ing [Poet.] open

OPEC (o̅′pek) Organization of Petroleum Exporting Countries

o·pen (o̅′p'n) *adj.* [OE.: for IE. base see UP¹] **1.** allowing someone or something to enter or exit; not closed or shut /open doors/ **2.** allowing freedom to see or pass through; not enclosed, fenced in, etc.; unobstructed /*open* country; *open* fields/ **3.** unsealed; unwrapped /an *open* package/ **4.** *a)* not covered /an *open* sewer/ *b)* unprotected or undefended /an *open* city/ **5.** spread out; unfolded /an *open* book/ **6.** having spaces, gaps, etc. /*open* ranks/ **7.** free from ice /the lake is *open*/ **8.** *a)* not keeping anyone out /an *open* meeting/ *b)* ready to admit customers, clients, etc. /the store is *open* now/ **9.** free to be argued; not settled /an *open* question/ **10.** *a)* not prejudiced or narrow-minded /an *open* mind/ *b)* liberal; generous /give with an *open* heart/ ☆**11.** *a)* free from legal restrictions /an *open* season on deer/ *b)* free from discrimination /*open* housing/ *c)* that does not enforce regulations on drinking, gambling, etc. /the city is wide *open*/ **12.** having political, civil, and social freedom /an *open* society/ **13.** in force or operation /an *open* account/ **14.** not already taken or engaged /the job is *open*/ **15.** accessible; available /there are three courses *open* to us/ **16.** not secret; public /an *open* quarrel/ **17.** frank; candid /an *open* manner/ **18.** *Math.* of a set whose every point has a neighborhood completely contained in the set **19.** *Music a)* not stopped by the finger: said of a string *b)* not closed at the top: said of an organ pipe *c)* produced by an open string or pipe or without a slide or key: said of a tone *d)* not muted **20.** *Phonetics a)* low *b)* fricative *c)* ending in a vowel or diphthong: said of a syllable —*vt.* **1.** to make open, or no longer closed, shut, obstructed, etc. /to *open* a door, drain, etc./ **2.** *a)* to make an opening in /to *open* an abscess/ *b)* to produce (a hole, way, etc.) **3.** to make spaces between; spread out; expand /to *open* ranks/ **4.** to expose (*to* an influence or action) **5.** to make available without restriction, fee, etc. /to *open* land for a park/ **6.** *a)* to free from prejudice /to *open* one's mind/ *b)* to make liberal and generous /to *open* one's heart/ **7.** to reveal; disclose /to *open* the records to the public/ **8.** to begin (bidding, a session, etc.) **9.** to start operating, going, etc. /to *open* a new shop/ —*vi.* **1.** to become open /the door *opened* slowly/ **2.** to spread out; expand; unfold /her hand began to *open*/ **3.** to become revealed, disclosed, etc. /a scenic view *opened* before us/ **4.** to give access (with *to, into, on,* etc.) /the door *opens* onto the porch/ **5.** to

begin; start /the program *opened* with a song/ **6.** to start operating, going, etc. /school will *open* in September/ **7.** to begin a series of performances, games, etc. /our season *opened* with a win/ —*n.* [*usually* O-] any of various golf tournaments for both professionals and amateurs —*see* SYN *at* FRANK — **open out 1.** to expand **2.** to develop **3.** to reveal —**open to 1.** willing to receive, discuss, etc. **2.** liable to **3.** available or accessible to or for —**open up 1.** to make or become open **2.** to spread out; unfold **3.** to start; begin **4.** [Colloq.] to begin firing a gun or guns **5.** [Colloq.] to speak freely or with great feeling **6.** [Colloq.] to go or make go faster —**the open 1.** any open, clear area **2.** the outdoors **3.** public knowledge —**o′pened** *adj.* —**o′pen·ly** *adv.* —**o′pen·ness** *n.*

open air the outdoors —**o′pen-air′** *adj.*

☆**o·pen-and-shut** (o̅′p'n 'n shut′) *adj.* easily decided; very simple or obvious /an *open-and-shut* case/

open chain the structural form of certain molecules in which the chain of atoms does not form a ring

open door 1. a policy of admitting everyone **2.** equal opportunity for all nations to trade with a given nation —**o′pen-door′** *adj.*

o·pen-end (-end′) *adj.* **1.** describing an investment company that does not limit the shares issued so that they can be sold or redeemed on demand **2.** allowing additional borrowing over a period of time on the original security /an *open-end* mortgage/ **3.** *same as* OPEN-ENDED

o·pen-end·ed (-en′did) *adj.* **1.** having no set limits as to length, direction, amount, etc. /an *open-ended* discussion/ **2.** open to change /an *open-ended* plan/ **3.** allowing for an answer worded as one chooses rather than one chosen from among fixed answers: said of a question —**o′pen-end′ed·ness** *n.*

o·pen·er (-ər) *n.* **1.** a person or thing that opens **2.** a device for opening bottles, cans, etc. **3.** the first game in a series, first act in a variety show, etc.

o·pen-eyed (-īd′) *adj.* with the eyes open or wide open, as in awareness or amazement

o·pen-faced (-fāst′) *adj.* **1.** having a frank, honest face ☆**2.** designating a sandwich without a top slice of bread: also **o′pen-face′**

o·pen·hand·ed (-han′did) *adj.* generous —**o′pen·hand′ed·ly** *adv.* —**o′pen·hand′ed·ness** *n.*

o·pen-heart·ed (-här′tid) *adj.* **1.** not reserved; candid; frank **2.** kindly; generous —**o′pen·heart′ed·ly** *adv.* —**o′pen·heart′ed·ness** *n.*

o·pen-hearth (-härth′) *adj.* designating or using a furnace with a wide, saucer-shaped hearth and a low roof, for making steel

o·pen-heart surgery (-härt′) heart surgery done with the chest opened and while the blood is being recirculated and oxygenated by mechanical means

open house 1. an informal party at one's home, with guests coming and going freely **2.** a time when a school, business, etc. is open to visitors

o·pen·ing (-iŋ) *n.* **1.** a becoming or making open **2.** an open place; hole; gap ☆**3.** a clearing in a wooded area **4.** *a)* a beginning /the *opening* of a new store/ *b)* a first performance /the *opening* of a play/ **5.** an opportunity /at the first *opening* in the conversation, he made his suggestion/ **6.** a job available /the company has no *openings* now/ **7.** *Chess, Checkers,* etc. the series of first moves

OPEN-HEARTH FURNACE (A, lining; B, metal; C, heater ports; D, gas; E, air: fired alternately from either end)

open letter a letter written as to a specific person but published in a newspaper, etc. for all to read

open market *same as* FREE MARKET

o·pen-mind·ed (-mīn′did) *adj.* open to new ideas; not biased —**o′pen-mind′ed·ly** *adv.* —**o′pen-mind′ed·ness** *n.*

o·pen-mouthed (-mouthd′, -moutht′) *adj.* **1.** having the mouth open **2.** staring with the mouth open, as in surprise or confusion

☆**open primary** a primary election in which voters need not declare their party but may vote for candidates of any party

fat, āpe, cär, ten, ēven, is, bīte; gō, hôrn, to̅o̅l, look; oil, out; up, fur; get; joy; yet; chin; she; thin, then; zh, leisure; ŋ, ring; ə for a in ago, e in agent, i in sanity, o in comply, u in focus; ′ as in able (ā′b'l); Fr. bál; ë, Fr. coeur; ö, Fr. feu; Fr. mon; δ, Fr. coq; ü, Fr. duc; r, Fr. cri; H, G. ich; kh, G. doch; ‡foreign; ☆ Americanism; < derived from. See inside front cover.

open sea 1. the large area of sea away from coastlines, bays, inlets, etc. **2.** *same as* HIGH SEAS

open secret something supposed to be secret but known to almost everyone

open sesame 1. magic words spoken to open the door of the thieves' den in the story of Ali Baba **2.** any sure means of getting what or where one wants

☆**open shop** a factory, business, etc. employing workers regardless of whether or not they belong to the union

open stock merchandise, as dishes, available in sets, with individual pieces kept in stock

o·pen·work (-wurk′) *n.* ornamental work, as in cloth, with openings in the material

op·er·a[1] (äp′ər ə, äp′rə) *n.* [It. < L., a work: for IE. base see OPUS] **1.** a play with most or all of the text sung, accompanied by an orchestra, and usually with costuming, sets, and dances **2.** the art of such plays **3.** the score, libretto, or performance of an opera **4.** a theater for operas

o·pe·ra[2] (ō′pə rə, äp′ər ə) *n. pl. of* OPUS

op·er·a·ble (äp′ər ə b'l) *adj.* [< ML.: see OPERATE & -ABLE] **1.** that can be done; practicable [*an operable* plan] **2.** that can be treated by surgery [*an operable* hernia] —**op′er·a·bil′i·ty** *n.*

‡**o·pé·ra bouffe** (ȯ pä rȧ bo͞of′; *E.* äp′ər ə bo͞of′) [Fr.] comic opera; esp., an operatic farce

opera glasses a pair of small telescopes fastened together, used at the opera, in theaters, etc.

opera hat a man's tall, collapsible silk hat

opera house a theater chiefly for the performance of operas

op·er·ant (äp′ər ənt) *adj.* operating, or producing an effect or effects —*n.* one that operates

op·er·ate (äp′ə rāt′) *vi.* **-at′ed, -at′ing** [< L. pp. of *operari,* to work < *operis,* genitive of *opus:* see OPUS] **1.** to be in action; work [his car isn't *operating* well] **2.** to produce a certain effect [this drug *operates* on the heart] **3.** to carry on military movements **4.** to perform a surgical operation [to *operate* on diseased tonsils] —*vt.* **1.** [Now Rare] to effect **2.** *a)* to put or keep in action; work (a machine, etc.) *b)* to conduct or manage (a business, etc.) **3.** [Colloq.] to do a surgical operation on

OPERA GLASSES

op·er·at·ic (äp′ə rat′ik) *adj.* of, like, or fit for opera —**op′er·at′i·cal·ly** *adv.*

op·er·a·tion (äp′ə rā′shən) *n.* **1.** the act, process, or method of operating [explain the *operation* of a typewriter] **2.** the condition of being in action or at work [the new factory will be in *operation* soon] **3.** a process or action that is part of a series in some work [many *operations* are involved in automobile manufacture] **4.** any strategic military movement **5.** any specific plan, project, etc. [*Operation* Cleanup] **6.** a treatment by surgery to heal or correct an injury or defect **7.** *Math.* any process, as addition or division, involving a change in quantity —**in operation 1.** in action; working **2.** in force

op·er·a·tion·al (-'l) *adj.* **1.** of the operation of a device, system, process, etc. **2.** *a)* that can be used or operated *b)* in use; operating **3.** of or ready for use in a military operation —**op′er·a′tion·al·ly** *adv.*

op·er·a·tion·al·ize (-'l īz′) *vt.* **-ized′, -iz′ing** to make operational; put into operation —**op′er·a′tion·al·i·za′tion** *n.*

op·er·a·tive (äp′ə rā′tiv, äp′ər ə-) *adj.* **1.** capable of or in operation [our new factory will be *operative* next month] **2.** producing the results wanted; effective [an *operative* law] **3.** connected with physical work or mechanical action [low *operative* expenses] **4.** of or resulting from a surgical operation —*n.* **1.** a worker, esp. a skilled industrial worker ☆**2.** a detective or spy —**op′er·a′tive·ly** *adv.*

op·er·a·tor (äp′ə rāt′ər) *n.* **1.** one who operates; specif., *a)* a person who brings something about; agent ☆*b)* a person who works a machine or device [a telephone *operator*] *c)* a person engaged in commercial or industrial operations or enterprises ☆**2.** [Slang] a clever person who generally manages to achieve his ends

o·per·cu·lum (ō pur′kyo͞o ləm) *n., pl.* **-la** (-lə), **-lums** [ModL. < L., lid, dim. < *operire,* to close] any of various covering flaps or lidlike structures in plants and animals, as the bony covering protecting the gills of fishes: see illustration at FISH —**o·per′cu·lar** *adj.* —**o·per′cu·late** (-lit, -lāt′), **o·per′cu·lat′ed** *adj.*

op·er·et·ta (äp′ə ret′ə) *n.* [It., dim. of *opera,* OPERA[1]] a light, amusing opera with spoken dialogue

o·phid·i·an (ō fid′ē ən) *n.* [< ModL. < Gr. *ophis,* a snake + -AN] a snake or serpent —*adj.* of or like a snake

oph·thal·mi·a (äf thal′mē ə) *n.* [< LL. < Gr. < *ophthalmos,* the eye] severe inflammation of the eyeball or conjunctiva

oph·thal·mic (-mik) *adj.* of the eye; ocular

oph·thal·mo- [< Gr. *ophthalmos,* the eye] *a combining form meaning* the eye: also **oph·thalm-**

oph·thal·mol·o·gy (äf′thal mäl′ə jē, äp′-; -thə-) *n.* the branch of medicine dealing with the structure, functions, and diseases of the eye —**oph′thal·mo·log′i·cal** (-mə läj′i k'l) *adj.* —**oph′thal·mol′o·gist** *n.*

oph·thal·mo·scope (äf thal′mə skōp′, äp′-) *n.* [OPHTHALMO- + -SCOPE] an instrument for examining the interior of the eye —**oph′thal·mo·scop′ic** (-skäp′ik) *adj.* —**oph′thal·mos′co·py** (-thəl mäs′kə pē) *n.*

-o·pi·a (ō′pē ə) [< Gr. < *ōps,* an EYE] *a combining form meaning* a (specified kind of) eye defect [*myopia*]

o·pi·ate (ō′pē it, -āt′) *n.* **1.** any medicine containing opium or any of its derivatives, and that is used to bring sleep, reduce pain, etc. **2.** anything quieting, soothing, etc. —*adj.* **1.** containing opium **2.** bringing sleep, quiet, etc.; narcotic

o·pine (ō pīn′) *vt., vi.* **o·pined′, o·pin′ing** [< MFr. < L. *opinari:* see OPINION] to hold or express (some opinion): now usually humorous

o·pin·ion (ə pin′yən) *n.* [< OFr. < L. < *opinari,* to think: for IE. base see OPTION] **1.** a belief not based on what is known to be true or certain but on what seems true, valid, or probable [in my *opinion,* it will rain before dark] **2.** a judgment or impression about something [what is your *opinion* of her work?] **3.** an expert's formal judgment [it would be better to get several medical *opinions*]

SYN.—**opinion** is used of a conclusion or judgment which seems true or probable to one's own mind even though it may still be argued [it's my *opinion* that he'll agree]; **belief** refers to the acceptance by the mind of an idea, esp. a doctrine or dogma that others accept [religious *beliefs*]; a **view** is an opinion affected by the personal way one looks at things [she gave us her *views* on life]; a **conviction** is a strong belief about whose truth one has no doubts [I have a *conviction* of his innocence]; **sentiment** refers to an opinion that is the result of careful thought but that is influenced by emotion; **persuasion** refers to a strong belief that cannot be shaken because one wishes to believe in its truth

o·pin·ion·at·ed (-āt′id) *adj.* holding unreasonably or stubbornly to one's own opinions —**o·pin′ion·at′ed·ly** *adv.* —**o·pin′ion·at′ed·ness** *n.*

o·pin·ion·a·tive (-āt′iv, -ə tiv) *adj.* **1.** of, or of the nature of, opinion **2.** opinionated —**o·pin′ion·a′tive·ly** *adv.* —**o·pin′ion·a′tive·ness** *n.*

o·pi·um (ō′pē əm) *n.* [L. < Gr. < *opos,* vegetable juice] a narcotic drug made from the juice of the seed capsules of the opium poppy, used in medicine to relieve pain and bring sleep: opium and the drugs derived from it (morphine, codeine, and heroin) are habit-forming

opium poppy an annual poppy with large, white or purple flowers, the source of opium

O·por·to (ō pôr′tō) seaport in N Portugal: pop. 305,000

☆**o·pos·sum** (ə päs′əm) *n., pl.* **-sums, -sum:** see PLURAL, II, D, 1 [< Algonquian, lit., white beast] any of several American marsupials; esp., the American (or Virginian) opossum, a small, tree-dwelling mammal: it is active at night and seems to become paralyzed or to be pretending to be dead when trapped

opp. 1. opposed **2.** opposite

op·po·nent (ə pō′nənt) *n.* [< L. prp. of *opponere* < *ob-* (see OB-) + *ponere,* to set] one who opposes, as in a fight, game, etc.; adversary —*adj.* opposing; antagonistic

SYN.—**opponent** refers to anyone who is opposed to one, as in a fight, game, debate, etc.; **antagonist** implies more active opposition, esp. in a struggle for control or power; **adversary** usually suggests that there is ill will or hostility in the conflict; **enemy** may imply actual hatred of the opponent and a desire to injure him, or it may simply refer to any member of the opposing group, nation, etc., whether or not there is personal dislike or ill will involved; **foe** is now a somewhat literary synonym for enemy —**ANT.** ally, confederate

OPOSSUM (body 12–20 in. long; tail 10–21 in. long)

op·por·tune (äp′ər to͞on′, -tyo͞on′) *adj.* [< MFr. < L. *opportunus,* lit., before the port < *ob-* (see OB-) + *portus,* PORT[1]] **1.**

right for the purpose: said of time *[the letter arrived at the opportune moment]* **2.** happening or done at the right time; timely *[an opportune remark]* —see SYN. at TIMELY —**op′por·tune′ly** *adv.* —**op′por·tune′ness** *n.*

op·por·tun·ism (-iz′m) *n.* the act or practice of taking advantage of every opportunity, as in politics, for one's own benefit without considering what is right or proper —**op′por·tun′ist** *n.* —**op′por·tun·is′tic** *adj.* —**op′por·tun·is′ti·cal·ly** *adv.*

op·por·tu·ni·ty (äp′ər tōō′nə tē, -tyōō′-) *n., pl.* **-ties** **1.** a combination of circumstances favorable for the purpose *[their arrival created an opportunity to show his paintings]* **2.** a good chance or occasion, as to advance oneself

op·pos·a·ble (ə pō′zə b'l) *adj.* **1.** that can be resisted or opposed **2.** that can be placed opposite something else *[human beings have an opposable thumb]* —**op·pos′a·bil′i·ty** *n.*

op·pose (ə pōz′) *vt.* **-posed′, -pos′ing** *[< OFr. < L. opponere:* see OB- & POSITION*]* **1.** to set against; place opposite, in balance or contrast *[to each of my arguments she opposed one of her own]* **2.** to speak or act against; resist *[he opposes raising taxes]* —*vi.* to act in opposition —**op·pos′er** *n.*

SYN.—**oppose** implies attacking something that threatens or interferes with one; **resist** implies defending against something that is already actively opposed to one *[one opposes a legislative act under consideration, one resists a law already passed by refusing to obey it]*; **withstand** usually implies resistance that keeps the attack from being successful *[can they withstand the heavy bombing?]* —ANT. submit, succumb, comply

op·po·site (äp′ə zit) *adj.* *[OFr. < L. pp. of opponere:* see prec.*]* **1.** set against, facing, or back to back; at the other end or side *[the opposite end of a table; the opposite side of a coin]* **2.** unfriendly; resistant **3.** entirely different; exactly contrary *[hot is opposite to cold]* **4.** *Bot.* growing in pairs, but separated by a stem —*n.* anything opposed or opposite *[love is the opposite of hate]* —*adv.* on opposing sides or in an opposite position —*prep.* facing; across from *[we sat opposite each other]* —**op′po·site·ly** *adv.* —**op′po·site·ness** *n.*

SYN.—**opposite** is applied to things that are directly against each other in position, direction, etc. *[they sat at opposite ends of the room]*; **contrary** adds to this notions of disagreement or unfriendliness *[they hold contrary views]*; **antithetical** implies that the contrasted things are as far apart as possible, as though at the opposite ends of a pole *[their tastes are completely antithetical]* —ANT. same, identical, like

op·po·si·tion (äp′ə zish′ən) *n.* **1.** an opposing or the condition of being opposed *[ideas that are in opposition]* **2.** resistance or a struggle against *[his plan met opposition]* **3.** anything that opposes; specif., *[often O-]* a political party opposing the party in power **4.** *Astrol., Astron.* the position of two heavenly bodies 180° apart in longitude —**op′po·si′tion·al** *adj.* —**op′po·si′tion·ist** *n., adj.*

op·press (ə pres′) *vt.* *[< OFr. < ML. < L. pp. of opprimere < ob-* (see OB-) *+ premere,* PRESS¹*]* **1.** to weigh heavily on the mind, spirits, or senses of; trouble *[oppressed by a feeling of fear]* **2.** to keep down by the cruel or unjust use of power; tyrannize over *[the king oppressed his subjects]* —**op·pres′sor** *n.*

op·pres·sion (ə presh′ən) *n.* **1.** an oppressing or being oppressed **2.** a thing that oppresses **3.** a feeling of being weighed down, as with worries or problems

op·pres·sive (ə pres′iv) *adj.* **1.** hard to put up with; burdensome *[oppressive tasks]* **2.** cruel and unjust; harsh *[the dictator's oppressive laws]* **3.** weighing heavily on the mind, etc.; distressing *[an oppressive fear of death]* —see SYN. at ONEROUS —**op·pres′sive·ly** *adv.* —**op·pres′sive·ness** *n.*

op·pro·bri·ous (ə prō′brē əs) *adj.* **1.** expressing scorn or dislike; abusive *[opprobrious names]* **2.** [Now Rare] disgraceful *[opprobrious behavior]* —**op·pro′bri·ous·ly** *adv.* —**op·pro′bri·ous·ness** *n.*

op·pro·bri·um (-əm) *n.* *[L. < opprobare,* to reproach *< ob-* (see OB-) *+ probrum,* a disgrace*]* **1.** the disgrace or scorn brought on by conduct viewed as very shameful **2.** anything bringing shame or disgrace **3.** scorn or contempt for something thought of as inferior

op·so·nin (äp′sə nin) *n.* *[< L. < Gr. opsōnion,* food *+ -IN¹]* a substance in blood serum that acts on bacteria and foreign cells in such a way that they are more easily destroyed by white blood cells —**op·son′ic** (-sän′ik) *adj.*

opt (äpt) *vi.* *[< Fr. < L. optare:* see OPTION*]* to make a choice (often with *for*) —**opt out (of)** to choose not to be or continue in (an activity, group, etc.)

opt. 1. optical **2.** optician **3.** optics **4.** optional

op·ta·tive (äp′tə tiv) *adj.* *[< Fr. < LL. < L. optare:* see OPTION*]* expressing wish or desire *[Greek grammar has an optative mood]* —*n.* the optative mood, or a verb in this mood —**op′ta·tive·ly** *adv.*

op·tic (äp′tik) *adj.* *[< Fr. < ML. < Gr. optikos:* for IE. base see EYE*]* of the eye or sense of sight

op·ti·cal (-'l) *adj.* **1.** of the sense of sight; visual *[an optical illusion]* **2.** of optics **3.** for aiding vision *[eyeglasses are optical instruments]* —**op′ti·cal·ly** *adv.*

op·ti·cian (äp tish′ən) *n.* a person who makes or deals in optical instruments, esp. one who prepares eyeglasses according to the prescriptions of an ophthalmologist or optometrist

optic nerve a nerve that connects the retina of the eye with the brain: see illustration at EYE

op·tics (äp′tiks) *n.pl.* *[with sing. v.]* *[< OPTIC]* the branch of physics dealing with the nature and properties of light and vision

op·ti·mal (äp′tə məl) *adj.* most favorable or desirable; best; optimum —**op′ti·mal·ly** *adv.*

op·ti·mism (äp′tə miz′m) *n.* *[< Fr. < L. optimus,* best (see OPTIMUM)*]* **1.** *Philos. a)* the doctrine that the existing world is the best possible *b)* the belief that in the long run good prevails over evil **2.** the tendency to take the most hopeful or cheerful view of matters —**op′ti·mist** (-mist) *n.* —**op′ti·mis′tic** (-mis′tik), **op′ti·mis′ti·cal** *adj.* —**op′ti·mis′ti·cal·ly** *adv.*

op·ti·mum (-məm) *n., pl.* **-mums, -ma** (-mə) *[L.,* neut. of *optimus,* best *< ops,* riches: see OPUS*]* the best or most favorable degree, condition, amount, etc. *[the balance of trade was at an optimum]* —*adj.* most favorable or desirable; best

op·tion (äp′shən) *n.* *[Fr. < L. optio < optare,* to wish *< IE.* base *op-,* to choose*]* **1.** a choosing; choice *[he had no option but to go]* **2.** the right or liberty of choosing *[give me the option of buying your share or selling mine]* **3.** something that is or can be chosen **4.** the right to buy, sell, or lease at a fixed price, sign a contract, etc. within a specified time —see SYN. at CHOICE

op·tion·al (-'l) *adj.* left to one's option, or choice; elective *[a book list of optional readings]* —**op′tion·al·ly** *adv.*

☆**op·tom·e·trist** (äp täm′ə trist) *n.* a specialist in optometry

op·tom·e·try (äp täm′ə trē) *n.* *[see* OPTIC *& -METRY]* the profession of examining the eyes for errors in vision and of prescribing glasses to correct such weaknesses —**op·to·met·ric** (äp′tə met′rik), **op′to·met′ri·cal** *adj.*

op·u·lent (äp′yə lənt) *adj.* *[< L. < ops:* see OPUS*]* **1.** wealthy; rich *[an opulent nation]* **2.** abundant; profuse *[an opulent growth of hair]* —see SYN. at RICH —**op′u·lence, op′u·len·cy** *n.* —**op′u·lent·ly** *adv.*

o·pun·ti·a (ō pun′shē ə, -shə) *n.* *[ModL. < L. (herba) Opuntia,* (plant) of *Opus,* city in Greece*]* any of various cactus plants; esp., *same as* PRICKLY PEAR

o·pus (ō′pəs) *n., pl.* **o·pe·ra** (ō′pə rə, äp′ər ə), **o′pus·es** *[L.,* a work *< IE.* base *op-,* to work, from which also comes L. *ops,* riches*]* a work; composition; esp., any of the musical works of a composer numbered in the order in which they appeared

-o·py (ō′pē) *same as* -OPIA

or¹ (ôr; *unstressed* ər) *conj.* *[ME.,* in form a contr. of *other,* either, but actually *< OE. oththe]* a coordinating conjunction introducing: *a)* another choice or possibility *[beer or wine, either go or stay]* *b)* a term having the same meaning *[ill, or sick]*

or² (ôr) *n.* *[Fr. < L. aurum,* gold*]* *Heraldry* gold or yellow

-or (ər; *occas.* ôr) *[< OFr. < L. -or]* a suffix meaning: **1.** a person or thing that *[inventor]* **2.** quality or condition *[error]*: in Brit. usage, often **-our**

OR Oregon

‡**o·ra** (ôr′ə) *n. pl.* of OS²

or·a·cle (ôr′ə k'l, är′-) *n.* *[OFr. < L. oraculum < orare,* to pray *< os:* see ORAL*]* **1.** in ancient Greece and Rome, *a)* a place or priest through which gods were consulted for the answers to questions *b)* the answer or message as given by such a priest **2.** *a)* any person or agency believed to be in communication with a deity *b)* any person of great wisdom *c)* opinion or statements of any such oracle

o·rac·u·lar (ô rak′yoo lər) *adj.* of or like an oracle; wise, mysterious, etc. —**o·rac′u·lar′i·ty** (-yə lar′ə tē) *n.* —**o·rac′u·lar·ly** *adv.*

o·ral (ôr′əl) *adj.* *[< L. oris,* genitive of *os,* the mouth *< IE.* base *ous-,* mouth*]* **1.** uttered; spoken, not written **2.** of or using

---

fat, āpe, cär; ten, ēven; is, bīte; gō, hôrn, tōōl, look; oil, out; up, fur; get; joy; yet; chin; she; thin, then; zh, leisure; ŋ, ring; ə for *a* in *ago, e* in *agent, i* in *sanity, o* in *comply, u* in *focus;* ′ as in *able* (ā′b'l); Fr. bal; ë, Fr. coeur; ö, Fr. feu; Fr. mon; ô, Fr. coq; ü, Fr. duc; r, Fr. cri; H, G. ich; kh, G. doch; ‡foreign; ☆ Americanism; < derived from. See inside front cover.

speech **3.** of, at, or near the mouth [*oral surgery*] —☆ *n.* an examination, as in a college, in which the questions and answers are spoken, not written —**o'ral·ly** *adv.*

SYN. —**oral** refers to that which is spoken, rather than written, to communicate something [an *oral* promise, request, etc.]; **verbal,** though sometimes used in the same way as **oral,** in careful discrimination refers to the use of words, either written or oral, rather than pictures, symbols, etc. to communicate an idea or feeling [a *verbal* image, portrait, etc.]

oral history 1. historical information consisting of personal memories, usually in the form of tape-recorded interviews **2.** such an interview

O·ran (ō rän′) seaport in N Algeria, on the Mediterranean: pop. 325,000

Or·ange[1] (ôr′inj, är′-) ruling family of the Netherlands: see NASSAU

Or·ange[2] (ôr′inj, är′-) **1.** [prob. after the *orange* groves there] city in SW Calif.: suburb of Los Angeles: pop. 77,000 **2.** river in South Africa, flowing from NE Lesotho into the Atlantic

or·ange (ôr′inj, är′-) *n.* [< OFr. < Pr. *auranja* < Sp. *naranja* < Ar. < Per. < Sans. *naranga*] **1.** a reddish-yellow, round, edible citrus fruit with a sweet, juicy pulp **2.** the evergreen tree it grows on **3.** reddish yellow —*adj.* **1.** reddish-yellow **2.** made with or flavored like orange

or·ange·ade (-ād′) *n.* a drink made of orange juice and water, usually sweetened

Orange Free State province of South Africa, west of Lesotho

Or·ange·man (ôr′inj mən, är′-) *n., pl.* **-men** [after the Prince of *Orange,* later WILLIAM III] a member of a secret society organized in northern Ireland in 1795 to support Protestantism

orange pekoe a black tea of Ceylon and India

or·ange·wood (ôr′inj wood′, är′-) *n.* the wood of the orange tree —*adj.* of orangewood

o·rang·u·tan (ō raŋ′oo tan′, ə-; -taŋ′) *n.* [< Malay < *oran,* man + *utan,* forest] an ape of Borneo and Sumatra, with shaggy, reddish-brown hair, very long arms, small ears, and a hairless face: also sp. **o·rang'ou·tang'** (-taŋ′)

o·rate (ô rāt′, ôr′āt) *vi.* **o·rat'ed, o·rat'ing** [< ORATION] to speak like some orators, in an exaggerated or self-important way

o·ra·tion (ô rā′shən) *n.* [< L. *oratio* < *orare,* to speak < IE. base *or-,* speak] a formal speech, as at a ceremony —see **SYN.** at SPEECH

or·a·tor (ôr′ət ər, är′-) *n.* **1.** a person who delivers an oration **2.** a skillful public speaker

or·a·tor·i·cal (ôr′ə tôr′i k'l, är′-) *adj.* of or characteristic of orators or oratory —**or'a·tor'i·cal·ly** *adv.*

or·a·to·ri·o (ôr′ə tôr′ē ō′, är′-) *n., pl.* **-os'** [It., small chapel: so called because first performed at a chapel in Rome] a long, dramatic musical work, usually on a religious theme, consisting of arias, recitatives, choruses, etc. with orchestral accompaniment but without stage action, scenery, etc.

or·a·to·ry (ôr′ə tôr′ē, är′-) *n., pl.* **-ries** [L. *oratoria*] **1.** the art of an orator; skill in public speaking **2.** [< LL. < L. *oratorius,* of prayer < *orator*] a small chapel, esp. for private prayer

orb (ôrb) *n.* [L. *orbis,* a circle] **1.** a globe; sphere **2.** any heavenly sphere, as the moon or a planet **3.** a small globe with a cross on top, as a royal symbol **4.** [Poet.] the eye —*vt.* **1.** to form into a sphere or circle **2.** [Poet.] to enclose —**orbed** *adj.*

or·bic·u·lar (ôr bik′yoo lər) *adj.* [< LL. < L. dim. of *orbis,* a circle] **1.** in the form of an orb; spherical or circular **2.** *Bot.* round and flat, as some leaves Also **or·bic'u·late** (-lit, -lāt′), **or·bic'u·lat'ed** (-lāt′id) —**or·bic'u·lar'i·ty** (-lar′ə tē) *n.*

or·bit (ôr′bit) *n.* [< MFr. < ML. < L. *orbita,* path < *orbis,* a circle] **1.** the bony cavity containing the eye; eye socket **2.** *a)* the path of a heavenly body revolving around another *b)* the path of an artificial satellite or spacecraft around a heavenly body **3.** the range of one's experience or activity —*vi.* to move in an orbit or circle —*vt.* **1.** to put (a spacecraft, etc.) into an orbit in space **2.** to move in an orbit around [the moon *orbits* the earth] —**or'bit·al** *adj.* —**or'bit·er** *n.*

or·chard (ôr′chərd) *n.* [< OE. *ortgeard,* ult. < L. *hortus,* a garden + OE. *geard,* YARD[2]] **1.** an area of land where fruit trees or nut trees are grown **2.** the trees in an orchard

or·ches·tra (ôr′kis trə, -kes′-) *n.* [L. < Gr. *orchēstra,* space for the chorus in front of the stage < *orcheisthai,* to dance: for IE. base see RUN] **1.** the space in front of and below the stage,

where the musicians sit: in full, **orchestra pit** ☆**2.** *a)* the main-floor seats of a theater, esp. the front section *b)* the main floor itself **3.** *a)* a group of musicians playing together; esp., *same as* SYMPHONY ORCHESTRA *b)* their instruments

or·ches·tral (ôr kes′trəl) *adj.* of, for, by, or like an orchestra

or·ches·trate (ôr′kis trāt′) *vt., vi.* **-trat'ed, -trat'ing 1.** to compose or arrange (music) for an orchestra **2.** to provide an orchestral score for (a ballet, etc.) —**or'ches·tra'tion** *n.* —**or'ches·tra'tor, or'ches·trat'er** *n.*

or·chid (ôr′kid) *n.* [< L.: see ORCHIS] **1.** any of a large group of plants having bulbous roots and flowers with three petals, of which the middle one is larger and lip-shaped **2.** the flower **3.** a light bluish red —*adj.* of this color

or·chis (ôr′kis) *n.* [L. < Gr. *orchis,* lit., testicle: from the shape of the roots] an orchid, specif. one with small flowers growing in spikes

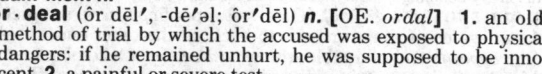

ord. 1. order **2.** ordinal **3.** ordinance

or·dain (ôr dān′) *vt.* [< OFr. < L. *ordinare* < *ordo,* ORDER] **1.** to decree; order; establish; enact [to believe that fate *ordains* one's future] **2.** to appoint as a minister, priest, or rabbi, often by a special ceremony —*vi.* to command; decree —**or·dain'ment** *n.*

ORCHID

or·deal (ôr dēl′, -dē′əl; ôr′dēl) *n.* [OE. *ordal*] **1.** an old method of trial by which the accused was exposed to physical dangers: if he remained unhurt, he was supposed to be innocent **2.** a painful or severe test

or·der (ôr′dər) *n.* [< OFr. < L. *ordo,* straight row: for IE. base see ART[1]] **1.** social position [for people of all *orders*] **2.** a state of peace; orderly conduct ["law and *order*"] **3.** arrangement of things or events; series [names in alphabetical *order*] **4.** a fixed or definite plan; system [the *order* of the universe] **5.** a group set off from others by some quality **6.** a group of persons joined together for religious or social purposes, etc. [the Jesuit *Order;* the Masonic *Order*] **7.** *a)* a group of persons distinguished by having received a certain award or citation [the *Order* of the Purple Heart] *b)* the group's insignia **8.** a condition in which everything is in its right place and functioning properly [the house is in *order*] **9.** condition in general [in working *order*] **10.** a command, direction, etc., usually backed by authority [the general's *orders* were quickly obeyed] **11.** class; kind; sort [intelligence of a high *order*] **12.** an established method, as of conduct in meetings, court, etc. **13.** *a)* a request or authorization to make or supply something [an *order* for merchandise or services] *b)* the goods supplied [this store will deliver your *order*] ☆*c)* a single portion of some food, as in a restaurant [an *order* of cole slaw] **14.** *Archit. a)* any of several classical styles of structure, esp. as shown by the type of column and entablature [the Doric *order*] *b)* a style of building **15.** *Biol.* a classification ranking above a family and below a class [whales and dolphins belong to the same *order* of mammals] **16.** *Finance* written instructions to pay money or hand over property [a money *order*] **17.** *Theol. a)* any of the nine grades of angels *b)* any rank in the Christian clergy *c)* [*pl.*] the position of ordained minister —*vt.* **1.** to put or keep in order; arrange [I must *order* my affairs before I leave] **2.** *a)* to command [the captain *ordered* his men to charge] *b)* to command to go (*to, out of,* etc.) [she *ordered* him out of the room] **3.** to request or direct (something to be supplied) [*order* some art supplies for the class] —*vi.* **1.** to give a command **2.** to request that something be supplied —see **SYN.** at COMMAND —**by order of** according to the command of —**call to order** to request to be quiet, as to start a (meeting) —**in** (or **out of**) **order 1.** in (or not in) proper arrangement or position **2.** in (or not in) good condition **3.** in (or not in) accordance with the rules, as for conducting a meeting ☆**4.** being (or not being) suitable to the occasion [that remark was *out of order*] —**in order that** so that; to the end that —**in order to** for the purpose of; as a means to —**in short order** without delay —**on order** ordered but not yet supplied —**on the order of 1.** similar to; somewhat resembling **2.** approximately —☆**tall order** [Colloq.] a difficult task or requirement —**to order** as specified by the buyer [a suit made *to order*] —**or'der·er** *n.*

or·der·ly (ôr′dər lē) *adj.* **1.** *a)* neatly arranged; in order [an *orderly* closet] *b)* following some regular order; systematic [an *orderly* arrangement of seats] **2.** well-behaved; obeying the rules [an *orderly* crowd] —*adv.* in proper order; methodically —*n., pl.* **-lies 1.** *Mil.* an enlisted man assigned to an officer as a servant, messenger, etc. or given a specific task [a latrine *order-ly*] **2.** a male hospital attendant —**or′der·li·ness** *n.*

SYN.—**orderly** implies freedom from disorder or confusion as by following a proper arrangement, a set rule, etc. [an *orderly* desk, crowd, meeting, etc.]; **methodical** implies the close following of a fixed plan in every detail [a *methodical* investigation, worker, etc.]; **systematic** often adds the idea of thoroughness in planning and emphasizes the overall purpose, design, etc. [a *systematic* assault on civil liberties] —**ANT.** disorderly, haphazard, chaotic

or·di·nal (ôr′d'n əl) *adj.* [< LL. *ordinalis* < L. *ordo*, ORDER] **1.** showing order, specif. of a number in a series: see ORDINAL NUMBER **2.** of an order of animals or plants —*n.* **1.** *same as* ORDINAL NUMBER **2.** [*often* **O-**] a book of religious rituals

ordinal number a number used to indicate order (e.g., ninth, 25th, etc.) in a series: distinguished from CARDINAL NUMBER

or·di·nance (ôr′d'n əns) *n.* [< OFr. < *ordener*: see ORDAIN] **1.** a command given by authority **2.** an established practice, rite, etc. ☆**3.** a statute or law, esp. one made by a city government

or·di·nar·i·ly (ôr′d'n er′ə lē) *adv.* **1.** usually; as a rule **2.** in an ordinary way

or·di·nar·y (ôr′d'n er′ē) *n., pl.* **-nar′ies** [< OFr. < ML. < L. *ordinarius*, an overseer < *ordo*, ORDER] **1.** an official of church or court who has primary power, not that of a deputy **2.** [Brit.] *a)* a set meal at a fixed price *b)* an inn, etc. serving such meals **3.** *Eccles.* [*often* **O-**] the part of the Mass that does not vary —*adj.* **1.** customary; usual [the *ordinary* price is $10] **2.** *a)* unexceptional; common; average [a man of *ordinary* ability] *b)* below average; inferior [a very *ordinary* piece of merchandise] —**in ordinary** in regular service —**out of the ordinary** unusual; extraordinary —**or′di·nar′i·ness** *n.*

or·di·nate (ôr′d'n it, -āt′) *n.* [< ModL. (*linea*) *ordinate* (*applicata*), line applied in an ordered manner] *Math.* in a system of coordinates, the distance of a point from the horizontal axis as measured along a line parallel to the vertical axis: see ABSCISSA

or·di·na·tion (ôr′d'n ā′shən) *n.* an ordaining or being ordained, as to the ministry

ord·nance (ôrd′nəns) *n.* [contr. < ORDINANCE] **1.** cannon or artillery **2.** all military weapons together with ammunition, vehicles, equipment, etc. **3.** a military unit supplying and storing ordnance

Or·do·vi·cian (ôr′də vish′ən) *adj.* [< L. *Ordovices*, a tribe in Wales] designating or of the second period of the Paleozoic Era —**the Ordovician** the Ordovician Period or its rocks: see GEOLOGIC TIME CHART

or·dure (ôr′jər, -dyoor) *n.* [OFr. < *ord*, filthy < L. *horridus*, HORRID] dung; filth; excrement

ore (ôr) *n.* [OE. *ar*, brass, copper, identified with *ora*, metal not yet wrought] **1.** any natural combination of minerals, esp. one from which a metal or metals can be readily separated **2.** a natural substance from which a nonmetallic material, as sulfur, can be separated

ö·re (ö′rə) *n., pl.* **ö′re** [Sw., ult. < L. *aurum*, gold] *see* MONETARY UNITS, table (Sweden)

ø·re (ö′rə) *n., pl.* **ø′re** [Dan. & Norw.: see prec.] *see* MONETARY UNITS, table (Denmark, Norway)

o·reg·a·no (ô reg′ə nō, ə-) *n.* [Sp. *orégano*, ult. < Gr. *origanon*] any of several plants of the mint family, with fragrant leaves used for seasoning

Or·e·gon (ôr′i gən, är′-; *also, but not locally,* -gän′) [prob. < AmInd. name for the Columbia River] NW State of the U.S.: 96,981 sq. mi.; pop. 2,091,000; cap. Salem: abbrev. **Oreg., OR** —**Or′e·go′ni·an** (-gō′nē ən) *adj., n.*

☆**Oregon Trail** former route used by pioneers going west, from the Missouri River to the Columbia River in Oregon

O·res·tes (ô res′tēz, ə-) *Gr. Myth.* brother of Electra: see ELECTRA

or·gan (ôr′gən) *n.* [< OFr. & OE. < L. *organum* < Gr. *organon*, an instrument < *ergon*, work: for IE. base see WORK] **1.** *a)* a large wind instrument consisting of various sets of pipes which, opened by keys on one or

OREGON TRAIL

more keyboards, allow compressed air to enter, causing sound by vibration: also called **pipe organ** *b)* any of several musical instruments producing similar sounds, as a reed organ or an electronic organ **2.** in animals and plants, a part made up of specialized tissues and having a special purpose [the heart, liver, and eyes are *organs* of the body] **3.** a means for performing some action [the city council is an *organ* of local government] **4.** a means of communicating ideas, as a newspaper or magazine

or·gan·dy, or·gan·die (ôr′gən dē) *n., pl.* **-dies** [Fr. *organdi* < ?] a very sheer, crisp cotton fabric, used for dresses, curtains, etc.

or·gan·elle (ôr′gə nel′) *n.* [ult. < L. *organum*, a tool + -*ella*, dim. suffix] any structure within a cell that has a specialized function, such as a chloroplast

organ grinder a person who makes a living by playing a barrel organ in the streets

or·gan·ic (ôr gan′ik) *adj.* **1.** of or having to do with an organ of the body [an *organic* disorder] **2.** having to do with the basic makeup of a thing; inherent [music and drama, both *organic* parts of opera] **3.** made up of parts related in a systematic way; organized [the *organic* structure of society] **4.** *a)* designating or of any chemical compound containing carbon *b)* designating or of the branch of chemistry dealing with carbon compounds **5.** of, like, or derived from living organisms [coal is *organic* rather than mineral in origin] ☆**6.** grown with only animal or vegetable fertilizers and without the use of chemical pesticides, etc. [*organic* vegetables] —**or·gan′i·cal·ly** *adv.*

or·gan·ism (ôr′gə niz'm) *n.* **1.** any animal or plant with organs and parts that function together to maintain life **2.** anything like a living thing in having many parts that function together in a complex way [a nation is a political *organism*] —**or·gan·is′mic** *adj.* —**or·gan·is′mi·cal·ly** *adv.*

or·gan·ist (ôr′gə nist) *n.* one who plays the organ

or·gan·i·za·tion (ôr′gə ni zā′shən, -nī-) *n.* **1.** an organizing or being organized **2.** the way in which the parts of a thing are organized **3.** any group operating as a whole; esp., *a)* a group organized for a certain purpose, as a club, union, etc. *b)* the administration or management of a business or political party —**or·gan′i·za′tion·al** *adj.* —**or·gan′i·za′tion·al·ly** *adv.*

or·gan·ize (ôr′gə nīz′) *vt.* **-ized′, -iz′ing** [< ML. *organizare* < L. *organum:* see ORGAN] **1.** *a)* to arrange in an orderly way [to *organize* books in a library according to subject] *b)* to put together in a clear way, with all parts properly connected [to *organize* an essay] *c)* to make plans and arrange for [to *organize* a campaign] **2.** to bring into being; establish [to *organize* a club] **3.** *a)* to enlist in, or cause to form, a labor union [to *organize* crop workers] ☆*b)* to enlist the employees of (an industry, business, etc.) in a labor union **4.** [Colloq.] to set (oneself) into an orderly state of mind —*vi.* **1.** to become organized ☆**2.** to form an organization, esp. a labor union —**or′gan·iz′a·ble** *adj.* —**or′gan·iz′er** *n.*

☆**or·gan·za** (ôr gan′zə) *n.* [< ?] a stiff, sheer fabric of rayon, silk, etc.

or·gasm (ôr′gaz'm) *n.* [< Fr. < Gr. *orgasmos* < *organ*, to swell with moisture] the climax of sexual excitement, as in intercourse —**or·gas′mic, or·gas′tic** (-gas′tik) *adj.*

or·gy (ôr′jē) *n., pl.* **-gies** [< Fr. < L. < Gr. *orgia*, pl., secret rites] **1.** [*usually pl.*] in ancient Greece and Rome, wild celebration in worship of certain gods **2.** any wild merrymaking in a group, esp. with sexual activity **3.** an engaging in any activity in an uncontrolled way [an *orgy* of eating] —**or·gi·as′tic** (-as′tik) *adj.* —**or·gi·as′ti·cal·ly** *adv.*

o·ri·el (ôr′ē əl) *n.* [< OFr. < ? ML. *oriolum*, porch] a large window built out from a wall and resting on a bracket or corbel

o·ri·ent (ôr′ē ənt; *also, and for v. usually,* -ent′) *n.* [OFr. < L. *oriens*, direction of the rising sun, prp. of *oriri*, to arise: for IE. base see RUN] the east: now rare, except [**O-**] the East, or Asia; esp., the Far East —*adj.* **1.** shining, as pearls **2.** [Poet.] *a)* eastern; oriental *b)* rising, as the sun —*vt.* **1.** to arrange with reference to the east [to *orient* a church by placing the altar at the eastern end] **2.** to set (a map or chart) in agreement with the points of the compass **3.** to adjust

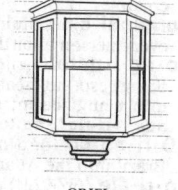

ORIEL

or adapt to a particular situation (often used reflexively) *[to orient oneself in a new job]*

o·ri·en·tal (ôr′ē en′t'l) *adj.* **1.** [Poet.] eastern **2.** [O-] of the Orient, its people, or their culture; Eastern —*n.* *[usually O-]* a native of the Orient or a member of a people native to that region

o·ri·en·tal·ism (-iz'm) *n.* **1.** any trait, quality, etc. associated with people of the East **2.** study of Eastern culture —**O′ri·en′tal·ist** *n.*

Oriental poppy a perennial poppy often grown for its red, pink, or white flowers

Oriental rug (or **carpet**) a carpet hand-woven in the Orient, usually with complicated, colorful designs

o·ri·en·tate (ôr′ē en tāt′, -en-) *vt.* **-tat′ed, -tat′ing** *same as* ORIENT —*vi.* **1.** to face east, or in any specified direction **2.** to adjust to a situation

o·ri·en·ta·tion (ôr′ē ən tā′shən, -en-) *n.* **1.** an orienting or being oriented **2.** *a)* a being aware of where one is in space and time and of one's surroundings *b)* a period of becoming adjusted to some situation

or·i·fice (ôr′ə fis, är′-) *n.* [Fr. < LL. *orificium* < L. *os*, mouth (see ORAL) + *facere*, to make, DO¹] an opening or mouth, as of a tube or cavity

or·i·flamme (ôr′ə flam′, är′-) *n.* [Fr. < OFr. < L. *aurum*, gold + *flamma*, flame] **1.** the ancient royal standard of France, a red silk banner with flame-shaped streamers **2.** any battle standard

orig. **1.** origin **2.** original **3.** originally

o·ri·ga·mi (ôr′ə gä′mē) *n.* [Jap.] **1.** a traditional Japanese art of folding paper to form flowers, animal figures, etc. **2.** an object so made

or·i·gin (ôr′ə jin, är′-) *n.* [< MFr. < L. *origo* < *oriri*, to rise: see ORIENT] **1.** a coming into existence or use; beginning **2.** parentage; birth; lineage **3.** source; root *[etymology deals with the *origins* of words]* **4.** *Math.* the point at which coordinate axes intersect

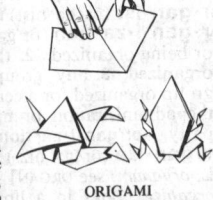

ORIGAMI

SYN.—**origin** is applied to that from which a person or thing has its very beginning *[the word "rodeo" has its *origin* in Spanish]*; **source** is applied to the point or place from which something arises, comes, or develops *[the sun is our *source* of energy]*; **beginning** is the general term for a starting point or place *[the *beginning* of a friendship]*; **inception** is specifically applied to the beginning of an undertaking, organization, etc. *[Smith headed the business from its *inception*]*; **root** suggests an origin so deep and basic as to be the very first cause from which something stems *[an error in arithmetic was the *root* of all our trouble]*

o·rig·i·nal (ə rij′ə n'l) *adj.* **1.** having to do with an origin; first; earliest *[the *original* inhabitants of an area]* **2.** never having been before; new; novel *[an *original* idea]* **3.** capable of creating something new, or thinking or acting in an independent, fresh way; inventive *[an *original* composer]* **4.** coming from someone as the originator, maker, author, etc. *[an *original* Picasso painting]* **5.** being that from which copies, translations, etc. have been made *[the *original* letter and two carbons]* —*n.* **1.** the form from which other varieties have developed *[eohippus was the *original* of the modern horse]* **2.** an original work of art, writing, etc., as distinguished from a copy, etc. **3.** the person or thing pictured in a painting, etc. **4.** a person with an original and creative mind —see SYN. at NEW —**o·rig′i·nal·ly** *adv.*

o·rig·i·nal·i·ty (ə rij′ə nal′ə tē) *n.* **1.** the quality or condition of being original **2.** the ability to be original, inventive, or creative

original sin sinfulness which Christians believe is present in every person at birth as a direct result of Adam's sin

o·rig·i·nate (ə rij′ə nāt′) *vt.* **-nat′ed, -nat′ing** to bring into being; esp., to create (something original); invent —*vi.* to come into being; begin; start —**o·rig′i·na′tion** *n.* —**o·rig′i·na′tive** *adj.* —**o·rig′i·na′tor** *n.*

O·ri·no·co (ôr′ə nō′kō) river in Venezuela, flowing from N Brazil into the Atlantic: c. 1,700 mi.

o·ri·ole (ôr′ē ōl′) *n.* [< OFr. < ML. < L. *aureolus*, golden < *aurum*, gold] **1.** any of a family of yellow-and-black birds found from Europe to Australia ☆**2.** any of a group of American birds, including the Baltimore oriole, that have orange and black plumage and build hanging nests

O·ri·on (ō rī′ən, ô-) a constellation on the celestial equator near Taurus, containing the bright stars Rigel and Betelgeuse

or·i·son (ôr′i z'n, är′-; -s'n) *n.* [< OFr. < LL. *oratio*, a prayer < L.: see ORATION] a prayer

Ork·ney Islands (ôrk′nē) group of islands that form a county of N Scotland

Or·lan·do (ôr lan′dō) [after *Orlando* Reeves, an Indian runner] city in C Fla.: pop. 99,000

Or·lé·ans (ôr lā än′; *E.* ôr′lē ənz) city in NC France, on the Loire: pop. 96,000

☆**Or·lon** (ôr′län) [coined after (NYL)ON] *a trademark for* a synthetic acrylic fiber somewhat like nylon, or a fabric made from this fiber —*n.* [o-] this fiber or fabric

Or·mazd (ôr′mazd) [Per.] *Zoroastrianism* the supreme deity and creator of the world: also sp. **Or′muzd**

or·mo·lu (ôr′mə lōō′) *n.* [< Fr. *or moulu*, ground gold] an imitation gold consisting of an alloy of copper and tin, used as decoration, etc.

or·na·ment (ôr′nə mənt; *for v.* -ment′) *n.* [< OFr. < L. *ornamentum* < *ornare*, to adorn] **1.** anything added to make something look better; decoration; embellishment **2.** a person whose character or talent makes his surroundings, group, etc. seem better *[he is an *ornament* to his profession]* **3.** an adorning or being adorned **4.** *Music* a trill, arpeggio, etc., added to notes as a kind of decoration —*vt.* to furnish with ornaments or be an ornament to; decorate —see SYN. at ADORN —**or′na·ment′er** *n.*

or·na·men·tal (ôr′nə men′t'l) *adj.* serving as an ornament; decorative *[ornamental* fringe] —*n.* something ornamental; specif., a decorative plant —**or′na·men′tal·ly** *adv.*

or·na·men·ta·tion (-men tā′shən) *n.* **1.** an ornamenting or being ornamented **2.** the things used as ornaments; decoration

or·nate (ôr nāt′) *adj.* [< L. pp. of *ornare*, to adorn] **1.** having much or too much decoration **2.** showy or flowery, as some kinds of writing —**or·nate′ly** *adv.* —**or·nate′ness** *n.*

or·ner·y (ôr′nər ē) *adj.* [altered < ORDINARY] [Chiefly Dial.] **1.** having an ugly or mean disposition **2.** obstinate; stubborn **3.** base; low —☆**or′ner·i·ness** *n.*

or·ni·thol·o·gy (ôr′nə thäl′ə jē) *n.* [< ModL. < Gr. *ornithos*, genitive of *ornis*, bird + -LOGY] the branch of zoology dealing with birds —**or·ni·tho·log·i·cal** (ôr′ni thə läj′i k'l) *adj.* —**or′ni·tho·log′i·cal·ly** *adv.* —**or·ni·thol′o·gist** *n.*

o·ro·tund (ôr′ə tund′) *adj.* [< L. *ore rotundo*, lit., with round mouth] **1.** clear, strong, and deep: said of the voice **2.** too solemn and dignified; pompous, as speech —**o′ro·tun′di·ty** *n.*

O·roz·co (ô rôs′kô), **Jo·sé Cle·men·te** (hô se′ kle men′te) 1883–1949; Mex. painter

or·phan (ôr′fən) *n.* [< LL. < Gr. *orphanos*] a child whose parents are dead; sometimes, a child who has lost only one parent by death —*adj.* **1.** being an orphan *[an *orphan* child]* **2.** of or for orphans *[an *orphan* home]* —*vt.* to cause to become an orphan *[children *orphaned* by war]* —**or′phan·hood′** *n.*

or·phan·age (-ij) *n.* **1.** the state of being an orphan **2.** an institution that is a home for orphans

Or·phe·us (ôr′fē əs, -fyōōs) *Gr. Myth.* a poet-musician with magic musical powers who lost his chance to lead his wife, Eurydice, out from the world of the dead when he looked back at her

Or·phic (ôr′fik) *adj.* **1.** of or characteristic of Orpheus **2.** [also o-] *a)* like the music of Orpheus; enchanting; entrancing *b)* mystic; occult

or·pi·ment (ôr′pi mənt) *n.* [< OFr. < L. *auripigmentum:* see ORPINE] a lemon-yellow sulfide of arsenic, used as a pigment

or·pine (ôr′pin) *n.* [< MFr. < OFr. < L. *auripigmentum*, pigment of gold] a plant with fleshy leaves and white, yellow, or purple flowers

Or·ping·ton (ôr′piŋ tən) *n.* [after *Orpington*, village in England] a breed of large, heavy chickens

or·ris (ôr′is, är′-) *n.* [prob. < MIt. < L. *iris*, iris] any of several European irises, esp. a species from which orrisroot is got

or·ris·root (-rōōt′) *n.* the rootstock of the orris, which is powdered for use in perfumes, tooth powders, etc.

Or·te·ga y Gas·set (ôr te′gä ē gä set′), **Jo·sé** (hô se′) 1883–1955; Sp. philosopher & writer of essays

or·tho- [< Gr. *orthos*, straight] *a combining form meaning:* **1.** straight *[orthodontics]* **2.** right angle *[orthoclase]* **3.** correct or standard *[orthography]* **4.** *Med.* correction of deformities *[orthopedics]* Also, before a vowel, **orth-**

or·tho·clase (ôr′thə klās′, -klāz′) *n.* [< G. < Gr. *orthos* (see ORTHO-) + *klasis*, fracture: it has a 90° cleavage] potassium feldspar, commonly found in granite

or·tho·don·tics (ôr′thə dän′tiks) *n.pl.* [with sing. v.] [< ModL.: see ORTH(O)-, -ODONT, & -ICS] the branch of dentistry concerned with correcting teeth that grow irregularly and cause

poor occlusion: also **or′tho·don′ti·a** (-dän′shə, -shē ə) —**or′-tho·don′tic** *adj.* —**or′tho·don′tist** *n.*

or·tho·dox (ôr′thə däks′) *adj.* [< Fr. < LL. < LGr. < Gr. *orthos*, correct + *doxa*, opinion < *dokein*, to think] **1.** keeping to the usual beliefs or fixed doctrines, as in religion, politics, etc.; conventional; specif., *a*) keeping to the Christian faith as expressed in the early creeds *b*) [O-] strictly observing the rites and traditions of Judaism, such as kashrut, the Sabbath, etc. **2.** [O-] designating or of any church in the Orthodox Eastern Church —**or′tho·dox′y** *n.*, *pl.* **-dox′ies**

Orthodox Eastern Church the main Christian church in E Europe, W Asia, and N Africa, that does not recognize the Pope as its head and that includes the self-ruling churches of the Soviet Union, Greece, Romania, Bulgaria, etc.

or·tho·e·py (ôr thō′ə pē, ôr′thō-) *n.* [< ModL. < Gr. < *orthos*, right + *epos*, a word] **1.** the study of pronunciation; phonology **2.** the standard pronunciation of a language —**or-tho·ep·ic** (ôr′thō ep′ik), **or′tho·ep′i·cal** *adj.* —**or′tho·ep′i-cal·ly** *adv.* —**or′tho·e·pist** *n.*

or·tho·gen·e·sis (ôr′thə jen′ə sis) *n.* [ModL.: see ORTHO- & -GENESIS] the theory that the evolution of certain organisms follows a fixed course that has been determined in advance and that is not affected by environment or other influences

or·thog·o·nal (ôr thäg′ə n'l) *n.* [< L. < Gr. *orthogōnios*: see ORTHO- & -GON] having to do with right angles; rectangular

or·thog·ra·phy (ôr thäg′rə fē) *n.*, *pl.* **-phies** [< MFr. < L. < Gr.: see ORTHO- & -GRAPHY] **1.** spelling that follows the accepted standard of usage **2.** any method of spelling [the unstandardized *orthography* of earlier times] **3.** spelling as a subject for study —**or·thog′ra·pher** *n.* —**or·tho·graph·ic** (ôr′thə graf′ik), **or′tho·graph′i·cal** *adj.* —**or′tho·graph′i·cal·ly** *adv.*

or·tho·pe·dics, or·tho·pae·dics (ôr′thə pē′diks) *n.pl.* [with sing. v.] [< Fr. < Gr. *orthos*, straight + *paideia*, training of children < *pais*, child] the branch of surgery dealing with the treatment of deformities, diseases, and injuries of the bones, joints, etc. —**or·tho·pe′dic, or·tho·pae′dic** *adj.* —**or′-tho·pe′dist, or′tho·pae′dist** *n.*

or·thop·ter·an (ôr thäp′tər ən) *n.* [< ORTHO- + Gr. *pteron*, wing] any of a large group of insects, including crickets, grasshoppers, roaches, etc., having chewing mouthparts and hard forewings that fold back to cover membranous hind wings —**or·thop′ter·ous** *adj.*

or·tho·rhom·bic (ôr′thə räm′bik) *adj.* [ORTHO- + RHOMBIC] designating a crystal form having three axes unequal in length and at right angles to one another

or·to·lan (ôr′t'l ən) *n.* [Fr. < Pr. < It. < L. *hortulanus*, dim. of *hortus*, a garden] **1.** an old-world bunting, eaten as a delicacy ☆**2.** same as BOBOLINK

Or·well (ôr′wel, -wəl), **George** (pseud. of *Eric Arthur Blair*) 1903–50; Eng. writer —**Or·well′i·an** *adj.*

-o·ry (ôr′ē, ər ē) [< OFr. < L. *-orius*, *-oria*, *-orium*] a suffix meaning: **1.** of, having the nature of [contradictory] **2.** a place or thing for [laboratory]

o·ryx (ôr′iks, är′-) *n.*, *pl.* **o′ryx·es, o′ryx:** see PLURAL, II, D, 1 [ModL. < L., wild goat < Gr., lit., pickax] any of a group of large African and Asian antelopes, including the gemsbok, with long horns that slant backward

‡**os**[1] (äs) *n.*, *pl.* **os·sa** (äs′ə) [L.] a bone

‡**os**[2] (äs) *n.*, *pl.* **o·ra** (ôr′ə) [L.] a mouth; opening

Os *Chem.* osmium

OS, O.S. Old Style

OS., OS, O.S. Old Saxon

☆**O·sage orange** (ō sāj′, ō′sāj) [< *Osage*, AmInd. tribe] **1.** a thorny tree of the mulberry family, used for hedges, etc. and having hard, yellow wood used in tanning, etc. **2.** its yellowish, orangelike fruit that cannot be eaten

O·sa·ka (ō′sä kä′; *E.* ō sä′kə) seaport in S Honshu, Japan: pop. 3,156,000

Os·car (äs′kər) [< OE. < *os*, a god + *gar*, a spear] a masculine

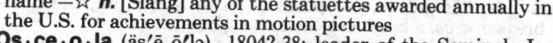

ORYX
(to 7 ft. high at shoulder; horns to 4 ft. long)

name —☆ *n.* [Slang] any of the statuettes awarded annually in the U.S. for achievements in motion pictures

Os·ce·o·la (äs′ē ō′lə) 1804?-38; leader of the Seminole Indians

os·cil·late (äs′ə lāt′) *vi.* **-lat′ed, -lat′ing** [< L. pp. of *oscillare*, to swing] **1.** to swing back and forth, as a pendulum do **2.** to be uncertain in an opinion, feeling, etc.; vacillate **3.** *Physics* to vary between maximum and minimum values, as electric current —*vt.* to cause to oscillate —**see SYN.** at SWING —**os′cil·la-to′ry** (-lə tôr′ē) *adj.*

os·cil·la·tion (äs′ə lā′shən) *n.* **1.** an oscillating **2.** a changing back and forth; fluctuation **3.** *Physics a*) variation between maximum and minimum values, as of current *b*) a single swing of an oscillating object, from one extreme to the other

os·cil·la·tor (äs′ə lāt′ər) *n.* **1.** a person or thing that oscillates **2.** *Physics* a device, as an electron tube, that produces electrical oscillations, or alternating current

os·cil·lo·graph (ä sil′ə graf′, ə-) *n.* [< L. *oscillare*, to swing + -GRAPH] an instrument for displaying or recording electrical oscillations in a wavy line (**oscillogram**)

os·cil·lo·scope (-skōp′) *n.* [< L. *oscillare*, to swing + -SCOPE] a type of oscillograph that displays an electrical wave on a fluorescent screen, as of a cathode-ray tube —**os·cil′lo-scop′ic** (-skäp′ik) *adj.*

os·cine (äs′in, -īn) *adj.* [< ModL. < L. *oscen*, bird whose notes were used in divining < *ob-*, toward + *canere*, sing] designating or of a group of perching birds, as the finches, larks, etc., mostly with well-developed vocal organs —*n.* an oscine bird

os·cu·late (äs′kyə lāt′) *vt.*, *vi.* **-lat′ed, -lat′ing** [< L. pp. of *osculari* < *osculum*, kiss, dim. of *os*, a mouth: see ORAL] **1.** to kiss **2.** to touch closely —**os′cu·lant** *adj.* —**os′cu·la′tion** *n.* —**os′cu·la·to′ry** (-lə tôr′ē) *adj.*

-ose[1] (ōs) [Fr. < (*gluc*)*ose*: see GLUCOSE] a suffix designating: **1.** a carbohydrate [sucrose] **2.** the product of a protein hydrolysis [protease]

-ose[2] (ōs) [L. *-osus*] a suffix meaning full of, having the qualities of, like [verbose]

OSHA Occupational Safety and Health Administration

Osh·a·wa (äsh′ə wə, -wô) city in SE Ontario, Canada, on Lake Ontario: pop. 107,000

Osh·kosh (äsh′käsh) [after *Oshkosh* (1795–1850), Am. Indian chief] city in E Wis.: pop. 53,000

o·sier (ō′zhər) *n.* [< OFr. < ML. *ausaria*, bed of willows] **1.** any of several willows whose branches or stems are used for baskets and furniture **2.** a willow branch used for wickerwork ☆**3.** any of several N. American dogwoods

O·si·ris (ō sī′ris) the ancient Egyptian god of the lower world, brother and husband of Isis

-o·sis (ō′sis) [L. < Gr. *-ōsis*] a suffix meaning: **1.** state, condition, action [osmosis] **2.** an abnormal or diseased condition [neurosis]

-os·i·ty (äs′ə tē) [< Fr. < L. *-ositas*] a suffix used to form nouns from adjectives ending in -OSE[2] or -OUS

Os·ler (ōs′lər), **Sir William** 1849–1919; Canad. physician

Os·lo (äs′lō, äz′-; *Norw.* ōōs′lōō) capital of Norway; seaport in the SE part: pop. 487,000

Os·man·li (äz man′lē, äs-) *n.* [Turk. < *Osman* (1259–1326), founder of Ottoman Empire] **1.** *pl.* **-lis** a Turk of the tribe that founded the Ottoman Empire **2.** same as TURKISH (*n.* 1) —*adj.* same as TURKISH

os·mics (äz′miks) *n.pl.* [with sing. v.] [< Gr. *osmē*, odor + -ICS] the science dealing with smells and the sense of smell

os·mi·um (äz′mē əm) *n.* [ModL. < Gr. *osmē*, odor: after the odor of one of its oxides] a very hard, bluish-white, metallic chemical element that occurs in the form of an alloy with platinum and iridium: symbol, Os; at. wt., 190.2; at. no., 76

os·mose (äs′mōs, äz′-) *vt.*, *vi.* **-mosed, -mos·ing** to undergo or make undergo osmosis

os·mo·sis (äs mō′sis, äz-) *n.* [ModL., ult. < Gr. *ōsmos*, impulse < *ōthein*, to push] **1.** the tendency of a solvent to pass through a semipermeable membrane, as the wall of a living cell, into a solution, so as to become mixed and equal in strength on both sides of the membrane **2.** any gradual spreading or absorbing of something [customs learned by cultural *osmosis*] —**os·mot·ic** (-mät′ik) *adj.* —**os·mot′i·cal·ly** *adv.*

os·prey (äs′prē) *n., pl.* **-preys** [< L. *ossifraga*, lit., the bone-breaker < *os*, a bone (see OSSIFY) + *frangere*, to break] a large diving bird of prey of the hawk family, with a blackish back and white breast, that feeds solely on fish

Os·sa (äs′ə) mountain in Thessaly, NE Greece: see PELION

‡**os·sa** (äs′ə) *n. pl. of* os[1]

os·se·ous (äs′ē əs) *adj.* [< L. *os*, a bone (see OSSIFY)] composed of, containing, or like bone; bony

OSPREY
(20–24 in. long)

os·si·fy (äs′ə fī′) *vt., vi.* **-fied′, -fy′ing** [< L. *os*, a bone (< IE. base *ost-*, bone) + -FY] 1. to change or develop into bone 2. to make or become fixed or set in a practice, custom, belief, etc. [a mind *ossified* by prejudice] —**os′si·fi·ca′tion** *n.*

os·te·al (äs′tē əl) *adj.* osseous; bony

os·te·i·tis (äs′tē īt′əs) *n.* [OSTE(O)- + -ITIS] inflammation of the bone or bony tissue

os·ten·si·ble (äs ten′sə b'l, əs-) *adj.* [Fr. < ML. < L. *ostendere*, to show < *ob(s)-*, against + *tendere*, to stretch: see TEND[2]] seeming or claimed, but not necessarily real [what was her *ostensible* reason for calling?] —**os·ten′si·bly** *adv.*

os·ten·sive (äs ten′siv) *adj.* 1. directly pointing out; clearly demonstrative 2. *same as* OSTENSIBLE —**os·ten′sive·ly** *adv.*

os·ten·ta·tion (äs′tən tā′shən) *n.* [< L., ult. < *ostendere*: see OSTENSIBLE] a showing off, as of wealth, knowledge, etc.; pretentiousness [they live in a house of great *ostentation*] —**os′ten·ta′tious** *adj.* —**os′ten·ta′tious·ly** *adv.*

os·te·o- [ModL. < Gr. *osteon*: for IE. base see OSSIFY] a combining form meaning a bone or bones [*osteopath*]: also, before a vowel, **oste-**

os·te·oid (äs′tē oid′) *adj.* [OSTE(O)- + -OID] like bone

os·te·ol·o·gy (äs′tē äl′ə jē) *n.* [ModL.: see OSTEO- & -LOGY] the study of the structure and function of bones —**os′te·o·log′i·cal** (-ə läj′i k'l) *adj.* —**os′te·ol′o·gist** *n.*

os·te·o·ma·la·cia (äs′tē ō mə lā′shə) *n.* [ModL. < OSTEO- + *malacia*, a softness of tissue] a bone disease in which there is a softening of the bones because of a lack of calcium salts

os·te·o·my·e·li·tis (äs′tē ō mī′ə līt′əs) *n.* [ModL.: see OSTEO- & MYELITIS] infection of bone marrow or other parts of the bone, usually caused by a bacterium

☆**os·te·op·a·thy** (äs′tē äp′ə thē) *n.* [ModL.: see OSTEO- & -PATHY] a system of medicine and surgery that emphasizes the interrelationship of the skeleton and muscle system with all other body parts —**os′te·o·path′** (-ə path′) *n.* —**os′te·o·path′ic** *adj.* —**os′te·o·path′i·cal·ly** *adv.*

os·te·o·po·ro·sis (äs′tē ō pô rō′sis) *n.* [ModL. < OSTEO- + *porosis*, a porous condition] a disease in which the bones become porous and brittle because of a loss of calcium

Ös·ter·reich (ös′tər rīH′) Ger. name of AUSTRIA

Os·ti·a (äs′tē ə) ancient city that was the port of Rome, at the mouth of the Tiber

ost·ler (äs′lər) *n. same as* HOSTLER

os·tra·cism (äs′trə siz'm) *n.* [see OSTRACIZE] 1. in ancient Greece, the temporary banishment of a citizen by popular vote 2. the action of a group or of society in deciding to have nothing to do with someone who is disliked, etc.

os·tra·cize (-sīz′) *vt.* **-cized′, -ciz′ing** [Gr. *ostrakizein*, to exile by votes written on potsherds < *ostrakon*, a potsherd: for IE. base see OSSIFY] to banish, keep out, etc. by ostracism

Os·tra·va (ôs′trä vä) city in N Moravia, Czechoslovakia: pop. 272,000

os·trich (ôs′trich, äs′-) *n., pl.* **-trich·es, -trich** see PLURAL, II, D, 1 [< OFr. < VL. < L. *avis*, bird + *struthio*, ostrich < Gr. *strouthos*] 1. a swift-running, nonflying bird of Africa and the Near East, the largest living bird, with a long neck and legs and small wings 2. *same as* RHEA (see RHEA *n.*)

Os·tro·goth (äs′trə gäth′) *n.* an East Goth; esp., a member of the tribe which conquered Italy, 5th cent. A.D. —**Os′tro·goth′ic** *adj.*

Oś·wię·cim (ôsh vyän′tsim) Pol. name of AUSCHWITZ

OT., OT, O.T. Old Testament

O·thel·lo (ə thel′ō, ô-) a tragedy by Shakespeare in which the title character, made madly jealous by the villainous Iago, kills his faithful wife, Desdemona

oth·er (uth′ər) *adj.* [OE.] 1. being the

OSTRICH
(to 8 ft. high)

remaining one or ones of two or more [Bill and the *other* boy(s)] 2. different or distinct from that or those implied [some *other* girl won it] 3. different [it is *other* than you think] 4. additional [to have no *other* coat] 5. former [in *other* times] —*pron.* 1. the other one [each loved the *other*] 2. some other person or thing [to do as *others* do] —*adv.* otherwise; differently [he can't do *other* than go] —**of all others** above all others —**the other day** (or **night,** etc.) not long ago —**oth′er·ness** *n.*

oth·er·wise (-wīz′) *adv.* 1. in another manner; differently [to believe *otherwise*] 2. in all other respects [an *otherwise* intelligent man] 3. in other circumstances Often used as a conjunction meaning "or else" [please help me; *otherwise* I'll be late] —*adj.* different [her answer could not be *otherwise*]

other world a supposed world after death

oth·er·world·ly (-wurld′lē) *adj.* being apart from interests of this world; concerned with life in a future or imaginary world —**oth′er·world′li·ness** *n.*

-ot·ic [Gr. *-ōtikos*] a suffix meaning: 1. of or affected with [*sclerotic*] 2. producing [*narcotic*]

o·ti·ose (ō′shē ōs′, ōt′ē-) *adj.* [< L. < *otium*, leisure] 1. idle; indolent; lazy 2. ineffective; futile 3. useless; superfluous —**o′ti·ose′ly** *adv.* —**o′ti·os′i·ty** (-äs′ə tē) *n.*

O·tis (ōt′əs) 1. [orig. family name] a masculine name 2. **James,** 1725–83; Am. Revolutionary statesman

o·ti·tis (ō tīt′əs) *n.* [ModL.: see OTO- & -ITIS] inflammation of the ear

o·to- [< Gr. *ōtos*, genitive of *ous*, EAR[1]] a combining form meaning the ear [*otology*] : also, before a vowel, **ot-**

o·to·lar·yn·gol·o·gy (ōt′ə lar′in gäl′ə jē) *n.* [OTO- + LARYNGO- + -LOGY] the branch of medicine dealing with problems of the ear, nose, and throat —**o′to·lar′yn·gol′o·gist** *n.*

☆**o·tol·o·gy** (ō täl′ə jē) *n.* [OTO- + -LOGY] the branch of medicine dealing with problems of the ear —**o·to·log′i·cal** (ōt′ə läj′i k'l) *adj.* —**o·tol′o·gist** *n.*

o·to·scle·ro·sis (ōt′ō skli rō′sis) *n.* [OTO- + SCLEROSIS] a growth of spongy bone in the inner ear causing deafness

O·tran·to (ō trän′tō), **Strait of** strait between Italy & Albania, connecting the Adriatic & Ionian seas

Ot·ta·wa[1] (ät′ə wə, -wä′) *n.* 1. *pl.* **-was, -wa** a member of a tribe of Indians of SE Canada and Michigan 2. their Algonquian language —*adj.* of the Ottawas

Ot·ta·wa[2] (ät′ə wə, -wä′) capital of Canada, in SE Ontario: pop. 304,000

ot·ter (ät′ər) *n., pl.* **-ters, -ter** see PLURAL, II, D, 1 [OE. *oter*: for IE. base see WATER] 1. a furry, flesh-eating mammal related to the weasel and mink, with webbed feet used in swimming and a long tail 2. its fur 3. *same as* SEA OTTER

Ot·to (ät′ō) [< OHG. < *auda*, rich] 1. a masculine name 2. **Otto I** 912–973 A.D.; king of Germany (936–973) & emperor of the Holy Roman Empire (962–973): called *the Great*

Ot·to·man (ät′ə mən) *adj.* [ult. < Ar. *'Uthmāni*, of Osman: see OSMANLI] *same as* TURKISH —*n., pl.* **-mans** 1. a Turk 2. [o-] *a)* a low, cushioned seat or couch without a back or arms *b)* an upholstered, padded footstool

Ottoman Empire empire (c.1300–1918) of the Turks, which at one time included much of SE Europe, SW Asia, & NE Africa

Oua·ga·dou·gou (wä′gə dōō′gōō) capital of Upper Volta, in the C part: pop. 110,000

ouch (ouch) *interj.* an exclamation of pain

ought[1] (ôt) *v.aux.* [orig., pt. of OWE < OE. pp. of *agan*, OWE] a helping verb used with infinitives and meaning: 1. to be obliged or have the duty [she *ought* to pay her debts] 2. to be bound by what is wise or desirable [you *ought* to eat more] 3. to be probable or expected [it *ought* to be over soon] Past tense is expressed by combining *ought* with the perfect infinitive of the verb being used [I *ought* to have told you]

OTTOMAN EMPIRE (16th cent.)

ought[2] (ôt) *n., adv. var. of* AUGHT

ought[3] (ôt) *n.* [by faulty separation of *a nought* into *an ought*] a nought; the figure zero (0)

ought·n't (ôt′'nt) ought not

‡**oui** (wē) *adv.* [Fr.] yes

☆**Oui·ja** (wē′jə, -jē) [Fr. *oui*, yes + G. *ja*, yes] *a trademark for* a device consisting of a planchette, or pointer, and a board bearing the alphabet and other symbols, used for supposedly spelling out answers and messages, as from spirits

ounce[1] (ouns) *n.* [< OFr. < L. *uncia*, a twelfth] **1.** a unit of weight equal to 1/16 pound avoirdupois, or 1/12 pound troy **2.** *same as* FLUID OUNCE **3.** any small amount [an *ounce* of care] Abbrev. **oz.** (*sing. & pl.*)

ounce[2] (ouns) *n.* [< OFr. *lonce* (mistaken as *l'once*) < VL. < L. *lynx*, lynx] *same as* SNOW LEOPARD

our (our, är) *adj.* [OE. *ure*] of, belonging to, made by, or done by us [*our* home, *our* mistake]

Our Father *same as* LORD'S PRAYER

Our Lady Mary, the mother of Jesus; Virgin Mary

ours (ourz, ärz) *pron.* that or those belonging to us: used without a following noun [*ours* are better]: also used after *of* to indicate possession [a friend of *ours*]

our·self (our self′, är-) *pron.* myself: used as by a monarch or editor who is referring to himself as *we*

our·selves (-selvz′) *pron.* a form of the 1st person plural pronoun, used: *a*) as an intensive [we went *ourselves*] *b*) as a reflexive [we hurt *ourselves*] *c*) as a kind of noun meaning "our real or true selves" [we are not *ourselves* today]

-ous (əs) [< OFr. < L. *-osus*] *a suffix meaning:* **1.** having, full of, characterized by [*dangerous*] **2.** *Chem.* having a lower valence than is indicated by the suffix *-ic* [*nitrous*]

ou·sel (o͞o′z'l) *n. same as* OUZEL

oust (oust) *vt.* [< Anglo-Fr. < OFr. *ouster* < L. *ostare* < *ob-*, against + *stare*, to STAND] to force or drive out; expel, dispossess, eject, etc. —see SYN. at EJECT

oust·er (ou′stər) *n.* **1.** a person or thing that ousts **2.** *Law* an ousting or being ousted; esp., a forcing or being forced from one's property by unlawful means

out (out) *adv.* [OE. *ut* < IE. base *ud-*, up, up away] **1.** *a*) away or forth from a place, position, etc. [they live ten miles *out*] *b*) away from home [let's eat *out*] *c*) away from shore [a ship ten miles *out*] *d*) on strike [the miners went *out* last week] **2.** into the open air [come *out* and play] **3.** into existence or activity [disease broke *out*] **4.** *a*) to a conclusion [argue it *out*] *b*) completely [tired *out*] *c*) in full bloom, or in leaf **5.** into sight or notice [the moon came *out*] **6.** *a*) into or in circulation [to put *out* a new style] *b*) into or in society [debutantes who come *out*] **7.** from existence or activity [fade *out*] **8.** so as to remove from power or office [vote them *out*] **9.** aloud [sing *out*] **10.** beyond a regular surface, condition, etc. [stand *out*, eke *out*] **11.** away from the interior or midst [spread *out*] **12.** from one state, as of harmony, to another, as of disagreement [friends may fall *out*] **13.** into disuse, discard, etc. [long skirts went *out*] **14.** from a number or stock [pick *out* a hat] **15.** [Slang] into unconsciousness [to pass *out*] ☆**16.** *Baseball*, etc. in a manner that results in an out [to fly *out*] —*adj.* **1.** external: usually in combination [*outpost*] **2.** not inside nor in the usual limits [lock the door after all are *out*] **3.** outlying **4.** directed outward [an *out* flight] **5.** away from work, etc. **6.** not right; in error [he is *out* in his estimate] **7.** not working or in use [the lights are *out*] **8.** not to be considered; not possible [that idea is *out*] **9.** not in power [the *out* group] ☆**10.** trying to reach a verdict [the jury is still *out*] **11.** for outgoing mail [the *out* basket] ☆**12.** [Colloq.] having suffered a loss [*out* five dollars] **13.** [Colloq.] no longer popular; outmoded [wide cuffs are *out* this year] ☆**14.** *Baseball* having failed to get on base —*prep.* **1.** out of; through to the outside [walk *out* the door] **2.** along the way of [to drive *out* a driveway] **3.** [Poet.] forth from: usually after *from* —*n.* **1.** something that is out **2.** a person, group, etc. that is not in power, office, etc.: *usually used in pl.* ☆**3.** [Slang] a way out; means of avoiding [he has an *out* and won't have to go] ☆**4.** *Baseball* the failure of a batter or runner to reach base safely **5.** *Tennis*, *Squash*, etc. a service or return that lands out of bounds —*vi.* to come out; esp., to become known [the truth will *out*] —*vt.* to put out —*interj.* **1.** get out! **2.** message completed: used in ending a radio communication —**all out** completely; wholeheartedly —**on the outs** [Colloq.] on unfriendly terms: also **at outs** —**out and away** by far; without comparison —**out and out** completely; thoroughly —☆**out for** making a determined effort to get or do —**out of** **1.** from inside of **2.** from the number of [chosen *out of* the crowd] **3.** beyond [*out of* sight] **4.** from (material, etc.) [made *out of* stone] **5.** because of [*out of* spite] **6.** given birth by: said of animals **7.** having no [*out of* gas] **8.** not in a condition of [*out of* order] **9.** so as to deprive [cheat *out of* money] —**out one's way** [Colloq.] to or near one's neighborhood —**out to** making a determined effort to

out- [< OUT] *a combining form meaning:* **1.** at or from a point away, outside [*outbuilding*] **2.** going away or forth, outward [*outbound*] **3.** better, greater, or more than [*outdo*]: commonly used, as in the following self-explanatory terms:

outact	outhit	outscore
outbox	outperform	outshout
outfight	outproduce	outspend

☆**out·age** (out′ij) *n.* [OUT- + -AGE] an accidental interruption of electric power

out-and-out (out′'n out′) *adj.* complete; thorough [an *out-and-out* scoundrel]

out·back (out′bak′) *n.* [*also* O-] the flat, dry, wild inland region of Australia

out·bal·ance (out′bal′əns) *vt.* -anced, -anc·ing to be greater than in weight, value, etc.

out·bid (-bid′) *vt.* -bid′, -bid′ding to bid or offer more than (someone else)

out·board (out′bôrd′) *adj.*, *adv.* **1.** outside the hull or bulwarks of a ship or boat ☆**2.** away from the fuselage or hull of an aircraft ☆**3.** outside the main body of a spacecraft —*n.* **1.** *same as* OUTBOARD MOTOR **2.** a boat with an outboard motor

☆**outboard motor** a portable gasoline engine with propeller, mounted outboard on the stern of a boat to propel it

out·bound (-bound′) *adj.* outward bound

out·break (-brāk′) *n.* a breaking out; sudden occurrence, as of disease, war, rioting, etc.

out·build·ing (-bil′diŋ) *n.* a structure, as a garage or shed, separate from the main building

out·burst (-burst′) *n.* a sudden release, as of feeling, energy, etc.

out·cast (-kast′) *adj.* driven out; rejected —*n.* a person cast out or rejected, as by society

OUTBOARD MOTOR

out·class (out′klas′) *vt.* to be better than; surpass; excel

out·come (out′kum′) *n.* the way something turns out; result [the *outcome* of the election] —see SYN. at EFFECT

out·crop (out′kräp′; *for v.* out′kräp′) *n.* **1.** the breaking forth of a mineral from the earth so as to be exposed on the surface **2.** the exposed part of such a mineral —*vi.* -cropped′, -crop′ping to break forth in this way

out·cry (-krī′) *n.*, *pl.* -cries′ **1.** a crying out **2.** a strong protest or objection

out·dat·ed (out′dāt′id) *adj.* no longer current or popular; behind the times [*outdated* ideas]

out·dis·tance (-dis′təns) *vt.* -tanced, -tanc·ing to leave behind or get ahead of, as in a race

out·do (-do͞o′) *vt.* -did′, -done′, -do′ing to do better or more than; exceed or surpass —**outdo oneself** to do one's best or better than expected

out·door (out′dôr′) *adj.* **1.** being or taking place outdoors [an *outdoor* wedding] **2.** of, or fond of, the outdoors

☆**out·doors** (-dôrz′) *adv.* in or into the open; outside [they strolled *outdoors*] —*n.* **1.** any area outside a building **2.** countryside, etc. where there are few houses [he loves the *outdoors*]

out·er (out′ər) *adj.* **1.** located farther out; exterior **2.** relatively far removed [the *outer* regions]

Outer Banks chain of long, narrow, sandy islands along the coast of N.C.

out·er·coat (-kōt′) *n.* a topcoat, overcoat, etc.

Outer Mongolia *former name of* MONGOLIAN PEOPLE'S REPUBLIC: see MONGOLIA

out·er·most (-mōst′) *adj.* located farthest out

outer space **1.** space beyond the atmosphere of the earth **2.** space outside the solar system

out·er·wear (-wer′) *n.* outer garments, as topcoats

---

out·face (out'fās') *vt.* **-faced', -fac'ing** **1.** to overcome with a look or stare **2.** to defy or resist

out·field (out'fēld') *n.* ☆*Baseball* **1.** the playing area beyond the infield **2.** the outfielders as a group

☆**out·field·er** (-ər) *n. Baseball* a player whose position is in the outfield; right fielder, center fielder, or left fielder

out·fit (-fit') *n.* **1.** a set of articles or equipment used in some work or activity [a camping *outfit*] ☆**2.** articles of clothing worn together [a new spring *outfit*] ☆**3.** a group of people associated in some activity, as a military unit —*vt.* **-fit'ted, -fit'ting** to supply with what is needed [a store which *outfits* hunting parties] —*vi.* to obtain an outfit —see **SYN.** at FURNISH —**out'fit'ter** *n.*

out·flank (out'flaŋk') *vt.* **1.** to go around and beyond the flank of (enemy troops) **2.** to thwart; outwit

out·flow (out'flō') *n.* **1.** the act of flowing out **2.** *a)* that which flows out *b)* the amount flowing out

☆**out·fox** (out'fäks') *vt.* to outwit; outsmart

out·gen·er·al (-jen'ər əl) *vt.* **-aled** or **-alled, -al·ing** or **-al·ling** to be a better general or leader than

out·go (out'gō'; *for n.* out'gō') *vt.* **-went', -gone', -go'ing** to surpass; go beyond —*n., pl.* **-goes'** **1.** a going out **2.** that which goes out or is paid out; outflow or money spent

out·go·ing (out'gō'iŋ) *adj.* **1.** going out; leaving [the *outgoing* train] **2.** sociable, friendly, etc. [an *outgoing* personality] —*n.* the act of going out

out·grow (out'grō') *vt.* **-grew', -grown', -grow'ing** **1.** to grow faster or larger than [she *outgrew* her twin sister] **2.** to lose or get rid of by becoming mature [to *outgrow* an interest in dolls] **3.** to grow too large for [to *outgrow* a suit]

out·growth (out'grōth') *n.* **1.** a growing out **2.** a result; consequence; development [astronomy was an *outgrowth* of astrology] **3.** an offshoot

out·guess (out'ges') *vt.* to outwit by guessing the plans of

out·house (out'hous') *n.* an outbuilding; specif., a small shed over a pit, used as a toilet

out·ing (-iŋ) *n.* **1.** a pleasure trip or holiday away from home **2.** an outdoor walk, ride, etc.

out·land·er (-lan'dər) *n.* a foreigner; stranger

out·land·ish (out lan'dish) *adj.* **1.** very odd; fantastic, as though from a foreign land [dressed in *outlandish* clothes] **2.** remote; out-of-the-way [an *outlandish* corner of the world] —see **SYN.** at STRANGE —**out·land'ish·ly** *adv.*

out·last (-last') *vt.* **1.** to endure longer than [these soles will *outlast* the shoes] **2.** to outlive —see **SYN.** at OUTLIVE

out·law (out'lô') *n.* [OE. *utlaga* < ON. *utlagr,* outlawed: see OUT & LAW] **1.** orig., a person who had lost the rights and protection of the law **2.** a notorious criminal who is a fugitive from the law —*vt.* **1.** orig., to declare to be an outlaw **2.** to make (a contract, etc.) no longer binding **3.** to declare illegal [to *outlaw* parking on the streets] —**out'law'ry** *n., pl.* **-ries**

out·lay (out'lā'; *for v., usually* out'lā') *n.* **1.** a spending (of money, energy, etc.) **2.** money, etc. spent —*vt.* **-laid', -lay'ing** to spend (money)

out·let (out'let') *n.* **1.** a passage for letting something out [a flue is an *outlet* for fumes] **2.** a means of expression [her letters are an *outlet* for her rage] **3.** a stream, river, etc. that flows out from a lake **4.** *a)* a market for goods *b)* a store, etc. that sells the goods of a specific manufacturer or wholesaler ☆**5.** a point in a wiring system at which electric current may be taken by inserting a plug

out·line (-līn') *n.* **1.** a line following the outer limits of an object and showing its shape **2.** a sketch showing only the outer lines of an object **3.** [*also pl.*] a general plan without details **4.** a systematic listing of the important points of a subject [first prepare an *outline* of your talk] —*vt.* **-lined', -lin'ing** **1.** to draw in outline **2.** to list the main points of

out·live (out'liv') *vt.* **-lived', -liv'ing** **1.** to live or endure longer than **2.** to live through; outlast

SYN.—**outlive, outlast,** and **survive** all mean a continuing to exist longer than others or after a particular event, but **outlive** stresses power to endure, as in overcoming a difficulty [to *outlive* one's enemies, a disgrace, etc.], **outlast** suggests a remaining in existence for a time [to *outlast* one's usefulness], and **survive** implies a remaining alive after another's death [a son *survives* the deceased] or in spite of some danger or difficulty [we *survived* the flood]

out·look (out'look') *n.* **1.** *a)* a place for looking out *b)* the view from such a place **2.** one's way of thinking; point of view; attitude [she has a cheerful *outlook*] **3.** what is likely for the future; probable outcome [the business *outlook* for the coming year]

out·ly·ing (-lī'iŋ) *adj.* relatively far out from a certain point or center; remote [the *outlying* suburbs]

out·man (out'man') *vt.* **-manned', -man'ning** to have more men than [their troops were *outmanned* by the enemy]

out·ma·neu·ver, out·ma·noeu·vre (-mə nōō'vər) *vt.* **-vered** or **-vred, -ver·ing** or **-vring** to maneuver with better effect than; outwit

out·mod·ed (out'mōd'id) *adj.* no longer in style or common use; obsolete [*outmoded* clothes; *outmoded* methods]

out·most (out'mōst') *adj.* most remote; outermost

out·num·ber (out'num'bər) *vt.* to be greater in number than [the orchestra *outnumbered* its audience]

out-of-date (out'əv dāt') *adj.* no longer in style or use; outmoded; old-fashioned

out-of-door (-dôr') *adj. same as* OUTDOOR

out-of-doors (-dôrz') *adv., n. same as* OUTDOORS

out-of-pock·et (-päk'it) *adj.* designating minor expenses, or ready cash paid out, as for small items not included in a budget

out-of-the-way (-thə wā') *adj.* **1.** away from crowded centers, main roads, etc.; secluded [an *out-of-the-way* cabin] **2.** unusual; not well known [we saw some *out-of-the-way* movies]

out·pace (out'pās') *vt.* **-paced', -pac'ing** to surpass; exceed

out·pa·tient (out'pā'shənt) *n.* a patient coming in for treatment at a hospital but not kept in a bed there overnight

out·play (out'plā') *vt.* to play better than

out·point (-point') *vt.* to score more points than

out·post (out'pōst') *n.* **1.** *Mil. a)* a small group stationed at a distance from the main force, to prevent a surprise attack *b)* the place where it is stationed *c)* any military base away from the home country **2.** a settlement on a frontier

out·pour (out'pôr'; *for v.* out'pôr') *n.* **1.** a pouring out [he received an *outpour* of criticism] **2.** that which pours out; outflow Also **out'pour'ing** —*vt., vi.* to pour out

out·put (out'poot') *n.* **1.** the work done or amount produced, esp. over a given period **2.** in computers, *a)* information delivered according to coded instructions *b)* the act or process of delivering this information *c)* any of various devices involved in this process **3.** *Elec. a)* the useful current delivered by amplifiers, generators, etc. or by a circuit *b)* the terminal where such energy is delivered

out·rage (out'rāj') *n.* [< OFr. < *outre,* beyond < L. *ultra*] **1.** an extremely vicious or violent act **2.** a deep insult or offense **3.** great anger, indignation, etc. aroused by such an act or offense —*vt.* **-raged', -rag'ing** **1.** to commit an outrage upon; specif., *a)* to offend, insult, or wrong *b)* to rape **2.** to cause great anger, etc. in

out·ra·geous (out rā'jəs) *adj.* **1.** involving or doing great injury or wrong [the *outrageous* killing of hostages] **2.** so wrong or uncontrolled as to be shocking [to charge *outrageous* prices] —**out·ra'geous·ly** *adv.* —**out·ra'geous·ness** *n.*

SYN.—**outrageous** applies to that which is so much against what is right, moral, decent, etc. that it hurts or shocks [the *outrageous* massacre of the villagers]; **flagrant** is used of that which is openly bad or evil in persons or their acts [a *flagrant* sinner; a *flagrant* violation of the law]; **monstrous** and **atrocious** are applied to that which is extremely or shockingly wrong, bad, evil, cruel, etc. [a *monstrous* vice, lie, etc.; *atrocious* cruelty, manners, etc.]; **heinous** implies wickedness that is so extreme as to be revolting and arouse the strongest hatred [a *heinous* crime]

☆**out·rank** (out'raŋk') *vt.* to be of higher rank than

‡**ou·tré** (ōō trā'; *E.* -trā') *adj.* [Fr.] **1.** exaggerated **2.** odd or queer; eccentric; bizarre

out·reach (out'rēch'; *for n. & adj.* out'rēch') *vt., vi.* **1.** to reach farther (than); surpass **2.** to reach out; extend —*n.* a reaching out —☆*adj.* that is a branch office, as of a social agency, that serves those who cannot come to the main office

out·ride (out'rīd') *vt.* **-rode', -rid'den, -rid'ing** **1.** to ride better than **2.** to get through successfully [to *outride* a storm]

out·rid·er (out'rīd'ər) *n.* **1.** an attendant on horseback who rides ahead of or beside a carriage ☆**2.** a cowboy who rides over a range to prevent cattle from straying

out·rig·ger (-rig'ər) *n.* **1.** any framework reaching out beyond the rail of a ship, as a brace for an oarlock **2.** a timber or other float rigged out from the side of certain canoes to prevent tipping; also, a canoe of this type

out·right (out'rīt'; *for adv.* out'rīt') *adj.* **1.** being wholly such; thorough; complete; downright [an *outright* lie; an *outright*

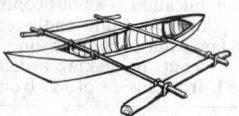

OUTRIGGER

fool] **2.** straightforward [an *outright* denial] —*adv.* **1.** entirely; wholly [the farm was sold *outright*] **2.** without holding back; openly [she laughed *outright*] **3.** at once [he was hired *outright*] —**out′right·ness** *n.*

out·run (out′run′) *vt.* **-ran′, -run′, -run′ning 1.** to run faster or farther than **2.** to go beyond; exceed [his expenses *outran* his income] **3.** to escape (a pursuer) as by running

out·sell (-sel′) *vt.* **-sold′, -sell′ing 1.** to sell in greater amounts than [a brand of tea that *outsells* all others] **2.** to sell more than (another salesman)

out·set (out′set′) *n.* a setting out; beginning; start [things went smoothly at the *outset* of the project]

out·shine (out′shīn′) *vt.* **-shone′** or **-shined′, -shin′ing 1.** to shine brighter or longer than (another) **2.** to be better than; surpass; excel [Eddie *outshines* the other players]

out·shoot (out′shoot′; *for n.* out′shoot′) *vt., vi.* **-shot′, -shoot′ing** to shoot better than (another) —*n.* that which shoots out or protrudes; projection

out·side (out′sīd′, out′-; *for prep. & adv., usually* out′sīd′) *n.* **1.** the outer side, part, or surface; exterior [wash the windows on the *outside*] **2.** outward look or appearance [a man who seems jolly on the *outside*] **3.** any place or area not inside [the prisoners got little news from the *outside*] —*adj.* **1.** of or on the outside; outer [the *outside* layer] **2.** coming from or situated beyond given limits; from some other place, person, group, etc. [to accept no *outside* help] **3.** extreme; maximum [an *outside* estimate] **4.** mere; slight [an *outside* chance] —*adv.* **1.** on or to the outside **2.** beyond certain limits **3.** outdoors [go play *outside*] —*prep.* **1.** on or to the outer side of [leave it *outside* the door] **2.** beyond the limits of [traveling *outside* the country] —**at the outside** at the very most —**outside of 1.** outside **2.** [Colloq.] other than; except for

out·sid·er (out′sīd′ər) *n.* one who is outside or not included; esp., one not a member of a given group

out·sit (-sit′) *vt.* **-sat′, -sit′ting** to sit longer than or beyond the time of

out·size (out′sīz′) *n.* **1.** an odd size; esp., an unusually large size **2.** a garment, etc. of such a size —*adj.* of nonstandard size; esp., unusually large: also **out′sized′**

out·skirts (-skurts′) *n.pl.* the outer areas, as of a city

☆**out·smart** (out′smärt′) *vt.* to overcome by cunning or cleverness; outwit —**outsmart oneself** to fail by trying too hard to be cunning or clever

out·spo·ken (out′spō′kən) *adj.* **1.** speaking in a free, unrestrained way; frank [an *outspoken* critic] **2.** spoken boldly or candidly [*outspoken* criticism] —see **SYN.** at FRANK —**out′spo′ken·ly** *adv.* —**out′spo′ken·ness** *n.*

out·spread (out′spred′; *for adj. & n.* out′spred′) *vt., vi.* **-spread′, -spread′ing** to spread out; extend; expand —*n.* a spreading out —*adj.* spread out; extended; expanded [the *outspread* branches of the tree]

out·stand·ing (out′stand′iŋ) *adj.* **1.** that stands out as very unusual; prominent; distinguished [an *outstanding* feat] **2.** unsettled [talks to settle *outstanding* issues] **3.** unpaid [*outstanding* debts] **4.** that have been issued and sold: said of stocks and bonds —see **SYN.** at NOTICEABLE —**out′stand′ing·ly** *adv.*

out·stare (-ster′) *vt.* **-stared′, -star′ing** to overcome with a look or stare; outface

out·sta·tion (out′stā′shən) *n.* a post or station in a remote or unsettled area

out·stay (out′stā′) *vt.* **1.** to stay longer than **2.** to stay beyond the time of; overstay [to *outstay* one's welcome]

out·stretch (-strech′) *vt.* **1.** to extend **2.** to stretch beyond —**out′stretched′** *adj.*

out·strip (-strip′) *vt.* **-stripped′, -strip′ping 1.** to go at a faster pace than; get ahead of **2.** to do better than; surpass; excel [to *outstrip* one's competitors]

out·talk (-tôk′) *vt.* to talk more skillfully, loudly, or forcibly than; surpass in talking

out·think (-thiŋk′) *vt.* **-thought′, -think′ing 1.** to think deeper, faster, or more cunningly than **2.** to outwit in this way

out·vote (-vōt′) *vt.* **-vot′ed, -vot′ing** to defeat in a vote

out·ward (out′wərd) *adj.* **1.** having to do with the outside; outer **2.** readily seen; visible [he showed no *outward* sign of fear] **3.** to or toward the outside [an *outward* glance] —*adv.*

toward the outside; away, as from port [they were *outward* bound]: also **out′wards** —*n.* that which is outward —**out′ward·ness** *n.*

out·ward·ly (-lē) *adv.* **1.** toward or on the outside **2.** in looks or appearance; seemingly [he was *outwardly* contented]

out·wear (out′wer′) *vt.* **-wore′, -worn′, -wear′ing 1.** to wear out or use up **2.** to be more lasting than [these shoes will *outwear* any others]

out·weigh (-wā′) *vt.* **1.** to weigh more than **2.** to be more important, valuable, etc. than [but hope *outweighed* his fear]

out·wit (-wit′) *vt.* **-wit′ted, -wit′ting** to get the better of by cunning or cleverness

out·work (out′wurk′; *for v.* out′wurk′) *n.* a lesser fortification built out beyond the main defenses —*vt.* **-worked′** or **-wrought′, -work′ing** to work better or harder than

ou·zel (ōō′z'l) *n.* [OE. *osle*] any of several perching birds including the dippers, of Europe, Asia, and the New World; esp., *same as* WATER OUZEL

o·va (ō′və) *n. pl. of* OVUM

o·val (ō′v'l) *adj.* [< Fr. < L. *ovum*, an egg] **1.** shaped like the cross section of an egg lengthwise; elliptical **2.** having the form of an egg —*n.* anything oval —**o′val·ly** *adv.* —**o′val·ness** *n.*

o·va·ry (ō′vər ē) *n., pl.* **-ries** [< ModL. < L. *ovum,* an egg] **1.** *Anat., Zool.* either of the pair of female reproductive glands producing eggs and, in vertebrates, sex hormones **2.** *Bot.* the enlarged hollow part of the pistil, containing ovules —**o·var·i·an** (ō ver′ē ən) *adj.*

o·vate (ō′vāt) *adj.* [< L. < *ovum,* an egg] **1.** egg-shaped **2.** *Bot.* shaped like the cross section of an egg lengthwise, esp. with the broader end at the base, as some leaves —**o′vate·ly** *adv.*

OVARIES
(A, ovary;
B, Fallopian
tube; C, uterus)

o·va·tion (ō vā′shən) *n.* [L. *ovatio* < *ovare,* to celebrate a triumph] loud and long applause or cheering by a crowd to show approval or welcome

ov·en (uv′ən) *n.* [OE. *ofen*] a compartment, as in a stove, for baking or roasting food or for heating or drying things

ov·en·bird (-burd′) *n.* ☆a N. American warbler that builds a domelike nest on the ground in the woods

o·ver (ō′vər) *prep.* [OE. *ofer* < IE. base *uper*] **1.** *a)* in, at, or to a position up from; above [the canopy *over* their bed] *b)* across and down from [to fall *over* a cliff] **2.** while engaged in [discuss it *over* dinner] **3.** upon the surface of [spread icing *over* the cake] **4.** so as to cover [shutters *over* the windows] **5.** so as to have an effect on [he cast a spell *over* us] **6.** with care, concern, etc. for [watch *over* the flock] **7.** above in authority, power, etc. [the officers *over* him] **8.** along or across, or above and to the other side of [fly *over* the lake] **9.** on the other side of [a city *over* the border] **10.** through all or many parts of [*over* the whole State] **11.** during [*over* the years] **12.** more than [*over* ten dollars] **13.** up to and including [stay *over* Easter] **14.** rather than [choose red *over* blue] **15.** concerning; about [don't fight *over* it] **16.** through the medium of [*over* the radio] —*adv.* **1.** *a)* above, across, or to the other side [jump *over*] *b)* across the brim or edge [the soup boiled *over*] **2.** more; beyond [three hours or *over*] **3.** longer or till a time later [please stay *over*] **4.** covering the entire area [the wound healed *over*] **5.** from start to finish [count the money *over*] **6.** *a)* from an upright position [he fell *over*] *b)* upside down [turn the cup *over*] **7.** again [do it *over*] **8.** at or on the other side, as of an intervening space [*over* in Spain] **9.** from one side, viewpoint, person, etc. to another [they won him *over*] —*adj.* **1.** upper, outer, superior, excessive, or extra: often in combination [*overcoat, overseer, oversupply*] **2.** finished; past [his life is *over*] **3.** having reached the other side **4.** [Colloq.] as a surplus; extra [an hour *over* for the week] —*n.* something in addition; surplus —*interj.* **1.** turn the page, etc. over **2.** channel turned over to you for reply: used in radio communication —**over again** another time; anew —**over all** over the whole extent; from end to end —**over and above** more than —**over and over (again)** repeatedly

o·ver- *a combining form meaning:* **1.** above in position, outer, upper, superior [*overhead, overlord*] **2.** passing across or beyond [*overrun*] **3.** downward from above [*overflow*] **4.** excessive, too much [*overload, oversell*]: the list below includes some common compounds formed with *over-* that can be understood if *too* or *too much* is added to the meaning of the base word

o'ver·a·bun'dance	o'ver·has'ty
o'ver·a·bun'dant	o'ver·heat'
o'ver·ac'tive	o'ver·i·mag'i·na·tive
o'ver·ag·gres'sive	o'ver·in·dulge'
o'ver·am·bi'tious	o'ver·in·vest'
o'ver·an·a·lyt'i·cal	o'ver·jeal'ous
o'ver·anx'ious	o'ver·kind'
o'ver·at·ten'tive	o'ver·lad'en
o'ver·bold'	o'ver·long'
o'ver·buy'	o'ver·mod'est
o'ver·care'ful	o'ver·nice'
o'ver·care'less	o'ver·op'ti·mis'tic
o'ver·cau'tious	o'ver·or'ga·nize'
o'ver·com·pet'i·tive	o'ver·par·tic'u·lar
o'ver·con·fi'dent	o'ver·pay'
o'ver·con·sci·en'tious	o'ver·praise'
o'ver·con·ser'va·tive	o'ver·pre·cise'
o'ver·cook'	o'ver·re·fined'
o'ver·crit'i·cal	o'ver·re·li'gious
o'ver·dec'o·rate	o'ver·ripe'
o'ver·de·pen'dent	o'ver·sen'si·tive
o'ver·ea'ger	o'ver·sen'ti·men'tal
o'ver·eat'	o'ver·skep'ti·cal
o'ver·e·lab'o·rate	o'ver·so·lic'i·tous
o'ver·e·mo'tion·al	o'ver·spe'cial·ize'
o'ver·em'pha·size'	o'ver·spend'
o'ver·en·thu'si·as'tic	o'ver·stim'u·late'
o'ver·ex·cite'	o'ver·stretch'
o'ver·ex'er·cise'	o'ver·strict'
o'ver·ex·ert'	o'ver·sub'tle
o'ver·ex·pand'	o'ver·sus·pi'cious
o'ver·ex·tend'	o'ver·tire'
o'ver·fa·mil'iar	o'ver·use'
o'ver·fed'	o'ver·val'ue
o'ver·fond'	o'ver·war'y
o'ver·gen'er·ous	o'ver·wind'
o'ver·greed'y	o'ver·zeal'ous

o·ver·a·chieve (ō'vər ə chēv') *vi.* **-chieved', -chiev'ing** to do better, as in one's studies, than it is thought one is able to do —**o'ver·a·chiev'er** *n.*

o·ver·act (ō'vər akt') *vt., vi.* to act (a part in a play) in an exaggerated way

o·ver·age[1] (ō'vər āj') *adj.* **1.** over the age fixed as a standard **2.** so old as to be of no use

o·ver·age[2] (ō'vər ij) *n.* [OVER- + -AGE] a surplus, as of goods

o·ver·all (ō'vər ôl'; *for adv.* -ôl') *adj.* **1.** from end to end [the *overall* length of a boat] **2.** including everything; total [the *overall* cost] —*adv.* **1.** from end to end **2.** in general [a good contract *overall*]

☆**o·ver·alls** (-ôlz') *n.pl.* loose-fitting trousers, often with a part coming up over the chest, worn over other clothing to protect against dirt and wear

o·ver·arch (ō'vər ärch') *vt., vi.* to form an arch over (something)

o·ver·arm (ō'vər ärm') *adj.* done by raising the arm above the shoulder, as a swimming stroke

o·ver·awe (ō'vər ô') *vt.* **-awed', -aw'ing** to overcome or make feel humble by filling with awe

o·ver·bal·ance (ō'vər bal'əns; *for n.* ō'vər bal'əns) *vt.* **-anced, -anc·ing 1.** *same as* OUTWEIGH **2.** to throw off balance —*n.* something that overbalances

o·ver·bear (ō'vər ber') *vt.* **-bore', -borne', -bear'ing 1.** to press or bear down by weight or physical power **2.** to overcome, override, or be domineering over —*vi.* to be too fruitful

o·ver·bear·ing (-iŋ) *adj.* **1.** ordering others about in a harsh, bullying way; arrogant or domineering **2.** dominant or overriding —see SYN. at PROUD —**o'ver·bear'ing·ly** *adv.* —**o'ver·bear'ing·ness** *n.*

o·ver·bid (ō'vər bid'; *for n.* ō'vər bid') *vt., vi.* **-bid', -bid'ding 1.** to bid more than (another person) **2.** to bid more than the worth of (a thing, as one's hand in bridge) —*n.* a higher or excessive bid

o·ver·blown[1] (ō'vər blōn') *adj.* past the stage of full bloom

o·ver·blown[2] (ō'vər blōn') *adj.* **1.** stout; obese **2.** *a)* overdone; excessive *b)* pompous; bombastic

o·ver·board (ō'vər bôrd') *adv.* **1.** over a ship's side **2.** from a ship into the water [he fell *overboard*] —**go overboard** ☆[Colloq.] to go to extremes; esp., to be wildly enthusiastic —**throw overboard** to get rid of

o·ver·build (ō'vər bild') *vt., vi.* **-built', -build'ing** to build more houses or other buildings than are needed or wanted in (an area)

o·ver·bur·den (-bur'd'n) *vt.* to place too heavy a burden on; weigh down; oppress

o·ver·cap·i·tal·ize (-kap'ə tə līz') *vt., vi.* **-ized', -iz'ing** to furnish too much capital for or set too high a capital value on (a business) —**o'ver·cap'i·tal·i·za'tion** *n.*

o·ver·cast (ō'vər kast'; *for v. 1, usually* ō'vər kast') *n.* a covering, esp. of clouds —*adj.* **1.** cloudy: said of the sky or weather **2.** *Sewing* made with overcasting —*vt., vi.* **-cast', -cast'ing 1.** to overcloud; darken **2.** *Sewing* to sew over (an edge) with long, loose stitches to prevent raveling

o·ver·charge (ō'vər chärj'; *for n.* ō'vər chärj') *vt., vi.* **-charged', -charg'ing 1.** to charge too high a price **2.** to overload —*n.* **1.** too high a charge **2.** too full or heavy a load

o·ver·cloud (-kloud') *vt., vi.* **1.** to darken or cover with clouds; dim **2.** to make or become gloomy, angry, etc. in appearance

☆**o·ver·coat** (ō'vər kōt') *n.* a coat, esp. a heavy coat, worn over the usual clothing for warmth

o·ver·come (ō'vər kum') *vt.* **-came', -come', -com'ing 1.** to get the better of in competition, etc.; conquer [to *overcome* an enemy] **2.** to master, triumph over, or get the better of [to *overcome* obstacles] **3.** to make weak or helpless; overpower or overwhelm [*overcome* by laughter] —*vi.* to win —see SYN. at CONQUER

o·ver·com·pen·sate (-käm'pən sāt') *vt.* **-sat'ed, -sat'ing** to give too much compensation to —*vi.* to react to a real or imagined physical or psychological defect by an exaggerated drive to compensate for it —**o'ver·com'pen·sa'tion** *n.*

o·ver·crowd (-kroud') *vt.* to crowd with too many people or things

o·ver·de·vel·op (-di vel'əp) *vt.* **1.** to develop too much **2.** *Photog.* to develop (a film, plate, etc.) too long or in too strong a developer —**o'ver·de·vel'op·ment** *n.*

o·ver·do (-doo') *vt.* **-did', -done', -do'ing 1.** to do too much, or to excess [he *overdid* the campaigning] **2.** to spoil the effect of by exaggeration [to *overdo* an apology] **3.** to cook too long —*vi.* to do too much

o·ver·dose (ō'vər dōs'; *for v.* ō'vər dōs') *n.* too large a dose, now especially of a narcotic —*vt., vi.* **-dosed', -dos'ing** to give or take too large a dose See also OD (*n.*)

o·ver·draft (ō'vər draft') *n.* **1.** an overdrawing of money from a bank **2.** the amount overdrawn

o·ver·draw (ō'vər drô') *vt.* **-drew', -drawn', -draw'ing 1.** to spoil the effect of by exaggeration [villains are *overdrawn* in melodramas] **2.** to write checks for more money than one has in his bank account

o·ver·dress (-dres') *vt., vi.* to dress too warmly, too showily, or too formally for the occasion

o·ver·drive (ō'vər drīv') *n.* a gear that at a certain speed automatically reduces an engine's power output without reducing its driving speed

o·ver·due (ō'vər doo', -dyoo') *adj.* **1.** past or delayed beyond the time set for payment, arrival, etc. [an *overdue* bill] **2.** that should have come about sooner [*overdue* reforms]

o·ver·es·ti·mate (-es'tə māt'; *for n.* -mit) *vt.* **-mat'ed, -mat'ing** to set too high an estimate on or for —*n.* an estimate that is too high —**o'ver·es'ti·ma'tion** *n.*

o·ver·ex·pose (-ik spōz') *vt.* **-posed', -pos'ing** to expose too much or too long —**o'ver·ex·po'sure** (-spō'zhər) *n.*

o·ver·flow (ō'vər flō'; *for n.* ō'vər flō') *vt.* **1.** to flow or spread across; flood [water *overflowed* the streets] **2.** to flow over the brim or edge of [the river *overflowed* its banks] **3.** to cause to overflow by filling beyond capacity [he *overflowed* the glass with ice water] —*vi.* **1.** to flow or spread beyond the limits; run over [the sink is *overflowing*] **2.** to be superabundant; be more than full [she is *overflowing* with kindness] —*n.* **1.** an overflowing or being overflowed **2.** the amount that overflows; surplus **3.** an outlet for draining off overflowing liquids, as near the top of a bathtub

o·ver·fly (ō'vər flī') *vt.* **-flew', -flown', -fly'ing** to fly an aircraft over (a specified area) or beyond (a specified place), as for military spying —**o'ver·flight'** *n.*

o·ver·grow (-grō') *vt.* **-grew', -grown', -grow'ing 1.** to spread with growth or foliage so as to cover up [the lawn is *overgrown* with weeds] **2.** to outgrow —*vi.* **1.** to grow too large or too fast **2.** to grow beyond normal size [he is *over-grown* for his age] —**o′ver·growth′** *n.*

o·ver·hand (ō′vər hand′) *adj.* **1.** with the hand over the object it grasps **2.** done with the arm raised above the shoulder [an *overhand* pitch] **3.** designating or of sewing in which the stitches are passed over two edges to sew them together —*adv.* in an overhand manner [to throw a ball *overhand*] —☆*vt.* to sew overhand —*n. Sports* an overhand stroke

overhand knot a kind of knot: see illustration at KNOT

o·ver·hang (ō′vər haŋ′; *for n.* ō′vər haŋ′) *vt.* **-hung′, -hang′-ing 1.** to hang or project over or beyond [the roof *overhangs* the house] **2.** to loom over; threaten —*vi.* to project or jut out over something —*n.* **1.** the projection of one thing over or beyond another **2.** an overhanging or projecting part

o·ver·haul (ō′vər hôl′; *for n.* ō′vər hôl′) *vt.* **1.** to haul over, as for examination **2.** *a*) to check thoroughly for needed repairs, adjustments, etc. *b*) to make such repairs, etc. on **3.** to catch up with —*n.* an overhauling

o·ver·head (ō′vər hed′; *for adv.* ō′vər hed′) *adj.* **1.** located or operating above the level of the head [an *overhead* light] **2.** in the sky [the clouds *overhead*] **3.** on a higher level, with reference to related objects [a machine with an *overhead* drive] —*n.* the general, continuing costs of running a business, as of rent, maintenance, taxes, etc. —*adv.* above the head; aloft

o·ver·hear (ō′vər hir′) *vt.* **-heard′, -hear′ing** to hear (something spoken or a speaker) without the speaker's knowledge or intention

o·ver·joy (-joi′) *vt.* to give great joy to; delight

☆**o·ver·kill** (-kil′) *n.* the capacity of a nation's nuclear weapon stockpile to kill many times the total population of any given nation

o·ver·land (-land′, -lənd) *adv., adj.* by, on, or across land

O·ver·land Park (ō′vər lənd) [after the *Overland*, or Santa Fe, Trail which passed through the area] city in NE Kans.: suburb of Kansas City: pop. 77,000

o·ver·lap (ō′vər lap′; *for n.* ō′vər lap′) *vt., vi.* **-lapped′, -lap′ping** to lap over; extend over (something or each other) so as to occupy some part of the same space or time [the scales on fish *overlap* one another; the two events *overlapped* in time] —*n.* **1.** an overlapping **2.** a part that overlaps **3.** the extent or place of overlapping

o·ver·lay (ō′vər lā′; *for n.* ō′vər lā′) *vt.* **-laid′, -lay′ing 1.** to lay or spread over **2.** to cover, as with a decorative layer [the box was *overlaid* with ivory] —*n.* **1.** a covering **2.** a decorative layer or covering **3.** a transparent flap showing additional details, areas of color, etc. placed over a map, art work, etc.

OVERLAY (sense 3)

o·ver·leap (ō′vər lēp′) *vt.* **1.** to leap over or across **2.** to omit; pass over **3.** to overreach (oneself) by leaping too far

o·ver·lie (-lī′) *vt.* **-lay′, -lain′, -ly′ing 1.** to lie on or over **2.** to smother by lying on

o·ver·load (ō′vər lōd′; *for n.* ō′vər lōd′) *vt.* to put too great a load in or on —*n.* too great a load

o·ver·look (ō′vər look′; *for n.,* ō′vər look′) *vt.* **1.** to look at from above **2.** to give a view of from above; rise above [the high building *overlooks* the city] **3.** *a*) to look beyond and not see; fail to notice [I *overlooked* that detail] *b*) to ignore; neglect **4.** to pass over indulgently; excuse [can you *overlook* his rudeness?] —*n.* a height or the view from it

o·ver·lord (ō′vər lôrd′) *n.* a lord ranking above other lords, esp. in the feudal system

o·ver·ly (-lē) *adv.* too or too much; excessively

o·ver·man (ō′vər man′) *vt.* **-manned′, -man′ning** to supply with more men than necessary

o·ver·mas·ter (-mas′tər) *vt.* to overcome; conquer

o·ver·match (-mach′) *vt.* **1.** to be more than a match for **2.** to match against a superior opponent

o·ver·much (-much′) *adj., adv., n.* too much

o·ver·night (ō′vər nīt′; *for adj.* ō′vər nīt′) *adv.* **1.** during or through the night [plan on staying with us *overnight*] **2.** on or during the previous evening [the carnival had moved out over-night] **3.** very suddenly [his attitude changed *overnight*] —*adj.* **1.** done or going on during the night [an *overnight* snow] **2.** of the previous evening **3.** for one night [an *overnight* guest] ☆**4.** of or for a brief trip [an *overnight* bag]

o·ver·pass (ō′vər pas′) ☆*n.* a bridge or other passageway over a road, railway, etc.

o·ver·play (ō′vər plā′) *vt.* **1.** to overact, overdo, or overemphasize **2.** *Card Games* to overestimate the strength of (one's hand)

o·ver·pop·u·late (-päp′yə lāt′) *vt.* **-lat′ed, -lat′ing** to populate (an area) too heavily for the available resources —**o′ver·pop′u·la′tion** *n.*

o·ver·pow·er (-pou′ər) *vt.* **1.** to get the better of; make helpless; subdue; overwhelm **2.** to supply with more power than is needed —**o′ver·pow′er·ing** *adj.* —**o′ver·pow′er·ing·ly** *adv.*

o·ver·print (ō′vər print′; *for n.* ō′vər print′) *vt.* to print over (a previously printed surface) —*n.* anything overprinted, as (on) a stamp

o·ver·pro·duce (ō′vər prə doōs′, -dyoōs′) *vt., vi.* **-duced′, -duc′ing** to produce in a quantity that exceeds the need or demand —**o′ver·pro·duc′tion** *n.*

o·ver·pro·tect (-prə tekt′) *vt.* to protect more than is necessary; specif., to seek to shield (one's child, etc.) from normal hurts or conflicts —**o′ver·pro·tec′tive** *adj.*

o·ver·rate (-rāt′) *vt.* **-rat′ed, -rat′ing** to rate or estimate too highly

o·ver·reach (-rēch′) *vt.* **1.** to reach beyond or above **2.** to reach too far for and miss **3.** to outwit or cheat —*vi.* to reach too far —**overreach oneself 1.** to fail because of trying more than one can do **2.** to fail because of being too crafty or eager —**o′ver·reach′er** *n.*

o·ver·re·act (-rē akt′) *vi.* to react in a highly emotional way, often with violence

o·ver·ride (-rīd′) *vt.* **-rode′, -rid′den, -rid′ing 1.** to ride over **2.** to trample down **3.** to put down or prevail over [the tyrant *overrode* the wishes of the people] **4.** to disregard, overrule, or nullify [Congress *overrode* the President's veto] **5.** to fatigue (a horse, etc.) by riding too long

o·ver·rule (-roōl′) *vt.* **-ruled′, -rul′ing 1.** to set aside or decide against, as by higher authority; rule against or rule out [the higher court *overruled* the judge's decision] **2.** to win out or prevail over

o·ver·run (ō′vər run′; *for n.* ō′vər run′) *vt.* **-ran′, -run′, -run′ning 1.** to spread out over so as to cover [weeds *overran* the garden] **2.** to swarm over, doing harm [a house *overrun* with mice] **3.** to invade or conquer by a rapid advance [the enemy *overran* our positions] **4.** to spread swiftly throughout, as ideas **5.** to run beyond (certain limits) [to *overrun* second base] —*vi.* **1.** to overflow **2.** to run beyond certain limits —*n.* **1.** an act or instance of overrunning [an *overrun* in the cost of production] **2.** the amount that overruns

o·ver·seas (ō′vər sēz′) *adv.* over or beyond the sea [food was sent *overseas*] —*adj.* **1.** foreign [an *overseas* visitor] **2.** over or across the sea [an *overseas* flight] Also, chiefly Brit., **o′ver·sea′**

o·ver·see (ō′vər sē′) *vt.* **-saw′, -seen′, -see′ing** to watch over and direct; supervise; superintend [he *oversaw* the work]

o·ver·se·er (ō′vər sē′ər) *n.* a person who directs the work of others; supervisor

o·ver·sell (ō′vər sel′) *vt.* **-sold′, -sell′ing 1.** to sell more than can be supplied ☆**2.** to promote to an extreme degree that defeats one's purposes

o·ver·set (ō′vər set′; *for n.* ō′vər set′) *vt.* **-set′, -set′ting 1.** to upset **2.** to overturn or overthrow —*vi.* to tip over —*n.* an overturning

o·ver·shad·ow (ō′vər shad′ō) *vt.* **1.** *a*) to cast a shadow over *b*) to darken or spread gloom over **2.** to be more significant or important than by comparison [good times *overshadow* the bad ones]

☆**o·ver·shoe** (ō′vər shoō′) *n.* a kind of boot of rubber or fabric worn over the regular shoe to protect against cold or dampness; galosh

o·ver·shoot (ō′vər shoōt′) *vt.* **-shot′, -shoot′ing 1.** to shoot or pass over or beyond (a target, mark, etc.) **2.** to go farther than (an intended or normal limit); exceed —*vi.* to shoot or go too far

o·ver·shot (ō'vər shät') *adj.* **1.** with the upper part or half extending past the lower [an *overshot* jaw] **2.** driven by water flowing onto the upper part [an *overshot* water wheel]

o·ver·sight (-sīt') *n.* **1.** a failure to notice or do something; careless mistake or omission **2.** an overseeing; supervision

o·ver·sim·pli·fy (ō'vər sim'plə fī') *vt., vi.* **-fied', -fy'ing** to make (something) seem to be much more simple than it really is —**o'ver·sim'pli·fi·ca'tion** *n.*

o·ver·size (ō'vər sīz') *adj.* **1.** too large **2.** larger than the normal or usual [*oversize* shoes] Also **o'ver·sized'** —*n.* a size larger than regular sizes

☆**o·ver·skirt** (-skʉrt') *n.* an outer skirt

o·ver·sleep (ō'vər slēp') *vi.* **-slept', -sleep'ing** to sleep past the intended time for getting up

o·ver·spread (-spred') *vt.* **-spread', -spread'ing** to spread over; cover the surface of [a blush *overspread* her face]

o·ver·state (-stāt') *vt.* **-stat'ed, -stat'ing** to give an exaggerated account of (facts, truth, etc.) —**o'ver·state'ment** *n.*

o·ver·stay (-stā') *vt.* to stay beyond the time or limits of [the guest *overstayed* his welcome]

o·ver·step (-step') *vt.* **-stepped', -step'ping** to go beyond the limits of; exceed [to *overstep* one's authority]

o·ver·stock (ō'vər stäk'; *for n.* ō'vər stäk') *vt.* to stock more of than is needed or can be used —*n.* too large a stock

o·ver·strung (ō'vər struŋ') *adj.* very high-strung; too nervous

o·ver·stuff (-stuf') *vt.* **1.** to stuff with too much of something **2.** to upholster (furniture) with deep stuffing —**o'ver·stuffed' adj.**

o·ver·sub·scribe (-səb skrīb') *vt., vi.* **-scribed', -scrib'ing** to subscribe for more (of) than is available or asked —**o'ver·sub·scrip'tion** (-skrip'shən) *n.*

o·ver·sup·ply (-sə plī') *vt.* **-plied', -ply'ing** to supply with more than is needed —*n., pl.* **-plies** too great a supply

o·vert (ō vʉrt', ō'vʉrt) *adj.* [< MFr. pp. of *ovrir* < L. *aperire*, to open] **1.** not hidden; open [crying is an *overt* display of grief] **2.** *Law* done publicly, without attempt at concealment — **o·vert'ly** *adv.* —**o·vert'ness** *n.*

o·ver·take (ō'vər tāk') *vt.* **-took', -tak'en, -tak'ing** **1.** to catch up with and, often, go beyond [the tortoise *overtook* the hare] **2.** to come upon unexpectedly or suddenly [a sudden storm *overtook* us]

o·ver·tax (-taks') *vt.* **1.** to tax too heavily **2.** to make excessive demands on; put too much strain on [the work *overtaxed* his strength]

o·ver·throw (ō'vər thrō'; *for n.* ō'vər thrō') *vt.* **-threw', -thrown', -throw'ing** **1.** to throw or turn over; upset **2.** to overcome; conquer; end [the rebels *overthrew* the government] **3.** to throw a ball, etc. beyond (the intended receiver or target) —*n.* **1.** an overthrowing or being overthrown **2.** destruction; end; downfall —see **SYN.** *at* CONQUER

o·ver·time (ō'vər tīm'; *for v.* -tīm') *n.* **1.** time beyond the established limit, as of working hours **2.** pay for work done in such time **3.** *Sports* an extra period added to the game to decide a tie —*adj., adv.* of, for, or during (an) overtime —*vt.* **-timed', -tim'ing** to allow too much time for (a photographic exposure, etc.)

o·ver·tone (ō'vər tōn') *n.* **1.** any of the higher tones heard along with a fundamental musical tone **2.** something implied; nuance: *usually used in pl.* [a reply full of *overtones*]

o·ver·top (ō'vər täp') *vt.* **-topped', -top'ping** **1.** to rise above **2.** to excel; surpass

o·ver·train (-trān') *vt., vi.* to train too long or too hard

o·ver·trick (ō'vər trik') *n. Card Games* any trick won above the number bid

o·ver·trump (ō'vər trump') *vt., vi. Card Games* to trump with a higher trump than has been played

o·ver·ture (ō'vər chər, ō'və-) *n.* [< OFr. < L. *apertura*, APERTURE] **1.** an opening proposal or move made to get someone to do something **2.** a musical introduction, as to an opera

o·ver·turn (ō'vər tʉrn'; *for n.* ō'vər tʉrn') *vt.* **1.** to turn over; upset **2.** to overthrow; conquer —*vi.* to tip over; capsize —*n.* an overturning or being overturned

o·ver·view (ō'vər vyo͞o') *n.* a general review or survey

o·ver·ween·ing (ō'vər wē'niŋ) *adj.* [< OE. *oferwenan*: see

OVER- & WEEN] **1.** arrogant; too proud **2.** exaggerated; excessive [he has *overweening* ambition] —**o'ver·ween'ing·ly** *adv.*

o·ver·weigh (-wā') *vt.* **1.** *same as* OUTWEIGH **2.** to weigh down; burden; oppress

o·ver·weight (ō'vər wāt'; *for adj. & v.,* ō'vər wāt') *n.* more weight than is needed or allowed; extra weight —*adj.* above the normal, desirable, or allowed weight —*vt. same as* OVERWEIGH

o·ver·whelm (ō'vər hwelm', -welm') *vt.* [see OVER- & WHELM] **1.** to pour down on and bury beneath [floods *overwhelmed* the farm] **2.** to overcome completely; crush; overpower [our team *overwhelmed* theirs] —**o'ver·whelm'ing** *adj.* —**o'ver·whelm'ing·ly** *adv.*

o·ver·work (ō'vər wʉrk'; *for n.* ō'vər wʉrk') *vt.* to work or use too much [to *overwork* a horse; to *overwork* an excuse] —*vi.* to work too hard or too long —*n.* work that is too harsh or heavy

o·ver·write (ō'vər rīt') *vt., vi.* **-wrote', -writ'ten, -writ'ing** **1.** to write over (other writing) **2.** to write too much, or in a labored style, about (some subject) **3.** to receive a commission on the sales of (a subagent)

o·ver·wrought (ō'vər rôt') *adj.* **1.** very nervous or excited **2.** with the surface decorated **3.** having too much decoration; showy [an *overwrought* design]

o·vi- [< L. *ovum*, an egg] *a combining form meaning* egg or ovum [*oviduct, oviform*]

Ov·id (äv'id) (L. name, *Publius Ovidius Naso*) 43 B.C.–17? A.D., Rom. poet

o·vi·duct (ō'vi dukt') *n.* [< ModL.: see OVI- & DUCT] a duct or tube through which the ovum passes from an ovary to the uterus or to the outside

o·vi·form (-fôrm') *adj.* [OVI- & -FORM] egg-shaped

o·vip·a·rous (ō vip'ər əs) *adj.* [< L.: see OVI- & -PAROUS] producing eggs which hatch after leaving the body, as birds: opposed to VIVIPAROUS —**o·vip'a·rous·ly** *adv.*

o·vi·pos·i·tor (ō'vi päz'i tər) *n.* [ModL. < OVI- + L. *positor*, one who places < *ponere*, to place] an organ of many female insects, usually at the end of the abdomen, for depositing eggs

o·void (ō'void) *adj.* [OV(I)- + -OID] egg-shaped: also **o·void'al** —*n.* anything of ovoid form

o·vo·vi·vip·a·rous (ō'vō vī vip'ər əs) *adj.* [< OVI- + VIVIPAROUS] designating various animals, as some reptiles, fishes, and snails, which produce eggs with enclosing membranes, that are hatched within the body so that the young are born alive

o·vu·late (ō'vyə lāt', äv'yə-) *vi.* **-lat'ed, -lat'ing** [OVUL(E) + -ATE] to produce and discharge ova from the ovary —**o'vu·la'tion** *n.* —**o'vu·la·to·ry** (-lə tôr'ē) *adj.*

o·vule (ō'vyo͞ol, äv'yo͞ol) *n.* [Fr. < ModL. dim. of L. *ovum*, egg] a small egg or seed, esp. one in an early stage of development; specif., *a)* *Bot.* the part of a plant which develops into a seed *b)* *Zool.* the immature ovum —**o'vu·lar** *adj.*

o·vum (ō'vəm) *n., pl.* **o·va** (ō'və) [L., an egg] *Biol.* a mature female germ cell

ow (ou) *interj.* a cry of pain

owe (ō) *vt.* **owed, ow'ing** [OE. *agan*, to own < IE. base *eik-*, to possess] **1.** to be indebted to someone for (a specified amount or thing) [he still *owes* the bank $200 on his loan; I *owe* my life to that doctor] **2.** to feel the need or have the obligation to do, give, etc. [I *owe* my aunt a letter; we *owe* her our respect] **3.** to harbor (a feeling) toward another: only in **owe a grudge** —*vi.* to be in debt

O·wens·bor·o (ō'ənz bʉr'ō) [after a Col. *Owens* (1769–1811)] city in NW Ky., on the Ohio: pop. 50,000

ow·ing (ō'iŋ) *adj.* **1.** that owes **2.** due; unpaid [ten dollars *owing* on a bill] —**owing to** because of; as a result of

owl (oul) *n.* [OE. *ule*] a night bird of prey found throughout the world, having a large face, large eyes, a short, hooked beak, and feathered legs with sharp talons: the owl is thought of as having a wise or solemn look —**owl'like' adj.**

owl·et (oul'it) *n.* a young or small owl

owl·ish (-ish) *adj.* like or characteristic of an owl —**owl'ish·ly** *adv.* —**owl'ish·ness n.**

own (ōn) *adj.* [OE. *agen*, pp. of *agan*, to possess: see OWE] belonging or relating to oneself or itself: used to strengthen a preceding possessive [his *own* book] —*n.* that which belongs to oneself [the car is his *own*] —*vt.* **1.** to possess; have [he *owns* three houses] **2.** to admit; acknowledge [he *owned* that he was wrong] —*vi.* to

SAW-WHET
OWL (to
8 in. long)

OVERSHOT
WATER WHEEL

confess (*to*) [*she owned to a feeling of shame*] —**come into one's own** to receive what properly belongs to one, esp. fame or success —see SYN. at ACKNOWLEDGE —**of one's own** belonging strictly to oneself —**on one's own** [Colloq.] by one's own efforts; independent —**own up (to)** to confess (to) —**own′er** *n.* —**own′er·less** *adj.*

own·er·ship (ō′nər ship′) *n.* **1.** the state or fact of being an owner **2.** legal right of possession; lawful title (to something)

ox (äks) *n., pl.* **ox·en,** rarely **ox**: see PLURAL, II, D, 1 [OE. *oxa*] **1.** any of several bovine mammals, as the buffalo, bison, yak, etc. **2.** a castrated bull, used as a draft animal —**ox′like′** *adj.*

ox·a·late (äk′sə lāt′) *n.* a salt or ester of oxalic acid

ox·al·ic acid (äk sal′ik) [< Fr. < L. < Gr. *oxalis,* sorrel < *oxys,* acid] a colorless, poisonous, crystalline acid, (COOH)₂, found in many plants and used in dyeing, bleaching, etc.

ox·a·lis (äks′ə lis) *n.* [see prec.] *same as* WOOD SORREL

ox·blood (äks′blud′) *n.* a deep-red color

ox·bow (-bō′) *n.* **1.** the U-shaped part of an ox yoke which passes under and around the animal's neck ☆**2.** something shaped like this, as a bend in a river

ox·en (äk′s'n) *n. pl. of* OX

ox·eye (äks′ī′) *n.* **1.** any of several composite plants, ☆as a tall plant of eastern N. America that resembles the sunflower **2.** any of various birds, as the dunlin

ox·eyed (-īd′) *adj.* having large, full eyes

☆**oxeye daisy** *same as* DAISY (sense 1)

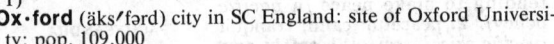

OXBOWS

Ox·ford (äks′fərd) city in SC England: site of Oxford University: pop. 109,000

ox·ford (äks′fərd) *n.* [after prec.] [*sometimes* O-] **1.** a low shoe laced over the instep: also **oxford shoe 2.** a cotton or cottonlike fabric with a basket weave, used for shirts, etc.: also **oxford cloth**

Oxford gray a very dark gray, nearly black

ox·heart (äks′härt′) *n.* ☆a large, heart-shaped cherry

ox·i·dant (äk′sə dənt) *n.* an oxidizing agent

ox·i·da·tion (äk′sə dā′shən) *n.* an oxidizing or being oxidized —**ox′i·da′tive** *adj.*

ox·i·da·tion-re·duc·tion (-ri duk′shən) *n.* a chemical reaction in which one of the substances is reduced (gains one or more electrons) and another substance is oxidized (loses one or more electrons)

ox·ide (äk′sīd) *n.* [Fr. < Gr. *oxys,* sour + Fr. (*ac*)*ide,* acid] a binary compound of oxygen with another element or a radical

ox·i·dize (äk′sə dīz′) *vt.* -**dized**, -**diz′ing** [OXID(E) + -IZE] **1.** to unite with oxygen, as in burning or rusting **2.** to increase the positive valence or decrease the negative valence of (an element or ion) —*vi.* to become oxidized —**ox′i·diz′a·ble** *adj.* —**ox′i·diz′er** *n.*

ox·lip (äks′lip′) *n.* [< OE. < *oxa,* ox + *slyppe,* dropping] a perennial plant related to the primrose, having yellow flowers in early spring

Ox·nard (äks′närd) [after H. *Oxnard,* local businessman] city in SW Calif.: pop. 71,000

Ox·o·ni·an (äk sō′nē ən) *adj.* of Oxford (England) or Oxford University —*n.* **1.** a student or alumnus of Oxford University **2.** a native or inhabitant of Oxford, England

ox·tail (äks′tāl′) *n.* the tail of an ox or steer, esp. when skinned and used in soup or stew

ox·y-¹ [< OXY(GEN)] *a combining form meaning* containing oxygen

ox·y-² [< Gr. *oxys,* sharp] *a combining form meaning* sharp, pointed, or acid [*oxymoron, oxygen*]

ox·y·a·cet·y·lene (äk′sē ə set′'l ēn′) *adj.* of or using a mixture of oxygen and acetylene, as for producing an extremely hot flame used in welding or cutting metals [*oxyacetylene* torch]

ox·y·gen (äk′si jən) *n.* [< Fr.: see OXY-² & -GEN] a colorless, odorless, and tasteless gas that is a chemical element: it is the most abundant of all elements and occurs free in the atmosphere, forming one fifth of its volume; it is able to combine with nearly all other elements and is essential to life processes and to combustion: symbol, O; at. wt., 15.9994; at. no., 8 —**ox′y·gen·ic** (-jen′ik, -zē′nik) *adj.*

ox·y·gen·ate (äk′si jə nāt′) *vt.* -**at′ed**, -**at′ing** to mix, treat, or combine with oxygen: also **ox′y·gen·ize′**, -**ized′**, -**iz′ing** —**ox′y·gen·a′tion** *n.* —**ox′y·gen·a′tor** *n.*

oxygen tent a transparent enclosure into which oxygen is released, fitted around a bed patient to help him breathe

ox·y·hem·o·glo·bin (äk′si hē′mə glō′bin) *n.* [OXY-¹ + HEMOGLOBIN] the bright-red substance in arterial blood, formed in the lungs when oxygen loosely unites with hemoglobin

ox·y·hy·dro·gen (äk′si hī′drə jən) *adj.* of or using a mixture of oxygen and hydrogen, as for producing a hot flame used in welding [*oxyhydrogen* torch]

ox·y·mo·ron (äk′si môr′än) *n., pl.* -**mo′ra** (-ə) [LGr. < *oxys,* sharp + *moros,* dull] a figure of speech in which contradictory ideas or terms are combined, as "sweet sorrow"

o·yez, o·yes (ō′yez′, -yes′, -yā′) *interj.* [Anglo-Fr., hear ye, ult. < L. *audire,* to hear] hear ye! attention!: usually cried out three times by an official to command silence before a proclamation is made —*n.* a cry of "oyez"

oys·ter (oi′stər) *n.* [< OFr. < L. *ostrea* < Gr. *ostreon:* for IE. base see OSSIFY] **1.** a marine mollusk with two rough shells hinged together, found esp. on the ocean floor and widely used as food **2.** any of several similar bivalve mollusks

oyster bed a natural or artificially prepared place on the ocean floor for breeding oysters

oyster crab any of various small crabs that live in the gill cavities of oysters, clams, etc.

☆**oyster cracker** a small, round, salted soda cracker

oyster plant ☆*same as* SALSIFY

oz. *pl.* **oz.**, **ozs.** ounce

O·zark Mountains (ō′zärk) [< Fr. *aux Arcs,* to the (region of the) Arc (Arkansas) Indians, a Siouan-speaking tribe] highland region in NW Ark., SW Mo., & NE Okla.: also **Ozarks**

o·zone (ō′zōn) *n.* [Fr. < Gr. *ozein,* to smell] **1.** a pale-blue gas, O₃, with a sharp odor: it is a form of oxygen produced by a silent electrical discharge in air and used as a bleaching agent, water purifier, etc. **2.** [Slang] pure, fresh air —**o·zon′ic** (-zän′ik, -zō′nik) *adj.*

o·zon·ize (ō′zō nīz′) *vt.* -**ized′**, -**iz′ing** **1.** to change (oxygen) into ozone **2.** to treat with ozone —**o′zon·i·za′tion** *n.* —**o′zon·iz′er** *n.*

o·zo·no·sphere (ō zō′nə sfir′) *n.* [< OZONE + -SPHERE] the atmospheric layer, extending from a height of about 6 miles to about 30 miles, in which there is a measurable amount of ozone that prevents some heat loss from earth

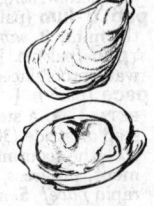

OYSTER
(upper, closed; lower, open)

P

P, p (pē) *n., pl.* **P's, p's 1.** the sixteenth letter of the English alphabet **2.** the sound of *P* or *p* —**mind one's p's and q's** to be careful what one does

P 1. *Chess* pawn **2.** *Chem.* phosphorus **3.** police **4.** *Physics* power or pressure

p [Brit.] penny; pennies

P., p. 1. pitcher **2.** power **3.** pressure

p. 1. *pl.* **pp.** page **2.** participle **3.** past **4.** penny **5.** per **6.** piano **7.** pint

pa (pä; *dial. often* pô) *n.* [Colloq.] father; papa

Pa *Chem.* protactinium

Pa., PA Pennsylvania

P.A. public address (system)

p.a. 1. participial adjective **2.** per annum

pa·'an·ga (pä äŋ'ä) *n., pl.* **pa·'an'ga** [Polynesian (Tongan), a kind of seedpod] *see* MONETARY UNITS, table (Tonga)

☆**Pab·lum** (pab'ləm) [< PABULUM] *a trademark for* a soft, bland cereal food for infants —*n.* [p-] any oversimplified or tasteless writing, ideas, etc.

pab·u·lum (pab'yoo ləm) *n.* [L.] **1.** food **2.** nourishment for the mind **3.** *same as* PABLUM

☆**pac** (pak) *n.* [< AmInd. *pacu,* moccasin] a high, insulated, waterproof, laced boot

pace (pās) *n.* [< OFr. *pas* < L. *passus,* a step: for IE. base see PETAL] **1.** a step in walking, running, etc. **2.** the length of a step or stride (30 in. to 40 in.) **3.** the rate of speed in walking, etc. [the scoutmaster set the *pace* in the hike] **4.** rate of movement, progress, development, etc. [science goes forward at a rapid *pace*] **5.** a particular way of walking, etc.; gait [a halting *pace*] **6.** the gait of a horse in which both legs on the same side are raised together —*vt.* **paced, pac'ing 1.** to walk back and forth across [we *paced* the floor nervously] **2.** to measure by paces (often with *off*) [*pace* off 30 yards] **3.** to train or guide the pace of (a horse) **4.** to set the pace for (a runner, etc.) **5.** to go before and lead [electronics industries *paced* others in the 1960's] **6.** to cover (a certain distance) —*vi.* **1.** to walk with regular steps **2.** to raise both legs on the same side at the same time in moving: said of a horse —**change of pace 1.** variation in tempo or mood **2.** *Baseball* a slowly pitched ball thrown with the same arm movement as another ball —**keep pace (with)** to maintain the same speed or rate of progress (as) —**put through one's paces** to test one's abilities, etc. —**set the pace 1.** to go at a speed that others try to equal **2.** to do or be something for others to equal or surpass —**pac'er** *n.*

pace·mak·er (pās'mā'kər) *n.* **1.** *a)* a runner, horse, etc. that sets the pace for others, as in a race *b)* a person, group, or thing that serves as a model Also **pace'set'ter 2.** *Med.* an electronic device implanted in the body and connected, as through an artery, to the heart: it provides regular, mild electric shocks that regulate the heartbeat —**pace'mak'ing** *n.*

pa·chi·si (pə chē'zē) *n.* [< Hindi < *pacīs,* twenty-five (the highest throw)] **1.** in India, a game in which the moves of pieces around a board are determined by the throwing of cowrie shells **2.** *same as* PARCHEESI

pach·y·derm (pak'ə durm') *n.* [< Fr. < Gr. < *pachys,* thick + *derma,* a skin] **1.** a large, thick-skinned,

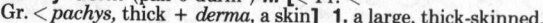
PACEMAKER

hoofed animal, as the elephant, rhinoceros, or hippopotamus **2.** an insensitive, stolid person —**pach'y·der'mal, pach'y·der'mic** *adj.* —**pach'y·der'ma·tous, pach'y·der'mous** *adj.*

☆**pach·y·san·dra** (pak'ə san'drə) *n.* [ModL. < Gr. *pachys,* thick + ModL. *-andrus, -*ANDROUS] a low, dense-growing, hardy evergreen plant, often used for a ground cover

Pa·cif·ic (pə sif'ik) [< its pacific (that is, calm) appearance] largest of the earth's oceans, between Asia and the American continents —*adj.* of, in, on, or near this ocean

pa·cif·ic (pə sif'ik) *adj.* [< Fr. < L. < *pacificare,* PACIFY] **1.** making or tending to make peace [a *pacific* policy] **2.** peaceful; calm; tranquil [*pacific* skies] —**pa·cif'i·cal·ly** *adv.*

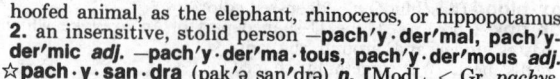
PACHYSANDRA

pac·i·fi·ca·tion (pas'ə fi kā'shən) *n.* a pacifying or being pacified —**pa·cif'i·ca·to·ry** (pə sif'ə kə tôr'ē) *adj.*

Pacific Islands, Trust Territory of the U.S. trust territory in the W Pacific, consisting of the Caroline & Marshall islands: 420 sq. mi.; pop. 95,000

☆**Pacific Standard Time** *see* STANDARD TIME

pac·i·fi·er (pas'ə fī'ər) *n.* **1.** a person or thing that pacifies ☆**2.** a rubber or plastic nipple or teething ring for babies

pac·i·fism (pas'ə fiz'm) *n.* [< Fr.: see PACIFIC & -ISM] opposition to the use of force under any circumstances; specif., refusal for reasons of conscience to participate in war or any military activity —**pac'i·fist** *n., adj.* —**pac'i·fis'tic** *adj.* —**pac'i·fis'ti·cal·ly** *adv.*

pac·i·fy (pas'ə fī') *vt.* **-fied', -fy'ing** [< Fr. < L. *pacificare* < *pax,* PEACE + *facere,* to make] **1.** to make peaceful or calm; appease; tranquilize [apologies *pacified* her neighbors] **2.** *a)* to secure peace in (a nation, etc.) *b)* to seek to neutralize or win over (people in occupied areas) —**pac'i·fi'a·ble** *adj.*

SYN.—pacify implies a making quiet and peaceful that which has become noisy or disorderly [to *pacify* a crying child]; **appease** suggests a pacifying by giving in to demands [to *appease* one's hunger]; **mollify** suggests a soothing of wounded feelings or calming of anger [his compliments failed to *mollify* her]; **placate** implies the changing of an unfriendly or angry attitude to a friendly or favorable one [to *placate* an offended colleague]; **propitiate** implies a calming or preventing of hostile feeling by winning the good will of higher power [to *propitiate* a deity]; **conciliate** implies the use of arbitration, concession, persuasion, etc. in an attempt to win someone over —ANT. anger, enrage

pack[1] (pak) *n.* [MDu. *pak* < MFl. *pac*] **1.** a bundle of things tied up for carrying, as on the back; load; burden **2.** a container in which something may be stored compactly [parachute *pack*] **3.** a group or set [a *pack* of lies or liars]; specif., *a)* a package of a standard number [a *pack* of cigarettes] *b)* a set of playing cards; deck *c)* a set of hunting hounds *d)* a group of wild animals living and hunting together **4.** *same as* ICE PACK **5.** *a)* treatment by wrapping a patient in sheets, etc. that are wet or dry and hot or cold *b)* the sheets so used **6.** a cosmetic paste applied to the skin and left to dry [mudpack] **7.** *a)* the amount of food put in cans, etc. in a season or year *b)* a method of packing or canning [cold *pack*] —*vt.* **1.** to make a pack of **2.** *a)* to put together in a box, trunk, etc. for carrying or storing [to *pack* away summer clothes] *b)* to fill (a box, trunk, etc.) for carrying or storing **3.** to put (food) in (cans, etc.) for preservation **4.** *a)* to crowd; cram [the stadium was *packed*] *b)* to crowd (people) together **5.** to fill in tightly, as for prevention of leaks [to *pack* valves] **6.** to press together firmly [*packed* earth] **7.** to load (an animal) with a pack **8.** to carry (goods, etc.) in a pack: said of an animal **9.** to send (*off*), usually in haste [to *pack* a boy off to school] ☆**10.** [Slang] to wear or carry (a gun, etc.) as part of one's equipment **11.** [Slang] *a)* to deliver (a blow, punch, etc.) with force *b)* to provide or contain [a play that *packs* a message] —*vi.* **1.** to make up packs **2.** to put one's clothes, etc. into luggage for a trip [an hour in which to *pack*] **3.** to crowd together in a small space **4.** to admit of being folded compactly, put in a container, etc. [this suit *packs* well] ☆**5.** to settle into a compact mass [the snow on the road *packed* fast] —*adj.* **1.** used in or suitable for packing **2.** formed into packs **3.** used for carrying packs, loads, etc. [a *pack* animal] —see SYN. at GROUP —**send packing** to dismiss (a person) abruptly —**pack′a·bil′i·ty** *n.* —**pack′a·ble** *adj.*

pack² (pak) *vt.* [? related to prec.] to choose (a jury, court, etc.) dishonestly so as to get desired results

☆**-pack** (pak) *a combining form meaning* a carton of (a specified number of) bottles or cans, as of beer

pack·age (pak′ij) *n.* **1.** orig., the act or process of packing **2.** a wrapped or boxed thing; parcel **3.** a container, wrapping, etc., esp. one in which a commodity is packed for sale ☆**4.** a number of items, plans, etc. offered together as a unit —☆*vt.* **-aged, -ag·ing** to put into a package —☆*adj.* designating or of a plan, offer, etc. by which a number of items are offered for acceptance as a unit [*package* deal; *package* tour] —**pack′ag·er** *n.*

☆**package store** a store where alcoholic liquor is sold by the bottle to be drunk off the premises

pack·er (pak′ər) *n.* a person or thing that packs; specif., *a)* one who packs goods for shipping, sale, etc. ☆*b)* one who owns or manages a packing house

pack·et (pak′it) *n.* **1.** a small package **2.** *same as* PACKET BOAT —*vt.* to make up into a packet

packet boat a boat that travels a regular route carrying passengers, freight, and mail

pack·ing (pak′iŋ) *n.* **1.** the act or process of a person or thing that packs; specif., the large-scale processing and packaging of meats, fruits, etc. **2.** any material used to pack

☆**packing house** a plant where meats are processed and packed for sale; also, a similar plant for packing fruits and vegetables

☆**pack rat** a N. American rat that often hides small articles in its nest

pack·sad·dle (-sad′'l) *n.* a saddle with fastenings to hold the load carried by a pack animal

pack·thread (-thred′) *n.* strong, thick thread or twine for tying bundles, packages, etc.

☆**pack train** a group of pack animals moving in a line

pact (pakt) *n.* [< OFr. < L. < pp. of *paciscere*, to agree < *pax*, PEACE] an agreement between persons, groups, or nations; compact

pad¹ (pad) *n.* [echoic, but infl. by PAD³] the dull sound made by a footstep or staff on the ground

pad² (pad) *n.* [? var. of POD] **1.** a soft, stuffed saddle **2.** anything made of or stuffed with soft material to fill out a shape, protect from friction, jarring, blows, etc.; cushion [a shoulder *pad;* a seat *pad*] **3.** a piece of folded gauze, etc. used as a dressing on a wound, etc. **4.** *a)* the foot of certain animals, as the wolf, fox, etc. *b)* any of the cushionlike parts on the underside of such a foot ☆**5.** the floating leaf of a water plant, as the waterlily **6.** a number of sheets of paper for writing or drawing, glued together along one edge; tablet **7.** a small cushion soaked with ink for inking a rubber stamp: in full, **stamp pad** or **ink pad** **8.** *same as* LAUNCH PAD **9.** [Slang] *a)* a bed *b)* the room, apartment, etc. where one lives —*vt.* **pad′ded, pad′ding** **1.** to stuff, cover, or line with a pad or padding **2.** to lengthen (a speech or writing) with unnecessary material ☆**3.** to put on (an expense account, etc.) items that are made up or raised above the true amount

pad³ (pad) *vi.* **pad′ded, pad′ding** [< Du. *pad*, path] **1.** to travel on foot; walk **2.** to walk or run with a soft step

pad·ding (pad′iŋ) *n.* **1.** the action of one who pads **2.** any soft material used to pad, as cotton, felt, etc. **3.** unnecessary material put into a speech, writing, etc. to make it longer

pad·dle¹ (pad′'l) *n.* [< ?] **1.** a short oar with a wide blade, used, without an oarlock, to make a canoe go **2.** any of various things shaped like this and used for stirring, mixing, beating, spanking, etc. ☆**3.** a flat, rounded piece of wood with a short handle, used to hit a ball, as in table tennis **4.** any of the boards in a water wheel or paddle wheel —*vt., vi.* **-dled, -dling** **1.** to move (a canoe, etc.) with a paddle **2.** to punish by beating as with a paddle; spank **3.** to stir, work, etc. with a paddle —☆**paddle one's own canoe** to depend entirely on oneself —**pad′dler** *n.*

PADDLE

pad·dle² (pad′'l) *vi.* **-dled, -dling** [prob. PAD³ + -LE²] **1.** to move the hands or feet about in the water; dabble **2.** to walk like a small child; toddle —**pad′dler** *n.*

☆**paddle ball** a game similar to squash, played in a walled court with short-handled rackets

☆**pad·dle·fish** (-fish′) *n., pl.* **-fish′, -fish′es:** see FISH a large fish of the Mississippi and Yangtze river systems, with a paddle-shaped snout

☆**paddle tennis** an outdoor game played with paddles and a rubber ball on a raised platform surrounded by a screen, combining rules of tennis, handball, and squash

paddle wheel a wheel with paddles around it for moving a steamboat through the water

pad·dock (pad′ək) *n.* [< OE. *pearruc*, enclosure] **1.** a small, fenced-off field near a stable, in which horses are exercised **2.** an enclosed place at a race track, where horses are saddled and walked before a race

pad·dy (pad′ē) *n., pl.* **-dies** [Malay *padi*] **1.** rice in the husk, growing or gathered **2.** a rice field: often **rice paddy**

☆**paddy wagon** *slang name for* PATROL WAGON

Pa·de·rew·ski (pä′de ref′skē; *E.* pad′ə ref′skē), **I·gnace (Jan)** (ē′nyàs′) 1860–1941; Pol. pianist & composer

pad·lock (pad′läk′) *n.* [< ME. < *pad* (< ?) + *lokke*, LOCK¹] a removable lock with a hinged, U-shaped arm to be passed through a staple, chain, or eye —*vt.* to fasten or keep shut as with a padlock

pa·dre (pä′drā, -drē; *It.* -dre; *Sp.* -thre) *n., pl.* **-dres** (-dräz, -drēz; *It.* -thres); *It.* **pa′dri** (-drē) [Sp., It., Port. < L. *pater*, a FATHER] **1.** father: the title of a priest in Italy, Spain, Portugal, and Latin America **2.** [Slang] a priest or chaplain

pa·dro·ne (pə drō′nē) *n.* [It. < L. *patronus*, PATRON] master; boss; patron

Pad·u·a (paj′ōō ə, pad′yōō ə) city in N Italy: pop. 226,000: It. name **Pa·do·va** (pä′dô vä) —**Pad′u·an** *adj., n.*

pae·an (pē′ən) *n.* [L. < Gr. < *Paian*, epithet of Apollo] a song of joy, triumph, praise, etc.

pae·do- *same as* PEDO-¹: also **paed-**

pa·el·la (pä yel′ə; *Sp.* pä e′lyä) *n.* [Catalonian, lit., cooking pot < OFr. < L. *patella*, a small pan] a Spanish dish of rice cooked with chicken, seafood, etc. and seasoned with saffron

pa·gan (pā′gən) *n.* [LL. *paganus*, a heathen < L., a peasant < *pagus*, country] **1.** anyone not a Christian, Moslem, or Jew **2.** a person who has no religion —*adj.* **1.** of pagans **2.** not religious —**pa′gan·dom** *n.* —**pa′gan·ish** *adj.* —**pa′gan·ism** *n.* SYN.—**pagan** and **heathen** are both applied to peoples who do not believe in God, but **pagan** specifically refers to one of the ancient peoples who believed in many gods, esp. the Greeks and Romans, and **heathen** is applied to any peoples thought of as primitive idol worshipers

Pa·ga·ni·ni (pä′gä nē′nē; *E.* pag′ə nē′nē), **Ni·co·lò** (nē′kô-lô′) 1782–1840; It. violinist & composer

pa·gan·ize (pā′gə nīz′) *vt., vi.* **-ized′, -iz′ing** to make or become pagan —**pa′gan·iz′er** *n.*

page¹ (pāj) *n.* [Fr. < L. *pagina* < base of *pangere*, to fasten: for IE. base see PEACE] **1.** *a)* one side of a leaf of a book, newspaper, etc. *b)* the printing or writing on it [the sports *pages*] *c)* an entire leaf in a book, etc. **2.** [often *pl.*] a record of events *[the *pages* of history]* **3.** an event or series of events that might fill a page *[a colorful *page* in his life]* —*vt.* **paged, pag'ing** to number the pages of —*vi.* to turn pages in looking quickly (*through* a book, etc.)

page[2] (pāj) *n.* [OFr. < It. *paggio*] **1.** formerly, a boy training for knighthood **2.** a boy attendant, esp. one serving a person of high rank, as in court **3.** a boy, or sometimes a girl, who runs errands, carries messages, etc., as in a hotel, legislature, etc. —*vt.* **paged, pag'ing 1.** to attend as a page ☆**2.** to try to find or summon (a person) by calling his name, as a hotel page does

pag·eant (paj'ənt) *n.* [Anglo-L. *pagina*, scene displayed on a stage, stage < L., PAGE[1]] **1.** a spectacular exhibition, elaborate parade, etc., as a procession with floats **2.** a drama, often staged outdoors, celebrating a historical event or events **3.** empty show or display

pag·eant·ry (-ən trē) *n., pl.* **-ries 1.** pageants as a group **2.** grand spectacle; gorgeous display **3.** empty show or display

pag·i·nate (paj'ə nāt) *vt.* **-nat'ed, -nat'ing** to number the pages of (a book, etc.)

pag·i·na·tion (paj'ə nā'shən) *n.* **1.** the numbering of the pages of a book, etc. **2.** the figures with which pages are numbered in order

pa·go·da (pə gō'də) *n.* [< Port., prob. < Per. < *but*, idol + *kadah*, house, prob. infl. by Prakrit *bhagodī*, divine] in the Orient, a temple that is a tapering tower with rooflike, upward curving projections between its several stories

PAGODA

Pa·go Pa·go (päŋ'ō päŋ'ō, pä'gō pä'gō) seaport on the S coast of Tutuila Island, American Samoa: pop. 2,500

paid (pād) *pt. & pp.* of PAY

pail (pāl) *n.* [OE. *pægel*, small measure < LL. *pagella* (dim. of L. *pagina*, PAGE[1]) in VL. a measure of area or volume] **1.** a cylindrical container, usually with a hoop-shaped handle, for carrying liquids, etc.; bucket **2.** the amount held by a pail: also **pail'ful'**, *pl.* **-fuls'**

pain (pān) *n.* [< OFr. < L. *poena*, punishment: see PENAL] **1.** orig., penalty or punishment **2.** a feeling of hurting caused by injury, disease, etc. *[a sharp *pain* in the chest]* **3.** the distress or suffering caused by worry, grief, disappointment, etc. *[the memory of the loss brought her *pain*]* **4.** *[pl.]* the labor of childbirth **5.** *[pl.]* great care or effort *[to take *pains* with one's work]* **6.** [Slang] an annoyance or nuisance: often used in phrases specifying a part of the body, as in **pain in the neck** —*vt.* to cause pain to; hurt *[his wound *pains* him]* —see SYN. at EFFORT —**on** (or **upon** or **under**) **pain of** at the risk of bringing upon oneself (punishment, death, etc.)

Paine (pān), **Thomas** 1737–1809; Am. Revolutionary patriot, writer, & political theorist, born in England

pained (pānd) *adj.* **1.** hurt or distressed; having the feelings hurt; offended **2.** showing hurt feelings or resentment *[a *pained* expression]*

pain·ful (pān'fəl) *adj.* **1.** causing pain; hurting; distressing *[a *painful* situation]* **2.** having pain; aching *[a *painful* finger]* **3.** exacting and difficult *[to take *painful* care]* **4.** annoying; unpleasant *[a long, *painful* lecture]* —**pain'ful·ly** *adv.* —**pain'ful·ness** *n.*

☆**pain·kill·er** (-kil'ər) *n.* [Colloq.] a medicine that relieves pain; analgesic

pain·less (-lis) *adj.* **1.** free from or without pain **2.** not causing or involving pain *[painless* childbirth]* —**pain'less·ly** *adv.* —**pain'less·ness** *n.*

pains·tak·ing (pānz'tā'kiŋ) *n.* great care or diligence —*adj.* requiring, using, or showing great care and effort *[painstaking* work]* —**pains'tak'ing·ly** *adv.*

paint (pānt) *vt.* [< OFr. pp. of *peindre* < L. *pingere* < IE. base *peig-*, to mark] **1.** *a)* to make (a picture, etc.) in colors applied to a surface *b)* to make a picture of with paints *[to *paint* a landscape]* **2.** to describe colorfully; picture in words **3.** to cover or decorate with paint *[to *paint* a wall]* **4.** to apply such cosmetics as lipstick, rouge, etc. to **5.** to apply (a medicine, etc.) with a brush or swab —*vi.* **1.** to practice the art of painting pictures **2.** to use cosmetics —*n.* **1.** a mixture of coloring matter with oil, water, etc. used for coating a surface or for making pictures on canvas, etc. **2.** a dried coat of paint **3.** *a)* coloring matter, as lipstick, rouge, etc., used as a cosmetic *b)* *same as* GREASEPAINT ☆**4.** [Dial.] a spotted horse; pinto —**paint out** to cover up as with a coat of paint —☆**paint the town (red)** [Slang]

to go on a spree in nightclubs, bars, etc. —**paint'a·ble** *adj.* —**paint'y** *adj.* **paint'i·er, paint'i·est**

paint·brush (pānt'brush') *n.* a brush used for applying paint

painted cup ☆*same as* INDIAN PAINTBRUSH

Painted Desert [so named from the colorful rock strata] desert plateau in NC Ariz., east of the Colorado River

paint·er[1] (pānt'ər) *n.* **1.** an artist who paints pictures **2.** a person whose work is covering surfaces, as walls, with paint

paint·er[2] (pānt'ər) *n.* [< OFr., ult. < L. *pendere*, to hang] a rope attached to the bow of a boat for tying it to a dock, etc.

☆**paint·er**[3] (pānt'ər) *n.* [< PANTHER] *dial. var. of* COUGAR

paint·er·ly (pān'tər lē) *adj.* having the quality of the techniques special to the art of painting, as in brushwork and the use of color masses rather than lines to achieve form

paint·ing (pānt'iŋ) *n.* **1.** the work or art of one who paints **2.** a picture made with paints

pair (per) *n., pl.* **pairs;** sometimes, after a number, **pair** [< OFr. < L. neut. pl. of *par*, equal] **1.** two things of the same kind that are used together; set of two *[a *pair* of shoes]* **2.** a single thing with two joined corresponding parts *[a *pair* of pants]* **3.** two persons or animals; specif., *a)* a married, engaged, or courting couple *b)* two mated animals *c)* two people with something in common *[a *pair* of thieves]* *d)* two animals that form a team *[a *pair* of oxen]* *e)* two legislators on opposing sides of a question who agree to withhold their vote so as to offset each other; also, such an agreement **4.** two playing cards of the same denomination —*vt.* **1.** to make a pair of (two persons or things) or of (one *with* another) by matching, joining, etc. **2.** to arrange in pairs —*vi.* **1.** to form a pair; match **2.** to mate —**pair off 1.** to join (two people or things) in a pair **2.** to separate into pairs

pair·ing (per'iŋ) *n.* **1.** the grouping of contestants in a tournament into competing pairs **2.** *[pl.]* the list of such pairs

pai·sa (pī'sä) *n., pl.* **-se** (-se) [Hindi *paisā*] *see* MONETARY UNITS, table (Bangladesh, India, Oman, Pakistan)

Pais·ley (pāz'lē) city in SC Scotland, near Glasgow: pop. 96,000

pais·ley (pāz'lē) *adj.* [after PAISLEY, where orig. made] *[also* P-] **1.** of or having an elaborate, colorful pattern of curved figures **2.** made of cloth having such a pattern —*n. [also* P-] a paisley cloth, shawl, necktie, etc.

Pai·ute (pī'yōōt, pī yōōt') *n.* [< Shoshonean *pah-ute*, lit., water Ute] **1.** *pl.* **-utes, -ute** a member of any of various groups of N. American Indians living in Nevada, California, Utah, and Arizona **2.** any of their Shoshonean dialects

pa·ja·mas (pə jam'əz, -jä'məz) *n.pl.* [< Hindi < Per. *pāi*, a leg + *jāma*, garment] a loosely fitting sleeping or lounging suit consisting of a jacket, or pullover blouse, and trousers —**pa·ja'·ma** *adj.*

PAISLEY PATTERN

Pa·ki·stan (pä'ki stän', pak'i stan') country in S Asia, on the Arabian Sea: 310,403 sq. mi.; pop. 42,900,000; cap. Islamabad

Pa·ki·stan·i (pä'ki stä'nē, pak'i stan'ē) *adj.* of Pakistan or its people —*n.* a native or inhabitant of Pakistan

pal (pal) *n.* [Eng. Romany < Sans. *bhrātr*, BROTHER] [Colloq.] a close friend; comrade; chum —*vi.* **palled, pal'ling** [Colloq.] **1.** to go about together as pals **2.** to be a pal (*with* another)

pal·ace (pal'is) *n.* [< OFr. < L. < *Palatium*, one of the seven hills of Rome, where Augustus lived] **1.** the official residence of a king, emperor, etc. **2.** any large, magnificent house or building

pal·a·din (pal'ə din) *n.* [< Fr. < It. < L. *palatinus*, a palace officer: see PALACE] **1.** any of the twelve legendary knights of Charlemagne's court **2.** a knight or heroic champion

pa·lae·o- *same as* PALEO-: also **pa·lae-**

pal·an·quin, pal·an·keen (pal'ən kēn') *n.* [< Port. < Jav. < Sans. *palyaṅka*] formerly in eastern Asia, a covered couch for one person, carried by poles on men's shoulders

pal·at·a·ble (pal'it ə b'l) *adj.* [PALAT(E) + -ABLE] **1.** pleasant or acceptable to the taste *[a *palatable* meal]* **2.** pleasing or acceptable to the mind *[a *palatable* idea]* —**pal·at·a·bil'i·ty, pal'at·a·ble·ness** *n.* —**pal'at·a·bly** *adv.*

pal·a·tal (pal'it 'l) *adj.* **1.** of the palate **2.** pronounced with the tongue raised against or near the hard palate, as *y* in *yes* —*n.* a palatal sound —**pal'a·tal·ly** *adv.*

pal·a·tal·ize (-īz') *vt.* **-ized', -iz'ing** to pronounce as a palatal *[the *t* in *nature* is palatalized to *ch*]* —**pal'a·tal·i·za'tion** *n.*

pal·ate (pal′it) *n.* [L. *palatum*] **1.** the roof of the mouth, consisting of a hard, bony forward part (the *hard palate*) and a soft, fleshy back part (the *soft palate*) **2.** taste [the food was delicious to his *palate*] **3.** liking

PALATE

pa·la·tial (pə lā′shəl) *adj.* [see PALACE] **1.** of, suitable for, or like a palace **2.** large and splendid; grand; magnificent —**pa·la′tial·ly** *adv.*

pa·lat·i·nate (pə lat′′n āt′, -it) *n.* the territory ruled by a palatine

pal·a·tine (pal′ə tīn, -tin) *adj.* [< OFr. < L. *palatium*, palace] **1.** of a palace **2.** having royal powers in his own territory [a count *palatine*] **3.** of or belonging to a palatine or palatinate —*n.* a medieval vassal lord having the rights of royalty in his own territory, or palatinate —[P-] one of the SEVEN HILLS OF ROME

pa·lav·er (pə lav′ər) *n.* [Port. *palavra*, a word, speech < LL. *parabola*, PARABLE] **1.** a conference, as orig. between African natives and European explorers or traders **2.** talk; esp., idle chatter **3.** flattery; cajolery —*vi.* **1.** to talk, esp. idly or flatteringly **2.** to confer —*vt.* to flatter or wheedle

Pa·la·wan (pä lä′wän) island in the W Philippines, southwest of Mindoro: 4,550 sq. mi.

pale[1] (pāl) *adj.* pal′er, pal′est [OFr. < L. < *pallere*, to be pale] **1.** having little color in the face [*pale* after a sunless winter; *pale* with fright] **2.** lacking intensity or brilliance; dim; faint: said of color, light, etc. **3.** feeble; weak [a *pale* imitation] —*vi.* paled, pal′ing **1.** to become pale; lose color [her face *paled* at the news] **2.** to seem weaker or less important [my work *paled* beside his] —*vt.* to make pale — **pale′ly** *adv.* —**pale′ness** *n.* —**pal′ish** *adj.*

SYN.—**pale** is the most general of the words describing an unnatural whiteness or lack of color, often temporary, of the complexion; **pallid** suggests a paleness resulting from exhaustion, faintness, emotional strain, etc.; **wan** suggests the paleness resulting from a serious illness; **ashen** implies the grayish paleness of the skin as in death; **livid** refers to a grayish-blue complexion, as of one in great rage or fear —ANT. **ruddy, rosy**

pale[2] (pāl) *n.* [< MFr. < L. *palus*, a stake: for IE. base see PEACE] **1.** a narrow, pointed stake used in fences; picket **2.** a fence; enclosure; boundary: now chiefly figurative [outside the *pale* of the law] **3.** a district enclosed within bounds

☆ **pale·face** (pāl′fās′) *n.* a white person: a term said to be first used by N. American Indians

Pa·lem·bang (pä′lem bäŋ′) seaport in SE Sumatra, Indonesia: pop. 723,000

pa·le·o- [< Gr. *palaios*, ancient] *a combining form meaning* ancient, prehistoric, primitive, etc. [*Paleozoic, paleolithic*]: also, before a vowel, **pale-**

Pa·le·o·cene (pā′lē ə sēn′, pal′ē-) *adj.* [< PALEO- + Gr. *kainos*, recent] designating or of the first epoch of the Tertiary Period in the Cenozoic Era —**the Paleocene** the Paleocene Epoch or its rocks: see GEOLOGIC TIME CHART

pa·le·og·ra·phy (pā′lē äg′rə fē, pal′ē-) *n.* **1.** ancient writing or forms of writing **2.** the science of identifying or translating ancient writings —**pa·le·og′ra·pher** *n.* —**pa·le·o·graph·ic** (-ə graf′ik), **pa′le·o·graph′i·cal** *adj.*

pa·le·o·lith·ic (pā′lē ə lith′ik, pal′ē-) *adj.* [PALEO- + -LITHIC] designating or of the middle part of the early Stone Age, during which stone and bone tools were used

pa·le·on·tol·o·gy (-än täl′ə jē) *n.* [< Fr.: see PALE(O)- & ONTO- & -LOGY] the branch of geology that deals with prehistoric life through the study of fossils —**pa′le·on′to·log′i·cal** (-tə läj′i k′l), **pa′le·on′to·log′ic** *adj.* —**pa′le·on·tol′o·gist** *n.*

Pa·le·o·zo·ic (-ə zō′ik) *adj.* [PALEO- + ZO- + -IC] designating or of the era between the Precambrian and the Mesozoic —**the Paleozoic** the Paleozoic Era or its rocks: see GEOLOGIC TIME CHART

Pa·ler·mo (pə lur′mō; *It.* pä ler′mô) seaport on the N coast of Sicily: pop. 659,000

Pal·es·tine (pal′əs tīn′) **1.** region on the E coast of the Mediterranean, the country of the Jews in Biblical times **2.** territory in this region, west of the Jordan River, held by the British as a mandate from 1923 until the establishment of the state of Israel in 1948 —**Pal·es·tin′i·an** (-tin′ē ən) *adj., n.*

Pal·es·tri·na (pä′les trē′nä; *E.* pal′ə strē′nə), **Gio·van·ni (Pierluigi) da** (jô vän′nē dä) 1525?–94; It. composer

pal·ette (pal′it) *n.* [Fr. < L. *pala*, a shovel] **1.** a thin board with a hole for the thumb at one end, on which an artist arranges and mixes his paints **2.** the colors used, as by a particular artist

palette knife a flexible steel blade on a handle, used by artists for mixing, scraping, and applying paints

pal·frey (pôl′frē) *n., pl.* -freys [< OFr. < ML., ult. < Gr. *para*, beside + L. *veredus*, post horse] [Archaic] a saddle horse, esp. a gentle one for a woman

PALETTE

Pa·li (pä′lē) *n.* the Old Indic dialect which has become the religious language of Buddhism

pal·imp·sest (pal′imp sest′) *n.* [< L. < Gr. *palin*, again + *psēn*, to rub smooth] a parchment, tablet, etc. that has been written upon several times, with previous, erased texts still partly visible

pal·in·drome (pal′in drōm′) *n.* [< Gr. < *palin*, again + *dramein*, to run] a word, phrase, or sentence that reads the same backward or forward, as the word *madam*

pal·ing (pāl′iŋ) *n.* **1.** a fence made of pales **2.** the action of making such a fence **3.** a pale, or a number of pales

pal·i·sade (pal′ə sād′, pal′ə sād′) *n.* [< Fr. < Pr. < L. *palus*, a stake, PALE[2]] **1.** any of a row of large pointed stakes set in the ground to form a fence as for fortification **2.** such a fence ☆ **3.** [*pl.*] a line of steep cliffs, usually along a river —*vt.* -sad′ed, -sad′ing to fortify or defend with a palisade

pall[1] (pôl) *vi.* palled, pall′ing [ME. *pallen*, short for *appallen*, APPALL] **1.** to become tiresome, boring, dull, etc. [his jokes are beginning to *pall* on me] **2.** to become tired or surfeited [his interest in stamps soon *palled*] —*vt.* to bore after a time

pall[2] (pôl) *n.* [< OE. < L. *pallium*, a cover] **1.** a piece of velvet, etc. used to cover a coffin, hearse, or tomb **2.** a dark or gloomy covering [a *pall* of smoke] **3.** a cloth, or cardboard covered with cloth, used to cover the chalice in some Christian churches —*vt.* palled, pall′ing to cover as with a pall

Pal·la·dio (päl lä′dyô), **An·dre·a** (än dre′ä) (born *Andrea di Pietro*) 1518–80; It. architect —**Pal·la·di·an** (pə lā′dē ən, -lä′-) *adj.*

Pal·la·di·um (pə lā′dē əm) *n., pl.* -di·a (-ə) **1.** the legendary statue of Pallas Athena in Troy on which the safety of the city was supposed to depend **2.** [p-] anything supposed to ensure the safety of something; safeguard

pal·la·di·um (pə lā′dē əm) *n.* [ModL., ult. < Gr. *Pallas*, the goddess] a rare, silvery-white, metallic chemical element: it is used as a catalyst, or in alloys with gold, silver, etc.: symbol, Pd; at. wt., 106.4; at. no., 46

Pal·las (pal′əs) *Gr. Myth.* Athena, goddess of wisdom: also **Pallas Athena** —**Pal·la·di·an** (pə lā′dē ən) *adj.*

pall·bear·er (pôl′ber′ər) *n.* [PALL[2] + BEARER] one of the persons who bear the coffin at a funeral

pal·let[1] (pal′it) *n.* [< MFr.: see PALETTE] **1.** a wooden tool consisting of a flat blade with a handle; esp., such a tool for smoothing pottery **2.** same as PALETTE (sense 1) **3.** a low, portable platform for storing goods in warehouses, etc. **4.** any of the clicks or pawls in the escapement of a clock, etc. which engage the teeth of a ratchet wheel to regulate the speed: see illustration at PAWL

pal·let[2] (pal′it) *n.* [< MFr. < OFr. *paille*, straw < L. *palea*, chaff] a small, crude bed or a mattress filled as with straw and used on the floor

pal·li·ate (pal′ē āt′) *vt.* -at′ed, -at′ing [< LL. pp. of *palliare*, to conceal < *pallium*, a cloak] **1.** to lessen the pain or severity of without curing; alleviate [aspirin *palliates* a fever] **2.** to make appear less serious or offensive; excuse [to *palliate* an error] —**pal′li·a′tion** *n.* —**pal′li·a′tor** *n.*

pal·li·a·tive (-āt′iv, -ə tiv) *adj.* that palliates, eases, or excuses —*n.* something that palliates, as a drug

pal·lid (pal′id) *adj.* [L. *pallidus*, PALE[1]] lacking in normal or natural color or brightness [a *pallid* face] —see SYN. at PALE[1] —**pal′lid·ly** *adv.* —**pal′lid·ness** *n.*

fat, āpe, cär; ten, ēven; is, bīte; gō, hôrn, tōol, look; oil, out; up, fur; get; joy; yet; chin; she; thin, then; zh, leisure; ŋ, ring; ə for a in ago, e in agent, i in sanity, o in comply, u in focus; ' as in able (ā′b'l); Fr. bal; ë, Fr. coeur; ö, Fr. feu; Fr. mon; ô, Fr. coq; ü, Fr. duc; r, Fr. cri; H, G. ich; kh, G. doch; ‡foreign; ☆ Americanism; < derived from. See inside front cover.

pal·lor (pal'ər) *n.* [L. < *pallere:* see PALE[1]] lack of color; unnatural paleness, esp. of the face of someone who is sick, tired, frightened, etc.

palm[1] (päm; *occas.* pälm) *n.* [OE. < L. *palma:* from its handlike fronds] **1.** any of a family of tropical or subtropical trees with a tall, branchless trunk and a bunch of large leaves at the top **2.** a leaf of this tree carried as a symbol of victory, triumph, etc. **3.** victory; triumph —*adj.* designating or of a family of plants including the coconut palm, date palm, etc. —**bear** (or **carry off**) **the palm** to be the winner —**palma·ceous** (pal mā'shəs, pä-) *adj.*

palm[2] (päm; *occas.* pälm) *n.* [< OFr. < L. *palma:* for IE. base see FIELD] **1.** the inner surface of the hand between the fingers and wrist **2.** the part of a glove, etc. that covers the palm **3.** the broad, flat part of an antler, as of a moose **4.** a unit of measure based either on the width of the hand (3 to 4 inches) or its length (7 to 9 inches) **5.** any broad, flat part at the end of an arm, handle, etc. —*vt.* to hide (something) in the palm or between the fingers, as in a sleight-of-hand trick —**have an itching palm** [Colloq.] to desire money greedily —**palm off** to get something sold, accepted, etc. by fraud or trickery —**palm·ar** (pal'mər, pä'-) *adj.*

DATE PALM
(tree & fruit)

Pal·ma (päl'mä) seaport on Majorca: chief city of the Balearic Islands: pop. 208,000: in full, **Palma de Mallorca**

pal·mate (pal'māt, pä'-) *adj.* [< L. < *palma,* PALM[2]] shaped like a hand with the fingers spread; specif., *a*) *Bot.* having veins or lobes spreading out from a common center, as some leaves *b*) *Zool.* web-footed, as many water birds Also **pal'mat·ed** —**pal'mate·ly** *adv.* —**pal·ma'tion** *n.*

Palm Beach resort town on the SE coast of Fla.

palm·er (päm'ər, päl'mər) *n.* **1.** a pilgrim who carried a palm leaf as a sign that he had been to the Holy Land **2.** any pilgrim

Palm·er·ston (päm'ər stən), 3d Viscount, (*Henry John Temple*) 1784–1865; Brit. statesman; prime minister (1855–58; 1859–65)

pal·met·to (pal met'ō) *n., pl.* **-tos, -toes** [Sp. *palmito,* dim. < *palma* < L., PALM[1]] any of several new-world palms with fan-shaped leaves, as the cabbage palm

palm·is·try (päm'is trē, päl'mis-) *n.* [< ME., prob. contr. < *paume,* PALM[2] + *maistrie,* mastery] the pretended art of telling a person's fortune by the lines, etc. on the palm of his hand —**palm'ist** *n.*

pal·mit·ic acid (pal mit'ik, pä-) [< Fr.] a fatty acid found in many natural fats and oils

palm leaf the leaf of a palm tree, esp. of a palmetto, used to make fans, hats, etc.

palm oil an oil obtained from the fruit of certain palms, used in making soap, candles, etc.

Palm Springs resort city in S Calif.

Palm Sunday the Sunday before Easter, commemorating Jesus' triumphal entry into Jerusalem

palm·y (päm'ē, päl'mē) *adj.* **palm'i·er, palm'i·est** **1.** having many palm trees **2.** of or like a palm **3.** prosperous; flourishing [in his *palmy* days, he was one of the richest men in town]

Pal·my·ra (pal mī'rə) ancient city in central Syria

pal·my·ra (pal mī'rə) *n.* [< Port. < *palma* < L., PALM[1]] a palm tree grown in India, Ceylon, and Africa for its durable wood, its leaves used for thatching, etc.

Pal·o Al·to (pal'ō al'tō) [Sp., lit., tall tree (the redwood)] city in W Calif., near San Francisco: pop. 56,000

☆**pal·o·mi·no** (pal'ə mē'nō) *n., pl.* **-nos** [AmSp. < Sp., dove-colored, ult. < L. *palumbes,* pigeon] a cream, golden, or light-chestnut horse with white mane and tail

palp (palp) *n. same as* PALPUS —**pal'pal** *adj.*

pal·pa·ble (pal'pə b'l) *adj.* [< LL. < L. *palpare,* to touch] **1.** that can be touched, felt, or handled [a small but *palpable* lump under the skin] **2.** easy to see, hear, recognize, notice, etc.; obvious [*palpable* dampness; a *palpable* sound; *palpable* lies] —see SYN. at EVIDENT, PERCEPTIBLE —**pal'pa·bil'i·ty** *n.* —**pal'pa·bly** *adv.*

pal·pate (pal'pāt) *vt.* **-pat·ed, -pat·ing** [< L. pp. of *palpare,* to touch] to examine by touching, as for medical diagnosis —**pal·pa'tion** *n.*

pal·pi·tate (pal'pə tāt') *vi.* **-tat·ed, -tat·ing** [< L. pp. of *palpitare* < *palpare,* to feel] **1.** to beat rapidly or flutter: said of the heart **2.** to throb; quiver; tremble —**pal'pi·tant** *adj.* —**pal'pi·ta'tion** *n.*

pal·pus (pal'pəs) *n., pl.* **pal'pi** (-pī) [ModL. < L. *palpus,* the soft palm of the hand] a jointed organ or feeler for touching or tasting, attached to one of the head parts of insects, lobsters, etc.

pal·sy (pôl'zē) *n., pl.* **-sies** [< OFr. < L. *paralysis,* PARALYSIS] paralysis in some part of the body, often with a shaking or trembling that cannot be controlled —*vt.* **-sied, -sy·ing** to affect with or as with palsy; paralyze

pal·ter (pôl'tər) *vi.* [< dial. *palt,* a rag + -ER] **1.** to talk or act insincerely; prevaricate **2.** to trifle with facts, decisions, etc. **3.** to quibble or haggle —**pal'ter·er** *n.*

pal·try (pôl'trē) *adj.* **-tri·er, -tri·est** [prob. < LowG. *paltrig* < *palte,* a rag] very small and almost worthless; trifling; petty [a *paltry* wage] —see SYN. at PETTY —**pal'tri·ness** *n.*

Pa·mirs (pä mirz') mountain system in central Asia, mostly in the Tadzhik S.S.R.: highest peak, c. 25,000 ft.

Pam·li·co Sound (pam'li kō') [< Algonquian tribal name] sound between the coast of N.C. and narrow offshore islands

pam·pas (pam'pəz; *for adj., usually* -pəs) *n.pl.* [AmSp., pl. of *pampa* < Quechua, plain] the broad treeless plains of S. America, esp. of Argentina —*adj.* of the pampas

pampas grass a tall grass of S. America, with a plumelike, silvery or pinkish top, used in dried bouquets

pam·per (pam'pər) *vt.* [< LowG. source] to give in easily to the wishes of; be too gentle and giving with [to *pamper* a child] —see SYN. at INDULGE —**pam'per·er** *n.*

pam·phlet (pam'flit) *n.* [< OFr. *Pamphilet,* popular name of a ML. poem] **1.** a small, unbound booklet, usually with a paper cover **2.** a piece of writing published in this form, as on some topic of current interest

pam·phlet·eer (pam'flə tir') *n.* a writer of pamphlets, esp. those dealing with political or social issues —*vi.* to write or publish pamphlets

Pan (pan) *Gr. Myth.* a god of fields, forests, wild animals, flocks, and shepherds, represented with the legs of a goat

pan[1] (pan) *n.* [OE. *panne*] **1.** any broad, shallow container, usually of metal and without a cover, used in cooking, etc.: often in combination [a frying *pan*; a *saucepan*] **2.** a pan-shaped part or object; specif., ☆*a*) a container for washing out gold, etc. from gravel *b*) either holder in a pair of scales **3.** *same as* HARDPAN (sense 1) **4.** the part holding the powder in a flintlock ☆**5.** [Slang] a face —*vt.* **panned, pan'ning 1.** to cook in a pan ☆**2.** [Colloq.] to criticize unfavorably, as in reviewing [to *pan* a play] ☆**3.** *Mining a*) to wash (gravel) in a pan *b*) to separate (gold, etc.) from gravel in this way —*vi. Mining* ☆**1.** to wash gravel in a pan ☆**2.** to yield gold in this process —☆**pan out 1.** *Mining* to yield gold, as gravel, a mine, etc. **2.** [Colloq.] to turn out; esp., to turn out well

pan[2] (pan) *vt., vi.* **panned, pan'ning** [< PAN(ORAMA)] to move (a motion-picture or television camera) so as to get a panoramic effect or follow a moving object —*n.* the act of panning

pan- [< Gr. *pan,* neut. of *pas,* all, every: for IE. base see CAVE] a combining form meaning: **1.** all [*pantheism*] **2.** [P-] *a*) of, including, or common to every [*Pan*-American] *b*) (belief in) the union or cooperation of all members of (a specified group) [*Pan*-Americanism] In sense 2, usually with a hyphen, as in the following words:

Pan-Af'ri·can	**Pan'-Eu·ro·pe'an**
Pan-Ar'a·bic	**Pan'-Is·lam'ic**
Pan-A·si·at'ic	**Pan-Slav'ic**

pan·a·ce·a (pan'ə sē'ə) *n.* [L. < Gr. < *pan,* all + *akeisthai,* to cure] a supposed remedy or cure for all diseases or ills; cure-all —**pan'a·ce'an** *adj.*

pa·nache (pə nash', -näsh') *n.* [Fr., ult. < LL. *pinnaculum,* plume] **1.** a plume on a helmet **2.** carefree self-confidence; dashing elegance of manner; flair

Pan·a·ma (pan'ə mä', -mô') **1.** country in Central America, on the Isthmus of Panama: 29,201 sq. mi.; pop. 1,425,000 **2.** its capital, on the Pacific: pop. 412,000: also **Panama City 3. Isthmus of,** strip of land connecting South America & Central America —**Pan·a·ma·ni·an** (-mä'nē ən) *adj., n.*

Panama Canal ship canal across the Isthmus of Panama, connecting the Caribbean Sea & the Pacific Ocean: 50.7 mi. long

Panama (**hat**) [< *Panama* (city)] a fine, hand-woven hat made from the leaves of a Central and South American plant

☆**Pan-A·mer·i·can** (pan'ə mer'ə kən) *adj.* of North, Central, and South America

☆**Pan-A·mer·i·can·ism** (-iz'm) *n.* a policy of political and economic cooperation, mutual cultural understanding, etc. among the Pan-American nations

☆**pan·a·tel·a, pan·a·tel·la** (pan′ə tel′ə) *n.* [AmSp., orig. a long biscuit < It., dim. of *pane*, bread] a long, slender cigar

Pa·nay (pä nī′; *E.* pə nī′) island of the C Philippines, between Mindoro & Negros: 4,446 sq. mi.

pan·broil (pan′broil′) *vt.* to fry in a pan with little or no fat

pan·cake (pan′kāk′) *n.* **1.** a thin, flat cake of batter fried on a griddle or in a pan; griddlecake; flapjack **2.** a landing in which the airplane levels off, stalls, then drops almost vertically: in full, **pancake landing** —*vi., vt.* **-caked′, -cak′ing** to make, or cause to make, a pancake landing

☆**pancake makeup** a thin cake of compressed powder used as cosmetic or theatrical makeup

pan·chro·mat·ic (pan′krō mat′ik) *adj.* sensitive to light of all colors [*panchromatic* film] —**pan·chro·ma·tism** (pan krō′mə-tiz′m) *n.*

pan·cre·as (pan′krē əs, paŋ′-) *n.* [ModL. < Gr. < *pan*, all + *kreas*, flesh] a large gland that secretes an alkaline digestive juice (**pancreatic juice**) into the small intestine and a hormone (**insulin**) into the bloodstream: the pancreas of animals, used as food, is called *sweetbread*: see illustration at ALIMENTARY CANAL —**pan′cre·at′ic** (-at′ik) *adj.*

pan·da (pan′də) *n.* [Fr. < native name in Nepal] *same as:* **1.** GIANT PANDA **2.** LESSER PANDA

pan·dect (pan′dekt) *n.* [< Fr. < LL. < Gr. < *pan*, all (see PAN-) + *dechesthai*, to contain, receive] **1.** [often *pl.*] a complete body of laws; legal code **2.** a complete digest —**the Pandects** a digest of Roman civil law in fifty books, made for Justinian in the 6th cent. A.D.

pan·dem·ic (pan dem′ik) *adj.* [< LL. < Gr. < *pan*, all + *dēmos*, the people] epidemic over a large region —*n.* a pandemic disease

Pan·de·mo·ni·um (pan′də mō′nē əm) [ModL. < Gr. *pan-* + *daimōn*, demon] the capital of Hell in Milton's *Paradise Lost* —*n.* [**p-**] wild disorder, noise, or confusion, or a place where this exists

pan·der (pan′dər) *n.* [< L. *Pandarus*, who, in the story of Troilus and Cressida, acts as their go-between] **1.** a person who arranges meetings between others for sexual purposes; pimp **2.** one who provides the means of helping to satisfy the ambitions, vices, etc. of another Also **pan′der·er** —*vi.* to act as a pander (*to*)

pan·dit (pun′dit, pan′-) *n.* [var. of PUNDIT] in India, a learned man: used [**P-**] as a title of respect

P. and L., P. & L. profit and loss

Pan·do·ra (pan dôr′ə) [L. < Gr. < *pan*, all + *dōron*, a gift] *Gr. Myth.* the first mortal woman, who in curiosity opened a box and let out all human ills into the world

☆**pan·dow·dy** (pan dou′dē) *n., pl.* **-dies** [prob. < obs. E. dial. *pandoulde*, custard] deep-dish apple pie, having a top crust only

pane (pān) *n.* [< OFr. < L. *pannus*, piece of cloth] **1.** a flat piece, side, or face **2.** *a)* a single division of a window, etc., consisting of a sheet of glass in a frame *b)* such a sheet of glass **3.** a panel, as of a door

pan·e·gyr·ic (pan′ə jir′ik) *n.* [< Fr. < L. < Gr. *panēgyris*, public meeting < *pan*, all + *ageirein*, to bring together] **1.** a formal speech or writing praising a person or event **2.** high or exaggerated praise —see SYN. at TRIBUTE —**pan′e·gyr′i·cal** *adj.* —**pan′e·gyr′i·cal·ly** *adv.* —**pan′e·gyr′ist** *n.* —**pan′e·gy·rize′** (-jə rīz′) *vt., vi.* **-rized′, -riz′ing**

pan·el (pan′'l) *n.* [< OFr., ult. < L. *pannus*, piece of cloth] **1.** a section or division of a surface; specif., *a)* a flat piece, usually rectangular, forming a part of the surface of a wall, door, etc., usually raised, sunk in, framed, etc. *b)* a similar piece used as a cover, a light diffuser, a built-in heating element, etc. *c)* a pane of a window *d)* a board, or flat surface, for instruments or controls, as of an airplane **2.** *a)* a thin board for an oil painting *b)* a painting on such a board *c)* a picture much longer than it is wide **3.** *a)* a list of persons called for jury duty *b)* the jury itself **4.** a group of persons selected for a specific purpose, as for judging a contest, discussing an issue, etc. **5.** a lengthwise strip, as of different material, in a skirt or dress —*vt.* **-eled** or **-elled, -el·ing** or **-el·ling** to provide, decorate, etc. with panels

panel discussion a discussion carried on by a selected group of speakers before an audience

pan·el·ing, pan·el·ling (-iŋ) *n.* **1.** panels as a group; series of panels in a wall, etc. **2.** sections of plastic, wood, etc. from which to cut panels

pan·el·ist (-ist) *n.* a member of a panel (*n.* 4)

☆**panel truck** a small, enclosed pickup truck

☆**pan·e·tel·a, pan·e·tel·la** (pan′ə tel′ə) *n. same as* PANATELA

☆**pan fish** a fish that can be fried whole in a pan

pan-fry (pan′frī′) *vt.* **-fried′, -fry′ing** to fry in a shallow skillet or frying pan

pang (paŋ) *n.* [< ?] a sudden, sharp, brief pain, physical or emotional; sudden feeling of distress [hunger *pangs*; a *pang* of homesickness]

pan·go·lin (paŋ gō′lin) *n.* [Malay *pĕngulin*, roller < *gulin*, to roll] any of various toothless, scaly mammals of Asia and Africa, able to roll into a ball when attacked

PANGOLIN
(to 6 ft. long, including tail)

pan·han·dle[1] (pan′han′d'l) *n.* **1.** the handle of a pan ☆**2.** [often **P-**] a strip of land like the handle of a pan, as the northern extension of Texas

☆**pan·han·dle**[2] (pan′han′d'l) *vt., vi.* **-dled, -dling** [ult. < PAN[1] + HANDLE, *vt.*] [Colloq.] to beg from (passers-by) on the streets —**pan′han′dler** *n.*

Pan·hel·len·ic (pan′hə len′ik) *adj.* **1.** of all the Greek peoples **2.** of all Greek-letter fraternities and sororities

pan·ic[1] (pan′ik) *n.* [L. *panicum*, kind of millet < *panus*, a swelling] any of several related grasses, as millet, used as fodder: also **panic grass**

pan·ic[2] (pan′ik) *adj.* [< Fr. < Gr. *panikos*, of Pan] **1.** literally, of Pan or of sudden fear supposedly inspired by him **2.** like, showing, or resulting from, panic [*panic* selling on the stock market] —*n.* **1.** a sudden, wild fear that is not controlled and can spread quickly [the fire caused *panic* in the theater] **2.** a widespread fear of financial collapse, resulting in a sharp drop in the stock market, withdrawals of bank deposits, etc. **3.** [Slang] a very comical person or thing —*vt.* **-icked, -ick·ing 1.** to fill with panic [the loud noise *panicked* the hens] **2.** [Slang] to stir (an audience, etc.) to great laughter, delight, etc. —*vi.* to give way to or show panic [he *panicked* at the sight of the mob] —☆**push** (or **press, hit,** etc.) **the panic button** [Slang] to react to a crisis by some wild action that could be disastrous —**pan′i·cal·ly** *adv.* —**pan′ick·y** *adj.*

pan·i·cle (pan′i k'l) *n.* [< L. dim. of *panus*, a swelling, ear of millet] a loose, irregularly branched flower cluster; compound raceme —**pan′i·cled**, **pa·nic·u·late** (pa nik′yə lit, -lāt′) *adj.*

pan·ic-strick·en (pan′ik strik′'n) *adj.* filled with panic; badly frightened: also **panic-struck**

pan·jan·drum (pan jan′drəm) *n.* [a made-up word] a self-important, pompous official

pan·nier, pan·ier (pan′yər, -ē ər) *n.* [< MFr. < L. *panarium*, breadbasket < *panis*, bread] **1.** *a)* a large basket for carrying loads on the back *b)* either of a pair of baskets hung across the back of a donkey, horse, etc. **2.** *a)* a framework, as of wire, used formerly to puff out a skirt at the hips *b)* a skirt so puffed

PANICLE
OF OATS

pan·ni·kin (pan′ə kin) *n.* [Chiefly Brit.] a small pan or cup

☆**pa·no·cha** (pə nō′chə) *n.* [AmSp. < Sp. *pan*, bread < L. *panis*] **1.** a coarse Mexican sugar **2.** *var. of* PENUCHE

pan·o·ply (pan′ə plē) *n., pl.* **-plies** [< Gr. < *pan*, all + *hopla*, arms] **1.** a complete suit of armor **2.** any complete or magnificent covering or display —**pan′o·plied** *adj.*

pan·o·ra·ma (pan′ə ram′ə) *n.* [< PAN- + Gr. *horama*, a view: for IE. base see GUARD] **1.** *a)* a picture unrolled in such a way as to give the impression of a continuous view *b) same as* CYCLORAMA (sense 1) **2.** an open view in all directions **3.** a full review of a subject **4.** a constantly changing scene [the *panora-*

ma of the waterfront] **—pan′o·ram′ic** *adj.* **—pan′o·ram′i·cal·ly** *adv.*

pan·pipe (pan′pīp′) *n.* [*also* P-] a primitive musical instrument made of a row of reeds or tubes of different lengths, played by blowing across the open ends: also **panpipes, Pan's pipes**

pan·sy (pan′zē) *n., pl.* **-sies** [Fr. *pensée,* a thought < *penser,* to think] a small, flowering plant with flat, broad, velvety petals in many colors

pant[1] (pant) *vi.* [prob. < OFr. *pantaisier,* ult. < L. *phantasia,* nightmare: see FANTASY] **1.** to breathe rapidly and heavily, as from running fast **2.** to beat rapidly, as the heart; throb **3.** to feel strong desire; yearn eagerly (with *for* or *after*) [*to pant after fame and fortune*] **—vt.** to gasp out [*he rushed up and panted out the news*] **—n.** **1.** any of a series of rapid, heavy breaths; gasp **2.** a throb, as of the heart **3.** a puff of an engine

PANSIES

pant[2] (pant) *n., adj. see* PANTS

pan·ta·lets, pan·ta·lettes (pan′t'l ets′) *n.pl.* [dim. of PANTALOON] **1.** long, loose drawers showing below the skirt, worn by women in the 19th cent. **2.** detachable ruffles for the legs of drawers

pan·ta·loon (pan′t'l ōōn′) [< Fr. < It., ult. after the Venetian patron saint *Pantalone*] [P-] **1.** a foolish old man in early Italian comedy, typically slender and in tightfitting trousers **2.** a similar buffoon in modern pantomime **—n.** [*pl.*] trousers, esp. of an earlier closefitting kind

pant·dress (pant′dres′) *n.* a woman's garment with the lower part like pants instead of a skirt

pan·the·ism (pan′thē iz'm) *n.* **1.** the belief that God is the sum of all beings, things, forces, etc. in the universe **2.** the worship of all gods **—pan′the·ist** *n.* **—pan′the·is′tic, pan′the·is′ti·cal** *adj.* **—pan′the·is′ti·cal·ly** *adv.*

pan·the·on (pan′thē än′, -ən) *n.* [< L. < Gr. < *pan,* all + *theos,* a god] **1.** a temple for all the gods; esp., [P-] a temple built in Rome in 27 B.C.: used since 609 A.D. as a Christian church **2.** all the gods of a people **3.** [*often* P-] a building in which the famous dead of a nation are buried or honored

pan·ther (pan′thər) *n., pl.* **-thers, -ther:** see PLURAL, II, D, 1 [< OFr. < L. < Gr. *panthēr*] **1.** a leopard; specif., *a)* a black leopard *b)* a leopard that is very large or fierce **2.** *same as: a)* COUGAR *b)* JAGUAR **—pan′ther·ess** *n.fem.*

☆**pant·ies** (pan′tēz) *n.pl.* women's or children's short underpants: also **pant′ie** (-tē) *n.*

pan·to- [< Gr. *pantos,* genitive of *pan:* see PAN-] *a combining form meaning* all or every: also, before a vowel, **pant-**

pan·to·graph (pan′tə graf′) *n.* [< Fr. < PANTO- & -GRAPH] a mechanical device for reproducing a drawing on the same or a different scale

pan·to·mime (pan′tə mīm′) *n.* [< L. < Gr. < *pantos* (see PANTO-) + *mimos,* a mimic] **1.** *a)* a play, skit, etc. performed without words, using actions and gestures only *b)* the art of acting in this way **2.** the use of actions and gestures without words to tell something **—vt., vi.** **-mimed′, -mim′ing** to express or act in pantomime **—pan′to·mim′ic** (-mim′ik) *adj.* **—pan′to·mim′ist** (-mī′mist, -mim′ist) *n.*

pan·to·then·ic acid (pan′tə then′ik) [< Gr. *pantothen,* from every side] a thick, yellow oil, $C_9H_{17}O_5N$, a member of the vitamin B complex, found in all living tissues

pan·try (pan′trē) *n., pl.* **-tries** [< OFr. < ML. *panetaria* < L. *panis,* bread] **1.** a small room off the kitchen, where cooking ingredients and utensils, china, etc. are kept **2.** *same as* BUTLER'S PANTRY

☆**pants** (pants) *n.pl.* [abbrev. of PANTALOON(s)] **1.** an outer garment extending from the waist to the knees or ankles and covering each leg separately; trousers **2.** drawers or panties As an adjective or in compounds, usually **pant** [*pant legs, pantdress*]

pant·suit (pant′sōōt′) *n.* a woman's outfit of a matched jacket and pants: also **pants suit**

☆**pant·y** (pan′tē) *n., pl.* **pant′ies** *same as* PANTIES

panty girdle a girdle with a crotch or legs like panties

panty hose a woman's undergarment combining panties with hose: also **pant′y·hose′** (-hōz′)

pant·y·waist (-wāst′) *n.* **1.** orig., a child's two-piece undergarment **2.** [Slang] a sissy

pan·zer (pan′zər; *G.* pän′tsər) *adj.* [G., armor] armored [*a panzer division*]

Pao·tou (bou′dō′) city in NE China: pop. 1,500,000

pap[1] (pap) *n.* [prob. orig. < baby talk] [Archaic] a nipple or teat

pap[2] (pap) *n.* [orig. < baby talk] **1.** any soft food for babies or invalids **2.** any oversimplified or tasteless writing, ideas, etc.

pa·pa (pä′pə; *now less freq.* pə pä′) *n.* [< baby talk, as also in Fr. & L. *papa*] father: a child's word

pa·pa·cy (pā′pə sē) *n., pl.* **-cies** [< ML. < LL. *papa,* pope] **1.** the position or authority of the Pope **2.** the period during which a pope rules **3.** the line or succession of popes **4.** [*also* P-] the government of the Roman Catholic Church, headed by the Pope

pa·pal (pā′pəl) *adj.* [< MFr. < ML.: see POPE & -AL] **1.** of the Pope or the papacy **2.** of the Roman Catholic Church

Papal States former territory in C & NC Italy, ruled by the papacy from the 8th cent. until 1870

pa·paw (pô′pô, pə pô′) *n.* [prob. < PAPAYA] **1.** *same as* PAPAYA ☆**2.** *a)* a tree of central and southern U.S. having a yellowish, edible fruit with many seeds *b)* its fruit

pa·pa·ya (pə pä′yə) *n.* [Sp. < Carib name] **1.** a palmlike tropical American tree bearing a large, yellowish-orange fruit like a melon **2.** its fruit

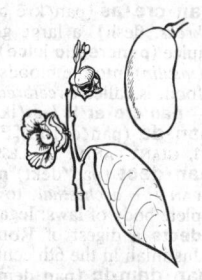

PAPAW (flower, leaf & fruit)

Pa·pe·e·te (pä′pē ā′tä) seaport & chief town on Tahiti; capital of French Polynesia: pop. 22,000

pa·per (pā′pər) *n.* [< OFr. < L. *papyrus,* PAPYRUS] **1.** a thin, flexible material usually in sheets, made from wood pulp, rags, etc., and used for writing or printing on, for packaging, etc. **2.** a single piece or sheet of this **3.** a printed or written paper; specif., *a)* an official document *b)* an article, essay, dissertation, etc. [*to read a paper* at a science conference] *c)* a written examination, report, etc. **4.** *same as: a)* COMMERCIAL PAPER *b)* PAPER MONEY **5.** *clipped form of: a)* NEWSPAPER *b)* WALLPAPER **6.** a small wrapper of paper, usually including its contents [*a paper* of pins] **7.** any material like paper, as papyrus **8.** [*pl.*] *a)* documents identifying a person; credentials *b)* a collection of letters, writings, etc. [the Lincoln *papers*] **—adj.** **1.** of paper; made of paper [*paper* flowers] **2.** like paper; thin [*paper* walls in an apartment] **3.** existing only in written form; theoretical [*paper* profits] **—vt.** **1.** to cover with paper, esp. wallpaper **2.** to wrap in paper **—vi.** to hang wallpaper **—on paper** **1.** in written or printed form **2.** in theory **—pa′per·er** *n.* **—pa′per·like′** *adj.*

pa·per·back (pā′pər bak′) *n.* a book bound in paper **—pa′per·backed′, pa′per·bound′** (-bound′) *adj.*

☆**paper birch** the N. American birch having white or ash-colored paperlike bark

pa·per·board (-bôrd′) *n.* ☆a relatively stiff, heavy material made from paper pulp

pa·per·boy (-boi′) *n.* a boy or man who sells or delivers newspapers

☆**paper clip** a flexible clasp of metal wire for holding loose sheets of paper together

paper cutter **1.** *same as* PAPER KNIFE **2.** a device for cutting and trimming a number of sheets of paper at a time

pa·per·hang·er (-haŋ′ər) *n.* a person whose work is covering walls with wallpaper **—pa′per·hang′ing** *n.*

paper knife a knifelike blade, as of metal, used to slit sealed envelopes and uncut book pages

☆**paper money** printed notes, as dollar bills, issued by a government or its banks, for use as money along with metal coins

paper nautilus an eight-armed mollusk related to the octopus: the female has a paperlike shell in which the young develop

paper tiger a person, nation, etc. that seems to present a threat but is actually powerless

pa·per·weight (-wāt′) *n.* any small, heavy object set on papers to keep them from being scattered

paper work the keeping of records, filing of reports, etc. that must done as part of some work or task

pa·per·y (pā′pər ē) *adj.* thin, light, etc., like paper

Pa·phos (pā′fäs) ancient city in SW Cyprus, founded by the Phoenicians

pa·pier-mâ·ché (pā′pər mə shā′) *n.* [Fr. *papier,* paper + pp. of *mâcher,* to chew] a material made of paper pulp mixed with size, glue, etc., that is easily molded when moist and dries strong and hard **—adj.** made of papier-mâché

pa·pil·la (pə pil′ə) *n., pl.* **-lae** (-ē) [L., dim. of *papula,* pimple] **1.** a small bulge of flesh, as at the root of a hair or on the surface of the tongue **2.** any tiny, bulging part like this —**pap·il·lar·y** (pap'ə ler'ē, pə pil'ə rē) *adj.* —**pap·il·late** (pap'ə lāt', pə pil'it) *adj.*

pap·il·lo·ma (pap'ə lō'mə) *n., pl.* **-ma·ta** (-mə tə), **-mas** [ModL.: see PAPILLA & -OMA] a harmless tumor of the skin or mucous membrane, consisting of a thickened and enlarged papilla or group of papillae, as a corn or wart

pa·pist (pā'pist) *n.* [< ModL. < LL. *papa*, POPE] **1.** one who believes in the supreme power of the Pope **2.** a Roman Catholic —*adj.* Roman Catholic An unfriendly term

☆**pa·poose** (pa pōōs', pə-) *n.* [< Algonquian *papoos*] a North American Indian baby

pap·pus (pap'əs) *n., pl.* **pap'pi** (-ī) [ModL. < L. < Gr. *pappos*, old man] *Bot.* a tuft of bristles, hairs, etc., as on dandelion seeds —**pap'pose** (-ōs), **pap'pous** (-əs) *adj.*

pap·py (pap'ē) *n., pl.* **-pies** [Dial. or Colloq.] father

pa·pri·ka (pa prē'kə, pə-; pap'ri kə) *n.* [Hung. < Serb. < Gr. *peperi*, pepper] a mild, red seasoning ground from the dried fruit of certain peppers

☆**Pap test** (pap) [after G. *Papanicolaou* (1883–1962), U.S. anatomist] the microscopic examination of a smear (**Pap smear**) taken from the cervix of a woman: a test for cancer

Pap·u·a (pap'yoo wə, pä'poo wə) **1.** *same as* NEW GUINEA **2. Territory of,** former Australian territory consisting of the SE section of the island of New Guinea & nearby islands

Papua New Guinea country occupying the E half of the island of New Guinea & nearby islands, including the former Territory of Papua & the former Trust Territory of New Guinea: c. 180,000 sq. mi.; pop. 2,756,000

pap·ule (pap'yōōl) *n.* [L. *papula*] a pimple —**pap'u·lar** (-yoo lər) *adj.* —**pap'u·lose'** (-lōs') *adj.*

pa·py·rus (pa pī'rəs) *n., pl.* **-ri** (-rī), **-rus·es** [L. < Gr. *papyros*, prob. < Egypt.] **1.** a tall water plant abundant in the Nile region in Egypt **2.** a writing material made from the pith of this plant by the ancient Egyptians, Greeks, and Romans **3.** any ancient document or manuscript on papyrus

par (pär) *n.* [L., an equal < IE. base *per-*, to sell] **1.** the established value of the money of one country in terms of the money of another **2.** an equal status, footing, level, etc.: usually in **on a par (with) 3.** the average state, condition, etc. [work that is above *par*] **4.** *Commerce* the face value of stocks, bonds, etc. **5.** *Golf* the number of strokes established as a skillful score for a hole or course —*adj.* **1.** of or at par **2.** average; normal —*vt.* **parred, par'ring** *Golf* to score par on (a given hole or course)

par. 1. paragraph **2.** parallel **3.** parenthesis **4.** parish

Pa·rá (pä rä') river in NE Brazil; an estuary of the Amazon

pa·ra (pä rä', pär'ə) *n.* [Turk. < Per. *pārah*, a piece] *see* MONETARY UNITS, table (Yugoslavia)

par·a- [< Gr. < *para*, at the side of: for IE. base see FAR] *a prefix meaning:* **1.** by or at the side of, beyond, aside from [*paramilitary*] **2.** *Med. a)* in a secondary capacity *b)* functionally disordered, abnormal *c)* like or resembling [*paratyphoid*] Also, before a vowel, **par-**

par·a·a·mi·no·ben·zo·ic acid (par'ə ə mē'nō ben zō'ik, -am'ə nō'-) a crystalline compound, $C_7H_7NO_2$, considered a member of the vitamin B complex

par·a·ble (par'ə b'l) *n.* [< MFr. < LL. < L. < Gr. *parabolē*, a comparing: ult. < *para-*, beside + *ballein*, to throw] a short, simple story teaching a moral or religious lesson, as in the Bible

pa·rab·o·la (pə rab'ə lə) *n.* [ModL. < Gr. *parabolē*: see prec.] *Geom.* a plane curve formed by cutting through a cone with a plane parallel to its side

par·a·bol·ic¹ (par'ə bäl'ik) *adj.* of, like, or expressed by a parable: also **par'a·bol'i·cal** —**par'a·bol'i·cal·ly** *adv.*

par·a·bol·ic² (par'ə bäl'ik) *adj.* **1.** of or like a parabola **2.** concave with the regular outline of a parabola, as a reflector —**par'a·bol'i·cal·ly** *adv.*

Par·a·cel·sus (par'ə sel'səs), **Phi·lip·pus Au·re·o·lus** (fi lip'əs ô rē'ə ləs) (born *Theophrastus Bombastus von Hohenheim*) 1493–1541; Swiss physician & alchemist

par·a·chute (par'ə shōōt') *n.* [Fr. < *para-* (< It. *parare*, to ward off) + *chute*, a fall] **1.** a large cloth device shaped like an

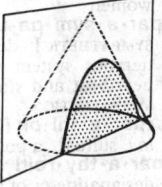

PARABOLA

umbrella when it opens up, used to slow up the fall of a person or thing dropping from an airplane, etc. **2.** something shaped like or having the effect of a parachute —*vt., vi.* **-chut'ed, -chut'ing** to drop or descend by parachute —**par'a·chut'ist** *n.*

pa·rade (pə rād') *n.* [Fr. < Sp. *parada*, ult. < L. *parare*, to prepare] **1.** a boastful show; a showing off [she makes a *parade* of her beauty] **2.** *a)* a military assembly for display or inspection; esp., a ceremony of troops marching, as for review *b)* a place where troops assemble regularly for parade **3.** any organized procession or march [a Mardi gras *parade*] **4.** *a)* a public walk; place for promenading *b)* persons promenading; strollers **5.** a succession of persons or things [a *parade* of suspects] —*vt.* **-rad'ed, -rad'ing 1.** to bring together (troops, etc.) for inspection or display **2.** to march or walk through (the streets, etc.), as for display **3.** to show off [he *parades* his knowledge] —*vi.* **1.** to march in a parade **2.** to walk about in a showy way **3.** to assemble in military formation for review or display —**on parade** on display —**pa·rad'er** *n.*

par·a·digm (par'ə dim, -dīm') *n.* [< Fr. < LL. < Gr. < *para*, PARA- + *deigma*, example < *deiknynai*, to show: for IE. base see DICTION] **1.** a pattern, example, or model **2.** *Gram.* an example of the inflection of a noun, verb, etc., giving all the inflected forms of the word —**par'a·dig·mat'ic** (-dig mat'ik) *adj.*

par·a·dise (par'ə dīs') *n.* [< OFr. < LL. < L. < Gr. *paradeisos*, a garden] **1.** [P-] the garden of Eden **2.** *Theol.* the place of the blessed after death; heaven **3.** any place that is very beautiful or seems exactly as one would wish [a fisherman's *paradise*] **4.** any place or state of great happiness —**par'a·di·si'a·cal** (-di sī'ə k'l), **par'a·dis'i·ac'** (-dis'ē ak') *adj.*

par·a·dox (par'ə däks') *n.* [< L. < Gr. < *para-*, beyond + *doxa*, opinion < *dokein*, to think] **1.** a statement that seems contradictory, absurd, etc. but may be true in fact (Example: "water, water, everywhere, and not a drop to drink") **2.** a statement that contradicts itself and is false (Example: the sun was so hot we nearly froze to death) **3.** a person, situation, etc. that seems inconsistent or full of contradictions —**par'a·dox'i·cal** *adj.* —**par'a·dox'i·cal·ly** *adv.* —**par'a·dox'i·cal·ness** *n.*

par·af·fin (par'ə fin) *n.* [G. < L. *parum*, too little + *affinis*, akin: from its chemical inertness] **1.** a white, waxy substance consisting of a mixture of hydrocarbons, distilled from petroleum and used for making candles, sealing jars, etc.: also called **paraffin wax 2.** *Chem.* any hydrocarbon of the methane series —*vt.* to coat or fill with paraffin

par·a·gon (par'ə gän', -gən) *n.* [MFr. < It. *paragone*, touchstone < Gr. < *para-*, PARA- + *akonē*, whetstone: for IE. base see ACID] a model of perfection or excellence [a *paragon* of virtue]

par·a·graph (par'ə graf') *n.* [< OFr. < ML. < Gr. *paragraphos* < *para-*, PARA- + *graphein*, to write (see GRAPHIC)] **1.** a separate section of a chapter, letter, etc., dealing with a particular point and made up of one or more sentences: it is begun on a new line, often indented **2.** a mark (¶) used as by proofreaders to indicate the beginning of a paragraph **3.** a brief item in a newspaper or magazine —*vt.* **1.** to write about in paragraphs **2.** to arrange in paragraphs —**par'a·graph'er, par'a·graph'ist** *n.* —**par'a·graph'ic** *adj.*

Par·a·guay (par'ə gwā', -gwī'; *Sp.* pä rä gwī') **1.** inland country in south central S. America: 157,042 sq. mi.; pop. 2,396,000; cap. Asunción **2.** river flowing from S Brazil through Paraguay into the Paraná —**Par'a·guay'an** *adj., n.*

par·a·keet (par'ə kēt') *n.* [MFr. *paroquet*, prob. < *perrot*, parrot] any of various small, slender parrots with a long, tapering tail

par·a·le·gal (par'ə lē'gəl) *adj.* [PARA- + LEGAL] designating or of persons trained to aid lawyers but not licensed to practice law —*n.* a person doing paralegal work

par·al·lax (par'ə laks') *n.* [< Fr. < Gr. < *para-*, beyond + *allassein*, to change] **1.** the change that seems to occur in the position of an object due to a change in the viewer's position **2.** the amount of such change; esp., *Astron.* the apparent difference in the position of a star, planet, etc. as it is

PARAKEET
(to 8 in. long, including tail)

seen from some point on the surface of the earth and as it might be seen from some other point, as the center of the earth — **par·al·lac·tic** *adj.*

par·al·lel (par'ə lel', -ləl) *adj.* [< Fr. < L. < Gr. < *para-*, side by side + *allēlos*, one another] **1.** extending in the same direction and always at the same distance apart, so as never to meet, as lines, planes, etc. **2.** having parallel parts or movements **3.** *a)* similar, alike, or corresponding, as in purpose, time, or essential parts [their lives followed *parallel* courses] *b)* having a balanced arrangement, esp. of phrases or clauses [*parallel* structure] **4.** *Elec.* designating a circuit in parallel —*adv.* in a parallel manner —*n.* **1.** a parallel line, surface, etc. **2.** any person or thing similar or corresponding to another; counterpart [your experience is a *parallel* to mine] **3.** a being parallel or similar **4.** any comparison showing likeness [he drew a *parallel* between the two books] **5.** *a)* any of the imaginary lines parallel to the equator and representing degrees of latitude *b)* such a line drawn on a map or globe: in full, **parallel of latitude 6.** [*pl.*] a sign (∥) used as a reference mark **7.** *Elec.* a circuit connection in which the negative terminals are joined to one conductor and the positive terminals to another: usually in phrase, **in parallel** —*vt.* **-al·leled'** or **-al·lelled', -al·lel'ing** or **-al·lel'ling 1.** *a)* to make (one thing) parallel to another *b)* to make parallel to each other **2.** to be parallel with [the road *parallels* the river] **3.** to compare (things) in order to show similarity **4.** to be or find something that is like or similar to; match [nothing can *parallel* that discovery]

parallel bars two parallel, horizontal bars set on adjustable upright posts: used in gymnastics

par·al·lel·e·pi·ped (par'ə lel'ə pī'pid, -pip'id) *n.* [< Gr. *parallēlos*, parallel + *epipedos*, plane] a solid with six faces, each of which is a parallelogram: also **par·al·lel·e·pip'e·don'** (-pip'ə dän')

par·al·lel·ism (par'ə lel iz'm, -ləl-) *n.* **1.** the state of being parallel **2.** close resemblance; similarity **3.** use of parallel structure in writing

par·al·lel·o·gram (par'ə lel'ə gram') *n.* [< Fr. < L. < Gr. < *parallēlos*, PARALLEL + *grammē*, a line] a plane figure with four sides, having the opposite sides parallel and of equal length

PARALLEL BARS

pa·ral·y·sis (pə ral'ə sis) *n.*, *pl.* **-ses'** (-sēz') [L. < Gr. < *paralyein*, to loosen at the side < *para-*, beside + *lyein*, to loose] **1.** a loss of the power to move or feel in any part of the body, as because of injury to the nervous system **2.** any condition of helpless inactivity or inability to act [a *paralysis* of industry]

par·a·lyt·ic (par'ə lit'ik) *adj.* of or having paralysis —*n.* a person having paralysis

par·a·lyze (par'ə līz) *vt.* **-lyzed', -lyz'ing 1.** to cause paralysis in **2.** to make helpless or powerless; bring activity to a stop [heavy snows *paralyzed* the city] —see SYN. at SHOCK[1] —**par'a·ly·za'tion** *n.* —**par'a·lyz'er** *n.*

par·a·mag·net·ic (par'ə mag net'ik) *adj.* designating or of a substance, as aluminum, having low magnetic permeability that varies little with the magnetizing force

Par·a·mar·i·bo (par'ə mar'i bō') seaport & capital of Surinam: pop. c.150,000

par·a·me·ci·um (par'ə mē'shē əm, -sē əm) *n.*, *pl.* **-ci·a** (-ə) [ModL. < Gr. *paramēkēs*, oval] a one-celled, long and narrow protozoan that moves by means of cilia

☆**par·a·med·ic[1]** (par'ə med'ik) *n.* [< PARA(CHUTE) + MEDIC[1]] a medic, esp. a medical corpsman, who parachutes to combat or rescue areas

☆**par·a·med·ic[2]** (par'ə med'ik) *n.* [< PARAMEDICAL] a person in paramedical work

☆**par·a·med·i·cal** (par'ə med'i k'l) *adj.* [PARA- + MEDICAL] designating or of auxiliary medical personnel, as midwives, corpsmen, nurses' aides, laboratory technicians, etc.

pa·ram·e·ter (pə ram'ə tər) *n.* [< ModL. < Gr. *para*, alongside + *metron*, measure] **1.** *Math.* a quantity whose value varies with that part of a system to which the quantity is applied **2.** a variable that is given a fixed value during the investigation of other variables —**par·a·met·ric** (par'ə met'rik) *adj.*

PARALLELOGRAMS

par·a·mil·i·tar·y (par'ə mil'ə ter'ē) *adj.* [PARA- + MILITARY] designating or of forces working along with, or in place of, a regular military organization, often as a semiofficial or secret auxiliary

par·a·mount (par'ə mount') *adj.* [< Anglo-Fr. < OFr. *par* (L. *per*), by + *amont* (< L. *ad montem*), uphill] ranking higher than any other; chief; supreme; most important [of *paramount* concern to us]

par·a·mour (par'ə moor') *n.* [< OFr. *par amour*, with love] **1.** the lover of a person married to another **2.** [Archaic] a sweetheart

Pa·ra·ná (pä'rä nä') river flowing from S Brazil through NE Argentina into the Río de la Plata

par·a·noi·a (par'ə noi'ə) *n.* [ModL. < Gr. < *para-*, beside + *nous*, the mind] a mental disorder in which a person thinks that others are persecuting him and also has false feelings of importance

par·a·noid (par'ə noid') *adj.* of, like, having, or seeming to have paranoia: also **par'a·noi'dal** —*n.* a person having paranoia Also **par'a·noi'ac** (-noi'ak)

par·a·pet (par'ə pit, -pet') *n.* [Fr. < It. < *parare*, to guard + *petto*, breast < L. *pectus*] **1.** a wall or bank for protecting troops from enemy fire **2.** a low wall or railing, as on a balcony or bridge

par·a·pher·na·li·a (par'ə fər nāl'yə, -fə nāl'-; -nā'lē ə) *n.pl.* [often with sing. v.] [ML. < LL. *parapherna* < Gr. < *para-*, beyond + *phernē*, a dowry] **1.** personal belongings **2.** all the things used in some activity; equipment; apparatus; gear [fishing *paraphernalia*]

par·a·phrase (par'ə frāz') *n.* [Fr. < L. < Gr. *paraphrasis*, ult. < *para-*, beyond + *phrazein*, to tell] a putting of something spoken or written into different words having the same meaning —*vt.*, *vi.* **-phrased', -phras'ing** to express in a paraphrase —**par'a·phras'er, par'a·phrast'** (-frast') *n.*

par·a·ple·gi·a (par'ə plē'jē ə, -jə) *n.* [ModL. < Gr. *paraplēgia*, a stroke at one side: see PARA- & -PLEGIA] paralysis of the entire lower half of the body

par·a·ple·gic (par'ə plē'jik, -plej'ik) *adj.* of or having paraplegia —*n.* a person having paraplegia

par·a·psy·chol·o·gy (-sī käl'ə jē) *n.* [PARA- + PSYCHOLOGY] the study of such psychic phenomena as telepathy, ESP, etc. —**par'a·psy·chol'o·gist** *n.*

par·a·site (par'ə sīt') *n.* [< L. < Gr. *parasitos*, one who eats at the table of another < *para-*, beside + *sitos*, food] **1.** a person who lives at others' expense without making any useful return **2.** a plant or animal that lives on or within another from which it gets food, as mistletoe, fleas, etc.

par·a·sit·ic (par'ə sit'ik) *adj.* **1.** of or like a parasite; living at the expense of others **2.** caused by parasites, as a disease Also **par'a·sit'i·cal** —**par'a·sit'i·cal·ly** *adv.*

par·a·sit·i·cide (par'ə sit'ə sīd') *n.* [< PARASITE + -CIDE] anything used to destroy parasites —**par'a·sit'i·ci'dal** *adj.*

par·a·sit·ism (par'ə sīt'iz'm) *n.* **1.** *Biol.* the living together of two kinds of organisms in which the parasite is benefited and the host is usually harmed **2.** *Med.* the condition of being overrun with parasites

par·a·sit·ize (-si tīz', -sī-) *vt.* **-ized', -iz'ing 1.** to live on, in, or with as a parasite **2.** to overrun with parasites

par·a·si·tol·o·gy (par'ə sī täl'ə jē, -si-) *n.* the science dealing with parasites —**par'a·si·tol'o·gist** *n.*

par·a·sol (par'ə sôl', -säl') *n.* [Fr. < It. < *parare*, to ward off + *sole*, the sun] a light umbrella carried as a sunshade, esp. by women

par·a·sym·pa·thet·ic (par'ə sim'pə thet'ik) *adj.* [PARA- + SYMPATHETIC] designating or of that part of the autonomic nervous system whose functions include the slowing of the heartbeat and stimulation of certain digestive glands: see also SYMPATHETIC

☆**par·a·thi·on** (par'ə thī'än) *n.* [< Gr. *para-*, alongside + *theion*, sulfur] a poisonous insecticide, $C_{10}H_{14}O_5NPS$

par·a·thy·roid (par'ə thī'roid) *adj.* [PARA- + THYROID] designating or of any of four small glands located on or near the thyroid gland: they secrete a hormone that controls the body's calcium and phosphorus balance —*n.* a parathyroid gland

par·a·troops (par'ə trōōps') *n.pl.* [< PARA(CHUTE) + TROOP] troops trained and equipped to parachute into a combat area —**par'a·troop'** *adj.* —**par'a·troop'er** *n.*

par·a·ty·phoid (par'ə tī'foid) *adj.* [PARA- + TYPHOID] designating, of, or causing a disease similar to typhoid fever but milder and caused by various bacteria —*n.* paratyphoid fever

‡**par a·vion** (pȧr ȧ vyōn') [Fr.] by air mail

par·boil (pär′boil′) *vt.* [< OFr. < *par* (< L. *per*), through + *boullir* (< L. *bullire*), to boil: meaning infl. by Eng. *part*] **1.** to boil until partly cooked, as before roasting **2.** to make uncomfortably hot

par·buck·le (pär′buk′′l) *n.* [altered (after BUCKLE¹) < Early ModE. *parbunkel*] a sling for a log, barrel, etc. made by passing a doubled rope around the object and pulling the ends through the loop or by fastening the doubled rope at its midpoint and looping it over the object to be raised or lowered —*vt.* -led, -ling to raise or lower by using a parbuckle

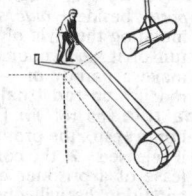

PARBUCKLES

Par·cae (pär′sē) *n.pl. Rom. Myth.* the three Fates

par·cel (pär′s′l) *n.* [< MFr., ult. < L. *particula*: see PARTICLE] **1.** a small, wrapped bundle; package **2.** a quantity of items put up for sale **3.** a group; pack [*a parcel* of fools] **4.** a piece, as of land —*vt.* -celed or -celled, -cel·ing or -cel·ling **1.** to separate into parts and give away or sell (with *out*) **2.** to make up in or as a parcel

parcel post a postal service for carrying and delivering parcels (fourth-class mail)

parch (pärch) *vt.* [< ?] **1.** to expose (corn, beans, etc.) to great heat, so as to dry **2.** to make hot and dry [fields *parched* by the sun] **3.** to make very thirsty **4.** to dry up and shrivel with cold —*vi.* to become very hot, dry, thirsty, etc.

Par·chee·si (pär chē′zē) *a trademark for* a game like pachisi, in which dice are thrown —*n.* [p-] this game or the game of pachisi: also sp. **par·che′si, par·chi′si**

parch·ment (pärch′mənt) *n.* [< OFr., ult. < L. (*charta*) *Pergamena,* (paper) of Pergamum, city in Asia Minor] **1.** an animal skin, as of a sheep or goat, prepared as a surface for writing or painting **2.** paper treated to resemble this **3.** a manuscript, diploma, etc. on parchment

pard (pärd) *n.* [< OFr. < L. < Gr. *pardos*] [Archaic or Poet.] a leopard, or panther

☆**pard·ner** (pärd′nər) *n.* [altered < PARTNER] [Chiefly Dial.] a partner: often shortened to **pard**

par·don (pär′d′n) *vt.* [< OFr. < LL. < L. *per-*, through + *donare,* to give] **1.** to release (a person) from punishment **2.** to cancel penalty for (a crime); forgive **3.** to excuse (a person) for (a minor fault, discourtesy, etc.) —*n.* **1.** a pardoning or being pardoned; forgiveness **2.** an official document granting a pardon **3.** *R.C.Ch. same as* INDULGENCE —**see SYN.** at ABSOLVE —**par′don·a·ble** *adj.* —**par′don·a·bly** *adv.*

par·don·er (-ər) *n.* **1.** in the Middle Ages, a person authorized to sell ecclesiastical pardons, or indulgences **2.** a person who pardons

pare (per) *vt.* pared, par′ing [< MFr. < L. *parare,* to PREPARE] **1.** to cut or trim away (the rind, skin, covering, etc.) of (anything); peel **2.** to reduce (costs, etc.) gradually (often with *down*) —**par′er** *n.*

par·e·gor·ic (par′ə gôr′ik, -gär′-) *n.* [< LL. < Gr. < *parēgoros,* speaking, soothing < *para-,* beside + *agora,* assembly] a camphorated tincture of opium, used to relieve diarrhea

paren. *pl.* **parens.** parenthesis

pa·ren·chy·ma (pə ren′ki mə) *n.* [ModL. < Gr., ult. < *para-,* beside + *en-,* in + *cheein,* to pour] **1.** *Anat.* the basic tissue of an organ, as distinguished from its connective tissue, blood vessels, etc. **2.** *Bot.* a soft tissue of thin-walled cells in plant leaves and stems, fruit pulp, etc. —**pa·ren′chy·mal, par·en·chym·a·tous** (par′ən kim′ə təs) *adj.*

par·ent (per′ənt, par′-) *n.* [OFr. < L. *parens,* parent, orig. prp. of *parere,* to beget: see -PAROUS] **1.** a father or mother **2.** any organism in relation to its offspring **3.** a source; origin [Latin is the *parent* of various languages] —**pa·ren·tal** (pə ren′t′l) *adj.* —**pa·ren′tal·ly** *adv.* —**par′ent·hood′** *n.*

par·ent·age (-ij) *n.* **1.** descent or derivation from parents or ancestors; family line; lineage; origin **2.** the position or relation of a parent; parenthood

par·en·ter·al (pa ren′tər əl) *adj.* [PAR(A)- + ENTER(O)- + -AL] **1.** outside the intestine **2.** brought into the body in some way other than through the digestive tract, as by intravenous injection —**par·en′ter·al·ly** *adv.*

pa·ren·the·sis (pə ren′thə sis) *n., pl.* **-ses′** (-sēz′) [LL. < Gr., ult. < *para-,* beside + *entithenai,* to insert] **1.** a word, clause, remark, etc. added as an explanation or comment within a complete sentence and usually marked off by curved lines, commas, etc. **2.** either or both of the curved lines ( ) so used **3.** an episode or interlude

pa·ren·the·size (-sīz′) *vt.* **-sized′, -siz′ing 1.** to insert (a word, etc.) as a parenthesis **2.** to put into parentheses (sense 2)

par·en·thet·i·cal (par′ən thet′i k′l) *adj.* **1.** *a)* of, or having the nature of, a parenthesis *b)* marked off by parentheses **2.** put in as an added note or explanation **3.** using parentheses Also **par′en·thet′ic** —**par′en·thet′i·cal·ly** *adv.*

par·ent·ing (per′ənt iŋ, par′-) *n.* the work or skill of a parent in raising a child or children

pa·re·sis (pə rē′sis, par′ə sis) *n., pl.* **-ses** (-sēz) [ModL. < Gr. < *parienai,* to relax] **1.** partial or slight paralysis **2.** a brain disease caused by syphilis and marked by dementia, paralytic attacks, etc.: in full, **general paresis** —**pa·ret·ic** (pə ret′ik, -rē′tik) *n., adj.*

par ex·cel·lence (pär ek′sə läns′) [Fr.] in the greatest degree of excellence; beyond comparison

par·fait (pär fā′) *n.* [Fr., lit., perfect] **1.** a frozen dessert of cream, eggs, syrup, etc. in a tall, slender, short-stemmed glass **2.** a dessert of layers of ice cream, fruit, etc. in such a glass

par·he·li·on (pär hē′lē ən, -hēl′yən) *n., pl.* **-li·a** (-ə, -ya) [< L. < Gr. < *para-,* beside + *hēlios,* the sun] a bright, colored spot of light on a solar halo —**par·he′lic** *adj.*

pa·ri·ah (pə rī′ə) *n.* [< Tamil *paraiyan,* a drummer: the pariah was a hereditary drumbeater] **1.** a member of one of the lowest social castes in India **2.** any person despised or rejected by others; outcast

Pa·ri·cu·tín (pä rē kōō tēn′) volcanic mountain in WC Mexico: c. 9,000 ft.: also **Pa·ri·cu·tin** (pä rē′kōō tēn)

pa·ri·e·tal (pə rī′ə t′l) *adj.* [< Fr. < LL. < L. *paries,* a wall] ☆**1.** of or having to do with life within a college [*parietal* regulations] **2.** *Anat.* of, pertaining to, or forming the walls of a cavity, etc.; esp., designating either of two bones forming part of the top and sides of the skull

par·i·mu·tu·el (par′ə myōō′choo wəl) *n.* [Fr., lit., a mutual bet] **1.** a system of betting on races in which the winning bettors share the total amount bet, minus a percentage for the track operators, taxes, etc. **2.** a machine for recording such bets and figuring the payoffs; totalizator

par·ing (per′iŋ) *n.* a thin piece or strip pared off

‡**pa·ri pas·su** (per′ē pas′ōō, pär′ē) [L.] **1.** with equal speed **2.** in equal proportion

Par·is¹ (par′is) *Gr. Legend* a son of Priam: he kidnapped Helen, thus causing the Trojan War

Par·is² (par′is; *Fr.* pȧ′rē′) capital of France, on the Seine: pop. 2,591,000 (urbanized area, 8,197,000) —**Pa·ri·sian** (pə rizh′ən, -rē′zhən) *adj., n.*

Paris green a poisonous, bright-green chemical powder used chiefly as an insecticide

par·ish (par′ish) *n.* [< OFr. < LL. < LGr. *paroikia,* diocese, ult. < Gr. *para-,* beside + *oikos,* dwelling] **1.** a district of British local government **2.** an administrative district of various churches, esp. a part of a diocese, under the charge of a priest or minister **3.** *a)* the members of a church congregation *b)* the territory they live in ☆**4.** a local subdivision in Louisiana, like a county in other States

pa·rish·ion·er (pə rish′ə nər) *n.* a member of a parish

par·i·ty (par′ə tē) *n., pl.* **-ties** [< Fr. < L. < *par,* equal] **1.** the condition of being the same in power, value, etc.; equality **2.** resemblance; similarity **3.** equivalence in value of a currency in terms of another country's currency **4.** equality of value at a given ratio between different kinds of money, commodities, etc. ☆**5.** a controlled price for farm products, to keep the farmers' purchasing power at a specified level

park (pärk) *n.* [< OFr. < ML. *parricus*] **1.** land with woods, lakes, etc., forming part of a private estate or used as a hunting preserve **2.** an area of public land; specif., *a)* an area for public recreation, usually with walks, playgrounds, etc. *b)* an open square in a city, with benches, trees, etc. *c) same as* AMUSEMENT PARK *d)* a large area known for its natural scenery, preserved for public recreation by a government ☆**3.** *same as* BALLPARK **4.** an arrangement in an automatic transmission of a motor vehicle that holds the vehicle in place when it is parked **5.** an area for parking motor vehicles **6.** *Mil.* an area for storing and servicing vehicles and other equipment —*vt.* **1.** to assemble (military equipment) in a park ☆**2.** to leave (a vehicle) in a certain place temporarily ☆**3.** to maneuver (a vehicle) into a space where it can be left temporarily ☆**4.** [Colloq.] to put, leave, or deposit in a certain place —*vi.* to park a vehicle

Park (pärk), **Mun·go** (muŋ′gō) 1771–1806; Scot. explorer in W Africa

☆**par·ka** (pär′kə) *n.* [Aleutian < Russ.] **1.** a hip-length pullover fur garment with a hood, worn in arctic regions **2.** a similar hooded jacket

☆**par·ker·house roll** (pär′kər hous′) [< *Parker House*, Boston hotel where first served] a yeast roll shaped by folding over a flat, round piece of buttered dough

☆**parking lot** an area for parking motor vehicles

☆**parking meter** a coin-operated timing device installed at a parking space to show the length of time that a parked vehicle may occupy that space

Par·kin·son's disease (pär′kin sənz) [after J. *Parkinson* (1755–1824), Eng. physician] a brain disease that causes a tremor and makes muscles become rigid

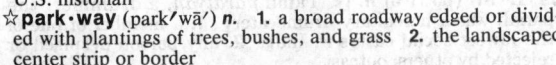

PARKA

Park·man (pärk′mən), **Francis** 1823–93; U.S. historian

☆**park·way** (park′wā′) *n.* **1.** a broad roadway edged or divided with plantings of trees, bushes, and grass **2.** the landscaped center strip or border

Parl. **1.** Parliament **2.** Parliamentary

parl·ance (pär′ləns) *n.* [< Anglo-Fr. < OFr. < *parler*, to speak] a style or manner of speaking or writing; language; idiom [military *parlance*]

par·lan·do (pär län′dō) *adj., adv.* [It.] *Music* to be sung in a style suggesting or very much like speech

☆**par·lay** (pär′lā, -lē; *for v.*, *also* pär lā′) *vt., vi.* [< Fr. < It. < *paro*, an equal < L. *par*] **1.** to bet (an original wager plus its winnings) on another race, etc. **2.** to use (an asset) in a successful way [to *parlay* one's voice into fame] —*n.* a bet or series of bets made by parlaying

par·ley (pär′lē) *vi.* [< Fr. *parler*, to speak < LL. < *parabola*, PARABLE] to hold a talk or conference, esp. with an enemy —*n., pl.* **-leys** a conference; specif., a military conference with an enemy to discuss terms

par·lia·ment (pär′lə mənt) *n.* [< OFr. *parlement* < *parler*: see prec.] **1.** an official conference or council concerned with public affairs **2.** [P-] the national legislative body of Great Britain, composed of the House of Commons and the House of Lords **3.** [P-] a similar body in other countries

par·lia·men·tar·i·an (pär′lə men ter′e ən, -mən-) *n.* a person skilled in parliamentary rules or debate

par·lia·men·ta·ry (pär′lə men′tər ē, -trē) *adj.* **1.** of, like, or established by a parliament **2.** conforming to the rules of a parliament or other public assembly [*parliamentary* procedure] **3.** having or governed by a parliament; specif., of a government in which the prime minister holds office only so long as he is supported by a majority in the parliament

par·lor (pär′lər) *n.* [< OFr. < *parler*: see PARLEY] **1.** *a)* orig., a room set aside for the entertainment of guests *b)* any living room: old-fashioned term **2.** a small, semiprivate room in a hotel, club, etc., used as for conferences **3.** a business establishment, esp. one with specialized services [a beauty *parlor*] Brit. sp. **parlour**

par·lous (pär′ləs) *adj.* [ME., contr. of *perilous*] [Chiefly Archaic] **1.** perilous; dangerous **2.** cunning, shrewd, etc. —*adv.* [Chiefly Archaic] extremely; very

Par·ma (pär′mə; *for 1, also* It. pär′mä) **1.** city in N Italy: pop. 172,000 **2.** [after prec.] city in NE Ohio: suburb of Cleveland: pop. 100,000

Par·men·i·des (pär men′ə dēz′) 5th cent. B.C.; Gr. philosopher

Par·me·san (cheese) (pär′mə zän′, -zən, -zan′) [Fr. < It. < PARMA, Italy] a very hard, dry Italian cheese made from skim milk and usually grated for sprinkling on spaghetti, soup, etc.

Par·nas·sus (pär nas′əs) mountain in C Greece: sacred to Apollo and the Muses in ancient times —*n.* any center of poetic or artistic activity —**Par·nas′si·an** (-ē ən) *adj.*

Par·nell (pär′n'l, pär nel′), **Charles Stewart** 1846–91; Ir. nationalist leader

pa·ro·chi·al (pə rō′kē əl) *adj.* [OFr. < ML. < LL. *parochia*: see PARISH] **1.** of or in a parish or parishes **2.** narrow; provincial; limited [a *parochial* outlook] —**pa·ro′chi·al·ism** *n.* —**pa·ro′chi·al·ist** *n.* —**pa·ro′chi·al·ly** *adv.*

parochial school ☆a school supported and controlled by a church

par·o·dy (par′ə dē) *n., pl.* **-dies** [< Fr. < L. < Gr. *parōidia* < *para-*, beside + *ōidē*, song] **1.** a literary or musical composition imitating the style of a writer or composer in a way that makes fun of it **2.** a poor or weak imitation —*vt.* **-died, -dy·ing** to make a parody of —see SYN. at CARICATURE —**pa·rod·ic** (pə räd′ik), **pa·rod′i·cal** *adj.* —**par′o·dist** *n.* —**par′o·dis′tic** *adj.*

pa·role (pə rōl′) *n.* [Fr. < LL. *parabola*, PARABLE] **1.** word of honor; esp., the promise of a prisoner of war not to fight further if released **2.** the condition of being on parole ☆**3.** *a)* the release of a prisoner before he has served his full sentence, on condition he will obey certain required rules *b)* the freedom thus granted, or the time it lasts —*vt.* **-roled′, -rol′ing** ☆to release on parole —**on parole** at liberty under conditions of parole

☆**pa·rol·ee** (pə rō′lē′) *n.* a person on parole from prison

par·o·no·ma·si·a (par′ə nō mā′zhə, -zhē ə) *n.* [L. < Gr. < *para-*, beside + *onomazein*, to name] the act or practice of punning —**par′o·no·mas′tic** (-mas′tik) *adj.*

Par·os (per′äs; *Gr.* pä′rôs) island of the Cyclades, in the SC Aegean

pa·rot·id (pə rät′id) *adj.* [< ML. < L. < Gr. *parōtis* < *para-*, beside + *ōtos*, genitive of *ous*, EAR¹] designating or of either of the salivary glands below and in front of each ear —*n.* a parotid gland

-par·ous (pər əs) [< L. < *parere*, to bear < IE. base *per-*] a combining form meaning bringing forth, producing, bearing [*viviparous*]

par·ox·ysm (par′ək siz'm) *n.* [< Fr. < ML. < Gr. < *para-*, beyond + *oxynein*, to sharpen < *oxys*, sharp] **1.** a sudden attack of a disease or an increase in the intensity of its symptoms, usually occurring at intervals **2.** a sudden outburst of laughter, rage, etc.; fit; spasm —**par′ox·ys′mal** (-siz′m'l) *adj.*

par·quet (pär kā′) *n.* [Fr. < MFr. dim. of *parc*, a park] ☆**1.** the main floor of a theater, esp. from the orchestra pit to the parquet circle: usually called *orchestra* **2.** a flooring of parquetry —*vt.* **-queted′** (-kād′), **-quet′ing** (-kā′iŋ) **1.** to use parquetry to make (a floor, etc.) **2.** to decorate the floor of (a room) with parquetry

☆**parquet circle** the part of a theater beneath the balcony and behind the parquet

par·quet·ry (pär′kə trē) *n.* inlaid woodwork, or pieces of wood fitted together to form a pattern: used esp. in flooring

parr (pär) *n., pl.* **parrs, parr:** see PLURAL, II, D, 1 [< ?] a young salmon before it enters salt water

par·ra·keet (par′ə kēt′) *n. alt. sp. of* PARAKEET

par·ri·cide (par′ə sīd′) *n.* [Fr. < L. *parricida*] **1.** a person who murders his parent or another near relative **2.** the act of a parricide —**par′ri·ci′dal** *adj.*

PARQUETRY

par·rot (par′ət) *n.* [Fr. dial. *perrot*] **1.** any of several related tropical birds with a hooked bill, brightly colored feathers, and feet having two toes pointing forward and two backward: some parrots can learn to imitate human speech **2.** a person who just repeats or copies what others do or say without understanding —*vt.* to repeat or imitate, esp. without full understanding

parrot fever *same as* PSITTACOSIS

parrot fish any of various related, brightly colored, tropical ocean fishes with parrotlike jaws

par·ry (par′ē) *vt.* **-ried, -ry·ing** [prob. < imper. of Fr. *parer* < It. *parare*, to ward off < L. *parare*, to PREPARE] **1.** to ward off or turn aside (a blow, sword thrust, etc.) **2.** to turn aside (a question, etc.) as by answering in a clever, indirect, or tricky way —*vi.* to make a parry —*n., pl.* **-ries** **1.** a warding off of a blow, etc. **2.** a clever, indirect, or tricky answer

parse (pärs) *vt., vi.* **parsed, pars′ing** [< L. *pars (orationis)*, part (of speech)] [Now Rare] **1.** to separate (a sentence) into its parts, explaining the grammatical form, function, etc. of each part **2.** to describe the form, part of speech, etc. of (a word in a sentence)

par·sec (pär′sek′) *n.* [PAR(ALLAX) + SEC(OND)²] a unit of measure of astronomical distance, equal to 3.26 light years, or 19.2 trillion miles

Par·see, Par·si (pär′sē, pär sē′) *n.* [Per. *Pārsī*, a Persian] a member of a Zoroastrian religious sect in India descended from Persian refugees from the Moslem persecutions of the 7th and 8th cent. —**Par′see·ism, Par′si·ism n.**

Par·si·fal (pär′si fäl′, -fəl) the title character in Wagner's opera (1882) about the knights of the Holy Grail

par·si·mo·ni·ous (pär′sə mō′nē əs) *adj.* too careful in spending; overly thrifty; miserly —see SYN. at STINGY —**par′si·mo′ni·ous·ly adv.** —**par′si·mo′ni·ous·ness n.**

par·si·mo·ny (pär′sə mō′nē) *n.* [< L. *parcimonia* < *parcere*, to spare] a tendency to be overly careful in spending; stinginess

pars·ley (pärs′lē) *n.* [< OE. & OFr. < L. *petroselinum* < Gr. < *petros*, a rock + *selinon*, celery] a plant of the parsley family, with spicy, often curled leaves used to flavor or garnish some foods —*adj.* designating a family of hollow-stemmed plants having umbels, including the parsnip, carrot, etc.

pars·nip (pär′snip) *n.* [altered (after ME. *nepe*, turnip) < OFr. < L. *pastinaca* < *pastinare*, to dig up] 1. a plant of the parsley family, with a long, thick, sweet, white root used as a vegetable 2. its root

par·son (pär′s'n) *n.* [< OFr. < ML. *persona*, orig., person < L.; see PERSON] 1. a clergyman in charge of a parish 2. any clergyman

PARSLEY

par·son·age (-ij) *n.* the dwelling provided by a church for the use of its parson

part (pärt) *n.* [OE. & OFr., both < L. *partis*, genitive of *pars*, part: for IE. base see PAR] 1. a division or portion of a whole; specif., *a)* any of several equal quantities, numbers, pieces, etc. into which something can be divided [a cent is a 100th *part* of a dollar] *b)* a necessary element which can be replaced [radio *parts*] *c)* a certain amount but not all [to lose *part* of one's fortune] *d)* a segment or organ as of the body 2. a share assigned or given; specif., *a)* a share of work or duty [to do one's *part*] *b)* interest; concern [to have some *part* in a matter] *c)* [*usually pl.*] talent; ability [a man of *parts*] *d)* a role in a play *e)* *Music* any voice or instrument in an ensemble, or the score for it 3. a region; esp., [*usually pl.*] a portion of a country; district [are you from these *parts?*] 4. one of the sides in a transaction, dispute, etc. [I won't take his *part* in the quarrel] ☆5. the dividing line made by combing the hair in different directions —*vt.* [< OFr. < L. *partire* < the *n.*] 1. to break or divide into parts [the strain *parted* the rope] 2. to comb (the hair) so as to leave a part 3. to break up or separate; break or hold apart [a passer-by *parted* the struggling boys] 4. [Archaic] to divide into parts or shares —*vi.* 1. to break or divide into parts [the rope *parted* in the middle] 2. to separate and go different ways [the stream *parted*] 3. to cease associating [they *parted* in anger] 4. *a)* to go away; depart (*from*) *b)* to die —*adj.* not total; partial [*part* owner of a factory] —*adv.* in part; partly [it was *part* red, *part* blue] —**for one's part** as far as one is concerned —**for the most part** mostly; generally —**in good part** good-naturedly —**in part** to some extent or degree; partly —**on the part of one** 1. as far as one is concerned 2. by or coming from one Also **on one's part** —**part with** to give up; relinquish —**play a part** 1. to behave unnaturally in trying to deceive 2. to participate: also **take part**

SYN.—**part** is the general word for any of the components of a whole [a *part* of one's life]; **portion** often suggests a part given or assigned as a share [his *portion* of the inheritance]; a **piece** is either a part separated from the whole [a *piece* of pie] or a single unit from a collection of related things [only one *piece* missing from her set of china]; a **division** is a part formed by cutting, partitioning, classifying, etc. [the fine-arts *division* of a library]; **section** means much the same as **division** but usually suggests a smaller part [a *section* of a bookcase]; **segment** implies a part separated along natural lines of division [a *segment* of a tangerine]; a **fraction** is strictly a part contained by the whole a certain number of times without remainder, but generally it suggests a small, unimportant part [he received only a *fraction* of the benefits he was entitled to]; a **fragment** is a relatively small part separated as by breaking [a *fragment* of rock] —ANT. whole

part. 1. participial 2. participle

par·take (pär tāk′) *vi.* -took′, -tak′en, -tak′ing [< *partaker*,

contr. of *part taker*] 1. to take part (*in* an activity); participate 2. to take a portion; specif., to eat or drink, esp. with others (usually with *of*) 3. to have or show a trace (*of*); have some of the qualities (*of*) [his dealings *partake* of fraud] —**par·tak′er n.**

part and parcel a necessary part (*of* something)

part·ed (pär′tid) *adj.* 1. divided; separated 2. *Bot.* divided almost to the base, as some leaves

par·terre (pär ter′) *n.* [Fr. < *par*, on + *terre*, earth] 1. an ornamental garden area ☆2. *same as* PARQUET CIRCLE

par·the·no·gen·e·sis (pär′thə nō jen′ə sis) *n.* [ModL. < Gr. *parthenos*, virgin + *genesis*, origin] reproduction by the development of an unfertilized ovum, seed, or spore, as in certain insects, algae, etc. —**par′the·no·ge·net′ic** (-jə net′ik) *adj.* —**par′the·no·ge·net′i·cal·ly adv.**

Par·the·non (pär′thə nän′, -nən) [L. < Gr. < *parthenos*, a virgin (that is, Athena)] the Doric temple of Athena built (5th cent. B.C.) on the Acropolis in Athens

Par·thi·a (pär′thē ə) ancient country southeast of the Caspian Sea —**Par′thi·an adj., n.**

Parthian shot any hostile gesture or remark made in leaving: Parthian cavalrymen shot at the enemy while retreating or pretending to retreat

par·tial (pär′shəl) *adj.* [MFr. < ML. < L. *pars*, PART] 1. favoring one person, faction, etc. more than another; biased [a judge should not be *partial*] 2. not complete or total [a *partial* eclipse of the sun] —**partial to** fond of [he's *partial* to strawberries] —**par′tial·ly adv.**

par·ti·al·i·ty (pär′shē al′ə tē, pär shal′-) *n.* 1. the state or quality of being partial; bias 2. particular fondness or liking —see SYN. at PREJUDICE

par·tic·i·pant (pär tis′ə pənt, pər-) *adj.* participating —*n.* a person who participates

par·tic·i·pate (pär tis′ə pāt′, pər-) *vi.* -pat′ed, -pat′ing [< L. pp. of *participare* < *pars*, PART + *capere*, to take] to have or take a share with others (*in* an activity, etc.) —**par·tic′i·pa′tion n.** —**par·tic′i·pa′tive adj.** —**par·tic′i·pa′tor n.** —**par·tic′i·pa·to′ry** (-pə tôr′ē) *adj.*

par·ti·cip·i·al (pär′tə sip′ē əl) *adj.* of, based on, or having the nature and use of a participle —**par′ti·cip′i·al·ly adv.**

par·ti·ci·ple (pär′tə sip′'l) *n.* [OFr. < L. < *particeps*, partaking < *pars*, PART + *capere*, to take] a verbal form having the qualities of both verb and adjective Participles are used: *a)* in verb phrases (are *asking*) *b)* as verbs (*seeing* her, he stopped) *c)* as adjectives (the *beaten* path) *d)* as nouns (*seeing* is *believing*) *e)* as adverbs (*raving* mad) *f)* as connectives (*saving* those present)

par·ti·cle (pär′ti k'l) *n.* [< MFr. < L. *particula*, dim. of *pars*, PART] 1. *a)* a tiny fragment [a dust *particle*] *b)* the slightest trace; speck [not a *particle* of truth in the story] 2. *Gram. a)* a short, usually uninflected part of speech used to show relationships between words, as an article, preposition, conjunction, or interjection *b)* an uninflected stem 3. *Physics* a piece of matter so small as to be considered without magnitude

par·ti·col·ored (pär′tē kul′ərd) *adj.* [< Fr. pp. of *partir*: see PARTY] having different colors in different parts

par·tic·u·lar (pər tik′yə lər, pär-) *adj.* [< MFr. < LL. < L. *particula*, PARTICLE] 1. of or belonging to a single, definite person, group, or thing [his own *particular* set of beliefs] 2. regarded separately; specific [to have a *particular* color in mind] 3. unusual; special [no *particular* reason for going] 4. itemized; detailed 5. hard to please; exacting [very *particular* about her food] —*n.* 1. a distinct fact, item, or instance 2. a detail; item —see SYN. at SPECIAL —**in particular** particularly; especially

par·tic·u·lar·i·ty (pər tik′yə lar′ə tē, pär-) *n., pl.* -ties 1. the state, quality, or fact of being particular; specif., *a)* relation to one of a group rather than to all *b)* a being detailed, as a description *c)* attention to detail 2. something particular; specif., *a)* a peculiarity *b)* a minute detail

par·tic·u·lar·ize (pər tik′yə lə rīz′, pär-) *vt.* -ized, -iz′ing to specify; itemize —*vi.* to give particulars or details —**par·tic′u·lar·i·za′tion n.**

par·tic·u·lar·ly (pər tik′yə lər lē, pär-) *adv.* 1. in detail 2. especially; unusually 3. specifically

par·tic·u·late (pär tik′yə lit, -lāt′) *adj.* [< L. *particula*, PARTICLE + -ATE¹] of or pertaining to tiny, separate particles [*particulate* matter from incomplete burning] —*n.* a tiny particle

part·ing (pärt'iŋ) *adj.* **1.** dividing; separating **2.** departing **3.** given, spoken, done, etc. at parting [a *parting* remark] —*n.* **1.** a breaking or separating **2.** a dividing point or line **3.** something that separates or divides **4.** a leave-taking or departure **5.** death

par·ti·san (pärt'ə z'n, -s'n) *n.* [MFr. < It. *partigiano* < L. *pars,* PART] **1.** a strong supporter of a side, party, or person; often, specif., an unreasoning, emotional supporter **2.** any of a group of guerrilla fighters; esp., a member of an organized civilian force fighting to drive out occupying enemy troops —*adj.* of, like, or typical of a partisan Also sp. **par'ti·zan** —**par'ti·san·ship'** *n.*

par·ti·ta (pär tēt'ə) *n.* [It. < fem. pp. of *partire,* to divide < L. *pars,* part] *Music* **1.** a kind of suite, esp. of the 18th cent. **2.** an air with variations

par·tite (pär'tīt) *adj.* [< L. pp. of *partire,* to part] in parts: often in compounds [*tripartite*]

par·ti·tion (pär tish'ən, pər-) *n.* [< L. *partitio*] **1.** division into parts [the *partition* of Ireland in 1925] **2.** something that divides, as a wall separating rooms **3.** a part or section —*vt.* **1.** to divide into parts **2.** to divide by a partition —**par·ti'-tioned** *adj.* —**par·ti'tion·er** *n.*

par·ti·tive (pärt'ə tiv) *adj.* [< ML.: see PARTITE & -IVE] **1.** making a division **2.** *Gram.* restricting to or involving only a part of a whole —*n.* a partitive word —**par'ti·tive·ly** *adv.*

part·ly (pärt'lē) *adv.* in part; not fully or completely

part·ner (pärt'nər) *n.* [altered (after *part*) < *parcener,* joint inheritor] one who takes part in an activity with another or others; specif., *a)* one of two or more persons heading the same business enterprise and sharing its profits and risks *b)* a husband or wife *c)* either of two persons dancing together *d)* either of two players on the same side or team playing against two others —*vt.* **1.** to join (others) together as partners **2.** to be or provide a partner for

part·ner·ship (-ship') *n.* **1.** the state of being a partner **2.** the relationship of partners; joint interest **3.** *a)* an association of partners in a business enterprise *b)* the contract for this

part of speech any of the classes of words of a given language, variously based on form, function, meaning, etc.: in traditional English grammar, the parts of speech are noun, verb, adjective, adverb, pronoun, preposition, conjunction, and interjection

par·took (pär took') *pt. of* PARTAKE

par·tridge (pär'trij) *n., pl.* **-tridg·es, -tridge** : see PLURAL, II, D, 1 [< OFr. < L. < Gr. *perdix*] **1.** a European game bird with an orange-brown head, a grayish neck, and a rust-colored tail: successfully introduced into N. America **2.** any of various game birds like the partridge, as the pheasant

☆**par·tridge·ber·ry** (-ber'ē) *n., pl.* **-ries** **1.** a trailing N. American evergreen, with pinkish flowers and red berries **2.** its berry

part song a song for several voices singing in harmony, usually unaccompanied: also **part'-song** *n.*

PARTRIDGE
(to 14 in. long; wingspread to 13 in.)

part-time (pärt'tīm') *adj.* designating, of, or engaged in work, study, etc. for periods regarded as taking less time than a full schedule

part time as a part-time employee, student, etc. [to work *part time*]

par·tu·ri·ent (pär tyoor'ē ənt, -toor'-) *adj.* [< L. prp. of *parturire,* to be in labor < *parere:* see -PAROUS] **1.** giving birth for about to give birth to young **2.** of childbirth —**par·tu'ri·en·cy** *n.*

par·tu·ri·tion (pär'choo rish'ən, -tyoo-, -too-) *n.* [< L.: see PARTURIENT] the act of giving birth to offspring; childbirth

part·way (pärt'wā') *adv.* to some point, degree, or extent less than full, complete, etc. [*partway* done]

par·ty (pär'tē) *n., pl.* **-ties** [< OFr. < *partir,* to divide < L. < *pars,* PART] **1.** a group working to establish or promote certain principles or policies of government; esp., a political group which tries to elect its candidates to office **2.** any group acting together to accomplish or do something [a surveying *party*] **3.** a gathering of people to have a good time, usually with food and drinks served [a cocktail *party*] **4.** a participant in an action, plan, etc. (often with *to*) [he is a *party* to the plan] **5.** either of the persons or sides concerned in a legal matter **6.** [Colloq.] a person [the *party* who telephoned] —*adj.* **1.** of a political party [a *party* leader] **2.** for a social gathering [*party* clothes] —*vi.* **-tied, -ty·ing** ☆to attend or hold social parties —*vt.* ☆to be host to at a party

party line ☆**1.** a single circuit connecting two or more telephone users with the exchange **2.** the line of policy followed by a political party —**par'ty-lin'er** *n.*

par value the value of a stock, bond, etc. fixed at the time of its issue; face value

par·ve·nu (pär'və noo', -nyoo') *n.* [Fr., pp. of *parvenir* < L. *parvenire,* to arrive] a person who has suddenly acquired wealth or power and is not fully accepted socially by the class into which he has risen —*adj.* like or characteristic of a parvenu

pas (pä) *n., pl.* **pas** (päz; *Fr.* pä) [Fr. < L. *passus,* a step] a step or series of steps in dancing: in ballet, a **pas de deux** (pä'də doo') is a dance for two, a **pas de trois** (pät trwä') is for three, a **pas de qua·tre** (pät kå'tr') is for four

Pas·a·de·na (pas'ə dē'nə) **1.** [< Ojibwa, lit., valley town] city in SW Calif., near Los Angeles: pop. 113,000 **2.** [after prec.] city in SE Tex., near Houston: pop. 89,000

Pas·cal (pás kál'; *E.* pas kal'), **Blaise** (blez) 1623-62; Fr. mathematician, physicist, & philosopher

Pas·cal celery (pas'k'l) [< ?] a large, dark-green variety of celery with firm stalks

Pasch (pask) *n.* [< OFr. < LL. < Gr. *pascha* < Heb. *pesaḥ,* the Passover] *same as:* **1.** PASSOVER **2.** EASTER —**pas'chal** (pas'k'l) *adj.*

paschal lamb **1.** among the ancient Hebrews, the lamb slain and eaten at the Passover **2.** [P- L-] among Christians, Jesus, esp. when represented symbolically as a lamb

pasch flower (pask) *same as* PASQUEFLOWER

pa·sha (pə shä', pä'shə, pash'ə) *n.* [Turk. *pasha*] formerly, in Turkey, **1.** a title of honor placed after the name **2.** a high official

Pash·to (push'tō, päsh'-) *n.* an Iranian language of Afghanistan and Pakistan

pasque·flow·er (pask'flou'ər) *n.* [< MFr. < *passer,* PASS² + *fleur,* a flower, altered after Fr. *pasque,* PASCH] any of several plants of the buttercup family; esp., a N. American wildflower with hairy leaves and cup-shaped, bluish flowers

pass¹ (pas) *n.* [see PACE] a narrow passage or opening, esp. between mountains; gap; defile

pass² (pas) *vi.* [< OFr. *passer,* ult. < L. *passus,* a step: see PACE] **1.** to go forward, through, or out [the sentry let no one *pass*] **2.** to extend; lead [a road *passing* around the hill] **3.** to be handed on from person to person **4.** to go or be conveyed from one place, condition, owner, etc. to another **5.** to be exchanged between persons, as greetings [the fever *passed*] *b)* to go away; depart **7.** to die (usually with *away* or *on*) **8.** to go by or past [we saluted as the flag *passed*] **9.** to slip by or elapse [an hour *passed*] **10.** to make a way (with *through* or *by*) **11.** to take place or be accepted without question [we'll let that *pass* for the time being] **12.** to be sanctioned or approved, as by a lawmaking body **13.** *a)* to go through a test, course, etc. successfully; satisfy requirements *b)* to be barely acceptable as a substitute **14.** to take place; happen [no one knows what *passed* behind those locked doors] **15.** to give a judgment, opinion, etc.; decide (*on* or *upon*) **16.** to be rendered or pronounced [the judgment *passed* against us] **17.** *Card Games* to give up one's chance to bid, play, etc. **18.** *Sports* to make a pass of the ball, puck, etc. —*vt.* **1.** to go by, beyond, past, over, or through; specif., *a)* to leave behind [to *pass* others in a race] *b)* to undergo (usually with *through*) *c)* to go by without noticing ☆*d)* to omit paying (a regular dividend) *e)* to go through (a test, course, etc.) successfully *f)* to surpass; excel **2.** to cause or allow to go or move; specif., *a)* to send; dispatch *b)* to guide into position [to *pass* a rope around a stake] *c)* to cause to go through *d)* to make move past [he *passed* his hand in front of her eyes] *e)* to cause or allow to get by an obstacle, etc. *f)* to ratify, enact, or approve [Congress *passed* the bill] *g)* to cause or allow to go through a test, course, etc. successfully *h)* to spend (time) *i)* to excrete; void [to *pass* urine] ☆*j)* *Baseball* to walk (a batter) **3.** to make move from place to place or person to person; specif., *a)* to hand to another [*pass* the salt] *b)* to put into circulation [to *pass* a bad check] *c)* to throw or hit (a ball, puck, etc.) from one player to another **4.** *a)* to give (an opinion or judgment) *b)* to utter (a remark) —*n.* **1.** an act of passing; passage **2.** *a)* the successful completion of a course or test in school, esp. without honors *b)* a mark indicating this **3.** condition or situation [a strange *pass*] **4.** *a)* a ticket, etc. that allows a person to come and go freely or without charge *b)* a ticket that permits unlimited rides on a bus, etc. for a specified period *c)* *Mil.* a written leave of absence for a brief period **5.** a motion of the hands meant to deceive, as in card tricks **6.** a motion of the hand, as in hypnotism **7.** *a)* a motion of the hand as if to strike *b)* an uncertain attempt *[to make a* pass *at repairing something]* **8.** [Slang] an attempt to be intimate in a sexual way **9.** *Aeron.* a flight over a specified point or at a target **10.** *Card Games* a giving up of one's chance to bid, play, etc. **11.** *Sports* *a)* a passing of the ball, puck, etc. to another player during play *b)* a lunge or thrust in fencing ☆c) a walk in baseball—see **SYN.** at DIE¹ —**bring to pass** to make happen —**come to pass** to happen —**pass for** to be accepted or looked upon as *[it is a sham but* passes *for the real thing]* —**pass off** **1.** to cease **2.** to take place, as a transaction **3.** to be or cause to be accepted as genuine, etc., esp. through deceit *[to* pass *himself* off *as a police officer]* —**pass out** **1.** to distribute **2.** to faint —**pass over** **1.** to disregard; ignore; omit **2.** to not consider (someone) for a promotion, etc. —☆**pass up** [Colloq.] to reject, refuse, or let go by, as an opportunity —**pass′er** *n.*

pass. **1.** passenger **2.** passim **3.** passive

pass·a·ble (pas′ə b'l) *adj.* **1.** that can be passed, traveled over, or crossed *[muddy but* passable *roads]* **2.** that can be circulated, as coin **3.** barely satisfactory; fair *[a* passable *meal]* **4.** that can be enacted, as a proposed law —**pass′a·ble·ness** *n.* —**pass′a·bly** *adv.*

pass·a·ca·glia (päs′ə käl′yə, pas′-) *n.* [< It. < Sp. < *pasar,* to pass + *calle,* street: so named from dancing in the street] a musical form based on a former Italian dance, in 3/4 time

pas·sage (pas′ij) *n.* [OFr. < *passer:* see PASS² & -AGE] **1.** the act of passing; specif., *a)* movement from one place to another; migration *[birds of* passage*]* *b)* transition *[the* passage *of day into night]* *c)* the passing of a law by a legislature **2.** permission, right, or a chance to pass *[granted* passage *through the enemy lines]* **3.** a journey, esp. by water; voyage *[a* passage *to India]* **4.** *a)* passenger accommodations, esp. on a ship *[to book* passage *on a steamer]* *b)* the charge for this **5.** a way or means of passing; specif., *a)* a road or path *b)* a channel, duct, etc. *c)* a passageway **6.** an exchange, as of blows or words **7.** a short section of something written or spoken or of a musical composition *[a* passage *from the Bible]*

pas·sage·way (-wā′) *n.* a narrow way for passage, as a hall, corridor, or alley; passage

Pas·sa·ic (pə sā′ik) [after *Passaic* River (on which the city is located) < Delaware *passajeck,* valley] city in northeastern N.J.: pop. 55,000

pass·book (pas′book′) *n. same as* BANKBOOK

pas·sé (pa sā′, pas′ā) *adj.* [Fr., lit., past] out-of-date; old-fashioned

☆**passed ball** *Baseball* a pitch that the catcher should have caught but that gets by him, allowing a base runner to advance

pas·sel (pas′'l) *n.* [< PARCEL] [Colloq. or Dial.] a group or collection, esp. a fairly large one

pas·sen·ger (pas′'n jər) *n.* [< MFr. < OFr. *passage,* PASSAGE] a person traveling in a train, boat, automobile, etc., esp. one having no part in its operation

☆**passenger pigeon** a N. American pigeon formerly abundant but now extinct

passe-par·tout (pas′pär tōō′, päs′-) *n.* [Fr., lit., passes everywhere] **1.** a passkey **2.** a picture mounting in which glass, picture, backing, and often a mat are bound together, as by strips of gummed paper along the edges

pass·er-by (pas′ər bī′) *n., pl.* **pass′ers-by′** a person who passes by

pas·ser·ine (pas′ər in, -ə rīn′) *adj.* [< L. < *passer,* a sparrow] of the order of perching songbirds to which most birds belong —*n.* a bird of this order

‡**pas·sim** (pas′im) *adv.* [L.] here and there; in various parts (of a book, etc.)

pass·ing (pas′iŋ) *adj.* **1.** going by, beyond, past, over, or through *[a* passing *train]* **2.** only brief; momentary *[a* passing *fancy]* **3.** casual; incidental *[a* passing *remark]* **4.** satisfying requirements *[a* passing *grade]* —*adv.* [Chiefly Archaic] very *[it was* passing *strange]* —*n.* **1.** the act of one that passes; specif., death **2.** a means or place of passing —**in passing** **1.** casually **2.** incidentally

pas·sion (pash′ən) *n.* [OFr. < LL. < L. pp. of *pati,* to suffer < IE. base *pe-,* to harm] **1.** orig., suffering, as of a martyr **2.** [P-] the suffering of Jesus during the Crucifixion or after the Last Supper **3.** *a)* any emotion, as hate, grief, love, etc. *b)* [pl.] all

of these emotions **4.** extreme emotion; specif., *a)* rage; fury *b)* enthusiasm *[a* passion *for music]* *c)* strong love or affection *d)* sexual desire; lust **5.** that for which a strong desire or liking is felt *[golf is his* passion*]* —**pas′sion·less** *adj.*

SYN.—passion usually implies an emotion so strong that it may overcome a person's ability to think clearly and make him behave in a way he would normally avoid; **fervor** and **ardor** both imply emotion of burning intensity, **fervor** suggesting a steady, long-lasting glow of feeling *[religious* fervor*],* and **ardor** suggesting a restless, excited, flamelike emotion *[the* ardors *of youth];* **enthusiasm** implies strong feelings in favor of an object or cause and usually suggests eager participation *[his* enthusiasm *for golf];* **zeal** implies intense enthusiasm for an object or cause, usually as displayed in energetic and devoted activity in support of it *[a* zeal *for reform]*

pas·sion·ate (pash′ən it) *adj.* **1.** having or showing strong emotions **2.** hot-tempered **3.** resulting from, expressing, or tending to arouse strong feeling; ardent *[a* passionate *speech]* **4.** readily aroused sexually **5.** very strong; intense *[a* passionate *rage]* —**pas′sion·ate·ly** *adv.*

SYN.—passionate implies very strong emotion that may lead to violent action *[a* passionate *rage];* **impassioned** suggests an expression of emotion that is deeply and sincerely felt *[an* impassioned *plea for tolerance];* **ardent** and **fervent** both imply an intense, glowing feeling of eagerness, dedication, devotion, etc., with **fervent** often suggesting a somewhat more profound, deep-seated, or long-lasting emotion *[an* ardent *interest in football;* a *fervent* prayer];* **fervid** differs from **fervent** in often suggesting a feverish outburst of intense feeling *[a vengeful,* fervid *hatred]*

pas·sion·flow·er (pash′ən flou′ər) *n.* [from the supposed resemblance of parts of the flowers to Jesus' wounds, crown of thorns, etc.] any of a number of tropical plants with variously colored flowers and yellow or purple, egglike fruit (**passion fruit**)

PASSIONFLOWER

Passion play a religious play representing the Passion of Jesus

Passion Sunday the fifth Sunday in Lent, two weeks before Easter Sunday

Passion Week **1.** the week beginning with Passion Sunday **2.** formerly, the week before Easter; Holy Week

pas·sive (pas′iv) *adj.* [< L. *passivus* < pp. of *pati,* to suffer: see PASSION] **1.** acted upon without acting in return *[passive* viewers of a play] **2.** not resisting; submissive *[the* passive *subjects of a tyrant]* **3.** taking no active part; inactive *[a* passive *member of his political party]* **4.** *Gram.* denoting the voice or form of a verb whose subject is the receiver (object) of the action of the verb *[in the sentence "I was hit by the ball," "was hit" is in the* passive *voice]* —*n. Gram.* the passive voice —**pas′sive·ly** *adv.* —**pas′sive·ness, pas·siv·i·ty** (pa siv′ə tē) *n.*

passive immunity **1.** immunity (to a disease) acquired by the injection of antibodies from an animal or person with active immunity **2.** temporary immunity acquired by a child in the womb from antibodies it gets from the mother

passive resistance opposition to a government or to its policies by refusal to pay certain taxes, obey certain laws, etc. or by such nonviolent acts as fasting, peaceful demonstrations, etc.

pass·key (pas′kē′) *n.* **1.** *same as:* a) MASTER KEY b) SKELETON KEY **2.** any private key

Pass·o·ver (pas′ō′vər) *n.* [PASS² & OVER] a Jewish holiday (*Pesach*) of eight (or more) days beginning on the 14th of Nisan and commemorating the ancient Hebrews' deliverance from slavery in Egypt: Ex. 12

pass·port (pas′pôrt′) *n.* [< Fr. < *passer,* PASS² & *port,* PORT¹] **1.** a government document issued to a citizen for travel abroad, stating who he is and giving him the right to protection in foreign countries **2.** anything that makes it possible for a person to be accepted or successful *[a college degree is often a* passport *to a good job]*

☆**pass-through** (-thrōō′) *n.* an opening in a wall, as for passing food, etc. from a kitchen to another room

pass·word (-wurd′) *n.* **1.** a secret word or phrase that must be said to a guard or sentry by someone wishing to get past him **2.** any means of gaining entrance, etc.

past (past) *rare pp. of* PASS² —*adj.* **1.** gone by; ended *[what is* past *is finished]* **2.** of a former time *[based on* past *experience]*

3. just gone by [the *past* week] 4. having served formerly [a *past* chairman] 5. *Gram.* indicating a time or condition gone by or an action completed or in progress at a former time [the *past* tense of "walk" is "walked"] —*n.* 1. time gone by 2. the history or former life of a person, group, etc.: often used to indicate a hidden or questionable past [a woman with a *past*] 3. *Gram.* a) the past tense b) a verb form in this tense —*prep.* 1. later than [ten minutes *past* two] 2. farther on than [*past* the city limits] 3. beyond in amount or degree [her older sister is *past* twenty] 4. beyond the extent, power, etc. of [such claims are *past* belief] —*adv.* to and beyond a point in time or space —**not put it past someone** to believe someone is not unlikely (to do a certain thing) [I would *not put it past* him to lie]

pas·ta (päs'tə) *n.* [It. < LL.: see PASTE] 1. dough made as of semolina and shaped and dried in the form of spaghetti, macaroni, etc. 2. spaghetti, macaroni, etc. cooked in some way

paste (pāst) *n.* [OFr. < LL. *pasta* < Gr. *pastē*, barley porridge] 1. *a)* dough for making rich pastry *b)* same as PASTA 2. any soft, moist, smooth-textured substance [*toothpaste*] 3. a foodstuff, pounded or ground until creamy [almond *paste*] 4. a mixture of flour or starch, water, resin, etc., put on paper or anything light to make it stick to something else 5. the moistened clay used to make pottery or porcelain 6. *a)* a hard, brilliant glass for making artificial gems *b)* such a gem or gems 7. [Slang] a blow or punch —*vt.* **past'ed, past'ing** 1. to fasten or make stick as with paste 2. to cover with pasted material [to *paste* a wall with posters] 3. [Slang] to hit; punch —**past'er** *n.*

paste·board (pāst'bôrd') *n.* a stiff material made of layers of paper pasted together or of pressed and dried paper pulp —*adj.* 1. of pasteboard 2. flimsy

pas·tel (pas tel') *n.* [Fr. < It. *pastello* < LL. *pasta*, PASTE] 1. *a)* ground coloring matter formed into a crayon *b)* such a crayon 2. a picture drawn with such crayons 3. drawing with pastels as an art form 4. a soft, pale shade of any color —*adj.* 1. soft and pale: said of colors 2. of pastel 3. drawn with pastels —**pas·tel'ist, pas·tel'list** *n.*

pas·tern (pas'tərn) *n.* [< MFr. < *pasture*, a tether, ult. < L. *pastor*: see PASTOR] the part of a horse's foot between the fetlock and the hoof

Pas·teur (pas tur'; *Fr.* pȧs tër'), **Louis** 1822–95; Fr. chemist & bacteriologist

pas·teur·i·za·tion (pas'chər i zā'shən, pas'tər-) *n.* a method of destroying and checking bacteria in milk, beer, etc. by heating the liquid to a specified temperature for a specified period of time

pas·teur·ize (pas'chə rīz', pas'tə-) *vt.* **-ized', -iz'ing** [after L. PASTEUR] to subject (milk, beer, etc.) to pasteurization —**pas'teur·iz'er** *n.*

Pasteur treatment Pasteur's method of preventing rabies by giving a series of inoculations of the virus that causes rabies, each one stronger than the one before

pas·tiche (pas tēsh') *n.* [Fr. < It. *pasticcio*] 1. *a)* a literary, artistic, or musical composition made up of bits from various sources; potpourri *b)* such a composition intended to imitate or ridicule another artist's style 2. a jumbled mixture; hodgepodge

pas·tie (pas'tē) *n.* same as PASTY[2]

pas·tille (pas tēl') *n.* [Fr. < L. *pastillus*, lozenge < *pascere*, to feed] 1. a small tablet or lozenge containing medicine, flavoring, etc. 2. a little ball of paste with a strong odor, burned for fumigating or deodorizing Also **pas·til** (pas'til)

pas·time (pas'tīm') *n.* [transl. of Fr. *passe-temps*] a way of spending spare time pleasantly

past master 1. a former master, as in a lodge 2. an expert —**past mistress** *fem.*

pas·tor (pas'tər) *n.* [< OFr. < L., a shepherd < *pascere*, to feed: for IE. base see FOOD] a clergyman in charge of a church or congregation —**pas'tor·ship'** *n.*

pas·to·ral (pas'tər əl) *adj.* [< L. < *pastor*, a shepherd: see PASTOR] 1. of shepherds or their work, etc. 2. of or characteristic of rural life, esp. when thought of as being peaceful, simple, and natural 3. of a pastor or his duties —*n.* 1. a poem, play, etc. with a rural setting, esp. one dealing with shepherds and their lives in an idealized, artificial way 2. a pastoral picture or scene 3. a letter from a pastor or bishop to those in his charge 4. *same as* PASTORALE —see SYN. at RURAL —**pas'to·ral·ly** *adv.*

pas·to·rale (pas'tə ral', -rä'lē) *n.* [It., lit., pastoral] *Music* a composition suggesting rural scenes or life

pas·tor·ate (pas'tər it) *n.* 1. the position, rank, or term of office of a pastor 2. a group of pastors

past participle a participle used: *a)* with helping verbs to show completed action or a time or state gone by (as *started* in "he has started") *b)* as an adjective (as *grown* in "a grown man")

past perfect 1. a tense indicating an action or state as completed before a specified or implied time in the past 2. a verb form in this tense (Example: he *had gone* before we arrived)

pas·tra·mi (pə strä'mē) *n.* [Yid. < Romanian < *pastra*, to preserve] highly spiced, smoked beef

pas·try (pās'trē) *n., pl.* **-tries** [see PASTE & -ERY] 1. *a)* flour dough made with shortening and used for pie crust, tarts, etc. *b)* foods made with this 2. all fancy baked goods 3. a single pie, cake, etc.

pas·tur·age (pas'chər ij) *n.* same as PASTURE

pas·ture (pas'chər) *n.* [OFr. < LL. *pastura* < L. *pascere*, to feed: see PASTOR] 1. grass or other growing plants used as food by grazing animals 2. ground suitable for grazing, or a field set aside for grazing —*vt.* **-tured, -tur·ing** 1. to put (cattle, etc.) out to graze in a pasture 2. to provide with pasture: said of land [grassy fields that will *pasture* many cattle] —*vi.* to graze —**put out to pasture** 1. to put in a pasture to graze 2. to cause to retire from work —**pas'tur·er** *n.*

past·y[1] (pās'tē) *adj.* **past'i·er, past'i·est** of or like paste in color or texture [a *pasty* complexion] —**past'i·ness** *n.*

pas·ty[2] (pas'tē, päs'-, pās'-) *n., pl.* **pas'ties** [< OFr. < *paste*, PASTE] [Chiefly Brit.] a meat pie

pat[1] (pat) *adj.* [prob. < next entry] 1. at the right time; apt; timely 2. exactly suitable [a *pat* hand in poker] 3. smooth and clever but superficial [a *pat* solution to a complex problem] —*adv.* in a pat manner —**have (down) pat** [Colloq.] to know or have memorized thoroughly —☆**stand pat** to refuse to change an opinion, way of acting, etc. —**pat'ly** *adv.* —**pat'ness** *n.*

pat[2] (pat) *n.* [prob. echoic] 1. a gentle tap or stroke with the hand or other flat surface 2. the sound made by this 3. a small lump, as of butter —*vt.* **pat'ted, pat'ting** 1. *a)* to tap or stroke gently, esp. with the hand, as in affection, sympathy, etc. *b)* to tap lightly with a flat surface 2. to shape, apply, etc. by patting —*vi.* 1. to pat a surface 2. to move along with a patting sound

pat. 1. patent 2. patented

Pat·a·go·ni·a (pat'ə gō'nē ə, -gōn'yə) dry, grassy region in the S parts of Argentina & Chile, east of the Andes — **Pat'a·go'ni·an** *adj., n.*

patch (pach) *n.* [prob. < OFr. *pieche*, PIECE] 1. a piece of material to cover or mend a hole or tear or to strengthen a weak spot 2. a dressing for a wound 3. a shield worn over an injured eye 4. a differing part of a surface area [*patches* of blue sky] 5. a small plot of ground [a potato *patch*] 6. a scrap of material; remnant 7. *Mil.* a cloth insignia worn high on the sleeve, which tells what unit a serviceman is in —*vt.* 1. to put a patch on [to *patch* a torn coat] 2. to be a patch for 3. to make (a quilt, etc.) out of patches 4. to make or put together crudely or hurriedly (often with *up* or *together*) [to *patch* together a speech] —**patch up** to end or settle (differences, a quarrel, etc.) —**patch'er** *n.*

PATAGONIA

patch·ou·li, patch·ou·ly (pach'oo lē, pə choo'lē) *n.* [Fr., altered < E. *patch leaf* < Tamil < *paccu*, green + *ilai*, leaf] 1. an East Indian plant that yields a heavy, dark-brown, fragrant oil 2. a perfume made from this oil

patch pocket a pocket made by sewing a patch of shaped material to the outside of a garment

patch test a test for finding out whether a person is allergic to a specific substance, made by attaching a sample of the substance to the skin and observing the reaction

patch·work (pach'wurk') *n.* 1. anything made of odd, miscellaneous parts; jumble 2. needlework, as a quilt, made of odd patches of cloth sewn together at the edges 3. any design or surface like this

patch·y (pach'ē) *adj.* **patch'i·er, patch'i·est** 1. of or like patches 2. not consistent or uniform in quality; irregular [he has a *patchy* education] —**patch'i·ly** *adv.* —**patch'i·ness** *n.*

patd. patented

pate (pāt) *n.* [< ?] the head, esp. the top of the head: a humorous term

pâ·té (pä tā′) *n.* [Fr.] **1.** a pie **2.** a meat paste

pâ·té de foie gras (pä tā′ də fwä′ grä′, pät′ā) [Fr.] a paste made of the livers of fattened geese

pa·tel·la (pə tel′ə) *n., pl.* **-las, -lae** (-ē) [L., dim. of *patina,* a pan < Gr. *patanē*] *same as* KNEECAP: see illustration at SKELE-TON —**pa·tel′lar** *adj.*

pat·en (pat′'n) *n.* [< OFr. < L. *patina:* see prec.] a metal plate, esp. for the Eucharistic bread

pa·ten·cy (pāt′'n sē, pat′-) *n.* the state or quality of being patent, or obvious

pat·ent (pat′'nt; *Brit.,* & *for adj.* 2, 3, & 4, *usually* pāt′-) *adj.* [MFr. < L. prp. of *patere,* to be open: for IE. base see PETAL] **1.** *a)* open to public inspection: said of a document granting a right, esp. to an invention [letters *patent*] *b)* granted or appointed by letters patent **2.** generally accessible or available **3.** obvious; evident [a *patent* lie] **4.** open or unobstructed **5.** *a)* protected by a patent; patented *b)* of or having to do with patents or the granting of patents [*patent* law] *c)* made or sold under a patent —*n.* **1.** an official document granting a right or privilege; letters patent; esp., a document granting to someone the right to be the only one to produce, sell, or get a profit from an invention, process, etc. for a certain number of years **2.** *a)* the right so granted *b)* the thing so protected **3.** a right or license that belongs to only one individual —*vt.* **1.** to grant a patent to or for **2.** to get a patent for —**pat′ent·a·ble** *adj.*

pat·ent·ee (pat′'n tē′) *n.* a person who has been granted a patent

☆**patent leather** leather with a hard, glossy, usually black finish: made by a process that was formerly patented

pa·tent·ly (pāt′'nt lē, pat′-) *adv.* in a patent manner; clearly; obviously; openly [*patently* false]

patent medicine a trademarked medical preparation that can be bought without a physician's prescription

pat·en·tor (pat′'n tər) *n.* the grantor of a patent

pa·ter (pāt′ər) *n.* [L.] [Chiefly Brit. Colloq.] father

Pa·ter (pāt′ər), **Walter (Horatio)** 1839–94; Eng. essayist & critic

pa·ter·fa·mil·i·as (pāt′ər fə mil′ē əs, pät′-) *n.* [L.] the father of a family

pa·ter·nal (pə tur′n'l) *adj.* [< ML. < L. < *pater,* FATHER] **1.** of or like a father; fatherly **2.** derived or inherited from a father **3.** related through the father's side of the family [*paternal* grandparents] —**pa·ter′nal·ly** *adv.*

pa·ter·nal·ism (pə tur′n'l iz'm) *n.* a system of controlling a country, group of employees, etc. like that used by a father in dealing with his children —**pa·ter′nal·ist** *n., adj.* —**pa·ter′nal·is′tic** *adj.* —**pa·ter′nal·is′ti·cal·ly** *adv.*

pa·ter·ni·ty (pə tur′nə tē) *n.* **1.** the state of being a father **2.** male parentage **3.** origin in general

pa·ter·nos·ter (pāt′ər nôs′tər; pat′ər näs′tər, pät′-) *n.* [L., our father] **1.** the Lord's Prayer, esp. in Latin: often **Pater Noster 2.** each large bead on a rosary

Pat·er·son (pat′ər s'n) [after W. *Paterson* (1745–1806), State governor] city in northeastern N.J.: pop. 145,000

path (path) *n.* [OE. *pæth:* for IE. base see FIND] **1.** a way worn by footsteps **2.** a walk for use by people on foot, as in a park **3.** a course along which something moves [the *path* of the meteor] **4.** a course of conduct or procedure [to follow the *path* of duty] —**path′less** *adj.*

path. 1. pathological **2.** pathology

Pa·than (pə tän′, pət hän′) *n.* a member of a Moslem, Pashto-speaking people of Afghanistan and N West Pakistan

pa·thet·ic (pə thet′ik) *adj.* [< LL. < Gr. *pathētikos,* akin to *pathos,* suffering] **1.** expressing or arousing pity, sympathy, etc.; pitiful [the wounded bird's *pathetic* cries] **2.** pitifully unsuccessful, ineffective, etc. [a *pathetic* attempt to be witty] **3.** of the emotions: now only in PATHETIC FALLACY —see SYN. at MOVING —**pa·thet′i·cal·ly** *adv.*

pathetic fallacy the literary custom of describing nonhuman things as if they had human feelings, etc. (Example: the angry sea)

☆**path·find·er** (path′fīn′dər) *n.* one who makes a way where none had existed, as in a wilderness

-path·i·a (path′ē ə) [ModL.] *same as* -PATHY

-path·ic (path′ik) *a combining form used to form adjectives from nouns ending in* -PATHY

path·o- [< Gr. *pathos,* suffering] *a combining form meaning* suffering, disease, feeling: also, before a vowel, **path-**

path·o·gen (path′ə jən) *n.* [PATHO- + -GEN] any microorganism or virus that can cause disease —**path′o·gen′ic** (-jen′ik) *adj.* —**path′o·gen′i·cal·ly** *adv.*

path·o·gen·e·sis (path′ə jen′ə sis) *n.* [ModL.: see PATHO- & GENESIS] the development of a disease: also **pa·thog·e·ny** (pə-thäj′ə nē) —**path′o·ge·net′ic** (-jə net′ik) *adj.*

path·o·log·i·cal (path′ə läj′i k'l) *adj.* **1.** of pathology; of or concerned with diseases **2.** caused by or having to do with disease **3.** compelled by an irrational impulse; compulsive [a *pathological* liar] Also **path′o·log′ic** —**path′o·log′i·cal·ly** *adv.*

pa·thol·o·gy (pə thäl′ə jē, pa-) *n., pl.* **-gies** [< Fr. or ModL. < Gr.: see PATHOS & -LOGY] **1.** the branch of medicine dealing with the nature of disease, esp. with the structural and functional changes caused by disease **2.** all the conditions, processes, or results of a particular disease —**pa·thol′o·gist** *n.*

pa·thos (pā′thäs, -thôs) *n.* [Gr., suffering] **1.** the quality in some happening, story, etc. which arouses feelings of pity, sorrow, sympathy, or compassion **2.** the feeling aroused

path·way (path′wā′) *n. same as* PATH

-pa·thy (pə thē) [< ModL. < Gr. < *pathos,* suffering] *a combining form meaning:* **1.** feeling, suffering [*antipathy*] **2.** disease, treatment of disease [*osteopathy*]

pa·tience (pā′shəns) *n.* [< OFr. < L. *patientia < pati,* to suffer: see PASSION] **1.** the state, quality, or fact of being patient **2.** [Chiefly Brit.] any game of solitaire

pa·tient (pā′shənt) *adj.* [< OFr. < L. prp. of *pati:* see PATIENCE] **1.** enduring pain, trouble, etc. without complaining or losing self-control **2.** refusing to be angered, as by an insult; forbearing **3.** putting up with delay, confusion, etc. calmly **4.** showing calm endurance [a *patient* face] **5.** working steadily without giving up [a *patient* craftsman] —*n.* a person receiving medical care —**pa′tient·ly** *adv.*

pat·i·na (pat′'n ə, pə tē′nə) *n.* [Fr. < It.] **1.** a fine greenish crust formed by oxidation on bronze or copper, often valued as ornamental **2.** any color change due to age, as on the surface of old wood

pa·ti·o (pat′ē ō′, pät′-) *n., pl.* **-ti·os′** [Sp.] ☆**1.** a courtyard or inner area open to the sky, as in Spanish and Spanish-American architecture ☆**2.** a paved area, as one next to a house, with chairs, tables, etc. for outdoor lounging, dining, etc.

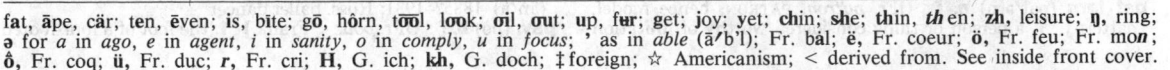

PATIO

Pat·mos (pat′məs, pät′-) island of the Dodecanese, in the SE Aegean

Pat·na (put′nə, pat′-) city in NE India, on the Ganges: pop. 364,000

pat·ois (pat′wä; *Fr.* pà twä′) *n., pl.* **-ois** (-wäz; *Fr.* -twä′) [Fr.] **1.** a form of a language differing from the accepted standard, as a local dialect **2.** *same as* JARGON (sense 4)

pat. pend. patent pending

Pa·tras (pə träs′) seaport in the NW Peloponnesus, Greece, on the Ionian Sea: pop. 95,000: Gr. name **Pá·trai** (pä′trē)

pat·ri- [L. < Gr. < *patēr,* FATHER] *a combining form meaning* father

pa·tri·arch (pā′trē ärk′) *n.* [< OFr. < LL. < Gr., ult. < *patēr,* FATHER + *archein,* to rule] **1.** the father and ruler of a family or tribe: in the Bible, Abraham, Isaac, Jacob, and Jacob's twelve sons were patriarchs **2.** a person thought of as the founder of a religion, business, etc. **3.** a man of great age and dignity **4.** [often P-] *a)* any of certain bishops in the early Christian Church *b)* R.C.Ch. the Pope (**Patriarch of the West**), or any of certain Eastern bishops *c)* Orthodox Eastern Ch. the highest-ranking bishop at Constantinople, Alexandria, Antioch, Jerusalem, Moscow, etc. —**pa′tri·ar′chal** *adj.*

pa·tri·ar·chate (-är′kit, -kāt) *n.* **1.** the position, rank, territory, etc. of a patriarch **2.** *same as* PATRIARCHY

pa·tri·ar·chy (-är′kē) *n., pl.* **-chies 1.** a form of social organization in which the father is the head of the family or tribe, descent being traced through male ancestors **2.** rule or control by men —**pa·tri·ar'chic** *adj.*

Pa·tri·cia (pə trish'ə, -trē'shə) [L., fem. of *patricius:* see PATRICK] a feminine name: dim. *Pat, Patty*

pa·tri·cian (pə trish'ən) *n.* [< MFr. < L. *patricius* < *patres,* pl. of *pater,* FATHER] **1.** in ancient Rome, *a*) orig., a member of the family of any of the earliest Roman citizens *b*) later, a member of the nobility **2.** a person of high social rank; aristocrat —*adj.* **1.** of or characteristic of patricians **2.** noble; aristocratic

pat·ri·cide (pat'rə sīd') *n.* [< ML.: see PATRI- & -CIDE] **1.** the act of killing one's father **2.** a person who kills his or her father —**pat'ri·ci'dal** *adj.*

Pat·rick (pat'rik) [L. *patricius,* patrician] **1.** a masculine name **2.** Saint, 385?-461? A.D.; Brit. missionary in, and patron saint of, Ireland

pat·ri·mo·ny (pat'rə mō'nē) *n., pl.* **-nies** [< OFr. < L. *patrimonium* < *pater,* FATHER] **1.** property inherited from one's father or ancestors **2.** property given to a church, etc. to provide income **3.** anything inherited; heritage —**pat'ri·mo'ni·al** *adj.*

pa·tri·ot (pā'trē ət, -ät'; *chiefly Brit.* pat'rē-) *n.* [< Fr. < LL. < Gr. < *patris,* fatherland] one who loves and loyally supports one's country —**pa'tri·ot'ic** *adj.* —**pa'tri·ot'i·cal·ly** *adv.*

pa·tri·ot·ism (-ə tiz'm) *n.* love and loyal support of one's own country

pa·tris·tic (pə tris'tik) *adj.* [< G. < L. *patres,* pl. of *pater,* FATHER] of the early leaders, or fathers, of the Christian Church or their writings: also **pa·tris'ti·cal** —**pa·tris'ti·cal·ly** *adv.*

pa·trol (pə trōl') *vt., vi.* **-trolled', -trol'ling** [Fr. *patrouiller* < OFr. *patouiller,* to paddle] to make regular, repeated trips around (an area, camp, etc.), as in guarding —*n.* **1.** a patrolling **2.** a person or group patrolling **3.** a group of ships, airplanes, soldiers, etc. used to guard an area or get information about the enemy **4.** a subdivision of a troop of Boy Scouts or Girl Scouts —**pa·trol'er** *n.*

☆**pa·trol·man** (-mən) *n., pl.* **-men** a policeman assigned to patrol a specific area

☆**patrol wagon** a small, enclosed truck used by the police in transporting prisoners

pa·tron (pā'trən) *n.* [< OFr. < ML., ult. < L. *pater,* FATHER] **1.** a person who is like a father in some respects; protector; benefactor **2.** a person, usually a wealthy or important one, who sponsors and supports some person, activity, etc. [the *patrons* of the orchestra] **3.** a regular customer —**pa'tron·al** *adj.* —**pa'tron·ess** *n.fem.*

pa·tron·age (pā'trən ij, pat'rən-) *n.* **1.** support, sponsorship, etc. given by a patron **2.** favor, courtesy, etc. shown to people considered inferior; condescension **3.** *a*) customers as a group *b*) the regular business or trade of customers **4.** *a*) the power to appoint people to office or give other political favors *b*) the giving out of such offices or favors *c*) the offices, etc. thus given

pa·tron·ize (pā'trə nīz', pat'rə-) *vt.* **-ized', -iz'ing 1.** to act as a patron toward; sponsor; support **2.** to be kind or helpful to, but in a haughty or snobbish way, as if dealing with an inferior **3.** to be a regular customer of (a store, etc.)

patron saint a saint looked upon as the special guardian of a person, place, institution, etc.

pat·ro·nym·ic (pat'rə nim'ik) *n.* [< LL. < Gr. < *patēr,* FATHER + *onyma,* a NAME] a name showing descent from a given person as by the addition of a prefix or suffix (e.g., *Stevenson,* son of Steven, *O'Brien,* descendant of Brien)

pa·troon (pə trōōn') *n.* [Du., protector < Fr. *patron,* PATRON] ☆a person who held an estate that he could rent to others, under the old Dutch governments of New York and New Jersey

pat·sy (pat'sē) *n., pl.* **-sies** [prob. < It. *pazzo,* a lunatic] ☆[Slang] a person easily taken advantage of or cheated

pat·ten (pat'n) *n.* [MFr. *patin,* a clog < *pate,* a paw] a thick wooden sandal or clog

pat·ter¹ (pat'ər) *vi.* [< PAT² + -ER (sense 4)] to make, or move so as to make, a patter —*n.* a series of quick, light taps [the *patter* of rain on the window]

pat·ter² (pat'ər) *vt., vi.* [< *pater,* in PATERNOSTER] to speak rapidly or easily; recite (prayers, etc.) mechanically —*n.* **1.** the special words and phrases used by a certain group, class, etc.; jargon **2.** smooth, rapid speech, as of salesmen, comedians, etc. **3.** idle, meaningless chatter

pat·ter³ (pat'ər) *n.* a person or thing that pats

pat·tern (pat'ərn) *n.* [< OFr. *patron,* PATRON, hence model, pattern] **1.** a person or thing considered worthy of imitation or copying [a government that is a *pattern* of skillful organization] **2.** a model, plan, or set of forms used as a guide in making things [a dress *pattern*] **3.** a typical example of a class or type; sample [Sir Galahad was a *pattern* of the noble knight] **4.** an arrangement of parts; design [wallpaper *patterns;* the *pattern* of a novel] **5.** a regular or habitual way of acting [behavior *patterns*] **6.** a predictable route, movement, etc. or one that has been established by rule or order [traffic *pattern;* landing *pattern*] —*vt.* to make, do, shape, or plan in imitation of a model or pattern (with *on, upon,* or *after*) [she *patterned* her life on that of her teacher] —**pat'tern·mak'er** *n.*

pat·ty (pat'ē) *n., pl.* **-ties** [Fr. *pâté,* a pie] **1.** a small pie **2.** a small, flat cake of ground meat, fish, etc., usually fried **3.** any disk-shaped piece, as of candy

patty shell a small, baked pie crust in which an individual portion of a creamed food, etc. is served

pau·ci·ty (pô'sə tē) *n.* [< MFr. < L. < *paucus,* few] **1.** fewness; small number [the *paucity* of good novels] **2.** small amount; scarcity [*paucity* of rain in July]

Paul (pôl) [L. *Paulus,* Rom. surname, prob. < *paulus,* small] **1.** a masculine name **2.** *Bible* the apostle of Christianity to the Gentiles, author of many Epistles: also *Saint Paul* **3. Paul III** 1468-1549; Pope (1534-49) **4. Paul VI** 1897-1978; Pope (1963-78)

Paul·a (pôl'ə) [L., fem. of PAUL] a feminine name

☆**Paul Bun·yan** (bun'yən) *American Folklore* a giant lumberjack, who, with the help of his blue ox, Babe, performed various superhuman feats

paul·dron (pôl'drən) *n.* [< MFr. < *espaule,* the shoulder] a piece of plate armor to protect the shoulder: see illustration at ARMOR

Paul·ine¹ (pô lēn') [L. *Paulina,* fem. of *Paulinus:* see next entry] a feminine name

Paul·ine² (pôl'īn, -ēn) *adj.* [ModL. *Paulinus*] of the Apostle Paul, his writings, or doctrines

Paul·ing (pôl'iŋ), **Li·nus (Carl)** (lī'nəs) 1901- ; U.S. chemist

Paul·ist (pôl'ist) *n.* ☆a Roman Catholic priest belonging to the Missionary Society of St. Paul the Apostle, founded in New York in 1858

paunch (pônch) *n.* [< MFr. < L. *pantex,* belly] the abdomen, or belly; esp., a large belly that sticks out; potbelly —**paunch'i·ness** *n.* —**paunch'y** *adj.*

pau·per (pô'pər) *n.* [L., poor person] **1.** a person who lives on charity, esp. public charity **2.** an extremely poor person —**pau'per·ism, pau'per·dom** *n.*

pau·per·ize (pô'pə rīz') *vt.* **-ized', -iz'ing** to make a pauper of —**pau'per·i·za'tion** *n.*

pause (pôz) *n.* [MFr. < L. < Gr. *pausis,* a stopping < *pauein,* to stop] **1.** a temporary stop or rest, as in working or speaking **2.** hesitation; delay [pursuit without *pause*] **3.** a stop or break in reading or speaking, as in order to make the meaning clearer **4.** *Music same as* FERMATA **5.** *Prosody* a break in the rhythm of a line of poetry or a caesura —*vi.* **paused, paus'ing 1.** to make a pause; stop; hesitate [he *paused* to catch his breath] **2.** to dwell or linger (*on* or *upon*) [the singer *paused* upon the low note] —**give one pause** to cause one to hesitate or be uncertain —**paus'er** *n.*

pav·ane (pə vän', -van') *n.* [Fr. < OIt. *pavana* < (*danza*) *Pavana,* lit., Paduan (dance)] **1.** a slow, dignified dance for couples, popular in the 17th century **2.** the music for this Also **pav·an** (pav'ən)

pave (pāv) *vt.* **paved, pav'ing** [< OFr. *paver,* ult. < L. *pavire,* to beat] **1.** to cover the surface of (a road, etc.), as with concrete, asphalt, etc. **2.** to be the top surface of —**pave the way (for)** to prepare the way (for) —**pav'er** *n.*

pave·ment (pāv'mənt) *n.* **1.** a paved surface, as of concrete, brick, etc.; specif., a paved street or road **2.** the material used in paving

pa·vil·ion (pə vil'yən) *n.* [< OFr. < L. *papilio,* butterfly, also tent] **1.** a large tent, usually with a pointed top **2.** a building, often partly open, for exhibits, dancing, etc., as at a fair or park **3.** part of a building sticking out from the main part **4.** any of the separate or connected parts of a group of related buildings, as of a hospital —*vt.* to furnish with or shelter in a pavilion

pav·ing (pā'viŋ) *n.* **1.** a pavement **2.** material for a pavement

Pav·lov (päv'lôf; *E.* pav'lôv), **I·van Pe·tro·vich** (i vän' pye trô'vich) 1849-1936; Russ. physiologist —**Pav·lov·i·an** (pav lô've ən) *adj.*

Pav·lo·va (päv'lô vä; *E.* päv lō'və), **An·na (Matveyevna)** (än'ä) 1885?-1931; Russ. ballet dancer

paw (pô) *n.* [< OFr. *poue* < Frank.] **1.** the foot of a four-footed animal having claws **2.** [Colloq.] a hand —*vt., vi.* **1.** to touch, dig, strike at, etc. with the paws or feet [*the horse pawed the air*] **2.** to handle clumsily or roughly, or caress in too familiar a way [*the angry man pawed through the papers on his desk*] —**paw′-er** *n.*

pawl (pôl) *n.* [akin ? to Du. *pal*, pole] a mechanical device allowing rotation in only one direction, as a hinged bar which catches in the notches of a ratchet wheel, preventing backward motion

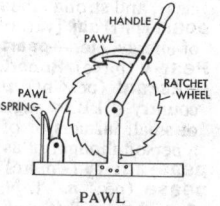

HANDLE
PAWL
RATCHET WHEEL
PAWL SPRING
PAWL

pawn[1] (pôn) *n.* [< MFr. *pan*] **1.** anything given as security, as in exchange for a loan; pledge **2.** the state of being held as security, as for a loan [*his ring was in pawn*] —*vt.* **1.** to put in pawn **2.** to stake or risk [*to pawn one's honor*] —**pawn′age** *n.* —**pawn′er, paw′nor** *n.*

pawn[2] (pôn) *n.* [< OFr. < ML. *pedo*, foot soldier, ult. < L. *pes*, FOOT] **1.** a chessman of the lowest value **2.** a person used to advance another's purposes; tool

pawn·bro·ker (pôn′brō′kər) *n.* a person licensed to lend money at interest on personal belongings left with him as security —**pawn′bro′king** *n.*

Paw·nee (pô nē′) *n.* [< ? Algonquian *pani*, slave] **1.** *pl.* **-nees′, -nee′** a member of an Indian tribe formerly living in Nebraska and now in northern Oklahoma **2.** the language of this tribe —*adj.* of this tribe or their language

pawn·shop (pôn′shäp′) *n.* a pawnbroker's shop

pawn ticket a receipt for goods in pawn

paw·paw (pô′pô′) *n.* same as PAPAW

Paw·tuck·et (pə tuk′it) [< Algonquian, little falls] city in northeastern R.I., adjacent to Providence: pop. 77,000

‡pax vo·bis·cum (paks vō bis′kəm, päks) [L.] peace (be) with you

pay[1] (pā) *vt.* **paid** or obs. (except in phrase *pay out*, sense 2) **payed, pay′ing** [< OFr. < L. *pacare*, to pacify < *pax*, PEACE] **1.** to give to (a person) what is due, as for goods or services; remunerate [*he paid the milkman*] **2.** to give (what is due) in return, as for goods or services [*she paid $10 for the hat*] **3.** to make a deposit or transfer of (money) [*to pay $10 into savings*] **4.** to settle (a debt, etc.) **5.** *a)* to give (a compliment, respects, etc.) *b)* to make (a visit, etc.) **6.** to bring as wages or salary [*this job pays $90*] **7.** to be profitable or worthwhile to [*it will pay him to listen*] —*vi.* **1.** to give what is due or owed; make payment **2.** to be profitable or worthwhile **3.** to produce return as specified [*that stock pays poorly*] —*n.* **1.** a paying or being paid; payment **2.** money paid; esp., wages or salary [*he gets his pay on Friday*] **3.** anything given or done in return [*your gratitude is my pay*] —*adj.* **1.** operated or made available by depositing a coin [*a pay telephone*] **2.** designating a service, facility, etc. paid for by subscription, fees, etc. [*pay TV*] —**in the pay of** employed and paid by —☆**pay as you go** to pay expenses as they arise —**pay back 1.** to repay **2.** to get even with —**pay for 1.** to undergo punishment because of **2.** to make up for —**pay off 1.** to pay all that is owed **2.** to take revenge on (a wrongdoer) or for (a wrong done) **3.** [Colloq.] to succeed —**pay out 1.** to give out (money, etc.) **2.** to let out a rope, cable, etc. gradually —**pay up** to pay in full or on time

SYN.—*pay* is the simple, direct word meaning to give money, etc. due for services provided, goods received, etc.; **compensate** implies a return, whether of money or something else, thought of as equal to the service given, the effort made, or the loss suffered [*he could never be compensated for the loss of his son*]; **remunerate** emphasizes the idea of pay for a service provided, but it often also implies a reward [*a bumper crop remunerated the farmer for his labors*]; to **reimburse** is to pay back what has been spent [*the salesman was reimbursed for his traveling expenses*] —see also SYN. at WAGE

pay[2] (pā) *vt.* **payed, pay′ing** [ONormFr. *peier* < L. < *pix*, pitch] to coat (the seams of a vessel, etc.) as with tar, in order to make waterproof

pay·a·ble (pā′ə b'l) *adj.* **1.** that can be paid **2.** that is to be paid (on a specified date); due

☆**pay·check** (-chek′) *n.* a check in payment of wages or salary

pay·day (-dā′) *n.* the day on which wages, etc. are paid

☆**pay dirt** soil, gravel, ore, etc. rich enough in minerals to make mining profitable —**hit** (or **strike**) **pay dirt** [Colloq.] to discover a source of wealth, success, etc.

pay·ee (pā ē′) *n.* the person to whom a check, note, money, etc. is to be paid

pay·er (pā′ər) *n.* the person who pays or is to pay

pay·load (pā′lōd′) *n.* **1.** a cargo, or the part of a cargo, producing income: also **pay load 2.** *a)* the warhead of a ballistic missile, the spacecraft launched by a rocket, etc. *b)* the weight of this

pay·mas·ter (-mas′tər) *n.* the official in charge of paying employees —**pay′mis′tress** *n.fem.*

pay·ment (-mənt) *n.* **1.** a paying or being paid [*the payment of taxes*] **2.** something paid [*a monthly car payment of $75*] **3.** penalty or reward

pay·nim (pā′nim) *n.* [< OFr. < LL. *paganismus*, paganism] [Archaic] **1.** a pagan or the pagan world **2.** a non-Christian; esp., a Moslem

☆**pay·off** (pā′ôf′) *n.* **1.** the act or time of payment **2.** settlement, as of bills, rewards, etc. **3.** that which is paid off; recompense **4.** [Colloq.] a bribe **5.** [Colloq.] a climax or outcome, esp. when unexpected or unlikely [*and the payoff was that despite all his injuries he managed to win*]

☆**pay·o·la** (pā ō′lə) *n.* [PAY[1] + -*ola*, as in *Pianola* (trademark for a player piano)] [Slang] **1.** the paying of bribes or graft for special favors, as to a disc jockey for promoting a song unfairly **2.** such a bribe or graft

☆**pay·roll** (pā′rōl′) *n.* **1.** a list of employees to be paid, with the amount due to each **2.** the total amount needed for this for a given period

payt., pay't payment

☆**pa·zazz** (pə zaz′) *n.* same as PIZAZZ

Pb [L. *plumbum*] *Chem.* lead

PBS Public Broadcasting Service

PBX, P.B.X. [< *p(rivate) b(ranch) ex(change)*] the telephone connections on the switchboard of an office, company, etc.

pc. 1. piece **2.** price(s)

p.c. 1. percent **2.** postal card **3.** post card

pct. percentage

Pd *Chem.* palladium

pd. paid

P.D. 1. per diem: also **p.d. 2.** Police Department **3.** postal district

P.E. 1. Physical Education **2.** Protestant Episcopal

pea (pē) *n., pl.* **peas,** archaic or Brit. dial. **pease** [< ME. *pese*, a pea, taken as pl. < OE. *pise* < L. < Gr. *pison*] **1.** a climbing plant with white or pinkish flowers and green seedpods **2.** its small, round seed, eaten as a vegetable **3.** any similar plant —**as like as two peas (in a pod)** exactly alike

peace (pēs) *n.* [< OFr. *pais* < L. *pacis*, genitive of *pax* < IE. base *pak-*, to fasten] **1.** freedom from war or fighting [*to live in peace with all countries*] **2.** a treaty or agreement to end war **3.** freedom from public disturbance; law and order [*the rioters were disturbing the peace*] **4.** freedom from disagreements or quarrels; harmony; concord [*peace in our household at last*] **5.** an undisturbed state of mind; serenity: in full, **peace of mind 6.** calm; quiet [*the peace of the forest*] —*vi.* [Obs. except in giving an order, making a strong request, etc.] to be or become silent or quiet —**at peace** free from war, fighting, etc. —**hold** (or **keep**) **one's peace** to be silent —**keep the peace** to maintain law and order —**make peace** to end war, fighting, etc.

peace·a·ble (pēs′ə b'l) *adj.* **1.** fond of or tending to bring about peace; not quarrelsome **2.** at peace; peaceful —**peace′a·bly** *adv.*

☆**Peace Corps** an agency of the U.S., established to provide volunteers skilled in teaching, construction, etc. to assist the people of underdeveloped areas abroad

peace·ful (-fəl) *adj.* **1.** not quarrelsome; peaceable [*a peaceful people*] **2.** free from noise or disorder; quiet; calm; tranquil [*a peaceful countryside*] **3.** of or characteristic of a time of peace [*peaceful trade between nations*] —see SYN. at CALM —**peace′-ful·ly** *adv.* —**peace′ful·ness** *n.*

peace·mak·er (-mā′kər) *n.* a person who makes peace, as by stopping a fight or quarrel —**peace′mak′ing** *n., adj.*

peace offering an offering, as a gift, made in order to bring about a peaceful or friendly relationship

peace officer an officer with the duty of keeping law and order, as a sheriff, constable, policeman, etc.

☆**peace pipe** *same as* CALUMET

peace·time (-tīm′) *n.* a time of peace —*adj.* of or characteristic of such a time

peach[1] (pēch) *n.* [< OFr. < VL., ult. < L. *Persicum (malum)*, Persian (apple)] **1.** a small tree with pink blossoms and round, juicy, orange-yellow fruit with a fuzzy skin and a rough pit **2.** its fruit **3.** the color of this fruit ☆**4.** [Slang] a very fine or excellent person or thing —**peach′like′** *adj.*

peach[2] (pēch) *vi.* [ult. < OFr. *empechier*, IMPEACH] [Old Slang] to inform on another; turn informer

peach·y (pē′chē) *adj.* **peach′i·er, peach′i·est** **1.** peachlike, as in color or texture ☆**2.** [Old Slang] fine; excellent — **peach′i·ness** *n.*

☆**pea·coat** (pē′kōt′) *n. same as* PEA JACKET

pea·cock (pē′käk′) *n., pl.* **-cocks′, -cock′:** see PLURAL, II, D, 1 [< OE. *pea* < L. *pavo*, peacock + *cok*, COCK[1]] **1.** the male of a species of peafowls, with a crest and long tail feathers having rainbow-colored, eyelike spots: these feathers can be raised and fanned out **2.** any male peafowl **3.** a vain, strutting person —*vi.* to behave, dress, etc. in a vain, showy way

PEACOCK
(to 6 ft. long, including tail)

peacock blue a greenish blue

pea·fowl (-foul′) *n., pl.* **-fowls′, -fowl′:** see PLURAL, II, D, 1 any of a group of pheasantlike birds of southern Asia and the East Indies, including the peacock that is widely domesticated

pea green a light yellowish green

pea·hen (-hen′) *n.* a female peafowl

☆**pea jacket** [< Du. < *pij*, coarse cloth + *jekker*, jacket] a hip-length, heavy woolen coat worn as by seamen

peak (pēk) *n.* [< Brit. dial. *pike*, summit] **1.** a pointed end or top, as of a cap, roof, etc. **2.** *a)* the pointed top of a mountain *b)* a mountain with such a top **3.** the highest point or degree; maximum [the *peak* of production] **4.** *Naut. a)* the top rear corner of a fore-and-aft sail *b)* the upper end of the gaff *c)* the narrowed part of the hull, front or rear —*adj.* maximum [*peak* production] —*vi.* to come to a peak; reach a high point [his popularity *peaked* in early June] —see SYN. at SUMMIT

peaked[1] (pēkt; *occas.* pē′kid) *adj.* having a peak

peak·ed[2] (pē′kid) *adj.* [< ?] thin and tired-looking, or weak and pale, as from illness —**peak′ed·ness** *n.*

peal (pēl) *n.* [ME. *pele* < *apele*, appeal] **1.** the loud ringing of a bell or bells **2.** a set of bells; chimes **3.** any loud, echoing or long-lasting sound, as of gunfire, laughter, etc. —*vt., vi.* to sound in a peal; resound; ring

pe·an (pē′ən) *n. alt. sp. of* PAEAN

☆**pea·nut** (pē′nut′) *n.* **1.** an annual vine of the legume family, with dry pods that ripen underground and contain edible seeds **2.** the pod or one of its seeds **3.** [*pl.*] [Slang] a small or unimportant sum of money

☆**peanut butter** a food paste or spread made by grinding roasted peanuts

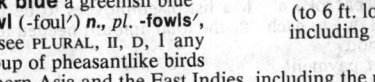

pear (per) *n.* [< OE. < VL. *pira* < L. pl. of *pirum*] **1.** a tree with soft, juicy fruit, round at the base and narrowing toward the stem **2.** this fruit

Pearl (purl) [< PEARL (the gem)] a feminine name

PEANUT PLANT

pearl (purl) *n.* [< MFr., ult. < L. *perna*, a sea mussel] **1.** a smooth, hard, roundish growth formed around a foreign body within the shell of some oysters and other mollusks: it is usually white or bluish-gray and is used as a gem **2.** *same as* MOTHER-OF-PEARL **3.** anything like a pearl in size, color, beauty, value, etc. **4.** the color of some pearls, a bluish gray —*vt.* to cover with pearls or drops that look like pearls —*vi.* to fish for pearl-bearing mollusks —*adj.* **1.** of or having pearls [a *pearl* necklace] **2.** like a pearl in shape or color **3.** made of mother-of-pearl [*pearl* buttons] —**cast pearls before swine** to offer something of great value to someone who is not able to understand or enjoy it —**pearl′er** *n.* —**pearl′i·ness** *n.* — **pearl′y** *adj.* **-i·er, -i·est**

pearl diver a person who dives for pearl-bearing mollusks

pearl gray a pale bluish gray

Pearl Harbor [after the *pearl* oysters once there] inlet on the S coast of Oahu, Hawaii, near Honolulu: site of a U.S. naval base bombed by Japan, Dec. 7, 1941

Pearly Gates [Colloq.] the gates of heaven: Rev. 21:21

pear-shaped (per′shāpt′) *adj.* **1.** shaped like a pear **2.** full, clear, and strong [the singer's *pear-shaped* tones]

peart (pirt) *adj.* [var. of PERT] [Dial.] lively, in good spirits, full of energy, etc. —**peart′ly** *adv.* —**peart′ness** *n.*

Pear·y (pir′ē), Robert Edwin 1856–1920; U.S. arctic explorer

peas·ant (pez′'nt) *n.* [< Anglo-Fr. < MFr. < OFr. < *païs*, country < LL. < *pagus*: see PAGAN] **1.** any person of the class of small farmers or of farm laborers, as in Europe or Asia **2.** a person thought of as being coarse, rude, ignorant, etc.

peas·ant·ry (-'n trē) *n.* peasants as a group

pease (pēz) *n. pl.* **peas′es, peas′en** (-'n) [Obs.] a pea **2.** *archaic or Brit. dial. pl. of* PEA

pease·cod, peas·cod (pēz′käd′) *n.* [Archaic] the pod of the pea plant

pea·shoot·er (pē′shōōt′ər) *n.* a toy consisting of a tube through which dried peas, etc. are blown, as at a target

peat (pēt) *n.* [ML. *peta*, piece of turf < Celt.] **1.** partly decayed plant matter found in ancient bogs and swamps **2.** a dried block of this used as fuel —**peat′y** *adj.* **peat′i·er, peat′i·est**

peat moss **1.** *same as* SPHAGNUM **2.** peat formed from mosses, used as a mulch

☆**pea·vey** (pē′vē) *n., pl.* **-veys** [prob. after J. *Peavey*, said to be its inventor, c. 1872] a heavy wooden lever with a pointed metal tip and hinged hook near the end: used by lumbermen in handling logs: also sp. **pea′vy**, *pl.* **-vies**

peb·ble (peb′'l) *n.* [< OE. *papol(stan)*, pebble (stone)] **1.** a small stone worn smooth and round, as by the action of water **2.** clear, transparent quartz or a lens made from it **3.** a surface treated to make it uneven or indented, as on leather (**pebble leather**), paper, etc. —*vt.* **-bled, -bling** **1.** to cover as with pebbles **2.** to stamp (leather) so as to give it a pebbly surface

peb·bly (-lē) *adj.* **-bli·er, -bli·est** **1.** having many pebbles [a *pebbly* stream] **2.** rough and uneven [*pebbly* leather]

☆**pe·can** (pi kan′, -kän′; pē′kan, -kän) *n.* [< Algonquian *pakan*] **1.** an oval, edible nut with a thin, smooth shell **2.** the N. American tree on which it grows

pec·ca·dil·lo (pek′ə dil′ō) *n., pl.* **-loes, -los** [< Sp. dim. of *pecado* < L. < *peccare*, to sin] a minor or petty sin; slight fault

pec·cant (pek′ənt) *adj.* [< L. prp. of *peccare*, to sin] sinful; sinning —**pec′can·cy** *n., pl.* **-cies** —**pec′cant·ly** *adv.*

pec·ca·ry (pek′ər ē) *n., pl.* **-ries, -ry:** see PLURAL, II, D, 1 [AmSp. *pecari* < native Carib name] an animal like a pig with sharp tusks, found in N. and S. America

peck[1] (pek) *vt.* [< ME. var. of *picken*, PICK[2]] **1.** to strike with a pointed object, as a beak **2.** to make by doing this [to *peck* a hole] **3.** to pick up with the beak; get by pecking [chickens *peck* corn] —*vi.* to make strokes as with a pointed object —*n.* **1.** a stroke so made, as with the beak **2.** a mark made by pecking **3.** [Colloq.] a quick, light kiss —**peck at** **1.** to make a pecking motion at **2.** [Colloq.] to eat very little of **3.** [Colloq.] to criticize constantly —**peck′er** *n.*

PECCARY
(to 2 ft. high at shoulder)

peck[2] (pek) *n.* [< OFr. *pek*] **1.** a unit of dry measure equal to 1/4 bushel, or eight quarts **2.** any container that will hold a peck **3.** [Colloq.] a large amount, as of trouble

☆**peck·ing order** (pek′iŋ) **1.** an arrangement within a flock of hens or other birds, in which each bird pecks those members of the flock which are less aggressive than it is and allows itself to be pecked by the more aggressive birds **2.** any arrangement of the members of a group according to relative power, importance, etc. [the office *pecking order*] Also **peck order**

Pe·cos (pā′kōs, -kəs) [< native name of a nearby pueblo] river in southwestern U.S., flowing into the Rio Grande: 735 mi.

pec·ten (pek′tən) *n., pl.* **pec′ti·nes** (-tə nēz′) [< L. < *pectere*, to comb] *Zool.* **1.** a tissue that looks somewhat like the teeth of a comb, around the transparent, jellylike part of the eye in many birds and reptiles **2.** *same as* SCALLOP (*n.* 1)

pec·tin (pek′tin) *n.* [< Gr. *pēktos*, congealed + -IN[1]] a water-soluble carbohydrate obtained from certain ripe fruits, which yields a gel that is the basis of jellies and jams —**pec′tic, pec′-tin·ous** adj.

pec·ti·nate (pek′tə nāt′) adj. [see PECTEN] having toothlike parts like those on a comb: also **pec′ti·nat′ed**

pec·to·ral (pek′tər əl) adj. [< L. < pectoris, genitive of pectus, breast] **1.** of or located in or on the breast or chest [a pectoral muscle] **2.** worn on the chest or breast [a bishop's pectoral cross] —n. a pectoral fin or muscle

pectoral fin either of a pair of fins just behind the head of a fish: see illustration at FISH

pectoral girdle the structures of bone or cartilage to which the forelimbs (or arms) of a vertebrate are attached

pec·u·late (pek′yə lāt′) vt., vi. **-lat′ed -lat′ing** [< L. pp. of peculari, to embezzle < peculium: see PECULIAR] to steal or misuse (money or property in one's care); embezzle —**pec′u·la′tion** n. —**pec′u·la′tor** n.

pe·cu·liar (pi kyōōl′yər) adj. [< L. < peculium, private property: for IE. base see FEE] **1.** of only one person, thing, group, etc.; exclusive [markings peculiar to the oriole] **2.** particular; special [a matter of peculiar interest] **3.** queer; odd; strange [things look peculiar through these dark glasses] —see SYN. at STRANGE —**pe·cul′iar·ly** adv.

pe·cu·liar·i·ty (pi kyōō′lē ar′ə tē, -kyōōl′yar′-) n. **1.** a being peculiar **2.** pl. **-ties** something that is peculiar, as a habit or trait

pe·cu·ni·ar·y (pi kyōō′nē er′ē) adj. [< L. < pecunia, money: see FEE] **1.** of or involving money [pecuniary aid] **2.** involving a money penalty, or fine [a pecuniary offense] —see SYN. at FINANCIAL —**pe·cu′ni·ar′i·ly** adv.

ped- same as: **1.** PEDO- **2.** PEDI- Used before a vowel

ped·a·gog·ic (ped′ə gäj′ik, -gō′jik) adj. [see PEDAGOGUE] of or characteristic of teachers or of teaching: also **ped′a·gog′i·cal** —**ped′a·gog′i·cal·ly** adv.

ped·a·gogue, ped·a·gog (ped′ə gäg′, -gôg′) n. [< OFr. < L. < Gr. < pais, a child + agein, to lead] a teacher, often specif. one who is boring and overly formal and who pays too much attention to minor details

ped·a·go·gy (-gō′jē, -gäj′ē) n. [see prec.] **1.** the profession of teaching **2.** the art or science of teaching; esp., instruction in teaching methods

ped·al (ped′'l; also, for adj. 1, pēd′-) adj. [< L. < pedis, genitive of pes, a FOOT] **1.** of the foot or feet **2.** of or operated by a pedal —n. a lever operated by the foot to transmit motion, as in a bicycle, or to change the tone or volume of an organ, harp, etc. —vt., vi. **-aled** or **-alled, -al·ing** or **-al·ling** to move or operate by means of a pedal or pedals [to pedal a bicycle]

☆**pedal pushers** calf-length pants for women or girls, used originally for bicycle riding

ped·ant (ped′'nt) n. [< Fr. < It. pedante, ult. < Gr. paidagōgos: see PEDAGOGUE] **1.** a person who shows off his learning in a boring way or who pays too much attention to the minor details of a subject **2.** a narrow-minded teacher who insists on following the rules exactly —**pe·dan·tic** (pi dan′tik) adj. —**pe·dan′ti·cal·ly** adv.

ped·ant·ry (ped′'n trē) n., pl. **-ries 1.** the qualities, practices, etc. of a pedant; showy display of knowledge, or an instance of this **2.** a rigid, unimaginative following of formal rules

ped·ate (ped′āt) adj. [< L. < pes, FOOT] **1.** Bot. designating a leaf having three main divisions growing from a common center **2.** Zool. a) having a foot or feet b) like a foot

ped·dle (ped′'l) vi. **-dled, -dling** [back-formation < peddler < ? ME. ped, a basket] to go from place to place selling small articles —vt. **1.** to carry from place to place and offer for sale [to peddle magazines] **2.** to give out or circulate (gossip, ideas, etc.) —**ped′dler** n.

-pede (pēd) [< L. pes, a FOOT] a combining form meaning foot or feet [centipede]: also **-ped** (ped)

ped·er·as·ty (ped′ə ras′tē, pē′dər ə-) n. [< ModL. < Gr. < paidos, genitive of pais, boy + eran, to love] sexual relations between males, esp. between a man and a boy —**ped′er·ast′** n.

ped·es·tal (ped′is t'l) n. [< Fr. < It. piè (< L. pes), a FOOT + di, of chest. **1.** the bottom support of a column, statue, etc. **2.** any foundation, base, etc. —vt. **-taled** or **-talled, -tal·ing** or **-tal·ling** to place on or furnish with a pedestal —**put (or set) on a pedestal** to think of with great or excessive admiration; idolize

pe·des·tri·an (pə des′trē ən) adj. [< L. pedester < pedis, genitive of pes, a FOOT + -IAN] **1.** going or done on foot **2.** of or for pedestrians [a pedestrian crossing] **3.** lacking interest or imagination; prosaic; dull [a pedestrian lecture] —n. one who goes on foot; a walker —**pe·des′tri·an·ism** n.

ped·i- [< L. pedis, genitive of pes, a FOOT] a combining form meaning foot or feet [pedicure]

pe·di·a·tri·cian (pē′dē ə trish′ən) n. a specialist in pediatrics: also **pe′di·at′rist** (-at′rist)

pe·di·at·rics (-at′riks) n.pl. [with sing. v.] [< PED(O)-[1] + -IATRICS] the branch of medicine dealing with the care of infants and children and the treatment of their diseases —**pe′di·at′ric** adj.

ped·i·cab (ped′i kab′) n. [PEDI- + CAB] a three-wheeled passenger vehicle, esp. in southeastern Asia, which is pedaled like a bicycle by the driver

ped·i·cel (ped′i s'l) n. [< ModL. dim. of L. pediculus, dim. of pes, a FOOT] **1.** Bot. the stalk of a single flower, fruit, grass spikelet, etc.: see illustration at FLOWER **2.** Zool. a) a small, stalklike structure b) a small, footlike part Also **ped′i·cle** (-k'l) —**ped′i·cel′late** (-sel′it, -āt) adj.

PEDICAB

pe·dic·u·lo·sis (pi dik′yə lō′sis) n. [< L. dim. of pedis, a louse + -OSIS] infestation with lice —**pe·dic′u·lous** (-ləs) adj.

☆**ped·i·cure** (ped′i kyoor′) n. [< Fr. < L. pes, a FOOT + cura, care] **1.** early term for PODIATRIST **2.** care of the feet; esp., a trimming, polishing, etc. of the toenails —**ped′i·cur′ist** n.

ped·i·gree (ped′ə grē′) n. [< MFr. piè de grue, lit., crane's foot: from the lines in the genealogical tree] **1.** a list of ancestors; family tree **2.** descent; lineage **3.** a recorded line of descent, esp. of a purebred animal —**ped′i·greed′** adj.

ped·i·ment (ped′ə mənt) n. [altered (after L. pedis, genitive of pes, a FOOT) < earlier periment, prob. < PYRAMID] **1.** a part in the shape of a low triangle on the front of some buildings of Grecian architecture **2.** any piece like this used as an ornament over a doorway, etc. —**ped′i·men′tal** adj.

PEDIMENT

ped·i·palp (ped′i palp′) n. [< ModL.: see PEDI- & PALPUS] either of the second pair of legs of spiders and other arachnids, used as for grasping or sensing

ped·lar, ped·ler (ped′lər) n. one who peddles; peddler

pe·do-[1] (< Gr. paidos, genitive of pais, a child: for IE. base see FEW] a combining form meaning child, children

ped·o-[2] [< Gr. pedon, the ground: for IE. base see FOOT] a combining form meaning ground, soil, earth

☆**pe·dol·o·gy**[1] (pi däl′ə jē) n. [PEDO-[1] + -LOGY] the scientific study of the behavior and development of children —**pe·do·log·i·cal** (pē′də läj′i k'l) adj. —**pe·dol′o·gist** n.

pe·dol·o·gy[2] (pi däl′ə jē) n. [PEDO-[2] + -LOGY] the scientific study of soils —**ped·o·log·i·cal** (ped′ə läj′i k'l) adj. —**pe·dol′o·gist** n.

pe·dom·e·ter (pi däm′ə tər) n. [< Fr. < L. pes FOOT + Gr. metron, a measure] an instrument carried by a walker to measure the distance he walks

pe·dun·cle (pi dun′k'l, pē′dun k'l) n. [< ModL. dim. of L. pes, FOOT] **1.** Anat., Med., Zool. a stalklike part **2.** Bot. a stalk, esp. of a flower cluster —**pe·dun′cu·lar** (-kyə lər) adj.

pe·dun·cu·late (pi dun′kyə lit, -lāt′) adj. growing on or having a peduncle: also **pe·dun′cu·lat′ed**

peek (pēk) vi. [< ?] to take a quick, sly or secret look, as through an opening —n. such a look

peek·a·boo (pēk′ə bōō′) n. a child's game in which someone hides his face, as behind his hands, and then suddenly reveals it, calling "peekaboo!" —☆adj. made of openwork or sheer fabric, as a blouse

peel[1] (pēl) vt. [< OFr. < L. pilare, to make bald < pilus: see PILE[2]] to cut away or strip off (the rind, skin, surface, etc.) of

fat, āpe, cär; ten, ēven; is, bīte; gō, hôrn, tōōl, look; oil, out; up, fur; get; joy; yet; chin; she; thin, then; zh, leisure; ŋ, ring; ə for a in ago, e in agent, i in sanity, o in comply, u in focus; ' as in able (ā′b'l); Fr. bal; ë, Fr. coeur; ö, Fr. feu; ô, Fr. mon; ô, Fr. coq; ü, Fr. duc; r, Fr. cri; H, G. ich; kh, G. doch; ‡foreign; ☆ Americanism; < derived from. See inside front cover.

(anything); pare —*vi.* **1.** to shed skin, bark, etc. [my back is *peeling* from a sunburn] **2.** to come off in layers or flakes [the paint on the house is *peeling*] **3.** [Slang] to undress —*n.* the rind or skin of fruit —**peel off** to turn sharply out of its place in a formation of airplanes —☆**peel rubber** (or **tires**) [Slang] to accelerate an automobile quickly —**peel′er** *n.*

peel² (pēl) *n.* [< OFr. < L. *pala*, a spade] a tool like a long shovel, used by bakers for moving bread into and out of ovens

Peel (pēl), Sir **Robert** 1788–1850; Brit. statesman; prime minister (1834–35; 1841–46)

peel·ing (pēl′iŋ) *n.* a peeled-off strip, as of apple skin

peen (pēn) *n.* [prob. < Scand.] the part of certain hammerheads opposite to the flat striking surface: often ball-shaped (**ball peen**) or wedge-shaped —*vt.* to hammer, bend, etc. with a peen

peep¹ (pēp) *vi.* [orig. echoic] **1.** to make the short, high-pitched cry of a young bird **2.** to speak in a small, weak voice, as from fear —*n.* **1.** a short, high-pitched sound; chirp **2.** a slight vocal sound [I told him not to make a *peep*, whatever happened]

peep² (pēp) *vi.* [? akin to ME. *piken*, peek] **1.** to look through a small opening or from a place of hiding **2.** to take a quick, sly or secret look **3.** to show or appear gradually or partially [stars *peeped* through the clouds] —*vt.* to cause to appear or stick out —*n.* **1.** a brief look; secret or sly glimpse **2.** the first appearance, as of dawn

peep·er¹ (pēp′ər) *n.* **1.** a person who peeps or spies **2.** [Slang] [*pl.*] the eyes

peep·er² (pēp′ər) *n.* **1.** one that peeps, cheeps, chirps, etc. ☆**2.** any of various tree frogs that peep in early spring

peep·hole (-hōl′) *n.* a hole to peep through

Peeping Tom 1. *Eng. Legend* the tailor who was struck blind after peeping at Lady Godiva **2.** [**p- T-**] a person who gets pleasure, esp. sexual pleasure, from secretly watching others

peer¹ (pir) *n.* [< OFr. *per* < L. *par*, an equal: see PAR] **1.** one that has the same rank, value, etc. as another; specif., an equal before the law [she has no *peer* as a poet; tried by a jury of his *peers*] **2.** a noble; esp., a British duke, marquess, earl, viscount, or baron —**peer of the realm** a British peer

peer² (pir) *vi.* [? short for APPEAR] **1.** to look closely, as in trying to see more clearly [to *peer* into a dark room] **2.** to come partly into sight [the moon *peered* over the hill]

peer·age (pir′ij) *n.* **1.** all the peers of a particular country **2.** the rank of a peer **3.** a book or list of peers with their lineage

peer·ess (-is) *n.* **1.** the wife of a peer **2.** a woman having the rank of peer in her own right

peer group a group of people of about the same age and status and having the same set of values

peer·less (-lis) *adj.* without equal; better than the rest [her *peerless* beauty] —**peer′less·ly** *adv.* —**peer′less·ness** *n.*

☆**peeve** (pēv) *vt.* **peeved**, **peev′ing** [back-formation < PEEVISH] [Colloq.] to make cross or annoyed [Mother will be *peeved* if I'm late] —*n.* [Colloq.] **1.** a thing that annoys one [a pet *peeve*] **2.** a peevish state

pee·vish (pē′vish) *adj.* [< ?] **1.** irritable; fretful; cross [illness made her *peevish*] **2.** showing ill humor or impatience [a *peevish* remark] —**pee′vish·ly** *adv.* —**pee′vish·ness** *n.*

☆**pee·wee** (pē′wē′) *n.* [prob. < WEE] [Colloq.] an unusually small person or thing

peg (peg) *n.* [prob. < LowG. source] **1.** a short pin or bolt used to hold parts together, close an opening, hang things on, fasten ropes to, mark the score in a game, etc. **2.** a step or degree [the promotion moved me up a few *pegs*] **3.** any of the pins that hold the strings of a violin, etc. and are used to tighten or loosen them: see illustration at VIOLIN **4.** [Colloq.] the foot or leg [it knocked his *pegs* out from under him] **5.** [Colloq.] a throw [a good *peg* from the outfield] —*vt.* **pegged**, **peg′ging 1.** to put a peg or pegs into so as to fasten, mark, etc. **2.** to maintain (prices, etc.) at a fixed level **3.** [Colloq.] to identify or put in a category [she quickly *pegged* him as a fool] **4.** [Colloq.] to throw [to *peg* the ball to first base] —*vi.* to move quickly (with *along*, etc.) —**peg away (at)** to work hard and steadily (at) —**round peg in a square hole** one in a position, etc. for which he is unfitted: also **square peg in a round hole** —**take down a peg** to make less proud or vain; humble

Peg·a·sus (peg′ə səs) **1.** a winged horse in Greek myths: it is a symbol of poetic inspiration **2.** a large northern constellation

peg·board (peg′bôrd′) *n.* **1.** a small board with holes in it for inserting scoring pegs for cribbage ☆**2.** a piece of boardlike material with rows of holes into which hooks to hold displays, tools, etc. may be inserted: as a trademark, **Peg-Board**

Peg·gy (peg′ē) [dim. of MARGARET] a feminine name

peg leg [Colloq.] **1.** a wooden leg **2.** a person with a wooden leg

peg·ma·tite (peg′mə tīt′) *n.* [< Gr. *pēgma*, a framework + -ITE¹] a very hard igneous rock containing large crystals of quartz, mica, etc. —**peg′ma·tit′ic** (-tit′ik) *adj.*

peg-top (peg′täp′) *adj.* designating trousers that are full at the hips and narrow at the cuffs

P.E.I. Prince Edward Island

peign·oir (pān wär′, pen-; pān′wär, pen′-) *n.* [Fr. < *peigner*, to comb, ult. < L. *pecten*, a comb] a negligee

Pei·ping (bā′piŋ′) *former name of* PEKING

Peirce (purs), **Charles San·ders** (san′dərz) 1839–1914; U.S. philosopher & mathematician

pe·jo·ra·tive (pi jôr′ə tiv, pej′ə rāt′iv) *adj.* [< L. pp. of *pejorare*, to make worse < *pejor*, worse: for IE. base see FOOT] showing scorn or disrespect; disparaging ["old-fashioned" is often used with a *pejorative* meaning] —*n.* a pejorative word —**pe·jo′ra·tive·ly** *adv.*

Pe·king (pē′kiŋ′; *Chin.* bā′jiŋ′) capital of China, in the NE part: pop. c. 7,000,000

Pe·king·ese (pē′kiŋ ēz′; *for n. 3, usually* -kə nēz′) *adj.* of Peking or its people —*n., pl.* **Pe′king·ese′ 1.** a native or inhabitant of Peking **2.** the Chinese dialect of Peking **3.** a small dog with long, silky hair, short legs, and a pug nose Also **Pe′kin·ese′** (-kə nēz′)

Peking man a type of early man of the Pleistocene age, known from fossil remains found near Peking

pe·koe (pē′kō) *n.* [< Chin. *pek-ho*, lit., white down (on the young leaves used)] a black tea of Ceylon and India

PEKINGESE
(to 6 in. high
at shoulder)

pel·age (pel′ij) *n.* [Fr. < L. *pilus*, hair] the coat, or covering, of a mammal, as hair or fur

pe·lag·ic (pi laj′ik) *adj.* [< L. < Gr. < *pelagos*, the sea] of the open sea or ocean

pel·ar·go·ni·um (pel′är gō′nē əm) *n.* [ModL. < Gr. *pelargos*, stork] any of a group of plants, including the geranium, with lobed leaves and showy flowers

pelf (pelf) *n.* [akin to MFr. *pelfre*, booty] **1.** orig., booty **2.** money or wealth looked upon with contempt

pel·i·can (pel′i kən) *n.* [< OE. < LL. < Gr. *pelekan*] a large water bird with webbed feet and a pouch that hangs from the lower bill and is used for scooping up fish

Pe·li·on (pē′lē ən) mountain in NE Greece: in Greek mythology, the Titans piled Pelion on Ossa and both on Olympus in a futile attempt to attack the gods

pe·lisse (pə lēs′) *n.* [Fr., ult. < L. *pellicius*, made of skins < *pellis*, a skin] a long cloak or outer coat, esp. one made or lined with fur

pel·la·gra (pə lag′rə, -lā′grə) *n.* [It. < *pelle* (< L. *pellis*, skin + -*agra* < Gr. *agra*, seizure] a chronic disease caused by a lack of niacin in the diet and characterized by a skin rash and mental disorders —**pel·la′grous** *adj.*

pel·let (pel′ət) *n.* [< OFr. *pelote* < VL. dim. of L. *pila*, a ball: for IE. base see PILE²] **1.** a little ball, as of clay, paper, medicine, compressed food, etc. **2.** *a)* a projectile of stone, etc. used in a catapult or early cannon *b)* a bullet *c)* a small lead shot —*vt.* **1.** to make pellets of **2.** to shoot or hit with pellets

pel·let·ize (-īz′) *vt.* -**ized′**, -**iz′ing** to make pellets of the iron-containing particles recovered from low-grade iron (ore) —**pel′let·i·za′tion** *n.*

pel·li·cle (pel′i k'l) *n.* [< L. dim. of *pellis*, skin] a thin skin or film —**pel·lic·u·lar** (pə lik′yə lər), **pel·lic′u·late** (-lit, -lat′) *adj.*

pell-mell, pell·mell (pel′mel′) *adv., adj.* [< Fr. < OFr. *pesle mesle < mesler*, to mix] **1.** in a jumbled, confused mass or manner [the clothes were tossed *pell-mell* into the suitcase] **2.** in reckless haste; headlong [he ran *pell-mell* down the hill] —*n.* confusion; disorder

pel·lu·cid (pə lōō′sid) *adj.* [< L. < *pellucere < per*, through + *lucere*, to shine] **1.** transparent or translucent; clear [a *pellucid* stream] **2.** easy to understand; clear and simple [a *pellucid* explanation] —**pel·lu·cid·i·ty** (pel′ōō sid′ə tē, -yōō-), **pel·lu′cid·ness** *n.* —**pel·lu′cid·ly** *adv.*

Pel·o·pon·ne·sus, Pel·o·pon·ne·sos (pel′ə pə nē′səs) peninsula forming the S part of the mainland of Greece —**Pel′o·pon·ne′sian** (-shən, -zhən) *adj., n.*

pe·lo·rus (pə lôr′əs) *n.* [? after *Pelorus*, name of Hannibal's pilot] a device used on ships for taking bearings, consisting of a movable ring fitted with sights that is mounted over a gyrocompass on a stand

pe·lo·ta (pə lōt′ə) *n.* [Sp., lit., a ball, ult. < L. *pila*, a ball] *Spanish name for* JAI ALAI

pelt[1] (pelt) *vt.* [? ult. < L. *pillare*, to drive] **1.** to throw things at; strike with missiles [we *pelted* each other with snowballs] **2.** to hit heavily and repeatedly [rain *pelted* the roof] **3.** to throw (missiles) —*vi.* **1.** to strike heavily or steadily, as hard rain **2.** to rush [he came *pelting* down the hall] —*n.* a blow —(at) full pelt at full speed

pelt[2] (pelt) *n.* [prob. < PELTRY] the skin of a fur-bearing animal, esp. after it is stripped from the carcass

pel·tate (pel′tāt) *adj.* [< L. *pelta*, light shield + -ATE[1]] *Bot.* shaped like a shield: said of a leaf —**pel′tate·ly** *adv.*

pelt·ry (pel′trē) *n., pl.* **-ries** [< OFr. < *peletier*, furrier < *pel*, a skin] pelts, or fur-bearing skins

pel·vic (pel′vik) *adj.* of or near the pelvis

pelvic fin either of a pair of fins corresponding to the hind limbs of a higher vertebrate and attached to the pelvic girdle in fishes: see illustration at FISH

pelvic girdle the structures of bone or cartilage to which the hind limbs or fins of a vertebrate are attached

pel·vis (pel′vis) *n., pl.* **-vis·es**, **-ves** (-vēz) [ModL. < L., a basin] *Anat., Zool.* any structure shaped like a hollow basin; specif., *a)* the cavity formed by a ring of bones in the rear part of the trunk in many vertebrates: in man, these bones rest on the legs and support the spinal column *b)* these bones; pelvic girdle

PELVIS

Pem·ba (pem′bə) island of Tanzania in the Indian Ocean, off the E coast of Africa

pem·mi·can (pem′i kən) *n.* [< Cree *pemikkân*, fat meat < *pimiy*, fat] **1.** dried lean meat pounded into a paste with fat and preserved in pressed cakes **2.** a concentrated food of dried beef, suet, dried fruit, etc., used as by arctic explorers

pen[1] (pen) *n.* [OE. *penn*] **1.** a small yard or enclosed place for animals **2.** the animals inside it **3.** any small enclosed place [a play*pen* for a baby] —*vt.* **penned** or **pent**, **pen′ning** to shut up or enclose as in a pen

pen[2] (pen) *n.* [< OFr. < L. *penna*, a feather: for IE. base see FEATHER] **1.** orig., a heavy quill or feather trimmed to a split point, used for writing with ink **2.** any of various devices used in writing or drawing with ink, often with a split metal point: see also BALL POINT PEN, FOUNTAIN PEN **3.** the metal point for this device **4.** *a)* writing as a profession ["the *pen* is mightier than the sword"] *b)* literary style [her witty *pen*] —*vt.* **penned**, **pen′ning** to write as with a pen

☆**pen**[3] (pen) *n.* [Slang] a penitentiary

pen[4] (pen) *n.* [< ?] a female swan

pen. peninsula

pe·nal (pē′n'l) *adj.* [< L. < *poena*, punishment < Gr. *poinē*, penalty < IE. base *kwei-*, to avenge] of, for, dealing with, or involving punishment, esp. legal punishment [*penal* laws; a *penal* offense] —**pe′nal·ly** *adv.*

penal code an organized set of laws dealing with various crimes or offenses and their legal penalties

pe·nal·ize (pē′n'l īz′, pen′'l-) *vt.* **-ized′**, **-iz′ing** **1.** to set a penalty for [how shall we *penalize* cheating?] **2.** to put a penalty on, as for breaking some rule [to *penalize* a boxer for a foul blow] **3.** to put at a disadvantage [he was *penalized* by his poor education] —**pe′nal·i·za′tion** *n.*

pen·al·ty (pen′'l tē) *n., pl.* **-ties** **1.** a punishment fixed by law, as for a crime **2.** the handicap, fine, forfeit, etc. put upon an offender or one who does not fulfill a contract or obligation **3.** any unfortunate result [indigestion is often the *penalty* for eating fast] **4.** any disadvantage, as a loss of yardage or the removal of a player, put on one side in a contest for breaking a rule

pen·ance (pen′əns) *n.* [< OFr. < L. *paenitens:* see PENITENT] **1.** *R.C.Ch. & Orthodox Eastern Ch.* a sacrament involving the confession of sin, repentance, and the acceptance of certain penalties followed by absolution **2.** any suffering that a person agrees to undergo to show that he is sorry for having done wrong —**do penance** to perform an act of penance

Pe·nang (pi naŋ′) seaport in Malaysia, on an island (**Penang**) off the NW coast of the Malay Peninsula: pop. 325,000

pe·na·tes (pi nāt′ēz) *n.pl.* [L.] the household gods of the ancient Romans: see LARES AND PENATES

pence (pens) *n.* [Brit.] *pl. of* PENNY

pen·chant (pen′chənt) *n.* [Fr. < *pencher*, to incline, ult. < L. *pendere:* see PENDANT] a strong liking or fondness; inclination [a *penchant* for baseball]

pen·cil (pen′s'l) *n.* [< MFr. < L. *penicillus* < dim. of *penis*, a tail] **1.** orig., an artist's brush **2.** the style of a given artist **3.** a pointed, rod-shaped instrument with a center stick of graphite or crayon, used for writing, drawing, etc. **4.** something shaped or used like a pencil [a styptic *pencil*] **5.** a series of lines coming to or spreading out from a point —*vt.* **-ciled** or **-cilled**, **-cil·ing** or **-cil·ling** **1.** to write, draw, etc. as with a pencil **2.** to use a pencil on —**pen′cil·er, pen′cil·ler** *n.*

pend (pend) *vi.* [< OFr. < L. *pendere:* see PENDANT] to await judgment or decision

pend·ant (pen′dənt) *n.* [< OFr. prp. of *pendre* < L. *pendere*, to hang < IE. base (*s*)*pen(d)-*, to stretch] **1.** an ornament that hangs down, as from an earring **2.** anything hanging, as the pull chain on a lamp **3.** something that matches, or serves as a companion piece or sequel to, something else —*adj. same as* PENDENT —**pend′ant·ly** *adv.*

pend·ent (pen′dənt) *adj.* [see prec.] **1.** hanging down or supported from above [a *pendent* lamp] **2.** overhanging [a *pendent* cliff] **3.** undecided; pending —*n. same as* PENDANT —**pend′en·cy** *n.* —**pend′ent·ly** *adv.*

pend·ing (pen′diŋ) *adj.* **1.** not decided or established [patent *pending*] **2.** about to happen; impending [*pending* dangers] —*prep.* **1.** throughout the course of; during [*pending* this discussion] **2.** while awaiting; until [*pending* his arrival]

pen·drag·on (pen drag′ən) *n.* [W. *pen*, head + *dragon*, leader < L. *draco*, cohort's standard] supreme chief or leader: a title used in ancient Britain

pen·du·lous (pen′joo ləs, -dyoo-) *adj.* [L. *pendulus* < *pendere*, to hang: see PENDANT] **1.** hanging loosely; free to swing [*pendulous* willow branches] **2.** drooping [*pendulous* jowls] — **pen′du·lous·ly** *adv.* —**pen′du·lous·ness** *n.*

pen·du·lum (pen′joo ləm, -dyoo-, -d'l əm) *n.* [ModL. < L.: see prec.] a weight hung from a fixed point so as to swing freely to and fro under the combined forces of gravity and momentum: often used to regulate clock movements — **pen′du·lar** *adj.*

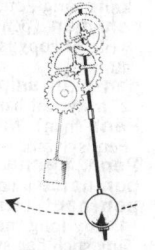

Pe·nel·o·pe (pə nel′ə pē) [L. < Gr. *Pēnelopē*] **1.** a feminine name: dim. *Penny* **2.** Odysseus' wife, who waited faithfully for his return from the Trojan War

☆**pe·ne·plain, pe·ne·plane** (pē′nə-plān′) *n.* [L. *pene, paene*, almost + PLAIN, PLANE[2]] land worn down by erosion almost to a level plain

pen·e·tra·ble (pen′i trə b'l) *adj.* that can be penetrated —**pen′e·tra·bil′i·ty** *n.* — **pen′e·tra·bly** *adv.*

PENDULUM

pen·e·trate (pen′ə trāt′) *vt.* **-trat′ed, -trat′ing** [< L. pp. of *penetrare* < base of *penitus*, inward] **1.** to find or force a way into or through; enter as by piercing [the needle *penetrated* her arm] **2.** to see into [no eye can *penetrate* such darkness] **3.** to have an effect throughout; spread through; permeate [smoke *penetrated* the whole room] **4.** to affect or move deeply **5.** to understand [I finally *penetrated* the meaning of the riddle] —*vi.* **1.** to make a way into or through something; pierce **2.** to have a marked effect on the mind or emotions

pen·e·trat·ing (-trāt′iŋ) *adj.* **1.** that can penetrate [a *penetrating* oil] **2.** sharp; piercing [a *penetrating* sound or smell] **3.** that has entered deeply [a *penetrating* wound] **4.** keen or shrewd; discerning [a *penetrating* mind] Also **pen′e·tra′tive** —**pen′e·trat′ing·ly, pen′e·tra′tive·ly** *adv.*

pen·e·tra·tion (pen′ə trā′shən) *n.* **1.** a penetrating **2.** the depth to which something penetrates, as a military force into enemy territory **3.** keenness of mind; insight

pen·guin (peŋ′gwin, pen′-) *n.* [prob. < W. *pen gwyn*, lit., white head] any of a group of birds of the Southern Hemisphere, having webbed feet and flippers for swimming and diving: penguins cannot fly

pen·hold·er (pen′hōl′dər) *n.* **1.** the holder into which a pen point fits **2.** a container for a pen

pen·i·cil·lin (pen′ə sil′in) *n.* [< ff. + -IN¹] any of several antibiotic compounds obtained from certain molds or produced synthetically

pen·i·cil·li·um (-ē əm) *n., pl.* **-li·ums, -li·a** (-ə) [ModL. < L. *penicillus*, a brush: from the tuftlike ends] any of a group of fungi growing as green mold on stale bread, decaying fruit, etc.: penicillin is obtained from some types

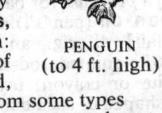

PENGUIN
(to 4 ft. high)

pen·in·su·la (pə nin′sə lə, -syoo-) *n.* [< L. < *paene*, almost + *insula*, island] **1.** a piece of land almost entirely surrounded by water, connected with the mainland by an isthmus **2.** any piece of land sticking out into the water —**pen·in′su·lar** *adj.*

pe·nis (pē′nis) *n., pl.* **-nis·es, -nes** (-nēz) [L., a tail, penis] the male organ of sexual intercourse: in mammals it is also the organ through which urine leaves the bladder —**pe′nile** (-nīl, -nil) *adj.*

pen·i·tence (pen′ə təns) *n.* the state of being penitent

SYN.—**penitence** implies sorrow over having done wrong and a willingness to make up for one's wrongful act; **repentance** implies a full understanding of one's wrongs and a will to change one's ways; **contrition** implies a deep sorrow for one's wrongs, with a firm determination to change for the better; **compunction** suggests a sharp but passing feeling of uneasiness about one's wrongdoing; **remorse** implies a deep and torturing sense of guilt; **regret** may refer to sorrow over any unfortunate happening as well as over a fault or act of one's own

pen·i·tent (pen′ə tənt) *adj.* [< OFr. < L. prp. of *paenitere*, to repent] sorry for having done wrong and willing to make up for one's wrongful act; repentant —*n.* **1.** a penitent person **2.** *R.C.Ch.* a person undergoing penance —**pen′i·tent·ly** *adv.*

pen·i·ten·tial (pen′ə ten′shəl) *adj.* of, having to do with, or expressing penitence or penance —**pen′i·ten′tial·ly** *adv.*

pen·i·ten·tia·ry (pen′ə ten′shə rē) *adj.* [< ML. < L.: see PENITENT] **1.** of or for penance **2.** used in punishing and reforming **3.** making one liable to imprisonment in a penitentiary [*a penitentiary* crime] **4.** of or in a penitentiary [*penitentiary* inmates] —*n., pl.* **-ries** a prison; specif., ☆a State or Federal prison for persons convicted of serious crimes

pen·knife (pen′nīf′) *n., pl.* **-knives** (-nīvz′) a small pocketknife; orig., one used in making quill pens

pen·man (pen′mən) *n., pl.* **-men 1.** a person employed to write or copy; scribe **2.** a person skilled in penmanship **3.** an author

pen·man·ship (-ship′) *n.* **1.** handwriting as an art or skill **2.** a style of handwriting

Penn (pen), **William** 1644–1718; Eng. Quaker leader: founder of Pennsylvania

Penn., Penna. Pennsylvania

pen name a name used by an author in place of his real name

pen·nant (pen′ənt) *n.* [< PENNON, altered after PENDANT] **1.** any long, narrow flag, usually in the shape of a triangle **2.** any such flag symbolizing a championship, esp. in baseball

pen·nate (pen′āt) *adj.* [< L. < *penna*, a feather] *Bot. same as* PINNATE

pen·ni (pen′ē) *n., pl.* **-ni·a** (-ə), **-nis, -ni** [Finn., akin to PENNY] *see* MONETARY UNITS, table (Finland)

pen·ni·less (pen′i lis) *adj.* without even a penny; extremely poor —**pen′ni·less·ness** *n.*

Pen·nine Alps (pen′īn, -in) division of the W Alps, along the Swiss-Italian border

pen·non (pen′ən) *n.* [< OFr. < *penne*: see PEN²] **1.** a long, narrow, triangular or swallow-tailed flag once carried by knights or lancers **2.** any flag or pennant **3.** a pinion; wing

Penn·syl·va·nia (pen′s'l vān′yə, -vā′nē ə) [after Wm. PENN + L. *sylvania*, wooded (land), ult. < *sylva*, forest] State of the northeastern U.S.: 45,333 sq. mi.; pop. 11,794,000; cap. Harrisburg: abbrev. **Pa., PA**

☆**Pennsylvania Dutch 1.** the descendants of early German immigrants, who settled mainly in eastern Pennsylvania **2.** their High German dialect: also called **Pennsylvania German 3.** their folk art, featuring carved or painted decorations of flowers, birds, etc., as on furniture —**Penn′syl·va′ni·a-Dutch** *adj.*

☆**Penn·syl·va·ni·an** (pen′s'l vān′yən, -vā′nē ən) *adj.* **1.** of Pennsylvania **2.** designating or of the sixth period of the Paleozoic Era in N. America —*n.* a native or inhabitant of Penn-

sylvania —**the Pennsylvanian** the Pennsylvanian Period or its rocks: see GEOLOGIC TIME CHART

pen·ny (pen′ē) *n., pl.* **-nies;** for 1, usually **pence** [OE. *pening*, ult. < L. *pannus*, cloth (a medium of exchange)] **1.** in the United Kingdom and certain Commonwealth countries, *a)* formerly, a unit of currency equal to one twelfth of a shilling *b)* a unit of currency equal to one 100th part of a pound: in full, **new penny** ☆**2.** a U.S. or Canadian cent **3.** a sum of money —**a pretty penny** [Colloq.] a large sum of money

penny arcade a public amusement hall with various coin-operated game and vending machines

penny pincher a person who is extremely frugal or stingy —**pen′ny-pinch′ing** *n., adj.*

pen·ny·roy·al (pen′ē roi′əl) *n.* [< Anglo-Fr. < OFr. *poliol* (< L. *pulegium*, fleabane) + *real*, royal] **1.** a European mint with lavender flowers **2.** a similar N. American mint that yields a sweet-smelling oil

pen·ny·weight (pen′ē wāt′) *n.* a unit of weight, equal to 24 grains or 1/20 ounce troy weight

pen·ny·wise (pen′ē wīz′) *adj.* careful or thrifty in small matters —**penny-wise and pound-foolish** thrifty in small matters but wasteful in major ones

pen·ny·worth (pen′ē wurth′) *n.* **1.** the amount that can be bought for one penny **2.** the value in money of something paid for **3.** a small amount

pe·nol·o·gy (pē näl′ə jē) *n.* [Gr. *poinē*, penalty (see PENAL) + -LOGY] the study of prison management and of ways to try to reform criminals and turn them into useful citizens —**pe·no·log′i·cal** (pē′nə läj′i k'l) *adj.* —**pe·nol′o·gist** *n.*

pen pal a person, esp. a stranger in another country, with whom one arranges a regular exchange of letters

Pen·sa·co·la (pen′sə kō′lə) [< Choctaw, hair people < *pansha*, hair + *okla*, people] seaport in NW Fla., on the Gulf of Mexico: pop. 60,000

pen·sile (pen′sil) *adj.* [L. *pensilis* < pp. of *pendere*: see PENDANT] **1.** hanging **2.** having or building a hanging nest, as the Baltimore oriole

pen·sion (pen′shən; *for n. 3*, pän′sē än′, *Fr.* pän syōn′) *n.* [< MFr. < L. *pensio* < pp. of *pendere*, to pay: see PENDANT] **1.** a regular payment, not wages, to one who has fulfilled certain requirements, as by having worked a certain number of years, lived to a certain age, become disabled, etc. **2.** a regular payment, not a fee, given to an artist, etc. by his patron; subsidy **3.** in France and other continental countries, *a)* a boardinghouse *b)* room and board —*vt.* to grant a pension to —**pension off** to dismiss from service with a pension

pen·sion·er (pen′shən ər) *n.* a person who receives a pension

pen·sive (pen′siv) *adj.* [< OFr. < *penser* < L. *pensare*, to consider < *pendere*, to weigh: see PENDANT] **1.** thinking deeply, often of sad or melancholy things **2.** expressing deep thoughtfulness, often with some sadness —**pen′sive·ly** *adv.* —**pen′sive·ness** *n.*

SYN.—**pensive** suggests deep thought as in a dreamlike state, often of sad or melancholy matters [*a pensive* look in her eye]; **contemplative** implies very deep thought, as on a subject of great concern, often as a form of discipline [a *contemplative* student of religion]; **reflective** suggests the turning over of a matter in the mind in a careful, orderly way in order to reach some conclusion [after a *reflective* pause he answered]; **meditative** implies the spending of time in quiet thought without intending to reach some conclusion [a *meditative* walk alone in the woods]

pen·stock (pen′stäk′) *n.* [PEN¹ + STOCK] **1.** a sluice for controlling the flow of water ☆**2.** a tube or trough for carrying water to a water wheel

pent (pent) *alt. pt. & pp. of* PEN¹ —*adj.* held or kept in; penned (often with *up*) [they enjoyed playing in the park after being *pent* up in the house]

pen·ta- [Gr. *penta-* < *pente*, FIVE] *a combining form meaning* five: also, before a vowel, **pent-**

pen·ta·gon (pen′tə gän′) *n.* [< L. < Gr.: see PENTA- & -GON] a plane figure with five angles and five sides —☆**the Pentagon** a five-sided building in Arlington, Va., housing the Department of Defense; hence, the U.S. military establishment —**pen·tag·o·nal** (pen tag′ə n'l) *adj.*

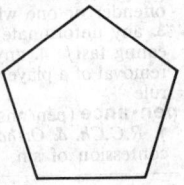

PENTAGON

pen·ta·he·dron (pen′tə hē′drən) *n., pl.* **-drons, -dra** (-drə) [ModL.: see PENTA- & -HEDRON] a solid figure with five plane surfaces —**pen′ta·he′dral** *adj.*

pen·tam·er·ous (pen tam′ər əs) *adj.* [PENTA- + -MEROUS] *Biol.* made up of five parts: also written **5-merous**

pen·tam·e·ter (pen tam′ə tər) *n.* [L. < Gr.: see PENTA- & ME-TER[1]] **1.** a line of verse containing five metrical feet (Example: "Hĕ jĕsts / ăt scărs / whŏ nĕv / ĕr fĕlt / ă wóund") **2.** verse consisting of pentameters —*adj.* having five metrical feet

pen·tane (pen′tān) *n.* [PENT(A)- + -ANE] any of three isomeric, colorless hydrocarbons, C_5H_{12}, of the methane series: used as a solvent, in low-temperature thermometers, etc.

Pen·ta·teuch (pen′tə to͞ok′, -tyo͞ok′) *n.* [< LL. < Gr. < *penta-*, five + *teuchos*, a book] the first five books of the Bible

pen·tath·lon (pen tath′län, -län) *n.* [< Gr. < *penta-*, five + *athlon*, a contest] **1.** an athletic contest in which each contestant takes part in five track and field events **2.** in the Olympic games, a contest consisting of five events (in horseback riding, running, swimming, fencing, and pistol shooting): in full, **modern pentathlon**

pen·ta·va·lent (pen′tə vā′lənt) *adj.* **1.** having a valence of five **2.** *same as* QUINQUEVALENT (sense 1)

Pen·te·cost (pen′tə kôst′, -käst′) *n.* [< LL. < Gr. *pentēkostē* (*hēmera*), the fiftieth (day) after Passover] **1.** *same as* SHAVUOT **2.** a Christian festival on the seventh Sunday after Easter, celebrating the descent of the Holy Spirit upon the Apostles; Whitsunday —**Pen′te·cos′tal** *adj.*

pent·house (pent′hous′) *n.* [< MFr. *apentis*, ult. < L. *appendere*, APPEND] **1.** a small structure with a sloping roof, or such a roof, attached to the side of a building **2.** an apartment or houselike structure built on the roof of a building

pen·to·bar·bi·tal sodium (pen′tə bär′bi tôl′) [*pento-* for PENTA- + BARBITAL] an odorless, white powder soluble in water: taken as a medicine to cause sleep

pen·tode (pen′tōd) *n.* [PENT(A)- + -ODE] an electron tube containing five electrodes, usually a cathode, anode, and three grids

☆**Pen·to·thal Sodium** (pen′tə thôl′) *a trademark for* THIOPENTAL SODIUM: often clipped to **Pentothal**

pent-up (pent′up′) *adj.* held in check; curbed; confined [*pent-up* emotion]

☆**pe·nu·che, pe·nu·chi** (pə no͞o′chē) *n.* [var. of PANOCHA] a fudgelike candy made of brown sugar, milk, butter, and, sometimes, nuts

pe·nult (pē′nult, pi nult′) *n.* [< L. < *paene*, almost + *ultimus*, last] the one next to the last; specif., the second last syllable in a word

pe·nul·ti·mate (pi nul′tə mit) *adj.* **1.** next to the last **2.** of the penult —*n. same as* PENULT —**pe·nul′ti·mate·ly** *adv.*

pe·num·bra (pi num′brə) *n., pl.* **-brae** (-brē), **-bras** [ModL. < L. *paene*, almost + *umbra*, shade] **1.** the partly lighted area surrounding the complete shadow of a body, as the moon, in full eclipse: see illustration at ECLIPSE **2.** the less dark region around the central area of a sunspot **3.** a vague, indefinite, or borderline area —**pe·num′bral** *adj.*

pe·nu·ri·ous (pə nyoor′ē əs, -noor′-) *adj.* **1.** unwilling to part with money or possessions; miserly; stingy **2.** of or in great poverty; destitute —see SYN. at STINGY —**pe·nu′ri·ous·ly** *adv.* —**pe·nu′ri·ous·ness** *n.*

pen·u·ry (pen′yə rē) *n.* [< L. *penuria*, want] lack of money, property, or necessities; great poverty; destitution —see SYN. at POVERTY

pe·on (pē′än, -ən) *n.* [< Sp. < ML. *pedo*, foot soldier: see PAWN[2]] **1.** in Latin America, a person of the laboring class ☆**2.** in the southwestern U.S., formerly, a person forced to work for someone in order to pay off a debt **3.** an unskilled or exploited laborer

pe·on·age (pē′ə nij) *n.* the condition of a peon

pe·o·ny (pē′ə nē) *n., pl.* **-nies** [< OE. & OFr. < L. < Gr. *Paiōn*, a name given to Apollo, god of medicine: from its former medicinal use] **1.** any of a group of plants with large pink, white, red, or yellow, showy flowers **2.** the flower

peo·ple (pē′p'l) *n., pl.* **-ple;** for 1 & 10, **-ples** [< Anglo-Fr. < OFr. < L. *populus*, nation] **1.** all the persons of a racial, national, religious, linguistic, or cultural group; nation, race, ethnic group, etc. **2.** the persons belonging to a certain place, community, or class [the *people* of Ohio, *people* of wealth] **3.** the persons under the leadership or control of a particular person or body **4.** the members of (someone's) occupation, social class or set, race, etc. [the miner spoke for his *people*] **5.** one's relatives or ancestors; family **6.** persons without wealth, special position, etc.; the public generally **7.** the electorate of a

state **8.** persons considered indefinitely [what will *people* say?] **9.** human beings, as distinct from other animals **10.** a group of creatures [the ant *people*] —*vt.* **-pled, -pling** to fill with people; populate [the pioneers *peopled* the West]

people's front *same as* POPULAR FRONT

Pe·o·ri·a (pē ôr′ē ə) [< Fr. < Algonquian *piwarea*, ? he carries a pack] city in C Ill.: pop. 127,000

☆**pep** (pep) *n.* [< PEPPER] [Colloq.] energy; vigor; liveliness —*vt.* **pepped, pep′ping** [Colloq.] to fill with pep; invigorate; stimulate (with *up*)

Pep·in the Short (pep′in) 715–768 A.D.; king of the Franks (751–768): father of CHARLEMAGNE

pep·lum (pep′ləm) *n., pl.* **-lums, -la** (-lə) [L. < Gr. *peplos*, a shawl] a flounce attached at the waist of a dress, coat, etc. and extending around the hips

pe·po (pē′pō) *n., pl.* **-pos** [L., a large melon] any fleshy gourd fruit with a hard rind and many seeds, as the melon, squash, etc.

pep·per (pep′ər) *n.* see PLURAL, II, D, 3 [< OE. < L. *piper* < Gr. *peperi*] **1.** *a)* a hot-tasting seasoning made by grinding the small, dried berries of an East Indian plant: see BLACK PEPPER, WHITE PEPPER *b)* the plant itself **2.** any of various plants with a strong, sweet, or spicy smell, used as flavoring **3.** *a)* *same as* CAPSICUM *b)* the fruit of the capsicum: see RED PEPPER, GREEN PEPPER, SWEET PEPPER **4.** any of various strong spices, as cayenne pepper ☆**5.** *Baseball* a warm-up session in which the ball is repeatedly thrown to a batter close by, who bunts it back to be fielded: in full, **pepper game** —*vt.* **1.** to season with ground pepper **2.** to sprinkle thickly **3.** to shower with many small objects [a roof *peppered* with hailstones] **4.** to beat or hit with quick jabs

PEPPER
(left, sense 1b; right, sense 3a)

pep·per-and-salt (-'n sôlt′) *adj.* speckled with contrasting colors, esp. black and white

pep·per·corn (-kôrn′) *n.* [OE. *piporcorn*] the dried berry of the black PEPPER (*n.* 1)

pep·per·grass (-gras′) *n.* a plant of the mustard family, with small, whitish flowers and flattened pods

pepper mill a hand mill used to grind peppercorns

pep·per·mint (-mint′, -mənt) *n.* **1.** a plant of the mint family, with lance-shaped leaves and whitish or purplish flowers **2.** an oil with a sharp, cool taste that is pressed from this plant and used for flavoring **3.** a candy flavored with this oil

☆**pep·per·o·ni** (pep′ə rō′nē) *n., pl.* **-nis, -ni** [< It. *peperoni*, cayenne pepper] a highly spiced Italian sausage

pepper pot ☆**1.** a hotly seasoned stew of vegetables, dumplings, tripe, etc. **2.** a soup of meat and vegetables flavored with hot spices

pepper shaker a container with holes in the top, for sprinkling ground pepper: also **pep′per·box′** (-bäks′) *n.*

pepper tree a S. American ornamental tree with loose clusters of yellowish flowers and pinkish-red berries

pep·per·y (pep′ər ē) *adj.* **1.** of, like, or highly seasoned with pepper **2.** sharp or fiery, as speech or writing **3.** easily made angry; hot-tempered; irritable —**pep′per·i·ness** *n.*

☆**pep pill** [Slang] any of various pills containing a stimulant, esp. amphetamine

☆**pep·py** (pep′ē) *adj.* **-pi·er, -pi·est** [Colloq.] full of pep, or energy; brisk; vigorous —**pep′pi·ly** *adv.* —**pep′pi·ness** *n.*

pep·sin (pep′s'n) *n.* [G. < Gr. *peptein*, to digest: for IE. base see COOK] **1.** an enzyme produced in the stomach, aiding in the digestion of proteins by splitting them into simpler compounds **2.** an extract of pepsin from the stomachs of calves, etc., formerly used to help in digesting food

☆**pep talk** a talk, as to an athletic team by its coach, intended to make a team or group enthusiastic, eager to win, etc.

pep·tic (pep′tik) *adj.* [< L. < Gr. *peptein*: see PEPSIN] **1.** of or aiding digestion **2.** of or relating to pepsin **3.** caused to some extent by digestive juices [a *peptic* ulcer]

---

fat, āpe, cär; ten, ēven; is, bīte; gō, hôrn, to͞ol, look; oil, out; up, fur; get; joy; yet; chin; she; thin, then; zh, leisure; ŋ, ring; ə for *a* in *ago, e* in *agent, i* in *sanity, o* in *comply, u* in *focus;* ' as in *able* (ā′b'l); Fr. bàl; ë, Fr. coeur; ö, Fr. feu; Fr. mon; ô, Fr. coq; ü, Fr. duc; r, Fr. cri; H, G. ich; kh, G. doch; ‡foreign; ☆ Americanism; < derived from. See inside front cover.

pep·tide (pep′tīd) *n.* [PEPT(ONE) + -IDE] a compound formed of two or more amino acids linked together

pep·tone (pep′tōn) *n.* [< G. < Gr. *peptos*, digested] any of a group of proteins soluble in water that are formed by the action of enzymes on proteins, as in digestion —**pep·ton′ic** (-tän′ik) *adj.*

Pepys (pēps; *occas.* peps, pep′is, pē′pis), **Samuel** 1633–1703; Eng. government official, known for his diary

Pe·quot (pē′kwät) *n.* [< Algonquian *paquatanog*, destroyers] **1.** *pl.* **-quots, -quot** any member of a tribe of Indians in Connecticut until scattered in 1637 **2.** their Algonquian language —*adj.* of this tribe

per (pur; *unstressed* pər) *prep.* [L.: for IE. base see FAR] **1.** through; by; by means of [*delivery per* messenger] **2.** for each [*fifty cents per* yard] **3.** [Colloq.] according to [*per* his instructions]

per- [< L. *per*, through: see PER] a prefix meaning: **1.** through, throughout [*perceive, percolate*] **2.** thoroughly, very [*persuade*] **3.** *Chem.* containing a specified element or radical in its maximum valence or in a relatively high valence [*peroxide*]

Per. 1. Persia **2.** Persian

per. 1. period **2.** person

per·ad·ven·ture (pur′əd ven′chər) *adv.* [< OFr. < *par*, by + *aventure*, chance] [Archaic] **1.** possibly **2.** by chance —*n.* chance; doubt

per·am·bu·late (pər am′byoo lāt′) *vt.* **-lat′ed, -lat′ing** [< L. pp. of *perambulare* < *per*, through + *ambulare*, to walk] to walk through, over, around, etc., as in inspecting —*vi.* to stroll —**per·am′bu·la′tion** *n.* —**per·am′bu·la·to′ry** (-lə tôr′ē) *adj.*

per·am·bu·la·tor (-lāt′ər) *n.* **1.** a person who perambulates **2.** [Chiefly Brit.] a baby carriage; buggy

per an·num (pər an′əm) [L.] by the year; yearly

per·cale (pər kāl′, -kal′) *n.* [Fr. < Per. *pargāla*] closely woven cotton cloth, used for sheets, etc.

per cap·i·ta (pər kap′ə tə) [ML., lit., by heads] for each person [the *per capita* cost of education]

per·ceive (pər sēv′) *vt., vi.* **-ceived′, -ceiv′ing** [< OFr. < L. *percipere* < *per*, through + *capere*, to take] **1.** to grasp or take in mentally [he quickly *perceived* the joke] **2.** to become aware (of) through sight, hearing, touch, taste, or smell —see SYN. at DISCERN —**per·ceiv′a·ble** *adj.* —**per·ceiv′a·bly** *adv.* —**per·ceiv′er** *n.*

per·cent (pər sent′) *adv., adj.* [< It. < L. *per centum*] in or for every hundred [a 20 *percent* rate means 20 in every hundred]: symbol, %: also **per cent** or, now rare, **per cent., per cen·tum** (sen′təm) —*n.* **1.** a hundredth part **2.** [Colloq.] percentage **3.** [*pl.*] bonds, etc. bearing regular interest of a (stated) percentage [the four *percents*]

per·cent·age (-ij) *n.* **1.** a given part or amount in every hundred **2.** any amount, as of interest, stated in percent **3.** part; portion [a *percentage* of the audience] ☆**4.** [Colloq.] *a)* use; advantage [no *percentage* in worrying] *b)* [*usually pl.*] a risk based on favorable odds

per·cen·tile (pər sen′tīl, -sent′'l) *n. Statistics* **1.** any value in a series dividing the distribution of its members into 100 groups of equal frequency **2.** any of these groups —*adj.* of a percentile

per·cept (pur′sept) *n.* [< PERCEPTION] a recognizable sensation or impression received by the mind through the senses

per·cep·ti·ble (pər sep′tə b'l) *adj.* that can be perceived — **per·cep′ti·bil′i·ty** *n.* —**per·cep′ti·bly** *adv.*

SYN.—perceptible is applied to anything that one can be aware of through the senses but often suggests that the thing can just barely be seen, heard, etc. [a *perceptible* change in his tone]; **sensible** applies to that which can clearly be perceived [a *sensible* difference in their size]; **palpable** refers to anything that can be perceived by or as by the sense of touch [a *palpable* fog]; **tangible** applies to that which can be grasped, either with the hand or the mind [*tangible* assets, reasons, results, etc.]; **appreciable** is used of that which is sufficiently perceptible to be measured, estimated, etc. or to have significance [an *appreciable* increase]. —**ANT. imperceptible**

per·cep·tion (pər sep′shən) *n.* [< L. < pp. of *percipere*: see PERCEIVE] **1.** *a)* the act of perceiving or the ability to perceive; awareness *b)* insight or intuition **2.** the understanding, knowledge, etc. or a specific idea, concept, etc. got by perceiving [he has a clear *perception* of his duty] —**per·cep′tion·al** *adj.* —**per·cep′tu·al** (-choo əl) *adj.*

per·cep·tive (-tiv) *adj.* **1.** of or capable of perception **2.** able to perceive quickly and easily —**per·cep′tive·ly** *adv.* —**per·cep′tive·ness, per·cep·tiv·i·ty** (pur′sep tiv′ə tē) *n.*

perch¹ (purch) *n., pl.* **perch, perch′es:** see PLURAL, II, D, 2 [< OFr. < L. < Gr. *perkē*] **1.** a small, spiny-finned, freshwater food fish **2.** any of various bony, spiny-rayed, usually saltwater fishes

perch² (purch) *n.* [< OFr. < L. *pertica*, a pole] **1.** a branch on a tree, or a bar in a cage, for a bird to roost on **2.** any resting place, esp. a high or insecure one **3.** *a)* a measure of length, equal to 5½ yards *b)* a measure of area, equal to 30¼ square yards —*vi.* to come to rest on a perch —*vt.* to place on a perch —**perch′er** *n.*

per·chance (pər chans′) *adv.* [< OFr. *par*, by + *chance*, chance] [Archaic] **1.** by chance **2.** perhaps; possibly

Per·che·ron (pur′chə rän′, -shə-) *n.* [Fr. < *Perche*, region in France] a breed of large, fast-trotting draft horses: also **Percheron Norman**

PERCHERON

per·cip·i·ent (pər sip′ē ənt) *adj.* perceiving, esp. keenly or readily —*n.* a person who perceives —**per·cip′i·ence, per·cip′i·en·cy** *n.* —**per·cip′i·ent·ly** *adv.*

Per·ci·val (pur′sə v'l) [< OFr., prob. < *perce val*, pierce valley] **1.** a masculine name **2.** a knight in Arthurian legend, who saw the Holy Grail: usually **Per′ci·vale** (-v'l)

per·co·late (pur′kə lāt′) *vt.* **-lat′ed, -lat′ing** [< L. pp. of *percolare* < *per*, through + *colare*, to strain] **1.** to pass (a liquid) gradually through a substance that is porous, or has many tiny holes; filter **2.** to drain or ooze through (a porous substance); permeate **3.** to brew (coffee) in a percolator —*vi.* **1.** to ooze through a porous substance **2.** to spread throughout; permeate **3.** to become active or start bubbling up, as percolated coffee —**per′co·la′tion** *n.*

per·co·la·tor (-lāt′ər) *n.* a coffeepot in which boiling water bubbles up through a tube and filters back down through the ground coffee, which is held in a container with many little holes

per·cuss (pər kus′) *vt.* to tap gently and firmly, as in doing percussion (sense 4)

per·cus·sion (pər kush′ən) *n.* [< L. < pp. of *percutere*, to strike] **1.** the hitting of one body against another, as the hammer of a firearm against a powder cap **2.** the impact of sound waves on the ear **3.** percussion instruments as a group **4.** *Med.* the tapping of the chest, back, etc. with the fingers to determine from the sound produced the condition of internal organs —**per·cus′sive** *adj.* —**per·cus′sive·ly** *adv.* —**per·cus′sive·ness** *n.*

percussion cap a small paper or metal container holding a charge that explodes when struck

percussion instrument a musical instrument in which the tone is produced when some part is struck, as the drums, cymbals, xylophone, etc.

per·cus·sion·ist (-ist) *n.* a musician who plays percussion instruments

Per·cy (pur′sē) **1.** a masculine name: see PERCIVAL **2.** Sir **Henry,** 1364–1403; Eng. soldier & rebel against Henry IV

per di·em (pər dē′əm, dī′əm) [L.] **1.** by the day; daily ☆**2.** a daily allowance, as for expenses

per·di·tion (pər dish′ən) *n.* [< OFr. < LL. < L. pp. of *perdere*, to lose] **1.** [Archaic] complete and irreparable loss; ruin **2.** *Theol. a)* the loss of the soul; damnation *b) same as* HELL

per·dur·a·ble (pər door′ə b'l, -dyoor′-) *adj.* [< OFr. < LL. < L. *perdurare* < *per-*, thoroughly + *durare*, to last] very durable or lasting a long time

‡père (per) *n.* [Fr.] father: often used after the surname, like English *Senior* [Dumas *père*]

per·e·gri·nate (per′ə gri nāt′) *vt., vi.* **-nat′ed, -nat′ing** [< L. pp. of *peregrinari* < *peregrinus*: see PILGRIM] to travel, esp. walk (along or through) —**per′e·gri·na′tion** *n.*

per·e·grine (falcon) (per′ə grin, -grēn′) [see prec.] a very swift European falcon with a spotted breast: used in falconry

per·emp·to·ry (pə remp′tər ē) *adj.* [< L. < L. < pp. of *perimere*, to destroy < *per-*, thoroughly + *emere*, to take] **1.** *Law a)* barring further action, debate, etc.; final; decisive *b)* not requiring that any cause be shown [a *peremptory* challenge of a juror will keep him off a jury] **2.** that cannot be denied, delayed, etc. [a *peremptory* command] **3.** forcing one's wishes or opinions on another in a bullying way [a *peremptory* manner] —**per·emp′to·ri·ly** *adv.* —**per·emp′to·ri·ness** *n.*

per·en·ni·al (pə ren′ē əl) *adj.* [< L. < *per*, through + *annus*, a year: see PER & ANNUAL] **1.** lasting or active throughout the whole year **2.** continuing for a long time [*perennial* youth] **3.** becoming active again and again; perpetual [a *perennial* problem] **4.** having a life cycle of more than two years: said of plants —*n.* a perennial plant —**per·en·ni·al·ly** *adv.*

perf. 1. perfect **2.** perforated

per·fect (pur′fikt; *for v., usually* pər fekt′) *adj.* [< OFr. < L. pp. of *perficere* < *per*, through + *facere*, to DO¹] **1.** complete in all respects; flawless [a *perfect* specimen] **2.** in a condition of excellence, as in skill or quality [*perfect* health] **3.** completely accurate; exact [a *perfect* copy] **4.** utter; absolute [*perfect* strangers] **5.** *Bot.* same as MONOCLINOUS **6.** *Gram.* expressing a state or action completed at the time of speaking or at the time indicated: verbs have three perfect tenses: present perfect, past perfect, and future perfect **7.** *Music* designating an interval, as an octave, whose character is not altered by inversion and which has no alternative major and minor forms —*vt.* **1.** to bring to completion **2.** to make perfect or more nearly perfect according to a given standard, as by training, practice, etc. [to *perfect* one's serve in tennis] —*n.* **1.** the perfect tense **2.** a verb form in this tense —**per·fect′er** *n.* —**per′fect·ness** *n.*

per·fect·i·ble (pər fek′tə b'l) *adj.* that can become, or be made, perfect or more nearly perfect —**per·fect′i·bil′i·ty** *n.*

per·fec·tion (pər fek′shən) *n.* **1.** the act or process of perfecting [to work at the *perfection* of a skill] **2.** the condition of being perfect [*perfection* in spelling is her goal] **3.** a person or thing that is perfect or excellent —**to perfection** completely; perfectly

☆**per·fec·tion·ism** (-iz′m) *n.* a devoted or fanatic striving to reach absolute perfection, as in one's work —**per·fec′tion·ist** *n., adj.* —**per·fec′tion·is′tic** *adj.*

per·fect·ly (pur′fikt lē) *adv.* **1.** to a perfect degree **2.** completely; fully

perfect number a positive integer which is equal to the sum of all its factors, excluding itself (Example: 28 = 1 + 2 + 4 + 7 + 14)

☆**per·fec·to** (pər fek′tō) *n., pl.* **-tos** [Sp., perfect] a cigar of a standard shape, thick in the center and tapering to a point at each end

perfect participle same as PAST PARTICIPLE

perfect pitch a popular term for ABSOLUTE PITCH

per·fer·vid (pər fur′vid) *adj.* extremely fervid

per·fid·i·ous (pər fid′ē əs) *adj.* showing treachery or perfidy; treacherous —see SYN. at FAITHLESS —**per·fid′i·ous·ly** *adv.*

per·fi·dy (pur′fə dē) *n., pl.* **-dies** [< Fr. < L. *perfidia* < *per fidem* (*decipi*), to (deceive) through faith] betrayal of the trust that others put in one; treachery

per·fo·li·ate (pər fō′lē it, -āt′) *adj.* [< ModL. < L. *per*, through + *folium*, a leaf] having a stem that seems to pass through it: said of a leaf —**per·fo′li·a′tion** *n.*

per·fo·rate (pur′fə rāt′; *for adj., usually* -rit) *vt., vi.* **-rat′ed, -rat′ing** [< L. pp. of *perforare* < *per*, through + *forare*, to bore] **1.** to make a hole or holes through, as by punching or boring **2.** to pierce with holes in a row, as a pattern, computer tape, etc. —*adj.* pierced with holes, esp. in a row, for easy tearing: also **per′fo·rat′ed** —**per′fo·ra·ble** *adj.* —**per′fo·ra′tor** *n.*

PERFOLIATE LEAVES

per·fo·ra·tion (pur′fə rā′shən) *n.* **1.** a perforating or being perforated **2.** a hole made by piercing, ulceration, etc. **3.** any of a series of punched holes, as those between postage stamps on a sheet

per·force (pər fôrs′) *adv.* [< OFr.: see PER & FORCE] by or through necessity; necessarily

per·form (pər fôrm′) *vt.* [< Anglo-Fr. < OFr. *parfournir*, to consummate < *par* (< L. *per-*, thoroughly) + *fornir*, to accomplish] **1.** to act on so as to complete; do (a task, process, etc.) **2.** to fulfill (a promise, etc.) **3.** to play, render, or enact (a piece of music, a dramatic role, etc.) —*vi.* to do something; carry out an action or process; esp., to act in a play, dance, etc. before an audience —**per·form′a·ble** *adj.* —**per·form′er** *n.*

SYN.—**perform**, often just a formal substitute for **do**, is usually used of a more or less involved process rather than a single act [to *perform* an experiment]; **execute** implies a putting into effect or completing that which has been planned or ordered [to *execute* a plan]; **accomplish** suggests effort and determination in carrying out a plan or purpose [to *accomplish* a mission]; **achieve** implies the overcoming of obstacles in accomplishing something worthwhile or important [to *achieve* a lasting peace]; **effect** also

suggests the overcoming of difficulties but emphasizes what has been done to bring about the result [his cure was *effected* by the use of certain drugs]; **fulfill** implies the successful bringing about of what is expected or demanded [to *fulfill* a promise]

per·form·ance (pə fôr′məns) *n.* **1.** the act of performing; execution, accomplishment, etc. [faithful in the *performance* of one's duty] **2.** functioning, usually with regard to effectiveness, as of a machine **3.** a deed or feat **4.** *a)* a formal exhibition or presentation before an audience, as a play, musical program, etc.; show *b)* one's part in this

performing arts arts, such as drama, dance, and music, that are performed before an audience

per·fume (pər fyōōm′; *for n., usually* pur′fyōōm) *vt.* **-fumed′, -fum′ing** [< MFr. < It. < L. *per-*, thoroughly + *fumare*, to smoke: for IE. base see DOWN²] **1.** to fill with a pleasing odor **2.** to put perfume on —*n.* **1.** a sweet smell; pleasing odor; fragrance **2.** a substance producing a pleasing odor; esp., such a substance as an oil pressed from flowers, to be put on the body

per·fum·er (pər fyōō′mər) *n.* **1.** one who makes or sells perfumes **2.** a person or thing that perfumes

per·fum·er·y (-ē) *n., pl.* **-er·ies 1.** the business or art of a perfumer **2.** perfumes as a group **3.** a place where perfume is made or sold

per·func·to·ry (pər funk′tər ē) *adj.* [< LL. < L. pp. of *perfungi* < *per-*, thoroughly + *fungi*, to perform] **1.** done merely as a routine; superficial [a *perfunctory* examination] **2.** not having any real concern; careless; indifferent [a *perfunctory* worker] —**per·func′to·ri·ly** *adv.* —**per·func′to·ri·ness** *n.*

per·fuse (pər fyōōz′) *vt.* **-fused′, -fus′ing** [< L. pp. of *perfundere* < *per*, through + *fundere*, to pour] **1.** to sprinkle, cover over, or soak with a liquid **2.** to pour or spread (a liquid, etc.) through or over something —**per·fu′sion** *n.*

Per·ga·mum (pur′gə məm) **1.** ancient Greek kingdom occupying most of W Asia Minor **2.** capital of this kingdom

per·go·la (pur′gə lə) *n.* [It., arbor < L. *pergula*, projecting cover] an arbor, esp. one with an open roof of cross rafters supported on columns, usually with climbing vines

Per·go·le·si (per′gō le′zē, -sē), **Gio·van·ni Bat·tis·ta** (jō vän′nē bät tēs′tä) 1710-36; It. composer

per·haps (pər haps′, -aps′) *adv.* [PER + *haps*, pl. of HAP] possibly; maybe

pe·ri (pir′ē) *n.* [Per. *parī*] *Persian Myth.* **1.** a fairy or elf **2.** any fairylike being

per·i- [< Gr. < *peri*: for IE. base see FAR] *a prefix meaning:* **1.** around, about [*periscope*] **2.** near [*perigee*]

per·i·anth (per′ē anth′) *n.* [< ModL. < Gr. *peri-*, around + *anthos*, a flower] the outer envelope of a flower, including the calyx and corolla

per·i·car·di·tis (per′ə kär dīt′is) *n.* inflammation of the pericardium

per·i·car·di·um (-kär′dē əm) *n., pl.* **-di·a** (-ə) [ModL. < Gr. < *peri-*, around + *kardia*, heart] in vertebrates, the thin, membranous sac around the heart —**per′i·car′di·al, per′i·car·di·ac′** *adj.*

per·i·carp (per′ə kärp′) *n.* [< ModL. < Gr.: see PERI- & -CARP] *Bot.* the wall of a ripened ovary —**per′i·car′pi·al** *adj.*

Per·i·cles (per′ə klēz′) 495?-429 B.C.; Athenian statesman & general —**Per′i·cle′an** (-klē′ən) *adj.*

per·i·cra·ni·um (per′ə krā′nē əm) *n., pl.* **-ni·a** (-ə) [ModL. < Gr. < *peri-*, around + *kranion*, skull] the tough membrane covering the skull

per·i·derm (per′ə durm′) *n.* [< ModL.: see PERI- & DERMIS] the outer bark and the layer of soft, growing tissue between the bark and the wood in plants —**per′i·der′mal, per′i·der′mic** *adj.*

per·i·gee (per′ə jē′) *n.* [< Fr. < ModL. < Gr. < *peri-*, near + *gē*, earth] **1.** the point nearest to the earth, the moon, or another planet, in the orbit of a satellite or spacecraft around it **2.** the lowest or nearest point —**per′i·ge′an, per′i·ge′al** *adj.*

per·i·he·li·on (per′ə hē′lē ən, -hēl′yən) *n., pl.* **-li·ons, -li·a** (-ə) [ModL. < Gr. *peri-*, around + *hēlios*, the sun] the point nearest the sun in the orbit around it of a planet, comet, or man-made satellite: see illustration at APHELION

per·il (per′əl) *n.* [OFr. < L. *periculum*, danger] **1.** exposure to harm or injury; danger [the flood put many lives in *peril*] **2.** something that may cause harm or injury [speeders are a *peril*

PERIODIC TABLE OF THE ELEMENTS

GROUP	I	II	III	IV	V	VI	VII	VIII	0
Type of Hydride	RH	RH_2	RH_3	RH_4	RH_3	RH_2	RH		
Type of Oxide	R_2O	RO	R_2O_3	RO_2	R_2O_5	RO_3	R_2O_7	RO_4	
SUBGROUP	A B	A B	A B	A B	A B	A B	A B		

PERIOD

Period	I	II	III	IV	V	VI	VII	VIII	0
1	1[a] H[b] 1.00797[c]								2 He 4.0026
2	3 Li 6.939	4 Be 9.0122	5 B 10.811	6 C 12.01115	7 N 14.0067	8 O 15.9994	9 F 18.9984		10 Ne 20.183
3	11 Na 22.9898	12 Mg 24.312	13 Al 26.9815	14 Si 28.086	15 P 30.9738	16 S 32.064	17 Cl 35.453		18 Ar 39.948
4 (A)	19 K 39.102	20 Ca 40.08	21 Sc 44.956	22 Ti 47.90	23 V 50.942	24 Cr 51.996	25 Mn 54.9380	26 Fe 55.847 — 27 Co 58.9332 — 28 Ni 58.71	
4 (B)	29 Cu 63.546	30 Zn 65.37	31 Ga 69.72	32 Ge 72.59	33 As 74.9216	34 Se 78.96	35 Br 79.909		36 Kr 83.80
5 (A)	37 Rb 85.47	38 Sr 87.62	39 Y 88.905	40 Zr 91.22	41 Nb 92.906	42 Mo 95.94	43 Tc (97)	44 Ru 101.07 — 45 Rh 102.905 — 46 Pd 106.4	
5 (B)	47 Ag 107.868	48 Cd 112.40	49 In 114.82	50 Sn 118.69	51 Sb 121.75	52 Te 127.60	53 I 126.9044		54 Xe 131.30
6 (A)	55 Cs 132.905	56 Ba 137.34	57* La 138.91	72 Hf 178.49	73 Ta 180.948	74 W 183.85	75 Re 186.2	76 Os 190.2 — 77 Ir 192.2 — 78 Pt 195.09	
6 (B)	79 Au 196.967	80 Hg 200.59	81 Tl 204.37	82 Pb 207.19	83 Bi 208.980	84 Po 210.05	85 At (210)		86 Rn 222.00
7	87 Fr (223)	88 Ra 226.00	89** Ac (227)	104	105	106			

*58–71 LANTHANIDE SERIES	58 Ce 140.12	59 Pr 140.907	60 Nd 144.24	61 Pm (145)	62 Sm 150.35	63 Eu 151.96	64 Gd 157.25	65 Tb 158.924	66 Dy 162.50	67 Ho 164.930	68 Er 167.28	69 Tm 168.934	70 Yb 173.04	71 Lu 174.97
**90–103 ACTINIDE SERIES	90 Th 232.038	91 Pa 231.10	92 U 238.03	93 Np 237.00	94 Pu 239.00	95 Am 243.13	96 Cm (247)	97 Bk (248)	98 Cf (251)	99 Es (252)	100 Fm (257)	101 Md (258)	102 No (255)	103 Lr (256)

Key at element 1., H a atomic number b chemical symbol c atomic weight ( ) encloses mass number of longest half-life isotope (if no exact atomic weight has been determined)

on the highway] —*vt.* **-iled** or **-illed**, **-il·ing** or **-il·ling** to expose to danger; imperil —see SYN. at DANGER

per·il·ous (-əs) *adj.* involving peril or risk; dangerous —**per′il·ous·ly** *adv.* —**per′il·ous·ness** *n.*

pe·rim·e·ter (pə rim′ə tər) *n.* [< L. < Gr. < *peri-*, around + *metron*, a measure] **1.** the outer boundary of a figure or area **2.** the total length of this —**per·i·met·ric** (per′ə met′rik), **per′i·met′ri·cal** *adj.* —**per′i·met′ri·cal·ly** *adv.*

per·i·ne·um (per′ə ne′əm) *n., pl.* **-ne′a** (-ə) [ModL. < LL. < Gr. < *peri-*, around + *inein*, to discharge] the region between the thighs; specif., the small area between the anus and the genital organs —**per′i·ne′al** *adj.*

pe·ri·od (pir′ē əd) *n.* [< MFr. < L. < Gr. *periodos*, a cycle < *peri-*, around + *hodos*, way] **1.** the time that goes by between happenings in a cycle involving a heavenly body, as between two full moons **2.** the time that goes by between two specified happenings **3.** a portion of time during which certain events, processes, conditions, etc. go on or exist; stage [a *period* of change] **4.** any of the portions of time into which a game, school day, etc. is divided **5.** the full course, or one of the stages, of a disease **6.** the menses **7.** an end or conclusion [death put a *period* to his plans] **8.** a subdivision of a geologic era **9.** *Gram.* a) a sentence, esp. a well-balanced sentence b) the pause in speaking or a mark of punctuation (.) used at the end of a declarative sentence c) the dot (.) following many abbreviations **10.** *Physics* the interval of time necessary for a complete cycle of a regularly recurring motion —*adj.* of or like that of an earlier period or age [*period* furniture] —*interj.* an exclamation used to give emphasis at the end of a statement [he hates cats, *period!*]

pe·ri·od·ic (pir′ē äd′ik) *adj.* **1.** appearing or coming again at regular intervals [a *periodic* fever] **2.** occurring from time to time; intermittent [*periodic* tests to measure the students' progress] **3.** of or characterized by periods **4.** describing a sentence written so that the full meaning cannot be understood until the very end —see SYN. at INTERMITTENT

pe·ri·od·i·cal (-i k′l) *adj.* **1.** *same as* PERIODIC **2.** published at regular intervals, as weekly, monthly, etc. **3.** of a periodical —*n.* a periodical publication

pe·ri·od·i·cal·ly (-ik ′l ē, -ik lē) *adv.* **1.** at regular intervals **2.** from time to time; recurrently

pe·ri·o·dic·i·ty (pir′ē ə dis′ə tē) *n., pl.* **-ties** **1.** the tendency of appearing or recurring at regular intervals **2.** *Chem.* the occurrence of similar properties in elements occupying similar positions in the periodic table

periodic law the law that properties of chemical elements recur periodically when the elements are arranged in order of their atomic numbers

periodic table an arrangement of the chemical elements according to their atomic numbers, so as to show the periodic law: see table on opposite page

per·i·o·don·tal (per′ē ə dän′t′l) *adj.* [PERI- + -ODONT- + -AL] occurring around a tooth or affecting the gums

per·i·o·don·tics (-tiks) *n.pl.* [*with sing. v.*] [SEE PERIODONTAL & -ICS] the branch of dentistry concerned with diseases of the bone and tissue supporting the teeth: also **per′i·o·don′ti·a** (-dän′shə, -shē ə) —**per′i·o·don′tic** *adj.* —**per′i·o·don′tist** *n.*

per·i·os·te·um (per′i äs′tē əm) *n., pl.* **-te·a** (-ə) [ModL. < L. < Gr. < *peri-*, around + *osteon*, a bone] the membrane of tough, fibrous connective tissue covering all bones except at the joints —**per′i·os′te·al** *adj.*

per·i·pa·tet·ic (per′i pə tet′ik) *adj.* [< Fr. < L. < Gr., ult. < *peri-*, around + *patein*, to walk] **1.** [P-] of the philosophy or followers of Aristotle, who walked about while he was teaching **2.** walking or moving about; itinerant —*n.* **1.** [P-] a follower of Aristotle **2.** a person who walks from place to place —**per′i·pa·tet′i·cal·ly** *adv.*

pe·riph·er·al (pə rif′ər əl) *adj.* **1.** of, belonging to, or forming a periphery **2.** *Anat.* of, at, or near the surface of the body **3.** only slightly connected with what is essential or important; merely incidental [of *peripheral* interest] —**pe·riph′er·al·ly** *adv.*

peripheral vision the area of vision lying just outside the line of direct sight

pe·riph·er·y (-ē) *n., pl.* **-er·ies** [< MFr. < LL. < Gr. < *peri-*, around + *pherein*, to BEAR¹] **1.** a boundary line or outside surface, esp. of something round **2.** surrounding space or area; outer parts; environs or outskirts

pe·riph·ra·sis (pə rif′rə sis) *n., pl.* **-ses′** (-sēz′) [L. < Gr. < *peri-*, around + *phrazein*, to speak] the use of many words where a few would do; roundabout way of speaking: also **per·i·phrase** (per′ə frāz′)

per·i·phras·tic (per′ə fras′tik) *adj.* **1.** of, like, or expressed in periphrasis **2.** *Gram.* formed with a particle or a helping verb instead of by inflection, as the phrase *did sing* used for *sang* —**per′i·phras′ti·cal·ly** *adv.*

☆**pe·rique** (pə rēk′) *n.* [AmFr.] a strong, rich black tobacco grown in Louisiana, used in blending

per·i·sarc (per′ə särk′) *n.* [< PERI- + Gr. *sarx*, flesh] the tough, nonliving, outer skeleton layer of many hydroid colonies: see illustration at POLYP

per·i·scope (per′ə skōp′) *n.* [PERI- + -SCOPE] an optical instrument consisting of a tube equipped with lenses and mirrors or prisms, so arranged that a person looking through one end can see objects reflected at the other end: used on submarines under the water —**per′i·scop′ic** (-skäp′ik) *adj.*

per·ish (per′ish) *vi.* [< OFr. < L. *perire*, to perish < *per-*, thoroughly + *ire*, to go: see YEAR] **1.** to be destroyed, ruined, or wiped out **2.** to die; esp., to die a violent or untimely death —see SYN. at DIE¹ —**perish the thought!** do not even consider such a possibility!

per·ish·a·ble (-ə b′l) *adj.* that may perish; esp., liable to spoil, as some foods —*n.* something, esp. a food, liable to spoil or deteriorate —**per′ish·a·bil′i·ty**, **per′ish·a·ble·ness** *n.*

PERISCOPE

per·i·stal·sis (per′ə stōl′sis, -stal′-) *n., pl.* **-ses** (-sēz) [ModL. < Gr. < *peri-*, around + *stellein*, to place] the wavelike motion of the walls of the alimentary canal and certain other hollow organs, caused by muscles in the walls that keep expanding and contracting and so move the contents onward —**per′i·stal′tic** *adj.*

per·i·style (per′ə stīl′) *n.* [< Fr. < L. < Gr. < *peri-*, around + *stylos*, a column] **1.** a row of columns forming an enclosure or supporting a roof **2.** any area so formed, as a court

per·i·to·ne·um (per′it ′n ē′əm) *n., pl.* **-ne′a** (-ə), **-ne′ums** [LL. < Gr. < *peri-*, around + *teinein*, to stretch] the serous membrane lining the abdominal cavity and covering the visceral organs —**per′i·to·ne′al** *adj.*

per·i·to·ni·tis (-′n ī′tis) *n.* inflammation of the peritoneum

per·i·wig (per′ə wig′) *n.* [earlier *perwyke* < Fr. *perruque*, PERUKE] a wig, esp. one of a type formerly worn by men

per·i·win·kle¹ (per′ə wiŋ′k′l) *n.* [< OE. < L. *pervinca*] a European creeping plant with blue, white, or pink flowers, grown as a ground cover

per·i·win·kle² (per′ə wiŋ′k′l) *n.* [OE. *pinewincle*] **1.** any of various small saltwater snails having a thick, cone-shaped shell **2.** such a shell

PERIWIG

per·jure (pur′jər) *vt.* **-jured**, **-jur·ing** [< OFr. < L. < *per*, through + *jurare*, to swear: see JURY¹] to make (oneself) guilty of perjury —**per′jur·er** *n.*

per·jured (-jərd) *adj.* **1.** guilty of perjury [a *perjured* witness] **2.** characterized by perjury [*perjured* testimony]: also **per·ju·ri·ous** (pər jur′ē əs)

per·ju·ry (-jər ē) *n., pl.* **-ries** [< OFr. < L. < *perjurus*, false] **1.** the telling of a lie on purpose, after one has taken an oath to tell the truth **2.** the breaking of any oath or formal promise

perk¹ (purk) *vt.* [< ? ONormFr. *perquer*, to perch] **1.** to raise (the head, ears, etc.) briskly (often with *up*) **2.** to make jaunty or stylish in appearance (often with *up* or *out*) **3.** to give or restore freshness, liveliness, etc. to (usually with *up*) —*vi.* **1.** to straighten one's posture jauntily **2.** to become lively or recover one's spirits (with *up*)

perk[2] (purk) *vt., vi.* [Colloq.] *clipped form of* PERCOLATE

perk[3] (purk) *n.* [Chiefly Brit. Colloq.] *clipped form of* PERQUISITE

perk·y (pur′kē) *adj.* **perk′i·er, perk′i·est** **1.** aggressive; self-confident **2.** gay or lively; saucy —**perk′i·ly** *adv.* —**perk′i·ness** *n.*

Perm (perm) city in E European R.S.F.S.R.: pop. 850,000

per·ma·frost (pur′mə frôst′, -fräst′) *n.* [PERMA(NENT) + FROST] permanently frozen subsoil

per·ma·nence (pur′mə nəns) *n.* the state or quality of being permanent

per·ma·nen·cy (-nən sē) *n.* **1.** *same as* PERMANENCE **2.** *pl.* **-cies** something permanent

per·ma·nent (-nənt) *adj.* [MFr. < L. prp. of *permanere* < *per*, through + *manere*, to remain] lasting or intended to last indefinitely or for a relatively long time —*n.* [Colloq.] *clipped form of* PERMANENT WAVE —**per′ma·nent·ly** *adv.*

permanent magnet a magnet, usually of hard steel, which keeps most of its magnetism after it has once been magnetized

permanent tooth any of the 32 adult human teeth including those that replace the milk teeth

permanent wave a hair wave that is produced by applying heat or chemical preparations and that is relatively long lasting

per·man·ga·nate (pər man′gə nāt′) *n.* a salt of permanganic acid, generally dark purple and a strong oxidizing agent

per·man·gan·ic acid (pur′man gan′ik) an unstable acid, HMnO₄, that is an oxidizing agent

per·me·a·bil·i·ty (pur′mē ə bil′ə tē) *n.* **1.** a being permeable **2.** *Physics a)* the measure of ease with which magnetic lines of force are carried by a particular material *b)* the rate of diffusion of a fluid through a porous body

per·me·a·ble (pur′mē ə b'l) *adj.* that can be permeated, as by liquids —**per′me·a·bly** *adv.*

per·me·ate (-āt′) *vt.* **-at′ed, -at′ing** [< L. pp. of *permeare* < *per*, through + *meare*, to glide] to pass into or through and affect every part of; spread through [ink *permeates* blotting paper; a society *permeated* with idealism] —*vi.* to spread or diffuse (with *through* or *among*) —**per′me·a′tion, per′me·ance** *n.* —**per′me·a′tive** (-āt′iv) *adj.*

Per·mi·an (pur′mē ən) *adj.* [after *Perm*, former province of Russia] designating or of the seventh and last period of the Paleozoic Era —**the Permian** the Permian Period or its rocks: see GEOLOGIC TIME CHART

per·mis·si·ble (pər mis′ə b'l) *adj.* that can be permitted; allowable —**per·mis′si·bil′i·ty** *n.* —**per·mis′si·bly** *adv.*

per·mis·sion (pər mish′ən) *n.* the act of permitting; esp., formal consent; leave [he has my *permission* to go]

per·mis·sive (-mis′iv) *adj.* **1.** giving permission **2.** allowing freedom; esp., tolerant of behavior or practices disapproved of by others; indulgent; lenient —**per·mis′sive·ly** *adv.* —**per·mis′sive·ness** *n.*

per·mit (pər mit′; *for n., usually* pur′mit) *vt.* **-mit′ted, -mit′ting** [< L. < *per*, through + *mittere*, to send: see MISSION] **1.** to allow; consent to [smoking is not *permitted*] **2.** to give permission to; authorize [to *permit* women to vote] **3.** to give opportunity for [to *permit* light to enter] —*vi.* to give opportunity [if time *permits*] —*n.* **1.** *same as* PERMISSION **2.** a document granting permission; license —see SYN. at LET¹ —**per·mit′ter** *n.*

per·mu·ta·tion (pur′myoo tā′shən) *n.* **1.** any radical alteration; total transformation **2.** *Math.* any one of the total number of groupings, or subsets, into which a group, or set, of elements can be arranged: the permutations of 1, 2, and 3 taken two at a time are 12, 21, 13, 31, 23, 32 —**per′mu·ta′tion·al** *adj.*

per·mute (pər myoot′) *vt.* **-mut′ed, -mut′ing** [< L. *permutare* < *per-*, thoroughly + *mutare*, to change] **1.** to make different; alter **2.** to rearrange the order or sequence of —**per·mut′a·ble** *adj.*

Per·nam·bu·co (pur′nəm boo′kō; *Port.* per′nänm boo′koo) *same as* RECIFE

per·ni·cious (pər nish′əs) *adj.* [< Fr. < L. < *pernecare* < *per*, thoroughly + *necare*, to kill < *necis*, genitive of *nex*, death: see NECRO-] **1.** causing great injury, destruction, or ruin **2.** [Rare] wicked; evil —**per·ni′cious·ly** *adv.* —**per·ni′cious·ness** *n.*

SYN.—**pernicious** applies to that which does great harm by undermining or weakening in a slow way not easily noticed [*pernicious* anemia; a *pernicious* teaching]; **baneful** implies a harming by or as by poisoning [a *baneful* superstition]; **noxious** refers to anything that is injurious to physical or mental health [*noxious* fumes]; **deleterious** implies something that injures health slowly but may be remedied [the *deleterious* effects of an unbalanced diet]; **detrimental** implies a causing of damage, loss, or disadvantage to something specified [his interference was *detrimental* to our cause] —ANT. harmless, innocuous

pernicious anemia a form of anemia in which there is a reduction in the number of the red blood cells and which causes disturbances of the digestive and nervous systems

per·nick·et·y (pər nik′ə tē) *adj. same as* PERSNICKETY

per·o·rate (per′ə rāt′) *vi.* **-rat′ed, -rat′ing** **1.** to make a speech, esp. a lengthy oration **2.** to sum up or conclude a speech

per·o·ra·tion (per′ə rā′shən) *n.* [< L. < pp. of *perorare* < *per*, through + *orare*, to speak] **1.** the concluding part of a speech, including a summing up of the main ideas **2.** a bombastic speech

per·ox·ide (pə räk′sīd) *n.* [PER- + OXIDE] any oxide containing the oxygen (O₂) group linked by a single bond; specif., hydrogen peroxide —*vt.* **-id·ed, -id·ing** to bleach (hair, etc.) with hydrogen peroxide —*adj.* bleached with hydrogen peroxide

per·pen·dic·u·lar (pur′pən dik′yə lər) *adj.* [< OFr. < L. < *perpendiculum*, plumb line < *per-*, thoroughly + *pendere*, to hang] **1.** at right angles to a given plane or line [the wall should be *perpendicular* to the floor] **2.** exactly upright; vertical **3.** very steep —*n.* **1.** a line at right angles to another line or plane **2.** a perpendicular position —**per′pen·dic′u·lar′i·ty** (-lar′ə tē) *n.* —**per′pen·dic′u·lar·ly** *adv.*

PERPENDICULAR

per·pe·trate (pur′pə trāt′) *vt.* **-trat′ed, -trat′ing** [< L. pp. of *perpetrare* < *per*, thoroughly + *patrare*, to effect] **1.** to do (something evil, criminal, or offensive); be guilty of **2.** to commit (a blunder), impose (a hoax), etc. —**per′pe·tra′tion** *n.* —**per′pe·tra′tor** *n.*

per·pet·u·al (pər pech′oo wəl) *adj.* [< OFr. < L. < *perpetuus*, constant] **1.** lasting forever or for an indefinitely long time **2.** continuing indefinitely without interruption; constant [a *perpetual* nuisance] —see SYN. at CONTINUAL —**per·pet′u·al·ly** *adv.*

perpetual calendar a calendar so arranged that one can find the correct day of the week for any given date over a wide range of years

perpetual motion the motion of an imaginary device which, after it has been set in motion, would operate indefinitely by creating by itself the energy needed to keep on going

per·pet·u·ate (pər pech′oo wāt′) *vt.* **-at′ed, -at′ing** to make perpetual; cause to continue or be remembered [the Rhodes scholarships *perpetuate* the memory of Cecil Rhodes] —**per·pet′u·a′tion** *n.* —**per·pet′u·a′tor** *n.*

per·pe·tu·i·ty (pur′pə too′ə tē, -tyoo′-) *n., pl.* **-ties** **1.** a being perpetual **2.** something perpetual, as a pension to be paid indefinitely **3.** unlimited time; eternity —**in perpetuity** forever

per·plex (pər pleks′) *vt.* [< MFr. < L. *perplexus*, confused < *per*, through + pp. of *plectere*, to twist: for IE. base see COMPLICATE] **1.** to make (a person) uncertain, hesitant, etc.; confuse **2.** to make intricate or complicated; make confusing or hard to understand [to *perplex* an issue] —see SYN. at PUZZLE —**per·plexed′** *adj.* —**per·plex′ed·ly** (-plek′sid lē) *adv.* —**per·plex′ing** *adj.* —**per·plex′ing·ly** *adv.*

per·plex·i·ty (-plek′sə tē) *n.* **1.** the state of being perplexed; bewilderment; confusion **2.** *pl.* **-ties** something that confuses or puzzles, as a complication or intricacy

per·qui·site (pur′kwə zit) *n.* [< ML. < pp. of *perquirere*, to obtain < L. < *per-*, thoroughly + *quaerere*, to seek] **1.** something additional to regular profit or pay, resulting from one's employment, esp. something customary or expected **2.** a tip or gratuity **3.** a privilege or benefit to which a person, institution, etc. is entitled because of status, position, etc.; right

Per·ry (per′ē) **1.** [? < Fr. < L. *Petrus*, Peter] a masculine name **2.** Matthew Cal·braith (kal′breth), 1794–1858; U.S. naval officer **3.** Oliver Haz·ard (haz′ərd), 1785–1819; U.S. naval officer: brother of *Matthew*

Pers. **1.** Persia **2.** Persian

pers. **1.** person **2.** personal

per se (pur′ sē′, sā′) [L.] by (or in) itself; intrinsically

per second per second for each second every second: used of a rate of acceleration: a body accelerating from rest at 20 ft. per second per second would travel 90 ft. in 3 seconds, since it would travel 10 ft. in the first second, 30 ft. in the second, and 50 ft. in the third

per·se·cute (pur′sə kyoot′) *vt.* **-cut′ed, -cut′ing** [< MFr. < L. < *persequi*, to pursue < *per*, through + *sequi*, to follow] **1.** to cause continual pain or suffering to, esp. for reasons of religion, politics, or race **2.** to annoy constantly [*persecuted* by mosquitoes] —**per′se·cu′tion** *n.* —**per′se·cu′tive** *adj.* —**per′se·cu′tor** *n.*

Per·seph·o·ne (pər sef′ə nē) *Gr. Myth.* the daughter of Zeus and Demeter, abducted by Hades (Pluto) to be his wife in the lower world: identified with the Roman goddess Proserpina

Per·sep·o·lis (pər sep′ə lis) capital of the ancient Persian Empire, in what is now SC Iran

Per·seus (pur′syo͞os, -sē əs) **1.** *Gr. Myth.* a son of Zeus and slayer of Medusa: he married Andromeda after rescuing her from a sea monster **2.** a N constellation

per·se·ver·ance (pur′sə vir′əns) *n.* **1.** the act of persevering; continued, patient effort **2.** persistence; steadfastness
SYN.—perseverance implies a continuing to do something in spite of difficulties, obstacles, etc.; **persistence** may imply either steadfast perseverance that is usually admired or stubborn continuance that is usually annoying; **tenacity** and **pertinacity** both imply firmness in holding to some purpose, action, or belief but **tenacity** suggests that such firmness is admirable while **pertinacity** suggests a being obstinate in a way that annoys

per·sev·er·ate (pər sev′ə rāt′) *vi.* **-at·ed, -at·ing** to show or display perseveration

per·sev·er·a·tion (pər sev′ə rā′shən) *n.* the tendency of an idea, experience, or response to persist or the tendency of an individual to continue a particular mental activity without being able to shift easily to another in response to a new stimulus

per·se·vere (pur′sə vir′) *vi.* **-vered′, -ver′ing** [< OFr. < L. < *perseverus* < *per-*, thoroughly + *severus*, severe] to continue in some effort, course of action, etc. in spite of difficulty, opposition, etc.; persist **—per′se·ver′ing·ly** *adv.*

Per·shing (pur′shiŋ), **John Joseph** 1860-1948; U.S. general: commander of U.S. forces in World War I

Per·sia (pur′zhə, -shə) **1.** *former official name of* IRAN **2.** *same as* PERSIAN EMPIRE

Per·sian (-zhən, -shən) *adj.* of Persia, its people, their language, etc.; Iranian **—n. 1.** a native or inhabitant of Persia **2.** the Iranian language of Iran

Persian cat a variety of domestic cat with long, silky hair

Persian Empire ancient empire in SW Asia, including at its peak the area from the Indus River to the W borders of Asia Minor & Egypt: founded by Cyrus the Great & conquered by Alexander the Great

Persian Gulf arm of the Arabian Sea, between SW Iran & Arabia

Persian lamb 1. the lamb of the karakul sheep **2.** the black or gray pelt of new-born karakul lambs, having small, tight curls

PERSIAN EMPIRE (500 B.C.)

Persian rug (or **carpet**) an Oriental rug made in Persia, with a richly colored, intricate pattern

per·si·flage (pur′sə fläzh′) *n.* [Fr. < *persifler*, to banter < *per-* (see PER-) + *siffler*, to whistle] **1.** a light, playful style of writing or speaking **2.** talk or writing of this kind

☆**per·sim·mon** (pər sim′ən) *n.* [< AmInd.] **1.** any of various trees with white flowers, hard wood, and yellow, plumlike fruit **2.** the fruit, sour when green, but sweet for eating when ripe

per·sist (pər sist′, -zist′) *vi.* [< MFr. < L. < *per*, through + *sistere*, to cause to stand < *stare*, STAND] **1.** to refuse to give up, esp. when faced with opposition [the team *persisted* until they won] **2.** to say or do over and over again [he *persists* in telling that stale joke] **3.** to last for some time; continue; remain [the pain *persisted* all day]•—see SYN. at CONTINUE

per·sist·ence (pər sis′təns, -zis′-) *n.* **1.** a persisting; stubborn continuance **2.** a persistent or lasting quality; tenacity: also **per·sist′en·cy 3.** the continuance of an effect after the removal of its cause [the *persistence* of vision causes visual images to continue upon the retina for a brief time] —see SYN. at PERSEVERANCE

per·sist·ent (-tənt) *adj.* **1.** continuing, esp. in the face of opposition, etc.; stubborn [*persistent* effort] **2.** continuing to exist or endure [a *persistent* headache] **3.** constantly repeated; continued [*persistent* appeals] **—per·sist′ent·ly** *adv.*

per·snick·e·ty (pər snik′ə tē) *adj.* [< Scot. dial.] [Colloq.] **1.** too particular or precise; fussy **2.** showing or requiring careful treatment

per·son (pur′s'n) *n.* [< OFr. < L. *persona*, lit., actor's mask, hence a person] **1.** a human being; individual man, woman, or child **2.** *a)* a living human body *b)* bodily appearance [to be neat about one's *person*] **3.** personality; self **4.** *Gram. a)* division into three sets of pronouns (**personal pronouns**), and, usually, verb forms that go with them, to show who or what the subject is: see FIRST PERSON, SECOND PERSON, THIRD PERSON *b)* any of these sets **5.** *Law* an individual or incorporated group having certain legal rights and responsibilities **6.** *Theol.* any of the three beings (Father, Son, and Holy Ghost) in the Trinity **—in person** actually present

-per·son (pur′s'n) *a combining form meaning* person (of either sex) in a certain activity: used to coin words that avoid the masculine notions implied by *-man* ["chair*person*"]

per·so·na (pər sō′nə) *n., pl.* **-nae** (-nē); for sense 2, **-nas** [L.: see prec.] **1.** [*pl.*] the characters of a drama, novel, etc. **2.** *Psychol.* the outer personality presented to others by an individual

per·son·a·ble (pur′s'n ə b'l) *adj.* having a pleasing appearance and personality; attractive **—per′son·a·ble·ness** *n.* **—per′son·a·bly** *adv.*

per·son·age (-ij) *n.* **1.** an important person **2.** any person **3.** a character in history, a play, novel, etc.

‡**per·so·na gra·ta** (pər sō′nə grät′ə, grät′ə) [L.] a person who is acceptable or welcome; esp., a foreign diplomat acceptable to the government to which he is sent

per·son·al (pur′s'n əl) *adj.* **1.** of one's own; private; individual [his *personal* secretary] **2.** done in person or by oneself [he had a *personal* interview with the mayor] **3.** involving human beings [*personal* relationships] **4.** of the body or physical appearance [*personal* hygiene] **5.** *a)* having to do with the character, conduct, etc. of a certain person [he made *personal* remarks about her] *b)* tending to make personal remarks [to get *personal* in an argument] **6.** of or like a person or rational being **7.** *Gram.* having to do with person [*personal* pronouns] **8.** *Law* describing property (**personal property**) that is movable or not attached to the land **—n.** ☆**1.** a local news item about a person or persons ☆**2.** a classified advertisement about a personal matter

personal effects personal or intimate belongings of an individual, esp. those worn or carried on the person

personal equation variation in the way individuals judge or observe something, that may cause an error in relation to an expected result and that should be allowed for

☆**personal foul** in certain team games, a foul involving body contact with an opponent, such as unnecessary roughness or hindering

per·son·al·i·ty (pur′sə nal′ə tē) *n., pl.* **-ties 1.** the quality or fact of being a person **2.** the quality or fact of being a particular person; individuality **3.** *a)* all the special qualities of a person which make him different from other people *b)* such qualities applied to a group, nation, etc. **4.** *a)* the sum of such qualities that attract others to one *b)* personal attractiveness **5.** a person; esp., a famous person **6.** [*pl.*] any offensive remarks finding fault with another person [let's avoid *personalities*] —see SYN. at DISPOSITION

per·son·al·ize (pur′s'n ə līz′) *vt.* **-ized′, -iz′ing 1.** to intend or understand in a personal way [he *personalized* her comments about bachelors as meant for him] **2.** *same as* PERSONIFY **3.** to have marked with one's name or initials [*personalized* checks]

per·son·al·ly (-ə lē) *adv.* **1.** without the help of others; in person [to attend to a matter *personally*] **2.** as a person [I dislike him *personally*, but admire his art] **3.** in one's own opinion **4.** as though directed at oneself [to take a remark *personally*]

per·son·al·ty (-əl tē) *n., pl.* **-ties** *same as* PERSONAL PROPERTY: see PERSONAL (sense 8)

‡**per·so·na non gra·ta** (pər sō′nə nän grät′ə, grät′ə) [L.] a person who is not acceptable or welcome; esp., a foreign diplomat not acceptable to the government to which he is sent

per·son·ate (pur′sə nāt′) *vt.* **-at·ed, -at·ing 1.** to act the part of, as in a drama **2.** *Law* to pretend to be (someone else) in order to deceive or cheat others; impersonate **—per′son·a′tion** *n.* **—per′son·a′tive** *adj.* **—per′son·a′tor** *n.*

per·son·i·fi·ca·tion (pər sän′ə fi kā′shən) *n.* **1.** a personifying or being personified **2.** a person or thing thought of as representing some quality, idea, etc.; perfect example [Cupid is the *personification* of love] **3.** a figure of speech in which a thing or idea is represented as a person

per·son·i·fy (pər sän′ə fī′) *vt.* **-fied′, -fy′ing 1.** to think or speak of (a thing) as a person [to *personify* a ship by referring to it as "she"] **2.** to symbolize (an abstract idea) by a human figure, as in art [this statue *personifies* liberty] **3.** to be a symbol or perfect example of (something); typify [Tom Sawyer *personifies* the spirit of boyhood] —**per·son′i·fi′er** *n.*

per·son·nel (pur′sə nel′) *n.* [Fr.] **1.** persons employed in any work, enterprise, service, etc. [office *personnel*] **2.** a personnel department or office for hiring employees, etc. —*adj.* of or in charge of personnel [*personnel* department]

per·spec·tive (pər spek′tiv) *adj.* [< LL. < L. perspicere < *per*, through + *specere*, to look: see SPY] **1.** of perspective **2.** drawn in perspective —*n.* **1.** the art of picturing objects or a scene, esp. by lines that come together, so as to show them as they appear to the eye to be close or far away, big or small, etc. **2.** the appearance of objects as viewed from a given point according to their shape, size, distance, etc. [*perspective* makes things far away seem small]

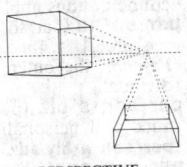

PERSPECTIVE

3. the relationship of the parts of a whole, regarded from a particular standpoint or point in time **4.** *a)* a specific point of view in judging things or events *b)* the ability to see things in a true relationship **5.** a distant view; vista —**per·spec′tive·ly** *adv.*

per·spi·ca·cious (pur′spə kā′shəs) *adj.* [L. perspicax < *perspicere*: see prec.] able to understand and judge things clearly; discerning —see SYN. at SHREWD —**per′spi·ca′cious·ly** *adv.* —**per′spi·cac′i·ty** (-kas′ə tē), **per′spi·ca′cious·ness** *n.*

per·spic·u·ous (pər spik′yoo wəs) *adj.* [L. perspicuus, transparent < *perspicere*: see PERSPECTIVE] clear in statement or expression; easily understood —**per·spi·cu·i·ty** (pur′spə kyoo′ə tē), **per·spic′u·ous·ness** *n.* —**per·spic′u·ous·ly** *adv.*

per·spi·ra·tion (pur′spə rā′shən) *n.* [Fr.] **1.** a perspiring; sweating **2.** sweat —**per·spir·a·to·ry** (pər spīr′ə tôr′ē) *adj.*

per·spire (pər spīr′) *vt., vi.* **-spired′, -spir′ing** [< Fr. < L. perspirare < *per*, through + *spirare*, to breathe: see PER- & SPIRIT] to give forth (a characteristic salty moisture) through the pores of the skin; sweat

per·suade (pər swād′) *vt.* **-suad′ed, -suad′ing** [< MFr. < L. persuadere < *per*-, thoroughly + *suadere*, to urge: for IE. base see SWEET] to cause to do or believe something, esp. by reasoning, urging, etc.; induce; convince —**per·suad′a·ble, per·sua′si·ble** (-swā′sə b'l) *adj.* —**per·suad′er** *n.* —**per·sua′si·bil′i·ty** *n.*

SYN.—**persuade** implies an influencing of a person to do or believe something by a direct appeal to his reason or emotions [after some coaxing, pleading, and arguing, we *persuaded* him to go]; **induce** suggests such a clever leading of a person to a course of action that the decision seems finally to be his own [he was *induced* to accept the position]; **prevail on**, which can be used in place of either **persuade** or **induce**, often suggests stronger resistance that can be overcome only after much argument, etc. [he could not be *prevailed on* to change his mind]

per·sua·sion (pər swā′zhən) *n.* **1.** a persuading or being persuaded **2.** power of persuading **3.** a strong belief; conviction **4.** *a)* a particular religious belief or system; religion [a man of the Moslem *persuasion*] *b)* a particular sect, group, etc. **5.** [Colloq.] kind, sex, etc.: used in a joking way —see SYN. at OPINION

per·sua·sive (-siv) *adj.* having the power to persuade; tending to persuade —**per·sua′sive·ly** *adv.* —**per·sua′sive·ness** *n.*

pert (purt) *adj.* [short for *apert* < OFr. < L. apertus, open] **1.** bold or impudent in speech or behavior; saucy **2.** chic and jaunty **3.** [Dial.] lively; brisk —**pert′ly** *adv.* —**pert′ness** *n.*

per·tain (pər tān′) *vi.* [< OFr. < L. pertinere, to reach < *per*-, thoroughly + *tenere*, to hold: see TEND²] **1.** to belong; be connected or associated; be a part, etc. [lands *pertaining* to an estate] **2.** to be appropriate [conduct that *pertains* to a lady] **3.** to have reference; be related [laws *pertaining* to the case]

Perth (purth) capital of Western Australia: pop. 626,000

per·ti·na·cious (pur′tə nā′shəs) *adj.* [< L. pertinax, firm < *per*-, thoroughly + *tenax* < *tenere*, to hold: see TEND²] **1.** holding firmly or stubbornly to some purpose, belief, or action [a *pertinacious* opponent of the government] **2.** hard to get rid of; persistent [a *pertinacious* salesman] —see SYN. at STUBBORN —**per′ti·na′cious·ly** *adv.*

per·ti·nac·i·ty (-nas′ə tə) *n.* a being pertinacious; stubborn persistence —see SYN. at PERSEVERANCE

per·ti·nent (pur′t'n ənt) *adj.* [< MFr. < L. prp. of pertinere: see PERTAIN] having some connection with the matter at hand; relevant; to the point [a *pertinent* question] —see SYN. at RELEVANT —**per′ti·nence, per′ti·nen·cy** *n.* —**per′ti·nent·ly** *adv.*

per·turb (pər turb′) *vt.* [< MFr. < L. < *per*-, thoroughly + *turbare*, to disturb: for IE. base see STORM] **1.** to cause to be worried or upset; disturb or trouble greatly **2.** to cause confusion in —**per·turb′a·ble** *adj.* —**per·turb′ed·ly** *adv.* —**per·turb′er** *n.*

per·tur·ba·tion (pur′tər bā′shən) *n.* **1.** a perturbing or being perturbed **2.** something that perturbs; disturbance **3.** *Astron.* an irregularity in the orbit of a heavenly body, caused by the attraction of a body other than the one around which it orbits —**per·tur·ba′tion·al** *adj.*

per·tus·sis (pər tus′is) *n.* [ModL. < L. *per*-, thoroughly + *tussis*, a cough] same as WHOOPING COUGH

Pe·ru (pə roo′) country in western S.America, on the Pacific: 496,222 sq. mi.; pop. 13,586,000; cap. Lima —**Pe·ru·vi·an** (pə roo′vē ən) *adj., n.*

Pe·ru·gi·no (pe′roo jē′nô) ‖ (ēl) (born *Pietro Vannucci* 1446?–1523?; It. painter

pe·ruke (pə rook′) *n.* [< Fr. *perruque*] same as PERIWIG

pe·rus·al (pə roo′z'l) *n.* the act of perusing

pe·ruse (pə roo′z′) *vt.* **-rused′, -rus′ing** [prob. < L. *per*-, thoroughly + ME. usen, to use] to read, esp. thoroughly or carefully —**pe·rus′er** *n.*

Peruvian bark same as CINCHONA (sense 2)

per·vade (pər vād′) *vt.* **-vad′ed, -vad′ing** [< L. pervadere < *per*, through + *vadere*, to go] **1.** to pass through; spread throughout [the smell of cooking *pervaded* the house] **2.** to occur generally throughout [joy *pervades* his poems] —**per·va′sion** (-vā′zhən) *n.*

per·va·sive (-vā′siv) *adj.* tending to pervade or spread throughout [a *pervasive* odor] —**per·va′sive·ly** *adv.* —**per·va′sive·ness** *n.*

per·verse (pər vurs′) *adj.* [< OFr. < L. pp. of pervertere: see PERVERT] **1.** turning aside from what is considered right or good; improper, wicked, etc. [cruelty to animals is a *perverse* act] **2.** continuing in a stubborn way to do what is wrong or harmful [the *perverse* man continued to smoke, against his doctor's orders] **3.** obstinate; stubborn [her *perverse* unwillingness to believe the truth] —**per·verse′ly** *adv.* —**per·verse′ness** *n.*

per·ver·sion (-vur′zhən, -shən) *n.* **1.** a perverting or being perverted **2.** something perverted **3.** any sexual act or practice considered abnormal

per·ver·si·ty (-sə tē) *n.* **1.** a being perverse **2.** *pl.* **-ties** an instance of this

per·vert (pər vurt′; *for n.* pur′vərt) *vt.* [< OFr. < L. < *per*-, completely + *vertere*, to turn: see VERSE] **1.** to lead away from what is right or good; misdirect; corrupt [they *perverted* the course of justice] **2.** to turn to an improper use; misuse [an artist who has *perverted* his talent] **3.** to give a wrong meaning to; misinterpret; distort [political enemies *perverted* his remarks] **4.** to bring into a worse condition; debase —*n.* a perverted person; esp., one who practices sexual perversion —see SYN. at DEBASE —**per·ver′sive** (-vur′siv) *adj.* —**per·vert′ed** *adj.* —**per·vert′er** *n.*

per·vi·ous (pur′vē əs) *adj.* [< L. < *per*, through + *via*, way] allowing passage through; permeable [a surface *pervious* to water] —**per′vi·ous·ly** *adv.* —**per′vi·ous·ness** *n.*

Pe·sach (pä′säkh) *n.* [Heb. *pesaḥ*, a passing over] same as PASSOVER

pe·se·ta (pə sāt′ə; *Sp.* pe se′tä) *n.* [Sp., dim. of *peso*, PESO] the monetary unit and a coin of Spain and Equatorial Guinea: see MONETARY UNITS, table

pes·e·wa (pes′ə wä) *n., pl.* **-e·was, -e·wa** [< native word *kpesaba*, a seed] see MONETARY UNITS, table (Ghana)

pes·ky (pes′kē) *adj.* **-ki·er, -ki·est** [prob. var. of *pesty* < PEST + -Y²] [Colloq.] annoying; troublesome —**pes′ki·ly** *adv.* —**pes′ki·ness** *n.*

pe·so (pā′sō; *Sp.* pe′sô) *n., pl.* **-sos** [Sp. < L. pp. of *pendere*, to weigh: see PENDANT] the monetary unit of Argentina, Colombia, Cuba, Mexico, the Philippines, etc.: see MONETARY UNITS, table

peso bo·liv·i·a·no (bô lē′vyä′nô) *pl.* **pesos bolivianos** see MONETARY UNITS, table (Bolivia)

pes·si·mism (pes′ə miz'm) *n.* [< Fr. < L. pessimus, superl. of *pejor*, worse: see PEJORATIVE] **1.** *Philos. a)* the doctrine that the existing world is the worst possible *b)* the belief that the evil in life outweighs the good **2.** the tendency to expect things to turn out badly; a looking on the dark side of things —**pes′si-**

mist (-mist) *n.* —**pes'si·mis'tic** (-mis'tik) *adj.* —**pes'si·mis'·ti·cal·ly** *adv.*

pest (pest) *n.* [< Fr. < L. *pestis*, a plague] **1.** a person or thing that causes trouble, annoyance, etc.; specif., any destructive insect, small animal, weed, etc. **2.** [Rare] bubonic plague

pes·ter (pes'tər) *vt.* [< OFr. *empestrer*, orig., to hobble a horse: infl. by PEST] to annoy repeatedly with petty irritations; bother [to *pester* someone with questions] —**pes'ter·er** *n.*

pest·hole (pest'hōl') *n.* a place overrun or likely to be overrun with an epidemic disease

pes·ti·cide (pes'tə sīd') *n.* [< PEST + -CIDE] any chemical used for killing insects, weeds, etc. —**pes'ti·ci'dal** *adj.*

pes·tif·er·ous (pes tif'ər əs) *adj.* [< L. < *pestis*, a plague + *ferre*, to bear] **1.** orig., *a)* bringing or carrying disease *b)* overrun with an epidemic disease **2.** dangerous to the welfare of society; evil **3.** [Colloq.] annoying or mischievous —**pes·tif'er·ous·ly** *adv.* —**pes·tif'er·ous·ness** *n.*

pes·ti·lence (pes't'l əns) *n.* [see PESTILENT] **1.** any disease that is fatal or very harmful and that spreads rapidly from person to person, esp. an epidemic of such disease, as bubonic plague **2.** anything, as a doctrine, believed to be harmful —**pes'ti·len'tial** (-lən'shəl) *adj.* —**pes'ti·len'tial·ly** *adv.*

pes·ti·lent (-ənt) *adj.* [< L. < *pestis*, plague] **1.** likely to cause death; deadly [a *pestilent* disease] **2.** dangerous to the security and welfare of society; pernicious [the *pestilent* threat of war] **3.** annoying; troublesome —**pes'ti·lent·ly** *adv.*

pes·tle (pes''l) *n.* [< OFr. < L. *pistillum* < *pinsere*, to pound] a tool used to pound or grind substances, as in a mortar: see illustration at MORTAR —*vt., vi.* -**tled**, -**tling** to pound, grind, crush, etc. as with a pestle

pet[1] (pet) *n.* [orig. Scot. dial.] **1.** an animal that is tamed and kept as a companion or treated with fondness **2.** a person who is liked or treated better than others; favorite [a teacher's *pet*] —*adj.* **1.** kept or treated as a pet [a *pet* turtle] **2.** especially liked; favorite [a *pet* project of hers] **3.** greatest; particular [one's *pet* peeve] **4.** showing fondness [a *pet* name] —*vt.* **pet'·ted, pet'ting 1.** to stroke or pat gently; fondle; caress [to *pet* a dog] **2.** to be overly kind to; pamper —☆ *vi.* [Colloq.] to kiss, caress, etc. as lovers do —**pet'ter** *n.*

pet[2] (pet) *n.* [< ?] a sulky, cross mood

Pet. Peter

pet·al (pet''l) *n.* [< ModL. < Gr. < *petalos*, outspread: from IE. base *pet*-, to stretch out] any of the parts, or leaves, that make up a corolla: see illustration at FLOWER —**pet'aled, pet'alled** (-'ld) *adj.* —**pet'al·like'** *adj.* —**pet'al·ous** *adj.*

pe·tard (pi tärd') *n.* [< Fr. < *péter*, ult. < L. *pedere*, to break wind] a metal cone filled with explosives: formerly used to break open a wall or gate —**hoist with** (or **by**) **one's own petard** destroyed by the very means with which one meant to destroy others

pet·cock (pet'käk') *n.* [< obs. *pet*, breaking wind + COCK[1]] a small valve for draining excess water or air from pipes, radiators, boilers, etc.

Pe·ter (pēt'ər) [< LL. < Gr. < *petros*, a rock] **1.** a masculine name: dim. **Pete 2.** *Bible a)* ?-64? A.D.; one of the Twelve Apostles, a fisherman who is believed to be the author of the Epistles of Peter: also called *Simon Peter b)* either of the two Epistles of Peter **3. Peter I** 1672-1725; czar of Russia (1682-1725): called *Peter the Great*

pe·ter (pēt'ər) *vi.* [< ?] [Colloq.] ☆to become gradually smaller, weaker, etc. and then stop or disappear (with *out*)

Pe·ter·bor·ough (pēt'ər bʉr'ō) city in SE Ontario, Canada, near Toronto: pop. 60,000

pet·i·ole (pet'ē ōl') *n.* [< ModL. < L. *petiolus*, dim. of *pes*, a FOOT] **1.** *Bot.* the slender part of a leaf, which supports the blade and is attached to the stem; leafstalk **2.** *Zool.* a stalklike part; peduncle —**pet'i·o·lar** (-ə lər) *adj.* —**pet'i·o·late'** (-ə lāt', -lit) *adj.*

PETIOLE

pet·it (pet'ē; *Fr.* pə tē') *adj.* [< OFr.: see PETTY] small or of less importance: now used chiefly in law

pe·tite (pə tēt') *adj.* [Fr., fem. of *petit*] small and dainty: said of a woman —**see** SYN. at SMALL —**pe·tite'ness** *n.*

pe·tit four (pet'ē fôr'; *Fr.* pə tē fōōr') *pl.* **pe·tits fours** (pet'ē

fôrz'; *Fr.* pə tē fōōr'), **pe·tit fours** (pet'ē fôrz') [Fr. < *petit*, small + *four*, lit., oven] a small cake cut from spongecake, etc. and decorated with icing

pe·ti·tion (pə tish'ən) *n.* [< OFr. < L. *petitio* < *petere*, to ask: for IE. base see FEATHER] **1.** a solemn, earnest request to a superior or to those in authority; entreaty **2.** a formal document making such a request, often signed by a number of persons **3.** something that is asked or entreated [to grant a *petition*] **4.** *Law* a written plea asking for specific court action [a *petition* for rehearing] —*vt.* **1.** to address a petition to [to *petition* Congress for aid] **2.** to ask for; solicit —*vi.* to make a petition —**see** SYN. at APPEAL —**pe·ti'tion·ar'y** *adj.* —**pe·ti'tion·er** *n.*

petit jury a group of twelve citizens picked to weigh evidence in and decide the issues of a trial in court: see GRAND JURY

petit larceny *see* LARCENY

pe·tit mal (pə tē' mäl') [Fr., lit., small ailment] a type of epilepsy in which there are brief periods of unconsciousness without convulsions

Pe·trarch (pē'trärk) (It. name *Francesco Petrarca*) 1304-74; It. lyric poet & scholar

Pe·trar·chan sonnet (pi trär'kən) a sonnet made up of a group of eight lines (*octave*) that rhyme *abba, abba*, and a group of six lines (*sestet*) that rhyme in various ways, as *cdc dcd* or *cde cde*

pet·rel (pet'rəl) *n.* [? a dim. of PETER, in allusion to St. Peter's walking on the sea] any of various related small, dark sea birds with long wings; esp., *same as* STORMY PETREL

pe·tri dish (pē'trē) [after J. *Petri* (1852-1921), G. bacteriologist] [*also* P- d-] a shallow, cylindrical, transparent dish with a cover, used for the culture of microorganisms

pet·ri·fac·tion (pet'rə fak'shən) *n.* [< PETRIFY] **1.** a petrifying or being petrified **2.** something petrified Also **pet'ri·fi·ca'tion** (-fi kā'shən) —**pet'ri·fac'tive** *adj.*

Petrified Forest National Park national park in EC Ariz., containing petrified trunks of several coniferous forests

pet·ri·fy (pet'rə fī') *vt.* -**fied'**, -**fy'ing** [< Fr. < L. *petra*, a rock + *facere*, to make] **1.** to replace the normal cells of (organic matter) with silica, etc.; re-form as a stony substance **2.** to harden or deaden [dull routine has *petrified* his imagination] **3.** to paralyze, as with fear —*vi.* to become petrified

pet·ro- [< Gr. *petra* or *petros*] *a combining form meaning* rock or stone: also, before a vowel, **petr-**

pet·ro·chem·i·cal (pet'rō kem'i k'l) *n.* [PETRO(LEUM) + CHEMICAL] a chemical derived ultimately from petroleum

pet·ro·dol·lars (pet'rō däl'ərz) *n.pl.* [PETRO(LEUM) + DOLLARS] the money accumulated by oil-exporting countries, seen as affecting the financial balance of the world

Pet·ro·grad (pet'rə grad; *Russ.* pyet'rô grät') *former name* (1914-24) *of* LENINGRAD

pe·trog·ra·phy (pi träg'rə fē) *n.* [< ModL.: see PETRO- & -GRAPHY] the science of the description or classification of rocks —**pe·trog'ra·pher** *n.* —**pet·ro·graph·ic** (pet'rə graf'ik), **pet'ro·graph'i·cal** *adj.* —**pet'ro·graph'i·cal·ly** *adv.*

pet·rol (pet'rəl) *n.* [< Fr. < ML. *petroleum*: see PETROLEUM] *Brit.* term for GASOLINE

☆**pet·ro·la·tum** (pet'rə lāt'əm, -lät'-) *n.* [ModL.: see -ATE[2]] a greasy, jellylike substance consisting of a mixture of hydrocarbons obtained from petroleum: used in ointments, etc.

pe·tro·le·um (pə trō'lē əm) *n.* [ML. < L. *petra*, a rock + *oleum*, oil] an oily, liquid solution of hydrocarbons, yellowish-green to black in color, found in the earth in layers of certain rock: it yields paraffin, fuel oil, kerosene, gasoline, benzine, etc.

☆**petroleum jelly** *same as* PETROLATUM

pe·trol·o·gy (pi träl'ə jē) *n.* [PETRO- + -LOGY] the study of the composition, structure, and origin of rocks —**pet·ro·log·ic** (pet'rə läj'ik), **pet'ro·log'i·cal** *adj.* —**pe·trol'o·gist** *n.*

pet·rous (pet'rəs, pē'trəs) *adj.* [< L. < *petra*, a rock] **1.** of or like rock; hard **2.** designating or of that part of the temporal bone which surrounds and protects the internal ear

pet·ti·coat (pet'i kōt') *n.* [< PETTY + COAT] **1.** a skirt, now esp. an underskirt, worn by women and girls **2.** [Colloq.] a woman or girl —*adj.* of or by women [*petticoat* government]

pet·ti·fog·ger (pet'ē fäg'ər, -fôg'-) *n.* [PETTY + obs. *fogger* < ?] **1.** a lawyer who handles petty cases, esp. one who uses unethical methods **2.** a person who quibbles over petty details —**pet'ti·fog'** *vi.* -**fogged'**, -**fog'ging** —**pet'ti·fog'ger·y** *n.*

pet·tish (pet′ish) *adj.* [< PET[2] + -ISH] peevish; petulant; cross —**pet′tish·ly** *adv.* —**pet′tish·ness** *n.*

pet·ty (pet′ē) *adj.* **-ti·er, -ti·est** [OFr. *petit*] **1.** relatively unimportant; trivial or minor **2.** small-minded, mean, etc. [full of *petty* spite] **3.** relatively low in rank; subordinate [a *petty* official] —**pet′ti·ly** *adv.* —**pet′ti·ness** *n.*

SYN.—**petty** is applied to that which is small, minor, unimportant, etc. compared to others of its kind, and it is frequently used to imply small-mindedness [*petty* cash; a *petty* grudge]; **trivial** applies to that which, because it is both petty and ordinary, has no special value [a *trivial* remark]; **trifling** applies to something so small and unimportant that it can be ignored [a *trifling* matter]; **paltry** applies to something so small or worthless that it deserves contempt [a *paltry* wage]; **picayune** is used of a person or thing thought of as small, mean, or insignificant [a *picayune* objection] —**ANT.** important, significant

petty cash a cash fund kept on hand to pay minor expenses

petty jury same as PETIT JURY

petty larceny see LARCENY

petty officer an enlisted person in the navy whose grade corresponds to that of a noncommissioned officer in the army

pet·u·lant (pech′oo lənt) *adj.* [< L. *petulans* < *petere*, to attack: see PETITION] showing anger or annoyance over little things; peevish —**pet′u·lance, pet′u·lan·cy** *n.* —**pet′u·lant·ly** *adv.*

pe·tu·ni·a (pə tōōn′yə, -tyōōn′-; -ē ə) *n.* [ModL. < Fr. < Tupi *petun*, tobacco] a plant of the nightshade family, with variously colored, funnel-shaped flowers

pew (pyōō) *n.* [< OFr. *puie* < L. pl. of *podium*, balcony < Gr. *podion* < *pous*, a FOOT] **1.** any of the benches with a back that are fixed in rows in a church **2.** any of the boxlike enclosures with seats, in some churches, for the use of one family, etc.

☆**pe·wee** (pē′wē) *n.* [echoic of its call] any of several small flycatchers

pe·wit (pē′wit, pyōō′it) *n.* [echoic of its call] *same as:* **1.** LAPWING ☆**2.** PEWEE

PETUNIA

pew·ter (pyōōt′ər) *n.* [< OFr. *peautre*] **1.** a dull, silvery-gray alloy of tin with brass, copper, or, esp., lead **2.** articles made of pewter, esp. dishes, tableware, etc. —**adj.** made of pewter

☆**pe·yo·te** (pā ōt′ē; *Sp.* pe yô′te) *n.* [AmSp. < Nahuatl *peyotl*, caterpillar: the cactus has a downy center] *same as* MESCAL (sense 3): also **pe·yo′tl** (-′l; *Sp.* -t′l)

pf. **1.** perfect **2.** pfennig: also **pfg.** **3.** preferred: also **pfd.**

Pfc, Pfc., PFC Private First Class

pfen·nig (fen′ig; *G.* pfen′iH) *n., pl.* **-nigs,** *G.* **-ni·ge** (-i gə) [G., akin to PENNY] *see* MONETARY UNITS, table (Germany)

☆**PG** parental guidance suggested: a motion-picture rating indicating that the film contains certain parts that parents may find unsuitable for children

pg. page

pH (pē′āch′) [< Fr. *p(ouvoir)* *h(ydrogène)*, lit., hydrogen power] *a symbol for* the degree of acidity or alkalinity of a solution, expressed as the logarithm of the reciprocal of the hydrogen-ion concentration: pH7 indicates a neutral solution, values from 7 to 0 increasing acidity, and values from 7 to 14 increasing alkalinity

Phae·dra (fē′drə) *Gr. Myth.* wife of Theseus: she loved her stepson, Hippolytus, who rejected her

Pha·ë·thon (fā′ə thən) *Gr. & Rom. Myth.* son of Helios: he tried to drive his father's sun chariot and would have set the world on fire had not Zeus struck him down with a thunderbolt

pha·e·ton, pha·ë·ton (fā′ət 'n) *n.* [< Fr. < L.: see prec.] **1.** a light, four-wheeled carriage with front and back seats and, usually, a folding top ☆**2.** *same as* TOURING CAR

-phage (fāj) [< Gr. *phagein*, to eat] *a combining form meaning* eating or destroying [bacteriophage]

phag·o- [< Gr. *phagein*, to eat] *a combining form meaning:* **1.** eating or destroying [phagocyte] **2.** phagocyte Also, before a vowel, **phag-**

phag·o·cyte (fag′ə sīt′) *n.* [PHAGO- + -CYTE] any leukocyte that absorbs and destroys other cells, microorganisms, etc. in the blood and tissues —**phag′o·cyt′ic** (-sit′ik) *adj.*

phag·o·cy·to·sis (fag′ō sī tō′sis) *n.* [ModL.: see PHAGOCYTE & -OSIS] the absorption and destruction of cells, microorganisms, etc. by phagocytes —**phag′o·cy·tot′ic** (-tät′ik) *adj.*

-pha·gous (fə gəs) [< Gr. *phagein*, to eat] *a combining form meaning* that eats (a thing specified)

-pha·gy (fə jē) [< ModL. < Gr. *phagein*, to eat] *a combining form meaning* the practice of eating (a thing specified): also **-pha·gi·a** (fā′jē ə, -jē)

pha·lan·ger (fə lan′jər) *n.* [ModL. < Gr. *phalanx*, bone between two joints: with reference to the structure of the hind feet] any of various small Australian marsupials with a long, bushy tail

pha·lanx (fā′laŋks, fal′aŋks) *n., pl.* **-lanx·es;** also, & for 4 always, **pha·lan·ges** (fə lan′jēz) [L. < Gr., line of battle: see BALK] **1.** an ancient military formation of infantry in close ranks with shields together **2.** a group of individuals massed close together **3.** a group of individuals joined together for a common purpose **4.** any of the bones of the fingers or toes: see illustration at SKELETON —**pha·lan·ge·al** (fə lan′jē əl) *adj.*

PHALANGER
(to 3 ft. long, including tail)

phal·a·rope (fal′ə rōp′) *n.* [Fr. < ModL. < Gr. *phalaris*, coot + *pous*, foot] a small swimming and wading bird that resembles the sandpiper

phal·lus (fal′əs) *n., pl.* **-li** (-ī), **-lus·es** [L. < Gr. *phallos*] the penis, esp. as a symbol of reproduction in certain religions —**phal′lic** (-ik) *adj.*

phan·tasm (fan′taz'm) *n.* [< OFr. < L. < Gr. *phantasma* < *phantazein*, to show: see FANTASY] **1.** something that one imagines is real, but that exists only in the mind; esp., a specter, or ghost **2.** a deceptive likeness —**phan·tas′mal** (-taz′m'l), **phan·tas′mic** *adj.*

phan·tas·ma·go·ri·a (fan taz′mə gôr′ē ə) *n.* [< Fr. < Gr. *phantasma*, phantasm + *ageirein*, to assemble] **1.** a rapidly changing series of things seen or imagined, as in a dream **2.** any rapidly changing scene —**phan·tas′ma·go′ric, phan·tas′ma·go′ri·cal** *adj.*

phan·ta·sy (fan′tə sē) *n., pl.* **-sies** *same as* FANTASY

phan·tom (fan′təm) *n.* [< OFr. *fantosme:* see PHANTASM] **1.** something not real that one seems to see; apparition; specter **2.** something feared [the *phantom* of poverty] **3.** something that exists only in the mind; illusion [the cynical belief that happiness is a mere *phantom*] **4.** a person or thing that is not really what it seems to be or should be [a *phantom* of a leader] —**adj.** of, like, or constituting a phantom; illusory [*phantom* ships in the fog]

Phar·aoh (fer′ō) *n.* [ult. < Egypt. *pr-′o*, great house] the title of the rulers of ancient Egypt

Phar·i·sa·ic (far′ə sā′ik) *adj.* **1.** of the Pharisees **2.** [p-] *a)* observing the letter but not the spirit of religious law *b)* pretending to be highly moral without actually being so; hypocritical: also **phar′i·sa′i·cal** —**phar′i·sa′i·cal·ly** *adv.*

Phar·i·sa·ism (far′ə sā′iz'm) *n.* **1.** the beliefs and practices of the Pharisees **2.** [p-] pharisaic behavior, principles, character, etc.

Phar·i·see (far′ə sē′) *n.* **1.** a member of an ancient Jewish party that carefully observed the written law but also accepted the oral, or traditional, law **2.** [p-] a pharisaic person —**Phar′i·see′ism** *n.*

Pharm., pharm. **1.** pharmaceutical **2.** pharmacist **3.** pharmacopeia **4.** pharmacy

phar·ma·ceu·ti·cal (fär′mə sōōt′i k'l, -syōōt′-) *adj.* [< LL. < Gr., ult. < *pharmakon*, a medicine] **1.** of pharmacy or pharmacists **2.** of or by drugs Also **phar′ma·ceu′tic** —*n.* a pharmaceutical product; drug —**phar′ma·ceu′ti·cal·ly** *adv.*

phar·ma·ceu·tics (-iks) *n.pl.* [*with sing. v.*] *same as* PHARMACY (sense 1)

phar·ma·cist (fär′mə sist) *n.* a person licensed to practice pharmacy; druggist

phar·ma·col·o·gy (fär′mə käl′ə jē) *n.* [< ModL. < Gr. *pharmakon*, a drug] **1.** orig., the study of the preparation, qualities, and uses of drugs **2.** the science dealing with the effects of drugs —**phar′ma·co·log′i·cal** (-kə läj′i k'l) *adj.* —**phar′ma·co·log′i·cal·ly** *adv.* —**phar′ma·col′o·gist** *n.*

phar·ma·co·pe·ia, phar·ma·co·poe·ia (fär′mə kə pē′ə) *n.* [ModL. < Gr. < *pharmakon*, a drug + *poiein*, to make] an official book containing a list of drugs and medicines and the lawful standards for their production, distribution, etc. —**phar′ma·co·pe′ial, phar′ma·co·poe′ial** *adj.*

phar·ma·cy (fär′mə sē) *n., pl.* **-cies** [< MFr. < LL. < Gr. < *pharmakon*, a drug] **1.** the art or profession of preparing and giving out drugs and medicines **2.** a place where this is done; drugstore

Pha·ros (fer′äs) small peninsula at Alexandria, Egypt: in ancient times it was an island with a large lighthouse on it

phar·yn·gi·tis (far′in jīt′əs) *n.* inflammation of the mucous membrane of the pharynx; sore throat

phar·ynx (far′iŋks) *n., pl.* **phar′ynx·es, pha·ryn·ges** (fə rin′jēz) [ModL. < Gr. *pharynx:* for IE. base see BORE¹] the cavity leading from the mouth and nasal passages to the larynx and esophagus: see illustration at EPIGLOTTIS —**pha·ryn·ge·al** (fə rin′jē əl, far′ən jē′əl), *adj.*

phase (fāz) *n.* [< ModL. < Gr. *phasis < phainesthai,* to appear: for IE. base see BEACON] **1.** any stage in the illumination or appearance of the moon or a planet **2.** any stage or form in a series of changes, as in development [adolescence is a *phase* we all go through] **3.** any of the ways in which something may be looked at, thought about, or shown; aspect [to study all *phases* of the problem] **4.** *Chem.* a solid, liquid, or gaseous homogeneous form [ice is a *phase* of H₂O] **5.** *Physics* the part of a cycle through which a periodic wave, as of light, sound, etc., has advanced at any instant, measured from a given starting point —*vt.* **phased, phas′ing** to plan, introduce, carry out, etc. in phases, or stages (often with *in, into,* etc.) —*vi.* to move by phases —**in** (or **out of**) **phase** *Physics* having (or not having) the same rate and phase, as sound waves —☆**phase out** to bring or come to an end, or withdraw from use, by stages —**pha·sic** (fā′zik) *adj.*

phase modulation *Radio* variation in the phase of a carrier wave in accordance with some signal, as speech

☆**phase-out** (fāz′out′) *n.* a phasing out; gradual ending, withdrawal, etc.

Ph.D. [L. *Philosophiae Doctor*] Doctor of Philosophy

pheas·ant (fez′'nt) *n., pl.* **-ants, -ant:** see PLURAL, II, D, 1 [< Anglo-Fr. < OFr. < L. < Gr. *phasianos,* lit., (bird) of *Phasis,* river in Asia] **1.** a game bird with a long tail and brightly colored feathers ☆**2.** any of various birds resembling the pheasant, as the ruffed grouse

RING-NECKED PHEASANT
(to 35 in. long, including beak and tail)

phel·lem (fel′em) *n.* [< Gr. *phellos*] same as CORK (n. 4)

phel·lo·gen (fel′ə jən) *n.* [< Gr. *phellos,* cork + -GEN] same as CORK CAMBIUM —**phel′lo·ge·net′ic** (-jə net′ik), **phel′lo·gen′ic** (-jen′ik) *adj.*

phen- [< Fr. < Gr. *phainein,* to show] *a combining form meaning* of or derived from benzene: also **phe·no-**

phe·nac·e·tin (fi nas′ə tin) *n.* [PHEN- + ACET(O)- + -IN¹] same as ACETOPHENETIDIN

phe·no·bar·bi·tal (fē′nə bär′bə tôl′, fē′nō-) *n.* [PHEN(O)- + BARBITAL] an odorless, white powder, C₁₂O₃N₂H₁₂, used as a sedative and for relieving spasms

phe·no·cop·y (fē′nə käp′ē) *n., pl.* **-ies** [PHENO(TYPE) + COPY] *Genetics* a change in an organism that is brought about by the environment and that is similar to a mutation but is not hereditary

phe·nol (fē′nōl, -nôl, -näl) *n.* [PHEN- + -OL¹] **1.** a white, crystalline compound, C₆H₅OH, produced from coal tar and used in making explosives, etc.: a weak solution of phenol in water is commonly called carbolic acid **2.** any of a group of hydroxyl derivatives of benzene similar in structure to phenol —**phe·no·lic** (fi nō′lik, -näl′ik) *adj.*

phenolic resin any of a group of thermosetting resins formed by condensing phenol with various aldehydes, as formaldehyde

phe·nol·phthal·ein (fē′nōl thal′ēn, -nôl-; -fthal′-; -ē ən) *n.* [< PHENOL + NAPHTHALENE] a white to pale-yellow, crystalline powder, C₂₀H₁₄O₄, used as a laxative, in making dyes, and as an acid-base indicator in chemical analysis: it is red in a solution containing a base and colorless in an acid solution

phe·nom·e·na (fi näm′ə nə) *n. pl. of* PHENOMENON

phe·nom·e·nal (fi näm′ə n'l) *adj.* **1.** of or making up a phenomenon or phenomena **2.** very unusual; extraordinary [a *phenomenal* success] —**phe·nom′e·nal·ly** *adv.*

phe·nom·e·non (fi näm′ə nän′, -nən) *n., pl.* **-na** (-nə); also, esp. for 2 and 3, **-nons′** [< LL. < Gr. *phainomenon,* neut. prp. of *phainesthai,* to appear: see FANTASY] **1.** any fact or experience that can be seen, heard, etc. and scientifically described, as an eclipse **2.** anything extremely unusual **3.** [Colloq.] a person who is extraordinary in some way

phe·no·type (fē′nə tīp′) *n.* [G. *phänotypus*] *Biol.* all of the observable characteristics of an organism, resulting from both its heredity and its environment —**phe′no·typ′ic** (-tip′ik), **phe′no·typ′i·cal** *adj.* —**phe′no·typ′i·cal·ly** *adv.*

phen·yl (fen′il, fē′nil) *n.* [PHEN- + -YL] the monovalent radical, C₆H₅, forming the basis of phenol, benzene, aniline, and some other compounds

phen·yl·al·a·nine (fen′il al′ə nēn′, fē′nil-) *n.* an essential amino acid, C₉H₁₁O₂N, occurring in proteins

phen·yl·ke·to·nu·ri·a (-kēt′ə nyoor′ē ə) *n.* [PHENYL + KETON(E) + -URIA] an inherited disorder in which phenylalanine accumulates in the body and which, if untreated, causes severe mental retardation in infants

phew (fyoo, fyoo) *interj.* a breathy sound expressing disgust, surprise, relief, etc.

phi (fī, fē) *n.* [MGr.] the 21st letter of the Greek alphabet (Φ, φ)

phi·al (fī′əl) *n.* [< OFr. < Pr. < ML. < L. < Gr. *phialē,* shallow bowl] a small glass bottle; vial

☆**Phi Be·ta Kap·pa** (fī′ bāt′ə kap′ə, bēt′ə) **1.** an honorary society of U.S. college students of high scholastic rank **2.** a member of this society

Phid·i·as (fid′ē əs) 5th cent. B.C.; Gr. sculptor —**Phid′i·an** *adj.*

Phil. **1.** Philippians **2.** Philippine

Phil·a·del·phi·a (fil′ə del′fē ə, -fyə) [Gr. *philadelphia,* brotherly love < *philos,* loving + *adelphos,* brother] city & port in SE Pa.: pop. 1,949,000 (met. area 4,818,000) —**Phil′a·del′phi·an** *adj., n.*

phi·lan·der (fi lan′dər) *vi.* [< Gr. < *philos,* loving + *andros,* genitive of *anēr,* a man] to take part casually in one quick love affair after another: said of a man —**phi·lan′der·er** *n.*

phil·an·throp·ic (fil′ən thräp′ik) *adj.* of, showing, or consisting of philanthropy; charitable; benevolent; humane: also **phil′an·throp′i·cal** —**phil′an·throp′i·cal·ly** *adv.*

phi·lan·thro·py (fi lan′thrə pē) *n.* [< LL. < Gr. < *philein,* to love + *anthrōpos,* man] **1.** a desire to help mankind, as by gifts to charitable or humanitarian institutions **2.** *pl.* **-pies** a philanthropic act, gift, institution, etc. —**phi·lan′thro·pist** *n.*

phi·lat·e·ly (fi lat′'l ē) *n.* [< Fr. < Gr. *philos,* loving + *ateleia,* a being free from tax (that is, with "postage prepaid")] the collection and study of postage stamps, postmarks, etc., usually as a hobby —**phil·a·tel·ic** (fil′ə tel′ik) *adj.* —**phil′a·tel′i·cal·ly** *adv.* —**phi·lat′e·list** *n.*

-phile (fīl, fil) [< Gr. *philos,* loving] *a combining form meaning* one who loves or likes [Anglophile]: also **-phil** (fil)

Phi·le·mon (fi lē′mən, fī-) a book of the New Testament, an epistle from the Apostle Paul to his friend Philemon: abbrev. **Philem.**

phil·har·mon·ic (fil′här män′ik, fil′ər-) *adj.* [< Fr. < Gr. *philos,* loving + *harmonia,* harmony] loving or devoted to music: used in the title of some symphony orchestras —*n.* **1.** a society formed to sponsor a symphony orchestra **2.** [Colloq.] such an orchestra or one of its concerts

-phil·i·a (fil′ē ə, fil′yə) [< Gr. *philos,* loving] *a combining form meaning:* **1.** tendency toward [hemophilia] **2.** strong or abnormal attraction to [Anglophilia, coprophilia]

Phil·ip (fil′əp) [< L. < Gr. < *philos,* loving + *hippos,* a horse] **1.** a masculine name: dim. *Phil:* also sp. **Phil′lip 2.** *Bible* one of the twelve apostles **3. Philip II** *a)* 382–336 B.C.; king of Macedonia (359–336): father of ALEXANDER THE GREAT *b)* 1165–1223; king of France (1180–1223) *c)* 1527–98; king of Spain (1556–98): sent the Armada against England (1588)

Phi·lip·pi (fi lip′ī) ancient city in Macedonia —**Phi·lip′pi·an** (-ē ən) *adj., n.*

Phi·lip·pi·ans (-ē ənz) a book of the New Testament, an epistle from the Apostle Paul to the Christians of Philippi

Phi·lip·pic (fi lip′ik) *n.* **1.** any of the speeches of Demosthenes against Philip, king of Macedon **2.** [p-] any bitter verbal attack

Phil·ip·pine (fil′ə pēn′) *adj.* of the Philippine Islands or their people

Philippine mahogany the reddish wood of various trees of the Philippines and southeastern Asia

Phil·ip·pines (fil′ə pēnz′) country occupying a group of c. 7,100 islands (**Philippine Islands**) in the SW Pacific off the SE coast of Asia: 114,830 sq. mi.; pop. 43,751,000; cap. Manila

Phi·lis·ti·a (fə lis′tē ə) country of the Philistines, in ancient SW Palestine

Phil·is·tine (fil′is tēn′; fi lis′tin, -tēn) *n.* **1.** a member of a non-Semitic people who lived in Philistia and repeatedly warred with the Israelites **2.** [*often* p-] a person thought of as narrow-minded and conventional, with no interest in cultural values, etc. —*adj.* **1.** of the ancient Philistines **2.** [*often* p-] narrow-minded and conventional, lacking in culture, etc. — **Phil′is·tin·ism** *n.*

Phil·lips (fil′əps) [after H. *Phillips* (?–1958), its U.S. developer] ☆*a trademark for* a screwdriver (**Phillips screwdriver**) with a tip that can be used on a screw (**Phillips screw**) that has two slots crossing at the center of the head

phil·o- [< Gr. *philos*, loving] *a combining form meaning* loving, liking, having a preference for [*philology*] : also, before a vowel, **phil-**

phil·o·den·dron (fil′ə den′drən) *n.* [ModL. < Gr. *philos*, loving + *dendron*, a tree] a tropical American vine of the arum family, often with heart-shaped leaves

PHILLIPS SCREW & SCREWDRIVER

phi·lol·o·gy (fi läl′ə jē) *n.* [< Fr. < L. < Gr. *philologia*, love of literature < *philein*, to love + *logos*: see LOGIC] **1.** the study of literary texts and other written records in order to determine their genuineness, meaning, etc. **2.** *earlier term for* LINGUISTICS —**phil·o·log·i·cal** (fil′ə läj′i k′l), **phil′o·log′ic** *adj.* —**phil′o·log′i·cal·ly** *adv.* —**phi·lol′o·gist** *n.*

philos. philosophy

phi·los·o·pher (fi läs′ə fər) *n.* [< OFr. < L. < Gr. *philos*, loving + *sophos*, wise] **1.** a person who studies or is an expert in philosophy **2.** a person who lives by a system of philosophy **3.** a person who meets difficulties in a calm, brave way

philosophers' (or **philosopher's**) **stone** an imaginary substance that alchemists believed would change base metals such as lead and iron into gold or silver

phil·o·soph·ic (fil′ə säf′ik) *adj.* **1.** of or according to a philosophy or philosopher **2.** like or suited for a philosopher **3.** calm, as in a difficult situation; reasonable [she was *philosophic* about losing her purse] Also **phil′o·soph′i·cal** — **phil′o·soph′i·cal·ly** *adv.*

phi·los·o·phize (fi läs′ə fīz′) *vi.* -phized′, -phiz′ing **1.** to think or reason like a philosopher **2.** to talk or write about philosophic ideas, matters of right and wrong, etc., esp. in a rambling or superficial way —**phi·los′o·phiz′er** *n.*

phi·los·o·phy (-fē) *n., pl.* -phies [< OFr. < L. < Gr.: see PHILOSOPHER] **1.** the study of the basic nature of conduct, thought, knowledge, existence, and reality [*philosophy* includes ethics, logic, metaphysics, etc.] **2.** the general principles of a field of knowledge [the *philosophy* of economics] **3.** a particular system of principles for the conduct of life [Plato's *philosophy*] **4.** *a*) a study of human morals, character, and behavior *b*) calmness of mind or manner thought of as resulting from this

-phi·lous (fi ləs) [< Gr. *philos*, loving] *a combining form meaning* loving, liking

phil·ter (fil′tər) *n.* [< MFr. < L. < Gr. *philtron* < *philein*, to love] **1.** a potion or charm that is supposed to arouse sexual love, esp. toward a specific person **2.** any magic potion

phle·bi·tis (fli bīt′is) *n.* [see PHLEBO- & -ITIS] inflammation of a vein —**phle·bit′ic** (-bit′ik) *adj.*

phleb·o- [< Gr. *phlebos*, genitive of *phleps*, a vein] *a combining form meaning* vein: also, before a vowel, **phleb-**

phle·bot·o·my (fli bät′ə mē) *n., pl.* -mies [< OFr. < LL. < Gr.: see prec. & -TOMY] the act of opening a vein and letting out blood in certain medical procedures —**phle·bot′o·mist** *n.*

phlegm (flem) *n.* [< MFr. < LL. < Gr. *phlegma*, inflammation < *phlegein*, to burn: for IE. base see BLACK] **1.** the thick, stringy substance secreted by the mucous glands of the breathing passages and coughed up, as during a cold **2.** [Obs.] that one of the four humors believed to cause sluggishness **3.** *a*) sluggishness *b*) calmness; composure —**phlegm′y** *adj.*

phleg·mat·ic (fleg mat′ik) *adj.* [ult. < Gr. *phlegma*, inflam-

mation: see PHLEGM (sense 2)] hard to make excited or active; specif., *a*) sluggish; dull *b*) calm; cool —see **SYN.** at IMPASSIVE — **phleg·mat′i·cal·ly** *adv.*

phlo·em (flō′em) *n.* [G. < Gr. *phloos*, bark] the cell tissue serving as a path for the distribution of food material in a plant

phlo·gis·ton (flō jis′tän, -tən) *n.* [ModL., ult. < Gr. *phlegein*, to burn] an imaginary element formerly believed to cause burning and to be given off by anything burning

phlox (fläks) *n.* [ModL. < L. < Gr. *phlox*, a flame < *phlegein*, to burn] any of a group of chiefly N. American plants, with opposite leaves and white, pink, red, or bluish flowers

Phnom Penh (p′nôm′ pen′) capital of Cambodia, on the Mekong River: pop. c. 600,000: also **Pnom-Penh**

-phobe (fōb) [Fr. < L. < Gr. < *phobos*, a fear] *a suffix meaning* one who fears or hates [*Francophobe*]

pho·bi·a (fō′bē ə) *n.* [< Gr. *phobos*, a fear] a strong, unreasonable, continuing fear of some particular thing or situation —**pho′bic** *adj.*

-pho·bi·a (fō′bē ə) [see prec.] *a combining form meaning* fear, dread, hatred [*claustrophobia*]

PHLOX

Phoe·be (fē′bē) [L. < Gr. < *phoibos*, bright] **1.** a feminine name **2.** *Gr. Myth.* same as ARTEMIS

☆**phoe·be** (fē′bē) *n.* [echoic, but spelling influenced by the prec.] any of several American flycatchers with a gray or brown back, a light-yellow breast, and a short tuft of feathers on its head

Phoe·bus (fē′bəs) *Gr. Myth.* same as APOLLO

Phoe·ni·cia (fə nish′ə, -nē′shə) ancient region of city-states at the E end of the Mediterranean, in the region of present-day Syria & Lebanon

Phoe·ni·cian (-nish′ən, -nē′shən) *adj.* of Phoenicia, its people, their language, etc. —*n.* **1.** a native of Phoenicia **2.** the ancient Semitic language of the Phoenicians, related to Hebrew

Phoe·nix (fē′niks) [in allusion to the bird (see next entry)] capital of Ariz., in the SC part: pop. 582,000 (met. area 968,000)

phoe·nix (fē′niks) *n.* [< OE. & OFr. *fenix* < L. *phoenix* < Gr. *phoinix*] *Egyptian Myth.* a beautiful bird which lived for 500 or 600 years and then burned itself to death and rose out of its own ashes to start another long life: a symbol of immortality

phon (fän) *n.* [< Gr. *phōnē*, a sound] a measure of the apparent loudness of a sound

phone¹ (fōn) *n.* [Gr. *phōnē*, a sound] any single speech sound: a phoneme is composed of phones

☆**phone²** (fōn) *n., vt., vi.* phoned, phon′ing *shortened form of* TELEPHONE

-phone (fōn) [< Gr. *phōnē*, a sound] *a combining form meaning*: **1.** a device producing or transmitting sound [*saxophone*] **2.** a telephone [*radiophone*]

pho·neme (fō′nēm) *n.* [< Fr. < Gr. *phōnēma*, a sound < *phōnē*, a voice] *Linguis.* a set of similar but slightly different sounds in a language that are heard as the same sound and represented by the same symbol, as the sounds of *p* in *pin*, *spin*, and *tip* —**pho·ne·mic** (fə nē′mik, fō-) *adj.*

pho·ne·mics (fə nē′miks, fō-) *n.pl.* [with *sing. v.*] **1.** the branch of language study dealing with the phonemic systems of languages **2.** the description and classification of the phonemes of a language —**pho·ne′mi·cist** (-mə sist) *n.*

pho·net·ic (fə net′ik, fō-) *adj.* [< ModL. < Gr. < *phōnētos*, to be spoken, ult. < *phōnē*, a sound] **1.** of or showing speech sounds [*phonetic* symbols] **2.** of phonetics **3.** according to pronunciation ["tuf" is a *phonetic* spelling of "tough"] —**pho·net′i·cal·ly** *adv.*

pho·net·ics (-iks) *n.pl.* [with *sing. v.*] **1.** the branch of language study dealing with speech sounds and with their representation by written symbols **2.** the system of speech sounds of a particular language —**pho·ne·ti·cian** (fō′nə tish′ən) *n.*

☆**pho·ney** (fō′nē) *adj., n.* [Colloq.] same as PHONY

phon·ic (fän′ik) *adj.* [< Gr. *phōnē*, a sound] **1.** of, or having the nature of, sound; esp., of speech sounds **2.** of or having to do with phonics —**phon′i·cal·ly** *adv.*

phon·ics (fän′iks) *n.pl.* [with *sing. v.*] [< prec.] a method of teaching beginners to read by learning the usual sounds of certain letters or groups of letters

pho·no- [< Gr. *phōnē*, a sound] *a combining form meaning* sound, speech: also, before a vowel, **phon-**

pho·no·gram (fō′nə gram′) *n.* [PHONO- + -GRAM] a symbol representing a word, syllable, or sound, as in shorthand —**pho′-no·gram′ic, pho′no·gram′mic** *adj.* —**pho′no·gram′i·cal·ly, pho′no·gram′mi·cal·ly** *adv.*

pho·no·graph (fō′nə graf′) *n.* [PHONO- + -GRAPH] ☆an instrument for reproducing sound that has been transcribed in a spiral groove on a disk: a needle or stylus follows the groove in the revolving disk and picks up and transmits the sound vibrations

pho·no·graph·ic (fō′nə graf′ik) *adj.* ☆1. of a phonograph or the sounds made by one 2. of phonography —**pho′no·graph′i·cal·ly** *adv.*

pho·nog·ra·phy (fō näg′rə fē) *n.* [PHONO- + -GRAPHY] 1. a written representation of the sounds of speech 2. any system of shorthand based on a phonetic transcription of speech

pho·nol·o·gy (fō näl′ə jē, fə-) *n.* [PHONO- + -LOGY] 1. phonetics or phonemics or, esp., both considered as a system of the speech sounds of a language 2. the study of the changes in speech sounds in the development of a language or dialect —**pho·no·log·i·cal** (fō′nə läj′i k'l), pho′no·log′ic *adj.* —**pho′no·log′i·cal·ly** *adv.* —**pho·nol′o·gist** *n.*

pho·non (fō′nän) *n.* [PHON(O)- + -on, as in PHOTON] a quantum of sound energy that is a carrier of heat

☆**pho·ny** (fō′nē) *adj.* **-ni·er, -ni·est** [< Brit. thieves' argot *fawney,* a gilt ring (passed off as gold) < Ir. *fáinne*] [Colloq.] not genuine; false, counterfeit, insincere, etc. —*n., pl.* **-nies** [Colloq.] 1. something not genuine; fake 2. a person who deceives, behaves hypocritically, is insincere, etc.; fraud —**pho′ni·ness** *n.*

-phore (fôr) [< ModL. < Gr. *-phoros* < *pherein,* to BEAR¹] *a combining form meaning* bearer, producer

-phor·ous (fər əs) [see prec.] *a combining form meaning* bearing, producing

phos·gene (fäs′jēn) *n.* [< Gr. *phōs,* light + *-gene* (for -GEN)] a colorless, volatile liquid, COCl₂, used as a poison gas, in making dyes, etc.

phos·pha·tase (fäs′fə tās′) *n.* [< PHOSPHATE + -ASE] an enzyme found in body tissues and fluids that frees phosphate ions from certain organic compounds

phos·phate (fäs′fāt) *n.* [Fr.] 1. a salt or ester of phosphoric acid 2. a fertilizer containing phosphates ☆3. a soft drink made with soda water, syrup, and, originally, a few drops of phosphoric acid —**phos·phat′ic** (-fat′ik) *adj.*

phos·pha·tide (fäs′fə tīd′) *n.* [PHOSPHAT(E) + -IDE] any of a group of fatty compounds, as lecithin, found in animal and plant cells

phos·phide (-fīd) *n.* a compound consisting of trivalent phosphorus and another element or a radical

phos·phite (-fīt) *n.* [Fr.] a salt or ester of phosphorous acid

phos·pho- [< PHOSPHORUS] *a combining form meaning* phosphorus or phosphoric acid: also, before a vowel, **phosph-**

phos·pho·lip·id (fäs′fō lip′id) *n.* [PHOSPHO- + LIPID] *same as* PHOSPHATIDE: also **phos′pho·lip′ide** (-īd)

Phos·phor (fäs′fər) [see PHOSPHORUS] [Poet.] the morning star, esp. Venus —*n.* [p-] 1. *same as* PHOSPHORUS: now esp. in **phosphor bronze,** a bronze with a small amount of phosphorus in it 2. a phosphorescent or fluorescent substance

phos·pho·resce (fäs′fə res′) *vi.* **-resced′, -resc′ing** to show or undergo phosphorescence

phos·pho·res·cence (-res′'ns) *n.* [Fr.: see PHOSPHORUS & -ESCENT] 1. *a)* the condition or property of giving off light after exposure to radiant energy, as light, X-rays, etc. *b)* such light 2. a giving off of light without noticeable heat, as phosphorus does —**phos′pho·res′cent** *adj.*

phos·pho·ret·ed, phos·pho·ret·ted (fäs′fə ret′id) *adj.* combined with phosphorus: also **phos′phu·ret′ed** (-fyoo-), **phos′phu·ret′ted**

phos·phor·ic (fäs fôr′ik, -fär′-) *adj.* of, like, or containing phosphorus, esp. with a valence of five

phosphoric acid any of several oxygen acids of phosphorus

phos·pho·rous (fäs′fər əs, fäs fôr′əs) *adj.* of, like, or containing phosphorus, esp. with a valence of three

phosphorous acid a white or yellowish, crystalline acid, H₃PO₃, that absorbs oxygen readily

phos·pho·rus (fäs′fər əs) *n.* [ModL. < L. *Phosphorus,* morning star < Gr. < *phōs,* a light + *pherein,* to bear] 1. orig., any phosphorescent substance or object 2. a nonmetallic chemical element, normally a white, phosphorescent, waxy solid that becomes yellow when exposed to light: it is poisonous and starts burning at room temperature: when heated in sealed tubes it is changed into a red form which is nonpoisonous and less flammable than the white: symbol, P; at. wt., 30.9738; at. no., 15: a radioactive isotope (**phosphorus 32**) is used in medical treatment, as a tracer in research, etc.

pho·tic (fōt′ik) *adj.* [< Gr. *phōtos,* genitive of *phōs,* a light + -IC] of light, esp. in its effect on organisms

photic zone the uppermost layer in a body of water into which daylight enters in amounts large enough to influence living organisms, esp. by allowing photosynthesis

pho·to (fōt′ō) *n., pl.* **-tos** *clipped form of* PHOTOGRAPH

pho·to- [< Gr. *phōtos,* genitive of *phōs,* a light] *a combining form meaning:* 1. of or produced by light [*photograph*] 2. of a photograph or photography

pho·to·cell (fōt′ə sel′) *n. same as* PHOTOELECTRIC CELL

pho·to·chem·is·try (fōt′ō kem′is trē) *n.* the branch of chemistry having to do with the effect of light or other forms of radiant energy in producing chemical action —**pho′to·chem′i·cal** (-i k'l) *adj.*

pho·to·co·ag·u·la·tion (-kō ag′yoo lā′shən) *n.* a technique using intense light energy, as from a laser, to produce scar tissue: used in treating certain eye disorders, in medical and biological research, etc. —**pho′to·co·ag′u·la′tor** *n.*

pho·to·com·po·si·tion (-käm′pə zish′ən) *n.* any of various methods of preparing matter for printing by projecting light images of the letters on a photosensitive surface to produce a negative from which plates can be made —**pho′to·com·pose′** (-kəm pōz′) *vt.* **-posed′, -pos′ing**

pho·to·con·duc·tive (-kən duk′tiv) *adj.* designating or of a substance, as selenium, with an ability to conduct electricity that varies depending on the amount of radiation striking it —**pho′to·con·duc′tor** *n.*

pho·to·cop·y (fōt′ə käp′ē) *n., pl.* **-cop′ies** a photographic copy of printed or other graphic material —*vt.* **-cop′ied, -cop′y·ing** to make a photocopy of

pho·to·e·lec·tric (fōt′ō i lek′trik) *adj.* of or having to do with the electric effects produced by light or other radiation, esp. as in the discharge of electrons by certain substances when subjected to radiation of suitable wavelength

☆**photoelectric cell** any device in which light controls the discharge of electrons from a cathode, the electrical resistance of an element, etc.: usually used in an electric circuit for mechanical devices, as for opening doors, setting off alarms, etc.; electric eye

pho·to·e·lec·tron (-i lek′trän) *n.* an electron discharged by a photoelectric effect

pho·to·en·grav·ing (-in grā′viŋ) *n.* 1. a photomechanical process by which photographs are reproduced in relief on printing plates 2. a plate so made 3. a print from such a plate —**pho′to·en·grave′** *vt.* **-graved′, -grav′ing** —**pho′to·en·grav′er** *n.*

photo finish 1. a race so close that the winner can be determined only by means of a photograph taken at the finish line 2. any close finish of a game, contest, etc.

pho·to·fin·ish·ing (-fin′ish iŋ) *n.* the process of developing exposed photographic film, making prints, etc. —**pho′to·fin′ish·er** *n.*

pho·to·flash (fōt′ə flash′) *adj. Photog.* designating or of a light, esp. a flashbulb, electrically synchronized with the shutter —*n.* a photoflash bulb, lamp, photograph, etc.

pho·to·flood (-flud′) *adj. Photog.* designating or of a high-intensity electric lamp used in photography for sustained illumination —*n.* a photoflood bulb, lamp, photograph, etc.

PHOTO FINISH

photog. 1. photographic 2. photography

pho·to·gen·ic (fōt′ə jen′ik) *adj.* [PHOTO- + -GENIC] 1. giving off light 2. that looks or is likely to look attractive in photographs: said esp. of a person —**pho′to·gen′i·cal·ly** *adv.*

pho·to·gram·me·try (-gram′ə trē) *n.* [*photogram* (var. of PHOTOGRAPH) + -METRY] the art or process of surveying or measuring an area of land by taking aerial photographs

pho·to·graph (fōt′ə graf′) *n.* a picture made by photography —*vt.* to take a photograph of —*vi.* **1.** to take photographs **2.** to appear (as specified) in photographs [it will *photograph* better in direct sunlight] —**pho·tog·ra·pher** (fə täg′rə fər) *n.*

pho·to·graph·ic (fōt′ə graf′ik) *adj.* **1.** of or like a photograph or photography [in *photographic* detail] **2.** used in or made by photography [*photographic* equipment] **3.** able to remember in exact detail [a *photographic* mind] —**pho′to·graph′i·cal·ly** *adv.*

pho·tog·ra·phy (fə täg′rə fē) *n.* [PHOTO- + -GRAPHY] the art or process of producing images of objects upon a photosensitive surface (as film in a camera) by the chemical action of light or other radiant energy

pho·to·gra·vure (fōt′ə grə vyoor′) *n.* [Fr.] **1.** a photomechanical process by which photographs are reproduced on intaglio printing plates **2.** a plate so made **3.** a print from such a plate, usually with a satinlike finish

pho·to·jour·nal·ism (-jur′n'l iz'm) *n.* journalism in which news stories, etc. are presented mainly through photographs — **pho′to·jour′nal·ist** *n.*

pho·to·li·thog·ra·phy (-li thäg′rə fē) *n.* a printing process combining photography and lithography

pho·tol·y·sis (fō täl′ə sis) *n.* [see PHOTO- & -LYSIS] chemical separation into basic parts due to the action of light

pho·to·me·chan·i·cal (fōt′ə mə kan′i k'l) *adj.* designating or of any process by which printing plates are made by a photographic method —**pho′to·me·chan′i·cal·ly** *adv.*

pho·tom·e·ter (fō täm′ə tər) *n.* [PHOTO- + -METER] a device used to measure the intensity of light

pho·tom·e·try (-trē) *n.* the measurement of the intensity of light, esp. as a branch of optics —**pho·to·met·ric** (fōt′ə met′rik) *adj.* —**pho′to·met′ri·cal·ly** *adv.*

pho·to·mi·cro·graph (fōt′ə mī′krə graf′) *n.* [PHOTO- + MICROGRAPH] a photograph taken through a microscope —**pho′to·mi·cro·graph′ic** *adj.* —**pho′to·mi·crog′ra·phy** (-mī kräg′rə fē) *n.*

pho·to·mon·tage (fōt′ə män täzh′, -mōn-) *n.* montage done in or with photographs

pho·to·mul·ti·pli·er (-mul′tə plī′ər) *n.* an electron tube sensitive to light or other radiation and designed to amplify the electrons emitted from the cathode and convert them into brighter light, an electric signal, etc.

pho·to·mu·ral (-myoor′əl) *n.* a very large photograph used as a mural

☆**pho·ton** (fō′tän) *n.* [PHOT(O)- + (ELECTR)ON] a quantum of electromagnetic energy, as of light, X-rays, etc., having both particle and wave behavior

pho·to·off·set (fōt′ō ôf′set′) *n.* a method of offset printing in which the text or pictures are photographically transferred to a metal plate from which inked impressions are made on the rubber roller

pho·to·pi·a (fō tō′pē ə) *n.* [< PHOTO- + -OPIA] adjustment of the eye to bright light —**pho·to′pic** (-tō′pik, -täp′ik) *adj.*

pho·to·re·cep·tor (-ri sep′tər) *n.* Biol. a sense organ, as an eye, specialized to detect light —**pho′to·re·cep′tive** *adj.*

pho·to·re·con·nais·sance (-ri kän′ə səns) *n.* Mil. reconnaissance by means of aerial photographs

pho·to·sen·si·tive (-sen′sə tiv) *adj.* reacting or sensitive to radiant energy, esp. to light —**pho′to·sen′si·tiv′i·ty** *n.* —**pho′to·sen′si·tize′** (-tīz′) *vt.* **-tized′, -tiz′ing**

pho·to·sphere (fōt′ə sfir′) *n.* [PHOTO- + SPHERE] the visible surface of the sun —**pho′to·spher′ic** (-sfer′ik) *adj.*

☆**Pho·to·stat** (-stat′) [PHOTO- + -STAT] *a trademark for* a device for making photographic copies of printed matter, drawings, etc. directly as positives upon special paper —*n.* [p-] a copy so made —*vt.* [p-] **-stat′ed** *or* **-stat′ted, -stat′ing** *or* **-stat′ting** to make a photostat of —**pho′to·stat′ic** *adj.*

pho·to·syn·the·sis (fōt′ə sin′thə sis) *n.* the formation in green plants of organic substances, chiefly sugars, from carbon dioxide and water in the presence of light and chlorophyll —**pho·to·syn′the·size′** (-sīz′) *vt., vi.* **-sized′, -siz′ing** —**pho·to·syn·thet′ic** (-sin thet′ik) *adj.* —**pho′to·syn′thet′i·cal·ly** *adv.*

pho·tot·ro·pism (fō tät′rə piz'm) *n.* Bot. movement of a part of a plant toward or away from light sources: see HELIOTROPISM —**pho·to·trop·ic** (fōt′ə träp′ik) *adj.*

phrase (frāz) *n.* [< L. *phrasis*, diction < Gr. < *phrazein*, to speak] **1.** a short, colorful or forceful expression [“it's raining cats and dogs” is a well-known *phrase*] **2.** *Gram.* a sequence of

---

two or more words conveying a single thought or forming a distinct part of a sentence but not containing a subject and predicate (Examples: giving parties; of mine; ham and eggs): see CLAUSE **3.** *Linguis.* a linguistic unit consisting of two or more words spoken between two distinct pauses and having a single primary stress **4.** *Music* a short, distinct passage, usually of two, four, or eight measures —*vt.* **phrased, phras′ing 1.** to express in words or in a phrase [he *phrased* his answer carefully] **2.** *Music* to mark off or group (notes) in phrases —**phras′al** *adj.* —**phras′al·ly** *adv.*

phra·se·ol·o·gy (frā′zē äl′ə jē) *n., pl.* **-gies** [< ModL.: see PHRASE & -LOGY] choice and arrangement of words; way of speaking or writing [legal *phraseology*]

phras·ing (frā′ziŋ) *n.* **1.** way of speaking or writing **2.** the manner in which one phrases musical passages

phre·net·ic (fri net′ik) *adj.* [< OFr. < L. < Gr. *phrenētikos*, mad] *earlier sp. of* FRENETIC

☆**phre·nol·o·gy** (fri näl′ə jē) *n.* [< Gr. *phrēn*, mind + -LOGY] a system, now rejected, by which character and mental abilities are analyzed by studying the shape of the skull —**phren·o·log·i·cal** (fren′ə läj′i k'l) *adj.* —**phre·nol′o·gist** *n.*

Phryg·i·a (frij′ē ə) ancient country in WC Asia Minor: see map at TROY —**Phryg′i·an** *adj., n.*

PHS, P.H.S. Public Health Service

phthi·sis (thī′sis, tī′-, fthī′-) *n.* [L. < Gr. < *phthiein*, to waste away] *old term for* any wasting disease, esp. tuberculosis of the lungs —**phthis·ic** (tiz′ik) *adj., n.* —**phthis′i·cal** *adj.*

phy·co·my·cete (fī′kō mī′sēt, -mī sēt′) *n.* [< Gr. *phykos*, seaweed + -MYCETE] any of a class of fungi resembling the algae —**phy′co·my·ce′tous** (-mī sēt′əs) *adj.*

Phyfe (fīf), **Duncan** (born *Duncan Fife*) 1768–1854; U.S. cabinetmaker & furniture designer, born in Scotland

phy·la (fī′lə) *n. pl. of* PHYLUM

phy·lac·ter·y (fi lak′tər ē, -trē) *n., pl.* **-ter·ies** [< ML. < LL. < Gr. *phylaktērion*, a safeguard < *phylassein*, to guard] a small leather case holding slips inscribed with Scripture passages: one is worn on the forehead and one on the left arm by Orthodox or Conservative Jewish men during morning prayer

PHYLACTERIES

phy·let·ic (fi let′ik) *adj.* [< ModL. < Gr. *phylē*, tribe] *Biol.* of or relating to a phylum or to an evolutionary line of descent —**phy·let′i·cal·ly** *adv.*

-phyll (fil) [Gr. < *phyllon*, a leaf] *a combining form meaning* leaf [*chlorophyll*]

Phyl·lis (fil′is) [< Gr. *Phyllis*, lit., a leaf] a feminine name

phyl·lo- [< Gr. *phyllon*, a leaf] *a combining form meaning* leaf: also, before a vowel, **phyll-**

phyl·lo·tax·is (fil′ə tak′sis) *n.* [ModL. < PHYLLO- + Gr. *taxis*, arrangement] *Bot.* **1.** the arrangement of leaves on a stem **2.** the study or principles of such arrangement Also **phyl′lo·tax′y** (-sē) —**phyl′lo·tac′tic** (-tik) *adj.*

-phyl·lous (fil′əs) [see PHYLLO- & -OUS] *a combining form meaning* having (a specified number or kind of) leaves, leaflets, etc.

phyl·lox·e·ra (fil′ək sir′ə, fi läk′sər ə) *n., pl.* **-rae** (-ē), **-ras** [ModL. < Gr. *phyllon*, a leaf + *xēros*, dry] any of various plant lice that attack the leaves and roots of certain plants, as grapevines

phy·lo- [< Gr. *phylon*, tribe] *a combining form meaning* tribe, race, phylum, etc.: also, before a vowel, **phyl-**

phy·log·e·ny (fī läj′ə nē) *n., pl.* **-nies** [< G.: see PHYLO- & -GENY] the history of the evolution of a species or kind of animal or plant: distinguished from ONTOGENY Also **phy·lo·gen·e·sis** (fī′lə jen′ə sis) —**phy·lo·ge·net′ic** (-jə net′ik), **phy·lo·gen′ic** (-jen′ik) *adj.* —**phy·lo·ge·net′i·cal·ly** *adv.*

phy·lum (fī′ləm) *n., pl.* **-la** (-lə) [< Gr. *phylon*, tribe] **1.** any main division of the animal kingdom: sometimes, unofficially, a main subdivision of the plant kingdom **2.** *a)* a language stock *b)* loosely, a language family

phys. 1. physical **2.** physician **3.** physics

phys. ed. physical education

phys·i·at·rics (fiz′ē at′riks) *n.pl.* [*with sing. v.*] [PHYS(IO)- + -IATRICS] the branch of medicine that deals with physical therapy: also **phys′i·at′ry** (-rē) *n.*

phys·i·at·rist (fiz′ē at′rist) *n.* a doctor who specializes in physiatrics

phys·ic (fiz′ik) *n.* [< OFr. < L. *physica*, natural science < Gr. < *physis*, nature < *phyein*, to produce] **1.** [Archaic] medical science **2.** a medicine, esp. one for making the bowels move —*vt.* **-icked, -ick·ing** to dose with a physic

phys·i·cal (fiz′i k'l) *adj.* [< ML. < L.: see prec.] **1.** of nature and all matter; natural; material [the *physical* universe] **2.** of natural science **3.** of or according to the laws of nature **4.** of, or produced by the forces of, physics **5.** of or concerned with the body as opposed to the mind [*physical* exercise] —*n.* a general medical examination: in full, **physical examination** —see SYN. at BODILY and MATERIAL —**phys·i·cal·i·ty** (fiz′ə kal′ə tē) *n.* —**phys′i·cal·ly** *adv.*

physical chemistry the branch of chemistry dealing with the physical properties of substances as they relate to the chemical properties and changes

☆**physical education** instruction in the exercise, care, hygiene, etc. of the human body; esp., a course in gymnastics, athletics, etc., as in a school or college

physical geography the study of the features and nature of the earth's surface, atmosphere, climate, etc.

physical science any science dealing with nonliving matter or energy, as physics, chemistry, etc.

physical therapy the treatment of disease, injury, etc. by the use of exercise, massage, heat, etc. where it might be helpful —**physical therapist**

phy·si·cian (fə zish′ən) *n.* [< OFr. < L.: see PHYSIC] **1.** a person licensed to practice medicine; doctor of medicine **2.** a medical doctor other than a surgeon **3.** any person or thing that heals or relieves

phys·i·cist (fiz′ə sist) *n.* a specialist in physics

phys·ics (fiz′iks) *n.pl.* [*with sing. v. in senses 1 & 2*] [transl. of L. *physica*, physics] **1.** orig., natural science **2.** *a)* the science dealing with the properties, interactions, etc. of matter and energy, with energy considered as given off in an unbroken stream (**classical physics**, including electricity, heat, optics, mechanics, etc.) or in a stream of separate units (**quantum physics**, including atomic, nuclear, and solid-state physics) *b)* a specific system of physics **3.** physical properties or processes [the *physics* of flight]

phys·i·o- [< Gr. *physis*, nature] *a combining form meaning:* **1.** nature; natural [*physiography*] **2.** physical [*physiotherapy*] Also, before a vowel, **physi-**

phys·i·og·no·my (fiz′ē äg′nə mē; *chiefly Brit.* -än′ə-) *n.* [< MFr. < ML. < Gr. < *physis*, nature + *gnōmōn*, one who knows] **1.** the practice of trying to judge character and intelligence by studying the features of the face **2.** facial features, esp. as supposedly showing character [the *physiognomy* of an honest man] **3.** outward features [the *physiognomy* of the city] —see SYN. at FACE —**phys′i·og·nom′ic** (-äg näm′ik, -ə näm′-), **phys′i·og·nom′i·cal** *adj.* —**phys′i·og′no·mist** *n.*

phys·i·og·ra·phy (fiz′ē äg′rə fē) *n.* [PHYSIO- + -GRAPHY] **1.** a description of the features and phenomena of nature **2.** *same as* PHYSICAL GEOGRAPHY —**phys′i·og′ra·pher** *n.* —**phys′i·o·graph′ic** (-ə graf′ik), **phys′i·o·graph′i·cal** *adj.*

physiol. 1. physiological **2.** physiology

phys·i·o·log·i·cal (fiz′ē ə läj′i k'l) *adj.* **1.** of physiology **2.** characteristic of, normal, or healthy, functioning Also **phys′i·o·log′ic** —**phys′i·o·log′i·cal·ly** *adv.*

phys·i·ol·o·gy (fiz′ē äl′ə jē) *n.* [< Fr. < L. < Gr.: see PHYSIO- & -LOGY] **1.** the study of the functions of living things and the ways in which their parts and organs work [plant *physiology*] **2.** the functions and vital processes (*of* an animal or plant, or of any of its parts) [the *physiology* of the digestive tract] —**phys′i·ol′o·gist** *n.*

phys·i·o·ther·a·py (fiz′ē ō ther′ə pē) *n. same as* PHYSICAL THERAPY —**phys′i·o·ther′a·pist** *n.*

phy·sique (fi zēk′) *n.* [Fr.] the form or build of one's body [a muscular *physique*]

-phyte (fīt) [< Gr. *phyton*, a plant] *a combining form meaning:* **1.** a plant growing in a (specified) way or place [*sporophyte*] **2.** plantlike [*zoophyte*]

phy·to- [< Gr. *phyton*, a plant] *a combining form meaning* a plant, vegetation: also, before a vowel, **phyt-**

phy·to·hor·mone (fīt′ə hôr′mōn) *n. same as* PLANT HORMONE

phy·to·plank·ton (fīt′ə plaŋk′tən) *n.* [PHYTO- + PLANKTON] plankton consisting of plants, as algae

pi¹ (pī) *n., pl.* **pies** [see PIE²] **1.** a mixed, disordered collection of printing type **2.** any jumble or mixture —*vt.* **pied, pie′ing**

pi′ing to make jumbled; mix up (type) The following line is pied: The gared nis in bloom

pi² (pī) *n.* [Gr.] **1.** the sixteenth letter of the Greek alphabet (Π, π) **2.** *a)* the symbol (π) designating the ratio of the circumference of a circle to its diameter *b)* this ratio, equal to 3.14159265+

pi·a ma·ter (pī′ə māt′ər, pē′ə mät′ər) [ML., lit., gentle mother < L.] the vascular membrane that is the innermost of the three membranes around the brain and spinal cord

pi·an·ism (pē an′iz'm, pē′ən-) *n.* a pianist's technique

pi·a·nis·si·mo (pē′ə nis′ə mō′) *adj., adv.* [It., superl. of *piano*, soft] *Music* very soft: a direction to the performer —*n., pl.* **-mos′, -mi′** (-mē′) a pianissimo note or passage

pi·an·ist (pē an′ist, pyan′-, pē′ən-) *n.* a person who plays the piano, esp. skillfully

pi·an·o¹ (pē an′ō, pyan′ō) *n., pl.* **-os** [It., contr. < *pianoforte*] a large musical instrument with many wire strings in a case, played from a keyboard: each key operates a felt-covered hammer that strikes and vibrates a corresponding rigid steel wire or set of wires to sound a tone

pi·a·no² (pē ä′nō, pyä′-) *adj., adv.* [It., soft, smooth < L. *planus*, smooth] *Music* soft: a direction to the performer —*n., pl.* **-nos** a note or passage played softly

pi·an·o·for·te (pē an′ə fôrt′, pē an′ə fôr′tē) *n.* [It. < *piano*, soft + *forte*, strong] *same as* PIANO¹

pi·as·ter (pē as′tər) *n.* [< Fr. < It., ult. < L. *emplastrum*, plaster] **1.** a unit of currency in Lebanon, Sudan, Syria, and Egypt **2.** the monetary unit of South Vietnam See MONETARY UNITS, table Also, Brit. sp., **pi·as′tre**

pi·az·za (pē az′ə; *It.* pyät′tsä) *n.* [It. < L. *platea:* see PLACE] **1.** in Italy, an open public square, esp. with buildings around it ☆**2.** a large, covered porch

pi·broch (pē′bräk) *n.* [< Gael. *piobaireachd*, ult. < *piob*, bagpipe] a piece of music for the bagpipe, usually a march but sometimes a piece sounding like a funeral hymn

pi·ca (pī′kə) *n.* [< ? ML., directory: perhaps in reference to the type used in printing it] **1.** a size of type, 12 point **2.** the height of this type, about 1/6 inch: used as a unit of measure in printing

pic·a·dor (pik′ə dôr′) *n.* [Sp. < *picar*, to prick] in bullfighting, any of the horsemen who prick the bull's neck with a lance to weaken him

Pic·ar·dy (pik′ər dē) region & former province of N France: Fr. **Pi·car·die** (pē kár dē′)

pic·a·resque (pik′ə resk′) *adj.* [< Sp. < *pícaro*, a rascal] of or dealing with sharp-witted vagabonds or rogues and their adventures [a *picaresque* novel]

Pi·cas·so (pi kä′sō, -kas′ō), **Pa·blo** (pä′blō) 1881–1973; Sp. painter & sculptor in France

☆**pic·a·yune** (pik′ē ōōn′, -ə yōōn′) *n.* [Fr. *picaillon*, small coin < Pr.] **1.** a coin of small value **2.** anything trivial or worthless —*adj.* trivial; petty; small or small-minded: also **pic′a·yun′ish** —see SYN. at PETTY

pic·ca·lil·li (pik′ə lil′ē) *n.* [prob. < PICKLE] a relish of chopped vegetables, mustard, vinegar, spices, etc.

Pic·card (pē kár′; *E.* pi kärd′) **1. Au·guste** (ō′güst′), 1884–1962; Swiss physicist: known for balloon ascents & descents in a bathyscaph **2. Jean Fé·lix** (zhän fā lēks′), 1884–1963; U.S. aeronautical engineer, born in Switzerland: also known for balloon ascents: twin brother of *Auguste*

pic·co·lo (pik′ə lō′) *n., pl.* **-los′** [It., small] a small flute, pitched an octave above the ordinary flute —**pic′co·lo′ist** *n.*

pice (pīs) *n., pl.* **pice** [Hindi *paisā*] see MONETARY UNITS, table (Nepal)

pick¹ (pik) *n.* [var. of PIKE⁴] **1.** a heavy tool with a long, pointed metal head set at a right angle to the handle, used for breaking up soil, rock, etc. **2.** a pointed instrument for picking [*toothpick*] **3.** *same as* PLECTRUM **4.** a pin used to hold hair rollers in place

pick² (pik) *vt.* [ME. *picken*, akin to ON. *pikka*, to pierce] **1.** to break up, pierce, or dig up (soil, rock, etc.) with something pointed **2.** to make (a hole)

PICCOLO

---

fat, āpe, cär; ten, ēven; is, bīte; gō, hôrn, tōōl, lŏŏk; oil, out; up, fur; get; joy; yet; chin; she; thin, *th*en; zh, leisure; ŋ, ring; ə for *a* in *ago*, *e* in *agent*, *i* in *sanity*, *o* in *comply*, *u* in *focus*; ' as in *able* (ā′b'l); Fr. bál; ë, Fr. coeur; ö, Fr. feu; Fr. mo*n*; ô, Fr. coq; ü, Fr. duc; r, Fr. cri; H, G. ich; kh, G. doch; ‡foreign; ☆ Americanism; < derived from. See inside front cover.

with something pointed 3. *a)* to dig, probe, or scratch at in trying to remove *b)* to clear something from (the teeth, etc.) in this way 4. to remove by pulling; specif., to gather (flowers, berries, etc.) 5. to clear in this way (a fowl) of its feathers, (a tree) of its fruit, etc. 6. to take up (food) in small bits, as a bird with its bill 7. to pull (fibers, rags, etc.) apart 8. to choose or select [the judges *picked* the winner] 9. to find occasion for (a quarrel or fight) 10. to search out [to *pick* flaws] ☆11. *a)* to pluck (the strings on a guitar, etc.) *b)* to play (a guitar, etc.) in this way 12. to open (a lock) with a wire, etc. instead of a key 13. to steal from (another's pocket, etc.) —*vi.* 1. to eat sparingly or fussily 2. to thieve 3. to use a pick 4. to gather growing berries, flowers, etc. 5. to be picked [grapes *pick* easily] 6. to choose or select, esp. in a fussy way ☆7. to play the guitar, banjo, etc. —*n.* 1. a stroke or blow with something pointed 2. the act of choosing or a thing chosen [take your *pick* of these books] 3. the best or most desirable one or ones [this kitten is the *pick* of the litter] 4. the amount of a crop gathered at one time —see SYN. at CHOOSE —**pick and choose** to choose or select carefully —**pick at** 1. to eat small portions of, esp. in a fussy way 2. [Colloq.] to find fault with 3. to toy with; finger — **pick off** 1. to pluck 2. to hit with a carefully aimed shot ☆3. *Baseball* to throw out (a base runner taking a lead) —**pick on** 1. to choose 2. [Colloq.] to single out for abuse, criticism, etc.; annoy; tease —**pick one's way** to move slowly and cautiously —**pick out** 1. to choose 2. to single out from among a group; distinguish 3. to make out (meaning or sense) 4. to play (a tune) note by note —**pick over** to examine or sort out, item by item —**pick up** 1. to grasp and lift 2. to get, find, or learn with little or no effort [he *picks up* languages easily] 3. to stop for and take along 4. to take into custody; arrest 5. to gain (speed) 6. to regain (health, power, etc.); improve 7. to resume (an activity, etc.) after a pause 8. to bring into range of sight, hearing, radio or TV reception, etc. ☆9. to make (a room, etc.) tidy 10. [Colloq.] to strike up an acquaintance with, esp. for sexual purposes —**pick′er** *n.*

pick·a·back (pik′ə bak′, pik′ē-) *adv., adj.* [var. of *pickapack*, redupl. of PACK¹] *same as* PIGGYBACK

pick·ax, pick·axe (pik′aks′) *n.* [altered (after *ax*) < OFr. *picquois*] a pick with a point at one end of the head and an edge like a chisel at the other —*vt., vi.* **-axed′, -ax′ing** to use a pickax (on)

picked (pikt) *adj.* [< PICK²] 1. selected with care [*picked* men] 2. gathered directly from plants, as berries

pick·er·el (pik′ər əl, pik′rəl) *n., pl.* **-el, -els**: see PLURAL, II, D, 2 [dim. of PIKE³] 1. any of various small N. American freshwater fishes related to the pike 2. *a local name for* WALLEYED PIKE

pick·er·el·weed (-wēd′) *n.* ☆any of certain N. American aquatic plants, esp. a shallow-water plant with arrow-shaped leaves and bluish flowers

PICKAX

pick·et (pik′it) *n.* [< Fr. dim. of *pic*, PIKE²] 1. a pointed stake used in a fence, as a hitching post, etc. 2. a soldier or soldiers stationed to guard troops from surprise attack 3. a ship or airplane patrol 4. a person, as a member of a labor union on strike, standing or walking outside a factory, store, public building, etc. to show protest, keep strikebreakers out, etc. —*vt.* 1. to enclose with a picket fence 2. to hitch (an animal) to a picket 3. *a)* to post as a military picket *b)* to guard (troops) with a picket 4. to place pickets, or serve as a picket, at (a factory, etc.) —*vi.* to serve as a picket (sense 4) —**pick′et·er** *n.*

☆**picket fence** a fence made of upright stakes

picket line a line of people serving as pickets

Pick·ett (pik′it), **George Edward** 1825–75; Confederate general

pick·ing (pik′iŋ) *n.* 1. the act of one that picks 2. [*usually pl.*] something picked, or the amount of this; specif., *a)* small scraps that may be collected bit by bit *b)* something got by effort, often dishonestly; returns or spoils

pick·le (pik′'l) *n.* [< MDu. *pekel*] 1. any brine, vinegar, or spicy solution used to preserve or marinate food 2. a vegetable, specif. a cucumber, so preserved 3. a chemical bath to clean metal of scale, preserve wood, etc. 4. [Colloq.] an awkward or difficult situation —*vt.* **-led, -ling** to treat or preserve in a pickle solution —**pick′ler** *n.*

pick·led (-'ld) *adj.* [Slang] intoxicated; drunk

☆**pick-me-up** (pik′mē up′) *n.* [Colloq.] an alcoholic drink taken to raise one's spirits

pick·pock·et (-päk′it) *n.* a thief who steals from the pockets of persons, as in crowds

pick·up (pik′up′) *n.* 1. a picking up [the shortstop made a good *pickup* of the ball] 2. an increasing in speed; acceleration [a car with good *pickup*] ☆3. a small, open truck for light loads 4. [Colloq.] *a)* a casual acquaintance, esp. one formed for sexual purposes *b)* the person with whom such an acquaintance is formed ☆5. [Colloq.] improvement, as in business ☆6. [Colloq.] *a)* a stimulant *b)* stimulation 7. *a)* in an electric phonograph, a device that causes the vibrations picked up by the needle in a record groove to be changed into electrical signals, which are then changed into sound *b)* the pivoted arm holding this 8. *Radio & TV a)* reception of sound or light for change into electrical signals in the transmitter *b)* the apparatus used *c)* any place outside a studio where a broadcast originates *d)* the electrical system connecting this place to the broadcasting station —*adj.* [Colloq.] assembled, organized, etc. informally or hastily [a *pickup* jazz band]

☆**pick·y** (pik′ē) *adj.* **pick′i·er, pick′i·est** [Colloq.] overly critical or demanding; fussy

pic·nic (pik′nik) *n.* [< Fr., prob. < *piquer*, to pick + *nique*, a trifle] 1. a pleasure outing during which a meal is eaten outdoors ☆2. a shoulder cut of pork, cured like ham: also **picnic ham, picnic shoulder** 3. [Slang] *a)* a pleasant experience *b)* an easy task —*vi.* **-nicked, -nick·ing** to hold or go on a picnic —**pic′nick·er** *n.*

pi·co- [prob. < It. *piccolo*, small] a combining form meaning one trillionth; the factor 10^{-12}

Pi·co Ri·ver·a (pē′kō rə ver′ə) [after P. *Pico*, gov. of Mexican Calif. + *Rivera*, from its being between two rivers] city in SW Calif.: suburb of Los Angeles: pop. 54,000

pi·cot (pē′kō) *n., pl.* **-cots** (-kōz) [Fr., dim. of *pic*, a point] any of the small loops forming a fancy edge on lace, ribbon, etc. —*vt., vi.* **-coted** (-kōd), **-cot·ing** (-kō iŋ) to edge with these

pic·ric acid (pik′rik) [< Fr. < Gr. *pikros*, bitter] a poisonous, yellow, crystalline, bitter acid, $C_6H_3O_7N_3$, used in dyes, explosives, etc.

Pict (pikt) *n.* any of an ancient people of Great Britain, driven into Scotland by the Britons and Romans —**Pict′ish** *adj., n.*

pic·to·graph (pik′tə graf′) *n.* [< L. *pictus* (see PICTURE) + -GRAPH] 1. a picture or picturelike symbol representing an idea, as in ancient writing 2. a diagram using pictured objects to show ideas, data, etc. —**pic′to·graph′ic** *adj.* —**pic′to·graph′i·cal·ly** *adv.* —**pic·tog′ra·phy** (-täg′rə fē) *n.*

pic·to·ri·al (pik tôr′ē əl) *adj.* 1. of, containing, or expressed in pictures [the *pictorial* page of a newspaper; a *pictorial* graph] 2. suggesting a picture to the mind; vivid; graphic [a *pictorial* description] —☆*n.* a periodical featuring many pictures —**pic·to′ri·al·i·za′tion** *n.* —**pic·to′ri·al·ize′** *vt.* **-ized′, -iz′ing** —**pic·to′ri·al·ly** *adv.*

pic·ture (pik′chər) *n.* [< L. *pictura* < *pictus*, pp. of *pingere*, to PAINT] 1. *a)* a likeness of an object, person, or scene produced on a flat surface, as by painting or photography *b)* a printed reproduction of this 2. any likeness, image, or good example [she's the *picture* of her mother; he's the *picture* of health] 3. anything thought of as having artistic beauty [the garden in bloom was a *picture*] 4. a mental image; idea 5. a vivid description [a *picture* of the times] 6. all the facts of an event; situation 7. *same as: a)* TABLEAU *b)* MOTION PICTURE 8. the image on a TV screen —*vt.* **-tured, -tur·ing** 1. to make a picture of by painting, drawing, etc. 2. to make visible; show clearly [joy was *pictured* in his face] 3. to describe or explain [Dickens *pictured* life in England] 4. to imagine [you can *picture* how pleased I was] —**in** (or **out of**) **the picture** considered as involved (or not involved) in a situation

picture card *same as* FACE CARD

pic·tur·esque (pik′chə resk′) *adj.* 1. like a picture; specif., *a)* having a wild or natural beauty, as mountain scenery *b)* pleasantly unfamiliar; quaint [a *picturesque* village] 2. suggesting a mental picture; vivid [a *picturesque* description] —**pic′tur·esque′ly** *adv.* —**pic′tur·esque′ness** *n.*

☆**picture tube** *same as* KINESCOPE (sense 1)

picture window a large window, esp. in a living room, that seems to frame the outside view

picture writing 1. writing consisting of pictures or figures representing ideas 2. the pictures or figures so used

pic·tur·ize (pik′chə rīz′) *vt.* **-ized′, -iz′ing** to make a picture of, esp. a motion picture —**pic′tur·i·za′tion** *n.*

pid·dle (pid′'l) *vi., vt.* **-dled, -dling** [child's word for URINATE] to dawdle or trifle [to *piddle* the time away] —**pid′dler** *n.*

pid·dling (pid′liŋ) *adj.* trifling; petty

pidg·in (pij′in) *n.* [a supposed Chin. pronun. of BUSINESS] a mixed language, or jargon, as pidgin English, combining a simple vocabulary and grammar of two or more languages

pidgin English 1. a simplified form of English used in some parts of the Orient as a trade language 2. any jargon of English like this

pie[1] (pī) *n.* [akin ? to PIE[3]] 1. a baked dish consisting of fruit, meat, etc. with an under or upper crust, or both 2. a layer cake with a filling of custard, jelly, etc. ☆3. [Slang] something extremely good or easy —(**as**) **easy as pie** [Colloq.] extremely easy

pie[2] (pī) *n., vt.* [< ? prec.] *chiefly Brit. sp. of* PI[1]

pie[3] (pī) *n.* [OFr.] *same as* MAGPIE

pie·bald (pī′bôld′) *adj.* [PIE[3] + BALD] covered with patches or spots of two colors, esp. white and black —*n.* a piebald horse or other animal

piece (pēs) *n.* [OFr. *pece,* prob. < Gaul.] 1. a part broken or separated from the whole [a *piece* of shattered glass] 2. a section or quantity of a whole, thought of as complete in itself [a *piece* of meat; a *piece* of land] 3. a single thing, specimen, etc.; specif., *a*) a work of music, writing, or art *b*) an action or its result [a *piece* of business] *c*) a firearm, as a rifle [an old shooting *piece*] *d*) a coin or token [a fifty-cent *piece*] *e*) one of a set, as of china *f*) a counter as used in games [a chess *piece*] *g*) a single instance or example [a *piece* of gossip] 4. the amount of a thing made up as a unit [to sell cloth by the *piece*] 5. an amount or unit of work making up a single job 6. [Archaic or Dial.] an amount of time or space ☆7. [Slang] a financial interest; share —*vt.* **pieced, piec′ing** 1. to add pieces to, as in repairing or enlarging [to *piece* a pair of trousers] 2. to join (*together*) the pieces of, as in mending or forming a whole [to *piece* together a broken jug; to *piece* a book together from magazine articles] —*vi.* [Colloq.] to eat a snack between meals —see SYN. at PART —**go to pieces** 1. to fall apart 2. to lose all self-control, morally or emotionally —**of a** (or **one**) **piece** of the same sort; alike —**piec′er** *n.*

‡pièce de ré·sis·tance (pyes′ də rā zēs täns′) [Fr., piece of resistance] 1. the main dish of a meal 2. the main item or event in a series

piece goods *same as* YARD GOODS

piece·meal (pēs′mēl′) *adv.* [< ME. < *pece,* PIECE + *-mele,* a measure] 1. piece by piece; in small amounts or degrees 2. into pieces —*adj.* made or done in pieces or one piece at a time

piece of eight the obsolete Spanish dollar

piece·work (pēs′wurk′) *n.* work paid for at a fixed rate (**piece rate**) per piece —**piece′work′er** *n.*

pie chart a graph showing the proportions of the parts of a whole as sectors of a circle

pied (pīd) *adj.* covered with spots or patches of two or more colors; piebald; variegated

Pied·mont (pēd′mänt) 1. hilly, upland region of the eastern U.S., between the Atlantic coastal plain & the Appalachians 2. region of NW Italy, on the border of Switzerland & France: chief city, Turin: see map at LIGURIA

pied·mont (pēd′mänt) *adj.* [< PIEDMONT, Italy] at the base of mountains [a *piedmont* stream] —*n.* a piedmont area, etc.

☆**pie·plant** (pī′plant′) *n.* rhubarb: so called from use in pies

pier (pir) *n.* [ML. *pera,* ult. < ? akin to L. *petra,* stone] 1. a heavy structure supporting the spans of a bridge 2. a structure built out over water and supported by pillars: used as a landing place, a walk, etc. 3. *Archit. a*) a heavy supporting column, as at the end of an arch *b*) the part of a wall between windows or other openings *c*) a buttress

pierce (pirs) *vt.* **pierced, pierc′ing** [OFr. *percer,* ult. < L. *per,* through + *tundere,* to strike: for IE. base see STEEP[1]] 1. to pass into or through as a pointed instrument does; stab [the needle *pierced* her finger] 2. to affect sharply the senses or feelings of [*pierced* by the cold] 3. to make a hole in; perforate; bore [to *pierce* one's ears for earrings] 4. to make (a hole), as by boring 5. to break into or through [the explorer *pierced* the jungle] 6. to sound sharply through [a shriek *pierced* the air] 7. to see through or understand [to *pierce* a mystery] —*vi.* to force a way (*to, into,* or *through* something) —**pierc′er** *n.* —**pierc′ing·ly** *adv.*

Pierce (pirs), **Franklin** 1804–69; 14th president of the U.S. (1853–57)

Pi·e·ri·an (pī ir′ē ən) *adj.* 1. of a region (**Pieria**) in northern Greece, where the Muses were worshiped 2. of the Muses or the arts

Pi·erre[1] (pē er′; *Fr.* pyer) [Fr., var. of PETER] a masculine name

Pierre[2] (pir) [after *Pierre* Chonteau, early fur trader] capital of S.Dak., on the Missouri River: pop. 10,000

Pi·er·rot (pē′ə rō′; *Fr.* pye rō′) [Fr., dim. of *Pierre,* PETER] a stock comic character in old French pantomime, having a whitened face and wearing loose white pantaloons and jacket

Pie·ter·mar·itz·burg (pē′tər mer′its burg′) city in E South Africa: pop. 113,000

pi·e·tism (pī′ə tiz′m) *n.* religious piety, esp. when exaggerated —**pi·e·tis′tic, pi·e·tis′ti·cal** *adj.* —**pi·e·tis′ti·cal·ly** *adv.*

pi·e·ty (pī′ə tē) *n., pl.* **-ties** [< OFr. < LL. *pietas* < L. < *pius,* pious] 1. devotion to religious duties and practices 2. loyalty and devotion to parents, family, etc. 3. a pious act, belief, etc.

piezoelectric effect the property that certain crystals have of producing voltage when subjected to stress and undergoing stress when subjected to voltage: such crystals can be ground and cut to a particular size to oscillate or vibrate at a particular frequency

pi·e·zo·e·lec·tric·i·ty (pē ā′zō ə lek′tris′ə tē) *n.* [< Gr. *piezein,* to press + ELECTRICITY] electricity resulting from the piezoelectric effect —**pi·e·zo·e·lec′tric, pi·e·zo·e·lec′tri·cal** *adj.* —**pi·e·zo·e·lec′tri·cal·ly** *adv.*

pif·fle (pif′'l) *n.* [< Brit. dial.] [Colloq.] talk, action, etc. thought of as unimportant or foolish —*interj.* nonsense! —**pif′-fling** *adj.*

pig (pig) *n., pl.* **pigs, pig:** see PLURAL, II, D, 1 [ME. *pigge,* orig., young pig] 1. an animal with a long, broad snout and a thick, fat body covered with coarse bristles: it is raised for its meat; swine; hog 2. a young hog of less than about 100 lbs. 3. pork 4. a person thought of as piggish or like a pig; greedy or filthy person 5. *a*) a long and narrow casting of iron, etc. poured from the smelting furnace *b*) the mold used *c*) clipped form of PIG IRON —*vi.* **pigged, pig′ging** 1. to give birth to pigs 2. to live like a pig, esp. in the phrase **pig it** —**buy a pig in a poke** to buy or accept something without knowing what it really is

pi·geon[1] (pij′ən) *n., pl.* **-geons, -geon:** see PLURAL, II, D, 1 [< MFr. < LL. *pipio,* chirping bird < *pipire,* to peep] 1. any of various related birds with a small head, plump body, and short legs: see also DOVE[1] ☆2. *same as* CLAY PIGEON 3. [Slang] a person easily tricked; dupe

pi·geon[2] (pij′ən) *n. same as* PIDGIN

pigeon breast a deformity of the human chest, as from rickets, in which the breastbone sticks out sharply like that of a pigeon —**pi′geon-breast′ed** *adj.*

pigeon hawk ☆a small N. American falcon

pi·geon·hole (-hōl′) *n.* 1. a small hole, usually one of a series, for pigeons to nest in 2. a small, open compartment, as in a desk, for filing papers —*vt.* **-holed′, -hol′ing** 1. to put in the pigeonhole of a desk, etc. 2. to put aside indefinitely, as if meaning to ignore or forget; shelve [the mayor *pigeonholed* the park plan] 3. to put in a particular category or categories; classify

pi·geon-toed (-tōd′) *adj.* having the toes or feet turned in

pig·ger·y (pig′ər ē) *n., pl.* **-ger·ies** *chiefly Brit. var. of* PIGPEN

pig·gish (pig′ish) *adj.* like a pig; greedy or filthy —**pig′gish·ly** *adv.* —**pig′gish·ness** *n.*

pig·gy (pig′ē) *n., pl.* **-gies** a little pig: also sp. **pig′gie** —*adj.* **-gi·er, -gi·est** *same as* PIGGISH

pig·gy·back (pig′ē bak′) *adv., adj.* [alt. of PICKABACK] 1. on the shoulders or back [to carry a child *piggyback*] ☆2. of or by a system in which loaded truck trailers are carried on railroad flatcars —☆*vt.* to carry or transport piggyback

☆**piggy bank** any small savings bank, often in the form of a pig, with a slot for coins

pig·head·ed (pig′hed′id) *adj.* stubborn; obstinate —**pig′head′ed·ly** *adv.* —**pig′head′ed·ness** *n.*

CHILD RIDING PIGGYBACK

pig iron [see PIG, *n.* 5] crude iron, as it comes from the blast furnace

pig Latin a playful code in speaking, in which end syllables are formed using initial consonants (Ex.: "etslay artstay" for "let's start")

pig·let (pig′lit) *n.* a little pig, esp. a suckling

pig·ment (pig′mənt) *n.* [< L. *pigmentum* < base of *pingere*, to PAINT] **1.** coloring matter, usually a powder, mixed with oil, water, etc. to make paints **2.** coloring matter in the cells and tissues of plants or animals —*vi.*, *vt.* to color or become colored with pigment: also **pig′ment·ize′ -ized′, -iz′ing** —**pig′men·tar′y** (-mən ter′ē) *adj.*

pig·men·ta·tion (pig′mən tā′shən) *n.* coloration in plants or animals due to pigment in the tissue

Pig·my (pig′mē) *adj.*, *n.*, *pl.* **-mies** same as PYGMY

pig·nut (pig′nut′) *n.* ☆**1.** any of several bitter-tasting hickory nuts ☆**2.** any tree they grow on

pig·pen (pig′pen′) *n.* a pen where pigs are kept

pig·skin (-skin′) *n.* **1.** the skin of a pig **2.** leather made from this ☆**3.** [Colloq.] a football

pig·stick·ing (-stik′iŋ) *n.* the hunting of wild boars, esp. on horseback with spears —**pig′stick′er** *n.*

pig·sty (-stī′) *n.*, *pl.* **-sties** same as PIGPEN

pig·tail (-tāl′) *n.* **1.** tobacco in a twisted roll **2.** a braid of hair hanging at the back of the head

pig·weed (-wēd′) *n.* ☆**1.** any of several coarse weeds with thick, bristly clusters of small green flowers **2.** any of several goosefoots; esp., same as LAMB'S-QUARTERS

pi·ka (pī′kə) *n.* [< E. Siberian name] any of various small, rabbitlike mammals of rocky, usually high areas in western N. America and in Asia

pike[1] (pīk) *n. shortened form of* TURNPIKE

pike[2] (pīk) *n.* [< Fr. < *piquer*, to pierce < ? L. *picus*, woodpecker] a weapon, formerly used by foot soldiers, with a metal spearhead on a long, wooden shaft —*vt.* **piked, pik′ing** to stab with a pike

pike[3] (pīk) *n.*, *pl.* **pike, pikes**: see PLURAL, II, D, 2 [prob. < *pike* (see PIKE[4]), from the pointed head] **1.** a slender, freshwater game fish of northern waters, with a narrow, pointed head and sharp teeth: also **northern pike 2.** any of several related fishes, as the pickerel and the muskellunge **3.** a fish resembling the true pike, as the walleyed pike

pike[4] (pīk) *n.* [OE. *pic*, a pickax] a spike or point, as the pointed tip of a spear

pike·man (pīk′mən) *n.*, *pl.* **-men** a soldier armed with a pike

pike·perch (pīk′purch′) *n.*, *pl.* **-perch′, -perch′es**: see PLURAL, II, D, 2 a fish that looks like a pike, as the walleyed pike

pik·er (pī′kər) *n.* [orig., prob. one from *Pike* County, Mo.] ☆[Slang] a person who does things in a petty, stingy, or very cautious way

Pikes Peak (pīks) [after Z. *Pike* (1779–1813), Am. explorer] mountain in C Colo.: 14,110 ft.

pike·staff (pīk′staf′) *n.*, *pl.* **-staves** (-stāvz′) **1.** the shaft of a pike **2.** a traveler's staff with a sharp point

pi·laf, pi·laff (pi läf′, pē′läf) *n.* [Pers. & Turk. *pilāw*] a dish of rice boiled in a seasoned liquid, and usually containing meat or fish

pi·las·ter (pi las′tər) *n.* [< Fr. < It. *pilastro* < L. *pila*, a pile] a rectangular support sticking out partially from a wall and treated architecturally as a column, with a base, shaft, and capital

Pi·late (pī′lət), **Pon·tius** (pän′shəs, -chəs, -tē əs) 1st cent. A.D.; Rom. governor of Judea & Samaria (26?–36?) who condemned Jesus to be crucified

pi·lau, pi·law (pi lô′) *n.* same as PILAF

pil·chard (pil′chərd) *n.* [earlier *pilcher* < ?] **1.** a small saltwater fish of the herring family, the commercial sardine of western Europe **2.** any of several related fishes; esp., the **Pacific sardine,** found off the western coast of the U.S.

Pil·co·ma·yo (pēl′kô mä′yô) river flowing from Bolivia along the Argentine-Paraguay border into the Paraguay River

PILASTER

pile[1] (pīl) *n.* [< MFr. < L. *pila*, a pillar] **1.** a mass of things heaped together [a *pile* of leaves] **2.** a heap of wood, etc. on which a corpse or sacrifice is burned **3.** a large building or group of buildings **4.** [Colloq.] *a)* a large amount or number [a *pile* of work] ☆*b)* a lot of money [he made a *pile* in his youth] **5.** *Elec.* *a)* orig., a series of alternate plates of unlike metals with acid-soaked cloth or paper between them, for mak-

ing an electric current *b)* any similar arrangement that produces an electric current; battery ☆**6.** *an earlier name for* NUCLEAR REACTOR —*vt.* **piled, pil′ing 1.** to put in a pile; heap up [to *pile* rubbish] **2.** to cover with a pile; load [he *piled* the cart with hay; she *piled* the table with books] **3.** to accumulate [she *piled* up points in the game] Often with *up* —*vi.* **1.** to form a pile or heap [the letters *piled* up on his desk] **2.** to move confusedly in a mass (with *in, out, on,* etc.) [the football fans *piled* into the stadium]

pile[2] (pīl) *n.* [< L. *pilus,* a hair < IE. base *pilo-,* hair] **1.** a soft, velvety, raised surface on a rug, fabric, etc., consisting of yarn loops that are often sheared **2.** soft, fine hair, as on wool, fur, etc. —**piled** *adj.*

pile[3] (pīl) *n.* [OE. *pil*] **1.** a long, heavy beam driven into the ground, sometimes under water, to support a bridge, dock, etc. **2.** any similar support —*vt.* **piled, pil′ing 1.** to drive piles into **2.** to support with piles

pi·le·ate (pī′lē it, pil′ē-; -āt′) *adj.* [< L. < *pileus,* cap] having a crest extending from the bill to the nape, as some birds Also **pi′le·at′ed** (-āt′id)

☆**pileated woodpecker** a N. American woodpecker with a black and white body and a red crest

pile driver (or **engine**) a machine with a heavy weight that is raised and then dropped, for driving piles

pi·le·ous (pī′lē əs, pil′ē-) *adj.* [< L. *pilus,* a hair + -EOUS] hairy or furry

piles (pīlz) *n.pl.* [< L. *piloe,* pl. of *pila,* a ball] same as HEMORRHOIDS (see HEMORRHOID)

pi·le·um (pī′lē əm, pil′ē-) *n., pl.* **-le·a** (-ə) [ModL. < L. *pileum,* felt cap] the top of a bird's head from the bill to the nape

pile·up (pīl′up′) *n.* **1.** a piling up **2.** [Colloq.] a collision involving several vehicles

pi·le·us (pī′lē əs, pil′ē-) *n., pl.* **-le·i′** (-ī′) [< L. *pileus* (or *pileum*), felt cap] *Bot.* the cap of a mushroom, or a similar part of other fungi

pil·fer (pil′fər) *vt., vi.* [MFr. *pelfrer* < *pelfre,* booty] to steal (esp. small sums, petty objects, etc.) —**pil′fer·age** *n.* —**pil′fer·er** *n.*

pil·grim (pil′grəm) *n.* [< OFr. < LL. < L. *peregrinus,* foreigner, ult. < *per,* through + *ager,* country (see ACRE)] **1.** a wanderer **2.** a traveler to a shrine or holy place ☆**3.** [P-] any member of the band of English Puritans who founded Plymouth Colony in 1620

pil·grim·age (-ij) *n.* **1.** a pilgrim's journey, esp. to a shrine, etc. **2.** any similar long journey

☆**Pilgrim Fathers** the Pilgrims of Plymouth Colony

Pilgrim's Progress a religious allegory by John Bunyan (1678)

pil·ing (pī′liŋ) *n.* **1.** piles used for docks, bridges, etc. **2.** a structure of piles

Pil·i·pi·no (pil′ə pē′nô) *n.* [Tag. < obs. Sp. *Philippino,* FILIPINO] same as TAGALOG (sense 2): official national language of the Philippines

pill (pil) *n.* [contr. < L. *pilula,* dim. of *pila,* a ball] **1.** a small ball, tablet, or capsule of medicine to be swallowed whole **2.** a thing that is unpleasant but unavoidable [the criticism was a bitter *pill* for him to take] **3.** [Slang] a baseball, golf ball, etc. **4.** [Slang] an unpleasant person —*vt.* to dose with pills —*vi.* to form into small balls of fuzz on a fabric —**the pill** ☆[Colloq.] any contraceptive drug for women, taken in the form of a pill

pil·lage (pil′ij) *n.* [< MFr. < *piller,* to rob] **1.** a plundering **2.** booty; loot —*vt.* **-laged, -lag·ing 1.** to take away money or property by violence; loot **2.** to take as booty or loot —*vi.* to take loot —**pil′lag·er** *n.*

pil·lar (pil′ər) *n.* [< OFr., ult. < L. *pila,* a column] **1.** a slender, vertical structure used as a support; column **2.** a column standing alone as a monument **3.** anything like a pillar in form or use [a *pillar* of smoke] **4.** a person who is a main support of an institution, movement, etc. [a *pillar* of society, of the church, etc.] —*vt.* to support as with pillars —**from pillar to post** from one difficulty, place of appeal, etc. to another

Pillars of Hercules two headlands on either side of the Strait of Gibraltar, one at Gibraltar and the other in Morocco, on the coast of Africa

pill·box (pil′bäks′) *n.* **1.** a small, shallow box, often round, for pills **2.** a low, enclosed gun emplacement of concrete and steel **3.** a woman's small, round hat, flat on top and brimless

☆**pill bug** a land crustacean with a flat body, capable of rolling into a ball, often found in damp places

pil·lion (pil′yən) *n.* [< Gael. < *peall,* a hide, ult. < L. *pellis,* a skin] **1.** a cushion behind a saddle for an extra rider, esp. a woman **2.** an extra saddle behind the driver's on a motorcycle

pil·lo·ry (pil′ər ē) *n., pl.* **-ries** [OFr. *pilori*] **1.** a wooden board with holes for the head and hands, in which petty offenders were formerly locked to shame them in public **2.** any laying open to public scorn —*vt.* **-ried, -ry·ing 1.** to punish by placing in a pillory **2.** to lay open to public ridicule, scorn, or abuse

pil·low (pil′ō) *n.* [OE. *pyle*] **1.** a cloth case filled with feathers, foam rubber, etc., used as a support, as for the head in sleeping **2.** anything like a pillow in form or use —*vt.* **1.** to rest as on a pillow **2.** to be a pillow for —*vi.* to rest the head as on a pillow

PILLORY

pil·low·case (-kās′) *n.* a removable cloth case to cover a pillow: also **pil′low·slip′** (-slip′)

☆**pillow sham** a fancy cover laid over a bed pillow

pil·low·y (-ē) *adj.* like a pillow; soft; yielding

pi·lose (pī′lōs) *adj.* [< L. < *pilus*, a hair] covered with hair, esp. fine, soft hair: also **pi′lous** (-ləs) —**pi·los·i·ty** (pī läs′ə tē) *n.*

pi·lot (pī′lət) *n.* [< MFr. < It. *pilota*, ult. < Gr. *pēdon*, oar blade] **1.** a steersman; specif., a person whose work is directing or steering ships into or out of a harbor or through difficult waters **2.** a person who handles the controls of an aircraft or spacecraft **3.** a guide; leader **4.** a device guiding the action of a machine or machine part **5.** *same as: ☆a)* COWCATCHER *b)* PILOT LIGHT *c)* PILOT FILM (or TAPE) —*vt.* **1.** to act as a pilot of, on, in, or over **2.** to guide; lead [to *pilot* a team to a championship] —*adj.* **1.** that guides or activates **2.** that serves as a testing unit [a *pilot* project] —see SYN. at GUIDE —**pi′lot·less** *adj.*

pi·lot·age (-ij) *n.* a piloting, or the fee for it

pilot balloon a small balloon sent up to determine the direction and speed of the wind

☆**pilot biscuit** (or **bread**) *same as* HARDTACK

pilot film (or **tape**) a film (or videotape) of a single episode of a proposed television series, for showing to possible commercial sponsors

pilot fish 1. a small, spiny-finned fish with a widely forked tail, often seen swimming near sharks ☆**2.** a N. America whitefish found in deep, cold, freshwater lakes from the Great Lakes to Alaska

☆**pi·lot·house** (-hous′) *n.* an enclosed place on the upper deck of a ship, in which the helmsman stands while steering and from which the ship is usually guided

pi·lot·ing (-iŋ) *n.* the directing of a ship's movements near land, using landmarks, buoys, soundings, etc.

pilot lamp an electric lamp placed in an electric circuit to show when the current is on

pilot light 1. a small gas burner kept burning for use in lighting a main burner when needed: also **pilot burner 2.** *same as* PILOT LAMP

Pil·sener, Pil·sner (pilz′nər, pils′-) *adj.* [after *Pilsen* (*Plzeň*), city in Bohemia, where first made] [*often* p-] designating a light, Bohemian lager beer often served in a tall, cone-shaped glass (**Pilsener glass**)

Pilt·down man (pilt′doun′) a supposed species of prehistoric man presumed on the basis of bone fragments found in Piltdown (Sussex, England) in 1911 and exposed as a hoax in 1953

☆**Pi·ma** (pē′mə) *n.* [< Sp. < Pima] **1.** *pl.* **-mas, -ma** any member of a N. American Indian tribe in Arizona **2.** their language —**Pi′man** *adj.*

☆**Pima cotton** [< *Pima* County, Ariz.] a strong, smooth cotton grown in the southwestern U.S.

pi·men·to (pi men′tō) *n., pl.* **-tos** [< Sp. < L. *pigmentum*, lit., PIGMENT (in VL. & ML., spice)] **1.** a sweet variety of the capsicum pepper, or its red fruit, used as a relish, etc. **2.** *same as* ALLSPICE

pimento cheese a cheese containing pimentos

pi·mien·to (pi myen′tō, -men′-) *n. same as* PIMENTO

pimp (pimp) *n.* [prob. < or akin to MFr. *pimper*, to allure] a man who is an agent for prostitutes and lives off their earnings —*vi.* to act as a pimp

pim·per·nel (pim′pər nel′, -nəl) *n.* [< OFr. < LL., ult. < L. *piper*, PEPPER: its fruit resembles peppercorns] any of certain related plants with clustered flowers and leafless stems; esp., the **scarlet pimpernel**, with red, white, or blue, starlike flowers which close in bad weather

pim·ple (pim′p'l) *n.* [prob. < or akin to OE. *piplian*, to break out in pimples] any small, rounded, usually inflamed swelling of the skin

pim·ply (pim′plē) *adj.* **-pli·er, -pli·est** having pimples: also **pim′pled** (-p'ld)

pin (pin) *n.* [OE. *pinn*] **1.** a peg of wood, metal, etc., used for fastening things together, as a support to hang things, etc. **2.** a little piece of stiff wire with a pointed end and flattened or rounded head, for fastening things together **3.** something worthless or unimportant; trifle **4.** *clipped form of* CLOTHESPIN, SAFETY PIN, COTTER PIN, etc. **5.** anything like a pin in form, use, etc. **6.** an ornament, badge, or emblem with a pin or clasp for fastening to clothes **7.** a peg for regulating the tension of a string in a piano, harp, etc. **8.** [Colloq.] the leg: *usually used in pl.* **9.** *Bowling* any of the bottle-shaped, wooden clubs at which the ball is rolled **10.** *Golf* a pole with a flag attached, placed in and marking the hole of a green **11.** *Naut. a) same as* THOLE *b)* a peg or bolt used in fastening the rigging —*vt.* **pinned, pin′ning 1.** to fasten with or as with a pin **2.** to pierce with a pin **3.** to hold firmly in one position [the wrestler *pinned* his opponent to the floor] —**pin down 1.** to get (someone) to commit himself as to his opinion, plans, etc. **2.** to determine or prove the truth of (a fact, details, etc.) —☆**pin someone's ears back** [Colloq.] to beat, defeat, or scold someone soundly —**pin (something) on someone** [Colloq.] to lay the blame for (something) on someone

PIMPERNEL

pin·a·fore (pin′ə fôr′) *n.* [PIN + AFORE] **1.** a sleeveless, apron-like garment worn by little girls over the dress **2.** a sleeveless housedress

☆**pin·ball machine** (pin′bôl′) a game machine with a sloping board having pins, holes, etc., marked with scores, for a spring-driven ball to contact

pince-nez (pans′nā′, pins′-; Fr. paɴs nā′) *n., pl.* **pince′nez′** (-nāz′; Fr. -nā′) [Fr., nose-pincher] eyeglasses without sidepieces, kept in place by a spring gripping the bridge of the nose

pin·cers (pin′sərz) *n.pl.* [occas. with sing. v.] [< OFr. *pincier*, to pinch] **1.** a tool with two pivoted parts for gripping or nipping things **2.** a grasping claw, as of a crab —**pin′cer·like′** *adj.*

pinch (pinch) *vt.* [ult. < OFr. *pincier*] **1.** to squeeze as between finger and thumb or between two edges [he *pinched* the baby's cheek; she *pinched* her finger in the door] **2.** to nip off the end of (a plant shoot) **3.** to press painfully upon (a part of the body) [the new shoes *pinch* my toes] **4.** to cause distress or discomfort to **5.** to make thin, cramped, etc., as by hunger or cold [the illness had *pinched* his face] **6.** to restrict closely; straiten: usually in the passive [they were *pinched* for funds to expand the business] **7.** [Slang] *a)* to steal *b)* to arrest —*vi.* **1.** to squeeze painfully **2.** to be stingy or thrifty [he *pinched* and saved for years to buy the house] —*n.* **1.** a pinching; squeeze [a *pinch* on the arm] **2.** a quantity that may be grasped between finger and thumb; small amount [a *pinch* of salt] **3.** distress; hardship [the *pinch* of poverty] **4.** an emergency; urgent situation [she will help us in a *pinch*] **5.** [Slang] *a)* a theft *b)* an arrest —**pinch pennies** to be very thrifty —**pinch′er** *n.*

PINCERS

pinch·beck (pinch′bek′) *n.* [after C. *Pinchbeck*, 18th-cent. Eng. jeweler] **1.** an alloy of copper and zinc used to imitate gold in jewelry **2.** anything cheap or imitation —*adj.* of or like pinchbeck

pinch·cock (pinch′käk′) *n.* [PINCH + COCK¹] a clamp used on a flexible tube to control the flow of fluid through the tube

pinch·ers (pin′chərz) *n.pl. same as* PINCERS

☆**pinch-hit** (pinch′hit′) *vi.* **-hit′, -hit′ting 1.** *Baseball* to bat in place of the batter whose turn it is, esp. when a hit is particularly needed   **2.** to act as a substitute (*for*) in an emergency —**pinch hitter**

pin curl a strand of hair formed into a curl and held in place with a bobby pin while it sets

pin·cush·ion (pin′koŏsh′ən) *n.* a small cushion to stick pins and needles in, to keep them handy

Pin·dar (pin′dər) 522?–438? B.C.; Gr. lyric poet —**Pin·dar·ic** (pin dar′ik) *adj.*

pine[1] (pīn) *n.* see PLURAL, II, D, 3 [OE. *pin* < L. *pinus*, pine tree < IE. base *pi-*, fat] **1.** any of various evergreen trees of a family having needlelike leaves and woody cones: many pines are valuable for their wood and their resin, from which turpentine, tar, etc. are obtained   **2.** the wood

pine[2] (pīn) *vi.* pined, pin′ing [OE. *pinian*, to torment < *pin* < L. *poena*, a pain: see PENAL] **1.** to waste (*away*) with grief, longing, etc.   **2.** to have a strong longing; yearn [to *pine* for the old days]

pin·e·al body (pin′ē əl) [< Fr. < L. *pinea*, a pine cone] a small, cone-shaped body in the brain of vertebrates: its function is not known

pine·ap·ple (pīn′ap′'l) *n.* [ME. *pinappel*, pine cone (see PINE[1] & APPLE)] **1.** a juicy tropical fruit looking somewhat like a pine cone   **2.** the plant it grows on, with spiny-edged leaves

Pine Bluff city in central Ark., on the Arkansas River: pop. 57,000

pine cone the cone of a pine tree: see illustration at CONE

pine needle the needlelike leaf of a pine tree

pine nut ☆the sweet, edible seed of any of several pines found chiefly in the southwestern U.S. and in Mexico

☆**pine siskin** a small, brown finch of N. America, with yellow markings on the wings and tail: also called **pine finch**

pine tar a thick, dark liquid obtained by the destructive distillation of pine wood, used in ointments, tar paints, etc.

PINEAPPLE

pin·ey (pī′nē) *adj.* pin′i·er, pin′i·est **1.** filled with pines **2.** of or like pines [a *piney* fragrance]

pin·feath·er (pin′feth′ər) *n.* an undeveloped feather that is just coming through the skin

pin·fold (pin′fōld′) *n.* [OE. *pundfald* < *pund*, POUND[3] + *fald*, FOLD[2]] a place where stray animals are kept

ping (piŋ) *n.* [echoic] a sharp sound, as of a bullet striking, an engine knocking, etc. —*vi., vt.* to make or cause to make such a sound

Ping-Pong (piŋ′pôŋ′, -päŋ′) [echoic] *a trademark for* table tennis equipment —*n.* [p- p-] *same as* TABLE TENNIS

pin·head (pin′hed′) *n.* **1.** the head of a pin **2.** anything tiny or unimportant ☆**3.** a stupid or silly person —☆**pin′head′ed** *adj.*

pin·hole (-hōl′) *n.* **1.** a tiny hole made as by a pin **2.** a hole into which a pin or peg goes

pin·ion[1] (pin′yən) *n.* [< Fr., ult. < L. *pinna*, bucket of a paddle wheel, lit., feather] a small cogwheel with teeth that fit into a gearwheel or rack

pin·ion[2] (pin′yən) *n.* [< OFr. < L. *pinna*, a feather: see PEN[2]] **1.** the end joint of a bird's wing **2.** a bird's wing **3.** any wing feather —*vt.* **1.** to cut off or bind the pinions of (a bird) to keep it from flying **2.** to bind (the wings) **3.** to keep from moving by binding the arms of **4.** to bind (the arms) firmly

pink[1] (piŋk) *n.* [< ?] **1.** any of a group of plants of the pink family, with white, pale-red, or deep-red flowers that have a spicy smell **2.** the flower **3.** pale red **4.** the finest example, degree, etc. [the *pink* of perfection] **5.** [Colloq.] a person of somewhat radical political views —*adj.* **1.** designating a family of plants with bright-colored flowers, as the carnation, sweet william, etc. **2.** pale-red **3.** [Colloq.] somewhat radical —**in the pink** [Colloq.] in good physical condition; healthy —**pink′ish** *adj.* —**pink′ness** *n.*

pink[2] (piŋk) *vt.* [akin ? to OE. *pyngan*, to prick] **1.** to decorate (cloth, paper, etc.) with small holes in a pattern **2.** to cut a saw-toothed edge on (cloth, etc.) to prevent unraveling or for decoration **3.** to prick or stab, as with a sword **4.** to adorn or decorate —**pink′er** *n.*

pink·eye (piŋk′ī′) *n.* a severe form of conjunctivitis that can easily be spread from person to person

pink·ie, pink·y (piŋk′kē) *n., pl.* **pink′ies** [prob. < Du. dim. of *pink*, little finger] the fifth, or smallest, finger

pink·ing shears (piŋ′kiŋ) shears with notched blades, for pinking the edges of cloth, etc.

☆**pink salmon** a widespread species of salmon, often canned

☆**pink tea** [Colloq.] a social gathering at which nothing important is said or done

pink money **1.** orig., an allowance given to a wife for small personal expenses **2.** any small sum of money, as for minor expenses

pin·na (pin′ə) *n., pl.* **-nae** (-ē), **-nas** [L., a feather: see PEN[2]] **1.** *Anat.* the external ear **2.** *Bot.* a leaflet of a pinnate leaf **3.** *Zool.* a feather, wing, fin, etc.

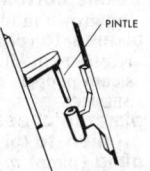

PINKING SHEARS

pin·nace (pin′is) *n.* [< Fr. < Sp., ult. < L. *pinus*, PINE[1]] **1.** a small sailing ship **2.** a ship's boat

pin·na·cle (pin′ə k'l) *n.* [< MFr. < LL. dim. of L. *pinna*, wing: see PEN[2]] **1.** a small turret or spire on a buttress, etc. **2.** a slender, pointed formation, as a mountain peak **3.** the highest point; acme [the *pinnacle* of success] —*vt.* **-cled, -cling 1.** to set on a pinnacle **2.** to furnish with pinnacles **3.** to form the pinnacle of —see SYN. at SUMMIT

pin·nate (pin′āt, -it) *adj.* [ModL. < L. < *pinna*, a feather: see PEN[2]] **1.** resembling a feather **2.** *Bot.* with leaflets on each side of the leafstalk —**pin′nate·ly** *adv.* —**pin·na′tion** *n.*

pin·ni·ped (pin′ə ped′) *adj.* [< ModL. < L. < *pinna*, a feather + *pes*, foot] belonging to a group of sea animals having flippers, including the seals and walruses —*n.* a pinniped animal

pin·nule (pin′yōōl) *n.* [ModL. < L., dim. of *pinna*, a wing, feather] **1.** any of the smallest divisions of a leaf which is doubly pinnate, esp. in ferns **2.** any of the side branches of the arm of a crinoid —**pin′nu·late** (-yoo lāt′), **pin′nu·lat′ed** *adj.*

☆**pi·noch·le, pi·noc·le** (pē′nuk′'l, -näk′'l) *n.* [earlier *binochle* < G. dial. < Fr. *binocle*, eyeglasses] **1.** a card game using a 48-card deck made up of two of every card above the eight, including the ace, in every suit **2.** the scoring combination of the queen of spades and the jack of diamonds in this game

☆**pi·ñon** (pin′yən, -yōn; *Sp.* pē nyôn′) *n., pl.* **-ñons;** *Sp.* **-ño′nes** (-nyô′nes) [< AmSp. < Sp., ult. < L. *pinus*, PINE[1]] **1.** any of several small pines with large, edible seeds, found in western N. America **2.** the seed

pin·point (pin′point′) *vt.* **1.** to show the location of (a place on a map, etc.) by sticking in a pin **2.** to locate, define, or focus on exactly [their research finally *pinpointed* the problem] —*n.* **1.** the point of a pin **2.** something small or unimportant [a *pinpoint* of light came through the curtain] —*adj.* minute, exact, precise, etc. [*pinpoint* accuracy]

pin·prick (-prik′) *n.* **1.** a tiny hole made as by a pin **2.** a minor irritation or annoyance

pins and needles a prickling feeling as in a numb arm or leg —**on pins and needles** in a state of anxious suspense

☆**pin·set·ter** (-set′ər) *n.* **1.** a person that sets up bowling pins on the alley **2.** a device that does this automatically Also **pin′spot′ter** (-spät′ər)

pin stripe **1.** a very thin stripe, as in some suits **2.** a pattern of such stripes in parallel

pint (pīnt) *n.* [< MFr. < ML. *pinta*: orig. prob. a painted spot marking the level in a measure] **1.** a measure of capacity (liquid or dry) equal to 1/2 quart **2.** a container holding a pint Abbrev. **pt., p.**

pin·tail (pin′tāl′) *n., pl.* **-tails′, -tail′:** see PLURAL, II, D, 1 **1.** any of several ducks, esp. one with long, pointed tail feathers ☆**2.** a grouse with a long, pointed tail —**pin′tailed′** *adj.*

pin·tle (pin′t'l) *n.* [OE. *pintel*, penis] a pin or bolt upon which some other part pivots or turns

☆**pin·to** (pin′tō) *adj.* [AmSp. < Sp., ult. < L. pp. of *pingere*, to PAINT] marked with patches of white and another color —*n., pl.* **-tos 1.** a pinto horse **2.** *same as* PINTO BEAN

PINTLE

☆**pinto bean** a spotted kidney bean grown in the southwestern U.S. for food and fodder

pint-size (pīnt′sīz′) *adj.* ☆small; tiny: also **pint′-sized′**

pin·up (pin′up′) *adj.* **1.** that is or can be pinned up on or fastened to a wall [a *pinup* lamp] ☆**2.** [Colloq.] designating or of a person whose sexual attractiveness makes her or him a suitable subject for the kind of pictures often pinned up on walls —☆*n.* [Colloq.] such a person, picture, etc.

pin·wheel (-hwēl′, -wēl′) *n.* **1.** a small wheel with colored vanes of paper, etc., pinned to a stick so as to spin in the wind **2.** a firework that spins and sends out colored lights when set off

pin·worm (-wurm′) *n.* a small, unsegmented worm sometimes found as a parasite in the large intestine and rectum, esp. in children

pin·y (pī′nē) *adj.* **pin′i·er, pin′i·est** same as PINEY

pi·on (pī′än) *n.* [PI² + (MES)ON] any of three mesons, positive, negative, or neutral, with a mass approximately 270 times that of an electron

pi·o·neer (pī′ə nir′) *n.* [< Fr. < OFr. *peonier*, foot soldier < *peon:* see PEON] ☆one who goes before, preparing the way for others, as an early settler or a scientist in research —*adj.* of or being a pioneer —*vi.* **1.** to prepare or open (a way, etc.) ☆**2.** to be a pioneer in (a region, undertaking, etc.)

pi·ous (pī′əs) *adj.* [L. *pius*] **1.** having or showing religious devotion **2.** coming from actual or pretended religious devotion **3.** pretending to be virtuous without really being so —**pi′ous·ly** *adv.* —**pi′ous·ness** *n.*

pip[1] (pip) *n.* a small seed, as of an apple, pear, etc.

pip[2] (pip) *n.* [earlier *peep* < ?] **1.** any of the spots on playing cards, dice, etc. **2.** same as BLIP (sense 1)

pip[3] (pip) *vi.* **pipped, pip′ping** [prob. var. of PEEP¹] to peep or chirp, as a young bird —*vt.* to break through (the shell): said of a hatching bird

pip[4] (pip) *n.* [< MDu., ult. < L. *pituita*, phlegm] **1.** a contagious disease of fowl, characterized by the secretion of mucus in the throat **2.** [Colloq.] any unspecified human illness: a humorous usage

pipe (pīp) *n.* [OE., ult. < L. *pipare*, to chirp] **1.** a cylindrical tube, as of wood or metal, into which air is blown to make musical sounds; specif., [*pl.*] same as: *a)* PANPIPE *b)* BAGPIPE **2.** any of the tubes in an organ that produce the tones **3.** a boatswain's whistle **4.** a high, shrill sound, as of a birdcall **5.** [often *pl.*] the vocal organs, esp. as used in singing **6.** a long tube of concrete, metal, etc., for carrying water, oil, etc. from one place to another **7.** a tube-shaped organ of the body; esp., [*pl.*] the breathing organs **8.** anything shaped like a tube **9.** *a)* a tube with a small bowl at one end, in which tobacco, etc. is smoked *b)* enough tobacco, etc. to fill such a bowl **10.** *a)* a cask holding about 126 gallons *b)* this volume as a unit of measure —*vi.* **piped, pip′ing 1.** to play on a pipe **2.** to utter shrill sounds —*vt.* **1.** to play (a tune, etc.) on a pipe **2.** to utter in a shrill voice **3.** to bring, call, etc. by piping ☆**4.** to move (water, oil, etc.) from one place to another by pipes ☆**5.** to provide with pipes **6.** to trim (a dress, etc.) with piping **7.** [Slang] to look at —**pipe down** ☆[Slang] to become quiet, stop shouting, etc. —**pipe up 1.** to begin to play or sing (music) **2.** to speak up or say, esp. in a piping voice

pipe clay a white, plastic clay used for making tobacco pipes, whitening leather, etc.

pipe cleaner a short length of thin wires twisted together to hold tiny tufts of yarn, used to clean the stem of a tobacco pipe

pipe cutter a tool with a curved jaw containing sharp disks that is rotated around a metal pipe in order to cut it

☆**pipe dream** [Colloq.] a fantastic idea or vain hope, such as an opium smoker might have

pipe·fish (pīp′fish′) *n., pl.* **-fish′, -fish′es:** see FISH a long, narrow fish with bony scales and a tubelike snout, related to the sea horses

pipe fitter a mechanic who installs and maintains plumbing pipes, etc. —**pipe fitting**

pipe·ful (pīp′fool′) *n., pl.* **-fuls′** the amount (of tobacco, etc.) put in a pipe at one time

☆**pipe·line** (-līn′) *n.* **1.** a line of pipes for moving water, gas, oil, etc. **2.** any means whereby something is passed on [a *pipeline* of information] —*vt.* **-lined′, -lin′ing** to move by, or supply with, a pipeline

☆**pipe of peace** same as CALUMET

☆**pipe organ** same as ORGAN (sense 1 *a*)

pip·er (pīp′ər) *n.* a person who plays on a pipe; esp., a bagpiper —**pay the piper** to suffer the consequences of doing as one pleases

pipe·stem (-stem′) *n.* **1.** the slender stem of a tobacco pipe **2.** anything like this in form

pi·pette, pi·pet (pī pet′, pi-) *n.* [Fr., dim. of *pipe*, a pipe] a slender tube for measuring or transferring small amounts of liquids

pip·ing (pīp′iŋ) *n.* **1.** the act of one who pipes **2.** music made by pipes **3.** a shrill sound **4.** a system of pipes **5.** material used for pipes **6.** a narrow, rounded fold of material with which edges or seams are trimmed —*adj.* **1.** playing on a pipe **2.** high and shrill [a *piping* voice] —**piping hot** so hot as to sizzle; very hot

pip·it (pip′it) *n.* [echoic of its cry] a small songbird with a slender bill and streaked breast

pip·kin (pip′kin) *n.* [? dim. of PIPE, *n.* 10] a small earthenware pot

pip·pin (pip′in) *n.* [OFr. *pepin*, seed, pip] any of a number of varieties of apple

☆**pip·sis·se·wa** (pip sis′ə wə) *n.* [< Algonquian] a N. American evergreen plant with jagged, leathery leaves formerly used in medicine

pip·squeak (pip′skwēk′) *n.* [PIP³ + SQUEAK] [Colloq.] anything or anyone regarded as small or insignificant

pi·quant (pē′kənt, -känt; *now occas.* -kwänt) *adj.* [Fr. prp., of *piquer*, to prick] **1.** pleasantly sharp or spicy to the taste [a *piquant* sauce] **2.** exciting interest; stimulating; provocative [a *piquant* remark] —**pi′quan·cy** (-kən sē), **pi′quant·ness** *n.* —**pi′quant·ly** *adv.*

pique (pēk) *n.* [Fr. < *piquer*, to prick] **1.** resentment at being ignored or treated impolitely; ruffled pride **2.** a fit of displeasure —*vt.* **piqued, piqu′ing 1.** to arouse resentment in, as by slighting; offend **2.** to arouse (one's curiosity, etc.) —see SYN. at OFFENSE

pi·qué (pē kā′) *n.* [Fr., pp. of *piquer*, to prick] a firmly woven cotton fabric with ribbed weave

pi·quet (pi ket′, -kā′) *n.* [Fr. < *pic*, orig., a sting] a game of cards for two, played with 32 cards

pi·ra·cy (pī′rə sē) *n., pl.* **-cies** [< ML.: see PIRATE] **1.** robbery of ships on the high seas **2.** the unauthorized publication or use of a copyrighted or patented work

Pi·rae·us (pī rē′əs) seaport in SE Greece: part of Athens metropolitan area: pop. 184,000

Pi·ran·del·lo (pir′ən del′ō; *It.* pē′rän del′lô), **Lu·i·gi** (loo-ē′jē) 1867–1936; It. playwright & novelist

pi·ra·nha (pi rän′yə, -ran′-) *n.* [Braz. Port. < Tupi, toothed fish] a small, fiercely hungry freshwater fish of South America that in schools will attack any animal

pi·rate (pī′rət) *n.* [< L. < Gr. *peiratēs* < *peirān*, to attack: for IE. base see FARE] **1.** a person who practices piracy; esp., a robber of ships on the high seas **2.** a pirates' ship —*vt., vi.* **-rat·ed, -rat·ing 1.** to practice piracy (upon) **2.** to take (something) by piracy **3.** to publish or reproduce without authorization (a literary work, musical recording, etc.), esp. in violation of a copyright —**pi·rat·i·cal** (pī rat′i k'l), **pi·rat′ic** *adj.* —**pi·rat′i·cal·ly** *adv.*

PIRANHA
(to 2 ft. long)

pi·rogue (pi rōg′) *n.* [< Fr. < Sp. *piragua* < Carib] a canoe made by hollowing out a log

pir·ou·ette (pir′oo wet′) *n.* [Fr., spinning top; prob. < dial. *piroue*, a top] a whirling around on one foot or the point of the toe, esp. in ballet —*vi.* **-et′ted, -et′ting** to do a pirouette

Pi·sa (pē′zə; *It.* pē′sä) city in W Italy: famous for its Leaning Tower, a bell tower which leans more than 17 ft. from the perpendicular: pop. 103,000

pis·ca·to·ri·al (pis′kə tôr′ē əl) *adj.* [< L. < *piscator*, fisherman] of fishermen or fishing: also **pis′ca·to·ry**

Pis·ces (pis′ēz, pis′ēz) [L., pl. of *piscis*, a FISH] **1.** a constellation S of Andromeda **2.** the twelfth sign of the zodiac: see ZODIAC

pis·ci- [< L. *piscis*, a FISH] *a combining form meaning* fish [*pisciculture*]

pis·ci·cul·ture (pis′i kul′chər) *n.* [prec. + CULTURE] the breeding of fish as a science or industry

pis·cine (pis′īn, -ēn; pī′sēn) *adj.* [< L. *piscis*, a FISH] of or resembling fish

Pi·sis·tra·tus (pī sis′trə təs, pi-) 600?–527 B.C.; tyrant of Athens (560–527, with two interruptions)

pis·mire (pis′mīr′, piz′-) *n.* [< ME. < *pisse*, urine + *mire*, ant: from the odor of ants' formic acid] an ant

Pis·sar·ro (pē sà rō′; *E.* pi sär′ō), **Ca·mille** (kà mē′y′) 1830–1903; Fr. painter

pis·ta·chi·o (pi stä′shē ō′, -stash′ē ō′, -stash′ō) *n., pl.* -chi·os′ [< It. < L. < Gr. *pistakē* < OPer. *pistah*] **1.** a small tree related to the cashew **2.** its edible, greenish seed (**pistachio nut**) **3.** the flavor of this nut **4.** a light yellow-green color

pis·til (pis′t'l) *n.* [Fr. < L. *pistillum*, PESTLE] the seed-bearing organ of a flowering plant, consisting of one carpel or of several united carpels

pis·til·late (pis′tə lit, -lāt′) *adj.* having a pistil or pistils; specif., having pistils but no stamens

pis·tol (pis′t'l) *n.* [< Fr. < G. < Czech *pišt'al*, prob. < *pisk*, a whistling sound] **1.** a small firearm held and fired with one hand **2.** such a firearm in which the chamber is part of the barrel: see also REVOLVER —*vt.* **-toled** or **-tolled, -tol·ing** or **-tol·ling** to shoot with a pistol

pis·tole (pis tōl′) *n.* [Fr.] **1.** a former Spanish gold coin **2.** any similar obsolete European coin

☆**pis·tol-whip** (pis′t'l hwip′, -wip′) *vt.* **-whipped′, -whip′ping** to beat with a pistol, esp. about the head

pis·ton (pis′t'n) *n.* [Fr. < It. < *pistare*, to beat, ult. < L. *pinsere*, to pound] **1.** a disk or short cylinder closely fitted in a hollow cylinder and moved back and forth by the pressure of a fluid so as to move the rod (**piston rod**) attached to it, or moved by the rod so as to exert pressure on the fluid **2.** *Music* a sliding valve moved in the cylinder of a brass-wind instrument to change the pitch

Pis·ton (pis′t'n), **Walter** 1894– ; U.S. composer

piston ring a split metal ring placed around a piston to make it fit the cylinder closely

☆**pit¹** (pit) *n.* [Du. < MDu. *pitte*] the hard stone in the center of a plum, peach, etc., which contains the seed —*vt.* **pit′ted, pit′ting** to remove the pit from

pit² (pit) *n.* [OE. *pytt*, ult. < L. *puteus*, a well] **1.** a hole in the ground **2.** an abyss **3.** hell: used with *the* **4.** a covered hole used to trap wild animals; pitfall **5.** any concealed danger; trap **6.** an enclosed area in which animals are kept or made to fight [a bear *pit*] **7.** *a*) the shaft of a coal mine *b*) the mine itself **8.** a hollow on a part of the human body [an *armpit*] **9.** a small hollow in a surface; specif., a smallpox scar on the skin **10.** [Brit.] *a*) the rear part of the ground floor of a theater *b*) the spectators in that section **11.** the sunken section in front of the stage, where the orchestra sits ☆**12.** the part of the floor of an exchange where a special branch of business is transacted [the corn *pit*] ☆**13.** an area off the side of a racing speedway for servicing racing cars **14.** *Bot.* a thin area in a plant cell wall —*vt.* **pit′ted, pit′ting** **1.** to put or store in a pit **2.** to make pits in **3.** to mark with small scars [a face *pitted* by smallpox] **4.** to set (cocks, etc.) in a pit to fight **5.** to set in competition (*against*) [which team is *pitted* against ours?] —*vi.* to become marked with pits

pit·a·pat (pit′ə pat′) *adv.* [echoic] with rapid beating; palpitatingly [her heart went *pitapat*] —*n.* a rapid succession of beats or taps —*vi.* **-pat′ted, -pat′ting** to go pitapat

Pit·cairn Island (pit′kern) Brit. island in Polynesia, South Pacific: settled by Brit. mutineers in 1790

pitch¹ (pich) *n.* [OE. *pic* < L. *pix:* for IE. base see PINE¹] **1.** a black, sticky substance formed in the distillation of coal tar, petroleum, etc. and used for waterproofing, pavements, etc. **2.** natural asphalt **3.** a resin from certain evergreen trees —*vt.* to cover or smear as with pitch

pitch² (pich) *vt.* [ME. *picchen*] **1.** to set up [to *pitch* a tent] **2.** to throw; fling; toss **3.** to fix or set at a particular point, level, degree, etc. ☆**4.** *a*) to throw (the baseball) to the batter *b*) to serve as pitcher for (a game) **5.** to hit (a golf ball) in a high curve, esp. in making an approach **6.** to set the key of (a tune, an instrument, or the voice) —*vi.* **1.** to encamp **2.** to take up one's position; settle **3.** to hurl or toss anything, as hay, a baseball, etc. **4.** to fall or plunge forward or headlong **5.** to incline downward; dip [the roof *pitches* sharply] **6.** to toss with the

bow and stern rising and falling: said of a ship **7.** to move in a like manner in the air: said of an aircraft **8.** to act as pitcher in a ball game —*n.* **1.** act or manner of pitching **2.** a throw; toss **3.** the pitching of a ship or aircraft in rough sea or air **4.** anything pitched [the *pitch* hit the batter] **5.** a point or degree [emotion was at a high *pitch*] **6.** the degree of slope or inclination **7.** *a*) the blade angle of a propeller *b*) the distance advanced by a propeller in one revolution ☆**8.** a card game in which the suit of the first card led becomes trump ☆**9.** [Colloq.] a line of talk, such as a salesman or hawker uses to persuade or sell **10.** the distance between corresponding points, as on two adjacent gear teeth or on two adjacent threads of a screw, measured along the axis **11.** *a*) that quality of a tone or sound determined by the frequency of vibration of the sound waves: the greater the frequency, the higher the pitch *b*) a standard of pitch for tuning instruments —see SYN. at THROW —☆**make a pitch for** [Slang] to speak in favor of —**pitch in** [Colloq.] **1.** to set to work energetically **2.** to make a contribution —**pitch into** [Colloq.] to attack

pitch-black (pich′blak′) *adj.* very black

pitch-blende (pich′blend′) *n.* [< G. < *pech*, PITCH¹ + *blende*, BLENDE] a brown to black lustrous mineral, the chief ore of uranium

pitch-dark (pich′därk′) *adj.* very dark

pitched battle (picht) **1.** a battle in which placement of troops and the line of combat are fixed before the action **2.** a hard-fought battle

pitch·er¹ (pich′ər) *n.* [< OFr. < VL. *bicarium*, a jug, cup; see BEAKER] a container, usually with a handle and lip, for holding and pouring liquids —**pitch′er·ful′** (-fool′) *n., pl.* **-fuls′**

pitch·er² (pich′ər) *n.* [PITCH² + -ER] *Baseball* the player who pitches the ball to opposing batters

pitcher plant a plant with pitcherlike leaves which attract and trap insects

pitch·fork (pich′fôrk′) *n.* a large, long-handled fork used for lifting and tossing hay, etc. —*vt.* to lift and toss as with a pitchfork

☆**pitch·man** (-mən) *n., pl.* **-men** **1.** a person who sells novelties, jewelry, etc., as at a carnival, by keeping up a loud sales talk **2.** [Slang] any high-pressure salesman or advertiser

☆**pitch·out** (-out′) *n.* **1.** *Baseball* a ball pitched away from the plate on purpose so that the catcher can try to throw out a runner who is off base **2.** *Football* a lateral pass behind the line of scrimmage, usually from the quarterback to another back

PITCHFORK

☆**pitch pine** a resinous pine of eastern N. America from which pitch or turpentine is obtained

pitch pipe a small pipe which produces a fixed tone used as a standard for tuning instruments, etc.

pitch·y (pich′ē) *adj.* **pitch′i·er, pitch′i·est** **1.** full of or smeared with pitch **2.** thick and sticky like pitch **3.** black —**pitch′i·ness** *n.*

pit·e·ous (pit′ē əs) *adj.* arousing or deserving pity [*piteous* cries] —see SYN. at PITIFUL —**pit′e·ous·ly** *adv.* —**pit′e·ous·ness** *n.*

pit·fall (pit′fôl′) *n.* [< ME. < *pit*, PIT² + *falle*, a trap < OE. *fealle*] **1.** a lightly covered pit used as a trap for animals **2.** any hidden danger or difficulty

pith (pith) *n.* [OE. *pitha*] **1.** the soft, spongy tissue in the center of certain plant stems **2.** any soft core, as of a bone **3.** the essential part; gist [the *pith* of an argument] **4.** importance: now usually in the phrase **of great pith and moment** —*vt.* to remove the pith from (a plant stem)

Pith·e·can·thro·pus e·rec·tus (pith′ə kan′thrə pəs i-rek′təs, -kan thrō′pəs) [ModL. < Gr. *pithēkos*, an ape + *anthrōpos*, man] an earlier name for JAVA MAN

pith·y (pith′ē) *adj.* **pith′i·er, pith′i·est** **1.** of, like, or full of pith **2.** brief and full of substance or meaning —see SYN. at CONCISE —**pith′i·ly** *adv.* —**pith′i·ness** *n.*

pit·i·a·ble (pit′ē ə b'l) *adj.* arousing or deserving pity, sometimes mixed with scorn or contempt —see SYN. at PITIFUL —**pit′i·a·ble·ness** *n.* —**pit′i·a·bly** *adv.*

pit·i·ful (pit′i fəl) *adj.* **1.** exciting or deserving pity **2.** deserving contempt; pitiable; despicable —**pit′i·ful·ly** *adv.* —**pit′i·ful·ness** *n.*

SYN.—pitiful is applied to that which arouses or deserves pity because it is sad or pathetic [the suffering of the starving refugees was *pitiful*]; **pitiable**

(Illustrations labeled PISTIL and PISTON appear in the left column.)

is usually used when contempt is mixed with feelings of pity [the opposition was reduced to a *pitiable* minority]; **piteous** stresses the nature of the thing calling for pity rather than its effect on an observer [her *piteous* pleas for help were ignored]

pit·i·less (pit′i lis) *adj.* without pity; merciless —see SYN. at CRUEL —**pit′i·less·ly** *adv.* —**pit′i·less·ness** *n.*

pi·ton (pē′tän; *Fr.* pē tōn′) *n., pl.* **-tons** (-tänz; *Fr.* -tōn′) [Fr. < MFr., a spike] a metal spike that is driven into rock or ice for support in mountain climbing: it has an eye to which a rope can be secured

Pitt (pit), **William** **1.** 1st Earl of Chatham, 1708–78; Eng. statesman; prime minister (1766–68) **2.** 1759–1806; Eng. statesman; prime minister (1783–1801; 1804–06): son of *prec.*

pit·tance (pit′′ns) *n.* [< OFr. *pitance*, food allowed a monk, ult. < L. *pietas*, PIETY] **1.** a meager allowance of money **2.** a small amount or share

pit·ter-pat·ter (pit′ər pat′ər) *n.* [echoic] a rapid succession of light beating or tapping sounds, as of raindrops —*adv.* with a pitter-patter —*vi.* to fall, move, etc. with a pitter-patter

Pitts·burgh (pits′bərg) [after Wm. PITT (the father)] city in SW Pa.: pop. 520,000 (met. area 2,401,000)

Pitts·field (pits′fēld′) [after Wm. PITT (the father)] city in W Mass.: pop. 57,000

pi·tu·i·tar·y (pi tōō′ə ter′ē, -tyōō′-) *adj.* [< L. < *pituita*, phlegm: for IE. base see PINE¹] of the pituitary gland —*n., pl.* **-tar′ies** same as PITUITARY GLAND

pituitary gland (or **body**) a small, oval endocrine gland attached to the base of the brain: it secretes hormones influencing body growth, the activity of other endocrine glands, etc.

pit viper any of a family of poisonous snakes, as the rattlesnake, copperhead, etc., with a pit on each side of the head

pit·y (pit′ē) *n., pl.* **pit′ies** [< OFr. < L. *pietas*, PIETY] **1.** sorrow for another's suffering or misfortune; compassion **2.** a cause for sorrow or regret [it's a *pity* that you weren't there] —*vt., vi.* **pit′ied, pit′y·ing** to feel pity (for) —**have** (or **take**) **pity on** to show pity for —**pit′i·er** *n.* —**pit′y·ing·ly** *adv.*

SYN.—**pity** implies sorrow felt for another's suffering or misfortune and sometimes suggests slight contempt as well, because the person's troubles are considered to be the result of his own weakness or inferiority [she felt *pity* for a person so ignorant]; **compassion** implies pity along with an urge to help or spare [he was moved by *compassion* and did not demand payment of the debt]; **sympathy** implies a feeling of such closeness to another that one is able to understand and even share emotionally his sorrow, etc. [he always turned to his wife for *sympathy*]

‡**più** (pyōō) *adv.* [It.] more: a direction in music, as in *più allegro*, more quickly

Pi·us (pī′əs) name of twelve popes; esp., **Pius XII** 1876–1958; Pope (1939–58)

piv·ot (piv′ət) *n.* [Fr.] **1.** a point, shaft, etc. on which something turns **2.** a person or thing on which something turns or depends [that point is the *pivot* of his whole argument] **3.** a movement made as if turning on a pivot —*adj.* same as PIVOTAL —*vt.* to provide with or mount on a pivot —*vi.* to turn as on a pivot [he *pivoted* on his heel and walked away]

piv·ot·al (-'l) *adj.* **1.** of or acting as a pivot **2.** on which something turns or depends; crucial [a *pivotal* decision]

pix·ie, pix·y (pik′sē) *n., pl.* **pix′ies** [< Brit. dial.] a fairy or sprite, esp. one that is mischievous —**pix′ie·ish, pix′y·ish** *adj.*

Pi·zar·ro (pē thär′rō; *E.* pi zä′rō), **Fran·cis·co** (frän thēs′kō) 1470?–1541; Sp. conqueror of Peru

☆**pi·zazz, pi·zzazz** (pə zaz′) *n.* [< ?] [Slang] **1.** energy, vitality, spirit, etc. **2.** smartness, style, flair, etc.

☆**piz·za** (pēt′sə) *n.* [It.] an Italian dish made by baking a thin layer of dough covered with a spiced preparation of tomatoes, cheese, etc.

☆**piz·ze·ri·a** (pēt′sə rē′ə) *n.* [It.] a place where pizzas are prepared and sold

piz·zi·ca·to (pit′sə kät′ō; *It.* pēt′tsē kä′tô) *adj.* [It.] *Music* plucked: a direction to pluck the strings of a violin, viola, etc. —*adv.* in a pizzicato manner —*n., pl.* **-ca′ti** (-ē; *It.* -tē) a note or passage played in this way

☆**pj's** (pē′jāz′) *n.pl.* [< P(A)J(AMA)S] *colloq. var. of* PAJAMAS

pk. *pl.* **pks.** **1.** pack **2.** park **3.** peak **4.** peck

pkg. package; packages

PKU phenylketonuria

pkwy. parkway

pl. **1.** place **2.** plate **3.** plural

plac·a·ble (plak′ə b'l, plā′kə-) *adj.* [< OFr. < L. < *placare*: see PLACATE] capable of being placated; forgiving —**plac′a·bil′i·ty** *n.* —**plac′a·bly** *adv.*

plac·ard (plak′ärd, -ərd) *n.* [< MFr. < MDu. *placke*, a piece] **1.** a notice for display in a public place; poster **2.** a small card or plaque —*vt.* **1.** to place placards on or in [to *placard* a fence with advertising posters] **2.** to advertise by means of placards —*vi.* to set up placards

pla·cate (plā′kāt, plak′āt) *vt.* **-cat·ed, -cat·ing** [< L. pp. of *placare*, to appease: for IE. base see FLAKE] to stop from being angry; appease; pacify —see SYN. at PACIFY —**pla′cat·er** *n.* —**pla·ca′tion** *n.* —**pla′ca·tive** (plā′kāt·iv, -kət-; plak′āt′-) *adj.* —**pla′ca·to·ry** *adj.*

place (plās) *n.* [OFr. < L. *platea* < Gr. *plateia*, a street < *platys*, broad: for IE. base see PLANT] **1.** a square or court in a city **2.** a short street **3.** space; room **4.** a region or locality **5.** *a)* the part of space occupied by a person or thing [one cannot be in two *places* at one time] *b)* situation or state [if I were in her *place*] **6.** a city, town, or village **7.** a residence; dwelling [staying overnight at his *place*] **8.** a building or space devoted to a special purpose [a *place* of amusement] **9.** a particular spot on or part of something [a sore *place* on the leg] **10.** a particular passage or page in a book, etc., esp. the point where one has temporarily stopped reading [to mark one's *place*] **11.** position or standing, esp. one of importance [one's *place* in history] **12.** a step or point in a sequence [in the first *place*] **13.** the customary or proper position, time, or character [this is not the *place* for loud talking] **14.** a space reserved or occupied by a person, as a seat in a theater, etc. **15.** a job or position; employment [he's looking for a *place* in government] **16.** official position **17.** the duties of any position **18.** one's duty or business [it's not her *place* to discipline my child] **19.** *Arith.* the position of a figure, as in noting decimals [the third decimal *place*] **20.** *Racing* the first, second, or third position at the finish, specif. the second position —*vt.* **placed, plac′ing 1.** *a)* to put in a particular place, condition, or relation ☆*b)* to identify by associating with the correct place or circumstances [I can't *place* that man's face] **2.** to find employment or a position for **3.** to arrange for [to *place* an order] **4.** to assign (a value) **5.** to offer for consideration, etc. [to *place* the problem before the Board of Trustees] **6.** to repose (trust, etc.) *in* a person or thing **7.** to finish in (a specified position) in a competition —*vi.* to finish among the first three in a contest; specif., to finish second in a horse or dog race —**give place 1.** to make room **2.** to yield ☆**go places** [Slang] to achieve success —**in** (or **out of**) **place 1.** in (or out of) the customary or proper place **2.** being (or not being) fitting or timely —**in place of** instead of; as a substitute for —**put someone in his place** to let someone know he has been too bold, friendly, arrogant, etc. —**take place** to happen; occur —**take the place of** to be a substitute for

pla·ce·bo (plə sē′bō) *n., pl.* **-bos, -boes** [L., I shall please] *Med.* a sugar pill or like given as a medicine to a patient to humor him, or such a preparation used as a control in an experiment

☆**place card** a small card with the name of a guest, set at the place that he is to occupy at a table

place kick *Football* a kick made while the ball is held in place on the ground, as in kicking off or in attempting a field goal —**place′-kick′** *vi.*

place mat a small mat serving as an individual table cover for a person at a meal

place·ment (plās′mənt) *n.* **1.** a placing or being placed **2.** the finding of employment for a person **3.** location or arrangement **4.** *Football a)* the position of the ball on the ground for a place kick *b) same as* PLACE KICK

pla·cen·ta (plə sen′tə) *n., pl.* **-tas, -tae** [ModL. < L., lit., a cake, ult. < Gr. *plax*, a flat object: for IE. base see FLAKE] **1.** a vascular organ developed within the uterus, connected by the umbilical cord to the fetus and supplying it with nourishment **2.** *Bot.* that part of the lining of the ovary which bears the ovules —**pla·cen′tal** *adj.*

plac·er¹ (plās′ər) *n.* a person who places

☆**plac·er**² (plas′ər) *n.* [AmSp. < Catalan < *plassa*, a place] a waterborne or glacial deposit of gravel or sand containing particles of gold, platinum, etc. that can be washed out

---

fat, āpe, cär; ten, ēven; is, bīte; gō, hôrn, tōōl, lŏŏk; ôil, out; up, fur; get; joy; yet; chin; she; thin, then; zh, leisure; ŋ, ring; ə for *a* in *ago*, *e* in *agent*, *i* in *sanity*, *o* in *comply*, *u* in *focus*; ' as in *able* (ā′b'l); Fr. bál; ë, Fr. coeur; ö, Fr. feu; ô, Fr. mon; ô, Fr. coq; ü, Fr. duc; r, Fr. cri; H, G. ich; kh, G. doch; ‡ foreign; ☆ Americanism; < derived from. See inside front cover.

☆**plac·er mining** (plas′ər) mining of placer deposits by washing, dredging, etc.

place setting the china, silverware, etc. for setting one place at a table for a meal

plac·id (plas′id) *adj.* [L. *placidus*] undisturbed; tranquil; calm [a *placid* village; a *placid* disposition] —see SYN. at CALM —**pla·cid·i·ty** (plə sid′ə tē), **plac′id·ness** *n.* —**plac′id·ly** *adv.*

plack·et (plak′it) *n.* [prob. < PLACARD, in related obs. sense] a slit at the waist of a skirt or dress to make it easier to put the garment on and take it off

plac·oid (plak′oid) *adj.* [< Gr. *plax*, flat plate + -OID] of or having the horny scales found in cartilaginous fishes, as the sharks, rays, etc.

pla·gia·rism (plā′jə riz′m, -jē ə riz′m) *n.* [< L. *plagiarius*, kidnapper] **1.** the act of plagiarizing **2.** an idea, plot, piece of writing, etc. that has been plagiarized —**pla′gia·rist** *n.* —**pla·gia·ris′-tic** *adj.*

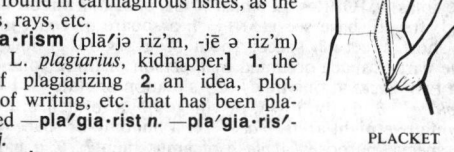

PLACKET

pla·gia·rize (plā′jə rīz′, plā′jē ə-) *vt., vi.* -rized′, -riz′ing [see prec.] to take (ideas, writings, etc.) from (another) and pass them off as one's own —**pla′gia·riz′er** *n.*

pla·gi·o·clase (plā′jē ə klās′) *n.* [< G. < Gr. *plagios*, oblique + *klasis*, a cleaving] any of a series of common rock-forming feldspars

plague (plāg) *n.* [< MFr. < L. *plaga* < Gr. *plēgē*, misfortune] **1.** anything that causes suffering or trouble; calamity **2.** any deadly epidemic disease; specif., *same as* BUBONIC PLAGUE **3.** [Colloq.] a nuisance —*vt.* **plagued**, **plagu′ing 1.** to afflict with a plague **2.** to vex; torment [mosquitoes *plagued* the picnickers] —see SYN. at ANNOY —**plagu′er** *n.*

pla·guy, pla·guey (plā′gē) *adj.* [Dial. or Colloq.] annoying; disagreeable —*adv.* [Dial. or Colloq.] annoyingly; disagreeably: also **pla′gui·ly**

plaice (plās) *n., pl.* **plaice, plaic′es**: see PLURAL, II, D, 2 [< OFr. < LL. *platessa*, flatfish < Gr. *platys*, broad] any of various related American or European flatfishes

plaid (plad) *n.* [Gael. *plaide*, a blanket] **1.** a long woolen cloth with a crossbarred pattern, worn over the shoulder by Scottish Highlanders **2.** a fabric with stripes or bars of various colors and widths that cross at right angles **3.** any pattern of this kind —*adj.* having such a pattern: also **plaid′ed**

plain (plān) *adj.* [OFr. < L. *planus*, flat: for IE. base see FIELD] **1.** orig., flat; level; plane **2.** not obstructed; open [in *plain* view] **3.** clearly understood; obvious [his meaning was *plain*] **4.** *a)* outspoken; frank [*plain* talk] *b)* downright; absolute; utter [*plain* nonsense] **5.** *a)* not luxurious or elegant [a *plain* way of life] *b)* not fancy; with little or no decoration [a *plain* coat] **6.** not complicated; simple [*plain* sewing] **7.** not good-looking; homely [a *plain* face] **8.** not having a pattern, markings, etc. on it [a *plain* sheet of paper] **9.** pure; unmixed [*plain* soda] **10.** common; ordinary [a *plain* man] —*n.* an extent of level country —*adv.* clearly or simply [just *plain* tired] —see SYN. at EVIDENT —**plain′ly** *adv.* —**plain′ness** *n.*

plain·clothes man (plān′klōz′, -klōthz′) a police detective who wears civilian clothes on duty: also **plain′clothes′man** (-mən) *n., pl.* -**men**

☆**Plains Indian** a member of any of the American Indian tribes who lived on the Great Plains, where they followed the bison herds

☆**plains·man** (plānz′mən) *n., pl.* -**men** an inhabitant of the plains; esp., a frontiersman on the Great Plains

Plains of Abraham a plain near Quebec: site of a battle (1759) of the French and Indian War in which the British under Wolfe defeated the French under Montcalm

plain·song (plān′sôŋ′) *n.* early Christian church music, still used in some churches, in free rhythm and sung in unison: also **plain′chant** (-chant′)

plain-spo·ken (plān′spō′k'n) *adj.* speaking or spoken plainly or frankly —**plain′-spo′ken·ness** *n.*

plaint (plānt) *n.* [< OFr. < L. pp. of *plangere*, to lament] **1.** [Poet.] a wail of sorrow; lament **2.** a complaint

plain·tiff (plān′tif) *n.* [< OFr. < *plaindre*, to complain: see prec.] a person who brings a suit into a court of law; complainant

plain·tive (plān′tiv) *adj.* [< OFr.: see PLAINT] expressing sorrow or melancholy; mournful; sad —**plain′tive·ly** *adv.* —**plain′tive·ness** *n.*

plait (plāt; *chiefly Brit.* plat) *n.* [< OFr. < L. pp. of *plicare*, to fold: see COMPLICATE] **1.** *same as* PLEAT **2.** a braid of hair, ribbon, etc. —*vt.* **1.** *same as* PLEAT **2.** to braid or make by braiding —**plait′er** *n.*

plan (plan) *n.* [Fr., plan: merging of *plan* (< L. *planus*, flat) with MFr. *plant* < It. *pianta* < L. *planta*, sole of the foot: see PLANT] **1.** a diagram showing the arrangement in horizontal section of a structure, piece of ground, etc. [floor *plans* of the house] **2.** *a)* a scheme or program for making, doing, or arranging something; project; schedule, etc. [vacation *plans*] *b)* a method of proceeding [it would be a good *plan* to stop halfway and eat] —*vt.* **planned**, **plan′ning 1.** to make a plan of (a structure, piece of ground, etc.) **2.** to think out a way of doing, making, etc. [he *planned* his escape carefully] **3.** to have in mind as a project or purpose [we *plan* to visit Canada next year] —*vi.* to make plans —**plan′ner** *n.*

SYN.—**plan** refers to any detailed method, thought out ahead of time, for doing or making something [plans for the merger of the companies]; **design** stresses the outcome aimed at in a plan and implies the use of skill or craft, sometimes in an underhanded way [it was his *design* to separate us]; **project** suggests an ambitious or large-scale plan [a housing *project*]; **scheme** often suggests a plan that is vague and impractical or one that is crafty or underhanded [a *scheme* for getting rich quick]

pla·nar (plā′nər) *adj.* of, having to do with, or lying in one plane

pla·nar·i·an (plə ner′ē ən) *n.* [< ModL. < LL. *planarius*, flat < L. *planus*] any of a group of small, soft-bodied, free-living flatworms moving by means of cilia

plan·chette (plan chet′, -shet′) *n.* [Fr., dim. of *planche*, PLANK] a small, three-cornered device used on a Ouija board: it points to letters or words as it moves, supposedly without the guidance of the fingers resting on it

Planck (plāŋk), **Max** (mäks) 1858–1947; Ger. physicist

plane[1] (plān) *n.* [< MFr. < L. < Gr. < *platys*, broad: from its broad leaves] any of several trees with maplelike leaves and bark that comes off in large patches: also **plane tree**

plane[2] (plān) *adj.* [L. *planus*: see PLAIN] **1.** flat; level **2.** *Math. a)* on a surface that is a plane *b)* of such surfaces —*n.* **1.** a surface that wholly contains every straight line joining any two points lying in it **2.** a flat or level surface **3.** a level of achievement, existence, etc. [on a high *plane* of civilization] **4.** clipped form of AIRPLANE **5.** any airfoil; esp., a wing of an airplane

plane[3] (plān) *n.* [< OFr. < LL. < *planare*, to make level < L. *planus*: see PLAIN] a carpenter's tool for shaving a wood surface to make it smooth, level, etc. —*vt.* **planed**, **plan′ing 1.** to make smooth or level with a plane **2.** to remove with a plane (with *off* or *away*) —*vi.* **1.** to work with a plane **2.** to do the work of a plane —**plan′er** *n.*

PLANE

plane[4] (plān) *vi.* **planed**, **plan′ing** [Fr. *planer* < OFr. (term used in falconry)] **1.** to soar or glide **2.** to rise partly out of the water while moving at a high speed, as a hydroplane does **3.** to travel by airplane

plane angle an angle formed by two straight lines that lie in the same plane

plane geometry the branch of geometry dealing with plane figures

plan·et (plan′it) *n.* [< OFr. < LL. < Gr. *planētēs*, wanderer < *planan*, to wander: for IE. base see FIELD] **1.** any heavenly body shining by reflected sunlight and revolving about the sun: the major planets, in their order from the sun, are Mercury, Venus, Earth, Mars, Jupiter, Saturn, Uranus, Neptune, and Pluto: see also ASTEROID **2.** *Astrol.* any heavenly body regarded as influencing human lives

plan·e·tar·i·um (plan′ə ter′ē əm) *n., pl.* -**i·ums**, -**i·a** (-ə) [ModL. < LL. *planeta*, PLANET + L. (*sol*)*arium*, SOLARIUM] **1.** an arrangement for projecting images of the sun, moon, planets, and stars on the inside of a large dome by means of a complicated optical instrument that is revolved to show the celestial motions **2.** the room or building containing this

plan·e·tar·y (plan′ə ter′ē) *adj.* **1.** of or having to do with a planet or the planets **2.** terrestrial; global **3.** wandering; erratic **4.** moving in an orbit, like a planet **5.** designating or of a train of gears for changing speeds, as in an automobile transmission **6.** *Astrol.* under the influence of a planet

plan·e·tes·i·mal (plan′ə tes′i m'l) *adj.* [PLANET + (IN-FINIT)ESIMAL] of very small bodies in space that move in planetary orbits: according to the **planetesimal hypothesis** the planets were formed by the uniting of planetesimals —*n.* any of these bodies

plan·et·oid (plan′ə toid′) *n.* [PLANET + -OID] *same as* ASTEROID (*n.* 1)

plan·gent (plan′jənt) *adj.* [< L. prp. of *plangere*, to beat] **1.** beating with a loud or deep sound, as breaking waves **2.** loud or resonant, and, often, mournful-sounding —**plan′gen·cy** (-jən sē) *n.* —**plan′gent·ly** *adv.*

plank (plaŋk) *n.* [< ONormFr. < OFr. < LL. *planca*, ult. < Gr. *phalanx*, PHALANX] **1.** a long, broad, thick board **2.** something that supports or forms a foundation ☆**3.** any of the principles in a platform, as of a political party —*vt.* **1.** to cover, lay, etc. with planks ☆**2.** to broil and serve (steak, etc.) on a board **3.** [Colloq.] *a*) to lay or set (*down*) with force ☆*b*) to pay (usually with *down* or *out*) —**walk the plank** to walk off a plank jutting out from a ship's side, as pirates' victims were forced to do

plank·ing (plaŋk′iŋ) *n.* **1.** the act of laying planks **2.** the planks in a structure

plank·ton (plaŋk′tən) *n.* [G. < Gr. *planktos*, wandering < *plazesthai*, to wander] the microscopic animal and plant life floating in bodies of water, used as food by fish —**plank·ton′ic** (-tän′ik) *adj.*

pla·no- [< L. *planus*, flat] *a combining form meaning:* **1.** plane, flat **2.** having one side plane and (the other as specified)

pla·no-con·cave (plā′nō kän kāv′, -kän′kāv) *adj.* having one side plane and the other concave

pla·no-con·vex (-kän veks′, -kän′veks) *adj.* having one side plane and the other convex

plan position indicator a circular radarscope on which the center represents the location of the transmitter and echoes represent the location of objects as on a chart

plant (plant) *n.* [OE. *plante* < L. *planta*, a sprout, ult. < *planta*, sole of the foot < IE. base *pla-*, flat] **1.** a living organism that, unlike an animal, cannot move about by itself, has no sense organs, and usually makes its own food by photosynthesis **2.** a young tree, shrub, or herb, ready to put into other soil to mature **3.** a soft-stemmed organism of this kind, as distinguished from a tree or shrub **4.** the machinery, buildings, etc. of a factory **5.** the equipment, buildings, etc. of an institution, as a school **6.** the apparatus for a certain mechanical operation [a ship's power *plant*] **7.** [Slang] a person placed, or thing used, to trick or trap —*vt.* **1.** *a*) to put into the ground to grow [to *plant* flower seeds] *b*) to set plants in (a piece of ground) [to *plant* a garden] **2.** to set firmly in position [he *planted* his feet and pushed against the door] **3.** to fix in the mind; implant **4.** to settle; found; establish [to *plant* a colony] ☆**5.** to put a stock of (fish, etc.) in a body of water **6.** [Slang] to deliver (a punch, etc.) with force **7.** [Slang] *a*) to place (a person or thing) in such a way as to trick, trap, etc. [to *plant* a spy in their organization] *b*) to place (an apparent news item) in a newspaper, etc., as in order to mold public opinion **8.** [Slang] to hide or conceal [police *planted* a microphone in his room] —**plant′like′** *adj.*

Plan·tag·e·net (plan taj′ə nit) the ruling family of England (1154–1399), or any member of it

plan·tain¹ (plan′tin) *n.* [OFr. < L. *plantago*] any of various related plants with clusters of leaves at the base of the stem and spikes of tiny, greenish flowers, esp. a common lawn weed

plan·tain² (plan′tin) *n.* [< Sp. *plá(n)tano*, lit., plane tree < L. *platanus*: see PLANE¹] **1.** a tropical banana plant with a coarse fruit eaten as a cooked vegetable **2.** this fruit

plantain lily a plant of the lily family, with broad leaves and white or bluish flowers

PLANTAIN

plan·tar (plan′tər) *adj.* [< L. *planta*, sole of the foot: see PLANT] of or on the sole of the foot [a *plantar* wart]

plan·ta·tion (plan tā′shən) *n.* [< L. < *plantare*, to plant] **1.** formerly, a colony ☆**2.** an area growing cultivated crops **3.** an estate, as in a warm or hot region, cultivated by workers living on it [a sugar *plantation*] **4.** a large, cultivated planting of trees [a rubber *plantation*]

plant·er (plan′tər) *n.* ☆**1.** the owner of a plantation **2.** a person or machine that plants **3.** a decorative container for house plants

plant hormone an organic chemical produced by plant cells and regulating growth, food use, etc. in plants

plan·ti·grade (plan′tə grād′) *adj.* [Fr. < L. *planta*, sole + Fr. -*grade*, -GRADE] walking on the whole sole of the foot, as a bear, man, etc. —*n.* a plantigrade animal

plant louse *same as* APHID

plan·u·la (plan′yoo lə) *n.*, *pl.* **-u·lae′** (-lē′) [ModL., ult. < L. *planus*, flat] the young, ciliated, usually free-swimming larva of a coelenterate —**plan′u·loid′** (-loid′) *adj.*

plaque (plak) *n.* [Fr. < MDu. *placke*, a disk] **1.** *a*) any thin, flat piece of metal, wood, etc. with a design, etc., used to decorate a wall *b*) a wall tablet with lettering on it to commemorate or identify something **2.** a platelike brooch **3.** *a*) an abnormal patch on the skin, mucous membrane, etc. *b*) a thin, transparent film on a tooth surface, which, if not removed, hardens into tartar

plash¹ (plash) *n.* [OE. *plæsc*, prob. echoic] a pool or puddle —**plash′y** *adj.* **plash′i·er**, **plash′i·est**

plash² (plash) *vt.*, *vi.*, *n.* [echoic] *same as* SPLASH

-pla·si·a (plā′zhə ə) [ModL. < Gr. < *plassein*, to mold: see PLASTIC] *a combining form meaning* change, development [hyperplasia]

-plasm (plaz′m) [see PLASMA] *a combining form meaning:* **1.** the fluid substances of an animal or vegetable cell **2.** protoplasm [cytoplasm]

plas·ma (plaz′mə) *n.* [G. < Gr., something molded < *plassein*: see PLASTIC] **1.** the fluid part of blood, without the corpuscles **2.** the fluid part of lymph, milk, or intramuscular liquid **3.** *same as* PROTOPLASM **4.** a high-temperature, ionized gas composed of nearly equal numbers of electrons and positive ions —**plas·mat′ic** (-mat′ik) *adj.*

plas·ma·gel (plaz′mə jel′) *n.* [PLASMA + GEL] protoplasm in its more firm and jellylike state

plasma membrane a very thin living membrane surrounding the cytoplasm of a plant or animal cell

plas·ma·sol (plaz′mə sôl′, -säl′) *n.* [PLASMA + SOL³] protoplasm in its more liquid or fluid state

plas·mol·y·sis (plaz mäl′ə sis) *n.* [ModL.: see PLASMA & -LYSIS] a shrinking of the protoplasm of a living cell due to loss of water by osmosis

plas·ter (plas′tər) *n.* [< OE. & OFr. < LL. *plastrum* < L. *emplastrum* < Gr. < *emplassein*, to daub over] **1.** a pasty mixture of lime, sand, and water, hard when dry, for coating walls, ceilings, etc. **2.** *same as* PLASTER OF PARIS **3.** a pasty preparation spread on cloth and applied to the body as a medicine [a mustard *plaster*] —*vt.* **1.** to cover, smear, etc. with or as with plaster **2.** to apply or put on like a plaster [to *plaster* posters on walls] **3.** to make lie smooth and flat [to *plaster* one's hair down] **4.** [Colloq.] to affect or strike with force —**plas′ter·er** *n.* —**plas′ter·y** *adj.*

☆**plas·ter·board** (-bôrd′) *n.* a thin board formed of layers of plaster and paper, used in wide sheets as a lath or substitute for plaster in walls, etc.

plaster cast **1.** a copy or mold of a statue or other object, cast in plaster of Paris **2.** a rigid cast, as for holding a fractured bone in place, made with a bandage of gauze soaked in wet plaster of Paris

plaster of Paris [from use of gypsum from Paris, France] a heavy white powder, calcined gypsum, which, when mixed with water, forms a thick paste that sets quickly: used for casts, statuary, etc.

plas·tic (plas′tik) *adj.* [< L. < Gr. *plastikos* < *plassein*, to form: for IE. base see FIELD] **1.** molding or shaping matter; formative **2.** *a*) that can be molded or shaped [clay is a *plastic* material] *b*) made of a plastic [a *plastic* comb] ☆*c*) artificial, synthetic, fake, phony, etc. [a *plastic* culture or society] **3.** in a flexible state; impressionable [the personality of a young child is quite *plastic*] **4.** dealing with molding or modeling [sculpture is a *plastic* art] **5.** *Physics* capable of change of shape without breaking apart —*n.* any of various nonmetallic compounds, synthetically produced, which can be molded and hardened, and formed into pliable sheets, etc. —SEE SYN. at PLIABLE —**plas′ti·cal·ly** *adv.* —**plas·tic′i·ty** (-tis′ə tē) *n.*

-plas·tic (plas′tik) [< Gr.: see prec.] *a combining form meaning* forming, developing

plastic arts any of the arts concerned with molding or modeling, as sculpture, ceramics, etc.

plastic bomb a puttylike substance containing explosives, that will stick to walls, etc. and is exploded by fuse or electricity, as in acts of terrorism

Plas·ti·cine (plas′tə sēn′) [PLASTIC + -INE⁴] *a trademark for* an oil-base modeling paste, used like clay or wax —*n.* [p-] this paste: also **plas′ti·cene** (-sēn)

plas·ti·cize (plas′tə sīz′) *vt., vi.* -cized′, -ciz′ing to make or become plastic

plas·ti·ciz·er (-sī′zər) *n.* any substance added to a plastic material to keep it soft and pliable

plastic surgery surgery intended to repair or restore injured, deformed, or destroyed parts of the body or to improve the appearance —**plastic surgeon**

plas·tid (plas′tid) *n.* [< G. < Gr. < *plastēs,* molder < *plassein,* to form] a specialized bit of protoplasm structure in the cytoplasm of some plant cells

plas·tron (plas′trən) *n.* [Fr. < It. < *piastra,* thin plate of metal] **1.** a metal breastplate **2.** a chest protector for a fencer **3.** the under shell of a turtle

-plas·ty (plas′tē) [< Gr. < *plastos,* formed < *plassein,* to mold] *a combining form meaning* plastic surgery

plat¹ (plat) *vt.* **plat′ted, plat′ting** [see PLAIT] [Dial.] to plait or braid —*n.* [Dial.] a plait or braid

plat² (plat) *n.* [var. of PLOT] **1.** a small piece of ground **2.** a map or plan, esp. of a piece of land divided into building lots —*vt.* **plat′ted, plat′ting** to make a map or plan of

Pla·ta, Rí·o de la (plä′tä, rē′ō̇ de lä) estuary of the Paraná & Uruguay rivers, between Argentina & Uruguay

plate (plāt) *n.* [OFr., flat object, ult. < Gr. *platys:* see PLATY-] **1.** a smooth, flat, thin piece of metal, etc. **2.** *same as* SHEET METAL **3.** *a)* any of the thin sheets of metal used in one kind of armor (**plate armor**) *b)* such armor **4.** *a)* a thin, flat piece of metal on which an engraving is cut *b)* an impression taken from this **5.** a print of a woodcut, lithograph, etc. **6.** a full-page book illustration printed on special paper **7.** dishes, utensils, etc. of, or plated with, gold or silver **8.** a shallow dish from which food is eaten **9.** *same as* PLATEFUL **10.** the food in a dish; course [a fruit *plate*] **11.** food and service for an individual at a meal [lunch at a dollar a *plate*] **12.** a dish or other container passed in churches, etc. for donations of money **13.** a thin cut of beef from the forequarter, just below the short ribs: see illustration at BEEF **14.** *Anat., Zool.* a thin layer or scale, as of horny tissue, etc. **15.** *Archit.* a horizontal wooden girder that supports the trusses or rafters of a roof ☆**16.** *Baseball* short for HOME PLATE **17.** *Dentistry a)* that part of a denture which fits to the mouth and holds the teeth *b)* [often pl.] loosely, a full set of false teeth **18.** *Elec. same as* ANODE (sense 1) **19.** *Philately* the impression surface from which a sheet of stamps is printed **20.** *Photog.* a sheet of glass, metal, etc. coated with a film sensitive to light, upon which the image is formed **21.** *Printing* a piece of flat metal or other material prepared for use as a printing surface —*vt.* **plat′ed, plat′ing 1.** to coat with gold, tin, etc. **2.** to cover with metal plates for protection **3.** to make a printing plate from —**plat′er** *n.*

pla·teau (pla tō′) *n., pl.* -**teaus′, -teaux′** (-tōz′) [Fr. < OFr. < *plat:* see PLATE] **1.** an elevated area of more or less level land **2.** a period of little change or progress, as shown by a flat extent on a graph, etc. [to reach a *plateau* in learning]

plat·ed (plāt′id) *adj.* **1.** protected with plates, as of armor **2.** coated with a metal [silver-*plated*]

plate·ful (plāt′fool′) *n., pl.* -**fuls′** as much as a plate will hold

plate glass polished, clear glass in thick sheets, used for shop windows, mirrors, etc.

plate·let (plāt′lit) *n.* [PLATE + -LET] any of certain roundish disks, smaller than a red blood cell, found in the blood of mammals and associated with blood clotting

plat·en (plat′'n) *n.* [< OFr. *platine,* flat plate < *plat:* see PLATE] **1.** a flat metal plate, as that in a printing press which presses the paper against the inked type ☆**2.** in a typewriter, the roller against which the keys strike

plate tec·ton·ics (tek tän′iks) [see TECTONIC] the theory that the earth's surface consists of plates, or large slabs of crust, that are in constant motion, causing the continents to drift, mountains to be built up, etc.

plat·form (plat′fôrm′) *n.* [Fr. *plate-forme,* lit., flat form: see PLATE & FORM] **1.** a raised horizontal surface; specif., *a)* a raised flooring beside railroad tracks, etc. ☆*b)* a vestibule at the end of a railroad car *c)* a raised stage for performers, speakers, etc. ☆**2.** a statement of principles and policies, as of a political party —*adj.* **1.** *a)* designating a woman's shoe with a thick sole of cork, leather, etc. *b)* designating such a sole ☆**2.** designating a rocking chair (**platform rocker**) that rocks atop an attached, stationary base

plat·ing (plāt′in) *n.* **1.** the act of one that plates **2.** an outer layer of metal plates **3.** a thin coating of gold, silver, etc.

plat·i·nize (plat′'n īz′) *vt.* -nized′, -niz′ing to coat or combine with platinum —**plat′i·ni·za′tion** *n.*

plat·i·num (plat′'n əm) *n.* [ModL. < Sp. *platina* < *plata,* silver] a silvery-white, ductile metallic chemical element that resists tarnishing, acids, and heat: used as a chemical catalyst, for electrical contacts, jewelry, dental alloys, etc.: symbol, Pt; at. wt., 195.09; at. no., 78

☆**platinum blonde 1.** a girl or woman with very light, silvery blonde hair **2.** such a color

plat·i·tude (plat′ə tōōd′, -tyōōd′) *n.* [Fr. < *plat,* flat (see PLATE), after *latitude,* etc.] **1.** dullness or triteness of ideas, things said, etc. **2.** a trite or obvious remark, esp. one uttered as though it were fresh or original —**plat′i·tu′di·nous** (-tōō′d'n əs) *adj.* —**plat′i·tu′di·nous·ly** *adv.*

plat·i·tu·di·nize (plat′ə tōō′d'n īz′, -tyōō′-) *vi.* -nized′, -niz′-ing to write or speak platitudes

Pla·to (plā′tō) 427?–347? B.C.; Gr. philosopher

Pla·ton·ic (plə tän′ik, plā-) *adj.* **1.** of or characteristic of Plato or his philosophy **2.** idealistic or impractical **3.** [usually p-] not amorous or sexual, but purely spiritual or intellectual [platonic love] —**pla·ton′i·cal·ly** *adv.*

Pla·to·nism (plāt′'n iz'm) *n.* the philosophy of Plato or his school, based on his theory of ideas (see IDEA, sense 6); Platonic idealism —**Pla′to·nist** *n.* —**Pla′to·nis′tic** *adj.*

pla·toon (plə tōōn′) *n.* [Fr. *peloton,* a ball, group < *pelote,* a ball: see PELLET] **1.** a military unit composed of two or more squads **2.** a group like this [a *platoon* of police] ☆**3.** any of the specialized squads on a team, as an offensive or defensive squad in football —*vt.* to divide into, or use as or on, a platoon

Platt·deutsch (plät′doich′, plat′-) *n.* [G. < Du. *plat,* clear, lit., flat + *duitsch,* German, Dutch] any Low German vernacular dialect of N Germany

Platte (plat) [< Fr. *Rivière Platte,* lit., flat river] river formed in C Nebr. & flowing east into the Missouri

plat·ter (plat′ər) *n.* [< Anglo-Fr. < OFr. *plat:* see PLATE] **1.** a large, shallow dish, usually oval, from which food, esp. meat or fish, is served ☆**2.** [Slang] a phonograph record

plat·y (plat′ē) *n., pl.* **plat′y, plat′ys,** or **plat′ies** [< ModL. < PLATY- + Gr. *poikilos,* many-colored] any of a number of brightly colored freshwater fishes of Central America used in tropical aquariums

plat·y- [< Gr. *platys,* flat: for IE. base see FIELD] *a combining form meaning* broad or flat: also, before a vowel, **plat-**

plat·y·hel·minth (plat′ē hel′minth) *n.* [PLATY- + HELMINTH] any of a large group of flattened worms, as the tapeworms, liver flukes, etc.: many are parasitic —**plat′y·hel·min′thic** *adj.*

plat·y·pus (plat′ə pəs) *n., pl.* -**pus·es, -pi′** (-pī′) [ModL. < Gr. < *platys,* flat + *pous,* a foot] a small, aquatic, egg-laying mammal of Australia and Tasmania, with webbed feet, a tail like a beaver's, and a bill like a duck's: in full, **duckbill platypus**

plau·dit (plô′dit) *n.* [< L. pl. imper. of *plaudere,* to applaud] [usually pl.] **1.** a round of applause **2.** any strong expression of approval or praise

plau·si·ble (plô′zə b'l) *adj.* [< L. *plausibilis* < *plaudere,* to applaud] **1.** seemingly true, acceptable, etc.: often implying disbelief **2.** seemingly honest or reliable: often implying distrust —**plau′si·bil′i·ty, plau′si·ble·ness** *n.* —**plau′si·bly** *adv.*

PLATYPUS
(16–24 in. long,
including tail)

SYN.—**plausible** and **specious** both apply to that which at first glance seems to be reasonable, correct, etc., but **plausible** suggests that it may not be so, while **specious** stresses that it really is not so and strongly suggests intent to deceive [she presented a *plausible* case for lowering taxes; he used *specious* reasoning in his argument]; **credible** is used of that which is believable because it is supported by evidence, sound logic, etc. [a *credible* explanation of his behavior] —ANT. **genuine, actual**

Plau·tus (plô′təs), (**Titus Maccius**) 254?-184 B.C.; Rom.writer of comic dramas

play (plā) *vi.* [OE. *plegan*] **1.** to move lightly, rapidly, etc. [*sunlight playing on the waves*] **2.** to have fun; amuse oneself [*a time to work and a time to play*] **3.** to take part in a game or sport [*not playing because of an injury*] **4.** to gamble **5.** to handle or treat carelessly or lightly; trifle (*with* a thing or person) [*playing with the food on her plate*] **6.** to perform on a musical instrument **7.** to give out musical sounds, etc.: said of an instrument, phonograph record, etc. **8.** *a*) to act in a specified way [*to play fair*] *b*) to pretend to be [*to play dumb*] **9.** to perform on the stage, etc. **10.** to be performed in a theater, on the radio, etc. [*what movie is playing?*] **11.** to be directed or kept in motion (with *on, over,* or *along*) [*beams from the spotlights played over the buildings*] **12.** to impose (*on* another's feelings or weaknesses) [*propaganda that played on their fears*] —*vt.* **1.** *a*) to take part in (a game or sport) [*to play golf*] *b*) to be stationed at (a specified position) in a sport **2.** to oppose (a person, team, etc.) in a game or contest **3.** to use (a player, etc.) in a game **4.** to do (something), as in fun or to deceive [*to play tricks*] **5.** *a*) to bet ☆*b*) to bet on [*to play the horses*] ☆*c*) to act on the basis of [*to play a hunch*] ☆**6.** to speculate in (the stock market) **7.** to cause to move, act, etc.; wield **8.** to put (a specified card) into play [*to play an ace*] **9.** to cause or effect [*to play havoc*] **10.** to perform (music, a drama, etc.) **11.** *a*) to perform on (an instrument) *b*) to put (a phonograph, a recording, etc.) into operation **12.** to act the part of [*to play Juliet*] **13.** to imitate the activities of, as children do for amusement [*to play teacher, house, etc.*] ☆**14.** to give performances in [*to play Boston for a week*] **15.** to direct (a light, a stream of water, etc.) repeatedly or continuously (*on, over,* or *along*) **16.** to let (a hooked fish) tire itself by tugging at the line ☆**17.** to use or exploit (a person) [*played him for a fool*] — *n.* **1.** motion or activity, esp. when free and rapid [*bringing his full strength into play*] **2.** freedom or looseness of movement in a mechanical part [*too much play in a wheel*] **3.** activity for amusement or recreation; sport, games, etc. [*she has little time for play*] **4.** fun; joking [*to do a thing in play*] **5.** the playing of, or the way of playing, a game [*rain halted play*] **6.** a move or act in a game [*it's your play*] **7.** gambling **8.** a dramatic composition or performance; drama —**in** (or **out of**) **play** *Sports* in (or not in) the condition for continuing play: said of a ball, etc. —**make a play for** [Colloq.] to use one's arts or skills to get, win, attract, etc. —**play along** (**with**) to cooperate (with), often for selfish reasons —**play around 1.** to behave in a frivolous way **2.** to be sexually unfaithful or promiscuous —**play at 1.** to pretend to be engaged in **2.** to work at halfheartedly —**play down** to make seem not too important; minimize —**played out 1.** finished **2.** tired out; exhausted —**play into** (**someone's**) **hands** to act in a way that gives the advantage to (someone) —**play it** to act in a (specified) manner [*to play it* smart] —**play off 1.** to set (one) against another, as in a fight or contest ☆**2.** to break (a tie) by playing once more —**play out 1.** to play to the finish; end **2.** to pay out (a rope, etc.) —☆**play up** to give prominence to; emphasize —**play up to** [Colloq.] to try to please by flattery, etc. —**play'a·ble** *adj.*

☆**pla·ya** (plä′yə) *n.* [Sp., lit., beach] a desert basin that temporarily becomes a shallow lake after heavy rains

play·act (plā′akt′) *vi.* **1.** to act in a play **2.** to pretend **3.** to behave in an artificial or showy way —**play′act′ing** *n.*

play·back (-bak′) *n.* the playing of a phonograph record or tape just after recording on it, to check the quality of the performance or reproduction

play·bill (-bil′) *n.* **1.** a poster or circular advertising a play **2.** a program of a play

play·boy (-boi′) *n.* ☆ a man, esp. a wealthy man, who spends much time in irresponsible, pleasure-seeking activities

☆**play-by-play** (-bī plā′) *adj.* describing each play of a game or incident of a happening as it occurs or occurred

play·er (-ər) *n.* **1.** a person who plays a game **2.** an actor **3.** a person who plays a musical instrument **4.** a gambler ☆**5.** a thing that plays; specif., a RECORD PLAYER

☆**player piano** a piano that can play mechanically

play·ful (-fəl) *adj.* **1.** fond of play or fun; frisky; frolicsome [*a playful puppy*] **2.** said or done in fun; jocular [*a playful shove*] —**play′ful·ly** *adv.* —**play′ful·ness** *n.*

play·go·er (-gō′ər) *n.* a person who goes to the theater frequently —**play′go′ing** *n., adj.*

play·ground (-ground′) *n.* a place, often part of a schoolyard, for outdoor games and play

☆**play hook·y** (hook′ē) [*hooky* prob. < *hook it,* to run away] to stay away from school without permission

play·house (plā′hous′) *n.* **1.** a theater ☆**2.** a small house for children to play in

playing cards cards used in playing various games, arranged in four suits (spades, hearts, diamonds, and clubs): a standard deck has 52 cards

playing field ground for playing games on, esp. as marked out for the playing of a particular game

play·let (-lit) *n.* a short drama

play·mate (-māt′) *n.* a companion in games and recreation: also **play′fel′low** (-fel′ō)

play-off (-ôf′) *n.* a game or any of a series of games played to break a tie or to decide a championship

play on words a pun or punning

play·pen (-pen′) *n.* a small, portable enclosure in which an infant can play, crawl, etc.

play·thing (-thiŋ′) *n.* a toy

play·time (-tīm′) *n.* time for play or recreation

play·wright (-rīt′) *n.* a writer of plays; dramatist

pla·za (plä′zə, plaz′ə) *n.* [Sp. < L. *platea:* see PLACE] **1.** a public square in a city or town **2.** *same as* SHOPPING CENTER **3.** an area along a superhighway, with a restaurant, service station, etc.: also **service plaza**

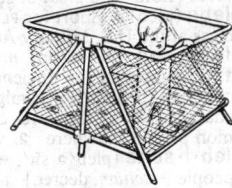

PLAYPEN

plea (plē) *n.* [< OFr. < L. *placitum,* an opinion < pp. of *placere,* to PLEASE] **1.** a statement in defense; excuse [*illness was his plea for being absent*] **2.** an urgent request; appeal [*a plea for mercy*] **3.** *Law* a defendant's statement, answering the charges against him or showing why he should not answer [*to enter a plea of not guilty*]

☆**plea bargaining** bargaining before a trial that if the defendant will plead guilty to a lesser charge, then more serious charges will be dropped to avoid the trial

pleach (plēch) *vt.* [< ONormFr. *plechier* for OFr. *plessier,* to weave] to bend and intertwine (branches of trees or shrubs) so as to form an archway or a hedge

plead (plēd) *vi.* **plead′ed** or **pled, plead′ing** [< OFr.: see PLEA] **1.** to present a case or a plea in a law court **2.** to make an appeal; beg [*to plead for mercy*] —*vt.* **1.** to argue (a law case) **2.** to declare oneself to be (guilty or not guilty) of a charge **3.** to offer as an excuse [*to plead ignorance*] —**see SYN** at APPEAL —**plead′a·ble** *adj.* —**plead′er** *n.*

plead·ings (plēd′iŋz) *n.pl.* the statements setting forth to the court the claims of the plaintiff and the answer of the defendant

pleas·ance (plez′'ns) *n.* [< MFr. < *plaisant:* see PLEASANT] a pleasant area or garden, as on an estate

pleas·ant (plez′'nt) *adj.* [< MFr. prp. of *plaisir,* to PLEASE] **1.** giving satisfaction or delight; agreeable [*a pleasant evening*] **2.** having an agreeable manner, appearance, etc.; likable [*a pleasant person*] —**pleas′ant·ly** *adv.* —**pleas′ant·ness** *n.*

SYN. —**pleasant** and **pleasing** are both applied to the effect of giving satisfaction or delight, but **pleasant** stresses the effect produced [*a pleasant smile*] and **pleasing,** the ability to produce such an effect [*her pleasing ways*]; **agreeable** is used of that which suits one's personal likes, mood, etc. [*agreeable music*]; **enjoyable** implies the ability to give enjoyment or pleasure [*an enjoyable picnic*]; **gratifying** implies the ability to give pleasure by satisfying one's wishes, hopes, etc. [*a gratifying experience*] —**ANT. unpleasant, disagreeable**

pleas·ant·ry (plez′'n trē) *n., pl.* -**ries 1.** the quality or state of being pleasant or playful in conversation **2.** *a*) a humorous remark *b*) a jesting or playful social remark [*to exchange pleasantries*]

please (plēz) *vt.* **pleased, pleas′ing** [MFr. *plaisir* < L. *placere:* for IE. base see FLAKE] **1.** to be agreeable to; give pleasure to; satisfy [*the compliment pleased her*] **2.** to be the will or wish of [*it pleased him to remain*] —*vi.* **1.** to be agreeable; satisfy [*to aim to please*] **2.** to have the will or wish; like [*to do as one pleases*] *Please* is also used for politeness in requests to mean "be obliging enough (to)" [*please* sit down] —**if you please** if you wish or like

pleas·ing (plē′zin) *adj.* giving pleasure; agreeable; pleasant; gratifying —see SYN. at PLEASANT —**pleas′ing·ly** *adv.* —**pleas′-ing·ness** *n.*

pleas·ur·a·ble (plezh′ər ə b'l) *adj.* pleasant; enjoyable — **pleas′ur·a·ble·ness** *n.* —**pleas′ur·a·bly** *adv.*

pleas·ure (plezh′ər, plā′zhər) *n.* **1.** a pleased feeling; enjoyment; delight [to get *pleasure* from walking] **2.** one's wish, will, or choice [what is your *pleasure?*] **3.** a thing that gives delight or satisfaction [her performance was a *pleasure* to see] **4.** sensual satisfaction **5.** amusement; fun —**pleas′ure·ful** *adj.*
SYN.—**pleasure** is a broad term for any feeling of satisfaction, from quiet enjoyment to happy excitement; **delight** suggests a feeling of great pleasure, openly shown [a child's *delight* with a new toy]; **joy** suggests a more deeply felt and longer-lasting happiness than **delight** does [their *joy* at their child's safe return]; **enjoyment** suggests a rather quiet feeling of satisfaction with that which pleases [our *enjoyment* of the recital] —ANT. **displeasure, sorrow, vexation**

pleat (plēt) *n.* [ME. *pleten:* see PLAIT] a flat double fold in cloth or other material, pressed or stitched in place —*vt.* to lay and press (cloth) in a pleat or series of pleats —**pleat′er** *n.*

plebe (plēb) *n.* [short for PLEBIAN] ☆a member of the freshman class at the U.S. Military Academy or Naval Academy

ple·be·ian (pli bē′ən) *n.* [< L. < *plebs*, common people] **1.** a member of the ancient Roman lower class **2.** one of the common people **3.** a vulgar, coarse person —*adj.* **1.** of or characteristic of the lower class in ancient Rome or of the common people anywhere **2.** vulgar, coarse, or common

pleb·i·scite (pleb′ə sīt′, -sit) *n.* [< Fr. < L. < *plebs*, common people + *scitum*, decree] a direct vote of the people on a political issue, as on a choice between independence for their region or union with another nation

plebs (plebz) *n., pl.* **ple·bes** (plē′bēz) [L.] **1.** the lower class in ancient Roman society **2.** the common people

plec·trum (plek′trəm) *n., pl.* **-trums**, **-tra** (-trə) [L. < Gr. *plēktron* < *plēssein*, to strike] a thin piece of metal, bone, plastic, etc., used for plucking the strings of a guitar, mandolin, etc.

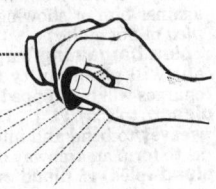

PLECTRUM

pled (pled) *alt. pt. & pp. of* PLEAD

pledge (plej) *n.* [< OFr. or ML., prob. < OS. *plegan*, to guarantee] **1.** the condition of being given or held as security for a contract, payment, etc. [a thing held in *pledge*] **2.** a person or thing given or held as such security; something pawned; hostage **3.** a token or symbol of something [he gave her a locket as a *pledge* of his love] **4.** the drinking of a toast to someone **5.** a promise or agreement [the *pledge* of allegiance to the flag] **6.** something promised, esp. money to be donated ☆**7.** a person serving a trial period before he is initiated into a fraternity —*vt.* **pledged, pledg′ing 1.** to present as security, esp. for the repayment of a loan; pawn **2.** to drink a toast to **3.** to bind by a promise [he is *pledged* to marry her] **4.** to promise to give (loyalty, a donation, etc.) ☆**5.** *a)* to become a pledge (*n.* 7) in (a fraternity) *b)* to accept as a pledge (*n.* 7) —**take the pledge** to vow not to drink alcoholic liquor —**pledg′er** *n.*
SYN.—**pledge** applies to anything given as a guarantee that something promised will be done, that a debt will be paid, etc. [he gave them a sum of money as a *pledge* that he would buy their business later]; **earnest**, in current usage, applies to anything given or done that shows, promises, or assures that more will follow [his early triumphs are an *earnest* of his success]; **token** is used of anything done or given as a sign or symbol of authority, genuineness, good faith, etc. [this watch is a *token* of our gratitude]

pledg·ee (plej ē′) *n.* a person to whom a pledge is delivered: distinguished from PLEDGOR

pledg·or (plej′ər, plej′ôr′) *n. Law* a person who delivers something as security

-ple·gia (plē′jē ə, -jə) [ModL. < Gr. *plēgē*, a stroke] *a combining form meaning* paralysis [paraplegia]

Ple·ia·des (plē′ə dēz′, plī′-) *n.pl., sing.* **Ple′iad** (-ad) **1.** *Gr. Myth.* the seven daughters of Atlas, placed by Zeus among the stars **2.** *Astron.* a cluster of stars in the constellation Taurus

Plei·o·cene (plī′ə sēn′) *adj. & n.* same as PLIOCENE

Pleis·to·cene (plīs′tə sēn′) *adj.* [< Gr. *pleistos*, most + *kainos*, recent] designating or of the first epoch of the Quaternary Period in the Cenozoic Era —**the Pleistocene** the Pleistocene Epoch or its rocks: see GEOLOGIC TIME CHART

ple·na·ry (plē′nə rē, plen′ə-) *adj.* [< LL. < L. *plenus*, FULL¹] **1.** full; complete [*plenary* power] **2.** for attendance by all members [a *plenary* session] —**ple′na·ri·ly** (-rə lē) *adv.*

plenary indulgence *R.C.Ch.* an indulgence that completely does away with the temporal punishment due a sinner

plen·i·po·ten·ti·ar·y (plen′i pə ten′shē er′ē, -shə rē) *adj.* [< ML. < LL. < L. *plenus*, full + *potens*, powerful] having or giving full authority [an ambassador *plenipotentiary*] —*n., pl.* **-ar′ies** a person given full authority to act as diplomatic representative of a government

plen·i·tude (plen′ə tood′, -tyood′) *n.* [OFr. < L. < *plenus*, FULL¹] **1.** fullness; completeness **2.** abundance; plenty — **plen′i·tu′di·nous** *adj.*

plen·te·ous (plen′tē əs) *adj.* plentiful; abundant —**plen′te·ous·ly** *adv.* —**plen′te·ous·ness** *n.*

plen·ti·ful (plen′ti fəl) *adj.* **1.** having or providing plenty **2.** more than enough; abundant [a *plentiful* food supply] — **plen′ti·ful·ly** *adv.* —**plen′ti·ful·ness** *n.*
SYN.—**plentiful** implies a large or full supply of goods [a *plentiful* supply of books]; **abundant** implies a very plentiful or very large supply [a forest *abundant* in wild game]; **copious**, now used chiefly to refer to quantity produced, used, etc., implies a rich or continuing abundance [a *copious* harvest, discharge, etc.]; **profuse** implies a giving or pouring forth abundantly or very generously, often beyond what is needed or wanted [*profuse* in his thanks]; **ample** applies to that which is large enough to meet all demands [his savings are *ample* to see him through this crisis] —ANT. **scarce, scant**

plen·ty (plen′tē) *n., pl.* **-ties** [< MFr. < L. *plenitas* < *plenus*, FULL¹] **1.** prosperity; abundance [a time of *plenty*] **2.** a supply that is large enough; all that is needed [we have *plenty* of help] **3.** a large number [*plenty* of errors] —*adj.* [Colloq.] ample; enough; plentiful [*plenty* work to be done] —*adv.* [Colloq.] very; quite [*plenty* good]

ple·o·nasm (plē′ə naz'm) *n.* [< LL. < Gr. *pleonazein*, to be in excess < *pleōn*, more, compar. of *polys:* see POLY-] **1.** the use of more words than are necessary for the meaning; redundancy (Example: "plenty enough") **2.** a word or words of this kind —**ple′o·nas′tic** *adj.*

ple·si·o·saur (plē′sē ə sôr′) *n.* [ModL. < Gr. *plēsios*, near + *sauros*, lizard] a large water reptile that lived in the Mesozoic Era, having a small head, long neck, short tail, and four paddle-like limbs

pleth·o·ra (pleth′ə rə) *n.* [ML. < Gr. < *plēthos*, fullness] **1.** the state of being too full; overabundance; excess [a *plethora* of words] **2.** an abnormal condition in which there is too much blood in the circulatory system —**ple·thor·ic** (plə thôr′ik, pleth′ə rik) *adj.*

pleu·ra (ploor′ə) *n., pl.* **-rae** (-ē) [ML. < Gr. *pleura*, a rib] the thin membrane lining each half of the chest cavity and covering a lung —**pleu′ral** *adj.*

pleu·ri·sy (ploor′ə sē) *n.* [< MFr. < LL. < L. < Gr. *pleura*, a rib] inflammation of the pleura, causing painful breathing — **pleu·rit·ic** (ploo rit′ik) *adj.*

pleu·ro- [< Gr. *pleura*, a rib] *a combining form meaning:* **1.** on or near the side **2.** of, involving, or near the pleura Also, before a vowel, **pleur-**

pleu·ro·pneu·mo·ni·a (ploor′ō noo mōn′yə, ploor′ō nyoo-; -mō′nē ə) *n.* pneumonia complicated by pleurisy

☆**Plex·i·glas** (plek′sə glas′) [< L. *plexus*, a twining + GLASS] *a trademark for* a lightweight, transparent, thermoplastic resin, used for lenses, windows, etc. —*n.* this material: also **plex′i·glass′**

plex·us (plek′səs) *n., pl.* **-us·es**, **-us** [ModL. < L. < pp. of *plectere*, to twine] a network; specif., *Anat.* a network of blood vessels, nerves, etc.

pli·a·ble (plī′ə b'l) *adj.* [< MFr. < *plier*, to bend < L. *plicare*, to fold: see PLY¹] **1.** easily bent; flexible [a *pliable* stem or stalk] **2.** easily influenced or persuaded [a *pliable* personality] **3.** adjusting readily; adaptable [a *pliable* attitude] —**pli′a·bil′i·ty, pli′a·ble·ness** *n.* —**pli′a·bly** *adv.*
SYN.—**pliable** and **pliant** both suggest something that can be easily bent, as a thin wooden stick, and in a more general way, a nature that gives in or adapts easily; **plastic** is used of substances, such as plaster or clay, that can be molded into various shapes which they keep after they become hard, and is also used of persons who can be easily influenced or persuaded; **ductile** suggests that which can be drawn or stretched out [copper is a *ductile* metal]; **malleable** suggests that which can be hammered, beaten, or pressed into various forms [copper is *malleable* as well as ductile] —ANT. **inflexible, rigid, brittle**

pli·ant (plī′ənt) *adj.* [see prec.] **1.** easily bent; pliable **2.** adaptable or compliant —see SYN. at PLIABLE —**pli′an·cy, pli′ant·ness** *n.* —**pli′ant·ly** *adv.*

pli·cate (plī′kāt) *adj.* [< L. pp. of *plicare*, to fold: see PLY¹] having lengthwise folds like a fan [a *plicate* leaf] —**pli·ca′tion** *n.*

pli·er (plī′ər) *n.* a person or thing that plies

pli·ers (plī'ərz) *n.pl.* [< PLY[1]] small pincers for gripping small objects, bending wire, etc.

plight1 (plīt) *n.* [< Anglo-Fr. *plit*, for OFr. *pleit*, a fold] a condition or state of affairs; esp., an awkward, sad, or dangerous situation [the *plight* of the men trapped in the mine]

plight2 (plīt) *vt.* [OE. *plihtan*, to pledge < *pliht*, danger] to pledge or bind by a pledge —**plight one's troth** to make a promise of marriage

Plim·soll mark (or **line**) (plim'səl, -säl, -sôl) [after S. *Plimsoll* (1824–98), Eng. statesman] a line or set of lines on the outside of merchant ships, showing the water level to which they may legally be loaded

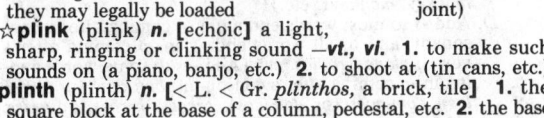

PLIERS
(A, slip joint; B, needle nose; C, arc joint)

☆**plink** (pliŋk) *n.* [echoic] a light, sharp, ringing or clinking sound —*vt., vi.* 1. to make such sounds on (a piano, banjo, etc.) 2. to shoot at (tin cans, etc.)

plinth (plinth) *n.* [< L. < Gr. *plinthos*, a brick, tile] 1. the square block at the base of a column, pedestal, etc. 2. the base on which a statue rests

Plin·y (plin'ē) 1. (L. name *Gaius Plinius Secundus*) 23–79 A.D.; Rom. naturalist & writer: called *the Elder* 2. (L. name *Gaius Plinius Caecilius Secundus*) 62?–113? A.D.; Rom. writer & statesman: called *the Younger*: nephew of *Pliny the Elder*

Pli·o·cene (plī'ə sēn') *adj.* [< Gr. *pleōn*, more + *kainos*, new] designating or of the last epoch of the Tertiary Period in the Cenozoic Era —**the Pliocene** the Pliocene Epoch or its rocks: see GEOLOGIC TIME CHART

☆**Pli·o·film** (plī'ə film') [< PLIABLE + FILM] *a trademark for* a sheeting of rubber hydrochloride used for raincoats, as a covering for packages, etc.

plis·sé, plis·se (pli sā') *n.* [< Fr. < pp. of *plisser*, to pleat] 1. a crinkled finish given to cotton, nylon, etc. with a caustic soda solution 2. a fabric with this finish

PLO, P.L.O. Palestine Liberation Organization

plod (pläd) *vi.* **plod'ded, plod'ding** [prob. echoic] 1. to walk or move heavily and with effort; trudge [the old horse *plodded* along the street] 2. to work steadily and monotonously; drudge [to *plod* away at one's work] —*n.* 1. the act of plodding 2. the sound of a heavy step —**plod'der** *n.* —**plod'ding·ly** *adv.*

-ploid (ploid) [< Gr. *-ploos*, -fold + -OID] *a combining form meaning* of or being a (specified) multiple of the basic (haploid) number of chromosomes characteristic of a group of related organisms [diploid]

plonk (pläŋk, pluŋk) *vt., vi., n. same as* PLUNK

plop (pläp) *vt., vi.* **plopped, plop'ping** [echoic] 1. to drop with a sound like that of something flat falling into water 2. to drop heavily —*n.* the act of plopping or the sound made by this —*adv.* with a plop

plo·sive (plō'siv) *adj.* [< (EX)PLOSIVE] *Phonet.* produced by stopping and suddenly releasing the breath, as the sounds of *k, p,* and *t* used at the beginning of words —*n.* a plosive sound

plot (plät) *n.* [OE., a piece of land] 1. a small area of ground [a garden *plot*] 2. a chart or diagram, as of a building or estate 3. a secret, usually evil, scheme 4. the plan of action of a play, novel, etc. —*vt.* **plot'ted, plot'ting** 1. a) to draw a plan of (a ship's course, etc.) b) to mark the position or course of on a map 2. to make secret plans for [to *plot* a robbery] 3. to plan the action of (a story, etc.) 4. a) to determine the location of (a point) on a graph by means of coordinates b) to represent (an equation) by joining points on a graph to form a curve —*vi.* to plan together secretly; scheme [to *plot* against the queen] —**plot'less** *adj.* —**plot'less·ness** *n.* —**plot'ter** *n.*

SYN. —**plot** is used of a secret, usually evil, project or scheme the details of which have been carefully worked out [a *plot* to keep her from getting her inheritance]; **intrigue**, implying more complicated scheming, suggests hidden, underhanded dealing often of an illegal nature [the *intrigues* of the royal court]; **machination** emphasizes trickery and slyness in forming plots intended to harm someone [the *machinations* of the villain]; **conspiracy** suggests a plot in which a number of people plan and act together secretly for an unlawful or harmful purpose [a *conspiracy* to seize the throne]; **cabal** suggests a small group of persons involved in a political intrigue

plough (plou) *n., vt., vi. chiefly Brit. sp. of* PLOW

plov·er (pluv'ər, plō'vər) *n., pl.* **plov'ers, plov'er:** see PLURAL, II, D, 1 [< OFr., ult. < L. *pluvia,* rain] a shore bird with a short tail, long, pointed wings, and a short beak

plow (plou) *n.* [ME. *ploh* < Late OE.] 1. a farm implement used to cut and turn up the soil ☆2. anything like this; specif., a SNOWPLOW —*vt.* 1. to cut and turn up (soil) with a plow 2. to make furrows in with or as with a plow 3. to make as if by plowing [he *plowed* his way through the crowd] 4. to cut a way through (water) —*vi.* 1. to use a plow in tilling the soil 2. to cut a way (*through* water, etc.) 3. to go forward with effort; plod 4. to begin work vigorously (with *into*) 5. to strike against forcefully (with *into*) —**plow back** to reinvest (profits) in the same business enterprise —**plow up** 1. to remove with a plow 2. to till (soil) thoroughly —**plow'a·ble** *adj.* —**plow'er** *n.*

PLOVER
(to 11 in. high)

plow·boy (plou'boi') *n.* 1. formerly, a boy who led a team of horses drawing a plow 2. a country boy

plow·man (plou'mən) *n., pl.* **-men** 1. a man who guides a plow 2. a farm worker

plow·share (-sher') *n.* the share, or cutting blade, of a moldboard plow

ploy (ploi) *n.* [? < (EM)PLOY] an action or maneuver intended to outwit and get the better of another person

pluck (pluk) *vt.* [OE. *pluccian:* for IE. base see PILE[2]] 1. to pull off or out; pick [to *pluck* an apple from a tree] 2. to drag or snatch; grab [she *plucked* a burning stick from the fire] 3. to pull feathers or hair from [to *pluck* a chicken, *pluck* eyebrows] 4. to pull at (the strings of a musical instrument) and release quickly to sound tones 5. [Slang] to rob or swindle —*vi.* 1. to pull; tug; snatch (often with *at*) [he *plucked* at his long mustache] 2. to pluck a musical instrument —*n.* 1. a pulling; tug 2. courage to meet danger or difficulty; fortitude —**pluck up** to stir up one's (courage); take heart —**pluck'er** *n.*

pluck·y (pluk'ē) *adj.* **pluck'i·er, pluck'i·est** brave; spirited — see SYN. at BRAVE —**pluck'i·ly** *adv.* —**pluck'i·ness** *n.*

plug (plug) *n.* [MDu. *plugge*] 1. an object used to stop up a hole, drain, etc. 2. *a*) a cake of pressed tobacco *b*) a piece of chewing tobacco 3. a device, as with prongs that stick out, for fitting into an electric outlet, etc. to make electrical contact 4. *same as: a*) SPARK PLUG *b*) FIREPLUG 5. [Colloq.] a defective or shopworn article ☆6. [Slang] an old, worn-out horse ☆7. [Colloq.] a boost, advertisement, etc., esp. one slipped into the entertainment part of a radio or TV program, a magazine article, etc. —*vt.* **plugged, plug'ging** 1. to stop up (a hole, etc.) with a plug (often with *up*) 2. to insert (something) as a plug [she *plugged* the putty in the hole] 3. [Colloq.] *a*) to promote (a song) by frequent performance ☆*b*) to promote with a plug (*n.* 7) 4. [Slang] to shoot a bullet into —*vi.* [Colloq.] to work or study hard and steadily; plod —**plug in** to connect (an electrical device) with an outlet, etc. by inserting a plug in a socket or jack —**pull the plug** [Colloq.] ☆1. to shut off a device being used to keep alive a patient dying of a fatal disease ☆2. to put an end to something —**plug'ger** *n.*

☆**plug hat** [Old Slang] a man's high silk hat

☆**plug·o·la** (plug'ō lə) *n.* [PLUG, *n.* 7 + (PAY)OLA] [Slang] the paying of a bribe, or a bribe paid, for the dishonest promotion of something or someone on radio or TV

☆**plug-ug·ly** (-ug'lē) *n., pl.* **-lies** [Old Slang] a ruffian or gangster

plum (plum) *n.* [OE. *plume*] 1. *a*) any of various small trees bearing a smooth-skinned fruit with a flattened stone *b*) the fruit eaten as food 2. a raisin, when used in pudding or cake [*plum* pudding] 3. the dark bluish-red or reddish-purple color of some plums 4. something excellent or desirable [the new contract is a rich *plum* for the company]

plum·age (plōō'mij) *n.* [MFr. < L. *pluma,* a feather] a bird's feathers

plu·mate (-māt, -mit) *adj.* [< L. *pluma,* a feather] *Zool.* resembling a feather, esp. in structure

plumb (plum) *n.* [< MFr. < L. *plumbum,* LEAD²] a lead weight (**plumb bob**) hung at the end of a line (**plumb line**), used to find out how deep water is or whether a wall, etc. is vertical —*adj.* perfectly vertical —*adv.* **1.** straight down; directly [to fall *plumb* to the ground] **2.** [Colloq.] entirely; absolutely [*plumb* crazy] —*vt.* **1.** to test or sound with a plumb **2.** to discover the facts of; solve [to *plumb* a mystery] **3.** to make vertical —**out of** (or **off**) **plumb** not vertical

plum·ba·go (plum bā'gō) *n., pl.* **-gos** [L. < *plumbum,* LEAD²] *same as* GRAPHITE

plumb·er (plum'ər) *n.* [< MFr. < L. < *plumbarius,* lead-worker < *plumbum,* LEAD²] a skilled worker who installs and repairs pipes, fixtures, etc., as of water or gas systems in a building

plumb·ing (plum'iŋ) *n.* **1.** the using of a plumb **2.** the work of a plumber **3.** the pipes and fixtures with which a plumber works

plume (plōōm) *n.* [OFr. < L. *pluma*] **1.** *a)* a feather, esp. a large, showy one *b)* a cluster of these **2.** an ornament made of such a feather or feathers, or a feathery tuft of hair, esp. when worn on a hat, helmet, etc. **3.** a token of worth or achievement; prize **4.** something like a plume in shape or lightness [a *plume* of smoke] —*vt.* **plumed, plum'ing** **1.** to provide, cover, or adorn with plumes **2.** to preen (its feathers): said of a bird **3.** to pride (oneself) —**plume'let** *n.*

plum·met (plum'it) *n.* [< MFr. dim. of *plombe:* see PLUMB] **1.** a plumb **2.** a thing that weighs heavily —*vi.* to fall or drop straight downward [the plane *plummeted* to earth]

plu·mose (plōō'mōs) *adj.* [< L. < *pluma,* a feather] **1.** feathered **2.** like a feather —**plu'mose·ly** *adv.* —**plu·mos·i·ty** (plōō mäs'ə tē) *n.*

plump¹ (plump) *adj.* [< MDu. *plomp,* bulky] full and rounded in form; chubby [a *plump* girl] —*vt., vi.* to make plump; fill out (sometimes with *up* or *out*) [to *plump* up a pillow] —**plump'ish** *adj.* —**plump'ly** *adv.* —**plump'ness** *n.*

plump² (plump) *vi.* [< MDu. *plompen:* orig. echoic] **1.** to fall or bump (*against*) suddenly or heavily **2.** to offer strong support (*for* someone or something) —*vt.* to drop, throw, or put down heavily or all at once [he *plumped* himself down in the chair] —*n.* a sudden or heavy fall or the sound of this —*adv.* **1.** suddenly or heavily [he fell *plump* to the ground] **2.** straight down **3.** in plain words; bluntly —*adj.* blunt; direct

plum pudding [orig. made with plums] a rich pudding made of raisins, currants, flour, suet, etc., boiled or steamed, as in a linen bag

plu·mule (plōōm'yōōl) *n.* [< L. dim. of *pluma,* a feather] **1.** the growing stem tip of the embryo of a plant seed **2.** a soft down feather

plum·y (plōō'mē) *adj.* **plum'i·er, plum'i·est** **1.** covered or decorated with plumes **2.** like a plume; feathery

plun·der (plun'dər) *vt.* [< G. *plunder,* baggage] **1.** to rob (a person or place) by force, esp. in warfare **2.** to take (property) by force or fraud —*vi.* to engage in plundering —*n.* **1.** the act of plundering; pillage **2.** goods taken by force or fraud; loot; booty —**plun'der·er** *n.* —**plun'der·ous** *adj.*

☆**plunge** (plunj) *vt.* **plunged, plung'ing** [< OFr. *plongier,* ult. < L. *plumbum,* LEAD²] to thrust or throw suddenly (*into* a liquid, hole, condition, etc.) [to *plunge* an oar into the water; to *plunge* a country into debt] —*vi.* **1.** to dive or rush, as into water, a fight, etc. **2.** to move violently and rapidly downward or forward [the car *plunged* over the cliff] **3.** to pitch, as a ship **4.** to extend far down in a revealing way [a *plunging* neckline] **5.** [Colloq.] to spend, gamble, or speculate heavily —*n.* **1.** *a)* a dive or downward leap *b)* a swim **2.** any sudden, violent plunging motion **3.** [Colloq.] a heavy, reckless investment [a *plunge* in the stock market] —**take the plunge** to start on some new and uncertain enterprise, esp. after some hesitation

plung·er (plun'jər) *n.* **1.** a person who plunges **2.** a large, rubber suction cup with a long handle, used to open up clogged drains **3.** any cylindrical device that operates with a plunging motion, as a piston

plunk (pluŋk) *vt.* [echoic] **1.** to pluck or strum (a banjo, guitar, etc.) **2.** to throw or put down heavily; plump —*vi.* **1.** to give out a twanging sound, as a banjo **2.** to fall heavily [the stone *plunked* into the water] —*n.* the act or sound of plunking —*adv.* with a twang or thud —☆**plunk down** [Colloq.] to pay —**plunk'er** *n.*

plu·per·fect (plōō pur'fikt) *adj.* [abbrev. of L. *plus quam perfectum,* more than perfect] describing a tense in any of certain languages that is like the past perfect in English —*n.* a pluperfect tense or a form in this tense

plu·ral (ploor'əl) *adj.* [L. *pluralis* < *pluris,* genitive of *plus,* more: see PLUS] **1.** of or including more than one **2.** of or involving a number of persons or things [*plural* marriage] **3.** *Gram.* showing that more than one is meant —*n. Gram.* **1.** the plural number **2.** a plural form of a word **3.** a word in plural form The plurals of nouns are formed in English in the ways listed below.

I. REGULAR ENGLISH PLURALS
   A. Add -*s* in all cases except as noted below
   B. Add -*es* after final -*ss, -sh, -ch, -s, -x, -z,* and -*zz: glasses, ashes, witches, gases, boxes, adzes, buzzes*
   C. Add -*es* after -*y* when it follows a consonant or -*qu-,* and change the -*y* to -*i: fly, flies; soliloquy, soliloquies;* etc. (Add -*s* after -*y* when it follows a vowel: *day, days; monkey, monkeys;* etc.)
   D. Add -*s* to most words ending in -*o* coming after a consonant, and to all words ending in -*o* coming after a vowel: *pianos, radios,* etc. (Add -*es* to some words ending in -*o* coming after a consonant: *buffaloes* (or *buffalos*), *dominoes* (or *dominos*), *echoes, heroes, potatoes,* etc.)

II. OTHER ENGLISH PLURALS
   A. Change -*f* to -*v* in many words, and add -*es: half, halves; life, lives; leaf, leaves; scarf¹, scarves* (or *scarfs*); etc.
   B. Plural formed by:
      1. -*en: oxen*
      2. -*ren: children*
      3. Vowel change: *man, men; foot, feet; mouse, mice;* etc.
   C. Plural the same as singular: *alms, barracks, Chinese, deer* (occas. *deers*), *forceps, gross, means, moose, sheep,* etc.
   D. Plural either different from or the same as the singular:
      1. Plural usually different, but sometimes the same, esp. in the usage of hunters and fishermen: *antelope, badger, brant, buffalo, cougar, giraffe, mullet, shrimp, sturgeon, tarpon,* etc.
      2. Plural usually the same, but different if referring to different kinds, species, varieties, etc. [the *fishes* of the South Pacific]: *cod, elk, gar, mackerel, shad, springbok, trout,* etc.
      3. Plural usually not used except when different kinds are referred to [the many *steels* produced]: *brass, coffee, fruit, iron, linen, wool,* etc.
      4. Plural and collective singular interchangeable: *seeds, seed;* etc.

III. FORMS SINGULAR OR PLURAL ONLY
   A. Singular only: *clearness, fishing, information, knowledge, luck, music, nonsense,* etc.
   B. Plural only (even when singular in meaning), including certain senses of nouns otherwise singular: *Balkans, blues* (depression), *overalls, pliers, remains* (corpse), *scissors, tongs, trousers,* etc.
   .C. Plural in form but used with singular verbs: *checkers* (game), *measles, mumps, news,* etc.
   D. Nouns ending in -*ics* are singular when they denote scientific subjects, as *mathematics, physics,* etc., and plural when they denote activities or qualities, as *acrobatics, acoustics,* etc.

IV. FOREIGN PLURALS
   A. Some plurals keep the foreign form only, as because the word is a technical term (*bronchus, bronchi*), because the plural form had early become in English the more commonly used form (*datum, data*), because adding a regular English plural form would result in too many *s* sounds (*analysis, analyses*), because a distinction in sex is being made (*alumnus, alumni; alumna, alumnae*), etc.
   B. Some plurals have both a foreign form and a regular English form (with either form correct and a tendency more and more to favor the regular English form): *formula, formulae, formulas; index, indices, indexes; criterion, criteria, criterions; beau, beaux, beaus; virtuoso, virtuosi, virtuosos;* etc.

V. PLURALS OF NUMBERS, LETTERS, SIGNS, WORDS (when thought of as things), etc. add -*'s* (or now often -*s*): *8's* (or *8s*), *B's* (or *Bs*), *&'s* (or *&s*), *but's* (or *buts*), etc.

plu·ral·ism (ploor'əl iz'm) *n.* **1.** a being plural, or existing in more than one part or form **2.** the existence within a society of groups that differ in ethnic origins, cultural patterns, etc. **3.** *Philos.* the theory that reality is made up of a number of fundamental beings, principles, or substances —**plu′ral·ist** *n., adj.* — **plu′ral·is′tic** *adj.*

plu·ral·i·ty (ploo ral′ə tē) *n., pl.* **-ties** **1.** a being plural or numerous **2.** a great number; multitude ☆**3.** the number of votes that the leading candidate of more than two obtains over the next highest candidate *[if Smith gets 65 votes, Jones gets 40, and Brown gets 35, then Smith has a *plurality* of 25]* **4.** *same as* MAJORITY

plu·ral·ize (ploor′ə līz′) *vt., vi.* **-ized′, -iz′ing** to make or become plural in form or number —**plu′ral·i·za′tion** *n.* —**plu′ral·iz′er** *n.*

plu·ral·ly (-əl ē) *adv.* in the plural number

plu·ri- [L. < *pluris*, genitive of *plus*, several: see PLUS] *a combining form meaning* several or many

plus (plus) *prep.* [L., more: for IE. base see FULL¹] **1.** added to *[2 plus 2 equals 4]* **2.** in addition to *[salary plus bonus]* —*adj.* **1.** designating a sign (**plus sign**) indicating addition *[+ is a plus sign]* **2.** positive *[a plus quantity]* **3.** somewhat higher than *[a grade of B plus]* **4.** involving extra gain or advantage *[a plus factor]* **5.** [Colloq.] and more *[she has personality plus]* ☆**6.** *Elec. same as* POSITIVE *[the plus terminal]* —*adv.* [Colloq.] moreover *[he has the time plus he has the money]* —*n., pl.* **plus′es, plus′ses 1.** a plus sign **2.** an added or favorable quantity or thing **3.** a positive quantity

plus fours [orig. indicating added length of material for overlap below the knee] loose knickerbockers worn, esp. formerly, for active sports

plush (plush) *n.* [< Fr. < *peluche*, ult. < L. *pilus*, hair] a fabric with a soft, thick, deep pile —*adj.* **1.** of plush **2.** [Slang] luxurious, as in furnishings —**plush′i·ly** *adv.* —**plush′i·ness** *n.* — **plush′y** *adj.* **plush′i·er, plush′i·est**

Plu·tarch (ploo′tärk) 46?-120? A.D.; Gr. biographer & historian

Plu·to (ploot′ō) **1.** *Gr. & Rom. Myth.* the god ruling the lower world **2.** the outermost planet of the solar system: diameter, c. 3,700 mi. —**Plu·to′ni·an** *adj.*

plu·toc·ra·cy (ploo täk′rə sē) *n., pl.* **-cies** [< Gr. < *ploutos*, wealth + *kratein*, to rule] **1.** government by the wealthy **2.** a group of wealthy people who control or greatly influence a government

plu·to·crat (ploot′ə krat′) *n.* **1.** a member of a wealthy ruling class **2.** a person whose wealth gives him control or great influence —**plu′to·crat′ic** *adj.* —**plu′to·crat′i·cal·ly** *adv.*

plu·ton·ic (ploo tän′ik) *adj.* [after PLUTO] *Geol.* formed far below the surface of the earth by intense heat and slow cooling, as some rocks

☆**plu·to·ni·um** (ploo tō′nē əm) *n.* [ModL. after *Pluto* (planet)] a radioactive, metallic chemical element found in uranium ores: its most important isotope (**plutonium 239**) is used in nuclear weapons and as a reactor fuel: symbol, Pu; at. wt., 239.05; at. no., 94

plu·vi·al (ploo′vē əl) *adj.* [< L. < *pluvia*, rain: for IE. base see FULL¹] **1.** *a)* of or having to do with rain *b)* having much rain **2.** *Geol.* formed by the action of rain

ply¹ (plī) *vt.* **plied, ply′ing** [< OFr. < L. *plicare*, to fold: for IE. base see COMPLICATE] [Now Rare] to bend, twist, fold, or mold —*n., pl.* **plies 1.** a single thickness or layer, as of plywood, doubled cloth, etc. **2.** one of the twisted strands in rope, yarn, etc. —*adj.* having (a specified number of) layers, strands, etc. *[three-ply]*

ply² (plī) *vt.* **plied, ply′ing** [ME. *plien*, short for *applien*, APPLY] **1.** to work with; wield or use (a tool, faculty, etc.), esp. with energy **2.** to work at (a trade) **3.** to speak to (someone) urgently (*with* questions, etc.) **4.** to keep supplying (*with* gifts, food, etc.) **5.** to sail regularly back and forth across *[boats ply the channel]* —*vi.* **1.** to keep busy or work (*at* something or *with* a tool, etc.) **2.** to travel regularly (*between* places): said of ships, buses, etc.

Ply·mouth (plim′əth) **1.** seaport in SW England, on the English Channel: pop. 257,000 **2.** village on the SE coast of Mass.: settled by the Pilgrims (1620) as **Plymouth Colony**

☆**Plymouth Rock 1.** boulder at Plymouth, Mass., where the Pilgrims are said to have landed **2.** any of a breed of American chickens

ply·wood (plī′wood′) *n.* [PLY¹ + WOOD] a material made of thin layers of wood glued and pressed together, usually with the grains at right angles to one another

PLYWOOD

Plzeň (p′l zen y′) city in W Bohemia, Czechoslovakia: pop. 144,000

Pm *Chem.* promethium

pm. 1. phase modulation **2.** premium

P.M. 1. Paymaster **2.** Postmaster **3.** Prime Minister

P.M., p.m., PM [L. *post meridiem*] after noon: used to designate the time from noon to midnight

p.m. post-mortem

pmk. postmark

pneu·mat·ic (noo mat′ik, nyoo-) *adj.* [< L. < Gr. < *pneuma*, breath] **1.** of or containing wind, air, or gases **2.** *a)* filled with compressed air *[pneumatic tire]* *b)* worked by compressed air *[pneumatic drill]* —**pneu·mat′i·cal·ly** *adv.*

pneu·mat·ics (-iks) *n.pl.* [*with sing. v.*] the branch of physics dealing with such properties of air and other gases as pressure, density, etc.

pneu·mo·coc·cus (noo′mə käk′əs, nyoo′-) *n., pl.* **-coc′ci** (-käk′sī) [ModL. < Gr. *pneumōn*, a lung + COCCUS] a bacterium that is a cause of pneumonia —**pneu′mo·coc′cal** (-käk′′l), **pneu′mo·coc′cic** (-käk′sik) *adj.*

pneu·mo·co·ni·o·sis (noo′mə kō′nē ō′sis, nyoo′-) *n.* [ModL. < Gr. *pneumōn*, a lung + *konia*, dust + -OSIS] a disease of the lungs, causing fibrosis and resulting from continually breathing in mineral dusts, esp. silica and asbestos

pneu·mo·en·ceph·a·lo·gram (noo′mə en sef′ə lō gram′, nyoo′-) *n.* [< Gr. *pneumōn*, a lung + *en-*, in + *kephalē*, the head + -GRAM] an X-ray photograph of the brain made after cerebrospinal fluid has been replaced with air or oxygen

pneu·mo·ni·a (noo mōn′yə, nyoo-; -mō′nē ə) *n.* [ModL. < Gr. < *pneumōn*, a lung < *pnein*, to breathe] inflammation or infection of the alveoli of the lungs, caused by any of various agents, such as bacteria or viruses —**pneu·mon′ic** (-män′ik) *adj.*

Pnom-Penh (p′nôm′pen′) *same as* PHNOM PENH

Po (pō) river in N Italy, flowing from the Alps east into the Adriatic

Po *Chem.* polonium

po, p.o. *Baseball* putout; putouts

P.O., p.o. 1. petty officer: also **PO 2.** post office **3.** post office box

poach¹ (pōch) *vt.* [< MFr. < *poche*, a pocket: the yolk is "pocketed" in the white] to cook (an egg without its shell, a fish, etc.) in water or other liquid near the boiling point, or in a small container put over boiling water —**poach′er** *n.*

poach² (pōch) *vt.* [< Fr. < OFr. *pochier*, to tread upon < MHG. *puchen*, to plunder] **1.** to trample **2.** *a)* to trespass on (private property), esp. for hunting or fishing *b)* to hunt or catch (game or fish) illegally, esp. by trespassing **3.** to steal —*vi.* to hunt or fish illegally, esp. as a trespasser —**poach′er** *n.*

Po·ca·hon·tas (pō′kə hän′təs) 1595?-1617; Am. Indian princess who is said to have saved Captain John Smith from execution

po·chard (pō′chərd, -kärd) *n., pl.* **-chards, -chard:** see PLURAL, II, D, 1 [< ? Fr. *pocher*, to pocket] a European, diving sea duck with a brownish-red head

pock (päk) *n.* [OE. *pocc:* for IE. base see BIG] **1.** a small pimple, esp. one caused by smallpox **2.** *same as* POCKMARK —**pocked** *adj.* —**pock′y** *adj.* **pock′i·er, pock′i·est**

pock·et (päk′it) *n.* [< Anglo-Fr. < ONormFr. dim. of *poque,* a bag] **1.** *a)* a little bag or pouch, now usually sewn into or on clothing, for carrying money and small articles *b)* any usually small container, compartment, pouch, etc. **2.** a hollow space for holding something **3.** a small area or group *[a pocket of poverty]* **4.** a confining or frustrating situation **5.** funds *[a drain on one's pocket]* **6.** *Aeron. same as* AIR POCKET **7.** any of the pouches at the sides and corners of a billiard or pool table **8.** *Geol. a)* a hollow space filled with ore, oil, gas, or water *b)* a small deposit of ore, etc. —*adj.* **1.** *a)* that is or can be carried in a pocket *[a pocket watch]* *b)* smaller than standard **2.** not widespread; isolated *[pocket resistance]* —*vt.* **1.** to put into a pocket [he *pocketed* his change] **2.** to provide with pockets **3.** to surround; enclose [the airport is *pocketed* in fog] **4.** to take dishonestly; appropriate (money, etc.) for one's own use **5.** to put up with (an insult, etc.) without answering or showing anger **6.** to hide, suppress, or set aside [*pocket* one's pride] —**in one's pocket** completely under one's influence —**out of pocket** from money at hand

☆**pocket billiards** *same as* POOL[2] (*n.* 2)

pock·et·book (-book′) *n.* **1.** a case, as of leather, for carrying money and papers in one's pocket; billfold ☆**2.** a woman's purse **3.** one's supply of money, funds, etc.

pocket book a book small enough to be carried in one's pocket

pock·et·ful (-fool′) *n., pl.* **-fuls′** as much as a pocket will hold

☆**pocket gopher** *same as* GOPHER (sense 1)

pock·et·knife (-nīf′) *n., pl.* **-knives** (-nīvz′) a knife with blades that fold into the handle

pocket money cash for small expenses

pock·et·size (-sīz′) *adj.* of a small size; esp., of a size to fit in a pocket: also **pock′et·sized′**

☆**pocket veto** the indirect veto by the President of the U.S. of a bill presented to him by Congress within ten days of its adjournment, by his failing to sign and return the bill before Congress adjourns

pock·mark (päk′märk′) *n.* a scar or pit left by a small pimple, as of smallpox, or any mark like this —*vt.* to cover with pockmarks —**pock′marked′** *adj.*

POCKET-
KNIFE

po·co (pō′kō) *adv.* [It.] *Music* somewhat; to a slight degree

pod (päd) *n.* [< ?] **1.** the case or shell that holds the seeds of certain plants, as the pea and bean ☆**2.** a part shaped to enclose something else, as the housing of a jet engine —*vi.* **pod′ded, pod′ding 1.** to bear pods **2.** to swell out into a pod —**pod′like′** *adj.*

-pod (päd) [< Gr. *podis,* genitive of *pous,* a FOOT] *a combining form meaning:* **1.** foot **2.** (one) having (a specified number or kind of) feet [*tripod*] Also **-pode** (pōd)

podg·y (päj′ē) *adj.* **podg′i·er, podg′i·est** *var. of* PUDGY

po·di·a·trist (pō dī′ə trist, pə-) *n.* a person who practices podiatry

☆**po·di·a·try** (pō dī′ə trē, pə-) *n.* [< Gr. *pous* (see -POD) + -IATRY] the profession dealing with the care of the feet and with the treatment of foot disorders —**po′di·at′ric** (-dē at′rik) *adj.*

po·di·um (pō′dē əm) *n., pl.* **-di·a** (-ə); for 1 usually, **-di·ums** [L. < Gr. *podion,* dim. of *pous* (see -POD)] **1.** a low platform, esp. for the conductor of an orchestra **2.** *Zool.* a foot or footlike structure

Po·dunk (pō′duŋk′) [after a village in Mass. or Conn.] [Colloq.] any typically dull small town in the U.S.

Poe (pō), **Edgar Allan** 1809–49; U.S. poet, short-story writer, & critic

po·em (pō′əm) *n.* [< MFr. < L. < Gr. *poiēma* < *poiein,* to make < IE. base *kwei-,* to build] **1.** an arrangement of words written or spoken having rhythm and, often, rhyme, usually in language that shows more imagination and deep feeling than ordinary speech: some poems are in meter, some in free verse **2.** anything suggesting a poem in its effect

po·e·sy (pō′ə sē′, -zē′) *n., pl.* **-sies** [< OFr. < L. < Gr. *poiēsis* < *poiein,* to make: see POEM] **1.** *old-fashioned var. of* POETRY **2.** [Obs.] a poem

po·et (pō′ət) *n.* [< OFr. < L. < Gr. *poiētēs* < *poiein:* see POEM] **1.** a person who writes poems **2.** a person who expresses himself with beauty of thought and language —**po′et·ess** [Now Rare] *n.fem.*

poet. 1. poetic **2.** poetry

po·et·as·ter (pō′ə tas′tər) *n.* [see POET & -ASTER] a writer of inferior verse; would-be poet

po·et·ic (pō et′ik) *adj.* **1.** of, like, or fit for a poet or poetry [*poetic* language] **2.** written in verse [*poetic* drama] **3.** having the beauty, imaginative quality, etc. of good poetry [a *poetic* film] **4.** imaginative or creative [*poetic* talent] Also **po·et′i·cal** —**po·et′i·cal·ly** *adv.*

po·et·i·cize (-ə sīz′) *vt.* **-cized′, -ciz′ing 1.** to make poetic **2.** to express in poetry, or deal with in poetry —*vi.* to write poetry

poetic justice justice, as in some plays, etc., in which good is rewarded and evil punished

poetic license 1. disregard of strict fact or of rigid form, as by a poet, for artistic effect **2.** freedom to do this

po·et·ics (pō et′iks) *n.pl.* [with sing. v.] **1.** a) the theory or

structure of poetry *b*) an article or book on this **2.** the poetic theory or practice of a specific poet

po·et·ize (pō′ə tīz′) *vt., vi.* **-ized′, -iz′ing** *same as* POETICIZE

poet laureate *pl.* **poets laureate, poet laureates 1.** the court poet of England, appointed for life by the monarch to write poems celebrating official occasions, national events, etc. **2.** any official poet of any nation, region, etc.

po·et·ry (pō′ə trē) *n.* [< OFr. < ML. < L. *poeta,* POET] **1.** the art, theory, or structure of poems **2.** poems [the *poetry* of Walt Whitman] **3.** *a*) poetic qualities; the rhythm, spirit, feelings, etc. of poems *b*) the expression of such qualities in any of the arts [there is *poetry* in her dancing]

☆**po·go stick** (pō′gō) [a made-up word] a stilt with pedals and a spring at one end, used as a toy on which one can move along in a series of bounds

POGO
STICK

po·grom (pō gräm′, -grum′; pō′grəm) *n.* [Russ., devastation] an organized persecution and massacre of a minority group, esp. of Jews (as in Czarist Russia)

☆**poi** (poi, pō′ē) *n.* [Haw.] a Hawaiian food made of mashed, fermented taro root

poign·ant (poin′yənt; *chiefly Brit.* -ənt) *adj.* [MFr. prp. of *poindre* < L. *pungere,* to prick: see POINT] **1.** *a*) sharp or piercing to the smell or, formerly, the taste *b*) keenly affecting the other senses [*poignant* beauty] **2.** *a*) sharply painful to the feelings [a *poignant* memory] *b*) drawing forth pity, compassion, etc. [a *poignant* scene of poverty] **3.** sharp, biting, etc. [*poignant* wit] —see SYN. at MOVING —**poign′an·cy** *n.* —**poign′ant·ly** *adv.*

poi·kil·o·ther·mal (poi kil′ō thur′m'l) *adj.* [< Gr. *poikilos,* variant + THERMAL] *Zool. same as* COLDBLOODED (sense 1)

poin·ci·a·na (poin′sē an′ə, -ā′nə) *n.* [ModL., after M. de Poinci, a governor of the Fr. West Indies] any of various small tropical trees with showy red, orange, or yellow flowers

☆**poin·set·ti·a** (poin set′ē ə, -set′ə) *n.* [ModL., after J. R. Poinsett (d. 1851), U.S. ambassador to Mexico] a Mexican and Central American plant with yellow flowers surrounded by petallike red leaves

point (point) *n.* [OFr., a dot, prick < L. < *punctus,* pp. of *pungere,* to prick < IE. base *peug-,* to prick] **1.** a very small mark or dot **2.** a dot in print or writing, as a period, decimal point, etc. **3.** *a*) an element in geometry having definite position, but no size, shape, or extension *b*) a particular position, location, spot, etc. [*points* on a journey] **4.** *a*) the position of a player, as in cricket *b*) the player **5.** the exact moment [at the *point* of death] **6.** a stage, condition, level, or degree reached [a boiling *point*] **7.** a particular detail or part; item [explain it *point* by *point*] **8.** *a*) a special quality or characteristic [generosity is one of his good *points*] *b*) a physical characteristic of an animal, used as a standard in judging breeding **9.** a unit, as of measurement, value, game scores, etc. [a touchdown is worth six *points*] **10.** *a*) a sharp end; tip [the *point* of a needle] *b*) something with a sharp end **11.** needlepoint lace **12.** a piece of land that sticks out; cape **13.** a branch of a deer's antler [a ten-*point* buck] **14.** *a*) the essential fact or idea under consideration [our discussion finally came to the *point*] *b*) the main idea or feature of a story, etc. [the *point* of a joke] **15.** aim; purpose; object [there's no *point* in going] **16.** *a*) an impressive argument or fact [he has a *point* there!] ☆*b*) a helpful hint ☆**17.** the number that the thrower must make to win in craps **18.** *Ballet* the position of being on the tips of the toes ☆**19.** *Education* a unit of academic credit based on grades and class hours **20.** *Elec.* either of the two tungsten or platinum contacts that make or break the circuit in a distributor **21.** *Finance a*) a standard unit of value, equal to $1, used in quoting prices, as of stocks *b*) a percentage of a mortgage required to be paid in advance by the borrower **22.** *Navigation a*) any of the 32 marks showing direction on a compass card *b*) the angle between two successive compass points **23.** *Printing* a measuring unit for type bodies and printed matter, equal to about 1/72 of an inch —*vt.* **1.** *a*) to put punctuation marks in *b*) to mark (off a sum, etc.) with (decimal) points **2.** to sharpen (a pencil, etc.) to a point **3.** to give (a story, remark, etc.) emphasis (usually with *up*) [he raised his voice to *point* up his meaning] **4.** to show or call attention to (usually with *out*) [*point* the way; *point* out a person's mistakes] **5.** to aim or direct (a gun, finger, etc.) **6.** to extend the foot so as to bring (the toe) more nearly in line with the leg **7.** to show the location of (game) by standing still and facing toward it: said of hunting dogs **8.** *Masonry* to rake out mortar from the joints of (brickwork) and finish with fresh mortar —*vi.* **1.** to direct one's finger or the like (*at* or *to*) [she *pointed* to the book she wanted] **2.** to call attention (*to*); hint (*at*) [everything *points* to a happy ending] **3.** to aim or be directed (*to* or *toward*) [our house *points* toward the park] **4.** to point game: said of a hunting dog —**at the point of** very close to —**beside the point** not having to do with the subject at hand —**in point** appropriate; pertinent; apt [a case *in point*] —**in point of** in the matter of; as concerns [*in point of* fact] —**make a point of 1.** to make (something) one's strict rule, practice, etc. **2.** to call special attention to —**on** (or **upon**) **the point of** almost in the act of; on the verge of —**stretch** (or **strain**) **a point** to make an exception or concession —**to the point** having much to do with the subject; pertinent; apt —**point′a·ble** *adj.*

point-blank (-blaŋk′) *adj.* [POINT + BLANK (white center of the target)] **1.** aimed horizontally, straight at a mark, as a gun **2.** straightforward; plain [a *point-blank* answer] —*adv.* **1.** in a direct line; straight [to fire a gun *point-blank*] **2.** without quibbling; directly; bluntly [to refuse *point-blank*]

point·ed (poin′tid) *adj.* **1.** *a)* having a point, or sharp end *b)* coming to a point; tapering **2.** sharp and to the point [a *pointed* saying] **3.** aimed at someone [a *pointed* remark] **4.** very obvious; emphasized [he showed his regret in a very *pointed* way] —**point′ed·ly** *adv.* —**point′ed·ness** *n.*

point·er (-tər) *n.* **1.** a person or thing that points **2.** a long, tapered rod for pointing to things, as on a map **3.** a hand or needle on a clock, meter, etc. **4.** a large, lean hunting dog with a smooth coat: it smells out game and then points **5.** [Colloq.] a helpful hint [*pointers* from the coach on how to hold a bat] —**the Pointers** *Astron.* the two stars in the Big Dipper that are almost in a line with the North Star

POINTER
(26 in. high
at shoulder)

poin·til·lism (pwan′t'l iz'm, -tē iz'm; point′'l-) *n.* [< Fr. < *pointille*, a dot < It. < L. *punctus*: see POINT] a method used in certain French impressionist paintings, in which a white background is covered with tiny points of pure color that blend together when seen from a distance

point lace needlepoint lace

point·less (point′lis) *adj.* **1.** without a point **2.** without meaning, purpose, or force; senseless [a *pointless* remark] —**point′less·ly** *adv.* —**point′less·ness** *n.*

point of honor a matter affecting one's honor

point of order a question as to whether the rules of parliamentary procedure are being followed

point of view 1. the place from which, or way in which, something is viewed; standpoint [a liberal *point of view*] **2.** a mental attitude

point·y (point′tē) *adj.* **point′i·er, point′i·est 1.** that comes to a sharp point **2.** having many points

poise (poiz) *n.* [< OFr. < VL. < L. *pensum*, something weighed < *pendere*, to weigh: see PENDANT] **1.** balance; stability [the scales are in *poise*] **2.** ease and dignity of manner; composure [he lost his *poise* when we laughed at him] **3.** the condition of being calm or serene [*poise* of mind] **4.** manner of carrying oneself; bearing, as of the body [the perfect *poise* of a tiger ready to spring] —*vt.* **poised, pois′ing 1.** to balance; keep steady **2.** to suspend (usually passive or reflexive) [the earth is *poised* in space] —*vi.* **1.** to be suspended or balanced **2.** to hover [the helicopter *poised* over the landing strip]

poi·son (poi′z'n) *n.* [< OFr. < L. *potio*, POTION] **1.** a substance causing illness or death when eaten, drunk, or absorbed in small quantities **2.** anything harmful to happiness or welfare [the *poison* of his hate] —*vt.* **1.** to harm or destroy by means of poison [to *poison* rats] **2.** to put poison on or into [to *poison* bait] **3.** to influence wrongfully [to *poison* one's mind] —*adj.* poisonous or poisoned [*poison* gas] —**poi′son·er** *n.*

☆**poison dogwood** *same as* POISON SUMAC

poison gas any poisonous chemical substance, in the form of a gas or vapor-forming liquid or solid, esp. one used in war to kill or injure when it is breathed in or touches the body

☆**poison hemlock** *same as* HEMLOCK (sense 1)

☆**poison ivy 1.** any of several plants having leaves of three leaflets and ivory-colored berries: the oil in the plant can cause a severe rash when it touches the skin **2.** such a rash

☆**poison oak** *name variously used for:* **1.** POISON IVY. **2.** POISON SUMAC

poi·son·ous (poi′z'n əs) *adj.* capable of injuring or killing by or as by poison; full of poison; venomous —**poi′son·ous·ly** *adv.* —**poi′son·ous·ness** *n.*

POISON IVY

☆**poison sumac** a swamp plant with clusters of grayish fruit and leaves made up of 7 to 13 leaflets: the oil in the plant can cause a severe rash when it touches the skin

poke¹ (pōk) *vt.* **poked, pok′ing** [MDu. or LowG. *poken*] **1.** *a)* to push or jab with a stick, finger, etc. *b)* [Slang] to hit with the fist **2.** to make (a hole, etc.) by poking **3.** to stir up (a fire) **4.** to thrust (something) forward; intrude [to *poke* one's head out a window] —*vi.* **1.** to jab with a stick, poker, etc. (*at*) **2.** to intrude; meddle [he *poked* into my affairs] **3.** to search (sometimes with *about* or *around*) [she *poked* around the attic looking for old letters] **4.** to stick out; protrude [his toe *poked* through the hole in his sock] **5.** to move slowly or lazily; loiter (often with *along*) —*n.* **1.** *a)* a poking; jab; thrust *b)* [Slang] a blow with the fist **2.** *same as* SLOWPOKE **3.** a poke bonnet —**poke fun** (**at**) to make jokes about; ridicule or deride

poke² (pōk) *n.* [OFr. *poke, poque* < Frank.: for IE. base see BIG] **1.** [Dial.] a sack or bag **2.** [Slang] *a)* a wallet or purse *b)* all of one's money

☆**poke³** (pōk) *n.* [< AmInd. *puccoon*] *same as* POKEWEED: also ☆**poke′ber′ry** (-ber′ē), *pl.* **-ries**

poke bonnet a bonnet with a wide front brim

☆**pok·er¹** (pō′kər) *n.* [< ?] a card game in which the players bet on the value of their hands, forming a pool to be taken by the winner: see DRAW POKER, STUD POKER

pok·er² (pō′kər) *n.* **1.** a person or thing that pokes **2.** a bar, as of iron, for stirring a fire

☆**poker face** [Colloq.] an expressionless face, as of a poker player trying to conceal from the other players what sort of hand he has

☆**poke·weed** (pōk′wēd′) *n.* [see POKE³] a N. American plant with purplish-white flowers, reddish-purple berries, and poisonous roots

pok·ey (pō′kē) *n., pl.* **pok′eys, pok′ies** [< ?] [Slang] a jail: also **pok′y**

pok·y (pō′kē) *adj.* **pok′i·er, pok′i·est** [POKE¹ + -Y²] **1.** slow; dull [a *poky* town] **2.** small; stuffy [a *poky* room] **3.** shabbily dressed Also **pok′ey** —**pok′i·ly** *adv.* —**pok′i·ness** *n.*

pol (päl) *n.* [Slang] an experienced politician

Pol. 1. Poland **2.** Polish

Po·land (pō′lənd) country in C Europe, on the Baltic Sea: 120,625 sq. mi.; pop. 33,130,000; cap. Warsaw

☆**Poland China** an American breed of large hog, usually black and white

po·lar (pō′lər) *adj.* [< ML. < L. *polus*: see POLE²] **1.** of or near the North or South Pole **2.** of a pole or poles **3.** having polarity **4.** opposite in character, direction, etc. [they took *polar* positions in the argument] **5.** central and guiding, like the polestar

polar bear a large, white bear of the arctic regions

polar body either of two very small cells cast off during the formation of an ovum

polar circle *same as:* **1.** ARCTIC CIRCLE **2.** ANTARCTIC CIRCLE

polar coordinate either of two numbers that locate a point in a plane: one is the distance of the point from a fixed point on a fixed line, and the other is the angle made by the fixed line with the line connecting the two points

Po·la·ris (pō lar′is) [ModL. < ML. (*stella*) *polaris*, polar (star)] *same as* NORTH STAR

POLAR BEAR
(to 5 ft. high
at shoulder)

po·lar·i·scope (pō lar′ə skōp′) *n.* [POLARI(ZE) + -SCOPE] an instrument for demonstrating or detecting the polarization of light, or for looking at things in polarized light —**po·lar′i·scop′ic** (-skäp′ik) *adj.*

po·lar·i·ty (pō lar′ə tē) *n., pl.* **-ties** **1.** the tendency of bodies having opposite magnetic poles to arrange themselves so that their two outer ends point to the two magnetic poles of the earth **2.** any tendency to turn, feel, etc. in a certain way, as if magnetized **3.** the having of qualities, powers, etc. opposed to each other **4.** the condition of being positive or negative with respect to some reference point or object

po·lar·i·za·tion (pō′lər i zā′shən) *n.* **1.** the producing or acquiring of polarity **2.** the collection of gases around the electrodes of an electric cell during electrolysis, causing a reduction in the flow of current **3.** *Optics* a condition, or the production of a condition, of light in which the transverse vibrations of the waves are in one plane or direction only

po·lar·ize (pō′lə rīz′) *vt.* **-ized′, -iz′ing** [< Fr. < *polaire,* POLAR] to give polarity to; produce polarization in —*vi.* to take on polarity; specif., to separate into completely opposed groups, viewpoints, etc. —**po′lar·iz′a·ble** *adj.* —**po′lar·iz′er** *n.*

☆**Po·lar·oid** (pō′lə roid′) [POLAR + -OID] *a trademark for:* **1.** a transparent material capable of polarizing light **2.** a camera that takes snapshots and also develops and prints them: in full, **Polaroid (Land) camera**

Pole (pōl) *n.* a native or inhabitant of Poland

pole[1] (pōl) *n.* [OE. *pal* < L. *palus,* a stake: see PALE[2]] **1.** a long, slender piece of wood, metal, etc. [a tent *pole*] **2.** a unit of measure, equal to one rod or one square rod **3.** the innermost position on a race track —*vt., vi.* **poled, pol′ing** ☆**1.** to push along (a boat or raft) with a pole **2.** to force, support, etc. (something) as with a pole

pole[2] (pōl) *n.* [L. *polus* < Gr. *polos:* for IE. base see COLLAR] **1.** either end of any axis, as of the earth, or the celestial sphere, etc. **2.** the region around the North Pole or South Pole **3.** either of two opposed forces, parts, etc., such as the ends of a magnet, the terminals of a battery, etc. or two completely opposed groups, viewpoints, etc. —**poles apart** widely separated

pole·ax, pole·axe (pōl′aks′) *n., pl.* **-ax′es** (-ak′siz) [< *pol,* POLL + *ax,* AX] **1.** a long-handled battle-ax **2.** any ax with a spike, hook, etc. opposite the blade —*vt.* **-axed′, -ax′ing** to attack with a poleax

☆**pole bean** any of certain varieties of the common garden bean that grow as vines twining about poles or other supports

pole·cat (pōl′kat′) *n., pl.* **-cats′, -cat′:** see PLURAL, II, D, 1 [prob. < OFr. *poule:* see PULLET & CAT] **1.** a small, weasellike animal of Europe ☆**2.** *same as* SKUNK

po·lem·ic (pə lem′ik, pō-) *adj.* [< Fr. < Gr. *polemikos* < *polemos,* a war] **1.** of or involving dispute; controversial **2.** inclined to argue Also, esp. for 2, **po·lem′i·cal** —*n.* **1.** an argument or controversial discussion **2.** a person who likes to argue —**po·lem′i·cal·ly** *adv.*

po·lem·ics (-iks) *n.pl.* [*with sing. v.*] the art or practice of formal discussion or debate —**po·lem′i·cist** (-ə sist) *n.*

pole·star (pōl′stär′) *n.* **1.** Polaris, the North Star **2.** a guiding principle **3.** a center of attraction

pole vault **1.** a contest in track and field in which the contestants leap for height, vaulting over a bar with the aid of a long, flexible pole to push themselves off the ground **2.** such a leap —**pole′-vault′** *vi.* —**pole′-vault′er** *n.*

po·lice (pə lēs′) *n.* [Fr. < LL. < Gr. *politeia,* the state < *politēs,* citizen < *polis,* city < IE. base *pel-,* fortress] **1.** the regulation of morals, safety, etc.; law enforcement **2.** the governmental department (of a city, state, etc.) for keeping order, enforcing the law, making arrests, and preventing crimes **3.** [*with pl. v.*] the members of such a department, or of a private organization like this [security *police*] ☆**4.** *U.S. Army* *a)* the duty of keeping a camp, etc. clean and orderly *b)* [*with pl. v.*] the soldiers charged with this —*vt.* **-liced′, -lic′ing** **1.** to control, protect, etc. with police or the like [to *police* the streets] ☆**2.** to keep (a military camp, etc.) clean and orderly

police dog a dog specially trained to assist police; esp., in popular usage, a German shepherd dog

po·lice·man (-mən) *n., pl.* **-men** a member of a police force —**po·lice′wom′an** *n.fem., pl.* **-wom′en**

police state a government that uses a secret police force to put down or crush political opposition

police station the headquarters of a local or district police force

pol·i·clin·ic (päl′i klin′ik) *n.* [< G. < Gr. *polis,* city + G. *klinik,* clinic] the department of a hospital where outpatients are treated

pol·i·cy[1] (päl′ə sē) *n., pl.* **-cies** [< OFr. < L. < Gr. *politeia:* see POLICE] **1.** wise or careful management **2.** any principle, plan, etc. as followed by a government, organization, individual, etc. [foreign *policy*]

pol·i·cy[2] (päl′ə sē) *n., pl.* **-cies** [< MFr. < It. *polizza* < ML., ult. < Gr. *apodeixis,* proof < *apodeiknynai,* to display] a written contract (**insurance policy**) in which one party guarantees to insure another against a specified loss, injury, etc.

pol·i·cy·hold·er (-hōl′dər) *n.* a person to whom an insurance policy is issued

☆**policy (racket)** *same as* THE NUMBERS (see NUMBER)

po·li·o (pō′lē ō′) *n. clipped form of* POLIOMYELITIS

po·li·o·my·e·li·tis (pō′lē ō mī′ə līt′əs) *n.* [ModL. < Gr. *polios,* gray + MYELITIS] a serious infectious disease, esp. of children, caused by a virus that inflames the gray matter of the spinal cord, often resulting in muscular paralysis

Pol·ish (pō′lish) *adj.* of Poland, its people, their language, or culture —*n.* the West Slavic language of the Poles

pol·ish (päl′ish) *vt.* [< OFr. < L. *polire:* for IE. base see FELT[1]] **1.** *a)* to smooth and brighten, as by rubbing *b)* to coat with wax, etc. and make glossy **2.** to improve or refine (manners, etc.) by removing crudeness **3.** to complete or perfect [to *polish* a piece of writing] —*vi.* to take a polish; become glossy, refined, etc. —*n.* **1.** a surface brightness or shine [your car has a nice *polish*] **2.** elegance; refinement, as in speech or manners **3.** a substance used for polishing [shoe *polish*] **4.** a polishing or being polished —**polish off** [Colloq.] **1.** to finish (a meal, job, etc.) completely and quickly **2.** to get rid of (a competitor, enemy, etc.) —**polish up** [Colloq.] to improve —**pol′ished** *adj.* —**pol′ish·er** *n.*

Po·lit·bu·ro (päl′it byoor′ō, pō′lit-) *n.* [< Russ. < *Polit(icheskoe) Byuro,* political bureau] the executive committee of the Communist Party of the Soviet Union and of certain other countries

po·lite (pə līt′) *adj.* [< L. pp. of *polire,* to polish] **1.** polished; cultured; refined [*polite* society] **2.** having or showing good manners; courteous [a *polite* note of thanks] —see SYN. at CIVIL —**po·lite′ly** *adv.* —**po·lite′ness** *n.*

pol·i·tesse (päl′ə tes′) *n.* [Fr.] politeness; courtesy

pol·i·tic (päl′ə tik) *adj.* [< MFr. < L. < Gr. *politēs:* see POLICE] **1.** having practical wisdom; prudent **2.** clever or cunning; crafty [a *politic* answer to the reporter's questions] **3.** worked out in a careful or crafty way to fit the situation; expedient [a *politic* plan] **4.** [Rare] political: see BODY POLITIC —*vi.* **-ticked, -tick·ing** to engage in political campaigning —see SYN. at SUAVE —**pol′i·tic·ly** *adv.*

po·lit·i·cal (pə lit′i k'l) *adj.* **1.** of or concerned with government, politics, etc. [*political* science] **2.** having a definite governmental organization **3.** engaged in politics [*political* parties] **4.** of or characteristic of political parties or politicians [*political* pressure] —**po·lit′i·cal·ly** *adv.*

political economy *earlier name for* ECONOMICS

political science the science of the principles, organization, and methods of government —**political scientist**

pol·i·ti·cian (päl′ə tish′ən) *n.* a person actively engaged in politics, often one holding or seeking political office: often used to show contempt for one who seeks only to advance himself or his party, as by scheming: see also STATESMAN

po·lit·i·co (pə lit′i kō′) *n., pl.* **-cos′** [Sp. or It.] *same as* POLITICIAN

pol·i·tics (päl′ə tiks) *n.pl.* [*with sing. or pl. v.*] **1.** the science of government; political science **2.** political affairs **3.** participation in political affairs, often as a profession [to enter *politics*] **4.** political methods, tactics, etc.; sometimes, specif., crafty or unprincipled methods **5.** political opinions, principles, etc. [what are your *politics?*] **6.** scheming for power within a group by its members [office *politics*]

pol·i·ty (päl′ə tē) *n., pl.* **-ties** [< MFr. < L. *politia:* see POLICY[1]] **1.** the government organization of a state, church, etc. **2.** a society or institution with a government; state

Polk (pōk), **James Knox** 1795–1849; 11th president of the U.S. (1845–49)

pol·ka (pōl′kə) *n.* [Czech < Pol. fem. of *Polak,* a Pole] **1.** a fast dance for couples **2.** music for this dance, in duple time —*vi.* to dance the polka

☆**pol·ka dot** (pō′kə) **1.** one of the small round dots regularly spaced to form a pattern on cloth **2.** a pattern or cloth with such dots —**pol′ka-dot′** *adj.*

poll (pōl) *n.* [< or akin to MDu. *pol,* head] **1.** the head; esp., the crown, back, or hair of the head **2.** a counting, listing, etc. of persons, esp. of voters **3.** the number of votes recorded ☆**4.** [*pl.*] a place where votes are cast and recorded ☆**5.** *a)* the act of contacting a selected or random group to collect information, or to attempt to discover public opinion *b*) a report on this *[a* **poll** *of our class shows that most of us want a party]* —*vt.* **1.** to cut off or cut short **2.** to trim the wool, branches, etc. of **3.** *a*) to register the votes of ☆*b*) to require each member of (a jury, etc.) to declare his vote individually **4.** to receive (a certain number of votes) **5.** to cast (a vote) **6.** to contact for the purposes of a poll (*n.* 5) —*vi.* to vote in an election —**poll′er** *n.*

pol·lack (päl′ək) *n., pl.* **-lack, -lacks:** see PLURAL, II, D, 2 [< early Scot. *podlok* < ?] any of several related saltwater food fishes of the cod family, having tiny scales and a lower jaw that sticks out: also sp. **pollock**

pol·len (päl′ən) *n.* [ModL. < L., dust < IE. base *pel-*, dust] the yellow, powderlike male sex cells on the stamens of a flower

pol·li·nate (päl′ə nāt′) *vt.* **-nat′ed, -nat′ing** to transfer pollen from a stamen to a pistil of (a flower) —**pol′li·na′tion** *n.* — **pol′li·na′tor** *n.*

pol·li·wog (päl′ē wäg′, -wôg′) *n.* [prob. < *pol,* POLL + *wigelen,* to WIGGLE] *same as* TADPOLE: also sp. **pol′ly·wog′**

Pol·lock (päl′ək), **Jackson** 1912–56; U.S. abstract painter

☆**poll·ster** (pōl′stər) *n.* a person whose work is taking public opinion polls

poll tax a tax per head: in some States a person is required to pay a poll tax in order to vote in State or local elections

pol·lu·tant (pə lōot′′nt) *n.* something that pollutes, as a chemical harmful to life that gets into the air or water as a waste product from incinerators, factories, etc.

pol·lute (pə lōot′) *vt.* **-lut′ed, -lut′ing** [< L. pp. of *polluere*] to make unclean, impure, or corrupt; defile *[the river is polluted with raw sewage]* —**pol·lut′er** *n.* —**pol·lu′tion** *n.*

Pol·lux (päl′əks) **1.** *Gr. 6 Rom. Myth.* the immortal twin of Castor **2.** the brightest star in the constellation Gemini

☆**Pol·ly·an·na** (päl′ē an′ə) *n.* [the heroine of novels by Eleanor H. Porter (1868–1920), U.S. writer] an overly optimistic person who always looks on the bright side of things

po·lo (pō′lō) *n.* [prob. < Tibet. *pulu,* the ball] **1.** a game played on horseback by two teams who try to drive a small wooden ball through the opponents' goal with long-handled mallets **2.** *same as* WATER POLO —**po′lo·ist** *n.*

Po·lo (pō′lō), **Mar·co** (mär′kō) 1254?–1324?; Venetian traveler in eastern Asia

po·lo·naise (päl′ə nāz′, pō′lə-) *n.* [Fr. < fem. of *polonais,* Polish] **1.** a stately Polish dance in triple time **2.** music for this dance

po·lo·ni·um (pə lō′nē əm) *n.* [ModL. < ML. *Polonia,* Poland: coinage of Marie Curie, its co-discoverer] a radioactive chemical element formed by the disintegration of radium: symbol, Po; at. wt., 210.05; at. no., 84

☆**polo shirt** a knitted pullover sport shirt

Pol·ska (pôl′skä) Polish name of POLAND

pol·ter·geist (pōl′tər gīst′) *n.* [G. < *poltern,* to rumble + *geist,* GHOST] a ghost supposed to cause table rappings and other mysterious noisy disturbances

pol·troon (päl trōon′) *n.* [< Fr. < It. *poltrone,* coward < *poltro,* colt] a thorough coward —*adj.* cowardly —**pol·troon′er·y** *n.*

pol·y- [ModL. < Gr. *poly-* < *polys,* much, many: for IE. base see FULL[1]] *a combining form meaning* much, many, more than one

pol·y·an·drous (päl′ē an′drəs) *adj.* **1.** practicing polyandry **2.** of or characterized by polyandry **3.** *Bot.* having many stamens

pol·y·an·dry (päl′ē an′drē, päl′ē an′-) *n.* [< Gr. < *poly-,* many + *anēr,* a man] **1.** the state or practice of having two or more husbands at the same time **2.** *Bot.* the presence of many stamens in one flower **3.** *Zool.* the mating of one female animal with more than one male —**pol′y·an′dric** *adj.* —**pol′y·an′drist** *n.*

pol·y·an·thus (päl′ē an′thəs) *n.* [ModL. < *poly-,* many + *anthos,* a flower] **1.** any of various primroses with many flowers **2.** a sweet-scented narcissus with clusters of star-shaped flowers

pol·y·cen·tric (päl′i sen′trik) *adj.* [POLY- + CENT(E)R + -IC]

POLO PLAYER

of or relating to independent centers of power within a political system —**pol′y·cen′trism** *n.* —**pol′y·cen′trist** *adj., n.*

pol·y·chaete (päl′i kēt′) *n.* [ModL. < Gr. < *polys,* much + *chaitē,* hair] any of a group of annelid worms, having on most segments a pair of fleshy, leglike parts covered with bristles — **pol′y·chae′tous** *adj.*

pol·y·chro·mat·ic (päl′i krō mat′ik) *adj.* [POLY- + CHROMATIC] having various or changing colors

pol·y·chrome (päl′i krōm′) *adj.* [Fr. < Gr. *polychrōmos:* see POLY- & -CHROME] **1.** *same as* POLYCHROMATIC **2.** done or decorated in several colors —*n.* a polychrome work of art

pol·y·clin·ic (päl′i klin′ik) *n.* [POLY- + CLINIC] a clinic or hospital treating various kinds of diseases

pol·y·es·ter (päl′ē es′tər) *n.* [POLY(MER) + ESTER] any of several polymeric synthetic resins used in making plastics, fibers, etc.

☆**pol·y·eth·yl·ene** (päl′ē eth′ə lēn′) *n.* [POLY(MER) + ETHYLENE] any of several thermoplastic resins, $(C_2H_4)_n$, used in making plastics, films, etc.

po·lyg·a·mous (pə lig′ə məs) *adj.* **1.** of, engaging in, or characterized by polygamy **2.** *Bot.* having bisexual flowers and unisexual flowers on the same plant or on different plants —**po·lyg′a·mous·ly** *adv.*

po·lyg·a·my (pə lig′ə mē) *n.* [< Fr. < Gr.: see POLY- & -GAMY] **1.** the practice of having two or more wives or husbands at the same time **2.** *Zool.* the practice of mating with more than one of the opposite sex —**po·lyg′a·mist** *n.*

pol·y·glot (päl′i glät′) *adj.* [< Gr. < *poly-,* many + *glōtta,* the tongue] **1.** speaking or writing several languages **2.** containing or written in several languages —*n.* **1.** a polyglot person **2.** a polyglot book

pol·y·gon (päl′i gän′) *n.* [< LL. < Gr.: see POLY- & -GON] a closed plane figure, esp. one with more than four sides and angles —**po·lyg·o·nal** (pə lig′ə n′l) *adj.*

pol·y·graph (päl′i graf′) *n.* **1.** an early device for making copies of writings or drawings **2.** an instrument for recording changes in blood pressure, pulse rate, etc.: see LIE DETECTOR — **pol′y·graph′ic** *adj.*

po·lyg·y·ny (pə lij′ə nē) *n.* [ModL. < POLY- + Gr. *gynē,* a woman] the practice of having two or more wives or concubines at the same time —**po·lyg′y·nous** (-nəs) *adj.*

pol·y·he·dron (päl′i hē′drən) *n., pl.* **-drons, -dra** (-drə) [ModL. < Gr.: see POLY- & -HEDRON] a solid figure, esp. one with more than six plane surfaces —**pol′y·he′dral** *adj.*

Pol·y·hym·ni·a (päl′ə him′nē ə) *Gr. Myth.* the Muse of sacred poetry: also **Po·lym′ni·a** (pə lim′-)

pol·y·math (päl′i math′) *n.* [< Gr. < *poly-* (see POLY-) + *manthanein,* to learn] a person of great and varied learning — **pol′y·math′ic** *adj.*

pol·y·mer (päl′i mər) *n.* [G. < Gr.: see POLY- & -MEROUS] a naturally occurring or synthetic substance made up of giant molecules formed by polymerization

pol·y·mer·ic (päl′i mer′ik) *adj.* made up of the same chemical elements in the same proportions by weight, but differing in molecular weight —**pol′y·mer′i·cal·ly** *adv.*

po·lym·er·i·za·tion (pə lim′ər i zā′shən, päl′i mər-) *n.* the process of joining two or more like molecules to form a large molecule whose molecular weight is a multiple of the original and whose physical properties are different —**po·lym′er·ize′** (-īz′) *vt., vi.* **-ized′, -iz′ing**

pol·y·mor·phism (päl′i môr′fiz′m) *n.* [POLYMORPH(OUS) + -ISM] **1.** *Chem., Mineralogy* the property of certain substances of crystallizing in two or more different forms **2.** *Zool.* the condition in which an organism has two or more very different morphological forms, as the castes of social insects

pol·y·mor·phous (päl′i môr′fəs) *adj.* [< Gr.: see POLY- & -MORPH] having, occurring in, or passing through several or various forms: also **pol′y·mor′phic** —**pol′y·mor′phous·ly** *adv.*

Pol·y·ne·sia (päl′ə nē′zhə, -shə) a major division of the Pacific islands east of the international date line, including Hawaii, Samoa, Tonga, Society Islands, etc.

Pol·y·ne·sian (-zhən, -shən) *adj.* of Polynesia, its people, their language, etc. —*n.* **1.** a member of the brown-skinned people of Polynesia, including the Hawaiians, Tahitians, Samoans, and Maoris **2.** the group of Malayo-Polynesian languages of Polynesia

pol·y·no·mi·al (päl′i nō′mē əl) *n.* [POLY- + (BI)NOMIAL] **1.** *Algebra* an expression consisting of two or more terms (Example: x³ + 3x + 2) **2.** *Biol.* a species or subspecies name having two or more terms —*adj.* consisting of polynomials

pol·yp (päl′ip) *n.* [< Fr. < L. < Gr. < *poly-*, many + *pous*, a foot] **1.** any of various coelenterates having a mouth fringed with tentacles at the top of a tubelike body, as the sea anemone, hydra, etc. **2.** a bulging growth of mucous membrane inside the nose, bladder, etc. —**pol′yp·ous** *adj.*

pol·y·pet·al·ous (päl′i pet′'l əs) *adj.* [POLY- + PETAL + -OUS] *Bot.* having separate petals

pol·y·phase (päl′i fāz′) *adj.* *Elec.* having, generating, or using alternating currents differing in phase [a *polyphase* system]

pol·y·phon·ic (päl′i fän′ik) *adj.* [< Gr.: see POLY- & -PHONE] **1.** having or making many sounds **2.** *Music* of or characterized by polyphony; contrapuntal Also **po·lyph·o·nous** (pə lif′ə-nəs) —**pol′y·phon′i·cal·ly** *adv.*

po·lyph·o·ny (pə lif′ə nē) *n.* **1.** a great number of sounds, as in an echo **2.** *Music* a combining of a number of individual but harmonious melodies; counterpoint

pol·y·ploid (päl′i ploid′) *adj.* [POLY- + -PLOID] having the number of chromosomes in the somatic cells three or more times the haploid number —*n.* a polyploid cell or organism —**pol′y·ploi′dy** *n.*

pol·y·pro·pyl·ene (päl′i prō′pə lēn′) *n.* [POLY(MER) + PROPYLENE] polymerized propylene, a very light thermoplastic resin used in packaging, tubing, etc.

pol·y·sac·cha·ride (päl′i sak′ə rīd′) *n.* [POLY- + SACCHARIDE] any of a group of complex carbohydrates, as starch, that break down by hydrolysis into a large number of monosaccharide units

pol·y·some (päl′i sōm′) *n.* [POLY- + -SOME³] a group of ribosomes in which protein synthesis occurs

pol·y·so·mic (päl′i sō′mik) *adj.* [< prec. + -IC] *Genetics* having extra chromosomes, not in a set

pol·y·sty·rene (päl′i stī′rēn) *n.* a tough plastic, a polymer of styrene, used to make containers, etc.

pol·y·syl·lab·ic (päl′i si lab′ik) *adj.* **1.** having several syllables, esp. four or more (Ex.: elementary) **2.** using polysyllables [he uses *polysyllabic* language] Also **pol′y·syl·lab′i·cal** —**pol′y·syl·lab′i·cal·ly** *adv.*

pol·y·syl·la·ble (päl′i sil′ə b'l) *n.* a polysyllabic word

pol·y·tech·nic (päl′i tek′nik) *adj.* [< Fr. < Gr. < *poly-*, many + *technē*, an art] of or providing instruction in many scientific and technical subjects —*n.* a polytechnic school

pol·y·the·ism (päl′i thē iz'm) *n.* [< Fr. < Gr. < *poly-*, many + *theos*, god] belief in more than one god or in many gods —**pol′y·the·ist** *adj., n.* —**pol′y·the·is′tic, pol′y·the·is′ti·cal** *adj.* —**pol′y·the·is′ti·cal·ly** *adv.*

pol·y·un·sat·u·rat·ed (päl′i un sach′ə rāt′id) *adj.* [POLY- + UNSATURATED] containing more than one double or triple bond in the molecule, as certain vegetable and animal fats and oils

pol·y·u·re·thane (-yoor′ə thān′) *n.* [POLY- + *urethane*, a chemical compound with the basic structure of polyurethane] any of certain synthetic rubber polymers used in cushions, molded products, etc.

pol·y·va·lent (-vā′lənt) *adj.* **1.** designating a vaccine for two or more strains of the same microorganism **2.** *Chem.* a) having a valence of more than two b) having more than one valence —**pol′y·va′lence** *n.*

pol·y·vi·nyl (-vī′n'l) *adj.* describing or of any of a group of polymerized vinyl compounds

☆**pol·y·wa·ter** (-wôt′ər, -wät′-) *n.* [POLY(MERIC) + WATER] a sticky substance variously identified as a new form of water, highly contaminated water, etc.

pom·ace (pum′is) *n.* [ML. *pomacium*, cider < L. *pomum*, a fruit] **1.** the crushed pulp of apples or other fruit pressed for juice **2.** the crushed matter of anything pressed, as seeds for oil

po·ma·ceous (pō mā′shəs) *adj.* [< L. *pomum*, a fruit] of or like apples or other pomes

po·made (pä mād′, pō-, pə-; -mäd′) *n.* [< Fr. < It. *pomata*, ult. < L. *pomum*, fruit: orig. perfumed with apple pulp] a perfumed preparation, as for grooming the hair: also **po·ma·tum** (pō māt′əm) —*vt.* **-mad′ed, -mad′ing** to apply pomade to

pome (pōm) *n.* [OFr., ult. < L. *pomum*, fruit] any fleshy fruit with a core and seeds, as the apple, pear, etc.

pome·gran·ate (päm′gran′it, päm′ə-; pum′-) *n.* [< OFr. < *pome*, apple + *granade* < L. *granatum*, lit., having seeds] **1.** a round fruit with a thick, red rind and many seeds covered with red, juicy pulp that can be eaten **2.** the bush or small tree that bears it

Pom·er·a·ni·a (päm′ə rā′nē ə) region in C Europe, on the Baltic, now divided between Poland & East Germany

Pom·er·a·ni·an (-ən) *adj.* of Pomerania or its people —*n.* **1.** a native or inhabitant of Pomerania **2.** any of a breed of small dog with long, silky hair, pointed ears, and a bushy tail

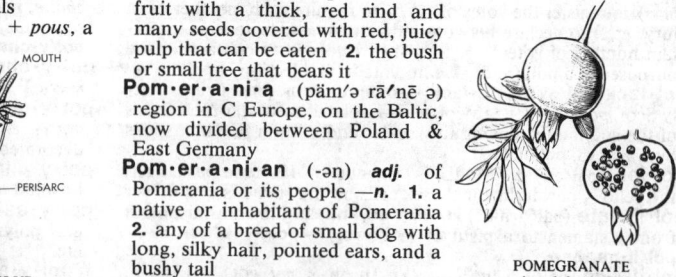

POMEGRANATE
(and fruit in cross section)

pom·mel (pum′'l; *also, for n.,* päm′'l) *n.* [< OFr. dim. of *pome*: see POME] **1.** a round knob on the end of some sword hilts **2.** the rounded part that sticks up on the front of a saddle—*vt.* **-meled** or **-melled, -mel·ing** or **-mel·ling** *same as* PUMMEL

po·mol·o·gy (pō mäl′ə jē) *n.* [< ModL.: see POME & -LOGY] the science of growing fruit —**po·mol′o·gist** *n.*

Po·mo·na (pə mō′nə) [after *Pomona*, Rom. goddess of fruits & fruit trees] city in S Calif., east of Los Angeles: pop. 87,000

pomp (pämp) *n.* [< MFr. < L. < Gr. *pompē*, solemn procession] **1.** dignified or stately display; splendor [the *pomp* of a coronation] **2.** showy display

pom·pa·dour (päm′pə dôr′) *n.* [after the marquise de POMPADOUR] a hairdo in which the hair is swept or brushed up high from the forehead

Pom·pa·dour (päm′pə dôr′, -door′; *Fr.* pōn pà doōr′), marquise de (də) 1721–64; mistress of Louis XV

☆**pom·pa·no** (päm′pə nō′) *n., pl.* **-no′, -nos′:** see PLURAL, II, D, 2 [Sp. *pámpano*] a spiny-finned, saltwater food fish of N. America and the West Indies

Pom·pei·i (päm pā′ē, -pā′) ancient city on the S coast of Italy: destroyed by the eruption of Mount Vesuvius (79 A.D.) —**Pom·pei′an** (-pā′ən) *adj., n.*

Pom·pey (päm′pē) (L. name *Gnaeus Pompeius*) 106–48 B.C.; Rom. general & statesman: called *the Great* (L. *Magnus*)

POMPANO
(to 18 in. long)

pom-pom (päm′päm′) *n.* [echoic] **1.** any of several rapid-firing automatic weapons **2.** *same as* POMPON (sense 1): also **pom′pom′**

pom·pon (päm′pän′, -päm′) *n.* [Fr.] **1.** a ball or tuft as of silk or wool, worn as a decoration on hats or waved by cheerleaders **2.** a) a kind of chrysanthemum, dahlia, etc. with small, round flowers b) the flower

pom·pos·i·ty (päm päs′ə tē) *n.* **1.** the quality of being pompous; self-importance **2.** *pl.* **-ties** a pompous act, remark, etc.

pom·pous (päm′pəs) *adj.* **1.** full of pomp; magnificent **2.** pretending to be important in a showy way —**pom′pous·ly** *adv.* —**pom′pous·ness** *n.*

Pon·ce (pôn′se) seaport on the S coast of Puerto Rico: pop. 126,000

Pon·ce de Le·ón (pôn′the the le ôn′; *E.* päns′ də lē′ən), **Juan** (hwän) 1460?–1521; Sp. explorer: discovered Florida

pon·cho (pän′chō) *n., pl.* **-chos** [< SAmInd.] **1.** a cloak like a blanket with a hole in the middle for the head **2.** a garment, esp. a raincoat, like this

pond (pänd) *n.* [ME. var. of POUND³] a body of standing water smaller than a lake, often man-made

pon·der (pän′dər) *vt., vi.* [< MFr. < L. *ponderare*, to weigh < *pondus*, a weight: see POUND¹] to think deeply (about); consider carefully —**pon′der·a·bil′i·ty** *n.* —**pon′der·a·ble** *adj.*

SYN.—**ponder** implies a weighing mentally and suggests careful consideration of a matter from all sides [to *ponder* over a problem]; **meditate** suggests quiet, deep study or thought [he *meditated* on the state of the world] or careful thinking about some plan [to *meditate* revenge]; **muse** implies a dreamlike series of thoughts [to *muse* over the past]; **ruminate** suggests turning a matter over and over in the mind [the loser *ruminated* on the cause of his defeat]

☆**pon·der·o·sa (pine)** (pän′də rō′sə) [< ModL. (*Pinus*) *ponderosa*, lit., heavy (pine)] **1.** a yellow pine of western N. America **2.** its wood

pon·der·ous (pän′dər əs) *adj.* [< L. < *ponderis*, genitive of *pondus*, a weight: see POUND[1]] **1.** very heavy **2.** difficult to handle because of weight **3.** heavy in a clumsy way; bulky [the *ponderous* truck lumbered down the road] **4.** dull or tiresome [a *ponderous* style] —see SYN. at HEAVY —**pon′der·ous·ly** *adv.* —**pon′der·ous·ness, pon′der·os′i·ty** (-äs′ə tē) *n.*

☆**pond lily** *same as* WATERLILY

pond·weed (pänd′wēd′) *n.* any of various related water plants, with its leaves under water or floating on the surface

☆**pone** (pōn) *n.* [< Algonquian] [Chiefly Southern] **1.** corn bread in small, oval loaves **2.** such a loaf

pon·gee (pän jē′) *n.* [< Chin. dial. *pen-chi*, domestic loom] **1.** a soft, thin silk cloth, usually left in its natural light-brown color **2.** a cloth like this

pon·iard (pän′yərd) *n.* [< Fr., ult. < L. *pugnus*, fist] a dagger —*vt.* to stab with a poniard

pons (pänz) *n., pl.* **pon·tes** (pän′tēz) [L., a bridge: for IE. base see FIND] *Anat., Zool.* a piece of connecting tissue

Pont·char·train (pän′chər trān′), **Lake** [after J. P. *Pontchartrain* (1674–1747), Fr. minister of colonies] shallow, saltwater lake in SE La., north of New Orleans

Pon·ti·ac[1] (pän′tē ak′) 1720?–69; Ottawa Indian chief

Pon·ti·ac[2] (pän′tē ak′) [after prec.] city in SE Mich., just north of Detroit: pop. 85,000

pon·ti·fex (pän′tə feks′) *n., pl.* **pon·tif·i·ces** (pän tif′ə sēz′) [L.: see PONTIFF] in ancient Rome, a member of the supreme college of priests

pon·tiff (pän′tif) *n.* [< Fr. < LL. *pontifex*, bishop < L., high priest] **1.** a bishop; specif., [P-] the Pope (in full, **Supreme Pontiff**) **2.** a high priest

pon·tif·i·cal (pän tif′i k'l) *adj.* **1.** having to do with a high priest **2.** celebrated by a bishop or other high-ranking prelate [a *pontifical* Mass] **3.** papal **4.** acting as if one had the dignity and power of a pontiff; often, specif., arrogant or haughty —*n.* **1.** [*pl.*] a pontiff's vestments and insignia **2.** a book of rites as performed by a bishop —**pon·tif′i·cal·ly** *adv.*

pon·tif·i·cate (-kit; *also, and for v. always,* -kāt′) *n.* the office or term of office of a pontiff —*vi.* **-cat′ed, -cat′ing 1.** to carry out the duties as a pontiff **2.** to speak in a pompous or arrogant way —**pon·tif′i·ca′tor** *n.*

pon·toon (pän tōōn′) *n.* [Fr. < *ponto* < *pons*, a bridge (see PONS)] **1.** a flat-bottomed boat **2.** any of a number of these boats, or of hollow, floating cylinders, etc., used to support a temporary bridge (**pontoon bridge**) **3.** a float on an aircraft

Pon·tus (pän′təs) ancient kingdom in NE Asia Minor, on the Black Sea

Pontus Eux·i·nus (yook sī′nəs) *Latin name of* BLACK SEA

po·ny (pō′nē) *n., pl.* **-nies** [< Scot., prob. < OFr. dim of *poulain*, a colt, ult. < L. *pullus*, foal: for IE. base see FEW] **1.** a small horse of any of several breeds, usually not over 58 in. high at the withers **2.** something small of its kind; specif., ☆a small liqueur glass or its contents ☆**3.** [Colloq.] a word-for-word translation of a foreign work, used in doing schoolwork, often dishonestly ☆**4.** [Slang] a racehorse —☆*vt., vi.* **-nied, -ny·ing** [Slang] to pay (money), as to settle an account (with *up*)

☆**pony express** a former system of carrying and delivering mail by riders on swift ponies

☆**po·ny·tail** (pō′nē tāl′) *n.* a hairdo in which long hair, tied tight high at the back of the head, hangs free

☆**pooch** (pōōch) *n.* [Slang] a dog

poo·dle (pōō′d'l) *n.* [G. *pudel* < LowG. < *pudeln*, to splash] any of a breed of dog with a curly coat of hair in a solid color of black, white, gray, etc.

POODLE
(to 20 in. high
at shoulder)

pooh[1] (pōō) *interj.* [prob. echoic] an exclamation of scorn, disbelief, or impatience

pooh[2] (pōō) *vt.* [Slang] *same as* POOP[2]

pooh-pooh (pōō′pōō′) *vt.* [see POOH[1]] to treat as unimportant; make light of; belittle [to *pooh-pooh* an idea]

pool[1] (pōōl) *n.* [OE. *pol*] **1.** a small pond, as in a garden **2.** a puddle **3.** *same as* SWIMMING POOL **4.** a deep, still spot in a river ☆**5.** a natural underground deposit of oil or gas —*vi.* to form, or gather in, a pool

pool[2] (pōōl) *n.* [Fr. *poule* < LL. *pulla*, hen: associated in E. with prec.] **1.** the total stakes played for, as in a single deal of a card game **2.** a game of billiards played with object balls numbered 1 to 15 and a cue ball, on a table with six pockets **3.** *a)* a combination of resources, funds, etc. for some common purpose [a *pool* formed to buy an office building] *b)* the persons or parties forming it ☆**4.** a combination of business firms for creating a monopoly **5.** a supply of equipment, personnel, etc. shared by a group [the company owns a *pool* of cars for its employees] —*vt., vi.* ☆to contribute to a common fund; form a pool (of) [we *pooled* our money and rented a cottage]

☆**pool·room** (pōōl′rōōm′) *n.* a room or place where pool is played: also **pool hall**

pool table a billiard table with a pocket at each corner and at the middle of both sides, for playing pool

Poo·na (pōō′nə) city in W India: pop. 598,000

poop[1] (pōōp) *n.* [< MFr., ult. < L. *puppis*] **1.** orig., the stern of a ship **2.** on sailing ships, a raised deck at the stern, sometimes forming the roof of a cabin: also **poop deck** —*vt.* to break over the poop or stern of: said of waves

poop[2] (pōōp) *vt.* [echoic] [Slang] to cause to be exhausted; tire: usually in the passive voice —☆**poop out** [Slang] **1.** to become exhausted **2.** to stop working

poop[3] (pōōp) *n.* [prob. < *poop*, feces] [Slang] **1.** a foolish or worthless person **2.** the facts worth knowing [give me all the *poop*]

poor (pōōr) *adj.* [< OFr. < L. *pauper*, poor: for IE. base see FEW] **1.** *a)* having little or no means to support oneself; needy *b)* indicating or characterized by poverty **2.** lacking in some quality or thing; specif., *a)* lacking abundance; scanty; inadequate [*poor* crops] *b)* lacking productivity; barren; sterile [*poor* soil] *c)* lacking nourishment; feeble [a *poor* body] *d)* lacking excellence; inferior [*poor* grades] *e)* mean-spirited; worthy of contempt [a *poor* attitude] *f)* lacking pleasure or comfort [to have a *poor* time] *g)* lacking skill [a *poor* cook] **3.** worthy of pity; unfortunate [the *poor* bird had broken its wing] —**the poor** poor, or needy, people —**poor′ness** *n.*

SYN.—**poor** is the simple, direct term for one who has no means for living or a very limited income; **impoverished** is applied to one who was at one time well-off but who is now very poor [an *impoverished* aristocrat]; **destitute** implies such great poverty that one must do without the bare necessities, such as food and shelter [left *destitute* by the war]; **impecunious** applies to one who usually has no regular or steady income, often because of his own weaknesses or failures [an *impecunious* gambler]; **indigent** implies a being so poor that one cannot afford any luxuries and must endure hardships [new clothes for *indigent* children] —ANT. **rich, wealthy**

☆**poor-boy sandwich** (pōōr′boi′) *same as* HERO SANDWICH

poor·house (pōōr′hous′) *n.* formerly, an institution for paupers, supported from public funds

poor·ly (-lē) *adv.* **1.** in a poor manner **2.** with a low opinion [thought *poorly* of it] —*adj.* [Colloq.] in poor health

poor-mouth (-mouth′) *vi.* [Colloq.] to complain about one's lack of money: also **talk** (or **cry**) **poor-mouth**

☆**poor white** a white person, esp. in the South, who lives in great poverty: often an offensive term

pop[1] (päp) *n.* [echoic] **1.** a sudden, short, light explosive sound **2.** a shot with a revolver, rifle, etc. **3.** any carbonated, nonalcoholic beverage ☆**4.** *Baseball* a ball popped into the infield: also **pop′-up′** —*vi.* **popped, pop′ping 1.** to make, or burst with, a pop **2.** to move, go, come, etc. suddenly and quickly [she *popped* out of bed] **3.** to open wide suddenly, or bulge: said of the eyes **4.** to shoot a pistol, etc. ☆**5.** *Baseball* to hit the ball high in the air into the infield (often with *up*) —*vt.* ☆**1.** to cause (corn) to pop, as by roasting, etc. **2.** *a)* to fire (a pistol, etc.) *b)* to shoot **3.** to put suddenly or quickly [to *pop* one's head in the door] ☆**4.** *Baseball* to hit (the ball) high in the air into the infield —*adv.* with or like a pop —**pop off** [Slang] **1.** to die suddenly ☆**2.** to speak or write emotionally, etc. **3.** [Chiefly Brit.] to leave quickly —**pop the question** [Colloq.] to propose marriage

☆**pop**[2] (päp) *n.* [< PAPA] [Slang] father: also used in a friendly way in speaking to any elderly man

pop[3] (päp) *adj.* *clipped form of* POPULAR [*pop* music]

pop. **1.** popular **2.** popularly **3.** population

☆**pop (art)** (päp) a realistic style of painting and sculpture, using techniques and popular subjects from commercial art and mass media, such as comic strips

pop concert a popular concert, chiefly of semiclassical and light classical music

☆**pop·corn** (päp′kôrn′) *n.* **1.** a variety of Indian corn with small ears and hard grains which pop open in a white, puffy mass when heated **2.** the popped grains, often salted for eating

pope (pōp) *n.* [OE. *papa* < LL., ult. < Gr. *pappas*, father] [*usually* P-] *R.C.Ch.* the bishop of Rome and head of the Church —**pope′dom** (-dəm) *n.*

Pope (pōp), **Alexander** 1688–1744; Eng. poet

pop·er·y (pōp′ər ē) *n.* the doctrines and rituals of the Roman Catholic Church: a term used to show hostility

☆**pop·eyed** (päp′īd′) *adj.* having wide eyes that bulge out

pop·gun (-gun′) *n.* a toy gun using compressed air to shoot little corks, etc. with a popping sound

pop·in·jay (päp′in jā′) *n.* [< MFr. *papagai* < Ar. *babaghā*, parrot] a talkative, conceited person

pop·ish (pōp′ish) *adj.* having to do with popery: a term used to show hostility —**pop′ish·ly** *adv.* —**pop′ish·ness** *n.*

pop·lar (päp′lər) *n.* [< OFr. *poplier*, ult. < L. *populus*] **1.** any of various tall, fast-growing trees with small leaves **2.** the wood of any of these **3.** *same as: a)* TULIP TREE *b)* TULIPWOOD (sense 1)

pop·lin (päp′lin) *n.* [Fr. *papeline*, prob. < (*draps de*) *Poperinghes*, (cloths from) Poperinge, city in Flanders] a strong fabric of cotton, rayon, etc. with fine ridges on the surface

Po·po·ca·té·petl (pō′ pō′kä te′pet′l; *E.* pō′pə kat′ə pet′l) volcano in SC Mexico

☆**pop·o·ver** (päp′ō′vər) *n.* a puffy, hollow muffin

pop·per (-ər) *n.* **1.** a person or thing that pops ☆**2.** a covered wire basket or pan for popping corn

pop·pet (päp′it) *n.* [var. of PUPPET] a valve that moves up from and down into its seat, as in a gasoline engine: in full, **poppet valve**

pop·py (päp′ē) *n., pl.* **-pies** [OE. *popæg* < L. *papaver*] **1.** any of various related plants with a milky juice and showy, variously colored flowers **2.** the flower of any of these **3.** a substance, as opium, made from poppy juice **4.** yellowish red, the color of some poppies: also **poppy red**

☆**pop·py·cock** (-käk′) *n.* [Du. *pappekak*, dung] [Colloq.] nonsense

poppy seed the small, dark seed of the poppy, used in baking, etc. as a flavoring or topping

☆**Pop·si·cle** (päp′si k'l) [blend < POP¹ + (I)CICLE] *a trademark for* a flavored ice frozen around a stick for eating —*n.* [p-] such a flavored ice

pop·u·lace (päp′yə lis) *n.* [Fr. < It. < L. *populus*, PEOPLE] **1.** the common people; the masses **2.** all the people in a country, etc; population

pop·u·lar (päp′yə lər) *adj.* [< L. < *populus*, PEOPLE] **1.** of or carried on by people generally [elected by *popular* vote] **2.** suitable or intended for the general public [*popular* music] **3.** that most people can afford [*popular* prices] **4.** common; widespread [a *popular* notion] **5.** liked by very many people [a *popular* actor] **6.** having many friends —**pop′u·lar′i·ty** (-lar′ə tē) *n.* —**pop′u·lar·ly** *adv.*

popular front a political coalition of leftist and liberal groups, as in France (1936–39) to combat fascism

pop·u·lar·ize (päp′yə lə rīz′) *vt.* **-ized′, -iz′ing 1.** to make popular **2.** to make understandable to the general public —**pop′u·lar·i·za′tion** *n.* —**pop′u·lar·iz′er** *n.*

pop·u·late (päp′yə lāt′) *vt.* **-lat′ed, -lat′ing** [< ML. pp. of *populare* < L. *populus*, PEOPLE] **1.** to be or become the inhabitants of; inhabit [the English *populated* Australia] **2.** to supply with inhabitants [New York is densely *populated*]

pop·u·la·tion (päp′yə lā′shən) *n.* **1.** *a)* all the people in a country, region, etc. *b)* the number of these *c)* a (specified) part of the people in a given area [the Japanese *population* of Hawaii] **2.** a populating or being populated [the gold rush speeded the *population* of California] **3.** *Biol.* all the organisms living in a given area **4.** *Statistics* a group of persons or things

☆**population explosion** the very great and continuing increase in human population in modern times

☆**Pop·u·list** (päp′yə list) *n.* [< L. *populus*, PEOPLE] a member of a U.S. political party (**Populist party** or **People's party**, 1891–1904) in favor of free coinage of gold and silver, public ownership of utilities, an income tax, etc. —*adj.* of this party: also **Pop′u·lis′tic** —**Pop′u·lism** *n.*

pop·u·lous (päp′yə ləs) *adj.* full of people; thickly populated —**pop′u·lous·ly** *adv.* —**pop′u·lous·ness** *n.*

por·ce·lain (pôr′s'l in, pôrs′lin) *n.* [< Fr. < It. *porcellana*, a kind of shell, shaped like a pig, ult. < L. *porcus*, pig] **1.** a hard,

white, nonporous, translucent ceramic ware, made of kaolin, feldspar, and quartz or flint **2.** porcelain dishes or ornaments, as a group —*adj.* made of porcelain —**por′ce·la′ne·ous, por′cel·la′ne·ous** (-sə lā′nē əs) *adj.*

por·ce·lain·ize (-īz′) *vt.* **-ized′, -iz′ing** to coat with porcelain or a substance like it

porch (pôrch) *n.* [< OFr. < L. *porticus* < *porta*, a gate: see PORT⁵] **1.** a covered entrance to a building, usually with a roof that is held up by posts **2.** an open or enclosed room on the outside of a building **3.** [Obs.] a portico

por·cine (pôr′sīn, -sin) *adj.* [< Fr. < L. < *porcus*, a hog] of or like pigs or hogs

por·cu·pine (pôr′kyə pīn′) *n., pl.* **-pines′, -pine′:** see PLURAL, II, D, I [< MFr. < OIt. < L. *porcus*, a pig + *spina*, a spine] any of various large, related rodents having coarse hair mixed with long, stiff, sharp spines

pore¹ (pôr) *vi.* **pored, por′ing** [< ?] **1.** to read or study carefully (with *over*) [to *pore* over a book] **2.** to think deeply and thoroughly; ponder (with *over*)

pore² (pôr) *n.* [< L. < Gr. *poros*, a passage: for IE. base see FARE] **1.** a tiny opening, as in plant leaves, skin, etc., through which fluids may go in or come out **2.** a similar tiny opening in rocks or other substances

PORCUPINE
(2½–4 ft. long, including tail)

☆**por·gy** (pôr′gē) *n., pl.* **-gies, -gy:** see PLURAL, II, D, I [prob. < Sp. or Port. *pargo* < L. *pagrus* < Gr. *phagros*, sea bream] **1.** a saltwater food fish having spiny fins and a wide body, as the scup **2.** any of various other fishes, as the menhaden

pork (pôrk) *n.* [< OFr. < L. *porcus*, a pig] the flesh of a pig or hog used, fresh or cured, as food

☆**pork barrel** [Colloq.] government money spent for political favors, as for local improvements to please the voters in a district

pork·er (pôr′kər) *n.* a hog, esp. a young one, fattened for use as food

CUTS OF PORK

pork pie 1. a meat pie made with chopped pork **2.** a man's soft hat with a round, flat crown: now often **pork′pie′** *n.,* **porkpie hat**

pork·y (pôr′kē) *adj.* **pork′i·er, pork′i·est 1.** of or like pork **2.** fat, as though overfed **3.** [Slang] rude, disrespectful, etc.

por·nog·ra·phy (pôr näg′rə fē) *n.* [< Gr. < *porne*, a prostitute + *graphein*, to write] writings, pictures, etc. intended primarily to arouse sexual desire —**por·nog′ra·pher** *n.* —**por′no·graph′ic** (-nə graf′ik) *adj.* —**por′no·graph′i·cal·ly** *adv.*

po·rous (pôr′əs) *adj.* full of pores, through which fluids, air, or light may pass —**po·ros·i·ty** (pô räs′ə tē, pə-), **po′rous·ness** *n.* —**po′rous·ly** *adv.*

por·phy·ry (pôr′fər ē) *n., pl.* **-ries** [< OFr. < ML., ult. < Gr. *porphyros*, purple] **1.** orig., an Egyptian rock with large feldspar crystals in a purplish rock mass **2.** any igneous rock resembling this —**por′phy·rit′ic** (-fə rit′ik) *adj.*

por·poise (pôr′pəs) *n., pl.* **-pois·es, -poise:** see PLURAL, II, D, I [< OFr. *porpeis* < L. *porcus*, a pig + *piscis*, a fish] **1.** any of a number of small, toothed whales with a blunt snout, found in most seas, esp. the **harbor porpoise 2.** a dolphin or any of several other small cetaceans

por·ridge (pôr′ij, pär′-) *n.* [altered < POTTAGE by confusion with ME. *porrey* < OFr. < VL. *porrata*, leek broth < L. *porrum*, leek] [Chiefly Brit.] a soft food of cereal or meal boiled in water or milk until thick

por·rin·ger (-in jər) *n.* [< Fr. *potager*, soup dish: altered after prec.] a bowl for porridge, cereal, etc., esp. one of metal used by children

port¹ (pôrt) *n.* [OFr. & OE. < L. *portus*, a haven: for IE. base see FARE] **1.** a harbor **2.** a city with a harbor where ships can load and unload cargo **3.** *same as* PORT OF ENTRY

port² (pôrt) *n.* [< *Oporto*, city in Portugal] a sweet, fortified, usually dark-red wine

port³ (pôrt) *vt.* [< MFr. < L. *portare*, to carry: see FARE] to hold or place (a rifle or sword) diagonally in front of one, as for inspection —*n.* the manner one carries one's head and body

port⁴ (pôrt) *n.* [prob. < PORT¹] the left-hand side of a ship or airplane as one faces forward, toward the bow: opposed to STARBOARD —*adj.* of or on the port —*vt., vi.* to move or turn (the helm) to the port side

port⁵ (pôrt) *n.* [< OFr. < L. *porta*, a door, akin to *portus*: see PORT¹] **1.** *a)* *same as* PORTHOLE *b)* a porthole covering **2.** an opening, as in a valve face, for the passage of steam, gas, etc.

Port. 1. Portugal **2.** Portuguese

port·a·ble (pôr′tə b'l) *adj.* [< MFr. < LL. < L. *portare*, to carry: see FARE] **1.** that can be carried **2.** *a)* easily carried or moved, esp. by hand [a *portable* TV] *b)* that can be used anywhere because battery-operated [a *portable* radio] —*n.* something portable —**port′a·bil′i·ty** *n.*

por·tage (pôr′tij; *for n. 2 & v., also Canad.* pôr tãzh′) *n.* [MFr. < ML. *portaticum* < L. *portare*: see PORTABLE] **1.** the act of carrying ☆**2.** *a)* a carrying of boats and supplies overland from one river or lake to another *b)* any route over which this is done —*vt., vi.* -**taged, -tag·ing** ☆to carry (boats, supplies, etc.) over a portage

por·tal (pôr′t'l) *n.* [MFr. < ML. < L. *porta*: see PORT⁵] a doorway, gate, or entrance, esp. a large or splendid one —*adj.* describing or of the vein carrying blood from the intestines, stomach, etc. to the liver

☆**por·tal-to-por·tal pay** (-tə pôr′t'l) wages paid to workers for the total time spent from the moment of entering the mine, factory, etc. until the moment of leaving it

Port Arthur [after *Arthur* Stilwell, local philanthropist] seaport in SE Tex.: pop. 57,000

Port-au-Prince (pôrt′ō prins′; *Fr.* pôr tō prans′) capital of Haiti; seaport on the Caribbean: pop. 250,000

port authority a government commission in charge of the traffic, regulations, etc. of a port

port·cul·lis (pôrt kul′is) *n.* [< MFr. < *porte*, a gate + *coleïce*, sliding < L. *colare*, to filter] a heavy iron grating hung from chains and lowered between grooves to bar the gateway of a castle or fortified town

porte-co·chere, porte-co·chère (pôrt′kō sher′) *n.* [Fr., coach gate] **1.** a large gateway into a courtyard **2.** a kind of porch roof sticking out over a driveway at an entrance to a house, etc.

Port Elizabeth seaport in S Cape Province, South Africa: pop. 381,000

por·tend (pôr tend′) *vt.* [< L. *portendere* < *por-*, through + *tendere*, to stretch: see TEND²] **1.** to be an omen or warning of; foreshadow **2.** to be an indication of; signify

PORTCULLIS

por·tent (pôr′tent) *n.* **1.** something that is thought to be a sign of an event about to occur, esp. an unfortunate event; omen [the Romans thought comets were *portents* of disaster] **2.** a portending; significance [a howl of dire *portent*] **3.** something amazing; marvel

por·ten·tous (pôr ten′təs) *adj.* **1.** being a sign of something about to happen, esp. something bad; ominous **2.** marvelous; amazing [*portentous* ability] **3.** pompous; self-important —**see** SYN· at OMINOUS —**por·ten′tous·ly** *adv.* —**por·ten′tous·ness** *n.*

por·ter¹ (pôr′tər) *n.* [< OFr. < LL. *portarius* < L. *porta*, a gate] a doorman or gatekeeper

por·ter² (pôr′tər) *n.* [< OFr. < LL. < L. *portare*, to carry: see FARE] **1.** a man whose work is to carry luggage, as for guests at a hotel ☆**2.** a man who sweeps, cleans, does errands, etc. in a bank, store, etc. ☆**3.** a railroad employee who waits on passengers in a sleeper or parlor car **4.** [short for *porter's ale*] a dark-brown beer

Por·ter (pôr′tər) **1. Katherine Anne,** 1890– ; U.S. short-story writer, essayist, & novelist **2. William Sydney,** *see* O. HENRY

por·ter·house (pôr′tər hous′) *n.* **1.** formerly, a place serving beer, porter, etc. (and sometimes steaks and chops) ☆**2.** a choice cut of beef from the loin just before the sirloin: in full, **porterhouse steak**

port·fo·li·o (pôrt fō′lē ō′) *n., pl.* -**li·os′** [< It. *portafoglio* < L. *portare*, to carry + *folium*, a leaf] **1.** a flat, portable case for carrying loose papers, drawings, etc. **2.** such a case for state documents **3.** the office of a minister of state [a minister without *portfolio* is a cabinet member who is not the head of a department] **4.** a list of an investor's stocks, bonds, etc.

port·hole (pôrt′hōl′) *n.* **1.** an opening in a ship's side, as for letting in light and air **2.** an opening to shoot through, as in the wall of a fort; embrasure **3.** any similar opening, as in a furnace door

por·ti·co (pôr′tə kō′) *n., pl.* -**coes′**, -**cos′** [It. < L. *porticus*: see PORCH] a porch or covered walk, consisting of a roof supported by columns

PORTICO

por·tiere, por·tière (pôr tyer′, -tē er′) *n.* [Fr. < *porte*, a door] a curtain hung in a doorway

por·tion (pôr′shən) *n.* [< OFr. < L. *portionis*, genitive of *portio*, a part] **1.** a part, esp. as given to a person, set aside for some purpose, etc.; share [the *portion* of one's time spent in study] **2.** the part of an estate received by an heir **3.** a dowry [a marriage *portion*] **4.** one's lot; destiny **5.** a helping of food —*vt.* **1.** to divide into portions [she *portioned* out the food] **2.** to give as a portion to **3.** to give a portion to —**see** SYN· at FATE and PART —**por′tion·er** *n.* —**por′tion·less** *adj.*

Port·land (pôrt′land) **1.** [after the seaport in Maine] city & port in NW Oreg., on the Columbia River: pop. 383,000 (met. area 1,009,000) **2.** [after *Portland*, town in England] seaport on the coast of SW Maine: pop. 65,000

portland cement [concrete made from it resembles stone from the Isle of *Portland*, England] [*sometimes* P-] a kind of cement that hardens under water, made by burning limestone and clay

Port Louis capital of Mauritius; seaport on the NW coast: pop. 139,000

port·ly (pôrt′lē) *adj.* -**li·er, -li·est** [PORT³ + -LY¹] **1.** large and heavy in a dignified or stately way [a *portly* judge] **2.** stout; fat —**port′li·ness** *n.*

port·man·teau (pôrt man′tō, pôrt′man tō′) *n., pl.* -**teaus, -teaux** (-tōz) [< Fr. < *porter*, to carry + *manteau*, a cloak] a stiff leather suitcase that opens like a book into two compartments

portmanteau word a word formed by combining parts of other words (Example: *smog*, from *smoke* and *fog*)

Port Mores·by (môrz′bē) seaport in SE New Guinea; capital of Papua New Guinea: pop. 42,000

Pôr·to (pôr′too) Portuguese name of OPORTO

Pôr·to A·le·gre (ä le′grə) seaport in S Brazil, on the Atlantic: pop. 886,000

port of call a port that is a regular stopover for ships

port of entry any place where customs officials check people and foreign goods entering a country

Port-of-Spain (pôrt′əv spān′) seaport on NW Trinidad; capital of Trinidad and Tobago: pop. 98,000

Por·to No·vo (pôr′tō nō′vō) capital of Benin; seaport on the Gulf of Guinea: pop. 100,000

Por·to Ri·co (pôr′tə rē′kō) *former name of* PUERTO RICO — **Por′to Ri′can**

por·trait (pôr′trit, -trāt) *n.* [MFr., pp. of *portraire*: see PORTRAY] **1.** a painting, photograph, etc. of a person, esp. of the face **2.** a description or portrayal of a person in a story, play, etc. —**por′trait·ist** *n.*

por·trai·ture (pôr′tri chər) *n.* **1.** the making of portraits **2.** a portrait

por·tray (pôr trā′) *vt.* [MFr. *portraire* < L. < *pro-*, forth + *trahere*, to DRAW] **1.** to make a picture or portrait of **2.** to make a word picture of; describe [the writer *portrays* life in New York] **3.** to play the part of in a play, movie, etc. [she *portrayed* a doctor] —**por·tray′a·ble** *adj.* —**por·tray′er** *n.*

por·tray·al (-əl) *n.* **1.** the act of portraying **2.** a portrait or description

Port Sa·id (sä ēd′, sä′id) seaport in NE Egypt, at the Mediterranean end of the Suez Canal: pop. 244,000

Ports·mouth (pôrts′məth) **1.** seaport in S England, on the English Channel: pop. 212,000 **2.** [after *prec.*] seaport in SE Va., on Hampton Roads: pop. 111,000

Por·tu·gal (pôr′chə gəl; *Port.* pôr′too gäl′) country in SW Europe, on the Atlantic, including the Azores & Madeira: 35,509 sq. mi.; pop. 9,526,000; cap. Lisbon

Por·tu·guese (pôr′chə gēz′) *adj.* of Portugal, its people, their

language, etc. —*n.* **1.** *pl.* **-guese′** a native or inhabitant of Portugal **2.** the Romance language spoken in Portugal and Brazil
Portuguese Guinea *former name of* GUINEA-BISSAU
Portuguese man-of-war a large, warm-sea animal having long, dangling tentacles that sting, and a large, bladderlike sac that enables it to float on water
por·tu·lac·a (pôr′chə lak′ə) *n.* [ModL. < L., purslane] a fleshy annual plant with yellow, pink, or purple flowers
pose[1] (pōz) *vt.* **posed, pos′ing** [< OFr. *poser* < VL. < LL. *pausare,* to pause: infl. by L. *positus,* pp. of *ponere,* to place] **1.** to put forth; assert *[to pose a claim]* **2.** to propose or present (a question, problem, etc.) **3.** to put (a model, photographic subject, etc.) in a certain position —*vi.* **1.** to take a certain position, as in modeling for an artist **2.** to behave in an affected or theatrical way in order to impress others *[look at her posing]* **3.** to pretend to be what one is not *[to pose as an officer]* —*n.* **1.** a bodily position, esp. one held for an artist, photographer, etc. **2.** behavior or speech put on to impress others; pretense *[his gruff manner is just a pose]*
pose[2] (pōz) *vt.* **posed, pos′ing** [< APPOSE, OPPOSE] to puzzle or confuse, as by a difficult question; baffle
Po·sei·don (pō sī′d'n, pə-) *Gr. Myth.* god of the sea: identified with the Roman god Neptune
pos·er[1] (pō′zər) *n.* **1.** a person who poses **2.** a person who behaves in an affected or theatrical way in order to impress others: also **po·seur** (pō zur′)
pos·er[2] (pō′zər) *n.* a baffling question or problem
posh (päsh) *adj.* [prob. < obs. Brit. slang *posh,* a dandy] [Colloq.] luxurious and fashionable; elegant —**posh′ly** *adv.* —**posh′ness** *n.*
pos·it (päz′it) *vt.* [< L. *positus,* pp. of *ponere,* to place] **1.** to set in place or position; situate **2.** to set down or accept as fact; postulate
po·si·tion (pə zish′ən) *n.* [MFr. < L. *positio* < pp. of *ponere,* to place] **1.** the manner in which a person or thing is placed or arranged; attitude *[a sitting position]* **2.** one's attitude toward or opinion on a subject; stand *[her position on foreign aid]* **3.** the place where a person or thing is, esp. in relation to others; location or situation *[the ship radioed its position]* **4.** the usual or proper place; station *[the players are in position]* **5.** a location or condition that gives one an advantage *[to jockey for position]* **6.** a person's relative place, as in society; rank; status **7.** a place of high rank in society, business, etc. *[a man of position]* **8.** a post of employment; job; office *[to apply for a teaching position]* —*vt.* to put in a particular position; place —**po·si′tion·al** *adj.* —**po·si′tion·er** *n.*
SYN.—**position** is used of any kind of work done for salary or wages, but often only of work done by a white-collar or professional worker; **situation** now usually refers to a position that needs to be filled or to one that is desired *[situation wanted as salesman];* **office** refers to a position that gives one authority or power, esp. in government, a corporation, etc.; a **post** is a position or office that carries important responsibilities, esp. one to which a person is appointed; **job** is now the common, basic term which can be used in place of any of the preceding terms
pos·i·tive (päz′ə tiv) *adj.* [< OFr. < L. *positivus* < pp. of *ponere,* to place] **1.** *a)* definitely set; explicit; specific *[positive instructions] b)* allowing no doubt; certain; sure *[I'm positive I locked the front door]* **2.** *a)* sure in mind; confident; assured *[a positive person] b)* too sure or too confident in oneself **3.** showing agreement; affirmative *[a positive answer]* **4.** tending in the direction thought of as that of increase, progress, etc. *[clockwise motion is positive]* **5.** making a definite contribution; that does some good or helps; constructive *[positive criticism]* **6.** unrelated to anything else; absolute; unqualified **7.** having real existence in itself *[a positive good]* **8.** based on reality or facts *[positive proof]* **9.** concerned only with real things and experience; empirical; practical **10.** [Colloq.] complete; downright *[a positive fool]* **11.** *Biol.* directed toward the source of a stimulus *[positive tropism]* ☆**12.** *Elec. a)* of, generating, or charged with POSITIVE ELECTRICITY *b)* having a shortage of electrons **13.** *Gram.* being the simple form of an adjective or adverb; not showing comparison: see also COMPARATIVE, SUPERLATIVE **14.** *Math.* designating a quantity greater than zero, or one to be added; plus **15.** *Med.* indicating the presence of a specific disease, condition, etc. **16.** *Photog.* with the relation of light and shade the same as in the thing photographed —*n.* something positive, as a degree, quality, etc.; specif., *a)* the plate in a voltaic battery where the higher potential is *b) Gram.* the positive degree, or a word in it *c) Math.* a positive quantity *d) Photog.* a positive print —**see SYN.** at SURE —**pos′i·tive·ly** *adv.* —**pos′i·tive·ness** *n.*
☆**positive electricity** the kind of electricity in a piece of glass

that has been rubbed with silk: it is deficient in electrons
pos·i·tiv·ism (päz′ə tiv iz′m) *n.* **1.** a being positive; certainty; assurance **2.** a being too confident or self-assured **3.** a system of philosophy based solely on scientific facts that can be observed and rejecting speculation about ultimate origins, esp. such a system originated by Auguste Comte —**pos′i·tiv·ist** *n., adj.* —**pos′i·tiv·is′tic** *adj.*
☆**pos·i·tron** (päz′ə trän′) *n.* [POSI(TIVE) + (ELEC)TRON] the positive antiparticle of an electron, with about the same mass and magnitude of charge
poss. 1. possession **2.** possessive **3.** possibly
pos·se (päs′ē) *n.* [ML., short for *posse comitatus,* power of the county] a body of men called together by a sheriff, to assist him in keeping the peace
pos·sess (pə zes′) *vt.* [< MFr. < L. pp. of *possidere* < *potis,* able (see POTENT) + *sedere,* SIT] **1.** to have as something that belongs to one; own *[to possess great wealth]* **2.** to have as a characteristic, quality, etc. *[to possess wisdom]* **3.** to gain or keep influence or control over; dominate *[possessed by an idea]* **4.** to cause (someone) to have property, facts, etc. (usually with *of) [we possessed her of the facts]* **5.** [Archaic] to seize; gain —**pos·ses′sor** *n.*
pos·sessed (pə zest′) *adj.* **1.** owned **2.** controlled as if by an evil spirit; crazed —**possessed of** having
pos·ses·sion (pə zesh′ən) *n.* **1.** a possessing or being possessed; ownership; hold, etc. **2.** anything possessed **3.** *[pl.]* property; wealth **4.** territory ruled by an outside country **5.** *Sports* actual control of the ball or puck in play
pos·ses·sive (pə zes′iv) *adj.* **1.** of possession, or ownership **2.** showing or desiring possession *[a possessive person]* **3.** *Gram.* designating or of a case, form, or construction expressing possession (Ex.: *men's, of men, her, whose)* —*n. Gram.* **1.** the possessive case **2.** a possessive form —**pos·ses′sive·ly** *adv.* —**pos·ses′sive·ness** *n.*
pos·set (päs′it) *n.* [< ?] a hot drink made of milk and ale, wine, etc., usually spiced
pos·si·bil·i·ty (päs′ə bil′ə tē) *n.* **1.** a being possible **2.** *pl.* **-ties** something that is possible
pos·si·ble (päs′ə b'l) *adj.* [OFr. < L. < *posse,* to be able: see POTENT] **1.** that can be *[the highest possible score in bowling is 300]* **2.** that may or may not happen *[colder tomorrow, with possible showers]* **3.** that can be done, known, chosen, etc., depending on circumstances *[a possible candidate]* **4.** that may be the truth *[only one possible explanation]* **5.** [Colloq.] that can be put up with; tolerable *[he is barely possible as a partner]*
SYN.—**possible** is used of anything that may exist, occur, be done, etc. depending on circumstances *[a possible solution to a problem];* **practicable** applies to that which can easily be brought about under the existing conditions or by the means available *[a practicable plan];* **feasible** is used of anything that is likely to be carried through to a successful conclusion and, thus, may seem worth doing *[a feasible enterprise]* —**see also SYN.** at PROBABLE
pos·si·bly (-blē) *adv.* **1.** by any possible means *[it can't possibly work]* **2.** perhaps; maybe *[possibly it's true]*
☆**pos·sum** (päs′əm) *n.* [Colloq.] *same as* OPOSSUM —**play possum** to pretend to be asleep, dead, unaware, etc.: opossums lie still as if paralyzed or pretending to be dead when they are attacked
post[1] (pōst) *n.* [OE. < L. *postis*] **1.** a piece of wood, metal, etc., usually long and square or in the shape of a cylinder, set upright to support a building, sign, fence, etc. **2.** the starting point of a horse race —*vt.* **1.** to put up (a poster, notice, etc.) on (a wall, post, etc.) **2.** to announce or publicize by posting notices, signs, etc. *[post a reward]* ☆**3.** to warn persons against trespassing on (grounds, etc.) by posted notices **4.** to put (a name) on a posted or published list ☆**5.** *Sports* to record (a specified score)
post[2] (pōst) *n.* [< Fr. < It., ult. < L. *positum,* neut. pp. of *ponere,* to place] **1.** the place where a soldier, guard, etc. is stationed **2.** *a)* a place where troops are stationed *b)* the troops there; garrison ☆**3.** a local unit of a veterans' organization **4.** a place where a person or group is stationed, as at a machine **5.** an assigned or appointed position, job, or duty ☆**6.** clipped form of TRADING POST —*vt.* **1.** to station at or assign to a post *[guards were posted at every exit]* ☆**2.** to put up or deposit (a bond, etc.) —**see SYN.** at POSITION
post[3] (pōst) *n.* [< Fr. < It. < L. fem. pp. of *ponere:* see POST[2]] **1.** formerly, *a)* any of a number of riders or runners stationed at intervals to carry mail, etc. in relays along a route *b)* a stage of a post route *c)* a post horse *d)* a packet boat **2.** [Chiefly

Brit.] *a)* (the) mail *b)* a post office *c)* a mailbox —*vi.* **1.** formerly, to travel in posts or stages **2.** to travel fast **3.** to rise and sink back in the saddle in rhythm with the horse's trot —*vt.* **1.** formerly, to send by post **2.** [Chiefly Brit.] to mail ☆**3.** to inform, as of events: usually passive [keep me *posted*] **4.** *Bookkeeping a)* to transfer (an item) to the ledger *b)* to enter all necessary items in (a ledger, etc.) —*adv.* speedily

post- [L. < *post*, after] *a prefix meaning:* **1.** after in time, following [*postglacial*] **2.** after in space, behind

post·age (pōs′tij) *n.* [< POST³ + -AGE] the amount charged for mailing a letter or package, esp. as shown by using stamps or printed markings

☆**postage meter** a machine that prints markings on mail, showing that postage has been paid

postage stamp a government stamp for a letter or package, showing that postage has been paid

post·al (pōs′t'l) *adj.* having to do with mail or post offices —*n.* ☆[Colloq.] a postal card

☆**postal card** **1.** a card with a postage stamp printed on it, issued by a government at a rate lower than that for letters **2.** *same as* POST CARD

post·bel·lum (pōst bel′əm) *adj.* [L.] occurring after the war, ☆specif., after the American Civil War

post·box (pōst′bäks′) *n. chiefly Brit. var. of* MAILBOX

post card **1.** an unofficial card, often a card with a picture on it, for mailing when a postage stamp is put on it **2.** *same as* POSTAL CARD

post chaise a closed, four-wheeled coach drawn by fast horses, formerly used to carry mail and passengers

post·date (pōst′dāt′) *vt.* -dat′ed, -dat′ing **1.** to give a later date to than the actual or current date **2.** to put such a date on **3.** to follow in time

post·er (pōs′tər) *n.* **1.** a person who posts notices, signs, etc. **2.** a large advertisement or notice, often with a picture on it, put up in a public place

pos·te·ri·or (päs tir′ē ər, pōs-) *adj.* [L., compar. of *posterus*, following < *post*, after] **1.** later; following after **2.** coming after in order; succeeding **3.** at or toward the rear; hinder; back: opposed to ANTERIOR —*n.* [formerly also *pl.*] the buttocks —**pos·te′ri·or′i·ty** (-ôr′ə tē) *n.* —**pos·te′ri·or·ly** *adv.*

pos·ter·i·ty (päs ter′ə tē) *n.* [< MFr. < L. < *posterus*: see prec.] **1.** all of a person's descendants **2.** all future generations [his music will be admired by *posterity*]

pos·tern (pōs′tərn, päs′-) *n.* [< OFr. < LL. *posterula* < *posterus*: see POSTERIOR] a back door or gate; private entrance at the side or rear —*adj.* of a postern; rear, etc.

☆**post exchange** a nonprofit general store at an army post, selling merchandise, as to servicemen

post·gla·cial (pōst′glā′shəl) *adj.* existing or happening after the disappearance of glaciers from a specific area

☆**post·grad·u·ate** (-graj′oo wit, -wāt′) *adj.* of or taking a course of study after graduation —*n.* a postgraduate student

post·haste (pōst′hāst′) *adv.* with great haste

post horse formerly, a horse kept at an inn (**post house**) for couriers or for hire to travelers

post·hu·mous (päs′choo məs, -tyoo-) *adj.* [< LL. < L. *postumus*, last, superl. of *posterus* (see POSTERIOR): altered after *humare*, to bury] **1.** born after the father's death [a *posthumous* child] **2.** published after the author's death [a collection of her *posthumous* poems] **3.** coming or continuing after one's death [*posthumous* fame] —**post′hu·mous·ly** *adv.*

post·hyp·not·ic (pōst′hip nät′ik) *adj.* of, or carried out in, the period following a hypnotic trance [*posthypnotic* suggestion]

pos·til·ion, pos·til·lion (pōs til′yən, päs-) *n.* [Fr. < It. < *posta*, POST³] a person riding the left-hand leading horse of a four-horse carriage or the left-hand horse of a two-horse carriage

post·im·pres·sion·ism (pōst′im presh′ən iz′m) *n.* the theory or practice of some late 19th-cent. painters reacting against impressionism and emphasizing the subjective viewpoint of the artist or the formal style of the painting —**post′im·pres′sion·ist** *adj., n.* —**post′im·pres′sion·is′tic** *adj.*

post·lude (pōst′lood′) *n.* [POST- + (PRE)LUDE] **1.** a solo on the organ at the end of a church service **2.** a concluding musical section

post·man (-mən) *n., pl.* -men *same as* MAIL CARRIER

post·mark (-märk′) *n.* a post-office mark stamped on a piece of mail, canceling the postage stamp and recording the date and place —*vt.* to stamp with a postmark

post·mas·ter (-mas′tər) *n.* a person in charge of a post office —**post′mas′ter·ship′** *n.* —**post′mis′tress** *n.fem.*

postmaster general *pl.* **postmasters general, postmaster generals** the head of a government's postal system

post·me·rid·i·an (pōst′mə rid′ē ən) *adj.* [< L.: see POST- & MERIDIAN] of or in the afternoon

post me·ri·di·em (mə rid′ē əm) [L.] after noon: abbrev. **P.M., p.m., PM**

post·mor·tem (pōst′môr′təm) *adj.* [L., after death] **1.** happening or done after death **2.** designating of or an examination of a human body after death —*n.* **1.** a post-mortem examination: see AUTOPSY **2.** a detailed analysis or evaluation of some event just ended [a *post-mortem* on the recent election]

post·na·sal drip (pōst′nā′z'l) a dripping of mucus from behind the nose onto the pharynx

post·na·tal (pōst′nāt′'l) *adj.* after birth; esp., of the period immediately after birth

post office **1.** the governmental department in charge of the mails **2.** an office or building where mail is sorted, postage stamps are sold, etc.

post·op·er·a·tive (pōst′äp′ər ə tiv, -äp′rə-; -ə rāt′iv) *adj.* of or in the period after surgery —**post′op′er·a·tive·ly** *adv.*

post·paid (pōst′pād′) *adj.* with the postage prepaid

post·par·tum (pōst′pär′təm) *adj.* [L. < *post*-, POST- + *partum* < *parere*, to bear] of the period following childbirth

post·pone (pōst pōn′, pōs-) *vt.* -poned′, -pon′ing [< L. *post*, after + *ponere*, to put] to put off until later; defer; delay [I *postponed* my trip because of illness] —**post·pon′a·ble** *adj.* —**post·pone′ment** *n.* —**post·pon′er** *n.*

post·pran·di·al (pōst′pran′dē əl) *adj.* [< POST- + L. *prandium*, noonday meal] taking place after a meal; esp., after dinner —**post′pran′di·al·ly** *adv.*

post road a road over which the post, or mail, is or formerly was carried

post·script (pōst′skript′, pōs′-) *n.* [< ModL. < L. pp. of *postscribere* < *post*-, after + *scribere*, to write: see SCRIBE] a note, paragraph, etc. added below the signature of a letter, or to a book, speech, etc., to give more facts, ideas, etc.

☆**post time** the scheduled starting time of a horse race

pos·tu·lant (päs′chə lənt) *n.* [Fr. < L. prp. of *postulare*: see POSTULATE] **1.** a person who asks for something **2.** a candidate for admission into a religious order

pos·tu·late (päs′chə lāt′; *for n. usually* -lit) *vt.* -lat′ed, -lat′ing [< L. pp. of *postulare*, to demand] **1.** to claim; demand; require **2.** to assume without proof to be true, real, or necessary, esp. as a basis for argument **3.** to take for granted; assume —*n.* **1.** something postulated, or assumed to be true, as a first step in proving something; axiom [the *postulates* of Euclidean geometry] **2.** a basic principle [the democratic *postulate* that all persons are born equal] —see SYN. at PRESUME —**pos′tu·la′tion** *n.*

pos·ture (päs′chər) *n.* [MFr. < It. < L. *positura* < *ponere*, to place] **1.** the way one holds the body in sitting or standing; bearing; carriage [good *posture* with the back held straight] **2.** a special way of holding the body, as in posing for an artist [he doubled up his fist in a *posture* of defiance] **3.** the way things stand; condition [the *posture* of foreign affairs] **4.** *a)* frame of mind; mental attitude *b)* an attitude taken on merely for effect **5.** an official stand on an issue —*vt.* -tured, -turing to place in a posture; pose —*vi.* to take on a certain bodily or mental posture, esp. a showy, artificial one that will make an impression; pose —**pos′tur·al** *adj.* —**pos′tur·er** *n.*

post·war (pōst′wôr′) *adj.* after the (or a) war

po·sy (pō′zē) *n., pl.* -sies [contr. < POESY] **1.** orig., a line of poetry or a motto inscribed inside a ring, etc. **2.** a flower or bouquet: an old-fashioned usage

pot (pät) *n.* [OE. *pott*] **1.** a round vessel of metal, earthenware, etc., for holding liquids, cooking food, etc. **2.** a pot with its contents **3.** *same as* POTFUL **4.** a pot of liquor **5.** *shortened form for* FLOWERPOT, LOBSTER POT, etc. **6.** a toilet: a coarse usage **7.** [Colloq.] *a)* all the money bet at a single time *b)* a large amount of money **8.** [Colloq.] a potshot **9.** [Slang] *same as:* ☆*a)* MARIJUANA *b)* POTBELLY —*vt.* **pot′ted, pot′ting 1.** to put into a pot [to *pot* a plant] **2.** to cook or preserve in a

fat, āpe, cär; ten, ēven; is, bīte; gō, hôrn, tool, look; oil, out; up, fur; get; joy; yet; chin; she; thin, then; zh, leisure; ŋ, ring; ə for a in ago, e in agent, i in sanity, o in comply, u in focus; ′ as in able (ā′b'l); Fr. bal; ë, Fr. coeur; ö, Fr. feu; Fr. mon; ô, Fr. coq; ü, Fr. duc; r, Fr. cri; H, G. ich; kh, G. doch; ‡foreign; ☆ Americanism; < derived from. See inside front cover.

pot [to pot fruit] **3.** to shoot (game) for food, not for sport **4.** to hit or get as by a potshot —**go to pot** to go to ruin; fall apart

po·ta·ble (pōt′ə b'l) *adj.* [Fr. < LL. < L. *potare*, to drink] fit to drink; drinkable —*n.* something drinkable; beverage —**po′ta·bil′i·ty, po′ta·ble·ness** *n.*

‡**po·tage** (pô täzh′) *n.* [Fr.] soup or broth

pot·ash (pät′ash′) *n.* [< Du. < *pot*, pot + *asch*, ash] **1.** *same as: a*) POTASSIUM CARBONATE (esp. when obtained from wood ashes) *b*) POTASSIUM HYDROXIDE **2.** any substance containing potassium; esp., any potassium compound used in fertilizers

po·tas·si·um (pə tas′ē əm) *n.* [ModL. < Du.: see prec.] a soft, silver-white, waxlike metallic chemical element: its natural salts are used in fertilizers, glass, etc.: symbol, K; at. wt., 39.102; at. no., 19 —**po·tas′sic** *adj.*

potassium bromide a white, crystalline compound, KBr, used in photography, medicine, etc.

potassium carbonate an alkaline, crystalline compound, K_2CO_3, used in making soap, glass, etc.

potassium chlorate a crystalline salt, $KClO_3$, a strong oxidizing agent used in medicine and in making explosives, etc.

potassium chloride a crystalline salt, KCl, used in fertilizers, as a source of potassium salts, etc.

potassium cyanide an extremely poisonous, crystalline compound, KCN, used in metallurgy, in electroplating, etc.

potassium hydroxide a strongly alkaline, crystalline compound, KOH, used in making soap, glass, etc.

potassium iodide a crystalline salt, KI, added to animal feed and used in medicine, photography, etc.

potassium nitrate a crystalline compound, KNO_3, used in fertilizers, gunpowder, etc. and as an oxidizing agent

potassium permanganate a dark-purple, crystalline compound, $KMnO_4$, used as an oxidizing agent, disinfectant, etc.

po·ta·tion (pō tā′shən) *n.* [< MFr. < L. < *potare*, to drink] **1.** the act of drinking **2.** a drink or draft, esp. of liquor

po·ta·to (pə tāt′ō, -ə) *n., pl.* -**toes** [Sp. *patata* < WInd. name] **1.** orig., *same as* SWEET POTATO **2.** *a*) the starchy tuber of a widely cultivated plant of the nightshade family, cooked as a vegetable *b*) the plant

☆**potato beetle** (or **bug**) *same as* COLORADO BEETLE

☆**potato chip** a very thin slice of potato, fried until crisp and then salted: also, Brit., **potato crisp**

pot·bel·lied (pät′bel′ēd) *adj.* **1.** having a potbelly **2.** having rounded, bulging sides [a *potbellied* stove]

pot·bel·ly (pät′bel′ē) *n., pl.* -**lies** a belly that sticks out

pot·boil·er (-boil′ər) *n.* a piece of writing, painting, etc., usually inferior, done quickly and for money only

☆**pot cheese** a type of dry cottage cheese with large curds

Po·tem·kin (pä tyòm′kin; *E.* pō tem′kin), **Gri·go·ri A·lek·san·dro·vich** (grē gô′rē ä′lyek sän′drô vich) 1739–91; Russian field marshal & statesman; favorite of Catherine II

po·ten·cy (pōt′'n sē) *n., pl.* -**cies** **1.** the state of being potent, or the degree of this; power; strength **2.** ability to develop; potentiality

po·tent (pōt′'nt) *adj.* [L. *potentis* < prp. of *posse*, to be able < *potis*, able (< IE. base *potis*, master) + *esse*, to be (see ESSENCE)] **1.** having authority or power; mighty [a *potent* monarch] **2.** forceful and to the point; convincing [a *potent* argument] **3.** effective or powerful in action, as a drug **4.** able to engage in sexual intercourse: said of a male —**po′tent·ly** *adv.*

po·ten·tate (pōt′'n tāt′) *n.* a person having great power; ruler; monarch

po·ten·tial (pə ten′shəl) *adj.* [< ML. < L.: see POTENT] **1.** that can be, but is not yet; possible; latent [a *potential* leader; a *potential* source of trouble] **2.** *Gram.* expressing possibility, capability, etc. ["I can go" is in the *potential* mood] —*n.* **1.** something potential; possibility of growing, developing, becoming powerful or skillful, etc. [a baseball team with *potential*] **2.** *Elec.* the relative voltage at a point in an electric circuit or field with respect to some reference point in the same circuit or field —**po·ten′tial·ly** *adv.*

potential energy energy in an inactive form, resulting from position or structure instead of motion, as in a coiled spring

po·ten·ti·al·i·ty (pə ten′shē al′ə tē) *n.* **1.** possibility or capability of becoming, developing, etc.; latency **2.** *pl.* -**ties** something potential; a possibility

po·ten·ti·ate (pə ten′shē āt′) *vt.* -**at′ed, -at′ing** [< L. *potentia*, potency + -ATE¹] to increase (the effect of a drug or poison) by previous or simultaneous use of another drug or poison —**po·ten′ti·a′tion** *n.* —**po·ten′ti·a′tor** *n.*

po·ten·ti·om·e·ter (pə ten′shē äm′ə tər) *n.* [< POTENTIAL + -METER] an instrument for measuring, comparing, or controlling electric potentials

pot·ful (pät′fool′) *n., pl.* -**fuls** as much as a pot will hold

pot·head (pät′hed′) *n.* ☆[Slang] a regular user of marijuana

poth·er (päth′ər) *n.* [< ?] **1.** a cloud of smoke, dust, etc. **2.** a noisy confusion; fuss —*vt., vi.* to fuss or bother

pot·herb (pät′urb′, -hurb′) *n.* any herb whose leaves and stems are boiled for food or used as a flavoring

pot·hold·er (-hōl′dər) *n.* a small pad, or piece of thick cloth, for handling hot pots, pans, etc.

pot·hole (-hōl′) *n.* **1.** a deep hole or pit, as in the rock of a river bed **2.** *chiefly Brit. var. of* CHUCKHOLE

pot·hook (-hook′) *n.* **1.** an S-shaped hook for hanging a pot or kettle over a fire **2.** a hooked rod for lifting hot pots, etc. **3.** a curved mark in writing

pot·house (-hous′) *n.* [Brit.] a small tavern

po·tion (pō′shən) *n.* [< OFr. < L. < *potare*, to drink: for IE. base see IMBIBE] a drink or liquid dose, as of medicine or a substance that is supposed to do magic

pot liquor [Dial.] the liquid left after meat or vegetables have been cooked: also **pot′lik′ker**

pot·luck (pät′luk′) *n.* whatever the family meal happens to be [invited in to take *potluck*]

pot marigold a cultivated calendula with showy yellow or orange flowers

Po·to·mac (pə tō′mək) [< Algonquian town name, lit., ? where tribute is brought] river forming a boundary of W.Va., Md., & Va., and flowing into Chesapeake Bay

☆**pot·pie** (pät′pī′) *n.* **1.** a meat pie made in a pot or deep dish, usually with only a top crust **2.** a stew with dumplings

pot·pour·ri (pō′poo rē′, pät poor′ē) *n.* [Fr. < *pot*, a pot + pp. of *pourrir*, to rot] **1.** a mixture of dried flower petals with spices, kept in a jar for its sweet smell **2.** a mixture or collection of things not usually placed together

pot roast meat, usually a large cut of beef, cooked slowly in a covered pan with a little liquid

Pots·dam (päts′dam′; *G.* pôts däm′) city in East Germany, near Berlin: pop. 111,000

pot·sherd (pät′shurd′) *n.* [see POT & SHARD] a piece of broken pottery

pot·shot (-shät′) *n.* **1.** an easy shot, as one fired at close range **2.** a shot taken without careful aim **3.** a hasty, unplanned criticism or attack

pot·tage (pät′ij) *n.* [< MFr. < *pot*, a pot < Du.] a thick soup or stew made of vegetables, or meat and vegetables

pot·ted (pät′id) *adj.* **1.** put into a pot [*potted* plants] **2.** cooked or preserved in a pot or can [*potted* meat] ☆**3.** [Slang] drunk

pot·ter¹ (pät′ər) *n.* a person who makes earthenware pots, dishes, etc.

pot·ter² (pät′ər) *vi., vt.* [< OE. *potian*, to push] *chiefly Brit. var. of* PUTTER³

potter's field [see Matt. 27:7] ☆a burial ground for persons who die poor or unknown

potter's wheel a rotating horizontal disk upon which clay is molded into bowls, etc.

pot·ter·y (pät′ər ē) *n., pl.* -**ter·ies** [< MFr. < *potier*, a potter < *pot*, a pot] **1.** a potter's workshop or factory **2.** the art of a potter **3.** pots, bowls, etc. made of clay hardened by heat; earthenware

pot·ty¹ (pät′ē) *n., pl.* -**ties 1.** a small pot used as a toilet by a child **2.** a child's chair for toilet training, having an open seat with a pot beneath: in full, **potty chair 3.** a toilet: a child's word

pot·ty² (pät′ē) *adj.* -**ti·er, -ti·est** [Brit. Colloq.] **1.** trivial; petty **2.** odd; slightly crazy —**pot′ti·ness** *n.*

pouch (pouch) *n.* [MFr. *poche*, var. of *poque*, POKE²] **1.** a small bag or sack, as for pipe tobacco ☆**2.** a mailbag **3.** any space, part, etc. shaped like a pouch **4.** *a*) a saclike structure on the belly of some animals, as the kangaroo, used to carry young; marsupium *b*) a baglike part, as of a gopher's cheeks, for carrying food —*vt.* **1.** to put into a

POTTER'S WHEEL

POTBELLIED STOVE

pouch 2. to make into a pouch —*vi.* to form a pouch [his cheeks *pouched* out] —**pouched** *adj.*

Pou·lenc (pŏŏ laŋk′), **Fran·cis** (frän sēs′) 1899–1963; Fr. composer

poul·ter·er (pōl′tər ər) *n.* [Brit.] a dealer in poultry and game: also [Archaic] **poul′ter**

poul·tice (pōl′tis) *n.* [ML. *pultes*, a thick, soft food, orig. pl. of L. *puls:* see PULSE²] a hot, soft, wet mass, as of flour, mustard, etc., applied, sometimes on a cloth, to a sore part of the body —*vt.* **-ticed, -tic·ing** to apply a poultice to

poul·try (pōl′trē) *n.* [< MFr. < OFr. *poulet:* see PULLET] domestic fowls raised for meat or eggs; chickens, turkeys, ducks, geese, etc.

poul·try·man (-mən) *n., pl.* **-men** 1. a person who raises poultry, esp. commercially 2. a dealer in poultry

pounce¹ (pouns) *n.* [< ? MFr. *poinçon:* see PUNCHEON¹] 1. a claw or talon of a bird of prey 2. the act of pouncing; swoop, leap, etc. —*vi.* **pounced, pounc′ing** to swoop down, spring, or leap (*on, upon,* or *at*) as in attacking —**pounc′er** *n.*

pounce² (pouns) *n.* [< Fr. < L. *pumex,* pumice] 1. a fine powder, as of cuttlefish bone, formerly used to keep ink from blotting 2. a fine powder sprinkled over a stencil to make a design, as on cloth —*vt.* **pounced, pounc′ing** to use pounce on

pound¹ (pound) *n., pl.* **pounds,** sometimes **pound** [OE. *pund* < L. *pondo,* abl. of *pondus,* weight, akin to *pendere:* see PENDANT] 1. a unit of weight, equal to 16 oz. (7,000 grains) avoirdupois or 12 oz. (5,760 grains) troy: abbrev. **lb.** 2. *a)* the monetary unit of the United Kingdom (in full, **pound sterling**) equal to 100 (new) pennies or, in the earlier system, to 20 shillings: symbol £ *b)* the monetary unit of various other countries, as of Ireland, Israel, etc. See MONETARY UNITS, table

pound² (pound) *vt.* [OE. *punian*] 1. to beat to a pulp, powder, etc. [to *pound* corn into meal] 2. to strike or drive with repeated heavy blows [to *pound* nails into a board] 3. to make by pounding [he *pounded* a cabinet together] —*vi.* 1. to deliver repeated, heavy blows (*at* or *on* a door, etc.) 2. to move with heavy steps, thumps, etc. [he *pounded* down the hall] 3. to beat heavily; throb [her heart *pounded* from the exercise] —*n.* a pounding, or the sound of it —see SYN. at BEAT —☆**pound one's ear** [Slang] to sleep —**pound out** 1. to flatten, smooth, etc. by pounding 2. to produce (musical notes, typed copy, etc.) with a very heavy touch —☆**pound the pavement** [Slang] to walk the streets, as in looking for work —**pound′er** *n.*

pound³ (pound) *n.* [< OE. *pund-*] 1. an enclosed place for keeping animals, esp. stray animals [the city dog *pound*] 2. a place of confinement, as for arrested persons 3. an enclosed area for catching or keeping fish

Pound (pound), **Ezra** (**Loomis**) 1885–1972; U.S. poet, in Italy (1924–45; 1958–72)

pound·age (poun′dij) *n.* 1. a tax, etc. per pound (monetary unit or weight) 2. weight in pounds

pound·al (poun′d'l) *n.* [< POUND¹] a unit of force producing an acceleration of one foot per second every second on a one-pound mass

pound·cake (pound′kāk′) *n.* a rich cake made with a pound each of flour, butter, sugar, etc.

-pound·er (poun′dər) *a combining form meaning* something weighing or worth (a specified number of) pounds [the trout he caught was a five-*pounder*]

pound-fool·ish (pound′fōōl′ish) *adj.* not handling large sums of money wisely: see PENNY-WISE

pour (pôr) *vt.* [< ?] 1. to make flow in a continuous stream [to *pour* milk into a glass] 2. to send out, say, etc. steadily or in large amounts or great detail [he *poured* out his troubles to me] —*vi.* 1. to flow freely, continuously, or abundantly [wet salt will not *pour*] 2. to rain heavily 3. to rush in a crowd; swarm [fans *poured* out of the stadium] ☆4. to act as a hostess by pouring tea, coffee, etc. for guests at a reception —*n.* 1. an act of pouring 2. a heavy rain —☆**pour it on** [Slang] 1. to flatter 2. to try or work very hard 3. to go very fast —**pour′er** *n.*

‡pour·boire (pōōr bwȧr′) *n.* [Fr. < *pour,* for + *boire,* to drink] a tip, or gift of money

Pous·sin (pōō san′), **Ni·co·las** (nē kô lä′) 1594–1665; Fr. painter

pout¹ (pout) *vi.* [ME. *pouten*] 1. to thrust out the lips, as in showing that one is annoyed or hurt has feelings 2. to be silent and unfriendly; sulk 3. to stick out: said of the lips —*vt.* to thrust out (the lips) —*n.* 1. the act of pouting 2. a fit of sulking: also **the pouts**

pout² (pout) *n., pl.* **pout, pouts:** see PLURAL, II, D, 2 [OE. *-pute*] any of several stout-bodied fishes, as the horned pout, eelpout, etc.

pout·er (pout′ər) *n.* 1. a person who pouts 2. any of a breed of pigeon that can make its crop swell out: also **pouter pigeon**

pov·er·ty (päv′ər tē) *n.* [< OFr. < L. < *pauper,* poor] 1. the condition or quality of being poor; need 2. the condition of being poor in quality or lacking in something; inferiority; inadequacy [*poverty* of the soil; her *poverty* of imagination] 3. smallness in amount; scarcity [a *poverty* of good books]
SYN.—**poverty** implies a lack of what is needed to live fairly comfortably; **destitution** and **want** imply such great poverty that basic items, such as food and shelter, are lacking; **indigence,** a somewhat milder term, implies a lack of luxuries which one was formerly able to enjoy; **penury** suggests such harsh poverty as to cause misery, or a loss of self-respect —**ANT.** wealth, affluence

pov·er·ty-strick·en (-strik′'n) *adj.* very poor

pow (pou) *interj.* an exclamation suggesting the sound of a shot, blow, explosion, etc.

POW, P.O.W. prisoner of war

pow·der (pou′dər) *n.* [< OFr. *poudre* < L. *pulvis:* for IE. base see POLLEN] 1. any dry substance in the form of fine, dustlike particles, produced by crushing, grinding, etc. 2. a specific kind of powder [face *powder*] 3. same as GUNPOWDER —*vt.* 1. to sprinkle or cover as with powder [snow *powdered* the rooftops] 2. to apply cosmetic powder to (the body, face, etc.) 3. to make into powder —*vi.* 1. to be made into powder 2. to use powder as a cosmetic —☆**take a powder** [Slang] to run away; leave —**pow′der·er** *n.*

powder blue pale blue —**pow′der-blue′** *adj.*

powder burn a skin burn caused by gunpowder exploding at close range

pow·dered sugar (pou′dərd) granulated sugar ground into a powder

powder horn a container made of an animal's horn, for carrying gunpowder

powder puff a soft pad for applying cosmetic powder

powder room ☆a lavatory for women

pow·der·y (pou′dər ē) *adj.* 1. of, like, or in the form of, powder [*powdery* snow] 2. easily made into powder [soft, *powdery* rock] 3. covered with or as if with powder

POWDER HORN

pow·er (pou′ər) *n.* [< OFr. *poeir,* earlier *poter,* ult. < L. *posse,* to be able: see POTENT] 1. ability to do, act, or produce [lobsters have the power to grow new claws] 2. a specific ability or faculty [the *power* of sight] 3. great ability to do, act, or affect strongly; strength or force [the *power* of a boxer's blows] 4. *a)* the ability or right to control others; authority; influence [the *power* of the law] *b)* legal authority [the *power* of the President to call out troops] 5. *a)* physical force or energy that can be put to work [water *power*] *b)* the capacity to use such force, specif. in terms of the rate at which it can be used [60-watt *power*] 6. a person or thing of great influence, force, or authority [he is a *power* in the community] 7. a nation, esp. one having influence over others [the great *powers*] 8. a spirit or divinity 9. military strength [air *power*] 10. *Math. a)* the result of multiplying a quantity by itself [4 is the second *power* of 2 (2^2)] *b)* same as EXPONENT (sense 3) 11. *Optics* the degree of magnification of a lens, telescope, etc. —*vt.* to supply with power [the car is *powered* by a 200-horsepower engine] —*adj.* 1. operated by electricity, a fuel engine, etc. [*power* tools] 2. using an additional, engine-powered system [*power* steering] 3. carrying electricity [*power* lines] —**in power** 1. in authority 2. in office —**the powers that be** the persons in control —**pow′-ered** *adj.*
SYN.—**power** refers to the natural ability or recognized right to rule, govern, determine, etc. [the limited *power* of a president]; **authority** refers to the power one has, because of one's rank or office, to give commands, force obedience, make decisions, etc. [the *authority* of a teacher]; **jurisdiction** refers to the power to rule or decide within certain set limits [a court with *jurisdiction* over criminal cases only]; **dominion** implies supreme authority [*dominion* over a dependent state]; **control** implies authority to guide or re-

strain the activities of persons or things [children under the *control* of a guardian]; **command** implies the kind of authority that one has when one's orders must be obeyed [in *command* of a regiment]

☆**pow·er·boat** (-bōt′) *n. same as* MOTORBOAT

power dive a dive by an airplane in which the engine is used to increase the speed of descent —**pow′er-dive′** *vi., vt.* **-dived′, -div′ing**

pow·er·ful (-fəl) *adj.* having much power; strong or influential —*adv.* [Dial.] very [a *powerful* sick cat] —**pow′er·ful·ly** *adv.* —**pow′er·ful·ness** *n.*

☆**pow·er·house** (-hous′) *n.* **1.** a building where electric power is generated **2.** [Colloq.] a powerful person, team, etc.

pow·er·less (-lis) *adj.* without power; weak, feeble, unable, etc. —**pow′er·less·ly** *adv.* —**pow′er·less·ness** *n.*

power of attorney a written statement giving a person legal power to act for one

power pack a unit, as in a radio or TV amplifier, that converts power-line or battery voltage to required voltages

power plant 1. the apparatus that is the source of power for some particular operation [the *power plant* of an automobile] ☆**2.** a building where power, esp. electric power, is generated

☆**power structure** those persons or groups in a nation, organization, etc. who hold the actual ruling power because of their official position or because of their wealth or social standing

Pow·ha·tan (pou′ə tan′) 1550?-1618; Algonquian Indian chief in eastern Va.: father of POCAHONTAS

☆**pow·wow** (pou′wou′) *n.* [< Algonquian *powwaw*, priest] **1.** a N. American Indian ceremony to bring about, as by magic, the cure of disease, success in war, etc. **2.** a conference of or with N. American Indians **3.** [Colloq.] any conference or gathering —*vi.* **1.** to hold a powwow **2.** [Colloq.] to have a talk

pox (päks) *n.* [for *pocks:* see POCK] **1.** a disease in which blisters form on the skin, as smallpox or chicken pox **2.** syphilis

Poz·nan (pôz′nän′y′) city in W Poland: pop. 462,000

pp, pp. *Music* pianissimo

pp. 1. pages **2.** past participle

P.P., p.p. 1. parcel post **2.** past participle **3.** postpaid **4.** prepaid

ppd. 1. postpaid **2.** prepaid

PPI plan position indicator

ppm, p.p.m., PPM parts per million

ppr., p.pr. present participle

P.P.S., p.p.s. [L. *post postscriptum*] an additional postscript

P.Q. Province of Quebec

Pr *Chem.* praseodymium

Pr. 1. Prince **2.** Provençal

pr. 1. pair(s) **2.** present **3.** price **4.** pronoun

P.R., PR 1. Puerto Rico **2.** public relations

prac·ti·ca·ble (prak′ti kə b'l) *adj.* [< Fr. < *pratiquer:* see PRACTICE] **1.** that can be done or put into practice; feasible [a *practicable* plan] **2.** that can be used; usable [a *practicable* tool] —see SYN. at POSSIBLE and PRACTICAL —**prac′ti·ca·bil′i·ty, prac′ti·ca·ble·ness** *n.* —**prac′ti·ca·bly** *adv.*

prac·ti·cal (prak′ti k'l) *adj.* [obs. *practic* < LL. *practicus:* see PRACTICE] **1.** of or learned through practice or action [*practical* knowledge] **2.** *a)* usable; workable; useful and sensible [*practical* proposals] *b)* designed for use; utilitarian [*practical* shoes] **3.** concerned with application to useful ends, rather than with theory, speculation, etc. [*practical* science] **4.** given to actual practice [a *practical* farmer] **5.** of, concerned with, or realistic and sensible about everyday activities, work, etc. [it would be more *practical* to sell the boat and buy a car now] **6.** that is so in practice; virtual [the *practical* head of England is the prime minister] **7.** matter-of-fact; unimaginative —**prac′ti·cal′i·ty** (-kal′ə tē), *pl.* **-ties, prac′ti·cal·ness** *n.*

SYN.—practical is used of something that has been tested in actual experience and found to work or that seems certain, from a completely realistic viewpoint, to accomplish what it is meant to accomplish; **practicable** is used of something that, at least in theory, seems able to be put into effect, but that has not yet been developed or tried [before the era of electronics, television seemed merely *practicable;* today it is just one of many *practical* applications of the science] —ANT. impractical, impracticable

practical joke a trick played on someone but meant in fun —**practical joker**

prac·ti·cal·ly (prak′tik lē, -tik ′l ē) *adv.* **1.** in a practical way **2.** from a practical viewpoint [let's look at the problem *practically*] **3.** in effect; really; virtually [*practically* a dictator] **4.** [Colloq.] nearly [we're *practically* home]

☆**practical nurse** a nurse with less training than a registered nurse, often one licensed by the State

prac·tice (prak′tis) *vt.* **-ticed, -tic·ing** [< MFr. < *pratiquer* < ML. < LL. < Gr. *praktikos*, practical < *prassein*, to do] **1.** to

do or engage in regularly; make a habit of [to *practice* thrift] **2.** to do repeatedly so as to gain skill [to *practice* batting] **3.** *a)* to work at, esp. as a profession [to *practice* law] *b)* to be guided by (beliefs, ideals, etc.) [to *practice* one's religion] —*vi.* **1.** to do something repeatedly so as to gain skill [he *practices* six hours a day on the piano] **2.** to work at a profession, as medicine, law, etc. —*n.* **1.** the act, result, etc. of practicing; specif., *a)* a usual action; habit [to make a *practice* of being early] *b)* a usual method or custom; convention [the *practice* of tipping for services] **2.** *a)* the doing of something over and over again to gain skill [batting *practice*] *b)* the resulting condition of being skilled [to be out of *practice*] **3.** knowledge put into action [the *practice* of a theory] **4.** *a)* exercise of a profession [the *practice* of law] *b)* a business based on this [to buy another's law *practice*] —see SYN. at HABIT —**prac′tic·er** *n.*

prac·ticed (-tist) *adj.* **1.** skilled through practice [a *practiced* artist] **2.** learned or perfected by practice [her *practiced* cooking skills]

practice teacher *same as* STUDENT TEACHER —**practice teaching**

☆**prac·ti·cum** (prak′ti kəm) *n.* [< Gr. < LL. < *practicus*, active] a course or group session emphasizing the practical application of theory, esp. one in which a student gains practical experience in a field of study

prac·tise (-tis) *vt., vi.* **-tised, -tis·ing** *chiefly Brit. sp. of* PRACTICE

prac·ti·tion·er (prak tish′ə nər) *n.* a person who practices a profession, art, etc. [a medical *practitioner*]

prae- [L.: see PRE-] *same as* PRE-

prae·no·men (prē nō′mən) *n., pl.* **-no′mens, -nom′i·na** (-näm′i nə) [L. < *prae-*, before + *nomen*, a name] the first name of an ancient Roman

prae·tor (prēt′ər) *n.* [L., ult. < *prae-*, before + *ire*, to go] an ancient Roman official, next below a consul in rank —**prae·to·ri·al** (pri tôr′ē əl) *adj.*

prae·to·ri·an (pri tôr′ē ən) *adj.* **1.** of a praetor **2.** [often P-] designating or of the bodyguard (**Praetorian Guard**) of a Roman emperor —*n.* [often P-] a member of the Praetorian Guard

prag·mat·ic (prag mat′ik) *adj.* [< L. < Gr. *pragmatikos* < *pragma*, business < *prassein*, to do] **1.** concerned with actual practice, not with theory; practical **2.** of philosophical pragmatism Also **prag·mat′i·cal** —**prag·mat′i·cal·ly** *adv.*

pragmatic sanction any of various royal decrees that had the force of fundamental law

prag·ma·tism (prag′mə tiz'm) *n.* **1.** the quality or condition of being pragmatic ☆**2.** a method in philosophy that tests the truth of all concepts by their practical results —**prag′ma·tist** *n., adj.*

Prague (präg) capital of Czechoslovakia, in the W part: pop. 1,034,000: Czech name **Pra·ha** (prä′hä)

☆**prai·rie** (prer′ē) *n.* [Fr. < OFr. *praerie* < *pré* (< L. *pratum*), meadow + *-erie*, -ERY] a large area of level or slightly rolling, grassy land without many trees

☆**prairie chicken** either of two brown-and-white, henlike grouse, with a short, rounded tail, found on the N. American prairies and along the coast of the Gulf of Mexico: also **prairie hen**

☆**prairie dog** a small, squirrellike, burrowing rodent of N. America, with a barking cry

Prairie Provinces Canad. provinces of Manitoba, Saskatchewan, & Alberta

☆**prairie schooner** a large covered wagon used by pioneers to cross the American prairies

☆**prairie wolf** *same as* COYOTE

praise (prāz) *vt.* **praised, prais′ing** [< OFr. < LL. < L. *pretium*, worth] **1.** to express approval or admiration of [to *praise* someone's work] **2.** to worship (God, etc.), as in song; glorify —*n.* a praising or being praised; words that show approval; glorification —**sing someone's praise** (or **praises**) to praise someone highly —**prais′er** *n.*

PRAIRIE DOG
(to 15 in. long, including tail)

SYN.—praise is the simple, basic word that refers to the expressing of approval, respect, or admiration [to *praise* a student's work]; **laud** implies great, sometimes excessive praise [the critics *lauded* the actor to the skies]; **extol** implies high, often formal praise that is meant to make the one who receives it feel proud and happy [the scientist was *extolled* for his work]; **eulogize** suggests formal praise in a speech or writing, esp. of someone who has recently died

praise·wor·thy (-wur′thē) *adj.* deserving praise; laudable —**praise′wor′thi·ly** *adv.* —**praise′wor′thi·ness** *n.*

Pra·krit (prä′krit) *n.* [Sans. *prākṛta*, natural < *pra-*, before + *kṛ*, to do] any of several Old Indic languages not of Sanskrit origin, spoken in ancient India

☆**pra·line** (prä′lēn; *chiefly South* prä′-) *n.* [Fr., after Marshal Duplessis-*Praslin* (1598-1675), whose cook created it] 1. a crisp candy made of a pecan, almond, etc. browned in boiling sugar 2. a candy patty made of pecans, brown sugar, etc.

pram (pram) *n.* [Brit. Colloq.] a perambulator

prance (prans) *vi.* **pranced, pranc′ing** [< ?] 1. to rise up on the hind legs in a lively way, esp. while moving along: said of a horse 2. to ride on a prancing horse 3. to move about in a way that suggests a prancing horse; caper 4. to swagger; strut —*vt.* to make (a horse) prance —*n.* 1. an act of prancing 2. a prancing movement —**pranc′er** *n.* —**pranc′ing·ly** *adv.*

prank[1] (praŋk) *n.* [< ? or akin to PRANK[2]] a playful trick, often one causing some mischief —**prank′ster** *n.*

prank[2] (praŋk) *vt., vi.* [prob. < LowG. source] to dress up or adorn showily

prank·ish (praŋ′kish) *adj.* 1. full of pranks; mischievous 2. like a prank —**prank′ish·ly** *adv.* —**prank′ish·ness** *n.*

pra·se·o·dym·i·um (prä′zē ō dim′ē əm, -sē-) *n.* [ModL. < Gr. *prasios*, green + (DI)DYMIUM] a metallic chemical element of the rare-earth group, whose salts are generally green: symbol, Pr; at. wt., 140.907; at. no., 59

prat (prat) *n.* [< ?] [Slang] the buttocks

prate (prāt) *vi.* **prat′ed, prat′ing** [< MDu. *praten;* prob. echoic] to talk on and on in a foolish way; chatter —*vt.* to tell idly; blab —*n.* idle talk; chatter —**prat′er** *n.* —**prat′ing·ly** *adv.*

☆**prat·fall** (prat′fôl′) *n.* [Slang] a fall on the buttocks, esp. for comic effect, as in burlesque

prat·tle (prat′'l) *vi., vt.* **-tled, -tling** [MLowG. *pratelen*] 1. *same as* PRATE 2. to speak in a childish way; babble —*n.* 1. foolish chatter 2. childish talk —**prat′tler** *n.*

prau (prou, prä′ōō) *n. same as* PROA

prawn (prôn) *n.* [< ?] a shellfish like a large shrimp; also, sometimes, a large shrimp

Prax·it·e·les (prak sit′ə lēz′) 4th cent. B.C.; Athenian sculptor

pray (prā) *vt.* [< OFr. < LL. < L. *precari* < *precis,* genitive of *prex,* prayer] 1. to beg or ask for seriously: no longer used except in a shortened form of direct request [(I) *pray* (you) tell me] 2. to ask for by prayer; beg for 3. to recite (a prayer) 4. to effect, get, etc. by praying —*vi.* 1. to make a humble request, as to a deity [to *pray* for rain] 2. to worship God, as by saying prayers —see SYN. at APPEAL

prayer[1] (prer) *n.* [< OFr. < ML. < L. *precarius,* got by begging < *precari,* to entreat] 1. the act of praying 2. a serious request; entreaty 3. *a)* a humble and sincere request to God *b)* an expression of praise, thanksgiving, etc. to God *c)* a set of words used in praying [evening *prayer*] 4. [often *pl.*] a religious prayer service 5. something prayed for ☆6. [Slang] a chance to succeed [he doesn't have a *prayer*]

pray·er[2] (prā′ər) *n.* a person who prays

prayer book a book of formal religious prayers

prayer·ful (prer′fəl) *adj.* 1. praying often; devout [a *prayerful* monk] 2. of or like a prayer [a *prayerful* request] —**prayer′-ful·ly** *adv.* —**prayer′ful·ness** *n.*

praying mantis *same as* MANTIS

pre- [< Fr. *pré-* or L. *prae-* < L. *prae,* before: for IE. base see FAR] a prefix meaning: 1. before in time, place, or rank [*prewar*] 2. leading up to, in preparation for [*preschool*]

preach (prēch) *vi.* [< OFr. < LL. < L. *prae-,* before + *dicare,* to proclaim] 1. to speak in public on a religious subject; give a sermon 2. to give moral or religious advice, esp. in a tiresome way —*vt.* 1. to teach, support, or urge as by preaching [to *preach* the word of God; to *preach* peace] 2. to deliver (a sermon)

preach·er (prē′chər) *n.* a person who preaches; esp., a clergyman

preach·i·fy (-chə fī′) *vi.* **-fied′, -fy′ing** [Colloq.] to preach or give moral advice in a tiresome way

preach·ment (prēch′mənt) *n.* a preaching or sermon, esp. a long, tiresome one

preach·y (prē′chē) *adj.* **preach′i·er, preach′i·est** [Colloq.] full of, or fond of giving, moral advice

pre·am·ble (prē′am′b'l, prē am′-) *n.* [< MFr., ult. < L. < *prae-,* before + *ambulare,* to go] 1. an introduction, esp. to a constitution, statute, etc., stating its background and purpose 2. an introductory fact, event, etc.; preliminary

pre·am·pli·fi·er (prē am′plə fī′ər) *n.* in a radio, phonograph, etc., an amplifier to boost the voltage of a weak signal before it reaches the main amplifier

pre·ar·range (prē′ə rānj′) *vt.* **-ranged′, -rang′ing** to arrange beforehand —**pre′ar·range′ment** *n.*

preb·end (preb′ənd) *n.* [< MFr. < LL. *praebenda,* state support to a private person < L. *praebere,* to give] 1. the amount paid a clergyman by his cathedral or collegiate church 2. the church property that provides the revenue to pay this amount 3. *same as* PREBENDARY

preb·en·dar·y (preb′ən der′ē) *n., pl.* **-dar′ies** a person receiving a prebend

prec. preceding

Pre·cam·bri·an (prē kam′brē ən) *adj.* designating or of the geologic era covering all the time before the Cambrian Period, often divided into a **Late Precambrian Era** and an **Early Precambrian Era** —**the Precambrian** the Precambrian Era or its rocks: see GEOLOGIC TIME CHART

pre·can·cel (prē kan′s'l) *vt.* **-celed** or **-celled, -cel·ing** or **-cel·ling** to cancel (a postage stamp) before use in mailing —*n.* a precanceled stamp

pre·can·cer·ous (-kan′sər əs) *adj.* that may become or is likely to become cancerous [a *precancerous* mole]

pre·car·i·ous (pri ker′ē əs) *adj.* [L. *precarius:* see PRAYER[1]] 1. dependent upon chance or circumstances; insecure; uncertain [a *precarious* living] 2. unsafe; dangerous; risky [a *precarious* foothold] 3. not based on facts or good evidence [a *precarious* theory] —**pre·car′i·ous·ly** *adv.* —**pre·car′i·ous·ness** *n.*

pre·cast concrete (prē′kast) blocks, slabs, etc. of concrete cast into form before being put into position

pre·cau·tion (pri kô′shən) *n.* [< Fr. < LL. < L. pp. of *praecavere* < *prae-,* before + *cavere,* to take care: for IE. base see HEAR] 1. care taken beforehand; careful foresight 2. a measure taken beforehand against possible danger, failure, etc. [he took the *precaution* of locking the door before he left] —**pre·cau′tion·ar′y** *adj.*

pre·cede (pri sēd′) *vt., vi.* **-ced′ed, -ced′ing** [< MFr. < L. < *prae-,* before + *cedere,* to go] to be, come, or go before in time, order, rank, importance, etc. [she *preceded* him into the room; a colonel *precedes* a major]

prec·e·dence (pres′ə dəns, pri sēd′'ns) *n.* 1. the act, right, or fact of preceding, or coming before in time, order, rank, etc. [the election of officers will take *precedence* at the next meeting] 2. a ranking of officials, etc. in order of importance Also **prec′e·den·cy**

prec·e·dent (pri sēd′'nt; *for n.* pres′ə dənt) *adj.* that precedes —*n.* 1. an act, decision, etc. that may serve as an example, reason, or rule for a later one 2. a practice based upon earlier precedents

pre·ced·ing (pri sēd′iŋ) *adj.* that precedes; going or coming before —see SYN. at PREVIOUS

pre·cen·tor (pri sen′tər) *n.* [< LL. < L. < *prae-,* before + *canere,* to sing] a person who directs a church choir or congregation in singing —**pre·cen·to·ri·al** (prē′sen tôr′ē əl) *adj.*

pre·cept (prē′sept) *n.* [< L. < *praecipere,* to teach < *prae-,* before + *capere,* to take] 1. a direction meant as a rule of action or conduct (Example: Look before you leap) 2. a rule of moral conduct 3. a rule or direction, as in technical matters [medical *precepts*] —**pre·cep′tive** *adj.*

pre·cep·tor (pri sep′tər) *n.* [see prec.] a teacher —**pre·cep·to·ri·al** (prē′sep tôr′ē əl) *adj.* —**pre·cep′tress** *n.fem.*

pre·ces·sion (pri sesh′ən) *n.* 1. a preceding; precedence 2. *Mech.* a change in direction of the rotational axis of a spinning body, which causes the axis to describe a cone —**pre·ces′sion·al** *adj.*

pre·cinct (prē′siŋkt) *n.* [< ML. < L. pp. of *praecingere,* to encompass < *prae-,* before + *cingere,* to surround (see CINCH)]

PRAWN
(from 1 in. to
2 ft. long)

1. [*usually pl.*] an enclosed place between buildings, walls, etc. **2.** [*pl.*] environs; neighborhood ☆**3.** *a)* a division of a city, as for police administration *b)* a subdivision of a ward, as for voting **4.** any limited area, as of thought **5.** a boundary

pre·ci·os·i·ty (presh′ē äs′ə tē) *n., pl.* **-ties** [see PRECIOUS] a being overly refined, delicate, or affected, esp. in language

pre·cious (presh′əs) *adj.* [< OFr. < L. *pretiosus* < *pretium*, a PRICE] **1.** of great price or value; costly [diamonds are *precious* gems; freedom is *precious*] **2.** much loved or cherished; dear [her *precious* child] **3.** too delicate or refined; not natural [a *precious* style of writing] **4.** very great [a *precious* liar] —*adv.* [Colloq.] very [we had *precious* little time] —**pre′cious·ly** *adv.* —**pre′cious·ness** *n.*

precious stone a rare and costly gem

prec·i·pice (pres′ə pis) *n.* [< Fr. < L. < *praeceps*, headlong < *prae-*, before + *caput*, a HEAD] **1.** a vertical, almost vertical, or overhanging rock face; steep cliff **2.** the brink of disaster, defeat, etc.

pre·cip·i·tan·cy (pri sip′ə tən sē) *n., pl.* **-cies** a being precipitate; great haste; rashness: also **pre·cip′i·tance**

pre·cip·i·tant (pri sip′ə tənt) *adj.* [< L. prp. of *praecipitare*] *same as* PRECIPITATE —*n.* a substance which, when added to a solution, causes the formation of a precipitate

pre·cip·i·tate (pri sip′ə tāt′; *also, for adj. & n.,* -tit) *vt.* **-tat′ed, -tat′ing** [< L. pp. of *praecipitare* < *praeceps:* see PRECIPICE] **1.** to throw headlong; hurl downward **2.** to make happen before expected, needed, etc.; hasten [to *precipitate* a crisis] **3.** *Chem.* to cause (a dissolved substance) to become insoluble and separate out from a solution **4.** *Meteorol.* to condense (vapor) and cause to fall as rain, snow, etc. —*vi.* **1.** *Chem.* to be precipitated **2.** *Meteorol.* to condense and fall as rain, snow, etc. —*adj.* **1.** falling steeply, rushing headlong, flowing swiftly, etc. **2.** acting, happening, or done very hastily or rashly; impetuous [her *precipitate* departure] **3.** very sudden; abrupt [his *precipitate* downfall] —*n.* a substance precipitated out from a solution —**pre·cip′i·tate·ly** *adv.* —**pre·cip′i·tate·ness** *n.* —**pre·cip′i·ta·tive** *adj.* —**pre·cip′i·ta·tor** *n.*

pre·cip·i·ta·tion (pri sip′ə tā′shən) *n.* **1.** a throwing or falling headlong **2.** sudden or rash haste **3.** a bringing on suddenly [the *precipitation* of a crisis] **4.** *Chem.* a precipitating or being precipitated from a solution **5.** *Meteorol. a)* rain, snow, etc. *b)* the amount of this

pre·cip·i·tous (pri sip′ə təs) *adj.* **1.** steep like a precipice **2.** having precipices **3.** rapid, reckless, or sudden —see SYN. at STEEP¹ —**pre·cip′i·tous·ly** *adv.* —**pre·cip′i·tous·ness** *n.*

pré·cis (prā sē′, prā′sē) *n., pl.* **pré·cis′** (-sēz′, -sēz) [Fr.: see PRECISE] a concise summary —*vt.* to make a précis of

pre·cise (pri sīs′) *adj.* [MFr. *precis* < L. pp. of *praecidere*, to cut off < *prae-*, before + *caedere*, to cut] **1.** strictly defined; accurately stated; definite [a *precise* explanation of her responsibilities] **2.** speaking definitely or distinctly **3.** minutely exact [the *precise* amount] **4.** *a)* very careful or strict in following a procedure, rules, etc. *b)* too refined or sensitive; finicky —see SYN. at CORRECT —**pre·cise′ly** *adv.* —**pre·cise′ness** *n.*

pre·ci·sion (pri sizh′ən) *n.* **1.** the quality of being precise; exactness, accuracy, etc. [the *precision* of a watch] **2.** the degree of this —*adj.* characterized by precision, as in measurement, operation, etc. [a *precision* instrument] —**pre·ci′sion·ist** *n.*

pre·clin·i·cal (prē klin′i k'l) *adj.* of or in the stage of a disease before any of the symptoms appear

pre·clude (pri klōōd′) *vt.* **-clud′ed, -clud′ing** [< L. *praecludere* < *prae-*, before + *claudere*, to CLOSE²] to make impossible, esp. in advance; prevent [his care *precluded* any chance of failure] —see SYN. at PREVENT —**pre·clu′sion** (-klōō′zhən) *n.* —**pre·clu′sive** (-siv) *adj.* —**pre·clu′sive·ly** *adv.*

pre·co·cious (pri kō′shəs) *adj.* [L. *praecox*, ult. < *prae-*, before + *coquere*, to COOK] **1.** developed or matured beyond normal for one's age, esp. in mental capacity, talent, etc. [a *precocious* child] **2.** of or showing premature development —**pre·co′cious·ly** *adv.* —**pre·co′cious·ness**, **pre·coc′i·ty** (-käs′ə tē) *n.*

pre·cog·ni·tion (prē′käg nish′ən) *n.* the supposed awareness or knowledge of an event, condition, etc. before it occurs, esp. by extrasensory powers —**pre·cog′ni·tive** (-nə tiv) *adj.*

pre·con·ceive (prē′kən sēv′) *vt.* **-ceived′, -ceiv′ing** to form an idea or opinion of beforehand [a juror should have no *preconceived* views about a case he will hear] —**pre′con·cep′tion** *n.*

pre·con·cert·ed (-kən sur′tid) *adj.* arranged or agreed upon beforehand [a *preconcerted* attack] —**pre′con·cert′ed·ly** *adv.*

pre·con·di·tion (-kən dish′ən) *vt.* to prepare (someone or something) to behave, react, etc. in a certain way under certain conditions —*n.* anything which must exist or is required before something else can occur, be done, etc.

pre·cook (prē kook′) *vt.* to cook partially or completely, for final preparation later

pre·cur·sor (pri kur′sər) *n.* [< L. < *praecurrere*, to run ahead] **1.** a person or thing that comes before and shows, or prepares the way for, what will follow; forerunner [the harpsichord was a *precursor* of the piano] **2.** a predecessor, as in office

pre·cur·so·ry (-sə rē) *adj.* **1.** acting as a precursor; being a sign of something to follow **2.** introductory; preliminary

pred. predicate

pre·da·cious, **pre·da·ceous** (pri dā′shəs) *adj.* [< L. *praedari*, to prey upon < *praeda*, a prey + -ACEOUS] preying on other animals; predatory —**pre·dac′i·ty** (-das′ə tē), **pre·da′cious·ness**, **pre·da′ceous·ness** *n.*

pre·date (prē dāt′) *vt.* **-dat′ed, -dat′ing** **1.** to give an earlier date to than the actual or current date **2.** to come before in time

pre·da·tion (pri dā′shən) *n.* [< L. < pp. of *praedari:* see PREDACIOUS] **1.** a plundering or preying **2.** the method of existence of predatory animals

pred·a·tor (pred′ə tər) *n.* a predatory person or animal

pred·a·to·ry (-tôr′ē) *adj.* [< L. < *praeda*, a prey] **1.** that plunders, robs, or takes advantage of others [a *predatory* band of wanderers] **2.** living by killing and feeding upon other animals —**pred′a·to′ri·ly** *adv.* —**pred′a·to′ri·ness** *n.*

pre·de·cease (prē′di sēs′) *vt., vi.* **-ceased′, -ceas′ing** to die before (someone else)

pred·e·ces·sor (pred′ə ses′ər; *chiefly Brit.* prē′di-) *n.* [< MFr. < LL. < L. *prae-*, before + *decessor*, retiring officer < *decessus:* see DECEASE] **1.** a person coming before another, as in office **2.** a thing replaced by another thing, as in use

pre·des·ti·nate (prē des′tə nit; *for v.* -nāt′) *adj.* predestined or foreordained —*vt.* **-nat′ed, -nat′ing** *Theol.* to order or decide beforehand by divine decree —**pre·des′ti·na′tor** *n.*

pre·des·ti·na·tion (prē des′tə nā′shən) *n.* **1.** *Theol.* the act by which God decided beforehand everything that would happen, specif. which souls were to be saved and which to be condemned **2.** one's fate in life; destiny

pre·des·tine (prē des′tin) *vt.* **-tined, -tin·ing** to destine, decide, or decree beforehand; foreordain [he seemed *predestined* to be a poet]

pre·de·ter·mine (prē′di tur′mən) *vt.* **-mined, -min·ing** **1.** to determine or decide beforehand [a *predetermined* route] **2.** to bias or prejudice beforehand —**pre′de·ter′mi·nate** (-mə nit) *adj.* —**pre′de·ter′mi·na′tion** *n.*

pred·i·ca·ble (pred′i kə b'l) *adj.* that can be predicated —*n.* something predicable —**pred′i·ca·bil′i·ty**, **pred′i·ca·ble·ness** *n.* —**pred′i·ca·bly** *adv.*

pre·dic·a·ment (pri dik′ə mənt) *n.* [< LL. *praedicamentum* < L. *praedicare:* see PREACH] a situation that is difficult, embarrassing, or comical [he is in the *predicament* of having locked himself out]

pred·i·cate (pred′ə kāt′; *for n. and adj.,* -kit) *vt.* **-cat′ed, -cat′ing** [< L. pp. of *praedicare:* see PREACH] **1.** orig., to proclaim; affirm **2.** *a)* to declare to be a quality, attribute, or property of something [to *predicate* the honesty of his motives] *b)* *Logic* to put forth as a predicate in a proposition **3.** to base (something) on or upon facts, conditions, etc. [the decisions of the courts are *predicated* upon the Constitution] **4.** to imply or connote —*n.* **1.** the word or words that say something about the subject of a sentence or clause: a predicate may be a verb (the wind *blows*), a verb and adverb (the wind *blows hard*), a verb and its object (the wind *blows the leaves down*), or a linking verb and its complement (he *is the happiest man I know*) **2.** *Logic* something that is said to be true or denied about the subject of a proposition (Example: *green* in "grass is green") —*adj. Gram.* of, or having the nature of, a predicate [a *predicate* adjective] —**pred′i·ca′tion** *n.* —**pred′i·ca′tive** *adj.* —**pred′i·ca′tive·ly** *adv.*

pre·dict (pri dikt′) *vt., vi.* [< L. pp. of *praedicere* < *prae-*, before + *dicere*, to tell] to state (what one believes will happen); foretell [I *predict* that you will win] —see SYN. at FORETELL —**pre·dict′a·bil′i·ty** *n.* —**pre·dict′a·ble** *adj.* —**pre·dict′a·bly** *adv.* —**pre·dic′tive** *adj.* —**pre·dic′tive·ly** *adv.* —**pre·dic′tor** *n.*

pre·dic·tion (pri dik′shən) *n.* **1.** a predicting or being predicted **2.** something predicted

pre·di·gest (prē′di jest′, -dī-) *vt.* to digest beforehand; specif., to treat (food) as with enzymes for easier digestion —**pre′di·ges′tion** *n.*

pre·di·lec·tion (pred′'l ek′shən, prēd′-) *n.* [< Fr. < ML. < L. *prae-*, before + *diligere*, to prefer] a special liking; partiality or preference (*for*)

pre·dis·pose (prē′dis pōz′) *vt.* **-posed′, -pos′ing** to make more likely to accept, get, etc.; incline [fatigue *predisposes* one to illness] —**pre·dis·po·si′tion** (-pə zish′ən) *n.*

☆**pred·ni·sone** (pred′nə sōn′) *n.* [< *pre(gnane)*, a steroid + *-d(ie)n(e)*, having a double bond + (CORT)ISONE] a substance obtained from cortisone, used to treat arthritis, allergies, etc.

pre·dom·i·nant (pri däm′ə nənt) *adj.* **1.** having authority or influence over others; superior [he had the *predominant* voice in the discussion] **2.** most frequent; prevailing [cotton is the *predominant* choice for summer dresses] —**pre·dom′i·nance, pre·dom′i·nan·cy** *n., pl.* **-cies, pre·dom′i·nant·ly** *adv.*

pre·dom·i·nate (-nāt′; *for adj.* -nit) *vi.* **-nat′ed, -nat′ing** **1.** to have controlling influence or power (*over* others); hold sway **2.** to be greatest in amount, number, etc.; prevail [yellow *predominates* in the pattern] —*adj.* same as PREDOMINANT —**pre·dom′i·nate·ly** *adv.* —**pre·dom′i·na′tion** *n.*

pre·e·lec·tion, pre-e·lec·tion (prē′i lek′shən) *adj.* occurring before an election: also **pre′ë·lec′tion**

☆**pree·mie** (prē′mē) *n.* [< PREM(ATURE) + -IE] [Colloq.] a prematurely born infant, esp. one weighing less than 5½ pounds

pre·em·i·nent, pre-em·i·nent (prē em′ə nənt) *adj.* eminent above others; most outstanding in worth, rank, fame, etc. [he is *preeminent* among modern painters]: also **pre·ëm′i·nent** —**pre·em′i·nence, pre-em′i·nence** *n.* —**pre·em′i·nent·ly, pre-em′i·nent·ly** *adv.*

☆**pre·empt, pre-empt** (prē empt′) *vt.* [back-formation < PREEMPTION] **1.** to acquire (some public land) before **2.** to take before anyone else can; appropriate [they came early and *preempted* the best seats] **3.** *Radio & TV* to replace (a regularly scheduled program) —*vi. Bridge* to make a preemptive bid Also **pre·ëmpt′** —**pre·emp′tor, pre-emp′tor** *n.*

☆**pre·emp·tion, pre-emp·tion** (prē emp′shən) *n.* [< ML. pp. of *preemere* < L. *prae-*, before + *emere*, to buy] **1.** the act or right of buying land, etc. before, or in preference to others; esp., such a right given to a settler on public land **2.** the taking of something before others can Also **pre·ëmp′tion**

pre·emp·tive, pre-emp·tive (-emp′tiv) *adj.* **1.** having to do with preemption **2.** *Bridge* designating a high bid intended to shut out opposing bids Also **pre·ëmp′tive** —**pre·emp′tive·ly, pre-emp′tive·ly** *adv.*

preen (prēn) *vt.* [< OE. < *proinen*] **1.** to clean and trim (the feathers) with the beak: said of birds **2.** to make (oneself) trim and neat; groom (oneself) **3.** to show satisfaction with or vanity in (oneself) —*vi.* to dress up with great care; primp —**preen′er** *n.*

pre·ex·ist, pre-ex·ist (prē′ig zist′) *vt., vi.* [< LL.] to exist previously or before (another person or thing): also **pre′ëx·ist′** —**pre′ex·ist′ence, pre′-ex·ist′ence** *n.* —**pre′ex·ist′ent, pre′-exist′ent** *adj.*

pref. **1.** preface **2.** preferred **3.** prefix

pre·fab (prē′fab′) *n.* [Colloq.] a prefabricated building

pre·fab·ri·cate (prē fab′rə kāt′) *vt.* **-cat′ed, -cat′ing** **1.** to fabricate beforehand **2.** to make (houses, etc.) in standardized sections for shipment and quick assembly —**pre′fab·ri·ca′tion** *n.*

pref·ace (pref′is) *n.* [< MFr. < ML. < L. *prae-*, before + pp. of *fari*, to speak: see BAN¹] **1.** an introductory statement to an article, book, or speech, telling its subject, purpose, etc. **2.** something introductory —*vt.* **-aced, -ac·ing** **1.** to furnish or introduce with a preface [he *prefaced* his talk with a joke] **2.** to be or serve as a preface to —see SYN. at INTRODUCTION

pref·a·to·ry (pref′ə tôr′ē) *adj.* of, like, or serving as a preface; introductory: also **pref′a·to′ri·al** —**pref′a·to′ri·ly** *adv.*

pre·fect (prē′fekt) *n.* [< OFr. < L. pp. of *praeficere*, to set over < *prae-*, before + *facere*, to make] **1.** in ancient Rome, any of various officials in charge of governmental or military departments. *a)* the head official of a department in France *b)* the chief of the Paris police

pre·fec·ture (prē′fek chər) *n.* the office, authority, territory, or residence of a prefect —**pre·fec′tur·al** *adj.*

pre·fer (pri fur′) *vt.* **-ferred′, -fer′ring** [< MFr. < L. < *prae-*, before + *ferre*, BEAR¹] **1.** to promote or advance in position or status **2.** to put before a magistrate, court, etc. to be considered

[to *prefer* charges against an attacker] **3.** to choose first; like better [he *prefers* baseball to football] **4.** to give preference or priority to (a creditor, etc.) —see SYN. at CHOOSE —**pre·fer′rer** *n.*

pref·er·a·ble (pref′ər ə b'l, pref′rə-) *adj.* to be preferred; more desirable —**pref′er·a·bil′i·ty, pref′er·a·ble·ness** *n.* —**pref′er·a·bly** *adv.*

pref·er·ence (pref′ər əns, pref′rəns) *n.* **1.** a preferring or being preferred; greater liking [he has a *preference* for lively music] **2.** the right, power, etc. of prior choice or claim [he was given *preference* in settling the debt] **3.** something preferred; one's choice [what is your *preference* in sports?] **4.** a giving of advantage to one person, country, etc. over others, as in granting credit or setting tariff rates —see SYN. at CHOICE

pref·er·en·tial (pref′ə ren′shəl) *adj.* **1.** of, giving, or receiving preference [*preferential* treatment] **2.** offering a preference [a *preferential* ballot] ☆**3.** designating a union shóp which gives preference to union members in hiring, layoffs, etc. —**pref′er·en′tial·ly** *adv.*

pre·fer·ment (pri fur′mənt) *n.* **1.** a preferring **2.** an advancement in rank or office; promotion **3.** an office, rank, or honor to which a person is advanced

☆**preferred stock** stock on which dividends must be paid before those of common stock

pre·fig·u·ra·tion (prē′fig yə rā′shən, prē fig′-) *n.* **1.** the act of prefiguring **2.** something in which something else is prefigured; prototype

pre·fig·ure (prē fig′yər) *vt.* **-ured, -ur·ing** [< LL. < L. *prae-*, before + *figurare*, to fashion] **1.** to be a type of or foreshadow (something that will appear later) **2.** to imagine beforehand —**pre·fig′ur·a·tive** *adj.* —**pre·fig′ur·a·tive·ly** *adv.* —**pre·fig′ur·a·tive·ness** *n.* —**pre·fig′ure·ment** *n.*

pre·fix (prē′fiks; *also, for v.,* prē fiks′) *vt.* [< MFr. < L. pp. of *praefigere* < *prae-*, before + *figere*, to FIX] to put before a word, name, etc.; esp., to add as a prefix —*n.* **1.** a syllable or group of syllables joined to the beginning of a word to change its meaning or make a new word [*pre-* is a prefix added to *cool* to form *precool*] **2.** a title before a person's name, as *Dr.* —**pre′fix·al** *adj.*

pre·flight (prē′flīt′) *adj.* coming before a flight or the flying of aircraft [*preflight* instructions]

pre·fron·tal (prē frunt′'l) *adj.* of or situated near the front of the brain or of the head of a vertebrate

preg·na·ble (preg′nə b'l) *adj.* [< MFr. < *prendre*, to take] that can be captured or attacked; vulnerable —**preg′na·bil′i·ty** *n.*

preg·nan·cy (preg′nən sē) *n., pl.* **-cies** the condition, quality, or period of being pregnant

preg·nant (preg′nənt) *adj.* [< L. *pregnans* < *prae-*, before + base of OL. *gnasci*, to be born: see NATURE] **1.** having (an) offspring developing in the uterus; with young or with child **2.** mentally fertile; full of ideas; inventive **3.** productive of results; fruitful [a *pregnant* year] **4.** full of meaning, significance, etc. [a *pregnant* silence] **5.** filled (*with*) or rich (*in*); abounding [a book *pregnant* with ideas] —**preg′nant·ly** *adv.*

pre·heat (prē hēt′) *vt.* to heat ahead of time [*preheat* the oven to 350° before putting in the roast]

pre·hen·sile (pri hen′s'l) *adj.* [< Fr. < L. pp. of *prehendere*, to grasp < IE. base *ghend-*] adapted for seizing or grasping, esp. by wrapping itself around something as a monkey's tail does —**pre·hen·sil·i·ty** (prē′hen sil′ə tē) *n.*

pre·his·tor·ic (prē′his tôr′ik, -tär′-) *adj.* of the period before recorded history [dinosaurs were *prehistoric* creatures]: also **pre′his·tor′i·cal** —**pre′his·tor′i·cal·ly** *adv.*

pre·judge (prē juj′) *vt.* **-judged′, -judg′ing** [< Fr. < L.: see PRE- & JUDGE] to judge beforehand or before one knows enough to judge fairly —**pre·judg′ment, pre·judge′ment** *n.*

prej·u·dice (prej′ə dis) *n.* [< MFr. < L. < *prae-*, before + *judicium*, judgment] **1.** an opinion formed before the facts are known, usually one that is unfavorable **2.** *a)* an opinion held while ignoring facts that disagree with it; unreasonable bias *b)* the holding of such opinions **3.** dislike or distrust of people just because they are of another race, religion, country, etc. **4.** harm resulting as from some judgment or action of another [he gave evidence to the *prejudice* of the defendant] —*vt.* **-diced, -dic·ing** **1.** to harm or damage, as by some judgment or action [one low grade *prejudiced* his chances for a scholarship] **2.** to

---

fat, āpe, cär; ten, ēven; is, bīte; gō, hôrn, too͞l, look; oil, out; up, fur; get; joy; yet; chin; she; thin, then; zh, leisure; ŋ, ring; ə for *a* in *ago*, *e* in *agent*, *i* in *sanity*, *o* in *comply*, *u* in *focus*; ′ as in *able* (ā′b'l); Fr. bál; ë, Fr. coeur; ö, Fr. feu; Fr. mon; ô, Fr. coq; ü, Fr. duc; r, Fr. cri; H, G. ich; kh, G. doch; ‡foreign; ☆ Americanism; < derived from. See inside front cover.

cause to have prejudice; bias [she *prejudiced* her sister against their aunt]

SYN.—prejudice implies an unfair or unreasonable opinion formed without knowing or caring about the facts and showing one's fear, suspicion, hatred, etc. of someone or something [a *prejudice* against foreigners; a *prejudice* against modern art]; **bias** implies a mental leaning in favor of or against someone or something [few of us are without *bias* of any kind]; **partiality** implies an inclination to favor a person or thing because of strong fondness or attachment [the conductor has a *partiality* for the works of Brahms]

prej·u·di·cial (prej′ə dish′əl) *adj.* causing prejudice, or harm; injurious; detrimental **—prej′u·di·cial·ly** *adv.*

prel·a·cy (prel′ə sē) *n., pl.* **-cies** 1. *a*) the office or rank of a prelate *b*) prelates as a group Also **prel′a·ture** (-chər) 2. church government by prelates: often a hostile term: also **prel′a·tism** (-it iz′m)

prel·ate (-it) *n.* [< OFr. < LL. < L. pp. of *praeferre*, to PREFER] a high-ranking clergyman, as a bishop **—prel′ate·ship′** *n.* — **pre·lat·ic** (pri lat′ik) *adj.*

pre·lim (prē′lim) *n.* [Slang] *clipped form of* PRELIMINARY **prelim.** preliminary

pre·lim·i·nar·y (pri lim′ə ner′ē) *adj.* [< Fr. or ModL. < L. *prae-*, before + *liminaris* < *limen*, threshold] leading up to the main action, business, etc.; introductory; preparatory [the *preliminary* matches before the main bout] **—n., pl.** **-nar′ies** 1. a preliminary step, procedure, etc. [when the *preliminaries* were over, the meeting began] 2. a preliminary examination 3. a contest before the main one **—pre·lim′i·nar′i·ly** *adv.*

pre·lit·er·ate (prē lit′ər it) *adj.* [PRE- + LITERATE] of or belonging to a society not developed to the stage of having a written language

prel·ude (prel′yood; prā′lood, prē′-) *n.* [< Fr. < ML. < L. < *prae-*, before + *ludere*, to play: see LUDICROUS] 1. a part that comes before or leads up to what follows [the calm was a *prelude* to the storm] 2. *Music a*) an introductory section of a suite, fugue, etc. *b*) since the 19th cent., any short, romantic composition **—vt., vi.** **-ud·ed, -ud·ing** 1. to serve as or be a prelude (to) 2. to introduce by or play (as) a prelude **—pre·lu·di·al** (prā lōō′dē əl, prē-) *adj.*

pre·mar·i·tal (prē mar′ə t'l) *adj.* before marriage

pre·ma·ture (prē′mə toor′, -choor′, -tyoor′) *adj.* [< L.: see PRE- & MATURE] happening, done, arriving, or existing before the proper or usual time; specif., born before the full period of pregnancy **—pre′ma·ture′ly** *adv.* **—pre′ma·tu′ri·ty, pre′ma·ture′ness** *n.*

☆**pre·med** (prē′med′) *adj. clipped form of* PREMEDICAL **—n.** a premedical student

pre·med·i·cal (prē med′i k'l) *adj.* designating or of the studies preparatory to the study of medicine

pre·med·i·tate (pri med′ə tāt′) *vt.* **-tat′ed, -tat′ing** to think out or plan beforehand [a *premeditated* murder] **—vi.** to meditate beforehand **—pre·med′i·tat′ed** *adj.* **—pre·med′i·tat′ed·ly** *adv.* **—pre·med′i·ta′tive** *adj.* **—pre·med′i·ta′tor** *n.*

pre·med·i·ta·tion (pri med′ə tā′shən, prē′med-) *n.* 1. a premeditating 2. *Law* enough planning and thinking ahead on one's part to show that one intended to do a particular thing, as commit a crime

pre·mier (pri mir′, -myir′; prē′mē ər) *adj.* [MFr. < L. *primarius* < *primus*, PRIME] 1. first in importance; chief 2. first in time **—n.** a chief official; specif., *the title of a*) the prime minister in certain countries *b*) the governor of a Canadian province **—pre·mier′ship** *n.*

pre·mière, pre·miere (pri myer′, -mir′, -mē er′) *n.* [Fr., fem. of *premier*: see prec.] a first performance of a play, movie, etc. **—adj.** 1. being the leading woman performer, as in ballet 2. *same as* PREMIER **—vt., vi.** **-mièred′** or **-miered′, -mièr′ing** or **-mier′ing** to exhibit (a play, movie, etc.) for the first time

prem·ise (prem′is; *for v. also*, pri miz′) *n.* [< ML. < L. pp. of *praemittere* < *prae-*, before + *mittere*, to send] 1. a statement or belief taken for granted and serving as a basis for an argument; specif., either of the two propositions of a syllogism from which the conclusion is drawn [the democratic *premise* that all citizens have equal rights]: also sp. **prem′iss** 2. [*pl.*] *a*) the part of a deed or lease that states the parties and property involved, etc. *b*) the property so mentioned 3. [*pl.*] a piece of real estate; building and its land [keep off the *premises*] **—vt.** **-ised, -is·ing** 1. to state as a premise 2. to preface with some explanation **—vi.** to make a premise

pre·mi·um (prē′mē əm, prēm′yəm) *n.* [< L. < *prae-*, before + *emere*, to take] 1. a reward or prize, esp. one offered free or at a special, low price as an added reason to buy or do something [a valuable *premium* inside the box] 2. an amount paid in ad-

dition to the regular charge, interest, wages, etc. [extra pay as a *premium* for risky work] 3. a payment, as for an insurance policy 4. very high value [to put a *premium* on honesty] 5. the amount by which one form of money exceeds another (of the same nominal value), as in exchange value **—adj.** rated as superior and higher in price [*premium* beers] **—at a premium** 1. at a value or price higher than normal 2. very valuable, as because hard to get

pre·mo·lar (prē mō′lər) *adj.* designating or of any bicuspid tooth in front of the molars **—n.** a premolar tooth

pre·mo·ni·tion (prē′mə nish′ən, prem′ə-) *n.* [< MFr. < LL. < L. < *prae-*, before + *monere*, to warn] 1. a warning in advance; forewarning 2. a feeling that something bad will happen; foreboding **—pre·mon·i·to·ry** (pri män′ə tôr′ē) *adj.*

pre·na·tal (prē nāt′'l) *adj.* [PRE- + NATAL] existing or taking place before birth **—pre·na′tal·ly** *adv.*

pre·nup·tial (prē nup′shəl, -chəl) *adj.* 1. before a marriage or wedding 2. *Zool.* before mating

pre·oc·cu·pa·tion (prē äk′yə pā′shən) *n.* a preoccupying or being preoccupied, esp. mentally: also **pre·oc′cu·pan·cy,** *pl.* **-cies**

pre·oc·cu·pied (-äk′yə pīd′) *adj.* 1. previously or already occupied 2. wholly occupied with or absorbed in one's thoughts; engrossed **—see SYN.** at ABSENT-MINDED

pre·oc·cu·py (-äk′yə pī′) *vt.* **-pied′, -py′ing** [< MFr. < L.: see PRE- & OCCUPY] 1. to occupy or take up completely the thoughts of; engross; absorb [he is *preoccupied* with vacation plans] 2. to occupy or take possession of before someone else or beforehand

pre·or·dain (prē′ôr dān′) *vt.* to ordain or decree beforehand **—pre′or·di·na′tion** (-d'n ā′shən) *n.*

prep (prep) *adj.* ☆[Colloq.] *clipped form of* PREPARATORY [a *prep* school] **—☆vi.** **prepped, prep′ping** [Colloq.] to prepare oneself by study, etc. **—vt.** to prepare (one) for something; specif., to prepare (a patient) as for surgery

prep. 1. preparation 2. preparatory 3. preposition

☆**pre·pack·age** (prē pak′ij) *vt.* **-aged, -ag·ing** to package (goods, esp. foods) in certain amounts or weights before selling

pre·paid (prē pād′) *pt. & pp. of* PREPAY

prep·a·ra·tion (prep′ə rā′shən) *n.* 1. a preparing or being prepared 2. something done to prepare, or get ready; preparatory measure 3. something prepared for a special purpose, as a medicine, cosmetic, etc.

pre·par·a·tive (pri par′ə tiv) *adj. same as* PREPARATORY **—n.** *same as* PREPARATION (sense 2, 3)

pre·par·a·to·ry (-tôr′ē) *adj.* 1. that prepares or serves to prepare; introductory [*preparatory* training] ☆2. undergoing preparation, esp. for college entrance [a *preparatory* student] **— pre·par′a·to′ri·ly** *adv.*

preparatory school a private secondary school for preparing students to enter college

pre·pare (pri par′, -per′) *vt.* **-pared′, -par′ing** [< MFr. < L. < *prae-*, before + *parare*, to get ready] 1. to make ready or suitable [to *prepare* ground for planting] 2. to make able to receive, take in, etc. [to *prepare* someone for bad news] 3. to equip or furnish; fit out [to *prepare* an expedition] 4. to put together or make out of parts or ingredients; compound [to *prepare* a dinner or a medicine] **—vi.** 1. to make things ready 2. to make oneself ready [to *prepare* for a test] **—pre·par′ed·ly** (-id lē) *adv.*

pre·par·ed·ness (-id nis) *n.* the state of being prepared, esp. for waging war, as by stockpiling weapons

pre·pay (prē pā′) *vt.* **-paid′, -pay′ing** to pay or pay for in advance **—pre·pay′ment** *n.*

pre·pense (pri pens′) *adj.* [< OFr. < *pur-*, pro- + *penser*, to think] planned beforehand; premeditated

pre·pon·der·ant (pri pän′dər ənt) *adj.* greater in amount, power, influence, etc.; predominant [the *preponderant* religion in a country] **—pre·pon′der·ance, pre·pon′der·an·cy** *n.* **— pre·pon′der·ant·ly** *adv.*

pre·pon·der·ate (-də rāt′) *vi.* **-at′ed, -at′ing** [< L. pp. of *praeponderare* < *prae-*, before + *ponderare*, to weigh < *pondus*, a weight] to be greater in amount, power, influence, etc.; predominate **—pre·pon′der·a′tion** *n.*

prep·o·si·tion (prep′ə zish′ən) *n.* [< L. < pp. of *praeponere* < *prae-*, before + *ponere*, to place] 1. a relation word, as *in, by, for, with, to,* etc., that connects a noun or pronoun, or a noun phrase, to another noun (the sound of rain), to a verb (he went *to* the store), or to an adjective (late *for* the tea party) 2. any construction having a similar use (Example: *in back of,* used for *behind*) **—prep′o·si′tion·al** *adj.* **—prep′o·si′tion·al·ly** *adv.*

prepositional phrase a preposition and its object

pre·pos·sess (prē'pə zes') *vt.* **1.** orig., to occupy beforehand or before another **2.** to preoccupy so as to keep out other thoughts, feelings, etc. **3.** to prejudice or bias **4.** to impress favorably at once —**pre'pos·ses'sion** *n.*

pre·pos·sess·ing (-iŋ) *adj.* that prepossesses, or impresses favorably; pleasing [a *prepossessing* manner] —**pre'pos·sess'·ing·ly** *adv.* —**pre'pos·sess'ing·ness** *n.*

pre·pos·ter·ous (pri päs'tər əs) *adj.* [< L. < *prae-*, before + *posterus*, coming after < *post*, after] so contrary to nature, common sense, etc. as to be laughable; absurd [the idea that the earth is flat now strikes us as *preposterous*] —see **SYN.** at ABSURD —**pre·pos'ter·ous·ly** *adv.* —**pre·pos'ter·ous·ness** *n.*

pre·puce (prē'pyōōs) *n.* [< MFr. < L. *praeputium*] the fold of skin covering the end of the penis; foreskin —**pre·pu'tial** (-pyōō'shəl) *adj.*

Pre-Raph·a·el·ite (prē raf'ē ə līt', -rä'fē-) *n.* **1.** a member of a society of artists (**Pre-Raphaelite Brotherhood**) formed in England in 1848 to revive the qualities of Italian art before Raphael **2.** any artist with similar aims —*adj.* of or like Pre-Raphaelites —**Pre-Raph'a·el·it'ism** *n.*

pre·re·cord (prē'ri kôrd') *vt.* *Radio & TV* to record (an announcement, program, etc.) in advance, for later broadcasting

pre·req·ui·site (pri rek'wə zit) *adj.* required beforehand, esp. as a necessary condition for something following —*n.* something prerequisite [mathematics is a *prerequisite* for a career in science]

pre·rog·a·tive (pri räg'ə tiv) *n.* [< MFr. < L. *praerogativa*, called upon to vote first, ult. < *prae-*, before + *rogare*, to ask] **1.** a prior or special privilege, esp. of a rank, class, etc. [most governors have the *prerogative* of pardoning prisoners] **2.** a superior advantage —*adj.* of or having a prerogative

Pres. **1.** Presbyterian: also **Presb.** **2.** President

pres. **1.** present **2.** presidency

pres·age (pres'ij; *for v., usually* pri sāj') *n.* [< MFr. < L. *prae-*, before + *sagire*, to perceive] **1.** a sign or warning of a future event; portent; omen **2.** a feeling that something is going to happen; something bad; foreboding **3.** foreshadowing quality [of ominous *presage*] —*vt.* **-aged', -ag'ing** **1.** to give a sign or warning of; portend [dark clouds *presaging* a storm] **2.** to have a foreboding of **3.** to predict or foretell (something) —*vi.* to make a prediction —see **SYN.** at FORETELL —**pres·ag'er** *n.*

pres·by·ter (prez'bi tər, pres'-) *n.* [LL.: see PRIEST] **1.** in the early Christian church and in the Presbyterian Church, an elder **2.** in the Episcopal Church, a priest or minister

pres·by·te·ri·al (prez'bə tir'ē əl, pres'-) *adj.* of or having to do with a presbyter or presbytery

pres·by·te·ri·an (prez'bə tir'ē ən, pres'-) *adj.* **1.** having to do with church government by presbyters **2.** [P-] designating or of a church of a Calvinistic Protestant denomination governed by presbyters, or elders —*n.* [P-] a member of a Presbyterian church —**Pres'by·te'ri·an·ism** *n.*

pres·by·ter·y (prez'bə ter'ē, pres'-) *n., pl.* **-ter'ies** **1.** *a)* in Presbyterian churches, a governing body made up of all the ministers and an equal number of elders from all the churches in a district *b)* such a district **2.** the part of a church reserved for the officiating clergy

pre·school (prē'skōōl') *adj.* designating, of, or for a child between infancy and school age, usually between the ages of two and five (or six) —**pre·school'er** *n.*

pre·sci·ence (prē'shē əns, presh'əns) *n.* [< OFr. < LL., ult. < L. *prae-*, before + *scire*, to know] apparent knowledge of things before they happen; foreknowledge —**pre'sci·ent** *adj.* —**pre'sci·ent·ly** *adv.*

Pres·cott (pres'kət), **William H**(ickling) 1796–1859; U.S. historian

pre·scribe (pri skrīb') *vt.* **-scribed', -scrib'ing** [< L. < *prae-*, before + *scribere*, to write] **1.** to set down as a rule or direction; order [the penalty *prescribed* by law] **2.** to order or advise as a medicine or treatment [the doctor *prescribed* an antibiotic and bed rest] —*vi.* **1.** to set down or impose rules **2.** to give medical advice or prescriptions —**pre·scrib'er** *n.*

pre·script (pri skript'; *also, and for n. always*, prē'skript) *adj.* prescribed —*n.* something prescribed; direction; rule

pre·scrip·tion (pri skrip'shən) *n.* **1.** a prescribing **2.** some-

thing prescribed; order, rule, or direction **3.** *a)* a doctor's written direction for the preparation and use of a medicine, the grinding of eyeglass lenses, etc. *b)* a medicine so prescribed —*adj.* made according to, or purchasable only with, a doctor's prescription [*prescription* lenses; a *prescription* drug] —**pre·scrip'·tive** *adj.* —**pre·scrip'tive·ly** *adv.*

pres·ence (prez''ns) *n.* **1.** the fact or condition of being present [his *presence* at the meeting] **2.** the place where a person is; immediate surroundings [admitted to his *presence*] **3.** one that is present, esp. a person of high station or imposing appearance **4.** *a)* a person's looks, manner, etc. [a man of stately *presence*] *b)* poised and confident bearing, as that of a performer before an audience (**stage presence**) **5.** a spirit or ghost felt to be present

presence of mind ability to think clearly and act quickly and intelligently in an emergency

pres·ent (prez''nt; *for v.* pri zent') *adj.* [OFr. < L. *praesens*, prp. of *praeesse* < *prae-*, before + *esse*, to be (see ESSENCE)] **1.** *a)* being at the specified place; in attendance [is everyone *present* today?] *b)* existing (*in* a particular thing) [nitrogen is *present* in the air] **2.** existing or happening now [my *present* needs are few] **3.** now being discussed, considered, etc. [the *present* writer] **4.** *Gram.* showing action as now taking place (he *goes*) or state as now existing (the plums *are* ripe), action that is habitual (he *speaks* with an accent), or action that is always true (two and two is four) —*n.* **1.** the present time [at *present*, I am in school] **2.** the present occasion **3.** *Gram.* the present tense or a verb in it **4.** [*pl.*] *Law* this very document [know by these *presents*] **5.** something presented, or given; gift [Christmas *presents*] —*vt.* [< L. *praesentare*, to place in the presence of < *praesens*: see the *adj.*] **1.** to introduce (a person *to* someone), esp. in a formal way **2.** to offer for viewing or notice; exhibit; show [to *present* a play on Broadway] **3.** to offer for consideration [to *present* a plan, an opportunity, etc.] **4.** *a)* to give as a gift, award, etc. [to *present* a trophy to the winner] *b)* to make a gift to [he *presented* the school with a piano] **5.** to hand over, send, etc. (a bill, credentials, etc.) to **6.** to point, direct, or aim (a weapon, etc.) —**present arms** *Mil.* **1.** to hold a rifle vertically in front of the body: a position of salute **2.** *a)* this position *b)* the command to assume it —**pre·sent'er** *n.*

SYN.—present and **gift** both refer to something given to show one's friendship, love, respect, concern, etc., as on certain occasions [a birthday *present*; *gifts* for graduates], but **gift** is the word preferred when the giving is more formal or public in nature [the painting was a *gift* to the museum]; **donation** applies to a gift of money, esp. as asked for in a public drive for funds [*donations* to charities; a *donation* to the orchestra fund] —see also **SYN.** at GIVE and OFFER

pre·sent·a·ble (pri zen'tə b'l) *adj.* **1.** that can be presented; fit to be shown, given, etc. to others [he's putting his talk in *presentable* form] **2.** properly dressed for meeting people —**pre·sent'a·bil'i·ty, pre·sent'a·ble·ness** *n.* —**pre·sent'a·bly** *adv.*

pre·sen·ta·tion (prē'zen tā'shən, prez''n-) *n.* **1.** a presenting or being presented [a *presentation* of awards] **2.** something presented, as a theatrical performance, a gift, etc. —**pre'sen·ta'tion·al** *adj.*

pres·ent-day (prez''nt dā') *adj.* of the present time

pre·sen·ti·ment (pri zen'tə mənt) *n.* [MFr. < L.: see PRE- & SENTIMENT] a feeling that something, esp. of an unfortunate nature, is about to take place; foreboding

pres·ent·ly (prez''nt lē) *adv.* **1.** in a little while; soon [I'll join you *presently*] **2.** at present; now [he is *presently* on vacation] **3.** [Archaic] instantly

pre·sent·ment (pri zent'mənt) *n.* **1.** *same as* PRESENTATION **2.** a grand-jury report of an offense based on the jury's own knowledge and observations and without their having received a bill of indictment

present participle a participle used: *a)* with helping verbs to show present or continuing action or state of being Example: *going* in "I am going" *b)* as an adjective Example: *going* in "a going concern"

present perfect **1.** a tense indicating an action or state as completed at the time of speaking but not at any definite time in the past **2.** a verb form in this tense (Example: has gone)

pres·er·va·tion (prez'ər vā'shən) *n.* a preserving or being preserved

pre·serv·a·tive (pri zur′və tiv) *adj.* preserving —*n.* anything that preserves; esp., a substance added to food to keep it from spoiling

pre·serve (pri zurv′) *vt.* **-served′, -serv′ing** [< MFr. < L. *prae-*, before + *servare*, to keep] **1.** to keep from harm, damage, etc.; protect; save [to *preserve* our national forests] **2.** to keep from spoiling or rotting **3.** to prepare (food), as by canning, salting, etc., for future use **4.** to keep up; maintain [to *preserve* liberty] —*vi.* to preserve fruit, etc. —*n.* **1.** [*usually pl.*] fruit preserved whole or in large pieces by cooking with sugar **2.** a place where game, fish, etc. are protected or kept for controlled hunting and fishing **3.** any area of activity or influence thought of as belonging to some person or group —see SYN. at DEFEND —**pre·serv′a·ble** *adj.* —**pre·serv′er** *n.*

pre·set (prē set′) *vt.* **-set′, -set′ting** to set (the controls of an automatic apparatus) beforehand

pre·shrunk (prē′shruŋk′) *adj.* shrunk by a special process in manufacture so as to reduce shrinkage in laundering or dry cleaning to a minimum

pre·side (pri zīd′) *vi.* **-sid′ed, -sid′ing** [< Fr. < L. *praesidere* < *prae-*, before + *sedere*, to SIT] **1.** to be in charge of an assembly or meeting; act as chairman [the Vice President *presides* over the U.S. Senate] **2.** to have authority, control, etc. (usually with *over*) —**pre·sid′er** *n.*

pres·i·den·cy (prez′i dən sē) *n., pl.* **-cies** **1.** the office, function, or term of president ☆**2.** [*often* P-] the office of President of the U.S.

pres·i·dent (prez′i dənt) *n.* [< MFr. < L. prp. of *praesidere:* see PRESIDE] ☆**1.** the highest executive officer of a company, society, university, club, etc. **2.** [*often* P-] the chief executive, or sometimes the formal head, of a republic **3.** any presiding officer —**pres′i·den′tial** (-den′shəl) *adj.* —**pres′i·den′tial·ly** *adv.*

☆**pres·i·dent-e·lect** (-i lekt′) *n.* an elected president who has not yet taken office

☆**pre·sid·i·o** (pri sid′ē ō′) *n., pl.* **-i·os** [Sp. < L. *praesidium*] a military post, esp. in the southwestern U.S.

pre·sid·i·um (pri sid′ē əm) *n., pl.* **-i·a** (-ə), **-i·ums** [< Russ. < L. *praesidium*, a presiding over] **1.** in the Soviet Union, *a)* any of a number of permanent administrative committees *b)* [P-] the permanent administrative committee of the Supreme Soviet **2.** [P-] a chief administrative committee as in Albania, Romania, etc.

pre·sig·ni·fy (prē sig′nə fī′) *vt.* **-fied′, -fy′ing** to indicate beforehand; foreshadow

press¹ (pres) *vt.* [< MFr. < L. *pressare* < *premere*, to press < IE. base *per-*, to strike] **1.** to act on with steady force or weight; push steadily against; squeeze [to *press* a doorbell] **2.** to squeeze (juice, etc.) from (grapes, etc.) **3.** *a)* to squeeze so as to make smooth, compact, etc.; compress *b)* to iron (clothes, etc.) with a heavy iron or a steam machine **4.** to embrace closely [he *pressed* the child in his arms] **5.** to force; compel; constrain **6.** to keep on asking or urging [the store *pressed* her for the money she owed] **7.** to try to force acceptance of [she *pressed* the gift on us] **8.** to lay stress on; emphasize [he kept on *pressing* his point] **9.** to distress or trouble [to be *pressed* for time] **10.** to urge on **11.** to shape (a phonograph record, plastic item, etc.), using a form **12.** [Archaic] to crowd; throng **13.** [Obs.] *same as* OPPRESS —*vi.* **1.** to exert pressure; specif., *a)* to weigh down; bear heavily *b)* to go forward with determined effort [the soldiers *pressed* on through the night] *c)* to force one's way *d)* to crowd; throng [thousands *pressed* into the arena] *e)* to be urgent or insistent *f)* to try too hard **2.** to iron clothes, etc. **3.** to undergo pressing in a specified way —*n.* **1.** a pressing or being pressed; pressure, urgency, etc. [the *press* of business kept him away for a time] **2.** a crowd; throng **3.** an instrument or machine by which something is crushed, stamped, smoothed, etc. by pressure [a cider *press*] **4.** the condition of clothes as to smoothness, creases, etc. after pressing **5.** *a)* shortened form of PRINTING PRESS *b)* a printing or publishing establishment *c)* the art or business of printing *d)* newspapers, magazines, etc. or the persons who write for them *e)* publicity, criticism, etc., as in newspapers [to receive a bad *press*] **6.** an upright closet for clothes, etc. —see SYN. at URGE —**go to press** to start to be printed —**press′er** *n.*

press² (pres) *vt.* [altered (after prec.) < obs. *prest*, to enlist for military service by advance pay < OFr., ult. < L. *praes*, surety + *stare*, to stand] **1.** to force into service, esp. military or naval service **2.** to use in a way different from the ordinary, esp. in an emergency

☆**press agent** a person whose work is to get publicity for an individual, organization, etc. —**press′-a′gent·ry** *n.*

☆**press box** a place reserved for reporters at sports events, etc.

☆**press conference** an interview granted to a group of newsmen as by a celebrity or personage

press gang [for *prest gang:* see PRESS²] a group of men who round up other men and force them into military or naval service: also **press′gang′** *n.*

press·ing (pres′iŋ) *adj.* calling for immediate attention; urgent [a *pressing* problem] —*n.* something stamped, squeezed, etc. with a press, often a series or one of a series of identical articles [a *pressing* of phonograph records] —**press′ing·ly** *adv.*

press·man (pres′mən) *n., pl.* **-men** **1.** an operator of a printing press **2.** [Brit.] a newspaperman

press of sail (or **canvas**) the maximum amount of sail that a ship can safely carry under given conditions

pres·sure (presh′ər) *n.* [OFr. < L. *pressura* < pp. of *premere*, to PRESS¹] **1.** a pressing or being pressed; force of pushing or of weight; compression; squeezing [the *pressure* of the foot on the brake] **2.** a state of trouble or strain that is hard to bear [overcome by the *pressure* of his grief] **3.** a feeling as though a part of the body is being compressed **4.** influence or force to make someone do something [social *pressure*] **5.** pressing demands; urgency [a news story written under *pressure* of time] **6.** shortened form of: *a)* AIR PRESSURE *b)* BLOOD PRESSURE **7.** *Physics* the force distributed over a surface, expressed in units of force per unit of area —*vt.* **-sured, -sur·ing** ☆to exert pressure, or compelling influence, on [they were *pressured* into agreeing to the proposal]

☆**pressure cooker** an airtight container for quick cooking by steam under pressure —**pres′sure-cook′** *vt.*

pressure gauge a gauge for measuring the pressure of steam, water, gas, etc.

pressure group any group putting pressure on legislators and the public through lobbies, propaganda, etc. to influence legislation, etc.

pressure point any of a number of points on the body where pressure on an artery will stop bleeding from an injured part

pres·sur·ize (presh′ər īz′) *vt.* **-ized′, -iz′ing** **1.** to keep nearly normal air pressure inside of (an airplane, spacesuit, etc.), as at high altitudes **2.** to put under high pressure —**pres′sur·i·za′tion** *n.* —**pres′sur·iz′er** *n.*

press·work (pres′wurk′) *n.* **1.** the operation of a printing press **2.** work done by a printing press

pres·ti·dig·i·ta·tion (pres′tə dij′i tā′shən) *n.* [Fr. < *preste* < It. *presto*, quick + L. *digitus*, a finger] the doing of tricks by quick, skillful use of the hands; sleight of hand —**pres′ti·dig′i·ta′tor** *n.*

pres·tige (pres tēzh′, -tēj′) *n.* [Fr. < LL. *praestigium*, illusion, ult. < L. *praestringere*, to blind] **1.** the power to impress or influence, as because of success, wealth, etc. **2.** reputation based on high achievement, character, etc. —**pres·tige′ful, pres·ti′gious** (-tij′əs, -tē′jəs) *adj.*

pres·tis·si·mo (pres tis′ə mō′) *adv., adj.* [It., superl. of PRESTO] *Music* very fast —*n., pl.* **-mos′** a prestissimo passage or movement

pres·to (pres′tō) *adv., adj.* [It., quick < L. *praestus*, ready] **1.** fast **2.** *Music* in fast tempo —*n., pl.* **-tos** *Music* a presto passage or movement

☆**pre·stressed concrete** (prē′strest′) concrete containing steel cables, wires, etc. under tension to produce compressive stress and lend greater strength

pre·sum·a·ble (pri zoōm′ə b'l, -zyoōm′-) *adj.* that may be presumed, or taken for granted; probable —**pre·sum′a·bly** *adv.*

pre·sume (pri zoōm′, -zyoōm′) *vt.* **-sumed′, -sum′ing** [< OFr. < L. < *prae-*, before + *sumere*, to take] **1.** to take upon oneself without permission or authority; dare (to say or do something); venture [I wouldn't *presume* to tell you what to do] **2.** to take for granted, lacking proof; suppose [I *presume* you know the risk you are taking] **3.** to serve as reasonable evidence for supposing [a signed invoice *presumes* receipt of goods] —*vi.* **1.** to act too boldly; take liberties **2.** to rely too much (*on* or *upon*), as in taking liberties [to *presume* on another's friendship] —**pre·sum′ed·ly** *adv.* —**pre·sum′ing·ly** *adv.* —**pre·sum′er** *n.*

SYN.—**presume** implies a taking something for granted or accepting it as true, usually on the basis of probable evidence in its favor and the absence of proof against it [the man is *presumed* to be of sound mind]; **presuppose** suggests a taking something for granted without good reason [this writer *presupposes* too large a vocabulary in children]; **assume** implies the taking of something for granted as a basis for argument or action [let us *assume* his motives were good]; **postulate** implies the assuming of something as an underlying factor, often something that cannot be proved [his argument *postulates* the natural goodness of man]

pre·sump·tion (pri zump′shən) *n.* **1.** a presuming; specif., *a)* an overstepping of proper bounds; effrontery [his *presumption* in ordering us to leave] *b)* a taking of something for granted **2.** the thing presumed; supposition [because of the dark clouds, the *presumption* is that it will rain] **3.** a ground or reason for presuming **4.** *Law* the inference that a fact exists, based on other known facts

pre·sump·tive (-tiv) *adj.* **1.** giving reasonable ground for belief [*presumptive* evidence] **2.** based on probability; presumed [an heir *presumptive*] —**pre·sump′tive·ly** *adv.*

pre·sump·tu·ous (-choo wəs) *adj.* too bold or forward; overstepping proper bounds; showing presumption —**pre·sump′tu·ous·ly** *adv.* —**pre·sump′tu·ous·ness n.**

pre·sup·pose (prē′sə pōz′) *vt.* **-posed′, -pos′ing** **1.** to suppose or assume beforehand; take for granted [let's *presuppose* that we win the game] **2.** to require or imply as a condition coming beforehand [an effect *presupposes* a cause] —see **SYN.** at PRESUME —**pre′sup·po·si′tion** (-sup ə zish′ən) *n.*

pret. preterit

☆**pre·teen** (prē′tēn′) *n.* a child nearly a teen-ager

pre·tend (pri tend′) *vt.* [< MFr. < L. < *prae-*, before + *tendere*, to stretch: see TEND²] **1.** to claim; profess [I don't *pretend* to know much on the subject] **2.** to claim or profess falsely; feign [to *pretend* illness] **3.** to make believe, as in play [to *pretend* to be astronauts] —*vi.* **1.** to lay claim (with *to*) [to *pretend* to a throne] **2.** to make believe in play or deception [let's stop *pretending*] —*adj.* [Colloq.] make-believe [*pretend* jewelry] —**pre·tend′ed adj.**

pre·tend·er (-ten′dər) *n.* **1.** a person who pretends **2.** a person who lays claim to something, esp. to a throne

pre·tense (pri tens′, prē′tens) *n.* [< Anglo-Fr., ult. < L. pp. of *praetendere*: see PRETEND] **1.** a claim; pretension [making no *pretense* to being rich] **2.** a false claim or profession [a *pretense* of friendship] **3.** a false show of something [a *pretense* of being ill] **4.** a pretending, as at play; make-believe **5.** a pretext **6.** a showing off; pretentiousness [a simple person, without *pretense*] Also, Brit. sp., **pretence.**

pre·ten·sion (pri ten′shən) *n.* [< ML. < L.: see prec.] **1.** a false claim or excuse **2.** a claim, as to a right, title, distinction, etc. [*pretensions* to the championship] **3.** declaration of a claim **4.** a showing off; pretentiousness

pre·ten·tious (-shəs) *adj.* [< Fr.] **1.** claiming or pretending to be more important, elegant, etc. than is really so [a *pretentious* person] **2.** affectedly grand; ostentatious [a *pretentious* house] —**pre·ten′tious·ly** *adv.* —**pre·ten′tious·ness n.**

pret·er·it, pret·er·ite (pret′ər it) *adj.* [< MFr. < L. pp. of *praeterire* < *praeter-*, beyond + *ire*, to go] *Gram.* expressing past action or state —*n.* **1.** the past tense **2.** a verb in the past tense

pre·ter·mit (prē′tər mit′) *vt.* **-mit′ted, -mit′ting** [< L. < *praeter-*, beyond + *mittere*, to send] **1.** to leave out or undone; neglect or omit **2.** to let pass unnoticed; overlook —**pre′ter·mis′sion n.**

pre·ter·nat·u·ral (prē′tər nach′ər əl) *adj.* [< ML. < L. *praeter-*, beyond + *naturalis*, natural] **1.** differing from or beyond what is natural; abnormal [*preternatural* strength] **2.** same as SUPERNATURAL —**pre′ter·nat′u·ral·ism n.** —**pre′ter·nat′u·ral·ly adv.**

pre·test (prē′test′; *for v.* prē′test′) *n.* a test of a product, etc. before making it available for use —*vt., vi.* to test in advance

pre·text (prē′tekst) *n.* [< L. pp. of *praetexere*, to pretend: see PRE- & TEXTURE] **1.** a false reason or motive put forth to hide the real one; excuse [she was bored but left on the *pretext* of being ill] **2.** a cover-up; front [the pool hall is only a *pretext* for the gambling operation]

pre·tor (prēt′ər) *n.* same as PRAETOR —**pre·to·ri·al** (pri tôr′ē-əl) *adj.* —**pre·to′ri·an adj., n.**

Pre·to·ri·a (pri tôr′ē ə) capital of the Transvaal & the seat of the government of South Africa: pop. 493,000

pre·tri·al (prē′trī′əl) *adj.* occurring, presented, etc. before a court trial begins [a *pretrial* motion]

pret·ti·fy (prit′ē fī′) *vt.* **-fied′, -fy′ing** to make pretty

pret·ty (prit′ē, pur′tē) *adj.* **-ti·er, -ti·est** [< OE. *prættig*, crafty < *prætt*, a trick] **1.** pleasing or attractive, esp. in a delicate, dainty, or graceful way [a *pretty* girl; a *pretty* voice; a *pretty* garden] **2.** *a)* fine; nice: often used ironically [a *pretty* fix] *b)* skillful in a clever way [a *pretty* move] **3.** [Colloq.] considerable; quite large [a *pretty* price] —*adv.* **1.** fairly; somewhat; quite [*pretty* sure] **2.** [Colloq.] prettily [to talk *pretty*] —*n., pl.* **-ties** a pretty person or thing —*vt.* **-tied, -ty·ing** to make pretty (usually with *up*) —see **SYN.** at BEAUTIFUL —☆**sitting pretty** [Slang] in a favorable position —**pret′ti·ly** *adv.* —**pret′ti·ness n.** —**pret′ty·ish adj.**

☆**pret·zel** (pret′s'l) *n.* [G. *brezel* < OHG., ult. < L. *brachium*, an arm] a hard, brittle biscuit usually in the form of a loose knot or a stick, sprinkled with salt

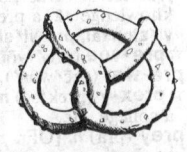

PRETZEL

pre·vail (pri vāl′) *vi.* [< L. < *prae-*, before + *valere*, to be strong: see VALUE] **1.** to gain the advantage or mastery; be victorious (*over* or *against*) [to *prevail* over an enemy] **2.** to be effective; succeed **3.** to be or become stronger or more widespread; predominate [his ideas *prevail* in the group] **4.** to exist widely; be prevalent, as a custom or practice —**prevail on** (or **upon, with**) to persuade; induce —see **SYN.** at PERSUADE

pre·vail·ing (-iŋ) *adj.* **1.** superior in strength, influence, or effect [*prevailing* winds] **2.** most frequent; predominant **3.** widely existing; prevalent [a *prevailing* style] —**pre·vail′ing·ly adv.**

SYN.—**prevailing** applies to that which leads all others in being accepted, used, believed, etc. at a given time and in a given place [the *prevailing* religion in Spain]; **prevalent** implies widespread occurrence or acceptance but not to a greater degree than others [*prevalent* customs]; **current** refers to that which is commonly used, known, or accepted at the present time or at some specified time [*current* styles in dress]; **rife** applies to that which has spread rapidly and is causing excitement or alarm [rumors about the plague were *rife*]

prev·a·lent (prev′ə lənt) *adj.* [see PREVAIL] **1.** [Rare] dominant **2.** widely existing, practiced, or accepted; common [a *prevalent* belief] —see **SYN.** at PREVAILING —**prev′a·lence n.** —**prev′a·lent·ly adv.**

pre·var·i·cate (pri var′ə kāt′) *vi.* **-cat′ed, -cat′ing** [< L. pp. of *praevaricari*, lit., to walk crookedly < *prae-*, before + *vari·care*, to straddle, ult. < *varus*, bent] **1.** to turn aside from, or try to hide, the truth; equivocate **2.** to tell an untruth; lie —see **SYN.** at LIE² —**pre·var′i·ca′tion n.** —**pre·var′i·ca′tor n.**

pre·vent (pri vent′) *vt.* [< L. pp. of *praevenire* < *prae-*, before + *venire*, to come: for IE. base see BASIS] **1.** to stop or keep (*from* doing something) [a storm *prevented* us from going] **2.** to keep from happening; make impossible by earlier action; hinder [careful driving *prevents* accidents] —**pre·vent′a·ble, pre·vent′i·ble adj.** —**pre·vent′er n.**

SYN.—**prevent** implies a stopping or keeping from happening, as by some earlier action or by putting an obstacle or hindrance in the way [to *prevent* disease]; **forestall** suggests the stopping of a particular thing that is about to happen by making some clever or shrewd move [to *forestall* a vote on the question by sending it back to committee]; **preclude** implies a making impossible by shutting off every possibility of occurrence [locked doors *precluded* his escape]; **obviate** suggests the preventing of some unfavorable outcome by taking the necessary actions beforehand [his frankness *obviated* objections]; **avert** suggests a taking action just in time to keep away danger or misfortune [diplomacy can *avert* war] —**ANT.** permit, allow

pre·ven·tion (pri ven′shən) *n.* **1.** a preventing [*prevention* of crime] **2.** [Now Rare] a means of preventing; preventive

pre·ven·tive (pri ven′tiv) *adj.* preventing or used to prevent; esp., preventing disease [*preventive* medicine] —*n.* anything that prevents disease, trouble, etc. Also **pre·vent′a·tive** —**pre·ven′tive·ly adv.** —**pre·ven′tive·ness n.**

pre·view (prē′vyoo) *vt.* to view or show beforehand —*n.* ☆**1.** a previous or preliminary view or survey ☆**2.** *a)* an advance showing, as of a movie, before exhibition to the public generally *b)* a showing of scenes from a movie, TV show, etc. to advertise it

pre·vi·ous (prē′vē əs) *adj.* [< L. < *prae-*, before + *via*, a way] **1.** occurring before in time or order; earlier [at a *previous* meeting; on the *previous* page] ☆**2.** [Colloq.] too soon; premature —**previous to** before —**pre′vi·ous·ly adv.**

SYN.—**previous** generally implies a coming before in time or order [a *previous* meeting]; **prior** adds to this the idea of greater importance or claim as a result of being first [a *prior* obligation]; **preceding,** esp. when used with the definite article, implies a coming just before [the *preceding* night]; **antecedent** adds to the meaning of **previous** the idea of directly causing what follows [events *antecedent* to the war]; **foregoing** applies specif. to something previously said or written [the *foregoing* examples]; **former** always implies comparison between the first and the last (called *latter*) of two persons or things just mentioned —**ANT.** following

previous question a motion made to bring the question under consideration by a group to an immediate vote without further debate

pre·vi·sion (prē vizh′ən) *n.* [< Fr. < ML. < L. pp. of *praevidere* < *prae-*, before + *videre*, to see] **1.** foresight or foreknowledge **2.** a prediction or prophecy —*vt.* to foresee —**pre·vi′sion·al, pre·vi′sion·ar′y** *adj.*

☆**pre·vue** (prē′vyōō) *n.* same as PREVIEW (esp. sense 2)

pre·war (prē′wôr′) *adj.* before a (or the) war

☆**prex·y** (prek′sē) *n., pl.* **prex′ies** [Slang] the president, esp. of a college, etc.

prey (prā) *n.* [OFr. *preie* < L. *praeda*: for IE. base see PREHENSILE] **1.** orig., plunder; booty **2.** an animal hunted for food by another animal **3.** a person or thing that falls victim to someone or something **4.** the way of living by preying on other animals [a bird of *prey*] —*vi.* **1.** to plunder; rob [the pirates *preyed* upon helpless ships] **2.** to hunt other animals for food **3.** to profit by cheating [swindlers *prey* on foolish people] **4.** to have a wearing or harmful influence [debts *prey* upon my mind] Generally used with *on* or *upon* —**prey′er** *n.*

Pri·am (prī′əm) *Gr. Legend* the last king of Troy, who reigned during the Trojan War: father of Hector and Paris

pri·ap·ic (prī ap′ik) *adj.* [< PRIAPUS + -IC] **1.** same as PHALLIC **2.** overly concerned with one's virility

Pri·a·pus (prī ā′pəs) [L. < Gr.] *Gr. & Rom. Myth.* the god personifying male sexual potency

Prib·i·lof Islands (prib′ə läf′) group of four Alaskan islands in the Bering Sea, north of the Aleutian Islands

price (prīs) *n.* [< OFr. < L. *pretium*: for IE. base see FAR] **1.** the amount of money, etc. asked or paid for something; cost **2.** value or worth [a painting of great *price*] **3.** a reward for the capture or death of a person [a *price* on his head] **4.** the cost, as in life, labor, etc., of obtaining some benefit [he gained success at the *price* of his health] —*vt.* **priced, pric′ing** **1.** to put a price on; fix the price of [the rug was *priced* at $10] **2.** [Colloq.] to ask or find out the price of [he *priced* all the models before he bought a car] —**at any price** no matter what the cost —**beyond** (or **without**) **price** priceless; invaluable —**price out of the market** to force (oneself or one's product) out of competition by charging prices that are too high —**pric′er** *n.*

price control the setting of ceiling prices on basic commodities by a government, as to fight inflation

price index see INDEX (sense 5 *b*)

price·less (prīs′lis) *adj.* **1.** too valuable to be measured by price [a *priceless* painting] **2.** [Colloq.] very amusing or absurd [the little boy said something *priceless*]

☆**price support** support of certain price levels at or above market values, esp. by government action

prick (prik) *n.* [OE. *prica*, a dot] **1.** a very small hole or dot made by a sharp point **2.** [Archaic] a pointed object, as a thorn **3.** a pricking [a *prick* of a pin] **4.** a sharp pain caused as by being pricked —*vt.* **1.** to make (a tiny hole) in (something) with a sharp point **2.** to pain sharply [*pricked* by remorse] **3.** to mark by dots, points, or small holes [to *prick* a design in leather] **4.** to cause to point or stick up (with *up*) [the dog *pricked* up his ears] **5.** [Archaic] to goad —*vi.* **1.** to cause or feel a slight, sharp pain **2.** to point or stick up: said esp. of ears —**prick up one's ears** to listen closely —**prick′er** *n.*

prick·le (prik′'l) *n.* [OE. *pricel* < base of *prica*, prick] **1.** any sharp point; specif., a small, sharp point growing out of the stem on a plant **2.** a prickly sensation; tingling —*vt.* **-led, -ling** **1.** to prick as with a thorn **2.** to cause to feel a tingling sensation —*vi.* to tingle

prick·ly (-lē) *adj.* **-li·er, -li·est** **1.** full of prickles **2.** stinging; tingling —**prick′li·ness** *n.*

☆**prickly heat** an itching skin disease with small rashes caused by inflammation of the sweat glands

☆**prickly pear** **1.** any of various cactus plants, some of which have barbed spines **2.** its pear-shaped, edible fruit

pride (prīd) *n.* [OE. *pryte* < *prut*, PROUD] **1.** *a)* an overhigh opinion of oneself; exaggerated self-esteem [his *pride* blinded him to his own faults] *b)* haughty behavior resulting from this; arrogance **2.** a sense of one's own dignity; self-respect [he has too much *pride* to go begging] **3.** delight or satisfaction in

one's own or another's achievements, etc. [he takes *pride* in his cabinetmaking] **4.** a person or thing that one is proud of [he is his mother's *pride*] **5.** the best of a class, group, etc.; pick **6.** the best part; prime [in the *pride* of manhood] **7.** *a)* a group or family (of lions) *b)* [Colloq.] any impressive group —*vt.* **prid′ed, prid′ing** [Rare] to make proud —see SYN. at GROUP —**pride oneself on** to be proud of —**pride′ful** *adj.* —**pride′ful·ly** *adv.* —**pride′ful·ness** *n.*

prie-dieu (prē′dyōō′) *n.* [Fr. < *prier*, to pray + *dieu*, God] a narrow, upright frame with a ledge for kneeling on at prayer and an upper ledge, as for a book

pri·er (prī′ər) *n.* a person who pries

priest (prēst) *n.* [OE. *preost* < LL. *presbyter*, an elder < Gr. < *presbys*, old < IE. base *per-* (see FAR) + *gwow-*, ox (see BEEF): hence, orig., lead-ox] **1.** a person of special rank who performs religious rites in a temple of God or a god **2.** in some Christian churches, a clergyman authorized to administer the sacraments **3.** any clergyman —**priest′hood** *n.*

PRIE-DIEU

priest·ess (prēs′tis) *n.* a girl or woman priest, esp. of a pagan religion

Priest·ley (prēst′lē), **Joseph** 1733–1804; Eng. scientist & theologian: discoverer of oxygen

priest·ly (prēst′lē) *adj.* **-li·er, -li·est** of, like, or suitable for a priest or priests —**priest′li·ness** *n.*

prig (prig) *n.* [< 16th-c. slang] an annoying person who is very proper and acts as though he were better than others in manners, morals, etc. —**prig′ger·y, prig′gism** *n.* —**prig′gish** *adj.* —**prig′gish·ly** *adv.* —**prig′gish·ness** *n.*

prim (prim) *adj.* **prim′mer, prim′mest** [< ? MFr. *prim*, prime, sharp, neat < L. *primus*, first] stiffly formal, precise, moral, etc.; proper, prudish, prissy, etc. —*vt., vi.* **primmed, prim′ming** to get a prim look on (one's face or mouth) —**prim′ly** *adv.* —**prim′ness** *n.*

prim. **1.** primary **2.** primitive

pri·ma ballerina (prē′mə) [It., lit., first ballerina] the leading woman dancer in a ballet company

pri·ma·cy (prī′mə sē) *n., pl.* **-cies** [< MFr. < ML. < LL. *primas*: see PRIMATE] **1.** the state of being first in time, order, rank, etc. **2.** the rank or authority of a primate in a church

pri·ma don·na (prē′mə dän′ə, prim′ə) *pl.* **pri′ma don′nas** [It., lit., first lady] **1.** the most important woman singer, as in an opera **2.** [Colloq.] a very conceited, excitable person; esp., such a woman

pri·ma fa·ci·e (prī′mə fā′shi ē′, fā′shē) [L.] at first sight: used to describe legal evidence (**prima facie evidence**) that is enough to establish a fact unless proved wrong

pri·mal (prī′m'l) *adj.* [< ML. < L. *primus*, first] **1.** first in time; original **2.** first in importance; chief

☆**pri·ma·quine** (prī′mə kwēn′) *n.* a synthetic chemical compound, $C_{15}H_{21}N_3O$, used as a cure for malaria

pri·ma·ri·ly (prī mer′ə lē, prī′mer′-) *adv.* **1.** at first; originally [*primarily* honest, he was in time çorrupted] **2.** for the most part; mainly [a concert *primarily* for children]

pri·ma·ry (prī′mer′ē, -mər ē) *adj.* [< L. *primarius* < *primus*, first] **1.** *a)* first in time or order of development; primitive; original [the *primary* instinct of suckling in newborn mammals] *b)* first in a series or succession [the *primary* grades in school] **2.** *a)* from which others are derived; fundamental; basic [the *primary* design in a line of prefabricated houses] *b)* designating colors regarded as basic, from which all others are formed: see COLOR (*n.* 2 & 3) **3.** first in importance; chief; principal [our *primary* concern] **4.** firsthand; direct [a *primary* source of information] **5.** *Elec.* designating or of an inducing current, input circuit, or input coil in a transformer, etc. **6.** *Zool.* of the large feathers on the end joint of a bird's wing —*n., pl.* **-ries** **1.** something first in order, quality, importance, etc. ☆**2.** in the U.S., *a)* a local meeting of voters of a given political party to nominate candidates for public office, etc. *b)* same as DIRECT PRIMARY ELECTION **3.** any of the primary colors **4.** *Elec.* a primary coil **5.** *Zool.* a primary feather

primary accent (or **stress**) **1.** the heavier stress or force given to one syllable in a spoken word or to one word in a series of spoken words **2.** the mark to show this (′)

primary cell a battery cell whose energy comes from an electro-chemical reaction that cannot be reversed: such a cell is not rechargeable

primary school same as ELEMENTARY SCHOOL

pri·mate (prī′māt; *also, for 1,* -mit) *n.* [< OFr. < LL. *primatis,* genitive of *primas,* chief < L. *primus,* first: see PRIME] **1.** an archbishop, or the highest-ranking bishop in a province, etc. **2.** any of an order of mammals, including man, the apes, monkeys, lemurs, etc. —**pri′mate·ship′** *n.* —**pri·ma·tial** (prī mā′shəl) *adj.*

prime (prīm) *adj.* [MFr. < L. *primus,* first < OL. *pri,* before: for IE. base see FAR] **1.** first in time; original; primitive **2.** first in rank; chief [*prime* minister] **3.** first in importance; principal [a *prime* advantage] **4.** first in quality; first-rate [*prime* beef] **5.** from which others are derived; fundamental **6.** *Finance* designating the most favorable interest rate on bank loans **7.** *Math. a)* of or being a prime number *b)* having no factor in common except 1 [9 and 16 are *prime* to each other] —*n.* [OE. *prim* < L. *prima* (*hora*), first (hour): see the *adj.*] **1.** [*often* P-] the canonical hour that follows lauds **2.** the first or earliest part; dawn, springtime, youth, etc. **3.** *a)* the best or most vigorous period or stage of a person or thing [an athlete in his *prime*] *b)* the best part; pick **4.** a mark (′) used to indicate minutes of a degree, feet in a measure of length, etc.: it is also used to distinguish a letter, etc. from another of the same kind, as A′ **5.** *Math.* same as PRIME NUMBER **6.** *Music* same as UNISON —*vt.* **primed, prim′ing 1.** to make ready; prepare **2.** to prepare (a gun) for firing or (a charge) for exploding by providing with priming or a primer **3.** *a)* to get (a pump) to work by pouring in water *b)* to get (an empty carburetor) to work by pouring in gasoline **4.** to undercoat, size, etc. (a surface) for painting **5.** to provide (a person) beforehand with information, answers, etc. —*vi.* to prime a person or thing —**prime′ness** *n.*

prime meridian the meridian from which longitude is measured both east and west; 0° longitude: see GREENWICH TIME

prime minister in parliamentary governments, the chief executive and, usually, head of the cabinet —**prime ministry**

prime number an integer that can be evenly divided by no other whole number than itself and 1, as 2, 3, 5, or 7

prim·er¹ (prim′ər; *Brit.* prī′mər) *n.* [< ML. < L. *primus,* first: see PRIME] **1.** a simple book for first teaching children to read **2.** a textbook giving the first principles of any subject

prim·er² (prī′mər) *n.* a person or thing that primes; specif., *a)* a small cap, tube, etc. containing an explosive, used to set off the main charge *b)* a first coat of paint, sizing, etc.

prime ribs a choice cut of beef consisting of the seven ribs immediately before the loin

☆**prime time** *Radio & TV* the hours, esp. the evening hours, when the largest audience is readily available

pri·me·val (prī mē′v'l) *adj.* [< L. *primaevus* (< *primus,* first + *aevum,* an age) + -AL] of the earliest times or ages; primordial —**pri·me′val·ly** *adv.*

prim·ing (prī′miŋ) *n.* **1.** the gunpowder or other explosive used to set off the charge in a gun, etc. **2.** paint, sizing, etc. used as a primer

prim·i·tive (prim′ə tiv) *adj.* [< MFr. < L. *primitivus* < *primus,* first: see PRIME] **1.** of or existing in the earliest times or ages; original [some *primitive* peoples worshiped the sun] **2.** *a)* like that of earliest times [*primitive* art] *b)* crude, simple, etc. [*primitive* sanitary facilities] **3.** not derivative; primary [the *primitive* source of knowledge] —*n.* **1.** a primitive person or thing **2.** *a)* an artist or a work of art of an early culture *b)* an artist or a work of art characterized by lack of formal training —**prim′i·tive·ly** *adv.* —**prim′i·tive·ness** *n.*

prim·i·tiv·ism (-iz'm) *n.* **1.** belief in or practice of primitive ways, living, etc. **2.** the qualities, etc. of primitive art or artists —**prim′i·tiv·ist** *n., adj.*

pri·mo·gen·i·tor (prī′mō jen′i tər) *n.* [LL. < L. *primus,* first + *genitor,* a father] **1.** an ancestor; forefather **2.** the earliest ancestor of a family, race, etc.

pri·mo·gen·i·ture (-chər) *n.* [< ML. < L. *primus,* first + *genitura,* a begetting] **1.** the condition or fact of being the firstborn of the same parents **2.** *Law* the right of the eldest son to inherit his father's complete estate

pri·mor·di·al (prī môr′dē əl) *adj.* [< LL. < L. *primordium,* the beginning < *primus,* first + *ordiri,* to begin] **1.** existing at or from the beginning; primitive **2.** fundamental; original —**pri·mor′di·al·ly** *adv.*

primp (primp) *vt., vi.* [prob. extension of PRIM] to groom or dress up in a fussy way

prim·rose (prim′rōz′) *n.* [< MFr. altered (after *rose,* ROSE¹) < OFr. *primerole* < ML. *primula* < L. *primus,* first] **1.** any of a number of related plants having variously colored, tubelike flowers: also **prim′u·la** (-yoo lə) **2.** the flower of any of these plants **3.** the light yellow of some primroses —*adj.* **1.** of the primrose **2.** light-yellow

primrose path [see *Hamlet* I, iii] the path of pleasure, self-indulgence, etc.

prin. 1. principal **2.** principle

prince (prins) *n.* [OFr. < L. *princeps,* chief < *primus* (see PRIME) + *capere,* to take] **1.** orig., any male monarch; esp., a king **2.** a ruler whose rank is below that of a king; head of a principality **3.** a nonruling male member of some royal families **4.** in Great Britain, a son or grandson of the sovereign ☆**5.** *a)* a very important person in any group [a merchant *prince*] *b)* [Colloq.] a fine, generous, helpful fellow —**prince′dom** *n.*

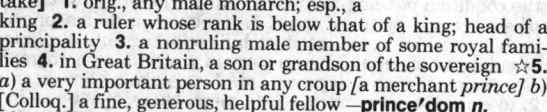
PRIMROSE

Prince Albert ☆ a long, double-breasted frock coat

prince consort the husband of a queen or empress ruling in her own right

Prince Edward Island island province of SE Canada, in the Gulf of St. Lawrence: 2,184 sq. mi.; pop. 118,000; cap. Charlottetown: abbrev. **P.E.I.**

prince·ling (prins′liŋ) *n.* a young, small, or lesser prince

prince·ly (-lē) *adj.* **-li·er, -li·est 1.** of a prince; royal **2.** characteristic or worthy of a prince; magnificent; generous —**prince′li·ness** *n.*

Prince of Darkness *a name sometimes given to* SATAN

Prince of Peace *a name sometimes given to* JESUS

Prince of Wales *title given to* the oldest son and heir apparent of a British king or queen

prince royal the oldest son of a king or queen

prin·cess¹ (prin′sis, -ses) *n.* **1.** orig., any female monarch **2.** a nonreigning female member of a royal family **3.** in Great Britain, a daughter of the sovereign or of a son of the sovereign **4.** the wife of a prince

prin·cess² (prin′sis, prin ses′) *adj.* [< Fr. *princesse,* a princess] of or describing a woman's one-piece, closefitting, gored dress, coat, etc., unbroken at the waistline and with a flared skirt: also **prin·cesse′** (-ses′)

princess royal the oldest daughter of a king or queen

Prince·ton (prins′tən) [after the *Prince* of Orange, later WILLIAM III] borough in central N.J., near Trenton: scene of a battle of the Revolutionary War: pop. 12,000

prin·ci·pal (prin′sə pəl) *adj.* [OFr. < L. *principalis* < *princeps:* see PRINCE] **1.** first in rank, authority, importance, etc.; chief; main [the *principal* cities in Europe] **2.** that is or has to do with principal (*n.* 3) —*n.* **1.** a principal person or thing; specif., *a)* a chief; head *b)* a governing officer, as of a school *c)* a main actor or other kind of performer **2.** any of the main end rafters of a roof **3.** *Finance a)* the amount of a debt, investment, etc. minus the interest, or on which interest is figured *b)* the face value of a stock or bond *c)* the main portion of an estate, etc., as distinguished from income **4.** *Law a)* one who employs another to act as his agent *b)* the one primarily responsible for an obligation *c)* one who commits a crime: see also ACCESSORY —**prin′ci·pal·ly** *adv.* —**prin′ci·pal·ship′** *n.*

prin·ci·pal·i·ty (prin′sə pal′ə tē) *n., pl.* **-ties 1.** the rank or jurisdiction of a prince **2.** the territory ruled by a prince **3.** a country with which a prince's title is identified

principal parts the principal inflected forms of a verb, from which the other forms may be derived: in English, they are the present infinitive, the past tense, the past participle, and, sometimes, the present participle (Examples: *drink, drank, drunk, drinking; go, went, gone, going*)

prin·ci·ple (prin′sə pəl) *n.* [< MFr. < L. *principium < princeps:* see PRINCE] **1.** the ultimate or basic source or cause [ancient philosophers considered earth, air, fire, and water to be the *principles* of life] **2.** a natural or original tendency, faculty, etc. **3.** a fundamental truth, law, etc., upon which others are based [the *principles* of democracy] **4.** *a)* a rule of conduct, esp. of right conduct [it's against her *principles* to lie] *b)* all such rules *c)* a sticking to them; honesty and fairness; integrity [a man of *principle*] **5.** an essential element or quality *[the active *principle* of a medicine]* **6.** a) the scientific law that explains a natural action *[the *principle* of cell division]* b) the method of a thing's operation *[the *principle* of the gasoline engine]* —**in principle** theoretically or in essence —**on principle** because of a principle, or rule of conduct

prin·ci·pled (-pəld) *adj.* having or based on principles, as of conduct

prink (priŋk) *vt., vi.* [prob. < PRANK²] *same as* PRIMP

print (print) *n.* [< OFr. < pp. of *preindre* < L. *premere*, to PRESS¹] **1.** a mark made on a surface by pressing, stamping, or hitting with an object; imprint *[the *print* of a heel]* **2.** an object for making such a mark, as a stamp, die, etc. **3.** a cloth printed with a design, or a dress, blouse, etc. made of this **4.** the condition of being printed **5.** printed lettering **6.** the impression made by inked type **7.** a picture or design printed from a plate, block, etc., as an etching or lithograph **8.** printed or published material *[to see a story in *print*]* **9.** a photograph, esp. one made from a negative —*vt.* **1.** to make a print on or in **2.** to stamp or draw, trace, etc. (a mark, letter, etc.) on or in a surface **3.** to produce on (paper, etc.) the impression of inked type, plates, etc. by means of a printing press **4.** to produce (a book, etc.) by typesetting, presswork, etc. **5.** to publish in print *[to *print* a story]* **6.** to write in letters resembling printed ones **7.** to produce (a photograph) from (a negative) **8.** in computers, to deliver (information) by means of a printer: often with *out* **9.** to impress upon the mind, memory, etc. —*vi.* **1.** to practice the trade of a printer **2.** to produce an impression, photograph, etc. *[a negative that *prints* well]* **3.** to write in letters resembling printed ones **4.** to produce newspapers, books, etc. by means of a printing press —**in** (or **out of**) **print** still (or no longer) for sale by the publisher: said of books, etc.

print·a·ble (print'ə b'l) *adj.* **1.** that can be printed or printed from **2.** fit to print —**print'a·bil'i·ty** *n.*

printed circuit an electrical circuit formed by stamping or electroplating conductive material in fine lines or other shapes on an insulating surface

print·er (-ər) *n.* **1.** one whose work or business is printing **2.** a device that prints; esp., in computers, a device that produces information in printed or typewritten form

printer's devil an apprentice in a printing shop

print·ing (-iŋ) *n.* **1.** the act of a person or thing that prints **2.** the production of printed matter **3.** the art of a printer **4.** something printed **5.** all the copies of a book, etc. printed at one time **6.** written letters made like printed ones

printing press a machine for printing from inked type, plates, or rolls

print·out (-out') *n.* the output of a computer presented in printed or typewritten form

print shop ☆**1.** a shop where printing is done: also **printing office 2.** a shop where prints, etchings, etc. are sold

pri·or (prī'ər) *adj.* [L., former, superior] **1.** preceding in time; earlier **2.** preceding in order or importance *[a *prior* choice]* —*n.* [OE. & OFr., both < ML. < L.] **1.** the head of a priory or other religious house **2.** in an abbey, the person in charge next below the abbot —**see** SYN at PREVIOUS —**prior to** before in time

pri·or·ess (prī'ər.is) *n.* **1.** the woman head of a priory of nuns, etc. **2.** in an abbey of nuns, the woman in charge next below the abbess

pri·or·i·tize (prī ôr'ə tīz', -är'-) *vt.* -**tized'**, -**tiz'ing** to arrange (items) in order of priority

pri·or·i·ty (prī ôr'ə tē, -är'-) *n., pl.* -**ties 1.** a being prior; precedence *[the *priority* of his claim to the land]* **2.** a) a right to get, buy, or do something before others b) an order granting this **3.** something given or to be given prior attention *[high on her list of *priorities*]*

pri·o·ry (prī'ər ē) *n., pl.* -**ries** a monastery governed by a prior, or a convent governed by a prioress

Pris·cil·la (pri sil'ə) [L., ult. < *priscus*, ancient] a feminine name

prise (prīz) *vt.* **prised**, **pris'ing** [Chiefly Brit.] to prize, or pry, as with a lever

prism (priz'm) *n.* [< LL. < Gr. *prisma*, lit., something sawed < *prizein*, to saw] **1.** a solid figure whose ends are equal and parallel polygons and whose sides are parallelograms **2.** anything that refracts light, as a drop of water **3.** *Optics* a) a transparent body, as of glass, whose ends are equal and parallel triangles, and whose three sides are parallelograms: used for refracting or dispersing light, as into the spectrum b) any similar body of three or more sides

TRIANGULAR PRISM

pris·mat·ic (priz mat'ik) *adj.* **1.** of or like a prism **2.** that refracts light as a prism **3.** that forms prismatic colors **4.** many-colored; brilliant —**pris·mat'i·cal·ly** *adv.*

prismatic colors the colors of the visible spectrum produced by passing white light through a prism; red, orange, yellow, green, blue, indigo, and violet

pris·on (priz''n) *n.* [OFr. < L. *prensio*, for *prehensio* < *prehendere*, to take: see PREHENSILE] **1.** a place where persons are confined **2.** a building, usually with cells, where persons convicted by trial or awaiting trial are confined; specif., such a building maintained by a State or the Federal government **3.** imprisonment

pris·on·er (priz'nər, -'n ər) *n.* **1.** a person confined in prison, as for some crime **2.** a person held in custody **3.** a person captured or held captive *[a *prisoner* of love]*

prisoner of war a member of the armed forces of a nation at war held captive by the enemy

☆**pris·sy** (pris'ē) *adj.* -**si·er**, -**si·est** [prob. PR(IM) + (S)ISSY] [Colloq.] very prim or precise; fussy, prudish, etc. —**pris'si·ly** *adv.* —**pris'si·ness** *n.*

pris·tine (pris'tēn, -tin; pris tēn') *adj.* [L. *pristinus*, former] **1.** characteristic of the earliest period or condition; original **2.** still pure; uncorrupted; unspoiled *[*pristine* beauty]*

prith·ee (prith'ē) *interj.* [< *pray thee*] [Archaic] I pray thee; please

pri·va·cy (prī'və sē; *Brit. also* priv'ə-) *n., pl.* -**cies 1.** the quality or condition of being private; withdrawal from public view; seclusion *[seeking *privacy* in a cabin in the woods]* **2.** secrecy *[told in strict *privacy*]* **3.** one's private life or personal affairs *[an invasion of one's *privacy*]*

pri·vate (prī'vit) *adj.* [< L. *privatus*, belonging to oneself, ult. < *privus*, separate] **1.** of or concerning only one particular person or group; not general *[*private* property, her *private* affairs]* **2.** not open to or controlled by the public *[a *private* school]* **3.** for an individual person *[a *private* room in a hospital]* **4.** not holding public office *[a *private* citizen]* **5.** away from public view; secluded *[a *private* dining room]* **6.** secret; confidential *[a *private* matter]* **7.** not connected with an institution or organization; independent *[*private* medical practice; a *private* detective]* —*n.* an enlisted man of either of the two lowest ranks in the U.S. Army or of the lowest rank in the U.S. Marine Corps —**in private** not publicly —**pri'vate·ly** *adv.*

private enterprise *same as* FREE ENTERPRISE

pri·va·teer (prī'və tir') *n.* [< PRIVAT(E) + -EER] **1.** a privately owned and manned armed ship commissioned in a war to attack and capture enemy ships, esp. merchant ships **2.** a commander or crew member of a privateer: also ☆ **pri'va·teers'man** (-tirz'mən), *pl.* -**men** —*vi.* to sail as a privateer

☆**private eye** [Slang] a private detective

☆**private first class** an enlisted man ranking just below a corporal in the U.S. Army and just below a lance corporal in the U.S. Marine Corps

pri·va·tion (prī vā'shən) *n.* [< L. *privatio*: see PRIVATE] **1.** deprivation; the loss or absence of some quality or condition **2.** lack of the ordinary necessities of life; want *[the troops at Valley Forge faced severe *privation*]*

priv·a·tive (priv'ə tiv) *adj.* **1.** depriving or tending to deprive **2.** *Gram.* showing negation, absence, or loss —*n. Gram.* a privative prefix or suffix, as *a-*, *un-*, or *-less* —**priv'a·tive·ly** *adv.*

priv·et (priv'it) *n.* [< ?] any of various shrubs of the olive family, with bluish-black berries and white flowers, often used for hedges

priv·i·lege (priv''l ij, priv'lij) *n.* [< OFr. < L. *privilegium*, a law for or against an individual < *privus*, separate + *legis*, genitive of *lex*, a law] **1.** a right, advantage, favor, etc. specially granted to a certain person, group, or class **2.** a basic civil right, guaranteed by a government *[the *privilege* of trial by jury]* —*vt.* -**leged**, -**leg·ing** to grant a privilege to

priv·i·leged (-ijd, -lijd) *adj.* having one or more privileges

privileged communication information that one cannot legally be forced to reveal, as that given to a lawyer by his client or by a patient to his doctor

priv·y (priv'ē) *adj.* [< OFr. < L. *privatus*, PRIVATE] **1.** orig., private; personal **2.** [Archaic] hidden, secret, etc. —*n., pl.* **priv'ies** a toilet; esp., an outhouse —**privy to** privately informed about —**priv'i·ly** *adv.*

privy council a body of advisers or confidential counselors appointed by or serving a ruler —**privy councilor**

privy seal in Great Britain, the seal placed on documents which later receive the great seal or which are not important enough to receive it

prize[1] (prīz) *vt.* **prized, priz′ing** [see PRICE] **1.** formerly, to price or appraise **2.** to value highly; esteem [he *prizes* your friendship] —*n.* **1.** something offered or given to the winner of a contest, lottery, etc. **2.** a reward, premium, etc. **3.** anything worth striving for; any highly valued possession —*adj.* **1.** that has received a prize [last year's *prize* novel] **2.** worthy of a prize [planning to retire and raise *prize* cattle] **3.** given as a prize [the first-place *prize* ribbon] —see SYN. at APPRECIATE

prize[2] (prīz) *n.* [< OFr. *prise*, fem. pp. of *prendre* < L. *prehendere*, to take: see PREHENSILE] something taken by force, as in war; esp., a captured enemy warship —*vt.* **prized, priz′ing 1.** to seize as a prize of war **2.** to pry, as with a lever

prize·fight (prīz′fīt′) *n.* a professional boxing match —**prize′-fight′er** *n.* —**prize′fight′ing** *n.*

prize ring 1. a square platform, enclosed by ropes, for prizefights **2.** prizefighting

pro[1] (prō) *adv.* [L., for] on the affirmative side; favorably [to discuss the matter *pro* and con] —*adj.* favorable —*prep.* in favor of; for —*n., pl.* **pros** a reason, vote, position, etc. in favor of something

pro[2] (prō) *adj., n., pl.* **pros** *clipped form of* PROFESSIONAL

pro-[1] [Gr. < *pro*, before] *a prefix meaning* before in place or time [prologue]

pro-[2] [L. < *pro*, forward] *a prefix meaning:* **1.** forward or ahead [progress] **2.** forth [produce] **3.** substituting for, acting for [pronoun] **4.** supporting, favoring [prolabor]

pro·a (prō′ə) *n.* [Malay *prau*] a Malayan boat having a triangular sail and one outrigger

prob. 1. probable **2.** probably **3.** problem

prob·a·bil·i·ty (präb′ə bil′ə tē) *n., pl.* **-ties 1.** the quality or state of being probable; likelihood **2.** a probable thing or event **3.** *Math.* the ratio of the number of times a particular event can occur to the total number of likely events involved [the *probability* of cutting the ace of clubs is one in fifty-two] —**in all probability** very likely

PROA

prob·a·ble (präb′ə b'l) *adj.* [MFr. < L. < *probare*, to prove] **1.** likely to occur or be; that can reasonably but not certainly be expected [the *probable* winner] **2.** reasonably so, as on the basis of evidence, but not proved [the *probable* cause of a disease] —**prob′a·bly** *adv.*

SYN.—**probable** applies to that which seems reasonable to expect on the basis of evidence or logic although it is neither certain nor proved; **possible** applies to that which, although not probable, can conceivably exist, happen, be done, etc.; **likely** is an informal word for **probable** and applies to that which is apt to be, happen, etc. —**ANT.** improbable, unlikely

pro·bate (prō′bāt) *n.* [< L. pp. of *probare*: see PROBE] **1.** the act or process of proving or establishing that a document submitted for official certification and registration, as a will, is genuine ☆**2.** all matters coming under the jurisdiction of probate courts —*adj.* having to do with probate or a probate court —*vt.* **-bat·ed, -bat·ing 1.** to establish officially the genuineness or validity of (a will) ☆**2.** popularly, to certify in a probate court as mentally unsound

☆**probate court** a court having jurisdiction over the probating of wills, the administration of estates, and, usually, the guardianship of minors and incompetents

pro·ba·tion (prō bā′shən) *n.* [< OFr. < L. < *probare*: see PROBE] **1.** a testing or trial, as of a person's character, fitness for a position, etc. **2.** the suspension of sentence of a person convicted but not imprisoned, on condition of continued good behavior and regular reporting to a probation officer **3.** *a)* the status of a person being tested or on trial [a student on *probation* because of low grades] *b)* the period of testing or trial —**pro·ba′tion·ar′y, pro·ba′tion·al** *adj.*

pro·ba·tion·er (-ər) *n.* a person on probation

☆**probation officer** an officer appointed by a court to supervise persons placed on probation

pro·ba·tive (prō′bə tiv, präb′ə-) *adj.* [< L. < *probare*: see PROBE] **1.** serving to test or try **2.** providing proof or evidence Also **pro′ba·to′ry** (-tôr′ē)

probe (prōb) *n.* [LL. *proba*, proof < L. *probare*, to test < *probus*, proper] **1.** a slender, blunt surgical instrument for exploring a wound, tissues, etc. **2.** the act of probing **3.** a searching examination; specif., ☆*a)* an investigation, as by a legislative committee, into corruption, etc. *b)* an exploratory survey ☆**4.** a spacecraft equipped with instruments, for exploring the upper atmosphere, outer space, another planet, etc. —*vt.* **probed, prob′ing 1.** to explore (a wound, etc.) with a probe **2.** to examine or investigate thoroughly —*vi.* to search; investigate —**prob′er** *n.*

prob·i·ty (prō′bə tē, präb′ə-) *n.* [< L. < *probus*, good] uprightness; honesty; integrity —see SYN. at HONESTY

prob·lem (präb′ləm) *n.* [< MFr. < L. < Gr. *problēma* < *pro-*, forward + *ballein*, to throw] **1.** a question or matter to be thought about or worked out [a math *problem*] **2.** a matter, person, etc. that is perplexing or difficult [feeding that many people will be a *problem*] —*adj.* **1.** depicting a social problem [a *problem* play] **2.** very difficult to deal with; esp., very difficult to train or discipline [a *problem* child]

prob·lem·at·ic (präb′lə mat′ik) *adj.* **1.** having the nature of a problem; hard to solve or deal with **2.** not settled; uncertain [our vacation plans remain *problematic*] Also **prob′lem·at′i·cal** —see SYN. at DOUBTFUL —**prob′lem·at′i·cal·ly** *adv.*

‡**pro bo·no pu·bli·co** (prō bō′nō pub′li kō′) [ML.] for the public good or welfare

pro·bos·cis (prō bäs′is) *n., pl.* **-cis·es, -ci·des′** (-ə dēz′) [L. < Gr. < *pro-*, before + *boskein*, to feed] **1.** an elephant's trunk, or a long, flexible snout, as of a tapir **2.** any tubular organ for sucking, food-gathering, sensing, etc., as of some insects, worms, and mollusks **3.** a person's nose, esp. if large: a humorous usage

pro·caine (prō′kān) *n.* [PRO-[2] + (CO)CAINE] a synthetic crystalline compound used as a local anesthetic

pro·cam·bi·um (prō kam′bē əm) *n.* [ModL.: see PRO-[2] + CAMBIUM] *Bot.* the growing layer in the tip of a stem or root which produces primary phloem, primary xylem, and cambium

pro·ce·dure (prə sē′jər, prō-) *n.* **1.** the act, method, or manner of proceeding in some action; esp., the order of steps to be followed [the *procedure* to follow during a fire drill] **2.** a particular course or method of action [an illegal *procedure*] **3.** the established way of carrying on the business of a legislature, law court, etc. —**pro·ce′dur·al** *adj.* —**pro·ce′dur·al·ly** *adv.*

pro·ceed (prə sēd′, prō-) *vi.* [< MFr. < L. < *pro-*, forward + *cedere*, to go] **1.** to advance or go on, esp. after stopping **2.** to go on speaking, esp. after an interruption **3.** to begin and carry on some action [to *proceed* to build a fire] **4.** to move along or be carried on [things *proceeded* smoothly] **5.** to take legal action (often with *against*) **6.** to come forth, issue, or arise (*from*) [smoke *proceeded* from the chimney]

pro·ceed·ing (-iŋ) *n.* **1.** an advancing or going on with what one has been doing **2.** the carrying on of an action or course of action **3.** a particular action or course of action **4.** [*pl.*] a record of the matters dealt with, as at a meeting of a scholarly group **5.** [*pl.*] legal action [to start *proceedings* against someone]

pro·ceeds (prō′sēdz) *n.pl.* the money or profit from a sale, business venture, etc.

proc·ess (präs′es; *chiefly Brit. & Canad.,* prō′ses) *n.* [< OFr. < L. pp. of *procedere:* see PROCEED] **1.** a series of changes by which something develops or is brought about [the *process* of digestion, growth, etc.] **2.** a particular method of making or doing something, in which there are a number of steps [the refining *process* used in making gasoline from crude oil] **3.** *Biol.* a projecting part of a structure or organism [a bony *process* on his heel] **4.** *Law a)* an action or suit *b)* a written order, as a summons to appear in court —*vt.* **1.** to prepare by or subject to a special process [to *process* food for storage by quick-freezing] —*adj.* prepared by a special process —**in process** in the course of being done —**in (the) process of** in or during the course of —**proc′es·sor, proc′ess·er** *n.*

process cheese a cheese made by heating and blending together several natural cheeses with an emulsifying agent: also **proc′essed cheese**

pro·ces·sion (prə sesh′ən, prō-) *n.* [OFr. < L. < *procedere:* see PROCEED] **1.** the act of proceeding, esp. in an orderly manner **2.** a number of persons or things moving forward, as in a parade, in an orderly, formal way

---

fat, āpe, cär; ten, ēven; is, bīte; gō, hôrn, tōōl, look; oil, out; up, fŭr; get; joy; yet; chin; she; thin, *th*en; zh, leisure; ŋ, ring; ə for *a* in *ago*, *e* in *agent*, *i* in *sanity*, *o* in *comply*, *u* in *focus*; ' as in *able* (ā′b'l); Fr. bàl; ë, Fr. coeur; ö, Fr. feu; Fr. mon; ô, Fr. coq; ü, Fr. duc; r, Fr. cri; H, G. ich; kh, G. doch; ‡foreign; ☆ Americanism; < derived from. See inside front cover.

pro·ces·sion·al (-'l) *adj.* of or relating to a procession —*n.* 1. a hymn sung at the beginning of a church service during the entrance of the clergy 2. any musical composition to accompany a procession

pro·claim (prō klām', prə-) *vt.* [< MFr. < L. < *pro-*, before + *clamare*, to cry out: see CLAMOR] 1. to announce to the public officially; announce to be ["*proclaim* liberty throughout all the land"] 2. to show to be [acts that *proclaimed* him a friend]

proc·la·ma·tion (präk'lə mā'shən) *n.* 1. a proclaiming or being proclaimed 2. something that is proclaimed, or announced officially

pro·cliv·i·ty (prō kliv'ə tē) *n., pl.* **-ties** [L. *proclivitas* < *pro-*, before + *clivus*, a slope] a natural or habitual tendency or inclination [his well-known *proclivity* to falsehood]

pro·con·sul (prō kän's'l) *n.* [L. < *pro consule*, (acting) for the consul] a Roman official with consular authority who commanded an army in the provinces, often acting as provincial governor —**pro·con'sul·ar** (-ər) *adj.* —**pro·con'sul·ate** (-it), **pro·con'sul·ship'** *n.*

pro·cras·ti·nate (prō kras'tə nāt', prə-) *vi., vt.* **-nat'ed, -nat'ing** [< L. pp. of *procrastinare*, ult. < *pro-*, forward + *cras*, tomorrow] to put off doing (something) until later; delay —**pro·cras'ti·na'tion** *n.* —**pro·cras'ti·na'tor** *n.*

pro·cre·ate (prō'krē āt') *vt., vi.* **-at'ed, -at'ing** [< L. pp. of *procreare* < *pro-*, before + *creare*, to create] 1. to produce (young); beget 2. to produce or bring into existence —**pro'cre·a'tion** *n.* —**pro'cre·a'tor** *n.*

Pro·crus·te·an (prō krus'tē ən) *adj.* 1. of or like Procrustes or his actions 2. forcing persons or things to conform; drastic

Pro·crus·tes (prō krus'tēz) *Gr. Myth.* a giant who seized travelers, tied them to a bedstead, and either stretched them or cut off their legs to make them fit it

proc·tol·o·gy (präk täl'ə jē) *n.* [< Gr. *prōktos*, anus + -LOGY] the branch of medicine dealing with the rectum and anus and their diseases —**proc'to·log'ic** (-tə läj'ik), **proc'to·log'i·cal** *adj.* —**proc·tol'o·gist** *n.*

proc·tor (präk'tər) *n.* [< ME., contr. < *procuratour:* see PROCURATOR] a college or university official who maintains order, supervises students at written examinations, etc. —*vt.* to supervise (an examination) —**proc·to'ri·al** (präk tôr'ē əl) *adj.* —**proc'tor·ship'** *n.*

pro·cum·bent (prō kum'bənt) *adj.* [< L. prp. of *pro cumbere*, ult. < *pro-*, forward + *cubare*, to lie down] 1. lying face down 2. *Bot.* trailing along the ground: said of a stem

proc·u·ra·tor (präk'yə rāt'ər) *n.* [< OFr. < L. < *procurare:* see PROCURE] 1. in the Roman Empire, an administrator of a province 2. a person employed to manage another's affairs; agent —**proc'u·ra·to'ri·al** (-yər ə tôr'ē əl) *adj.*

pro·cure (prō kyoor', prə-) *vt.* **-cured', -cur'ing** [< MFr. < L. < *pro*, for + *curare*, to attend to < *cura*, a care] 1. to get or bring about by some effort; obtain; secure [to *procure* works; to *procure* supplies] 2. to obtain (women) for the purpose of prostitution —see SYN. at GET —**pro·cur'a·ble** *adj.* —**pro·cure'ment, pro·cur'ance, pro·cur'al** *n.*

pro·cur·er (-kyoor'ər) *n.* a person who procures; specif., a man who obtains women for the purpose of prostitution; pimp —**pro·cur'ess** *n.fem.*

Pro·cy·on (prō'sē än') [L. < Gr. < *pro-*, before + *kyōn*, dog: it rises before the Dog Star] a star of the first magnitude in Canis Minor

prod (präd) *vt.* **prod'ded, prod'ding** [< ?] 1. to jab or poke as with a pointed stick 2. to urge or stir into action [questioning him in order to *prod* his memory] —*n.* 1. a prodding; jab, poke, thrust, etc. 2. something that prods; specif., a rod or pointed stick used in driving cattle —**prod'der** *n.*

prod·i·gal (präd'i gəl) *adj.* [MFr. < L. < *prodigere*, to waste < *pro-*, forth + *agere*, to drive: see ACT] 1. wasteful in a reckless way [*prodigal* with our natural resources] 2. very generous; lavish [*prodigal* with his praise] 3. very abundant; profuse [*prodigal* jungle growth] —*n.* a person who recklessly wastes his wealth, resources, etc.; spendthrift —**prod'i·gal'i·ty** (-gal'ə tē) *n., pl.* **-ties** —**prod'i·gal·ly** *adv.*

prodigal son *Bible* a son who is sorry for having led a wild, wasteful life and is welcomed home: Luke 15:11–32

pro·di·gious (prə dij'əs) *adj.* [< L.: see PRODIGY] 1. wonderful; amazing; impressive, esp. because grand, large in scope, etc. [a *prodigious* display of learning] 2. enormous; huge [a *prodigious* appetite] —**pro·di'gious·ly** *adv.* —**pro·di'gious·ness** *n.*

prod·i·gy (präd'ə jē) *n., pl.* **-gies** [L. *prodigium*, omen] a person or thing so extraordinary as to cause wonder; specif., a child who is amazingly talented or intelligent

pro·duce (prə doos', -dyoos'; *for n.* präd'oos, -yoos; prō'doos, -dyoos) *vt.* **-duced', -duc'ing** [L. *producere* < *pro-*, forward + *ducere*, to lead: see DUKE] 1. to bring to view; offer for inspection [to *produce* identification] 2. to bring forth; bear; yield [a well that *produces* oil] 3. *a*) to make or manufacture [a company that *produces* bicycles] *b*) to create [he worked for years to *produce* a great novel] 4. to cause; give rise to [war *produces* devastation] 5. to be the producer of (a play, movie, etc.) 6. *Econ.* to create (anything having exchange value) 7. *Geom.* to extend (a line or plane) —*vi.* to bear, yield, create, manufacture, etc. something —*n.* something produced; yield; esp., fresh fruits and vegetables —**pro·duc'i·bil'i·ty** *n.* —**pro·duc'i·ble** *adj.*

pro·duc·er (prə doos'ər, -dyoos'-) *n.* 1. a person or thing that produces; specif., one who produces goods and services: opposed to CONSUMER 2. a person in charge of the financing and managing of all activities in connection with the staging or filming of a play, movie, etc.

producer gas a fuel gas that is a mixture of nitrogen, carbon monoxide, and hydrogen, made by passing air or a mixture of air and steam over red hot coal or coke

producer goods goods, such as raw materials and machines, that are used in producing consumer goods

prod·uct (präd'əkt) *n.* [< ML. < L. pp. of *producere:* see PRODUCE] 1. something produced by nature or by man 2. result; outgrowth [a *product* of her imagination] 3. *Chem.* any substance resulting from a chemical change 4. *Math.* the quantity obtained by multiplying two or more quantities together

pro·duc·tion (prə duk'shən) *n.* 1. the act or process of producing 2. the rate of producing or the amount produced [the new machinery increased *production*] 3. *a*) something produced; product *b*) a work of art, literature, etc. *c*) a show, movie, etc. 4. the creation of things having economic value; producing of goods and services —☆**make a production (out) of** [Colloq.] to dwell on or fuss over needlessly

pro·duc·tive (-tiv) *adj.* 1. producing much; fertile [*productive* soil; a *productive* mind] 2. marked by abundant production or effective results [a *productive* day] 3. bringing as a result (with *of*) [war is *productive* of much misery] 4. producing goods or wealth [*productive* labor] —**pro·duc'tive·ly** *adv.* —**pro·duc·tiv·i·ty** (prō'dək tiv'ə tē, präd'ək-, prə duk'-), **pro·duc'tive·ness** *n.*

pro·em (prō'em) *n.* [< MFr. < L. < Gr. < *pro-*, before + *oimē*, song] a brief introduction; preface

☆**prof** (präf) *n.* [Colloq.] *shortened form of* PROFESSOR

Prof. Professor

prof·a·na·tion (präf'ə nā'shən) *n.* a profaning or being profaned; desecration —**pro·fan·a·to·ry** (prə fan'ə tôr'ē, prō-) *adj.*

pro·fane (prə fān', prō-) *adj.* [< MFr. < L. < *pro-*, before (that is, "outside of") + *fanum*, a temple] 1. not connected with religion; secular [*profane* art] 2. not holy or hallowed 3. showing disrespect or contempt for sacred things, as by curses or vulgar words; irreverent [*profane* language] —*vt.* **-faned', -fan'ing** 1. to treat (sacred things) with disrespect or contempt 2. to put to an unworthy or improper use [to *profane* Bach's music by using it in a silly commercial] —**pro·fane'ly** *adv.* —**pro·fane'ness** *n.* —**pro·fan'er** *n.*

pro·fan·i·ty (-fan'ə tē) *n.* 1. the state or quality of being profane 2. *pl.* **-ties** something profane; esp., profane language or the use of profane language

pro·fess (prə fes', prō-) *vt.* [< L. pp. of *profiteri* < *pro-*, before + *fateri*, to avow] 1. to make an open declaration of; affirm [to *profess* one's love] 2. to claim to have (some feeling, knowledge, etc.): often implying insincerity or pretense [to *profess* a friendship one does not really feel] 3. to practice as one's profession 4. to declare one's belief in [to *profess* Christianity]

pro·fessed (-fest') *adj.* 1. openly declared; avowed [a *professed* liberal] 2. insincerely declared; pretended [his *professed* friendship] 3. having made one's profession (sense 3) 4. professing to be qualified as such [a *professed* economist] —**pro·fess'ed·ly** (-id lē) *adv.*

pro·fes·sion (prə fesh'ən) *n.* 1. the act of professing, or openly declaring; avowal, as of love, religious belief, etc. 2. *a*) an occupation requiring advanced education and involving intellectual skills, as medicine, law, theology, engineering, or teaching *b*) all the people in such an occupation [the legal *profession* denounced the proposal] *c*) loosely, any occupation 3. the act or ceremony of taking vows on entering a religious order

pro·fes·sion·al (-'l) *adj.* **1.** of, engaged in, or worthy of the standards of, a profession ☆**2.** designating or of a school, esp. a graduate school, offering instruction in a profession **3.** earning one's living from an activity, such as a sport, not normally thought of as an occupation [a *professional* golfer] **4.** engaged in by professional players [*professional* hockey] **5.** engaged in a specified occupation for pay [a *professional* writer] **6.** being such in the manner of one practicing a profession [a *professional* hatemonger] —*n.* **1.** a person who is professional (esp. in sense 3) **2.** a person who does something with great skill — **pro·fes′sion·al·ism** *n.* —**pro·fes′sion·al·ly** *adv.*

pro·fes·sion·al·ize (-'l īz′) *vt.* **-ized**, **-iz′ing** to cause to have professional qualities, status, etc. —**pro·fes′sion·al·i·za′tion** *n.*

pro·fes·sor (prə fes′ər) *n.* **1.** a person who professes something **2.** a teacher; specif., a teacher of the highest rank in a college or university —**pro·fes·so·ri·al** (prō′fə sôr′ē əl) *adj.* —**pro′fes·so′ri·al·ly** *adv.* —**pro·fes′sor·ship′**, **pro·fes′sor·ate** (-it) *n.*

prof·fer (präf′ər) *vt.* [< Anglo-Fr. & OFr. < *por-*, PRO-² + *offrir*, ult. < L. *offerre*, to offer] to offer (advice, friendship, etc.) —*n.* an offer or proposal —see SYN. at OFFER

pro·fi·cient (prə fish′ənt) *adj.* [< L. prp. of *proficere*, to advance < *pro-*, forward + *facere*, to make] highly competent; skilled [he practiced hard and became quite a *proficient* golfer] —**pro·fi′cien·cy** (-ən sē) *n., pl.* **-cies** —**pro·fi′cient·ly** *adv.*

pro·file (prō′fīl; *chiefly Brit.* -fēl) *n.* [< It. < *profilare*, to outline < *pro-* (< L. *pro-*), before + *filo* (< L. *filum*), a thread] **1.** *a)* a side view of the face *b)* a drawing of this **2.** outline [the *profile* of a distant hill] ☆**3.** a short, vivid biographical and character sketch **4.** a graph, summary, etc. presenting data about a particular subject **5.** *Archit.* a side or sectional elevation of a building, etc. —*vt.* **-filed**, **-fil·ing** to sketch, write, or make a profile of

prof·it (präf′it) *n.* [OFr. < L. pp. of *proficere*, to profit: see PROFICIENT] **1.** advantage; gain; benefit [it would be to his *profit* to read more] **2.** [*often pl.*] income from money invested in stocks, bonds, real estate, etc. **3.** [*often pl.*] the sum remaining after all costs are deducted from the income of a business —*vi.* **1.** to make a financial profit **2.** to benefit; gain [she will *profit* from the experience] —*vt.* to be of profit or advantage to [speaking so frankly seldom *profits* a politician] —**prof′it·er** *n.* —**prof′it·less** *adj.*

prof·it·a·ble (-ə b'l) *adj.* yielding profit, gain, or benefit — **prof′it·a·bil′i·ty, prof′it·a·ble·ness** *n.* —**prof′it·a·bly** *adv.*

prof·it·eer (präf′ə tir′) *n.* [PROFIT + -EER] a person who makes an unfair profit by charging very high prices when there is a short supply of something needed —*vi.* to be a profiteer

profit sharing the practice of dividing a share of the profits of a business among employees, in addition to paying them their wages —**prof′it-shar′ing** *adj.*

prof·li·gate (präf′lə git) *adj.* [< L. pp. of *profligare*, to rout, ruin < *pro-*, forward + *fligere*, to drive] **1.** immoral and shameless; dissolute [a *profligate* life] **2.** recklessly extravagant [a *profligate* spender] —*n.* a profligate person —**prof′li·ga·cy** (-gə sē), **prof′li·gate·ness** *n.* —**prof′li·gate·ly** *adv.*

pro·found (prə found′) *adj.* [< OFr. < L. *profundus* < *pro-*, forward + *fundus*, bottom] **1.** very deep or low [a *profound* abyss, sigh, etc.] **2.** marked by intellectual depth; showing great knowledge, thought, etc. [*profound* talk] **3.** deeply or intensely felt [*profound* grief] **4.** thoroughgoing [*profound* changes] **5.** unbroken [a *profound* silence] —**pro·found′ly** *adv.* —**pro·found′ness** *n.*

pro·fun·di·ty (prə fun′də tē) *n., pl.* **-ties** **1.** great depth **2.** intellectual depth; deep wisdom, knowledge, etc. **3.** a profound idea, matter, etc.

pro·fuse (prə fyoos′) *adj.* [< L. pp. of *profundere* < *pro-*, forth + *fundere*, to pour] **1.** giving freely; generous [*profuse* in her apologies] **2.** given or poured forth freely and abundantly [a *profuse* flow of water] —see SYN. at PLENTIFUL —**pro·fuse′ly** *adv.* —**pro·fuse′ness** *n.*

pro·fu·sion (-fyoo′zhən) *n.* **1.** a pouring forth freely or too freely **2.** the quality of being lavish or extravagant **3.** rich or lavish supply; abundance [lilies in *profusion*]

pro·gen·i·tor (prō jen′ə tər, prə-) *n.* [< MFr. < L., ult. < *pro-*, forth + *gignere*, to beget] **1.** a forefather; ancestor in direct line **2.** an originator or precursor [the *progenitor* of the atomic theory]

prog·e·ny (präj′ə nē) *n., pl.* **-nies** [< MFr. < L. < *progignere*: see prec.] children, descendants, or offspring

pro·ges·ter·one (prō jes′tə rōn′) *n.* [PRO-¹ + GE(STATE) + STER(OL) + -ONE] a steroid hormone, $C_{21}H_{30}O_2$, that prepares the uterus for the fertilized ovum and the mammary glands for milk secretion

prog·na·thous (präg′nə thəs, präg nā′-) *adj.* [< PRO-¹ + Gr. *gnathos*, a jaw] having the jaws projecting beyond the upper face: also **prog·nath′ic** (-nath′ik) —**prog′na·thism** (-thiz′m) *n.*

prog·no·sis (präg nō′sis) *n., pl.* **-no·ses** (-sēz) [< LL. < Gr. < *pro-*, before + *gignōskein*, to know] a forecast or forecasting; esp., a prediction of the probable course of a disease in an individual and the chances of recovery

prog·nos·tic (-näs′tik) *n.* [see prec.] **1.** a sign; omen **2.** a forecast —*adj.* **1.** foretelling **2.** *Med.* of, or serving as a basis for, prognosis

prog·nos·ti·cate (-näs′tə kāt′) *vt.* **-cat′ed**, **-cat′ing** [see PROGNOSIS] **1.** to foretell or predict **2.** to indicate beforehand —see SYN. at FORETELL —**prog·nos′ti·ca′tion** *n.* —**prog·nos′ti·ca′tive** (-kāt′iv) *adj.* —**prog·nos′ti·ca′tor** *n.*

pro·gram (prō′gram, -grəm) *n.* [< Fr. < LL. < Gr. *programma*, an edict < *pro-*, before + *graphein*, to write] **1.** *a)* the acts, speeches, musical pieces, etc. that make up an entertainment, ceremony, etc. *b)* a printed list of these **2.** a scheduled broadcast on radio or television **3.** a plan or procedure [a government *program* to help farmers] **4.** all the activities offered at a camp, resort, etc. **5.** *a)* a sequence of operations to be performed by a digital computer, as in solving a problem *b)* the coded instructions and data for such a sequence —*vt.* **-grammed** or **-gramed**, **-gram·ming** or **-gram·ing** **1.** to schedule in a program ☆**2.** to prepare (a textbook) for use in programmed learning **3.** *a)* to furnish (a computer) with a program *b)* to plan a computer program for (a particular problem, specific data, etc.) —*vi.* to prepare a program Also, Brit. sp., **pro′gramme** —**pro·gram·mat·ic** (prō′grə mat′ik) *adj.* —**pro′gram·mer, pro′gram·er** *n.*

☆**programmed learning** learning that a pupil may get on his own, step by step, from a textbook that has a series of questions with the answers given elsewhere in the book

program music instrumental music that is meant to suggest a particular scene, story, etc.

prog·ress (präg′res, -rəs; *chiefly Brit.* prō′gres; *for v.* prə gres′) *n.* [< L. pp. of *progredi* < *pro-*, before + *gradi*, to step: see GRADE] **1.** a moving forward or onward [the boat's *progress* downstream] **2.** forward course; development [a chart on which the *progress* of the disease was noted] **3.** advance toward a better state; improvement [the *progress* of mankind] —*vi* **1.** to move forward or onward **2.** to move toward completion, a goal, etc. **3.** to advance toward a better state; improve [science has helped man *progress*] —**in progress** going on

pro·gres·sion (prə gresh′ən) *n.* **1.** a moving forward or onward **2.** a succession, as of acts, happenings, etc. [a *progression* of lucky events led to his success] **3.** *Math.* a series of numbers increasing or decreasing by a constant difference between terms: see ARITHMETIC PROGRESSION, GEOMETRIC PROGRESSION **4.** *Music a)* the movement forward from one tone or chord to another *b)* a succession of tones or chords —**pro·gres′sion·al** *adj.*

pro·gres·sive (prə gres′iv) *adj.* **1.** moving forward or onward **2.** continuing by successive steps [a *progressive* decline] **3.** of, or concerned with, progression **4.** designating a tax whose rate increases as the base increases **5.** favoring or working for progress, as through political or social reform [a *progressive* senator] ☆**6.** of education that stresses individuality, self-expression, etc. **7.** *Gram.* showing continuing action: said of certain verb forms, such as *am working* **8.** *Med.* becoming more severe: said of a disease —*n.* **1.** a person who is progressive, esp. one who favors political progress or reform **2.** [P-] a member of a Progressive Party —see SYN. at LIBERAL —**pro·gres′sive·ly** *adv.* —**pro·gres′sive·ness** *n.*

Progressive Party ☆any of several former U.S. political parties; specif., *a)* one formed in 1912 by followers of Theodore Roosevelt *b)* one formed in 1924 and led by Robert LaFollette *c)* one formed in 1948, orig. led by Henry Wallace (1888–1965)

pro·hib·it (prō hib′it, prə-) *vt.* [< L. pp. of *prohibere* < *pro-*, before + *habere*, to have: see HABIT] **1.** to refuse to permit; forbid by law or by an order [smoking is *prohibited* in the building] **2.** to prevent; hinder [a high wall *prohibited* us from going farther] —**pro·hib′it·er, pro·hib′i·tor** *n.*

pro·hi·bi·tion (prō′ə bish′ən) *n.* **1.** a prohibiting or being prohibited **2.** an order or law that forbids ☆**3.** the forbidding by law of the manufacture or sale of alcoholic liquors; specif., [P-] in the U.S., the period (1920–1933) of prohibition by Federal law —**pro′hi·bi′tion·ist** *n.*

pro·hib·i·tive (prō hib′ə tiv, prə-) *adj.* **1.** prohibiting or tending to prohibit something **2.** such as to prevent purchase, use, etc. [*prohibitive* prices] Also **pro·hib′i·to·ry** (-tôr′ē) —**pro·hib′i·tive·ly** *adv.*

proj·ect (präj′ekt, -ikt; *for v.* prə jekt′) *n.* [< L. pp. of *projicere* < *pro-*, before + *jacere*, to throw: see JET[1]] **1.** a proposal; plan ☆**2.** an organized undertaking, as a special unit of work, research, etc. in school ☆**3.** a planned group of apartments or houses, in a specific location, esp. one that is owned or supported by the government and provides housing for those with low incomes: in full, **housing project** —*vt.* **1.** to propose (an act or plan of action); plan [our *projected* trip to Europe] **2.** to throw forward **3.** *a)* to cause (one's voice) to be heard clearly and at a distance *b)* to get (ideas, feelings, etc.) across to others effectively **4.** to send forth in one's imagination [to *project* oneself into the future] **5.** to cause to jut out **6.** to cause (a shadow, image, etc.) to fall upon a surface **7.** to predict on the basis of known facts, data, etc.; extrapolate [to *project* sales for next year] **8.** *Geom.* to draw lines from the points of (a geometric figure) to form the points of another figure that is larger, smaller, etc., keeping the space relations between the points constant —*vi.* **1.** to jut out **2.** to project one's voice, ideas, etc. —see SYN. at PLAN

pro·jec·tile (prə jek′t'l, -tīl) *n.* **1.** an object made to be shot with force through the air, as a cannon shell, bullet, or rocket **2.** anything thrown forward —*adj.* **1.** that can be hurled forward or thrust outward **2.** hurling forward [*projectile* force]

pro·jec·tion (prə jek′shən) *n.* **1.** a projecting or being projected **2.** something that projects, or juts out **3.** something that is projected; specif., in map making, the representation on a plane of all or part of the earth's surface or of the celestial sphere **4.** a prediction based on known facts, data, etc. **5.** *Psychiatry* the act of unconsciously ascribing to others one's own ideas, impulses, or emotions **6.** *Photog.* the process of projecting an image, as from a transparent slide, upon a screen, etc. —**pro·jec′tion·al** *adj.* —**pro·jec′tive** *adj.*

SYN.—**projection** implies a jutting out abruptly beyond the rest of the surface [the *projection* of the eaves beyond the sides of the house]; **protrusion** suggests a thrusting or pushing out that is abnormal or disfiguring [*protrusion* of the eyeballs]; **protuberance** suggests a swelling out, usually in rounded form [the tumor on his arm formed a *protuberance*]; **bulge** suggests an outward swelling that may result from internal pressure [the *bulge* in the can resulted from the fermentation of its contents]

☆**pro·jec·tion·ist** (-ist) *n.* the operator of a motion-picture or slide projector

pro·jec·tor (prə jek′tər) *n.* a person or thing that projects; specif., a machine for throwing an image on a screen, as from a transparent slide or motion-picture film

Pro·kof·iev (prô kôf′yef; *E.* prə kō′fē ef′), **Ser·gei** (**Sergeevich**) (syer gyä′) 1891–1953; Russ. composer

pro·lac·tin (prō lak′tin) *n.* [PRO-[1] + LACT(O)- + -IN[1]] a pituitary hormone stimulating milk secretion in mammals

pro·lapse (prō′laps; *also, and for v. usually,* prō laps′) *n.* [< ModL. < LL. < pp. of L. *prolabi* < *pro-*, forward + *labi*, to fall] *Med.* the slipping out of place of an internal organ, as the uterus: also **pro·lap′sus** (-lap′səs) —*vi.* **-lapsed′, -laps′ing** *Med.* to slip out of place

pro·late (prō′lāt) *adj.* [< L. pp. of *proferre*, to bring forward] extended or elongated at the poles [a *prolate* spheroid]

pro·leg (prō′leg′) *n.* [PRO-[1] + LEG] any of the fleshy limbs attached to the abdomen of certain insect larvae

pro·le·tar·i·an (prō′lə ter′ē ən) *adj.* of the proletariat —*n.* a member of the proletariat; worker

pro·le·tar·i·at (prō′lə ter′ē ət) *n.* [< Fr. < L. *proletarius*, a citizen of the poorest class, who served the state only by having children < *proles*, offspring] **1.** [Rare] the class of lowest status in any society **2.** the working class; esp., the industrial working class

pro·lif·er·ate (prō lif′ə rāt′, prə-) *vt., vi.* **-at′ed, -at′ing** [ult. < ML. < L. *proles*, offspring + *ferre*, to BEAR[1]] **1.** to reproduce or grow rapidly [the cells *proliferated*] **2.** to multiply rapidly; increase profusely [problems and difficulties are *proliferating*] —**pro·lif′er·a′tion** *n.* —**pro·lif′er·ous** (-rəs) *adj.*

pro·lif·ic (prə lif′ik, prō-) *adj.* [< Fr. < ML. < L. *proles*, offspring + *facere*, to make] **1.** producing many young or much fruit [mice are *prolific* animals] **2.** creating many products of the mind [a *prolific* poet] **3.** fruitful; abounding (often with *in* or *of*) —see SYN. at FERTILE —**pro·lif′i·ca·cy** (-i kə sē) *n.* —**pro·lif′i·cal·ly** *adv.*

pro·lix (prō liks′, prō′liks) *adj.* [< L. *prolixus*, extended < *pro-*, forth + base of *liquere*, to flow] containing or using more words than are necessary; verbose or long-winded [a *prolix* style] —see SYN. at WORDY —**pro·lix′i·ty** *n.* —**pro·lix′ly** *adv.*

pro·logue (prō′lôg, -läg) *n.* [< MFr. < L. < Gr. < *pro-*, before + *logos*, a discourse: see LOGIC] **1.** an introduction to a poem, play, etc.; esp., introductory lines spoken by an actor before a dramatic performance **2.** the actor speaking such lines **3.** any preliminary act, event, etc. [the Spanish Civil War was a *prologue* to World War II]

pro·long (prə lôŋ′) *vt.* [< MFr. < LL. < L. *pro-*, forth + *longus*, long] to lengthen in time or space [we *prolonged* our visit by another day; don't *prolong* the suspense]: also **pro·lon′gate** (-gāt) **-gat·ed, -gat·ing** —see SYN. at EXTEND —**pro·lon·ga·tion** (prō′lôŋ gā′shən) *n.* —**pro·long′er** *n.*

☆**prom** (präm) *n.* [< PROMENADE] [Colloq.] a ball or dance, as of a particular class at a school or college

prom·e·nade (präm′ə nād′, -näd′) *n.* [Fr. < *promener*, to take for a walk < LL. < L. *pro-*, forth + *minare*, to herd] **1.** a leisurely walk taken for pleasure, to show off one's fine clothing, etc. **2.** a public place for such a walk, as an avenue or the deck of a ship **3.** *a)* a ball, or formal dance *b)* a march of all the guests, beginning a formal ball —*vi., vt.* **-nad′ed, -nad′ing** to take a promenade (along or through); parade —**prom′e·nad′er** *n.*

Pro·me·the·an (prə mē′thē ən) *adj.* **1.** of or like Prometheus **2.** creative or original, esp. in a daring way

Pro·me·theus (prə mē′thyōōs, -thē əs) *Gr. Myth.* a Titan who stole fire from heaven to benefit mankind: in punishment, Zeus chained him to a rock where a vulture ate away at his liver

☆**pro·me·thi·um** (-thē əm) *n.* [ModL. < prec.] a metallic chemical element of the rare-earth group: symbol, Pm; at. wt., 145(?); at. no., 61

prom·i·nence (präm′ə nəns) *n.* **1.** the state or quality of being prominent **2.** something that is prominent or sticks out, as a hill

prom·i·nent (präm′ə nənt) *adj.* [< L. prp. of *prominere*, to project] **1.** sticking out; projecting [a *prominent* chin] **2.** noticeable at once; conspicuous [a bird with *prominent* markings] **3.** widely and favorably known [a *prominent* artist] —see SYN. at NOTICEABLE —**prom′i·nent·ly** *adv.*

pro·mis·cu·ous (prə mis′kyoo wəs) *adj.* [< L. < *pro-*, forth + *miscere*, to mix] **1.** consisting of different elements mixed together without sorting [a *promiscuous* collection of books] **2.** showing little or no taste or care in choosing; specif., engaging in sexual intercourse with many persons casually **3.** without plan or purpose; casual [her *promiscuous* club activities] —**prom·is·cu·i·ty** (präm′is kyoo′ə tē, prō′mis-), *pl.* **-ties, pro·mis′cu·ous·ness** *n.* —**pro·mis′cu·ous·ly** *adv.*

prom·ise (präm′is) *n.* [< L. *promissum*, ult. < *pro-*, forth + *mittere*, to send: see MISSION] **1.** an agreement to do or not to do something; vow [to make a *promise*] **2.** a sign that gives reason for expecting success [she shows *promise* as a singer] **3.** something promised —*vi.* **-ised, -is·ing** **1.** to make a promise **2.** to give a basis for expectation —*vt.* **1.** to make a promise to give (something) *to* somebody [I *promised* help to my friends; he *promised* her a gift] **2.** to engage or pledge (with an infinitive or clause) [to *promise* to go] **3.** to give a basis for expecting [clear skies *promise* good weather] **4.** [Colloq.] to assure —**prom′is·er,** *Law* **prom′i·sor′** (-i sôr′) *n.*

Promised Land 1. *Bible* Canaan, promised by God to Abraham and his descendants: Gen. 17:8 **2.** [p- l-] a place where one expects to have a better life

prom·is·ing (präm′i siŋ) *adj.* showing promise of success, excellence, etc. [a *promising* young poet] —**prom′is·ing·ly** *adv.*

prom·is·so·ry (präm′i sôr′ē) *adj.* containing a promise

promissory note a written promise to pay a certain sum of money to a certain person or bearer on demand or on a specified date

prom·on·to·ry (präm′ən tôr′ē) *n., pl.* **-ries** [< LL. < L. *pro-*

munturium, prob. < *prominere,* to project] a peak of high land that juts out into a body of water; headland

pro·mote (prə mōt′) *vt.* **-mot′ed, -mot′ing** [< L. pp. of *promovere* < *pro-,* forward + *movere,* to MOVE] **1.** to raise or advance to a higher position or rank [she was *promoted* to manager] **2.** to help bring about or further the growth or establishment of [to *promote* the general welfare] ☆**3.** to further the popularity, sales, etc. of by publicizing and advertising [to *promote* a product] ☆**4.** to move forward a grade in school —**pro·mot′a·ble** *adj.*

pro·mot·er (-mōt′ər) *n.* a person or thing that promotes; specif., a person who begins, gets financing for, and helps to organize an undertaking, as a business or a sports event

pro·mo·tion (-mō′shən) *n.* an act or instance of promoting; specif., *a)* advancement in rank, grade, or position *b)* furtherance of an enterprise, cause, etc. —**pro·mo′tion·al** *adj.*

prompt (prämpt) *adj.* [< MFr. < L. < pp. of *promere,* forth + *emere,* to take] **1.** quick to act or to do what is required; ready, punctual, etc. [prompt in paying his bills] **2.** done, spoken, etc. at once or without delay [a *prompt* reply] —*vt.* **1.** to urge into action [tyranny *prompted* them to revolt] **2.** to remind (a person) of something he has forgotten; specif., to help (an actor, etc.) with a cue **3.** to move or inspire by suggestion [cheerful music *prompts* happy thoughts] —see SYN. at QUICK —**prompt′ly** *adv.* —**prompt′ness** *n.*

prompt·er (prämp′tər) *n.* a person who prompts; specif., one who cues performers when they forget their lines

promp·ti·tude (prämp′tə tōōd′, -tyōōd′) *n.* the quality of being prompt; promptness

prom·ul·gate (präm′əl gāt′, prō mul′gāt) *vt.* **-gat′ed, -gat′ing** [< L. pp. of *promulgare,* to publish, altered < ? *pro-,* before + *vulgus,* the people] **1.** to publish or make known officially (a decree, law, dogma, etc.) **2.** to make widespread [to *promulgate* culture] —**prom′ul·ga′tion** *n.* —**prom′ul·ga′tor** *n.*

pron. 1. pronominal **2.** pronoun **3.** pronounced **4.** pronunciation

prone (prōn) *adj.* [< L. *pronus* < *pro,* before] **1.** lying or leaning face downward **2.** lying flat or prostrate **3.** having a natural bent; disposed or inclined (*to*) [prone to error] —**prone′ly** *adv.* —**prone′ness** *n.*

SYN.—**prone,** in strict use, implies a position in which one lies on one's belly [he fell *prone* upon the ground and drank from the brook]; **supine** implies a position in which one lies on one's back, and may suggest a listless feeling or passive attitude [lying *supine* on the grass and gazing lazily at the clouds]; **prostrate** implies the position of one thrown or lying flat in a prone or supine position or the state of one completely beaten, helpless, exhausted, etc. [the victim lay *prostrate* at his attacker's feet]; **recumbent** suggests a lying down or back in any position one might assume for rest or sleep [she was *recumbent* upon the couch] —see also SYN. at LIKELY —**ANT.** erect

prong (prôŋ) *n.* [akin to MLowG. *prangen,* to pinch] **1.** any of the pointed ends of a fork; tine **2.** any pointed projecting part, as the tip of an antler —*vt.* to pierce or break up with a prong —**pronged** *adj.*

☆**prong·horn** (prôŋ′hôrn′) *n., pl.* **-horns′, -horn′:** see PLURAL, II, D, 1 an antelopelike deer of Mexico and the western U.S., having curved horns

pro·nom·i·nal (prō näm′i n'l) *adj. Gram.* of, or having the function of, a pronoun —**pro·nom′i·nal·ly** *adv.*

pro·noun (prō′noun) *n.* [< MFr. < L. *pronomen* < *pro,* for + *nomen,* noun] *Gram.* a word used as a substitute for a noun and often referring to a noun used earlier in a sentence: *I, you, them, it, ours, who, which, myself, anybody,* etc. are pronouns

pro·nounce (prə nouns′) *vt.* **-nounced′, -nounc′ing** [< OFr. < L. < *pro-,* before + *nuntiare,* to announce < *nuntius,* messenger] **1.** to say or declare officially, solemnly, etc. [to *pronounce* a couple man and wife] **2.** to declare to be as specified [to *pronounce* a man guilty] **3.** *a)* to utter or

PRONGHORN
(to 3½ ft. high at shoulder)

articulate (a sound or word) *b)* to utter in the accepted or standard manner [he couldn't *pronounce* my name] —*vi.* **1.** to state or pass a judgment **2.** to pronounce words, syllables, etc. —**pro·nounce′a·ble** *adj.* —**pro·nounc′er** *n.*

pro·nounced (-nounst′) *adj.* **1.** spoken or uttered **2.** clearly marked; unmistakable; decided [a *pronounced* change] —**pro·nounc′ed·ly** (-noun′sid lē) *adv.*

pro·nounce·ment (-nouns′mənt) *n.* a formal statement of a fact, opinion, or judgment

☆**pron·to** (prän′tō) *adv.* [Sp. < L. *promptus:* see PROMPT] [Slang] at once; quickly; immediately

pro·nun·ci·a·men·to (prə nun′sē ə men′tō, prō-) *n., pl.* **-tos** [< Sp. < L.: see PRONOUNCE] **1.** a public declaration; proclamation **2.** *same as* MANIFESTO

pro·nun·ci·a·tion (prə nun′sē ā′shən) *n.* **1.** the act or manner of pronouncing words **2.** *a)* any of the accepted or standard pronunciations of a word *b)* the representation in phonetic symbols of such a pronunciation —**pro·nun′ci·a′tion·al** *adj.*

proof (prōōf) *n.* [< OFr. *prueve* < LL. *proba:* see PROBE] **1.** a proving, testing, or trying of something **2.** anything serving to establish the truth of something; conclusive evidence [do they have *proof* of his guilt?] **3.** the establishment of the truth of something [to work on the *proof* of a theory] **4.** a test or trial of the truth, worth, quality, etc. of something [the *proof* of the pudding is in the eating] **5.** the state of having been tested or proved **6.** tested or proved strength, as of armor **7.** the percentage of alcohol in an alcoholic liquor, as measured on a scale in which, in the U.S., 100 indicates 50% alcohol by volume [90 *proof* whiskey contains 45% alcohol] **8.** *Law* all the facts, admissions, and conclusions drawn from evidence which together operate to determine a verdict **9.** *Photog.* a trial print of a negative **10.** *Printing* an impression of composed type taken for checking errors and making changes —*adj.* **1.** of tested and proved strength **2.** able to resist, withstand, etc. (with *against*) [*proof* against criticism] **3.** used in proving or testing —*vt.* **1.** to make a proof of **2.** clipped form of PROOFREAD

-proof (prōōf) *a combining form meaning:* **1.** that cannot be penetrated by [waterproof] **2.** protected from [rustproof] **3.** resistant to [fireproof]

☆**proof·read** (prōōf′rēd′) *vt., vi.* to read and mark corrections on (printers' proofs, etc.) —**proof′read′er** *n.*

prop[1] (präp) *n.* [MDu. *proppe,* a prop] **1.** a support, as a stake or pole, placed under or against a structure or part **2.** a person or thing that gives support to a person, institution, etc. —*vt.* **propped, prop′ping 1.** to support or hold up, as with a prop (often with *up*) [to *prop* up a sagging roof] **2.** to place or lean (something) against a support [he *propped* his bike against the wall] **3.** to strengthen or bolster [to *prop* up one's spirits]

prop[2] (präp) *n. same as* PROPERTY (sense 5)

prop[3] (präp) *n.* clipped form of PROPELLER

prop. 1. proper(ly) **2.** property **3.** proposition **4.** proprietor

prop·a·gan·da (präp′ə gan′də, prō′pə-) *n.* [ModL., short for *congregatio de propaganda fide,* congregation for propagating the faith] **1.** [P-] *R.C.Ch.* a committee of cardinals in charge of the foreign missions **2.** intense effort to spread a certain set of ideas, doctrines, etc. that will help one's own cause or damage an opposing one: also **prop·a·gan′dism 3.** ideas, doctrines, or allegations so spread, esp. if regarded as false or deliberately misleading —**prop′a·gan′dist** *n., adj.* —**prop′a·gan·dis′tic** *adj.* —**prop′a·gan·dis′ti·cal·ly** *adv.*

prop·a·gan·dize (-dīz) *vt., vi.* **-dized, -diz·ing 1.** to spread (certain ideas or propaganda) **2.** to subject (people) to propaganda

prop·a·gate (präp′ə gāt′) *vt.* **-gat′ed, -gat′ing** [< L. pp. of *propagare,* to peg down < *propago,* slip (of a plant)] **1.** to cause (a plant or animal) to reproduce itself; raise or breed **2.** to reproduce (itself): said of a plant or animal **3.** to spread (ideas, customs, etc.) **4.** to extend or transmit (sound waves, etc.) through air or water —*vi.* to reproduce, as plants or animals —**prop′a·ga·ble** (-gə b'l) *adj.* —**prop′a·ga′tion** *n.* —**prop′a·ga′tive** *adj.* —**prop′a·ga′tor** *n.*

pro·pane (prō′pān) *n.* [PROP(YL) + (METH)ANE] a heavy, gaseous hydrocarbon, C_3H_8, of the methane series, used as a fuel, in refrigerants, etc.

‡**pro pa·tri·a** (prō pā′trē ə) [L.] for (one's) country

pro·pel (prə pel′) *vt.* -pelled′, -pel′ling [< L. < *pro*-, forward + *pellere*, to drive: for IE. base see FELT¹] to push, drive, or make go onward, forward, or ahead [a rocket *propelled* by liquid fuel] —see **SYN.** at PUSH

pro·pel·lant (-ənt) *n.* a person or thing that propels; specif., *a*) the explosive charge that propels a projectile from a gun ☆*b*) the fuel and oxidizer used to propel a rocket

pro·pel·lent (-ənt) *adj.* propelling or tending to propel —*n.* *same as* PROPELLANT

pro·pel·ler (-ər) *n.* a person or thing that propels; specif., a device (**screw propeller**) consisting of blades twisted to move in a spiral as they rotate with the hub, for driving a ship or aircraft forward

pro·pen·si·ty (prə pen′sə tē) *n.*, *pl.* -ties [< L. pp. of *propendere*, to hang forward + -ITY] a natural inclination or tendency; bent [he has a *propensity* for saving things]

prop·er (präp′ər) *adj.* [< OFr. < L. *proprius*, one's own] **1.** specially adapted or suitable; appropriate [the *proper* tool for a job] **2.** naturally belonging or peculiar

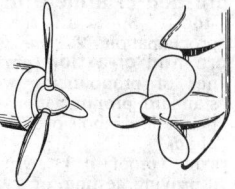

PROPELLERS
(left, air propeller;
right, water propeller)

(*to*) [weather *proper* to May] **3.** agreeing with an accepted standard or with good usage; correct [a *proper* spelling] **4.** fitting; seemly; right [*proper* modesty] **5.** decent or in good taste or very respectable [*proper* manners] **6.** in its most restricted sense; strictly so called [Chicago *proper* (that is, apart from its suburbs)] **7.** [Chiefly Brit. Colloq.] complete; thorough [a *proper* scoundrel] **8.** [Archaic or Dial.] *a*) fine; excellent *b*) handsome **9.** *Gram.* designating a noun that names a specific individual, place, etc., is not used with an article, and is normally capitalized, as *Donald*, *Boston*, etc. — *adv.* [Dial.] completely; thoroughly —see **SYN.** at FIT¹ —**prop′er·ly** *adv.* —**prop′er·ness** *n.*

proper fraction *Math.* a fraction in which the numerator is less than the denominator, as 2/5

proper subset a subset that does not include all the members of the set to which it belongs

prop·er·tied (präp′ər tēd) *adj.* owning property

prop·er·ty (präp′ər tē) *n.*, *pl.* -ties [< L. *proprietas* < *proprius*, one's own] **1.** *a*) the right to possess, use, and get rid of something; ownership [*property* in land] *b*) something, as a piece of writing, in which copyright or other rights are held **2.** a thing or things owned; possessions; esp., land or real estate owned [much loss of *property* during the fire] **3.** a specific piece of land or real estate [a fence around our *property*] **4.** any special characteristic or basic quality [the *properties* of a chemical compound] **5.** any of the movable articles used as part of a stage setting or in a piece of stage business, except the costumes, backdrops, etc. —see **SYN.** at QUALITY —**prop′er·ty·less** *adj.*

property man a person in charge of the properties in a theatrical production

proph·e·cy (präf′ə sē) *n.*, *pl.* -cies [< OFr. < LL. < Gr. *prophētēs*: see PROPHET] **1.** prediction of the future by a prophet, as supposedly influenced by the guidance of God or a god **2.** any prediction **3.** something prophesied

proph·e·sy (-sī′) *vt.*, *vi.* -sied′, -sy′ing **1.** to declare or predict (something) by or as by the influence of divine guidance; utter (prophecies) **2.** to predict (a future event) in any way —see **SYN.** at FORETELL —**proph′e·si′er** *n.*

proph·et (präf′it) *n.* [< OFr. < LL. < Gr. *prophētēs*, interpreter of a god's will < *pro*-, before + *phanai*, to speak] **1.** a person who claims to speak for God **2.** a religious leader who claims to be, or is thought to be, divinely inspired **3.** a spokesman for some cause, group, etc. **4.** a person who predicts the future —**the Prophet** *a name used for* MOHAMMED (by Moslems) *or for* ☆Joseph SMITH (by Mormons) —**the Prophets 1.** the prophetic books of the Bible that include Amos, Ezekiel, Hosea, Isaiah, Jeremiah, etc. **2.** the authors or subjects of these books — **proph′et·ess** *n.fem.*

proph·et·ic (prə fet′ik) *adj.* **1.** of, or having the powers of, a prophet **2.** of or containing a prophecy [a *prophetic* warning] **3.** that predicts Also **pro·phet′i·cal** —**pro·phet′i·cal·ly** *adv.*

pro·phy·lac·tic (prō′fə lak′tik) *adj.* [< Gr., ult. < *pro*-, before + *phylassein*, to guard] preventive or protective; esp., preventing disease —*n.* a prophylactic medicine, device, etc.; ☆esp., a condom

pro·phy·lax·is (-sis) *n.*, *pl.* -lax′es (-sēz) the prevention of disease or protection from disease; prophylactic treatment; specif., a cleaning of the teeth by a dentist, to remove plaque and tartar

pro·pin·qui·ty (prō piŋ′kwə tē) *n.* [< MFr. < L. < *propinquus*, near] **1.** nearness in time or place **2.** nearness of relationship; kinship

pro·pi·ti·ate (prə pish′ē āt′, prō-) *vt.* -at·ed, -at·ing [< L. pp. of *propitiare* < *propitius*: see PROPITIOUS] to win or regain the good will of; appease or conciliate [sacrifices made to *propitiate* the gods] —see **SYN.** at PACIFY —**pro·pi′ti·a·ble** *adj.* — **pro·pi′ti·a′tion** *n.* —**pro·pi′ti·a′tor** *n.* —**pro·pi′ti·a·to′ry** (-ə tôr′ē), **pro·pi′ti·a′tive** (-āt′iv) *adj.*

pro·pi·tious (prə pish′əs, prō-) *adj.* [< OFr. < L. *propitius* < *pro*-, before + *petere*, to seek] **1.** favorably inclined; gracious [the *propitious* gods] **2.** favorable; auspicious [a *propitious* sign] **3.** that favors or furthers [*propitious* winds] —**pro·pi′tious·ly** *adv.* —**pro·pi′tious·ness** *n.*

☆**prop·jet** (präp′jet′) *n. same as* TURBOPROP

pro·po·nent (prə pō′nənt) *n.* [< L. prp. of *proponere* < *pro*-, forth + *ponere*, to place] **1.** a person who makes a proposal or proposition **2.** a person who takes up or supports a cause, etc. [a *proponent* of lower taxes]

Pro·pon·tis (prə pän′tis) *ancient name of* the Sea of MARMARA

pro·por·tion (prə pôr′shən) *n.* [< MFr. < L. < *pro*-, for + *portio*, a part] **1.** the comparative relation of one thing to another with respect to size, amount, etc.; ratio [the *proportion* of girls to boys in our class is three to two; there are three girls to every two boys] **2.** a part, share, etc., esp. in its relation to the whole; quota [a large *proportion* of the earth is covered with water] **3.** a pleasing or proper arrangement or balance of parts [the small desk and large chair are not in *proportion*] **4.** size, degree, etc. relative to a standard **5.** [*pl.*] dimensions, as length, width, and height [a building of large *proportions*] **6.** *Math. a*) a relationship between four numbers, in which the first two are in the same relationship as the last two (Example: 2 is to 6 as 3 is to 9): also called **geometrical proportion** *b*) *same as* RULE OF THREE —*vt.* **1.** to cause to be in proper relation, balance, etc. [*proportion* the penalty to the crime] **2.** to arrange the parts of (a whole) so as to be harmonious or properly balanced [a well-*proportioned* statue] —see **SYN.** at SYMMETRY —**pro·por′tion·a·ble** *adj.* —**pro·por′tioned** *adj.* —**pro·por′tion·ment** *n.*

pro·por·tion·al (-′l) *adj.* **1.** of or determined by proportion; relative **2.** in proportion [pay *proportional* to work done] **3.** *Math.* having the same ratio —*n.* a quantity in a mathematical proportion —see **SYN.** at PROPORTIONATE —**pro·por′tion·al′i·ty** (-al′ə tē) *n.* —**pro·por′tion·al·ly** *adv.*

proportional representation a system of voting that allows each political party to be represented in a legislature in proportion to its share of the popular vote

pro·por·tion·ate (prə pôr′shə nit; *for v.* -nāt′) *adj.* in proper proportion; proportional —*vt.* -at′ed, -at′ing to make proportionate —**pro·por′tion·ate·ly** *adv.*

SYN.—*proportionate* and *proportional* both imply a being in proper proportion, the former usually being preferred when referring to two things that seem to have a cause-and-effect relationship [the output was *proportionate* to the work done], and the latter, when referring to things that are intended to be in a certain relationship [*proportional* representation]; **commensurable** applies to things that can be measured by the same standard or to things properly proportioned; **commensurate**, in addition, implies a being equal or suitable of things that are alike or related to each other [a reward *commensurate* with his heroism] —**ANT.** disproportionate

pro·pos·al (prə pō′z'l) *n.* **1.** a proposing **2.** a plan or action proposed **3.** an offer of marriage

SYN.—*proposal* refers to a plan, offer, etc. presented for acceptance or rejection [his *proposal* for a decrease in taxes was approved]; **proposition**, commonly used in place of **proposal** when referring to business dealings, etc., in a narrow sense applies to a statement, theorem, etc. set forth for argument, demonstration, proof, etc. [the *proposition* that all men are created equal]

pro·pose (prə pōz′) *vt.* -posed′, -pos′ing [< OFr. < L. pp. of *proponere*: see PROPONENT] **1.** to put forth for consideration or acceptance [we *propose* that the city build a zoo] **2.** to plan or intend [he *proposes* to leave] **3.** to present as a toast in drinking **4.** to nominate (someone) for membership, office, etc. —*vi.* **1.** to make a proposal; form a purpose, etc. **2.** to offer marriage —see **SYN.** at INTEND —**pro·pos′er** *n.*

prop·o·si·tion (präp′ə zish′ən) *n.* **1.** a proposing **2.** *a*) something proposed; plan [I accepted his *proposition* to share expenses] ☆*b*) [Colloq.] an immoral proposal, esp. in sexual relations ☆**3.** [Colloq.] a proposed deal, as in business ☆**4.** [Colloq.] a person, problem, etc. to be dealt with **5.** a subject to be discussed **6.** *Logic* an expression in which the predicate affirms or denies something about the subject **7.** *Math.* a theorem to be demonstrated or a problem to be solved —☆*vt.* to make a proposition, esp. an improper one, to —see SYN. at PROPOSAL —**prop′o·si′tion·al** *adj.*

pro·pound (prə pound′) *vt.* [< L. *proponere:* see PROPONENT] to put forth for consideration; propose [to *propound* a new theory] —**pro·pound′er** *n.*

pro·pri·e·tar·y (prə prī′ə ter′ē) *n., pl.* -**tar′ies** [< LL. < L. *proprietas:* see PROPERTY] **1.** a proprietor **2.** a group of proprietors **3.** proprietorship or ownership —*adj.* **1.** belonging to a proprietor **2.** holding property [the *proprietary* classes] **3.** of property or proprietorship [*proprietary* rights] **4.** privately owned and operated [a *proprietary* nursing home] **5.** held under patent, trademark, or copyright [a *proprietary* medicine]

pro·pri·e·tor (prə prī′ə tər) *n.* [< PROPRIET(ARY) + -OR] **1.** a person who is the only one who has the legal right to some property; owner **2.** one who owns and operates a business establishment —**pro·pri′e·tor·ship′** *n.* —**pro·pri′e·tress** (-tris) *n.fem.*

pro·pri·e·ty (-ə tē) *n., pl.* -**ties** [< OFr.: see PROPERTY] **1.** the quality of being proper, fitting, etc.; fitness [people question the *propriety* of a judge accepting such gifts] **2.** agreement with what is proper or fitting or with accepted standards of behavior —**the proprieties** accepted standards of behavior in polite society

pro·pri·o·cep·tor (prō′prē ə sep′tər) *n.* [< L. *proprius,* one's own + (RE)CEPTOR] any of the end organs in the muscles, tendons, etc. that are sensitive to the stimuli originating from within the tissues by the movement of the body —**pro·pri·o·cep′tive** *adj.*

prop root a root growing down from the plant stem into the ground, as on the mangrove, and helping to support the stem

pro·pul·sion (prə pul′shən) *n.* [< L. pp. of *propellere* (see PROPEL) + -ION] **1.** a propelling or being propelled **2.** something that propels; propelling or driving force —**pro·pul′sive, pro·pul′so·ry** *adj.*

pro·pyl (prō′pil) *n.* [< PRO(TO)- + Gr. *piōn,* fat + -YL] the monovalent radical C_3H_7, occurring in two isomeric forms —**pro·pyl′ic** *adj.*

pro·pyl·ene (prō′pə lēn′) *n.* [prec. + -ENE] a flammable, colorless gas, used in making polypropylene, synthetic glycerol, etc.

propylene glycol a colorless, thick liquid used as antifreeze, in making polyester resins, etc.

pro ra·ta (prō rāt′ə, rät′ə) [L. *pro rata (parte),* according to the calculated (share)] in proportion; proportionate or proportionately

☆**pro·rate** (prō rāt′, prō′rāt′) *vt., vi.* -**rat′ed, -rat′ing** [< prec.] to divide, assess, or distribute proportionately —**pro·rat′a·ble** *adj.* —**pro·ra′tion** *n.*

pro·rogue (prō rōg′) *vt., vi.* -**rogued′, -rogu′ing** [< MFr. < L. *prorogare,* to defer < *pro-,* for + *rogare,* to ask] to discontinue or end a session of (a legislative assembly) —**pro·ro·ga′tion** (-rō gā′shən) *n.*

pro·sa·ic (prō zā′ik) *adj.* [< ML. < L. *prosa,* PROSE] **1.** of or like prose; unpoetic **2.** commonplace; dull [to lead a *prosaic* life] —**pro·sa′i·cal·ly** *adv.* —**pro·sa′ic·ness** *n.*

pro·sce·ni·um (prō sē′nē əm) *n., pl.* -**ni·ums, -ni·a** (-ə) [L. < Gr. < *pro-,* before + *skēnē,* a tent] **1.** the apron of a stage **2.** the area separating the main part of the stage from the audience and including the arch (proscenium arch) and its curtain

pro·sciut·to (prə shōōt′ō) *n.* [It. < *prosciugare,* to dry out] a spicy Italian ham, cured by drying and served in very thin slices

pro·scribe (prō skrīb′) *vt.* -**scribed′, -scrib′ing** [< L. < *pro-,* before + *scribere,* to write] **1.** in ancient Rome, to publish the name of (a person) condemned to death, banishment, etc. **2.** to deprive of the protection of the law; outlaw **3.** to banish; exile **4.** to forbid or talk against as being wrong or harmful [candy is *proscribed* for children by most dentists] —**pro·scrib′er** *n.*

pro·scrip·tion (-skrip′shən) *n.* **1.** a proscribing or being proscribed **2.** prohibition —**pro·scrip′tive** *adj.* —**pro·scrip′tive·ly** *adv.*

prose (prōz) *n.* [MFr. < L. *prosa,* for *prorsa (oratio),* direct (speech), ult. < pp. of *provertere,* to turn forward] **1.** the ordinary form of language, without rhyme or meter: see also VERSE, POETRY **2.** dull, commonplace talk —*adj.* **1.** of or in prose

2. dull; unimaginative; prosaic —*vt., vi.* prosed, pros′ing to speak or write in prose —**pros′er** *n.*

pros·e·cute (präs′ə kyōōt′) *vt.* -**cut′ed, -cut′ing** [< L. pp. of *prosequi* < *pro-,* before + *sequi,* to follow] **1.** to follow up (something) to a conclusion [to *prosecute* a war] **2.** to carry on; keep at [to *prosecute* one's studies] **3.** *a)* to put on trial in a court of law for a crime or wrongdoing *b)* to try to get, enforce, etc. by legal process [to *prosecute* a claim] —*vi.* to begin and carry on a legal suit —**pros′e·cut′a·ble** *adj.*

☆**prosecuting attorney** a public official who acts for the State or the people in prosecuting persons for crimes, etc.; prosecutor

pros·e·cu·tion (präs′ə kyōō′shən) *n.* **1.** a prosecuting, or following up **2.** the conducting of a lawsuit **3.** the State as the party that begins and carries on criminal proceedings in court

pros·e·cu·tor (präs′ə kyōōt′ər) *n.* **1.** a person who prosecutes **2.** *Law a)* a person who begins a prosecution in court *b) same as* PROSECUTING ATTORNEY

pros·e·lyte (präs′ə līt′) *n.* [< LL. < Gr. *prosēlytos*] a person who has been converted from one religion, belief, etc. to another —*vt., vi.* -**lyt′ed, -lyt′ing** **1.** to try to change (a person) from one religion, political party, etc. to another **2.** to persuade to do or join something —**pros′e·lyt′er** *n.* —**pros′e·lyt·ism** (-li·tiz′m, -līt iz′m) *n.*

pros·e·lyt·ize (-li·tīz′) *vi., vt.* -**ized′, -iz′ing** *same as* PROSELYTE —**pros′e·lyt·iz′er** *n.*

Pro·ser·pi·na (prō sur′pi nə) *Rom. Myth.* the daughter of Ceres and wife of Pluto: identified with the Greek goddess Persephone: also **Pro·ser′pi·ne′** (-nē′, präs′ər pīn′)

‡**pro·sit** (prō′zit; *E.* prō′sit) *interj.* [G. < L. *prodesse,* to do good] to your health: a toast, esp. among Germans

pros·o·dy (präs′ə dē) *n., pl.* -**dies** [< L. < Gr. *prosōidia,* tone, accent < *pros,* to + *ōidē,* song] **1.** the science or art of composing verse or poetry, including the study of meter, rhyme, etc. **2.** a system of versification [Poe's *prosody*] —**pro·sod·ic** (prə·säd′ik), **pro·sod′i·cal** *adj.* —**pro·sod′i·cal·ly** *adv.* —**pros′o·dist** *n.*

pros·pect (präs′pekt) *n.* [L. *prospectus,* lookout, ult. < *pro-,* forward + *specere,* to look: see SPY] **1.** *a)* a broad view, as from a tower; scene *b)* a place from which one can see such a view **2.** a mental view; survey **3.** the view from any particular point; outlook **4.** a looking forward; anticipation [the happy *prospect* of a party] **5.** *a)* something hoped for *b)* [*usually pl.*] the likely chance for success [a team with no *prospects* of winning the pennant] **6.** a likely customer, candidate, etc. —*vt., vi.* ☆to explore or search (for) [to *prospect* for gold] —see SYN. at VIEW —**in prospect** expected

pro·spec·tive (prə spek′tiv, prä-) *adj.* **1.** looking toward the future **2.** expected; likely [a *prospective* inheritance] —**pro·spec′tive·ly** *adv.*

☆**pros·pec·tor** (präs′pek tər) *n.* a person who prospects for valuable ores, oil, etc.

pro·spec·tus (prə spek′təs, prä-) *n.* [L.: see PROSPECT] a statement outlining the main features of a new work, business enterprise, etc. or of an established institution

pros·per (präs′pər) *vi.* [< MFr. < L. < *prosperus,* favorable] to succeed, thrive, grow, etc. vigorously —*vt.* [Archaic] to cause to prosper

pros·per·i·ty (prä sper′ə tē) *n.* prosperous condition; good fortune, wealth, success, etc.

pros·per·ous (präs′pər əs) *adj.* **1.** prospering; flourishing [a *prosperous* business] **2.** well-to-do; well-off **3.** leading to success; favorable —**pros′per·ous·ly** *adv.*

pros·tate (präs′tāt) *adj.* [< ML. < Gr. *prostatēs,* one standing before, ult. < *pro-,* before + *histanai,* to stand] of or relating to the prostate gland: also **pros·tat′ic** (-tat′ik) —*n. same as* PROSTATE GLAND

pros·ta·tec·to·my (präs′tə tek′tə mē) *n., pl.* -**mies** the removal by surgery of all or part of the prostate gland

prostate gland a partly muscular gland surrounding the urethra at the base of the bladder in most male mammals

pros·ta·ti·tis (präs′tə tīt′is) *n.* inflammation of the prostate gland

pros·the·sis (präs′thə sis; *for 2, often* präs thē′-) *n., pl.* -**the·ses′** (-sēz′) [< LL. < Gr. < *pros,* to + *tithenai,* to place] *Med.* **1.** the replacement of a missing limb, eye, etc. by an artificial substitute **2.** such a substitute —**pros·thet′ic** (-thet′ik) *adj.*

---

fat, āpe, cär; ten, ēven; is, bīte; gō, hôrn, tōōl, look; oil, out; up, fur; get; joy; yet; chin; she; thin, then; zh, leisure; ŋ, ring; ə for a in ago, e in agent, i in sanity, o in comply, u in focus; ′ as in able (ā′b'l); Fr. bal; ë, Fr. coeur; ö, Fr. feu; Fr. mon; ô, Fr. coq; ü, Fr. duc; r, Fr. cri; H, G. ich; kh, G. doch; ‡foreign; ☆ Americanism; < derived from. See inside front cover.

pros·ti·tute (präs′tə to͞ot′, -tyo͞ot′) *vt.* **-tut′ed, -tut′ing** [< L. pp. of *prostituere* < *pro-*, before + *statuere*, to make stand] **1.** to sell the services of (oneself or another) for purposes of sexual intercourse **2.** to sell (oneself, one's integrity, etc.) for unworthy purposes —*n.* **1.** a person, esp. a woman, who is available to engage in sexual intercourse for pay **2.** a writer, artist, etc. who sells his services for unworthy purposes —**pros′-ti·tu′tion** *n.* —**pros′ti·tu′tor** *n.*

pros·trate (präs′trāt) *adj.* [< L. pp. of *prosternere* < *pro-*, before + *sternere*, to stretch out] **1.** lying with the face downward to show one's humility, reverence, etc. [worshipers *prostrate* before an idol] **2.** lying flat, either on one's face or on one's back [the boxer was laid *prostrate* by the blow] **3.** thrown or fallen to the ground **4.** *a)* laid low; overcome [*prostrate* with terror] *b)* physically weak or exhausted [*prostrate* from the heat] **5.** *Bot.* trailing on the ground —*vt.* **-trat·ed, -trat·ing 1.** to lay flat on the ground **2.** to lay low; overcome or exhaust [*prostrated* by illness] —see **SYN.** at PRONE —**pros·tra′tion** *n.*

pro·style (prō′stīl) *adj.* [< L. < Gr. < *pro*, before + *stylos*, pillar] having a portico with columns, usually four, across the front only —*n.* such a portico

pros·y (prō′zē) *adj.* **pros′i·er, pros′i·est 1.** like, or having the nature of, prose **2.** prosaic, dull, etc. —**pros′i·ly** *adv.* —**pros′i·ness** *n.*

Prot. Protestant

pro·tac·tin·i·um (prō′tak tin′ē əm) *n.* [ModL.: see PROTO- & ACTINIUM] a rare, radioactive, metallic chemical element: symbol, Pa; at. wt., 231.10; at. no., 91

pro·tag·o·nist (prō tag′ə nist) *n.* [< Gr. *prōtos*, first + *agōnistēs*, actor] **1.** the main character in a drama, novel, or story around whom the action centers **2.** a person playing a leading or active part

Pro·tag·o·ras (prō tag′ər əs) 481?–411? B.C.; Gr. philosopher

pro·te·an (prōt′ē ən, prō tē′ən) *adj.* **1.** [P-] of or like Proteus **2.** readily taking on different shapes or forms

pro·te·ase (prōt′ē ās′) *n.* [PROTE(IN) + (DIAST)ASE] an enzyme that breaks down proteins into simpler compounds

pro·tect (prə tekt′) *vt.* [< L. pp. of *protegere* < *pro-*, before + *tegere*, to cover] **1.** to shield from injury, danger, or loss; defend [armor to *protect* the knight's body] **2.** to set aside funds for paying (a note, draft, etc.) when it matures **3.** *Econ.* to guard (domestic goods) by tariffs on imports —see **SYN.** at DEFEND —**pro·tect′a·ble** *adj.*

pro·tec·tion (prə tek′shən) *n.* **1.** a protecting or being protected [the night watchman carried a gun for *protection*] **2.** a person or thing that protects [insurance is a *protection* against loss in case of accidents] **3.** a passport ☆**4.** [Colloq.] *a)* money demanded by racketeers from those they threaten with violence *b)* bribes paid by racketeers to avoid being arrested **5.** *Econ.* the system of protecting domestic goods by taxing imports

pro·tec·tion·ism (-iz′m) *n. Econ.* the system, theory, or policy of protection —**pro·tec′tion·ist** *n., adj.*

pro·tec·tive (prə tek′tiv) *adj.* **1.** protecting or intended to protect [a *protective* gesture; *protective* custody] **2.** *Econ.* intended to protect domestic products, industries, etc. in competition with foreign ones [a *protective* tariff] —**pro·tec′tive·ly** *adv.* —**pro·tec′tive·ness** *n.*

protective coloration (or **coloring**) natural coloration of certain animals allowing them to blend in with the natural environment and escape being noticed by their enemies

pro·tec·tor (prə tek′tər) *n.* **1.** one that protects; guardian **2.** *a)* a person ruling a kingdom during the time when the sovereign is unable to rule *b)* [P-] the title (in full **Lord Protector**) held by Oliver Cromwell (1653–1658) and his son Richard (1658–1659), during the Protectorate —**pro·tec′tor·ship′** *n.* —**pro·tec′tress** (-tris) *n.fem.*

pro·tec·tor·ate (-it) *n.* **1.** government by a protector **2.** the office or term of a protector **3.** [P-] the government of England under the Protectors (1653–1659) **4.** *a)* the relation of a strong state to a weaker state under its control and protection *b)* a state so controlled

pro·té·gé (prōt′ə zhā′, prōt′ə zhā′) *n.* [Fr., pp. of *protéger* < L.: see PROTECT] a person who is guided and helped in his career by another person with money or influence —**pro·té·gée** (-zhā′, -zhā′) *n.fem.*

pro·tein (prō′tēn, prōt′ē in) *n.* [G. < Fr. < Gr. *prōteios*, prime < *prōtos*, first] any of a class of complex substances containing nitrogen which are found in all animal and vegetable matter and are necessary to the diet of animals

pro tem·po·re (prō tem′pə rē′) [L.] for the time (being); temporary or temporarily: shortened to **pro tem**

pro·te·ol·y·sis (prōt′ē äl′ə sis) *n.* [ModL.: see PROTEIN & -LYSIS] *Biochem.* the breaking down of proteins, as by gastric juices, to form simpler substances —**pro′te·o·lyt′ic** (-ə lit′ik) *adj.*

pro·te·ose (prōt′ē ōs′) *n.* [PROTE(IN) + -OSE¹] any of a class of water-soluble products, formed in the hydrolysis of proteins, that can be broken down into peptones

pro·test (prə test′; *for n.* prō′test) *vt.* [< MFr. < L. < *pro-*, forth + *testari*, to affirm < *testis*, a witness] **1.** to state positively; declare or affirm strongly [he *protested* that he was innocent] ☆**2.** to speak strongly against [to *protest* injustice] **3.** to make a written declaration of the nonpayment of (a promissory note, check, etc.) —*vi.* **1.** to make a solemn or truthful statement about something **2.** to express disapproval; object [they *protested* against the high taxes] —*n.* **1.** the act or an instance of protesting; objection [they ignored his *protest* and continued hammering] **2.** a document formally objecting to something **3.** *Law* a formal declaration that a bill or note has not been honored by the drawer —see **SYN.** at OBJECT —**under protest** while expressing one's objections; unwillingly —**pro·test′er, pro·tes′tor** *n.*

Prot·es·tant (prät′is tənt; *for n. 2 & adj. 2, also* prə tes′tənt) *n.* [Fr. < G. < L. prp. of *protestari*: see prec.] **1.** a member of any of the Christian churches that grew out of the Reformation under the leadership of Luther, Calvin, Wesley, etc. **2.** [p-] a person who protests —*adj.* **1.** of Protestants or Protestant beliefs, practices, etc. **2.** [p-] protesting —**Prot′es·tant·ism** *n.*

☆**Protestant Episcopal Church** the Protestant church in the U.S. that follows the practices and principles of the Church of England

prot·es·ta·tion (prät′is tā′shən, prō′tes-) *n.* **1.** a strong declaration or positive statement [*protestations* of love] **2.** the act of protesting **3.** a protest; objection

Pro·te·us (prōt′ē əs, prō′tyo͞os) *Gr. Myth.* a sea god who could change his own form whenever he pleased

pro·thal·li·um (prō thal′ē əm) *n., pl.* **-li·a** (-ə) [ModL. < Gr. *pro-*, before + *thallos*, a shoot] the part of a fern that bears the sex organs, a small, flat, greenish disc usually attached to the ground by hairlike roots: also **pro·thal′lus** (-əs), *pl.* **-li** (-ī), **-lus·es**

pro·throm·bin (prō thräm′bin) *n.* [PRO-¹ + THROMBIN] a factor in the blood plasma that combines with calcium to form thrombin during blood clotting

pro·tist (prōt′ist) *n.* [< Gr. *prōtos*, first] *Biol.* any of a large group of one-celled organisms having characteristics found in both plants and animals and including algae, yeasts, bacteria, etc. —**pro·tis·tan** (prō tis′tən) *adj., n.*

pro·ti·um (prōt′ē əm, prō′shē-) *n.* [ModL.: see PROTO- & -IUM] the most common isotope of hydrogen, H¹, having a mass number of 1

pro·to- [< Gr. < *prōtos*, first] *a combining form meaning:* **1.** first in time, original, primitive [*prototype*] **2.** first in importance, chief [*protagonist*] **3.** [P-] primitive, original: said of people, their language, etc. [*Proto-Germanic*] Also, before a vowel, **prot-**

pro·to·col (prōt′ə kôl′, -käl′) *n.* [< MFr. < ML. < LGr. *prōtokollon*, first leaf glued to a manuscript (noting the contents) < Gr. *prōtos*, first + *kolla*, glue] **1.** an original draft or record of a document, negotiation, etc. **2.** the code of manners and courtesies that are accepted as polite and proper in official dealings, as between heads of state or diplomats —*vt., vi.* **-colled′** or **-coled′, -col′ling** or **-col′ing** to draw up a protocol, or state in a protocol

pro·ton (prō′tän) *n.* [ModL. < Gr. neut. of *prōtos*, first] a fundamental particle in the nucleus of all atoms: it carries a unit positive charge of electricity and has a mass approximately 1836 times that of an electron: see NEUTRON

☆**proton synchrotron** a synchrotron for giving very high energies to protons and other heavy particles

pro·to·plasm (prōt′ə plaz′m) *n.* [< G.: see PROTO- & PLASMA] a semifluid, colloidal substance that is the necessary living matter of all animal and plant cells —**pro′to·plas′mic** *adj.*

pro·to·type (prōt′ə tīp′) *n.* [see PROTO- & TYPE] **1.** the first thing or being of its kind; original [the U.S. Constitution was the *prototype* of other democratic constitutions] **2.** a model for another of its kind [this movie was the *prototype* for many later movies] **3.** a perfect example of a particular type [he is the *prototype* for the meek clerk] —**pro′to·typ′al** (-tī′p'l), **pro′to·typ′ic** (-tip′ik), **pro′to·typ′i·cal** *adj.*

pro·to·zo·an (prōt′ə zō′ən) *n.* [ModL. *Protozoa* (see PROTO- & -ZOA) + -AN] any of a large group of mostly microscopic, one-celled animals living chiefly in water, sometimes as parasites: also **pro′to·zo′on** (-än), *pl.* **-zo′a** (-ə) —*adj.* of the protozoans: also **pro′to·zo′ic** (-ik)

pro·tract (prō trakt′) *vt.* [< L. pp. of *protrahere* < *pro-*, forward + *trahere*, to draw] **1.** to draw out in time; prolong [*protracted* arguments] **2.** to draw to scale, using a protractor and scale **3.** *Zool.* to thrust out; extend —see SYN. at EXTEND —**pro·tract′ed·ly** *adv.* —**pro·tract′ed·ness** *n.* —**pro·tract′i·ble** *adj.* —**pro·trac′tion** *n.* —**pro·trac′tive** *adj.*

pro·trac·tile (prō trak′t′l) *adj.* capable of being protracted or thrust out; extensible

pro·trac·tor (-tər) *n.* [ML.] **1.** a person or thing that protracts **2.** an instrument in the form of a half-circle marked with degrees, for plotting and measuring angles

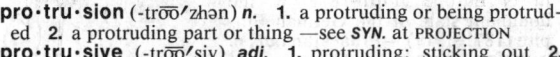

PROTRACTOR
(DAC, angle measured)

pro·trude (prō trōōd′) *vt., vi.* **-trud′ed, -trud′ing** [< L. < *pro-*, forth + *trudere*, to thrust] to thrust or jut out; project [*protruding* front teeth]

pro·tru·sile (prō trōō′s′l) *adj.* that can be protruded, or thrust out, as a tentacle, etc.: also **pro·tru′si·ble**

pro·tru·sion (-trōō′zhən) *n.* **1.** a protruding or being protruded **2.** a protruding part or thing —see SYN. at PROJECTION

pro·tru·sive (-trōō′siv) *adj.* **1.** protruding; sticking out **2.** *same as* OBTRUSIVE —**pro·tru′sive·ly** *adv.* —**pro·tru′sive·ness** *n.*

pro·tu·ber·ance (prō tōō′bər əns, -tyōō′-) *n.* **1.** a being protuberant **2.** a part or thing that sticks out; projection; bulge; swelling Also **pro·tu′ber·an·cy** (-ən sē), *pl.* **-cies** —see SYN. at PROJECTION

pro·tu·ber·ant (-ənt) *adj.* [< LL. prp. of *protuberare*, to bulge out < L. *pro-*, forth + *tuber*, a bump] bulging or swelling out; protruding; prominent —**pro·tu′ber·ant·ly** *adv.*

proud (proud) *adj.* [OE. *prud* < OFr. < LL. *prode*, beneficial < L. *prodesse*, to be useful < *pro-*, PRO-[2] + *esse*, to be: for IE. base see IS] **1.** having or showing a proper pride in oneself, one's position, etc. [he is too *proud* to ask for help] **2.** having or showing too high an opinion of oneself; haughty; arrogant [too *proud* to greet us] **3.** feeling or causing great pride or joy [his *proud* parents, a *proud* moment] **4.** caused by pride; presumptuous [he looks down on us with *proud* contempt] **5.** stately; splendid [a *proud* fleet] **6.** spirited [a *proud* stallion] —**do oneself proud** [Colloq.] to do extremely well —**proud of** highly pleased with —**proud′ly** *adv.*

SYN.—**proud** has a broad range of meaning, from having proper self-respect or pride to having too high an opinion of one's importance [too *proud* to beg]; **arrogant** implies the forceful presenting of oneself as having superior importance or privileges [the *arrogant* colonel]; **haughty** implies great awareness of one's high position, rank, etc. that shows itself in scorn for those one considers beneath one [a *haughty* aristocrat]; **overbearing** implies extreme, domineering haughtiness and contempt made clear in insulting behavior [an *overbearing* supervisor]; **supercilious** emphasizes a haughty, scornful manner toward others, thought of as inferiors [a *supercilious* snob]; **disdainful** implies very strong and obvious feelings of scorn for that which is beneath one —ANT. humble

proud flesh [< the notion of swelling up] an abnormal growth of flesh around a healing wound

Proust (prōōst), **Mar·cel** (mär sel′) 1871–1922; Fr. novelist —**Proust′i·an** *adj.*

Prov. 1. Provençal **2.** Proverbs **3.** Province

prov. 1. province **2.** provincial **3.** provisional **4.** provost

prove (prōōv) *vt.* **proved, proved** or **prov′en, prov′ing** [< OFr. *prover* < L.: see PROBE] **1.** to test by experiment, a standard, etc.; try out [a *proving* ground for new aircraft] **2.** to establish as true; demonstrate to be a fact [your grades *prove* that you know how to study] **3.** to establish the validity of (a will, etc.) **4.** to show (oneself) to be capable, dependable, etc. **5.** *Math.* to test the correctness of (a calculation, etc.) —*vi.* to be found by experience or trial; turn out to be [a guess that *proved* right] —**prov′a·bil′i·ty, prov′a·ble·ness** *n.* —**prov′a·ble** *adj.* —**prov′a·bly** *adv.* —**prov′er** *n.*

prov·e·nance (präv′ə nəns) *n.* [Fr. < L. < *pro-*, forth + *venire*, to come] origin; derivation; source

Pro·ven·çal (prō′vən säl′, präv′ən-) *adj.* of Provence, its people, their language, etc. —*n.* **1.** the common language of S France, a Romance language which, in its medieval form, was an important literary language **2.** a native or inhabitant of Provence

Pro·vence (prō väns′) region & former province of SE France, on the Mediterranean

prov·en·der (präv′ən dər) *n.* [< MFr. < ML. *praebenda*: see PREBEND] **1.** dry food for livestock, as hay, corn, etc. **2.** [Colloq.] provisions; food

prov·erb (präv′ərb) *n.* [< OFr. < L. < *pro-*, before + *verbum*, a word: see VERB] **1.** a short, popular saying that expresses some obvious truth; adage; maxim **2.** a person or thing that has become commonly recognized as a type; byword —see SYN. at SAYING

pro·ver·bi·al (prə vʉr′bē əl) *adj.* **1.** of, like, or expressed in, a proverb [*proverbial* wisdom] **2.** well-known because commonly referred to [the *proverbial* glamour of Paris] —**pro·ver′bi·al·ly** *adv.*

Prov·erbs (präv′ərbz) a book of the Bible containing maxims supposed to have been said by Solomon and others

pro·vide (prə vīd′) *vt.* **-vid·ed, -vid′ing** [< L. < *pro-*, before + *videre*, to see: for IE. base see VISION] **1.** to make available; supply [the school *provides* free books] **2.** to supply (someone with something) **3.** to state as a condition; stipulate [our lease *provides* that rent will be paid monthly] —*vi.* **1.** to prepare (for or *against* a possible situation, event, etc.) [to *provide* for rain by taking umbrellas] **2.** to furnish the means of support (for) [he has a large family to *provide* for] —**pro·vid′er** *n.*

pro·vid·ed (-vīd′id) *conj.* on the condition or understanding; if (often with *that*) [you may watch TV, *provided* you do your homework first]

Prov·i·dence (präv′ə dəns) [named by Roger WILLIAMS] capital of Rhode Island, on Narragansett Bay: pop. 179,000 (met. area 914,000)

prov·i·dence (präv′ə dəns) *n.* [< MFr. < L. < prp. of *providere*: see PROVIDE] **1.** a looking ahead to the future or preparing for it; provision [the *providence* of a nation in saving its natural resources] **2.** skill in management; prudence **3.** *a)* the care or help of God or nature [a special *providence* seemed to guide the weary travelers] *b)* an instance of this **4.** [P-] God

prov·i·dent (-dənt) *adj.* [< L. *providens*, prp. of *providere*: see PROVIDE] **1.** providing for future needs or events **2.** prudent or economical —see SYN. at THRIFTY —**prov′i·dent·ly** *adv.*

prov·i·den·tial (präv′ə den′shəl) *adj.* of, by, or as if ordered by divine providence —see SYN. at LUCKY —**prov′i·den′tial·ly** *adv.*

pro·vid·ing (prə vīd′iŋ) *conj.* on the condition or understanding; provided (often with *that*)

prov·ince (präv′ins) *n.* [< OFr. < L. *provincia*] **1.** an outside territory governed by ancient Rome **2.** an administrative division of a country; specif., any of the ten main divisions of Canada **3.** *a)* a territorial district; territory *b)* [pl.] the parts of a country away from the capital and major cities **4.** range of duties or functions [enforcing laws falls within the *province* of a police department] **5.** a field of knowledge, activity, etc. [the *province* of medicine] **6.** a division of a country under the jurisdiction of an archbishop or metropolitan

pro·vin·cial (prə vin′shəl) *adj.* **1.** of or belonging to a province **2.** having the ways, speech, attitudes, etc. of a certain province **3.** rural; countrified; rustic [*provincial* manners] **4.** narrow or limited in outlook; unsophisticated [a *provincial* attitude] —*n.* **1.** a native of a province **2.** a provincial person, esp. one who is unsophisticated —**pro·vin′cial·ly** *adv.*

pro·vin·cial·ism (-iz′m) *n.* **1.** a being provincial **2.** narrowness of outlook. **3.** a provincial custom, characteristic, etc. **4.** a word, phrase, etc. used in a certain province Also **pro·vin′ci·al′i·ty** (-shē al′ə tē), *pl.* **-ties** —**pro·vin′cial·ist** *n.*

proving ground a place for testing new equipment, new theories, etc.

pro·vi·sion (prə vizh′ən) *n.* [MFr. < L. < pp. of *providere*: see PROVIDE] **1.** a providing or supplying **2.** something provided for the future; specif., [pl.] a stock of food **3.** a preparatory arrangement or measure taken in advance [his savings are a *provi-*

sion for his old age] **4.** a statement, as in a will, that makes a condition [he was left the money with the *provision* that it be for his education] —*vt.* to supply with provisions [to *provision* an army] —**pro·vi'sion·er** *n.*

pro·vi·sion·al (-'l) *adj.* conditional or temporary, until a permanent arrangement can be set up [a *provisional* government] —**pro·vi'sion·al·ly** *adv.*

pro·vi·so (prə vī'zō) *n., pl.* **-sos, -soes** [ML. *proviso* (*quod*), provided that] **1.** a statement, as in a document, making some condition **2.** a condition or stipulation [you may borrow it, with the *proviso* that you return it promptly]

pro·vi·so·ry (-zər ē) *adj.* **1.** containing a proviso; conditional **2.** *same as* PROVISIONAL —**pro·vi'so·ri·ly** *adv.*

pro·vi·ta·min (prō vīt'ə min) *n.* any substance which can be changed into a vitamin when taken within the organism

Pro·vo (prō'vō) [after Étienne *Provot*, early fur trader] city in NC Utah: pop. 53,000

prov·o·ca·tion (präv'ə kā'shən) *n.* **1.** a provoking **2.** something that provokes; esp., a cause of anger or irritation [his noisy parties are a *provocation* to the neighbors]

pro·voc·a·tive (prə väk'ə tiv) *adj.* provoking or tending to provoke; that arouses one to be excited, angry, irritated, curious, etc. [her *provocative* remark] —*n.* something that provokes —**pro·voc'a·tive·ly** *adv.* —**pro·voc'a·tive·ness** *n.*

pro·voke (prə vōk') *vt.* **-voked', -vok'ing** [< MFr. < L. < *pro-*, forth + *vocare*, to call < *vox*, VOICE] **1.** to excite to some action or feeling [he was *provoked* into a fist fight] **2.** to anger or irritate [it *provoked* me to see such waste] **3.** to stir up (action or feeling) [to *provoke* interest] **4.** to call forth; evoke [his antics *provoked* laughter —see SYN. at IRRITATE —**pro·vok'er** *n.*

pro·vok·ing (-vō'kiŋ) *adj.* that provokes; esp., annoying or vexing —**pro·vok'ing·ly** *adv.*

pro·vo·lo·ne (prō'və lō'nē, präv'ə-) *n.* [It.] a hard, light-colored Italian cheese, usually smoked

pro·vost (prō'vōst; präv'əst; *esp. military* prō'vō) *n.* [< OE. & OFr., both < ML. *propositus*, for L. *praepositus*, chief, ult. < *prae-*, before + *ponere*, to place] **1.** a superintendent; official in charge **2.** the chief magistrate of a Scottish burgh **3.** the head of a cathedral chapter or principal church ☆**4.** an administrative official in certain American universities —**pro'vost·ship'** *n.*

☆**pro·vost guard** (prō'vō) a detail of military police under the command of an officer (**provost marshal**)

prow (prou) *n.* [< Fr., ult. < L. < Gr. *prōira*] **1.** the forward part of a ship **2.** anything like this

prow·ess (prou'is, prō'-) *n.* [< OFr. *prouesse* < *prou*, brave, var. of *prud:* see PROUD] **1.** bravery; valor **2.** superior ability, skill, etc. [his *prowess* in archery]

prowl (proul) *vi., vt.* [ME. *prollen* < ?] to roam about in a quiet, secret way, as in search of prey —*n.* a prowling —**on the prowl** prowling about —**prowl'er** *n.*

☆**prowl car** *same as* SQUAD CAR

prox. proximo

prox·i·mal (präk'sə m'l) *adj.* **1.** proximate; next or nearest **2.** *Anat.* located near the point of attachment of a limb, etc. —**prox'i·mal·ly** *adv.*

prox·i·mate (präk'sə mit) *adj.* [< LL. pp. of *proximare*, to come near < L. *proximus*, nearest, superl. of *prope*, near] **1.** next or nearest in space, order, time, etc. **2.** approximate —**prox'i·mate·ly** *adv.*

prox·im·i·ty (präk sim'ə tē) *n.* [< MFr. < L. < *proximus:* see prec.] nearness in space, time, etc.

☆**proximity fuze** an electronic fuze that sets off a bomb, missile, etc. when it gets close to the target

prox·i·mo (präk'sə mō') *adv.* [L. *proximo* (*mense*), in the next (month)] in or of the next month [on the 9th *proximo*]

prox·y (präk'sē) *n., pl.* **prox'ies** [ME. *prokecie* < *procuracie*, office of a procurator] **1.** the authority to act for another [voting by *proxy*] **2.** a person given this authority **3.** a document giving this authority, as in voting at a stockholders' meeting

prs. pairs

prude (prood) *n.* [Fr. < *prudefemme*, excellent woman] a person who is overly modest or proper in behavior, dress, speech, etc., esp. in a way that annoys others

pru·dence (prood''ns) *n.* **1.** the quality or fact of being prudent **2.** careful management; economy

pru·dent (prood''nt) *adj.* [OFr. < L. *prudens*, for *providens*, PROVIDENT] **1.** using sound judgment in practical matters, esp. as concerns one's own interests **2.** cautious in conduct; sensible; not rash **3.** managing carefully and with economy —see SYN. at WISE[1] —**pru'dent·ly** *adv.*

pru·den·tial (proo den'shəl) *adj.* **1.** characterized by or using

prudence ☆**2.** acting as an adviser [a *prudential* committee] —**pru·den'tial·ly** *adv.*

prud·er·y (prood'ər ē) *n.* a being prudish

prud·ish (prood'ish) *adj.* of or like a prude; too modest or proper —**prud'ish·ly** *adv.* —**prud'ish·ness** *n.*

prune[1] (proon) *n.* [< MFr. < VL. < L. < Gr. *proumnon*, plum] **1.** a plum dried for eating ☆**2.** [Slang] a dull or otherwise unpleasant person

prune[2] (proon) *vt.* **pruned, prun'ing** [< MFr., prob. ult. < *provain* (< L. *propago*), a slip] **1.** to remove dead or living parts from (a plant), as to increase fruit or flower production **2.** to cut out as being unnecessary **3.** to shorten by removing unnecessary parts [to *prune* a novel] —*vi.* to remove unnecessary parts —**prun'er** *n.*

pruning hook a long tool or shears with a hooked blade, for pruning plants

pru·ri·ent (proor'ē ənt) *adj.* [L. *pruriens* < *prurire*, to itch, long for] **1.** having lustful ideas or desires **2.** full of or causing lust; lascivious; lewd —**pru'ri·ence, pru'ri·en·cy** *n.* —**pru'ri·ent·ly** *adv.*

pru·ri·tus (proo rīt'əs) *n.* [< L. pp. of *prurire*, to itch] intense itching without a rash —**pru·rit'ic** (-rit'ik) *adj.*

Prus·sia (prush'ə) former kingdom in N Europe (1701–1871) & the dominant state of the German Empire (1871–1919) —**Prus'sian** *adj., n.*

Prussian blue any of a group of dark-blue powders used in paints, printing inks, etc.

PRUNING HOOK

prus·sic acid (prus'ik) *same as* HYDROCYANIC ACID

pry[1] (prī) *n., pl.* **pries** [back-formation < PRIZE[2]] **1.** a lever or crowbar **2.** leverage —*vt.* **pried, pry'ing** **1.** to raise or move with a lever or crowbar **2.** to draw forth or get with difficulty [to *pry* money from a miser]

pry[2] (prī) *vi.* **pried, pry'ing** [ME. *prien* < ?] to look (*into*) closely or curiously; peer or snoop [don't *pry* into my affairs] —*n., pl.* **pries** **1.** a prying **2.** a person who is too curious

pry·er (prī'ər) *n. same as* PRIER

pry·ing (-iŋ) *adj.* improperly curious or inquisitive —see SYN. at CURIOUS —**pry'ing·ly** *adv.*

Ps., Psa. Psalm; Psalms

ps. pieces

P.S. **1.** Privy Seal **2.** Public School

P.S., p.s., PS postscript

psalm (säm) *n.* [OE. *sealm* < LL. < Gr. *psalmos* < *psallein*, to pluck (a harp)] **1.** a sacred song or poem **2.** [*usually* P-] any of the sacred songs in praise of God that make up the Book of Psalms in the Bible

psalm·book (säm'book') *n.* a collection of psalms for use in religious worship

psalm·ist (-ist) *n.* a composer of psalms —**the Psalmist** King David, who is thought to have written some or all of the Psalms

psal·mo·dy (säm'ə dē, sal'mə-) *n.* [< LL. < Gr. < *psalmos* (see PSALM) + *ōidē*, a song] **1.** the singing of psalms **2.** psalms as a group **3.** the arrangement of psalms for singing —**psal'mo·dist** *n.*

Psalms (sämz) a book of the Bible, consisting of 150 psalms: also **Book of Psalms**

Psal·ter (sôl'tər) [< OE. & OFr., both < L. < Gr. *psaltērion*, psaltery < *psallein*, to pluck] the Book of Psalms —*n.* [also p-] a version of the Psalms for use in religious services

psal·ter·y (sôl'tər ē, sôl'trē) *n., pl.* **-ter·ies** [< OFr. < L.: see PSALTER] an ancient stringed instrument with a shallow sound box, played by plucking the strings

pseud. pseudonym

pseu·do (soo'dō, syoo'-) *adj.* [see next entry] sham; false; spurious; pretended; counterfeit

pseu·do- [< LL. < Gr. < *pseudēs*, false < *pseudein*, to deceive] *a combining form meaning:* **1.** fictitious, pretended, or sham [*pseudonym*] **2.** counterfeit, spurious, false [a *pseudoscience*] **3.** closely or falsely similar to (a specified thing): also, before a vowel, **pseud-**

PSALTERY

pseu·do·nym (sōō′də nim′, syōō′-) *n.* [< Fr. < Gr. < *pseudēs*, false + *onyma*, a name] a made-up name, esp. one taken by an author in place of his real name; pen name —**pseu·do·nym′i·ty** *n.* —**pseu·don′y·mous** (-dän′ məs) *adj.* —**pseu·don′y·mous·ly** *adv.*

pseu·do·po·di·um (sōō′də pō′dē əm, syōō′-) *n., pl.* **-di·a** (-ə) [ModL.: see PSEUDO- & PODIUM] a temporary sticking out of a part of a single cell, as in an amoeba, by means of which it can move about or take in food: also **pseu′do·pod′** (-päd′) —**pseu·dop′o·dal** (-däp′ə dəl) *adj.*

pseu·do·sci·ence (-dō sī′əns) *n.* any system of theories that claims to be a science but has no scientific basis —**pseu′do·sci·en′tif′ic** *adj.*

psf, p.s.f. pounds per square foot

pshaw (shô) *interj., n.* an exclamation expressing impatience, disgust, contempt, etc.

psi (sī, psē) *n.* [LGr. < Gr.] the twenty-third letter of the Greek alphabet (Ψ, ψ)

psi, p.s.i. pounds per square inch

psi·lo·cy·bin (sī′lə sī′bin, sil′ə-) *n.* [< ModL., genus name] a drug made from certain mushrooms that causes hallucinations

psit·ta·co·sis (sit′ə kō′sis) *n.* [ModL. < L. < Gr. *psittakos*, a parrot + -OSIS] an infectious virus disease of birds of the parrot family, often passed on to human beings, in whom it is characterized by fever and pneumonia

pso·ri·a·sis (sə rī′ə sis) *n.* [ModL. < Gr. < *psōra*, an itch] a chronic skin disease in which scaly, reddish patches are formed —**pso·ri·at·ic** (sôr′ē at′ik) *adj.*

psst (pst) *interj.* a sound made to get someone's attention quickly and quietly

PST, P.S.T. Pacific Standard Time

☆**psych** (sīk) *vt.* **psyched, psych′ing** [shortened from PSYCHOANALYZE] [Slang] to figure out the motives of, esp. in order to outwit, control, etc. (often with *out*)

psych. 1. psychological 2. psychology

Psy·che (sī′kē) [L. < Gr. < *psychē*, the soul] *Rom. Myth.* a maiden who becomes the wife of Cupid and is made immortal

psy·che (sī′kē) *n.* [L. < Gr. < *psychē*, the soul] 1. the human soul 2. *Psychiatry* the mind as a complex functional entity

☆**psy·che·del·ic** (sī′kə del′ik) *adj.* [< PSYCHE + Gr. *delein*, to make manifest] 1. of or causing extreme changes in the conscious mind, with hallucinations, delusions, etc. 2. of or like the intense, distorted sights, sounds, colors, etc. produced by such changes in the mind —*n.* a psychedelic drug —**psy·che·del′i·cal·ly** *adv.*

psy·chi·a·trist (sə kī′ə trist, sī-) *n.* a doctor of medicine specializing in psychiatry

psy·chi·a·try (sə kī′ə trē, sī-) *n.* [ModL.: see PSYCHO- & -IATRY] the branch of medicine dealing with the treatment of mental illness, including psychoses and neuroses —**psy·chi·at·ric** (sī′kē at′rik), **psy·chi·at′ri·cal** *adj.* —**psy·chi·at′ri·cal·ly** *adv.*

psy·chic (sī′kik) *adj.* [< Gr. < *psychē*, the soul] 1. of the psyche, or mind [*psychic* processes] 2. that cannot be explained by natural or known physical laws; supernatural [people used to think that an eclipse was due to *psychic* forces] 3. that seems to be sensitive to supernatural forces [a *psychic* person who appears to read your mind] Also **psy·chi·cal** —*n.* a person who seems to be sensitive to supernatural forces —**psy·chi·cal·ly** *adv.*

psy·cho (sī′kō) *adj., n. colloq.* clipped form of PSYCHOTIC, PSYCHOPATHIC, PSYCHOPATH

psy·cho- [< Gr. *psychē*, soul] *a combining form meaning* the mind or mental processes [*psychology*]: also, before a vowel, **psych-**

psy·cho·ac·tive (sī′kō ak′tiv) *adj.* [PSYCHO- + ACTIVE] designating or of a drug, chemical, etc. that has a strong or specific effect on the mind

psy·cho·a·nal·y·sis (sī′kō ə nal′ə sis) *n.* [ModL.: see PSYCHO- & ANALYSIS] a method or practice, originated by Freud, of treating neuroses and some other forms of mental illness through analysis of emotional conflicts, repressions, etc. by getting the patient to talk freely, analyzing his dreams, etc. —**psy·cho·an·a·lyt′ic** (-an′ə lit′ik), **psy·cho·an·a·lyt′i·cal** *adj.* —**psy·cho·an·a·lyt′i·cal·ly** *adv.*

psy·cho·an·a·lyst (-an′əl ist) *n.* a specialist in psychoanalysis

psy·cho·an·a·lyze (-an′ə līz′) *vt.* **-lyzed′, -lyz′ing** to treat by means of psychoanalysis

☆**psy·cho·dra·ma** (sī′kə drä′mə) *n.* a form of psychotherapy in which each patient in a group acts out situations related to his problem —**psy·cho·dra·mat′ic** (-drə mat′ik) *adj.*

psy·cho·dy·nam·ics (sī′kō dī nam′iks) *n.pl.* [with *sing. v.*] the study of the basic mental and emotional drives that make people think and behave in certain ways —**psy·cho·dy·nam′ic** *adj.* —**psy·cho·dy·nam′i·cal·ly** *adv.*

psy·cho·gen·ic (sī′kə jen′ik) *adj.* [PSYCHO- + -GENIC] caused by mental conflicts or emotional problems —**psy·cho·gen′i·cal·ly** *adv.*

psy·cho·ki·ne·sis (sī′kō ki nē′sis) *n.* [PSYCHO- + Gr. *kinēsis*, motion] the supposed ability to make things move or make things happen only by thinking about them —**psy·cho·ki·net′ic** (-net′ik) *adj.*

psy·cho·log·i·cal (sī′kə läj′i k'l) *adj.* 1. of or using psychology [*psychological* tests] 2. of the mind; mental [*psychological* development] 3. affecting or intended to affect the mind [*psychological* torture] Also **psy·cho·log′ic** —**psy·cho·log′i·cal·ly** *adv.*

psychological moment 1. the moment when one is mentally ready for something 2. the right moment for doing something successfully

psychological warfare the use of psychological means, as propaganda, to influence the thinking of the enemy or to weaken its morale

psy·chol·o·gist (sī käl′ə jist) *n.* a specialist in psychology

psy·chol·o·gize (-ə jīz′) *vi.* **-gized′, -giz′ing** 1. to study psychology 2. to reason psychologically —*vt.* to analyze psychologically

psy·chol·o·gy (-jē) *n., pl.* **-gies** [< ModL.: see PSYCHO- & -LOGY] 1. *a)* the science that studies the mind and the reasons for the ways that people think and act *b)* the science that studies human and animal behavior 2. the sum of the actions, traits, thoughts, etc. of a person or group [the *psychology* of the adolescent] 3. a particular system of psychology

psy·chom·e·try (sī käm′ə trē) *n.* [PSYCHO- + -METRY] the measurement of mental processes, as by psychological tests: also **psy·cho·met·rics** (sī′kə met′riks) *n.pl.* [with *sing. v.*]

psy·cho·neu·ro·sis (sī′kō nōō rō′sis, -nyōō-) *n., pl.* **-ro′ses** (-sēz) [ModL.: see PSYCHO- & NEUROSIS] *same as* NEUROSIS —**psy·cho·neu·rot′ic** (-rät′ik) *adj., n.*

psy·cho·path (sī′kə path′) *n. same as* PSYCHOPATHIC PERSONALITY (sense 1)

psy·cho·path·ic (sī′kə path′ik) *adj.* characterized by psychopathy; mentally ill —**psy·cho·path′i·cal·ly** *adv.*

psychopathic personality 1. a person with serious personality problems, whose behavior is amoral and asocial (often criminal), generally without seeming to be psychotic 2. the personality of such a person

psy·cho·pa·thol·o·gy (sī′kō pa thäl′ə jē) *n.* 1. the science dealing with mental illness 2. the behavior of the mentally ill —**psy·cho·path′o·log′i·cal** (-path′ə läj′i k'l) *adj.* —**psy·cho·pa·thol′o·gist** *n.*

psy·chop·a·thy (sī käp′ə thē) *n.* [PSYCHO- + -PATHY] mental illness

psy·cho·phar·ma·col·o·gy (sī′kō fär′mə käl′ə jē) *n.* the study of the effects of drugs on the mind —**psy·cho·phar′ma·co·log′i·cal** (-kə läj′i k'l), **psy·cho·phar′ma·co·log′ic** *adj.*

psy·cho·sex·u·al (-sek′shōō wəl) *adj.* having to do with the psychological aspects of sexuality in contrast to the physical aspects —**psy·cho·sex′u·al′i·ty** (-wal′ə itē) *n.*

psy·cho·sis (sī kō′sis) *n., pl.* **-cho′ses** (-sēz) [ModL.: see PSYCHO- & -OSIS] a major mental illness in which there is sudden, noticeable change in the personality and in which usually one's sense of reality is so confused that one cannot deal with ordinary situations —see SYN. at INSANITY

psy·cho·so·cial (sī′kō sō′shəl) *adj.* of the psychological development of an individual in relation to his social environment

psy·cho·so·mat·ic (-sō mat′ik) *adj.* [PSYCHO- + SOMATIC] 1. describing or of a physical disorder that is caused by or made worse by one's mental or emotional problems 2. describing a system of medicine using both a psychological and a physiological approach toward such disorders —**psy·cho·so·mat′i·cal·ly** *adv.*

---

fat, āpe, cär; ten, ēven; is, bīte; gō, hôrn, tōōl, look; oil, out; up, fur; get; joy; yet; chin; she; thin, then; zh, leisure; ŋ, ring; ə for *a* in *ago, e* in *agent, i* in *sanity, o* in *comply, u* in *focus*; ′ as in *able* (ā′b'l); Fr. bâl; ë, Fr. coeur; ö, Fr. feu; Fr. mon; ô, Fr. coq; ü, Fr. duc; r, Fr. cri; H, G. ich; kh, G. doch; ‡ foreign; ☆ Americanism; < derived from. See inside front cover.

psy·cho·ther·a·py (-ther′ə pē) *n.* [PSYCHO- + THERAPY] treatment of mental illness by counseling, psychoanalysis, etc. —**psy′cho·ther′a·peu′tic** (-ther′ə pyōō′tik) *adj.* —**psy′cho·ther′a·pist** *n.*

psy·chot·ic (sī kät′ik) *adj.* of or having a psychosis —*n.* a person having a psychosis —**psy·chot′i·cal·ly** *adv.*

psy·chot·o·mi·met·ic (sī kät′ō mị met′ik) *adj.* [< PSYCHOT-(IC) + -o- + MIMETIC] designating or of certain drugs, as LSD and mescaline, that produce hallucinations, psychotic symptoms, etc. —*n.* a psychotomimetic drug

psy·cho·tox·ic (sī′kō täk′sik) *adj.* [PSYCHO- + TOXIC] of or relating to substances that can damage the brain

psy·chrom·e·ter (sī kräm′ə tər) *n.* [< Gr. *psychros*, cold & -METER] an instrument for measuring the amount of water in the air by comparing the readings on two thermometers, one of which is left uncovered, while the bulb of the other is cooled by the evaporation of water from a wet cloth wrapped around it

Pt *Chem.* platinum

pt. *pl.* **pts.** 1. part 2. pint 3. point

p.t. 1. past tense: also **pt.** 2. pro tempore

P.T.A. Parent-Teacher Association

ptar·mi·gan (tär′mə gən) *n., pl.* **-gans, -gan:** see PLURAL, II, D, 1 [altered (after PTERO-) < Scot. *tarmachan*] any of several varieties of northern or alpine grouse, having feathered legs and changing in color with the season

☆**PT boat** [*p*(*atrol*) *t*(*orpedo*) *boat*] a high-speed motorboat equipped with torpedoes and machine guns

pter·i·do·phyte (ter′ə dō fīt′, tə rid′ə-) *n.* [< Gr. *pteris*, a fern + -PHYTE] any of a group of plants that reproduce by means of spores, as the ferns —**pter′i·do·phyt′ic** (-fit′ik), **pter′i·doph′y·tous** (-däf′i təs) *adj.*

pter·o- [ModL. < Gr. *pteron*] *a combining form meaning* feather, wing [*pterodactyl*]

pter·o·dac·tyl (ter′ə dak′t′l) *n.* [< ModL.: see prec. & DAC-TYL] an extinct flying reptile, having wings of skin stretched between the hind limb and a long finger of the forelimb —**pter′o·dac′tyl·oid′, pter′o·dac′tyl·ous** *adj.*

-pter·ous (tər əs) [see PTERO- & -OUS] *a combining form meaning* having (a specified number or kind of) wings [*homopterous*]

Ptol·e·ma·ic (täl′ə mā′ik) *adj.* 1. of Ptolemy, the astronomer, or his theory that the earth is the center of the universe and that the heavenly bodies move around it 2. of the Ptolemies who ruled Egypt

PTERODACTYL
(wingspread to 20 ft.)

Ptol·e·my (täl′ə mē) 1. (L. *Claudius Ptolemaeus*) 2d cent. A.D.; Gr. astronomer, mathematician, & geographer of Alexandria 2. *pl.* **-mies** Macedonian family whose members formed the ruling dynasty of Egypt (305?-30 B.C.); esp., *a*) **Ptolemy I** 367?-283; 1st king of this dynasty (305?-285) *b*) **Ptolemy II** 309?-247?; king of Egypt (285-247?)

pto·maine (tō′mān) *n.* [< It. < Gr. *ptōma*, a corpse < *piptein*, to fall] any of a class of alkaloid substances, some of which are poisonous, formed in decaying animal or vegetable matter by bacteria

ptomaine poisoning *earlier term for* FOOD POISONING (wrongly thought to be from ptomaines)

pty·a·lin (tī′ə lin) *n.* [< Gr. < *ptyein*, to spit + -IN¹] an enzyme in the saliva of man (and some animals) that changes starch into dextrin and maltose

Pu *Chem.* plutonium

pub (pub) *n. chiefly Brit. colloq. clipped form of* PUBLIC HOUSE (sense 2)

pub. 1. public 2. published 3. publisher 4. publishing

pu·ber·ty (pyōō′bər tē) *n.* [< L. < *puber*, adult] the state of physical development when sexual reproduction first becomes possible: the age is generally fixed in common law at 14 for boys and 12 for girls —**pu′ber·tal** *adj.*

pu·bes¹ (pyōō′bēz) *n.* [L., pubic hair] 1. the body hair appearing at puberty; esp., the hair surrounding the genitals 2. the region of the abdomen covered by such hair

pu·bes² (pyōō′bēz) *n. pl. of* PUBIS

pu·bes·cence (pyōō bes′'ns) *n.* 1. the quality or state of being pubescent 2. the soft down that covers the surface of many plants and insects

pu·bes·cent ('nt) *adj.* [Fr. < L. prp. of *pubescere*, to reach puberty < *pubes*, adult] 1. reaching or having reached puberty 2. covered with a soft down, as many plants and insects

pu·bic (pyōō′bik) *adj.* of or in the region of the pubes

pu·bis (-bis) *n., pl.* **pu′bes** (-bēz) [ModL. < L.: see PUBES¹] that part of either hipbone forming, with the other, the front arch of the pelvis

pub·lic (pub′lik) *adj.* [L. *publicus*, ult. < *populus*, the people] 1. of, belonging to, or concerning the people as a whole; of the community at large [the *public* welfare] 2. for the use or benefit of all; esp., government-supported [a *public* park] 3. acting officially for the people as a whole [the *public* prosecutor] 4. known by all or most people [a *public* figure] —*n.* 1. the people as a whole; community at large [what the *public* wants] 2. a specific part of the people [the reading *public*] —**go public** *Finance* to offer corporation stock for sale to the public —**in public** openly; not in privacy or secret —**pub′lic·ly** *adv.*

☆**pub·lic-ad·dress system** (pub′lik ə dres′) an electronic system, used in auditoriums, etc., for making announcements, music, etc. sound loud enough to be heard easily by a large audience

pub·li·can (pub′li kən) *n.* 1. in ancient Rome, a tax collector 2. [Brit.] a saloonkeeper; innkeeper

pub·li·ca·tion (pub′lə kā′shən) *n.* [< L. < *publicare*: see PUBLISH] 1. a publishing or being published; public notification 2. the printing and distribution, usually for sale, of books, magazines, newspapers, etc. 3. something published, esp. a magazine or newspaper

☆**public defender** a lawyer paid from public funds to defend poor persons accused of crimes who cannot afford to pay a lawyer

☆**public domain** 1. public lands, for the use of everyone 2. the condition of being free from copyright or patent, and available to anyone

public enemy a hardened criminal or other person who is a menace to society

public house 1. an inn 2. [Brit.] a place where alcoholic drinks are sold and served; bar

pub·li·cist (pub′lə sist) *n.* 1. a specialist in international law 2. a journalist who writes about public affairs 3. a person whose business is to publicize persons, organizations, etc.

pub·lic·i·ty (pə blis′ə tē) *n.* 1. a being public, or commonly known ☆2. *a*) any information that makes a person, place, etc. known or well-known to the public [the newspapers gave much *publicity* to our play] *b*) the work of handling such information 3. a being noticed by the public [a politician seeks *publicity*] 4. any procedure or act intended to gain public attention [he hired an agent to handle his *publicity*]

pub·li·cize (pub′lə sīz′) *vt.* **-cized′, -ciz′ing** to give publicity to; draw public attention to

public opinion the opinion held by people generally, esp. as a force that influences social and political action

☆**public relations** relations of an organization with the public through publicity seeking to form public opinion

public school ☆1. in the U.S., an elementary or secondary school that is part of a system of free schools supported by public taxes and run by local authorities 2. in England, any of several private, expensive, endowed boarding schools for boys, preparing them for the universities or the public service

public servant a person who serves the public, as anyone elected or appointed to a position or work in government

pub·lic-spir·it·ed (pub′lik spir′i tid) *adj.* concerned about and working for the public welfare

public utility an organization that supplies water, electricity, transportation, etc. to the public: it may be operated either by a private corporation (☆**public-service corporation**) under governmental regulation or by the government itself

public works ☆works constructed by the government for public use or service, as highways or dams

pub·lish (pub′lish) *vt.* [< OFr. < L. *publicare* < *publicus*, PUBLIC] 1. to make publicly known; announce; proclaim [to *publish* a secret] 2. *a*) to prepare and bring out (a book, newspaper, magazine, etc.), as for sale to the public *b*) to be the publisher of (a certain writer) —*vi.* 1. to publish books, newspapers, etc. 2. to write books, etc. that are published —**pub′lish·a·ble** *adj.*

pub·lish·er (-ər) *n.* a person or business company that publishes books, newspapers, magazines, etc.

Puc·ci·ni (pōōt chē′nē), **Gia·co·mo** (jä′kô mô′) 1858-1924; It. operatic composer

puce (pyōōs) *n.* [Fr., lit., a flea] brownish purple

puck¹ (puk) *n.* [akin to POKE¹] *Ice Hockey* a hard rubber disk which the players try to drive into the opponents' goal

puck² (puk) *n.* [OE. *puca:* for IE. base see BIG] a mischievous sprite or elf, as [P-] the one in Shakespeare's *A Midsummer Night's Dream*

puck·a (puk/ə) *adj.* same as PUKKA

puck·er (puk/ər) *vt., vi.* [< POKE²] to draw up into wrinkles or small folds [*to pucker* the brow in a frown; *to pucker* cloth by pulling a thread] —*n.* such a wrinkle or fold —**pucker up** to pull one's lips together as in getting ready to kiss —**puck/er·y** *adj.*

puck·ish (puk/ish) *adj.* [PUCK² + -ISH] full of mischief; impish —**puck/ish·ly** *adv.* —**puck/ish·ness** *n.*

pud·ding (pood/iŋ) *n.* [akin ? to OE. *puduc,* a swelling] **1.** [Scot.] a kind of boiled sausage **2.** a soft, mushy food, usually made with a base of flour, cereal, etc. and boiled or baked **3.** a sweetened dessert of this kind, variously containing eggs, milk, fruit, etc.

pud·dle (pud/'l) *n.* [dim. < OE. *pudd,* a ditch: for IE. base see BIG] **1.** a small pool of water, esp. stagnant or muddy water **2.** a thick mixture of clay, and sometimes sand, with water —*vt.* **-dled, -dling** **1.** to make muddy **2.** to make a thick mixture of (wet clay and sand) **3.** to treat (iron) by the puddling process —*vi.* to wade or wallow in muddy water —**pud/dler** *n.* —**pud/-dly** *adj.* **-dli·er, -dli·est**

pud·dling (-liŋ) *n.* the process of making wrought iron from pig iron by heating and stirring it in the presence of oxidizing agents

pu·den·dum (pyōo den/dəm) *n., pl.* **-den/da** (-də) [ModL., ult. < L. *pudere,* to be ashamed] [*usually pl.*] the external human sex organs, esp. of the female —**pu·den/dal** (-d'l) *adj.*

pudg·y (puj/ē) *adj.* **pudg/i·er, pudg/i·est** [prob. < Scot. *pud,* belly] short and fat —**pudg/i·ness** *n.*

Pueb·lo (pweb/lō) [see next entry] city in SC Colo., on the Arkansas River: pop. 97,000

☆**pueb·lo** (pweb/lō) *n., pl.* **-los;** also, for 2, **-lo** [Sp. < L. *populus,* people] **1.** an Indian village of the southwestern U.S.; specif., one in which the Indians live together in one or more flat-roofed structures of stone or adobe, arranged in terraces **2.** [P-] an Indian, as a Hopi, living in a pueblo

pu·er·ile (pyōo/ər əl, pyoor/əl; -īl) *adj.* [< Fr. < L. < *puer,* boy: for IE. base see FEW] childish; silly; immature —see SYN. at YOUNG —**pu/er·ile·ly** *adv.* —**pu/er·il/i·ty** (-ə ril/ə tē) *n., pl.* **-ties**

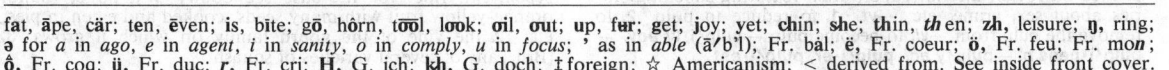

PUEBLO

pu·er·per·al (pyōo ur/pər əl) *adj.* [< L. < *puer,* boy + *parere,* to bear] of or connected with childbirth

Puer·to Ri·co (pwer/tə rē/kō, pôr/-) island in the West Indies that is a commonwealth associated with the U.S.: 3,421 sq. mi.; pop. 2,712,000; cap. San Juan: abbrev. **P.R., PR** —**Puer/to Ri/-can**

puff (puf) *n.* [OE. *pyff* < the *v.*] **1.** *a)* a short, sudden burst or gust, as of wind, or a forcing out, as of breath *b)* a small quantity of vapor, smoke, etc. forced out at one time **2.** a drawing into the mouth of smoke from a cigarette, etc. **3.** a swelling or a bulging part **4.** a shell of light pastry filled with whipped cream, etc. **5.** a soft, bulging mass of material, gathered in at the edges **6.** a soft roll of hair on the head **7.** a soft pad for dabbing powder on the skin or hair **8.** a quilted bed covering with a filling of down, etc. **9.** exaggerated praise, as in a book review —*vi.* [OE. *pyffan:* for IE. base see BIG] **1.** to blow in puffs, as the wind **2.** *a)* to give forth puffs of smoke, steam, etc. *b)* to breathe rapidly and hard, as after running **3.** to move (*away, out, in,* etc.), giving forth puffs [the steam engine *puffed* uphill] **4.** to fill, become inflated, or swell (*out* or *up*), as with air or pride [the sails *puffed* out in the wind; her skin *puffed up*] **5.** to take a puff or puffs on a cigarette, etc. —*vt.* **1.** to blow, drive, etc. in or with a puff or puffs [the wind *puffed* out the flame] **2.** to inflate; swell [she *puffed* out her cheeks when playing the trumpet] **3.** to praise too greatly, as in a book review **4.** to smoke (a cigarette, etc.) **5.** to set (the hair) in puffs —**puff/i·ly** *adv.* —**puff/i·ness** *n.* —**puff/y** *adj.* **puff/i·er, puff/i·est**

puff adder **1.** a large, poisonous African snake which hisses or puffs loudly when irritated ☆**2.** same as HOGNOSE SNAKE

puff·ball (puf/bôl/) *n.* any of various round, white-fleshed fungi that burst when mature if they are touched

puff·er (-ər) *n.* **1.** one that puffs ☆**2.** any of various fishes that can make the body larger by swallowing air or water

puff·er·y (puf/ər ē) *n.* exaggerated praise, esp. in publicity, advertising, etc.

puf·fin (puf/in) *n.* [ME. *poffin* < ?] a northern sea bird with a short neck, ducklike body, and brightly colored triangular beak

puff paste a rich dough for light, flaky pastries

pug¹ (pug) *n.* [< ? PUCK²] **1.** a small, short-haired dog with a wrinkled face, snub nose, and curled tail **2.** *same as* PUG NOSE

pug² (pug) *vt.* **pugged, pug/ging** [< dial.: prob. echoic of pounding] **1.** to mix (wet, plastic clay) for making bricks, earthenware, etc. **2.** to fill in with clay, mortar, etc. for soundproofing —*n.* wet, plastic clay

pug³ (pug) *n.* [Slang] a pugilist

Pu·get Sound (pyōo/jit) [after P. *Puget,* Eng. explorer] inlet of the Pacific, extending southward into NW Wash.

pug·ging (pug/iŋ) *n.* **1.** the mixing of pug (wet clay) **2.** clay, mortar, etc. used for soundproofing

pu·gil·ism (pyōo/jə liz'm) *n.* [< L. *pugil,* boxer, akin to *pugnare,* to fight + -ISM] *same as* BOXING —**pu/gil·ist** *n.* —**pu/gil·is/tic** *adj.*

pug·na·cious (pug nā/shəs) *adj.* [< L. < *pugnare,* to fight (for IE. base see POINT) + -OUS] eager and ready to fight; quarrelsome —see SYN. at BELLIGERENT —**pug·na/cious·ly** *adv.* —**pug·nac/i·ty** (-nas/ə tē), pug·na/cious·ness *n.*

pug nose a short, thick, turned-up nose —**pug/-nosed/** (-nōzd/) *adj.*

pu·is·sant (pyōo/i sənt, pyōo is/'nt, pwis/'nt) *adj.* [OFr. < *poeir:* see POWER] [Archaic] powerful; strong —**pu/is·sance** *n.* —**pu/is·sant·ly** *adv.*

puke (pyōok) *n., vi., vt.* **puked, puk/ing** [akin ? to G. *spucken,* to spit] *same as* VOMIT: avoided by some as a vulgar term

puk·ka (puk/ə) *adj.* [Hindi *pakkā,* ripe] [Anglo-Indian] **1.** good or first-rate of its kind **2.** genuine; real

pul (pool) *n., pl.* **puls, pul** [< Per., ult. < L., orig., bellows, hence bag, moneybag] *see* MONETARY UNITS, table [Afghanistan]

Pu·las·ki (poo las/kē; *Pol.* poo lä/skē), **Cas·i·mir** (kaz/i mir) 1748–79; Pol. general in the Am. Revolutionary army

pul·chri·tude (pul/krə tōōd/, -tyōōd/) *n.* [< L. < *pulcher,* beautiful] physical beauty —☆**pul/chri·tu/di·nous** (-'n əs) *adj.*

pule (pyōol) *vi.* **puled, pul/ing** [echoic] to whine or whimper, as a sick or fretful child

Pul·it·zer (pool/it sər; *now often* pyōo/lit-), **Joseph** 1847–1911; U.S. newspaper owner & philanthropist, born in Hungary

☆**Pulitzer Prize** any of various yearly prizes established by Joseph Pulitzer, for outstanding work in journalism, literature, and music

pull (pool) *vt.* [OE. *pullian,* to pluck] **1.** to use force or influence on so as to make move toward or after the source of the force; drag, tug, draw, etc. [to *pull* a sled; to *pull* up a sock] **2.** *a)* to draw or pluck out; extract (a tooth, etc.) *b)* to pick or uproot (weeds, etc.) **3.** to draw apart; tear [to *pull* a seam] ☆**4.** to stretch (taffy, etc.) back and forth repeatedly **5.** to strain or injure [to *pull* a muscle] ☆**6.** [Colloq.] to carry out; perform [to *pull* a raid] **7.** [Colloq.] to hold back; restrain [to *pull* one's punches] **8.** [Colloq.] ☆*a)* to take out (a gun, etc.) so as to threaten *b)* to force (a wheel, etc.) off or out **9.** *Baseball, Golf* to hit (the ball) so it goes to the left or, if left-handed, to the right **10.** *Printing* to take (a proof) on a hand press **11.** *Rowing* *a)* to work (an oar) by drawing it toward one *b)* to be rowed normally by [this boat *pulls* four oars] —*vi.* **1.** to use force in or for dragging, tugging, or attracting something [he *pulled* on the oar for over an hour] **2.** to take a deep draft of a drink, a puff on a cigarette, etc. **3.** to be capable of being pulled [this wagon *pulls* easily] **4.** to move or go (*away, ahead, out,* etc.) [the car *pulled* out of the driveway] —*n.* **1.** the act or force of pulling;

specif., *a)* a dragging, tugging, attracting, etc [one more *pull* brought the car out of the ditch] *b)* a drink, a puff on a cigarette, etc. *c)* a hard, steady effort [it's a long *pull* to the top] *d)* the force to move something, measured in pounds **2.** something to be pulled, as a drawer handle ☆**3.** [Colloq.] *a)* influence or special advantage *b)* drawing power; appeal —**pull apart** to find fault with; criticize —**pull down 1.** to tear down or overthrow **2.** to degrade; humble **3.** to reduce **4.** [Colloq.] to get (a specified wage, grade, etc.) —☆**pull for** [Colloq.] to cheer on, or hope for the success of —**pull in 1.** to arrive **2.** to draw in or hold back **3.** [Slang] to arrest and take to police headquarters —**pull off** [Colloq.] to accomplish or do —**pull oneself together** to regain one's self-control, courage, etc. —**pull out** ☆**1.** to depart ☆**2.** to withdraw or retreat ☆**3.** to escape from a responsibility, etc. —**pull over** to drive (a vehicle) to or toward the curb —**pull through** to get over (an illness, difficulty, etc.) —**pull up 1.** to uproot **2.** to bring or come to a stop **3.** to drive (a vehicle) to a specified place **4.** to check or scold —**pull′er** *n.*

SYN.—**pull** is a term broadly used in the sense of using force to make something move; **draw** suggests a smoother, more even motion than pull [he *drew* his sword from its scabbard]; **drag** implies the slow pulling of something heavy, especially something that resists being pulled [he *dragged* the desk across the floor]; **tug** may suggest hard, continued effort in pulling something, sometimes without being able to move it [he *tugged* at the rope in vain] or it may refer to a series of quick pulls on something [*tugging* at her skirt]; **haul** implies continued effort in transporting something heavy, often by mechanical means [to *haul* furniture in a truck] —**ANT. push, shove**

pull·back (pool′bak′) *n.* **1.** a pulling back; esp., a planned withdrawal by a military force **2.** something that hinders **3.** a device for pulling something back

pul·let (pool′it) *n.* [< OFr. dim. of *poule*, hen < L. *pullus*, chicken: for IE. base see FEW] a young hen, usually not more than a year old

pul·ley (pool′ē) *n., pl.* **-leys** [< OFr. < ML. *poleia*, ult. < Gr. dim. of *polos*, axis: for IE. base see COLLAR] **1.** a small wheel with a grooved rim in which a rope or chain runs, as to raise a weight attached at one end by pulling on the other end **2.** a combination of such wheels and ropes, used to increase the power being applied **3.** a wheel that turns or is turned by a belt, rope, chain, etc., so as to pass power on

☆**Pull·man** (pool′mən) *n.* **1.** [after G.M. *Pullman* (1831–1897), U.S. inventor] a railroad car with small private rooms or seats that can be made up into berths for sleeping: also **Pullman car 2.** [*often* p-] a suitcase that opens flat and has a hinged divider inside: also **pullman case**

☆**Pullman kitchen** [*also* p-] a small, compact kitchen, typically built into an alcove, as in some apartments

pull·out (pool′out′) *n.* **1.** a pulling out; esp., a removal, withdrawal, etc. **2.** something to be pulled out, as a section or a gatefold in a magazine

pull·o·ver (-ō′vər) *adj.* that is put on by being pulled over the head —*n.* a pullover sweater, shirt, etc.

pul·lu·late (pul′yoo lāt′) *vi.* **-lat·ed, -lat·ing** [< L. pp. of *pullulare*, to sprout < *pullus*, chicken] **1.** to sprout out; germinate **2.** to breed quickly **3.** to spring up in abundance; teem —**pul′lu·la′tion** *n.*

pull-up (pool′up′) *n.* the act of chinning oneself in gymnastics

pul·mo·nar·y (pul′mə ner′ē, pool′-) *adj.* [< L. < *pulmonis*, genitive of *pulmo*, a lung: for IE. base see FLOW] **1.** of, like, or affecting the lungs **2.** having lungs **3.** designating the artery carrying blood from the heart to the lungs or any of the veins carrying blood from the lungs to the heart: see illustration at HEART Also **pul·mon·ic** (-män′ik)

☆**Pul·mo·tor** (pool′mōt′ər, pul′-) [< L. *pulmo*, a lung + MO-TOR] *a trademark for* a device that gives artificial respiration by forcing oxygen into the lungs —*n.* [p-] such a device

pulp (pulp) *n.* [< Fr. < L. *pulpa*, flesh] **1.** a soft, moist, formless mass **2.** the soft, juicy part of a fruit **3.** the soft pith of a plant stem **4.** the soft, sensitive substance under the dentin of a tooth: see illustration at TOOTH **5.** ground-up, moistened fibers of wood, rags, etc., from which paper is made ☆**6.** a magazine printed on rough, inferior paper, often featuring shocking stories about sex, crime, etc. —*vt.* **1.** to reduce to pulp **2.** to remove the pulp from —*vi.* to become pulp —**pulp′i·ly** *adv.* —**pulp′i·ness** *n.* —**pulp′y** *adj.* **pulp′i·er, pulp′i·est**

pul·pit (pool′pit, pul′-) *n.* [L. *pulpitum*, a stage] **1.** a raised platform from which a clergyman preaches in a church **2.** preachers as a group

pulp·wood (pulp′wood′) *n.* **1.** soft wood for making paper **2.** wood ground to pulp for paper

☆**pul·que** (pool′kē; *Sp.* pōōl′ke) *n.* [AmSp., prob. of Mex.Ind. origin] an alcoholic drink, popular in Mexico, made from the juice of an agave

pul·sar (pul′sär, -sər) *n.* [PULS(E)¹ + -AR] any of several small objects in the Milky Way that send out radio pulses at regular intervals

pul·sate (pul′sāt) *vi.* **-sat·ed, -sat·ing** [< L. pp. of *pulsare*, to beat] **1.** to beat or throb rhythmically, as the heart **2.** to vibrate; quiver —**pul′sa·tive** (-sə tiv) *adj.* —**pul′sa·tor** *n.* —**pul′sa·to·ry** *adj.*

pul·sa·tion (pul sā′shən) *n.* **1.** a pulsating; rhythmical beating or throbbing **2.** a beat; throb; vibration

pulse¹ (puls) *n.* [< OFr., ult. < L. pp. of *pellere*, to beat: for IE. base see FELT¹] **1.** the regular beating in the arteries, caused by the contractions of the heart **2.** any regular or rhythmical beat, signal, etc. **3.** the underlying feelings of a group, the public, etc. **4.** a brief surge of electric current **5.** a very short burst of radio waves —*vi.* **pulsed, puls′ing** to beat or throb [the music *pulsed* in his ears] —*vt.* to cause to pulse —**puls′er** *n.*

pulse² (puls) *n.* [< OFr. < L. *puls*, a pottage: for IE. base see POLLEN] **1.** the seeds of peas, beans, lentils, and similar plants having pods and used as food **2.** any such plant

pulse·jet (**engine**) (puls′jet′) a jet engine in which the valves that bring air into the combustion chamber open and close in a pulselike manner

pul·ver·ize (pul′və rīz′) *vt.* **-ized′, -iz′ing** [< MFr. < LL. < L. *pulvis*, dust: for IE. base see POLLEN] **1.** to crush, grind, etc. into a powder or dust **2.** to destroy completely; demolish [the bombs *pulverized* the city] —*vi.* to be pulverized into a powder or dust —**pul′ver·iz′a·ble, pul′ver·a·ble** (-vər ə b'l) *adj.* —**pul′ver·i·za′tion** *n.* —**pul′ver·iz′er** *n.*

pu·ma (pyōō′mə, pōō′-) *n., pl.* **-mas, -ma:** see PLURAL, II, D, 1 [AmSp. < Quechua] *same as* COUGAR

pum·ice (pum′is) *n.* [< OFr. < L. *pumex*] a spongy, light rock formed from the lava of a volcano and used in solid or powdered form to scour, smooth, and polish: also **pumice stone** —*vt.* **-iced, -ic·ing** to clean, polish, etc. with pumice —**pu·mi·ceous** (pyōō mish′əs) *adj.*

pum·mel (pum′'l) *vt.* **-meled** or **-melled, -mel·ing** or **-mel·ling** [< POMMEL] to beat or hit with repeated blows, esp. with the fist —see **SYN.** at BEAT

pump¹ (pump) *n.* [< MDu. *pompe* < Sp. *bomba*, prob. of echoic origin] any of various machines that force a liquid or gas into or through, or draw it out of, something, as by suction or pressure —*vt.* **1.** to raise or move (fluids) with a pump [to *pump* water from a well] **2.** to remove water, etc. from, as with a pump [to *pump* out a flooded basement] **3.** to drive air into, as with a pump [to *pump* up a tire] **4.** to force in, draw out, move up and down, etc. in the manner of a pump [they *pumped* money into the building program] **5.** to apply force to with a pumping motion [she *pumped* the pedals of the bicycle] **6.** [Colloq.] *a)* to question closely and repeatedly [the police *pumped* the suspect] *b)* to get (information) in this way —*vi.* **1.** to work a pump **2.** to move water, etc. with a pump **3.** to move or go up and down like a pump handle **4.** to flow in, out, or through by, or as if by, being pumped [the blood was *pumping* through his veins] —**pump′er** *n.*

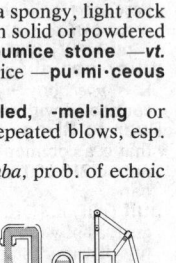

pump² (pump) *n.* [< ? Fr. *pompe*, an ornament] a low-cut shoe without straps or ties

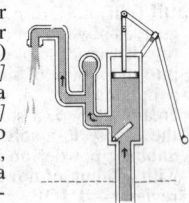

PUMP

☆**pump·er·nick·el** (pum′pər nik′'l) *n.* [G.] a coarse, dark, sour bread made of unsifted rye

pump·kin (pum′kin, pump′-, puŋ′-) *n.* [< MFr. < L. < Gr. *pepōn*, lit., ripe: for IE. base see COOK] **1.** a large, round, orange-yellow fruit with many seeds, cooked and eaten in pies, etc. **2.** the vine of the gourd family on which it grows **3.** [Brit.] any of several varieties of squash

PULPIT

PULLEYS
(A, anchor;
E, energy;
W, weight)

pump·kin·seed (-sēd´) *n.* **1.** the seed of the pumpkin ☆**2.** a small, freshwater sunfish of N. America, greenish-yellow above and orange-yellow below

pun (pun) *n.* [< ? It. *puntiglio*, fine point] the humorous use of words that have the same sound or spelling, but have different meanings; a play on words [there is a *pun* in the name of a restaurant called the "Dewdrop Inn"] —*vi.* **punned, pun´ning** to make a pun or puns —**pun´ner** *n.*

Punch (punch) [< PUNCHINELLO] the hero of the puppet show **Punch and Judy,** a humpbacked figure with a hooked nose, constantly fighting with his wife, Judy —**pleased as Punch** greatly pleased

punch¹ (punch) *n.* [see PUNCHEON¹] **1.** *a)* a tool driven or pressed against a surface that is to be shaped or stamped *b)* a tool driven against a nail, bolt, etc. that is to be worked in or out **2.** a device or machine for making holes, cuts, etc. [a paper *punch*] **3.** the hole, cut, etc. so made —*vt.* **1.** to pierce, stamp, etc. with a punch **2.** to make (a hole, etc.) with a punch — **punch´er** *n.*

punch² (punch) *vt.* [ME. *punchen*] **1.** to prod or poke with a stick ☆**2.** to herd (cattle) as by prodding **3.** to strike with the fist —*n.* **1.** a thrusting blow with the fist ☆**2.** [Colloq.] force or vigor that has a strong effect —**pull one's punches** [Colloq.] to give blows, criticisms, etc. intended to have little or no effect —☆**punch a (time) clock** to put a timecard into a time clock when arriving at or leaving work —☆**punch in** (or **out**) to make a record that one has arrived (or left) by punching a time clock —**punch´er** *n.*

punch³ (punch) *n.* [Hindi *pāc*, five: it orig. had five ingredients] a sweet drink of fruit juices, carbonated beverages, sherbet, etc., often mixed with wine or liquor, and served in cups from a large bowl (**punch bowl**)

☆**punch·board** (punch´bôrd´) *n.* a board or card with covered holes to be punched out, used as a game of chance: the holes contain slips or disks with hidden numbers, etc. usually naming prizes to be won

☆**punch card** a card with holes or notches put in certain places in it, used by a key punch for data processing

punch-drunk (-druŋk´) *adj.* dazed, walking unsteadily, confused in speech, etc., as because of many blows to the head in boxing

pun·cheon¹ (pun´chən) *n.* [< MFr., ult. < L. pp. of *pungere*, to prick] **1.** a short, upright wooden post used in framework ☆**2.** a heavy piece of timber roughly trimmed with one side flat **3.** a device for punching, stamping, etc.

pun·cheon² (pun´chən) *n.* [OFr. *poinçon*] **1.** a large cask of varying capacity (72–120 gal.), for beer, wine, etc. **2.** as much as such a cask will hold

pun·chi·nel·lo (pun´chə nel´ō) *n., pl.* **-los** [< a character's name in a Neapolitan puppet play] a buffoon; clown

punching bag a stuffed or inflated leather bag hung up in order to be punched for exercise or practice

☆**punch line** the line carrying the point of a joke

punch press a press in which dies are fitted for cutting, shaping, or stamping metal

punch·y (pun´chē) *adj.* **punch´i·er, punch´i·est** [Colloq.] ☆**1.** forceful; vigorous ☆**2.** *same as* PUNCH-DRUNK

punc·til·i·o (puŋk til´ē ō´) *n., pl.* **-os´** [< Sp. or It., ult. < L. *punctum*, a POINT] **1.** a small detail of conduct, ceremony, etc. **2.** a being punctilious

punc·til·i·ous (-ē əs) *adj.* **1.** very careful about every detail of behavior, ceremony, etc. [a *punctilious* host] **2.** very exact; careful about details [to keep *punctilious* records] — **punc·til´i·ous·ly** *adv.* —**punc·til´i·ous·ness** *n.*

punc·tu·al (puŋk´choo wəl) *adj.* [< ML. *punctualis* < L. *punctus*, a POINT] on time; prompt —**punc·tu·al´i·ty** (-wal´ə tē) *n.* —**punc´tu·al·ly** *adv.* —**punc´tu·al·ness** *n.*

punc·tu·ate (puŋk´choo wāt´) *vt.* **-at´ed, -at´ing** [< ML. pp. of *punctuare* < L. *punctus*, a POINT] **1.** *a)* to insert punctuation marks in *b)* to function as a punctuation mark in **2.** to break in on here and there [a speech *punctuated* with applause] **3.**

to emphasize; accentuate [he *punctuated* his protest by shouting] —*vi.* to use punctuation marks —**punc´tu·a´tor** *n.*

punc·tu·a·tion (puŋk´choo wā´shən) *n.* **1.** a punctuating; specif., the use of standardized marks in writing and printing to separate sentences or parts of a sentence or to make meaning clearer **2.** a punctuation mark or marks

punctuation mark any of the marks used in punctuation, as a period, comma, question mark, colon, semicolon, dash, etc.

punc·ture (puŋk´chər) *n.* [< L. < *pungere*, to pierce: see POINT] **1.** a making of a hole with a sharp point; piercing **2.** a hole made by a sharp point —*vt.* **-tured, -tur·ing** **1.** to make a hole with a sharp point; pierce [to *puncture* a balloon] **2.** to reduce or put an end to, as if by piercing [to *puncture* one's pride] —*vi.* to be punctured —**punc´tur·a·ble** *adj.*

pun·dit (pun´dit) *n.* [< Hindi < Sans. *paṇḍita*] **1.** in India, a Brahman learned in Sanskrit, Hindu philosophy, etc. **2.** a person who has great learning

pun·gent (pun´jənt) *adj.* [< L. prp. of *pungere*, to prick: see POINT] **1.** producing a sharp sensation of taste or smell; acrid [a *pungent* chili sauce] **2.** sharp to the mind; poignant [a *pungent* sermon] **3.** very keen and direct, sometimes painfully so; biting [*pungent* language] **4.** keenly clever [*pungent* wit] — **pun´gen·cy** *n.* —**pun´gent·ly** *adv.*

Pu·nic (pyoo´nik) *adj.* [L. *Punicus* < *Poeni*, the Carthaginians] **1.** of ancient Carthage or its people **2.** like the Carthaginians, thought of by the Romans as faithless and treacherous

pun·ish (pun´ish) *vt.* [< OFr. < L. *punire*, to punish < *poena*, punishment: see PENAL] **1.** to cause to undergo pain, loss, or suffering for a crime or wrongdoing **2.** to set a penalty for [to *punish* murder with life imprisonment] **3.** to treat harshly or harmfully [the *punishing* rays of the sun] **4.** [Colloq.] to consume or use up [he *punished* a whole pie] —*vi.* to deal out punishment —**pun´ish·a·bil´i·ty** *n.* —**pun´ish·a·ble** *adj.* — **pun´ish·er** *n.*

SYN.—**punish** implies making a wrongdoer suffer for his wrongdoing by paying a penalty, usually with no idea of reforming or correcting him [to *punish* a murderer by hanging him]; **discipline** suggests punishment that is intended to control the wrongdoer or to establish in him habits of self-control [to *discipline* a naughty child]; **correct** suggests punishment of a wrongdoer for the purpose of overcoming his faults [to *correct* unruly pupils]; **chastise** implies punishment, usually physical punishment, along with an attempt to correct the wrongdoer

pun·ish·ment (-mənt) *n.* **1.** a punishing or being punished **2.** what is done to a person to make him pay for his crime or wrongdoing **3.** harsh treatment

pu·ni·tive (pyoo´ni tiv) *adj.* that punishes or has to do with punishment: also **pu´ni·to·ry** (-tôr´ē) —**pu´ni·tive·ly** *adv.* — **pu´ni·tive·ness** *n.*

punitive damages *same as* EXEMPLARY DAMAGES

Pun·jab (pun jäb´, pun´jäb, -jab) **1.** region in NW India & NE Pakistan, between the Indus & Jumna rivers **2.** state of India, in this region: 19,403 sq. mi.; pop. 11,147,000

☆**punk¹** (puŋk) *n.* [var. of SPUNK] any substance, as decayed wood, that burns very slowly without a flame, used as tinder; esp., a fungous substance shaped into slender, fragile sticks and used to light fireworks, etc.

punk² (puŋk) *n.* [< ?] [Slang] ☆**1.** a young hoodlum ☆**2.** anyone, esp. a youngster, regarded as inexperienced, insignificant, etc. —☆*adj.* [Slang] poor or bad in quality, condition, etc.

PUNCHING BAG

PUNJAB

pun·kah, pun·ka (puŋ´kə) *n.* [Hindi *pankhā*] in India, a large fan made from the palmyra leaf, or a large, swinging fan hung from the ceiling

☆**punk·ie** (puŋ´kē) *n.* [ult. < Algonquian] a tiny fly with piercing and sucking mouthparts

pun·ster (pun´stər) *n.* a person who is fond of making puns

punt¹ (punt) *n.* [< slang of Rugby School, England] *Football* a kick in which the ball is dropped from the hands and then kicked

fat, āpe, cär; ten, ēven; is, bīte; gō, hôrn, to͞ol, lo͝ok; oil, out; up, fur; get; joy; yet; chin; she; thin, then; zh, leisure; ŋ, ring; ə for a in ago, e in agent, i in sanity, o in comply, u in focus; ' as in able (ā´b'l); Fr. bal; ë, Fr. coeur; ö, Fr. feu; Fr. mon; ô, Fr. coq; ü, Fr. duc; r, Fr. cri; H, G. ich; kh, G. doch; ‡foreign; ☆ Americanism; < derived from. See inside front cover.

before it strikes the ground —*vt., vi.* to kick (a football) in this way —**punt′er** *n.*

punt² (punt) *n.* [OE. < L. *ponto:* see PONTOON] a flat-bottomed boat with square ends, usually pushed along by a long pole —*vt.* **1.** to move (a boat) along by pushing with a pole against the bottom of a shallow river or lake **2.** to carry in a punt —*vi.* to go in a punt —**punt′er** *n.*

punt³ (punt) *vi.* [< Fr. < Sp. *punto* < L. *punctum,* a point] **1.** in certain card games, to bet against the banker **2.** [Brit.] to gamble; bet —**punt′er** *n.*

Pun·ta A·re·nas (pōōn′tä ä re′näs) seaport in S Chile, on the Strait of Magellan: pop. 68,000

pu·ny (pyōō′nē) *adj.* **-ni·er, -ni·est** [< Fr. < OFr. *puis,* after + *né,* born] of inferior size, strength, or importance; weak —**pu′·ni·ness** *n.*

pup (pup) *n.* **1.** *a)* a young dog; puppy **2.** a young fox, wolf, seal, whale, etc. —*vi.* **pupped, pup′ping** to give birth to pups

pu·pa (pyōō′pə) *n., pl.* **-pae** (-pē), **-pas** [ModL. < L., a girl, doll] an insect in the stage between the larval and adult forms: some pupae are enclosed in cocoons —**pu′pal** *adj.*

PUPA

pu·pate (-pāt) *vi.* **-pat·ed, -pat·ing** to go through the pupal stage —**pu·pa′tion** *n.*

pu·pil¹ (pyōō′p'l) *n.* [< MFr. < L. *pupillus* (dim. of *pupus,* boy), *pupilla* (dim. of *pupa,* girl), ward] a person being taught by a teacher or tutor, as in a school —**pu′pil·age, pu′pil·lage** *n.*

SYN.—**pupil** is applied either to a child in school or to a person who is receiving personal instruction or lessons from a particular teacher [he is the *pupil* of a famous violinist]; **student** is applied either to one attending an educational institution above the elementary level or to one who is making a study of a particular problem [a *student* of social problems]

pu·pil² (pyōō′p'l) *n.* [< Fr. < L. *pupilla,* one's figure reflected in another's eye: special use of *pupilla:* see prec.] the dark, circular opening in the center of the iris of the eye: it grows larger or smaller to let in more or less light

pup·pet (pup′it) *n.* [< OFr., ult. < L. *pupa,* a girl, doll] **1.** orig., a doll **2.** a small, usually jointed figure, in the form of a human being, animal, etc., moved with the hands or by strings, wires, or rods, usually in a puppet show **3.** a person who does, says, and thinks what another tells him to

pup·pet·eer (pup′i tir′) *n.* a person who operates or designs puppets or produces puppet shows

pup·pet·ry (pup′i trē) *n.* the art or work of a puppeteer

puppet show a play or performance with puppets

pup·py (pup′ē) *n., pl.* **-pies** [< MFr. *popee,* doll < OFr.: see PUPPET] **1.** a young dog **2.** a disrespectful, conceited, or silly young man —**pup′py·ish** *adj.*

☆ **puppy love** immature, childish love between a boy and a girl

☆ **pup tent** *same as* SHELTER TENT

pur·blind (pur′blīnd′) *adj.* [ME. *pur blind,* quite blind] **1.** orig., completely blind **2.** partly blind **3.** slow in seeing or understanding what something is about —**pur′blind′ness** *n.*

Pur·cell (pur′s'l), **Henry** 1659?-95; Eng. composer

pur·chase (pur′chəs) *vt.* **-chased, -chas·ing** [< OFr. < *pour,* for + *chacier,* to chase] **1.** to get for money; buy [to *purchase* a car] **2.** to get at a cost, as of suffering [the hero *purchased* fame with his life] **3.** *a)* to move or raise by applying mechanical power *b)* to get a fast hold on so as to do this —*n.* **1.** anything obtained by buying [she carried her *purchases* home in a bag] **2.** a buying [his *purchase* of a house] **3.** *a)* a fast hold applied to move something mechanically or to keep from slipping [the tires can't get a good *purchase* on ice] *b)* an apparatus for applying such a hold —**pur′chas·a·ble** *adj.* —**pur′chas·er** *n.*

pur·dah (pur′də) *n.* [Hindi & Per. *pardah,* a veil] a curtain or veil used by some Hindus and Moslems to hide their women from strangers; also, this practice of hiding women

pure (pyoor) *adj.* [< OFr. < L. *purus* < IE. base *peu-,* to purify] **1.** *a)* not mixed with something else [*pure* maple syrup] *b)* free from anything harmful [*pure* water or air] **2.** simple; mere [*pure* luck] **3.** complete; absolute [*pure* joy] **4.** free from mistakes; perfect [he spoke *pure* English] **5.** free from sin or guilt; innocent [he is *pure* in heart] **6.** virgin or chaste [a *pure* body] **7.** of unmixed stock; purebred [the dog is a *pure* collie] **8.** abstract or dealing only with theory [*pure* physics] **9.** *Phonet.* remaining unchanged in sound [a *pure* vowel] —**pure′ly** *adv.* —**pure′ness** *n.*

pure·bred (pyoor′bred′) *adj.* belonging to a recognized breed through generations of unmixed descent —*n.* such a plant or animal

pu·rée (pyoo rā′; pyoor′ā, -ē) *n.* [Fr. < OFr. < L. < *purus,* pure] **1.** food prepared by putting cooked vegetables, fruits, etc. through a sieve or blender **2.** a thick, smooth soup made with this —*vt.* **-réed′, -rée′ing** to make a purée of Also sp. **puree**

pure line *Genetics* a breed or strain of animals or plants in which certain characteristics remain very much the same as a result of continued inbreeding for generations

pur·ga·tion (pur gā′shən) *n.* the act of purging

pur·ga·tive (pur′gə tiv) *adj.* **1.** that purges **2.** causing bowel movement —*n.* a substance that purges; specif., a cathartic —**pur′ga·tive·ly** *adv.*

pur·ga·to·ry (pur′gə tôr′ē) *n., pl.* **-ries** [< OFr. < ML. < LL. < L. *purgare:* see PURGE] **1.** [*often* P-] in R.C. and other Christian doctrine, a state or place in which those who have died in the grace of God suffer for a certain time for their sins **2.** any state or place of temporary punishment —**pur′ga·to′ri·al** *adj.*

purge (purj) *vt.* **purged, purg′ing** [< OFr. < L. *purgare* < *purus,* PURE + *agere,* to do: see ACT] **1.** to cleanse or rid of impurities, foreign matter, or anything undesirable [to *purge* a city of slums] **2.** to cleanse of guilt, sin, etc. **3.** to remove by cleansing; clear (*away, off,* or *out*) **4.** *a)* to rid (a nation, political party, etc.) of individuals thought of as disloyal or undesirable *b)* to kill or otherwise get rid of (such individuals) **5.** *Med. a)* to empty (the bowels) *b)* to make the bowels of (a person) become empty —*vi.* **1.** to become clean, clear, or pure **2.** to have or cause a thorough bowel movement —*n.* **1.** a purging **2.** that which purges; esp., a medicine that moves the bowels —**purg′er** *n.*

pu·ri·fy (pyoor′ə fī′) *vt.* **-fied′, -fy′ing** [< OFr. < L. *purificare* < *purus,* PURE + *facere,* to make, DO¹] **1.** to rid of impurities or pollution [to *purify* water by filtering it through sand] **2.** to free from guilt, sin, corruption, etc. —*vi.* to become purified —**pu′ri·fi·ca′tion** *n.* —**pu·rif·i·ca·to·ry** (pyoo rif′ə kə tôr′ē) *adj.* —**pu′ri·fi′er** *n.*

Pu·rim (poor′im, pōō rēm′) *n.* [Heb. *pūrīm,* pl., lit., lots] a Jewish holiday celebrated on the 14th day of Adar, commemorating the deliverance of the Jews by Esther from a massacre: also called **Feast of Lots**

pu·rine (pyoor′ēn, -in) *n.* [< G. < L. *purus,* pure + ModL. *uricum,* uric acid + *-in,* -INE⁴] **1.** a colorless, crystalline, organic compound, $C_5H_4N_4$, the substance from which the uric-acid group of compounds comes **2.** a substance produced when a nucleoprotein breaks down, which has a purine-type molecule, as caffeine

pur·ism (pyoor′iz'm) *n.* **1.** a being very careful or precise in usage or style, as in applying formal rules of grammar, art, etc. **2.** an instance of this —**pur′ist** *n.* —**pu·ris′tic, pu·ris′ti·cal** *adj.* —**pu·ris′ti·cal·ly** *adv.*

Pu·ri·tan (pyoor′ə t'n) *n.* [see PURITY & -AN] **1.** a member of a Protestant group in England and America who, in the 16th and 17th centuries, wanted to make the Church of England simpler in its services and stricter about morals **2.** [p-] a person thought of as overly strict in morals and religion —*adj.* **1.** of the Puritans **2.** [p-] puritanical —**Pu′ri·tan·ism, pu′ri·tan·ism** *n.*

pu·ri·tan·i·cal (pyoor′ə tan′i k'l) *adj.* **1.** [P-] of the Puritans **2.** overly strict in morals and religion Also **pu′ri·tan′ic** —**pu′ri·tan′i·cal·ly** *adv.*

pu·ri·ty (pyoor′ə tē) *n.* [< MFr. < LL. < L. *purus,* PURE] the quality or condition of being pure; specif., *a)* freedom from harmful or inferior matter *b)* cleanness; clearness *c)* innocence or chastity *d)* freedom from elements thought of as corrupting

purl¹ (purl) *vi.* [< ? Scand.] **1.** to move in ripples or with a murmuring sound, as a shallow brook or small stream **2.** to eddy; swirl —*n.* a stream or brook that purls, or its murmuring sound

purl² (purl) *vt., vi.* [prob. < a Romance source] **1.** to edge (lace) with small loops **2.** to make (stitches) in knitting that are looped opposite to the usual stitches —*n.* **1.** metal thread, for embroidery **2.** a small loop or chain of loops on the edge of lace **3.** a knitting stitch that is looped opposite to the usual stitch

pur·lieu (pur′lōō, purl′yōō) *n.* [< Anglo-Fr. < OFr. < *pur-,* through + *aler,* to go] **1.** orig., an outlying part of a royal forest, returned to private owners **2.** a place one visits often **3.** [*pl.*] *a)* bounds; limits *b)* surrounding area; environs **4.** an outlying part, as of a city

pur·lin, pur·line (pur′lin) *n.* [< ?] a horizontal timber supporting rafters of a roof

pur·loin (pər loin′, pur′loin) *vt., vi.* [< OFr. < *pur-,* for + *loin,* far] to steal; filch —**pur·loin′er** *n.*

pur·ple (pʉr′p'l) *n.* [OE. < L. *purpura* < Gr. *porphyra*, shellfish yielding purple dye] **1.** a dark color that is a mixture of red and blue **2.** esp. formerly, *a)* deep crimson *b)* cloth or clothing of such color: a symbol of royalty or high rank —*adj.* **1.** of the color purple **2.** imperial; royal **3.** *a)* flowery [*purple* prose] *b)* strong and often offensive [*purple* language] —*vt., vi.* **-pled, -pling** to make or become purple —**born to** (or **in**) **the purple** of royal or high birth —**pur′plish, pur′ply** *adj.*

☆**Purple Heart** a decoration awarded to members of the U.S. armed forces wounded in action

☆**purple martin** a large N. American swallow with bluish-black feathers

pur·port (pər pôrt′; *also, & for n. always,* pʉr′pôrt) *vt.* [< Anglo-Fr. < OFr. < *por-*, forth + *porter*, to bear] to seem or claim to be, mean, etc., often falsely [a book that *purports* to give the true facts] —*n.* meaning; main idea [what is the *purport* of his message?] —see SYN. at MEANING —**pur·port′ed** *adj.* —**pur·port′ed·ly** *adv.*

pur·pose (pʉr′pəs) *vt., vi.* **-posed, -pos·ing** [< OFr. var. of *proposer*, to PROPOSE] to plan, intend, or resolve —*n.* **1.** what one plans to get or do; intention; aim [his *purpose* in life] **2.** firm intention; determination [a man of *purpose*] **3.** the reason or use for something [a room with no *purpose*] —**on purpose** not by accident; intentionally —**to good purpose** with a good result; advantageously —**to little** (or **no**) **purpose** with little or no effect —**to the purpose** apt; relevant —**pur′pose·less** *adj.* —**pur′pose·less·ly** *adv.* —**pur′pose·less·ness** *n.*

pur·pose·ful (-fəl) *adj.* **1.** firmly aiming at a specific goal **2.** directed toward a specific end; not meaningless —**pur′pose·ful·ly** *adv.* —**pur′pose·ful·ness** *n.*

pur·pose·ly (-lē) *adv.* with a definite purpose; intentionally; deliberately

pur·pos·ive (pʉr′pə siv) *adj.* **1.** used for some purpose **2.** having purpose —**pur′pos·ive·ly** *adv.*

purr (pʉr) *n.* [echoic] **1.** a low, soft, rumbling sound made by a cat when it seems to be pleased **2.** any sound like this —*vi., vt.* to make such a sound or express by such a sound

purse (pʉrs) *n.* [OE. *purs* < ML. *bursa*, a bag < LL., a hide < Gr. *byrsa*] **1.** a small bag or pouch for carrying money **2.** finances; money **3.** a sum of money given as a present or prize ☆**4.** a woman's handbag —*vt.* **pursed, purs′ing** to draw tightly together or pucker (one's lips, brows, etc.)

purs·er (pʉr′sər) *n.* [ME., a purse bearer] a ship's officer in charge of accounts, freight, tickets, etc., esp. on a passenger vessel

purse strings a drawstring for certain purses —**hold the purse strings** to be in control of the money —**tighten** (or **loosen**) **the purse strings** to make funds less (or more) readily available

purs·lane (pʉrs′lin, -lān) *n.* [< MFr. < LL. *porcilaca* < L. *portulaca*] any of a number of trailing weeds with pink, fleshy stems and small, yellow flowers; esp., an annual used as a potherb and in salads

pur·su·ance (pər sōō′əns, -syōō′-) *n.* a pursuing, or carrying out, as of a project, plan, etc.

pur·su·ant (-ənt) *adj.* [Now Rare] pursuing —**pursuant to 1.** following upon **2.** according to [he will leave now, *pursuant* to our plans]

pur·sue (pər sōō′, -syōō′) *vt.* **-sued′, -su′ing** [< OFr. < VL. < L. < *pro-*, forth + *sequi*, to follow: see SEQUENT] **1.** to follow in order to overtake, capture, etc.; chase [to *pursue* a runaway horse] **2.** to follow or go on with (a specified course, action, etc.) **3.** to try to find; seek after [to *pursue* success] **4.** to have as one's occupation or chief activity, interest, etc. [to *pursue* dentistry] **5.** to keep on troubling; hound [bad luck *pursued* him] —*vi.* **1.** to chase **2.** to go on; continue —**pur·su′a·ble** *adj.* —**pur·su′er** *n.*

pur·suit (-sōōt′, -syōōt′) *n.* **1.** a pursuing [the *pursuit* of truth] **2.** a career, activity, interest, etc. to which one devotes oneself [golf is his favorite *pursuit*]

pursuit plane a fighter plane: see FIGHTER (sense 3)

PURPLE MARTIN
(to 8 in. long)

pur·sui·vant (pʉr′si vənt, -swi-) *n.* [< OFr. < *poursuir:* see PURSUE] **1.** in England, an officer ranking below a herald **2.** a follower; attendant

pur·sy[1] (pʉr′sē) *adj.* **-si·er, -si·est** [< Anglo-Fr. *pursif*, for OFr. *polsif* < *polser*, to push, pant < L. *pulsare*, to beat] **1.** short-winded, esp. from being fat **2.** fat —**pur′si·ness** *n.*

pur·sy[2] (pʉr′sē) *adj.* [< ME.] pursed; puckered

pu·ru·lent (pyoor′ə lənt, -yoo lənt) *adj.* [Fr. < L. < *puris*, genitive of *pus*, PUS] of, like, containing, or giving off pus —**pu′ru·lence, pu′ru·len·cy** *n.* —**pu′ru·lent·ly** *adv.*

Pu·rús (poo roos′) river in S. America, flowing from E Peru through NW Brazil into the Amazon: c. 2,000 mi.

pur·vey (pər vā′) *vt.* [< Anglo-Fr. < OFr. < L. *providere:* see PROVIDE] to supply (esp. food or provisions) —**pur·vey′or** *n.*

pur·view (pʉr′vyōō) *n.* [< Anglo-Fr. *purveu* (it is) provided, ult. < L. *providere:* see PROVIDE] **1.** the body and scope of a legislative act or bill **2.** extent or range of control, activity, concern, etc.; province **3.** range of sight or understanding

pus (pus) *n.* [L.: for IE. base see FOUL] the thick, yellowish-white liquid matter that oozes from a sore or is found in a boil, consisting of bacteria, white corpuscles, serum, etc.

Pu·san (poo′sän′) seaport on the SE coast of South Korea: pop. 1,879,000

push (poosh) *vt.* [< MFr. < OFr. < L. *pulsare*, to beat < pp. of *pellere*, to drive: for IE. base see FELT[1]] **1.** *a)* to use pressure or force against, esp. so as to move [to *push* a stalled car] *b)* to move in this way *c)* to thrust, shove, or drive (*up, down, in, out,* etc.) [to *push* a stake into the ground] **2.** *a)* to urge on; impel; force [he *pushed* the men to work harder] *b)* to follow up vigorously; promote (a campaign, claim, etc.) *c)* to extend or expand (business activities, etc.) **3.** to bring into a critical state; press [to be *pushed* for time] **4.** to urge or promote the use, sale, etc. of [the company is *pushing* its new product] ☆**5.** [Colloq.] to be near or close to [*pushing* sixty years] —*vi.* **1.** to press against a thing so as to move it [they *pushed* on the door] **2.** to try hard to advance, succeed, etc. [to *push* to the top] **3.** to move forward against opposition [to *push* through a crowd] **4.** to move by being pushed [the window *pushes* in] —*n.* **1.** a pushing; shove [one hard *push* opened the door] **2.** a vigorous effort, campaign, etc. [a big *push* to reelect the mayor] **3.** pressure of circumstances [in the *push* of daily life] **4.** [Colloq.] the energy to get things done; drive [a leader with plenty of *push*] —**push off** [Colloq.] to set out; depart —**push on** to go forward; proceed

SYN.—**push** implies the use of force or pressure by a person or thing in contact with the object to be moved ahead, aside, etc. [to *push* a baby carriage]; **shove** implies a pushing of something so as to force it to slide along a surface, or it suggests rough handling in pushing [*shove* the box into the corner]; to **thrust** is to push with sudden, often violent force, sometimes so as to put one thing into another [he *thrust* his hand into the water]; **propel** implies a driving forward of something by a force that makes it move [the wind *propelled* the sailboat] —**ANT.** pull, draw

☆**push-but·ton** (poosh′but′'n) *adj.* controlled by push buttons, as warfare using long-range, automated missiles

☆**push button** a small knob or button that is pushed to cause something to operate, as by closing an electric circuit

☆**push·cart** (poosh′kärt′) *n.* a cart pushed by hand, esp. one used by street vendors

push·er (-ər) *n.* **1.** a person or thing that pushes ☆**2.** [Slang] a person peddling drugs, esp. narcotics, illegally

push·ing (-iŋ) *adj.* **1.** aggressive; enterprising; energetic **2.** rude; forward; officious —**push′ing·ly** *adv.*

Push·kin (poosh′kin; *E.* poosh′-), **A·lek·san·dr** (Ser·geyevich) (ä′lyik sän′dr′) 1799–1837; Russ. poet

☆**push·o·ver** (poosh′ō′vər) *n.* [Slang] **1.** anything very easy to do **2.** a person, group, etc. easily persuaded, defeated, etc.

Push·tu (push′tōō) *n.* same as PASHTO

push-up, push·up (poosh′up′) *n.* an exercise in which a person lying face down, with hands palm down under the shoulders, pushes the body up by straightening the arms and lowers it by bending the arms

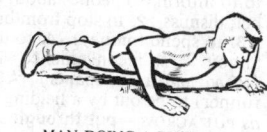

MAN DOING A PUSH-UP

☆**push·y** (poosh′ē) *adj.* **push′i·er, push′i·est** [Colloq.] aggressive and rude in a way that annoys others —see SYN. at AGGRESSIVE —**push′i·ness** *n.*

pu·sil·lan·i·mous (pyōō's'l an'ə məs) *adj.* [< LL. < L. *pusil·lus*, tiny + *animus*, the mind] **1.** timid or cowardly **2.** showing a lack of courage —**pu'sil·la·nim'i·ty** (-ə nim'ə tē) *n.* —**pu'sil·lan'i·mous·ly** *adv.*

puss[1] (poos) *n.* [orig. ? echoic of the spitting of a cat] **1.** a cat: used as a pet name **2.** a girl: used as a term of affection

puss[2] (poos) *n.* [prob. < IrGael. *pus*, mouth] [Slang] ☆**1.** the face ☆**2.** the mouth

pus·sy[1] (pus'ē) *adj.* **-si·er, -si·est** containing or like pus

puss·y[2] (poos'ē) *n., pl.* **puss'ies** [dim. of PUSS[1]] a cat, esp. a kitten: also **puss'y·cat'** (-kat')

☆**puss·y·foot** (-foot') *vi.* [Colloq.] **1.** to move quietly and carefully, like a cat **2.** to keep away from giving a definite opinion, taking a firm stand, etc. [the candidate *pussyfooted* on the subject of taxes] —**puss'y·foot'er** *n.*

☆**pussy willow** any of several willows bearing silvery, velvetlike catkins before the leaves appear

pus·tu·lant (pus'chə lənt) *adj.* making pustules form

pus·tu·lar (-lər) *adj.* of, like, or covered with pustules: also **pus'tu·lous** (-ləs)

pus·tu·late (-lāt'; *for adj.* -lit) *vt., vi.* **-lat'ed, -lat'ing** [< LL. pp. of *pustulare* < *pustula*, a pustule] to form into pustules — *adj.* covered with pustules —**pus'tu·la'tion** *n.*

pus·tule (pus'chool) *n.* [L. *pustula*] **1.** a small swelling in the skin, containing pus **2.** any small swelling like a blister or pimple

put (poot) *vt.* **put, put'ting** [< or akin to OE. *potian*, to push] **1.** *a)* to drive or send by a blow, shot, or thrust [to *put* nails in wood] *b)* to throw with an overhand thrust from the shoulder [*put* the shot] **2.** to make do something; impel; force [to *put* them to work] **3.** to make be in a specified place, condition, relation, etc.; place; set [*put* the box here; *put* her at ease] **4.** to make undergo; subject [*put* it through tests] **5.** to impose (a burden, tax, etc.) **6.** *a)* to bring to bear (*on*); apply (*to*) [to *put* one's mind on one's work] *b)* to bring in; add; inject [to *put* life into a party] *c)* to bring about; effect [to *put* a stop to cheating] **7.** to set down as belonging to; assign; ascribe [*put* the blame on him] **8.** to express; state [*put* it plainly] **9.** to translate [he *put* the book into English] **10.** to present for consideration, decision, etc. [*put* the question] **11.** *a)* to estimate as being (with *at*) [to *put* the cost at $50] *b)* to fix or set (a price, value, etc.) *on* **12.** to fit (words) to music **13.** *a)* to bet (money) *on* *b)* to invest (money) *in* or *into* —*vi.* to go (*in, out, back,* etc.) —*n.* a cast or thrust; esp., the act of putting the shot —*adj.* [Colloq.] fixed [stay *put*] —**put about 1.** to change a ship's course from one tack to another **2.** to move in another direction —**put across** [Colloq.] ☆**1.** to make understood or accepted **2.** to carry out with success **3.** to carry out by trickery —**put aside** (or **by**) **1.** to keep for later **2.** to give up; discard —**put away 1.** *same as* PUT ASIDE **2.** [Colloq.] *a)* to put in a jail, etc. *b)* to consume (food or drink) *c)* to kill (a pet) to prevent suffering —**put down 1.** *a)* to overcome with force; crush; repress *b)* to strip of power, rank, etc.; degrade **2.** to write down; record **3.** to set down as belonging (to) **4.** to consider as; classify **5.** to land (an aircraft) ☆**6.** [Slang] to belittle, reject, criticize, or humiliate —**put forth 1.** to grow (leaves, etc.) **2.** to bring into action; exert (effort, etc.) **3.** to propose; offer **4.** to leave port —**put forward** to present or propose (a plan, etc.) —**put in 1.** to enter a port or haven **2.** to enter (a claim, etc.) **3.** [Colloq.] to spend (time) in a specified way —**put in for** to apply for —☆**put it (or something) over on** [Colloq.] to deceive; trick —**put off 1.** to leave until later; postpone; delay; evade **2.** to confuse, mislead, make wait, etc. **3.** to disturb greatly; upset —**put on 1.** to clothe, adorn, or cover oneself with **2.** to take on; add [to *put on* a few pounds] **3.** to pretend [she *put on* an air of innocence] **4.** to apply (a brake, etc.) **5.** to stage (a play) ☆**6.** [Slang] to fool (someone) by taking advantage of his readiness to believe; hoax —☆**put on to** to inform (someone) about (something) —**put out 1.** to expel; dismiss **2.** to stop from burning; extinguish (a fire or light) ☆**3.** to spend (money) **4.** to upset or confuse **5.** to distress or annoy **6.** to inconvenience **7.** to publish, produce, or supply [to *put out* a newspaper] ☆**8.** *Baseball* to cause (a batter or runner) to be out by a fielding play —**put over** ☆[Colloq.] *same as* PUT ACROSS —**put through** ☆**1.** to carry out successfully [to *put through* a business deal] **2.** to cause to do or undergo [he was *put through* an ordeal] **3.** to connect (someone) by telephone with someone else —**put to it** to place in a difficult situation; press hard —**put up 1.** to offer, as for consideration, decision, sale, etc. **2.** to offer as a candidate **3.** to preserve or can (fruits, etc.) **4.** to erect; build **5.** to lodge, or provide lodgings for **6.** ☆*a)* to advance or provide (money) *b)* [Slang] to do or produce what is needed or wanted **7.** to arrange (the hair) with curlers, bobby pins, etc. **8.** to carry on [to *put up* a struggle] **9.** [Colloq.] to urge (a person) *to* some action —**put upon** to impose on; take advantage of —**put up with** to bear with patience; tolerate

pu·ta·tive (pyōō'tə tiv) *adj.* [< L. < *putare*, to suppose] generally considered or believed to be such; reputed [a *putative* ancestor] —**pu'ta·tive·ly** *adv.*

☆**put-down** (poot'doun') *n.* [Slang] a belittling remark or crushing reply

put-on (poot'än') *adj.* feigned; pretended [a *put-on* smile] —*n.* [Slang] a fooling of someone by taking advantage of his readiness to believe; also, something meant to fool someone by this means

☆**put-out** (-out') *n. Baseball* a play in which the batter or runner is retired, or put out

☆**put-put** (put'put') *n., vi.* **put'-put'ted, put'-put'ting** *same as* PUTT-PUTT

pu·tre·fac·tion (pyōō'trə fak'shən) *n.* [see PUTREFY] the rotting of organic matter by bacteria, fungi, and oxidation, with the result that it has a bad smell —**pu'tre·fac'tive** *adj.*

pu·tre·fy (pyōō'trə fī') *vt., vi.* **-fied', -fy'ing** [< L. *putrefacere* < *putris,* PUTRID + *facere,* to make, DO[1]] to make or become putrid or rotten —see SYN. at DECAY —**pu'tre·fi'er** *n.*

pu·tres·cent (pyōō tres''nt) *adj.* [L. prp. of *putrescere,* to become rotten < *putris,* rotten] **1.** becoming putrid; rotting **2.** of or relating to putrefaction —**pu·tres'cence** *n.*

pu·trid (pyōō'trid) *adj.* [< Fr. < L. *putridus* < *putrere,* to be rotten: for IE. base see FOUL] **1.** rotten and smelling bad [*putrid* garbage] **2.** of or from decay [a *putrid* smell] **3.** morally corrupt or depraved [a *putrid* society] **4.** [Colloq.] very unpleasant [a *putrid* movie] —see SYN. at STINKING —**pu·trid'i·ty, pu'trid·ness** *n.* —**pu'trid·ly** *adv.*

‡**Putsch** (pooch) *n.* [G.] an uprising or rebellion, esp. an unsuccessful one

putt (put) *n.* [< PUT, *v.*] *Golf* a light stroke made on the putting green in trying to put the ball into the hole —*vt., vi.* to hit (the ball) with a putt

put·tee (pu tē', put'ē) *n.* [< Hindi *paṭṭī,* a bandage < Sans. *paṭṭa,* a strip of cloth] a cloth or leather legging or a cloth strip wound round and round up the leg from ankle to knee

put·ter[1] (poot'ər) *n.* a person or thing that puts

putt·er[2] (put'ər) *n. Golf* **1.** a short, straight-faced club used in putting **2.** a person who putts

putt·er[3] (put'ər) *vi.* [var. of POTTER[2]] to busy oneself without getting anything worthwhile done; dawdle (often with *around,* etc.) —*vt.* to dawdle or fritter (*away*)

putt·ing green (put'iŋ) *Golf* the area of smooth, closely mowed turf in which the hole is sunk

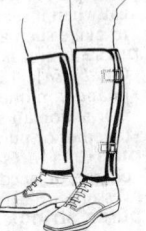
PUTTEES

☆**putt-putt** (put'put') *n.* [echoic] **1.** the chugging or popping sounds of a motorboat engine, etc. **2.** [Colloq.] a boat, etc. making such sounds —*vi.* **putt'-putt'ed, putt'-putt'ing** to make, move along, or operate with such sounds

put·ty (put'ē) *n.* [< Fr. *potée,* lit., potful < *pot,* a pot] **1.** a soft, plastic mixture of powdered chalk and linseed oil, used to hold panes of glass in windows, to fill small cracks, etc. **2.** any similar substance —*vt.* **-tied, -ty·ing** to cement, fill, etc. with putty —**put'ti·er** *n.*

Pu·tu·ma·yo (pōō'tōō mä'yô) river flowing from SW Colombia into the Amazon in NW Brazil

put-up (poot'up') *adj.* [Colloq.] planned secretly beforehand [a *put-up* job]

puz·zle (puz''l) *vt.* **-zled, -zling** [< ?] to confuse; perplex; bewilder [her strange behavior *puzzled* them] —*vi.* **1.** to be confused, perplexed, etc. **2.** to keep one's mind busy, as on a problem —*n.* **1.** a puzzled state **2.** a puzzling problem, etc. [it's a *puzzle* to me how he got here] **3.** a toy or problem to test skill or cleverness [a crossword *puzzle*] —**puzzle out** to solve by deep thought —**puzzle over** to give deep thought to —**puz'zle·ment** *n.* —**puz'zler** *n.*

SYN.—**puzzle** implies that a problem, situation, etc. is so involved or complicated that it is very hard or difficult to understand or solve; **perplex,** in addition, implies uncertainty or even worry as to what to think, say, or do; **confuse** implies a being mixed up mentally to a greater or lesser degree; **confound** implies a being so confused that one is completely frustrated or greatly astonished; **bewilder** implies such complete confusion in one's mind that one can no longer think clearly

Pvt. *Mil.* Private

PW Prisoner of War

PWA, P.W.A. Public Works Administration

pwt. pennyweight(s)

PX post exchange

pya (pyä) *n., pl.* **pyas** [Burmese] *see* MONETARY UNITS, table (Burma)

pyc·nom·e·ter (pik näm′ə tər) *n.* [< Gr. *pyknos*, thick, tight + -METER] a device used to measure the specific gravity of liquids or solids

py·e·mi·a (pī ē′mē ə) *n.* [ModL.: see PYO- & -EMIA] blood poisoning caused by pus-producing organisms —**py·e′mic** *adj.*

Pyg·ma·li·on (pig māl′yən, -mā′lē ən) *Gr. Legend* a sculptor who fell in love with his statue of a maiden, later brought to life as Galatea by Aphrodite

Pyg·my (pig′mē) *n., pl.* **-mies** [< L. < Gr. *pygmaios*, of the length of the *pygmē*, forearm and fist] **1.** a member of any of several African and Asian peoples who are very short **2.** [p-] any very small or unimportant person or thing —*adj.* **1.** of Pygmies **2.** [p-] very small —*see* SYN. at DWARF

py·ja·mas (pə jam′əz, -jä′məz) *n.pl. Brit. sp.* of PAJAMAS

py·lon (pī′län) *n.* [Gr. *pylon*, gateway] **1.** a gateway, as of an Egyptian temple **2.** a towerlike structure, as for supporting electric lines, marking an aircraft course, etc.

py·lo·rus (pī lôr′əs, pə-) *n., pl.* **-ri** (-ī) [LL. < Gr. *pylōros*, gatekeeper < *pylē*, a gate + *ouros*, watchman] the opening from the stomach into the first section of the small intestine —**py·lor′ic** *adj.*

Pym (pim), **John** 1583?-1643; Eng. parliamentary leader

py·o- [< Gr. *pyon*, PUS] a combining form meaning: **1.** pus **2.** pus-forming Also, before a vowel, **py-**

Pyong·yang (pyuŋ′yäŋ′) capital of North Korea, in the W part: pop. 1,500,000

py·or·rhe·a, py·or·rhoe·a (pī′ə rē′ə) *n.* [ModL.: see PYO- & -RRHEA] a giving off of pus; specif., *short for* PYORRHEA ALVEOLARIS —**py′or·rhe′al, py′or·rhoe′al** *adj.*

pyorrhea al·ve·o·la·ris (al vē′ə ler′is) an infection of the gums and tooth sockets, in which pus forms and the teeth become loose

pyr·a·mid (pir′ə mid) *n.* [L. *pyramidis*, genitive of *pyramis*, pyramid < Gr.] **1.** any huge structure with a square base and four sloping, triangular sides meeting at the top, as those built for royal tombs in ancient Egypt **2.** anything shaped like this **3.** *Geom.* a solid figure the base of which is a polygon whose sides are the bases of triangular surfaces meeting at a common vertex —*vi., vt.* to build up or grow as in the form of a pyramid —**py·ram·i·dal** (pi ram′-ə d'l) *adj.* —**py·ram′i·dal·ly** *adv.* —**pyr′a·mid′ic, pyr′a·mid′i·cal** *adj.*

EGYPTIAN PYRAMID

pyre (pīr) *n.* [< L. < Gr. < *pyr*, a FIRE] a pile, esp. of wood, for burning a corpse in a funeral rite

Pyr·e·nees (pir′ə nēz′) mountain range along the border between France & Spain —**Pyr′e·ne′an** (-nē′ən) *adj.*

py·re·thrum (pī rē′thrəm) *n.* [ModL. < L. < Gr. *pyrethron*, feverfew] **1.** any of several chrysanthemums, with white, pink, red, or purple flower heads **2.** an insecticide made from the dried flower heads of certain chrysanthemums

py·ret·ic (pī ret′ik) *adj.* [< ModL. < Gr. *pyretos*, fever < *pyr*, a FIRE] of or causing fever

☆**Py·rex** (pī′reks) [a made-up word < PIE[1] + -r- + -ex] a trademark for a heat-resistant glassware for cooking, etc.

pyr·i·dine (pir′ə dēn′, -din) *n.* [PYR(O)- + -ID + -INE[4]] a liquid base, C_5H_5N, with a sharp odor, produced by distilling coal tar, etc. and used in making vitamins and drugs, etc. synthetically

pyr·i·dox·ine (pir′ə däk′sēn′, -sin) *n.* [PYRID(INE) + OX(Y)[-1] + -INE[4]] a pyridine derivative, $C_8H_{11}O_3N$, a vitamin of the B complex, found in cereal grains, liver, yeast, etc.

py·rim·i·dine (pi rim′ə dēn′, pī-; pir′im-) *n.* [< G] **1.** a colorless, liquid, organic compound, $C_4H_4N_2$, the common form of a group of bases, some of which are found in

nucleic acid **2.** any of several basic substances produced when nucleoproteins break down

py·rite (pī′rīt) *n., pl.* **py·ri·tes** (pə rīt′ēz, pi-; pī′rīts) [< L. < Gr. *pyritēs*, flint < *pyr*, a FIRE] iron sulfide, FeS_2, a shiny, yellow mineral that is an important ore of sulfur

py·ri·tes (pə rīt′ēz, pī-; pī′rīts) *n.* any of various metallic sulfides as found in nature, as pyrite —**py·rit′ic** (-rit′ik), **py·rit′i·cal** *adj.*

py·ro- [< Gr. *pyr*, a FIRE] a combining form meaning fire, heat [*pyromania*]: also, before a vowel, **pyr-**

☆**Py·ro·ce·ram** (pī′rō sə ram′) [PYRO- + CERAM(IC)] a trademark for a heavy, glasslike, ceramic material highly resistant to heat and breakage: used for cooking utensils, rocket nose cones, etc.

py·rog·ra·phy (pī räg′rə fē) *n.* [PYRO- + -GRAPHY] **1.** the art of burning designs on wood or leather with heated tools **2.** a design so made —**py·rog′ra·pher** *n.* —**py′ro·graph′ic** (-rə-graf′ik) *adj.*

py·rol·y·sis (pī räl′ə sis) *n.* [ModL.: see PYRO- & -LYSIS] chemical breaking down of a substance by heat —**py·ro·lyt·ic** (pī′rə lit′ik) *adj.* —**py′ro·lyt′i·cal·ly** *adv.*

py·ro·ma·ni·a (pī′rə mā′nē ə, -mān′yə) *n.* [ModL.: see PYRO- & -MANIA] an uncontrollable desire to start destructive fires —**py′ro·ma′ni·ac′** (-nē ak′) *n., adj.* —**py′ro·ma·ni′a·cal** (-mə nī′ə k'l) *adj.*

py·rom·e·ter (pī räm′ə tər) *n.* [PYRO- + -METER] an instrument for measuring unusually high temperatures —**py′ro·met′·ric** (-ə met′rik) *adj.* —**py′ro·met′ri·cal·ly** *adv.* —**py·rom′e·try** (-trē) *n.*

py·ro·tech·nic (pī′rə tek′nik) *adj.* [< Fr. < Gr. *pyr*, FIRE + *technē*, art] **1.** of fireworks **2.** describing or of spacecraft devices or materials that ignite or explode to set off propellants, etc. **3.** brilliant; dazzling [*pyrotechnic* wit] Also **py′ro·tech′ni·cal** —**py′ro·tech′ni·cal·ly** *adv.*

py·ro·tech·nics (-niks) *n.pl.* **1.** [*with sing. v.*] the art of making and using fireworks: also **py′ro·tech′ny** (-nē) **2.** *a)* a display of fireworks *b)* fireworks; esp., rockets, flares, etc., as for signaling *c)* pyrotechnic devices in spacecraft **3.** a brilliant or dazzling display, as of skill in playing a musical instrument —**py′ro·tech′nist** *n.*

py·rox·y·lin, py·rox·y·line (pī räk′sə lin) *n.* [< Fr. < Gr. *pyr*, fire + *xylon*, wood] nitrocellulose, esp. in less explosive forms than guncotton, used in making paints, lacquers, celluloid, etc.

Pyr·rhic victory (pir′ik) [after *Pyrrhus*, king of Epirus, who defeated the Romans in 280 and 279 B.C., suffering extremely heavy losses] a victory that is too costly

py·ru·vic acid (pī roo′vik) [< PYR(O)- + L. *uva*, grape + -IC] a colorless, liquid or crystalline organic acid that is formed during carbohydrate metabolism in the cell

Py·thag·o·ras (pi thag′ər əs) 6th cent. B.C.; Gr. philosopher & mathematician —**Py·thag′o·re′an** (-ə rē′ən) *adj., n.*

Pythagorean theorem the theorem that the square of the hypotenuse of a right triangle is equal to the sum of the squares of the lengths of the other two sides

Pyth·i·an (pith′ē ən) *adj.* [< L. < Gr. *Pythios*, of *Pythō*, older name for DELPHI] **1.** of Apollo as patron of Delphi and the Delphic oracle **2.** designating or of the games held at Delphi every four years in ancient Greece in honor of Apollo

Pythias *see* DAMON AND PYTHIAS

py·thon (pī′thän, -thən) *n.* [< L. < Gr. *Pythōn*, a serpent slain by Apollo] **1.** any of a group of large, nonpoisonous snakes of Asia, Africa, and Australia, that crush their prey to death **2.** popularly, any large snake that crushes its prey

py·tho·ness (pī′thə nis) *n.* [< MFr. < ML. < LL. < Gr. *Pythō*: see PYTHIAN] **1.** a priestess of Apollo at Delphi **2.** any woman soothsayer; prophetess

pyx (piks) *n.* [< L. < Gr. *pyxis*, a box < *pyxos*, the box tree] the container in which the consecrated wafer of the Eucharist is kept or carried

pyx·is (pik′sis) *n., pl.* **pyx′i·des′** (-sə dēz′) [L.: see prec.] **1.** a vase with a cover, used by the ancient Greeks and Romans **2.** *Bot.* a dry fruit whose upper portion splits off, forming a part that resembles a lid: also **pyx·id·i·um** (pik sid′ē əm), *pl.* **-i·a** (-ə)

PYXIS
(sense 2)

---

fat, āpe, cär; ten, ēven; is, bīte; gō, hôrn, tōōl, lŏŏk; oil, out; up, fur; get; joy; yet; chin; she; thin, *th*en; zh, leisure; ŋ, ring; ə for *a* in *ago, e* in *agent, i* in *sanity, o* in *comply, u* in *focus*; ′ as in *able* (ā′b'l); Fr. bal; ë, Fr. coeur; ö, Fr. feu; Fr. mon; ô, Fr. coq; ü, Fr. duc; r, Fr. cri; H, G. ich; kh, G. doch; ‡foreign; ☆ Americanism; < derived from. See inside front cover.

Q, q (ky$\overline{oo}$) *n.*, *pl.* **Q's, q's** **1.** the seventeenth letter of the English alphabet **2.** the sound of *Q* or *q*

Q *Chess* queen

Q. **1.** Quebec **2.** Queen **3.** Question

q. **1.** quart **2.** quarter **3.** quarto **4.** queen **5.** question **6.** quetzal **7.** quintal: also **ql. 8.** quire

Qa·tar (kä'tär) independent Arab sheikdom occupying a peninsula in E Arabia on the Persian gulf: 8,500 sq. mi.; pop. 130,000; cap. Doha

Q.C. Queen's Counsel

Q.E.D. [L. *quod erat demonstrandum*] which was to be proved

qin·tar (kin tär') *n.* [Alb., ult. < L. *centum*, cent] *see* MONETARY UNITS, table (Albania)

QM, Q.M. Quartermaster

qr. *pl.* **qrs.** **1.** quarter **2.** quire

qt. **1.** quantity **2.** quart(s)

Q.T., q.t. [Slang] quiet: usually in **on the Q.T.** (or **q.t.**), in secret

qto. quarto

qua (kwā, kwä) *adv.* [L. < *qui*, WHO] in the function or capacity of; as *[the President qua Commander in Chief]*

quack[1] (kwak) *vi.* [echoic] to utter the sound or cry of a duck, or a sound like it —*n.* the sound made by quacking

quack[2] (kwak) *n.* [short for QUACKSALVER] **1.** a person without proper training or skill who pretends to be a doctor **2.** any person who pretends to have knowledge or skill that he does not have; charlatan —*adj.* making claims that have little or no foundation; not genuine; fake *[a quack healer, medicine, etc.]* — **quack'ish** *adj.* —**quack'ish·ly** *adv.*

quack·er·y (kwak'ər ē) *n.* the claims or methods of a quack

☆**quack grass** [ult. < OE. *cwicu*, alive] *same as* COUCH GRASS

quack·sal·ver (-sal'vər) *n.* [< MDu. < *quacken*, to brag + *zalf*, salve] [Now Rare] a quack; charlatan

quad[1] (kwäd) *n.* *same as:* **1.** QUADRANGLE (of a college) **2.** QUADRUPLET ☆**3.** QUADRAPHONIC

quad[2] (kwäd) *n.* [< QUAD(RAT)] *Printing* a piece of type metal lower than the face of the type, used for spacing, to fill blank lines, etc. —*vt.* **quad'ded, quad'ding** to fill out (a line) with quads

Quad·ra·ges·i·ma (kwäd'rə jes'i mə) *n.* [LL. < fem. of L. *quadragesimus*, fortieth] the first Sunday in Lent: also **Quadragesima Sunday**

quad·ran·gle (kwäd'raŋ'g'l) *n.* [< MFr. < LL. < L.: see QUADRI- & ANGLE[1]] **1.** a plane figure with four angles and four sides **2.** *a)* an area, as of a college campus, surrounded on four sides by buildings *b)* the buildings themselves —**quad·ran·gu·lar** (-gyə lər) *adj.*

quad·rant (kwäd'rənt) *n.* [< L. *quadrans*, fourth part] **1.** a fourth part of the circumference of a circle; an arc of 90° **2.** a quarter section of a circle **3.** an instrument for measuring altitudes or angular elevations in astronomy and navigation **4.** any of the four parts into which a plane surface is divided by two axes intersecting at right angles —**quad·ran'tal** (-ran't'l) *adj.*

☆**quad·ra·phon·ic** (kwäd'rə fän'ik) *adj.* [< L. *quadra*, a square + PHONIC] designating or of sound reproduction, as on records or tapes or in broadcasting, using four channels to carry and reproduce through separate speakers a blend of sounds from separate sources: also **quad'ra·son'ic** (-sän'ik)

quad·rat (kwäd'rat) *n.* [var. of QUADRATE] **1.** *same as* QUAD[2] **2.** *Ecology* a plot of ground used to study and analyze plant and animal life

quad·rate (kwäd'rāt; *also, for adj. & n.*, -rit) *adj.* [< L. pp. of *quadrare*, to make square, ult. < *quattuor*, FOUR] **1.** square or nearly square **2.** *Zool.* describing a bone or cartilage of the skull, as in birds, bony fishes, and reptiles, to which the lower jaw is joined —*n.* **1.** a square or rectangle **2.** a square or rectangular space, thing, etc. **3.** *Zool.* the quadrate bone —*vi.* **-rat·ed, -rat·ing** to square; agree (*with*) —*vt.* to make square; make (something) conform

quad·rat·ic (kwäd rat'ik) *adj.* [< QUADRATE + -IC] *Algebra* involving a quantity or quantities that are squared but none that are raised to a higher power —*n.* *Algebra* a quadratic term, expression, or equation —**quad·rat'i·cal·ly** *adv.*

quadratic equation *Algebra* an equation in which the second power, or square, is the highest to which the unknown quantity is raised

quad·ra·ture (kwäd'rə chər) *n.* [< LL. < L. pp. of *quadrare*: see QUADRATE] **1.** the act of squaring **2.** the determining of the dimensions of a square equal in area to a given surface **3.** *Astron.* the relative position of two heavenly bodies when 90° distant from each other

quad·ren·ni·al (kwäd ren'ē əl) *adj.* [< L. < *quadri-*, QUADRI- + *annus*, a year] **1.** lasting four years **2.** occurring once every four years —*n.* a quadrennial event —**quad·ren'ni·al·ly** *adv.*

quad·ri- [< L. < base of *quattuor*, FOUR] *a combining form meaning* four times, fourfold: also, before a vowel, **quadr-**

quad·ri·ceps (kwäd'ri seps') *n.* [ModL. < QUADRI- + L. *caput*, the head] the large muscle at the front of the thigh, which extends the leg

quad·ri·lat·er·al (kwäd'rə lat'ər əl) *adj.* [< L.: see QUADRI- & LATERAL] four-sided —*n.* **1.** *Geom.* a plane figure having four sides and four angles **2.** a four-sided area —**quad'ri·lat'er·al·ly** *adv.*

qua·drille (kwə dril', kwä-) *n.* [Fr. < Sp. *cuadrilla*, dim. < *cuadro*, a square] **1.** a square dance performed by four couples **2.** music for this dance

quad·ril·lion (kwäd ril'yən) *n.* [Fr. < *quadri-* (see QUADRI-) + (MI)LLION] **1.** in the U.S. and France, the number represented by 1 followed by 15 zeros **2.** in Great Britain and Germany, the number represented by 1 followed by 24 zeros —*adj.* amounting to one quadrillion in number —**quad·ril'lionth** *adj., n.*

quad·ri·ple·gi·a (kwäd'rə plē'jē ə, -jə) *n.* [ModL.: see QUADRI- & -PLEGIA] total paralysis of the body from the neck down —**quad'ri·ple'gic** (-plē'jik, -plej'ik) *adj., n.*

quad·ri·va·lent (kwäd'rə vā'lənt, kwä driv'ə-) *adj.* **1.** having four valences **2.** *same as* TETRAVALENT (sense 1) —**quad'ri·va'lence, quad'ri·va'len·cy** *n.*

quad·ru·ped (kwäd'roo ped') *n.* [< L. < *quadru-* (for QUADRI-), four + *pes*, a FOOT] an animal, esp. a mammal, with four feet —*adj.* having four feet —**quad·ru·pe·dal** (kwä droo'pi d'l, kwäd'rə ped'l) *adj.*

quad·ru·ple (kwä droo'p'l, -drup''l; kwäd'roo-) *adj.* [MFr. < L. < *quadru-* (see prec.) + *-plus*, -fold] **1.** consisting of four **2.** four times as much or as many; fourfold **3.** *Music* having four beats to the measure *[quadruple time]* —*n.* an amount four

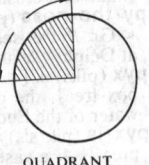

QUADRANT

QUADRILATERALS

782

times as much or as many —*vt., vi.* **-pled, -pling** to make or become four times as much or as many

quad·ru·plet (kwä drup′lit, -drōō′plit; kwäd′roo plit) *n.* [dim. of prec.] **1.** any of four offspring born at a single birth **2.** a group of four, usually of one kind

quad·ru·pli·cate (kwä drōō′plə kāt′; *for adj. & n., usually* -kit) *vt.* **-cat′ed, -cat′ing** [< L. pp. of *quadruplicare* < *quadru-* (see QUADRUPED) + *plicare*, to fold] to make four identical copies of —*adj.* **1.** fourfold **2.** designating the fourth of identical copies —*n.* any of four identical copies —**in quadruplicate** in four identical copies —**quad·ru·pli·ca′tion** *n.*

quaes·tor (kwes′tər, kwēs′-) *n.* [L. < pp. of *quaerere*, to inquire] **1.** in ancient Rome, orig., a judge in certain criminal cases **2.** later, any of certain state treasurers —**quaes·to′ri·al** (-tôr′ē əl) *adj.* —**quaes′tor·ship′** *n.*

quaff (kwäf, kwaf) *vt., vi.* [prob. (by misreading of *-ss-* as *-ff-*) < LowG. *quassen*, to overindulge] to drink deeply in a hearty or thirsty way —*n.* **1.** a quaffing **2.** a drink that is quaffed —**quaff′er** *n.*

quag·ga (kwag′ə) *n., pl.* **-ga, -gas** see PLURAL, II, D, 2 [Afrik. < native name] a striped wild ass of Africa, resembling the donkey and the zebra: it is now extinct

quag·gy (kwag′ē) *adj.* **-gi·er, -gi·est 1.** like a quagmire; boggy; miry **2.** soft; flabby

quag·mire (kwag′mīr′) *n.* [< earlier *quag*, a bog + MIRE] **1.** wet, boggy ground, yielding under the feet **2.** a difficult or dangerous situation from which it is hard to escape [a *quagmire* of debts]

☆**qua·hog, qua·haug** (kwô′hôg, kō′-; -häg) *n.* [< AmInd. name] an edible clam of the eastern coast of N. America, having a very hard, solid shell

quail[1] (kwāl) *vi.* [prob. < OFr. *coaillier* < L. *coagulare*, to coagulate] to draw back in fear; lose courage; cower

quail[2] (kwāl) *n., pl.* **quails, quail:** see PLURAL, II, D, 1 [< OFr. < ML. *cuacula*, prob. < Gmc. echoic name] **1.** any of various small game birds, resembling partridges ☆**2.** *same as* BOBWHITE

quaint (kwānt) *adj.* [< OFr. *cointe* < L. *cognitus*, known: see COGNITION] **1.** unusual or old-fashioned in a pleasing way [a *quaint* old inn] **2.** unusual; curious [a *quaint* attitude] **3.** fanciful; whimsical [*quaint* notions] —see SYN. at STRANGE — **quaint′ly** *adv.* —**quaint′ness** *n.*

quake (kwāk) *vi.* **quaked, quak′ing** [OE. *cwacian*] **1.** to tremble or shake, as the ground does in an earthquake **2.** to shudder or shiver, as from fear or cold —*n.* **1.** a shaking or tremor **2.** an earthquake —see SYN. at SHAKE

Quak·er (kwāk′ər) *n.* [orig. mocking: said to be from founder's urging of those to whom he preached to "quake" at the word of the Lord] *a popular name for* a member of the Society of Friends: see SOCIETY OF FRIENDS —**Quak′er·ess** [Now Rare] *n.fem.* —**Quak′er·ish** *adj.* —**Quak′er·ism** *n.*

☆**quaking aspen** a poplar with small, flat-stemmed leaves that tremble in the slightest breeze

quak·y (kwā′kē) *adj.* **quak′i·er, quak′i·est** inclined to quake; shaky —**quak′i·ly** *adv.* —**quak′i·ness** *n.*

qual·i·fi·ca·tion (kwäl′ə fi kā′shən) *n.* **1.** a qualifying or being qualified **2.** a thing or condition that qualifies or limits; modification or restriction [to recommend a book without any *qualification*] **3.** any skill, knowledge, experience, etc. that fits a person for a position, office, etc. **4.** a condition that must be met in order to make use of certain rights [to meet the *qualifications* for voting]

qual·i·fied (kwäl′ə fīd′) *adj.* **1.** having met conditions or requirements set [a *qualified* voter] **2.** having the necessary or desirable qualities; competent [a highly *qualified* candidate] **3.** limited; modified [*qualified* approval] —see SYN. at ABLE —**qual′i·fied′ly** *adv.* —**qual′i·fied′ness** *n.*

qual·i·fi·er (-fī′ər) *n.* one that qualifies; specif., *a)* a person who meets set requirements *b)* a word, as an adjective or adverb, that modifies or limits the meaning of another word

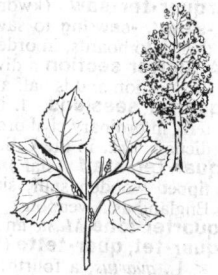

QUAKING ASPEN
(tree & leaves)

qual·i·fy (-fī′) *vt.* **-fied′, -fy′ing** [< Fr. < ML. < L. *qualis*, of what kind + *facere*, to make] **1.** to describe by giving the qualities or characteristics of **2.** to make fit for an office, position, etc. [his training *qualifies* him for the job] **3.** to make legally capable; license [*qualified* to vote at the age of 18] **4.** to modify; restrict; limit [to *qualify* one's approval] **5.** to moderate; soften [to *qualify* a punishment] **6.** *Gram.* to limit or modify the meaning of (a word) [adjectives *qualify* nouns] —*vi.* to be or become qualified [43 golfers *qualified* for the final round of the tournament] —**qual′i·fi′a·ble** *adj.* —**qual′i·fy′ing·ly** *adv.*

qual·i·ta·tive (kwäl′ə tāt′iv) *adj.* having to do with quality or qualities —**qual′i·ta′tive·ly** *adv.*

qualitative analysis the branch of chemistry dealing with the testing of substances to find out what elements or ingredients are in them

qual·i·ty (kwäl′ə tē) *n., pl.* **-ties** [< OFr. < L. < *qualis*, of what kind] **1.** any of the features that make something what it is; characteristic; attribute [coldness is one *quality* of ice cream] **2.** basic nature; character [soap with an oily *quality*] **3.** the degree of excellence which a thing possesses [a poor *quality* of paper] **4.** excellence; superiority [to look for *quality* in a product] **5.** [Archaic] *a)* high social position [a lady of *quality*] *b)* people of such position **6.** the property of a tone determined by its overtones; timbre

SYN.—**quality** refers to that which forms the basic nature of a thing or is one of its distinguishing features [the *quality* of mercy]; **property** applies to any of the special qualities, actions, or effects by which a thing is known [elasticity is a *property* of rubber]; **character** may refer to the total of qualities, actions, etc. that makes one person or thing different from others or, in scientific use, to a particular hereditary feature passed on by the genes; an **attribute** is a quality or feature that is thought of as a natural part of a person or thing [omnipotence is an *attribute* of God]; **trait** specifically applies to a distinguishing quality of personality [enthusiasm is one of her outstanding *traits*]

☆**quality control** a system for keeping up desired standards in a product, esp. by inspecting samples

qualm (kwäm) *n.* [OE. *cwealm*, disaster] **1.** a sudden feeling of sickness, faintness, or nausea **2.** a sudden feeling of uneasiness or doubt; misgiving [to feel *qualms* about sailing in rough weather] **3.** a twinge of conscience; scruple [a hardened grafter who took bribes without a *qualm*] —**qualm′ish·ly** *adj.* — **qualm′ish·ly** *adv.* —**qualm′ish·ness** *n.*

SYN.—**qualm** implies a painful feeling of uneasiness coming from an awareness that one is or may be acting wrongly [having such reverence for all living things that she felt *qualms* about eating meat]; **scruple** implies doubt or hesitation coming from difficulty in making up one's mind about what is right, proper, just, etc. [a lawyer with *scruples* about using evidence gathered by wiretapping]; **compunction** implies a twinge of conscience for wrongdoing, now often for a slight offense [to have no *compunctions* about telling a white lie]; **misgiving** implies a troubled state of mind resulting from not being sure about whether what one is doing is right [the builder had *misgivings* about tearing down the stately old house]

quan·da·ry (kwän′drē, -dər ē) *n., pl.* **-ries** [< ? L. *quande*, how much] a condition of being doubtful or confused about what to do; dilemma [in a *quandary* as to whether to sell now or wait for a higher offer]

quan·ta (kwän′tə) *n. pl. of* QUANTUM

quan·ti·fy (kwän′tə fī′) *vt.* **-fied′, -fy′ing** [ML. < L. *quantus*, how much + *facere*, to make] to find out or show the quantity of; measure —**quan′ti·fi′a·ble** *adj.* —**quan′ti·fi·ca′tion** *n.* — **quan′ti·fi′er** *n.*

quan·ti·ta·tive (kwän′tə tāt′iv) *adj.* **1.** having to do with quantity **2.** capable of being measured —**quan′ti·ta′tive·ly** *adv.* —**quan′ti·ta′tive·ness** *n.*

quantitative analysis the branch of chemistry dealing with the measurement of the amounts or percentages of the various elements or ingredients in a substance

quan·ti·ty (kwän′tə tē) *n., pl.* **-ties** [< OFr. < L. < *quantus*, how great < *quam*, how, how much] **1.** an amount; portion [a small *quantity* of oil] **2.** any bulk, weight, or number not definitely specified [various *quantities* of surplus foods] **3.** the exact amount of something **4.** [*also pl.*] a great amount or number [the factory makes toys in *quantity*] **5.** that property of anything which can be determined by measurement **6.** the relative length of a vowel, syllable, musical tone, etc. **7.** *Math. a)* a thing that has the property of being measurable in dimensions, amounts, etc. *b)* a number or symbol expressing a quantity

quan·tum (kwän′təm) *n., pl.* **-ta** (-tə) [L., neut. sing. of *quantus*, how much] **1.** quantity; amount **2.** in the quantum theory, any of the small, separate bits or amounts of energy that are given off or absorbed

quantum mechanics the branch of physics that deals with atomic structure and phenomena by the methods of the quantum theory

quantum theory the theory that radiant energy, as light, is not given off or absorbed in a continuous flow but in a series of small, separate bits, each bit being an amount of energy called a quantum

quar·an·tine (kwôr′ən tēn′, kwär′-) *n.* [It. *quarantina*, lit., forty days, ult. < L. *quadraginta*, forty] **1.** *a)* the period, orig. 40 days, during which a vessel suspected of carrying contagious disease is kept in a port in isolation *b)* the place where such a vessel is stationed **2.** any isolation or restriction on travel to keep contagious diseases, insect pests, etc. from spreading **3.** a place where persons, animals, or plants having such diseases, etc. are isolated **4.** the state of being quarantined —*vt.* **-tined′, -tin′ing 1.** to place under quarantine **2.** to cut off politically, commercially, socially, etc. from dealings with others — **quar′an·tin′a·ble** *adj.*

quark (kwôrk) *n.* [orig. a word coined by James Joyce in *Finnegan's Wake*] ☆any of three proposed particles thought of as the building blocks of baryons and mesons

quar·rel¹ (kwôr′əl, kwär′-) *n.* [< OFr., ult. < dim. of L. *quadrus*, a square] **1.** a square-headed arrow shot from a crossbow **2.** a small, diamond-shaped or square pane of glass

quar·rel² (kwôr′əl, kwär′-) *n.* [< OFr. < L. *querela*, complaint < *queri*, to complain] **1.** a cause for dispute [I have no *quarrel* with the way things are being run] **2.** a dispute, esp. one marked by anger and resentment **3.** a breaking up of friendly relations —*vi.* **-reled** or **-relled, -rel·ing** or **-rel·ling 1.** to find fault; complain [I *quarrel* with his methods, not with his results] **2.** to dispute heatedly **3.** to have a breach in friendship — **quar′rel·er, quar′rel·ler** *n.*

SYN.—quarrel implies a sharp disagreement full of angry words and feeling and often suggests that those arguing become unfriendly; **wrangle** suggests a noisy, fairly lengthy dispute in which each person stubbornly refuses to change his mind; **altercation** suggests a heated argument which may or may not come to blows; **squabble** implies undignified, childish arguing over a small matter; **spat** is the colloquial word for a petty quarrel and suggests a brief, angry outburst that has little lasting effect —**ANT.** agreement, harmony

quar·rel·some (-səm) *adj.* inclined or ready to quarrel —see **SYN.** at BELLIGERENT —**quar′rel·some·ly** *adv.* —**quar′rel·some·ness** *n.*

quar·ry¹ (kwôr′ē, kwär′ē) *n., pl.* **-ries** [< OFr. *cuiree*, altered (after *cuir*, a hide) < pp. of *curer*, to eviscerate] **1.** an animal that is being hunted down, esp. with dogs or hawks **2.** anything being hunted or pursued

quar·ry² (kwôr′ē, kwär′ē) *n., pl.* **-ries** [< ML., ult. < L. *quarare*, to square] a place where building stone, marble, or slate is excavated —*vt.* **-ried, -ry·ing 1.** to excavate from a quarry **2.** to make a quarry in (land)

quar·ry·man (-mən) *n., pl.* **-men** a person who works in a stone quarry: also **quar·ri·er** (kwôr′ē ər, kwär′-)

quart (kwôrt) *n.* [< MFr. < OFr. < L. *quartus*, fourth < base of *quattuor*, FOUR] **1.** a liquid measure, equal to two pints or 1/4 gallon (57.75 cu. in.) **2.** a dry measure, equal to 1/8 peck **3.** any container that can hold one quart Abbrev. **qt., q.**

quar·tan (kwôr′t'n) *adj.* [< MFr. < L. (*febris*) *quartana*, (fever) occurring every fourth day] occurring every fourth day, counting both days of occurrence: said of a fever —*n.* a type of malaria in which the attacks occur every fourth day

quar·ter (kwôr′tər) *n.* [< OFr. < L. *quartarius*, a fourth < *quartus*, fourth: see QUART] **1.** any of the four equal parts of something; fourth **2.** *a)* one fourth of a year; three months *b)* a school or college term lasting about twelve weeks **3.** *a)* one fourth of an hour; 15 minutes *b)* the moment marking the end of each fourth of an hour ☆**4.** *a)* one fourth of a dollar; 25 cents *b)* a coin of the U.S. and Canada equal to 25 cents: in the U.S., made of cupronickel **5.** any leg of a four-legged animal, with the adjoining parts [a *quarter* of beef] **6.** *a)* any of the four main points of the compass *b)* any of the four divisions of the horizon as marked off by these points *c)* any of the regions of the earth thought of as under these divisions **7.** a particular district in a city [the Latin *Quarter*] **8.** [*pl.*] lodgings; place to live in, often just for a while **9.** mercy, specif., mercy granted to a surrendering foe **10.** a particular person, group, place, etc., esp. one serving as a source [news from the highest

quarters] **11.** *a)* the period of time in which the moon makes one fourth of its revolution around the earth *b)* a phase of the moon when it is half lighted ☆**12.** *Football, Basketball*, etc. any of the four periods into which a game is divided **13.** *Heraldry a)* any of the four equal divisions of a shield *b)* the charge occupying such a division **14.** *Naut. a)* the after part of a ship's side, between the beam and the stern *b)* [*pl.*] an assembly of crew members as for muster or at assigned stations for a drill —*vt.* **1.** to divide into four equal parts **2.** loosely, to separate into any number of parts **3.** to dismember (the body of a person put to death) into four parts **4.** to provide lodgings for; specif., to assign (soldiers) to lodgings **5.** to pass back and forth over (an area) in many directions, as hounds do in searching for game **6.** *Heraldry* to place (different coats of arms) on the quarters of a shield, or to add (a coat of arms) to a shield thus —*vi.* **1.** to be lodged or stationed (*at* or *with*) **2.** to range over a field, etc., as hounds in hunting **3.** *Naut.* to blow on the quarter of a ship: said of the wind —*adj.* constituting or equal to a quarter [a *quarter* share of the profits] —**at close quarters** at close range —**cry quarter** to beg for mercy —**quar′ter·ing** *adj., n.*

☆**quar·ter·back** (-bak′) *n. Football* the offensive back who calls the signals and directs the plays —*vt., vi.* **1.** to act as quarterback for (a team) **2.** to direct or lead; manage

quarter day any of the four days regarded as beginning a new quarter of the year, when quarterly payments of interest, rent, etc. are due

quar·ter·deck (-dek′) *n.* **1.** the after part of a ship's upper deck, usually reserved for officers **2.** *U.S. Navy* the part of a ship's upper deck reserved for official ceremonies

quar·tered (kwôr′tərd) *adj.* **1.** divided into quarters **2.** provided with quarters or lodgings **3.** quartersawed

quar·ter·fi·nal (kwôr′tər fī′n'l; *for n. usually* kwôr′tər fī′n'l) *adj.* coming just before the semifinals, as of a tournament —*n.* **1.** a quarterfinal match **2.** [*pl.*] a quarterfinal round —**quar′ter·fi′nal·ist** *n.*

☆**quarter horse** an American breed of horse with a low, compact, muscular body and great sprinting speed for distances up to a quarter of a mile

quar·ter-hour (kwôr′tər our′) *n.* **1.** fifteen minutes **2.** the point on a clock marking the first quarter or the third quarter of an hour

quar·ter·ly (kwôr′tər lē) *adj.* **1.** occurring or appearing at regular intervals four times a year **2.** consisting of a quarter —*adv.* once every quarter of the year —*n., pl.* **-lies** a publication issued every three months

quar·ter·mas·ter (-mas′tər) *n.* **1.** *Mil.* an officer whose duty it is to provide troops with quarters, clothing, equipment, etc. **2.** a ship's petty officer who attends to navigation, signals, etc.

quar·tern (kwôr′tərn) *n.* [< OFr.: see QUART] **1.** orig., a fourth part **2.** [Brit.] one fourth of a pint, a peck, etc.

quarter note *Music* a note held one fourth as long as a whole note; crotchet: see illustration at NOTE

☆**quar·ter·saw** (kwôr′tər sô′) *vt.* **-sawed′, -sawed′** or **-sawn′, -saw′ing** to saw (a log) into quarters lengthwise and then into boards, in order to show off the grain of the wood

☆**quarter section** a division of public lands that is one fourth of a section and is half a mile square: equal to 160 acres

quarter sessions 1. in England, a local court that sits quarterly in ordinary civil proceedings and has limited criminal jurisdiction ☆**2.** in the U.S., any of various courts that sit quarterly

quar·ter·staff (-staf′) *n., pl.* **-staves′** (-stāvz′) a stout, iron-tipped wooden staff, six to eight feet long, formerly used in England as a weapon

quarter tone *Music* an interval of one half of a semitone

quar·tet, quar·tette (kwôr tet′) *n.* [< Fr. < It. dim. of *quarto* < L. *quartus*, a fourth: see QUART] **1.** any group of four **2.** *Music a)* a composition for four voices or four instruments *b)* the four performers of such a composition

quar·to (kwôr′tō) *n., pl.* **-tos** [< L. (*in*) *quarto*, (in) a fourth] **1.** the page size (about 9 by 12 in.) of a book made up of printer's sheets folded into four leaves **2.** a book with pages of this size —*adj.* with pages of this size

quartz (kwôrts) *n.* [G. *quarz* < ?] a brilliant, crystalline mineral, silicon dioxide, SiO_2, occurring most often in a colorless, transparent form, but also as variously colored semiprecious stones —**quartz·ose** (kwôrt′sōs) *adj.*

quartz crystal *Electronics* a thin plate or rod cut from quartz and ground so as to vibrate at a particular frequency

quartz·ite (kwôrt′sīt′) *n.* [QUARTZ + -ITE] a very hard sandstone

☆**quartz lamp** a mercury-vapor lamp with a quartz tube for transmitting ultraviolet rays

☆**qua·sar** (kwā′sär, -zär, -sər) *n.* [< *quas(i-stell)ar (radio source)*] any of a number of extremely distant starlike objects that emit powerful radio waves

quash¹ (kwäsh) *vt.* [< MFr. < LL. *cassare*, to destroy < L. *cassus*, empty: for IE. base see CASTRATE] *Law* to annul or set aside (an indictment)

quash² (kwäsh) *vt.* [< MFr. < L. *quassare*, to shatter < pp. of *quatere*, to break] to put down or overcome as by force; suppress; quell [to *quash* an uprising]

qua·si (kwā′sī, -zī) *adv.* [L. < *quam*, as + *si*, if] as if; seemingly; in part —*adj.* seeming Often hyphenated as a prefix [a *quasi*-legal document]

quas·si·a (kwäsh′ē ə, kwäsh′ə) *n.* [ModL. < Graman *Quassi*, Surinam Negro who prescribed it for fever, c. 1730] **1.** any of a group of tropical trees related to the ailanthus **2.** the wood of certain of these or a drug extracted from it

qua·ter·na·ry (kwät′ər ner′ē, kwə tur′nər ē) *adj.* [< L. < *quaterni*, four each] **1.** consisting of four **2.** [Q-] designating or of the geologic period following the Tertiary in the Cenozoic Era —**the Quaternary** the Quaternary Period or its rocks: see GEOLOGIC TIME CHART

quat·rain (kwä′trān) *n.* [Fr. < *quatre* < L. *quattuor*, FOUR] a stanza or poem of four lines

quat·re·foil (kat′ər foil′, kat′rə-) *n.* [< MFr. < *quatre* < L. *quattuor*, four + *feuille* (< L. *folium*), a leaf] **1.** a flower with four petals or a leaf with four leaflets **2.** *Archit.* a circular design made up of four arcs joined together

qua·ver (kwā′vər) *vi.* [ME. *cwafien*] **1.** to shake or tremble **2.** to be shaky or tremulous: said of the voice **3.** to make a trill in singing or playing —*vt.* **1.** to utter in a shaky voice **2.** to sing or play with a trill —*n.* **1.** a tremulous quality in a voice or tone **2.** [Brit.] *same as* EIGHTH NOTE —**qua′ver·er** *n.* —**qua′ver·ing·ly** *adv.* —**qua′ver·y** *adj.*

quay (kē) *n.* [MFr. *cai* < Celt.] a wharf for loading and unloading ships, usually one of stone or concrete

quea·sy (kwē′zē) *adj.* **-si·er, -si·est** [ME. *qwesye* < Scand.] **1.** causing or feeling nausea **2.** squeamish; easily nauseated **3.** uncomfortable; uneasy — **quea′si·ly** *adv.* —**quea′si·ness** *n.*

QUATREFOILS

Que·bec (kwi bek′) **1.** province of E Canada: 594,860 sq. mi.; pop. 6,234,000; abbrev. **Que., P.Q. 2.** its capital, on the St. Lawrence River: pop. 177,000 (met. area 413,000) Fr. **Qué·bec** (kā bek′)

Que·bec·ois (ke′be kwä′) *n., pl.* **-ois′** [< CanadFr.] a French-speaking native or inhabitant of the province of Quebec

que·bra·cho (kā brä′chō) *n., pl.* **-chos** [AmSp. < *quebrar*, to break + *hacha*, an ax] **1.** a tropical American tree with hard wood that yields an extract used in tanning **2.** its wood or bark

Quech·ua (kech′wä, -wə) *n.* [Sp. < Quechua name] **1.** *pl.* **-uas, -ua** a member of any of a group of S. American Indian tribes dominant in the former Inca Empire **2.** their language, still widely spoken —**Quech′uan** *adj., n.*

queen (kwēn) *n.* [OE. *cwen*] **1.** the wife of a king **2.** a woman who rules over a monarchy in her own right **3.** a woman who is famous or honored for something [beauty *queen*] **4.** a place or thing regarded as the best or most beautiful of its kind [queen among cities of Asia] **5.** the fully developed, egg-laying female in a colony of bees, ants, or termites **6.** a playing card with a picture of a queen on it **7.** *Chess* the most powerful piece: it can move in any straight or diagonal direction —*vt. Chess* to make a queen of (a pawn that has been moved to the opponent's end of the board) —**queen it** to act like a queen; domineer —**queen′hood** *n.* —**queen′like** *adj.*

☆**Queen Anne's lace** *same as* WILD CARROT

queen consort the wife of a reigning king

queen dowager the widow of a king

queen·ly (kwēn′lē) *adj.* **-li·er, -li·est** of, like, or fit for a queen; royal; regal —**queen′li·ness** *n.*

queen mother a queen dowager who is mother of a reigning sovereign

queen post *Carpentry* either of two vertical posts set between the rafters and the base of a truss, at equal distances from the apex

Queens (kwēnz) [after *Queen* Catherine, wife of CHARLES II of England] borough of New York City, on W Long Island: pop. 1,987,000

☆**queen-size** (kwēn′sīz′) *adj.* [Colloq.] larger than usual, but less than king-size [a *queen-size* bed is 60 by 80 inches]

Queens·land (kwēnz′land′, -lənd) state of NE Australia

queer (kwir) *adj.* [< ? G. *quer*, crosswise] **1.** differing from what is usual or ordinary; odd; strange [a *queer* custom] **2.** slightly ill; giddy, queasy, etc. [he felt *queer* after eating the day-old food] **3.** [Colloq.] doubtful; suspicious [her *queer* behavior in refusing to testify] **4.** [Colloq.] having mental quirks; eccentric **5.** [Slang] counterfeit; not genuine —*vt.* [Slang] **1.** to spoil the success of **2.** to put (oneself) into an unfavorable position —*n.* [Slang] **1.** counterfeit money **2.** a strange or eccentric person —**see SYN.** at STRANGE —**queer′ish** *adj.* —**queer′ly** *adv.* —**queer′ness** *n.*

quell (kwel) *vt.* [OE. *cwellan*, to kill] **1.** to crush; subdue; put an end to [to *quell* a mutiny] **2.** to quiet; allay [to *quell* fears] —**quell′er** *n.*

Que·moy (kē′moi′) island off the SE coast of China, held by the government on Taiwan: 62 sq. mi.

quench (kwench) *vt.* [OE. *cwencan*, caus. of *cwincan*, to go out] **1.** to extinguish; put out [water *quenched* the fire] **2.** to overcome; subdue **3.** to satisfy; slake [he *quenched* his thirst] **4.** to cool (hot steel, etc.) suddenly by plunging into water, oil, or other liquid —**quench′a·ble** *adj.* —**quench′er** *n.* —**quench′less** *adj.*

quern (kwurn) *n.* [OE. *cweorn*] a primitive hand mill, esp. for grinding grain

quer·u·lous (kwer′ə ləs, -yə-) *adj.* [< L. < *queri*, to complain] **1.** inclined to find fault; always complaining **2.** showing ill humor or impatience; peevish [a *querulous* comment] —**quer′u·lous·ly** *adv.* —**quer′u·lous·ness** *n.*

que·ry (kwir′ē) *n., pl.* **-ries** [< L. *quaere*, 2d pers. sing., imper., of *quaerere*, to ask] **1.** a question; inquiry **2.** a doubt **3.** a question mark (?) —*vt.* **-ried, -ry·ing 1.** to call in question; ask about [she *queried* my reasons for leaving] **2.** to question (a person) **3.** to question the accuracy of (written or printed matter) by marking with a question mark —*vi.* to ask questions or express doubt —**see SYN.** at ASK —**que′rist** *n.*

ques. question

quest (kwest) *n.* [< OFr. < ML., ult. < L. *quaesitus*, pp. of *quaerere*, to seek] **1.** a seeking; hunt; search [a student in *quest* of knowledge] **2.** a journey in search of adventure, etc., as those undertaken by knights-errant in medieval times **3.** the persons taking part in a quest —*vi.* to go in search or pursuit —**quest′er** *n.*

ques·tion (kwes′chən) *n.* [< Anglo-Fr. < OFr. < L. *quaestio* < pp. of *quaerere*, to ask] **1.** an asking; inquiry **2.** something asked; interrogative sentence **3.** doubt; uncertainty [there is no *question* about her honesty] **4.** something in controversy before a court **5.** a problem; matter open to discussion or inquiry [the *question* of who really discovered America] **6.** a matter or case of difficulty [it's not a *question* of money] **7.** *a)* a point being debated or a resolution brought up before an assembly *b)* the putting of such a matter to a vote —*vt.* **1.** to ask questions of; interrogate [to *question* the witness] **2.** to express uncertainty about; doubt [to *question* the value of censorship] **3.** to dispute; challenge [to *question* her right to vote] —*vi.* to ask a question or questions —**see SYN.** at ASK —**beside the question** not related to what is being discussed —**beyond (all) question** without any doubt —**in question** being considered, debated, etc. —**out of the question** impossible; not to be considered —**ques′tion·er** *n.* —**ques′tion·ing·ly** *adv.*

ques·tion·a·ble (-ə b′l) *adj.* **1.** that can or should be questioned; open to doubt [a *questionable* story] **2.** suspected with good reason of being immoral, dishonest, etc. [a man of *questionable* character] **3.** uncertain [of *questionable* excellence] —**see SYN.** at DOUBTFUL —**ques′tion·a·ble·ness** *n.* —**ques′tion·a·bly** *adv.*

QUEEN POSTS

question mark **1.** a mark of punctuation (?) put after a sentence, word, etc. to indicate a direct question, and also used to express doubt, uncertainty, etc. ☆**2.** an unknown factor

ques·tion·naire (kwes′chə ner′) *n.* [Fr.] a written or printed list of questions used in gathering information from one or more persons

quet·zal (ket säl′) *n.* [AmSp. < Nahuatl < *quetzalli*, tail feather] **1.** a Central American bird, usually brilliant green above and red below, with long, streaming tail feathers in the male **2.** *pl.* **-zal′es** (-sä′les) *see* MONETARY UNITS, table (Guatemala)

QUETZAL
(length, including plumes, to 42 in.)

queue (kyōō) *n.* [Fr. < OFr. *coue* < L. *cauda*, tail] **1.** a pigtail **2.** [Chiefly Brit.] a line, as of persons waiting to be served —*vi.* **queued,** **queu′ing** [Chiefly Brit.] to form in a line (often with *up*) *[to queue up at the bus stop]*

Que·zon (ke′sôn; *E.* kā′zän), **Man·uel Lu·is** (mä nwel′ lōō ēs′) 1878–1944; Philippine statesman

Que·zon City (ke′sôn; *E.* kā′zän) former capital of the Philippines, which became a part of Manila in 1975

quib·ble (kwib′'l) *n.* [< L. *quibus* (formerly common in legal documents), abl. pl. of *qui*, who, which] **1.** an avoiding of the main point as by arguing about some unimportant detail **2.** a petty objection or criticism —*vi.* **-bled,** **-bling** to use or engage in quibbles; cavil —**quib′bler** *n.*

quick (kwik) *adj.* [OE. *cwicu*, living < IE. base *gwei-*, to live] **1.** [Archaic] living **2.** *a)* rapid in action; swift *[a quick walk, a quick worker] b)* prompt *[a quick reply]* **3.** lasting a short time *[a quick look]* **4.** able to understand or learn rapidly **5.** sensitive *[a quick sense of smell]* **6.** easily stirred; fiery *[a quick temper]* —*adv.* quickly; rapidly *[come quick!]* —*n.* **1.** the living, esp. in **the quick and the dead** **2.** the sensitive flesh under a fingernail or toenail **3.** the deepest feelings *[cut to the quick by the insult]* —**quick′ly** *adv.* —**quick′ness** *n.*

SYN.—**quick** implies a natural ability or tendency to respond rapidly in action, thought, or feeling *[a quick mind];* **prompt** suggests a being willing or a being disciplined to respond immediately to a demand, request, etc. *[prompt to obey;* a *prompt acceptance];* **ready** implies a being prepared, inclined, or willing to act at once in a specified way *[her ready wit]* —**see also SYN.** at AGILE and FAST —**ANT.** slow

☆**quick bread** any bread, as muffins, corn bread, etc., leavened with baking powder, soda, etc. so that it can be baked as soon as the batter or dough is mixed

quick·en (kwik′ən) *vt.* **1.** to make alive; animate; enliven **2.** to stir; arouse; stimulate *[the news quickened his interest]* **3.** to make move more rapidly; speed up *[the horse quickened its pace]* —*vi.* **1.** to become enlivened; revive **2.** *a)* to begin to show signs of life *b)* to enter the stage of pregnancy in which the movement of the fetus can be felt **3.** to become more rapid; speed up *[the pulse quickens with fear]* —**quick′en·er** *n.*

☆**quick-freeze** (kwik′frēz′) *vt.* **-froze′, -froz′en, -freez′ing** to process (food) by sudden freezing so that flavor and natural juices are kept and the food can be stored at low temperatures for a long time

☆**quick·ie** (-ē) *n.* [Slang] anything done or made quickly —*adj.* [Slang] done or made quickly

quick·lime (-līm′) *n.* lime, or calcium oxide, which gives off much heat in combining with water; unslaked lime

quick·sand (-sand′) *n.* [see QUICK & SAND] a deep deposit of loose, wet sand in which a person or heavy object may be easily swallowed up

quick·set (-set′) *n.* [Chiefly Brit.] **1.** a live slip or cutting, as of hawthorn, planted, as for a hedge **2.** a hedge, as of hawthorn

quick·sil·ver (-sil′vər) *n.* [< OE., lit., living silver (see QUICK): from its liquid form] the metal mercury

quick·step (-step′) *n.* **1.** the step used for marching in quick time **2.** a march in the rhythm of quick time

quick-tem·pered (kwik′tem′pərd) *adj.* easily angered

quick time the normal rate of marching: in the U.S. Army, 120 (30-inch) paces a minute

quick-wit·ted (kwik′wit′id) *adj.* nimble of mind; alert —**quick′-wit′ted·ly** *adv.* —**quick′-wit′ted·ness** *n.*

quid[1] (kwid) *n.* [var. of *cud*] a piece, as of tobacco, to be chewed

quid[2] (kwid) *n., pl.* **quid** [Brit. Slang] a pound sterling

quid pro quo (kwid′ prō kwō′) [L.] **1.** one thing in return for another **2.** something equivalent; substitute

qui·es·cent (kwī es′'nt) *adj.* [< L. prp. of *quiescere*, to become

quiet: see QUIET] quiet; still; inactive —**qui·es′cence** *n.* —**qui·es′cent·ly** *adv.*

qui·et (kwī′ət) *adj.* [< OFr. < L. *quietus*, pp. of *quiescere*, to keep quiet < *quies* (gen. *quietis*), rest, genitive of *quies*, rest < IE. base *kweye-*, to rest] **1.** still; calm; motionless **2.** *a)* not noisy; hushed *[a quiet motor] b)* not speaking; silent **3.** not agitated; gentle *[a quiet sea]* **4.** not easily excited *[a quiet disposition]* **5.** not bright or showy *[quiet colors]* **6.** not forward; reserved *[a quiet manner]* **7.** secluded *[a quiet den]* **8.** peaceful; relaxing *[a quiet evening at home]* **9.** *Commerce* not busy *[a quiet day on the stock market]* —*n.* **1.** a quiet state; calmness, stillness, etc. *[the quiet of the night]* **2.** a quiet or peaceful quality —*vt., vi.* to make or become quiet —*adv.* in a quiet manner —*see* **SYN.** at STILL¹ —**qui′et·er** *n.* —**qui′et·ly** *adv.* —**qui′et·ness** *n.*

qui·et·en (-'n) *vt., vi.* [Brit. or Dial.] to make or become quiet

qui·e·tude (kwī′ə tōōd′, -tyōōd′) *n.* a state of being quiet; rest; calmness

qui·e·tus (kwī ēt′əs) *n.* [< ME. *quietus* (*est*) < ML., (he is) quit < L., QUIET] **1.** discharge or release from debt, obligation, etc. **2.** discharge or release from life; death **3.** anything that kills **4.** anything that quiets, controls, or ends an activity

quill (kwil) *n.* [prob. < MLowG. or MDu.] **1.** any of the large, stiff wing or tail feathers of a bird **2.** *a)* the hollow, horny stem of a feather *b)* anything made from this, as a pen or plectrum **3.** any of the spines of a porcupine or hedgehog

QUILL PEN

quilt (kwilt) *n.* [< OFr. < L. *culcita*, a bed] **1.** a bedcover made of two layers of cloth filled with down, wool, etc. and stitched together in lines or patterns to keep the filling in place **2.** anything like or used as a quilt —*vt.* **1.** to stitch as or like a quilt *[to quilt a potholder]* **2.** to fasten between two pieces of material **3.** to line or pad with quilting —☆ *vi.* to make a quilt or quilts

quilt·ing (kwilt′iŋ) *n.* **1.** the act of making quilts **2.** material for quilts, or quilted work ☆ same as QUILTING BEE

☆**quilting bee** (or **party**) a social gathering of women at which they work together sewing quilts

quince (kwins) *n.* [orig. pl. of ME. *quyn* < OFr. < L. < Gr. *kydōnion*] **1.** a golden or greenish-yellow, hard, apple-shaped fruit used in preserves **2.** the tree that bears this fruit

Quin·cy (kwin′zē) [after J. *Quincy* (1689–1767), a local official] city in E Mass.: suburb of Boston: pop. 88,000

qui·nine (kwī′nīn; *chiefly Brit.* kwi nēn′) *n.* [< *quina*, cinchona bark (< Sp. < Quechua name) + -INE⁴] **1.** a bitter, crystalline substance, $C_{20}H_{24}N_2O_2$, got from cinchona bark **2.** any compound of this used as a medicine, esp. for malaria

quinine water *same as* TONIC (*n.* 2)

Quin·qua·ges·i·ma (kwiŋ′kwə jes′i mə) *n.* [LL. *quinquagesima* (*dies*), fiftieth (day), that is, before Easter] the Sunday before Lent: also **Quinquagesima Sunday**

quin·quen·ni·al (kwiŋ kwen′ē əl) *adj.* [< L. < *quinque*, five + *annus*, year] **1.** lasting five years **2.** taking place every five years —*n.* a quinquennial event —**quin·quen′ni·al·ly** *adv.*

quin·que·va·lent (kwiŋ′kwə vā′lənt) *adj.* [L. *quinque*, five + -VALENT] **1.** having five valences **2.** *same as* PENTAVALENT (sense 1) —**quin′que·va′lence, quin′que·va′len·cy** *n.*

quin·sy (kwin′zē) *n.* [< ML. *quinancia* < LL. *cynanche* < Gr. *kynanchē*, lit., dog-choking < *kyōn*, dog + *anchein*, to choke] an earlier term for TONSILLITIS

quint (kwint) *n.* shortened form of QUINTUPLET

quin·tal (kwint′'l) *n.* [< MFr. < ML. < Ar. *qintār*, ult. < L. *centenarius*: see CENTENARY] **1.** a hundredweight (100 lbs. in U.S., 112 lbs. in Great Britain) **2.** a metric unit of weight, equal to 100 kilograms (220.46 lbs.)

quin·tes·sence (kwin tes′'ns) *n.* [< MFr. < ML. *quinta essentia*, fifth *essence*, or *ultimate substance:* see ELEMENT (sense 1)] **1.** the essence of something in its purest form **2.** the perfect type or example of something *[the movie was the quintessence of horror]* —**quin′tes·sen′tial** (-tə sen′shəl) *adj.*

quin·tet, quin·tette (kwin tet′) *n.* [< Fr. < It. dim. of *quinto* < L. *quintus*, a fifth] **1.** any group of five **2.** *Music a)* a composition for five voices or five instruments *b)* the five performers of such a composition

Quin·til·ian (kwin til′yən, -ē ən) (L. name *Marcus Fabius Quintilianus*) 30?–96? A.D.; Rom. rhetorician, born in Spain

quin·til·lion (-yən) *n.* [< L. *quintus*, a fifth + (M)ILLION] **1.** in the U.S. and France, the number represented by 1 followed by 18 zeros **2.** in Great Britain and Germany, the number represented by 1 followed by 30 zeros —*adj.* amounting to one quintillion in number —**quin·til'lionth** *adj., n.*

quin·tu·ple (kwin tōō'p'l, -tyōō'-, -tup'l; kwin'tōō p'l) *adj.* [MFr. < LL. < L. *quintus,* a fifth + *-plex,* -fold] **1.** consisting of five **2.** five times as much or as many; fivefold —*n.* an amount five times as much or as many —*vt., vi.* **-pled, -pling** to make or become five times as much or as many

quin·tu·plet (kwin tup'lit, -tōō'plit, -tyōō'-; kwin'tōō plit) *n.* [dim. of prec.] **1.** any of five offspring born at a single birth **2.** a group of five, usually of one kind

quip (kwip) *n.* [< L. *quippe,* indeed] a witty or, esp. formerly, sarcastic remark; jest —*vi.* **quipped, quip'ping** to utter quips — **quip'ster** *n.*

quire[1] (kwīr) *n.* archaic var. of CHOIR

quire[2] (kwīr) *n.* [< OFr. < VL. *quaternum,* paper in sets of four pages < L. *quaterni,* four each] a set of 24 or 25 sheets of paper of the same size and stock

quirk (kwʉrk) *n.* [< ? ON. *kverk,* a bird's crop] **1.** *a)* a sudden twist, turn, etc. [a *quirk* of fate] *b)* a flourish in writing **2.** a peculiar trait or mannerism —**quirk'i·ly** *adv.* —**quirk'i·ness** *n.* —**quirk'y** *adj.* **quirk'i·er, quirk'i·est**

☆**quirt** (kwʉrt) *n.* [AmSp. *cuarta*] a riding whip with a braided leather lash and a short handle —*vt.* to strike with a quirt

quis·ling (kwiz'liŋ) *n.* [after Vidkun *Quisling* (1887-1945), Norw. politician who betrayed his country to the Nazis and ruled it from within] a traitor

quit (kwit) *vt.* **quit** or **quit'ted, quit'ting** [< OFr. < ML. *quietus,* free: see QUIET] **1.** formerly, to acquit or conduct (oneself) in a specified way **2.** to pay up (a debt); repay **3.** to leave; go away from [to *quit* the country] **4.** to stop, discontinue, or resign from [to *quit* smoking; to *quit* one's job] —*vi.* **1.** *a)* to stop doing something *b)* to give up, as in discouragement **2.** to give up one's job; resign —*adj.* clear, free, or rid [quit of all debts] —see SYN. at STOP

quitch (kwich) *n.* [< OE. *cwicu,* alive] same as COUCH GRASS

quit·claim (kwit'klām') *n.* [< Anglo-Fr. & OFr.: see QUIT & CLAIM] **1.** the giving up of a claim, right, title, etc. **2.** a legal paper in which a person gives up to another his claim or title to some property or right: in full, **quitclaim deed** —*vt.* to give up a claim or title to, esp. by a quitclaim deed

quite (kwīt) *adv.* [ME. form of QUIT, *adj.*] **1.** completely; entirely [not *quite* done] **2.** really; truly [quite a hero] **3.** to a considerable degree or extent; very or fairly [quite warm outside] —☆**quite a few** (or **bit,** etc.) [Colloq.] more than a few (or bit, etc.) —**quite (so)!** certainly! I agree!

Qui·to (kē'tō) capital of Ecuador: pop. 463,000

quit·rent (kwit'rent') *n.* a rent paid in place of feudal services: also **quit rent**

quits (kwits) *adj.* [prob. contr. < ML. *quittus,* var. of *quietus:* see QUIETUS] on even terms, as by paying a debt, getting revenge, etc. —☆**call it quits** [Colloq.] **1.** to stop working, playing, etc. **2.** to end a close association or friendship

quit·tance (kwit''ns) *n.* [see QUIT] **1.** *a)* payment of a debt or obligation *b)* a document certifying this; receipt **2.** repayment or reprisal [to give him fair *quittance* for the injury]

quit·ter (kwit'ər) *n.* ☆[Colloq.] a person who quits or gives up easily, without trying hard

quiv·er[1] (kwiv'ər) *vi.* [ME. *quiveren:* for IE. base see QUICK] to shake with a tremulous motion; tremble —*n.* the act or condition of quivering; tremble —see SYN. at SHAKE —**quiv'er·y** *adj.*

quiv·er[2] (kwiv'ər) *n.* [OFr. *coivre* < Gmc.] **1.** a case for holding arrows **2.** the arrows in it

‡**qui vive?** (kē vēv') [Fr., (long) live who? (or, whose side are you on?)] who goes there?: a sentry's challenge —**on the qui vive** on the lookout; on the alert

Quixote, Don see DON QUIXOTE

quix·ot·ic (kwik sät'ik) *adj.* **1.** [often Q-] of or like Don Quixote **2.** foolishly kind, noble, or idealistic; visionary; impractical —**quix·ot'i·cal·ly** *adv.* —**quix'ot·ism** (-sə tiz'm) *n.*

quiz (kwiz) *n., pl.* **quiz'zes** [prob. arbitrary use of L. *quis,* what?] **1.** former-

QUIVER

ly, a practical joke; hoax ☆**2.** a questioning; esp., a short examination to test one's knowledge —*vt.* **quizzed, quiz'zing** **1.** formerly, to make fun of ☆**2.** *a)* to ask questions of [to *quiz* the suspect] *b)* to give a quiz to [to *quiz* the class] —**quiz'zer** *n.*

☆**quiz program** (or **show**) a radio or TV program in which a group of people compete in answering questions asked by a master of ceremonies (**quizmaster**)

quiz·zi·cal (kwiz'i k'l) *adj.* **1.** gently mocking or teasing [a *quizzical* smile] **2.** perplexed; questioning [a *quizzical* look on the student's face] —**quiz'zi·cal/i·ty** (-kal'ə tē), **quiz'zi·cal·ness** *n.* —**quiz'zi·cal·ly** *adv.*

Qum·ran (koom rän') region in Palestine, near the Dead Sea: site of caves in which Dead Sea Scrolls have been found

quoin (koin, kwoin) *n.* [var. of COIN] **1.** an outer corner of a building; esp., any of the large, squared stones in such a corner **2.** a wedgelike piece of stone, etc., such as the keystone of an arch **3.** a wedge-shaped wooden or metal block used to hold something in place

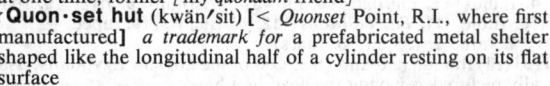

QUOINS

quoit (kwoit; *chiefly Brit.* koit) *n.* [< Anglo-Fr., prob. < OFr. *coite,* a cushion] **1.** a ring of rope or metal thrown, in a game like horseshoes, at an upright peg in an attempt to encircle it **2.** [*pl., with sing. v.*] this game

quon·dam (kwän'dəm) *adj.* [L.] that was at one time; former [my *quondam* friend]

☆**Quon·set hut** (kwän'sit) [< *Quonset* Point, R.I., where first manufactured] *a trademark for* a prefabricated metal shelter shaped like the longitudinal half of a cylinder resting on its flat surface

quo·rum (kwôr'əm) *n.* [L., genitive pl. of *qui,* WHO] the minimum number of members required to be present at an assembly or meeting before it can validly proceed to carry on its business

quot. quotation

quo·ta (kwōt'ə) *n.* [ML., short for L. *quota pars,* how large a part] **1.** a share which each of a number is asked to give or allowed to get; proportional share ☆**2.** the number or proportion that is allowed to be admitted [former nationality *quotas* for immigrants to the U.S.]

quot·a·ble (kwōt'ə b'l) *adj.* worthwhile quoting or suitable for quotation —**quot'a·bil/i·ty** *n.* —**quot'a·bly** *adv.*

quo·ta·tion (kwō tā'shən) *n.* **1.** the act of quoting **2.** the words or passage quoted [a talk full of *quotations* from the Bible] **3.** the current quoted price of a stock, bond, commodity, etc.

quotation mark either of a pair of punctuation marks (". . .") used to enclose a direct quotation, or of single marks ('. . .') for enclosing a quotation within a quotation

quote (kwōt) *vt.* **quot'ed, quot'ing** [< ML. *quotare,* to number (chapters, etc.) < L. *quotus,* of what number] **1.** to repeat a passage from or statement of [to *quote* Shakespeare] **2.** to repeat (a passage, statement, etc.) [to *quote* Hamlet's first soliloquy from memory] **3.** to cite as an example or authority [she *quoted* case after case that seemed to prove her point] **4.** to state (the price of something) —*vi.* to make a quotation, as from a book or author —*n.* [Colloq.] *same as:* **1.** QUOTATION **2.** QUOTATION MARK —*interj.* I shall quote: used in speech before a quotation —**quot'er** *n.*

quoth (kwōth) *vt.* [< OE. < *cwethan,* to speak] [Archaic] said: the past tense, followed by a subject in the first or third person ["*Quoth* the raven, 'Nevermore.' "]

quoth·a (kwōth'ə) *interj.* [< *quoth he*] [Archaic] indeed!

quo·tid·i·an (kwō tid'ē ən) *adj.* [< OFr. < L. < *quotidie,* daily < *quot,* as many as + *dies,* day] **1.** daily; recurring every day **2.** everyday; ordinary —*n.* anything, esp. a fever, that recurs daily

quo·tient (kwō'shənt) *n.* [< L. *quoties,* how often < *quot,* how many] *Arith.* the result obtained when one number is divided by another [in 32 ÷ 8 = 4, the number 4 is the *quotient*]

quo war·ran·to (kwō wô ran'tō) *pl.* **quo war·ran·tos** [ML., by what warrant] a legal proceeding with the purpose of recovering an office, franchise, etc. from the one in possession

qursh (koorsh) *n., pl.* **qu·rush** (koo'rəsh) [< Ar. *taqrush,* to earn < *qrsh,* to collect] *see* MONETARY UNITS, table (Saudi Arabia)

q.v. [L. *quod vide*] which see

R

R, r (är) *n., pl.* **R's, r's** **1.** the eighteenth letter of the English alphabet **2.** a sound of *R* or *r*

R **1.** *Chem.* radical **2.** *Math.* ratio **3.** *Elec.* resistance **4.** *Chess* rook —**the three R's** reading, writing, and arithmetic, regarded as the basic studies

☆**R** restricted: a motion-picture rating meaning that no one under the age of seventeen will be admitted unless accompanied by a parent or guardian

r **1.** *Math.* radius **2.** roentgen(s) **3.** ruble

R. **1.** Radical **2.** Republic(an)

R., r. **1.** [L. *Rex*] king **2.** [L. *Regina*] queen **3.** rabbi **4.** radius **5.** railroad **6.** railway **7.** right **8.** river **9.** road **10.** ruble **11.** *Baseball* runs **12.** *pl.* **Rs., Rs, rs.** rupee

r. **1.** rare **2.** retired **3.** rod(s)

Ra[1] (rä) the sun god and chief god of the ancient Egyptians, usually pictured as having the head of a hawk

Ra[2] *Chem.* radium

Ra·bat (rä bät′, rə-) capital of Morocco, on the NW coast: pop. 435,000

ra·bat (rab′ē, rə bat′) *n.* [MFr.] a plain, black dickey worn with a clerical collar by some clergymen

rab·bet (rab′it) *n.* [< OFr. < *rabattre*: see REBATE] a groove or cut made in the edge of a board, etc. so that another piece may be fitted into it to form a joint (**rabbet joint**) —*vt.* **1.** to cut a rabbet in **2.** to join by means of a rabbet —*vi.* to be joined by a rabbet

rab·bi (rab′ī) *n., pl.* **-bis, -bies** [< LL. < Gr. < Heb. *rabbī*, my master] a teacher of the Jewish law, now usually one who is ordained and is the spiritual head of a congregation

rab·bin·ate (rab′i nit, -nāt′) *n.* **1.** the position or office of rabbi **2.** rabbis as a group

Rab·bin·ic (rə bin′ik) *adj.* **1.** designating the Hebrew language as used in the writings of rabbis of the Middle Ages **2.** [r-] *same as* RABBINICAL

rab·bin·i·cal (rə bin′i k'l) *adj.* **1.** of the rabbis, their doctrines, learning, language, etc., esp. in the early Middle Ages **2.** of or for the rabbinate —**rab·bin′i·cal·ly** *adv.*

rab·bit (rab′it) *n., pl.* **-bits, -bit**: see PLURAL, II, D, 1 [ME. *rabette*] **1.** a burrowing mammal that has soft fur, long ears, and a stubby tail: rabbits are related to hares but are usually smaller and bear unfurred young **2.** the fur of a rabbit **3.** *same as* WELSH RABBIT —*vi.* to hunt rabbits

☆**rabbit ears** [Colloq.] an indoor TV antenna with two adjustable rods that swivel apart at a V-shaped angle

☆**rabbit fever** *same as* TULAREMIA

rabbit punch *Boxing* a sharp blow to the back of the neck

rab·ble (rab′'l) *n.* [< ? or akin to ML. *rabulus*, noisy < L. *rabula*, a pettifogger] a noisy, disorderly crowd; mob —*vt.* **-bled, -bling** to attack as a rabble; mob —**the rabble** the common people; the masses: a term of contempt

rab·ble-rous·er (-rouz′ər) *n.* a person who tries to stir up people to violent action by appeals to emotions, prejudices, etc.; demagogue —**rab′ble-rous′ing** *adj., n.*

Rab·e·lais (rà blē′; *E.* rab′ə lā′), **Fran·çois** (frän swà′) 1495?–1553; Fr. writer

Rab·e·lai·si·an (rab′ə lā′zhən, -zē ən) *adj.* of or like Rabelais or his works; humorous in a way that is coarse, lusty, satirical, etc.

rab·id (rab′id; *for 3 occas.* rā′bid) *adj.* [< L. < *rabere*, to rage]

RABBETS

1. violent; raging [*rabid* with anger] **2.** holding certain ideas, opinions, etc. in a strong, unreasonable way; fanatical [a *rabid* reactionary] **3.** of or having rabies [a *rabid* dog] —**ra·bid′i·ty** (rə bid′ə tē), **rab′id·ness** *n.* —**rab′id·ly** *adv.*

ra·bies (rā′bēz) *n.* [L., madness] an infectious virus disease of mammals, passed on to man by the bite of an infected animal: it causes choking, convulsions, etc.

☆**rac·coon** (ra kōōn′) *n., pl.* **-coons′, -coon′**: see PLURAL, II, D, 1 [< Algonquian *äräkun*, lit., scratcher] **1.** a small, tree-climbing, chiefly flesh-eating mammal of N. America, active largely at night and having long, yellowish-gray fur and a long, black-ringed tail **2.** its fur

RACCOON
(2–3 ft. long,
including tail)

race[1] (rās) *n.* [< ON. *rās*, a running < IE. base *eras-*, to flow] **1.** a competition of speed in running, riding, etc. [let's have a *race* to the corner] **2.** [*pl.*] a series of such competitions for horses, cars, etc., on a regular race track **3.** any contest likened to a race [the *race* for mayor] **4.** a steady onward movement [the *race* of events] **5.** *a*) a swift current of water *b*) a channel for this, esp. one built to use the water in running machinery [a *millrace*] —*vi.* **raced, rac′ing** **1.** to take part in a race [how many boats are *racing*?] **2.** to go or move very fast or too fast [a people *racing* to their destruction] —*vt.* **1.** to compete with in a race [I'll *race* you to the house?] **2.** to enter or run (a horse, etc.) in a race **3.** to make go very fast or too fast **4.** to run (an engine) at high speed with the transmission system not engaged

race[2] (rās) *n.* [Fr. < It. *razza*] **1.** any of the various groups of mankind, mainly the Caucasoid, Mongoloid, or Negroid groups, distinguished by kind of hair, color of skin, height, etc.: now often replaced in scientific use by *ethnic stock* or *group* **2.** any group of people having the same ancestry, nationality, place of origin, etc. **3.** any group of people having the same habits, ideas, interests, activities, etc. [a *race* of heroes] **4.** *Biol. a*) a subspecies, or variety of plant or animal *b*) *same as* BREED (*n.* 1) —**the (human) race** mankind

race·course (rās′kôrs′) *n. same as* RACE TRACK

race·horse (-hôrs′) *n.* a horse bred and trained for racing

ra·ceme (rā sēm′, rə-) *n.* [L. *racemus*, cluster of grapes] a flower cluster with individual flowers growing on small stems along the length of one central stem, as in the lily of the valley —**rac·e·mose** (ras′ə mōs′) *adj.*

rac·er (rās′ər) *n.* **1.** any person, animal, vehicle, etc. that takes part in races ☆**2.** any of several slim, swift, harmless snakes, as the American blacksnake

☆**race riot** violence and fighting in a community brought on by racial conflicts and hatreds

race track a track laid out for racing, usually in a circle or oval

☆**race·way** (rās′wā′) *n.* **1.** a narrow channel for water **2.** a race track for harness racing **3.** a race track for drag races, racing stock cars, etc.

Ra·chel (rā′chəl) [LL. < Gr. < Heb. *rāhēl*, lit., ewe] **1.** a feminine name **2.** *Bible* the younger of the two wives of Jacob: Gen. 29–35

ra·chis (rā′kis) *n., pl.* **ra·chis·es, ra·chi·des** (rak′ə dēz′, rā′kə-) [ModL. < Gr. *rhachis*, spine] **1.** the spinal column

RA-
CEME

2. *Bot.* the axis of an inflorescence or of a compound leaf **3.** *Zool.* the shaft of a feather

ra·chi·tis (rə kīt'əs, ra-) *n.* [ModL. < Gr. *rhachitis*, inflammation of the spine < *rhachis*, spine] *same as* RICKETS —**ra·chit'ic** (-kit'ik) *adj.*

Rach·ma·ni·noff (räkh mä'nü nôf; *E.* räk mä'ni nôf'), **Ser·gei V(assilievich)** (syer gā') 1873-1943; Russ. composer, conductor, & pianist: also sp. **Rachmaninov**

ra·cial (rā'shəl) *adj.* **1.** of a race, or ethnic group **2.** of or between races —**ra'cial·ly** *adv.*

ra·cial·ism (-iz'm) *n.* **1.** a doctrine or teaching, without scientific support, that claims to find racial differences in character, intelligence, etc. and that seeks to maintain the supposed superiority and purity of some one race **2.** *same as* RACISM (sense 2) —**ra'cial·ist** *n., adj.*

Ra·cine (rə sēn') [Fr., root, after the nearby Root River] city in SE Wis., on Lake Michigan: pop. 95,000

Ra·cine (ra sēn'; *E.* rə sēn'), **Jean Bap·tiste** (zhän bá tēst') 1639-99; Fr. poet & dramatist

rac·ism (rā'siz'm) *n.* **1.** *same as* RACIALISM (sense 1) **2.** the practice of racial discrimination, segregation, etc., based on racialism —**rac'ist** *n., adj.*

rack¹ (rak) *n.* [prob. < MDu. *rek* < *recken*, to stretch] **1.** a framework, stand, etc. for holding things [clothes *rack*] **2.** the triangular device in which the balls are set up at the start of a pool game **3.** a device for lifting an automobile for repairs from below **4.** a bar having teeth into which the teeth of a cogwheel, etc. fit as the wheel moves along **5.** a frame on which a victim is tortured by stretching his limbs out of place **6.** any great pain or suffering, or its cause **7.** a wrenching or upheaval, as by a storm —*vt.* **1.** to put in or on a rack **2.** to torture on a rack **3.** to cause pain or suffering to [a body *racked* with disease] **4.** to oppress, as by demanding excessive rent —**off the rack** ready-made: said of clothing —**on the rack** in a very difficult or painful situation —**rack one's brains** (or **memory,** etc.) to try very hard to think of something —**rack up** [Slang] **1.** to gain or score [to *rack up* a victory] **2.** to beat decisively

rack² (rak) *n., vi.* [< ?] *same as* SINGLE-FOOT

rack³ (rak) *n.* [var. of WRACK] destruction: now only in **go to rack and ruin,** to become ruined

rack⁴ (rak) *n.* [prob. < Scand.] a broken mass of clouds blown by the wind

rack·et¹ (rak'it) *n.* [prob. echoic] **1.** loud and confused talk or activity; noisy confusion; uproar ☆**2.** *a)* a scheme for getting money illegally, as by organized dealings in bootlegging, extortion, narcotics, etc. *b)* [Colloq.] any dishonest scheme ☆**3.** [Slang] *a)* an easy, profitable source of income *b)* any business, profession, etc. —*vi.* to make a racket, or uproar —**see SYN.** at NOISE —**rack'et·y** *adj.*

rack·et² (rak'it) *n.* [MFr. *raquette* < ML. *rasceta* < Ar. *rāḥah*, palm of the hand] **1.** a light bat for tennis, etc., with a network of catgut, nylon, etc. in an oval or round frame attached to a handle **2.** loosely, a table-tennis paddle **3.** [*pl.*, *with sing. v.*] the game of racquets

☆**rack·et·eer** (rak'ə tir') *n.* [see -EER] a person who works in or runs a racket (see RACKET¹, *n.* 2a) —*vi.* to be a racketeer —**rack'et·eer'ing** *n.*

rac·on·teur (rak'än tur') *n.* [Fr. < *raconter*, to recount] a person skilled at telling stories or anecdotes

☆**ra·coon** (ra kōōn') *n., pl.* **-coons,** **-coon':** see PLURAL, II, D, 1 *same as* RACCOON

rac·quet (rak'it) *n.* **1.** *same as* RACKET² **2.** [*pl.*, *with sing. v.*] a game similar to court tennis: see TENNIS

☆**rac·quet·ball** (-bôl') *n.* a game like handball, but played with a short-handled racket

rac·y (rā'sē) *adj.* **rac'i·er, rac'i·est** [RACE² + -Y²] **1.** having the taste or quality required to be genuine [*racy* fruit] **2.** lively; spirited [a *racy* style of writing] **3.** producing a sharp

RACKETS
(A, squash; B, tennis; C, badminton; D, racquetball)

taste or smell; pungent [*racy* flavor] ☆**4.** somewhat indecent; risqué [a *racy* story] —**rac'i·ly** *adv.* —**rac'i·ness** *n.*

rad (rad) *n.* [< *rad(iation)*] the unit of absorbed dose of ionizing radiation, equal to 100 ergs of energy per gram of matter

rad. 1. radical **2.** radius

☆**ra·dar** (rā'där) *n.* [*ra(dio) d(etecting) a(nd) r(anging)*] a system or device for sending out radio waves in order to detect an object, as a ship or aircraft, by the waves reflected back from the object and thus find out its direction, distance, height, or speed: used also in storm detection, mapping, navigation, etc. —**ra'dar·man** (-mən) *n., pl.* **-men**

☆**radar beacon** a beacon that sends out radar waves for receiving and display, showing its range or location, or both

☆**ra·dar·scope** (rā'där skōp') *n.* an instrument that displays on a screen the reflected radio waves picked up by radar

ra·di·al (rā'dē əl) *adj.* [< ML.: see RADIUS] **1.** of or like a ray or rays; branching out in all directions from a common center **2.** of or like a radius **3.** *Anat.* of or near the radius, or bone of the forearm —*n.* a radial part —**ra'di·al·ly** *adv.*

radial engine an internal-combustion engine with cylinders arranged radially like wheel spokes

radial (ply) tire a tire with the ply cords extending to the beads almost at right angles to the center line of the tread

ra·di·an (rā'dē ən) *n.* [< RADIUS] a unit of measure equal to 57.295+ degrees, the angle formed at the center of a circle by two radii cutting off an arc equal in length to the radius of the circle

ra·di·ant (rā'dē ənt) *adj.* [< L. prp. of *radiare*: see RADIATE] **1.** shining brightly **2.** filled with light [a *radiant* morning] **3.** showing joy, love, well-being, etc. [a *radiant* smile] **4.** coming (from a source) in or as in rays [*radiant* energy] —*n.* a source of heat or light rays —**see SYN.** at BRIGHT —**ra'di·ance,** **ra'di·an·cy** *n.* —**ra'di·ant·ly** *adv.*

radiant energy any form of energy traveling in waves; esp., electromagnetic radiation, as heat, light, X-rays, etc.

radiant heating heating by means of electric coils, hot-water or steam pipes, etc. that are set into the floor or walls

ra·di·ate (rā'dē āt') *vi.* **-at'ed, -at'ing** [< L. pp. of *radiare* < *radius*: see RADIUS] **1.** to send out rays of heat, light, etc. **2.** to spread out in rays [heat *radiating* from a stove] **3.** to branch out in lines from a center [highways *radiating* from a city] —*vt.* **1.** to send out (heat, light, etc.) in rays **2.** to give forth (happiness, love, etc.) as if from a center —*adj.* having rays or raylike parts; radial —**ra'di·ate·ly** *adv.*

ra·di·a·tion (rā'dē ā'shən) *n.* **1.** a radiating; specif., the process in which radiant energy is sent out from atoms and molecules as they undergo change **2.** such radiant energy **3.** *Nuclear Physics* rapidly moving nuclear particles, as alpha and beta particles —**ra'di·a'tion·al** *adj.* —**ra'di·a'tive** *adj.*

radiation sickness sickness produced by being exposed too long to radiation from X-rays, nuclear explosions, etc. and resulting in nausea, diarrhea, bleeding, etc.

ra·di·a·tor (rā'dē āt'ər) *n.* anything that radiates; specif., ☆*a)* a series of pipes with hot water or steam circulating in them so as to radiate heat into a room, etc. ☆*b)* a device of tubes and fins, as in a motor vehicle, through which circulating water passes so as to remove heat and so cool the engine

rad·i·cal (rad'i k'l) *adj.* [< LL. < L. *radicis*, genitive of *radix*, ROOT¹] **1.** *a)* of, from, or going to the root or source; fundamental; basic [a *radical* principle] *b)* extreme; thorough [a *radical* change in one's life] **2.** *a)* favoring basic or extreme change, as in the social or economic structure *b)* [R-] designating or of any of various modern political parties, as in Europe, ranging from moderate to conservative —*n.* **1.** *a)* a basic part of something *b)* a fundamental **2.** *a)* a person having radical views *b)* [R-] a member of a Radical party **3.** *Chem.* a group of two or more atoms that acts as a single atom and goes through a reaction unchanged, or is replaced by a single atom **4.** *Math. a)* an expression showing that a root is to be figured *b)* *same as* RADICAL SIGN —**see SYN.** at LIBERAL —**rad'i·cal·ly** *adv.*

rad·i·cal·ism (-iz'm) *n.* **1.** the quality or state of being radical **2.** radical principles, methods, or practices

rad·i·cal·ize (-īz') *vt., vi.* **-ized', -iz'ing** to make or become politically radical —**rad'i·cal·i·za'tion** *n.*

radical sign *Math.* the sign (√ or √⎺) used before a quantity to show that a root is to be figured

---

rad·i·cand (rad′i kand′) *n. Math.* a quantity from which a root is to be figured, shown with a radical sign

rad·i·ces (rad′ə sēz′, rā′də-) *n. alt. pl. of* RADIX

rad·i·cle (rad′i k′l) *n.* [< L. dim. of *radix*, ROOT¹] **1.** *Anat.* the rootlike beginning of a nerve, vein, etc. **2.** *Bot.* the root part of a plant embryo

ra·di·i (rā′dē ī′) *n. alt. pl. of* RADIUS

☆**ra·di·o** (rā′dē ō′) *n., pl.* -os′ [shortened from RADIOTELE-GRAPH] **1.** a way of communicating over a distance by changing sounds or signals into electromagnetic waves that are sent through space, without wires, to a receiving set, which changes them back into sounds or signals **2.** such a receiving set **3.** broadcasting by radio as an industry, entertainment, etc. —*adj.* **1.** of, using, used in, or sent by radio **2.** of electromagnetic wave frequencies from c.10 kilohertz to c.300,000 megahertz —*vt., vi.* **-oed′, -o′ing** to send (a message, etc.) or communicate with (a person, etc.) by radio

ra·di·o- [Fr. < L. *radius*, ray: see RADIUS] *a combining form meaning:* **1.** ray, raylike **2.** by radio **3.** by means of radiant energy [*radiotherapy*] **4.** radioactive [*radioisotope*]

ra·di·o·ac·tive (rā′dē ō ak′tiv) *adj.* giving off radiant energy in particles or rays as a result of the breaking up of the atomic nuclei: said of such elements as radium and uranium —**ra·di·o·ac′tive·ly** *adv.* —**ra·di·o·ac·tiv′i·ty** (-ak tiv′ə tē) *n.*

radioactive series the series of isotopes of various elements successively formed by a radioactive substance before it comes to a stable state, usually lead

radio astronomy astronomy dealing with radio waves in space in order to get data about certain regions in the universe

☆**radio beacon** a radio transmitter that gives off special signals to help ships or aircraft determine their positions or come in safely, as in a fog

ra·di·o·bi·ol·o·gy (-bī äl′ə jē) *n.* [RADIO- + BIOLOGY] the branch of biology dealing with the effects of radiation on living organisms and with biological studies using radioactive tracers —**ra′di·o·bi′o·log′i·cal** (-bī′ə läj′i k′l) *adj.* —**ra′di·o·bi·ol′o·gist** *n.*

☆**ra·di·o·broad·cast** (-brôd′kast′) *n.* a broadcast by radio —*vt., vi.* **-cast′** or **-cast′ed, -cast′ing** to broadcast by radio —**ra′di·o·broad′cast′er** *n.*

☆**ra·di·o·car·bon** (-kär′bən) *n. same as* CARBON 14: see CARBON

radio frequency any frequency between normally audible sound waves and infrared light, from c.10 kilohertz to c.300,000 megahertz

ra·di·o·gram (rā′dē ō gram′) *n.* **1.** a message sent by radio: also **ra′di·o·tel′e·gram′** **2.** *same as* RADIOGRAPH

ra·di·o·graph (-graf′) *n.* a picture made on a sensitized film or plate by X-rays —**ra′di·og′ra·pher** (-äg′rə fər) *n.* —**ra′di·o·graph′ic** *adj.* —**ra′di·og′ra·phy** *n.*

ra·di·o·i·so·tope (rā′dē ō ī′sə tōp′) *n.* a natural or artificial radioactive isotope of a chemical element

ra·di·o·lar·i·an (rā′dē ō ler′ē ən) *n.* [< ModL. name of the order < dim. of L. *radius*, ray] any of various deep-sea protozoans with long, radiating pseudopodia and a spiny skeleton of silica

ra·di·ol·o·gy (rā′dē äl′ə jē) *n.* [RADIO- + -LOGY] the science dealing with X-rays and other forms of radiant energy, esp. as used in medicine for X-raying parts of the body and for diagnosing and treating disease —**ra′di·o·log′i·cal** (-ə läj′i k′l) *adj.* —**ra′di·o·log′i·cal·ly** *adv.* —**ra′di·ol′o·gist** *n.*

ra·di·om·e·ter (-äm′ə tər) *n.* an instrument for measuring radiant energy —**ra′di·om′e·try** *n.*

☆**ra·di·o·phone** (rā′dē ō fōn′) *n. same as* RADIOTELEPHONE

ra·di·o·pho·to (rā′dē ō fōt′ō) *n., pl.* **-tos** a photograph or picture transmitted by radio: also **ra′di·o·pho′to·graph′**

ra·di·os·co·py (-äs′kə pē) *n.* [RADIO- + -SCOPY] the direct examination of the inside structure of opaque objects by radiation, as by X-rays —**ra′di·o·scop′ic** (-ə skäp′ik) *adj.*

☆**ra·di·o·sonde** (rā′dē ō sänd′) *n.* [Fr. < *radio*, RADIO + *sonde*, a sounding line] a compact package made up of a radio transmitter and meteorological instruments sent into the upper atmosphere, as by balloon, to record and radio back temperature, pressure, and humidity data

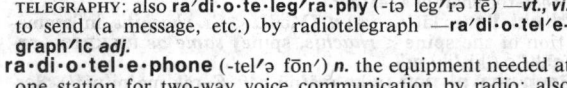

RADIOM-ETER

radio spectrum the complete range of frequencies of electromagnetic radiation useful in radio, from c.10 kilohertz to c.300,000 megahertz

ra·di·o·tel·e·graph (rā′dē ō tel′ə graf′) *n. same as* WIRELESS TELEGRAPHY: also **ra′di·o·te·leg′ra·phy** (-tə leg′rə fē) —*vt., vi.* to send (a message, etc.) by radiotelegraph —**ra′di·o·tel′e·graph′ic** *adj.*

ra·di·o·tel·e·phone (-tel′ə fōn′) *n.* the equipment needed at one station for two-way voice communication by radio: also **ra′di·o·phone′** —**ra′di·o·tel′e·phon′ic** (-fän′ik) *adj.* —**ra′di·o·te·leph′o·ny** (-tə lef′ə nē) *n.*

radio telescope a radio antenna or set of antennas for use in radio astronomy

ra·di·o·ther·a·py (-ther′ə pē) *n.* the treatment of disease by X-rays or by rays from a radioactive substance

radio wave any electromagnetic wave at a radio frequency

rad·ish (rad′ish) *n.* [OE. *rædic* < L. *radix*, a ROOT¹] **1.** an annual plant of the mustard family, with a small, round or long root **2.** the root, which has a sharp taste and is eaten raw as a relish or in a salad

ra·di·um (rā′dē əm) *n.* [ModL. < L. *radius*, a ray] a radioactive metallic chemical element, found in uranium minerals: symbol, Ra; at. wt., 226.00; at. no., 88

radium therapy the treatment of cancer or other diseases by the use of radium

ra·di·us (rā′dē əs) *n., pl.* **-di·i′** (-ī′), **-us·es** [L., a spoke (of a wheel), hence ray (of light), prob. akin to *radix*, ROOT¹] **1.** a raylike part, as a spoke of a wheel **2.** *a)* a straight line from the center to the outside of a circle or sphere *b)* its length **3.** *a)* the circular area or distance within the sweep of such a line [no house within a *radius* of five miles] *b)* the distance a ship or airplane can go and still get back without refueling **4.** any limited extent, scope, etc. [within the *radius* of one's experience] **5.** the shorter and thicker of the two bones of the forearm on the same side as the thumb: see illustration at ULNA

ra·dix (rā′diks) *n., pl.* **ra·di·ces** (rad′ə sēz′, rā′də-), **ra′dix·es** [L., a ROOT¹] **1.** the root of a plant **2.** *same as* RADICLE **3.** *Math.* the base of a number system

RAdm Rear Admiral

ra·dome (rā′dōm′) *n.* [RA(DAR) + DOME] a domed housing for a radar antenna, esp. on aircraft

ra·don (rā′dän) *n.* [RAD(IUM) + -ON] a radioactive gaseous chemical element formed in the atomic breakup of radium: symbol, Rn; at. wt., 222.00; at. no., 86

rad·u·la (raj′oo lə) *n., pl.* **-lae** (-lē′) [ModL. < L. < *radere*, to scrape] in most mollusks, a ribbonlike part with rows of small teeth, used to tear up food and take it into the mouth

RAF, R.A.F. Royal Air Force

raf·fi·a (raf′ē ə) *n.* [< Malagasy native name] **1.** a palm tree of Madagascar, with large, pinnate leaves **2.** fiber from its leaves, woven into baskets, hats, etc.

raff·ish (raf′ish) *adj.* [(RIFF)RAFF + -ISH] **1.** not respectable; rakish; dissolute **2.** cheap and showy; vulgar; low —**raff′ish·ly** *adv.* —**raff′ish·ness** *n.*

raf·fle (raf′'l) *n.* [MFr. *rafle*, dice game < OHG. *raffel*, a rake] a lottery in which a chance or chances to win a prize are bought —*vt.* **-fled, -fling** to offer as a prize in a raffle (often with *off*) —**raf′fler** *n.*

raft¹ (raft) *n.* [< ON. *raptr*, a log] **1.** a flat structure of logs, boards, etc. fastened together and floated on water **2.** an inflatable boat or pad, as of rubber, for floating on water —*vt.* to carry on a raft —*vi.* to travel, work, etc. on a raft —**rafts′man** (rafts′mən) *n., pl.* **-men**

raft² (raft) *n.* [< Brit. Dial. *raff*, rubbish] [Colloq.] a large number, collection, or quantity; lot

raft·er (raf′tər) *n.* [OE. *ræfter*] any of the beams that slope from the ridge of a roof to the eaves and serve to support the roof

rag¹ (rag) *n.* [ult. < ON. *rögg*, tuft of hair: for IE. base see RUPTURE] **1.** a waste piece of cloth, esp. an old or torn one **2.** a small cloth for dusting, washing, etc. **3.** anything thought of as having as little value as a rag **4.** [*pl.*] *a)* old, worn clothes *b)* any clothes: humorous term **5.** [Slang] any newspaper thought of with contempt —*adj.* made of rags [a *rag* doll] —**chew the rag** [Slang] to talk together; chat

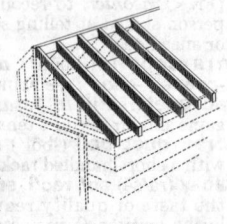

RAFTERS

rag² (rag) *vt.* **ragged, rag′ging** [< ?] [Slang] **1.** to tease **2.** to scold

☆**rag³** (rag) *n.* **1.** *clipped form of* RAGTIME **2.** a composition in ragtime —*vt.* **ragged, rag′ging** to play in ragtime

ra·ga (rä′gə) *n.* [Sans. *rāga*, lit., color] any of various traditional melodies used in improvising by Hindu musicians

rag·a·muf·fin (rag′ə muf′in) *n.* [ME. *Ragamoffyn*, name of a demon in *Piers Plowman*, a poem attributed to William Langland] a dirty, ragged person; esp., a poor, ragged child

rag·bag (rag′bag′) *n.* 1. a bag for rags 2. a collection of odds and ends

rage (rāj) *n.* [< OFr. < LL. < L. *rabies*, madness] 1. furious, uncontrolled anger; esp., a brief spell of raving fury 2. violence or great force, as of the wind 3. strong emotion, enthusiasm, or desire —*vi.* **raged, rag′ing** 1. to show violent anger in action or speech 2. to be violent, uncontrolled, etc. [a *raging* sea] 3. to spread without being stopped, as a disease —see SYN. at ANGER —**(all) the rage** anything thought of as a fad

rag·ged (rag′id) *adj.* 1. shabby or torn from wear [a *ragged* shirt] 2. wearing shabby or torn clothes [a *ragged* man] 3. uneven; rough [a *ragged* edge] 4. shaggy; unkempt [*ragged* hair] 5. not finished; imperfect [a *ragged* style] 6. harsh; grating [a *ragged* voice] —☆**run ragged** to wear (someone) out by keeping up pressure to get things done, etc. —**rag′ged·ly** *adv.* —**rag′ged·ness** *n.*

☆**ragged edge** the farthest edge, like that of a steep cliff; verge [the *ragged edge* of poverty] —**on the ragged edge** dangerously close to loss of self-control, normal state of mind, etc.

rag·ged·y (rag′i dē) *adj.* somewhat ragged, or tattered

rag·lan (rag′lən) *n.* [after Lord *Raglan* (1788–1855), Brit. general] a loose overcoat or topcoat without shoulder seams, each sleeve (**raglan sleeve**) continuing in one piece to the collar

rag·man (rag′man′) *n., pl.* **-men′** a man who collects, buys, and sells rags, old paper, etc.

ra·gout (ra gōō′) *n.* [< Fr. < *ragoûter*, to revive the appetite of] a highly seasoned stew of meat and vegetables —*vt.* **-gouted′** (-gōōd′), **-gout′ing** (-gōō′iŋ) to make into a ragout

rag·pick·er (rag′pik′ər) *n.* a person who makes his living by picking up and selling rags and junk

☆**rag rug** a rug of rag strips woven or sewn together

rag·tag (and bobtail) (rag′tag′) [RAG¹ + TAG] the lowest classes; the rabble: term of contempt

☆**rag·time** (rag′tīm′) *n.* [prob. < *ragged time*] 1. a type of strongly syncopated American music in fast, even time, popular orig. from 1890 to 1915 2. its rhythm

rag·weed (rag′wēd′) *n.* [from the tattered appearance of the leaves] any of a group of chiefly N. American plants of the composite family, having tassellike, greenish flowers with a pollen that is a major cause of hay fever

rag·wort (-wurt′) *n.* [see prec.] *same as* GROUNDSEL

☆**rah** (rä) *interj.* hurrah: used as a cheer

raid (rād) *n.* [< ROAD, in obs. sense "a riding"] 1. *a)* a sudden, hostile attack, as by troops, aircraft, bandits, etc. *b)* any act of entering to remove something [a *raid* on a refrigerator] 2. any sudden entering of a place by police, to discover and deal with violations of the law ☆3. an attempt to get employees away from a competing employer 4. an attempt by speculators to cause a quick, unexpected fall in stock-market prices —*vt., vi.* to make a raid (on) —**raid′er** *n.*

rail¹ (rāl) *n.* [< OFr. < L. *regula*, a rule] 1. a bar of wood, metal, etc. placed horizontally between posts as in a fence 2. a fence or railing 3. any of a series of parallel metal bars laid on crossties, etc. to make a track for trains, etc. 4. a railroad as a means of transportation [travel by *rail*] 5. the rim of a billiard table 6. a narrow wooden piece at the top of a ship's bulwarks —*vt.* to supply with rails or a railing; fence

rail² (rāl) *vi.* [< MFr. *railler* < Pr., ult. < LL. *ragere*, to bellow] to complain violently (with *against* or *at*) [to *rail* at one's fate] —**rail′er** *n.*

rail³ (rāl) *n., pl.* **rails, rail:** see PLURAL, II, D, 1 [< MFr. < *raaler*, to screech] any of a number of small, cranelike wading birds living in marshes and having short wings and tail, long toes, and a harsh cry

rail·ing (rāl′iŋ) *n.* 1. material for rails 2. rails collectively 3. a fence or balustrade made of rails and posts

rail·ler·y (rāl′ər ē) *n., pl.* **-ler·ies** [Fr. *raillerie:* see RAIL² & -ERY] 1. a joking or teasing in a friendly, playful way; banter 2. a teasing act or remark

rail·road (rāl′rōd′) *n.* 1. a road laid with parallel steel rails along which locomotives draw cars in a train 2. a complete system of such roads, including cars, engines, stations, etc. 3. the corporation owning such a system —*vt.* ☆1. to transport by railroad ☆2. [Colloq.] to rush through quickly, so as to prevent careful thought and attention [to *railroad* a bill through Congress] ☆3. [Slang] to cause to go to prison on a false charge or after a hasty trial —*vi.* ☆to work on a railroad —**rail′road′er** *n.* —**rail′road′ing** *n.*

☆**rail-split·ter** (-split′ər) *n.* a person who splits logs into rails, as for fences —**the Rail-Splitter** *nickname of* Abraham LINCOLN

rail·way (-wā′) *n.* 1. *a)* a railroad for light vehicles [a street *railway*] *b)* [Brit.] any railroad 2. any track with rails for guiding wheels

rai·ment (rā′mənt) *n.* [ME. *rayment* < *arayment:* see ARRAY & -MENT] [Archaic] clothing; wearing apparel

rain (rān) *n.* [OE. *regn*] 1. water falling in drops condensed from the moisture in the atmosphere 2. the falling of such drops; shower 3. *a)* rainy weather *b)* [*pl.*] the rainy season (preceded by *the*) 4. a rapid falling of many small pieces or things [a *rain* of ashes] —*vi.* 1. to fall: said of rain [it is *raining*] 2. to fall like rain [bullets *rained* about him] 3. to cause rain to fall: said of the heavens, clouds, etc. —*vt.* 1. to pour down (rain or something likened to rain) 2. to give in large quantities [to *rain* praises on someone] —☆**rain out** to cause (an event) to be postponed or canceled because of rain —**rain′less** *adj.*

rain·bow (rān′bō′) *n.* [see RAIN & BOW²] a huge arc containing the colors of the spectrum in bands, formed in the sky when the sun's rays pass through falling rain or mist —*adj.* of many colors

☆**rainbow trout** a game fish native to the mountain streams and rivers of the Pacific coast of N. America

☆**rain check** 1. the stub of a ticket to a ball game, etc., permitting the holder to be admitted to a future date if the original event is rained out 2. a chance at a future invitation in place of one turned down [he said he was busy that night but asked for a *rain check*]

☆**rain·coat** (rān′kōt′) *n.* a waterproof or water-repellent coat for giving protection from rain

rain·drop (-dräp′) *n.* a single drop of rain

rain·fall (-fôl′) *n.* 1. a falling of rain; shower 2. the amount of water falling as rain, snow, etc. over a given area in a given period of time: measured in inches of depth in an instrument (**rain gauge**) into which the water falls

rain forest a dense, evergreen forest in a tropical region having abundant rainfall throughout the year

Rai·nier (rā nir′, rā′nir), **Mount** [after an 18th-cent. Brit. Adm. *Rainier*] mountain of the Cascade Range, in WC Wash.: 14,410 ft.: the central feature of a national park (**Mount Rainier National Park**)

☆**rain·mak·er** (rān′mā′kər) *n.* a person who tries to make rain fall; specif., *a)* an American Indian medicine man who used certain rituals to influence the rain gods *b)* [Colloq.] a meteorologist or aircraft pilot involved in seeding clouds or the like —**rain′mak′ing** *n.*

rain·proof (rān′prōōf′) *adj.* not letting rain through —*vt.* to make rainproof

rain·storm (-stôrm′) *n.* a storm with a heavy rain

rain·wa·ter (-wôt′ər, -wät′ər) *n.* water that falls or has fallen as rain and is soft and fairly free of mineral matter

rain·wear (-wer′) *n.* rainproof clothing

rain·y (rā′nē) *adj.* **rain′i·er, rain′i·est** 1. that has rain or much rain [the *rainy* season] 2. wet with rain 3. bringing rain [*rainy* winds] —**rain′i·ness** *n.*

rainy day a possible future time of difficulty or need [to save for a *rainy day*]

raise (rāz) *vt.* **raised, rais′ing** [< ON. *reisa:* for IE. base see RUN] 1. *a)* to make rise; lift [*raise* the window] *b)* to put upright [to *raise* a pillar into place] 2. to construct (a building, etc.) 3. to stir up; arouse; incite [to *raise* a revolt] 4. to increase in size, value, amount, etc. [to *raise* prices] 5. to increase in degree, force, etc. [to *raise* one's voice] 6. to improve the position or rank of [to *raise* oneself from poverty] 7. to cause to arise, appear, or come; esp., to bring back as from death [to *raise* the dead] 8. to bring about; produce; cause [the joke *raised* a laugh] 9. to bring up for thinking about [to *raise* a question] 10. to collect or get together (an army, money, etc.) 11. to utter (a cry, shout, etc.) 12. to bring to an end [to *raise* a siege] **13.** to cause to become light; leaven (bread, etc.) **14.** *a)* to cause to grow [to *raise* corn] *b)* to breed (cattle, etc.) *c)* to bring up or rear (children or a family) **15.** to contact by radio **16.** to make (a blister) form **17.** to make (a nap on cloth) with teasels, etc. ☆**18.** *Bridge* to increase (one's partner's bid in a suit) **19.** *Naut.* to come within sight of (land, etc.) **20.** *Phonet.* to change the sound of (a vowel) by putting the tongue in a higher position ☆**21.** *Poker* to bet more than (the highest preceding bet or bettor) —*vi.* **1.** [Dial.] to rise or arise ☆**2.** *Poker* to increase the bet —*n.* **1.** a raising **2.** an increase in amount; specif., ☆an increase in salary or wages —see **SYN.** at LIFT —**raise Cain** (or **the devil, hell, a rumpus, the roof,** etc.) [Slang] to create a disturbance; cause trouble

raised (rāzd) *adj.* **1.** made in low relief; embossed **2.** having a napped surface **3.** leavened with yeast

rai·sin (rā′z'n) *n.* [< OFr. < L. *racemus,* cluster of grapes] a sweet, dried grape, usually seedless

rai·son d'être (rā′zōn det′, det′rə; *Fr.* re zōn de′tr′) [Fr.] reason for being; justification for existence

raj (räj) *n.* [see RAJAH] in India, rule; sovereignty; dominion

ra·jah, ra·ja (rä′jə) *n.* [< Hindi < Sans. *rājan* < *rāj,* to rule: for IE. base see REGAL] **1.** formerly, a prince or chief in India **2.** esp. formerly, a Malay chief

Raj·pu·ta·na (räj′pσσ tä′nə) region in NW India, on the border of Pakistan

rake¹ (rāk) *n.* [OE. *raca:* for IE. base see REGAL] a long-handled tool with teeth or prongs at one end, used for gathering loose grass, leaves, etc. —*vt.* **raked, rak′ing 1.** *a)* to gather with or as with a rake [to *rake* leaves] *b)* to make (a lawn, etc.) tidy with a rake **2.** to scratch or smooth as with a rake [to *rake* a gravel path] **3.** to search through carefully **4.** to direct gunfire along (a line of troops, the deck of a ship, etc.): often used figuratively —*vi.* **1.** to use a rake **2.** to search as if with a rake [he *raked* through the old papers looking for a letter] **3.** to scrape or sweep (with *over, across,* etc.) —**rake in** to gather fast a great deal of [to *rake in* money] —**rake up** to uncover facts or gossip about (the past, a scandal, etc.)

rake² (rāk) *n.* [shortened from *rakehell,* prob. < ME. *rakel,* rash] a man who leads a wild, dissolute life: also **rake′hell** (-hel′)

RAKES
(A, leaf rake;
B, garden rake)

rake³ (rāk) *vi., vt.* **raked, rak′ing** [? akin to Sw. *raka,* to project] to be or make slightly inclined, as a ship's masts; slant —*n.* a slanting or inclining

☆**rake-off** (rāk′ôf′) *n.* [Slang] a commission, rebate, or share, esp. one gained in a shady deal

rak·ish¹ (rā′kish) *adj.* [< RAKE³ + -ISH] **1.** having a trim, neat appearance suggesting speed: said of a ship **2.** having a gay, careless look; jaunty [a hat worn at a *rakish* angle] —**rak′ish·ly** *adv.* —**rak′ish·ness** *n.*

rak·ish² (rā′kish) *adj.* like a rake; wild and dissolute —**rak′ish·ly** *adv.* —**rak′ish·ness** *n.*

Ra·leigh (rô′lē, rä′-) [after Sir Walter RALEIGH] capital of N.C., in the C part: pop. 122,000

Ra·leigh (rô′lē, rä′-), Sir **Walter** 1552?-1618; Eng. statesman, explorer, & poet: also sp. **Ralegh**

ral·len·tan·do (räl′ən tän′dō) *adj., adv.* [It., prp. of *rallentare,* to slow down] *Music* gradually slower: abbrev. **rall.**

ral·ly¹ (ral′ē) *vt.* **-lied, -ly·ing** [< Fr. < OFr. < *re-,* again + *alier,* to join: see ALLY] **1.** to gather together (esp. retreating troops) and bring back to a state of order **2.** to bring (persons) together for a common purpose **3.** to revive (one's spirits, etc.) —*vi.* **1.** to return to a state of order: said esp. of retreating troops **2.** to come together for a common purpose [the students *rallied* to cheer the football team] **3.** to come in order to help [to *rally* to a friend] **4.** to revive; recover [to *rally* from an illness] **5.** *Commerce* to rise in price after having fallen: said of stocks, etc. **6.** *Sports* to come from behind in scoring **7.** *Tennis,* etc. to take part in a rally —*n., pl.* **-lies 1.** a rallying or being rallied; specif., a mass meeting [a political *rally*] **2.** an organized run of sports cars over a course of public roads, with travel time set between points and with traffic rules observed: also sp. **ral′lye 3.** *Tennis,* etc. an exchange of several strokes before the point is won —**ral′li·er** *n.*

ral·ly² (ral′ē) *vt., vi.* **-lied, -ly·ing** [Fr. *rallier,* to RAIL²] to tease or mock playfully; banter

Ralph (ralf; *Brit. usually* rāf) [< ON. < *rath,* counsel + *ulfr,* a wolf] a masculine name

ram (ram) *n.* [OE. *ramm*] **1.** a male sheep **2.** *same as* BATTERING RAM **3.** *a)* formerly, a sharp part sticking out from a prow, for piercing enemy vessels *b)* a ship with this **4.** *same as* HYDRAULIC RAM **5.** the striking part of a pile driver **6.** the plunger of a force pump —[**R-**] *same as* ARIES —*vt.* **rammed, ram′ming 1.** to strike against with great force [the car *rammed* the fence] **2.** to force into place [to *ram* a charge into a gun] **3.** to force acceptance of (an idea, legislative bill, etc.): often with *across* or *through* **4.** to stuff or cram (*with* something) —*vi.* **1.** to strike with force; crash **2.** to move rapidly [the motorcycle *rammed* past us] —**ram′mer** *n.*

Ram·a·dan (ram′ə dän′) *n.* [Ar. *ramaḍān,* lit., the hot month < *ramaḍa,* to be hot] the ninth month of the Moslem year, a period of daily fasting from sunrise to sunset

Ra·ma·ya·na (rä mä′yə nə) one of the two great epics of India, written in Sanskrit after the Mahabharata and telling the story of the seventh incarnation of the god Vishnu

ram·ble (ram′b'l) *vi.* **-bled, -bling** [< ME. *romblen* < *romen,* to roam] **1.** to roam about; esp., to stroll about idly **2.** to talk or write aimlessly, without sticking to any point **3.** to spread in all directions, as a vine —*vt.* to roam through —*n.* a rambling, esp. a stroll —see **SYN.** at ROAM

ram·bler (ram′blər) *n.* **1.** a person or thing that rambles **2.** any of certain climbing roses

☆**ram·bunc·tious** (ram buŋk′shəs) *adj.* [altered < *robustious* < *robust*] wild, boisterous, unruly, etc. —**ram·bunc′tious·ly** *adv.* —**ram·bunc′tious·ness** *n.*

ram·e·kin, ram·e·quin (ram′ə kin) *n.* [Fr. *ramequin* < MDu. *rammeken,* cheese dish] **1.** a food mixture, specif. of bread crumbs, cheese, and eggs, baked in individual baking dishes **2.** a baking dish of this kind

Ram·e·ses (ram′ə sēz) *var. of* RAMSES

ram·ie (ram′ē) *n.* [Malay *rami*] **1.** a woody plant grown in warm climates for the strong bast fiber of the stems **2.** this fiber, used in making fine cloth

ram·i·fi·ca·tion (ram′ə fi kā′shən) *n.* **1.** a ramifying or being ramified **2.** *a)* a branch or offshoot *b)* an effect, result, or development of something [the *ramifications* of an act]

ram·i·fy (ram′ə fī′) *vt., vi.* **-fied′, -fy′ing** [< Fr. < ML. < L. *ramus,* a branch + *facere,* to make] to divide or spread out into branches or branchlike divisions

ram·jet (engine) (ram′jet′) a jet engine in which the air for burning the fuel is compressed by being rammed into the inlet by the aircraft's speed

ra·mose (rā′mōs, rə mōs′) *adj.* [< L. < *ramus,* a branch] **1.** bearing many branches **2.** branching —**ra′mose·ly** *adv.*

ra·mous (rā′məs) *adj.* **1.** *same as* RAMOSE **2.** branchlike

ramp¹ (ramp) *n.* [Fr. *rampe* < OFr.: see next entry] **1.** a sloping walk, road, plank, etc. joining different levels ☆**2.** a wheeled staircase rolled up to an airplane for use in getting on or off

ramp² (ramp) *vi.* [OFr. *ramper,* to climb] **1.** to rear up on the hind legs; specif., *Heraldry* to be shown rampant **2.** to rampage or rage —*n.* a ramping

ram·page (ram pāj′; *also, and for n. always,* ram′pāj) *vi.* **-paged′, -pag′ing** [prob. < RAMP²] to rush violently or wildly about; rage —*n.* a rampaging: chiefly in **on the** (or **a**) **rampage** —**ram·pa′geous** *adj.* —**ram·pag′er** *n.*

ramp·ant (ram′pənt) *adj.* [< OFr.: see RAMP²] **1.** growing or spreading unchecked; rife [the plague was *rampant* in Europe in the Middle Ages] **2.** violent and uncontrollable in action, manner, speech, etc. **3.** standing up on the hind legs; specif., *Heraldry* shown so in profile, one forepaw above the other [a lion *rampant*] —**ramp′an·cy** *n.* —**ramp′ant·ly** *adv.*

LION
RAMPANT

ram·part (ram′pärt, -pərt) *n.* [Fr. < *re-,* again + *emparer* < Pr. *amparer* < L. *ante,* before + *parare,* to prepare] **1.** a defensive embankment around a castle, fort, etc., with a parapet at the top **2.** any defense or bulwark

ram·rod (ram′räd′) *n.* a rod for ramming down the charge in a gun loaded through the muzzle

Ram·ses (ram′sēz) any of a number of Egyptian kings who ruled from c. 1315 to c. 1090 B.C.; esp., *a)* **Ramses II** ?-1225; king (1292-25) *b)* **Ramses III** ?-1167; king (1198-67)

ram·shack·le (ram′shak′'l) *adj.* [< RANSACK + -LE²] loose and rickety; likely to fall to pieces [a *ramshackle* old building]

ran (ran) *pt. of* RUN

☆**ranch** (ranch) *n.* [< RANCHO] **1.** a large farm, esp. in western States, for raising many cattle, horses, or sheep **2.** any large farm for raising a particular crop or livestock [a fruit *ranch;* a turkey *ranch*] **3.** *same as* RANCH HOUSE —*vi.* to work on or manage a ranch —**ranch′er** *n.* —**ranch′man** (-mən) *n., pl.* -**men**

☆**ran·che·ro** (ran cher′ō, rän-) *n., pl.* -**ros** (-ōz) [AmSp.] in the southwestern U.S. and Mexico, a person who owns or works on a ranch

☆**ranch house 1.** the owner's residence on a ranch **2.** a house with all the rooms on one floor, usually with a garage attached

☆**ran·cho** (ran′chō, rän′-) *n., pl.* -**chos** [AmSp.] in Spanish America, *same as* RANCH

ran·cid (ran′sid) *adj.* [< L. < *rancere,* to be rank] having the bad smell or taste of spoiled fats or oils —**ran·cid′i·ty** (-sid′ə-tē), **ran′cid·ness** *n.* —**ran′cid·ly** *adv.*

ran·cor (raŋ′kər) *n.* [OFr. < LL. < L. *rancere,* to be rahk] a long-lasting and bitter hate or ill will; deep spite: also, Brit. sp., **ran′cour** —see SYN. at MALICE —**ran′cor·ous** *adj.* —**ran′cor·ous·ly** *adv.*

rand (rand, ränd) *n., pl.* **rand** [Afrik., orig., shield] *see* MONETARY UNITS, table [Botswana, Lesotho, South Africa, Swaziland]

Rand (rand), **the** *same as* WITWATERSRAND

R & B, r & b rhythm and blues

R & D, R. and D. research and development

Ran·dolph (ran′dälf, -dôlf) [< ML. < OE. *randwulf,* lit., shield wolf] a masculine name

ran·dom (ran′dəm) *n.* [< OFr. *randon,* violence, speed < *randir,* to run violently] aimless or unplanned movement: now only in **at random,** without careful choice, aim, plan, etc.; haphazardly —*adj.* **1.** made, done, etc. in an aimless or unplanned way; haphazard [a *random* choice] **2.** not uniform; esp., of different sizes [a *random* assortment of dresses] **3.** with each in a set or group having an equal opportunity of occurring [a *random* sample] —**ran′dom·ly** *adv.* —**ran′dom·ness** *n.*

SYN.—**random** applies to that which happens or is done without careful choice, aim, plan, etc. [a *random* remark]; **haphazard** applies to that which is done, made, etc. without regard to whether it is appropriate or to its possible results and so emphasizes the idea of accident or chance [a *haphazard* selection of books]; **casual** implies a happening by chance without intention or purpose and often suggests a lack of real interest [a *casual* acquaintance]; **desultory** suggests a lack of method or attention, as in jumping from one thing to another [his *desultory* reading in the textbook]; **chance** implies a happening by accident without any arranging or planning beforehand [a *chance* encounter] —ANT. deliberate

ran·dom·ize (-īz′) *vt.* -**ized**′, -**iz**′**ing** to pick at random so as to get an unbiased result —**ran′dom·i·za′tion** *n.*

R & R, R and R *Mil.* rest and recuperation (leave)

ran·dy (ran′dē) *adj.* -**di·er**, -**di·est** [prob. < *rand,* dial. var. of RANT + -Y²] sexually aroused; lustful

ra·nee (rä′nē) *n. alt. sp. of* RANI

rang (raŋ) *pt. of* RING¹

range (rānj) *vt.* **ranged**, **rang′ing** [< OFr. var. of *rengier* < *renc,* a row < Frank.] **1.** to put in a certain order, esp. in a row or rows [the tulips were *ranged* along the path] **2.** to classify **3.** to place with others in a cause, party, etc. [to *range* oneself with the rebels] **4.** to aim (a gun, telescope, etc.) properly **5.** to roam over or through [bears *ranged* the forests] **6.** to move along parallel to [*ranging* the coastline] ☆**7.** to put out (cattle, etc.) to graze on a range —*vi.* **1.** to extend in a given direction [hills *ranging* south] **2.** to wander about; roam [*ranging* through the hills] **3.** to vary between stated limits [ages *ranging* from 1 to 7] **4.** *Biol., Zool.* to be native to a specified region —*n.* **1.** a row, line, or series; rank **2.** a class, kind, or order **3.** a chain or single system of mountains [the Appalachian *range*] **4.** *a)* the horizontal distance from a weapon to a particular target or to the farthest target its projectile can reach [a cannon with a twenty-mile *range*] *b)* the flight path of a missile or rocket **5.** the farthest distance a plane, etc. can go without refueling **6.** *a)* a place for shooting practice [a rifle *range*] *b)* a place for testing rockets in flight **7.** the full extent over which something moves or is heard, seen, effective, etc.; scope [within *range* of my voice] **8.** the full extent of pitch, from highest to lowest tones, of a voice, instrument, etc. [she

has a *range* of three octaves] ☆**9.** a large, open area of land for grazing livestock **10.** the limits within which there are changes or differences in amount, degree, etc. [a wide *range* in price] **11.** a cooking unit typically with an oven and surface heating units **12.** *Biol., Zool.* the region to which a plant or animal is native **13.** *Math.* the set of all distinct values that may be taken on a given function **14.** *Statistics* the difference between the largest and smallest values in a sample —☆*adj.* of a range (sense 9) [*range* livestock]

SYN.—**range** refers to the full extent over which something is recognizable, effective, etc. [the *range* of his knowledge]; **reach** refers to the furthest limit of effectiveness, influence, etc. [beyond the *reach* of my understanding]; **scope** is used of the area covered by a particular activity, written work, etc. having set limits [does it fall within the *scope* of this dictionary?]; **compass** suggests completeness within limits thought of as the outer edge of a circle [he did all within the *compass* of his power]; **gamut**, in this connection, refers to the full range of shades, tones, etc. within the limits of something [the full *gamut* of emotions] —see also SYN. at ROAM

range finder any of various instruments used to determine the distance of a target or object from a gun, camera, etc.

rang·er (rān′jər) *n.* **1.** one who ranges; roamer **2.** *a)* a member of a special military or police force that patrols a region ☆*b)* [often R-] a soldier of a group trained for raiding **3.** *a)* in England, the chief official of a royal park or forest ☆*b)* in the U.S., a warden patrolling government forests

Ran·goon (raŋ gōōn′) capital of Burma, a seaport in the S part, on the Irrawaddy: pop. 1,759,000

rang·y (rān′jē) *adj.* **rang′i·er**, **rang′i·est 1.** ranging about ☆**2.** long-limbed and slender [a *rangy* adolescent] ☆**3.** having an open range —**rang′i·ness** *n.*

ra·ni (rä′nē) *n.* [< Hindi < Sans. fem. of *rājan:* see RAJAH] the wife of a rajah

rank¹ (raŋk) *n.* [< MFr. < OFr. *renc:* see RANGE] **1.** a row, line, or series; specif., a set of organ pipes of the same kind **2.** an orderly arrangement **3.** a social class [people from all *ranks* of life] **4.** a high position in society [a man of *rank*] **5.** an official grade [the *rank* of captain] **6.** a relative position as measured by quality, etc. [a poet of the first *rank*] **7.** a row of soldiers, etc., side by side **8.** [*pl.*] all those in an organization, as the army, who are not officers or leaders [to rise from the *ranks*]: also **rank and file** —*vt.* **1.** to place in a rank or ranks **2.** to assign a relative position to [he *ranked* this school among the best] ☆**3.** to have a higher rank than; outrank [a colonel *ranks* a major] —*vi.* to hold a certain position [to *rank* third] —☆**pull (one's) rank** [Slang] to use one's higher rank to get others to obey, etc.

rank² (raŋk) *adj.* [OE. *ranc,* strong: for IE. base see REGAL] **1.** growing vigorously and coarsely; too luxuriant [*rank* grass] **2.** producing or covered with a luxuriant crop **3.** very bad in smell or taste [*rank* fish] **4.** coarse; indecent [*rank* talk] **5.** of the worst or most extreme kind [*rank* injustice] —see SYN. at STINKING —**rank′ly** *adv.* —**rank′ness** *n.*

rank·ing (raŋ′kiŋ) *adj.* ☆**1.** of the highest rank [the *ranking* officer] ☆**2.** prominent or outstanding [a *ranking* composer]

ran·kle (raŋ′k'l) *vi., vt.* -**kled**, -**kling** [< OFr. < *draoncle* < ML. *dracunculus,* a fester < L. dim. of *draco,* dragon] **1.** orig., to fester **2.** to cause or fill with long-lasting hate, ill will, resentment, etc.

ran·sack (ran′sak) *vt.* [< ON. < *rann,* a house + *sækja,* to search] **1.** to search through every part of [to *ransack* one's pockets for a key] **2.** to search through for loot [bandits *ransacked* the town] —**ran′sack·er** *n.*

ran·som (ran′səm) *n.* [< OFr. *raençon* < L. *redemptio,* REDEMPTION] **1.** the act of getting a captive or seized property released by paying money or meeting other demands **2.** the price so paid or demanded —*vt.* to get (a captive, etc.) released by paying the demanded price —**ran′som·er** *n.*

rant (rant) *vi., vt.* [< obs. Du. *ranten,* to rave] to talk or say in a loud, wild way; declaim violently; rave —*n.* ranting talk —**rant′er** *n.* —**rant′ing·ly** *adv.*

rap¹ (rap) *vt.* **rapped**, **rap′ping** [prob. echoic] **1.** to strike quickly and sharply; tap ☆**2.** [Slang] to criticize sharply —*vi.* **1.** to knock quickly and sharply [to *rap* on a door] ☆**2.** [Slang] to talk; chat —*n.* **1.** a quick, sharp knock; tap ☆**2.** [Slang] a talking; chat ☆**3.** [Slang] blame or punishment; specif., a being charged with or sentenced for a crime: usually in beat (escape) or **take** (receive) **the rap,** or **bum** (unfair) **rap** —**rap out** to say sharply [to *rap out* orders] —**rap′per** *n.*

rap² (rap) *n.* [< ?] [Colloq.] the least bit: in **not care** (or **give**) **a rap,** not care anything at all

ra·pa·cious (rə pā′shəs) *adj.* [< L. *rapacis,* genitive of *rapax* < *rapere,* to seize: see RAPE¹] **1.** taking by force; plundering [a *rapacious* army] **2.** greedy or grasping **3.** living on captured prey; predatory [a *rapacious* animal] —**ra·pa′cious·ly** *adv.* —**ra·pac·i·ty** (rə pas′ə tē), **ra·pa′cious·ness** *n.*

rape¹ (rāp) *n.* [ME. < L. *rapere,* to seize < IE. base *rep-,* to seize] **1.** *a)* the crime of forcing a woman or girl to have sexual intercourse with one against her will: see also STATUTORY RAPE *b)* any sexual attack upon a person **2.** [Now Rare] a seizing and carrying away by force **3.** any violent attack or outrageous plunder [the *rape* of the cities] —*vt., vi.* **raped, rap′ing** to commit rape (on) —☆**rap′ist** *n.*

rape² (rāp) *n.* [L. *rapa, rapum,* turnip] an annual old-world plant of the mustard family, with seed (**rape′seed′**) from which an oil (**rape oil, rapeseed oil**) is pressed and with leaves used for fodder

Raph·a·el (rā′fē əl; *also, and for* 2 *usually,* raf′ē-) [LL. < Gr. < Heb. *repha′ēl,* lit., God hath healed] **1.** an archangel mentioned in the Apocrypha **2.** (born *Raffaello Santi* or *Sanzio*) 1483–1520; It. painter & architect

ra·phe (rā′fē) *n.* [ModL. < Gr. < *rhaptein,* to stitch together] **1.** *Anat.* a seamlike ridge or crease between the halves of an organ, as of the tongue **2.** *Bot. a)* a ridge along the side of an ovule *b)* a line running along the center of a diatom

rap·id (rap′id) *adj.* [L. *rapidus* < *rapere,* to rush: see RAPE¹] moving, occurring, or acting with speed; swift; fast; quick —☆*n.* **1.** [*usually pl.*] a part of a river where the current is swift, as because of a narrowing of the river bed **2.** a rapid transit car, train, or system —see SYN. at FAST¹ —**ra·pid·i·ty** (rə pid′ə tē), **rap′id·ness** *n.* —**rap′id·ly** *adv.*

rap·id-fire (-fīr′) *adj.* **1.** firing shots in rapid succession: said of guns **2.** done, carried on, etc. in a swift, sharp way [*rapid-fire* talk]

☆**rapid transit** a system of rapid public transportation in a city, using electric trains running along a clear right of way

ra·pi·er (rā′pē ər, rāp′yər) *n.* [Fr. *rapière*] **1.** orig., a slender, two-edged sword with a large cup hilt **2.** later, a light, sharp-pointed sword used only for thrusting

rap·ine (rap′in) *n.* [OFr. < L. *rapina* < *rapere,* to seize: see RAPE¹] the act of seizing and carrying off by force others' property; plunder; pillage

Rap·pa·han·nock (rap′ə han′ək) [< Algonquian, the ebb-and-flow stream] river in NE Va., flowing into Chesapeake Bay

rap·pel (ra pel′, rə-) *n.* [Fr., lit., a recall] a descent down a steep cliff by a mountain climber using a double rope secured above —*vi.* **-pelled′, -pel′ling** to make such a descent

rap·pen (räp′ən) *n., pl.* **-pen** [G. < *rappe,* raven: after the eagle on an earlier Alsatian coin] see MONETARY UNITS, table (Liechtenstein, Switzerland)

rap·port (ra pôr′, -pôrt′) *n.* [Fr. < OFr. < *re-,* again + *aporter* < L. < *ad-,* to + *portare,* to carry: see PORT³] relationship, esp. of a sympathetic kind; agreement; harmony

rap·proche·ment (ra prōsh′män; *Fr.* rȧ prȯsh män′) *n.* [Fr.] an establishing, or esp. a restoring, of harmony and friendly relations

rap·scal·lion (rap skal′yən) *n.* [< earlier *rascallion,* extension of RASCAL] a rascal; rogue

rapt (rapt) *adj.* [< L. pp. of *rapere,* to seize: see RAPE¹] **1.** carried away with joy, love, etc.; full of or showing rapture [a *rapt* look on his face] **2.** completely absorbed (*in* meditation, study, etc.)

rap·to·ri·al (rap tôr′ē əl) *adj.* [< L. < pp. of *rapere:* see RAPE¹] **1.** of or belonging to a group of birds of prey with a strong notched beak and sharp talons, as the eagle **2.** adapted for seizing prey [*raptorial* claws]

rap·ture (rap′chər) *n.* [RAPT + -URE] **1.** the state of being carried away with joy, love, etc.; feeling of ecstasy [the music filled him with *rapture*] **2.** an expression of great joy, pleasure, etc. [she went into *raptures* thanking us] —see SYN. at ECSTASY —**rap′tur·ous** *adj.* —**rap′tur·ous·ly** *adv.*

MAN RAPPELLING

rare¹ (rer) *adj.* **rar′er, rar′est** [MFr. < L. *rarus*] **1.** not often seen, done, found, etc.; uncommon [radium is a *rare* element] **2.** unusually good; excellent [we had a *rare* time at the party] **3.** not dense; thin [*rare* atmosphere] —**rare′ness** *n.*

SYN.—**rare** is applied to something of which there are not many instances or examples and usually suggests, therefore, great value [a *rare* gem]; **infrequent** applies to that which occurs only once in a long while [his *infrequent* trips]; **uncommon** and **unusual** refer to that which does not ordinarily happen and is therefore remarkable or worthy of notice [her *uncommon* generosity; this *unusual* heat]; **scarce** applies to something of which there is, at the moment, not enough [potatoes are *scarce* these days] **ANT.** frequent, common, abundant

rare² (rer) *adj.* **rar′er, rar′est** [OE. *hrere*] not fully cooked; partly raw: said esp. of meat —**rare′ness** *n.*

rare³ (rer) *vi.* **rared, rar′ing** **1.** *dial. var. of* REAR² *vi.* ☆**2.** [Colloq.] to be eager, enthusiastic, etc.: used in present participle [*raring* to go]

rare·bit (rer′bit) *n.* same as WELSH RABBIT

rare earth *n.* **1.** any of certain similar basic oxides; specif., any of the oxides of the rare-earth metals **2.** any of the rare-earth metals

rare-earth metals (or **elements**) (rer′urth′) a group of rare metallic chemical elements with atomic numbers 57 to 71 inclusive and also scandium and yttrium

rar·e·fy (rer′ə fī′) *vt., vi.* **-fied′, -fy′ing** [< MFr. < L. < *rarus,* rare + *facere,* to make] **1.** to make or become thin, or less dense [the air at high altitudes is *rarefied*] **2.** to make or become more refined, subtle, or lofty [a *rarefied* sense of humor] —**rar·e·fac·tion** (-fak′shən) *n.*

rare·ly (rer′lē) *adv.* **1.** not often; seldom **2.** beautifully, excellently, etc. **3.** uncommonly; unusually

rar·i·ty (rer′ə tē) *n.* **1.** a being rare; specif., *a)* uncommonness; scarcity [the *rarity* of whooping cough] *b)* excellence [the *rarity* of her performance] *c)* lack of density; thinness [the *rarity* of air] **2.** *pl.* **-ties** a rare or uncommon thing [this old coin is a *rarity*]

ras·cal (ras′k'l) *n.* [OFr. *rascaille,* scrapings, ult. < L. pp. of *radere,* to scrape: for IE. base see RAT] a scoundrel; rogue; scamp: often used playfully, as of a mischievous child

ras·cal·i·ty (ras kal′ə tē) *n.* **1.** the character or behavior of a rascal **2.** *pl.* **-ties** a low, mean, or dishonest act

ras·cal·ly (ras′k'l ē) *adj.* of or like a rascal; base; dishonest; mean —*adv.* in a rascally way

rase (rāz) *vt.* **rased, ras′ing** *alt. Brit. sp. of* RAZE

rash¹ (rash) *adj.* [ME. *rasch*] too hasty and careless; reckless —**rash′ly** *adv.* —**rash′ness** *n.*

rash² (rash) *n.* [MFr. *rasche:* for IE. base see RAT] **1.** a breaking out of red spots on the skin **2.** a sudden outbreak of a large number [a *rash* of complaints]

rash·er (rash′ər) *n.* [< ? obs. *rash,* to cut] **1.** a thin slice of bacon or, rarely, ham, for frying or broiling ☆**2.** a serving of several such slices

rasp (rasp) *vt.* [< OFr. < OHG. *raspon,* to scrape together] **1.** to scrape or rub as with a file **2.** to say in a rough, grating tone [the sergeant *rasped* out a command] **3.** to grate upon; irritate [her giggling *rasped* his nerves] —*vi.* **1.** to scrape; grate **2.** to make a rough, grating sound [the old hinges *rasped* as the door opened] —*n.* **1.** a type of rough file with sharp, projecting points **2.** a rough, grating sound —**rasp′er** *n.* —**rasp′ing·ly** *adv.*

rasp·ber·ry (raz′ber′ē, -bər ē) *n., pl.* **-ries** [earlier *raspis berry* < *raspis,* raspberry] **1.** the small, juicy, edible fruit of various brambles of the rose family: it is a cluster of red, purple, or black drupelets **2.** the bramble bearing this **3.** [Slang] a jeering sound made by blowing out so as to vibrate the tongue between the lips

Ras·pu·tin (räs poō′tin; *E.* ras pyoot′'n), **Gri·go·ri E·fi·mo·vich** (gri gô′ri ye fē′mə vich) 1871?–1916; Russ. religious mystic & faith healer: assassinated

rasp·y (ras′pē) *adj.* **rasp′i·er, rasp′i·est** **1.** rasping; grating **2.** easily irritated —**rasp′i·ness** *n.*

ras·sle (ras′'l) *n., vi., vt.* **-sled, -sling** *dial. or colloq. var. of* WRESTLE

rat (rat) *n.* [OE. *ræt* < IE. base *rod-,* to scratch] **1.** *a)* any of numerous long-tailed rodents resembling, but larger than, the mouse, very destructive, and carriers of disease *b)* any of various ratlike rodents **2.** [Slang] a sneaky, contemptible person,

RASP

esp. one who informs on or betrays others —*vi.* **rat′ted, rat′-
ting** **1.** to hunt rats **2.** [Slang] *a)* to desert or betray a cause,
movement, etc. *b)* to act as an informer (with *on*) —☆*vt.* to
tease (the hair) —☆**rats!** [Slang] an exclamation of disgust,
disappointment, etc. —**smell a rat** to suspect a trick, plot, etc.
rat·a·ble (rāt′ə b'l) *adj.* **1.** that can be rated, or estimated,
etc. **2.** figured at a certain rate; proportional **3.** [Brit.] taxable
Also sp. **rate′a·ble** —**rat′a·bly, rate′a·bly** *adv.*
ra·tan (ra tan′) *n. alt. sp. of* RATTAN
rat-a-tat (rat′ə tat′) *n.* [echoic] a series of sharp, quick rapping sounds: also **rat′-a-tat′-tat′**
ratch·et (rach′it) *n.* [< Fr. < It. *rocchetto*, dim. of *rocca*, distaff]
1. a toothed wheel (in full, **ratchet wheel**)
or bar whose teeth slope in one direction
so as to catch and hold a pawl, which thus
prevents backward movement **2.** such a
pawl **3.** such a wheel (or bar) and pawl as
a unit

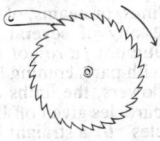

RATCHET WHEEL

rate¹ (rāt) *n.* [OFr. < L. *rata* (*pars*), reckoned (part) < pp. of *reri*, to reckon: for IE.
base see ART¹] **1.** the amount, degree, etc.
of anything in relation to units of some-
thing else [the *rate* of pay per month] **2.** a fixed ratio; proportion [the *rate* of exchange] **3.** a price or value; specif., the cost
per unit of some commodity, service, etc. [insurance *rate*] **4.**
speed of movement or action [he works at a fast *rate*] **5.** a
class or rank [of the first *rate*] **6.** [Brit.] a local property tax
7. *U.S. Navy* any of the grades of an enlisted man with a rating
—*vt.* **rat′ed, rat′ing** **1.** to estimate the value, capacity, skill,
etc. of; appraise [the dealer *rated* the diamond at $8,000] **2.**
a) to put into a particular class or rank *b)* *U.S. Navy* to assign
a rate to **3.** to consider; esteem [the show is *rated* as being very
entertaining] **4.** to fix or determine the rates for **5.** [Colloq.]
to deserve [to *rate* an increase in salary] —*vi.* **1.** to be classed
or ranked **2.** to have value, status, or rating —see SYN. at ESTI-
MATE —**at any rate 1.** in any event **2.** anyway
rate² (rāt) *vt., vi.* **rat′ed, rat′ing** [ME. *raten*] to scold harshly;
chide
rate·pay·er (rāt′pā′ər) *n.* [Brit. & Canad.] one who pays rates,
or local taxes
-rat·er (rāt′ər) *a combining form meaning* one of a (specified)
rate, or class [first-*rater*]
rath·er (rath′ər; *for interj.* ra′thʉr′) *adv.* [OE. *hrathor*, compar.
of *hrathe*, quickly] **1.** more willingly; preferably [would you
rather have tea?] **2.** with more justice, reason, etc. [one might
rather say] **3.** more accurately; more precisely [his sister, or
rather, stepsister] **4.** on the contrary [not a help, *rather* a hin-
drance] **5.** to some degree; somewhat [*rather* hungry] —*interj.*
[Chiefly Brit.] certainly —**had (or would) rather 1.** would
choose to **2.** would prefer that —**rather than** instead of
☆**raths·kel·ler** (rät′skel′ər, rath′-) *n.* [G. < *rat*, council + *kel-
ler*, cellar] a restaurant of the German type, usually below
street level, where beer is served
rat·i·fy (rat′ə fī′) *vt.* **-fied′, -fy′ing** [< MFr. < ML. < L. *ratus*
(see RATE¹) + *facere*, to make] to approve or confirm, esp. in an
official way [the Senate *ratified* the treaty] —**rat′i·fi·ca′tion** *n.*
—**rat′i·fi′er** *n.*
rat·ing (rāt′iŋ) *n.* **1.** *a)* a rank, class, or grade; specif., a classification of military or naval personnel according to specialties
[the *ratings* of yeoman and quartermaster in the U.S. Navy]
b) [Brit.] an enlisted man in the Navy **2.** a placement in a certain rank or class **3.** a judgment as to how good or bad the
credit or financial standing of a businessman, firm, etc. is **4.**
an amount determined as a grade ☆**5.** *Radio & TV* the
popularity of a program as compared with other programs by
taking polls or surveys
ra·tio (rā′shō, -shē ō′) *n., pl.* **-tios** [L.: see REASON] **1.** a fixed
relation in degree, number, etc. between two similar things; proportion [a *ratio* of two boys to three girls] **2.** *Math.* the quotient of one quantity divided by another of the same kind,
usually expressed as a fraction [1/3 and 5/15 are equal
ratios]
ra·ti·o·ci·nate (rash′ē ō′sə nāt′, rat′ē-; -äs′ə nāt′) *vi.*
-nat′ed, -nat′ing [< L. pp. of *ratiocinari* < *ratio*: see REASON]
to reason; esp., to reason using formal logic —**ra′ti·o′ci·na′-
tion** *n.* —**ra′ti·o′ci·na′tive** *adj.* —**ra′ti·o′ci·na′tor** *n.*

ra·tion (rash′ən, rā′shən) *n.* [MFr. < ML. < L. *ratio*: see REA-
SON] **1.** a fixed portion; share; allowance **2.** a fixed allowance
of food or provisions, esp. a daily allowance, as for a soldier
3. [*pl.*] food or food supply —*vt.* **1.** to give rations to **2.** to
give out (food, clothing, etc.) in rations, as in times when these
are scarce [gasoline was *rationed* during World War II] —**ra′-
tion·ing** *n.*
ra·tion·al (rash′ən 'l) *adj.* [L. *rationalis* < *ratio*: see REASON]
1. of or based on reasoning [man's *rational* powers] **2.** able to
reason; reasoning [he was too angry to be *rational*] **3.** showing
reason; sensible [a *rational* plan] **4.** *Math.* designating or of a
number that can be expressed as the quotient of two integers or
as an integer —**ra′tion·al·i·ty** (-ə nal′ə tē) *n., pl.* **-ties** —**ra′-
tion·al·ly** *adv.*
SYN.—**rational** implies the ability to reason in an orderly, carefully controlled way so as to reach conclusions logically without being swayed by
emotion [Holmes's *rational* explanation of the mysterious events]; **reasonable** suggests the calm, careful use of the mind in making decisions,
choices, etc. that are fair and practical [the teacher was *reasonable* in the
amount of homework she required]; **sensible** implies the use of common
sense based on sound judgment and practical experience [a *sensible* man
who bought no more than he needed] —ANT. **irrational, absurd**
ra·tion·ale (rash′ə nal′, -nä′lē) *n.* [L., neut. of *rationalis*, RA-
TIONAL] **1.** the rational basis for something **2.** an explanation
of reasons or principles [a book which offers a *rationale* of the
country's foreign policy]
ra·tion·al·ism (rash′ən 'l iz'm) *n.* the principle or practice of
accepting reason as the only source of knowledge and as the
only basis for forming one's opinions, beliefs, or course of action —**ra′tion·al·ist** *n., adj.* —**ra′tion·al·is′tic** *adj.* —**ra′tion-
al·is′ti·cal·ly** *adv.*
ra·tion·al·ize (rash′ən ə līz′) *vt.* **-ized′, -iz′ing** **1.** to make
rational; make conform to reason **2.** to explain on the basis of
reason or logic **3.** *Math.* to remove the radical signs from (an
equation) without changing the value **4.** *Psychol.* to give a reasonable explanation of (one's acts, beliefs, etc.), usually without
being aware that it is not the real one —*vi.* **1.** to think in a
rational or rationalistic manner **2.** to rationalize one's acts, beliefs, etc. —**ra′tion·al·i·za′tion** *n.* —**ra′tion·al·iz′er** *n.*
rat·ite (rat′īt) *n.* [< L. < *ratis*, a raft] any flightless bird with a
flat breastbone, as the ostrich
rat·line (rat′lin) *n.* [altered by folk etym. < LME. *ratling* < ?]
any of the small, thin pieces of tarred rope that
join the shrouds of a ship and serve as the
steps of a ladder for climbing the rigging: also
sp. **rat′lin**
☆**rat race** [Slang] a mad scramble or intense
struggle in competing with others, as in the
business world
rats·bane (rats′bān′) *n.* [see BANE] rat poison
rat·tail (rat′tāl′) *adj.* shaped like a rat's tail;
slim and tapering: also **rat′tailed′**
rat·tan (ra tan′) *n.* [Malay *rotan* < *raut*, to
strip] **1.** a climbing palm with long, slender,
tough stems **2.** these stems, used in making
wickerwork, etc. **3.** a cane or switch made
from such a stem

RATLINES

rat·ter (rat′ər) *n.* **1.** a dog or cat skilled at catching rats **2.**
[Slang] a betrayer or informer
rat·tle (rat′'l) *vi.* **-tled, -tling** [ME. *ratelen*: prob. echoic] **1.**
to make a rapid series of sharp, short sounds **2.** to move with
such sounds [a cart *rattled* over the stones] **3.** to talk in a rapid, thoughtless way; chatter (often with *on*) —*vt.* **1.** to cause to
rattle [he *rattled* the handle] **2.** to say or perform rapidly (usually with *off*) [she *rattled* off the names of the 50 States] ☆**3.**
to confuse or upset [catcalls *rattled* the speaker] —*n.* **1.** a
quick succession of short, sharp sounds **2.** a rattling noise in
the throat, as of a dying person **3.** a noisy uproar ☆**4.** the series of horny rings at the end of a rattlesnake's tail **5.** a device,
as a baby's toy, intended to rattle when shaken —see SYN. at
EMBARRASS —**rattle around in** to occupy (a place too big for
one's needs) —**rat′tly** *adj.*
rat·tle·brain (rat′'l brān′) *n.* a silly, talkative person: also
rat′tle·pate (-pāt′) —**rat′tle·brained′** *adj.*
rat·tler (rat′lər) *n.* **1.** a person or thing that rattles ☆**2.** a rattlesnake

fat, āpe, cär; ten, ēven; is, bīte; gō, hôrn, tōōl, look; oil, out; up, fʉr; get; joy; yet; chin; she; thin, then; zh, leisure; ŋ, ring;
ə for *a* in *ago*, *e* in *agent*, *i* in *sanity*, *o* in *comply*, *u* in *focus*; ′ as in *able* (ā′b'l); Fr. bal; ë, Fr. coeur; ö, Fr. feu; Fr. mon;
ô, Fr. coq; ü, Fr. duc; ɼ, Fr. cri; H, G. ich; kh, G. doch; ‡foreign; ☆ Americanism; < derived from. See inside front cover.

☆**rat·tle·snake** (rat′'l snāk′) *n.* any of various poisonous American pit vipers having a series of horny rings at the end of the tail that rattle when shaken

rat·tle·trap (-trap′) *n.* anything worn out, rickety, or rattling; esp., an old, worn-out automobile

rat′tling (rat′liŋ) *adj.* 1. that rattles 2. [Colloq.] very fast, good, etc. —*adv.* [Colloq.] very [*a rattling* good time]

rat·ty (rat′ē) *adj.* -ti·er, -ti·est 1. of, like, or full of rats 2. [Slang] shabby or run-down

rau·cous (rô′kəs) *adj.* [L. *raucus*] 1. hoarse; rough-sounding [*a raucous* shout] 2. loud and rowdy [*a raucous* party] —**rau′cous·ly** *adv.* —**rau′cous·ness** *n.*

☆**raun·chy** (rôn′chē, rän′-) *adj.* -chi·er, -chi·est [< ?] [Slang] 1. dirty, cheap, sloppy, etc. 2. appealing to sexual interest; risqué, lustful, etc. —**raun′chi·ly** *adv.* —**raun′chi·ness** *n.*

rau·wol·fi·a (rô woŏl′fē ə, rou-) *n.* [ModL., after L. *Rauwolf*, 16th-c. G. botanist] 1. any of a group of tropical trees and shrubs, some of which yield medicinal substances 2. the root of one of these trees, a source of reserpine

rav·age (rav′ij) *n.* [Fr. < *ravir*: see RAVISH] 1. the act or practice of violently destroying 2. a result of such destruction [the *ravages* of war] —*vt.* -**aged**, -**ag·ing** to destroy violently; devastate; ruin [floods had *ravaged* the land] —*vi.* to commit ravages —**rav′ag·er** *n.*

rave (rāv) *vi.* **raved, rav′ing** [prob. < OFr. *raver*] 1. to talk wildly or without making sense as when delirious or insane 2. to talk with great or excessive enthusiasm (*about*) [she *raved* about the movie] 3. to rage, as a storm —*vt.* to utter in a wild way that does not make sense —*n.* 1. a raving ☆2. [Colloq.] a highly or overly enthusiastic recommendation: often used before a noun [a *rave* review] —**rav′er** *n.*

rav·el (rav′'l) *vt.* -**eled** or -**elled**, -**el·ing** or -**el·ling** [MDu. *ravelen*] 1. to make complicated or tangled (often with *up*) 2. to separate the parts, esp. threads, of; untwist 3. to make clear; disentangle —*vi.* to become raveled in its parts, esp. threads; fray (*out*) —*n.* 1. a raveled part in knitted or woven fabric; raveling 2. a tangled mass —**rav′el·er, rav′el·ler** *n.*

Ra·vel (ra vel′; E. ra vel′), **Mau·rice (Joseph)** (mô rēs′) 1875–1937; Fr. composer

rav·el·ing, rav·el·ling (rav′'l iŋ, rav′liŋ) *n.* anything raveled; esp., a thread raveled from knitted or woven fabric

ra·ven[1] (rā′vən) *n.* [OE. *hræfn* < IE. base *ker*-, imitative of harsh sounds] a large black bird of the crow family, with shiny black feathers and a sharp beak —*adj.* black and shiny

rav·en[2] (rav′'n) *vt.* [< OFr. < L. *rapere*, to seize: see RAPE[1]] to devour greedily —*vi.* 1. to prowl hungrily 2. to devour food or prey greedily

rav·en·ing (rav′'n iŋ) *adj.* greedily searching for prey

Ra·ven·na (rə ven′ə; *It.* rä ven′nä) city in NC Italy: pop. 131,000

rav·e·nous (rav′ə nəs) *adj.* [see RAVEN[2]] 1. greedily hungry 2. greedy [*ravenous* for praise] —**rav′e·nous·ly** *adv.* —**rav′e·nous·ness** *n.*

ra·vine (rə vēn′) *n.* [Fr., flood < OFr.: see RAVEN[2]] a long, deep hollow in the earth's surface, worn by a stream; gorge

rav·ing (rāv′iŋ) *adj.* 1. raging; delirious [a *raving* madman] ☆2. [Colloq.] causing raving admiration; outstanding [a *raving* beauty] —*adv.* so as to cause raving [*raving* mad] —*n.* delirious speech that does not make sense

ra·vi·o·li (rav′ē ō′lē) *n.pl.* [*with sing. v.*] [It.] small casings of dough containing seasoned ground meat, cheese, etc., boiled and served usually in a spicy tomato sauce

rav·ish (rav′ish) *vt.* [< stem of OFr. *ravir*, ult. < L. *rapere*, to seize: see RAPE[1]] 1. to seize and carry away by force 2. to rape 3. to overcome with joy or delight —**rav′ish·er** *n.* —**rav′ish·ment** *n.*

rav·ish·ing (-iŋ) *adj.* causing great joy or delight; entrancing —**rav′ish·ing·ly** *adv.*

raw (rô) *adj.* [OE. *hreaw*: for IE. base see CRUDE] 1. not cooked 2. in its natural condition; not changed by art, manufacture, etc. [*raw* silk] 3. not processed, edited, interpreted, etc. [*raw* data] 4. not yet trained; inexperienced [a *raw* recruit] 5. with the

RATTLESNAKE
(to 5½ ft. long)

skin rubbed off; sore and inflamed [a *raw* cut] 6. uncomfortably cold and damp [a *raw* wind] ☆7. *a*) brutal or coarse in frankness *b*) indecent; bawdy 8. [Colloq.] harsh or unfair [a *raw* deal] —**in the raw 1.** in the natural state ☆2. naked —**raw′ly** *adv.* —**raw′ness** *n.*

Ra·wal·pin·di (rä′wəl pin′dē) city in NE Pakistan: pop. 340,000

raw·boned (rô′bōnd′) *adj.* having little fat; lean; gaunt

raw·hide (-hīd′) *n.* 1. an untanned or partially tanned cattle hide ☆2. a whip made of this —☆*vt.* -**hid′ed**, -**hid′ing** to beat or drive with such a whip

Ray (rā) [dim. of RAYMOND] a masculine name

ray[1] (rā) *n.* [< OFr. < L. *radius*: see RADIUS] 1. any of the thin lines, or beams, of light that appear to come from a bright source 2. any of several lines coming out from a center 3. a tiny amount [a *ray* of hope] 4. *Bot., Zool.* any part of a structure with parts coming like rays from a center, as the petals of certain flowers, the limbs of a starfish, etc. 5. *Physics a*) a stream of particles given off by a radioactive substance, or any of the particles *b*) a straight line along which any part of a wave of radiant energy is regarded as traveling —*vi.* 1. to shine forth in rays 2. to radiate [streets that *ray* out from a central square] —*vt.* 1. to send out in rays 2. to supply with rays or radiating lines —**ray′less** *adj.* —**ray′like** *adj.*

ray[2] (rā) *n.* [< MFr. < L. *raia*] any of several fishes, as the stingray, electric ray, skate, etc., having a broad, flat body with both eyes on top, wide fins at each side, and a slender or whip-like tail

ray flower any of the flowers around the margin of the flower head of certain composite plants, as the daisy: also **ray floret**

Ray·mond (rā′mənd) [< ONormFr. < Frank. *Raginmund*, lit., wise protection] a masculine name

☆**ray·on** (rā′än) *n.* [a made-up word < RAY[1]] 1. any of various synthetic textile fibers produced by pressing a cellulose solution through very small holes and solidifying it in the form of filaments 2. any fabric woven or knitted from such fibers

raze (rāz) *vt.* **razed, raz′ing** [< OFr. *raser*, ult. < L. pp. of *radere*, to scrape: for IE. base see RAT] to tear down completely; level to the ground; demolish [wreckers *razed* the old building] —see SYN. at DESTROY

ra·zor (rā′zər) *n.* [< OFr. < *raser*: see prec.] 1. a sharp-edged cutting instrument for shaving off or cutting hair 2. *same as* SHAVER (sense 2)

ra·zor·back (-bak′) *n.* 1. a wild or semiwild hog of the southern U.S., with a ridged back and long legs 2. a sharp, narrow ridge

☆**razz** (raz) *vt., vi.* [shortened from RASPBERRY] [Slang] to tease, ridicule, etc. —*n.* [Slang] *same as* RASPBERRY (sense 3)

☆**raz·zle-daz·zle** (raz′'l daz′'l) *n.* [Slang] a flashy display intended to confuse, bewilder, or deceive

☆**razz·ma·tazz** (raz′mə taz′) *n.* [Slang] 1. lively spirit; excitement 2. flashy display; showiness

Rb *Chem.* rubidium

rbi, RBI, r.b.i. *Baseball* run(s) batted in

R.C. 1. Red Cross 2. Roman Catholic

R.C.Ch. Roman Catholic Church

Rd., rd. 1. road 2. rod 3. round

R.D. Rural Delivery

re[1] (rā) *n.* [It. < L. *re(sonare)*: see GAMUT] *Music* a syllable representing the second tone of the diatonic scale

re[2] (rē, rā) *prep.* [L., ablative of *res*, thing] in the case or matter of; as regards: short for *in re* [I am writing *re* your inquiry of last week]

re- [< Fr. *re-, ré-* < L. *re-, red-*, back] *a prefix meaning:* 1. back [*repay*] 2. again, anew [*reappear*] It is used with a hyphen: 1) to distinguish between a word in which the prefix means *again* or *anew* and a word having a special meaning (Ex.: *re-sound, resound*) 2) to avoid misunderstanding in spelling newly coined or unusual words [*re-urge*] 3) esp. formerly, before words beginning with an *e* [*re-edit*]: now usually written as a solid word [*reedit*] The list at the bottom of this page and the following pages contains some of the more common words in which *re-* means *again* or *anew*

Re *Chem.* rhenium

reach (rēch) *vt.* [OE. *ræcan*] 1. to thrust out or extend (the hand, etc.) 2. to extend to, or touch, by thrusting out, etc. [can you *reach* the limb with a pole?] 3. to obtain and hand over [*reach* me the salt] 4. to go as far as; get to [we'll *reach* Paris tonight] 5. to carry as far as [the news *reached* him late] 6.

to add up to [the bill will *reach* hundreds of dollars] **7.** to influence; affect [his songs *reached* the hearts of millions] **8.** to get in touch with, as by telephone —*vi.* **1.** to thrust out the hand, foot, etc. **2.** to stretch, or be extended, in amount, influence, space, time, etc. [Roman power *reached* into many lands] **3.** to carry, as sight, sound, etc. **4.** to try to get or touch something [he *reached* for his wallet] **5.** to try too hard to make a point, joke, etc. **6.** *Naut.* to sail on a reach —*n.* **1.** a stretching or thrusting out **2.** the power of stretching, obtaining, etc. **3.** the distance or extent covered in stretching, obtaining, etc. [out of the *reach* of danger] **4.** a continuous extent or stretch, esp. of water **5.** *Naut.* a tack sailed when the wind is blowing toward the side of a ship —**reach′a·ble** *adj.* —**reach′er** *n.*
SYN.—**reach** implies an arriving at some goal, destination, point in development, etc. [he has *reached* the age of 60]; **gain** suggests the reaching of a goal through great effort [she has *gained* a place on her country's Olympic team]; **achieve** suggests the reaching of a goal through great effort and, usually, the use of skill [she worked for years to *achieve* success]; **attain** suggests the gaining of an end that is considered very difficult or unusual [statesmen striving to *attain* a lasting peace]—see also **SYN.** at RANGE

re·act (rē akt′) *vi.* **1.** to act in return or reciprocally [do wages and prices *react* on each other in going up and down?] **2.** to act in opposition [he *reacted* strongly against his parents' way of life] **3.** to go back to a former condition, stage, etc. **4.** to respond to a stimulus, influence, etc. [she *reacted* to the news by fainting] **5.** *Chem.* to act with another substance in producing a chemical change —*vt.* to produce a chemical change in
re-act (rē′akt′) *vt.* to act or do again
re·act·ance (rē ak′təns) *n. Elec.* opposition to the flow of alternating current, caused by inductance or capacitance
re·act·ant (rē ak′tənt) *n.* any of the substances involved in a chemical reaction
re·ac·tion (rē ak′shən) *n.* **1.** an action, influence, etc. in return or in response to some other action, influence, etc. **2.** a response, as to a stimulus [what was his *reaction* to your suggestion?] **3.** a movement back to a former or less advanced condition, stage, etc.; esp., such a movement in politics [a party of *reaction* opposed to the forces of progress] **4.** *Chem. a)* the mutual action of substances undergoing chemical change *b)* a process that produces changes in an atomic nucleus **5.** *Med. a)* an action brought about by resistance to another action *b)* the effect produced by an allergen *c)* depression or exhaustion following nervous tension, overstimulation, etc. *d)* increased activity following depression —**re·ac′tion·al** *adj.*
re·ac·tion·ar·y (rē ak′shə ner′ē) *adj.* of, showing, or favoring reaction, esp. in politics —*n., pl.* **-ar′ies** a reactionary person
reaction engine an engine, as a jet or rocket engine, that develops thrust in reaction to the stream of gases forced from it
reaction time *Psychol.* the time between stimulation and the beginning of the response
re·ac·ti·vate (rē ak′tə vāt′) *vt.* **-vat′ed, -vat′ing** to make active again; ☆specif., to restore to active military status —*vi.* to be reactivated —**re·ac′ti·va′tion** *n.*
re·ac·tive (rē ak′tiv) *adj.* **1.** tending to react **2.** of, caused by, or showing reaction or reactance —**re·ac′tive·ly** *adv.* —**re·ac′tive·ness, re·ac·tiv′i·ty** *n.*
re·ac·tor (rē ak′tər) *n.* **1.** a person or thing that reacts **2.** *same as* NUCLEAR REACTOR
read¹ (rēd) *vt.* **read** (red), **read′ing** (rēd′iŋ) [OE. *rædan*, to counsel: for IE. base see ART¹] **1.** to get the meaning of (something written or printed) by understanding its characters or signs [to *read* books, music, Braille, etc.] **2.** to utter aloud (something written or printed) **3.** to watch the movements of the lips of a person speaking) so as to understand what he says **4.** to know (a language) well enough to understand its written form **5.** to understand the nature, significance, or thinking of as if by reading [to *read* his character in his face] **6.** to find meaning in (dreams, omens, etc.) or foretell (the future) **7.** to give to (a printed passage, a signal, etc.) a particular meaning [I *read* her nod as indicating agreement] **8.** to have or give as a reading in a certain passage [this edition reads "shew," not "show"] **9.** to

study [to *read* law] **10.** to register [the thermometer *reads* 80°] **11.** to put into a specified state by reading [to *read* a child to sleep] **12.** to get (information) from (punch cards, tape, etc.): said of a computer **13.** [Slang] to hear and understand [I *read* you loud and clear] —*vi.* **1.** to read something written or printed **2.** to learn by reading (with *about* or *of*) **3.** to study **4.** to have a particular meaning when read [a poem that *reads* several ways] **5.** to be put in certain words [the sentence *reads* as follows] **6.** to lend itself to being read [the book *reads* easily] —**read into** (or **in**) to think of as meaning [he *read into* what she said things she didn't intend] —**read out** to display or record with a readout device —**read out of** to expel from (a political party, society, etc.) —**read up** (**on**) to become well-informed (about) by reading
read² (red) *pt. & pp. of* READ¹ —*adj.* having knowledge got from reading; informed [well-*read*]
read·a·ble (rēd′ə b'l) *adj.* **1.** interesting or easy to read **2.** capable of being read; legible —**read′a·bil′i·ty, read′a·ble·ness** *n.* —**read′a·bly** *adv.*
Reade (rēd), **Charles** 1814–84; Eng. novelist
read·er (rēd′ər) *n.* **1.** a person who reads **2.** a person who reads lessons, prayers, etc. aloud in church **3.** *a)* a schoolbook containing stories, poems, etc. for use in teaching how to read *b)* an anthology of stories, essays, etc.
read·er·ship (-ship′) *n.* all the people who read a particular publication, author, etc.
Read·ing (red′iŋ) **1.** city in SC England: pop. 127,000 **2.** [after the city in England] city in SE Pa.: pop. 88,000
read·ing (rēd′iŋ) *adj.* **1.** inclined to read or study [a *reading* family] **2.** of or for reading [a *reading* lamp] —*n.* **1.** the act or practice of one who reads **2.** the reciting of a literary work in public **3.** material read or to be read [Dickens' novels were her summer *reading*] **4.** the extent to which a person has read **5.** the amount measured by a barometer, thermometer, etc. **6.** the form of a certain word, passage, etc. in a particular edition of a literary work **7.** a particular interpretation or performance [a superb *reading* of Hamlet]
read·out (rēd′out′) *n.* **1.** a retrieving of information from storage in a digital computer **2.** this information, displayed visually or recorded, as by typewriter or on tape, for immediate use **3.** information immediately displayed or recorded from various electronic instruments
read·y (red′ē) *adj.* **read′i·er, read′i·est** [OE. *ræde*: for IE. base see RIDE] **1.** prepared to act or be used immediately [ready to go, *ready* for occupancy] **2.** unhesitant; willing [a *ready* worker] **3.** *a)* likely or liable immediately [*ready* to cry] *b)* apt; inclined [always *ready* to blame others] **4.** done without delay; prompt [a *ready* reply] **5.** available immediately [*ready* cash] —*vt.* **read′ied, read′y·ing** to make ready; prepare [to *ready* the house for visitors] —see SYN. at QUICK —**at the ready** available for immediate use [to keep a gun *at the ready*] —**make ready** to prepare —**read′i·ly** *adv.* —**read′i·ness** *n.*
read·y-made (red′ē mād′) *adj.* made so as to be ready for immediate use or sale; not made-to-order: also, as applied to clothing, **read′y-to-wear** (-tə wer′)
☆**ready room** a room where aircraft crews gather so that they can be briefed before making flights
re·a·gent (rē ā′jənt) *n.* [RE- + AGENT] *Chem.* a substance used to detect or measure another substance or to convert one substance into another by means of the reaction which it causes
re·a·gin (rē ā′jin) *n.* [REAG(ENT) + -IN¹] a type of antibody in the blood associated with some allergic diseases and with syphilis
re·al¹ (rē′əl, rēl) *adj.* [OFr. < ML. *realis* < L. *res*, thing] **1.** existing or happening as or in fact; actual, true, etc. [hard to believe that such good luck is *real*] **2.** *a)* authentic; genuine [*real* pearls] *b)* not pretended; sincere [to feel *real* grief] **3.** describing wages or income as measured by purchasing power **4.** *Law* of or relating to permanent, immovable things [*real* property] **5.** *Philos.* existing objectively; actual (not merely possible or ideal) —*adv.* [Colloq.] very —see SYN. at TRUE —**for real** [Slang] real or really

re′ac·quaint′	re′ad·dress′	re′ad·mis′sion	re′a·dopt′
re′ac·quire′	re′ad·just′	re′ad·mit′	re′af·firm′
re′a·dapt′	re′ad·just′ment	re′ad·mit′tance	re′af·fir·ma′tion

fat, āpe, cär; ten, ēven; is, bīte; gō, hôrn, tōōl, look; oil, out; up, fur; get; joy; yet; chin; she; thin, then; zh, leisure; ŋ, ring; ə for *a* in *ago, e* in *agent, i* in *sanity, o* in *comply, u* in *focus*; ' as in *able* (ā′b'l); Fr. bal; ë, Fr. coeur; ö, Fr. feu; Fr. mon; ô, Fr. coq; ü, Fr. duc; r, Fr. cri; H, G. ich; kh, G. doch; ‡foreign; ☆ Americanism; < derived from. See inside front cover.

re·al² (rē′əl; *Sp.* re äl′) *n., pl.* **re′als;** *Sp.* **re·al′es** (-ä′les) [Sp. & Port., lit., royal < L. *regalis:* see REGAL] a former silver coin of Spain

re·al³ (re äl′) *n. sing. of* REIS

real estate land, including the buildings or improvements on it and its natural assets, as minerals, water, timber, etc.

re·a·lign (rē′ə līn′) *vt., vi.* to align again; specif., to readjust alliances (between) —**re′a·lign′ment** *n.*

re·al·ism (rē′ə liz′m) *n.* **1.** a tendency to face facts and be practical **2.** the picturing in art and literature of people and things as they really appear to be, without idealizing **3.** *Philos.* the doctrine that material objects really exist in themselves, apart from the mind's being aware of them —**re′al·ist** *n.*

re·al·is·tic (rē′ə lis′tik) *adj.* **1.** of, having to do with, or in the style of, realism or realists **2.** tending to face facts and be practical —**re′al·is′ti·cal·ly** *adv.*

re·al·i·ty (rē al′ə tē) *n., pl.* **-ties 1.** the quality or fact of being real [discussing the possible *reality* of ghosts] **2.** a person or thing that is real; fact [his dream of fame became a *reality*] **3.** the quality of being true to life **4.** *Philos.* that which is real —**in reality** in fact; actually

re·al·ize (rē′ə līz′) *vt.* **-ized′, -iz′ing 1.** to make real; bring into being; achieve [to *realize* one's ambitions] **2.** to make appear real **3.** to understand fully or clearly [only then did he *realize* that he was lost] **4.** to convert (assets, rights, etc.) into money **5.** to gain; obtain [to *realize* a profit] **6.** to be sold for, or bring as profit (a specified sum) —**re′al·i·za′tion** *n.*

re·al·ly (rē′ə lē, rēl′ē) *adv.* **1.** in reality; in fact [did you *really* visit him?] **2.** truly or genuinely [*really* hot] —**interj.** indeed

realm (relm) *n.* [< OFr. *reaume* < L. *regimen,* rule < L. *regalis,* REGAL] **1.** a kingdom **2.** a region; sphere; area [the *realm* of imagination]

real number *Math.* any rational or irrational number

☆**real time 1.** time in which the occurrence and recording of an event take place almost together **2.** the actual time used by a computer to solve a problem the answer to which is immediately available to control a process that is going on at the same time

☆**Re·al·tor** (rē′əl tər) *n.* [< REALTY & -OR] a real estate broker who is a member of the National Association of Real Estate Boards

re·al·ty (rē′əl tē) *n.* [REAL¹ + -TY¹] *same as* REAL ESTATE

ream¹ (rēm) *n.* [< MFr. < Ar. *rizma,* a bale] **1.** a quantity of paper varying from 480 sheets (20 quires) to 516 sheets **2.** [*pl.*] [Colloq.] a great amount

ream² (rēm) *vt.* [OE. *reman,* akin to *ryman,* lit., to make roomy < base of *rum,* ROOM] **1.** *a)* to enlarge or taper (a hole) *b)* to enlarge the bore of (a gun) **2.** to remove (a defect) by reaming ☆**3.** to squeeze the juice from (an orange, lemon, etc.) with a reamer **4.** [Slang] ☆*a)* to cheat or deceive ☆*b)* to blame sharply; rebuke (often with *out*)

ream·er (rēm′ər) *n.* a person or thing that reams; specif., *a)* a sharp-edged tool for enlarging or tapering holes *b)* a device with a ridged cone-shaped part on which oranges, etc. are squeezed for juice

re·an·i·mate (rē an′ə māt′) *vt.* **-mat′ed, -mat′ing** to give new life, power, vigor, courage, etc. to —**re·an′i·ma′tion** *n.*

REAMER

reap (rēp) *vt.* [OE. *ripan:* for IE. base see ROW¹] **1.** to cut (grain) with a scythe, machine, etc. **2.** to gather (a crop, harvest, etc.) by cutting **3.** to harvest grain from (a field) **4.** to get as the result of action, work, etc. [to *reap* a reward] —**vi.** to reap a harvest, reward, etc. [as you sow, so shall you *reap*]

reap·er (rē′pər) *n.* **1.** a person who reaps **2.** a machine for reaping grain —**the (Grim) Reaper** death

re·ap·por·tion (rē′ə pôr′shən) *vt.* to apportion again, as with the intent of having all legislative districts contain about the same number of people —**re′ap·por′tion·ment** *n.*

re·ap·praise (rē′ə prāz′) *vt.* **-praised′, -prais′ing** to make a fresh appraisal of; reconsider —**re′ap·prais′al** *n.*

rear¹ (rir) *n.* [< ARREAR(S)] **1.** the back part of something **2.** the place or position behind or at the back [at the *rear* of the house] **3.** the part of an army, navy, etc. farthest from the battle front ☆**4.** [Slang] the buttocks: also **rear end** —*adj.* of, at, or in the rear [a *rear* entrance] —**bring up the rear** to come at the end, as of a procession

rear² (rir) *vt.* [OE. *ræran* < *risan,* to RISE] **1.** to put upright; elevate; raise [the cobra *reared* its head] **2.** to build; erect [*rearing* altars to pagan gods] **3.** to grow or breed (animals or plants) **4.** to bring to maturity by educating, nourishing, etc. [to *rear* children] —*vi.* **1.** to rise on the hind legs, as a horse **2.** to rise (*up*) in anger, etc. —see SYN. at LIFT

rear admiral a naval officer next in rank above a captain and below a vice admiral

rear guard a military body of troops put at the rear of a main force or body to protect it

re·arm (rē ärm′) *vt., vi.* **1.** to arm again **2.** to arm with new or more effective weapons —**re·ar′ma·ment** *n.*

rear·most (rir′mōst′) *adj.* farthest in the rear

re·ar·range (rē′ə rānj′) *vt.* **-ranged′, -rang′ing** to arrange again or in a different manner —**re′ar·range′ment** *n.*

rear·ward (rir′wərd) *adj.* at, in, or toward the rear —*adv.* toward the rear: also **rear′wards** (-wərdz)

rea·son (rē′z'n) *n.* [< OFr. < L. *ratio,* a reckoning < pp. of *reri,* to think: for IE. base see ART¹] **1.** an explanation or justification of an act, idea, etc. [write the *reasons* for your answer] **2.** a cause or motive [she had no *reason* for behaving that way] **3.** the ability to think, draw conclusions, etc. [man is the only animal that truly possesses *reason*] **4.** sound thought or judgment; good sense [he won't listen to *reason*] **5.** normal mental powers; sanity [to lose one's *reason*] —*vi.* **1.** to think logically; draw conclusions from facts known or assumed **2.** to argue or talk in a logical way [to *reason* with a child] —*vt.* **1.** to think logically about; analyze [we'll have to *reason* it out] **2.** to argue, conclude, or infer [he *reasoned* that the method was too costly] **3.** to justify with reason **4.** to persuade by reasoning (*into* or *out of* something) —see SYN. at CAUSE and THINK¹ —**by reason of** because of —**in (or within) reason** in accord with what is reasonable —**out of all reason** unreasonable —**stand to reason** to be logical or reasonable —**with reason** justifiably; rightly —**rea′son·er** *n.*

rea·son·a·ble (-ə b'l) *adj.* **1.** capable of reasoning or being reasoned with **2.** using or showing reason, or sound judgment; sensible [a *reasonable* decision] **3.** *a)* not extreme or excessive [*reasonable* demands] *b)* not expensive —see SYN. at RATIONAL —**rea′son·a·ble·ness** *n.* —**rea′son·a·bly** *adv.*

rea·son·ing (-iŋ) *n.* **1.** the drawing of inferences or conclusions from known or assumed facts **2.** the reasons, proofs, etc. used in this process

re·as·sure (rē′ə shoor′) *vt.* **-sured′, -sur′ing 1.** to assure again or anew **2.** to restore to confidence **3.** [Brit.] to insure anew —**re′as·sur′ance** *n.* —**re′as·sur′ing·ly** *adv.*

reave (rēv) *vt.* **reaved** or **reft, reav′ing** [OE. *reafian*] [Archaic] to take away by violence; seize; rob

re·bate (rē′bāt; *also for v.* ri bāt′) *vt.* **-bat·ed, -bat·ing** [< OFr. < *re-,* re- + *abattre:* see ABATE] **1.** to give back (part of an amount paid) **2.** to make a deduction from (a bill) —*n.* a return of part of the amount paid, as for goods

re·bec, re·beck (rē′bek) *n.* [Fr. < OFr. *rebebe* < Ar. *rabab*] a medieval pear-shaped instrument played with a bow like that used in playing a violin

Re·bec·ca (ri bek′ə) [LL. < Gr. < Heb. *ribbqāh,* lit., noose] **1.** a feminine name **2.** *Bible* the wife of Isaac and mother of Jacob and Esau: usually sp. **Rebekah**

reb·el (reb′'l; *for v.* ri bel′) *n.* [< OFr. < L. < *re-,* again + *bellare,* to war < *bellum:* see DUEL] **1.** a person who takes up arms against the government of his own country **2.** a person who resists any

REBEC

authority or controls ☆**3.** [often **R-**] a name given to a Confederate soldier —adj. **1.** rebellious **2.** of rebels —vi. **-elled′, -el′ling 1.** to be a rebel against the government of one's country **2.** to resist any authority or controls **3.** to feel or show strong dislike; be repelled [his mind rebels at the thought]

re·bel·lion (ri bel′yən) n. [< MFr. < L.: see prec.] **1.** an act or state of armed resistance to one's government **2.** a fight or struggle against any authority or controls

SYN.—rebellion implies organized, armed, open resistance to the authority or government in power, and, when applied to a historical event, suggests that it failed [Shay's Rebellion]; **revolution** applies to a rebellion that succeeds in overthrowing an old government and establishing a new one [the American Revolution] or to any movement that brings about a drastic change in society [the Industrial Revolution]; **insurrection** suggests an outbreak that is smaller in scope and less well organized than a rebellion [the Philippine Insurrection]; **revolt** stresses a casting off of allegiance or a refusal to submit to established authority [a revolt of students against the dress code]; **mutiny** applies to a forcible revolt of soldiers or, especially, sailors against their officers [mutiny on the Bounty]; **uprising** is a simple, direct term for any outbreak against a government and applies specifically to a small, limited action or to the beginning of a general rebellion [local uprisings against the Stamp Act]

re·bel·lious (ri bel′yəs) adj. **1.** resisting authority; engaged in rebellion **2.** of or like rebels or rebellion **3.** opposing any controls; defiant **4.** difficult to treat or handle [a rebellious cowlick] —**re·bel′lious·ly** adv. —**re·bel′lious·ness** n.

re·birth (rē burth′, rē′burth′) n. **1.** a new or second birth, as through reincarnation **2.** a reawakening; revival [a rebirth of interest in the arts]

re·bound (ri bound′; also, & for n. usually, rē′bound′) vi. **1.** to bound back, as after hitting a surface **2.** to revive or recover, as after defeat or disappointment [his spirits rebounded] —vt. to make bound or spring back —n. **1.** a rebounding; recoil ☆**2.** a basketball that bounces off the backboard or basket rim, or the act of recovering such a rebound —**on the rebound 1.** after bouncing off the ground, a wall, etc. **2.** while still reacting to being rejected [he married Jane on the rebound when Betty jilted him]

☆**re·bo·zo** (ri bō′zō; Sp. re bô′thô, -sô) n., pl. **-zos** (-zōz; Sp. -thôs, -sôs) [Sp., a shawl] a long scarf worn by women around the head and shoulders, as in Mexico

re·broad·cast (rē brôd′kast′) vt., vi. **-cast′** or **-cast′ed, -cast′ing 1.** to broadcast again **2.** to broadcast (a program, etc. received in a relay system from another station) —n. **1.** a rebroadcasting **2.** a program that is being or has been rebroadcast

re·buff (ri buf′) n. [< MFr. < It. rabbuffo, ult. < Gmc.] **1.** a blunt refusal of offered help, advice, etc. **2.** any check or repulse —vt. **1.** to refuse bluntly; snub **2.** to check or repulse

re·buke (ri byook′) vt. **-buked′, -buk′ing** [< Anglo-Fr. < OFr. < re-, back + buchier, to beat] to blame or scold in a sharp way; reprimand —n. a sharp scolding or reprimand —**re·buk′er** n. —**re·buk′ing·ly** adv.

re·bus (rē′bəs) n. [L., lit., by things] a puzzle consisting of pictures of things combined so as to suggest words or phrases

re·but (ri but′) vt., vi. **-but′ted, -but′ting** [< Anglo-Fr. < OFr. < re-, back + buter, to push: see BUTT²] to prove or try to prove (someone or something) to be wrong, esp. in a formal manner by argument, proof, etc. —**re·but′ta·ble** adj. —**re·but′ter** n.

re·but·tal (-'l) n. a rebutting, as in law

REBUS
(Look before you leap.)

☆**rec** (rek) n. shortened form of RECREATION in such compounds as **rec room, rec hall**

rec. 1. receipt **2.** recipe **3.** record(ed) **4.** recording

re·cal·ci·trant (ri kal′si trənt) adj. [< L. prp. of recalcitrare < re-, back + calcitrare, to kick < calx, a heel] **1.** refusing to obey authority or rules, follow orders, etc.; stubborn and disobedient; defiant **2.** hard to handle or deal with [an old,

recalcitrant can opener] —n. a recalcitrant person —**re·cal′ci·trance, re·cal′ci·tran·cy** n. —**re·cal′ci·trant·ly** adv.

re·call (ri kôl′; for n. also rē′kôl′) vt. **1.** to call back; order to return [the ambassador was recalled to Paris] **2.** to bring back to mind; remember [I can't recall her name] **3.** to take back; revoke [they recalled his license] ☆**4.** to remove from office by the process of recall **5.** to bring back in awareness, attention, etc. [her cry for help recalled him to his senses] —n. **1.** a recalling **2.** the ability to remember; memory ☆**3.** the process of removing, or the right to remove, a public official from office by popular vote, usually after using petitions to call for such a vote —see SYN. at REMEMBER —**re·call′a·ble** adj.

re·cant (ri kant′) vt., vi. [< L. < re-, back + cantare, to sing < canere, to sing] to take back (statements one has made) or confess being wrong about (beliefs, etc. one has held), esp. formally or publicly —**re·can·ta·tion** (rē′kan tā′shən) n.

re·cap¹ (rē kap′; also, & for n. always, rē′kap′) vt. **-capped′, -cap′ping** [RE- + CAP] ☆to cement, mold, and vulcanize a strip of rubber on the outer surface of (a worn pneumatic tire); retread —☆n. a recapped tire

re·cap² (rē′kap′) n. a recapitulation, or summary —vi., vt. **-capped′, -cap′ping**

re·ca·pit·u·late (rē′kə pich′ə lāt′) vi., vt. **-lat′ed, -lat′ing** [see RE- & CAPITULATE] to tell again briefly, as in an outline; summarize

re·ca·pit·u·la·tion (-pich′ə lā′shən) n. **1.** a recapitulating **2.** a summary, or brief restatement —**re·ca·pit·u·la·tive, re·ca·pit·u·la·to·ry** (-lə tôr′ē) adj.

re·cap·ture (rē kap′chər) vt. **-tured, -tur·ing 1.** to capture again; retake; reacquire **2.** to bring back by remembering [to recapture a feeling] —n. a recapturing or being recaptured

re·cast (rē kast′; for n. rē′kast′) vt. **-cast′, -cast′ing 1.** to cast again or anew **2.** to improve the form of by redoing; reconstruct [to recast a sentence] —n. a recasting

recd., rec'd. received

re·cede¹ (ri sēd′) vi. **-ced′ed, -ced′ing** [< L.: see RE- & CEDE] **1.** to go or move back [the flood receded] **2.** to slope backward [her chin recedes] **3.** to lessen, dim, etc. [as early memories recede]

☆**re·cede²** (rē′sēd′) vt. **-ced′ed, -ced′ing** to cede back

re·ceipt (ri sēt′) n. [< Anglo-Fr. < ML. < L. < pp. of recipere: see RECEIVE] **1.** old-fashioned var. of RECIPE **2.** a receiving or being received **3.** a written acknowledgment that something, as goods, money, etc., has been received **4.** a) something received b) [pl.] the amount of money taken in, as by a business —vt. **1.** to mark (a bill) paid ☆**2.** to write a receipt for (goods, etc.)

re·ceiv·a·ble (ri sē′və b'l) adj. **1.** that can be received **2.** suitable for acceptance **3.** due in payment from one's customers [accounts receivable] —n. [pl.] accounts or bills receivable

re·ceive (ri sēv′) vt. **-ceived′, -ceiv′ing** [< Anglo-Fr. < OFr. < L. recipere < re-, back + capere, to take] **1.** to take or get (something given, offered, sent, etc.) **2.** to meet with; experience [to receive acclaim] **3.** to undergo; suffer [to receive a blow] **4.** to take the force of; bear [each wheel receives equal weight] **5.** to react to as specified [the song was well received] **6.** to get knowledge of; learn [to receive news] **7.** to accept as authentic, valid, etc. [received truths] **8.** a) to let enter; admit b) to have room for; contain **9.** to greet (visitors, etc.) —vi. **1.** to take or get something **2.** to greet guests or visitors **3.** Radio & TV to change incoming electromagnetic waves into sound or light, thus reproducing the sounds or images being transmitted **4.** Sports to catch a ball or be prepared to return a thrown, kicked, etc. ball

re·ceiv·er (ri sē′vər) n. **1.** a person who receives; specif., a) a football player who receives or, according to the rules, may receive a forward pass b) Law a person appointed by the court to administer or take care of property involved in a lawsuit **2.** a thing that receives; specif., a) a receptacle or container b) an apparatus that changes electromagnetic waves or electrical signals into sound or light, as a radio or television receiving set, or ☆that part of a telephone held to the ear

| re·bid′ | re·bind′ | re·build′ | re·cal·cu·late′ |
| re·bill′ | re·born′ | re·bur′y | re·car′ry |

re·ceiv·er·ship (-ship′) *n. Law* **1.** the duties or office of a receiver **2.** the state of being administered or held by a receiver

☆**receiving blanket** a small, lightweight blanket, usually of cotton, for wrapping around a baby

receiving line at formal gatherings, the host, hostess, guests of honor, etc., who stand in a row to greet guests

receiving set an apparatus for receiving radio or television signals; receiver

re·cent (rē′s'nt) *adj.* [MFr. < L. *recens* < *re-*, again + base akin to Gr. *kainos*, new] **1.** done, made, etc. just before the present time; modern; new **2.** of a time just before the present **3.** [R-] designating or of the present epoch, extending from the close of the Pleistocene —**the Recent** the Recent Epoch or its rocks: see GEOLOGIC TIME CHART —**re′cent·ly** *adv.* —**re′cent·ness, re′cen·cy** *n.*

re·cep·ta·cle (ri sep′tə k'l) *n.* [L. *receptaculum* < *recipere:* see RECEIVE] **1.** anything used to contain or hold something else; container **2.** an electrical wall outlet designed for use with a plug **3.** *Bot. a)* the part of the stalk from which the flower grows *b)* a cuplike or disklike part supporting spores, seeds, etc.

re·cep·tion (ri sep′shən) *n.* [OFr. < L. < pp. of *recipere:* see RECEIVE] **1.** *a)* a receiving or being received *b)* the manner of this [a friendly *reception*] **2.** a social function, often formal, for the receiving of guests [a wedding *reception*] **3.** *Radio & TV* the manner of receiving, as regards how well the programs come through [poor *reception*]

re·cep·tion·ist (-ist) *n.* an office employee who receives callers, gives information, etc.

re·cep·tive (ri sep′tiv) *adj.* **1.** receiving or tending to receive, admit, or contain **2.** able or ready to receive requests, suggestions, new ideas, etc. **3.** of reception or receptors —**re·cep′tive·ly** *adv.* —**re·cep′tiv·i·ty, re·cep′tive·ness** *n.*

re·cep·tor (ri sep′tər) *n. Physiol.* a nerve ending specialized for the reception of stimuli; sense organ

re·cess (rē′ses; *also, and for v. usually,* ri ses′) *n.* [< L. pp. of *recedere,* to recede] **1.** a receding or hollow place, as in a wall; niche **2.** a hidden or inner place [the *recesses* of the subconscious] **3.** a temporary halting of work, study, etc. —*vt.* **1.** to place in a recess [a *recessed* door] **2.** to form a recess in ☆**3.** to halt temporarily [to *recess* the hearing] —☆*vi.* to stop work, study, etc. temporarily [Congress *recessed* until Tuesday]

re·ces·sion[1] (ri sesh′ən) *n.* [L. *recessio* < pp. of *recedere,* to recede] **1.** a going backward; withdrawal **2.** a departing procession, as of clergy and choir after a church service **3.** a receding part, as of a wall **4.** a temporary falling off of business activity during a generally prosperous period

re·ces·sion[2] (rē sesh′ən) *n.* [RE- + CESSION] a ceding back, as to a former owner

re·ces·sion·al (-'l) *adj.* of a recession —*n.* a hymn or other piece of music sung or played during a church recession

re·ces·sive (ri ses′iv) *adj.* **1.** receding or tending to recede **2.** *Genetics* designating or of that one of any pair of allelic characters which, when both are present in the germ plasm, remains latent: opposed to DOMINANT —*n. Genetics* a recessive character or factor —**re·ces′sive·ly** *adv.* —**re·ces′sive·ness** *n.*

re·cher·ché (rə sher′shā, -sher′shā′) *adj.* [Fr., pp. of *rechercher:* see RESEARCH] **1.** sought out with care; rare; choice **2.** having refinement or carefully planned elegance **3.** too refined; too specialized; lacking popular appeal

re·cid·i·vism (ri sid′ə viz′m) *n.* [< L. < *recidere* < *re-*, back + *cadere,* to fall + -ISM] habitual relapse or falling back into former ways, esp. into crime or antisocial behavior —**re·cid′i·vist** *n., adj.* —**re·cid′i·vis′tic, re·cid′i·vous** *adj.*

Re·ci·fe (re sē′fə) seaport in NE Brazil, on the Atlantic: pop. 1,079,000

rec·i·pe (res′ə pē) *n.* [L., imperative of *recipere:* see RECEIVE] **1.** formerly, a prescription for medicine **2.** a list of ingredients and directions for making something to eat or drink [a *recipe* for Irish stew] **3.** any method used for bringing about a desired result [his *recipe* for success is hard work]

re·cip·i·ent (ri sip′ē ənt) *n.* [< L. prp. of *recipere:* see RECEIVE] a person or thing that receives —*adj.* receiving, or ready or able to receive —**re·cip′i·ence, re·cip′i·en·cy** *n.*

re·cip·ro·cal (ri sip′rə k'l) *adj.* [< L. *reciprocus,* returning] **1.** done, felt, given, etc. in return [hoping for a *reciprocal* favor] **2.** on both sides; mutual [their *reciprocal* affection] **3.** corre-

sponding but reversed **4.** acting or working together; complementary [*reciprocal* action of the parts of the machine] **5.** *Gram.* expressing mutual action or relation [*each other* is a *reciprocal* pronoun] **6.** *Math.* of reciprocals —*n.* **1.** anything that has a reciprocal relation to another; counterpart **2.** *Math.* the quantity resulting from the division of 1 by the given quantity [the *reciprocal* of 7 is 1/7] —**re·cip′ro·cal′i·ty** (-kal′ə tē) *n.* —**re·cip′ro·cal·ly** *adv.*

re·cip·ro·cate (ri sip′rə kāt′) *vt., vi.* **-cat′ed, -cat′ing** [< L. pp. of *reciprocare* < *reciprocus:* see prec.] **1.** *a)* to give and get reciprocally [they *reciprocated* cheerful greetings] *b)* to give, do, feel, etc. (something similar) in return [when someone shows you hospitality, you should *reciprocate*] **2.** to move alternately back and forth [a *reciprocating* engine is one in which the pistons move back and forth] —**re·cip′ro·ca′tion** *n.* —**re·cip′ro·ca′tive, re·cip′ro·ca·to′ry** (-kə tôr′ē) *adj.*

rec·i·proc·i·ty (res′ə präs′ə tē) *n., pl.* **-ties** [< Fr.] **1.** reciprocal state or relationship **2.** mutual exchange; esp., exchange of special privileges between two countries, as when each country lowers the duty or tariff on goods that the other wants to buy

re·cit·al (ri sīt′'l) *n.* **1.** *a)* a reciting; specif., a telling in detail [a lengthy *recital* of his troubles] *b)* the account, story, etc. told **2.** a musical or dance program given by a soloist, soloists, or a small ensemble —**re·cit′al·ist** *n.*

rec·i·ta·tion (res′ə tā′shən) *n.* **1.** a recital (sense 1) **2.** *a)* the speaking aloud in public of something memorized *b)* the piece so presented ☆**3.** *a)* a reciting by pupils of answers to questions on a prepared lesson, etc. *b)* a class meeting in which this occurs

rec·i·ta·tive (res′ə tə tēv′) *n.* [It. *recitativo* < L. *recitare,* to RECITE] *Music* **1.** a type of singing having the rhythm and tempo of speech but uttered in musical tones, used in the dialogue of operas **2.** a work or passage in this style **3.** music for such passages —*adj.* in the style of recitative

re·cite (ri sīt′) *vt., vi.* **-cit′ed, -cit′ing** [< OFr. < L. *recitare:* see RE- & CITE] **1.** to speak aloud, as from memory, (a lesson) in class or (a poem, etc.) before an audience **2.** to tell in detail or narrate (something) —**re·cit′er** *n.*

reck (rek) *vi., vt.* [OE. *reccan*] [Archaic] **1.** to have care or concern (*for*) or take heed (*of*) [he *recks* not of the peril] **2.** to concern or be of concern; matter (to)

reck·less (rek′lis) *adj.* [see RECK & -LESS] **1.** careless; heedless; taking chances [a *reckless* driver] **2.** showing no concern for consequences; irresponsible [the *reckless* spending of public funds] —**reck′less·ly** *adv.* —**reck′less·ness** *n.*

reck·on (rek′ən) *vt.* [OE. *-recenian:* for IE. base see REGAL] **1.** to count; figure up; compute [to *reckon* the bill] **2.** *a)* to consider as; regard as being [*reckon* them friends] *b)* to judge; estimate **3.** [Colloq. or Dial.] to suppose [I *reckon* I ought to go] —*vi.* **1.** to count up; figure **2.** [Colloq.] to rely (with *on*) [she *reckoned* on his being early] **3.** [Colloq.] to suppose —see SYN. at CALCULATE —**reckon with** to take into consideration [factors we must *reckon with* in making our plans] —**reck′on·er** *n.*

reck·on·ing (-iŋ) *n.* **1.** the act of one who reckons; count or computation **2.** a calculated guess **3.** *a)* a bill; account *b)* the payment of an account **4.** the giving of rewards or punishments [day of *reckoning*] **5.** *Naut.* the determination of the position of a ship; esp., *short for* DEAD RECKONING

re·claim (ri klām′) *vt.* [< OFr. < L. *reclamare:* see RE- & CLAIM] **1.** to rescue or bring back (someone) from a life of sin, crime, etc.; reform **2.** to make (wasteland, desert, etc.) capable of being cultivated or lived on, as by filling or irrigating **3.** to recover (useful materials) from waste products —*n.* reclamation [beyond *reclaim*] —**re·claim′a·ble** *adj.* —**re·claim′ant, re·claim′er** *n.*

re-claim (rē′klām′) *vt.* to claim back; demand the return of; try to get back

rec·la·ma·tion (rek′lə mā′shən) *n.* a reclaiming or being reclaimed, as of wasteland or of useful materials from waste products

re·cline (ri klīn′) *vi., vt.* **-clined′, -clin′ing** [< L. < *re-*, back + *clinare,* to lean (see INCLINE)] to lie down or lean back, or cause to do so —**rec·li·na·tion** (rek′lə nā′shən) *n.*

re·clin·er (-klī′nər) *n.* **1.** one that reclines **2.** an upholstered armchair with a movable back and seat that can be adjusted for reclining: also **reclining chair**

---

rec·luse (rek′lōōs, ri klōōs′) *adj.* [< OFr. < LL. < L. pp. of *recludere* < *re-*, back + *claudere*, to shut] secluded; solitary —*n.* a person who chooses to live alone and to have little or nothing to do with others —**re·clu·sion** (ri klōō′zhən) *n.* —**re·clu′sive** *adj.*

rec·og·ni·tion (rek′əg nish′ən) *n.* [< L. < pp. of *recognoscere*: see next entry] **1.** *a)* a recognizing or being recognized; acknowledgment *b)* acknowledgment and approval, gratitude, etc. [in *recognition* of his services] **2.** formal acceptance by a government of the sovereignty of a newly established state or government **3.** identification of a person or thing as being known to one **4.** notice, as in passing; greeting —**re·cog·ni·to·ry** (ri käg′nə tôr′ē), **re·cog′ni·tive** *adj.*

re·cog·ni·zance (ri käg′ni zəns, -kän′i-) *n.* [< OFr. < L. < *re-*, again + *cognoscere*, to know: see COGNITION] *Law* **1.** a bond or obligation of record binding a person to do a certain thing, as to appear in court **2.** a sum of money that one must forfeit if one does not meet this obligation

rec·og·nize (rek′əg nīz′) *vt.* -nized′, -niz′ing [altered (after prec.) < OFr.: see prec.] **1.** to be aware of as something or someone known before [she *recognized* the street] **2.** to know by some detail, as of appearance [to *recognize* a butterfly by its coloring] **3.** to be aware of the significance of [to *recognize* symptoms] **4.** to acknowledge the existence, validity, etc. of [to *recognize* a claim] **5.** to accept as a fact; admit [to *recognize* defeat] **6.** to acknowledge as worthy of appreciation or approval [to *recognize* his years of faithful service] **7.** to acknowledge the legal standing of (a government or state), as by starting to do business with it **8.** to show acquaintance with (a person) by greeting ☆**9.** to grant (a person) the right to speak, as in a meeting [the chair *recognizes* the delegate from Ohio] —**rec′og·niz′a·bil′i·ty** *n.* —**rec′og·niz′a·ble** *adj.* —**rec′og·niz′a·bly** *adv.* —**rec′og·niz′er** *n.*

re·coil (ri koil′; *also for n., esp. of weapons*, rē′koil) *vi.* [< OFr. < *re-*, back + *cul* < L. *culus*, the buttocks] **1.** to draw, start, or shrink back, as in fear, surprise, disgust, etc. **2.** to fly back when let go, as a spring, or kick back when fired, as a gun **3.** to return as to the starting point or source; react (*on* or *upon*) —*n.* **1.** a recoiling **2.** the state of having recoiled **3.** the distance through which a gun, spring, etc. recoils —**re·coil′er** *n.* —**re·coil′less** *adj.*

rec·ol·lect (rek′ə lekt′) *vt.* [< L.: see RE- & COLLECT¹] **1.** to call back to mind; remember, esp. with some effort **2.** to recall to (oneself) something temporarily forgotten —*vi.* to remember —see SYN. at REMEMBER

re·col·lect (rē′kə lekt′) *vt.* **1.** to collect again (what has been scattered) **2.** to rally (one's courage, etc.) **3.** to make (oneself) calm again; compose (oneself): in this sense sometimes written **recollect**

rec·ol·lec·tion (rek′ə lek′shən) *n.* **1.** the act or power of recollecting, or calling back to mind; remembrance **2.** what is recollected [jotting down his *recollections* of the past] —see SYN. at MEMORY —**rec′ol·lec′tive** *adj.*

re·com·bi·na·tion (rē käm′bə nā′shən) *n.* a combining again; specif., *Genetics* the appearance in offspring of new combinations of allelic genes not present in either parent, produced from the mixing of genetic material, as by crossing-over

rec·om·mend (rek′ə mend′) *vt.* [< ML.: see RE- & COMMEND] **1.** to turn over; entrust [funds *recommended* to his care] **2.** to suggest favorably as being suitable for some purpose or use [to *recommend* a book, a doctor, etc.] **3.** to make acceptable or pleasing [his charm *recommends* him] **4.** to advise; counsel [I *recommend* that we stop here] —**rec′om·mend′a·ble** *adj.* —**rec′om·mend′a·to·ry** *adj.* —**rec′om·mend′er** *n.*

rec·om·men·da·tion (-mən dā′shən) *n.* **1.** a recommending **2.** anything that recommends or makes a favorable or pleasing impression; specif., a letter recommending a person or thing **3.** advice; counsel

re·com·mit (rē′kə mit′) *vt.* -mit′ted, -mit′ting **1.** to commit again **2.** to refer (a question, bill, etc.) back to a committee —**re′com·mit′ment, re′com·mit′tal** *n.*

rec·om·pense (rek′əm pens′) *vt.* -pensed′, -pens′ing [< MFr. < LL.: see RE- & COMPENSATE] **1.** to repay (a person, etc.); reward **2.** to make up for (a loss, injury, etc.); compensate —*n.* **1.** something given or done in return for something else; requital, reward, etc. **2.** something given or done to make up for a loss, injury, etc.; compensation

rec·on·cile (rek′ən sīl′) *vt.* -ciled′, -cil′ing [< OFr. < L.: see RE- & CONCILIATE] **1.** to make friendly again [to *reconcile* feuding families] **2.** to settle (a quarrel, etc.) **3.** to make (facts, ideas, texts, etc.) agree or fit together **4.** to make ready to put up with [to become *reconciled* to one's fate] —**rec′on·cil′a·bil′i·ty** *n.* —**rec′on·cil′a·ble** *adj.* —**rec′on·cil′a·bly** *adv.* —**rec′on·cil′i·a′tion** (-sil′ē ā′shən), **rec′on·cile′ment** *n.* —**rec′on·cil′i·a·to·ry** (-sil′ē ə tôr′ē) *adj.*

rec·on·dite (rek′ən dīt′, ri kän′dīt) *adj.* [< L. pp. of *recondere* < *re-*, back + *condere*, to store up, hide] **1.** very hard to understand; profound **2.** dealing with subjects very hard to understand **3.** hard to see or hidden —**rec′on·dite′ly** *adv.* —**rec′on·dite′ness** *n.*

re·con·di·tion (rē′kən dish′ən) *vt.* to put back in good condition by cleaning, repairing, etc.

re·con·nais·sance (ri kän′ə səns, -zəns) *n.* [Fr.: see RECOGNIZANCE] a survey or examination, as in seeking out information about enemy positions

rec·on·noi·ter (rē′kə noit′ər, rek′ə-) *vt., vi.* [< Fr. < OFr.: see RECOGNIZANCE] to make a reconnaissance (of): also, chiefly Brit. sp., **rec′on·noi′tre** -tred, -tring —**rec′on·noi′ter·er, rec′on·noi′trer** (-noi′trər) *n.*

re·con·sid·er (rē′kən sid′ər) *vt., vi.* to consider again; think over, as with the idea of changing one's mind —**re′con·sid′er·a′tion** *n.*

re·con·sti·tute (rē kän′stə tōōt′, -tyōōt′) *vt.* -tut′ed, -tut′ing to constitute or form again or anew; specif., to restore (a dehydrated or condensed substance) to its full liquid form by adding water —**re′con′sti·tu′tion** *n.*

re·con·struct (rē′kən strukt′) *vt.* **1.** to construct again; make over **2.** to build up again (something in its original form), as from remaining parts —**re′con·struc′tive** *adj.*

re·con·struc·tion (-struk′shən) *n.* **1.** *a)* a reconstructing *b)* something reconstructed ☆**2.** [R-] the period (1867–77) or the process, after the Civil War, of bringing back the Southern States into the Union

re·con·vert (rē′kən vurt′) *vt., vi.* to change back, as to a former status, form, religion, opinion, etc. —**re′con·ver′sion** *n.*

re·cord (ri kôrd′; *for n. & adj.,* rek′ərd) *vt.* [< OFr. < L. *recordari*, to remember < *re-*, again + *cordis*, genitive of *cor*, HEART, mind] **1.** *a)* to put in writing, print, etc. for future use [to *record* the day's events] *b)* to make an official note of [to *record* a vote] **2.** *a)* to indicate automatically and permanently, as on a graph [a seismograph *records* earthquakes] *b)* to show, as on a dial [a thermometer *records* temperatures] **3.** to remain as evidence of [metal tools *record* a developed culture] **4.** *a)* to register (sound or visual images) in some permanent form, as on a phonograph disc, magnetic tape, etc. for reproduction on a playback device *b)* to register the performance of (a musician, actor, composition, etc.) in this way —*vi.* **1.** to record something **2.** to lend itself to being recorded —*n.* **1.** the condition of being recorded **2.** *a)* an account of events *b)* anything that serves as evidence of an event, etc. *c)* an official report of public proceedings, as in a court **3.** anything that written evidence is put on or in, as a register, monument, etc. ☆**4.** *a)* the known facts about anyone or anything, as about one's career [his fine *record* as mayor] *b)* the recorded crimes of a person who has been arrested one or more times ☆**5.** a thin, flat, grooved disc for playing on a phonograph **6.** the best performance, highest speed, greatest amount, etc. achieved, esp. when officially recorded [the *record* for the high jump is over

---

re·code′	re′com·pose′	re′con·firm′	re′con·sol′i·date′
re·coin′	re′com·press′	re′con·nect′	re′con·tam′i·nate′
re·col′or	re′com·pute′	re′con·quer′	re′con·vene′
re′com·bine′	re′con·dense′	re′con·quest′	re′con·vey′
re′com·mence′	re′con·duct′	re′con·se·crate′	re·cook′
re′com·mis′sion	re′con·fine′	re′con·sign′	re·cop′y

---

seven feet] —**adj.** establishing a record as the best, largest, etc. [a *record* crop] —☆**go on record** to state one's opinions publicly or officially —☆**off the record** confidential(ly); not for publication —**on (the) record** publicly or officially declared or known

☆**record changer** a phonograph device that automatically sets in place each record from a stack of records placed on the turntable spindle

re·cord·er (ri kôr′dər) *n.* 1. a public officer who keeps records of deeds or other official papers 2. a machine or device that records; esp., *same as* TAPE RECORDER 3. an early form of flute

re·cord·ing (ri kôr′diŋ) *adj.* that records —*n.* 1. the act of one that records 2. *a)* what is recorded, as on a disc or tape *b)* the record itself

record player a phonograph having the pickup, turntable, amplifier, speaker, etc. operate electrically or electronically

re·count (ri kount′) *vt.* [< Anglo-Fr.: see RE- & COUNT[1]] to tell in detail; narrate [he *recounted* his adventures] —see SYN. at TELL —**re·count′al** *n.*

RECORDER

re-count (rē′kount′; *for n.* rē′kount′) *vt.* to count again —*n.* a second or additional count, as of votes: also written **recount**

re·coup (ri kōōp′) *vt.* [< Fr. < *re-*, again + *couper*, to cut] 1. *a)* to make up for [to *recoup* a loss] *b)* to regain [to *recoup* one's health] 2. to pay back —*n.* a recouping —**re·coup′a·ble** *adj.* —**re·coup′ment** *n.*

re·course (rē′kôrs, ri kôrs′) *n.* [< OFr. < L. *recursus*, a running back: see RE- & COURSE] 1. a turning for aid, safety, etc. [he had *recourse* to the law] 2. that to which one turns seeking aid, safety, etc. [one's last *recourse*]

re·cov·er (ri kuv′ər) *vt.* [< OFr. < L. *recuperare*: see RECUPERATE] 1. *a)* to get back (something lost, stolen, etc.) *b)* to regain (health, etc.) 2. to make up for [to *recover* losses] 3. *a)* to get (oneself) back to a state of control, balance, etc. *b)* to save (oneself) from stumbling, showing one's feelings, etc. 4. to reclaim (land from the sea, useful substances from waste, etc.) 5. *Law* to get or get back by final judgment in a court [to *recover* damages] —*vi.* 1. to regain health, balance, control, etc. 2. to save oneself from a slip, self-betrayal, etc. 3. *Law* to receive judgment in one's favor —**re·cov′er·a·ble** *adj.*

SYN.—**recover** implies a finding or getting back something that one has lost in any manner [to *recover* stolen property, one's self-control, etc.]; **regain** emphasizes a struggle to win back something that has been taken from one [to *regain* a hill from the enemy]; **retrieve** suggests that something is beyond easy reach and requires some effort to get it back [he was determined to *retrieve* his honor]

re-cov·er (rē′kuv′ər) *vt.* to cover again or anew

re·cov·er·y (ri kuv′ər ē) *n., pl.* **-er·ies** the act or an instance of recovering; specif., *a)* a regaining of something lost or stolen *b)* a return to health, consciousness, etc. *c)* a regaining of balance, self-control, etc. *d)* a retrieval of a capsule, nose cone, etc. after a spaceflight *e)* the removal of valuable substances from waste material, byproducts, etc.

☆**recovery room** a hospital room where patients are kept for close observation and care after having operations

rec·re·ant (rek′rē ənt) *adj.* [OFr. prp. of *recreire*, to surrender allegiance < ML. < L. *re-*, back + *credere*, to believe] 1. *a)* orig., crying for mercy *b)* cowardly 2. disloyal; traitorous —*n.* 1. a coward 2. a disloyal person; traitor —**rec′re·an·cy, rec′re·ance** *n.* —**rec′re·ant·ly** *adv.*

rec·re·ate (rek′rē āt′) *vt.* **-at′ed, -at′ing** [< L. pp. of *recreare*: see RE- & CREATE] to refresh in body or mind, esp. after work, by play, amusement, or relaxation —*vi.* to take recreation —**rec′re·a′tive** *adj.*

re-cre·ate (rē′krē āt′) *vt.* **-at′ed, -at′ing** to create anew —**re′-cre·a′tion** *n.* —**re′-cre·a′tive** *adj.*

rec·re·a·tion (rek′rē ā′shən) *n.* [see RECREATE] 1. refreshment in body or mind, as after work, by some form of play, amusement, or relaxation 2. any form of play, amusement, etc. used for this purpose, as games, sports, etc. —**rec′re·a′tion·al** *adj.*

rec·rim·i·nate (ri krim′ə nāt′) *vi.* **-nat′ed, -nat′ing** [< ML.: see RE- & CRIMINATE] to answer an accuser by accusing him in return —**re·crim′i·na′tion** *n.* —**re·crim′i·na·to·ry** (-nə tôr′ē) *n.* **re·crim′i·na·tive** *adj.*

re·cru·desce (rē′krōō des′) *vi.* **-desced′, -desc′ing** [< L. *re-*, again + *crudescere*, to become harsh < *crudus*, raw] to break out again after being relatively inactive, as a disease, crime, etc. —**re·cru·des′cence** *n.* —**re·cru·des′cent** *adj.*

re·cruit (ri krōōt′) *vt.* [< Fr. < pp. of *recroître*, to grow again < L. *re-*, again + *crescere*, to grow: see CRESCENT] 1. to raise or strengthen (an army, navy, etc.) by enlisting personnel 2. to enlist (personnel) into an army or navy 3. *a)* to enlist (new members) for a party, organization, etc. *b)* to hire or engage the services of [to *recruit* new salespersons] —*vi.* to enlist new personnel, esp. for a military force —*n.* 1. a recently enlisted or drafted soldier, sailor, etc. 2. a new member of any group, etc. —**re·cruit′er** *n.* —**re·cruit′ment** *n.*

rec. sec. recording secretary

rect. 1. receipt 2. rectangle 3. rector 4. rectory

rec·tal (rek′t'l) *adj.* of, for, or near the rectum —**rec′tal·ly** *adv.*

rec·tan·gle (rek′taŋ'g'l) *n.* [Fr. < ML.: see RECTI- & ANGLE[1]] any four-sided plane figure with four right angles

rec·tan·gu·lar (rek taŋ′gyə lər) *adj.* 1. shaped like a rectangle 2. having right-angled corners, as a building 3. right-angled —**rec·tan′gu·lar′i·ty** (-lar′ə tē) *n.* —**rec·tan′gu·lar·ly** *adv.*

RECTANGLES

rectangular coordinates the coordinates in a rectangular Cartesian coordinate system

rec·ti- [LL. < L. *rectus*] *a combining form meaning* straight, right [*rectilinear*]: also, before a vowel, **rect-**

rec·ti·fi·er (rek′tə fī′ər) *n.* 1. a person or thing that rectifies 2. *Elec.* a device that converts alternating current into direct current

rec·ti·fy (rek′tə fī′) *vt.* **-fied′, -fy′ing** [< MFr. < LL.: see RECTI- & -FY] 1. to put right; correct [to *rectify* an error] 2. *Chem.* to refine or purify (a liquid) by distillation 3. *Elec.* to convert (alternating current) to direct current —**rec′ti·fi′a·ble** *adj.* —**rec′ti·fi·ca′tion** *n.*

rec·ti·lin·e·ar (rek′tə lin′ē ər) *adj.* [< LL. < *rectus*, straight + *linea*, LINE[1]] 1. in or forming a straight line 2. bounded, formed, or characterized by straight lines Also **rec′ti·lin′e·al** —**rec′ti·lin′e·ar·ly** *adv.*

rec·ti·tude (rek′tə tōōd′, -tyōōd′) *n.* [MFr. < LL. < L. *rectus*, straight] 1. strict honesty; uprightness of character 2. correctness of judgment or method

rec·to (rek′tō) *n., pl.* **-tos** [< ModL. (*folio*) *recto*, on (the page) to the right] *Printing* any right-hand page of a book; front side of a leaf: opposed to VERSO

rec·tor (rek′tər) *n.* [L. < pp. of *regere*, to rule: see REGAL] 1. a clergyman or minister in charge of a parish, esp. in the Protestant Episcopal Church or an Anglican Church 2. *R.C.Ch.* *a)* a priest in charge of a seminary, college, etc. *b)* [Brit.] the head priest of a parish 3. in certain schools, colleges, etc., the head or headmaster —**rec′tor·ate** (-it) *n.* —**rec·to·ri·al** (-tôr′ē əl) *adj.*

rec·to·ry (rek′tər ē) *n., pl.* **-ries** the residence or dwelling of a clergyman who is a rector

rec·tum (rek′təm) *n., pl.* **-tums, -ta** (-tə) [ModL. < L. *rectum* (*intestinum*), straight (intestine)] the lowest, or last, section of the large intestine, ending at the anus: see illustration at ALIMENTARY CANAL

re·cum·bent (ri kum′bənt) *adj.* [< L. < *re-*, back + *cumbere*, to lie down] 1. lying down; reclining [a *recumbent* figure on the sofa] 2. resting; idle —see SYN. at PRONE —**re·cum′ben·cy** *n.* —**re·cum′bent·ly** *adv.*

re·cu·per·ate (ri kōō′pə rāt′, -kyōō′-) *vt.* **-at′ed, -at′ing** [< L. pp. of *recuperare*, to recover] to get back, or recover (losses, health, etc.) —*vi.* 1. to get well again 2. to recover losses, etc. —**re·cu′per·a′tion** *n.* —**re·cu′per·a·tive** (-pə rāt′iv, -pər ə-tiv), **re·cu′per·a·to·ry** (-ə tôr′ē) *adj.* —**re·cu′per·a′tor** *n.*

re·cur (ri kur′) *vi.* **-curred′, -cur′ring** [< L. < *re-*, back + *currere*, to run: see CURRENT] 1. to turn for aid, safety, etc. (*to*) 2. to return in thought, talk, etc. [to *recur* to a topic] 3. to occur again, as in memory 4. to happen or appear again or from time to time [his fever *recurs* every few months]

re·cur·rent (ri kur′ənt) *adj.* 1. appearing again or from time to time [a *recurrent* dream] 2. turning back in the opposite direction, as some nerves —see SYN. at INTERMITTENT —**re·cur′rence** *n.* —**re·cur′rent·ly** *adv.*

---

re·cross′   re·crown′   re·crys′tal·lize′   re·cul′ti·vate′

re·curve (ri kurv′) **vt., vi. -curved′, -curv′ing** to curve or bend back or backward —**re·cur·vate** (ri kur′vit, -vāt) *adj.*

re·cy·cle (rē sī′k'l) **vt., vi. -cled, -cling 1.** to pass through a cycle again, as for treating **2.** to use again and again, as a single supply of water

red[1] (red) *n.* [OE. *read* < IE. base *reudh-*, red] **1.** a primary color varying in hue from that of blood to pink **2.** a pigment producing this color **3.** [*often* R-] a political radical; esp., a communist ☆**4.** [*often* R-] [*pl.*] N. American Indians **5.** anything colored red, as a red checker piece —*adj.* **red′der, red′dest 1.** of the color red **2.** having red hair **3.** *a)* having a reddish skin *b)* flushed or blushing *c)* bloodshot *d)* sore **4.** [R-] *a)* politically radical; esp., communist *b)* of the Soviet Union — ☆**in the red** in debt or losing money —**see red** [Colloq.] to be or become angry —**red′dish** *adj.* —**red′ness** *n.*

red[2] (red) *vt., vi.* **red, red′ding** *var. of* REDD

re·dact (ri dakt′) *vt.* [< L. pp. of *redigere*, to reduce to order] to arrange in proper form for publication; edit —**re·dac′tor** *n.*

re·dac·tion (ri dak′shən) *n.* **1.** the preparation of written work for publication; editing **2.** an edited work; esp., a reissue or new edition

red algae a group of red, brownish-red, pink, or purple algae that form shrublike masses in the depths of the oceans

red·bait (red′bāt′) *vi., vt.* to accuse publicly (a person or group) of being communist, esp. with little or no valid evidence

red·bird (-burd′) *n.* any of several largely red-colored birds, as the cardinal, scarlet tanager, etc.

red blood cell (or **corpuscle**) *same as* ERYTHROCYTE

red-blood·ed (red′blud′id) *adj.* high-spirited and strong-willed; vigorous, lusty, etc.

red·breast (-brest′) *n.* any of several birds with a reddish breast; esp., the American robin and the European robin

☆**red·bud** (-bud′) *n. same as* JUDAS TREE

red·cap (-kap′) *n.* ☆a porter at a railway station, airport, etc.

red carpet 1. a long red carpet laid out for important guests to walk on, as at a reception ☆**2.** a very grand welcome and entertainment (with *the*) —**roll out the red carpet** (for) to welcome and entertain in a very grand style —**red′-car′pet** *adj.*

☆**red cedar 1.** any of a number of juniper trees or shrubs with bluish, berrylike fruit and red wood **2.** this wood

red clover a kind of clover with flowers in reddish, ball-shaped heads, grown for feeding cattle, horses, sheep, etc.

red·coat (red′kōt′) *n.* a British soldier in a uniform with a red coat, as during the American Revolution

Red Cross 1. a red cross on a white ground, emblem of neutrality in war, used since 1864 to mark hospitals, ambulances, etc. **2.** *a)* an international society (in full, **International Red Cross**) set up to help people in time of war or floods, earthquakes, etc. *b)* any branch of this in various countries

redd (red) *vt., vi.* **redd** or **redd′ed, redd′ing** [< ? OE. *hreddan*, to free] [Colloq.] to make (a place) tidy; put in order (usually with *up*)

red deer 1. a deer native to Europe and Asia ☆**2.** the white-tailed deer when it has its reddish summer coloring

red·den (red′'n) *vt.* to make red —*vi.* to become red; esp., to blush or flush

re·deem (ri dēm′) *vt.* [< MFr. < L. *redimere* < *re(d)-*, back + *emere*, to get] **1.** to get or buy back; recover [he *redeemed* his watch from the pawnshop] **2.** to pay off (a mortgage, etc.) ☆**3.** *a)* to exchange (paper money) for coin or bullion *b)* to exchange (stocks, bonds, etc.) for cash *c)* to turn in (trading stamps or coupons) for a prize, premium, etc. **4.** *a)* to set free by paying a ransom *b)* to rescue from sin and from being punished for one's sins **5.** to carry out or fulfill (a promise or pledge) **6.** *a)* to make up for [her brave act *redeemed* her faults] *b)* to restore (oneself) to favor by making amends *c)* to make worthwhile [a dull book *redeemed* by beautiful illustrations] —**re·deem′a·ble** *adj.* —**re·deem′er** *n.*

re·demp·tion (ri demp′shən) *n.* [OFr. < L. < pp. of *redimere*: see prec.] **1.** a redeeming or being redeemed **2.** something

that redeems —**re·demp′tive, re·demp′to·ry** *adj.*

re·de·ploy (rē′di ploi′) *vt., vi.* to move (troops, etc.) from one front or area to another —**re′de·ploy′ment** *n.*

☆**red fox 1.** the common European fox with reddish fur **2.** the similar related fox of N. America

red-hand·ed (red′han′did) *adv., adj.* **1.** with hands covered with a victim's blood **2.** in the very act of committing a crime **3.** in a situation that makes one seem guilty

red·head (red′hed′) *n.* **1.** a person with red hair ☆**2.** a N. American duck related to the canvasback: the male has a red head —**red′head′ed** *adj.*

☆**redheaded woodpecker** a N. American woodpecker with a bright-red head and neck

red heat 1. the temperature at which a substance is red-hot **2.** the state of being at this temperature

red herring 1. a smoked herring **2.** something used to turn attention away from the basic issue: from the act of drawing a herring across the trace in hunting, to confuse the hounds

red-hot (red′hät′) *adj.* **1.** hot enough to glow; very hot **2.** very excited, angry, etc. **3.** very new; up-to-the-minute [*red-hot* news] —☆*n.* [Colloq.] a frankfurter

red·in·gote (red′iŋ gōt′) *n.* [Fr., altered < E. *riding coat*] **1.** formerly, a man's long, full-skirted overcoat **2.** a long, unlined, lightweight coat, open down the front, worn by women

red·in·te·grate (red in′tə grāt′, ri din′-) *vt.* **-grat·ed, -grat′ing** [< L. pp. of *redintegrare*: see RE- & INTEGRATE] to make whole again; reunite; reestablish —**red·in′te·gra′tion** *n.*

re·di·rect (rē′di rekt′, -dī-) *vt.* to direct again or to a different place —☆*adj. Law* designating the examination of one's own witness again, after his cross-examination by the opposing lawyer —**re′di·rec′tion** *n.*

re·dis·count (rē dis′kount) *vt.* to discount (esp. commercial paper) for a second time —*n.* **1.** a rediscounting **2.** rediscounted commercial paper —**re′dis·count′a·ble** *adj.*

☆**re·dis·trict** (rē dis′trikt) *vt.* to divide anew into districts, esp. so as to reapportion representatives

red lead red oxide of lead, Pb_3O_4, used in making paint, in glassmaking, etc.

red-let·ter (red′let′ər) *adj.* designating a memorable or joyous day or event: from the custom of marking holidays on the calendar in red ink

red light 1. any danger or warning signal **2.** a red stoplight

☆**red·lin·ing** (red′lī′niŋ) *n.* [from the practice of outlining such areas in red on a map] the refusal as by some banks and insurance companies to issue mortgage loans or insurance on property in certain neighborhoods thought of by them as dropping in value

red man ☆a North American Indian

red meat meat that is red before cooking; esp., beef or mutton as distinguished from pork, veal, poultry, etc.

re·do (rē dōō′) *vt.* **-did′, -done′, -do′ing 1.** to do again or do over **2.** to redecorate (a room, etc.)

☆**red oak 1.** any of several oaks having leaves with sharp-tipped lobes, dark bark, and reddish wood **2.** this wood

red ocher a red, earthy hematite, used as a pigment

red·o·lent (red′'l ənt) *adj.* [OFr. < L. prp. of *redolere* < *re(d)-*, thoroughly + *olere*, to smell] **1.** sweet-smelling **2.** smelling (*of*) [*redolent* of tar] **3.** suggestive (*of*) [a song *redolent* of young love] —**red′o·lence** *n.* —**red′o·lent·ly** *adv.*

Re·don·do Beach (rə dän′dō) [< Sp. *redondo*, circular] city in SW Calif., on the Pacific: suburb of Los Angeles: pop. 56,000

re·dou·ble (rē dub′'l) *vt.* **-bled, -bling** [MFr. *redoubler*: see RE- & DOUBLE] **1.** *a)* to increase fourfold *b)* to make twice as much or twice as great *c)* to make much greater [to *redouble* one's efforts] **2.** to refold —*vi.* **1.** *a)* to become twice as great or twice as much *b)* to increase fourfold **2.** [Archaic] to re-

REDIN-
GOTE

---

fat, āpe, cär, ten, ēven, is, bīte; gō, hôrn, tōōl, look; oil, out; up, fur; get; joy; yet; chin; she; thin, then; zh, leisure; ŋ, ring; ə for *a* in *ago*, *e* in *agent*, *i* in *sanity*, *o* in *comply*, *u* in *focus*; ′ as in *able* (ā′b'l); Fr. bal; ë, Fr. coeur; ö, Fr. feu; Fr. mon; ô, Fr. coq; ü, Fr. duc; r, Fr. cri; H, G. ich; kh, G. doch; ‡foreign; ☆ Americanism; < derived from. See inside front cover.

echo **3.** to turn sharply backward [to *redouble* on one's tracks] **4.** *Bridge* to double a bid that an opponent has already doubled —*n.* a redoubling

re·doubt (ri dout′) *n.* [< Fr. < It. *ridotto* < ML. *reductus*, orig. pp. of L. *reducere*: see REDUCE] **1.** a breastwork outside or within a fortification **2.** any stronghold

re·doubt·a·ble (ri dout′ə b'l) *adj.* [< MFr. < *redouter*, to fear < L. *re-*, thoroughly + *dubitare*, to doubt] **1.** causing fear [a *redoubtable* enemy] **2.** commanding respect [a *redoubtable* planner] —**re·doubt′a·bly** *adv.*

re·dound (ri dound′) *vi.* [< MFr. < L. *redundare*, to overflow < *re(d)-*, thoroughly + *undare*, to surge] **1.** to have a result (*to* the credit or discredit of someone or something) **2.** to come back; recoil (*upon*): said of honor or disgrace

red pepper **1.** a plant of the nightshade family with a red, many-seeded fruit, as the cayenne **2.** the fruit **3.** the ground fruit or seeds, used for seasoning

red·poll (red′pōl′) *n.* any of a number of finches the males of which usually have a red crown

re·dress (ri dres′; *for n., usually* rē′dres) *vt.* [< OFr.: see RE- & DRESS] **1.** to set right; rectify, as by making up for (a wrong, injury, etc.) **2.** [Now Rare] to make amends to —*n.* **1.** something done to make up for a wrong, injury, etc. **2.** a redressing —**re·dress′a·ble** *adj.* —**re·dress′er** *n.*

re-dress (rē′dres′) *vt.* to dress again

Red River **1.** river flowing along the Tex.-Okla. border, through Ark. & La. into the Mississippi **2.** river flowing along the N.Dak.-Minn. border into Lake Winnipeg in Manitoba: in full, **Red River of the North**

red salmon *same as* SOCKEYE

Red Sea sea between NE Africa & W Arabia, connected with the Mediterranean Sea by the Suez Canal

☆**red·shirt** (red′shʉrt′) *vt.* [from red shirts worn by a scrimmage team] [Slang] to withdraw (a player) from the varsity team so that he will be eligible to play an extra year later —*n.* such a player

☆**red snapper** a reddish, deep-water food fish, found in the Gulf of Mexico and in nearby Atlantic waters

red spider a small, red mite that eats green plants

☆**red squirrel** a N. American tree squirrel, with reddish fur

red·start (red′stärt′) *n.* [RED¹ + obs. *start*, tail] ☆**1.** an American fly-catching warbler **2.** a small European warbler with a reddish tail

red tape [from the tape used to tie official papers] **1.** official forms and routines **2.** too great attention to routine and regulations, causing delay in getting business done

☆**red tide** a reddish coloring found in sea waters, caused by large numbers of certain red protozoans that release poisons that kill fishes and other organisms

red·top (-täp′) *n.* ☆a grass grown in the cooler parts of N. America for hay, pastures, and lawns

re·duce (ri dōōs′, -dyōōs′) *vt.* -duced′, -duc′ing [< L. < *re-*, back + *ducere*, to lead: for IE. base see DUKE] **1.** *a)* to lessen in any way, as in size, amount, value, price, etc. [to *reduce* taxes] *b)* to put into a simpler form [to *reduce* the lecture to a brief summary] **2.** to bring into a certain order; systematize [he *reduced* his research to a series of articles] **3.** to change into a different form, as by melting, grinding, etc. [to *reduce* almonds to a paste] **4.** to lower, as in rank; demote [the sergeant was *reduced* to a private] **5.** *a)* to bring to order, obedience, etc., as by persuasion or force *b)* to subdue or conquer [the army *reduced* the enemy fort] **6.** *a)* to bring into difficult circumstances [they were *reduced* to poverty] *b)* to force to do something because one is poor, needy, etc. [he was *reduced* to stealing] **7.** to make thin [she is *reduced* to skin and bones] **8.** *Arith.* to change in denomination or form without changing in value [to *reduce* 4/8 to 1/2] **9.** *Chem. a)* to decrease the positive valence of (an atom or ion) *b)* to increase the number of electrons of (an atom or ion) *c)* to remove the oxygen from *d)* to combine with hydrogen *e)* to bring into the metallic state by removing nonmetallic elements **10.** *Photog.* to weaken the density of (a negative) **11.** *Surgery* to restore to normal position [to *reduce* a fracture] —*vi.* **1.** to become reduced **2.** to lose weight, as by being on a diet —see SYN. at DECREASE —**re·duc′er** *n.* —**re·duc′i·bil′i·ty** *n.* —**re·duc′i·ble** *adj.* —**re·duc′i·bly** *adv.*

reducing agent *Chem.* any substance that reduces another substance and is itself oxidized in the process

‡**re·duc·ti·o ad ab·sur·dum** (ri duk′tē ō′ ad ab sʉr′dəm, -shē ō′) [L., lit., reduction to absurdity] *Logic* the disproof of a proposition by showing the logical conclusions drawn from it to be absurd

re·duc·tion (ri duk′shən) *n.* **1.** *a)* a reducing or being reduced *b)* the amount of this [a ten-pound *reduction* in weight] **2.** anything made or brought about by reducing, as a smaller copy —**re·duc′tion·al** *adj.* —**re·duc′tive** *adj.* —**re·duc′tive·ly** *adv.*

re·dun·dan·cy (ri dun′dən sē) *n., pl.* -**cies** **1.** a being redundant **2.** an overabundance **3.** the use of redundant or unnecessary words **4.** the part of a statement that is redundant or unnecessary Also **re·dun′dance**

re·dun·dant (-dənt) *adj.* [< L. prp. of *redundare*: see REDOUND] **1.** more than enough; excess; superfluous **2.** using more words than are needed; wordy [it is *redundant* to say "take daily doses every day"] **3.** unnecessary to the meaning: said of words and affixes —see SYN. at WORDY —**re·dun′dant·ly** *adv.*

re·du·pli·cate (ri dōō′plə kāt′, -dyōō′-; *for adj. & n., usually* -kit) *vt.* -cat′ed, -cat′ing [< ML.: see RE- & DUPLICATE] **1.** to redouble, double, or repeat **2.** to double (a syllable or word) to form a new word (as *tom-tom*), sometimes with changes (as *chitchat*) —*vi.* to become reduplicated —*adj.* reduplicated; doubled —*n.* something reduplicated —**re·du′pli·ca′tion** *n.* —**re·du′pli·ca′tive** *adj.*

red·wing (red′wiŋ′) *n.* **1.** a small European thrush with an orange-red patch on the underside of the wings ☆**2.** *same as* RED-WINGED BLACKBIRD

☆**red-winged blackbird** a N. American blackbird with a bright-red patch on the top surface of the wings in the male: also **redwing blackbird**

red·wood (-wood′) *n.* ☆**1.** a giant evergreen having long-lasting, soft wood, found on the coast of California and southern Oregon ☆**2.** *same as* BIG TREE **3.** the wood of these trees

Redwood City [< the *redwoods* orig. there] city in W Calif., on San Francisco Bay: suburb of San Francisco: pop. 56,000

Redwood National Park national park in NW Calif., containing groves of redwood trees

re·ech·o, re-ech·o (rē ek′ō) *vt., vi.* -ech′oed, -ech′o·ing to echo back or again; resound —*n., pl.* -ech′oes the echo of an echo Also **re-ech′o**

reed (rēd) *n.* [OE. *hreod*] **1.** *a)* any of various tall, slender grasses growing in wet or marshy land *b)* the stem of any of these *c)* such plants as a group **2.** a musical pipe made from a hollow stem **3.** *Music a)* a thin strip of some flexible substance placed within the opening of the mouthpiece of certain wind instruments, as the clarinet: when vibrated by the breath, it produces a musical tone *b)* an instrument with a reed *c)* in some organs, a similar device that vibrates in a current of air

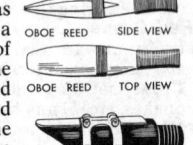

OBOE REED   SIDE VIEW
OBOE REED   TOP VIEW
CLARINET REED   SIDE VIEW
REEDS

Reed (rēd), **Walter** 1851–1902; U.S. army surgeon & bacteriologist

reed organ an organ with a set of free metal reeds instead of pipes to produce the tones

re·ed·u·cate, re-ed·u·cate (rē ej′ə kāt′) *vt.* -cat′ed, -cat′ing to educate anew, esp. so as to rehabilitate or adapt to new situations: also **re·ĕd′u·cate′** —**re·ed′u·ca′tion, re-ed′u·ca′tion** *n.* —**re·ed′u·ca′tive, re-ed′u·ca′tive** *adj.*

reed·y (rēd′ē) *adj.* **reed′i·er, reed′i·est** **1.** full of reeds **2.** made of reed or reeds **3.** like a reed; slender, fragile, etc. **4.** sounding like a reed instrument; thin; piping [a high, *reedy* voice] —**reed′i·ly** *adv.* —**reed′i·ness** *n.*

reef¹ (rēf) *n.* [prob. < ON. *rif*, a rib] a ridge of rock, coral, or sand lying at or near the surface of the water —see SYN. at SHOAL²

reef² (rēf) *n.* [< or akin to prec.] **1.** a part of a sail which can be folded and tied down to reduce the area exposed to the wind **2.** the act of reefing —*vt.* **1.** to reduce (a sail) by taking in part of it **2.** to lower (a spar or mast) or reduce the projection of (a bowsprit)

reef·er (rē′fər) *n.* **1.** a person who reefs **2.** a short, thick, double-breasted coat like a seaman's jacket ☆**3.** [from the rolled appearance of a *reef* (of a sail)] [Slang] a marijuana cigarette

reef knot a square knot used for reefing

reek (rēk) *n.* [OE. *rec*] **1.** vapor; fume **2.** a strong, unpleasant smell; stench —*vi.* **1.** to give off steam or smoke; fume **2.** to have a strong, unpleasant smell **3.** to be spread through with anything very unpleasant [her remark *reeked* of jealousy] —*vt.* to send out or give off (vapor, fumes, etc.) —**reek′y** *adj.*

reel[1] (rēl) *vi.* [< the *n.*] **1.** to give way or fall back; sway or stagger as from being struck **2.** to move in an unsteady way, as from dizziness **3.** to go around and around; whirl [the room seemed to *reel* before his eyes] **4.** to feel dizzy —*vt.* to cause to reel —*n.* [OE. *hreol*] a reeling motion; whirl, stagger, etc. —see **SYN.** at STAGGER

reel[2] (rēl) *n.* [prob. < REEL[1], *n.*] **1.** *a*) a lively Scottish dance *b*) same as VIRGINIA REEL **2.** music for either of these

reel[3] (rēl) *n.* [OE. *hreol*] **1.** a frame or spool on which thread, wire, film, etc. is wound **2.** such a frame on a fishing rod for winding line **3.** the quantity of wire, thread, film, etc. usually wound on one reel **4.** in a lawn mower, a set of spiral steel blades turning on a horizontal bar —*vt., vi.* to wind on a reel —**reel in 1.** to wind on a reel **2.** to pull in (a fish) by winding a line on a reel —**reel off** to tell, write, etc. easily and quickly —**reel out** to unwind from a reel —☆(**right**) **off the reel** without hesitation or pause

re·en·force, re·en·force (rē′in fôrs′) *vt.* **-forced′, -forc′ing** same as REINFORCE: also **re′ën·force′**

re-en·try, re-en·try (rē en′trē) *n., pl.* **-tries 1.** a reentering; specif., a coming back, as of a space vehicle, into the earth's atmosphere **2.** a second or repeated entry **3.** *Bridge, Whist* a card that will win a trick and regain the lead Also **re·ën′try**

reeve[1] (rēv) *n.* [OE. *gerefa*] **1.** in English history, *a*) the chief officer of a town or district *b*) the overseer of a manor; steward **2.** the elected head of a town council in certain Canadian provinces

reeve[2] (rēv) *vt.* **reeved** or **rove, rove** or **rov′en, reev′ing** [prob. < Du. *reven*] *Naut.* **1.** to slip (a rope, etc.) through a block, ring, etc. **2.** *a*) to pass in, through, or around something *b*) to fasten by so doing **3.** to pass a rope through (a block or pulley)

ref (ref) *n., vt., vi. same as* REFEREE

ref. **1.** referee **2.** reference **3.** reformed

re·fec·tion (ri fek′shən) *n.* [OFr. < L. < pp. of *reficere* < *re-*, again + *facere*, to make] **1.** food or drink taken to refresh oneself **2.** a light meal

re·fec·to·ry (ri fek′tər ē) *n., pl.* **-ries** a dining hall in a monastery, convent, college, etc.

re·fer (ri fur′) *vt.* **-ferred′, -fer′ring** [< MFr. < L. *referre* < *re-*, back + *ferre*, to BEAR[1]] **1.** to assign or trace back (to) something as being the cause or origin [she *referred* her headaches to her accident] **2.** to assign or think of as belonging (*to* a kind, class, etc.) [he *referred* that type of bacteria to the second group] **3.** to present (*to*), as for help in settling [we *referred* our argument to the teacher] **4.** to direct (*to* someone or something) for aid, information, etc. —*vi.* **1.** to relate or apply (*to*) **2.** to direct attention, or make reference (*to*) [to *refer* to an earlier event] **3.** to turn for information, aid, etc. (*to*) [to *refer* to a map] —**ref·er·a·ble** (ref′ər ə b′l), **re·fer′ra·ble, re·fer′ri·ble** (ri fur′-) *adj.* —**re·fer′rer** *n.*

SYN.—*refer* implies the direct mentioning of something in an open, deliberate way [he *referred* in detail to their dishonest practices]; *allude* implies the indirect mentioning of something, as by a hint, a figure of speech, etc. [although he used different names, he was *alluding* to his parents]

ref·er·ee (ref′ə rē′) *n.* **1.** a person to whom something is referred for help in settling **2.** an official who sees to it that the rules are followed in certain sports contests **3.** *Law* a person appointed by a court to study, and report on, a matter —*vt., vi.* **-eed′, -ee′ing** to act as referee (in)

ref·er·ence (ref′ər əns, ref′rəns) *n.* **1.** a referring or being referred **2.** relation; connection; regard [in *reference* to his let-

ter] **3.** *a*) the direction of attention to a person or thing *b*) a mention or allusion [she made no *reference* to the accident] **4.** *a*) a mention, as in a book, of some other work where information can be found *b*) the work so mentioned *c*) a number or symbol (in full, **reference mark**) directing the reader to a footnote, etc. **5.** *a*) the giving of the name of a person who can offer information or recommendation *b*) the person so indicated *c*) a written statement giving the qualifications, abilities, etc. of someone seeking a position, etc. **6.** *a*) a source of information: often used like an adjective [*reference* books] *b*) a book, etc. used for reference —*vt.* **-enced, -enc·ing** to provide with references —**make reference to** to refer to; mention —**ref·er·en′tial** (-ə ren′shəl) *adj.* —**ref′er·en′tial·ly** *adv.*

ref·er·en·dum (ref′ə ren′dəm) *n., pl.* **-dums** or **-da** (-də) [ModL. < L., gerund of *referre:* see REFER] ☆**1.** the placing of a law, proposed or already in effect, before the people for a direct vote ☆**2.** the right of the people to vote on such laws, thus overruling the legislature ☆**3.** the vote itself

ref·er·ent (ref′ər ənt) *n.* something referred to; specif., *Linguis.* the thing referred to by a term or expression

re·fer·ral (ri fur′əl) *n.* **1.** a referring or being referred, as to someone for professional service **2.** a person who is referred or directed to another person, an agency, etc.

re·fill (rē fil′; *for n.* rē′fil) *vt., vi.* to fill again —*n.* a new filling; esp., *a*) a unit to replace the used-up contents of a container [a *refill* for a ball point pen] *b*) any additional filling of a prescription for medicine —**re·fill′a·ble** *adj.*

re·fi·nance (rē′fə nans′, rē fī′nans) *vt.* **-nanced, -nanc′ing** to finance again; specif., to provide or obtain a new loan or more capital for

re·fine (ri fīn′) *vt., vi.* **-fined′, -fin′ing** [RE- + FINE[1], *v.*] **1.** to free or become free from impurities, dross, etc.; purify [to *refine* sugar] **2.** to free or become free from imperfection, coarseness, etc.; make or become more polished [to *refine* one's style of writing] **3.** to make or become more subtle or exact [to *refine* one's technique] —**refine on** (or **upon**) to improve, as by adding refinements —**re·fin′er** *n.*

re·fined (ri fīnd′) *adj.* **1.** made free from impurities; purified [*refined* sugar] **2.** free from coarseness; cultivated; elegant [*refined* manners] **3.** characterized by great subtlety, exactness, etc.

re·fine·ment (ri fīn′mənt) *n.* **1.** *a*) a refining or being refined *b*) the result of this **2.** delicacy or elegance of language, speech, manners, etc.; polish [a woman of *refinement*] **3.** a development; improvement; elaboration [he made several *refinements* in his plan] **4.** a subtle or precise point of difference

re·fin·er·y (ri fīn′ər ē) *n., pl.* **-er·ies** a place or plant where some raw material, such as oil, metal, sugar, etc., is refined or purified

re·fin·ish (rē fin′ish) *vt.* to give a new surface to (wood, etc.) —**re·fin′ish·er** *n.*

re·fit (rē fit′; *also for n.* rē′fit′) *vt., vi.* **-fit′ted, -fit′ting** to make or be made ready or fit for use again, as by repairing, reequipping, etc. —*n.* an act or instance of refitting

refl. **1.** reflection **2.** reflex **3.** reflexive

re·flect (ri flekt′) *vt.* [< MFr. < L. < *re-*, back + *flectere*, to bend] **1.** to bend or throw back (light, heat, or sound) **2.** to give back an image of; mirror or reproduce [the calm lake *reflected* the trees on the shore] **3.** to bring back as a result (with *on*) [deeds that *reflect* honor on him] **4.** to express or show [skills that *reflect* years of training] **5.** to recollect or realize after thought (*that*) [he *reflected* that he had left the door unlocked] **6.** to fold or turn back [a *reflected* leaf] —*vi.* **1.** to be thrown back [light *reflecting* from the water] **2.** to throw back light, heat, etc. [a *reflecting* surface] **3.** *a*) to give back an image *b*) to be mirrored **4.** to think seriously; contemplate (*on*

---

fat, āpe, cär; ten, ēven; is, bīte; gō, hôrn, tōōl, look; oil, out; up, fur; get; joy; yet; chin; she; thin, *th*en; zh, leisure; ŋ, ring; ə for *a* in *ago*, *e* in *agent*, *i* in *sanity*, *o* in *comply*, *u* in *focus*; ′ as in *able* (ā′b'l); Fr. bal; ë, Fr. coeur; ö, Fr. feu; Fr. mon; ô, Fr. coq; ü, Fr. duc; *r*, Fr. cri; H, G. ich; kh, G. doch; ‡foreign; ☆ Americanism; < derived from. See inside front cover.

or *upon*) [he *reflected* on his past mistakes] **5.** to bring blame or discredit (*on* or *upon*) [that act *reflects* on his honesty] —see **SYN.** at CONSIDER and THINK[1]

re·flec·tance (-flek′t’ns) *n. Physics* the ratio of the total electromagnetic radiation, usually light, reflected by a surface to the total striking the surface

re·flec·tion (ri flek′shən) *n.* **1.** a reflecting or being reflected **2.** the throwing back by a surface of sound, light, etc. **3.** anything reflected; specif., an image; likeness [one's *reflection* in a mirror] **4.** *a*) serious thought; contemplation [after much *reflection*, he began to write] *b*) an idea, remark, etc. that comes from such thought **5.** *a*) blame; discredit *b*) a statement or action bringing blame or discredit [that joke was not meant as a *reflection* on his skill] **6.** *Anat.* a bending back on itself —**re·flec′tion·al** *adj.*

re·flec·tive (-tiv) *adj.* **1.** reflecting **2.** of or produced by reflection **3.** meditative; thoughtful [a *reflective* poem] —see **SYN.** at PENSIVE —**re·flec′tive·ly** *adv.* —**re·flec′tive·ness, re′flec·tiv′i·ty** *n.*

re·flec·tor (-tər) *n.* **1.** a person or thing that reflects; esp., a surface, object, or device that reflects radiant energy, as light, sound, etc. **2.** a reflecting telescope: see TELESCOPE

re·flex (rē′fleks; for v. ri fleks′) *n.* [< L. pp. of *reflectere*: see REFLECT] **1.** reflection, as of light **2.** a reflected image or reproduction **3.** an action of the muscles or glands caused by a stimulus sent through nerves in an automatic way, without being controlled by the mind or by thinking [when the doctor strikes a patient's knee to see if the lower leg will jerk, he is testing a *reflex*] **4.** any quick, automatic or habitual response **5.** [*pl.*] ability to react quickly and effectively [a boxer with good *reflexes*] —*adj.* **1.** turned or bent back **2.** coming in reaction; esp., of or having to do with a reflex (sense 3) **3.** *Geom.* designating an angle greater than a straight angle (180°) —*vt.* to bend, turn, or fold back —**re′flex·ly** *adv.*

REFLEX ANGLE

reflex arc the entire nerve path involved in a reflex (sense 3)

reflex camera a camera in which the image formed by the lens is reflected by a mirror onto a glass plate to help in focusing the lens

re·flex·ion (ri flek′shən) *n. Brit. var. of* REFLECTION

re·flex·ive (-siv) *adj.* **1.** [Rare] reflex **2.** *Gram. a*) designating a verb whose subject and direct object refer to the same person or thing (Example: *wash* in "I wash myself") *b*) designating a pronoun used as the direct object of such a verb, as *myself* in the above example —*n.* a reflexive verb or pronoun —**reflex′ive·ly** *adv.* —**re·flex′ive·ness, re·flex·iv·i·ty** (rē′fleksiv′ə tē) *n.*

ref·lu·ent (ref′loo wənt) *adj.* [< L. prp. of *refluere*, to flow back] flowing back; ebbing, as the tide to the sea —**ref′lu·ence** *n.*

re·flux (rē′fluks′) *n.* [< L. pp. of *refluere*: see prec.] a flowing back; ebb

re·for·est (rē fôr′ist, -fär′-) *vt., vi.* to plant new trees on (land once forested) —**re′for·est·a′tion** *n.*

re·form (ri fôrm′) *vt.* [< OFr. < L. *reformare*: see RE- & FORM] **1.** to make better by removing faults; correct [to *reform* a calendar] **2.** *a*) to make better by stopping wrongs, introducing better procedures, etc. [to *reform* working conditions in a factory] *b*) to put a stop to (wrongs, etc.) **3.** to cause (a person) to give up bad conduct and behave better —*vi.* to become better; give up one's bad ways [the outlaw *reformed* and became a useful citizen] —*n.* **1.** a correction of faults or evils, as in government or society **2.** an improvement in character and conduct —*adj.* ☆[R-] designating or of a movement in Judaism that emphasizes its ethical aspects rather than a strict observance of traditional ritual —**re·form′a·ble** *adj.* —**re·form′a·tive** *adj.* —**re·formed′** *adj.*

re-form (rē′fôrm′) *vt., vi.* to form again

ref·or·ma·tion (ref′ər mā′shən) *n.* **1.** a reforming or being reformed **2.** [R-] the 16th-cent. religious movement that aimed at reforming the Roman Catholic Church and resulted in establishing the Protestant churches —**ref′or·ma′tion·al** *adj.*

☆**re·form·a·to·ry** (ri fôr′mə tôr′ē) *adj.* reforming or aiming at reform —*n., pl.* -**ries** **1.** an institution to which young people who have broken the law are sent for training and discipline intended to reform them: also **reform school** **2.** a prison for women

reformed spelling any of various systems suggested for simplifying the spelling of English words, esp. by spelling them according to the way they sound and by dropping those letters that are not pronounced

re·form·er (ri fôr′mər) *n.* a person who seeks to bring about reform, esp. political or social reform

re·form·ism (-miz′m) *n.* the practice or support of reform, esp. political or social reform —**re·form′ist** *n., adj.*

re·fract (ri frakt′) *vt.* [< L. *refractus*, pp. of *refringere* < *re-*, back + *frangere*, to break] **1.** to cause (a ray or wave of light, heat, or sound) to bend by refraction **2.** *Optics* to measure the degree of refraction of (an eye or lens) —**re·frac′tive** *adj.* —**re·frac′tive·ly** *adv.* —**re·frac·tiv·i·ty** (rē′frak tiv′ə tē), **re·frac′tive·ness** *n.*

re·frac·tion (ri frak′shən) *n.* **1.** the bending of a ray or wave of light, heat, or sound, as it passes on a slant from one medium to another of different density **2.** *Optics* the ability of the eye to refract light entering it, so as to form an image on the retina

refractive index *same as* INDEX OF REFRACTION

re·frac·tor (ri frak′tər) *n.* **1.** something that refracts **2.** a refracting telescope: see TELESCOPE

re·frac·to·ry (ri frak′tər ē) *adj.* [< L. < *refractus*: see REFRACT] **1.** hard to manage; stubborn; obstinate [a *refractory* horse] **2.** resistant to heat; hard to melt or work: said of ores or metals **3.** not responding to treatment, as a disease —**re·frac′to·ri·ly** *adv.* —**re·frac′to·ri·ness** *n.*

re·frain[1] (ri frān′) *vi.* [< OFr. < L. < *re-*, back + *frenare*, to curb < *frenum*, a rein] to hold back; keep oneself (*from* doing something); forbear

SYN.—refrain usually suggests the curbing of an impulse in keeping oneself from saying or doing something [although angered, he *refrained* from answering]; **abstain** implies voluntary self-denial or the giving up of something on purpose [to *abstain* from liquor]; **forbear** suggests self-control showing patience and an ability to stay calm when irritated [to *forbear* becoming angry]

re·frain[2] (ri frān′) *n.* [MFr., ult. < L. *refringere*: see REFRACT] **1.** a phrase or verse repeated from time to time in a song or poem, as after each stanza **2.** music for this

re·fran·gi·ble (ri fran′jə b'l) *adj.* [< RE- + L. *frangere*, to break + -IBLE] that can be refracted, as light rays —**re·fran′gi·bil′i·ty, re·fran′gi·ble·ness** *n.*

re·fresh (ri fresh′) *vt.* [< OFr.: see RE- & FRESH[1]] **1.** to make fresh by cooling, wetting, etc. [rains *refreshing* parched plants] **2.** to make (another or oneself) feel cooler, stronger, etc., as by food, drink, or sleep **3.** to make full or complete again, as by new supplies, etc. **4.** to stimulate (the memory, etc.) —*vi.* **1.** to become fresh again; revive **2.** to take refreshment, as food or drink —**re·fresh′er** *n.* —**re·fresh′ing** *adj.* —**re·fresh′ing·ly** *adv.*

refresher course a course of study reviewing material previously studied

re·fresh·ment (ri fresh′mənt) *n.* **1.** a refreshing or being refreshed **2.** something that refreshes, as food, drink, etc. **3.** [*pl.*] food or drink or both, esp. when not a full meal

re·frig·er·ant (ri frij′ər ənt) *adj.* **1.** that refrigerates; cooling or freezing **2.** reducing heat or fever —*n.* **1.** a substance used to reduce fever **2.** a substance used in refrigeration; specif., any of various liquids that become vapor at a low temperature, used in mechanical refrigeration

re·frig·er·ate (-ə rāt′) *vt.* -**at′ed, -at′ing** [< L. pp. of *refrigerare* < *re-*, thoroughly + *frigerare*, to cool < *frigus*, cold] **1.** to make or keep cool or cold; chill **2.** to preserve (food, etc.) by keeping cold or freezing —**re·frig′er·a′tion** *n.* —**re·frig′er·a′tive, re·frig′er·a·to′ry** *adj.*

re·frig·er·a·tor (-rāt′ər) *n.* something that refrigerates; esp., a box, cabinet, or room in which food, etc. is kept cool, as by ice or mechanical refrigeration

reft (reft) *alt. pt. & pp. of* REAVE —*adj.* robbed or deprived (*of* something); bereft

ref·uge (ref′yōoj) *n.* [< OFr. < L., ult. < *re-*, back + *fugere*, to flee] **1.** shelter or protection from danger, difficulty, etc. [he

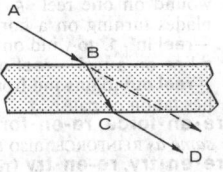
REFRACTION
(AB, entering light ray; BC, refracted ray; CD, emerging ray)

sought *refuge* from his enemies*]* **2.** a place of safety; shelter; safe retreat *[a wildlife *refuge]*

ref·u·gee (ref′yoo jē′, ref′yoo jē′) *n.* a person who flees from his home or country to seek refuge elsewhere, as in a time of war, persecution, etc.

re·ful·gent (ri ful′jənt) *adj.* [< L. prp. of *refulgere:* see RE- & FULGENT] shining; radiant; glowing —**re·ful′gence, re·ful′gen·cy** *n.* —**re·ful′gent·ly** *adv.*

re·fund[1] (ri fund′; *for n.* rē′fund′) *vt., vi.* [< MFr. < L. < *re-,* back + *fundere,* to pour] to give back (money, etc.); repay *[they *refunded* her tuition when she had to leave school]* —*n.* the act of refunding or the amount refunded; repayment —**re·fund′a·ble** *adj.*

re·fund[2] (rē′fund′) *vt.* to fund again or anew; specif., *Finance* to use borrowed money, as from the sale of a bond issue, to pay back (a loan)

re·fur·bish (ri fur′bish) *vt.* [RE- + FURBISH] to brighten, freshen, or polish up again; renovate —**re·fur′bish·ment** *n.*

re·fus·al (ri fyoo′z'l) *n.* **1.** the act of refusing **2.** the right or chance to accept or refuse something before it is offered to another; option *[he has first *refusal* on her car if she sells it]*

re·fuse[1] (ri fyooz′) *vt.* **-fused′, -fus′ing** [< OFr. *refuser,* ult. < L. pp. of *refundere:* see REFUND[1]] **1.** to say that one will not accept; reject *[to *refuse* a gift; to *refuse* a suggestion]* **2.** to say that one will not do, give, grant, obey, etc.; deny *[to *refuse* a request; to *refuse* to go]* **3.** to stop short at (a fence, etc.) without jumping it: said of a horse —*vi.* to say that one will not accept, agree to, or do something —see SYN. at DECLINE —**re·fus′er** *n.*

ref·use[2] (ref′yoos, -yooz) *n.* [< OFr. pp. of *refuser:* see prec.] anything thrown away or rejected as worthless or useless; waste; rubbish —*adj.* thrown away or rejected as worthless or useless

ref·u·ta·tion (ref′yə tā′shən) *n.* **1.** the act of refuting **2.** something that refutes, as an argument Also **re·fut·al** (ri fyoot′'l)

re·fute (ri fyoot′) *vt.* **-fut′ed, -fut′ing** [L. *refutare,* to repel: see RE- & CONFUTE] **1.** to prove (a person) to be wrong; confute **2.** to prove (an argument or statement) to be false or wrong, by argument or evidence —see SYN. at DISPROVE —**re·fut′a·ble** (-fyoot′ə b'l, ref′yoot tə-) *adj.* —**re·fut′a·bly** *adv.* —**re·fut′er** *n.*

reg. 1. regiment **2.** region **3.** register **4.** registered **5.** registrar **6.** regular **7.** regulation

re·gain (ri gān′) *vt.* **1.** to get back again; recover *[he *regained* his health slowly]* **2.** to succeed in reaching again; get back to *[the boat *regained* the harbor]* —see SYN. at RECOVER

re·gal (rē′gəl) *adj.* [MFr. < L. *regalis* < *regis,* genitive of *rex,* a king < IE. base *reg-,* straight, direct] **1.** of a king; royal **2.** characteristic of, like, or fit for a king; splendid, stately, etc. —**re·gal·i·ty** (rē gal′ə tē) *n.* —**re′gal·ly** *adv.*

re·gale (ri gāl′) *vt.* **-galed′, -gal′ing** [< Fr. < *ré-* (see RE-) + OFr. *gale,* joy] **1.** to entertain by providing a splendid feast **2.** to delight with something pleasing or amusing *[to *regale* listeners with jokes]* —*vi.* to feast —**re·gale′ment** *n.*

re·ga·li·a (ri gāl′yə, -gā′lē ə) *n.pl.* [L., neut. pl. of *regalis:* see REGAL] **1.** the emblems and symbols of kingship, as a crown, scepter, etc. **2.** the special decorations worn by a member of a certain order, society, etc. **3.** splendid clothes; finery

re·gard (ri gärd′) *n.* [< OFr. < *regarder:* see RE- & GUARD] **1.** a firm, fixed look; gaze **2.** consideration; attention; concern *[have *regard* for your health]* **3.** respect and affection; esteem *[to have high *regard* for one's teachers]* **4.** reference; respect; relation *[in *regard* to your plan]* **5.** *[pl.]* good wishes; respects *[give my *regards* to Sue]* —*vt.* **1.** to look at with a firm, steady gaze **2.** to take into account; consider *[he never *regards* the feelings of others]* **3.** [Archaic] to give attentive heed to **4.** to hold in affection and respect *[to *regard* one's friends highly]* **5.** to think of in a certain way *[to *regard* taxes as a burden]* **6.** to have relation to; concern *[this *regards* your welfare]* —**as regards** concerning —**without regard to** without considering

SYN. —regard usually implies a judging of someone or something according to its worth or value *[the book is highly *regarded* by critics]*; **respect** implies a judging to have great worth or high value, as shown by courtesy or honor *[a jurist *respected* by lawyers]*; **esteem,** in addition, suggests that the person or object is highly prized or desired *[a friend es-

teemed for his loyalty]*; **admire** suggests a feeling of enthusiastic delight in appreciating something or someone that is superior *[one must *admire* such courage]*

re·gard·ful (-fəl) *adj.* **1.** observant; heedful; mindful (*of*) **2.** showing regard; respectful —**re·gard′ful·ly** *adv.*

re·gard·ing (-iŋ) *prep.* with regard to; concerning; about

re·gard·less (-lis) *adj.* without regard; heedless; careless —☆ *adv.* [Colloq.] without regard for objections, difficulties, etc.; anyway *[we protested, but she went *regardless]* —**regardless of** in spite of; notwithstanding *[*regardless* of the cost]*

re·gat·ta (ri gät′ə, -gat′-) *n.* [It.] **1.** a boat race **2.** a series of such races

re·gen·cy (rē′jən sē) *n., pl.* **-cies 1.** the position, function, or authority of a regent or group of regents **2.** a group of persons serving as regents **3.** a country governed by a regent or a group of regents **4.** the time during which a regent or regency governs; specif., [R-] in England, the period between 1811 and 1820

re·gen·er·ate (ri jen′ər it; *for v.* -ə rāt′) *adj.* [< L. pp. of *regenerare:* see RE- & GENERATE] **1.** spiritually reborn **2.** renewed or restored *[a *regenerate* society]* —*vt.* **-at′ed, -at′ing 1.** to cause to be spiritually reborn **2.** to cause to be completely reformed or improved **3.** to bring into existence again; reestablish *[to *regenerate* a former fashion]* **4.** *Biol.* to grow anew (a part to replace one hurt or lost) **5.** *Electronics* to increase the amplification of (a signal) by feeding energy back from an amplifier output to its input **6.** *Physics* to restore (a battery, etc.) to its original state or properties —*vi.* **1.** to form again, or be made anew **2.** to be regenerated, or spiritually reborn —**re·gen′er·a·cy** (-ə sē) *n.* —**re·gen′er·a′tion** *n.* —**re·gen′er·a′tive** *adj.* —**re·gen′er·a′tor** *n.*

re·gent (rē′jənt) *adj.* [MFr. < ML. < L. prp. of *regere,* to rule: see REGAL] acting in place of a king or ruler *[a prince *regent]* —*n.* **1.** a person appointed to rule a monarchy when the king or queen is sick, absent, too young, etc. ☆**2.** a member of a governing board, as of a State university or a State system of schools —**re′gent·ship′** *n.*

reg·i·cide (rej′ə sīd′) *n.* [< ML. < L. *rex* (see REGAL) + *-cida:* see -CIDE] **1.** a person who kills a king **2.** the killing of a king —**reg′i·ci′dal** *adj.*

re·gime, ré·gime (rə zhēm′, rā-) *n.* [< Fr. < L. *regimen:* see REGIMEN] **1.** *a)* a political system *b)* a form of government or rule **2.** a social system or order **3.** the period of time that a person or system is in power **4.** *same as* REGIMEN

reg·i·men (rej′ə mən) *n.* [L., rule < *regere,* to rule] a controlled system of diet, exercise, rest, etc. for keeping one healthy

reg·i·ment (rej′ə mənt; *for v.* -ment′) *n.* [< MFr. < LL. *regimentum,* government < L. *regere,* to rule: see REGAL] **1.** a military unit consisting of two or more battalions **2.** a large number (of persons, etc.) —*vt.* **1.** to form into regiments **2.** to assign to a regiment **3.** to organize systematically, as into uniform groups **4.** to organize in a rigid system under strict discipline and control *[life in a prison is *regimented]* —**reg′i·men′tal** *adj.* —**reg′i·men′tal·ly** *adv.* —**reg′i·men·ta′tion** *n.*

reg·i·men·tals (rej′ə men′t'lz) *n.pl.* **1.** a regiment's uniform and insignia **2.** military uniform

Re·gi·na (ri jī′nə) [L., a queen] capital of Saskatchewan, Canada, in the S part: pop. 150,000 —*n.* [*also* r-] queen

Reg·i·nald (rej′i nəld) [ult. < Gmc. bases meaning "wise ruler"] a masculine name: dim. *Reggie*

re·gion (rē′jən) *n.* [< Anglo-Fr. < OFr. < L. *regio* < *regere,* to rule: see REGAL] **1.** a part of the earth's surface, esp. a part having a specified position or feature *[a coastal *region,* tropical *regions]* **2.** any area, place, space, etc. or sphere, realm, etc. *[the upper *regions* of the air, a *region* of research]* **3.** an administrative division of a country, as in Italy or the U.S.S.R. **4.** a division or part of the body *[the abdominal *region]*

re·gion·al (-'l) *adj.* **1.** of a whole region, not just a local place **2.** of some particular region, district, etc. *[a *regional* dialect]* —**re′gion·al·ly** *adv.*

re·gion·al·ism (-'l iz'm) *n.* **1.** regional quality or character **2.** the tendency of a writer to emphasize the qualities of life in a particular region **3.** a word, expression, etc. commonly used in a certain region

---

re·fur′nish   **re·gath′er**   **re·gear′**   **re·gild′**

---

reg·is·ter (rej′is tər) *n.* [< MFr. < ML. *registrum* < LL. < L. pp. of *regerere*, to record] **1.** *a)* a record or list of names, events, items, etc. *b)* a book in which this is kept [a hotel *register*] *c)* an entry in such a record **2.** registration; enrollment **3.** a device, as a meter or counter, for recording fares paid, money deposited, etc. [a cash *register*] ☆**4.** an opening into a room by which the amount of air passing, as from a furnace, can be controlled **5.** *Music a)* a part of a range of tones of the human voice or of an instrument having a specified quality *b)* an organ stop, or the tone quality it produces **6.** *Printing* exact placing of lines, pages, colors, etc. —*vt.* ☆**1.** to enter in or as in a record or list; enroll [to *register* a birth] **2.** to indicate as on a scale [a thermometer *registers* temperature] **3.** to show, as by a look on the face [to *register* surprise] **4.** to protect (mail) by paying a fee to have its delivery recorded at a post office **5.** *Printing* to cause to be in register —*vi.* **1.** to enter one's name, as in a hotel register, a list of eligible voters, etc. **2.** to enroll in a school, college, etc. **3.** to make an impression —**reg′is·tra·ble** (-trə b'l) *adj.* —**reg′is·trant** (-trənt) *n.*

reg·is·tered (-tərd) *adj.* officially or legally recorded, enrolled, or certified

☆**registered nurse** a nurse who has completed thorough training and has passed a State examination so as to qualify for performing complete nursing services

reg·is·trar (rej′i strär′, rej′i strär′) *n.* **1.** an official who keeps records, as of the students in a college **2.** a trust company that keeps the records of stock transfers, etc.

reg·is·tra·tion (rej′i strā′shən) *n.* **1.** a registering or being registered **2.** an entry in a register **3.** the number of persons registered

reg·is·try (rej′is trē) *n., pl.* -**tries** **1.** *same as* REGISTRATION **2.** an office where registers are kept **3.** an official record or list; register **4.** a certificate showing the nationality of a merchant ship as recorded in an official register

reg·nant (reg′nənt) *adj.* [< L. prp. of *regnare*, to reign] **1.** reigning; ruling **2.** of greatest power; predominant **3.** prevalent; widespread —**reg′nan·cy** *n.*

re·gorge (ri gôrj′) *vt.* -**gorged**′, -**gorg**′**ing** [< Fr.: see RE- & GORGE] to throw up or back; disgorge

re·gress (rē′gres; *for v.* ri gres′) *n.* [< L. pp. of *regredi* < *re-*, back + *gradi*, to go: see GRADE] **1.** a going or coming back **2.** backward movement; retrogression —*vi.* **1.** to go back; move backward **2.** to return to an earlier form or to earlier or childlike ways of behaving —**re·gres′sor** *n.*

re·gres·sion (ri gresh′ən) *n.* **1.** a regressing, or going back; return; movement backward **2.** a going back to an earlier or simpler form or to a general or common type **3.** a going back to earlier or childlike ways of behaving

re·gres·sive (ri gres′iv) *adj.* **1.** regressing or tending to regress **2.** of or like regression **3.** designating a tax, as a sales tax, that becomes proportionately lower as the tax base increases —**re·gres′sive·ly** *adv.*

re·gret (ri gret′) *vt.* -**gret**′**ted**, -**gret**′**ting** [< OFr. *regreter*, to mourn < a Gmc. base] **1.** to be sorry about or mourn for (a person or thing gone, lost, etc.) **2.** to feel troubled or guilty over (something that has happened, that one has done, etc.) —*n.* **1.** a troubled feeling or guilt, esp. over something one has done or failed to do **2.** sorrow over a person or thing gone, lost, etc. —see SYN. at PENITENCE —(one's) **regrets** a polite expression of regret, as at refusing an invitation —**re·gret′ful** *adj.* —**re·gret′-ful·ly** *adv.* —**re·gret′ful·ness** *n.* —**re·gret′ta·ble** *adj.* —**re·gret′ta·bly** *adv.* —**re·gret′ter** *n.*

re·group (rē grōōp′) *vt., vi.* to group again; specif., *Mil.* to reorganize (one's forces), as after a battle

reg·u·lar (reg′yə lər) *adj.* [< MFr. < L. < *regula*: see RULE] **1.** keeping close in form or arrangement to a rule, principle, type, etc.; orderly; symmetrical [*regular* features] **2.** that follows a fixed principle or procedure [a *regular* schedule of work] **3.** *a)* usual; customary [he sat in his *regular* place] ☆*b)* not a substitute; established [the *regular* quarterback] **4.** consistent, habitual, steady, etc. [a *regular* customer] **5.** happening again at set times or functioning in a normal way [a *regular* pulse] **6.** following a generally accepted rule of conduct; proper [to lead a *regular* life] **7.** properly qualified [a *regular* doctor] **8.** *same as* CUBIC (sense 3) **9.** [Colloq.] thorough; absolute [a *regular* nuisance] ☆**10.** [Colloq.] pleasant, friendly, etc. [a

regular fellow] **11.** *Bot.* having all similar parts of the same shape and size: said of flowers **12.** *Eccles.* belonging to a religious order, etc. and following its rule **13.** *Gram.* being the usual type, as in inflection ["walk" is a *regular* verb, but "swim" is not] **14.** *Math.* having all angles and sides equal, as a polygon, or all faces equal, as a polyhedron **15.** *Mil. a)* designating or of the standing army of a country *b)* designating soldiers recognized in international law as legitimate combatants in warfare ☆**16.** *Politics* designating, of, or loyal to the party leadership, candidates, etc. —*n.* **1.** a member of a religious order **2.** a member of a regular army ☆**3.** a regular member of an athletic team **4.** a clothing size for men of average height **5.** [Colloq.] one that is regular, as in attendance ☆**6.** *Politics* one who is loyal to the party leadership, candidates, etc. —see SYN. at STEADY —**reg′u·lar′i·ty** (-lar′ə tē) *n., pl.* -**ties** —**reg′u·lar·ly** *adv.*

reg·u·late (reg′yə lāt′) *vt.* -**lat**′**ed**, -**lat**′**ing** [< LL. pp. of *regulare* < L. *regula*: see RULE] **1.** to control or direct according to a rule, system, etc. [to *regulate* employment practices] **2.** to adjust to a standard, rate, degree, etc. [*regulate* the heat] **3.** to adjust (a clock, etc.) so as to make operate accurately **4.** to make uniform, orderly, etc. —**reg′u·la′tive, reg′u·la·to′ry** (-lə tôr′ē) *adj.*

reg·u·la·tion (reg′yə lā′shən) *n.* **1.** a regulating or being regulated **2.** a rule or law by which conduct, etc. is regulated [safety *regulations*] —*adj.* **1.** required by regulation [a *regulation* uniform] **2.** usual; normal —see SYN. at LAW

reg·u·la·tor (reg′yə lāt′ər) *n.* a person or thing that regulates; specif., *a)* a mechanism for controlling the movement of machinery, fluids, etc. *b)* the device in a watch or clock by which its speed is adjusted

Reg·u·lus (reg′yōō ləs) [ML. < L., dim. of *rex*, king] a first-magnitude star, the brightest in the constellation Leo

re·gur·gi·tate (ri gur′jə tāt′) *vi., vt.* -**tat**′**ed**, -**tat**′**ing** [< ML. pp. of *regurgitare* < *re-*, back + LL. *gurgitare*, to surge] to surge or flow back, or cause to do this; specif., to bring (partly digested food) from the stomach back to the mouth —**re·gur′gi·tant** *adj.* —**re·gur′gi·ta′tion** *n.*

re·ha·bil·i·tate (rē′hə bil′ə tāt′, rē′ə-) *vt.* -**tat**′**ed**, -**tat**′**ing** [< ML. < L. *re-*, back + *habilitare*, to make suitable] **1.** to restore to rank, privileges, reputation, etc. which one has lost **2.** to put back in good condition [to *rehabilitate* a slum area] **3.** *a)* to restore to a normal state of health, etc. as by medical treatment *b)* to prepare (the handicapped or disadvantaged) for useful employment by special training —**re′ha·bil′i·ta′tion** *n.* —**re′ha·bil′i·ta′tive** *adj.*

re·hash (rē hash′; *for n.* rē′hash) *vt.* [RE- + HASH[1]] to work up again or go over again [to *rehash* the same old arguments] —*n.* the act or result of rehashing [a *rehash* of an earlier book]

re·hear (rē hir′) *vt.* -**heard**′ (-hurd′), -**hear**′**ing** *Law* to hear (a case) a second time —**re·hear′ing** *n.*

re·hears·al (ri hur′s'l) *n.* a rehearsing; specif., a practice performance of a play, concert, etc.

re·hearse (ri hurs′) *vt.* -**hearsed**′, -**hears**′**ing** [< OFr. < *re-*, again + *herser*, to harrow < *herse*, a harrow] **1.** to repeat aloud as heard or read; recite **2.** to tell in detail [he *rehearsed* all his troubles to me] **3.** to perform (a play, concert, etc.) for practice in preparation for a public performance **4.** to drill (a person) in what he is to do or say —*vi.* to rehearse a play, concert, etc.

re·heat (rē hēt′) *vt.* to heat again; specif., to add heat to (a fluid), as in an afterburner —**re·heat′er** *n.*

Reich (rīk; *G.* rīH) *n.* [G.] Germany or the German government; specif., the German fascist state under the Nazis from 1933 to 1945 (**Third Reich**)

reichs·mark (rīks′märk′; *G.* rīHs′märk′) *n., pl.* -**marks**′, -**mark**′ [G.] the monetary unit of Germany from 1924 to 1948

Reichs·tag (rīks′täg′; *G.* rīHs′täkh′) *n.* [G.] formerly, the legislative assembly of Germany

reign (rān) *n.* [< OFr. < L. *regnum* < *regere*, to rule: see REGAL] **1.** royal power or rule **2.** widespread influence; prevalence [the *reign* of fashion] **3.** the period of rule, influence, etc. —*vi.* **1.** to rule as a sovereign [Henry VIII *reigned* for 38 years] **2.** to be widespread; prevail [peace *reigns*]

Reign of Terror the period of the French Revolution from 1793 to 1794, during which many persons were executed

---

re·glaze′	re·grade′	re·han′dle	re·hos′pi·tal·ize′
re·glo′ri·fy′	re·grind′	re·hang′	re·house′
re·glue′	re·grow′	re·hire′	re·ig′nite′

re·im·burse (rē′im burs′) *vt.* **-bursed′**, **-burs′ing** [RE- + archaic *imburse*, to pay, after Fr. *rembourser*] **1.** to pay back (money spent) **2.** to repay (a person) for expenses, damages, losses, etc. —see SYN. at PAY[1] —**re′im·burs′a·ble** *adj.* —**re′im·burse′ment** *n.*

Reims (rēmz; *Fr.* rans) city in NE France: pop. 153,000

rein (rān) *n.* [< OFr. *resne*, ult. < L. *retinere*: see RETAIN] **1.** a narrow strip of leather attached to each end of a horse's bit and held by the rider or driver to control the animal: *usually used in pl.* **2.** [*pl.*] a means of guiding, controlling, etc. [*the reins of government*] —*vt.* to guide, control, etc. as with reins —*vi.* to stop or slow down a horse, etc. as with reins (with *in* or *up*) —**draw rein** to slow down or stop: also **draw in the reins** —**give (free) rein to** to allow to act freely

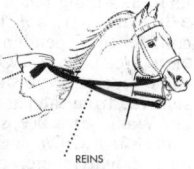

REINS

re·in·car·nate (rē′in kär′nāt) *vt.* **-nat·ed**, **-nat·ing** to cause to undergo reincarnation

re·in·car·na·tion (-kär nā′shən) *n.* **1.** a rebirth of the soul in another body, as in Hindu religious belief **2.** a new incarnation or bodily form **3.** the doctrine that the soul reappears after death in another and different bodily form

rein·deer (rān′dir) *n., pl.* **-deer′**, occas. **-deers′** [< ON. < *hreinn*, reindeer (for IE. base see HORN) + *dyr*, deer] a large deer with branching antlers in both sexes, found in northern regions: it is tamed and used as a beast of burden and for its milk, meat, and leather

reindeer moss an arctic lichen eaten by grazing animals

re·in·force (rē′in fôrs′) *vt.* **-forced′**, **-forc′ing** [RE- + var. of ENFORCE] **1.** to strengthen (a military or naval force) with more troops, ships, planes, etc. **2.** to strengthen, as by propping, adding new material, etc. **3.** to make stronger or more forceful [*to reinforce an argument*] —**re′in·forc′er** *n.*

reinforced concrete concrete masonry containing steel bars or mesh to increase its tensile strength

re·in·force·ment (-mənt) *n.* **1.** a reinforcing or being reinforced **2.** anything that reinforces; specif., [*pl.*] additional troops, ships, etc.

re·in·state (rē′in stāt′) *vt.* **-stat′ed**, **-stat′ing** to instate again; restore to a former condition, position, etc. —**re′in·state′ment** *n.*

reis (rās) *n.pl.*, *sing.* **re·al** (re äl′) [Port.] a former Portuguese and Brazilian money of account

re·it·er·ate (rē it′ə rāt′) *vt.* **-at′ed**, **-at′ing** [< L. pp. of *reiterare*: see RE- & ITERATE] to say or do again or repeatedly [*the prisoner reiterated his innocence*] —**re·it′er·a′tion** *n.* —**re·it′er·a′tive** (-ə rāt′iv, -ər ə tiv) *adj.* —**re·it′er·a′tive·ly** *adv.*

re·ject (ri jekt′; *for n.* rē′jekt) *vt.* [< L. pp. of *rejicere* < *re-*, back + *jacere*, to throw: see JET[1]] **1.** to refuse to take, agree to, use, believe, etc. [*to reject advice*] **2.** to discard or throw out as worthless, useless, or below standard **3.** to vomit (food) **4.** to deny love or acceptance to (someone) [*a rejected child*] **5.** *Physiol.* to be unable to make (a transplanted organ, etc.) a living part of the body —*n.* a rejected thing or person —see SYN. at DECLINE —**re·ject′ee′** *n.* —**re·ject′er**, **re·jec′tor** *n.* —**re·jec′tion** *n.* —**re·jec′tive** *adj.*

re·joice (ri jois′) *vi.* **-joiced′**, **-joic′ing** [< OFr. *rejoir* < *re-*, again + *joir* < L. *gaudere*, to rejoice: see JOY] to be glad or happy [*we rejoiced at the news*] —*vt.* to make glad; delight —**re·joic′ing·ly** *adv.*

re·join[1] (rē join′) *vt.* [< MFr.: see next entry] **1.** to come into the company of again [*to rejoin one's friends after an absence*] **2.** to join together again; reunite [*to rejoin the ends of a broken wire*] **3.** to renew membership in (an organization) —*vi.* to become joined together again

re·join[2] (ri join′) *vt.* [< Anglo-Fr. < MFr. *rejoindre*: see RE- & JOIN] to say in answer [*"That's not so!" he rejoined*] —*vi.* to answer —see SYN. at ANSWER

re·join·der (-dər) *n.* [< Anglo-Fr. use of *rejoindre* as a noun: see prec.] **1.** *a)* an answer to a reply *b)* any answer **2.** *Law* the defendant's answer to the plaintiff's replication

re·ju·ve·nate (ri jōō′və nāt′) *vt.* **-nat·ed**, **-nat·ing** [< RE- + L. *juvenis*, young + -ATE[1]] **1.** to make feel or seem young again; bring back to youthful strength, appearance, etc. **2.** to make seem new or fresh again —**re·ju′ve·na′tion** *n.* —**re·ju′ve·na′tor** *n.*

rel. 1. relating **2.** relative **3.** relatively **4.** religion

re·lapse (ri laps′; *for n., also* rē′laps) *vi.* **-lapsed′**, **-laps′ing** [< L. pp. of *relabi*, to slip back: see RE- & LAPSE] to slip back into a former condition, esp. after improving or seeming to improve —*n.* **1.** a relapsing **2.** the reappearance of a disease after apparent improvement —**re·laps′er** *n.*

re·late (ri lāt′) *vt.* **-lat·ed**, **-lat·ing** [< L. pp. of *referre*, to bring back: see REFER] **1.** to tell the story of; narrate [*relate to us what you did*] **2.** to connect, as in thought or meaning; show a relation between [*to relate theory and practice*] —*vi.* **1.** *a)* to have a connection or relation (*to*) [*proper diet relates to good health*] *b)* to show sympathy and understanding [*not able to relate to strangers*] **2.** to have reference (*to*) [*this example relates to my first statement*] —see SYN. at TELL —**re·lat′a·ble** *adj.* —**re·lat′er**, **re·la′tor** *n.*

re·lat·ed (-lāt′id) *adj.* connected or associated, as by origin, kinship, marriage, etc.; of the same family or kind [*oranges, lemons, and related fruits; a man related to the king*] —**re·lat′ed·ness** *n.*

re·la·tion (ri lā′shən) *n.* **1.** a narrating, telling, etc. **2.** what is narrated; account **3.** connection, as in thought, meaning, etc. [*his remark had no relation to the discussion*] **4.** connection of persons by blood or marriage; kinship **5.** a person related to others by blood or marriage; relative **6.** [*pl.*] the connections between or among persons, groups, nations, etc. [*labor relations; foreign relations*] —**in** (or **with**) **relation to** concerning; regarding —**re·la′tion·al** *adj.*

re·la·tion·ship (-ship′) *n.* **1.** the state or an instance of being related **2.** connection by blood or marriage; kinship

rel·a·tive (rel′ə tiv) *adj.* **1.** related each to the other; referring to each other [*to stay in the same relative positions*] **2.** having to do with; relevant [*documents relative to his life*] **3.** as compared with something else; comparative [*the relative importance of an idea*] **4.** meaningful only in relationship; not absolute [*"cold" is a relative term*] **5.** *Gram.* *a)* designating a word that introduces a subordinate clause and refers to an antecedent [*"which" is a relative pronoun in "the hat which you bought"*] *b)* introduced by such a word [*a relative clause*] —*n.* **1.** a relative word or thing **2.** a person related to others by blood or marriage; member of the same family —**relative to 1.** concerning; about **2.** corresponding to; in proportion to —**rel′a·tive·ness** *n.*

relative humidity see HUMIDITY

rel·a·tive·ly (-lē) *adv.* in a relative manner; in relation to or compared with something else; not absolutely [*a relatively unimportant matter*]

rel·a·tiv·ism (-iz′m) *n.* any theory of ethics or knowledge based on the idea that all values or judgments are relative, differing according to circumstances, persons, etc. —**rel′a·tiv·ist** *n.* —**rel′a·tiv·is′tic** *adj.*

rel·a·tiv·i·ty (rel′ə tiv′ə tē) *n.* **1.** the condition or fact of being relative **2.** *Physics* the fact, principle, or theory of the relative, rather than absolute, nature of motion, mass, time, etc.: as developed esp. by Albert Einstein, the theory includes the statements that: 1) the velocity of light is constant; 2) the mass of a body in motion varies with its velocity; 3) matter and energy

re′im·pose′	re′in·form′	re′in·struct′	re′in·vig′or·ate′
re′im·pris′on·ment	re′in·fuse′	re′in·sure′	re′in·vite′
re′in·cor′po·rate′	re′in·oc′u·late′	re′in·ter′pret′	re′in·volve′
re′in·cur′	re′in·sert′	re′in·ter′ro·gate′	re·is′sue
re′in·duce′	re′in·spect′	re′in·tro·duce′	re·kin′dle
re′in·fect′	re′in·spire′	re′in·tro·duc′tion	re·knit′
re′in·fec′tion	re′in·stall′	re′in·vest′	re·la′bel
re′in·flate′	re·in′sti·tute′	re′in·ves′ti·gate′	re·lace′

are equivalent; 4) space and time are interdependent and form a four-dimensional continuum

re·lax (ri laks′) *vt., vi.* [< L. < *re-*, back + *laxare*, to loosen < *laxus*, loose: see LAX] **1.** to make or become looser, or less firm, stiff, or tense [the body *relaxes* in sleep] **2.** to make or become less strict, severe, or intense, as discipline, effort, etc. **3.** to rest, as from work, worry, etc. [he reads to *relax* his mind] —re·laxed′ *adj.* —re·lax′ed·ly (-lak′sid lē) *adv.* —re·lax′er *n.*

re·lax·ant (-ənt) *adj.* of or causing relaxation, esp. of muscular tension —*n.* a relaxant drug or agent

re·lax·a·tion (rē′lak sā′shən) *n.* **1.** a relaxing or being relaxed; loosening, lessening of harshness, etc. **2.** *a)* a lessening of or rest from work, worry, etc. *b)* recreation or other activity for bringing this about

re·lay (rē′lā; *for v., also* ri lā′) *n.* [MFr. *relais* (pl.), orig. relays of hunting hounds < *re-*, back + *laier*, to leave] **1.** a fresh supply of horses, etc. ready to take over for others, as for a part of a journey **2.** a crew of workers taking over for others; shift **3.** *a) same as* RELAY RACE *b)* any of the laps of a relay race **4.** a passing on or transmitting as by relays **5.** *same as* SERVOMOTOR **6.** *Elec.* a device activated by variations in conditions in one electric circuit and controlling a larger current or activating other devices in the same or another circuit: used in telegraphy, etc. —*vt.* -layed, -lay·ing **1.** to convey by or as by relays; get and pass on [to *relay* news] **2.** *Elec.* to control, operate, or send on by a relay

re·lay (rē′lā′) *vt.* -laid′, -lay·ing to lay again or anew [to *re-lay* a cable]: also written **re′lay′**

relay race a race between teams, in which each member of a team goes only a certain part of the total distance

re·lease (ri lēs′) *vt.* -leased′, -leas·ing [< OFr. < L. *relaxare*: see RELAX] **1.** to set free, as from confinement, duty, work, etc. **2.** to let go; let loose [he *released* his hold on the rope] **3.** to grant freedom from a tax, obligation, etc. **4.** to set free from pain, worries, etc. ☆**5.** to permit to be issued, published, broadcast, etc. [to *release* information to reporters] **6.** *Law* to give up (a claim, right, etc.) to someone else —*n.* **1.** a freeing or being freed, as from prison, pain, a debt, etc. **2.** relief from emotional tension as by expressing one's feelings freely **3.** a document authorizing release, as from prison, a debt, etc. **4.** a letting loose of something caught, held, etc. **5.** a device for releasing a catch, etc., as on a machine ☆**6.** *a)* the act of releasing a book, film, news story, etc. to the public *b)* the book, film, news story, etc. released **7.** *Law a)* a giving up of a claim or right *b)* the document by which this is done

re·lease (rē′lēs′) *vt.* -leased′, -leas·ing to lease again

☆**released time** periods during school time when pupils in a public school may leave the school in order to receive religious instruction elsewhere

rel·e·gate (rel′ə gāt′) *vt.* -gat·ed, -gat·ing [< L. pp. of *relegare* < *re-*, away + *legare*, to send] **1.** to exile or banish (*to* a specified place) **2.** to put in or assign to a less important position [the manager of the team was *relegated* to the job of assistant coach] **3.** to assign to a class, sphere, etc. [it was *relegated* to the category of unsolved problems] **4.** to assign or hand over for decision or action [he *relegated* the task to his assistant] —rel′e·ga′tion *n.*

re·lent (ri lent′) *vi.* [ult. < L. < *re-*, again + *lentus*, pliant] to become less harsh, strict, or stubborn; soften [he *relented* and let us go] —re·lent′ing·ly *adv.*

re·lent·less (-lis) *adj.* **1.** not relenting; having no pity; harsh [a *relentless* foe] **2.** going on without stopping; persistent [the *relentless* pounding of the waves on the beach] —re·lent′less·ly *adv.* —re·lent′less·ness *n.*

rel·e·vant (rel′ə vənt) *adj.* [< ML. prp. of *relevare*: see RELIEVE] having to do with the matter at hand; pertinent; to the point —rel′e·vance, rel′e·van·cy *n.* —rel′e·vant·ly *adv.*
SYN.—**relevant** implies a close logical relationship with, and importance to, the matter being considered [*relevant* testimony]; **germane** implies such close natural connection as to be highly suitable or fitting [your memories are not really *germane* to this discussion]; **pertinent** implies an immediate and direct bearing on the matter at hand [a *pertinent* suggestion]; **apposite** applies to that which is both relevant and happily suitable or fitting [referring to an *apposite* passage in Shakespeare]; **apropos** is used of that which is right for the purpose as well as relevant [an *apropos* remark] —**ANT.** inappropriate, extraneous

re·li·a·ble (ri lī′ə b'l) *adj.* that can be relied on; dependable —re·li·a·bil′i·ty, re·li′a·ble·ness *n.* —re·li′a·bly *adv.*
SYN.—**reliable** is used of a person or thing that can be counted upon to do

what is expected or required [his *reliable* assistant]; **dependable** refers to a person or thing that can be depended on as in an emergency and often suggests personal loyalty, levelheadedness, or steadiness [she is a *dependable* friend]; **trustworthy** applies to a person, or sometimes a thing, whose truthfulness, honesty, carefulness, etc. one has complete confidence in [a *trustworthy* source of information]; **trusty** applies to a person or thing that has in the past always been trustworthy or dependable [his *trusty* horse]

re·li·ance (-əns) *n.* **1.** the act of relying **2.** trust, dependence, or confidence [air travelers put complete *reliance* in the pilot] **3.** a thing relied on

re·li·ant (-ənt) *adj.* having or showing trust, dependence, or confidence; dependent (*on*) —re·li′ant·ly *adv.*

rel·ic (rel′ik) *n.* [< OFr. < L. *reliquiae* (pl.), remains < *relinquere*: see RELINQUISH] **1.** *a)* an object, custom, etc. that has survived from the past [this cannon is a *relic* of the Revolutionary War] *b)* a keepsake or souvenir **2.** [*pl.*] remaining parts; ruins **3.** *R.C.Ch. & Orthodox Eastern Ch.* the bodily remains of a saint, martyr, etc., or an object associated with him, kept as a memorial

rel·ict (rel′ikt) *n.* [< L. pp. of *relinquere*: see RELINQUISH] [Archaic] a widow

re·lief (ri lēf′) *n.* [< OFr. *relever*: see RELIEVE] **1.** an easing, as of pain, anxiety, a burden, etc. [a salve giving *relief* from itching] **2.** anything that lessens tension, or offers a pleasing change [it's a *relief* to get out of that stuffy hall] **3.** aid in the form of goods or money given, as by a government agency, to those unable to support themselves **4.** any aid given in times of need, danger, or disaster, as supplies sent into a flooded area **5.** *a)* rest from work or duty [working six hours with only a ten-minute *relief*] *b)* the person or persons bringing such rest by taking over a post [the guard's *relief* arrived at midnight] **6.** *a)* a way of carving or molding figures and forms so that they stand out from a flat surface *b)* a work of art so made **7.** *a)* the differences in height of land forms in any particular area *b)* these differences as shown by lines, colors, or raised areas on a map (**relief map**) **8.** *Law* the assistance sought by a person who makes a complaint as in a court of equity **9.** *a) Painting* the apparent three-dimensional quality of objects *b)* distinctness of outline; contrast —*adj. Baseball* designating a pitcher regularly used to replace another during a game —**in relief** carved or molded so as to stand out from a surface —**on relief** receiving government aid, as when out of work

re·lieve (ri lēv′) *vt.* -lieved′, -liev·ing [< OFr. < L. < *re-*, again + *levare*, to raise < *levis*: see LIGHT²] **1.** *a)* to ease, lighten, or reduce (pain, worry, etc.) *b)* to free (a person) from pain, worry, etc. **2.** to lighten (pressure, stress, etc.) on (something) **3.** to give or bring aid or assistance to [to *relieve* a besieged city] **4.** *a)* to set free from a burden, debt, etc. *b)* to remove (a burden, etc.) **5.** to set free from duty or work by replacing with oneself or another [to *relieve* the guard every four hours]; specif., ☆*Baseball* to take the place of (another pitcher) during a game **6.** to make less boring, monotonous, etc. by providing a pleasing change [a long, dry play *relieved* by a few funny scenes] **7.** to set off by contrast; make stand out **8.** to ease (oneself) by urinating or defecating —re·liev′er *n.*
SYN.—**relieve** implies enough lessening of misery, discomfort, or boredom to make it bearable [playing games to *relieve* the monotony of the trip]; **alleviate** implies temporary relief brought about without removing the cause of the misery [drugs to *alleviate* the pain]; **lighten** implies a comforting or cheering as by reducing the weight of something depressing or burdensome [nothing can *lighten* her grief]; **assuage** suggests a softening or soothing influence in lessening pain, calming passion, etc. [her kind words *assuaged* his anger]; **mitigate** implies a making milder of that which is likely to cause pain [to *mitigate* a punishment]; **allay** suggests temporary or partial calming or quieting [we've *allayed* his suspicions] —see also SYN. at COMFORT

re·lie·vo (ri lē′vō, ril yev′ō) *n., pl.* -vos *same as* RELIEF (sense 6)

re·li·gion (ri lij′ən) *n.* [< OFr. < L. *religio* < ? < *re-*, back + *ligare*, to bind] **1.** *a)* belief in a superhuman power or powers to be obeyed and worshiped as the creator(s) and ruler(s) of the universe *b)* expression of this belief in conduct and ritual **2.** any specific system of belief, worship, etc., often involving a code of ethics [the Christian *religion*] **3.** any object that is respected and sought after [success is a *religion* with him]

re·li·gi·os·i·ty (ri lij′ē äs′ə tē) *n.* the quality of being overly religious or religious in a sentimental way —re·li′gi·ose′ (-ōs′) *adj.*

re·li·gious (ri lij′əs) *adj.* **1.** that believes in or supports a religion; devout; pious **2.** of or concerned with religion [*religious* books] **3.** belonging to a community of monks, nuns, etc. **4.** very careful; exact; scrupulous [paying *religious* attention to one's diet] —*n.*, *pl.* -**gious** a member of a community of monks, nuns, etc. —**re·li′gious·ly** *adv.* —**re·li′gious·ness** *n.*

re·line (rē līn′) *vt.* -**lined′**, -**lin′ing** 1. to mark with new lines 2. to provide with a new lining

re·lin·quish (ri liŋ′kwish) *vt.* [< OFr. < L. < *re-*, from + *linquere*, to leave: for IE. base see LOAN] 1. to give up; abandon (a plan, policy, etc.) 2. to surrender (something owned, a right, etc.) 3. to let go (a grasp, hold, etc.) —**re·lin′quish·ment** *n.*

SYN.—**relinquish** implies a giving up of something desirable, often because of being forced or required to [he will not *relinquish* his advantage]; **abandon**, in this connection, implies a complete and final giving up of something, as because of being tired, discouraged, etc. [do not *abandon* hope]; **waive** suggests a voluntary giving up of something by refusing to insist on one's right or claim to it [to *waive* a jury trial]—see also SYN. at SURRENDER —ANT. keep, retain

rel·i·quar·y (rel′ə kwer′ē) *n.*, *pl.* -**quar′ies** [< Fr. < L.: see RELIC] a small box, casket, or shrine in which religious relics are kept and shown

rel·ique (rel′ik, re lēk′) *n. archaic var. of* RELIC

rel·ish (rel′ish) *n.* [< OFr. *relais*, something remaining < *relaisser*: see RELEASE] 1. the distinctive flavor something has [a *relish* of garlic in the stew] 2. a trace or touch (of some quality) [a *relish* of anger in his speech] 3. an appetizing flavor; pleasing taste [salt adds *relish* to the meat] 4. *a*) pleasure; enjoyment [to listen with *relish*] *b*) liking or craving [showing little *relish* for the job] 5. anything that gives pleasure, zest, etc. 6. pickles, olives, etc. served with a meal to add flavor or as an appetizer —*vt.* to enjoy; like [to *relish* ice cream; to *relish* a good joke]

re·live (rē liv′) *vt.* -**lived′**, -**liv′ing** to experience again (a past event) as in the imagination

☆**re·lo·cate** (rē lō′kāt) *vt.*, *vi.* -**cat·ed**, -**cat·ing** 1. to locate again 2. to move to a new location —**re·lo·ca′tion** *n.*

re·luc·tance (ri luk′təns) *n.* 1. a being reluctant; unwillingness 2. *Elec.* resistance offered to the passage of magnetic lines of force by a magnetic circuit

re·luc·tant (ri luk′tənt) *adj.* [< L. prp. of *reluctari* < *re-*, against + *luctari*, to struggle: for IE. base see LOCK¹] 1. not wanting (*to* do something); unwilling 2. showing unwillingness [a reluctant answer] —**re·luc′tant·ly** *adv.*

SYN.—**reluctant** implies an unwillingness to do something, as because of dislike, uncertainty, etc. [she was *reluctant* to marry]; **disinclined** suggests a lack of desire for something, as because it fails to suit one's taste [I feel *disinclined* to argue]; **hesitant** implies a holding back from action, as because of caution, uncertainty, etc. [don't be *hesitant* about asking]; **loath** suggests a strong feeling of unwillingness [I am *loath* to depart]; **averse** suggests a deep-seated, long-lasting unwillingness [she is *averse* to borrowing money]—ANT. inclined, disposed, eager

re·ly (ri lī′) *vi.* -**lied′**, -**ly′ing** [< OFr. < L. *religare*: see RELIGION] to have confidence; depend (with *on* or *upon*) [you can *rely* on me to be on time]

REM (rem) *n.*, *pl.* **REMs** [r(apid) e(ye) m(ovement)] the rapid, jerky movement of the eyeballs occurring from time to time under closed lids during sleep accompanied by dreaming

rem (rem) *n.*, *pl.* **rem** [r(oentgen) e(quivalent), m(an)] a dosage of ionizing radiation with a biological effect equal to that produced by one roentgen of X-ray or gamma-ray radiation

re·main (ri mān′) *vi.* [< OFr. < L. < *re-*, back + *manere*, to stay] 1. to be left over when the rest has been taken away, destroyed, etc. [only a few columns of the ancient temple *remain*] 2. to stay while others go [to *remain* at home] 3. to go on being [to *remain* a cynic] 4. to continue to exist; persist [hope *remains*] 5. to be left to be taken care of, done, etc. [that *remains* to be seen] —see SYN. at STAY³

re·main·der (-dər) *n.* 1. those remaining 2. what is left when a part is taken away [I sold some of my records and gave the *remainder* away] 3. a copy or copies of a book still held by the publisher when the sale has fallen off, usually sold at a very low price 4. *Arith. a*) what is left when a smaller number is subtracted from a larger [when 3 is subtracted from 10 the *remainder* is 7] *b*) what is left undivided when one number is not evenly divisible by another [9 divided by 2 gives 4 with a *remainder* of 1] —*vt.* to sell (books, etc.) as remainders

re·mains (ri mānz′) *n.pl.* 1. what is left after part has been used, destroyed, etc. 2. a dead body; corpse 3. writings left unpublished by an author at his death

re·make (rē māk′; *for n.* rē′māk′) *vt.* -**made′**, -**mak′ing** to make again or anew —*n.* 1. the act of remaking 2. something remade, as a motion picture

re·mand (ri mand′) *vt.* [< OFr., ult. < L. *re-*, back + *mandare*, to order] 1. to send back 2. *Law a*) to send (a prisoner or accused person) back into custody, as to await trial *b*) to send (a case) back to a lower court for further action —*n.* a remanding or being remanded

re·mark (ri märk′) *vt.* [Fr. *remarquer* < *re-*, again + *marquer*, to mark: for IE. base see MARK¹] 1. to notice or observe; perceive [to *remark* a difference in quality] 2. to say or write as an observation or comment —*vi.* to make an observation or comment (with *on* or *upon*) [she *remarked* on his good humor] —*n.* 1. a noticing or observing [a woman worthy of *remark*] 2. something said briefly; comment [an unkind *remark*]

SYN.—**remark** applies to a brief, more or less casual statement of opinion, etc., as in calling attention to something [a *remark* about her clothes]; an **observation** is an expression of opinion on something to which one has given special attention and thought [the warden's *observations* on prison reform]; a **comment** is a remark or observation made in explaining, criticizing, or interpreting something [*comments* on a novel]

re·mark·a·ble (-ə b'l) *adj.* 1. worthy of remark or notice 2. unusual; extraordinary —see SYN. at NOTICEABLE —**re·mark′a·ble·ness** *n.* —**re·mark′a·bly** *adv.*

re·match (rē′mach′) *n.* a second match or contest involving the same contestants

Rem·brandt (Harmensz) van Rijn (rem′brant van rīn′; Du. rem′bränt vän rīn′) 1606-69; Du. painter & etcher

re·me·di·a·ble (ri mē′dē ə b'l) *adj.* that can be remedied —**re·me′di·a·ble·ness** *n.* —**re·me′di·a·bly** *adv.*

re·me·di·al (-əl) *adj.* 1. providing, or intended to provide, a remedy [*remedial* treatment] ☆2. *Educ.* of or being a course for helping students who are having difficulty in the subject [*remedial* reading] —**re·me′di·al·ly** *adv.*

rem·e·dy (rem′ə dē) *n.*, *pl.* -**dies** [< Anglo-Fr. < OFr. < L. *remedium* < *re-*, again + *mederi*, to heal: for IE. base see MEDICAL] 1. any medicine or treatment that cures or relieves a disease or tends to restore health 2. something that corrects or removes an evil or wrong or that helps make things better [a *remedy* for unemployment] —*vt.* -**died**, -**dy·ing** to act as a remedy for; cure, make better, correct, etc. [to *remedy* a situation] —see SYN. at CURE —**rem′e·di·less** *adj.*

re·mem·ber (ri mem′bər) *vt.* [< OFr. < LL. < L. *re-*, again + *memorare*, to bring to mind < *memor*, mindful: see MEMORY] 1. to have (an event, thing, person, etc.) come to mind again; think of again [suddenly *remembering* an appointment] 2. to bring back to mind by an effort; recall [I can't *remember* your name] 3. to bear in mind; be careful not to forget [*remember* to lock the door] 4. to keep (a person) in mind for a present, inheritance, etc. [he always *remembers* me on my birthday] 5. to mention as sending greetings [*remember* me to your sister] —*vi.* 1. to bear in, or call back to, mind 2. to have memory

SYN.—**remember** implies a putting oneself in mind of something, often suggesting that the thing stays so vividly alive in the memory that one becomes conscious of it without effort [he'll *remember* this day]; **recall** and **recollect** both imply some effort to bring something back to mind, **recall**, in addition, often suggesting that one tells others what is brought back [let me *recall* what was said; to *recollect* the days of one's childhood] —ANT. forget

re·mem·brance (-brəns) *n.* 1. a remembering or being remembered 2. the power to remember 3. a memory [he had no *remembrance* of what happened] 4. the length of time over which one can remember 5. a souvenir or keepsake 6. commemoration [in *remembrance* of the dead] 7. [*pl.*] greetings —see SYN. at MEMORY

Remembrance Day a British and Canadian holiday in November, equivalent to VETERANS DAY

re·mind (ri mīnd′) *vt.*, *vi.* [RE- + MIND, *v.*] to put (a person) in mind (*of* something); cause to remember —**re·mind′er** *n.*

Rem·ing·ton (rem′iŋ tən), **Frederic** 1861-1909; U.S. painter, sculptor, & illustrator

---

re·load′
re·man′

re·mar′riage
re·mar′ry

re·meas′ure
re·melt′

re·merge′
re·mil′i·ta·rize′

---

fat, āpe, cär; ten, ēven; is, bīte; gō, hôrn, too̅l, look; oil, out; up, fur; get; joy; yet; chin; she; thin, then; zh, leisure; ŋ, ring; ə for a in ago, e in agent, i in sanity, o in comply, u in focus; ′ as in able (ā′b'l); Fr. bal; ë, Fr. coeur; ö, Fr. feu; Fr. mon; ō, Fr. coq; ü, Fr. duc; r, Fr. cri; H, G. ich; kh, G. doch; ‡ foreign; ☆ Americanism; < derived from. See inside front cover.

rem·i·nisce (rem′ə nis′) *vi.* **-nisced′, -nisc′ing** [see next entry] to think, talk, or write about one's past experiences

rem·i·nis·cence (-'ns) *n.* [Fr. < LL. < L. prp. of *reminisci* < *re-*, again + *memini*, to remember: for IE. base see MIND] **1.** a remembering of past experiences [his eyes grew bright in *reminiscence*] **2.** a memory or recollection **3.** [*pl.*] an account, written or spoken, of remembered experiences —see SYN. at MEMORY

rem·i·nis·cent (-'nt) *adj.* **1.** characterized by or given to reminiscence [an old man in a *reminiscent* mood] **2.** bringing to mind something else; suggestive (*of*) [a perfume *reminiscent* of an old-fashioned garden] —**rem′i·nis′cent·ly** *adv.*

re·miss (ri mis′) *adj.* [see REMIT] **1.** careless in, or negligent about, doing one's work or duty **2.** showing carelessness or negligence —**re·miss′ness** *n.*

SYN.—**remiss** implies the failure to do a task or duty for which one is responsible, or carelessness in doing it [the waitress was *remiss* in forgetting our water]; **negligent** and **neglectful** both imply failure to do something adequately or properly, but **negligent** often emphasizes this as a habit or trait [*negligent* in dress] and **neglectful** suggests a deliberate disregard of that for which one is responsible [a mayor *neglectful* of his pledges to the voters]; **derelict** implies a very serious neglect of a duty or obligation, deserving criticism or blame; **lax** implies looseness in enforcing requirements, following standards or rules, etc. [*lax* discipline]

re·mis·si·ble (-ə b'l) *adj.* that can be remitted or forgiven

re·mis·sion (ri mish′ən) *n.* the act or an instance of remitting; forgiveness of sins or debts, lessening or disappearance of pain or symptoms, etc. —**re·mis′sive** *adj.*

re·mit (ri mit′) *vt.* **-mit′ted, -mit′ting** [< L. *remittere* (pp. *remissus*) < *re-*, back + *mittere*, to send: see MISSION] **1.** to forgive or pardon (sins, etc.) **2.** to free someone from (a debt, tax, penalty, etc.) **3.** to make less or weaker; slacken [without *remitting* one's efforts] **4.** to refer (a matter) for consideration, judgment, etc.; specif., *Law* same as REMAND **5.** to send (money) in payment —*vi.* **1.** *a)* to become less or weaker; slacken *b)* to have its symptoms lessen or disappear: said of an illness **2.** to send money in payment —**re·mit′ment** *n.* —**re·mit′ta·ble** *adj.* —**re·mit′ter** *n.*

re·mit·tal (-'l) *n.* same as REMISSION

re·mit·tance (-'ns) *n.* **1.** the sending of money, as by mail **2.** the money sent

re·mit·tent (-'nt) *adj.* remitting; lessening for a while or at intervals, as a fever —**re·mit′tent·ly** *adv.*

rem·nant (rem′nənt) *n.* [< OFr. prp. of *remaindre*: see REMAIN] **1.** what is left over; remainder **2.** [*often pl.*] a small remaining part, amount, or number **3.** a trace; last remaining sign of what has been [a *remnant* of his former pride] **4.** a piece of cloth, ribbon, etc. left over, as at the end of the bolt

re·mod·el (rē mäd′'l) *vt.* **-eled** or **-elled, -el·ing** or **-el·ling 1.** to model again **2.** to make over; rebuild [to *remodel* a kitchen]

re·mon·strance (ri män′strəns) *n.* a remonstrating; protest, complaint, etc., or a statement of this

re·mon·strant (-strənt) *adj.* remonstrating or objecting —*n.* a person who remonstrates —**re·mon′strant·ly** *adv.*

re·mon·strate (-strāt) *vt.* **-strat·ed, -strat·ing** [< ML. pp. of *remonstrare* < L. *re-*, again + *monstrare*, to show] to say or plead in protest, objection, etc. —*vi.* to present and urge reasons in opposition or complaint; protest [to *remonstrate* against his country's foreign policy] —see SYN. at OBJECT —**re·mon·stra·tion** (rē′män strā′shən, rem′ən-) *n.* —**re·mon′stra·tive** (-strətiv) *adj.* —**re·mon′stra·tive·ly** *adv.* —**re·mon′stra·tor** (-strāt ər) *n.*

rem·o·ra (rem′ər ə) *n.* [L., lit., hindrance] an ocean fish with a sucking disc on the head, by which it clings to sharks, ships, etc.

re·morse (ri môrs′) *n.* [< OFr. < LL. < L. pp. of *remordere* < *re-*, again + *mordere*, to bite: for IE. base see MORBID] **1.** a deep, torturing sense of guilt over a wrong one has done; self-reproach [he felt *remorse* at having lied to his father] **2.** pity: now only in **without remorse**, pitilessly —see SYN. at PENITENCE —**re·morse′ful** *adj.* —**re·morse′ful·ly** *adv.* —**re·morse′ful·ness** *n.* —**re·morse′less** *adj.* —**re·morse′less·ly** *adv.* —**re·morse′less·ness** *n.*

re·mote (ri mōt′) *adj.* **-mot′er, -mot′est** [< L. pp. of *removere*, to REMOVE] **1.** distant in space or time; far off [a *remote* star in our galaxy] **2.** far off and hidden; secluded [a *remote* valley in

the Alps] **3.** not closely connected, related, etc. [a question *remote* from the subject; a *remote* cousin] **4.** not warm and friendly; aloof **5.** slight; faint [a *remote* chance] —**re·mote′ly** *adv.* —**re·mote′ness** *n.*

remote control control of aircraft, missiles, or other apparatus from a distance, as by radio waves

re·mount (rē mount′; *for n. usually* rē′mount′) *vt., vi.* to mount again —*n.* a fresh horse to replace another

re·mov·a·ble (ri mōō′və b'l) *adj.* that can be removed —**re·mov′a·bil′i·ty** *n.* —**re·mov′a·bly** *adv.*

re·mov·al (ri mōō′v'l) *n.* a removing or being removed; esp., *a)* a taking away *b)* dismissal from an office or position *c)* a moving to a new location

re·move (ri mōō′v′) *vt.* **-moved′, -mov′ing** [< OFr. < L. *removere*: see RE- & MOVE] **1.** to move (something) from where it is; take away **2.** to take off [*remove* your hat] **3.** *a)* to kill *b)* to dismiss, as from an office *c)* to get rid of [to *remove* the causes of war] **4.** to take, draw out, or separate (someone or something *from*) [most of the butterfat is *removed* from skim milk] —*vi.* **1.** [Poet.] to go away **2.** to move away, as to another place of residence **3.** to be removable [paint that *removes* easily] —*n.* **1.** the act of removing **2.** the distance between one thing and another [living at a far *remove* from here] **3.** any step, interval, or degree [just one *remove* from war] —**re·mov′er** *n.*

re·moved (ri mōōvd′) *adj.* **1.** distant by (a specified number of degrees of relationship) [one's first cousin once *removed* is the child of one's first cousin] **2.** remote; distant (*from*)

re·mu·ner·ate (ri myōō′nə rāt′) *vt.* **-at′ed, -at′ing** [< L. pp. of *remunerari*, to reward < *re-*, again + *munus*, a gift] to pay (a person) for (a service, loss, etc.); reward or repay —see SYN. at PAY[1] —**re·mu′ner·a·ble** *adj.* —**re·mu′ner·a′tor** *n.*

re·mu·ner·a·tion (ri myōō′nə rā′shən) *n.* **1.** the act of remunerating **2.** that which remunerates; reward, pay, compensation, etc.

re·mu·ner·a·tive (ri myōō′nə rāt′iv, -nər ə tiv) *adj.* **1.** remunerating **2.** giving profit or reward [a *remunerative* business] —**re·mu′ner·a′tive·ly** *adv.* —**re·mu′ner·a′tive·ness** *n.*

Re·mus (rē′məs) [L.] *see* ROMULUS

ren·ais·sance (ren′ə säns′, -zäns′; *chiefly Brit.* ri nā′s'ns) *n.* [Fr. < *re-*, again + *naître* (ult. < L. *nasci*), to be born] **1.** a rebirth; revival **2.** [**R-**] *a)* the great revival of art, literature, and learning in Europe in the 14th, 15th, and 16th centuries *b)* the period of this revival *c)* the style of art, literature, architecture, etc. of this period *d)* any similar revival —*adj.* [**R-**] of, like, or in the style of, the Renaissance

re·nal (rē′n'l) *adj.* [< Fr. < L. *renalis* < *renes*, kidneys] of or near the kidneys

re·nas·cence (ri nas′'ns, -nās′-) *n.* [*also* **R-**] same as RENAISSANCE

re·nas·cent (-'nt) *adj.* [< L.: see RE- & NASCENT] having or showing new life, strength, or vigor

rend (rend) *vt.* **rent, rend′ing** [OE. *rendan*] **1.** to tear or pull with violence (with *from*, *off*, etc.) **2.** to tear apart or split with violence [the tree was *rent* by lightning] —*vi.* to tear; split apart —see SYN. at TEAR[1]

ren·der (ren′dər) *vt.* [< OFr., ult. < L. < *re-*, back + *dare*, to give] **1.** to hand over, or submit, as for approval, consideration, payment, etc. [*render* an account of your actions; *render* a bill] **2.** to give (*up*); surrender [to *render* up a city to the enemy] **3.** to give in return [*render* good for evil] **4.** to give or pay as due [to *render* thanks] **5.** to cause to be; make [to *render* one helpless] **6.** *a)* to give (aid, etc.) *b)* to do (a service, etc.) **7.** to represent, as in a drawing; depict **8.** to recite (a poem, etc.), play (music), act (a role), etc. **9.** to translate [to *render* a Spanish song into English] **10.** to deliver (a judgment, verdict, etc.) **11.** to melt down (fat) —**ren′der·a·ble** *adj.* —**ren′der·er** *n.* —**ren′der·ing** *n.*

ren·dez·vous (rän′dā vōō′, -dē-, -də-) *n.*, *pl.* **-vous′** (-vōōz′) [< Fr. *rendez vous*, betake yourself] **1.** a place set for a meeting, as of troops, ships, spacecraft, etc. **2.** a place where people gather; meeting place [the drive-in restaurant is our favorite *rendezvous*] **3.** *a)* an agreement to meet at a certain time or place *b)* the meeting itself —*vi., vt.* **-voused′** (-vōōd′), **-vous′ing** (-vōō′iŋ) to bring or come together at a rendezvous

ren·di·tion (ren dish′ən) *n.* a rendering or result of rendering; specif., ☆*a)* a performance (*of* a piece of music, a role, etc.) *b)* a translation

ren·e·gade (ren′ə gād′) *n.* [< Sp. pp. of *renegar*, to deny, ult.

REMORA
(7 in. to 3 ft. long)

< L. *re-*, again + *negare*, to deny] a person who abandons his religion, party, principles, etc. to join the other side; apostate; traitor —*adj.* disloyal; traitorous

re·nege (ri nig′, -neg′, -nēg′) *vi.* **-neged′, -neg′ing** [ML. *renegare:* see prec.] **1.** to back out of an agreement; go back on a promise **2.** *Card Games* to play a card of another suit, against the rules, when holding any of the suit called for —*n. Card Games* an act of reneging —**re·neg′er** *n.*

re·new (ri nōō′, -nyōō′) *vt.* **1.** to make new or as if new again; make fresh or strong again [*renew* your old car by painting it] **2.** to cause to exist again; reestablish [we must *renew* our former high standards] **3.** to begin again; resume [to *renew* negotiations] **4.** to go over again; repeat [to *renew* one's objections] **5.** to replace as by a fresh supply of [to *renew* provisions] **6.** to give or get an extension of [to *renew* a lease] —**re·new′a·bil/i·ty** *n.* —**re·new′a·ble** *adj.* —**re·new′al** *n.* —**re·new′ed·ly** *adv.* —**re·new′er** *n.*

ren·i- [< L. *renes*, kidneys] *a combining form meaning* kidney, kidneys

ren·i·form (ren′ə fôrm′, rē′nə-) *adj.* [< ModL.: see RENI- & -FORM] shaped liked a kidney

Rennes (ren) city in NW France: pop. 181,000

ren·net (ren′it) *n.* [< OE. *gerennan*, to coagulate] **1.** *a)* membrane lining the stomach of an unweaned animal, esp. the fourth stomach of a calf *b)* the contents of such a stomach **2.** *a)* a substance obtained from this membrane or from the stomach contents, used to curdle milk, as in making cheese or junket *b)* any substance used to curdle milk

ren·nin (ren′in) *n.* [RENN(ET) + -IN¹] a coagulating enzyme that can curdle milk, found in rennet

Re·no (rē′nō) [after U.S. Gen. J. L. *Reno* (1823–62)] city in W Nev.: pop. 73,000

Re·noir (rə nwàr′; *E.* ren′wär), **Pierre Au·guste** (ô güst′) 1841–1919; Fr. painter

re·nounce (ri nouns′) *vt.* **-nounced′, -nounc′ing** [OFr. < L. < *re-*, back + *nuntiare*, to tell < *nuntius*, messenger] **1.** to give up formally (a claim, right, etc.) [the king *renounced* the throne] **2.** to give up (a pursuit, practice, belief, etc.) **3.** to refuse to have anything more to do with; cast off or disown [to *renounce* a son] —**re·nounce′ment** *n.*

ren·o·vate (ren′ə vāt′) *vt.* **-vat′ed, -vat′ing** [< L. pp. of *renovare* < *re-*, again + *novare*, to make new < *novus*, NEW] to make fresh or sound again, as though new; clean up, replace worn parts in, repair, rebuild, etc. [to *renovate* a sofa] —**ren′o·va′tion** *n.* —**ren′o·va′tive** *adj.* —**ren′o·va′tor** *n.*

re·nown (ri noun′) *n.* [< Anglo-Fr. < OFr. < *re-*, again + *nom(m)er*, to name < L. < *nomen*, a name] great fame

re·nowned (-nound′) *adj.* famous —see SYN. at FAMOUS

rent¹ (rent) *n.* [< OFr. < LL. word thought to be a form of L. *reddita* (*pecunia*), paid (money)] **1.** a stated payment for the temporary use of a house, land, etc., made at regular times by the tenant or user to the owner **2.** *Econ.* income from the use of land —*vt.* **1.** to get or give temporary possession of (a house, land, etc.) in return for rent **2.** to get or give temporary use of (a car, tool, etc.) in return for a fee —*vi.* ☆to be leased or let for rent or a fee [this room *rents* for $10 a week] —see SYN. at HIRE —☆for rent that may be rented —**rent′a·ble** *adj.* —**rent′er** *n.*

rent² (rent) *pt. & pp.* of REND

rent³ (rent) *n.* [n. use of obs. var. of REND] **1.** a hole or gap made by tearing or splitting, as a torn place in cloth **2.** a split in an organization; schism

rent·al (ren′t'l) *n.* **1.** an amount paid or received as rent **2.** a house, car, etc. for rent **3.** the act of renting —*adj.* of, in, or for rent

re·nun·ci·a·tion (ri nun′sē ā′shən) *n.* [< L.: see RENOUNCE] the act of renouncing a right, claim, pursuit, etc. —**re·nun′ci·a·tive** (-ə tiv), **re·nun′ci·a·to·ry** (-ə tôr′ē) *adj.*

re·or·der (rē ôr′dər) *n.* a repeated order for the same goods —*vt.* **1.** to order again **2.** to put in order again —*vi.* to order goods again

re·or·gan·i·za·tion (rē ôr′gə ni zā′shən, rē′ôr-) *n.* **1.** a reorganizing or being reorganized **2.** a complete rebuilding of the structure of a business corporation as after, or in anticipation of, a failure

re·or·gan·ize (rē ôr′gə nīz′) *vt., vi.* **-ized′, -iz′ing** to organize again or anew; bring about a reorganization (of) —**re·or′gan·iz′er** *n.*

rep (rep) *n.* [Fr. *reps* < Eng. *ribs*] a ribbed fabric of silk, wool, cotton, rayon, etc.

Rep. **1.** Representative **2.** Republic **3.** Republican

rep. **1.** repeat **2.** report(ed) **3.** reporter

re·pack·age (rē pak′ij) *vt.* **-aged, -ag·ing** to package again or anew, as in a sturdier or more attractive package

re·paid (ri pād′) *pt. & pp.* of REPAY

re·pair¹ (ri per′) *vt.* [< OFr. < L. < *re-*, again + *parare*, to prepare] **1.** to put back in good condition after damage, decay, etc.; fix [to *repair* a broken toy] **2.** to renew; restore [to *repair* one's health] **3.** to set right; remedy [to *repair* a mistake] **4.** to make amends for; make up for (a wrong, injury, etc.) —*n.* **1.** the act or process of repairing **2.** [*usually pl.*] an instance of, or work done in, repairing [to make *repairs* on a house] **3.** the state of being repaired, or fit for use [a car kept in *repair*] **4.** condition with respect to being repaired [in bad *repair*] —see SYN. at MEND —**re·pair′a·ble** *adj.* —**re·pair′er** *n.*

re·pair² (ri per′) *vi.* [< OFr. < LL. *repatriare* < L. *re-*, back + *patria*, one's native country] to go (*to* a place) [after class, they *repaired* to the library]

re·pair·man (-mən, -man′) *n., pl.* **-men** (-mən, -men′) a man whose work is repairing things

rep·a·ra·ble (rep′ər ə b'l) *adj.* that can be repaired, remedied, etc. —**rep′a·ra·bly** *adv.*

rep·a·ra·tion (rep′ə rā′shən) *n.* [< MFr. < LL. < pp. of L. *reparare:* see REPAIR¹] **1.** a repairing or being repaired **2.** a making up for a wrong or injury **3.** anything paid or done to make up for something else; compensation; specif., [*usually pl.*] compensation by a defeated nation for damage done by it in a war

rep·ar·tee (rep′ər tē′; -är-; -tā′) *n.* [< Fr. pp. of *repartir*, to reply < *re-*, back + *partir*, to part] **1.** a quick, witty reply **2.** a series of such replies; banter **3.** skill in making witty replies

re·past (ri past′) *n.* [< OFr. < *re-*, RE- + *past*, food < L. < pp. of *pascere*, to feed] food and drink; a meal

re·pa·tri·ate (rē pā′trē āt′; *for n. usually* -it) *vt., vi.* **-at′ed, -at′ing** [< LL. pp. of *repatriare:* see REPAIR²] to send back or return to the country of birth or citizenship [to *repatriate* prisoners of war] —*n.* a person who has been repatriated —**re·pa′tri·a′tion** *n.*

re·pay (ri pā′) *vt.* **-paid′, -pay′ing** [OFr. *repaier*] **1.** *a)* to pay back (money) *b)* to pay back (a person) **2.** to make some return for [*repay* a kindness] **3.** to make some return to (a person), as for some service —*vi.* to make a repayment or return —**re·pay′a·ble** *adj.* —**re·pay′ment** *n.*

re·peal (ri pēl′) *vt.* [< OFr. *rapeler:* see RE- & APPEAL] to withdraw officially or formally; revoke; cancel; annul [to *repeal* a law] —*n.* the act of repealing —see SYN. at ABOLISH —**re·peal′a·ble** *adj.* —**re·peal′er** *n.*

re·peat (ri pēt′) *vt.* [< OFr. < L. < *re-*, again + *petere*, to seek] **1.** to say or utter again [to *repeat* a remark] **2.** to say from memory; recite **3.** to say (something) as said by someone else **4.** to tell to others [to *repeat* a secret] **5.** to do or make again [*repeat* an operation] **6.** to say again what has been said before by (oneself) —*vi.* to say or do again what has been said or done before —*n.* **1.** the act of repeating **2.** *a)* anything said or done again *b)* a rebroadcast of a radio or TV program **3.** *Music a)* a passage repeated in playing *b)* a symbol for this —**re·peat′a·bil/i·ty** *n.* —**re·peat′a·ble** *adj.*

re·peat·ed (-id) *adj.* said, made, or done again, or again and again —**re·peat′ed·ly** *adv.*

re·peat·er (-ər) *n.* **1.** a person or thing that repeats ☆**2.**

---

re·ne·go/ti·ate′   re·oc/cu·py′   re·o/ri·ent′   re·pa/per
re·nom/i·nate′   re·oc/cur′   re·out/fit′   re·park/
re·no/ti·fy′   re·oc·cur/rence   re·pack/   re·par·ti/tion
re·num/ber   re·o/pen   re·paint/   re·pave/
re·ob·tain/   re·op·pose/   re·pan/el   re·pay/

---

same as REPEATING FIREARM ☆**3.** a person who has been convicted a number of times for breaking the law ☆**4.** a person who illegally votes more than once in the same election ☆**5.** a student who repeats a course or grade in school

repeating decimal a decimal in which some digit or group of digits is repeated continuously (Examples: .3333, .037037037)

☆**repeating firearm** a firearm that can fire a number of shots (from a magazine or clip) without being reloaded

re·pel (ri pel′) *vt.* **-pelled′, -pel′ling** [< L. < *re-*, back + *pellere*, to drive: see PULSE¹] **1.** to drive back or force back [to *repel* an attack] **2.** to refuse, reject, or spurn [she *repelled* his attentions] **3.** to cause dislike in; disgust [the odor *repels* me] **4.** *a)* to be resistant to, or present an opposing force to [plastic *repels* water] *b)* to fail to mix with [water *repels* oil] —*vi.* to cause distaste, dislike, aversion, etc. —**re·pel′ler** *n.*

re·pel·lent (-ənt) *adj.* **1.** that repels; pushing away or driving back **2.** causing distaste, dislike, etc.; repulsive [a *repellent* odor] **3.** able to resist the absorption of liquid, esp. water, to a limited extent [a water-*repellent* raincoat] —*n.* something that repels; specif., *a)* a solution applied to fabric to make it water-repellent *b)* any substance used to keep insects away Also sp. **re·pel′lant** —**re·pel′len·cy** *n.* —**re·pel′lent·ly** *adv.*

re·pent (ri pent′) *vi., vt.* [< OFr. < VL. < L. *re-*, again + *paenitere*, to repent: for IE. base see PASSION] **1.** to feel sorry for (a past error, sin, failure to do something, etc.) **2.** to feel such regret over (some past act, intention, etc.) that one changes one's mind [to *repent* of one's generosity; to *repent* one's kindness] —**re·pent′er** *n.*

re·pent·ance (-'ns) *n.* a repenting or being penitent; feeling of sorrow, etc., esp. for wrongdoing; remorse —see SYN. at PENITENCE —**re·pent′ant** *adj.* —**re·pent′ant·ly** *adv.*

re·peo·ple (rē pē′p'l) *vt.* **-pled, -pling** to people anew; provide with new inhabitants

re·per·cus·sion (rē′pər kush′ən, rep′ər-) *n.* [< L. pp. of *repercutere:* see RE- & PERCUSSION] **1.** formerly, a recoil **2.** reflection, as of sound **3.** an effect of or reaction to some event or action: *usually used in pl.* [his death had *repercussions* all over the world] —**re′per·cus′sive** *adj.*

rep·er·toire (rep′ər twär′, rep′ə-) *n.* [< Fr. < LL. *repertorium:* see REPERTORY] **1.** the stock of plays, operas, roles, songs, etc. that a company, actor, singer, etc. knows and is ready to perform ☆**2.** the stock of special skills of a certain person or group

rep·er·to·ry (rep′ər tôr′ē, rep′ə-) *n., pl.* **-ries** [LL. *repertorium* < L. pp. of *reperire,* to discover] **1.** a storehouse, or the things in it **2.** *same as* REPERTOIRE **3.** the system of play production used by a repertory theater

repertory theater a theater whose acting company performs several plays a season, alternating them at regular intervals

rep·e·ti·tion (rep′ə tish′ən) *n.* [< MFr. < L. *repetitio*] **1.** a repeating; a doing or saying again, or again and again **2.** something repeated **3.** a copy or imitation

rep·e·ti·tious (-əs) *adj.* full of or using repetition, esp. tiresome or boring repetition —**rep′e·ti′tious·ly** *adv.* —**rep′e·ti′tious·ness** *n.*

re·pet·i·tive (ri pet′ə tiv) *adj.* of or marked by repetition —**re·pet′i·tive·ly** *adv.*

re·phrase (rē frāz′) *vt.* **-phrased′, -phras′ing** to phrase again, esp. in a different way

re·pine (ri pīn′) *vi.* **-pined′, -pin′ing** [RE- + PINE²] to feel or express unhappiness or dissatisfaction; complain; fret —**re·pin′er** *n.* —**re·pin′ing·ly** *adv.*

re·place (ri plās′) *vt.* **-placed′, -plac′ing** **1.** to put back in a former or the proper place or position [*replace* the tools when you are done] **2.** to take the place of [workers *replaced* by automated equipment] **3.** to provide an equivalent for [*replace* a worn tire] **4.** to put back or pay back; restore [*replace* stolen goods] —**re·place′a·ble** *adj.* —**re·plac′er** *n.*

SYN.—**replace** implies a taking the place of someone or something that is now lost, gone, destroyed, worn out, etc. [we *replace* defective tubes]; **displace** suggests the forcing or driving out of a person or thing by another that replaces it [he had been *displaced* in her affections by another man]; **supersede** implies a replacing with something superior, more up-to-date, etc. [the steamship *superseded* the sailing ship]; **supplant** suggests a displacing that involves force, trickery, or an introduction of new methods [the prince had been *supplanted* by an impostor]

re·place·ment (-mənt) *n.* **1.** a replacing or being replaced **2.** a person or thing that takes the place of another that is lost, worn out, dismissed, etc.

re·plen·ish (ri plen′ish) *vt.* [< OFr. < L. *re-*, again + *plenus,*

full: for IE. base see FULL] **1.** to make full or complete again, as with a new supply [to *replenish* a stock of goods] **2.** to supply again with fuel, etc. [to *replenish* a furnace with more coal] —**re·plen′ish·er** *n.* —**re·plen′ish·ment** *n.*

re·plete (ri plēt′) *adj.* [< OFr. < L. pp. of *replere* < *re-*, again + *plere*, to fill] **1.** well-filled; plentifully supplied [a play *replete* with jokes] **2.** stuffed with food and drink —**re·ple′tion** *n.*

re·plev·in (ri plev′in) *n.* [< OFr. *re-*, again + *plevir*, to pledge] *Law* **1.** the recovery by a person of goods claimed to be his, on his promise to test the matter in court and give up the goods if defeated **2.** the writ by which this is done —*vt.* to take back (goods) under such a writ: usually **re·plev′y** (-ē) **-plev′ied, -plev′y·ing**

rep·li·ca (rep′li kə) *n.* [It. < ML. < L. *replicare:* see REPLY] a reproduction or close copy, as of a work of art —see SYN. at COPY

rep·li·cate (rep′li kāt′) *vt.* **-cat′ed, -cat′ing** [< L. pp. of *replicare:* see REPLY] **1.** to fold; bend back **2.** to repeat or duplicate

rep·li·ca·tion (rep′lə kā′shən) *n.* [< MFr. < L. < pp. of *replicare:* see REPLY] **1.** the act or process of replicating **2.** a reply, or answer **3.** repetition of a sound; echo **4.** a copy; reproduction **5.** *Law* the plaintiff's answer to the plea of the defendant

re·ply (ri plī′) *vi.* **-plied′, -ply′ing** [< OFr. < L. < *re-*, back + *plicare,* to fold: see PLY¹] **1.** to answer in speech or writing [to *reply* to a question] **2.** to respond by some action [to *reply* to enemy fire] **3.** *Law* to answer a defendant's plea —*vt.* to say in answer [she *replied* that she agreed] —*n., pl.* **-plies′** **1.** an answer in speech or writing **2.** a response by some action —see SYN. at ANSWER —**re·pli′er** *n.*

re·port (ri pôrt′) *vt.* [< OFr. < L. < *re-*, back + *portare,* to carry: see PORT³] **1.** to give an account of; give information about; recount [to *report* the condition of the crops] **2.** to carry and repeat (a message, etc.) [*report* these requests to your leader] **3.** to give an account of in a newspaper or on a newscast **4.** to make known the presence, approach, etc. of [to *report* strange aircraft overhead] **5.** to give an official account of (the results of an investigation, etc.) **6.** to present (something referred for study, etc.) with conclusions, recommendations, etc. (often with *out*) [the committee *reported* the bill out] **7.** to make a charge about (an offense or offender) to a person in authority [to *report* a rudeness; to *report* a thief] —*vi.* **1.** to make a report [to *report* on our field trip] **2.** to work as a reporter [he *reports* for a national news organization] **3.** to present oneself or make one's presence known [to *report* for duty] **4.** to be responsible (*to* a superior) —*n.* **1.** rumor; gossip [*report* has it that he will resign] **2.** reputation [a man of good *report*] **3.** a statement or account brought in and presented, often for publication [a *report* of a battle] **4.** a formal or official presentation of facts or of the record of an investigation, court case, etc. **5.** a loud noise, esp. one made by an explosion —see SYN. at TELL —**re·port′a·ble** *adj.*

re·port·age (-ij) *n.* the reporting of news events

☆**report card** a written report of a student's grades, etc. sent to his parents or guardian at regular intervals

re·port·ed·ly (-id lē) *adv.* according to report or reports

re·port·er (-ər) *n.* a person who reports; specif., *a)* a person who makes official reports of legal or legislative proceedings [a court *reporter*] *b)* a person who gathers information and writes reports for a newspaper, magazine, etc. *c)* a person who reports news on radio or TV —☆**rep·or·to·ri·al** (rep′ər tôr′ē əl) *adj.* —☆**rep′or·to′ri·al·ly** *adv.*

re·pose¹ (ri pōz′) *vt.* **-posed′, -pos′ing** [< OFr. < LL. < L. *re-*, again + LL. *pausare,* to rest] to lay down; place for rest [to *repose* oneself on a bed] —*vi.* **1.** to lie at rest [to *repose* on a couch] **2.** to rest from work, travel, etc. **3.** to rest in death or a grave **4.** to rest or be supported [the shale *reposes* on limestone] —*n.* **1.** a reposing, or resting **2.** *a)* rest *b)* sleep **3.** ease of manner; composure **4.** calm; peace —**re·pose′ful** *adj.* —**re·pose′ful·ly** *adv.*

re·pose² (ri pōz′) *vt.* **-posed′, -pos′ing** [< L. *repositus:* see REPOSITORY] **1.** to place (trust, etc.) in someone **2.** to place (power, etc.) in the control of someone

re·pos·i·to·ry (ri päz′ə tôr′ē) *n., pl.* **-ries** [< L. < pp. of *reponere* < *re-*, back + *ponere,* to place] **1.** a box, chest, closet, or room in which things may be placed for safekeeping **2.** a center for storing [a *repository* of information] **3.** a person to whom something is confided [he is the *repository* of all her secrets]

---

re·pho′to·graph′   re·plant′   re·plate′   re·pol′ish
re·plan′   re·plas′ter   re·play′   re·pop′u·late′

re·pos·sess (rē′pə zes′) *vt.* to get possession of again; specif., to take back from a buyer who has failed to keep up payments —re′pos·ses′sion (-zesh′ən) *n.*

repp (rep) *n. alt. sp. of* REP

rep·re·hend (rep′ri hend′) *vt.* [< L. < *re-*, back + *prehendere*, to take: see PREHENSILE] **1.** to scold or blame (a person) **2.** to find fault with (something done) —see SYN. at CRITICIZE —rep·re·hen·sion (-hen′shən) *n.* —rep′re·hen′sive *adj.* —rep′re·hen′sive·ly *adv.*

rep·re·hen·si·ble (-hen′sə b'l) *adj.* deserving to be scolded, blamed, etc. [a *reprehensible* act or person] —rep′re·hen′si·bil′i·ty *n.* —rep′re·hen′si·bly *adv.*

rep·re·sent (rep′ri zent′) *vt.* [< OFr. < L.: see RE- & PRESENT, *v.*] **1.** to present or picture to the mind **2.** to show or picture [the artist *represented* America as a woman holding a torch] **3.** to describe or set forth, often in order to influence, persuade, etc. [he *represented* himself as an authority] **4.** *a)* to be a sign or symbol for [x *represents* the unknown] *b)* to express by symbols, characters, etc. [to *represent* quantities by letters] **5.** to be the equivalent of; serve as or be like [a cave *represents* home to them] **6.** to act the part of (a character), as in a play **7.** to act in place of; be a substitute for [my lawyer will *represent* me in court] **8.** to speak and act for by the authority given to one, as a legislator for his constituents **9.** to serve as a specimen, example, type, etc. of [he *represents* the youth of America] —rep′re·sent′a·ble *adj.*

rep·re·sen·ta·tion (rep′ri zen tā′shən) *n.* **1.** a representing or being represented; specif., the fact of representing or being represented in a legislative assembly **2.** legislative representatives as a group **3.** a likeness, image, picture, etc. **4.** [*often pl.*] an account or statement of facts, arguments, etc., esp. one meant to influence action, make protest, etc. **5.** the production or performance of a play, etc.

rep·re·sen·ta·tion·al (-'l) *adj.* **1.** of representation **2.** designating or of art that represents objects in nature in recognizable form —rep′re·sen·ta′tion·al·ly *adv.*

rep·re·sen·ta·tive (rep′rə zen′tə tiv) *adj.* **1.** representing; specif., *a)* picturing; portraying [a sculptured figure *representative* of justice] *b)* acting in the place of or on behalf of another or others; esp., serving as an elected delegate **2.** of or based on representation of the people by elected delegates [*representative* government] **3.** being an example of a certain kind of thing; typical [this building is *representative* of modern architecture] —n. **1.** a typical example **2.** a person chosen to act or speak for others, as an elected legislator or a salesman, agent, etc. ☆**3.** [R-] a member of the lower house of Congress or of a State legislature —rep′re·sent′a·tive·ly *adv.* —rep′re·sent′a·tive·ness *n.*

re·press (ri pres′) *vt.* [< L. pp. of *reprimere*: see RE- & PRESS¹] **1.** to hold back; restrain [to *repress* a sigh] **2.** to put down; subdue [to *repress* an uprising] **3.** to control so strictly or harshly as to keep from developing or behaving naturally [to *repress* a child] **4.** *Psychiatry a)* to force (ideas, impulses, etc. that are painful to the conscious mind) into the unconscious *b)* to prevent (unconscious ideas, etc.) from becoming conscious —re·press′er, re·pres′sor *n.* —re·pres′sive *adj.* —re·pres′sive·ly *adv.* —re·pres′sive·ness *n.*

re-press (rē′pres′) *vt.* ☆to press again; esp., to make new copies of (a recording) from the original master

re·pres·sion (ri presh′ən) *n.* **1.** a repressing or being repressed **2.** *Psychiatry a)* the process by which ideas, impulses, etc. are repressed *b)* a repressed idea, impulse, etc.

re·prieve (ri prēv′) *vt.* -prieved′, -priev′ing [ult. < Fr. pp. of *reprendre*, to take back] **1.** to delay the punishment of; esp., to delay the execution of (a person condemned to death) **2.** to give temporary relief to, as from pain —n. a reprieving or being reprieved; specif., *a)* a delaying of a penalty, esp. of execution *b)* a temporary relief, as from trouble or pain

rep·ri·mand (rep′rə mand′; *also for v.,* rep′rə mand′) *n.* [< Fr. < L. *reprimendus*, that is to be repressed < *reprimere*, RE- PRESS] a harsh or formal scolding —vt. to scold harshly or formally

re·print (rē′print′; *for n. usually* rē′print′) *vt.* to print an additional impression of (an earlier book, pamphlet, etc.), usually without changes —n. something reprinted

re·pris·al (ri prī′z'l) *n.* [< MFr. < It. < *riprendere*, to take back < L. *reprehendere*: see REPREHEND] **1.** the use of force, short of war, against another nation to get satisfaction or compensation for injuries **2.** injury done in return for injury received, esp. in war, as the killing of prisoners

re·prise (ri prēz′) *n.* [< OFr. pp. of *reprendre*, to take back] in a musical play, the repetition of all or part of a song performed earlier —vt. -prised′, -pris′ing to present a reprise of (a song)

re·proach (ri prōch′) *vt.* [OFr. *reprochier*: ult. < L. *re-*, back + *prope*, near] to accuse of and blame for a fault so as to make feel ashamed; rebuke; reprove [she *reproached* me for spending too much] —n. **1.** shame, disgrace, or blame, or a source or cause of this [slums are a *reproach* to a city] **2.** a blaming, or an expression of blame; rebuke —re·proach′a·ble *adj.* —re·proach′er *n.* —re·proach′ing·ly *adv.*

re·proach·ful (-fəl) *adj.* full of or expressing reproach —re·proach′ful·ly *adv.* —re·proach′ful·ness *n.*

rep·ro·bate (rep′rə bāt′) *vt.* -bat′ed, -bat′ing [< LL. pp. of *reprobare*: see REPROVE] **1.** to disapprove of strongly; condemn **2.** to reject or abandon —adj. **1.** without principles; depraved; corrupt **2.** *Theol.* lost in sin; rejected by God —n. a very bad or immoral person; scoundrel —rep′ro·ba′tion *n.* —rep′ro·ba′tive *adj.*

re·pro·duce (rē′prə dōōs′, -dyōōs′) *vt.* -duced′, -duc′ing to produce again; specif., *a)* to bring forth others of (its kind), esp. by sexual intercourse *b)* to make (a lost part or organ) grow again *c)* to make a copy, imitation, etc. of (a picture, sound, etc.) *d)* to repeat —vi. **1.** to produce offspring, esp. by sexual intercourse **2.** to undergo copying, duplication, etc. —re′pro·duc′er *n.* —re′pro·duc′i·ble *adj.*

re·pro·duc·tion (rē′prə duk′shən) *n.* **1.** a reproducing or being reproduced **2.** something made by reproducing; copy [a *reproduction* of an ancient statue] **3.** the process by which animals and plants produce new individuals —see SYN. at COPY

re·pro·duc·tive (-tiv) *adj.* **1.** reproducing **2.** of or for reproduction —re′pro·duc′tive·ly *adv.* —re′pro·duc′tive·ness *n.*

re·proof (ri prōōf′) *n.* a reproving or something said in reproving; rebuke: also **re·prov·al** (-prōō′v'l)

re·prove (ri prōōv′) *vt.* -proved′, -prov′ing [< OFr. < LL. *reprobare*: see RE- & PROVE] **1.** to speak to in disapproval; rebuke; scold [she *reproved* him for being so rude] **2.** to express disapproval of (something done or said) —re·prov′a·ble *adj.* —re·prov′er *n.* —re·prov′ing·ly *adv.*

rep·tant (rep′tənt) *adj.* [< L. prp. of *reptare*, to crawl] *Biol.* creeping or crawling

rep·tile (rep′t'l, -tīl) *n.* [LL. < neut. of L. *reptilis*, crawling < pp. of *repere*, to creep] **1.** any of a group of coldblooded vertebrates having a body covered with scales or horny plates and including snakes, lizards, turtles, crocodiles, etc. and dinosaurs **2.** a mean, sneaky person —adj. of or like a reptile

rep·til·i·an (rep til′ē ən, -til′yən) *adj.* **1.** of, like, or characteristic of reptiles **2.** sneaky, mean, etc. —n. *same as* REPTILE

re·pub·lic (ri pub′lik) *n.* [< MFr. < L. < *res*, thing + *publica*, public] **1.** a nation in which the supreme power rests in all the citizens entitled to vote and is exercised by representatives elected by them **2.** the government of such a state **3.** a nation with a president as its head **4.** any of certain divisions of the U.S.S.R. or Yugoslavia

re·pub·li·can (ri pub′li kən) *adj.* **1.** of or like a republic **2.** favoring a republic ☆**3.** [R-] of the Republican Party —n. **1.** a person who favors a republican form of government ☆**2.** [R-] a member of the Republican Party

re·pub·li·can·ism (-iz'm) *n.* **1.** republican government **2.** republican principles, or support of them ☆**3.** [R-] the principles, policies, etc. of the Republican Party

☆**Republican Party** one of the two major political parties in the U.S., organized in 1854

re·pu·di·ate (ri pyōō′dē āt′) *vt.* -at′ed, -at′ing [< L. pp. of *repudiare*, to divorce < *repudium*, separation] **1.** to refuse to have anything to do with **2.** *a)* to refuse to accept or support (a belief, treaty, etc.) *b)* to deny the truth of (a charge, etc.)

re·pot′	re′-pre·sent′	re·proc′ess	re′pub·li·ca′tion
re·pour′	re·price′	re·prove′	re·pub′lish

3. to refuse to acknowledge or pay (a debt, etc.) —**re·pu′di·a′tion** *n.* —**re·pu′di·a′tor** *n.*

re·pug·nance (ri pug′nəns) *n.* [< MFr. < L. < prp. of *repugnare* < *re-*, back + *pugnare*, to fight: see PUGNACIOUS] **1.** inconsistency or contradiction **2.** extreme dislike or distaste Also **re·pug′nan·cy** —see SYN. at AVERSION

re·pug·nant (-nənt) *adj.* **1.** contradictory or opposed [actions *repugnant* to his words] **2.** causing repugnance; offensive; disgusting [a *repugnant* odor] —**re·pug′nant·ly** *adv.*

re·pulse (ri puls′) *vt.* -pulsed′, -puls′ing [< L. pp. of *repellere*, REPEL] **1.** to drive back; repel (an attack, etc.) **2.** to act toward in a cold or unfriendly way; rebuff [she *repulsed* her former friends] **3.** to be repulsive or disgusting to [the greasy food *repulsed* him] —*n.* **1.** a repelling or being repelled **2.** a refusal or rebuff

re·pul·sion (ri pul′shən) *n.* **1.** a repelling or being repelled **2.** strong dislike, distaste, or disgust **3.** *Physics* the mutual action by which bodies or particles of matter tend to repel each other: opposed to ATTRACTION

re·pul·sive (-siv) *adj.* **1.** tending to repel **2.** causing strong dislike or disgust [*repulsive* manners] **3.** of repulsion —**re·pul′sive·ly** *adv.* —**re·pul′sive·ness** *n.*

rep·u·ta·ble (rep′yoo tə b′l) *adj.* having a good reputation; respected [a *reputable* lawyer] —**rep′u·ta·bil′i·ty** *n.* —**rep′u·ta·bly** *adv.*

rep·u·ta·tion (rep′yoo tā′shən) *n.* [< L. < pp. of *reputare*: see REPUTE] **1.** what people generally think about the character of a person or thing; repute [he has a *reputation* for being lazy] **2.** good character in the opinion of others; good name [to lose one's *reputation*] **3.** fame; distinction [his *reputation* as a writer has grown]

re·pute (ri pyoot′) *vt.* -put′ed, -put′ing [< MFr. < L. < *re-*, again + *putare*, to think] to think or consider to be as specified; suppose [he is *reputed* to be rich] —*n. same as* REPUTATION (senses 1, 3)

re·put·ed (-id) *adj.* generally thought of as being such [the *reputed* owner] —**re·put′ed·ly** *adv.*

re·quest (ri kwest′) *n.* [< OFr. < ML., ult. < L. *requirere*: see REQUIRE] **1.** an asking for something; petition [a *request* for help] **2.** something asked for [will he grant our *request*?] **3.** state of being asked for; demand [a song much in *request*] —*vt.* **1.** to ask for, esp. in a polite or formal way [to *request* a hearing] **2.** to ask (a person) to do something [I *requested* her to come] —**by request** in response to a request

Re·qui·em (rek′wē əm, rāk′-, rēk′-) *n.* [L., acc. of *requies*, rest: first word of the Mass for the Dead] [*also* r-] **1.** *R.C.Ch. a)* a Mass for the dead *b)* a musical setting for this **2.** a dirge

‡**ré·qui·es·cat in pa·ce** (rāk′wē es′kät in pä′chā, rek′-) [L.] may he (or she) rest in peace

re·quire (ri kwīr′) *vt.* -quired′, -quir′ing [< OFr. < L. *requirere* < *re-*, again + *quaerere*, to ask] **1.** to ask or insist upon, as by right or authority; demand [to *require* obedience] **2.** to order; command [to *require* him to go] **3.** to be in need of; need [to *require* help] **4.** to call for as necessary [the work *requires* skill] —*vi.* to make a demand —see SYN. at LACK

re·quire·ment (-mənt) *n.* **1.** the act of requiring **2.** something required or demanded, as a condition [to meet the *requirements* for the job] **3.** something needed; necessity [vitamins are a *requirement* in the diet]

req·ui·site (rek′wə zit) *adj.* [< L. pp. of *requirere*: see REQUIRE] required, as by circumstances; necessary for some purpose [the *requisite* supplies for a journey] —*n.* something requisite —see SYN. at ESSENTIAL and NEED

req·ui·si·tion (rek′wə zish′ən) *n.* **1.** a requiring, as by authority **2.** a formal written request, as for equipment [do you have a *requisition* for these supplies?] **3.** the state of being demanded for use [horses were in *requisition*] —*vt.* **1.** to demand or take, as by authority [to *requisition* food for troops] **2.** to submit a written request for (equipment, etc.)

re·quite (ri kwīt′) *vt.* -quit′ed, -quit′ing [RE- + *quite*, obs. var. of QUIT] to repay or make return to (a person, group, etc.) for (a benefit, service, etc. or an injury, wrong, etc.) —**re·quit′al** *n.* —**re·quit′er** *n.*

rere·dos (rir′däs, rer′ə-) *n.* [< Anglo-Fr. < OFr. *arere* (see ARREARS) + *dos*, back] an ornamental screen or partition wall behind an altar in a church

re·route (rē root′, -rout′) *vt.* -rout′ed, -rout′ing to send by a new or different route

re·run (rē run′; *for n.* rē′run′) *vt.* -ran′, -run′ning to run again —*n.* **1.** a rerunning; esp., ☆a repeat showing of a movie, taped TV program, etc. ☆**2.** the movie, etc. so shown

res. **1.** reserve **2.** residence **3.** resides **4.** resolution

re·sal·a·ble (rē sāl′ə b′l) *adj.* that can be sold again

re·sale (rē′sāl′) *n.* the act of selling again

re·scind (ri sind′) *vt.* [L. *rescindere* < *re-*, back + *scindere*, to cut] to withdraw, repeal, or cancel (a law, order, etc.) —see SYN. at ABOLISH —**re·scind′a·ble** *adj.* —**re·scind′er** *n.*

re·scis·sion (ri sizh′ən) *n.* the act of rescinding

re·script (rē′skript) *n.* [< L. < pp. of *rescribere* < *re-*, back + *scribere*, to write] an official decree or order

res·cue (res′kyoo) *vt.* -cued, -cu·ing [< OFr. < *re-*, again + *escorre*, to shake < L. < *ex-*, off + *quatere*, to shake] **1.** to free or save from danger, evil, etc. **2.** *Law* to take out of legal custody by force —*n.* a rescuing —**res′cu·a·ble** *adj.* —**res′cu·er** *n.*

re·search (ri surch′; *for n. equally* rē′surch) *n.* [< MFr.: see RE- & SEARCH] [*sometimes pl.*] systematic study or investigation in a field of knowledge, to discover or establish facts or principles —*vi., vt.* to do research (on or in) [to *research* the subject for a term paper] —*vt.* to search for —**re·search′a·ble** *adj.* —**re·search′er** *n.*

re·seat (rē sēt′) *vt.* **1.** to seat again or in another seat **2.** to supply with a new seat or seats

re·sect (ri sekt′) *vt.* [< L. pp. of *resecare* < *re-*, back + *secare*, to cut] *Surgery* to remove part of (an organ, bone, etc.) —**re·sec′tion** *n.*

re·sem·blance (ri zem′bləns) *n.* **1.** the state or fact of resembling; likeness **2.** a point, degree, or sort of likeness —see SYN. at LIKENESS

re·sem·ble (ri zem′b′l) *vt.* -bled, -bling [< OFr. < *re-*, again + *sembler* < L. *simulare*: see SIMULATE] to be like or similar to in appearance or nature [rabbits *resemble* hares but are smaller]

re·sent (ri zent′) *vt.* [< Fr. < OFr. < *re-*, again + *sentir* < L. *sentire*, to feel: for IE. base see SEND] to feel or show bitter hurt or anger at (some act, etc.) or toward (a person) [he *resented* being called a coward]

re·sent·ful (-fəl) *adj.* feeling or showing resentment —**re·sent′ful·ly** *adv.* —**re·sent′ful·ness** *n.*

re·sent·ment (-mənt) *n.* a feeling of bitter hurt or anger at being insulted, slighted, etc. [his great *resentment* at being left out] —see SYN. at OFFENSE

re·ser·pine (ri sur′pin, -pēn; res′ər pēn′) *n.* [G. *reserpin*] a crystalline alkaloid, $C_{33}H_{40}N_2O_9$, obtained from the root of a rauwolfia: used in treating hypertension and as a sedative

res·er·va·tion (rez′ər vā′shən) *n.* **1.** a reserving or the thing reserved; specif., ☆*a*) public land set aside for some special use [an Indian *reservation*] ☆*b*) an arrangement by which a hotel room, theater ticket, etc. is set aside for use at a certain time or until called for ☆*c*) anything set aside in this way **2.** an objection or qualification, expressed or implied [I support his position on tax reform, but with certain *reservations*]

re·serve (ri zurv′) *vt.* -served′, -serv′ing [< OFr. < L. < *re-*, back + *servare*, to hold: see OBSERVE] **1.** to keep back, store up, or set apart for later use or a special purpose [to *reserve* part of one's pay for emergencies] **2.** to hold over to a later time [to *reserve* comment] **3.** to set aside or have set aside for someone [to *reserve* a hotel room] **4.** to keep back for oneself [to *reserve* the right to refuse] —*n.* **1.** something kept back or stored up, as for later use **2.** a limitation: now rare except in **without reserve** (see below) **3.** the practice of keeping one's thoughts, feelings, etc. to oneself; aloofness; reticence; silence **4.** restraint in artistic expression; freedom from exaggeration **5.** [*pl.*] *a*) manpower kept out of action and ready for emergency use or for replacing others, as in sports or warfare *b*) military forces not on active duty but subject to call; militia (with *the*) **6.** cash, or assets easily turned into cash, kept aside by a bank, business, etc. to meet expected or unexpected demands ☆**7.** land set apart for special use [a forest *reserve*] —*adj.* being, or having the nature of, a reserve [a *reserve* supply] —**in reserve** reserved for later use —**without reserve** under no limitation

☆**reserve bank** a bank in which the reserves of other banks are deposited; specif., *same as* FEDERAL RESERVE BANK

re·served (ri zurvd′) *adj.* **1.** set apart for some purpose, person, etc. [*reserved* seats] **2.** keeping one's thoughts to oneself;

---

aloof or reticent —see **SYN.** at SILENT —**re·serv′ed·ly** (-zɜr′vid-lē) *adv.* —**re·serv′ed·ness n.**

re·serv·ist (ri zɜr′vist) *n.* a member of a country's military reserves

res·er·voir (rez′ər vwär′, rez′ə-; -vwôr′, -vôr′) *n.* [< Fr. < *réserver:* see RESERVE] **1.** a place where anything is collected and stored; esp., a natural or artificial lake in which water is stored for use **2.** a container for a fluid [the ink *reservoir* in a fountain pen] **3.** an extra or reserve supply

re·set (rē set′; *for n.* rē′set′) *vt.* **-set′, -set′ting** to set again (a broken bone, type, a gem, etc.) —*n.* **1.** a resetting **2.** something reset **3.** a device for resetting something

re·ship (rē ship′) *vt.* **-shipped′, -ship′ping 1.** to ship again **2.** to transfer to another ship —**re·ship′ment n.**

re·shuf·fle (rē shuf′'l) *vt.* **-fled, -fling 1.** to shuffle again **2.** to rearrange or reorganize —*n.* a reshuffling or being reshuffled, or the result of this

re·side (ri zīd′) *vi.* **-sid′ed, -sid′ing** [< MFr. < L. *residere* < *re-*, back + *sedere*, to SIT] **1.** to dwell for a long time; live (*in* or *at*) **2.** to be present or exist (*in*): said of qualities, etc. [the beauty that *resides* in natural forms] **3.** to be vested (*in*): said of rights, powers, etc. [the power to tax *resides* in Congress]

res·i·dence (rez′i dəns) *n.* **1.** the act or fact of residing **2.** the fact or status of living or staying in a place while working, going to school, etc., esp. long enough to qualify for certain rights **3.** the place where one resides; dwelling place; esp., a house or mansion **4.** the time during which a person resides in a place

res·i·den·cy (-dən sē) *n., pl.* **-cies 1.** *same as* RESIDENCE ☆**2.** a period of advanced, specialized medical or surgical training at a hospital

res·i·dent (-dənt) *adj.* **1.** having a residence (*in* or *at*); residing **2.** being in residence (sense 2) [a *resident* physician of a hospital] **3.** present or existing (*in*) **4.** not migratory: said of birds, etc. —*n.* **1.** a person who lives in a place, not just a visitor ☆**2.** a doctor who is serving a residency **3.** a bird or animal that is not migratory

res·i·den·tial (rez′ə den′shəl) *adj.* **1.** of or having to do with residence [a *residential* requirement for voting] **2.** of or suitable for residences, or homes [a *residential* area] ☆**3.** chiefly for residents rather than for persons staying only a short time [a *residential* hotel] —**res′i·den′tial·ly adv.**

re·sid·u·al (ri zij′ōō wəl) *adj.* of or like a residue; leftover; remaining —*n.* **1.** something remaining, as at the end of a process ☆**2.** [*pl.*] extra fees paid to performers, writers, etc. for reruns, as on TV **3.** *Math.* the difference between an actual and an estimated value —**re·sid′u·al·ly adv.**

re·sid·u·ar·y (-ōō wer′ē) *adj.* **1.** residual; leftover **2.** *Law* *a*) relating to the residue of an estate [a *residuary* clause in a will] *b*) receiving such a residue [a *residuary* legatee]

res·i·due (rez′ə dōō′, -dyōō′) *n.* [< MFr. < L. neut. of *residuus*, remaining < *residere:* see RESIDE] **1.** what is left after part is removed; remainder **2.** *Chem.* matter remaining at the end of a process, as after evaporation, combustion, etc. [a *residue* of ashes] **3.** *Law* the part of an estate that is left after heirs and creditors have received what is due to them

re·sid·u·um (ri zij′ōō wəm) *n., pl.* **-u·a** (-wə) [L.] *same as* RESIDUE

re·sign (ri zīn′) *vt., vi.* [< MFr. < L. < *re-*, back + *signare*, to sign] to give up or relinquish (a claim, office, position, etc.), esp. by formal notice [he *resigned* from the club] —see **SYN.** at SURRENDER —**resign oneself (to)** to accept (something) without complaining; submit or become reconciled (to)

res·ig·na·tion (rez′ig nā′shən) *n.* **1.** *a*) the act of resigning *b*) formal notice of this, esp. in writing **2.** patient acceptance of something without complaining [to endure trouble with *resignation*]

re·signed (ri zīnd′) *adj.* feeling or showing resignation; accepting what happens patiently —**re·sign′ed·ly** (-zīn′id lē) *adv.* —**re·sign′ed·ness n.**

re·sil·ience (ri zil′yəns, -ē əns) *n.* the quality of being resil-

ient; esp., *a*) the ability to spring back into shape *b*) the ability to recover strength, good spirits, etc. quickly Also **re·sil′-ien·cy**

re·sil·ient (-yənt, -ē ənt) *adj.* [< L. prp. of *resilire* < *re-*, back + *salire*, to jump: see SALIENT] **1.** springing back into shape, position, etc. after being stretched, bent, or squeezed **2.** recovering strength, good spirits, etc. quickly —**re·sil′ient·ly adv.**

res·in (rez′'n) *n.* [< MFr. < L. *resina*] **1.** a solid or semisolid, sticky, organic substance that comes out of various plants and trees, as the pines: natural resins are used in varnishes and lacquers **2.** *same as: a*) SYNTHETIC RESIN *b*) ROSIN —*vt.* to treat or rub with resin: also **res′in·ate′** (-ə nāt′) **-at′ed, -at′ing**

res·in·ous (-əs) *adj.* **1.** of or like resin **2.** obtained from resin **3.** containing resin Also **res′in·y**

re·sist (ri zist′) *vt.* [< MFr. < L. < *re-*, back + *sistere*, to set < *stare*, to STAND] **1.** to withstand; fend off; stand firm against [stainless steel *resists* rust] **2.** *a*) to oppose actively; fight or work against [to *resist* an invasion] *b*) to refuse to cooperate with, submit to, etc. [to *resist* conscription] **3.** to keep from yielding to or enjoying [to *resist* temptation] —*vi.* to oppose or withstand someone or something; offer resistance —*n.* a resistant substance, as a protective coating —see **SYN.** at OPPOSE —**re·sist′er n.**

re·sist·ance (ri zis′təns) *n.* **1.** a resisting; opposition **2.** power or ability to resist; specif., the ability of an organism to ward off disease **3.** opposition of some force, thing, etc. to another [the fabric's *resistance* to wear] **4.** a force that slows down or opposes motion **5.** [*often* R-] the underground movement in a country fighting against a foreign occupying power, a dictatorship, etc. **6.** *Elec. a*) the property of a conductor by which it opposes the flow of a current and thus generates heat *b*) *same as* RESISTOR

re·sist·ant (-tənt) *adj.* offering resistance; resisting

re·sist·i·ble (-tə b'l) *adj.* that can be resisted —**re·sist′i·bil′i·ty n.**

re·sis·tive (ri zis′tiv) *adj.* resisting or capable of resistance

re·sis·tiv·i·ty (rē′zis tiv′ə tē, ri zis′-) *n.* **1.** property of or capacity for resistance **2.** *Elec.* the resistance between opposite faces of a unit cube of a substance

re·sist·less (ri zist′lis) *adj.* **1.** that cannot be resisted; irresistible [a *resistless* force] **2.** without power to resist [he was *resistless* against her charm] —**re·sist′less·ly adv.** —**re·sist′-less·ness n.**

re·sis·tor (ri zis′tər) *n.* *Elec.* a device, as a coil of wire, used to provide resistance in a circuit

re·sole (rē·sōl′) *vt.* **-soled′, -sol′ing** to put a new sole on (a shoe, etc.) —*n.* a new sole for a shoe, etc.

re·sol·u·ble (ri zäl′yōō b'l) *adj.* that can be resolved

res·o·lute (rez′ə lōōt′) *adj.* [< L. pp. of *resolvere:* see RE- & SOLVE] having or showing a fixed, firm purpose; determined; unwavering —**res′o·lute′ly adv.** —**res′o·lute′ness n.**

res·o·lu·tion (rez′ə lōō′shən) *n.* **1.** *a*) a resolving of something or breaking it up into its separate parts *b*) the result of this **2.** *a*) a determining or deciding *b*) a decision as to future action [his *resolution* to work harder] **3.** a resolute quality of mind; determination [don't hesitate—act with *resolution*] **4.** a formal statement of opinion adopted by a group **5.** a solving or answering; solution [the *resolution* of a problem] **6.** the part of a novel, play, etc. in which the plot is explained or made clear **7.** *Med.* the lessening or disappearance of swelling, fever, etc. **8.** *Music* the passing of a dissonant chord (or tone) to a consonant chord (or tone)

re·solve (ri zälv′, -zôlv′) *vt.* **-solved′, -solv′ing** [< L.: see RE- & SOLVE] **1.** to break up into separate parts; analyze [to *resolve* water into hydrogen and oxygen] **2.** to change or transform [the conversation *resolved* itself into an argument] **3.** to cause to decide [this *resolved* him to go] **4.** to reach as a decision; determine [to *resolve* to go] **5.** *a*) to find an answer to (a problem); solve *b*) to make a decision about, as by vote or in a formal way [to *resolve* the points at issue] *c*) to explain or make clear (a problem, a fictional plot, etc.) *d*) to remove

re·set′tle	re·shine′	re·sign′	re·smooth′
re·sew′	re·show′	re·sil′ver	re·sol′der
re·shape′	re·shuf′fle	re·sit′u·ate′	re′so·lid′i·fy′
re·sharp′en	re·sift′	re·sketch′	re·solve′

(doubt, etc.) **6.** *Med.* to cause (a swelling, fever, etc.) to lessen or disappear **7.** *Music* to make (a dissonant chord or tone) become consonant —*vi.* **1.** to be resolved, as by analysis **2.** to come to a decision —*n.* **1.** a fixed purpose or intention [his *resolve* to be a teacher] **2.** a formal resolution, as by a group —see SYN. at DECIDE —**re·solv′a·ble** *adj.* —**re·solv′er** *n.*

re·solved (-zälvd′, -zôlvd′) *adj.* with one's mind made up; determined —**re·solv′ed·ly** (-zäl′vid lē, -zôl′-) *adv.*

res·o·nance (rez′ə nəns) *n.* **1.** a being resonant **2.** the strengthening and lengthening of a sound or musical tone when it is reflected or when it causes some object to vibrate **3.** *Chem.* the property of certain molecules of having two or more structures in which only the positions of electrons differ **4.** *Elec.* the condition in a circuit when an incoming current is at the same, or nearly the same, frequency as the circuit, thus producing much greater currents **5.** *Phonet.* the quality a vocal sound has when it vibrates in a resonating space, as the mouth or nose **6.** *Physics* the effect produced when the natural vibration frequency of a body is greatly amplified by vibrations at this same frequency from another body

res·o·nant (-nənt) *adj.* [< L. prp. of *resonare*, to resound] **1.** resounding or reechoing [a *resonant* sound] **2.** producing resonance [*resonant* walls] **3.** of, full of, or intensified by resonance [a *resonant* voice] —**res′o·nant·ly** *adv.*

res·o·nate (-nāt′) *vi., vt.* -**nat′ed**, -**nat′ing** to be or make resonant

res·o·na·tor (-nāt′ər) *n.* **1.** a device for producing resonance or increasing sound by resonance **2.** *Electronics* an apparatus or system that can be put into oscillation by oscillations in another system

re·sorb (ri sôrb′) *vt.* [< L. < *re-*, again + *sorbere*, to suck up] to absorb again —**re·sorp′tion** (-sôrp′shən) *n.*

res·or·cin·ol (ri zôr′si nōl′, -nôl′) *n.* [< RES(IN) & It. *orcello*, a kind of lichen] a colorless crystalline compound, $C_6H_4(OH)_2$, used in making dyes, celluloid, medicines, etc.: also **res·or′cin** (-sin)

re·sort (ri zôrt′) *vi.* [< OFr. < *re-*, again + *sortir*, to go out] **1.** to go; esp., to go often **2.** to have recourse; turn (*to*) for help, support, etc. [to *resort* to harsh measures] —*n.* **1.** a place people often go to for rest or recreation, as on a vacation [a winter *resort* for skiing] **2.** a frequent getting together or visiting [a place of general *resort*] **3.** a person or thing one turns to for help, support, etc. [a good doctor is your best *resort*] **4.** a turning for help, support, etc.; recourse [a *resort* to threats] —see SYN. at RESOURCE —**as a (or the) last resort** as the last available means

re·sound (ri zound′) *vi.* [< OFr. < L. < *re-*, again + *sonare*, to sound: for IE. base see SOUND¹] **1.** to echo or be filled with sound; reverberate [the hall *resounded* with music] **2.** to make a loud, echoing sound; be echoed [her shout *resounded* throughout the cave] **3.** to be praised [an act of bravery that has *resounded* through the ages] —*vt.* **1.** to give back (sound); echo **2.** to give forth or utter loudly

re·sound·ing (-iŋ) *adj.* **1.** reverberating; echoing **2.** thoroughgoing; complete [a *resounding* victory] **3.** sounding important; impressive —**re·sound′ing·ly** *adv.*

re·source (rē′sôrs, -zôrs; ri sôrs′, -zôrs′) *n.* [< Fr. < OFr. < *re-*, again + *sourdre*, to spring up < L. *surgere*, to rise] **1.** something ready for use or available as needed **2.** [*pl.*] wealth; assets **3.** [*pl.*] something that a country, state, etc. has and can use to its advantage [natural *resources* such as oil and coal] **4.** something that can be done when help is needed; expedient [he applied for a loan as his last *resource*] **5.** [*pl.*] a source of strength or ability within oneself: in full, **inner resources** **6.** skill in solving problems or getting out of trouble [it takes great *resource* to survive a shipwreck]

SYN.—**resource** applies to any thing, person, action, etc. to which one turns for aid in time of need or in an emergency [what *resource* is left us?]; **resort** is usually used with *last* and refers to a resource one turns to when everything else has failed [we'll take the train only as a last *resort*]; **expedient** refers to something used to bring about a desired end and specifically to something used as a substitute for the usual means [the daybed was an excellent *expedient* for unexpected guests]; **makeshift** applies to a quick expedient and is a somewhat scornful term, suggesting an inferior substitute, carelessness, etc. [she served sandwiches as a *makeshift* for dinner]; **stopgap** refers to a temporary substitute that is to be replaced as soon as possible [he's just a *stopgap* until a new manager is named]

re·source·ful (ri sôrs′fəl, -zôrs′-) *adj.* full of resource; skillful at solving problems or getting out of trouble —**re·source′ful·ly** *adv.* —**re·source′ful·ness** *n.*

re·spect (ri spekt′) *vt.* [< L. pp. of *respicere* < *re-*, back + *specere*, to look at: see SPY] **1.** *a*) to think highly of; show honor or courtesy to *b*) to have proper or prudent regard for [politicians *respect* the power of the press] **2.** to show consideration for; avoid interfering with [*respect* others' privacy] **3.** to concern; have to do with —*n.* **1.** a feeling of high regard; esteem [to have *respect* for a great artist] **2.** a state of being held in honor [to have *respect* of one's sons] **3.** regard based on a sense of what is proper or prudent [a healthy *respect* for the rules of traffic safety] **4.** courteous consideration [to have *respect* for the feelings of others] **5.** [*pl.*] courteous expressions of regard: now chiefly in **pay one's respects**, to show polite regard as by visiting **6.** a particular point or detail [right in every *respect*] **7.** reference; relation [with *respect* to this] —see SYN. at REGARD —**in respect of with reference to** —**respect′er** *n.*

re·spect·a·ble (ri spek′tə b'l) *adj.* **1.** worthy of respect or esteem **2.** socially acceptable; proper **3.** fairly good in quality [a *respectable* meal] **4.** fairly large [a *respectable* score] **5.** good enough to be seen, worn, etc. [a *respectable* pair of shoes] —**re·spect′a·bil′i·ty** *n.* —**re·spect′a·bly** *adv.*

re·spect·ful (ri spekt′fəl) *adj.* full of or showing respect; polite —**re·spect′ful·ly** *adv.* —**re·spect′ful·ness** *n.*

re·spect·ing (ri spek′tiŋ) *prep.* concerning; about [I know little *respecting* their plans]

re·spec·tive (-tiv) *adj.* as relates separately to each of two or more [we went our *respective* ways]

re·spec·tive·ly (-tiv lē) *adv.* in regard to each in the order named [the first and second prizes went to Mary and George, *respectively*]

re·spell (rē spel′) *vt.* to spell again; specif., to spell differently in an attempt to show the pronunciation [to respell the word "calf" as (kaf)]

Re·spi·ghi (re spē′gē), **Ot·to·ri·no** (ôt′tô rē′nô) 1879–1936; It. composer

res·pi·ra·tion (res′pə rā′shən) *n.* **1.** act or process of respiring; breathing **2.** the processes by which a living organism or cell takes in oxygen, distributes and uses it in oxidation, and gives off carbon dioxide, etc. **3.** a similar process in anaerobic organisms —**res′pi·ra′tion·al** *adj.*

res·pi·ra·tor (res′pə rāt′ər) *n.* **1.** a device worn over the mouth and nose to prevent the breathing in of harmful substances **2.** an apparatus for giving artificial respiration

res·pi·ra·to·ry (res′pər ə tôr′ē, ri spīr′ə-) *adj.* of, for, or involving respiration

respiratory pigment a colored protein substance, as hemoglobin, in the circulatory system of animals and some plants, that combines with oxygen that is carried to the tissues

re·spire (ri spīr′) *vi., vt.* -**spired′**, -**spir′ing** [< OFr. < L. < *re-*, back + *spirare*, to breathe: see SPIRIT] to breathe; inhale and exhale (air)

res·pite (res′pit) *n.* [< OFr. < L. pp. of *respicere*: see RESPECT] **1.** a delay or postponement, esp. in carrying out a death sentence; reprieve **2.** a period of temporary relief or rest, as from pain, work, etc. —*vt.* -**pit·ed**, -**pit·ing** to give a respite to

re·splend·ent (ri splen′dənt) *adj.* [< L. prp. of *resplendere* < *re-*, again + *splendere*, to shine] shining brightly; dazzling —**re·splend′ence, re·splend′en·cy** *n.* —**re·splend′ent·ly** *adv.*

re·spond (ri spänd′) *vi.* [< OFr. < L. < *re-*, back + *spondere*, to pledge: see SPONSOR] **1.** to answer; reply **2.** to act in return, as if in answer [she *responded* with a smile] **3.** to react favorably, as to medical treatment —*vt.* to say in answer —see SYN. at ANSWER

re·spond·ent (-spän′dənt) *adj.* responding; answering —*n.* **1.** a person who responds **2.** *Law* a defendant

re·sponse (ri späns′) *n.* [< ML. < L. pp. of *respondere*: see RESPOND] **1.** something said or done in answer; reply or reaction **2.** *Eccles.* a word, phrase, etc. sung or spoken as by the congregation or choir in answer to the clergyman during worship **3.** *Electronics* the ratio of output to input of a device or system **4.** *Physiol., Psychol.* a reaction to a stimulus

re·spon·si·bil·i·ty (ri spän′sə bil′ə tē) *n., pl.* -**ties** **1.** the condition of being responsible [he accepted *responsibility* for the error] **2.** a person or thing that one is responsible for [her education is my *responsibility*] —see SYN. at DUTY

re·spon·si·ble (ri spän′sə b'l) *adj.* [< MFr. < L.: see RESPONSE] **1.** expected or obliged to account (*for* something, *to* someone); answerable **2.** that requires one to make important decisions and perform important duties [a *responsible* job] **3.**

that is the cause of something [dampness is *responsible* for the rust] **4.** able to tell the difference between right and wrong and hence expected to account for one's actions **5.** dependable or reliable [a *responsible* person] —**re·spon′si·ble·ness** *n.* —**re·spon′si·bly** *adv.*

SYN.—**responsible** applies to one who has been given a duty or responsibility by someone in authority and who is subject to penalty in case of failure [he is *responsible* to the mayor for making out the reports]; **answerable** implies a legal or moral obligation for which one must answer to someone sitting in judgment [he is not *answerable* for the crimes of his parents]; **accountable** is used of someone who may properly be called upon to explain something [I am not *accountable* for what my associates may say]

re·spon·sive (-siv) *adj.* **1.** answering [a *responsive* nod] **2.** reacting quickly and easily, as to suggestion [a *responsive* audience] **3.** containing responses [*responsive* reading in church] —**re·spon′sive·ly** *adv.* —**re·spon′sive·ness** *n.*

rest[1] (rest) *n.* [OE.] **1.** *a)* peace, ease, and refreshment as produced by sleep *b)* sleep or a lying still **2.** refreshing inactivity after work or exercise, or a period of this **3.** *a)* freedom from worry, trouble, pain, etc. *b)* peace of mind **4.** the repose of death **5.** absence of motion; condition of being still [the golf ball came to *rest* near the hole] **6.** a place for resting; lodging place, as for travelers **7.** a thing that supports [a *footrest*] **8.** *Music a)* a measured interval of silence between tones *b)* a symbol for this —*vi.* **1.** *a)* to become refreshed by sleeping, lying down, stopping work, etc. *b)* to sleep **2.** to be at ease or at peace [he couldn't *rest* until he found it] **3.** to be dead **4.** to be or become quiet or still for a while **5.** to remain unchanged [let the matter *rest*] **6.** *a)* to lie, sit, or lean [the hoe *rested* against a tree] *b)* to be placed or based (*in, on,* etc.) [his faith *rested* on human goodness] **7.** to be or lie (where specified) [the fault *rests* with him] **8.** to be fixed [his eyes *rested* on her] **9.** to rely; depend [success often *rests* on luck] ☆**10.** *Law* to end voluntarily the introduction of evidence in a case —*vt.* **1.** to give rest to; refresh by rest [he *rested* his horse] **2.** to put or lay for ease, support, etc. [*rest* your head on the pillow] **3.** to base; ground [to *rest* an argument on facts] **4.** to fix (the eyes, etc.) ☆**5.** *Law* to end voluntarily the introduction of evidence in a (case) —**at rest 1.** asleep **2.** not moving **3.** free from distress, care, etc. **4.** dead —**lay to rest** to bury —**rest′er** *n.*

MUSICAL RESTS
(A, whole; B, half; C, quarter; D, eighth; E, sixteenth)

rest[2] (rest) *n.* [< OFr. < L. *restare,* to remain < *re-,* back + *stare,* to STAND] **1.** the part left over; remainder **2.** [*with pl. v.*] those that are left; the others Used with *the* —*vi.* to go on being [*rest* assured we will go]

re·state (rē stāt′) *vt.* **-stat′ed, -stat′ing** to state again, esp. in a different way —**re·state′ment** *n.*

☆**res·tau·rant** (res′tə rənt, -ränt′) *n.* [Fr. < prp. of *restaurer:* see RESTORE] a place where meals can be bought and eaten

res·tau·ra·teur (res′tər ə tur′) *n.* [Fr.] a person who owns or operates a restaurant

rest·ful (rest′fəl) *adj.* **1.** full of or giving rest [a *restful* vacation] **2.** having a soothing effect; quiet; peaceful [*restful* music] —**rest′ful·ly** *adv.* —**rest′ful·ness** *n.*

rest·ing (res′tiŋ) *adj.* **1.** being in a state of rest **2.** *Biol.* remaining dormant for a period of time, as certain spores, eggs, etc. **3.** *Physiol.* not actively dividing: said of a cell, etc.

res·ti·tu·tion (res′tə tōō′shən, -tyōō′-) *n.* [< MFr. < L. < pp. of *restituere,* to restore < *re-,* again + *statuere,* to set up: see STORE] **1.** a giving back to the rightful owner of something lost or taken away **2.** a making good for loss or damage

res·tive (res′tiv) *adj.* [< OFr. < *rester:* see REST[2]] **1.** hard to control; unruly; balky, etc. [a *restive* mob] **2.** nervous; restless —**res′tive·ly** *adv.* —**res′tive·ness** *n.*

rest·less (rest′lis) *adj.* **1.** unable to rest or relax [a *restless* child] **2.** giving no rest or relaxation; disturbed [*restless* sleep]

3. never or seldom still; always moving [the *restless* wind] **4.** seeking change; discontented —**rest′less·ly** *adv.* —**rest′less·ness** *n.*

rest mass *Physics* the mass of a body at absolute rest when its speed is zero

res·to·ra·tion (res′tə rā′shən) *n.* **1.** a restoring or being restored, as of a person or thing to a former condition or position, or of something taken away or lost to its rightful owner **2.** a reconstruction of the original form of a building, fossil animal, etc. **3.** something restored, as by rebuilding —**the Restoration 1.** reestablishment of the monarchy in England in 1660 under Charles II **2.** the period of the reign of Charles II (1660–85)

re·stor·a·tive (ri stôr′ə tiv) *adj.* **1.** of restoration **2.** restoring or able to restore health, consciousness, etc. [a *restorative* medicine] —*n.* a thing that is restorative

re·store (ri stôr′) *vt.* **-stored′, -stor′ing** [< OFr. < L. < *re-,* again + *-staurare,* to place: see STORE] **1.** to give back (something taken away, lost, etc.) **2.** to bring back to a former or normal condition, as by repairing, rebuilding, etc. [to *restore* a building, painting, etc.] **3.** to put (a person) back into a position, rank, etc. [to *restore* a king to his throne] **4.** to bring back to health, strength, etc. **5.** to bring back into being, use, etc. [to *restore* order] —**re·stor′a·ble** *adj.* —**re·stor′er** *n.*

restr. restaurant

re·strain (ri strān′) *vt.* [< OFr. < L. < *re-,* back + *stringere,* to draw tight: see STRICT] **1.** to hold back from action; check; curb **2.** to keep under control [*restrain* your temper] **3.** to deprive of liberty, as by arresting **4.** to limit; restrict [laws that *restrain* the powers of local officials] —**re·strain′a·ble** *adj.* —**re·strain′ed·ly** *adv.* —**re·strain′er** *n.*

SYN.—**restrain** suggests the use of strong force or authority either in preventing, or in putting down or controlling, some action [try to *restrain* your enthusiasm]; **curb, check,** and **bridle** get their meanings from the various uses of a horse's harness, **curb** implying a sudden, sharp action to bring something under control [to curb one's tongue], **check** implying a slowing up of action or progress [to *check* inflationary trends], and **bridle** suggesting a holding in of emotion, feelings, etc. [to *bridle* one's envy]; **inhibit,** as used in psychology, implies a holding down or keeping back of some thought or emotion [her natural warmth and affection had become *inhibited*]

re·straint (ri strānt′) *n.* **1.** a restraining or being restrained **2.** a restraining influence or action **3.** a means of restraining **4.** loss or limitation of liberty; confinement [kept in *restraint*] **5.** control of emotions, impulses, etc.; reserve [showing great *restraint* in the crisis]

restraint of trade restriction or prevention of business competition, as by monopoly, price fixing, etc.

re·strict (ri strikt′) *vt.* [< L. pp. of *restringere:* see RESTRAIN] to keep within certain limits; limit; confine [the use of the pool is *restricted* to members]

re·strict·ed (ri strik′tid) *adj.* limited; confined; specif., ☆*a)* that may be seen only by authorized personnel [a *restricted* document] ☆*b)* keeping out certain groups, esp. minorities

re·stric·tion (-shən) *n.* **1.** restricting or being restricted **2.** something that restricts; limitation [to place *restrictions* on the sale of drugs]

re·stric·tive (ri strik′tiv) *adj.* **1.** restricting or tending to restrict [*restrictive* laws] **2.** *Gram.* designating a clause, phrase, or word that is needed for the full meaning of the sentence and so is not set off with commas (Example: the man *who spoke to us* is my uncle) —**re·stric′tive·ly** *adv.* —**re·stric′tive·ness** *n.*

☆**rest·room** (rest′rōōm′) *n.* a room or rooms in a public building, with toilets, washbowls, and, sometimes, couches, etc.: also **rest room**

re·struc·ture (rē struk′chər) *vt.* **-tured, -tur·ing** to plan or provide a new structure or organization for

re·sult (ri zult′) *vi.* [< ML. < L. *resultare,* to rebound < *resilire:* see RESILIENT] **1.** to happen because of something else; follow as an effect (often with *from*) [floods *resulting* from heavy rains] **2.** to end as an effect (*in* something) [heavy rains *resulting* in floods] —*n.* **1.** *a)* what comes about from an action,

re·spread′	re·start′	re·strength′en	re·stud′y
re·sta′bi·lize′	re·stim′u·late′	re·stretch′	re·style′
re·staff′	re·stitch′	re·strike′	re′sub·merge′
re·stage′	re·stock′	re·string′	re′sub·mit′
re·stamp′	re·straight′en		re′sub·scribe′

process, etc.; consequence; outcome *[his skill is a result of practice]* **b)** *[pl.]* desired effects *[a man who gets results]* **2.** the number, quantity, etc. obtained by mathematical calculation —see SYN. at EFFECT and FOLLOW

re·sult·ant (-'nt) *adj.* that results *[war and its resultant agony]* —*n.* **1.** a result **2.** *Physics* a force, velocity, etc. with an effect equal to that of two or more such forces, etc. acting together

re·sume (ri zōōm', -zyōōm') *vt.* **-sumed', -sum'ing** *[< MFr. < L. < re-, again + sumere, to take]* **1.** to take or occupy again *[to resume one's seat]* **2.** to begin again or go on with again after interruption *[to resume a conversation]* —*vi.* to begin again or go on again after interruption

ré·su·mé (rez'ōō mā', rā'zōō-; rā'zōō mā') *n.* [Fr., pp. of *résumer:* see prec.] a summary; specif., ☆a statement of a job applicant's previous employment experience, education, etc.: also written **resume, resumé**

re·sump·tion (ri zump'shən) *n.* *[< L. < pp. of resumere]* the act of resuming *[resumption of classes after vacation]*

☆**re·sur·face** (rē sur'fis) *vt.* **-faced, -fac·ing** to put a new surface on —*vi.* to come to the surface again

re·sur·gent (ri sur'jənt) *adj.* *[< L. prp. of resurgere, to rise again]* rising or tending to rise again *[resurgent hopes]* —**re·sur'gence** *n.*

res·ur·rect (rez'ə rekt') *vt.* *[< RESURRECTION]* **1.** *Theol.* to bring back to life **2.** to bring back into notice, use, etc. *[to resurrect an old custom]* —*vi.* *Theol.* to rise from the dead

res·ur·rec·tion (rez'ə rek'shən) *n.* *[< OFr. < LL. < L. resurrectus, pp. of resurgere, to rise again]* **1.** *Theol.* **a)** a rising from the dead, or coming back to life **b)** the state of having so risen **2.** a return to notice, use, etc.; revival —**the Resurrection** *Theol.* **1.** the rising of Jesus from the dead **2.** the rising of all the dead at the Last Judgment —**res'ur·rec'tion·al** *adj.*

re·sus·ci·tate (ri sus'ə tāt') *vt., vi.* **-tat·ed, -tat·ing** *[< L. pp. of resuscitare < re-, again + suscitare, to revive]* to bring or come back to life or consciousness; revive *[the fireman resuscitated the man overcome by smoke]* —**re·sus'ci·ta'tion** *n.* —**re·sus'ci·ta'tive** *adj.*

re·sus·ci·ta·tor (-tāt'ər) *n.* a person or thing that resuscitates; esp., an apparatus for giving artificial respiration by forcing air or oxygen into the lungs

ret (ret) *vt.* **ret'ted, ret'ting** [MDu. *reten*] to dampen or soak (flax, hemp, etc.) in water in order to separate the fibers from woody tissue

ret. 1. retain **2.** retired **3.** return(ed)

re·tail (rē'tāl; *for vt. 2, usually* ri tāl') *n.* *[< OFr. retailler, to cut up < re-, again + tailler, to cut]* the sale of goods in small quantities directly to the consumer: see WHOLESALE —*adj.* having to do with the selling of goods in this way —*adv.* in small amounts or at a retail price —*vt.* **1.** to sell directly to the consumer **2.** to repeat or pass on (gossip, secrets, etc.) —*vi.* to be sold directly to the consumer *[books that retail for a dollar]* —**re'tail·er** *n.*

re·tain (ri tān') *vt.* *[< OFr. < L. < re-, back + tenere, to hold: see TEND²]* **1.** to keep in one's possession *[retain these for future use]* **2.** to continue to hold in *[to retain heat]* **3.** to continue to practice, use, etc. *[to retain the old traditions]* **4.** to keep in mind; remember *[he retains what he reads]* **5.** to hire (a lawyer, etc.) by paying a fee to —**re·tain'ment** *n.*

re·tain·er (ri tā'nər) *n.* **1.** a person or thing that retains **2.** a servant to a wealthy person or family **3.** a device for holding teeth in position after they have been adjusted by orthodontics **4.** *Law* **a)** the act of retaining the services of a lawyer, consultant, etc. **b)** a fee paid in advance to make such services available when needed

retaining wall a wall built to keep a bank of earth from sliding or water from flooding

re·take (rē tāk'; *for n.* rē'tāk') *vt.* **-took', -tak'en, -tak'ing 1.** to take again, take back, or recapture ☆**2.** to photograph again —*n.* **1.** a retaking ☆**2.** a movie scene, etc. rephotographed or to be rephotographed

RETAINER
(upper shows it in position in mouth)

re·tal·i·ate (ri tal'ē āt') *vi.* **-at'ed, -at'ing** *[< L. pp. of retaliare < re-, back + talio, punishment of the same kind]* to return like for like; esp., to pay back injury for injury —*vt.* to return an injury, wrong, etc. for (an injury, wrong, etc. suffered) —**re·tal'i·a'tion** *n.* —**re·tal'i·a·tive, re·tal'i·a·to'ry** *adj.*

re·tard (ri tärd') *vt.* *[< OFr. < L. < re-, back + tardare, to make slow < tardus, slow]* to hinder, delay, or slow the advance or progress of —*n.* a retarding; delay

re·tard·ant (-'nt) *n.* something that retards; esp., a substance that delays a chemical reaction: also **re·tard'er** —*adj.* tending to retard

☆**re·tard·ate** (ri tär'dāt) *n.* a mentally retarded person

re·tar·da·tion (rē'tär dā'shən) *n.* **1.** a retarding or being retarded **2.** something that retards **3.** *same as* MENTAL RETARDATION —**re·tard·a·tive** (ri tär'də tiv), **re·tard'a·to'ry** (-tôr'ē) *adj.*

re·tard·ed (ri tär'did) *adj.* slowed or delayed in development or progress, esp. because of mental retardation

retch (rech) *vi.* [OE. *hræcan*, to clear the throat: for IE. base see RAVEN¹] to undergo the straining action of vomiting, esp. without bringing anything up

retd. 1. retained **2.** retired **3.** returned

re·te (rēt'ē) *n., pl.* **-ti·a** (-ē ə) *[< L. rete, a net]* *Anat.* a network or plexus, as of blood vessels or nerve fibers

re·ten·tion (ri ten'shən) *n.* **1.** a retaining or being retained **2.** power of or capacity for retaining *[cloth with high color retention]* **3. a)** memory **b)** ability to remember

re·ten·tive (-tiv) *adj.* **1.** retaining or able to retain **2.** having good recall or a good memory *[a retentive mind]* —**re·ten'tive·ly** *adv.* —**re·ten'tive·ness, re·ten·tiv·i·ty** (rē'ten tiv'ə tē) *n.*

re·think (rē think') *vt.* **-thought', -think'ing** to think over again, with a view to changing; reconsider

ret·i·cence (ret'ə s'ns) *n.* the quality or state, or an instance, of being reticent; reserve: also **ret'i·cen·cy**

ret·i·cent (-s'nt) *adj.* *[< L. prp. of reticere < re-, again + tacere, to be silent]* not willing to say much; tending to keep one's thoughts, etc. to oneself; reserved —see SYN. at SILENT —**ret'i·cent·ly** *adv.*

re·tic·u·lar (ri tik'yə lər) *adj.* [see RETICULE] **1.** like a net **2.** intricate; entangled —**re·tic'u·lar·ly** *adv.*

re·tic·u·late (-lit; *also, and for v. always,* -lāt') *adj.* *[< L. reticulum: see RETICULE]* like a net or network; specif., *Bot.* having the veins arranged like the threads of a net *[a reticulate leaf]*: also **re·tic'u·lat'ed** —*vt., vi.* **-lat'ed, -lat'ing** to divide, mark, or be marked so as to look like network —**re·tic'u·late·ly** *adv.* —**re·tic'u·la'tion** *n.*

ret·i·cule (ret'ə kyōōl') *n.* *[< Fr. < L. reticulum, dim. of rete, a net]* a woman's drawstring handbag, orig. made of net

re·tic·u·lum (ri tik'yə ləm) *n., pl.* **-la** (-lə) [L.: see RETICULE] **1.** a network **2.** the second division of the stomach of cud-chewing animals, as cows: see illustration at RUMINANT

ret·i·na (ret''n ə) *n., pl.* **-nas, -nae'** (-ē') [ML., prob. < L. *rete*, a net] a layer of cells sensitive to light that forms the innermost coat of the back part of the eyeball, on which the image is formed by the lens: see illustration at EYE —**ret'i·nal** *adj.*

ret·i·nue (ret''n ōō', -yōō') *n.* *[< OFr. < pp. of retenir: see RETAIN]* the servants or followers of a person of rank or importance

re·tire (ri tīr') *vi.* **-tired', -tir'ing** *[< Fr. < re-, back + tirer, to draw]* **1.** to withdraw to a private or quiet place *[he retired to the library after dinner]* **2.** to go to bed **3.** to retreat, as in battle **4.** to give up one's work, career, etc., esp. because of advanced age **5.** to move back or away —*vt.* **1.** to withdraw (troops) from action **2.** to take (money, paid-off bonds, etc.) out of circulation **3.** to cause to retire from a job, etc. *[to retire a general]* **4.** to withdraw from use *[to retire worn-out machinery]* ☆**5.** *Baseball,* etc. to end the batting turn of (a batter, side, etc.)

re·tired (ri tīrd') *adj.* **1.** hidden or private *[a retired cabin]* **2. a)** that has given up one's work, business, career, etc., esp. because of advanced age *[a retired fireman]* **b)** of or for such retired persons

☆**re·tir·ee** (ri tīr'ē') *n.* one who has retired from work, business, etc.: also **re·tir'ant** (-ənt)

re·tire·ment (ri tīr'mənt) *n.* **1.** a retiring or being retired, specif. from work, business, etc. **2.** privacy; isolation

re·tir·ing (-iŋ) *adj.* **1.** that retires **2.** drawing back from being with others, from publicity, etc.; reserved; shy

re·took (rē took′) *pt. of* RETAKE

☆**re·tool** (rē tōōl′) *vt., vi.* to adapt the machinery of (a factory) for making a different product by changing the tools and dies

re·tort¹ (ri tôrt′) *vt., vi.* [< L. *retortus,* pp. of *retorquere* < *re-,* back + *torquere,* to twist: see TORT] **1.** to respond to (an insult, argument, etc.) with a reply of the same kind **2.** to answer back, esp. in a sharp, quick, or clever way —*n.* a sharp or clever reply —see SYN. at ANSWER

re·tort² (ri tôrt′) *n.* [< Fr. < ML. *retorta* < L. fem. of *retortus:* see prec.] **1.** a container in which substances are distilled, usually made of glass and having a long tube **2.** a vessel in which ore is heated to remove a metal, coal is heated to produce gas, etc.

re·touch (rē tuch′; *for n., also* rē′tuch′) *vt.* to touch up or change details in (a painting, the negative or print of a photograph, etc.) in order to improve it —*n.* the act of retouching or a change made in retouching —**re·touch′er** *n.*

RETORT

re·trace (ri trās′) *vt.* **-traced′, -trac′ing** [Fr. *retracer:* see RE- & TRACE¹] **1.** to go back over again, esp. in the reverse direction [to *retrace* one's steps] **2.** to trace again the story of, from the beginning

re·trace (rē′trās′) *vt.* **-traced′, -trac′ing** to trace the lines of (a drawing, engraving, etc.) over again

re·tract (ri trakt′) *vt., vi.* [< L.: ult. < *re-,* back + *trahere,* to DRAW] **1.** to draw back or in [the cat *retracted* its claws] **2.** to withdraw or take back (a statement, promise, offer, charge, etc.); recant or revoke —**re·tract′a·bil′i·ty** *n.* —**re·tract′a·ble** *adj.*

re·trac·tile (ri trak′t'l, -tīl) *adj.* [Fr.] that can be retracted, or drawn back or in, as the claws of a cat

re·trac·tion (-shən) *n.* a retracting or being retracted; specif., *a)* withdrawal, as of a statement, promise, charge, etc. *b)* a drawing or being drawn back or in

re·trac·tor (-tər) *n.* one that retracts; esp., *a)* a muscle that retracts an organ, part that sticks out, etc. *b)* a surgical device for retracting a part or organ

re·tread (rē tred′; *for n.* rē′tred′) *vt., n. same as* RECAP¹

re·tread (rē′tred′) *vt.* **-trod′, -trod′den** or **-trod′, -tread′ing** to tread again

re·treat (ri trēt′) *n.* [< OFr., ult. < L. *re-,* back + *trahere,* to DRAW] **1.** a going back or backward; withdrawal in the face of opposition, etc. **2.** withdrawal to a safe or private place **3.** a safe, quiet, or hidden place **4.** a period of isolation, esp. one used for religious contemplation, often as part of a group **5.** *Mil. a)* the forced withdrawal of troops under attack, or a signal for this *b)* a signal given by bugle or drum at sunset for lowering the national flag, or the ceremony at which this is done —*vi.* **1.** to withdraw; go back [we *retreated* from the swarm of bees] **2.** to slope backward —**beat a retreat** to retreat or withdraw in a hurry

re·trench (rē trench′) *vt., vi.* [< MFr.: see RE- & TRENCH] to cut down or reduce (esp. expenses); curtail, economize, etc. —**re·trench′ment** *n.*

re·tri·al (rē′trī′əl, -trīl′) *n.* a second trial, as of a case in a law court

ret·ri·bu·tion (ret′rə byōō′shən) *n.* [< OFr. < LL., ult. < L. < *re-,* back + *tribuere,* to pay] punishment that one deserves for a wrong he has done —**re·trib·u·tive** (ri trib′yoo tiv), **re·trib′u·to·ry** (-tôr′ē) *adj.* —**re·trib′u·tive·ly** *adv.*

re·triev·al (ri trē′v'l) *n.* **1.** the act of retrieving **2.** possibility of being retrieved [beyond *retrieval*]

re·trieve (ri trēv′) *vt.* **-trieved′, -triev′ing** [< OFr. < *re-,* again + *trouver,* to find] **1.** to get back; recover [to *retrieve* a kite from a tree] **2.** to restore; revive [to *retrieve* one's spirits] **3.** to rescue or save **4.** to set right or make good (a loss, error, etc.) **5.** to recall to mind ☆**6.** to recover (information) from data stored in a computer **7.** *Hunting* to find and bring back (killed or wounded game): said of dogs **8.** *Tennis,* etc. to re-

turn (a ball that is hard to reach) —*vi. Hunting* to retrieve game —*n.* a retrieving —see SYN. at RECOVER —**re·triev′a·ble** *adj.*

re·triev·er (-ər) *n.* **1.** a person or thing that retrieves **2.** a dog trained to retrieve game; specif., any of several breeds of dog developed for this purpose

ret·ro (ret′rō) *n., pl.* **-ros** *clipped form of* RETROROCKET

ret·ro- [< L. *retro,* backward] *a combining form meaning* backward, back, behind [*retroactive*]

ret·ro·ac·tive (ret′rō ak′tiv) *adj.* applying to, or going into effect as of, a period or date in the past [a *retroactive* pay increase] —**ret′ro·ac′tive·ly** *adv.* —**ret′ro·ac·tiv′i·ty** *n.*

ret·ro·cede (ret′rə sēd′) *vi.* **-ced′ed, -ced′ing** [< L. < *retro-,* back + *cedere,* to yield, go] to go back; recede —*vt.* to cede or give (territory) back —**ret′ro·ces′sion** (-sesh′ən) *n.*

☆**ret·ro·fire** (ret′rə fīr′) *vi., vt.* **-fired′, -fir′ing** to ignite: said of a retrorocket —*n.* the igniting of a retrorocket

☆**ret·ro·fit** (-fit′) *n.* [RETRO- + FIT¹] a change in design, construction, etc., as of an aircraft, to include later improvements —*vt., vi.* **-fit′ted, -fit′ting** to alter with a retrofit

ret·ro·flex (-fleks′) *adj.* [< L.: see RETRO- & FLEX²] **1.** bent or turned backward **2.** *Phonet.* pronounced with the tip of the tongue raised and bent slightly backward Also **ret′ro·flexed′** —*n. Phonet.* a retroflex sound

ret·ro·grade (ret′rə grād′) *adj.* [< L. *retrogradi:* see RETRO- & GRADE] **1.** moving or directed backward **2.** going back to an earlier, esp. worse, condition —*vi.* **-grad′ed, -grad′ing** **1.** to go or move backward **2.** to become worse; deteriorate

ret·ro·gress (ret′rə gres′, ret′rə gres′) *vi.* [< L. pp. of *retrogradi:* see prec.] to move backward, esp. into an earlier or worse condition —**ret′ro·gres′sion** (-gresh′ən) *n.* —**ret′ro·gres′sive** *adj.* —**ret′ro·gres′sive·ly** *adv.*

☆**ret·ro·rock·et, ret·ro-rock·et** (ret′rō räk′it) *n.* a small rocket on a larger rocket or spacecraft, used to produce thrust opposite to the direction of flight so as to reduce speed

re·trorse (ri trôrs′) *adj.* [< L. < *retro-,* back + *versus,* pp. of *vertere,* to turn] *Biol.* bent or turned backward or downward

ret·ro·spect (ret′rə spekt′) *n.* [< L. pp. of *retrospicere* < *retro-,* back + *specere,* to look: see SPY] a looking back on or thinking about things past —**in retrospect** in thinking back over the past —**ret′ro·spec′tion** *n.*

ret·ro·spec·tive (ret′rə spek′tiv) *adj.* **1.** looking back on or directed to the past, past events, etc. **2.** applying to the past; retroactive —*n.* an exhibition of typical works from the whole career of an artist —**ret′ro·spec′tive·ly** *adv.*

ret·rous·sé (ret′rōō sā′) *adj.* [Fr., turned up] turned up at the tip [a *retroussé* nose]

ret·si·na (ret′si nə) *n.* [ModGr.] a wine of Greece, flavored with pine resin

re·turn (ri turn′) *vi.* [< OFr. *retourner:* see RE- & TURN] **1.** to go or come back, as to a former place, condition, opinion, etc. **2.** to answer; retort —*vt.* **1.** to bring, send, carry, or put back [to *return* the book to the shelf] **2.** to pay back by doing or giving the same; reciprocate [to *return* a visit, a compliment, etc.] **3.** to produce (a profit, revenue, etc.); yield **4.** to report or declare officially [the jury *returned* a verdict] **5.** to elect or re-elect, as to a legislature **6.** *Sports* to hit, run, or throw back (a ball) —*n.* **1.** a coming or going back [the *return* of summer] **2.** a bringing, sending, carrying, or putting back **3.** something returned **4.** repayment; reciprocation [the *return* of a favor] **5.** *a)* profit made on an exchange of goods *b)* [*often pl.*] yield or profit, as from investments **6.** an answer; retort **7.** *a)* an official or formal report *b)* [*usually pl.*] a report on a vote count [election *returns*] *c)* a form for reporting income tax due: in full, **(income) tax return** **8.** *Sports* a hitting, throwing, or running back of a ball —*adj.* **1.** of or for returning [a *return* ticket] **2.** given, sent, done, etc. again or in return [a *return* visit] **3.** returning or returned —**in return** as a return; as an equivalent, response, etc. —**re·turn′a·ble** *adj.* —**re·turn′er** *n.*

☆**re·turn·ee** (ri tur′nē′) *n.* a person who returns, as one who returns home from military service

re·tuse (ri tōōs′, -tyōōs′) *adj.* [< L. pp. of *retundere* < *re-,* back + *tundere,* to strike] *Bot.* having a blunt or rounded tip with a small notch, as some leaves

---

re·ti′tle	re′trans·fer′	re·treat′	re·try′
re·train′	re′trans·late′	re·trim′	re·tune′

Reu·ben (rōō'bin) [via LL. < Gr. < Heb. *rĕ'ūbēn*, lit., behold, a son] **1.** a masculine name: dim. *Rube* **2.** *Bible a)* the eldest son of Jacob *b)* the tribe of Israel descended from him

re·u·ni·fy (rē yōō'nə fī') *vt., vi.* **-fied', -fy'ing** to unify again after being divided —**re·u'ni·fi·ca'tion** *n.*

Ré·u·ni·on (rā ü nyôn'; *E.* rē yōōn'yən) French island possession in the Indian Ocean, east of Madagascar

re·un·ion (rē yōōn'yən) *n.* **1.** the act of reuniting **2.** a gathering of persons after separation *[a family reunion]*

re·u·nite (rē'yōō nīt') *vt., vi.* **-nit'ed, -nit'ing** to unite again; bring or come together again

rev (rev) *n.* [Colloq.] a revolution, as of an engine —*vt.* **revved, rev'ving** [Colloq.] to speed up (an engine, motor, etc.): usually with *up*

Rev. 1. *Bible* Revelation **2.** *pl.* **Revs.** Reverend

rev. 1. revenue **2.** reverse **3.** review(ed) **4.** revise(d) **5.** revision **6.** revolution **7.** revolving

re·val·u·ate (rē val'yōō wāt') *vt.* **-at'ed, -at'ing** to make a new valuation or appraisal of —**re·val'u·a'tion** *n.*

☆**re·vamp** (rē vamp') *vt.* **1.** to put a new vamp on (a shoe or boot) **2.** to make over; revise *[to revamp an old plot for a play]* —*n.* a revamping

re·vanch·ism (rə vänsh'iz'm, -vänch'-) *n.* [< Fr. *revanche*, revenge + -ISM] the revengeful spirit moving a defeated nation to consider going to war to get back its lost territories, etc. —**re·vanch'ist** *adj., n.*

re·veal (ri vēl') *vt.* [< OFr. < L. *revelare*, lit., to draw back the veil < *re-*, back + *velum*, a veil] **1.** to make known (something hidden or secret); disclose **2.** to expose to view; show; display *[she took off her hat, revealing her golden hair]* —**re·veal'a·ble** *adj.* —**re·veal'er** *n.* —**re·veal'ment** *n.*

SYN.—**reveal** implies a making known of something hidden or secret, as if by drawing back a veil *[to reveal one's identity]*; **disclose** suggests a laying open of what has previously been kept hidden *[he refuses to disclose his plans]*; **divulge** suggests that what has been disclosed should properly have been kept secret or private *[do not divulge the contents of this letter]*; **tell** usually suggests the making known of necessary or requested information *[tell me what to do]*; **betray** implies either disloyalty in divulging something *[betrayed by an informer]* or an unintentional revealing of something *[her blush betrayed embarrassment]* —**ANT. conceal, hide**

re·veil·le (rev'ə lē) *n.* [< Fr. imper. of *(se) réveiller*, to wake up, ult. < L. *re-*, again + *vigilare*, to watch: for IE. base see WAKE¹] *Mil.* **1.** an early morning signal, as on a bugle, to wake soldiers or sailors or call them to the first assembly of the day **2.** this assembly

rev·el (rev'l) *vi.* **-eled** or **-elled, -el·ing** or **-el·ling** [< MFr. < L. *rebellare*: see REBEL] **1.** to have fun in a noisy way; make merry **2.** to take much pleasure (*in*) *[to revel in sports]* —*n.* **1.** merrymaking; revelry **2.** [often *pl.*] a noisy, happy celebration —**rev'el·er, rev'el·ler** *n.*

rev·e·la·tion (rev'ə lā'shən) *n.* **1.** a revealing, or making known *[her revelation of the secret]* **2.** something revealed or made known, especially when it comes as a great surprise **3.** *Theol.* God's revealing of himself and his will to man —[R-] the last book of the New Testament (in full, **The Revelation of Saint John the Divine**): also **Revelations** —**rev'e·la'tor** *n.* —**rev'e·la·to·ry** (-lə tôr'ē) *adj.*

rev·el·ry (rev'l rē) *n., pl.* **-ries** the act of reveling; noisy merrymaking; boisterous festivity

re·venge (ri venj') *vt.* **-venged', -veng'ing** [< OFr. < *re-*, again + *vengier*, to take vengeance < L. *vindicare*: see VINDICATE] **1.** to inflict injury or punishment in return for (an injury, insult, etc.) **2.** to get even for a wrong or injury done to (a person, oneself, etc.); avenge —*n.* **1.** a revenging; vengeance **2.** what is done in revenging **3.** desire to take vengeance *[motivated by revenge]* **4.** a chance to get even, as by a return match after a defeat —**be revenged** to get revenge —see SYN. at AVENGE —**re·veng'er** *n.* —**re·veng'ing·ly** *adv.*

re·venge·ful (-fəl) *adj.* full of or desiring revenge —see SYN. at VINDICTIVE —**re·venge'ful·ly** *adv.* —**re·venge'ful·ness** *n.*

rev·e·nue (rev'ə nōō', -nyōō') *n.* [< MFr. < *re-*, back + *venir* < L. *venire*, to COME] **1.** the income or return from property or investment **2.** an item or source of income **3.** the income of a government from taxes, licenses, etc.

☆**rev·e·nu·er** (-ər) *n.* [Colloq.] a Treasury Department revenue agent, esp. one working to stop the illegal distilling of alcohol and bootlegging

revenue stamp a stamp, as on a box of cigars, that shows a tax has been paid

re·ver·ber·ant (ri vur'bər ənt) *adj.* reverberating

re·ver·ber·ate (ri vur'bə rāt') *vt.* **-at'ed, -at'ing** [< L. < *re-*, again + *verberare*, to beat < *verber*, a lash] **1.** to cause (a sound) to reecho **2.** to reflect (light, heat, etc.) —*vi.* **1.** to echo back; resound *[the low note reverberated in the empty auditorium]* **2.** to be reflected, as light or heat

re·ver·ber·a·tion (ri vur'bə rā'shən) *n.* **1.** a reverberating or being reverberated; reflection of light or sound waves, etc. **2.** something reverberated, as reechoed sound —**re·ver'ber·a'tive** (-bə rāt'iv, -bər ə tiv) *adj.* —**re·ver'ber·a'tive·ly** *adv.*

re·ver·ber·a·to·ry (ri vur'bər ə tôr'ē) *adj.* **1.** operating or produced by reverberation **2.** describing or of a furnace or kiln in which ore, metal, etc. is heated by very hot gases from the burning fuel which are reflected downward from the arched roof —*n., pl.* **-ries** such a furnace or kiln

Re·vere (ri vir'), **Paul** 1735–1818; Am. patriot

re·vere¹ (ri vir') *vt.* **-vered', -ver'ing** [< Fr. < L. < *re-*, again + *vereri*, to fear: for IE. base see GUARD] to regard with deep respect, love, and awe; venerate

SYN.—**revere** implies a regarding with great respect, affection, honor, deference, etc. *[a poet revered by all of his countrymen]*; **reverence**, having nearly the same meaning, is more often applied to a thing or abstract idea than to a person *[brought up to reverence the ideals of truth and loyalty]*; **venerate** is applied to something regarded as holy or sacred *[to venerate saints, relics, etc.]* but may also suggest the deep respect felt for that which is very old and dignified, honorable, etc. *[to venerate the traditions of one's ancestors]*; **worship** implies the use of prayer and ritual in paying honor to a divine being, but broadly suggests very great, sometimes uncritical, love or admiration of any kind *[he worships his wife]*

re·vere² (ri vir') *n. same as* REVERS

rev·er·ence (rev'ər əns, rev'rəns) *n.* **1.** a feeling or attitude of deep respect, love, and awe; veneration **2.** an indication of this; specif., a bow or curtsy **3.** the state of being revered **4.** [R-] a title used in speaking to or of a clergyman: preceded by *your* or *his* —*vt.* **-enced, -enc·ing** to treat with reverence —see SYN. at AWE and HONOR and REVERE¹

rev·er·end (rev'ər ənd, -rənd) *adj.* [< MFr. < L. *reverendus*, gerundive of *revereri*: see REVERE¹] worthy of reverence: [usually R-] used as a title of respect for a clergyman, usually preceded by *the* and followed by the name *[the Reverend John Jones]* —*n. colloq. term for* CLERGYMAN

rev·er·ent (rev'ər ənt, -rənt) *adj.* feeling or showing reverence —**rev'er·ent·ly** *adv.*

rev·er·en·tial (rev'ə ren'shəl) *adj.* showing or caused by reverence —**rev'er·en'tial·ly** *adv.*

rev·er·ie (rev'ər ē) *n.* [< Fr. < MFr. < *rever*, to wander] **1.** dreamy thinking, esp. about pleasant things; daydreaming **2.** a dreamy, unrealistic notion; daydream

re·vers (ri vir', -ver') *n., pl.* **-vers'** (-virz', -verz') [Fr. < L. *reversus*: see REVERSE] a part (of a garment) turned back to show the reverse side or facing, as a lapel

re·ver·sal (ri vur's'l) *n.* a reversing or being reversed *[the reversal of the lower court's decision]*

re·verse (ri vurs') *adj.* [< OFr. < L. pp. of *revertere*: see REVERT] **1.** *a)* turned backward; opposite or contrary, as in position, direction, etc. *[in reverse order]* *b)* with the back showing **2.** acting or moving in a way opposite or contrary to the usual **3.** causing movement backward or in the opposite direction *[reverse gear]* —*n.* **1.** the opposite or contrary *[just the reverse of what he said is true]* **2.** the back, as the side of a coin or medal that does not show the main design **3.** a reversing; esp., a change from good fortune to bad; defeat; check *[the army suffered a reverse]* **4.** an arrangement of gears, or some other device in an automatic transmission, that causes a machine or motor vehicle to run backward ☆**5.** *Football* a play in which a back moving in one direction hands the ball to another back moving in the opposite direction —*vt.* **-versed', -vers'ing 1.** to turn in an opposite position or direction, upside down, or inside out **2.** to change to the opposite *[to reverse an opinion, policy, trend, etc.]* **3.** to cause to go in an opposite direction **4.** to transfer (the charges for a telephone call) to the party being called **5.** *Law* to revoke or annul (a decision, etc.) —*vi.* **1.** to go or turn in the opposite direction **2.** to put a motor, engine, etc. in reverse —**re·vers'ed·ly** *adv.* —**re·vers'er** *n.*

re·vers·i·ble (ri vur'sə b'l) *adj.* **1.** that can be reversed, as cloth, coats, etc. finished so that either side can be used as the

re·twist'	re·us'a·ble	re·vac'ci·nate'	re·var'nish
re·type'	re·use'	re·val'u·a'tion	re·ver'i·fi·ca'tion
re·up·hol'ster	re·u'ti·lize'	re·val'ue	re·ver'i·fy'

outer side **2.** that can reverse or go in either direction, as a chemical reaction —**n.** a reversible coat, jacket, etc. —**re·vers′i·bil′i·ty** n. —**re·vers′i·bly** adv.

re·ver·sion (ri vur′zhən, -shən) n. **1.** a return, as to a former state, custom, etc. [the half-tamed animal's *reversion* to nature] **2.** *Biol.* a return to a former or primitive type; atavism **3.** *Law* a) the right of succession, future possession, etc. b) the return of an estate to the grantor and his heirs after the period of a grant is over —**re·ver′sion·ar′y, re·ver′sion·al** adj.

re·vert (ri vurt′) vi. [< OFr. < L. < *re-*, back + *vertere*, to turn: see VERSE] **1.** to go back; return, as to a former condition, practice, subject, etc. [his thoughts *reverted* to what she had said when she left] **2.** *Biol.* to return to an earlier type **3.** *Law* to go back to a former owner or his heirs —**re·vert′i·ble** adj.

rev·er·y (rev′ər ē) n., pl. **-er·ies** same as REVERIE

re·vet·ment (ri vet′mənt) n. [< Fr. < OFr., ult. < L. *re-*, again + *vestire*, to clothe] **1.** a facing of stone, cement, etc., as to protect an embankment **2.** same as RETAINING WALL **3.** an embankment or wall of sandbags, earth, etc. for protection against shell fragments, strafing, etc.

re·view (ri vyoo′) n. [< MFr. < L. < *re-*, again + *videre*, to see: see WISE[1]] **1.** a looking at or looking over again **2.** a general survey or report **3.** a looking back, as on past events **4.** reexamination, as by a higher court of the decision of a lower court **5.** a report, as in a newspaper, telling about a recent book, play, concert, etc. and giving one's opinion of it **6.** a magazine containing articles of criticism and evaluation, often in a specific field [a law *review*] **7.** the act of going over a lesson again, as in studying **8.** same as REVUE **9.** a formal inspection, as of troops on parade —vt. **1.** to look back on (past events, etc.) **2.** to survey in thought, speech, or writing **3.** to inspect (troops, etc.) formally **4.** to give or write a review of (a recent book, play, etc.) **5.** to reexamine (a lower court's decision) **6.** to go over (lessons, a subject, etc.) again —vi. to review books, plays, etc.

re·view·er (-ər) n. a person who reviews; esp., one who reviews books, plays, etc. as for a newspaper

re·vile (ri vīl′) vt. **-viled′, -vil′ing** [< OFr. *reviler*, to treat as vile: see RE- & VILE] to say harsh or abusive things to or about [the fisherman *reviled* the thieves who stole his nets] —see SYN. at SCOLD —**re·vile′ment** n. —**re·vil′er** n.

re·vise (ri vīz′) vt. **-vised′, -vis′ing** [< Fr. < L. < *re-*, back + *visere*, to survey < *videre*, to see: see WISE[1]] **1.** to read over carefully and correct, improve, or bring up to date where necessary [to *revise* a history textbook] **2.** to change or amend [to *revise* one's opinion] —n. a revising or a revision —**re·vis′al** n. —**re·vis′er, re·vi′sor** n.

Revised Standard Version a mid-20th-cent. revision of an earlier version of the Bible, made by a group of U.S. scholars

Revised Version a late-19th-cent. revision of the Authorized, or King James, Version of the Bible

re·vi·sion (ri vizh′ən) n. **1.** act, process, or work of revising **2.** a revised form, as of a book, etc. —**re·vi′sion·ar′y, re·vi′sion·al** adj.

re·vi·sion·ist (-ist) n. a person who favors the revision of some accepted theory, doctrine, etc. —adj. of revisionists —**re·vi′sion·ism** n.

re·vi·so·ry (ri vī′zər ē) adj. of, or having the nature or power of, revision [a *revisory* committee]

re·viv·al (ri vī′v'l) n. a reviving or being revived; specif., a) a bringing or coming back into use, being, etc. [a *revival* of classic style in architecture] b) a new presentation of an earlier play, movie, etc. c) restoration to vigor and activity d) a bringing or coming back to life or consciousness e) a stirring up of religious feelings, usually by the excited preaching of evangelists at public meetings ☆f) a series of such meetings

re·viv·al·ist (-ist) n. a person who promotes or conducts religious revivals —**re·viv′al·ism** n. —**re·viv′al·is′tic** adj.

re·vive (ri vīv′) vi., vt. **-vived′, -viv′ing** [< L. < *re-*, again + *vivere*, to live: for IE. base see QUICK] **1.** to come or bring back to life or consciousness [to *revive* after fainting] **2.** to come or bring back to health and vigor [a shower and some food *revived* them after the tiring trip] **3.** to come or bring back into use, operation, or attention [to *revive* an ancient custom] **4.** to come or bring to mind again **5.** to present (a play or mov-

ie) again after a time —**re·viv′a·bil′i·ty** n. —**re·viv′a·ble** adj. —**re·viv′er** n.

re·viv·i·fy (ri viv′ə fī′) vt., vi. **-fied′, -fy′ing** to give or acquire new life or vigor; revive [the music *revivified* our drooping spirits] —**re·viv′i·fi·ca′tion** n. —**re·viv′i·fi′er** n.

rev·o·ca·ble (rev′ə kə b'l) adj. that can be revoked: also **re·vok·a·ble** (ri vō′kə b'l) —**rev′o·ca·bil′i·ty** n. —**rev′o·ca·bly** adv.

rev·o·ca·tion (rev′ə kā′shən) n. a revoking or being revoked; repeal; annulment

rev·o·ca·to·ry (rev′ə kə tôr′ē) adj. revoking or tending to revoke

re·voke (ri vōk′) vt. **-voked′, -vok′ing** [< MFr. < L. < *re-*, back + *vocare*, to call: for IE. base see VOICE] to withdraw, repeal, or cancel (a law, permit, etc.) —vi. same as RENEGE (sense 2) —n. same as RENEGE —see SYN. at ABOLISH —**re·vok′er** n.

re·volt (ri vōlt′) n. [< Fr. < It., ult. < L. *revolvere*: see REVOLVE] **1.** a rising up against the government; rebellion **2.** any refusal to obey rules, customs, authority, etc. [her *revolt* against the dictates of fashion] **3.** the state of a person or persons revolting —vi. **1.** to rise up against the government **2.** to refuse to submit to authority; rebel **3.** to be disgusted or shocked (with *at* or *against*) [his stomach *revolted* at the smell] —vt. to disgust [such cruelty *revolts* her] —see SYN. at REBELLION —**re·volt′er** n.

re·volt·ing (-vōl′tiŋ) adj. **1.** engaged in revolt; rebellious **2.** causing disgust or revulsion; disgusting —**re·volt′ing·ly** adv.

rev·o·lute (rev′ə loot′) adj. [< L. pp. of *revolvere*: see REVOLVE] rolled backward at the tips or margins, as some leaves

rev·o·lu·tion (rev′ə loo′shən) n. [< OFr. < LL. < L. pp. of *revolvere*: see REVOLVE] **1.** a) movement of a body, as of a star or planet, in an orbit or circle: in this sense, distinguished from ROTATION b) the time taken for a body to go around an orbit **2.** a) a turning motion of a body around its center or axis; rotation b) one complete turn of such a rotating body **3.** a complete cycle of events [the *revolution* of the seasons] **4.** a complete or radical change of any kind [a *revolution* in modern physics] **5.** overthrow of a government or social system, with another taking its place —see SYN. at REBELLION

rev·o·lu·tion·ar·y (-er′ē) adj. **1.** of, like, favoring, or causing a revolution in a government or social system **2.** bringing about a very great change [a *revolutionary* discovery in biology] ☆**3.** [R-] having to do with the American Revolution **4.** revolving or rotating —n., pl. **-ar·ies** a person who favors or takes part in a revolution

☆**Revolutionary War** see AMERICAN REVOLUTION

rev·o·lu·tion·ist (-ist) n. a person who favors or takes part in a revolution

rev·o·lu·tion·ize (-īz′) vt. **-ized′, -iz′ing 1.** to make a complete and basic change in [automation has *revolutionized* industry] **2.** [Rare] to bring about a political revolution in

re·volve (ri välv′) vt. **-volved′, -volv′ing** [< L. < *re-*, back + *volvere*, to roll: see WALK] **1.** to turn over in the mind; reflect on **2.** to cause to travel in a circle or orbit **3.** to cause to rotate, or spin around an axis —vi. **1.** to move in a circle or orbit **2.** to spin or turn around a center or axis; rotate **3.** to seem to move (*around* or *about* something) [her life *revolves* around her family] **4.** to recur at intervals **5.** to be thought over —see SYN. at TURN —**re·volv′a·ble** adj.

re·volv·er (ri väl′vər) n. ☆a handgun with a revolving cylinder holding several bullets which can be fired without reloading

re·volv·ing (-viŋ) adj. **1.** that revolves ☆**2.** a) designating a fund that is regularly refilled, for making loans, payments, etc. b) designating credit, as for a charge account, that is renewed for a certain amount if regular payments are made

☆**revolving door** a door having four panels hung on a central axle, and turned around by pushing on a panel

REVOLVER

re·vue (ri vyoo′) n. [Fr.: see REVIEW] a musical show consisting of skits, songs, and dances, often making fun of well-known people and of current events, plays, etc.

---

re·vis′it   **re·vis′u·al·ize′**   **re·vi′tal·ize′**   **re·vote′**

---

fat, āpe, cär; ten, ēven; is, bīte; gō, hôrn, too̅l, look; oil, out; up, fur; get; joy; yet; chin; she; thin, then; zh, leisure; ŋ, ring; ə for a in ago, e in agent, i in sanity, o in comply, u in focus; ' as in able (ā′b'l); Fr. bal; ë, Fr. coeur; ö, Fr. feu; Fr. mon; ô, Fr. coq; ü, Fr. duc; r, Fr. cri; H, G. ich; kh, G. doch; ‡foreign; ☆ Americanism; < derived from. See inside front cover.

re·vul·sion (ri vul′shən) *n.* [< Fr. < L. < pp. of *revellere* < *re-*, back + *vellere*, to pull] **1.** a sudden, complete, and violent change of feeling **2.** extreme disgust; loathing [filled with *revulsion* at the sight of the worm in the apple] —see SYN. at AVERSION —**re·vul′sive** *adj.*

re·ward (ri wôrd′) *n.* [< ONormFr. (for OFr. *regarde*) < *regarder:* see REGARD] **1.** something given in return for something done, esp. for something good **2.** money offered, as for the capture of a criminal, the return of something lost, etc. **3.** a result that satisfies or benefits [increased skill is the *reward* of long practice] —*vt.* **1.** to give a reward to [to *reward* the hero] **2.** to give a reward for [to *reward* his bravery] **3.** to serve as a reward to or for [a splendid view *rewards* the weary hiker] —**re·ward′a·ble** *adj.* —**re·ward′er** *n.*

re·ward·ing (-iŋ) *adj.* giving a sense of reward; satisfying, beneficial, etc. [a *rewarding* experience] —**re·ward′ing·ly** *adv.*

re·wind (rē wīnd′) *vt.* -wound′, -wind′ing to wind again; specif., to wind (film, tape, etc.) back on the original reel —*n.* **1.** something rewound **2.** a rewinding

re·wire (rē wīr′) *vt., vi.* -wired′, -wir′ing to wire again; specif., to put new wires in or on (a house, motor, etc.)

re·word (rē wurd′) *vt.* to state again in other words; change the wording of

re·work (rē wurk′) *vt.* to work again; specif., *a)* to rewrite or revise *b)* to process (something used) for use again

re·write (rē rīt′; *for n.* rē′rīt′) *vt., vi.* -wrote′, -writ′ten, -writ′ing **1.** to write again **2.** to revise ☆**3.** to write (news turned in by a reporter) in a different form for publication —☆*n.* an article so written —**re·writ′er** *n.*

Rex (reks) [L., a king] a masculine name —*n.* [*also* r-] ′king: the official title of a reigning king [George *Rex*]

Rey·kja·vik (rā′kyə vēk′) capital of Iceland: seaport on the SW coast: pop. 81,000

Reyn·ard (ren′ərd, rā′nərd, rā′närd) [OFr. *Renard* < OHG.] the fox in the medieval beast epic *Reynard the Fox;* hence, a name for the fox in folk tales, etc.

Reyn·olds (ren′əldz), Sir **Joshua** 1723–92; Eng. portrait painter

Rey·no·sa (rā nō′sä) city in N Mexico, on the Rio Grande: pop. 107,000

RF, R.F., r.f. **1.** radio frequency **2.** rapid-fire

rf., rf *Baseball* right field (or fielder)

RFD, R.F.D. Rural Free Delivery

Rh **1.** *see* RH FACTOR **2.** *Chem.* rhodium

r.h. relative humidity

r.h., R.H., RH right hand

Rhad·a·man·thus (rad′ə man′thəs) *Gr. Myth.* a son of Zeus who after he died became a judge of the dead in the lower world

Rhae·ti·a (rē′shē ə, -shə) ancient Roman province in the region of modern Bavaria, E Switzerland, & the N Tirol —**Rhae′tian** (-shən) *adj., n.*

rhap·sod·ic (rap säd′ik) *adj.* of, or having the nature of, rhapsody; extravagantly enthusiastic [*rhapsodic* praise]: also **rhap·sod′i·cal** —**rhap·sod′i·cal·ly** *adv.*

rhap·so·dize (rap′sə dīz′) *vi., vt.* -dized′, -diz′ing to speak, write, or recite in a rhapsodic manner or form —**rhap′so·dist** *n.*

rhap·so·dy (-dē) *n., pl.* -dies [< Fr. < Gr. *rhapsōidia*, ult. < *rhaptein*, to stitch together + *ōidē*, song] **1.** a speech or writing showing very great enthusiasm or very strong feeling [she went into *rhapsodies* of delight over the gift] **2.** a musical composition that is free in form and full of feeling

Rhe·a (rē′ə) *Gr. Myth.* the daughter of Uranus and Gaea, wife of Cronus, and mother of Zeus, Hera, etc. —*n.* [r-] a large S. American nonflying bird, resembling the African ostrich but smaller and having a feathered neck and head

Rheims (rēmz; *Fr.* raⁿs) *former sp. of* REIMS

Rhen·ish (ren′ish) *adj.* [< L. *Rhenus*, Rhine] of the Rhine or the regions around it —*n.* [Now Rare] *same as* RHINE WINE

rhe·ni·um (rē′nē əm) *n.* [ModL. < L. *Rhenus*, Rhine] a rare metallic chemical element resembling manganese: symbol, Re; at. wt., 186.2; at no., 75

rhe·o- [< Gr. *rheos*, current < *rhein*, to flow] *a combining form meaning* a flow, current [rheostat]

rhe·o·stat (rē′ə stat′) *n.* [RHEO- + -STAT] a device for varying the resistance of an electric circuit without interrupting the circuit, used to dim or brighten electric lights —**rhe′o·stat′ic** *adj.*

rhe·sus (rē′səs) *n.* [ModL. < L. < Gr. *Rhēsos*, proper name] a brownish-yellow macaque of India, often kept in zoos and used in medical research: in full, **rhesus monkey**

rhet·o·ric (ret′ər ik) *n.* [< OFr. < L. < Gr. *rhētorikē* (*technē*), oratorical (art) < *rhētōr*, orator] **1.** the art of using words effectively in speaking or writing; esp., now, the art of prose composition **2.** a book on this **3.** a way of speaking or writing that is filled with showy or impressive expressions but is often empty of ideas

rhe·tor·i·cal (ri tôr′i k'l, -tär′-) *adj.* **1.** of, having the nature of, or according to rhetoric [his *rhetorical* skill] **2.** using rhetoric; showy or impressive in speech or writing —**rhe·tor′i·cal·ly** *adv.*

rhetorical question a question asked only for effect, not because an answer is expected (Example: who wouldn't be happy on a beautiful day like this?)

rhet·o·ri·cian (ret′ə rish′ən) *n.* **1.** a person skilled in using or teaching the art of rhetoric **2.** a person who speaks or writes in a showy, elaborate way

rheum (rōōm) *n.* [< OFr. < L. < Gr. *rheuma*, a flow] **1.** any watery discharge from the mucous membranes, as of the mouth, eyes, or nose **2.** a cold; rhinitis —**rheum′y** *adj.* **rheum′i·er**, **rheum′i·est**

rheu·mat·ic (rōō mat′ik) *adj.* of, caused by, or having rheumatism —*n.* a person who has rheumatism —**rheu·mat′i·cal·ly** *adv.*

rheumatic fever a disease in which there is fever, pain and swelling of the joints, and inflammation of the heart, typically occurring in children and young adults

rheu·ma·tism (rōō′mə tiz'm) *n.* [< L. < Gr. *rheumatismos:* see RHEUM] *a popular term for* any of various painful conditions in which the joints and muscles become inflamed and stiff, including rheumatoid arthritis, bursitis, etc.

rheu·ma·toid (-toid′) *adj.* of or like rheumatism

rheumatoid arthritis a chronic disease in which the joints become inflamed, painful, and swollen often to the extent that fingers, toes, etc. become deformed

☆**Rh factor** (är′ach′) [RH(ESUS): first discovered in rhesus monkeys] a group of antigens, often present in human red blood cells, which can cause complications during pregnancy in some cases: people who have this factor are **Rh positive**; those who lack it are **Rh negative**

rhi·nal (rī′n'l) *adj.* [RHIN(O)- + -AL] of the nose; nasal

Rhine (rīn) river in W Europe, flowing from E Switzerland through Germany & the Netherlands into the North Sea

Rhine·land (rīn′land′, -lənd) that part of Germany west of the Rhine

rhine·stone (rīn′stōn′) *n.* [transl. of Fr. *caillou du Rhin:* so called because orig. made at Strasbourg (on the Rhine)] a bright, artificial gem made of hard, colorless glass, often cut to look like a diamond

Rhine wine **1.** any of various wines produced in the Rhine Valley, esp. any such light, dry white wine **2.** a wine like this produced elsewhere

rhi·ni·tis (rī nīt′əs) *n.* [ModL.: see RHINO- & -ITIS] inflammation of the mucous membrane of the nose

rhi·no (rī′nō) *n., pl.* -nos, -no shortened form of RHINOCEROS

rhi·no- [< Gr. *rhinos*, genitive of *rhis*, the nose] *a combining form meaning* nose: also, before a vowel, **rhin-**

rhi·noc·er·os (rī näs′ər əs) *n., pl.* -os·es, -os: see PLURAL, II, D, 1 [< L. < Gr. < *rhis* (see prec.) + *keras*, HORN] any of various large, thick-skinned, plant-eating mammals of Africa and Asia, with one or two upright horns on the snout

rhi·zo- [< Gr. *rhiza*, a root] *a combining form meaning* root: also, before a vowel, **rhiz-**

rhi·zoid (rī′zoid) *adj.* [RHIZ(O)- + -OID] rootlike —*n.* any of the rootlike filaments in a moss, fern, etc. that attach the plant to the soil, etc. —**rhi·zoi′dal** *adj.*

RHESUS
MONKEY
(head & body
to 18 in.; tail
to 8 in.)

INDIAN
RHINOCEROS
(3–6½ ft. high
at shoulder)

rhi·zome (rī′zōm) *n.* [ModL. < Gr., ult. < *rhiza,* a root] a creeping stem lying at or under the surface of the soil: it has scale leaves, bears leaves or aerial shoots near its tips, and produces roots from its undersurface — **rhi·zom′a·tous** (-zäm′ə təs, -zō′mə-) *adj.*

rhi·zo·pod (rī′zə päd′) *n.* [RHIZO- + -POD] any of a class of one-celled animals with pseudopodia, including the amoebas, foraminifers, etc. —**rhi·zop′o·dous** (-zäp′ə dəs) *adj.*

☆**Rh negative** *see* RH FACTOR

rho (rō) *n.* [Gr.] the seventeenth letter of the Greek alphabet (P, ρ)

RHIZOME OF GRASS

Rho·da (rō′də) [< L. < Gr. < *rhodon,* a rose, prob. akin to L. *rosa*] a feminine name

Rhode Island (rōd) [< ? Du. *Roodt Eylandt,* red island, or < ? RHODES] New England State of the U.S.: 1,214 sq. mi.; pop. 950,000; cap. Providence: abbrev. **R.I., RI** —**Rhode Islander**

☆**Rhode Island Red** any of a breed of American chickens with reddish-brown feathers and a black tail

☆**Rhode Island White** any of a breed of chickens similar to Rhode Island Reds, but with white feathers

Rhodes (rōdz) largest island of the Dodecanese, in the Aegean: 545 sq. mi. —**Rho·di·an** (rō′dē ən) *adj., n.*

Rhodes (rōdz), **Cecil John** 1853–1902; Brit. financier & administrator in S Africa

Rho·de·sia (rō dē′zhə, -zhē ə) *former name* (1965–79) *of* ZIMBABWE: before 1965 (as *Southern Rhodesia*) a Brit. territory — **Rho·de′sian** *adj., n.*

Rhodesian man [skeletal remains found in Northern *Rhodesia*] a form of primitive man of the later Pleistocene, with massive brow ridges

rho·di·um (rō′dē əm) *n.* [ModL. < Gr. *rhodon,* a rose: from the color of its salts in solution] a hard, gray-white metallic chemical element, used in alloys with platinum and gold: symbol, Rh; at. wt., 102.905; at. no., 45

rho·do- [< Gr. *rhodon,* a rose] *a combining form meaning* rose, rose-red: also, before a vowel, **rhod-**

rho·do·den·dron (rō′də den′drən) *n.* [L. < Gr. < *rhodon,* a rose + *dendron,* a tree] any of a group of trees and shrubs, mainly evergreen, with showy flowers of pink, white, or purple

rho·dop·sin (rō däp′sin) *n.* [< Gr. *rhodon,* rose + *ōps,* EYE + -IN¹] a purplish pigment in the rods of the retina, needed for seeing in dim light

RHOMBOID

rhom·ben·ceph·a·lon (räm′ben sef′ə län′) *n.* [< ModL.] *same as* HINDBRAIN

rhom·bic (räm′bik) *adj.* **1.** of, or having the form of, a rhombus **2.** orthorhombic, as some crystals

rhom·bo·he·dron (räm′bə hē′drən) *n., pl.* **-drons, -dra** (-drə) [ModL.: see RHOMBUS & -HEDRON] a six-sided prism each face of which is a rhombus —**rhom·bo·he′dral** *adj.*

rhom·boid (räm′boid) *n.* [< Fr. < L. < Gr.: see RHOMBUS & -OID] a parallelogram with oblique angles and only the opposite sides equal —*adj.* shaped like a rhomboid or rhombus: also **rhom·boi′dal**

rhom·bus (räm′bəs) *n., pl.* **-bus·es, -bi** (-bī) [L. < Gr. *rhombos,* turnable object] an equilateral parallelogram, esp. one with oblique angles: also **rhomb**

Rhon·dda (rän′də) city in SE Wales: pop. 94,000

Rhone, Rhône (rōn) river flowing from SW Switzerland south through France into the Mediterranean

RHOMBUS

☆**Rh positive** *see* RH FACTOR

rhu·barb (rōō′bärb) *n.* [< OFr. < ML. < LL. < Gr. *rhēon,* rhubarb + *barbaron,* foreign] **1.** a perennial plant having large leaves whose long, thick, sour stalks are cooked into a sauce or baked in pies ☆**2.** [Slang] a heated argument

rhumb (rum, rumb) *n.* [< Port. & Sp. *rumbo,* prob. < L. *rhombus,* RHOMBUS] any of the points of a mariner's compass

☆**rhum·ba** (rum′bə) *n. alt. sp. of* RUMBA

rhumb line the course of a ship that keeps a constant compass

direction, charted as a line cutting all meridians at the same angle

rhyme (rīm) *n.* [< OFr. < *rimer,* to rhyme, prob. < Frank. word thought to be *rim,* a row (for IE. base see ART¹): form < L. *rhythmus,* rhythm] **1.** likeness of sounds at the ends of words or lines of verse **2.** a word that has the same end sound as another [''lazy'' is a *rhyme* for ''daisy''] **3.** a poem, or verse in general, using such end sounds —*vi.* **rhymed, rhym′ing 1.** to make verse, esp. rhyming verse **2.** to form a rhyme [''more'' *rhymes* with ''door''] **3.** to be in metrical form with rhymes; have rhymes [blank verse does not *rhyme*] —*vt.* **1.** to put into rhyme **2.** to compose in metrical form with rhymes **3.** to use as a rhyme [to *rhyme* ''new'' with ''true''] —**rhyme or reason** order or sense: preceded by *without, no,* etc. —**rhym′er** *n.*

rhyme scheme the pattern of rhymes used in a piece of verse, as the pattern *ababbcc* in the **rhyme royal** stanza of Chaucer

rhyme·ster (rīm′stər) *n.* a writer of light, simple verses

rhythm (ri‍th′m, ri‍th′əm) *n.* [< Fr. < L. < Gr. *rhythmos,* measure < *rhein,* to flow] **1.** *a)* flow or movement having a regularly repeated pattern of accents, beats, etc. [the *rhythm* of the waves, of dancing, of the heartbeat, etc.] *b)* the pattern of this **2.** the repeated occurrence at regular times of certain events, changes, etc. [the *rhythm* of the menstrual periods] **3.** *Music a)* regular, repeated grouping of strong and weak beats, or heavily and lightly accented tones *b)* the form or pattern of this [waltz *rhythm*] **4.** *Prosody* the form or pattern of the regularly repeated stressed and unstressed or long and short syllables [iambic *rhythm*] —**rhyth′mic** (ri‍th′mik), **rhyth′mi·cal** *adj.* —**rhyth′mi·cal·ly** *adv.*

☆**rhythm and blues** a form of popular U.S. Negro music, influenced by the blues and having a strong beat

rhythm method a method of seeking birth control by not having sexual intercourse during the probable period of ovulation

rhythm section those instruments in a band, as the drums, bass viol, etc., that mainly supply rhythm

R.I., RI Rhode Island

ri·al (rī′əl) *n.* [Per. < Ar. < Sp. *real,* REAL²] *see* MONETARY UNITS, table (Iran and Oman)

ri·al·to (rē al′tō) *n., pl.* **-tos** [< *Rialto,* a bridge in Venice, Italy] a trading area or marketplace

☆**ri·a·ta** (rē ät′ə) *n.* [AmSp. *reata,* ult. < L. *re-,* again + *aptare,* to fit] *Western term for* LARIAT

rib (rib) *n.* [OE. *rib*] **1.** any of the curved bones attached to the backbone and enclosing the chest cavity: in man there are twelve pairs of such bones: see TRUE RIBS, FALSE RIBS, FLOATING RIBS: see illustration at SKELETON **2.** *a)* a cut of meat having one or more ribs *b)* [*pl.*] shortened form of SPARERIBS **3.** a ridge in woven or knitted material **4.** any riblike piece used to form a framework, or to shape or strengthen something [an umbrella *rib*] **5.** any of the main veins of a leaf **6.** [Slang] a playfully teasing remark —*vt.* **ribbed, rib′bing 1.** to provide, form, or strengthen with ribs **2.** [Slang] to tease or make fun of; kid —**ribbed** *adj.* —**rib′ber** *n.* —**rib′less** *adj.*

rib·ald (rib′əld) *adj.* [< OFr. *ribaud,* debauchee, ult. < OHG. *riban,* to copulate] joking or humorous in a coarse or vulgar way —**see SYN.** at COARSE

rib·ald·ry (-əl drē) *n.* ribald language or humor

rib·and (rib′ənd, -ən) *n. archaic var. of* RIBBON

rib·bing (rib′in̊) *n.* an arrangement or series of ribs, as in knitted fabric, a ship's framework, etc.

rib·bon (rib′ən) *n.* [MFr. *riban*] **1.** a narrow strip as of silk or rayon, used for decorating or tying, for badges, etc. **2.** anything suggesting such a strip [a *ribbon* of blue sky] **3.** [*pl.*] torn strips or shreds; tatters [a sleeve torn to *ribbons*] ☆**4.** a narrow strip of cloth inked for use in a typewriter, etc. —*vt.* to decorate, trim, or mark with ribbons —**rib′bon·like′** *adj.*

rib·bon·fish (-fish′) *n., pl.* **-fish′, -fish′es:** see FISH any of several sea fishes with a long, narrow body

rib cage the cagelike part of the body formed by the ribs

ri·bo·fla·vin (rī′bə flā′vin) *n.* [RIBO(SE) + FLAVIN] a factor of the vitamin B complex, found in milk, eggs, liver, fruits, leafy vegetables, etc.: lack of riboflavin in the diet causes stunted growth, loss of hair, etc.

ri·bo·nu·cle·ase (rī′bō nōō′klē ās′, -nyōō′-) *n.* [RIBO(SE) + NUCLEASE] any of various enzymes that split ribonucleic acids

ri·bo·nu·cle·ic acid (rī′bō nōō klē′ik, -nyōō-) [RIBO(SE) +

NUCLEIC ACID] an essential substance in all living cells, mainly in the cytoplasm: it is made up of long chains of phosphate and ribose connected by several bases and it carries the genetic information needed to form protein in the cell: commonly called *RNA*

ri·bose (rī′bōs) *n*. [< G. *rib(onsäure)*, an acid containing four OH radicals + -OSE¹] a sugar, $C_5H_{10}O_5$, derived from nucleic acids

ri·bo·some (rī′bə sōm′) *n*. [RIBO(SE) + -SOME³] any of the minute particles composed of RNA and proteins, found in cell cytoplasm and functioning in the production of proteins —**ri′bo·so′mal** *adj*.

rice (rīs) *n*. [OFr. *ris* < It. < L. < Gr. *oryza*: of Oriental origin] **1.** a cereal grass of warm climates, planted in ground under water **2.** its starchy seeds or grain, used as food —*vt*. **riced, ric′-ing** to form (cooked potatoes, etc.) into strands the thickness of rice by pressing through a ricer

rice·bird (rīs′burd′) *n*. ☆chiefly *Southern* name for BOBOLINK

rice paper 1. a thin paper made from the straw of rice **2.** a fine, delicate paper made by cutting and pressing the pith of an Asian plant (the **rice-paper plant**)

☆**ric·er** (rī′sər) *n*. a utensil for ricing cooked potatoes, etc. by forcing them through small holes

rich (rich) *adj*. [OE. *rice*, noble, powerful < OFr. < Gmc.: for IE. base see REGAL] **1.** having much money or property; wealthy **2.** having abundant natural resources [a *rich* region] **3.** well-supplied (*with*); abounding (*in*) [*rich* in vitamin C] **4.** valuable [a *rich* prize] **5.** costly and elegant; sumptuous [*rich* gifts] **6.** *a*) full of fats, or fats and sugar [*rich* pastries] *b*) strong and flavorful [*rich* wine] **7.** *a*) full and mellow: said of sounds, the voice, etc. *b*) deep; vivid: said of colors *c*) very fragrant: said of odors **8.** abundant; ample [a *rich* fund of stories] **9.** yielding in abundance, as soil, etc. **10.** having a high proportion of fuel to air [a *rich* fuel mixture] **11.** [Colloq.] *a*) very amusing *b*) absurd —**the rich** wealthy people as a group —**rich′ness** *n*.

SYN.—**rich** is the general word for one who has much more money or income than he needs and can afford a life of luxury; **wealthy** may in addition suggest that a person's wealth gives him advantages such as social position, financial power, etc.; **affluent** suggests a continuing increase in wealth, accompanied by free or lavish spending of money for goods and services [an *affluent* community in which most families own their own homes]; **opulent** suggests a display of great wealth in luxurious or showy living [an *opulent* mansion]; **well-to-do** suggests that one has enough wealth to provide a comfortable living —ANT. poor

Rich·ard (rich′ərd) [< OFr. < OHG. *Richart* < Gmc. bases meaning "strong king"] **1.** a masculine name **2. Richard I,** 1157-99; king of England (1189-99): called **Richard the Lion-Hearted** (Fr. *Richard Coeur de Lion*) **3. Richard II,** 1367-1400; king of England (1377-99) **4. Richard III,** 1452-85; king of England (1483-85)

Rich·ard·son (rich′ərd sən), **Samuel** 1689-1761; Eng. novelist

Ri·che·lieu (rish′ə lōō′; *Fr.* rēsh lyö′), duc de (*Armand Jean du Plessis*) 1585-1642; Fr. cardinal & statesman

rich·en (rich′'n) *vt*. to make rich or richer

rich·es (rich′iz) *n.pl*. [ME. *richess*, n. *sing.* < OFr. *richesse*] valuable possessions; much money, property, etc.; wealth

rich·ly (rich′lē) *adv*. **1.** in a rich manner **2.** amply; fully [a reward she *richly* deserved]

Rich·mond (rich′mənd) **1.** [after Duke of *Richmond*, son of CHARLES II] borough of New York City, including Staten Island: pop. 295,000 **2.** [after *Richmond*, city in SE England] *a*) capital of Va.; port on the James River: pop. 250,000 (met. area 518,000) *b*) seaport in W Calif., on San Francisco Bay: pop. 79,000

☆**Rich·ter scale** (rik′tər) [devised by C. *Richter* (1900-), U.S. seismologist] a scale for measuring the force of earthquakes, with each of its 10 steps about 60 times greater than the preceding step

rick (rik) *n*. [OE. *hreac*] a stack of hay, straw, etc. in a field, esp. one covered for protection from rain —*vt*. to pile (hay, etc.) into ricks

rick·ets (rik′its) *n*. [altered < ? RACHITIS] a disease, chiefly of children, characterized by a softening and, often, bending of the bones: it is caused by lack of vitamin D

☆**rick·ett·si·a** (ri ket′sē ə) *n., pl.* **-si·ae′** (-ē′), **-si·as** [ModL., after H. T. *Ricketts* (1871-1910), U.S. pathologist] any of a genus of microorganisms that cause certain diseases, as typhus, and are transmitted by the bite of certain lice and ticks —**rick·ett′si·al** *adj*.

rick·et·y (rik′it ē) *adj*. **1.** of or having rickets **2.** weak in the joints; tottering **3.** liable to fall apart or break down; shaky [a *rickety* table] —**rick′et·i·ness** *n*.

☆**rick·rack** (rik′rak′) *n*. [redupl. of RACK¹] flat, zigzag braid for trimming dresses, etc.

rick·shaw, rick·sha (rik′shô) *n. same as* JINRIKISHA

ric·o·chet (rik′ə shā′, rik′ə shā′; *also, chiefly Brit.,* -shet′) *n*. [Fr.] **1.** the rebound or skipping of a bullet, stone, etc. after striking a surface at an angle **2.** a bullet, etc. that ricochets —*vi*. **-cheted** (-shād′) or **-chet′ted** (-shet′id), **-chet′ing** (-shā′iŋ) or **-chet′ting** (-shet′iŋ) to move with such a motion

ri·cot·ta (ri kät′ə; *It.* rē kôt′tä) *n*. [It. < L. pp. of *recoquere*, to boil again] a soft, dry or moist Italian cheese made from whey left from making other cheeses

RICKRACK

rid (rid) *vt*. **rid** or **rid′ded, rid′ding** [ON. *rythja*, to clear (land): for IE. base see RUPTURE] to free, clear, or relieve, as of something undesirable [to *rid* a garden of weeds] —**be rid of** to be freed from —**get rid of 1.** to get free from **2.** to do away with; dispose of

rid·dance (rid′'ns) *n*. a ridding or being rid; clearance or removal, as of something undesirable —**good riddance** welcome relief or deliverance: often used as an exclamation of joy at getting rid of someone or something

rid·den (rid′'n) *pp*. of RIDE —*adj*. controlled or obsessed (by the thing specified) [fear-*ridden*]

rid·dle¹ (rid′'l) *n*. [OE. *rædels*, akin to *rædan*, to guess, READ¹] **1.** a puzzle in the form of a question or statement with a tricky meaning or answer that is hard to guess; conundrum **2.** any puzzling person or thing; enigma —*vt*. **-dled, -dling** to solve or explain (something that is a riddle) —*vi*. to speak in or ask riddles —see SYN. at MYSTERY¹ —**rid′dler** *n*.

rid·dle² (rid′'l) *n*. [OE. *hriddel*: for IE. base see CARNAGE] a coarse sieve —*vt*. **-dled, -dling 1.** to sift through a riddle **2.** *a*) to make many holes in, as with buckshot or bullets *b*) to affect every part of; spread throughout [*riddled* with errors]

ride (rīd) *vi*. **rode** or archaic **rid** (rid), **rid′den** or archaic **rid** or **rode, rid′ing** [OE. *ridan* < IE. base *reidh-*, to go] **1.** *a*) to sit on and control a horse or other animal in motion *b*) to be carried along (*in* a vehicle, *on* a bicycle, etc.) *c*) to move along as if so carried *d*) to be carried or supported in motion (*on* or *upon*) [tanks *ride* on treads] **2.** to carry a rider, passengers, etc. [the car *rides* smoothly] **3.** to move, lie, or float on the water **4.** to be dependent (*on*) [the change *rides* on his approval] **5.** to be placed as a bet (*on*) [he has $5 *riding* on the favorite] ☆**6.** [Colloq.] to continue undisturbed, with no action taken [let the matter *ride*] —*vt*. **1.** to sit on or in and control so as to move along [to *ride* a horse] **2.** to move along on or be carried or supported on [to *ride* the waves] **3.** to move over, along, or through (a road, area, etc.) by horse, car, etc. **4.** to cover (a specified distance) by riding **5.** to engage in by riding [to *ride* a race] **6.** to cause to ride; carry [I'll *ride* you home on my bike] **7.** to control, dominate, or oppress [*ridden* by fear] **8.** [Colloq.] to torment or tease, as with ridicule, criticism, etc. —*n*. **1.** *a*) a riding; esp., a journey by horse, car, bicycle, etc. *b*) a way or chance to ride [she's looking for a *ride* to Chicago] *c*) the way a car, etc. rides **2.** a road, etc. for riding **3.** a roller coaster, Ferris wheel, or other thing to ride, as at a carnival —see SYN. at BAIT —**ride down 1.** to knock down by riding against **2.** to overtake by riding **3.** to overcome —**ride out** to withstand or endure (a storm, crisis, etc.) successfully —**ride up** to move upward out of place, as an article of clothing —☆**take for a ride** [Slang] to cheat or swindle —**rid′a·ble, ride′a·ble** *adj*.

rid·er (rīd′ər) *n*. **1.** a person who rides **2.** *a*) an addition or amendment to a contract, etc. *b*) a clause, usually dealing with an unrelated matter, added to a proposed law before it is voted on —**rid′er·less** *adj*.

rid·er·ship (-ship′) *n*. the passengers using a particular system of public transportation over a given period of time, or the estimated number of these

ridge (rij) *n*. [OE. *hrycg*: for IE. base see CIRCUS] **1.** the long, narrow top or crest of something, as of an animal's back, a wave, etc. **2.** a long, narrow elevation of land or similar range of hills or mountains **3.** any narrow, raised strip, as on fabric **4.** the horizontal line formed by the meeting of two sloping surfaces [the *ridge* of a roof] —*vt., vi.* **ridged, ridg′ing** to form into or mark with a ridge or ridges —**ridge′like′** *adj*. —**ridg′y** *adj*.

ridge·pole (rij'pōl') *n.* the horizontal timber or beam at the ridge of a roof: also **ridge'piece'**

rid·i·cule (rid'i kyool') *n.* [Fr. < L. *ridiculum*, a jest, ult. < *ridere*, to laugh: for IE. base see VERSE] **1.** the act of making a person or thing seem foolish, as by making fun of, mocking, laughing, etc. **2.** words or actions used in doing this —*vt.* **-culed', -cul'ing** to make fun of or make others laugh at; deride; mock

RIDGEPOLE

SYN.—ridicule implies a making fun of a person or thing by way of showing disapproval [he *ridiculed* her new hat]; deride suggests contempt for or a strong dislike of what is being made fun of [to *deride* another's beliefs]; mock suggests a ridiculing by the unkind imitation of another's mannerisms or habits [it is cruel to *mock* his lisp]; taunt implies insulting ridicule, esp. as shown by jeering at another and harping on something that makes him feel ashamed [they *taunted* him about his failure]

ri·dic·u·lous (ri dik'yə ləs) *adj.* deserving ridicule; absurd —see SYN. at ABSURD —**ri·dic'u·lous·ly** *adv.* —**ri·dic'u·lous·ness** *n.*

rid·ing[1] (rīd'iŋ) *adj.* **1.** that rides **2.** of or for riders on horseback [jodhpurs and boots are parts of a *riding* habit] ☆**3.** designed to be worked by a rider [a *riding* mower] —*n.* the act of one that rides

rid·ing[2] (rīd'iŋ) *n.* [OE. *-thrithing*, a third part] any of the three administrative divisions of Yorkshire, England

ri·el (rē el', rēl) *n.* [see RIAL, REAL[2]] *see* MONETARY UNITS, table (Cambodia)

Rif (rif) mountain range along the Mediterranean coast of Morocco: also **Er Rif** (er)

rife (rīf) *adj.* [OE. *ryfe*] **1.** happening frequently or commonly; widespread [gossip was *rife*] **2.** *a)* abundant *b)* abounding; filled [*rife* with error] —see SYN. at PREVAILING —**rife'ness** *n.*

Riff (rif) *same as* RIF —*n., pl.* **Riffs, Riff'i** (-ē) a member of a Berber people living in or near the Rif

☆**riff** (rif) *n.* [prob. altered < REFRAIN[2]] *Jazz* a short musical phrase played again and again —*vi.* Jazz to play a riff

rif·fle (rif'l) *n.* [< ? or akin to G. *riffel*, a groove: for IE. base see ROW[1]] ☆**1.** *a)* a shoal, reef, etc. in a stream, producing a stretch of ruffled or choppy water *b)* a stretch of such water, or a ripple on it **2.** the act or a method of riffling cards —*vt., vi.* **-fled, -fling 1.** to ruffle or ripple **2.** to leaf rapidly through (a book, etc.) by letting the edges of the pages slip lightly across the thumb **3.** to shuffle (playing cards) in a way like this by holding part of the deck in each hand

riff·raff (rif'raf') *n.* [< OFr. *rif et raf* < *rifler*, to scrape + *rafle*, a raking in] **1.** those people regarded as worthless, low, coarse, etc.; rabble **2.** [Dial.] trash

ri·fle[1] (rī'f'l) *vt.* **-fled, -fling** [Fr. *rifler*, to scrape < OFr. < MHG. *riffeln*, to scratch] **1.** to cut spiral grooves on the inside of (a gun barrel, etc.) ☆**2.** to hurl or throw with great speed —*n.* ☆**1.** a shoulder gun with spiral grooves cut into the inner surface of the barrel: see RIFLING **2.** [*pl.*] troops armed with rifles

ri·fle[2] (rī'f'l) *vt.* **-fled, -fling** [< OFr. *rifler*, to plunder, orig. to scratch: see prec.] **1.** to ransack in order to rob; pillage; plunder [to *rifle* a safe] **2.** to take as plunder; steal —**ri'fler** *n.*

☆**ri·fle·man** (-mən) *n., pl.* **-men 1.** a soldier armed with a rifle **2.** a man who uses, or is skilled in using, a rifle

rifle range a place for target practice with a rifle

☆**ri·fle·ry** (-rē) *n.* the skill or practice of shooting at targets with rifles

ri·fling (rī'fliŋ) *n.* **1.** the cutting of spiral grooves within a gun barrel, to make the projectile spin when fired **2.** a system of such grooves

rift (rift) *n.* [Dan., a fissure < *rive*, to tear: see RIVE] **1.** an opening caused by splitting; fissure; cleft **2.** an open break in friendly relations —*vt., vi.* to burst open; split

rig (rig) *vt.* **rigged, rig'ging** [< Scand.] **1.** *a)* to fit (a ship, mast, etc.) with sails, shrouds, etc. *b)* to fit (a ship's sails, shrouds, etc.) to the masts, yards, etc. **2.** to fit (*out*); equip **3.** to put together or prepare for use, esp. in a makeshift or hasty way (often with *up*) [to *rig* up a table out of old boxes] **4.** to arrange in a dishonest way; fix [to *rig* an election] **5.** [Colloq.]

to dress; clothe (usually with *out*) [all *rigged* out in a cowboy suit] —*n.* **1.** the arrangement of sails, masts, etc. on a vessel ☆**2.** equipment for a special purpose; gear [a ham radio operator's *rig*] ☆**3.** equipment for drilling an oil well ☆**4.** *a)* a carriage, etc. with its horse or horses *b)* a tractor-trailer or, sometimes, the tractor alone **5.** [Colloq.] dress or costume, esp. if odd or showy —**rig'ger** *n.*

Ri·ga (rē'gə) capital of the Latvian S.S.R.; seaport on the Baltic Sea: pop. 733,000

rig·a·ma·role (rig'ə mə rōl') *n. var. of* RIGMAROLE

rig·a·to·ni (rig'ə tō'nē; *It.* rē'gä tô'nē) *n.* [It., pl. < pp. of *rigare*, to mark with lines] short, ridged casings of pasta, often stuffed with ground meat, cheese, etc.

Ri·gel (rī'j'l, -g'l) [Ar. *rijl*, foot: in the left foot of Orion] a bright, bluish star, brightest in the constellation Orion

rig·ging (rig'iŋ) *n.* **1.** the chains, ropes, etc. used for supporting and working the masts, sails, etc. of a vessel ☆**2.** equipment; gear

right (rīt) *adj.* [OE. *riht*: for IE. base see REGAL] **1.** orig., straight: now only in mathematics [a *right* line] **2.** *a)* formed by a straight line perpendicular to a base [a *right* angle] *b)* having the axis perpendicular to the base [a *right* cylinder] **3.** in accordance with justice, law, morality, etc.; virtuous [*right* conduct] **4.** in accordance with fact, reason, etc.; correct; true [the *right* answer] **5.** fitting; suitable [the *right* dress for a dance] **6.** designating the side meant to be seen [the *right* side of cloth] **7.** *a)* physically or mentally healthy [he doesn't look *right*] *b)* in a satisfactory condition; in good order [to make things *right* again] **8.** *a)* designating or of that side of one's body which is toward the east when one faces north, the side of the more-used hand in most people *b)* designating or of the corresponding side of anything *c)* closer to the right side of a person facing the thing mentioned [the top *right* drawer] **9.** of the bank of a river on the right of a person facing downstream **10.** of the political right; conservative or reactionary —*n.* **1.** what is right, or just, lawful, proper, etc. [to know *right* from wrong] **2.** *a)* a power, privilege, etc. that a person has or gets by law, nature, tradition, etc. [the *right* of free speech] *b)* [often *pl.*] an interest in property, real or intangible **3.** the true or correct report, as of a happening (with *the*) **4.** *a)* the right side [the first door on the *right*] *b)* a turn toward the right side [take a *right* at the corner] **5.** *Boxing a)* the right hand *b)* a blow delivered with the right hand **6.** [often R-] *Politics* a conservative or reactionary position, party, etc. (often with *the*): from the seating (on the right) of conservatives in some European legislatures —*adv.* **1.** in a straight line; directly [go right home] **2.** in a way that is correct, proper, just, favorable, etc.; well [do it *right*] **3.** completely [soaked *right* through his coat] **4.** exactly [*right* here] ☆**5.** immediately [come right down] **6.** on or toward the right hand or side **7.** very [he knows *right* well]: colloquial except in certain titles [the *right* reverend] —*interj.* agreed! I understand! —*vt.* **1.** to put in or restore to an upright position [to *right* a capsized boat] **2.** to correct [to *right* an error] **3.** to put in order [she *righted* the room] **4.** to make amends for [to *right* a wrong] —*vi.* to regain an upright position —**by right** (or **rights**) in justice; properly —**in one's own right** through one's own status, ability, etc. —**in the right** on the side supported by truth, justice, etc. —**right away** (or **off**) without delay; at once —**to rights** [Colloq.] in or into proper condition or order —**right'er** *n.* —**right'ness** *n.*

right·a·bout (rīt'ə bout') *n. same as* RIGHTABOUT-FACE —*adv., adj.* with, in, or by a rightabout-face

right·a·bout-face (-fās') *n.* **1.** a turning directly about so as to face in the opposite direction **2.** a complete turnabout, as of belief —*interj.* a military command to do a rightabout-face

right angle an angle of 90 degrees, made by the meeting of two straight lines perpendicular to each other

right-an·gled (rīt'aŋ'g'ld) *adj.* having or forming one or more right angles; rectangular: also **right'-an'gle**

right·eous (rī'chəs) *adj.* [altered < OE. *rihtwis*: see RIGHT & -WISE] **1.** acting justly; doing what is right; upright; virtuous [a *righteous* man] **2.** morally right or having a sound moral basis [*righteous* anger] —see SYN. at MORAL —**right'eous·ly** *adv.* —**right'eous·ness** *n.*

RIGHT ANGLE

☆**right field** *Baseball* the right-hand part of the outfield (as viewed from home plate)

right·ful (rīt′fəl) *adj.* **1.** fair and just; right [*a rightful act*] **2.** having or based on a just, lawful claim, or right [*the rightful owner; his rightful share*] **3.** proper; fitting [*harsh sounds that have no rightful place in such music*] —**right′ful·ly** *adv.* —**right′ful·ness** *n.*

right-hand (rīt′hand′) *adj.* **1.** on or directed toward the right **2.** of, for, or with the right hand **3.** most helpful or reliable [*the president's right-hand man*]

right-hand·ed (-han′did) *adj.* **1.** using the right hand more skillfully than the left **2.** done with the right hand [*a right-handed throw*] **3.** made for use with the right hand [*a right-handed catcher's mitt*] **4.** turning from left to right; worked by clockwise motion —*adv.* with the right hand [*to throw right-handed*] —**right′-hand′ed·ly** *adv.* —**right′-hand′ed·ness** *n.* —**right′-hand′er** *n.*

right·ist (rīt′ist) *n.* a person whose political position is conservative or reactionary; member of the right —*adj.* conservative or reactionary —**right′ism** *n.*

right·ly (rīt′lē) *adv.* **1.** with justice; fairly **2.** properly; suitably **3.** correctly

right-mind·ed (rīt′mīn′did) *adj.* thinking or believing what is right; having correct views or sound principles —**right′-mind′ed·ly** *adv.* —**right′-mind′ed·ness** *n.*

right of way **1.** the legal right to go first or to cross in front of another, as at a traffic intersection **2.** the right to use a certain route, as over another's property ☆**3.** *a)* a strip of land used by a railroad for its tracks *b)* land over which a public road, an electric power line, etc. passes Also **right′-of-way′** *n.*

☆**right-to-work** (rīt′tə wurk′) *adj.* designating or of laws prohibiting the union shop

right triangle a triangle with a right angle

right·ward (rīt′wərd) *adv., adj.* on or toward the right: also **right′wards** *adv.*

☆**right whale** a large-headed whalebone whale without teeth or dorsal fin

right wing [see RIGHT, *n.* 6] the more conservative or reactionary section of a political party, group, etc. —**right′-wing′** *adj.* —**right′-wing′er** *n.*

rig·id (rij′id) *adj.* [< L. < *rigere*, to be stiff] **1.** not bending or flexible; stiff [*a rigid metal girder*] **2.** not moving; set **3.** severe, strict, or rigorous [*a rigid taskmaster, a rigid rule*] **4.** *Aeron.* having a rigid framework that encloses containers for the gas, as a dirigible —see SYN. at STRICT —**ri·gid·i·ty** (ri jid′ə tē), **rig′id·ness** *n.* —**rig′id·ly** *adv.*

ri·gid·i·fy (ri jid′ə fī′) *vt., vi.* **-fied′, -fy′ing** to make or become rigid —**ri·gid′i·fi·ca′tion** *n.*

rig·ma·role (rig′mə rōl′) *n.* [< *ragman roll* < ME. *rageman rolle*, a long list] **1.** rambling talk; nonsense **2.** a foolish or unnecessarily complicated way of doing things

rig·or (rig′ər; *for 4, also* rī′gôr) *n.* [< MFr. < L. < *rigere*, to be rigid] **1.** harshness or severity; specif., *a)* strictness [*the rigor of martial law*] *b)* extreme hardship [*the rigors of pioneer life*] **2.** extreme precision or accuracy [*the rigor of the philosopher's reasoning*] **3.** a severe, harsh, or oppressive act, etc. **4.** stiffness or rigidity, esp. in body tissues Also, Brit. sp., **rig′our** —see SYN. at DIFFICULTY

rig·or mor·tis (rig′ər môr′tis, rī′gôr) [ModL., stiffness of death] the stiffening of the muscles after death

rig·or·ous (rig′ər əs) *adj.* **1.** very strict or stern [*rigorous rules*] **2.** very severe or harsh; hard to bear [*a rigorous climate*] **3.** exactly precise or accurate [*rigorous scholarship*] —see SYN. at STRICT —**rig′or·ous·ly** *adv.* —**rig′or·ous·ness** *n.*

Ri·je·ka (rē ye′kä) seaport in NW Yugoslavia, on the Adriatic: pop. 101,000

rile (rīl) *vt.* **riled, ril′ing** [var. of ROIL] [Colloq. or Dial.] **1.** *same as* ROIL **2.** to make angry; irritate

Ri·ley (rī′lē), **James Whit·comb** (hwit′kəm, wit′-) 1849–1916; U.S. poet

Ril·ke (ril′kə), **Rai·ner Ma·ri·a** (rī′nər mä rē′ä) 1875–1926; Austrian poet, born in Prague

rill[1] (ril) *n.* [< Du. *ril* or LowG. *rille*] a little brook

rille, rill[2] (ril) *n.* [G. *rille*, a groove] *Astron.* any of several long, narrow valleys on the moon's surface

rim (rim) *n.* [OE. *rima*, an edge] **1.** an edge, border, or margin, esp. of something circular **2.** *a)* the outer part of a wheel *b)* the metal flange of an automobile wheel, on which the tire is mounted ☆**3.** *Basketball* the metal hoop to which the net is attached —*vt.* **rimmed, rim′ming** **1.** to put a rim on or around **2.** to roll around the rim of [*the golf ball rimmed the hole*]

Rim·baud (ran bō′), **(Jean Nicolas) Ar·thur** (àr tür′) 1854–91; Fr. poet

rime[1] (rīm) *n., vt., vi.* **rimed, rim′ing** *same as* RHYME —**rim′er** *n.*

rime[2] (rīm) *n.* [OE. *hrim*] a white frost on grass, leaves, etc.; hoarfrost —*vt.* **rimed, rim′ing** to coat with rime

Rim·sky-Kor·sa·kov (rēm′skē kôr′sä kôf′; *E.* rim′skē kôr′sə kôf′), **Ni·ko·lai (Andreyevich)** (nē kô lī′) 1844–1908; Russ. composer: also sp. **Rimsky-Korsakoff**

rim·y (rīm′ē) *adj.* **rim′i·er, rim′i·est** covered with rime; frosty

rind (rīnd) *n.* [OE.] a thick, hard, or tough outer layer or coating, as on fruit, cheese, bacon, etc.

rin·der·pest (rin′dər pest′) *n.* [G. *rinder*, cattle + *pest*, a plague] an acute infectious disease of cattle and, often, sheep and goats

ring[1] (riŋ) *vi.* **rang** or now chiefly dial. **rung, rung, ring′ing** [OE. *hringan:* for IE. base see RAVEN[1]] **1.** to give forth the clear, resonant sound of a bell **2.** to produce, as by sounding, a specified impression [*promises that ring false*] **3.** to cause a bell to sound, esp. as a summons [*to ring for a maid*] **4.** to sound loudly or be full of sound; resound [*the room rang with laughter*] **5.** to have a sensation of ringing, humming, etc.: said of the ears or head —*vt.* **1.** to cause (a bell, etc.) to ring **2.** to sound (a peal, knell, etc.) as by ringing a bell **3.** to signal, announce, etc. as by ringing [*chimes rang the hours*] **4.** to call by telephone (often with *up*) —*n.* **1.** the sound of a bell **2.** any sound like this, esp. when loud and continued [*the ring of applause*] **3.** the way something sounds in showing a certain feeling [*the ring of sincerity in his voice*] **4.** the act of ringing a bell, etc. **5.** a telephone call: chiefly in **give (someone) a ring,** to telephone (someone) —**ring a bell** ☆to cause one to remember; sound familiar —**ring down** (or **up**) **the curtain** **1.** to signal for a theater curtain to be lowered (or raised) **2.** to end (or begin) something —**ring in** [Slang] to bring in or put in by a trick —**ring up** ☆to record (a specified amount) on a cash register

ring[2] (riŋ) *n.* [OE. *hring:* for IE. base see CIRCUS] **1.** a small, circular band, esp. of precious metal, to be worn on the finger **2.** any similar band used for some special purpose, as for holding or fastening things [*a key ring*] **3.** a circular line, edge, mark, or figure **4.** any of the circular marks seen in the cross section of a tree trunk: each ring represents a year's growth: in full, **annual ring** **5.** a circular course, as in dancing **6.** a number of people or things grouped in a circle ☆**7.** a group of people joined together, esp. to do something dishonest or illegal [*a spy ring*] **8.** an enclosed area, often circular, for contests, exhibitions, etc. [*a circus ring*] **9.** *a)* an enclosure, now a square, in which boxing and wrestling matches are held *b)* prizefighting (with *the*) **10.** a contest: often used in **throw one's hat into the ring,** to enter a contest, esp. one for political office **11.** *Chem.* a number of atoms united in such a way that they can be represented as a ring **12.** *Geom.* the space between two concentric circles —*vt.* **ringed, ring′ing** **1.** to encircle as with a ring [*hills ring the pasture*] **2.** to form into, or furnish with, a ring or rings **3.** in some games, to toss a ring, horseshoe, etc. so that it encircles (a peg) **4.** to cut a ring of bark from around (a tree); girdle —*vi.* to form in a ring or rings —**run rings around** [Colloq.] **1.** to run much faster than **2.** to do much better than —**ringed** *adj.*

ring·bolt (riŋ′bōlt′) *n.* a bolt with a ring at the head

ring·er[1] (riŋ′ər) *n.* **1.** a horseshoe, quoit, etc. thrown so that it encircles the peg **2.** such a throw

ring·er[2] (riŋ′ər) *n.* **1.** a person or thing that rings a bell, chime, etc. ☆**2.** [Slang] *a)* a horse, player, etc. fraudulently entered, or substituted for another, in a competition *b)* a person or thing very closely resembling another

ring·lead·er (riŋ′lēd′ər) *n.* a person who leads others, esp. in unlawful acts, etc.

ring·let (-lit) *n.* **1.** a little ring **2.** a curl of hair, esp. a long one —**ring′let·ed** *adj.*

ring·mas·ter (riŋ′mas′tər) *n.* a man who directs the performances in a circus ring

ring-necked pheasant (-nekt′) an Asian game fowl with a whitish collar around the neck in the male, now widespread in N. America: see illustration at PHEASANT

ring·side (-sīd′) *n.* **1.** the space just outside the ring, as at a boxing match or circus **2.** any place that provides a close view of something

ring-tailed (-tāld′) *adj.* having the tail marked with rings

ring·worm (-wurm′) *n.* any contagious skin disease caused by a fungus that produces itchy, ring-shaped patches

rink (riŋk) *n.* [< Scot. < OFr. *renc*, RANK[1]] **1.** a smooth area of ice, often enclosed, for ice-skating or for playing hockey **2.** a smooth floor, usually of wood and enclosed, for roller-skating **3.** a building enclosing either of such rinks

rinse (rins) *vt.* **rinsed, rins′ing** [< OFr. *rincer*, ult. < L. *recens*, fresh] **1.** to wash lightly, as by dipping into clear water **2.** *a)* to remove soap, scum, etc. from by such washing *b)* to remove (soap, scum, etc.) by such washing **3.** to flush (the mouth or teeth), as with clear water **4.** to use a rinse on (the hair) —*n.* **1.** a rinsing **2.** the water or solution used in rinsing **3.** a substance mixed with water and used to tint hair —**rins′er** *n.*

Ri·o de Ja·nei·ro (rē′ō dā′ zhə ner′ō, dē′, də; jə nir′ō) seaport in SE Brazil, on the Atlantic: pop. 4,694,000

Ri·o Grande (rē′ō grand′, gran′dē, grän′dā) river flowing from S Colo. through N.Mex., then southeast as the boundary between Texas & Mexico into the Gulf of Mexico: 1,885 mi.

ri·ot (rī′ət) *n.* [OFr. *riote* < *rihoter*, to make a disturbance] **1.** wild or violent disorder, confusion, etc.; tumult **2.** a violent, public disturbance of the peace by a number of persons (in law, usually three or more) assembled together **3.** a brilliant display [a *riot* of color] **4.** [Now Rare] *a)* debauchery *b)* wild merrymaking or a wild good time ☆**5.** [Colloq.] a very amusing person, thing, or event —*vi.* **1.** to take part in a riot or public disturbance **2.** [Now Rare] to have a wild good time —**read the riot act** to give strict orders to so as to make obey; warn sternly —**run riot 1.** to act in a wild way **2.** to grow wild in great number —**ri′ot·er** *n.*

☆**riot gun** a short-barreled repeating shotgun used to disperse rioters

ri·ot·ous (rī′ət əs) *adj.* **1.** *a)* having the nature of a disturbance of the peace *b)* engaging in rioting **2.** disorderly or boisterous **3.** debauched; immoral [*riotous* living] **4.** luxuriant or profuse —**ri′ot·ous·ly** *adv.* —**ri′ot·ous·ness** *n.*

rip[1] (rip) *vt.* **ripped, rip′ping** [prob. < or akin to Fl. *rippen*, to tear: for prob. IE. base see ROW[1]] **1.** *a)* to cut or tear apart roughly *b)* to remove as by cutting or tearing (with *off*, *out*, etc.) *c)* to make (a hole) in this way *d)* to slash with a sharp instrument *e)* to cut or tear (stitches) so as to open (a seam, hem, etc.) **2.** to saw or split (wood) along the grain —*vi.* **1.** to become torn or split apart **2.** [Colloq.] to move with speed or violence —*n.* **1.** a torn place or split seam **2.** the act of ripping —see SYN. at TEAR[1] —**rip into** [Colloq.] to attack violently, often with words —**rip off** ☆[Slang] **1.** to steal or rob **2.** to cheat, exploit, or take advantage of —**rip out** [Colloq.] to utter sharply, as in anger —**rip′per** *n.*

☆**rip**[2] (rip) *n.* [< ? prec.] an extent of rough water caused by cross currents or tides meeting

rip[3] (rip) *n.* [var. of *rep*, prob. abbrev. of REPROBATE] [Colloq.] a wild, immoral, pleasure-seeking person

R.I.P. *abbrev. of* REQUIESCAT IN PACE

ri·par·i·an (ri per′ē ən, rī-) *adj.* [< L. < *ripa*, a bank] of, adjacent to, or living on the bank of a river or, sometimes, of a lake, pond, etc.

rip cord a cord, etc. pulled to open a parachute during descent

ripe (rīp) *adj.* [OE.: for IE. base see ROW[1]] **1.** fully grown or developed; specif., ready to be harvested for food, as grain or fruit **2.** like ripe fruit, as in being well filled out or plump [*ripe* lips] **3.** ready to be used [*ripe* cheese] **4.** fully or highly developed; mature [*ripe* wisdom] **5.** advanced in years [the *ripe* age of ninety] **6.** ready to do or undergo something; fully prepared [a student *ripe* for specialized training] **7.** far enough along (*for* some purpose) [the time is *ripe* for reform] —**ripe′ly** *adv.* —**ripe′ness** *n.*

rip·en (rī′pən) *vi., vt.* to become or make ripe; mature, age, cure, etc. —**rip′en·er** *n.*

☆**rip-off** (rip′ôf′) *n.* [Slang] **1.** a stealing, robbing, cheating, exploiting, etc. **2.** something by means of which people are cheated or otherwise taken advantage of

ri·poste, ri·post (ri pōst′) *n.* [< Fr. < It. *risposta* < L. *respondere*: see RESPOND] **1.** *Fencing* a swift thrust made after parrying an opponent's lunge **2.** a sharp, swift retort —*vi.* **-post′ed, -post′ing** to make a riposte

rip·ping (rip′iŋ) *adj.* **1.** that rips or tears **2.** [Chiefly Brit. Slang] excellent; fine —**rip′ping·ly** *adv.*

rip·ple (rip′'l) *vi.* **-pled, -pling** [prob. < RIP[1] + -LE[2]] **1.** *a)* to form or have little waves on the surface, as water stirred by a breeze *b)* to flow with such waves on the surface *c)* to be

formed or set in small folds or waves, as cloth or hair **2.** to give the effect of rippling water, as by alternately rising and falling [laughter *rippling* through the hall] —*vt.* to cause to ripple —*n.* **1.** a small wave, as on the surface of water **2.** a movement, appearance, etc. like this [*ripples* in a field of grain] **3.** a sound like that of rippling water [a *ripple* of applause] —**rip′pler** *n.* —**rip′ply** (-lē) *adj.* **-pli·er, -pli·est**

rip·rap (rip′rap′) *n.* [echoic redupl. of RAP[1]] ☆**1.** a foundation or wall made of broken stones thrown together loosely, as in water ☆**2.** stones used for this

☆**rip-roar·ing** (rip′rôr′iŋ) *adj.* [Slang] very lively and noisy; boisterous; uproarious

rip·saw (rip′sô′) *n.* [RIP[1] + SAW[1]] a saw with coarse teeth, for cutting wood along the grain

rip·tide (rip′tīd′) *n.* [RIP[2] + TIDE] a tide opposing another tide, producing rough waters

Rip van Win·kle (rip′ van wiŋ′k'l) the main character in Washington Irving's story (1819) of the same name: Rip awakens after sleeping for twenty years and finds everything changed

rise (rīz) *vi.* **rose, ris·en** (riz′'n), **ris′ing** [OE. *risan*: for IE. base see RUN] **1.** to stand or assume an erect or nearly erect position after sitting, lying, etc. **2.** to get up after sleeping or resting **3.** to rebel; revolt [the peasants *rose* against the king] **4.** to end an official assembly or meeting **5.** to return to life after dying, as in the Resurrection **6.** to go to a higher place or position; ascend **7.** to appear above the horizon [the moon *rose*] **8.** to reach a higher level [the river is *rising*] **9.** to advance in status, rank, etc. [he *rose* to be president of the company] **10.** to become erect or rigid, as bristling hair on a dog **11.** to extend or incline upward [hills *rising* steeply] **12.** to increase in amount, degree, etc. [the temperature *rose*] **13.** to become louder, shriller, etc. **14.** to become stronger, more vivid, etc. [her spirits *rose*] **15.** to become larger and puffier, as dough containing yeast **16.** to originate; begin **17.** to have its source [the Mississippi *rises* in Minnesota] **18.** to happen; occur **19.** to become apparent to the senses or the mind [land *rising* ahead of the ship] —*n.* **1.** the appearance of the sun, moon, etc. above the horizon **2.** upward motion; ascent **3.** an advance in status, rank, etc. **4.** a piece of ground higher than that around it **5.** a slope upward **6.** the vertical height of something, as of a flight of stairs or a single step **7.** *a)* an increase in height, as of water level *b)* an increase in pitch of a sound *c)* an increase in degree, amount, etc. **8.** a beginning, origin, etc. —**get a rise out of** [Slang] to draw a desired response from, as by teasing —**give rise to** to bring about; be the cause of —**rise to** to prove oneself capable of dealing with [to *rise to* the occasion]

SYN.—**rise** and **arise** both imply a coming into being, action, notice, etc., but **rise** carries an added suggestion of upward movement [empires *rise* and fall] and **arise** is often used to show a cause-and-effect relationship [accidents *arise* from carelessness]

ris·er (rīz′ər) *n.* **1.** one that rises [an early *riser*] **2.** any of the vertical pieces between the steps in a stairway

ris·i·bil·i·ty (riz′ə bil′ə tē) *n., pl.* **-ties 1.** the quality or state of being risible ☆**2.** [*usually pl.*] a sense of the ridiculous or amusing

ris·i·ble (riz′ə b'l) *adj.* [Fr. < LL. < L. pp. of *ridere*, to laugh] **1.** able or inclined to laugh **2.** of or connected with laughter **3.** causing laughter; laughable; funny

ris·ing (rī′ziŋ) *adj.* **1.** that rises; ascending, advancing, etc. **2.** growing; maturing [the *rising* generation] **3.** [Colloq. or Dial.] ☆somewhat more than; also, approaching [a man *rising* fifty]: in these senses sometimes regarded as a preposition —*n.* the act of one that rises; esp., an uprising; revolt

risk (risk) *n.* [Fr. *risque* < It. *risco*] **1.** the chance of injury, damage, or loss; dangerous chance; hazard **2.** *a)* the chance or likelihood that a person or thing insured may suffer injury, damage, or loss *b)* the person or thing insured, in relation to such chance or likelihood [that old barn is a poor fire-insurance *risk*] —*vt.* **1.** to expose to risk; hazard [to *risk* one's life] **2.** to take the chance of [to *risk* a fight] —see SYN. at DANGER —**risk′er** *n.*

risk·y (ris′kē) *adj.* **risk′i·er, risk′i·est** involving risk; hazardous; dangerous —**risk′i·ly** *adv.* —**risk′i·ness** *n.*

ris·qué (ris kā′) *adj.* [Fr., pp. of *risquer*, to risk] very close to being improper or indecent; daring; suggestive

Ri·ta (rēt′ə) [It.] a feminine name

fat, āpe, cär; ten, ēven; is, bīte; gō, hôrn, tōōl, look; oil, out; up, fur; get; joy; yet; chin; she; thin, *th*en; zh, leisure; ŋ, ring; ə for *a* in *ago*, *e* in *agent*, *i* in *sanity*, *o* in *comply*, *u* in *focus*; ′ as in *able* (ā′b'l); Fr. bäl; ë, Fr. coeur; ö, Fr. feu; ô, Fr. mon; ô, Fr. coq; ü, Fr. duc; r, Fr. cri; H, G. ich; kh, G. doch; ‡foreign; ☆ Americanism; < derived from. See inside front cover.

ri·tar·dan·do (rē′tär dän′dō) *adj., adv.* [It., gerund of *ritardare*, to delay: see RETARD] *Music* becoming gradually slower

rite (rīt) *n.* [L. *ritus:* for IE. base see ART¹] **1.** a formal act or ceremony carried out according to fixed rules, as in religious use [marriage *rites*] **2.** any formal, customary observance, practice, or procedure [the *rites* of courtship] **3.** a particular system or form of ceremonial procedure; ritual [the Scottish *rite* of Freemasonry] **4.** [*often* R-] liturgy; specif., any of the set forms or ritual for worship service (esp. the Eucharistic service) in certain Christian churches [the Latin *Rite*]

rit·u·al (rich′ōō wəl) *adj.* [L. *ritualis*] of, having the nature of, or done as a rite [*ritual* dances] —*n.* **1.** a set form or system of rites, religious or otherwise **2.** the observance of set forms or rites, as in worship **3.** a book containing rites **4.** a practice, service, or procedure done as a rite —**rit′u·al·ly** *adv.*

rit·u·al·ism (-iz′m) *n.* **1.** the observance of ritual **2.** an excessive devotion to ritual —**rit′u·al·ist** *n., adj.* —**rit′u·al·is′tic** *adj.* —**rit′u·al·is′ti·cal·ly** *adv.*

rit·u·al·ize (-īz′) *vt.* -ized′, -iz′ing to make a ritual of —**rit′u·al·i·za′tion** *n.*

☆**ritz·y** (rit′sē) *adj.* ritz′i·er, ritz′i·est [< the *Ritz* hotels] [Old Slang] luxurious, fashionable, elegant, etc. —**ritz′i·ness** *n.*

ri·val (rī′v'l) *n.* [Fr. < L. *rivalis*, orig., one using the same stream as another < *rivus*, a brook: for IE. base see RUN] **1.** a person who tries to get the same thing as another, or to equal or surpass another; competitor **2.** an equal or a satisfactory substitute [plastics are *rivals* of many metals] —*adj.* acting as a rival or rivals; competing [*rival* teams] —*vt.* -**valed** or -**valled**, -**val·ing** or -**val·ling** **1.** to try to equal or surpass; compete with [they *rivaled* each other for her love] **2.** to equal or be as good as [her paintings now *rival* those of her old teacher]

ri·val·ry (-rē) *n., pl.* -**ries** the act of rivaling or the fact or state of being a rival or rivals; competition —see SYN. at COMPETITION

rive (rīv) *vt., vi.* rived, riv·en (riv′'n) or rived, riv′ing [ON. *rifa:* for IE. base see ROW¹] **1.** to tear apart; rend **2.** to split; cleave [a giant oak riven by lightning]

riv·er (riv′ər) *n.* [< OFr. < VL. < L. *riparius:* see RIPARIAN] **1.** a natural stream of water larger than a creek and emptying into an ocean, a lake, or another river **2.** any plentiful stream or flow [a *river* of lava] —☆**sell down the river** to betray, deceive, etc.: from the former selling of slaves to plantations on the lower Mississippi where life for them was harshest

Ri·ve·ra (rē ve′rä; *E.* ri ver′ə), **Die·go** (dye′gô) 1886-1957; Mex. painter, esp. of murals

river basin the area drained by a river and its tributaries

riv·er·bed (riv′ər bed′) *n.* the channel in which a river flows or has flowed

Riv·er·side (riv′ər sīd′) [< Santa Ana *River*, near which it is located] city in S Calif.: pop. 140,000

riv·er·side (riv′ər sīd′) *n.* the bank of a river —*adj.* on or near the bank of a river

riv·et (riv′it) *n.* [MFr. < *river*, to clinch] **1.** a metal bolt with a head on one end, used to fasten metal plates or beams together by being inserted through holes: the plain end is then hammered into a head **2.** a similar device used to strengthen seams, as on work clothes —*vt.* **1.** to fasten with rivets **2.** to hammer the end of (a bolt, etc.) into a head **3.** to fasten firmly **4.** to hold (the eyes, attention, etc.) firmly —**riv′et·er** *n.*

Riv·i·er·a (riv′ē er′ə; *It.* rē vye′rä) coastal strip of the Mediterranean in SE France & NW Italy: a famous resort area

riv·u·let (riv′yōō lit) *n.* [< It. *rivoletto*, ult. < L. *rivus*, a brook] a little stream

Ri·yadh (rē yäd′) political capital of Saudi Arabia: pop. c. 300,000: see MECCA

ri·yal (rē yäl′, -yôl′) *n., pl.* -**yals** [Ar. *riyāl* < Sp. *real:* see REAL²] *see* MONETARY UNITS, table (Qatar, Saudi Arabia, Yemen)

rm. *pl.* **rms. 1.** ream **2.** room

Rn *Chem.* radon

R.N. 1. Registered Nurse: also **RN 2.** Royal Navy

RNA ribonucleic acid

☆**roach¹** (rōch) *n.* **1.** same as COCKROACH **2.** [Slang] the butt of a marijuana cigarette

roach² (rōch) *n., pl.* **roach, roach′es:** see PLURAL, II, D, 2 [OFr. *roche*, prob. < Gmc.] **1.** a freshwater fish of the carp family, found in N Europe **2.** any of various similar American fishes

road (rōd) *n.* [OE. *rad*, a ride < *ridan*, to RIDE] **1.** *a*) a way made for traveling between places by automobile, horseback,

RIVETS
(A, rivet holding steel beams together; B, C, D, rivets)

etc.; highway *b*) same as ROADBED (sense 2) **2.** a way; path; course [the *road* to fortune] ☆**3.** same as RAILROAD **4.** [*often pl.*] a protected place near shore, not as enclosed as a harbor, where ships can ride at anchor —**on the road 1.** traveling, as a salesman **2.** on tour, as actors —**take to the road** to start traveling

road·a·bil·i·ty (rōd′ə bil′ə tē) *n.* the degree of operating ease and riding comfort of a vehicle on the road

☆**road·bed** (rōd′bed′) *n.* **1.** a layer of crushed rock, cinders, etc. on which the ties and rails of a railroad are laid **2.** the foundation and surface of a road, or highway

road·block (-bläk′) *n.* **1.** a blockade set up in a road to stop vehicles **2.** any obstacle in one's way

☆**road hog** a driver who keeps his car, truck, etc. in or near the middle of the road so that it is hard or impossible for others to pass

road·house (-hous′) *n.* a tavern, inn, or, esp., nightclub along a country road, as in the 1920's

road map a map for motorists, showing the roads of a given region, their route numbers, condition, etc.

☆**road runner** a long-tailed, crested desert bird of the southwestern U.S. and northern Mexico, that can run swiftly

road·side (-sīd′) *n.* the side of a road —*adj.* on or at the side of a road [a *roadside* park]

road·stead (-sted′) *n.* same as ROAD (sense 4)

road·ster (-stər) *n.* ☆an earlier type of open automobile with a single seat for two or three persons and, sometimes, a rumble seat

road test a test of a vehicle, tires, etc. under actual driving conditions —**road′-test′** *vt.*

road·way (-wā′) *n.* **1.** a road **2.** that part of a road meant for cars, trucks, and other vehicles to travel on

road·work (-wurk′) *n.* the exercise of jogging or running distances, as along a road, esp. by a prizefighter in training

roam (rōm) *vi.* [ME. *romen:* for IE. base see RUN] to travel from place to place, esp. with no special plan or purpose; wander —*vt.* to wander over or through [to *roam* the streets] —*n.* the act of roaming; ramble —**roam′er** *n.*

SYN.—**roam** implies a traveling about without a fixed goal over a large area and carries suggestions of freedom, pleasure, etc. [to *roam* about the country]; **ramble** implies an idle moving or walking about, esp. in a carefree or aimless way [we *rambled* through the woods]; **rove** suggests a wandering over a wide area, but usually implies a special purpose or activity [a *roving* reporter; *roving* bands of looters]; **range** stresses the wide area covered and sometimes suggests a search for something [hunters *ranging* the western plains]; **meander** is used of streams, paths, etc., and, less often, of people and animals, that follow a winding, seemingly aimless course

roan (rōn) *adj.* [OFr. < OSp. *roano*, ult. < *ravus*] of a solid color, as reddish-brown, black, etc., with a thick sprinkling of white hairs: said chiefly of horses —*n.* **1.** a roan color **2.** a roan horse or other animal

Ro·a·noke (rō′ə nōk′) [< Algonquian *Roanok*, northern people] **1.** city in SW Va.: pop. 92,000 **2.** island off the NE coast of N.C.: site of an unsuccessful Eng. colony (1585-87)

roar (rôr) *vi.* [OE. *rarian*] **1.** to utter a loud, deep, rumbling sound, as a lion or a person in pain, anger, etc. **2.** to talk or laugh loudly and boisterously **3.** to make a loud, deep or echoing noise, as a motor or gun **4.** to resound with a noisy din —*vt.* **1.** to utter with a roar **2.** to make, put, etc. by roaring [to *roar* oneself hoarse] —*n.* **1.** a loud, deep, rumbling sound, as of a lion, bull, crowd shouting, etc. **2.** a loud burst of laughter **3.** a loud noise, as of waves, a motor, etc.; din —**roar′er** *n.*

roast (rōst) *vt.* [OFr. *rostir* < Frank.] **1.** to cook (something) with little or no liquid, as in an oven or over an open fire **2.** to dry, parch, or brown (coffee, etc.) by exposure to heat **3.** to expose to great heat **4.** to heat (ore, etc.) in a furnace in order to remove impurities or cause oxidation **5.** [Colloq.] to criticize or ridicule severely —*vi.* **1.** to be cooked by being roasted **2.** to be or become very hot —*n.* **1.** roasted meat **2.** a cut of meat for roasting ☆**3.** a picnic at which food is roasted [a steer *roast*] —*adj.* roasted [*roast* pork] —**roast′ing** *adj.*

roast·er (rōs′tər) *n.* **1.** a person or thing that roasts **2.** a pan, oven, etc. for roasting meat **3.** a young pig, chicken, etc. suitable for roasting

rob (räb) *vt.* **robbed, rob′bing** [OFr. *rober* < Gmc.: for IE. base see RUPTURE] **1.** *a*) *Law* to take personal property, money, etc. from unlawfully by using or threatening force *b*) popularly, to steal something from in any way **2.** to deprive (someone) *of* something belonging to or due him [the accident *robbed* him of health] —*vi.* to commit robbery —**rob′ber** *n.*

rob·ber·y (räb′ər ē) *n., pl.* -**ber·ies** a robbing; specif., *Law* the committing of a felony by using violence or the threat of violence to take another's property while he is present

Robbia see DELLA ROBBIA

robe (rōb) *n.* [OFr., a robe, orig., booty < Gmc.] **1.** a long, loose outer garment; specif., *a*) such a garment worn on formal occasions or to show one's rank or office *[the judge's robe]* *b*) a bathrobe or dressing gown ☆**2.** short for LAP ROBE —*vt.*, *vi.* **robed, rob′ing** to dress in or cover with a robe

Rob·ert (räb′ərt) [< OFr. < OHG. < *hruod-*, fame + *perht*, bright] **1.** a masculine name: dim. *Bob, Rob* **2. Robert I** see BRUCE (sense 2)

Ro·ber·ta (rə bur′tə, rō-) [fem. of ROBERT] a feminine name

Ro·bes·pierre (rō bes pyer′; *E.* rōbs′pyer, -pir), **Max·i·mi·lien (Francois Marie Isidore de)** (måk sē mē lyan′) 1758–94; Fr. revolutionist & Jacobin leader: guillotined

rob·in (räb′in) *n.* [< OFr. dim. of *Robert*] ☆**1.** a large N. American thrush with a dull-red breast and belly **2.** a small European warbler with a yellowish-red breast Also **robin redbreast**

Robin Good·fel·low (good′fel′ō) *Eng. Folklore* a mischievous elf or fairy: identified with Puck

Robin Hood *Eng. Legend* an outlaw of the 12th cent. who lived with his followers in Sherwood Forest and robbed the rich to help the poor

☆**rob·in's-egg blue** (räb′inz eg′) a light greenish blue

Rob·in·son (räb′in s'n), **Edwin Ar·ling·ton** (är′liŋ tən) 1869–1935; U.S. poet

Robinson Cru·soe (krōō′sō) the hero of Defoe's novel (1719) of the same name, a sailor who is shipwrecked on a tropical island

ro·bot (rō′bət, -bät) *n.* [< Czech *robota*, forced labor < OBulg. < *rabu*, servant] **1.** *a*) any manlike mechanical being, as of the kind in Karel Capek's play *R.U.R.* *b*) any mechanical device operated automatically, esp. by remote control, to perform in a seemingly human way **2.** an automaton; esp., a person who acts or works in an automatic or mechanical way

robot bomb a small, jet-propelled bomb with wings, steered by an automatic pilot and carrying high explosives

Rob·son (räb′sən), **Mount** mountain in E British Columbia: highest peak of the Canadian Rockies: 12,972 ft.

ro·bust (rō bust′, rō′bust) *adj.* [L. *robustus* < *robur*, hard variety of oak] **1.** *a*) strong and healthy; hardy *b*) strongly built; muscular or sturdy **2.** suited to or requiring physical strength *[robust work]* **3.** rough; coarse; boisterous **4.** full and rich, as in flavor *[a robust port wine]* —see SYN. at HEALTHY —**ro·bust′ly** *adv.* —**ro·bust′ness** *n.*

roc (räk) *n.* [< Ar. < Per. *rukh*] *Arabian & Persian Legend* a fabulous bird, so huge and strong that it could carry off large animals

Ro·cham·beau (rō shän bō′), **comte de** (*Jean Baptiste Donatien de Vimeur*) 1725–1807; Fr. general: commanded Fr. forces against the Brit. in the Am. Revolutionary War

Ro·chelle salt (rō shel′) [after La *Rochelle*, France] a colorless, crystalline compound, $KNaC_4H_4O_6 \cdot 4H_2O$, used as a laxative and as a piezoelectric material

Roch·es·ter (rä′ches′tər, räch′is-) **1.** [after N. *Rochester*, Revolutionary officer] city in western N.Y., on Lake Ontario: pop. 296,000 (met. area 883,000) **2.** [after the city in N.Y.] city in SE Minn.: pop. 54,000

roch·et (räch′it) *n.* [< OFr. < *roc*, a cloak < MHG. < OHG. *roch*] a vestment of lawn or linen, like a surplice, worn by bishops

rock¹ (räk) *n.* [< OFr. *roche*] **1.** a large mass of stone forming a peak or cliff **2.** *a*) a large stone detached from the mass; boulder *b*) broken pieces of such rock **3.** *a*) mineral matter formed in masses in the earth's crust *b*) a particular kind or mass of this **4.** anything like a rock, as in strength; esp., a firm support, basis, etc. **5.** [Colloq. or Dial.] any stone **6.** [Slang] a diamond or other gem —**on the rocks** [Colloq.] **1.** in or into a condition of ruin or catastrophe **2.** bankrupt ☆**3.** served undiluted over ice cubes: said of liquor, wine, etc.

rock² (räk) *vt.* [OE. *roccian*] **1.** to move (a cradle, a child in the arms, etc.) back and forth or from side to side **2.** to make or put by moving in this way *[to rock a baby to sleep]* **3.** *a*) to cause to tremble or vibrate; shake *[the explosion rocked the house]* *b*) to upset emotionally —*vi.* **1.** to move back and forth or from side to side **2.** to sway strongly; shake —*n.* **1.** a rocking motion ☆**2.** *a*) same as ROCK-AND-ROLL *b*) popular music developed from rock-and-roll, containing elements of the blues, folk music, country music, etc.

☆**rock·a·bil·ly** (räk′ə bil′ē) *n.* [ROCK² (*n.* 2*b*) + -*a*- + (HILL)BILLY] a form of popular music that combines some of the features of rock and country music

☆**rock-and-roll** (räk′'n rōl′) *n.* a form of popular music, which has a strong and regular rhythm and which developed from jazz and the blues: also sp. **rock 'n' roll**

☆**rock bottom** the lowest level or point; very bottom

rock-bound (-bound) *adj.* surrounded by or covered with rocks *[a rock-bound coast]*

rock candy large, hard, clear crystals of sugar

Rock Cornish (hen) same as CORNISH (sense 2 *b*)

rock crystal a transparent quartz, esp. when colorless

rock dove the European wild pigeon: also **rock pigeon**

Rock·e·fel·ler (räk′ə fel′ər) **John D(avison)**, 1839–1937; U.S. industrialist & philanthropist

rock·er (räk′ər) *n.* **1.** either of the curved pieces on the bottom of a cradle, rocking chair, etc. ☆**2.** same as ROCKING CHAIR **3.** any of various devices that work with a rocking motion —**off one's rocker** [Slang] crazy; insane

rocker panel any of the sections of body paneling below the doors of an automobile

rock·et (räk′it) *n.* [It. *rocchetta*, a spool, orig. dim. of *rocca*, a distaff < OHG.] **1.** any of various devices having a cylindrical body and containing a substance which when ignited produces a jet of gases that push through a rear vent and drive the container forward: rockets are used as fireworks and weapons and to propel spacecraft **2.** a spacecraft, missile, etc. propelled by a rocket —*vi.* **1.** to shoot ahead like a rocket **2.** to travel in a rocket **3.** to soar; rise rapidly *[prices rocketed]* —*vt.* to carry in a rocket —**rock·e·teer** (räk′ə tir′) *n.*

rock·et·ry (räk′ə trē) *n.* **1.** the science of designing, building, and launching rockets **2.** rockets collectively

rocket ship same as SPACESHIP

rock·fish (räk′fish′) *n., pl.* **-fish′, -fish·es:** see FISH any of a large number of unrelated fishes that stay among rocks offshore or in rocky beds, as the striped bass

Rock·ford (räk′fərd) [so named after the *rocky*-bottomed *ford* there] city in N Ill.: pop. 147,000

rock garden a garden with rocks arranged for flowers and plants to grow among them

Rock·ies (räk′ēz) same as ROCKY MOUNTAINS

☆**rocking chair** a chair mounted on rockers or springs, so that it can rock

rocking horse a toy horse mounted on rockers or springs and big enough for a child to ride

Rock Island [< the name of the *rocky island* in the river] city in NW Ill., on the Mississippi: pop. 50,000

rock lobster same as SPINY LOBSTER

rock-ribbed (räk′ribd′) *adj.* **1.** having rocky ridges *[rock-ribbed coasts]* ☆**2.** firm; unyielding *[a rock-ribbed policy]*

rock salt common salt as mined in solid masses and used in the form of large, coarse crystals

rock wool a fibrous material that looks like spun glass, made from molten rock or slag through which steam is forced: it is used for insulation, esp. in buildings

rock·y¹ (räk′ē) *adj.* **rock′i·er, rock′i·est** **1.** full of rocks **2.** consisting of rock **3.** like a rock; firm, hard, unfeeling, etc. **4.** full of obstacles *[the rocky road to success]* —**rock′i·ness** *n.*

rock·y² (räk′ē) *adj.* **rock′i·er, rock′i·est** **1.** *a*) that is inclined to rock, or sway; wobbly *b*) uncertain; shaky **2.** [Slang] weak or dizzy, as from illness —**rock′i·ness** *n.*

☆**Rocky Mountain goat** a white, goatlike antelope of the mountains of northwest N. America

ROCKY MOUNTAIN GOAT
($2^1/_2$–$3^1/_2$ ft. high at shoulder)

Rocky Mountain National Park national park in a range of the Rocky Mountains in NC Colo.

Rocky Mountains mountain system in western North America, extending from central N.Mex. to northern Alas.

Rocky Mountain sheep *same as* BIGHORN

☆**Rocky Mountain spotted fever** an acute infectious disease caused by a rickettsia

ro·co·co (rə kō′kō; *occas.* rō′kə kō′) *n.* [Fr. < *rocaille,* ornamentation with a pattern resembling shells] a style of architecture and decoration using elaborate ornamentation that imitates leaves, shells, scrolls, etc.: popular in the 18th cent. —*adj.* 1. of or in rococo 2. too elaborate; showy and tasteless [a *rococo* style of writing]

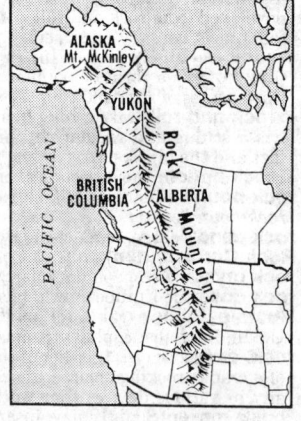

ROCKY MOUNTAINS

rod (räd) *n.* [OE. *rodd*] 1. *Bible* a branch of a family or tribe 2. any straight stick, bar, etc. of wood, metal, etc. [curtain *rods*] 3. *a)* a stick for beating as punishment *b)* such punishment 4. *a)* a staff, scepter, etc., carried as a symbol of office or rank *b)* power; authority 5. *same as* FISHING ROD 6. a stick used to measure something 7. *a)* a measure of length equal to 5½ yards *b)* a square rod, equal to 30¼ square yards 8. [Slang] a pistol or revolver ☆9. [Slang] *same as* HOT ROD 10. *Anat.* any of the rod-shaped cells in the retina that are sensitive to dim light 11. *Biol.* a rod-shaped microorganism —**rod′like′** *adj.*

rode (rōd) *pt. & archaic pp. of* RIDE

ro·dent (rōd′'nt) *adj.* [< L. prp. of *rodere,* to gnaw: for IE. base see RAT] 1. gnawing 2. of or like rodents —*n.* any of various gnawing mammals, including rats, mice, beavers, etc., that have constantly growing incisors; esp., a rat or mouse

☆**ro·de·o** (rō′dē ō′, rō dā′ō) *n., pl.* **-de·os′** [Sp. < *rodear,* surround < L. *rotare:* see ROTATE] 1. [Now Rare] a roundup of cattle 2. a public exhibition of the skills of cowboys, as broncobusting, lassoing, etc.

Ro·din (rô dan′; *E.* rō dan′), (François) **Au·guste** (René) (ô güst′) 1840–1917; Fr. sculptor

rod·o·mon·tade (räd′ə män tād′, rō′də-; -täd′) *n.* [Fr. < It. *Rodomonte,* boastful Saracen leader in *Orlando Furioso,* 16th-c. epic] arrogant boasting or blustering talk

roe[1] (rō) *n.* [akin to or < ? ON. *hrogn*] fish eggs, esp. when still massed in the ovarian membrane

roe[2] (rō) *n., pl.* **roe, roes:** see PLURAL, II, D, 2 [OE. *ra*] a small, agile, graceful deer found in Europe and Asia

roe·buck (rō′buk′) *n., pl.* **-bucks′, -buck′:** see PLURAL, II, D, 1 the male of the roe deer

roent·gen (rent′gən, ren′chən) *n.* [after W. K. *Roentgen* (1845–1923), Ger. physicist who discovered X-rays] the international unit used in measuring ionizing radiation, as X-rays or gamma rays, equal to the quantity of radiation that will produce in one cubic centimeter of dry air ions carrying one electrostatic unit of electricity of either sign

Roentgen ray [*also* r-] *same as* X-RAY

ro·ga·tion (rō gā′shən) *n.* [< L. < *rogare,* to ask] a supplication or prayer, esp. as chanted in church ceremonies during Rogation days

Rogation days the three days before Ascension Day, during which supplications are chanted

Rog·er (räj′ər) [OFr. < OHG. < *hruod-,* fame + base meaning "spear"] a masculine name —*interj.* [< conventional name of international signal flag for *R*] [*also* r-] 1. received: term used in two-way voice communication by radio to indicate reception of a message 2. [Colloq.] right! OK!

Ro·get (rō zhā′), **Peter Mark** 1779–1869; Eng. writer: compiler of a thesaurus

rogue (rōg) *n.* [< ? L. *rogare,* to ask] 1. formerly, a vagabond or tramp 2. a scoundrel 3. a fun-loving, mischievous person 4. an elephant or other animal that wanders alone and is fierce and wild

ro·guer·y (rō′gər ē) *n., pl.* **-guer·ies** the behavior of a rogue; specif., *a)* trickery; cheating *b)* playful mischief

☆**rogues' gallery** a collection of photographs of criminals, as used by police in identification

ro·guish (rō′gish) *adj.* of or like a rogue; specif., *a)* dishonest; unscrupulous *b)* playfully mischievous —**ro′guish·ly** *adv.* —**ro′guish·ness** *n.*

roil (roil) *vt.* [< Fr. < OFr. *rouil,* rust, ult. < L. *robigo,* rust] 1. to make (a liquid) cloudy, muddy, etc. by stirring up the sediment 2. to stir up; agitate 3. to make angry or irritable —*vi.* to be agitated —**roil′y** *adj.* **roil′i·er, roil′i·est**

roist·er (rois′tər) *vi.* [< OFr. < L. *rusticus:* see RUSTIC] 1. to boast or swagger 2. to be lively and noisy; revel boisterously —**roist′er·er** *n.* —**roist′er·ous** *adj.*

Ro·land (rō′lənd) [Fr. < OHG. < *hruod-,* fame + *land,* land] 1. a masculine name 2. a hero famous for his courage who appears in legends about Charlemagne

role, rôle (rōl) *n.* [Fr. *rôle,* a roll: from roll containing actor's part] 1. a part, or character, that an actor plays 2. a function assumed by someone [an advisory *role*]

roll (rōl) *vi.* [OFr. *roller,* ult. < L. *rotula* (or *rotulus*), dim. of *rota,* wheel < IE. base *ret(h)-,* to run] 1. to move by turning on an axis or over and over 2. *a)* to move on wheels *b)* to travel in a wheeled vehicle 3. to pass [the years *rolled* by] 4. to rotate about its axis lengthwise, as a spacecraft in flight 5. *a)* to flow, as water, in a full, sweeping motion *b)* to be carried in a flow 6. to extend in gentle swells or undulations [the *rolling* plains] 7. to make a loud, rising and falling sound [thunder *rolls*] 8. to rise and fall in a full, mellow cadence, as speech 9. to trill or warble 10. to be wound into a ball or cylinder, as yarn 11. to turn in a circular motion [with eyes *rolling*] 12. to rock from side to side [the ship pitched and *rolled*] 13. to walk by swaying 14. to become spread under a roller [this paint *rolls* on easily] 15. to make progress; advance [the campaign is finally beginning to *roll*] 16. to start operating [the presses *rolled*] 17. [Colloq.] to have plenty; abound (*in*) [*rolling* in wealth] ☆18. *Football* to move parallel to the line of scrimmage: said of the passer: in full, **roll out** —*vt.* 1. to move by turning on an axis or over and over 2. to move on wheels or rollers 3. to cause to start operating 4. to beat (a drum) with light, rapid blows 5. to utter with a full, flowing sound [to *roll* one's words] 6. to say with a trill [to *roll* one's r's] 7. to give a swaying motion to 8. to move around or from side to side [to *roll* one's eyes] 9. to wind into a ball or cylinder [to *roll* up the rug] 10. to wrap or enfold 11. to make flat or spread out by using a roller, rolling pin, etc. ☆12. [Slang] to rob (a drunken or sleeping person) —*n.* 1. the act or an instance of rolling 2. *a)* a scroll *b)* something that is or looks as if it is rolled up 3. a register; catalog 4. a list of names for checking attendance 5. a standard length of something rolled into a cylinder [a roll of wallpaper] 6. a cylindrical mass of something [a sausage *roll*] 7. bread baked in a small, shaped piece 8. a roller (in various senses) 9. a swaying motion 10. a rapid succession of light blows on a drum 11. a loud, echoing sound, as of thunder 12. a slight rise on the surface of something, as land ☆13. [Slang] money; esp., a wad of paper money —**roll back** 1. to force back ☆2. to reduce (prices) to a previous level by government action —**roll in** to arrive or appear, usually in large numbers or amounts —**roll out** to spread out by unrolling —**roll up** 1. to increase by accumulation [to *roll up* a big score] 2. [Colloq.] to arrive in a vehicle —**strike off** (or **from**) **the rolls** to expel from membership

☆**roll·a·way** (rōl′ə wā′) *adj.* having rollers for easy moving and storing when not in use [a *rollaway* bed]

☆**roll bar** a heavy metal bar reinforcing the roof of a motor vehicle to protect passengers if the vehicle should roll over

roll call the reading aloud of a roll, as in military formations, to find out who is absent

roll·er (rō′lər) *n.* 1. a person or thing that rolls 2. *a)* a cylinder of metal, wood, etc. over which something is rolled for easier movement *b)* a cylinder on which something is rolled up [a hair *roller*] *c)* a rolling cylinder used to crush, smooth, or spread something [a lawn *roller;* a paint *roller*] 3. a long, heavy wave that breaks on the shoreline 4. a canary that trills

☆**roller bearing** a bearing in which the shaft turns on rollers in a ringlike track

☆**roller coaster** an amusement ride in which small, open cars move on tracks that dip and curve sharply

☆**roller skate** a skate with wheels: see SKATE[1] (sense 2) —**roll′er-skate′** *vi.* **-skat′ed, -skat′ing** —**roller skater**

rol·lick (räl′ik) *vi.* [< ? FROLIC] to play or behave in a happy, carefree way; romp —**rol′lick·ing, rol′lick·some** (-səm) *adj.*

roll·ing (rōl′iŋ) *adj.* that rolls; specif., rotating or revolving, recurring, swaying, surging, resounding, trilling, etc. —*n.* the action, motion, or sound of something that rolls

rolling mill 1. a factory in which metal bars, sheets, etc. are rolled out 2. a machine used for such rolling

rolling pin a smooth cylinder of wood, glass, etc., usually with a handle at each end, used to roll out dough

rolling stock all the locomotives, cars, etc. of a railroad, or the trucks, trailers, etc. of a trucking company

☆**roll-top** (rōl′täp′) *adj.* made with a flexible top of parallel slats that slides back [a *roll-top* desk]

ro·ly-po·ly (rō′lē pō′lē) *adj.* [redupl. of ROLL] short and plump; pudgy —*n., pl.* **-lies** 1. a rolypoly person or thing 2. [Chiefly Brit.] a pudding made of rich dough spread with jam, rolled up, and boiled, steamed, etc.

rom, rom. roman (type)

Rom. 1. Roman 2. Romance 3. Romania 4. Romanian 5. Romanic 6. Romans (Epistle to the Romans)

ROLL-TOP DESK

Ro·ma (rō′mä) *It.* name of ROME

Ro·ma·ic (rō mā′ik) *n.* the everyday language of modern Greece —*adj.* of this language

ro·maine (rō mān′, rō′mān) *n.* [Fr. < fem. of *romain,* Roman] a kind of lettuce with long leaves that form a somewhat loose head: also **romaine lettuce**

Ro·man (rō′mən) *adj.* 1. of or characteristic of ancient or modern Rome, its people, etc. 2. of the Roman Catholic Church 3. [*usually* r-] designating or of the usual upright style of printing types; not italic —*n.* 1. a native, citizen, or inhabitant of ancient or modern Rome 2. [*usually* r-] roman type or characters

Roman alphabet the alphabet of the ancient Romans, used with little change in most modern European languages

Roman arch a semicircular arch

Roman candle a firework consisting of a long tube that sends out balls of fire, sparks, etc.

Roman Catholic 1. of the Roman Catholic Church 2. a member of this church —**Roman Catholicism**

Roman Catholic Church the Christian church headed by the Pope

Ro·mance (rō mans′, rō′mans) *adj.* [see next entry] designating or of any of the languages derived from Vulgar Latin, as Italian, Spanish, French, etc. —*n.* these languages

ro·mance (rō mans′; *also, for n.,* rō′mans) *n.* [OFr. *romanz,* Roman (that is, the everyday speech, not Latin), ult. < L. *Romanicus,* Roman] 1. a long verse or prose narrative, orig. written in one of the Romance languages, about knights and chivalry, adventure, and love 2. a novel of love, adventure, etc. 3. excitement, love, and adventure of the kind found in such literature 4. the tendency to enjoy romantic adventures 5. an exaggeration or made-up story 6. a love affair —*vi.* **-manced′, -manc′ing** 1. to make up false or exaggerated stories 2. to think or talk about romantic things —*vt.* [Colloq.] to try to get the love of; woo; court —**ro·manc′er** *n.*

Roman Curia *R.C.Ch.* see CURIA (sense 3)

Roman Empire empire established by Augustus, including, at its peak, W & S Europe, Britain, Asia Minor, N Africa, & the lands at the E end of the Mediterranean: it existed from 27 B.C. until 395 A.D.

Ro·man·esque (rō′mə nesk′) *adj.* designating or of a style of European architecture of the 11th and 12th cent., based on ancient Roman architecture and using round arches and vaults, massive walls, etc. —*n.* this style of architecture

Roman holiday [after the ancient Roman gladiatorial contests] entertainment at the expense of others' suffering, or a spectacle providing such entertainment

ROMAN EMPIRE (100 A.D.)

Ro·ma·ni·a, Ro·mâ·ni·a (rō mān′yə, -mä′nē ə; *Romanian* rô mu′nyä) country in SE Europe, on the Black Sea: 91,700 sq. mi.; pop. 20,470,000; cap. Bucharest

Ro·ma·ni·an (-mān′yən, -mä′nē ən) *adj.* of Romania, its people, language, etc. —*n.* 1. a native or inhabitant of Romania 2. the Romance language of the Romanians

Ro·man·ic (-man′ik) *adj., n.* same as ROMANCE

Roman nose a nose with a prominent bridge

Roman numerals the Roman letters used as numerals until the 10th cent. A.D.: in Roman numerals I = 1, V = 5, X = 10, L = 50, C = 100, D = 500, and M = 1,000 The value of a symbol following another that is the same or greater in value is added (III = 3, XV = 15); the value of a symbol coming before one of greater value is subtracted (IX = 9)

ROMAN NOSE

Ro·ma·no (rō mä′nō) *n.* [It., ROMAN] a dry, sharp, very hard Italian cheese, usually grated

Ro·ma·nov (rō mä′nôf; *E.* rō′mə nôf′) ruling family of Russia from 1613 to 1917: also sp. **Romanoff**

Ro·mans (rō′manz) a book of the New Testament, an epistle from the Apostle Paul to the Christians of Rome

ro·man·tic (rō man′tik) *adj.* 1. of, like, or characterized by romance 2. without a basis in fact; fanciful or fictitious 3. not practical; visionary [a *romantic* scheme] 4. full of thoughts, feelings, etc. of romance [a *romantic* youth] 5. describing or having to do with lovemaking or wooing in an idealized way [a *romantic* novel] 6. [*often* R-] of the ROMANTIC MOVEMENT —*n.* 1. a romantic person 2. [*often* R-] a poet, composer, etc. of the Romantic Movement —see SYN. at SENTIMENTAL —**ro·man′ti·cal·ly** *adv.*

ro·man·ti·cism (rō man′tə siz'm) *n.* 1. romantic spirit, outlook, etc. 2. *a*) *same as* ROMANTIC MOVEMENT *b*) the spirit, style, etc. of the Romantic Movement or adherence to this —**ro·man′ti·cist** *n.*

ro·man·ti·cize (rō man′tə sīz′) *vt.* **-cized′, -ciz′ing** to deal with or think about in a romantic way —*vi.* to have romantic ideas, attitudes, etc. —**ro·man′ti·ci·za′tion** *n.*

Romantic Movement the revolt in the 18th and 19th cent. against the formal style and spirit of the revival of classicism in literature, music, art, etc.: it stressed free expression of the artist's feelings, ideas, etc. and began to deal with the common man, primitive nature, etc.

Rom·a·ny (räm′ə nē, rō′mə-) *n.* [Romany *romani,* Gypsy < *rom,* a man < Sans.] 1. *pl.* **-ny, -nies** a Gypsy 2. the Indic language of the Gypsies —*adj.* of the Gypsies, their language, etc. Also sp. **Rom′ma·ny**

Rom. Cath. Roman Catholic

Rome (rōm) 1. capital of Italy, on the Tiber River: formerly, the capital of the Roman Empire: pop. 2,731,000 2. [after prec.] city in central N.Y., near Utica: pop. 50,000 3. *same as* ROMAN CATHOLIC CHURCH

Ro·me·o (rō′mē ō′) the hero of Shakespeare's tragedy *Romeo and Juliet* (c. 1595), lover of Juliet —*n., pl.* **-os′** a man who is a great lover

Rom·ney (räm′nē, rum′-), **George** 1734-1802; Eng. painter

romp (rämp) *n.* [< earlier *ramp,* hussy, prob. < OFr. *ramper:* see RAMP²] 1. a person who romps, esp. a girl 2. the act of playing in a rough, lively way 3. an easy victory —*vi.* 1. to play in a rough, lively way; frolic 2. to win with ease in a race, contest, etc.

romp·er (räm′pər) *n.* 1. one who romps 2. [*pl.*] a young child's loose-fitting, one-piece outer garment with bloomerlike pants

Rom·u·lus (räm′yoo ləs) *Rom. Myth.* the founder and first king of Rome: he and his twin brother Remus were raised by a she-wolf

Ron·ald (rän′ld) [Scot. < ON. *Rögnvaldr:* see REGINALD] a masculine name

ron·deau (rän′dō) *n., pl.* **-deaux** (-dōz) [Fr. < *rondel* < *rond,* round] a short lyrical poem of thirteen (or ten) lines and an unrhymed refrain that consists of the opening words and is used in two places

ron·do (rän′dō) *n., pl.* **-dos** [It. < Fr.: see RONDEAU] *Music* a composition or movement having its principal theme stated three or more times, separated by subordinate themes

rood (rōōd) *n.* [OE. *rod*] **1.** a crucifix **2.** in England, a measure of area equal to 1/4 acre

roof (rōōf, roof) *n., pl.* **roofs** [OE. *hrof*] **1.** the outside top covering of a building **2.** such a covering over a house, often a symbol of a place to live **3.** anything like a roof in position or use [the *roof* of the mouth] —*vt.* to cover as with a roof —**raise the roof** [Slang] to be very noisy, as in anger or joy —**roof′less** *adj.*

roof·er (rōōf′ər, roof′-) *n.* a person who builds or repairs roofs

roof·ing (-iŋ) *n.* **1.** the act of covering with a roof **2.** material for roofs

roof·top (-täp′) *n.* the roof of a building

roof·tree (-trē′) *n.* **1.** the ridgepole of a roof **2.** a roof

rook[1] (rook) *n.* [OE. *hroc*] a European crow —*vt., vi.* to swindle; cheat

rook[2] (rook) *n.* [< OFr. *roc* < Ar. < Per. *rukh*] a chess piece shaped like a castle tower which can move parallel to the sides of the board across any number of empty squares: also called **castle**

rook·er·y (rook′ər ē) *n., pl.* **-er·ies** a breeding place or colony of rooks, or of seals, penguins, etc.

rook·ie (rook′ē) *n.* [altered < ? RECRUIT] [Slang] **1.** a new recruit in the army ☆**2.** any beginner or novice, as on a police force or in a professional sport

room (rōōm, room) *n.* [OE. *rum* < IE. base *rewe-*, to open] **1.** space to contain something or in which to do something [room for one more] **2.** opportunity or occasion [room for doubt] **3.** a space within a building enclosed or set apart by walls **4.** [*pl.*] living quarters; lodgings **5.** the people in a room [the whole room was silent] —☆ *vi.* to have lodgings; lodge [to room with friends] —*vt.* to provide with lodgings

room and board lodging and meals

room clerk a clerk at a hotel or motel who registers guests, assigns them rooms, etc.

☆**room·er** (rōōm′ər, room′-) *n.* a person who rents a room or rooms to live in; lodger

☆**room·ette** (rōō met′, roo-) *n.* a small compartment for one person in a railroad sleeping car

room·ful (rōōm′fool′, room′-) *n., pl.* **-fuls′** **1.** as much or as many as will fill a room **2.** all of the people or objects in a room

☆**rooming house** a house with furnished rooms for rent

☆**room·mate** (-māt′) *n.* a person with whom one shares a room or rooms: also [Colloq.] **room′ie** (-ē)

room·y (-ē) *adj.* **room′i·er, room′i·est** having plenty of room; spacious —**room′i·ly** *adv.* —**room′i·ness** *n.*

Roo·se·velt (rō′zə velt′, -vəlt; rōz′velt′) **1. Franklin Del·a·no** (del′ə nō′), 1882–1945; 32d president of the U.S. (1933–45) **2. Theodore,** 1858–1919; 26th president of the U.S. (1901–09)

roost (rōōst) *n.* [OE. *hrost*] **1.** a perch on which birds, esp. domestic fowls, can rest or sleep **2.** a place with perches for birds **3.** a place for resting, sleeping, etc. —*vi.* **1.** to sit, sleep, etc. on a perch **2.** to settle down, as for the night —**come home to roost** to come back in an unfavorable way to the doer; boomerang —**rule the roost** to be master

roost·er (rōōs′tər) *n.* the male of the chicken

root[1] (rōōt, root) *n.* [Late OE. *rote* < ON. *rot* < IE. base *wrad-*, a twig, from which also comes L. *radix*, a root] **1.** the part of a plant, usually below the ground, that lacks nodes, shoots, and leaves, holds the plant in place, and draws water and food from the soil **2.** loosely, any underground part of a plant, as a tuber **3.** the attached or embedded part of a tooth, hair, etc. **4.** the source or cause of an action, quality, condition, etc. [″the love of money is the *root* of all evil″] **5.** an ancestor **6.** [*pl.*] the close ties one has with some place or people as through birth, upbringing, long association, etc. **7.** a supporting part; base **8.** an essential or basic part; core [the *root* of the matter] **9.** *Math. a)* a quantity that, multiplied by itself a specified number of times, produces a given quantity [4 is the square *root* (4 x 4) of 16 and the cube *root* (4 x 4 x 4) of 64] *b)* a number that, when substituted for the unknown quantity in an equation, will satisfy the equation **10.** *Music* the basic tone of a chord **11.** *Linguis.* a word or part of a word that

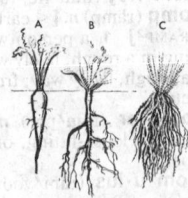

ROOTS
(A, B, taproot; C, fibrous)

is used as a base for making other words [the word "body" is the *root* for the words "bodily," "disembody," etc.] —*vi.* **1.** to begin to grow by putting out roots **2.** to become fixed, settled, etc. —*vt.* **1.** to fix the roots of in the ground **2.** to put firmly in place; settle —**see SYN.** at ORIGIN —**root up** (or **out, away**) to pull out by or as by the roots; remove completely —**take root** **1.** to begin growing by putting out roots **2.** to become settled

root[2] (rōōt, root) *vt.* [OE. *wrotan* < *wrot*, snout] to dig (*up* or *out*) with or as with the snout [wild pigs *rooting* up acorns] —*vi.* **1.** to dig in the ground, as with the snout **2.** to search about; rummage [to *root* through a drawer] ☆**3.** [Colloq.] to encourage a contestant or team by applauding and cheering; also, to support a candidate, cause, etc.: usually with *for* —**root′er** *n.*

Root (rōōt, root), **E·li·hu** (el′ə hyōō′) 1845–1937; U.S. statesman; secretary of state (1905–09)

☆**root beer** a sweet carbonated drink flavored with juices from the roots and bark of certain plants

root canal a small channel, normally filled with pulp, in the root of a tooth

root crop a crop, as turnips, beets, etc., grown for the roots that are used as vegetables

root hair any of the hairlike outgrowths from a growing root, which absorb water and minerals from the soil

root·less (rōōt′lis, root′-) *adj.* having no roots or ties [a *rootless* wanderer] —**root′less·ly** *adv.* —**root′less·ness** *n.*

root·let (-lit) *n.* a little root

root·stock (-stäk′) *n. Bot.* **1.** *same as* RHIZOME **2.** a plant onto which another is grafted as a new top

rope (rōp) *n.* [OE. *rap:* for IE. base see ROW[1]] **1.** a thick, strong cord made of strands of fiber, wires, etc. twisted together **2.** *a)* a noose for hanging a person *b)* death by hanging: with the ☆**3.** *same as* LASSO **4.** a ropelike string of things [a *rope* of pearls] **5.** a ropelike, sticky formation, as in wine —*vt.* **roped, rop′ing** **1.** to fasten or tie with a rope **2.** to connect by a rope **3.** to mark off or enclose with a rope (usually with *in, off,* or *out*) [to *rope* off a statue in a museum] ☆**4.** to catch with a lasso [to *rope* steers] —*vi.* to become ropelike and sticky [to cook candy until it *ropes*] —**know the ropes** [Colloq.] to know the details or procedures, as of a job —☆**rope in** [Slang] to trick into doing something —**the end of one's rope** the end of one's endurance, resources, etc. —**rop′er** *n.*

rope·walk (rōp′wôk′) *n.* a long, low, narrow building, shed, etc. in which ropes are made

rope·walk·er (-wôk′ər) *n.* a performer who walks or does tricks on a tightrope: also **rope′danc′er** (-dan′sər)

rop·y (rō′pē) *adj.* **rop′i·er, rop′i·est** **1.** forming sticky threads, as some liquids **2.** like rope —**rop′i·ness** *n.*

Roque·fort (cheese) (rōk′fərt) [< *Roquefort,* France, where made] *a trademark for* a strong cheese with a bluish mold, made from goats' and ewes' milk

ror·qual (rôr′kwəl) *n.* [Fr. < Norw. *röyrkval* < ON. *reytharhvalr,* lit., red whale] any of the whalebone whales with a well-developed dorsal fin, esp. a finback whale with lengthwise furrows on its belly and throat

Ror·schach test (rôr′shäk) [after H. *Rorschach* (1884–1922), Swiss psychiatrist] a psychological test in which the person being tested tells what is suggested to him by a standard series of inkblot designs: his responses are then interpreted

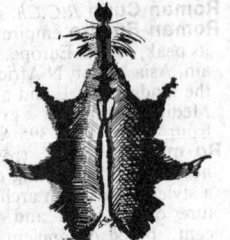

RORSCHACH DESIGN

ro·sa·ceous (rō zā′shəs) *adj.* **1.** of the rose family of plants, as the strawberry, plum, etc. **2.** like a rose **3.** rose-colored

Ros·a·lie (rō′zə lē′, räz′ə-) [Fr., prob. ult. < L. *rosa,* rose] a feminine name

Ros·a·lind (räz′ə lind) [Sp. *Rosalinda,* as if from *rosa linda,* pretty rose] a feminine name

Ro·sa·rio (rō sä′ryδ) city & port in EC Argentina, on the Paraná River: pop. 672,000

ro·sa·ry (rō′zər ē) *n., pl.* **-ries** [L. *rosarium,* ult. < *rosa,* a rose] *R.C.Ch.* **1.** a string of beads used to keep count in saying certain prayers [*also* R-] the prayers said with these beads **2.**

Rose (rōz) [after the flower] a feminine name

rose[1] (rōz) *n.* [OE. < L. *rosa*] **1.** any of a large group of shrubs with prickly stems and usually fragrant flowers of red, pink, white, yellow, etc. **2.** the flower of any of these **3.** any of several related plants **4.** pinkish red or purplish red **5.** anything like a rose in form, as a rosette or the form of a gem, esp. a diamond, cut with many facets and a flat base **6.** *same as* COMPASS CARD; also, a representation of this, as on maps —*adj.* **1.** of or having to do with a rose or roses **2.** rose-colored **3.** rose-scented **4.** designating a large family of wild and cultivated flowers, shrubs, and trees, including the hawthorns, roses, strawberries, apples, peaches, almonds, etc. —**rose′like** *adj.*

rose² (rōz) *pt. of* RISE

ro·sé (rō zā′) *n.* [Fr., lit., pink] a light, pink wine made by removing the grape husks after partial fermentation

ro·se·ate (rō′zē it, -āt′) *adj.* **1.** rose-colored; rosy **2.** cheerful or optimistic —**ro′se·ate·ly** *adv.*

rose·bud (rōz′bud′) *n.* the bud of a rose

rose·bush (-boosh′) *n.* a shrub that bears roses

rose chafer ☆a small N. American beetle that feeds on the leaves and flowers of roses and other plants: also called **rose bug**

rose-col·ored (-kul′ərd) *adj.* **1.** pinkish-red or purplish-red **2.** cheerful or optimistic —**through rose-colored glasses** with optimism, esp. too much optimism

☆**rose fever** a kind of hay fever believed to be caused by the pollen of roses: also **rose cold**

rose hip *same as* HIP²

rose mallow a mallow that grows in marshes, having large pink, red, or white flowers

Rose·mar·y (rōz′mer′ē) [after the plant] a feminine name

rose·mar·y (rōz′mer′ē) *n.* [altered (after ROSE¹ & MARY), ult. < L. *ros marinus*, lit., dew of the sea] an evergreen plant of the mint family, with small, light-blue flowers and fragrant leaves used in cooking, making perfume, etc.

rose of Sharon ☆**1.** a plant with white, red, pink, or purplish, bell-shaped flowers **2.** [Chiefly Brit.] a Saint Johnswort shrub with large, yellow flowers

ro·se·o·la (rō zē′ə lə, rō′zē ō′lə) *n.* [ModL., dim. < L. *roseus*, rosy] any of various rose-colored skin rashes

Ro·set·ta stone (rō zet′ə) a stone tablet, found in 1799 at Rosetta, Egypt, bearing inscriptions that provided a key for understanding Egyptian hieroglyphics

ro·sette (rō zet′) *n.* [Fr. < OFr., dim. of *rose*, ROSE¹] **1.** an ornament, arrangement, etc. resembling or suggesting a rose [a *rosette* of ribbon] **2.** *Archit.* a painted or sculptured ornament, usually circular, with petals and leaves radiating from the center **3.** *Bot.* a circular cluster of leaves, petals, etc.

Rose·ville (rōz′vil) [after W. *Rose*, 1st local postmaster (1836)] city in SE Mich.: suburb of Detroit: pop. 61,000

rose water a preparation consisting of water mixed with oil made from rose petals, used as a perfume

rose window a circular window with roselike tracery or mullions arranged like the spokes of a wheel

rose·wood (rōz′wood′) *n.* [from its odor] **1.** any of a number of valuable hard, reddish, black-streaked woods, used in making furniture, etc. **2.** a tropical tree producing such wood

Rosh Ha·sha·na (rōsh′ hə shō′nə, -shä′-; *Heb.* rōsh′ hä shä nä′) the Jewish New Year, celebrated on the 1st and 2d days of Tishri: also sp. **Rosh Hashona, Rosh Hashanah,** etc.

ros·in (räz′'n) *n.* [altered < MFr. *resine*, RESIN] the hard, brittle resin, light-yellow to almost black, left after the distillation of crude turpentine: it is rubbed on violin bows, used in making varnish, etc. —*vt.* to rub with rosin; put rosin on —**ros′in·ous, ros′in·y** *adj.*

ROSE WINDOW

Ross (rôs) **1. Bet·sy** (bet′sē), (*Mrs. Elizabeth Griscom Ross*) 1752-1836; Am. woman said to have made the first Am. flag **2.** Sir **James Clark,** 1800-62; Brit. polar explorer **3.** Sir **John,** 1777-1856; Brit. arctic explorer, born in Scotland: uncle of Sir *James Clark* **4.** Sir **Ronald,** 1857-1932; Eng. pathologist

Ros·set·ti (rō zet′ē, -set′ē) **1. Chris·ti·na (Georgina)** (kris-tē′nə), 1830-94; Eng. poet **2. Dante Gabriel,** 1828-82; Eng. painter & poet: brother of *Christina*

Ross Ice Shelf frozen S section of the Ross Sea: also called **Ross Shelf Ice**

Ros·si·ni (rôs sē′nē; *E.* rō sē′nē), **Gio·ac·chi·no (Antonio)** (jô′ä kē′nō) 1792-1868; It. composer

Ross Sea arm of the Pacific, along the coast of Antarctica

Ros·tand (rôs tän′; *E.* räs′tand), **Ed·mond** (ed môn′) 1868-1918; Fr. dramatist & poet

ros·ter (räs′tər) *n.* [Du. *rooster*, orig., gridiron, hence a list (from ruled paper used for lists)] **1.** a list of military or naval personnel, telling what work each person is to do for a certain period of time **2.** any list; roll

Ros·tock (rôs′tôk; *E.* räs′täk) seaport in N East Germany, on the Baltic: pop. 195,000

Ros·tov (rô stôf′; *E.* räs′täv) seaport in southwestern R.S.F.S.R., at the mouth of the Don: pop. 789,000: also called **Ros′tov-on-Don′**

ros·trum (räs′trəm) *n., pl.* **-trums, -tra** (-trə) [L., (ship's) beak, hence the speakers' platform in the Forum, decorated with ramming beaks taken from captured ships] **1.** any platform on which a person stands while making a public speech **2.** public speaking, or public speakers as a group —**ros′tral** *adj.*

ros·y (rō′zē) *adj.* **ros′i·er, ros′i·est 1.** like a rose, esp. in color; rose-red or pink [*rosy* cheeks] **2.** [Archaic] made with roses **3.** bright, promising, cheerful, etc. [a *rosy* future] —**ros′i·ly** *adv.* —**ros′i·ness** *n.*

SYN.—**rosy** suggests the warm pink or red color of a rose in bloom [*rosy* cheeks]; **rubicund** implies a flushed, unnatural redness of the face that results from too much eating, drinking, etc. [a *rubicund* nose]; **ruddy** implies such healthy redness as results from an outdoor life [the *ruddy* face of the forest ranger]; **florid** implies the deep, often splotchy redness of face of someone suffering from high blood pressure, strong emotional excitement, etc. [his face grew *florid* as he shouted]

rot (rät) *vi.* **rot′ted, rot′ting** [OE. *rotian:* for IE. base see RUPTURE] **1.** to fall apart gradually by the action of bacteria, etc.; decay **2.** to become unhealthy, etc. [to *rot* in prison] **3.** to become morally corrupt —*vt.* **1.** to cause to rot, or fall apart **2.** *same as* RET —*n.* **1.** a rotting or being rotten; decay **2.** something rotting or rotten **3.** any of various plant and animal diseases, esp. of sheep, causing decay **4.** [Slang] nonsense —*interj.* an exclamation showing disgust, anger, etc. —see SYN. at DECAY

ro·ta·ry (rōt′ər ē) *adj.* [< ML. < L. *rota*, a wheel: see ROLL] **1.** turning around a central point or axis, as a wheel; rotating **2.** *a)* having a rotating part or parts *b)* having blades that rotate on a hub [a *rotary* lawn mower] **3.** occurring around an axis [*rotary* motion] —*n., pl.* **-ries** a rotary machine or engine

☆**Rotary Club** any local organization of an international club (**Rotary International**) of business and professional men, founded in 1905 to promote community welfare —**Ro·tar·i·an** (rō ter′ē ən) *n., adj.* —**Ro·tar′i·an·ism** *n.*

rotary engine 1. an engine, such as a steam turbine, in which rotary motion is produced directly, without reciprocating parts **2.** an early type of radial engine with the cylinders rotating around a stationary crankshaft

rotary press a printing press with curved plates mounted on rotating cylinders, for printing on paper fed from a roll

ro·ta·ry-wing aircraft (-wiŋ′) an aircraft, as the helicopter, kept up in the air by rotors

ro·tate (rō′tāt) *vi., vt.* **-tat·ed, -tat·ing** [< L. pp. of *rotare* < *rota*, a wheel: see ROLL] **1.** to move or turn around a center point or axis, as a wheel **2.** to change by turns in regular order; alternate [to *rotate* crops] —see SYN. at TURN —**ro′tat·a·ble** *adj.* —**ro·ta·tive** (rō′tāt iv, rōt′ə tiv) *adj.* —**ro′ta·tor** *n.*

ro·ta·tion (rō tā′shən) *n.* **1.** a rotating or being rotated [the daily *rotation* of the earth]: distinguished from REVOLUTION **2.** a changing by turns in regular order [a *rotation* of duties] —**ro·ta′tion·al** *adj.*

rotation of crops a system of rotating in a fixed order the kinds of crops grown in the same field, to keep the soil fertile

ro·ta·to·ry (rō′tə tôr′ē) *adj.* **1.** of, or having the nature of, rotation **2.** rotating; rotary **3.** going or following in rotation **4.** causing rotation

ROTC, R.O.T.C. Reserve Officers' Training Corps

rote (rōt) *n.* [< ?] a fixed, mechanical way of doing something; routine —**by rote** by memory alone, without thought

ro·te·none (rōt′'n ōn′) *n.* [Jap. *roten*, an East Indian plant + -ONE] a white, odorless, crystalline substance, $C_{23}H_{22}O_6$, used in insecticides

rot·gut (rät′gut′) *n.* [ROT + GUT] ☆[Slang] raw, low-grade whiskey or other liquor

---

fat, āpe, cär; ten, ēven; is, bīte; gō, hôrn, tōōl, look; oil, out; up, fur; get; joy; yet; chin; she; thin, *th*en; zh, leisure; ŋ, ring; ə for *a* in ago, *e* in agent, *i* in sanity, *o* in comply, *u* in focus; ′ as in able (ā′b'l); Fr. bàl; ë, Fr. coeur; ö, Fr. feu; Fr. mon; ô, Fr. coq; ü, Fr. duc; *r*, Fr. cri; H, G. ich; kh, G. doch; ‡ foreign; ☆ Americanism; < derived from. See inside front cover.

Roth·schild (rôth′chīld′, räths′-; *G.* rōt′shilt) family of European bankers since the 18th cent., originally of Germany

ro·ti·fer (rōt′ə fər) *n.* [ModL. < L. *rota*, wheel + -FER] any of various microscopic, invertebrate freshwater animals, having a ring or rings of cilia at the front end of the body —**ro·tif·er·al** (rō tif′ər əl), **ro·tif′er·ous, ro·tif′er·an** *adj.*

☆**ro·tis·se·rie** (rō tis′ər ē) *n.* [Fr. < MFr., ult. < *rostir*, to ROAST] 1. a shop where roasted meats are sold 2. a grill with an electrically turned spit

☆**ro·to** (rōt′ō) *n., pl.* -**tos** *shortened form of* ROTOGRAVURE

☆**ro·to·gra·vure** (rōt′ə grə vyoor′) *n.* [< L. *rota*, a wheel + GRAVURE] 1. a printing process using photogravure cylinders on a rotary press 2. a print or newspaper pictorial section printed by this process

ro·tor (rōt′ər) *n.* [< ROTATE] 1. the rotating part of a motor, dynamo, etc. 2. a rotating device, as on a helicopter, consisting of generally horizontal blades with their hub

☆**Ro·to·till·er** (rōt′ə til′ər) *a trademark for* a motorized cultivator with rotary blades —*n.* [*also* r-] such a cultivator —**ro′to·till′** *vt.*

rot·ten (rät′'n) *adj.* [ON. *rotinn*: for IE. base see RUPTURE] 1. fallen apart; decayed; spoiled [*rotten* apples] 2. smelling of decay; putrid [a *rotten* odor] 3. morally corrupt or offensive; dishonest, etc. [*rotten* politics] 4. unsound or weak, as if decayed within [a *rotten* floor] 5. [Slang] very bad, disagreeable, unsatisfactory, etc. [a *rotten* show] —**rot′ten·ly** *adv.* —**rot′ten·ness** *n.*

rot·ten·stone (rät′'n stōn′) *n.* a sandy limestone used for polishing metals

rot·ter (rät′ər) *n.* [< ROT] [Chiefly Brit. Slang] a fellow deserving scorn; cad; bounder

Rot·ter·dam (rät′ər dam′; *Du.* rôt′ər däm′) seaport in SW Netherlands, in the Rhine delta: pop. 687,000

ro·tund (rō tund′) *adj.* [L. *rotundus*, akin to *rota*: see ROLL] 1. round or rounded out; plump or stout 2. full-toned; sonorous [a *rotund* voice] —**ro·tun′di·ty, ro·tund′ness** *n.* —**ro·tund′ly** *adv.*

ro·tun·da (rō tun′də) *n.* [< It. < L. fem. of *rotundus*, ROTUND] a round building, hall, or room, esp. one with a dome

Rou·ault (roo ō′), **Georges** (zhôrzh) 1871-1958; Fr. painter

rou·ble (roo′b'l) *n. same as* RUBLE

rou·é (roo ā′) *n.* [Fr., pp. of *rouer*, to break on the wheel < L. *rota*: see ROLL] a man who leads a wild, dissolute life; debauchee; rake

Rou·en (roo än′; *Fr.* rwän) city & port in NW France, on the Seine: pop. 120,000

rouge (roozh) *n.* [Fr., red < L. *rubeus*, RUBY] 1. any of various reddish cosmetic powders, pastes, etc. for coloring the cheeks and lips 2. a reddish powder, mainly ferric oxide, for polishing jewelry, metal, etc. —*vi., vt.* **rouged, roug′ing** to use cosmetic rouge (on)

rough (ruf) *adj.* [OE. *ruh*: for IE. base see RUPTURE] 1. *a)* not smooth or level; uneven [a *rough* surface] *b)* not easily traveled; overgrown, wild, etc. [*rough* country] 2. shaggy [an animal with a *rough* coat] 3. moving violently; agitated; specif., *a)* stormy; tempestuous [*rough* weather] *b)* noisy or disorderly [*rough* play] 4. harsh, rude, brutal, etc. [a *rough* temper] 5. sounding, feeling, or tasting harsh 6. lacking comforts and conveniences [the *rough* life of pioneers] 7. not refined or polished [a *rough* diamond] 8. not finished, perfected, etc. [a *rough* sketch, a *rough* estimate] 9. needing strength rather than skill or intelligence [*rough* labor] 10. [Colloq.] difficult, unpleasant, etc. [a *rough* time] 11. *Phonet.* pronounced with an aspirate; having the sound of *h* —*n.* 1. rough ground 2. rough material or condition ☆3. a rough sketch or draft 4. [Chiefly Brit.] a rough person; rowdy 5. *Golf* any part of the course where grass, weeds, etc. grow uncut —*adv.* in a rough manner —*vt.* 1. to make rough; roughen [to *rough* up metal with a file] 2. to treat roughly (often with *up*) [the street gang *roughed* up their victim] 3. to make or shape roughly (usually with *in* or *out*) [*rough* out a scheme] —*vi.* to behave roughly —**In the rough** in a rough or crude state —**rough it** to live without comforts and conveniences —**rough′ish** *adj.* —**rough′ly** *adv.* —**rough′ness** *n.*

☆**rough·age** (ruf′ij) *n.* rough or coarse substance; specif., coarse food or fodder, as bran, straw, vegetable peel, etc., that helps to move waste products through the intestines

rough-and-read·y (ruf′'n red′ē) *adj.* 1. rough, or crude, rude, etc., but effective [*rough-and-ready* methods] 2. characterized by rough strength rather than refinement, formality, etc. [a *rough-and-ready* fellow]

rough-and-tum·ble (-tum′b'l) *adj.* violent and disorderly, with no concern for rules [a *rough-and-tumble* fight] —*n.* a fight or struggle of this kind

rough·cast (ruf′kast′) *n.* 1. a coarse plaster for covering outside surfaces, as walls 2. a rough pattern or crude model —*vt.* -**cast′, -cast′ing** 1. to cover (walls, etc.) with roughcast 2. to make or shape in a rough form

rough-dry (-drī′) *vt.* -**dried′, -dry′ing** to dry (washed laundry) without ironing: also **rough′dry′** —*adj.* washed and dried but not ironed

rough·en (ruf′'n) *vt., vi.* to make or become rough

rough-hew (ruf′hyoo′) *vt.* -**hewed′, -hewed′** or -**hewn′, -hew′ing** 1. to hew (timber, stone, etc.) roughly, or without finishing or smoothing 2. to form roughly; give crude shape or outline to Also **rough′hew′**

☆**rough·house** (ruf′hous′) *n.* [Slang] rough or rowdy play, fighting, etc. —*vt.* -**housed′, -hous′ing** [Slang] to treat (a person) in a rough or rowdy way —*vi.* [Slang] to take part in rough-house

☆**rough·neck** (-nek′) *n.* [Slang] a rough person; rowdy

rough·rid·er (-rīd′ər) *n.* 1. a person who breaks horses for riding 2. a person who does much hard, rough riding ☆3. [R-] a member of Theodore Roosevelt's volunteer cavalry regiment in the Spanish-American War: also **Rough Rider**

rough·shod (-shäd′) *adj.* shod with horseshoes that have metal points to prevent slipping —**ride roughshod over** to treat in a harsh, overbearing, thoughtless manner

rou·lade (roo läd′) *n.* [Fr. < *rouler*, to ROLL] 1. a rapid series of tones sung to one syllable 2. a slice of meat rolled and cooked

rou·lette (roo let′) *n.* [Fr. < OFr. dim. of *roele*, a small wheel, ult. < L. *rota*: see ROLL] 1. a gambling game played by rolling a small ball around a shallow bowl with a revolving inner disk (**roulette wheel**) with red and black numbered compartments 2. a small toothed wheel for making rows of marks or dots, as between postage stamps on a sheet —*vt.* -**let′ted, -let′ting** to make marks, dots, etc. in with a roulette

ROULETTE WHEEL

Rou·ma·ni·a (roo mān′yə, -mä′nē ə) *same as* ROMANIA — **Rou·ma′ni·an** *adj., n.*

round (round) *adj.* [< OFr. < L. *rotundus*, ROTUND] 1. shaped like a ball; spherical 2. *a)* shaped like a circle, ring, etc.; circular or curved *b)* shaped like a cylinder; cylindrical 3. plump or stout [*round* cheeks] 4. with or involving a circular motion [a *round* dance] 5. full; complete [a *round* dozen] 6. expressed by a whole number, or in tens, hundreds, etc. [500 is a *round* number for 498, 503, etc.] 7. large in amount, size, etc. [a *round* sum] 8. mellow and full in tone; sonorous [rich *round* tones] 9. brisk; lively [a *round* pace] 10. outspoken; plain and blunt [a *round* denial] 11. *Phonet.* pronounced with the lips forming an oval [a *round* vowel] —*n.* 1. something round; thing that is spherical, circular, curved, etc. 2. a rung of a ladder or a chair 3. the part of a beef animal between the rump and the leg: in full, **round of beef**: see illustration at BEEF 4. movement in a circular course 5. *same as* ROUND DANCE 6. a series of actions, events, etc. of a similar kind [a *round* of parties] 7. the complete extent; whole range [the *round* of human beliefs] 8. [*often pl.*] a course or route taken regularly, as by a watchman in his work 9. a single serving, as of drinks, for each in a group 10. *a)* a single shot from a rifle, etc. or from a number of rifles fired together *b)* ammunition for such a shot 11. a single outburst, as of applause 12. *Games & Sports* a single period or division of action [a *round* of poker]; specif., *a)* *Boxing* any of the timed periods of a fight *b)* *Golf* a number of holes as a unit of competition 13. *Music* a short song for two or more persons or groups, in which the second starts when the first reaches the second phrase, etc. —*vt.* 1. to make round (often with *off*) [*round* off the corners of the board] 2. to pronounce with rounded lips [to *round* a vowel] 3. to make plump (usually with *out*) 4. to express as a round number (usually with *off*) 5. to complete; finish (usually with *out* or *off*) [to *round* out the day] 6. to go or pass around [we *rounded* the island] 7. to make a turn about [the car *rounded* the corner] —*vi.* 1. to make a complete or partial circuit 2. *a)* to turn; reverse direction *b)* to attack suddenly; turn (*on*) 3. to become round or plump —*adv.* 1. in a circle; along a circular course 2. through a complete cycle of time; throughout [to work the year *round*] 3. from one person or place to another [the peddler came *round*] **4.** for everyone [not enough to go *round*] **5.** in circumference **6.** on all sides; in every direction **7.** about; near **8.** in a roundabout way **9.** here and there; in various places **10.** with a rotating movement **11.** in or to the opposite direction, belief, viewpoint, etc. —**prep. 1.** so as to encircle or surround **2.** on the circumference or border of **3.** on all sides of **4.** close to **5.** in a circuit or course through **6.** in various places in or on **7.** so as to make a curve or circuit about In the U.S., *round* (*adv. & prep.*) is generally replaced by *around;* in Great Britain, *round* is preferred for most senses —**go the round (or rounds) 1.** to be talked about widely, as a story, rumor, etc. **2.** to walk over a route regularly taken in one's work: also **make one's rounds** —**in the round 1.** with the audience, etc. seated all around a central stage, etc. **2.** in full and completely rounded form, not in relief: said of sculpture **3.** in full detail —**out of round** not having perfect roundness —**round about 1.** in or to the opposite direction **2.** in every direction around —**round up** ☆**1.** to drive (cattle, etc.) together in a herd, group, etc. ☆**2.** [Colloq.] to gather or assemble —**round′ish** *adj.* —**round′ness** *n.*

SYN.—**round** applies to anything shaped like a circle, sphere, or cylinder, or like a part of any of these; **spherical** applies to a round body or mass having the surface equally distant from the center at all points; **globular** is used of things that are ball-shaped but not necessarily perfect spheres; **circular** is applied to round lines, or round flat surfaces, in the shape of a ring or disk, which may or may not form a perfect circle

round·a·bout (round′ə bout′) *adj.* not straight or straightforward; indirect [*roundabout* methods] —*n.* **1.** something that is not direct ☆**2.** a short, tight jacket formerly worn by men or boys **3.** *Brit. var. of* MERRY-GO-ROUND

☆**round clam** *same as* QUAHOG

round dance 1. a dance with the dancers moving in a circle **2.** any of several dances, as the waltz, polka, etc., in which the couples make circular movements

round·ed (roun′did) *adj.* **1.** made round **2.** having variety in tastes, abilities, etc. [a well-*rounded* person]

roun·de·lay (roun′də lā′) *n.* [< MFr. dim. of *rondel*, a rondel] a simple song in which some phrase, line, etc. is continually repeated

round·er (roun′dər) *n.* **1.** a person or thing that rounds, as a tool for rounding edges **2.** [*pl.*, *with sing. v.*] a British game somewhat like baseball ☆**3.** [Colloq.] an immoral and shameless person or drunkard

Round·head (round′hed′) *n.* a member of the Parliamentary, or Puritan, party in England during the English civil war (1642–52)

round·house (-hous′) *n.* ☆**1.** a building, generally circular, with a turntable in the center, for storing and repairing locomotives **2.** a cabin at the rear of a ship's quarter-deck ☆**3.** *a) Baseball* a pitch with a wide curve *b) Boxing* a wide swing or hook, as to the head

round·ly (-lē) *adv.* **1.** in a round form **2.** in a round manner; specif., *a)* sharply, harshly, etc. [he was *roundly* scolded] *b)* fully; completely [*roundly* defeated]

round robin 1. a petition, protest, etc. with the signatures written in a circle to conceal the order of signing **2.** a tournament in which every player or team is matched with every other one **3.** a letter passed or sent among the members of a group, forwarded by each in turn, often with added comments

round·shoul·dered (-shōl′dərd) *adj.* stooped because the shoulders are bent forward

round steak a cut from a round of beef: see ROUND (*n.* 3)

Round Table 1. the table around which King Arthur and his knights sat **2.** King Arthur and his knights, as a group **3.** [r-t-] *a)* an informal discussion group *b)* the informal discussion —**round′-ta′ble** *adj.*

round-the-clock (-thə kläk′) *adj., adv.* throughout the day and night; continuously

☆**round trip** a trip to a place and back again —**round′-trip′** *adj.*

round turn a kind of knot making one complete turn around something: see illustration at KNOT

round·up (-up′) *n.* ☆**1.** *a)* the act of driving cattle, etc. together on the range and collecting in a herd, as for branding *b)* the cowboys, horses, etc. that do this work ☆**2.** any similar driving together or collecting [a *roundup* of suspected persons] ☆**3.** a summary, as of news

round·worm (-wurm′) *n.* **1.** *same as* NEMATODE **2.** a type of nematode worm, living as a parasite, esp. in the intestines of man and other mammals

rouse (rouz) *vt.* **roused, rous′ing** [prob. < Anglo-Fr. or OFr.] **1.** to cause (game) to fly up from cover, come out of a lair, etc. **2.** to stir up, as to anger or action; excite **3.** to bring out of sleep; wake —*vi.* **1.** to leave cover, a lair, etc.: said of game **2.** to come out of sleep; wake **3.** to become active —*n.* a rousing —see SYN. at STIR¹ —**rous′er** *n.* —**rous′ing·ly** *adv.*

Rous·seau (rōō sō′) **1. Hen·ri** (än rē′), 1844–1910; Fr. painter **2. Jean Jacques** (zhän zhäk), 1712–78; Fr. political philosopher & writer, born in Switzerland

roust·a·bout (roust′ə bout′) *n.* [*roust*, dial. var. of ROUSE + ABOUT] ☆**1.** a deckhand or waterfront laborer ☆**2.** an unskilled or temporary laborer, as in a circus or on a ranch

rout¹ (rout) *n.* [< OFr. < L. *rupta:* see ROUTE] **1.** a disorderly crowd; rabble **2.** a disorderly flight, as of defeated troops [to be put to *rout*] **3.** an overwhelming defeat **4.** [Archaic] a group of people; company —*vt.* **1.** to put to disorderly flight [to *rout* enemy troops] **2.** to defeat overwhelmingly —see SYN. at CONQUER

rout² (rout) *vi.* [var. of ROOT²] **1.** to dig for food with the snout, as a pig **2.** to poke or rummage about —*vt.* **1.** to dig up with the snout **2.** to force out —**rout out 1.** to expose to view **2.** to scoop, gouge, or hollow out ☆**3.** to make (a person) get out —**rout up 1.** to get by poking about ☆**2.** to make (a person) get up —**rout′er** *n.*

route (rōōt; *also, and for n.* 2 *usually*, rout) *n.* [OFr. < L. *rupta* (*via*), broken (path) < pp. of *rumpere:* see RUPTURE] **1.** a road, etc. for traveling; esp., a highway ☆**2.** *a)* a regular course traveled as in delivering mail, milk, etc. *b)* a set of customers to whom one regularly makes deliveries —*vt.* **rout′ed, rout′ing** ☆**1.** to send by a specified route [to *route* goods through Omaha] ☆**2.** to fix the order of procedure of [to *route* orders through the sales department] —☆**go the route** [Colloq.] *Baseball* to pitch an entire game

rou·tine (rōō tēn′) *n.* [Fr. < *route:* see prec.] **1.** a regular, unvarying procedure, fixed by custom, rules, or habit [the *routine* of preparing breakfast] **2.** a theatrical skit ☆**3.** a series of dance steps **4.** a set of coded instructions for a computer —*adj.* having the nature of or using routine [a *routine* task] —**rou·tine′ly** *adv.*

roux (rōō) *n.* [Fr. *roux* (*beurre*), reddish-brown (butter)] a cooked mixture of butter (or other fat) and flour, used for thickening sauces, soups, gravies, etc.

rove¹ (rōv) *vi.* **roved, rov′ing** [< ?] **1.** to wander about; roam **2.** to look around: said of the eyes —*vt.* to wander over; roam through [he *roved* the woods] —*n.* a roving; ramble —see SYN. at ROAM —**rov′er** *n.*

rove² (rōv) *vt.* [< ?] to twist (fibers) together and draw out into a strand (*roving*) before spinning

rove³ (rōv) *alt. pt. & pp. of* REEVE²

rov·en (rōv′'n) *alt. pp. of* REEVE²

row¹ (rō) *n.* [OE. *ræw* < IE. base *rei-*, to split, tear] **1.** a number of people or things arranged in a line **2.** any of the lines of seats side by side in a theater, etc. **3.** a street with a line of buildings, as of a specified kind, on either side [fraternity *row*] —*vt.* to arrange or put in rows —☆**hard** (or **long**) **row to hoe** anything hard or tiring to do —**in a row** one after the other

row² (rō) *vt.* [OE. *rowan*] **1.** to move (a boat, etc.) on water by using oars **2.** to carry in a rowboat [*row* us across the lake] **3.** to use (oarsmen, a stroke, etc. as specified) in rowing **4.** to take part in (a race) by rowing —*vi.* **1.** to use oars in moving a boat **2.** to be moved by oars: said of a boat —*n.* **1.** a rowing **2.** a trip made by rowboat —**row′er** *n.*

row³ (rou) *n.* [< ? ROUSE] a noisy quarrel, dispute, or disturbance; squabble or brawl —*vi.* to take part in a row

row·an (rō′ən, rou′-) *n.* [< Scand.] **1.** the mountain ash, a tree with white flowers and reddish berries **2.** its fruit: also **row′an·ber′ry**, *pl.* **-ries**

row·boat (rō′bōt′) *n.* a boat made to be rowed

☆**row·dy** (rou′dē) *n.*, *pl.* **-dies** [< ? ROW³] a person whose behavior is rough, quarrelsome, and disorderly; hoodlum —*adj.* **-di·er, -di·est** of or like a rowdy; rough, quarrelsome, etc. —**row′di·ly** *adv.* —**row′di·ness** *n.* —**row′dy·ish** *adj.* —**row′dy·ism** *n.*

row·el (rou′əl) *n.* [< OFr. *roele:* see ROULETTE] a small wheel with sharp points, forming the end of a spur —*vt.* **-eled** or **-elled, -el·ing** or **-el·ling** to spur or prick (a horse) with a rowel

row·lock (rul′ək, räl′-; rō′läk′) *n.* [altered (after ROW²) < OARLOCK] *chiefly Brit.* term for OARLOCK

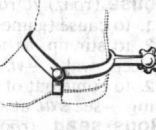

ROWEL

Roy (roi) [as if < OFr. *roy* (Fr. *roi*), a king, but prob. < Gael. *rhu,* red] a masculine name

roy·al (roi′əl) *adj.* [< OFr. < L. *regalis:* see REGAL] **1.** of a king, queen, or other sovereign [a *royal* edict, the *royal* family] **2.** having the rank of a king or queen **3.** of a kingdom, its government, etc. [the *royal* fleet] **4.** founded or supported by a king or queen [the *Royal* Society] **5.** like or fit for a king or queen; magnificent, stately, etc. [a *royal* carriage] **6.** unusually large, fine, etc. [a *royal* meal] —*n.* a small sail set on the royal mast —**roy′al·ly** *adv.*

royal blue a deep, bright reddish or purplish blue

☆**royal flush** the highest poker hand, consisting of the ace, king, queen, jack, and ten of the same suit

roy·al·ist (-ist) *n.* a person who supports a king or a monarchy, esp. in times of revolution —**roy′al·ism** *n.*

royal mast a small mast above the topgallant mast

Royal Oak [after an oak in which CHARLES II is said to have hidden] city in SE Mich.: suburb of Detroit: pop. 85,000

☆**royal palm** any of a group of tall, ornamental palm trees

roy·al·ty (roi′əl tē) *n., pl.* **-ties 1.** the rank, status, or power of a king or queen **2.** a royal person, or royal persons as a group **3.** a kingdom **4.** royal quality or character; regalness, nobility, etc. **5.** [*usually pl.*] a right, privilege, etc. of a monarch **6.** *a)* a share of the earnings paid to the owner of a right, as a patent, for its use *b)* such a share paid to one who leases out lands rich in oil or minerals *c)* a share of the earnings from his work paid to an author, composer, etc.

rpm, r.p.m. revolutions per minute

R.R. 1. railroad: also **RR 2.** Right Reverend

-rrha·gi·a (rā′jē ə) [ModL. < Gr. < *rhēgnynai,* to burst] *a combining form meaning* abnormal discharge or flow: also **-rrhage** (rij), **-rrhag′y** (rā′jē)

-rrhe·a, -rrhoe·a (rē′ə) [ModL. < Gr. < *rhein,* to flow] *a combining form meaning* a flow, discharge

Rs, rs. rupees

R.S.F.S.R., RSFSR Russian Soviet Federated Socialist Republic

RSV, R.S.V. Revised Standard Version (of the Bible)

R.S.V.P., r.s.v.p. [Fr. *répondez s'il vous plaît*] please reply

rt. right

rte. route

Ru *Chem.* ruthenium

rub (rub) *vt.* **rubbed, rub′bing** [ME. *rubben,* akin to Dan. *rubbe:* for IE. base see RUPTURE] **1.** to move (one's hand, a cloth, etc.) back and forth over (something) firmly **2.** to spread or apply (polish, salve, etc.) on a surface **3.** to move (a thing) against something else, or move (things) over each other with pressure and friction **4.** to put into a specified condition by applying pressure and friction [*rub* it dry] **5.** to make sore by rubbing [the shoe *rubbed* his heel] **6.** to remove by rubbing (*out, off,* etc.) [the eraser will *rub* out the mark] —*vi.* **1.** to move with pressure and friction (*on, against,* etc.) [the tire *rubbed* against the fender] **2.** to rub something **3.** to lend itself to being rubbed or removed by rubbing (often with *off, out,* etc.) [the paint will not *rub* off easily] —*n.* **1.** a rubbing; specif., a massage **2.** trouble or difficulty [she may not even know—there's the *rub*] **3.** something that irritates, annoys, etc. —**rub down 1.** to massage **2.** to smooth, polish, etc. by rubbing —**rub it in** [Slang] to keep reminding someone of his failure or mistake —☆**rub off on** to be left on as a mark, as by rubbing or by close contact —**rub the wrong way** to annoy or irritate

ru·ba·to (rᴏᴏ bät′ō) *adj., adv.* [It. < (*tempo*) *rubato,* stolen (time)] *Music* with some notes lengthened and others shortened in ignoring exact tempo for a desired effect —*n., pl.* **-toes 1.** a rubato effect **2.** a rubato passage, phrase, etc.

rub·ber¹ (rub′ər) *n.* **1.** a person or thing that rubs **2.** [from use as an eraser] an elastic or springy substance produced from the milky sap of various tropical plants, or synthetically **3.** something made of this substance; specif., *a*) an eraser ☆*b*) a low-cut overshoe ☆**4.** *Baseball* an oblong piece of rubber, etc. set into the pitcher's mound —*adj.* made of rubber —**rub′ber·like′** *adj.* —**rub′ber·y** *adj.*

rub·ber² (rub′ər) *n.* [< ?] **1.** *Bridge* a series limited to three games, two of which must be won to win the series **2.** any game played to break a tie in games won: usually **rubber game**

rubber band a narrow, ringlike band of rubber, often put around small objects for holding them together

rubber cement an adhesive made of rubber dissolved in a liquid that evaporates quickly

rub·ber·ize (-īz′) *vt.* **-ized′, -iz′ing** to coat or fill with rubber [to *rubberize* cloth]

☆**rub·ber·neck** (-nek′) *n.* [Old Slang] a person who looks around to see everything he can, as a sightseer does —*vi.* [Old Slang] to look around at things in this way

rubber plant 1. any plant producing latex from which crude rubber is formed **2.** a house plant with large, shiny, leathery leaves

rub·ber-stamp (rub′ər stamp′) *vt.* **1.** to mark with a rubber stamp ☆**2.** [Colloq.] to approve in a routine way —☆ *adj.* approved or approving in a routine way

rubber stamp 1. a stamp made of rubber, pressed down on an inked pad and used for printing signatures, dates, etc. ☆**2.** [Colloq.] *a)* a person, bureau, etc. that approves something in a routine way, without questioning or objecting *b)* any routine approval

rub·bing (rub′iŋ) *n.* a picture made of a raised or engraved design, etc. by placing a piece of paper over it and rubbing with graphite, wax, etc.

RUBBER PLANT (sense 2)

rub·bish (rub′ish) *n.* [ult. < base of RUB] **1.** any material thrown away as worthless; trash **2.** worthless, foolish ideas, statements, etc.; nonsense

rub·ble (rub′'l) *n.* [akin to RUBBISH, RUB] **1.** rough, broken pieces of stone, brick, etc. **2.** masonry made of such pieces: also **rub′ble·work′ 3.** broken pieces from buildings, etc., resulting from earthquake, bombing, etc. —**rub′bly** *adj.*

rub·down (rub′doun′) *n.* a massage

☆**rube** (rᴏᴏb) *n.* [< REUBEN] [Slang] a country person thought of as simple, unrefined, easily fooled, etc.

ru·bel·la (rᴏᴏ bel′ə) *n.* [ModL. < L. *rubellus* < *ruber,* red] a contagious virus disease causing swollen glands in the neck and small red spots on the skin; German measles

Ru·bens (rᴏᴏ′bənz), **Peter Paul** 1577-1640; Fl. painter

ru·be·o·la (rᴏᴏ bē′ə lə, rᴏᴏ′bē ō′lə) *n.* [ModL., neut. pl. dim. of L. *rubeus,* red] *same as* MEASLES (sense 1)

Ru·bi·con (rᴏᴏ′bi kän′) small river in N Italy crossed by Caesar to march on Rome with his army (49 B.C.), starting a civil war —**cross the Rubicon** to make an important move that cannot be undone

ru·bi·cund (rᴏᴏ′bi kund′) *adj.* [< Fr. < L. < *ruber,* red] reddish; ruddy —**see SYN. at ROSY —ru′bi·cun′di·ty** *n.*

ru·bid·i·um (rᴏᴏ bid′ē əm) *n.* [ModL. < L. *rubidus,* red (from red lines in its spectrum)] a soft, silvery-white metallic chemical element, resembling potassium: symbol, Rb; at. wt., 85.47; at. no., 37

ru·ble (rᴏᴏ′b'l) *n.* [Russ. *rubl'*] the monetary unit of the U.S.S.R.: see MONETARY UNITS, table

ru·bric (rᴏᴏ′brik) *n.* [< MFr. < L. *rubrica,* rubric < *ruber,* red] **1.** in early books and manuscripts, a chapter heading, initial letter, etc. printed or written in red, decorative lettering, etc. **2.** a heading, title, etc., as of a chapter, a law, etc. **3.** a direction in a prayer book **4.** a note of comment; gloss **5.** an established rule of procedure —**ru′bri·cal** *adj.* —**ru′bri·cal·ly** *adv.*

ru·by (rᴏᴏ′bē) *n., pl.* **-bies** [< OFr. *rubi,* ult. < L. *rubeus,* red: for IE. base see RED¹] **1.** a clear, deep-red variety of corundum, valued as a precious stone **2.** deep red —*adj.* deep-red

ruche (rᴏᴏsh) *n.* [Fr., lit., beehive < OFr. < Celt.] a fluting or pleating of lace, ribbon, net, etc. for trimming garments, esp. at the neck or wrist

ruch·ing (rᴏᴏ′shiŋ) *n.* **1.** trimming made of ruches **2.** material used to make ruches

ruck (ruk) *n.* [< ON. *hroki,* a heap] the mass of ordinary people or things

ruck·sack (ruk/sak′, rook/-) *n.* [G. < *rücken*, the back + *sack*, a sack] a kind of knapsack

☆**ruck·us** (ruk/əs) *n.* [prob. a merging of RUCTION & RUMPUS] [Colloq.] noisy confusion; uproar; row; disturbance

ruc·tion (ruk/shən) *n.* [altered < INSURRECTION] [Colloq.] a noisy disturbance or quarrel

rud·der (rud/ər) *n.* [OE. *rother*, steering oar] **1.** a broad, flat, movable piece of wood or metal hinged vertically at the stern of a boat or ship, used for steering **2.** a piece like this on an aircraft, etc. —**rud′der·less** *adj.*

rud·der·post (-pōst′) *n.* the sternpost to which the rudder is fastened

rud·dy (rud/ē) *adj.* **-di·er, -di·est** [OE. *rudig*: for IE. base see RED[1]] **1.** having a healthy red color [a *ruddy* complexion] **2.** red or reddish —see SYN. at ROSY —**rud′di·ness** *n.*

RUDDER

☆**ruddy duck** a small, N. American duck, the adult male of which has a brownish-red upper body

rude (rood) *adj.* **rud′er, rud′est** [OFr. < L. *rudis*: for IE. base see RUPTURE] **1.** crude or rough in form [a *rude* hut] **2.** uncivilized or ignorant [*rude* savages] **3.** lacking refinement; coarse, vulgar, etc. [*rude* table manners] **4.** discourteous; impolite [a *rude* reply] **5.** rough; harsh [a *rude* awakening] **6.** harsh in sound; discordant [*rude* tones] **7.** simple or primitive [*rude* drawings] **8.** not carefully worked out or finished [a *rude* analysis] —**rude′ly** *adv.* —**rude′ness** *n.*

SYN.—**rude** implies being purposely thoughtless of others' feelings and connotes, esp., being shamelessly bold and disrespectful [it was *rude* of you to ignore your uncle]; **ill-mannered** suggests not knowing or following the courtesies of polite behavior [a well-meaning but *ill-mannered* fellow]; **boorish** is applied to one who is rude or ill-mannered in a coarse, loud or overbearing way; **impolite** implies merely a failure to practice good manners [it would be *impolite* to leave so early]; **discourteous** suggests a lack of dignified thoughtfulness for others [a *discourteous* reply]; **uncivil** implies paying little attention to even the basic rules of good manners [her *uncivil* treatment of the waiter] —ANT. polite, civil

ru·di·ment (roo/də mənt) *n.* [L. *rudimentum* < *rudis*, RUDE] **1.** something to be learned first, as any basic principle of a subject [the *rudiments* of physics] **2.** a first slight beginning of something [the *rudiments* of a plan] **3.** *Biol.* an incompletely developed or vestigial organ or part

ru·di·men·ta·ry (roo/də men/tər ē, -men/trē) *adj.* **1.** of rudiments or basic principles; elementary [*rudimentary* studies] **2.** not fully or completely developed [a tadpole has *rudimentary* legs] Also **ru′di·men/tal** —**ru′di·men/ta·ri·ness** *n.*

Ru·dolf (roo/dälf), **Lake** lake in NW Kenya, on the border of Ethiopia

Ru·dolf I (roo/dälf, -dôlf) 1218-91; Ger. king & emperor of the Holy Roman Empire (1273-91)

Ru·dolph (roo/dälf, -dôlf) [< G. < OHG. < *hruod-*, fame + *wolf*, a wolf] a masculine name: dim. **Rudy**

rue[1] (roo) *vt., vi.* **rued, ru′ing** [OE. *hreowan*] to feel sorrow or remorse for (a sin or something one wishes undone); regret; repent [he *rued* his angry words] —*n.* [Archaic] sorrow or regret

rue[2] (roo) *n.* [< OFr. < L. *ruta* < Gr. *rhytē*] a strong-smelling herb with yellow flowers and bitter-tasting leaves formerly used in medicine

rue·ful (roo/fəl) *adj.* **1.** causing sorrow or pity [*rueful* news] **2.** feeling or showing sorrow or regret, esp. in a wry way [a *rueful* look] —**rue′ful·ly** *adv.* —**rue′ful·ness** *n.*

ruff[1] (ruf) *n.* [contr. of RUFFLE[1], *n.*] **1.** a high, frilled, stiff collar worn by men and women in the 16th and 17th cents. **2.** a ring of feathers or fur standing out about the neck of a bird or animal **3.** a Eurasian sandpiper the male of which grows a ruff in the breeding season —**ruffed** *adj.*

ruff[2] (ruf) *n.* [< OFr. *roffle*] *Card Games* the act of trumping —*vt., vi. Card Games* to trump

RUFF

☆**ruffed grouse** a N. American game bird with neck feathers that can be spread into a ruff: also called *partridge* in the northern U.S. and *pheasant* in the southern U.S.: see illustration at GROUSE

ruf·fi·an (ruf/ē ən, ruf/yən) *n.* [< Fr. < It. *ruffiano*, a pander] a brutal, lawless person; hoodlum —*adj.* brutal and lawless: also **ruf′fi·an·ly** —**ruf′fi·an·ism** *n.*

ruf·fle[1] (ruf/'l) *vt.* **-fled, -fling** [< ON. or MLowG.] **1.** to disturb the smoothness of; ripple [wind *ruffling* the water] **2.** to gather into ruffles **3.** to put ruffles on **4.** to make (feathers, etc.) stand up as in a ruff **5.** to disturb or annoy [their questions *ruffled* him] **6.** *a)* to turn (pages) rapidly *b)* to shuffle (cards) —*vi.* **1.** to become uneven **2.** to become disturbed, annoyed, etc. —*n.* **1.** a strip of cloth, lace, etc. gathered in pleats or puckers and used for trimming **2.** a bird's ruff **3.** a disturbance; annoyance **4.** a ripple —**ruf′fly** *adj.* **-fli·er, -fli·est**

ruf·fle[2] (ruf/'l) *n.* [prob. echoic] a low, continuous beating of a drum —*vi., vt.* **-fled, -fling** to beat (a drum, etc.) with a ruffle

ru·fous (roo/fəs) *adj.* [L. *rufus*, red] brownish-red

rug (rug) *n.* [< Scand.: for IE. base see RUPTURE] **1.** a piece of thick, often napped fabric, woven strips of rag, an animal skin, etc. used as a floor covering **2.** *chiefly Brit.* term for LAP ROBE

Rug·by (rug/bē) *n.* [first played at *Rugby*, a boys' school in C England] a kind of football in which there are 15 players on each side and the oval ball may be kicked, thrown (but not forward), or run with

rug·ged (rug/id) *adj.* [< Scand.] **1.** having a surface that is uneven, rough, craggy, etc. [*rugged* ground] **2.** strong, irregular, and lined [a *rugged* face] **3.** stormy [*rugged* weather] **4.** sounding harsh [*rugged* tones] **5.** harsh; hard [a *rugged* life] **6.** not polished or refined; rude [*rugged* manners] ☆**7.** strong; robust; vigorous; hardy [a *rugged* man] **8.** [Colloq.] requiring skill, endurance, etc. [a *rugged* game] —**rug′ged·ly** *adv.* —**rug′ged·ness** *n.*

Ruhr (roor; *G.* roor) **1.** river in C West Germany, flowing west into the Rhine **2.** major coal-mining & industrial region in the valley of this river: also called **Ruhr Basin**

ru·in (roo/in) *n.* [< OFr. < L. *ruina* < *ruere*, to fall: for IE. base see RUN] **1.** [*pl.*] the remains of a fallen building, city, etc., or of something destroyed, decayed, etc. **2.** anything that has been destroyed, etc. **3.** the state of being destroyed, broken down, etc. [the house fell into *ruin*] **4.** downfall, destruction, decay, etc., as of a thing or person, or the cause of this [gambling was his *ruin*] —*vt.* to bring to ruin; specif., *a)* to destroy, or damage greatly [the mud *ruined* her shoes] *b)* to make bankrupt *c)* to seduce (a chaste woman) —*vi.* to go or come to ruin

RUHR BASIN

ru·in·a·tion (roo/ə nā/shən) *n.* **1.** a ruining or being ruined **2.** anything that ruins

ru·in·ous (roo/ə nəs) *adj.* **1.** falling or fallen into ruin **2.** bringing ruin; disastrous [*ruinous* floods] —**ru′in·ous·ly** *adv.* —**ru′in·ous·ness** *n.*

rule (rool) *n.* [< OFr. < L. *regula*, straightedge < *regere*, to lead straight: for IE. base see REGAL] **1.** *a)* an authoritative regulation for conduct, method, procedure, etc. [the *rules* of the game] *b)* an established practice that serves as a guide [*rules* of grammar] **2.** a set of regulations in a religious order **3.** a habit; custom [to make it a *rule* never to hurry] **4.** the usual or expected thing [famine is the *rule* following war] **5.** *a)* government; reign; control *b)* the period of a particular reign [during the *rule* of Elizabeth I] **6.** a ruler or straightedge **7.** *Law a)* a court regulation *b)* a decision, order, etc. made by a judge or court concerning a specific question or point *c)* a legal principle **8.** *Printing* a thin, metal strip as high as a piece of type, used to print lines —*vt.* **ruled, rul′ing 1.** to have an influence over; guide [to be *ruled* by the wishes of one's friends] **2.** to keep under control [try to *rule* your temper] **3.** to have authority over; govern [to *rule* a country] **4.** to settle by decree; determine [the court *ruled* that Jones was at fault] **5.** to mark (lines) on (paper, etc.) as with a ruler —*vi.* **1.** to govern [to *rule* as king] **2.** to be at a specified rate or level; prevail: said of prices, etc. **3.** to issue a formal decree about a question —see **SYN.** at GOVERN and LAW —**as a rule** usually —**rule out** to decide to leave out or ignore

rule of three *Math.* the method of finding the fourth term of a proportion when three terms are given: the product of the first and last is equal to the product of the second and third

rule of thumb **1.** a rule based on experience or practice rather than on scientific knowledge **2.** any practical, though not exact, method of estimating

rul·er (r$\overline{oo}$ʹlər) *n.* **1.** a person or thing that rules or governs **2.** a thin strip of wood, metal, etc. with a straight edge, used in drawing lines, measuring, etc. —**rulʹer·ship** *n.*

rul·ing (-liŋ) *adj.* that rules; governing, controlling, etc. —*n.* **1.** a governing or controlling **2.** a decision made by a court **3.** *a)* the making of ruled lines *b)* the lines so made

rum[1] *n.* [short for *rumbullion*, orig. a dial. term, tumult < ?] **1.** an alcoholic liquor distilled from fermented sugar cane, molasses, etc. ☆**2.** any strong alcoholic liquor

rum[2] (rum) *adj.* [< obs. *rum*, good] [Chiefly Brit. Colloq.] **1.** odd; strange **2.** bad, poor, etc. [a *rum* joke]

rum[3] (rum) *n.* ☆*same as* RUMMY[1]

Ru·ma·ni·a (r$\overline{oo}$ mānʹyə, -māʹnē ə) *same as* ROMANIA —**Ru·maʹni·an** *adj., n.*

rum·ba (rumʹbə, room′-; *Sp.* r$\overline{oo}$mʹbä) *n.* [AmSp., prob. of Afr. origin] **1.** a dance of Cuban Negro origin **2.** a ballroom dance like this, with rhythmic movements of the lower part of the body **3.** music for this dance —*vi.* to dance the rumba

rum·ble (rumʹb'l) *vi.* **-bled, -bling** [prob. < MDu. *rommelen*] **1.** to make a deep, heavy rolling sound, as thunder **2.** to move with such a sound [the truck *rumbled* across the bridge] —*vt.* **1.** to cause to make, or move with, such a sound **2.** to say with such a sound —*n.* **1.** a deep, heavy rolling sound **2.** a widespread expression of discontent ☆**3.** [Slang] a fight between gangs, esp. of teen-agers —**rumʹbler** *n.* —**rumʹbling·ly** *adv.* —**rumʹbly** *adj.*

☆**rumble seat** in some earlier automobiles, an open rear seat that could be folded shut when not in use

ru·men (r$\overline{oo}$ʹmin) *n., pl.* **-mi·na** (-mi nə) [ModL. < L., gullet] the first stomach of a ruminant: see illustration at RUMINANT

Rum·ford (rumʹfərd), Count *see* Benjamin THOMPSON

ru·mi·nant (r$\overline{oo}$ʹmə nənt) *adj.* [< L. prp. of *ruminare*, to ruminate < *rumen*, RUMEN] **1.** chewing the cud **2.** of the cud-chewing animals **3.** tending to think deeply; thoughtful —*n.* any of a large group of cud-chewing mammals that have four feet with hoofs and an even number of toes, as the cattle, sheep, goat, deer, camel, etc. —**ruʹmi·nant·ly** *adv.*

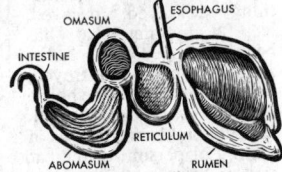

ESOPHAGUS
OMASUM
INTESTINE
RETICULUM
ABOMASUM
RUMEN

STOMACH OF A RUMINANT

ru·mi·nate (-nātʹ) *vt., vi.* **-natʹed, -natʹing** [< L. pp. of *ruminare*: see prec.] **1.** to chew (the cud), as a cow does **2.** to turn (something) over in the mind; meditate (on) —see **SYN.** at PONDER —**ruʹmi·naʹtion** *n.* —**ruʹmi·naʹtive** *adj.* —**ruʹmi·naʹtive·ly** *adv.*

rum·mage (rumʹij) *n.* [< MFr. < *arrumer*, to stow cargo < *run*, ship's hold < Frank.] **1.** odds and ends **2.** a rummaging search —*vt.* **-maged, -mag·ing** **1.** to search through (a place, etc.) thoroughly by moving the contents about **2.** to get or turn up by searching thoroughly (with *up* or *out*) —*vi.* to make a thorough search, as through the contents of a container —**rumʹmag·er** *n.*

rummage sale a sale of various kinds of articles, used or new, to raise money for a charity, an organization, etc.

rum·my[1] (rumʹē) *adj.* **-mi·er, -mi·est** [RUM[2] + -Y[2]] [Chiefly Brit. Colloq.] odd; strange; queer —☆*n.* any of certain card games in which the object is to match cards into sets of the same denomination or sequences of the same suit

rum·my[2] (rumʹē) *n., pl.* **-mies** [RUM[1] + -Y[2]] ☆[Slang] a drunkard —*adj.* **-mi·er, -mi·est** of or like rum

ru·mor (r$\overline{oo}$ʹmər) *n.* [< OFr. < L., noise] **1.** general talk not based on definite knowledge; hearsay [according to *rumor*, they're going to move] **2.** a report, story, etc. that may or may not be true and is passed on from person to person —*vt.* to tell or spread by rumor Also, Brit. sp., **ruʹmour**

ru·mor·mon·ger (-muŋʹgər, -mäŋʹ-) *n.* a person who spreads rumors

rump (rump) *n.* [ON. *rumpr*] **1.** the hind part of an animal, where the legs and back join **2.** a cut of beef from this part,

behind the loin and above the round: see illustration at BEEF **3.** the buttocks **4.** the last and unimportant part; remnant

Rum·pel·stilts·kin (rumʹp'l stiltʹskin) *German Folklore* a dwarf who agrees to spin flax into gold to save the life of a king's bride: in return she agrees to give him her first child, unless she can guess his name, but she does

rum·ple (rumʹp'l) *n.* [< MDu. < *rompe*, a wrinkle: for IE. base see CIRCUS] an uneven fold or crease; wrinkle —*vt., vi.* **-pled, -pling** **1.** to make rumples (in); crumple [*rumpled* clothing] **2.** to make or become tousled [*rumpled* hair] —**rumʹply** *adj.*

rum·pus (rumʹpəs) *n.* [< ?] [Colloq.] noisy disturbance

☆**rum·run·ner** (rumʹrunʹər) *n.* a person, ship, etc. engaged in smuggling alcoholic liquor —**rumʹrunʹning** *n.*

run (run) *vi.* **ran** or dial. **run, run, runʹning** [ON. *rinna* & OE. *rinnan* < IE. base *er-*, to set in motion] **1.** to go by moving the legs faster than in walking **2.** *a)* to move swiftly [we *ran* to her aid] *b)* to go (*to*) for help [*run* to the doctor] **3.** to associate (*with*) [he *runs* with a bad crowd] **4.** to go, move, etc. easily and freely, without hindrance [a breeze *ran* through the trees] **5.** to flee [*run* for your life!] **6.** to make a quick trip (*up to, down to,* etc.) for a brief stay **7.** *a)* to take part in a contest or race ☆*b)* to be a candidate in an election [she *ran* for senator] **8.** to swim in migration: said of fish **9.** to go, as on a schedule [a bus *runs* between Chicago and Detroit] **10.** to pass lightly and rapidly [his eyes *ran* over the page] **11.** to be told repeatedly [a rumor *ran* through the town] **12.** to climb or creep, as a vine **13.** to ravel [her stocking *ran*] **14.** to operate with parts that revolve or slide [the machine is *running*] **15.** to flow [rivers *run* to the sea] **16.** to melt and flow, as wax **17.** *a)* to spread over cloth, etc. when moistened, as colors *b)* to be likely to have this spreading, as fabric **18.** to be wet with a flow [her eyes *ran* with tears] **19.** *a)* to let out pus, mucus, etc. *b)* to leak, as a faucet **20.** *a)* to appear in print, as in a newspaper *b)* to appear continuously [the play *ran* for a year] **21.** *a)* to continue in effect [the law *runs* for ten years] *b)* to continue to occur [talent *runs* in the family] **22.** to show a preference for (with *to*) [his taste *runs* to sweets] **23.** *a)* to extend in a continuous line [a fence *runs* through the woods] *b)* to extend in scope (*from* one thing *to* another) **24.** to pass into a specified condition, etc. [to *run* into trouble] **25.** to be written, expressed, etc. in a specified way [the proverb *runs* like this] **26.** to be or continue at a specified size, price, etc. [apples *running* four to the pound] —*vt.* **1.** to follow (a specified course) **2.** to travel over [horses *ran* the range] **3.** to perform as by running [to *run* a race] **4.** to take on (a risk) ☆**5.** *a)* to get past [to *run* a blockade] *b)* to go through without making a required stop [to *run* a red light] **6.** to hunt (game, etc.) **7.** to compete with as in a race **8.** *a)* to enter (a horse, etc.) in a race ☆*b)* to put up as a candidate for election [the independents *ran* Smith] **9.** *a)* to make run, move, etc. *b)* to cause to go between points, as on a schedule *c)* to cause (an engine, etc.) to idle for a while **10.** to bring or force into a specified condition by running [to *run* oneself into debt] **11.** *a)* to transport, as in a vehicle *b)* to smuggle **12.** to drive or force (an object) into, against, etc. (something) [he *ran* his car into a tree] **13.** to make pass, flow, etc., esp. rapidly, in a specified way, place, etc. [to *run* water into a glass] **14.** ☆*a)* to manage [to *run* a household] *b)* to perform the steps of (a test, etc.) *c)* to cause to undergo a test, etc. **15.** to cost (an amount) [boots that *run* $20] **16.** to mark or draw (lines, as on a map) **17.** to trace [to *run* a story back to its source] **18.** to undergo (a fever, etc.) **19.** to melt or smelt (ore) **20.** to cast or mold; found ☆**21.** to publish (a story, etc.) as in a newspaper **22.** *Billiards,* etc. to complete successfully (a series of shots, etc.) **23.** *Bridge* to lead (a suit) taking a series of tricks —*n.* **1.** *a)* an act or period of running [a *run* around the block] *b)* a running pace [going at a *run*] **2.** the distance covered or time spent in running **3.** a trip; journey; esp., *a)* a regular trip, as of a plane *b)* a route for making deliveries **4.** *a)* movement onward; progression [the *run* of events] *b)* a continuous course or period [a *run* of good luck] **5.** a continuous course of performances, etc., as of a play **6.** a continued series of demands, as for specified goods **7.** a continuous series or extent **8.** *a)* flow or rush of water, etc., as of the tide **9.** a small, swift stream **10.** *a)* a period during which some fluid flows readily *b)* the amount of flow **11.** *a)* a period of operation of a machine *b)* the output during this period **12.** *a)* a kind or class [a better *run* of apples] *b)* the usual or average kind [it's no better than the *run*] **13.** *a)* an inclined pathway or course [a ski *run*] *b)* an enclosed area for domestic animals [a dog *run*] **14.** freedom to move about at will [to have the *run* of the house] **15.** *a)* a large number of fish migrating together *b)* such migration ☆**16.** a ravel, as in a stocking ☆**17.** *Baseball* a scoring point, made by touching all the bases in order **18.** *Billiards*, etc. a series of successful shots, etc. **19.** *Mil.* the approach to the target made by an airplane in bombing, etc. **20.** *Music* a rapid series of tones —*adj.* **1.** melted **2.** poured while in a melted state [*run metal]* —**a run for one's money 1.** powerful competition **2.** satisfaction for the money or effort spent —**in the long run** in the final outcome; ultimately —**on the run 1.** running **2.** running away —☆**run across** to come upon by chance —**run along** to leave or depart —**run away 1.** to flee **2.** to desert one's home or family **3.** to escape and run loose, as a horse —**run away with 1.** to steal **2.** to carry out of control [*his anger ran away with* him] **3.** *a)* to outdo all others in (a contest, etc.) *b)* to get (a prize, etc.) in this way —**run down 1.** to stop operating **2.** to run or drive against so as to knock down **3.** to pursue and capture or kill **4.** to search out the source of **5.** to speak of with disapproval **6.** to lessen or lower in worth, quality, etc. **7.** to read through rapidly —**run for it** to run to escape something —**run in 1.** to include (something additional) **2.** [Colloq.] to make a quick visit ☆**3.** [Slang] to arrest —**run into 1.** to come upon by chance **2.** to bump or crash into **3.** to add up to (a large sum of money): also **run to** —**run off** ☆**1.** to print, make copies of, etc. **2.** to cause to be run, played, etc. **3.** to drive (trespassers) away **4.** to flow off; drain **5.** *same as* RUN AWAY —**run on 1.** to continue or be continued **2.** to add (something) at the end **3.** to talk continuously —**run out 1.** to come to an end; expire **2.** to drive out —**run out of** to use up —**run out on** [Colloq.] to abandon or desert —**run over 1.** to ride or drive over **2.** to overflow **3.** to go beyond a limit **4.** to examine, rehearse, etc. rapidly —**run scared** [Slang] to behave as if expecting to fail —**run through 1.** to use up or spend quickly or recklessly **2.** to pierce **3.** to examine, rehearse, etc. rapidly —**run up 1.** to raise, rise, or make rapidly **2.** to let (bills, etc.) go without paying them **3.** to sew with a rapid series of stitches

run·a·bout (run'ə bout') *n.* **1.** a person who runs about from place to place **2.** a light, one-seated, open carriage or automobile ☆**3.** a light motorboat

run·a·round (-ə round') ☆*n.* [Colloq.] a series of excuses, delays, etc. used to avoid granting a request: usually in **get** (or **give**) **the runaround**

run·a·way (-ə wā') *n.* **1.** a person that runs away; fugitive **2.** a horse, etc. that runs away **3.** a running away —*adj.* **1.** running away or having run away [a *runaway* horse] **2.** of or done by runaways [a *runaway* marriage] **3.** easily won, as a race **4.** *a)* rising rapidly, as prices *b)* having an uncontrolled rise of prices [*runaway* inflation]

☆**run·back** (-bak') *n.* *Football* the act of running back with the ball, as after receiving the kickoff or intercepting a forward pass

run·ci·nate (run'si nit, -nāt') *adj.* [< L. pp. of *runcinare*, to plane off < *runcina*, a plane (formerly understood as "saw")] *Bot.* irregularly saw-toothed, with the teeth or lobes curved backward, as some leaves

run-down (-doun') *adj.* **1.** not wound and therefore not running, as a clock **2.** in poor physical condition, as from overwork **3.** in need of repair; falling apart [a *run-down* house]

run·down (-doun') *n.* a concise summary; quick report

rune (rōōn) *n.* [OE. *run*] **1.** any of the characters of an ancient Germanic alphabet **2.** something inscribed in such characters **3.** *a)* a Finnish or Old Norse poem or canto *b)* [Poet.] any poem, song, etc. that is mystical or difficult to understand

rung¹ (ruŋ) *n.* [OE. *hrung*, a staff] **1.** any strong stick, bar, or rod used as a crossbar, support, etc.; specif., *a)* any of the steps of a ladder *b)* a crosspiece between the legs of a chair, or across the back, etc. **2.** a degree, as of social status, success, etc.

rung² (ruŋ) *pp. & chiefly dial. pt. of* RING¹

ru·nic (rōō'nik) *adj.* **1.** consisting of or set down in runes **2.** like runes in decorative effect **3.** difficult to understand; mystical

run-in (run'in') *adj.* *Printing* made continuous without a break or paragraph —*n.* **1.** *Printing* run-in matter ☆**2.** [Colloq.] a quarrel, fight, etc.

run·nel (run''l) *n.* [OE. *rynel* < *rinnan*, to run] a small stream; little brook: also **run'let** (-lit)

run·ner (run'ər) *n.* **1.** one that runs; specif., *a)* a racer ☆*b)* *same as* BASE RUNNER **2.** a messenger, as for a bank or broker **3.** a smuggler **4.** a person who operates a machine, etc. **5.** a long, narrow cloth or rug **6.** a long ravel, as in hose; run **7.** a long, trailing stem, as of a strawberry, that puts out roots along the ground, thus producing new plants **8.** something on or in which something else moves ☆**9.** either of the long, narrow pieces on which a sled or sleigh slides ☆**10.** the blade of a skate

RUNNER
(wild strawberry)

run·ner-up (-up') *n.*, *pl.* **-ners-up'** a person or team that finishes second in a race, contest, etc.

run·ning (run'iŋ) *n.* **1.** the act of one that runs; racing, managing, etc. **2.** that which runs, or flows —*adj.* **1.** moving or advancing rapidly **2.** flowing [*running* water] **3.** flowing; cursive: said of handwriting **4.** melting; becoming liquid **5.** letting out pus [a *running* sore] **6.** creeping or climbing: said of plants **7.** in operation, as machinery **8.** in a straight line [a *running* foot] **9.** without interruption; continuous [a *running* commentary] **10.** in progress; current [a *running* account] **11.** going on at the same time; simultaneous [a *running* translation] **12.** moving easily or smoothly **13.** slipping or sliding easily, as a knot **14.** moving when pulled, as a rope **15.** done in or by a run [a *running* jump] **16.** of the normal run (of a train, bus, etc.) [the *running* time is two hours] —*adv.* in succession [for ten days *running*] —**in** (or **out of**) **the running** having (or not having) a chance to win

☆**running board** esp. formerly, a footboard along the lower part of the side of some automobiles

running fire a rapid series of shots fired, remarks made, questions asked, etc.

☆**running gear** the wheels, axles, springs, and frame of a motor vehicle

running head (or **title**) a heading or title printed at the top of every page or every other page

running knot *same as* SLIPKNOT

running lights the lights that a ship or aircraft traveling at night is required to display

☆**running mate** a candidate for a lesser office, as for the vice-presidency, running together with his party's candidate for the greater office

run·ny (run'ē) *adj.* **-ni·er, -ni·est** **1.** that flows, esp. too freely **2.** that keeps on letting out mucus [a *runny* nose]

Run·ny·mede (run'ē mēd') meadow on the south bank of the Thames, southwest of London: see MAGNA CHARTA

run-off (run'ôf') *n.* ☆**1.** something that runs off, as rain that is more than the amount that soaks into the ground **2.** a final race, election, etc. run off to decide who wins, as in case of a tie

run-of-the-mill (run'əv thə mil') *adj.* [see RUN, *n.*, 12 *b]* not selected or special; ordinary

run-on (run'än') *adj.* *Printing* continuous without a break or new paragraph —*n.* run-on matter

runt (runt) *n.* [< ?] **1.** a stunted or undersized animal, plant, thing, or (usually in showing contempt) person **2.** the smallest animal of a litter —**runt'i·ness** *n.* —**runt'y** *adj.* **runt'i·er, runt'i·est**

run-through (run'thrōō') *n.* a full rehearsal, as of a play, without stopping

☆**run·way** (-wā') *n.* a channel, track, chute, etc. in, on, or along which something moves; specif., *a)* a strip of flat, usually paved ground for use by airplanes in taking off and landing *b)* a narrow extension of a stage out into the audience

ru·pee (rōō pē', rōō'pē) *n.* [< Hindi < Sans. *rūpya*, wrought silver] the monetary unit of India, Pakistan, Ceylon, etc.: see MONETARY UNITS, table

ru·pi·ah (rōō pē'ə) *n.* [< Hindi] *see* MONETARY UNITS, table (Indonesia)

rup·ture (rup'chər) *n.* [< MFr. < L. < pp. of *rumpere*, to break < IE. base *reu-*, to tear apart] **1.** a breaking apart or being broken apart [a *rupture* in a gas line] **2.** a breaking off of friendly or peaceful relations, as between nations **3.** a hernia

—vt., vi. -tured, -tur·ing **1.** to break apart or burst **2.** to have a rupture or cause to have a rupture

ru·ral (roor′əl) **adj.** [< MFr. < LL. *ruralis* < L. *ruris*, genitive of *rus*, the country: for IE. base see ROOM] **1.** of or like the country, country folk, etc.; rustic **2.** living in the country **3.** having to do with farming **—ru′ral·ly adv.**

SYN.—**rural** is the general word referring to life on the farm or in the country as distinguished from life in the city [*rural* schools]; **rustic** emphasizes the contrast between the supposed crudeness and lack of sophistication of country people and the polish and refinement of city people [*rustic* humor]; **pastoral** suggests an ideally simple sort of life as lived in the country, originally by shepherds; **bucolic**, in contrast, suggests a down-to-earth rustic simplicity or crudeness [her *bucolic* suitor] —**ANT.** urban

☆**rural delivery** delivery of mail by carriers on routes in rural areas: formerly **rural free delivery**

ru·ral·ism (-iz′m) **n.** **1.** rural quality **2.** rural life **3.** a rural idiom, feature, etc. Also **ru·ral·i·ty** (roo ral′ə tē), *pl.* **-ties** **—ru′ral·ist** (-ist) **n.**

ru·ral·ize (roor′ə līz′) **vt.** **-ized′, -iz′ing** to make rural **—ru′ral·i·za′tion n.**

ruse (rooz) **n.** [< MFr. < OFr. *reuser*, to deceive < L. *recusare*, to refuse] a trick or plan for fooling someone —see SYN. at TRICK

rush[1] (rush) **vi.** [< Anglo-Fr. < MFr. < OFr. *reuser:* see prec.] **1.** to move swiftly [he *rushed* from the room] **2.** to act in haste, without careful thought [she *rushed* into marriage] **3.** to pass, come, go, etc. swiftly or suddenly [a thought *rushing* into the mind] ☆**4.** *Football* to advance the ball by a running play **—vt.** **1.** to move, send, push, etc. swiftly or violently [we *rushed* him to the hospital] **2.** to do, make, move, etc. with unusual speed or haste [to *rush* an order, a person at work, etc.] **3.** *a)* to attack suddenly [the troops *rushed* the fort] *b)* to overcome or capture in this way ☆**4.** [Colloq.] *a)* to give much attention to, as in courting *b)* to entertain with parties, etc. before inviting to join a fraternity or sorority **—n.** **1.** a rushing [the *rush* of the wind] **2.** an eager movement of many people to get to a place [the *rush* to California for gold] **3.** intense activity; haste; hurry [the *rush* of modern life] **4.** a sudden attack ☆**5.** a scrimmage contest between groups of college students **6.** great pressure, as of much business requiring quick or hasty attention **7.** [*usually pl.*] *Motion Pictures* a first print of a scene or scenes, shown for the director, etc. to inspect **—adj.** requiring haste [*rush* orders] **—with a rush** suddenly and forcefully **—rush′er n.**

rush[2] (rush) **n.** [OE. *risc*] **1.** any of a group of grasslike plants usually growing in wet places and having, in some types, round stems and easily bent leaves used in making baskets, mats, etc. **2.** any of various similar plants, as bulrushes **—rush′y adj.** **rush′i·er, rush′i·est**

rush candle a candle made with the soft center of the stem of a rush as the wick: also **rush′light′ n., rush light**

☆**rush·ee** (rush ē′) **n.** a college student who is being rushed by a fraternity or sorority

☆**rush hour** a time of the day when business, traffic, etc. are especially heavy **—rush′-hour′ adj.**

Rush·more (rush′môr′), **Mount** [after C. E. *Rushmore*, N.Y. mining attorney] mountain in the Black Hills, western S.Dak., on which are carved huge heads of Washington, Jefferson, Lincoln, & Theodore Roosevelt

rusk (rusk) **n.** [Sp. *rosca*, twisted bread roll] **1.** sweet, raised bread or cake toasted in an oven until crisp, usually after being sliced **2.** a piece of this

Rus·kin (rus′kin), **John** 1819–1900; Eng. writer, art critic, & social reformer

Russ. **1.** Russia **2.** Russian

Rus·sell (rus′'l) [< surname *Russell*, orig. dim. of Fr. *roux*, red] **1.** a masculine name: dim. *Russ* **2. Bertrand (Arthur William)**, 3d Earl Russell, 1872–1970; Brit. philosopher, mathematician, & writer, born in Wales **3. Lord John**, 1st Earl Russell, 1792–1878; Eng. statesman; prime minister (1846–52; 1865–66): grandfather of *Bertrand*

rus·set (rus′it) **n.** [< OFr. < L. *russus*, reddish] **1.** yellowish brown or reddish brown **2.** a coarse, brownish cloth, formerly used for clothing by country folk **3.** a winter apple with a rough, spotted skin **—adj.** yellowish-brown or reddish-brown

Rus·sia (rush′ə) **1.** former empire (**Russian Empire**) in E Europe & N Asia, 1547–1917, ruled by the czars: cap. St. Petersburg **2.** popular name for the UNION OF SOVIET SOCIALIST REPUBLICS

Russia leather a fine, smooth leather, usually dyed dark red, orig. made in Russia: used in bookbinding, etc.

Rus·sian (rush′ən) **adj.** of Russia, its people, their language, etc. **—n.** **1.** *a)* a native or inhabitant of Russia, specif. of the R.S.F.S.R. *b)* popularly, any citizen of the U.S.S.R. **2.** a member of the chief Slavic people of Russia **3.** the East Slavic language of the Russians; esp., its principal dialect (**Great Russian**), the official language of the U.S.S.R.

☆**Russian dressing** mayonnaise mixed with chili sauce, chopped pickles, pimentos, etc.: used on salads, etc.

Rus·sian·ize (-īz′) **vt.** **-ized′, -iz′ing** to make Russian in character **—Rus′sian·i·za′tion n.**

Russian olive a small, strong tree with silvery leaves and sweet-smelling, yellow flowers

Russian Revolution the revolution of 1917 in Russia in which the Czar's government was overthrown

☆**Russian roulette** a deadly game of chance in which a person spins the cylinder of a revolver holding only one bullet, aims at his head, and pulls the trigger

Russian Soviet Federated Socialist Republic largest republic of the U.S.S.R., stretching from the Baltic Sea to the Pacific: 6,592,000 sq. mi.; pop. 130,100,000; cap. Moscow

☆**Russian thistle** a large weed with spiny branches: it matures into a tumbleweed

Russian wolfhound *same as* BORZOI

Rus·si·fy (rus′ə fī′) **vt.** **-fied′, -fy′ing** *same as* RUSSIANIZE

Rus·so- *a combining form meaning:* **1.** Russia or Russian **2.** Russian and [*Russo*-Japanese]

rust (rust) **n.** [OE.: for IE. base see RED[1]] **1.** the reddish-brown coating (mainly ferric oxide) formed on iron or steel by oxidation, as during exposure to air and moisture **2.** any similar coating on other metals **3.** any stain or formation resembling iron rust **4.** any habit, influence, etc. harmful to the mind, character, etc. **5.** inactivity; idleness **6.** a reddish brown **7.** *a)* any of various plant diseases caused by parasitic fungi that produce reddish spots on stems and leaves *b)* such a fungus: in full, **rust fungus** **—vi., vt.** **1.** to have or cause to have a rust fungus **2.** to become or cause to be coated with rust **3.** to spoil, as from lack of use [a mind that has *rusted*] **4.** to become or make rust-colored **—rust′-col′ored adj. —rust′less adj.**

rus·tic (rus′tik) **adj.** [< MFr. < L. *rusticus* < *rus:* see RURAL] **1.** of or living in the country, as distinguished from cities or towns; rural **2.** not refined or sophisticated; specif., *a)* simple, plain, or natural *b)* awkward, rough, or boorish [*rustic* manners] **3.** made of bark-covered branches or roots [*rustic* furniture] **—n.** a country person, esp. one regarded as simple, awkward, rough, etc. —see SYN. at RURAL **—rus′ti·cal·ly adv. —rus·tic′i·ty** (-tis′ə tē) **n.**

rus·ti·cate (rus′ti kāt′) **vi.** **-cat′ed, -cat′ing** **1.** to go to the country **2.** to live in the country **—vt.** **1.** to send to live in the country **2.** [Brit.] to suspend (a student) for a time from a university **—rus′ti·ca′tion n. —rus′ti·ca′tor n.**

rus·tle[1] (rus′'l) **vi., vt.** **-tled, -tling** [ult. < WGmc. echoic base] to make or cause to make soft sounds, as of leaves moved by a breeze or of papers being shuffled **—n.** a series of such sounds **—rus′tling·ly adv.**

rus·tle[2] (rus′'l) **vi., vt.** **-tled, -tling** [< ? RUSH[1] + HUSTLE] [Colloq.] **1.** to work with, or move or get by, forceful action ☆**2.** to steal (cattle, etc.) **—**☆**rustle up** [Colloq.] to collect or get together, as by searching around [to *rustle* up a meal from leftovers] **—rus′tler n.**

rust·proof (rust′proof′) **adj.** resistant to rust **—vt.** to make rustproof

rust·y (rus′tē) **adj.** **rust′i·er, rust′i·est** **1.** coated with rust, as a metal, or affected by rust, as a plant **2.** of or caused by rust **3.** not working freely because of or as if because of rust [a *rusty* lock] **4.** *a)* made worse, weaker, etc. by disuse, neglect, etc. [to find one's golf swing *rusty*] *b)* having lost one's skill through lack of practice [he's a little *rusty* in chess] **5.** rust-colored **6.** faded, old-looking, or shabby [a *rusty* suit] **—rust′i·ly adv. —rust′i·ness n.**

rut[1] (rut) **n.** [< ? MFr. *route*, ROUTE] **1.** a track or furrow, esp. one made by wheeled vehicles **2.** a fixed, routine procedure, way of acting, thinking, etc. [to get into a *rut*] **—vt.** **rut′ted, rut′ting** to make a rut or ruts in

rut[2] (rut) **n.** [< OFr. < L. < *rugire*, to roar] **1.** the sexual excitement of certain mammals, esp. males, occurring at regular intervals **2.** the period of this **—vi. rut′ted, rut′ting** to be in rut

ru·ta·ba·ga (root′ə bā′gə, root′ə bā′gə) **n.** [Sw. dial. *rotabagge*] a turnip with a large, yellow root

Ruth (rooth) [LL. < Heb. *rûth*, prob. contr. < *re'uth*, companion] **1.** a feminine name **2.** *Bible* *a)* a Moabite widow deeply devoted to her mother-in-law, Naomi *b)* the book of the

Bible that tells her story **3. George Herman,** (nicknamed "*Babe*") 1895–1948; U.S. baseball player

ruth (rōōth) *n.* [ult. < OE. *hreowan,* to rue] [Now Rare] **1.** pity; compassion **2.** sorrow; grief; remorse

Ru·the·ni·a (rōō thē′nē ə) region in W Ukrainian S.S.R. —**Ru·the′ni·an** *adj., n.*

ru·the·ni·um (rōō thē′nē əm) *n.* [ModL. < ML. *Ruthenia,* Russia, where first found] a rare, very hard metallic chemical element that is silvery-gray in color, used in alloys and as a catalyst: symbol, Ru; at. wt., 101.07; at. no., 44

Ruth·er·ford (ruth′ər fərd), **Ernest,** 1st Baron Rutherford of Nelson, 1871–1937; Brit. physicist, born in New Zealand

ruth·ful (rōōth′fəl) *adj.* [Now Rare] full of ruth, or pity, sorrow, etc. —**ruth′ful·ly** *adv.* —**ruth′ful·ness** *n.*

ruth·less (-lis) *adj.* without ruth; showing no pity or kindness, as in seeking some goal —see SYN. at CRUEL —**ruth′less·ly** *adv.* —**ruth′less·ness** *n.*

Rut·ledge (rut′lij), **Anne** 1813?–35; young woman to whom Abraham Lincoln is believed to have been engaged

rut·ty (rut′ē) *adj.* **-ti·er, -ti·est** having or full of ruts [*a rutty road*] —**rut′ti·ness** *n.*

Ru·wen·zo·ri (rōō′wen zō′rē) group of mountains in EC Africa, on the border of Uganda & Zaire

☆**RV** (är′vē′) *n., pl.* **RVs** [*R(ecreational) V(ehicle)*] any of various vehicles, as campers and trailers, outfitted as a place to live, as when camping out

Rwan·da (ʉr wän′dä, rʊʊ wän′də) country in EC Africa, east of Zaire: 10,169 sq. mi.; pop. 3,724,000; cap. Kigali —**Rwan′dan** *adj., n.*

Rwy., Ry. Railway

Rx [< *Rx,* symbol for L. *recipe:* see RECIPE] *symbol for* PRESCRIPTION (sense 3) —*n.* a prescription for any disorder

-ry (rē) *shortened form of* -ERY [*dentistry, jewelry*]

Ry·der (rī′dər), **Albert Pink·ham** (piŋk′əm) 1847–1917; U.S. painter

rye (rī) *n.* see PLURAL, II, D, 3 [OE. *ryge*] **1.** a hardy cereal grass widely grown for its grain and straw **2.** the grain or seeds of this plant, used for making flour and whiskey, and as feed for livestock ☆**3.** *a*) whiskey distilled from this grain *b*) in the eastern U.S., a blended whiskey

rye bread bread made altogether or partly of rye flour, often with caraway seeds added

rye·grass (rī′gras′) *n.* any of various grasses that are annuals or that live for only a few years

Ryu·kyu Islands (ryōō′kyōō′) chain of Japanese islands in the W Pacific, between Kyushu & Taiwan

---

fat, āpe, cär; ten, ēven; is, bīte; gō, hôrn, tōōl, look; oil, out; up, fʉr; get; joy; yet; chin; she; thin, then; zh, leisure; ŋ, ring; ə for *a* in *ago, e* in *agent, i* in *sanity, o* in *comply, u* in *focus;* ' as in *able* (ā′b'l); Fr. bàl; ë, Fr. coeur; ö, Fr. feu; Fr. mon; ô, Fr. coq; ü, Fr. duc; r, Fr. cri; H, G. ich; kh, G. doch; ‡foreign; ☆ Americanism; < derived from. See inside front cover.

S

S, s (es) *n.*, *pl.* **S's, s's** **1.** the nineteenth letter of the English alphabet **2.** a sound of *S* or *s*

S (es) *n.* **1.** something shaped like an *S* **2.** *Chem.* sulfur —*adj.* shaped like *S*

-s [alt. form of -ES] **1.** the plural ending of most nouns [*hips, shoes*] **2.** the ending of the third person singular, in the present tense, of verbs [*gives, runs*] **3.** a suffix used to form some adverbs [*betimes, days*]

-'s¹ [OE. *-es*] the ending of the possessive singular of nouns (and some pronouns) and of the possessive plural of nouns not ending in *s* [*boy's, one's, women's*]

-'s² *the unstressed and contracted form of:* **1.** is [*he's here*] **2.** has [*she's eaten*] **3.** does [*what's it matter?*] **4.** us [*let's go*]

S, S., s, s. **1.** south **2.** southern

S. **1.** Saturday **2.** September **3.** Sunday

S., s. **1.** *pl.* **SS., ss.** saint **2.** school

s. **1.** second(s) **2.** shilling(s) **3.** singular

SA Seaman Apprentice

S.A. **1.** Salvation Army **2.** South America

Saar (sär, zär) **1.** river flowing from NE France north into the Moselle River, SW West Germany **2.** rich coal-mining region in the valley of this river: also called **Saar Basin**

Saar·land (sär′land, zär′-; *G.* zär′länt′) state of SW West Germany, in the Saar River Basin

Sa·ba (sä′bə) ancient kingdom in S Arabia in the region of modern Yemen: Biblical name, *Sheba*

Sab·ba·tar·i·an (sab′ə ter′ē ən) *adj.* of the Sabbath as a day of rest and worship —*n.* **1.** a person, esp. a Christian, who regards Saturday as the Sabbath **2.** a Christian who favors strict observance of Sunday as the Sabbath —**Sab′ba·tar′i·an·ism** *n.*

Sab·bath (sab′əth) *n.* [< OFr. & OE. *sabat*, both < L. < Gr. < Heb. < *shābath*, to rest] **1.** the seventh day of the week (Saturday), regarded as a day of rest and worship by Jews and some Christian sects **2.** Sunday as the usual Christian day of rest and worship —*adj.* of the Sabbath

Sab·bat·i·cal (sə bat′i k'l) *adj.* [< Fr. < LL. < Gr. *sabbatikos*: see SABBATH] **1.** of or suited to the Sabbath ☆**2.** [s-] describing a year or other period given with pay to some college teachers as a time for study, rest, or travel: orig. given every seven years —*n.* [s-] a sabbatical year or period Also **Sab·bat′ic**

sa·ber (sā′bər) *n.* [< Fr. < G. *sabel* < MHG. < Pol. & Hung.] **1.** a heavy sword with a slightly curved blade **2.** a fencing weapon, heavier than a foil, used for slashing as well as thrusting movements —*vt.* to cut, wound, or kill with a saber

sa·ber-toothed tiger (-tōōtht′) an animal no longer living that was very much like the tiger, but with a larger body, shorter legs and tail, and long, curved upper canine teeth

Sa·bin (sā′bin), **Albert B(ruce)** 1906– ; U.S. bacteriologist: developed an oral vaccine to prevent poliomyelitis

Sa·bine (sā′bīn) *n.* a member of an ancient tribe living in central Italy, conquered by the Romans, 3d century B.C.

sa·ble (sā′b'l) *n.*, *pl.* **-bles, -ble**: see PLURAL, II, D, 1 [OFr. < ML. *sabelum*, ult. < Russian *sobol'*] **1.** *same as* MARTEN; esp., *a)* the **European marten**, with light-colored underfur *b)* the

SABER

American marten, with a darker pelt **2.** *a)* the costly fur of the sable *b)* [*pl.*] a coat, etc. of this **3.** *Heraldry* the color black —*adj.* **1.** made of or with the fur of the sable **2.** black or dark brown; dark

sa·bot (sab′ō, sa bō′) *n.* [Fr., ult. < Ar. *sabbât*, sandal] **1.** a shoe shaped from a single piece of wood **2.** a heavy leather shoe with a wooden sole

sab·o·tage (sab′ə täzh′) *n.* [Fr. < *saboter*, to damage < *sabot*: see SABOT & -AGE: from damage done to machinery by wooden shoes] **1.** the destruction of machines, work materials, etc., as by workers during labor disputes **2.** the destruction of railroads, bridges, etc. as by enemy agents or by civilians resisting an invader **3.** any deliberate harm or damage done to any cause, effort, etc. —*vt.* **-taged′, -tag′ing** to injure or destroy by sabotage —*vi.* to do acts of sabotage

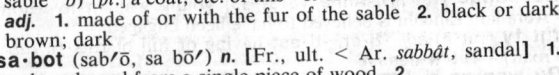

SABOT

sab·o·teur (sab′ə tʉr′) *n.* [Fr.] a person who sabotages

sa·bra (sä′brə) *n.* [ModHeb. *sābrāh*, lit., prickly fruit of a native cactus] a native-born Israeli

sa·bre (sā′bər) *n.*, *vt.* **-bred, -bring** *same as* SABER

sac (sak) *n.* [Fr. < L. *saccus*: see SACK¹] a pouchlike part in a plant or animal, esp. one filled with fluid —**sac′like′** *adj.*

SAC, S.A.C. Strategic Air Command

sac·cha·ride (sak′ə rīd′) *n.* [see SACCHARIN] any of the carbohydrates; esp., any of the sugars, as glucose

sac·cha·rin (sak′ə rin) *n.* [< L. *saccharum*, sugar < Gr. *sakcharon*, ult. < Sans.] ☆a white, crystalline compound, $C_7H_5O_3NS$, made from coal tar: it is about 500 times sweeter than cane sugar and is used as a substitute for sugar in diabetic diets.

sac·cha·rine (-rin, -rīn′) *adj.* [see SACCHARIN] **1.** of, like, or producing sugar ☆**2.** too sweet or syrupy [*a saccharine voice*] —☆*n. same as* SACCHARIN —**sac′cha·rine·ly** *adv.* —**sac′cha·rin′i·ty** (-rin′ə tē) *n.*

Sac·co (sak′ō; *It.* säk′kô), **Ni·co·la** (nē kô′lä) 1891–1927; It. anarchist in the U.S.: with B. VANZETTI, charged with murder in 1920; their conviction & execution, regarded as the result of prejudice, aroused international protest

sac·cule (sak′yool) *n.* [< L. *sacculus*, dim. of *saccus*, a SACK¹] a small sac; esp., the smaller of the two divisions of the inner ear: also **sac′cu·lus** (-yoo ləs), *pl.* **-li′** (-lī′)

sac·er·do·tal (sas′ər dōt′'l, sak′-) *adj.* [< MFr. < L. < *sacerdos*, priest] of priests or the office of priest; priestly —**sac′er·do′tal·ly** *adv.*

☆**sa·chem** (sā′chəm) *n.* [< Algonquian *sâchimau*] among some N. American Indian tribes, the chief

sa·chet (sa shā′; *chiefly Brit.* sash′ā) *n.* [Fr. < OFr., dim. of *sac*: see SAC] **1.** a small bag, pad, etc. filled with perfumed powder or dried herbs and put in dresser drawers, etc. to make clothing smell sweet **2.** such powder: also **sachet powder**

sack¹ (sak) *n.* [OE. *sacc* < L. *saccus* < Gr. < Heb. *śaq*] **1.** *a)* a bag, esp. a large bag of coarse cloth, for holding grain, foodstuffs, etc. *b)* the contents of a sack or the amount it will hold **2.** a loose-fitting jacket or dress **3.** [Slang] dismissal from a job (with *the*) ☆**4.** [Slang] a bed, bunk, etc. ☆**5.** *Baseball* a base —*vt.* **1.** to put into sacks **2.** [Slang] to dismiss from a job; fire —☆**hit the sack** [Slang] to go to bed

sack² (sak) *n.* [< MFr. < It. *sacco*, plunder, lit., bag < L. *saccus*: see prec.] the plundering or looting of a captured city, etc. —*vt.* to plunder or loot (a city, etc.)

sack³ (sak) *n.* [< Fr. (*vin*) *sec*, dry (wine) < L. *siccus*, dry] any of various dry white wines from Spain or the Canary Islands

sack·but (sak′but′) *n.* [Fr. *saquebute* < OFr. *saquer*, to pull + *bouter*, to push] a medieval wind instrument that came before the trombone: the word is also incorrectly used in the King James Version of the Bible to translate an Aramaic word for a kind of lyre

sack·cloth (sak′klôth′, -kläth′) *n.* 1. *same as* SACKING 2. a rough cloth worn as a symbol of mourning or penitence —**in sackcloth and ashes** in a state of great mourning or penitence

☆ **sack coat** a man's loose-fitting, straight-backed coat, usually part of a business suit

sack·ful (sak′fool′) *n., pl.* **-fuls′** 1. the amount a sack holds 2. a large quantity

sack·ing (-iŋ) *n.* a cheap, coarse cloth of flax, hemp, jute, etc., used esp. for sacks

sacque (sak) *n.* [pseudo-Fr.] 1. a loose-fitting jacket or dress; sack ☆2. a baby's jacket

sa·cral (sā′krəl) *adj.* [< ModL.: see SACRUM & -AL] of, or in the region of, the sacrum

sac·ra·ment (sak′rə mənt) *n.* [< OFr. < LL. *sacramentum*, ult. < L. *sacer*, sacred] 1. any of certain very sacred ceremonies that Christians believe were ordained by Jesus, as baptism, Holy Communion, etc. 2. [*sometimes* S-] the Eucharist, or Holy Communion; also, the consecrated bread and wine, or sometimes the bread alone 3. something thought of as sacred

sac·ra·men·tal (sak′rə men′t'l) *adj.* of, like, or used in a sacrament —*n.* R.C.Ch. something like a sacrament but established by the Church, as holy water —**sac′ra·men′tal·ly** *adv.*

Sac·ra·men·to (sak′rə men′tō) [Sp., sacrament] 1. river in C Calif., flowing south into San Francisco Bay 2. capital of Calif., on this river: pop. 254,000 (met. area 801,000)

sa·cred (sā′krid) *adj.* [< OFr. < L. < *sacer*, holy] 1. consecrated to a god or deity; holy [a *sacred* temple] 2. having to do with religion or religious rites [a *sacred* song] 3. given the respect that holy things receive; venerated [a *sacred* martyr] 4. dedicated to a person, place, purpose, etc. [*sacred* to his memory] 5. that must not be broken, ignored, etc.; inviolate [a *sacred* promise] —see SYN. at HOLY —**sa′cred·ly** *adv.* —**sa′cred·ness** *n.*

Sacred College *same as* COLLEGE OF CARDINALS

☆ **sacred cow** any person or thing thought of as above criticism or attack

sac·ri·fice (sak′rə fīs′) *n.* [< OFr. < L. *sacrificium* < *sacer*, sacred + *facere*, to make] 1. *a)* an offering of the life of a person or animal, or of an object, to God or a god *b)* the thing offered 2. *a)* a giving up, destroying, etc. of one thing for the sake of another [the *sacrifice* of principles to gain power] *b)* the thing given up, etc. 3. *a)* a selling or giving up of a thing at less than its value *b)* the loss resulting [he traded in his car at a *sacrifice*] ☆4. Baseball *same as* SACRIFICE BUNT —*vt.* **-ficed′, -fic′-ing** 1. to offer as a sacrifice to God or a god 2. to give up, destroy, etc. (something valued) for the sake of another thing 3. to sell at a loss ☆4. Baseball to advance (a base runner) by a sacrifice —*vi.* to make a sacrifice

☆ **sacrifice bunt** *Baseball* a bunt by the batter hit so that while he is being put out a base runner advances: also **sacrifice hit**

☆ **sacrifice fly** *Baseball* a play in which the batter flies out and a runner scores from third base after the catch

sac·ri·fi·cial (sak′rə fish′əl) *adj.* of, like, or used in a sacrifice —**sac′ri·fi′cial·ly** *adv.*

sac·ri·lege (sak′rə lij) *n.* [< MFr. < L. < *sacrilegus*, temple robber < *sacer*, sacred + *legere*, to take away] 1. misuse or violation of what is thought to be sacred, holy, or consecrated to God 2. the disrespectful treatment of anything thought of as sacred

sac·ri·le·gious (sak′rə lij′əs, -lē′jəs) *adj.* 1. that is or involves sacrilege 2. guilty of sacrilege —**sac′ri·le′gious·ly** *adv.* —**sac′ri·le′gious·ness** *n.*

sac·ris·tan (sak′ris tən) *n.* a person in charge of a sacristy

sac·ris·ty (-tē) *n., pl.* **-ties** [< Fr. < ML. < L. < *sacrista*, sacristan] a room in a church where the sacred vessels, robes, etc. are kept

sa·cro·il·i·ac (sā′krō il′ē ak′, sak′rō-) *adj.* [< SACRUM + ILIAC] of the sacrum and the ilium; esp., designating the joint between them —*n.* the sacroiliac joint

sac·ro·sanct (sak′rō saŋkt′) *adj.* [< L. < *sacer*, sacred + *sanc-tus*, holy] very sacred or holy [a *sacrosanct* shrine] —**sac′ro·sanc′ti·ty** *n.*

sa·crum (sā′krəm, sak′rəm) *n., pl.* **-cra** (-krə, -rə) or **-crums** [ModL. < LL. (*os*) *sacrum*, sacred (bone): ? from former use in sacrifices] a thick, triangular bone at the lower end of the spinal column, where it joins both hipbones to form the rear part of the pelvis

sad (sad) *adj.* **sad′der, sad′dest** [OE. *sæd*, sated < IE. base *sa-*, satisfied] 1. having or expressing low spirits or sorrow; unhappy; sorrowful 2. causing or characterized by sorrow, depression, etc. [*sad* music] 3. dark or dull in color; drab 4. [Colloq.] very bad; deplorable 5. [Dial.] heavy or soggy [a *sad* cake] —**sad′ly** *adv.* —**sad′ness** *n.*

SYN.—**sad** is the simple, general term, implying anything from a mild unhappiness that is over quickly to a feeling of great, deep grief; **sorrowful** implies a sadness caused by some specific loss, disappointment, etc. [her death left him *sorrowful*]; **melancholy** suggests a more or less continuing mournfulness or gloominess, or, often, merely a deep thoughtfulness [a *melancholy* view of life and its misfortunes]; **dejected** implies discouragement or a sinking of spirits, as because of frustration; **depressed** suggests a mood of worry and hopelessness, as because of feeling tired or useless [the unhappy ending left him feeling *depressed*]; **doleful** implies a mournful, often exaggerated, sadness [the *doleful* look on a lost child's face] —**ANT. happy, cheerful**

sad·den (sad′'n) *vt., vi.* to make or become sad

sad·dle (sad′'l) *n.* [OE. *sadol*: for IE. base see SIT] 1. a seat, usually of padded leather, for a rider on a horse, bicycle, etc. 2. a padded part of a harness worn over a horse's back 3. the part of an animal's back where a saddle is put 4. anything like a saddle in form, position, etc. 5. a ridge between two peaks 6. a cut of lamb, etc. including part of the backbone and the two loins —*vt.* **-dled, -dling** 1. to put a saddle upon 2. to weigh down (a person) with (a debt, responsibility, duty, etc.) —*vi.* to put a saddle on a horse and mount it (often with *up*) —**in the sad-dle** 1. seated on a saddle 2. having control

ENGLISH SADDLE

sad·dle·bag (-bag′) *n.* 1. a large bag, usually one of a pair, carried on either side of the back of a horse, etc., just behind the saddle ☆2. a similar bag carried over the back wheel of a motorcycle, etc.

sad·dle·bow (-bō′) *n.* the arched front part of a saddle, the top of which is the pommel

sad·dle·cloth (-klôth′, -kläth′) *n.* a thick cloth placed under a saddle on an animal's back

saddle horse a horse trained to be ridden

sad·dler (sad′lər) *n.* a person whose work is making, repairing, or selling saddles, harnesses, etc.

saddle roof a roof with a ridge running between two gables

sad·dler·y (sad′lə rē) *n., pl.* **-dler·ies** 1. the work of a saddler 2. articles made by a saddler 3. a shop where such articles are sold

☆ **saddle shoes** white oxford shoes with a band of different-colored leather across the instep

☆ **saddle soap** a mild soap with neat's-foot oil in it, for cleaning and softening leather

Sad·du·cee (saj′oo sē′, sad′yoo-) *n.* a member of an ancient Jewish party accepting only the written law and rejecting the oral, or traditional, law —**Sad′du·ce′an** *adj.*

SADDLE SHOES

Sade (säd), marquis de (full name, comte Donatien Alphonse François de Sade) 1740–1814; Fr. soldier & novelist

sa·dhu (sä′doo) *n.* [Sans. < *sādhu*, straight] a Hindu holy man

sad·i·ron (sad′ī′ərn) *n.* [SAD (sense 5) + IRON] a heavy flat-iron, pointed at both ends

sad·ism (sad′iz'm, sā′diz'm) *n.* [Fr., after marquis de SADE] the getting of pleasure, specif. sexual pleasure, from hurting or mistreating another or others —**sad′ist** *n.* —**sa·dis·tic** (sə-dis′tik, sā-) *adj.* —**sa·dis′ti·cal·ly** *adv.*

sad·o·mas·o·chism (sā'dō mas'ə kiz'm, sad'ō-; -maz'-) *n.* sadism and masochism existing together in the same individual —**sad'o·mas'o·chist** *n.* —**sad'o·mas'o·chis'tic** *adj.*

☆**sad sack** [Slang] a person who means well but is always making mistakes and getting into trouble

sa·fa·ri (sə fär'ē) *n., pl.* -ris [Swahili < Ar. < *safara,* to travel] a journey or hunting expedition, esp. in eastern Africa

safe (sāf) *adj.* **saf'er, saf'est** [OFr. *sauf* < L. *salvus* < IE. base *solo-,* whole] **1.** *a)* free from danger, damage, etc.; secure [he's *safe* in bed] *b)* having escaped injury; unharmed [he was *safe* after the battle] **2.** *a)* giving protection [a *safe* hiding place] *b)* that can be trusted or relied on [a *safe* adviser] **3.** unable to cause trouble or damage [*safe* in jail] **4.** taking or involving no risks [a *safe* driver] ☆**5.** *Baseball* having reached base without being put out —*n.* **1.** a strong metal container with a lock, for keeping valuables **2.** any compartment, box, etc. to store food, etc. —**safe'ly** *adv.* —**safe'ness** *n.*

SYN. —**safe** implies freedom from damage, danger, or injury or from the risk of damage, etc. [is it *safe* to leave?]; **secure,** often used instead of **safe,** is now usually applied to something about which there is no need to feel fear or anxiety [she is *secure* in her job] —**ANT. dangerous, precarious, unsure**

safe-con·duct (sāf'kän'dukt) *n.* **1.** permission to travel through a dangerous area, as in time of war, with protection against arrest or harm **2.** a written pass giving this

safe·crack·ing (-krak'iŋ) *n.* the breaking open and robbing of safes —**safe'crack'er** *n.*

☆**safe-de·pos·it** (-di päz'it) *adj.* describing or of a box or vault, esp. in a bank, for storing valuables: also **safe'ty-de·pos'it**

safe·guard (-gärd') *n.* any person or thing that protects or guards against loss or injury; a precaution or protection —*vt.* to protect or guard

safe·keep·ing (-kēp'iŋ) *n.* a keeping or being kept in safety; protection or custody

safe·ty (sāf'tē) *n., pl.* -ties **1.** a being safe; security **2.** a device to prevent an accident, as a locking device (also **safety catch, safety lock**) on a firearm ☆**3.** *Football a)* a play in which a player grounds the ball behind his own goal line when the ball was caused to pass the goal line by his own team: it scores two points for the opponents *b)* a player of a defensive backfield whose position is deep, behind the cornerbacks: in full, **safety man** —*adj.* giving safety

safety belt 1. *same as* LIFE BELT **2.** a belt attaching a person working at heights to something to keep him from falling **3.** *same as* SEAT BELT

safety glass glass made to resist being shattered by fastening together two sheets of glass with a transparent, plastic substance between them

safety lamp a miner's lamp designed so as not to cause a fire, etc.

safety match a match that will light only when it is struck on a prepared surface

safety pin a pin bent back on itself so as to form a spring, the point being held with a guard

☆**safety razor** a razor with a blade that fits into a holder with guards to protect the skin from cuts

safety valve 1. a valve for a steam boiler, etc., to release steam automatically if the pressure becomes too great **2.** any outlet for emotion, energy, etc.

saf·fi·an leather (saf'ē ən) [G. *saffian,* ult. < Per. *säht,* hard] leather of sheepskin or goatskin tanned with sumac and usually dyed a bright color

saf·flow·er (saf'lou'ər) *n.* [< Du. or MFr., ult. < Ar. *aṣ far,* a yellow plant] a thistlelike annual plant of the composite family, with orange flower heads producing a dyestuff and with seeds producing an oil used in paints, foods, etc.

saf·fron (saf'rən) *n.* [< OFr. *safran,* ult. < Ar. *za'farān*] **1.** a perennial old-world plant with funnel-shaped, purplish flowers having orange stigmas **2.** the dried stigmas, used in flavoring and coloring foods **3.** orange yellow: also **saffron yellow** —*adj.* orange-yellow

S. Afr. 1. South Africa **2.** South African

sag (sag) *vi.* **sagged, sag'ging** [prob. < Scand.] **1.** to sink or bend, esp. in the middle, from weight or pressure [shelves that *sag*] **2.** to hang down in a loose or uneven way [*sagging* flesh] **3.** to lose firmness, strength, etc.; weaken [school spirit *sagged*] **4.** to decline in price, sales, etc. —*vt.* to cause to sag —*n.* **1.** a sagging ☆**2.** a sunken place

sa·ga (sä'gə) *n.* [ON., a tale: for IE. base see SAY] **1.** a medieval Scandinavian story of battles, etc., generally telling the leg-endary history of a Norse family **2.** any long story telling about heroic deeds

sa·ga·cious (sə gā'shəs) *adj.* [< L. *sagacis,* genitive of *sagax,* wise] having or showing good judgment; wise —see SYN. at SHREWD —**sa·ga'cious·ly** *adv.* —**sa·ga'cious·ness** *n.*

sa·gac·i·ty (sə gas'ə tē) *n., pl.* -ties the quality or an instance of being sagacious

☆**sag·a·more** (sag'ə môr') *n.* [< AmInd. *sāgimau*] a chief of second rank among certain tribes of N. American Indians

sage[1] (sāj) *adj.* **sag'er, sag'est** [< OFr., ult. < L. *sapiens,* orig. prp. of *sapere,* to know < IE. base *sap-,* to taste] having or showing wisdom or good judgment [a *sage* comment] —*n.* a very wise man, esp. an old man respected for his wisdom, experience, judgment, etc. —see SYN. at WISE[1] —**sage'ly** *adv.*

sage[2] (sāj) *n.* [< OFr. < L. < *salvus,* SAFE: it was believed to have healing powers] **1.** any of various plants of the mint family, as the **scarlet sage,** with bright red flowers, or the **garden sage,** with leaves dried for seasoning meats, etc. ☆**2.** *same as* SAGEBRUSH

Sage (sāj), **Russell** 1816–1906; U.S. financier

☆**sage·brush** (sāj'brush') *n.* any of certain plants of the composite family, common in dry, alkaline areas of the western U.S.; esp., the **big sagebrush,** with sweet-smelling leaves

☆**sage grouse** a large grouse living on the sagebrush plains of western N. America: also, esp. for the female, **sage hen**

sag·gy (sag'ē) *adj.* **-gi·er, -gi·est** likely to sag

Sag·i·naw (sag'ə nô') [< Ojibway village name, lit., at the mouth of a river] city in EC Mich.: pop. 92,000

Sag·it·ta·ri·us (saj'i ter'ē əs) [L., archer] **1.** a large southern constellation in the Milky Way **2.** the ninth sign of the zodiac: see ZODIAC

sag·it·tate (saj'ə tāt') *adj.* [< ModL. < L. *sagitta,* arrow] in the shape of an arrowhead, as some leaves

sa·go (sā'gō) *n., pl.* -gos [Malay *sāgū*] **1.** a starch used as food that is prepared from certain palm trees and other plants **2.** a palm tree producing this starch: also **sago palm**

☆**sa·gua·ro** (sə gwä'rō, -wä'-) *n., pl.* -ros [MexSp. < native name] a giant cactus with a thick, spiny stem and white flowers, native to the southwestern U.S. and northern Mexico: also **sa·hua'ro** (-wä'-)

Sa·ha·ra (sə har'ə, -her'ə, -hä'rə) [Ar. *ṣahrā,* a desert] very large desert region in N Africa —**Sa·ha'ran** *adj.*

sa·hib (sä'ib, -hib, -ēb, -hēb) *n.* [< Hindi < Ar. *ṣāhib,* master] sir; master: title formerly used by natives in colonial India when speaking to or of a European

said (sed) *pt.* & *pp.* of SAY —*adj.* aforesaid; named before

Sai·gon (sī gän') seaport in S Vietnam: capital of the former South Vietnam: now called **Ho Chi Minh City**

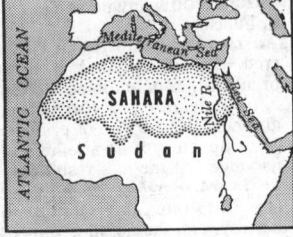

SAHARA

sail (sāl) *n.* [OE. *segl*] **1.** any of the shaped sheets of canvas, etc. spread to catch the wind and so drive a ship or boat forward **2.** sails as a group **3.** a sailing vessel or vessels **4.** a trip in a ship or boat **5.** anything like a sail, as an arm of a windmill —*vi.* **1.** to be moved forward by means of sails or a propeller, etc. **2.** to travel on water: said of a vessel or its passengers **3.** to begin a trip by water [we *sail* at noon] **4.** to manage a sailboat, as in racing **5.** to glide through the air [a hawk *sailing* in the sky] **6.** to move smoothly, like a ship sailing [the bride *sailed* down the aisle] **7.** [Colloq.] to move quickly [arrows *sailed* through the air] ☆**8.** [Colloq.] to throw oneself (*into*) with energy [he *sailed* into his new work] ☆**9.** [Colloq.] to attack or criticize someone harshly (with *into*) —*vt.* **1.** to move through or upon (a body of water) in a boat or ship **2.** to manage or navigate (a boat or ship) —**in sail** with sails set —**make sail 1.** to spread out a ship's sail **2.** to begin a trip by water —**set sail 1.** to raise the sails for departure **2.** to begin a trip by water —**take in sail** to lower sails —**under sail** sailing; with sails set —**sail'ing** *n., adj.*

sail·boat (sāl'bōt') *n.* a boat having a sail or sails

sail·cloth (-klôth', -kläth') *n.* canvas or other cloth used in making sails, tents, etc.

sail·er (-ər) *n.* a ship or boat, esp. one with sails, specif. with reference to its speed, etc. [a swift *sailer*]

sail·fish (-fish′) n., pl. **-fish′, -fish′es**: see FISH a large, tropical sea fish with a large, saillike fin on its back and a sword-shaped upper jaw

sail·or (-ər) n. **1.** a person who makes his living by sailing; seaman **2.** a) an enlisted man in the navy b) anyone in the navy **3.** a person on a ship or boat thought of in terms of whether or not he gets seasick [a good or bad *sailor*] **4.** a straw hat with a low, flat crown and flat brim —**sail′or·ing** n. —**sail′or·ly** adj.

sail·plane (sāl′plān′) n. a light glider designed for flying along without engine power —vi. **-planed′, -plan′ing** to fly a sailplane

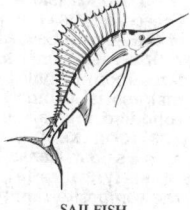

SAILFISH
(to 11 ft. long)

saint (sānt) n. [< OFr. < LL. < L. sanctus, holy] **1.** a holy person **2.** a person who is very humble, unselfish, patient, etc. **3.** [pl.] those, esp. holy persons, who have died and are believed to be with God **4.** a) in the New Testament, any Christian b) [S-] a member of any religious group calling themselves Saints **5.** in certain Christian churches, a dead person officially recognized as having lived an unusually holy life and thus as being in heaven —vt. to make a saint of For names of saints see the given name (as JOHN, PAUL, etc.); for other terms, see ST. and the following entries —**saint′hood′** n.

Saint Agnes's Eve the night of January 20, when a girl's future husband might appear to her as in a dream if she performed certain magic rites

Saint Ber·nard (bər närd′) a large, reddish-brown and white dog of a breed formerly trained by monks at the St. Bernard hospice, in the Swiss Alps, to rescue travelers

saint·ed (sān′tid) adj. **1.** of or fit for a saint; saintly **2.** thought of as a saint **3.** holy; sacred

Saint El·mo's fire (or **light**) (el′mōz) [after St. Elmo, patron saint of sailors] a visible electric discharge from tips of masts, spires, trees, etc.: seen sometimes during electrical storms

Saint-Ex·u·pé·ry (san teg zü pā rē′), **An·toine de** (än-twän′ də) 1900–44; Fr. aviator & writer

Saint-Gau·dens (sānt gô′d'nz), **Augustus** 1848–1907; U.S. sculptor, born in Ireland

Saint Johns·wort (jänz′wurt′) [< Saint JOHN + WORT²: reason for name uncertain] any of various plants with usually yellow flowers and spotted leaves

saint·ly (sānt′lē) adj. **-li·er, -li·est** like or fit for a saint; very good or holy —**saint′li·ness** n.

Saint Patrick's Day March 17, observed by the Irish in honor of Saint Patrick, the patron saint of Ireland

Saint-Saëns (san säns′), **Charles Ca·mille** (shårl kà mē′y′) 1835–1921; Fr. composer

Saint-Si·mon (san sē mōn′), **comte de** (Claude Henri de Rouvroy) 1760–1825; Fr. social philosopher

Saint Valentine's Day February 14, observed in honor of a martyr of the 3d cent.: it has become a custom to send valentines to sweethearts, etc. on this day

Saint Vi·tus' dance (vī′təs) [after St. Vitus, patron saint of persons having chorea] same as CHOREA

Sai·pan (sī pan′, -pän′) island of the Mariana Islands, in the W Pacific

saith (seth; now also sā′ith) archaic third person singular in the present tense of SAY

sake¹ (sāk) n. [OE. sacu, suit at law < IE. base sag-, to seek out] **1.** purpose or reason; motive [for the *sake* of peace] **2.** advantage; behalf; benefit [for my *sake*] —**for heaven's** (or **gosh** or **Pete's**) **sake!** a mild exclamation of surprise, annoyance, etc.

sa·ke² (sä′kē) n. [Jap.] a Japanese alcoholic beverage made from fermented rice: also sp. **sa′ki**

Sa·kha·lin (sä khä lēn′; E. sak′ə lēn′) island of the U.S.S.R., off the E coast of Siberia

sal (sal) n. [L.] Pharmacy salt

sa·laam (sə läm′) n. [Ar. salām, peace] **1.** a Moslem greeting ("peace") **2.** an Oriental greeting made by bowing low with the palm of the right hand placed on the forehead **3.** a greeting showing respect —vt., vi. to greet with, or make, a salaam

sal·a·ble (sāl′ə b'l) adj. that can be sold; fit to buy

sa·la·cious (sə lā′shəs) adj. [< L. salire, to leap: for IE. base see SALIENT] **1.** lecherous; lustful **2.** obscene; pornographic

—**sa·la′cious·ly** adv. —**sa·la′cious·ness, sa·lac′i·ty** (-las′ə-tē) n.

sal·ad (sal′əd) n. [< MFr. < Pr. < L. pp. of salare, to salt < sal, salt: for IE. base see SALT] **1.** a dish, usually cold, of vegetables, usually raw, or fruits, fish, eggs, etc., served with a dressing, or molded in gelatin **2.** any green plant or herb used for such a dish ☆**3.** a finely chopped or ground food, as egg, ham, or chicken, mixed with mayonnaise and served on a bed of lettuce or in a sandwich

salad days time when one is young and inexperienced

salad dressing a preparation of olive oil or other vegetable oil, vinegar, spices, etc. served with a salad

Sal·a·din (sal′ə din) (born Salah-ed-Din Yusuf ibn-Ayub) 1137–93; sultan of Egypt & Syria (1174–93)

Sa·la·do (sä lä′thō) river in N Argentina, flowing from the Andes southeast into the Paraná: c. 1,100 mi.

sal·a·man·der (sal′ə man′dər) n. [< OFr. < L. salamandra < Gr.] **1.** a reptile in myths that was said to live in fire **2.** any of a group of animals that look like lizards but are related to frogs and toads and have a soft, wet skin

sa·la·mi (sə lä′mē) n. [It., pl., preserved meat, ult. < L. sal, salt] a highly spiced, salted sausage, orig. Italian, of pork and beef, or of beef alone

Sal·a·mis (sal′ə mis; Gr. sä lä mēs′) **1.** Gr. island in the Aegean, near Athens **2.** ancient ruined city on the E coast of Cyprus

sal ammoniac same as AMMONIUM CHLORIDE

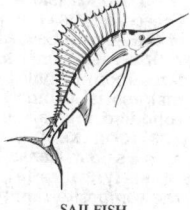

SALAMANDER
(to 4 in. long)

sal·a·ried (sal′ə rēd) adj. **1.** receiving a salary **2.** that gives one a salary [a *salaried* position]

sal·a·ry (sal′ə rē) n., pl. **-ries** [< L. salarium, orig., part of a Roman soldier's pay for buying salt < sal, salt: for IE. base see SALT] a fixed amount of money paid at regular times for work done, esp. for clerical or professional work —see SYN. at WAGE

sale (sāl) n. [< OE. < ON. sala: for IE. base see SELL] **1.** the act of selling or exchanging something or some service for an agreed sum of money [the clerk made ten *sales* today] **2.** opportunity to sell; market **3.** an auction **4.** a special selling of goods at prices lower than usual [a clearance *sale*] **5.** [pl.] receipts in business **6.** [pl.] the work, department, etc. of selling [a job in *sales*] —**for** (or **on**) **sale** to be sold

sale·a·ble (sāl′ə b'l) adj. same as SALABLE

Sa·lem (sā′ləm) [< Biblical place name] **1.** capital of Oreg., in the NW part: pop. 68,000 **2.** city on the NE coast of Mass.: suburb of Boston: pop. 41,000

Sa·ler·no (sä ler′nō; E. sə lur′nō) seaport in S Italy, on the Tyrrhenian Sea: pop. 151,000

☆**sales·clerk** (sālz′klurk′) n. a person employed to sell goods in a store

sales·man (sālz′mən) n., pl. **-men 1.** a man who is a salesclerk ☆**2.** a traveling agent who sells goods or services

sales·man·ship (-ship′) n. the ability, skill, or technique of selling

☆**sales·per·son** (sālz′pur′s'n) n. a person employed to sell goods; esp., a salesclerk —**sales′peo′ple** (-pē′p'l) n.pl.

☆**sales resistance** resistance of possible customers to efforts aimed at getting them to buy

☆**sales·room** (-room′) n. a room in which goods are shown and offered for sale

☆**sales talk** any persuasion or argument used in trying to sell something or to persuade one to do something

☆**sales tax** a tax on sales and, sometimes, services, added to the price paid by the customer

sales·wom·an (-woom′ən) n., pl. **-wom′en** (-wim′in) a woman salesclerk: also **sales′la′dy** (-lā′dē), pl. **-dies, sales′girl′** (-gurl′)

Sal·ic law (sal′ik, sā′lik) [< ML. < LL. Salii, a tribe of Franks] **1.** a code of laws of Germanic tribes, or any of these laws **2.** a law that barred women from any right to the throne in the French and Spanish monarchies

sa·lic·y·late (sə lis′ə lāt′; sal′ə sil′āt, -it) n. any salt or ester of salicylic acid

sal·i·cyl·ic acid (sal'ə sil'ik) [< Fr. *salicyle* (radical of the acid) < L. *salix*, willow + -IC] a white, crystalline compound, $C_7H_6O_3$, used in making aspirin, as a food preservative, etc.

sa·li·ent (sāl'yənt, sā'lē ənt) *adj.* [< L. prp. of *salire*, to leap < IE. base *sel-*, to jump] 1. leaping 2. pointing outward; projecting 3. standing out; noticeable; prominent /the *salient* idea in a plan/ —*n.* 1. the part of a battle line, fort, etc. standing out farthest toward the enemy 2. an angle, part, etc. pointing outward —**sa'lience** *n.* —**sa'lien·cy** *n., pl.* -cles —**sa'lient·ly** *adv.*

sa·li·en·ti·an (sā'lē en'shē ən, -shən) *n.* [ModL. *Salientia*, name of the order] any of a group of tailless amphibians, with a broad body and well-developed hind legs: it includes frogs, toads, and tree toads —*adj.* of the salientians

Sa·li·nas (sə lē'nəs) [ult. < L. *salina*, salty < *sal*, SALT] city in WC Calif., near San Jose: pop. 59,000

sa·line (sā'līn, -lēn; *for n. 1 also* sə lēn') *adj.* [< L. < *sal*, salt: for IE. base see SALT] of, like, or containing salt; salty —*n.* 1. a salt lick, salt marsh, etc. 2. a salt of an alkali metal or of magnesium, used as a cathartic 3. a saline solution —**sa·lin·i·ty** (sə lin'ə tē) *n.*

Sal·in·ger (sal'in jər), **J(erome) D(avid)** 1919– ; U.S. novelist & short-story writer

Salis·bur·y (sôlz'ber'ē, -bə rē) 1. city in SC England: noted for its 13th-cent. cathedral: pop. 36,000 2. capital of Zimbabwe, in the NE part: pop. 385,000

Salisbury, 3d Marquis of, (*Robert Arthur Talbot Gascoyne-Cecil*) 1830–1903; Eng. statesman

☆**Salisbury steak** *same as* HAMBURGER (sense 2)

sa·li·va (sə lī'və) *n.* [L.] the thin, watery, slightly sticky fluid produced by the salivary glands: it aids digestion by making food soft and wet, and contains an enzyme that changes starch to dextrin and maltose

sal·i·var·y (sal'ə ver'ē) *adj.* of or producing saliva

sal·i·vate (-vāt') *vt.* -vat'ed, -vat'ing [< L. pp. of *salivare*] to produce too great a flow of saliva in —*vi.* to produce saliva —**sal·i·va'tion** *n.*

Salk (sôlk), **Jonas E(dward)** 1914– ; U.S. bacteriologist: developed a vaccine for injection to prevent poliomyelitis

sal·low¹ (sal'ō) *adj.* [OE. *salu*] of or having an unhealthy, pale-yellow look /a *sallow* complexion/ —*vt.* to make sallow —**sal'low·ness** *n.*

sal·low² (sal'ō) *n.* [ME. *salwe*] 1. a kind of willow with large flowers which appear before the leaves 2. a willow twig

Sal·lust (sal'əst) (L. name *Gaius Sallustius Crispus*) 86–35? B.C.; Rom. historian

Sal·ly (sal'ē) [dim. of SARAH] a feminine name

sal·ly (sal'ē) *n., pl.* -lies [MFr. *saillie*, ult. < L. *salire*, to leap] 1. a sudden rushing forth, as of troops to attack the enemy 2. any sudden start into activity 3. a short, witty remark; quip 4. a trip or jaunt —*vi.* -lied, -ly·ing 1. to make a sally 2. *a)* to go outdoors *b)* to set out on a trip Used with *forth* or *out*

sal·ma·gun·di (sal'mə gun'dē) *n.* [Fr. *salmigondis* < ? It. *salame conditi*, pickled meat] 1. a dish of chopped meat, eggs, etc. flavored with onions, anchovies, etc. 2. any mixture or medley

salm·on (sam'ən) *n., pl.* -on, -ons: see PLURAL, II, D, 2 [< MFr. < OFr. *saumon* < L. *salmo*] 1. any of various bony fishes; specif., any of various game and food fishes of the Northern Hemisphere, with silver scales and flesh that is pink when cooked: salmon usually live in salt water but swim up rivers to lay their eggs 2. yellowish pink: also **salmon pink**

☆**sal·mo·nel·la** (sal'mə nel'ə) *n., pl.* -nel'lae (-ē), -nel'la, -nel'las [ModL.: after D. *Salmon* (d. 1914), U.S. veterinarian] any of certain rod-shaped bacteria that cause various diseases, as typhoid fever, food poisoning, etc.

Sa·lo·me (sə lō'mē; *occas.* sal'ə mā') *traditional name of* the stepdaughter of Herod Antipas: her dancing pleased Herod so much that he granted her request for the head of John the Baptist: Matt. 14:8

Sal·o·mon (sal'ə mən), **Haym** (hīm) 1740–85; Am. financier & patriot, born in Poland: helped finance the Am. Revolutionary War

sa·lon (sə län', sal'än; *Fr.* sa lōn') *n.* [Fr.: see SALOON] 1. large reception hall 2. a drawing room of a French private home 3. a regular gathering of famous persons, writers, artists, etc. in a well-known person's home 4. *a)* an art gallery *b)* an

art exhibition 5. a shop or business place specially equipped for performing some personal service; parlor /beauty *salon*/

Sa·lo·ni·ka (sal'ə nē'kə, -nī'-; sə län'i kə) 1. seaport in N Greece, on the Gulf of Salonika: pop. 251,000 2. Gulf of, N arm of the Aegean Sea Also sp. **Salonica**

sa·loon (sə lōōn') *n.* [Fr. *salon* < It. < *sala*, a hall] 1. any large room or hall for receptions, exhibitions, etc.; specif., the main social cabin of a passenger ship ☆2. a place where alcoholic drinks are bought and drunk: an old-fashioned term

☆**sa·loon·keep·er** (-kēp'ər) *n.* a person who owns or manages a saloon (sense 2)

sal·si·fy (sal'sə fē', -fī') *n.* [< Fr. < It. *sassefrica*] a plant of the composite family, with white, fleshy roots: it is used as a vegetable and has an oysterlike flavor

sal soda crystallized sodium carbonate

salt (sôlt, sält) *n.* [OE. *sealt* < IE. base *sal-*, salt] 1. sodium chloride, NaCl, a white, crystalline substance found in deposits in the earth, in sea water, etc., and used for seasoning and preserving food, etc. 2. a chemical compound formed from an acid by replacing hydrogen, wholly or partly, with a metal or an electropositive radical 3. that which makes something else interesting /his talk was livened by the *salt* of his wit/ 4. *same as* SALTCELLAR 5. [*pl.*] mineral salts used to help move the bowels (as **Epsom salts**), to soften bath water (**bath salts**), to revive a person (**smelling salts**), etc. 6. [Colloq.] a sailor —*adj.* 1. containing salt /*salt* water/ 2. preserved with salt /*salt* pork/ 3. tasting or smelling of salt /*salt* breezes/ 4. *a)* flooded with salt water *b)* growing in salt water —*vt.* 1. to sprinkle, season, or preserve with salt /to *salt* meat/ 2. to put salt on (streets, etc.) to melt snow and ice 3. to make interesting /to *salt* a speech with humor/ ☆4. to put minerals in (a mine), oil in (a well), etc. so as to trick possible buyers —**salt away** (or **down**) 1. to pack and preserve with salt ☆2. [Colloq.] to store or save (money, etc.) —**salt of the earth** a person or persons thought of as the finest or best —**with a grain** (or **pinch**) **of salt** with some doubt in believing; skeptically —**worth one's salt** worth one's wages, etc. —**salt'er** *n.* —**salt'ish** *adj.* —**salt'like'** *adj.* —**salt'ness** *n.*

☆**SALT** (sôlt, sält) Strategic Arms Limitation Talks

salt-and-pep·per (sôlt'n pep'ər) *adj. same as* PEPPER-AND-SALT

salt·box (sôlt'bäks') *n.* 1. a box for salt, with a sloping lid ☆2. a house shaped like this, with two stories in front and one at the rear and a gable roof Also **salt box**

salt·cel·lar (-sel'ər) *n.* [< ME. < salt, salt + MFr. *salière*, saltcellar] 1. a small dish for salt at the table 2. *same as* SALTSHAKER

Sal·til·lo (säl tē'yō) city in N Mexico: pop. 192,000

☆**salt·ine** (sôl tēn') *n.* [SALT + -INE⁴] a flat, crisp cracker sprinkled with salt

Salt Lake City capital of Utah, near the SE end of the Great Salt Lake: pop. 176,000 (met. area 558,000)

☆**salt lick** 1. an exposed natural deposit of rock salt which animals come to lick 2. a block of rock salt placed in a pasture for cattle, etc. to lick

salt marsh grassland over which salt water flows from time to time

salt·pe·ter (sôlt'pēt'ər) *n.* [< MFr. < ML. < L. *sal*, salt + *petra*, a rock] 1. *same as* POTASSIUM NITRATE 2. *see* CHILE SALTPETER

salt pork pork cured in salt

☆**salt·shak·er** (sôlt'shā'kər) *n.* a container for salt, with holes in the top for shaking out the salt

salt·wa·ter (-wôt'ər, -wät'ər) *adj.* of, having to do with, or living in salt water or the sea

salt·works (-wurks') *n., pl.* -works' a place where salt is made, as by evaporating water full of salt

salt·wort (-wurt') *n.* any of a group of plants of the goosefoot family, growing on seashores or salty soils

salt·y (sôl'tē) *adj.* **salt'i·er, salt'i·est** 1. of, tasting of, or containing salt 2. smelling of or suggesting the sea 3. *a)* witty and witty /a *salty*, amusing story/ *b)* coarse or earthy /the *salty* language of the factory workers/ *c)* highly critical or sarcastic /a movie review full of *salty* comments/ —**salt'i·ly** *adv.* —**salt'i·ness** *n.*

sa·lu·bri·ous (sə lōō'brē əs) *adj.* [L. *salubris* < *salus*, health] promoting health or welfare; healthful, wholesome, etc. /a *salubrious* climate/ —**sa·lu'bri·ous·ly** *adv.* —**sa·lu'bri·ty** (-brə tē), **sa·lu'bri·ous·ness** *n.*

sal·u·tar·y (sal'yoo ter'ē) *adj.* [< Fr. < L. < *salutis*, genitive of *salus*, health] 1. promoting health; healthful /running is a *salutary* pastime] **2.** promoting some good purpose; beneficial [a *salutary* lesson] —**sal′u·tar′i·ly** *adv.* —**sal′u·tar′i·ness** *n.*

sal·u·ta·tion (sal′yoo tā′shən) *n.* [< MFr. < L. < pp. of *salutare:* see SALUTE] **1.** the act of greeting, addressing, etc. by gestures or words [he waved to us in *salutation*] **2.** certain words used as a greeting or as the opening words of a letter, as "Dear Sir"

☆**sa·lu·ta·to·ri·an** (sə loōt′ə tôr′ē ən) *n.* in some schools and colleges, the student, usually the one ranking second highest in the class in scholarship, who gives the salutatory

sa·lu·ta·to·ry (sə loōt′ə tôr′ē) *adj.* of or expressing a salutation —*n., pl.* -**ries** ☆an opening address, esp. at a school or college commencement exercise

sa·lute (sə loōt′) *vt.* -**lut′ed**, -**lut′ing** [< L. *salutare < salus:* see SALUTARY] **1.** to greet in a friendly way, as by bowing, tipping the hat, etc. **2.** to show honor and respect for in an official way by firing cannon, raising the right hand to the forehead, etc. **3.** to present itself to, as if in greeting [the crowing rooster *saluted* the dawn] **4.** to praise or commend [he *saluted* her accomplishments in his speech] —*vi.* to make a salute —*n.* **1.** an act, remark, or gesture made in saluting **2.** *Mil.* the position of the hand, etc. used in saluting —**sa·lut′er** *n.*

sal·va·ble (sal′və b'l) *adj.* that can be saved or salvaged

Sal·va·dor (sal′və dôr′; *Port.* säl′və-dôr′) seaport in E Brazil, on the Atlantic: pop. 1,001,000

Sal·va·do·ran (sal′və dôr′ən) *adj.* of El Salvador, its people, or culture —*n.* a native or inhabitant of El Salvador Also **Sal′va·do·ri·an** (-dôr′ē ən)

sal·vage (sal′vij) *n.* [Fr. < MFr. < *salver*, to SAVE[1]] **1.** *a)* the rescue of a ship and cargo at sea from fire, shipwreck, etc. *b)* money paid to those who help in such rescue *c)* the ship or cargo so rescued *d)* the bringing up of a sunken ship or its cargo by divers, caissons, etc. **2.** *a)* the saving of any goods, etc. from destruction or waste *b)* goods, etc. so saved *c)* the money received from sale of such goods, etc., taken into account in settling insurance claims —*vt.* -**vaged**, -**vag·ing** to save or rescue from shipwreck, fire, flood, etc.; take part or succeed in the salvage of (ships, goods, etc.) —**sal′vage·a·bil′i·ty** *n.* —**sal′vage·a·ble** *adj.* —**sal′vag·er** *n.*

sal·va·tion (sal vā′shən) *n.* [< OFr. < LL. < L. pp. of *salvare*, to SAVE[1]] **1.** a saving or being saved **2.** a person or thing that saves or rescues **3.** in Christian belief, the saving of the soul from the results of sin —**sal·va′tion·al** *adj.*

Salvation Army a Christian organization that works to bring religion and help to the very poor

salve[1] (sav) *n.* [OE. *sealf*] **1.** any soothing or healing ointment used on wounds, burns, sores, etc. **2.** anything that soothes or heals; balm [her smile was a *salve* to his anger] —*vt.* **salved**, **salv′ing** to soothe or make quiet; smooth over [praise *salved* his wounded pride]

salve[2] (salv) *vt.* **salved**, **salv′ing** same as SALVAGE

sal·ver (sal′vər) *n.* [< Fr. < Sp. *salva < salvar*, to taste (so as to prove food wholesome) < L. *salvare*, to SAVE[1]] a tray on which something is served or presented

sal·vi·a (sal′vē ə) *n.* [ModL., genus name < L.] same as SAGE[2] (sense 1)

sal·vo (sal′vō) *n., pl.* -**vos**, -**voes** [< It. < L. *salve*, hail!] **1.** a firing of a number of guns one after another or at the same time, either in salute or at a target **2.** the release of a load of bombs or the launching of several rockets at the same time **3.** a burst of cheers or applause

sal vo·la·ti·le (sal′vō lat′'l ē′) [ModL., volatile salt] a solution of ammonium carbonate, used in smelling salts

Sal·ween (sal wēn′) river in SE Asia, flowing from Tibet through Burma into the Indian Ocean

Salz·burg (zälts′boŏrkh; *E.* sôlz′bərg) city in C Austria: pop. 108,000

SAM (sam) surface-to-air missile

Sam. Samuel

Sa·mar (sä′mär) island of the E Philippines, southeast of Luzon: 5,181 sq. mi.

sam·a·ra (sam′ər ə, sə mer′ə) *n.* [ModL. < L., elm seed] a dry fruit, as of the maple, that contains a seed and has a winglike part that helps carry it through the air

Sa·mar·i·a (sə mer′ē ə, -mar′-) in ancient times, **1.** the capital of the N kingdom of Israel **2.** a district of Palestine between Galilee & Judea

Sa·mar·i·tan (-ə t'n) *n.* **1.** a native or inhabitant of Samaria **2.** *see* GOOD SAMARITAN —*adj.* of Samaria or its people

sa·mar·i·um (sə mer′ē əm, -mar′-) *n.* [ModL. < *samarskite*, a mineral < Col. *Samarski*, Russ. mining official] a metallic chemical element of the rare-earth group: symbol, Sm; at. wt., 150.35; at. no., 62

Sam·ar·kand (sam′ər kand′; *Russ.* sä mär känt′) city in E Uzbek S.S.R.: pop. 267,000

sam·ba (sam′bə, säm′-) *n.* [Port., prob. of Afr. origin] **1.** a Brazilian dance based on an African dance **2.** music for this dance —*vi.* to dance the samba

Sam Browne belt (sam′ broun′) [after 19th-c. Brit. Gen. *Samuel J. Browne*] a military officer's belt with a diagonal strap across the right shoulder

same (sām) *adj.* [ON. *samr* < IE. base *sem-*, one, from which also comes Gr. *homos*, alike] **1.** being the very one; identical [he is the *same* man who spoke to me] **2.** alike in kind, quality, amount, etc.; similar [both rugs are of the *same* color] **3.** unchanged; not different [he looks the *same* healthy man as ever] **4.** mentioned earlier; just spoken of [and he then chose the *same* dinner] —*pron.* the same person or thing [I'll have the *same*] —*adv.* in the same way [treat her the *same* as us] The *adj. & pron.* are usually used with *the*, *this*, or *that*; the *adv.*, with *the* —**same′ness** *n.*

SYN.—same, in one sense, agrees with **selfsame** and **very** in implying that what is referred to is one thing and not two or more distinct things [that is the *same* (or *selfsame* or *very*) house we once lived in]; in another sense, it implies that the things referred to are distinct but not really different in kind, appearance, amount, etc. [I eat the *same* food every day]; **identical**, in one sense, also expresses the first idea [this is the *identical* bed where he slept] and, in another, implies that the things are exactly similar in all details [the signatures are *identical*]; **equal** implies that there is no difference in quantity, size, value, degree, etc. [*equal* weights; an *equal* advantage]; **equivalent** implies of things that they amount to the same thing in value, force, meaning, etc. [$5 or an *equivalent* amount of merchandise] —**ANT. different**

sam·i·sen (sam′ə sen′) *n.* [Jap. < Chin. *san hsien*, three strings] a Japanese musical instrument somewhat like a banjo, but with three strings

sam·ite (sam′īt, sā′mīt) *n.* [< MFr. < ML. < MGr. < *hexamitos*, woven with six threads] a heavy silk fabric interwoven with gold or silver threads, worn in the Middle Ages

Sa·mo·a (sə mō′ə) group of islands in the South Pacific, north of Tonga: seven of these islands make up a possession (**American Samoa**) of the U.S., 76 sq. mi., pop. 28,000: see also WESTERN SAMOA —**Sa·mo′an** *adj., n.*

Sa·mos (sā′mäs; *Gr.* sä′môs) Gr. island in the Aegean, off the W coast of Turkey —**Sa·mi·an** (sā′mē ən) *adj., n.*

Sam·o·thrace (sam′ə thrās′) Gr. island in the NE Aegean

sam·o·var (sam′ə vär′, sam′ə vär′) *n.* [Russ., lit., self-boiler] a metal urn, used esp. in Russia, having a spigot and an inside tube that holds the fuel for heating water in making tea

Sam·o·yed, Sam·o·yede (sam′ə yed′) *n.* [Russ.] **1.** any of a Uralic people of Siberia **2.** their language **3.** any of a strong breed of Siberian dog, with a thick, white coat —*adj.* of the Samoyeds or their language: also **Sam′o·yed′ic**

☆**samp** (samp) *n.* [< Algonquian *nasaump*, softened by water] coarse cornmeal or a porridge made from this

sam·pan (sam′pan) *n.* [Chin. *san-pan* < ? *san*,

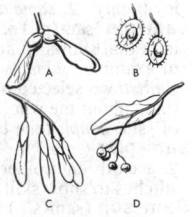

SAMARAS
(A, maple; B, elm;
C, ash; D, basswood)

SAMOVAR

three + *pan*, a plank] any of various small boats used in China and Japan, rowed with an oar at the stern, and often having a sail and a small cabin formed of mats

sam·phire (sam′fīr′) *n.* [< Fr. (*herbe de*) *Saint Pierre*, St. Peter's (herb)] **1.** a fleshy, old-world, seashore plant of the parsley family **2.** *same as* GLASSWORT

sam·ple (sam′p'l) *n.* [< OFr.: see EXAMPLE] **1.** a part, piece, or item that shows what the whole or group is like; specimen or example [*samples* of wallpaper, a *sample* of his humor] ☆**2.** *Statistics* a selected part of the population studied to learn something about the whole —*vt.* **-pled, -pling** to take or test a sample of [she *sampled* the basket of grapes]

sam·pler (-plər) *n.* **1.** a person who prepares or tests samples **2.** a cloth embroidered with designs, mottoes, etc. in different stitches to show skill in embroidery

Sam·son (sam′s'n) [LL. < Gr. < Heb. *shimshōn* < ? *shemesh*, sun] *Bible* an Israelite judge noted for his great strength: betrayed to the Philistines by Delilah: Judges 13–16

Sam·u·el (sam′yōō wəl, -yool) [LL. < Gr. < Heb. *shěmū′ĕl*, lit., name of God] **1.** a masculine name: dim. *Sam, Sammy* **2.** *Bible* a) a Hebrew judge and prophet b) either of two books (I Samuel, II Samuel) telling of Samuel, Saul, and David

sam·u·rai (sam′ə rī′) *n., pl.* **-rai′** [Jap.] a member of a military class in feudal Japan

‡**-san** (sän) [Jap.] a Japanese suffix meaning "honorable," added to names, titles, etc.

Sa·n'a (sä nä′) capital of the Yemen Arab Republic, in the central part: pop. 89,000: also sp. **Sana, Sanaa**

San An·ge·lo (san an′jə lō′) [after *Santa Angela*, a Mex. nun] city in WC Tex.: pop. 64,000

San An·to·ni·o (san′ ən tō′nē ō′, an-) [Sp., St. Anthony, 13th-c. Franciscan friar of Padua] city in SC Tex.: site of the Alamo: pop. 654,000 (met. area 864,000)

san·a·tive (san′ə tiv) *adj.* [< OFr. < LL. < L. pp. of *sanare*, to heal] having the power to heal or cure; curative

san·a·to·ri·um (san′ə tôr′ē əm) *n., pl.* **-ri·ums, -ri·a** (-ə) [ModL. < LL. *sanatorius*, giving health < L. *sanare*, to heal] *chiefly Brit. var. of* SANITARIUM

San Ber·nar·di·no (san′ bur′nər dē′nō, -nə-) [Sp., St. Bernardine (of Siena)] city in S Calif., near Los Angeles: pop. 104,000

sanc·ti·fied (saŋk′tə fīd′) *adj.* **1.** made holy; consecrated **2.** pretending to be holy; sanctimonious

sanc·ti·fy (saŋk′tə fī′) *vt.* **-fied′, -fy′ing** [< OFr. < LL. *sanctificare:* see SAINT & -FY] **1.** to make holy; specif., *a)* to set apart as holy; consecrate [to *sanctify* a new altar] *b)* to make free from sin; purify **2.** to make seem morally right or binding [a practice *sanctified* by custom] —**sanc′ti·fi·ca′tion** *n.* —**sanc′ti·fi′er** *n.*

sanc·ti·mo·ni·ous (saŋk′tə mō′nē əs) *adj.* pretending to be very holy, religious, or righteous —**sanc′ti·mo′ni·ous·ly** *adv.* —**sanc′ti·mo′ni·ous·ness** *n.*

sanc·ti·mo·ny (saŋk′tə mō′nē) *n.* [< OFr. < L. *sanctimonia* < *sanctus*, holy] pretended holiness or righteousness; a being pious in a hypocritical way

sanc·tion (saŋk′shən) *n.* [< Fr. < L. < *sanctus*, holy] **1.** the approving or permitting of an action by a recognized authority; authorization [the club was formed with the school's *sanction*] **2.** support; approval **3.** something that gives binding force to a law, as the penalty for breaking it or a reward for carrying it out **4.** something, as a moral principle, that makes a rule of conduct binding **5.** [*usually pl.*] a boycott, blockade, or similar measure backed up by force as against a nation that is considered to have violated international law —*vt.* to give sanction to; specif., *a)* to give official approval to *b)* to allow or permit [I cannot *sanction* such rudeness] —see SYN. at APPROVE —**sanc′tion·a·ble** *adj.*

sanc·ti·ty (saŋk′tə tē) *n., pl.* **-ties** [< L. < *sanctus*, holy] **1.** saintliness or holiness **2.** a being sacred [the *sanctity* of a chapel] **3.** the state of being regarded as something not to be violated [the *sanctity* of a person's home] **4.** anything held to be sacred

sanc·tu·ar·y (saŋk′chōō wer′ē) *n., pl.* **-ar′ies** [< MFr. < LL. < L. *sanctus*, sacred] **1.** a holy place, as a building set aside for worship; specif., *a)* the ancient Temple at Jerusalem *b)* any church, temple, etc. *c)* a holy place within a church, temple, etc., as the part around the altar, the holy of holies, etc. **2.** a place of refuge or protection **3.** a being safe from punishment or arrest, as by taking refuge in a church **4.** a reservation where animals or birds are sheltered for breeding purposes and may not be hunted or trapped

sanc·tum (saŋk′təm) *n., pl.* **-tums, -ta** (-tə) [L., neut. of *sanctus*, holy] **1.** a sacred place **2.** a study or private room where one is not to be disturbed

sanctum sanc·to·rum (saŋk tôr′əm) [LL.] **1.** *same as* HOLY OF HOLIES **2.** a highly private place where one is never to be disturbed

sand (sand) *n.* [OE.] **1.** loose, gritty grains worn away from rock, as on beaches, in deserts, etc. **2.** [*usually pl.*] an area of sand; beach **3.** [< the sand in an hourglass] [*pl.*] moments; particles of time ☆**4.** [Old Slang] grit; courage —*vt.* **1.** to sprinkle, fill, or mix with sand **2.** to smooth or polish with sand, sandpaper, or a similar substance —**sand′ed** *adj.* —**sand′er** *n.*

Sand (sand; *Fr.* sänd), **George** (pen name of *Amandine Aurore Lucie Dupin*, Baronne *Dudevant*) 1804–76; Fr. novelist

san·dal[1] (san′d'l) *n.* [< L. < Gr. dim. of *sandalon*] **1.** a kind of footwear consisting of a sole fastened to the foot by straps over the instep or toes, or around the ankles **2.** a type of low slipper —**san′daled, san′dalled** *adj.*

san·dal[2] (san′d'l) *n. same as* SANDALWOOD

san·dal·wood (-wood′) *n.* [< MFr. < ML., ult. < Sans. *candana*] **1.** the hard, sweet-smelling heartwood of any of certain Asiatic trees, used for carving and cabinetmaking or burned as incense **2.** any of these trees

san·da·rac (san′də rak′) *n.* [< L. < Gr. *sandarake*] **1.** any of several African and Australian trees of the pine family, producing a brittle, transparent resin used in varnishes **2.** this resin

sand·bag (sand′bag′) *n.* **1.** a bag filled with sand and used for ballast or in building or strengthening walls against floods, attack, etc. ☆**2.** a small, sand-filled bag used as a hitting weapon —*vt.* **-bagged′, -bag′-ging** **1.** to place sandbags in or around ☆**2.** to hit with a sandbag ☆**3.** [Colloq.] to force into doing something —**sand′-bag′ger** *n.*

sand·bank (-baŋk′) *n.* **1.** *same as* SAND BAR **2.** a large mass of sand, as on a hillside

☆**sand bar** a ridge of sand formed in a river or along a shore by the action of currents or tides

sand·blast (-blast′) *n.* **1.** a current of air or steam carrying sand at a high speed, used in etching glass and in cleaning surfaces as of metals, stone, etc. **2.** the machine used to apply this blast —*vt.* to engrave, clean, etc. with a sandblast —**sand′-blast′er** *n.*

sand·box (-bäks′) *n.* ☆a box containing sand for children to play in

Sand·burg (sand′bərg, san′-), **Carl** 1878–1967; U.S. poet, writer, & ballad collector

sand dab a small flatfish used as food; ☆esp., a flounder found along the Pacific coast of N. America

☆**sand dollar** a flat, round sea animal of the echinoderm group, that lives on sandy ocean beds

sand flea **1.** a small crustacean found on sandy beaches, that leaps like a flea **2.** *same as* CHIGGER

sand fly any of various tiny, two-winged, biting flies, some of which carry disease

san·dhi (sän′dē, san′-, sun′-) *n.* [< Sans. *samdhi*, a linking] the change of a speech sound by the influence of the sounds next to it (for example, the pronunciation of *t* as (ch) in *picture*)

☆**sand·hog** (sand′hôg′, -häg′) *n.* a person who works on underwater construction projects under compressed air, as in a caisson

San Di·e·go (san′ dē ā′gō) [after *San Diego* (St. Didacus), 15th-cent. Sp. friar] seaport in S Calif., on the Pacific: pop. 697,000 (met. area 1,358,000)

☆**sand·lot** (sand′lät′) *adj.* having to do with games, esp. baseball, played by amateurs, originally on a sandy lot or field —**sand′lot′ter** *n.*

sand·man (-man′) *n.* a make-believe man, as in fairy tales, supposed to make children sleepy by dusting sand in their eyes

sand·pa·per (-pā′pər) *n.* a strong paper with sand glued on one side, used for smoothing and polishing —*vt.* to smooth or polish with sandpaper

sand·pip·er (-pī′pər) *n., pl.* **-pip′ers, -pip′er:** see PLURAL, II, D, 1 a small shore bird with a long, soft-tipped bill

SANDALS

SAND DOLLAR
(to 4 in. wide)

San·dra (san′drə, sän′-) [< *Alexandra*, fem. of ALEXANDER] a feminine name

sand·stone (sand′stōn′) *n.* a common sedimentary rock much used for building, made up largely of sand grains, mainly quartz, cemented together by silica, etc.

sand·storm (-stôrm′) *n.* a windstorm in which sand is blown about in large clouds

☆ **sand trap** a pit filled with sand to serve as a hazard on a golf course

sand·wich (sand′wich, san′-) *n.* [< 4th Earl of *Sandwich* (1718–1792): it is said he ate these while gambling so that he would not need to leave for meals] two or more slices of bread with a filling of meat, cheese, etc. between them: see also OPEN-FACED (sense 2) —*vt.* to place between other persons, things, materials, etc. [a shed *sandwiched* between two houses]

Sandwich Islands [after the 4th Earl of *Sandwich:* see prec.] *former name of the* HAWAIIAN ISLANDS (see HAWAII)

sandwich man a man who walks the streets with two sign-boards (**sandwich boards**) hung from his shoulders, front and back, as for advertising something

sand·wort (sand′wurt′) *n.* a low-growing plant of the pink family, growing in sandy soil and forming a mosslike mat

sand·y (san′dē) *adj.* **sand′i·er, sand′i·est** **1.** made up of, full of, or covered with sand [a *sandy* shore] **2.** pale brown or dull yellow [*sandy* hair] —**sand′i·ness** *n.*

sane (sān) *adj.* **san′er, san′est** [L. *sanus,* healthy] **1.** having a normal, healthy mind; able to make sound, reasonable judgments **2.** showing good sense; sensible [a *sane* policy] —**sane′ly** *adv.* —**sane′ness** *n.*

☆ **San·for·ized** (san′fə rīzd′) [after *Sanford* L. Cluett (1874–1968), the inventor] *a trademark* applied to cloth preshrunk by a patented process before it is made into garments

San Fran·cis·co (san′ frən sis′kō) [Sp., prob. after St. FRAN-CIS OF ASSISI] seaport on the coast of C Calif., on an inlet (**San Francisco Bay**) of the Pacific: pop. 716,000 (met. area, incl. Oakland, 3,110,000)

sang (saŋ) *pt. of* SING

Sang·er (saŋ′ər), **Margaret** (born *Margaret Higgins*) 1883–1966; U.S. nurse: leader in birth-control education

sang-froid (saŋ′frwä′; Fr. sän frwà′) *n.* [Fr., lit., cold blood] cool control of oneself in a difficult situation; calmness of manner —see SYN. at EQUANIMITY

san·gui·nar·y (saŋ′gwi ner′ē) *adj.* [< L. < *sanguis:* see SAN-GUINE] **1.** with much bloodshed or killing [a *sanguinary* revolt] **2.** of or stained with blood **3.** eager for bloodshed; bloodthirsty —**san′gui·nar′i·ly** *adv.* —**san′gui·nar′i·ness** *n.*

san·guine (saŋ′gwin) *adj.* [< OFr. < L. < *sanguinis,* genitive of *sanguis,* blood] **1.** of the color of blood; ruddy **2.** [from the medieval belief that those in whom blood is the main humor are cheerful] cheerful; confident; optimistic —**san′guine·ly** *adv.* —**san′guine·ness** *n.*

san·guin·e·ous (saŋ gwin′ē əs) *adj.* same as: **1.** SANGUI-NARY **2.** SANGUINE

San·he·drin (san hed′rin, sän-; -hē′drin) *n.* [< Heb. < Gr. < *syn-,* together + *hedra,* seat] the highest religious and civil court of the ancient Jewish nation

san·i·tar·i·an (san′ə ter′ē ən) *adj.* same as SANITARY —*n.* a specialist in public health and sanitation

san·i·tar·i·um (-ē əm) *n., pl.* **-i·ums, -i·a** (-ə) [ModL. < *sani-tas,* health] an institution for the care of invalids or those recovering from an illness, esp. one for treating a specific disease, such as tuberculosis

san·i·tar·y (san′ə ter′ē) *adj.* [< Fr. < L. *sanitas,* health] **1.** of health or the rules and conditions of health; esp., promoting health by getting rid of dirt and of things that bring disease [the *sanitary* department] **2.** free from dirt, etc. that could bring disease; clean [a *sanitary* restaurant] —**san′i·tar′i·ly** *adv.* —**san′i·tar′i·ness** *n.*

☆ **sanitary belt** a narrow elastic belt for holding a sanitary napkin in place

☆ **sanitary napkin** an absorbent pad of cotton, etc. worn by women during menstruation

san·i·ta·tion (san′ə tā′shən) *n.* **1.** the science and work of bringing about healthful and sanitary conditions **2.** the system of carrying away and getting rid of sewage

san·i·tize (san′ə tīz′) *vt.* **-tized′, -tiz′ing** to make sanitary, as by sterilizing —**san′i·tiz′er** *n.*

san·i·ty (san′ə tē) *n.* [< OFr. < L. *sanitas,* health] **1.** the condition of being sane; soundness of mind; mental health **2.** soundness of judgment

San Joa·quin (san′ wô kēn′, wä-) [Sp., St. Joachim, reputed father of the Virgin Mary] river in C Calif., flowing south into the Sacramento River

San Jo·se (san′ hō zā′, ə zā′) [Sp. *San José,* St. Joseph] city in WC Calif.: pop. 446,000 (met. area 1,065,000)

San Jo·sé (sän′ hō se′) capital of Costa Rica, in the C part: pop. 203,000

☆ **San Jo·se scale** (san′ hō zā′) [< *San Jose,* Calif., where first seen in the U.S.] a scale insect very harmful to fruit trees

San Juan (san′ hwän′, wôn′; *Sp.* sän′ hwän′) [Sp., St. John] capital of Puerto Rico; seaport on the Atlantic: pop. 445,000 (met. area 851,000)

sank (saŋk) *alt. pt. of* SINK

San Le·an·dro (san′ lē an′drō) [Sp., St. Leander, archbishop of Seville] city in W Calif., on San Francisco Bay: suburb of Oakland: pop. 69,000

San Ma·ri·no (sän′ mä rē′nō; *E.* san′ mə rē′nō) independent country within E Italy: 23 sq. mi.; pop. 19,000

San Mar·tín (sän′ mär tēn′), **Jo·sé de** (hō se′ de) 1778–1850; S. American revolutionary leader, born in Argentina

San Ma·te·o (san′ mə tā′ō) [Sp., St. Matthew] city in W Calif.: suburb of San Francisco: pop. 79,000

sans (sanz; *Fr.* sän) *prep.* [< OFr. *sanz* (Fr. *sans*) < L. *sine,* without] without; lacking

Sans. Sanskrit

San Sal·va·dor (san sal′və dôr′; *Sp.* sän säl′vä *thô*r′) **1.** capital of El Salvador: pop. 341,000 **2.** island of the E Bahamas: prob. the place of Columbus' first landing (1492)

sans-cu·lotte (sanz′kσo lät′, -kyσo-) *n.* [Fr., without breeches] a revolutionary: term of contempt as used in the French Revolution by aristocrats of the poorly dressed republicans

san·se·vi·e·ri·a (san′sə vir′ē ə, -vi ē′rē ə) *n.* [ModL., after the Prince of *Sanseviero* (1710–71), a scholar of Naples] any of a group of succulent plants with thick, lance-shaped leaves

San·skrit (san′skrit) *n.* [< Sans. *samskrta,* lit., made together, well arranged] an ancient Indic language, the literary language of India: important in the study of Indo-European linguistics —*adj.* of or written in Sanskrit Also sp. **San′-scrit** —**San·skrit′ic** *adj.* —**San′skrit·ist** *n.*

sans-ser·if (san ser′if) *n.* [see SANS & SERIF] a style of printing type with no serifs: the entry words of this dictionary are in sans-serif

San·ta (san′tə, -ti; *for adj., also* sän′tä) ☆ *short for* SANTA CLAUS —*adj.* [Sp. & It., female saint] holy or saint: used in combinations [*Santa* Maria]

San·ta An·a (san′tə an′ə) [Sp., St. Anne] city in SW Calif.: suburb of Los Angeles: pop. 157,000

San·ta An·na (sän′tä ä′nä), **An·to·nio Ló·pez de** (än tô′nyô lô′pes de) 1795?–1876; Mex. revolutionist & president

San·ta Bär·ba·ra (san′tə bär′bə rə) [Sp., St. Barbara] city on the coast of SW Calif.: pop. 70,000

Santa Cat·a·li·na (kat′'l ē′nə) island off the SW coast of Calif.: a tourist resort

Santa Cla·ra (kler′ə) [Sp., St. Clare (of Assisi)] city in W Calif., near San Jose: pop. 88,000

☆ **San·ta Claus, San·ta Klaus** (san′tə klôz′, -ti) [< Du. dial. < *Sant Nikolass,* St. NICHOLAS] *Folklore* a fat, white-bearded, jolly old man in a red suit, who distributes gifts at Christmas time: also called **Saint Nicholas, Saint Nick**

San·ta Fe (san′tə fā′) [Sp., holy faith] capital of N.Mex., in the NC part: pop. 41,000

SANDWICH MAN

SANSEVIERIA

Santa Fe Trail trade route between Santa Fe, N.Mex., & Independence, Mo.: important from 1821 to 1880

San·ta Is·a·bel (sän′tä ē sä bel′) capital of Equatorial Guinea, on an island in the Gulf of Guinea: pop. 20,000

San·ta Mon·i·ca (sän′tə män′i kə) [Sp., St. Monica, mother of St. AUGUSTINE (of North Africa)] city in SW Calif., on the Pacific: suburb of Los Angeles: pop. 88,000

SANTA FE TRAIL

San·ta Ro·sa (sän′tə rō′zə) [Sp., holy rose] city in W Calif., north of San Francisco: pop. 50,000

San·ta·ya·na (san′tē an′ə, -ä′nə; Sp. sän′tä yä′nä), **George** 1863–1952; Sp. philosopher & writer in English

San·ti·a·go (sän′tē ä′gō; E. san′tē ä′gō) capital of Chile, in the C part: pop. 2,566,000 (met. area 3,120,000)

San·to Do·min·go (sän′tō dō min′gō; E. san′tō dō min′gō) capital of the Dominican Republic: pop. 577,000

Saône (sōn) river in E France, flowing south into the Rhone

São Pau·lo (soun pou′loo) city in SE Brazil: pop. 5,902,000

São To·mé and Prín·ci·pe (tō mā′ ənd prin′sə pē′) country off the W coast of Africa, made up of two islands (São Tomé and Príncipe): 372 sq. mi.; pop. 75,000

sap[1] (sap) **n.** [OE. sæp: for IE. base see SAGE[1]] **1.** the juice that circulates through a plant, esp. a woody plant, bearing water, food, etc. **2.** any fluid considered vital to life or health **3.** vigor; energy **4.** [Old Slang] a stupid person: in full, **sap′head′** (-hed′) —**vt. sapped, sap′ping** to drain of sap

sap[2] (sap) **n.** [MFr. sappe, a hoe < It. zappe] a trench for approaching or undermining an enemy position —**vt. sapped, sap′ping 1.** to weaken or wear down by digging away foundations [flood waters sapped the canal wall] **2.** to weaken or wear down in any way; exhaust [a bad cold sapped her energy] —**vi. 1.** to dig saps **2.** to approach a position by saps

sa·pi·ent (sā′pē ənt) **adj.** [< L. sapere, to taste, know: for IE. base see SAGE[1]] full of knowledge; wise —**sa′pi·ence n.**

sap·ling (sap′liŋ) **n. 1.** a young tree **2.** a youth

sap·o·dil·la (sap′ə dil′ə) **n.** [< Sp. < Nahuatl tzapotl] **1.** a tropical American evergreen tree, yielding chicle and having an edible, brown fruit with a yellowish pulp **2.** the fruit

sap·o·na·ceous (sap′ə nā′shəs) **adj.** [< ModL. < L. sapo, soap] soapy or soaplike

sa·pon·i·fy (sə pän′ə fī′) **vt. -fied′, -fy′ing** [< Fr. < L. saponis, genitive of sapo, soap + facere, to make] to turn (a fat) into soap by treating with an alkali —**sa·pon′i·fi·ca′tion n.**

sap·per (sap′ər) **n. 1.** a soldier whose work is digging saps, laying mines, etc. **2.** a person or thing that saps

sap·phire (saf′īr) **n.** [< OFr. < L. < Gr. sappheiros < Heb. sappir < Sans. sanipriya, lit., dear to (the planet) Saturn] **1.** a hard, transparent precious stone of a clear, deep-blue corundum **2.** its color **3.** any of various other varieties of corundum, varying in color, used as a gem —**adj.** deep-blue

Sap·pho (saf′ō) 7th cent. B.C.; Gr. lyric poetess of Lesbos —**Sap′phic** (-ik) **adj.**

Sap·po·ro (sä′pō rō′) chief city on the island of Hokkaido, Japan: pop. 821,000

sap·py (sap′ē) **adj. -pi·er, -pi·est 1.** full of sap; juicy **2.** [Old Slang] foolish; silly; fatuous —**sap′pi·ness n.**

sap·ro- [< Gr. sapros, rotten] a combining form meaning dead, decaying: also, before a vowel, **sapr-**

sa·proph·a·gous (sa prä′fə gəs) **adj.** [SAPRO- + -PHAGOUS] feeding on decaying organic matter

sap·ro·phyte (sap′rə fīt′) **n.** [SAPRO- + -PHYTE] any organism that lives on dead or decaying organic matter, as some fungi —**sap′ro·phyt′ic** (-fit′ik) **adj.**

☆**sap·suck·er** (sap′suk′ər) **n.** any of several small American woodpeckers that often drill holes in maples, apple trees, etc. for the sap

SAPSUCKER (to 9 in. long, including tail)

sap·wood (sap′wood′) **n.** the soft wood through which the sap flows, between the inner bark of a tree and the heartwood

sar·a·band (sar′ə band′) **n.** [< Fr. < Sp., ult. < Per. sarband, kind of dance] **1.** a graceful, stately, slow Spanish dance in triple time **2.** music for this dance

Sar·a·cen (sar′ə s′n) **n.** an Arab or Moslem; esp., a Moslem at the time of the Crusades —**adj.** of the Saracens

Sar·ah (ser′ə, sar′ə) [Heb. śārāh, lit., princess] **1.** a feminine name: dim. Sadie, Sally; var. Sara **2.** Bible the wife of Abraham and mother of Isaac: also **Sa·rai** (ser′ī)

Sa·ra·je·vo (sä′rä′ye vō; E. sar′ə yä′vō) city in C Yugoslavia where an Austrian archduke was assassinated (June 28, 1914) setting off World War I: pop. 175,000

☆**sa·ran** (sə ran′) **n.** [a made-up word] any of various thermoplastic resins used to make transparent wrappings, etc.

Sa·ra·tov (sä rä′tôf) city & port in SC European R.S.F.S.R., on the Volga: pop. 758,000

sar·casm (sär′kaz′m) **n.** [< LL. < Gr. < sarkazein, to tear flesh like dogs < sarx, flesh] **1.** a mocking or sneering remark meant to hurt someone or make him seem foolish; gibe or jeer **2.** the act of making such a remark ["I only explained it five times," she replied in sarcasm] **3.** sarcastic quality

sar·cas·tic (sär kas′tik) **adj. 1.** of, like, or full of sarcasm; sneering **2.** using sarcasm —**sar·cas′ti·cal·ly adv.**
SYN.—**sarcastic** implies a deliberate attempt to hurt by ridicule, mocking, sneers, etc. [a sarcastic reminder that work begins at 9:00 A.M.]; **ironical** or **ironic** is used of a form of sarcasm in which the meaning of what is said is directly opposite to the usual sense ["My, you're early," was his ironical taunt to the latecomer]; **sardonic** implies sneering or mocking bitterness in a person, or, more often, in what he says or how he looks [a sardonic smile]; **caustic** implies a cutting, biting, or stinging wit or sarcasm [a caustic tongue]

sar·co·ma (sär kō′mə) **n., pl. -mas, -ma·ta** (-mə tə) [ModL. < Gr. < sarx, flesh] any of various cancers that begin in connective tissue —**sar·co′ma·to′sis** (-tō′sis) **n.**

sar·coph·a·gus (sär käf′ə gəs) **n., pl. -gi′** (-jī′), **-gus·es** [L. < Gr. < sarx, flesh + phagein, to eat: because the limestone formerly used caused faster disintegration] a stone coffin, esp. one on display, as in a large tomb

sard (särd) **n.** [L. sarda < Gr. sardios, ? lit., stone of SARDIS] a very hard, deep orange-red variety of chalcedony, used in jewelry, etc.

sar·dine (sär dēn′) **n., pl. -dines, -dine′:** see PLURAL, II, D, 1 [< MFr. < L. < sarda, kind of fish, prob. < Gr. Sardō, SARDINIA] any of various small ocean fishes preserved in tightly packed cans for eating; specif., same as PILCHARD

Sar·din·i·a (sär din′ē ə, -din′yə) It. island in the Mediterranean, south of Corsica: c.9,196 sq. mi.: It. name **Sar·de·gna** (sär dā′nyä) —**Sar·din′i·an adj., n.**

Sar·dis (sär′dis) capital of ancient Lydia

sar·don·ic (sär dän′ik) **adj.** [< Fr. < L. < Gr. < sardanios, bitter, scornful] scornfully or bitterly sneering or sarcastic [a sardonic smile] —see SYN. at SARCASTIC —**sar·don′i·cal·ly adv.**

sar·do·nyx (sär dän′iks, sär′də niks) **n.** [L. < Gr. < sardios, sard + onyx, onyx] a variety of onyx made up of layers of white chalcedony and sard, used as a gem

Sar·gas·so Sea (sär gas′ō) part of the N Atlantic, northeast of the West Indies, filled with sargassum

sar·gas·sum (sär gas′əm) **n.** [ModL. < Port. < sarga, kind of grape] any of various floating, brown seaweeds having special branches with berrylike air sacs: also **sar·gas′so** (-ō), **pl. -sos**, **sargasso weed**

Sar·gent (sär′jənt), **John Sing·er** (siŋ′ər) 1856–1925; U.S. painter in Europe

Sar·gon II (sär′gän) ?-705 B.C.; king of Assyria (722–705)

sa·ri (sä′rē) **n.** [< Hindi < Sans.] an outer garment of Hindu women, a long cloth wrapped around the body with one end over the shoulder: also sp. **sa′ree**

Sar·ni·a (sär′nē ə) city & port in SE Ontario, Canada, at the S end of Lake Huron: pop. 55,000

sa·rod, sa·rode (sə rōd′) **n.** [Hindi sarod < Per.] a musical instrument of India, like a lute, with many strings

sa·rong (sə rôŋ′, -räŋ′) **n.** [Malay sārung] a garment of men and women in the Malay Archipelago, the East Indies, etc., consisting of a long cloth, often brightly colored and printed, worn like a skirt

SARI

sar·sa·pa·ril·la (sas′pə ril′ə, särs′-, sär′sə-) **n.** [Sp. zarzaparilla < zarza, bramble + dim. of parra, vine] **1.** a tropical American plant with sweet-smelling roots **2.** its root, dried for use as a flavoring **3.** an extract of this root ☆**4.** a carbonated drink flavored with sarsaparilla

Sar·to (sär′tô), **An·dre·a del** (än dre′ä del) 1486–1531; Florentine painter

sar·to·ri·al (sär tôr′ē əl) *adj.* [< LL. *sartor*, a tailor < pp. of L. *sarcire*, to patch, mend] **1.** of tailors or their work **2.** of men's clothing or dress —**sar·to′ri·al·ly** *adv.*

sar·to·ri·us (sär tôr′ē əs) *n.* [ModL. < LL. *sartor*, a tailor: because tailors traditionally sat cross-legged at work] a long, narrow muscle of the thigh that helps to rotate the leg to the position used when sitting cross-legged

Sar·tre (sár′tr′; *E.* särt), **Jean-Paul** (zhän pôl) 1905–80; Fr. philosopher, playwright, & novelist

sash¹ (sash) *n.* [Ar. *shāsh*, muslin] a broad ribbon or scarf worn over one shoulder or around the waist as a decoration

sash² (sash) *n.* [thought by mistake to be the sing. of earlier *shashes* < Fr. *châssis*, a frame: see CHASSIS] a frame for holding the glass pane of a window or door, esp. a sliding frame —*vt.* to furnish with sashes

☆**sa·shay** (sa shā′) *vi.* [altered < *chassé* (a gliding dance step)] [Colloq.] to move, walk, or go, esp. in a casual way

sash cord a cord attached to either side of a sliding sash, having balancing weights (**sash weights**) for raising or lowering the window easily

sa·shi·mi (sä shē′mē) *n.pl.* [Jap., raw fish] a Japanese appetizer of thin slices of raw fish, usually dipped in a sauce

Sas·katch·e·wan (sas kach′ə wän′, -wən) province of SC Canada: 251,700 sq. mi.; pop. 921,000; cap. Regina: abbrev. **Sask.**

Sas·ka·toon (sas′kə tōōn′) city in C Saskatchewan, Canada: pop. 134,000

sass (sas) *n.* [var. of SAUCE] [Colloq.] back talk; impudent replies —*vt.* [Colloq.] to talk back to in an impudent way

☆**sas·sa·fras** (sas′ə fras′) *n.* [Sp. *sasafras*] **1.** a small eastern N. American tree having leaves with two or three fingerlike lobes and bearing small, bluish fruits **2.** the dried root bark of this tree, used as a flavoring or to brew a kind of tea

sass·y (sas′ē) *adj.* **sass′i·er**, **sass′i·est** [dial. var. of SAUCY] [Colloq.] talking back; impudent; saucy —**sass′i·ly** *adv.* —**sass′i·ness** *n.*

sat (sat) *pt.* & *pp. of* SIT

SAT, S.A.T. Scholastic Aptitude Test

Sat. **1.** Saturday **2.** Saturn

Sa·tan (sāt′n) [OE., ult. < Heb. *ṣāṭān*, enemy < *sāṭan*, to plot against] *Christian Theol.* the chief evil spirit; the Devil

SASSAFRAS (leaves & fruit)

sa·tang (sä täng′) *n., pl.* **-tang′** [Siamese *satāṅ*] *see* MONETARY UNITS, table (Thailand)

sa·tan·ic (sä tan′ik, sə-) *adj.* of or like Satan; devilish; wicked: also **sa·tan′i·cal** —**sa·tan′i·cal·ly** *adv.*

satch·el (sach′əl) *n.* [< OFr. < L. dim. of *saccus*, a sack] a small bag for carrying clothes, books, etc.

sate¹ (sāt) *vt.* **sat′ed**, **sat′ing** [prob. < L. *satiare*, to fill full, SATIATE] **1.** to satisfy (an appetite, desire, etc.) to the full **2.** to supply with so much that it becomes boring or disgusting; surfeit; glut —*see* SYN. *at* SATIATE

sate² (sat, sāt) *archaic pt.* & *pp. of* SIT

sa·teen (sa tēn′, sə-) *n.* [< SATIN] a smooth, glossy cotton cloth, made to look like satin

sat·el·lite (sat′′l īt′) *n.* [Fr. < L. *satelles*, an attendant] **1.** a follower of some important person, esp. one who obeys in an eager or slavish way **2.** *a)* a small planet revolving around a larger one *b)* a man-made object put into orbit around the earth, the moon, or some other heavenly body **3.** a small state that depends on and is controlled by a larger state

sa·tia·ble (sā′shə b′l, sā′shē ə-) *adj.* that can be sated or satiated —**sa′tia·bil′i·ty** *n.* —**sa′tia·bly** *adv.*

sa·ti·ate (sā′shē āt′) *vt.* **-at′ed**, **-at′ing** [< L. pp. of *satiare*, to satisfy < *satis*, enough: for IE. base see SAD] **1.** [Rare] to satisfy fully **2.** to provide with more than enough, so as to make bored or disgusted; glut; surfeit —**sa′ti·a′tion** *n.*

SYN.—**satiate** and **sate** both mean to satisfy completely, but in modern-

day use **satiate** almost always implies, and **sate** often does, a being filled or stuffed so full that all pleasure or desire is lost [*satiated*, or *sated*, with food, success, etc.]; **surfeit** implies a being filled or supplied with so much that it nauseates or disgusts [*surfeited* with pleasure]; **cloy** emphasizes the distaste one feels for something too sweet, rich, etc., of which one has had enough [*cloying*, sentimental music]; **glut** implies an overloading by filling or supplying too much [to *glut* the market]

Sa·tie (sä tē′), **E·rik** (e rēk′) 1866–1925; Fr. composer

sa·ti·e·ty (sə tī′ə tē) *n.* the feeling of having had more than one wants; surfeit

sat·in (sat′′n) *n.* [< MFr. < Sp. < Ar. *zaitūnī*, of *Zaitūn*, former name of a Chinese seaport] a fabric of silk, nylon, rayon, etc. with a smooth, glossy finish on one side —*adj.* of or like satin; smooth and glossy —**sat′in·y** *adj.*

sat·in·wood (sat′′n wood′) *n.* **1.** any of several smooth, hard woods used in fine furniture, etc. **2.** a tree producing such wood, esp. one in the East Indies or one in the West Indies

sat·ire (sa′tīr) *n.* [Fr. < L. *satira*, a medley in poetry, orig. a dish of fruits, prob. < Etruscan] **1.** the use of irony, sarcasm, and humor to criticize or make fun of foolish or immoral actions, customs, etc. of people **2.** *a)* a novel, play, etc. in which this is done *b)* such literary works as a group —*see* SYN. *at* CARICATURE

sa·tir·i·cal (sə tir′i k′l) *adj.* **1.** of, like, or containing satire **2.** fond of using satire Also **sa·tir′ic** —**sa·tir′i·cal·ly** *adv.*

sat·i·rist (sat′ə rist) *n.* **1.** a writer of satires **2.** a person who uses satire

sat·i·rize (-rīz′) *vt.* **-rized′**, **-riz′ing** to attack, make fun of, or criticize with satire —**sat′i·riz′er** *n.*

sat·is·fac·tion (sat′is fak′shən) *n.* **1.** a satisfying or being satisfied **2.** something that satisfies; specif., *a)* anything that brings pleasure or contentment *b)* a paying or settling of something owed [the *satisfaction* of a debt] *c)* anything paid or done to make up for injury or insult —**give satisfaction 1.** to satisfy **2.** to accept a challenge to duel or fight

sat·is·fac·to·ry (-fak′tə rē, -trē) *adj.* good enough to satisfy a need, wish, requirement, etc.; adequate —**sat′is·fac′to·ri·ly** *adv.* —**sat′is·fac′to·ri·ness** *n.*

sat·is·fy (sat′is fī′) *vt.* **-fied′**, **-fy′ing** [< OFr. < L. < *satis*, enough (see SATIATE) + *facere*, to make; DO] **1.** to meet the needs or desires of; please [only first prize will *satisfy* her] **2.** to meet (requirements) **3.** to act in agreement with (rules or obligations) **4.** *a)* to free from doubt; convince [the jury was *satisfied* that he was innocent] *b)* to answer (a doubt, etc.) adequately **5.** *a)* to give what is due to *b)* to pay off (a debt, etc.) **6.** to make up to for an injury or wrong done —*vi.* to be adequate, sufficient, etc. —**sat′is·fi′a·ble** *adj.* —**sat′is·fi′er** *n.*

SYN.—**satisfy** implies the fact of meeting wishes, needs, expectations, etc. fully; **content** implies a filling of needs to the degree that one is not disturbed by a desire for something more [it takes great wealth to *satisfy* him, but she is *contented* with their modest but steady income]

sa·to·ri (sä tôr′ē) *n.* [Jap.] a condition of high self-awareness and spiritual knowledge that is sought in Zen Buddhism

sa·trap (sā′trap, sat′rap) *n.* [< L. < Gr. *satrapēs* < OPer. *xsathrapāvan*, lit., protector of the land] **1.** the governor of a province in ancient Persia **2.** a minor ruler, as of a colony, esp. one who is a tyrant

sa·trap·y (sā′trə pē, sat′rə-) *n., pl.* **-trap·ies** the government, authority, or province of a satrap

sat·u·ra·ble (sach′ə ə b′l) *adj.* that can be saturated —**sat′u·ra·bil′i·ty** *n.*

sat·u·rate (sach′ə rāt′) *vt.* **-rat′ed**, **-rat′ing** [< L. pp. of *saturare*, to fill up < *satur*, full: for IE. base see SAD] **1.** to cause to be thoroughly soaked [the baby's bib was *saturated* with milk] **2.** to cause to be so completely filled or supplied that no more can be taken up [the town was *saturated* with used-car lots] **3.** *Chem. a)* to cause (a substance) to combine with another to the greatest extent possible *b)* to dissolve the maximum amount of (a gas, liquid, or solid) in a solution —*see* SYN. *at* SOAK —**sat′u·ra′tor** *n.*

sat·u·rat·ed (-id) *adj. Chem.* **1.** containing so much dissolved substance that no more will dissolve at a given temperature **2.** designating an organic compound having no double or triple bonds and no free valence

sat·u·ra·tion (sach′ə rā′shən) *n.* **1.** a saturating or being saturated **2.** the degree to which a color is free from mixture with white; intensity of hue

saturation point 1. the point at which the maximum amount of something has been absorbed 2. the limit beyond which something cannot be continued, endured, etc.

Sat·ur·day (sat′ər dē, -dā′) *n.* [OE. *Sæterdæg*, Saturn's day] the seventh and last day of the week

Sat·ur·days (-dēz, -dāz′) *adv.* on or during every Saturday [*Saturdays* he mows the lawn]

Sat·urn (sat′ərn) 1. the Roman god of agriculture, who is identified with the Greek god Cronus 2. a planet in the solar system, sixth in distance from the sun: diameter, c.72,000 mi.: it has three rings made up of very many small particles that revolve around its equator —**Sa·tur·ni·an** (sə tur′nē ən) *adj.*

Sat·ur·na·li·a (sat′ər nā′lē ə, -nāl′yə) *n.pl.* 1. the ancient Roman festival of Saturn, held about December 17, with feasting and merrymaking 2. [s-] [*often with sing. v. & with a pl. -li·as*] any period of uncontrolled merrymaking; orgy —**Sat′ur·na′li·an** *adj.*

sat·ur·nine (sat′ər nīn′) *adj.* [< SATURN: in astrology, people born under its sign are supposed to be gloomy] quiet in a gloomy or solemn way —**sat′ur·nine′ly** *adv.*

sat·yr (sāt′ər, sat′-) *n.* [< L. < Gr. *satyros*] 1. *Gr. Myth.* any of a number of minor woodland gods serving Bacchus and pictured as a lustful man having pointed ears, short horns, and the legs of a goat 2. a lustful man 3. a butterfly with gray or brown wings often marked with eyelike spots

sau (sou) *n.* [Vietnamese] *see* MONETARY UNITS, table (North Vietnam)

sauce (sôs) *n.* [< OFr. < L. *salsa*, salted food, ult. < *sal*, salt: see SALT] 1. *a*) a liquid or soft dressing served with food as a relish *b*) a flavored syrup put on ice cream ☆2. stewed or preserved fruit, often mashed [*applesauce*] 3. something that adds interest or excitement 4. [Dial.] garden vegetables eaten as a side dish 5. [Colloq.] impudence ☆6. [Slang] alcoholic liquor —*vt.* **sauced, sauc′ing** 1. to flavor with a sauce 2. to give flavor or interest to 3. [Colloq.] to be impudent or saucy to

sauce·pan (sôs′pan′) *n.* a small pot with a projecting handle, used for cooking

sau·cer (sô′sər) *n.* [MFr. *saussier* < *sause*, SAUCE] 1. a small, round, shallow dish, esp. one to hold a cup 2. anything round and shallow like a saucer

sau·cy (sô′sē) *adj.* **-ci·er, -ci·est** [SAUC(E) + -Y²] 1. rude; impudent 2. lively and bold; pert [a *saucy* smile] —see SYN. at IMPERTINENT —**sau′ci·ly** *adv.* —**sau′ci·ness** *n.*

Sa·u·di Arabia (sä ōō′dē, sou′dē) kingdom occupying most of Arabia: c. 873,000 sq. mi.; pop. 6,036,000; cap. Riyadh

☆**sau·er·bra·ten** (sour′brät′'n, zou′ər-) *n.* [G. < *sauer*, sour + *braten*, a roast] a dish made of beef marinated in vinegar with onion, spices, etc. before cooking

☆**sau·er·kraut** (sour′krout′) *n.* [G. *sauer*, sour + *kraut*, cabbage] chopped cabbage allowed to ferment in its own juice, to which salt has been added

☆**sau·ger** (sô′gər) *n.* [< ?] a small American pikeperch

Saul (sôl) [< LL. < Gr. < Heb. *shā′ūl*, lit., asked (of God)] 1. a masculine name 2. *Bible a*) the first king of Israel *b*) orig. name of the Apostle PAUL

Sault Ste. Ma·rie (sōō′ sānt′ mə rē′) [< Fr. *Sault de Sainte Marie*, lit., falls of St. Mary] 1. city in N Mich., on a river (*St. Marys River*) flowing from Lake Superior into Lake Huron: pop. 15,000 2. city opposite it, in Ontario, Canada: pop. 75,000 Also **Sault Sainte Marie** See also Soo

sau·na (sou′nə, sô′-) *n.* [Finn.] 1. a kind of Finnish bath, in which the body is exposed to very hot, relatively dry air, and the skin is beaten lightly with birch or cedar branches 2. the room or other enclosure for such a bath

saun·ter (sôn′tər) *vi.* [< ?] to walk about idly; stroll —*n.* 1. a leisurely and aimless walk 2. a slow, leisurely way of walking —**saun′ter·er** *n.*

sau·ri·an (sôr′ē ən) *n.* [< Gr. *sauros*, a lizard] any of those reptiles that are lizards —*adj.* of or like lizards

-sau·rus (sôr′əs) [see prec.] *a combining form meaning* lizard

sau·sage (sô′sij) *n.* [< ONormFr. < VL. < L. *salsus:* see SAUCE] pork or other meat, chopped fine, highly seasoned, and either stuffed into a tube made of thin skin or made into patties for cooking

sau·té (sō tā′, sô-) *adj.* [Fr., pp. of *sauter*, to leap] fried quickly in a little fat —*vt.* **-téed′, -té′ing** to fry quickly in a pan with a little fat —*n.* a sautéed food

sau·terne (sō turn′, sô-) *n.* [< *Sauternes*, town in France] a white, usually sweet table wine

Sa·va (sä′vä) river in N Yugoslavia, flowing from the Alps eastward into the Danube: c. 450 mi.

sav·age (sav′ij) *adj.* [< OFr. < VL. < L. *silvaticus*, wild < *silva*, a wood] 1. wild; uncultivated [a *savage* jungle] 2. fierce; untamed [a *savage* tiger] 3. in an early stage of civilization; primitive [a *savage* tribe] 4. cruel; pitiless [*savage* warfare] —*n.* 1. a member of a primitive society or savage tribe 2. a fierce, brutal person 3. a crude person without fine manners —*vt.* **-aged, -ag·ing** to attack violently —see SYN. at BARBARIAN —**sav′age·ly** *adv.* —**sav′age·ness** *n.*

sav·age·ry (-rē) *n., pl.* **-ries** 1. the condition of being savage, wild, primitive, etc. 2. savage act or behavior

sa·van·na, sa·van·nah (sə van′ə) *n.* [< Sp. < *zavana* < a S. American native name] a treeless plain or a grassland with scattered trees, esp. in or near the tropics

Sa·van·nah (sə van′ə) [< the native name of the Shawnees] 1. river forming the border between Ga. & S.C., flowing southeast into the Atlantic: 314 mi. 2. seaport in SE Ga.: pop. 118,000

sa·vant (sə vänt′, sav′ənt) *n.* [Fr., orig. prp. of *savoir* < L. *sapere*, to know: see SAGE¹] a learned person; scholar

save¹ (sāv) *vt.* **saved, sav′ing** [< OFr. *salver* < L. < *salvus*, SAFE] 1. to rescue or keep from harm or danger [to *save* a child from drowning] 2. to keep for future use (often with *up*) [she *saved* up her money for a vacation] 3. to keep from being lost or wasted [to *save* a game; to *save* time] 4. to prevent or make less [to *save* wear and tear] 5. to treat carefully in order to keep from being damaged, lessen wear, etc. [*save* your dress by wearing this apron] 6. *Theol.* to free from sin and punishment —*vi.* 1. to avoid expense, loss, waste, etc. [she *saves* on food by buying less meat] 2. to keep something or someone from danger, harm, etc. 3. to put aside money or goods for later use —*n. Sports* an action that keeps an opponent from scoring or winning —**sav′a·ble, save′a·ble** *adj.* —**sav′er** *n.*

save² (sāv) *prep.* [< OFr. *sauf*, lit., SAFE (that is, not involved)] except; but [I've asked everyone *save* you two] —*conj.* 1. except; but 2. [Archaic] unless

sav·in, sav·ine (sav′in) *n.* [< OE. & OFr. < L. (*herba*) *Sabina*, lit., Sabine (herb)] a low, spreading juniper of eastern N. America and Europe whose leaves and tops produce an oil (**savin oil**) used in making perfumes

sav·ing¹ (sā′viŋ) *adj.* that saves; specif., *a*) rescuing *b*) avoiding waste; economical [a time-*saving* device] *c*) containing an exception [a *saving* clause] *d*) making up for something; redeeming [a *saving* grace] —*n.* 1. the act of one that saves 2. any reduction in expense, time, etc. [a *saving* of 10%] 3. *a*) anything saved *b*) [*pl.*] sums of money saved [one's life *savings*]

sav·ing² (sā′viŋ) *prep.* [Now Rare] 1. with due respect for [*saving* your presence] 2. except; save —*conj.* [Now Rare] save

savings account an account in a bank or savings association, to which a person deposits savings that draw interest

☆**savings and loan association** an association of persons who deposit savings that are used for making real-estate loans and so earn interest for the depositors

sav·ior, sav·iour (sāv′yər) *n.* [< OFr. < LL. *salvator* < *salvare*, to SAVE¹] a person who saves —**the Saviour** (or **Savior**) Jesus Christ

sa·voir-faire (sav′wär fer′) *n.* [Fr., to know (how) to do] knowledge of the right thing to do or say, and of when and how to do or say it; poise and tact, esp. in a social situation

Sa·vo·na·ro·la (sä′vō nä rō′lä; E. sav′ə nə rō′lə), **Gi·ro·la·mo** (jē rô′lä mô′) 1452–98; It. monk & religious reformer, who was burned at the stake for heresy

sa·vor (sā′vər) *n.* [< OFr. < L. *sapor:* for IE. base see SAGE¹] 1. the taste or smell of something; flavor [a dressing with a *savor* of garlic] 2. characteristic quality [a musical piece with the *savor* of jazz] 3. power to excite interest, enjoyment, etc. [golf has lost all its *savor* for him] —*vi.* 1. to have the particular taste, smell, or quality; smack (*of*) [a drink that *savors* of nutmeg] 2. to show traces or signs (*of*) [his action *savors* of rudeness] —*vt.* 1. to season or flavor 2. to taste or smell, esp. with relish 3. to dwell on with delight; relish [he *savored* his success as an actor] Also, Brit. sp., **savour** —**sa′vor·er** *n.* —**sa′vor·less** *adj.* —**sa′vor·ous** *adj.*

sa·vor·y¹ (sā′vər ē) *adj.* **-vor·i·er, -vor·i·est** [< OFr. pp. of *savourer*, to taste < *savour*, SAVOR] 1. pleasing to the taste or smell [a *savory* stew] 2. morally right or respectable [not a very *savory* character] 3. salty or sharp; not sweet [a *savory* relish] —*n., pl.* **-vor·ies** in England, a small, highly seasoned portion of food served at the end of a meal or as an appetizer Also, Brit. sp., **savoury** —**sa′vor·i·ness** *n.*

sa·vor·y[2] (sā′vər ē) *n.* [< OFr. *savoreie*, altered (prob. after *savour*) < L. *satureia*, savory] a sweet-smelling herb of the mint family, used in cooking

Sa·voy (sə voi′) region in SE France, on the borders of Italy & Switzerland: formerly, a duchy

sa·voy (sə voi′) *n.* [Fr., after prec.] a kind of cabbage with crinkled leaves and a solid head

Sa·voy·ard (sə voi′ərd, sav′oi yärd′) *n.* 1. a native or inhabitant of Savoy 2. [< the *Savoy*, London theater] an actor, producer, or admirer of Gilbert and Sullivan operas

☆**sav·vy** (sav′ē) *vi.* **-vied, -vy·ing** [altered < Sp. *sabe* (*usted*), do (you) know? < *saber*, to know < L. *sapere*: see SAGE[1]] [Slang] to understand; get the idea —*n.* [Slang] 1. shrewd understanding 2. skill or know-how —*adj.* [Slang] shrewd or wise

saw[1] (sô) *n.* [OE. *sagu* < IE. base *sek-*, to cut] 1. a cutting tool having a thin, metal blade or disk with sharp teeth along the edge 2. a machine that operates a saw —*vt.* **sawed, sawed** or chiefly Brit. **sawn, saw′ing** 1. to cut or shape with a saw 2. *a*) to make sawlike cutting motions through (the air, etc.) *b*) to produce with such motions [to *saw* a tune on a fiddle] —*vi.* 1. to cut with a saw or as a saw does [he *sawed* through the pipe] 2. to be cut with a saw [wood that *saws* easily] 3. to make sawlike cutting motions — ☆**saw wood** [Slang] to snore or sleep —**saw′er** *n.*

SAWS
(A, keyhole; B, hacksaw; C, handsaw; D, crosscut)

saw[2] (sô) *n.* [OE. *sagu*: for IE. base see SAY] an old saying; maxim —see SYN. at SAYING

saw[3] (sô) *pt. of* SEE[1]

saw·bones (sô′bōnz′) *n.* [Old Slang] a surgeon

☆**saw·buck** (-buk′) *n.* 1. [Du. *zaagbok*] a sawhorse, esp. one with the legs sticking up above the crossbar 2. [from resemblance of the crossed legs of a sawbuck to an X (Roman numeral for 10)] [Slang] a ten-dollar bill

saw·dust (-dust′) *n.* tiny bits of wood formed in sawing

sawed-off (sôd′ôf′) *adj.* ☆1. having the barrel cut off short [a *sawed-off* shotgun] ☆2. [Colloq.] short in height

saw·fish (sô′fish′) *n., pl.* **-fish′, -fish′es:** see FISH any of a group of tropical giant rays having a long, flat, sawlike snout edged with teeth on both sides

saw·fly (-flī′) *n., pl.* **-flies′** any of a group of four-winged insects having (in the female) a pair of sawlike organs: with these she cuts into plants and then deposits her eggs in the cuts

saw·horse (-hôrs′) *n.* a rack on which wood is placed while being sawed

saw·mill (-mil′) *n.* 1. a place where logs are sawed into boards 2. a large sawing machine

sawn (sôn) *chiefly Brit. pp. of* SAW[1]

☆**saw palmetto** a dwarf palm with fan-shaped leaves and spiny leafstalks, that grows in the southeastern U.S.

saw-toothed (sô′tootht′) *adj.* having notches like the teeth of a saw; serrate: also **saw′tooth′**

☆**saw-whet owl** (sô′hwet′, -wet′) [echoic] a very small N. American owl with a harsh cry and brown-and-white feathers: see illustration at OWL

saw·yer (sô′yər) *n.* 1. a person whose work is sawing wood, as into planks and boards ☆2. a brown-and-gray beetle whose larvae burrow into wood

☆**sax** (saks) *n.* [Colloq.] a saxophone

sax·horn (saks′hôrn′) *n.* [after A. J. *Sax* (1814–1894), Belgian inventor] any of a group of brass-wind instruments with valves, that have a full, even tone and a wide range

sax·ic·o·lous (sak sik′ə ləs) *adj.* [< L. *saxum*, a rock + *colere*, to dwell + -OUS] living or growing on or among rocks: also **sax·ic′o·line′** (-līn′, -lin)

sax·i·frage (sak′sə frij) *n.* [MFr. < L. < *saxum*, a rock + base of *frangere*, to break: the plant grows in rock crevices] any of a group of plants with white, yellow, purple, or pinkish small flowers, and leaves growing in clusters often at the base of the plant

Sax·on (sak′s'n) *n.* 1. a member of an ancient Germanic people of northern Germany: some Saxons conquered parts of England in the 5th & 6th cent. A.D. 2. same as ANGLO-SAXON (*n.* 1 & 4) 3. a native or inhabitant of modern Saxony 4. any of the Low German dialects of the Saxon peoples —*adj.* 1. of the Saxons, their language, etc. 2. of Saxony

Sax·on·y (sak′sə nē) 1. region in S East Germany: formerly, a kingdom 2. former duchy at the base of Jutland: now part of a West German state called *Lower Saxony*

sax·o·phone (sak′sə fōn′) *n.* [Fr., after A. J. *Sax* (see SAXHORN) & -PHONE] a wind instrument with a single-reed mouthpiece, keys for the fingers, and a metal body, usually curved —**sax′o·phon′ist** *n.*

SAXOPHONE

say (sā) *vt.* **said, say′ing** [OE. *secgan* < IE. base *sekw-*, to note, say] 1. to utter (a word or words); speak ["Hello," he *said*] 2. to express in words; state; declare [the newspaper *says* it will rain tomorrow] 3. to state positively or as an opinion [who can *say* what will be?] 4. to indicate or show [the clock *says* ten] 5. to recite; repeat [to *say* one's prayers] 6. to estimate or assume [he is, I'd *say*, forty] 7. to declare without proof; report [they *say* he's guilty] 8. to communicate (an idea, feeling, etc.) [the painting *says* nothing to me] —*vi.* to make a statement; speak; express an opinion —*n.* 1. a chance to speak [everyone has now had his *say*] 2. the power to decide: often with *the* [who has the final *say* about that?] —*adv.* 1. for example [any fish, *say* perch] 2. about; nearly [costing, *say*, $5] —*interj.* an exclamation expressing surprise, admiration, etc. —**go without saying** to be so clear as to need no explanation —**that is to say** in other words; that means —**to say the least** to say less strongly than the truth allows; understate —**say′er** *n.*

say·ing (sā′iŋ) *n.* something said; statement; esp., an adage, proverb, or maxim

SYN.—**saying** is the simple, direct term for any short statement that is considered to express some wisdom or truth; a **saw** is an old, homely saying that has become stale from being repeated often [the preacher filled his sermon with wise *saws*]; a **maxim** is a saying that states a rule of conduct taken from practical experience (Example: "Waste not, want not"); an **adage** is a saying that has been popularly accepted over a long period of time (Example: "Where there's smoke, there's fire"); a **proverb** is a wise saying stated in a simple, practical way (Example: "A penny saved is a penny earned"); a **motto** is a saying accepted as a principle to guide one's behavior (Example: "Honesty is the best policy"); an **aphorism** is a short saying that tells a general truth and that shows deep thought rather than wit (Example: "He is a fool that cannot hide his wisdom"); an **epigram** is a short, witty statement that often makes its point by using opposite ideas (Example: "The only way to get rid of a temptation is to yield to it")

‡**sa·yo·na·ra** (sä′yō nä′rä) *n., interj.* [< Jap.] farewell

says (sez) *third person singular in the present tense of* SAY

say-so (sā′sō′) *n.* [Colloq.] 1. (one's) word, opinion, assurance, etc. 2. the power or right to decide; authority

Sb [L. *stibium*] *Chem.* antimony

Sc *Chem.* scandium

SC, S.C. South Carolina

Sc. 1. Scotch 2. Scots 3. Scottish

sc. 1. scene 2. science 3. scilicet

s.c. *Printing* small capitals

scab (skab) *n.* [ON. *skabb*: for IE. base see SHAPE] 1. a crust that forms over a sore or wound as it is healing 2. a mangy skin disease, esp. of sheep 3. a plant disease causing rough, scablike spots 4. *a*) [Old Slang] a scoundrel ☆*b*) a worker who refuses to join a union *c*) a worker who refuses to strike, or who takes the place of a striking worker —*vi.* **scabbed, scab′bing** 1. to become covered with a scab ☆2. to work or act as a scab

fat, āpe, cär; ten, ēven; is, bīte; gō, hôrn, tool, look; oil, out; up, fur; get; joy; yet; chin; she; thin, then; zh, leisure; ŋ, ring; ə for *a* in *ago*, *e* in *agent*, *i* in *sanity*, *o* in *comply*, *u* in *focus*; ′ as in *able* (ā′b'l); Fr. bal; ë, Fr. coeur; ö, Fr. feu; Fr. mon; ô, Fr. coq; ü, Fr. duc; r, Fr. cri; H, G. ich; kh, G. doch; ‡ foreign; ☆ Americanism; < derived from. See inside front cover.

scab·bard (skab′ərd) *n.* [< Anglo-Fr. *escaubers,* scabbards < ? OHG. *scar,* sword + *bergan,* to hide] a sheath or case to hold the blade of a sword, dagger, etc. —*vt.* to sheathe

scab·by (skab′ē) *adj.* **-bi·er, -bi·est** 1. covered with or consisting of scabs 2. diseased with scab [a *scabby* sheep] 3. low; base; mean —**scab′bi·ly** *adv.* —**scab′bi·ness** *n.*

sca·bies (skā′bēz, -bē ēz) *n.* [L., itch < *scabere,* to scratch] a contagious skin disease caused by mites that burrow under the skin to deposit eggs, causing much itching

sca·bi·o·sa (skā′bē ō′sə) *n.* [ModL., genus name < ML. < L. *scabies* (see SCABIES): it was once considered a remedy for scabies] any of various related plants having showy flowers in flattened or dome-shaped heads: also **sca′bi·ous** (-əs)

scab·rous (skab′rəs, skā′brəs) *adj.* [< LL. < L. *scabere,* to scratch] 1. rough, like a file; scaly, scabby, etc. 2. full of difficulties 3. indecent, improper, shocking, etc. —**scab′rous·ly** *adv.* —**scab′rous·ness** *n.*

scad[1] (skad) *n., pl.* **scad, scads:** see PLURAL, II, D, 2 [related to SHAD] any of several saltwater food fishes

scad[2] (skad) *n.* [< ?] [*usually pl.*] ☆[Colloq.] a very large number or amount [*scads* of money]

scaf·fold (skaf′'ld, -ōld) *n.* [OFr. *escafalt:* prob. related to CATAFALQUE] 1. a temporary framework for holding workmen and materials during the erecting, repairing, or painting of a building, etc. 2. a raised platform on which criminals are executed, as by hanging 3. any raised framework —*vt.* to furnish or support with a scaffold

scaf·fold·ing (-'l diŋ) *n.* 1. the materials that form a scaffold 2. a scaffold or scaffolds

☆**scag** (skag) *n.* [< ?] [Slang] heroin

sca·lar (skā′lər) *adj.* 1. in, on, or of a scale 2. *Math.* describing or of a quantity that can be measured but has no direction in space, as volume or temperature —*n.* a scalar quantity

☆**sca·la·re** (skə ler′ē, -lär′-) *n.* [ModL. < L., neut. of *scalaris,* ladderlike] a freshwater fish of S. America, with a flattened body and transparent fins, often kept in aquariums

☆**scal·a·wag** (skal′ə wag′) *n.* [< ?] 1. a person full of tricks; rascal 2. a white Southern Republican during the Reconstruction: a term used to show contempt Also sp. **scallawag**

scald[1] (skôld) *vt.* [< ONormFr. < OFr. < LL. *excaldare* < L. *ex-,* very + *calidus,* hot: for IE. base see CALDRON] 1. to burn with hot liquid or steam 2. to heat almost to the boiling point [to *scald* milk for a custard] 3. to use boiling liquid on, as in sterilizing, etc. —*vi.* to be or become scalded —*n.* 1. a burn caused by scalding 2. the act or an instance of scalding 3. any of various plant diseases in which there is a whitening or browning of tissues

scald[2] (skôld, skäld) *n. var. of* SKALD —**scald′ic** *adj.*

scale[1] (skāl) *n.* [< LL. *scala* < L., a ladder] 1. orig., a ladder or flight of stairs 2. *a)* a series of marks along a line, as at regular intervals, used in measuring or registering something [the *scale* of a thermometer] *b)* any instrument or ruler so marked 3. *a)* the proportion that a map, model, etc. bears to the thing that it represents [a *scale* of one inch to a mile] *b)* a line marked off on a map to show this proportion 4. a system of classifying in a series of steps or degrees according to size, amount, rank, etc. [a wage *scale*] 5. *Math.* a number system having a specified base [the binary *scale*] 6. *Music* a series of tones, esp. an octave, arranged in order from highest to lowest or from lowest to highest, with fixed intervals between the notes —*vt.* **scaled, scal′ing** 1. to climb up or over [to *scale* a wall] 2. to make or set according to a scale [the pay is *scaled* according to skill] 3. to measure as by a scale —**on a large** (or **small**) **scale** to a relatively large (or small) degree or extent —☆**scale down** (or **up**) to reduce (or increase) according to a ratio —**scal′er** *n.*

scale[2] (skāl) *n.* [< OFr. *escale,* husk & *escaille,* shell: both < Gmc.: for IE. base see CUTLASS] 1. any of the thin, flat, overlapping, hard plates forming the outer covering of many fishes and reptiles 2. *same as* SCALE INSECT 3. any thin layer or piece, as of dry skin 4. a flaky film of oxide that forms on heated or rusted metals 5. a coating that forms on the inside of boilers, kettles, etc. in which water is heated 6. any small, scalelike leaf or bract, esp. one covering the bud of a seed plant

—*vt.* **scaled, scal′ing** 1. to strip or scrape scales from [to *scale* a fish] 2. to remove in thin layers; pare down 3. to throw (a thin, flat object) so that its edge cuts the air or so that it skips across water —*vi.* 1. to flake or peel off in scales 2. to become covered with scale or scales —**scale′less** *adj.*

scale[3] (skāl) *n.* [ON. *skāl,* bowl] 1. either of the shallow dishes or pans of a balance 2. [*often pl.*] a balance or other device for weighing things —*vt.* **scaled, scal′ing** 1. to weigh in scales 2. to have a weight of [she *scales* 110 pounds]: in this sense, sometimes thought of as a *vi.* —**the Scales** *same as* LIBRA —**turn the scales** to determine; decide

scale insect any of a large group of small insects that are harmful to plants: the females secrete a round, wax scale under which they live and lay their eggs

sca·lene (skā lēn′, skā′lēn) *adj.* [< LL. < Gr. *skalēnos,* uneven] *Geom.* 1. having unequal sides and angles: said of a triangle 2. having the axis not perpendicular to the base: said of a cone, etc.

scal·lion (skal′yən) *n.* [< ONormFr. *escalogne,* ult. < L. (*caepa*) *Ascalonia,* (onion of) Ascalon (in Philistia)] any of three varieties of onion; specif., *a)* the shallot *b)* the leek *c)* a green onion with a small, underdeveloped bulb

scal·lop (skäl′əp, skal′-) *n.* [OFr. *escalope* < *escale:* see SCALE[2]] 1. a kind of mollusk with two deeply grooved, curved shells: it swims by means of a large muscle that rapidly snaps its shells together 2. this muscle, used as food 3. a single shell of such a mollusk, or a dish shaped like such a shell, specif. one in which seafood is baked and served 4. any of a series of curves, projections, etc. forming a decoration on an edge of cloth, lace, etc. —*vt.* 1. to cut the edge or border of in scallops 2. to bake with a milk sauce and bread crumbs; escallop —*vi.* to gather scallops —**scal′lop·er** *n.*

SCALLOP (sense 1)

☆**scal·ly·wag** (skal′ē wag′) *n. same as* SCALAWAG

scal·op·pi·ne (skal′ə pē′nē, skäl′-) *n.* [< It. < dim. of *scaloppo,* thin slice] thin slices of meat, esp. veal, sautéed slowly with herbs and, usually, wine: also sp. **scal′lo·pi′ni, scal′lop·pe′ni**

scalp (skalp) *n.* [< Scand.: for IE. base see CUTLASS] 1. the skin on the top and back of the head, usually covered with hair 2. a part of this, cut or torn from the head of an enemy for a trophy, as orig. by a few N. American Indian tribes: frontiersmen later spread the practice among western tribes 3. any symbol of victory, strength, etc. —☆*vt.* 1. to cut or tear the scalp from 2. *a)* to cheat or rob *b)* to defeat decisively 3. [Colloq.] to buy and sell in order to make small, quick profits 4. [Colloq.] to buy (theater tickets, etc.) and sell later at higher than regular prices —☆*vi.* [Colloq.] to scalp tickets, etc. —**scalp′er** *n.*

scal·pel (skal′pəl) *n.* [< L. dim. of *scalprum,* a knife < *scalpere,* to cut] a small, light, straight knife with a very sharp blade, used esp. by surgeons

☆**scalp lock** formerly, a tuft of hair left on the shaved head by certain N. American Indian warriors

scal·y (skā′lē) *adj.* **scal′i·er, scal′i·est** having, covered with, or resembling scales —**scal′i·ness** *n.*

scamp[1] (skamp) *n.* [< obs. *scamp,* to roam < MFr. *escamper,* to flee, ult. < L. *ex-,* out + *campus,* battlefield: see CAMPUS] a person who often gets into mischief or trouble; rogue; rascal —**scamp′ish** *adj.*

scamp[2] (skamp) *vt.* [akin to or < ON. *skammr,* short] to do in a careless, hurried way —**scamp′er** *n.*

scam·per (skam′pər) *vi.* [prob. < obs. *scamp:* see SCAMP[1]] to run or go hurriedly or quickly [squirrels *scampering* through the trees] —*n.* the act of scampering —**scam′per·er** *n.*

scam·pi (skam′pē) *n., pl.* **-pi, -pies** [It., pl. of *scampo*] a large kind of prawn or shrimp, valued as food

scan (skan) *vt.* **scanned, scan′ning** [< L. *scandere,* to climb] 1. to analyze the meter of (verse) by counting accents and syllables and marking off the feet 2. to look at closely or in a broad, searching way; scrutinize [to *scan* the horizon] ☆3. to glance at quickly [to *scan* the headlines] 4. in computers, to examine (data) in sequence, esp. with an electronic device 5. *Radar* to pass a series of radar beams over (an area) 6. *TV* to pass a beam of light or electrons across (a surface) in transmitting or reproducing an image —*vi.* 1. to scan verse 2. to have a regular poetic meter [this line doesn't *scan*] —*n.* a scanning

Scan., Scand. 1. Scandinavia 2. Scandinavian

scan·dal (skan′d'l) *n.* [< OFr. < LL. *scandalum,* cause for stumbling < Gr. *skandalon,* a snare] 1. any act, person, or thing that offends or shocks the moral feelings of people and leads to disgrace [the bribes became a national *scandal*] **2.** a feeling of shame, outrage, etc. caused by such an act, person, etc. [behavior that caused *scandal* in the neighborhood] **3.** disgrace or dishonor [he brought *scandal* upon his office] **4.** talk that harms a reputation; wicked gossip —see SYN. at DISGRACE

scan·dal·ize (skan'də līz') *vt.* **-ized', -iz'ing** to shock the feelings of by immoral conduct; outrage [the lies he told *scandalized* his listeners] —**scan'dal·iz'er** *n.*

scan·dal·mon·ger (skan'd'l muŋ'gər, -mäŋ'-) *n.* a person who gossips in a harmful way and spreads scandal

scan·dal·ous (-əs) *adj.* **1.** causing scandal; shocking to people's moral feelings; shameful [the *scandalous* acts of the administration] **2.** consisting of or spreading slander; libelous [*scandalous* reports] —**scan'dal·ous·ly** *adv.*

Scan·di·na·vi·a (skan'də nā'vē ə) **1.** region in N Europe, including Norway, Sweden, & Denmark and, sometimes, Iceland **2.** peninsula in N Europe, consisting of Norway & Sweden: in full, **Scandinavian Peninsula**

Scan·di·na·vi·an (-ən) *adj.* of Scandinavia, its people, their languages, etc. —*n.* **1.** any of the people of Scandinavia **2.** the Germanic languages spoken by them; North Germanic

scan·di·um (skan'dē əm) *n.* [ModL. < ML. *Scandia*, Scandinavia: because it was first found there] a rare metallic chemical element: symbol, Sc; at. wt., 44.956; at. no., 21

scan·ner (skan'ər) *n.* one that scans; esp., any device used in computers, television, etc. for scanning

scan·sion (skan'shən) *n.* the act of scanning verse

scant (skant) *adj.* [< ON. < *skammr*, short] **1.** too little in size or amount; not enough; meager [a *scant* water supply] **2.** not quite up to full measure [the recipe calls for a *scant* teaspoon of salt] —*vt.* **1.** to limit in size or amount; stint **2.** to fail to give full measure of **3.** to treat in a careless or hasty way —*adv.* [Dial.] scarcely; barely —see SYN. at MEAGER —**scant'ly** *adv.* — **scant'ness** *n.*

scant·ling (skant'liŋ) *n.* [< ONormFr. < OFr. *eschandillon*, a measure] a small beam or timber; esp., a small upright timber, as in the frame of a structure

scant·y (skan'tē) *adj.* **scant'i·er, scant'i·est** [SCANT + -Y²] barely enough or not enough; meager or insufficient [a *scanty* crop] —see SYN. at MEAGER —**scant'i·ly** *adv.* —**scant'i·ness** *n.*

scape¹ (skāp) *n.* [L. *scapus*, shaft] **1.** a leafless flower stalk growing directly from the root, as that of the narcissus or dandelion **2.** something like a stalk, as the shaft of a feather or of an insect's antenna **3.** the shaft of a column

scape² (skāp) *n., vt., vi.* **scaped, scap'ing** [Archaic] same as ESCAPE: also **'scape**

-scape (skāp) [< (LAND)SCAPE] *a combining form meaning* a view or scene, or a drawing, painting, etc. of it [*cityscape*]

scape·goat (skāp'gōt') *n.* [SCAPE² + GOAT] **1.** a goat over which the high priest of the ancient Jews confessed the sins of the people, after which it was allowed to escape: Lev. 16:7–26 **2.** a person, group, or thing that is blamed for the mistakes or crimes of others

scape·grace (-grās') *n.* [SCAPE² + GRACE] a person without strong principles; rascal or rogue

scaph·o·pod (skaf'ə päd') *n.* [< Gr. *skaphos*, a ship, hollow shell + -POD] any of a group of mollusks that live in muddy or sandy sea bottoms and have slightly curved, tube-shaped shells open at both ends

scap·u·la (skap'yōō lə) *n., pl.* **-lae'** (-lē'), **-las** [ModL. < L., orig. prob. shovel: from the use of the bone as a spade] either of two flat bones in the back of the shoulder; shoulder blade

scap·u·lar (skap'yōō lər) *adj.* of the shoulder or scapula —*n.* **1.** a long, sleeveless outer garment falling from the shoulders, worn by monks **2.** two small pieces of cloth joined by strings, worn on the chest and back, under the clothes, by some Roman Catholics as a token of religious devotion **3.** any of the feathers growing in the region of a bird's shoulders

scar (skär) *n.* [< MFr. < LL. < Gr. *eschara*, orig., fireplace] **1.** a mark left

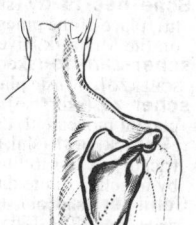

SCAPULA

after a wound, burn, ulcer, etc. has healed **2.** any mark like this, as on a plant where a leaf was attached **3.** the effects left on the mind or emotions as a result of suffering —*vt., vi.* **scarred, scar'ring** to mark with or form a scar

scar·ab (skar'əb) *n.* [< Fr. < L. *scarabaeus*] **1.** any of a large group of beetles, mostly with a thick body, often brilliantly colored **2.** *a)* the black, winged dung beetle, which was sacred to the ancient Egyptians *b)* an image of this beetle, cut from a stone or gem and formerly worn as a charm

scar·a·bae·id (skar'ə bē'id) *n.* [< ModL. family name] same as SCARAB (sense 1) —*adj.* of the scarab beetles

scarce (skers) *adj.* [ONormFr. *escars*, ult. < L. *excerpere*, to select: for IE. base see CARNAGE] **1.** not common; rarely seen [the black bear is *scarce* in settled areas] **2.** not plentiful; hard to get [gasoline was *scarce* in wartime] —*adv.* now rare var. of SCARCELY [I could *scarce* believe my eyes] —see SYN. at RARE¹ — **make oneself scarce** [Colloq.] to go or stay away —**scarce'·ness** *n.*

scarce·ly (skers'lē) *adv.* **1.** hardly; barely; only just [I can *scarcely* hear you] **2.** probably not or certainly not [you can *scarcely* expect us to believe that]

scar·ci·ty (skers'sə tē) *n., pl.* **-ties 1.** the condition of being scarce; inadequate supply **2.** rarity; uncommonness

scare (sker) *vt.* **scared, scar'ing** [ON. *skirra*, to scare < *skjarr*, timid] to fill with fear or terror; esp., to frighten suddenly —*vi.* to become frightened, esp. suddenly [he *scares* easily] —*n.* **1.** a sudden fear or panic **2.** a state of widespread fear or panic [a war *scare*] —see SYN. at AFRAID —☆ **scare up** [Colloq.] to produce or gather quickly [try to *scare up* some help]

scare·crow (sker'krō') *n.* **1.** a figure of a man made with sticks, old clothes, etc., put in a field to scare birds away from crops **2.** anything that frightens one but is harmless **3.** a person who looks or is dressed like a scarecrow

scare·head (-hed') *n.* [Colloq.] an especially large newspaper headline giving sensational news

scarf¹ (skärf) *n., pl.* **scarfs, scarves** [ONormFr. *escarpe*, a purse hung from the neck < ML. *scirpa*, a pouch made of rushes < L. < *scirpus*, a bulrush] **1.** a long or broad piece of cloth worn about the neck, head, etc. for warmth or decoration **2.** a long, narrow covering for a table, dresser, etc.; runner **3.** a sash worn by soldiers or officials

scarf² (skärf) *n., pl.* **scarfs** [prob. < Scand.] **1.** a joint made by notching, grooving, or otherwise cutting the ends of two pieces and fastening them so that they join firmly into one continuous piece: also **scarf joint 2.** the ends of a piece so cut —*vt.* **1.** to join by a scarf **2.** to make a scarf in the end of

scar·i·fy (skar'ə fī') *vt.* **-fied', -fy'ing** [< MFr., ult. < Gr. *skariphasthai*, to scratch < *skariphos*, a stylus, related to L. *scribere*, write: see SCRIBE] **1.** to make a series of small cuts or punctures in (the skin), as in surgery **2.** to criticize sharply **3.** to loosen or scratch the surface of (soil) —**scar'i·fi·ca'tion** *n.*

scar·la·ti·na (skär'lə tē'nə) *n.* [ModL. < ML. (*febris*) *scarlatina*, scarlet (fever)] *popular term for a mild form of* SCARLET FEVER

Scar·lat·ti (skär lät'tē) **1. A·les·san·dro** (ä'les sän'drô), 1660?–1725; It. composer **2. (Giuseppe) Do·me·ni·co** (dô me'nē kô'), 1685–1757; It. composer: son of *Alessandro*

scar·let (skär'lit) *n.* [< OFr. < ML. *scarlatum*, scarlet cloth < Per. *säqirlät*, red dress < Ar.] **1.** very bright red with a slightly orange tinge **2.** cloth or clothing of this color —*adj.* **1.** of this color **2.** sinful

scarlet fever a highly contagious disease, esp. of children, that causes a sore throat, fever, and a scarlet rash

scarlet runner (bean) a climbing bean plant of tropical America, having scarlet flowers, and pods with red-and-black seeds

☆ **scarlet tanager** a songbird native to the U.S., the male of which has a scarlet body and black wings and tail

scarp (skärp) *n.* [< It. *scarpa*] **1.** a steep slope; specif., an es-

SCARF JOINTS

carpment or cliff along the edge of a plateau 2. the outer slope of a rampart, or a rear slope of a ditch below the rampart —**vt.** to make into a steep slope

scar tissue the thick, fibrous connective tissue that makes up a scar

scarves (skärvz) *n. alt. pl. of* SCARF[1]

scar·y (sker′ē) *adj.* **scar′i·er, scar′i·est** [Colloq.] **1.** causing fear; frightening [a *scary* ghost story] **2.** easily frightened —**scar′i·ness** *n.*

scat[1] (skat) *vi.* **scat′ted, scat′ting** [? a hiss + CAT] [Colloq.] to go away [she saw the unfamiliar cat and said, "*Scat!*"]

☆**scat[2]** (skat) *adj.* [one of the syllables orig. used] describing jazz singing in which meaningless syllables are used —*n.* such singing —*vi.* **scat′ted, scat′ting** to engage in scat singing

scathe (skā*th*) *vt.* **scathed, scath′ing** [< ON. < *skathi*, harm] **1.** [Archaic or Dial.] *a)* to injure *b)* to wither or sear **2.** to criticize or denounce fiercely —*n.* [Archaic or Dial.] injury or harm —**scathe′less** *adj.*

scath·ing (skā′*thi*ŋ) *adj.* very harsh or bitter [*scathing* remarks] —**scath′ing·ly** *adv.*

sca·tol·o·gy (skə täl′ə jē) *n.* [< Gr. *skatos*, genitive of *skōr*, excrement + -LOGY] great interest in or concern with body wastes or the excreting of body wastes, esp. in literature —**scat·o·log·i·cal** (skat′ə läj′i k'l), **scat′o·log′ic** *adj.*

scat·ter (skat′ər) *vt.* [ME. *skateren*: for IE. base see SAW[1]] **1.** to throw here and there or strew loosely; sprinkle [the truck *scattered* salt on the icy road] **2.** to separate and drive in many directions; disperse [a people *scattered* by war] **3.** *Physics* to reflect, refract, diffuse, etc. in an irregular manner —*vi.* to separate and go off in several directions [the crowd *scattered*] —*n.* something scattered about [a *scatter* of snowflakes] —**scat′ter·er** *n.*

SYN.—**scatter** implies a tossing about over a wide area [to *scatter* seeds] or a driving apart in many directions [the wind *scattered* the leaves]; **disperse** implies a scattering which completely breaks up a group and spreads the individuals far and wide [royalists were forced into exile and *dispersed* throughout Europe]; **dissipate** suggests a breaking up of something so completely that it disappears [the sun *dissipated* the fog; a fortune *dissipated* by reckless spending]; **dispel** suggests a scattering that drives away something which hides, confuses, worries, etc. [hope that *dispelled* their fears] —**ANT.** assemble, gather, collect

scat·ter·brain (skat′ər brān′) *n.* a person who is flighty and not able to think or concentrate in a serious way —**scat′ter·brained′** *adj.*

scat·ter·ing (-iŋ) *n.* **1.** the act of one that scatters **2.** a small amount or number spread out here and there [an audience of children with a *scattering* of adults]

☆**scatter rug** a small rug for covering only a limited area

scaup (skôp) *n., pl.* **scaups, scaup:** see PLURAL, II, D, 1 [obs. form of dial. *scalp*, mussel bed: the ducks feed on mussels] any of several wild ducks related to the canvasback and redhead: also **scaup duck**

scav·enge (skav′inj) *vt.* **-enged, -eng·ing** [< SCAVENGER] **1.** to remove rubbish from (streets, etc.) **2.** to salvage (things that can be used) by rummaging through things that have been discarded —*vi.* **1.** to act as a scavenger **2.** to look for food

scav·eng·er (skav′in jər) *n.* [< Anglo-Fr. *scawage*, inspection < Fl. *scawen* or OFrank. *scouwon*, to peer at: for IE. base see HEAR] **1.** a person who gathers things that have been discarded by others **2.** any animal that feeds on rotting meat or plants

☆**scavenger hunt** a party game in which persons go out to bring back odd items on a list, without buying them

sce·nar·i·o (si ner′ē ō′, -när′-) *n., pl.* **-i·os′** [It. < L. < *scaena*, stage, SCENE] **1.** an outline of the plot of a opera, play, etc. ☆**2.** the script from which a motion picture is made; screenplay **3.** an outline for any proposed or planned series of events, real or imagined —☆**sce·nar′ist** *n.*

scene (sēn) *n.* [< MFr. < L. < Gr. *skēnē*, tent, stage: for IE. base see SHINE] **1.** the place in which any event occurs [the *scene* of the crime] **2.** the setting of the action of a play, story, etc. [the *scene* of *Hamlet* is Denmark] **3.** a division of a play, usually part of an act **4.** a part of a play, story, etc. that is a single, continuous unit of action [a deathbed *scene*] **5.** *same as* SCENERY (sense 1) **6.** a view, landscape, etc. [a peaceful autumn *scene*] **7.** a show of strong feeling before others [she made a *scene* in court] **8.** a real or imaginary event, esp. as described [she witnessed a distressing *scene* on her way home] **9.** [Colloq.] a particular area of interest or activity [the poetry *scene*] —see SYN. at VIEW —**behind the scenes 1.** backstage **2.** in private or in secrecy —☆**make the scene** [Slang] **1.** to be present **2.** to participate actively or successfully

sce·ner·y (sē′nər ē) *n., pl.* **-ner·ies 1.** painted screens, back-

drops, hangings, etc., used on the stage to represent places **2.** the general appearance of a place; features of a landscape

sce·nic (sē′nik, sen′ik) *adj.* **1.** of the stage; esp., of stage scenery [the *scenic* effects included a waterfall] **2.** *a)* having to do with natural scenery [a *scenic* route] *b)* having beautiful scenery **3.** representing an action, event, etc. [a *scenic* mural] —**sce′ni·cal·ly** *adv.*

scent (sent) *vt.* [< OFr. < L. *sentire*, to feel: for IE. base see SEND] **1.** to smell [the dog *scented* game] **2.** to get a hint of; suspect [to *scent* trouble] **3.** to fill with an odor; perfume [to *scent* a handkerchief] —*vi.* to hunt by the sense of smell —*n.* **1.** a smell; odor [the *scent* of new-mown hay] **2.** the sense of smell [lions hunt partly by *scent*] **3.** a perfume **4.** an odor left by an animal, by which it is tracked **5.** a track followed in hunting **6.** any series of clues, by which something is followed or uncovered; trail [she was hot on the *scent* of the anonymous writer] —**scent′ed** *adj.* —**scent′less** *adj.*

scep·ter (sep′tər) *n.* [< OFr. < L. < Gr. *skēptron*, staff] **1.** a staff held by rulers at certain ceremonies as a symbol of power **2.** royal authority; sovereignty —*vt.* to give a scepter or royal power to

scep·tic (skep′tik) *n., adj. chiefly Brit. sp. of* SKEPTIC —**scep′ti·cal** *adj.* —**scep′ti·cal·ly** *adv.* —**scep′ti·cism** *n.*

scep·tre (sep′tər) *n., vt.* **-tred, -tring** *chiefly Brit. sp. of* SCEPTER

SCEPTER

sched·ule (skej′ool; *Brit. & often Canad.* shed′yool, shej′ool) *n.* [< OFr. < LL. dim. of L. *scheda*, a leaf of paper < Gr. *schidē*, splinter of wood] **1.** a list or catalog of details [a *schedule* of freight charges] ☆**2.** a list of the times at which certain things are to happen; timetable [a bus *schedule* showing departure times] ☆**3.** a plan for a project, usually one showing when parts are to be begun and completed [following the *schedule* closely] —*vt.* **-uled, -ul·ing 1.** to place in a schedule [to *schedule* a work program] ☆**2.** to plan for a certain time [*schedule* my speech for 8:00 P.M.]

Sche·he·ra·za·de (shə her′ə zä′də, -zäd′) in *The Arabian Nights*, the Sultan's bride, who saves her own life by keeping the Sultan's interest in tales that she tells for 1001 nights

Scheldt (skelt) river flowing from N France through Belgium & the Netherlands into the North Sea: Du. name **Schel·de** (skhel′də)

sche·ma (skē′mə) *n., pl.* **-ma·ta** (-mə tə) [Gr.: SEE SCHEME] an outline, diagram, scheme, plan, etc.

sche·mat·ic (skē mat′ik) *adj.* of or being a scheme, schema, plan, etc. [a *schematic* diagram] —*n.* a diagram, as of the wiring of an electric circuit —**sche·mat′i·cal·ly** *adv.*

scheme (skēm) *n.* [< L. < Gr. *schēma*, a form: for IE. base see SCHOOL[1]] **1.** *a)* a carefully arranged plan for doing something [a *scheme* to prevent flooding] *b)* a secret or underhanded plan; plot [a *scheme* to get control of a company] **2.** an orderly combination of things on a definite plan [the color *scheme* of a painting] **3.** an outline showing different parts of an object or system —*vt.* **schemed, schem′ing** to plan as a scheme; devise; contrive; plot [they *schemed* to depose the king] —*vi.* **1.** to make schemes **2.** to plot; intrigue —see SYN. at PLAN —**schem′er** *n.*

schem·ing (skē′miŋ) *adj.* forming schemes or plots; crafty, tricky, etc. —**schem′ing·ly** *adv.*

Sche·nec·ta·dy (skə nek′tə dē) [< Du. < Iroquoian name (? lit., place of the pines) + Du. *stede*, place] city in eastern N.Y., on the Mohawk River: pop. 78,000

scher·zan·do (sker tsän′dō, -tsan′-) *adj.* [It. < *scherzo*: see SCHERZO] *Music* playful —*adv. Music* playfully

scher·zo (sker′tsō) *n., pl.* **-zos, -zi** (-tsē) [It., a jest] a lively, playful movement, as of a sonata or symphony, in 3/4 time

☆**Schick test** (shik) [after B. *Schick* (1877–1967), U.S. pediatrician] a test to find out if one is immune to diphtheria, made by injecting dilute diphtheria toxin just under the skin

Schil·ler (shil′ər), (Johann Christoph) **Fried·rich von** (frē′driH fôn) 1759–1805; Ger. dramatist & poet

schil·ling (shil′iŋ) *n.* [G.] *see* MONETARY UNITS, table (Austria)

schism (siz′m, skiz′m) *n.* [< OFr. < LL. < Gr. *schisma* < *schizein*, to cleave: see SCHIZO-] **1.** a split or division in an organized group, esp. a church, caused by a difference of opinion **2.** the offense of trying to cause a split in a church

schis·mat·ic (siz mat′ik, skiz-) *adj.* **1.** of or having the nature of schism **2.** tending to cause or causing schism Also

schis·mat'i·cal —n. a person who causes or tries to cause schism —**schis·mat'i·cal·ly** adv.

schist (shist) n. [< Fr. < L. < Gr. schistos, easily cleft < schizein, to cleave: see SCHIZO-] any metamorphic rock of a type that splits easily into thin leaves —**schist'ose** (-ōs) adj.

schis·to·some (shis'tə sōm') n. [ModL. < Gr. schistos, cleft + sōma, body] a flatworm that lives as a parasite in the blood vessels of mammals and birds

schis·to·so·mi·a·sis (shis'tə sō mī'ə sis) n. [ModL.: see prec. & -IASIS] a chronic disease caused by schistosomes, that produces disorders of the liver, bladder, lungs, etc.

schiz·o- [ModL. < Gr. schizein, to cleave < IE. base skei-, to cut, from which also come SCIENCE & SCISSORS] a combining form meaning split, division: also, before a vowel, **schiz-**

schiz·o·carp (skiz'ə kärp', skit'sə-) n. [prec. + -CARP] Bot. a dry fruit, as of the maple, that splits into one-seeded carpels — **schiz'o·car'pous, schiz'o·car'pic** adj.

schiz·oid (skit'soid, skiz'oid) adj. of, like, having, or tending to have schizophrenia —n. a schizoid person

schiz·o·my·cete (skiz'ō mī sēt', skit'sə-) n. [SCHIZO- + -MYCETE] any of the group of microorganisms consisting of the bacteria; bacterium —**schiz'o·my·ce'tous** (-sēt'əs) adj.

schiz·o·phre·ni·a (skit'sə frē'nē ə, skiz'ə-) n. [ModL. < SCHIZO- + Gr. phrēn, the mind] a major mental disorder in which there is a separation of the thought processes and the emotions, along with a breakdown of personality, and the sense of reality is distorted by delusions and hallucinations, etc. — **schiz'o·phren'ic** (-fren'ik, -frē'nik) adj., n.

schiz·o·phyte (skiz'ə fīt', skit'sə-) n. [SCHIZO- + -PHYTE] any of a group of plants each made up of a single cell or a colony of cells, including the bacteria and blue-green algae —**schiz'o·phyt'ic** (-fit'ik) adj.

☆**schle·miel** (shlə mēl') n. [< Yid. < Heb. proper name Shelumiël] [Slang] a bungling person who regularly fails or is easily fooled or cheated: also sp. **schle·mihl'**

Schles·wig-Hol·stein (shles'wig hōl'stīn; G. shläs'viH hōl'-shtīn) state of N West Germany, at the base of Jutland

☆**schmaltz** (shmälts, shmôlts) n. [< Yid. < G. schmalz, lit., melted fat] [Slang] 1. highly sentimental and trite music, literature, etc. 2. extreme sentimentalism Also sp. **schmalz** — **schmaltz'y** adj. **schmaltz'i·er, schmaltz'i·est**

schnapps (shnäps, shnaps) n., pl. **schnapps** [G., a dram] any strong alcoholic liquor; specif., gin made in the Netherlands: also sp. **schnaps**

schnau·zer (shnou'zər) n. [G. < schnauzen, to snarl] any of three breeds of sturdy, active dog with a close, wiry coat

☆**schnit·zel** (shnit's'l) n. [G. < schnitz, a piece cut off] a cutlet, esp. of veal

☆**schnook** (shnook) n. [< Yid.] a meek person who is easily fooled or cheated

schnoz·zle (shnäz''l) n. [< Yid. < G. schnauze, related to SNOUT] [Slang] the nose: also **schnoz**

SCHNAUZER
(17—20 in. high
at shoulder)

schol·ar (skäl'ər) n. [< OE. or OFr., both ult. < L. schola, a SCHOOL¹] 1. a) a person who has learned much through study; learned person b) a specialist in a particular branch of learning, esp. in the humanities [a famous Mark Twain scholar] 2. a student given scholarship aid 3. any student or pupil

schol·ar·ly (-lē) adj. 1. of or relating to scholars 2. showing much knowledge and learning [a scholarly book] 3. devoted to learning; studious [a scholarly girl]

schol·ar·ship (-ship') n. 1. the quality of knowledge and learning shown by a student [that report shows faulty scholarship] 2. the carefully organized knowledge of a learned person, or of scholars as a group [well-read in modern Shakespearean scholarship] 3. a gift of money or other aid to help pay for a student's education

scho·las·tic (skə las'tik) adj. [< L. < Gr. < scholazein, to be at leisure < scholē, a SCHOOL¹] 1. of schools, colleges, students, teachers, etc.; academic [scholastic honors] 2. [also S-] of or relating to scholasticism 3. too much concerned with petty de-

tails of scholarship; pedantic —n. [also S-] 1. same as SCHOOLMAN (sense 1) 2. a person who follows the teachings of Scholasticism —**scho·las'ti·cal·ly** adv.

scho·las·ti·cism (skə las'tə siz'm) n. 1. [often S-] a medieval system of Christian thought based on the methods of logic used by Aristotle 2. a close following of traditional doctrines and methods

scho·li·ast (skō'lē əst) n. [< ModL. < MGr. < Gr. scholion, a comment < scholē, a SCHOOL¹] a scholar who wrote commentaries on the classics in ancient times —**scho'li·as'tic** adj.

Schön·berg (shān'bərg, shōn'-; G. shön'berkh), **Arnold** 1874-1951; U.S. composer, born in Austria

school¹ (skool) n. [OE. scol < L. schola < Gr. scholē, leisure (esp. as used for study), school < IE. base segh-, to hold] 1. a place or institution for teaching and learning [a public school, dancing school] 2. a) the building or buildings, classrooms, etc. of a school b) all of its students and teachers [most of the school attends the games] c) a regular session of teaching at a school [school begins next week] 3. a) attendance at a school [to miss school for a week] b) the process of being educated at a school [she finished school at seventeen] 4. any situation or experience through which one gains knowledge, training, etc. [the school of hard knocks] 5. a particular division of an institution of learning, esp. of a university [the school of law] 6. a group following the same teachings, beliefs, methods, etc. [the Impressionist school] 7. a way of life [a gentleman of the old school] —vt. 1. to teach; instruct; educate [he was schooled in the old methods] 2. to discipline or control [to school oneself to be patient] —adj. of a school or schools —see SYN. at TEACH

school² (skool) n. [Du., a crowd] a large number of fish or water animals of the same kind swimming or feeding together —vi. to move together in such a school —see SYN. at GROUP

school board a group of people, elected or appointed, who are in charge of local public schools

school·book (skool'book') n. a book used for study in schools; textbook

school·boy (-boi') n. a boy attending school

☆**school bus** a vehicle for taking children to or from school or on trips related to school

school·child (-chīld') n., pl. **-chil·dren** (-chil'drən) a child attending school

school·fel·low (-fel'ō) n. same as SCHOOLMATE

school·girl (-gurl') n. a girl attending school

school guard a person whose duty it is to direct and watch over children as they cross streets near schools

school·house (-hous') n. a building used as a school

school·ing (-iŋ) n. 1. training or education; esp., formal instruction at school 2. cost of attending school

school·man (-mən; for 2, often -man') n., pl. **-men** (-mən; for 2, often -men') 1. [often S-] any of the medieval teachers of scholasticism 2. a teacher or educator

☆**school·marm** (-märm', -mäm') n. [Colloq.] a woman schoolteacher, esp. one who tends to be old-fashioned, strict, and fussy: also **school'ma'am'** (-mäm', -mam')

school·mas·ter (-mas'tər) n. 1. a man who teaches in a school: an old-fashioned term 2. [Brit.] a headmaster or master in a school —**school'mis'tress** (-mis'tris) n.fem.

school·mate (-māt') n. a person going to the same school at the same time as another

school·room (-room') n. a classroom

school·teach·er (-tē'chər) n. a person whose work is teaching in a school

school·work (-wurk') n. lessons worked on in classes at school or done as homework

school·yard (-yärd') n. the ground around or near a school, often used as a playground, playing field, etc.

school year the part of a year when school is in session, usually from September to June

☆**schoon·er** (skoo'nər) n. [< ? Scot. dial. scun, to skip a flat stone across water] 1. a ship with two or more masts, rigged fore and aft 2. short for PRAIRIE SCHOONER 3. a large beer glass

Scho·pen·hau·er (shō'pən hou'ər), **Arthur** 1788-1860; Ger. philosopher —**Scho'pen·hau'er·ism** n.

schot·tische (shät'ish) n. [< G. (der) schottische (tanz), (the) Scottish (dance)] 1. a form of round dance in 2/4 time, similar to the polka, but with a slower tempo **2.** music for this —*vi.* **-tisched, -tisch·ing** to dance a schottische

Schu·bert (shoo′bərt; *G.* shoo′bert), **Franz** (**Peter**) (fränts) 1797–1828; Austrian composer

Schu·mann (shoo′män), **Robert** (**Alexander**) 1810–56; Ger. composer

schuss (shoos) *n.* [G., lit., shot, rush] a straight run at full speed down a hill in skiing —*vi.* to make such a run

schwa (shwä) *n.* [G. < Heb. *sh'wa*, a mark showing an absence of vowel sound] **1.** the neutral vowel sound of most unstressed syllables in English; sound of *a* in *ago, e* in *agent*, etc. **2.** the symbol (ə) for this sound

Schwarz·wald (shvärts′vält′) *Ger. name of the* BLACK FOREST

Schweit·zer (shvīt′sər; *E.* shwīt′sər), **Al·bert** (äl′bert) 1875–1965; Alsatian medical missionary, philosopher, & musician in Africa

sci. **1.** science **2.** scientific

sci·at·ic (sī at′ik) *adj.* [< MFr. < ML. < L. < Gr. *ischiadikos* < *ischion*, the hip] of, near, or affecting the hip or its nerves

sci·at·i·ca (sī at′i kə) *n.* pain in the region of the hip and thighs caused by neuritis of the long nerve (**sciatic nerve**) passing down the back of the thigh

sci·ence (sī′əns) *n.* [< OFr. < L. < prp. of *scire*, to know, orig., to distinguish, separate: for IE. base see SCHIZO-] **1.** orig., the state or fact of knowing **2.** knowledge made up of an orderly system of facts gotten by means of observation, study, and experimentation [*science* has in three centuries changed the way man lives and thinks] **3.** a branch of such knowledge [the *science* of mathematics] **4.** *a)* the organized knowledge of nature and the physical world *b)* any branch of this See NATURAL SCIENCE **5.** skill based upon systematic training [the *science* of cooking] ☆**6.** [**S-**] shortened form of CHRISTIAN SCIENCE

science fiction fiction based on real or imagined scientific developments, often with an imaginary or fantastic view of the future

sci·en·tif·ic (sī′ən tif′ik) *adj.* **1.** of, dealing with, or used in science [*scientific* study, *scientific* apparatus] **2.** *a)* based on, or using, the principles and methods of science; systematic and exact [to use a *scientific* procedure] *b)* describing a method in which theories are based on data collected in a systematic way and which are then tested by objective experiments **3.** learned or learning by training carried out in a systematic way [*scientific* boxing; a *scientific* boxer] —**sci·en·tif′i·cal·ly** *adv.*

sci·en·tism (sī′ən tiz′m) *n.* **1.** the techniques and attitudes of scientists **2.** the principle that scientific methods can and should be used in all areas of study —**sci·en·tis′tic** (-tis′tik) *adj.*

sci·en·tist (sī′ən tist) *n.* a specialist in science; esp., a person whose profession is investigating in one of the natural sciences, as biology, chemistry, physics, etc.

☆**sci-fi** (sī′fī′) *adj., n. same as* SCIENCE FICTION

scil·i·cet (sil′i set′) *adv.* [L., contr. of *scire licet*, it is permitted to know] namely; that is to say

scim·i·tar, scim·i·ter (sim′ə tər) *n.* [It. *scimitarra* < ?] a short, curved sword with an edge on the convex side, used chiefly by Turks, Arabs, etc.

scin·til·la (sin til′ə) *n.* [L.] **1.** a spark **2.** the least trace [not a *scintilla* of hope]

scin·til·late (sin′t'l āt′) *vi.* **-lat′ed, -lat′ing** [< L. pp. of *scintillare* < *scintilla*, a spark] **1.** to give off sparks; flash; sparkle **2.** to sparkle with wit [such *scintillating* conversation] **3.** to twinkle, as a star —**scin′til·lant** *adj.* —**scin′til·la′tor** *n.*

scin·til·la·tion (sin′t'l ā′shən) *n.* **1.** a scintillating, or flashing, twinkling, sparkling, etc. **2.** a spark or flash **3.** the flash of light made by radiation when it strikes a crystal detector or a phosphor, as in an instrument (**scintillation counter**) used to detect and measure radiation

sci·o·lism (sī′ə liz′m) *n.* [< L. dim. of *scius*, knowing < *scire*, to know] superficial knowledge, esp. of one who pretends to be learned —**sci′o·list** *n.* —**sci′o·lis′tic** *adj.*

sci·on (sī′ən) *n.* [OFr. *cion* < ?] **1.** a shoot or bud of a plant, esp. one for grafting **2.** a descendant; offspring

Scip·i·o (sip′ē ō) **1.** 237?–183? B.C.; Rom. general: defeated Hannibal (202): called *Major* or *the Elder* **2.** 184?–129? B.C.; Rom. general & statesman: destroyed Carthage (146): grandson of *prec.*: called *Minor* or *the Younger*

scis·sile (sis′il) *adj.* [< L. < pp. of *scindere*, to cut] that can be cut or split smoothly and easily

scis·sion (sizh′ən, sish′-) *n.* [Fr. < LL. < L. pp. of *scindere*, to cut] a cutting or splitting, or the state of being cut

scis·sor (siz′ər) *vt.* to cut with scissors —*n. same as* SCISSORS

scis·sors (siz′ərz) *n.pl.* [< OFr. < LL. pl. of *cisorium*, cutting tool < L. *caedere*, to cut: for IE. base see SCHIZO-] **1.** [*also with sing. v.*] a cutting instrument, smaller than shears, with two opposing blades which are pivoted together so that they work against each other: also **pair of scissors 2.** [*with sing. v.*] *a)* an exercise in gymnastics in which the legs are moved in a way that suggests the blades of scissors *b) same as* SCISSORS HOLD

scissors hold a wrestling hold in which one contestant clasps a part of the other's body with his legs

scissors kick a swimming kick in which one leg is bent forward at the knee, the other is thrust backward, and then both are brought together with a snap

☆**scis·sor·tail** (siz′ər tāl′) *n.* a pale gray-and-pink variety of flycatcher of the southern U.S. and Mexico, having a forked tail

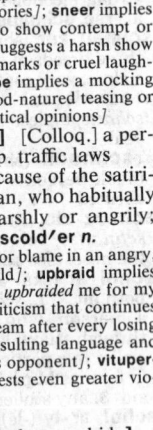

SCISSORS KICK
(seen from above)

SCLC, S.C.L.C. Southern Christian Leadership Conference

scle·ra (sklir′ə) *n.* [< Gr. *skleros*, hard] the tough, white, fibrous membrane covering all of the eyeball except the area covered by the cornea: see illustration at EYE

scle·ren·chy·ma (skli ren′kə mə) *n.* [ModL. < Gr. *skleros*, hard + *enchyma*, infusion] *Bot.* plant tissue made up of thick-walled, dead cells, as in nut shells

scle·ro- [< Gr. *skleros*, hard] *a combining form meaning:* **1.** hard **2.** of the sclera Also, before a vowel, **scler-**

scler·oid (sklir′oid) *adj.* [< SCLERO- + -OID] *Biol.* hard or hardened; indurated

scle·ro·sis (skli rō′sis) *n., pl.* **-ses** (-sēz) [< ML. < Gr. *skleros*, hard] **1.** an abnormal hardening of body tissues, esp. of the nervous system or the walls of arteries **2.** a hardening of the cell wall of a plant, as by an increase of lignin

scle·rot·ic (skli rät′ik) *adj.* **1.** hard **2.** of, characterized by, or having sclerosis **3.** of the sclera

scoff (skôf, skäf) *n.* [prob. < Scand.] a rude or mocking expression or remark; jeer —*vi.* to show scorn or mockery; jeer (*at*) —**scoff′er** *n.* —**scoff′ing·ly** *adv.*

SYN.—**scoff** suggests a showing of scorn or contempt that results from doubt, lack of respect, etc. [scientists *scoffed* at his theories]; **sneer** implies a tone of scorn in the voice, a mocking smile, etc. to show contempt or disrespect ["You call this a dinner?" he *sneered*]; **jeer** suggests a harsh show of scorn or disapproval by means of loud, insulting remarks or cruel laughter [the crowd *jeered* at the awkward performer]; **gibe** implies a mocking or making fun of someone and may suggest either good-natured teasing or sarcastic criticism [always *gibing* at her about her political opinions]

☆**scoff·law** (skôf′lô, skäf′-) *n.* [SCOFF + LAW] [Colloq.] a person who regularly breaks laws on purpose, esp. traffic laws

scold (skōld) *n.* [< ON. *skald*, poet (prob. because of the satirical poems they wrote)] a person, esp. a woman, who habitually scolds, nags, etc. —*vt.* to find fault with harshly or angrily; rebuke —*vi.* to find fault harshly or angrily —**scold′er** *n.*

SYN.—**scold** is the common term meaning to criticize or blame in an angry, often nagging way [a mother *scolds* a naughty child]; **upbraid** implies sharp or bitter criticism, esp. when it is justified [she *upbraided* me for my carelessness]; **berate** suggests violent or excessive criticism that continues for some time [an emotional coach who *berates* his team after every losing game]; **revile** implies the use of very coarse and insulting language and often suggests the use of slander [bitterly *reviling* his opponent]; **vituperate** has much the same meaning as **revile**, but suggests even greater violence and hatred

scol·lop (skäl′əp) *n., vt. var. of* SCALLOP

sconce (skäns) *n.* [< OFr., ult. < L. *abscondere*, to hide] a bracket attached to a wall for holding a candle, candles, etc.

scone (skōn) *n.* [Scot. < ? MDu. *schoonbrot*, fine bread] a small, flat cake, somewhat like a baking powder biscuit but sweeter, orig. baked on a griddle and served with butter

scoop (skoop) *n.* [< MDu. *schope*, bailing vessel & *schoppe*, a shovel: for IE. base see SHAPE] **1.** any of various tools shaped like a small shovel; specif., *a)* a kitchen utensil used to take up sugar, flour, etc. *b)* a small utensil with a round bowl, for dishing up ice cream, mashed potatoes, etc. **2.** the deep shovel of a dredge or steam shovel, which takes up sand, dirt, etc. **3.** the act or motion of taking up with or as with a scoop [he grabbed the ball with a *scoop* of his

SCONCE

glove] **4.** the amount taken up at one time by a scoop [two *scoops* of ice cream] **5.** a hollowed-out place ☆**6.** [Colloq.] *a)* advantage gained over a competitor by being first, specif. in reporting a news item *b)* such a news item *c)* current information [give her the *scoop* on our plans] —*adj.* describing a rounded, somewhat low neckline in a dress, etc. —*vt.* **1.** to take up or out as with a scoop **2.** to dig (*out*); hollow (*out*) **3.** to make by digging out **4.** to gather (*in* or *up*) as if with a scoop [he *scooped* up the money and ran] ☆**5.** [Colloq.] to report a news item before (a competitor) —**scoop′er** *n.*

scoop·ful (skōōp′fool′) *n., pl.* **-fuls′** as much as a scoop will hold

scoot (skōōt) *vi., vt.* [prob. < ON. *skjōta,* to SHOOT] [Colloq.] to go quickly; hurry (off); dart —*n.* [Colloq.] the act of scooting

scoot·er (skōōt′ər) *n.* [< SCOOT] **1.** a child's toy for riding on, consisting of a low board for one foot, with a wheel or wheels at each end, and a raised handlebar for steering: it is moved by pushing the other foot against the ground **2.** a two-wheeled vehicle with a seat, like a small motorcycle, propelled by a motor: in full, **motor scooter**

scope (skōp) *n.* [< It. < L. < Gr. *skopos,* distant object viewed, watcher: for IE. base see SPY] **1.** the extent of the mind's ability to grasp something; range of understanding [the problem is beyond his *scope*] **2.** the range within which something is carried on, dealt with, covered, etc. [the *scope* of a dictionary] **3.** room or opportunity for action or thought [it leaves little *scope* for the imagination] **4.** *short for* TELESCOPE, MICROSCOPE, RADARSCOPE, etc. —see SYN. at RANGE

-scope (skōp) [< Gr. < *skopein,* to see: see SCOPE] *a combining form meaning an instrument, etc. for seeing or observing* [telescope]

sco·pol·a·mine (skō päl′ə mēn′, -min) *n.* [< G. < ModL. *Scopolia,* a genus of plants, after G. A. *Scopoli* (1723–1788), It. naturalist + G. *amin, amine*] an alkaloid drug used in medicine as a sedative, to cause sleep, to relieve pain, etc.

-sco·py (skə pē) [< Gr. < *skopein,* to see] *a combining form meaning a seeing, observing* [bioscopy]

scor·bu·tic (skôr byōōt′ik) *adj.* [< ModL. < ML. *scorbutus,* scurvy < Russ. *skórbnut,* to wither] of, like, or having scurvy: also **scor·bu′ti·cal**

scorch (skôrch) *vt.* [< ? Scand.] **1.** *a)* to burn slightly in a way that chars or discolors the surface [I forgot about the iron and *scorched* the shirt] *b)* to parch or shrivel by heat [the sun *scorched* the plants] **2.** to criticize very sharply —*vi.* to become scorched —*n.* **1.** a slight burn on the surface **2.** a browning of plant tissues because of heat, fungi, etc. —see SYN. at BURN[1]

scorched-earth policy (skôrcht′urth′) the strategy of destroying crops, buildings, etc. in the path of an advancing enemy

scorch·er (skôrch′ər) *n.* anything that scorches; esp., [Colloq.] *a)* a very hot day *b)* a sharply critical remark

score (skôr) *n.* [OE. *scoru* < ON. *skor:* for IE. base see CARNAGE] **1.** *a)* a scratch, mark, incision, etc. *b)* notches, marks, etc. made to keep tally or account **2.** an amount due; debt **3.** a wrong one seeks to get even for [to settle an old *score*] **4.** a reason or ground [his absences can be excused on that *score*] **5.** the number of points made in a game or contest by one team or contestant; also, the record of all the points made **6.** a grade or rating, as on a test **7.** *a)* twenty people or things *b)* [*pl.*] very many [*scores* of customers appeared] **8.** [Colloq.] a successful action, remark, etc. ☆**9.** [Colloq.] the way things really are: chiefly in **know the score** **10.** [Slang] the victim of a swindle; mark **11.** *Music a)* a written or printed copy of a composition, showing all parts for the instruments or voices *b)* the music for a stage production, motion picture, etc. —*vt.* **scored, scor′ing 1.** to mark or mark out with notches, lines, gashes, etc. [*score* the ham before baking] **2.** to keep account of by lines or notches **3.** *a)* to make (runs, hits, goals, etc.) in a game *b)* to record the score of *c)* to add (points) to one's score ☆*d)* *Baseball* to bring (a runner) home [his bunt *scored* the man on third] **4.** to win or achieve [to *score* a success] **5.** *a)* to grade (a test, etc.) *b)* to get (a specified score) on a test **6.** *a)* to raise welts on by lashing ☆*b)* to criticize sharply; berate **7.** *Music* to arrange in a score —*vi.* **1.** to make a point or points, as in a game **2.** to get a specified kind of score [he *scored* poorly on the test] **3.** to keep score in a game **4.** to succeed in getting what one wants —**scor′er** *n.*

score·board (skôr′bôrd′) *n.* ☆a large board for posting the score and other details of a game, as in a baseball stadium

☆**score card** a card for recording the score of a game, match, etc.: also **score′card′** *n.*

☆**score·keep·er** (-kēp′ər) *n.* a person keeping score, esp. an official who does so at a game, competition, etc.

score·less (-lis) *adj.* with no points scored

sco·ri·a (skôr′ē ə) *n., pl.* **-ri·ae′** (-ē′) [L. < Gr. < *skōr,* dung] **1.** the slag or refuse left after metal has been smelted from ore **2.** cinderlike lava —**sco′ri·a′ceous** (-ā′shəs) *adj.*

scorn (skôrn) *n.* [< OFr. < *escharnir,* to scorn] **1.** great contempt for someone or something, often with some indignation [to feel *scorn* for those who take bribes] **2.** a showing of this feeling [the *scorn* in his smile] **3.** a person or thing that meets with scorn —*vt.* **1.** to feel scorn for; treat with contempt **2.** to refuse or reject as wrong or disgraceful [he *scorned* to tell a lie] —**scorn′er** *n.*

scorn·ful (skôrn′fəl) *adj.* filled with or showing scorn or contempt —**scorn′ful·ly** *adv.* —**scorn′ful·ness** *n.*

Scor·pi·o (skôr′pē ō′) [L.] **1.** a southern constellation: also **Scor′pi·us** (-əs) **2.** the eighth sign of the zodiac: see ZODIAC

scor·pi·oid (skôr′pē oid′) *adj.* **1.** of, like, or having to do with scorpions **2.** with a curved end, like a scorpion's tail

scor·pi·on (skôr′pē ən) *n.* [OFr. < L. < Gr. *skorpios*] any of a group of arachnids found in warm regions, with a long tail ending in a curved, poisonous sting —[**S-**] *same as* SCORPIO

Scot (skät) *n.* **1.** any member of a Gaelic tribe of northern Ireland that migrated to Scotland in the 5th cent. A.D. **2.** a native or inhabitant of Scotland

scot (skät) *n.* [ON. *skot,* tribute] money that must be paid, as a tax or levy

Scot. 1. Scotch **2.** Scotland **3.** Scottish

SCORPION
(to 10 in. long)

Scotch (skäch) *adj.* of Scotland, its people, their language, etc.: see SCOTTISH —*n. same as:* **1.** SCOTTISH **2.** SCOTCH WHISKY —**the Scotch** the people of Scotland

scotch (skäch) *vt.* [< ?] **1.** to wound without killing; maim **2.** to put an end to; stifle [to *scotch* a rumor]

☆**Scotch-I·rish** (skäch′ī′rish) *adj.* of or being any of those people of northern Ireland who are descended from Scottish settlers

Scotch·man (-mən) *n., pl.* **-men** *var. of* SCOTSMAN

Scotch pine a hardy pine with yellow or orange wood

☆**Scotch tape** [< *Scotch,* a trademark] a thin, transparent, cellulose tape with adhesive on one side

Scotch terrier *same as* SCOTTISH TERRIER

Scotch whisky whiskey, often having a smoky flavor, distilled in Scotland from malted barley

sco·ter (skōt′ər) *n., pl.* **-ters, -ter:** see PLURAL, II, D, 1 [< ?] any of several large, dark-colored sea ducks found chiefly along the N coasts of Europe and N. America

scot-free (skät′frē′) *adj.* **1.** free from payment of scot, or tax **2.** unharmed or unpunished; free from injury or penalty

Scot·land (skät′lənd) division of the United Kingdom, made up of the northern half of Great Britain & nearby islands: 30,405 sq. mi.; pop. 5,217,000; cap. Edinburgh

Scotland Yard 1. headquarters of the metropolitan London police: officially, **New Scotland Yard 2.** the London police, esp. the detective bureau

sco·to·pi·a (skə tō′pē ə) *n.* [ModL. < Gr. *skotos,* darkness + *ōps,* EYE] the adjustment of the eye to dim light —**sco·to′pic** (-tō′pik, -täp′ik) *adj.*

Scots (skäts) *adj., n. same as* SCOTTISH

Scots·man (skäts′mən) *n., pl.* **-men** a person, esp. a man, born or living in Scotland, or one whose ancestors were Scottish: *Scotsman* or *Scot* is preferred to *Scotchman* in Scotland — **Scots′wom′an** *n.fem., pl.* **-wom′en**

Scott (skät) **1. Dred** (dred), 1795–1858; U.S. slave, whose suit for freedom resulted in a Supreme Court decision (1857) that extended slavery into Federal territories **2. Robert Fal·con** (fôl′kən), 1868–1912; Eng. antarctic explorer **3. Sir Walter,** 1771–1832; Scot. poet & novelist **4. Win·field** (win′fēld), 1786–1866; U.S. general

Scot·ti·cism (skät′ə siz'm) *n.* a Scottish idiom, expression, word, pronunciation, etc.

Scot·tie, Scot·ty (skät′ē) *n., pl.* **-ties** *colloq. name for* SCOTTISH TERRIER

Scot·tish (skät′ish) *adj.* of Scotland, its people, their English dialect, etc. *Scottish* is preferred in formal usage, but with some words, *Scotch* is almost always used (as, Scotch tweed, Scotch whisky), with others, *Scots* (as, Scots law) —*n.* the dialect of English spoken in Scotland —**the Scottish** the Scottish people

Scottish Gaelic the Celtic language of the Scottish Highlands: see GAELIC

Scottish terrier any of a breed of terrier with short legs, a squarish muzzle, rough, wiry hair, and pointed, erect ears

Scotts·dale (skäts′dāl′) [after Rev. W. *Scott*, chaplain in the Civil War] city in SC Ariz.: suburb of Phoenix: pop. 68,000

Scotus *see* DUNS SCOTUS

scoun·drel (skoun′drəl) *n.* [prob. < Anglo-Fr. *escoundre*, ult. < L. *abscondere*, ABSCOND] a mean, immoral, or wicked person; villain; rascal —**scoun′drel·ly** *adj.*

scour[1] (skour) *vt.* [MDu. *scuren* < ? OFr. *escurer* < VL. < L. *ex-*, thoroughly + *curare*, to take care of] 1. to clean or polish by hard rubbing, as with something rough or gritty [to *scour* a pan with steel wool] 2. to remove dirt and grease from (wool, etc.) 3. *a*) to wash or clear as by a swift current of water; flush *b*) to wash away —*vi.* 1. to clean things by rubbing and polishing 2. to become clean and bright by being scoured —*n.* 1. the act of scouring 2. [*usually pl.*, *with sing. v.*] dysentery in cattle, etc. —**scour′er** *n.*

scour[2] (skour) *vt.* [< ? OFr. *escourre*, to run forth < VL. < L. *ex-*, out + *currere*, to run] to go over or through quickly but thoroughly, as in searching or hunting [to *scour* a town for an escaped convict] —*vi.* to go about quickly, as in searching for something —**scour′er** *n.*

scourge (skurj) *n.* [< OFr. < L. *ex*, off + *corrigia*, a whip] 1. a whip 2. any means of harsh punishment 3. a cause of great suffering [the *scourge* of war] —*vt.* **scourged, scourg′ing** 1. to whip or flog 2. to punish or make suffer severely —**scourg′er** *n.*

scour·ings (skour′iŋz) *n.pl.* dirt, refuse, or remains removed by or as if by scouring

scout[1] (skout) *n.* [< OFr. < *escouter*, to hear < L. *auscultare*, to listen] 1. a soldier, plane, etc. sent to spy out the strength, movements, etc. of the enemy ☆2. a person sent out to get information about a competitor, to search for new talent, etc. [a baseball *scout*] 3. a member of the Boy Scouts or Girl Scouts 4. the act of scouting, or reconnoitering 5. [Colloq.] fellow; guy [be a good *scout* and help me lift this] —*vt.* 1. to explore or observe closely in seeking information [two planes out *scouting* the area] 2. to find by looking around (often with *out, up*) [see if you can *scout* up some tools] —*vi.* 1. to go out in search of information about the enemy; reconnoiter 2. to go in search of something [*scout* around for some firewood] ☆3. to work as a scout (*n.* 2) 4. to be active in the Boy Scouts or Girl Scouts —**scout′er** *n.* —**scout′ing** *n.*

scout[2] (skout) *vt.* [prob. < ON. *skuti*, a taunt] to reject (an idea, suggestion, theory, etc.) as absurd; scoff at —*vi.* to scoff (*at*)

scout·mas·ter (-mas′tər) *n.* the adult leader of a troop of Boy Scouts

☆**scow** (skou) *n.* [Du. *schouw*] a large, flat-bottomed boat with square ends, used for carrying coal, sand, etc. and often towed by a tug

scowl (skoul) *vi.* [prob. < Scand.] to draw the eyebrows together and lower the corners of the mouth in showing displeasure; look angry, sullen, etc. —*vt.* to express with a scowl —*n.* the act or expression of scowling; angry frown —**scowl′er** *n.*

scrab·ble (skrab′l) *vi.* **-bled, -bling** [Du. *schrabbelen < schrabben*, to scrape] 1. to scratch, scrape, or paw as though looking for something 2. to struggle [he's still *scrabbling* to make ends meet] 3. to scribble —*vt.* 1. to scrape together quickly 2. to scribble —*n.* a scrabbling; a scramble, scribble, etc. —☆[S-] *a trademark for* a word game played like anagrams with lettered tiles on a board —**scrab′bler** *n.*

scrab·bly (skrab′lē) *adj.* **-bli·er, -bli·est** [Colloq.] 1. having a scratching sound 2. scrubby, sparse, poor, etc.

scrag (skrag) *n.* [prob. < ON.] 1. a thin, scrawny person, animal, or plant 2. [Slang] the neck —*vt.* **scragged, scrag′ging** [Slang] to choke or wring the neck of

scrag·gly (skrag′lē) *adj.* **-gli·er, -gli·est** [see SCRAG & -LY[1]] sparse, scrubby, irregular, uneven, ragged, etc. [a *scraggly* beard] —**scrag′gli·ness** *n.*

scrag·gy (skrag′ē) *adj.* **-gi·er, -gi·est** [< SCRAG] 1. rough or jagged 2. lean; bony; skinny —**scrag′gi·ly** *adv.*

☆**scram** (skram) *vi.* **scrammed, scram′ming** [< SCRAMBLE] [Old Slang] to leave or get out, esp. in a hurry

scram·ble (skram′b′l) *vi.* **-bled, -bling** [< ? SCAMPER + SCRABBLE] 1. to climb, crawl, or clamber hurriedly 2. to scuffle or struggle for something in an eager, confused way [to *scramble* for scattered pennies; to *scramble* for political office] —*vt.* 1. *a*) to throw together in a disorderly way; jumble [clothing all *scrambled* together in the drawer] *b*) *Electronics* to change (transmitted signals) so that they cannot be made understandable without special receiving equipment ☆2. to cook (eggs) while stirring the mixed whites and yolks —*n.* 1. a hard, hurried climb or advance as over difficult ground 2. a disorderly struggle or rush, as for something many people want [they were caught up in the *scramble* for seats] 3. a jumble —**scram′bler** *n.*

Scran·ton (skrant′'n) [family name of the founders of a local ironworks] city in NE Pa.: pop. 104,000

scrap[1] (skrap) *n.* [< ON. *skrap*, scraps, trifles < *skrapa*, to SCRAPE: for IE. base see CARNAGE] 1. a small piece; fragment; bit [a *scrap* of paper; a *scrap* of information] 2. *a*) metal pieces, as old auto parts, bits of machinery, etc., collected for reprocessing *b*) articles of rubber, leather, paper, etc. that have been thrown away as useless 3. [*pl.*] bits of leftover food —*adj.* in the form of pieces, leftovers, etc. [*scrap* iron] —*vt.* **scrapped, scrap′ping** 1. to make into scrap 2. to get rid of as useless; discard; junk [she *scrapped* the story and started all over] —**scrap′per** *n.*

scrap[2] (skrap) *n.* [prob. < SCRAPE, *n.* 5] [Colloq.] a fight or quarrel —*vi.* **scrapped, scrap′ping** [Colloq.] to fight or quarrel —**scrap′per** *n.*

scrap·book (skrap′book′) *n.* a book of blank pages on which clippings, pictures, souvenirs, etc. are mounted for keeping

scrape (skrāp) *vt.* **scraped, scrap′ing** [< ON. *skrapa*: see SCRAP[1]] 1. to rub over the surface of with something rough or sharp [the bushes *scraped* his car] 2. to make smooth or clean by rubbing with a tool or something rough 3. to remove by rubbing with something sharp or rough (with *off, out,* etc.) [*scrape* off the old paint] 4. to scratch or injure by a rough, rubbing contact [she fell and *scraped* her knee] 5. to rub with a harsh, grating sound [chalk *scraping* a blackboard] 6. to gather slowly and with difficulty [to *scrape* up some money] —*vi.* 1. to rub against something harshly; grate 2. to give out a harsh, grating noise [the old gate *scraped* as he opened it] 3. to gather goods or money slowly and with difficulty 4. to manage to get by (with *through, along, by*) [they *scrape* by on very little money] 5. to draw the foot back along the ground in bowing —*n.* 1. the act of scraping 2. a scraped place; abrasion 3. a harsh, grating sound 4. a hard or disagreeable situation; predicament 5. a fight or conflict —**scrap′er** *n.*

scrap·heap (skrap′hēp′) *n.* a pile of scrap, or discarded things —**throw** (or **toss**) **on the scrapheap** to get rid of as useless

scrap·ing (skrā′piŋ) *n.* 1. the act of a person or thing that scrapes 2. the sound of this 3. [*usually pl.*] something scraped off, together, or up

scrap iron discarded or waste pieces of iron, to be recast

☆**scrap·ple** (skrap′'l) *n.* [dim. of SCRAP[1]] cornmeal boiled with scraps of pork, allowed to set, and then sliced and fried

scrap·py[1] (skrap′ē) *adj.* **-pi·er, -pi·est** [SCRAP[1] + -Y[2]] 1. made of scraps 2. broken up into unconnected parts [*scrappy* memories] —**scrap′pi·ly** *adv.* —**scrap′pi·ness** *n.*

scrap·py[2] (skrap′ē) *adj.* **-pi·er, -pi·est** [SCRAP[2] + -Y[2]] [Colloq.] fond of fighting —**scrap′pi·ly** *adv.* —**scrap′pi·ness** *n.*

scratch (skrach) *vt.* [prob. altered < ME. *scratten*, to scratch, after *cracchen*] 1. to mark or cut the surface of slightly with something pointed or sharp [thorns *scratched* our legs] 2. to tear or dig with the nails or claws [our cat *scratched* the chair] 3. *a*) to rub or scrape lightly, as with the fingernails, to relieve itching, etc. [to *scratch* a mosquito bite] *b*) to make sore by rubbing; chafe 4. to rub or scrape with a grating noise [the chalk *scratched* the blackboard] 5. to write or draw hurriedly or carelessly [to *scratch* off a letter] 6. to cross out or erase (writing, etc.) 7. to gather with difficulty; scrape (*together* or *up*) 8. *Sports* to withdraw (an entry) from a contest, specif. from a horse race —*vi.* 1. to use nails or claws in digging or wounding 2. to scrape the skin lightly to relieve itching, etc. 3. to manage to get by; survive 4. to make a harsh, scraping noise [the pen *scratched* when she wrote] 5. *Billiards, Pool* to commit a scratch —*n.* 1. the act of scratching 2. a mark, tear, or slight wound made by scratching 3. a grating or scraping sound 4. a scribble 5. the starting line of a race ☆6. [Slang] money 7. *Billiards, Pool a*) a shot that results in a penalty *b*) a miss **8.** *Sports* an entry withdrawn from a contest —*adj.* ☆**1.** used for hasty notes, figuring, etc. [*scratch paper*] **2.** put together in haste and without much selection [*a scratch team*] ☆**3.** *Baseball* designating a chance hit credited to the batter for a ball not hit sharply —**from scratch** from little or nothing; without advantage [*a business built up from scratch*] —**scratch the surface** to do or deal with something in a hasty, shallow way —**up to scratch** [Colloq.] up to a standard; acceptable —**scratch′er** *n.*

scratch test a test for finding out what substances a person is allergic to, made by rubbing allergens into small scratches or punctures in the skin

scratch·y (skrach′ē) *adj.* **scratch′i·er, scratch′i·est 1.** made as if with scratches [*scratchy* handwriting] **2.** making a scratching noise [*a scratchy* pen] **3.** that chafes, itches, etc. [*scratchy* cloth] —**scratch′i·ly** *adv.* —**scratch′i·ness** *n.*

scrawl (skrôl) *vt., vi.* [< ?] to write, draw, or mark hastily, carelessly, or awkwardly —*n.* **1.** sprawling handwriting, often hard to read **2.** something scrawled —**scrawl′er** *n.* —**scrawl′y** *adj.* **scrawl′i·er, scrawl′i·est**

scraw·ny (skrô′nē) *adj.* **-ni·er, -ni·est** [prob. < Scand.] **1.** very thin; skinny and bony **2.** stunted or scrubby [*a scrawny* tree] —see SYN. at LEAN[2] —**scraw′ni·ness** *n.*

scream (skrēm) *vi.* [akin to WFl. *schreemen,* to scream, G. *schrei,* a cry: for IE. base see RAVEN[1]] **1.** to utter or make a shrill, piercing cry or sound **2.** to laugh loudly or hysterically **3.** to have a startling effect [*headlines that scream* out at the reader] **4.** to shout or yell in anger, hysteria, etc. —*vt.* **1.** to utter with or as with a scream **2.** to bring into a specified state by screaming [*to scream* oneself hoarse] —*n.* **1.** a sharp, piercing cry or sound **2.** [Colloq.] a very funny person or thing **SYN.—scream** is the general word for a loud, high, piercing cry, made as in fear, pain, or anger; **shriek** suggests a sharper, more sudden or anguished cry than **scream** and is also used of loud, high-pitched, uncontrolled laughter; **screech** suggests a shrill or harsh cry that is painful or unpleasant to hear

scream·er (skrēm′ər) *n.* **1.** a person who screams ☆**2.** [Slang] a startling headline **3.** any of various long-toed S. American wading birds

scream·ing (-iŋ) *adj.* **1.** that screams **2.** startling in effect [*screaming* colors] **3.** causing screams of laughter —**scream′-ing·ly** *adv.*

screech (skrēch) *vi.* [ON. *skraekja:* for IE. base see RAVEN[1]] to utter or make a shrill, high-pitched, harsh shriek or sound —*vt.* to utter with a screech —*n.* a shrill, high-pitched, harsh shriek or sound —see SYN. at SCREAM —**screech′er** *n.* —**screech′y** *adj.* **screech′i·er, screech′i·est**

screech owl ☆**1.** a small owl with feathered ear tufts and an eerie, wailing cry **2.** [Brit.] *same as* BARN OWL

screed (skrēd) *n.* [ME. *screde,* var. of *schrede,* shred] a long, tiresome speech or piece of writing

screen (skrēn) *n.* [< OFr. *escren* < Gmc.: for IE. base see CARNAGE] **1.** a curtain or movable, covered frame, used to separate, hide, protect, etc. **2.** anything that protects, hides, etc. [*a smoke screen*] **3.** a coarse mesh of wire, etc. used as a sieve for separating smaller pieces of coal, stone, etc. from larger ones **4.** a system for screening or testing persons **5.** a frame covered with a wire or plastic mesh used, as on a window, to keep insects out **6.** *a*) a white surface upon which movies, slides, etc. are shown *b*) the movie industry or art **7.** the surface area of a television or radar receiver on which the light pattern is traced —*vt.* **1.** to separate, hide, or protect, as with a screen [*a* hedge *screens* the yard] **2.** to enclose or provide with a screen [*the* porch was *screened* in] **3.** to sift through a screen **4.** *a*) to interview or test in order to separate according to skills, personality, etc. *b*) to separate in this way (usually with *out*) **5.** *a*) to show (movies, etc.) upon a screen *b*) to make a movie of (a story, play, etc.) —*vi.* to be screened or suitable for screening, as in movies —**screen′a·ble** *adj.* —**screen′er** *n.*

screen·ing (skrēn′iŋ) *n.* **1.** the act of one that screens **2.** *a*) a screen or set of screens *b*) mesh used in a screen **3.** [*pl.*] material separated out by a sifting screen

☆**screen pass** *Football* a short forward pass to a receiver who is protected by blockers

☆**screen·play** (-plā′) *n.* a story written, or adapted from a novel, etc., for production as a movie

screen test a short film made to test a person's suitability as a movie actor or actress

screw (skrōō) *n.* [MFr. *escroue,* hole in which a screw turns < L. *scrofa,* sow, infl. by *scrobis,* vulva] **1.** *a*) a piece of metal like a nail with a ridge winding around it in a spiral and usually with a slot across its head: it is forced into things, by turning, in order to hold them together: also called **male** (or **external**) **screw** *b*) the internal thread, as of a nut, into which a male screw can be turned: also called **female** (or **internal**) **screw** *c*) the act of turning a screw **2.** any of various devices operating or threaded like a screw, as a screw propeller **3.** [Slang] a prison guard **4.** [Chiefly Brit. Colloq.] a stingy person **5.** [Brit. Colloq.] a salary —*vt.* **1.** to screw; turn; tighten [*screw* the lid on tight] **2.** to fasten, tighten, insert, etc. as with a screw or screws [*he screwed* the bookshelf to the wall] **3.** to twist out of shape; contort [*to screw* up one's face] **4.** to make stronger (often with *up*) [*he screwed* up his courage] **5.** [Slang] to cheat; swindle —*vi.* **1.** to go together or come apart by being turned like a screw [*a* lid *screws* on] **2.** to be fastened with screws [*this hinge screws* to the door] **3.** to twist; turn; wind [*it screws* on easily] **4.** to cheat; swindle —**have a screw loose** [Slang] to be eccentric, odd, etc. —**put the screws on** (or **to**) to use force or great pressure on —**screw up** [Slang] to make a mess of, as by ineptness; bungle

☆**screw·ball** (skrōō′bôl′) *n.* **1.** *Baseball* a ball thrown by a right-handed pitcher that curves to the right, or by a left-handed pitcher that curves to the left **2.** [Slang] a person who seems eccentric, unconventional, crazy, etc. —*adj.* [Slang] eccentric, crazy, etc.

screw·driv·er (-drī′vər) *n.* **1.** a tool used for turning screws, having an end that fits into the slot in the head of a screw ☆**2.** a cocktail of orange juice and vodka

screw eye a screw with a loop for a head

screw hook a screw with a hook for a head

screw pine a southeast Asian tree or shrub with daggerlike leaves and, often, prop roots

screw propeller *see* PROPELLER

screw thread the spiral ridge of a screw

☆**screw·worm** (skrōō′wurm′) *n.* a larva of any of several American flies, found swarming over wounds, the nostrils, etc. of mammals, often causing illness

screw·y (skrōō′ē) *adj.* **screw′i·er, screw′i·est** [Slang] ☆**1.** mentally unbalanced; crazy ☆**2.** peculiar, odd, etc. in a confusing way —**screw′i·ness** *n.*

scrib·ble (skrib′'l) *vt., vi.* **-bled, -bling** [< ML. < L. *scribere:* see SCRIBE] **1.** to write carelessly or hastily **2.** to cover with or make marks that are meaningless or hard to read —*n.* scribbled writing, marks, etc.; scrawl —**scrib′bler** *n.*

scribe (skrīb) *n.* [L. *scriba,* public writer < *scribere,* to write: for IE. base see CARNAGE] **1.** a penman who copied manuscripts before the invention of printing **2.** a writer; author **3.** a person learned in the Jewish law who makes handwritten copies of the Torah **4.** a person employed by the public to write letters, etc. —*vi.* **scribed, scrib′ing** to work as a scribe —**scrib′al** *adj.*

scrim (skrim) *n.* [< ?] **1.** a light, sheer, loosely woven cotton or linen cloth ☆**2.** a hanging of such cloth used in the theater as a backdrop or as a semitransparent curtain

scrim·mage (skrim′ij) *n.* [altered < SKIRMISH] **1.** a rough, confused fight or struggle ☆**2.** *Football a*) the play that follows the pass from center *b*) football practice in the form of actual play between two units —*vi.* **-maged, -mag·ing** to take part in a scrimmage

scrimp (skrimp) *vt.* [prob. < Scand.] **1.** to make too small, short, etc.; skimp **2.** to treat stingily; stint —*vi.* to spend or use as little as possible; be sparing and frugal [*to scrimp* on food] —**scrimp′er** *n.* —**scrimp′ing·ly** *adv.*

scrimp·y (skrim′pē) *adj.* **scrimp′i·er, scrimp′i·est 1.** not quite enough; scanty; meager **2.** frugal or economical

☆**scrim·shaw** (skrim′shô′) *n.* [< ?] **1.** carving done on shells, bone, ivory, etc., esp. by sailors **2.** an article or articles so made

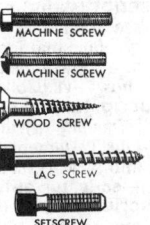

MACHINE SCREW

MACHINE SCREW

WOOD SCREW

LAG SCREW

SETSCREW

scrip (skrip) *n.* [contr. < SCRIPT] **1.** a note, list, receipt, etc. **2.** a certificate of a right to receive something; specif., *a)* a certificate representing a fraction of a share of stock ☆*b)* a certificate of indebtedness, issued as currency, as by a local government without funds

script (skript) *n.* [< MFr. < L. *scriptum*, neut. pp. of *scribere:* see SCRIBE] **1.** handwriting, or a style of this **2.** *Printing* a typeface that looks like handwriting **3.** an original manuscript **4.** a copy of the text of a play or movie, or of a radio or television show —*vt.* [Colloq.] to write the script for (a movie, etc.)

scrip·ture (skrip/chər) *n.* [< L. < *scriptus:* see SCRIPT] **1.** [S-] [*often pl.*] *a)* the sacred writings of the Jews, identical with the Old Testament of the Christians *b)* the Christian Bible; Old and New Testaments **2.** any sacred writing —**scrip/tur·al** *adj.* —**scrip/tur·al·ly** *adv.*

script·writ·er (skript/rīt′ər) *n.* a person who writes scripts for movies, television shows, etc.

scriv·ner (skriv/nər, -'n ər) *n.* [< OFr., ult. < L. *scriba*, SCRIBE] [Archaic] **1.** a scribe or clerk **2.** a notary

☆**scrod** (skräd) *n.* [prob. < MDu. *schrode*, strip] a young codfish or haddock, esp. one split and prepared for cooking

scrof·u·la (skräf/yə lə) *n.* [ML. < L. < dim. of *scrofa*, a sow] tuberculosis of the lymphatic glands, esp. of the neck, in which the glands become enlarged —**scrof/u·lous** *adj.* —**scrof/u·lous·ly** *adv.* —**scrof/u·lous·ness** *n.*

scroll (skrōl) *n.* [altered (? after *roll*) < ME. *scrowe* < OFr. *escroue*, roll of writings] **1.** a roll of parchment, paper, etc., usually with writing on it **2.** anything having the form of a loosely rolled sheet of paper, as an ornamental design in coiled or spiral form —**scrolled** *adj.*

SCROLL

scroll saw a thin, ribbonlike saw for cutting thin wood into spiral or ornamental designs (**scroll/work′**)

Scrooge (skrōōj) *n.* [after *Scrooge*, a character in Dickens' *A Christmas Carol*] [*also* **s-**] a hardhearted, miserly old man

scro·tum (skrōt/əm) *n., pl.* **-ta** (-ə), **-tums** [L.] in most male mammals, the pouch of skin containing the testicles —**scro/tal** *adj.*

scrounge (skrounj) *vt.* **scrounged, scroung/ing** [< ?] [Colloq.] **1.** to get or find by hunting around [*to scrounge up some kindling*] **2.** to get by begging or sponging [*to scrounge a meal*] —*vi.* [Colloq.] to search (*around*) for something —**scroung/er** *n.*

scrub¹ (skrub) *n.* [dial. var. of *shrub*, infl. ? by ON. *skroppa*, a lean creature] **1.** *a)* short, stunted trees or bushes growing thickly together *b)* land covered with such growth **2.** any person, animal, or thing smaller than the usual, or thought of as inferior ☆**3.** *Sports a)* a player not on the regular team *b)* [*pl.*] a secondary team made up of such players —*adj.* **1.** of poor quality; inferior **2.** undersized; stunted ☆**3.** *Sports* of or for the scrubs

scrub² (skrub) *vt.* **scrubbed, scrub/bing** [prob. < Scand.] **1.** to clean or wash by rubbing hard *b)* to remove (dirt, etc.) by rubbing **2.** to rub hard **3.** to cleanse (a gas) of impurities **4.** [Colloq.] *a)* to cancel or call off (esp. a rocket launch just before or during the countdown) *b)* to get rid of —*vi.* to clean something by rubbing, as with a brush —*n.* the act of scrubbing —**scrub/ber** *n.*

scrub·by (skrub/ē) *adj.* **-bi·er, -bi·est 1.** undersized or inferior; stunted [*scrubby* bushes] **2.** covered with or made up of small trees and bushes [*scrubby* land] **3.** shabby, almost worthless, etc. —**scrub/bi·ly** *adv.* —**scrub/bi·ness** *n.*

scrub typhus *same as* TSUTSUGAMUSHI DISEASE

scrub·wom·an (-woom/ən) *n., pl.* **-wom/en** *same as* CHARWOMAN

scruff (skruf) *n.* [< ON. *skrufr*, tuft of hair] the back of the neck; nape

scruff·y (skruf/ē) *adj.* **scruff/i·er, scruff/i·est** [< dial. *scruff*, var. of SCURF + -Y²] shabby, unkempt, or untidy; grubby —**scruff/i·ly** *adv.* —**scruff/i·ness** *n.*

scrump·tious (skrump/shəs) *adj.* [< SUMPTUOUS] [Colloq.] very pleasing, attractive, etc., esp. to the taste —**scrump/tious·ly** *adv.*

scrunch (skrunch) *vt., vi.* [< CRUNCH] **1.** to crunch or crumple **2.** to hunch or squeeze [all *scrunched* together on the short bench] —*n.* a crunching sound

scru·ple (skrōō/p'l) *n.* [< MFr. < L. *scrupulus*, small sharp stone] **1.** a very small quantity **2.** an apothecaries' weight equal to 1/3 dram (20 grains) **3.** a doubt that comes from difficulty in deciding what is right, proper, etc.; uneasy feeling about something one thinks is wrong [he has *scruples* about telling even a small lie] —*vi.* **-pled, -pling** to hesitate because of doubt; have scruples [he *scrupled* at asking for more] —see SYN. at QUALM

scru·pu·lous (skrōō/pyə ləs) *adj.* **1.** having or showing scruples; very honest [*scrupulous* in his business dealings] **2.** demanding or marked by precision, care, and exactness [her *scrupulous* attention to details] —**scru/pu·los/i·ty** (-läs/ə tē), *pl.* **-ties, scru/pu·lous·ness** *n.* —**scru/pu·lous·ly** *adv.*

scru·ti·nize (skrōōt/'n īz′) *vt.* **-nized′, -niz′ing** to look at carefully or examine closely —**scru/ti·niz′er** *n.*

scru·ti·ny (-'n ē) *n., pl.* **-nies** [< LL. < L. *scrutari*, to search into carefully] **1.** a close examination **2.** a careful, continuous watch **3.** a lengthy, searching look

☆**scu·ba** (skōō/bə) *n.* [*s*(elf-)*c*(ontained) *u*(nderwater) *b*(reathing) *a*(pparatus)] a diver's apparatus for breathing under water, consisting of compressed-air tanks connected to a mouthpiece

scud (skud) *vi.* **scud/ded, scud/ding** [prob. < ON.] **1.** to move swiftly **2.** to be driven by the wind, as clouds —*n.* **1.** the act of scudding **2.** spray, rain, or snow driven by the wind **3.** very low, dark, swiftly moving clouds

scuff (skuf) *vt.* [prob. < or akin to ON. *skufa*, to shove] **1.** to scrape (the ground, floor, etc.) with the feet **2.** to wear a rough place on the surface of (a shoe, etc.) **3.** to scrape (one's feet) on the ground, etc. —*vi.* **1.** to walk without lifting the feet; shuffle [to *scuff* along] **2.** to become scraped or worn in patches —*n.* **1.** a noise or act of scuffing **2.** a worn or rough spot **3.** a loose-fitting house slipper, esp. one without a counter

scuf·fle (skuf/'l) *vi.* **-fled, -fling** [SCUFF + -LE²] **1.** to struggle or fight in a rough, confused way **2.** to move in a confused hurry **3.** to drag one's feet —*n.* **1.** a rough, confused fight **2.** the sound of feet shuffling

scull (skul) *n.* [prob. < Scand.] **1.** an oar mounted at the stern and worked from side to side to move a boat forward **2.** either of a pair of light oars used by a single rower **3.** a light racing boat for one, two, or four rowers —*vt., vi.* to propel (a boat) with a scull or sculls —**scull/er** *n.*

scul·ler·y (skul/ər ē) *n., pl.* **-ler·ies** [< OFr., ult. < *escuelle*, a dish < L. *scutella*, a tray] a room adjoining the kitchen, where pots and pans are cleaned or where the rough, dirty kitchen work is done

scul·lion (skul/yən) *n.* [< OFr. < L. *scopa*, a broom] [Archaic] a domestic servant doing the rough, dirty work in a kitchen

ONE-MAN SCULL

scul·pin (skul/pin) *n., pl.* **-pin, -pins:** see PLURAL, II, D, 2 [prob. < Fr. *scorpene* < L. *scorpaena*: see SCORPION] any of certain spiny sea fishes with a big head and wide mouth

sculpt (skulpt) *vt.* [Fr. *sculpter*, ult. < L. *sculpere:* see SCULPTURE] to represent, carve, shape, etc. by means of sculpture [to *sculpt* a head in bronze] —*vi.* to make sculptures; be a sculptor Also **sculp**

sculp·tor (skulp/tər) *n.* [L. < *sculpere*, to carve] an artist who shapes, carves, or otherwise makes figures or forms of clay, stone, metal, wood, etc. —**sculp/tress** [Now Rare] *n.fem.*

sculp·ture (-chər) *n.* [< L. < pp. of *sculpere*, to carve] **1.** the art of carving wood, chiseling stone, casting or welding metal, modeling clay, etc. into statues, figures, or the like **2.** any work or works of sculpture —*vt.* **-tured, -tur·ing 1.** to carve, chisel, etc. into statues, figures, etc. **2.** to represent in sculpture **3.** to form like sculpture **4.** to decorate with sculpture —*vi.* to work as a sculptor —**sculp/tur·al** *adj.* —**sculp/tur·al·ly** *adv.*

scum (skum) *n.* [< MDu. *schum:* for IE. base see HIDE¹] **1.** a thin layer of dirt or waste matter which forms on the top of liquids **2.** worthless parts or things; refuse **3.** a low, contemptible person, or such people as a group —*vi.* **scummed,** **scum/ming** to become covered with scum

scum·my (skum/ē) *adj.* **-mi·er, -mi·est 1.** of, like, or covered with scum **2.** [Colloq.] worthy of contempt; low; mean

☆**scup** (skup) *n., pl.* **scup, scups:** see PLURAL, II, D, 2 [< AmInd.] a brown-and-white porgy of the N Atlantic

scup·per (skup/ər) *n.* [< ?] an opening in a ship's side to allow water to run off the deck

☆**scup·per·nong** (skup/ər nôŋ, -näŋ′) *n.* [< the *Scuppernong*

River, N. Carolina] **1.** a golden-green grape of the southern U.S. **2.** a sweet wine made from this grape

scurf (skurf) *n.* [< ON. word thought to be *skurfr*] **1.** little, dry scales shed by the skin, as dandruff **2.** any scaly coating —**scurf′y** *adj.* **scurf′i·er, scurf′i·est**

scur·ril·i·ty (skə ril′ə tē) *n.* **1.** coarseness of language, esp. in joking **2.** *pl.* **-ties** a scurrilous act or remark

scur·ril·ous (skur′ə ləs) *adj.* [< L. < *scurra*, buffoon] using or containing coarse, vulgar, or insulting language —**scur′ril·ous·ly** *adv.* —**scur′ril·ous·ness** *n.*

scur·ry (skur′ē) *vi.* **-ried, -ry·ing** [< HURRY-SCURRY] to run quickly; scamper —*n.* the act of scurrying

scur·vy (skur′vē) *adj.* **-vi·er, -vi·est** [< SCURF] low; mean; worthy of contempt [a *scurvy* trick] —*n.* a disease resulting from a lack of vitamin C in the body and causing weakness, anemia, swollen and bleeding gums, etc. —**scur′vi·ly** *adv.* —**scur′vi·ness** *n.*

scut (skut) *n.* [< ?] a short, stumpy tail, esp. of a rabbit or deer

scu·tate (skyōō′tāt) *adj.* [ModL. < L. < *scutum*, a shield] **1.** *Bot.* same as PELTATE **2.** *Zool.* covered by bony or horny plates or scales

scutch (skuch) *vt.* [prob. < OFr., ult. < L. *ex-*, from + *quatere*, to shake] to free the fibers of (flax, cotton, etc.) from the woody parts by beating —*n.* an instrument for doing this: also **scutch′er**

scutch·eon (skuch′ən) *n.* same as ESCUTCHEON

scute (skyōōt) *n.* [L. *scutum*, a shield] *Zool.* any external bony or horny plate, as on some fishes and many reptiles

scu·tel·late[1] (skyōōt′'l āt′, skyōō tel′it) *adj.* covered with scutella, or small scales or plates

scu·tel·late[2] (skyōōt′'l āt′, skyōō tel′it) *adj.* [< ModL., ult. < dim. of *scutum*, a shield] *Biol.* shaped like a shield

scu·tel·lum (skyōō tel′əm) *n., pl.* **-tel′la** (-ə) **1.** [ModL., mistaken for L. dim. of *scutum*, a shield] *Bot.* any of various shield-shaped parts **2.** [ModL. < L. *scutella*: see SCUTTLE[1]] *Zool.* a small, horny scale or plate

scut·tle[1] (skut′'l) *n.* [OE. *scutel*, a dish < L. *scutella*] a bucket for holding or carrying coal: in full, **coal scuttle**

scut·tle[2] (skut′'l) *vi.* **-tled, -tling** [prob. akin to SCUD] to run quickly, esp. away from danger, trouble, etc.; scurry or scamper —*n.* a scurry or scamper

scut·tle[3] (skut′'l) *n.* [< MFr. < Sp. *escotilla*, dim. of *escote*, a notch] **1.** an opening in a wall or roof, fitted with a cover **2.** a small, covered opening in the hull or deck of a ship **3.** the cover for such an opening —*vt.* **-tled, -tling 1.** to sink (a ship) by making or opening holes in the hull below the waterline **2.** to abandon (a plan, undertaking, etc.)

scut·tle·butt (skut′'l but′) *n.* [orig. < *scuttled butt*, cask with an opening for a dipper] **1.** *Naut.* a drinking fountain on shipboard ☆**2.** [Colloq.] rumor or gossip

scu·tum (skyōōt′əm) *n., pl.* **scu′ta** (-ə) [L.] **1.** the long, leather-covered, wooden shield of Roman infantrymen **2.** *Zool.* a heavy, horny scale, as on certain reptiles or insects

Scyl·la (sil′ə) a dangerous rock on the southern Italian coast, opposite the whirlpool Charybdis —**between Scylla and Charybdis** between two dangers or evils, neither of which can be avoided without facing the other

scy·pho·zo·an (sī′fə zō′ən) *n.* [< ModL. class name < Gr. *skyphos*, a cup + *zōion*, an animal] any of a group of sea coelenterates consisting of the true jellyfishes

scythe (sīth) *n.* [altered (after L. *scindere*, to cut) < OE. *sithe*: for IE. base see SAW[1]] a tool with a long, single-edged blade on a long, curved handle, used in cutting tall grass, grain, etc. by hand —*vt.* **scythed, scyth′ing** to cut with a scythe

Scyth·i·a (sith′ē ə) ancient region in SE Europe, on the N coast of the Black Sea —**Scyth′i·an** *adj., n.*

S.Dak., SD South Dakota

Se *Chem.* selenium

SE, S.E., s.e. 1. southeast **2.** southeastern

sea (sē) *n.* [OE. *sæ*] **1.** the ocean **2.** a large body of salt water wholly or partly enclosed by land [the Red *Sea*]

SCYTHE

3. a large body of fresh water [the *Sea* of Galilee] **4.** the condition of the ocean's surface [a calm *sea*] **5.** a large swell or wave [almost swamped by heavy *seas*] **6.** a very great amount or number [a *sea* of debt] **7.** *Astron.* same as MARE[2] (sense 2) —*adj.* of, connected with, or for use at sea —**at sea 1.** on the open sea **2.** uncertain; confused —**go to sea** to become a sailor —**put (out) to sea** to sail away from land

sea anchor a large, canvas-covered frame, usually cone-shaped, let out from a ship as a drag to slow down drifting or to keep the ship heading into the wind

sea anemone a sea polyp having a firm, jellylike body topped with colored tentacles that look like petals

sea bag a large, cylindrical canvas bag in which a sailor carries his clothes and personal belongings

☆**sea bass 1.** any of numerous sea fishes; esp., *a)* the **black sea bass**, a food fish with large scales and a wide mouth, found along the Atlantic coast of the U.S. *b)* the **giant sea bass**, found along the California coast **2.** any of various similar fishes, as the **white sea bass**, a drum found along the California coast

☆**Sea·bee** (sē′bē′) *n.* [< CB, short for *Construction Battalion*] a member of any of the construction and engineering battalions of the U.S. Navy

sea bird a bird living on or near the sea: also **sea fowl**

sea·board (-bôrd′) *n.* land or coastal region bordering on the sea —*adj.* bordering on the sea

sea·borne (-bôrn′) *adj.* **1.** carried on or by seagoing ships **2.** afloat: said of ships

sea bream same as BREAM[1] (sense 2); ☆esp., a porgy of the Atlantic coast of the U.S.

sea breeze a breeze blowing inland from the sea

sea·coast (-kōst′) *n.* land bordering on the sea

sea cow 1. any of several sea mammals, as the dugong or manatee **2.** earlier name for WALRUS

sea cucumber an echinoderm with a cucumber-shaped, flexible body and long tentacles around the mouth

sea dog 1. an experienced sailor **2.** any of various seals

sea fan any of several fan-shaped corals; esp., a horny coral of the West Indies and Florida Keys

sea·far·er (-fer′ər) *n.* a traveler by sea; esp., a sailor

sea·far·ing (-fer′iŋ) *adj.* of or engaged in life at sea —*n.* **1.** the occupation of a sailor **2.** travel by sea

☆**sea·food** (-fōōd′) *n.* food prepared from or consisting of salt-water fish or shellfish

sea·front (-frunt′) *n.* the part of a town or other built-up area facing on the sea

sea·girt (-gurt′) *adj.* surrounded by the sea

sea·go·ing (-gō′iŋ) *adj.* **1.** made for use on the open sea [a *seagoing* schooner] **2.** same as SEAFARING

sea green a pale bluish green —**sea′-green′** *adj.*

sea gull same as GULL[1]; esp., any gull living along a seacoast

sea horse 1. a small, semitropical marine fish with a slender tail, plated body, and a head somewhat like that of a horse **2.** a mythical sea creature, half fish and half horse

Sea Islands chain of islands off the coasts of S.C., Ga., & N Fla.

seal[1] (sēl) *n.* [< OFr. < L. *sigillum*, a seal, dim. of *signum*, a SIGN] **1.** a design, initials, etc. placed on a letter, document, etc. to prove it is genuine: letters were once commonly sealed with molten wax stamped with such a design **2.** a stamp or signet ring for making such a design **3.** a piece of wax, paper, etc. stamped with a design recognized as official **4.** something that closes or fastens tightly or securely, or that prevents the passage of air or water **5.** anything that guarantees; pledge **6.** a sign; token [a handshake as a *seal* of friendship] ☆**7.** an ornamental paper stamp [a Christmas *seal*] —*vt.* **1.** to mark with a seal **2.** to protect the contents of (a letter, etc.) by closing with a wax seal, a gummed flap, etc. **3.** to confirm the genuineness of (a promise, etc.) by some action [to *seal* a bargain with a handshake] **4.** to certify as being official, accurate, exact, etc. by or as by fixing a seal to **5.** to settle or decide finally [to *seal* one's fate] **6.** *a)* to close, fasten, etc. as with a seal [to *seal* one's lips] *b)* to close completely so

SEA HORSE (to 6 in. long)

as to make airtight or watertight c) to apply a coating to (a porous surface, as a wood) so as to block the passage of fluids —**seal off 1.** to close completely **2.** to surround (an area, etc.) with barriers, a cordon, etc. —**set one's seal to 1.** to mark with one's seal **2.** to endorse; approve —**seal′a·ble** *adj.* —**seal′er** *n.*

seal[2] (sēl) *n., pl.* **seals, seal:** see PLURAL, II, D, 1 [OE. *seolh*] **1.** a sea mammal with four flippers that lives in cold waters and eats fish **2.** the fur of a fur seal **3.** leather made from sealskin —*vi.* to hunt seals

☆**Sea·lab** (sē′lab′) *n.* [SEA + LAB(ORATORY)] any of a series of underwater laboratories of the U.S. Navy for undersea exploration and research

sea lamprey a parasitic lamprey of the N Atlantic that spawns in streams and is now landlocked in the Great Lakes

sea lane a commonly used route for travel by sea

FUR SEAL
(5–7 ft. long)

seal·ant (sēl′ənt) *n.* [SEAL[1] + -ANT] a substance, as a wax, plastic, silicone, etc., used for sealing

sea lavender a stiff plant with white, pink, lavender, or yellow flowers and many branches

sea legs the ability to walk without loss of balance on board ship, esp. in a rough sea

seal·er·y (sēl′ər ē) *n., pl.* **-er·ies 1.** a place where seals are hunted **2.** the work of hunting seals Also **seal fishery**

sea level the level of the surface of the sea, esp. the mean level between high and low tide: used as a standard in measuring heights and depths

sea lily a stalked and attached crinoid

sealing wax a hard mixture of resin and turpentine used for sealing letters, dry cells, etc.: it softens when heated

sea lion a large seal of the N Pacific

seal ring *same as* SIGNET RING

seal·skin (sēl′skin′) *n.* **1.** the skin of the seal; esp., the soft undercoat dyed dark-brown or black **2.** a garment made of this —*adj.* made of sealskin

Sea·ly·ham terrier (sē′lē ham′, -əm) [< *Sealyham*, an estate in Wales] a small, white terrier with short legs and square jaws

seam (sēm) *n.* [OE. *seam:* for IE. base see SEW] **1.** the line formed by sewing together two pieces of material **2.** a line marking adjoining edges, as of boards **3.** a mark, line, etc. like this, as a scar, wrinkle, etc. **4.** a layer or stratum of ore, coal, etc. —*vt.* **1.** to join together so as to form a seam **2.** to mark with a line, crack, etc. like a seam [a face *seamed* with wrinkles] —**seam′less** *adj.*

sea·man (sē′mən) *n., pl.* **-men 1.** a sailor **2.** *U.S. Navy* a nonrated enlisted man whose duties are concerned with deck maintenance, equipment, etc. —**sea′man·like′** *adj.*

sea·man·ship (-ship′) *n.* skill in sailing, navigating, or working a ship

sea·mark (sē′märk′) *n.* any easily seen object, as a lighthouse, serving as an aid to navigation

seam·stress (sēm′stris) *n.* a woman who sews expertly or who makes her living by sewing

seam·y (sē′mē) *adj.* **seam′i·er, seam′i·est 1.** having or showing seams **2.** unpleasant, dirty, or wretched [the *seamy* side of life] —**seam′i·ness** *n.*

sé·ance (sā′äns) *n.* [Fr. < L. *sedere,* to sit] a meeting at which spiritualists seek or claim to communicate with the dead

sea otter a web-footed sea mammal found along the northern Pacific coast: its dark-brown fur is valuable

sea·plane (sē′plān′) *n.* any airplane designed to land on and take off from water

sea·port (-pôrt′) *n.* **1.** a port or harbor used by ocean ships **2.** a town or city having such a port

sea power 1. naval strength **2.** a nation having great naval strength

sea purse the horny egg case or egg capsule of certain skates, rays, and sharks

sear (sir) *adj.* [OE.] dried up; withered; sere —*vt.* **1.** to dry up; wither [the hot sun *seared* the crops] **2.** to scorch or burn the surface of [hot grease *seared* her arm] **3.** to make hard or unfeeling [a *seared* conscience] —*n.* a mark produced by searing —see SYN. at BURN[1] —**sear′ing·ly** *adv.*

search (surch) *vt.* [< OFr. *cercher* < LL. *circare,* to go about < *circus,* ring: see CIRCUS] **1.** to go over and look through in order to find something [to *search* the house] **2.** to examine (a person) for something hidden **3.** to examine carefully; probe [to *search* one's soul] —*vi.* to make a search [to *search* for an answer] —*n.* the act of searching; examination —**in search of** trying to find —☆**search me** [Slang] I do not know —**search out** to seek or find by searching —**search′a·ble** *adj.* —**search′er** *n.*

search·ing (surch′iŋ) *adj.* **1.** examining thoroughly [a *searching* test] **2.** sharp; piercing [a *searching* wind] —**search′ing·ly** *adv.*

search·light (-līt′) *n.* **1.** a device on a swivel for throwing a far-reaching beam of light in any direction **2.** such a beam

search warrant a legal document authorizing a police search, as for stolen articles

☆**sea robin** any of a number of spiny-finned sea fishes having a broad head covered with plates of bone, and large, winglike chest fins; esp., any of a group with reddish coloring

sea·scape (sē′skāp′) *n.* [SEA + (LAND)SCAPE] **1.** a view of the sea **2.** a drawing, painting, etc. of such a view

sea serpent any large, unidentified or imaginary serpentlike animal reported to have been seen in the sea

sea·shell (-shel′) *n.* the shell of any saltwater mollusk

sea·shore (-shôr′) *n.* land along the sea; seacoast

sea·sick·ness (-sik′nis) *n.* nausea, dizziness, etc. caused by the movement of a ship at sea —**sea′sick′** *adj.*

sea·side (-sīd′) *n.* land along the sea; seashore —*adj.* at or of the seaside

sea snake any of various poisonous snakes with a flattened tail, living in tropical seas

sea·son (sē′z'n) *n.* [< OFr. < VL. *satio,* sowing time < L. < base of *serere,* to sow] **1.** any of the four divisions into which the year is divided; spring, summer, fall (or autumn), or winter **2.** the time of the year when something specified takes place, is popular, permitted, at its best, etc. [the harvest *season,* the hunting *season*] **3.** a period of time [the busy *season* in a factory] **4.** the fitting or convenient time **5.** the time of a specified festival or holiday [the Easter *season*] —*vt.* **1.** to make (food) more tasty by adding salt, spices, etc. **2.** to add excitement or interest to [to *season* a speech with humor] **3.** to make more fit for use, as by aging, drying, etc. [to *season* lumber] **4.** to give experience to or make used to [a *seasoned* actor, traveler, etc.] **5.** to make less harsh; soften [discipline *seasoned* with kindness] —*vi.* to become seasoned, as wood by drying —**for a season** for a while —**in season 1.** available fresh for use as food [apples are *in season*] **2.** at the legally established time for being hunted or caught: said of game, etc. **3.** in or at the proper time **4.** early enough: also **in good season 5.** in heat: said of animals —**out of season** not in season —**sea′son·er** *n.*

sea·son·a·ble (-ə b'l) *adj.* **1.** suitable to or usual for the time of year [*seasonable* weather] **2.** coming at the right time; timely [*seasonable* advice] —see SYN. at TIMELY —**sea′son·a·bly** *adv.*

sea·son·al (-əl) *adj.* of or depending on a season or the seasons [*seasonal* rains, *seasonal* work] —**sea′son·al·ly** *adv.*

sea·son·ing (-iŋ) *n.* anything that adds flavor or interest; esp., salt, spices, etc. added to food to make it more tasty

season ticket a ticket or set of tickets as for a series of concerts, sports events, etc. or for transportation, etc. for a given period of time

sea spider any of various small saltwater arthropods with very long legs attached to a relatively tiny body

sea squirt *same as* ASCIDIAN

seat (sēt) *n.* [ON. *sæti:* for IE. base see SIT] **1.** the manner of sitting, as on horseback **2.** *a)* a place to sit, or the right to sit a place, esp. as shown by a ticket *b)* a thing to sit on; chair, bench, etc. **3.** *a)* the buttocks *b)* the part of a garment covering the buttocks *c)* the part of a chair, etc. that supports the buttocks **4.** the right to sit as a member; membership [a *seat* on the stock exchange] **5.** a part or surface on which another part rests or fits **6.** the chief location; a center [the *seat* of government; a *seat* of learning] —*vt.* **1.** to put or set in or on a seat [*seat* yourself quickly] **2.** to lead to a seat [the usher will *seat* you] **3.** to have seats for [the car *seats* six] **4.** to put a seat in or on; repair the seat of **5.** to put in a certain place, position, etc. [*seat* the washer carefully to prevent leaking] —**be seated 1.** to get in a seat; sit down: also **take a seat 2.** to be sitting **3.** to be located, settled, etc. —**seat′less** *adj.*

seat belt a device consisting of straps that buckle across the hips of a passenger in an automobile, airplane, etc. to hold him securely in his seat, as in an accident

-seat·er (sēt′ər) *a combining form meaning* a vehicle, etc. having (a specified number of) seats [a two-*seater*]

seat·ing (-iŋ) *n.* **1.** a providing with a seat or seats **2.** material for covering chair seats, etc. **3.** the arrangement or number of seats [a theater with limited *seating*]

☆**seat·mate** (-māt′) *n.* a person in an adjoining seat in an airplane, bus, etc.

SEATO (sē′tō) Southeast Asia Treaty Organization

sea trout any of various saltwater fishes related to the drums and including several weakfishes

Se·at·tle (sē at′′l) [after *Seathl*, an Indian chief] seaport in WC Wash., on Puget Sound: pop. 531,000 (met. area 1,422,000)

sea urchin a small sea animal with a round body in a shell covered with long, movable spines

sea wall a wall made to break the force of the waves and to protect the shore from erosion

sea·ward (sē′wərd) *adj., adv.* toward the sea: also **sea′wards** *adv.* —*n.* a seaward direction or position

sea·way (-wā′) *n.* **1.** a route for travel on the sea **2.** a ship's headway **3.** a rough sea **4.** an inland waterway to the sea for ocean ships

sea·weed (-wēd′) *n.* **1.** any sea plant or plants; esp., any marine alga, as kelp: in full, **marine seaweed** **2.** any similar freshwater plant: in full, **freshwater seaweed**

SEA URCHIN
(1½–10 in. in
diameter)

sea·wor·thy (-wur′thē) *adj.* fit to travel in on the open sea; sturdy: said of a ship —**sea′wor′thi·ness** *n.*

se·ba·ceous (si bā′shəs) *adj.* [< L. < *sebum*, tallow] of or like fat, tallow, or sebum; greasy; oily; esp., designating certain skin glands that give out sebum

Se·bas·tian (si bas′chən) [L. < Gr. < *Sebastia*, ancient city in Asia Minor] **1.** a masculine name **2.** Saint, ?–288? A.D.; Christian martyr of Rome

se·bum (sē′bəm) *n.* [L., tallow] the greasy, lubricating liquid given out by the sebaceous glands

‡**sec** (sek) *adj.* [Fr.] dry; not sweet: said of wine

SEC, S.E.C. Securities and Exchange Commission

sec secant

sec. **1.** second(s) **2.** secondary **3.** secretary **4.** section(s) **5.** sector **6.** security

se·cant (sē′kənt, -kant) *adj.* [< L. prp. of *secare*, to cut] cutting; intersecting —*n.* **1.** *Geom.* any straight line intersecting a curve at two or more points **2.** *Trigonometry* the ratio of the hypotenuse of a right triangle to either of the other two sides with reference to the enclosed angle

se·cede (si sēd′) *vi.* **-ced′ed, -ced′ing** [< L. < *se-*, apart + *cedere*, to go] to withdraw formally from membership in a group or organization, esp. a political one —**se·ced′er** *n.*

se·ces·sion (si sesh′ən) *n.* **1.** an act of seceding ☆**2.** [often S-] the withdrawal of the Southern States from the Federal Union at the start of the Civil War —**se·ces′sion·al** *adj.*

☆**se·ces·sion·ist** (-ist) *n.* a person who favors or takes part in secession; specif., [often S-] one who favored the secession of the Southern States —**se·ces′sion·ism** *n.*

☆**Seck·el (pear)** (sek′′l) [after the Pa. fruit grower who originated it] a small, sweet, juicy, reddish-brown pear

se·clude (si klo͞od′) *vt.* **-clud′ed, -clud′ing** [< L. < *secludere* < *se-*, apart + *claudere*, to shut] **1.** to keep away or shut off from others; isolate [nuns *secluded* in a convent] **2.** to make private or hidden

se·clud·ed (-klo͞od′id) *adj.* **1.** shut off or kept apart from others; isolated; withdrawn **2.** hidden from view [a *secluded* garden] —**se·clud′ed·ly** *adv.*

se·clu·sion (si klo͞o′zhən) *n.* a secluding or being secluded; isolation [to live in *seclusion*] —see SYN. at SOLITUDE

sec·ond[1] (sek′ənd) *adj.* [OFr. < L. *secundus* < *sequi*, to follow: see SEQUENT] **1.** coming next after the first in order; 2d or 2nd **2.** other; additional [a *second* helping] **3.** being of the same kind as another [a *second* Caesar] **4.** alternate [every *second* day] **5.** next below the first in rank, value, merit, etc. [*second* prize] **6.** *Music a)* lower in pitch *b)* performing a part lower in pitch [*second* violin] —*n.* **1.** any person, thing, class, place, etc. that is second [the *second* to arrive] **2.** the next after the first [the *second* to arrive] **3.** an article of merchandise that is not of the first quality **4.** an aid or assistant, as to a duelist or boxer **5.** the second forward gear ratio of a motor vehicle **6.** the act of

seconding a motion, etc. **7.** [Slang] [pl.] a second helping of food —*vt.* **1.** to act as an aid to; assist **2.** to give support or encouragement to; reinforce [to *second* a cause by giving money] **3.** to indicate formal support of (a motion, nomination, etc.) so that it may be discussed or voted on —*adv.* in the second place, group, etc. —**sec′ond·er** *n.*

sec·ond[2] (sek′ənd) *n.* [ML. (*pars minuta*) *secunda*, second (small part): from being a further division (i.e., beyond the minute)] **1.** 1/60 of a minute of time **2.** 1/60 of a minute of angular measurement **3.** a very short time; instant [wait just a *second*] **4.** a specific point in time [come here this *second*]

sec·ond·ar·y (sek′ən der′ē) *adj.* **1.** second, or below the first, in rank, importance, place, etc.; subordinate; minor [a matter of *secondary* interest] **2.** *a)* coming from something considered primary or original; derivative *b)* secondhand; not original [a *secondary* source of information] *c)* designating colors derived by mixing two primary colors: see COLOR (*n.* 3) **3.** coming after the first in a series of processes, events, stages, etc. [*secondary* education] **4.** *Elec.* designating of or an induced current or its circuit in a transformer, induction coil, etc. **5.** *Zool.* designating or of the long flight feathers on the second joint of a bird's wing —*n., pl.* **-ar′ies** **1.** a person or thing that is secondary **2.** *Elec.* an output winding of a transformer from which the power is taken ☆**3.** *Football* the defensive backfield —**sec′ond·ar′i·ly** *adv.*

secondary accent (or **stress**) **1.** any accent, or stress, that is weaker than the full, or primary, accent **2.** a mark (in this dictionary, ′) to show this

secondary cell a battery cell in which the electrochemical reaction can be reversed so that it is possible to recharge the cell economically by an electric current

secondary emission the emission of electrons (**secondary electrons**) from a material, after it has been struck by high-speed electrons

☆**secondary school** a school, as a high school, coming after elementary school

secondary sex ̶̶̶̶̶̶̶̶̶̶ any physical characteristic, such as the growth of hair on the face or the development of breasts, that is different in men and women and is not directly related to reproduction

☆**second banana** [Slang] **1.** a less important performer in a show, esp. burlesque, as one who plays straight man to the top banana, or star comedian **2.** any person in a less important position

☆**second base** *Baseball* the base between first base and third base, located behind the pitcher

sec·ond-best (sek′ənd best′) *adj.* next below the best

second childhood the condition of an old person who is weak and childish

sec·ond-class (sek′ənd klas′) *adj.* **1.** of the class, rank, quality, etc. next below the highest **2.** designating of or accommodations next below the best [a *second-class* cabin on a ship] ☆**3.** designating or of a class of mail consisting of newspapers, periodicals, etc. **4.** of poor quality, standing, etc. —*adv.* **1.** with second-class accommodations [to travel *second-class*] **2.** as or by second-class mail

Second Coming in the theology of some Christian sects, the expected return of Christ, at the Last Judgment

second cousin the child of one's parent's first cousin

second growth ☆trees growing on land that had its original trees cut down or burned

sec·ond-guess (sek′ənd ges′) *vt., vi.* [Colloq.] to use hindsight in criticizing (someone or something), remaking (a decision), etc. —**sec′ond-guess′er** *n.*

sec·ond·hand (-hand′) *adj.* **1.** not direct from the original source; not original [*secondhand* news] **2.** used or worn previously by another; not new [a *secondhand* coat] **3.** of or dealing in merchandise that is not new [a *secondhand* store] —*adv.* not firsthand; not directly [I heard it *secondhand*]

second hand the hand (of a clock or watch) that shows the seconds and moves around the dial once every minute

second lieutenant a commissioned officer of the lowest rank in the U.S. Army, Air Force, or Marine Corps

sec·ond·ly (sek′ənd lē) *adv.* in the second place; second

second nature a habit that is fixed so deeply as to seem part of a person's nature

---

second person that form of a pronoun (as *you*) or verb (as *are*) which refers to the person or persons spoken to

sec·ond-rate (-rāt′) *adj.* **1.** second in quality, rank, etc.; second-class **2.** inferior; mediocre —**sec′ond-rat′er** *n.*

second sight the supposed ability to see things not physically present, to foresee the future, etc.

sec·ond-string (-striŋ′) *adj.* [Colloq.] **1.** *Sports* chosen second or as a substitute to play at a specified position [*our second-string* catcher] **2.** second-rate; inferior —**sec′ond-string′er** *n.*

second wind **1.** the return of normal ease in breathing during hard exercise after one has at first been out of breath **2.** recovered ability to continue any effort

se·cre·cy (sē′krə sē) *n., pl.* **-cies** **1.** the condition of being secret **2.** the practice or habit of keeping things secret

se·cret (sē′krit) *adj.* [< OFr. < L. pp. of *secernere* < *se-*, apart + *cernere*, to sift, discern] **1.** kept from the knowledge of others [a *secret* formula] **2.** remote; secluded [a *secret* hideaway] **3.** keeping one's affairs to oneself; secretive **4.** beyond general understanding; mysterious [*secret* knowledge] **5.** concealed from sight or notice; hidden [a *secret* drawer] **6.** acting in secret [a *secret* society] —*n.* **1.** something known only to some and kept from the knowledge of others **2.** something not understood or explained; mystery [nature's *secrets*] **3.** the true explanation, thought of as not obvious [the *secret* of success] —**in secret** without the knowledge of others; secretly —**se′cret·ly** *adv.*

SYN.—**secret** implies a hiding or keeping from the knowledge of others, for whatever reason [my *secret* opinion of him]; **covert** implies a hiding as by disguising or veiling [a *covert* threat]; **clandestine** suggests that what is being kept secret is illegal, immoral, or forbidden [the spies' *clandestine* meetings]; **stealthy** implies slow, secret movement in an attempt to escape notice and may suggest dishonest activity [the thief's *stealthy* approach]; **furtive** suggests the quick, sneaky movements of someone who feels guilty or is afraid of getting caught [her *furtive* glance through the curtain]; **surreptitious** suggests the slyness or watchfulness of one who is doing something forbidden [a *surreptitious* reading of someone else's mail]; **underhanded** implies sly and dishonest secrecy [*underhanded* business dealings] —**ANT.** open, obvious

secret agent a person who serves as a spy or does similar secret work, as for a government

sec·re·tar·i·at (sek′rə ter′ē ət) *n.* **1.** the office, position, or quarters of a secretary of high position, as in a government **2.** a staff headed by a secretary-general

sec·re·tar·y (sek′rə ter′ē) *n., pl.* **-tar′ies** [ML. *secretarius*, one entrusted with secrets < L. *secretum:* see SECRET] **1.** *a)* a person whose work is keeping records, taking care of correspondence, etc. as for an executive in a business office *b)* an officer of a company, club, etc. having somewhat similar duties ☆**2.** an official in charge of a department of government [*Secretary* of the Treasury] **3.** a writing desk, esp. one with a small bookcase built on top —**sec′re·tar′i·al** *adj.* —**sec′re·tar′y·ship′** *n.*

secretary bird [from the penlike feathers of its crest] a large, grayish-blue and black African bird of prey with a long neck and long legs

sec·re·tar·y-gen·er·al (-jen′ər əl) *n., pl.* **-tar′ies-gen′er·al** the chief administrative officer of an organization, in charge of a secretariat

se·crete (si krēt′) *vt.* **-cret′ed, -cret′ing** [< L. pp. of *secernere:* see SECRET] **1.** to hide; conceal **2.** to form and release (a specified secretion) as a gland, etc. does —see SYN. at HIDE[1]

se·cre·tion (si krē′shən) *n.* **1.** the act of hiding or concealing something **2.** *a)* the process by which a substance is formed from the blood or sap and then released into the organism or as a waste product *b)* such a substance

se·cre·tive (sē′krə tiv; *also, & for 2 always,* si krēt′iv) *adj.* [SECRET + -IVE] **1.** keeping one's thoughts, feelings, etc. to oneself; not frank; reticent **2.** *same as* SECRETORY —see SYN. at SILENT —**se′cre·tive·ly** *adv.* —**se′cre·tive·ness** *n.*

se·cre·to·ry (si krēt′ər ē) *adj.* of, or having the function of, secretion —*n.* a secretory gland, etc.

secret police a police force that operates secretly, esp. in order to put down opposition to the government

secret service a government service that carries on secret investigation; specif., ☆[S- S-] a division of the U.S. Treasury Department for uncovering counterfeiters, protecting the President, etc.

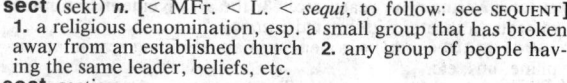

SECRETARY BIRD (to 4 ft. high)

sect (sekt) *n.* [< MFr. < L. < *sequi*, to follow: see SEQUENT] **1.** a religious denomination, esp. a small group that has broken away from an established church **2.** any group of people having the same leader, beliefs, etc.

sect. section

sec·tar·i·an (sek ter′ē ən) *adj.* **1.** of or relating to a sect **2.** devoted to some sect **3.** narrow-minded —*n.* **1.** a member of any religious sect **2.** a person who is blindly devoted to a sect —**sec·tar′i·an·ism** *n.*

sec·ta·ry (sek′tər ē) *n., pl.* **-ries** a member of a sect

sec·tile (sek′t'l, -tīl) *adj.* [Fr. < L. < *secare*, to cut] **1.** capable of being cut smoothly with a knife **2.** *Bot.* cut into small divisions —**sec·til′i·ty** (-til′ə tē) *n.*

sec·tion (sek′shən) *n.* [< L. < pp. of *secare*, to cut: for IE. base see SAW[1]] **1.** a cutting or separating by cutting; specif., an incision in surgery **2.** a part separated by cutting; slice; division **3.** *a)* a division of a book, newspaper, etc. *b)* a numbered paragraph of a law, etc. **4.** any distinct or separate part [a bookcase in *sections*] **5.** a segment of an orange, grapefruit, etc. **6.** *a)* a part of a city, country, etc.; district or region [a hilly *section;* the business *section*] ☆*b)* a division of public lands that is a mile square (640 acres) **7.** a drawing, etc. of a thing as it would appear if cut straight through in a given plane **8.** any of the distinct groups of instruments or voices in an orchestra or chorus [the woodwind *section*] ☆**9.** any one of two or more buses, trains, or airplanes used for a particular run or flight ☆**10.** *Railroading* several miles of track maintained by a single crew —*vt.* **1.** to cut or divide into sections **2.** to show in sections —see SYN. at PART

sec·tion·al (sek′shən 'l) *adj.* **1.** of or devoted to a given section or district; regional **2.** made up of or divided into sections —☆*n.* a sectional sofa, bookcase, etc. —**sec′tion·al·ly** *adv.*

☆**sec·tion·al·ism** (-iz'm) *n.* narrow-minded concern shown for one section of a country —**sec′tion·al·ist** *adj., n.*

sec·tor (sek′tər) *n.* [LL. < L., cutter < *secare:* see SECTION] **1.** part of a circle bounded by any two radii and the arc between them **2.** any of the districts into which an area is divided for military operations **3.** a distinct part of a society or of an economy, group, etc. [the public *sector* of the economy] —*vt.* to divide into sectors

sec·u·lar (sek′yə lər) *adj.* [< OFr. < LL. < L. < *saeculum*, age, generation] **1.** *a)* not related to church or religion; not sacred or religious; temporal; worldly [*secular* schools] *b)* of secularism **2.** living in the outside world and not bound by a monastic vow [the *secular* clergy] —*n.* a member of the secular clergy —**sec′u·lar·ly** *adv.*

sec·u·lar·ism (-iz'm) *n.* **1.** worldly spirit, views, etc.; esp., a system of beliefs and practices that rejects any form of religious faith **2.** the belief that religion should be kept separate from the activities of government, esp. from public education —**sec′u·lar·ist** *n., adj.* —**sec′u·lar·is′tic** *adj.*

sec·u·lar·ize (sek′yə lə rīz′) *vt.* **-ized′, -iz′ing** **1.** to change from religious to civil ownership or use **2.** to take away the religious character, influence, etc. of **3.** to convert to secularism —**sec′u·lar·i·za′tion** *n.*

se·cure (si kyoor′) *adj.* [< L. < *se-*, free from + *cura*, care: see CURE] **1.** free from fear, care, doubt, etc.; not worried, troubled, etc. [to feel *secure* about the future] **2.** free from danger; safe [a *secure* hiding place] **3.** in safekeeping or custody [the prisoner is *secure*] **4.** firm; stable [make the knot *secure*] **5.** reliable; dependable [a *secure* investment] —*vt.* **-cured′, -cur′ing** **1.** to make secure, or safe; protect [to *secure* one's house against burglars] **2.** to make sure or certain; guarantee, as with a pledge [to *secure* a loan with collateral] **3.** to make firm, fast, etc. [*secure* the bolt] **4.** to obtain; acquire; get [to *secure* aid] —*vi.* to give security [a policy that *secures* against loss] —see SYN. at GET and SAFE —**se·cur′ance** *n.* —**se·cure′ly** *adv.* —**se·cur′er** *n.*

se·cu·ri·ty (si kyoor′ə tē) *n., pl.* **-ties** **1.** the state of being or feeling free from fear, anxiety, danger, doubt, etc. **2.** protection or defense, as against attack, espionage, etc. [funds for national *security*] **3.** *a)* something given as a pledge of repayment, etc. [a car may be used as *security* for a loan] *b)* a person who promises to pay another's debt if he fails to pay it **4.** a stock certificate or bond: *usually used in pl.*

security blanket a small blanket or other soft cloth, as clutched or stroked by a child for the feeling of comfort and security it gives

Security Council the United Nations council responsible for maintaining international peace and security

secy., sec′y. secretary

se·dan (si dan′) *n.* [< ? L. *sedere*, to sit] **1.** *same as* SEDAN CHAIR ☆**2.** a closed automobile with two or four doors, and two wide seats, front and rear

sedan chair an enclosed chair for one person, carried on poles by two men

se·date[1] (si dāt′) *adj.* [< L. pp. of *sedare*, to settle: see SIT] calm or quiet; esp., serious and unemotional; decorous —see SYN. at SERIOUS —**se·date′ly** *adv.* —**se·date′ness** *n.*

☆**se·date**[2] (si dāt′) *vt.* **-dat′ed, -dat′ing** [< SEDATIVE] to give a dose of sedative to

se·da·tion (si dā′shən) *n.* *Med.* **1.** the reducing of excitement, nervousness, or irritation by means of sedatives **2.** the calm state produced by sedatives

SEDAN CHAIR

sed·a·tive (sed′ə tiv) *adj.* [see SEDATE[1]] tending to soothe or quiet; specif., *Med.* producing sedation —*n.* a sedative medicine

sed·en·tar·y (sed′'n ter′ē) *adj.* [< Fr. < L. < prp. of *sedere*, to SIT] **1.** *a)* tending to sit much of the time [a *sedentary* old man] *b)* keeping one seated much of the time [a *sedentary* job] **2.** *a)* not migratory: said of birds *b)* fixed to one spot, as a barnacle —**sed′en·tar′i·ly** *adv.* —**sed′en·tar′i·ness** *n.*

Se·der (sā′dər) *n., pl.* **Se·dar·im** (sə där′im), **Se′ders** [Heb. *sēdher*, arrangement] *Judaism* the Passover feast commemorating the exodus of the Jews from Egypt

sedge (sej) *n.* [OE. *secg*] any of several coarse, grasslike plants often found on wet ground or in water —**sedg′y** *adj.*

sed·i·ment (sed′ə mənt) *n.* [< Fr. < L. < *sedere*, to SIT] **1.** matter that settles to the bottom of a liquid; dregs **2.** *Geol.* matter deposited by water or wind, as sand or soil

sed·i·men·ta·ry (sed′ə men′tər ē) *adj.* **1.** of, like, or containing sediment **2.** formed by the deposit of sediment, as certain rocks —**sed′i·men·ta·ri·ly** *adv.*

sed·i·men·ta·tion (sed′ə men tā′shən, -mən-) *n.* the depositing or formation of sediment

se·di·tion (si dish′ən) *n.* [OFr. < L. < *sed-*, apart + *itio*, a going < *ire*, to go] a stirring up of rebellion against a government —**se·di′tion·ist** *n.*

se·di·tious (si dish′əs) *adj.* **1.** of or like sedition **2.** stirring up rebellion —**se·di′tious·ly** *adv.* —**se·di′tious·ness** *n.*

se·duce (si dōōs′, -dyōōs′) *vt.* **-duced′, -duc′ing** [< LL. < L. < *se-*, apart + *ducere*, to lead: see DUKE] **1.** *a)* to persuade to do something disloyal, disobedient, etc. *b)* to tempt to do something evil or wrong; lead astray *c)* to persuade to take part in unlawful sexual intercourse, esp. for the first time **2.** to entice; tempt —**se·duce′ment** *n.* —**se·duc′er** *n.* —**se·duc′i·ble** *adj.*

se·duc·tion (si duk′shən) *n.* **1.** a seducing or being seduced **2.** something that seduces

se·duc·tive (-tiv) *adj.* likely to seduce; very tempting or attractive —**se·duc′tive·ly** *adv.* —**se·duc′tive·ness** *n.*

se·duc·tress (-tris) *n.* a woman who seduces

sed·u·lous (sej′oo ləs) *adj.* [L. *sedulus*, ult. < *se-*, apart + *dolus*, trickery] working hard and with care; diligent —see SYN. at BUSY —**se·du·li·ty** (si dyōōl′ə tē, -dōōl′-), **sed′u·lous·ness** *n.* —**sed′u·lous·ly** *adv.*

se·dum (sē′dəm) *n.* [ModL., genus name < L.] any of a group of plants found on rocks and walls, with fleshy stalks and leaves and white, yellow, or pink flowers

see[1] (sē) *vt.* **saw, seen, see′ing** [OE. *seon:* for IE. base see SAY] **1.** *a)* to get knowledge of through the eyes; look at *b)* to picture mentally **2.** *a)* to grasp mentally; understand [to *see* the point of a joke] *b)* to accept as right, fitting, or proper [I can't *see* him as president] *c)* to consider; judge [he *saw* it as his duty] **3.** to find out; learn [*see* who's there] **4.** to undergo or live through; experience [the town has *seen* better days] **5.** to look over; inspect [let me *see* the scar] **6.** to make sure [*see* that he goes] **7.** *a)* to go along with; accompany; escort [to *see* someone home] *b)* to keep company with [they have been *seeing* each other for three months] **8.** to encounter; meet [I saw Bill on my way out] **9.** to call on; visit or consult [*see* a lawyer] **10.** to receive as a visitor [too ill to *see* anyone] **11.** to be a spectator at; view or attend [*see* a show] **12.** *Card*

Games to meet (a bet) of (another) by staking an equal sum —*vi.* **1.** to have the power of sight **2.** to be aware of objects, colors, etc. by using the eyes [able to *see* far] **3.** *a)* to take a look [go and *see*] *b)* to find out about something; inquire [*see* if he's ready] **4.** to understand [it's a simple matter, can't you *see*] **5.** to think something over; reflect [let's *see*, where is it?] —*interj.* behold! look! —**see about 1.** to inquire into **2.** to take care of; attend to: also **see after** —**see fit (to)** to think it is right or proper (to do something) —**see into 1.** to look into **2.** to understand the true meaning or nature of —**see off** to go with and watch (another) leave by plane, boat, bus, etc. —**see out 1.** to go through with; finish **2.** to wait till the end of —**see through 1.** to understand the true meaning or character of **2.** to carry out to the end; finish **3.** to help through a time of difficulty —**see to** to take care of; attend to —**see′a·ble** *adj.*

SYN.—**see** is the basic term for the use of the eyes; **behold** is a formal word that implies a directing of the eyes on something and holding it in view [he never *beheld* a sight more beautiful]; **view** implies a seeing or looking at what lies before one, as in inspection or examination [the jury *viewed* the evidence]

see[2] (sē) *n.* [< OFr. *sie* < L. *sedes*, a seat] the office or district of a bishop

seed (sēd) *n., pl.* **seeds, seed:** see PLURAL, II, D, 4 [OE. *sæd*] **1.** the part of a flowering plant that contains the embryo and will grow into a new plant under the right conditions **2.** loosely, *a)* any part, as a bulb, from which a new plant will grow *b)* a small, seedlike fruit **3.** seeds used for sowing [to scatter grass *seed*] **4.** a source or beginning [the *seeds* of revolt] **5.** family stock; ancestry **6.** descendants; posterity **7.** *same as* SPAT[4] **8.** seed-bearing condition [in *seed*] **9.** *same as* SPORE (*n.* 2) **10.** sperm or semen **11.** something tiny, like a seed; esp., ☆*a)* a tiny crystal or particle, as one added to a solution to start it crystallizing *b)* a tiny bubble, as in glassware ☆**12.** *Sports* a seeded player —*vt.* **1.** to plant with seeds [to *seed* a lawn] **2.** to sow (seeds of a specified kind) **3.** to remove the seeds from [to *seed* grapes] ☆**4.** to sprinkle particles of dry ice, silver iodide, etc. into (clouds), as in trying to produce rainfall **5.** to provide with the means or stimulus for growing or developing ☆**6.** *Sports a)* to distribute the names of contestants in the draw for position in (a tournament) so as to avoid matching the most skilled together too early, as in tennis *b)* to rank (the most skilled players) in this way —*vi.* **1.** to become ripe and produce seeds **2.** to shed seeds **3.** to sow seeds —**go** (or **run**) **to seed 1.** to develop and shed seeds after flowering **2.** to become weak, useless, etc. —**seed′ed** *adj.* —**seed′er** *n.* —**seed′less** *adj.*

seed·bed (sēd′bed′) *n.* a bed of soil, usually covered with glass, in which seedlings are grown for transplanting

seed·cake (-kāk′) *n.* any cake or cookie containing spicy seeds, as of caraway

seed·case (-kās′) *n. same as* SEED VESSEL

seed coat the protective outer layer or coating of a seed

seed coral pieces of coral used in ornaments

seed leaf *same as* COTYLEDON

seed·ling (-lin) *n.* **1.** a plant grown from a seed, rather than from a cutting, etc. **2.** any young plant; esp., a young tree less than three feet high

☆**seed money** money made available to begin the financing of, or to attract additional funds for, a long-term project

seed oysters oyster spat; very young oysters, esp. when ready to be moved to another place

seed pearl a very small pearl, often imperfect

seed plant *same as* SPERMATOPHYTE

seed·pod (-päd′) *n.* a carpel or pistil, enclosing ovules or seeds in angiosperms

seeds·man (sēdz′mən) *n., pl.* **-men 1.** a sower of seeds **2.** a dealer in seeds Also **seed′man**

seed·time (sēd′tīm′) *n.* the season for sowing seeds

seed vessel any dry, hollow fruit, as a pod, containing seed

seed·y (sēd′ē) *adj.* **seed′i·er, seed′i·est 1.** containing many seeds **2.** gone to seed **3.** shabby, run-down, or looking bad, ill, etc. —**seed′i·ly** *adv.* —**seed′i·ness** *n.*

see·ing (sē′in) *n.* **1.** the sense or power of sight **2.** the use of the eyes to see —*adj.* having the sense of sight —*conj.* in view of the fact; inasmuch as; considering [*seeing* that he's here, let's begin eating]

---

fat, āpe, cär; ten, ēven; is, bīte; gō, hôrn, tōōl, look; oil, out; up, fur; get; joy; yet; chin; she; thin, *th*en; zh, leisure; ŋ, ring; ə for *a* in *ago*, *e* in *agent*, *i* in *sanity*, *o* in *comply*, *u* in *focus*; ′ as in *able* (ā′b'l); Fr. bal; ë, Fr. coeur; ö, Fr. feu; Fr. mon; ô, Fr. coq; ü, Fr. duc; r, Fr. cri; H, G. ich; kh, G. doch; ‡foreign; ☆ Americanism; < derived from. See inside front cover.

☆**Seeing Eye dog** [*also* s- e-] a guide dog, specif. one trained by Seeing Eye, Inc., near Morristown, N.J.

seek (sēk) *vt.* **sought, seek′ing** [OE. *secan:* for IE. base see SAKE[1]] **1.** to try to find; look for [to *seek* gold] **2.** to go to; resort to [to *seek* the woods for peace] **3.** *a)* to try to get or find out by asking or searching [to *seek* an answer] *b)* to request; ask for [to *seek* advice] **4.** to try for; aim at [*seeking* perfection] **5.** to try: used with an infinitive [to *seek* to please] —*vi.* to look for someone or something —**seek′er** *n.*

seem (sēm) *vi.* [prob. < ON. *sæma,* to conform to: for IE. base see SAME] **1.** *a)* to have the look of being; appear to be [he *seems* glad; the soil *seems* dry] *b)* to appear: usually used with an infinitive [he *seems* to know] *c)* to have the impression; think: used with an infinitive [I *seem* to recall] **2.** to appear to exist [there *seems* no end] **3.** to appear to be true [it *seems* he was right]

seem·ing (sēm′iŋ) *adj.* that seems real, true, etc. without necessarily being so; apparent [her *seeming* anger] —*n.* outward appearance; semblance —**seem′ing·ly** *adv.*

seem·ly (sēm′lē) *adj.* **-li·er, -li·est** [< ON. < *sæmr,* fitting] **1.** pleasing in appearance **2.** as it should be; suitable, proper, etc. [*seemly* behavior] —*adv.* in a seemly way —**seem′li·ness** *n.*

seen (sēn) *pp. of* SEE[1]

seep (sēp) *vi.* [OE. *sipian,* to soak < IE. base *seip-,* to run out] to leak, drip, or flow out slowly through small openings; ooze —*n. same as* SEEPAGE —**seep′y** *adj.*

seep·age (sēp′ij) *n.* **1.** a seeping; leakage **2.** liquid that seeps

seer (sē′ər *for 1;* sir *for 2*) *n.* **1.** a person who sees **2.** a person with the supposed power to foretell the future

seer·suck·er (sir′suk′ər) *n.* [< Hindi < Per. *shir u shakar,* lit., milk and sugar] a light, crinkled fabric of cotton, etc., usually with a striped pattern

see·saw (sē′sô′) *n.* [redupl. of SAW[1]] **1.** a plank balanced at the middle, used by children at play, who ride the ends so that when one goes up, the other comes down **2.** such a riding **3.** any up-and-down or back-and-forth movement or change [a *seesaw* in prices] —*adj.* moving up and down or back and forth —*vt., vi.* to move up and down or back and forth on a seesaw or like a seesaw

seethe (sēth) *vt.* **seethed, seeth′ing** [OE. *sēothan*] **1.** to cook by boiling **2.** to soak or saturate in liquid —*vi.* **1.** to boil or to surge, foam, etc. as if boiling [the *seething* waves] **2.** to be in a very excited or upset state [*seething* with rage] —*n.* a seething

seg·ment (seg′mənt; *for v.* -ment) *n.* [L. *segmentum* < *secare,* to cut: see SECTION] **1.** any of the parts into which something is divided or can be separated; section [the *segments* of an earthworm] **2.** *Geom.* any part, esp. of a circle or sphere, cut off by a line or plane, as a part of a circle bounded by an arc and its chord —*vt., vi.* to divide into segments —see SYN. at PART —**seg′men·tar′y** *adj.*

seg·men·tal (seg men′t'l) *adj.* **1.** having the form of a segment of a circle **2.** of, like, or made up of a segment or segments —**seg·men′tal·ly** *adv.*

segmental phonemes the vowel, consonant, and semivowel sounds of a language: see SUPRASEGMENTAL PHONEMES

seg·men·ta·tion (seg′mən tā′shən, -men-) *n.* **1.** a dividing or being divided into segments **2.** *Biol.* the progressive growth and splitting of a single cell into many others to form a new organism

☆**se·go** (sē′gō) *n., pl.* **-gos** [< AmInd.] **1.** a bulb plant with trumpet-shaped flowers, found in western N. America: in full, **sego lily 2.** its edible bulb

Se·go·via (se gô′vyä; *E.* sə gō′vē ə), **An·drés** (än dres′) 1894– ; Sp. guitarist & composer

seg·re·gate (seg′rə gāt′; *for adj. usually* -git) *adj.* [< L. pp. of *segregare* < *se-,* apart + *gregis,* genitive of *grex,* a flock] separate; set apart —*vt.* **-gat′ed, -gat′ing** to set apart from others; isolate; specif., to place or force a system of segregation on (racial groups, social facilities, etc.) —*vi.* to become segregated —**seg′re·gat′ive** *adj.*

seg·re·gat·ed (seg′rə gāt′id) *adj.* ☆following a system that segregates racial groups [*segregated* housing]

seg·re·ga·tion (seg′rə gā′shən) *n.* a segregating or being segregated; specif., the policy or practice of forcing racial groups to live apart from each other, go to separate schools, etc. —**seg′re·ga′tion·ist** *n., adj.*

se·gue (seg′wā, sā′gwä) *vi.* **-gued, -gue·ing** [< It., ult. < L. *sequi,* to follow] to continue without break (*to* or *into*) the next part or what follows —*n.* a segueing

sei·del (zī′d'l, sī′-) *n., pl.* **-dels, -del** [G. < MHG. < L. *situla,* a bucket] a large beer mug, often with a hinged lid

Seid·litz powders (sed′lits) [after a mineral spring in Czechoslovakia] a laxative made up of sodium bicarbonate, Rochelle salt, and tartaric acid: also **Seidlitz powder**

sei·gneur (sen yur′, sān-, sen-) *n.* [Fr. < MFr.: see SEIGNIOR] **1.** *same as* SEIGNIOR **2.** the owner of a seigneury (sense 2) —**sei·gneur′i·al** (-ē əl) *adj.*

sei·gneur·y (sen′yər ē, sān′-, sen′-) *n., pl.* **-gneur·ies 1.** *same as* SEIGNIORY (sense 1) **2.** in French Canada, an estate granted by royal decree to 17th-cent. French settlers

sei·gnior (sēn′yər) *n.* [< Anglo-Fr. < OFr. < L. *senior:* see SENIOR] a lord or noble; specif., the lord of a feudal estate or manor

sei·gnio·ri·al (sēn yôr′ē əl) *adj.* of or relating to a seignior

sei·gnior·y (sēn′yər ē) *n., pl.* **-gnior·ies 1.** the estate of a seignior **2.** the rights or authority of a feudal lord

Seine (sān; *Fr.* sen) river in N France, flowing through Paris into the English Channel

seine (sān) *n.* [OE. *segne,* ult. < L. < Gr. *sagēnē*] a large fishing net with floats along the top edge and weights along the bottom —*vt., vi.* **seined, sein′ing** to fish with a seine

seis·mic (sīz′mik, sīs′-) *adj.* [< Gr. *seismos,* an earthquake < *seiein,* to shake] of, relating to, or caused by an earthquake or earthquakes or similar, but man-made, tremors —**seis′mi·cal·ly** *adv.*

seis·mo- [< Gr. *seismos:* see prec.] *a combining form meaning* earthquake [*seismogram*]

seis·mo·gram (sīz′mə gram′, sīs′-) *n.* the chart of an earthquake as recorded by a seismograph

seis·mo·graph (-graf′) *n.* an instrument that records the force and time of earthquakes and similar tremors —**seis·mog·ra·pher** (sīz mäg′rə fər, sīs-) *n.* —**seis′mo·graph′ic** *adj.* —**seis·mog′ra·phy** *n.*

seis·mol·o·gy (sīz mäl′ə jē, sīs-) *n.* [SEISMO- + -LOGY] the science dealing with earthquakes and related phenomena —**seis·mo·log′ic** (-mə läj′ik), **seis′mo·log′i·cal** *adj.* —**seis′mo·log′i·cal·ly** *adv.* —**seis·mol′o·gist** *n.*

seize (sēz) *vt.* **seized, seiz′ing** [< OFr. *saisir* < ML. *sacire,* prob. < Frank.: for IE. base see SAKE[1]] **1.** *a)* orig., to give a feudal holding to *b)* in the passive voice: to invest with ownership of: in the passive voice [*seized* of the lands] **2.** *a)* to take possession of by legal power; confiscate [to *seize* contraband] *b)* to capture and put into custody; arrest; apprehend [to *seize* a criminal suspect] **3.** to take forcibly or quickly; grasp [to *seize* a weapon, to *seize* power] **4.** *a)* to suddenly fill the mind of [an idea *seized* him] *b)* to grasp with the mind, esp. suddenly [*seized* their purpose] **5.** to take quick advantage of (an opportunity, etc.) **6.** ☆to afflict suddenly [*seized* with tremors] **7.** *Naut.* to bind (ropes, etc.), as with a cord —**seize on** (or **upon**) **1.** to grasp or take eagerly **2.** to turn eagerly to (an idea, plan, etc.) —**seiz′a·ble** *adj.* —**seiz′er** *n.*

sei·zin (sē′zin) *n.* [< OFr.: see prec.] legal possession, esp. of a freehold estate —**sei′zor** *n.*

sei·zure (sē′zhər) *n.* **1.** a seizing or being seized **2.** a sudden attack, as of illness

sel. 1. selected **2.** selection(s)

se·lah (se′lə, se lä′) *n.* [Heb. *selāh*] a Hebrew word of unknown meaning at the end of verses in the Psalms, perhaps a musical direction or a word of blessing

sel·dom (sel′dəm) *adv.* [OE. *seldan*] not often; rarely —*adj.* rare; infrequent —**sel′dom·ness** *n.*

se·lect (sə lekt′) *adj.* [L. *selectus,* pp. of *seligere* < *se-,* apart + *legere,* to choose] **1.** chosen for excellence or some special quality; specially picked [a *select* group of players from various teams] **2.** choice; excellent [a *select* cut of meat] **3.** careful in choosing; discriminating [very *select* in the movies he sees] **4.** limited to certain people or groups; exclusive [a *select* country club] —*vt., vi.* to choose as best, most suitable, etc.; pick out [*select* a tie to go with the suit] —see SYN. at CHOOSE —**se·lect′ness** *n.* —**se·lec′tor** *n.*

☆**se·lect·ee** (sə lek′tē′) *n.* a person inducted into the armed forces under selective service

se·lec·tion (sə lek′shən) *n.* **1.** a selecting or being selected **2.** *a)* a thing, person, or group chosen *b)* a group of things to choose from [a *selection* of colors] **3.** *Biol.* any process by which certain organisms or genetic characters naturally survive over others or are bred to do so: see NATURAL SELECTION

se·lec·tive (-tiv) *adj.* **1.** of or characterized by selection **2.** having the power of selecting, or tending to select **3.** *Radio* keeping out undesired frequencies when tuned to a specific station —**se·lec′tive·ly** *adv.* —**se·lec′tive·ness** *n.*

☆**selective service** compulsory military training and service according to age, physical fitness, etc.

se·lec·tiv·i·ty (sə lek′tiv′ə tē) *n.* **1.** the state or quality of being selective **2.** the degree to which a radio receiver is selective

☆**se·lect·man** (sə lekt′mən; *locally, also* sē′lekt man′) *n., pl.* **-men** (-mən, -men′) any of a board of officers elected in most New England towns to manage municipal affairs

Se·le·ne (si lē′nē) the Greek goddess of the moon

sel·e·nite (sel′ə nīt′) *n.* [< L. < Gr. *selēnitēs* (*lithos*), lit., moon (stone)] a kind of gypsum in crystalline form

se·le·ni·um (sə lē′nē əm) *n.* [ModL. < Gr. *selēnē*, the moon] a nonmetallic chemical element whose power to conduct electricity varies with the brightness of light: used in photoelectric devices, etc.: symbol, Se; at. wt., 78.96; at. no., 34

sel·e·nog·ra·phy (sel′ə näg′rə fē) *n.* [< ModL. < Gr. *selēnē*, the moon + -GRAPHY] the study of the surface and physical features of the moon —**sel′e·nog′ra·pher** *n.*

Se·leu·cid (sə loo′sid) *n., pl.* **-cids, -ci·dae** (-si dē′) a member of a dynasty founded by Seleucus I and ruling (312–64? B.C.) over S Asia Minor and the region between the Mediterranean and the Indus River —*adj.* of the Seleucids

Se·leu·cus I (sə loo′kəs) (*Seleucus Nicator*) ?–280 B.C.; Macedonian general & founder of the Seleucid dynasty

self (self) *n., pl.* **selves** [OE.] **1.** the identity, character, or essential qualities of a person or thing **2.** one's own person or being as apart from all others **3.** one's own well-being or advantage [too much concern with *self*] —**pron.** [Colloq.] myself, himself, herself, or yourself [tickets for *self* and wife] —*adj.* of the same kind, color, material, etc. as the rest [a *self* lining]

self- a prefix used in hyphenated compounds, meaning: **1.** of oneself or itself [*self*-restraint] **2.** by oneself or itself [*self*-starting] **3.** in oneself or itself [*self*-centered] **4.** to, with, or for oneself or itself [*self*-addressed, *self*-pity]

self-a·base·ment (self′ə bās′mənt) *n.* a humbling of oneself

self-ab·ne·ga·tion (-ab′nə gā′shən) *n.* lack of thought for oneself; self-denial

self-ab·sorp·tion (-əb zôrp′shən, -sôrp′-) *n.* a being absorbed in or all taken up with one's own interests, affairs, etc. —**self′-ab·sorbed′** *adj.*

self-a·buse (-ə byoos′) *n.* a word used in place of MASTURBATION

self-act·ing (-ak′tiŋ) *adj.* working by itself; automatic

self-ad·dressed (-ə drest′) *adj.* addressed to oneself [a *self*-addressed envelope]

self-ad·vance·ment (-əd vans′mənt) *n.* the advancing or promoting of one's own interests

self-ap·point·ed (-ə poin′tid) *adj.* acting as such on one's own, but not recognized as such by others [a *self*-appointed censor]

self-as·ser·tion (-ə sur′shən) *n.* the act of demanding recognition for oneself or of insisting upon one's rights, claims, etc. —**self′-as·ser′tive, self′-as·sert′ing** *adj.*

self-as·sur·ance (-ə shoor′əns) *n.* confidence in oneself, one's own ability, talent, etc. —**self′-as·sured′** *adj.*

self-cen·tered (-sen′tərd) *adj.* taken up or concerned only with one's own affairs; egocentric; selfish

self-clos·ing (-klōz′iŋ) *adj.* closing automatically

self-col·ored (-kul′ərd) *adj.* **1.** of only one color **2.** of the natural or original color, as a fabric

self-com·mand (-kə mand′) *n.* same as SELF-CONTROL

self-com·pla·cent (-kəm plā′s'nt) *adj.* self-satisfied, esp. in a smug way —**self′-com·pla′cen·cy** *n.*

self-con·ceit (-kən sēt′) *n.* too high an opinion of oneself; conceit —**self′-con·ceit′ed** *adj.*

self-con·fessed (-kən fest′) *adj.* being such by one's own admission [a *self*-confessed thief]

self-con·fi·dence (-kän′fə dəns) *n.* confidence in oneself, one's own abilities, talents, etc. —**self′-con′fi·dent** *adj.* —**self′-con′fi·dent·ly** *adv.*

self-con·scious (-kän′shəs) *adj.* **1.** too conscious of oneself so that one feels or acts embarrassed or ill at ease when with others **2.** showing embarrassment [a *self*-conscious cough] —**self′-con′scious·ly** *adv.* —**self′-con′scious·ness** *n.*

self-con·tained (-kən tānd′) *adj.* **1.** keeping one's thoughts and feelings to oneself; reserved **2.** showing self-control **3.** having all working parts, complete with motive power, in an enclosed unit: said of machinery **4.** having within oneself or itself all that is necessary; self-sufficient, as a community —**self′-con·tain′ment** *n.*

self-con·tent·ed (-kən ten′tid) *adj.* contented with what one is or has —**self′-con·tent′, self′-con·tent′ment** *n.*

self-con·tra·dic·tion (-kän′trə dik′shən) *n.* **1.** contradiction of oneself or itself **2.** any statement or idea containing elements that contradict each other —**self′-con′tra·dic′to·ry** *adj.*

self-con·trol (-kən trōl′) *n.* control of, or of one's own emotions, desires, actions, etc.

self-de·cep·tion (-di sep′shən) *n.* the deceiving of oneself as to one's true feelings, motives, circumstances, etc.: also **self′-de·ceit′, self′-de·lu′sion** (-di loo′zhən) —**self′-de·ceiv′ing** *adj.*

self-de·feat·ing (-di fēt′iŋ) *adj.* that defeats its own purpose or interests

self-de·fense (-di fens′) *n.* **1.** defense of oneself, one's rights, etc. **2.** boxing: usually in **manly art of self-defense** —**self′-de·fen′sive** *adj.*

self-de·ni·al (-di nī′əl) *n.* the act of giving up one's own desires or pleasures, often for the benefit of others —**self′-de·ny′ing** *adj.*

☆**self-de·struct** (-di strukt′) *vi.* same as DESTRUCT

self-de·struc·tion (-di struk′shən) *n.* destruction of oneself or itself; specif., suicide —**self′-de·struc′tive** *adj.*

self-de·ter·mi·na·tion (-di tur′mə nā′shən) *n.* **1.** the act or power of making up one's own mind about what to think or do **2.** the right of a people to decide upon its own political status or form of government —**self′-de·ter′mined** *adj.* —**self′-de·ter′min·ing** *adj.*

self-dis·ci·pline (-dis′ə plin) *n.* the disciplining or controlling of oneself, one's desires, actions, etc. —**self′-dis′ci·plined** *adj.*

self-doubt (-dout′) *n.* lack of self-confidence

self-ed·u·cat·ed (-ej′ə kāt′id) *adj.* educated by oneself, with little or no formal schooling

self-ef·face·ment (-i fās′mənt) *n.* the practice of keeping oneself modestly in the background —**self′-ef·fac′ing** *adj.*

self-em·ployed (-im ploid′) *adj.* working for oneself, with direct control over work, services, fees, charges, etc. —**self′-em·ploy′ment** *n.*

self-es·teem (-ə stēm′) *n.* **1.** belief in oneself; self-respect **2.** much pride in oneself; conceit

self-ev·i·dent (-ev′ə dənt) *adj.* plain to see without need of proof or explanation —**self′-ev′i·dent·ly** *adv.*

self-ex·am·i·na·tion (-ig zam′ə nā′shən) *n.* examination or analysis of oneself and one's conduct, motives, etc.

self-ex·ist·ent (-ig zis′tənt) *adj.* existing of or by itself without outside cause —**self′-ex·ist′ence** *n.*

self-ex·plan·a·to·ry (-ik splan′ə tôr′ē) *adj.* explaining itself: also **self′-ex·plain′ing**

self-ex·pres·sion (-ik spresh′ən) *n.* expression of one's own personality or emotions, as in the arts

self-fer·til·i·za·tion (-fur′t'l i zā′shən) *n.* fertilization of a plant by its own pollen or of an animal by its own sperm

self-ful·fill·ing (-fəl fil′iŋ) *adj.* **1.** bringing about self-fulfillment **2.** brought to fulfillment chiefly as a result of having been expected [a *self*-fulfilling prophecy]

self-ful·fill·ment (-fəl fil′mənt) *n.* fulfillment of one's ambitions, hopes, etc. through one's own efforts

self-gov·ern·ment (-guv′ər mənt, -ərn-) *n.* government of a group by its own members, as in electing representatives to make its laws —**self′-gov′ern·ing** *adj.*

self-hate (-hāt′) *n.* hate directed against oneself or one's own people, often in despair: also **self′-ha′tred**

self-heal (-hēl′) *n.* any of various plants supposed to have healing properties; esp., a common old-world weed of the mint family

self-help (-help′) *n.* care or betterment of oneself by one's own efforts, as through study

self·hyp·no·sis (-hip nō′sis) *n.* a hypnotizing of oneself; autohypnosis

self·im·age (-im′ij) *n.* one's idea of oneself and one's identity, abilities, worth, etc.

self·im·por·tant (-im pôr′t'nt) *adj.* having or showing an exaggerated opinion of one's own importance; pompous or officious —**self′-im·por′tance** *n.*

self·im·posed (-im pōzd′) *adj.* placed on oneself by oneself, as a duty

self·im·prove·ment (-im prōōv′mənt) *n.* improvement of one's status, mind, etc. by one's own efforts

self·in·crim·i·na·tion (-in krim′ə nā′shən) *n.* incrimination of oneself by one's own statements or answers —**self′-in·crim′i·nat′ing** *adj.*

self·in·duced (-in dōōst′) *adj.* 1. induced by oneself or itself 2. produced by self-induction

self·in·duc·tion (-in duk′shən) *n.* induction of a voltage in a circuit by the variation of current in that circuit

self·in·dul·gence (-in dul′jəns) *n.* a giving in to one's own desires, impulses, etc. —**self′-in·dul′gent** *adj.*

self·in·flict·ed (-in flik′tid) *adj.* inflicted on oneself by oneself, as an injury

self·in·ter·est (-in′trist, -in′tər ist) *n.* 1. one's own interest or advantage 2. a selfish and exaggerated concern for this

self·ish (sel′fish) *adj.* 1. caring too much for one's own welfare or interests, with little or no thought or care for others 2. showing or caused by self-interest —**self′ish·ly** *adv.* —**self′ish·ness** *n.*

self·jus·ti·fi·ca·tion (self′jus′tə fi kā′shən) *n.* the justifying or explaining away of one's actions or motives

self·less (self′lis) *adj.* caring more about others than about oneself; unselfish; self-sacrificing —**self′less·ly** *adv.* —**self′less·ness** *n.*

self·load·ing (self′lōd′iŋ) *adj.* loading again by its own action [a *self-loading* gun]

self·love (-luv′) *n.* love of self or concern for oneself and one's own interests

self·made (-mād′) *adj.* 1. made by oneself or itself 2. successful, rich, etc. through one's own efforts

self·o·pin·ion·at·ed (-ə pin′yə nāt′id) *adj.* stubborn or conceited about one's own opinions

self·pit·y (-pit′ē) *n.* pity for oneself

self·pol·li·na·tion (-päl′ə nā′shən) *n.* pollination of a flower by itself or by another flower on the same plant —**self′-pol′li·nat′ed** *adj.*

self·por·trait (-pôr′trit, -trāt) *n.* a painting, drawing, etc. of oneself, done by oneself

self·pos·ses·sion (-pə zesh′ən) *n.* full control of one's feelings, actions, etc.; self-control; self-command; composure —**self′-pos·sessed′** *adj.*

self·pres·er·va·tion (-prez′ər vā′shən) *n.* the act or instinct of keeping oneself safe and alive

self·pro·nounc·ing (-prə noun′siŋ) *adj.* showing pronunciation by marks added to the original spelling, not by a separate phonetic spelling

self·pro·pelled (-prə peld′) *adj.* moving by its own power; driven by its own motor: also **self′-pro·pel′ling**

self·re·al·i·za·tion (-rē′ə li zā′shən) *n.* fulfillment of oneself, one's capabilities, etc.

self·re·cord·ing (-ri kôr′diŋ) *adj.* recording its own operations automatically, as a seismograph

self·re·gard (-ri gärd′) *n.* 1. concern for oneself and one's own interests 2. *same as* SELF-RESPECT

self·reg·u·lat·ing (-reg′yə lāt′iŋ) *adj.* regulating oneself or itself automatically or without outside control —**self′-reg′u·la′tion** *n.*

self·re·li·ance (-ri lī′əns) *n.* reliance on one's own judgment, abilities, etc. —**self′-re·li′ant** *adj.*

self·re·proach (-ri prōch′) *n.* blame of oneself; guilt feeling —**self′-re·proach′ful** *adj.*

self·re·spect (-ri spekt′) *n.* proper respect for oneself and one's worth as a person —**self′-re·spect′ing** *adj.*

self·re·straint (-ri strānt′) *n.* restraint of oneself; self-control —**self′-re·strained′** *adj.*

self·re·veal·ing (-ri vēl′iŋ) *adj.* revealing one's innermost thoughts, feelings, etc.: also **self′-rev′e·la·to·ry** (-rev′ə lə tôr′ē) —**self′-rev′e·la′tion** *n.*

self·right·eous (-rī′chəs) *adj.* thinking oneself more righteous or moral than others —**self′-right′eous·ly** *adv.* —**self′-right′eous·ness** *n.*

☆**self·ris·ing** (-rīz′iŋ) *adj.* rising by itself: said specif. of flour

sold with a leavening agent, as baking powder, blended in for quick breads or cakes

self·rule (-rōōl′) *n.* *same as* SELF-GOVERNMENT

self·sac·ri·fice (-sak′rə fīs′) *n.* sacrifice of oneself or one's interests to benefit others —**self′-sac′ri·fic′ing** *adj.*

self·same (-sām′) *adj.* exactly the same; identical; (the) very same [we were born on the *selfsame* day] —see SYN. at SAME —**self′same′ness** *n.*

self·sat·is·fied (-sat′is fīd′) *adj.* pleased with oneself or with what one has done —**self′-sat′is·fac′tion** *n.*

self·sat·is·fy·ing (-sat′is fī′iŋ) *adj.* satisfying to oneself

self·seal·ing (-sēl′iŋ) *adj.* 1. automatically sealing punctures, etc., as some tires 2. that can be sealed by pressure alone, as some envelopes

self·seek·er (-sē′kər) *n.* a person seeking only or mainly to further his own interests —**self′-seek′ing** *n.,* *adj.*

☆**self·serv·ice** (-sur′vis) *adj.* set up so that customers serve themselves [a *self-service* store; a *self-service* gas station]

self·serv·ing (-sur′viŋ) *adj.* furthering one's own selfish interests, esp. at the expense of others

self·sown (-sōn′) *adj.* sown by wind, water, or other natural means, as some weeds

self·styled (-stīld′) *adj.* so named by oneself [he is a *self-styled* expert]

self·suf·fi·cient (-sə fish′ənt) *adj.* able to get along without help; independent —**self′-suf·fi′cien·cy** *n.*

self·sup·port (-sə pôrt′) *n.* support of oneself or itself without outside help —**self′-sup·port′ing** *adj.*

self·sus·tain·ing (-sə stān′iŋ) *adj.* 1. supporting or able to support oneself or itself 2. able to continue once begun

self·taught (-tôt′) *adj.* 1. having taught oneself without help from others 2. learned by oneself without instruction

self·ward (-wərd) *adv.* toward oneself: also **self′wards** —*adj.* directed toward oneself

self·willed (-wild′) *adj.* stubborn about getting one's own way; willful —**self′-will′** *n.*

self·wind·ing (-wīn′diŋ) *adj.* winding automatically, as certain wristwatches

sell (sel) *vt.* **sold, sell′ing** [OE. *sellan,* to give < IE. base *sel-,* to take] 1. to give up (property, goods, services, etc.) in return for money 2. *a)* to offer for sale; deal in [this store *sells* radios; to *sell* real estate] *b)* to make or try to make sales in or to [to *sell* chain stores] 3. *a)* to give up (a person) to his enemies, into slavery, etc. *b)* to betray (a country, cause, etc.) 4. to give up (one's honor, etc.) for profit, etc. 5. to promote the sale of [television *sells* many products] ☆6. [Colloq.] *a)* to establish confidence or belief in [to *sell* oneself to the public] *b)* to persuade (someone) of the value of something (with *on*) [*sell* him on the idea] 7. [Slang] to cheat or trick —*vi.* 1. to sell something 2. to work or act as a salesman or salesperson 3. to be a popular item on the market [his new book is *selling*] 4. to be sold (*for* or *at*) [belts *selling* for two dollars] 5. [Colloq.] to be accepted, approved, etc. [a scheme that won't *sell*] —*n.* [Slang] 1. a trick or hoax ☆2. selling or salesmanship —**sell out** 1. to sell all that one has of ☆2. [Colloq.] to betray (someone, a cause, etc.) —☆**sell short** 1. to sell (securities, etc. not yet owned), expecting to cover later at a lower price 2. to undervalue

sell·er (sel′ər) *n.* 1. a person who sells 2. something that sells, referring to its rate of sale [a good *seller*]

sell·off (-ôf′) *n.* a price decline for all or certain stocks and bonds, due to pressure to sell

☆**sell·out** (-out′) *n.* [Colloq.] 1. a selling out, or betrayal 2. a show, etc. for which all seats have been sold

Sel·ma (sel′mə) [< ? Gr. *selma,* a ship] a feminine name

Selt·zer (selt′sər) *n.* [< *Niederselters,* village near Wiesbaden, Germany] 1. natural mineral water that gives off gas bubbles 2. [*often* s-] any carbonated water Also **Seltzer water**

sel·vage, sel·vedge (sel′vij) *n.* [< SELF + EDGE, after MDu. *selfegge*] 1. a specially woven edge to keep cloth from raveling 2. an edge of fabric or paper that is to be trimmed off or covered

selves (selvz) *n. pl. of* SELF

Sem. 1. Seminary 2. Semitic

sem. 1. semester 2. semicolon

se·man·tic (sə man′tik) *adj.* [Gr. *sēmantikos,* significant < *sēmainein,* to show < *sēma,* a sign] 1. of meaning, esp. in language 2. of semantics —**se·man′ti·cal·ly** *adv.*

se·man·tics (-tiks) *n.pl.* [*with sing. v.*] [see prec.] 1. the branch of linguistics dealing with the meanings given to words and the changes that occur to these meanings as time goes on 2. the relationships between symbols and the ideas associated with them by their users **3.** loosely, the twisting of meaning to mislead or confuse, as in some advertising and propaganda —**se·man'ti·cist** (-tə sist) **n.**

sem·a·phore (sem'ə fôr') **n.** [< Fr. < Gr. *sēma*, a sign + *-phoros:* see -PHOROUS] any device or system for signaling, as by lights, flags, mechanical arms, etc. —**vt., vi.** -**phored'**, -**phor'ing** to signal by semaphore — **sem'a·phor'ic** adj. —**sem'a·phor'ist** n.

Se·ma·rang (sə mä'räŋ) seaport in N Java, Indonesia: pop. 503,000

sem·blance (sem'bləns) **n.** [< OFr. < *sembler*, to seem, appear, ult. < L. *similis*, like] **1.** outward look or show; seeming likeness [a *semblance* of order] **2.** a likeness, image, or representation [a *semblance* of a bird in the abstract painting] **3.** a false, assumed, or deceiving form or appearance —see SYN. at APPEARANCE

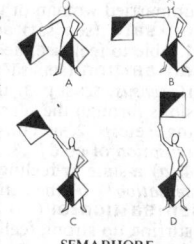

SEMAPHORE
(signals for letters A, B, C, D)

se·men (sē'mən) **n.** [ModL. < L., a seed] the fluid that is produced by the male sex organs and that contains the spermatozoa

se·mes·ter (sə mes'tər) **n.** [G. < L. *semestris*, half-yearly < *sex*, six + *mensis*, month] either of the two terms which usually make up a school or college year —**se·mes'tral** adj.

☆**sem·i** (sem'ī) **n.** [< SEMITRAILER] [Colloq.] a semitrailer and the tractor (sense 2) to which it is connected

sem·i- (sem'ī; *also variously* -ē, -ī, -ə) [L.] *a prefix meaning:* **1.** half [*semicircle*] **2.** partly [*semiskilled*] **3.** twice in a (specified period) [*semiannually*]

sem·i·an·nu·al (sem'ī an'yoo wəl) adj. **1.** happening, presented, etc. every half year [*semiannual* interest] **2.** lasting only half a year, as some plants —**sem'i·an'nu·al·ly** adv.

sem·i·a·quat·ic (-ə kwät'ik, -kwat'-) adj. Biol. **1.** growing in or near water, as certain plants **2.** spending some time in water, as muskrats

sem·i·au·to·mat·ic (-ôt'ə mat'ik) adj. **1.** partly automatic and partly hand-controlled: said of machinery **2.** operating like an automatic firearm but requiring a trigger pull for each shot fired —**n.** a semiautomatic firearm

sem·i·breve (sem'ī brēv') **n.** [It.] [Brit.] *same as* WHOLE NOTE

sem·i·cir·cle (sem'ī sur'k'l) **n.** a half circle —**sem'i·cir'cu·lar** (-kyə lər) adj.

semicircular canal any of the three loop-shaped tubes of the inner ear that help the body keep its balance

sem·i·co·lon (sem'ī kō'lən) **n.** a mark of punctuation (;) showing more separation than that marked by the comma and less than that marked by the period: usually used between certain closely related independent clauses

sem·i·con·duc·tor (sem'ī kən duk'tər) **n.** a substance, as silicon, whose conductivity is improved by very small additions of certain substances or by application of heat, light, or voltage: used in transistors, etc.

sem·i·con·scious (-kän'shəs) adj. not fully conscious or awake —**sem'i·con'scious·ness** n.

sem·i·de·tached (-di tacht') adj. partly separate, as two houses joined by a common wall

sem·i·fi·nal (sem'ī fī'n'l; *for n., usually* sem'ī fī'n'l) adj. coming just before the final match, as of a tournament —**n.** **1.** a semifinal match **2.** [*pl.*] a semifinal round —**sem'i·fi'nal·ist** n.

sem·i·flu·id (sem'ī floo'id) adj. heavy or thick but able to flow —**n.** a semifluid substance

sem·i·for·mal (-fôr'm'l) adj. less than strictly formal but not informal

sem·i·hard (-härd') adj. somewhat hard, but easily cut

sem·i·lit·er·ate (-lit'ər it) adj. knowing how to read and write a little, or knowing only how to read

sem·i·lu·nar valve (-loo'nər) adj. either of two crescent-shaped valves between the ventricles and the aorta or the pulmonary artery that keep blood from flowing back into the ventricles

☆**sem·i·month·ly** (-munth'lē) adj. coming, happening, done, etc. twice a month —**n.**, pl. **-lies** something coming, appearing, issued, etc. twice a month —**adv.** twice a month

sem·i·nal (sem'ə n'l) adj. [< MFr. < L. < *semen*, a seed] **1.** of or containing seed or semen **2.** of reproduction [*seminal*

power] **3.** like a seed in being a source from which much can develop or has developed [a *seminal* idea]

sem·i·nar (sem'ə när') **n.** [G. < L.: see SEMINARY] **1.** a group of supervised students doing advanced study **2.** a) a course for such a group b) the room where the group meets **3.** any similar group discussion

sem·i·nar·y (sem'ə ner'ē) **n.**, pl. **-nar'ies** [< L. neut. of *seminarius*, of seed < *semen*, a seed] **1.** a school, esp. a private school for young women: an old-fashioned term **2.** a school or college where priests, ministers, or rabbis are trained —**sem'i·nar'i·an** (-e ən) n.

sem·i·nif·er·ous (sem'ə nif'ər əs) adj. [< L. *semen*, a seed + -FEROUS] **1.** seed-bearing **2.** containing or carrying semen

sem·i·niv·o·rous (sem'ə niv'ər əs) adj. [< L. *semen*, a seed + -VOROUS] feeding on seeds

Sem·i·nole (sem'ə nōl') **n.** [Creek *Simanóle*, lit., runaway] **1.** pl. **-noles', -nole'** any of an American Indian people of southern Florida and Oklahoma **2.** their Muskogean language

sem·i·of·fi·cial (sem'ē ə fish''l) adj. having some, but not full, official authority —**sem'i·of·fi'cial·ly** adv.

se·mi·ot·ics (sē'mē ät'iks) n.pl. [< Gr. < *sēmeion*, a sign] [with sing. v.] Philos. a general theory of signs and symbols; esp., the analysis of signs used in language —**se'mi·ot'ic** adj.

sem·i·per·me·a·ble (sem'ī pur'mē ə b'l) adj. allowing some substances to pass; permeable to smaller molecules but not to larger ones

sem·i·pre·cious (-presh'əs) adj. designating gems, as garnets and opals, of lower value than precious gems

sem·i·pri·vate (-prī'vit) adj. partly but not completely private; specif., designating or of a hospital room with two, three, or, sometimes, four beds

☆**sem·i·pro** (sem'ī prō') adj., n. *shortened form of* SEMIPROFESSIONAL

sem·i·pro·fes·sion·al (sem'ī prə fesh'ən 'l) adj. not fully professional; specif., a) taking part in a sport, etc. for pay but not as a regular occupation b) taken part in by semiprofessional players, etc. —**n.** a semiprofessional player, etc. —**sem'i·pro·fes'sion·al·ly** adv.

sem·i·qua·ver (sem'ī kwā'vər) **n.** [Brit.] *same as* SIXTEENTH NOTE

sem·i·rig·id (sem'ī rij'id) adj. somewhat or partly rigid; specif., designating an airship with a rigid internal keel

sem·i·skilled (-skild') adj. **1.** partly skilled **2.** of or doing manual work that requires only limited training

sem·i·soft (-sôft') adj. soft but firm and easily cut

sem·i·sol·id (-säl'id) adj. thick and slowly flowing, as asphalt —**n.** a semisolid substance

Sem·ite (sem'īt; *chiefly Brit.* sē'mīt) **n.** [prob. < Fr. < ModL. < *Semiticus*, SEMITIC] a member of any people speaking a Semitic language, as a Hebrew, Arab, etc.

Se·mit·ic (sə mit'ik) adj. [< G. < ModL. *Semiticus*, ult. < Gr. *Sem* < Heb. *Shēm*, SHEM] **1.** of or like the Semites **2.** designating or of a major division of a family of languages of southwestern Asia and northern Africa, including Hebrew, Arabic, etc. —**n.** this division, or any member of it

Sem·i·tism (sem'ə tiz'm) **n.** **1.** a Semitic word or idiom **2.** traits, customs, etc. of the Semites

sem·i·tone (sem'ī tōn') **n.** Music the difference in pitch between any two keys next to each other on the piano; half of a whole tone —**sem'i·ton'ic** (-tän'ik), **sem'i·ton'al** (-tō'n'l) adj.

☆**sem·i·trail·er** (-trā'lər) **n.** **1.** a trailer designed to be attached by a coupling to the rear part of a tractor (sense 2), on which it is partly supported **2.** a truck made up of such a trailer and tractor

sem·i·trop·i·cal (sem'ī träp'i k'l) adj. somewhat like the tropics; nearly tropical: also **sem'i·trop'ic**

sem·i·vow·el (sem'ī vou'əl) **n.** Phonet. a glide at the beginning of a syllable, as the sound of w in *wall*

☆**sem·i·week·ly** (sem'ī wēk'lē) adj. appearing, happening, done, etc. twice a week —**n.**, pl. **-lies** a semiweekly publication —**adv.** twice a week

sem·i·year·ly (-yir'lē) adj. coming, happening, done, etc. twice a year —**adv.** twice a year

sem·o·li·na (sem'ə lē'nə) **n.** [< It. dim. of *semola*, bran] particles of coarsely ground durum, used in making macaroni, puddings, etc.

‡**sem·per fi·de·lis** (sem′pər fi dā′lis) [L.] always faithful: motto of the U.S. Marine Corps

‡**semper pa·ra·tus** (pə rät′əs, -rāt′əs) [L.] always prepared: motto of the U.S. Coast Guard

sem·pi·ter·nal (sem′pi tur′n′l) *adj.* [< ML. < L. < *semper*, always + *aeternus*, ETERNAL] everlasting; eternal —**sem′pi·ter′nal·ly** *adv.* —**sem′pi·ter′ni·ty** *n.*

sen (sen) *n., pl.* **sen** [Jap.] *see* MONETARY UNITS, table (Cambodia, Indonesia, Japan)

Sen., sen. 1. senate 2. senator 3. senior

sen·ate (sen′it) *n.* [< OFr. < L. *senatus* < *senex*, old] 1. the supreme council of the ancient Roman state 2. a lawmaking assembly 3. [S-] ☆a) the upper branch of the legislature of the U.S., or of most of the States of the U.S. b) a similar body in other countries 4. a governing body, as in some schools

sen·a·tor (sen′ə tər) *n.* a member of a senate —**sen′a·to′ri·al** (-tôr′ē əl) *adj.*

send (send) *vt.* **sent, send′ing** [OE. *sendan* < IE. base *sent-*, to go, find out] 1. a) to cause to go or be carried; convey [food was *sent* by plane] b) to cause (a message) to go or be transmitted by mail, radio, etc. 2. to direct or command to go [*send* him home] 3. to provide with the means for going [to *send* one's son to college] 4. to cause to move by hitting, throwing, etc. [he *sent* the ball over the fence] 5. to drive into some condition [greed *sent* him to his ruin] 6. to cause to happen, come, etc. [joy *sent* by the gods] ☆7. [Slang] to excite; thrill —*vi.* 1. to send a message, messenger, etc. [to *send* for help] 2. to transmit, as by radio —**send away** to cause to go away, leave, etc. —**send down** [Brit.] to suspend or expel from a university —**send flying** 1. to dismiss hurriedly 2. to cause to stagger, as with a blow 3. to put to flight 4. to scatter suddenly in all directions —**send for** 1. to order to come; summon 2. to request or order delivery of —**send forth** to give out or forth; produce, emit, etc. —**send in** 1. to hand in or send to one receiving 2. to put (a player) in a game —**send off** 1. to mail or dispatch (a letter, gift, etc.) 2. to dismiss 3. to give a send-off to —**send up** 1. to cause to rise ☆2. [Colloq.] to sentence to prison —**send′er** *n.*

☆**send-off** (send′ôf′) *n.* [Colloq.] 1. something done to show friendly feeling toward someone starting out on a trip, career, etc. 2. a start given to someone or something

Sen·e·ca[1] (sen′i kə) *n.* [< Oneida Indian name meaning "people of the standing rock"] 1. *pl.* **-cas, -ca** any of a N. American Indian people of New York and Ontario 2. their Iroquoian language —**Sen′e·can** *adj.*

Sen·e·ca[2] (sen′i kə) (*Lucius Annaeus Seneca*) 4? B.C.–65 A.D.; Rom. philosopher, dramatist, & statesman

Sen·e·gal (sen′i gôl′) 1. country in W Africa, on the Atlantic: 76,124 sq. mi.; pop. 3,780,000; cap. Dakar 2. river flowing from W Mali, along the Senegal border into the Atlantic —**Sen′e·ga·lese′** (-gə lēz′) *adj., n., pl.* **-lese′**

se·nes·cent (sə nes′′nt) *adj.* [< L. prp. of *senescere*, to grow old] growing old; aging —**se·nes′cence** (-′ns) *n.*

sen·es·chal (sen′ə shəl) *n.* [< OFr. < Frank. *siniskalk*, oldest servant] a steward in a medieval household

se·nile (sē′nīl, sen′īl) *adj.* [L. *senilis* < *senex*, old] 1. of or typical of old age 2. showing the weaknesses, esp. the mental confusion, memory loss, etc., often found in old people —**se′nile·ly** *adv.* —**se·nil·i·ty** (si nil′ə tē) *n.*

sen·ior (sēn′yər) *adj.* [L., compar. of *senex*, old] 1. of the greater age; older: written *Sr.* after the name of a father whose son bears the same name 2. of higher rank or longer service [a *senior* partner] ☆3. of or for seniors in a high school or college [the *senior* class] —*n.* 1. a person older than another or others 2. a person of greater rank or longer service ☆3. a student in the last year of a high school or college —**one's senior** a person older than oneself

senior citizen an elderly person, esp. one who is retired

☆**senior high school** high school, following junior high school: it usually includes the 10th, 11th, and 12th grades

sen·ior·i·ty (sēn yôr′ə tē, -yär′-) *n., pl.* **-ties** 1. the condition or fact of being senior, as in age or rank 2. certain rights, esp. the right to continue to hold a certain job, based on length of service

sen·i·ti (sen′ə tē) *n., pl.* **sen′i·ti** [Tongan, altered < CENT] *see* MONETARY UNITS, table (Tonga)

sen·na (sen′ə) *n.* [< ML. < Ar. *sanā*] 1. any of a group of plants of the legume family, with yellow flowers 2. the dried leaflets of various sennas, used, esp. formerly, as a laxative

Sen·nach·er·ib (sə nak′ər ib) ?–681 B.C.; king of Assyria (705–681): son of SARGON II

‡**se·ñor** (se nyôr′) *n., pl.* **se·ño′res** (-nyô′res) [Sp. < *senior*: see SENIOR] a man; gentleman: Spanish title used like *Mr.* or *sir*

‡**se·ño·ra** (se nyô′rä) *n., pl.* **se·ño′ras** (-räs) [Sp.] a married woman: Spanish title used like *Mrs.* or *madam*

‡**se·ño·ri·ta** (se′nyô rē′tä) *n., pl.* **se·ño·ri′tas** (-täs) [Sp.] an unmarried woman or girl: Spanish title used like *Miss*

sen·sate (sen′sāt) *adj.* [< LL. < L. *sensus*: see SENSATION] 1. able to feel, see, hear, etc. 2. known through the senses

sen·sa·tion (sen sā′shən) *n.* [< LL. < *sensatus*, intelligent < L. *sensus*, SENSE] 1. the power or process of receiving impressions through the senses [the *sensations* of hearing, seeing, feeling, etc.] 2. a conscious feeling or sense impression [a *sensation* of cold] 3. a generalized feeling [a *sensation* of joy] 4. a) a state or feeling of general excitement [the play caused a *sensation*] b) the action, event, person, etc. causing this

sen·sa·tion·al (-'l) *adj.* 1. of the senses or sensation 2. a) stirring up strong feeling or great excitement [a *sensational* new theory] b) meant to startle, shock, thrill, etc. [a *sensational* novel] 3. [Colloq.] unusually good, fine, etc. —**sen·sa′tion·al·ize′** (-'l īz′) *vt.* **-ized′, -iz′ing** —**sen·sa′tion·al·ly** *adv.*

sen·sa·tion·al·ism (-'l iz′m) *n.* 1. the use of subject matter, style, etc. meant to shock, thrill, etc. 2. *Philos.* the belief that all knowledge is acquired through the senses —**sen·sa′tion·al·ist** *n.* —**sen·sa′tion·al·is′tic** *adj.*

sense (sens) *n.* [< Fr. < L. *sensus* < *sentire*, to feel: for IE. base see SEND] 1. ability to receive and react to stimuli, as light, sound, etc.; specif., any of five special powers of receiving impressions through certain body organs (sight, touch, taste, smell, and hearing) 2. [Now Rare] these powers as a group 3. a) feeling, impression, or awareness through the senses [a *sense* of warmth] b) a generalized feeling [a *sense* of longing] 4. an ability to judge external conditions, sounds, etc. [a *sense* of direction, pitch, etc.] 5. an ability to feel, appreciate, or understand some quality [a *sense* of humor, honor, etc.] 6. a) sound thinking; normal intelligence and judgment [he showed good *sense* in his decision] b) something wise or reasonable [to talk *sense*] 7. [pl.] normal ability to think or reason soundly [to come to one's *senses*] 8. a) meaning; esp., any of several meanings of the same word or phrase b) essential meaning; gist 9. the general opinion or attitude of a group —*vt.* **sensed, sens′ing** 1. to be aware of; perceive [to *sense* another's hostility] 2. to understand 3. to detect automatically, as by sensors —see SYN. at MEANING —**in a sense** from one aspect; to a limited degree —**make sense** to be understandable or logical

sense·less (sens′lis) *adj.* 1. unconscious [knocked *senseless* by a blow] 2. not showing good sense; stupid; foolish [*senseless* behavior] 3. having no real point; meaningless [a *senseless* reply] —**sense′less·ly** *adv.* —**sense′less·ness** *n.*

sense organ any organ or structure, as an eye or a taste bud, that receives specific stimuli which are sent to the brain

sen·si·bil·i·ty (sen′sə bil′ə tē) *n., pl.* **-ties** [< MFr. < LL. < L.: see SENSIBLE] 1. the ability to feel or become aware of sensations [the *sensibility* of the skin to heat or cold] 2. [often pl.] a) sensitive or refined feelings [that remark wounded her *sensibilities*] b) a delicate awareness or appreciation of something

sen·si·ble (sen′sə b'l) *adj.* [< MFr. < L. *sensibilis* < pp. of *sentire*, to feel: see SENSE] 1. that can be felt or noticed by the senses or the mind [*sensible* stimuli] 2. easily felt or noticed; marked [a *sensible* rise in temperature] 3. capable of receiving sensation [the eye is *sensible* to light rays] 4. having appreciation or understanding; aware [*sensible* of his embarrassment] 5. having or showing good sense or sound judgment; wise; reasonable [*sensible* advice] —see SYN. at AWARE and PERCEPTIBLE and RATIONAL —**sen′si·ble·ness** *n.* —**sen′si·bly** *adv.*

sen·si·tive (sen′sə tiv) *adj.* [< MFr. < ML. *sensitivus* < L. *sensus*: see SENSE] 1. of the senses or sensation; sensory 2. receiving and responding to stimuli [the skin is *sensitive* to touch] 3. quick to react to stimuli [a *sensitive* ear] 4. easily hurt; tender [a *sensitive* bruise] 5. quick to notice, appreciate, or react to the things around one [*sensitive* to beauty; *sensitive* to his wife's moods] 6. easily offended, shocked, irritated, etc. [*sensitive* about being criticized] 7. showing, measuring, or reacting to small changes or differences [*sensitive* instruments] ☆8. of or dealing with secret or delicate government matters [*sensitive* negotiations] —**sen′si·tive·ly** *adv.* —**sen′si·tive·ness** *n.*

sensitive plant a tropical American plant with purplish flowers, whose leaflets fold and leafstalks droop when touched

sen·si·tiv·i·ty (sen′sə tiv′ə tē) *n.* the condition or degree of being sensitive

☆**sensitivity training** a kind of group therapy in which the members of the group, under the guidance of a leader, seek a deeper understanding of themselves and others, as by letting one another know of their private feelings and experiences

sen·si·tize (sen′sə tīz′) *vt.* **-tized′, -tiz′ing** to make sensitive [to *sensitize* film to light] —**sen′si·ti·za′tion** *n.* —**sen′si·tiz′er** *n.*

sen·sor (sen′sər, -sôr) *n.* [< L. pp. of *sentire,* to feel + -OR] a device designed to detect, measure, or record light, heat, radio waves, etc. and to respond, as by transmitting information or operating controls

sen·so·ri·mo·tor (sen′sə rē mōt′ər) *adj.* [< SENSORY + MO-TOR] *Physiol., Psychol.* of or involving both sensory and motor functions

sen·so·ry (sen′sər ē) *adj.* **1.** of the senses or sensation **2.** having to do with the receiving and transmitting of sense impressions Also **sen·so′ri·al** (-sôr′ē əl)

sen·su·al (sen′shoo wəl) *adj.* [L. *sensualis* < *sensus,* SENSE] **1.** of the body and the senses as apart from the mind or spirit [*sensual* pleasures] **2.** *a)* having to do with or giving oneself up to bodily or sexual pleasures; voluptuous *b)* lustful; lewd —see SYN. at SENSUOUS —**sen′su·al·ly** *adv.*

sen·su·al·ism (-iz′m) *n.* a giving oneself up to sensual pleasures; sensuality —**sen′su·al·ist** *n.*

sen·su·al·i·ty (sen′shoo wal′ə tē) *n.* **1.** the quality or condition of being sensual **2.** a fondness for or a giving oneself up to sensual pleasures

sen·su·al·ize (sen′shoo wə līz′) *vt.* **-ized′, -iz′ing** to make sensual —**sen′su·al·i·za′tion** *n.*

sen·su·ous (sen′shoo wəs) *adj.* **1.** coming from, acting on, or appealing to the senses **2.** getting a special pleasure from sights, sounds, tastes, etc. —**sen′su·ous·ly** *adv.* —**sen′su·ous·ness** *n.*

SYN.—**sensuous** suggests the strong appeal of that which is pleasing to the eye, ear, touch, and other senses [soft, *sensuous* music]; **sensual** refers to that which stimulates or satisfies the needs and desires of the body

sent (sent) *pt. & pp. of* SEND

sen·tence (sen′t'ns) *n.* [< OFr. < L. *sententia,* opinion, ult. < prp. of *sentire,* to feel: see SENSE] **1.** *a)* a decision or judgment, esp. by a court of a convicted person's punishment *b)* the punishment [a life *sentence* in prison] **2.** *Gram.* a word or group of words stating, asking, commanding, or exclaiming something, usually having a subject and predicate and, in writing, beginning with a capital letter and ending with a period, question mark, etc. —*vt.* **-tenced, -tenc·ing** to pass sentence on (a convicted person); condemn (*to* a specified punishment) —**sen·ten′tial** (-ten′shəl) *adj.*

sen·ten·tious (sen ten′shəs) *adj.* [< L. < *sententia:* see prec.] **1.** expressing much in few words; short and pithy **2.** full of, or fond of using, maxims, proverbs, etc., esp. in a pompously boring or moralizing way [a *sententious* sermon] —**sen·ten′tious·ly** *adv.* —**sen·ten′tious·ness** *n.*

sen·tient (sen′shənt, -shē ənt) *adj.* [< L. prp. of *sentire:* see SENTIMENT] having senses or feelings; conscious [a *sentient* being] —**sen′tience, sen′tien·cy** *n.* —**sen′tient·ly** *adv.*

sen·ti·ment (sen′tə mənt) *n.* [< OFr. < ML. < L. *sentire,* to feel: see SENSE] **1.** a group of feelings and thoughts connected with and stirred up by an idea [the *sentiment* of romantic love] **2.** an opinion, attitude, etc. [what are your *sentiments* about the election?] **3.** feelings, esp. tender feelings, as apart from reason or judgment [he claims there is no room for *sentiment* in business] **4.** gentle or tender feelings of a weak or foolish kind [a novel full of *sentiment*] **5.** a short sentence, etc. expressing some thought or wish, as in a toast or on a greeting card **6.** the real thought or meaning behind something said, done, etc. —see SYN. at OPINION

sen·ti·men·tal (sen′tə men′t'l) *adj.* **1.** having or showing tender, gentle feelings, often in a weak or foolish way [a *sentimental* song] **2.** influenced more by feeling than reason **3.** of or resulting from sentiment [to save a picture for *sentimental* reasons] —**sen′ti·men′tal·ism** *n.* —**sen′ti·men′tal·ist** *n.* —**sen′ti·men′tal·ly** *adv.*

SYN.—**sentimental** suggests emotion of a kind that is felt in a longing or tender mood [*sentimental* music] or emotion that is exaggerated, artificial, foolish, etc. [a trashy, *sentimental* novel]; **romantic** suggests emotion stirred up by that which appeals to the imagination as it is influenced by stories of love and adventure [a *romantic* girl waiting for her knight in shining armor]; that is **mawkish** which is sentimental in a disgustingly weak, insincere, or exaggerated way [the *mawkish* lyrics of a popular love song]; that is **maudlin** which is tearfully or weakly sentimental in a foolish way [to become *maudlin* when drunk]

sen·ti·men·tal·i·ty (sen′tə men tal′ə tē) *n.* **1.** the quality or condition of being sentimental, esp. in a weak or foolish way **2.** *pl.* **-ties** any expression of this

sen·ti·men·tal·ize (-men′tə līz′) *vi.* **-ized′, -iz′ing** to be sentimental —*vt.* to think of or treat sentimentally —**sen′ti·men′tal·i·za′tion** *n.*

sen·ti·nel (sen′ti n'l) *n.* [< Fr. < It. *sentinella,* ult. < L *sentire,* to feel: see SENSE] a person or animal set to guard a group; specif., a sentry —*vt.* **-neled** or **-nelled, -nel·ing** or **-nel·ling** **1.** to guard as a sentinel **2.** to furnish with a sentinel **3.** to post as a sentinel

sen·try (sen′trē) *n., pl.* **-tries** [< ? obs. *centery,* guardhouse] a sentinel; esp., any member of a military guard posted to guard against, and warn of, danger

Se·oul (sōl; *Korean* syö′ool′) capital of South Korea, in the NW part: pop. 5,510,000

Sep. **1.** September **2.** Septuagint

se·pal (sē′p'l; *chiefly Brit.* sep′'l) *n.* [< Fr. < ModL. *sepalum* < Gr. *skepē,* a covering + L. *petalum,* petal] *Bot.* any of the usually green, leaflike parts of the calyx —**se′paled, se′palled** *adj.* —**se′pal·oid** (-oid′) *adj.*

-sep·al·ous (sep′'l əs) *a combining form meaning* having (a specified number or kind of) sepals

sep·a·ra·ble (sep′ər ə b'l, sep′rə-) *adj.* that can be separated —**sep′a·ra·bil′i·ty** *n.* —**sep′a·ra·bly** *adv.*

sep·a·rate (sep′ə rāt′; *for adj. & n.* sep′ər-it, sep′rit) *vt.* **-rat′ed, -rat′ing** [< L. pp. of *separare* < *se-,* apart + *parare,* to arrange] **1.** to set apart into groups, sets, units, etc.; cause to be no longer together; disunite; divide **2.** to tell apart; distinguish between [I cannot *separate* the twins] **3.** to keep apart by being between [a wall that *separates* the yards] **4.** to bring about a separation between (a husband and wife) **5.** to set apart from others; segregate [to *separate* contagious patients in a special ward] **6.** to take away (a part or ingredient) from a combination or mixture **7.** *a)* to discharge from military service ☆*b)* to dismiss from a job —*vi.* **1.** to withdraw or secede [to *separate* from a party] **2.** to part, come apart, become disconnected, etc. [the strands of the rope *separated*] **3.** to part company; go in different directions [the friends *separated* at the crossroads] **4.** to stop living together as husband and wife but without getting a divorce **5.** to become distinct or separate, as from a mixture —*adj.* **1.** set apart or divided from the rest or others; not joined or united [a *separate* garage] **2.** not associated with others; distinct; individual [the President has powers *separate* from those of Congress] **3.** having individual form or function [the *separate* parts of the body] **4.** not shared or held in common [*separate* lockers] —*n.* [*pl.*] articles of dress designed to be worn as a set or separately

sep·a·ra·tion (sep′ə rā′shən) *n.* **1.** a separating or being separated **2.** the place where this occurs; break; division **3.** something that separates **4.** an arrangement by which a husband and wife live apart by agreement or court decree

sep·a·ra·tism (sep′ər ə tiz′m) *n.* a policy of or movement for political, religious, or racial separation —**sep·a·ra·tist** (sep′ər-ə tist, -ə rāt′ist) *n., adj.*

sep·a·ra·tive (sep′ə rāt′iv, -ər ə tiv) *adj.* tending to separate or cause separation: also **sep′a·ra·to′ry** (-ər ə tôr′ē)

sep·a·ra·tor (sep′ə rāt′ər) *n.* a person or thing that separates, as a device for separating cream from milk

Se·phar·dim (sə fär′dim, -fär dēm′) *n.pl., sing.* **Se·phard** (sə-färd′), **Se·phar·di** (-fär′dē, -fär dē′) [< Heb.: see Obad., verse 20] the Jews of Spain and Portugal before the Inquisition, or their descendants —**Se·phar′dic** *adj.*

se·pi·a (sē′pē ə) *n.* [L., cuttlefish < Gr. *sēpia* < *sēpein,* to cause to rot (from the inky fluid)] **1.** a dark-brown pigment made from the inky fluid of cuttlefish **2.** a dark reddish-brown color **3.** a photographic print in this color —*adj.* **1.** of sepia **2.** dark reddish-brown

se·poy (sē′poi) *n.* [Port. *sipae* < Hindi & Per. *sipāhī* < *sipāh,* army] formerly, a native of India serving in the British army

sep·pu·ku (se poo′koo) *n.* [Jpn.] *same as* HARA-KIRI

sep·sis (sep′sis) *n.* [ModL. < Gr. < *sēpein,* to make putrid] poisoning caused by the spreading into the blood of certain bacteria and their products

Sept. 1. September 2. Septuagint

Sep·tem·ber (sep tem′bər, səp-) *n.* [< L. < *septem,* seven: the early Romans reckoned from March] the ninth month of the year, having 30 days

sep·te·nar·y (sep′tə ner′ē) *adj.* [< L. < *septem,* seven] consisting of seven —*n., pl.* **-nar′ies** a group or set of seven, esp. seven years

sep·ten·ni·al (sep ten′ē əl) *adj.* [< L. < *septem,* seven + *annus,* year] 1. lasting seven years 2. coming, happening, etc. every seven years —**sep·ten′ni·al·ly** *adv.*

sep·tet, sep·tette (sep tet′) *n.* [G. < L. *septem,* seven + G. (*du*)*ett*] 1. a group of seven persons or things 2. *Music* *a*) a composition for seven voices or instruments *b*) the performers of this

sep·tic (sep′tik) *adj.* [< L. < Gr. *sēptikos* < *sēpein,* to make putrid] caused by or involving microorganisms that are infecting or rotting —**sep′ti·cal·ly** *adv.*

sep·ti·ce·mi·a (sep′tə sē′mē ə) *n.* [< Gr. *sēptikos,* putrefactive + *haima,* blood] a disease caused by certain microorganisms and their poisonous products in the blood —**sep′ti·ce′mic** *adj.*

septic tank an underground tank in which waste matter is broken down and rotted away by bacteria

sep·til·lion (sep til′yən) *n.* [Fr. < L. *septem,* seven + Fr. (*m*)*illion*] ☆1. in the U.S. and France, the number represented by 1 followed by 24 zeros 2. in Great Britain and Germany, the number represented by 1 followed by 42 zeros —*adj.* amounting to one septillion in number

sep·tu·a·ge·nar·i·an (sep′too wə ji ner′ē ən) *adj.* [< LL. < L. *septuageni,* seventy each < *septuaginta,* seventy] seventy years old, or between the ages of seventy and eighty —*n.* a person of this age

Sep·tu·a·gint (sep′too wə jint, -tyoo-, -choo-) *n.* [< L. *septuaginta,* seventy: in tradition, done by 70 or 72 translators] a Greek translation of the Hebrew Scriptures made in the 3d cent. B.C.

sep·tum (sep′təm) *n., pl.* **-tums, -ta** (-tə) [ModL. < L. < *sepire,* to enclose < *saepes,* a hedge] *Biol.* a part that separates two cavities or masses of tissue, as in the nose, a fruit, etc.; partition —**sep′tal** *adj.*

SEPTUM

sep·tu·ple (sep too′p'l, -tyoo′-, -tup′'l; sep′too p'l) *adj.* [LL. *septuplus* < L. *septem,* seven] 1. consisting of seven 2. seven times as much or as many —*vt., vi.* **-pled, -pling** to multiply by seven

sep·ul·cher (sep′'l kər) *n.* [< OFr. < L. *sepulcrum* < *sepelire,* to bury] a vault or chamber for burial; tomb —*vt.* to bury in a sepulcher

se·pul·chral (sə pul′krəl) *adj.* 1. of sepulchers, burial, etc. 2. suggestive of the grave or burial; dismal; gloomy 3. deep and melancholy: said of sound —**se·pul′chral·ly** *adv.*

sep·ul·chre (sep′'l kər) *n., vt.* **-chred, -chring** *Brit. sp.* of SEPULCHER

sep·ul·ture (sep′'l chər) *n.* burial; interment

seq. [L. *sequentes* or *sequentia*] the following: also **seqq.**

se·quel (sē′kwəl) *n.* [< MFr. < L. *sequela* < *sequi,* to follow: see SEQUENT] 1. something that follows; continuation 2. a result or consequence [floods came as a *sequel* to the heavy rains] 3. a book that carries on a story begun in an earlier work ["Twenty Years After" is a *sequel* to "The Three Musketeers"]

se·que·la (si kwē′lə, -kwel′ə) *n., pl.* **-lae** (-lē, -ē) [L. < *sequi,* to follow] a thing that follows; consequence; specif., a diseased condition following and resulting from a previous disease

se·quence (sē′kwəns) *n.* [< MFr. < LL. < L. *sequens,* SEQUENT] 1. *a*) the following of one thing after another; succession or continuity [the *sequence* of events in his life] *b*) the order in which this occurs [line them up in *sequence* from small to large] 2. a continuous or related series [a *sequence* of misfortunes] 3. a resulting event; consequence 4. an ordered set of numbers, quantities, or elements 5. a part of a movie made up of a series of interrelated scenes —*vt.* **-quenced, -quencing** to arrange in a sequence —see SYN. at SERIES

se·quent (-kwənt) *adj.* [L. *sequens,* prp. of *sequi,* to follow < IE. base *sekw-,* to follow] 1. following in time or order; subsequent 2. following as a result; consequent —*n.* something sequent; consequence

se·quen·tial (si kwen′shəl) *adj.* 1. *same as* SEQUENT 2. having or forming a regular sequence of parts —**se·quen′tial·ly** *adv.*

se·ques·ter (si kwes′tər) *vt.* [< MFr. < LL. *sequestrare,* to remove < L. *sequester,* trustee] 1. to set apart; separate 2. to take possession of (property) as security for a debt, claim, etc. 3. to take over or seize, esp. by authority [to *sequester* illegal guns] 4. to hide or keep away from others; withdraw [he *sequestered* himself in a lonely cabin] —**se·ques′tered** *adj.*

se·ques·trate (-trāt) *vt.* **-trat·ed, -trat·ing** *same as* SEQUESTER —**se′ques·tra′tor** *n.*

se·ques·tra·tion (sē′kwes trā′shən, si kwes′-) *n.* 1. a sequestering or being sequestered; seclusion; separation 2. *a*) the legal seizure of property for security *b*) confiscation of property, as by court or government action

se·quin (sē′kwin) *n.* [Fr. < It. *zecchino* < *zecca,* a mint < Ar. *sikkah,* a stamp] 1. an obsolete Italian gold coin 2. a small, shiny spangle or disk, esp. one of many sewn on fabric for decoration —*vt.* **-quined** or **-quinned, -quin·ing** or **-quin·ning** to decorate with sequins

☆**se·quoi·a** (si kwoi′ə) *n.* [ModL., genus name: after *Sequoya,* Am. Indian (c. 1760–1843) who worked out the Cherokee syllabary] either of two giant evergreen trees; specif., *a*) BIG TREE *b*) REDWOOD

Sequoia National Park national park in EC Calif., containing giant sequoias

se·rag·lio (si ral′yō, -räl′-) *n., pl.* **-lios** [It. *serraglio,* enclosure (infl. by Turk. *serai,* palace), ult. < LL. *serare,* to lock < *sera,* a lock] 1. the part of a Moslem's household where his wives or concubines live; harem 2. the palace of a Turkish sultan Also **se·rail** (sə rī′, -rīl′, -rāl′)

☆**se·ra·pe** (sə rä′pē) *n.* [MexSp.] a woolen blanket, often brightly colored, worn as an outer garment by men in Spanish-American countries

ser·aph (ser′əf) *n., pl.* **-aphs, -a·phim′** (-ə fim′) [< LL. < Heb. *sĕrāphīm, pl.*] *Bible* one of the heavenly beings mentioned in Isaiah as surrounding the throne of God —**se·raph·ic** (sə raf′ik) *adj.* —**se·raph′i·cal·ly** *adv.*

Serb (surb) *n.* 1. a native or inhabitant of Serbia 2. *same as* SERBIAN (*n.* 1) —*adj. same as* SERBIAN

Ser·bi·a (sur′bē ə) republic of Yugoslavia, in the E part: 21,580 sq. mi.; cap. Belgrade

Ser·bi·an (-ən) *adj.* of Serbia, the Serbs, or their language —*n.* 1. Serbo-Croatian as spoken in Serbia 2. *same as* SERB (*n.* 1)

Ser·bo-Cro·a·tian (sur′bō krō ā′shən) *n.* the major South Slavic language of Yugoslavia: it is generally written in the Roman alphabet in Croatia and in the Cyrillic alphabet in Serbia —*adj.* of this language or the people who speak it

SERAPE

sere (sir) *adj.* [var. of SEAR] [Poet.] dried up; withered

ser·e·nade (ser′ə nād′) *n.* [< Fr. < It. *serenata,* ult. < L. *serenus,* clear] 1. the act of playing or singing music outdoors at night, esp. by a lover under the window of his sweetheart 2. a piece of music suitable for this —*vt., vi.* **-nad′ed, -nad′ing** to play or sing a serenade (*to*) —**ser′e·nad′er** *n.*

ser·en·dip·i·ty (ser′ən dip′ə tē) *n.* [after the princes in a Per. fairy tale, *The Three Princes of Serendip,* who make such discoveries] a seeming gift for finding good things accidentally —**ser′en·dip′i·tous** *adj.*

se·rene (sə rēn′) *adj.* [L. *serenus*] 1. clear; unclouded [a *serene* sky] 2. not troubled; calm, peaceful, etc. [a *serene* look] 3. [S-] exalted: in titles [His *Serene* Highness] —see SYN. at CALM —**se·rene′ly** *adv.* —**se·rene′ness** *n.*

se·ren·i·ty (sə ren′ə tē) *n., pl.* **-ties** [< Fr. < L. *serenitas*] the fact or condition of being serene; calmness, peacefulness, clearness, etc. —see SYN. at EQUANIMITY

serf (surf) *n.* [OFr. < L. *servus,* a slave] 1. a person in a slavelike condition under the feudal system, bound to his master's land and transferred with it 2. a person treated like a slave —**serf′dom, serf′hood′** *n.*

Serg., serg. sergeant

serge (surj) *n.* [< OFr. < L. *sericus,* silken, lit., of the *Seres,* prob. the Chinese, prob. ult. < Chin. *se,* silk] a strong, twilled fabric, esp. of wool —*vt.* **serged, serg′ing** to finish off (a cut or raveling edge) with overcast stitches

ser·gean·cy (sär′jən sē) *n., pl.* **-cies** the position or rank of a sergeant: also **ser′geant·ship′**

ser·geant (sär′jənt) *n.* [< OFr. < L. *serviens,* serving < *servire,* to serve] 1. *same as* SERGEANT-AT-ARMS ☆2. *a*) a noncommissioned officer of the fifth grade, ranking just above a corporal in the U.S. Army and Marine Corps *b)* generally, any of the noncommissioned officers in the U.S. armed forces with *sergeant* as part of the title of their rank **3.** a police officer ranking next below a captain or a lieutenant

ser·geant-at-arms (-ət ärmz′) *n., pl.* **ser′geants-at-arms′** an officer appointed to keep order in a legislature, court, social club, etc.

☆**sergeant first class** *U.S. Army* the seventh grade of enlisted man, ranking just below master sergeant

sergeant major *pl.* **sergeants major 1.** the chief administrative noncommissioned officer of a military headquarters: an occupational title, not a rank ☆**2.** *U.S. Army & Marine Corps* the highest ranking noncommissioned officer

se·ri·al (sir′ē əl) *adj.* [< ModL. < L. *series,* a row, SERIES] **1.** of, arranged in, or forming a series [*serial* numbers] **2.** appearing or published in a series of continuing parts at regular times **3.** of a serial or serials **4.** *same as* TWELVE-TONE —*n.* a story presented in serial form, as in magazines, movies, radio, TV, etc. —**se′ri·al·ly** *adv.*

se·ri·al·ize (-īz′) *vt.* **-ized′, -iz′ing** to put or publish (a story, etc.) in serial form —**se′ri·al·i·za′tion** *n.*

serial number any of a series of numbers given to a person (as a soldier) or thing (as an engine) for identification

se·ri·a·tim (sir′ē āt′im) *adv., adj.* [ML. < L. *series*] one after another in order; serial(ly)

ser·i·cul·ture (ser′i kul′chər) *n.* [< Fr. < L. *sericus,* silken + Fr. *culture,* farming] the raising of silkworms for the production of raw silk —**ser′i·cul′tur·ist** *n.*

se·ries (sir′ēz) *n., pl.* **-ries** [L. < *serere,* to join together: for IE. base see DESERT¹] **1.** a number of similar things arranged in a row [*a series* of arches] **2.** a number of similar persons, things, or events coming one after another; sequence [*a series* of concerts] **3.** a number of things produced as a related group; set [*a series* of illustrations for a book] **4.** *Elec.* a circuit connection in which the components are joined end to end, forming a single path for the current: usually in the phrase **in series 5.** *Geol.* a subdivision of a geologic system **6.** *Math.* a sequence, often infinite, of terms to be added or subtracted —*adj. Elec.* designating or of a circuit in series

SYN.—series applies to a number of similar, related things following one another in time or place [*a series* of concerts]; **sequence** emphasizes a relationship through logical connection, numerical order, etc. [*the sequence of events*]; **succession** merely implies a following of one thing after another, without any necessary connection between them [*a succession* of errors]; **chain** refers to a series that is connected physically or logically [*a chain* of ideas]

series winding the winding of an electric motor or generator so that the field and armature circuits are connected in series —**se′ries-wound′** (-wound′) *adj.*

ser·if (ser′if) *n.* [Du. *schreef,* a stroke < *schrijven,* to write < L. *scribere*] *Printing* a fine line across the top or bottom of a main stroke of a letter: see illustration at TYPE

ser·i·graph (ser′ə graf′) *n.* [< L. *sericum,* silk + -GRAPH] a color print made by the silk-screen process and printed by the artist himself —**se·rig·ra·phy** (sə rig′rə fē) *n.*

se·ri·o·com·ic (sir′ē ō käm′ik) *adj.* partly serious and partly comic —**se′ri·o·com′i·cal·ly** *adv.*

se·ri·ous (sir′ē əs) *adj.* [< ML. *seriosus* < L. *serius*] **1.** having or showing deep thought; earnest, solemn, etc. [*a serious* man] **2.** *a)* meaning what one says or does; not joking or fooling; sincere [*he's serious* about wanting to help] *b)* meant in earnest [*a serious* suggestion] **3.** having to do with important or difficult matters; weighty [*a serious* novel] **4.** needing careful thought or attention [*a serious* problem] **5.** giving cause for worry or concern; dangerous [*a serious* wound] —**se′ri·ous·ly** *adv.* —**se′ri·ous·ness** *n.*

SYN.—serious implies being taken up with deep thought or really important things rather than with light or frivolous matters [*a serious* interest in government reform]; **grave** applies to things of a very serious or critical nature [*grave* risks; *a grave* illness]; **solemn** suggests an impressive or awe-inspiring seriousness [*a solemn* ceremony]; **sedate** implies a dignified, proper, and calm seriousness [*a sedate* minister]; **earnest** suggests a seriousness of purpose marked by sincerity and enthusiasm [*an earnest* desire to help]; **sober** implies a seriousness marked by moderation, self-control, emotional balance, etc. [*a sober* criticism] —ANT. **frivolous, flippant**

se·ri·ous-mind·ed (-mīn′did) *adj.* having or showing serious-ness of purpose, etc.; not flighty, silly, etc. —**se′ri·ous-mind′ed·ly** *adv.* —**se′ri·ous-mind′ed·ness** *n.*

ser·jeant (sär′jənt) *n. Brit. var. of* SERGEANT

ser·mon (sur′mən) *n.* [OFr. < LL. < L. *sermo,* a discourse] **1.** a speech, esp. by a clergyman during services, on some religious topic or on morals **2.** any serious or boring talk on one's behavior, responsibilities, etc. —**ser·mon′ic** (-män′ik) *adj.*

ser·mon·ize (-mə nīz′) *vi., vt.* **-ized′, -iz′ing** to preach (to); lecture —**ser′mon·iz′er** *n.*

Sermon on the Mount the sermon given by Jesus to his disciples: Matt. 5–7, Luke 6:20–49

se·rol·o·gy (si räl′ə jē) *n.* [< SERUM + -LOGY] the science dealing with the properties and actions of serums —**se·ro·log′ic** (sir′ə läj′ik), **se·ro·log′i·cal** *adj.* —**se·rol′o·gist** *n.*

se·ro·sa (si rō′sə) *n., pl.* **-sas, -sae** (-sē) [ModL. < L. *serosus,* serous] *same as:* **1.** SEROUS MEMBRANE **2.** CHORION

se·rous (sir′əs) *adj.* **1.** of or containing serum **2.** like serum; thin and watery

serous membrane a thin membrane, as the peritoneum, lining a closed space of the body

ser·pent (sur′pənt) *n.* [OFr. < L. < prp. of *serpere,* to creep] **1.** a snake, esp. a large or poisonous one **2.** a sly, sneaky, or treacherous person

ser·pen·tine (sur′pən tēn′, -tīn′) *adj.* of or like a serpent; esp., *a)* sly or sneaky; treacherous *b)* coiled, twisted, or winding —*n.* **1.** a coil of thin paper thrown out to unwind as a streamer **2.** a green or brownish-red mineral, magnesium silicate

ser·rate (ser′āt, -it; *for v. usually* sə rāt′) *adj.* [L. *serratus* < *serra,* a saw] having sawlike notches along the edge, as some leaves or knives: also **ser·rat′ed** —*vt.* **-rat′ed, -rat′ing** to make serrate

ser·ra·tion (sə rā′shən) *n.* **1.** the condition of being serrate **2.** a single tooth or notch in a serrate edge **3.** a formation of these Also **ser·ra·ture** (ser′ə chər)

SERPENTINE WALL

ser·ried (ser′ēd) *adj.* [pp. of obs. *serry* < Fr. *serrer,* to crowd < L. *serare:* see SERAGLIO] placed close together; compact, as soldiers in ranks

ser·ru·late (ser′yoo lit, ser′ə-; -lāt′) *adj.* [< ModL. < L. dim. of *serra,* a saw] having very small, fine teeth or notched along the edge: also **ser′ru·lat′ed** —**ser′ru·la′tion** *n.*

ser·um (sir′əm) *n., pl.* **-rums, -ra** (-ə) [L., whey] **1.** any watery animal fluid, esp. the yellowish fluid that is left after blood clots: in full, **blood serum 2.** blood serum used as an antitoxin, taken from an animal made immune to a specific disease by inoculation **3.** whey **4.** watery plant fluid

serum albumin the main protein in blood serum, which controls osmotic pressure and is used in the treatment of shock

ser·val (sur′v'l) *n., pl.* **-vals, -val:** see PLURAL, II, D, 1 [Fr. < Port. *(lobo) cerval,* ult. < L. *lupus,* a wolf & *cervus,* a stag] an African wildcat with a black-spotted tan coat and long legs

ser·vant (sur′vənt) *n.* [OFr. < prp. of *servir* < L. *servire,* to serve] **1.** a person hired to work in another's home as a maid, cook, etc. **2.** a person who works for a government [a civil *servant*] **3.** a person who serves another for a cause, etc.

serve (surv) *vt.* **served, serv′ing** [< OFr. < L. *servire,* to serve < *servus,* a slave] **1.** to work for as a servant **2.** *a)* to do work or services for; aid; help [he *served* his clients well] *b)* to worship, obey, etc. [to *serve* God] **3.** to do military or naval service for **4.** to pass or spend (a term of office, imprisonment, military service, etc.) **5.** to be an assistant in the service of (Mass or Holy Communion) **6.** to provide (customers) with (goods or services) **7.** to offer or pass (food, drink, etc.) to (a person or persons) **8.** *a)* to meet the needs of [a tool to *serve* many purposes] *b)* to promote or further [to *serve* the national interest] **9.** to be used by [one hospital *serves* the town] **10.** to function or perform for [my memory *serves* me well] **11.** to treat [she was cruelly *served*] **12.** to deliver (a summons, subpoena, etc.) to (someone) **13.** to hit (a tennis ball, etc.) to one's opponent in order to start play **14.** to operate (a large gun) **15.** to have sexual intercourse with (the female): said of the male in the breeding of animals **16.** *Naut.* to put a binding around in order to strengthen (rope, etc.) —*vi.* **1.** to work as a servant [she *served* in their household five years] **2.** to be in service [to *serve* in the navy] **3.** to carry out the duties of an office or position [he *served* as mayor for two terms] **4.** to be used or usable; function [his idea *serves* perfectly] **5.** to meet needs or satisfy requirements [one nail will *serve* in hanging the picture] **6.** to wait on table **7.** to be suitable: said of weather, wind, etc. **8.** to start play in tennis, etc. by hitting the ball —*n.* the act or manner of serving the ball in tennis, etc., or one's turn to serve —**serve (someone) right** to be what (someone) deserves, as for doing something wrong

serv·er (sur'vər) *n.* **1.** a person who serves, as a waiter, etc. **2.** a thing used in serving, as a tray, cart, etc.

serv·ice (sur'vis) *n.* [< OFr. < L. *servitium* < *servus*, a slave] **1.** the condition or work of a servant [she was in *service* for many years] **2.** *a)* employment, esp. public employment [diplomatic *service*] *b)* a branch of this, including the people in it; specif., the army, navy, air force, etc. **3.** work done or duty performed for others [repair *service*] **4.** a religious ceremony, esp. a meeting for prayer **5.** *a)* an act of assistance *b)* the result of this; benefit *c)* [*pl.*] friendly help; also, professional aid [a fee for *services*] **6.** the act or manner of serving food [a restaurant with fine *service*] **7.** a set of utensils used in serving [a tea *service*] **8.** a system or method of providing people with electric power, water, transportation, etc. **9.** installation, maintenance, repairs, etc. provided to purchasers of equipment by a dealer or manufacturer **10.** the act or manner of serving the ball in tennis, etc., or one's turn to serve **11.** *Law* notification of legal action, esp. through the serving of a writ, etc. **12.** *Naut.* any material, as wire, used in serving (ropes, etc.) —*adj.* **1.** of, for, or in service [the *service* trades] **2.** of, for, or used by servants, tradespeople, etc. [a *service* entrance] —*vt.* **-iced, -ic·ing 1.** to furnish with a service [one gas company *services* the whole region] **2.** *same as* SERVE, *vt.* 15 ☆**3.** to make or keep fit for service, as by adjusting, repairing, etc. [we *service* television sets] —**at one's service 1.** ready to serve one **2.** ready for one's use —**in service 1.** in use; functioning **2.** in the armed forces **3.** working as a servant —**of service** helpful; useful

Ser·vice (sur'vis), **Robert (William)** 1874?-1958; Canad. writer, born in England

serv·ice·a·ble (sur'vis ə b'l) *adj.* **1.** that can be of service; ready for use; useful [a *serviceable* method] **2.** that will give good service; durable [*serviceable* clothing] —**serv'ice·a·bil'i·ty, serv'ice·a·ble·ness** *n.* —**serv'ice·a·bly** *adv.*

serv·ice·ber·ry (-ber'ē) *n., pl.* **-ries** ☆**1.** *same as* JUNEBERRY **2.** the fruit of any service tree

service line the line parallel to the net, as in tennis, beyond which a served ball may not be hit

serv·ice·man (sur'vis man', -mən) *n., pl.* **-men** (-men', -mən) **1.** a member of the armed forces **2.** a person whose work is servicing or repairing something [a television *serviceman*]: also **service man**

☆**service mark** a symbol, word, etc. used by a supplier of services, as transportation, laundry, etc., to distinguish the services from those of competitors: usually registered and protected by law: see TRADEMARK

☆**service station 1.** a place providing repair, parts, etc. as for electrical equipment **2.** a place providing such service, and selling gas and oil, for motor vehicles

☆**service stripe** a stripe, or any of the parallel diagonal stripes, worn on the left sleeve of a uniform to show years spent in the service

service tree either of two European trees of the rose family, related to the mountain ash and having small, edible fruit

ser·vi·ette (sur'vē et') *n.* [Fr. < MFr. < *servir*, to serve] a table napkin

serv·ile (sur'v'l, -vīl) *adj.* [< L. < *servus*, a slave] **1.** of a slave or slaves **2.** like that of slaves or servants [*servile* employment] **3.** too humble or submissive; cringing [a *servile* flatterer] —**ser'vile·ly** *adv.* —**ser·vil·i·ty** (sər vil'ə tē), *pl.* **-ties**, **ser'vile·ness** *n.*

serv·ing (-viŋ) *n.* a helping, or single portion, of food —*adj.* used for serving food [a *serving* spoon]

ser·vi·tor (sur'və tər) *n.* a servant, attendant, etc.

ser·vi·tude (sur'və tōōd', -tyōōd') *n.* [MFr. < L. < *servus*, a slave] **1.** slavery or bondage **2.** work that one is forced to do as punishment for crime

SERVICE STRIPES

ser·vo·mech·a·nism (sur'vō mek'ə niz'm) *n.* [SERVO(MOTOR) + MECHANISM] an automatic control system in which the output is compared with the input through feedback so that any error in control is corrected

ser·vo·mo·tor (sur'vō mōt'ər) *n.* [< Fr. *servo-moteur* < L. *servus*, slave + Fr. *moteur*, MOTOR] a device, as an electric motor, that is controlled by an amplified signal as from a servomechanism

ses·a·me (ses'ə mē') *n.* [< L. < Gr. *sēsamon*, of Sem. origin] **1.** an East Indian plant whose flat seeds yield an edible oil **2.** its seeds, used for flavoring bread, rolls, etc. See also OPEN SESAME

ses·qui- [< L. < *semis*, half + *que*, and] *a combining form meaning* one and a half [*sesquicentennial*]

☆**ses·qui·cen·ten·ni·al** (ses'kwi sen ten'ē əl) *adj.* of or ending a period of 150 years —*n.* a 150th anniversary or its celebration

ses·qui·pe·da·li·an (-pə dā'lē ən, -pə dāl'yən) *adj.* [< L. < *sesqui-* (see SESQUI-) + *pedalis* < *pes*, a foot] **1.** very long: said of words **2.** using long words

ses·sile (ses'il, -īl) *adj.* [< L. pp. of *sedere*, to SIT] **1.** *Anat., Zool.* attached directly by its base **2.** *Bot.* attached directly to the main stem, as some flowers and leaves

SESSILE LEAVES
(A, trillium; B,
Solomon's seal)

ses·sion (sesh'ən) *n.* [< L. *sessio* < *sedere*, to SIT] **1.** *a)* the sitting together or meeting of a court, legislature, council, etc. *b)* a continuous series of such meetings *c)* the period a session lasts **2.** a school term or period of study, classes, etc. **3.** the governing body of a Presbyterian church **4.** a period of activity or meeting of any kind [a *session* with one's lawyer] —**in session** meeting —**ses'sion·al** *adj.*

ses·tet (ses tet', ses'tet) *n.* [< It. dim. of *sesto*, sixth < L. < *sex*, six] **1.** *Music same as* SEXTET **2.** *a)* the final six lines of a sonnet *b)* a poem or stanza of six lines

set (set) *vt.* **set, set'ting** [OE. *settan* < base of SIT] **1.** to cause to sit; seat **2.** *a)* to cause (a fowl) to sit on eggs to hatch them *b)* to put (eggs) under a fowl to hatch them **3.** to put in a certain or designated place or position [*set* the book on the table, *set* the wheel on the axle] **4.** to bring (something) into contact with something else [to *set* a match to paper] **5.** to place (one's signature, etc.) on a document **6.** to cause to be in some condition or relation [to *set* a house on fire; to *set* a book on end] **7.** to cause to be in working or proper condition; arrange; fix; specif., *a)* to fix (a net, trap, etc.) to catch animals *b)* to fix (a sail) to catch the wind *c)* to adjust; regulate [to *set* a clock] *d)* to place (oneself) in readiness for action *e)* to arrange (a table) with tableware for a meal *f)* to put (a dislocated or fractured bone) into normal position **8.** *a)* to put into a fixed position [he *set* his jaw] *b)* to cause (one's mind, etc.) to be fixed, determined, etc. *c)* to cause to become firm [pectin *sets* jelly] *d)* to make (a color) fast in dyeing *e)* to mount (gems) in jewelry *f)* to decorate (jewelry) with gems *g)* to arrange (hair) in a certain style with lotion, rollers, etc. **9.** *a)* to cause to take a specified direction; direct [he *set* his face toward home] *b)* to direct (one's desires, hopes, heart, etc.) with serious attention (*in* or *on* someone or something) **10.** to appoint; establish; specif., *a)* to station (a person) for certain duties [to *set* sentries at a gate] *b)* to fix (limits or boundaries) *c)* to fix (a time) for (an event) *d)* to establish (a rule, record, etc.) *e)* to give or furnish (an example) for others *f)* to introduce (a fashion, etc.) *g)* to fix (a quota) for a given period *h)* to begin to apply (oneself) to a task **11.** *a)* to fix (the amount of a price, fine, etc.) *b)* to fix (a price, fine, etc.) at a specified amount *c)* to fix or put as an estimate [to *set* little store by someone] **12.** to point toward (game): said of dogs **13.** *Baking* to put aside (leavened dough) to rise **14.** *Bridge* to prevent (one's opponents) from making their bid **15.** *Music* to write or fit (words to music or music to words) **16.** *Printing a)* to arrange (type) for printing *b)* to put (manuscript) into type **17.** *Theater a)* to place (a scene) in a given locale *b)* to arrange the scenery and properties on (the stage) —*vi.* **1.** to sit on eggs: said of a fowl **2.** to become firm or hard [the cement *set*] **3.** to become fast, as a dye **4.** *a)* to begin to move, travel, etc. (with *out, forth, on, off*, etc.) *b)* to get started [to *set* to work] **5.** to have a certain direction; tend [the wind *sets* from the north] **6.** *a)* to sink below the horizon [the *setting* sun] *b)* to wane;

decline **7.** to hang or fit in a certain way [the jacket *sets* well]
8. to grow together: said of a broken bone **9.** [Now Dial.] to sit
10. *Bot.* to begin to develop into a fruit —*adj.* **1.** fixed in advance [a *set* time] **2.** established, as by authority [the *set* rules of the game] **3.** deliberate; intentional; purposeful **4.** conventional, stereotyped, or routine [a *set* speech] **5.** fixed; motionless; rigid [a *set* look on his face] **6.** determined or stubborn [*set* in his ways] **7.** firm or hard **8.** ready [get *set*] **9.** formed; built: usually used in combination [thickset; heavyset] —*n.* **1.** a setting or being set; specif., the act of a dog in setting game **2.** the way or position in which a thing is set; specif., *a)* direction or course, as of a current *b)* tendency; inclination *c)* change of form resulting from pressure, strain, etc.; warp; bend *d)* the way in which an article of clothing fits *e)* the position of a part of the body [the *set* of her head] **3.** something which is set; specif., *a)* a twig, slip, young bulb, etc. for planting or grafting *b)* the scenery for a play, movie, etc. **4.** *a)* the act or a style of arranging hair *b)* the lotion, etc. used for this: in full, **hair set 5.** a group of persons or things classed or belonging together [the social *set;* a *set* of tools, books, china, etc.] **6.** assembled equipment for radio or television reception **7.** *Math.* a collection of points, numbers, or other objects that satisfy a given condition **8.** *Tennis* a group of games of which the winner must win a specified number, usually (and at least) six —see **SYN.** at COTERIE —☆**all set** [Colloq.] prepared; ready —**set about** to begin; start doing —**set against 1.** to balance **2.** to compare **3.** to make unfriendly toward —**set aside 1.** to separate and keep for a purpose: also **set apart 2.** to get rid of; discard; reject **3.** to declare no longer legally binding; annul —**set back 1.** to reverse or hinder the progress of ☆**2.** [Slang] to cost (a person) a specified sum of money —**set down 1.** to put down **2.** to land (an airplane) **3.** to put in writing or print **4.** to establish (rules, etc.) **5.** to consider or ascribe [I *set* down his disloyalty as being due to weakness] —**set forth** to make known; state —**set in 1.** to begin [infection had *set* in] **2.** to insert —**set off 1.** to start (a person) doing something **2.** to make begin **3.** to make stand out by contrast **4.** to show to advantage; enhance **5.** to cause to explode —**set on 1.** to urge to attack [to *set* dogs *on* intruders] **2.** to attack: also **set upon** —**set out 1.** to display, as for sale **2.** to plant **3.** to take upon oneself; undertake [to *set* out to prove a theory] —**set to 1.** to get to work; begin **2.** to begin fighting —**set up 1.** to place in an upright position **2.** to raise to power, a high position, etc. **3.** to present (oneself) as being something specified [he *set* himself *up* as judge and jury] **4.** to put together or erect (a tent, machine, etc.) **5.** to establish; found [to *set* up a new business] **6.** to make detailed plans for [to *set* up a new football play] **7.** to begin **8.** to make successful, etc.

se·ta (sēt′ə) *n.,* pl. **-tae** (-ē) [ModL. < L., a stiff hair] *Bot., Zool.* a bristle or bristlelike part or organ

se·ta·ceous (si tā′shəs) *adj.* [ModL. < L. *seta:* see SETA] **1.** having bristles **2.** bristlelike Also **se·tose** (sēt′ōs)

set·back (set′bak′) *n.* **1.** the condition of being set back, or put behind; reversal or relapse **2.** an upper part of a wall or building, set back to form a steplike section

Seth (seth) [LL. < Gr. < Heb. *shēth,* lit., appointed] **1.** a masculine name **2.** *Bible* the third son of Adam

set·off (set′ôf′) *n.* **1.** a thing that makes up for something else; counterbalance **2.** *a)* a debt claimed by a debtor against his creditor *b)* a claim for this

set piece anything carefully planned beforehand

set·screw (set′skroō′) *n.* a machine screw passing through one part and against or into another to prevent movement, as of a ring around a shaft

set·tee (se tē′) *n.* [prob. altered < SETTLE¹] **1.** a seat or bench with a back **2.** a small or medium-sized sofa

set·ter (set′ər) *n.* **1.** a person who sets or a thing used in setting [pinsetter] **2.** any of several breeds of longhaired bird dog trained to find game and point it out by standing rigid: see ENGLISH SETTER, IRISH SETTER

set theory the branch of mathematics

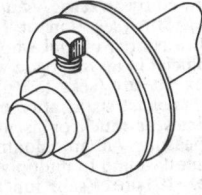

SETSCREW

that deals with the properties and relations of sets (see SET, *n.* 7)

set·ting (set′iŋ) *n.* **1.** the act of one that sets **2.** the position of something, as a dial, that has been set **3.** a thing in or on which something, as a gem, has been set **4.** time and place, environment, etc. of an event, story, play, etc. **5.** surroundings, or scenery that surrounds **6.** the music written for a set of words, as for a poem **7.** the eggs in the nest of a setting hen **8.** same as PLACE SETTING

set·tle¹ (set′l) *n.* [OE. *setl*] a long wooden bench with a back and armrests

set·tle² (set′l) *vt.* **-tled, -tling** [OE. < *setl,* a seat < base of SIT] **1.** to put in order; arrange as desired [to *settle* one's affairs] **2.** to set in place firmly or comfortably [to *settle* oneself in a chair] **3.** to establish as a resident or residents [he *settled* his family in London] **4.** to go to live in; colonize [New York was *settled* by the Dutch] **5.** to cause to sink and become more closely packed together [the rain *settled* the dust] **6.** to make (a liquid) clear by causing the sediment to sink to the bottom **7.** to calm or quiet (the mind, nerves, stomach, etc.) **8.** to establish in business, marriage, etc. **9.** to fix definitely; decide (something in doubt) **10.** to end (a dispute) **11.** to pay (a bill, debt, etc.) **12.** to make over (property, etc.) to someone by legal action (with *on* or *upon*) **13.** to decide (a legal dispute) without court action —*vi.* **1.** to stop moving and stay in one place; come to rest [the fly *settled* on the pie] **2.** to cast itself, as fog over a landscape or gloom over a person **3.** to become centered in a part of the body: said of pain or disease **4.** to take up permanent residence [they *settled* out west] **5.** to move downward; sink [the car *settled* in the mud] **6.** to become more dense by sinking, as sediment **7.** to become clearer by the settling of dregs [let the tea *settle* before pouring] **8.** to become more stable or calm **9.** *a)* to reach a decision (with *with, on,* or *upon*) [they *settled* on which route to take] ☆*b)* to accept something less than what is hoped for [he'll *settle* for any kind of work] **10.** to pay a bill or debt —see **SYN.** at DECIDE —**settle down 1.** to take up permanent residence, a regular job, etc. **2.** to become less nervous, erratic, etc. **3.** to apply oneself steadily

set·tle·ment (-mənt) *n.* **1.** a settling or being settled **2.** a new colony **3.** a village **4.** a community established by a religious or social group **5.** an agreement, adjustment, etc. [to reach a *settlement* in a dispute] **6.** *a)* the paying or agreement to pay an amount in money or property to another, as at marriage, divorce, or death *b)* this amount **7.** a place in a poor, crowded neighborhood, where people can go to get advice, take classes, have recreation, etc.: also **settlement house**

set·tler (set′lər) *n.* **1.** a person or thing that settles ☆**2.** one who settles in a new country

set·tlings (set′liŋz) *n.pl.* the solid matter that settles to the bottom of a liquid; sediment; dregs

set-to (set′tōō′) *n., pl.* **-tos** (-tōōz′) [Colloq.] **1.** a fight or struggle **2.** any brisk or vigorous contest

set·up (set′up′) *n.* **1.** the way in which something is set up; specif., *a)* plan, makeup, or arrangement, as of equipment, an organization, etc. *b)* the details of a situation, plan of action, etc. ☆**2.** bodily posture; carriage ☆**3.** the glass, ice, soda water, etc. for preparing an alcoholic drink ☆**4.** [Colloq.] *a)* a contest purposely arranged to result in an easy victory *b)* the contestant marked for defeat *c)* any undertaking that is, or is made, very easy *d)* a person easily tricked

Seu·rat (sö rà′), **Georges (Pierre)** (zhôrzh) 1859–91; Fr. painter

Se·vas·to·pol (sə vas′tə pōl; *Russ.* se′väs tô′pəl y′) seaport in SW Crimea, on the Black Sea: pop. 229,000

sev·en (sev′'n) *adj.* [OE. *seofon*] totaling one more than six —*n.* **1.** the cardinal number between six and eight; 7; VII **2.** anything having seven units or members, or numbered seven

sev·en·fold (-fōld′) *adj.* [see -FOLD] **1.** having seven parts **2.** having seven times as much or as many —*adv.* seven times as much or as many

Seven Hills of Rome seven low hills on the E bank of the Tiber, on & about which Rome was originally built

seven seas all the oceans of the world

sev·en·teen (sev′'n tēn′) *adj.* [OE. *seofentyne*] seven more than ten —*n.* the cardinal number between sixteen and eighteen; 17; XVII

---

fat, āpe, cär; ten, ēven; is, bīte; gō, hôrn, toōl, look; oil, out; up, fur; get; joy; yet; chin; she; thin, then; zh, leisure; ŋ, ring; ə for a in ago, e in agent, i in sanity, o in comply, u in focus; ' as in able (ā′b'l); Fr. bal; ë, Fr. coeur; ö, Fr. feu; Fr. mon; ô, Fr. coq; ü, Fr. duc; r, Fr. cri; H, G. ich; kh, G. doch; ‡foreign; ☆ Americanism; < derived from. See inside front cover.

sev·en·teenth (-tēnth′) *adj.* **1.** coming after sixteen others in a series; 17th **2.** designating any of the seventeen equal parts of something —*n.* **1.** the one following the sixteenth **2.** any of the seventeen equal parts of something; 1/17

☆**sev·en·teen-year locust** (sev′'n tēn′yir′) a cicada which lives underground as a larva for from thirteen to seventeen years before developing into an adult to live in the open for a short time

sev·enth (sev′'nth) *adj.* [< ME. < *seoven* + -TH²] **1.** coming after six others in a series; 7th **2.** designating any of the seven equal parts of something —*n.* **1.** the one following the sixth **2.** any of the seven equal parts of something; 1/7 **3.** *Music a)* the seventh tone of an ascending diatonic scale, or a tone six degrees above or below a given tone *b)* the interval between two such tones, or a combination of them —**sev′enth·ly** *adv.*

seventh heaven 1. in certain ancient beliefs, the outermost of the spheres enclosing the earth, in which God and his angels are **2.** a state of perfect happiness

sev·en·ti·eth (sev′'n tē ith) *adj.* **1.** coming after sixty-nine others in a series; 70th **2.** designating any of the seventy equal parts of something —*n.* **1.** the one following the sixty-ninth **2.** any of the seventy equal parts of something; 1/70

sev·en·ty (-tē) *adj.* seven times ten —*n., pl.* **-ties** the cardinal number between sixty-nine and seventy-one; 70; LXX —**the seventies** the numbers or years, as of a century, from seventy through seventy-nine

sev·er (sev′ər) *vt., vi.* [< OFr., ult. < L. *separare*] **1.** to separate; divide [*severed* from his family by the war] **2.** to part or break off; cut in two [to *sever* a cable, to *sever* a relationship]

sev·er·al (sev′ər əl, sev′rəl) *adj.* [< Anglo-Fr. < ML. < L. *separ*, separate] **1.** separate; distinct [the *several* clauses of the contract] **2.** different; respective [they parted and went their *several* ways] **3.** more than two but not many; few [*several* people left you messages] —*n.* [*with pl. v.*] an indefinite but small number (*of* persons or things) —*pron.* [*with pl. v.*] several persons or things; a few

sev·er·al·ly (-ē) *adv.* **1.** separately; distinctly **2.** respectively; individually

sev·er·ance (sev′ər əns, sev′rəns) *n.* a severing or being severed

☆**severance pay** extra pay given to an employee dismissed through no fault of his own

se·vere (sə vir′) *adj.* **-ver′er, -ver′est** [< MFr. < OFr. < L. *severus*] **1.** harsh or strict, as in treatment; stern [*severe* punishment; a *severe* critic] **2.** serious; grave [a *severe* glance; a *severe* wound] **3.** rigidly accurate or demanding **4.** very plain or simple [a *severe* style] **5.** keen, intense, violent, etc. [*severe* pain; a *severe* storm] **6.** hard to bear; difficult [a *severe* test] —**se·vere′ly** *adv.* —**se·vere′ness** *n.*

SYN.—*severe* applies to a person or thing that is strict and very firm and suggests a total lack of softness, looseness, humor, etc. [a *severe* judge; a *severe* scolding]; **stern** suggests firmness of a kind shown in a grim or forbidding appearance or manner [a *stern* guardian]; **austere** suggests harsh self-control, self-denial, utter simplicity [the *austere* diet of wartime], or a lack of warmth, feeling, decoration, etc. [an *austere* bedroom] —**ANT.** mild, lax, indulgent

se·ver·i·ty (sə ver′ə tē) *n.* **1.** a being severe; specif., *a)* strictness; harshness *b)* seriousness; gravity *c)* rigid accuracy *d)* extreme plainness, as in style *e)* keenness, as of pain *f)* extreme hardship; rigorousness **2.** *pl.* **-ties** something severe

Sev·ern (sev′ərn) river flowing from C Wales through England & into the Bristol Channel

Se·ville (sə vil′) city in SW Spain: pop. 622,000: Sp. name **Se·vil·la** (sā vē′lyä)

Sè·vres (sev′rə) *n.* [< *Sèvres*, suburb of Paris] a type of fine French porcelain

sew (sō) *vt.* **sewed, sewn** or **sewed, sew′ing** [OE. *siwian* < IE. base *siw-*, to sew] **1.** to join or fasten with stitches made with needle and thread **2.** to make, mend, etc. by such means —*vi.* to work with needle and thread or at a sewing machine —**sew up 1.** to close together the edges of with stitches ☆**2.** [Colloq.] *a)* to get or have complete control of *b)* to bring to a successful conclusion *c)* to make certain of success in [to *sew up* an election]

sew·age (sōo′ij, syōo′-) *n.* the waste matter carried off by sewers or drains

Sew·ard (sōo′ərd), **William Henry** 1801-72; U.S. statesman; secretary of state (1861-69)

sew·er¹ (sōo′ər, syōo′-) *n.* [MFr. *esseveur*, ult. < L. *ex*, out + *aqua*, water] a pipe or drain, usually underground, for carrying off water and waste matter

sew·er² (sō′ər) *n.* a person or thing that sews

sew·er·age (sōo′ər ij, syōo′-) *n.* **1.** removal of surface water and waste matter by sewers **2.** a system of sewers **3.** *same as* SEWAGE

sew·ing (sō′iŋ) *n.* **1.** the act or occupation of a person who sews **2.** material for sewing; needlework

☆**sewing circle** a group of women who meet regularly to sew, as for some charitable purpose

☆**sewing machine** a machine with a mechanically driven needle used for sewing and stitching

sewn (sōn) *alt. pp. of* SEW

sex (seks) *n.* [L. *sexus* < ? *secare*, to divide] **1.** either of the two divisions, male or female, of persons, animals, or plants, with reference to their reproductive functions **2.** the character of being male or female **3.** anything connected with sexual pleasure or reproduction; esp., the attraction of one sex for the other **4.** sexual intercourse —*adj.* of or having to do with sex [*sex* studies]

sex- [< L. *sex*, six] *a combining form meaning* six

sex·a·ge·nar·i·an (sek′sə ji ner′ē ən) *adj.* [< L. < *sexageni*, sixty each] sixty years old, or between the ages of sixty and seventy —*n.* a person of this age

☆**sex appeal** the body build and erotic charm that attracts members of the opposite sex

sex chromosome a chromosome in the germ cells that determines sex: the eggs carry an X chromosome and the spermatozoa either an X or Y chromosome, and an egg receiving an X chromosome at fertilization will develop into a female (XX) while one receiving a Y will develop into a male (XY)

sexed (sekst) *adj.* **1.** of or having sex **2.** having (a specified degree of) sexuality

sex hormone any hormone, as testosterone, estrogen, etc., having an effect upon the reproductive organs, sexual characteristics, etc.

☆**sex·ism** (sek′siz'm) *n.* [SEX + (RAC)ISM] social, political, or economic discrimination against members of one sex by the other, specif. against women by men —**sex′ist** *adj., n.*

sex·less (seks′lis) *adj.* **1.** lacking the characteristics of sex; asexual **2.** lacking in normal sexual desire or appeal —**sex′less·ly** *adv.* —**sex′less·ness** *n.*

sex linkage *Genetics* the condition in which certain inherited traits are controlled by a gene carried on a sex chromosome and are therefore linked with the sex of an individual [the *sex linkage* of colorblindness, which occurs mainly among males but is carried by females] —**sex′-linked′** (-liŋkt′) *adj.*

sex·ol·o·gy (sek säl′ə jē) *n.* the science dealing with human sexual behavior —**sex·ol′o·gist** *n.*

sex·pot (seks′pät′) *n.* [Slang] a woman with much sex appeal

sext (sekst) *n.* [< ML. < L. *sexta* (*hora*), sixth (hour)] [*often* S-] the fourth of the canonical hours

sex·tant (seks′tənt) *n.* [ModL. *sextans*, arc of a sixth part of a circle < L. < *sextus*, sixth] an instrument used by navigators for measuring the distance in degrees of an angle of the sun, a star, etc. from the horizon, as in finding the position of a ship

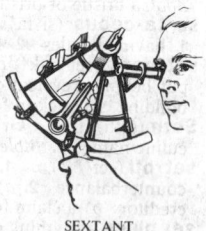

SEXTANT

sex·tet, sex·tette (seks tet′) *n.* [altered (after L. *sex*, six) < SESTET] **1.** any group of six **2.** *Music a)* a composition for six voices or instruments *b)* the six performers of this

sex·til·lion (seks til′yən) *n.* [Fr. < L. *sextus*, sixth + Fr. (*m*)*illion*] ☆**1.** in the U.S. and France, the number represented by 1 followed by 21 zeros **2.** in Great Britain and Germany, the number represented by 1 followed by 36 zeros —*adj.* amounting to one sextillion in number

sex·ton (seks′tən) *n.* [< OFr. < ML. *sacristanus*, SACRISTAN] **1.** a church official who takes care of church property ☆**2.** an official in a synagogue who manages its day-to-day affairs

sex·tu·ple (seks tōo′p'l, -tyōo′-, -tup′'l; seks′tōo p'l) *adj.* [< L. *sextus*, sixth, after QUADRUPLE] **1.** consisting of six **2.** six times as much or as many **3.** *Music* having six beats to the measure —*n.* an amount six times as much or as many —*vt., vi.* **-pled, -pling** to multiply by six

sex·tu·plet (seks tup′lit, -tōo′plit, -tyōo′-; seks′tōo plit) *n.* [dim. of prec.] **1.** any of six offspring born at a single birth **2.** a group of six, usually of one kind

sex·u·al (sek′shōo wəl) *adj.* **1.** of or involving sex, the sexes, the organs of sex and their functions, etc. **2.** *Biol. a)* having sex *b)* designating or of reproduction by the union of male and female germ cells —**sex′u·al·ly** *adv.*

sex·u·al·i·ty (sek'shoo wal'ə tē) *n.* **1.** the fact of being sexual **2.** *a)* interest in sex *b)* sexual drive or activity

sex·y (sek'sē) *adj.* **sex'i·er, sex'i·est** [Colloq.] causing or intended to cause sexual desire; erotic —**sex'i·ly** *adv.* —**sex'i·ness** *n.*

Sey·chelles (sā shel', -shelz') country on a group of islands in the Indian Ocean, northeast of Madagascar: a member of the Commonwealth: 107 sq. mi.; pop. 58,000

☆**sfer·ics** (sfir'iks, sfer'-) *n.pl.* [*with sing. v.*] *same as* ATMOS-PHERICS

sfor·zan·do (sfôr tsän'dō) *adj., adv.* [It. < *sforzare,* to force] *Music* with emphasis: abbrev. **sf., sfz.** —*n., pl.* **-dos** a sforzando note or chord Also **sfor·za'to** (-tsä'tō)

sg, s.g. **1.** senior grade **2.** specific gravity

sgd. signed

sgraf·fi·to (skra fē'tō) *n., pl.* **-fi'ti** (-tē) [It. < *sgraffiare,* to scratch] **1.** the producing of a design on ceramics, stuccoed façades, etc. by cutting into the outer coating to reveal a surface underneath of a different color **2.** such a design or the object bearing it

's Gra·ven·ha·ge (skhrä'vən hä'khə) *Du. name of* The HAGUE

Sgt, Sgt. Sergeant

sh (sh: *a lengthened sound*) *interj.* hush!

sh. **1.** share(s) **2.** shilling(s)

shab·by (shab'ē) *adj.* **-bi·er, -bi·est** [< dial. *shab,* scab < OE. *sceabb*] **1.** poorly taken care of; run-down [a *shabby* neighborhood] **2.** *a)* showing much wear; threadbare: said of clothing *b)* wearing such clothing **3.** beggarly; unworthy [a *shabby* offering] **4.** not proper; mean; shameful [*shabby* treatment] —**shab'bi·ly** *adv.* —**shab'bi·ness** *n.*

Sha·bu·oth (shä voo'ōt, shə voo'ōs) *n. var. of* SHAVUOT

☆**shack** (shak) *n.* [prob. < Scot. dial. *shachle,* a shanty] a small, crudely built cabin; shanty

shack·le (shak''l) *n.* [OE. *sceacul*] **1.** a metal fastening, usually one of a linked pair, for the wrist or ankle of a prisoner; fetter; manacle **2.** [*usually pl.*] anything that keeps one from acting, thinking, or developing freely [the *shackles* of ignorance] **3.** any of several devices for fastening or coupling —*vt.* **-led, -ling** to bind, fasten, or hinder with or as with shackles —**shack'ler** *n.*

Shack·le·ton (shak''l tən), Sir **Ernest Henry** 1874-1922; Brit. antarctic explorer, born in Ireland

shad (shad) *n., pl.* **shad, shads:** see PLU-RAL, II, D, 2 [OE. *sceadd*] **1.** any of several herringlike saltwater food fishes that spawn in rivers ☆**2.** any of various similar fishes, esp. the **giz-zard shad,** often stocked in fresh waters as food for other fish

☆**shad·ber·ry** (shad'ber'ē, -bər ē) *n., pl.* **-ries** *same as* JUNE-BERRY: also called **shad·bush** (-boosh')

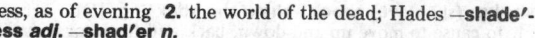
SHACKLES

shade (shād) *n.* [OE. *sceadu*] **1.** slight darkness caused by an opaque object cutting off rays of light, as from the sun **2.** an area less brightly lighted than its surroundings, as an open place sheltered from sunlight **3.** [Archaic] *a)* a shadow *b)* [*often pl.*] a secluded place **4.** a dark area in a painting, etc. **5.** degree of darkness of a color [various *shades* of blue] **6.** *a)* a small difference [*shades* of opinion] *b)* a slight amount or degree; trace [a *shade* of humor in her voice] **7.** [Chiefly Literary] *a)* a ghost *b)* anything lacking reality **8.** *a)* any device used to protect or screen from light [a window *shade*] *b)* a partial cover for an electric lamp, etc., for spreading out or directing light: in full, **lamp shade** ☆**9.** [*pl.*] [Slang] sunglasses —*vt.* **shad'ed, shad'ing** **1.** to protect or screen from light or heat [the trees *shade* the house] **2.** to provide with a shade **3.** to hide or screen as with a shadow **4.** to darken; dim [to *shade* the sun's rays] **5.** *a)* to show the effects of shade in (a painting, etc.) *b)* to mark with degrees of light or color **6.** to change by very slight degrees ☆**7.** to lessen (a price) slightly — *vi.* to change or vary slightly or by degrees [the drapes *shade* from purple to lavender] —**in** (or **into**) **the shade** **1.** in or into darkness or shadow **2.** in or into a position of being obscured — **shades of (something)!** how suggestive of (something past)! [*shades of* Prohibition!] —**the shades** **1.** the increasing dark-ness, as of evening **2.** the world of the dead; Hades —**shade'-less** *adj.* —**shad'er** *n.*

shad·ing (shād'iŋ) *n.* **1.** a shielding against light **2.** the use of darker colors or of lines, etc. to give the effect of shade or shadow in a picture **3.** any small difference, as in quality

sha·doof (shä doof') *n.* [Ar. *shādūf*] a long, pivoted pole with a bucket on one end and a weight on the other, used in Egypt, etc. for raising water, esp. in irrigating land

shad·ow (shad'ō) *n.* [< OE. *sceadu,* shade] **1.** the darkness or the dark shape cast upon a surface by something cutting off light from it [his hand cast a *shadow* on the wall; her face was hidden in *shadow*] **2.** [*pl.*] the growing darkness after sunset **3.** *a)* gloom, sadness, etc. *b)* anything causing gloom, doubt, etc. [the *shadow* of illness] **4.** a dark or shaded area, as in a picture **5.** *a)* something without substance or not real [is fame only a *shadow?*] *b)* a ghost; apparition **6.** a sign or indication of something to come **7.** *a)* a faint suggestion or appearance; trace [a *shadow* of hope] *b)* a slight or weakened remaining part; remnant; vestige [a mere *shadow* of his former self] **8.** a constant companion ☆**9.** a person who trails another closely, as a detective or spy —*vt.* **1.** to throw a shadow upon [hills *shadowed* the valley] **2.** to make dark or gloomy [a frown *shadowed* his face] **3.** to foreshadow (often with *forth*) **4.** to follow closely, esp. in secret —**in** (or **under**) **the shadow of** **1.** very close to **2.** under the influence of —**under the shadow of1.** *see prec. phrase* **2.** in danger of —**shad'ow·er** *n.* —**shad'ow·less** *adj.*

shad·ow·box (-bäks') *vi.* to box with an imaginary opponent, as in training —**shad'ow·box'ing** *n.*

☆**shadow box** a small, shallow, open box hung on the wall to display small objects

shad·ow·graph (-graf') *n.* an image or silhouette produced by throwing a shadow upon a lighted surface

shadow play a play produced by showing to the audience only the shadows of actors or puppets on a screen

shad·ow·y (shad'ə wē) *adj.* **1.** that is or is like a shadow; specif., *a)* without reality; illusory [a *shadowy* hope] *b)* not clear; dim [a *shadowy* figure in the fog] **2.** shaded or full of shadow [a *shadowy* corner of the room] —**shad'ow·i·ness** *n.*

shad·y (shād'ē) *adj.* **shad'i·er, shad'i·est** **1.** giving shade [a *shady* tree] **2.** shaded, as from the sun; full of shade [a *shady* path] **3.** [Colloq.] not clearly honest or proper [a *shady* business deal] —**on the shady side of** beyond (a given age) — **shad'i·ly** *adv.* —**shad'i·ness** *n.*

shaft (shaft) *n.* [OE. *sceaft:* see SHAPE] **1.** *a)* the long stem or handle of an arrow or spear *b)* an arrow or spear **2.** a missile or something like a missile [*shafts* of light, wit, etc.] **3.** a long, slender part or object; specif., *a)* the stem of a feather *b)* a column or obelisk; also, the main part between the ends of a column *c)* a flagpole *d)* a handle, as on some tools or implements *e)* either of the two poles between which an animal is harnessed to a vehicle *f)* a bar supporting, or passing on motion to, a mechanical part [the drive *shaft* of an engine] **4.** a long, narrow opening sunk into the earth [a mine *shaft*] **5.** a vertical opening through the floors of a building **6.** a passage for air, as in heating or ventilating —*vt.* [Slang] to cheat, trick, exploit, etc. —**get the shaft** [Slang] to be cheated, tricked, etc. —**give (someone) the shaft** [Slang] to cheat or trick (someone)

shag¹ (shag) *n.* [OE. *sceacga*] **1.** *a)* a long, heavy, coarse nap, as on some rugs *b)* fabric with such a nap **2.** any disordered, tangled mass, as of hair **3.** coarse, shredded tobacco —*vt.* **shagged, shag'ging** to make shaggy or rough

shag² (shag) *vt.* **shagged, shag'ging** [< ?] ☆to chase after (baseballs, esp. fly balls, hit in batting practice)

☆**shag·bark** (shag'bärk') *n.* **1.** a hickory tree with gray, shredding bark **2.** its wood **3.** its nut

shag·gy (shag'ē) *adj.* **-gi·er, -gi·est** **1.** covered with long, coarse hair or wool [a *shaggy* dog] **2.** carelessly groomed; unkempt [a *shaggy* head] **3.** of tangled, coarse growth; straggly **4.** having a heavy, coarse nap or surface —**shag'gi·ly** *adv.* — **shag'gi·ness** *n.*

sha·green (shə grēn') *n.* [Fr. *chagrin* < Turk. *saghri,* hide] **1.** rawhide with a rough, grainy surface, made from the skin of a horse, seal, etc. **2.** the hard, rough skin of the shark or dogfish

shah (shä) *n.* [Per. *shāh*] a title of the ruler of Iran

Shak. Shakespeare

---

fat, āpe, cär, ten, ēven, is, bīte; gō, hôrn, tool, look; oil, out; up, fur; get; joy; yet; chin; she; thin, then; zh, leisure; ŋ, ring; ə for *a* in *ago, e* in *agent, i* in *sanity, o* in *comply, u* in *focus;* ' as in *able* (ā'b'l); Fr. bál; ë, Fr. coeur; ö, Fr. feu; Fr. mon; ô, Fr. coq; ü, Fr. duc; r, Fr. cri; H, G. ich; kh, G. doch; ‡foreign; ☆ Americanism; < derived from. See inside front cover.

shake (shāk) *vt.* **shook, shak′en, shak′ing** [OE. *sceacan*] **1.** to cause to move up and down, back and forth, or from side to side with short, quick movements **2.** to bring, force, mix, scatter, etc. by short, quick movements [*shake* the medicine before taking it, *shake* salt on the steak] **3.** to cause to tremble [chills that *shook* his body] **4.** *a)* to cause to totter or become unsteady *b)* to weaken, disturb, or upset [he was *shaken* by the news] **5.** to wave in the air; brandish [he *shook* a gun in my face] **6.** to clasp (another's hand), as in greeting ☆**7.** [Colloq.] to get away from or rid of [to *shake* one's pursuers] **8.** *Music same as* TRILL —*vi.* **1.** to move quickly up and down, back and forth, etc.; vibrate **2.** to tremble, quiver, etc., as from cold or fear **3.** to become unsteady; totter **4.** to clasp each other's hand, as in greeting **5.** *Music same as* TRILL —*n.* **1.** an act of shaking [a *shake* of the fist] **2.** an unsteady or trembling movement or sound [a *shake* in his voice] **3.** a natural split in rock or timber **4.** a rough-hewn wood shingle **5.** [Colloq.] an earthquake ☆**6.** *short for* MILKSHAKE **7.** [*pl.*] [Colloq.] a violent trembling, as from chills, fear, etc. (usually with *the*) **8.** [Colloq.] a moment [be back in a *shake*] **9.** [Colloq.] a kind of treatment; deal [a fair *shake*] **10.** *Music same as* TRILL —**no great shakes** [Colloq.] not outstanding or unusual —**shake down 1.** to bring down or cause to fall by shaking **2.** to cause to settle by shaking **3.** to test or condition (new equipment, etc.) ☆**4.** [Slang] to get money from by using force or threats, as in blackmailing —**shake off** to get away from or rid of —**shake out** to make fall out, empty, straighten out, etc. by shaking —**shake up 1.** to shake, esp. so as to mix or loosen **2.** to disturb or stir up by or as by shaking **3.** to jar or shock **4.** to reorganize or redistribute by or as by shaking —**shak′a·ble, shake′a·ble** *adj.*

SYN.—**shake** is the general word for a moving up and down or back and forth with quick, short motions; **tremble** implies such a shaking of the body as to suggest a loss of control, as from fear, weakness, etc. [she *trembled* at the lion's roar]; **quake** usually suggests a somewhat violent trembling, as in terror [to *quake* in one's boots with dread]; **quiver** suggests a slight vibration, as of a tightly stretched string that has been plucked [the leaves *quivered* in the breeze]

shake·down (shāk′doun′) *n.* [Colloq.] ☆**1.** an illegal getting of money, as by blackmail ☆**2.** a thorough search of a person or place —☆*adj.* for testing the performance, getting the personnel to know their work, etc. [the *shakedown* cruise for a ship]

shak·en (-'n) *pp.* of SHAKE

shake·out (-out′) *n.* ☆**1.** any movement in the prices of securities that forces speculators to sell ☆**2.** any drop in economic activity that forces out some businesses, products, etc.

shak·er (shā′kər) *n.* **1.** a person or thing that shakes **2.** a device used in shaking [a cocktail *shaker*] ☆**3.** [S-] [short for earlier *Shaking Quaker:* from trembling under emotional stress of devotions] a member of a former religious sect that lived and worked together in communes and practiced celibacy

Shake·speare (shāk′spir), **William** 1564–1616; Eng. poet & dramatist: also sp. **Shakespere, Shakspere,** etc. —**Shakespear′e·an, Shake·spear′i·an** *adj., n.*

Shakespearean sonnet a sonnet made up of three quatrains and a final couplet

shake-up (shāk′up′) *n.* a shaking up; specif., ☆a wide reorganization, as in policy or personnel

shak·o (shak′ō) *n., pl.* **shak′os** [< Fr. < Hung. *csákó* < ? G. *zacke,* a peak] a stiff military dress hat in the shape of a cylinder, usually with a flat top and a plume

shak·y (shā′kē) *adj.* **shak′i·er, shak′i·est 1.** not firm or secure; weak, unsound, etc., as a structure or belief **2.** *a)* trembling *b)* nervous or jittery *c)* weak and slightly ill **3.** not dependable or reliable; questionable [*shaky* evidence] —**shak′i·ly** *adv.* —**shak′i·ness** *n.*

shale (shāl) *n.* [OE. *scealu,* a shell] a fine-grained rock formed largely by the hardening of clay: it splits easily into thin layers —**shal′y** *adj.* **shal′i·er, shal′i·est**

shale oil a dark mineral oil produced by the destructive distillation of bituminous shale or brown coal

shall (shal; *unstressed* shəl) *v., pt.* **should** [OE. *sceal,* inf. *sceolan*] **1.** a helping verb sometimes used to express the simple future in the first person [I *shall* tell him] and determination, obligation, etc. in the second and third persons [you *shall* obey]: see also WILL² **2.** a helping verb regularly used: *a)* in questions in the

SHAKO

first person asking for agreement [*shall* we dance?] *b)* in laws and resolutions [the fine *shall* not exceed $100]

shal·lop (shal′əp) *n.* [< Fr., prob. orig. fig. use of *chaloupe,* nutshell, ult. < OFr. *escalope,* SCALLOP] a small open boat of earlier times, fitted with oars or sails or both

shal·lot (shə lät′) *n.* [obs. Fr. *eschalotte,* altered < OFr. *eschaloigne,* scallion] **1.** a small onion with bulbs that grow in clusters, taste like garlic but milder, and are used for flavoring **2.** *same as* GREEN ONION

shal·low (shal′ō) *adj.* [ME. *shalow* < an OE. word no longer known] **1.** not deep [a *shallow* lake] **2.** lacking depth of character or intellect; superficial —*n.* [*usually pl., often with sing. v.*] a shallow place in a body of water; shoal —*vt., vi.* to make or become shallow —see SYN. at SUPERFICIAL —**shal′low·ly** *adv.* —**shal′low·ness** *n.*

sha·lom (shä lōm′) *n., interj.* [Heb. *shālōm,* lit., peace] a word used as the traditional Jewish greeting or farewell

shalt (shalt; *unstressed* shəlt) *archaic second person singular in the present tense of* SHALL: *used with* thou

sham (sham) *n.* [prob. < a dial. var. of SHAME] **1.** *a)* an imitation that is meant to deceive *b)* an action, appearance, etc. that is deliberately misleading **2.** a person who pretends to be what he is not ☆**3.** *short for* PILLOW SHAM —*adj.* not genuine or real; false; fake —*vt., vi.* to fake; pretend —see SYN. at FALSE —**sham′mer** *n.*

sha·man (shä′mən, shā′-; sham′ən) *n., pl.* **-mans** [Russ., ult. < Prakrit *śamana,* Buddhist monk] a priest or medicine man of shamanism —**sha·man·ic** (shə man′ik) *adj.*

sha·man·ism (-iz′m) *n.* **1.** a religion of northeast Asia, based on a belief in spirits who can be influenced only by shamans **2.** a similar religion of some American Indians —**sha′man·ist** *n.* —**sha′man·is′tic** *adj.*

sham·ble (sham′b'l) *vi.* **-bled, -bling** [orig. *adj.,* in *shamble legs,* prob. < SHAMBLES, in obs. sense of "stool"] to walk in a clumsy manner, barely lifting the feet —*n.* a shambling walk

sham·bles (sham′b'lz) *n.pl.* [*with sing. v.*] [OE. *scamol,* a bench, ult. < L. *scamellum,* dim. < *scamnum,* a bench] **1.** a slaughterhouse **2.** a scene of great slaughter or bloodshed **3.** any scene or condition of great destruction or disorder [the children left the room a *shambles*]

shame (shām) *n.* [OE. *scamu*] **1.** a painful feeling of having lost the respect of others because of something wrong, foolish, etc. done by oneself or another **2.** a tendency to have feelings of this kind [she has no *shame*] **3.** dishonor or disgrace [to bring *shame* to one's family] **4.** a person or thing that brings dishonor or disgrace **5.** something unfortunate or offensive [it's a *shame* that he wasn't told] —*vt.* **shamed, sham′ing 1.** to cause to feel shame **2.** to dishonor or disgrace **3.** to force by a sense of shame [*shamed* into apologizing] —see SYN. at DISGRACE —**for shame!** you ought to be ashamed! —**put to shame 1.** to cause to feel shame **2.** to do much better than; surpass

shame·faced (shām′fāst′) *adj.* [altered < OE. < *scamu,* shame + *fæst,* firm] **1.** shy or bashful **2.** showing a feeling of shame; ashamed —**shame·fac·ed·ly** (shām′fās′id lē, shām′fāst′ld) *adv.* —**shame′fac′ed·ness** *n.*

shame·ful (-fəl) *adj.* **1.** bringing or causing shame or disgrace; disgraceful **2.** not just, moral, or decent; offensive —**shame′ful·ly** *adv.* —**shame′ful·ness** *n.*

shame·less (-lis) *adj.* having or showing no shame, modesty, or decency; brazen [a *shameless* liar] —**shame′less·ly** *adv.* —**shame′less·ness** *n.*

sham·my (sham′ē) *n., pl.* **-mies;** *adj., vt.* **-mied, -my·ing** *same as* CHAMOIS (*n.* 2, *adj.* 1, *vt.*)

sham·poo (sham pōō′) *vt.* **-pooed′, -poo′ing** [Hindi *chāmpo,* imper. of *champnā,* to press] **1.** formerly, to massage **2.** to wash (the hair and scalp), esp. with a shampoo **3.** to wash the hair and scalp of **4.** to wash (a rug, upholstery, etc.) with a shampoo —*n.* **1.** the act of washing hair, a rug, etc. **2.** a special soap, or soaplike preparation, that produces suds —**shampoo′er** *n.*

sham·rock (sham′räk′) *n.* [< Ir. dim. of *seamar,* clover] any of certain clovers or cloverlike plants having compound leaves divided into three leaflets: the emblem of Ireland

☆**sha·mus** (shā′məs, shä′-) *n.* [prob. blend of Yid. *shamas,* servant & Ir. *Séamas,* James] [Slang] **1.** a policeman **2.** a private detective

Shang·hai (shaŋ′hī′, shäŋ′-) seaport in E China, near the mouth of the Yangtze: pop. c. 10,000,000

shang·hai (shaŋ′hī, shaŋ hī′) ☆*vt.* **-haied, -hai·ing** [< SHANGHAI, where such kidnapping was done to get crews on the China run] **1.** to kidnap, usually by drugging, and force to work as a sailor on board a ship **2.** [Slang] to cause (another) to do something through force or underhanded methods —**shang′hai·er** n.

Shan·gri-La (shaŋ′grə lä′) n. [< the scene of J. Hilton's novel, *Lost Horizon*] **1.** any imaginary place that is remote, peaceful, and utopian **2.** any very beautiful, secluded place

shank (shaŋk) n. [OE. *scanca*] **1.** the part of the leg between the knee and the ankle in man or a part like this in animals **2.** the whole leg **3.** a cut of meat from the leg of an animal **4.** a straight, narrow part between other parts, as *a*) the part of a tool or instrument between the handle and the working part; shaft *b*) the narrow part of a shoe sole **5.** a part that sticks out on some buttons by which they are sewn to fabric —**ride** (or **go**) **on shank's mare** to walk —**shank of the evening** the early part of the evening

Shan·non (shan′ən) river in WC Ireland, flowing southwestward into the Atlantic

shan't (shant) shall not

shan·tey (shan′tē) n., pl. **-teys** var. of CHANTEY

Shan·tung (shan′tuŋ′; also, for the Chinese province, shän′doοŋ′) province of NE China, on the Yellow Sea —n. [sometimes **s-**] a fabric of silk, rayon, etc. with an uneven surface

☆**shan·ty**[1] (shan′tē) n., pl. **-ties** [< CanadFr. *chantier*, workshop] a small, shabby dwelling; shack

shan·ty[2] (shan′tē) n., pl. **-ties** var. of CHANTEY

☆**shan·ty·town** (shan′tē toun′) n. the section of a city where there are many ramshackle houses

shape (shāp) n. [< OE. *(ge)sceap*, form, akin to *scieppan*, to create < IE. base *(s)kep-*, to cut, from which also come SHAFT, SHAVE] **1.** the way a thing looks because of its outline; outer form **2.** the form of a particular person or thing, or class of things **3.** the contour of the body; figure **4.** assumed appearance; guise [a foe in the *shape* of a friend] **5.** a phantom **6.** a mold used for shaping **7.** definite or regular form [to begin to take *shape*] ☆**8.** [Colloq.] *a*) condition; state [a patient in poor *shape*] *b*) good physical condition [exercises that keep one in *shape*] —vt. **shaped, shap′ing 1.** to give definite shape to; make **2.** to arrange, express, or devise (a plan, answer, etc.) in definite form **3.** to adapt or adjust [*shape* your plans to your abilities] **4.** to direct or conduct (one's life, the course of events, etc.) —vi. [Colloq.] to take shape (often with *into* or *up*) —see SYN. at MAKE —☆**shape up** [Colloq.] **1.** to develop to a definite form, condition, etc. **2.** to develop satisfactorily **3.** to behave as required —**take shape** to begin to have definite form —**shap′er** n.

shape·less (shāp′lis) adj. **1.** without distinct or regular form **2.** without a pleasing shape; unshapely —**shape′less·ly** adv. — **shape′less·ness** n.

shape·ly (-lē) adj. **-li·er, -li·est** having a pleasing shape; wellproportioned: used esp. of a woman —**shape′li·ness** n.

☆**shape-up** (-up′) n. a method of selecting a daily work crew, as, esp. formerly, of longshoremen, from a group present and available for the job

shard (shärd) n. [OE. *sceard*] a fragment or broken piece, esp. of pottery; potsherd

share[1] (sher) n. [OE. *scearu*: for IE. base see CARNAGE] **1.** a part or portion that belongs to an individual, or the part contributed by one **2.** a just or full part [to do one's *share* of work] **3.** any of the parts into which the ownership of a piece of property is divided; esp., any of the equal parts of the capital stock of a corporation —vt. **shared, shar′ing 1.** to divide and give out in shares **2.** to receive, use, experience, etc. in common with another or others [four of us *shared* a bedroom] —vi. **1.** to have a share; participate (often with *in*) **2.** to share or divide something equally (often with *with*) —**go shares** to take part together, as in a project —**share and share alike** with each having an equal share —**shar′er** n.

share[2] (sher) n. [OE. *scear*: see SHARECROP] the part of a plow or other agricultural tool that cuts the soil; plowshare

☆**share·crop** (sher′kräp′) vi., vt. **-cropped′, -crop′ping** to work (land) for a share of the crop, esp. as a tenant farmer —**share′-crop′per** n.

share·hold·er (sher′hōl′dər) n. a person who holds or owns a share or shares, esp. in a corporation

shark[1] (shärk) n. [prob. < G. *schurke*, scoundrel] a person who victimizes others, as by swindling or cheating [a card *shark*]

shark[2] (shärk) n. [? akin to SHARK[1]] any of many, usually large ocean fishes with a tough, slate-gray skin: most sharks are fish-eaters and some will attack man

shark·skin (shärk′skin′) n. **1.** leather made from the skin of a shark ☆**2.** a cloth of cotton, wool, rayon, etc. with a smooth, silky surface **3.** a fabric woven with a pebbly pattern

SHARK
(45 ft. maximum
length)

Shar·on (sher′ən) [? < ROSE OF SHARON] a feminine name

sharp (shärp) adj. [OE. *scearp*: for IE. base see CARNAGE] **1.** having a very thin edge or fine point, suitable for cutting or piercing; keen **2.** having a point or edge; not rounded [a *sharp* ridge] **3.** not gradual; abrupt [a *sharp* turn] **4.** clearly defined; distinct [a *sharp* contrast] **5.** quick or acute in perception or intellect; specif., *a*) acutely sensitive in seeing, hearing, etc. [*sharp* eyes] *b*) clever; shrewd [a *sharp* mind] **6.** attentive; alert [a *sharp* lookout] **7.** crafty; underhanded [*sharp* business practices] **8.** harsh, biting, or severe [*sharp* criticism] **9.** sudden and forceful; violent [a *sharp* attack] **10.** brisk; active [a *sharp* run] **11.** severe; intense [a *sharp* pain] **12.** strong; pungent, as in taste **13.** high-pitched; shrill [a *sharp* sound] **14.** cold and cutting [a *sharp* wind] **15.** [Slang] stylishly dressed or groomed **16.** *Music a*) higher in pitch by a half step [C *sharp*] *b*) above the true pitch —n. **1.** [Colloq.] same as SHARK[1], SHARPER **2.** *Music a*) a note or tone one half step above another *b*) the symbol (♯) indicating such a note —vt. *Music* to make sharp —vi. *Music* to sing or play above the true pitch —adv. **1.** in a sharp manner; specif., *a*) abruptly or briskly *b*) attentively or alertly [look *sharp!*] *c*) *Music* above the true pitch **2.** precisely; exactly [one o'clock *sharp*] —**sharp′ly** adv. —**sharp′ness** n.

SYN.—**sharp** and **keen** both apply to that which is cutting, biting, penetrating, or piercing, as because of having a very thin edge, but **sharp** may imply a harsh, disagreeable cutting quality [a *sharp* pain, tongue, etc.] and **keen**, a pleasantly biting or stimulating quality [*keen* wit, delight, etc.]; **acute** is used literally to describe an angle or end formed by lines or edges that meet in a sharp point, but may be used to suggest a very clear awareness of small differences [*acute* hearing; an *acute* intelligence] or the quality of being sharply painful to the feelings [*acute* distress]—**ANT.** dull

sharp·en (shär′p'n) vt., vi. to make or become sharp or sharper —**sharp′en·er** n.

sharp·er (-pər) n. a person, esp. a gambler, who is dishonest in dealing with others; swindler

☆**sharp·ie** (shär′pē) n. [< SHARP] **1.** a long, narrow, flatbottomed fishing boat with one or two masts, each with a triangular sail **2.** [Colloq.] a shrewd, cunning person

sharp·shoot·er (shärp′shοot′ər) n. a person who shoots with great accuracy; good marksman —**sharp′shoot′ing** n.

sharp-tongued (-tuŋd′) adj. using or full of sharp or harshly critical language

sharp-wit·ted (-wit′id) adj. having or showing keen intelligence; thinking quickly and effectively —**sharp′-wit′ted·ly** adv.

Shas·ta (shas′tə), **Mount** [< a tribal name] volcanic mountain in the Cascade Range, N Calif.

☆**Shasta daisy** [after prec.] a chrysanthemum with large flowers that look like daisies

Shatt-al-A·rab (shat′əl ä′räb) river in SE Iraq, formed by the joining of the Tigris & Euphrates rivers, that flows into the Persian Gulf

shat·ter (shat′ər) vt. [ME. *schateren*, to scatter] **1.** to break into pieces suddenly, as with a blow **2.** to damage badly; ruin or destroy [the news *shattered* her dreams] —vi. to burst into pieces —n. [pl.] broken pieces: chiefly in **in** (or **into**) **shatters** —see SYN. at BREAK

shat·ter·proof (-prοof′) adj. that will resist shattering

shave (shāv) vt. **shaved, shaved** or **shav′en, shav′ing** [OE. *sceafan*: see SHAPE] **1.** to cut away thin slices from [to *shave* the edge of a door] **2.** to scrape into thin sections or slices [*shaved* ham] **3.** *a*) to cut off (hair, esp. the beard) at the surface of the skin (often with *off* or *away*) *b*) to cut the hair to the surface of [to *shave* the chin, the legs, etc.] *c*) to cut the beard of (a person) **4.** to barely touch or almost touch in passing; graze **5.** to trim (grass, etc.) closely —vi. to cut off hair with a razor or shaver; shave oneself —n. **1.** a tool used for cutting off thin slices **2.** the act or result of shaving the beard

shav·er (shā′vər) *n.* **1.** a person who shaves **2.** an instrument used in shaving; esp., a device with a small electric motor that operates a set of cutters **3.** [Colloq.] a young boy

☆**shave·tail** (shāv′tāl′) *n.* [orig., an unbroken mule] [Slang] a second lieutenant, esp. one recently appointed

Sha·vi·an (shā′vē ən) *adj.* [< ModL. *Shavius*, Latinized < SHAW] of or characteristic of George Bernard Shaw

shav·ing (shā′viŋ) *n.* **1.** the act of one that shaves **2.** a thin piece of wood, metal, etc. shaved off

shaving cream a soap, cream, etc. used to make the beard soft and wet for shaving

Sha·vu·ot (shä vōō′ōt, shə vōō′ōs) *n.* [Heb. *shābhū'oth*, lit., weeks] a Jewish holiday, orig. celebrating the spring harvest, now chiefly in honor of the revelation of the Law at Mount Sinai

Shaw (shô), **George Bernard** 1856–1950; Brit. dramatist & critic, born in Ireland

shawl (shôl) *n.* [prob. via Urdu < Per. *shāl*] an oblong or square cloth worn, esp. by women, over the head or shoulders

shawm (shôm) *n.* [< MFr., ult. from L. *calamus*, a reed] an early double-reed wind instrument resembling the oboe

Shaw·nee (shô nē′, shô′nē) *n.* [< Algonquian < *shawun*, south + *ogi*, people] **1.** *pl.* **-nees′, -nee** any member of a tribe of N. American Indians living at various times in the East and Midwest, and now chiefly in Oklahoma **2.** their Algonquian language

shay (shā) *n.* [back-formation < CHAISE, incorrectly thought to be a pl.] [Dial.] a light carriage; chaise

Shays (shāz), **Daniel** 1747?–1825; Am. Revolutionary soldier: leader of an insurrection (**Shays' Rebellion**) in W Mass. (1786–87), protesting high land taxes

she (shē; *unstressed* shi) *pron. for pl. see* THEY [prob. after OE. *seo*, fem. def. article, replacing OE. *heo*, she] the woman, girl, or female animal (or the object regarded as female) being talked about: the case forms of the feminine third personal pronoun are: *she*, nominative; *her*, objective; *her* and *hers*, possessive; *herself*, intensive and reflexive —*n., pl.* **shes** a woman, girl, or female animal

she- *a combining form meaning* female: used in hyphenated compounds [*she-bear*]

sheaf (shēf) *n., pl.* **sheaves** [OE. *sceaf*] **1.** a bunch of cut stalks of grain, etc. bound together **2.** a collection, as of papers, bound in a bundle —*vt. same as* SHEAVE[2]

shear (shir) *vt.* **sheared, sheared** *or* **shorn, shear′ing** [OE. *scieran*: for IE. base see CARNAGE] **1.** to cut as with shears **2.** *a)* to remove (the hair, wool, etc.) by cutting *b)* to cut the hair, wool, etc. from **3.** to tear (*off*) by shearing stress [an avalanche *sheared* off the trees] **4.** to move through as if cutting **5.** to strip (*of* a power, right, etc.) —*vi.* **1.** to use shears, etc. in cutting wool, metal, etc. **2.** to break under a shearing stress **3.** to move as if by cutting [the plane *sheared* through the clouds] —*n.* **1.** a machine used in cutting metal **2.** *same as* SHEARING STRESS —**shear′er** *n.*

sheared (shird) *adj.* cut by shearing: said esp. of fur trimmed to give an even surface [*sheared* beaver]

shearing stress the force causing two contacting parts to slide upon each other in opposite directions parallel to their plane of contact

shears (shirz) *n.pl.* [*also with sing. v.*] **1.** large scissors: also called **pair of shears** **2.** any of several large tools or machines with two blades that can be brought together, used to cut metal, etc.

shear·wa·ter (shir′wôt′ər, -wät′-) *n.* any of various black-and-white sea birds, related to the albatrosses, that skim the water in flight

sheath (shēth) *n., pl.* **sheaths** (shēthz, shēths) [OE. *sceath*] **1.** a case for the blade of a knife, sword, etc. **2.** a covering resembling this, as the membrane around a muscle, etc. **3.** a woman's closefitting dress —*vt. same as* SHEATHE

sheathe (shēth) *vt.* **sheathed, sheath′ing 1.** to put into a sheath or scabbard **2.** to enclose in or protect with a case or covering [wood *sheathed* with tin] **3.** to retract (claws)

sheath·ing (shē′thiŋ) *n.* something that sheathes, as the inner covering of boards or waterproof material on the roof or outside wall of a frame house

sheath knife a knife carried in a sheath

sheave[1] (shēv, shiv) *n.* [ME. *scheve*: for IE. base see SCHIZO-] a wheel with a grooved rim, as one used to guide the rope in a pulley block

sheave[2] (shēv) *vt.* **sheaved, sheav′ing** [< SHEAF] to gather and bind up (grain, papers, etc.) in a sheaf or sheaves

sheaves[1] (shēvz) *n. pl. of* SHEAF

sheaves[2] (shēvz, shivz) *n. pl. of* SHEAVE[1]

She·ba (shē′bə) *Biblical name of* SABA

Sheba, Queen of *Bible* the queen who visited King Solomon to find out how wise he was: I Kings 10:1–13

☆**she·bang** (shə baŋ′) *n.* [Colloq.] an affair, business, contrivance, thing, etc.: chiefly in **the whole shebang**

She·bat (shə vät′) *n.* [Heb.] *see* JEWISH CALENDAR

shed[1] (shed) *n.* [OE. *scead*] **1.** a small, rough building or lean-to, used for shelter or storage **2.** a large, strongly built structure, often with open front or sides

shed[2] (shed) *vt.* **shed, shed′ding** [OE. *sceadan*, to separate: for IE. base see SCHIZO-] **1.** to pour out or send forth; emit [the sun *sheds* light] **2.** to cause to flow; let fall in drops [to *shed* tears] **3.** to cause to flow off without going through; repel [oilskin *sheds* water] **4.** *a)* to cast off (a natural growth or covering, as leaves, hair, etc.) *b)* to take off [he *shed* his coat and tie] *c)* to get rid of [trying to *shed* a few pounds] —*vi.* to shed leaves, hair, etc. —*n. same as* WATERSHED —**shed blood** to kill in a violent way —**shed′der** *n.*

she'd (shēd) **1.** she had **2.** she would

sheen (shēn) *n.* [< the adj.] brightness; shininess; luster [the *sheen* of well-brushed hair] —*adj.* [OE. *sciene*, beautiful] [Archaic] of shining beauty; bright

sheep (shēp) *n., pl.* **sheep** [OE. *sceap*] **1.** a cud-chewing mammal related to the goats, with heavy wool and with flesh, called mutton, that is used as food **2.** a person who is meek, stupid, timid, etc. —**make sheep's eyes at** to look shyly but lovingly at

sheep·cote (shēp′kōt′) *n.* [see COTE] *chiefly Brit. var. of* SHEEPFOLD: also **sheep′cot′** (-kät′)

sheep-dip (-dip′) *n.* any chemical preparation used as a bath to free sheep from vermin or to clean the fleece

sheep dog any dog trained to herd and protect sheep: also **sheep′dog′** (shēp′dôg′, -däg′)

sheep·fold (-fōld′) *n.* a pen or enclosed place for sheep

☆**sheep·herd·er** (-hur′dər) *n.* a person who herds or takes care of a large flock of grazing sheep —**sheep′herd′ing** *n.*

sheep·ish (-ish) *adj.* **1.** *a)* feeling or showing embarrassment when one is caught in a mistake, lie, etc. *b)* awkwardly shy or bashful **2.** meek, timid, etc. like sheep —**sheep′ish·ly** *adv.* —**sheep′ish·ness** *n.*

sheep·man (-man′, -mən) *n., pl.* **-men′** (-men′, -mən) ☆a person who raises sheep for the market

sheep·shank (-shaŋk′) *n.* a knot used for shortening a rope

sheeps·head (shēps′hed′) *n., pl.* **-head′, -heads′**: see PLURAL, II, D, 2 ☆any of several fishes; esp., *a)* a large food fish found in the ocean along the eastern coast of the U.S. *b)* the freshwater drum of central N. America

sheep·skin (shēp′skin′) *n.* **1.** the skin of a sheep, esp. with the fleece left on **2.** parchment or leather made from the skin of a sheep ☆**3.** [Colloq.] *same as* DIPLOMA

sheep sorrel a low-growing weed with reddish or yellowish flowers, often found on dry soils

sheer[1] (shir) *vi.* [var. of SHEAR] to turn aside sharply from a course; swerve —*vt.* to cause to sheer —*n.* **1.** a sudden change of course **2.** the upward curve of a ship's deck toward the bow and stern as seen from the side

sheer[2] (shir) *adj.* [ON. *skærr*: for IE. base see SHINE] **1.** very thin; fine enough to be seen through: said of textiles **2.** not mixed with anything else; pure [*sheer* ice] **3.** absolute; downright [*sheer* persistence] **4.** extremely steep, as the face of a cliff —*adv.* **1.** completely; utterly **2.** very steeply —see SYN. at STEEP[1] —**sheer′ly** *adv.* —**sheer′ness** *n.*

sheet[1] (shēt) *n.* [OE. *sceat*] **1.** a large piece of cotton, linen, etc., used on a bed, usually in pairs, one under and one over the body **2.** *a)* a single piece of paper *b)* a large piece of paper with a number of pages printed on it, to be folded into a signature for binding into a book: *usually used in pl.* *c)* [Colloq.] a newspaper [a scandal *sheet*] **3.** a broad, continuous surface or layer, as of flame, water, etc. **4.** a broad, thin piece of any material, as glass, metal, etc. **5.** a flat baking pan [a cookie *sheet*] **6.** [Chiefly Poet.] a sail —*vt.* to cover or provide with, or form into, a sheet or sheets —*adj.* in the form of a sheet or sheets [*sheet* iron] —**sheet′like′** *adj.*

sheet[2] (shēt) *n.* [short for OE. *sceatline*] **1.** a rope for controlling the set of a sail, attached to a lower corner **2.** [*pl.*] the spaces not occupied by thwarts, or cross seats, at the bow and stern of an open boat

sheet anchor a large anchor used only in emergencies

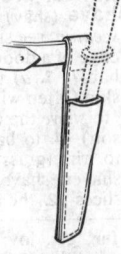

SHEATH

sheet bend a sailor's knot used in fastening a rope to the bight of another rope or to an eye

sheet·ing (shēt'iŋ) *n.* **1.** material made of cotton, linen, etc. and used for making sheets **2.** material used in covering or lining a surface [copper *sheeting*]

sheet metal metal rolled thin in the form of a sheet

sheet music music printed on unbound sheets of paper

Shef·field (shef'ēld) city in Yorkshire, NC England: pop. 525,000

sheik, sheikh (shēk) *n.* [Ar. *shaikh,* lit., old man] **1.** the chief of an Arab family, tribe, village, etc. **2.** an official in the Moslem religious organization

sheik·dom, sheikh·dom (shēk'dəm) *n.* a political unit ruled by a sheik

Shei·la (shē'lə) [Ir.] a feminine name

shek·el (shek''l) *n.* [< Heb. < *shāqal,* to weigh] **1.** among the ancient Hebrews, Babylonians, etc., a unit of weight (about half an ounce), or a gold or silver coin of this weight **2.** the monetary unit of Israel: see MONETARY UNITS, table

shel·drake (shel'drāk') *n., pl.* **-drakes', -drake':** see PLURAL, II, D, 1 [prob. < a ME. word related to MDu. *schillede,* marked with different colors + *drake,* drake] **1.** a large, old-world wild duck that feeds on fish, etc. and nests in burrows: the plumage is marked with different colors **2.** *same as* MERGANSER

shelf (shelf) *n., pl.* **shelves** [prob. < MLowG. *schelf:* for IE. base see CUTLASS] **1.** a thin, flat length of wood, metal, etc. fixed horizontally to a wall or built into a frame, as in a bookcase, and used for holding things **2.** the contents of a shelf, or the amount it will hold **3.** something like a shelf; specif., *a)* a flat ledge of rock *b)* a sand bar or reef —**on the shelf** not active, in use, etc. —**shelf'like'** *adj.*

shell (shel) *n.* [OE. *sciel:* for IE. base see CUTLASS] **1.** *a)* a hard outer covering, as of a turtle, egg, nut, etc. *b)* material of or like animal shell, used in making things **2.** something like a shell in being hollow, empty, a covering, etc., as the hull of a boat, an unfilled pie crust, the framework of a building, etc. **3.** a shy or reserved manner [to come out of one's *shell*] ☆**4.** a woman's pullover, sleeveless knit blouse ☆**5.** a light, long, narrow racing boat rowed usually by a team of oarsmen **6.** an explosive projectile containing powerful explosives and sometimes shrapnel, chemicals, etc. and fired from large guns ☆**7.** any cartridge for small firearms **8.** *Chem., Physics* any one of the orbits of electrons around the nucleus of an atom, all having nearly the same amount of energy —*vt.* **1.** to remove the shell or covering from [to *shell* peas] **2.** to separate (kernels of corn, etc.) from the ear **3.** to fire shells at from large guns; bombard —*vi.* to separate from the shell or covering [peanuts *shell* easily] —**shell out** [Colloq.] to pay out (money) —**shell'-like'** *adj.* —**shell'y** *adj.*

she'll (shēl; *unstressed* shil) **1.** she shall **2.** she will

shel·lac, shel·lack (shə lak') *n.* [SHEL(L) + LAC, used as transl. of Fr. *laque en écailles,* lac in fine sheets] **1.** refined lac, a resin usually produced in thin, flaky layers, used in making varnish, phonograph records, etc. **2.** a thin varnish containing this resin and alcohol —*vt.* **-lacked', -lack'ing 1.** to apply shellac to ☆**2.** [Slang] *a)* to beat *b)* to defeat thoroughly

shell·back (shel'bak') *n.* [prob. referring to the shell of the sea turtle] **1.** an old, experienced sailor **2.** anyone who has crossed the equator by ship

☆**shell·bark** (-bärk') *n.* same as SHAGBARK

-shelled (sheld) *a combining form meaning* having a (specified kind of) shell [soft-*shelled* crab]

Shel·ley (shel'ē) **1. Mary Woll·stone·craft** (wool'stən kraft'), 1797–1851; Eng. novelist: 2d wife of *Percy* **2. Percy Bysshe** (bish), 1792–1822; Eng. poet

shell·fire (shel'fir') *n.* the firing of large shells

shell·fish (-fish') *n., pl.* **-fish', -fish'es:** see FISH any animal that lives in the water and has a shell, esp. such an animal as the clam, lobster, etc., used as food

☆**shell game 1.** a swindling game in which the victim bets on the location of a small object under one of three shells moved about by sleight of hand **2.** any scheme for cheating people

shell·proof (-prōōf') *adj.* safe against damage from shells or bombs

shell shock *an earlier term used for* COMBAT FATIGUE —**shell'-shocked'** *adj.*

shel·ter (shel'tər) *n.* [< ? OE. *sceldtruma,* 'troop protected by interlocked shields < *scield,* shield + *truma,* a troop] **1.** something that covers or protects; place of protection from the weather, danger, etc. **2.** a being covered, protected, etc.; refuge [give us *shelter*] —*vt.* to provide shelter or refuge for; protect —*vi.* to find shelter or refuge [cattle *sheltering* beneath a tree] —**shel'ter·er** *n.* —**shel'ter·less** *adj.*

☆**shelter tent** a small, portable tent that shelters two people: it is made from two sections (**shelter halves**), just alike, one section being part of every soldier's field equipment

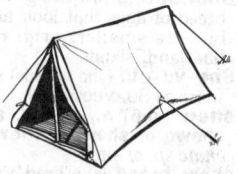

SHELTER TENT

shel·tie, shel·ty (shel'tē) *n., pl.* **-ties** [prob. < ON. *hjalti,* Shetland Islander] *same as:* **1.** SHETLAND PONY **2.** SHETLAND SHEEP-DOG

shelve (shelv) *vi.* **shelved, shelv'ing** [< SHELF] to slope gradually —*vt.* **1.** to equip with shelves **2.** to put on a shelf or shelves [to *shelve* books] **3.** *a)* to lay aside as if on a shelf [to *shelve* a discussion] *b)* to dismiss from active service

shelves (shelvz) *n. pl. of* SHELF

shelv·ing (shel'viŋ) *n.* **1.** material for shelves **2.** shelves as a group **3.** the condition or degree of sloping

Shem (shem) *Bible* the eldest of Noah's three sons: Gen. 5:32

Shen·an·do·ah (shen'ən dō'ə) [< AmInd., lit., ? spruce stream] river in N Va., flowing between the Blue Ridge & Allegheny mountains into the Potomac

Shenandoah National Park national park in the Blue Ridge Mountains of N Virginia

☆**she·nan·i·gan** (shi nan'i g'n) *n.* [altered < ? Ir. *sionna-chuighim,* I play the fox] [*usually pl.*] [Colloq.] nonsense; trickery; mischief

Shen·yang (shun'yäŋ') city in NE China: pop. c. 4,000,000

She·ol (shē'ōl, shē ōl') [< Heb. < *shā'al,* to dig] *Bible* a place deep in the earth where the dead are believed to go

shep·herd (shep'ərd) *n.* [OE. *sceaphyrde:* see SHEEP & HERD[2]] **1.** a person who herds sheep **2.** a leader of a group; esp., a clergyman —*vt.* to herd, look after, lead, etc. like a shepherd [to *shepherd* visiting parents through the classrooms] —**shep'herd·ess** *n.fem.*

shepherd dog *same as* SHEEP DOG

shepherd's pie a meat pie baked with a top crust of mashed potatoes

shepherd's purse a small weed of the mustard family, with triangular, pouchlike pods

Sher·a·ton (sher'ə tən) *adj.* [after T. *Sheraton* (1751–1806), Eng. cabinetmaker] describing or of a style of furniture that is simple in form and has straight, slender lines

sher·bet (shur'bət) *n.* [< Turk. < Ar. *sharbah,* a drink] **1.** [Brit.] a beverage made of watered fruit juice and sugar **2.** a frozen dessert like an ice but with gelatin and, often, milk added

Sher·brooke (shur'brook) city in S Quebec, Canada: pop. 76,000

Sher·i·dan (sher'i d'n) **1. Philip Henry,** 1831–88; Union general in the Civil War **2. Richard Brins·ley** (brinz'lē), 1751–1816; Brit. dramatist & politician, born in Ireland

she·rif (shə rēf') *n.* [Ar. *sharīf,* noble] **1.** a descendant of Mohammed through his daughter Fatima **2.** an Arab chief

sher·iff (sher'if) *n.* [< OE. < *scir,* shire + *gerefa,* a reeve] **1.** in England, esp. formerly, any of various officers of a shire, or county ☆**2.** in the U.S., the chief law-enforcement officer of a county, in charge of keeping the peace and carrying out court orders —**sher'iff·dom** *n.*

Sher·lock Holmes (shur'läk hōmz', hōlmz') a detective who is very clever in solving mysteries and crimes, in stories by A. Conan Doyle

Sher·man (shur'mən) **1. John,** 1823–1900; U.S. statesman: brother of *William* **2. William Tecumseh,** 1820–91; Union general in the Civil War

sher·ry (sher'ē) *n., pl.* **-ries** [< earlier *sherris* < *Xeres* (now Jerez), Spain] **1.** a strong, yellow or brownish wine from Spain **2.** any similar wine made elsewhere

Sher·wood Forest (shur'wood) forest in C England, near Nottingham, made famous in the Robin Hood legends

she's (shēz) **1.** she is **2.** she has

Shet·land Islands (shet'lənd) group of islands northeast of the Orkney Islands, forming a region (**Shetland**) of Scotland

Shetland pony any of a breed of sturdy ponies with a rough coat and long tail and mane, orig. from the Shetland Islands

Shetland sheepdog any of a breed of dogs that look like collies but are smaller: orig. from the Shetland Islands

She·vu·oth (shə voo'ōt) n. [Heb.] same as SHAVUOT

shew (shō) n., vt., vi. **shewed, shewn** or **shewed, shew'ing** archaic sp. of SHOW

shew·bread (shō'bred') n. [SHEW + BREAD, transl. of Heb. lehem pānīm, bread of display] the unleavened bread placed at the altar in the ancient Jewish Temple as an offering every Sabbath by the priests

WILD SHETLAND PONY
(to 40 in. high
at shoulder)

SHF, S.H.F., shf, s.h.f. superhigh frequency

shib·bo·leth (shib'ə ləth) n. [< LL. < Heb. shibbōleth, a stream] **1.** Bible the test word used by the men of Gilead to identify the escaping tribesmen of Ephraim who pronounced the initial (sh) as (s): Judg. 12:4-6 **2.** something said or done that is a sign or test of belonging to a certain group, class, etc.

shied (shīd) pt. & pp. of SHY

shield (shēld) n. [OE. scield: for IE. base see CUTLASS] **1.** a broad piece of armor carried in the hand or worn on the forearm to ward off blows or missiles **2.** any person or thing that guards or protects **3.** anything shaped like a triangular shield, broad at the top and with curved sides, as an escutcheon, badge, etc. **4.** a safety screen or guard, as over the moving parts of machinery **5.** a pad worn at the armpit to protect a garment from perspiration: also **dress shield** —vt. **1.** to be a shield for; protect **2.** to hide from view —**see SYN.** at DEFEND

shift (shift) vt. [OE. sciftan, to divide: for IE. base see SCHIZO-] **1.** to move or transfer from one person, place, direction, etc. to another [to shift the blame] **2.** to change or exchange [shift places with her] **3.** to change the arrangement of (gears) in driving a motor vehicle —vi. **1.** to change position, direction, form, etc. [the wind has shifted] **2.** to get along; manage [to shift for oneself] ☆**3.** to change from one gear arrangement to another **4.** in typing, to change from small letters, etc. to capitals, etc. by pushing down a key (**shift key**) —n. **1.** the act of shifting; change [a shift in public opinion] **2.** a plan of conduct, esp. for an emergency; stratagem **3.** a deceitful scheme; trick ☆**4.** short for GEARSHIFT **5.** a group of workers taking turns with other groups at the same jobs, or the work period involved [the night shift] **6.** a) [Now Rare] a woman's slip b) a loose dress that hangs straight with no waistline ☆**7.** Football a move from one place to another by members of the offensive backfield shortly before the ball is put in play —**make shift** to do the best one can (with the means at hand) —**shift'er** n.

shift·less (shift'lis) adj. lazy or careless —**shift'less·ly** adv. — **shift'less·ness** n.

shift·y (shif'tē) adj. **shift'i·er, shift'i·est** having or showing a tricky or dishonest nature —**shift'i·ly** adv. —**shift'i·ness** n.

Shih·chia·chuang (shu'jyä'jwäŋ') city in NE China, southwest of Peking: pop. 1,118,000

Shih Tzu (shē'dzoo') pl. **Shih Tzus, Shih Tzu** [< Chin. shih, lion + tzu, son] any of a Chinese breed of small dog with long, silky hair and short legs

Shi·ko·ku (shē'kô koo') smallest of the four major islands of Japan, south of Honshu: c. 6,860 sq. mi.

shill (shil) n. [< ?] [Slang] a person who works with a gambler, pitchman, auctioneer, etc., by pretending to buy, bet, or bid so as to lure others

shil·le·lagh, shil·la·lah (shi lā'lē, -lə) n. [< Shillelagh, Irish village] a club or cudgel: also sp. **shil·le'lah**

shil·ling (shil'iŋ) n. [OE. scylling] **1.** a) a British money of account and a silver coin, equal to 1/20 of a pound: symbol, /: coinage discontinued in 1971 b) any of several monetary units used in other countries: see MONETARY UNITS, table **2.** a coin of colonial America

shil·ly-shal·ly (shil'ē shal'ē) vi. **-lied, -ly·ing** [< repetition of sounds of shall I?] to be unable to make up one's mind; show indecision; vacillate —n. the act of shilly-shallying

Shi·loh (shī'lō) [after an ancient town in Israel] region in SW Tenn.: scene of a Civil War battle (1862)

shim (shim) n. [< ?] ☆a thin piece of wood, metal, etc. used for filling space, leveling, etc., as when building with brick or stone —☆ vt. **shimmed, shim'ming** to fit with a shim or shims

shim·mer (shim'ər) vi. [OE. scymrian] **1.** to shine with an unsteady light; glimmer **2.** to form a wavering image, as by reflection from waves of water or heat —n. a shimmering light; glimmer —**see SYN.** at FLASH —**shim'mer·y** adj.

shim·my (shim'ē) n. [< CHEMISE] ☆**1.** a jazz dance of the 1920's, with much shaking of the body ☆**2.** a shaking or wobbling, as in the front wheels of an automobile —☆ vi. **-mied, -my·ing 1.** to dance the shimmy **2.** to shake or wobble

shin (shin) n. [OE. scinu] **1.** the front part of the leg between the knee and the ankle **2.** the lower foreleg in beef —vt., vi. **shinned, shin'ning** to climb (a rope, pole, etc.) by gripping with both hands and legs: often with up

shin·bone (shin'bōn') n. same as TIBIA

☆**shin·dig** (shin'dig') n. [< colloq. shindy, commotion, changed by folk etymology to mean "dig or kick in the shin"] [Colloq.] a dance, party, or other social affair

shine (shīn) vi. **shone** or, esp. for vt. 2, **shined, shin'ing** [OE. scinan < IE. base skai-, to glimmer] **1.** to give off or reflect light; gleam; glow **2.** to excel; be outstanding [he shines in arithmetic] **3.** to show itself clearly [love shone from her face] —vt. **1.** to direct the light of [to shine a flashlight in his face] **2.** to make shiny by polishing [to shine shoes] —n. **1.** brightness; radiance **2.** luster; polish; gloss ☆**3.** short for SHOESHINE **4.** sunshine; fair weather [rain or shine] —☆**shine up to** [Slang] to use flattery, etc. in trying to get the approval of — ☆**take a shine to** [Slang] to take a liking to (someone)

shin·er (shīn'ər) n. **1.** a person or thing that shines ☆**2.** pl. **-ers, -er:** see PLURAL, II, D, 1 any of a number of freshwater minnows with silvery scales ☆**3.** [Slang] same as BLACK EYE

shin·gle[1] (shiŋ'g'l) n. [prob. < Scand.] [Chiefly Brit.] **1.** pebbles and small stones, as on a beach **2.** a beach covered with these —**shin'gly** adj. **-gli·er, -gli·est**

shin·gle[2] (shiŋ'g'l) n. [prob. altered < OE. scindel, ult. < L. scindula, a shingle] **1.** a thin piece of wood, slate, or composition material containing asphalt, asbestos, etc. laid with others in a series of overlapping rows as a covering for roofs, etc. ☆**2.** a woman's short haircut with the hair in back shaped close to the head ☆**3.** [Colloq.] a small signboard, as that of a doctor or lawyer —vt. **-gled, -gling 1.** to cover (a roof, etc.) with shingles ☆**2.** to cut (hair) in shingle style

shin·gles (shiŋ'g'lz) n. [< ML. < L. cingulum, a girdle < cingere, to gird] same as HERPES ZOSTER

shin·guard (shin'gärd') n. either of a pair of padded guards worn, as by a baseball catcher, to protect the shins

shin·ing (shīn'iŋ) adj. **1.** giving off or reflecting light; bright **2.** brilliant; splendid [a shining example] —**see SYN.** at BRIGHT

shin·ny[1] (shin'ē) n., pl. **-nies** [prob. < SHIN] **1.** a simple form of hockey played by children **2.** the curved stick used in this game

☆**shin·ny**[2] (shin'ē) vi. **-nied, -ny·ing** same as SHIN

☆**shin·plas·ter** (shin'plas'tər) n. **1.** a plaster for use on sore shins **2.** a piece of paper money made almost worthless by inflation or, formerly, one having a face value of less than a dollar

shin·splints (-splints') n.pl. [with sing. v.] [< SHIN + prob. splint, bony growth] painful strain of muscles in the lower leg, caused by running on a hard surface

Shin·to (shin'tō) n. [Jpn. < Chin. shin, god + tao, way] a religion of Japan, emphasizing worship of nature and of ancestors —**Shin'to·ism** n. —**Shin'to·ist** n., adj. —**Shin'to·is'tic** adj.

shin·y (shīn'ē) adj. **shin'i·er, shin'i·est 1.** bright; shining **2.** highly polished; glossy **3.** worn so smooth as to have a glossy look [a shiny suit] —**shin'i·ness** n.

ship (ship) n. [OE. scip: for IE. base see SCHIZO-] **1.** any large vessel for traveling on deep water **2.** a sailing vessel with a bowsprit and at least three square-rigged masts **3.** a ship's officers and crew **4.** an aircraft, spaceship, etc. —vt. **shipped, ship'ping 1.** to put or take on board a ship ☆**2.** to send or transport by any carrier [to ship coal by rail] **3.** to take in (wa-

SHINGUARDS
(on hockey goalie)

ter) over the side, as a ship in a stormy sea **4.** to put or fix in its proper place on a ship or boat [to *ship* the oars] **5.** [Colloq.] to send (*away, out,* etc.); get rid of —**vi.** **1.** to go aboard ship; embark **2.** to be hired to serve on a ship **3.** to travel by ship — **ship over** to reenlist in the U.S. Navy —**when** (or **if,** etc.) **one's ship comes in** (or **home**) when (or if, etc.) one becomes rich —**ship′pa·ble** *adj.*

-ship (ship) [OE. *-scipe*] *a suffix meaning:* **1.** the quality or state of [*friendship*] **2.** *a)* the rank or office of [*governorship*] *b)* one having the rank of [*lordship*] **3.** ability as [*leadership*] **4.** all individuals (of the specified class) [*readership*]

ship biscuit same as HARDTACK

ship·board (ship′bôrd′) *n.* a ship: chiefly in **on shipboard,** aboard a ship —*adj.* done, happening, used etc. on a ship [a *shipboard* romance]

ship·build·er (-bil′dər) *n.* one whose business is building ships —**ship′build′ing** *n.*

☆**ship canal** a canal large enough for seagoing ships

ship·load (-lōd′) *n.* the full load of a ship

ship·mas·ter (-mas′tər) *n.* the officer in command of a merchant ship; captain

ship·mate (-māt′) *n.* a fellow sailor on the same ship

ship·ment (-mənt) *n.* **1.** the shipping or transporting of goods **2.** goods shipped

ship of the line formerly, a warship of the largest class, having a position in the line of battle

ship·own·er (-ō′nər) *n.* an owner of a ship or ships

ship·per (-ər) *n.* a person who ships goods

ship·ping (-iŋ) *n.* **1.** the act or business of transporting goods **2.** all ships belonging to a certain nation, using a certain port, etc.

ship·shape (-shāp′) *adj.* having everything neatly in place, as on board ship; trim —*adv.* in a neat and orderly manner

ship·side (-sīd′) *n.* the area on a pier alongside a ship

ship·worm (-wurm′) *n.* any of various small mollusks with wormlike bodies: they burrow into wood under water

ship·wreck (-rek′) *n.* **1.** the remains of a wrecked ship **2.** the loss or destruction of a ship in a storm, collision, etc. **3.** any ruin or destruction —*vt.* **1.** to cause to undergo shipwreck **2.** to destroy, ruin, or wreck

ship·wright (-rīt′) *n.* a person, esp. a carpenter, whose work is the construction and repair of ships

ship·yard (-yärd′) *n.* a place where ships are built and repaired

shire (shīr) *n.* [OE. *scir,* office] **1.** any of the former districts in Great Britain coinciding generally with the modern county **2.** any of the counties of Great Britain with a name ending in *-shire*

shirk (shurk) *vt., vi.* [? akin to G. *schurke,* rascal] to get out of doing or leave undone (something that should be done) [don't *shirk*—do your homework now] —**shirk′er** *n.*

Shir·ley (shur′lē) [ult. < OE. *scire,* shire + *leah,* meadow] a feminine name

☆**shirr** (shur) *n.* [< ?] same as SHIRRING —*vt.* **1.** to make shirring in (cloth or a garment) **2.** to bake (eggs) with crumbs in small buttered dishes

☆**shirr·ing** (shur′iŋ) *n.* **1.** a gathering made in cloth by drawing the material up on parallel rows of short, running stitches **2.** any trim made by shirring

shirt (shurt) *n.* [OE. *scyrte:* for IE. base see CARNAGE] **1.** *a)* the usual garment worn by men on the upper part of the body, often under a suit coat, typically having a collar and a buttoned opening down the front *b)* a similar garment for women **2.** same as UNDERSHIRT —**lose one's shirt** [Slang] to lose everything

shirt·ing (shurt′iŋ) *n.* material for making shirts

shirt-sleeve (-slēv′) ☆*adj.* **1.** wearing, or suitable for wearing, a shirt without a coat over it [*shirt-sleeve* weather] **2.** plain; direct; informal [*shirt-sleeve* philosophy]

SHIRRING

☆**shirt·tail** (shurt′tāl′) *n.* the part of a shirt that hangs below the waist

☆**shirt·waist** (-wāst′) *n.* **1.** a woman's blouse tailored more or less like a shirt **2.** a dress with the upper part like a shirtwaist: also **shirtwaist dress, shirt′dress′** *n.*

shish ke·bab (shish′ kə bäb′) [< Arm., ult. < Ar. *shīsh,* skewer + *kabāb,* kebab] small chunks of meat, esp. lamb, placed on skewers alternately with tomatoes, onions, etc. and broiled: also **shish′ ka·bob′**

shiv (shiv) *n.* [prob. < Romany *chiv,* a blade] [Slang] a knife, esp. one with a narrow blade used as a weapon

Shi·va (shē′və) *var. of* SIVA

shiv·a·ree (shiv′ə rē′, shiv′ə rē′) *n.* [< Fr. *charivari* < LL. *caribaria,* headache] a mock serenade, as to newlyweds, with kettles, horns, etc.

shiv·er[1] (shiv′ər) *n.* [ME. *schivere*] a fragment or splinter of something broken, as glass —*vt., vi.* to break into many fragments or splinters; shatter

shiv·er[2] (shiv′ər) *vi.* [ME. *cheveren* < ? OE. *ceafl,* a jaw] to shake, tremble, etc., as from fear or cold —*n.* a shaking, trembling, etc., as from fear or cold —**the shivers** a fit of shivering

shiv·er·y (shiv′ər ē) *adj.* **1.** shivering; suffering from cold, fear, etc. **2.** causing or likely to cause shivering; terrifying

☆**shmaltz** (shmälts) *n.* [Slang] *var. of* SCHMALTZ —**shmaltz′y** *adj.*

shoal[1] (shōl) *n.* [OE. *scolu*] **1.** a large group; mass; crowd **2.** a large school of fish —*vi.* to come together in a shoal or move about as a shoal

shoal[2] (shōl) *n.* [OE. *sceald,* shallow] **1.** a shallow place in a river, sea, etc. **2.** a sand bar, etc. forming a shallow place that is a danger to navigation, esp. one that can be seen when the water is low —*vt., vi.* to make or become shallow —**shoal′y** *adj.*

SYN.—**shoal** applies to any place in a sea, river, etc. where the water is shallow and difficult for boats and ships to navigate; **bank** applies to a shallow place, formed by a raised shelf of ground, that is deep enough to be navigated safely by light boats and ships; a **reef** is a ridge of rock, coral, etc. lying at or very close to the surface of the sea, just offshore; **bar** applies to a ridge of sand, gravel, etc. that builds up at the mouth of a river or harbor and hinders navigation

shoat (shōt) *n.* [ME. *schote*] a young hog of between about 100 and 180 lbs.

shock[1] (shäk) *n.* [< Fr. < MFr. *choquer,* prob. < MDu. *schokken,* to collide] **1.** a sudden, powerful blow, shake, disturbance, etc. [the *shock* of an earthquake] **2.** *a)* a sudden and strong upsetting of the mind or feelings *b)* something causing this [her accident was a *shock* to us] **3.** the violent effect on the body of an electric current passed through it **4.** [Colloq.] short for SHOCK ABSORBER: used in pl. **5.** *Med.* a disorder caused by severe injury or damage to the body, loss of blood, etc., and marked by a sharp drop in blood pressure, a rapid pulse, etc. —*vt.* **1.** to disturb emotionally; astonish, horrify, etc. [her words *shocked* us] **2.** to cause a physical shock to **3.** to produce electric shock in —*vi.* to be shocked, distressed, etc. [one who does not *shock* easily] —**shock′er** *n.*

SYN.—**shock** suggests a violent disturbance of the mind or emotions caused by an unexpected, overwhelming event that comes as a blow [*shocked* by her sudden death]; **startle** implies a slight shock of surprise or alarm, often one that causes a person to jump or flinch [*startled* by the clap of thunder]; **paralyze** suggests such extreme shock as to make one unable to move for a time [*paralyzed* with fear]; to **stun** is to shock with such force as to make one numb, dazed, or speechless [*stunned* by the disaster]

shock[2] (shäk) *n.* [prob. via MDu. or MLowG. *schok*] a number of sheaves of grain, as corn or wheat, stacked together on end to cure and dry —*vt., vi.* to gather in shocks

shock[3] (shäk) *n.* [< ? SHOCK[2]] a thick, bushy or tangled mass, as of hair

shock absorber a device, as on the springs of a car, that lessens or absorbs the force of shocks

shock·ing (shäk′iŋ) *adj.* causing great surprise, horror, disgust, etc. —**shock′ing·ly** *adv.*

☆**shock·proof** (-prōof′) *adj.* able to take a shock, blow, etc. without being damaged [a *shockproof* watch]

SHOCKS OF CORN

shock therapy a method of treating certain severe mental illnesses by injecting the patient with certain drugs or applying electric current to the brain so as to produce convulsions or coma: also **shock treatment**

shock troops troops trained and equipped to lead an attack

shock wave a violent disturbance caused by the movement of a body, as an aircraft, at a speed greater than sound and producing a rapid increase in the pressure and temperature of the air

shod (shäd) *alt. pt. & pp. of* SHOE

shod·dy (shäd′ē) *n.* [< ?] **1.** an inferior woolen yarn or cloth made from fibers taken from used fabrics **2.** anything of less worth than it seems to have —*adj.* **shod′di·er, shod′di·est 1.** *a)* made of shoddy *b)* made of any inferior material *c)* poorly done or made **2.** not as good as it is said to be **3.** contemptible [a *shoddy* trick] —**shod′di·ly** *adv.* —**shod′di·ness** *n.*

shoe (shōō) *n.* [OE. *sceoh:* for IE. base see HIDE¹] **1.** an outer covering for the foot, made of leather, canvas, etc. and usually having a stiff sole and a heel **2.** something like a shoe in shape or use; specif., *a) short for* HORSESHOE, BRAKE SHOE *b)* the metal strip along the bottom of a sled runner *c)* the casing of a pneumatic tire —*vt.* **shod** or **shoed, shoe′ing** to furnish with shoes —**fill one's shoes** to take one's place —**in another's shoes** in another's position

shoe·horn (shōō′hôrn′) *n.* an implement of metal, horn, plastic, etc. with a curved blade, inserted at the back of a shoe to help in slipping the heel in

shoe·lace (-lās′) *n.* a length of cord, leather, etc. used for lacing and fastening a shoe

shoe·mak·er (-māk′ər) *n.* a person whose business is making or repairing shoes —**shoe′mak′ing** *n.*

☆**shoe·pac** (-pak′) *n.* [altered (after SHOE & PAC) < AmInd. *shipak* < *paku*, shoe] *same as* PAC

shoe·shine (-shīn′) *n.* the cleaning and polishing of shoes

shoe·string (-striŋ′) *n.* **1.** *same as* SHOELACE ☆**2.** a small amount of money as capital [the business was started on a *shoestring*] —☆ *adj.* at, near, or around the ankles [a *shoestring* catch of a ball; a *shoestring* tackle]

☆**shoestring potatoes** potatoes cut into long, very narrow strips and fried crisp in deep fat

shoe tree a form, as of wood or metal, put into a shoe to stretch it or preserve its shape

sho·far (shō′fər; *Heb.* shô fär′) *n., pl.* **-fars;** *Heb.* **-frot′** (-frōt′) [Heb. *shōphār*] a ram's horn used in ancient times as a signaling trumpet and still blown in synagogues on Rosh Hashana and at the end of Yom Kippur

sho·gun (shō′gun′, -gōōn′) *n.* [Jpn. < Chin. *chiang-chun,* leader of an army] any of the military governors of Japan who, until 1868, were the absolute rulers of the country —**sho′gun·ate** (-gə nit, -gə nāt′) *n.*

Sho·la·pur (shō′lə pōōr′) city in W India: pop. 338,000

Sho·lo·khov (shô′lô khôf), **Mi·kha·il (Aleksandrovich)** (mi khä ēl′) 1905– ; Russ. novelist

Sho·lom A·leich·em (shô′ləm ä läkh′əm) (pseud. of *Solomon Rabinowitz*) 1859–1916; Russ. writer in Yiddish

shone (shōn) *pt. & pp. of* SHINE

shoo (shōō) *interj.* [echoic] **1.** an exclamation used in driving away chickens and other animals **2.** go away! get out! —*vt.* to drive away, as by crying "shoo" [to *shoo* flies away]

☆**shoo-in** (shōō′in′) *n.* [SHOO + IN] [Colloq.] someone or something expected to win easily in an election, a race, etc.

shook (shook) *pt. and dial. pp. of* SHAKE —☆**shook up** [Slang] upset; disturbed

shoon (shōōn) *n. archaic or dial. pl. of* SHOE

shoot (shōōt) *vt.* **shot, shoot′ing** [OE. *sceotan* < IE. base *(s)keud-,* to throw] **1.** *a)* to move swiftly over, by, etc. [to *shoot* the rapids in a canoe] *b)* to make move with great force [to *shoot* an elevator upward] **2.** to pour, empty out, or dump, as down a chute **3.** *a)* to hurl or thrust out [volcanoes *shooting* molten rock into the air] ☆*b)* to throw away or spoil (an opportunity, chance, etc.) *c)* [Colloq.] to use up or waste (time, money, etc.) **4.** to slide (a door bolt) into or out of its fastening **5.** *a)* to streak or fleck (*with* another color or substance) [blue *shot* with orange] *b)* to vary (*with* something different) [a story *shot* with humor] **6.** *a)* to thrust out suddenly [snakes *shooting* out their tongues] *b)* to put forth (a branch, leaves, etc.) **7.** *a)* to launch (a rocket), discharge (a bullet, arrow, etc.), or fire (a gun, bow, etc.) *b)* to give off (rays) with force **8.** to put forth (a question, fist, etc.) swiftly or with force **9.** to hit, wound, kill, or destroy with a bullet, arrow, etc. **10.** to take the altitude of (a star), as with a sextant **11.** to photograph or film

12. [Slang] to inject (a narcotic drug, etc.) into one's bloodstream **13.** *Games, Sports a)* to throw or drive (a ball, etc.) toward the objective *b)* to score (a goal, points, etc.) *c)* to play (golf, pool, craps, etc.) *d)* to make (a specified bet), as in craps —*vi.* **1.** *a)* to move swiftly [a horse *shot* out of the barn] *b)* to spurt or gush **2.** to be felt suddenly and keenly [a pain *shot* across his back] **3.** to grow or sprout rapidly [she *shot* up in her early teens] **4.** to jut out; project **5.** to fire a missile, gun, etc. **6.** to use guns, bows and arrows, etc., as in hunting ☆**7.** *a)* to photograph a scene *b)* to start movie cameras working **8.** [Slang] to inject a narcotic drug, etc. into one's bloodstream: usually with *up* **9.** *Sports a)* to propel a ball, etc. toward the objective *b)* to roll dice —*n.* **1.** *a)* the act of shooting *b)* a shooting trip, party, or contest [a turkey *shoot*] **2.** a new growth; sprout **3.** the launching of a rocket, guided missile, etc. ☆**4.** a sloping trough; chute —*interj.* **1.** an exclamation of disgust, disappointment, etc. **2.** begin talking! —**shoot at** (or **for**) [Colloq.] to strive for —☆**shoot off one's** (or **at the**) **mouth** [Slang] **1.** to speak without caution; blab **2.** to boast; brag —**shoot′er** *n.*

shooting gallery a place, as a booth at an amusement park, for practice in shooting at targets that are usually moving on an endless belt

☆**shooting script** the final version of a movie or television script as it is to be filmed or taped

shooting star *same as* METEOR

shooting stick a canelike stick with a spike at one end and a narrow, folding seat at the top for resting on

☆**shoot-out, shoot·out** (shōōt′out′) *n.* [Slang] a battle with handguns, etc., as between police and criminals

shop (shäp) *n.* [OE. *sceoppa,* booth] **1.** *a)* a place where certain goods or services are offered for sale *b)* a specialized department in a large store [the gourmet *shop*] **2.** a place where a particular kind of work is done [a printing *shop*] ☆**3.** in some schools, a manual-training course, class, or department —*vi.* **shopped, shop′ping** to visit shops so as to examine or buy merchandise —*vt.* ☆[Colloq.] to shop at (a specified store) —**set up shop** to start a business —☆**shop around 1.** to go from shop to shop, looking for bargains, etc. **2.** to search for a good job, idea, etc. —**talk shop** to talk about one's work

shop·girl (shäp′gurl′) *n.* [Chiefly Brit.] *same as* SALESWOMAN

shop·keep·er (shäp′kē′pər) *n.* a person who owns or operates a shop, or small store —**shop′keep′ing** *n.*

shop·lift·er (-lif′tər) *n.* a person who steals articles displayed on counters, racks, etc. from a store during shopping hours —**shop′lift′ vt., vi.**

shoppe (shäp) *n. var. of* SHOP (sense 1)

shop·per (shäp′ər) *n.* **1.** a person who shops; esp., one hired by a store to shop for its customers **2.** a person hired by a store to compare competitors' merchandise and prices ☆**3.** a handbill containing advertisements of local stores

shopping center a number of stores, restaurants, etc. grouped together and having a common parking lot

shop steward a person elected by his fellow workers in a union shop to represent them in dealing with the employer

shop·talk (shäp′tôk′) *n.* **1.** the specialized vocabulary used by people having the same occupation, etc. **2.** conversation or talk about one's work, esp. after hours

shop·worn (-wôrn′) *adj.* **1.** soiled, faded, etc. from having been displayed in a shop **2.** drab, dull, trite, etc.

☆**Shor·an** (shôr′an) *n.* [*Sho*(rt) *Ra*(nge) *N*(avigation)] [also s-] a radar system for locating the position of a plane, etc. by signals from a pair of transponders on the ground

shore¹ (shôr) *n.* [< OE. word no longer known, akin to *scorian,* to jut out] **1.** land at the edge of a body of water **2.** land as opposed to water

shore² (shôr) *n.* [akin to MDu. *schore,* OIce. *skortha,* a prop] a beam, etc. placed under or against something as a support —*vt.* **shored, shor′ing** to support or make stable as with shores (usually with *up*)

shore bird any of the birds that feed or nest on the shores of the oceans, rivers, etc., as the curlews, sandpipers, etc.

☆**shore dinner** a meal with various kinds of seafood dishes

shore leave leave of absence granted to a ship's crew for going ashore

shore·line (shôr′līn′) *n.* the edge of a body of water

☆**shore patrol** a small group chosen

SHOFAR

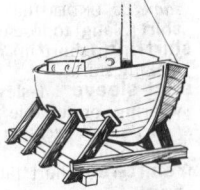

SHORES

from the U.S. Navy, Coast Guard, or Marine Corps to serve as military police on shore

shore·ward (-wərd) *adv.* toward the shore: also **shore′wards** —*adj.* moving toward the shore

shor·ing (shôr′iŋ) *n.* 1. the act of supporting with shores 2. a system of shores used for support

shorn (shôrn) *alt. pp. of* SHEAR

short (shôrt) *adj.* [OE. *scort:* for IE. base see CARNAGE] 1. not extending far from end to end; not long or not long enough [a *short* stick] 2. not great in range or scope [a *short* journey, view, etc.] 3. low in height; not tall [a *short* tree] 4. lasting but a little time; brief [a *short* meeting] 5. not holding in the mind for long [a *short* memory] 6. condensed or concise, as a story, speech, etc. 7. brief to the point of rudeness; curt [a *short* answer] 8. less or having less than what is enough or correct [*short* on money] 9. not far enough to reach the objective [the shot fell *short*] 10. having a tendency to crumble, as pastry ☆11. *a)* not possessing at the time of sale the commodity or security one is selling *b)* describing or of a sale of commodities or securities which the seller does not have but expects to buy later at a lower price 12. requiring a relatively short time to pronounce: said of a speech sound —*n.* 1. something short; specif., *a)* a short sound or syllable *b) same as* SHORT SUBJECT 2. a variation of clothing size shorter than the average for that size 3. [*pl.*] *a)* formerly, knee breeches *b)* short trousers reaching to the knee or above ☆*c)* a man's undergarment of similar form 4. [*pl.*] items needed to make up a shortage or lack 5. [*pl.*] a byproduct of wheat milling that consists of bran, germ, and coarse meal 6. *clipped form of:* ☆*a)* SHORTSTOP *b)* SHORT CIRCUIT —*adv.* 1. abruptly; suddenly [the car stopped *short*] 2. rudely; curtly [he cut her off *short*] 3. briefly; concisely 4. so as to be short [cut it off *short*] 5. by surprise; unawares [caught *short*] 6. by a short sale —*vt., vi.* 1. to give less than what is needed, usual, etc. 2. *clipped form of: a)* SHORTCHANGE *b)* SHORT-CIRCUIT —see SYN. at BRIEF —**fall** (or **come**) **short** 1. to be lacking 2. to fail to reach a given mark, objective, etc. —**for short** as a shorter form [call him Al *for short*] —**in short** 1. in summing up 2. briefly —**run short** to have less than enough —**short for** being a shorter form of — **short of** 1. not equal to or reaching; less than 2. lacking 3. without actually turning to —☆**the short end of the stick** the worst of a deal —**short′ish** *adj.* —**short′ness** *n.*

☆**short·age** (shôrt′ij) *n.* a lack in the quantity or amount needed or expected; deficit [a *shortage* of help]

short·bread (-bred′) *n.* a rich, crumbly cake or cookie made with much shortening

short·cake (-kāk′) *n.* a light biscuit or a sweet cake served with fruit, etc. as a dessert

☆**short·change** (-chānj′) *vt., vi.* -changed′, -chang′ing [Colloq.] 1. to give less money than is due in change 2. to cheat —**short′chang′er** *n.*

short-cir·cuit (-sur′kit) *vt.* 1. *Elec.* to make a short circuit in 2. to get around or avoid [to *short-circuit* debate by calling for a vote] 3. to frustrate or defeat [their plans were *short-circuited*] —*vi.* to develop a short circuit

short circuit 1. a usually accidental low-resistance connection between two points in an electric circuit that causes too much current flow 2. popularly, a broken electric circuit resulting from this

short·com·ing (-kum′iŋ) *n.* a falling short of what is expected or required; fault or weakness

short·cut (-kut′) *n.* 1. a shorter way to get to the same place 2. any way of saving time, effort, expense, etc.

short division the process of dividing one number by another without putting the steps down in full

short·en (shôrt′'n) *vt.* 1. to make short or shorter [to *shorten* a skirt] 2. to take in or roll up (a sail) 3. to add shortening to (pastry, etc.) for crispness or flakiness —*vi.* to become short or shorter —**short′en·er** *n.*

SYN.—**shorten** implies reduction in the length or scope of something or the time it takes [to *shorten* a rope, a visit, one's life, etc.]; **curtail** implies making reductions that are necessary, as to save time, money, or energy [the company *curtailed* overtime in order to cut costs]; **abridge** implies reduction in scope by condensing, leaving out parts, etc. but usually connotes that what is essential is kept [to *abridge* a dictionary] —ANT. lengthen, extend

short·en·ing (shôrt′'n iŋ, shôrt′niŋ) *n.* 1. a making or becoming short or shorter 2. fat used to make pastry, etc. crisp or flaky

short·hand (-hand′) *n.* any system of special symbols for letters, words, and phrases for taking notes, dictation, etc. rapidly —*adj.* written in or using shorthand

"THIS IS A SAMPLE OF SHORTHAND WRITING"

short-hand·ed (-han′did) *adj.* short of workers or helpers

short·head·ed (shôrt′hed′id) *adj.* having a short or broad head —**short′head′ed·ness** *n.*

short·horn (-hôrn′) *n.* any of a breed of cattle with short, curved horns: they are raised for both beef and milk

short-lived (-līvd′, -livd′) *adj.* having or tending to have a short life span or existence

short·ly (-lē) *adv.* 1. in a few words; briefly 2. in a short time; soon 3. abruptly and rudely; curtly

short order any food that can be cooked or served quickly when ordered, as at a lunch counter —**short′-or′der** *adj.*

short-range (shôrt′rānj′) *adj.* 1. having a range of short distance [a *short-range* missile] 2. not looking far into the future [*short-range* plans]

short ribs the rib ends of beef from the forequarter

short shrift very little care or attention, as from lack of patience or sympathy —**make short shrift of** to deal with quickly and impatiently: also **give short shrift**

short·sight·ed (shôrt′sīt′id) *adj.* 1. *same as* NEARSIGHTED 2. not looking ahead or planning for the future —**short′sight′ed·ly** *adv.* —**short′sight′ed·ness** *n.*

☆**short·stop** (-stäp′) *n. Baseball* the infielder stationed between second and third base

short story a kind of story shorter than the novel or novelette, developing a single theme and more limited in scope and number of characters

short subject any short film presentation shown along with the feature in a motion-picture program

short-tem·pered (-tem′pərd) *adj.* having a tendency to lose one's temper; easily or quickly angered

short-term (-turm′) *adj.* 1. for or extending over a short time 2. designating or of a loan, capital gain, etc. taking place over a relatively short period

short ton a ton that is 2,000 pounds avoirdupois

short-waist·ed (-wās′tid) *adj.* with a high waistline

short-wave (-wāv′) *n.* 1. a radio wave sixty meters or less in length 2. a radio or radio band for broadcasting or receiving shortwaves: in full, **shortwave radio**

short-wind·ed (-win′did) *adj.* 1. easily put out of breath by exercise 2. breathing with quick, forced breaths 3. brief or concise: said of speech or writing —**short′-wind′ed·ness** *n.*

short·y, short·ie (-ē) *n., pl.* **short′ies** [Colloq.] a person or thing of less than average height or size

Sho·sho·ne (shō shō′nē) *n.* [< ? Shoshonean *tsosoni,* curly head] 1. *pl.* **-sho′nes, -sho′ne** any member of a group of N. American Indians scattered over Idaho, Nevada, Utah, Wyoming, and California 2. their Shoshonean language Also sp. **Sho·sho′ni**

Sho·sho·ne·an (shō shō′nē ən, shō′shə nē′ən) *n.* a branch of the Uto-Aztecan languages —*adj.* 1. of Shoshonean 2. of the Shoshones

Sho·sta·ko·vich (shô′stä kô′vich; *E.* shäs′tə kō′vich), **Dmi·tri** (d′mē′trē) 1906–75; Russ. composer

shot[1] (shät) *n.* [OE. *sceot:* for IE. base see SHOOT] 1. the act of shooting; the firing of a missile, esp. from a gun [I heard a *shot*] 2. *a)* the distance a missile travels *b)* range; scope [within *ear-shot*] 3. an attempt to hit with a missile [the first *shot* missed] 4. *a)* any attempt or try *b)* a guess 5. an unkind or critical remark [a parting *shot*] 6. the flight or path of an object thrown, driven, etc. in any of several games 7. *a)* something to be fired from a gun, esp. a solid ball or bullet *b)* such balls or bullets as a group 8. a small pellet or pellets of lead, used for a charge of a shotgun 9. the ball used in the shot put: see SHOT PUT 10. a blast, as in mining 11. a marksman [he's a fair *shot*] ☆12. *a)* a single photograph *b)* a sequence or view taken by a single continuous run of a movie or TV camera ☆13. a hypodermic injection, as of vaccine ☆14. a drink of liquor 15. [Colloq.] a bet, with reference to the odds given [a ten-to-one *shot*] —*vt.* **shot′ted, shot′ting** to load or weight with shot —**a shot in the arm** something that stimulates, encourages, etc. —**call the shots 1.** to give orders **2.** to control what happens —**have (or take) a shot at** [Colloq.] to make a try at —**like a shot** quickly or suddenly

shot[2] (shät) *pt. & pp. of* SHOOT —*adj.* **1.** streaked with another color [a green dress *shot* with blue] **2.** varied with something different [a novel *shot* through with humor] ☆**3.** [Colloq.] ruined or worn out

shote (shōt) *n. var. of* SHOAT

☆**shot·gun** (shät′gun′) *n.* a smoothbore gun for firing a charge of small shot at short range —*vt., vi.* to shoot, force, etc. with a shotgun

shot put (poot′) **1.** a contest in which a heavy metal ball is thrown from above the level of the shoulder **2.** a single throw of this ball —**shot′-put′ter** *n.* —**shot′-put′ting** *n.*

SHOT-PUTTER

should (shood; *unstressed, often* shəd) *v.* [OE. *sceolde*, pt. of *sceal*, I am obliged] **1.** *pt. of* SHALL **2.** a helping verb used to express: *a)* necessity, duty, etc. [he *should* help her] *b)* expectation or probability [he *should* be here soon]: equivalent to *ought to c)* the future from the standpoint of the past in indirect quotations: replaceable by *would* [I said I *should* (or *would*) be home late] *d)* the future in polite requests or in statements implying doubt: replaceable by *would* [I *should* (or *would*) think he'd like it] *e)* a future condition [if I *should* die tomorrow] *f)* a past condition: replaceable by *would* [I *should* (or *would*) have gone had you asked me] In the usage of some grammarians, the distinctions between *should* and *would* are the same as those between *shall* and *will*: see WILL[2]

shoul·der (shōl′dər) *n.* [OE. *sculdor*: for IE. base see CUTLASS] **1.** *a)* the joint connecting the arm or forelimb with the body *b)* the part of the body including this joint, extending to the base of the neck **2.** [*pl.*] the two shoulders and the part of the back between them **3.** a cut of meat consisting of the upper foreleg and attached parts: see illustration at PORK **4.** the part of a garment that covers the shoulder **5.** a part that sticks out like a shoulder ☆**6.** the strip along the edge of a paved road; berm —*vt.* **1.** to push along or through, as with the shoulder [to *shoulder* one's way into the room] **2.** to carry upon the shoulder **3.** to take on the responsibility of [to *shoulder* a task] —*vi.* to push with the shoulder —**cry on someone's shoulder** to tell one's troubles to someone in seeking sympathy —**put one's shoulder to the wheel** to set to work with extra effort —**shoulder arms** to rest a rifle against the shoulder, supporting the butt with the hand —**shoulder to shoulder 1.** side by side and close together **2.** working together —**straight from the shoulder 1.** moving straight forward from the shoulder: said of a blow **2.** without reserve; frankly —**turn (or give) a cold shoulder to** to treat with scorn; avoid

shoulder blade either of two flat bones in the upper back: see illustration at SCAPULA

☆**shoulder harness** a strap passing over the shoulder and body to the hip, used for safety in a car

shoulder knot an ornament of braided cord worn on the shoulders of full-dress uniforms

☆**shoulder patch** a piece of cloth with insignia that identify the wearer's branch of military service, unit, etc., worn on the sleeve of a uniform, just below the shoulder

shoulder strap 1. a strap, usually one of a pair, worn over the shoulder to support a garment **2.** a strap worn over the shoulder for carrying an attached purse, camera, etc. **3.** a flap of cloth on the shoulder of a uniform, coat, etc.

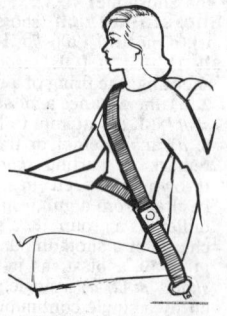

SHOULDER HARNESS

should·n't (shood′'nt) should not

shouldst (shoodst) *archaic second person singular in the past tense of* SHALL: *used with* thou: also **should·est** (shood′ist)

shout (shout) *n.* [ME. *schoute*] a loud, sudden cry, call, or out burst —*vt., vi.* to say or cry out in a loud voice —**shout down** to make be quiet by shouting at —**shout′er** *n.*

shove (shuv) *vt., vi.* **shoved, shov′ing** [OE. *scufan*] **1.** to push, as along a surface **2.** to push roughly —*n.* a push or thrust —see SYN. at PUSH —**shove off 1.** to push (a boat) away from shore ☆**2.** [Colloq.] to start off; leave —**shov′er** *n.*

shov·el (shuv′'l) *n.* [OE. *scofl*] **1.** *a)* a tool with a broad scoop or blade and a long handle: used in lifting and moving loose material *b)* any machine with a shovellike device **2.** *same as* SHOVELFUL —*vt.* **-eled** or **-elled, -el·ing** or **-el·ling 1.** to lift and move with a shovel **2.** to dig out (a path, etc.) with a shovel **3.** to put in large quantities [to *shovel* food in one's mouth] —*vi.* to use a shovel

shov·el·er, shov·el·ler (shuv′'l ər, shuv′lər) *n.* **1.** a person or thing that shovels **2.** a freshwater duck with a long, broad, flattened bill: also **shov′el·bill′**

shov·el·ful (shuv′'l fool′) *n., pl.* **-fuls′** as much as a shovel will hold

show (shō) *vt.* **showed, shown** or **showed, show′ing** [OE. *sceawian*, to look: for IE. base see HEAR] **1.** to bring or put in sight; make visible; exhibit; display [to *show* new fashions] **2.** to guide; conduct [*show* him to his room] **3.** to direct attention to; point out [we *showed* him the sights] **4.** to reveal or allow to be seen [to *show* anger] **5.** to explain, prove, or demonstrate [to *show* how it works] **6.** to register; indicate [a clock *shows* the time] **7.** to give or grant; bestow (favor, mercy, etc.) —*vi.* **1.** to be or become seen; appear [daylight began to *show* in the sky] **2.** to be noticeable [the scratch won't *show*] ☆**3.** to finish third in a horse or dog race: cf. PLACE **4.** [Colloq.] to come or arrive as expected —*n.* **1.** a showing or demonstration [a *show* of passion] **2.** a display or exhibition, esp. in public or for the public **3.** something meant to attract attention **4.** a trace as of metal, coal, etc. in the earth **5.** something false or pretended [her sorrow was mere *show*] **6.** a ridiculous spectacle or sight **7.** a presentation of entertainment, as a TV program or a movie ☆**8.** third position at the finish of a horse or dog race —**for show** in order to attract attention —☆**put (or get) the show on the road** [Slang] to start an activity, undertaking, etc. —**show off 1.** to make a display of **2.** to do something meant to attract attention —**show up 1.** to make easily seen; expose **2.** to be clearly seen; stand out **3.** to come; arrive **4.** [Colloq.] to be superior to; surpass

SYN.—**show** implies a putting or bringing something into view so that it can be seen or looked at [*show* us the garden]; to **display** something is to spread it out before one so that it is shown effectively [jewelry *displayed* on a sales counter]; **exhibit** implies display that stands out, often for the purpose of attracting public attention or examination [to *exhibit* products at a fair]; **expose** implies the laying open and displaying of something that has been covered or hidden [this bathing suit *exposes* her scar]; **flaunt** implies a flashy, rude, or bold display [to *flaunt* one's riches, vices, etc.]

☆**show·boat** (shō′bōt′) *n.* a boat with a theater in which plays are presented for people who live in river towns

show·bread (-bred′) *n. same as* SHEWBREAD

☆**show business** the theater, motion pictures, television, etc. as a business or industry: also **show biz**

☆**show·case** (-kās′) *n.* **1.** a glass-enclosed case for protecting things on display **2.** a means of displaying effectively [the revue was a *showcase* for new talent] —*vt.* **-cased′, -cas′ing** to display effectively

☆**show·down** (-doun′) *n.* [Colloq.] **1.** *Poker* the laying down of the cards face up to see who wins **2.** any action that brings matters to a final settlement

show·er[1] (shō′ər) *n.* a person who shows something

show·er[2] (shou′ər) *n.* [OE. *scur*: for IE. base see HIDE[1]] **1.** a brief fall of rain, hail, sleet, or snow **2.** a sudden, very full fall or flow, as of tears, sparks, praise, etc. ☆**3.** a party at which gifts are presented to the guest of honor ☆**4.** *a)* a bath in which the body is sprayed with fine streams of water from a nozzle with many holes in it: in full, **shower bath** *b)* an apparatus, or a room or enclosure, for such a bath —*vt.* **1.** to make wet as with a spray of water **2.** to pour forth as in a shower [*showered* with praise] —*vi.* **1.** to fall or come as a shower **2.** to bathe under a shower —**show′er·y** *adj.*

☆**show·girl** (shō′gurl′) *n. same as* CHORUS GIRL

show·ing (shō′iŋ) *n.* **1.** an exhibition or display [an art *showing*] ☆**2.** a performance or appearance [a good *showing* in the contest]

show·man (shō′mən) *n., pl.* **-men 1.** a person whose business is producing or presenting shows **2.** a person skilled at this or at presenting anything in an exciting manner —**show′man·ship′** *n.*

shown (shōn) *alt. pp. of* SHOW

show·off (shō′ôf′) *n.* **1.** a showing off to attract attention **2.** a person who shows off

show·piece (-pēs′) *n.* **1.** something exhibited **2.** something that is a fine example of its kind

show·place (-plās′) *n.* **1.** a place that is exhibited to the public for its beauty, etc. **2.** any place that is beautiful, expensively furnished, etc.

show·room (-rōōm′) *n.* a room where merchandise is displayed, as for advertising or sale

☆**show window** a store window for displaying goods

show·y (-ē) *adj.* **show′i·er, show′i·est 1.** of striking or attractive appearance [a *showy* flower] **2.** too bright or flashy; gaudy —see SYN. at GAUDY —**show′i·ly** *adv.* —**show′i·ness** *n.*

shrank (shraŋk) *alt. pt. of* SHRINK

shrap·nel (shrap′n′l) *n.* [after H. *Shrapnel* (1761–1842), Brit. general who invented it] **1.** an artillery shell filled with an explosive charge and many small metal balls, set to explode in the air **2.** these metal balls or the shell fragments scattered by any exploding shell

shred (shred) *n.* [OE. *screade:* for IE. base see CARNAGE] **1.** a long, narrow strip or piece cut or torn off **2.** a very small piece or amount; fragment [not a *shred* of truth] —*vt.* **shred′-ded** or **shred, shred′ding** to cut or tear into shreds —**shred′-der** *n.*

Shreve·port (shrēv′pôrt) [after H. M. *Shreve* (1785–1854), U.S. inventor] city in NW La.: pop. 182,000

shrew (shrōō) *n.* [OE. *screawa*] **1.** a small, mouselike mammal with soft, brown fur and a long snout: also **shrew′mouse**, *pl.* **-mice′ 2.** a nagging, bad-tempered woman — **shrew′ish** *adj.* —**shrew′ish·ly** *adv.* — **shrew′ness** *n.*

shrewd (shrōōd) *adj.* [< ME. pp. of *schrewen*, to curse < *schrewe*, shrew] keen-witted, clever, or sharp in practical affairs; astute —**shrewd′ly** *adv.* — **shrewd′ness** *n.*

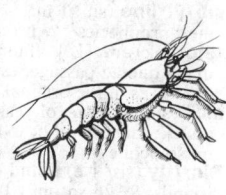

SHREW
(to 10 in. long, including tail)

SYN.—**shrewd** implies a keen mind, sharp insight, and often a crafty approach in practical matters [a *shrewd* comment, businessman, etc.]; **sagacious** implies a keen insight and farsighted judgment [a *sagacious* adviser]; **perspicacious** suggests the keen mental vision or judgment that helps one clearly to see and understand what is vague, hidden, etc. [a *perspicacious* judge of character]; **astute** implies shrewdness combined with wisdom [an *astute* politician] —see also SYN. at CLEVER

shriek (shrēk) *vi.* [prob. < ON.] to make a loud, sharp, shrill cry or sound; screech —*vt.* to say with a shriek —*n.* a loud, sharp, shrill cry or sound —see SYN. at SCREAM —**shriek′er** *n.*

shrift (shrift) *n.* [OE. *scrift* < *scrifan*, to shrive] [Archaic] **1.** confession to and absolution by a priest **2.** the act of shriving See also SHORT SHRIFT

shrike (shrīk) *n.* [OE. *scric*] any of several shrill-voiced birds with hooked beaks: most types feed on insects, some on small birds, frogs, etc., which the shrikes sometimes hang on thorns before eating them

shrill (shril) *adj.* [ME. *schrille:* echoic] **1.** having or producing a high, thin, sharp tone; high-pitched **2.** characterized or accompanied by shrill sounds **3.** forcing intrusion in a way that annoys [*shrill* demands] —*vt., vi.* to say with or make a shrill sound —**shrill′ness** *n.* —**shril′ly** *adv.*

shrimp (shrimp) *n., pl.* **shrimps, shrimp:** see PLURAL, II, D, 1 [< base of OE. *scrimman*, to shrink] **1.** a small, long-tailed crustacean, used as food **2.** [Colloq.] a small, slight person —*vi.* to fish for shrimp — **shrimp′er** *n.*

shrine (shrīn) *n.* [OE. *scrin* < L. *scrinium*, box: for IE. base see CIRCUS] **1.** a container holding sacred relics **2.** the tomb of a saint or honored person **3.** a place of worship, usually one whose center is a sacred scene or object **4.** a place or thing held sacred or honored because of someone or something important connected with it

SHRIMP
(to 9 in. long)

shrink (shriŋk) *vi.* **shrank** or **shrunk, shrunk** or **shrunk′en, shrink′ing** [OE. *scrincan:* for IE. base see CIRCUS] **1.** to become smaller or contract, as from heat, cold, wetness, etc. **2.** to lessen, as in amount, worth, etc. **3.** to draw back in fear, dislike, etc.; cower or flinch —*vt.* to cause to shrink or contract [to *shrink* wool by washing] —*n.* **1.** a shrinking ☆**2.** [< (*head*)*shrink*(*er*)] [Slang] a psychiatrist: also **shrink′er** —see SYN. at CONTRACT —**shrink′a·ble** *adj.*

shrink·age (shriŋ′kij) *n.* **1.** the act or process of shrinking, as of a fabric in washing **2.** decrease in value; depreciation **3.** the amount of shrinking, decrease, etc. [a *shrinkage* of 2%]

shrinking violet a very shy or modest person

shrive (shrīv) *vt., vi.* **shrived** or **shrove, shriv′en** (shriv′'n) or **shrived, shriv′ing** [OE. *scrifan*, ult. < L. *scribere*, to write] [Archaic] **1.** to hear the confession of (a person) and, usually after penance, give absolution **2.** to get absolution for (oneself) by confessing and doing penance

shriv·el (shriv′'l) *vt., vi.* **-eled** or **-elled, -el·ing** or **-el·ling** [prob. < Scand.] **1.** to shrink and make or become wrinkled or withered [the dry flowers *shriveled* up] **2.** to make or become helpless, useless, etc. —see SYN. at WITHER

shroud (shroud) *n.* [OE. *scrud:* for IE. base see CARNAGE] **1.** a cloth used to wrap a corpse for burial **2.** something that covers, protects, or screens; veil **3.** any of the ropes stretched from a ship's side to a masthead to help keep the mast straight **4.** any of the lines from a parachute's canopy to the harness: in full, **shroud line** —*vt.* **1.** to wrap (a corpse) in a shroud **2.** to hide; cover; screen [the town is *shrouded* in darkness]

shrove (shrōv) *alt. pt. of* SHRIVE

Shrove·tide (shrōv′tīd′) *n.* the three days before Ash Wednesday (**Shrove Sunday, Monday,** and **Tuesday**), formerly set aside as a period of confession and of festivity just before Lent

shrub[1] (shrub) *n.* [OE. *scrybb*, brushwood] a low, woody plant with several permanent stems instead of a single trunk; bush —**shrub′like** *adj.*

shrub[2] (shrub) *n.* [< Ar. *sharāb*, drink] a drink made of fruit juice, sugar, and, sometimes, rum or brandy

shrub·ber·y (shrub′ər ē) *n., pl.* **-ber·ies** a group or heavy growth of shrubs, as around a house

shrub·by (-ē) *adj.* **-bi·er, -bi·est 1.** covered with shrubs **2.** like a shrub —**shrub′bi·ness** *n.*

shrug (shrug) *vt., vi.* **shrugged, shrug′ging** [ME. *schruggen*, orig., to shiver] to draw up (the shoulders), as in expressing doubt, lack of concern, scorn, etc. —*n.* **1.** the gesture so made **2.** a woman's short jacket or sweater with wide, loose sleeves —**shrug off** to put out of one's mind in a carefree way

shrunk (shruŋk) *alt. pt. & pp. of* SHRINK

shrunk·en (shruŋk′'n) *alt. pp. of* SHRINK —*adj.* made smaller in size; shriveled

‡**shtet·l** (shtet′'l) *n., pl.* **shtet′lach** (-läkh); E. **shtet′ls** (-'lz) [Yid., dim. of *shtat*, city < G. *stadt*] any of the former Jewish villages of eastern Europe, esp. in Russia

☆**shtick** (shtik) *n.* [Yid., pranks, caprice] [Slang] **1.** a comic piece of business, as in a vaudeville act **2.** a special talent, quality, bit of behavior, etc.

shuck[1] (shuk) *n.* [< ?] **1.** a shell, pod, or husk ☆**2.** the shell of an oyster or clam —*vt.* **1.** to remove shucks from (corn, clams, etc.) **2.** to remove like a shuck [to *shuck* one's clothes] — **shuck′er** *n.*

☆**shuck**[2] (shuk) *vt., vi.* [< ?] to trick, fool, or hoax —*n.* **1.** a trick or hoax **2.** someone or something that shucks or tricks one

☆**shucks** (shuks) *interj.* an exclamation of mild disappointment, embarrassment, etc.

shud·der (shud′ər) *vi.* [ME. *schoderen*] to shake or tremble suddenly and violently, as in horror —*n.* a shuddering; sudden, strong tremor —**the shudders** a feeling of horror, disgust, etc. —**shud′der·ing·ly** *adv.* —**shud′der·y** *adj.*

shuf·fle (shuf′'l) *vt.* **-fled, -fling** [prob. < or akin to LowG. *schuffeln* < base of SHOVE] **1.** to move (the feet) with a dragging motion **2.** to mix (playing cards) so as to change their order **3.** to mix together in a jumbled mass [he *shuffled* his clothes into a bag] **4.** to shift (things) about from one place to another **5.** to bring, put, or thrust (*into* or *out of*) clumsily or trickily —*vi.* **1.** to move by dragging or scraping the feet, as in walking or dancing **2.** to act in a shifty, tricky, or dishonest manner **3.**

to shift repeatedly from one position or place to another **4.** to shuffle playing cards —*n.* **1.** the act of shuffling **2.** a tricky or deceptive action; evasion; trick **3.** *a)* a shuffling of the feet *b)* a way of walking, a dance, etc. in which one shuffles the feet **4.** *a)* a shuffling of playing cards *b)* one's turn at this —☆**lose in the shuffle** to leave out in the confusion of things —**shuffle off** to get rid of —**shuf′fler** *n.*

shuf·fle·board (-bôrd′) *n.* [< earlier *shovel board*, after the shape of the cues] **1.** a game in which large disks are pushed with a cue along a smooth lane toward numbered squares **2.** the surface on which it is played

shun (shun) *vt.* **shunned, shun′ning** [OE. *scunian*] to keep away from; avoid entirely —**shun′ner** *n.*

shunt (shunt) *vt., vi.* [? akin to SHUN] **1.** to move or turn to one side; turn aside or out of the way **2.** to switch (a train, etc.) from one track to another **3.** *Elec.* to turn aside or be turned aside by a shunt —*n.* **1.** a shunting **2.** a railroad switch **3.** *Elec.* a conductor connecting two points in a circuit and turning aside part of the current from the main circuit —**shunt′er** *n.*

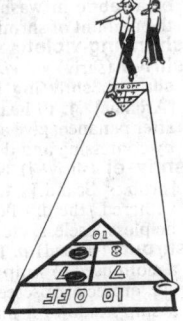

SHUFFLEBOARD

shush (shush) *interj.* [echoic] hush! be quiet! —*vt.* to say "shush" to; tell (another) to be quiet

shut (shut) *vt.* **shut, shut′ting** [OE. *scyttan* < base of *sceotan*, to SHOOT] **1.** *a)* to move (a door, window, lid, etc.) into a position that covers the opening to which it is fitted *b)* to fasten (a door, etc.) securely, as with a bolt or catch **2.** to close (an opening, container, etc.) **3.** *a)* to stop entrance to or exit from; bar *b)* to confine or enclose (in a room, cage, etc.) **4.** to fold up or close the parts of (an umbrella, a book, the eyes, etc.) **5.** to stop completely or for a time the operation of (a school, business, etc.) —*vi.* to be or become shut —*adj.* closed, fastened, etc. —*n.* the act or time of shutting —**shut down 1.** to close by lowering **2.** to settle over (a place) so as to hide, as fog **3.** to close (a factory, etc.), usually just for a time —**shut in** to surround or enclose —**shut off 1.** to keep (water, electricity, etc.) from moving, flowing, etc. through pipes, wires, etc. **2.** to stop or block (a road, faucet, etc.) from being used **3.** to separate; isolate —**shut out 1.** to refuse entrance to; keep out (sound, a view, etc.) ☆**2.** to keep (the opposing side or team) from scoring in a game —**shut up 1.** to enclose, confine, or imprison **2.** to close all the entrances to **3.** [Colloq.] *a)* to stop talking or cause to stop talking *b)* to keep from speaking or writing freely; censor

☆**shut·down** (shut′doun′) *n.* a stopping of work or activity completely or for a time, as in a factory

shut-eye (-ī′) *n.* [Slang] sleep

shut-in (-in′) ☆*n.* a person who is too ill, weak, etc. to go out —*adj.* not able to go out

shut-off (-ôf′) *n.* **1.** something that shuts off a flow, as a valve **2.** a stoppage or interruption

shut·out (-out′) *n.* ☆**1.** a preventing of the opposing team from scoring ☆**2.** a game in which this occurs

shut·ter (shut′ər) *n.* **1.** a person or thing that shuts **2.** a movable, usually hinged cover for a window **3.** anything used to cover an opening; specif., a device for opening and closing the hole in front of a camera lens to expose the film or plate —*vt.* to close or furnish with shutters

☆**shut·ter·bug** (-bug′) *n.* [< (CAMERA) SHUTTER + BUG] [Slang] a person whose hobby is photography

shut·tle (shut′'l) *n.* [OE. *scytel*, missile: from being cast back and forth] **1.** *a)* a device used to pass the woof thread back and forth between the warp threads that go up and down in weaving *b)* any of several devices having a similar use or motion, as the device that carries the lower thread back and forth on a sewing machine ☆**2.** a bus, train, helicopter, etc. making frequent trips back and forth over a short route —*vt., vi.* **-tled, -tling 1.** to move rapidly to and fro ☆**2.** to go by means of a shuttle

shut·tle·cock (-käk′) *n.* **1.** a rounded piece of cork having a flat end stuck with feathers: it is struck back and forth across a net by players in badminton or in battledore and shuttlecock **2.** the game of battledore and shuttlecock

shy¹ (shī) *adj.* **shy′er** or **shi′er, shy′est** or **shi′est** [OE. *sceoh*] **1.** easily frightened or startled; timid [a *shy* animal] **2.** not at ease with other people; bashful [a *shy* child] **3.** distrustful;

wary ☆**4.** [Slang] lacking in amount; short (*on* or *of*) [just before payday, he is *shy* on money] —*vi.* **shied, shy′ing 1.** to move or pull back suddenly when startled; start [the horse *shied* when the gun went off] **2.** to be or become cautious or unwilling; draw back (often with *at* or *from*) [she *shied* at going in the deep water] —*n., pl.* **shies** an act of shying; start, as of a horse —**fight shy of** to keep away from; avoid —**shy′er** *n.* —**shy′ly** *adv.* —**shy′ness** *n.*

SYN.—**shy** implies a drawing back from being noticed by others and an unwillingness to go near other people, especially strangers; **bashful** implies such shyness as is shown by behaving in an awkward way and being timid and embarrassed; **diffident** implies a lack of confidence in oneself that makes one unwilling to insist on one's rights; **modest** implies a humble or meek manner in one who, because of his ability, success, etc., might be expected to be bold or boastful; **demure**, in current use, suggests a very proper and modest manner, often one that is only pretended —ANT. **bold, confident**

shy² (shī) *vt., vi.* **shied, shy′ing** [< ? or akin to SHY¹] to throw or fling, esp. sidewise with a jerk [*shying* stones at a target] —*n., pl.* **shies** a shying; fling

Shy·lock (shī′läk′) the moneylender in Shakespeare's *Merchant of Venice* —*n.* a person who is without pity in business dealings

☆**shy·ster** (shī′stər) *n.* [prob. altered < G. *scheisser*, defecator] [Slang] a person, esp. a lawyer, who uses dishonest or tricky methods

si (sē) *n. Music* same as TI

‡**sí** (sē) *adv.* [Sp.] yes

‡**sì** (sē) *adv.* [It.] yes

Si *Chem.* silicon

Si·am (sī am′) former name of THAILAND

Si·a·mese (sī′ə mēz′, -mēs′) *n., pl.* **Si·a·mese** same as THAI —*adj.* same as THAI

Siamese cat a breed of short-haired cat with blue eyes and a fawn-colored coat that shades to a darker color at the face, ears, paws, and tail

Siamese twins [after such a pair born in Siam] any pair of twins born joined to each other

Si·an (shē′än′) city in NC China: pop. c. 1,500,000

SIAMESE CAT

sib (sib) *n.* [OE. *sibb*] **1.** a person related to one by birth; esp., a brother or sister **2.** a group of persons related to one another by birth or by descent from a common ancestor —*adj.* related by birth

Si·be·li·us (si bā′lē oos; *E.* sə bāl′yəs), **Jean (Julius Christian)** (zhän) 1865–1957; Finn. composer

Si·ber·i·a (sī bir′ē ə) region in N Asia, between the Urals & the Pacific; Asiatic section of the R.S.F.S.R. —**Si·ber′i·an** *adj., n.*

Siberian husky full name of HUSKY¹

sib·i·lant (sib′'l ənt) *adj.* [< L. < *sibilare*, to hiss] having or making a hissing sound —*n. Phonet.* a consonant that has a hissing sound, as (s), (z), (sh), (zh), (ch), and (j) —**sib′i·lance, sib′i·lan·cy** *n., pl.* **-cies** —**sib′i·lant·ly** *adv.*

sib·ling (sib′liŋ) *n.* [20th-c. readoption of OE. *sibling*, a relative] one of two or more persons born of the same parents, or, sometimes, having one parent in common; brother or sister

Sib·yl (sib′'l) [L. *Sibylla*: see next entry] a feminine name

sib·yl (sib′'l) *n.* [< L. < Gr. *sibylla*] **1.** any of certain women who acted as prophetesses or oracles for the ancient Greeks and Romans **2.** a prophetess; fortuneteller

sib·yl·line (sib′'l īn′, -ēn′, -in) *adj.* **1.** of or like the sibyls or their prophecies **2.** prophetic or mysterious

‡**sic¹** (sik) *adv.* [L.] thus; so: used within brackets, [*sic*], to show that a quoted passage, esp. one containing some error, is shown exactly as in the original

sic² (sik) *vt.* [var. of SEEK] **sicked, sick′ing 1.** to follow and attack: said esp. of or to a dog **2.** to urge to attack [to *sic* a dog on someone]

Sic·i·ly (sis′'l ē) island of Italy, off its S tip: with small nearby islands, 9,926 sq. mi.: It. name **Si·ci·lia** (sē chēl′yä) —**Si·cil·ian** (si sil′yən, -ē ən) *adj., n.*

sick¹ (sik) *adj.* [OE. *seoc*] **1.** suffering from disease; physically or mentally ill **2.** having a feeling that makes one vomit or want to vomit; nauseated **3.** indicating sickness [a *sick* expression] **4.** of or for sick people [*sick* leave] **5.** deeply disturbed, as by grief, failure, etc. [*sick* over the loss of his dog] **6.** disgusted by too much of something [she is *sick* of his excuses]: often **sick and tired 7.** in poor condition; unsound [a *sick*

motor] **8.** having a great longing (*for*) [he is *sick* for the hills]
9. of sickly color; pale **10.** menstruating **11.** [Colloq.] sadistic, very unwholesome, morbid, etc. [a *sick* joke] —**the sick** sick people as a group

SYN.—**sick** and **ill** both express the idea of being in bad health, having a disease, etc., but **sick** is more commonly used than **ill**, which is somewhat formal [he's a *sick* person; he is *sick*, or *ill*, with the flu]; **ailing** usually suggests poor health that lasts a long time or never improves [she has been *ailing* ever since her operation]; **indisposed** suggests a slight, brief illness or feeling of physical discomfort [*indisposed* with a headache] —**ANT.** well, healthy

sick² (sik) *vt. same as* SIC²
sick bay a ship's hospital or dispensary
sick·bed (sik′bed′) *n.* the bed of a sick person
sick call *Mil.* **1.** a daily formation made up of those who wish to receive medical attention **2.** a signal for or the time of such a formation
sick·en (sik′'n) *vt., vi.* to make or become sick, disgusted, etc. —**sick′en·er** *n.*
sick·en·ing (-iŋ) *adj.* **1.** causing sickness or making one want to vomit **2.** disgusting —**sick′en·ing·ly** *adv.*
sick headache 1. any headache that makes one want to vomit **2.** *same as* MIGRAINE
sick·ish (sik′ish) *adj.* **1.** somewhat sick or nauseated **2.** somewhat sickening or nauseating —**sick′ish·ly** *adv.*
sick·le (sik′'l) *n.* [OE. *sicol*, ult. < L. *secula* < *secare*, to cut: for IE. base see SAW¹] a tool consisting of a curved blade with a short handle, for cutting tall grass, etc.

SICKLE

sick leave leave or permission for a sick person to be absent from work, often with pay (**sick pay**) for a limited number of days
☆**sickle cell anemia** an inherited chronic anemia found chiefly among Negroes, in which there are abnormal red blood cells containing a faulty form of hemoglobin that causes these cells to become sickle-shaped: also **sickle cell disease**
sick·ly (sik′lē) *adj.* **-li·er, -li·est 1.** in poor health; sick much of the time **2.** of or caused by sickness [a *sickly* pallor] **3.** producing illness; unhealthful **4.** sickening, as an odor **5.** faint; feeble; weak [a *sickly* light; a *sickly* smile] —*adv.* in a sick manner: also **sick′li·ly** —*vt.* **-lied, -ly·ing** to make sickly, as in color, vigor, etc. —**sick′li·ness** *n.*
sick·ness (-nis) *n.* **1.** a being sick or diseased; illness **2.** a particular disease or illness **3.** a feeling that one is about to vomit; nausea
☆**sick·out** (-out′) *n.* a united action by a group of employees claiming illness and not reporting for work in order to force the granting of certain demands; esp., such an action by a group forbidden by law to strike
sick·room (-rōōm′) *n.* the room in which a sick person is kept
Sid·dhar·tha Gau·ta·ma (sid där′tə gout′ə mə, gôt′-) *see* BUDDHA
side (sīd) *n.* [OE.] **1.** the right or left half of a human or animal body [a pain in one's *side*] **2.** a position beside one [he never left my *side*] **3.** *a*) any of the lines or surfaces that bound something [a square has four *sides;* a cube has six *sides*] *b*) either of the two bounding surfaces of an object that are not the front, back, top, or bottom [a door at the *side* of the house] **4.** either of the two surfaces of paper, cloth, etc. **5.** a particular or specified surface [the inner *side* of a vase, the visible *side* of the moon] **6.** a particular part or quality of a person or thing [his cruel *side*, the bright *side* of life] **7.** the slope of a hill, bank, etc. **8.** any location, area, space, etc. as it is related to a central point or line, or to the speaker [this *side* of the street] **9.** the ideas, opinions, or position of one person or group opposing another [his *side* of the argument] **10.** any of the groups against each other in a contest, conflict, etc. [the judges voted for our *side* in the debate] **11.** all the relatives of either one's mother or one's father [an uncle on my mother's *side*] —*adj.* **1.** of, at, or on a side [a *side* door] **2.** to or from one side [a *side* glance] **3.** done, happening, etc. as something in addition [a *side* effect] **4.** not main; secondary [a *side* issue] —*vt.* **sid′ed, sid′ing** to furnish with sides or siding —☆**on the side 1.** in addition to the main thing, part, course, etc. **2.** in addi-

tion to one's main or regular occupation —**side by side** beside each other; together —**side with** to support (one side rather than the other) in a contest, conflict, etc. —**take sides** to support one person or group against the others in a dispute, conflict, etc.
☆**side·arm** (-ärm′) *adj., adv.* with a sweeping forward motion of the arm from the side of the body at or below shoulder level [a *sidearm* pitch]
side arms weapons of the kind that may be worn at the side or at the waist, as a sword, pistol, etc.
side·board (sīd′bôrd′) *n.* **1.** a piece of dining-room furniture for holding table linen, silver, china, etc. **2.** [*pl.*] *Hockey* the solid fence surrounding the ice rink
☆**side·burns** (-burnz′) *n.pl.* [reversed < BURNSIDES] **1.** *same as* BURNSIDES **2.** the hair growing on the sides of a man's face just in front of the ears, esp. when the rest of the beard is cut off
side·car (-kär′) *n.* a small car attached to the side of a motorcycle, for carrying a passenger, packages, etc.
sid·ed (sīd′id) *adj.* having (a specified number or kind of) sides [six-*sided*]
side dish any food served along with the main course, usually in a separate dish
side effect an effect in addition to the one intended or desired; specif., an effect, sometimes harmful, that a medicine, drug, etc. may have in addition to the effect for which it is taken
☆**side·kick** (-kik′) *n.* [Slang] **1.** a companion; close friend **2.** a partner; confederate
side·light (-līt′) *n.* **1.** a light coming from the side **2.** a less important piece of information on a subject **3.** a red light on the port side or a green light on the starboard side of a ship or boat
side·line (-līn′) *n.* a line along the side; specif., *a*) either of the two lines marking the side limits of a playing area, as in football or basketball *b*) [*pl.*] the areas just outside these lines ☆*c*) a line, as of merchandise or work, in addition to one's main line —*vt.* **-lined′, -lin′ing** ☆to remove from taking part actively in a sport, activity, etc., as because of injury —☆**on the sidelines 1.** outside the main area of action **2.** not actively participating —**side′lin′er** *n.*
side·ling (-liŋ) *adv.* sidelong; sideways —*adj.* **1.** directed or moving to the side **2.** sloping; inclined
side·long (-lôŋ′) *adv.* **1.** toward the side; obliquely **2.** on the side —*adj.* **1.** inclined; slanting **2.** directed to the side [a *sidelong* glance]
☆**side·man** (-man′) *n., pl.* **-men′** (-men′) [as distinguished from the *front man*, or leader] a member of a jazz or dance band other than the leader
side·piece (-pēs′) *n.* a piece forming the side of something, or attached to it
si·de·re·al (sī dir′ē əl) *adj.* [< L. < *sideris*, genitive of *sidus*, a star] **1.** of the stars or constellations **2.** measured by what seems to be the motion of the stars —**si·de′re·al·ly** *adv.*
sidereal day the time between two passages of the vernal equinox over the upper meridian: it measures one rotation of the earth and is equal to 23 hours, 56 minutes, 4.091 seconds of mean solar time
sidereal year *see* YEAR (sense 3)
sid·er·ite (sid′ə rīt′) *n.* [< G. < L. < Gr. < *sidēros*, iron] a yellowish to light-brown iron ore, $FeCO_3$ —**sid′er·it′ic** (-rit′ik) *adj.*
side·sad·dle (sīd′sad′'l) *n.* a saddle for women wearing skirts, upon which the rider sits with both legs on the same side of the animal —*adv.* on or as if on a sidesaddle
☆**side·show** (-shō′) *n.* **1.** a small show apart from the main show, as of a circus **2.** activity of minor importance
side·slip (-slip′) *vi.* **-slipped′, -slip′ping 1.** to slip sideways, as on skis **2.** to move in a sideslip: said of an airplane —*vt.* to cause to sideslip —*n.* **1.** a slip or skid to the side **2.** a sidewise and downward movement toward the inside of a turn by an airplane in a sharp bank
side·split·ting (-split′iŋ) *adj.* **1.** very hearty: said of laughter **2.** causing hearty laughter [a *sidesplitting* comedy]
☆**side·step** (-step′) *vt.* **-stepped′, -step′ping** to avoid by or as by stepping aside; dodge [to *sidestep* a difficulty] —*vi.* to step to one side
side step a step to one side, as to avoid something, or a step taken sidewise

side·stroke (-strōk′) *n.* a swimming stroke done with one side of the body uppermost, the arms moving back and forth, and the legs doing a scissors kick

☆**side·swipe** (-swīp′) *vt., vi.* -swiped′, -swip′ing to hit along the side in passing [the truck *sideswiped* his car] —*n.* a glancing blow made by hitting something while passing

☆**side·track** (-trak′) *vt., vi.* **1.** to switch (a train, etc.) to a siding **2.** to turn away from the main subject —*n.* a railroad siding

☆**side·walk** (-wôk′) *n.* a path for walking, usually paved, along the side of a street

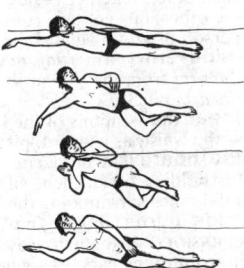

SIDESTROKE

☆**side·wall** (-wôl′) *n.* the side of an automobile tire between the tread and the rim of a wheel

side·ward (-wərd) *adv., adj.* directed or moving toward one side: also **side′wards** *adv.*

side·ways (-wāz′) *adv.* **1.** from the side [seen *sideways*, it looks thin] **2.** with one side forward [he turned his head *sideways* to show his profile] **3.** toward one side; obliquely [the car skidded *sideways* on the ice] —*adj.* turned or moving toward or from one side [a *sideways* glance] Also **side′way, side′wise′** (-wīz′)

☆**side·wheel** (sīd′hwēl′, -wēl′) *adj.* describing a steamboat having a paddle wheel on each side —**side′-wheel′er** *n.*

side whiskers whiskers growing at the side of the face

side·wind·er (sīd′wīn′dər) *n.* ☆a small desert rattlesnake of the southwestern U.S. that moves by looping its body sideways

sid·ing (sīd′iŋ) *n.* ☆**1.** shingles, boards, aluminum panels, etc. forming the outside covering of a frame building **2.** a short railway track connected with a main track by a switch and used for unloading, bypassing, etc.

si·dle (sī′d'l) *vi.* -dled, -dling [< *sideling*, sideways] to move sideways, esp. in a shy or stealthy manner —*vt.* to make go sideways —*n.* a sidling movement

SIDING

Sid·ney (sid′nē) **1.** [< the surname *Sidney*, prob. reduced from *St. Denis*] a masculine or feminine name: dim. **Sid 2.** Sir **Philip,** 1554–86; Eng. poet, soldier, & statesman

Si·don (sī′d'n) chief city of ancient Phoenicia, on the Mediterranean in what is now SW Lebanon

siege (sēj) *n.* [OFr., ult. < L. *obsidere,* to besiege < *ob-,* against + *sedere,* to SIT] **1.** the surrounding of a city, fort, etc. by an enemy army trying to capture it by continued blockade and attack **2.** any stubborn and continued effort to win or control something ☆**3.** a long, difficult period [a *siege* of illness] **4.** [Obs.] a seat; throne —*vt.* **sieged, sieg′ing** *same as* BESIEGE —**lay siege to** to force to undergo a siege; attempt to win, gain, overcome, etc.

Sieg·fried (sēg′frēd, sig′-) a hero of Germanic legend who wins the treasure of the Nibelungs

Si·en·a (sē en′ə; *It.* sye′nä) city in central Italy: pop. 66,000 — **Si′en·ese′** (-ə nēz′, -nēs′) *adj., n.*

si·en·na (sē en′ə) *n.* [It. *terra di Siena,* lit., earth of SIENA] **1.** a kind of clay containing iron and manganese and used as a yellowish-brown pigment **2.** a reddish-brown pigment made by burning this; burnt sienna **3.** either of these colors

si·er·ra (sē er′ə) *n.* [Sp. < L. *serra,* a saw] a range of mountains whose peaks look like the edge of a saw

Si·er·ra Le·one (sē er′ə lē ōn′) country in W Africa, on the Atlantic, between Guinea & Liberia: a member of the Commonwealth: 27,925 sq. mi.; pop. 2,600,000; cap. Freetown

Si·er·ra Ma·dre (sē er′ə mä′drä; *Sp.* sye′rä mä′dre) mountain system of Mexico, made up of three ranges bordering the central plateau

Sierra Nevada [Sp., lit., snowy range] mountain range in E Calif.: also called **the Si·er·ras** (sē er′əz)

si·es·ta (sē es′tə) *n.* [Sp. < L. *sexta* (*hora*), sixth (hour), noon] a brief nap or rest taken after the noon meal, esp. in Spain and some Latin American countries

sieve (siv) *n.* [OE. *sife:* for IE. base see SEEP] a utensil having many small openings, used to strain solids from liquids or to separate fine particles from coarser ones; strainer; sifter —*vt., vi.* **sieved, siev′ing** to pass through a sieve

sift (sift) *vt.* [OE. *siftan* < *sife,* a SIEVE] **1.** to pass through a sieve so as to separate the large pieces from the small ones, or to break up lumps, as of flour **2.** to scatter by or as by the use of a sieve [*sift* sugar over the cookies] **3.** to examine with care; weigh (evidence, etc.) **4.** to separate; screen [to *sift* fact from fable] —*vi.* **1.** to sift something **2.** to pass through or as through a sieve [sunshine *sifted* through the clouds] —**sift′er** *n.*

sift·ings (sift′iŋz) *n.pl.* sifted matter

sigh (sī) *vi.* [OE. *sican*] **1.** to take in and let out a long, deep, sounded breath, as to show that one is sad, tired, relieved, etc. **2.** to make a sound like a sigh [trees *sighing* in the wind] **3.** to feel sadness or longing [he *sighed* for the old days] —*vt.* to express with a sigh —*n.* the act or sound of sighing —**sigh′er** *n.*

sight (sīt) *n.* [OE. (ge)siht < base of *seon,* to SEE[1]] **1.** *a)* something seen; view *b)* a remarkable view; spectacle *c)* a thing worth seeing: *usually used in pl.* [the *sights* of the city] **2.** the act of seeing [our first *sight* of town] **3.** a look; glimpse **4.** any device used to aid the eyes in lining up a gun, optical instrument, etc. on its objective **5.** aim or an observation taken as with a sextant, gun, etc. [get a clear *sight* before firing] **6.** the ability to see; vision; eyesight [the operation restored his *sight*] **7.** range of vision [the jet passed beyond *sight*] **8.** one's thinking or opinion [a hero in her *sight*] **9.** a person or thing not pleasant to look at [his hair looks a *sight*] **10.** [Dial.] a large amount; lot [a *sight* better than fighting] —*vt.* **1.** to observe or examine by taking a sight 2. to catch sight of; see [the sailor *sighted* land] **3.** *a)* to furnish with a sighting device *b)* to adjust the sights of **4.** to aim (a gun, etc.) at (a target), using the sights —*vi.* **1.** to take aim or an observation with a sight **2.** to look carefully [*sight* along the line] —*adj.* **1.** read, done, understood, etc. as soon as seen ☆**2.** payable when presented [a *sight* draft] —**a sight for sore eyes** [Colloq.] a welcome sight —**at** (or **on**) **sight** when or as soon as seen —**by sight** by recognizing but not by knowing personally —**catch sight of** to see, esp. briefly; glimpse —**lose sight of 1.** to see no longer **2.** to forget —**not by a long sight 1.** not nearly **2.** not at all —**out of sight 1.** not in sight **2.** far off; remote **3.** [Colloq.] extremely high, as in price **4.** [Slang] excellent; wonderful —**sight unseen** without seeing (the thing) beforehand

TELESCOPIC SIGHT
ON RIFLE

sight·ed (sīt′id) *adj.* **1.** having sight; not blind **2.** having a specified kind of) sight: used in combination [*farsighted*]

sight·less (-lis) *adj.* **1.** blind **2.** unseen —**sight′less·ly** *adv.* —**sight′less·ness** *n.*

sight reading the act or skill of playing or singing readily upon sight written music unfamiliar to one —**sight′read′** *vt., vi.*

sight·see·ing (-sē′iŋ) *n.* the act of visiting places and things of interest —*adj.* for or engaged in seeing sights —**sight′se′er** *n.*

sig·ma (sig′mə) *n.* [Gr.] the eighteenth letter of the Greek alphabet (Σ, σ, ς)

sig·moid (-moid) *adj.* [< Gr.: see SIGMA & -OID] **1.** *a)* having a double curve like the letter S *b)* curved like the letter C **2.** of the sigmoid flexure Also **sig·moi′dal** —**sig·moi′dal·ly** *adv.*

sigmoid flexure 1. *Anat.* the last curving part of the colon, ending in the rectum **2.** *Zool.* an S-shaped curve

Sig·mund (sig′mənd) [< G. & ON.] a masculine name

sign (sīn) *n.* [< OFr. < L. *signum*] **1.** something that stands for something else; symbol [black is a *sign* of mourning] **2.** *a)* a gesture that tells something specified [a nod is a *sign* of approval] *b)* any of the gestures used in sign language **3.** a mark or symbol having a specific meaning [the *sign* ¢ for cent(s)] **4.** a publicly displayed board, placard, etc. bearing information, advertising, etc. **5.** anything that tells that something else is present or is coming [the first robin is a *sign* of spring] **6.** *same as* SIGN OF THE ZODIAC —*vt.* **1.** to mark with a sign, esp. of the cross as in blessing **2.** to write one's name on, as in agreeing to or authorizing something [to *sign* a contract] **3.** to write (one's name) as a signature **4.** to hire by getting to sign a contract [the baseball club *signed* five new players] —*vi.* **1.** to write one's signature, as in agreeing to something **2.** to make a sign; signal —**sign away** (or **over**) to give away or turn over (something) to someone else by signing a document —**sign in** (or **out**) to sign a register when arriving (or leaving) —**sign off** to stop broadcasting, as for the day —**sign on** to hire or be hired —**sign up** 1. *same as* SIGN ON 2. to enlist in military service —**sign'er** *n.*

sig·nal (sig'n'l) *n.* [< OFr. < VL. *signale*, ult. < L. *signum*, a sign] 1. any sign, event, etc. that is a call to some kind of action [a bugle *signal* to attack] 2. *a*) a sign given by a gesture, device, etc. to make known a command, direction, warning, etc. *b*) an object or device providing such a sign 3. *Card Games* a bid or play intended to guide one's partner 4. *Telegraphy, Radio & TV*, etc. the electrical impulses sent out or received as sounds or pictures —*adj.* 1. not ordinary; notable [a *signal* achievement] 2. used as a signal [a *signal* light] —*vt.* **-naled** or **-nalled**, **-nal·ing** or **-nal·ling** 1. to make a signal or signals to [he *signaled* her to stop] 2. to make known by signals [the ship *signaled* it was sinking] —*vi.* to make a signal or signals —**sig'nal·er**, **sig'nal·ler** *n.*

☆**signal corps** the part of an army in charge of communications, as by radio

sig·nal·ize (-īz') *vt.* **-ized'**, **-iz'ing** 1. to make worth noticing [a career *signalized* by great achievement] 2. to draw attention to [cheers *signalized* her arrival] —**sig'nal·i·za'tion** *n.*

sig·nal·ly (-ē) *adv.* in an unusual or outstanding way [*signally* honored]

sig·nal·man (-mən, -man') *n., pl.* **-men** (-mən, -men') a person responsible for signaling or receiving signals

signal word *Linguis.* a word having a particular form and showing by its clearly marked position in a sentence what the nature is of a structure that follows: conjunctions, pronouns, articles, and prepositions all may be used as signal words

sig·na·to·ry (sig'nə tôr'ē) *adj.* that has or have joined in the signing of something —*n., pl.* **-ries** any of the persons, states, etc. that have signed a document

sig·na·ture (sig'nə chər) *n.* [< LL. < L. *signare*, to sign] 1. a person's name written by himself 2. the act of signing one's name 3. an identifying characteristic or mark 4. *Music* a sign or signs placed at the beginning of a staff to show key or time 5. *Printing a*) a large sheet on which pages are printed in some multiple of four, and which, when folded to page size, forms one section of a book *b*) a letter or number on the first page of each sheet showing in what order that section is to be bound 6. *Radio & TV* a theme song, picture, etc. used to identify a program

sign·board (sīn'bôrd') *n.* a board bearing a sign, esp. one advertising a business, product, etc.

sig·net (sig'nit) *n.* [MFr. dim. of *signe*, a sign] 1. a small seal used in marking documents as official, etc. 2. a mark made by a signet

signet ring a finger ring containing a signet, often in the form of an initial or a monogram

sig·nif·i·cance (sig nif'ə kəns) *n.* 1. that which is signified; meaning [the *significance* of a remark] 2. the quality of being significant; suggestiveness; expressiveness 3. importance; consequence [a battle of great *significance*] Also **sig·nif'i·can·cy** —see SYN. at IMPORTANCE

sig·nif·i·cant (-kənt) *adj.* [< L. prp. of *significare*, to signify] 1. *a*) having or expressing a meaning *b*) full of meaning [a *significant* speech] 2. important; momentous [a *significant* occasion] 3. having or expressing a special or hidden meaning [a *significant* wink] 4. of a difference too large to be due to chance, as in statistics Also **sig·nif'i·ca'tive** (-kāt'iv) —**sig·nif'i·cant·ly** *adv.*

sig·ni·fi·ca·tion (sig'nə fi kā'shən) *n.* 1. significance; meaning 2. a signifying; indication —see SYN. at MEANING

sig·ni·fy (sig'nə fī') *vt.* **-fied'**, **-fy'ing** [< OFr. < L. *significare* < *signum*, a sign + *facere*, to make] 1. to be a sign or indication of; mean [the rags that *signify* their poverty] 2. to show or make known by a sign, words, etc. [to *signify* approval by saying "aye"] —*vi.* to be significant; matter —**sig'ni·fi'er** *n.*

sign language communication of thoughts or ideas by means of signs and gestures of the hands and arms

sign of the cross a movement of the hand or fingers made by some Christians to suggest an outline of the cross

sign of the zodiac any of the twelve divisions of the zodiac, each represented by a symbol: see ZODIAC

‡**si·gnor** (sē nyôr'; *E.* sēn'yôr) *n., pl.* **si·gno'ri** (-nyô'rē); *E.* **si'gnors** [It.] a gentleman; man: Italian title used like *Mr.* or *sir*

‡**si·gno·ra** (sē nyô'rä; *E.* sēn yôr'ə) *n., pl.* **si·gno're** (-re); *E.* **si·gno'ras** [It.] a married woman: Italian title used like *Mrs.* or *madam*

‡**si·gno·re** (sē nyô'rē) *n., pl.* **si·gno'ri** (-rē) [It.] a gentleman; man: Italian title used in speaking to a man without using his name

‡**si·gno·ri·na** (sē'nyô rē'nä; *E.* sēn'yə rē'nə) *n., pl.* **-ri'ne** (-ne); *E.* **-ri'nas** [It.] an unmarried woman: used in Italy as a title like *Miss*

sign·post (sīn'pōst') *n.* 1. a post with a sign on it, as for showing a route or direction; guidepost 2. a clear or obvious clue, symptom, etc.

Si·gurd (sig'ərd) a hero of Norse legend identified with the German SIEGFRIED

Sikh (sēk) *n.* [Hindi, a disciple] a member of a Hindu religious sect that believes in one God and rejects the caste system —*adj.* of Sikhs —**Sikh'ism** *n.*

Si Kiang (sē' kyäŋ'; *Chin.* shē' jyäŋ') river in S China, flowing eastward into the South China Sea: 1,250 mi.

Sik·kim (sik'im) state of India (until 1975, a protectorate), in the E Himalayas: 2,818 sq. mi.; pop. 250,000

si·lage (sī'lij) *n.* [contr. (after SILO) < ENSILAGE] green fodder stored in a silo

Si·las (sī'ləs) [LL. < Gr. < Aram. *sh'ilâ*, lit., asked for] a masculine name: dim. *Si*

sild (sild) *n., pl.* **sild**, **silds**: see PLURAL, II, D, 2 [Norw., herring] any of several small or young herrings canned as Norwegian sardines

si·lence (sī'ləns) *n.* 1. the state or fact of keeping silent or still 2. absence of any sound or noise; stillness 3. a withholding of knowledge or a not mentioning something [the author's *silence* on that point] 4. failure to communicate, write, etc. —*vt.* **-lenced**, **-lenc·ing** 1. to make silent 2. to put down; repress [to *silence* a revolt] 3. to put (enemy guns) out of action —*interj.* be silent!

si·lenc·er (sī'lən sər) *n.* 1. one that silences ☆2. a device attached to the muzzle of a firearm to muffle its sound when fired

si·lent (sī'lənt) *adj.* [< L. < prp. of *silere*, to be silent] 1. making no vocal sound; mute 2. seldom speaking; not talkative 3. free from sound or noise; quiet; still [a *silent* place to study] 4. not spoken, expressed, etc. [*silent* grief, the *silent* "b" in "debt"] 5. making no mention, explanation, etc. [the newspaper is *silent* on that matter] 6. not active [factories now *silent*] 7. designating or of motion pictures without synchronized sound recording —**si'lent·ly** *adv.*

SILESIA

SYN. —**silent** is the simple, direct word for one who is temporarily not speaking or who seldom speaks; **taciturn** applies to a somewhat gloomy and unsociable person who has a habit of not talking or expressing his feelings; **reserved** implies that one has a habit of being withdrawn in speech and self-controlled or cool in manner; **reticent** implies a lack of desire, sometimes temporary as from shyness or embarrassment, to express one's feelings or to speak freely about certain matters; **secretive** suggests the sneaky or overly cautious reticence of one who hides things even when there is no need to do so —**ANT.** **talkative, voluble**

☆**silent butler** a dish with a hinged cover and a handle, in which to empty ashtrays, brush crumbs, etc.

☆**silent partner** a partner who shares in financing but not in managing a business, firm, etc.

Si·le·sia (sī lē'shə, si-; -zhə) region in E Europe, mainly in SW Poland —**Si·le'sian** *adj., n.*

si·lex (sī'leks) *n.* [L.] 1. silica, esp. in the form of flint or quartz 2. heat-resistant glass made of fused quartz

---

fat, āpe, cär, ten, ēven, is, bīte; gō, hôrn, tool, look; oil, out; up, fur; get; joy; yet; chin; she; thin, then; zh, leisure; ŋ, ring; ə for *a* in *ago*, *e* in *agent*, *i* in *sanity*, *o* in *comply*, *u* in *focus*; ' as in *able* (ā'b'l); Fr. bál; ë, Fr. coeur; ö, Fr. feu; ô, Fr. mon; ŏ, Fr. coq; ü, Fr. duc; r, Fr. cri; H, G. ich; kh, G. doch; ‡foreign; ☆ Americanism; < derived from. See inside front cover.

sil·hou·ette (sil′oo wet′) *n.* [Fr., after E. de *Silhouette*, 18th-c. Fr. minister of finance] **1.** *a)* an outline drawing, esp. of a profile, in black or in some solid color, often a cutout mounted on a light background *b)* any dark shape seen against a light background **2.** the outline of a figure, garment, etc.; contour —*vt.* **-et′ted, -et′ting** to show in silhouette [birds *silhouetted* against the sky]

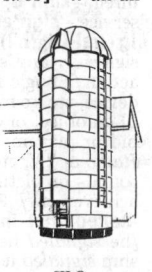

SILHOUETTE

sil·i·ca (sil′i kə) *n.* [ModL. < L. *silex*, flint] the dioxide of silicon, SiO₂, a hard, glassy mineral found in various forms, as in quartz, sand, opal, etc.

silica gel silica in the form of very small grains: it is highly adsorbent and is used as a drying agent, etc.

sil·i·cate (sil′i kit, -kāt′) *n.* a salt or ester produced from silica or a silicic acid

si·li·ceous (sə lish′əs) *adj.* **1.** of, containing, or like silica **2.** growing in soil that has much silica in it

si·lic·ic (sə lis′ik) *adj.* of, like, or produced from silica or silicon

silicic acid any of several jellylike substances formed by adding acid to sodium silicate solution

si·lic·i·fy (sə lis′ə fī′) *vt.* **-fied′, -fy′ing** [< L. *silex*, SILEX + -FY] to convert into or fill with silica; specif., same as PETRIFY (*vt.* 1) —**si·lic′i·fi·ca′tion** *n.*

sil·i·con (sil′i kən, -kän′) *n.* [ModL., ult. < L. *silex*, flint] a nonmetallic chemical element that is always found combined with something else, as in silica: only oxygen is found in greater supply in nature: symbol, Si; at. wt., 28.086; at. no., 14

silicon carbide a very hard, bluish-black crystalline substance, SiC, produced in an electric furnace

sil·i·cone (sil′i kōn′) *n.* [SILIC(ON) + -ONE] any of a group of polymerized, organic silicon compounds highly resistant to heat, water, etc. and used in oils, polishes, etc.

silicone rubber a rubberlike polymer made from certain silicones: it keeps its elasticity over a wide temperature range and is used in gaskets, insulation, etc.

sil·i·co·sis (sil′ə kō′sis) *n.* [ModL.: see SILICON & -OSIS] a chronic lung disease caused in miners, stonecutters, etc. by inhaling silica dust over a long period of time

silk (silk) *n.* see PLURAL, II, D, 3 [OE. *seoluc*, ult. < ? L. *sericus*: see SERGE] **1.** the fine, soft, shiny fiber produced by silkworms **2.** thread or fabric made from this **3.** a garment or other article made of such fabric **4.** any silklike filament or substance [corn *silk*] —*adj.* of or like silk

silk cotton same as KAPOK

silk·en (sil′k'n) *adj.* **1.** made of silk **2.** like silk; soft, smooth, glossy, etc. [*silken* hair, *silken* words]

silk hat a tall hat shaped like a cylinder and covered with silk or satin, worn by men in formal dress

silk-screen (silk′skrēn′) *adj.* **1.** designating or of a process of printing a design through a screen of silk or other fine cloth, parts of the screen being blocked as with a film through which the coloring cannot pass **2.** designating a print made by this process —*vt.* to print by this process

silk-stock·ing (-stäk′iŋ) *adj.* **1.** fashionably or richly dressed **2.** wealthy or aristocratic [a *silk-stocking* clientele]

silk·worm (-wurm′) *n.* any of certain moth caterpillars that produce cocoons of silk fiber

silk·y (sil′kē) *adj.* **silk′i·er, silk′i·est** **1.** of or like silk; soft, smooth, shiny, etc. [*silky* fur, a *silky* voice] **2.** having fine, soft hairs, as some leaves —**silk′i·ly** *adv.* —**silk′i·ness** *n.*

sill (sil) *n.* [OE. *syll*] **1.** a heavy, horizontal timber or line of bricks, stones, etc. supporting a house wall, etc. **2.** a horizontal piece forming the bottom frame of the opening into which a window or door is set **3.** *Geol.* a flattened sheet of igneous rock forced between beds of stratified rocks

sil·la·bub (sil′ə bub′) *n.* var. of SYLLABUB

sil·ly (sil′ē) *adj.* **-li·er, -li·est** [OE. *sælig*, happy, blessed < *sæl*, happiness (sense development: happy → blissful → unaware of reality → foolish)] **1.** not having or showing good sense or good judgment; foolish, absurd, etc. **2.** not important or serious [a *silly* novel] **3.** [Colloq.] dazed or stunned, as from a blow —*n., pl.* **-lies** a silly person —**sil′li·ly** (or **sil′ly**) *adv.* —**sil′li·ness** *n.*

SYN.—**silly** implies unthinking behavior that seems to show a lack of common sense, good judgment, or seriousness [it was *silly* of you to dress so lightly]; **stupid** implies slowness in thinking or a lack of normal intelligence [he is *stupid* to believe that]; **fatuous** suggests stupidity or dullness joined with smug, mistaken satisfaction with the way things are [a

fatuous smile]; **asinine** implies the extreme stupidity traditionally thought of as characteristic of the ass, or donkey [an *asinine* argument] —see also SYN. at ABSURD —ANT. wise, intelligent

si·lo (sī′lō) *n., pl.* **-los** [Fr. < Sp. < L. < Gr. *siros*] **1.** an airtight pit or tower in which green fodder is stored ☆**2.** an underground structure for storing and launching a long-range ballistic missile —*vt.* **-loed, -lo·ing** to store in a silo

silt (silt) *n.* [prob. < Scand.] fine particles of sand, soil, etc., carried along or deposited by moving water —*vt., vi.* to fill or choke up with silt, as a river bottom —**sil·ta·tion** (sil-tā′shən) *n.* —**silt′y** *adj.* **silt′i·er, silt′i·est**

Si·lu·ri·an (si loor′ē ən, sī-) *adj.* [< L. *Silures*, ancient tribe in Wales] designating or of the geological period after the Ordovician in the Paleozoic Era —**the Silurian** the Silurian Period or its rocks: see GEOLOGIC TIME CHART

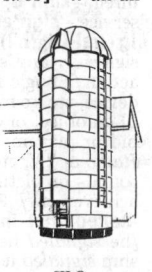

SILO

sil·van (sil′vən) *adj., n.* same as SYLVAN

sil·ver (sil′vər) *n.* [OE. *seolfor*] **1.** a white, metallic chemical element that is easily beaten or stretched into various shapes and takes a high polish: it is a precious metal and is used in coins, jewelry, etc.: symbol, Ag; at. wt., 107.868; at. no., 47 **2.** *a)* silver coins [two dollars in *silver*] *b)* money; riches **3.** articles, esp. tableware, made of or plated with silver **4.** the shiny, grayish-white color of silver **5.** something having this color, as the coating for a mirror —*adj.* **1.** of or containing silver; silvery [*silver* thread] ☆**2.** of or supporting silver as a currency standard **3.** having a silvery color, tone, etc. **4.** eloquent [a *silver* tongue] **5.** marking or celebrating the twenty-fifth year [a *silver* wedding anniversary] —*vt.* **1.** to cover with silver or something like silver **2.** to make silvery in color [hair *silvered* with age] —*vi.* to become silvery

☆**silver birch** same as PAPER BIRCH

silver bromide a yellow-white crystalline compound, AgBr, which becomes dark when exposed to light: used in photography

☆**silver certificate** formerly, a type of U.S. paper currency which could be exchanged for silver

silver chloride a white crystalline compound, AgCl, which becomes dark when exposed to light: used in photography

sil·ver·fish (-fish′) *n.* **1.** *pl.* **-fish′, -fish′es:** see FISH any of various unrelated fishes of silvery color, as the tarpon **2.** *pl.* **-fish′** a wingless insect with silvery scales and long feelers, found in damp, dark places

silver fox **1.** a variety of N. American red fox having black fur tipped with white **2.** this fur

silver iodide a yellow powder, AgI, that becomes dark when exposed to light: used in photography, to seed clouds, etc.

SILVERFISH
(to ½ inch long)

silver lining anything seen as hopeful or comforting in the midst of sadness, misfortune, etc.

silver nitrate a colorless crystalline salt, AgNO₃, used in silverplating, photography, medicine, etc.

sil·ver·plate (-plāt′) *vt.* **-plat′ed, -plat′ing** to coat with silver, esp. by electroplating

silver plate tableware made of, or plated with, silver

☆**sil·ver·side** (-sīd′) *n.* any of certain small, mostly saltwater fishes with silver stripes along the sides: also **sil′ver·sides′**

sil·ver·smith (-smith′) *n.* a skilled worker who makes articles of silver

silver standard a monetary standard in which the basic currency unit is made equal to and exchangeable for a specified quantity of silver

sil·ver·tongued (-tuŋd′) *adj.* eloquent [a *silver-tongued* orator]

☆**sil·ver·ware** (-wer′) *n.* **1.** articles, esp. tableware, made of or plated with silver **2.** any metal tableware

sil·ver·y (sil′vər ē) *adj.* **1.** like silver, as in color or luster **2.** covered with or containing silver **3.** soft and clear, like the sound of a silver bell —**sil′ver·i·ness** *n.*

sil·vi·cul·ture (sil′vi kul′chər) *n.* [< Fr. < L. *silva*, forest + *cultura*, culture] the art of cultivating a forest —**sil′vi·cul·tur·al** *adj.* —**sil′vi·cul·tur·ist** *n.*

Sim·e·on (sim′ē ən) *Bible* the second son of Jacob and Leah, or the tribe of Israel descended from him

Sim·fe·ro·pol (sim′fe rô′pôl y′) chief city of the Crimea, in the southwestern U.S.S.R.: pop. 250,000

Sim·hat To·rah (sim khät′ tō rä′, sim′khäs tō′rə) [< Heb., lit., rejoicing in the Torah] a Jewish festival in early fall marking the end of the annual cycle of Torah readings and the beginning of the next cycle: also sp. **Simchath Torah**

sim·i·an (sim′ē ən) *adj.* [< L. *simia,* an ape, prob. < *simus,* flat-nosed < Gr.] of or like an ape or monkey —*n.* an ape or monkey

sim·i·lar (sim′ə lər) *adj.* [< Fr. < L. *similis:* for IE. base see SAME] **1.** nearly but not exactly the same or alike [her ideas are *similar* to mine] **2.** *Geom.* having the same shape, but not the same size or position —**sim′i·lar·ly** *adv.*

sim·i·lar·i·ty (sim′ə lar′ə tē) *n.* **1.** a being similar; likeness **2.** *pl.* **-ties** a similar point, feature, or instance —**see** SYN·at LIKENESS

sim·i·le (sim′ə lē) *n.* [L., a likeness < *similis,* SIMILAR] a figure of speech in which one thing is compared to another, different thing by using the word *like* or *as* (Example: a voice like thunder): see also METAPHOR

si·mil·i·tude (sə mil′ə tōōd′, -tyōōd′) *n.* [MFr. < L. *similitudo*] **1.** a person or thing resembling another **2.** the form or likeness (*of* some person or thing) **3.** similarity

Si·mi Valley (sə mē′; *popularly,* sē′mē) [prob. < AmInd. *shimiji,* little white clouds] city in SW Calif., northwest of Los Angeles: pop. 56,000

sim·mer (sim′ər) *vi.* [of echoic origin] **1.** to remain at or just below the boiling point **2.** to be about to lose control or break forth [he *simmered* with rage] —*vt.* **1.** to make (a liquid) simmer **2.** to cook in such a liquid —*n.* the condition of simmering —**simmer down 1.** to simmer, as a liquid, until little is left ☆**2.** to become calm; cool off

Si·mon (sī′mən) [LL. < Gr. < Heb. *shim′ōn,* lit., heard] **1.** a masculine name **2.** *Bible* one of the twelve apostles, called *Peter* or *Simon Peter*

Simon Le·gree (lə grē′) **1.** the wicked slave overseer in H. B. STOWE's novel *Uncle Tom's Cabin* **2.** any cruel supervisor

Simon Ma·gus (mā′gəs) *Bible* a Samaritan magician who tried to buy information about spiritual matters: Acts 8:9–24

si·mon-pure (sī′mən pyoor′) *adj.* [after *Simon Pure,* a Quaker in S. Centlivre's play *A Bold Stroke for a Wife* (1718)] genuine; authentic

si·mo·ny (sī′mə nē, sim′ə-) *n.* [< OFr. < ML. *simonia* < SIMON MAGUS] the buying or selling of sacred or spiritual things, as church offices

si·moom (si mōōm′) *n.* [< Ar. < *samma,* to poison] a very strong, hot wind blowing sand in the African and Asiatic deserts: also **si·moon′** (-mōōn′)

sim·pa·ti·co (sim pät′i kō, -pat′-) *adj.* [< It. *simpatico* or Sp. *simpático*] that gets along well with or goes well with another or others; compatible or congenial

sim·per (sim′pər) *vi.* [akin to MDu. *simperlijc,* dainty, affected] to smile in a silly, coy, or self-conscious way —*n.* such a smile —**sim′per·er** *n.* —**sim′per·ing·ly** *adv.*

sim·ple (sim′p'l) *adj.* **-pler, -plest** [OFr. < L. *simplex*] **1.** having only one part, feature, etc.; not compound or complex **2.** having few parts, etc.; not complicated or involved [a *simple* pattern] **3.** easy to do, solve, or understand, as a task, question, etc. **4.** without anything added [the *simple* facts] **5.** a) not highly decorated; unadorned [*simple* clothes] b) not luxurious; plain [*simple* tastes] **6.** pure; unadulterated [*simple* honesty] **7.** without slyness or trickery **8.** a) not showy or pretended; natural [her easy, *simple* ways] b) not sophisticated; naive **9.** of low rank or position; lowly or ordinary [*simple* peasants] **10.** a) stupid or foolish b) uneducated or ignorant **11.** *Bot.* a) consisting of one piece; whole b) not branched c) developing from a single carpel [a *simple* fruit] **12.** *Chem.* elementary or unmixed **13.** *Law* unconditional [in fee *simple*] **14.** *Zool.* not divided into parts; not compounded [a *simple* eye] —*n.* **1.** an ignorant or foolish person **2.** something having only one part, substance, etc. **3.** [Archaic] a plant or herb used in making medicines or a medicine made from it — see SYN· at EASY —**sim′ple·ness** *n.*

simple fraction a fraction in which both numerator and denominator are whole numbers, as 1/2

simple fracture a bone fracture in which the broken ends of bone do not cut through the skin

sim·ple-heart·ed (-här′tid) *adj.* sincere; unsophisticated

simple interest interest computed on principal alone, not on principal plus interest

simple machine any of the basic mechanical devices, including the lever, wheel and axle, pulley, wedge, screw, and inclined plane, on which the operation of complex machines is based

sim·ple-mind·ed (-mīn′did) *adj.* **1.** not subtle or clever; unsophisticated **2.** foolish; stupid; silly **3.** mentally retarded — **sim′ple-mind′ed·ly** *adv.* —**sim′ple-mind′ed·ness** *n.*

simple sentence a sentence having one main clause and no subordinate clauses (Example: The girl ran home.)

sim·ple·ton (sim′p'l tən) *n.* [< SIMPLE] a person who is stupid or easily tricked; fool

sim·plex (sim′pleks) *adj.* [L., simple] having only one part; not complex or compound

sim·plic·i·ty (sim plis′ə tē) *n., pl.* **-ties 1.** the fact of being simple, not complicated, not difficult, etc. **2.** the condition of being plain, not fancy, without ornaments, etc. **3.** a sincere or natural quality **4.** lack of sense; foolishness

sim·pli·fy (sim′plə fī′) *vt.* **-fied′, -fy′ing** to make simpler, less complex, etc. —**sim′pli·fi·ca′tion** *n.* —**sim′pli·fi′er** *n.*

sim·plis·tic (sim plis′tik) *adj.* making complex problems seem too simple; oversimplifying or oversimplified —**sim·plis′ti·cal·ly** *adv.*

Sim·plon (sim′plän; *Fr.* san plōn′) **1.** mountain pass in the Alps of S Switzerland: 6,589 ft. high **2.** railway tunnel near this pass: 12.4 mi. long

sim·ply (sim′plē) *adv.* **1.** in a simple way [to speak *simply*] **2.** merely; only [*simply* trying to help] **3.** absolutely; completely [she was *simply* furious]

sim·u·la·crum (sim′yoo lā′krəm) *n., pl.* **-cra** (-krə) [L. < *simulare:* see SIMULATE] **1.** an image; likeness **2.** a vague likeness; semblance

sim·u·late (sim′yoo lāt′) *vt.* **-lat′ed, -lat′ing** [< L. pp. of *simulare,* to feign < *simul,* likewise: for IE. base see SAME] **1.** to pretend to have or feel; feign [to *simulate* anger] **2.** to look or act like [an insect *simulating* a twig] —**sim′u·la′tion** *n.*

sim·u·la·tor (-lāt′ər) *n.* one that simulates; specif., a training device, as for astronauts, that creates artificially the conditions likely to be found in a real operation

☆**si·mul·cast** (sī′m'l kast′) *vt.* **-cast′** or **-cast′ed, -cast′ing** [SIMUL(TANEOUS) + (BROAD)CAST] to broadcast (a program, event, etc.) simultaneously by radio and television —*n.* a program, etc. so broadcast

si·mul·ta·ne·ous (sī′m'l tā′nē əs, -tän′yəs) *adj.* [< ML., ult. < L. *simul,* at the same time: for IE. base see SAME] occurring, done, existing, etc. together or at the same time —**see** SYN· at CONTEMPORARY —**si′mul·ta·ne′i·ty** (-tə nē′ə tē), **si′mul·ta′ne·ous·ness** *n.* —**si′mul·ta′ne·ous·ly** *adv.*

simultaneous equations two or more equations that have common solutions and are satisfied by the same values of the unknowns

sin (sin) *n.* [OE. *synne*] **1.** a) the breaking of religious or moral law, esp. when done on purpose b) the state of committing sins **2.** any wrong or fault [a *sin* against good taste] —*vi.* **sinned, sin′ning** to commit a sin

sin sine

Si·nai (sī′nī; *occas.* sī′ni ī′), **Mount** *Bible* the mountain where Moses received the Law from God: Ex. 19

Sinai Peninsula peninsula in NE Egypt, between the Gulf of Suez & an arm of the Red Sea: see map at SUEZ CANAL

since (sins) *adv.* [< OE. *siththan,* ult. < *sith,* after + *thon,* instrumental form of *thæt,* that] **1.** from then until now [she came Monday and has been here ever *since*] **2.** at some or any time between then and now [he was ill last week but has *since* recovered] **3.** before now; ago [gone long *since*] —*prep.* **1.** continuously from (the time given) until now [out walking since noon] **2.** during the period following [Jo's written twice *since* May] —*conj.* **1.** after the time that [two years *since* he died] **2.** continuously from the time when [lonely ever *since* he left] **3.** inasmuch as; because [*since* you're tired, let's go home]

sin·cere (sin sir′) *adj.* **-cer′er, -cer′est** [< MFr. < L. *sincerus,* clean] **1.** not pretending or fooling; truthful; honest [*sincere* in wanting to help] **2.** genuine; real [*sincere* grief] —**sin·cere′ly** *adv.* —**sin·cere′ness** *n.*

SYN. —**sincere** implies a lack of dishonesty or hypocrisy and a sticking to the simple truth [a *sincere* desire to help]; **unaffected** implies a natu-

---

fat, āpe, cär, ten, ēven, is, bīte; gō, hôrn, tōōl, look; oil, out; up, fur; get; joy; yet; chin; she; thin, then; zh, leisure; ŋ, ring; ə for *a* in *ago, e* in *agent, i* in *sanity, o* in *comply, u* in *focus;* ′ as in *able* (ā′b'l); Fr. bál; ë, Fr. coeur; ö, Fr. feu; Fr. mon; ð, Fr. coq; ü, Fr. duc; r, Fr. cri; H, G. ich; kh, G. doch; ‡foreign; ☆ Americanism; < derived from. See inside front cover.

ral, genuine simplicity and a freedom from artificial behavior [an *unaffected* writing style]; **heartfelt** emphasizes depth as well as sincerity of feeling, esp. as expressed in warm words, acts, etc. [he extended his *heartfelt* sympathy] —**ANT. false**

sin·cer·i·ty (sin ser′ə tē) *n., pl.* **-ties** a being sincere; honesty, genuineness, etc.

Sin·clair (sin kler′), **Up·ton** (**Beall, Jr.**) (up′t'n) 1878–1968; U.S. novelist & socialist

Sind (sind) region in S Pakistan, in the lower Indus River valley

sine (sīn) *n.* [ML. *sinus* (< L., a curve), used as transl. of Ar. *jaib*, lit., bosom of a garment] *Trigonometry* the ratio between the side opposite a given acute angle in a right triangle and the hypotenuse

‡**si·ne** (sī′nē, sē′nā) *prep.* [L.] without

si·ne·cure (sī′nə kyoor, sin′ə-) *n.* [< ML. < L. *sine*, without + *cura*, care] **1.** a paid church office not involving spiritual care of members **2.** a job or position for which one is paid well without having to do much work or take much responsibility

si·ne di·e (sī′nē dī′ē, sin′ā dē′ā) [LL.] without (a) day (being set for meeting again); for an indefinite period of time [to adjourn an assembly *sine die*]

si·ne qua non (sī′nē kwä nän′, sin′ā kwä nōn′) [L., without which not] something absolutely necessary

sin·ew (sin′yoo) *n.* [OE. *seonu*] **1.** a tendon **2.** muscular power; strength [a man of *sinew*] **3.** [*often pl.*] any source of power or strength [schools are the *sinews* of democracy] —*vt.* to strengthen as with sinews

sin·ew·y (-yoo wē) *adj.* **1.** of or like sinew; tough **2.** having many sinews, as a cut of meat **3.** having good muscular development [*sinewy* shoulders] **4.** vigorous; powerful [a *sinewy* style of writing]

sin·ful (sin′fəl) *adj.* full of sin; wicked —**sin′ful·ly** *adv.* —**sin′ful·ness** *n.*

sing (siŋ) *vi.* **sang** or now rarely **sung, sung, sing′ing** [OE. *singan* < IE. base *sengwh-*, to sing] **1.** *a)* to produce musical sounds with the voice *b)* to perform musical selections vocally **2.** to use song in description, praise, etc. [of thee I *sing*] **3.** *a)* to make musical sounds like those of the human voice, as a songbird *b)* to whistle, buzz, hum, etc., as a teakettle, bee, etc. **4.** to admit of being sung [this piece does not *sing* well] **5.** to be happy; rejoice [his heart *sang*] —*vt.* **1.** to perform by singing [to *sing* a song] **2.** to chant (part of a church service, etc.) **3.** to describe, announce, etc. in song [to *sing* someone's praises] **4.** to bring or put by singing [to *sing* a baby to sleep] —*n.* [Colloq.] **1.** a singing by a group gathered for the purpose **2.** such a gathering of people —**sing out** [Colloq.] to speak or call out loudly —**sing′a·ble** *adj.* —**sing′er** *n.*

sing. singular

sing-a·long (siŋ′ə lôŋ′) *n.* [Colloq.] an informal gathering of people to join in the singing of songs

Sin·ga·pore (siŋ′gə pôr′, siŋ′ə-) **1.** island off the S tip of the Malay Peninsula **2.** country made up of this island & several nearby islets: a member of the Commonwealth: 225 sq. mi.; pop. 2,110,000 **3.** its capital, a seaport: pop. c.1,000,000

singe (sinj) *vt.* **singed, singe′ing** [OE. *sengan*] **1.** to burn slightly or on the surface only **2.** to hold in or near a flame so as to burn off bristles or feathers [to *singe* a chicken] —*n.* a slight burn —see SYN. at BURN¹ —**sing′er** *n.*

Sin·gha·lese (siŋ′gə lēz′, -lēs′) *adj., n., pl.* **-lese′** same as SINHALESE

sin·gle (siŋ′g'l) *adj.* [< OFr. < L. *singulus*: for IE. base see SAME] **1.** *a)* one only; one and no more [pulled by a *single* horse] *b)* distinct from others of the same kind [every *single* time] **2.** without another; alone [he faced the mob *single* and unarmed] **3.** of or for one person or family [a *single* bed; a *single* house] **4.** between two persons only [*single* combat] **5.** unmarried [the tax rate for *single* persons] **6.** having only one part; not double, compound, etc. **7.** the same for all; uniform [a *single* scale of pay] **8.** being a whole, or unbroken [forming a *single* front] **9.** having only one row of petals: said of flowers and plants **10.** honest; sincere [with steady, *single* dedication to the cause] —*vt.* **-gled, -gling** **1.** to select from others (usually with *out*) [the teacher *singled* him out for praise] ☆**2.** *Baseball* to advance (a runner) by hitting a single —*vi.* ☆*Baseball* to hit a single —*n.* **1.** a single person or thing; specif., *a)* a hotel room, a ticket, etc. for one person ☆*b)* a one-dollar bill *c)* [Colloq.] a phonograph record with a single, short performance, as of popular music, on each side ☆**2.** *Baseball* a hit by which the batter reaches first base **3.** [*pl.*] *Tennis*, etc. a match with only one player on each side —**sin′gle·ness** *n.*

sin·gle-breast·ed (-bres′tid) *adj.* overlapping over the breast just enough to be fastened with one button or one row of buttons, as a coat

single entry a system of bookkeeping in which a single account is kept, usually of cash and of debts owed to and by the company or firm in question

single file **1.** a single column of persons or things, one directly behind another **2.** in such a column [to march *single file*]

☆**sin·gle-foot** (-foot′) *n.* the gait of a horse in which the legs on the same side move together, but each foot falls separately —*vi.* to move with this gait

sin·gle-hand·ed (-han′did) *adj.* **1.** having only one hand **2.** using or requiring the use of only one hand [a *single-handed* sword] **3.** done or working alone [a *single-handed* victory] — *adv.* **1.** by means of only one hand **2.** without help [he won the fight *single-handed*] —**sin′gle-hand′ed·ly** *adv.* —**sin′gle-hand′ed·ness** *n.*

sin·gle-heart·ed (-här′tid) *adj.* honest; sincere —**sin′gle-heart′ed·ly** *adv.* —**sin′gle-heart′ed·ness** *n.*

sin·gle-mind·ed (-mīn′did) *adj.* **1.** *same as* SINGLE-HEARTED **2.** with only one aim or purpose —**sin′gle-mind′ed·ly** *adv.* — **sin′gle-mind′ed·ness** *n.*

sin·gle-space (-spās′) *vt., vi.* **-spaced′, -spac′ing** to type (copy) so that a blank line is not left between lines

☆**single standard** a moral code with the same standard of conduct for men and women alike, esp. in matters of sex

sin·gle·stick (-stik′) *n.* **1.** a swordlike stick formerly used for fencing **2.** the sport of fencing with such sticks

sin·glet (siŋ′glit) *n.* [Brit.] a man's undershirt or jersey

☆**single tax** **1.** a system of taxation with only one tax, as on the value of land **2.** such a tax —**sin′gle-tax′** *adj.*

sin·gle·ton (siŋ′g'l tən) *n.* **1.** the only playing card held by a player in a given suit **2.** a single thing, all by itself

☆**sin·gle-track** (-trak′) *adj. same as* ONE-TRACK

☆**sin·gle-tree** (-trē′) *n.* [< earlier *swingletree* < ME. *swingle*, a rod + *tre*, a tree] a crossbar at the front of a wagon, etc., to which the traces of a horse's harness are hooked

sin·gly (siŋ′glē) *adv.* **1.** as a single, separate person or thing; alone [dealing with each problem *singly*] **2.** one by one [they entered *singly*] **3.** without help; unaided

SINGLETREE

Sing Sing (siŋ′siŋ′) a N.Y. State penitentiary at Ossining

sing·song (siŋ′sôŋ′, -säŋ′) *n.* **1.** *a)* a steady, boring rise and fall of tone, as in speaking *b)* speech, tones, etc. marked by this **2.** monotonous rhyme or rhythm in verse —*adj.* in or like a singsong

sin·gu·lar (siŋ′gyə lər) *adj.* [< OFr. < L. < *singulus*, SINGLE] **1.** being the only one of its kind; unique [a *singular* specimen] **2.** extraordinary; remarkable [*singular* beauty] **3.** strange; odd [a *singular* remark] **4.** *Gram.* describing or of number when it refers to only one —*n. Gram.* **1.** the singular number **2.** the singular form of a word **3.** a word in singular form —**sin′gu·lar′i·ty** (-lar′ə tē) *n., pl.* **-ties** —**sin′gu·lar·ly** *adv.*

sin·gu·lar·ize (siŋ′gyə lə rīz′) *vt.* **-ized′, -iz′ing** to make singular

Sin·ha·lese (sin′hə lēz′, sin′ə-; -lēs′) *adj.* of Ceylon, its principal people, their language, etc. —*n.* **1.** *pl.* **-lese′** any member of the Sinhalese people **2.** their language

sin·is·ter (sin′is tər) *adj.* [< L. *sinister*, left-hand or unlucky (side)] **1.** of or on the left-hand side (on a coat of arms, the right of the viewer) **2.** threatening harm, evil, etc.; ominous [*sinister* storm clouds] **3.** evil or dishonest, esp. in a dark, mysterious way [a *sinister* plot] **4.** unfortunate or disastrous [a *sinister* fate] —**sin′is·ter·ly** *adv.* —**sin′is·ter·ness** *n.*

sin·is·tral (sin′is trəl) *adj.* [OFr. < L.: see prec.] **1.** on the left-hand side; left **2.** left-handed —**sin′is·tral·ly** *adv.*

sin·is·trorse (sin′is trôrs′) *adj.* [< ModL. < L. < *sinister*, left + pp. of *vertere*, to turn] *Bot.* twining upward to the left, as the stems of some vines

Si·nit·ic (si nit′ik) *n.* [see SINO-, -ITE, & -IC] a branch of Sino-Tibetan, including Chinese languages —*adj.* of China, the Chinese, their languages, etc.

sink (siŋk) *vi.* **sank** or **sunk, sunk** or obs. **sunk′en, sink′ing** [OE. *sincan*] **1.** to go beneath the surface of water, snow, etc.

and be partly or completely covered **2.** *a)* to go down slowly [the balloon *sank* to the earth] *b)* to seem to come down, as the sun **3.** to become lower in level, as a lake **4.** to decrease in degree, volume, or strength, as wind, flames, a sound, etc. **5.** to become less in value or amount, as prices **6.** to seem to become hollow or shrunken, as the cheeks **7.** to pass gradually (*into* sleep, despair, silence, etc.) **8.** to approach death; fail [the patient is *sinking* rapidly] **9.** *a)* to lose social position, reputation, wealth, etc. [he *sank* in her eyes] *b)* to lose or abandon one's moral values and lower oneself (*to* an unworthy action) **10.** to become absorbed; penetrate [the experience *sank* into his memory] —*vt.* **1.** to cause to sink; make go beneath a surface, make go down, etc. [he *sank* the spade into the ground] **2.** to make (a well, engraved design, etc.) by digging, drilling, or cutting **3.** *a)* to invest (money, capital, etc.) *b)* to lose by investing **4.** to hold back or hide (evidence, identity, etc.) **5.** to defeat; undo; ruin [if they find out, we're *sunk*] ☆**6.** *Sports* to put (a basketball) through the basket or (a golf ball) into the hole, and so score —*n.* **1.** a cesspool or sewer **2.** any place or thing thought of as morally bad **3.** a basin, as in a kitchen, with a drainpipe and, usually, a water supply ☆**4.** *Geol. a)* an area of slightly sunken land, esp. one in which water collects *b)* *same as* SINKHOLE (sense 2) —**sink in** [Colloq.] to be understood, esp. with difficulty —**sink′a·ble** *adj.*

sink·er (siŋ′kər) *n.* **1.** a person or thing that sinks **2.** a lead weight used in fishing ☆**3.** [Colloq.] a doughnut

sink·hole (siŋk′hōl′) *n.* **1.** *same as* CESSPOOL ☆ **2.** *Geol.* a hollow into which surface water flows to join an underground drainage system

Sin·kiang (sin′kyaŋ′; *Chin.* shin′jyäŋ′) autonomous region of NW China, between Tibet & U.S.S.R.: 635,830 sq. mi.

sinking fund a fund made up of sums of money set aside from time to time and usually invested at interest, to pay a debt, meet expenses, etc.

sin·less (sin′lis) *adj.* without sin; innocent —**sin′less·ly** *adv.* —**sin′less·ness** *n.*

sin·ner (-ər) *n.* a person who sins; wrongdoer

Sinn Fein (shin′ fān′) [Ir., we ourselves] an early 20th-cent. Irish revolutionary movement working for independence and to revive Irish culture —**Sinn′ Fein′er**

Si·no- [< Fr. < LL. < Gr. *Sinai*, an Oriental people] *a combining form meaning:* **1.** of the Chinese people or language **2.** Chinese and

Si·nol·o·gy (sī näl′ə jē, si-) *n.* [SINO- + -LOGY] the study of Chinese languages, customs, etc. —**Si·no·log·i·cal** (sī′nə läj′i-k'l, sin′ə-) *adj.* —**Si·nol′o·gist** *n.*

Si·no-Ti·bet·an (sī′nō ti bet′'n, sin′ō-) *adj.* designating or of a family of languages of central and southeastern Asia, including Sinitic, Tibetan, and Burmese —*n.* this family

sin·ter (sin′tər) *n.* [G., akin to CINDER] a mass of fine metal particles fused together by heating below the melting point —*vi., vt.* to become or make into a sinter

sin·u·ate (sin′yoo wit; *also, and for v. always,* -wāt′) *adj.* [< L. pp. of *sinuare*, to bend < *sinus*, a bend] **1.** *same as* SINUOUS **2.** *Bot.* having a notched, wavy margin, as some leaves —*vi.* -at′ed, -at′ing to wind in and out —**sin′u·ate·ly** *adv.*

sin·u·os·i·ty (sin′yoo wäs′ə tē) *n.* **1.** the state or quality of being sinuous **2.** *pl.* -ties a sinuous turn or movement

sin·u·ous (sin′yoo wəs) *adj.* [< L. < *sinus*, a bend] **1.** bending or winding in and out [a *sinuous* river] **2.** not straightforward or direct —**sin′u·ous·ly** *adv.*

si·nus (sī′nəs) *n.* [L., a bent surface] **1.** a bend or curve **2.** a cavity, hollow, or passage; specif., *Anat., Zool. a)* any air cavity in the skull opening into a nasal cavity *b)* a channel for venous blood **3.** a channel leading from a pus-filled cavity

si·nus·i·tis (sī′nə sīt′əs) *n.* [ModL.: see SINUS & -ITIS] inflammation of a sinus or sinuses, esp. of the skull

Si·on (sī′ən) *var. of* ZION

-sion (shən; *sometimes* zhən) [< L. *-sio*] *a suffix meaning* act, quality, condition, or result of [discussion, confusion]

Siou·an (sōō′ən) *adj.* designating or of a language family of N. American Indians of the west central U.S., central Canada, etc.: it includes Dakota, Crow, etc. —*n.* this family of languages

Sioux (sōō) *n., pl.* **Sioux** (sōō, sōōz) [Fr. < Ojibway dim. of *nadowe*, an adder, hence, an enemy] *same as* DAKOTA[1] (*n.* 1 & 2) —*adj. same as* DAKOTA[1] (*adj.* 1)

Sioux City city in W Iowa, on the Missouri River: pop. 86,000
Sioux Falls city in southeastern S.Dak.: pop. 72,000

sip (sip) *vt., vi.* **sipped, sip′ping** [akin to LowG. *sippen:* for IE. base see SUCK] to drink a little at a time —*n.* **1.** the act of sipping **2.** a small quantity sipped —**sip′per** *n.*

si·phon (sī′fən) *n.* [Fr. < L. < Gr. *siphōn*, a tube] **1.** a bent tube for carrying liquid out over the edge of a container to a lower level by means of the atmospheric pressure on the surface of the liquid: the tube must be filled, as by suction, before flow will start **2.** *same as* SIPHON BOTTLE **3.** a tubelike organ, as in a cuttlefish, for drawing in or forcing out liquids —*vt., vi.* to draw off, or pass, as through a siphon [to *siphon* gasoline from a tank] —**si′phon·al** (-'l) *adj.*

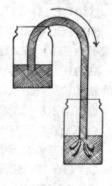

SIPHON

siphon bottle a heavy, sealed bottle containing carbonated water under pressure: the water can be squirted out by means of a valve and nozzle at the top

si·pho·no·phore (sī fän′ə fôr′, sī′fə ne-) *n.* [< Gr. *siphōn*, a tube + -PHORE] a small, transparent, often colored hydrozoan that swims or floats in the sea

Si·quei·ros (sē ke′rōs), (José) **Da·vid Al·fa·ro** (dä vēd′ äl fä′rō) 1896-1974; Mex. painter, esp. of murals

sir (sur) *n.* [< *sire:* see SIRE] **1.** [*sometimes* S-] a respectful term of address used to a man: not followed by the name and often used in the salutation of a letter [Dear *Sir*] **2.** [S-] the title used before the name of a knight or baronet [*Sir* Walter Raleigh] **3.** [Archaic] a term of address used with the title of a man's office, etc. [*sir* judge]

sire (sīr) *n.* [< OFr., a master < L. *senior:* see SENIOR] **1.** a title of respect used in talking to a king **2.** [Poet.] a father or forefather **3.** the male parent of an animal —*vt.* **sired, sir′ing** to be the male parent of: said esp. of animals

si·ren (sī′rən) *n.* [< OFr., ult. < Gr. *Seirēn*] **1.** *Gr. & Rom. Myth.* any of several sea nymphs whose sweet singing lured sailors to their death on rocky coasts **2.** a woman who attracts and tempts men **3.** a device using steam or air driven against a rotating disk to make a loud, wailing sound, esp. as a warning signal —*adj.* of or like a siren; dangerously attractive

si·re·ni·an (sī rē′nē ən) *n.* [ModL. *Sirenia*, name of the order + -AN] any of several large, vegetarian sea mammals, as the dugong, with a blunt snout and a large tail fluke

Si·ret (si ret′) river in SE Europe, flowing from the Carpathian Mountains southeast into the Danube: 450 mi.

Sir·i·us (sir′ē əs) [L. < Gr. *Seirios*, lit., the scorcher] *same as* DOG STAR (sense 1)

sir·loin (sur′loin) *n.* [< MFr. < OFr. *sur*, over < *loigne*, loin] a choice cut of meat, esp. of beef, from the loin end just in front of the rump

si·roc·co (sə räk′ō) *n., pl.* -cos [It. < Ar. *sharq*, the east] **1.** a hot, stifling wind blowing from the Libyan deserts into southern Europe **2.** any wind like this

sir·rah, sir·ra (sir′ə) *n.* [< SIR] [Archaic] a term showing contempt, used in speaking to a man

sir·up (sir′əp, sur′-) *n. same as* SYRUP —**sir′up·y** *adj.*

☆ **sis** (sis) *n. colloq. shortened form of* SISTER

si·sal (sī′s'l) *n.* [< *Sisal*, Yucatán, a former seaport] **1.** a strong fiber obtained from a widely grown agave native to southern Mexico, used for making rope, insulation, etc. **2.** the agave itself Also **sisal hemp**

☆ **sis·sy** (sis′ē) *n., pl.* -sies [dim. of SIS] [Colloq.] **1.** a man or boy who acts in a way that is considered not manly **2.** a timid person or coward —*adj.* [Colloq.] of or like a sissy: also **sis′si-fied′** (-ə fīd′) —**sis′sy·ish** *adj.*

sis·ter (sis′tər) *n.* [ON. *systir*] **1.** a female as she is related to other children of her parents **2.** a close friend who is like a sister **3.** a female fellow member of the same race, religion, profession, organization, etc. **4.** a member of a female religious order; nun **5.** a thing that is thought of as feminine and that resembles or is closely related to some other thing [the sun's pale *sister*, the moon] **6.** [Brit.] a nurse, esp. a head nurse —*adj.* related as sisters [*sister* ships]

sis·ter·hood (-hood′) *n.* **1.** the state of being a sister or sisters **2.** an association of women united in a common interest, work, belief, etc.

sis·ter-in-law (-in lô′) *n., pl.* **sis′ters-in-law′** **1.** the sister of one's husband or wife **2.** the wife of one's brother **3.** the wife of the brother of one's husband or wife

sis·ter·ly (-lē) *adj.* **1.** of or like that of a sister **2.** friendly, kind, loving, etc. —**sis′ter·li·ness** *n.*

Sis·tine Chapel (sis′tēn) [< It. (after Pope *Sixtus* IV)] the principal chapel in the Vatican, with frescoes by Michelangelo

Sis·y·phus (sis′ə fəs) *Gr. Myth.* a greedy king whose punishment in Hades was to roll a heavy stone uphill without success since it always rolled down again

sit (sit) *vi.* **sat, sit′ting** [OE. *sittan* < IE. base *sed-*, to sit, from which also comes L. *sedere*] **1.** *a)* to rest the body on the buttocks, as on a chair *b)* to rest on the haunches with forelegs braced [the dog *sat* perfectly still] *c)* to perch, as a bird **2.** to cover eggs with the body to hatch them [a *sitting* hen] **3.** *a)* to occupy a seat as a judge, legislator, etc. [to *sit* in the senate] *b)* to be in session, as a court **4.** to pose, as for a portrait **5.** to be or remain inactive [her bicycle *sits* all day in the garage] **6.** to be located [a house *sitting* on a hill] **7.** to hang on the wearer [the coat *sits* loosely at the back] **8.** to rest or lie as specified [cares *sit* lightly on him] ☆**9.** *same as* BABY-SIT —*vt.* **1.** to cause to sit [to *sit* oneself down] **2.** to stay seated on [she sits her horse well] **3.** to have seating space for [this table *sits* six] —*n.* [Colloq.] the time spent seated, esp. while waiting —**sit back 1.** to relax **2.** to be passive; do nothing —**sit down** to take a seat —**sit in** to take part; attend (often with *on*) —**sit on** (or **upon**) **1.** to be on (a jury, committee, etc.) **2.** to investigate **3.** [Colloq.] to hold back or conceal information about —**sit out 1.** to stay until the end of **2.** to stay seated during or take no part in (a dance, game, etc.) —**sit up 1.** to rise to a sitting position **2.** to sit with the back straight **3.** to put off going to bed **4.** [Colloq.] to become suddenly alert

si·tar (si tär′) *n.* [Hindi *sitār*] a musical instrument of India with a long, fretted neck, a gourd or gourds to make the tones deeper and fuller, and strings that are not plucked but that vibrate along with those that are —**si·tar′ist** *n.*

sit·com (sit′käm′) *n.* [Colloq.] *short for* SITUATION COMEDY

☆**sit-down** (sit′doun′) *n.* a strike in which strikers stay inside a factory, etc. refusing to work or leave until agreement is reached: in full, **sit-down strike**

site (sīt) *n.* [< L. *situs*, position < pp. of *sinere*, to put down] **1.** a piece of land for a certain purpose [a good *site* for a town] **2.** the place or scene of anything [a battle *site*] —*vt.* **sit′ed, sit′ing** to place on a site; locate

SITAR

sith (sith) *adv., conj., prep.* [OE. *siththa*] *archaic form of* SINCE

sit-in (sit′in′) *n.* a demonstration, as for civil rights, in which a group sits down in a public place and refuses to leave

sit·ter (sit′ər) *n.* one that sits; specif., ☆*a) short for* BABY SITTER *b)* a brooding hen

sit·ting (sit′iŋ) *n.* **1.** the act or position of one that sits **2.** a session or meeting, as of a court **3.** a period of being seated at some activity [to read a book in one *sitting*] **4.** *a)* a brooding upon eggs, as by a hen *b)* a clutch of eggs being hatched —*adj.* that sits; seated

Sitting Bull 1834?–90; Sioux Indian chief whose tribe killed all the attacking troops of General Custer (1876)

sitting duck [Colloq.] ☆an easy target

sitting room *same as* LIVING ROOM

sit·u·ate (sich′ōō wāt′) *vt.* **-at′ed, -at′ing** [< ML. pp. of *situare*, to place < L. *situs*, SITE] to put in a certain place or position; place; locate

sit·u·at·ed (-id) *adj.* **1.** placed with regard to site or position; located [situated in the suburbs] **2.** placed with regard to the conditions, esp. the financial conditions, that affect one [comfortably situated]

sit·u·a·tion (sich′ōō wā′shən) *n.* **1.** location; position **2.** a place; locality **3.** condition as caused by circumstances [the election has created an interesting *situation*] **4.** *a)* a combination of circumstances at a given time in real life or in the plot of a play, novel, etc. *b)* a difficult state of affairs **5.** a job [looking for a *situation* as a clerk] —**see SYN.** at POSITION

sit·u·a·tion·al (-'l) *adj.* of, resulting from, or changed to fit a specific situation [situational ethics] —**sit′u·a′tion·al·ly** *adv.*

situation comedy a comedy, esp. a TV comedy series, made up of episodes in the lives of stock characters

☆**sit-up, sit·up** (sit′up′) *n.* an exercise in which a person lying flat on the back rises to a sitting position without using the hands or bending the legs

si·tus (sīt′əs) *n.* [L.: see SITE] position or location; esp., the normal position, as of a bodily organ or plant part

sitz bath (sits, zits) [< G. *sitzbad*, a sitting bath] **1.** a bath in which only the hips and buttocks are covered, usually taken for medical reasons **2.** the tub or basin for this

Si·va (sē′və, shē′-) Hindu god of destruction and reproduction, a member of the supreme Hindu trinity: see BRAHMA, VISHNU —**Si′va·ism** *n.* —**Si′va·is′tic** *adj.*

Si·van (sē vän′, siv′ən) *n.* [Heb.] *see* JEWISH CALENDAR

six (siks) *adj.* [OE. *sex*] totaling one more than five —*n.* **1.** the cardinal number between five and seven; 6; VI **2.** anything having six units or members, or numbered six —**at sixes and sevens** [Colloq.] **1.** in confusion or disorder **2.** at odds; disagreeing

six·fold (siks′fōld′) *adj.* [see -FOLD] **1.** having six parts **2.** having six times as much or as many —*adv.* six times as much or as many

six·pence (-pəns) *n.* **1.** the sum of six British (old) pennies **2.** a British coin of this value, not minted since 1971

six·pen·ny (-pen′ē, -pə nē) *adj.* **1.** worth or costing sixpence **2.** of small worth; cheap **3.** designating a size of nails, two inches long

☆**six-shoot·er** (-shōōt′ər) *n.* [Colloq.] a revolver that fires six shots without reloading: also **six′-gun′**

six·teen (siks′tēn′) *adj.* [OE. *syxtene*] six more than ten —*n.* the cardinal number between fifteen and seventeen; 16; XVI

six·teenth (siks′tēnth′) *adj.* **1.** coming after fifteen others in a series; 16th **2.** designating any of the sixteen equal parts of something —*n.* **1.** the one following the fifteenth **2.** any of the sixteen equal parts of something; 1/16

sixteenth note *Music* a note held one sixteenth as long as a whole note: see illustration at NOTE

sixth (siksth) *adj.* [OE. *sixta*] **1.** coming after five others in a series; 6th **2.** designating any of the six equal parts of something —*n.* **1.** the one following the fifth **2.** any of the six equal parts of something; 1/6 **3.** *Music a)* the sixth tone of an ascending diatonic scale, or a tone five degrees above or below any given tone *b)* the interval between two such tones, or a combination of them —**sixth′ly** *adv.*

sixth sense the ability to know things by intuition, thought of as a sense in addition to the commonly accepted five senses

six·ti·eth (siks′tē ith) *adj.* **1.** coming after fifty-nine others in a series; 60th **2.** designating any of the sixty equal parts of something —*n.* **1.** the one following the fifty-ninth **2.** any of the sixty equal parts of something; 1/60

six·ty (siks′tē) *adj.* [OE. *sixtig*] six times ten —*n., pl.* **-ties** the cardinal number between fifty-nine and sixty-one; 60; LX —**the sixties** the numbers or years, as of a century, from sixty through sixty-nine

six·ty-fourth note (-fôrth′) *Music* a note held one sixty-fourth as long as a whole note: see illustration at NOTE

siz·a·ble (sī′zə b'l) *adj.* quite large or bulky: also **siz′a·ble** —**siz′a·ble·ness** *n.* —**siz′a·bly** *adv.*

size[1] (sīz) *n.* [< OFr. *sise*, short for *assise*: see ASSIZE] **1.** that quality of a thing which determines how much space it occupies; dimensions [the *size* of a room] **2.** any of a series of graded classifications of measure for goods [size ten shoes] **3.** *a)* extent, amount, etc. [an undertaking of great *size*] *b)* fairly large amount, dimensions, etc. [no park of any *size* in that city] **4.** [Colloq.] true state of affairs [that's the *size* of it] —*vt.* **sized, siz′ing 1.** to make according to a given size **2.** to arrange according to size —**of a size** of one or the same size —☆**size up** [Colloq.] **1.** to make an estimate of; judge **2.** to meet requirements —**siz′er** *n.*

size[2] (sīz) *n.* [ME. *syse*] any thin, pasty or gluey substance used to glaze or stiffen paper, cloth, etc. —*vt.* **sized, siz′ing** to apply size to

-sized (sīzd) *a combining form meaning* having (a specified) size [small-*sized*] : also **-size** [*life-size*]

siz·ing (sī′ziŋ) *n.* **1.** *same as* SIZE[2] **2.** the act or process of applying such size

siz·zle (siz′'l) *vi.* **-zled, -zling** [echoic] **1.** to make a hissing sound when in contact with heat, as water on hot metal **2.** to be extremely hot **3.** to simmer with barely controlled emotion, esp. with rage —*vt.* to make sizzle —*n.* a sizzling sound

☆**siz·zler** (-lər) *n.* [Colloq.] something hot (in various senses), as a very hot day

S.J. Society of Jesus

Skag·er·rak (skag'ə rak') arm of the North Sea, between Norway & Denmark

skald (skôld, skäld) *n.* [ON. *skáld*] any ancient Scandinavian poet, specif. of the Viking period —**skald'ic** *adj.*

skate[1] (skāt) *n.* [assumed sing. < Du. *schaats*, a skate < ONormFr. < OFr. *eschace*, stilt < Frank.] **1.** *a)* a long, narrow metal blade, or runner, in a frame that can be fastened to a shoe for gliding on ice *b)* a shoe with such a blade attached Also **ice skate 2.** a frame or shoe with two small wheels at the toe and two at the heel, for gliding on a sidewalk, etc.: also **roller skate 3.** the act of skating —*vi.* **skat'ed, skat'ing** to move along on skates —**skat'er** *n.*

skate[2] (skāt) *n., pl.* **skates, skate:** see PLURAL, II, D, I [ON. *skata*] any of various rays with a broad, flat body and short, spineless tail

☆ **skate·board** (skāt'bôrd') *n.* a short, narrow board with two wheels at each end, which one rides on, usually while standing

ske·dad·dle (ski dad''l) *vi.* **-dled, -dling** [coinage of Civil War period] [Colloq.] to run off; leave fast

☆ **skeet** (skēt) *n.* [ult. < ON. *skeyti*, a projectile] trapshooting in which the shooter fires from different angles, usually eight

skein (skān) *n.* [< MFr. *escaigne*] **1.** a quantity of thread or yarn wound in a coil **2.** a coil of hair, etc.

skel·e·ton (skel'ə t'n) *n.* [ModL. < Gr. *skeleton* (*sōma*), dried (body) < *skeletos*, dried up] **1.** the hard framework of an animal, supporting the tissues and protecting the organs; specif., all the bones or bony framework of a human being or other vertebrate **2.** anything like a skeleton; specif., *a)* a very lean or thin person or animal *b)* a supporting framework, as of a ship *c)* an outline, as of a novel —*adj.* of or like a skeleton; greatly reduced [a *skeleton* force] —**skeleton in the closet** some fact, as about a relative, kept secret because of shame —**skel'e·tal** (-t'l) *adj.*

skel·e·ton·ize (-īz') *vt.* **-ized', -iz'ing 1.** to reduce to a skeleton **2.** to outline (a story, report, etc.) **3.** to reduce (a work force, etc.) greatly in number or size

skeleton key a key with much of the bit filed away so that it can open any of various simple locks

Skel·ton (skel't'n), **John** 1460?-1529; Eng. poet

skep·tic (skep'tik) *adj.* [< L. < Gr. *skeptikos*, inquiring] of or being a skeptic —*n.* **1.** [S-] a member of any of the ancient Greek philosophical schools that denied the possibility of real knowledge **2.** a believer in philosophical skepticism **3.** one who habitually doubts or questions matters that most people accept **4.** one who doubts religious doctrines

skep·ti·cal (skep'ti k'l) *adj.* **1.** of or characteristic of skeptics or skepticism **2.** not easily convinced; doubting; questioning **3.** doubting the fundamental doctrines of religion —**skep'ti·cal·ly** *adv.*

skep·ti·cism (-siz'm) *n.* **1.** [S-] the doctrines of the ancient Greek Skeptics **2.** the philosophical doctrine that it is impossible to be certain of the truth of any knowledge **3.** skeptical or doubting attitude or state of mind, esp. about religious doctrines —see SYN. at UNCERTAINTY

sketch (skech) *n.* [Du. *schets* < It. *schizzo* < L. < Gr. *schedios*, extempore] **1.** a simple, rough drawing or design, done rapidly **2.** a brief description of main points; outline **3.** a short, light, informal story, description, skit, etc. —*vt., vi.* to make a sketch (of) —**sketch'a·ble** *adj.* —**sketch'er** *n.*

sketch·book (skech'book') *n.* **1.** a book of drawing paper for making sketches **2.** a book of literary sketches Also **sketch book**

sketch·y (-ē) *adj.* **sketch'i·er, sketch'i·est 1.** having the form of a sketch; not detailed **2.** not complete; inadequate [a *sketchy* report] —**sketch'i·ly** *adv.* —**sketch'i·ness** *n.*

skew (skyōō) *vi.* [< ONormFr. *eskiuer*, altered < OFr. < OHG.: see ESCHEW] to take a slanting course; swerve or twist —*vt.* **1.** to make slanting or oblique; set at a slant **2.** to present or describe in an unfair or inaccurate way; distort [to *skew* the facts] —*adj.* **1.** slanting; oblique **2.** not symmetrical [*skew* distribution] —*n.* **1.** a slant or twist **2.** a slanting part or movement —**skew'ness** *n.*

skew·er (skyōō'ər) *n.* [< ON. *skifa*, a slice] **1.** a long pin used to hold meat together while cooking or as a brochette **2.** any similar pin or rod —*vt.* to fasten or pierce as with skewers

ski (skē; *Brit. also* shē) *n., pl.* **skis, ski** [Norw. < ON. *skith*, snowshoe, strip of wood] **1.** either of a pair of long, thin runners of wood, metal, etc., fastened to the shoes for gliding over snow **2.** a water ski: see WATER-SKI —*vi.* **skied** (skēd), **ski'ing 1.** to glide on skis, as down snow-covered hills **2.** short for WATER-SKI —**ski'er** *n.*

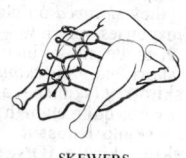

SKEWERS

skid (skid) *n.* [prob. < ON. *skith:* see SKI] ☆ **1.** a plank, log, etc. used as a support or as a track to slide or roll a heavy object on **2.** a low, movable platform for holding loads or stacks **3.** a runner in place of a wheel on an aircraft landing gear **4.** a sliding wedge or drag that acts as a brake when pressed against a wheel **5.** the act of skidding —*vt.* **skid'ded, skid'ding 1.** to brake or lock (a wheel) with a skid **2.** to support with or move on skids **3.** to cause (a wheel, vehicle, etc.) to skid —*vi.* **1.** to slide without turning, as a wheel when brakes are applied on a slippery surface **2.** to slide sideways, as a vehicle not gripping an icy road **3.** to slide sharply downward [prices *skidded* to a new low] —see SYN. at SLIDE —☆ **be on** (or **hit**) **the skids** [Slang] to be losing one's power or influence —☆ **put the skids under** [Slang] to hinder or cause to fail —**skid'der** *n.*

skid·dy (skid'ē) *adj.* **-di·er, -di·est** having a slippery surface on which vehicles are liable to skid

☆ **skid row** [altered < *skid road*, a trail for dragging logs, hence a section of town where loggers gathered] a section of a city where hobos, vagrants, derelicts, etc. gather

skiff (skif) *n.* [< MFr. < It. *schifo* < Gmc.] **1.** any light rowboat **2.** a long, narrow rowboat, esp. one with a centerboard, outrigger, and a small sail

☆ **ski jump 1.** a jump made by a skier after skiing down a long slope or track **2.** such a slope or track

☆ **ski lift** a motor-driven, endless cable, typically with seats attached, for carrying skiers up a slope

skill (skil) *n.* [ON. *skil*, distinction] **1.** great ability that comes from training, practice, etc.; expertness **2.** an art, craft, or science, esp. one involving the use of the hands or body **3.** ability in such an art, craft, or science

skilled (skild) *adj.* **1.** having skill; skillful **2.** having or requiring an ability gained by special experience or training [repairing watches is *skilled* work]

skil·let (skil'it) *n.* [< ? OFr. dim. of *escuelle*, basin < L. *scutella*, dim. of *scutra*, a dish] **1.** [Chiefly Brit.] a pot or kettle with a long handle **2.** a shallow pan with a handle, for frying food; frying pan

skill·ful, skil·ful (skil'fəl) *adj.* having or showing skill; expert [a *skillful* cook, performance, etc.] —**skill'ful·ly, skil'ful·ly** *adv.* —**skill'ful·ness, skil'ful·ness** *n.*

skim (skim) *vt.* **skimmed, skim'ming** [prob. akin to SCUM] **1.** *a)* to clear (a liquid) of floating matter *b)* to remove (floating matter) from a liquid **2.** to coat with a thin layer [a pond *skimmed* with ice] **3.** to look through (a book, etc.) quickly without reading carefully **4.** *a)* to glide swiftly over *b)* to throw so as to make bounce or ricochet lightly [*skim* a flat stone across water] —*vi.* **1.** to move along swiftly and lightly; glide [bugs *skimming* over the water] **2.** to read quickly or carelessly (*through* or *over* a book, etc.) **3.** to become thinly coated, as with scum —*n.* **1.** something skimmed **2.** the act of skimming **3.** a thin coating

SKI JUMP

HUMAN SKELETON

SKULL
VERTEBRAE
CLAVICLE
SCAPULA
STERNUM
HUMERUS
RIBS
VERTEBRAE
PELVIS
ULNA
RADIUS
CARPAL BONES
PHALANGES
FEMUR
PATELLA
TIBIA
FIBULA
TARSAL BONES
PHALANGES

fat, āpe, cär; ten, ēven; is, bīte; gō, hôrn, tōōl, look; oil, out; up, fur; get; joy; yet; chin; she; thin, then; zh, leisure; ŋ, ring; ə for a in ago, e in agent, i in sanity, o in comply, u in focus; ' as in able (ā'b'l); Fr. bàl; ë, Fr. coeur; ö, Fr. feu; Fr. mon; ô, Fr. coq; ü, Fr. duc; r, Fr. cri; H, G. ich; kh, G. doch; ‡foreign; ☆ Americanism; < derived from. See inside front cover.

skim·mer (skim′ər) *n.* **1.** one that skims **2.** a utensil for skimming liquids **3.** any of several sea birds that scoop up food while skimming over water ☆**4.** a hat, usually of straw, with a flat crown and a wide, straight brim

skim milk milk from which cream has been removed: also **skimmed milk**

skimp (skimp) *adj.* [prob. altered < SCRIMP] [Colloq.] *same as* SCANTY —*vi.* [Colloq.] **1.** to give or allow too little; be stingy [they *skimped* on clothes to save for a new home] **2.** to keep expenses very low —*vt.* [Colloq.] **1.** to do poorly or carelessly **2.** to be stingy in or toward; specif., to make too small, too short, etc. [she *skimped* material in making the dress]

skimp·y (skim′pē) *adj.* skimp′i·er, skimp′i·est [Colloq.] barely or not quite enough; scanty [a *skimpy* meal] —**skimp′i·ly** *adv.* —**skimp′i·ness** *n.*

skin (skin) *n.* [ON. *skinn:* for IE. base see SAW¹] **1.** the outer covering of the animal body **2.** this covering removed and prepared for use; pelt [a coat made of beaver *skins*] **3.** an outer layer somewhat like skin, as fruit rind, a film or scum, etc. **4.** a container made of animal skin, for holding liquids —*vt.* **skinned, skin′ning 1.** to cover as with skin **2.** *a*) to remove skin from [to *skin* a rabbit] *b*) to strip or peel off **3.** to injure by scraping (one's knee, etc.) **4.** [Colloq.] *a*) to cheat; swindle ☆*b*) to criticize harshly —*vi.* [Colloq.] **1.** to become covered with skin **2.** to climb (*up* or *down*) **3.** to move (*through*), pass (*by*), succeed, etc. by a tiny margin —☆**be no skin off one's nose** [Colloq.] to have no effect on one; be of no concern to one —**by the skin of one's teeth** by the tiniest margin; barely —☆**get under one's skin** [Colloq.] to anger or irritate one —**have a thick** (or **thin**) **skin** to be insensitive (or very sensitive) to criticism, etc. —**save one's skin** [Colloq.] to avoid death or injury —**skin alive** ☆**1.** [Colloq.] to scold or punish harshly **2.** [Colloq.] to defeat overwhelmingly —**skin′ner** *n.*

skin-deep (skin′dēp′) *adj.* **1.** penetrating no deeper than the skin [*skin-deep* cuts] **2.** without real significance; superficial [beauty is only *skin-deep*] —*adv.* so as to be skin-deep

skin diving underwater swimming in which the swimmer, without lines to the surface, is variously equipped with a face mask, flippers, a snorkel or scuba equipment, etc. —**skin′-dive′** (-dīv′) *vi.* -dived′, -div′ing —**skin diver**

skin·flint (-flint′) *n.* [lit., one who would skin a flint for economy] a stingy person; miser

☆**skin game** [Colloq.] **1.** a crooked gambling game **2.** any trick used in cheating people

skin grafting the surgical transplanting of skin (**skin graft**) to replace skin destroyed, as by burning

skink (skiŋk) *n.* [< L. < Gr. *skinkos*] a lizard with a very long, shiny body and short legs

skin·less (skin′lis) *adj.* without a skin, casing, etc.

skinned (skind) *adj.* having skin (of a specified kind) [dark-*skinned*]

skin·ny (skin′ē) *adj.* -ni·er, -ni·est **1.** of or like skin **2.** without much flesh; very thin —see SYN. at LEAN² —**skin′ni·ness** *n.*

☆**skin·ny-dip** (-dip′) *vi.* -dipped′, -dip′ping [Colloq.] to swim in the nude —*n.* [Colloq.] a swim in the nude

☆**skin-pop** (skin′päp′) *vt.* -popped′, -pop′ping [Slang] to inject (a narcotic drug) just beneath the skin: see also MAINLINE —**skin′-pop′per** *n.*

skin test any test for detecting the presence of a disease or allergy from the reaction of the skin to a test substance

skin·tight (skin′tīt′) *adj.* clinging closely to the skin; tightfitting [a *skintight* dress]

skip (skip) *vi.* skipped, skip′ping [prob. < Scand.] **1.** to leap, jump, etc. lightly; specif., to move along by hopping lightly on one foot and then the other **2.** to bounce off at an angle from a surface; ricochet **3.** to pass from one point to another, leaving out what lies between [*skip* from page 56 to page 64] ☆**4.** to be promoted in school beyond the next regular grade **5.** [Colloq.] to leave hurriedly; abscond —*vt.* **1.** to leap lightly over [to *skip* a brook] **2.** to pass over or leave out [I *skipped* lunch] **3.** to fail to attend a session of (school, church, etc.) **4.** to cause to skip or ricochet [to *skip* flat stones across a pond] ☆**5.** to promote to the school grade beyond the next regular one ☆**6.** [Colloq.] to leave (a town, etc.) hurriedly —*n.* **1.** *a*) an act of skipping; leap *b*) a skipping gait in which one makes light hops first on one foot and then on the other **2.** a passing over or leaving out —☆**skip it!** never mind! it doesn't matter!

SYN.—**skip** suggests a springing forward lightly and quickly, leaping first on one foot and then on the other, or, when used of nonliving things, a series of light, bouncing movements across a surface; **bound** implies longer leaps or bounces and more powerful, energetic movement than **skip** does;

hop suggests a single short jump, as on one leg, or a series of short, rather jerky jumps

ski pants pants that fit snugly at the ankles, worn for skiing and other winter sports

skip·jack (skip′jak′) *n., pl.* **-jacks′, -jack′:** see PLURAL, II, D, 1 any of several kinds of fish that leap out of, or play at the surface of, the water

ski·plane (skē′plān′) *n.* an airplane with skis for landing gear, for use on snow

ski pole either of a pair of light poles with a sharp tip, used by skiers as a help in climbing, keeping their balance, etc.

skip·per¹ (skip′ər) *n.* **1.** a person or thing that skips **2.** a small, heavy-bodied butterfly that darts about rapidly **3.** any of various skipping insects

skip·per² (skip′ər) *n.* [MDu. *schipper* < *schip,* a ship] **1.** the captain of a ship **2.** any leader, director, or captain —*vt.* to act as skipper of

skirl (skurl) *vt., vi.* [prob. < Scand.] [Scot. & Dial.] to sound out in shrill, piercing tones, as a bagpipe —*n.* a shrill sound, as of a bagpipe

skir·mish (skur′mish) *n.* [< MFr. < It. < *schermire,* to fight < Gmc.] **1.** a brief fight between small groups, usually a part of a battle **2.** any slight, unimportant conflict —*vi.* to take part in a skirmish —see SYN. at BATTLE —**skir′mish·er** *n.*

Skí·ros (skē′rôs) Gr. island of the N Sporades, in the Aegean Sea: c.80 sq. mi.

skirt (skurt) *n.* [ON. *skyrt,* shirt] **1.** that part of a dress, coat, robe, etc. that hangs below the waist **2.** a woman's garment that hangs down from the waist **3.** something like a skirt, as a flap covering the legs of a sofa or chair **4.** [*pl.*] the outer parts; outskirts, as of a city **5.** [Old Slang] a girl or woman —*vt.* **1.** to lie along or form the edge of **2.** *a*) to move along the edge of or pass around [the new highway will *skirt* our town] *b*) to miss narrowly **3.** to avoid (a difficult issue, problem, etc.) **4.** to border or edge with something —*vi.* to be on, or move along, the edge [a path *skirting* along the pond] —**skirt′er** *n.*

ski run a slope or course used for skiing

skit (skit) *n.* [prob. < Scand. var. of ON. *skjota,* to shoot] **1.** a short piece of satirical or humorous writing **2.** a short, comic theatrical sketch

☆**ski tow** a kind of ski lift for pulling skiers up a slope on their skis

skit·ter (skit′ər) *vi.* [< dial. *skite,* to dart about < Scand.] to skip or move along quickly or lightly, esp. over water

skit·tish (skit′ish) *adj.* [see SKIT & -ISH] **1.** lively or playful, esp. in a coy way **2.** easily frightened or very nervous [a *skittish* horse] **3.** fickle; undependable —**skit′tish·ly** *adv.* —**skit′tish·ness** *n.*

skit·tle (skit′'l) *n.* [prob. < Scand. word related to SHUTTLE] **1.** [*pl. with sing. v.*] a British form of ninepins in which a wooden disk or ball is used to knock down the pins **2.** any of these pins —**(not) all beer and skittles** (not) pure pleasure

skiv·vy (skiv′ē) *n., pl.* **-vies** [< ?] [Slang] **1.** a man's, esp. a sailor's, short-sleeved undershirt: usually **skivvy shirt 2.** [*pl.*] men's underwear

skoal (skōl) *interj.* [Dan. & Norw. *skaal,* a cup < ON. *skāl,* a bowl] to your health!: a toast

Sko·pje (skô′pye) city in SE Yugoslavia; capital of Macedonia: pop. 172,000

Skr., Skrt., Skt. Sanskrit

sku·a (skyōō′ə) *n.* [ModL., ult. < ON. *skūfr,* a tuft] any of several large, brown-and-white sea gulls, found in cold seas

☆**skul·dug·ger·y, skull·dug·ger·y** (skul dug′ər ē) *n.* [Early ModScot. *sculdudrie* < ?] [Colloq.] sneaky, dishonest behavior; trickery

skulk (skulk) *vi.* [prob. < LowG. *schulken* or Dan. *skulke*] to move about or hide in a sneaky, cowardly, or threatening way —*n.* a person who skulks —**skulk′er** *n.* —**skulk′ing·ly** *adv.*

skull (skul) *n.* [< Scand.] **1.** the bony framework of the head, enclosing the brain and sense organs **2.** the human head or mind [an empty *skull*]

skull and crossbones a picture of two crossed bones under a human skull, used as a symbol of death or danger, as on poisons

skull·cap (skul′kap′) *n.* a light, closefitting, brimless cap, usually worn indoors

☆**skunk** (skuŋk) *n.* [< AmInd. *segonku*] **1.** *a*) *pl.* **skunks, skunk:** see PLURAL, II, D, 1 a bushy-tailed mammal about the size of a cat: it has black fur with white stripes down its back, and sprays out a foul-smelling liquid when disturbed *b*) its fur **2.** [Colloq.] a mean, disgusting person —*vt.* [Slang] to defeat overwhelmingly in a game or contest

☆**skunk cabbage** a plant having large, cabbagelike leaves and a disagreeable smell

sky (skī) *n., pl.* **skies** [ON., a cloud: for IE. base see HIDE¹] **1.** [*often pl.*] the upper atmosphere, esp. with regard to its appearance [blue *skies,* a cloudy *sky*] **2.** the heavens, which seem to cover the earth like a dome; firmament **3.** heaven —*vt.* **skied** or **skyed, sky'ing** [Colloq.] to hit, throw, etc. high in the air —**out of a clear (blue) sky** without warning —**to the skies** without limits

sky blue a blue color like that of the sky on a clear day —**sky'-blue'** *adj.*

☆**sky·cap** (skī'kap') *n.* a porter, or red-cap, at an air terminal

☆**sky diving** the sport of jumping from an airplane and performing free-fall movements before opening the parachute —**sky'-dive'** (-dīv') *vi.* **-dived', -div'ing** —**sky diver**

Skye (skī), **Isle of** island of the Hebrides, off the W coast of Scotland: 643 sq. mi.

sky-high (skī'hī') *adj., adv.* **1.** very high **2.** so as to be completely blown apart; to pieces

☆**sky·jack** (skī'jak') *vt.* [Colloq.] to hijack (an aircraft) — **sky'jack'er** *n.* —**sky'jack'ing** *n.*

sky·lark (-lärk') *n.* a Eurasian lark, famous for the song it sings as it rises high into the sky —*vi.* [SKY + LARK²] to play or frolic

sky·light (-līt') *n.* a window in a roof or ceiling

sky·line (-līn') *n.* **1.** the line along which sky and earth seem to meet **2.** the outline, as of a city, seen against the sky

sky·rock·et (-räk'it) *n.* a firework rocket that explodes in mid-air in a shower of colored sparks —☆*vi., vt.* to rise or cause to rise rapidly [*meat prices skyrocketed*]

sky·sail (skī'sāl', -s'l) *n.* the small sail set above the royal at the top of a square-rigged mast

sky·scrap·er (-skrā'pər) *n.* ☆a very tall building

sky·ward (-wərd) *adv., adj.* toward the sky: also **sky'wards** *adv.*

sky·ways (-wāz') *n.pl.* routes of air travel

sky·writ·ing (-rīt'iŋ) *n.* the act or result of forming words, figures, etc. in the sky by trailing smoke from an airplane in flight —**sky'write'** *vi., vt.* **-wrote', -writ'ten, -writ'ing** —**sky'writ'er** *n.*

slab (slab) *n.* [ME. *slabbe*] **1.** a piece that is flat, broad, and fairly thick [a *slab* of concrete; a *slab* of bacon] **2.** a rough piece cut from the outside of a log

slack¹ (slak) *adj.* [OE. *slæc:* for IE. base see LAX] **1.** slow; sluggish [a *slack* pace] **2.** barely moving [a *slack* breeze] **3.** not busy or active; dull [a *slack* period] **4.** loose; not tight or taut [a *slack* tennis net] **5.** weak; lax [*slack* authority] **6.** careless or negligent [a *slack* workman] —*vt.* **1.** to make slack **2.** to slake —*vi.* **1.** to be or become slack; slacken **2.** to be idle, careless, or negligent [to *slack* on the job] —*adv.* in a slack manner —*n.* **1.** a part that is slack or hangs loose [take in the *slack* of the rope] **2.** a lack of tension; looseness **3.** a stopping of movement in a current; a dull period; lull —**slack off** to slacken —**slack up** to go more slowly —**slack'ness** *n.*

slack² (slak) *n.* [akin to Fl. *slecke,* dross, Du. *slak*] a mixture of small pieces of coal, coal dust, and dirt left from the screening of coal

slack·en (slak''n) *vt., vi.* **1.** to make or become less active, brisk, intense, etc. [*slacken* your pace] **2.** to relax or loosen [to *slacken* one's grip] —**slack'en·er** *n.*

slack·er (-ər) *n.* a person who avoids doing his work or duty

slacks (slaks) *n.pl.* trousers for men or women; esp., trousers that are not part of a suit

slack water the period between tides when the water is not moving in or out

slag (slag) *n.* [MLowG. *slagge*] **1.** the waste matter that is left after metal has been melted down from ore **2.** lava that looks like this —*vt., vi.* **slagged, slag'ging** to form into slag —**slag'gy** *adj.* **-gi·er, -gi·est**

slain (slān) *pp.* of SLAY

slake (slāk) *vt.* **slaked, slak'ing** [OE. *slacian* < *slæc,* SLACK¹] **1.** to make less strong by satisfying [to *slake* one's thirst with water] **2.** to put out (a fire) **3.** to produce a chemical change in (lime) by mixing it with water —*vi.* to become slaked

slaked lime *same as* CALCIUM HYDROXIDE

sla·lom (slä'ləm) *n.* [Norw., sloping trail] a downhill skiing race over a zigzag course —*vi.* to ski in a slalom

slam¹ (slam) *vt.* **slammed, slam'ming** [prob. < Scand.] **1.** to shut with force and noise [to *slam* a door] **2.** to hit, put, etc. with force and noise [to *slam* a baseball over the fence] ☆**3.** [Colloq.] to criticize harshly —*vi.* to shut, go into place, etc. with force and noise [the window *slammed* shut] —*n.* **1.** *a)* a heavy hitting, shutting, etc. *b)* the noise made by this ☆**2.** [Colloq.] a harsh criticism

slam² (slam) *n.* [< ?] *Bridge shortened form of* GRAND SLAM *or* LITTLE SLAM

slan·der (slan'dər) *n.* [< Anglo-Fr. < LL. *scandalum:* see SCANDAL] **1.** the speaking of a falsehood that harms a person's character or reputation: see LIBEL **2.** such a spoken falsehood —*vt.* to say something slanderous about —**slan'der·er** *n.*

slan·der·ous (-əs) *adj.* **1.** containing slander **2.** speaking slander —**slan'der·ous·ly** *adv.*

slang (slaŋ) *n.* [18th-c. cant < ?] **1.** orig., the specialized vocabulary of criminals, tramps, etc.: now usually called CANT¹ **2.** the specialized vocabulary of those in the same work, way of life, etc.: now usually called SHOPTALK, ARGOT, JARGON **3.** highly informal language that is usually avoided in formal speech and writing: it consists of both new words and existing words with new meanings and is usually fresh, colorful, or humorous and popular for only a short time —*vi.* to use slang or insulting talk

slang·y (slaŋ'ē) *adj.* **slang'i·er, slang'i·est 1.** of, like, or containing slang **2.** using much slang —**slang'i·ly** *adv.* —**slang'i·ness** *n.*

slant (slant) *vt., vi.* [< Scand.] **1.** to turn or lie in a direction that is not straight up and down or straight across; slope [the picture is hanging so that it *slants* to the left] ☆**2.** to write or tell so as to appeal to a particular point of view or to express a particular bias [this newspaper *slants* its news coverage] —*n.* **1.** *a)* a slanting surface, line, etc.; slope *b) same as* VIRGULE ☆**2.** *a)* a point of view or attitude [your advice gave me a new *slant* on life] *b)* a point of view that shows bias —*adj.* oblique; sloping —**slant'ing** *adj.* —**slant'ing·ly** *adv.*

slant rhyme rhyme in which the sounds are similar but not exactly the same, as in *lid* and *lad, wait* and *made*

slant·wise (slant'wīz') *adv.* so as to slant or slope; obliquely: also **slant'ways'** —*adj.* slanting; oblique

slap (slap) *n.* [LowG. *slapp:* echoic] **1.** *a)* a blow with something flat, as the palm of the hand *b)* the sound of this, or a sound like it **2.** an injury to pride, self-respect, etc., as an insult [a *slap* at her intelligence] —*vt.* **slapped, slap'ping 1.** to hit with something flat, specif. the palm of the hand **2.** to put, hit, etc. carelessly or with force [to *slap* a hat on one's head] —*vi.* to make a dull, sharp noise [waves *slapped* against the dock] —*adv.* **1.** [Colloq.] straight; directly [he ran *slap* into the wall] **2.** [Brit. Colloq.] abruptly —**slap down** [Colloq.] to blame, scold, or refuse sharply —**slap'per** *n.*

slap·dash (slap'dash') *n.* something done carelessly and hastily —*adv.* in a hasty, careless manner —*adj.* hasty, careless, etc.

☆**slap-hap·py** (-hap'ē) *adj.* [Slang] **1.** dazed, as by blows to the head **2.** silly or giddy

☆**slap·jack** (-jak') *n. same as* FLAPJACK

☆**slap·stick** (-stik') *n.* **1.** a device, formerly used by stage comedians, made of two wooden slats that slap together loudly when hit against something **2.** rough comedy full of noisy activity, horseplay, etc. —*adj.* characterized by such comedy

slash (slash) *vt.* [< ? OFr. *esclachier,* to break] **1.** to cut or wound with a sweeping stroke or strokes, as of a knife **2.** to whip viciously; lash **3.** to cut slits in (a fabric, dress, etc.), esp. so that underlying material shows through **4.** to reduce very much [to *slash* prices] **5.** to criticize harshly —*vi.* to make a sweeping motion with or as with something sharp —*n.* **1.** a sweeping stroke made as with a knife **2.** a cut made by such a stroke; gash **3.** *same as* VIRGULE **4.** a decorative slit in a fabric, dress, etc. ☆**5.** *a)* an open place in a forest, cluttered with branches, chips, etc. as from the cutting of timber *b)* such branches, chips, etc.

slash·ing (slash'iŋ) *adj.* **1.** harsh; violent **2.** dashing; spirited —*n.* **1.** the act of one that slashes **2.** *same as* SLASH (*n.* 4 & 5) —**slash'ing·ly** *adv.*

slat (slat) *n.* [OFr. *esclat,* fragment: for IE. base see CUTLASS]

1. a thin, narrow strip of wood, metal, etc. [*slats* of a Venetian blind] ☆**2.** [*pl.*] [Slang] *a*) the ribs *b*) the buttocks —*vt.* **slat′ted, slat′ting** to provide or make with slats

slate (slāt) *n.* [< OFr. fem. of *esclat*: see prec.] **1.** a hard, fine-grained rock that separates easily into thin, smooth layers **2.** its bluish-gray color: also **slate blue 3.** a thin piece of slate, esp. one used as a roofing tile or as a tablet for writing on with chalk ☆**4.** a list of candidates proposed for nomination or election —*vt.* **slat′ed, slat′ing 1.** to cover with slate ☆**2.** to choose or schedule, as for a list of candidates, appointments, etc. [he is *slated* to speak at the meeting] —**a clean slate** a record that shows no faults, mistakes, etc. —**slat′er** *n.* —**slat′y** *adj.*

slath·er (slath′ər) *vt.* [< ?] [Dial. or Colloq.] to cover or spread thickly [to *slather* toast with honey]

slat·tern (slat′ərn) *n.* [< dial. *slatter*, to slop] **1.** a woman who is careless and sloppy in her habits, appearance, etc. **2.** a slut —**slat′tern·li·ness** *n.* —**slat′tern·ly** *adj., adv.*

slaugh·ter (slôt′ər) *n.* [ON. *slātr*, slain flesh: for IE. base see SLAY] **1.** the killing of animals for food; butchering **2.** the cruel killing of a human being **3.** the killing of people in large numbers, as in battle —*vt.* **1.** to kill (animals) for food; butcher **2.** to kill (people) cruelly or in large numbers —**slaugh′ter·er** *n.* —**slaugh′ter·ous** *adj.*

SYN.—**slaughter** suggests the brutal killing of large numbers of people, as in battle or by deliberate acts of senseless cruelty; **massacre** implies the widespread and often total destruction of those who are defenseless or unable to resist; **butchery** implies in addition extreme cruelty and a cold-blooded lack of concern about the suffering that results; **carnage** stresses the result of bloody slaughter and often suggests that heaps of dead bodies are to be seen

slaugh·ter·house (-hous′) *n.* a place where animals are butchered for food; abattoir

Slav (släv, slav) *n.* a member of any of a group of Slavic-speaking peoples of eastern, southeastern, and central Europe, including the Russians, Ukrainians, Serbs, Croats, Bulgars, Czechs, Poles, Slovaks, etc. —*adj. same as* SLAVIC

Slav. Slavic

slave (slāv) *n.* [< OFr. < ML. *sclavus*, slave, orig. Slav < LGr. *Sklabos*: first applied to captive Slavs] **1.** a human being who is owned as property by another and is under his complete control **2.** a person who is completely controlled by some influence, habit, person, etc. [*slaves* to fashion] **3.** a person who works hard like a slave; drudge **4.** any ant captured and put to work by ants of other species: also **slave ant 5.** a device put into action or controlled by another, similar device —*vi.* **slaved, slav′ing 1.** to work hard like a slave; drudge [to *slave* in the kitchen all day] **2.** to deal in slaves —**slave′like′** *adj.*

Slave Coast W African coast between the Volta & Niger rivers, on the Gulf of Guinea: its ports were the former centers of the African slave trade

☆**slave driver 1.** a person who directs the work of slaves **2.** any cruel supervisor

slave·hold·er (-hōl′dər) *n.* a person who owns slaves —**slave′hold′ing** *adj., n.*

slav·er¹ (slav′ər) *vi.* [< Scand.] to let saliva run from the mouth; drool —*n.* saliva drooling from the mouth

slav·er² (slā′vər) *n.* **1.** a ship used in the slave trade: also **slave ship 2.** a person who deals in slaves

slav·er·y (slā′vər ē, slāv′rē) *n.* **1.** the practice of owning slaves **2.** the condition of being a slave; bondage **3.** a condition of being completely controlled by some influence, habit, etc. **4.** hard work or toil; drudgery

Slave State any of the States in which slavery was legal before the Civil War

slave trade traffic in slaves; specif., the former transportation of African Negroes to America for sale as slaves

slav·ey (slā′vē, slav′ē) *n., pl.* **-eys** [Brit. Colloq.] a female house servant who does the hard work

Slav·ic (släv′ik, slav′-) *adj.* of the Slavs, their languages, etc. —*n.* a main branch of the Indo-European family of languages, including Russian, Ukrainian, Byelorussian (**East Slavic**); Old Church Slavic, Bulgarian, Serbo-Croatian, Slovenian (**South Slavic**); and Polish, Sorbian, Czech, Slovak (**West Slavic**) Also **Sla·von·ic** (slə vän′ik)

slav·ish (slā′vish) *adj.* **1.** of or like slaves; specif., *a*) too humble *b*) involving hard work; laborious **2.** blindly dependent; not free or original [a *slavish* copier of the latest fads] —**slav′ish·ly** *adv.* —**slav′ish·ness** *n.*

Sla·vo·ni·a (slə vō′nē ə) region in Croatia, N Yugoslavia —**Sla·vo′ni·an** *adj., n.*

☆**slaw** (slô) *n. short for* COLESLAW

slay (slā) *vt.* **slew** or for 2 **slayed, slain, slay′ing** [OE. *slean* < IE. base *slak-*, to strike] **1.** to kill in a violent way **2.** [Slang] to impress, delight, amuse, etc. greatly —**slay′er** *n.*

slea·zy (slē′zē) *adj.* **-zi·er, -zi·est** [< *Silesia*, var. of SILESIA] **1.** flimsy or thin; not firm [a *sleazy* fabric] **2.** shoddy, cheap, inferior, morally low, etc. [a *sleazy* rooming house; a *sleazy* novel] —**slea′zi·ly** *adv.* —**slea′zi·ness** *n.*

sled (sled) *n.* [MLowG. or MDu. *sledde*] a vehicle mounted on runners for coasting or for carrying loads on snow, ice, etc. —☆*vt., vi.* **sled′ded, sled′ding** to carry, ride, or coast on a sled —**sled′der** *n.*

☆**sled·ding** (sled′iŋ) *n.* **1.** the act of riding or carrying on a sled **2.** the condition of the ground for this **3.** conditions affecting the progress of something [it looks like easy *sledding* for this project]

sledge¹ (slej) *n., vt., vi.* **sledged, sledg′ing** [OE. *slecge* < base of *slean*, to strike] *same as* SLEDGEHAMMER

sledge² (slej) *n.* [MDu. *sleedse*] a large, heavy sled for carrying loads over ice, snow, etc. —*vi., vt.* **sledged, sledg′ing** to go or take by sledge

sledge·ham·mer (slej′ham′ər) *n.* [see SLEDGE¹] a long, heavy hammer, usually held with both hands —*vt., vi.* to strike as with a sledgehammer —*adj.* extremely powerful; crushing

sleek (slēk) *adj.* [var. of SLICK] **1.** smooth and shiny; glossy [*sleek* fur] **2.** looking healthy and well-fed or well-groomed [fat, *sleek* pigeons] **3.** speaking or acting in a smooth but insincere way [a *sleek* villain] **4.** luxurious, elegant, etc. —*vt.* to make sleek —**sleek′ly** *adv.* —**sleek′ness** *n.*

sleep (slēp) *n.* [OE. *slæp:* for IE. base see LAP¹] **1.** *a*) a condition of rest for the body and mind at regular times, during which the eyes stay closed and there is dreaming *b*) a period of sleeping **2.** any state like sleep, as death or a coma —*vi.* **slept, sleep′ing 1.** to be in the state of sleep; slumber [to *sleep* eight hours each night] **2.** to be in a state like sleep, as hibernation **3.** [Colloq.] to have sexual intercourse (*with*) **4.** [Colloq.] to postpone a decision (*on*) [let me *sleep* on the matter and I'll give you an answer tomorrow] —*vt.* **1.** to have (a specified kind of) sleep [to *sleep* the sleep of the just] **2.** to provide sleeping accommodations for [the boat *sleeps* four] —**last sleep** death —**sleep away** to spend in sleep [to *sleep away* the morning] —**sleep in 1.** to sleep at the place where one is employed as a household servant **2.** to sleep later than usual in the morning —**sleep off** to get over the effects of by sleeping —**sleep over** [Colloq.] to spend the night at another's home

SLEDGE-HAMMER

sleep·er (slē′pər) *n.* **1.** one who sleeps, esp. as specified [a light *sleeper*] **2.** a beam laid flat for supporting something **3.** [Chiefly Brit.] a tie supporting a railroad track ☆**4.** *same as* SLEEPING CAR ☆**5.** something that unexpectedly becomes successful, important, etc. ☆**6.** [*usually pl.*] pajamas for a young child that enclose the feet ☆**7.** *Bowling* a pin hidden by one in front of it, in bowling for a spare

☆**sleeping bag** a large bag with a warm lining, for sleeping in, esp. outdoors

☆**sleeping car** a railroad car with berths, compartments, etc. for passengers to sleep in

☆**sleeping pill** a pill or capsule containing a drug, esp. a barbiturate, that helps put one to sleep

sleeping sickness 1. an infectious disease, esp. of tropical Africa, transmitted by the bite of the tsetse fly: it is characterized by fever, drowsiness, and coma, usually ending in death **2.** inflammation of the brain, caused by a virus and bringing on drowsiness, sluggishness, etc.

sleep·less (slēp′lis) *adj.* **1.** unable to sleep; wakeful **2.** with little or no sleep [a *sleepless* night] **3.** always alert or active [a *sleepless* guardian of our rights] —**sleep′less·ly** *adv.* —**sleep′less·ness** *n.*

sleep·walk·ing (slēp′wôk′iŋ) *n.* the act or practice of walking while asleep; somnambulism —**sleep′walk′** *vi.* —**sleep′walk′er** *n.*

sleep·wear (-wer′) *n.* clothes to be worn in bed, as pajamas

sleep·y (slēp′ē) *adj.* **sleep′i·er, sleep′i·est 1.** ready or likely to fall asleep; drowsy **2.** not very active; dull; quiet [a *sleepy* little town] **3.** of or showing drowsiness [*sleepy* eyes] —**sleep′i·ly** *adv.* —**sleep′i·ness** *n.*

sleet (slēt) *n.* [< an OE. word no longer known] **1.** rain that freezes as it falls **2.** a mixture of rain and snow **3.** the icy coating formed when rain freezes on trees, streets, etc. —*vi.* to shower in the form of sleet —**sleet′y** *adj.*

sleeve (slēv) *n.* [OE. *sliefe*] **1.** that part of a garment that covers an arm or part of an arm **2.** a tube or tubelike part fitting around another part **3.** a thin paper or plastic cover for protecting a phonograph record —*vt.* **sleeved, sleev′ing** to provide with sleeves —**up one's sleeve** hidden but ready at hand — **sleeved** *adj.* —**sleeve′less** *adj.*

☆**sleigh** (slā) *n.* [Du. *slee*, shortened from *slede*, sled] a light vehicle on runners, usually pulled by horses, for travel over snow and ice —*vi.* to ride in or drive a sleigh —**sleigh′ing** *n.*

sleight (slīt) *n.* [< ON. *slœgth* < *slœgr*, crafty] **1.** slyness or cunning used in tricking people **2.** skill or cleverness

sleight of hand **1.** skill in using the hands so as to confuse those watching, as in doing magic tricks **2.** tricks performed in this way

slen·der (slen′dər) *adj.* [< ?] **1.** long and thin **2.** having a slim, trim figure **3.** small in amount, size, degree, etc.; slight [*slender* earnings, *slender* hope] —see SYN. at THIN —**slen′der·ly** *adv.* —**slen′der·ness** *n.*

slen·der·ize (-īz′) *vt.* **-ized′, -iz′ing** to make or cause to seem slender —*vi.* to become slender

slept (slept) *pt. & pp. of* SLEEP

sleuth (slōōth) *n.* [ON. *sloth*, a track, spoor] **1.** a bloodhound: in full, **sleuth′hound′** ☆**2.** [Colloq.] a detective —☆*vi.* to act as a detective

☆**slew**[1] (slōō) *n. same as* SLOUGH[2] (sense 4)

slew[2] (slōō) *n., vt., vi. same as* SLUE[1]

☆**slew**[3] (slōō) *n.* [Ir. *sluagh*, a host] [Colloq.] a large number or amount; a lot

slew[4] (slōō) *pt. of* SLAY

slice (slīs) *n.* [OFr. *esclice*, ult. < Frank. *slizzan*, to slice] **1.** a thin, broad piece cut from something [a *slice* of cake] **2.** a part or share [a *slice* of the profits] **3.** a spatula or knife with a broad, flat blade **4.** *a)* the path of a hit ball that curves away to the right from a right-handed player or to the left from a left-handed player *b)* a ball that follows such a path —*vt.* **sliced, slic′ing** **1.** to cut into slices [to *slice* bread] **2.** *a)* to cut as a slice (with *off, from, away*, etc.) [*slice* off the crust] *b)* to cut through like a knife **3.** to separate into parts or shares [to *slice* up the loot] **4.** to hit (a ball) in a slice —*vi.* **1.** to cut (*through*) like a knife [the plow *sliced* through the soft earth] **2.** to be hit in a slice [the ball *sliced* foul into the seats] —**slic′er** *n.*

slick (slik) *vt.* [OE. *slician*: for IE. base see DELETE] **1.** to make sleek or smooth [*slick* down your hair with oil] **2.** [Colloq.] to make smart, neat, or tidy (with *up*) [*slick* yourself up before the party] —*adj.* **1.** sleek; smooth [*slick* hair] **2.** slippery; oily, as a surface **3.** clever or skillful, often in a sly or tricky way [a *slick* salesman] **4.** having or showing skill in technique but lacking depth or sincerity [a *slick* style] —*n.* ☆**1.** *a)* a smooth area on the surface of water, as one resulting from a film of oil *b)* an oily film on the surface of water ☆**2.** [Colloq.] a magazine printed on paper with a glossy finish —*adv.* smoothly, cleverly, etc. —**slick′ly** *adv.* —**slick′ness** *n.*

slick·er (slik′ər) *n.* ☆**1.** a loose, waterproof coat ☆**2.** [Colloq.] a person with smooth, tricky ways

slide (slīd) *vi.* **slid** (slid), **slid′ing** [OE. *slidan*: for IE. base see DELETE] **1.** to move along a smooth surface, as on ice **2.** to move quietly and smoothly; glide [the sword *slid* into the scabbard] **3.** to move secretly or without being noticed [he *slid* behind the bush] **4.** to slip [it *slid* from his hand] **5.** to pass gradually (*into* or *out of*) some condition [to *slide* into bad habits] ☆**6.** *Baseball* to drop down and slide along the ground toward a base to avoid being tagged out —*vt.* **1.** to cause to slide [*slide* the note under the door] **2.** to move or slip quietly or secretly (*in* or *into*) [the thief *slid* his hand into the drawer] —*n.* **1.** an act of sliding **2.** a smooth, sloping surface down which to slide [a playground *slide*] **3.** something that works by sliding **4.** a piece of film with a photograph on it, mounted for use with a viewer or projector **5.** a small glass plate on which objects are mounted for microscopic study **6.** *a)* the fall of a mass of rock, snow, etc. down a slope ☆*b)* the mass that falls **7.** a U-shaped section of tubing which is moved to change the pitch of a trombone, etc. —**let slide** to fail to take care of (some matter)

SYN.—**slide** implies easy movement, as over a smooth surface, and usually suggests continuous contact with it [to *slide* down the banister]; **slip** often suggests an abrupt, accidental movement in which contact with the surface is lost [to *slip* and fall on ice]; **glide** suggests a flowing, smooth, easy, usually silent movement [*gliding* dancers]; **skid** means to slide or slip sideways and out of control, as an automobile when its tires fail to grip an icy road

☆**slide fastener** a zipper or a zipperlike device having two grooved edges joined or separated by a slide

slid·er (slīd′ər) *n.* **1.** a person or thing that slides ☆**2.** *Baseball* a curve ball that breaks only slightly

slide rule an instrument consisting of a ruler with a central sliding piece, both marked with logarithmic scales: used for rapid mathematical calculations

sliding scale a scale or schedule, as of costs, wages, etc., that varies with given conditions or standards

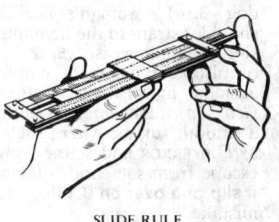

SLIDE RULE

slight (slīt) *adj.* [OE. *sliht*: for IE. base see DELETE] **1.** *a)* light in build; slender [most jockeys are short and *slight*] *b)* frail; fragile **2.** having little weight, strength, or importance [a *slight* criticism] **3.** small in amount or extent [a *slight* fever] —*vt.* **1.** to do carelessly or poorly; neglect [to *slight* one's homework] **2.** to be discourteous toward [to *slight* a neighbor] **3.** to treat as unimportant [we must not *slight* this crucial issue] —*n.* an insult, snub, discourteous act, etc. —see SYN. at THIN —**slight′ly** *adv.* —**slight′ness** *n.*

slight·ing (slīt′iŋ) *adj.* that is a slight; showing disrespect or an insulting lack of interest [a *slighting* remark] —**slight′ing·ly** *adv.*

sli·ly (slī′lē) *adv. var. of* SLYLY

slim (slim) *adj.* **slim′mer, slim′mest** [Du., crafty, bad] **1.** slender or thin **2.** small in amount, degree, or extent; slight; scant; meager [a *slim* crowd; *slim* hope] —*vt., vi.* **slimmed, slim′ming** to make or become slim [dieting to *slim* down] —see SYN. at THIN —**slim′ly** *adv.* —**slim′ness** *n.*

slime (slīm) *n.* [OE. *slim*: for IE. base see DELETE] any soft, moist, slippery, often sticky matter, as thin mud, the mucous coating on fish, etc.; specif., any such matter thought of as filthy or disgusting

slime mold an organism consisting of a large, naked lump of protoplasm that moves about to take in food: it has some characteristics of both plants and animals but is generally classified as a fungus

slim·y (slī′mē) *adj.* **slim′i·er, slim′i·est** **1.** of or like slime **2.** covered with slime **3.** filthy or disgusting —**slim′i·ly** *adv.* — **slim′i·ness** *n.*

sling (sliŋ) *n.* [ME. *slinge(n)*, prob. < ON. *slyngva*, to throw] **1.** *a)* a primitive device for throwing stones, etc., made of a piece of leather tied to cords ☆*b)* *same as* SLINGSHOT **2.** the act of slinging; a throw, fling, etc. **3.** *a)* a band or strap used in raising or lowering a heavy object, carrying a rifle, etc. *b)* a wide piece of cloth hanging down from around the neck, used to support an injured arm —*vt.* **slung, sling′ing** **1.** to throw (stones, etc.) with a sling **2.** to throw, hurl, fling, etc. **3.** to raise, lower, etc. in a sling **4.** to hang loosely or in a sling; suspend [he *slung* the hammock between two trees] —**sling′er** *n.*

☆**sling·shot** (sliŋ′shät′) *n.* a Y-shaped piece of wood, metal, etc. with an elastic band fastened to the upper tips for shooting stones, etc.

slink (sliŋk) *vi.* **slunk, slink′ing** [OE. *slincan*, to creep] to move in a fearful or sneaky way, or as if ashamed —**slink′ing·ly** *adv.*

slink·y (sliŋ′kē) *adj.* **slink′i·er, slink′i·est** **1.** sneaky in movement **2.** [Slang] curving and graceful in movement, line, etc. —**slink′i·ness** *n.*

slip[1] (slip) *vi.* **slipped, slip′ping** [MLowG. *slippen*: for IE. base see DELETE] **1.** to go quietly or secretly [to *slip* out of a room] **2.** *a)* to move or pass smoothly, quickly, or easily [a week *slipped* by] *b)* to get (*into* or *out of* clothes) quickly **3.** to pass gradually into or out of some condition, habit, etc. [to *slip* off to sleep] **4.** to escape from one's mind, power, etc. [to let a chance *slip* by] **5.** to shift or slide from position [the plate *slipped* from my hand] **6.** to slide accidentally, lose footing, etc. [*to slip on ice*] **7.** to make a mistake; err **8.** to become worse; weaken, fall off, etc. [*my memory is slipping*, prices have *slipped*] —**vt. 1.** to put or move smoothly, easily, or quickly [*to slip a bolt into place, to slip one's shoes off, to slip in a snide remark*] **2.** to escape (one's mind) **3.** to get loose from [*the dog slipped his leash*] **4.** to let loose (hounds) to follow game **5.** to transfer (a stitch) from one needle to another without knitting it, as in forming patterns **6.** to put out of joint; dislocate [*to slip a disk in one's back*] —**n. 1.** *a)* a ramp sloping down to water, on which ships are built or repaired ☆*b)* a space between piers or wharves where ships can dock **2.** a leash for a dog **3.** *a)* a woman's sleeveless undergarment, hanging from shoulder straps to the hemline of the skirt *b)* a petticoat or half slip **4.** a pillowcase **5.** a slipping or falling down **6.** an error or mistake in judgment, conduct, speech, etc., esp. one made by accident in speaking, writing, etc. [*a slip of the tongue*] **7.** *Geol. a)* a movement resulting in a small fault or landslide *b)* a smooth surface where such movement has taken place —see SYN. at ERROR and SLIDE —**give someone the slip** to avoid or escape from someone —**let slip** to say without meaning to — ☆**slip one over on** [Colloq.] to trick; fool —☆**slip up** to make a mistake

slip² (slip) *n.* [< MDu. < *slippen*, to cut] **1.** a stem, root, twig, etc. cut off for planting or grafting **2.** a young, slim person [*a slip of a girl*] **3.** a long, narrow piece; strip, as of cloth **4.** a small piece of paper, esp. one for a specific use [*an order slip*] —**vt. slipped, slip'ping** to take a slip from (a plant) for planting or grafting

slip³ (slip) *n.* [OE. *slypa*, a paste] *Ceramics* a thin paste of clay and water used for decorating, casting, or cementing

slip·case (slip'kās') *n.* a boxlike container for a book or set of books, open at one end

slip·cov·er (-kuv'ər) *n.* a fitted cloth cover for an armchair, sofa, etc. that can be taken off for washing —**vt.** to cover (a chair, etc.) with a slipcover

slip·knot (-nät') *n.* a knot made so that it will slip along the rope, etc. around which it is tied

slip·on (-än') *adj.* easily put on or taken off, as shoes without laces, or a garment to be slipped on or off over the head —**n.** a slip-on shoe or garment

slip·o·ver (-ō'vər) *adj., n.* same as PULLOVER

slip·page (slip'ij) *n.* **1.** a slipping, as of one gear past another **2.** the amount of this

slipped disk a disk that causes pain by protruding between two vertebrae, esp. in the lower part of the back

slip·per (slip'ər) *n.* a light, low shoe easily slipped on the foot, esp. one for indoor wear —**slip'pered** *adj.*

slip·per·y (slip'ər ē, slip'rē) *adj.* **-per·i·er, -per·i·est** [OE. *slipur*] **1.** causing or liable to cause slipping, as a wet surface **2.** tending to slip away, as from the grasp **3.** not reliable; tricky —**slip'per·i·ness n.**

☆**slippery elm 1.** a N. American elm with sticky inner bark and hard wood **2.** the wood or bark

slip·shod (slip'shäd') *adj.* [SLIP¹ + SHOD] **1.** wearing shoes with worn-down heels **2.** careless; not neat [*a slipshod job*] —see SYN. at SLOVENLY

slip·stream (-strēm') *n.* the current of air forced backward by the spinning propeller of an aircraft

slipt (slipt) *archaic pt. of* SLIP¹

☆**slip-up** (slip'up') *n.* [Colloq.] an error; mistake

slit (slit) *vt.* **slit, slit'ting** [akin to OE. *slitan*, to cut: for IE. base see CUTLASS] **1.** to cut or split open; esp., to make a long, straight cut in **2.** to cut lengthwise into strips —**n. 1.** a long, straight cut or tear **2.** a long, narrow opening or crack —**slit'-ter n.**

slith·er (slith'ər) *vi.* [< OE. *slidan*, to SLIDE] **1.** to slip or slide on a loose, broken surface, as a gravelly slope **2.** to move along by sliding or gliding, as a snake —**vt.** to cause to slither or slide —**n.** a slithering motion —**slith'er·y adj.**

sliv·er (sliv'ər) *n.* [OE. *slifan*, to cut] **1.** a thin, sharp piece that has been cut, split, or broken off; splinter **2.** a loose, thin, continuous fiber, as of flax, ready to be drawn and twisted —**vt., vi.** to cut or break into slivers

slob (släb) *n.* [Ir. *slab*, mud < Scand.] [Colloq.] a sloppy person or one with bad manners and poor taste

slob·ber (släb'ər) *vi.* [< or akin to LowG. *slubberen*, to swig] **1.** to let saliva, food, etc. run from the mouth; slaver **2.** to speak, write, etc. in a foolishly sentimental way —**n. 1.** saliva,

etc. running from the mouth **2.** foolishly sentimental talk or writing —**slob'ber·er n.** —**slob'ber·y adj.**

sloe (slō) *n.* [OE. *sla*] **1.** *same as* BLACKTHORN (sense 1) **2.** the small, blue-black, plumlike fruit of the blackthorn

sloe-eyed (slō'īd') *adj.* **1.** having large, dark eyes **2.** having almond-shaped eyes

slog¹ (släg) *vt., vi.* **slogged, slog'ging** [var. of SLUG⁴] to hit hard; slug —**slog'ger n.**

slog² (släg) *vt., vi.* **slogged, slog'ging** [ME. *sluggen*: see SLUGGARD] **1.** to make (one's) way with great effort; plod [*slogging up the mountain*] **2.** to work hard (*at* something); toil [*slogging away at his homework*] —**slog'ger n.**

slo·gan (slō'gən) *n.* [< Gael. < *sluagh*, a host + *gairm*, a call] **1.** orig., a battle cry of Scottish Highland and Irish clans **2.** a word or phrase used by a political party, business, etc. to get attention or to advertise a product

sloid, slojd (sloid) *n. same as* SLOYD

sloop (slōōp) *n.* [< Du. < LowG. < *slupen*, to glide] a fore-and-aft rigged sailing vessel with one mast

slop (släp) *n.* [ult. < OE. *slypa*, a paste] **1.** watery snow or mud; slush **2.** a splash or puddle of spilled liquid **3.** watery food that is thin and tasteless **4.** [*often pl.*] *a)* liquid waste of any kind ☆*b)* kitchen swill, used for feeding pigs **5.** [Slang] a sloppy person —*vi.* **slopped, slop'ping 1.** to spill or splash **2.** to walk or splash through slush or mud —*vt.* **1.** to spill liquid on **2.** to spill ☆**3.** to feed swill or slops to (pigs, etc.) —**slop over 1.** to overflow or spill ☆**2.** [Colloq.] to show exaggerated sentimentality; gush

SLOOP

slope (slōp) *n.* [< OE. pp. of *aslupan*, to slip away < *slupan*, to glide] **1.** ground that slants up or down, as a hillside **2.** any slanting line, surface, position, etc.; slant **3.** amount or degree of slant ☆**4.** the land area that drains into a given ocean **5.** the tangent of the angle formed by the intersection of a straight line with the x-axis of a rectangular coordinate system —*vi., vt.* **sloped, slop'ing** to slant or cause to slant up or down —**slop'er n.**

slop·py (släp'ē) *adj.* **-pi·er, -pi·est 1.** wet and splashy; muddy or slushy [*a sloppy road*] **2.** splashed or spotted with liquids [*a sloppy table*] **3.** *a)* very untidy; messy [*sloppy clothes*] *b)* careless; slipshod [*a sloppy job of construction*] **4.** [Colloq.] overly sentimental —see SYN. at SLOVENLY —**slop'pi·ly adv.** —**slop'pi·ness n.**

☆**sloppy Joe** ground meat cooked with tomato sauce, etc. and served on a bun

slosh (släsh) *vt.* [var. of SLUSH] **1.** to shake or stir up (a liquid or something in it) **2.** to apply (a liquid) carelessly or in great quantities —*vi.* **1.** to splash or move clumsily through water, mud, etc. **2.** to splash about: said of a liquid —*n.* **1.** *same as* SLUSH **2.** the sound of liquid splashing about —**slosh'y adj.**

slot (slät) *n.* [< OFr. *esclot*, the hollow between the breasts] **1.** a narrow notch, groove, or opening, as a slit for a coin in a vending machine ☆**2.** [Colloq.] a position in a group, series, sequence, etc. [*the game against North is in the third slot on our schedule*] —*vt.* **slot'ted, slot'ting 1.** to make a slot in ☆**2.** [Colloq.] to place in a series or sequence

sloth (slôth, slōth, släth) *n.* [OE. *slæwth* < *slaw*, slow] **1.** the condition of not liking to work or be active; indolence; laziness **2.** any of several slow-moving mammals of Central and South America that live in trees, often hanging upside down from the branches

sloth·ful (slôth'fal) *adj.* characterized by sloth; indolent; lazy —**sloth'ful·ly adv.** —**sloth'ful·ness n.**

slot machine a machine, esp. a gambling device, worked by putting a coin in a slot

SLOTH
(to 2 ft. long)

slouch (slouch) *n.* [ON. *slokr*, lazy fellow < *slōka*, to droop] ☆**1.** *a)* a person who is awkward or lazy *b)* [Colloq.] a person who lacks skill [*he's no slouch at golf*] **2.** *a)* a drooping or bending forward of the head and shoulders *b)* poor posture in general —*vi.* to sit, stand, walk, etc. in a slouch

slouch hat a soft hat with a broad, drooping brim

slouch·y (slouch′ē) *adj.* **slouch′i·er, slouch′i·est** slouching, esp. in posture —**slouch′i·ly** *adv.* —**slouch′i·ness** *n.*

slough[1] (sluf) *n.* [ME. *slouh*] **1.** the skin of a snake, esp. the outer, castoff layer **2.** any castoff layer, covering, etc. **3.** *Med.* the dead tissue that separates from living tissue or an ulceration —*vi.* **1.** to be shed, cast off, etc. **2.** to shed skin or other covering **3.** *Med.* to separate from the surrounding tissue: said of dead tissue Often with *off* —*vt.* to shed or throw (*off*); get rid of [he has *sloughed* off a number of bad habits] —**slough over** to think of or treat as unimportant —**slough′y** *adj.*

slough[2] (slou; *for 4* slō̄) *n.* [OE. *sloh*] **1.** a place full of soft, deep mud **2.** [< *Slough of Despond*, a swamp in Bunyan's *Pilgrim's Progress*] deep, hopeless discouragement **3.** a sinful or wicked state ☆**4.** a swamp, bog, etc., esp. one that is part of an inlet or backwater —**slough′y** *adj.*

Slo·vak (slō′väk, -vak) *n.* **1.** any of a Slavic people living chiefly in Slovakia **2.** their West Slavic language, related to Czech —*adj.* of Slovakia, the Slovaks, or their language

Slo·va·ki·a (slō vä′kē ə, -vak′ē ə) region of E Czechoslovakia —**Slo·va′ki·an** *adj., n.*

slov·en (sluv′ən) *n.* [prob. < MDu. *slof*, lax] a person who is careless in his appearance, habits, work, etc.; dirty or untidy person

Slo·ve·ni·a (slō vē′nē ə, -vēn′yə) republic of Yugoslavia, in the NW part: 7,896 sq. mi.; cap. Ljubljana

Slo·ve·ni·an (slō vē′nē ən, -vēn′yən) *n.* **1.** any of a Slavic people living chiefly in Slovenia **2.** their South Slavic language —*adj.* of Slovenia, the Slovenians, or their language Also **Slo·vene** (slō′vēn, slō vēn′)

SLOVAKIA

slov·en·ly (sluv′ən lē) *adj.* **-li·er, -li·est** of or like a sloven; careless in appearance, habits, work, etc.; untidy —*adv.* in a slovenly manner —**slov′en·li·ness** *n.*

SYN.—**slovenly** implies a general carelessness or laziness and a resulting lack of interest in keeping things clean, orderly, etc. [a *slovenly* housewife]; **slipshod** suggests a carelessness about details and a resulting lack of accuracy, thoroughness, etc. [*slipshod* work]; **untidy** implies a lack of neatness in appearance or arrangement [an *untidy* room]; **unkempt**, basically meaning uncombed, stresses untidiness that results from neglect [an *unkempt* beggar, lawn, etc.]; **sloppy** suggests a careless spilling over and therefore implies messiness, lack of control, etc. [a *sloppy* eater; *sloppy* thinking] —**ANT.** neat, tidy, fastidious

slow (slō) *adj.* [OE. *slaw*] **1.** not quick or clever in understanding; dull; obtuse [a *slow* learner] **2.** taking a longer time than is expected or usual [she was *slow* in answering me] **3.** marked by low speed, etc.; not fast [a *slow* train] **4.** making speed or progress difficult [a *slow* track] **5.** showing a time that is behind the correct time [his watch is *slow*] **6.** *a)* passing slowly or boringly [a *slow* afternoon] *b)* not lively; dull [a *slow* town] **7.** not active; slack [*slow* trading] **8.** burning so as to give off low heat [a *slow* fire] **9.** *Photog.* adapted to a relatively long exposure time —*vt., vi.* to make or become slow or slower (often with *up* or *down*) —*adv.* in a slow manner; slowly —see **SYN.** at STUPID —**slow′ly** *adv.* —**slow′ness** *n.*

slow burn ☆[Slang] a gradual working up or show of anger: often in the phrase **do a slow burn**

slow·down (slō′doun′) *n.* a slowing down, as of production

slow-mo·tion (-mō′shən) *adj.* **1.** moving at less than usual speed **2.** designating a part of a motion picture or television tape in which the action is made to appear much slower than the actual action

slow·poke (-pōk′) *n.* [Slang] a person who acts or moves slowly

slow time *same as* STANDARD TIME

slow-wit·ted (slō′wit′id) *adj.* having a mind that works slowly; not bright or alert; dull

sloyd (sloid) *n.* [Sw. *slöjd*, skill] a system of manual training originating in Sweden, based upon the use of hand tools in woodcarving

sludge (sluj) *n.* [var. of *slutch*, mud] **1.** mud, mire, or ooze **2.** spongy lumps of drift ice **3.** any heavy, slimy deposit or mass, as the waste resulting from oil refining, the sediment in a crankcase, etc. —**sludg′y** *adj.* **sludg′i·er, sludg′i·est**

sludge·worm (sluj′wurm′) *n.* a small, freshwater worm able to live where there is little oxygen, as in polluted waters

slue[1] (slō̄) *vt., vi.* **slued, slu′ing** [< ?] to turn or swing around a fixed point —*n.* **1.** the act of sluing **2.** the position to which a thing has been slued

slue[2] (slō̄) *n. same as* SLOUGH[2] (sense 4)

slue[3] (slō̄) *n. same as* SLEW[3]

slug[1] (slug) *n.* [ME. *slugge*, clumsy one < Scand.] **1.** a small mollusk that looks like a land snail, but usually has no outer shell **2.** rarely, a larva that looks like a slug **3.** a person, vehicle, etc. that moves slowly

slug[2] (slug) *n.* [prob. < prec.] **1.** a small piece of metal; specif., a bullet ☆**2.** a piece of metal used in place of a coin in automatic coin machines, esp. one used illegally ☆**3.** *Printing a)* a strip of nonprinting metal used to space between lines *b)* a line of type made in one piece, as by a linotype machine

slug[3] (slug) *n.* [prob. < or akin to Dan. *sluge*, to gulp] [Slang] a single drink, esp. of alcoholic liquor

slug[4] (slug) *vt.* **slugged, slug′ging** [ON. *slag*] [Colloq.] to hit hard, esp. with the fist or a bat —*n.* [Colloq.] a hard blow or hit

☆**slug·fest** (slug′fest′) *n.* [SLUG[4] + -FEST] [Colloq.] **1.** a fight or boxing match with much heavy punching **2.** a baseball game in which many hits are made

slug·gard (slug′ərd) *n.* [< ME. < *sluggen*, to be lazy] a lazy or idle person —*adj.* lazy or idle: also **slug′gard·ly**

☆**slug·ger** (-ər) *n.* [Colloq.] one who slugs; specif., *a)* a prizefighter who punches hard *b)* a baseball player who hits many home runs and other extra-base hits

slug·gish (-ish) *adj.* [SLUG[1] + -ISH] **1.** lacking energy or alertness; not active; lazy [a *sluggish* mind] **2.** slow or slow-moving [a *sluggish* engine] **3.** below normal [*sluggish* sales] —**slug′gish·ly** *adv.* —**slug′gish·ness** *n.*

sluice (slō̄s) *n.* [< OFr. *escluse* < LL. < pp. of L. *excludere*, EXCLUDE] **1.** an artificial channel for water, with a gate at its head to control the flow, as in a canal **2.** the water held back by or passing through such a gate **3.** such a gate: also **sluice gate 4.** any channel, esp. one for carrying off extra water ☆**5.** a sloping trough through which water is run, as in washing gold ore, carrying logs, etc. —*vt.* **sluiced, sluic′ing 1.** to draw off as by means of a sluice **2.** to wash with water from or as from a sluice [to *sluice* gravel for gold; to *sluice* a ship's deck with hoses] ☆**3.** to carry (logs, etc.) in a sluice —*vi.* to run or flow as in a sluice

☆**sluice·way** (slō̄s′wā′) *n.* an artificial channel for water, with or without a floodgate

slum (slum) *n.* [old slang, orig., a room < ?] a crowded area of a city having much poverty, poor housing, etc. —*vi.* **slummed, slum′ming** to visit or tour slums, esp. in order to amuse oneself —**slum′mer** *n.* —**slum′my** *adj.* **-mi·er, -mi·est**

slum·ber (slum′bər) *vi.* [< OE. < *sluma*, slumber] **1.** to sleep **2.** to be quiet or inactive [a *slumbering* volcano] —*n.* **1.** sleep **2.** an inactive state

slum·ber·ous (-əs) *adj.* **1.** sleepy; drowsy **2.** causing sleep [*slumberous* music] **3.** calm; quiet [a *slumberous* town] Also **slum′brous** (-brəs)

☆**slum·gul·lion** (slum′gul′yən) *n.* [*slum* (< ?) + dial. *gullion*, mud] [Colloq.] any inexpensive stew or hash

☆**slum·lord** (slum′lôrd′) *n.* [SLUM + (LAND)LORD] [Slang] an absentee landlord of slum dwellings, esp. one who charges rents that are too high and fails to make repairs

slump (slump) *vi.* [prob. < or akin to MLowG. *slumpen*, to come about by accident] **1.** to fall or sink suddenly [she *slumped* to the floor in a faint] **2.** to decline suddenly, as in value, etc. **3.** to have a drooping posture —*n.* **1.** a sudden or sharp fall **2.** a decline in business activity, prices, etc. [a sales *slump*]

SLUICE (sense 5)

3. a drooping posture ☆**4.** a period during which a player, team, etc. performs below normal

slung (sluŋ) *pt. & pp. of* SLING

slunk (sluŋk) *pt. & pp. of* SLINK

slur (slur) *vt.* **slurred, slur′ring** [prob. < MDu. *sleuren*, to drag] **1.** to pass (*over*) quickly and carelessly [he *slurred* over this point in his talk] **2.** to pronounce rapidly in an unclear way, as by combining or dropping sounds ["Gloucester" is *slurred* to (gläs′tər)] **3.** to say harmful things about; belittle **4.** *Music a)* to sing or play (two or more notes) by gliding from one to another without a break *b)* to mark (notes) with a slur —*n.* **1.** the act of slurring **2.** something slurred, as a pronunciation **3.** a remark that is harmful to a person's reputation; aspersion **4.** *Music* a curved symbol (⌢) or (⌣) connecting notes that are to be slurred — **slur′ring·ly** *adv.*

SLUR (sense 4)

slurp (slurp) *vt., vi.* [Du. *slurpen*, to sip] [Slang] to drink or eat noisily —*n.* [Slang] a loud sipping or sucking noise

slur·ry (slur′ē) *n., pl.* **-ries** [< MDu. *slore*, thin mud] a thin, watery mixture of a fine, insoluble material, as clay or cement

slush (slush) *n.* [prob. < Scand.] **1.** partly melted snow or ice **2.** soft mud; mire **3.** grease ☆**4.** overly sentimental talk or writing —*vi.* to walk or move through slush —**slush′i·ness** *n.* —**slush′y** *adj.* **slush′i·er, slush′i·est**

☆**slush fund** money used for bribery or other corrupt political purposes

slut (slut) *n.* [prob. akin to MLowG. *slote*, ditch] **1.** a dirty, untidy woman; slattern **2.** a sexually immoral woman —**slut′tish** *adj.* —**slut′tish·ly** *adv.* —**slut′tish·ness** *n.*

sly (slī) *adj.* **sli′er** or **sly′er, sli′est** or **sly′est** [ON. *slœgr*] **1.** [Dial.] skillful or clever **2.** skillful at tricking or deceiving others; cunning; crafty [a *sly* fox] **3.** tricking or teasing in a playful way [*sly* humor] —**on the sly** secretly —**sly′ly** *adv.* — **sly′ness** *n.*

SYN.—**sly** implies the use of subtle lies, sneaky tricks, evasiveness, etc. to get what one wants [a *sly* bargain]; **cunning** implies shrewd skillfulness in fooling others or getting around difficult situations [a *cunning* plot]; **crafty** implies skill in thinking up schemes and subtle tricks [a *crafty* diplomat]; **tricky** often suggests the shifty, unreliable quality associated with one who is always trying to deceive others; **foxy** suggests slyness and craftiness that have been sharpened by experience [a *foxy* old trader]; **wily** implies the deceiving or trapping of others by subtle tricks and schemes [*wily* compliments meant to soften her heart]

Sm *Chem.* samarium

smack¹ (smak) *n.* [OE. *smæc*] **1.** a slight but distinctive taste or flavor **2.** *a)* a small amount; bit *b)* a trace; touch —*vi.* to have a smack (*of*) [actions that *smack* of treason]

smack² (smak) *n.* [< ? or akin to MDu. *smack*, of echoic orig.] **1.** a sharp noise made by parting the lips suddenly **2.** a loud kiss **3.** *a)* a sharp blow with a flat object; slap *b)* the sound of this —*vt.* **1.** to part (the lips) suddenly so as to make a smack **2.** to kiss or slap loudly —*vi.* to make a loud, sharp noise, as when hitting something —*adv.* **1.** with a smack; violently [he ran *smack* into the wall] **2.** directly; squarely [she hit the target *smack* in the middle]: also [Colloq.] **smack′-dab′**

smack³ (smak) *n.* [prob. < Du. *smak*] **1.** a small sailboat, usually rigged as a sloop ☆**2.** a fishing boat with a well for keeping fish alive

smack⁴ (smak) *n.* [< ? Yid. *schmeck*, smell, sniff] [Slang] heroin

smack·ing (smak′iŋ) *adj.* brisk; lively [a *smacking* breeze]

small (smôl) *adj.* [OE. *smæl*] **1.** little in size, esp. when compared with others of the same kind; not large [a *small* city] **2.** *a)* little in quantity, length, value, time, etc. [a *small* income] *b)* consisting of relatively few units; low in numbers [a *small* crowd] **3.** of little importance; trivial [a *small* matter] **4.** young [*small* children] **5.** having relatively little investment, capital, etc. [a *small* business] **6.** small-minded; petty [a *small*, unpleasant nature] **7.** of low or inferior rank [a *small* official] **8.** gentle and low; soft, as a sound —*adv.* **1.** in small pieces **2.** in a low tone; softly **3.** in a small manner —*n.* **1.** the small or narrow part [the *small* of the back] **2.** [pl.] small articles — **feel small** to feel ashamed or humble —**small′ish** *adj.* —**small′ness** *n.*

SYN.—**small** and **little** are often used interchangeably, but **small** is preferred in referring to something of slightly less than the usual size, amount, value, importance, etc. [a *small* man, tax, matter, etc.] and **little** is more

often used when no comparison is being stressed [he has his *little* faults]; in expressing tenderness [his *little* sister], and in suggesting unimportance, pettiness, etc. [of *little* interest]; **diminutive** implies extreme, sometimes delicate, smallness or littleness [a *diminutive* teacup]; **minute** and the more informal **tiny** suggest that which is extremely diminutive, often to the degree that it can be noticed only by looking very closely [a *minute*, or *tiny*, difference]; **miniature** applies to a copy, model, etc. on a very small scale [*miniature* paintings]; **petite** refers specifically to a girl or woman who is small and trim in figure —**ANT.** large, big, great

small arms firearms of small caliber, held in the hand or hands when fired, as pistols, rifles, etc.

small change 1. coins, esp. those of low value **2.** something of little value or importance

small·clothes (smôl′klōz′, -klōthz′) *n.pl.* [Archaic] closefitting knee breeches worn during the 18th cent.

small game small wild animals, and sometimes birds, hunted as game

small hours the first few hours after midnight

small intestine the narrow upper part of the intestines, between the stomach and the large intestine

small-mind·ed (-mīn′did) *adj.* selfish, petty, prejudiced, narrow-minded, etc. —**small′-mind′ed·ly** *adv.* —**small′-mind′ed·ness** *n.*

☆**small potatoes** [Colloq.] a minor or unimportant person (or people) or thing (or things)

small·pox (-päks′) *n.* a highly contagious virus disease causing fever, vomiting, and pus-filled sores on the skin that often leave pitted scars, or pockmarks

small-scale (-skāl′) *adj.* **1.** drawn to a small scale **2.** of limited scope; not extensive [*small-scale* trading]

small screen, the [Colloq.] television

small talk light conversation about common, everyday things; chitchat

☆**small-time** (-tīm′) *adj.* [Colloq.] of little importance or significance; minor or petty [a *small-time* gambler]

smarm·y (smär′mē) *adj.* **smarm′i·er, smarm′i·est** [< ?] [Brit. Colloq.] flattering in an insincere way; unctuous

smart (smärt) *vi.* [OE. *smeortan*: for IE. base see MORBID] **1.** *a)* to cause sharp, stinging pain [a bee sting *smarts*] *b)* to feel such pain [smoke makes my eyes *smart*] **2.** to feel troubled or upset, as from sorrow, anger, etc. [the insult left him *smarting*] —*vt.* to cause to smart —*n.* **1.** a sharp, stinging pain or feeling ☆**2.** [pl.] [Slang] intelligence, shrewdness, or know-how; savvy: often the **smarts** —*adj.* **1.** causing sharp or stinging pain [a *smart* slap] **2.** sharp or stinging, as pain **3.** brisk; lively [moving at a *smart* pace] **4.** *a)* intelligent, alert, clever, witty, etc. *b)* shrewd or crafty, as in one's dealings **5.** neat; trim; spruce [the ship looked *smart* for inspection] **6.** in fashion; stylish [a *smart* new hat] **7.** [Colloq.] impertinent, flippant, or saucy [don't get *smart*] **8.** [Dial.] quite strong, intense, etc.; considerable [a right *smart* rain] —*adv.* in a smart way —see **SYN.** at INTELLIGENT —**smart′ly** *adv.* —**smart′ness** *n.*

☆**smart al·eck, smart al·ec** (al′ik) [SMART + *Aleck*, dim. of ALEXANDER] [Colloq.] a conceited, bumptious, cocky person — **smart′- al′eck, smart′-al′eck·y** *adj.*

☆**smart bomb** [Mil. Slang] a bomb directed to its target by a self-contained guidance system which responds to a laser beam or television signals, as from an aircraft

smart·en (smärt′n) *vt., vi.* to make or become smart or smarter; specif., *a)* to make or become neater or more stylish in appearance *b)* to make or become more alert, aware, etc. Usually with *up*

smart money [< SMART, *adj.* 4] ☆money bet or invested by those in the best position to know what might be advantageous

☆**smart set** sophisticated, fashionable people

smart·weed (-wēd′) *n.* a knotgrass whose bitter juice is thought to cause skin irritation

☆**smart·y** (smärt′ē) *n., pl.* **smart′ies** [Colloq.] *same as* SMART ALECK: also **smart′y-pants′**

smash (smash) *vt.* [prob. < *s-*, used to add emphasis + MASH] **1.** to break into pieces with noise or violence **2.** to hit (a tennis ball, etc.) with a hard overhand stroke **3.** to hit with a hard, heavy blow **4.** to ruin completely [to *smash* one's hopes] —*vi.* **1.** to break into pieces [the plate fell and *smashed*] **2.** to be destroyed **3.** to move or collide with force [the car *smashed* into a tree] —*n.* **1.** a hard, heavy blow; specif., a hard overhand stroke, as in tennis **2.** *a)* a violent, noisy breaking *b)* the sound of this **3.** *a)* a violent collision *b)* a wreck **4.** total failure, esp. in business ☆**5.** an overwhelming (popular) success [the play was a *smash*] —☆*adj.* that is a smash (n. 5) —see **SYN.** at BREAK —**go to smash** [Colloq.] **1.** to become smashed **2.** to fail completely —**smash′er** *n.*

smashed (smasht) *adj.* [Slang] drunk; intoxicated

smash·ing (smash′iŋ) *adj.* 1. that smashes 2. [Colloq.] extraordinary [a *smashing* success] —**smash′ing·ly** *adv.*

smash·up (-up′) *n.* 1. a violent wreck or collision 2. total failure; ruin 3. any disaster

smat·ter (smat′ər) *n.* [prob. akin to MHG. *smetern*, to chatter] *same as* SMATTERING

smat·ter·ing (-iŋ) *n.* 1. a slight or little knowledge [he has only a *smattering* of French] 2. a small number [a *smattering* of women in the audience]

smear (smir) *vt.* [OE. *smerian*, to anoint] 1. to cover or soil with something greasy, sticky, etc. [she *smeared* her face with cold cream] 2. to apply (something greasy, sticky, etc.) [to *smear* ointment on a cut] 3. to make an unwanted mark on, or make blurred or unclear, by rubbing [to *smear* wet paint accidentally] 4. to make a smear with (the hand, a rag, etc.) 5. to harm the reputation of; slander [he claimed that the newspaper had *smeared* him] 6. [Slang] to overwhelm or defeat decisively —*vi.* to be or become smeared —*n.* 1. a mark made by smearing 2. a small quantity of some substance smeared on a slide for microscopic study, etc. 3. the act of slandering

☆**smear·case** (smir′kās′) *n.* [< G. *schmierkäse* < *schmieren*, to spread + *käse*, cheese] *same as* COTTAGE CHEESE

smear·y (smir′ē) *adj.* **smear′i·er**, **smear′i·est** 1. covered with smears; smeared 2. tending to smear, as wet ink —**smear′i·ness** *n.*

smell (smel) *vt.* **smelled** or **smelt**, **smell′ing** [ME. *smellen*] 1. to be aware of by means of the nose and the olfactory nerves; notice the odor of 2. to sense the presence of [to *smell* trouble] 3. to test by the odor; sniff [*smell* the milk to tell if it's sour] —*vi.* 1. to use the sense of smell; sniff (often with *at* or *of*) 2. *a)* to have a scent or odor [some flowers don't *smell*] *b)* to have an unpleasant odor [something in this room *smells*] 3. to have the odor or a suggestion (*of*) [it *smells* of garlic] 4. [Colloq.] *a)* to be of poor quality [their new record *smells*] *b)* to be foul, corrupt, etc. [I say it's bribery and it *smells*] —*n.* 1. the sense by which a substance is perceived by means of nerves (*olfactory nerves*) inside the nose cavity 2. that quality of a thing which is noticed by the nose; odor; scent [the *smell* of coffee] 3. an act of smelling 4. that which suggests the presence of something; trace [not even a *smell* of scandal] —**smell out** to look for or find as by smelling —**smell up** to cause to stink —**smell′er** *n.*

smelling salts carbonate of ammonium, inhaled to relieve faintness, headaches, etc.

smell·y (smel′ē) *adj.* **smell′i·er**, **smell′i·est** having an unpleasant smell —**smell′i·ness** *n.*

smelt[1] (smelt) *n., pl.* **smelts**, **smelt**: see PLURAL, II, D, 1 [OE.] a small, silvery fish of northern seas, used as food

smelt[2] (smelt) *vt.* [MDu. or MLowG. *smelten*] 1. to melt or fuse (ore, etc.) so as to separate impurities from pure metal 2. to refine or extract (metal) in this way —*vi.* to be smelted

smelt[3] (smelt) *alt. pt. & pp. of* SMELL

smelt·er (smel′tər) *n.* 1. a person engaged in the work or business of smelting 2. a place where smelting is done: also **smelt′er·y**, *pl.* **-er·ies**

Sme·ta·na (sme′tȧ nȧ; *E.* smet′′n ə), **Be·drich** (bed′rzhikh) 1824–84; Czech composer

☆**smidg·en** (smij′ən) *n.* [prob. < dial. *smidge*, var. of *smitch*, a particle] [Colloq.] a small amount; a bit: also **smidg′in**, **smidg′eon**

smi·lax (smī′laks) *n.* [L. < Gr. *smilax*, bindweed] 1. *same as* CAT BRIER 2. a twining greenhouse vine of the lily family, with bright green leaves

smile (smīl) *vi.* **smiled**, **smil′ing** [ME. *smilen* < IE. base *smei-*, to smile] 1. to show pleasure, amusement, affection, irony, etc. by an upward curving of the corners of the mouth and a sparkling of the eyes 2. to look with favor (with *on* or *upon*) [fortune seemed to *smile* on her] —*vt.* to express with a smile [he *smiled* his thanks] —*n.* 1. the act of smiling 2. the look on one's face when one smiles —**smile away** to get rid of by smiling —**smil′er** *n.* —**smil′ing·ly** *adv.*

smirch (smurch) *vt.* [prob. < OFr. *esmorcher*, to hurt] 1. to soil or smear as with grime 2. to dishonor or disgrace [ugly rumors had *smirched* his reputation] —*n.* 1. a smudge; smear 2. a stain on a reputation

smirk (smurk) *vi.* [OE. *smearcian*, to smile: for IE. base see SMILE] to smile in a conceited or self-satisfied way —*n.* such a smile —**smirk′er** *n.* —**smirk′ing·ly** *adv.*

smite (smīt) *vt.* **smote**, **smit′ten** or **smote**, **smit′ing** [OE. *smitan*] *a)* to hit or strike hard *b)* to defeat, punish, or kill 2. to make a powerful attack on 3. to affect strongly and suddenly (*with*) [*smitten* with dread] 4. to disturb in the mind; distress [*smitten* by conscience] 5. to impress favorably [*smitten* with her charms] —*vi.* [Now Rare] to hit or strike hard —**smit′er** *n.*

Smith (smith) 1. **Adam**, 1723–90; Scot. economist 2. Captain **John**, 1580–1631; Eng. colonist in America 3. **Joseph**, 1805–44; U.S. founder of the Mormon Church 4. **Sydney**, 1771–1845; Eng. clergyman & essayist

smith (smith) *n.* [OE.] 1. a person who makes or repairs metal objects; metalworker: usually in combination [*silversmith*] 2. *shortened form of* BLACKSMITH

smith·er·eens (smith′ə rēnz′) *n.pl.* [Ir. *smidirin*] [Colloq.] small fragments; bits [blown to *smithereens*]

smith·y (smith′ē; *chiefly Brit.* smith′ē) *n., pl.* **smith′ies** [OE. *smiththe*] 1. the workshop of a smith, esp. a blacksmith ☆2. *same as* BLACKSMITH

smit·ten (smit′′n) *alt. pp. of* SMITE

smock (smäk) *n.* [OE. *smoc* or ON. *smokkr*] a loose, shirtlike, outer garment worn to protect the clothes —*vt.* 1. to dress in a smock 2. to decorate with smocking

smock·ing (smäk′iŋ) *n.* shirred, decorative stitching used in gathering cloth, as to make it hang in even folds

smog (smôg, smäg) *n.* [SM(OKE) + (F)OG] a harmful mixture of fog and smoke —**smog′gy** *adj.* **-gi·er, -gi·est**

smoke (smōk) *n.* [OE. *smoca*] 1. *a)* the gas and bits of carbon that rise from something burning *b)* a cloud of this 2. any vapor, fume, etc. resembling smoke 3. ☆*a)* an act or period of smoking tobacco, etc. [time for a *smoke*] *b)* something to smoke, as a cigarette 4. something that passes quickly, lacks reality, or makes things hard to understand —*vi.* **smoked**, **smok′ing** 1. to give off smoke or a smokelike substance 2. to give off too much smoke or make smoke go in the wrong place: said of a fuel, a fireplace, etc. 3. *a)* to draw smoke from a lighted cigar, cigarette, etc. into the mouth and blow it out again *b)* to be a habitual smoker —*vt.* 1. to stain or color with smoke 2. to cure (meat, fish, etc.) with smoke 3. to force out with smoke [to *smoke* an animal from its lair] 4. to use (tobacco, a pipe, etc.) in smoking —**smoke out** to force out into the open as with smoke —**smok′a·ble, smoke′a·ble** *adj.*

smoke·house (smōk′hous′) *n.* ☆a building where meats, fish, etc. are cured or flavored with smoke

smoke·less (-lis) *adj.* having or making little or no smoke [*smokeless* gunpowder]

smok·er (smō′kər) *n.* 1. a person or thing that smokes; specif., a person who habitually smokes tobacco ☆2. a railroad car or compartment reserved esp. for smoking: also **smoking car** ☆3. an informal party for men only

smoke screen 1. a cloud of smoke spread to hide the movements of troops, ships, etc. 2. anything said or done to conceal or mislead

☆**smoke·stack** (smōk′stak′) *n.* a pipe for the discharge of smoke from a steamship, factory, etc.

smoke tree a tree of the southwestern U.S. having feathery flower clusters that look like smoke

Smok·ies (smō′kēz) *same as* GREAT SMOKY MOUNTAINS

smoking jacket a man's dressy jacket for casual wear at home

smok·y (smō′kē) *adj.* **smok′i·er**, **smok′i·est** 1. giving off smoke, esp. too much smoke [a *smoky* fireplace] 2. like, of, or having the color of smoke [a *smoky* haze] 3. filled with smoke

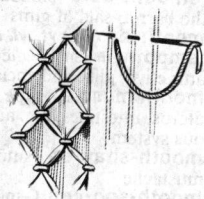

MAN
SMIRKING

SMOCKING

[a smoky room] 4. flavored by smoking 5. darkened or soiled by smoke *[smoky curtains]* —**smok′i·ly** *adv.* —**smok′i·ness** *n.*

Smoky Mountains *same as* GREAT SMOKY MOUNTAINS

smol·der (smōl′dər) *vi.* [ME. *smoldren* < Gmc.] 1. to burn and smoke without flame 2. to be present but kept under control *[his desire for revenge smoldered for years]* 3. to have or show feelings of controlled anger or hate *[she smoldered but said nothing]* —*n.* the act or condition of smoldering

Smol·lett (smäl′it), **To·bi·as George** (tō bī′əs) 1721–71; Brit. novelist, born in Scotland

smolt (smōlt) *n.* [LME. (Scot.)] a young salmon when it first leaves fresh water and descends to the sea

smooch (smōōch) *n.* [ult. akin to SMACK²] [Slang] a kiss —*vi., vt.* [Slang] 1. to kiss 2. to kiss and caress —**smooch′y** *adj.*

smooth (smōōth) *adj.* [OE. *smoth:* for IE. base see SAME] 1. having an even surface with no roughness or projections 2. without lumps *[a smooth paste]* 3. even or gentle in flow or movement *[a smooth voyage]* 4. free from interruptions, difficulties, etc. *[smooth progress]* 5. calm; serene *[a smooth temper]* 6. free from hair, beard, etc. 7. not harsh to the taste 8. having an easy, flowing rhythm or sound ☆9. polite, polished, or charming, esp. in an insincere way *[a smooth talker]* 10. *Phonet.* not aspirated —*vt.* 1. to make level or even 2. to remove the lumps from 3. to free from interruptions, difficulties, etc.; make easy *[friends smoothed his way to success]* 4. to make calm; soothe 5. to make crude; polish or refine —*vi.* to become smooth —*adv.* in a smooth manner —*n.* 1. a smooth part 2. an act of smoothing —see SYN. at EASY — **smooth away** to remove (difficulties, etc.) —**smooth down** to make or become smooth, or even, calm, etc. —**smooth over** to make (a fault, unpleasant situation, etc.) seem less serious or less bad —**smooth′er** *n.* —**smooth′ly** *adv.* —**smooth′ness** *n.*

☆**smooth·bore** (smōōth′bôr′) *adj.* not rifled or grooved inside the barrel: said of guns —*n.* a smoothbore gun

smooth·en (-′n) *vt., vi.* to make or become smooth

☆**smooth·ie** (smōō′thē) *n.* [Slang] a person, esp. a man, who is attractive, glib, and socially at ease: also sp. **smooth′y**

smooth muscle a type of muscle that occurs in the walls of the uterus, intestines, etc. and is controlled by the involuntary nervous system

smooth-shav·en (smōōth′shā′v′n) *adj.* wearing no beard or mustache

smooth-spo·ken (-spō′k′n) *adj.* speaking in a pleasing, persuasive, or polished manner

smooth-tongued (-tuŋd′) *adj.* smooth-spoken, esp. in an overly clever or flattering way

☆**smor·gas·bord, smör·gås·bord** (smôr′gəs bôrd′, smur′-) *n.* [Sw.] 1. a wide variety of appetizers, cheeses, fishes, meats, salads, etc., set out on a table from which people help themselves 2. a meal made up of such foods 3. a restaurant serving smorgasbord

smote (smōt) *pt. & alt. pp. of* SMITE

smoth·er (smuth′ər) *vt.* [ME. *smorthren* < *smorther*, dense smoke] 1. to keep from getting enough air to breathe, or to kill in this way; suffocate; stifle 2. to cover (a fire), causing it to smolder or go out 3. to cover over thickly *[liver smothered in onions]* 4. to hide or keep back as by covering *[to smother a yawn]* —*vi.* to be kept from getting enough air to breathe, or to die in this way —*n.* dense, suffocating smoke, dust, etc. — **smoth′er·er** *n.* —**smoth′er·y** *adj.*

smoul·der (smōl′dər) *vi., n. Brit. sp. of* SMOLDER

smudge (smuj) *n.* [prob. < ME. *smogen*] 1. a stain, smear, etc.; dirty spot 2. *a)* a fire made to produce dense smoke *b)* such smoke produced by burning a substance in containers (**smudge pots**), esp. for driving away insects or protecting plants from frost —*vt.* **smudged, smudg′ing** 1. to protect (an orchard, etc.) with smudge 2. to make dirty; soil —*vi.* 1. to blur or smear 2. to become smudged —**smudg′y** *adj.*

smug (smug) *adj.* **smug′ger, smug′gest** [prob. < LowG. *smuk*, trim] 1. orig., neat, trim, etc. 2. so pleased with oneself, one's opinions, etc. as to be annoying to others; too self-satisfied —**smug′ly** *adv.* —**smug′ness** *n.*

smug·gle (smug′'l) *vt.* **-gled, -gling** [< LowG. *smuggeln*] 1. to bring into or take out of a country secretly or illegally 2. to bring, take, etc. secretly *[he smuggled a saw into the jail]* —*vi.* to smuggle forbidden or taxable goods into or out of a country —**smug′gler** *n.*

smut (smut) *n.* [< or akin to LowG. *smutt*] 1. *a)* sooty matter *b)* a particle of this 2. a soiled spot 3. pornographic or obscene talk, pictures, writing, etc. 4. *Bot. a)* a plant disease in which certain fungi form masses of black spores that break up into a fine powder *b)* any fungus causing smut —*vt., vi.* **smut′ted, smut′ting** to affect with or be affected by smut

smutch (smuch) *vt.* [akin to prec.] to smudge; soil —*n.* 1. a dirty mark; smudge 2. soot, dirt, etc. —**smutch′y** *adj.*

smut·ty (smut′ē) *adj.* **-ti·er, -ti·est** 1. soiled with smut 2. affected with plant smut 3. pornographic or obscene —**smut′ti·ly** *adv.* —**smut′ti·ness** *n.*

Smyr·na (smur′nə) *former name of* IZMIR

Sn [L. *stannum*] *Chem.* tin

SN *U.S. Navy* Seaman

snack (snak) *n.* [prob. < MDu. *snacken*, to snap] a small amount of food; often, a light meal eaten between regular meals —*vi.* to eat a snack or snacks

snack bar a lunch counter, cafeteria, etc. serving snacks

snaf·fle (snaf′'l) *n.* [prob. < Du. < ODu. dim. of *snabbe*, bill of a bird] a bit for a horse's mouth, usually light and jointed, attached to a bridle and having no curb —*vt.* **-fled, -fling** to fit with or control by a snaffle

☆**sna·fu** (sna fōō′, snaf′ōō) *adj.* [orig. military slang for phrase *s(ituation) n(ormal), a(ll) f(ouled) u(p)*] [Slang] in disorder or confusion; completely mixed up —*vt.* **-fued′, -fu′ing** [Slang] to throw into confusion

SNAFFLE

snag (snag) *n.* [< Scand.] 1. a sharp part, point, etc. that sticks out and may catch on things ☆2. an underwater tree stump or branch that is dangerous to ships, boats, etc. 3. a tear in fabric or a pulled thread forming a loop, made by or as by a snag ☆4. an unexpected or hidden difficulty *[our vacation plans have hit a snag]* —*vt.* **snagged, snag′ging** 1. to catch, tear, etc. on a snag *[she snagged her hose]* 2. to hinder; impede 3. to catch with a quick motion *[the shortstop snagged the line drive]* —*vi.* 1. to strike a snag in water 2. to develop a snag —**snag′gy** *adj.*

snag·gle·tooth (snag′'l tōōth′) *n., pl.* **-teeth′** [SNAG + -LE² + TOOTH] 1. a tooth that sticks out beyond the others 2. a crooked or broken tooth —**snag′gle·toothed′** *adj.*

snail (snāl) *n.* [OE. *snægl*] 1. a slow-moving mollusk living on land or in water, having a spiral protective shell, and moving by means of a broad, fleshy, footlike part 2. any slow-moving person or animal

snake (snāk) *n.* [OE. *snaca*] 1. any of various crawling reptiles with a long, scaly body, lidless eyes, no legs, and a tapering tail: some species have a poisonous bite 2. a treacherous or deceitful person 3. a long, bending rod of wire in a spiral, used by a plumber to clear blocked pipes, etc. —*vi.* **snaked, snak′ing** to move, twist, etc. like a snake *[a soldier snaking along on his belly]* —*vt.* [Colloq.] ☆to drag, esp. lengthwise *[using horses to snake logs to the river]* —**snake′like′** *adj.*

SNAIL
(to 2 in. long)

snake·bite (snāk′bīt′) *n.* a bite by a snake, esp. a poisonous one, or the condition caused by it

☆**snake dance** an informal parade in which those taking part move along behind each other in a long, winding line

☆**snake fence** a zigzag fence of rails that cross each other at an angle

snake in the grass a treacherous person or harmful thing that is hidden or seems to be harmless

Snake River [transl. (prob. incorrect) of earlier *Shoshone River*] river in northwestern U.S., flowing from northwestern Wyo. into the Columbia River in Wash.: 1,038 mi.

☆**snake·root** (-rōōt′, -root′) *n.* 1. any of various plants supposed in folk medicine to cure snakebite 2. the roots of any of these

snake·skin (-skin′) *n.* a snake's skin or leather made from it

snak·y (snā′kē) *adj.* **snak′i·er, snak′i·est** 1. of or like a snake or snakes 2. sinuous; winding; twisting *[a snaky river]* 3. sly, treacherous, evil, etc. 4. full of snakes

snap (snap) *vi., vt.* **snapped, snap′ping** [< MDu. or MLowG. *snappen*] 1. to bite suddenly (often with *at*) 2. to snatch or grasp quickly or eagerly (often with *at* or *up*) *[snap at the chance; to snap up a bargain]* 3: to speak or say in a sharp, abrupt way *[to snap at a person in anger; to snap out orders]* 4. to break or part suddenly, esp. with a sharp, cracking sound *[the wire snapped under pressure]* 5. to break down suddenly under strain, as nerves, resistance, etc. **6.** to make or cause to make a sudden, sharp, cracking sound [to *snap* one's fingers] **7.** to close, fasten, etc. with a sound like this, as a lock **8.** to move or cause to move suddenly and smartly [to *snap* to attention, to *snap* the ball to first base] ☆**9.** to take a snapshot (of) —*n.* **1.** a sudden bite, grasp, snatch, etc. **2.** a sudden breaking or parting **3.** a sudden, sharp cracking or clicking sound [the *snap* of a whip] **4.** a short, angry utterance or way of speaking **5.** a brief period of cold weather **6.** any clasp or fastening that closes with a click [she broke the *snap* on her purse] **7.** a hard, thin cookie [gingersnaps] ☆**8.** same as SNAPSHOT ☆**9.** [Colloq.] alertness, vigor, or energy [a guitar solo with lots of *snap*] ☆**10.** [Slang] an easy job, problem, etc. [the test was a *snap*] —*adj.* ☆**1.** made or done quickly, without much thought [a *snap* decision] **2.** that fastens with a snap ☆**3.** [Slang] simple; easy [a *snap* course] —*adv.* with, or as with, a snap —**not a snap** not at all —**snap back** to recover quickly from an illness, disappointment, etc. —**snap out of it** to recover quickly or regain one's senses

snap bean any of various green beans or wax beans

snap·drag·on (snap'drag'ən) *n.* [SNAP + DRAGON: from the mouth-shaped flowers] a plant with spikes of white, yellow, or red flowers

snap·per (-ər) *n.* **1.** a person or thing that snaps **2.** *pl.* **-pers, -per:** see PLURAL, II, D, 1 ☆*a*) same as SNAPPING TURTLE *b*) any of various bony fishes of warm seas; esp., the red snapper

☆**snapping turtle** any of several large, freshwater turtles of N. America, with powerful jaws that snap with great force

SNAPDRAGON

snap·pish (snap'ish) *adj.* **1.** likely to snap or bite [a *snappish* dog] **2.** cross or irritable; sharp-tongued [feeling tired and *snappish*] —**snap'pish·ly** *adv.* —**snap'·pish·ness** *n.*

snap·py (snap'ē) *adj.* **-pi·er, -pi·est 1.** snappish; cross **2.** that snaps; snapping **3.** [Colloq.] *a*) brisk, vigorous, or lively [a *snappy* pace] *b*) sharply chilly [*snappy* weather] —☆**make it snappy** [Slang] be quick; hurry —**snap'pi·ly** *adv.* —**snap'pi·ness** *n.*

snap·shot (-shät') *n.* a photograph taken with brief exposure by snapping the shutter of a hand camera

snare (sner) *n.* [OE. *sneare* < ON. *snara*] **1.** a trap for small animals, usually made of a noose which jerks tight around the animal's body when it touches a trigger **2.** anything tempting or attractive by which a person is caught or trapped; trap **3.** *a*) a length of wire or of gut strung across the bottom of a snare drum to give more vibration *b*) [*pl.*] a set of snare drums —*vt.* **snared, snar'ing 1.** to catch in a trap or snare **2.** to lure into a situation that is dangerous, risky, etc. —**snar'er** *n.*

snare drum a small, double-headed drum with snares

snarl[1] (snärl) *vi.* [< earlier *snar*, to growl] **1.** to growl fiercely, showing the teeth [a *snarling* dog] **2.** to speak sharply or harshly, as in anger —*vt.* to utter with a snarl —*n.* **1.** a fierce, harsh growl **2.** a harsh, angry utterance —**snarl'er** *n.* —**snarl'ing·ly** *adv.* —**snarl'y** *adj.*

snarl[2] (snärl) *vt.* [ME. *snarlen*, akin to SNARE] **1.** to make (thread, hair, etc.) knotted or tangled **2.** to make disordered or confused [to *snarl* traffic] —*vi.* to become knotted or tangled —*n.* **1.** a tangle or knot [hair full of *snarls*] **2.** a confused state or situation —**snarl'y** *adj.*

SNARE DRUM

snatch (snach) *vt.* [prob. var. of ME. *snakken*, to seize] **1.** to grasp or seize suddenly, eagerly, or without permission, warning, etc.; grab [the thief *snatched* her purse and ran] **2.** to remove abruptly or hastily [he *snatched* off his coat and dived in] **3.** to take, get, etc. hastily or while there is a chance [to *snatch* a few hours of sleep] ☆**4.** [Slang] to kidnap —*vi.* to try to seize a thing suddenly; grasp (*at* something) [he *snatched* at the rope as he fell] —*n.* **1.** the act of snatching **2.** a short time [to sleep in *snatches*] **3.** a fragment; bit [*snatches* of gossip] —**snatch'er** *n.*

snatch·y (snach'ē) *adj.* **snatch'i·er, snatch'i·est** done in snatches; not complete or continuous; disconnected

☆**snaz·zy** (snaz'ē) *adj.* **-zi·er, -zi·est** [< ? SN(APPY) + (J)AZZY] [Slang] attractive in a stylish or showy way

sneak (snēk) *vi.* **sneaked** or colloq. **snuck, sneak'ing** [prob. < OE. word thought to be *snecan*, akin to *snican*, to crawl] **1.** to move in a quiet, sly, secret way so as to keep from being noticed **2.** to act in a secret, dishonest, or cowardly manner —*vt.* to give, put, take, etc. secretly or in a sneaking manner [she *sneaked* the gift into the house] —*n.* **1.** one who sneaks; sly, dishonest person **2.** an act of sneaking —*adj.* without warning [a *sneak* attack] —**sneak out of** to avoid (a duty, task, etc.) by sneaking

sneak·er (snē'kər) *n.* **1.** a person or animal that sneaks ☆**2.** a cloth shoe with a soft rubber sole and no heel

sneak·ing (-kiŋ) *adj.* **1.** cowardly, stealthy, dishonest, or furtive **2.** not admitted; secret [a *sneaking* fondness for candy] —**sneaking suspicion** a slight or growing suspicion —**sneak'ing·ly** *adv.*

☆**sneak preview** a showing of a movie one time, without advertising its title, before regular showings begin

☆**sneak thief** a person who commits thefts in a sneaking way, without the use of force or violence

sneak·y (snē'kē) *adj.* **sneak'i·er, sneak'i·est** of or like a sneak; stealthy, dishonest, etc. —**sneak'i·ly** *adv.* —**sneak'i·ness** *n.*

sneer (snir) *vi.* [ME. *sneren*] **1.** to look scornful or sarcastic, as by curling the lip **2.** to show scorn for or make fun of something in speech or writing —*vt.* to say in a sneering way —*n.* **1.** an act of sneering **2.** a sneering look, remark, etc. —see SYN. at SCOFF —**sneer'er** *n.* —**sneer'ing·ly** *adv.*

sneeze (snēz) *vi.* **sneezed, sneez'ing** [ME. *snesen*, altered < *fnesen* < OE. *fneosan*] to let out breath through the nose and mouth in a sudden, uncontrolled way, as because the mucous membrane of the nose has been irritated —*n.* an act of sneezing —**not to be sneezed at** not to be thought of as unimportant —**sneez'er** *n.* —**sneez'y** *adj.*

☆**snell** (snel) *n.* [U.S. dial. < ?] a short length of gut, nylon, etc. used to attach a fishhook to a fish line

snick[1] (snik) *n.* [prob. < *snick or snee*, combat with knives] a small cut or notch; nick —*vt.* to cut slightly; nick

snick[2] (snik) *n., vt., vi.* [echoic] same as CLICK

snick·er (snik'ər) *vi.* [echoic] to give a sly, partly held back laugh that shows embarrassment or lack of respect —*vt.* to say with a snicker —*n.* a snickering laugh —see SYN. at LAUGH —**snick'er·er** *n.* —**snick'er·ing·ly** *adv.*

snide (snīd) *adj.* [orig., counterfeit < thieves' slang, prob. of Du. dial. or G. origin] contemptuous or critical in a nasty, subtle way [a *snide* remark] —**snide'ly** *adv.* —**snide'ness** *n.*

sniff (snif) *vi.* [echoic] **1.** to draw air in through the nose with enough force to be heard, as when trying to smell something **2.** to express dislike, doubt, etc. by sniffing —*vt.* **1.** to draw (air, an inhalant, etc.) up the nose with some force **2.** to smell (a substance) by sniffing [he *sniffed* the milk to see if it was sour] **3.** to detect, perceive, etc. as by sniffing (often with *out*) [*sniffing* out hidden dangers] —*n.* **1.** an act or sound of sniffing **2.** something sniffed —**sniff'er** *n.*

snif·fle (snif''l) *vi.* **-fled, -fling** to sniff repeatedly, as in trying to keep mucus from running out of the nose —*n.* an act or sound of sniffling —**the sniffles** [Colloq.] a head cold, etc. in which there is much sniffling —**sniff'ler** *n.*

sniff·y (snif'ē) *adj.* **sniff'i·er, sniff'i·est** [Colloq.] characterized by or having a tendency to sniff, esp. as a sign of contempt; scornful: also **sniff'ish** —**sniff'i·ly** *adv.* —**sniff'i·ness** *n.*

snif·ter (snif'tər) *n.* ☆a globe-shaped goblet with a small opening, as for sniffing brandy before drinking it

snig·ger (snig'ər) *vi., vt., n.* [echoic] same as SNICKER

snip (snip) *vt.* **snipped, snip'ping** [Du. *snippen*] to cut with or as with scissors, shears, etc. in a short, quick stroke or strokes [to *snip* off the loose threads] —*vi.* to make a short, quick cut or cuts —*n.* **1.** a small cut made with scissors, etc. **2.** the sound of this **3.** a small piece cut off **4.** [*pl.*] heavy hand shears for cutting sheet metal, etc. **5.** [Colloq.] a young, small, or unimportant person, esp. one thought of as rude and disrespectful —**snip'per** *n.*

SNIFTER

snipe (snīp) *n.* [ON. *snipa*] **1.** *pl.* **snipes, snipe:** see PLURAL, II, D, 1 any of certain wading birds with a long, flexible bill, living chiefly in marshy places **2.** a shot from a hidden position —*vi.*

sniped, snip′ing 1. to hunt or shoot snipe **2.** to shoot from a hidden position at individuals of an enemy force **3.** to direct an attack (*at* someone) in a sly or underhanded way

snip·er (snī′pər) *n.* a person, esp. a soldier, who snipes

snip·pet (snip′it) *n.* [dim. of SNIP] **1.** a small scrap or fragment, specif. of information, a book, etc. [*snippets* from Chaucer] **2.** [Colloq.] *same as* SNIP (sense 5)

snip·py (snip′ē) *adj.* **-pi·er, -pi·est** [Colloq.] curt, sharp, etc., esp. in a rude or insolent way: also **snip′pet·y** (-it ē) —**snip′pi·ly** *adv.* —**snip′pi·ness** *n.*

snit (snit) *n.* [< ? SN(IPPY) + (F)IT²] a fit of anger, resentment, etc.: usually in the phrase **in** (or **into**) **a snit**

snitch (snich) *vt.* [< 18th-c. thieves' slang: orig. sense "a nose"] [Slang] to steal (usually something of little value); pilfer —*vi.* [Slang] to be an informer; tattle (*on*) —*n.* [Slang] an informer: also **snitch′er**

sniv·el (sniv′'l) *vi.* **-eled** or **-elled, -el·ing** or **-el·ling** [akin to OE. *snofl*, mucus] **1.** to have mucus running from the nose **2.** to sniff repeatedly, as from a head cold, crying, etc.; sniffle **3.** to cry and sniffle **4.** to complain or cry in a whining way —**sniv′el·er** *n.*

snob (snäb) *n.* [< ? ON. *snāpr*, dolt] **1.** a person who thinks that money, social position, etc. are very important and who looks down on those who are not wealthy, socially prominent, etc. **2.** a person who thinks that his tastes or interests are the best and feels superior to those who do not share them [an intellectual *snob*] —**snob′bish** *adj.* —**snob′bish·ly** *adv.* —**snob′bish·ness** *n.* —**snob′bism** *n.*

snob·ber·y (snäb′ər ē) *n.* snobbish behavior

snood (snood) *n.* [OE. *snod*] a baglike net worn at the back of a woman's head to hold the hair

snook (snook) *n., pl.* **snook, snooks:** see PLURAL, II, D, 2 [Du. *snoek*, pike] a fish that resembles a pike and lives in warm seas; esp., a game and food fish of the tropical Atlantic

snook·er (snook′ər) *n.* [< ?] a variety of the game of pool, played with fifteen red balls and six other balls

☆**snoop** (snoop) *vi.* [Du. *snoepen*, to eat snacks on the sly] [Colloq.] to look about in a sneaking, prying way —*n.* [Colloq.] **1.** one who snoops: also **snoop′er 2.** the act of snooping —**snoop′i·ness** *n.* —**snoop′y** *adj.* **snoop′i·er, snoop′i·est**

☆**snoop·er·scope** (snoop′ər skōp′) *n.* [see SNOOP & -SCOPE] an electronic viewing device using infrared radiation that allows an observer to see objects, areas, etc. in the dark

snoot (snoot) *n.* [see SNOUT] [Colloq.] the nose

☆**snoot·y** (snoot′ē) *adj.* **snoot′i·er, snoot′i·est** [SNOOT + -Y²] [Colloq.] having or showing a scornful or superior attitude toward others; haughty; snobbish —**snoot′i·ly** *adv.* —**snoot′i·ness** *n.*

snooze (snooz) *n.* [< ? LowG. *snusen*, to snore] [Colloq.] a brief sleep; nap —*vi.* **snoozed, snooz′ing** [Colloq.] to take a brief sleep; nap —**snooz′er** *n.*

snore (snôr) *vi.* **snored, snor′ing** [echoic] to breathe with noisy, rough sounds while sleeping, usually with the mouth open: the sounds are caused by the vibration of the soft palate —*n.* the act or sound of snoring —**snor′er** *n.*

☆**snor·kel** (snôr′k'l) *n.* [G. *schnörkel*, spiral] **1.** a device for submarines, with tubes for taking in fresh air and letting out stale air while the vessel is under water **2.** a breathing tube extending above the surface of the water, used in swimming just below the surface —*vi.* **-keled, -kel·ing** to move or swim under water using a snorkel —**snor′kel·er** *n.*

snort (snôrt) *vi.* [ME. *snorten*, akin to SNORE] **1.** to force breath from the nose in a sudden and noisy way **2.** to express anger, scorn, etc. by doing this **3.** to make a noise like a person doing this —*vt.* **1.** to express or say with a snorting sound ☆**2.** [Slang] to take (a narcotic drug) up into the nose by sniffing —*n.* **1.** the act or sound of snorting ☆**2.** [Slang] a drink of straight liquor, taken in one gulp —**snort′er** *n.* —**snort′ing·ly** *adv.*

snot (snät) *n.* [OE. (ge)*snot*, mucus] **1.** nasal mucus: a vulgar term **2.** [Slang] a person, esp. a young person, who is rude and disrespectful

SNORKEL

snot·ty (snät′ē) *adj.* **-ti·er, -ti·est 1.** of, like, or dirtied with snot **2.** [Slang] rude and disrespectful —**snot′ti·ly** *adv.* —**snot′ti·ness** *n.*

snout (snout) *n.* [prob. < MDu. *snute*] **1.** the nose and jaws of an animal when they stick out, as on a pig or dog **2.** something like an animal's snout, as a nozzle or spout **3.** [Colloq.] a human nose, esp. a large one

☆**snout beetle** *same as* WEEVIL

snow (snō) *n.* [OE. *snaw*] **1.** soft, white, crystalline flakes that fall to earth after being formed in the upper air when drops of water vapor freeze **2.** *a)* a falling of snow [we had a light *snow* today] *b)* snowy weather [expecting *snow* throughout January] **3.** a mass of fallen snow [playing in the *snow*] ☆**4.** flickering spots appearing on a TV screen as a result of a weak signal ☆**5.** [Slang] cocaine or heroin —*vi.* to fall as or like snow [it's *snowing*] —*vt.* **1.** to shower or let fall as or like snow [they *snowed* confetti onto the crowd below] ☆**2.** to cover, shut in, etc. with or as with snow (usually with *in, under*, etc.) [the blizzard *snowed* us in] ☆**3.** [Slang] to deceive, impress, win over, etc. by glib talk, flattery, etc. —☆**snow under** to overwhelm as with work or defeat

snow·ball (snō′bôl′) *n.* **1.** a mass of snow packed together into a ball ☆**2.** a kind of viburnum with round clusters of white or pinkish flowers —*vi.* to grow larger rapidly like a ball of snow rolling downhill [his debts *snowballed* after he lost his job] —*vt.* **1.** to throw snowballs at **2.** to cause to snowball

snow·bank (-baŋk′) *n.* a large mound of snow

snow·ber·ry (-ber′ē) *n., pl.* **-ries 1.** a hardy N. American plant with small, pink flowers and soft, white berries **2.** any of various other plants with white berries **3.** any of these berries

snow·bird (-burd′) *n.* **1.** a N. American junco with a white belly **2.** *same as* SNOW BUNTING

snow-blind (-blīnd′) *adj.* blinded temporarily by ultraviolet rays of the sun reflected from snow —**snow blindness**

☆**snow blower** a motorized, hand-guided machine on wheels, for removing snow as from walks: also **snow thrower**

snow·bound (-bound′) *adj.* shut in or blocked off by snow [the farmer's family was *snowbound* after the blizzard]

snow bunting a small finch living in cold regions in the Northern Hemisphere

snow·cap (-kap′) *n.* a cap of snow, as on a mountain, the top of a tree, etc. —**snow′capped′** *adj.*

snow·drift (-drift′) *n.* a smooth heap of snow blown together by the wind

snow·drop (-dräp′) *n.* a low-growing plant with small, bell-shaped white flowers

snow·fall (-fôl′) *n.* **1.** a fall of snow **2.** the amount of snow that falls in a given area or period of time [a 3-inch *snowfall*]

snow fence a light fence of lath and wire put up to control the drifting of snow

snow·field (-fēld′) *n.* a large expanse of snow

snow·flake (-flāk′) *n.* **1.** a single crystal of snow **2.** *same as* SNOW BUNTING **3.** a European plant with drooping white flowers

snow goose a white goose that breeds in the Arctic, having a red bill and black wing tips

snow leopard a large, whitish cat of the mountains of C Asia, having many dark blotches on its fur

SNOW FENCE

snow line (or **limit**) the lower boundary of a high region in which snow never melts

snow·man (-man′) *n., pl.* **-men** (-men′) a crude human figure made of snow packed together

snow·mo·bile (-mō bēl′) *n.* a motor vehicle for traveling over snow, usually with steerable runners at the front and tractor treads at the rear —*vi.* **-biled, -bil′ing** to travel by snowmobile

snow·mold (-mōld′) *n.* a fungus disease of grasses appearing as gray patches in lawns, near the edge of melting snow

snow-on-the-moun·tain (snō′än thə moun′t'n) *n.* ☆a widely cultivated spurge of the western U.S., with small flowers and the margins of the upper leaves white

☆**snow·plow** (snō′plou′) *n.* **1.** any machine equipped with a part shaped like a plow for clearing snow off a road, railroad, etc. **2.** *Skiing* a stemming of both skis, as for stopping, with the inside ski edges dug into the snow and the tips of the skis pointed at each other —*vi.* to stem with both skis

☆**snow·shoe** (-shoō′) *n.* a racket-shaped frame of wood criss-crossed with strips of leather, etc., worn on the feet to keep one from sinking in deep snow —*vi.* -**shoed**′, -**shoe·ing** to use snowshoes in walking —**snow′sho′er** *n.*

snowshoe hare a hare of northern N. America that is brown in summer and white in winter: also **snowshoe rabbit**

☆**snow·slide** (-slīd′) *n.* an avalanche of snow

☆**snow·storm** (-stôrm′) *n.* a storm with a heavy snowfall

☆**snow·suit** (-soōt′) *n.* a heavily lined one-piece garment or set of pants and jacket, often with a hood, worn by children in cold weather

SNOWSHOES

☆**snow tire** a tire with a deep tread, and sometimes studs that stick out, for getting a better grip on snow or ice

snow-white (-hwīt′, -wīt′) *adj.* white as snow

snow·y (snō′ē) *adj.* **snow′i·er, snow′i·est** 1. of or characterized by snow [a *snowy* day] 2. covered or filled with snow [a *snowy* valley] 3. like snow; specif., a) pure; spotless b) white — **snow′i·ly** *adv.* —**snow′i·ness** *n.*

snub (snub) *vt.* **snubbed, snub′bing** [ON. *snubba,* to chide] 1. orig., to check with sharp words 2. to treat in a scornful or unfriendly way, as by ignoring; slight 3. a) to check suddenly the movement of (a rope, etc.) by looping it around a post b) to make (a boat, etc.) fast in this way ☆4. to put out (a cigarette) by pressing the end against a surface —*n.* 1. scornful, slighting action or treatment 2. a snubbing, or checking —*adj.* short and turned up; pug [a *snub* nose] —**snub′ber** *n.*

snub·by (snub′ē) *adj.* **-bi·er, -bi·est** turned up; snub

snub-nosed (-nōzd′) *adj.* having a snub nose

☆**snuck** (snuk) *colloq. pt. & pp. of* SNEAK

snuff[1] (snuf) *n.* [< ?] the charred end of a candlewick —*vt.* 1. to trim off the charred end of (a candlewick) 2. to put out (a candle) with a snuffer or by pinching —**snuff out** 1. to put out (a candle, etc.); extinguish 2. to bring to an end or cause to die suddenly

snuff[2] (snuf) *vt.* [MDu. *snuffen*] 1. to inhale strongly through the nose; sniff 2. to smell or sniff at —*vi.* to sniff or snort —*n.* 1. the act or sound of snuffing; sniff 2. a preparation of powdered tobacco taken up into the nose by sniffing or put on the gums —**up to snuff** [Colloq.] as good as might be expected [not feeling *up to snuff*]

snuff·box (snuf′bäks′) *n.* a small box for holding snuff

snuff·er (-ər) *n.* 1. a device with a cone on the end of a handle, for putting out a burning candle: in full, **candle snuffer** 2. [pl.] an instrument like shears, for snuffing a candle: also **pair of snuffers**

snuf·fle (snuf′′l) *vi.* **-fled, -fling** [< SNUFF[2], *vi.* + -LE[2]] to breathe noisily and with difficulty or by constant sniffing, as a dog in trailing; sniffle —*n.* the act or sound of snuffling —**the snuffles** *same as* the SNIFFLES —**snuf′fler** *n.*

snug (snug) *adj.* **snug′ger, snug′gest** [prob. ult. < Scand.] 1. protected from the weather; warm and cozy [*snug* in their beds] 2. small but well-arranged and neat [a *snug* cottage] 3. large enough to live on in comfort [a *snug* income] 4. tight in fit [a *snug* coat] 5. well-built; seaworthy 6. hidden or concealed [to lie *snug*] —*adv.* so as to be snug —*vt.* **snugged, snug′ging** to make snug or secure —**snug′ly** *adv.* —**snug′ness** *n.*

snug·gle (snug′′l) *vi.* **-gled, -gling** [< SNUG & -LE[2]] to lie closely and comfortably; cuddle, as for warmth, in affection, etc. —*vt.* to hold or draw close; cuddle

so[1] (sō) *adv.* [OE. *swa*] 1. in the way shown, expressed, understood, etc. [hold the bat just *so*] 2. a) to such an extent [why are you *so* late?] b) very [they are *so* happy] c) [Colloq.] very much [she *so* wants to go] 3. for the reason specified; therefore [they were tired, and *so* left] 4. more or less; approximately [fifty dollars or *so*] : in this sense often regarded as a pronoun 5. also; likewise [I'm going and *so* are you] : also used colloquially in contradicting a negative statement [I did *so* tell the

truth!] 6. then [and *so* to bed] —*conj.* 1. in order that; with the purpose that: usually followed by *that* [talk louder *so* (that) all may hear] 2. [Colloq.] with the result that; therefore [he smiled, *so* I did too] 3. if only; as long as [I don't care, just *so* you don't stay too long] —*pron.* that which has been specified or named [she is a friend and will remain *so*] —*interj.* an exclamation of surprise, approval, dislike, etc. —*adj.* 1. true; in reality [that's *so*] 2. in proper order [everything must be just *so*] —**and so on** (or **forth**) and the rest; et cetera (etc.) —**so as** with the purpose or result [leave early *so as* to be on time] —**so much** to an unspecified but limited degree, amount, etc. [paid *so much* per day] —**so much for** no more need be said about [*so much for* that] —☆**so what?** [Colloq.] even if so, what then?: used to express disrespect, lack of interest, etc.

so[2] (sō) *n. Music same as* SOL[1]

So. 1. south 2. southern

soak (sōk) *vt.* [OE. *socian*] 1. to make thoroughly wet; drench or saturate [*soaked* to the skin by the rain] 2. to put into and keep in a liquid, as for thorough wetting, softening, soothing, etc. [*soak* the beans in water overnight] 3. a) to take in (liquid) by absorbing (usually with *up*) [*soak* up the water with a sponge] b) to absorb by exposure to it [to *soak* up sunshine] 4. to take in mentally [to *soak* up knowledge] ☆5. [Colloq.] to overcharge [some stores in resort areas *soak* the tourist] —*vi.* 1. to stay for a time in liquid for wetting, softening, etc. 2. to pass (*into* or *through*) as a liquid does [rain *soaking* through her coat] 3. to become absorbed mentally [the fact *soaked* into his head] —*n.* 1. a soaking or being soaked 2. liquid used for soaking 3. [Slang] a drunkard

SYN.—soak implies letting something stay in a liquid long enough for it to absorb the liquid, become soft, become completely wet, etc. [to *soak* bread in milk]; **saturate** implies the absorption of a liquid to the point where no more can be taken up [*air saturated* with moisture]; **drench** implies a thorough wetting as by a downpour [a garden *drenched* by the rain]; **steep** usually suggests soaking something for the purpose of getting its flavor, fragrance, etc. [to *steep* tea]; **impregnate** implies the passage of a fluid into something so as to spread through every part of it [a fence post *impregnated* with creosote to slow down rotting]

so-and-so (sō′ən sō′) *n., pl.* **so′-and-sos′** [Colloq.] 1. some person or thing whose name is not mentioned or not known 2. a person considered to be unpleasant, mean, hateful, etc. [what a *so-and-so* he has turned out to be]

soap (sōp) *n.* [OE. *sape*] 1. a substance used with water to produce suds for washing, usually produced by the action of an alkali, as caustic soda, on fats or oils 2. any metallic salt of a fatty acid ☆3. [Slang] *same as* SOAP OPERA —*vt.* to lather, scrub, etc. with soap —☆**no soap** [Slang] 1. (it is) not acceptable [I made an offer, but she said, "No soap"] 2. to no avail [I tried hard to convince them, but it was *no soap*]

soap·ber·ry (sōp′ber′ē) *n., pl.* **-ries** 1. any of various trees with fruits containing a soapy material 2. the globe-shaped fruit, with yellowish flesh and a large, round seed

soap·box (-bäks′) *n.* 1. a box for soap ☆2. anything that can be used as a platform by a person (**soapbox orator**) making an informal, often highly emotional speech to a street audience

☆**soap opera** [Colloq.] a radio or TV drama presented day after day in a series of melodramatic and sentimental episodes: originally, many of the sponsors were soap companies

☆**soap plant** any of various plants some parts of which can be used as soap

soap·stone (-stōn′) *n. same as* STEATITE

soap·suds (-sudz′) *n.pl.* 1. soapy water, esp. when stirred into a foam 2. the foam on soapy water

soap·y (sō′pē) *adj.* **soap′i·er, soap′i·est** 1. covered with or containing soap 2. of or like soap 3. [Slang] too smooth in speech or manner; oily —**soap′i·ly** *adv.* —**soap′i·ness** *n.*

soar (sôr) *vi.* [OFr. *essorer,* ult. < L. *ex-,* out + *aura,* air] 1. to rise or fly high into the air 2. to sail or glide along high in the air, as a glider does on air currents 3. to rise above the ordinary level [*soaring* prices] —*n.* the act of soaring —**soar′er** *n.*

sob (säb) *vi.* **sobbed, sob′bing** [ME. *sobben*] 1. to weep aloud with short, gasping breaths 2. to make a sound like this, as the wind —*vt.* 1. to put or bring (oneself) by sobbing [to *sob* oneself to sleep] 2. to say with sobs —*n.* the act or sound of sobbing —**sob′bing·ly** *adv.*

so·ber (sō′bər) *adj.* [< OFr. < L. *sobrius*] 1. showing self-control, esp. in the use of alcoholic liquor; temperate 2. not drunk **3.** serious, solemn, sedate, etc. /a worried, *sober* look on his face/ **4.** not bright or flashy; quiet; plain: said of color, clothes, etc. **5.** not distorted /the *sober* truth/ **6.** showing mental and emotional balance /his *sober* handling of the situation/ —*vt., vi.* to make or become sober (often with *up* or *down*) —see SYN. at SERIOUS —**so′ber·ly** *adv.* —**so′ber·ness** *n.*

so·ber-mind·ed (-mīn′did) *adj.* sensible and serious —**so′ber-mind′ed·ly** *adv.* —**so′ber-mind′ed·ness** *n.*

so·ber·sides (-sīdz′) *n., pl.* **-sides′** an unemotional, serious-minded person —**so′ber·sid′ed** *adj.*

so·bri·e·ty (sə brī′ə tē, sō-) *n.* a being sober; specif., *a)* temperance, esp. in the use of alcoholic liquor *b)* dignified seriousness

so·bri·quet (sō′brə kā′, sō′brə kā′) *n.* [Fr.] **1.** a nickname **2.** a name that one takes that is not one's real name

☆**sob story** [Colloq.] a very sad story; esp., a story about someone's personal troubles told in order to arouse sympathy

Soc., soc. 1. social **2.** socialist **3.** society

so-called (sō′kôld′) *adj.* **1.** popularly known by this term /the *so-called* nuclear powers/ **2.** incorrectly thought of as such /a *so-called* liberal/

soc·cer (säk′ər) *n.* [altered < (AS)SOC(IATION FOOTBALL)] a game played by two teams of eleven players with a round ball moved chiefly by kicking or by using any part of the body except the hands and arms

so·cia·ble (sō′shə b′l) *adj.* [Fr. < L. < *socius:* see SOCIAL] **1.** enjoying or requiring the company of others; friendly; affable /a *sociable* person/ **2.** characterized by pleasant, informal conversation and companionship /a *sociable* evening/ ☆a social, esp. a church social —**so′cia·bil′i·ty,** *pl.* **-ties, so′cia·ble·ness** *n.* —**so′cia·bly** *adv.*

so·cial (sō′shəl) *adj.* [< Fr. < L. *socialis* < *socius,* companion] **1.** of or having to do with human beings living together in a group so that their dealings with one another affect their common welfare /*social* problems/ **2.** living in this way /man as a *social* being/ **3.** of or having to do with the ranks of society, specif. the more fashionable of these /a *social* event/ **4.** getting along well with others; sociable /a warm, *social* nature/ **5.** of or for companionship /a *social* club/ **6.** of or engaged in welfare work /a *social* agency/ **7.** living in groups or communities /the ant is a *social* insect/ —*n.* an informal gathering of people for recreation; party /a church *social*/ —**so′cial·ly** *adv.*

☆**social climber** a person who seeks higher social status by getting acquainted with distinguished or wealthy people

social contract (or **compact**) in the political theories of Locke, Rousseau, etc., the agreement among individuals to unite, which marked the beginning of organized society

social disease any venereal disease

so·cial·ism (sō′shəl iz′m) *n.* **1.** any of various theories or systems in which the means of producing and distributing goods are owned and operated by society rather than by private individuals, with all members of society sharing in the work and the products **2.** [often **S-**] *a)* a political movement for establishing such a system *b)* the doctrines, methods, etc. of the Socialist parties **3.** the stage of society, in Marxist doctrine, coming between the capitalist stage and the communist stage (see COMMUNISM, sense 2), in which private ownership of the means of production and distribution has been done away with

so·cial·ist (sō′shəl ist) *n.* **1.** an advocate or supporter of socialism **2.** [**S-**] a member of a Socialist Party —*adj.* **1.** of or like socialism or socialists **2.** advocating or supporting socialism **3.** [**S-**] designating or of a political party advocating Socialism Also **so′cial·is′tic** —**so′cial·is′ti·cal·ly** *adv.*

☆**so·cial·ite** (sō′shə līt′) *n.* a person who is well-known in fashionable society and written about in society pages

so·ci·al·i·ty (sō′shē al′ə tē) *n.* **1.** a being sociable; sociability **2.** the tendency to form social groups

so·cial·ize (sō′shə līz′) *vt.* **-ized′, -iz′ing 1.** to make social or fit for living and getting along in a group **2.** to change so that it meets the needs of a social group **3.** to put under government ownership /to *socialize* the steel industry/ **4.** to cause to become socialist /to *socialize* a nation/ —☆*vi.* to take part in social activity, parties, etc. /they *socialize* only with members of their club/ —**so′cial·i·za′tion** *n.* —**so′cial·iz′er** *n.*

socialized medicine any system supplying complete medical and hospital care, through public funds, for all the people in a community, district, or nation

social science 1. the study of people living together in groups, families, etc. **2.** any of several studies, as economics or political science, dealing with society and the activity of its members —**social scientist**

social secretary a secretary employed by an individual to handle his social appointments and correspondence

☆**social security** a system of insurance managed by a government, by which the retired, the unemployed, the disabled, etc. receive regular payments from funds supplied by employees, employers, and the government

social service *same as* SOCIAL WORK —**so′cial-serv′ice** *adj.*

☆**social studies** a course of study, esp. in elementary and secondary schools, including history, civics, geography, etc.

social welfare 1. the welfare of society, esp. of those who are poor, unemployed, etc. **2.** *same as* SOCIAL WORK

social work any activity meant to improve the condition of people in a community, as through counseling services, health clinics, recreation and rehabilitation centers, aid for the needy and aged, etc. —**social worker**

so·ci·e·ty (sə sī′ə tē) *n., pl.* **-ties** [< MFr. < L. *societas* < *socius,* companion] **1.** a group of persons who have the same customs, beliefs, etc. or live under a common government and who are thought of as forming a single community **2.** the system or condition of living together in such a group /an urban *society*/ **3.** all people, when thought of as forming a community in which each person is partly dependent on all the rest /for the good of *society*/ **4.** company or companionship /seeking out the *society* of strangers/ **5.** any organized group of people with work, interests, etc. in common /a medical *society*/ **6.** the wealthy, fashionable class in a community /she made her debut into *society*/ —*adj.* of or involving society (*n.* 6) /the *society* page of a newspaper/ —**so·ci′e·tal** *adj.* —**so·ci′e·tal·ly** *adv.*

Society Islands group of French islands in the South Pacific: chief island, Tahiti

Society of Friends a Christian religious sect founded in England about 1650 by George Fox: the Friends have no formal creed, rites, liturgy, or priesthood, and reject violence in human relations, including war: see QUAKER

Society of Jesus see JESUIT

so·ci·o- (sō′sē ō′, -shē-; -ə) [Fr. < L. *socius,* companion] a combining form meaning social, society, sociological

☆**so·ci·o·bi·ol·o·gy** (sō′sē ō bī al′ə jē, -shē-) *n.* the scientific study of the biological basis for animal and human social behavior —**so′ci·o·bi·ol′o·gist** *n.*

☆**so·ci·o·ec·o·nom·ic** (-ē′kə näm′ik, -ek′ə-) *adj.* of or involving both social and economic factors

so·ci·ol·o·gy (sō′sē äl′ə jē, -shē-) *n.* [< Fr.: see SOCIO- & -LOGY] the science of human society and of social relations, organization, and change; specif., the study of the beliefs, values, etc. of groups in society —**so′ci·o·log′i·cal** (-ə läj′i k′l), **so′ci·o·log′ic** *adj.* —**so′ci·o·log′i·cal·ly** *adv.* —**so·ci·ol′o·gist** *n.*

so·ci·o·path (sō′sē ə path′, -shē-) *n.* [SOCIO- + (PSYCHO)PATH] a person suffering from a mental disorder that causes him to treat others in an irresponsible, often violently harmful way —**so′ci·o·path′ic** *adj.*

so·ci·o·po·lit·i·cal (sō′sē ō pə lit′i k′l, -shē-) *adj.* of or involving both social and political factors

sock¹ (säk) *n.* [OE. *socc* < L. *soccus,* a light, low-heeled shoe] **1.** a light shoe worn by comic characters in ancient Greek and Roman drama **2.** comic drama **3.** *pl.* **socks, sox** a stocking reaching only partway to the knee —☆**socked in** grounded (as an aircraft) or closed (as an airfield) as because of fog

sock² (säk) *vt.* [Slang] to hit with force, esp. with the fist —*n.* [Slang] a blow —*adv.* [Slang] directly; squarely —☆**sock away** to set aside (money)

sock·et (säk′it) *n.* [< Anglo-Fr., dim. < OFr. *soc,* plowshare < Gaul.] a hollow part into which something fits /an eye *socket,* the *socket* for a light bulb/

sock·eye (säk′ī′) *n.* [< AmInd. *sukkegh*] a salmon of the N Pacific with red flesh, often canned

☆**sock·o** (säk′ō) *adj.* [< SOCK²] [Slang] very successful

So·co·tra (sō kō′trə) island of the People's Democratic Republic of Yemen, off the E tip of Africa: 1,400 sq. mi.

Soc·ra·tes (säk′rə tēz′) 470?-399 B.C.; Athenian philosopher & teacher —**So·crat·ic** (sə krat′ik, sō-) *adj., n.*

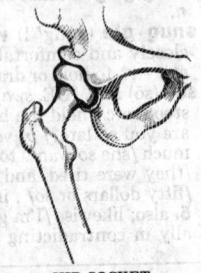

HIP SOCKET

Socratic method a method of teaching or discussion similar to the method used by Socrates, in which a series of questions and answers can lead to a logical conclusion or provide a thoughtful analysis of an idea, concept, etc.

sod (säd) *n.* [prob. < MDu. or MLowG. *sode*] **1.** a surface layer of earth containing grass with its roots; turf **2.** a piece of this layer —*vt.* **sod'ded, sod'ding** to cover with sod or sods

so·da (sō'də) *n.* [ML., ult. < Ar. *suwwād*, a plant burned to produce soda] **1.** *a)* sodium oxide, Na₂O *b)* *same as:* (1) SODIUM BICARBONATE (2) SODIUM CARBONATE (3) SODIUM HYDROXIDE **2.** *a)* *same as* SODA WATER (sense 1) *b)* [Chiefly Eastern] a drink of soda water flavored with syrup ☆*c)* a drink of soda water flavored with syrup, fruit, etc., served with ice cream in it

soda ash crude sodium carbonate (sense 1)

☆**soda biscuit 1.** a biscuit made with baking soda and sour milk or buttermilk **2.** [Chiefly Brit.] *same as* SODA CRACKER

☆**soda cracker** a light, crisp cracker, usually salted, made from a dough of flour, water, and leavening, orig. baking soda and cream of tartar

☆**soda fountain** a counter with equipment for making and serving soft drinks, sodas, sundaes, etc.

☆**soda jerk** [Slang] a person who works at a soda fountain: also **soda jerk·er** (jur'kər)

so·dal·i·ty (sō dal'ə tē) *n., pl.* **-ties** [< L. < *sodalis*, companion] an association or society, specif. one made up of Roman Catholic lay people joined together for devotional or charitable purposes

☆**soda pop** a flavored, carbonated soft drink, esp. as sold in tightly capped bottles or in cans

soda water 1. water charged under pressure with carbon dioxide gas, used in ice-cream sodas, as a chaser or mix, etc. **2.** *same as* SODA POP

sod·den (säd''n) *obs. pp. of* SEETHE —*adj.* **1.** filled with moisture; soaked [a lawn *sodden* with rain] **2.** soggy from improper baking or cooking, as bread **3.** dull or stupefied, as from drunkenness —**sod'den·ly** *adv.* —**sod'den·ness** *n.*

so·di·um (sō'dē əm) *n.* [ModL. < SODA] a silver-white, alkaline metallic chemical element, found in nature only in combined form: symbol, Na; at. wt., 22.9898; at. no., 11

sodium benzoate a sweet, white powder, the sodium salt of benzoic acid, used as a food preservative

sodium bicarbonate a white, crystalline compound, NaHCO₃, used in baking powder, as an antacid, etc.

sodium carbonate 1. the anhydrous sodium salt of carbonic acid, Na₂CO₃ **2.** any of the hydrated carbonates of sodium; esp., *same as* SAL SODA

sodium chloride common salt, NaCl

sodium cyanide a white, highly poisonous salt, NaCN, used in electroplating, as an insecticide, etc.

sodium hydroxide a white, strongly caustic substance, NaOH, used in chemistry, oil refining, etc.

sodium hyposulfite *see* SODIUM THIOSULFATE

sodium nitrate a clear, crystalline salt, NaNO₃, used in manufacturing explosives, fertilizers, etc.

sodium pentothal *same as* THIOPENTAL SODIUM

sodium thiosulfate a white, crystalline salt, Na₂S₂O₃, used as a fixing agent in photography, as a bleaching agent, etc.: popularly but wrongly called (*sodium*) *hyposulfite* or *hypo*

so·di·um-va·por lamp (sō'dē əm vā'pər) an electric lamp used for street lighting, fitted with two electrodes and filled with sodium vapor which gives off a soft yellow light

Sod·om (säd'əm) *Bible* a city destroyed by fire together with a neighboring city, Gomorrah, because of the sinfulness of the people: Gen. 18–19

Sod·om·ite (-īt') *n.* **1.** an inhabitant of Sodom **2.** [s-] a person who practices sodomy

sod·om·y (säd'əm ē) *n.* [< SODOM] any sexual intercourse considered to be unnatural, as between a person and an animal or between two persons of the same sex

so·ev·er (sō ev'ər) *adv.* **1.** in any way [how dark *soever* it may be] **2.** of any kind; at all [no rest *soever*]

-so·ev·er (sō ev'ər) a combining form added for emphasis to who, what, when, where, how, etc., *and meaning* any (person, thing, time, place, or manner) of all those possible

so·fa (sō'fə) *n.* [Fr. < Ar. *şuffah*, a cushion] an upholstered couch with a back and arms

sofa bed a sofa that can be opened into a double bed

sof·fit (säf'it) *n.* [< Fr. < It. *soffitta*] the underside of an arch, eave, etc.

So·fi·a (sō'fē ə, sō fē'ə; *Bulg.* sô'fē yä') capital of Bulgaria, in the W part: pop. 868,000

S. of Sol. Song of Solomon

soft (sôft, säft) *adj.* [OE. *softe*] **1.** giving way easily under pressure, as a feather pillow or moist clay **2.** easily cut, shaped, or worn away [a *soft* wood or metal] **3.** not as hard as is normal, desirable, etc. [*soft* butter] **4.** smooth to the touch [*soft* skin] **5.** *a)* bland; not acid, sour, or sharp *b)* easy to digest because free from roughage [a *soft* diet] **6.** containing no alcohol [a *soft* drink] **7.** having few or none of the mineral salts that keep soap from making a lather [*soft* water] **8.** mild or temperate [a *soft* summer breeze] **9.** *a)* not strong or vigorous; not able to endure hardship [*soft* from easy living] *b)* having flabby muscles **10.** requiring little effort; easy [a *soft* job] **11.** *a)* kind or lenient; not severe [too *soft* in dealing with offenders] *b)* easily influenced or imposed upon **12.** not bright; subdued [*soft* lights] **13.** showing little contrast or distinctness [a close-up of her filmed in *soft* focus] **14.** gentle; low [*soft* music] **15.** popularly, designating the letter *c* sounded as in *cent* or the letter *g* sounded as in *germ* **16.** unstable and declining: said of a market, prices, etc. —*adv.* softly; gently; quietly —*n.* something soft; soft part —*interj.* hush! stop! —**be soft on 1.** to treat gently **2.** to feel affectionate toward —**soft in the head** stupid or foolish —**soft'ish** *adj.* —**soft'ly** *adv.* —**soft'ness** *n.*

SYN.—**soft** suggests an absence or lessening of all that is harsh, rough, too intense, etc. so as to be pleasing to the senses [*soft* colors; a *soft* voice]; **bland** implies such a lack of what is spicy, irritating, stimulating, excessive, etc. as to be soothing, but also, often, dull and uninteresting [*bland* foods; a rather *bland* novel]; **mild** applies to that which is not as rough, harsh, irritating, etc. as it might be [a *mild* winter; *mild* criticism]; **gentle** is often used to mean just what **mild** does, but with a stronger suggestion of being pleasantly soothing or calming [a *gentle* breeze, voice, etc.] —**ANT.** harsh, rough

☆**soft·ball** (sôft'bôl', säft'-) *n.* **1.** a game like baseball played on a smaller diamond and with a larger and slightly softer ball, for seven innings **2.** the ball used

soft-boiled (-boild') *adj.* boiled only a short time so that the yolk is still soft: said of an egg

soft coal *same as* BITUMINOUS COAL

soft-cov·er (-kuv'ər) *n. same as* PAPERBACK —*adj.* bound as a paperback

soft drink a drink that contains no alcohol, esp. a carbonated drink

sof·ten (sôf''n, säf'-) *vt., vi.* **1.** to make or become soft or softer **2.** to make or become less able to resist (often with *up*) [*soften* him up with flattery] —**sof'ten·er** *n.*

soft·goods (sôft'goodz', säft'-) *n.pl.* goods that last a relatively short time, esp. products made of cloth: also **soft goods**

soft·head·ed (-hed'id) *adj.* stupid or foolish —**soft'head'ed·ly** *adv.* —**soft'head'ed·ness** *n.*

soft·heart·ed (-här'tid) *adj.* **1.** full of sympathy or tenderness **2.** not strict or severe, as in discipline —**soft'heart'ed·ly** *adv.* —**soft'heart'ed·ness** *n.*

☆**soft landing** a safe landing, as of a spacecraft on the moon, in which the craft and its contents remain unharmed

soft palate the soft, fleshy part at the rear of the roof of the mouth; velum

soft-ped·al (-ped''l) *vt.* **-aled** or **-alled, -al·ing** or **-al·ling 1.** to soften the tone of (a piano, etc.) by use of a special pedal (**soft pedal**) **2.** [Colloq.] to play down; give little attention to, make less noticeable, etc. [the newspaper has *soft-pedaled* its criticism of the mayor's policies]

☆**soft sell** selling that relies on indirect suggestion rather than high-pressure salesmanship —**soft'-sell'** *adj.*

☆**soft-shell** (-shel') *adj.* **1.** having a soft shell **2.** having an unhardened shell, as an animal that has just shed its old shell Also **soft'-shelled'**

soft-shoe (-shoo') *adj.* designating a kind of tap dancing done in shoes without metal taps

☆**soft shoulder** soft ground along the edge of a highway

soft-soap (-sōp') *vt.* [Colloq.] to flatter —**soft'-soap'er** *n.*

soft soap 1. soap in liquid or semifluid form **2.** [Colloq.] flattery or smooth talk

soft-spo·ken (-spō'k'n) *adj.* **1.** speaking or spoken with a soft, low voice **2.** smooth; polite and gracious

☆**soft touch** [Slang] a person who is easily persuaded to give or lend money

soft·ware (-wer′) *n.* ☆the programs, data, routines, etc. for a computer: see also HARDWARE (3 *b*)

soft wheat a kind of wheat with low protein content and soft kernels

soft·wood (-wood′) *n.* **1.** *a*) any light, easily cut wood *b*) a tree yielding such wood **2.** *Forestry* wood from a tree that has cones and needles, as a pine, spruce, etc.

soft·y, soft·ie (sôf′tē, säf′-) *n., pl.* **soft′ies** [Colloq.] **1.** a person who is overly sentimental or trusting **2.** a person whose body is soft or weak

sog·gy (säg′ē, sôg′ē) *adj.* **-gi·er, -gi·est** [prob. < or akin to ON. *sog*, lit., the act of sucking] **1.** saturated with moisture; soaked **2.** moist and heavy; sodden [a *soggy* cake] **3.** dull and boring [a *soggy* political speech] —**sog′gi·ly** *adv.* —**sog′gi·ness** *n.*

So·ho (sō′hō, sō hō′) district in central London: noted for its foreign restaurants, night life, etc.

soil[1] (soil) *n.* [Anglo-Fr. < OFr. < L. *solum*] **1.** the surface layer of earth, in which plants grow **2.** any place for growth or development [good political *soil* for the growth of democracy] **3.** land; country [foreign *soil*] **4.** ground or earth —**the soil** life and work on a farm

soil[2] (soil) *vt.* [< OFr., ult. < L. *suculus*, dim. of *sus*, pig] **1.** to make dirty; stain **2.** to bring disgrace upon [to *soil* one's honor by lying] **3.** to make impure; corrupt [such habits *soil* one's character] —*vi.* to become soiled —*n.* **1.** a soiled spot; stain **2.** excrement, sewage, etc. **3.** a soiling or being soiled

☆**soil bank** a Federal program under which subsidies are paid to farmers to stop growing certain surplus crops and to enrich the idle land by various methods

soi·ree, soi·rée (swä rā′) *n.* [Fr. *soirée* < *soir*, evening] a party or gathering in the evening

so·journ (sō′jurn; *also, for v.,* sō jurn′) *vi.* [< OFr. < L. *sub-*, under + *diurnus*, of a day < *dies*, day] to live somewhere temporarily; stay for a while [we *sojourned* in Italy] —*n.* a brief stay; visit —**so′journ·er** *n.*

Sol (säl) [L.] **1.** the Roman sun god, who is identified with the Greek god Helios **2.** the sun represented as a person

sol[1] (sōl; *Sp.* sôl) *n., pl.* **sols,** *Sp.* **so·les** (sô′les) [Sp., lit., sun] *see* MONETARY UNITS, table (Peru)

sol[2] (sōl) *n.* [< ML. *sol(ve)*: see GAMUT] *Music* a syllable representing the fifth tone of the diatonic scale

sol[3] (säl, sōl) *n.* [ult. < SOL(UTION)] a colloidal dispersion in a liquid

sol·ace (säl′is) *n.* [< OFr. < L. < *solari*, to comfort] **1.** an easing of grief, loneliness, etc. [seeking *solace* in travel] **2.** something that eases or relieves; comfort; relief [friends were his chief *solace*] —*vt.* **-aced, -ac·ing** **1.** to give solace to; comfort [attempting to *solace* the survivors] **2.** to lessen (grief, sorrow, etc.) —see SYN. at COMFORT —**sol′ac·er** *n.*

so·la·num (sō lā′nəm) *n.* [L., nightshade] any of a large genus of trees, vines, shrubs, and plants of the nightshade family: most are poisonous, but a few are cultivated for food, as the potato, eggplant, etc.

so·lar (sō′lər) *adj.* [L. *solaris* < *sol*, the sun] **1.** of or having to do with the sun **2.** produced by or coming from the sun [*solar* energy] **3.** depending upon the sun's light or energy [*solar* heating] **4.** measured by the earth's motion with relation to the sun [mean *solar* time]

☆**solar battery** a number of devices (**solar cells**) grouped together that change the energy of sunlight into electricity

solar flare a brief increase of intensity in the light of the sun, usually near a sunspot

so·lar·i·um (sō ler′ē əm, sə-) *n., pl.* **-i·a** (-ə) [L. < *sol*, the sun] a glassed-in porch, room, etc. where people sun themselves, as in treating illness

solar plexus **1.** a network of nerves in the abdominal cavity behind the stomach **2.** [Colloq.] the area of the belly just below the sternum

solar system the sun and all the heavenly bodies that revolve around it

solar wind streams of ionized gas particles constantly sent out from the sun

sold (sōld) *pt. & pp. of* SELL

sol·der (säd′ər) *n.* [< OFr. < L. *solidare*, to make firm] **1.** a metal alloy used when melted to join or patch metal parts or surfaces **2.** anything that joins or fuses; bond —*vt., vi.* **1.** to join or patch (things) with solder **2.** to unite or become united —**sol′der·er** *n.*

sol·der·ing iron (säd′ər iŋ) a pointed metal tool heated for use in melting and applying solder

sol·dier (sōl′jər) *n.* [< OFr. < *solde*, pay < LL. *solidus*, a coin] **1.** a member of an army **2.** an enlisted man, as distinguished from an officer **3.** a person who works for a specified cause [a *soldier* for peace] **4.** an ant or termite of a caste with a large head and jaws that fights in defense of the colony —*vi.* **1.** to serve as a soldier **2.** to shirk one's duty, as by pretending to work, to be ill, etc. —**sol′dier·li·ness** *n.* —**sol′dier·ly** *adj.*

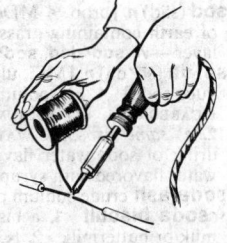

SOLDERING IRON

soldier of fortune a man who will serve as a soldier in any army for money or for adventure or excitement

sol·dier·y (-ē) *n., pl.* **-dier·ies** **1.** soldiers as a group **2.** military science: also **sol′dier·ship′**

sole[1] (sōl) *n.* [< OFr., ult. < L. *solum*, a base, bottom] **1.** the bottom surface of the foot **2.** the bottom surface of a shoe, sock, etc. **3.** the bottom surface of various objects, as a golf club —*vt.* **soled, sol′ing** to furnish (a shoe, etc.) with a sole, esp. a new sole

sole[2] (sōl) *adj.* [< OE. < L. *solus*] **1.** *a*) without another; single; one and only [the *sole* man present] *b*) acting, working, etc. alone without help [the *sole* support of her family] **2.** of or having to do with only one (specified) person or group; only [they are the *sole* survivors] **3.** not shared; exclusive [*sole* rights to a patent]

sole[3] (sōl) *n., pl.* **sole, soles:** see PLURAL, II, D, 2 [OFr. < L. *solea*, sole of a shoe, kind of fish: named from its shape] any of certain ocean flatfishes, most of which are highly valued as food

sol·e·cism (säl′ə siz'm) *n.* [< L. < Gr. < *soloikos*, speaking incorrectly < dialect used in Soloi, city in Asia Minor] **1.** a mistake in grammar or in the use of words, as "we done it" for "we did it" **2.** a mistake in etiquette —**sol′e·cist** (-sist) *n.* —**sol′e·cis′tic** (-sis′tik) *adj.* —**sol′e·cis′ti·cal·ly** *adv.*

SOLE
(to 24 in. long)

sole·ly (sōl′lē) *adv.* **1.** without another or others; alone [to be *solely* to blame] **2.** only, exclusively, merely, or altogether [to read *solely* for pleasure]

sol·emn (säl′əm) *adj.* [< OFr. < L. *sollemnis*, yearly < *sollus*, all + *annus*, year] **1.** *a*) observed or done according to ritual, as religious holidays, rites, etc. *b*) sacred **2.** according to strict rules; formal [a *solemn* ceremony] **3.** serious; deeply earnest [a *solemn* oath] **4.** awe-inspiring; very impressive [a *solemn* occasion] **5.** somber because dark in color —see SYN. at SERIOUS —**sol′emn·ly** *adv.* —**sol′emn·ness** *n.*

so·lem·ni·ty (sə lem′nə tē) *n., pl.* **-ties** **1.** solemn ceremony, ritual, etc. **2.** solemn feeling or quality; seriousness

sol·em·nize (säl′əm nīz′) *vt.* **-nized′, -niz′ing** **1.** to celebrate formally or according to ritual **2.** to perform the ceremony of (marriage, etc.) —see SYN. at CELEBRATE —**sol′em·ni·za′tion** *n.* —**sol′em·niz′er** *n.*

so·le·noid (sō′lə noid′, säl′ə-) *n.* [< Fr. < Gr. *sōlēn*, a channel + *eidos*, a form] a coil of wire that, when an electric current passes through it, acts like a magnet —**so′le·noi′dal** *adj.*

sole·plate (sōl′plāt′) *n.* [SOLE[1] + PLATE] the ironing surface of a flatiron

sol-fa (sōl′fä′) *n.* [It. *solfa* < *sol* + *fa*: see GAMUT] **1.** the syllables *do, re, mi, fa, sol, la, ti, do,* used for the tones of a scale, regardless of key **2.** the use of these syllables in vocal exercises —*vt., vi.* **-faed′** (-fäd′), **-fa′ing** to sing (a scale, song, etc.) to these syllables

sol·feg·gio (säl fej′ō, -fej′ē ō′) *n., pl.* **-feg′gios, -feg′gi** (-fej′ē) [It. < *solfa*: see prec.] **1.** voice practice in which scales are sung to the sol-fa syllables **2.** the use of these syllables in singing

so·lic·it (sə lis′it) *vt.* [< MFr. < L.: see SOLICITOUS] **1.** to ask or seek earnestly; appeal to or for [to *solicit* funds for charity] **2.** to entice (someone) to do wrong **3.** to approach for some immoral purpose, as a prostitute does —*vi.* to solicit someone or something —see SYN. at BEG —**so·lic′i·tant** (-i tənt) *n., adj.* —**so·lic′i·ta′tion** *n.*

so·lic·i·tor (-ər) *n.* **1.** a person who solicits; esp., one who tries to get customers for a business, money for a charity, etc. **2.** in England, a member of the legal profession who is not a barrister ☆**3.** in the U.S., a lawyer serving as official law officer as for a city —**see SYN.** at LAWYER

☆**solicitor general** *pl.* **solicitors general, solicitor generals 1.** a law officer (in the U.S., a member of the Department of Justice) ranking next below the attorney general **2.** the chief law officer in some States

so·lic·i·tous (sə lis′ə təs) *adj.* [L. *sollicitus* < *sollus,* whole + pp. of *ciere,* to set in motion] **1.** showing care, attention, or concern [*solicitous* for her child's welfare] **2.** showing anxious desire; eager [*solicitous* to make friends] **3.** full of anxiety — **so·lic′i·tous·ly** *adv.* —**so·lic′i·tous·ness** *n.*

so·lic·i·tude (-tōōd′, -tyōōd′) *n.* the state of being solicitous; care, concern, etc. —**see SYN.** at CARE

sol·id (säl′id) *adj.* [< MFr. < L. *solidus*] **1.** tending to keep its form rather than to flow or spread out like a liquid or gas; relatively firm or compact [ice is water in a *solid* form] **2.** not hollow [a *solid* block of wood] **3.** having the three dimensions of length, breadth, and thickness [prisms and other *solid* figures] **4.** firm, strong, sound, reliable, etc. [a *solid* structure; *solid* reasoning] **5.** serious; not trivial [*solid* reading] **6.** complete [*solid* satisfaction] **7.** having no breaks or divisions [a *solid* line of fortifications] **8.** with no pauses [to talk for a *solid* hour] **9.** of one or the same color, material, etc. throughout [a *solid* walnut table] ☆**10.** showing unity; unanimous [*solid* community support] **11.** thick or dense, as a fog ☆**12.** [Colloq.] having a firmly favorable relationship [to be in *solid* with someone] **13.** [Colloq.] healthful and filling [a *solid* meal] ☆**14.** [Old Slang] very good; excellent —*n.* **1.** a substance that is solid, not a liquid or gas **2.** an object or figure having length, breadth, and thickness —**see SYN.** at FIRM[1] —**sol′id·ly** *adv.* —**sol′id·ness** *n.*

sol·i·dar·i·ty (säl′ə dar′ə tē) *n., pl.* **-ties** agreement of all elements or individuals, as of a group; complete unity —**see SYN.** at UNITY

solid fuel a rocket fuel in solid form, consisting of both fuel and oxidizer combined or mixed

solid geometry geometry dealing with solid figures

so·lid·i·fy (sə lid′ə fī′) *vt., vi.* **-fied′, -fy′ing 1.** to make or become solid, firm, hard, etc. [fats *solidify* as they cool] **2.** to make or become solid, strong, or united [his speeches *solidified* his support among voters] —**so·lid′i·fi·ca′tion** *n.*

so·lid·i·ty (-tē) *n.* a being solid; firmness, hardness, etc.

sol·id-state (säl′id stāt′) *adj.* **1.** describing or of the branch of physics dealing with the fundamental properties of solids, as structure, binding forces, etc., and with their effects **2.** describing, of, or equipped with electronic devices, as semiconductors, that can control current without heated filaments, moving parts, etc.

sol·i·dus (säl′i dəs) *n., pl.* **-i·di′** (-dī′) [LL. < L.] **1.** a gold coin of the Late Roman Empire **2.** *same as* VIRGULE

so·lil·o·quize (sə lil′ə kwīz′) *vi.* **-quized′, -quiz′ing** to speak a soliloquy; talk to oneself —*vt.* to say in a soliloquy —**so·lil′o·quist** (-kwist) *n.*

so·lil·o·quy (sə lil′ə kwē) *n., pl.* **-quies** [< LL. < L. *solus,* alone + *loqui,* to speak] **1.** a talking to oneself **2.** lines in a drama in which a character reveals his thoughts to the audience by speaking as if to himself

sol·ip·sism (säl′ip siz′m) *n.* [< L. *solus,* alone + *ipse,* self + -ISM] the theory that the only knowledge one can have is knowledge of oneself or of one's own state of mind —**sol′ip·sist** *n.* —**sol′ip·sis′tic** *adj.*

sol·i·taire (säl′ə ter′) *n.* [< Fr. < L.: see SOLITARY] **1.** a diamond or other gem set by itself, as in a ring **2.** a card game played by one person

sol·i·tar·y (säl′ə ter′ē) *adj.* [< OFr. < L. *solitarius* < *solus,* alone] **1.** living or being alone [a *solitary* cow in a field] **2.** single; only [a *solitary* example] **3.** characterized by loneliness or lack of companions [a *solitary* existence] **4.** with few or no people; remote [a *solitary* place] **5.** *Bot.* growing singly rather than in a cluster **6.** *Zool.* living alone or in pairs —*n., pl.* **-tar′ies 1.** a person who lives by himself; esp., a hermit **2.** [Colloq.] *same as* SOLITARY CONFINEMENT —**see SYN.** at ALONE —**sol′i·tar′i·ly** *adv.* —**sol′i·tar′i·ness** *n.*

solitary confinement confinement of a prisoner away from all others, usually as extra punishment

sol·i·tude (säl′ə tōōd′, -tyōōd′) *n.* [< MFr. < L. *solitudo* < *solus,* alone] **1.** a being solitary, or alone; seclusion **2.** a lonely or secluded place

SYN.—**solitude** refers to the state of one who is completely alone, cut off from all human contact, and often stresses the loneliness of such a condition [the *solitude* of a hermit]; **isolation** suggests physical separation from others, often as the result of factors over which one has no control [the *isolation* of the farmer during the heavy snows]; **seclusion** suggests a deliberate staying away from others, as by not leaving one's home, by going off to a remote place, etc.

sol·ler·et (säl′ə ret′, säl′ə ret′) *n.* [< MFr. dim. of *soler,* a shoe] a kind of shoe made of hinged steel plates and worn with a suit of armor: see illustration at ARMOR

sol·mi·za·tion (säl′mi zā′shən) *n.* [< Fr. < *sol* + *mi:* see GAMUT] solfeggio, or any similar system of syllables in singing

so·lo (sō′lō) *n., pl.* **-los;** for *n.* 1 & 3, sometimes **-li** (-lē) [It. < L. *solus,* alone] **1.** a musical piece or passage to be played or sung by one person **2.** an airplane flight made by a pilot alone **3.** any performance by one person alone —*adj.* **1.** for or by a single voice or instrument **2.** performing a solo —*adv.* alone —*vi.* **1.** to perform a solo **2.** to make a solo flight —**so′lo·ist** *n.*

Sol·o·mon (säl′ə mən) [LL. < Gr. < Heb. *shĕlōmōh,* lit., peaceful < *shālōm,* peace] **1.** a masculine name: dim. **Sol 2.** *Bible* king of Israel; son & successor of DAVID: noted for his wisdom —*n.* a very wise man

Solomon Islands 1. country on a group of islands in the SW Pacific, east of New Guinea: c. 11,500 sq. mi.; pop. 206,000 **2.** group of islands including those which make up this country and others belonging to Papua New Guinea

Solomon's seal 1. the Star of David used as a mystic symbol in the Middle Ages **2.** any of various plants with broad, waxy leaves and blue or black berries

So·lon (sō′lən, -län) 640?-559? B.C.; Athenian statesman & lawgiver —*n.* [*sometimes* **s-**] a wise lawmaker

so long *colloq.* term for GOOD-BYE

sol·stice (säl′stis, sōl′-) *n.* [MFr. < L. *solstitium* < *sol,* the sun + *sistere,* to make stand still < *stare,* to stand] **1.** either of two points on the sun's ecliptic at which it is farthest north or farthest south of the celestial equator **2.** the time of reaching either of these points: see SUMMER SOLSTICE, WINTER SOLSTICE —**sol·sti′tial** (-stish′əl) *adj.*

SOLOMON'S SEAL

sol·u·bil·i·ty (säl′yōō bil′ə tē) *n., pl.* **-ties 1.** the condition or extent of being soluble **2.** the amount of a substance that can be dissolved in a given solvent under specified conditions

sol·u·ble (säl′yōō b'l) *adj.* [MFr. < L. *solubilis* < *solvere:* see SOLVE] **1.** that can be dissolved; capable of passing into solution [iodine is *soluble* in alcohol] **2.** that can be solved or explained [a *soluble* problem] —**sol′u·bly** *adv.*

sol·ute (säl′yōōt, sōl′ōōt) *n.* the substance dissolved in a solution —*adj.* dissolved; in solution

so·lu·tion (sə lōō′shən) *n.* [< OFr. < L. < pp. of *solvere:* see SOLVE] **1.** *a)* the solving of a problem *b)* the answer to a problem *c)* an explanation, etc. [the *solution* of a mystery] **2.** *a)* the dispersion of one or more substances in another, usually a liquid, so as to form a homogeneous mixture; a dissolving *b)* the state or fact of being dissolved [salt held in *solution* in water] *c)* the mixture so produced [a *solution* of sugar and vinegar]

solution set *Math.* the root or values that satisfy a given equation or inequality

solve (sälv) *vt.* **solved, solv′ing** [< L. *solvere,* to loosen < *se-,* apart + *luere,* to let go] to find a satisfactory answer for (a problem, mystery, etc.); make clear; explain —**solv′a·bil′i·ty** *n.* —**solv′a·ble** *adj.* —**solv′er** *n.*

sol·ven·cy (säl′vən sē) *n.* a solvent state or quality

sol·vent (säl′vənt) *adj.* [< L. prp. of *solvere:* see SOLVE] **1.** able to pay all one's debts **2.** that can dissolve another substance —*n.* **1.** a substance, usually liquid, that can dissolve another substance **2.** something that solves or explains

so·ma (sō′mə) *n., pl.* **so′ma·ta** (-mə tə) [ModL. < Gr. *sōma*, body] the entire body of an animal or plant, with the exception of the germ cells

So·ma·li (sō mä′lē, sə-) *n.* **1.** *pl.* **-lis, -li** a member of a Moslem people of Somalia and nearby regions, who raise sheep and goats **2.** their Eastern Cushitic language

So·ma·li·a (sō mä′lē ə, sə-; -mäl′yə) country of E Africa, on the Indian Ocean & the Gulf of Aden: 246,201 sq. mi.; pop. 2,864,000; cap. Mogadishu

So·ma·li·land (sō mä′lē land′, sə-) region in E Africa, including Somalia, Djibouti, & E Ethiopia

so·mat·ic (sō mat′ik) *adj.* [Gr. *sōmatikos* < *sōma*, the body] **1.** of the body; corporeal; physical **2.** of the cells (**somatic cells**) of an organism that develop into the various tissues, organs, etc. of the body **3.** of the outer walls of the body —see SYN. at BODILY —**so·mat′i·cal·ly** *adv.*

so·ma·to- [< Gr. *sōmatos*, genitive of *sōma*, body] *a combining form meaning* body [somatoplasm] : also, before a vowel, **somat-**

so·ma·to·plasm (sō′mə tə plaz′m′, sō mat′ə-) *n.* [SOMATO- + -PLASM] the body cells as distinguished from germ cells —**so′·ma·to·plas′tic** (-plas′tik) *adj.*

so·ma·to·type (-tīp′) *n.* [SOMATO- + -TYPE] body type or physique

som·ber (säm′bər) *adj.* [Fr. *sombre*, ult. < L. *sub*, under + *umbra*, shade] **1.** dark and gloomy or dull [somber skies] **2.** sad or serious; melancholy [somber thoughts] Also, chiefly Brit. sp., **som′bre** —**som′ber·ly** *adv.* —**som′ber·ness** *n.*

☆**som·bre·ro** (säm brer′ō, səm-) *n., pl.* **-ros** [Sp. < *sombra*, shade: see SOMBER] a broad-brimmed felt or straw hat, worn in Mexico, the Southwest, etc.

some (sum; *unstressed* səm) *adj.* [OE. *sum*] **1.** being a certain one or ones not specified or known [some people smoke] **2.** being of a certain unspecified quantity, degree, etc. [have some butter] ☆**3.** [Colloq.] remarkable, striking, etc. [it was some fight] —*pron.* **1.** a certain one or ones not specified or known [some agree] **2.** a certain unspecified number, quantity, etc. [take some] —*adv.* **1.** about [some ten men were hired] **2.** [Colloq.] to some extent [she slept some] ☆**3.** [Colloq.] to a great extent, at a great rate, etc. [you must run some to catch up] —☆**and then some** [Colloq.] and more than that

-some[1] (səm) [OE. -*sum*] *a suffix meaning* like, tending to, tending to be [tiresome, lonesome]

-some[2] (səm) [< ME. *sum*, SOME] *a suffix meaning* (a specified) number together [twosome]

-some[3] (sōm) [< Gr. *sōma*, body] *a combining form meaning* body [chromosome]

some·bod·y (sum′bud′ē, -bäd′ē, -bəd ē) *pron.* a person unknown or not named; some person; someone [somebody just left] —*n., pl.* **-bod′ies** a person of importance

some·day (-dā′) *adv.* at some future time

some·how (-hou′) *adv.* in a way not known, stated, or understood [it was somehow damaged] : often in **somehow or other**

some·one (-wun′, -wən) *pron. same as* SOMEBODY

some·place (-plās′) *adv.* in, to, or at some place; somewhere

som·er·sault (sum′ər sôlt′) *n.* [altered < MFr. *sombresault* < L. *supra*, over + *saltus*, a leap] an acrobatic stunt done by turning the body one full revolution, heels over head: often used as a figure of speech for a complete change of mind —*vi.* to do a somersault Also **som′er·set** (-set′)

Som·er·ville (sum′ər vil′) [? after Capt. R. *Somers* (1778-1804)] city in E Mass.: suburb of Boston: pop. 89,000

SOMERSAULT

some·thing (sum′thiŋ) *n.* **1.** a thing not definitely known, understood, etc. [something went wrong] **2.** some thing or things, definite but unspecified [have something to eat] **3.** a bit; a little [something over an hour] **4.** [Colloq.] a remarkable person or thing —*adv.* **1.** a little; somewhat [she looks something like me] **2.** [Colloq.] really [sounds something awful] Also used

SOMBRERO

after a figure to indicate a fraction beyond [the bus leaves at six *something*] —**make something of 1.** to find a use for **2.** treat as of great importance ☆**3.** [Colloq.] to have a quarrel or fight about —☆**something else** [Slang] a really remarkable person or thing

some·time (-tīm′) *adv.* **1.** at some time not known or specified [sometime last week] **2.** at some future time [come sometime soon] —*adj.* **1.** former [her sometime friend] **2.** only occasional; not regular [his wit is a sometime thing]

some·times (-tīmz′) *adv.* at times; occasionally [she sometimes goes to plays]

some·way (-wā′) *adv.* in some way or manner; somehow or other: also **some′ways′**

some·what (-hwut′, -hwät′, -wut′, -wət) *n.* some degree, amount, part, etc. [somewhat of a surprise] —*adv.* to some extent, degree, etc.; a little; rather [somewhat late]

some·where (-hwer′, -wer′) *adv.* **1.** in, to, or at some place not known or specified [he lives somewhere near here] **2.** at some time, degree, age, figure, etc. (with *about, around, in,* etc.) [somewhere around ten o'clock] —*n.* an unspecified or undetermined place Also [Chiefly Dial.] **some′wheres′**

Somme (sum; *Fr.* sôm) river in N France flowing west into the English Channel

som·me·lier (sum′əl yā′) *n.* [Fr. < MFr., orig., person in charge of pack animals] a waiter in a restaurant, club, etc. who is in charge of the wines

som·nam·bu·late (säm nam′byoo lāt′, səm-) *vi.* **-lat′ed, -lat′ing** [< L. *somnus*, sleep + *ambulare*, to walk] to walk about while asleep —**som·nam′bu·lant** *adj.* —**som·nam′bu·la′tion** *n.* —**som·nam′bu·la′tor** *n.*

som·nam·bu·lism (-liz′m) *n.* [see prec.] **1.** the act or practice of sleepwalking **2.** the dazed state of a sleepwalker —**som·nam′bu·list** *n.* —**som·nam′bu·lis′tic** *adj.*

som·nif·er·ous (säm nif′ər əs, səm-) *adj.* [< L. < *somnus*, sleep + *ferre*, to bring] causing sleep; soporific: also **som·nif′ic** —**som·nif′er·ous·ly** *adv.*

som·no·lent (säm′nə lənt) *adj.* [< MFr. < L. *somnolentus* < *somnus*, sleep] **1.** sleepy; drowsy **2.** causing drowsiness [a somnolent summer day] —**som′no·lence** *n.* —**som′no·lent·ly** *adv.*

son (sun) *n.* [OE. *sunu*] **1.** a boy or man as he is related to a parent or to both parents: sometimes also used of animals **2.** a male descendant **3.** *a)* a son-in-law *b)* a stepson **4.** a male thought of as having been influenced by something as a child is by a parent [sons of France] **5.** a friendly form of address to a boy or younger man —**the Son** Jesus Christ, as the second person of the Trinity

so·nant (sō′nənt) *adj.* [< L. prp. of *sonare*, to SOUND[1]] **1.** of sound **2.** having sound; sounding —**so′nance** *n.*

so·nar (sō′när) *n.* [so(und) n(avigation) a(nd) r(anging)] an apparatus that transmits high-frequency sound waves through water and registers the vibrations reflected back from an object: used to locate submarines, find depths, etc.

so·na·ta (sə nät′ə) *n.* [It. < L. *sonare*, to SOUND[1]] a musical composition for one or two instruments, usually in three or four movements in different tempos

sonata form a musical form consisting of the statement, development, and restatement of two themes and typically used for the first movement of a sonata, symphony, etc.

so·na·ti·na (sän′ə tē′nə) *n.* [It., dim. of *sonata*] a short or simplified sonata

☆**sonde** (sänd) *n.* [Fr., a sounding line] a device for measuring data about the weather during ascent and descent through the atmosphere and sending it back to earth as by radio

‡**son et lu·mière** (sôn nä lü myer′) [Fr., lit., sound and light] a historical spectacle at night before a monument, etc., using special lighting effects, narration, music, etc.

song (sôŋ) *n.* [OE. *sang*] **1.** the act or art of singing [to break into song] **2.** a piece of music sung or as if for singing **3.** *a)* poetry *b)* a poem that is or can be set to music, as a ballad **4.** a musical sound like singing [the song of the lark] —**for a song** for very little money; cheaply —**song′ful** *adj.* —**song′less** *adj.*

song·bird (sôŋ′burd′) *n.* **1.** a bird that makes vocal sounds that are like music **2.** a woman singer

☆**song·fest** (-fest′) *n.* [SONG + -FEST] an informal gathering of people for singing songs, esp. folk songs

Song of Solomon a book of the Bible that is a dramatic love poem, traditionally thought of as written by Solomon: also called **Song of Songs, Canticle of Canticles**

☆**song sparrow** a common N. American sparrow with a striped breast, noted for its sweet song

song·ster (sôŋ′stər) *n.* [OE. *sangestre*] **1.** a singer **2.** a song-bird —**song′stress** (-stris) *n.fem.*

song thrush a European songbird with brown wings and a white breast

song·writ·er (-rīt′ər) *n.* a person who writes words or music or both for songs, esp. popular songs

son·ic (sän′ik) *adj.* [< L. *sonus,* SOUND¹ + -IC] **1.** of or having to do with sound **2.** designating or of a speed equal to the speed of sound (about 1088 feet per second through air at sea level at 32°F or 0°C)

sonic barrier the large increase in drag met by an aircraft as it comes close to the speed of sound

sonic boom an explosive sound caused by the building up of pressure in a wave going ahead of an aircraft moving at or above the speed of sound

sonic depth finder *same as* FATHOMETER

son-in-law (sun′in lô′) *n., pl.* **sons′-in-law′** the husband of one's daughter

son·net (sän′it) *n.* [Fr. < It. < Pr. dim. of *son,* a song < L. *sonus,* SOUND¹] a poem of fourteen lines in any of several fixed verse and rhyme schemes: sonnets are usually in iambic pentameter: see PETRARCHAN SONNET, SHAKESPEAREAN SONNET

son·net·eer (sän′ə tir′) *n.* a person who writes sonnets

son·ny (sun′ē) *n., pl.* **-nies** little son: used in speaking to any young boy in a friendly way

son·o·buoy (sän′ō bōō′ē, sō′nō-; -boi′) *n.* [< L. *sonus,* SOUND¹ + BUOY] a buoy that picks up underwater sounds and transmits them by radio

so·no·rant (sə nôr′ənt, sō-) *n.* [SONOR(OUS) + (CONSON)ANT] a sound made when a speech organ, as the tongue, palate, etc., is moved in a way that does not restrict the air flow or compress it so that noise is produced

so·nor·i·ty (sə nôr′ə tē, sō-) *n., pl.* **-ties** the quality or state of being sonorous; resonance

so·no·rous (sə nôr′əs, sän′ər əs) *adj.* [< L. < *sonor,* a sound] **1.** producing or capable of producing sound, esp. sound that is full, deep, or rich; resonant [the *sonorous* bass viol] **2.** full, deep, or rich: said of sound **3.** sounding important or dignified; impressive [*sonorous* prose] —**so·no′rous·ly** *adv.* —**so·no′rous·ness** *n.*

Soo (sōō) [alteration of *Sault*] region in N Mich. & S Ontario, Canada, at the cities of Sault Ste. Marie & the ship canals (**Soo Locks**) that bypass a rapids of the St. Marys River: see SAULT STE. MARIE

Soo

soon (sōōn) *adv.* [OE. *sona,* at once] **1.** in a short time; shortly [we will *soon* be there] **2.** promptly; quickly [as *soon* as possible] **3.** ahead of time; early [he left too *soon*] **4.** readily; willingly [I would as *soon* go as stay] —**had sooner** would rather —**sooner or later** eventually

soot (soot, sōōt) *n.* [OE. *sot*] a black substance made up chiefly of tiny pieces of carbon formed when something, as wood or coal, burns without complete combustion —*vt.* to cover, soil, or treat with soot

sooth (sōōth) *adj.* [OE. *soth*] [Archaic] true —*n.* [Archaic] truth —**in sooth** [Archaic] in truth

soothe (sōōth) *vt.* **soothed, sooth′ing** [OE. *sothian* < *soth,* truth] **1.** to make calm or composed, as by gentleness, flattery, etc. **2.** to relieve (pain, etc.) —*vi.* to have a soothing effect —see SYN. at COMFORT —**sooth′er** *n.* —**sooth′ing** *adj.* —**sooth′ing·ly** *adv.*

sooth·say·er (sōōth′sā′ər) *n.* a person who claims that he can tell what is going to happen in the future —**sooth′say′ing** *n.*

soot·y (soot′ē, sōōt′ē) *adj.* **soot′i·er, soot′i·est 1.** of, like, or covered with soot **2.** dark or black like soot —**soot′i·ness** *n.*

sop (säp) *n.* [OE. *sopp*] **1.** a piece of food, as bread, soaked in milk, gravy, etc. **2.** *a*) something given to keep someone calm or satisfied *b*) a bribe —*vt.* **sopped, sop′ping 1.** to soak,

steep, etc. in or with liquid **2.** to take up (liquid) by absorption (usually with *up*) —*vi.* **1.** to soak (*in, into,* or *through* something) **2.** to be or become thoroughly wet

SOP, S.O.P. standing (or standard) operating procedure

sop. soprano

☆**soph** (säf) *n. shortened form of* SOPHOMORE

So·phi·a (sō fē′ə, -fī′-) [< Gr. *sophia,* wisdom < *sophos,* wise] a feminine name: var. *Sophie, Sophy*

soph·ism (säf′iz'm) *n.* [< OFr. < L. < Gr. *sophos,* clever] a clever and seemingly reasonable argument that is, however, faulty or misleading; fallacy or sophistry

soph·ist (säf′ist) *n.* [< L. < Gr. *sophistēs,* wise man] **1.** [*often* S-] in ancient Greece, any of a group of teachers of rhetoric, philosophy, etc., some of whom were widely known for their clever but misleading arguments **2.** any person practicing clever but misleading reasoning

so·phis·ti·cal (sə fis′ti k'l) *adj.* **1.** of or characteristic of sophists or sophistry **2.** clever and seemingly reasonable but misleading Also **so·phis′tic** —**so·phis′ti·cal·ly** *adv.*

so·phis·ti·cate (sə fis′tə kāt′; *for n. usually* -kit) *vt.* **-cat′ed, -cat′ing** [< ML. < L. *sophisticus,* sophistical] **1.** to change from being natural, simple, naive, etc. to being artificial, worldly-wise, etc. **2.** to bring to a more developed, complex, or refined form, level, etc. —*n.* a sophisticated person

so·phis·ti·cat·ed (-kāt′id) *adj.* **1.** not simple, natural, or naive; wise in the ways of the world; well-informed, subtle, etc. **2.** appealing to sophisticated people [*sophisticated* fashions] **3.** highly complex, refined, etc.; of an advanced form, technique, etc. [*sophisticated* equipment]

so·phis·ti·ca·tion (sə fis′tə kā′shən) *n.* **1.** the act of sophisticating **2.** the state or quality of being sophisticated

soph·is·try (säf′is trē) *n., pl.* **-tries** reasoning or an argument that is clever and seems correct but is faulty or misleading

Soph·o·cles (säf′ə klēz′) 496?–406 B.C.; Gr. writer of tragedies

soph·o·more (säf′ə môr′) *n.* [altered (after Gr. *sophos,* wise + *mōros,* foolish) < obs. *sophumer,* lit., sophist] **1.** a student in his second year of college or the tenth grade at high school ☆**2.** a person in his second year in some job, activity, etc. [a *sophomore* on the pro golf tour] —*adj.* of or for sophomores

☆**soph·o·mor·ic** (säf′ə môr′ik) *adj.* of or like sophomores, often thought of as overconfident, stubborn in holding to their opinions, etc. but immature —**soph′o·mor′i·cal·ly** *adv.*

-so·phy (sə fē) [< Gr. *sophia,* skill, wisdom] *a combining form meaning* knowledge [philosophy]

sop·o·rif·ic (säp′ə rif′ik, sō′pə-) *adj.* [< Fr. < L. *sopor,* sleep + -FIC] **1.** causing or tending to cause sleep **2.** sleepy, drowsy, dull, etc. —*n.* a drug, etc. that causes sleep

sop·ping (säp′iŋ) *adj.* thoroughly wet; drenched

sop·py (säp′ē) *adj.* **-pi·er, -pi·est 1.** very wet; sopping **2.** rainy **3.** [Colloq.] sentimental —**sop′pi·ness** *n.*

so·pra·no (sə pran′ō, -prä′nō) *n., pl.* **-nos, -ni** (-prä′nē) [It. < *sopra,* above] **1.** the range of the highest singing voice of women, girls, and young boys **2.** *a*) a voice or singer with this range *b*) a musical instrument with a similar range *c*) a part for such a voice or instrument —*adj.* of, for, or having this range

☆**so·ra** (sôr′ə) *n.* [< ? AmInd.] a small, short-billed wading bird of the rail family, living in marshes: also **sora rail**

sorb (sôrb) *n.* [< Fr. < L. < *sorbus,* service tree] **1.** any of a number of European trees of the rose family, as the service tree **2.** the fruit of any of these trees

sor·bic acid (sôr′bik) [SORB + -IC] a white, crystalline solid, $C_6H_8O_2$, used as a food preservative, fungicide, etc.

sor·bi·tol (sôr′bi tôl′, -tōl′) *n.* [SORB + -IT(E) + -OL¹] a white, sweet, crystalline alcohol, $C_6H_8(OH)_6$, used as a moistening agent in lotions, etc., and as a sugar substitute

Sor·bonne (sôr bän′; *Fr.* sôr bôn′) the liberal arts college of the University of Paris

sor·cer·er (sôr′sər ər) *n.* a person who practices sorcery; wizard —**sor′cer·ess** *n.fem.*

sor·cer·y (sôr′sər ē) *n., pl.* **-cer·ies** [< OFr. < *sorcier,* sorcerer < L. *sors,* lot, share] **1.** the supposed use of an evil supernatural power over people and their affairs; witchcraft; black magic **2.** seemingly magical power, influence, etc. —**sor′cer·ous** *adj.* —**sor′cer·ous·ly** *adv.*

sor·did (sôr′did) *adj.* [< Fr. < L. < *sordes,* filth] **1.** dirty, filthy, disgusting, etc. [*sordid* slums] **2.** *a)* base, low, dishonorable, etc. [a *sordid* scheme] *b)* selfish; eager for money —see **SYN.** at BASE² —**sor′did·ly** *adv.* —**sor′did·ness** *n.*

sore (sôr) *adj.* **sor′er, sor′est** [OE. *sar*] **1.** *a)* giving pain; painful [a *sore* throat] *b)* feeling pain, as from bruises, etc. [he is *sore* all over] **2.** *a)* filled with sadness, grief, etc. [*sore* at heart] *b)* causing sadness, grief, etc. [*sore* hardships] **3.** causing anger or irritation [a *sore* point] ☆**4.** [Colloq.] angry or irritated —*n.* **1.** a sore, usually infected spot on the body, as an ulcer or blister **2.** a source of pain, distress, etc. —*adv.* [Archaic] sorely —**sore′ness** *n.*

sore·head (sôr′hed′) *n.* ☆[Colloq.] a person who is angry, resentful, sulky, etc., or one easily made so

sore·ly (-lē) *adv.* **1.** painfully; severely [*sorely* vexed] **2.** urgently; extremely [*sorely* needed]

sor·ghum (sôr′gəm) *n.* [< It. *sorgo*] **1.** any of several tropical grasses grown for grain, syrup, fodder, etc. ☆**2.** a syrup made from the sweet juices of a variety (**sorgo**) of sorghum

so·ror·al (sə rôr′l) *adj.* [L. *soror*, sister + -AL] of or like a sister or sisters; sisterly —**so·ror′al·ly** *adv.*

so·ror·i·ty (sə rôr′ə tē) *n., pl.* **-ties** [< ML. < L. *soror*, sister] a group of women or girls joined together for social or professional reasons; ☆specif., a Greek-letter college organization

sor·rel¹ (sôr′əl, sär′-) *n.* [< OFr. < Frank. *sur*, sour] **1.** any of several plants with sour, fleshy leaves; dock **2.** *same as* WOOD SORREL

sor·rel² (sôr′əl, sär′-) *n.* [< OFr. < *sor*, light brown < ML. *saurus* < Gmc.] **1.** light reddish brown **2.** a horse, etc. of this color —*adj.* light reddish-brown

SORGHUM

sor·row (sär′ō, sôr′ō) *n.* [OE. *sorg*] **1.** mental suffering caused by loss, disappointment, etc.; sadness, grief, or regret **2.** that which produces such suffering; trouble, misfortune, etc. [her illness is a great *sorrow* to us] **3.** the outward expression of such suffering; mourning **4.** earnest repentance [*sorrow* for sin] —*vi.* to feel or show sorrow; grieve [*sorrowing* over her loss] —**sor′row·er** *n.* —**sor′row·ing·ly** *adv.*

SYN.—**sorrow** refers to the deep, long-lasting mental pain caused by loss, disappointment, etc. [his secret, lifelong *sorrow*]; **grief** suggests briefer, more intense mental pain resulting from a particular misfortune, disaster, etc. [her *grief* over the loss of her child]; **woe** suggests grief or misery so intense that it cannot be relieved [the war-torn nation's *woe*] —**ANT.** joy, happiness

sor·row·ful (-ə fəl) *adj.* feeling, causing, or expressing sorrow; sad —see **SYN.** at SAD —**sor′row·ful·ly** *adv.* —**sor′row·ful·ness** *n.*

sor·ry (sär′ē, sôr′ē) *adj.* **-ri·er, -ri·est** [OE. *sarig* < *sar*, sore] **1.** full of sorrow, pity, sympathy, etc.: also used in apologizing or in showing mild regret [*sorry* to be so late!] **2.** *a)* inferior in worth or quality; poor [a *sorry* performance] *b)* wretched, pitiful, etc. [a *sorry* sight] —**sor′ri·ly** *adv.* —**sor′ri·ness** *n.*

sort (sôrt) *n.* [< MFr., ult. < L. *sortis*, genitive of *sors*, a lot] **1.** any group related by having something in common; kind; class [a popular *sort* of music] **2.** quality or type; nature [remarks of that *sort*] **3.** [Archaic] manner or way —*vt.* to arrange according to class or kind (often with *out*) [to *sort* apples by weight] —*vi.* [Archaic] to harmonize or agree [such conduct does not *sort* well with her beliefs] —see **SYN.** at TYPE —**after a sort** in some way but not very well —**of sorts** of an inferior kind: also **of a sort** [a hat *of sorts*] —**out of sorts** [Colloq.] irritable or slightly ill —**sort of** [Colloq.] somewhat —**sort′a·ble** *adj.* —**sort′er** *n.*

sor·tie (sôr′tē) *n.* [Fr. < *sortir*, to issue] **1.** a sudden attack made by troops from a besieged place against the besiegers; sally **2.** one mission by a single military plane

so·rus (sō′rəs) *n., pl.* **-ri** (-rī) [ModL. < Gr. *sōros*, a heap] a cluster of spore cases on the undersurface of a fern frond, or a similar cluster or spot, as of fungus spores

SOS (es′ō′es′) **1.** a signal of distress in code (· · · — — — · · ·) used internationally in wireless telegraphy, as by ships **2.** [Colloq.] any urgent call for help

so-so (sō′sō′) *adv., adj.* neither very good nor very bad; fairly well or just fair **so so**

sos·te·nu·to (säs′tə nōōt′ō) *adj., adv.* [It. < L. *sustinere*, sustain] *Music* played at a slower tempo, with each note held for its full value

sot (sät) *n.* [< Late OE. *sott* or OFr. *sot*, a fool < VL. *sottus*] a drunkard —**sot′tish** *adj.* —**sot′tish·ly** *adv.*

sot·ted (sät′id) *adj.* besotted; intoxicated, foolish, etc.

sot·to vo·ce (sät′ō vō′chē) [It., under the voice] in a low tone of voice, so as not to be overheard

sou (sōō) *n., pl.* **sous** (sōōz; *Fr.* sōō) [Fr. < OFr. *sol* < LL. *solidus*, SOLIDUS] any of several former French coins, esp. one equal to five centimes

sou·brette (sōō bret′) *n.* [Fr. < Pr. < *soubret*, sly, ult. < L. *superare*, to be above] *Theater* **1.** the role of a lively, clever lady's maid or of any pretty, flirtatious young woman **2.** an actress who plays such roles

sou·bri·quet (sōō′brə kā′) *n. var. of* SOBRIQUET

sou·chong (sōō′shŏŋ′) *n.* [Chin. *hsiao*, small or young + *chung*, kind] a black tea with large leaves

souf·flé (sōō flā′, sōō′flā) *adj.* [Fr. < pp. of *souffler*, to blow] made light and puffy in cooking: also **souf·fléed** (-flād′) —*n.* a baked food made light and puffy by adding beaten egg whites before baking [a cheese *soufflé*]

sough (sou, suf) *n.* [< OE. *swogan*, to sound] a soft, murmuring, sighing, or rustling sound —*vi.* to make a sough

sought (sôt) *pt. & pp. of* SEEK

souk (sōōk) *n.* [Ar. *sūq*] an open-air marketplace in North Africa and the Middle East

soul (sōl) *n.* [OE. *sawol*] **1.** the part of one's being that is thought of as the center of feeling, thinking, will, etc. separate from the body: in some religions the soul is believed to go on after death **2.** the moral or emotional nature of man [an appeal for help that touched his *soul*] **3.** spiritual or emotional warmth, force, etc. [a cold painting, without *soul*] **4.** vital or essential part, quality, etc. ["brevity is the *soul* of wit"] **5.** the central or leading figure [Daniel Boone, *soul* of the frontier] **6.** a perfect example of some quality; embodiment [the very *soul* of kindness] **7.** a person [a town of 1,000 *souls*] ☆**8.** [Colloq.] *a)* among U.S. Negroes, a sense of racial pride *b)* short for SOUL MUSIC —☆*adj.* [Colloq.] of, for, like, or characteristic of U.S. Negroes —**upon my soul!** an exclamation of surprise

☆**soul food** [Colloq.] items of food popular orig. in the South esp. among Negroes, as chitterlings, ham hocks, yams, etc.

soul·ful (sōl′fəl) *adj.* full of or showing deep feeling [a *soulful* look] —**soul′ful·ly** *adv.* —**soul′ful·ness** *n.*

soul·less (-lis) *adj.* lacking soul, sensitivity, or deep feeling —**soul′less·ly** *adv.* —**soul′less·ness** *n.*

☆**soul music** [Colloq.] *a form of* RHYTHM AND BLUES (with added elements of U.S. Negro gospel singing)

soul-search·ing (-sur′chiŋ) *n.* a close, honest examination of one's true feelings, motives, etc.

sound¹ (sound) *n.* [< OFr. *son* < L. *sonus* < IE. base *swen-*, to sound] **1.** *a)* vibrations in air, water, etc. that act on the nerves of the inner ear and produce the sensation of hearing *b)* the sensation that these vibrations produce in the ear **2.** *a)* any identifiable noise, tone, vocal utterance, etc. [the *sound* of a violin, speech *sounds*] *b)* such effects transmitted by or recorded for radio, television, or movies **3.** the distance within which a sound may be heard; earshot [within *sound* of my voice] **4.** the impression made by something said or written; drift [the optimistic *sound* of his report] **5.** meaningless noise ["full of *sound* and fury, signifying nothing"] —*vi.* **1.** to make a sound [his voice *sounds* hoarse] **2.** to make a certain impression through sound or utterance; seem [that wind *sounds* dangerous] —*vt.* **1.** *a)* to cause to sound [*sound* your horn] *b)* to produce the sound of *c)* to utter distinctly [to *sound* one's r's] **2.** to express, signal, proclaim, etc. [the clock *sounds* the hour; *sound* his praises] **3.** to examine (the chest) by auscultation —**sound off** ☆**1.** to speak in turn, as in counting off ☆**2.** [Slang] *a)* to speak out freely in complaining, giving an opinion, etc. *b)* to speak in a loud or unpleasant way, as in boasting —**sound′er** *n.*

sound² (sound) *adj.* [OE. (ge)*sund*] **1.** free from defect, damage, or decay [*sound* timber] **2.** normal and healthy [a *sound* body and mind] **3.** firm and safe; stable; secure [put your savings in a *sound* bank] **4.** based on truth or good judgment; sensible; wise [*sound* advice] **5.** agreeing with established views or beliefs [*sound* doctrine] **6.** thorough, complete, etc. [a *sound* defeat] **7.** deep and undisturbed: said of sleep **8.** morally strong; honest, loyal, etc. **9.** *Law* valid —*adv.* completely; deeply [*sound* asleep] —see **SYN.** at HEALTHY —**sound′ly** *adv.* —**sound′ness** *n.*

sound³ (sound) *n.* [< OE. & ON. *sund*] **1.** a wide channel connecting two large bodies of water or separating an island from the mainland **2.** a long arm of the sea **3.** the air bladder of certain fishes

sound[4] (sound) *vt.* [< MFr. *sonder* < VL. *subundare* < L. *sub*, under + *unda*, a wave] **1.** *a)* to measure the depth of (water), esp. with a weighted line (**sounding line**) *b)* to examine (the bottom of the sea, etc.) with a line that brings up particles that stick to it *c)* to probe (the atmosphere or space) so as to gain data **2.** to try to find out the opinions of: often with *out* [let's *sound* him out on that matter] —*vi.* **1.** to sound water **2.** to dive suddenly downward through the water: said esp. of whales, etc. **3.** to try to find out something —**sound'er** *n.*

sound barrier *same as* SONIC BARRIER

sound effects sounds, as of thunder, animals, etc., produced artificially or by recording as for radio, TV, etc.

sound·ing[1] (soun'diŋ) *adj.* **1.** giving forth sound **2.** having a full, rich sound **3.** sounding important, but with little meaning

sound·ing[2] (soun'diŋ) *n.* **1.** *a)* the act of measuring the depth of water *b)* depth so measured *c)* [*pl.*] a place, usually less than 600 feet in depth, where a sounding line will touch bottom **2.** *a)* an examination of the atmosphere, as with a radiosonde *b)* a probe of space, as with a rocket **3.** [*pl.*] measurements or data learned by sounding **4.** [*often pl.*] a sampling, as of public opinion

sounding board **1.** a thin plate of wood, etc. built into a musical instrument to give a full, rich sound: also **sound'board'** *n.* **2.** any structure designed to reflect sound **3.** a person on whom to test one's ideas, opinions, etc.

sound·less[1] (sound'lis) *adj.* without sound; noiseless — **sound'less·ly** *adv.* —**sound'less·ness** *n.*

sound·less[2] (sound'lis) *adj.* so deep that it cannot be sounded or measured; unfathomable [the *soundless* deep]

sound·proof (-proof') *adj.* able to keep sound from coming through —*vt.* to make soundproof

sound track the area along one side of a motion-picture film, carrying the recording of the sound for the film

☆**sound truck** a motor truck with amplifiers, loudspeakers, etc. for broadcasting on the streets

SOUND TRACK.

sound wave *Physics* a pressure wave carried by an elastic medium, as air; esp., such a wave vibrating at a frequency that can be heard

soup (soop) *n.* [Fr. *soupe* < OFr., soup: of Gmc. origin] **1.** a liquid food made by cooking meat, vegetables, etc. in water, milk, etc. **2.** [Slang] a heavy fog ☆**3.** [Slang] nitroglycerin —**in the soup** [Slang] in trouble —**soup up** [Slang] to increase the power of (an engine, etc.) or its ability to go fast

soup·çon (soop sôn', soop'sôn') *n.* [Fr.] **1.** a suggestion or trace, as of a flavor **2.** a tiny amount; bit

soupe du jour (soop'doo zhoor') [Fr., lit., soup of the day] the featured soup on a menu for that day: also **soup du jour**

soup kitchen a place where soup, etc. is given to needy people

soup·spoon (soop'spoon') *n.* a large-bowled spoon for eating soup

soup·y (soop'pē) *adj.* **soup'i·er, soup'i·est** **1.** watery like soup **2.** [Colloq.] *a)* thick; dense [*soupy* fog] *b)* unpleasantly wet [*soupy* weather] ☆**3.** [Slang] very sentimental

sour (sour) *adj.* [OE. *sur*] **1.** having the sharp, acid taste of lemon juice, vinegar, etc. **2.** made acid or spoiled by fermentation [*sour* milk] **3.** cross, bad-tempered, bitter, etc. **4.** below what is usual; poor [his game has gone *sour*] **5.** distasteful or unpleasant **6.** gratingly wrong or off pitch [a *sour* note] **7.** excessively acid: said of soil —*n.* **1.** something sour ☆**2.** a cocktail made with lime or lemon juice [a whiskey *sour*] —*vt., vi.* to make or become sour —**sour'ish** *adj.* —**sour'ly** *adv.* —**sour'ness** *n.*

SYN.—**sour** usually implies an unpleasant sharpness of taste, often in something which has fermented or become rancid [*sour* milk]; **acid** suggests a sharpness of taste that is normal or natural [a lemon is an *acid* fruit]; **tart** implies a slightly sharp or stinging taste and usually suggests that it is pleasant or desirable [a *tart* cherry pie] —ANT. **sweet**

sour·ball (sour'bôl') *n.* a small ball of tart, hard candy

source (sôrs) *n.* [< OFr. < pp. of *sourdre* < L. *surgere*, to rise] **1.** a spring, etc. that is the starting point of a stream **2.** that from which something comes or is gotten [the sun is our *source*

of energy; a *source* of pleasure] **3.** a person, book, etc. that provides information [the scholar consulted various *sources*] **4.** the point from which light rays, sound waves, etc. come forth —see SYN. at ORIGIN

☆**source·book** (sôrs'book') *n.* a collection of selections from documents giving basic or firsthand information about a subject to be studied or written about; also, a diary, journal, etc. giving such information

sour·dough (sour'dō') *n.* **1.** [Dial.] fermented dough saved from one baking to the next, for use as leaven **2.** a prospector in the western U.S. or Canada: so called from his using sourdough

sour grapes [from Aesop's fable in which the fox, after many unsuccessful efforts to reach some grapes, scorns them as being sour] a scorning or belittling of something that one would like to have or do when one knows that it cannot be had or done

☆**sour gum** a hardy tree of eastern N. America, having purplish fruits and leaves that turn flaming red in autumn

☆**sour·puss** (sour'poos') *n.* [Slang] a gloomy or disagreeable person

sour·sop (-säp') *n.* **1.** a tropical American tree related to the custard-apple, with large, pulpy, acid fruit **2.** this fruit

Sou·sa (soo'zə, -sə), **John Philip** 1854–1932; U.S. bandmaster & composer of marches

☆**sou·sa·phone** (soo'zə fōn') *n.* [after J. P. SOUSA] a brasswind instrument similar to the tuba, used esp. in military bands

souse (sous) *n.* [< OFr. < OHG. *sulza*, brine] **1.** a pickled food, esp. the feet, ears, and head of a pig **2.** liquid for pickling; brine **3.** a plunging into a liquid ☆**4.** [Slang] a drunkard —*vt., vi.* **soused, sous'ing** **1.** to pickle **2.** to plunge or steep in a liquid **3.** to make or become soaking wet ☆**4.** [Slang] to make or become intoxicated

sou·tane (soo tan', -tän') *n.* [Fr. < It. *sottana*] *same as* CASSOCK

south (south) *n.* [OE. *suth*] **1.** the direction to the left of a person facing the sunset (180° on the compass, opposite north) **2.** a region or district in or toward this direction **3.** [*often* S-] the southern part of the earth, esp. the antarctic regions —*adj.* **1.** in, of, to, or toward the south **2.** from the south [a *south* wind] **3.** [S-] designating the southern part of a continent, country, etc. [*South* Asia] —*adv.* in or toward the south —**the South** ☆that part of the U.S. bounded on the north by Pennsylvania, the Ohio River, and N Missouri

South Africa country in southernmost Africa: 472,358 sq. mi.; pop. 22,987,000; caps. Cape Town, Pretoria —**South African**

South African Dutch **1.** the Boers **2.** *same as* AFRIKAANS

South America S continent in the Western Hemisphere: c. 6,864,000 sq. mi.; pop. 190,000,000 —**South American**

South·amp·ton (sou thamp'tən) seaport in S England: pop. 210,000

South Australia state of SC Australia

South Bend [from its being at the southernmost bend in the St. Joseph River] city in N Ind.: pop. 126,000

☆**south·bound** (south'bound') *adj.* going southward

South Carolina [see CAROLINA[1]] Southern State of the U.S., on the Atlantic: 31,055 sq. mi.; pop. 2,591,000; cap. Columbia: abbrev. **S.C., SC** —**South Carolinian**

South China Sea arm of the W Pacific, touching Taiwan, the Philippines, Borneo, & SE Asia

South Dakota [see DAKOTA[2]] Middle Western State of the U.S.: 77,047 sq. mi.; pop. 666,000; cap. Pierre: abbrev. **S.Dak., SD** —**South Dakotan**

south·east (south'ēst', sou-) *n.* **1.** the direction halfway between south and east; 45° east of due south **2.** a region or district in or toward this direction —*adj.* **1.** in, of, to, or toward the southeast **2.** from the southeast [a *southeast* wind] —*adv.* in, toward, or from the southeast —☆**the Southeast** the southeastern part of the U.S.

☆**south·east·er** (south'ēs'tər, sou-) *n.* a storm or strong wind from the southeast

south·east·er·ly (-tər lē) *adj., adv.* **1.** in or toward the southeast **2.** from the southeast [a *southeasterly* wind]

south·east·ern (-tərn) *adj.* **1.** in, of, or toward the southeast **2.** from the southeast [a *southeastern* wind] ☆**3.** [S-] of or characteristic of the Southeast —**South'east'ern·er** *n.*

south·east·ward (-ēst'wərd) *adv., adj.* toward the southeast:

also **south′east′wards** (-wərdz) *adv.* —*n.* a southeastward direction, point, or region

south·east·ward·ly (-wərd lē) *adj., adv.* **1.** toward the southeast **2.** from the southeast [a *southeastwardly* wind]

south·er (sou′thər) *n.* a storm or wind from the south

south·er·ly (suth′ər lē) *adj., adv.* **1.** toward the south **2.** from the south [a *southerly* wind]

south·ern (suth′ərn) *adj.* **1.** in, of, or toward the south **2.** from the south [a *southern* wind] ☆**3.** [S-] of or characteristic of the South

Southern Alps mountain range on South Island, New Zealand

Southern Cross a small S constellation with four bright stars in the form of a cross

south·ern·er (suth′ər nər, -ə nər) *n.* a native or inhabitant of the south, specif. ☆[S-] of the southern part of the U.S.

Southern Hemisphere that half of the earth south of the equator

southern lights *same as* AURORA AUSTRALIS

south·ern·most (suth′ərn mōst′) *adj.* farthest south

Southern Rhodesia *former name of* RHODESIA

Southern Yemen *former name of* YEMEN (sense 2)

Sou·they (suth′ē, sou′thē), **Robert** 1774–1843; Eng. poet & writer

South·field (south′fēld′) city in SE Mich.: suburb of Detroit: pop. 69,000

South Gate [< *South Gate Gardens,* south of Los Angeles] city in SW Calif.: suburb of Los Angeles: pop. 57,000

South Georgia group of Brit. islands in the South Atlantic, east of the Falkland Islands and administered with them as a single colony: 1,600 sq. mi.

South Island S island of the two main islands of New Zealand

south·land (south′land′, -lənd) *n.* [*also* S-] the southern region of a country —**south′land′er** *n.*

☆**south·paw** (-pô′) *n.* [SOUTH + PAW: in the Chicago ballpark (c. 1885) the pitcher's left arm was toward the south] [Slang] a person who is left-handed; esp., a left-handed baseball pitcher —*adj.* [Slang] left-handed

South Pole the southern end of the earth's axis

South Sea Islands islands in temperate or tropical parts of the South Pacific —**South Sea Islander**

South Seas 1. the South Pacific **2.** all the seas located south of the equator

south-south·east (south′south′ēst′, sou′sou′-) *n.* the direction halfway between due south and southeast; 22°30′ east of due south —*adj., adv.* **1.** in or toward this direction **2.** from this direction

south-south·west (-west′) *n.* the direction halfway between due south and southwest; 22°30′ west of due south —*adj., adv.* **1.** in or toward this direction **2.** from this direction

south·ward (south′wərd, suth′ərd) *adv., adj.* toward the south: also **south′wards** (-wərdz) *adv.* —*n.* a southward direction, point, or region

south·ward·ly (-lē) *adj., adv.* **1.** toward the south **2.** from the south [a *southwardly* wind]

south·west (south′west′, sou-) *n.* **1.** the direction halfway between south and west; 45° west of due south **2.** a district or region in or toward this direction —*adj.* **1.** in, of, to, or toward the southwest **2.** from the southwest [a *southwest* wind] —*adv.* in, toward, or from the southwest —☆**the Southwest** the southwestern part of the U.S., esp. Okla., Tex., N.Mex., Ariz., and S Calif.

South West Africa territory in S Africa, on the Atlantic, formerly a mandate of South Africa: revocation of mandate (1966) by UN not recognized by South Africa: 318,261 sq. mi.; pop. 574,000; cap. Windhoek See NAMIBIA

south·west·er (south′wes′tər, sou-) *n.* **1.** a storm or strong wind from the southwest **2.** a sailor's waterproof hat, having a broad brim in the back

south·west·er·ly (-tər lē) *adj., adv.* **1.** in or toward the southwest **2.** from the southwest [a *southwesterly* wind]

south·west·ern (-tərn) *adj.* **1.** in, of, or toward the southwest **2.** from the southwest [a *southwestern* wind] ☆**3.** [S-] of or characteristic of the Southwest —**South′west′ern·er** *n.*

south·west·ward (south′west′wərd, sou-) *adj., adv.* toward the southwest: also **south′west′wards** *adv.* —*n.* a southwestward direction, point, or region

SOUTHWESTER

south·west·ward·ly (-lē) *adj., adv.* **1.** toward the southwest **2.** from the southwest, as a wind

sou·ve·nir (sōō′və nir′, sōō′və nir′) *n.* [Fr., orig. inf., to remember < L. *subvenire,* to come to mind] something kept as a reminder of a place, person, or occasion; keepsake; memento

sou′·west·er (sou wes′tər) *n. same as* SOUTHWESTER

sov·er·eign (säv′rən, -ər in; *occas.* suv′-) *adj.* [< OFr. *soverain,* ult. < L. *super,* above] **1.** above or superior to all others; greatest [a problem of *sovereign* importance] **2.** supreme in power, rank, etc. **3.** of or being a ruler; reigning [a *sovereign* prince] **4.** independent of all others [a *sovereign* state] **5.** excellent; outstanding **6.** working very well, as a remedy —*n.* **1.** a monarch or ruler; king, queen, emperor, etc. **2.** a former British gold coin valued at 20 shillings or one pound sterling —**sov′er·eign·ly** *adv.*

sov·er·eign·ty (-tē) *n., pl.* **-ties 1.** the state of being sovereign **2.** the status, rule, power, etc. of a sovereign **3.** supreme and independent political authority **4.** a sovereign state

so·vi·et (sō′vē it, -et′; sō′vē et′) *n.* [Russ., lit., council] **1.** in the Soviet Union, any of various elected governing councils, ranging from village and town soviets to the Supreme Soviet of the whole country **2.** [S-] [*pl.*] the Soviet people or their officials —*adj.* **1.** of a soviet or soviets **2.** [S-] of or connected with the Soviet Union —**so′vi·et·ism** *n.*

so·vi·et·ize (sō′vē ə tīz′) *vt.* **-ized′, -iz′ing** [*often* S-] **1.** to change to a soviet form of government **2.** to bring under the Soviet system —**so′vi·et·i·za′tion** *n.*

Soviet Union *same as* UNION OF SOVIET SOCIALIST REPUBLICS: also **Soviet Russia**

sow[1] (sou) *n.* [OE. *sugu*] a full-grown female pig

sow[2] (sō) *vt.* **sowed, sown** (sōn) or **sowed, sow′ing** [OE. *sawan*] **1.** to scatter or plant (seed) for growing **2.** to plant (a field, etc.) with seed **3.** to spread or scatter; disseminate [to *sow* hate] **4.** to plant in the mind [to *sow* suspicion] —*vi.* to sow seed —**sow′er** *n.*

☆**sow·bel·ly** (sou′bel′ē) *n.* [Colloq.] *same as* SALT PORK

sow bug (sou) any of several small crustaceans with a flat, oval body, living in damp places, as under rocks

sox (säks) *n. alt. pl. of* SOCK[1] (sense 3)

soy (soi) *n.* [Jpn., colloq. for *shōyu* < Chin. < *chiang,* salted bean + *yu,* oil] **1.** a dark, salty sauce made from fermented soybeans soaked in brine, used esp. with Chinese and Japanese dishes: also **soy sauce 2.** the soybean plant or its seeds Also, chiefly Brit., **soy·a** (soi′ə)

soy·bean (soi′bēn′) *n.* **1.** a plant of the legume family, native to China and Japan but widely grown as a forage and cover crop, and for its seeds, which are rich in protein and oil **2.** its seed

SP, S.P. Shore Patrol

Sp. 1. Spain **2.** Spaniard **3.** Spanish

sp. 1. special **2.** *pl.* **spp.** species **3.** spelling

spa (spä) *n.* [< *Spa,* a health resort in Belgium] **1.** a spring of mineral water **2.** a place, esp. a health resort, with such a spring

space (spās) *n.* [< OFr. < L. *spatium*] **1.** *a)* the area that stretches in all directions, has no limits, and contains all things in the universe *b) same as* OUTER SPACE **2.** *a)* the distance, expanse, or area between, over, or within things [the *space* between desks] *b)* area or room for something [parking *space;* advertising *space* in a newspaper, etc.] **3.** length or period of time [the *space* of a week] ☆**4.** accommodations that can be had or reserved on a train, airplane, etc. **5.** *Math.* a set of points or elements that can be represented in a coordinate system by a single real number, a pair of numbers, etc. **6.** *Music* the open area between any two lines of a staff **7.** *Printing a)* a blank piece of type metal used to separate words, letters, etc. *b)* the area left vacant by this in a printed or typed line —*adj.* of space, esp. outer space —*vt.* **spaced, spac′ing** to arrange with spaces in between [trees *spaced* evenly; concerts *spaced* throughout the season] —**space′less** *adj.* —**spac′er** *n.*

SOYBEAN PLANT

Space Age [*also* s- a-] the period, since 1957, in which artificial satellites and manned space vehicles have been launched —**space′-age′** *adj.*

space bar a bar, as on a typewriter keyboard, pressed to leave a blank space or spaces between words, etc.

space·craft (spās′kraft′) *n., pl.* **-craft′** a spaceship or satellite for use in outer space

☆**spaced-out** (spāst′out′) *adj.* [Slang] intoxicated, dazed, etc., esp. from drugs: also **spaced**, **space′y**

☆**space·flight** (spās′flīt′) *n.* a flight through outer space

space heater a small heating unit for a room or small area

space·man (-man′, -mən) *n.*, *pl.* **-men′** (-men′, -mən) an astronaut or any of the crew of a spaceship

☆**space medicine** a branch of medicine dealing with diseases and disorders connected with flight in outer space

space·port (-pôrt′) *n.* a center where spacecraft are assembled, tested, and launched

space·ship (-ship′) *n.* a rocket-propelled vehicle for travel in outer space

☆**space shuttle** a spacecraft designed to transport persons and equipment between earth and an orbiting space station

space station (or **platform**) a structure designed to orbit in space as a launching pad or as an observation center

☆**space·suit** (-sōōt′) *n.* same as G-SUIT, esp. one adapted for use in spaceflights

space-time continuum (-tīm′) the universe thought of as a continuous whole, having the three dimensions of space along with a fourth dimension of time, in which any event can be located

☆**space·walk** (-wôk′) *n.* the act of an astronaut in moving about in space outside his spacecraft —*vi.* to engage in a spacewalk —**space′walk′er** *n.*

spa·cial (spā′shəl) *adj.* alt. sp. of SPATIAL

spac·ing (spā′siŋ) *n.* **1.** the arrangement of spaces **2.** space or spaces, as between printed words **3.** the act of a person or thing that spaces

spa·cious (spā′shəs) *adj.* **1.** having more than enough space or room; vast; extensive [a *spacious* hall] **2.** not confined or limited; large [the *spacious* heavens] —**spa′cious·ly** *adv.* —**spa′cious·ness** *n.*

☆**Spack·le** (spak′'l) [ult. < L. *spatula*, SPATULA] *a trademark for* a powdery substance (**spackling compound**) that is mixed with water and dries hard, to cover wall seams, nail holes, etc. —*n.* [s-] this substance —*vt.* **-led**, **-ling** [s-] to put spackle on

spade[1] (spād) *n.* [OE. *spadu*] a heavy, long-handled digging tool with a flat blade that is pressed with the foot —*vt.*, *vi.* **spad′ed**, **spad′ing** to dig or cut as with a spade —**call a spade a spade** to call something by its right name; use plain, blunt words —**spade′ful** *n.* —**spad′er** *n.*

spade[2] (spād) *n.* [Sp. *espada*, sword (sign used on Spanish cards) < L. *spatha*, SPATULA] **1.** the black figure (♠) marking one of the four suits of playing cards **2.** [*pl.*] this suit **3.** a card of this suit —**in spades** [Colloq.] in an extreme or emphatic way

spade·work (spād′wurk′) *n.* work done to get a project started, esp. when tiresome or difficult

spa·dix (spā′diks) *n.*, *pl.* **-dix·es**, **-di·ces′** (spā′də sēz′, spā dī′sēz) [ModL. < L., a palm branch < Gr. *spadix*] a fleshy spike of tiny flowers, usually enclosed in a spathe: see illustration at SPATHE

spa·ghet·ti (spə get′ē) *n.* [It., dim. pl. of *spago*, small cord] long, thin strings of pasta, cooked by boiling or steaming and served with a sauce

Spain (spān) country in SW Europe, on the Iberian Peninsula: 194,346 sq. mi.; pop. 34,134,000; cap. Madrid

spake (spāk) *archaic pt. of* SPEAK

span[1] (span) *n.* [OE. *sponn*] **1.** a measure of length, equal to nine inches, based on the distance between the tips of the extended thumb and little finger **2.** *a)* the full amount or extent between any two limits *b)* the distance between ends or supports [the *span* of an arch] *c)* the time that a thing continues or lasts [*span* of attention; the *span* of a man's life] **3.** a part between two supports [a bridge of four *spans*] **4.** *shortened form of* WINGSPAN ☆**5.** [borrowed in U.S. < Du. *span*, in same sense] a team of two animals used together —*vt.* **spanned**, **span′ning** **1.** to measure, esp. by the hand with the thumb and the little finger extended **2.** to encircle with the hand or hands, as in measuring **3.** to extend, reach, or pass over or across [a bridge *spans* the river]

span[2] (span) *archaic pt. of* SPIN

Span. **1.** Spaniard **2.** Spanish

span·dex (span′deks) *n.* [< EXPAND] a synthetic elastic fiber used in girdles, swimsuits, etc.

span·drel (span′drəl) *n.* [< dim. of Anglo-Fr. *spaundre* < OFr.

espandre, to expand] **1.** the space between the exterior curve of an arch and a rectangular frame enclosing it **2.** any of the spaces between a series of arches and a cornice above

span·gle (spaŋ′g'l) *n.* [< dim. of ME. *spang*, a clasp < OE.] **1.** a small piece of bright metal, esp. any of those sewn on fabric for decoration **2.** any small, glittering object —*vt.* **-gled**, **-gling** to cover with spangles —*vi.* to glitter as with spangles —**span′gly** *adj.* **-gli·er**, **-gli·est**

Span·iard (span′yərd) *n.* a native or inhabitant of Spain

span·iel (span′yəl) *n.* [< MFr. *espagnol*, lit., Spanish, ult. < L. *Hispania*, Spain] any of several breeds of dog with a silky coat, drooping ears, and short legs and tail

SPRINGER SPANIEL
(18 in. high at shoulder)

Span·ish (span′ish) *adj.* of Spain, its people, their language, etc. —*n.* the Romance language of Spain and of Spanish America —**the Spanish** the people of Spain

Spanish America Mexico and those countries in Central and South America and the West Indies in which Spanish is the chief language

Span·ish-A·mer·i·can (-ə mer′ə kən) *adj.* **1.** of both Spain and America **2.** of Spanish America or its people —*n.* a native or inhabitant of Spanish America, esp. one of Spanish descent

Spanish-American War the war between the U.S. and Spain (1898)

Spanish Armada see ARMADA (sense 1 *b*)

Spanish Civil War the civil war in Spain (1936–39)

Spanish Inquisition the Inquisition as reorganized in Spain in 1478: well-known for its cruel and extreme practices

Spanish Main **1.** orig., the coastal region of the Americas along the Caribbean Sea; esp., the N coast of S. America **2.** later, the Caribbean Sea itself, or that part of it adjacent to the N coast of S. America

☆**Spanish moss** a rootless plant often growing in long, graceful strands from the branches of trees in the southeastern U.S. and tropical America

☆**Spanish omelet** an omelet folded around a sauce of chopped onion, green pepper, and tomato

Spanish onion any of several large, globe-shaped, mild-flavored onions, often eaten raw

☆**Spanish rice** boiled rice cooked with tomatoes and chopped onions, green peppers, etc.

Spanish Sahara Sp. province at the W end of the Sahara, on the Atlantic: 109,000 sq. mi.; pop. 76,000

SPANISH MOSS

spank (spaŋk) *vt.* [echoic] to strike with something flat, as the open hand, esp. on the buttocks, as in punishment —*vi.* to move along swiftly —*n.* a smack given in spanking

spank·er (spaŋ′kər) *n.* **1.** a person or thing that spanks **2.** [Colloq.] an unusually fine, large, etc. person or thing **3.** *Naut.* *a)* a fore-and-aft sail on the after mast of a square-rigged vessel ☆*b)* the after mast and its sail on a vessel of more than three masts that is rigged like a schooner

spank·ing (-kiŋ) *adj.* **1.** rapid **2.** brisk: said of a breeze **3.** [Colloq.] unusually fine, large, etc. —*adv.* [Colloq.] altogether; completely [*spanking* new] —*n.* a series of smacks given by one who spanks

span·ner (span′ər) *n.* **1.** one that spans **2.** *chiefly Brit. term for* WRENCH (tool for turning nuts, bolts, etc.)

☆**Span·sule** (span′sool, -syool) [SPAN[1] + (CAP)SULE] *a trademark for* a long-acting medicinal capsule whose tiny beads of medicine dissolve at spaced periods of time —*n.* [often s-] such a capsule

☆**span·worm** (span′wurm′) *n. same as* MEASURING WORM

☆**Spar, SPAR** (spär) *n.* [< *s(emper) par(atus)*, (always prepared), L. motto of the Coast Guard] a woman member of the U.S. Coast Guard

fat, āpe, cär; ten, ēven; is, bīte; gō, hôrn, tōōl, look; oil, out; up, fur; get; joy; yet; chin; she; thin, then; zh, leisure; ŋ, ring; ə for a in ago, e in agent, i in sanity, o in comply, u in focus; ′ as in able (ā′b'l); Fr. bal, ë, Fr. coeur; ö, Fr. feu; Fr. mon; ô, Fr. coq; ü, Fr. duc; r, Fr. cri; H, G. ich; kh, G. doch; ‡foreign; ☆ Americanism; < derived from. See inside front cover.

spar[1] (spär) *n.* [< MDu. or MLowG. *spar*] any shiny, crystalline mineral that splits easily into chips or flakes —**spar′ry** *adj.* -ri·er, -ri·est

spar[2] (spär) *n.* [< ON. *sparri* or MDu. *sparre*] **1.** any pole, as a mast, yard, or boom, for supporting the sails on a ship **2.** a lengthwise support for the ribs of an airplane wing —*vt.* **sparred, spar′ring** to equip with spars

spar[3] (spär) *vi.* **sparred, spar′ring** [prob. < MFr. < It. *sparare*, to kick < *parare*, to parry] **1.** to fight with the feet and spurs: said of a fighting cock **2.** to box with jabbing or feinting movements, landing few heavy blows, as in practice matches **3.** to dispute or argue back and forth —*n.* a sparring match

spare (sper) *vt.* **spared, spar′ing** [OE. *sparian*] **1.** to treat with mercy; hold back from killing, hurting, etc. [to *spare* someone's life, feelings, etc.] **2.** to save or free (a person) from (something) [*spare* me the trouble] **3.** to omit, keep from using, or use with care [*spare* no effort] **4.** to part with or give up (money, time, some article, etc.) without trouble to oneself —*vi.* **1.** to practice careful economy; be frugal **2.** to show mercy —*adj.* **1.** not in regular use; extra [a *spare* room] **2.** not taken up by regular work or duties; free [*spare* time] **3.** small in amount; meager; scanty [*spare* rations] **4.** not fleshy; lean [a *spare*, old horse] —*n.* **1.** an extra part, thing, etc. ☆**2.** *Bowling* *a)* a knocking down of all the pins with two rolls of the ball *b)* a score so made —see **SYN.** at **LEAN**[2] and **MEAGER** — (**something**) **to spare** an amount of (something) over and above the amount needed or used [clearing the tunnel with no room *to spare*] —**spare′ly** *adv.* —**spare′ness** *n.* —**spar′er** *n.*

spare·ribs (sper′ribz′) *n.pl.* [altered (after **SPARE**, *adj.*) < MLowG. *ribbesper* < *ribbe*, rib + *sper*, a spit for roasting] a cut of meat, esp. pork, consisting of the thin end of the ribs with most of the meat cut away: see illustration at **PORK**

spar·ing (sper′iŋ) *adj.* **1.** that spares **2.** using or giving little; frugal [he was *sparing* in his praise] **3.** scanty or meager —see **SYN.** at **THRIFTY** —**spar′ing·ly** *adv.* —**spar′ing·ness** *n.*

spark[1] (spärk) *n.* [OE. *spearca*] **1.** a glowing bit of matter, esp. one thrown off by a fire **2.** any flash or sparkle of light like this **3.** a tiny beginning or trace, as of life, interest, etc.; bit **4.** a force that stirs something into action or being [the *spark* that touched off the mutiny] **5.** *Elec.* *a)* a very brief flash of light made by an electric discharge through air or some other insulating material *b)* such a discharge, as in a spark plug —*vi.* **1.** to make or throw off sparks **2.** to come forth as or like sparks —*vt.* to stir into action; be the force that enlivens [to *spark* one's interest] —**spark′er** *n.*

spark[2] (spärk) *n.* [ON. *sparkr*, lively] **1.** a dashing, gallant young man **2.** a beau or lover —*vt., vi.* ☆[Colloq.] to court, woo, pet, etc. An old-fashioned term

spark gap a space between two electrodes through which a spark discharge may take place

spar·kle (spär′k'l) *vi.* **-kled, -kling** [< ME. *sparken*, to **SPARK**[1]] **1.** to throw off sparks **2.** to shine with flashes of light; glitter, as jewels, sunlit water, etc. **3.** to be brilliant and lively [talk that *sparkles*] **4.** to bubble or effervesce, as some wines —*vt.* to make sparkle —*n.* **1.** a spark, or glowing particle **2.** a sparkling, or glittering [the *sparkle* of sequins] **3.** brilliance; liveliness —see **SYN.** at **FLASH**

spar·kler (-klər) *n.* one that sparkles; specif., *a)* a pencil-shaped firework that burns with bright sparks *b)* [*pl.*] [Colloq.] bright, clear eyes *c)* [Colloq.] a diamond or similar gem

☆**spark plug 1.** a piece fitted into a cylinder of an internal-combustion engine to make sparks that ignite the fuel mixture within **2.** [Colloq.] a person or thing that inspires, stirs into action, etc. —**spark′plug′** *vt.* **-plugged′, -plug′ging**

sparring partner any person with whom a prizefighter boxes for practice

spar·row (spar′ō) *n.* [OE. *spearwa*] **1.** any of several old-world weaverbirds, esp. of a group including the **ENGLISH SPARROW**, now common in the U.S. **2.** any of many finches native to both the Old and New Worlds; ☆esp., any of various American species, as the **SONG SPARROW**

sparrow hawk 1. a small European hawk with short wings ☆**2.** a small American falcon

sparse (spärs) *adj.* [< L. pp. of *spargere*, to scatter] thinly spread or scattered; not dense [a *sparse* crowd; *sparse* hair] —see **SYN.** at **MEAGER** —**sparse′ly** *adv.* —**sparse′ness, spar·si·ty** (spär′sə tē) *n.*

[spark plug diagram labels: TERMINAL, INSULATOR, ELECTRODES, GAP]
SPARK PLUG (cutaway model)

Spar·ta (spär′tə) city in the S Peloponnesus, Greece, a powerful military city in ancient Laconia: see map at **GREECE**

Spar·ta·cus (spär′tə kəs) ?–71 B.C.; Thracian slave & gladiator in Rome: leader of a slave revolt

Spar·tan (spär′t'n) *adj.* **1.** of ancient Sparta, its people, or their culture **2.** like or characteristic of the Spartans; brave, not complaining, not needing luxuries, highly disciplined, strict, etc. —*n.* **1.** a citizen of Sparta **2.** a person with Spartan traits — **Spar′tan·ism** *n.*

spar varnish a durable varnish for outdoor surfaces

spasm (spaz′m) *n.* [< MFr. < L. < Gr. *spasmos* < *span*, to pull] **1.** any sudden tightening of a muscle or muscles, that cannot be controlled **2.** any short, sudden burst of activity, feeling, etc. [a *spasm* of coughing, pity, etc.]

spas·mod·ic (spaz mäd′ik) *adj.* [ModL. *spasmodicus* < Gr. < *spasmos*: see prec.] of, like, or in a spasm or spasms; sudden, sharp, and irregular [his *spasmodic* pain; *spasmodic* efforts to reform] Also **spas·mod′i·cal** —**spas·mod′i·cal·ly** *adv.*

spas·tic (spas′tik) *adj.* [< L. < Gr. *spastikos*, pulling < *span*: see **SPASM**] of, marked by, or having spasms or spastic paralysis —*n.* a person with spastic paralysis —**spas′ti·cal·ly** *adv.*

spastic paralysis a condition, as in cerebral palsy, in which certain muscles stay tightened, causing some difficulty in movement

spat[1] (spat) *n.* [prob. echoic] **1.** a quick, slapping sound ☆**2.** [Colloq.] a small quarrel —*vi.* **spat′ted, spat′ting 1.** to strike with a spat ☆**2.** [Colloq.] to have a spat, or quarrel —see **SYN.** at **QUARREL**[2]

spat[2] (spat) *n.* [contr. < **SPATTERDASH**] a short gaiter of heavy cloth for the instep and ankle

spat[3] (spat) *alt. pt. & pp. of* **SPIT**[2]

spat[4] (spat) *n.* [Anglo-Fr. < ?] **1.** the spawn of the oyster or other bivalve shellfish **2.** a young oyster or young oysters —*vi.* **spat′ted, spat′ting** to spawn: said of oysters

spate (spāt) *n.* [ME.] **1.** [Chiefly Brit.] a sudden flood or heavy rain **2.** a large outpour, as of words

spathe (spāth) *n.* [< ModL. < L. < Gr. *spathē*, flat blade] a large, leaflike part or pair of such parts enclosing a flower cluster (esp. a spadix)

spa·tial (spā′shəl) *adj.* [< L. *spatium*, space] **1.** of space **2.** happening or existing in space —**spa·ti·al·i·ty** (-shē al′ə tē) *n.* —**spa′tial·ly** *adv.*

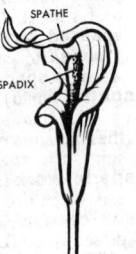
[labels: SPATHE, SPADIX]

spat·ter (spat′ər) *vt.* [akin to Fris. *spatten*, to splash] **1.** to scatter in drops or small blobs [to *spatter* red paint over blue] **2.** to splash or spot with such drops or blobs [a coat *spattered* with mud] **3.** to soil the reputation of; defame or slander —*vi.* **1.** to be scattered in drops, etc., as fat in frying **2.** to fall or strike as in a shower, as raindrops or pellets —*n.* **1.** *a)* a spattering *b)* its sound **2.** a mark made by spattering

spat·ter·dash (-dash′) *n.* [**SPATTER** + **DASH**] a long legging formerly worn to protect the stocking or trouser leg, as in wet weather

☆**spat·ter·dock** (-däk′) *n.* a N. American pond lily with thick roots, heart-shaped leaves, and yellow flowers

spat·u·la (spach′ə lə) *n.* [L., dim. of *spatha*, flat blade] a knifelike tool with a flat, flexible blade used for spreading icings, paints, etc., and for scraping, scooping, etc.

spat·u·late (-lit, -lāt′) *adj.* shaped like a spatula

spav·in (spav′in) *n.* [MFr. *esparvain*] a disease of horses in which there is a bony enlargement of the hock joint, usually causing lameness —**spav′ined** *adj.*

spawn (spôn) *vt., vi.* [< Anglo-Fr. < OFr. *espandre*, to shed < L.: see **EXPAND**] **1.** to produce or deposit (eggs, sperm, or young) **2.** to bring into being (esp. something thought of with contempt and produced in great quantity) —*n.* **1.** the eggs or young produced by fish, mollusks, amphibians, etc. **2.** something produced; specif., offspring or progeny: usually used with contempt

spay (spā) *vt.* [< Anglo-Fr. < OFr. < *espee*, sword < L. *spatha*: see **SPATHE**] to sterilize (a female animal) by removing the ovaries

speak (spēk) *vi.* **spoke** or archaic **spake**, **spo′ken** or archaic **spoke, speak′ing** [OE. *specan*, earlier *sprecan*] **1.** to say words with the ordinary voice; talk [I *spoke* to her over the telephone] **2.** to express opinions, feelings, ideas, etc. by or as by talking [he *speaks* well of her] **3.** to make a request or reservation (for): usually in the passive [a seat not yet *spoken* for] **4.** to make a speech; discourse [*speaking* first on the program] **5.** to be a spokesman (*for*) **6.** to hold a conversation; converse [I'll *speak* with her today] **7.** to give out sound, as a dog barking —*vt.* **1.** to make known by or as by speaking [*speak* your mind freely] **2.** to use or be able to use (a given language) in speaking **3.** to say (words) orally —**so to speak** that is to say —**speak for itself** to be clear without need of explanation —**speak out** (or **up**) **1.** to speak loudly or clearly **2.** to speak freely or forcefully —**speak well for** to show something favorable about —**to speak of** worthy of mention [no gains *to speak of*] —**speak′a·ble** *adj.*

SYN.—**speak** and **talk** generally can be substituted for one another, but **speak** often suggests formal speech, as to an audience [who will *speak* at the graduation?] and **talk** often suggests informal conversation [we were *talking* at dinner]; **converse** suggests a talking together by two or more people so as to exchange ideas, information, etc. [they are *conversing* in the parlor]; **discourse** suggests formal, lengthy talking of a scholarly kind [he was *discoursing* to us on Dickens]

☆**speak·eas·y** (spēk′ē′zē) *n., pl.* **-eas′ies** [SPEAK + EASY: so named from the secretive atmosphere] [Slang] a place selling alcoholic drinks illegally, esp. during Prohibition

speak·er (spē′kər) *n.* **1.** a person who speaks or makes speeches **2.** a person who serves as chairman of a lawmaking body; specif., ☆[S-] the chairman of the U.S. House of Representatives: in full, **Speaker of the House** **3.** a loudspeaker —**speak′er·ship′** *n.*

speak·ing (-kiŋ) *adj.* **1.** that speaks, or seems to speak; expressive; vivid [a *speaking* likeness] **2.** in or for speech [one's *speaking* voice; within *speaking* range] —*n.* **1.** the act or art of one who speaks **2.** that which is spoken; utterance —**on speaking terms** friendly enough to carry on conversation

speaking in tongues same as GLOSSOLALIA

spear (spir) *n.* [OE. *spere*] **1.** a weapon with a long shaft and sharp head, for thrusting or throwing **2.** any spearlike, often forked tool, as one used in fishing **3.** [var. of SPIRE] a long blade or shoot, as of grass —*vt.* **1.** to pierce or stab as with a spear **2.** to catch (fish, etc.) as with a spear —*vi.* **1.** to pierce like a spear **2.** to sprout into a long stem —**spear′er** *n.*

☆**spear·fish** (spir′fish′) *n., pl.* **-fish**[*, *-fish′es**: see FISH a deepsea fish with beaklike jaws, related to the marlin and sailfish —*vi.* to fish with a spear or spear-throwing device (**spear gun**)

spear·head (-hed′) *n.* **1.** the pointed head of a spear **2.** the person or persons leading an activity, esp. a military attack —*vt.* to lead (an attack, etc.)

spear·man (-mən) *n., pl.* **-men** a fighting man armed with a spear

spear·mint (-mint′) *n.* [from its flower spikes] a plant of the mint family, with a pleasant sharp smell, used for flavoring

spec. **1.** special **2.** specification **3.** speculation

spe·cial (spesh′əl) *adj.* [< OFr. < L. < *species*, kind] **1.** different, distinctive, or unique [a *special* process that was patented] **2.** unusual; extraordinary [a *special* treat] **3.** highly thought of [a *special* friend] **4.** of or for a particular occasion, purpose, etc. [a *special* celebration upon victory] **5.** not general or regular; specific [*special* legislation] —*n.* something special, as a featured item on a menu or in a sale, or a special TV program not part of a regular series —**spe′cial·ly** *adv.*

SYN.—**special** and **especial** both imply that the thing so described has qualities, aspects, uses, etc. which make it different from others of its kind, and the choice of word generally depends on which sounds better in a sentence, but **especial** is usually preferred in stressing importance [a matter of *especial* interest to you]; **specific** and **particular** are both applied to something that is singled out for attention, but **specific** suggests the statement of an example, illustration, etc. [he cited *specific* cases], and **particular** emphasizes the distinctness or individual nature of the thing so described [in this *particular* case] —**ANT.** general

☆**special delivery** delivery of mail by special postal messenger, for an extra fee

spe·cial·ist (-ist) *n.* **1.** a person who specializes in a particular branch of study, professional work, etc. [Dr. Gray is a *specialist* in skin diseases] ☆**2.** *U.S. Army* any of six grades above private first class for enlisted personnel with technical duties —*adj.* of a specialist: also **spe′cial·is′tic** —**spe′cial·ism′** *n.*

spe·ci·al·i·ty (spesh′ē al′ə tē) *n., pl.* **-ties** chiefly Brit. var. of SPECIALTY

spe·cial·ize (spesh′ə līz′) *vt.* **-ized′, -iz′ing** **1.** to make special or specific **2.** to direct toward a specific end [to *specialize*

one's studies] **3.** *Biol.* to adapt (parts or organs) to a special condition, use, etc. [a bat's wings are forelimbs *specialized* for flying] —*vi.* **1.** to make a specialty of some product, work, etc.; specif., to take up a special study or work in a special branch of a profession **2.** *Biol.* to become specialized —**spe′·cial·i·za′tion** *n.*

special jury *Law* a blue-ribbon jury

spe·cial·ty (-əl tē) *n., pl.* **-ties** **1.** a special quality, feature, etc. **2.** a special field of study, branch of a profession, etc. **3.** the state of being special **4.** a product, line of products, etc. given special attention and care to make it attractive, superior, etc. [a bakery whose *specialty* is pie]

☆**spe·ci·a·tion** (spē′shē ā′shən, -sē-) *n.* *Biol.* the process of developing new species through evolution —**spe′ci·ate′** (-āt′) *vi.* **-at′ed, -at′ing**

spe·cie (spē′shē, -sē) *n.* [abl. of L. *species*, kind: see use in phr. below] money made of metal, not paper; coin —**in specie** **1.** in kind **2.** in coin

spe·cies (spē′shēz, -sēz) *n., pl.* **-cies** [L., appearance, shape, kind, etc.] **1.** a distinct kind; sort; variety; class [a *species* of bravery] **2.** *Biol.* a group of highly similar plants or animals, part of a genus, that can reproduce fertile offspring only among themselves **3.** *Logic* a class of things with distinctive common qualities, grouped with similar classes in a genus **4.** *R.C.Ch.* *a)* the outward form or appearance of the consecrated Eucharistic bread and wine *b)* the bread or wine —**the species** the human race

specif. specifically

spe·cif·ic (spi sif′ik) *adj.* [LL. *specificus* < L. *species* (see SPECIES) + *-ficus*, -FIC] **1.** specifying or specified; definite; exact [no *specific* plans for the trip] **2.** of or forming a species **3.** peculiar to or characteristic of something [*specific* traits] **4.** of a particular sort [a *specific* solution to their problem] **5.** *Med.* *a)* specially effective as a cure for a particular disease [a *specific* remedy] *b)* produced by a particular microorganism [a *specific* disease] —*n.* **1.** something specially suited for a given use or purpose **2.** a specific cure or remedy **3.** a distinct item or detail; particular [give me the *specifics* on the new legislation] —see SYN. at SPECIAL —**spe·cif′i·cal·ly** *adv.* —**spec·i·fic·i·ty** (spes′ə fis′ə tē) *n.*

spec·i·fi·ca·tion (spes′ə fi kā′shən) *n.* **1.** a specifying; detailed mention **2.** [*usually pl.*] a statement of all necessary details as to size, materials, etc. [*specifications* for a new building] **3.** something specified; specified item, etc.

specific gravity the ratio of the weight or mass of a given volume of a substance to that of an equal volume of another substance (water for liquids and solids, air or hydrogen for gases) used as a standard

specific heat the quantity of heat needed to raise the temperature of a unit mass of a substance one degree

spec·i·fy (spes′ə fī′) *vt.* **-fied′, -fy′ing** [< OFr. < LL. < *specificus*, SPECIFIC] **1.** to mention or describe in detail; state definitely [to *specify* the time and place] **2.** to include as an item in a set of specifications [the plans *specified* hardwood floors in the house] —**spec′i·fi′a·ble** *adj.* —**spec′i·fi′er** *n.*

spec·i·men (spes′ə mən) *n.* [L. < *specere*, to see] **1.** a part of a whole, or one individual of a group, used as a sample of the rest [a *specimen* of handwriting] **2.** [Colloq.] a (specified kind of) individual or person [an odd *specimen*] **3.** *Med.* a sample, as of urine, for analysis

spe·cious (spē′shəs) *adj.* [< L. *speciosus* < *species*, appearance] seeming good, sound, etc., but not really so [*specious* logic] —see SYN. at PLAUSIBLE —**spe′cious·ly** *adv.* —**spe′cious·ness** *n.*

speck (spek) *n.* [OE. *specca*] **1.** a small spot or mark [a *speck* of paint on the rug] **2.** a tiny bit; particle [not a *speck* of food in the house] —*vt.* to mark with specks

speck·le (spek′'l) *n.* [dim. of ME. *specke*, SPECK] a small mark of a different color; speck —*vt.* **-led, -ling** to mark with speckles [the walls are white *speckled* with red]

specs (speks) *n.pl.* [Colloq.] **1.** eyeglasses ☆**2.** specifications: see SPECIFICATION (sense 2)

spec·ta·cle (spek′tə k'l) *n.* [< OFr. < L. < *spectare*, look at < *specere*, to see] **1.** something to look at, esp. a remarkable sight [the fireworks display was quite a *spectacle*] **2.** a public show on a grand scale **3.** [*pl.*] eyeglasses: old-fashioned term —**to**

make a spectacle of oneself to behave in a foolish or shocking way in public —**spec′ta·cled** *adj.*

spec·tac·u·lar (spek tak′yə lər) *adj.* of or like a spectacle; strikingly grand or unusual [a *spectacular* display of roses] —*n.* a grand or elaborate show —**spec·tac′u·lar·ly** *adv.*

spec·ta·tor (spek′tāt ər, spek tāt′-) *n.* [L. < pp. of *spectare*, to behold] a person who watches something without taking part; onlooker [*spectators* at sports events]

spec·ter (spek′tər) *n.* [< Fr. < L. *spectrum*, appearance, apparition < *spectare*, to behold] 1. a ghost; apparition 2. any object of dread Also, Brit. sp., **spec′tre**

spec·tra (spek′trə) *n. alt. pl. of* SPECTRUM

spec·tral (-trəl) *adj.* 1. of or like a specter; ghostly 2. of a spectrum [*spectral* colors] —**spec·tral′i·ty** (-tral′ə tē), **spec′tral·ness** *n.* —**spec′tral·ly** *adv.*

spec·tro- [< SPECTRUM] *a combining form meaning:* 1. of radiant energy as shown in a spectrum 2. of or by a spectroscope

spec·tro·gram (spek′trə gram′) *n.* a photograph of a spectrum

spec·tro·graph (-graf′) *n.* an instrument for breaking up light or other radiation into a spectrum and photographing the spectrum —**spec′tro·graph′ic** *adj.* —**spec′tro·graph′i·cal·ly** *adv.*

spec·trom·e·ter (spek träm′ə tər) *n.* an instrument for measuring spectral wavelengths —**spec′tro·met′ric** (-trə met′rik) *adj.* —**spec·trom′e·try** (-ə trē) *n.*

spec·tro·scope (spek′trə skōp′) *n.* an optical instrument for breaking up light from any source into a spectrum so that it can be studied —**spec′tro·scop′ic** (-skäp′ik) *adj.* —**spec′tro·scop′i·cal·ly** *adv.*

spec·tros·co·py (spek träs′kə pē) *n.* the study of spectra by use of the spectroscope —**spec·tros′co·pist** *n.*

spec·trum (spek′trəm) *n., pl.* **-tra** (-trə), **-trums** [ModL., special use of L. *spectrum:* see SPECTER] 1. the series of colored bands into which white light is broken up by passing through a prism, etc.: it is arranged according to wavelength, from red, the longest wave visible, to violet, the shortest 2. any like series of bands or lines formed from other kinds of radiant energy 3. a continuous range [a wide *spectrum* of opinion] 4. *same as* RADIO SPECTRUM

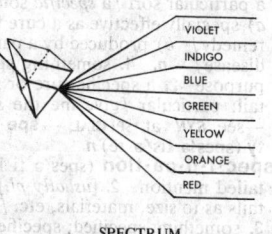

SPECTRUM

spec·u·late (spek′yə lāt′) *vi.* **-lat′ed, -lat′ing** [< L. pp. of *speculari*, to view < *specula*, watch tower < *specere*, to see] 1. to think about the various aspects of a subject; ponder; esp., to make guesses [scientists *speculate* about life on other planets] 2. to buy or sell stocks, land, etc., hoping to gain from price changes; also, to engage in any risky undertaking for possible huge profits —see SYN. at THINK¹ —**spec′u·la′tion** *n.*

spec·u·la·tive (spek′yə lāt′iv, -lə tiv) *adj.* 1. of, like, or taking part in speculation 2. having to do with theory only; not practical 3. uncertain; risky

spec·u·lum (spek′yə ləm) *n., pl.* **-la** (-lə), **-lums** [L. < *specere*, to look] 1. a mirror, esp. one of polished metal used as a reflector in a telescope, etc. 2. *Med.* an instrument used to make a passage wider for easier examination 3. *Zool.* a patch of color on the wings of certain birds, esp. ducks —**spec′u·lar** (-lər) *adj.*

sped (sped) *alt. pt. & pp. of* SPEED

speech (spēch) *n.* [OE. *spæc, spræc* < base of *sprecan*, to speak] 1. the act of speaking 2. the power or ability to speak [to lose one's *speech*] 3. the manner of speaking [his *speech* told us he was British] 4. what is spoken; utterance, talk, etc. 5. a talk given to an audience 6. the language or dialect used by a certain group of people 7. the study of the mechanics, techniques, and skills of speaking or practice in these

SYN.—**speech** is the general word for a piece on some subject spoken before an audience, with or without preparation; **address** implies a formal, carefully prepared speech and usually suggests that the speaker or the speech is important [an *address* to a legislature]; **oration** suggests an eloquent, sometimes merely pompous and showy speech, esp. one delivered on some special occasion [a Fourth of July *oration*]; a **lecture** is a carefully prepared speech intended to inform or instruct the audience [a *lecture* to a college class]; **talk** suggests informality and is applied either to an unprepared speech or to an address or lecture in which the speaker purposely uses a simple, conversational approach

speech community all the people speaking a particular language or dialect, whether together in a single area or spread out through various regions

speech·i·fy (spē′chə fī′) *vi.* **-fied′, -fy′ing** to make a speech: used with humor or contempt —**speech′i·fi′er** *n.*

speech·less (spēch′lis) *adj.* 1. not able to speak; mute 2. silent, as from shock [*speechless* with rage] 3. not expressed or expressible in words [*speechless* terror] —see SYN. at VOICELESS —**speech′less·ly** *adv.* —**speech′less·ness** *n.*

speed (spēd) *n.* [OE. *spæd*, success] 1. the act or state of moving rapidly; swiftness 2. *a)* the rate of movement; velocity [the *speed* of sound] *b)* the rate or swiftness of any action [reading *speed*] 3. an arrangement of gears as for the drive of an engine [a truck with five forward *speeds*] 4. [Colloq.] one's kind or level of taste, ability, etc. [tennis is not my *speed*] ☆5. [Slang] any of various amphetamine compounds 6. [Archaic] luck; success [to wish someone good *speed*] —*adj.* of speed —*vi.* **sped** or **speed′ed, speed′ing** 1. to go fast, ☆esp. at a speed greater than is safe or allowed by law [arrested for *speeding*] 2. [Archaic] *a)* to get along; fare *b)* to prosper —*vt.* 1. to help succeed; aid [a gift will *speed* the building program] 2. to wish Godspeed to [to *speed* the parting guest] 3. to cause to go, move, etc. swiftly [to *speed* a letter on its way] —see SYN. at HASTE —**speed up** to go or make go faster —**speed′er** *n.*

speed·boat (spēd′bōt′) *n.* a motorboat built for speed

speed·om·e·ter (spi däm′ə tər) *n.* [< SPEED + -METER] a device attached to a motor vehicle, etc. to show speed, as in miles per hour

☆**speed·ster** (spēd′stər) *n.* a person or thing that speeds

☆**speed trap** a strip of road where hidden police cars, electronic devices, etc. are used to catch speed violators

speed·up (-up′) *n.* an increase in speed; esp., an increase in the rate of output, etc., as required by an employer without any increase in pay

☆**speed·way** (-wā′) *n.* 1. a track for racing cars or motorcycles 2. a road for high-speed traffic

speed·well (-wel′) *n.* any of various plants of the figwort family, with spikes of white or bluish flowers

speed·y (spēd′ē) *adj.* **speed′i·er, speed′i·est** 1. rapid; swift [*speedy* runners] 2. without delay; prompt [a *speedy* reply] —see SYN. at FAST¹ —**speed′i·ly** *adv.* —**speed′i·ness** *n.*

spe·le·ol·o·gy (spē′lē äl′ə jē) *n.* [< L. < Gr. *spēlaion*, a cave + -LOGY] the scientific study and exploration of caves —**spe′le·ol′o·gist** *n.*

spell¹ (spel) *n.* [OE., a saying] 1. a word or words supposed to have some magic power 2. power or control that seems magical; charm; fascination —**cast a spell on** to enchant or charm by or as by magic —**under a spell** held in a spell or trance

spell² (spel) *vt.* **spelled** or **spelt, spell′ing** [< OFr. *espeller*, to explain < Frank. *spellōn*] 1. to say, write, or signal in order the letters of (a word, etc.) 2. to make up, or form (a word, etc.): said of specified letters 3. to mean [red *spells* danger] —*vi.* to spell words, etc. —**spell out** 1. to read letter by letter or with difficulty 2. to make out or recognize as if by close reading ☆3. to explain in detail [the supervisor *spelled* out his duties]

spell³ (spel) *vt.* **spelled, spell′ing** [OE. *spelian*] [Colloq.] to work in place of (another) while he rests; relieve —*n.* 1. a turn of working in place of another 2. any period of work, duty, etc. [a two-year *spell* as reporter] 3. a period (of being in some state) [a *spell* of gloom] 4. a period of specified weather [a cold *spell*] 5. [Colloq.] a period of time that is indefinite, short, etc. 6. [Colloq.] a period of some illness ☆7. [Dial.] a short distance

spell·bind (spel′bīnd′) *vt.* **-bound′, -bind′ing** to hold by or as by a spell; fascinate; enchant

☆**spell·bind·er** (-bīn′dər) *n.* a speaker who has great power to hold and sway his audience

spell·bound (-bound′) *adj.* held or influenced by or as by a spell; fascinated; enchanted

☆**spell·down** (-doun′) *n.* a spelling contest in which each contestant who misspells a word must drop out: also **spelling bee**

spell·er (-ər) *n.* 1. a person who spells words [a good *speller*] ☆2. an exercise book used to teach spelling

spell·ing (-iŋ) *n.* 1. the act of one who spells words 2. the way a word is spelled

spelt¹ (spelt) *alt. pt. & pp. of* SPELL²

spelt² (spelt) *n.* [OE. < LL. *spelta*] a kind of wheat with grains that do not thresh free of chaff

spel·ter (spel′tər) *n.* [< or related to MDu. *speauter*] crude zinc from the smelter, esp. as used in galvanizing

☆**spe·lunk·er** (spi luŋ′kər) *n.* [< obs. *spelunk*, a cave (ult. < Gr. *spēlynx*) + -ER] a person who explores caves as a hobby —**spe·lunk′ing** *n.*

Spen·cer (spen′sər), **Herbert** 1820–1903; Eng. philosopher

Spen·ce·ri·an (spen sir′ē ən) *adj.* **1.** of Herbert Spencer or his philosophy ☆**2.** of or in the style of penmanship taught by Platt Rogers Spencer (1800–64), characterized by rounded, well-formed letters —*n.* a follower of Herbert Spencer

spend (spend) *vt.* **spent**, **spend′ing** [< OE. *spendan* (in compounds) < ML. < L. *expendere*, to expend] **1.** to use up, exhaust, etc. [*his fury was spent*] **2.** to pay out (money) **3.** to give or devote (time, effort, etc.) to something **4.** to pass (time) [*spending hours alone*] **5.** to waste; squander —*vi.* to pay out or use up money, etc. —**spend′a·ble** *adj.* —**spend′er** *n.*

spend·thrift (spend′thrift′) *n.* a person who spends money carelessly; squanderer —*adj.* wasteful; extravagant

Spen·ser (spen′sər), **Edmund** 1552?–99; Eng. poet —**Spen·se′ri·an** (-sir′ē ən) *adj., n.*

spent (spent) *pt. & pp. of* SPEND —*adj.* **1.** tired out; physically exhausted **2.** used up; worn out

sperm[1] (spurm) *n.* [< MFr. < LL. < Gr. *sperma*, seed < *speirein*, to sow] **1.** the fluid from the male reproductive organs; semen **2.** same as SPERMATOZOON

sperm[2] (spurm) *n. shortened form of:* **1.** SPERMACETI **2.** SPERM OIL **3.** SPERM WHALE

-sperm (spurm) [see SPERM[1]] *a combining form meaning* seed [*gymnosperm*]

sper·ma·ce·ti (spur′mə set′ē, -sēt′ē) *n.* [ML. < LL. *sperma*, SPERM[1] + L. *ceti*, genitive of *cetus*, a whale] a white, waxlike substance from oil in the head of a sperm whale or dolphin, used in making cosmetics, ointments, candles, etc.

-sper·mal (spur′m′l) *same as* -SPERMOUS

sper·ma·the·ca (spur′mə thē′kə) *n.* [ModL.: see SPERM[1] & THECA] a small sac in the female reproductive tract in many invertebrates, esp. insects, for storing sperm

sper·mat·ic (spər mat′ik) *adj.* of, like, or having to do with sperm or sperm cells

spermatic cord a cord consisting of a vas deferens, nerves, and blood vessels and passing from a testicle into the body cavity of many mammals

sper·mat·o- [< Gr. *spermatos*, genitive of *sperma*, SPERM[1]] *a combining form meaning* seed or sperm

sper·ma·to·gen·e·sis (spər mat′ə jen′ə sis, spur′mə tō-) *n.* [ModL.: see SPERMATO- & -GENESIS] the process by which male germ cells are formed —**sper·mat′o·ge·net′ic** (-jə net′ik) *adj.*

sper·mat·o·phyte (spər mat′ə fīt′, spur′mə tə-) *n.* [SPERMATO- + -PHYTE] any seed-bearing plant —**sper·mat′o·phyt′ic** (-fit′ik) *adj.*

sper·mat·o·zo·id (-zō′id) *n.* [< SPERMATOZOON + -ID] *Bot.* in certain mosses, ferns, etc., a male germ cell that moves by means of whiplike parts

sper·mat·o·zo·on (spər mat′ə zō′än, -ən; spur′mə tə-) *n., pl.* **-zo′a** (-ə) [ModL. < SPERMATO- + Gr. *zōion*, animal] the male germ cell, found in semen: it enters and fertilizes the egg of the female —**sper·mat′o·zo′al**, **sper·mat′o·zo′an**, **sper·mat′o·zo′ic** *adj.*

sperm oil a lubricating oil from the sperm whale

-sper·mous (spur′məs) *a combining form meaning* having (a specified number or kind of) seed

sperm whale a large, toothed whale of warm seas: a closed cavity in its roughly square head contains sperm oil

spew (spyōō) *vt., vi.* [OE. *spiwan*] **1.** to throw up from or as from the stomach; vomit **2.** to flow or gush forth [*water spewed from the broken pipe*] —*n.* something spewed —**spew′er** *n.*

Spezia *see* LA SPEZIA

sp. gr. specific gravity

sphag·num (sfag′nəm) *n.* [ModL. < Gr. *sphagnos*, kind of moss] **1.** a spongelike moss found in bogs **2.** a mass of such mosses, used to improve soil, to pot plants, etc. —**sphag′nous** (-nəs) *adj.*

SPERMAT-OZOON

sphal·er·ite (sfal′ə rīt′) *n.* [< G. < Gr. *sphaleros*, deceptive] native zinc sulfide, ZnS, the main ore of zinc, usually brownish with a resinous shine

sphe·no·don (sfē′nə dän′) *n.* [< Gr. *sphēn*, a wedge + *odōn*, tooth] *same as* TUATARA

sphe·noid (sfē′noid) *adj.* [< ModL. < Gr. *sphēn*, a wedge + -OID] *Anat.* designating or of the wedge-shaped compound bone at the base of the skull: also **sphe·noi′dal** —*n.* the sphenoid bone

sphere (sfir) *n.* [< OFr. < L. < Gr. *sphaira*] **1.** any round body with a surface equally distant from the center at all points; globe; ball **2.** a star or planet **3.** the visible heavens; sky **4.** *short for* CELESTIAL SPHERE **5.** any of a series of transparent shells which ancient astronomers imagined as revolving one within another around the earth and containing the stars, planets, sun, and moon **6.** the place or range of action, knowledge, etc.; compass [a country's *sphere* of influence] **7.** place in society [the rich move in a different *sphere*] —*vt.* **sphered**, **spher′ing** [Chiefly Poet.] **1.** to put in or as in a sphere **2.** to put among the heavenly spheres **3.** to form into a sphere

-sphere (sfir) *a combining form meaning:* **1.** of or like a sphere [*hydrosphere*] **2.** of any of the layers of gas around the earth [*ionosphere*]

spher·i·cal (sfer′i k′l, sfir′-) *adj.* **1.** shaped like a sphere; globular **2.** of a sphere or spheres Also **spher′ic** —see SYN. at ROUND —**spher′i·cal·ly** *adv.* —**sphe·ric·i·ty** (sfi ris′ə tē) *n.*

spherical aberration distortion of an image resulting from the spherical shape of a lens or mirror

spherical angle an angle formed by the crossing arcs of two great circles on a sphere

spherical triangle a closed figure on the surface of a sphere bounded by the arcs of three great circles

sphe·roid (sfir′oid) *n.* a body that is almost but not quite a sphere —*adj.* of this shape: also **sphe·roi′dal**

spher·ule (sfer′ool, sfir′-, -yool) *n.* [< L. dim. of *sphaera*, sphere] a small sphere or spherical body —**spher′u·lar** *adj.*

spher·u·lite (-oo līt′, -yoo līt′) *n.* [SPHERULE + -ITE[1]] a rounded or spherical crystalline body found in some glassy volcanic rocks —**spher′u·lit′ic** (-lit′ik) *adj.*

sphinc·ter (sfink′tər) *n.* [LL. < Gr. *sphinktēr* < *sphingein*, to draw close] *Anat.* a ring-shaped muscle that surrounds a natural opening in the body and can open or close it by expanding or contracting —**sphinc′ter·al** *adj.*

sphinx (sfinks) *n., pl.* **sphinx′es**, **sphin′ges** (sfin′jēz) [L. < Gr. *sphinx*, lit., the strangler] **1.** any ancient Egyptian statue having a lion's body and the head of a man, ram, or hawk; specif., [S-] a huge statue of this kind with a man's head, near Cairo, Egypt **2.** *a*) *Gr. Myth.* a winged monster with a lion's body and a woman's head and breasts; specif., [S-] such a monster at Thebes, who strangled passers-by unable to solve its riddle *b*) a person who is hard to know or understand

sphyg·mo·ma·nom·e·ter (sfig′mō mə näm′ə tər) *n.* [< Gr. *sphygmos*, the pulse + MANOMETER] an instrument with an attached band that is wrapped around the upper arm and inflated to press against the artery, used to measure blood pressure

Spi·ca (spī′kə) [< L. *spica*, ear of grain, orig., a point] a first-magnitude star in the constellation Virgo

spi·cate (spī′kāt) *adj.* [L. *spicatus*, spiked] *Bot., Zool.* formed or arranged like a spike or spikes

spice (spīs) *n.* [OFr. *espice* < L. *species*, sort] **1.** *a*) any of several vegetable substances, as clove, cinnamon, pepper, etc., used to season food *b*) such substances as a group **2.** a spicy odor **3.** that which adds excitement or interest [the humor that added *spice* to his talk] —*vt.* **spiced**, **spic′ing** **1.** to season or flavor with spice **2.** to add excitement or interest to

☆**spice·bush** (spīs′boosh′) *n.* a spicy-smelling eastern N. American plant with small, yellowish flowers and red fruit

Spice Islands *former name of the* MOLUCCAS

spick-and-span (spik′'n span′) *adj.* [< *spick*, var. of SPIKE[1] +

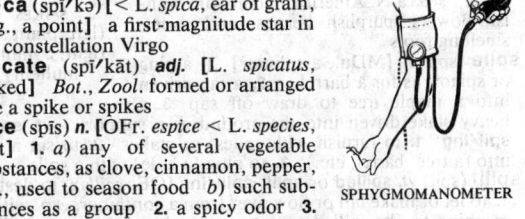

SPHYGMOMANOMETER

span-new < ON. < *spānn*, a chip + *nyr*, new] **1.** new or fresh **2.** neat and clean

spic·u·late (spik′yə lāt′) *adj.* **1.** shaped like a spicule; needlelike **2.** covered with or made up of spicules Also **spic′u·lar** (-lər)

spic·ule (spik′yōōl) *n.* [< ModL. < ML. < L. dim. of *spica*, a point] **1.** *Bot.* a small spike **2.** *Zool.* a small, hard, needlelike piece or growth, as in the skeleton of a sponge: also **spic′u·lum** (-yə ləm), *pl.* **-la** (-lə)

spic·y (spī′sē) *adj.* **spic′i·er, spic′i·est 1.** containing or full of spices **2.** having the flavor or smell of spice [a *spicy* perfume] **3.** lively, interesting, etc. [a *spicy* bit of gossip] **4.** suggestive; risqué; racy [a *spicy* novel] —**spic′i·ly** *adv.* —**spic′i·ness** *n.*

spi·der (spī′dər) *n.* [ME. *spithre*, ult. < OE. *spinnan*, to spin] **1.** any of various small arachnids with a body in two parts, the front part bearing the eight legs and the back part having organs that spin threads for making nests, cocoons, or webs ☆**2.** a cast-iron frying pan, orig. one with legs **3.** any of various devices with leglike extensions

spider crab any of a number of sea crabs with a pear-shaped body and long, thin legs

spider mite *same as* RED SPIDER

spider monkey a monkey of South and Central America with long, spidery limbs and a long tail

spi·der·wort (-wurt′) *n.* any of various fleshy perennial plants with grasslike leaves and showy purplish, white, or pink flowers

spi·der·y (-ē) *adj.* **1.** like a spider **2.** long and thin like a spider's legs **3.** filled with spiders

☆**spiel** (spēl) *n.* [G., play] [Slang] a talk, speech, or harangue, as in persuading or selling —*vi.* [Slang] to give a spiel —**spiel off** [Slang] to recite by rote —**spiel′er** *n.*

spi·er (spī′ər) *n.* a person who spies

spiff·y (spif′ē) *adj.* **spiff′i·er, spiff′i·est** [< dial. *spiff*, well-dressed person] [Old Slang] neat and trim; smart or dapper

spig·ot (spig′ət, spik′-) *n.* [ME. *spigote*] **1.** a plug or peg used to stop the hole in a barrel, etc. **2.** a faucet

spike[1] (spīk) *n.* [< ON. *spīkr* or < MDu. & MLowG. *spīker*] **1.** a long, heavy nail **2.** a sharp-pointed piece, as along the top of an iron fence **3.** *a)* any of the pointed pieces of metal on the bottoms of shoes used in baseball, golf, etc. *b)* [*pl.*] a pair of such shoes *c)* a high, very thin heel on a woman's shoe: also **spike heel** —*vt.* **spiked, spik′ing 1.** to fasten or provide with a spike or spikes **2.** to pierce, cut, etc. with a spike or spikes **3.** to stop or block (a scheme, etc.) **4.** [Slang] to add alcoholic liquor to (a drink) —**spik′y** *adj.*

spike[2] (spīk) *n.* [L. *spica*] **1.** an ear of grain **2.** a long flower cluster with flowers attached directly to the stalk —**spiked** *adj.*

spike lavender a European lavender mint that produces an oil used to perfume toiletries, thin out paints, etc.

spike·let (spīk′lit) *n.* a small spike, as in a flower cluster

spike·nard (-nərd, -närd) *n.* [< LL. < L. *spica*, ear of grain + *nardus*, NARD] **1.** a sweet-smelling ointment used in ancient times **2.** the Asiatic plant from which it is made ☆**3.** a N. American plant with whitish flowers, purplish berries, and sweet-smelling roots

SPIKES
(left, plantain; right, common mullein)

spile (spīl) *n.* [MDu., a splinter] **1.** a plug or spigot, as for a barrel ☆**2.** a tap driven into a maple tree to draw off sap **3.** a heavy stake driven into the ground as a support —*vt.* **spiled, spil′ing 1.** to furnish with spiles, or stakes **2.** to set a spile into (a tree, barrel, etc.) **3.** to plug (a hole) with a spile

spill[1] (spil) *vt.* **spilled** or **spilt, spill′ing** [OE. *spillan*, to destroy] **1.** to let or make fall or flow over from a container, esp. without meaning to [he *spilled* water on the table; try not to *spill* the sugar] **2.** to shed (blood) **3.** to lessen the pressure of (wind) on (a sail) **4.** [Colloq.] to let (a secret) become known **5.** [Colloq.] to make (a rider, load, etc.) fall off —*vi.* to flow over or run out [tears *spilled* from her eyes] —*n.* **1.** a spilling **2.** what is spilled **3.** a spillway **4.** [Colloq.] a fall or tumble, as from a horse —**spill over** to overflow

spill[2] (spil) *n.* [prob. via dial. *spil* < ON. *spila*, a splinter] **1.** a splinter **2.** a thin roll of paper, thin stick, etc. set on fire to light a pipe, candle, etc. **3.** a paper cone

☆**spill·way** (spil′wā′) *n.* [SPILL[1] + WAY] a channel to carry off an overflow of water, as around a dam

spin (spin) *vt.* **spun** or archaic **span, spun, spin′ning** [OE. *spinnan*] **1.** *a)* to draw out and twist fibers of (wool, cotton, etc.) into thread *b)* to make (thread, yarn, etc.) in this way **2.** to make (a web, cocoon, etc.) from a thick fluid coming from the body as a thread: said of spiders, etc. **3.** to produce in a way that suggests spinning [to *spin* a tale] **4.** to draw *out* (a story, etc.) to great length **5.** to make whirl [to *spin* a top] **6.** to make (wheels of a vehicle) rotate without gripping, as on ice **7.** to take out water from (clothes) in a washer by swift rotation —*vi.* **1.** to spin thread, etc. **2.** to fish with a spinning reel **3.** to whirl [the earth *spins* in space] **4.** to feel dizzy and seem to be spinning [my head is *spinning*] **5.** to go into a spin: said of an aircraft **6.** to move along swiftly and smoothly **7.** to rotate freely without gripping [wheels *spinning* on ice] —*n.* **1.** the spinning or rotating of something **2.** a moving along swiftly and smoothly **3.** a ride in a motor vehicle **4.** the falling or descent of an airplane, nose first, along a spiral path **5.** any sudden, steep downward movement —see SYN. at TURN —**spin off 1.** to produce as an outgrowth or secondary development **2.** to get rid of

spin·ach (spin′ich, -ij) *n.* [< MFr. < OSp. *espinaca* < Ar. < Per. *aspanākh*] **1.** a plant with large, dark-green leaves, usually eaten cooked **2.** the leaves

spi·nal (spī′n'l) *adj.* of the spine or spinal cord —*n.* a spinal anesthetic —**spi′nal·ly** *adv.*

spinal anesthesia anesthesia of the lower part of the body by injection of an anesthetic into the spinal cord, usually in the lumbar region —**spinal anesthetic**

spinal canal the canal, or tube, formed by the arches of the vertebrae and containing the spinal cord

spinal column the long row of connected bones that form the backbone

spinal cord the thick cord of nerve tissue of the central nervous system, in the spinal column

spin·dle (spin′d'l) *n.* [< OE. *spinel* < *spinnan*, to spin] **1.** a slender rod or pin for twisting, winding, or holding the thread in spinning by hand, on a spinning wheel, or in a spinning machine **2.** something spindle-shaped, as a thin, decorative rod in some chair backs **3.** any rod, pin, or shaft that turns, or on which something turns, as an axle **4.** in a lathe, a shaftlike part that rotates (**live spindle**) or does not rotate (**dead spindle**) while holding the thing to be turned ☆**5.** a metal spike on a base, to stick papers on for temporary filing: also **spindle file 6.** *Biol.* the spindle-shaped bundle of nuclear fibers formed during one stage of mitosis ☆**7.** *Naut.* a metal rod or pipe topped with a lantern, etc. and fastened to a rock, shoal, etc. to warn vessels —*adj.* of or like a spindle —*vi.* **-dled, -dling** to grow in or into a long, thin shape or stem —*vt.* **1.** to form into a spindle ☆**2.** to stick on a spindle (*n.* 5) for filing

spin·dle·legs (-legz′) *n.pl.* **1.** thin legs **2.** [*with sing. v.*] [Colloq.] a person with thin legs —**spin′dle-leg′ged** (-leg′id, -legd′) *adj.*

spin·dly (spin′dlē) *adj.* **-dli·er, -dli·est** long or tall and very thin or slender, often so as to seem frail or weak: also **spin′dling** (-dliŋ)

spin·drift (spin′drift′) *n.* [< Scot. var. of *spoondrift* < *spoon*, to scud (< ?) + DRIFT] spray blown from a rough sea or surf

spine (spīn) *n.* [< OFr. < L. *spina*, a thorn] **1.** a thin, sharp, stiff part that sticks out on certain plants and animals, as the cactus or porcupine; thorn or quill **2.** any of various pointed or projecting parts, as on bone **3.** the spinal column; backbone **4.** anything suggesting a backbone, as *a)* a ridge of ground or crest of a hill *b)* the narrow back part of a bound book, where the title and author's name usually appear

spi·nel (spi nel′, spin′'l) *n.* [< MFr. < It. dim. of *spina*, SPINE] a hard, crystalline mineral found in various colors: a red variety (**ruby spinel**) is used as a gem

spine·less (spīn′lis) *adj.* **1.** having no backbone; invertebrate **2.** having a weak backbone **3.** lacking courage, willpower, etc. **4.** having no spines or thorns —**spine′less·ly** *adv.* —**spine′less·ness** *n.*

spin·et (spin′it) *n.* [< MFr. < It. *spinetta*, prob. < *spina*, a thorn] **1.** a type of small harpsichord **2.** a small upright piano or electronic organ

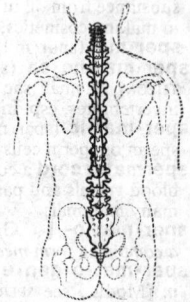

SPINAL COLUMN

spin·na·ker (spin′ə kər) *n.* [said to be altered < *Sphinx*, name of a yacht that carried the sail] a large, triangular forward sail used on some racing yachts

spin·ner (spin′ər) *n.* a person or thing that spins; specif., a fishing lure having blades that turn or flutter when drawn through the water; also, any of its blades

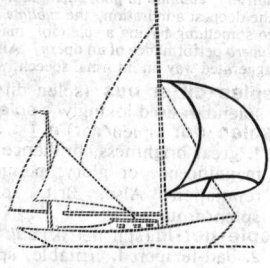

SPINNAKER

spin·ner·et (spin′ə ret′) *n.* [dim. of SPINNER] 1. the organ used by spiders, caterpillars, etc. to spin their silky threads 2. a device with tiny holes through which a solution is forced in making synthetic fibers

spin·ning (spin′iŋ) *n.* 1. the act of making thread, etc. from fibers or filaments 2. fishing done with a rod that has a fixed spool, a light line, and light lures —*adj.* that spins or is used in spinning

spinning jenny an early spinning machine with several spindles, for spinning more than one thread at a time

spinning wheel a simple spinning machine with a single spindle driven by a large wheel

spin·off (spin′ôf′) *n.* 1. distribution to a corporation's shareholders of stock held in a subsidiary corporation 2. a secondary benefit, development, etc., as a television series built around a character in an earlier series

SPINNING WHEEL

spi·nose (spī′nōs) *adj.* [< L. < *spina*, spine] full of or covered with spines: also **spi′nous** (-nəs) —**spi·nos′i·ty** (-näs′ə tē) *n.,* *pl.* **-ties**

Spi·no·za (spi nō′zə), **Ba·ruch** (bə rook′) or **Benedict** 1632-77; Du. philosopher —**Spi·no′zism** (-ziz′m) *n.*

spin·ster (spin′stər) *n.* [ME. < *spinnen,* to spin + -STER] 1. a woman who spins thread or yarn 2. an unmarried woman, esp. an older one; old maid —**spin′ster·hood′** *n.* —**spin′ster·ish** *adj.*

spi·nule (spī′nyōōl, spin′yōōl) *n.* [< L. dim. of *spina,* SPINE] a small, sharp spine —**spi·nu·lose** (spī′nyōō lōs′, spin′yōō-) *adj.*

spin·y (spī′nē) *adj.* **spin′i·er, spin′i·est** 1. covered with spines or thorns 2. full of difficulties; troublesome 3. spine-shaped —**spin′i·ness** *n.*

spiny anteater *same as* ECHIDNA

spin·y-finned (spī′nē find′) *adj.* having fins supported by pointed, stiff spines

spiny lobster a sea crustacean similar to the common lobster, but lacking large pincers and having a spiny shell

spin·y-rayed (-rād′) *adj.* 1. having pointed, stiff rays: said of a fin 2. *same as* SPINY-FINNED

spi·ra·cle (spī′rə k'l, spir′ə-) *n.* [L. *spiraculum* < *spirare,* to breathe] *Zool.* an opening for breathing, as any such opening on the sides of an insect's body, or the blowhole of a whale: see illustration at INSECT

spi·ral (spī′rəl) *adj.* [< ML. < L. *spira,* a coil < Gr. *speira*] circling or coiling around a central point in a flat or rising curve that keeps growing larger or smaller, as the mainspring of a watch or the thread of a screw, or that stays the same, as the thread of a bolt —*n.* 1. a spiral curve; coil or helix 2. something having a spiral form, as a wire for holding sheets in some notebooks 3. a spiral path or flight [the descending *spiral* of a falling leaf] 4. a section of a spiral 5. a continuous, quickening decrease or increase [an inflationary *spiral*] —*vi., vt.* **-raled** or **-ralled, -ral·ing** or **-ral·ling** to move in or form (into) a spiral —**spi′ral·ly** *adv.*

SPIRALS

spi·rant (spī′rənt) *n., adj.* [< L. prp. of *spirare,* to breathe] *same as* FRICATIVE

spire (spīr) *n.* [OE. *spir*] 1. a sprout, spike, or stalk of a plant, blade of grass, etc. 2. the top part of something that comes to a gradual point, as a mountain peak 3. anything that tapers to a point, as a pointed structure capping a tower or steeple —*vi.* **spired, spir′ing** to extend upward, tapering to a point

spi·re·a (spī rē′ə) *n.* [< ModL. genus name < L. < Gr. *speira,* a coil] any of several shrubs of the rose family, with thick clusters of small, pink or white flowers: also sp. **spi·rae′a**

spi·ril·lum (spī ril′əm) *n.,* *pl.* **-la** (-ə) [ModL., dim. of L. *spira* (see SPIRAL)] a bacterium having the form of a spiral thread: see illustration at BACTERIA

spir·it (spir′it) *n.* [< OFr. < L. *spiritus,* breath < *spirare,* to breathe < IE. base (*s*)*peis-,* to blow] 1. the life principle or the soul, esp. in man, frequently thought of as immortal 2. the thinking, feeling part of man; mind; intelligence 3. [*also* S-] life, will, thought, etc., regarded as separate from matter 4. a supernatural being, as a ghost, angel, demon, fairy, etc. 5. an individual person or personality [a brave *spirit*] 6. [*often pl.*] state of mind; mood [high *spirits;* in a *spirit* of fun] 7. liveliness, courage, enthusiasm, etc. [to answer with *spirit*] 8. enthusiasm and loyalty together [school *spirit*] 9. real meaning; true intention [to follow the *spirit* if not the letter of the law] 10. the main principle, quality, or influence [the *spirit* of the Renaissance] 11. [*usually pl.*] distilled alcoholic liquor 12. [*often pl.*] any liquid produced by distillation 13. [*often pl.*] an alcoholic solution of a substance [*spirits* of camphor] —*vt.* 1. to enliven, encourage, cheer, etc. 2. to carry (*away, off,* etc.) secretly and swiftly [the fox *spirited off* two chickens] —*adj.* 1. of spirits or spiritualism [the *spirit* world] 2. operating by the burning of alcohol [a *spirit* lamp] —**out of spirits** sad; depressed —**the Spirit** *same as* HOLY SPIRIT —**spir′it·less** *adj.* —**spir′it·less·ly** *adv.* —**spir′it·less·ness** *n.*

spir·it·ed (-id) *adj.* 1. full of spirit; lively; vigorous; animated [a *spirited* argument; *spirited* horses] 2. having a (specified) character, mood, or state of mind [low-*spirited*] —**spir′it·ed·ly** *adv.* —**spir′it·ed·ness** *n.*

spir·it·ism (-iz′m) *n.* *same as* SPIRITUALISM —**spir′it·ist** *n., adj.* —**spir′it·is′tic** *adj.*

spirit level *same as* LEVEL (*n.* 1)

spir·it·ous (spir′i təs) *adj. same as* SPIRITUOUS

spirits of ammonia a 10% solution of ammonia in alcohol: also **spirit of ammonia**

spir·it·u·al (spir′i chōō wəl, -chōōl) *adj.* 1. of the spirit or soul as distinguished from the body or material matters 2. of or having to do with the mind or feelings; intellectual or emotional [she considered Paris her *spiritual* home] 3. refined in thought or feeling 4. of religion or the church; sacred, devotional, etc. 5. of spirits; supernatural —*n.* ☆1. a religious folk song of the kind created by black Americans 2. [*pl.*] religious or church matters —**spir′it·u·al′i·ty** (-wal′ə tē), *pl.* **-ties, spir′it·u·al·ness** *n.* —**spir′it·u·al·ly** *adv.*

spir·it·u·al·ism (-iz′m) *n.* ☆1. *a*) the belief that the dead survive as spirits which can communicate with the living, esp. with the help of a medium *b*) practices based on this belief 2. the philosophy that all reality is basically spiritual; idealism 3. spiritual quality —**spir′it·u·al·ist** *n.* —**spir′it·u·al·is′tic** *adj.*

spir·it·u·al·ize (spir′i chōō wə līz′, -chōō līz′) *vt.* **-ized′, -iz′ing** 1. to make spiritual 2. to give a spiritual sense or meaning to —**spir′it·u·al·i·za′tion** *n.*

‡**spi·ri·tu·el** (spē rē tü el′; *E.* spir′i chōō wel′) *adj.* [Fr.] having or showing a refined nature or, esp., a quick, graceful wit or mind —**spi·ri·tu·elle′** *adj. fem.*

spir·it·u·ous (spir′i chōō wəs) *adj.* of, like, or containing alcohol: said of distilled liquors —**spir′it·u·os′i·ty** (-wäs′ə tē) *n.*

spi·ro·chete (spī′rə kēt′) *n.* [< ModL. < Gr. *speira,* a spiral + *chaitē,* hair] any of various spiral-shaped bacteria, some of which cause disease: also sp. **spi′ro·chaete**

spi·rom·e·ter (spī räm′ə tər) *n.* [< L. *spirare,* to breathe + -METER] an instrument for measuring the breathing capacity of the lungs —**spi′ro·met′ric** (-rə met′rik) *adj.*

spirt (spurt) *n., vt., vi. same as* SPURT

spir·y (spīr′ē) *adj.* **spir′i·er, spir′i·est** 1. of, or having the form of, a spire 2. having many spires

spit[1] (spit) *n.* [OE. *spitu*] 1. a thin, pointed rod on which meat is fixed for broiling or roasting over a fire or other direct heat 2. a narrow point of land, or a narrow reef or shoal, stretching out into a body of water —**vt. spit′ted, spit′ting** to fix as on a spit —**spit′ter** n.

spit[2] (spit) **vt. spit** or, esp. Brit., **spat, spit′ting** [OE. *spittan*] **1.** to force out from the mouth **2.** to throw (*out*), send out, or say with sudden force [he *spit* out an oath; the radiator valve is *spitting* steam] —**vi. 1.** to force out saliva from the mouth; expectorate **2.** to make an explosive hissing noise, as an angry cat **3.** to express contempt by or as if by spitting saliva (*on* or *at*) **4.** to sputter, as frying fat —**n. 1.** the act of spitting **2.** saliva **3.** a salivalike, frothy secretion of certain insects **4.** [Colloq.] the perfect likeness, as of a person: in **spit and image** (spit′n im′ij) —**spit up** to bring up from the stomach or throat —**spit′ter** n.

☆**spit·ball** (spit′bôl′) **n. 1.** a piece of paper chewed up into a wad for throwing **2.** *Baseball* a pitch, now illegal, made to curve by moistening one side of the ball as with saliva

spite (spīt) **n.** [short for DESPITE] **1.** a mean feeling toward another that makes one want to hurt or annoy him; malice **2.** an instance of this; a grudge —**vt. spit′ed, spit′ing** to show one's spite for by hurting, annoying, etc. [he built a high fence to *spite* his neighbors] —see SYN. at MALICE —**in spite of** regardless of

spite·ful (spīt′fəl) **adj.** full of or showing spite; purposefully annoying —see SYN. at VINDICTIVE —**spite′ful·ly** adv. —**spite′ful·ness** n.

spit·fire (spit′fīr′) **n.** a person, esp. a woman or girl, who has a quick and violent temper

Spits·ber·gen (spits′bur′gən) group of Norw. islands in the Arctic Ocean, east of Greenland

spit·ting im·age (spit′n im′ij) *same as* SPIT AND IMAGE: see SPIT[2]

spit·tle (spit′'l) **n.** [< OE. *spætl*, var. of *spatl*] saliva; spit

☆**spit·tle·bug** (-bug′) **n.** *same as* FROGHOPPER: also called **spit·tle insect**

☆**spit·toon** (spi tōōn′) **n.** a container to spit into

spitz (spits) **n.** [G. < *spitz*, pointed] a small Pomeranian dog with pointed muzzle and ears and a long, silky coat

splanch·nic (splaŋk′nik) **adj.** [< ModL. < Gr. < *splanchnon*, an entrail] of the viscera; visceral

splash (splash) **vt.** [stronger form of PLASH[2]] **1.** to cause (a liquid) to scatter and fall in drops **2.** to dash or scatter a liquid, mud, etc. on, so as to wet or soil [the car *splashed* her dress] **3.** to cause to splash a liquid [to *splash* the oars] **4.** to make (one's way) by splashing **5.** to mark as by splashing [*splashed* with sunlight] **6.** to display so as to attract attention [the scandal was *splashed* on the front page] —**vi. 1.** to dash or scatter a liquid about **2.** to move, fall, strike, or scatter with a splash [he *splashed* through the swamp] —**n. 1.** the act or sound of splashing **2.** water, mud, etc. splashed **3.** a spot or mark made as by splashing **4.** a patch of color, light, etc. —**make a splash** [Colloq.] to attract great, often brief, attention —**splash′er** n.

☆**splash·down** (splash′doun′) **n.** the landing of a spacecraft on water

splash·y (-ē) **adj. splash′i·er, splash′i·est 1.** making splashes **2.** wet, muddy, etc. **3.** covered or marked with splashes **4.** [Colloq.] attracting much notice or attention; showy —**splash′i·ly** adv. —**splash′i·ness** n.

splat[1] (splat) **n.** [via dial. < base of SPLIT] a thin, flat piece of wood, esp. as used in the back of a chair

splat[2] (splat) **n., interj.** a splattering or wet, slapping sound

splat·ter (splat′ər) **n., vt., vi.** [< SPATTER] spatter or splash

splay (splā) **vt., vi.** [< ME. *displaien*, to display] **1.** to spread out or apart; extend (often with *out*) **2.** to slope —**n. 1.** a sloping surface or angle **2.** a spreading; expansion —**adj. 1.** sloping, spreading, or turning outward **2.** broad and flat **3.** awkward

splay·foot (splā′foot′) **n., pl. -feet 1.** a foot that is flat and turned outward **2.** the condition of having such feet —**adj.** of or having splayfoot: also **splay′foot′ed**

spleen (splēn) **n.** [< OFr. < L. < Gr. *splen*, spleen] **1.** a large, vascular, lymphatic organ in the upper left part of the abdomen: it affects the blood structure and was once thought of as the cause of bad temper and mean feelings: see illustration at ALIMENTARY CANAL **2.** ill will; spite; bad temper —**spleen′ful, spleen′ish, spleen′y** adj.

splen·did (splen′did) **adj.** [L. *splendidus* < *splendere*, to shine] **1.** having or showing splendor; brilliant, magnificent, gorgeous, etc. **2.** worthy of high praise; grand; glorious; illustrious [his *splendid* courage] **3.** [Colloq.] very good; excellent [a *splendid* trip] —**splen′did·ly** adv. —**splen′did·ness** n.

SYN.—**splendid** applies to that which impresses or dazzles with its bril-

liance, magnificence, or grandness [a *splendid* palace; a *splendid* sunrise]; **glorious** refers to that which is radiantly beautiful or distinctive [a *glorious* sunset]; **sublime** implies such great beauty or splendor as to cause awe or the deepest admiration [the *sublime* art of Rembrandt]; **superb** is applied to something having a splendor, magnificence, etc. of the highest kind [a *superb* performance of an opera] All of these words are now used in an exaggerated way, in informal speech, with weakened effect

splen·dif·er·ous (splen dif′ər əs) **adj.** [Colloq.] gorgeous; splendid: used jokingly —**splen·dif′er·ous·ly** adv.

splen·dor (splen′dər) **n.** [< OFr. < L. < *splendere*, to shine] **1.** great brightness; brilliance [the *splendor* of a diamond] **2.** magnificence or glory; pomp; grandeur [the *splendor* of his reputation] Also, Brit. sp., **splen′dour** —**splen′dor·ous, splen′drous** adj.

sple·net·ic (spli net′ik) **adj.** [LL. *spleneticus*] **1.** of the spleen **2.** bad-tempered, irritable, spiteful, etc. Also **sple·net′i·cal** —**n.** a spleenful person —see SYN. at IRRITABLE —**sple·net′i·cal·ly** adv.

splen·ic (splen′ik, splēn′-) **adj.** [< L. < Gr. *splenikos*] **1.** of or having to do with the spleen **2.** in or near the spleen

splice (splīs) **vt. spliced, splic′ing** [MDu. *splissen*] **1.** to join (ropes or rope ends) by weaving together the end strands **2.** to join the ends of (timbers) by overlapping and binding or bolting together **3.** to fasten together the ends of (wire, motion-picture film, sound tape, etc.) **4.** [Slang] to join in marriage —**n.** the act or place of splicing —**splic′er** n.

splint (splint) **n.** [MDu. or MLowG. *splinte*] **1.** a thin strip of wood or cane woven together with others to make baskets, chair seats, etc. **2.** a thin, stiff strip of wood, metal, etc. used to keep a broken bone in place or to keep a part of the body in a fixed position —**vt.** to fit, support, or hold in place with a splint or splints

splin·ter (splin′tər) **vt., vi.** [< MDu., akin to *splinte*, splint] **1.** to break or split into thin, sharp pieces **2.** to break into groups with opposing views —**n. 1.** a thin, sharp piece of wood, bone, etc., made by splitting or breaking **2.** a splinter group —**adj.** designating a group that separates from a main group because of opposing views —see SYN. at BREAK

splin·ter·y (-ē) **adj. 1.** easily splintered **2.** of or like a splinter **3.** resulting in splinters, as a fracture **4.** full of splinters; jagged; rough

split (split) **vt. split, split′ting** [MDu. *splitten*] **1.** to separate, cut, or divide along the grain or length into two or more parts [to *split* a wiener bun] **2.** to break or rip apart by force [the crash *split* the wing off the plane] **3.** to divide into parts or shares [to *split* the cost] ☆**4.** to cast (one's vote) for candidates of more than one party **5.** to cause (a group, political party, etc.) to separate into opposing groups **6.** *a*) to break (a molecule) into atoms or into smaller molecules *b*) to produce nuclear fission (in an atom) **7.** *Finance* to divide (stock) by distributing one or more extra shares for each share outstanding —**vi. 1.** to separate lengthwise into two or more parts **2.** to break apart; burst **3.** to separate because of failure to agree (often with *up*) [the club *split* up after major disagreements] ☆**4.** [Slang] to leave a place; depart —**n. 1.** the act or result of splitting; specif., *a*) a break, crack, or tear [a *split* in the seam of her dress] *b*) a division in a group, between persons, etc. **2.** a splinter ☆**3.** a sweet dish made of a split banana or other fruit with ice cream, sauces, nuts, etc. **4.** [often pl.] the acrobatic act of spreading the legs apart until they lie flat on the floor, the body remaining upright **5.** [Colloq.] a small bottle of wine, etc., usually about six ounces **6.** [Colloq.] a share, as of loot **7.** *Bowling* an arrangement of pins after the first bowl, so separated as to make a spare extremely difficult —**adj. 1.** separated along the length or grain **2.** divided; separated —see SYN. at BREAK —**split off** to break off or separate as by splitting —**split′ter** n.

split infinitive *Gram.* an infinitive with the verb and the *to* separated by an adverb (Example: he promised *to always tell* the truth): although objected to by some people, often used deliberately to avoid confusion or wrong emphasis

split-lev·el (split′lev′'l) **adj.** designating or of a type of house with floor levels so arranged that each level is about a half story above or below the one next to it

☆**split pea** a green or yellow pea that has been shelled, dried, and split: used esp. for making soup

split personality *a popular name for* SCHIZOPHRENIA

split screen *Motion Pictures & Television* a technique in which two or more scenes are shown side by side on the same screen

split second a fraction of a second —**split′-sec′ond** adj.

SHORT SPLICE

☆**split shift** a shift, or work period, separated into two parts by a period longer than the usual one for a meal or rest

☆**split ticket** a ballot cast for candidates of more than one party

split·ting (split′iŋ) *adj.* **1.** that splits **2.** *a)* aching very much: said of the head *b)* very painful, as a headache

☆**split-up** (-up′) *n.* a breaking up or separating into two or more parts, units, groups, etc.

splotch (spläch) *n.* [prob. a fusion of SPOT & BLOTCH] a spot, splash, or stain, esp. one that is irregular —*vt., vi.* to mark or be marked with splotches —**splotch′y** *adj.*

☆**splurge** (splurj) *n.* [echoic] [Colloq.] **1.** any very showy display or effort **2.** a spending spree —*vi.* splurged, splurg′ing [Colloq.] **1.** to make a splurge **2.** to spend money extravagantly, as in buying or doing things to please oneself

splut·ter (splut′ər) *vi.* [var. of SPUTTER] **1.** to make hissing or spitting sounds; sputter [the kettle *spluttered* on the stove] **2.** to speak hurriedly and confusedly, as when excited —*vt.* **1.** to say hurriedly and confusedly [he *spluttered* out an excuse] **2.** to spatter —*n.* the act of spluttering —**splut′ter·er** *n.*

spoil (spoil) *vt.* **spoiled** or **spoilt, spoil′ing** [< MFr. < L. *spoliare* < *spolium*, plunder] **1.** to damage or injure so as to make useless, valueless, etc.; destroy [ink stains *spoiled* the paper] **2.** to lessen the enjoyment, quality, etc. of [rain *spoiled* the picnic] **3.** to let (a person) have his own way so much that he demands or expects it [to *spoil* a child] —*vi.* to be damaged or injured so as to become useless, valueless, etc.; decay, as food —*n.* [usually *pl.*] **1.** goods, territory, etc. taken by force, esp. in war; plunder; booty ☆**2.** public offices to which the political party that wins can appoint people —☆**be spoiling for a fight,** etc. to be eager for a fight, etc. —see SYN. at DECAY and INDULGE and INJURE —**spoil′a·ble** *adj.* —**spoil′er** *n.*

spoil·age (spoil′ij) *n.* **1.** a spoiling or being spoiled **2.** something spoiled or the amount spoiled

☆**spoils·man** (spoilz′mən) *n., pl.* **-men** a person who helps a political party in order to share in the spoils

spoil·sport (spoil′spôrt′) *n.* a person who behaves in such a way as to ruin the pleasure of others

☆**spoils system** the practice of treating public offices as the booty of the political party that wins an election, to be handed out to party workers

Spo·kane (spō kan′) [< ? AmInd. *spokanee*, sun] city in E Wash.: pop. 171,000

spoke[1] (spōk) *n.* [OE. *spaca*] **1.** any of the braces extending from the hub to the rim of a wheel **2.** a ladder rung **3.** any of the handholds along the rim of a ship's steering wheel —*vt.* **spoked, spok′ing** to equip with spokes

spoke[2] (spōk) *pt. & archaic pp. of* SPEAK

spo·ken (spō′k'n) *pp. of* SPEAK —*adj.* **1.** said aloud; oral [a *spoken* order] **2.** speaking or said in a (specified) kind of voice [soft-*spoken*]

spoke·shave (spōk′shāv′) *n.* a planing tool consisting of a blade with a handle at either end, used for shaping rounded surfaces, as, formerly, spokes

spokes·man (spōks′mən) *n., pl.* **-men** a person who speaks or gives information for another or for a group

spo·li·a·tion (spō′lē ā′shən) *n.* [L. *spoliatio*] **1.** robbery; plundering **2.** the act of spoiling or damaging

spon·dee (spän′dē) *n.* [< L. < Gr. < *spondē*, solemn libation (one accompanied by a solemn melody)] a metrical foot consisting of two long or a heavily accented syllables —**spon·da′ic** (-dā′ik) *adj.*

sponge (spunj) *n.* [OE. < L. < Gr. *spongia*] **1.** a plantlike sea animal having a structure full of holes and a tough, fibrous skeleton and growing fixed to surfaces under water **2.** the elastic skeleton of certain of these animals, light in weight and highly absorbent, used for washing surfaces, in bathing, etc. **3.** any substance like this; specif., *a)* a piece of spongy plastic, cellulose, etc., used like a natural sponge *b)* a pad of gauze or cotton, as used in surgery *c)* a light pudding full of holes *d)* a raised bread dough **4.** [Colloq.] *same as* SPONGER (sense 3) —*vt.* **sponged, spong′ing 1.** to use a sponge on so as to dampen, wipe clean, etc. **2.** to remove as with a damp sponge

SPONGES

(with *out, off,* etc.) **3.** to absorb with or like a sponge (often with *up*) **4.** [Colloq.] to get as by begging, taking advantage of friendship, etc. —*vi.* **1.** to gather sponges from the sea **2.** to take up liquid like a sponge **3.** [Colloq.] to be a sponger (sense 3): often with *off* or *on* —**throw** (or **toss,** etc.) **in the sponge** [Colloq.] to admit defeat; give up —**sponge′like** *adj.*

sponge bath a bath taken by using a wet sponge or cloth without getting into water or under a shower

sponge·cake (spunj′kāk′) *n.* a light, spongy cake made of flour, eggs, sugar, etc., but no shortening: also **sponge cake**

spong·er (spun′jər) *n.* **1.** a person or boat that gathers sponges **2.** a person who cleans, etc. with a sponge **3.** [Colloq.] a person who, though able to work, depends on others for food, money, etc.; parasite

sponge rubber spongy rubber that is firmer and denser than foam rubber: used for gaskets, etc.

spon·gy (spun′jē) *adj.* **-gi·er, -gi·est 1.** of or like a sponge; specif., *a)* light, soft, and elastic *b)* full of holes *c)* absorbent **2.** soft and completely soaked with moisture [*spongy* ground] —**spon′gi·ness** *n.*

spon·son (spän′sən) *n.* [altered < ? EXPANSION] **1.** a structure that sticks out over the side of a ship or boat, as a gun platform **2.** a winglike piece attached to the hull of a seaplane to steady it in the water

spon·sor (spän′sər) *n.* [L. < *spondere,* to promise solemnly < IE. base *spend-,* to vow] **1.** a person or agency that agrees to be responsible for, advise, or support a person, group, or activity **2.** a godparent; person who answers for a child, as at baptism, making the promises required ☆**3.** a business firm or other agency that alone or with others pays for a radio or TV program on which it advertises or promotes something —*vt.* to act as sponsor for —**spon·so′ri·al** (-sôr′ē əl) *adj.* —**spon′sor·ship′** *n.*

spon·ta·ne·i·ty (spän′tə nē′ə tē, -nā′-) *n.* **1.** the state or quality of being spontaneous **2.** *pl.* **-ties** spontaneous behavior, movement, action, etc.

spon·ta·ne·ous (spän tā′nē əs) *adj.* [< LL. < L. *sponte,* of free will] **1.** acting or done in a free, natural way, without effort or much thought [the audience broke into *spontaneous* applause] **2.** caused or brought about by its own force, without help [the *spontaneous* reaction of the morning glory to light] **3.** growing naturally; wild —**spon·ta′ne·ous·ly** *adv.* —**spon·ta′ne·ous·ness** *n.*

SYN.—**spontaneous** applies to that which is done so naturally that it seems to come without prompting or planning beforehand [a *spontaneous* demonstration]; **impulsive** applies to that which is caused by a sudden inner whim or mood rather than by a conscious decision [an *impulsive* reply]; **instinctive** suggests a sudden, unwilled response to something, as if caused by some natural tendency one has had since birth [an *instinctive* dread of snakes]; **involuntary** refers to that which is done without thinking about it or willing it, as a reflex action [an *involuntary* flicker of the eyelid]; **automatic** suggests a constant machinelike reaction to some thing or situation [an *automatic* response] —**ANT. deliberate, voluntary**

spontaneous combustion the catching on fire of matter as a result of heat built up in it by slow oxidation

spontaneous generation the theory, no longer accepted, that living organisms can originate from nonliving matter

spoof (spoof) *n.* [coined c. 1889] [Slang] **1.** a hoax, joke, or trick **2.** a light parody or satire —*vt., vi.* [Slang] **1.** to fool, joke, or trick **2.** to satirize in a playful manner

☆**spook** (spook) *n.* [Du.] [Colloq.] **1.** a ghost; specter **2.** any person thought of as being like a ghost, as a wierd or strange person, a secret agent, etc. —*vt., vi.* [Colloq.] to haunt, startle, etc. or be startled, frightened, etc.

☆**spook·y** (spook′ē) *adj.* **spook′i·er, spook′i·est** [Colloq.] **1.** of, like, or suggesting a spook or spooks; wierd; eerie **2.** easily spooked; nervous, fearful, jumpy, etc. —**spook′i·ly** *adv.* —**spook′i·ness** *n.*

spool (spool) *n.* [< MFr. < MDu. *spoele*] **1.** a cylinder, with a rim at either end, upon which thread, wire, etc. is wound **2.** something like a spool —*vt.* to wind on a spool

spoon (spoon) *n.* [OE. *spon,* a chip] **1.** a utensil consisting of a small, shallow bowl with a handle, used for picking up or stirring food, etc., as in eating or cooking **2.** something shaped like a spoon, as a shiny, curved fishing lure, usually of metal —*vt.* to take up as with a spoon —*vi.* [Colloq.] to make love, as by kissing, hugging, etc.: an old-fashioned term

---

spoon·bill (spoon′bil′) *n.* **1.** a wading bird with a broad, flat bill that is spoon-shaped at the tip **2.** any of various other birds with a bill like this ☆**3.** *same as* PADDLEFISH

☆**spoon bread** a soft, light, moist bread of cornmeal that is served with a spoon

spoon·drift (-drift′) *n.* early form of SPINDRIFT

spoon·er·ism (spoon′ər iz′m) *n.* [after Rev. W. A. *Spooner* (1844–1930), of Oxford Univ.] an accidental exchange of sounds in two or more words, as "a well-boiled icicle" for "a well-oiled bicycle"

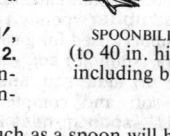

SPOONBILL
(to 40 in. high, including bill)

spoon·feed (spoon′fēd′) *vt.* **-fed′, -feed′ing 1.** to feed with a spoon **2.** to pamper; coddle **3.** to treat, instruct, etc. so as to discourage independent thought and action

spoon·ful (-fool′) *n., pl.* **-fuls′** as much as a spoon will hold

spoor (spoor, spôr) *n.* [Afrik. < MDu.] the track or trail of a wild animal hunted as game —*vt., vi.* to hunt by following a spoor

Spo·ra·des (spôr′ə dēz′; *Gr.* spô rä′thes) the Gr. islands along the W coast of Turkey, esp. the Dodecanese

spo·rad·ic (spô rad′ik, spə-) *adj.* [< ML. < Gr. *sporadikos* < *sporas,* scattered] **1.** happening from time to time; not regular [*sporadic* gunfire] **2.** appearing singly, apart, or in isolated instances [*sporadic* cases of smallpox] —**spo·rad′i·cal·ly** *adv.*

spo·ran·gi·um (spô ran′jē əm, spə-) *n., pl.* **-gi·a** (-ə) [ModL. < *spora,* SPORE + Gr. *angeion,* vessel] *Bot.* an organ or single cell producing spores —**spo·ran′gi·al** *adj.*

spore (spôr) *n.* [ModL. *spora* < Gr. *spora,* a seed] **1.** a tiny, usually single-celled body produced by bacteria, mosses, ferns, certain protozoans, etc. and capable of giving rise to a new plant or animal **2.** any seed, germ, cell, etc. that can develop into a new individual —*vi.* **spored, spor′ing** to develop spores

spore case *same as* SPORANGIUM

spo·ro- *a combining form meaning* spore [*sporophyte*]: also, before a vowel, **spor-**

spo·ro·go·ni·um (spôr′ə gō′nē əm) *n., pl.* **-ni·a** (-ə) [ModL.: see SPORO- & -GONIUM] the sporophyte in mosses and liverworts, usually a spore-bearing capsule on a stalk

spo·ro·phyll (spôr′ə fil) *n.* [SPORO- + -PHYLL] a leaf or leaf-like part producing one or more sporangia —**spo·ro·phyl·la·ry** (-fil′ə rē) *adj.*

spo·ro·phyte (-fīt′) *n.* [SPORO- + -PHYTE] the asexual spore-bearing phase of some plants: see GAMETOPHYTE —**spo·ro·phyt·ic** (-fit′ik) *adj.*

spo·ro·zo·an (spôr′ə zō′ən) *n.* [ModL. *Sporozoa* (see SPORO- & -ZOA) + -AN] any of a group of always parasitic protozoans that usually pass through phases of both sexual and asexual generation, frequently in different hosts: the malaria parasites belong to this group

spor·ran (spär′ən, spôr′-) *n.* [ScotGael. *sporan*] a leather pouch or purse, usually fur-covered, worn hanging from the belt in the dress costume of Scottish Highlanders

sport (spôrt) *n.* [shortened in ME. < DISPORT] **1.** any recreational activity; pastime **2.** active play, a game, etc. taken up for exercise or pleasure and, sometimes, as a profession [football, golf, bowling, swimming, etc. are *sports*] **3.** fun or play [he thought it great *sport* to fool others on the phone] **4.** *a)* an object of ridicule; laughingstock *b)* a thing or person thrown about, as though a plaything ☆**5.** [Colloq.] a gambler **6.** [Colloq.] *a)* a person who is sportsmanlike [be a *sport!*] *b)* a person judged by his ability to take defeat, teasing, etc. [a good (or poor) *sport*] ☆**7.** [Colloq.] a pleasure-loving, flashy person **8.** *Biol.* a plant or animal showing some marked difference from the normal type, as a white robin —*vt.* [Colloq.] to wear or display [to *sport* a loud tie] —*vi.* **1.** to play or frolic; have fun [to *sport* on a beach] **2.** *a)* to joke or jest *b)* to toy or play (*with*) *c)* to make fun of someone or something **3.** *Biol.* to differ markedly from the normal type —*adj.* **1.** of or for sports **2.** suitable for informal, casual wear [a *sport* coat] —**in** (or **for**) **sport** in fun; as

SPORRAN

a joke or jest —**make sport of** to make fun of; ridicule —**sport′er** *n.* —**sport′ful** *adj.* —**sport′ful·ly** *adv.*

sport·ing (spôrt′iŋ) *adj.* **1.** of, interested in, or taking part in sports **2.** sportsmanlike; fair ☆**3.** having to do with games, races, etc. involving gambling or betting —**sport′ing·ly** *adv.*

sporting chance [Colloq.] a fair or even chance

spor·tive (spôr′tiv) *adj.* **1.** playful **2.** done in fun or play, not seriously —**spor′tive·ly** *adv.* —**spor′tive·ness** *n.*

sports (spôrts) *adj. same as* SPORT [*sports* clothes]

sports (or **sport**) **car** a low, small automobile, typically with seats for two and a powerful engine

☆**sports·cast** (spôrts′kast′) *n.* a radio or TV broadcast of sports news —**sports′cast·er** *n.*

sports·man (-mən) *n., pl.* **-men 1.** a man who is interested in or takes part in sports, esp. in hunting, fishing, etc. **2.** a person who plays fair and can take defeat without complaint, or victory without boasting —**sports′man·like′, sports′man·ly** *adj.*

sports·man·ship (-mən ship′) *n.* **1.** skill in or fondness for sports **2.** qualities and behavior expected of a sportsman

sports·wear (-wer′) *n.* clothes worn while taking part in sports or for informal, casual wear

sports·wom·an (-woom′ən) *n., pl.* **-wom·en** (-wim′ən) a woman who is interested in or takes part in sports

sports·writ·er (-rīt′ər) *n.* a reporter who writes about sports or sports events

sport·y (spôrt′ē) *adj.* **sport′i·er, sport′i·est** [Colloq.] **1.** sportsmanlike **2.** characteristic of a sport or sportsman **3.** flashy or showy, as clothes —**sport′i·ly** *adv.* —**sport′i·ness** *n.*

spor·u·la·tion (spôr′yoo lā′shən) *n.* the formation or release of spores —**spor′u·late′** *vi.* **-lat′ed, -lat′ing**

spor·ule (spôr′yool) *n.* a small spore

spot (spät) *n.* [< or akin to MDu. *spotte*] **1.** a small area differing from the surrounding area, as in color **2.** a mark, stain, blot, speck, etc. **3.** a fault, as in character or reputation **4.** a locality; place [a good fishing *spot*] **5.** *shortened form of* SPOTLIGHT **6.** [Chiefly Brit. Colloq.] a small quantity; bit [a *spot* of tea] **7.** [Colloq.] a position or job [looking for a good *spot* on a newspaper staff] **8.** [Colloq.] a position in a schedule [an early evening *spot* on TV] —*vt.* **spot′ted, spot′ting 1.** to mark with spots **2.** to stain; blemish **3.** to place in or on a given spot or spots; locate [to *spot* guards at important points] **4.** to remove (spots or marks), as in dry cleaning **5.** *a)* to pick out; recognize [to *spot* someone in a crowd] *b)* to determine the location of (a target, the enemy, etc.) ☆**6.** [Colloq.] to allow as a handicap [I *spotted* him two points] —*vi.* **1.** to become marked with spots **2.** to make a stain, as ink, etc. —*adj.* **1.** *a)* ready; on hand [*spot* cash] *b)* involving immediate payment of cash **2.** made at random or by sampling [a *spot* survey] **3.** *a)* broadcast from the place where it happens [*spot* news] *b)* placed between regular radio or TV programs [a *spot* announcement] —**hit the spot** [Colloq.] to satisfy a desire —☆**in a (bad) spot** [Slang] in trouble —**on the spot 1.** at the place mentioned **2.** at once **3.** [Slang] in trouble or in a demanding situation ☆**4.** [Slang] in danger, esp. of being murdered

spot-check (spät′chek′) *vt.* to check or examine at random or by sampling —*n.* an act or instance of such checking

spot·less (-lis) *adj.* **1.** having no spots; perfectly clean **2.** free from shame or disgrace, as a reputation

☆**spot·light** (-līt′) *n.* **1.** a strong beam of light aimed at a particular person, thing, etc., as on a stage **2.** a lamp used to throw such a beam **3.** public notice [the governor is always in the *spotlight*] —*vt.* to put a spotlight on

spot·ted (-id) *adj.* **1.** marked with spots **2.** stained; blemished; sullied

spotted fever any of various diseases causing fever and skin rash

spot·ter (spät′ər) *n.* a person who spots; specif., *a)* a person whose work is removing spots, etc. in dry cleaning ☆*b)* a person hired to watch for dishonesty among employees, as in a store *c)* a person who watches for, and reports, enemy aircraft

spot·ty (-ē) *adj.* **-ti·er, -ti·est 1.** having, occurring in, or marked with spots **2.** not uniform or consistent, as in quality; uneven [*spotty* attendance] —**spot′ti·ly** *adv.* —**spot′ti·ness** *n.*

spot welding a process in which metal pieces are held together between two electrodes and welded by a powerful surge of current —**spot′-weld′** *vt., vi.* —**spot′-weld′er** *n.*

spous·al (spou′z'l) *n.* [< ESPOUSAL] [often *pl.*] [Now Rare] a marriage ceremony —*adj.* [Now Rare] of marriage

spouse (spous; *also, esp. for vt.,* spouz) *n.* [< OFr. < L. pp. of *spondere:* see SPONSOR] a partner in marriage —*vt.* **spoused, spous′ing** [Archaic] to marry

spout (spout) *n.* [ME. *spute* < *spouten*, to spout] **1.** a lip or tube, as of a teapot, drinking fountain, etc., by which a liquid is poured or let out **2.** a stream, jet, etc. as of liquid from a spout **3.** *same as: a)* DOWNSPOUT *b)* WATERSPOUT —*vt.* **1.** to shoot out (liquid, etc.) from a spout **2.** to say in a loud, pompous manner [he kept *spouting* poems learned in his youth] —*vi.* **1.** to shoot out with force in a jet: said of liquid, etc. **2.** to let out liquid, etc. as from a spout [the oil well began *spouting*] **3.** to spout words, esp. (usually **spout off**) in a hasty or careless way —**spout′er** *n.*

sprain (sprān) *vt.* [< ? OFr. *espreindre*, to strain < L. < *ex-*, out + *premere*, to press] to wrench or twist a ligament or muscle of (a joint, as the ankle) without dislocating the bones —*n.* **1.** an act of spraining **2.** an injury resulting from this

sprang (spraŋ) *alt. pt. of* SPRING

sprat (sprat) *n.* [OE. *sprott*] **1.** a small, sardinelike, European fish of the herring family **2.** any of several other small herrings

sprawl (sprôl) *vi.* [OE. *spreawlian*] **1.** *a)* to spread the limbs in a relaxed or awkward position [to *sprawl* in a chair] *b)* to sit or lie in such a position **2.** to crawl awkwardly **3.** to spread out awkwardly or unevenly, as handwriting, a line of men, etc. —*vt.* to cause to sprawl —*n.* a sprawling movement or position —**sprawl′er** *n.* —**sprawl′y** *adj.*

spray¹ (sprā) *n.* [< or akin to MDu. *spraeien*, to spray] **1.** a cloud or mist of fine liquid particles, as of water from breaking waves **2.** *a)* a stream of such particles, as from a spray gun or spray can *b)* a device for shooting out such a stream *c)* any liquid for spraying from such a device **3.** something like a spray [a *spray* of buckshot] —*vt., vi.* **1.** to direct a spray (upon) **2.** to shoot out in a spray —**spray′er** *n.*

spray² (sprā) *n.* [ME.] **1.** a small branch or sprig of a tree or plant, with leaves, berries, flowers, etc. **2.** a design or ornament like this

spray can a can in which gas under pressure is used to shoot out the contents as a spray

☆**spray gun** a gunlike device that shoots out a spray of liquid, as paint or insecticide, by air pressure from a compressor

spread (spred) *vt.* **spread**, **spread′ing** [OE. *sprǣdan*] **1.** to open or stretch out so as to cover more space; unfold; unfurl [*spread* out the tablecloth] **2.** to lay or place so as to be seen [he *spread* his paintings on the floor] **3.** to move apart (the fingers, arms, wings, etc.) **4.** *a)* to distribute over an area; scatter *b)* to distribute among a group [to *spread* the wealth] **5.** *a)* to distribute in a thin layer; smear [to *spread* butter on toast] *b)* to cover by smearing [to *spread* bread with jelly] **6.** to extend or stretch out in time [to *spread* payments over a two-year period] **7.** to cause to be widely or more widely known, felt, existent, etc. [to *spread* news, a disease, etc.] **8.** to cover or deck [the floor was *spread* with carpets] **9.** *a)* to set (a table) for a meal *b)* to set (food) on a table **10.** to push apart or farther apart —*vi.* **1.** to lie or extend; be expanded [a valley *spread* out before us] **2.** to become distributed **3.** to be made widely or more widely known, felt, etc. **4.** to be pushed apart or farther apart **5.** to be smeared [butter soft enough to *spread* easily] —*n.* **1.** the act of spreading; extension **2.** *a)* the amount or distance something can be spread [a six-foot wing *spread*] *b)* all the numbers between the highest and lowest figures of a set **3.** an expanse; extent ☆**4.** *a)* two facing pages of a magazine, etc., treated as a single sheet *b)* printed matter set across a page or several columns of a newspaper, etc. ☆**5.** a cloth cover for a table, bed, etc. ☆**6.** any soft substance, as jam, used for spreading on bread **7.** [Colloq.] a meal, esp. one with a wide variety of food ☆**8.** [Western] a ranch —☆**spread oneself** [Colloq.] **1.** to put forth effort in order to make a good impression, etc. **2.** to show off —☆**spread oneself thin** to try to do too many things at once —**spread′er** *n.*

spread-ea·gle (spred′ē′g′l) *adj.* having the figure of an eagle with the wings and legs spread —*vt.* **-gled**, **-gling** to stretch out in the form of a spread eagle, as for a whipping

spree (sprē) *n.* [18th-c. slang for earlier *spray* < ?] **1.** a lively, noisy time **2.** a period of drinking **3.** a period of uncontrolled activity [a shopping *spree*]

sprig (sprig) *n.* [ME. *sprigge*] **1.** *a)* a little twig or spray *b)* a design or ornament like this **2.** a young fellow; stripling —*vt.* **sprigged**, **sprig′ging** to decorate with a design of sprigs —**sprig′gy** *adj.* **-gi·er**, **-gi·est**

spright·ly (sprīt′lē) *adj.* **-li·er**, **-li·est** [< *spright*, var. of SPRITE + -LY¹] gay, light, and lively in movement, manner, style, etc. [a *sprightly* dance, tune, etc.] —*adv.* in a sprightly manner —see SYN. at AGILE —**spright′li·ness** *n.*

spring (spriŋ) *vi.* **sprang** or **sprung**, **sprung**, **spring′ing** [OE. *springan*] **1.** to move suddenly and rapidly; specif., *a)* to leap; bound [to *spring* to one's feet; to *spring* up the stairs] *b)* to appear suddenly [curses *springing* to her lips] *c)* to snap back into position or shape after being stretched, bent, or compressed; be resilient **2.** to arise as from some source; specif., *a)* to grow or develop [the plant *springs* from a seed] *b)* to come into being, usually quickly [towns *sprang* up] **3.** to become bent, warped, split, etc. [the door has *sprung*] **4.** to rise up above surrounding objects; tower [a steeple *springing* high above the town] Often followed by *up* —*vt.* **1.** to cause to leap forth suddenly **2.** to cause to snap shut, as by a spring [to *spring* a trap] **3.** *a)* to cause to warp, bend, split, etc., as by force *b)* to stretch (a spring, etc.) too far **4.** to make known suddenly [to *spring* a surprise] ☆**5.** [Slang] to get (someone) released from jail, as by paying bail —*n.* **1.** a springing; specif., *a)* a jump or leap, or the distance so covered *b)* a sudden darting or flying back **2.** *a)* the ability to snap back into position or shape [this elastic belt has lost its *spring*] *b)* energy or vigor, as in one's walk **3.** a device, as a coil of wire, that returns to its original shape when pressure on it is released: used to absorb shock, make clocks go, etc. **4.** *a)* a flow of water from the ground, often the source of a stream *b)* any source or origin **5.** *a)* that season of the year when plants begin to grow, between winter and summer *b)* any period of beginning **6.** *Naut.* a split or break, as in a mast —*adj.* **1.** of, for, appearing in, or planted in the spring [*spring* flowers] **2.** having, or supported on, springs [a *spring* mattress] **3.** coming from a spring [*spring* water] —**spring a leak** to begin to leak suddenly

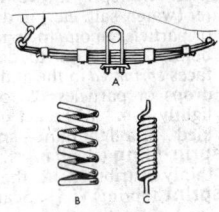

SPRINGS
(A, leaf; B, helical;
C, expansion)

spring·board (spriŋ′bôrd′) *n.* **1.** a flexible, springy board used by acrobats as a takeoff in leaping **2.** *same as* DIVING BOARD **3.** a starting point

spring·bok (-bäk′) *n.*, *pl.* **-bok′**, **-boks′**: see PLURAL, II, D, 2 [Afrik. < Du. *springen*, to spring + *bok*, a buck] a South African gazelle that leaps high in the air when startled: also **spring′buck′** (-buk′)

☆**spring chicken** **1.** a young chicken, esp. one only a few months old, used for broiling or frying **2.** [Slang] a young or inexperienced person, esp. such a woman

spring·er (-ər) *n.* **1.** a person or thing that springs **2.** *short for* SPRINGER SPANIEL ☆**3.** *same as* SPRING CHICKEN

springer spaniel a breed of spaniel used for driving game from cover

☆**spring fever** the lazy and listless feeling that many people get during the first warm days of spring

Spring·field (spriŋ′fēld′) [sense 1 after *Springfield*, village in SE England; others prob. after sense 1] **1.** city in SW Mass.: pop. 164,000 **2.** city in SW Mo.: pop. 120,000 **3.** capital of Ill., in the C part: pop. 92,000 **4.** city in WC Ohio: pop. 82,000

spring lock a lock in which the bolt is snapped into place automatically by a spring

☆**spring peeper** a small tree frog of the eastern U.S., that makes shrill, peeping sounds in early spring

spring·tail (-tāl′) *n.* a small, primitive, wingless insect, able to leap great distances by means of a springlike organ on the underside of the abdomen

spring tide **1.** a tide occurring at the new and the full moon, normally the highest tide of the month **2.** any great flow, rush, or flood

SPRINGBOK
(to 2½ ft. high at shoulder)

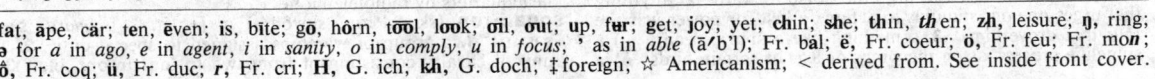

spring·time (spriŋ′tīm′) *n.* the season of spring: also **spring′tide′** (-tīd′)

spring·y (-ē) *adj.* **spring′i·er, spring′i·est** 1. flexible; elastic [*springy* wood for a bow] 2. having many springs of water — **spring′i·ly** *adv.* —**spring′i·ness** *n.*

sprin·kle (spriŋ′k'l) *vt.* **-kled, -kling** [ME. *sprinklen*] 1. to scatter (water, salt, etc.) in drops or particles 2. *a)* to scatter drops or particles upon [to *sprinkle* a lawn with water] *b)* to dampen before ironing 3. to distribute at random [she saw familiar faces *sprinkled* in the audience] —*vi.* 1. to scatter something in drops or particles 2. to fall in drops or particles 3. to rain lightly —*n.* 1. the act of sprinkling, or a small amount sprinkled 2. a light rain —**sprin′kler** *n.*

sprin·kling (-kliŋ) *n.* 1. a small number or amount, esp. when thinly distributed 2. the act of one that sprinkles

sprint (sprint) *vi.* [< Scand.] to run or race at full speed, esp. for a short distance —*n.* 1. the act of sprinting 2. a short race at full speed 3. a brief period of intense activity —**sprint′er** *n.*

sprit (sprit) *n.* [OE. *spreot*] a pole or spar extended diagonally upward from a mast to the topmost corner of a fore-and-aft sail

sprite (sprīt) *n.* [< OFr. *esprit* < L. *spiritus:* see SPIRIT] 1. an elf, pixie, fairy, or goblin 2. an elflike person

sprit·sail (sprit′sāl′, -s'l) *n.* a sail extended by a sprit

spritz (sprits; *G.* shprits) *vt., vi., n.* [ult. < MHG. *sprütze* < *sprützen,* to spray] squirt or spray

sprock·et (spräk′it) *n.* [< ?] 1. any of the teeth or points, as on the rim of a wheel, arranged to fit into the links of a chain 2. a wheel fitted with sprockets: in full, **sprocket wheel**

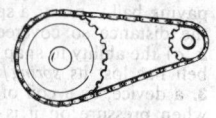

SPROCKET WHEELS

sprout (sprout) *vi.* [OE. *sprutan*] 1. to begin to grow or germinate; give off shoots or buds 2. to grow or develop rapidly [shopping centers *sprouted* up in the suburbs] —*vt.* to cause to sprout or grow —*n.* 1. a young growth on a plant, as a stem or branch; shoot 2. a new growth from a bud, rootstock, etc. 3. any offshoot or offspring 4. [*pl.*] shortened form of BRUSSELS SPROUTS

spruce[1] (sproos) *n.* [< OFr. < ML. *Prussia:* prob. because first known as coming from Prussia] 1. any of various evergreen trees of the pine family, having thin needles 2. its wood

spruce[2] (sproos) *adj.* **spruc′er, spruc′est** [ME. *Spruce,* Prussia, esp. in phr. *Spruce leather,* fine leather imported from Prussia] neat and trim; smart; dapper —*vt., vi.* **spruced, spruc′ing** to make or become spruce (usually with *up*) [new drapes will *spruce* up the room] —**spruce′ly** *adv.* —**spruce′ness** *n.*

sprue (sproo) *n.* [Du. *spruw*] a chronic, chiefly tropical disease characterized by anemia, difficulty in digestion, etc.

sprung (spruŋ) *pp. & alt. pt. of* SPRING —*adj.* 1. having the springs broken, overstretched, or loose 2. having the parts warped, bent, etc. so that they no longer fit together properly [a *sprung* suitcase]

spry (sprī) *adj.* **spri′er** or **spry′er, spri′est** or **spry′est** [< Scand.] full of life; active, brisk, and agile, esp. though elderly —see SYN. at AGILE —**spry′ly** *adv.* —**spry′ness** *n.*

spt. seaport

spud (spud) *n.* [prob. < Scand.] 1. a sharp spade for digging out weeds, etc. 2. [Colloq.] a potato —*vt., vi.* **spud′ded, spud′ding** to dig, etc. with a spud —**spud′der** *n.*

spue (spyoo) *n., vt., vi.* **spued, spu′ing** *same as* SPEW

spume (spyoom) *n.* [< MFr. < L. *spuma*] foam, froth, or scum —*vt., vi.* **spumed, spum′ing** to foam or froth —**spu′mous, spum′y** *adj.*

spu·mo·ni (spə mō′nē) *n.* [It.] an Italian frozen dessert of ice cream in layers of several flavors and colors, often containing bits of fruit and nuts: also sp. **spumone**

spun (spun) *pt. & pp. of* SPIN —*adj.* formed by or as if by spinning

spun glass fine glass fiber, made by forming liquid glass into a thread

spunk (spuŋk) *n.* [IrGael. *sponc,* tinder < L. *spongia,* sponge] 1. wood or fungus that smolders when ignited; punk 2. [Colloq.] courage; spirit

spunk·y (spuŋ′kē) *adj.* **spunk′i·er, spunk′i·est** [Colloq.] having spunk; courageous; spirited —**spunk′i·ly** *adv.* —**spunk′i·ness** *n.*

spur (spur) *n.* [OE. *spura*] 1. a pointed device worn on the heel by horsemen and used to urge the horse forward 2. anything that urges one on; stimulus to action [a lust for power was the *spur* that drove him] 3. something like a spur; specif., *a)* a spinelike process, as on the wings or legs of certain birds *b)* a

spinelike outgrowth of bone, as on the human heel, resulting from injury, disease, etc. *c)* a sharp metal device attached as a weapon to the leg of a gamecock *d)* a short branch or shoot of a tree, etc. 4. a ridge branching from the main mass of a mountain or mountain range 5. a short side track (**spur track**) connected with the main track of a railroad 6. *Bot.* a thin, tubelike structure formed by an extension of one or more petals or sepals, often holding nectar —*vt.* **spurred, spur′ring** 1. to prick with spurs 2. to urge on; stir up; stimulate [the prize money *spurred* her to greater efforts] 3. to provide with a spur or spurs —*vi.* 1. to spur one's horse 2. to hurry; hasten —**on the spur of the moment** quickly, without planning —**win one's spurs** to gain recognition or honor —**spur′like′** *adj.* —**spur′rer** *n.*

spurge (spurj) *n.* [< MFr. < *espurger,* to purge < L. *expurgare:* see EXPURGATE] any of a group of plants having a milky juice and tiny flowers often protected by showy, scalelike leaves — *adj.* designating a family of plants, usually with milky juice, including the poinsettia, cassava, rubber tree, etc.

spur gear 1. a gearwheel with teeth around the rim parallel to the axle: also **spur wheel** 2. gearing having this kind of gearwheel: also **spur gearing**

spu·ri·ous (spyoor′ē əs) *adj.* [L. *spurius*] 1. [Now Rare] illegitimate 2. not true or genuine; false; counterfeit [a *spurious* report] —**spu′ri·ous·ly** *adv.* —**spu′ri·ous·ness** *n.*

spurn (spurn) *vt.* [OE. *spurnan*] 1. to push or drive away as with the foot 2. to reject in a scornful way [he *spurned* my friendship] —*n.* 1. a kick 2. scornful treatment or rejection —see SYN. at DECLINE —**spurn′er** *n.*

spurred (spurd) *adj.* having, wearing, or fitted with spurs or spurlike parts

spurt (spurt) *vt.* [OE. *spryttan* < base of *sprutan,* to sprout] to force out suddenly in a stream or gushing flow; squirt; jet —*vi.* 1. to gush forth in a stream or jet [water *spurted* from the hose] 2. to show a sudden, brief burst of energy or increased activity, as near the end of a race —*n.* 1. a sudden, short stream or jet [the ketchup came out in *spurts*] 2. a sudden, brief burst of energy, etc. [to work in *spurts*]

sput·nik (spoot′nik, sput′-) *n.* [Russ., lit., co-traveler] an artificial satellite of the earth; specif., [**S-**] any of those put into orbit by the U.S.S.R. beginning in 1957

sput·ter (sput′ər) *vi.* [Du. *sputteren*] 1. to spit out bits of saliva, food, etc., as when talking excitedly; splutter 2. to talk in an excited, confused way, spitting out one's words 3. to make sharp, sizzling or spitting sounds, as frying fat —*vt.* 1. to spit out (bits or drops) noisily 2. to say by sputtering [he *sputtered* out an excuse] —*n.* 1. the act or noise of sputtering 2. matter thrown out in sputtering 3. hasty, confused talk —**sput′ter·ing·ly** *adv.*

spu·tum (spyoot′əm) *n., pl.* **spu′ta** (-ə) [< L. < pp. of *spuere,* to SPIT[2]] saliva, usually mixed with mucus from the breathing passages, spit out from the mouth

spy (spī) *vt.* **spied, spy′ing** [< OFr. < OHG. *spehōn,* to examine < IE. base *spek-,* to watch closely, from which also comes L. *specere,* to see] to catch sight of; see [I *spied* her in the distance] —*vi.* 1. to watch closely and secretly; act as a spy 2. to look carefully —*n., pl.* **spies** 1. a person who keeps close and secret watch on another or others 2. a person hired by a government to get secret information about the affairs, esp. military affairs, of another government, as of an enemy in wartime —**spy out** to discover or seek to discover by looking carefully

spy·glass (spī′glas′) *n.* a small telescope

sq. 1. squadron 2. square

sq. ft., sq. in., etc. square foot, square inch, etc.

squab (skwäb, skwôb) *n.* [prob. < Scand.] 1. a very young pigeon 2. a short, stout person 3. [Brit.] a stuffed cushion or couch —*adj.* short and stout: also **squab′by**

squab·ble (skwäb′'l, swôb′-) *vi.* **-bled, -bling** [< Scand.] to quarrel noisily over a small matter; wrangle —*n.* a noisy, petty quarrel; wrangle —see SYN. at QUARREL[2] —**squab′bler** *n.*

squad (skwäd, skwôd) *n.* [< Fr. < Sp. *escuadra,* or It. *squadra,* a square, both ult. < L.: see SQUARE] 1. a small group of soldiers assembled for drill, duty, etc. *a)* the smallest military unit, often part of a platoon ☆2. *a)* any small group of people working together [a police *squad*] *b)* an athletic team [a football *squad*] —*vt.* **squad′ded, squad′ding** 1. to form into a squad 2. to assign to a squad

☆**squad car** a police patrol car, usually communicating with headquarters by radiotelephone

squad·ron (skwäd′rən, skwôd′-) *n.* [< It. < *squadra:* see SQUAD] 1. a group of warships assigned to special duty 2. a unit of cavalry consisting of from two to four troops, etc. 3.

a) *U.S. Air Force* a unit consisting of two or more flights *b*) a formation of six or more aircraft **4.** any organized group

squal·id (skwäl'id, skwôl'-) *adj.* [< L. < *squalere*, to be foul] **1.** dirty; filthy [a *squalid* house] **2.** wretched; miserable [a *squalid* life] —**squa·lid'i·ty, squal'id·ness** *n.* —**squal'id·ly** *adv.*

squall[1] (skwôl) *n.* [< Scand.] **1.** a brief, violent windstorm, usually with rain or snow **2.** [Colloq.] a brief disturbance or commotion —*vi.* to storm briefly —**squall'y** *adj.*

squall[2] (skwôl) *vi., vt.* [ON. *skvala*, to cry out] to cry or scream loudly or harshly —*n.* a loud, harsh outcry or scream —**squall'er** *n.*

squal·or (skwäl'ər, skwôl'-) *n.* [L., foulness] a being squalid; filth and wretchedness

squa·ma (skwā'mə) *n., pl.* -**mae** (-mē) [L., a scale] a scale or scalelike part of an animal or plant

squa·mate (skwā'māt) *adj.* having or covered with scales

squa·mous (skwā'məs) *adj.* [< L. < *squama*, a scale] like, formed of, or covered with scales: also **squa'mose** (-mōs)

squan·der (skwän'dər, skwôn'-) *vt., vi.* [prob. < dial. *squander*, scatter] to spend or use (money, time, etc.) wastefully

square (skwer) *n.* [< OFr., ult. < L. *ex-*, out + *quadrare*, to square < *quadrus*, a square < *quattuor*, four] **1.** a plane figure having four equal sides and four right angles **2.** anything shaped like or nearly like this [a *square* of cloth] ☆**3.** an area bounded by streets on four sides; also, the distance along one side of such an area; block **4.** an open area bounded by, or at the meeting of, several streets, used as a park, plaza, etc. **5.** an instrument having two sides that form a 90° angle, used for drawing or testing right angles **6.** a solid piece with at least one face that is square [a cake cut into *squares*] **7.** the product of a number multiplied by itself [9 is the *square* of 3] ☆**8.** [Slang] a person who is square (*adj.* 11) —*vt.* **squared, squar'ing** **1.** *a*) to make into a square [to *square* a stone] *b*) to make into any rectangle **2.** to test or adjust for straightness or evenness [to *square* a surface with a ruler] **3.** to bring to or near the form of a right angle [*square* your shoulders] **4.** *a*) to make right or even; settle; adjust [to *square* accounts] *b*) to settle the accounts of [to *square* oneself with another] **5.** to make equal [to *square* the score of a game] **6.** to bring into agreement [to *square* a statement with the facts] **7.** to mark off (a surface) in squares **8.** to bring into the correct position, as with reference to a line, course, etc. **9.** to multiply (a quantity) by itself **10.** to determine the square that is equal in area to (a figure) —*vi.* to fit; agree; accord (*with*) [his story *squares* with mine] —*adj.* **1.** *a*) having four equal sides and four right angles *b*) more or less cubical, as a box **2.** forming a right angle, or having a rectangular part or cross section [a *square* corner] **3.** correctly adjusted; straight, level, even, etc. **4.** *a*) leaving no balance; balanced; even *b*) even in score; tied **5.** just; fair; honest [a *square* deal] **6.** clear; direct; straightforward [a *square* refusal] **7.** *a*) designating or of a unit of surface measure in the form of a square with sides of a specified length *b*) given or stated in terms of such measure **8.** having a shape broad for its length or height, with a solid, sturdy appearance [a *square* build] **9.** designating a number that is the product of another number multiplied by itself ☆**10.** [Colloq.] satisfying; solid [a *square* meal] ☆**11.** [Slang] not up on the latest styles, fads, slang, etc.; old-fashioned or unsophisticated —*adv.* **1.** honestly; fairly **2.** so as to be or form a square; at right angles **3.** directly; exactly **4.** so as to face **5.** firmly; solidly —**on the square** **1.** at right angles **2.** [Colloq.] honest(ly), fair(ly), genuine(ly), etc. —**square away** **1.** to bring a ship's yards around so as to sail before the wind **2.** *same as* SQUARE OFF **3.** [Colloq.] to get ready; put in order —☆**square off** to get into position for attacking or for defending —☆**square oneself** [Colloq.] to make up for a wrong one has done —**square the circle** **1.** to find a square equal in area to a given circle: a problem that cannot be solved **2.** to do or attempt something that seems impossible —**square up** to make a settlement, as by payment —**square'ly** *adv.* —**square'ness** *n.* —**squar'er** *n.* —**squar'ish** *adj.*

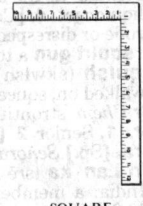

SQUARE
(sense 5)

square dance a lively dance with various steps and figures, in which the couples are grouped in squares or other specified forms —**square'-dance'** *vi.* **-danced', -danc'ing**

☆**square deal** [Colloq.] any dealing that is honest and fair

square knot a double knot in which the free ends run parallel to the standing parts: see illustration at KNOT

square measure a system of measuring area, esp. the system in which 144 square inches = 1 square foot or that in which 10,000 square centimeters = 1 square meter: see TABLES OF WEIGHTS AND MEASURES in Supplements

square-rigged (skwer'rigd') *adj.* having square sails as the principal sails —**square'-rig'ger** *n.*

square root the number that is multiplied by itself to produce a given number [3 is the *square root* of 9]

square sail a four-sided sail

☆**square shooter** [Colloq.] an honest, just person

square-shoul·dered (-shōl'dərd) *adj.* having shoulders that jut out squarely from the body

SQUARE-RIGGED
SHIP

squash[1] (skwäsh, skwôsh) *vt.* [< OFr. *esquasser*, ult. < L. *ex-*, thoroughly + pp. of *quatere*, to shake] **1.** *a*) to crush into a soft or flat mass *b*) to press tightly or too tightly [she was *squashed* in the crowd] **2.** to put down or suppress; quash [to *squash* a rebellion] **3.** [Colloq.] to silence (another) in a crushing way —*vi.* **1.** to be squashed by pressure, etc. [grapes *squash* easily] **2.** to make a sound of squashing **3.** to force one's way; squeeze —*n.* **1.** something squashed; crushed mass **2.** the act or sound of squashing [the tomatoes hit the floor with a *squash*] **3.** either of two games (**squash rackets, squash tennis**) played in a four-walled court with rackets and a rubber ball: see illustration at RACKET **4.** [Brit.] fruit juice or fruit-flavored syrup with soda water [lemon *squash*] —*adv.* with a squash

☆**squash**[2] (skwäsh, skwôsh) *n.* [< Algonquian] **1.** the fleshy fruit of various plants of the gourd family, cooked as a vegetable **2.** a plant, usually a vine, bearing this fruit

☆**squash bug** a large, dark-colored insect that attacks squash vines and similar plants

squash·y (skwäsh'ē, skwôsh'-) *adj.* **-i·er, -i·est** **1.** soft and wet; mushy [*squashy* mud] **2.** easily squashed, as overripe fruit —**squash'i·ness** *n.*

squat (skwät, skwôt) *vi.* **squat'ted, squat'ting** [< MFr. *esquatir*, ult. < L. *ex-*, very much + *coactus*, pp. of *cogere*, to force] **1.** to crouch, with the knees bent and the weight on the balls of the feet **2.** to crouch close to the ground, as an animal ☆**3.** to settle on land without any right or title to it ☆**4.** to settle on public land in order to get title to it from the government —*adj.* **1.** crouched in a squatting position **2.** short and thick [a *squat*, powerful man]: also **squat'ty** —*n.* the act or position of squatting —**squat'ly** *adv.* —**squat'ness** *n.* —**squat'ter** *n.*

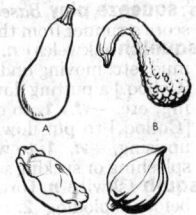

SQUASH
(A, butternut; B, crookneck; C, white bush; D, acorn)

☆**squaw** (skwô) *n.* [< Algonquian] a N. American Indian woman, esp. a wife: now sometimes felt to be a term of contempt

squawk (skwôk) *vi.* [echoic] **1.** to utter a loud, harsh cry, as a parrot or chicken ☆**2.** [Colloq.] to complain or protest loudly —*vt.* to utter in a squawk —*n.* **1.** a squawking cry ☆**2.** [Colloq.] a loud complaint —**squawk'er** *n.*

☆**squawk box** [Slang] an intercom speaker

☆**squaw man** a white man married to a N. American Indian woman, esp. such a man living with her tribe

squeak (skwēk) *vi.* [prob. akin to ON. *skvakka*, to gurgle] to make or utter a short, sharp, high-pitched sound or cry —*vt.* to utter with a squeak —*n.* a short, shrill sound or cry —**narrow (or close) squeak** [Colloq.] a narrow escape —**squeak through (or**

by, etc.) [Colloq.] to barely manage to succeed, survive, etc. —**squeak'i·ly** *adv.* —**squeak'y** *adj.* **-i·er, -i·est**

squeak·er (skwēk'ər) *n.* **1.** one that squeaks ☆**2.** [Colloq.] a narrow escape, victory, etc.

squeal (skwēl) *vi.* [prob. akin to ON. *skvala:* see SQUALL²] **1.** to make or utter a long, shrill sound or cry **2.** [Slang] to inform against, or tell on, someone (often with *on*) —*vt.* to utter with a squeal —*n.* a long, shrill sound or cry —**squeal'er** *n.*

squeam·ish (skwēm'ish) *adj.* [< Anglo-Fr. *escoimous,* orig., shy] **1.** easily nauseated; queasy [*squeamish* at the sight of blood] **2.** easily shocked or offended; prudish **3.** too sensitive —**squeam'ish·ly** *adv.* —**squeam'ish·ness** *n.*

squee·gee (skwē'jē) *n.* [prob. akin to SQUEEZE] a T-shaped tool with a blade of rubber, etc., for wiping liquid from a surface, as in washing windows —*vt.* **-geed, -gee·ing** to use a squeegee on

squeeze (skwēz) *vt.* **squeezed, squeez'ing** [OE. *cwysan,* to squeeze] **1.** to press hard or closely, esp. from two or more sides **2.** *a)* to press so as to force out liquid, etc. [to *squeeze* oranges] *b)* to force out (liquid, etc.) by pressure **3.** to force (into, out, etc.) as by pressing [he *squeezed* his hand into the jar] **4.** to get by force or unfair means [to *squeeze* money from poor people] **5.** to burden with taxes, heavy demands, etc. **6.** to put pressure on (someone) to do something, as to pay money **7.** to embrace closely; hug ☆**8.** *Baseball* to score (a run or runner) by a squeeze play —*vi.* **1.** to give way to pressure [a wet sponge *squeezes* easily] **2.** to use pressure **3.** to force one's way by pushing or pressing (*in, out, through,* etc.) [she *squeezed* through the narrow window] —*n.* **1.** a squeezing or being squeezed **2.** *a)* a close embrace; hug *b)* a firm handclasp **3.** the state of being closely pressed or packed; crush **4.** a difficult situation; pinch [in a financial *squeeze*] **5.** a quantity forced out by squeezing **6.** [Colloq.] pressure used, as in getting something by force or threats: esp. in ☆**put the squeeze on** ☆**7.** *short for* SQUEEZE PLAY —**squeeze through** (or **by,** etc.) [Colloq.] to barely manage to succeed, survive, etc. —**squeez'er** *n.*

SQUEEGEE

☆**squeeze play** *Baseball* a play in which a batter attempts to score a runner from third base by means of a bunt

squelch (skwelch) *n.* [prob. echoic] **1.** the sound of liquid, mud, etc. moving under pressure or suction, as in wet shoes **2.** [Colloq.] a putting down or silencing; esp., a harsh reply, scolding, etc. —*vt.* **1.** to crush as by stamping upon; squash **2.** [Colloq.] to put down or silence completely [to *squelch* an uprising] —*vi.* **1.** to walk heavily through mud, etc., making a splashing or sucking sound **2.** to make such a sound

squib (skwib) *n.* [prob. echoic] **1.** a firecracker that hisses before exploding **2.** a short, witty attack in words **3.** a short news article

squid (skwid) *n., pl.* **squids, squid:** see PLURAL, II, D, 1 [prob. akin to SQUIRT] a sea mollusk having a long, thin body and ten arms, two arms being much longer than the others

squig·gle (skwig''l) *n.* [SQU(IRM) + (W)IGGLE] **1.** a short curved or wavy line; curlicue **2.** an unclear or meaningless scribble —**squig'gly** *adj.*

squill (skwil) *n.* [< L. < Gr. *skilla*] **1.** *a)* the dried bulb of a plant of the lily family, formerly used in medicine *b)* this plant **2.** a variety of this plant having red bulbs used in making rat poison

☆**squinch** (skwinch) *vt.* [SQU(INT) + (P)INCH] **1.** *a)* to squint (the eyes) *b)* to pucker or screw up (the face, nose, etc.) **2.** to squeeze or compress —*vi.* **1.** to squint or pucker **2.** to crouch down or draw oneself together so as to seem smaller **3.** to flinch

squint (skwint) *vi.* [see ASQUINT] **1.** to look with the eyes partly closed, as in too strong light **2.** to look sideways **3.** to be cross-eyed —*vt.* to keep (the eyes) partly closed in peering —*n.* **1.** the act of squinting **2.** a being cross-eyed **3.** [Colloq.] a glance, often a sideways or hasty one —*adj.* **1.** looking sideways **2.** cross-eyed —**squint'er** *n.*

☆**squinting modifier** *Gram.* a misplaced adverb, etc. that can

SQUID
(small species to
8 in. long)

be interpreted as modifying either of two words (Example: *often* in "those who lie often are found out")

squire (skwīr) *n.* [< OFr. *esquier:* see ESQUIRE] **1.** a young man of high birth who attended a knight **2.** in England, a country gentleman who owns much land ☆**3.** a title of respect for a justice of the peace, etc., as in a rural district **4.** an attendant; esp., a man escorting a woman —*vt.* **squired, squir'ing** to escort [to *squire* her to the party]

squirm (skwurm) *vi.* [prob. echoic, infl. by WORM] **1.** to twist and turn the body as a snake does; wriggle; writhe **2.** to show or feel shame or embarrassment —*n.* a squirming motion —**squirm'y** *adj.* **-i·er, -i·est**

squir·rel (skwur'əl; *chiefly Brit.* skwir'-) *n., pl.* **-rels, -rel:** see PLURAL, II, D, 1 [< OFr., ult. < L. *sciurus* < Gr. < *skia,* a shadow + *oura,* tail] **1.** *a)* any of a group of small rodents that have a long, bushy tail and live in trees: they store up nuts and seeds for winter *b)* any of various related burrowing rodents, as chipmunks **2.** the heavy fur of some of these animals —*vt.* **-reled** or **-relled, -rel·ing** or **-rel·ling** to store (*away*)

squirt (skwurt) *vt.* [prob. < or akin to LowG. & Du. *swirtjen,* to squirt] **1.** to shoot out (a liquid) in a jet or narrow stream **2.** to wet with liquid thus shot out [she *squirted* us with a hose] —*vi.* to be squirted out; spurt —*n.* **1.** a device for squirting, as a syringe **2.** the act of squirting **3.** a small amount of squirted liquid; jet ☆**4.** [Colloq.] a small or young person, esp. one who is rude or disrespectful —**squirt'er** *n.*

☆**squirt gun** a toy gun that shoots a stream of water

squish (skwish) *vi.* to make a soft, splashing sound when walked on, squeezed, etc. —*n.* such a sound —**squish'y** *adj.*

Sr *Chem.* strontium

Sr. **1.** Senior **2.** [Sp.] *Señor* **3.** Sister

Sra. [Sp.] *Señora*

Sri Lan·ka (srē län'kə) country on an island off the SE tip of India: a member of the Commonwealth: 25,332 sq. mi.; pop. 13,942,000; cap. Colombo

S.R.O. standing room only

Srta. [Sp.] *Señorita*

SS. [L. *Sancti*] Saints

ss., ss *Baseball* shortstop

S.S., SS, S/S steamship

SSE, S.S.E., s.s.e. south-southeast

SSgt Staff Sergeant

S.S.R., SSR Soviet Socialist Republic

SSW, S.S.W., s.s.w. south-southwest

-st *same as* -EST

St. **1.** Saint: terms beginning with *St.* are entered in this dictionary as if spelled *St-* **2.** Strait **3.** Street

Sta. Station

stab (stab) *n.* [ME. *stabbe,* prob. < var. of *stubbe,* stub] **1.** a wound made by piercing with a knife, dagger, etc. **2.** a thrust, as with a knife **3.** a sudden, sharp hurt or pain —*vt.* **stabbed, stab'bing** **1.** to pierce or wound as with a knife **2.** to thrust (a knife, etc.) into something **3.** to have a sharp, painful effect on [her words *stabbed* his conscience] —*vi.* **1.** to make a thrust as with a knife **2.** to feel like a stabbing knife: said of pain —☆**make** (or **take**) **a stab at** to have a try at —**stab'ber** *n.*

sta·bile (stā'b'l, -bil; *also, and for n. usually,* -bēl) *adj.* [L. *stabilis:* see STABLE¹] stable; stationary —*n.* a large, stationary abstract sculpture, usually made of metal, wire, wood, etc.

sta·bil·i·ty (stə bil'ə tē) *n., pl.* **-ties** **1.** a being stable, or fixed; steadiness **2.** firmness of character, purpose, etc. **3.** resistance to change; permanence **4.** the ability of an object to return to a position after being tipped, etc.

sta·bi·lize (stā'bə līz') *vt.* **-lized', -liz'ing** **1.** to make stable, or firm **2.** to keep from changing, as in price **3.** to give stability to (an airplane, ship, etc.) with a stabilizer —*vi.* to become stabilized —**sta'bi·li·za'tion** *n.*

sta·bi·liz·er (-lī'zər) *n.* a person or thing that stabilizes; specif., *a)* an airfoil to keep an airplane steady in flight, specif. the horizontal part of the tail *b)* a gyrostabilizer or other device to steady a ship in rough waters *c)* anything added to a substance to keep it stable, slow down decay, etc.

STABILE

sta·ble¹ (stā'b'l) *adj.* **-bler, -blest** [< OFr. < L. *stabilis* < *stare,* to stand] **1.** *a)* not easily moved or put off balance; firm; steady [a *stable* floor lamp] *b)* not likely to break down, fall apart, etc. [a chair braced to make it *stable*] **2.** firm in character, purpose, etc.; steadfast [a *stable* person] **3.** not likely to change; lasting [a *stable* business] **4.** capable of returning to balance when tipped, tilted, etc. [a *stable* ship] **5.** *Chem.*, *Physics* not readily breaking down [a *stable* compound] —**sta′bly** *adv.*

sta·ble[2] (stā′b'l) *n.* [< OFr. < L. *stabulum* < *stare*, to stand] **1.** a building in which horses or cattle are sheltered and fed **2.** all the racehorses belonging to one owner **3.** [Colloq.] all the athletes, performers, etc. under one management —**vt., vi.** -**bled**, -**bling** to put, keep, or be kept in a stable

sta·ble·boy (-boi′) *n.* a boy who works in a stable

stac·ca·to (stə kät′ō) *adj.* [It., detached] **1.** *Music* with sharp breaks between tones **2.** made up of short, sharp elements or sounds [a *staccato* burst of gunfire] —*adv.* so as to be staccato —*n., pl.* -**tos** something staccato

stack (stak) *n.* [ON. *stakkr*] **1.** a large pile of straw, hay, etc., esp. one neatly arranged in the form of a cone **2.** any neat pile **3.** a number of arms, esp. three rifles, leaned together on end to form a cone **4.** a chimney or smokestack ☆**5.** [pl.] the main area and shelves for shelving books in a library **6.** [Colloq.] a large amount —*vt.* **1.** to pile in a stack **2.** to load with stacks [to *stack* a truck with boxes] **3.** to assign (aircraft) to various altitudes for circling before landing **4.** to arrange in a secret and unfair way so as to get a desired result [to *stack* a jury] — **stack up** ☆**1.** to add up; accumulate [new book orders were *stacking* up] ☆**2.** to compare (*with* or *against*) [how does he *stack up* with the other candidates?] —**stack′a·ble** *adj.*

stacked (stakt) *adj.* ☆[Slang] having a full, shapely figure; curvaceous: said of a woman

stack·up (stak′up′) *n.* an arrangement of circling aircraft at various altitudes awaiting their turn to land

sta·di·um (stā′dē əm) *n., pl.* -**di·a** (-ə); also, and for sense 2 usually, -**di·ums** [L. < Gr. *stadion*, fixed standard of length] **1.** in ancient Greece and Rome, a track for footraces, about 607 feet long, with rising rows of seats for spectators **2.** a large, usually open structure for football, baseball, etc. with rising rows of seats for spectators

Staël (stäl), Madame **de**, baronne de Staël-Holstein, (born *Anne Louise Germaine Necker*) 1766-1817; Fr. writer

staff (staf) *n., pl.* **staffs**; also, for senses 1 & 5, **staves** [OE. *stæf* < IE. base *stebh*-, pole] **1.** a stick, rod, or pole used as a support in walking, or as a weapon, a symbol of authority, a measure, etc. **2.** a group of people assisting a leader **3.** a group of military or naval officers serving a commanding officer as advisers and administrators **4.** a specific group of workers [a teaching *staff*] **5.** *Music* the five horizontal lines and four spaces between them on which music is written —*adj.* of, by, for, or on a staff —*vt.* to provide with a staff, as of workers

staff·er (staf′ər) *n.* a member of a staff

staff officer 1. an officer on a staff ☆**2.** *U.S. Navy* a commissioned officer with nonmilitary duties, as a surgeon, chaplain, etc.

staff of life bread, thought of as the basic food

staff sergeant ☆**1.** *U.S. Army & Marine Corps* an enlisted man ranking above sergeant ☆**2.** *U.S. Air Force* an enlisted man ranking above airman first class

stag (stag) *n., pl.* **stags, stag**: see PLURAL, II, D, 1 [OE. *stagga*] **1.** *a)* a full-grown male deer *b)* the male of various other animals **2.** a male animal, esp. a hog, castrated in maturity ☆**3.** *a)* a man who attends a social gathering unaccompanied by a woman *b)* a social gathering for men only —*adj.* ☆for men only [a *stag* dinner] —☆**go stag** [Colloq.] **1.** to go as a stag (sense 3 *a*) **2.** to go unescorted by a man

stage (stāj) *n.* [< OFr. *estage*, ult. < L. pp. of *stare*, to stand] **1.** a platform or dock [a landing *stage*] **2.** a workmen's scaffold **3.** a level, floor, or story **4.** *a)* a platform on which plays, speeches, etc. are presented *b)* any area, as in an arena theater, in which actors perform *c)* the theater as a profession [she left the *stage* to make movies] **5.** the scene of an event or events [Europe has been the *stage* of many wars] **6.** a stopping point on a route, esp., formerly, for a stagecoach **7.** the distance between two such points [to travel by short *stages*] **8.** *shortened form of* STAGECOACH **9.** a period or step in a process of development, change, etc. [a new *stage* in his career] **10.** any of the separate systems that work one after another in get-

ting a rocket into outer space —*vt.* **staged, stag′ing 1.** to present on or as on a stage [to *stage* a play] ☆**2.** to plan and carry out [*stage* an attack] —*vi.* to be presented on the stage [a play that *stages* well] —**by easy stages** a little at a time, with many stops to rest

stage·coach (stāj′kōch′) *n.* formerly, a horse-drawn coach carrying passengers and mail over a regular route

stage·craft (-kraft′) *n.* skill in writing or staging plays

stage door an outside door leading to the backstage part of a theater, used by actors, production staff, etc.

stage fright nervousness felt when appearing as a speaker or performer before an audience

stage·hand (-hand′) *n.* a person who helps to set and remove scenery and furniture, operate the curtain, etc. for a stage performance

stage-man·age (-man′ij) *vt.* -**aged**, -**ag·ing 1.** to be stage manager for **2.** to arrange or display with dramatic effect, esp. as if from behind the scenes

stage manager an assistant to the director of a play, in overall charge backstage during a performance

stage-struck (-struk′) *adj.* having a very strong desire to work in the theater, esp. as an actor or actress

stage whisper 1. a loud whisper by an actor on the stage, which the audience is to pretend the other actors cannot hear **2.** any similar loud whisper, meant to be overheard

stag·ger (stag′ər) *vi.* [ON. *stakra*, to totter] **1.** to walk or stand in an unsteady way, as if about to fall; sway; reel [the tired boxer *staggered* from the ring] **2.** to waver; hesitate —*vt.* **1.** to make stagger [the blow *staggered* him] **2.** to affect strongly, as with shock or confusion [*staggering* news] **3.** to set alternately, as on either side of a line; make zigzag [to *stagger* the teeth of a saw] **4.** to arrange (duties, vacations, etc.) so as to avoid crowding —*n.* **1.** the act of staggering, tottering, etc. **2.** a staggered arrangement **3.** [pl., with sing. v.] a nervous disease of horses, cattle, etc., causing them to stagger —**stag′ger·er** *n.* —**stag′ger·ing** *adj.* —**stag′ger·ing·ly** *adv.*

SYN.—**stagger** implies unsteady movement marked by loss of balance and inability to move in a straight line [to *stagger* under a heavy load]; **reel** suggests the swaying motion of one who seems almost ready to fall [the drunken man *reeled* down the hall]; **totter** suggests the weak, uncertain steps of a very old person or of an infant learning to walk

stag·ing (stā′jiŋ) *n.* **1.** a temporary structure used for support; scaffolding **2.** the act or process of presenting a play on the stage

staging area an area where troops are assembled before being transported elsewhere, as into a battle area

stag·nant (stag′nənt) *adj.* [< L. prp. of *stagnare*, to stagnate] **1.** not flowing or moving **2.** dirty and smelly from lack of movement: said of water, etc. **3.** not active, alert, etc.; sluggish [a *stagnant* mind] —**stag′nan·cy** (-nən sē) *n.* —**stag′nant·ly** *adv.*

stag·nate (-nāt) *vi., vt.* -**nat·ed**, -**nat·ing** [< L. pp. of *stagnare*, to stagnate < *stagnum*, a swamp] to become or make stagnant —**stag·na′tion** *n.*

stag·y (stā′jē) *adj.* **stag′i·er, stag′i·est 1.** of the stage; theatrical: usually used unfavorably **2.** affected; artificial [a *stagy* way of speaking] Also **stage′y** —**stag′i·ness** *n.*

staid (stād) *archaic pt. & pp. of* STAY[3] —*adj.* quiet, dignified, and serious —**staid′ly** *adv.* —**staid′ness** *n.*

stain (stān) *vt.* [< OFr. < L. *dis*-, from + *tingere*, to color] **1.** to spoil the appearance of by discoloring or spotting **2.** to disgrace or dishonor (one's character, reputation, etc.) **3.** to change the appearance of (wood, glass, etc.) by applying a dye, etc. **4.** to treat (material for microscopic study) with a coloring matter, as to make transparent parts visible —*vi.* to make a stain or become stained —*n.* **1.** a streak, spot, etc. resulting from staining **2.** a shame or disgrace [without a *stain* on his character] **3.** a dye, pigment, etc. for staining wood or material for microscopic study —**stain′a·ble** *adj.* —**stain′er** *n.*

stained glass glass colored in any of various ways and used as for church windows

stain·less (stān′lis) *adj.* **1.** without a stain; spotless **2.** that resists staining, rusting, etc. **3.** made of stainless steel —*n.* flatware made of stainless steel —**stain′less·ly** *adv.*

stainless steel steel alloyed with chromium, etc.: it is highly resistant to rust, stain, and corrosion

stair (ster) *n.* [OE. *stæger*] **1.** [*usually pl.*] a flight of steps; stair-case **2.** one of a series of steps leading from one level or floor to another

stair·case (ster′kās′) *n.* a flight of stairs with a supporting structure and a handrail: also **stair′way′** (-wā′)

stair·well (-wel′) *n.* a vertical shaft (in a building) containing a staircase: also **stair well**

stake (stāk) *n.* [OE. *staca*] **1.** a length of wood or metal pointed at one end for driving into the ground, as for marking a boundary **2.** *a)* the post to which a person was tied when being burned to death as a punishment *b)* execution by burning **3.** any of the posts fitted into sockets at the edge of a railway flatcar, truck bed, etc., to help hold a load **4.** [*often pl.*] something, esp. money, risked in a bet, game, or contest **5.** [*often pl.*] a prize given a winner, as in a race **6.** [*pl.*, *with sing. v.*] a race in which a prize is offered **7.** a share or interest [he has a *stake* in the business] ☆**8.** [Colloq.] a grubstake —*vt.* **staked**, **stak′ing** ☆**1.** *a)* to mark the boundaries of as with stakes [to *stake* out a building site] *b)* to establish (a claim) in this way **2.** to support (a plant, etc.) by tying to a stake **3.** to tie to a stake **4.** to bet; gamble [to *stake* one's life on the outcome] **5.** [Colloq.] *a)* to furnish with money or resources [he *staked* us to a meal] ☆*b)* to grubstake —**at stake** being risked — ☆**pull up stakes** [Colloq.] to change one's place of residence, business, etc. —**stake out** to station (police, etc.) at (a specified place) in an attempt to capture a suspected criminal

stake·hold·er (stāk′hōl′dər) *n.* one who holds money, etc. bet by others and pays it to the winner

☆**stake·out** (-out′) *n.* **1.** the staking out of police, etc. in an attempt to capture a suspected criminal **2.** the place where police, etc. are staked out

sta·lac·tite (stə lak′tīt; *chiefly Brit.* stal′ək tīt′) *n.* [ModL. < Gr. *stalaktos*, dripping < *stalassein*, to drip] an icicle-shaped deposit hanging from the roof of a cave, formed by dripping water full of lime —**stal·ac·tit·ic** (stal′ək tit′ik) *adj.*

sta·lag·mite (stə lag′mīt; *chiefly Brit.* stal′əg mīt′) *n.* [ModL. < Gr. *stalagmos*, a dropping < *stalassein*, to drip] a cone-shaped deposit built up on the floor of a cave by dripping water full of lime, often from a stalactite above —**stal·ag·mit·ic** (stal′əg mit′ik) *adj.*

STALACTITES

STALAGMITES

stale (stāl) *adj.* **stal′er**, **stal′est** [prob. < LowG.] **1.** having lost freshness; specif., *a)* flat; tasteless [*stale* beer] *b)* hard and dry, as bread *c)* having little oxygen; stagnant [*stale* air] *d)* beginning to decay, as eggs **2.** no longer new or interesting; trite [a *stale* joke] **3.** ineffective, weakened, bored, etc. from too much or too little activity [an actress gets *stale* if she plays the same part too often] —*vt.*, *vi.* **staled**, **stal′ing** to make or become stale —**stale′ly** *adv.* —**stale′ness** *n.*

stale·mate (stāl′māt′) *n.* [OFr. *estal*, a fixed location + MATE²] **1.** *Chess* any situation in which a player cannot move without placing his king in check: it results in a draw **2.** any unfinished situation in which further action is impossible or useless; deadlock —*vt.* **-mat′ed**, **-mat′ing** to bring into a stalemate

Sta·lin (stä′lin), **Joseph** (born *Iosif Vissarionovich Dzhugashvili*) 1879–1953; premier of the U.S.S.R. (1941–53) —**Sta′lin·ism** *n.* —**Sta′lin·ist** *adj.*, *n.*

Sta·lin·grad (stä′lin grät′; *E.* stä′lin grad′) *former name of* VOLGOGRAD

stalk¹ (stôk) *vi.* [OE. *stealcian* < *stealc*, steep] **1.** *a)* to walk in a stiff, haughty, or grim manner *b)* to advance or spread without stepping [plague *stalks* across the land] **2.** to pursue or approach game, etc. in a quiet, cautious way —*vt.* **1.** to pursue or approach (game, etc.) in a quiet, cautious way **2.** to advance or spread through [terror *stalks* the streets] —*n.* **1.** a slow, stiff, or haughty stride **2.** a stalking of game, etc. —**stalk′er** *n.*

stalk² (stôk) *n.* [akin to OE. *stela*, a stalk] **1.** any stem or part like a stem **2.** *Bot.* *a)* the main stem or axis of a plant *b)* a lengthened part on which an organ grows or is supported, as the petiole of a leaf **3.** *Zool.* a lengthened part that supports an animal organ or a whole body —**stalked** *adj.* —**stalk′less** *adj.*

stalk·ing-horse (stôk′iŋ hôrs′) *n.* **1.** a horse, or a figure of one, used as cover by a hunter stalking game **2.** anything used to hide one's real purposes, plans, etc.

stall¹ (stôl) *n.* [OE. *steall* < IE. base *stel-*, to place] **1.** *a)* formerly, a stable *b)* a compartment for one animal in a stable

2. any of various compartments, sections, etc.; specif., *a)* a booth, etc. where goods are sold, as at a fair *b)* an enclosed seat in a church *c)* [Brit.] a theater seat near the stage *d)* a small, enclosed space, as for taking a shower ☆*e)* any of the spaces marked off for parking cars in a garage, etc. **3.** a protective sheath for a finger; cot **4.** a stopping or standing still due to failure to work properly **5.** the condition of an aircraft when it tends to drop or go out of control because of loss of lift and increase of drag —*vt.*, *vi.* **1.** to put, keep, or be kept in a stall properly **2.** to stick fast, as in mud **3.** to stop, as from failure to work properly [the car *stalled* when the motor got wet] **4.** to put (an aircraft) into a stall, or go into a stall

stall² (stôl) *vi.* [< obs. *stale*, a decoy < Anglo-Fr. *estale*] to act or speak in a sly or hesitant way so as to trick or delay [to *stall* for time] —*vt.* to put off or delay by stalling (usually with *off*) [to *stall* off one's creditors] —*n.* [Colloq.] any trick used to deceive or delay

stal·lion (stal′yən) *n.* [OFr. *estalon* < Gmc. *stal*, a stall] an uncastrated male horse, esp. one used for breeding

stal·wart (stôl′wərt) *adj.* [OE. *stælwyrthe* < *stathol*, foundation + *wyrthe*, worth] **1.** strong and well-built; sturdy; robust [a *stalwart* athlete] **2.** brave; fearless [a *stalwart* soldier] **3.** not giving in easily; firm [the *stalwart* defense of a cause] —*n.* **1.** a stalwart person **2.** a faithful supporter, as of a political party —see SYN. at STRONG —**stal′wart·ly** *adv.* —**stal′wart·ness** *n.*

Stam·boul, Stam·bul (stäm bool′) **1.** *earlier name for* ISTANBUL **2.** the old section of Istanbul

sta·men (stā′mən) *n.*, *pl.* **-mens**, **stam·i·na** (stam′ə nə) [ModL. < L., a thread, orig., warp] a pollen-bearing organ in a flower, made up of a slender stalk (*filament*) and a pollen sac (*anther*): see illustration at FLOWER

Stam·ford (stam′fərd) [after *Stamford*, town in NE England] city in SW Conn.: pop. 109,000

stam·i·na (stam′ə nə) *n.* [L., pl. of *stamen*: see STAMEN] resistance to weariness, illness, hardship, etc.; endurance

stam·i·nate (stam′ə nit, -nāt′) *adj.* **1.** having stamens but no pistils, as male flowers **2.** having stamens

stam·mer (stam′ər) *vt.*, *vi.* [OE. *stamerian*] to speak or say with pauses that one cannot control, often repeating certain sounds, as because of excitement, embarrassment, fear, etc. —*n.* the act or habit of stammering —**stam′mer·er** *n.* —**stam′mer·ing·ly** *adv.*

stamp (stamp) *vt.* [ME. *stampen*] **1.** to bring (the foot) down forcibly on the ground, a floor, etc. **2.** *a)* to strike down on forcibly with the foot [to *stamp* the floor in anger] *b)* to beat, crush, etc. by pressing on heavily with the foot [to *stamp* the grass down to the earth] *c)* to remove by stamping the feet [*stamped* the snow from his boots] *d)* to grind or crush (ore, etc.) into powder or dust **3.** *a)* to imprint or cut out (a design, lettering, etc.) by bringing a form forcibly against a material [to *stamp* initials in leather] *b)* to cut out or make as by applying a die to metal [to *stamp* auto bodies] **4.** to mark or print with a design, etc., as to decorate, show ownership, etc. **5.** to mark clearly or permanently [a face *stamped* with grief] **6.** to put an official seal or a stamp on (a document, letter, etc.) **7.** to characterize or show clearly, as if by marking [the courage that *stamped* him as a hero] —*vi.* **1.** to bring the foot down forcibly on the ground, etc. **2.** to walk with loud, heavy steps, as in anger —*n.* **1.** the act of stamping **2.** a machine, tool, etc. for stamping or crushing ore, etc. **3.** *a)* any tool, as a die, that is brought forcibly against something to mark or shape it *b)* the mark or form so made **4.** a mark, seal, etc. used to show officially that a tax has been paid, authority given, etc. **5.** *a)* a small piece of paper printed and sold by a government, which must be put on a letter, parcel, document, etc. to show that the required fee has been paid *b)* any similar piece of paper, issued by an organization, business, etc. [trading *stamps*] **6.** a characteristic sign or mark [the *stamp* of truth] **7.** character; kind; class; type [women of her *stamp* are rare] —**stamp out 1.** to crush or put out (a fire, a cigarette, etc.) by pressing on forcibly with the foot **2.** to crush or put down (a revolt, rebellion, etc.) —**stamp′er** *n.*

☆**stam·pede** (stam pēd′) *n.* [AmSp. *estampida* < Sp. < *estampar*, to stamp < Gmc.] **1.** a sudden, headlong running away of a herd of frightened horses, cattle, etc. **2.** a confused, headlong rush of many people **3.** any sudden, spontaneous mass movement [a *stampede* to support a candidate] —*vi.* **-ped′ed**, **-ped′ing** to move in a stampede —*vt.* to cause to stampede —**stam·ped′er** *n.*

☆**stamp·ing ground** (stam′piŋ) [Colloq.] a regular or favorite gathering place or resort

stance (stans) *n.* [< OFr., ult. < L. prp. of *stare*, to stand] **1.** the way a person stands; specif., the position of the feet, as of a golfer or baseball batter [a wide *stance*, with the feet far apart] ☆**2.** an attitude taken on for dealing with a situation [a tough political *stance*]

stanch (stônch, stanch, stänch) *vt., vi., adj.* see STAUNCH

stan·chion (stan'chən, -shən) *n.* [< OFr. < *estance*: see STANCE] **1.** an upright bar, post, etc. used as a support ☆**2.** a device fitted loosely around the neck of a cow to keep it in its stall —*vt.* **1.** to support with stanchions ☆**2.** to hold (a cow) with a stanchion

stand (stand) *vi.* **stood, stand'ing** [OE. *standan* < IE. base *sta-*, to stand, from which also comes L. *stare*, to stand] **1.** *a)* to be or stay upright on the feet [*stand* by your desk] *b)* to be or stay upright on its base, bottom, etc. [the vase *stands* on the table] *c)* to grow upright: said of plants **2.** to rise to an upright position, as from a sitting or lying position **3.** *a)* to take, or be in, a (specified) upright position [*stand* straight] *b)* to take, keep, or be in a (specified) position or attitude [I *stand* opposed to that policy] **4.** to have a (specified) height when standing [he *stands* six feet] **5.** *a)* to be placed or situated [the house *stands* on a hill] *b)* to stay where situated, built, etc. [the statue *stands* there to-day] **6.** to gather and remain [sweat *stood* in drops on his brow] **7.** to remain unchanged, valid, etc. [the law still *stands*] **8.** to be in a (specified) condition [they *stood* in awe, he *stands* to lose ten dollars] **9.** to be of a (specified) rank, degree, etc. [to *stand* first in one's class] **10.** to maintain one's opinion, loyalty, etc.; remain firm **11.** to make resistance [to *stand* alone against the enemy] **12.** *a)* to halt *b)* to remain stationary **13.** to show the (specified) relative position of those involved [the score *stands* at 10 to 8] **14.** [Chiefly Brit.] to be a candidate, as for office; run **15.** *Naut.* to take or hold a certain course [*standing* out of the harbor] —*vt.* **1.** to make stand; put upright [*stand* the broom in the corner] **2.** to put up with; endure [to *stand* pain] **3.** to be unaffected by; withstand [it will *stand* years of hard use] **4.** to undergo [to *stand* trial] **5.** to do the duty of [*stand* watch] **6.** [Colloq.] *a)* to bear (the cost of a meal, etc.), as when treating *b)* to treat (a person) to food, drink, etc. —*n.* **1.** a standing; esp., a halt or stop; specif., *a)* a stopping to counterattack, resist, etc., as in retreat ☆*b)* a halt by a touring theatrical company to give a performance; also, the place stopped at **2.** the place where one stands or is supposed to stand; position [to take one's *stand* at the rear] **3.** a view, opinion, etc., as on an issue [to make one's *stand* clear] **4.** a structure to stand or sit on; specif., *a)* a raised platform for a band, etc. *b)* [*often pl.*] a set of benches in rising rows, as for spectators ☆*c)* the place where a witness testifies in a courtroom ☆**5.** *a)* a booth, stall, etc. where goods are sold [a cigar *stand*] *b)* a parking space reserved for taxicabs, etc. **6.** a rack, small table, etc. for holding things ☆**7.** a group of growing trees or plants [a *stand* of willows] —see SYN. at BEAR[1] —**make a stand 1.** to take a position for defense or opposition **2.** to support a definite position, opinion, etc. —**stand a chance** to have a chance —**stand by 1.** to be near and ready to act as needed **2.** to aid or support **3.** to keep (a promise, etc.) **4.** to be present, esp. as an onlooker **5.** *Radio & TV* to stay tuned in, as for a program to continue —**stand for 1.** to be a symbol for or sign of; represent ☆**2.** [Colloq.] to put up with; endure —**stand in for** to substitute for —**stand off 1.** to keep at a distance ☆**2.** to put off or avoid (a creditor or attacker) —**stand on 1.** to be founded on; depend on [to *stand on* principle] **2.** to insist upon (ceremony, one's rights, etc.) —**stand one's ground** to maintain one's position, as against attack —**stand out 1.** to stick out; project **2.** to show up clearly **3.** to be widely known or outstanding **4.** to refuse to give in —**stand up 1.** to rise to or be in a standing position **2.** to prove to be true, lasting, etc. [that theory won't *stand up* under testing] ☆**3.** [Slang] to fail to keep an appointment with —**stand up for** to defend or support —**stand up to** to meet or face fearlessly —**stand'er** *n.*

MUSIC STAND

stand·ard (stan'dərd) *n.* [OFr. *estendard*, ult. < Gmc.] **1.** a flag, banner, etc. used as an emblem or symbol of a leader, people, military unit, etc. **2.** something set up as a rule or basis of comparison in measuring or judging quantity, quality, value, etc. [*standards* of weight and measure] **3.** a usage or practice that is generally accepted or followed; criterion [moral *standards*] **4.** an upright support **5.** a piece of music that has remained popular for many years **6.** a tree or shrub with a single, tall stem —*adj.* **1.** used as, or meeting the requirements of, an established rule, model, etc. [the *standard* Canadian gallon is larger than the *standard* American one] **2.** generally accepted as reliable or worthwhile [*standard* reference books] **3.** regular or typical; not special or extra; ordinary [*standard* procedure] **4.** suitable to speech or writing that is more or less formal; not slang, dialectal, obsolete, etc. [*standard* English]

SYN.—**standard** applies to some measure, principle, model, etc. with which things of the same class are compared in order to determine their quantity, value, quality, etc. [*standards* of purity for drugs]; **criterion** refers to a test or rule for measuring the excellence, fitness, or correctness of something [mere memory is not an accurate *criterion* of intelligence]; **gauge** is used literally to refer to a scale or tool used in measuring thickness, force, etc. [a wire *gauge*], but it is also extended in meaning to refer to something used as a measure of a characteristic or quality [sales are an accurate *gauge* of a book's popularity]

stand·ard-bear·er (-ber'ər) *n.* **1.** a person carrying the standard, or flag, as of a military group **2.** the leader of a movement, political party, etc.

☆**stand·ard·bred** (-bred') *n.* [*often* S-] any horse of an American breed developed for trotting or pacing, esp. in harness racing

standard gauge 1. a width of 56½ inches between the rails of a railroad track **2.** a railroad having such a gauge —**stand'ard-gauge'** *adj.*

stand·ard·ize (stan'dər dīz') *vt.* **-ized', -iz'ing 1.** to make standard or uniform; make the same in all cases [television tends to *standardize* speech] **2.** to test by or adjust to a standard [to *standardize* test scores] —**stand'ard·i·za'tion** *n.* —**stand'ard·iz'er** *n.*

standard of living level of daily living, as of a nation or person, as measured by the availability of necessities and comforts

☆**standard time** the time in any of the 24 time zones, each an hour apart, into which the earth is divided: it is based on distance east or west of Greenwich, England: in North America there are eight such zones (see chart at TIME): standard time is the official time for each zone except when daylight-saving time is in effect

stand·by (stand'bī') *n., pl.* **-bys' 1.** a person or thing that can always be depended on, or one ready to be used if needed **2.** a person waiting to board a plane, etc. if space becomes available —*adj.* of, for, or being a standby —**on standby** ready or waiting as a standby

☆**stand·ee** (stan dē') *n.* a person who stands, usually because no seats are vacant

☆**stand-in** (stand'in') *n.* **1.** a person who takes the place of a movie or television actor while lights, cameras, etc. are being adjusted **2.** any substitute for another

stand·ing (stan'diŋ) *n.* **1.** the act, state, or position of one that stands **2.** *a)* status, rank, or reputation [in good *standing*] *b)* [*pl.*] a list showing rank or order [where is our team in the *standings*?] **3.** the time that something lasts; duration [a friendship of long *standing*] —*adj.* **1.** erect or upright [a *standing* position] **2.** in or from a standing position [a *standing* jump] **3.** not flowing; stagnant [*standing* water] **4.** going on regularly without change; lasting; permanent [a *standing* order] **5.** stationary; not movable [a *standing* machine] **6.** not in use [a *standing* machine]

standing army a permanent army

standing room room in which to stand, esp. when there are no vacant seats, as in a theater

standing wave a kind of vibration in which there are regularly spaced points where there is no motion, resulting from the meeting at these points of two equal sets of waves traveling in opposite directions

Stan·dish (stan'dish), **Miles** (or **Myles**) 1584?-1656; Eng. colonist; military leader of Plymouth Colony

stand·off (stand'ôf') *n.* **1.** a standing off or being stood off **2.** an equalizing effect **3.** a tie or draw in a contest —*adj.* **1.** that stands off **2.** *same as* STANDOFFISH

---

stand·off·ish (stand′ôf′ish) *adj.* reserved and cool; aloof — **stand′off′ish·ly** *adv.* —**stand′off′ish·ness** *n.*

☆**stand·out** (stand′out′) *n.* [Colloq.] a person or thing of outstanding superiority —*adj.* [Colloq.] outstandingly superior

☆**stand·pat** (-pat′) *adj.* [Colloq.] sticking firmly or stubbornly to an opinion, policy, etc. —**stand′pat′ter** *n.*

stand·pipe (-pīp′) *n.* a large vertical pipe or cylindrical tank for storing water

stand·point (-point′) *n.* the point or position from which something is seen or judged; point of view

stand·still (-stil′) *n.* a stop or halt

stand·up (-up′) *adj.* **1.** upright; erect **2.** done, taken, etc. in a standing position [a *stand-up* lunch] ☆**3.** designating or of a comedian who delivers monologues

☆**Stan·ford-Bi·net test** (stan′fərd bi nā′) a revision of the Binet-Simon test: developed at Stanford University (Calif.)

Stan·i·slav·sky (stan′i släf′skē, stän′-), **Kon·stan·tin** (kän′stən tēn′) (born *Konstantin Sergeyevich Alekseyev*) 1863-1938; Russ. actor, director, & teacher of acting

stank (staŋk) *alt. pt. of* STINK

Stan·ley (stan′lē) **1.** [< OE. *stan leah*, stone lea] a masculine name **2.** Sir **Henry Morton**, (born *John Rowlands*) 1841-1904; Brit. journalist & explorer in Africa

stan·nic (stan′ik) *adj.* [< LL. *stannum*, tin + -IC] of or containing tin, specif. with a valence of four

stan·nous (-əs) *adj.* [< LL. *stannum*, tin + -OUS] of or containing tin, specif. with a valence of two

stan·za (stan′zə) *n.* [It., room, ult. < L. *stare*, to stand] a group of lines of verse, usually regular in pattern, forming one of the divisions of a poem or song —**stan·za′ic** (-zā′ik) *adj.*

sta·pes (stā′pēz) *n., pl.* **sta′pes**, **sta·pe·des** (stə pē′dēz, stā′pə dēz′) [ModL. < ML., a stirrup, prob. < Gmc.] *Anat.* a small, stirrup-shaped bone, the innermost of the three bones in the middle ear: see illustration at EAR

staph (staf) *n. shortened form of* STAPHYLOCOCCUS

staph·y·lo·coc·cus (staf′ə lō käk′əs) *n., pl.* **-coc′ci** (-käk′sī) [ModL. < Gr. *staphylē*, bunch of grapes + -COCCUS] any of a group of spherical bacteria that generally occur in clusters or chains and cause pus to form in boils, etc. —**staph′y·lo·coc′cal** (-käk′′l), **staph′y·lo·coc′cic** (-käk′sik) *adj.*

sta·ple¹ (stā′p′l) *n.* [< OFr. < MDu. *stapel*, mart] **1.** the main product made, grown, etc. in a particular place [coffee is the *staple* of Brazil] **2.** a main item or element in anything [sports are the *staple* of his conversation] **3.** raw material **4.** any common, regularly stocked item of trade, as salt, flour, etc. **5.** the fiber of cotton, wool, etc. with regard to length and fineness —*adj.* **1.** produced or used regularly and in quantity [*staple* foods] **2.** chief; main [a *staple* industry] —*vt.* **-pled, -pling** to sort (wool, cotton, etc.) according to staple

sta·ple² (stā′p′l) *n.* [OE. *stapol*, a post] **1.** a U-shaped piece of metal with sharp-pointed ends, driven into a surface to hold a hook, wire, etc. in place **2.** a similar piece of thin wire driven through papers, etc. so that the ends bend over as a binding —*vt.* **-pled, -pling** to fasten with a staple or staples

sta·pler (stā′plər) *n.* a device for driving staples through paper, etc. or a heavier device (also called **staple gun**) for stapling insulation, upholstery fabric, etc. in place

star (stär) *n.* [OE. *steorra* < IE. base *ster-*, a star, from which also come L. *stella*, Gr. *astēr*] **1.** any heavenly body seen as a point of light in the night sky; specif., *Astron.* any such body that is gaseous and shaped like a slightly flattened ball and that produces its own light **2.** a flat figure with usually five or six points, representing a star **3.** a mark, emblem, etc. resembling such a figure, used as an award, symbol of rank, etc. **4.** an asterisk **5.** *a*) *Astrol.* a planet, etc. thought of as influencing human fate *b*) [*often pl.*] fate; destiny **6.** a person who is outstanding, esp. in a sport **7.** a leading actor or actress —*vt.* **starred, star′ring 1.** to decorate with stars **2.** to mark with a star or stars as a grade of quality **3.** to mark with an asterisk **4.** to present (a performer) in a leading role —*vi.* **1.** to be outstanding, esp. in a sport **2.** to have a leading role [she *stars* in his new movie] —*adj.* **1.** outstanding [a *star* athlete] **2.** of a star or stars —**star′less** *adj.* —**star′like′** *adj.*

star·board (stär′bərd, -bôrd′) *n.* [< OE. < *steoran*, to steer (with a large oar used on the ship's right side) + *bord*, board] the right-hand side of a ship or airplane as one faces forward,

toward the bow: opposed to PORT⁴ —*adj.* of or on the starboard —*vt., vi.* to move or turn (the helm) to the starboard side

starch (stärch) *n.* [ult. < OE. *stearc*, stiff] **1.** a white, tasteless, odorless food substance found in potatoes, grain, etc.: it is a complex carbohydrate $(C_6H_{10}O_5)_n$ **2.** a powdered form of this, used in laundering to stiffen cloth, etc. **3.** [*pl.*] starchy foods **4.** a stiff, formal way of behaving ☆**5.** [Colloq.] energy; vigor —*vt.* to stiffen with or as with starch [to *starch* a collar] — **starch′a·ble** *adj.* —**starch′less** *adj.*

Star Chamber 1. a royal English court or tribunal abolished in 1641, known for its harsh, unfair, and secret procedures **2.** [*also* s- c-] any similar tribunal, etc.

starch·y (stär′chē) *adj.* **starch′i·er, starch′i·est 1.** of, containing, or like starch **2.** stiffened with starch **3.** stiff or formal [a *starchy* manner] —**starch′i·ly** *adv.* —**starch′i·ness** *n.*

star-crossed (stär′krôst′) *adj.* [see STAR (*n.* 5)] sure to have an unhappy fate; ill-fated

star·dom (-dəm) *n.* **1.** the status of a star of stage, screen, sports, etc. **2.** such stars as a group

stare (ster) *vi.* **stared, star′ing** [OE. *starian* < IE. base (*s*)*ter-*, stiff] to look with a steady, fixed gaze, as in wonder, curiosity, dullness, etc. —*vt.* **1.** to look steadily at [to *stare* a person up and down] **2.** to affect in a given way by staring [to *stare* a person into confusion] —*n.* a long, steady look —**stare down** to stare back at (another) until he looks away —**stare one in the face** to be urgent or unavoidable —**star′er** *n.*

star·fish (stär′fish′) *n., pl.* **-fish′, -fish′es**: see FISH a small sea animal with a hard, spiny skeleton and five or more arms or rays arranged like the points of a star

star·gaze (-gāz′) *vi.* **-gazed′, -gaz′ing 1.** to gaze at the stars **2.** to daydream — **star′gaz′er** *n.*

stark (stärk) *adj.* [OE. *stearc*] **1.** *a*) stiff or rigid, as a corpse *b*) harsh; severe [*stark* discipline] **2.** sharply outlined [*winter* trees *stark* against the sky] **3.** lonely and bleak; desolate [a *stark* landscape] **4.** *a*) emptied; stripped [*stark* shelves] *b*) totally naked **5.** harshly honest; not softened, touched up, etc. [*stark* realism] **6.** complete; utter [*stark* terror] —*adv.* completely; entirely [*stark* mad] —**stark′ly** *adv.* —**stark′ness** *n.*

STARFISH
(to 9 in. across)

star·let (stär′lit) *n.* **1.** a small star ☆**2.** a young actress being promoted as a possible future star

star·light (-līt′) *n.* light from the stars

star·ling (stär′liŋ) *n.* [OE. *stærlinc*, dim. of *stær*, starling] any of a family of short-tailed, dark-colored birds, esp. the **common** starling, with shiny feathers, brought into the U.S. from Europe

star·lit (stär′lit′) *adj.* lighted by the stars

star-of-Beth·le·hem (-əv beth′lə hem′, -lē əm) *n., pl.* **stars′-of-Beth′le·hem′** a plant of the lily family, with white, star-shaped flowers and long, narrow leaves

star of Bethlehem *Bible* the bright star over Bethlehem at the birth of Jesus, guiding the Magi: Matt. 2:1–10

Star of David a six-pointed star formed of two equilateral triangles: a symbol of Judaism

star·ry (stär′ē) *adj.* **-ri·er, -ri·est 1.** set or marked with stars [a *starry* curtain] **2.** shining like stars; bright [*starry* eyes] **3.** starshaped **4.** lighted by or full of stars [a *starry* sky] **5.** of, from, or like stars [*starry* light] —**star′ri·ness** *n.*

☆**star·ry-eyed** (-īd′) *adj.* **1.** with the eyes sparkling in a glow of happiness, romance, dreams, wonder, etc. **2.** impractical, unrealistic, overly optimistic, etc. [a *starry-eyed* reformer]

STAPLER

STAR OF DAVID

☆**Stars and Bars** the original flag (1861) of the Confederacy, with three horizontal bars and a circle of stars

☆**Stars and Stripes** the red, white, and blue flag of the United States, with 13 stripes and 50 stars

star sapphire a sapphire cut with a surface that produces a star-shaped reflection of light in it

star-span·gled (stär′spaŋ′g′ld) *adj.* covered or decorated with stars

☆**Star-Spangled Banner 1.** the United States flag **2.** the United States national anthem: the words are by Francis Scott Key

start (stärt) *vi.* [OE. *styrtan* & cognate ON. *sterta*] **1.** to move suddenly, as when surprised; jump or jerk [the noise made her start] **2.** to become displaced, loose, warped, etc. **3.** to stick out or seem to stick out [eyes *starting* in fear] **4.** *a)* to go into action or motion; begin to do something or go somewhere [we *start* for Boston today] *b)* to make or have a beginning; commence [the show *starts* at 2:30] **5.** to be among the beginning entrants in a race, players in a game, etc. **6.** to spring into being, activity, etc. —*vt.* **1.** to make move suddenly; rouse or flush (game) **2.** to displace, loosen, warp, etc. [the crash *started* a seam] **3.** *a)* to enter upon; begin doing, etc. [I'll *start* the new course tomorrow] *b)* to set into motion, action, etc. [who *started* the fight?] **4.** to introduce (a topic, etc.) **5.** to cause to be among those starting in a race, game, etc. —*n.* **1.** a sudden, brief shock or fright [her frightened scream gave me quite a *start*] **2.** a sudden, startled movement; leap, jerk, etc. **3.** [*pl.*] brief bursts of activity: usually in *by fits and starts* **4.** *a)* a part that is loosened, warped, etc. *b)* the resulting break or gap **5.** the act of starting, or beginning **6.** *a)* the place or time of a beginning; starting point [he was ahead from the *start*] *b)* a lead or other advantage, as at the beginning of a race **7.** an opportunity to begin a career, etc. —see SYN. at BEGIN —☆**start in** to begin a task, activity, etc. —**start out** (or **off**) to begin a journey, action, etc. —**start up** **1.** to spring up **2.** to cause (a motor, etc.) to begin running

start·er (stärt′ər) *n.* a person or thing that starts; specif., *a)* the first in a series *b)* one starting in a race, etc. *c)* one giving the signal to start, as in a race *d)* one supervising departing trucks, buses, etc. *e)* any of various devices for starting an internal-combustion engine

star·tle (stärt′'l) *vt.* **-tled, -tling** [< ME. *sterten*, to start] to surprise, frighten, or alarm suddenly; esp., to make jump, jerk, etc. as from sudden fright —*vi.* to be startled —*n.* a start or shock, as of surprise or fright —see SYN. at SHOCK[1] —**star′tler** *n.* —**star′tling** *adj.* —**star′tling·ly** *adv.*

starve (stärv) *vi.* **starved, starv′ing** [OE. *steorfan*, to die] **1.** *a)* to die from lack of food *b)* to suffer or get weak from hunger *c)* [Colloq.] to be very hungry **2.** to suffer great need (with *for*) [*starving* for affection] —*vt.* **1.** to cause to starve **2.** to force by starving [to *starve* an enemy into submission] —**star·va′tion** *n.*

starve·ling (stärv′liŋ) *n.* a person or animal that is thin or weak from lack of food —*adj.* starving; weak from hunger

☆**stash** (stash) *vt.* [prob. a blend of STORE & CACHE] [Colloq.] to put or hide in a secret or safe place —*n.* [Slang] **1.** a place for hiding things **2.** something hidden away

sta·sis (stā′sis, stas′is) *n.*, *pl.* **-ses** (-sēz) [ModL. < Gr., a standing] **1.** a stopping of the flow of a bodily fluid, as blood **2.** a state of balance or motionlessness

-stat (stat) [< ModL. < Gr. -*statēs*] *a combining form meaning* stationary, making stationary [*thermostat*]

state (stāt) *n.* [< OFr. < L. *status* <·pp. of *stare*, to stand] **1.** a set of circumstances or qualities characterizing a person or thing at a given time; condition [a *state* of poverty] **2.** a particular mental or emotional condition [a *state* of bliss] **3.** condition with regard to structure, form, etc. [liquid *state*] **4.** wealthy and formal style or condition; pomp [we dined in *state*] **5.** [*sometimes* S-] *a)* a body of people politically organized under one government within a definite territory *b)* the authority represented by such a body of people ☆**6.** [*usually* S-] any of the political units that together form a federal government, as in the U.S. ☆**7.** the territory of a state (senses 5 *a* & 6) **8.** civil government [church and *state*] **9.** the level of highest governmental authority [matters of *state*] —*adj.* **1.** ceremonial; formal [a *state* occasion] **2.** [*sometimes* S-] of the government or a state [*state* papers] —*vt.* **stat′ed, stat′ing** **1.** to set or establish by specifying [let's *state* a time and place for meeting] **2.** to set forth or express in a specific, definite, or formal way [to *state* one's objections, *stating* a musical theme] —**in** (or **into**) **a state** [Colloq.] in (or into) an excited emotional condition —**lie in state** to be displayed formally to the public before burial —**the States** the United States —**stat′a·ble** *adj.* —**state′less** *adj.*

SYN.—**state** and **condition** both refer to the set of circumstances surrounding or characterizing a person or thing at a given time [what is his mental *state*, or *condition*?], but **condition** more strongly implies the relationship of such a set of circumstances to its causes or effects [a *condition* brought about by poverty and usually stirring up feelings of rebellion]; **situation**

implies a combination of related circumstances having a significant effect on a person or thing [to be in a difficult *situation*]; **status**, basically a legal term, refers to one's state as determined by age, sex, training, mentality, service, etc. [his *status* as a veteran gives him certain benefits]

state·craft (stāt′kraft′) *n.* same as STATESMANSHIP

☆**State·hood** (-hood′) *n.* the condition of being a State of the U.S. rather than a Territory

State·house (-hous′) *n.* ☆the official meeting place of the legislature of a State of the U.S.: also **State House** or **State Capitol**

state·ly (-lē) *adj.* **-li·er, -li·est** dignified, imposing, grand, or the like —**state′li·ness** *n.*

state·ment (-mənt) *n.* **1.** *a)* the act of stating *b)* the thing stated or said **2.** *a)* a summary of a financial account [a bank *statement*] *b)* a listing of charges for goods or services; bill

Stat·en Island (stat′'n) [< Du. *Staaten Eylandt*, States Island, after States-General, name of the legislative assembly of the Netherlands] island between New Jersey and Long Island, forming the borough of Richmond in New York City

☆**State prison** a prison maintained by a State for adult criminals, usually those convicted of serious crimes

state·room (stāt′room′) *n.* **1.** a private cabin on a ship ☆**2.** a private room in a railroad car

☆**state's evidence** *Law* evidence given by or for the prosecution in a criminal case, esp. by a criminal against his associates —**turn state's evidence** to give such evidence for the prosecution

☆**state·side** (stāt′sīd′) *adj.* [Colloq.] of or having to do with the U.S. (as viewed from abroad) [*stateside* newspapers] —*adv.* [Colloq.] in, to, or toward the U.S.

states·man (stāts′mən) *n.*, *pl.* **-men** a person who shows wisdom and skill in conducting state affairs or dealing with public issues, or one experienced in the business of government — **states′man·like′, states′man·ly** *adj.*

states·man·ship (-ship′) *n.* the ability, character, or methods of a statesman; skill in dealing with public affairs

state socialism the theory, doctrine, or practice of an economy planned and controlled by the state, based on state ownership of public utilities, basic industries, etc.

☆**States' rights** all the rights and powers which the Constitution neither grants to the Federal government nor denies to the State governments: also **State rights**

☆**state-wide** (stāt′wīd′) *adj.* all over or throughout a state [a *state-wide* vote on the issue]

stat·ic (stat′ik) *adj.* [< ModL. < Gr. *statikos*, causing to stand < *histanai*, to cause to stand] **1.** acting through weight only: said of the pressure exerted by a motionless body **2.** of masses, forces, etc. at rest or in equilibrium: opposed to DYNAMIC **3.** at rest; inactive; stationary [a *static* society, not a progressive one] **4.** *Elec.* describing, of, or producing stationary electrical charges, as those resulting from friction ☆**5.** *Radio* of or having to do with static —*n.* ☆**1.** *a)* electrical discharges in the atmosphere that disturb radio or TV reception, etc. *b)* disturbance or noises produced by such discharges **2.** [Slang] remarks showing disapproval —**stat′i·cal·ly** *adv.*

stat·ice (stat′ə sē′) *n.* [ModL. < L. < Gr. *statikē* < fem. of *statikos*, astringent] same as THRIFT (sense 3)

stat·ics (stat′iks) *n.pl.* [*with sing. v.*] [see STATIC] the branch of mechanics dealing with bodies, masses, or forces at rest or in equilibrium

sta·tion (stā′shən) *n.* [< OFr. < L. < pp. of *stare*, to stand] **1.** the place where a person or thing stands or is located, as one's post when on duty, a building for a special purpose, etc. [a sentry's *station*, a police *station*] **2.** in Australia, a sheep or cattle ranch **3.** *a)* a regular stopping place, as on a bus line or railroad *b)* the building or buildings at such a place **4.** social standing or position [a man of high *station*] **5.** *a)* a place equipped to transmit or receive radio waves; esp., the studios, equipment, etc. of an organization which broadcasts radio or television programs *b)* such an organization, or the broadcasting frequency or channel assigned to it —*vt.* to assign to a station; post [to *station* a guard at the door]

☆**station agent** an official in charge of a small railroad station, or of a department in a larger station

sta·tion·ar·y (stā′shə ner′ē) *adj.* [< L. < *statio*: see STATION] **1.** not moving or movable; fixed [a *stationary* engine] **2.** unchanging in condition, value, etc. [prices remained *stationary*]

fat, āpe, cär; ten, ēven; is, bīte; gō, hôrn, tōol, look; oil, out; up, fur; get; joy; yet; chin; she; thin, then; zh, leisure; ŋ, ring; ə for *a* in *ago*, *e* in *agent*, *i* in *sanity*, *o* in *comply*, *u* in *focus*; ′ as in *able* (ā′b'l); Fr. bal; ë, Fr. coeur; ö, Fr. feu; Fr. mon; ô, Fr. coq; ü, Fr. duc; r, Fr. cri; H, G. ich; kh, G. doch; ‡foreign; ☆ Americanism; < derived from. See inside front cover.

stationary engineer a person who operates and looks after stationary engines, such as steam boilers, turbines, etc.

stationary front *Meteorol.* a front that is not moving or is moving at a speed of less than five miles an hour

☆**station break** a pause in radio and television programs, during which the name of the station is given

sta·tion·er (stā′shə nər) *n.* [< ML. *stationarius* < L., STATIONARY] a person who sells office supplies, greeting cards, some books, etc.

sta·tion·er·y (stā′shə ner′ē) *n.* [see prec. & -ERY] writing materials; specif., paper and envelopes used for letters

station house a building used as a station, esp. by a company of police or firemen

☆**sta·tion·mas·ter** (stā′shən mas′tər) *n.* an official in charge of a large railroad station

Stations of the Cross [*also* s- c-] fourteen images or pictures, as along the walls of a church, representing the stages of Jesus' sufferings: before each one prayers are said by the devout

☆**station wagon** an automobile with folding or removable rear seats and a tailgate that opens for loading luggage, etc.

stat·ism (stāt′iz′m) *n.* the theory or practice of putting economic control and planning in the power of a centralized state government —**stat′ist** *n., adj.*

sta·tis·tic (stə tis′tik) *n.* a single statistical item or fact

sta·tis·ti·cal (-ti k′l) *adj.* of, having to do with, consisting of, or based on statistics —**sta·tis′ti·cal·ly** *adv.*

stat·is·ti·cian (stat′is tish′ən) *n.* an expert or specialist in statistics

sta·tis·tics (stə tis′tiks) *n.pl.* [< G. < ModL. *statisticus* < L. *status*: see STATE] **1.** facts or data in the form of numbers, collected and arranged so as to show certain information [*census statistics*] **2.** [*with sing. v.*] the science of collecting and arranging such facts

sta·tor (stāt′ər) *n.* [ModL. < L. < pp. of *stare*, to stand] the stationary part of the magnetic circuit in a motor, generator, etc.

stat·u·ar·y (stach′oo wer′ē) *n., pl.* -**ar′ies 1.** a group of statues **2.** the art of making statues —*adj.* of or for statues

stat·ue (stach′oo) *n.* [< OFr. < L. < *statuere*, to place < *stare*, to STAND] the form of a person or animal carved in stone, wood, etc., modeled in clay, etc., or cast in plaster, bronze, etc., esp. when done in the round

stat·u·esque (stach′oo wesk′) *adj.* like a statue; specif., *a)* tall and well-proportioned *b)* dignified and graceful —**stat′u·esque′ly** *adv.* —**stat′u·esque′ness** *n.*

stat·u·ette (stach′oo wet′) *n.* a small statue

stat·ure (stach′ər) *n.* [OFr. < L. *statura* < *statuere*: see STATUE] **1.** the height of the body in a natural standing position **2.** growth or level of achievement, esp. when considered worthy of respect [*moral stature*]

sta·tus (stāt′əs, stat′-) *n., pl.* -**tus·es** [L.: see STATE] **1.** condition or position according to law [the *status* of a minor] **2.** *a)* position; rank [high *status*] *b)* high position; prestige [seeking *status*] **3.** state or condition, as of affairs —see SYN. at STATE

status quo (kwō′) [L., lit., the state in which] the existing state of affairs: also **status in quo**

status symbol a possession, way of behaving, etc. regarded as a mark of high social status

stat·ute (stach′oot, -oot) *n.* [< OFr. < LL. < L. pp. of *statuere*: see STATUE] **1.** an established rule **2.** a law passed by a legislative body

statute law law established by a legislative body

statute mile a unit of measure (5,280 feet): see MILE

statute of limitations a statute limiting the period within which a specific legal action may be taken, so that a suit cannot be brought against a person in certain cases after a specified number of years have passed

stat·u·to·ry (stach′oo tôr′ē) *adj.* **1.** of, or having the nature of, a statute **2.** fixed by statute **3.** that the law or a statute says is an offense that is to be punished [*statutory* rape]

statutory rape sexual intercourse with a girl younger than an age set by law, whether she consents or not: it is a crime punishable by law

St. Augustine [after St. AUGUSTINE, sense 2 *a*] seaport in NE Fla.: oldest city in the U.S.: pop. 12,000

staunch (stônch, stänch) *vt.* [OFr. *estanchier*, ult. < L. *stans*: see STANCE] **1.** to stop or check (the flow of blood or of tears, etc.) from (a wound, opening, etc.) **2.** to stop or lessen (a drain of funds, resources, etc.) —*vi.* to cease flowing —*adj.* **1.** watertight; seaworthy [a *staunch* ship] **2.** firm; loyal [a *staunch* supporter] **3.** strong; solidly made Also **stanch** For the *adj.*,

staunch is now the more often used form; for the *v.*, **staunch** is used as often as **stanch** —see SYN. at FAITHFUL —**staunch′ly** *adv.* —**staunch′ness** *n.*

stave (stāv) *n.* [ME., taken as sing. of *staves*, pl. of *staf*, STAFF] **1.** *a)* any of the thin, shaped strips of wood, metal, etc. set edge to edge to form the wall of a barrel, bucket, etc. *b)* any similar slat, bar, rung, etc. **2.** a stick or staff **3.** a set of lines of a poem or song; stanza **4.** *Music* same as STAFF —*vt.* **staved** or **stove, stav′ing 1.** to puncture or smash, esp. by breaking in staves **2.** to furnish with staves —*vi.* to be or become stove in, as a boat —**stave in** to break or crush inward —**stave off** to ward off or hold off, as by force, cleverness, etc.

STAVE

staves (stāvz) *n.* **1.** *alt. pl.* of STAFF **2.** *pl. of* STAVE

stay¹ (stā) *n.* [OE. *stæg*] a heavy rope or cable, usually of wire, used as a brace, as for a mast of a ship; guy —*vt.* to brace or support with stays

stay² (stā) *n.* [MFr. *estaie* < Frank.] **1.** a support; prop **2.** a strip of stiffening material used in a corset, shirt collar, etc. —*vt.* **1.** to support, or prop up **2.** to strengthen or comfort in spirit [her faith *stayed* her in times of trouble] **3.** to cause to rest (*on, upon,* or *in*)

stay³ (stā) *vi.* **stayed** or archaic **staid, stay′ing** [< Anglo-Fr. < OFr. *ester* < L. *stare*, to stand] **1.** to continue in the place or condition specified; remain; keep [to *stay* at home, to *stay* healthy] **2.** to live, dwell, or reside, esp. temporarily [to *stay* with friends] **3.** to stop; halt **4.** to pause; wait; delay [time *stays* for no man] **5.** [Colloq.] to continue or endure; last [to *stay* with a project] **6.** [Colloq.] to keep up (*with* another contestant in a race, etc.) —*vt.* **1.** to stop, halt, or check [*stay* your anger] **2.** to hold back, hinder, or detain [with nothing to *stay* their departure] **3.** to postpone or delay (legal action) **4.** to satisfy for a time (thirst, appetite, etc.) **5.** *a)* to remain through (often with *out*) [to *stay* the week (out)] *b)* to be able to last through [to *stay* the distance in a race] —*n.* **1.** *a)* a stopping or being stopped *b)* a halt, check, or pause **2.** a postponement in legal action [a *stay* of execution] **3.** the action of remaining, or the time spent, in a place [a long *stay* in Spain] —☆**stay put** [Colloq.] to remain in place or unchanged

SYN.—**stay** implies a continuing in some place or position [he *stayed* on the police force twenty years]; **remain** often suggests a staying behind while others go [only she *remained* at home]; **wait** suggests a staying in a place until something happens [*waiting* for the signal to depart]; **tarry**, a slightly old-fashioned term, and **linger** both imply a staying on past the usual or expected time for leaving, with **linger** esp. suggesting that one stays on deliberately because of an unwillingness to leave [he *tarried* at his club, *lingering* over a pleasant meal] —ANT. **go, leave, depart**

staying power ability to last or endure; endurance

stay·sail (stā′sāl′, -s′l) *n.* a sail, esp. a triangular sail, fastened on a stay

St. Cath·a·rines (kath′rinz, -ər inz) city in SE Ontario, Canada, on the Welland Canal: pop. 123,000

St. Christopher island in the Leeward group of the West Indies: 65 sq. mi.: pop. 37,000: see ANGUILLA

St. Clair (kler), Lake [after Fr. *Sainte Claire* (St. Clare of Assisi, 1194–1253)] lake between SE Mich. & Ontario, Canada

St. Clair Shores city in SE Mich., on Lake St. Clair: suburb of Detroit: pop. 88,000

St. Croix (kroi) [Fr., holy cross] largest island of the Virgin Islands of the U.S.

std. standard

Ste. [Fr. *Sainte*] Saint (female)

stead (sted) *n.* [OE. *stede*] the place or position of a person or thing as filled by a substitute or successor [she came in my *stead*] —**stand (one) in good stead** to give (one) good use, service, etc.

stead·fast (sted′fast′, -fəst) *adj.* [OE. *stedefæste*] firm or fixed; not changing or wavering; constant [a *steadfast* friendship] —**stead′fast′ly** *adv.* —**stead′fast′ness** *n.*

stead·y (sted′ē) *adj.* **stead′i·er, stead′i·est** [see STEAD & -Y²] **1.** that does not shake, totter, etc.; firm; stable [a *steady* table] **2.** constant, regular, or continuous; not changing, faltering, etc. [a *steady* gaze] **3.** constant in behavior, loyalty, etc. **4.** habitual or regular [a *steady* customer] **5.** not easily excited; calm and controlled [*steady* nerves] **6.** serious and sensible; reliable [a *steady* young man] **7.** staying headed in the same direction: said of a ship —*interj.* keep calm! —*vt., vi.* **stead′ied, stead′y·ing** to make or become steady —*n.* ☆the only

person with whom one has dates —*adv.* in a steady manner —☆**go steady** [Colloq.] to date only one person and do so regularly; be sweethearts —**stead′i·ly** *adv.* —**stead′i·ness** *n.*
SYN.—**steady** implies a fixed regularity or dependability, esp. of movement, and an absence of wavering, faltering, etc. [*a steady breeze*]; **even,** often used in place of **steady,** emphasizes the absence of irregularity [*an even heartbeat*]; **uniform** implies a sameness or likeness of things, parts, events, etc., usually as the result of being patterned after a model or standard [*uniform traffic laws*]; **regular** stresses an orderliness or balance resulting from evenness or uniformity [*regular features, attendance, etc.*]; **equable** implies that the evenness or regularity is natural or basic [*a mild, equable climate*] —**ANT. changeable, jerky**

stead·y-state (-stāt′) *adj.* describing or of a system, process, mixture, etc. in which no change takes place or in which the proportions or relationships remain the same after a change

steady-state theory a theory holding that as the universe expands, new matter is continuously created

steak (stāk) *n.* [ON. *steik* < base of *steikja,* to roast on a spit] a slice of meat, esp. beef, or of a large fish, cut thick for broiling or frying

☆**steak·house** (stāk′hous′) *n.* a restaurant that specializes in steaks, especially of beef

☆**steak knife** a table knife with a very sharp steel blade often having sawlike notches

☆**steak tar·tare** (tär tär′) [*tartare,* imitation Fr. for TARTAR: hence, steak in Tartar style] raw sirloin or tenderloin steak ground up and mixed with chopped onion, raw egg, salt, and pepper, and eaten uncooked

steal (stēl) *vt.* **stole, stol′en, steal′ing** [OE. *stælan*] **1.** to take (another's property, etc.) dishonestly, esp. in a secret manner **2.** to get or take in a sly or secret way [to *steal* a look] **3.** to get in a tricky or clever way [he *stole* her heart] **4.** to be the outstanding performer in (a scene, act, etc.), esp. in a minor role **5.** to move, put, or convey quietly or secretly [in, *into, from, away, into,* etc.] ☆**6.** *Baseball* to gain (a base) safely without the help of a hit, error, etc.: said of a base runner —*vi.* **1.** to be a thief **2.** to move, pass, etc. secretly, quietly, etc. [to *steal* out of the house] —*n.* [Colloq.] **1.** an act of stealing **2.** something obtained at an unusually low cost —**steal′er** *n.*

stealth (stelth) *n.* [ME. *stelthe* < base of *stelen,* to steal] secret, sneaky, or quiet action or behavior

stealth·y (stel′thē) *adj.* **stealth′i·er, stealth′i·est** characterized by stealth; secret, sneaky, or quiet —see **SYN.** at SECRET — **stealth′i·ly** *adv.* —**stealth′i·ness** *n.*

steam (stēm) *n.* [OE.] **1.** orig., a vapor **2.** *a*) water changed into a vapor or gas by being heated to the boiling point: used for heating, as a source of power, etc. *b*) the power supplied by steam under pressure *c*) [Colloq.] energy; vigor [he ran out of *steam* late in the afternoon] **3.** condensed water vapor; mist [*steam* on the windows in winter] —*adj.* **1.** using steam; heated, operated, etc. by steam [a *steam* engine] **2.** containing steam or used for carrying steam [a *steam* pipe] —*vi.* **1.** to give off steam or a vapor **2.** to be given off as steam **3.** to become covered with condensed steam, as a window (usually with *up*) **4.** to move by or as if by steam power [the ship *steamed* out of the harbor] ☆**5.** [Colloq.] to be very angry; fume —*vt.* to expose to the action of steam, as in cooking —**let** (or **blow**) **off steam** [Colloq.] to express strong feeling

steam bath **1.** the act of bathing by exposing the body to steam, so as to cause sweating **2.** a room or place supplied with steam for such bathing

☆**steam·boat** (stēm′bōt′) *n.* a steamship, esp. a small one

steam boiler a tank in which water is heated to produce steam and hold it under pressure

steam engine 1. an engine using steam under pressure to supply mechanical energy **2.** a locomotive powered by steam

steam·er (stē′mər) *n.* **1.** something operated by steam power, as a steamship or, formerly, a steam-powered automobile **2.** a container in which things are cooked, cleaned, etc. with steam

☆**steamer trunk** a broad, low, rectangular trunk, originally designed to fit under a bunk on shipboard

steam fitter a mechanic whose work (**steam fitting**) is putting in and repairing steam boilers, pipes, etc.

steam heat heat given off by steam in a closed system of pipes and radiators

☆**steam iron** an electric iron that releases steam through vents in the soleplate onto material being pressed

steam·roll·er (stēm′rōl′ər) *n.* **1.** a heavy, steam-driven machine with rollers used to pack down and smooth the surface of roads **2.** power which crushes anything in its way —*vt.* to crush or force as if with a steamroller [to *steamroller* the opposition; to *steamroller* a bill through Congress] —*vi.* to move or act with overwhelming force or power Also **steam′roll′**

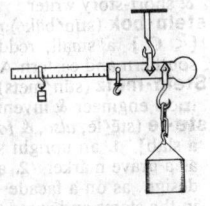
STEAMROLLER

steam·ship (-ship′) *n.* a ship driven by steam power

☆**steam shovel** a large, mechanically operated digger, powered by steam

steam table a serving table or counter, as in restaurants, having deep trays set in the surface over steaming water to keep foods in the trays warm

steam·y (stē′mē) *adj.* **steam′i·er, steam′i·est** **1.** of or like steam **2.** filled with steam **3.** giving off steam —**steam′i·ly** *adv.* —**steam′i·ness** *n.*

ste·ap·sin (stē ap′sin) *n.* [< Gr. *stea*(*r*), fat + (PE)PSIN] the lipase present in pancreatic juice

ste·a·rate (stē′ə rāt′, stir′āt) *n.* a salt or ester of stearic acid

ste·ar·ic acid (stē ar′ik, stir′ik) [< Fr. < Gr. *stear,* tallow] a colorless, waxlike fatty acid, $C_{18}H_{36}O_2$, found in many animal and vegetable fats, and used in making candles, soaps, etc.

ste·a·rin (stē′ə rin, stir′in) *n.* [< Fr. < Gr.: see prec. & -INE[4]] a white, crystalline substance, $(C_{18}H_{35}O_2)_3C_3H_5$, found in the solid portion of most animal and vegetable fats: also **ste′a·rine** (-rin, -rēn′)

ste·a·tite (stē′ə tīt′) *n.* [L. *steatitis* < Gr. *stear,* tallow] a compact, massive variety of talc; soapstone —**ste·a·tit′ic** (-tit′ik) *adj.*

sted·fast (sted′fast′, -fast) *adj.* earlier var. of STEADFAST

steed (stēd) *n.* [OE. *steda*] a horse; esp., a high-spirited riding horse: an older term now seldom used

steel (stēl) *n.* see PLURAL, II, D, 3 [OE. *stiele*] **1.** a hard, tough metal composed of iron alloyed with a small percentage of carbon and often with other metals, as nickel, chromium, etc., to produce hardness, resistance to rust, etc. **2.** something made of steel; specif., [Poet.] a sword or dagger **3.** great strength or hardness [muscles of *steel*] —*adj.* of or like steel —*vt.* **1.** to cover or edge with steel **2.** to make hard, tough, unfeeling, etc. [to *steel* himself for the shock]

steel blue a metallic blue color like that of tempered steel — **steel′-blue′** *adj.*

Steele (stēl), **Sir Richard** 1672–1729; Brit. essayist & dramatist, born in Ireland

steel gray a bluish-gray color —**steel′-gray′** *adj.*

☆**steel·head** (stēl′hed′) *n., pl.* **-head′, -heads′:** see PLURAL, II, D, 2 any of a variety of large rainbow trout found along the Pacific coast, that go up rivers to spawn

steel mill a mill where steel is made, processed, and shaped: also **steel′works′** *n.*

steel wool long, hairlike shavings of steel in a pad or ball, used for scouring, smoothing, and polishing

steel·work·er (stēl′wur′kər) *n.* a worker in a steel mill

steel·y (stē′lē) *adj.* **steel′i·er, steel′i·est** of or like steel, as in hardness, color, etc. —**steel′i·ness** *n.*

steel·yard (stēl′yärd′, stil′yard′) *n.* [STEEL & YARD[1] (in obs. sense of "rod")] a scale made up of a metal arm hanging from a hook: the object to be weighed is hung from the shorter end and a weight is moved along the longer end until it reaches a mark showing weight when the arm balances

Steen (stān), **Jan** (yän) 1626–79; Du. painter

steen·bok (stēn′bäk′, stān′-) *n., pl.* **-bok′, -boks′:** see PLURAL, II, D, 2 [Afrik. < Du. *steen,* a stone + *bok,* a buck] *same as* STEINBOK: also **steen′buck′** (-buk′)

STEELYARD

steep¹ (stēp) *adj.* [OE. *steap*, lofty < IE. base *steu-*, to strike] **1.** having a sharp rise or slope; precipitous [a *steep* incline] **2.** [Colloq.] too high or great; excessive [a *steep* price] —*n.* a steep slope —**steep′ly** *adv.* —**steep′ness** *n.*

SYN.—**steep** suggests a slope so sharp that it makes going up or down difficult [a *steep* hill]; **abrupt** implies a very sharp incline in a surface that breaks off suddenly from the level [an *abrupt* bank at the river's edge]; **precipitous** suggests the sudden, almost vertical drop of a precipice [*precipitous* canyon walls that few men could climb]; **sheer** indicates an incline that is straight up and down, or almost so, with a surface that is smooth and unbroken [cliffs falling *sheer* to the sea]

steep² (stēp) *vt.* [akin to ON. *steypa*] **1.** to soak in liquid, as in order to get the essence from **2.** to cause to be deeply involved, interested, or absorbed [to *steep* oneself in a subject] —*n.* **1.** a steeping or being steeped **2.** liquid in which something is steeped —*vi.* to be steeped, as tea leaves —see **SYN.** at **SOAK**

steep·en (stēp′'n) *vt., vi.* to make or become steep or steeper

stee·ple (stē′p'l) *n.* [OE. *stepel*] **1.** a tower rising above the main structure of a building, esp. of a church, usually capped with a spire **2.** *same as* **SPIRE** —**stee′pled** *adj.*

stee·ple·chase (-chās′) *n.* [the race orig. had as its goal a distant, visible steeple] **1.** orig., a horse race run across open country **2.** a horse race run over a prepared course with ditches, hedges, etc. placed so that they must be jumped —*vi.* -**chased′, -chas′ing** to race in a steeplechase

stee·ple·jack (-jak′) *n.* a person whose work is building, painting, or repairing steeples, smokestacks, etc.

steer¹ (stir) *vt.* [OE. *stieran*] **1.** to guide (a ship or boat) by means of a rudder **2.** to direct the movement of [to *steer* an automobile] **3.** to guide or direct [to *steer* a team to victory] **4.** to set and follow (a course) —*vi.* **1.** to steer a ship, automobile, etc. **2.** to be steered [the car *steers* easily] **3.** to set and follow a course —*n.* ☆[Colloq.] a suggestion; tip —see **SYN.** at GUIDE —**steer clear of** to avoid —**steer′a·ble** *adj.* —**steer′er** *n.*

steer² (stir) *n.* [OE. *steor*] **1.** a castrated male of the cattle family **2.** loosely, any male of beef cattle

steer·age (stir′ij) *n.* **1.** *a)* the act of steering *b)* the way in which a ship responds when being steered **2.** formerly, a section in some passenger ships occupied by passengers paying the lowest fare

steer·age·way (-wā′) *n.* the slowest forward speed at which a ship can move and still be steered

steers·man (stirz′mən) *n., pl.* -**men** a person who steers a ship or boat; helmsman

Ste·fans·son (stef′an sən), **Vil·hjal·mur** (vil′hyoul′mər) 1879–1962; U.S. arctic explorer, born in Canada

☆**steg·o·sau·rus** (steg′ə sôr′əs) *n., pl.* -**ri** (-ī) [ModL. < Gr. *stegos*, a roof + -SAURUS] a large dinosaur with a small head, heavy bony plates, and sharp spikes along the backbone

Stei·chen (stī′kən), **Edward** 1879–1973; U.S. photographer, born in Luxembourg

stein (stīn) *n.* [G.] **1.** an earthenware beer mug, or a similar mug of pewter, glass, etc. **2.** the amount that a stein will hold

Stein (stīn), **Gertrude** 1874–1946; U.S. writer in France

Stein·beck (stīn′bek′), **John (Ernst)** 1902–68; U.S. novelist & short-story writer

STEGOSAURUS
(to 24 ft. long)

stein·bok (stīn′bäk′) *n., pl.* -**bok′, -boks′**: see PLURAL, II, D, 2 [< G.] a small, reddish antelope found in grassy areas of southern and eastern Africa

Stein·metz (stīn′mets), **Charles Proteus** 1865–1923; U.S. electrical engineer & inventor, born in Germany

ste·le (stē′lē; *also, & for 2 & 3 usually,* stēl) *n.* [< L. < Gr. *stēlē*, a slab] **1.** an upright stone slab with an inscription or design, as a grave marker **2.** a prepared surface with an inscription or design, as on a façade **3.** a central cylinder of vascular tissues in the stems and roots of plants

Stel·la (stel′ə) [L. *stella*, a star] a feminine name

stel·lar (stel′ər) *adj.* [< LL. < L. *stella*, star] **1.** of the stars or a star **2.** like a star, as in shape **3.** by or as by a star performer; excellent [a *stellar* performance] **4.** leading; chief [a *stellar* role]

stel·late (stel′āt, -it) *adj.* [< L. pp. of *stellare*, to cover with

stars < *stella*, a star] star-shaped; coming out in rays or points from a center: also **stel·lat·ed** —**stel′late·ly** *adv.*

stem¹ (stem) *n.* [OE. *stemn*] **1.** the main stalk or trunk of a tree, shrub, or other plant, extending above the ground and bearing the leaves, flowers, etc. **2.** any stalk supporting leaves, flowers, or fruit **3.** a part like a stem; specif., *a)* the slender part of a tobacco pipe attached to the bowl *b)* a narrow supporting part above the foot of a wineglass, goblet, etc. *c)* the shaft projecting from a watch, with a knob for winding the spring *d)* the thick stroke of a letter, as in printing *e)* the vertical line of a musical note **4.** the forward part of a ship; bow **5.** a branch of a family **6.** the part of a word to which inflectional endings are added —*vt.* **stemmed, stem′ming 1.** to remove the stem from (a fruit, etc.) **2.** to move forward against [to row upstream, *stemming* the current] —*vi.* to originate or derive [all her troubles *stem* from her illness] —**from stem to stern 1.** from one end of a ship to another **2.** through the length of anything —**stem′less** *adj.* —**stem′like′** *adj.*

stem² (stem) *vt.* **stemmed, stem′ming** [ON. *stemma*] **1.** to stop or check by or as if by damming up [to *stem* the flow of water] **2.** to turn (a ski) in stemming —*vi.* to stop or slow down in skiing by turning the tip of the ski(s) inward —*n.* an act of stemming on skis

stemmed (stemd) *adj.* **1.** having a stem [a thin-*stemmed* goblet] **2.** with the stem or stems removed

☆**stem·ware** (stem′wer′) *n.* goblets, wineglasses, etc. having stems

☆**stem·wind·ing** (stem′wīn′diŋ) *adj.* wound, as a watch, by turning a knob at the outer end of the stem —**stem′-wind′er** *n.*

stench (stench) *n.* [OE. *stenc*] an offensive smell; stink

sten·cil (sten′s'l) *vt.* -**ciled** or -**cilled, -cil·ing** or -**cil·ling** [< OFr. < *estencele*, ult. < L. *scintilla*, a spark] to make, mark, or paint with a stencil —*n.* **1.** a thin sheet, as of paper or metal, with holes cut through in the shape of designs, letters, etc.: when ink, paint, etc. is applied to the sheet, the designs, letters, etc. are marked on the surface beneath **2.** a pattern, design, etc. made by stenciling —**sten′cil·er, sten′cil·ler** *n.*

Sten·dhal (sten′däl; *Fr.* stan däl′) (pseud. of *Marie Henri Beyle*) 1783–1842; Fr. novelist & essayist

sten·o- [< Gr. *stenos*, narrow] *a combining form meaning* narrow, thin, small, etc. [*stenography*]

☆**ste·nog·ra·pher** (stə näg′rə fər) *n.* a person skilled in stenography

ste·nog·ra·phy (stə näg′rə fē) *n.* [STENO- + -GRAPHY] shorthand writing; specif., the skill or work of writing down dictation, testimony, etc. in shorthand and later copying it out in full, as on a typewriter —**sten·o·graph·ic** (sten′ə graf′ik) *adj.* —**sten′o·graph′i·cal·ly** *adv.*

ste·no·sis (stə nō′sis) *n.* [ModL. < Gr. *stenōsis*: see STENO- & -OSIS] *Med.* a narrowing or constriction, of a passage, opening, etc. —**ste·not′ic** (-nät′ik) *adj.*

☆**sten·o·type** (sten′ə tīp′) *n.* [STENO- + -TYPE] a keyboard machine which types symbols representing sounds, words, or phrases in a kind of shorthand —*vt.* -**typed′, -typ′ing** to record by stenotype —**sten′o·typ′ist** *n.*

Sten·tor (sten′tôr) a Greek herald in the *Iliad* having a very loud voice

sten·to·ri·an (sten tôr′ē ən) *adj.* [< prec.] very loud [a *stentorian* voice]

step (step) *n.* [OE. *stepe*] **1.** the act of moving and placing the foot, as in walking, dancing, climbing, etc. **2.** the distance covered by such a movement [to move two *steps* closer] **3.** a short distance [only a *step* away] **4.** *a)* a manner of stepping; gait [light, skipping *steps*] *b)* any pace or stride in marching [the goose *step*] *c)* a set pattern of movements for a dance, usually done over and over [the waltz *step*] **5.** the sound of stepping; footfall **6.** a mark made by stepping; footprint **7.** a rest for the foot in climbing, as a stair or the rung of a ladder **8.** [*pl.*] a flight of stairs **9.** something resembling a stair step, as a raised frame supporting a mast **10.** a degree; rank; level; stage [a major is one *step* above a captain] **11.** any of a series of acts, processes, etc. [the next *step* is to add eggs] **12.** *Music a)* a degree of the staff or scale *b)* the interval between one degree and the next —*vi.* **stepped, step′ping 1.** to move by taking a step [*step* down] **2.** to walk, esp. a short distance [*step* outside] **3.** to move in a pattern of steps, as in dancing **4.** to move quickly: often with *along* **5.** to come or enter (*into* a situation, etc.) [to *step* into an argument] **6.** to put or press the foot down (*on* something) [*step* on the brake] —**vt. 1.** to take (one or more strides or paces) **2.** to set (the foot) down **3.** to do the steps of (a dance) **4.** to measure by taking steps: usually with *off* [*step* off ten yards] **5.** to provide with steps; specif., *a)* to cut steps in *b)* to arrange in a series of degrees or grades **6.** *Naut.* to set and fix (a mast) in its step —**break step** to stop marching in cadence —**in step 1.** keeping to a set rhythm in marching, dancing, etc. **2.** in conformity or agreement [in *step* with the times] —**keep step** to stay in step —**out of step** not in step —**step by step** by degrees; gradually —**step down** ☆**1.** to resign (*from* an office, etc.) ☆**2.** to decrease, as in rate —**step in** to come in so as to influence a situation; intervene —**step on it** [Colloq.] to go faster; hurry —**step out 1.** to leave a room, etc. for a short time **2.** to start to walk briskly ☆**3.** [Colloq.] to go out for a good time —**step up 1.** to approach **2.** to advance ☆**3.** to increase, as in rate —**take steps** to do certain things so as to get something done —☆**watch one's step** [Colloq.] to be careful

step·broth·er (step′bruth′ər) *n.* one's stepparent's son by a former marriage

step·child (-chīld′) *n., pl.* **-chil′dren** [OE. *steop-*, orphaned: orig. used of orphaned children] a child that one's husband or wife had by a former marriage

step·daugh·ter (-dôt′ər) *n.* a female stepchild

step-down (-doun′) *adj.* that steps down, or decreases, power, speed, etc., as a transformer, gear, etc. —*n.* a decrease, as in amount, intensity, etc.

step·fa·ther (-fä′thər) *n.* a male stepparent

steph·a·no·tis (stef′ə nōt′is) *n.* [ModL. < Gr. < *stephanos*, a crown] a woody vine grown for its white, waxy, sweet-scented flowers

Ste·phen (stē′vən) [L. *Stephanus* < Gr. < *stephanos*, a crown] a masculine name: dim. **Steve**

Ste·phen·son (stē′vən sən), **George** 1781–1848; Eng. engineer: developed the steam locomotive

step-in (step′in′) *adj.* put on by being stepped into —*n.* a step-in garment or [*pl.*], esp. formerly, undergarment

step·lad·der (-lad′ər) *n.* a four-legged ladder having broad, flat steps

step·moth·er (-muth′ər) *n.* a female stepparent

step·par·ent (-per′ənt, -par′-) *n.* [see STEPCHILD] the person who has married one's parent after the death or divorce of the other parent

steppe (step) *n.* [< Russ. *step′*] **1.** any of the great plains of southeastern Europe and Asia, having few trees **2.** any similar plain

☆**stepped-up** (stept′up′) *adj.* increased, as in tempo

step·per (step′ər) *n.* a person or animal that steps, usually in a specified manner, as a dancer or a horse

step·ping·stone (step′iŋ stōn′) *n.* **1.** a stone, usually one of a series, used to step on, as in crossing a stream, etc. **2.** a means of advancement [technical training was her *steppingstone* to success] Also **stepping stone**

step·sis·ter (step′sis′tər) *n.* one's stepparent's daughter by a former marriage

step·son (-sun′) *n.* a male stepchild

step-up (-up′) *adj.* that steps up, or increases, power, speed, etc., as a transformer, gear, etc. —*n.* an increase, as in amount, intensity, etc.

step·wise (-wīz′) *adv.* like a series of steps

-ster (stər) [OE. *-estre*, orig. a fem. agent suffix] *a suffix meaning:* **1.** a person who is, does, or creates (something specified) [*oldster, punster*] **2.** a person associated with (something specified) [*gangster*]

stere (stir) *n.* [Fr. *stère* < Gr. *stereos*, solid, cubic] a cubic meter

ster·e·o (ster′ē ō′, stir′-) *n., pl.* **-os′** ☆**1.** *a)* a stereophonic record player, radio, record, tape, etc. *b)* a stereophonic system or effect [to record in *stereo*] **2.** a stereoscopic effect, picture, etc. **3.** *shortened form of:* a) STEREOTYPE b) STEREOTYPY —*adj. shortened form of* STEREOPHONIC

ster·e·o- [< Gr. *stereos*, hard, firm] *a combining form meaning* solid, firm, three-dimensional [*stereoscope*]

ster·e·o·phon·ic (ster′ē ə fän′ik, stir′-) *adj.* [STEREO- + PHONIC] describing or of sound reproduction, as in motion pictures, records, tapes, or broadcasting, using two or more channels to carry and reproduce through separate speakers a blend of sounds from separate sources —**ster′e·o·phon′i·cal·ly** *adv.*

☆**ster·e·op·ti·con** (ster′ē äp′ti kən, -kän′) *n.* [< Gr. *stereos*, solid + *optikon*, of sight] a kind of slide projector that allows one view to fade out while the next is fading in

ster·e·o·scope (ster′ē ə skōp′, stir′-) *n.* [STEREO- + -SCOPE] an instrument that gives a three-dimensional effect to photographs viewed through it: it has two eyepieces, through which two slightly different views of the same scene are viewed side by side

STEREOSCOPE

ster·e·o·scop·ic (ster′ē ə skäp′ik, stir′-) *adj.* **1.** of or having to do with a stereoscope **2.** seeming to have three dimensions **3.** seeing things as in three dimensions —**ster′e·o·scop′i·cal·ly** *adv.*

ster·e·os·co·py (ster′ē äs′kə pē, stir′-) *n.* **1.** the science of stereoscopic effects and techniques **2.** the viewing of things as in three dimensions

ster·e·o·type (ster′ē ə tīp′, stir′-) *n.* [< Fr.: see STEREO- & -TYPE] **1.** a printing plate cast in type metal from a mold (*matrix*) taken as of a page of set type **2.** *same as* STEREOTYPY **3.** a fixed idea or popular conception, as about how a certain type of person looks, acts, etc. —*vt.* **-typed′, -typ′ing 1.** to make a stereotype of **2.** to print from stereotypes —**ster′e·o·typ′er, ster′e·o·typ′ist** *n.*

ster·e·o·typed (-tīpt′) *adj.* **1.** having the nature of a stereotype; esp., hackneyed; trite; not fresh or original **2.** printed from stereotype plates —see SYN. at TRITE

ster·e·o·typ·y (-tī′pē) *n.* the process of making or printing from stereotype plates

ster·ile (ster′'l; *Brit. & Canad., usually* -īl) *adj.* [L. *sterilis*] **1.** not able to reproduce; incapable of producing others of its kind; barren [a *sterile* woman] **2.** producing little or nothing [*sterile* soil] **3.** not lively, interesting, or imaginative [a *sterile* style] **4.** free from living microorganisms, esp. those that cause disease —**ster′ile·ly** *adv.* —**ste·ril′i·ty** (stə ril′ə tē) *n.*

ster·i·lize (ster′ə līz′) *vt.* **-lized′, -liz′ing** to make sterile; specif., *a)* to make incapable of producing others of its kind *b)* to free from living microorganisms, as by putting into boiling water or certain chemicals Also [Chiefly Brit.] **ster′i·lise′** —**ster′i·li·za′tion** *n.* —**ster′i·liz′er** *n.*

ster·ling (stur′liŋ) *n.* [ME. *sterlinge*, Norman silver penny < ?] **1.** sterling silver or articles made of it **2.** the standard of fineness of legal British coinage: for silver, 0.500; for gold, 0.91666 **3.** British money —*adj.* **1.** of standard quality: said of silver that is at least 92.5 percent pure **2.** of or payable in British money [ten pounds *sterling*] **3.** made of sterling silver **4.** very fine; excellent [a person of *sterling* character]

Ster·ling Heights (stur′liŋ) [? ult. after Lord *Sterling*, general in the Am. Revolutionary Army] city in SE Mich.: suburb of Detroit: pop. 61,000

stern[1] (sturn) *adj.* [OE. *styrne*] **1.** hard; severe; strict [*stern* measures] **2.** having an unsympathetic or disagreeable appearance; grim [a *stern* face] **3.** that cannot be changed [*stern* reality] **4.** unshakable; firm [*stern* determination] —see SYN. at SEVERE —**stern′ly** *adv.* —**stern′ness** *n.*

stern[2] (sturn) *n.* [ON. *stjorn*, steering < *styra*, to steer] **1.** the rear end of a ship, boat, etc. **2.** the rear end of anything

Sterne (sturn), **Laurence** 1713–68; Brit. novelist, born in Ireland

stern·most (sturn′mōst′) *adj.* **1.** nearest the stern **2.** last in a line of ships

stern·post (-pōst′) *n.* the main, upright piece at the stern of a vessel, usually supporting the rudder

ster·num (stur′nəm) *n., pl.* **ster′nums, ster′na** (-nə) [ModL. < Gr. *sternon*] a thin, flat structure of bone and cartilage to which most of the ribs are attached in front of the chest in most vertebrates; breastbone —**ster′nal** *adj.*

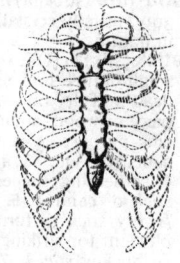

STERNUM

stern·ward (sturn′wərd) *adv., adj.* toward the stern; astern: also **stern′wards** *adv.*

---

stern·way (-wā′) *n.* backward movement of a ship

☆**stern-wheel·er** (-hwēl′ər, -wēl′ər) *n.* a steamer propelled by a paddle wheel at the stern

ster·oid (stir′oid, ster′-) *n.* [STER(OL) + -OID] any of a group of compounds including the sterols, sex hormones, etc., having a closed-chain structure —**ste·roi′dal** *adj.*

ster·ol (stir′ōl, ster′-; -ōl) *n.* [< (CHOLE)STEROL] any of a group of solid cyclic alcohols, as cholesterol, found in plant and animal tissues

ster·to·rous (stur′tə rəs) *adj.* [< L. *stertere*, to snore] characterized by loud, labored breathing, or snoring —**ster′to·rous·ly** *adv.* —**ster′to·rous·ness** *n.*

stet (stet) [L.] let it stand: a printer's term used to indicate that matter marked to be taken out is to remain —*vt.* **stet′ted**, **stet′ting** to cancel a change in or deletion of (a word, passage, etc.), as by writing "stet" in the margin of a manuscript

steth·o·scope (steth′ə skōp′) *n.* [< Fr. < Gr. *stēthos*, the chest + -SCOPE] *Med.* an instrument used by doctors to examine the heart, lungs, etc. by listening to the sounds they make —**steth′o·scop′ic** (-skäp′ik), **steth′o·scop′i·cal** *adj.* —**steth′o·scop′i·cal·ly** *adv.*

St-É·tienne (saṇ tā tyen′) city in SE France: pop. 213,000

Steu·ben (stōō′b'n; *G.* shtoi′bən), Baron **Frederick William Augustus von** 1730–94; Prussian military officer: served as Am. general in the Revolutionary War

☆**ste·ve·dore** (stē′və dôr′) *n.* [< Sp. < *estivar*, to stow < L. *stipare*, to cram] a person employed at loading and unloading ships —*vt.*, *vi.* **-dored**, **-dor·ing** to load or unload the cargo of (a ship)

STETHOSCOPE

Ste·ven (stē′vən) [see STEPHEN] a masculine name

Ste·ven·son (stē′vən s'n), **Robert Louis (Balfour)** 1850–94; Scot. novelist, poet, & essayist

stew (stōō, styōō) *vt.* [< MFr. *estuver*, ult. < L. *ex*, out + Gr. *typhos*, steam] to cook by simmering slowly for a long time —*vi.* **1.** to undergo cooking in this way **2.** to live in hot, overcrowded conditions **3.** to fret or worry —*n.* **1.** a dish, esp. of meat and vegetables, cooked by stewing **2.** a state of anxiety or worry —**stew in one's own juice** to suffer from one's own actions

stew·ard (stōō′ərd, styōō′-) *n.* [OE. *stiweard* < *stig*, enclosure + *weard*, a keeper] **1.** a person in charge of the affairs of a large household, who supervises the kitchen and servants, manages the accounts, etc. **2.** a person put in charge of the finances, property, etc. of another **3.** a person in charge of the food and drink, the service personnel, etc. in a club, restaurant, etc. **4.** a person in charge of arrangements for a ball, race, etc. **5.** an attendant on a ship, airplane, etc. who looks after the passengers' comfort **6.** *short for* SHOP STEWARD —*vi.* to act as a steward —**stew′ard·ship′** *n.*

stew·ard·ess (-ər dis) *n.* a woman steward (esp. sense 5)

Stew·art (stōō′ərt, styōō′-) [see STUART] a masculine name

stewed (stōōd) *adj.* **1.** cooked by stewing, as food **2.** [Slang] drunk; intoxicated

stew·pan (stōō′pan′, styōō′-) *n.* a pan for stewing

St. George's Channel strait between England & Wales, connecting the Irish Sea with the Atlantic

St. He·le·na (hə lē′nə, hel′i nə) Brit. island in the S Atlantic, c. 1,200 mi. from Africa: site of Napoleon's exile (1815–21)

stib·nite (stib′nīt) *n.* [< L. *stibium*, antimony + -ITE] the lead-gray, usually crystalline trisulfide of antimony, Sb_2S_3, as found in nature

stick (stik) *n.* [OE. *sticca* < IE. base *steig-*, a point] **1.** a twig or small branch broken or cut off, esp. a dead and dry one **2.** a long, slender piece of wood, often shaped for a specific purpose, as a wand, staff, club, cane, rod, etc. **3.** a stalk, as of celery **4.** something shaped like a stick [a *stick* of candy] **5.** a separate article [every *stick* of furniture] **6.** an implement for striking a ball, puck, etc. [a hockey *stick*] **7.** a stab or thrust **8.** [Colloq.] a dull, stiff, or unresponsive person ☆**9.** [Slang] a marijuana cigarette **10.** *Aeron.* a lever that controls the altitude and movement of an airplane: in full, **control stick** —*vt.* **stuck** or *for vt.* **8 sticked**, **stick′ing**

HOCKEY STICK

1. to pierce or puncture, as with a pointed instrument **2.** to kill by stabbing **3.** to pierce something with (a knife, pin, etc.) **4.** to thrust or push (*in, out*, etc.) [he *stuck* his hands in his pockets] **5.** to fasten or attach by gluing, pinning, etc. **6.** to fix on something pointed; impale **7.** to obstruct, bog down, etc.; also, to detain, delay, etc.: usually used in the passive [the wheels were *stuck*, he was *stuck* in town] **8.** to prop (a vine, etc.) with a stick **9.** [Colloq.] to place; put; set [just *stick* that table anyplace] **10.** [Colloq.] to puzzle; baffle [to be *stuck* by a question] **11.** [Slang] *a)* to make pay, often excessively *b)* to impose a disagreeable task, burden, etc. upon [to *stick* her with doing the dishes] —*vi.* **1.** to be fixed by a pointed end, as a nail, etc. **2.** to be attached by adhesion; adhere [the stamp won't *stick* to the paper] **3.** *a)* to remain in the same place; stay [to *stick* at home] *b)* to remain fixed in the memory *c)* to remain in effect [to make charges *stick*] **4.** to keep or stay close [friends *stick* together, *stick* to the trail] **5.** to persevere; persist [to *stick* at a job] **6.** to become fixed, blocked, embedded, jammed, etc. [my shoe *stuck* in the mud, the gears *stuck*] **7.** to be puzzled **8.** to hesitate; scruple [he'll *stick* at nothing] **9.** to protrude or extend (with *out, up*, etc.) —☆**on the stick** [Slang] alert, efficient, etc. —**stick around** [Slang] to stay near at hand —**stick by** (or **to**) to remain loyal to —**stick it out** [Slang] to endure something to the end —**stick up** [Slang] to commit armed robbery upon —**stick up for** [Colloq.] to uphold; defend —☆**the sticks** [Colloq.] the rural districts —**stick′like′** *adj.*

☆**stick·ball** (stik′bôl′) *n.* a game like baseball played by children, as on city streets, with whatever equipment is at hand, such as a broom handle and a soft rubber ball

stick·er (-ər) *n.* a person or thing that sticks; specif., ☆*a)* a bur, barb, or thorn ☆*b)* a gummed label *c)* [Colloq.] *same as* STICKLER

sticking plaster sticky material for covering a little scratch or wound, usually a thin cloth gummed on one side

stick insect any of a group of insects with a body that resembles a stick

stick-in-the-mud (stik′n thə mud′) *n.* [Colloq.] a person who resists change or progress, new ideas, etc.

stick·le (stik′'l) *vi.* **-led**, **-ling** [prob. < ME. *stightlen*, to dispose, ult. < OE. *stihtan*, to arrange] **1.** to raise objections, argue, etc., esp. in a stubborn way, usually about unimportant matters **2.** to have objections; scruple (*at*)

stick·le·back (stik′'l bak′) *n.* [< OE. *sticel*, a prick + ME. *bak*, back] a small, scaleless fish with sharp spines: the male builds a nest for the eggs

stick·ler (stik′lər) *n.* [see STICKLE] **1.** a person who insists on having things done in a certain way [a *stickler* for discipline] ☆**2.** [Colloq.] something puzzling to solve

☆**stick·pin** (stik′pin′) *n.* a pin, esp. one set with a gem, worn as an ornament in a cravat or necktie

☆**stick shift** a gearshift for a motor vehicle operated by hand, rather than automatically, by moving a lever, esp. one on the floor

☆**stick-to-it·ive·ness** (stik tōō′it iv nis) *n.* [Colloq.] persistence; perseverance

☆**stick-up** (stik′up′) *n.* *slang term for* HOLDUP (sense 2)

stick·y (-ē) *adj.* **stick′i·er**, **stick′i·est** **1.** that sticks; adhesive; clinging **2.** covered with a clinging substance [*sticky* fingers] **3.** [Colloq.] hot and humid ☆**4.** [Colloq.] difficult; troublesome [a *sticky* problem] ☆**5.** [Colloq.] overly sentimental —**stick′i·ly** *adv.* —**stick′i·ness** *n.*

stiff (stif) *adj.* [OE. *stif*] **1.** hard to bend or stretch; rigid; firm **2.** hard to move or operate; not free or limber **3.** sore or limited in movement: said of joints or muscles **4.** having such joints or muscles [I feel *stiff* this morning] **5.** not fluid or loose; thick [beat the egg whites until they are *stiff*] **6.** moving swiftly [a *stiff* breeze] **7.** containing much alcohol [a *stiff* drink] **8.** having a strong effect; potent [a *stiff* dose of medicine] **9.** harsh [a *stiff* punishment] **10.** difficult [a *stiff* climb] **11.** tense or awkward; not easy or relaxed [a *stiff* smile] **12.** determined or stubborn [to put up a *stiff* fight] **13.** [Colloq.] high [a *stiff* price] **14.** [Slang] drunk —*adv.* **1.** to a stiff condition **2.** [Colloq.] completely [scared *stiff*] —*n.* [Slang] ☆**1.** a corpse ☆**2.** a drunken person ☆**3.** a person [a working *stiff*] —☆*vt.* **stiffed**, **stiff′ing** [Slang] to cheat, as by leaving no tip —see SYN. at FIRM[1] —**stiff′ish** *adj.* —**stiff′ly** *adv.* —**stiff′ness** *n.*

stiff-arm (stif′ärm′) ☆*vt.* to push away (an opponent, etc.) with one's arm out straight —☆*n.* the act of stiff-arming

stiff·en (stif′'n) *vt.*, *vi.* to make or become stiff or stiffer —**stiff′en·er** *n.*

stiff-necked (stif′nekt′) *adj.* stubborn; obstinate

sti·fle[1] (stī'f'l) *vt.* **-fled, -fling** [ult. < MFr. *estouffer*, to smother] **1.** to suffocate; smother **2.** to hold back; check; stop [to *stifle* a sob] —*vi.* **1.** to die from lack of air **2.** to suffer from lack of fresh, cool air —**sti'fling** *adj.*

sti·fle[2] (stī'f'l) *n.* [ME.] the kneelike joint above the hock in the hind leg of a horse, dog, etc.: also **stifle joint**

stig·ma (stig'mə) *n., pl.* **-mas**; also, and for 4, 5, & 6 usually, **stig·ma·ta** (stig mät'ə, stig'mə te) [L. < Gr., lit., a prick with a pointed instrument] **1.** formerly, a mark burned or cut into the flesh of a criminal or slave **2.** something which harms the reputation of a person, group, etc.; mark of disgrace [the *stigma* of being a murderer] **3.** a mark, sign, etc. indicating that something is not considered normal **4.** a small mark, scar, opening, etc., as a pore, on the surface of a plant or animal **5.** a spot on the skin, esp. one that bleeds as the result of nervous tension **6.** [*pl.*] marks resembling the Crucifixion wounds of Jesus **7.** *Bot.* the upper tip of the style of a flower, on which pollen falls: see illustration at FLOWER —**stig·mat·ic** (-mat'ik) *adj.*

stig·ma·tize (stig'mə tīz') *vt.* **-tized', -tiz'ing 1.** to mark with a stigma **2.** to mark as disgraceful [his accident *stigmatized* him as a reckless driver] —**stig'ma·ti·za'tion** *n.*

stile (stīl) *n.* [OE. *stigel* < *stigan*, to climb] **1.** a step or set of steps used in climbing over a fence or wall **2.** *shortened form of* TURNSTILE

sti·let·to (sti let'ō) *n., pl.* **-tos, -toes** [It., dim. of *stilo*, a dagger < L. *stilus*: see STYLE] **1.** a small dagger with a slender, tapering blade **2.** a pointed instrument for making eyelet holes in cloth, etc. —*vt.* **-toed, -to·ing** to stab or kill with a stiletto

still[1] (stil) *adj.* [OE. *stille*] **1.** without sound; quiet; silent **2.** hushed, soft, or low in sound [a *still* small voice] **3.** not moving; motionless: following *stand, sit, lie*, etc., sometimes regarded as an adverb **4.** calm; tranquil; unruffled [*still* water] **5.** not effervescent or bubbling: said of wine **6.** *Motion Pictures* describing or of a single posed photograph or one made from a single frame of motion-picture film, for use in publicity —*n.* **1.** silence; quiet [in the *still* of the night] **2.** a still photograph —*adv.* **1.** at or up to the time indicated, whether past, present, or future [does she *still* work here?] **2.** even; yet [*still* colder] **3.** nevertheless; yet [rich but *still* unhappy] **4.** [Archaic] ever; constantly —*conj.* nevertheless; yet —*vt.* to make still; specif., *a)* to make silent *b)* to make motionless *c)* to calm; relieve [to *still* her fears] —*vi.* to become still —**still'ness** *n.*

SYN.—**still** implies the absence of sound and, usually, of movement also [the *still* hours before dawn]; **quiet** also implies the absence of sound, but usually stresses freedom from excitement, confusion, etc. [a *quiet* country town]; **noiseless** stresses the absence of noise and often suggests movement with little or no sound along with it [the *noiseless* flight of an owl]; **hushed** suggests the checking or softening of noise or sound [*hushed* hospital corridors; a *hushed* and reverent congregation] —**ANT.** noisy, stirring

still[2] (stil) *n.* [< obs. *still*, to DISTILL] **1.** an apparatus used for distilling liquids, esp. alcoholic liquors **2.** *same as* DISTILLERY —*vt., vi.* [Dial.] to distill (alcoholic liquor) illegally

still·birth (stil'burth') *n.* the birth of a stillborn fetus

still·born (stil'bôrn') *adj.* **1.** dead at birth **2.** unsuccessful from the beginning; abortive [a *stillborn* project]

still life 1. an arrangement of objects, as fruit in a bowl, flowers in a vase, etc., used as the subject of a painting, drawing, etc. **2.** *pl.* **still lifes** such a painting, etc. —**still'-life'** *adj.*

☆**Still·son wrench** (stil'sʼn) [after its U.S. inventor (in 1869), D. *Stillson*] *a trademark for* a wrench with a jaw that moves through a collar pivoted to the shaft, used for turning pipes, etc.: the jaw tightens as pressure is applied to the handle: see illustration at WRENCH

still·y (stil'ē; *for adv.* stil'lē) *adj.* **still'i·er, still'i·est** [Now Rare] still; silent; calm —*adv.* in a still manner; quietly

stilt (stilt) *n.* [prob. < MLowG. or MDu. *stelte*] **1.** either of a pair of poles, each with a footrest somewhere along its length,

used for walking with the feet above the ground, as in play **2.** any of a number of long posts used to hold a building, etc. above the ground or out of the water **3.** *pl.* **stilts, stilt:** see PLURAL, II, D, 1 any of several wading birds related to the avocet

stilt·ed (stil'tid) *adj.* **1.** raised on or as on stilts **2.** formal or dignified in a stiff, artificial way; pompous [a *stilted* prose style] —**stilt'ed·ly** *adv.* —**stilt'ed·ness** *n.*

Stil·ton (cheese) (stil't'n) [< *Stilton*, village in EC England] a rich, crumbly cheese with veins of blue-green mold

stim·u·lant (stim'yə lənt) *adj.* stimulating —*n.* anything that stimulates; specif., *a)* any drug, etc. that temporarily speeds up the activity of the heart or some other organ *b)* popularly, an alcoholic drink: actually alcohol is a depressant of the central nervous system

stim·u·late (-lāt') *vt.* **-lat'ed, -lat'ing** [< L. pp. of *stimulare*, to prick < *stimulus*, a goal] **1.** to make active or more active; stir up or spur on; arouse; excite [cooking smells *stimulate* my appetite] **2.** *Med., Physiol.* to excite (an organ, etc.) to activity or increased activity —*vi.* to act as a stimulant or stimulus —**stim·u·lat'er, stim·u·la'tor** *n.* —**stim'u·la'tion** *n.* —**stim·u·la'tive** *adj., n.*

stim·u·lus (-ləs) *n., pl.* **-u·li'** (-lī') [L., a goad] **1.** something that stirs to action or increased action; incentive [advertising can be a *stimulus* to business] **2.** *Physiol., Psychol.* any action or agent that causes or changes an activity in an organism, organ, etc.

sti·my (stī'mē) *n., pl.* **-mies, vt. -mied, -my·ing** *same as* STYMIE

sting (stiŋ) *vt.* **stung, sting'ing** [OE. *stingan*] **1.** to prick or wound with a sting: said of plants and insects **2.** to cause sharp, sudden, smarting pain to [cold wind *stings* the face] **3.** to cause to suffer mentally [his conscience *stung* him] **4.** to stimulate suddenly and sharply [*stung* into action] **5.** [Slang] to cheat; esp., to overcharge —*vi.* **1.** to prick or wound with a sting **2.** to cause or feel sharp, smarting pain, either physical or mental [my arm *stings* from the blow] —*n.* **1.** the act or power of stinging **2.** a pain or wound resulting from or as from stinging **3.** a thing that stimulates; goad **4.** a sharp-pointed organ, as in insects, used to prick, wound, or inject poison **5.** any of the stinging, hollow hairs on some plants, as nettles —**sting'ing·ly** *adv.* —**sting'less** *adj.*

sting·er (stiŋ'ər) *n.* a person or thing that stings; specif., a sharp-pointed organ of insects, etc., used for stinging

stinging hair *same as* STING (*n.* 5)

☆**sting·ray** (stiŋ'rā') *n.* a large ray (fish) having a whiplike tail with a sharp spine or spines that can inflict painful wounds: also **sting·a·ree** (stiŋ'ə rē', stiŋ'ə rē')

stin·gy (stin'jē) *adj.* **stin'gi·er, stin'gi·est** [akin to STING] **1.** not willing to give or spend; miserly **2.** less than needed or expected [a *stingy* serving of meat] —**stin'gi·ly** *adv.* —**stin'gi·ness** *n.*

SYN.—**stingy** implies a selfish unwillingness to part with anything, esp. money, that belongs to one; **close** suggests the keeping of a tight hold on what one has and a being careful to spend as little as possible; **parsimonious** implies great caution in spending, often to the point of being niggardly; **niggardly** implies a being so stingy that one is willing to spend only a very little or the least amount, as in helping others in need; **penurious** suggests that one is so tightfisted and close that one seems to be poverty-stricken; **miserly** implies a greedy desire to hoard money or goods for oneself, with little or no desire to share with others —**ANT.** generous, bountiful

stink (stiŋk) *vi.* **stank** or **stunk, stunk, stink'ing** [OE. *stincan*] **1.** to give off a strong, bad smell **2.** to be offensive or hateful [such immoral behavior *stinks*] **3.** [Slang] to be no good, or of low quality [his last novel *stank*] **4.** [Slang] to be supplied with to a degree that offends (with *of* or *with*) [he *stinks* with money] —*n.* **1.** a strong, bad smell; stench **2.** [Slang] a strong public reaction, as of outrage or protest [the bribery case raised quite a *stink*] —**stink out** to drive out by a strong, bad smell —**stink up** to cause to stink [cooking cabbage *stinks up* the house] —**stink'er** *n.*

stink bomb a device made to burn or explode and give off a foul smell

☆**stink·bug** (stiŋk'bug') *n.* any of various foul-smelling bugs

STINGRAY
(to 14 ft. long, including tail)

BOILING IMPURE LIQUID
COLD WATER
IN
DISTILLED LIQUID
OUT
STILL

stink·ing (-iŋ) *adj.* **1.** that stinks; bad-smelling **2.** [Slang] *a)* very bad, unsatisfactory, etc. *b)* offensive, disgusting, etc. — *adv.* [Slang] to an offensive degree —**stink′ing·ly** *adv.*

SYN.—**stinking** and the more formal **fetid** both imply foulness of odor [a *stinking* garbage can; the *fetid* smell of cigar butts]; **malodorous** is applied to smells that range from those that are unpleasant to those that are strongly offensive [*malodorous* cheeses]; **noisome** suggests that something that gives off a foul odor may be dangerous to one's health or harmful [the *noisome* stench of open sewers]; **putrid** stresses the sickening foul smell of rotting organic matter [buzzards feeding on *putrid* flesh]; **rank** implies a strong odor that may be slightly disagreeable or very disagreeable [the *rank* smell of a goat]

stink·weed (-wēd′) *n.* any of several foul-smelling plants, as the jimson weed

stint (stint) *vt.* [OE. *styntan,* to blunt] to limit to a certain, usually small, amount [she *stinted* herself on meals to save money] —*vi.* to be sparing in giving or using —*n.* **1.** restriction; limit [to help willingly and without *stint*] **2.** a task or share of work to be done [each child does a *stint* of housework] —**stint′er** *n.* —**stint′ing·ly** *adv.*

stipe (stīp) *n.* [Fr. < L. *stipes,* tree trunk] a stalk, as that supporting a mushroom cap, fern frond, etc.

sti·pend (stī′pend, -pənd) *n.* [L. *stipendium* < *stips,* small coin + *pendere,* to weigh out, pay] **1.** a regular or fixed payment for services, as a salary **2.** any periodic payment, as an allowance—see **SYN.** at WAGE

sti·pen·di·ar·y (stī pen′dē er′ē) *adj.* **1.** receiving, or performing services for, a stipend **2.** paid for by a stipend [*stipendiary* services] —*n., pl.* **-ar′ies** a person who receives a stipend

stip·ple (stip′'l) *vt.* **-pled, -pling** [< Du. < *stippel,* a speckle] **1.** to paint, draw, engrave, or apply in small dots rather than in lines or solid areas **2.** to mark with dots; fleck —*n.* **1.** *a)* the art of painting, drawing, etc. in dots *b)* the effect so produced, or an effect like it, as in nature **2.** stippled work Also **stip′pling** *n.* —**stip′pler** *n.*

stip·u·late (stip′yə lāt′) *vt.* **-lat′ed, -lat′ing** [< L. pp. of *stipulari,* to bargain] **1.** to include in the terms of a contract, etc. **2.** to specify as an essential condition of an agreement [he *stipulated* that the college use his gift for a new library] —*vi.* to make a specific demand (*for* something) as a condition of an agreement —**stip′u·la′tor** *n.* —**stip′u·la·to′ry** (-lə tôr′ē) *adj.*

stip·u·la·tion (stip′yə lā′shən) *n.* **1.** the act of stipulating **2.** something stipulated; point agreed upon, as in a contract

stip·ule (stip′yōōl) *n.* [ModL. *stipula* < L., a stalk] either of a pair of small, leaflike parts at the base of some leafstalks —**stip′u·lar** (-yōō lər) *adj.* —**stip′u·late** (-lit, -lāt′), **stip′u·lat′ed** *adj.*

stir¹ (stur) *vt.* **stirred, stir′ring** [OE. *styrian*] **1.** to move, shake, etc., esp. slightly [a breeze *stirred* the leaves] **2.** to rouse from sleep, drowsiness, boredom, etc. **3.** to make move or be active [*stirring* oneself to finish the work] **4.** to mix (a liquid, etc.) by moving a spoon, fork, spatula, etc. around **5.** to excite the feelings of; move deeply [his speech *stirred* the crowd] **6.** to incite or provoke (often with *up*) [to *stir* up trouble] **7.** to evoke, or call up [to *stir* memories] —*vi.* **1.** to move, esp. only slightly **2.** to be busy and active **3.** to begin to show signs of activity **4.** to undergo mixing —*n.* **1.** a stirring, or the sound of this **2.** movement; activity **3.** a state of excitement; commotion [a movie that has caused quite a *stir*] —**stir′rer** *n.*

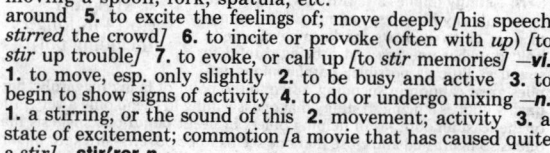
STIPULE

SYN.—**stir** (in this sense, often **stir up**) implies a bringing into action or activity by making excited, angry, etc. [the colonies were *stirred* to rebellion]; **arouse** and **rouse** are often used with exactly the same meaning, but **arouse** usually implies merely a bringing into a state of awareness or alertness, as from a state of sleep [*aroused* from daydreaming by the bell/ and **rouse** suggests a sudden stirring to vigorous or excited activity [a rifle shot *roused* the sleeping guard]; **awaken** and **waken** literally mean to arouse from sleep, but they also suggest the drawing forth of unused powers, hidden emotions, etc. [it *awakened,* or *wakened,* her maternal feelings]

stir² (stur) *n.* [prob. ult. < Romany] [Slang] a prison

☆**stir-cra·zy** (stur′krā′zē) *adj.* [see STIR²] [Slang] suffering nervous strain from being confined for a long time, specif. in prison

stir-fry (-frī′) *vt.* **-fried′, -fry′ing** in Chinese cooking, to fry (bits of meat, vegetables, etc.) very quickly in a wok, with a little oil, while stirring constantly

stirps (sturps) *n., pl.* **stir·pes** (stur′pēz) [L., lit., a root] **1.**

family or branch of a family **2.** *Law* the person from whom a family or branch of a family is descended

stir·ring (stur′iŋ) *adj.* **1.** active; busy **2.** that stirs one's feelings; moving; rousing [*stirring* music]

stir·rup (stur′əp, stir′-) *n.* [OE. *stigrap*] **1.** a flat-bottomed ring hung by a strap (**stirrup leather**) from a saddle and used as a footrest **2.** any of various stirruplike supports, clamps, etc.

stirrup (bone) *same as* STAPES

stitch (stich) *n.* [OE. *stice,* a puncture] **1.** *a)* a single complete in-and-out movement of a threaded needle in sewing *b)* *same as* SUTURE (*n.* 4 *c*) **2.** a single loop of yarn worked off a needle in knitting, crocheting, etc. **3.** a loop, knot, etc. made by stitching **4.** a particular kind of stitch or style of stitching **5.** a sudden, sharp pain, as in the side **6.** a bit, as of work, or piece, as of clothing [not wearing a *stitch*] —*vi.* to make stitches; sew —*vt.* to fasten, repair, etc. with stitches; sew —**in stitches** laughing uproariously —**stitch′er** *n.* —**stitch′ing** *n.*

stitch·er·y (stich′ər ē) *n.* **1.** decorative needlework, as embroidery, crewelwork, etc. **2.** *pl.* **-er·ies** something so decorated

sti·ver (stī′vər) *n.* [Du. *stuiver*] **1.** a former Dutch coin equal to 1/20 of a guilder **2.** a trifling sum

St. John 1. seaport in S New Brunswick, Canada: pop. 86,000 **2.** island of the Virgin Islands of the U.S.

St. John's capital of Newfoundland; seaport on the SE coast: pop. 87,000

St. Joseph city in NW Mo., on the Missouri River: pop. 73,000

St. Kitts (kits) *popular name of* ST. CHRISTOPHER

St-Lau·rent (san lô rän′) city in SW Quebec, Canada: suburb of Montreal: pop. 64,000

St. Lawrence [< Fr. *St. Laurent,* Rom. martyr (?-258)] **1.** river flowing from Lake Ontario into the Gulf of St. Lawrence **2. Gulf of,** inlet of the Atlantic in E Canada

St. Lawrence Seaway inland waterway for oceangoing ships, connecting the Great Lakes with the Atlantic: it consists of the St. Lawrence River & several locks & canals

stlg. sterling

St. Lou·is (lōō′is, lōō′ē) city & port in E Mo., on the Mississippi: pop. 622,000 (met. area 2,363,000)

St. Lu·ci·a (lōō′shē ə, -shə; lōō sē′ə) country on an island of the Windward group of the West Indies, south of Martinique: 238 sq. mi.; pop. 101,000

ST. LAWRENCE SEAWAY

St. Martin island of the Leeward group of the West Indies, south of Anguilla: the N part belongs to France, the S part to the Netherlands: 13 sq. mi.; pop. 11,000: Fr. name **St-Mar·tin** (san mȧr tan′); Du. name **St. Maar·ten** (sint mär′t'n)

St. Mo·ritz (sānt′ mō rits′; *Fr.* sȧn mô rēts′) mountain resort town in SE Switzerland

stoat (stōt) *n., pl.* **stoats, stoat:** see PLURAL, II, D, 1 [ME. *stote*] a large European weasel, esp. in its brown summer coat: see ERMINE (sense 1)

sto·chas·tic (stō kas′tik) *adj.* [< Gr. *stochastikos,* skillful in aiming < *stochos,* a target] **1.** of or due to chance **2.** describing or of a process in which each member of a set of items has a chance of occurring with equal frequency

stock (stäk) *n.* [OE. *stocc*] **1.** the trunk of a tree **2.** [Archaic] *a)* a tree stump *b)* a wooden log **3.** anything lacking life, motion, or feeling **4.** *a)* a plant stem into which a graft is inserted *b)* a plant from which cuttings are taken **5.** a rhizome or rootstock **6.** any of certain plants of the mustard family **7.** *a)* the individual that is the first of a line of descent *b)* a line of descent; ancestry or family *c)* a strain, race, or other related group of animals or plants *d)* a group of related languages or families of languages **8.** a supporting or main part, as of an implement, etc., to which the working parts are attached, as the butt of a whip, the frame of a plow, the part of a rifle holding the barrel, etc. **9.** [*pl.*] *a)* a framework, specif., *a)* a former means of punishment that was a wooden frame with holes for locking around an offender's ankles and, sometimes, his wrists *b)* a frame of timbers supporting a ship while it is being built **10.** raw material **11.** water in which meat, fish, etc. has been boiled, used as a base for soup or gravy **12.** paper of a specified weight, kind, etc. [heavy *stock*] **13.** a store or supply; specif., *a)* all the animals, equipment, etc. kept on a farm *b)* short for LIVESTOCK *c)* the total amount of goods on hand in a store, etc.; inventory   **14.** *a)* the capital invested in a company or corporation by individuals through the purchase of shares   *b)* the share that an individual stockholder has in the ownership of a corporation, as represented by shares of this capital in the form of certificates   **15.** a stock company (sense 2), or its plays   **16.** a large, wide, stiff neckband, worn in earlier times —*vt.* **1.** to attach to a stock [to *stock* a plow]   **2.** *a)* to furnish (a farm) with stock or (a shop, etc.) with stock   *b)* to supply with [to *stock* a pond with fish]   **3.** to get or keep a supply of, as for sale or for future use —*vi.* to put in a stock, or supply (often with *up*) —*adj.* **1.** always kept in stock [*stock* sizes]   **2.** common, hackneyed, or trite from being used again and again [a *stock* excuse]   **3.** that deals with stock [a *stock* boy]   **4.** of or relating to a stock company   **5.** for breeding [a *stock* mare]   **6.** of, or for the raising of, livestock [*stock* farming] —**in** (or **out of**) **stock** (not) available for sale or use —**take stock** **1.** to make an inventory of the stock on hand   **2.** to examine the situation before deciding or acting —☆**take** (or **put**) **stock in** to have confidence in, regard as important, etc.

stock·ade (stä kād′) *n.* [< Fr. < Pr. *estacado* < *estaca*, a stake] **1.** a barrier of stakes driven into the ground side by side, for defense against attack   ☆**2.** an enclosure, as a fort, made with such stakes   ☆**3.** an enclosure for military prisoners —*vt.* **-ad′ed, -ad′ing** to surround with a stockade

stock·bro·ker (stäk′brō′kər) *n.* a person who acts as an agent for others in buying and selling stocks and bonds —**stock′bro′ker·age, stock′bro′king** *n.*

☆**stock car** **1.** a railway car for carrying livestock   **2.** a passenger automobile of standard make, changed in various ways so it can be used in racing

stock company **1.** a company or corporation whose capital is divided into shares   **2.** a company of actors who put on a series of plays over a period of time, usually at one theater

stock dividend **1.** a dividend in the form of additional shares of the same stock   **2.** the payment of such a dividend

stock exchange **1.** a place where stocks and bonds are regularly bought and sold   **2.** an association of stockbrokers who meet together for buying and selling stocks and bonds according to regulations

stock·fish (stäk′fish′) *n., pl.* **-fish′, -fish′es:** see FISH [< MDu. < *stok*, stick + *visch*, fish] a fish split and dried without salt in the open air

stock·hold·er (-hōl′dər) *n.* a person owning stock or shares in a given company

Stock·holm (stäk′hōm′, -hōlm′; *Sw.* stôk′hôlm′) capital of Sweden, on the Baltic: pop. 768,000 (met. area 1,280,000)

stock·i·nette, stock·i·net (stäk′ə net′) *n.* [prob. for earlier *stocking net*] an elastic, machine-knitted cloth used for making stockings, underwear, etc.

stock·ing (stäk′iŋ) *n.* [< STOCK, in obs. sense of leg covering + -ING] **1.** a closefitting covering, usually knitted, for the foot and, usually, most of the leg   **2.** something like this, as a patch of color on an animal's leg —**in one's stocking feet** wearing stockings or socks but no shoes

stocking cap a long, tapered knitted cap

stock in trade **1.** merchandise stocked in a store   **2.** tools, materials, etc. used in carrying on a trade or business   **3.** any of the resources, practices, or devices always in use by a person or group

stock·man (-mən; *also, esp. for 2*, -man′) *n., pl.* **-men** (-mən, -men′) **1.** a man who owns or raises livestock   **2.** a man who works in a stockroom or warehouse

stock market **1.** *same as* STOCK EXCHANGE   **2.** the business carried on at a stock exchange   **3.** the prices of stocks and bonds as listed at a stock exchange

stock·pile (-pīl′) *n.* a supply of goods, raw material, etc., stored up to be sure of having enough for some future need or emergency —*vt., vi.* **-piled′, -pil′ing** to build up a stockpile (of)

stock·room (-rōōm′) *n.* a room in which a supply of goods, materials, etc. is kept: also **stock room**

stock split *Finance* the act or result of splitting stock by distributing one or more extra shares for each share outstanding

STOCKING
CAP

stock-still (stäk′stil′) *adj.* as still as a stock, or log; not moving at all; motionless

Stock·ton (stäk′tən) [after R. F. *Stockton* (1795–1866), U.S. naval officer]   city in C Calif.: pop. 108,000

stock·y (stäk′ē) *adj.* **stock′i·er, stock′i·est** [STOCK, *n.* 2 + -Y²] heavily built; sturdy; short and thickset —**stock′i·ness** *n.*

stock·yard (stäk′yärd′) *n.* **1.** an enclosed place for livestock on a farm   ☆**2.** an enclosure with pens, sheds, etc. where cattle, hogs, etc. are kept just before being slaughtered or shipped: usually used in pl.

stodg·y (stäj′ē) *adj.* **stodg′i·er, stodg′i·est** [< dial. *stodge*, heavy food + -Y²] **1.** heavily built; bulky and slow in movement   **2.** dull; uninteresting   **3.** drab, unfashionable, or unattractive   **4.** very old-fashioned or conventional —**stodg′i·ly** *adv.* —**stodg′i·ness** *n.*

☆**sto·gie, sto·gy** (stō′gē) *n., pl.* **-gies** [shortened from *Conestoga*, town in Pa.] a long, thin, inexpensive cigar

Sto·ic (stō′ik) *n.* [< L. < Gr. < *stoa*, colonnade: Zeno taught under a colonnade at Athens] **1.** a member of a Greek school of philosophy founded by Zeno about 308 B.C., holding that all things are governed by the laws of nature and that the wise man is led by his reason to accept calmly whatever happens, always controlling his emotions   **2.** [s-] a stoical person —*adj.* **1.** of the Stoics or their philosophy   **2.** [s-] *same as* STOICAL —see SYN. at IMPASSIVE

sto·i·cal (stō′i k'l) *adj.* **1.** sternly unconcerned and unemotional about joy, grief, pain, or pleasure; calm and unbothered in spite of suffering, bad fortune, etc.   **2.** [S-] *same as* STOIC — **sto′i·cal·ly** *adv.*

Sto·i·cism (-siz'm) *n.* **1.** the philosophy of the Stoics   **2.** [s-] stoical behavior or the state of being stoical

stoke (stōk) *vt., vi.* **stoked, stok′ing** [< STOKER] **1.** to stir up and feed fuel to (a fire)   **2.** to tend (a furnace, boiler, etc.)   **3.** to feed or eat large quantities of food; fill (*up*)

stoke·hold (stōk′hōld′) *n.* **1.** the room containing the boilers on a ship   **2.** *same as* STOKEHOLE (sense 2)

stoke·hole (-hōl′) *n.* **1.** the opening in a furnace or boiler through which the fuel is put   **2.** a space in front of a furnace or boiler from which the fire is tended, as on a ship   **3.** *same as* STOKEHOLD (sense 1)

Stoke-on-Trent (stōk′än trent′) city in WC England, on the Trent River: pop. 271,000

stok·er (stō′kər) *n.* [Du. < *stoken*, to poke < *stok*, a stick] **1.** a man who tends a furnace, esp. of a steam boiler   **2.** a machine that puts fuel into a furnace as it is needed

☆**STOL** (stōl) *adj.* [*s(hort) t(ake)o(ff and) l(anding)*] describing, of, or for an aircraft that can take off and land on a relatively short airstrip —*n.* a STOL aircraft, airstrip, etc.

stole¹ (stōl) *n.* [OE. < L. < Gr. *stolē*, a garment] **1.** a long, decorated strip of cloth worn like a scarf by officiating clergymen of various churches   **2.** a woman's long scarf of cloth or fur worn around the shoulders, with the ends hanging in front

stole² (stōl) *pt.* of STEAL

stol·en (stō′lən) *pp.* of STEAL

stol·id (stäl′id) *adj.* [L. *stolidus*, slow]   having or showing little or no emotion or sensitivity; unexcitable —see SYN. at IMPASSIVE —**sto·lid·i·ty** (stə lid′ə tē), **stol′id·ness** *n.* —**stol′id·ly** *adv.*

sto·lon (stō′län) *n.* [ModL. *stolonis*, genitive of *stolo* < L., a shoot] **1.** *Bot.* a runner; esp., a stem running underground   **2.** *Zool.* a stemlike structure that forms buds from which new individuals grow —**sto·lon·ic** (-län′ik) *adj.*

sto·ma (stō′mə) *n., pl.* **-ma·ta** (-mə tə), **-mas** [ModL. < Gr. *stoma*, mouth] **1.** a microscopic opening in the epidermis of plants, for letting gases in or out   **2.** *Zool.* a mouth or mouthlike opening —**sto·ma·tal** (stō′mə t'l, stäm′ə-) *adj.*

stom·ach (stum′ək) *n.* [< OFr. < L. < Gr. *stomachos*, gullet < *stoma*, mouth] **1.** the large hollow organ of vertebrate animals into which food passes from the esophagus or gullet to stay until it is partly digested: in cud-chewing animals it consists of four chambers: see illustration at ALIMENTARY CANAL   **2.** any hollow organ that digests food   **3.** the abdomen, or belly   **4.** appetite

STOLE

for food **5.** desire or inclination of any kind —*vt.* **1.** to be able to eat or digest **2.** to put up with; bear

stom·ach·ache (-āk′) *n.* pain in the stomach or abdomen

stom·ach·er (stum′ək ər) *n.* a decorated, triangular piece of cloth formerly worn, esp. by women, as a covering for the chest and abdomen

sto·mach·ic (stə mak′ik) *adj.* **1.** of or having to do with the stomach **2.** acting as a digestive tonic Also **sto·mach′i·cal** —*n.* a digestive tonic —**sto·mach′i·cal·ly** *adv.*

-stome (stōm) [< Gr. *stoma*, mouth] *a combining form meaning* mouth

-sto·mous (stə məs) [< Gr. *stoma*, mouth] *a combining form meaning* having a (specified kind of) mouth

stomp (stämp) *vt., vi. var. of* STAMP; esp., to injure or kill by stamping (on) —☆*n.* formerly, **1.** a jazz tune with a lively rhythm and a strong beat **2.** a dance to this music

-sto·my (stə mē) [< Gr. < *stoma*, mouth] *a combining form meaning* a surgical opening into (a specified part)

stone (stōn) *n.* [OE. *stan*] **1.** the hard, solid, nonmetallic mineral matter of which rock is composed **2.** a small piece of rock **3.** a piece of rock shaped for some purpose; specif., *a)* a block of this as for building *b)* a gravestone *c)* a milestone *d)* a grindstone **4.** *a)* the stonelike seed of certain fruits, as of a date *b)* the hard seed with its hard outer covering inside certain fruits, as of a peach **5.** *short for* PRECIOUS STONE **6.** *pl.* **stone** in Great Britain, a unit of weight equal to 14 pounds **7.** any abnormal stony substance formed in the body; calculus —*vt.* **stoned, ston′ing** **1.** to throw stones at or kill with stones **2.** to furnish, pave, line, etc. with stones **3.** to remove the stone from (a peach, etc.) —*adj.* of stone or stoneware —**cast the first stone** to be the first to blame or criticize —**leave no stone unturned** to do everything possible —**ston′er** *n.*

stone- [< prec., with the sense of "like a stone"] *a combining form used in hyphenated compounds, meaning* very, completely [*stone*-blind]

Stone (stōn), **Har·lan Fiske** (här′lən fisk) 1872-1946; U.S. jurist; chief justice of the U.S. (1941–46)

Stone Age the early period in human culture during which stone tools and weapons were used

stone-blind (stōn′blīnd′) *adj.* completely blind

stone-broke (-brōk′) *adj.* [Slang] having no money at all

stone·crop (-kräp′) *n. popular name for* SEDUM

stone·cut·ter (-kut′ər) *n.* a person or machine that cuts stone and makes it smooth —**stone′cut′ting** *n.*

stoned (stōnd) *adj.* **1.** having the stones removed [*stoned* peaches] ☆**2.** [Slang] *a)* drunk; intoxicated *b)* under the influence of a drug

stone-deaf (stōn′def′) *adj.* completely deaf

stone·fly (-flī′) *n., pl.* **-flies′** any of various soft-bodied, winged insects in an undeveloped stage that live under stones in swift streams

Stone·henge (stōn′henj′) [< ME. *ston*, stone + OE. *henge*, (something) hanging] a group of huge stone slabs in S England, arranged in a circle and dating from prehistoric times

stone·ma·son (-mā′s'n) *n.* a person who cuts stone to shape and uses it in making walls, buildings, etc. —**stone′ma′son·ry** (-rē) *n.*

stone's throw a relatively short distance

stone·ware (stōn′wer′) *n.* a coarse, dense pottery containing much silica or sand and flint

stone·work (-wurk′) *n.* **1.** the art or process of working in stone **2.** something made or built in stone **3.** [*pl.*] a place where stonecutting is done

ston·y (stō′nē) *adj.* **ston′i·er, ston′i·est** **1.** covered with or having many stones **2.** of or like stone; specif., *a)* hard *b)* unfeeling; pitiless [a *stony* heart] *c)* cold; fixed; rigid [a *stony* stare] Also **ston′ey** —**ston′i·ly** *adv.* —**ston′i·ness** *n.*

Stony Point village in southeastern N.Y., on the Hudson: site of a Brit. fort captured by Am. Revolutionary forces

stood (stood) *pt. & pp. of* STAND

☆**stooge** (stooj) *n.* [< ?] [Colloq.] **1.** an actor who aids a comedian in his performance, as by being the victim of pranks, jokes, etc. **2.** anyone who acts as a foil, underling, etc. —*vi.* **stooged, stoog′ing** [Colloq.] to be a stooge (*for* someone)

stool (stool) *n.* [OE. *stol*] **1.** *a)* a single seat having no back or arms *b)* same as FOOTSTOOL **2.** a toilet, or water closet **3.** the fecal matter passed out in a single bowel movement **4.** *a)* a root or tree stump sending out shoots *b)* a cluster of such shoots —*vi.* **1.** to put out shoots, as from a root ☆**2.** [Colloq.] to act as a stool pigeon

☆**stool pigeon** **1.** a pigeon or other bird used as a decoy

2. a person serving as a decoy **3.** [Colloq.] a spy or informer, esp. for the police: also **stool·ie** (stool′ē) *n.*

stoop¹ (stoop) *vi.* [OE. *stupian*] **1.** to bend the body forward or in a crouch [he *stooped* to tie his shoes] **2.** to carry the head and shoulders habitually bent forward **3.** to lower one's dignity or do something beneath one's dignity **4.** to swoop down, as a bird of prey —*vt.* to bend (the head, etc.) forward —*n.* **1.** the act or position of stooping the body, esp. habitually **2.** a lowering of one's dignity **3.** a swoop, as by a hawk at its prey —**stoop′er** *n.* —**stoop′ing·ly** *adv.*

SYN.—**stoop** implies a lowering oneself in dignity, as by doing something shameful or immoral [they *stooped* to cheating]; **condescend** implies an unbending by a person of high rank, great power, etc. so as to act in a charmingly polite or friendly way, or sometimes in a patronizing way, toward someone regarded as his inferior [the general *condescended* to talk with the private]; **deign** often connotes a condescending in an unwilling or proud way, esp. in sentences with *not, never, hardly*, etc. [he didn't *deign* to answer me]

☆**stoop²** (stoop) *n.* [Du. *stoep*] a small porch or platform with steps, at the door of a house

stop (stäp) *vt.* **stopped, stop′ping** [< OE. -*stoppian* (in compounds) < WGmc. *stoppon*, ult. < Gr. *styppe*, tow fibers] **1.** to close by filling, shutting off, covering, etc. [*stop* the cracks with putty] **2.** to staunch (a wound, etc.) **3.** to block up (a passage, pipe, etc.); obstruct: often with *up* **4.** to close (a bottle, etc.) as with a cork **5.** to cause to cease motion, activity, etc. **6.** to prevent the passage of (water, light, etc.); block **7.** to halt the progress of (a person, vehicle, etc.) **8.** *a)* to check (a blow, stroke, etc.); parry; counter *b)* to defeat (an opponent) **9.** to baffle; perplex **10.** to cease; desist from (with a gerund) [*stop* talking] **11.** to cause to end [*stop* that racket] **12.** to cause (an engine, machine, etc.) to cease operating or working **13.** to close (a finger hole of a wind instrument) or press down (a violin string, etc.) to produce a desired tone **14.** to keep from beginning, acting, etc.; prevent [can you *stop* them from getting married?] **15.** to notify one's bank to withhold payment on (one's check) —*vi.* **1.** to cease moving, walking, etc.; halt [cars *stopped* for the light] **2.** to leave off doing something; desist [if his humming bothers you ask him to *stop*] **3.** to cease operating or functioning [the motor *stopped*] **4.** to come to an end [the noise *stopped*] **5.** to become clogged [the drain *stopped* up] **6.** to spend a little time or stay for a while (often with *at* or *in*) —*n.* **1.** a stopping or being stopped; check; cessation; halt [he brought his car to a sudden *stop*] **2.** a finish; end [the war came to a *stop*] **3.** a stay or brief visit **4.** a place stopped at, as on a bus route **5.** something that stops; obstruction; specif., *a)* a plug or stopper *b)* an order to withhold payment on a check *c)* a mechanical part that stops or regulates motion *d)* [Chiefly Brit.] a punctuation mark, esp. a period **6.** *a)* a stopping of a violin string, finger hole of a wind instrument, etc. to produce a desired tone *b)* such a hole **7.** *a)* a tuned set of organ pipes, reeds, or electronic devices of the same type and tone quality *b)* a pull, lever, or key for putting such a set into or out of operation **8.** *Phonet.* *a)* a complete stopping of the outgoing breath, as with the lips, tongue, or velum *b)* a consonant formed in this way, as *p, b, k, g, t,* and *d* —*adj.* ☆that stops or is meant to stop [a *stop* signal] —**pull out all (the) stops** **1.** to use all the stops in playing an organ **2.** to make an all-out effort —**put a stop to** to cause to cease —☆**stop off** to stop for a short visit on the way to a place —☆**stop over** **1.** to visit for a while: also **stop in** (or **by**) **2.** to break a journey, as for rest

SYN.—**stop** implies a pause in, or an ending of, some motion, action, or progress [my watch *stopped*]; **cease** implies a pause in, or an ending of, a state, condition, or existence [her worry *ceased*]; **quit** implies a stopping for a time, or for good, of something being done or going on [please *quit* teasing; my watch has *quit* running] or a giving up of some activity, esp. of something regarded as undesirable, harmful, etc. [to *quit* eating so much]; **discontinue** suggests the giving up of a regular activity or of one's occupation, etc. [he has *discontinued* the practice of law]; **desist** implies the bringing to an end of an action or effort that is annoying, troublesome, or futile [he decided to *desist* from further questioning] —**ANT.** begin, start, commence

stop·cock (stäp′käk′) *n.* a valve for stopping or regulating the flow of a fluid, as through a pipe

stope (stōp) *n.* [prob. < MLowG. *stōpe*] a steplike excavation formed by removing ore from around a mine shaft —*vt., vi.* **stoped, stop′ing** to mine in stopes

stop·gap (stäp′gap′) *n.* a person or thing serving as a temporary substitute —*adj.* used as a stopgap —see **SYN.** at RESOURCE

☆**stop·light** (-līt′) *n.* **1.** a traffic light, esp. when red and signaling vehicles to stop **2.** a light at the rear of a vehicle, that lights up when the brakes are applied

☆**stop·o·ver** (-ō′vər) *n.* **1.** a brief stop or stay at a place during a trip **2.** a place for such a stop Also **stop′-off′**
stop·page (stäp′ij) *n.* **1.** a stopping or being stopped **2.** an obstructed condition; block
stop·per (stäp′ər) *n.* **1.** a person or thing that stops **2.** something put in to close an opening; plug —*vt.* to close with a plug or stopper
stop·ple (stäp′'l) *n.* [< ME. dim. < *stoppen*, to stop] a stopper, or plug —*vt.* **-pled, -pling** to close with a stopple
☆**stop street** a street intersection at which vehicles must come to a complete stop before going on
stop·watch (stäp′wäch′) *n.* a watch with a hand that can be started and stopped instantly so as to indicate fractions of seconds, as for timing races, etc.
stor·age (stôr′ij) *n.* **1.** a storing or being stored **2.** *a)* a place or space for storing goods *b)* the cost of keeping goods stored **3.** *same as* MEMORY (sense 7)
storage battery a battery of cells that generate electric current by means of chemical action: the cells can be recharged by passing a current through them in the direction opposite to the discharging flow of current
store (stôr) *vt.* **stored, stor′ing** [< OFr. *estorer* < L. *instaurare*, to restore < *in-*, IN-[1] + *-staurare* < IE. base *sta-*, STAND] **1.** to put or keep aside for use when needed [*storing* grain for the winter] **2.** to furnish with a supply or stock [a mind *stored* with knowledge] **3.** to put in a warehouse, etc. for safekeeping **4.** to be a place for the storage of **5.** to put or keep (information) in a computer memory unit —*vi.* to undergo storage in a specified way [potatoes *store* well] —*n.* **1.** a supply (of something) for use when needed; reserve [a *store* of coal] **2.** [*pl.*] supplies, esp. of food, clothing, etc. ☆**3.** a retail establishment where goods are regularly offered for sale **4.** a storehouse; warehouse **5.** a great amount; abundance [a *store* of information] —*adj.* of a kind sold in stores —**in store** set aside for the future or awaiting one in the future —**set** (or **put** or **lay**) **store by** to have a good opinion of; value —**stor′a·ble** *adj.*
☆**store·front** (stôr′frunt′) *n.* **1.** the front of a store **2.** a room at the ground front of a building, housing a retail store —*adj.* housed in a storefront [a *storefront* church]
store·house (-hous′) *n.* a place where things are stored; esp., a warehouse
store·keep·er (-kē′pər) *n.* **1.** a person in charge of stores, or supplies ☆**2.** a person who owns or manages a retail store
store·room (-rōōm′) *n.* a room where things are stored
sto·rey (stôr′ē) *n., pl.* **-reys** *Brit. sp. of* STORY[2]
sto·ried[1] (stôr′ēd) *adj.* **1.** decorated with designs showing scenes from history, a story, etc. **2.** famous in story or history
sto·ried[2] (stôr′ēd) *adj.* having stories, or floors: usually in hyphenated compounds [many-*storied*]
stork (stôrk) *n., pl.* **storks, stork:** see PLURAL, II, D, 1 [OE. *storc*] a large, long-legged wading bird, having a long neck and bill
storm (stôrm) *n.* [OE., < IE. base *(s)twer-*, to whirl] **1.** a disturbance of the atmosphere in which there is a strong wind usually along with rain, snow, etc. and often with thunder and lightning **2.** any heavy fall of snow, rain, etc. **3.** anything resembling a storm, as in force, violence, etc. [a *storm* of bullets] **4.** a strong emotional outburst **5.** a strong disturbance or upheaval of a political or social nature **6.** a sudden, strong attack on a fortified place **7.** *Meteorol.* a wind whose speed is 64 to 72 miles per hour —*vi.* **1.** to blow violently, rain, snow, etc. **2.** to rage; rant **3.** to rush or move violently

STORK
(to 4 ft. long)

[to *storm* into a room] —*vt.* **1.** to attack (someone) in a vigorous or angry outburst **2.** to capture or attempt to capture (a fortified place) with a sudden, strong attack
storm·bound (stôrm′bound′) *adj.* halted, delayed, or cut off by storms
☆**storm cellar** a deep cellar for shelter during heavy windstorms
☆**storm door** (or **window**) an extra door (or window) placed outside the regular one as added protection against winter weather
storm trooper a member of Hitler's Nazi party militia, notorious for their brutal and terroristic methods
storm·y (stôr′mē) *adj.* **storm′i·er, storm′i·est 1.** of, having, or characterized by storms **2.** violent, raging, wild, angry, etc. [a *stormy* debate] —**storm′i·ly** *adv.* —**storm′i·ness** *n.*
stormy petrel 1. any of several small petrels whose presence is thought to warn of coming storms: also **storm petrel 2.** a person thought to bring trouble wherever he goes
Stor·ting, Stor·thing (stôr′tiŋ′) *n.* [Norw. < *stor*, great + *ting*, assembly] the parliament of Norway
sto·ry[1] (stôr′ē) *n., pl.* **-ries** [< OFr. < L. < Gr. *historia:* see HISTORY] **1.** the telling of an event or series of events, whether true or made-up; account; narration **2.** an anecdote or joke **3.** a piece of fictional writing shorter than a novel; narrative; tale; specif., *same as* SHORT STORY **4.** the plot of a novel, play, etc. **5.** *a)* a report or rumor *b)* [Colloq.] a falsehood or fib **6.** romantic legend or history ☆**7.** a news event or a report of it, as in the newspapers —*vt.* **-ried, -ry·ing** to decorate with paintings, etc. of scenes from history or legend
SYN.—**story** is a general term for any informative or entertaining account, either oral or written, of something that really happened or that is partly or wholly made-up; **narrative**, a more formal term, is typically a prose account of a happening or series of happenings, either real or fictional; **tale** usually means a simple, leisurely story, more or less loosely organized, esp. one that is made-up or legendary; **anecdote** is a term applied to a short, entertaining, often instructive account of a single incident, usually personal or biographical
sto·ry[2] (stôr′ē) *n., pl.* **-ries** [ML. *historia*, a picture (< L.: see HISTORY): prob. from use of "storied" windows or friezes marking the outside of different floors] **1.** a horizontal division of a building extending from a floor to the ceiling directly above it; floor [ten *stories* high] **2.** all the rooms on the same level of a building
sto·ry·book (stôr′ē book′) *n.* a book of stories, esp. one for children —*adj.* typical of romantic tales in storybooks [a *storybook* ending]
sto·ry·tell·er (-tel′ər) *n.* **1.** a person who narrates stories **2.** [Colloq.] a fibber or liar —**sto′ry·tell′ing** *n.*
sto·tin·ka (stô tiŋ′kə) *n., pl.* **-tin·ki** (-kē) [Bulg.] *see* MONETARY UNITS, table (Bulgaria)
stoup (stōōp) *n.* [ON. *staup*] **1.** [Brit. Dial.] a drinking cup; tankard **2.** a basin for holy water in a church
stout (stout) *adj.* [OFr. *estout*, bold, prob. < Frank. *stolt*] **1.** courageous; brave [a *stout* heart] **2.** *a)* strong in body; sturdy *b)* firm; substantial [a *stout* wall] **3.** powerful, forceful [*stout* resistance] **4.** fat; thickset; corpulent —*n.* **1.** a fat person **2.** a garment in a size for a fat man **3.** a heavy, dark-brown brew like porter, with a higher percentage of hops —see SYN. at STRONG —**stout′ish** *adj.* —**stout′ly** *adv.* —**stout′ness** *n.*
stout·heart·ed (stout′här′tid) *adj.* courageous; brave —**stout′heart′ed·ly** *adv.* —**stout′heart′ed·ness** *n.*
stove[1] (stōv) *n.* [MDu., a heated room] an apparatus using fuel or electricity for heating, cooking, etc.
stove[2] (stōv) *alt. pt. & pp. of* STAVE
stove·pipe (stōv′pīp′) *n.* **1.** a metal pipe used to carry off smoke or fumes from a stove ☆**2.** [Colloq.] a man's tall silk hat: in full, **stovepipe hat**
stow (stō) *vt.* [OE. *stow*, a place] **1.** to pack or store, esp. in an orderly, compact way **2.** to fill by packing thus [to *stow* a box with books] **3.** to hold: said of a container, etc. **4.** [Slang] to stop [*stow* the chatter!] —**stow away 1.** to put or hide away **2.** to be a stowaway **3.** to consume (food or drink), esp. in large amounts
stow·age (stō′ij) *n.* **1.** a stowing or being stowed **2.** place or room for stowing **3.** the amount stowed **4.** charges for stowing

---

fat, āpe, cär; ten, ēven; is, bīte; gō, hôrn, tōōl, look; oil, out; up, fur; get; joy; yet; chin; she; thin, *th*en; zh, leisure; ŋ, ring; ə for *a* in *ago*, *e* in *agent*, *i* in *sanity*, *o* in *comply*, *u* in *focus*; ′ as in *able* (ā′b'l); Fr. bal; ë, Fr. coeur; ö, Fr. feu; ô, Fr. mon; ô, Fr. coq; ü, Fr. duc; r, Fr. cri; H, G. ich; kh, G. doch; ‡foreign; ☆ Americanism; < derived from. See inside front cover.

stow·a·way (-ə wā′) *n.* a person who hides aboard a ship, airplane, etc. so as to travel without paying or to get by officials without being caught

Stowe (stō), **Harriet (Elizabeth) Beecher** 1811–96; U.S. novelist: sister of Henry Ward BEECHER

St. Paul capital of Minn., on the Mississippi: pop. 310,000: see MINNEAPOLIS

St. Pe·ters·burg (pēt′ərz burg′) **1.** *former name of* LENINGRAD **2.** city in WC Fla., on Tampa Bay: pop. 216,000

St. Pierre and Mi·que·lon (mik′ə län′) Fr. territory in the Atlantic, south of Newfoundland, consisting of the islands of St. Pierre & Miquelon & six islets: 93 sq. mi.; pop. 6,000: Fr. name **St-Pierre et Mique·lon** (san pyer′ e mē klōn′)

stra·bis·mus (strə biz′məs) *n.* [ModL. < Gr. < *strabizein*, to squint < *strabos*, twisted] a disorder of the muscles of the eyes, as cross-eye, in which both eyes cannot be focused on the same point at the same time —**stra·bis′mal, stra·bis′mic** *adj.* —**stra·bis′mal·ly** *adv.*

Stra·bo (strā′bō) 63? B.C.–19? A.D.; Gr. geographer

Stra·chey (strā′chē), (**Giles) Lyt·ton** (lit′′n) 1880–1932; Eng. biographer

strad·dle (strad′′l) *vt.* **-dled, -dling** [< STRIDE + -LE²] **1.** to place oneself with a leg on either side of [to *straddle* a horse] **2.** to spread (the legs) wide apart ☆**3.** to take or appear to take both sides of (an issue); avoid committing oneself on —*vi.* **1.** to sit, stand, or walk with the legs wide apart **2.** to be spread apart: said of the legs ☆**3.** to straddle an issue, etc. —*n.* **1.** the act or position of straddling ☆**2.** a refusal to commit oneself definitely —**strad′dler** *n.*

Stra·di·va·ri (strä′dē vä′rē), **An·to·nio** (än tô′nyō) (L. name *Antonius Stradivarius*) 1644–1737; It. violin maker

Strad·i·var·i·us (strad′ə ver′ē əs) *n.* a string instrument, esp. a violin, made by A. Stradivari or his sons

strafe (strāf; *chiefly Brit.* sträf) *vt.* **strafed, straf′ing** [< G. phr. *Gott strafe England* (God punish England)] to attack with machine-gun fire from low-flying aircraft —**straf′er** *n.*

strag·gle (strag′′l) *vi.* **-gled, -gling** [prob. < ME. *straken*, to roam] **1.** to stray from the course or wander from the main group **2.** to be scattered over a wide area; ramble **3.** to leave, arrive, etc. from time to time **4.** to hang in an untidy way, as hair, clothes, etc. —*n.* a straggly arrangement or group —**strag′gler** *n.*

strag·gly (-lē) *adj.* **-gli·er, -gli·est** spread out in a straggling, irregular way [*straggly* hair]

straight (strāt) *adj.* [< ME. pp. of *strecchen*, to STRETCH] **1.** having the same direction throughout its length; without curves or angles [a *straight* line] **2.** not crooked, bent, wavy, etc. [*straight* hair] **3.** upright; erect [*straight* posture] **4.** level; even [a *straight* hemline] **5.** direct; undeviating, uninterrupted, etc. [to hold a *straight* course] ☆**6.** supporting fully the principles, candidates, etc. of a political party [to vote a *straight* ticket] **7.** following a direct course of reasoning, etc.; methodical [*straight* thinking] **8.** in order; properly arranged, etc. [to keep the files *straight*] **9.** *a)* honest; sincere *b)* reliable [*straight* information] **10.** outspoken; frank ☆**11.** *a)* without anything added; undiluted [a *straight* shot of whiskey] *b)* not blended with neutral grain spirits **12.** not qualified, slanted, etc. [a *straight* denial] ☆**13.** at a fixed price per unit regardless of the quantity bought [apples at ten cents *straight*] ☆**14.** [Slang] normal or conventional; specif., not homosexual, not addicted to drugs, etc. —*adv.* **1.** in a straight line or direction; unswervingly **2.** upright; erectly [walk *straight*] **3.** *a)* without detour, delay, etc. [go *straight* home] *b)* directly [tell it *straight*] *c)* without any changes, additions, etc. [read these lines *straight*] —*n.* **1.** a being straight **2.** something straight; specif., ☆*Poker* a hand consisting of any five cards in sequence: it ranks just below a flush —**straight away** (or **off**) at once; without delay —**the straight and narrow (path)** a strict code of morals —**straight′ly** *adv.* —**straight′ness** *n.*

straight angle an angle of 180 degrees

☆**straight-arm** (strāt′ärm′) *vt.* to push (someone) away with the arm outstretched —*n.* the act of straight-arming

☆**straight-ar·row** (-ar′ō, -er′ō) *adj.* [Slang] proper, righteous, highly moral, etc.: often used in a way that suggests dullness, conservatism, primness, or the like

☆**straight arrow** a person who is straight-arrow

straight·a·way (-ə wā′) *adj.* extending in a straight line —*n.* **1.** a race track, or part of a track, that extends in a straight line **2.** a straight and level stretch of highway

straight chair a chair with a back that is straight up and down or almost so, and not upholstered

straight·edge (-ej′) *n.* a piece of wood, etc. with a straight edge used in drawing straight lines, testing to see whether surfaces are flat, etc.

straight·en (-′n) *vt., vi.* to make or become straight —**straighten out 1.** to make or become less confused, easier to deal with, etc. ☆**2.** to correct or reform the behavior of —**straight′en·er** *n.*

straight face an expression of the face showing no amusement or other emotion —**straight′-faced′** *adj.*

straight flush *Poker* a flush in which all five cards are in sequence: it is the highest ranking hand

straight·for·ward (strāt′fôr′wərd) *adj.* **1.** moving or leading straight ahead; direct **2.** honest; frank; open —*adv.* in a straightforward manner: also **straight′for′wards** —**straight′for′ward·ly** *adv.* —**straight′for′ward·ness** *n.*

straight·jack·et (strāt′jak′it) *n. same as* STRAITJACKET

straight-laced *adj. same as* STRAIT-LACED (sense 2)

☆**straight man** an actor who serves as a foil for a comedian, saying lines for him to turn into jokes

straight-out (-out′) *adj.* [Colloq.] **1.** straightforward **2.** unrestrained ☆**3.** thoroughgoing; unqualified; absolute

☆**straight razor** a razor with a long blade sharp on one edge, that can be folded into the handle

straight·way (-wā′) *adv.* at once; without delay

strain¹ (strān) *vt.* [< OFr. < L. *stringere*, to draw tight] **1.** to draw or stretch tight **2.** to exert or use to the utmost [to *strain* every nerve] **3.** to injure or hurt by too much force or effort; wrench [to *strain* a muscle] **4.** to injure, weaken, or deform by force, pressure, etc. [the wind *strained* the roof] **5.** to stretch beyond the normal limits [*strain* the rule and let him play] **6.** *a)* to put through a screen, sieve, etc.; filter *b)* to remove by filtration, etc. **7.** to hug: now only in **to strain to one's bosom** (or **heart**, etc.) —*vi.* **1.** to make violent efforts; try very hard [she *strained* to hear him] **2.** to be or become strained **3.** to be subjected to great stress or pressure **4.** to pull or push with force [the dog *strained* at the leash] **5.** to filter, ooze, etc. —*n.* **1.** a straining or being strained **2.** great effort, hard work, etc. **3.** an injury to a part of the body as a result of too much effort [heart *strain*] **4.** stress or force [the *strain* of his weight on the chair made it break] **5.** a great or too great a demand on one's emotions, resources, etc.

strain² (strān) *n.* [OE. *streon*, procreation < base of *strynan*, to produce] **1.** ancestry; lineage **2.** the descendants of a common ancestor; race; stock; line **3.** a group of individuals within a species, different in one or more qualities from others in the species **4.** an inherited quality or tendency **5.** a trace; streak **6.** the style or tone of a speech, book, action, etc. **7.** [*often pl.*] a passage of music; tune; air

strained (strānd) *adj.* not natural or relaxed; forced

strain·er (strān′ər) *n.* a person or thing that strains; specif., a device, as a sieve, for straining, sifting, etc.

strait (strāt) *adj.* [< OFr. < L. pp. of *stringere*: see STRICT] **1.** [Archaic] *a)* narrow; tight *b)* strict; rigid **2.** [Now Rare] difficult; distressing —*n.* **1.** [*often pl.*] a narrow waterway connecting two large bodies of water **2.** [*often pl.*] difficulty; distress **3.** [Rare] an isthmus

strait·en (strāt′′n) *vt.* **1.** esp. formerly, *a)* to make strait or narrow *b)* to restrict or confine; hamper **2.** to bring into difficulties: usually in the phrase **in straitened circumstances**, not having enough money to live on

strait·jack·et (strāt′jak′it) *n.* a coatlike device that binds the arms tight against the body: used to restrain a person who is acting in a violent way

strait-laced (-lāst′) *adj.* **1.** formerly, tightly laced, as a corset **2.** narrowly strict in behavior or moral views

Straits Settlements former Brit. crown colony in SE Asia, including Singapore, Malacca, etc.

strake (strāk) *n.* [akin to STRETCH] a single line of planking or plating extending along the length of a ship

strand¹ (strand) *n.* [OE.] shore, esp. ocean shore —*vt., vi.* **1.** to run or drive aground [a ship *stranded* by the storm] **2.** to leave or be put in a difficult, helpless position [*stranded* in a strange city, with no money]

strand² (strand) *n.* [< ?] **1.** any of the threads, fibers, wires, etc. that are twisted together to form a string, rope, or cable **2.** a ropelike length of anything [a *strand* of pearls, *strands* of hair] **3.** any of the parts

STRAITJACKET

that are bound together to form a whole *[the strands of one's life]* —*vt.* to form (rope, etc.) by twisting strands together

strange (strānj) *adj.* **strang′er, strang′est** [< OFr. < L. *extraneus*, foreign < *extra*, outside] **1.** of another place or locality; foreign *[a strange city]* **2.** not previously known, seen, heard, etc.; unfamiliar *[a strange word]* **3.** unusual; extraordinary *[a strange animal]* **4.** peculiar; odd *[strange behavior]* **5.** lacking experience; unaccustomed *[strange to the job]* —*adv.* in a strange manner —**strange′ly** *adv.* —**strange′ness** *n.*
SYN.—**strange** is a general term applied to whatever is unfamiliar, out of the ordinary, curiously different, etc. *[strange customs; a strange idea; a strange movie]*; **odd** is also applied to anything unfamiliar, unusual, etc. especially if it is unconventional or unexpected *[an odd way of living]*; **peculiar** is used of anything strange or odd, especially if it is puzzling or difficult to describe or explain *[a peculiar smell]*; **queer** is also used of anything strange or odd, especially if it is thought to be not normal, acceptable, customary, etc. *[the blue lighting gave them a queer look]*; **outlandish** suggests something that is very odd or bizarre, fantastic, or outrageous *[an outlandish costume; an outlandish scheme]*; **quaint** is usually applied to something charmingly old-fashioned or pleasantly different from the usual *[a quaint old house]* —**ANT. familiar, ordinary**
stran·ger (strān′jər) *n.* **1.** an outsider, newcomer, or foreigner **2.** a person not known or familiar to one **3.** a person unaccustomed (*to* something) *[a stranger to hate]*
stran·gle (straŋ′g'l) *vt.* **-gled, -gling** [< OFr. < L. *strangulare* < Gr. < *strangalē*, halter] **1.** to kill by squeezing the throat as with the hands, a noose, etc., so as to shut off the breath **2.** to choke or suffocate in any way **3.** to suppress, stifle, or repress *[free speech strangled by censorship]* —*vi.* to be strangled; choke —**stran′gler** *n.*
stran·gle·hold (-hōld′) *n.* **1.** an illegal wrestling hold that chokes off an opponent's breath **2.** any force that restricts or suppresses freedom
stran·gu·late (straŋ′gyə lāt′) *vt.* **-lat′ed, -lat′ing** [< L. pp. of *strangulare*] **1.** *same as* STRANGLE **2.** *Med.* to cause (an intestine or other tube) to become squeezed so that a flow, as of blood, is cut off —*vi. Med.* to be strangulated —**stran′gu·la′tion** *n.*
strap (strap) *n.* [dial. form of STROP] **1.** a narrow strip of leather, plastic, cloth, etc. often with a buckle at one end, for tying or holding things together **2.** any of several straplike parts or things, as a shoulder strap, a razor strop, etc. —*vt.* **strapped, strap′ping 1.** to fasten with a strap **2.** to beat with a strap **3.** to strop (a razor) —**strap′less** *adj.* —**strap′per** *n.*
strap·hang·er (-haŋ′ər) *n.* [Colloq.] a standing passenger, as on a crowded bus, who supports himself by holding onto a hanging strap, etc.
strap hinge a hinge with long, usually triangular parts by which it is fastened: see illustration at HINGE
☆ **strapped** (strapt) *adj.* [Colloq.] in great need of money
strap·ping (strap′iŋ) *adj.* [Colloq.] tall and sturdy; robust
Stras·bourg (stras′bʉrg; *Fr.* strås bōōr′) city & port in NE France, on the Rhine: pop. 249,000
stra·ta (strāt′ə, strat′-) *n.* alt. pl. of STRATUM
strat·a·gem (strat′ə jəm) *n.* [< L. < Gr. *stratēgēma*, act of a general < *stratos*, army + *agein*, to lead] **1.** a trick, scheme, or plan for deceiving an enemy in war **2.** any trick or scheme for achieving some purpose —see **SYN.** at TRICK
stra·te·gic (strə tē′jik) *adj.* **1.** of or having to do with strategy **2.** using good strategy; showing sound planning **3.** *a)* needed for carrying out military strategy or carrying on war *[strategic materials]* ☆*b)* directed against the military bases and industrial centers of the enemy *[strategic bombing]* Also **stra·te′gi·cal** —**stra·te′gi·cal·ly** *adv.*
strat·e·gist (strat′ə jist) *n.* one skilled in strategy
strat·e·gy (-jē) *n., pl.* **-gies** [< Fr. < Gr. < *stratēgos*, general: see STRATAGEM] **1.** *a)* the science of planning and directing large-scale military operations *b)* a plan or action based on this **2.** *a)* skill in managing or planning, esp. by using stratagems *b)* a stratagem or clever means of bringing something about Also, esp. for sense 1, **stra·te·gics** (strə tē′jiks) *n.pl.*
Strat·ford-on-A·von (strat′fərd än ā′vän) town in C England, on the Avon River: birthplace & burial place of Shakespeare: pop. 19,000: also **Strat′ford-up·on-A′von**
strat·i·fy (strat′ə fī′) *vt.* **-fied′, -fy′ing** [< Fr. < ModL. < L. *stratum*, layer + *facere*, to make] **1.** to form or arrange in layers or strata **2.** to separate (people) into groups with levels of

social status according to social position, income, education, etc. *[a stratified society]* —*vi.* to become stratified —**strat′i·fi·ca′tion** (-fi kā′shən) *n.*
stra·tig·ra·phy (strə tig′rə fē) *n.* [< STRATUM + -GRAPHY] **1.** the arrangement of rocks in layers or strata **2.** the branch of geology that deals with the nature and relations of rocks that are found in layers in the earth's crust —**strat·i·graph·ic** (strat′ə-graf′ik) *adj.*
stra·to·cu·mu·lus (strāt′ō kyōōm′yə ləs, strat′-) *n., pl.* **-li′** (-lī′) [ModL.: see STRATUS & CUMULUS] a cloud formation with masses that are rounded, roll-shaped, etc. on a straight, usually unbroken base line
strat·o·sphere (strat′ə sfir′) *n.* [< Fr. < ModL. *stratum*, STRATUM + Fr. *sphère*, SPHERE] the part of the earth's atmosphere extending from about six miles to about fifteen miles above the earth's surface, in which the temperature ranges from about −45°C to −75°C —**strat′o·spher′ic** (-sfer′ik, -sfir′-) *adj.*
stra·tum (strāt′əm, strat′-) *n., pl.* **stra′ta** (-ə), **-tums** [ModL. < L. < *stratus*, pp. of *sternere*, to spread] **1.** a horizontal layer of material, esp. any of several lying one upon another; specif., *Geol.* a single layer of sedimentary rock **2.** a section, level, or division, as of the atmosphere or ocean, regarded as like a stratum **3.** any of the various levels of society regarded as separated according to social position, income, education, etc. —**stra·tal** (strāt′'l) *adj.*
stra·tus (strāt′əs, strat′-) *n., pl.* **stra′ti** (-ī) [L., a strewing: see STRATUM] a cloud formation extending in a long, low, gray layer with its base in a fairly straight line
Strauss (shtrous; *E.* strous) **1.** **Jo·hann** (yō′hän), 1825-99; Austrian composer, esp. of waltzes **2.** **Rich·ard** (riH′ärt), 1864-1949; Ger. composer & conductor
Stra·vin·sky (strə vin′skē; *Russ.* strå vēn′ski), **I·gor (Fedoro·vich)** (ē′gôr) 1882-1971; U.S. composer & conductor, born in Russia
straw (strô) *n.* [OE. *streaw*] **1.** hollow stalks of grain after threshing, used for bedding, for weaving hats, baskets, etc. **2.** a single one of such stalks **3.** a tube used for sucking beverages **4.** something, as a hat, made of straw **5.** a worthless trifle —*adj.* **1.** straw-colored; yellowish **2.** made of straw **3.** worthless; meaningless —**a straw in the wind** a sign of what may happen —**grasp (or clutch, catch) at a straw (or straws)** to try anything that offers even the slightest hope —**straw′y** *adj.*
straw·ber·ry (strô′ber′ē, -bər ē) *n., pl.* **-ries** [< OE. < *streaw*, straw + *berige*, berry: prob. so called from the small achenes on the fruit] **1.** the small, red, fleshy fruit of a low plant of the rose family that puts out runners **2.** this plant
☆ **strawberry blonde** reddish blonde
strawberry mark a small, red birthmark
straw·board (strô′bôrd′) *n.* a coarse cardboard made of straw pulp
☆ **straw boss** [Colloq.] **1.** an assistant to a boss or foreman **2.** an overseer of work who has little or no authority
straw color a pale-yellow color —**straw′-col′ored** *adj.*
straw·flow·er (-flou′ər) *n.* an annual plant whose brightly colored flower heads are dried for winter bouquets
☆ **straw-hat** (-hat′) *adj.* [from the practice, esp. formerly, of wearing straw hats in summer] describing or of a summer theater or summer theaters
straw man 1. a scarecrow made of straw **2.** a weak argument, opponent, etc. set up by one so that he may in attacking gain an easy, showy victory **3.** a person used to disguise another's activities, etc.; blind
☆ **straw vote** an unofficial vote or poll for sampling popular opinion on candidates or on an issue
stray (strā) *vi.* [< OFr. *estraier*, prob. ult. < L. *extra vagari*, to wander outside] **1.** to wander from a given place, course, etc.; roam **2.** to go wrong; deviate (*from* what is right) **3.** to wander from the subject; lose one's concentration or attention —*n.* a person or thing that strays; esp., a domestic animal wandering at large —*adj.* **1.** having strayed; lost **2.** isolated, occasional, or incidental *[a few stray words]* —**stray′er** *n.*
streak (strēk) *n.* [OE. *strica*] **1.** a line or long, thin mark; stripe or smear **2.** a ray of light or a flash, as of lightning **3.** a thin layer, as of fat in meat or ore in rock **4.** a tendency in one's nature *[a jealous streak]* ☆**5.** a period, spell, or run *[a streak of victories]* —*vt.* to mark with streaks —*vi.* **1.** to become

streaked **2.** to move swiftly ☆**3.** to dash naked through a public place as a prank —☆**like a streak** [Colloq.] swiftly — **streak′er** n.

streak·y (strē′kē) adj. **streak′i·er, streak′i·est** marked with or occurring in streaks; uneven —**streak′i·ness** n.

stream (strēm) n. [OE.] **1.** a current or flow of water; specif., a small river **2.** a steady flow of any fluid [a stream of cold air] or of rays of energy [a stream of light] **3.** a moving line of things [a stream of cars] **4.** a trend or course [the stream of events] —vi. **1.** to flow as in a stream **2.** to flow (with) [eyes streaming with tears] **3.** to move steadily or swiftly **4.** to float or fly, as a flag in the breeze —vt. to cause to stream

stream·er (strē′mər) n. **1.** something that streams **2.** a long, narrow flag **3.** any long, narrow, flowing strip of material **4.** a stream of light extending up from the horizon **5.** a newspaper headline across the full page

stream·let (strēm′lit) n. a small stream; rivulet

stream·line (-līn′) vt. **-lined′, -lin′ing** to make streamlined — adj. same as STREAMLINED

stream·lined (-līnd′) adj. **1.** having its shape designed so that it can move smoothly and easily through air, water, etc. [a streamlined boat] ☆**2.** arranged so as to be more efficient [a streamlined program] **3.** with no excess, as of weight, decoration, etc.; trim [a streamlined figure or design]

☆**stream of consciousness** the conscious experience of an individual regarded as having an unbroken flow: a principle made use of in novels, etc. in presenting the thoughts, inner feelings, etc. of a character in a natural, unrestrained flow

stream·y (strē′mē) adj. **stream′i·er, stream′i·est 1.** full of streams or currents **2.** flowing; streaming

street (strēt) n. [OE. strǣt < LL. < L. strata (via), paved (road)] **1.** a public road in a city or town; esp., a paved thoroughfare with sidewalks and buildings along the sides **2.** the group of people living, working, etc. in the buildings along a given street [the whole street gave money to the fund] —adj. **1.** of, in, on, or near the street [the street floor] **2.** suitable for everyday wear in public [street clothes]

☆**street·car** (strēt′kär′) n. a large car on rails that provides public transportation on city streets

street·walk·er (-wôk′ər) n. a prostitute who tries to get customers along the streets —**street′walk′ing** n.

strength (strenkth, strenth) n. [OE.] **1.** the state or quality of being strong; power; force; vigor [the strength of a blow] **2.** the power to resist strain, stress, etc.; toughness; durability [the strength of a steel beam] **3.** the power to resist attack **4.** legal, moral, or intellectual force [a mind of great strength] **5.** the degree to which something has an effect, as the potency of a drug or the intensity of a sound, color, odor, etc. **6.** force as measured in numbers [an army at full strength] **7.** vigor of feeling or expression **8.** a source of strength or support —**on the strength of** based or relying on

strength·en (strenkth′'n, strenth′-) vt., vi. to make or become stronger —**strength′en·er** n.

stren·u·ous (stren′yoo wəs) adj. [L. strenuus] **1.** requiring or needing great effort or energy [chopping wood is a strenuous task] **2.** vigorous, arduous, zealous, etc. [strenuous efforts] — **stren′u·ous·ly** adv. —**stren′u·ous·ness** n.

strep (strep) n. shortened form of STREPTOCOCCUS

strep·to·coc·cus (strep′tə käk′əs) n., pl. **-coc′ci** (-käk′sī) [ModL., genus name < Gr. streptos, twisted + COCCUS] any of a group of ball-shaped bacteria that occur generally in chains: some species cause serious diseases —**strep′to·coc′cal** (-käk′əl), **strep′to·coc′cic** (-käk′sik) adj.

☆**strep·to·my·cin** (-mī′sin) n. [< Gr. streptos, twisted + mykēs, fungus] an antibiotic drug, $C_{21}H_{39}N_7O_{12}$, used in the treatment of various bacterial diseases, as tuberculosis

stress (stres) n. [< OFr., ult. < L. strictus, STRICT] **1.** strain or straining force; specif., force exerted upon a body, that tends to strain or deform its shape **2.** special attention; emphasis; importance [to put stress on good health habits] **3.** a) mental or physical tension or strain [under the stress of a crisis] b) urgency, pressure, etc. causing this **4.** a) the relative force given a certain syllable or word in speaking it or in reciting a poem, according to the meter b) an accented syllable **5.** Music emphasis on a note or chord —vt. **1.** to put stress, pressure, or strain on **2.** to give stress or accent to **3.** to emphasize — **stress′ful** adj. —**stress′ful·ly** adv.

-stress (stris) [< -STER + -ESS] a suffix meaning female or woman and used like -STER [songstress]

stretch (strech) vt. [OE. streccan] **1.** to reach out; extend [to stretch out a helping hand] **2.** to cause (the body or limbs) to reach out to full length, as in relaxing, etc. **3.** to pull or spread out to full extent or to a greater size [keep the sheets stretched] **4.** to cause to extend over a given space, distance, or time [to stretch pipelines across a desert] **5.** a) to make extend farther or too far [don't stretch the collar] b) to strain or force the use or scope of beyond reasonable limits [to stretch a rule] **6.** to make tense with effort; strain (a muscle, etc.) —vi. **1.** a) to spread out to full extent or beyond normal limits [wings stretching out] b) to extend over a given space, distance, or time [the road stretches to the coast] **2.** a) to extend the body or limbs to full length, as in relaxing, etc. b) to lie down at full length (usually with out) [stretched out on the sofa] **3.** to become stretched to greater size, as any elastic substance [rubber easily stretches] —n. **1.** a stretching or being stretched [a stretch of the arms] **2.** a) an unbroken period [a stretch of ten days] b) [Slang] a term served in prison **3.** the extent to which something can be stretched [beyond the stretch of imagination] **4.** an unbroken length, tract, etc. [a stretch of beach] **5.** any of the sections of a race track; esp., short for HOMESTRETCH —adj. made of elasticized fabric [stretch pants] —**stretch′a·bil′i·ty** n. —**stretch′a·ble** adj.

stretch·er (strech′ər) n. **1.** one that stretches; specif., a) a brick or stone laid lengthwise in the face of a wall b) any of various devices for stretching or shaping garments, curtains, etc. **2.** a) a light frame covered with canvas, etc. and used for carrying the sick, injured, or dead b) any similar device, as a wheeled cot used in ambulances

stretch·y (-ē) adj. **stretch′i·er, stretch′i·est 1.** that can be stretched; elastic **2.** tending to stretch too far —**stretch′i·ness** n.

strew (stroo) vt. **strewed, strewed** or **strewn, strew′ing** [OE. streawian < IE. base ster-, to spread] **1.** to spread about here and there by or as by sprinkling; scatter [strewing birdseed] **2.** to cover by or as by scattering something on or over [strewed the ground with flowers] **3.** to be scattered over (a surface) [autumn leaves strewed the lawn]

STRETCHER

stri·a (strī′ə) n., pl. **stri′ae** (-ē) [L.] **1.** a narrow groove or channel **2.** any of a number of parallel lines, stripes, furrows, etc.; specif., any of the cylindrical fibers in voluntary muscles

stri·ate (strī′āt; for adj. usually -it) vt. **-at·ed, -at·ing** [< L. pp. of striare, to groove] to mark with striae; stripe, furrow, etc. — adj. same as STRIATED —**stri·a′tion** n.

stri·at·ed (strī′āt id) adj. marked with striae, as the voluntary muscles; striped, furrowed, etc.

strick·en (strik′'n) alt. pp. of STRIKE —adj. **1.** struck or wounded **2.** suffering, as from pain, trouble, etc.

strict (strikt) adj. [< L. pp. of stringere, to draw tight: for IE. base see STARE] **1.** exact or precise [a strict translation] **2.** perfect; absolute [the strict truth] **3.** a) enforcing rules with great care [a strict supervisor] b) closely enforced or rigidly maintained [strict regulations] c) disciplining severely [they are strict with their children] —**strict′ly** adv. —**strict′ness** n. **SYN.**—**strict** implies an exact, never-changing following of standards, rules, conditions, etc. [strict enforcement of the law]; **rigid** implies a being very stiff and unable or unwilling to bend, adjust, compromise, etc. [rigid rules]; **rigorous** implies such strictness or rigidity as to cause difficulties or hardship [rigorous training]; **stringent** implies a severe strictness that limits, binds, curbs, or confines [stringent censorship]

stric·ture (strik′chər) n. [< L. pp. of stringere, to draw tight] **1.** strong criticism; censure **2.** a limiting or restricting condition; restriction **3.** Med. an abnormal narrowing of a passage in the body —**stric′tured** adj.

stride (strīd) vi., vt. **strode, strid′den, strid′ing** [OE. stridan] **1.** to walk with long steps, esp. in a vigorous or swaggering manner **2.** to cross with a single, long step [he strode over the log] **3.** to straddle (a horse, etc.) —n. **1.** the act of striding **2.** a long step **3.** a) a full step in a gait, as of a horse b) the distance covered by such a step **4.** [usually pl.] progress; advancement [great strides in industry] —☆**hit one's stride** to reach one's normal level of skill or speed —**take in one's stride** to cope with easily and without great effort —**strid′er** n.

stri·dent (strīd′'nt) adj. [< L. prp. of stridere, to rasp] harsh-sounding; shrill; grating —see SYN. at VOCIFEROUS —**stri′dence, stri′den·cy** n. —**stri′dent·ly** adv.

strid·u·late (strij′ŏŏ lāt′) **vi. -lat′ed, -lat′ing [** < ModL. pp. of *stridulare* < L. < *stridere*, to rasp**]** to make a shrill, grating or chirping sound by rubbing certain body parts together, as some insects do **—strid′u·la′tion n.**

strid·u·lous (-ləs) **adj.** making a shrill, grating or chirping sound: also **strid′u·lant** (-lənt)

strife (strīf) **n. [**OFr. *estrif*] **1.** the act of striving; contention or competition **2.** the act or state of fighting or quarreling; struggle; conflict—see **SYN.** at DISCORD

strike (strīk) **vt. struck, struck** or occas. (but for *vt.* 12 commonly and for *vt.* 8 & 16 usually) **strick′en, strik′ing [**OE. *strican,* to go, proceed] **1.** *a)* to give a blow to; hit; smite *b)* to give (a blow, etc.) *c)* to remove as by a blow *[he struck the gun from her hand] d)* to make by stamping, printing, etc. *[to strike coins in a mint] e)* to pierce or penetrate *[struck in the head by a bullet]* **2.** to produce (a tone or chord) by hitting (a key or keys) or touching (a string or strings) on a musical instrument **3.** to announce (time), as with a bell: said of clocks, etc. *[the clock struck midnight]* **4.** *a)* to cause to come into forceful contact *[to strike one's head on a beam] b)* to thrust (a weapon, etc.) in or into something *[he struck the spear into the ground] c)* to set (a match) on fire as by rubbing it on something **5.** to produce (a light, etc.) by so rubbing **6.** to come into forceful contact with; crash into *[the stone struck his head]* **7.** to wound with the fangs: said of snakes **8.** to afflict, as with disease, pain, or death **9.** to attack *[bombers struck the city at dawn]* **10.** to come into contact with; specif., *a)* to fall on; shine on *[light striking the wall] b)* to reach (the eye or ear) *[a curious sight struck our eyes]* ☆*c)* to come upon *[we struck the main road]* ☆*d)* to discover, as after drilling *[to strike oil]* **11.** to affect as if by contact, a blow, etc.; specif., *a)* to occur to *[an idea struck him] b)* to impress (one's fancy, sense of humor, etc.) *c)* to seem to *[it strikes me as silly] d)* to cause to become suddenly *[to be struck dumb] e)* to overcome suddenly with strong feeling *[to be struck with amazement] f)* to cause (a feeling, etc.) to come suddenly *[to strike terror to the heart]* **12.** to remove (*from* a list, record, minutes, etc.) **13.** *a)* to make or reach, as by planning (a bargain, truce, etc.) *b)* to arrive at by figuring, etc. *[to strike a balance]* **14.** *a)* to lower (a sail, flag, etc.) *b)* to take down (a tent, etc.) *c)* to abandon (a camp) as by taking down tents **15.** to refuse to continue to work at (a factory, company, etc.) until certain demands have been met **16.** to level the top of (a measure of grain, etc.) as with a stick **17.** to assume (a pose, etc.) **18.** to put forth (roots): said of plants **19.** *Theater a)* to take apart and remove (a set) *b)* to turn (a light) down or off **—vi. 1.** to deliver or aim a blow; hit (*at*) **2.** to attack *[fearing the enemy would strike]* **3.** *a)* to make sounds as by being struck: said of a bell, clock, etc. *[do you hear the chimes striking?] b)* to be announced by the striking of a bell, etc.: said of the time *[one o'clock struck]* **4.** to hit; collide (*against, on,* or *upon*) *[the car struck against the wall]* **5.** to catch fire, as a match **6.** to seize a bait: said of a fish **7.** to dart in an attempt to wound, as a snake **8.** to penetrate or pierce (*to, through,* etc.) *[this strikes to the heart of the problem]* **9.** to come suddenly (*on* or *upon*) *[we struck on an idea]* **10.** to lower sail **11.** to lower a flag as a sign of surrender **12.** to refuse to continue to work until certain demands are met **13.** to take root: said of a plant **14.** to proceed, esp. in a new way or direction *[they struck northward]* ☆**15.** *U.S. Navy* to be in training (*for* a specified rating) **—n. 1.** the act of striking; blow; specif., a military attack **2.** *a)* a refusal by employees, as a group, to go on working, in an attempt to get higher wages, better working conditions, etc. *b)* any similar refusal to do something, done as a form of protest *[a hunger strike]* **3.** the discovery of a rich deposit of oil, coal, minerals, etc. ☆**4.** any sudden success *[a lucky strike in the stock market]* ☆**5.** the pull on the line by a fish seizing bait ☆**6.** *Baseball* a pitched ball which is struck at but missed, delivered across home plate between the batter's knees and armpits but not struck at, hit foul but not caught, etc.: three strikes put the batter out ☆**7.** *Bowling a)* the act of knocking down all the pins on the first bowl *b)* the score so made **—(out) on strike** striking; refusing to work **—strike dumb** to amaze; astound **—strike home 1.** to deliver an effective blow **2.** to have the desired effect *[his speech struck home]* **—☆strike it rich 1.** to discover a rich deposit of ore, oil, etc. **2.** to become rich or successful suddenly **—strike off 1.** to remove as by striking with a sword, etc. *[struck off his ear]* **2.** to remove from a record, etc.; erase **3.** to print, stamp, etc. **—strike out 1.** to remove from a record, etc.; erase **2.** to start out ☆**3.** *Baseball a)* to be put out by three strikes *b)* to put (a batter) out by pitching three strikes ☆**4.** to be a failure **—strike up 1.** to begin playing, singing, etc. *[the band struck up]* **2.** to begin (a friendship, etc.)

SYN.—strike and **hit** both mean to give a blow (to), aim a blow (at), and it often does not matter much which one is used *[the batter struck,* or *hit,* the ball]; but to express certain things **strike** is more likely to be used than **hit** *[lightning struck the barn]* or **hit** is more likely to be used than **strike** *[he hit the ball over the fence]*; **knock** implies a striking or hitting of something so as to move it from its usual or proper place *[he knocked the vase off the table]*, or it implies a striking or hitting several times or many times *[he knocked on the door]*

strike·bound (strīk′bound′) **adj.** closed because of employees who are on strike *[a strikebound plant]*

strike·break·er (-brā′kər) **n.** a person who tries to break up a strike, as by taking the place of a striking worker, threatening the strikers, etc. **—strike′break′ing n.**

strik·er (strī′kər) **n. 1.** a person who strikes; specif., a worker who is on strike **2.** a thing that strikes, as the clapper in a bell

strik·ing (strī′kiŋ) **adj. 1.** that strikes or is on strike **2.** getting attention because unusual or remarkable *[a striking hat]*—see **SYN.** at NOTICEABLE **—strik′ing·ly adv.**

Strind·berg (strind′burg, strin′-; *Sw.* strin′bar′y′), **(Johan) August** 1849-1912; Swed. dramatist & novelist

string (striŋ) **n. [**OE. *streng*] **1.** *a)* a thin length of twisted fiber or wire, nylon, etc. used for tying, pulling, etc. *b)* a narrow strip of leather or cloth for fastening shoes, clothing, etc. *[apron strings]* **2.** a length of things on a string *[a string of pearls]* **3.** a line, row, or series of things *[a string of houses, a string of victories]* **4.** a number of business enterprises under one ownership *[a string of motels]* ☆**5.** any of the groupings of players on a team according to ability: the **first string** is more skilled than the **second string,** etc. **6.** *a)* a thin cord of wire, gut, nylon, etc., stretched on a violin, guitar, etc., and bowed, plucked, or struck to make a musical sound *b)* [*pl.*] all the stringed instruments of an orchestra played with a bow, or the players of these **7.** a strong, thin, stringlike organ, structure, etc.; specif., a fiber of a plant ☆**8.** [Colloq.] a condition or limitation attached to a plan, offer, etc.: *usually used in pl.* *[an offer with no strings attached]* **—vt. strung, strung** or rare **stringed, string′ing 1.** to provide with strings *[to string a tennis racket]* **2.** to thread on a string *[to string beads]* **3.** to tie, pull, hang, etc. with a string **4.** to adjust or tune the strings of (a musical instrument) **5.** to make nervous or keyed (*up*) **6.** to remove the strings from (beans, etc.) **7.** to arrange in a row or series **8.** to stretch or extend like a string *[to string a cable]* **—vi. 1.** to form into a string or strings **2.** to stretch out in a line **—on a** (or **the**) **string** completely under one's control **—pull strings 1.** to get someone to use influence in one's behalf, often secretly **2.** to direct action of others, often secretly **—☆string along** [Colloq.] **1.** to agree **2.** to fool, trick, or keep in an uncertain state, as by promises **—string up** [Colloq.] to kill by hanging **—string′less adj. —string′like′ adj.**

string band a band of stringed instruments, as guitar, banjo, violin, etc., playing country music **—string′-band′ adj.**

☆**string bean** same as SNAP BEAN

string·board (striŋ′bôrd′) **n.** a board placed along the side of a staircase to cover the ends of the steps

string·course (-kôrs′) **n.** a decorative, horizontal band of brick or stone set in the wall of a building

stringed (striŋd) rare pp. of STRING **—adj.** having strings, as certain musical instruments

strin·gent (strin′jənt) **adj. [** < L. prp. of *stringere,* to draw tight] **1.** strict; severe *[a stringent rule]* ☆**2.** with money tight for loans or investments *[a stringent market]* **3.** forceful; convincing *[stringent reasons]* —see **SYN.** at STRICT **—strin′gen·cy n., pl. -cies —strin′gent·ly adv. —strin′gent·ness n.**

STRINGBOARD

string·er (striŋ′ər) **n. 1.** a person or thing that strings **2.** *a)* a long, horizontal timber used to connect upright posts in a framework, support floors, etc. *b)* a notched, sloping board that supports the treads and risers of stairs: also called **string** **3.** a long structural part of an airplane fuselage, wing, etc. ☆**4.** a team member in a specified group according to ability [*second-stringer*] ☆**5.** a person serving as a part-time, local correspondent for a newspaper, etc. published elsewhere

string·halt (striŋ'hôlt') *n.* a condition in horses causing the hind legs to jerk in walking

string·piece (-pēs') *n.* a long, horizontal timber for supporting a framework

string quartet a quartet of or for players on stringed instruments, usually first and second violins, a viola, and a violoncello

☆**string tie** a narrow necktie, usually tied in a bow

string·y (striŋ'ē) *adj.* **string'i·er, string'i·est** **1.** like a string or strings; long, thin, wiry, etc. **2.** consisting of strings or fibers **3.** having tough fibers [*stringy* meat, celery, etc.] **4.** forming strings; ropy [*stringy* molasses] —**string'i·ness** *n.*

strip¹ (strip) *vt.* **stripped, strip'ping** [OE. *strypan* (in compounds)] **1.** to remove (the clothing, covering, etc.) of or from (a person); make naked **2.** to deprive (a person) of (honors, titles, qualities, etc.) **3.** to plunder; rob [the soldiers *stripped* the city] **4.** to peel or take off (the covering, skin, etc.) from (something) [to *strip* bark from a tree] **5.** to make bare or clear by removing fruit, growth, removable parts, etc. [to *strip* a room of furniture] **6.** to take apart [to *strip* down a motor] **7.** to break or damage the thread of (a nut, bolt, etc.) or the teeth of (a gear) —*vi.* **1.** to take off all clothing; undress ☆**2.** to perform a striptease —**strip'per** *n.*

strip² (strip) *n.* [altered (after prec.) < STRIPE] **1.** a long, narrow piece, as of land, ribbon, wood, etc. ☆**2.** *short for* COMIC STRIP **3.** a runway for the takeoff and landing of airplanes; landing strip —*vt.* to cut or tear into strips

strip cropping crop planting of alternate rows of heavy-rooted and loose-rooted plants, as on a hillside to lessen erosion

stripe (strip) *n.* [MLowG. & MDu. *stripe*] **1.** a long, narrow band, mark, or streak, differing as in color from the area around it **2.** [*often pl.*] a fabric or garment with a pattern of parallel stripes **3.** a strip of cloth or braid worn on the sleeve of a uniform to show rank, years served, etc. **4.** type; kind; sort [a man of his *stripe*] —*vt.* **striped, strip'ing** to mark with stripes

striped (stript, strī'pid) *adj.* having a stripe or stripes

☆**striped bass** (bas) a silvery game and food fish with dark stripes along the sides, found along the coasts of N. America: it goes up rivers to spawn

strip·ling (strip'liŋ) *n.* a grown boy; youth

strip mining a method of mining, esp. for coal, by laying bare a mineral deposit near the earth's surface

stript (stript) *rare pt. & pp. of* STRIP¹

☆**strip·tease** (strip'tēz') *n.* an act, as in burlesque shows, in which a woman, or now sometimes a man, undresses gradually, usually while music is being played —**strip'tease'** *vi.* -**teased', -teas'ing** —**strip'teas'er** *n.*

strip·y (strī'pē) *adj.* **strip'i·er, strip'i·est** characterized by, like, or marked with stripes

strive (strīv) *vi.* **strove** or **strived, striv·en** (striv''n) or **strived, striv'ing** [< OFr. < *estrif*, effort < Gmc.] **1.** to make great efforts; try very hard [to *strive* to win] **2.** to struggle or fight [to *strive* against tyranny] —*see SYN.* at TRY —**striv'er** *n.*

strobe (strōb) *n.* **1.** *shortened form of* STROBOSCOPE **2.** an electronic tube that can send out very rapid, brief, and bright flashes of light: used in photography, the theater, etc.: also **strobe light**

stro·bi·lus (strō bī'ləs) *n., pl.* -li (-lī) [ModL. < LL. < Gr. *strobilos*, pine cone] *same as* CONE (*n.* 3): also **stro'bile** (-bīl, -bil)

stro·bo·scope (strō'bə skōp', sträb'ə-) *n.* [< Gr. *strobos*, a twisting around + -SCOPE] an instrument for studying the motion of objects as by means of a light that flashes on and off at a rapid, steady rate: when the flashing rate matches the rate at which the lighted object rotates, vibrates, etc. the motion appears to be stopped —**stro'bo·scop'ic** (-skäp'ik), **stro'bo·scop'i·cal** *adj.* —**stro'bo·scop'i·cal·ly** *adv.*

strode (strōd) *pt. of* STRIDE

stro·ga·noff (strō'gə nôf', strô'-) *adj.* [prob. after S. *Stroganoff*, 19th-c. Russ. gourmet] cooked with sour cream, bouillon, mushrooms, etc.: placed after the word it modifies [beef *stroganoff*]

stroke (strōk) *n.* [akin to OE. *strican*, to hit] **1.** a striking of one thing against another; blow of an ax, whip, etc. **2.** an action that comes with sudden force or has a special effect [a *stroke* of lightning, a *stroke* of luck] **3.** a sudden attack, esp. of paralysis caused by the breaking or blocking of a blood vessel in the brain

4. *a)* a single, strong effort or move to do something [he hasn't done a *stroke* of work] *b)* a deed, act, or idea that is striking or brilliant [a *stroke* of genius] **5.** the sound of striking, as of a clock **6.** *a)* a single movement, as with some tool [a *stroke* of a pen; a backhand *stroke* in tennis] *b)* any of a series of repeated rhythmic motions made against water, air, etc. [the *stroke* of a swimmer, rower, etc.] *c)* a type, manner, or rate of such a movement [a slow *stroke*] **7.** a mark made by a pen, brush, etc. **8.** a beat of the heart **9.** a gentle, caressing motion with the hand **10.** any of the continuous, back-and-forth movements of a piston, etc. **11.** the rower in a crew who sits nearest the stern and sets the rate of rowing —*vt.* **stroked, strok'ing** **1.** to draw one's hand, a tool, etc. gently over the surface of **2.** to mark with strokes **3.** to hit (a ball), as in tennis, pool, etc. **4.** to be stroke for (a crew or boat) in rowing —**strok'er** *n.*

stroll (strōl) *vi.* [prob. < SwissG. dial. *strolen*] **1.** to walk in a slow, easy manner; saunter **2.** to wander from place to place [a *strolling* musician] —*vt.* to stroll along or through (the streets, the countryside, etc.) —*n.* a strolling, slow, easy walk

stroll·er (strōl'ər) *n.* **1.** a person who strolls **2.** a strolling actor or player ☆**3.** a light, chairlike baby carriage

Strom·bo·li (sträm'bō lē') It. island in the Tyrrhenian Sea, north of Sicily: site of an active volcano

strong (strôŋ) *adj.* [OE. *strang*] **1.** *a)* physically powerful; having great muscular strength; robust [a *strong* man] *b)* healthy; sound; hale [feeling *stronger* after her illness] **2.** *a)* working well [a *strong* heart] *b)* not easily upset [a *strong* stomach] **3.** powerful in carrying out one's own wishes, decisions, etc. [a *strong* will or mind] **4.** having special ability (*in* a specified area) [to be *strong* in French] **5.** governing firmly; authoritarian [a *strong* ruler] **6.** *a)* tough; firm; durable; able to resist [a *strong* wall; a *strong* fabric] *b)* holding firmly [a *strong* grip] *c)* binding tightly [*strong* glue] **7.** having many resources; powerful in wealth, numbers, supplies, etc. [a *strong* nation] **8.** of a specified number [a force 6,000 *strong*] **9.** having a powerful effect; drastic [*strong* measures] **10.** having a large amount of its essential quality; not diluted [*strong* coffee] **11.** affecting the senses powerfully [*strong* light, odor, etc.] **12.** having a bad taste or smell; rank [*strong* butter] **13.** firm and loud [a *strong* voice] **14.** intense in degree or quality; specif., *a)* ardent; warm [*strong* affection] *b)* forceful; persuasive [*strong* reasons] *c)* felt deeply; decided [a *strong* opinion] *d)* very enthusiastic; zealous [a *strong* socialist] *e)* forceful; vigorous; forthright [*strong* language] *f)* clear; distinct; marked [a *strong* resemblance] *g)* having emphasis or stress [a *strong* beat] **15.** moving rapidly and with force [a *strong* wind] **16.** magnifying highly [*strong* lenses] **17.** tending toward higher prices [a *strong* market] **18.** *Chem.* having a high ion concentration, as some acids and bases **19.** *Gram.* showing change in tense by internal change of a vowel rather than by the addition of inflectional endings; irregular (Example: *swim, swam, swum*) —*adv.* in a strong manner; greatly; severely —☆**come on strong** [Slang] to do something in a way that is showy or too bold —**strong'ish** *adj.* —**strong'ly** *adv.*

SYN.—**strong** is the most general of these terms, implying power that can be used actively as well as power that resists destruction [a *strong* body, fortress, etc.]; **stout** implies ability to stand strain, pressure, wear, etc. without breaking down or giving way [a *stout* rope, heart, etc.]; **sturdy** suggests the strength of that which is solidly developed or built and thus difficult to shake, weaken, etc. [*sturdy* oaks, faith, etc.]; **tough** suggests the strength of that which is firm and resistant in quality [*tough* leather, opposition, etc.]; **stalwart** emphasizes firmness, loyalty, or reliability [a *stalwart* supporter] —*ANT.* weak

STROLLER

☆**strong-arm** (strôŋ'ärm') *adj.* [Colloq.] using force or violence —*vt.* [Colloq.] to use force upon, esp. in robbing

strong·box (-bäks') *n.* a heavily made box or safe for storing valuables

strong·hold (-hōld') *n.* **1.** a place made strong against attack; fortified place **2.** a place where there is much strong support for certain views, beliefs, ideas, etc. [a suburb that is a *stronghold* of conservative opinion]

strong-mind·ed (-mīn'did) *adj.* having a strong, firm mind or will; determined —**strong'-mind'ed·ly** *adv.* —**strong'-mind'ed·ness** *n.*

strong-willed (-wild') *adj.* having a strong or stubborn will

stron·ti·um (strän′shē əm, -shəm, -tē əm) *n.* [ModL. < *Strontian*, Scotland, where first found] a pale-yellow, metallic chemical element resembling calcium in properties: symbol, Sr; at. wt., 87.62; at. no., 38: a deadly radioactive isotope of strontium (**strontium 90**) is present in the fallout of nuclear explosions

strop (sträp) *n.* [OE., ult. < L. *struppus* < Gr. *strophos*, a twisted band] **1.** *same as* STRAP **2.** a thick leather band, used for putting a fine edge on razors —*vt.* **stropped, strop′ping** to sharpen on a strop —**strop′per** *n.*

stro·phe (strō′fē) *n.* [< Gr. < *strephein*, to turn] **1.** in the ancient Greek theater, *a)* a turning of the chorus from right to left *b)* that part of the song sung by the chorus during this **2.** a stanza; esp., any of the irregular divisions of an ode —**stroph·ic** (sträf′ik, strō′fik) *adj.*

strove (strōv) *alt. pt. of* STRIVE

strow (strō) *vt.* **strowed, strown** (strōn) or **strowed, strow′ing** *archaic form of* STREW

struck (struk) *pt. & pp. of* STRIKE —*adj.* closed or affected by a labor strike

struc·tur·al (struk′chər əl) *adj.* **1.** of, having, or characterized by structure [*structural* design] **2.** used in construction or building [*structural* steel] —**struc′tur·al·ly** *adv.*

structural formula a chemical formula that shows the arrangement of atoms and bonds in a molecule

struc·tur·al·ist (-ist) *n.* a supporter of structural principles, as in studying or using social, economic, or linguistic theory —*adj.* of structuralists or their theories —**struc′tur·al·ism** *n.*

structural linguistics the study of a language as a logical, regular system within itself, without comparing it to other languages or to its forms in early periods —**structural linguist**

struc·ture (struk′chər) *n.* [< L. < pp. of *struere*, to arrange] **1.** manner of building, constructing, or organizing **2.** something built or constructed, as a building or dam **3.** the arrangement of all the parts of a whole [the *structure* of the atom] **4.** something made up of parts related to each other [an organizational *structure*] —*vt.* **-tured, -tur·ing** to put together according to a system; construct; organize [society as it was *structured* under feudalism] —see SYN. at BUILDING —**struc′ture·less** *adj.*

stru·del (strōō′d'l; *G.* shtrōō′dəl) *n.* [G.] a kind of pastry made of a very thin sheet of dough filled with apple slices, cheese, etc., rolled up, and baked

strug·gle (strug′'l) *vi.* **-gled, -gling** [ME. *strogelen* < ?] **1.** to contend or fight violently with an opponent [the wrestlers *struggled* with one another] **2.** to make great efforts; strive [she *struggled* to learn French] **3.** to make one's way with difficulty [*struggling* through the thicket] —*n.* **1.** great effort put out to do or achieve something [the *struggle* for women's rights] **2.** a fight; conflict; strife —see SYN. at TRY —**strug′gler** *n.*

strum (strum) *vt., vi.* **strummed, strum′ming** [echoic] to play (a guitar, banjo, etc.), esp. with long strokes across the strings and often in a casual way —*n.* the act or sound of this —**strum′mer** *n.*

strum·pet (strum′pit) *n.* [ME. < ?] a prostitute

strung (strung) *pt. & alt. pp. of* STRING —☆**strung out** [Slang] suffering from the effects of being addicted to narcotic drugs

strut (strut) *vi.* **strut′ted, strut′ting** [OE. *strutian*, to stand rigid] to walk in a proud, stiff, swaggering manner —*vt.* **1.** to provide with a strut or brace **2.** to make a show of [*strutting* their newest clothes in the parade] —*n.* **1.** a vain, swaggering walk **2.** a brace fitted into a framework to resist pressure in the direction of its length —**strut′ter** *n.* —**strut′ting·ly** *adv.*

STRUT

strych·nine (strik′nin, -nīn, -nēn) *n.* [Fr. < ModL. genus name < L. < Gr. *strychnos*, nightshade] a highly poisonous crystalline alkaloid, obtained from nux vomica and related plants: used in small doses as a stimulant

St. Thomas second largest island of the Virgin Islands of the U.S.

Stu·art (stōō′ərt) [< ? OE. *stigweard*, chamberlain] **1.** a masculine name **2.** ruling family of Scotland (1371-1603) & of England & Scotland (1603-1714), except during the Common-

wealth (1649-60) **3.** **Gilbert (Charles)**, 1755-1828; U.S. portrait painter **4.** **J(ames) E(well) B(rown)**, (nicknamed *Jeb*) 1833-64; Confederate general

stub (stub) *n.* [OE. *stybb*] **1.** a tree stump **2.** a short piece remaining after the main part has been removed or used up [a cigar *stub*] **3.** any short, blunt part sticking out [a mere *stub* of a horn] **4.** a pen with a short, blunt point ☆**5.** a short piece of a ticket or of a leaf in a checkbook kept as a record —*vt.* **stubbed, stub′bing** **1.** to root out (weeds, etc.) **2.** to clear (land) of stumps **3.** to strike (one's toe, etc.) against something by accident **4.** to put out (a cigarette, etc.) by pressing the end against a surface: often with *out*

stub·ble (stub′'l) *n.* [OFr. *estouble* < VL. < L. *stipula*, a stalk] **1.** the short stumps of grain left standing after harvesting **2.** any short, uneven growth like this [a *stubble* of beard] —**stub′bled** *adj.* —**stub′bly** *adj.* **-bli·er, -bli·est**

stub·born (stub′ərn) *adj.* [prob. < OE. *stubb*, var. of *stybb*, STUB] **1.** refusing to give in; set on having one's way; obstinate **2.** done or carried on in this way [a *stubborn* campaign] **3.** hard to handle, treat, or deal with [a *stubborn* cold] —**stub′born·ly** *adv.* —**stub′born·ness** *n.*

SYN.—**stubborn** implies a being fixed in purpose, course, etc. in a way that strongly resists change, control, etc. [a *stubborn* child, belief, etc.]; **obstinate** applies to one who keeps sticking, often unreasonably, to his purpose, course, etc., against argument or persuasion [he was *obstinate* in his refusal to do homework]; **dogged** implies a steady, plodding effort to get something done or to have one's own way [the *dogged* pursuit of a goal]; **pertinacious** implies a strong firmness of purpose that is thought of unfavorably by others [a *pertinacious* critic] —ANT. compliant, tractable

stub·by (stub′ē) *adj.* **-bi·er, -bi·est** **1.** covered with stubs or stubble [*stubby* land] **2.** short and heavy or dense [a *stubby* beard] **3.** short and thick [*stubby* fingers] —**stub′bi·ly** *adv.* —**stub′bi·ness** *n.*

stuc·co (stuk′ō) *n., pl.* **-coes, -cos** [It., prob. < Gmc.] **1.** plaster or cement used for surfacing inside or outside walls, often in a rough or wavy finish **2.** the work done in this: also **stuc′co·work′** —*vt.* **-coed, -co·ing** to cover with stucco

stuck (stuk) *pt. & pp. of* STICK

stuck-up (stuk′up′) *adj.* [Colloq.] snobbish; conceited

stud¹ (stud) *n.* [OE. *studu*, post] **1.** any of a series of small knobs or rounded nailheads used to decorate a surface, as of leather **2.** a small, buttonlike device used as a decoration or fastener on a shirt front **3.** an upright piece in the frame of a building, to which panels, laths, etc. are nailed **4.** a metal crossbar bracing a link, as in a chain cable **5.** a pin or peg used as a support, pivot, etc., or, as in an automobile tire, to increase traction on ice —*vt.* **stud′ded, stud′ding** **1.** to set or decorate with studs or studlike objects **2.** to be set thickly on [rocks *stud* the hillside] **3.** to scatter or cluster (something) thickly [a crown *studded* with jewels] **4.** to provide (a building) with studs

stud² (stud) *n.* [OE. *stod*] **1.** *a)* a number of horses kept for breeding *b)* the place where these are kept ☆**2.** *a) same as* STUDHORSE *b)* any male animal used esp. for breeding **3.** [Slang] a man sexually active with many women —*adj.* of or having to do with a stud [a *stud* farm] —**at stud** available for breeding: said of male animals

stud·book (stud′book′) *n.* a register of purebred animals, esp. racehorses: also **stud book**

stud·ding (stud′iŋ) *n.* **1.** the studs in a wall or building **2.** material used for or as studs

stud·ding·sail (stud′iŋ sāl′, stun′s'l) *n.* [< ?] a light, auxiliary sail set at the edge of a working sail in light weather: also **studding sail**

stu·dent (stōōd′'nt, styōōd′-) *n.* [< OFr. < L. prp. of *studere*, to study] **1.** a person who studies something [a *student* of human behavior] **2.** a person who is enrolled for study in a school, college, etc. —see SYN. at PUPIL¹ —**stu′dent·ship′** *n.*

☆**student lamp** any of various lamps for use on a desk, as one with a gooseneck

☆**student teacher** a student in a college or university who teaches school under supervision as a requirement for a degree in education

stud·horse (stud′hôrs′) *n.* a stallion kept for breeding

stud·ied (stud′ēd) *adj.* **1.** prepared by careful study [a *studied* reply] **2.** planned beforehand; deliberate [*studied* indifference] —**stud′ied·ly** *adv.* —**stud′ied·ness** *n.*

fat, āpe, cär; ten, ēven; is, bīte; gō, hôrn, tōōl, look; oil, out; up, fur; get; joy; yet; chin; she; thin, then; zh, leisure; ŋ, ring; ə for *a* in *ago*, *e* in *agent*, *i* in *sanity*, *o* in *comply*, *u* in *focus*; ′ as in *able* (ā′b'l); Fr. bal; ë, Fr. coeur; ö, Fr. feu; Fr. mon; ô, Fr. coq; ü, Fr. duc; r, Fr. cri; H, G. ich; kh, G. doch; ‡ foreign; ☆ Americanism; < derived from. See inside front cover.

stu·di·o (stōō′dē ō′, styōō′-) *n., pl.* **-di·os′** [It. < L. *studium*, a study] **1.** a place where an artist or photographer does his work ☆**2.** a place where dancing or music lessons are given **3.** a place where motion pictures are made **4.** a place where radio or television programs are produced or where recordings are made

☆**studio couch** a kind of couch that can be opened into a full-sized bed

stu·di·ous (stōō′dē əs, styōō′-) *adj.* **1.** fond of study [a *studious* pupil] **2.** showing close attention [a *studious* look] **3.** very enthusiastic; wholehearted [*studious* efforts] —**stu′di·ous·ly** *adv.* —**stu′di·ous·ness** *n.*

☆**stud poker** a form of poker in which each player is dealt some cards face up

stud·y (stud′ē) *n., pl.* **stud·ies** [< OFr. < L. < *studere*, to study] **1.** the act of reading, thinking, etc. in order to learn something **2.** careful and serious examination of a subject, event, etc. [a *study* of traffic problems] **3.** a branch of learning [the *study* of medicine] **4.** [*pl.*] formal education; schooling [he continued his *studies* at college] **5.** an essay or thesis presenting results of an investigation **6.** a work of literature or art treating a subject in careful detail **7.** a first sketch for a story, picture, etc. **8.** *same as* ÉTUDE **9.** [Now Rare] an earnest effort or intention **10.** deep thought [he is lost in *study*] **11.** a room set apart for study, writing, etc. —*vt.* **stud′ied, stud′y·ing 1.** to try to learn by reading, thinking, etc. [to *study* law] **2.** *a)* to investigate carefully [to *study* the problem of crime] *b)* to look at carefully; scrutinize [to *study* a map] **3.** *a)* to read (a book, lesson, etc.) so as to know and understand it *b)* to memorize **4.** to take a course in at a school [all seniors must *study* history] **5.** to give attention or thought to [*studying* possible changes] —*vi.* **1.** to study something **2.** to be a student **3.** to try hard **4.** to meditate —see *SYN.* at CONSIDER —☆**study up on** [Colloq.] to make a careful study of

☆**study hall 1.** a room in a school for studying and doing homework **2.** an assigned period there

stuff (stuf) *n.* [< OFr. < *estoffer*, to cram, prob. < Frank.] **1.** the material out of which anything is or can be made **2.** basic nature or elements; essence; character [a man made of stern *stuff*] **3.** matter or substance of an unspecified kind **4.** cloth, esp. woolen cloth **5.** *a)* household goods *b)* personal belongings *c)* things; objects **6.** something to be drunk, swallowed, etc. **7.** worthless objects; junk **8.** *a)* talk or action of a specified kind *b)* foolish or worthless ideas, words, etc. [*stuff* and nonsense] **9.** [Colloq.] *a)* superior ability; also, ☆special skill or knowledge [to do or know one's *stuff*] ☆*b)* special control given to the ball in baseball, billiards, etc. —*vt.* **1.** to fill the inside of (something); pack; specif., *a)* to fill (a cushion, etc.) with padding *b)* to fill the skin of (a dead animal, etc.) in order to mount and preserve it *c)* to fill (a chicken, turkey, etc.) with seasoning, bread crumbs, etc. before roasting **2.** *a)* to fill too full; cram; overload [the suitcase was *stuffed* and would not close] *b)* to fill to excess with food **3.** to pack or crowd (something) into a container, etc. [she *stuffed* clothes into the drawer] **4.** to fill with information, ideas, etc. [to *stuff* one's head with facts] ☆**5.** to put illegal votes into (a ballot box) **6.** *a)* to plug; block [the drain was *stuffed* up] *b)* to choke or stop up, as with phlegm **7.** to force or push [he *stuffed* a pillow behind her head] ☆**8.** *Basketball* [Colloq.] to push (the ball) into the basket from above —*vi.* to eat too much —**stuff′er** *n.*

☆**stuffed shirt** [Slang] a pompous, stuffy person

stuff·ing (stuf′iŋ) *n.* **1.** the action of one that stuffs **2.** something used to stuff; specif., *a)* soft, springy material used as padding in cushions, etc. *b)* a seasoned mixture for stuffing fowl, roasts, etc.

stuff·y (stuf′ē) *adj.* **stuff′i·er, stuff′i·est 1.** poorly ventilated; having little fresh air; close [a *stuffy* room] **2.** having the nasal passages stopped up, as from a cold [a *stuffy* head] **3.** [Colloq.] *a)* dull, stodgy, old-fashioned, conservative, etc. *b)* prim; strait-laced *c)* pompous; self-important —**stuff′i·ly** *adv.* —**stuff′i·ness** *n.*

stul·ti·fy (stul′tə fī′) *vt.* **-fied′, -fy′ing** [< LL. < L. *stultus*, foolish + *facere*, to make] **1.** *a)* to cause to seem or be foolish, stupid, absurd, etc. *b)* to make dull or sluggish **2.** to make worthless or useless —**stul′ti·fi·ca′tion** *n.*

stum·ble (stum′b'l) *vi.* **-bled, -bling** [< Scand.] **1.** to trip in walking, running, etc. **2.** to walk in an unsteady way [the tired boy *stumbled* off to bed] **3.** to speak, act, etc. in a confused, blundering manner [he *stumbled* through his speech] **4.** to sin or err; do wrong **5.** to come by chance; happen [to *stumble* across a clue] —*vt.* to cause to stumble —*n.* a stumbling —**stum′bler** *n.* —**stum′bling·ly** *adv.*

☆**stum·ble·bum** (-bum′) *n.* [Slang] *same as* BUM (senses 1 & 2)

stumbling block something that gets in the way; obstacle or difficulty

stump (stump) *n.* [prob. < or akin to MLowG. *stump*] **1.** the lower end of a tree or plant left in the ground after most of the stem or trunk has been cut off **2.** *a)* the part of an arm, leg, tooth, etc. left after the rest has been removed *b)* a butt; stub [the *stump* of a pencil] ☆**3.** the place where a political speech is made **4.** *a)* the sound of a heavy, tramping step *b)* such a step **5.** *Cricket* any of the three upright sticks of a wicket —*vt.* **1.** to reduce to a stump; lop **2.** to remove stumps from (land) ☆**3.** to travel over (a district), making political speeches **4.** [Colloq.] to stub (one's toes, etc.) ☆**5.** [Colloq.] to puzzle; baffle [her question *stumped* the expert] —*vi.* **1.** to walk heavily or clumsily, as with a wooden leg ☆**2.** to travel about, making political speeches —**stump′er** *n.* —**stump′like′** *adj.*

stump·y (stum′pē) *adj.* **stump′i·er, stump′i·est** ☆**1.** covered with stumps **2.** like a stump; short and thick; stubby —**stump′i·ness** *n.*

stun (stun) *vt.* **stunned, stun′ning** [< OFr. *estoner*, to stun: see ASTONISH] **1.** to make senseless or unconscious, as by a blow **2.** to shock deeply; daze; astound [*stunned* by the news] **3.** to overpower as by a loud noise or explosion —*n.* the effect or condition of being stunned —see *SYN.* at SHOCK[1]

stung (stuŋ) *pt. & pp.* of STING

stunk (stuŋk) *pp. & alt. pt.* of STINK

stun·ner (stun′ər) *n.* one that stuns; specif., [Colloq.] a person or thing of striking beauty, excellence, etc.

stun·ning (-iŋ) *adj.* **1.** that stuns **2.** [Colloq.] remarkably attractive, excellent, etc. —**stun′ning·ly** *adv.*

stun·sail, stun·s'le (stun′s'l) *n. same as* STUDDINGSAIL

stunt[1] (stunt) *vt.* [OE. *stunt*, stupid] to keep from growing or developing fully; dwarf [poor soil *stunted* the plants] **2.** to hold back (growth or development) —*n.* **1.** a stunting **2.** something stunted

☆**stunt[2]** (stunt) *n.* [< ?] **1.** a show of skill or daring; trick **2.** something done to attract attention, etc. —*vi.* to perform a stunt or stunts

☆**stunt man** a person skilled in acrobatics, etc. who takes the place of an actor when dangerous scenes involving falls, leaps, etc. are filmed

stupe (stōōp) *n.* [< L. *stuppa*, tow fibers < Gr.] a soft cloth dipped in water, wrung dry, often medicated, and applied to the body as a compress

stu·pe·fac·tion (stōō′pə fak′shən, styōō′-) *n.* **1.** a stupefying or being stupefied **2.** stunned amazement; astonishment; bewilderment

stu·pe·fy (stōō′pə fī′, styōō′-) *vt.* **-fied′, -fy′ing** [< Fr. < L. < *stupere*, to be stunned + *facere*, to make] **1.** to make dull, senseless, or dazed [the drug *stupefied* her] **2.** to stun or astound [*stupefied* at the gory sight] —**stu′pe·fi′er** *n.*

stu·pen·dous (stōō pen′dəs, styōō-) *adj.* [< L. gerundive of *stupere*, to be stunned] **1.** astonishing; overwhelming [a *stupendous* development] **2.** astonishingly great or large [a *stupendous* success] —**stu·pen′dous·ly** *adv.* —**stu·pen′dous·ness** *n.*

stu·pid (stōō′pid, styōō′-) *adj.* [L. *stupidus* < *stupere*, to be stunned] **1.** dazed; stunned; stupefied **2.** lacking normal intelligence; slow-witted; dull **3.** showing or resulting from a lack of intelligence; foolish [a *stupid* idea] **4.** dull and boring [a *stupid* party] —*n.* a stupid person —**stu′pid·ly** *adv.* —**stu′pid·ness** *n.*

SYN.—**stupid** implies such lack of intelligence or inability to understand, learn, etc. as might be shown by one in a mental daze [a *stupid* answer]; **dull** implies a mental slowness that may be in one's makeup or may result from overfatigue, illness, etc. [the fever left him *dull* and listless]; **dense** suggests lack of sensitivity or an irritating failure to understand quickly or to react intelligently [too dense to take a hint]; **slow** suggests that the quickness to learn, but not necessarily the ability to learn, is below average [a pupil *slow* in his studies] —see also *SYN.* at SILLY —*ANT.* intelligent, bright

stu·pid·i·ty (stōō pid′ə tē, styōō-) *n.* **1.** a being stupid **2.** *pl.* **-ties** a stupid remark or act

stu·por (stōō′pər, styōō′-) *n.* [L.] **1.** a state in which the mind and senses are so dulled, as from shock or a drug, that one can barely think, act, feel, etc. **2.** mental or moral dullness or lack of interest —see *SYN.* at LETHARGY —**stu′por·ous** *adj.*

stur·dy (stur′dē) *adj.* **-di·er, -di·est** [OFr. *estourdi*, stunned] **1.** not giving in; firm; resolute; unyielding [*sturdy* defiance] **2.** strong; hardy [a *sturdy* oak] **3.** strongly built or constructed [a *sturdy* house] —see *SYN.* at STRONG —**stur′di·ly** *adv.* —**stur′di·ness** *n.*

stur·geon (stur′jən) *n.*, *pl.* **stur′geons**, **stur′geon**: see PLU-
RAL, II, D, 1 [OFr. *esturjon* < Frank.] any
of several large food fishes having rows of
spiny plates along the body and a long
snout: valuable as a source of caviar and
isinglass

stut·ter (stut′ər) *vt.*, *vi.* [< dial. *stut*, to
stutter < ME. *stutten* + -ER (sense 4)] **1.**
same as STAMMER **2.** to make (a series of
repeated sounds) [*stuttering* machine
guns] —*n.* the act or an instance of stuttering —**stut′ter·er** *n.*

Stutt·gart (stut′gärt; *G.* shtoot′gärt) city
in S West Germany: pop. 628,000

Stuy·ve·sant (stī′və s′nt), **Peter**
1592–1672; Du. governor of New Netherland (1646–64)

STURGEON
(to 7 ft. long)

St. Vincent 1. island of the Windward group of the West Indies **2.** country consisting of this island and a group of nearby
islands: 150 sq. mi.; pop. 100,000

sty[1] (stī) *n.*, *pl.* **sties** [OE. *sti*, *stig*] **1.** a pen for pigs **2.** any
filthy or disgusting place —*vt.*, *vi.* **stied, sty′ing** to keep or live
in or as in a sty

sty[2], **stye** (stī) *n.*, *pl.* **sties** [< obs. *styany* (taken as *sty on eye*) <
dial. *styan*, rising < OE. *stigan*, to climb] a small, inflamed
swelling of a sebaceous gland on the rim of the eyelid

Styg·i·an (stij′ē ən, stij′ən) *adj.* **1.** of or like the river Styx
and the mythical world of the dead **2.** [*also* **s-**] *a*) hellish *b*)
dark or gloomy

style (stīl) *n.* [L. *stilus*] **1.** a pointed instrument used by the
ancients in writing on wax tablets **2.** any device similar in
shape or use; specif., *a*) [Obs.] a pen *b*) an etching needle *c*) a
phonograph needle *d*) an engraving tool *e*) the pointer on a
dial, chart, etc. *f*) *Bot.* the stalklike part of a carpel between the
stigma and the ovary: see illustration at FLOWER **3.** *a*) the way
in which something is expressed in writing or speaking, as
apart from the ideas expressed *b*) characteristic manner of expression, design, etc. in any art, period, etc. [Gothic *style*] **4.**
excellence, originality, etc. in artistic or literary expression [this
author lacks *style*] **5.** the way in which anything is made or
done; manner [the player's batting *style*] **6.** *a*) the current,
fashionable way of dressing, acting, etc. *b*) something stylish;
esp., a garment of current, fashionable design *c*) a fashionable,
luxurious manner [to dine in *style*] **7.** elegance of manner and
bearing [she carries herself with *style*] **8.** form of address; title
[entitled to the *style* of Mayor] **9.** sort; kind; type [the old
style of politician] **10.** *Printing* a particular way of dealing
with spelling, punctuation, word division, etc. —*vt.* **styled,
styl′ing 1.** to name; call [Lincoln was *styled* the Great
Emancipator] ☆**2.** to design the style of [gowns *styled* in
Paris] **3.** to make fit a particular style [to *style* punctuation,
etc. in a newspaper] —*see* SYN. *at* FASHION —**style′less** *adj.*

style·book (stīl′book′) *n.* a book consisting of examples or
rules of style (esp. sense 10)

styl·ish (stī′lish) *adj.* in keeping with the current style in dress,
decoration, etc.; smart; fashionable —**styl′ish·ly** *adv.* —**styl′-
ish·ness** *n.*

styl·ist (-list) *n.* **1.** a writer, etc. whose work has style (sense 4)
2. a person who designs current styles, as in dress

sty·lis·tic (stī lis′tik) *adj.* of or having to do with style, esp.
literary style: also **sty·lis′ti·cal** —**sty·lis′ti·cal·ly** *adv.*

styl·ize (stī′līz) *vt.* **-ized, -iz·ing** to do in a certain style rather
than in a natural or realistic way [*stylized* flowers in a modern
design] —**styl′i·za′tion** *n.* —**styl′iz·er** *n.*

sty·lus (stī′ləs) *n.*, *pl.* **-lus·es, -li** (-lī) [L., for *stilus*, pointed
instrument] **1.** a style or other needlelike marking device **2.**
any of various pointed tools, as for marking mimeograph sten-
cils **3.** *a*) a sharp, pointed device for cutting the grooves of a
phonograph record *b*) a phonograph needle

sty·mie (stī′mē) *n.* [prob. < Scot. *stymie*, a person partially
blind] **1.** *Golf* the situation on a putting green when an
opponent's ball lies in a direct line between the player's ball
and the hole **2.** any frustrating situation —*vt.* **-mied, -mie·ing
1.** to get in the way of with a stymie **2.** to block; impede

sty·my (stī′mē) *n.*, *pl.* **-mies**, *vt.* **-mied, -my·ing** *same as* STY-
MIE

styp·tic (stip′tik) *adj.* [< L. < Gr. *styptikos* < *styphein*, to
contract] tending to stop bleeding by tightening the tissues or
blood vessels; astringent —*n.* any styptic substance

styptic pencil a small stick of a styptic substance, as alum,
used to stop bleeding from small cuts, as in shaving

sty·rene (stī′rēn, stir′ēn) *n.* [< L. *styrax*, a kind of tree +
-ENE] a colorless or yellowish liquid hydrocarbon used in the
manufacture of synthetic rubber and plastics

☆**Sty·ro·foam** (stī′rə fōm′) *a trademark for* rigid, lightweight, cellular polystyrene, used for containers that keep
things cold, for supporting and protecting articles in packaging,
etc. —*n.* [**s-**] this substance

Styx (stiks) [L., ult. < Gr. *stygein*, to hate] *Gr. Myth.* the river
of Hades across which Charon ferried the souls of the dead

su·a·ble (soo′ə b′l) *adj.* that can be or is liable to be sued

sua·sion (swā′zhən) *n.* [< L. < pp. of *suadere*, to persuade]
same as PERSUASION: now chiefly in **moral suasion**, a persuading by appealing to one's sense of morality —**sua′sive** (-siv)
adj. —**sua′sive·ly** *adv.* —**sua′sive·ness** *n.*

suave (swäv; *Brit. also* swāv) *adj.* [MFr. < L. *suavis*, sweet]
gracious or polite in a smooth way; polished; urbane —**suave′ly**
adv. —**suave′ness** *n.* —**suav·i·ty** (swä′və tē) *n.*, *pl.* **-ties**
SYN.—**suave** implies the smoothly gracious social manner of one who
deals with people easily and tactfully, sometimes suggesting a surface politeness too smooth to be convincing [his *suave* manner with waiters]; **urbane** suggests the social ease of a highly cultured person with much
worldly experience [an *urbane* conversation on European theater]; **diplomatic** implies skill and tact in dealing with people and handling delicate situations, sometimes in such a way as to gain one's own ends [a di-
plomatic answer]; **politic** also expresses this idea, often emphasizing the
immediate practical reasons for doing a thing [a *politic* move]

sub (sub) *n.* shortened form of: **1.** SUBMARINE **2.** SUBSCRIP-
TION **3.** SUBSTITUTE —*vi.* **subbed, sub′bing** [Colloq.] to be a
substitute (*for* someone)

sub- [< L. *sub*, under] *a prefix meaning:* **1.** under, beneath
[*subsoil*] **2.** lower in rank or position than [*subaltern*] **3.** to a
lesser degree than, somewhat [*subtropical*] **4.** by or forming a
division into smaller parts [*subsection*] **5.** *Chem.* with less
than the normal amount of (the specified substance) In words
of Latin origin, *sub-* is changed to *suc-* before *c*, *suf-* before *f*,
sug- before *g*, *sum-* before *m*, *sup-* before *p*, and *sur-* before *r*:
sub- often changes to *sus-* before *c*, *p*, and *t*

sub. 1. substitute(s) **2.** suburb(an)

sub·ac·id (sub as′id) *adj.* slightly acid, as certain fruits —
sub·a·cid·i·ty (-ə sid′ə tē) *n.* —**sub·ac′id·ly** *adv.*

sub·a·gent (-ā′jənt) *n.* a person representing an agent; agent
of an agent

sub·al·tern (səb ôl′tərn, sub′əl tərn) *adj.* [< Fr. < LL. < L.
sub-, under + *alternus*, alternate] **1.** of lower rank; subordinate **2.** [Brit.] holding an army commission below that of captain —*n.* **1.** a subordinate **2.** [Brit.] a subaltern officer

sub·ant·arc·tic (sub′ant ärk′tik, -är′-) *adj.* designating or of
the area surrounding the Antarctic Circle

sub·a·que·ous (sub ā′kwē əs, -ak′wē-) *adj.* [SUB- +
AQUEOUS] **1.** adapted for underwater use or existence **2.**
formed, living, or occurring under water

sub·arc·tic (sub ärk′tik, -är′-) *adj.* designating or of the area
surrounding the Arctic Circle

sub·a·tom·ic (sub′ə täm′ik) *adj.* of or relating to the inner
part of an atom or any particle smaller than an atom

sub·base·ment (sub′bās′mənt) *n.* any floor or room below
the main basement

sub·branch (-branch′) *n.* a division of a branch

sub·class (-klas′) *n.* **1.** a division of a class; specif., *Biol.* any
main natural subdivision of a class of plants or animals **2.**
Math. same as SUBSET

sub·cla·vi·an (sub klā′vē ən) *adj.* located under the clavicle
—*n.* a subclavian vein, artery, etc.

sub·clin·i·cal (sub klin′i k′l) *adj.* without clearly seen symptoms, as a disease in its early stages

sub·com·mit·tee (sub′kə mit′ē) *n.* any of the small committees with special duties into which a main committee may be
divided

☆**sub·com·pact** (-käm′pakt) *n.* a model of automobile
smaller than a compact

sub·con·scious (sub kän′shəs) *adj.* **1.** occurring with little or
no awareness on the part of the individual [a *subconscious*

fat, āpe, cär, ten, ēven, is, bīte; gō, hôrn, tōol, look; oil, out; up, fur; get; joy; yet; chin; she; thin, then; zh, leisure; ŋ, ring;
ə for *a* in *ago*, *e* in *agent*, *i* in *sanity*, *o* in *comply*, *u* in *focus*; ′ as in *able* (ā′b′l); Fr. bál; ë, Fr. coeur; ö, Fr. feu; Fr. mon;
δ, Fr. coq; ü, Fr. duc; r, Fr. cri; H, G. ich; kh, G. doch; ‡foreign; ☆ Americanism; < derived from. See inside front cover.

desire] **2.** not fully conscious —**the subconscious** subconscious activity of the mind —**sub·con′scious·ly** *adv.* —**sub·con′scious·ness** *n.*

sub·con·ti·nent (-kän′tə nənt) *n.* a large land mass, smaller than a continent; often, a subdivision of a continent

sub·con·tract (sub kän′trakt; *also, for v.,* sub′kən trakt′) *n.* a secondary contract undertaking one or more of the parts of a main contract [*construction companies often let subcontracts for the plumbing and electrical work*] —*vt., vi.* to make a subcontract (for) —**sub′con′trac·tor** *n.*

sub·cul·ture (sub′kul′chər) *n.* **1.** a group whose special interests, way of living, etc. are quite different from those of the society of which it is a part [*the hippie subculture of the 1960's*] **2.** the distinct cultural patterns of such a group —**sub·cul′tur·al** *adj.*

sub·cu·ta·ne·ous (sub′kyo͞o tā′nē əs) *adj.* being, used, or placed beneath the skin —**sub·cu·ta′ne·ous·ly** *adv.*

sub·dea·con (sub dē′k'n) *n.* a cleric ranking below a deacon

☆**sub·deb** (sub′deb′) *n.* [SUB- + DEB(UTANTE)] **1.** a girl in the years just before her debut into society **2.** any girl of such age —*adj.* of or suitable for a subdeb

sub·di·vide (sub′di vīd′, sub′di vīd′) *vt., vi.* -vid′ed, -vid′ing **1.** to divide again the parts into which something is already divided **2.** to divide (land) into lots to be sold for building homes, etc. —**sub′di·vid′er** *n.*

sub·di·vi·sion (sub′di vizh′ən, sub′di vizh′ən) *n.* **1.** a subdividing or being subdivided **2.** one of the parts resulting from subdividing **3.** an area of land subdivided into building lots

sub·dom·i·nant (sub däm′ə nənt) *n. Music* the fourth tone of a diatonic scale

sub·due (səb do͞o′, -dyo͞o′) *vt.* -dued′, -du′ing [< OFr. < L. *subducere*, to remove] **1.** to win control of; conquer; vanquish [*to subdue an invading army*] **2.** to overcome, as by persuading or training; control [*to subdue a bad habit*] **3.** to make less strong or harsh; diminish; soften [*talking in subdued tones; subdued colors, lighting, etc.*] **4.** to hold back or keep down (feelings, spirits, etc.) —see SYN. at CONQUER —**sub·du′a·ble** *adj.* —**sub·du′al** *n.* —**sub·du′er** *n.*

su·be·re·ous (so͞o bir′ē əs) *adj.* [< LL. < *suber*, cork < or akin to Gr. *syphar*, wrinkled skin] *Bot.* of or like cork: also **su′ber·ose′** (-bə rōs′)

su·ber·in (so͞o′bər in) *n.* [< Fr. < L. *suber*, cork + Fr. -*ine*, -INE⁴] a waxy or fatty substance that is the basic part of the cell walls of cork and gives it the property of keeping out water

su·ber·ize (-bə rīz′) *vt.* -ized′, -iz′ing [L. *suber*, cork + -IZE] *Bot.* to cause to become corky tissue by forming suberin in the cell walls —**su′ber·i·za′tion** *n.*

sub·fam·i·ly (sub′fam′ə lē) *n., pl.* -lies **1.** any main natural subdivision of a family of plants or animals **2.** a subdivision of a language family

sub·freez·ing (sub′frē′ziŋ) *adj.* below freezing

sub·group (-gro͞op′) *n.* a group that is part of a larger group

☆**sub·gum** (sub′gum′) *adj.* [Cantonese, lit., mixed vegetables] designating any of various Chinese-American dishes, as chow mein, prepared with mushrooms, almonds, etc.

sub·head (sub′hed′) *n.* **1.** the title of a subdivision of a chapter, article, etc. **2.** a subordinate heading or title, as of a newspaper article Also **sub′head′ing**

sub·hu·man (sub′hyo͞o′mən) *adj.* **1.** less than human **2.** nearly human

subj. 1. subject **2.** subjunctive

sub·ja·cent (sub jā′s'nt) *adj.* [< L. prp. of *subjacere* < *sub-*, under + *jacere*, to lie] located beneath; underlying —**sub·ja′cen·cy** *n.* —**sub·ja′cent·ly** *adv.*

sub·ject (sub′jikt; *for v.* səb jekt′) *adj.* [< OFr. < L. pp. of *subjicere* < *sub-*, under + *jacere*, to throw] **1.** under the authority or control of, or owing allegiance to, another [*subject peoples*] **2.** likely to have; liable (*to*) [*subject to fits of anger*] **3.** liable to receive [*subject to criticism*] **4.** depending on some action or condition [*subject to his approval*] —*n.* **1.** a person under the authority or control of another; esp., a person who owes allegiance to a particular ruler, government, etc. **2.** someone or something undergoing a treatment, experiment, etc. **3.** something dealt with in discussion, study, writing, painting, etc.; theme **4.** the main theme of a musical composition **5.** a branch of learning or course of study, as in a school **6.** *Gram.* the noun, noun phrase, or noun substitute in a sentence about which something is said **7.** *Philos.* the mind, or ego, that thinks or feels, as distinguished from everything outside the mind —*vt.* **1.** to bring under the authority or control of **2.** to lay open; make liable [*subject one to scorn*] **3.** to cause to undergo

something [*to subject to questioning*] —see SYN. at CITIZEN —**sub·jec′tion** *n.*

sub·jec·tive (səb jek′tiv) *adj.* **1.** of or resulting from the feelings of the subject, or person thinking; not objective; personal [*a subjective opinion*] **2.** determined by and emphasizing the ideas, feelings, etc. of the artist or writer [*subjective writing*] **3.** *Gram.* same as NOMINATIVE **4.** *Med.* describing or of a symptom of which only the patient is aware —**sub·jec′tive·ly** *adv.* —**sub·jec·tiv·i·ty** (sub′jek tiv′ə tē), **sub·jec′tive·ness** *n.*

subject matter the thing or things dealt with in a book, course of study, discussion, etc.

sub·join (səb join′) *vt.* [< MFr. < L.: see SUB- & JOIN] to add (something) at the end of a statement

sub·ju·gate (sub′jə gāt′) *vt.* -gat′ed, -gat′ing [< L. pp. of *subjugare* < *sub-*, under + *jugum*, a yoke] **1.** to bring under control or subjection; conquer **2.** to cause to give in; subdue —**sub′ju·ga′tion** *n.* —**sub′ju·ga′tor** *n.*

sub·junc·tive (səb juŋk′tiv) *adj.* [< LL. < L. pp. of *subjungere*, to SUBJOIN] designating or of that mood of a verb used to express supposition, desire, possibility, etc., rather than to state an actual fact [*were* in "if I *were* you" is in the *subjunctive* mood] —*n.* **1.** the subjunctive mood **2.** a verb in this mood —**sub·junc′tive·ly** *adv.*

sub·king·dom (sub′kiŋ′dəm) *n.* any main natural subdivision of the plant or animal kingdom

sub·lease (sub′lēs′; *for v.* sub lēs′) *n.* a lease for property given by a person who is himself leasing it from the owner —*vt.* -leased′, -leas′ing to give, receive, or hold a sublease of —**sub′les·see′** (-les ē′) *n.* —**sub·les·sor** (sub les′ôr, sub′les·ôr′) *n.*

sub·let (sub let′, sub′let′) *vt.* -let′, -let′ting **1.** to let to another (property which one is renting) **2.** to let out (work) to a subcontractor

sub·lieu·ten·ant (sub′lo͞o ten′ənt; *Brit. & Canad.* -lef ten′-) *n.* [Brit. & Canad.] a naval officer ranking below a lieutenant

sub·li·mate (sub′lə māt′; *for adj. & n., also* -mit) *vt.* -mat′ed, -mat′ing [< L. pp. of *sublimare*: see SUBLIME] **1.** to sublime (a substance) **2.** to have a purifying or refining effect on **3.** to use the energy associated with (sexual drives) in doing things that are useful, artistic, etc. —*vi.* to undergo subliming —*adj.* purified; sublimated —*n.* a substance that is the product of subliming —**sub′li·ma′tion** *n.*

sub·lime (sə blīm′) *adj.* [< L. < *sub-*, up to + *limen*, lintel] **1.** of the highest kind; great, noble, lofty, etc. [*a sublime philosophy*] **2.** inspiring awe or admiration through grandeur, beauty, etc. [*sublime scenery*] —*vt.* -limed′, -lim′ing **1.** to make sublime **2.** to purify (a solid) by heating directly to a gaseous state and condensing the vapor back into solid form —*vi.* to go through this process —see SYN. at SPLENDID —**the sublime** that which is noble, grand, etc. —**sub·lime′ly** *adv.* —**sub·lime′ness** *n.*

sub·lim·i·nal (sub lim′ə n'l) *adj.* [< SUB- + L. *limen*, threshold + -AL] below the threshold of consciousness; specif., using stimuli meant to take effect subconsciously through repetition —**sub·lim′i·nal·ly** *adv.*

sub·lim·i·ty (sə blim′ə tē) *n.* **1.** a sublime state or quality **2.** *pl.* -ties something sublime

☆**sub·ma·chine gun** (sub′mə shēn′) a lightweight, automatic or semiautomatic firearm fired from the shoulder or hip

sub·mar·gin·al (sub mär′ji n'l) *adj.* **1.** below minimum requirements or standards [*submarginal housing*] **2.** not producing a satisfactory return [*submarginal land*] —**sub·mar′gin·al·ly** *adv.*

sub·ma·rine (sub′mə rēn′; *for n. & v., usually* sub′mə rēn′) *adj.* being, living, used, etc. beneath the surface of the sea —*n.* **1.** a submarine plant or animal **2.** a kind of warship, armed with torpedoes, etc., that can operate under water —*vt.* -rined′, -rin′ing to attack or torpedo with a submarine

SUBMACHINE GUN

☆**submarine sandwich** same as HERO SANDWICH

sub·max·il·lar·y (sub mak′sə ler′ē) *adj.* [see SUB- & MAXILLARY] of or below the lower jaw; esp., designating of or either of two salivary glands, one on each side, beneath the lower jaw

sub·merge (səb murj′) *vt.* -merged′, -merg′ing [< L. < *sub-*, under + *mergere*, to plunge] **1.** to place under or as under water, etc. [*to submerge land in damming a river*] **2.** to cover over; suppress; hide [*to submerge anger under a calm appearance*]* **3.** to sink below a decent level of life *[the submerged people of the slums]* —*vi.* to sink or plunge beneath the surface of water, etc. —**sub·mer′gence** *n.* —**sub·mer′gi·ble** *adj.*

sub·merse (səb murs′) *vt.* **-mersed′, -mers′ing** [< L. pp. of *submergere*] *same as* SUBMERGE —**sub·mer′sion** (-mur′zhən, -shən) *n.*

sub·mers·i·ble (-mur′sə b′l) *adj.* that can be submerged —*n.* any of various ships that can operate under water

sub·mi·cro·scop·ic (sub′mī krə skäp′ik) *adj.* too small to be seen through an ordinary microscope

sub·mis·sion (səb mish′ən) *n.* [OFr. < L. < pp. of *submittere*] **1.** a submitting, giving up, or surrendering *[he brought the rebels to submission]* **2.** a being obedient or humble *[the queen's subject knelt in submission]* **3.** a submitting of something to another for decision or careful thought *[the submission of a petition to the President]*

sub·mis·sive (-mis′iv) *adj.* willing to give in to or obey another; humble; obedient —see SYN. at OBEDIENT —**sub·mis′sive·ly** *adv.* —**sub·mis′sive·ness** *n.*

sub·mit (səb mit′) *vt.* **-mit′ted, -mit′ting** [< L. < *sub-*, under + *mittere*, to send] **1.** to present to others for them to look over, decide about, etc. *[a new levy was submitted to the voters]* **2.** to give in to the control, power, etc. of another; also, to allow (oneself) to undergo treatment, analysis, etc. *[he submitted himself to their questioning]* **3.** to offer as an opinion; suggest *[I submit that we cannot accept his plan]* —*vi.* **1.** *a)* to give in to the power, control, etc. of another *[the enemy will never submit]* *b)* to give oneself up (*to* treatment, analysis, etc.) **2.** to give in to another's judgment or decision **3.** to be submissive, obedient, etc. —see SYN. at SURRENDER —**sub·mit′ta·ble** *adj.* —**sub·mit′tal** *n.* —**sub·mit′ter** *n.*

sub·nor·mal (sub nôr′m'l) *adj.* below the normal; less than normal, as in intelligence —*n.* a subnormal person —**sub′nor·mal′i·ty** (-mal′ə tē) *n.* —**sub·nor′mal·ly** *adv.*

sub·or·bit·al (sub ôr′bit 'l) *adj.* **1.** designating or of a spaceflight in which the spacecraft follows a steep, short path instead of going into orbit **2.** beneath the eye's orbit

sub·or·der (sub′ôr′dər) *n.* a subdivision of an order, esp. as a classification of plants or animals

sub·or·di·nate (sə bôr′də nit; *for v.* -nāt′) *adj.* [< ML. pp. of *subordinare* < L. *sub-*, under + *ordinare*, to order] **1.** below another in rank, power, importance, etc.; secondary *[a subordinate job]* **2.** under the power or authority of another *[the firemen are subordinate to their chief]* **3.** *Gram.* that is dependent on another part: see SUBORDINATE CLAUSE —*n.* a subordinate person or thing —*vt.* **-nat′ed, -nat′ing** to place in a lower position; treat as or make less important or secondary *[we subordinated our wishes to his]* —**sub·or′di·nate·ly** *adv.* —**sub·or′di·na′tion** *n.* —**sub·or′di·na′tive** (-nāt′iv) *adj.*

subordinate clause a clause that cannot stand alone and is being used as a noun, adjective, or adverb in a sentence; dependent clause (Example: she will visit us *if she can*)

subordinating conjunction a conjunction that is used at the beginning of a subordinate clause, as *if, as, so, unless, although, when*): also **subordinate conjunction**

sub·orn (sə bôrn′) *vt.* [< MFr. < L. *sub-*, under + *ornare*, to furnish] **1.** to get by bribery or other illegal methods **2.** to lead on or urge (another) to do something illegal, esp. to commit perjury —**sub·or·na·tion** (sub′ôr nā′shən) *n.* —**sub·or′na·tive** *adj.* —**sub·orn′er** *n.*

sub·plot (sub′plät′) *n.* a secondary or subordinate plot in a play, novel, etc.

sub·poe·na (sə pē′nə) *n.* [< ML. *sub poena*, lit., under penalty: see SUB- & PAIN] a written legal order telling a person to appear in court to give testimony, show certain records, etc. —*vt.* **-naed, -na·ing** **1.** to summon with such an order ☆**2.** to order that (certain records, documents, etc.) be brought to a court Also sp. **sub·pe′na**

sub·pop·u·la·tion (sub′päp yə lā′shən) *n.* a subdivision of a population, having certain characteristics in common

sub·ro·gate (sub′rə gāt′) *vt.* **-gat′ed, -gat′ing** [< L. pp. of *subrogare, surrogare:* see SURROGATE] to substitute (one person) for another; esp., to substitute (one creditor) for another —**sub′ro·ga′tion** *n.*

sub ro·sa (sub rō′zə) [L., under the rose, an ancient symbol of secrecy] secretly; privately

sub·rou·tine (sub′rōō tēn′) *n.* a short set of instructions, often used repeatedly, that directs a digital computer in the solution of part of a problem

sub·scribe (səb skrīb′) *vt.* **-scribed′, -scrib′ing** [L. *subscribere:* see SUB- & SCRIBE] **1.** to sign (one's name) at the end of a document, etc. **2.** to write one's signature on (a document, etc.) to show approval, agreement, etc. **3.** to promise to contribute (money) —*vi.* **1.** to sign one's name to a document, etc. **2.** to give support or approval (*to*) *[to subscribe to certain ideas]* **3.** to promise to contribute, or to give, a sum of money *[to subscribe to a building fund for a new hospital]* **4.** to agree to receive and pay for a magazine, theater tickets, etc. for a specified period (with *to*) —**sub·scrib′er** *n.*

sub·script (sub′skript) *adj.* [< L. pp. of *subscribere*, SUBSCRIBE] written below —*n.* a figure, letter, or symbol written below and to the side of another *[in Y_3 and X_a, 3 and *a* are subscripts]*

sub·scrip·tion (səb skrip′shən) *n.* **1.** the act of subscribing **2.** something subscribed; specif., *a)* a written signature at the end of a document *b)* a signed document *c)* agreement or approval, esp. in writing *d)* an amount of money subscribed *e)* a formal agreement to receive and pay for a magazine, theater tickets, etc. for a specified period

sub·sec·tion (sub′sek′shən) *n.* a subdivision of any of the sections into which a group, document, etc. is divided

sub·se·quent (sub′si kwənt, -kwent′) *adj.* [< L. prp. of *subsequi < sub-*, after + *sequi*, to follow] coming after; following in time, place, or order *[subsequent events]* —**subsequent to** after; following —**sub′se·quence′** *n.* —**sub′se·quent·ly** *adv.*

sub·serve (səb surv′) *vt.* **-served′, -serv′ing** to be useful or helpful to (a cause, etc.); serve; aid

sub·ser·vi·ent (-sur′vē ənt) *adj.* **1.** useful as a means to something more important **2.** very obedient and eager to please; submissive; obsequious —**sub·ser′vi·ence, sub·ser′vi·en·cy** *n.* —**sub·ser′vi·ent·ly** *adv.*

sub·set (sub′set′) *n.* a mathematical set containing some or all of the elements of a given set

sub·side (səb sīd′) *vi.* **-sid′ed, -sid′ing** [< L. < *sub-*, under + *sidere*, to settle] **1.** to sink to the bottom; settle, as sediment **2.** to sink to a lower level *[in June, the river began to subside]* **3.** to become quiet or less active; abate *[her anger subsided]* —see SYN. at WANE —**sub·sid′ence** (-sīd′'ns, sub′si dəns) *n.*

sub·sid·i·ar·y (səb sid′ē er′ē) *adj.* [< L. < *subsidium:* see SUBSIDY] **1.** giving aid, service, etc.; acting as a supplement; auxiliary **2.** being in a secondary position **3.** of, making up, or maintained by a subsidy or subsidies *[subsidiary payments]* —*n., pl.* **-ar′ies** a person or thing that is subsidiary; specif., a company (**subsidiary company**) controlled by another company that owns all or most of its shares —**sub·sid′i·ar′i·ly** *adv.*

sub·si·dize (sub′sə dīz′) *vt.* **-dized′, -diz′ing** **1.** to support with a subsidy *[college students subsidized by government funds]* **2.** to buy the aid of with a subsidy —**sub′si·di·za′tion** *n.* —**sub′si·diz′er** *n.*

sub·si·dy (sub′sə dē) *n., pl.* **-dies** [< Anglo-Fr. < L. *subsidium*, reserve troops, support] a grant of money; specif., a government grant to a private enterprise thought to be good for the public *[subsidies are given to farmers in crop-control programs]*

sub·sist (səb sist′) *vi.* [< L. < *sub-*, under + *sistere*, to stand] **1.** *a)* to continue to be or exist *b)* to continue to be in use, force, etc. **2.** to remain alive or continue to live (*on* specified foods, *by* specific means, etc.) **3.** to consist (*in*)

sub·sist·ence (-sis′təns) *n.* **1.** existence; being **2.** the act of providing food, etc. **3.** means of support or livelihood; specif., the barest means needed, as just enough food, to support life —**sub·sist′ent** *adj.*

sub·soil (sub′soil′) *n.* the layer of soil beneath the surface soil —*vt.* to turn up the subsoil of

sub·son·ic (sub sän′ik) *adj.* [SUB- + SONIC] **1.** designating, of, or moving at a speed in a surrounding fluid less than that of sound in the same fluid **2.** *same as* INFRASONIC

sub·spe·cies (sub′spē′shēz) *n.* any natural subdivision of a species that shows small differences in form from other subdivisions of the same species living in different regions

sub·stance (sub′stəns) *n.* [< OFr. < L. < *substare < sub-*, under + *stare*, to stand] **1.** the real or essential part of anything; essence **2.** *a)* the physical matter of which something is made; material *[a plastic substance much like leather]* *b)* matter of a particular kind or chemical composition [a sticky *substance*] **3.** solid or substantial quality; firmness, body, etc. [a gauzy fabric with no *substance*; a policy with little *substance*] **4.** the real content or meaning of something said or written [the *substance* of his remarks] **5.** material possessions; property; wealth [a man of *substance*] **—in substance 1.** basically; essentially [the movie is not changed *in substance* from the novel] **2.** actually; really

sub·stand·ard (sub stan′dərd) *adj.* below some standard set by law or custom [a *substandard* dwelling]

sub·stan·tial (səb stan′shəl) *adj.* **1.** of or having substance **2.** real; actual; true [his fears turned out not to be *substantial*] **3.** strong; solid; firm [the bridge did not look very *substantial*] **4.** more than average or usual; ample; large [a *substantial* share; a *substantial* meal] **5.** of considerable value; important [Einstein's *substantial* contribution to modern science **6.** wealthy or well-to-do [a *substantial* businessman] **7.** with regard to the main or basic parts [in *substantial* agreement] **—sub·stan′ti·al·i·ty** (-shē al′ə tē), **sub·stan′tial·ness** *n.* **—sub·stan′tial·ly** *adv.*

sub·stan·ti·ate (səb stan′shē āt′) *vt.* **-at′ed, -at′ing 1.** to give substance, real form, or body to **2.** to show to be true or real by giving evidence; prove [the experiments *substantiated* his theory] **—see** SYN. **at** CONFIRM **—sub·stan′ti·a′tion** *n.* **—sub·stan′ti·a′tive** *adj.* **—sub·stan′ti·a′tor** *n.*

sub·stan·tive (sub′stən tiv) *adj.* [< LL. < L. *substantia*, SUBSTANCE] **1.** having independent being or status **2.** of considerable amount **3.** actual; real **4.** *a)* basic; essential [a *substantive* part of a theory] *b)* having direct bearing on a matter [testimony *substantive* to the case] **5.** *Gram. a)* of or expressing existence [the *substantive* verb "to be"] *b)* of or used as a substantive **—n. 1.** something substantive **2.** a noun, or any word or group of words used as a noun in a sentence **—sub′stan·ti′val** (-tī′v'l) *adj.* **—sub′stan·ti′val·ly, sub·stan′tive·ly** *adv.* **—sub·stan′tive·ness** *n.*

sub·sta·tion (sub′stā′shən) *n.* a branch station, as of a post office

sub·sti·tute (sub′stə tōōt′, -tyōōt′) *n.* [< L. pp. of *substituere* < *sub-*, under + *statuere*, to put] a person or thing that takes the place of another **—vt. -tut′ed, -tut′ing** to put or use in place of another **—☆vi.** to act or serve in place of another [to *substitute* for an injured player] **—adj.** being a substitute **—sub′sti·tut′a·ble** *adj.* **—sub′sti·tu′tive** *adj.*

sub·sti·tu·tion (sub′stə tōō′shən, -tyōō′-) *n.* the substituting of one person or thing for another **—sub′sti·tu′tion·al, sub′sti·tu′tion·ar′y** *adj.*

sub·strate (sub′strāt) *n.* **1.** *same as* SUBSTRATUM **2.** *Biochem.* a substance acted upon, as by an enzyme

sub·stra·tum (sub′strāt′əm, -strat′-) *n., pl.* **-ta** (-ə), **-tums** [< L. pp. of *substernere* < *sub-*, under + *sternere*, to strew] **1.** a part, substance, etc. which lies beneath and supports another [land resting on a *substratum* of solid rock] **2.** any basis or foundation **3.** loosely, *same as* SUBSOIL

sub·struc·ture (-struk′chər) *n.* a structure acting as a support, base, or foundation **—sub·struc′tur·al** *adj.*

sub·sume (səb sōōm′, -syōōm′) *vt.* **-sumed′, -sum′ing** [< ModL. < L. *sub-*, under + *sumere*, to take] **1.** to include within a larger class, group, etc. **2.** to show (an idea, instance, etc.) to be covered by a rule, principle, etc.

sub·sur·face (sub′sur′fis) *adj.* lying below the surface, esp. of the earth, the oceans, etc. **—n.** a subsurface part

sub·sys·tem (-sis′təm) *n.* any system that is part of a larger system; component system

☆sub·teen (sub′tēn′) *n.* a child nearly a teen-ager; preteen

sub·tem·per·ate (sub tem′pər it) *adj.* of or occurring in the colder areas of the temperate zones

sub·ten·ant (-ten′ənt) *n.* one who rents from a tenant; tenant of a tenant **—sub·ten′an·cy** *n.*

sub·tend (səb tend′) *vt.* [< L. < *sub-*, under + *tendere*, to stretch] **1.** to extend under or be opposite to in position [each side of a triangle *subtends* the opposite angle] **2.** *Bot.* to enclose in an angle, as between a leaf and its stem

sub·ter·fuge (sub′tər fyōōj′) *n.* [< LL. < L. < *subter-*, below + *fugere*, to flee] any plan, action, etc. used to hide one's true purpose, avoid a difficult situation, etc.

sub·ter·ra·ne·an (sub′tə rā′nē ən) *adj.* [< L. < *sub-*, under + *terra*, earth] **1.** being, living, or working beneath the earth's surface; underground [a *subterranean* river] **2.** secret; hidden Also **sub′ter·ra′ne·ous** **—sub′ter·ra′ne·an·ly, sub′ter·ra′ne·ous·ly** *adv.*

sub·tile (sut′'l, sub′til) *adj. now rare var.* of SUBTLE **—sub′tile-**

ly *adv.* **—sub′tile·ness** *n.* **—sub′til·ty, sub·til·i·ty** (səb til′ə-tē) *n., pl.* **-ties**

sub·til·ize (sut′'l īz′, sub′t'l-) *vt., vi.* **-ized′, -iz′ing 1.** to make or become subtle **2.** to discuss or argue in a subtle way **—sub′-til·i·za′tion** *n.*

sub·ti·tle (sub′tīt′'l) *n.* **1.** a secondary title of a book, play, etc. **2.** one or more lines of dialogue or description flashed on a movie or TV screen, esp. at the bottom in translation **—vt.** **-ti′tled, -ti′tling** to add a subtitle or subtitles to

sub·tle (sut′'l) *adj.* **sub′tler** (-lər, -'l ər), **sub′tlest** (-list, -'l ist) [< OFr. < L. *subtilis*, orig., closely woven < *sub-*, under + *tela*, web] **1.** thin; not dense or heavy [a *subtle* gas] **2.** having or showing a keenness about small differences in meaning, etc. [a *subtle* thinker, *subtle* reasoning] **3.** hard to see or understand [a *subtle* problem] **4.** delicately skillful; deft or ingenious [a *subtle* design in lace] **5.** not open or direct; sly, clever, crafty, etc. or veiled, mysterious, etc. [a *subtle* hint, a *subtle* smile] **6.** not sharp or strong; delicate [a *subtle* shade of red, a *subtle* perfume] **—sub′tle·ness** *n.* **—sub′tly** *adv.*

sub·tle·ty (-tē) *n.* **1.** the quality or condition of being subtle **2.** *pl.* **-ties** something subtle, as a fine difference of meaning

sub·ton·ic (sub tän′ik) *n. Music* the seventh tone of a diatonic scale

sub·top·ic (sub′täp′ik) *n.* a topic that is a division of a main topic

sub·to·tal (-tōt′'l) *n.* a total forming part of a final, complete total **—vt., vi.** **-taled** or **-talled, -tal·ing** or **-tal·ling** to add up so as to form a subtotal

sub·tract (səb trakt′) *vt., vi.* [< L. pp. of *subtrahere* < *sub-*, under + *trahere*, to draw] to take away or deduct (a part from a whole) or (one number or quantity from another) [*subtracting* 2 from 7 leaves 5; the small mole on her face does not *subtract* from her beauty] **—sub·tract′er** *n.* **—sub·trac′tive** *adj.*

sub·trac·tion (-trak′shən) *n.* a subtracting or being subtracted; esp., the process of finding the difference between two numbers or quantities

sub·tra·hend (sub′trə hend′) *n.* [< L. gerundive of *subtrahere*: see SUBTRACT] a number or quantity to be subtracted from another

☆sub·treas·ur·y (sub′trezh′ər ē, sub trezh′-) *n., pl.* **-ur·ies** a branch treasury

sub·trop·i·cal (sub träp′i k'l) *adj.* designating, of, or belonging to regions bordering on the tropical zone; nearly tropical in climate, features, etc.: also **sub·trop′ic**

sub·trop·ics (-iks) *n.pl.* subtropical regions

sub·urb (sub′ərb) *n.* [< L. < *sub-*, under, near + *urbs*, town] **1.** a district, town, etc. on the outskirts of a city **2.** [*pl.*] a region of such districts (with *the*)

sub·ur·ban (sə bur′bən) *adj.* **1.** of or living in a suburb or the suburbs **2.** typical of the suburbs or suburbanites [*suburban* attitudes] **—sub·ur′ban·ize′** (-īz′) *vt., vi.* **-ized′, -iz′ing**

sub·ur·ban·ite (-īt′) *n.* a person living in a suburb

sub·ur·bi·a (sə bur′bē ə) *n.* the suburbs or suburbanites as a group: used to suggest suburban values, attitudes, etc.

sub·ven·tion (səb ven′shən) *n.* [< OFr. < LL. < L. < *sub-*, under + *venire*, to come] a grant of money; subsidy

sub·ver·sion (səb vur′zhən, -shən) *n.* a subverting or being subverted; ruin; overthrow

sub·ver·sive (-siv) *adj.* tending or seeking to subvert, overthrow, or destroy (an established government, institution, belief, etc.) **—n.** a person regarded as subversive **—sub·ver′sive·ly** *adv.* **—sub·ver′sive·ness** *n.*

sub·vert (səb vurt′) *vt.* [< MFr. < L. < *sub-*, under + *vertere*, to turn] **1.** to overthrow or destroy (something established) **2.** to weaken or undermine the beliefs, principles, or loyalty of; corrupt **—sub·vert′er** *n.*

sub·way (sub′wā′) *n.* ☆**1.** an underground electric railway in some large cities **2.** any underground way or passage

suc- *same as* SUB-: used before *c*

suc·ceed (sək sēd′) *vi.* [L. *succedere* < *sub-*, under + *cedere*, to go] **1.** *a)* to come next after another *b)* to follow another into office, possession, etc., as by election (often with *to*) [the prince *succeeded* to the throne] **2.** to happen or turn out as planned [a plan that *succeeded*] **3.** to manage to do something planned or tried [to *succeed* in convincing someone] **4.** to have success as in a career; gain wealth, fame, position, etc. [to *succeed* in business] **—vt. 1.** to follow into office, etc. [Harding *succeeded* Wilson as President] **2.** to come after; follow

suc·cess (sək ses′) *n.* [< L. < pp. of *succedere:* see SUCCEED] **1.** *a)* a favorable outcome; the result that was hoped for [*success* in training a dog] *b)* something having a favorable outcome *[our play was a success]* **2.** the gaining of wealth, fame, etc. *[her success did not change her]* **3.** a successful person

suc·cess·ful (-fəl) *adj.* **1.** turning out to be as was hoped for **2.** having gained wealth, fame, etc. —**suc·cess′ful·ly** *adv.* —**suc·cess′ful·ness** *n.*

suc·ces·sion (sək sesh′ən) *n.* **1.** a succeeding or coming after another in sequence or to an office, etc. *[the succession of a new king to the throne]* **2.** the right to succeed to an office, etc. **3.** a number of persons or things coming one after another; series; sequence *[a succession of delays]* **4.** *a)* a series of heirs or rightful successors *b)* the order or line of such a series *[the Vice President is first in succession to the President]* —see SYN. at SERIES —**in succession** one after another

suc·ces·sive (sək ses′iv) *adj.* **1.** coming one after another; consecutive *[winning six successive games]* **2.** of succession —**suc·ces′sive·ly** *adv.* —**suc·ces′sive·ness** *n.*

suc·ces·sor (-ər) *n.* a person or thing that succeeds, or follows, another; esp., one who succeeds to an office, etc.

suc·cinct (sək siŋkt′) *adj.* *[< L. pp. of succingere, to tuck up < sub-, under + cingere, to gird]* **1.** clearly and briefly stated; terse *[a succinct explanation]* **2.** concise and to the point in speaking —see SYN. at CONCISE —**suc·cinct′ly** *adv.* —**suc·cinct′ness** *n.*

suc·cor (suk′ər) *vt.* *[< OFr. < L. succurrere < sub-, under + currere, to run]* to help in time of need or distress —*n.* **1.** aid; help **2.** a person or thing that succors, or aids —see SYN. at HELP Also, Brit. sp., **suc′cour**

☆**suc·co·tash** (suk′ə tash′) *n.* *[< AmInd.]* a dish of lima beans and kernels of corn cooked together

Suc·coth (soo kôt′, sook′ōs) *n.* same as SUKKOT

suc·cu·bus (suk′yoo bəs) *n., pl.* **-bi′** (-bī′) *[< ML., ult. < L. sub-, under + cubare, to lie]* a female demon thought in medieval times to have sexual intercourse with sleeping men: also **suc′cu·ba** (-bə), *pl.* **-bae′** (-bē′)

suc·cu·lent (suk′yoo lənt) *adj.* *[L. succulentus < sucus, juice]* **1.** juicy, esp. in a way that is tasty or delicious *[a succulent peach]* **2.** pleasing, appealing, attractive, etc. **3.** *Bot.* having thick, fleshy tissues for storing water, as a cactus —*n.* a succulent plant —**suc′cu·lence, suc′cu·len·cy** *n.* —**suc′cu·lent·ly** *adv.*

suc·cumb (sə kum′) *vi.* *[L. succumbere < sub-, under + cumbere, to lie]* **1.** to give in (*to*); yield *[to succumb to curiosity]* **2.** to die *[to succumb to a plague]* —see SYN. at YIELD

such (such) *adj.* *[OE. swilc, swelc]* **1.** *a)* of the kind mentioned or implied *[one such as she]* *b)* of the same or a similar kind *[pens, pencils, and such supplies]* **2.** certain but not specified; whatever *[at such time as you go]* **3.** so great, so much, etc. *[such fun!]* *Such* is used, with *as* or *that*, in making comparisons *[such wit as his is rare]* An article may occur between *such* and the noun it modifies *[such a fool!]* —*adv.* to so great a degree *[such good news]* —*pron.* **1.** such a person or thing *[such as live by the sword]* **2.** that which has been mentioned or suggested *[such was her nature]* —**as such 1.** as being what is mentioned or meant *[he is the mayor and as such must be consulted]* **2.** in itself *[a name, as such, means nothing]* —**such as 1.** for example **2.** like or similar to *[poets such as Frost]*

such and such (being) someone or something particular but not specified *[he went to such and such a place]*

such·like (such′līk′) *adj.* of such a kind; of similar kind —*pron.* persons or things of such kind

suck (suk) *vt.* *[OE. sucan < IE. base seu-, juice]* **1.** *a)* to draw (liquid) into the mouth by pulling with the lips, cheeks, and tongue *b)* to draw up (water, oil, etc.) by the action of a pump **2.** to take up or in as by sucking; absorb, inhale, etc. *[to suck air into the lungs]* **3.** to suck liquid from (a breast, fruit, etc.) **4.** to hold (hard candy, ice, etc.) in the mouth so it dissolves **5.** to place (the thumb, etc.) in the mouth and draw on as if sucking —*vi.* **1.** to perform the action of sucking something *[to suck on a pipe; to suck at an orange]* **2.** to suck milk from the breast or udder **3.** to make a sucking sound or movement —*n.* **1.** the act or sound of sucking **2.** *a)* something drawn in by sucking *b)* [Colloq.] the amount sucked at one time —**suck in 1.** to tighten and pull inward *[to suck in one's belly]* **2.** [Slang] to fool, swindle, etc. —**suck up to** [Slang] to flatter or act humbly toward

suck·er (suk′ər) *n.* **1.** one that sucks ☆**2.** a carplike freshwater fish with a mouth adapted for sucking **3.** a part used for sucking; specif., *a)* a tube through which something is sucked *b)* the piston or piston valve of a suction pump *c)* an organ used by the leech, octopus, etc. for sucking or holding fast to a surface by suction ☆**4.** a lollipop ☆**5.** [Slang] *a)* a person easily fooled or cheated; dupe *b)* a person easily attracted to something specified *[a sucker for shaggy dogs]* **6.** *Bot.* a shoot from a root bud or stem bud —*vt.* **1.** to remove suckers, or shoots, from ☆**2.** [Slang] to make a sucker of; trick —*vi.* to bear suckers, or shoots

SUCKERS

suck·le (suk′'l) *vt.* **-led, -ling** *[prob. < SUCKLING]* **1.** to give milk to from a breast or udder; nurse **2.** to bring up; nourish; foster *[suckled on legends of heroes]* —*vi.* to suck milk from its mother

suck·ling (-liŋ) *n.* *[see SUCK & -LING¹]* a child or young animal that is not yet weaned

Su·cre (soo′kre) city in SC Bolivia; legal capital & seat of the judiciary (see LA PAZ): pop. 85,000

su·cre (soo′kre) *n.* *[AmSp. after A. J. de Sucre, 19th-c. S. American liberator]* see MONETARY UNITS, table (Ecuador)

su·crose (soo′krōs) *n.* *[< Fr. sucre, sugar + -OSE¹]* *Chem.* pure crystalline sugar, $C_{12}H_{22}O_{11}$, obtained from sugar cane or sugar beets: it can be broken down into glucose and fructose

suc·tion (suk′shən) *n.* *[OFr. < L. < suctus, pp. of sugere, to suck]* **1.** the act or process of sucking **2.** the drawing of air out of a space to make a vacuum that will suck in surrounding air, liquid, etc. or cause something to stick to the surface **3.** the sucking force so created —*adj.* causing or working by suction

suction pump a pump that draws liquid up by suction created by pistons fitted with valves

suc·to·ri·al (suk tôr′ē əl) *adj.* *[< ModL. < L.: see SUCTION]* sucking or adapted for sucking

Su·dan (soo dan′) **1.** vast plains region in NC Africa, south of the Sahara: see map at SAHARA **2.** country in the E part of this region, south of Egypt: 967,500 sq. mi.; pop. 16,489,000; cap. Khartoum —**Su′da·nese′** (-də nēz′) *adj., n., pl.* **-nese′**

☆**Sudan grass** *[after prec.]* a tall annual grass grown for summer pasture and hay

Sud·bur·y (sud′ber′ē, -bər ē) city in SE Ontario, Canada: pop. 98,000

sud·den (sud′'n) *adj.* *[OFr. sodain < L. subitaneus, ult. < sub-, under + ire, to go]* **1.** *a)* happening or coming unexpectedly; not foreseen *[a sudden storm came up]* *b)* sharp or abrupt *[a sudden turn]* **2.** done, coming, or taking place quickly; hasty *[she made a sudden change in her plans]* —**all of a sudden** without warning; quickly; unexpectedly —**sud′den·ly** *adv.* —**sud′den·ness** *n.*

sudden death an extra period added to a tied game in some sports, the game ending as soon as one side scores

Su·de·ten land (soo dāt′'n land′; *G.* zoo dā′tən länt′) region in the Sudetes Mountains, N Czechoslovakia

Su·de·tes Mountains (soo dēt′ēz) mountain range along the borders of N Czechoslovakia & SW Poland

su·dor·if·er·ous (soo′də rif′ər əs) *adj.* *[< ModL. < L. sudor, sweat: see -FEROUS]* secreting sweat

su·dor·if·ic (soo′də rif′ik) *adj.* *[< ModL. < L. sudor, sweat + facere, to make]* causing or increasing sweating —*n.* a sudorific drug, etc.

suds (sudz) *n.pl.* *[prob. < MDu. sudse, marsh water]* **1.** foamy, soapy water **2.** foam, froth, or lather ☆**3.** [Slang] beer or ale —*vt.* to make suds —☆*vi.* [Colloq.] to wash or soak in suds —☆**suds′y** *adj.* **-i·er, -i·est**

sue (soo) *vt.* **sued, su′ing** *[OFr. sivre, suir, ult. < L. sequi, to follow]* **1.** to appeal to; petition **2.** to bring a lawsuit in court against *[to sue a person for damages]* **3.** [Archaic] to woo —*vi.* **1.** make an appeal; ask in a formal way *[the weary enemy sued for peace]* **2.** [Archaic] to woo **3.** to bring legal suit —see SYN. at APPEAL —**su′er** *n.*

suede, suède (swād) *n.* *[Fr. Suède, Sweden, in gants de Suède, Swedish gloves]* **1.** tanned leather with the flesh side rubbed until the nap is very soft and fine **2.** a kind of cloth made to look like this: also **suede cloth**

su·et (sōō′it) *n.* [dim. < Anglo-Fr. *sue* < OFr. < L. *sebum*, fat] hard fat from around the kidneys and loins of cattle and sheep: used in cooking and to make tallow —**su′et·y** *adj.*

Su·ez (sōō ez′, sōō′ez) **1.** seaport in NE Egypt, on the Suez Canal: pop. 203,000 **2. Gulf of,** NW arm of the Red Sea **3. Isthmus of,** strip of land in NE Egypt, connecting Asia & Africa

Suez Canal ship canal across the Isthmus of Suez, joining the Mediterranean & the Gulf of Suez

suf- *same as* SUB-: used before *f*

suf·fer (suf′ər) *vt.* [< Anglo-Fr. < OFr. < L. *sufferre* < *sub-*, under + *ferre*, to bear] **1.** to undergo (something painful or unpleasant, as injury, a loss, etc.) **2.** to experience or undergo (any process, esp. change) **3.** to allow; tolerate [he won't *suffer* criticism] **4.** to bear up under; endure [he could not *suffer* opposition] —*vi.* **1.** to undergo pain, harm, loss, or penalty, etc. [she *suffered* in the heat; his grades *suffered* by comparison with hers] —see SYN. at BEAR¹ —**suf′fer·a·ble** *adj.* —**suf′fer·er** *n.* —**suf′fer·ing** *n.*

suf·fer·ance (suf′ər əns, suf′rəns) *n.* **1.** power or ability to bear up under pain, etc. **2.** permission, toleration, etc. implied by not stopping or forbidding —**on sufferance** allowed or tolerated but not supported or encouraged

suf·fer·ing (suf′ər iŋ, suf′riŋ) *n.* **1.** the undergoing of pain, distress, or injury **2.** something suffered; pain, distress, or injury —see SYN. at DISTRESS

suf·fice (sə fīs′, -fīz′) *vi.* -ficed′, -fic′ing [< OFr. < L. *sufficere* < *sub-*, under + *facere*, to make] to be enough [one cake should *suffice* for serving the guests] —*vt.* to be enough for

suf·fi·cien·cy (sə fish′ən sē) *n.* **1.** sufficient means, ability, or resources; an amount that is enough [a *sufficiency* of funds] **2.** a being sufficient; adequacy

suf·fi·cient (-′nt) *adj.* [see SUFFICE] as much as is needed; enough [*sufficient* supplies to last through the month] —**suf·fi′cient·ly** *adv.*

suf·fix (suf′iks; *also for v.* sə fiks′) *n.* [< ModL. < L. pp. of *suffigere* < *sub-*, under + *figere*, to fix] a letter, syllable, or group of syllables added at the end of a word or word base to change the meaning or give grammatical function (Examples: -*ish* in *smallish*, -*ed* in *walked*) —*vt.* to add as a suffix —**suf′fix·al** *adj.*

suf·fo·cate (suf′ə kāt′) *vt.* -cat′ed, -cat′ing [< L. pp. of *suffocare* < *sub-*, under + *fauces*, throat] **1.** to kill by cutting off the supply of oxygen to the lungs, gills, etc. **2.** to hinder the free breathing of **3.** to smother, put down, etc. —*vi.* **1.** to die by being suffocated **2.** to be unable to breathe freely; choke, etc. —**suf′fo·cat′ing·ly** *adv.* —**suf′fo·ca′tion** *n.* —**suf′fo·ca′tive** *adj.*

suf·fra·gan (suf′rə gən) *n.* [MFr. < ML. < L. *suffragari*, to support] **1.** a bishop assisting another bishop **2.** any bishop in relation to his archbishop —*adj.* **1.** designating or of such a bishop **2.** subordinate to a larger see

suf·frage (suf′rij) *n.* [MFr. < ML. < L. *suffragium*, a vote < *sub-*, under + *fragor*, loud applause] **1.** a short prayer of supplication **2.** a vote or voting ☆**3.** the right to vote in political elections

suf·fra·gette (suf′rə jet′) *n.* a woman who works for women's right to vote: term used in the early 20th cent. —**suf′fra·get′ism** *n.*

suf·fra·gist (suf′rə jist) *n.* a person who believes in extending the right to vote

suf·fuse (sə fyōōz′) *vt.* -fused′, -fus′ing [< L. pp. of *suffundere* < *sub-*, under + *fundere*, to pour] to spread over so as to fill with a glow, color, fluid, etc.: said of light, a blush, air, etc. —**suf·fu′sion** (-fyōō′zhən) *n.* —**suf·fu′sive** (-siv) *adj.*

Su·fi (sōō′fē) *n.* [Ar. *ṣūfī*, ascetic, lit., (a man) of wool < *ṣūf*, wool] a member of an Islamic group practicing a form of mysticism originated in Persia —**Su′fism** (-fiz′m) *n.*

sug- *same as* SUB-: used before *g*

sug·ar (shoog′ər) *n.* [OFr. *sucre*, ult. < Per. *šakar* < Sans. *śār-*

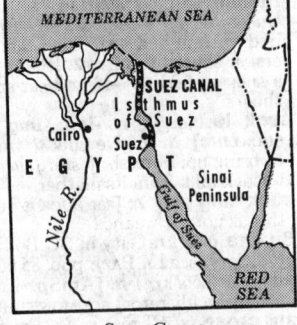

SUEZ CANAL

karâ] **1.** any of certain sweet substances in the form of crystals that dissolve in water, including sucrose, lactose, maltose, glucose, fructose, etc.: the sugars make up a class of carbohydrates **2.** sucrose in crystalline or powdered form: it is the common sugar used to sweeten food **3.** a bowl for sugar, specif. as forming a set with a creamer **4.** *short for* SUGAR DIABETES **5.** [Colloq.] sweetheart **6.** [Slang] money —*vt.* **1.** to put sugar on or in [*sugared* cookies] **2.** to make seem pleasant or less bad [*sugared* criticism] —*vi.* ☆**1.** to form sugar [the grape jelly *sugared*] ☆**2.** to boil down maple syrup to form maple sugar (usually with *off*) —**sug′ar·less** *adj.* —**sug′ar·like′** *adj.*

sugar beet a variety of beet with a white root from which common sugar is got

sug·ar·bush (-boosh′) *n.* a grove of sugar maples

sugar cane a very tall, tropical grass with thick, jointed stems, grown as the main source of common sugar

sug·ar·coat (-kōt′) *vt.* **1.** to cover or coat (pills, etc.) with sugar **2.** to make seem less unpleasant [to *sugarcoat* bad news]

☆**sug·ar·cured** (-kyoord′) *adj.* treated with a pickling preparation of sugar, salt, and nitrate or nitrite, as ham

sugar diabetes *popular name for* DIABETES MELLITUS

sugar loaf 1. a cone-shaped mass of crystallized sugar **2.** a similarly shaped hill, etc.

☆**sugar maple** an eastern N. American maple valued for its hard wood and for its sap, from which maple syrup is made

sugar of lead *same as* LEAD ACETATE

☆**sugar pine** a giant pine of the Pacific coast, with soft, reddish-brown wood, large cones, and sugarlike resin

sug·ar·plum (-plum′) *n.* a round or oval piece of sugary candy

sug·ar·y (shoog′ər ē) *adj.* **1.** of, like, or containing sugar; sweet, granular, etc. **2.** too sweet or sentimental; sweet in a false way [*sugary* words] —**sug′ar·i·ness** *n.*

sug·gest (səg jest′; *also, & Brit. usually,* sə jest′) *vt.* [< L. pp. of *suggerere* < *sub-*, under + *gerere*, to carry] **1.** to mention as something to think over, act on, etc.; bring to the mind for consideration [I *suggest* we meet again] **2.** to call to mind as something similar or somehow connected [objects *suggested* by the shapes of clouds] **3.** to propose (someone or something) as a possibility [to *suggest* a course of study] **4.** to show indirectly; imply; intimate [a silence that *suggested* agreement] —**sug·gest′er** *n.*

SYN.—**suggest** implies a putting of something into the mind either on purpose, as in making a proposal [I *suggest* you leave now], or through thinking of things that are alike or related in some way [the smell of ether *suggests* a hospital]; **imply** stresses the putting into the mind of something meant by, but not always directly stated in, a word, a remark, etc. [his answer *implied* a refusal]; **hint** applies to faint or indirect suggestion that is meant to be understood [he *hinted* that he would come]; **intimate** suggests a making known indirectly by a very slight hint [the news reporter *intimated* that the man was guilty]; **insinuate** implies the subtle hinting of something unpleasant or of that which one lacks the courage to say outright [are you *insinuating* that she is dishonest?]

sug·gest·i·ble (-jes′tə b'l) *adj.* easily influenced by suggestion —**sug·gest′i·bil′i·ty** *n.*

sug·ges·tion (səg jes′chən) *n.* **1.** the act of suggesting [it was done at her *suggestion*] **2.** something suggested **3.** the process by which one idea leads to another through thinking of things that are alike or related in some way **4.** a faint hint; trace [a *suggestion* of a smile crossed his face] **5.** *Psychol.* the bringing on of an idea that is accepted or acted on willingly without questioning, as in hypnosis

sug·ges·tive (-jes′tiv) *adj.* **1.** that suggests or tends to suggest ideas, etc. [a painting with abstract forms *suggestive* of faces] **2.** tending to suggest something considered improper or indecent —**sug·ges′tive·ly** *adv.* —**sug·ges′tive·ness** *n.*

su·i·ci·dal (sōō′ə sīd′əl) *adj.* **1.** of, involving, or leading to suicide **2.** having an urge to commit suicide **3.** rash to the point of being dangerous or disastrous [*suicidal* speeds] —**su′i·ci′dal·ly** *adv.*

su·i·cide (sōō′ə sīd′) *n.* [L. *sui*, of oneself + -CIDE] **1.** the act of killing oneself on purpose **2.** ruin of one's interests through one's own actions **3.** a person who commits suicide

su·i ge·ne·ris (sōō′ē jen′ər is, sōō′ī) [L., lit., of his (or her or its) own kind] like nothing or no one else; altogether unique

SUGAR CANE

suit (sōōt) *n.* [OFr. *suite,* ult. < L. *sequi,* to follow] **1.** *a)* a set of clothes to be worn together; esp., a coat and trousers (or skirt), usually of the same material *b)* any complete outfit [a *suit* of armor] **2.** a set or series of similar things; specif., any of the four sets of thirteen playing cards each (*spades, clubs, hearts, diamonds*) in a pack **3.** a lawsuit **4.** the act of suing, pleading, or wooing —*vt.* **1.** to meet the needs of; be right for or becoming to [this color *suits* your complexion] **2.** to make fit; adapt [a dance *suited* to the music] **3.** to please; satisfy [you can't *suit* everyone] **4.** to furnish with clothes, esp. with a suit —*vi.* to be suitable, convenient, or satisfactory —**bring suit** to start legal action; sue —**follow suit 1.** to play a card of the same suit as the card led **2.** to follow the example set —**suit oneself** to do as one pleases —☆**suit up** to put on a spacesuit, athletic uniform, etc. in getting ready for a particular activity

suit·a·ble (sōōt'ə b'l) *adj.* right for the purpose, occasion etc.; fitting; appropriate —see SYN. at FIT[1] —**suit'a·bil'i·ty, suit'a·ble·ness** *n.* —**suit'a·bly** *adv.*

suit·case (-kās') *n.* a travel case for clothes, etc., esp. a rectangular one that opens into two hinged compartments

suite (swēt; *for 2 b, occas.* sōōt) *n.* [Fr.: see SUIT] **1.** a group of attendants or servants; retinue **2.** a set or series of related things; specif., *a)* a unit of connected rooms [a hotel *suite*] *b)* a set of matched furniture for a room [a bedroom *suite*] **3.** *Music* an instrumental composition made up of several movements or, in earlier times, dances

suit·ing (sōōt'iŋ) *n.* cloth for making suits

suit·or (sōōt'ər) *n.* **1.** a person who sues, petitions, pleads, etc. **2.** a man courting a woman

☆**su·ki·ya·ki** (sōō'kē yä'kē) *n.* [Jpn.] a Japanese dish of thinly sliced meat, onions, and other vegetables cooked quickly, often at table, with soy sauce, sake, sugar, etc.

Suk·kot, Suk·koth (soo kōt', sook'ōs) *n.* [Heb. *sukkōth,* lit., tabernacles] a Jewish festival in early fall, celebrating the harvest and commemorating the desert wandering of the Hebrews during the Exodus: also **Suk'kos** (sook'ōs)

sul·cus (sul'kəs) *n., pl.* **-ci** (-sī) [< L.] a groove or furrow; esp., *Anat.* any of the shallow grooves separating the convolutions of the brain —**sul'cate** (-kāt), **sul'cat·ed** *adj.*

Su·lei·man (I) (sōō'lā män') 1494?–1566; sultan of the Ottoman Empire (1520–66)

sulf- *a combining form meaning* of or containing sulfur-

sul·fa (sul'fə) *adj.* designating or of a family of drugs that are sulfonamides, used in treating certain bacterial infections

sul·fa·di·a·zine (sul'fə dī'ə zēn', -zin) *n.* [prec. + DI-[1] + AZ(O) + -INE[4]] a sulfa drug, $C_{10}H_{10}N_4O_2S$, used in treating meningitis and certain infections of the intestines, etc.

sul·fa·nil·a·mide (-nil'ə mīd', -mid) *n.* [SULFA + ANIL(INE) + AMIDE] the earliest of the sulfa drugs, formerly used against certain infections

sul·fate (sul'fāt) *n.* a salt or ester of sulfuric acid

sul·fide (sul'fīd) *n.* a compound of sulfur with another element or a radical

sul·fite (-fīt) *n.* a salt or ester of sulfurous acid

sul·fon·a·mide (sul fän'ə mīd', -mid) *n.* [< *sulfon(yl),* the radical SO_2 + AMIDE] a compound, as sulfadiazine, containing the radical $-SO_2NH_2$; sulfa drug

sul·fur (sul'fər) *n.* [L. *sulphur, sulfur*] **1.** a pale-yellow, solid substance, often in the form of crystals, that is a nonmetallic chemical element: it burns with a blue flame and choking fumes: symbol, S; at. wt., 32.064; at. no., 16 **2.** any of numerous butterflies with dark-bordered, yellow or orange wings **3.** a greenish-yellow color —*vt.* to sulfurize

sul·fu·rate (sul'fyoo rāt', -fə-) *vt.* **-rat'ed, -rat'ing** *same as* SULFURIZE —**sul'fu·ra'tion** *n.*

sul·fur-bot·tom (sul'fər bät'əm) *n. same as* BLUE WHALE

sulfur dioxide a heavy, colorless, suffocating gas, SO_2, easily liquefied and used as a bleach, preservative, etc.

sul·fu·re·ous (sul fyoor'ē əs) *adj.* **1.** of, like, or containing sulfur **2.** greenish-yellow

sul·fu·ret (sul'fyoo ret') *vt.* **-ret'ed** or **-ret'ted, -ret'ing** or **-ret'ting** *same as* SULFURIZE

sul·fu·ric (sul fyoor'ik) *adj.* **1.** of or containing sulfur, esp. sulfur with a valence of six **2.** of or derived from sulfuric acid

sulfuric acid an oily, colorless liquid, H_2SO_4, that is a strong acid and is used in making explosives, fertilizers, chemicals, etc.

sul·fu·rize (sul'fyoo rīz', -fə-) *vt.* **-rized', -riz'ing** to combine or treat with sulfur or a sulfur compound —**sul'fu·ri·za'tion** *n.*

sul·fu·rous (sul'fər əs; *for 1 usually* sul fyoor'əs) *adj.* **1.** of or containing sulfur, esp. sulfur with a valence of four **2.** like burning sulfur in odor, color, etc. **3.** of or suggesting the fires of hell **4.** violently emotional; fiery —**sul'fu·rous·ly** *adv.* —**sul'fu·rous·ness** *n.*

sulfurous acid a colorless acid, H_2SO_3, known only in the form of its salts or in solution in water, and used as a chemical reagent, a bleach, etc.

sul·fur·y (sul'fər ē) *adj.* of or like sulfur

sulk (sulk) *vi.* [< SULKY] to be sulky —*n.* **1.** a sulky mood or state: also **the sulks 2.** a sulky person

sulk·y (sul'kē) *adj.* **sulk'i·er, sulk'i·est** [prob. < OE. *solcen,* idle] sullen in a pouting or cross way [a *sulky* child] —*n., pl.* **sulk'ies** a light, two-wheeled carriage for one person, esp., now, one used in harness races —**sulk'i·ly** *adv.* —**sulk'i·ness** *n.*

SULKY

Sul·la (sul'ə) (*Lucius Cornelius Sulla Felix*) 138?–78 B.C.; Rom. general; dictator of Rome (82–79)

sul·len (sul'ən) *adj.* [ult. < L. *solus,* alone] **1.** silent and keeping to oneself because one feels angry, bitter, hurt, etc. **2.** gloomy; dismal; depressing [a *sullen* day] **3.** somber; dull [*sullen* colors] —**sul'len·ly** *adv.* —**sul'len·ness** *n.*

Sul·li·van (sul'ə vən), Sir **Arthur Sey·mour** (sē'môr) 1842–1900; Eng. composer: see Sir William GILBERT

sul·ly (sul'ē) *vt.* **-lied, -ly·ing** [prob. < OFr. *souiller:* see SOIL[2]] to soil, stain, etc., now esp. by disgracing [to *sully* one's honor]

sulph- *now chiefly Brit. sp.* of SULF-: for words beginning **sulph-,** see forms under **sulf-**

sul·phur (sul'fər) *n. now chiefly Brit. sp.* of SULFUR

sul·tan (sul't'n) *n.* [Fr. < Ar. *sultān*] a Moslem ruler; esp., [S-] formerly, the ruler of Turkey

sul·tan·a (sul tan'ə, -tä'nə) *n.* **1.** a sultan's wife, mother, sister, or daughter: also **sul'tan·ess** (-tən is) **2.** a small, white, seedless grape or raisin

sul·tan·ate (sul't'n it, -āt') *n.* the authority, office, reign, or territory of a sultan

sul·try (sul'trē) *adj.* **-tri·er, -tri·est** [var. of *sweltry:* see SWELTER] **1.** uncomfortably hot and moist; sweltering [a *sultry* summer day] **2.** very hot; fiery **3.** suggesting or showing passion, lust, etc. —**sul'tri·ly** *adv.* —**sul'tri·ness** *n.*

Su·lu Archipelago (sōō'lōō) group of islands in the Philippines, southwest of Mindanao

sum (sum) *n.* [< MFr. < L. *summa,* fem. of *summus,* highest] **1.** an amount of money [we paid the *sum* asked for] **2.** the whole amount; totality [the *sum* of one's experiences] **3.** the gist or summary of something said, done, etc.: usually in **sum and substance 4.** *a)* the result gotten by adding numbers or quantities *b)* a series of numbers to be added up, or any problem in arithmetic —*vt.* **summed, sum'ming 1.** to add up **2.** to summarize —*vi.* to get, or come to, a total —**in sum** to put it briefly; in short —**sum up 1.** to add up or collect into a whole or total **2.** to review briefly; summarize

sum- *same as* SUB-: used before *m*

su·mac, su·mach (shōō'mak, sōō'-) *n.* [MFr. < Ar. *summāq*] **1.** *a)* any of a group of nonpoisonous plants with compound leaves and cone-shaped clusters of hairy, red fruit *b)* the powdered leaves of some of these plants, used in tanning and dyeing **2.** any of several poisonous plants, as poison ivy: see also POISON SUMAC

SUMAC

Su·ma·tra (soo mä'trə) large island of Indonesia, south of the Malay Peninsula: c. 165,000 sq. mi. —**Su·ma'tran** *adj., n.*

Su·mer (sōō'mər) ancient region in the lower valley of the Euphrates River

---

fat, āpe, cär; ten, ēven; is, bīte; gō, hôrn, tōōl, look; oil, out; up, fur; get; joy; yet; chin; she; thin, then; zh, leisure; ŋ, ring; ə for *a* in *ago,* e in *agent,* i in *sanity,* o in *comply,* u in *focus;* ' as in *able* (ā'b'l); Fr. bal; ë, Fr. coeur; ö, Fr. feu; ô, Fr. mo*n;* ô, Fr. coq; u, Fr. duc; r, Fr. cri; H, G. ich; kh, G. doch; ‡ foreign; ☆ Americanism; < derived from. See inside front cover.

Su·mer·i·an (sōō mir′ē ən, -mer′-) *adj.* designating or of an ancient, non-Semitic people of Sumer —*n.* **1.** any of the Sumerian people **2.** the language of the Sumerians

‡**sum·ma cum lau·de** (sōōm′ə kōōm lou′de, sum′ə kum lō′dē) [L.] with the greatest praise: phrase used to show graduation with the highest honors from a college or university

sum·ma·rize (sum′ə rīz′) *vt.* -rized′, -riz′ing to make or be a summary of; tell briefly; sum up —**sum′ma·ri·za′tion** *n.* —**sum′ma·riz′er** *n.*

sum·ma·ry (sum′ə rē) *adj.* [< ML. < L. *summa,* a sum] **1.** briefly giving the general idea; concise; condensed [a *summary* report] **2.** done quickly and without going through the usual procedures or forms [*summary* punishment; a *summary* dismissal] —*n., pl.* -ries a brief report covering the main points; digest —see SYN. at ABRIDGMENT —**sum·mar·i·ly** (sə mer′ə lē, sum′ə·rə lē) *adv.*

sum·ma·tion (sə mā′shən) *n.* **1.** a summing up, to find a total **2.** a total **3.** a final summing up of arguments, as in a court trial or debate

sum·mer (sum′ər) *n.* [OE. *sumor*] **1.** the warmest season of the year, following spring **2.** a year as marked by this season [a youth of sixteen *summers*] **3.** any period thought of, like summer, as a time of growth, full development, etc. —*adj.* of, typical of, or suitable for summer [*summer* activities] —*vi.* to pass the summer [we *summer* in Maine] —*vt.* to keep or feed during the summer —**sum′mer·y** *adj.*

sum·mer·house (-hous′) *n.* a small, open building with a roof in a garden, park, etc., for providing a shady rest

summer house a house or cottage, as in the country, used during the summer

sum·mer·sault (sum′ər sôlt′) *n., vi. var. of* SOMERSAULT

☆**summer sausage** a type of hard, dried and smoked sausage that does not spoil easily

☆**summer school** a session at a school or college during the regular summer vacation

summer solstice the time in the Northern Hemisphere when the sun is farthest north of the celestial equator; June 21 or 22

☆**summer squash** any of various small garden squashes grown in summer and eaten before fully ripe

sum·mer·time (-tīm′) *n.* the season of summer

sum·mit (sum′it) *n.* [< OFr., ult. < L. *summus,* highest] **1.** the highest point or part; top; apex [the *summit* of a hill] **2.** the highest degree or state; acme [the *summit* of success] ☆**3.** a top level of officials; specif., in diplomacy, the level limited to heads of government [a meeting at the *summit*] —*adj.* ☆of the heads of government [a *summit* conference]

SYN.—**summit** refers to the topmost point of a hill or similar high place or to the highest reachable level, as of achievement or rank; **peak** refers to the highest of a number of high points, as in a mountain range or in some changing action or condition [at the *peak* of his powers as a writer]; **climax** applies to the highest point in interest, force, excitement, etc. in a scale of rising values; **acme** refers to the highest possible point of perfection in the development or progress of something; **apex** suggests the highest point of a geometric figure or of a career, process, etc.; **pinnacle,** in its figurative uses, can be substituted for **summit** or **peak,** but sometimes suggests a dizzy or unsteady height [the *pinnacle* of success]; **zenith** refers to the highest point in the heavens and thus suggests fame or success reached by a spectacular rise

sum·mon (sum′ən) *vt.* [< OFr., ult. < L. *summonere,* to remind secretly < *sub-,* secretly + *monere,* to warn] **1.** to call together; order to meet [the President *summoned* his Cabinet] **2.** to call for or send for with authority or urgency [the boy was *summoned* to the office by the principal] **3.** to order, as by a summons, to appear in court **4.** to call upon to do something [to *summon* the city to withstand the enemy's siege] **5.** to call forth; rouse (often with *up*) [*summon* up strength] —see SYN. at CALL —**sum′mon·er** *n.*

sum·mons (-ənz) *n., pl.* -mons·es [< Anglo-Fr. *somonse* < OFr.: see prec.] **1.** an order to come or do something; specif., *Law* an official order to appear in court, specif. as a defendant; also, the writ containing such an order **2.** a call, knock, etc. that summons —*vt.* [Colloq.] to serve a court summons upon

‡**sum·mum bo·num** (sōōm′əm bō′nəm) [L.] the highest, or supreme, good

Sum·ner (sum′nər), **Charles** 1811–74; U.S. statesman & abolitionist

su·mo (**wrestling**) (sōō′mō) [Jap. *sumō*] [*sometimes* S-] a kind of Japanese wrestling taken part in by a hereditary class of large, very heavy men

sump (sump) *n.* [ME. *sompe,* a swamp] a pit, cistern, cesspool, etc. for liquid to drain into

sump pump a pump for removing liquid from a sump

sump·ter (sump′tər) *n.* [< OFr. *sometier* < LL. *sagma,* pack-saddle] a pack animal

sump·tu·ar·y (sump′chōō wer′ē) *adj.* [< L. < *sumptus,* expense < pp. of *sumere,* to take] of or controlling expenses or spending

sump·tu·ous (sump′chōō wəs) *adj.* [< OFr. < L. < *sumptus:* see prec.] **1.** involving great expense; costly; lavish [a *sumptuous* feast] **2.** magnificent; splendid [a *sumptuous* palace] —**sump′tu·ous·ly** *adv.* —**sump′tu·ous·ness** *n.*

sum total 1. the total arrived at by adding up a sum or sums **2.** everything involved or included

sum·up (sum′up′) *n.* [Colloq.] a summarizing or summary

sun (sun) *n.* [OE. *sunne*] **1.** *a)* the star about which the earth and other planets revolve and which furnishes light, heat, and energy for the solar system: it is about 93 million miles from earth and about 864,400 miles in diameter *b)* its heat or light [to lie in the *sun*] **2.** any star that is the center of a planetary system **3.** something bright or hot like the sun **4.** [Poet.] *a)* a day *b)* a year *c)* a clime; climate —*vt., vi.* **sunned, sun′ning** to place or lie in the sun so as to warm, tan, bleach, etc. —**place in the sun** the condition of being recognized as important, famous, etc. —**under the sun** on earth; in the world

Sun. Sunday

sun·baked (sun′bākt′) *adj.* **1.** baked by the sun's heat, as bricks **2.** very dry, cracked, etc. by the sun's heat

sun bath exposure of the body to sunlight or a sunlamp

sun·bathe (-bāth′) *vi.* -bathed′, -bath′ing to take a sun bath —**sun′bath′er** *n.*

sun·beam (-bēm′) *n.* a ray or beam of sunlight

sun·bon·net (-bän′it) *n.* a large-brimmed bonnet with a back flap, worn to shade the face and neck from the sun, esp. formerly, by women and girls

sun·burn (-burn′) *n.* a condition in which the skin is red and sore from being in the sun or under a sunlamp too long —*vi., vt.* **-burned′** or **-burnt′, -burn′ing** to get or give a sunburn

sun·burst (-burst′) *n.* **1.** a burst of sunlight, as between clouds **2.** a decoration suggesting the sun and its rays

☆**sun·cured** (-kyoord′) *adj.* cured, as meat or fruit, by drying in the sun

☆**sun·dae** (sun′dē, -dā) *n.* [prob. < SUNDAY] a dish of ice cream covered with syrup, fruit, nuts, etc.

Sun·da Islands (sun′də) islands of the W Malay Archipelago, making up most of Indonesia, stretching from the Malay Peninsula to and including Timor

Sun·day (sun′dē, -dā) *n.* [OE. *sun-nandæg,* lit., day of the sun] the first day of the week, observed by most Christians as a day of worship or as the Sabbath —*adj.* **1.** of or typical of Sunday **2.** done, worn, etc. on Sunday [a *Sunday* suit]

SUNBURST BROOCH

Sunday best [Colloq.] one's best clothes

Sun·days (-dēz, -dāz) *adv.* on or during every Sunday [*Sundays* he played golf]

Sunday school 1. a school giving religious instruction on Sunday at a church or synagogue **2.** the teachers and pupils of such a school

sun·der (sun′dər) *vt., vi.* [OE. *sundrian* < *sundor,* asunder] to break apart; separate; split —**in sunder** into parts or pieces —**sun′der·a·ble** *adj.* —**sun′der·ance** *n.*

Sun·der·land (sun′dər lənd) seaport in N England, on the North Sea: pop. 218,000

sun·dew (sun′dōō′) *n.* [transl. of ML. < L. *ros,* dew + *solis,* sun] a small plant having leaves covered with sticky hairs, that traps and feeds on insects

sun·di·al (sun′dī′əl, -dil′) *n.* an instrument that shows time by the shadow of a pointer or gnomon cast by the sun on a dial marked in hours

sun·dog (-dôg′) *n. same as* PARHELION

sun·down (-doun′) *n. same as* SUNSET

sun·dried (-drīd′) *adj.* dried by the sun

sun·dries (sun′drēz) *n.pl.* sundry items; things of various kinds

sun·dry (sun′drē) *adj.* [OE. *syndrig,* separate < *sundor,* apart] various; miscellaneous [*sundry* articles of clothing] —*pron.* [*with pl. v.*] sundry persons or things: chiefly in **all and sundry** everybody

SUNDIAL

sun·fast (sun′fast′) *adj.* that will not fade in sunlight

sun·fish (-fish′) *n., pl.* **-fish′, -fish′es:** see FISH ☆**1.** any of a large family of N. American freshwater fishes including the bluegill, black bass, etc. **2.** *same as* OCEAN SUNFISH

sun·flow·er (-flou′ər) *n.* any of various tall plants of the composite family, with large, yellow, daisylike flowers containing edible seeds from which an oil is extracted

Sung (sŏŏŋ) Chinese dynasty between 960 and 1279 A.D.: period noted for achievements in art and literature

sung (suŋ) *pp. & rare pt. of* SING

sun·glass (sun′glas′) *n.* **1.** *same as* BURNING GLASS **2.** [*pl.*] eyeglasses with special lenses, usually tinted, to protect the eyes from the sun's glare

sunk (suŋk) *pp. & alt. pt. of* SINK —*adj.* **1.** *same as* SUNKEN **2.** [Colloq.] utterly ruined, disgraced, etc.

sunk·en (suŋk′ən) *obs. pp. of* SINK —*adj.* **1.** sunk in water or other liquid; submerged [*a sunken* ship] **2.** below the level of the surrounding or adjoining area [*a sunken* patio] **3.** fallen in; hollow [*sunken* cheeks] **4.** depressed; dejected [*sunken* spirits]

☆**sun·lamp** (sun′lamp′) *n.* an electric lamp that radiates ultraviolet rays like those of sunlight

sun·less (-lis) *adj.* without sun or sunlight; dark

sun·light (-līt′) *n.* the light of the sun

sun·lit (-lit′) *adj.* lighted by the sun

sun·ny (sun′ē) *adj.* **-ni·er, -ni·est** **1.** bright with sunlight; full of sunshine [*a sunny* day] **2.** bright and cheerful [*a sunny* face] **3.** of or suggestive of the sun [*sunny* beams] —☆**on the sunny side of** somewhat younger than (a specified age) —**sun′ni·ly** *adv.* —**sun′ni·ness** *n.*

Sun·ny·vale (sun′ē vāl′) city in W Calif.: suburb of San Jose: pop. 95,000

☆**sun parlor** (or **porch** or **room**) a living room or enclosed porch with large windows to let sunlight in freely

sun·rise (-rīz′) *n.* **1.** the daily appearance of the sun above the eastern horizon **2.** the time of this **3.** the color of the sky at this time

sun·set (-set′) *n.* **1.** the daily disappearance of the sun below the western horizon **2.** the time of this **3.** the color of the sky at this time

sun·shade (-shād′) *n.* a parasol, awning, broad hat, etc. used for protection against the sun's rays

sun·shine (-shīn′) *n.* **1.** the shining of the sun, or its light and heat **2.** cheerfulness, joy, etc., or a source of this —**sun′shin′y** *adj.*

sun·spot (-spät′) *n.* any of the dark spots sometimes seen on the sun in regions there that are temporarily cooler: they are connected with magnetic disturbances on earth

sun·stroke (-strōk′) *n.* an illness caused by being in the sun too long on a hot day —**sun′struck′** (-struk′) *adj.*

sun·suit (-sŏŏt′) *n.* a garment consisting of short pants with a bib and shoulder straps, for babies and children

sun·tan (-tan′) *n.* a darkened condition of the skin resulting from being in the sun or under a sunlamp —**sun′-tanned′** *adj.*

sun·up (-up′) *n. same as* SUNRISE

Sun Valley resort city in SC Ida.

sun·ward (-wərd) *adv.* toward the sun: also **sun′wards** —*adj.* facing the sun

Sun Yat-sen (sŏŏn′ yät′sen′) 1866–1925; Chin. political & revolutionary leader

sup¹ (sup) *n., vt., vi.* **supped, sup′ping** [OE. *supan*, to drink] *same as* SIP

sup² (sup) *vi.* **supped, sup′ping** [< OFr. *souper* < *soupe*, soup] to have supper

sup- *same as* SUB-: used before *p*

sup. **1.** superior **2.** superlative **3.** supine **4.** supplement **5.** supplementary **6.** supply **7.** [L. *supra*] above

su·per (sŏŏ′pər) *n.* *shortened form of:* **1.** SUPERNUMERARY **2.** SUPERINTENDENT —*adj.* [< next entry] **1.** [Colloq.] excellent; outstanding; unusually fine **2.** being very great or too great

su·per- [L. < *super*, above] *a prefix meaning:* **1.** over, above, on top of [*superstructure*] **2.** higher in rank than, superior to [*superintendent*] **3.** *a)* greater in quality, amount, or degree than; surpassing [*superfine*] *b)* greater or better than others of its kind [*supermarket*] **4.** to a degree greater than normal [*supersaturate*] **5.** extra, additional [*supertax*]

su·per·a·ble (sŏŏ′pər ə b'l) *adj.* that can be overcome; surmountable —**su′per·a·bly** *adv.*

su·per·a·bound (sŏŏ′pər ə bound′) *vi.* to be superabundant

su·per·a·bun·dant (-ə bun′dənt) *adj.* very great or too great in amount —**su′per·a·bun′dance** *n.* —**su′per·a·bun′dant·ly** *adv.*

su·per·an·nu·ate (sŏŏ′pər an′yŏŏ wāt′) *vt.* **-at′ed, -at′ing** [< SUPERANNUATED] **1.** to set aside as old-fashioned or outdated **2.** to retire, esp. with a pension, because of old age —**su′per·an′nu·a′tion** *n.*

su·per·an·nu·at·ed (-id) *adj.* [< ML. pp. of *superannuari* < L. *super*, beyond + *annus*, year] **1.** *a)* too old for further work or use *b)* retired, esp. with a pension, because of old age **2.** obsolete; old-fashioned; outdated

su·perb (sŏŏ purb′, sŏŏ-) *adj.* [L. *superbus*, proud < *super*, above] **1.** noble, grand, or majestic **2.** rich; splendid **3.** of the finest kind; excellent [*superb* cooking] —see SYN. at SPLENDID —**su·perb′ly** *adv.* —**su·perb′ness** *n.*

su·per·car·go (sŏŏ′pər kär′gō) *n., pl.* **-goes, -gos** [< Sp. *sobrecargo* < *sobre*, over + *cargo*, CARGO] an officer on a merchant ship who has charge of the cargo and the business dealings of the voyage

su·per·charge (-chärj′) *vt.* **-charged′, -charg′ing** to increase the power of (an engine), as with a supercharger

su·per·charg·er (-chär′jər) *n.* a blower or compressor used to increase the power of an internal-combustion engine by increasing the supply of air or fuel mixture to the cylinders

su·per·cil·i·ar·y (sŏŏ′pər sil′ē er′ē) *adj.* [< ModL. < L. *supercilium*: see SUPERCILIOUS] of or near the eyebrow

su·per·cil·i·ous (sŏŏ′pər sil′ē əs) *adj.* [< L. < *supercilium*, eyebrow, hence (with reference to raised brows), haughtiness < *super-*, above + *cilium*, eyelid] proud and scornful; looking down on others; haughty [*a supercilious* snob] —see SYN. at PROUD —**su′per·cil′i·ous·ly** *adv.* —**su′per·cil′i·ous·ness** *n.*

su·per·con·duc·tiv·i·ty (-kän′dək tiv′ə tē) *n. Physics* the ability of certain metals and alloys to conduct electricity without resistance when cooled to near absolute zero: also **su′per·con·duc′tion** (-kən duk′shən) —**su′per·con·duct′ing, su′per·con·duc′tive** *adj.* —**su′per·con·duc′tor** *n.*

su·per·cool (-kŏŏl′) *vt.* to lower the temperature of (a liquid) to below its freezing point without its turning into a solid —*vi.* to become supercooled

su·per·e·go (sŏŏ′pər ē′gō) *n., pl.* **-gos** *Psychoanalysis* that part of the psyche which is thought of as seeking control by self-criticism, moral standards, etc.

su·per·em·i·nent (-em′ə nənt) *adj.* remarkable, distinguished, etc. beyond others —**su′per·em′i·nence** *n.* —**su′per·em′i·nent·ly** *adv.*

su·per·e·ro·ga·tion (sŏŏ′pər er′ə gā′shən) *n.* [< LL. < pp. of *supererogare* < *super*, above + *erogare*, to pay out] the act of doing more than is required or expected

su·per·e·rog·a·to·ry (-i räg′ə tôr′ē) *adj.* **1.** done beyond the degree required or expected **2.** superfluous

su·per·fam·i·ly (sŏŏ′pər fam′ə lē) *n., pl.* **-lies** a classification of plants and animals ranking above a family and below an order or suborder

su·per·fi·cial (sŏŏ′pər fish′əl) *adj.* [< L. < *superficies*, a surface < *super-*, above + *facies*, face] **1.** *a)* of or being on the surface [*a superficial* burn] *b)* of surface area; plane [*superficial* measurements] **2.** concerned with and understanding only the easily seen and obvious; shallow [*a superficial* mind] **3.** quick and with little attention to detail [*a superficial* reading] **4.** seeming such only at first glance [*a superficial* likeness] —**su′per·fi·ci·al′i·ty** (-ē al′ə tē) *n., pl.* **-ties** —**su′per·fi′cial·ly** *adv.* —**su′per·fi′cial·ness** *n.*

SYN.—**superficial** implies concern with the easily understood or surface features of a thing [*superficial* characteristics] and may suggest lack of thoroughness, deep thought, or real meaning [*superficial* judgments]; **shallow** in this connection always implies a lack of depth of character, intelligence, meaning, etc. [*shallow* writing]; **cursory** suggests the doing of something in a hurried or superficial way, with little attention to details [*a cursory* inspection] —ANT. deep, profound

su·per·fine (sŏŏ′pər fīn′, sŏŏ′pər fin′) *adj.* **1.** too subtle, delicate, or refined [*a superfine* distinction] **2.** of very fine quality [*superfine* glassware] **3.** extremely fine-grained [*superfine* sugar]

su·per·flu·i·ty (sōō′pər flōō′ə tē) *n., pl.* **-ties** **1.** a being superfluous **2.** a quantity beyond what is needed; excess **3.** something superfluous; thing not needed

su·per·flu·ous (soo pur′floo wəs) *adj.* [< L. < *superfluere* < *super-*, above + *fluere*, to flow] **1.** being more than is needed or wanted; excessive [a *superfluous* stock of goods] **2.** not needed; unnecessary [a *superfluous* explanation] —**su·per′flu·ous·ly** *adv.* —**su·per′flu·ous·ness** *n.*

su·per·gi·ant (sōō′pər jī′ənt) *n.* a very large star that has a diameter at least 100 times that of the sun and that is 100 to 10,000 times as bright

su·per·heat (sōō′pər hēt′; *for n.* sōō′pər hēt′) *vt.* **1.** to make too hot **2.** to heat (a liquid) above its boiling point without its turning into vapor **3.** to heat (steam not in contact with water) beyond its saturation point, so that a drop in temperature will not cause it to turn back to water

su·per·het·er·o·dyne (sōō′pər het′ə ə dīn′) *adj.* [SU-PER(SONIC) + HETERODYNE] designating or of radio reception in which some amplification is done at an intermediate supersonic frequency —*n.* a radio set for this kind of reception

su·per·high frequency (sōō′pər hī′) any radio frequency between 3,000 and 30,000 megahertz

☆**su·per·high·way** (sōō′pər hī′wā′) *n.* same as EXPRESSWAY

su·per·hu·man (-hyōō′mən) *adj.* **1.** having a nature above that of man; divine [a *superhuman* being] **2.** greater than normal for a human being [*superhuman* strength] —**su′per·hu′man·ly** *adv.* —**su′per·hu′man·ness** *n.*

su·per·im·pose (-im pōz′) *vt.* **-posed′, -pos′ing** **1.** to put or lay on top of something else **2.** to add as a feature that stands out above or does not properly fit with the rest

su·per·in·duce (-in dōōs′, -dyōōs′) *vt.* **-duced′, -duc′ing** to bring in as an addition —**su′per·in·duc′tion** (-duk′shən) *n.*

su·per·in·tend (-in tend′) *vt.* to act as superintendent of; direct or manage; supervise —**su′per·in·tend′ence, su′per·in·tend′en·cy** *n.*

su·per·in·tend·ent (-in ten′dənt) *n.* [< LL. prp. of *superintendere:* see SUPER- & INTEND] **1.** a person in charge of a department, institution, etc.; supervisor **2.** the custodian of a building —*adj.* that superintends

Su·pe·ri·or (sə pir′ē ər, soo-), **Lake** [orig. so called from its position above Lake Huron] largest & westernmost of the Great Lakes, between Mich. & Ontario, Canada: 32,483 sq. mi.

su·pe·ri·or (sə pir′ē ər, soo-) *adj.* [OFr. < L., compar. of *superus*, that is above] **1.** higher in space; placed higher up; upper **2.** high or higher in order, status, rank, etc. [a *superior* officer] **3.** greater in quality or value than (with *to*) [a wine *superior* to most] **4.** above average in quality; excellent [a *superior* grade of paper] **5.** refusing to give in to or be affected by (with *to*) [a man *superior* to temptation] **6.** showing a feeling of being better than others; haughty [a *superior* smirk] —*n.* **1.** a superior person or thing **2.** the head of a convent, monastery, etc. —**su·pe′ri·or′i·ty** (-ôr′ə tē) *n.*

superl. superlative

su·per·la·tive (sə pur′lə tiv, soo-) *adj.* [< MFr. < LL. < L. < *super-*, above + *latus*, pp. of *ferre*, to carry] **1.** of the highest kind; supreme **2.** being the form of adjectives and adverbs that shows the greatest degree in meaning: the superlative degree is usually shown by the suffix *-est* (*hardest*) or by the use of *most* (*most beautiful*) —*n.* **1.** the highest degree; acme **2.** something superlative **3.** *Gram. a*) the superlative degree *b*) a word or form in this degree —**su·per′la·tive·ly** *adv.* —**su·per′la·tive·ness** *n.*

su·per·man (sōō′pər man′) *n., pl.* **-men′** (-men′) **1.** in Nietzsche's philosophy, a type of superior man thought of as the goal of the struggle for survival in evolution **2.** a man who seems to have powers beyond those of a normal human being

☆**su·per·mar·ket** (-mär′kit) *n.* a large, self-service, retail food store or market, often one of a chain

su·per·nal (soo pur′n'l) *adj.* [MFr. < L. *supernus*, upper] celestial, heavenly, or divine —**su·per′nal·ly** *adv.*

su·per·na·tant (sōō′pər nāt′'nt) *adj.* [< L. prp. of *supernatare* < *super-*, above + *natare*, to swim] floating on the surface

su·per·nat·u·ral (sōō′pər nach′ər əl) *adj.* **1.** existing outside man's normal experience or the known laws of nature; specif., of or involving God or a god, or ghosts, the occult, etc. **2.** going beyond normal bounds; extraordinary [skating with *supernatural* grace] —**the supernatural** supernatural beings, forces, happenings, etc., esp. ghosts, spirits, and the like —**su′per·nat′u·ral·ly** *adv.*

su·per·nat·u·ral·ism (-iz'm) *n.* **1.** a supernatural quality or state **2.** a belief that some supernatural, or divine, force con-

trols nature and the universe —**su′per·nat′u·ral·ist** *n., adj.* —**su′per·nat′u·ral·is′tic** *adj.*

su·per·no·va (-nō′və) *n., pl.* **-vae** (-vē), **-vas** [ModL.: see SUPER- & NOVA] an extremely bright nova that suddenly increases 10 million or 100 million times in brightness

su·per·nu·mer·ar·y (-nōō′mə rer′ē, -nyōō′-) *adj.* [< LL. < L. *super*, above + *numerus*, number] beyond the regular or needed number; extra or superfluous —*n., pl.* **-ar′ies** **1.** a supernumerary person or thing **2.** *Theater* a person with a small, nonspeaking part, as in a mob scene

su·per·pa·tri·ot (-pā′trē ət) *n.* a person who is or claims to be a devoted patriot, often to the point of blind, unthinking loyalty —**su′per·pa′tri·ot′ic** (-pā′trē ät′ik) *adj.* —**su′per·pa′tri·ot·ism** *n.*

su·per·phos·phate (-fäs′fāt) *n.* an acid phosphate made by treating bone, phosphate rock, etc. with sulfuric acid and used as a fertilizer

su·per·pose (-pōz′) *vt.* **-posed′, -pos′ing** [< Fr. < L. pp. of *superponere:* see SUPER- & POSE[1]] **1.** to lay or place on, over, or above something else **2.** *Geom.* to place (one figure) on top of another that is congruent so that corresponding sides coincide —**su′per·pos′a·ble** *adj.* —**su′per·po·si′tion** *n.*

su·per·pow·er (sōō′pər pou′ər) *n.* any of the few most powerful nations of the world competing for influence over smaller nations

su·per·sat·u·rate (sōō′pər sach′ə rāt′) *vt.* **-rat′ed, -rat′ing** to saturate beyond the normal point for the given temperature —**su′per·sat′u·ra′tion** *n.*

su·per·scribe (-skrīb′) *vt.* **-scribed′, -scrib′ing** [< L.: see SUPER- & SCRIBE] to write or mark (an inscription, name, etc.) at the top or on an outer surface of (something)

su·per·script (sōō′pər skript′) *adj.* written above —*n.* a figure, letter, or symbol written above and to the side of another [in y^2 and x^n, *2* and *n* are superscripts]

su·per·scrip·tion (sōō′pər skrip′shən) *n.* **1.** the act of superscribing **2.** something superscribed; esp., an address on a letter

su·per·sede (sōō′pər sēd′) *vt.* **-sed′ed, -sed′ing** [< MFr. < L. *supersedere*, to preside over < *super-*, above + *sedere*, to sit] **1.** to replace or supplant; specif., to cause to be set aside as inferior or outdated [the automobile *superseded* the horse and buggy] **2.** to take the place or office of; succeed [Mr. Smith *superseded* Mr. Fox as principal] —see SYN. at REPLACE —☆**su′per·se′dure** (-sē′jər), **su′per·sed′ence** *n.*

su·per·sen·si·tive (-sen′sə tiv) *adj.* highly sensitive or too sensitive —**su′per·sen′si·tiv′i·ty** *n.*

su·per·ses·sion (-sesh′ən) *n.* [< L. pp. of *supersedere*] a superseding or being superseded

su·per·son·ic (-sän′ik) *adj.* [SUPER- + SONIC] **1.** designating, of, or moving at a speed in a surrounding fluid greater than that of sound in the same fluid: see SONIC **2.** same as ULTRASONIC

su·per·son·ics (-sän′iks) *n.pl.* [with sing. v.] the science dealing with supersonic phenomena

☆**su·per·star** (sōō′pər stär′) *n.* a very prominent performer, as in sports or the theater, considered to have outstanding skill and talent

su·per·sti·tion (sōō′pər stish′ən) *n.* [< MFr. < L. *superstitio*, ult. < *super-*, over + *stare*, to stand] **1.** any belief, based on fear or ignorance, that does not fit in with the known laws of science or with rational opinion; esp., such a belief in omens, supernatural forces, etc. **2.** any action or practice based on such a belief **3.** all such beliefs

su·per·sti·tious (-əs) *adj.* **1.** of, characterized by, or resulting from superstition **2.** having superstitions —**su′per·sti′tious·ly** *adv.* —**su′per·sti′tious·ness** *n.*

su·per·struc·ture (sōō′pər struk′chər) *n.* **1.** a structure built on top of another **2.** that part of a building above the foundation **3.** that part of a ship above the main deck

su·per·tax (-taks′) *n.* an additional tax; esp., a surtax

su·per·vene (sōō′pər vēn′) *vi.* **-vened′, -ven′ing** [< L. < *super-*, over + *venire*, to come] to come or happen as something added or not expected —**su′per·ven′ient** (-vēn′yənt) *adj.* —**su′per·ven′tion** (-ven′shən), **su′per·ven′ience** (-vēn′yəns) *n.*

su·per·vise (sōō′pər vīz′) *vt., vi.* **-vised′, -vis′ing** [< ML. pp. of *supervidere* < L. *super-*, over + *videre*, to see] to oversee, direct, or manage (work, workers, a project, etc.); superintend —**su′per·vi′sion** (-vizh′ən) *n.*

su·per·vi·sor (-vī′zər) *n.* **1.** a person who supervises; manager; director ☆**2.** in certain school systems, an official in charge of the courses and teachers for a particular subject —**su′per·vi′so·ry** *adj.*

su·pine (soo pīn′) *adj.* [L. *supinus*] **1.** lying on the back, face upward **2.** showing no concern or doing nothing about matters; lazy; listless —see SYN. at PRONE —**su·pine′ly** *adv.* —**su·pine′ness** *n.*

supp., suppl. 1. supplement **2.** supplementary

sup·per (sup′ər) *n.* [OFr. *souper,* to SUP²] **1.** an evening meal, as a dinner, or a late, light meal, as one eaten after attending the theater ☆**2.** an evening social gathering at which a meal is served [a church *supper*] —**sup′per·less** *adj.*

sup·plant (sə plant′) *vt.* [< OFr. < L. *supplantare,* to trip up < *sub-,* under + *planta,* sole of the foot] **1.** to take the place of, esp. through force or plotting [revolutionaries scheming to *supplant* the government] **2.** to remove and replace with something else [we must *supplant* the old methods with new techniques] —see SYN. at REPLACE —**sup·plan·ta·tion** (sup′lan tā′shən) *n.* —**sup·plant′er** *n.*

sup·ple (sup′'l) *adj.* [< OFr. < L. *supplex,* humble] **1.** easily bent; flexible [*supple* leather] **2.** able to bend and move easily; lithe; limber [a *supple* body] **3.** changing easily, as under new conditions or strong influences; adaptable or yielding [a *supple* mind] —**sup′ple·ly** *adv.* —**sup′ple·ness** *n.*

sup·ple·ment (sup′lə mənt; *for v.* -ment′) *n.* [< L. < *supplere:* see SUPPLY¹] **1.** something added, esp. to make up for a lack [a vitamin *supplement* for a poor diet] **2.** a section added to a book, etc., as to give additional information ☆**3.** a separate section of a newspaper, containing feature stories, etc. **4.** *Math.* the number of degrees to be added to an angle or arc to make 180 degrees —*vt.* to provide a supplement to; add to [to *supplement* the fire department with volunteers] —**sup′ple·men·ta′tion** *n.* —**sup′ple·ment′er** *n.*

sup·ple·men·ta·ry (sup′lə men′tər ē) *adj.* supplying what is lacking; additional: also **sup′ple·men′tal**

supplementary angle either of two angles that together form 180 degrees

sup·pli·ant (sup′lē ənt) *n.* [MFr., prp. of *supplier* < L.: see SUPPLICATE] a person who supplicates —*adj.* asking in a humble way; supplicating; beseeching [a *suppliant* look] —**sup′pli·ance** *n.* —**sup′pli·ant·ly** *adv.*

SUPPLEMENTARY ANGLES (angle BCA and angle DCB are supplementary)

sup·pli·cant (sup′lə kənt) *adj., n. same as* SUPPLIANT

sup·pli·cate (sup′lə kāt′) *vt.* -cat′ed, -cat′ing [< L. pp. of *supplicare,* to kneel down < *sub-,* under + *plicare,* to fold] **1.** to ask for humbly, as by prayer **2.** to make a humble request of (someone) —*vi.* to make a humble request, esp. in prayer —see SYN. at APPEAL —**sup′pli·ca′tor** *n.* —**sup′pli·ca·to′ry** (-kə tôr′ē) *adj.*

sup·pli·ca·tion (sup′lə kā′shən) *n.* **1.** the act of supplicating **2.** a humble request, prayer, petition, etc.

sup·ply¹ (sə plī′) *vt.* -plied′, -ply′ing [< MFr. < L. *supplere,* to fill up < *sub-,* under + *plere,* to fill] **1.** to give, furnish, or provide (what is needed) [to *supply* tools to workers] **2.** to meet the needs or requirements of [to *supply* workers with tools] **3.** to make up for (a lack, loss, etc.) —*n., pl.* -plies′ **1.** the act of supplying **2.** an amount available for use; stock; store [a large *supply* of new cars] **3.** [*pl.*] materials, provisions, etc. for supplying an army, a business, etc. **4.** *Econ.* the amount of a certain product available for purchase at a given price —*adj.* having to do with a supply or supplies [the *supply* boat arrives at noon] —**sup·pli′er** *n.*

sup·ply² (sup′lē) *adv.* in a supple manner; supplely

sup·port (sə pôrt′) *vt.* [< MFr. < LL. < L. < *sub-,* under + *portare,* to carry] **1.** *a)* to carry or bear the weight of; hold up [the ladder will *support* you] *b)* to carry or bear (a specified weight, pressure, etc.) [the rope *supports* 100 pounds] **2.** to give courage or faith to; help; comfort [she *supported* him in his time of need] **3.** to give approval to or be in favor of; uphold [to *support* a cause] **4.** to provide for (a person, institution, etc.) with money or means of livelihood **5.** to help prove or defend [evidence to *support* a claim] **6.** to bear; endure; tolerate **7.** to keep up; maintain; specif., to maintain (the price of a certain product) as by purchases **8.** *Theater* to act a secondary role in the same play with (a specified star) —*n.* **1.** a supporting

or being supported [this wall needs *support*] **2.** a person or thing that supports; specif., *a)* a prop, base, brace, etc. *b)* a means of livelihood *c)* an elastic device to support or bind a part of the body —**sup·port′a·ble** *adj.* —**sup·port′a·bly** *adv.*

SYN.—**support,** the broadest of these terms, suggests a favoring of someone or something, either by giving active help or merely by giving approval [to *support* a candidate for office]; **uphold** suggests that what is being supported is under attack [to *uphold* civil rights for all]; **sustain** implies full active support so as to strengthen or keep from failing [*sustained* by his faith in the future]; **maintain** suggests a continuing support so as to keep strong, secure, or in good condition [to *maintain* the law, a family, etc.]; **advocate** implies support in speech or writing and sometimes suggests the use of persuasion or argument [to *advocate* a change in policy]; **back** (often **back up**) suggests support, as financial aid, encouragement, etc., given to prevent failure [I'll *back* you up in your demands]

sup·port·er (-ər) *n.* **1.** a person who supports; advocate; adherent **2.** a thing that supports; esp., *a)* an elastic device to support the back, abdomen, etc. ☆*b) same as* JOCKSTRAP: in full, **athletic supporter** ☆*c) same as* GARTER —see SYN. at FOLLOWER

sup·port·ive (-iv) *adj.* that gives support, help, or approval

sup·pose (sə pōz′) *vt.* -posed′, -pos′ing [< MFr. < ML. *supponere,* ult. < L. *sub-,* under + *ponere,* to place] **1.** to take to be true, as for the sake of argument, etc. [*suppose* A equals B] **2.** to believe, think, guess, etc. [I *suppose* you're right] **3.** *same as* PRESUPPOSE (sense 2) **4.** to consider as a suggested possibility [*suppose* he doesn't come] **5.** to expect: always in the passive [she's *supposed* to telephone] —*vi.* to think or guess; conjecture —**sup·pos′a·ble** *adj.* —**sup·pos′a·bly** *adv.* —**sup·pos′er** *n.*

sup·posed (sə pōzd′) *adj.* **1.** thought of as true, possible, etc., without actual knowledge [her *supposed* wealth] **2.** merely imagined —**sup·pos′ed·ly** *adv.*

sup·po·si·tion (sup′ə zish′ən) *n.* **1.** the act of supposing **2.** something supposed; assumption Also **sup·pos·al** (sə pōz′'l) —**sup′po·si′tion·al** *adj.* —**sup′po·si′tion·al·ly** *adv.*

sup·po·si·tious (-əs) *adj. same as* SUPPOSITITIOUS

sup·pos·i·ti·tious (sə päz′ə tish′əs) *adj.* **1.** substituted with the intention of deceiving; counterfeit **2.** based on a supposition; hypothetical

sup·pos·i·to·ry (sə päz′ə tôr′ē) *n., pl.* -ries [< ModL. < L. < pp. of *supponere:* see SUPPOSE] a small piece of medicine for insertion into the rectum, vagina, etc., where body heat causes it to melt

sup·press (sə pres′) *vt.* [< L. pp. of *supprimere* < *sub-,* under + *premere,* to press] **1.** to put down by force or authority; crush [to *suppress* a mutiny] **2.** to keep from appearing or being known, published, etc. [to *suppress* a news story, a book, etc.] **3.** to keep back; restrain; check [to *suppress* a laugh, cough, etc.] **4.** to check the flow, secretion, etc. of **5.** *Electronics, Radio,* etc. to get rid of (an unwanted signal, etc.) **6.** *Psychiatry* to consciously put (unacceptable ideas, impulses, etc.) out of the mind —**sup·press′i·ble** *adj.* —**sup·pres′sive** *adj.* —**sup·pres′sive·ly** *adv.* —**sup·pres′sor** *n.*

sup·pres·sion (sə presh′ən) *n.* **1.** a suppressing or being suppressed **2.** *Psychiatry a)* the mental process by which unacceptable ideas, impulses, etc. are suppressed *b)* something suppressed in this way

sup·pu·rate (sup′yoo rāt′) *vi.* -rat′ed, -rat′ing [< L. pp. of *suppurare* < *sub-,* under + *puris,* genitive of *pus,* pus] to form or discharge pus; fester, as a wound —**sup′pu·ra′tion** *n.* —**sup′pu·ra′tive** *adj.*

su·pra- [< L. *supra,* above, over] *a prefix meaning* above, over, beyond [*suprarenal*]

su·pra·na·tion·al (soo′prə nash′ə n'l) *adj.* of, for, involving, or over all or a number of nations [*supranational* authority] —**su′pra·na′tion·al·ism** *n.*

su·pra·re·nal (-rē′n'l) *adj.* [< ModL.: see SUPRA- & RENAL] on or above the kidney; specif., designating or of an adrenal gland —*n.* an adrenal gland

su·pra·seg·men·tal phonemes (-seg men′t'l) those features of speech, such as pitch, stress, and juncture, which affect the meaning of segmental phonemes

su·prem·a·cist (sə prem′ə sist, soo-) *n.* a person who believes in or promotes the supremacy of a particular group [a white *supremacist*]

su·prem·a·cy (sə prem′ə sē, soo-) *n., pl.* -cies **1.** the quality or state of being supreme **2.** supreme power or authority

---

fat, āpe, cär; ten, ēven; is, bīte; gō, hôrn, tōōl, lŏŏk; ôil, ŏut; up, fur; get; joy; yet; chin; she; thin, then; zh, leisure; ŋ, ring; ə for a in ago, e in agent, i in sanity, o in comply, u in focus; ' as in able (ā′b'l); Fr. bal; ë, Fr. coeur; ö, Fr. feu; Fr. mon; ô, Fr. coq; ü, Fr. duc; r, Fr. cri; H, G. ich; kh, G. doch; ‡ foreign; ☆ Americanism; < derived from. See inside front cover.

su·preme (sə prēm', sŏō-) *adj.* [L. *supremus,* superl. of *superus,* that is above] **1.** highest in rank, power, etc. [the *supreme* commander] **2.** highest in quality, achievement, etc.; most excellent [a *supreme* honor] **3.** highest in degree; utmost [a *supreme* fool] **4.** final; ultimate [the *supreme* sacrifice is giving one's life for another] —**su·preme'ly** *adv.*

Supreme Being God

Supreme Court ☆**1.** the highest Federal court, made up of nine judges ☆**2.** the highest court in most States

Supreme Soviet the parliament of the Soviet Union

Supt., supt. Superintendent

sur-[1] [OFr. < L. *super,* over, above] *a prefix meaning* over, upon, above, beyond [*surcharge*]

sur-[2] *same as* SUB-: used before *r*

Su·ra·ba·ja (sōō'rä bä'yä) seaport in NE Java, Indonesia: pop. 1,008,000

su·rah (soor'ə) *n.* [< *Surat,* a seaport in India] a soft, twilled fabric of silk or rayon

sur·cease (sur sēs'; *for n. usually* sur'sēs) *vt., vi.* -ceased', -ceas'ing [< OFr. *sursis,* pp. of *surseoir,* to pause < L. *supersedere,* to refrain from] [Archaic] to stop; end —*n.* end; cessation

sur·charge (sur'chärj; *also for v.* sur chärj') *vt.* -charged', -charg'ing [< OFr.: see SUR-[1] & CHARGE] **1.** to overcharge **2.** to overload **3.** to fill too full **4.** to mark (a postage stamp) with a surcharge —*n.* **1.** *a)* an additional charge *b)* an overcharge **2.** an extra load or overload **3.** a new face value overprinted on a postage stamp

sur·cin·gle (sur'siŋ'g'l) *n.* [< MFr. < *sur-,* over + L. *cingulum,* a belt] a strap passed around a horse's body to hold on a saddle, pack, etc.

sur·coat (sur'kōt') *n.* [< MFr.: see SUR-[1] & COAT] an outer coat; esp., a short cloak worn over a knight's armor

surd (surd) *adj.* [L. *surdus,* deaf, mute] *same as:* **1.** *Math.* IRRATIONAL **2.** *Phonet.* VOICELESS —*n.* **1.** *Math.* an irrational number or quantity; specif., a root that can be expressed only approximately [√5 is a *surd*] **2.** *Phonet.* a voiceless sound

sure (shoor) *adj.* **sur'er, sur'est** [< OFr. < L. *securus:* see SECURE] **1.** orig., secure or safe **2.** that will not fail; always effective [a *sure* method] **3.** that can be relied upon; trustworthy [a *sure* friend] **4.** that cannot be doubted, questioned, etc.; absolutely true [*sure* information] **5.** having no doubt; positive; confident [to be *sure* of the facts] **6.** that can be counted on to be or happen [a *sure* defeat] **7.** bound to do, experience, etc. [*sure* to lose] **8.** never missing [a *sure* aim] —*adv.* [Colloq.] **1.** surely; inevitably **2.** certainly; indeed: used as an intensive [*sure,* I'll go] —**for sure** certain(ly); without doubt —**make sure** to be or cause to be certain —**sure enough** [Colloq.] certainly; without doubt —**to be sure** surely; certainly —**sure'ness** *n.*

SYN·—**sure** suggests merely a lack of doubt [I'm *sure* you don't mean it]; **certain** usually suggests a feeling of sureness based on convincing evidence [this letter makes me *certain* of her innocence]; **confident** emphasizes the firmness of one's certainty or sureness, esp. in believing that something will happen [he's *confident* he'll win]; **positive** implies unshakable confidence, esp. in the correctness of one's opinions or conclusions, and sometimes suggests stubborn confidence felt even without evidence or proof [she's too *positive* in her beliefs] —ANT· **doubtful**

☆**sure-fire** (shoor'fīr') *adj.* [Colloq.] sure to be successful or as expected; that will not fail

sure-foot·ed (-foot'id) *adj.* not likely to stumble, slip, fall, or make a mistake —**sure'-foot'ed·ly** *adv.*

sure·ly (-lē) *adv.* **1.** with confidence; in a sure, unhesitating manner **2.** without a doubt; certainly [*surely* you don't believe that!] **3.** without risk of failing: chiefly in **slowly but surely**

☆**sure thing** [Colloq.] **1.** something certain to win, succeed, etc. **2.** all right; O.K.: used as an interjection

sur·e·ty (shoor'ə tē, shoor'tē) *n., pl.* -**ties 1.** a being sure; assurance **2.** something sure; certainty **3.** something that makes sure or gives assurance, as against loss or failure to do something when required; security **4.** a person who makes himself responsible for another; specif., *Law* one who makes himself responsible for another's debts if the other fails to pay them — **sur'e·ty·ship'** *n.*

surf (surf) *n.* [earlier *suffe,* prob. var. of SOUGH] **1.** the waves of the sea breaking on the shore or a reef **2.** the foam or spray caused by this —*vi.* to take part in the sport of surfing —**surf'er** *n.*

sur·face (sur'fis) *n.* [Fr. < *sur-* (see SUB-) + *face,* a face] **1.** *a)* the outside or outer face of a thing [the *surface* of the earth] *b)* any side of a thing having several sides [the *surfaces* of a box] *c)* the area of such a side **2.** outward appearance [all smiles on the *surface*] **3.** *Aeron.* an airfoil **4.** *Geom.* a space or area having length and breadth, but no thickness —*adj.* **1.** of, on, or at the surface [the *surface* temperature of the lake] **2.** working, used, or carried on land or sea, rather than in the air or under water [*surface* forces, *surface* mail] **3.** seeming such on the surface; superficial [a *surface* friendliness] —*vt.* **-faced, -facing 1.** to treat the surface of, esp. so as to make smooth **2.** to give a surface to, as in paving **3.** to bring (a submarine, etc.) to the surface of the water —*vi.* **1.** to rise to the surface of the water **2.** to become known, esp. after being hidden

sur·face-ac·tive (-ak'tiv) *adj. Chem.* designating or of a substance, as a detergent, that lowers the surface tension of the solvent in which it is dissolved

surface tension a property of liquids in which the surface tends to become reduced to the smallest possible area, so that the surface seems like a thin, elastic film under tension

surf·board (surf'bôrd') *n.* a long, narrow board used in the sport of surfing —*vi.* to take part in this sport —**surf'board'er** *n.* —**surf'board'ing** *n.*

surf·boat (-bōt') *n.* a sturdy, light boat used in heavy surf

☆**surf-cast** (-kast') *vi.* **-cast', -cast'ing** to fish by casting into the ocean surf from or near the shore —**surf'cast'er** *n.*

sur·feit (sur'fit) *n.* [< OFr. *sorfaire,* to overdo < *sur-* (< L. *super*), over + *faire* (< L. *facere*), to make] **1.** too great an amount or supply; excess [a *surfeit* of compliments] **2.** the act of eating, drinking, etc. too much **3.** disgust, nausea, etc. resulting from any kind of excess —*vt.* to cause to feel sick or disgusted by giving too much of something to [*surfeited* with pleasures] —*vi.* [Rare] to eat, drink, etc. too much —**see SYN· at** SATIATE

SURFBOARD

surf·ing (sur'fiŋ) *n.* the sport of riding in toward shore on the crest of a wave, esp. on a surfboard

surf·rid·ing (surf'rīd'iŋ) *n. same as* SURFING

surg. **1.** surgeon **2.** surgery **3.** surgical

surge (surj) *n.* [prob. < OFr. < L. *surgere,* to rise] **1.** a large wave of water, or the swelling or rushing motion of such a wave or series of waves **2.** any sudden strong increase or rush [a *surge* of energy; the *surge* of the crowd] —*vi.* **surged, surg'ing** to move in a surge [the mob *surged* into the room]

sur·geon (sur'jən) *n.* a doctor who specializes in surgery

sur·ger·y (sur'jər ē) *n., pl.* -**ger·ies** [< OFr. *cirurgie* < L. < Gr. *cheirourgia,* handicraft < *cheir,* the hand + *ergein,* to work] **1.** *a)* the treatment of disease, injury, etc. by operations with the hands or instruments, as the removal of diseased parts by cutting, the setting of broken bones, etc. *b)* the branch of medicine dealing with this **2.** the operating room of a surgeon or hospital **3.** [Brit.] a doctor's office

sur·gi·cal (-ji k'l) *adj.* **1.** of surgeons or surgery [*surgical* experience] **2.** used in or connected with surgery [*surgical* gauze] **3.** resulting from surgery [*surgical* complications] — **sur'gi·cal·ly** *adv.*

Su·ri·nam (soor'i näm', soor'i nam') country on the NE coast of S. America: formerly part of the Netherlands: 55,144 sq. mi.; pop. 385,000

sur·ly (sur'lē) *adj.* **-li·er, -li·est** [earlier *sirly,* imperious < *sir,* SIR] bad-tempered; rude and unfriendly —**sur'li·ness** *n.*

sur·mise (sər mīz'; *for n. also* sur'mīz) *n.* [< OFr. pp. of *surmettre* < *sur-* (< L. *super*), upon + *mettre,* to put < L. *mittere,* to send] **1.** an idea or opinion that is only a guess, based on a few facts; conjecture [my *surmise* is that they were delayed by the storm] **2.** the act of surmising —*vt., vi.* **-mised', -mis'ing** to form (an opinion, conclusion, etc.) without much evidence; guess —**see SYN· at** GUESS —**sur·mis'er** *n.*

sur·mount (sər mount') *vt.* [OFr. *surmonter:* see SUR-[1] & MOUNT[2]] **1.** to get the better of; overcome [to *surmount* a difficulty] **2.** to be or lie at the top of [a crown *surmounted* his head] **3.** to climb up and across (a height, obstacle, etc.) —**surmount'a·ble** *adj.*

sur·name (sur'nām'; *for v. also* sur'nām') *n.* [< OFr. < *sur-*

SURCOAT

(see SUR-¹) + *nom* < L. *nomen*, name] **1.** the family name, or last name **2.** a special name added to a person's given name, often to describe him (Example: Ivan *the Terrible*) —*vt.* **-named′, -nam′ing** to give a surname to

sur·pass (sər pas′) *vt.* [< MFr. < *sur-* (see SUR-¹) + *passer*, to PASS²] **1.** to be better or greater than; excel [she *surpasses* her sisters in charm] **2.** to go beyond in quantity, degree, etc. [production has *surpassed* estimates] **3.** to go beyond the limit, capacity, range, etc. of [riches *surpassing* belief] —**sur·pass′a·ble** *adj.* —**sur·pass′er** *n.*

sur·pass·ing (-iŋ) *adj.* that surpasses the average; much better than the usual; unusually excellent —*adv.* [Archaic] exceedingly —**sur·pass′ing·ly** *adv.*

sur·plice (sur′plis) *n.* [< Anglo-Fr. < OFr. < ML. < L. *super-*, above + *pelliceum*, fur robe] a loose, white, wide-sleeved gown worn by the clergy and choir in some churches —**sur′pliced** *adj.*

sur·plus (sur′plus, -pləs) *n.* [OFr. < *sur-*, above + L. *plus*, more] **1.** a quantity over and above what is needed or used; excess [a grain *surplus* stored in silos] **2.** the amount by which the assets of a business are greater than its liabilities [a surplus; ex-cess [*surplus* material left over from making drapes] —*adj.* that is a surplus; ex-cess [*surplus* material left over from making drapes]

SURPLICE

sur·plus·age (-ij) *n.* **1.** surplus; excess **2.** unnecessary words

sur·prise (sər prīz′) *vt.* **-prised′, -pris′ing** [< OFr. pp. of *sorprendre* < *sur-* (see SUR-¹) + *prendre* < L. *prehendere*, to take] **1.** to come upon suddenly or unexpected-ly; take unawares [I *surprised* him in the act of stealing] **2.** to attack or capture without warning **3.** *a)* to cause to feel aston-ishment by being unexpected [her sudden anger *surprised* us] *b)* to present (someone) unexpectedly with a gift, etc. **4.** *a)* to cause (a person) by some unexpected action to do or say some-thing he had not meant to do or say [to *surprise* someone into admitting guilt] *b)* to bring out by such means [to *surprise* an admission of guilt from someone] —*n.* **1.** [Rare] a surprising **2.** an unexpected seizure or attack **3.** a being surprised; aston-ishment [much to our *surprise*, it began snowing] **4.** something that surprises because unexpected, unusual, etc. [his answer was quite a *surprise*] —**take by surprise 1.** to come upon suddenly or without warning **2.** to amaze; astound —**sur·pris′ed·ly** *adv.* —**sur·pris′er** *n.*

SYN.—surprise, in this connection, implies a causing wonder because unexpected, unusual, etc. [I'm *surprised* at your concern]; **astonish** im-plies a surprising with something that seems unbelievable [to *astonish* with magic tricks]; **amaze** suggests an astonishing that causes confusion [*amazed* at the sudden turn of events]; **astound** suggests shocking aston-ishment that leaves one unable to act or think [I was *astounded* when he offered me a bribe]

sur·pris·ing (-iŋ) *adj.* causing surprise; amazing —**sur·pris′ing·ly** *adv.*

sur·re·al·ism (sə rē′ə liz′m) *n.* [< Fr.: see SUR-¹ & REALISM] a modern movement in art and literature, in which an attempt is made to show the workings of the subconscious mind, as by arranging material in unexpected, fantastic ways —**sur·re′al, sur·re′al·is′tic** *adj.* —**sur·re′al·ist** *adj., n.* —**sur·re′al·is′ti·cal·ly** *adv.*

sur·ren·der (sə ren′dər) *vt.* [< MFr. < *sur-* (see SUR-¹) + *ren-dre*, to RENDER] **1.** to give up possession of or power over; yield to another on demand [to *surrender* a town to the enemy] **2.** to give up or abandon [to *surrender* all hope] **3.** to yield or resign (oneself) to an emotion, influence, etc. [she *surrendered* herself to grief] —*vi.* **1.** to give oneself up, esp. as a prisoner; yield [the troops *surrendered*] **2.** to give in (to) [to *surrender* to temptation] —*n.* the act of surrendering —**sur·ren′der·er** *n.*

SYN.—surrender commonly implies the giving up, under pressure, of something after attempting to keep it [to *surrender* a fort, one's freedom, etc.]; **yield** is close to **surrender** in meaning but often suggests milder pres-sure [to *yield* one's agreement]; **relinquish** is the general word implying an abandoning, giving up, or letting go of something held [to *relinquish* one's grasp, a claim, etc.]; to **submit** is to give in to authority or superior force [to *submit* to a conqueror]; **resign** implies either a willing, formal giving up of something [to *resign* an office] or a giving in or accepting without a struggle [to *resign* oneself to failure]

sur·rep·ti·tious (sur′əp tish′əs) *adj.* [< L. < pp. of *surripere*

< *sub-*, under + *rapere*, to seize] **1.** done, got, made, etc. in a secret, sly way; stealthy [a *surreptitious* wink] **2.** acting in a se-cret, sly way —see SYN. at SECRET —**sur′rep·ti′tious·ly** *adv.* —**sur′rep·ti′tious·ness** *n.*

sur·rey (sur′ē) *n., pl.* **-reys** [< *Surrey*, county in England] ☆a light pleasure carriage having four wheels, two seats, and usually a flat top

Sur·rey (sur′ē), Earl of, (*Henry Howard*) 1517?-47; Eng. poet

sur·ro·gate (sur′ə gāt′, sur′-; *for n. also* -git) *n.* [< L. pp. of *sur-rogare* < *sub-*, in place of + *rogare*, to elect] **1.** a deputy or substitute for another person ☆**2.** in some States, probate court, or a judge of this court

SURREY

sur·round (sə round′) *vt.* [< OFr. < LL. < L. *super*, over + *undare*, to rise < *unda*, a wave] **1.** to en-circle on all or nearly all sides; enclose [trees *surround* the house] **2.** to cut off (a military unit, etc.) from communication or retreat by encircling —*n.* [Chiefly Brit.] something that sur-rounds

sur·round·ing (-roun′diŋ) *n.* that which surrounds; esp., [*pl.*] the things, conditions, influences, etc. around a place or person; environment —*adj.* that surrounds

sur·tax (sur′taks) *n.* an extra tax on something already taxed

sur·tout (sər tōō′, -tōōt′) *n.* [Fr. < *sur*, over + *tout*, all] a man's long, closefitting overcoat of the 19th century

sur·veil·lance (sər vāl′əns, -vāl′yəns) *n.* [Fr. < *sur-* (see SUR-¹) + *veiller*, to watch < L. *vigilare*, to watch] **1.** watch kept over a person, esp. a suspect **2.** supervision —**sur·veil′lant** *n.*

sur·vey (sər vā′; *also, & for n. usually*, sur′vā) *vt.* [< Anglo-Fr. < OFr. < *sur-* (see SUR-¹) + *veoir* < L. *videre*, to see] **1.** to examine or inspect carefully **2.** to look at or study in a broad, general way [to *survey* the future prospects of the business] **3.** to find the location, shape, or boundaries of (a piece of land) by measuring lines and angles with a chain, transit, etc. [to *sur-vey* a farm] —*vi.* to survey land —*n., pl.* **-veys 1.** a detailed study made by gathering and analyzing information [a *survey* of public opinion] **2.** a general study or examination [a *survey* of Italian art] **3.** *a)* the process of surveying a piece of land *b)* a plan or written description of the area surveyed

sur·vey·ing (sər vā′iŋ) *n.* **1.** the act of one who surveys **2.** the science or work of surveying land

sur·vey·or (-ər) *n.* a person who surveys, esp. one whose work is surveying land

surveyor's measure a system of measurement used in survey-ing, based on the chain (**surveyor's chain**) as a unit: see CHAIN (*n.* 3)

sur·viv·al (sər vī′v'l) *n.* **1.** the act, state, or fact of surviving [a threat to our *survival*] **2.** someone or something that sur-vives, esp. an ancient belief, custom, usage, etc.

survival of the fittest popular term for NATURAL SELECTION

sur·vive (sər vīv′) *vt.* **-vived′, -viv′ing** [< OFr. < L. < *super-*, above + *vivere*, to live] **1.** to live or exist longer than; outlive [he *survived* his brother] **2.** to continue to live after or in spite of [to *survive* a wreck] —*vi.* to continue living or existing [Thanksgiving is a Pilgrim custom that *survives* today] —see SYN. at OUTLIVE —**sur·vi′vor** *n.*

Su·sa (sōō′sä) capital of ancient Elam, now a ruined city in W Iran

Su·san (sōō′z'n) [Fr. *Susanne* < LL. < Gr. < Heb. *shōshannāh*, lily] a feminine name: dim. *Sue*; var. *Susanna, Susannah*

sus·cep·ti·bil·i·ty (sə sep′tə bil′ə tē) *n., pl.* **-ties 1.** the quality or state of being susceptible **2.** [*pl.*] sensitive feelings

sus·cep·ti·ble (sə sep′tə b'l) *adj.* [< ML. < L. pp. of *sus-cipere*, to receive < *sus-* (see SUB-), under + *capere*, to take] easily affected emotionally; having sensitive feelings —**suscep-tible of** that gives a chance for; allowing [an answer *suscep-tible of* being understood in two different ways] —**susceptible to** easily influenced by or affected with [*susceptible to* disease] —**sus·cep′ti·ble·ness** *n.* —**sus·cep′ti·bly** *adv.*

su·shi (sōō′shē) *n.* [Jap.] a Japanese dish consisting of strips of raw fish wrapped about cakes of cold cooked rice

---

sus·pect (sə spekt′; *for adj. usually, & for n. always,* sus′pekt) *vt.* [< L. pp. of *suspicere* < *sus-* (see SUB-), under + *spicere,* to look] **1.** to believe to be guilty of something, although there is little or no evidence [*the detective suspected* him of murder] **2.** to have no trust in; have doubts about; distrust [I *suspect* his honesty] **3.** to think it likely; guess; suppose [I *suspect* that you are right] —*vi.* to be suspicious —*adj.* viewed with suspicion; suspected [his excuse remains *suspect*] —*n.* a person who is suspected, esp. one suspected of a crime, etc.

sus·pend (sə spend′) *vt.* [< OFr. < L. < *sus-* (see SUB-), under + *pendere,* to hang] **1.** to punish (someone) by removing from a position, school, team, etc., usually for a certain length of time **2.** to stop from operating for a time [to *suspend* bus service, a rule, etc.] **3.** to put off or hold back (judgment, a sentence, etc.) **4.** to hang by a support from above [the keys were *suspended* by a chain from his belt] **5.** to hold in place as though hanging [dust particles *suspended* in the air] —*vi.* to stop temporarily —**sus·pend′i·ble** *adj.*

sus·pend·ed animation (sə spen′did) a state resembling death, in which normal breathing, functioning by bodily organs, etc. slow down or stop temporarily

sus·pend·ers (sə spen′dərz) *n.pl.* **1.** a pair of straps or bands passed over the shoulders to hold up trousers or a skirt **2.** [Brit.] garters for holding up stockings

sus·pense (sə spens′) *n.* [< MFr. < ML. < L. pp. of *suspendere,* to SUSPEND] **1.** the state of being undecided **2.** the state of being anxious and uncertain, as while awaiting a decision **3.** the growing excitement felt as a story, play, etc. builds to a climax

sus·pen·sion (sə spen′shən) *n.* **1.** a suspending or being suspended; specif., *a)* a temporary removal from a position, school, etc. *b)* a temporary stopping of payment, service, etc. *c)* a temporary canceling, as of rules *d)* a holding back of a judgment, etc. **2.** a supporting device upon or from which something is suspended **3.** the system of springs, etc. supporting a vehicle upon its undercarriage **4.** *Chem. a)* the condition of a substance whose particles are spread through a fluid but not dissolved in it *b)* a substance in this condition *c)* a mixture of tiny, solid particles that are suspended in a liquid and that will settle out if the liquid is allowed to stand

suspension bridge a bridge suspended from cables anchored at either end and supported by a series of towers

sus·pen·sive (-siv) *adj.* **1.** that suspends, puts off, or temporarily stops something [a *suspensive* veto] **2.** tending to suspend judgment; undecided **3.** of, characterized by, expressing, or in suspense —**sus·pen′sive·ly** *adv.*

sus·pen·so·ry (-sə rē) *adj.* **1.** suspending, supporting, etc. [a *suspensory* muscle] **2.** suspending or delaying, esp. so as to leave something undecided —*n.,* pl. **-ries** a suspensory muscle, bandage, support, etc.: also **sus·pen′sor**

SUSPENSION BRIDGE

sus·pi·cion (sə spish′ən) *n.* [< OFr. < LL. < L. < *suspicere,* to SUSPECT] **1.** the act of suspecting guilt, a wrong, etc. with little or no evidence **2.** the feeling or idea of a person who suspects [I have a *suspicion* you are right] **3.** a very small amount or degree; trace [a salad with just a *suspicion* of garlic] —*vt.* [Dial.] to suspect —**above suspicion** not to be suspected; honorable —**on suspicion** because suspected —**under suspicion** suspected

sus·pi·cious (-əs) *adj.* **1.** causing or likely to cause suspicion [*suspicious* behavior] **2.** showing suspicion [a *suspicious* look] **3.** *a)* feeling suspicion *b)* tending habitually to suspect evil, etc. [her *suspicious* nature] —**sus·pi′cious·ly** *adv.* —**sus·pi′cious·ness** *n.*

Sus·que·han·na (sus′kwi han′ə) [< Iroquoian tribal or stream name] river flowing from central N.Y. through Pa. & Md. into Chesapeake Bay

sus·tain (sə stān′) *vt.* [< OFr. < L. *sustinere* < *sus-* (see SUB-), under + *tenere,* to hold] **1.** to keep in existence; maintain or prolong [to *sustain* a mood] **2.** to provide for the support of; specif., to provide nourishment for **3.** to support; carry the weight of [heavy piers *sustain* the bridge] **4.** to strengthen the spirits, courage, etc. of; comfort; encourage [hope of rescue *sustained* the shipwrecked sailors] **5.** to bear up under; withstand [that plant can *sustain* only a certain amount of heat] **6.** to undergo; suffer (an injury, loss, etc.) **7.** to uphold as true, correct, etc. [a higher court *sustained* the verdict] **8.** to support or help to prove; corroborate [some of the facts *sustain* her theory, but some do not] —see SYN. at SUPPORT —**sus·tain′a·ble** *adj.* —**sus·tain′er** *n.* —**sus·tain′ment** *n.*

sus·te·nance (sus′ti nəns) *n.* **1.** a sustaining or being sustained **2.** one's means of livelihood; maintenance; support **3.** that which sustains life; nourishment; food

Sut·lej (sut′lej) river flowing from SW Tibet across the Punjab, into the Indus River in Pakistan: c. 900 mi.

sut·ler (sut′lər) *n.* [< ModDu. < *soetelen,* to do dirty work] formerly, a person following an army to sell food, liquor, etc. to its soldiers

sut·tee (su tē′, sut′ē) *n.* [< Hindi < Sans. *satī,* virtuous wife] **1.** a Hindu widow who threw herself alive, and was cremated, on her husband's funeral pyre **2.** the former custom of burning oneself to death in this way: also **sut·tee′ism**

su·ture (sōō′chər) *n.* [< L. < pp. of *suere,* to sew] **1.** *a)* the act of joining together by or as by sewing *b)* the line along which such a joining is made **2.** *Anat.* the line where two bones, esp. of the skull, join together **3.** *Bot. a)* a seam formed when two parts unite *b)* a line of dehiscence along which a fruit, as a pod or capsule, splits **4.** *Surgery a)* the stitching together of the two edges of a wound or incision *b)* the gut, thread, wire, etc. used in such stitching *c)* any of the stitches so made —*vt.* **-tured, -tur·ing** to join together as with sutures —**su′tur·al** *adj.*

Su·va (sōō′vä) seaport & capital of Fiji: pop. 54,000

Su·wan·nee (sə wôn′ē, -wän′-; swô′nē, swä′-) [< AmInd. name] river flowing from S Ga. across N Fla. into the Gulf of Mexico

su·ze·rain (sōō′zə rin, -rān′) *n.* [Fr. < *sus,* above < L. *sursum,* upward + ending of Fr. *souverain,* SOVEREIGN] **1.** a feudal lord **2.** a state in its relation to another state over which it has political control

su·ze·rain·ty (-tē) *n.,* pl. **-ties** the position or power of a suzerain

s.v. [L. *sub verbo*] under the word (specified)

svelte (svelt, sfelt) *adj.* [Fr. < It., ult. < L. *evellere,* to pluck out] **1.** slender and graceful **2.** smoothly gracious, sophisticated, etc.

Sverd·lovsk (sferd lôfsk′) city in western R.S.F.S.R., in the Ural Mountains: pop. 1,026,000

SW, S.W., s.w. **1.** southwest **2.** southwestern

Sw. **1.** Sweden **2.** Swedish

swab (swäb) *n.* [< *swabber* < ModDu. *zwabber* < *zwabben,* to do dirty work] **1.** a mop used with water to clean decks, floors, etc. **2.** *a)* a small piece of cotton, sponge, etc. used to apply medicine to, or clean matter from, the throat, mouth, etc. *b)* matter collected in this way **3.** a brush for cleaning the barrel of a gun **4.** [Slang] *a)* a clumsy, stupid person *b)* a sailor, ☆esp. an enlisted man in the U.S. Navy: also **swab′bie,** **swab′by** (-ē) —*vt.* **swabbed, swab′bing** to clean, medicate, etc. with a swab —**swab′ber** *n.*

Swa·bi·a (swā′bē ə) region in SW West Germany, formerly a duchy —**Swa′bi·an** *adj., n.*

swad·dle (swäd′'l) *vt.* **-dled, -dling** [OE. *swethel*] **1.** to wrap (a newborn baby) in long, narrow bands of cloth (**swaddling clothes** or **bands**), as in former times **2.** to bind in or as in bandages; swathe —*n.* a cloth or bandage used for swaddling

swag (swag) *n.* [< or akin to Norw. *svagga,* to sway] **1.** a swaying or lurching **2.** a valance, garland, chain, etc. hanging decoratively in a loop or curve **3.** [Slang] stolen money or goods; loot; plunder

swage (swāj) *n.* [OFr. *souage*] **1.** a tool for bending or shaping metal **2.** a die or stamp for shaping metal by hammering —*vt.* **swaged, swag′ing** to shape, etc. with a swage

swag·ger (swag′ər) *vi.* [prob. < Norw. dial. *svagra* < *svagga,* to sway] **1.** to walk with a bold, showy stride; strut **2.** to boast, brag, or show off in a loud, superior manner —*n.* swaggering walk, manner, or behavior —*adj.* [Brit. Colloq.] stylish, esp. in an elegant way —see SYN. at BOAST —**swag′ger·er** *n.* —**swag′ger·ing·ly** *adv.*

swagger stick a short stick or cane as carried by some army officers, etc.: also [Brit.] **swagger cane**

Swa·hi·li (swä hē′lē) *n.* [< Ar. *sawāhil,* pl. of *sāhil,* coast + *-i,* belonging to] **1.** pl. **-lis, -li** any of a Bantu people of Zanzibar and the nearby mainland **2.** their Bantu language, widely used in eastern and central Africa

swain (swān) *n.* [< ON. *sveinn,* boy] [Poet. or Archaic] **1.** a country youth **2.** a lover

swale (swāl) *n.* [prob. < ON. *svalr*, cool] a hollow or low area of land; ☆specif., such a place in a wet, marshy area

swal·low[1] (swäl′ō) *n.* [OE. *swealwe*] **1.** any of various small, swift-flying birds with long, pointed wings and a forked tail, known for their regular migrations **2.** any of certain large swifts resembling swallows — **swal′low·like′** *adj.*

swal·low[2] (swäl′ō) *vt.* [OE. *swelgan*] **1.** to pass (food, etc.) from the mouth through the throat into the stomach **2.** to take in; absorb; engulf (often with *up*) [the waters of the lake *swallowed* her up] **3.** to take back (words said); retract **4.** to put up with; tolerate [to *swallow* insults] **5.** to keep from showing; hold back [to *swallow* one's pride] **6.** to say (words) unclearly **7.** [Colloq.] to accept as true without question [surely he didn't *swallow* that story] — *vi.* to move the muscles of the throat as in swallowing, esp. when emotionally upset — *n.* **1.** the act of swallowing **2.** the amount swallowed at one time — **swal′low·er** *n.*

BARN SWALLOW
(to 7½ in. long)

swal·low·tail (-tāl′) *n.* **1.** something having a forked shape like that of a swallow's tail **2.** a butterfly having taillike points on the hind wings

swal·low-tailed coat (-tāld′) a man's full-dress coat, with long, tapering tails at the back

swam (swam) *pt. of* SWIM[1] & SWIM[2]

swa·mi (swä′mē) *n., pl.* **-mis** [< Hindi < Sans. *svāmin*, a lord] **1.** master: a title of respect for a Hindu religious teacher **2.** a learned man   Also sp. **swa′my** *pl.* **-mies**

swamp (swämp, swômp) *n.* [< dial. var. of ME. *sompe*, SUMP] a piece of wet, spongy land; marsh; bog: also ☆**swamp′land** —*adj.* of, living in, or growing in a swamp —*vt.* **1.** to plunge in a swamp, deep water, etc. **2.** to flood with or as with water [the street was *swamped* in the flood] **3.** to overwhelm [*swamped* by debts] **4.** to sink (a boat) by filling with water ☆**5.** to clear of underbrush —*vi.* to sink as in a swamp

☆**swamp buggy** an automotive vehicle for traveling over swampy or muddy ground

☆**swamp fever** *same as* MALARIA

swamp·y (swäm′pē, swôm′-) *adj.* **swamp′i·er**, **swamp′i·est** **1.** of or made up of a swamp or swamps **2.** like a swamp; wet and spongy; marshy — **swamp′i·ness** *n.*

swan (swän, swôn) *n., pl.* **swans, swan:** see PLURAL, II, D, 1 [OE.] a large-bodied water bird with webbed feet, a long, graceful neck, and, usually, pure white feathers —[S-] the constellation Cygnus — **swan′like′** *adj.*

☆**swan dive** a forward dive in which the legs are held straight and together, the back is arched, and the arms are stretched out to the sides until just before the diver enters the water, when the arms are brought forward and together

Swa·nee (swô′nē, swä′-) *same as* SUWANNEE

swang (swaŋ) *archaic or dial. pt. of* SWING

SWAN DIVE

swank (swaŋk) *n.* [akin to OE. *swancor*, pliant, supple] [Colloq.] **1.** stylish display or showiness in dress, etc. **2.** swaggering, showy behavior, speech, etc. —*adj.* [Colloq.] stylish in a showy way —*vi.* [Slang] to show off; boast; swagger

swank·y (swaŋ′kē) *adj.* **swank′i·er**, **swank′i·est** [Colloq.] stylish or expensive in a showy way —**swank′i·ly** *adv.* —**swank′i·ness** *n.*

swan's-down (swänz′doun′, swônz′-) *n.* **1.** the soft, fine underfeathers, or down, of a swan, used for trimming clothes, etc. **2.** a soft, thick fabric of wool and silk, rayon, or cotton, used for making baby clothes, etc. **3.** a soft cotton flannel   Also **swans′down′**

Swan·sea (swän′sē, -zē) seaport in S Wales, on Bristol Channel; pop. 171,000

swan song 1. the sweet song supposed in ancient legend to be sung by a dying swan **2.** the last act, final creative work, etc. of a person

swap (swäp, swôp) *vt., vi.* **swapped, swap′ping** [ME. *swappen*, to strike: hands were struck to conclude a bargain] [Colloq.] to exchange, trade, or barter [to *swap* a horse for a cow] —*n.* [Colloq.] an exchange, trade, or barter —**swap′per** *n.*

sward (swôrd) *n.* [OE. *sweard*, a skin] grass-covered soil; turf

swarm[1] (swôrm) *n.* [OE. *swearm*] **1.** a large number of bees, led by a queen, leaving a hive to start a new colony **2.** a colony of bees in a hive **3.** a moving mass or crowd [a *swarm* of flies, visitors, etc.] —*vi.* **1.** to fly off in a swarm: said of bees **2.** to move, gather, etc. in large numbers; throng [*shoppers* swarmed into the store] **3.** to be filled or crowded; teem [the beach is *swarming* with people] —*vt.* to crowd; throng —see SYN. at CROWD and GROUP —**swarm′er** *n.*

swarm[2] (swôrm) *vi., vt.* [orig. nautical word < ?] to climb (a tree, mast, etc.) using the hands and feet; shin (*up*)

swart (swôrt) *adj.* [OE. *sweart*] *dial. var. of* SWARTHY

swarth (swôrth) *n. dial. var. of* SWARD *adj. same as* SWARTHY

swarth·y (swôr′thē, -thē) *adj.* **swarth′i·er**, **swarth′i·est** [< dial. *swarth*, var. of SWART + -Y[2]] having a dark complexion; dusky —**swarth′i·ly** *adv.* —**swarth′i·ness** *n.*

swash (swäsh, swôsh) *vi.* [echoic] **1.** to dash, strike, wash, etc. with a splashing sound; splash [the waves *swashed* against the pier] **2.** to swagger —*vt.* to splash (a liquid), as in a container —*n.* **1.** a channel of water cutting through or behind a sandbank **2.** the splashing of water **3.** a swaggering action

swash·buck·ler (-buk′lər) *n.* [prec. + BUCKLER] a fighting man who brags and swaggers —**swash′buck′ling** *n., adj.*

swas·ti·ka (swäs′ti ka) *n.* [< Sans. < *svasti*, well-being] **1.** a design or ornament of ancient origin in the form of a cross with four equal arms, each bent in a right-angle extension **2.** this design with the extensions bent clockwise: used as the Nazi emblem

swat (swät) *vt.* **swat′ted, swat′ting** [echoic] [Colloq.] to hit with a quick, sharp blow —*n.* [Colloq.] a quick, sharp blow —**swat′ter** *n.*

swatch (swäch) *n.* [orig., a cloth tally < ?] **1.** a sample piece of cloth or other material **2.** a small amount or number in a cluster, bunch, or patch

swath (swäth, swôth) *n.* [OE. *swathu*, a track] **1.** the space or width covered with one cut of a scythe or other mowing device **2.** the strip or band of grass, wheat, etc. cut in a single trip across a lawn or field by a mower, etc. **3.** any long strip —☆**cut a wide swath** to make a big or showy impression

swathe[1] (swāth) *vt.* **swathed, swath′ing** [OE. *swathian*] **1.** to wrap or bind up in a cloth or bandage **2.** to wrap (a bandage, etc.) around something **3.** to surround or envelop [a city *swathed* in fog] —*n.* a bandage or wrapping —**swath′er** *n.*

swathe[2] (swāth) *n. same as* SWATH

sway (swā) *vi.* [ON. *sveigja*, to bend] **1.** *a)* to swing or move from side to side or to and fro [the flowers *swayed* in the breeze] *b)* to waver between one opinion, etc. and another **2.** to lean or go to one side; veer [the car *swayed* to the right on the curve] —*vt.* **1.** to cause to sway, or swing to and fro, waver, lean to one side, etc. **2.** to change the thinking or actions of; influence in a certain direction [*swayed* by promises] **3.** [Archaic] to rule over; control —*n.* **1.** a swaying or being swayed; a swinging, leaning, etc. **2.** influence or control [under the *sway* of emotion] **3.** rule; dominion [under the king's *sway*] —**hold sway** to rule or be widespread —see SYN. at SWING —**sway′er** *n.*

sway·backed (swā′bakt′) *adj.* having an abnormal sagging of the spine, usually as a result of strain or overwork [a *swaybacked* horse] —**sway′back′** *n.*

Swa·zi·land (swä′zē land′) country in SE Africa, surrounded on three sides by South Africa: 6,705 sq. mi.; pop. 421,000; cap. Mbabane

SWAYBACKED HORSE

swear (swer) *vi.* **swore, sworn, swear′ing** [OE. *swerian*] **1.** to make a serious statement, supporting it with an appeal to God or to something held sacred [to *swear* on one's honor] **2.** to make a serious promise; vow **3.** to use profane or vulgar, offensive

fat, āpe, cär; ten, ēven; is, bīte; gō, hôrn, tōol, look; oil, out; up, fur; get; joy; yet; chin; she; thin, then; zh, leisure; ŋ, ring; ə for *a in ago, e in agent, i in sanity, o in comply, u in focus*; ′ as in able (ā′b'l); Fr. bàl; ë, Fr. coeur; ö, Fr. feu; Fr. mon; ô, Fr. coq; ü, Fr. duc; r, Fr. cri; H, G. ich; kh, G. doch; ‡foreign; ☆ Americanism; < derived from. See inside front cover.

language; curse **4.** *Law* to give evidence under oath —*vt.* **1.** to declare seriously in the name of God or of something held sacred **2.** to pledge or vow on oath [to *swear* loyalty to the party] **3.** to say or promise in a serious way or with great feeling [he *swore* that he would always love her] **4.** to take (an oath) by swearing **5.** to give a legal oath to —**swear by 1.** to name (something held sacred) in taking an oath **2.** to have great faith in [the cook *swears by* this recipe] —**swear for** to give a guarantee for —**swear in** to give an oath to (a person taking office, a witness, etc.) —**swear off** to promise to give up [to *swear off* smoking] —☆**swear out** to get (a warrant for someone's arrest) by making a charge under oath —**swear′er** *n.*

☆**swear·word** (swer′wurd′) *n.* a word or phrase used in swearing or cursing; profane or vulgar, offensive word

sweat (swet) *vi.* **sweat** or **sweat′ed, sweat′ing** [OE. *swǣtan* < *swat*, sweat < IE. base *sweid-*, to sweat] **1.** to give out a salty liquid through the pores of the skin; perspire [running fast made him *sweat*] **2.** *a)* to give out moisture in droplets on its surface, as a ripening cheese *b)* to form water in droplets on its surface [a glass of iced tea *sweats* in a warm room] **3.** to ferment: said of tobacco leaves, etc. **4.** to come out in drops through pores; ooze **5.** to work hard enough to cause sweating [*sweating* over an examination] **6.** [Colloq.] to suffer distress, great worry, etc. [*sweating* until the money arrived] —*vt.* **1.** *a)* to give out (moisture) through a porous surface *b)* to form (moisture) on the surface **2.** to cause to perspire, as by drugs, exercise, etc. **3.** to cause to give out moisture; esp., to ferment [to *sweat* tobacco leaves] **4.** to make wet with perspiration **5.** to heat (an alloy) so as to get an easily melted substance **6.** to unite (metal parts) by heating the solder applied to the ends until it melts **7.** *a)* to cause to work so hard as to sweat; overwork *b)* to cause (employees) to work long hours at low wages under poor working conditions ☆**8.** [Colloq.] *a)* to get information from by torture or exhausting questioning *b)* to get (information) in this way **9.** [Slang] to try hard or too hard to get or achieve —*n.* **1.** the clear, salty liquid given out through the pores in the skin **2.** moisture given out or collected in droplets on a surface **3.** the act or condition of sweating [the long run left him in a *sweat*] **4.** a condition of eagerness, worry, impatience, etc. [in a *sweat* over car payments that were due] **5.** hard work; drudgery —**sweat blood** [Slang] **1.** to work very hard; overwork **2.** to be impatient, anxious, etc. —**sweat off** to get rid of (weight) by sweating —☆**sweat out** [Slang] **1.** to suffer through (something) **2.** to wait for in a worried or impatient way

☆**sweat·band** (swet′band′) *n.* a band of leather, etc. inside a hat to protect it against sweat from the brow

sweat·er (swet′ər) *n.* **1.** a person or thing that sweats **2.** a knitted outer garment for the upper part of the body, styled as a pullover or a jacket

sweat gland any of the many tiny, tubelike glands just beneath the skin that secrete sweat

☆**sweat shirt** a heavy, long-sleeved cotton jersey, worn to absorb sweat during or after exercise: it is sometimes worn with loose trousers (**sweat pants**) of the same material, forming a combination (**sweat suit**)

☆**sweat·shop** (-shäp′) *n.* a shop where employees work long hours at low wages under poor working conditions

sweat·y (-ē) *adj.* **sweat′i·er, sweat′i·est** **1.** wet with sweat; sweating **2.** of sweat [a *sweaty* odor] **3.** causing sweat [*sweaty* work] —**sweat′i·ly** *adv.* —**sweat′i·ness** *n.*

SWEAT SUIT

Swed. 1. Sweden **2.** Swedish

Swede (swēd) *n.* a native or inhabitant of Sweden

Swe·den (swē′d'n) country in N Europe, in the E part of the Scandinavian Peninsula: 173,620 sq. mi.; pop. 8,115,000; cap. Stockholm

Swe·den·borg (swēd′'n bôrg′; *Sw.* sväd′'n bôr′y′), **E·man·u·el** (i man′yoo wəl) (born *Emanuel Swedberg*) 1688–1772; Swed. mystic & religious philosopher —**Swe′den·bor′gi·an** (-bôr′jē ən, -gē-) *adj., n.*

Swed·ish (swē′dish) *adj.* of Sweden, its people, their language, etc. —*n.* the North Germanic language of the Swedes —**the Swedish** the people of Sweden

sweep (swēp) *vt.* **swept, sweep′ing** [akin to (or ? altered <) OE. *swapan*: see SWOOP] **1.** to clear or clean as by brushing with a broom [to *sweep* a floor] **2.** to remove or clear away (dirt, debris, etc.) as with a broom or brushing movement **3.**

to strip, carry away, or destroy with forceful movement [the tornado *swept* the shed away] **4.** to carry along with a sweeping movement [he *swept* the cards into a pile] **5.** to touch or brush in moving across [her dress *sweeps* the ground] **6.** to pass swiftly over or across [his glance *swept* the crowd] **7.** to win overwhelmingly [to *sweep* an election] —*vi.* **1.** to clean a surface, room, etc. as with a broom **2.** to move or progress steadily and with speed or grace [planes *swept* across the sky] **3.** to trail, as skirts or the train of a gown **4.** to reach in a long curve or line [the road *sweeps* up the hill] —*n.* **1.** the act of sweeping, as with a broom **2.** a steady sweeping movement or stroke [the *sweep* of a scythe] **3.** a trailing, as of skirts **4.** the space covered; range [within the *sweep* of their guns] **5.** an unbroken stretch [a *sweep* of meadow] **6.** a long, smooth line, contour, curve, etc. [the graceful *sweep* of the draperies] **7.** a person whose work is sweeping; specif., *short for* CHIMNEY SWEEP **8.** [*usually pl.*] sweepings **9.** complete victory or success, as the winning of all of the contests in a series **10.** a long oar **11.** a long pole mounted on a pivot, with a bucket at one end, used for raising water, as from a well —**sweep′er** *n.*

sweep·ing (swēp′iŋ) *adj.* **1.** reaching in a long curve or line **2.** reaching over a wide range [a *sweeping* look] **3.** *a)* including a great deal; very broad [the ad made *sweeping* claims] *b)* complete [a *sweeping* defeat] —*n.* **1.** [*pl.*] things swept up, as dirt from a floor **2.** the act, work, etc. of one that sweeps —**sweep′ing·ly** *adv.*

sweep·stakes (-stāks′) *n., pl.* **-stakes′** **1.** a lottery in which each participant puts money into a common fund from which the money for the winners comes **2.** *a)* a contest, esp. a horse race, which determines the winners of such a lottery *b)* the prize or prizes won **3.** any of various other lotteries Also **sweep′stake′, sweeps**

sweet (swēt) *adj.* [OE. *swete* < IE. base *swad-*, pleasing to the taste] **1.** *a)* having a taste of, or like that of, sugar *b)* containing sugar in some form [*sweet* wines] **2.** *a)* pleasant in taste, smell, sound, looks, etc. [*sweet* perfume] *b)* agreeable [*sweet* praise] *c)* having a friendly, pleasing manner [a *sweet* child] *d)* sentimental *e)* [Slang] good, delightful, nice, etc. [she hit a *sweet* drive right down the fairway] **3.** *a)* not rancid, spoiled, or sour [*sweet* milk] *b)* not salty or salted: said of water or butter *c)* free from sourness or acidity: said of soil —*n.* **1.** a being sweet; sweetness **2.** something sweet; specif., *a)* [Chiefly Brit.] a candy; sweetmeat *b)* [Brit.] a sweet dessert **3.** a sweet or beloved person; darling —*adv.* in a sweet manner —**be sweet on** [Colloq.] to be in love with —**sweet′ish** *adj.* —**sweet′ly** *adv.* —**sweet′ness** *n.*

sweet alyssum a short garden plant with small spikes of tiny flowers

sweet basil *same as* BASIL

sweet bay 1. *same as* LAUREL (*n.* 1) ☆**2.** a N. American magnolia with fragrant white flowers

sweet·bread (swēt′bred′) *n.* the thymus (**heart**, or **throat, sweetbread**) or the pancreas (**stomach sweetbread**) of a calf, lamb, etc., when used as food

sweet·bri·er, sweet·bri·ar (-brī′ər) *n. same as* EGLANTINE

sweet cherry 1. an old-world cherry, widely grown for its sweet fruit **2.** its fruit

sweet clover any of various plants of the legume family, with small white or yellow flowers and leaflets in groups of three: grown for hay, forage, etc.

☆**sweet corn** a kind of Indian corn with kernels rich in sugar, cooked for eating, often on the cob

sweet·en (swēt′'n) *vt.* **1.** to make sweet with or as with sugar **2.** to make pleasant or agreeable, as in odor **3.** to make less acidic [lime *sweetens* the soil] —*vi.* to become sweet

sweet·en·er (-ər) *n.* a sweetening agent, esp. a synthetic substance, such as saccharin

sweet·en·ing (-iŋ) *n.* **1.** the process of making sweet **2.** something that sweetens

sweet flag a perennial marsh plant with sword-shaped leaves, small, green flowers, and a sweet-scented rhizome

☆**sweet gum 1.** a large N. American tree with leaves shaped like those of the maple, and spiny fruit balls **2.** the wood of this tree **3.** the sweet-smelling balsam of this tree, used in medicine

sweet·heart (swēt′härt′) *n.* **1.** *a)* a person with whom one is in love *b)* darling: a term showing affection **2.** [Slang] a very agreeable person or an excellent thing

sweet·ing (-iŋ) *n.* a kind of sweet apple

sweet marjoram *see* MARJORAM

sweet·meat (-mēt′) *n.* a bit of sweet food, esp. a candy, candied fruit, or the like

sweet pea a climbing plant of the legume family, with sweet-smelling flowers of many colors

sweet pepper 1. a variety of the red pepper producing a large, mild-tasting fruit **2.** the fruit

☆**sweet potato 1.** a tropical vine with purplish flowers and a thick orange or yellow root used as a vegetable **2.** its root **3.** [Colloq.] *same as* OCARINA

☆**sweet-talk** (-tôk′) *vt., vi.* [Colloq.] to talk in a flattering way (to) in an effort to get what one wants

sweet tooth [Colloq.] a fondness or craving for sweets

sweet william, sweet William a plant of the pink family, with clusters of small flowers of many colors

SWEET POTATO
PLANT

swell (swel) *vi.* **swelled, swelled** or **swol′len, swell′ing** [OE. *swellan*] **1.** to become larger as a result of pressure from within; expand **2.** to curve out; bulge; protrude [the vase *swells* into a graceful curve] **3.** to extend above the normal level [all the creeks *swelled* after the thaw] **4.** to form swells, or large waves: said of the sea **5.** to be filled (*with* pride, etc.) [her heart *swelled* with joy] **6.** to increase within one [his anger *swelled*] **7.** to increase in size, force, intensity, etc. [membership *swelled* to a thousand] **8.** to increase in loudness [the music *swelled* to a climax] —*vt.* to cause to swell; specif., *a)* to cause to increase in size, volume, etc. [water *swells* cork] *b)* to cause to bulge [wind *swelled* the sails] *c)* to fill with pride, anger, etc. *d)* to cause to increase in loudness —*n.* **1.** a part that swells; bulge; specif., *a)* a large wave that moves steadily without breaking *b)* a piece of rising ground **2.** a swelling or being swollen **3.** an increase in size, amount, degree, etc. **4.** [Colloq.] a wealthy person who dresses in a stylish way: an old-fashioned term **5.** *Music a)* a gradual increase in loudness of sound usually followed by a gradual decrease *b)* a sign (< >) indicating this *c)* a device for controlling the loudness of tones, as in an organ —*adj.* [Slang] fine, excellent, enjoyable, etc. —see SYN. at EXPAND

swelled head [Colloq.] too high an opinion of oneself

swell·ing (swel′iŋ) *n.* **1.** an increase in size, volume, etc. **2.** a swollen part, as on the body

swel·ter (swel′tər) *vi.* [OE. *sweltan*, to die] to be or feel uncomfortably hot; sweat, feel weak, etc. from great heat —*n.* a sweltering condition

swel·ter·ing (-iŋ) *adj.* very hot, sweaty, sticky, etc.: also **swel′try** (-trē), **-tri·er, -tri·est** —**swel′ter·ing·ly** *adv.*

swept (swept) *pt. & pp. of* SWEEP

swept·back (swept′bak′) *adj.* having a backward slant, as the wings of an aircraft

swept·wing (-wiŋ′) *adj. Aeron.* having sweptback wings

swerve (swurv) *vi., vt.* **swerved, swerv′ing** [OE. *sweorfan*, to scour] to turn aside suddenly from a straight line, course, etc. [the car *swerved* off the road] —*n.* the act or degree of swerving —see SYN. at DEVIATE —**swerv′er n.**

swift (swift) *adj.* [OE.] **1.** moving or capable of moving with great speed; fast **2.** coming, happening, or done quickly [a *swift* reply] **3.** acting or responding quickly; prompt [she was *swift* to help us] —*adv.* in a swift manner —*n.* a swift, insect-eating bird that looks like the swallow, as the chimney swift —see SYN. at FAST[1] —**swift′ly** *adv.* —**swift′ness n.**

Swift (swift), **Jonathan** 1667–1745; Eng. satirist, born in Ireland

swig (swig) *vt., vi.* **swigged, swig′ging** [< ?] [Colloq.] to drink in big gulps or amounts —*n.* [Colloq.] a big gulp, esp. of liquor —**swig′ger n.**

swill (swil) *vt.* [OE. *swilian*] **1.** to flood with water so as to wash **2.** to drink greedily [*swilling* down beer] **3.** to feed swill to (pigs, etc.) —*vi.* to drink liquor in large quantities —*n.* **1.** garbage, table scraps, etc. mixed with liquid and fed to pigs, etc. **2.** garbage or slop **3.** the act of swilling **4.** a swig

swim[1] (swim) *vi.* **swam, swum, swim′ming** [OE. *swimman*] **1.** to move through water by movements of the arms and legs, or of flippers, fins, etc. **2.** to move along smoothly; glide **3.** to float on the surface of a liquid **4.** to be covered with a liquid [food *swimming* in butter] **5.** to overflow [eyes *swimming* with tears] —*vt.* **1.** to move in or across (a body of water) by swimming [to *swim* a river] **2.** to cause to swim [*swim* the horses across] **3.** to perform (a specified stroke) in swimming [to *swim* the backstroke] —*n.* an act, time, or distance of swimming [a short *swim*] —**in the swim** doing what is popular at the moment, or active in current affairs —**swim′ma·ble adj.** —**swim′mer n.**

swim[2] (swim) *n.* [OE. *swima*] the condition of being dizzy —*vi.* **swam, swum, swim′ming 1.** to be dizzy [the fumes made his head *swim*] **2.** to have a hazy or whirling appearance [the room *swam* before her]

swim bladder a gas-filled sac in the body cavity of most bony fishes, giving buoyancy to the body

swim·mer·et (swim′ə ret′) *n.* any of the small parts growing on the abdomen in certain crustaceans, used for swimming and for carrying eggs

☆**swimming hole** a deep place in a river, creek, etc. used for swimming

swim·ming·ly (swim′iŋ lē) *adv.* easily and with success [everything went *swimmingly* at the party]

☆**swimming pool** a pool of water for swimming; esp., a tank specially built for swimming

swim·suit (swim′sōōt′) *n.* a garment worn for swimming

Swin·burne (swin′bərn), **Algernon Charles** 1837–1909; Eng. poet & critic

swin·dle (swin′d'l) *vt.* **-dled, -dling** [< G. *schwindeln*, to cheat] **1.** to cheat or trick (someone) out of money or property; defraud **2.** to get (money or property) in this way —*vi.* to engage in swindling others —*n.* an act of swindling —see SYN. at CHEAT —**swin′dler n.**

swine (swīn) *n., pl.* **swine** [OE. *swin*] **1.** a pig or hog **2.** a mean or disgusting person

swine·herd (swīn′hurd′) *n.* one who tends swine

swing (swiŋ) *vi.* **swung, swing′ing** [OE. *swingan*] **1.** to sway or move backward and forward, as something hanging loosely [a sign *swinging* in the wind] **2.** to walk, trot, etc. with loose, swaying movements [we *swung* off down the road] **3.** to aim a blow; strike (*at*) **4.** *a)* to turn, as on a hinge or swivel [the door *swung* open] *b)* to move in a curve [the driver *swung* right] **5.** *a)* to hang; be suspended *b)* [Colloq.] to be put to death by hanging **6.** to move backward and forward on a swing (*n.* 10) **7.** to have an exciting rhythmic quality [music that really *swings*] ☆**8.** [Slang] to be very fashionable, active, sophisticated, etc.; esp., to have sexual relations freely with a number of persons —*vt.* **1.** *a)* to move (a weapon, bat, etc.) with a sweeping motion; flourish *b)* to lift with a sweeping motion [he *swung* the child up to his shoulder] **2.** to cause (a hanging object) to move backward and forward **3.** to cause to turn or pivot, as on a hinge [*swing* the door shut] **4.** to cause to hang freely [to *swing* a scaffold from the roof] **5.** to cause to move in a curve [to *swing* a car around a corner] ☆**6.** [Colloq.] to manage to do, get, win, etc. [to *swing* an election] —*n.* **1.** the act of swinging **2.** the curved path through which something swings [the *swing* of a pendulum] **3.** the manner of swinging, as with a golf club, baseball bat, etc. [a smooth *swing*] **4.** freedom to do as one wishes [to have full *swing* in the matter] **5.** a relaxed motion, as in walking **6.** a sweeping blow or stroke [he took a *swing* at my jaw] **7.** the course or movement of some activity, etc. [business took a *swing* upward] **8.** the force behind something swung **9.** rhythm, as of poetry or music **10.** a seat hanging from ropes or chains, on which one can sit and swing **11.** a trip or tour [a *swing* around the country] ☆**12.** a style of jazz music of about 1935 to 1945, characterized by the use of large bands, strong rhythms, etc. —☆*adj.* of, in, or playing swing (music) —**in full swing** in full, active operation —**swing′er n.**

SYN.—**swing** suggests the to-and-fro motion of something that is hanging, hinged, pivoted, etc. so that it is free to turn or swivel at the point where it is attached [a *swinging* door]; **sway** suggests the slow, graceful, back-and-forth movement of something flexible, often something standing upright [willow trees *swaying* in the wind]; to **oscillate** is to swing back and forth in a regular way between two points, as the pendulum of a clock does

swin·gle (swiŋ′g'l) *vt.* **-gled, -gling** [< MDu. < *swinghel*, a swingle] to beat and clean (flax or hemp) with a swingle —*n.* a wooden, swordlike tool for beating and cleaning flax or hemp

swin·gle·tree (-trē′) *n. same as* SINGLETREE

☆**swing shift** [Colloq.] the evening work shift in some factories, from midafternoon to about midnight

swin·ish (swīn′ish) *adj.* of, like, or fit for swine; beastly, disgusting, etc. —**swin′ish·ly** *adv.* —**swin′ish·ness** *n.*

swipe (swīp) *n.* [prob. var. of SWEEP] [Colloq.] a hard, sweeping blow —*vt.* **swiped, swip′ing** 1. [Colloq.] to hit with a hard, sweeping blow ☆2. [Slang] to steal

swirl (swurl) *vi.* [ME. swyrl, prob. < Norw. dial. *sverra*, to whirl] to move with a whirling motion [the snow kept *swirling* down] —*vt.* to cause to swirl —*n.* 1. a swirling motion; whirl; eddy 2. a twist; curl 3. dizzy confusion —**swirl′ing·ly** *adv.* —**swirl′y** *adj.*

swish (swish) *vi.* [echoic] 1. to move with a sharp, hissing sound, as a cane swung through the air 2. to rustle, as skirts —*vt.* to cause to swish —*n.* 1. a hissing or rustling sound 2. a movement that makes this sound —*adj.* 1. [Chiefly Brit. Colloq.] fashionable ☆2. [Slang] of, like, or for effeminate male homosexuals —**swish′y** *adj.* **swish′i·er, swish′i·est**

Swiss (swis) *adj.* of Switzerland, its people, or its culture —*n.* 1. *pl.* **Swiss** a native or inhabitant of Switzerland 2. [s-] a type of sheer fabric —**the Swiss** the people of Switzerland

Swiss chard *same as* CHARD

Swiss (**cheese**) a pale-yellow, hard cheese with many large holes, originally made in Switzerland

☆**Swiss steak** a thick cut of round steak, pounded with flour and braised, usually with tomatoes, onions, etc.

switch (swich) *n.* [prob. < MDu. or LowG.] 1. a thin, flexible twig, stick, etc. used for whipping 2. the bushy part of the tail of a cow, etc. 3. a tress of real or false hair used by women in arranging the hair in certain styles 4. a sharp, lashing movement, as with a whip 5. a device used to open, close, or change the path of an electric circuit 6. a movable section of railroad track used in transferring a train from one track to another 7. a shift or change, esp. if sudden [a *switch* in attitude] —*vt.* 1. to whip as with a switch 2. to jerk or swing sharply [a cow *switches* its tail] 3. to shift; change; turn aside [they *switched* the subject to sports] 4. *a*) to operate the switch of (an electric circuit) *b*) to turn (an electric light, etc.) *on* or *off* in this way ☆5. to transfer (a train, etc.) from one track to another by means of a switch 6. [Colloq.] to change or exchange [to *switch* places] —*vi.* ☆1. to move as from one track to another 2. to shift; transfer [he *switched* to a new school] 3. to swing sharply; lash [the tiger's tail *switched* back and forth] —**switch′er** *n.*

☆**switch·back** (swich′bak′) *n.* a zigzag road or railroad up a steep grade

☆**switch-blade knife** (-blād′) a large jackknife that snaps open when a release button on the handle is pressed

☆**switch·board** (-bôrd′) *n.* a panel equipped with apparatus for controlling the operation of a system of electric circuits, as in a telephone exchange

☆**switch-hit·ter** (-hit′ər) *n.* a baseball player who bats sometimes right-handed and sometimes left-handed

switch·man (-mən) *n., pl.* **-men** a railroad employee who operates switches

☆**switch·yard** (-yärd′) *n.* a railroad yard where cars are shifted from one track to another by means of a system of switches, as in making up trains

Switz·er·land (swit′sər lənd) country in WC Europe, in the Alps: 15,941 sq. mi.; pop. 6,270,000; cap. Bern

swiv·el (swiv′'l) *n.* [< base of OE. *swifan*, to revolve] a fastening that allows the parts attached to it to turn freely; specif., a chain link in two parts, one piece fitting like a collar below the bolt head of the other and turning freely about it —*vt.* **-eled** or **-elled, -el·ing** or **-el·ling** 1. to cause to turn as on a swivel 2. to fit or support with a swivel —*vi.* to turn as on a swivel [she *swiveled* around and faced me]

☆**swivel chair** a chair whose seat turns horizontally on a pivot in the base

swiz·zle stick (swiz′'l) [*swizzle*, an early alcoholic drink < ?] a small rod for stirring mixed drinks

swob (swäb) *n., vt.* **swobbed, swob′bing** *var. sp. of* SWAB

swol·len (swō′lən) *alt. pp. of* SWELL —*adj.* bulging, expanded, etc., as from inner pressure

swoon (swoon) *vi.* [< OE. *geswogen*, unconscious] 1. to faint 2. to feel strong, esp. joyous emotion —*n.* an act of swooning —**swoon′er** *n.* —**swoon′ing·ly** *adv.*

swoop (swoop) *vt.* [OE. *swapan*, to sweep

along] to snatch or seize suddenly [the hawk *swooped* up its prey] —*vi.* to come down suddenly and swiftly (with *down* or *upon*) [the plane *swooped* down over our house] —*n.* the act of swooping

swoosh (swoosh, swōōsh) *vi., vt.* [var. of SWISH] to move with a rustling, liquid, or whistling sound [the car *swooshed* along the wet street] —*n.* such a sound

swop (swäp) *n., vt., vi.* **swopped, swop′ping** *var. sp. of* SWAP

sword (sôrd) *n.* [OE. *sweord*] 1. a hand weapon having a long, sharp, pointed blade, set in a hilt 2. *a*) power; esp., military power [''the pen is mightier than the *sword*''] *b*) war —**at swords' points** ready to quarrel or fight —**cross swords** 1. to fight 2. to argue —**put to the sword** 1. to kill with a sword 2. to slaughter, esp. in war —**sword′like′** *adj.*

sword·fish (sôrd′fish′) *n., pl.* **-fish′, -fish′es:** *see* FISH a large ocean fish with an upper jawbone like a long, pointed sword

sword grass any of a number of sedges or grasses with leaves shaped like swords or having jagged edges

sword knot a loop of leather, ribbon, etc. tied to a sword hilt as an ornament

sword·play (-plā′) *n.* the act or skill of using a sword in fencing or fighting

swords·man (sôrdz′mən) *n., pl.* **-men** 1. a person who uses a sword in fencing or fighting 2. a person skilled in using a sword —**swords′man·ship′** *n.*

swore (swôr) *pt. of* SWEAR

sworn (swôrn) *pp. of* SWEAR —*adj.* bound, pledged, promised, etc. by or as by an oath [*sworn* to secrecy]

swot (swät) *n., vt.* **swot′ted, swot′ting** *var. sp. of* SWAT

swum (swum) *pp. of* SWIM[1] & SWIM[2]

swung (swung) *pp. & pt. of* SWING

syb·a·rite (sib′ə rīt′) *n.* [< *Sybarite*, a native of Sybaris, an ancient Greek city in S Italy, famed for its luxury] anyone very fond of luxury, comfort, and costly pleasures —**syb·a·rit·ic** (-rit′ik) *adj.* —**syb′a·rit′i·cal·ly** *adv.*

Syb·il (sib′'l) [< SIBYL] a feminine name

syc·a·more (sik′ə môr′) *n.* [< OFr. < L. < Gr. *sykomoros*] 1. a shade tree of Egypt and Asia Minor, with edible fruit somewhat like the fig ☆2. *same as* PLANE[1]

syc·o·phant (sik′ə fənt) *n.* [< L. < Gr. *sykophantēs*, informer < *sykon*, a fig + *phainein*, to show] a person who flatters wealthy or important people in order to get things from them; toady —**syc′o·phan·cy** (-fən sē) *n., pl.* **-cies** —**syc′o·phan′tic** (-fan′tik), **syc′o·phant′ish** *adj.* —**syc′o·phant′ish·ly** *adv.*

Syd·ney (sid′nē) 1. [< SIDNEY] a masculine name 2. seaport in SE Australia: pop. 2,713,000

syl- *same as* SYN-: used before *l*

syl·la·bar·y (sil′ə ber′ē) *n., pl.* **-bar′ies** [< ModL. < L. *syllaba*: see SYLLABLE] 1. a table of syllables 2. a set of written characters representing the syllables of a language

syl·lab·ic (si lab′ik) *adj.* 1. of a syllable or syllables 2. forming a syllable by itself without a full vowel sound coming before or after [the sound of *l* in *tattle* (tat′'l) is *syllabic*] 3. designating a form of poetry based on the number of syllables in a line rather than on rhythm or stress 4. pronounced so that each of the syllables is clearly heard —*n.* a syllabic sound —**syl·lab′i·cal·ly** *adv.*

syl·lab·i·cate (si lab′ə kāt′) *vt.* **-cat′ed, -cat′ing** *same as* SYLLABIFY —**syl·lab′i·ca′tion** *n.*

syl·lab·i·fy (si lab′ə fī′) *vt.* **-fied′, -fy′ing** [< *syllabification* < L. *syllaba*, syllable + -FICATION] to form or divide into syllables —**syl·lab′i·fi·ca′tion** *n.*

syl·la·ble (sil′ə b'l) *n.* [< OFr. < L. < Gr. *syllabē*, ult. < *syn-*, together + *lambanein*, to hold] 1. a word or part of a word spoken with a single sounding of the voice, without a pause or break 2. any of the parts into which a written word is divided to show where the word may be broken at the end of a line: these parts of a word are related fairly closely to its spoken syllables 3. the slightest detail [don't mention a *syllable* of this] —*vt., vi.* **-bled, -bling** to pronounce in or as in syllables

syl·la·bub (sil′ə bub′) *n.* [< ?] a dessert or beverage made of sweetened milk or cream mixed with wine or cider and beaten to a froth

syl·la·bus (sil′ə bəs) *n., pl.* **-bus·es, -bi′** (-bī′) [LL., a list < L. < Gr. *sillybos*, parchment label] a summary or outline, esp. of a course of study

SWORDFISH
(to 15 ft. long)

SWIVEL CHAIR

syl·lo·gism (sil′ə jiz′m) *n.* [< MFr. < L. < Gr. *syn-*, together + *logizesthai*, to reason] **1.** a form of reasoning in which two statements or premises are made and a logical conclusion is drawn from them Ex.: All mammals are warmblooded (*major premise*); whales are mammals (*minor premise*); therefore, whales are warmblooded (*conclusion*) **2.** reasoning from the general to the particular —**syl′lo·gis′tic** *adj.* —**syl′lo·gis′ti·cal·ly** *adv.*

sylph (silf) *n.* [ModL. *sylphus* < L., a spirit < ?] **1.** an imaginary being supposed to live in the air **2.** a slender, graceful woman or girl —**sylph′like′** *adj.*

syl·van (sil′vən) *adj.* [< ML. < L. *silva*, a woods] **1.** of or characteristic of the woods or forest [*sylvan* beauty] **2.** living, found, or carried on in the woods or forest [a *sylvan* cottage] **3.** wooded [a *sylvan* valley]

Syl·vi·a (sil′vē ə) [< L. < *silva*, a woods] a feminine name

sym- *same as* SYN-: used before *m*, *p*, and *b*

sym·bi·o·sis (sim′bī ō′sis, -bē-) *n.* [ModL. < Gr. < *symbioun* < *syn-*, together + *bioun*, to live] **1.** *Biol.* the intimate living together of two kinds of organisms, esp. when such living together is useful to each **2.** a similar relationship in which persons or groups are dependent on each other —**sym′bi·ot′ic** (-ät′ik) *adj.*

sym·bol (sim′b'l) *n.* [< Fr. < L. < Gr. *symbolon*, token, ult. < *syn-*, together + *ballein*, to throw] **1.** something that stands for another thing; esp., an object that stands for an idea, quality, etc. [the dove is a *symbol* of peace] **2.** a mark, letter, abbreviation, etc. standing for an object, quality, process, quantity, etc., as in music, chemistry, or mathematics

sym·bol·ic (sim bäl′ik) *adj.* **1.** of or expressed in a symbol or symbols [the painting has a *symbolic* meaning] **2.** that serves as a symbol (*of* something) [white is *symbolic* of purity] **3.** using symbolism [*symbolic* poetry] Also **sym·bol′i·cal** —**sym·bol′i·cal·ly** *adv.*

symbolic logic a modern type of formal logic using special mathematical symbols to stand for propositions and for the relationships among propositions

sym·bol·ism (sim′b'l iz′m) *n.* **1.** the use of symbols to stand for things, esp. in art or literature **2.** a system of symbols **3.** symbolic meaning

sym·bol·ist (-ist) *n.* a person who uses symbols, esp. in art or literature —**sym′bol·is′tic** *adj.* —**sym′bol·is′ti·cal·ly** *adv.*

sym·bol·ize (-īz′) *vt.* -**ized′**, -**iz′ing** **1.** to be a symbol of; typify; stand for [a heart *symbolizes* love] **2.** to represent by a symbol or symbols [how does this poet *symbolize* hope?] —*vi.* to use symbols —**sym′bol·i·za′tion** *n.* —**sym′bol·iz′er** *n.*

sym·met·ri·cal (si met′ri k'l) *adj.* having symmetry; balanced [a *symmetrical* design] Also **sym·met′ric** —**sym·met′ri·cal·ly** *adv.*

sym·me·try (sim′ə trē) *n.*, *pl.* -**tries** [< MFr. < L. < Gr., ult. < *syn-*, together + *metron*, a measure] **1.** similarity of form or arrangement on either side of a dividing line or plane; correspondence of opposite parts in size, shape, and position **2.** balance or beauty of form resulting from such correspondence

SYN.—**symmetry** implies an exact correspondence in the form, size, arrangement, etc. of parts on either side of a line or plane going down the center; **proportion** suggests a pleasing relationship, in shape or arrangement, among parts which together form a graceful whole; **balance** implies a contrasting of parts in such a way as to make a stable, orderly whole; **harmony** suggests such an agreement of parts in size, color, form, etc. as to produce a feeling of unity in the whole

Top, symmetrical arrangement; bottom, nonsymmetrical arrangement

sym·pa·thet·ic (sim′pə thet′ik) *adj.* **1.** of, resulting from, feeling, or showing sympathy; sympathizing [*sympathetic* words] **2.** in agreement with one's tastes, mood, etc.; congenial [*sympathetic* surroundings] **3.** showing favor, approval, etc. [to be *sympathetic* to a plan] **4.** *Physiol.* designating or of that part of the autonomic nervous system which has to do with such involuntary response of the body to alarm as the speeding up of the heart rate and the enlargement of the pupils of the eyes **5.** *Physics* designating or of vibrations caused by other vibra-tions transmitted from a neighboring vibrating body —**sym′pa·thet′i·cal·ly** *adv.*

sym·pa·thize (sim′pə thīz′) *vi.* -**thized′**, -**thiz′ing** **1.** to share or understand the feelings or ideas of another; be in sympathy [she was able to *sympathize* with her daughter's longings] **2.** to feel or show sympathy, esp. in pity or compassion; commiserate [to *sympathize* with a friend whose brother died] —**sym′pa·thiz′er** *n.* —**sym′pa·thiz′ing·ly** *adv.*

sym·pa·thy (sim′pə thē) *n.*, *pl.* -**thies** [< L. < Gr. < *syn-*, together + *pathos*, feeling] **1.** sameness of feeling [the *sympathy* between fellow countrymen with regard to their land] **2.** a liking or understanding of each other based on sameness of feeling **3.** a sharing of, or the ability to share, another person's mental state, emotions, etc.; esp., [often pl.] pity or compassion felt for another's trouble, suffering, etc. [he showed *sympathy* for my loss] **4.** a feeling of approval of an idea, cause, etc. [in *sympathy* with the strikers] —see SYN. at PITY

sympathy (or **sympathetic**) **strike** a strike by a group of workers in support of another group on strike

sym·phon·ic (sim fän′ik) *adj.* **1.** of, like, or for a symphony or symphony orchestra **2.** of or having to do with harmony of sound —**sym·phon′i·cal·ly** *adv.*

symphonic poem a composition for a full symphony orchestra, meant to suggest the theme, story, mood, etc. of a certain poem, painting, etc.

sym·pho·ny (sim′fə nē) *n.*, *pl.* -**nies** [< OFr. < L. < Gr. < *syn-*, together + *phōnē*, a sound] **1.** harmony of sounds, esp. of instruments **2.** any harmony, as of color **3.** *Music a)* a long composition for a full orchestra, having several (usually four) movements with different rhythms and themes *b) short for* SYMPHONY ORCHESTRA *c)* [Colloq.] a concert by a symphony orchestra

symphony orchestra a large orchestra made up of string, wind, and percussion sections and playing symphonic works

sym·phy·sis (sim′fə sis) *n.*, *pl.* -**phy·ses′** (-sēz′) [ModL. < Gr. < *syn-*, with + *phyein*, to grow] a growing together, as of bones or parts of a plant

sym·po·si·um (sim pō′zē əm) *n.*, *pl.* -**si·ums**, -**si·a** (-ə) [L. < Gr. *syn-*, together + *posis*, a drinking] **1.** any meeting or social gathering at which ideas are freely exchanged **2.** a conference organized for the discussion of some particular subject **3.** a collection of opinions, esp. a group of essays, on a given subject —**sym·po′si·ac′** (-ak′) *adj.*

symp·tom (simp′təm) *n.* [< ML. < LL. < Gr. *symptōma*, ult. < *syn-*, together + *piptein*, to fall] something which shows that something else exists; indication; sign; specif., *Med.* any condition accompanying a disease or a physical disorder and helping in its diagnosis

symp·to·mat·ic (simp′tə mat′ik) *adj.* **1.** of or having to do with symptoms **2.** that is a symptom [the yellow skin *symptomatic* of jaundice; such behavior is often *symptomatic* of fear] —**symp′to·mat′i·cal·ly** *adv.*

symp·tom·a·tize (simp′tə mə tīz′) *vt.* -**tized′**, -**tiz′ing** to be a symptom or sign of: also **symp′tom·ize′**

syn- [Gr. < *syn*, with] *a prefix meaning* with, together with, at the same time, by means of: *syn-* is changed to *syl-* before *l*; *sym-* before *m*, *p*, and *b*; and *sys-* before *s* and aspirate *h*

syn. **1.** synonym **2.** synonymous **3.** synonymy

syn·a·gogue (sin′ə gäg′, -gôg′) *n.* [< OFr. < LL. < Gr. *synagōgē*, an assembly, ult. < *syn-*, together + *agein*, to bring] **1.** a group of Jews meeting for worship and religious study **2.** a building or place used by Jews for worship and religious study Also **syn′a·gog′** —**syn′a·gog′al** (-gäg′'l, -gôg′-), **syn′a·gog′i·cal** (-gäj′i k'l) *adj.*

syn·apse (si naps′) *n.* [see SYNAPSIS] the point of contact between two neurons, where nerve impulses pass from one to the other

syn·ap·sis (si nap′sis) *n.*, *pl.* -**ses** (-sēs) [ModL. < Gr. < *syn-*, together + *apsis*, a joining < *haptein*, to join] **1.** *Genetics* the pairing of corresponding chromosomes in the early stages of the formation of germ cells **2.** *Physiol.* same as SYNAPSE —**syn·ap′tic** (-tik) *adj.*

sync, synch (siŋk) *vt.*, *vi.* shortened form of SYNCHRONIZE —*n.* shortened form of SYNCHRONIZATION

syn·chro- a combining form meaning synchronized, synchronous [synchromesh]

---

fat, āpe, cär; ten, ēven; is, bīte; gō, hôrn, tōōl, look; oil, out; up, fur; get; joy; yet; chin; she; thin, then; zh, leisure; ŋ, ring; ə for *a* in *ago*, *e* in *agent*, *i* in *sanity*, *o* in *comply*, *u* in *focus*; ′ as in *able* (ā′b'l); Fr. bäl; ë, Fr. coeur; ö, Fr. feu; Fr. mon; ô, Fr. coq; ü, Fr. duc; r, Fr. cri; H, G. ich; kh, G. doch; ‡foreign; ☆ Americanism; < derived from. See inside front cover.

☆**syn·chro·cy·clo·tron** (siŋ′krō sī′klə trän′) *n.* a kind of cyclotron in which the frequency of the accelerating voltage changes as the particles reach high energy levels

syn·chro·mesh (siŋ′krə mesh′) *adj.* designating or using a device by which gears to be meshed are automatically brought to the same speed of rotation before the shift is completed —*n.* a synchromesh gear system

syn·chro·nism (siŋ′krə niz′m) *n.* **1.** the fact or state of being synchronous; occurrence at the same time **2.** a chronological listing of persons or events in history, showing existence or occurrence at the same time —**syn′chro·nis′tic** (-nis′tik) *adj.* —**syn′chro·nis′ti·cal·ly** *adv.*

syn·chro·nize (siŋ′krə nīz′) *vi.* **-nized′, -niz′ing** [< Gr. < *syn-chronos*, contemporary < *syn-*, together + *chronos*, time] to move or happen at the same time or rate; be synchronous —*vt.* **1.** to cause to agree in time or rate of speed; regulate (clocks, motion-picture action and dialogue, etc.) so as to make synchronous **2.** to assign (events, etc.) to the same date or period — **syn′chro·ni·za′tion** *n.* —**syn′chro·niz′er** *n.*

syn·chro·nous (-nəs) *adj.* [< LL. < Gr.: see prec.] **1.** happening at the same time; simultaneous **2.** having the same period of time between movements, occurrences, etc.; having the same rate and phase, as vibrations Also **syn′chro·nal, syn·chron·ic** (sin krän′ik, siŋ-)—see SYN. at CONTEMPORARY — **syn′chro·nous·ly** *adv.* —**syn′chro·nous·ness** *n.*

☆**syn·chro·tron** (siŋ′krə trän′) *n.* [SYNCHRO(NOUS) + (ELEC)TRON] a circular machine for accelerating charged particles, esp. electrons, to very high energies through the use of a low-frequency magnetic field in combination with a high-frequency electrostatic field

syn·cline (siŋ′klīn) *n.* [< Gr. < *syn-*, together + *klinein*, to incline] *Geol.* a fold of stratified rock in which the strata slope upward in opposite directions from the central axis: opposed to ANTICLINE —**syn·cli·nal** (sin klī′n′l, siŋ′kli n′l) *adj.*

syn·co·pate (siŋ′kə pāt′) *vt.* **-pat′ed, -pat′ing** [< ML. pp. of *syncopare*, to cut short < LL., to swoon < *syncope*: see SYNCOPE] **1.** to shorten (a word) by syncope **2.** *Music* to shift (the regular accent) as by beginning a tone on an unaccented beat and continuing it through the next accented beat, or on the last half of a beat and continuing it through the first half of the following beat *b)* to use such shifted accents in (a composition, etc.) —**syn′co·pa′tor** *n.*

syn·co·pa·tion (siŋ′kə pā′shən) *n.* **1.** a syncopating or being syncopated **2.** syncopated music, a syncopated rhythm, etc.

syn·co·pe (siŋ′kə pē) *n.* [LL. < Gr. < *syn-*, together + *koptein*, to cut] **1.** the dropping of sounds or letters from the middle of a word, as in *Gloster* for *Gloucester* **2.** a loss of consciousness caused by an inadequate flow of blood to the brain

SYNCOPATION

syn·dic (sin′dik) *n.* [Fr. < LL. < Gr. *syndikos*, advocate < *syn-*, together + *dikē*, justice] **1.** [Brit.] a business manager, esp. of a university **2.** a civil magistrate —**syn′di·cal** *adj.*

syn·di·cal·ism (sin′di k′l iz′m) *n.* a theory according to which all means of production and distribution would be brought under the control of federations of labor unions by the use of direct action, such as general strikes —**syn′di·cal·ist** *adj., n.*

syn·di·cate (sin′də kit; *for v.* -kāt′) *n.* [Fr. *syndicat* < *syndic*, SYNDIC] **1.** a council of syndics **2.** *a)* an association of individuals or corporations formed to carry out some project requiring much capital *b)* any group organized to carry out some project; ☆specif., an association of criminals set up to control vice, gambling, etc. *c)* a group of similar organizations, ☆as of newspapers, owned as a chain ☆**3.** an organization that sells articles or features for publication by many newspapers or periodicals —*vt.* **-cat′ed, -cat′ing** **1.** to manage as or form into a syndicate ☆**2.** to sell (an article, comic strip, etc.) through a syndicate for publication in many newspapers or periodicals —*vi.* to form a syndicate —see SYN. at MONOPOLY —**syn′di·ca′tion** *n.* —**syn′di·ca′tor** *n.*

syn·drome (sin′drōm) *n.* [ModL. < Gr. < *syn-*, with + *dramein*, to run] **1.** a set of symptoms characterizing a certain disease **2.** any set of characteristics identifying a certain type, condition, etc.

syne (sīn) *adv., conj., prep.* [Scot.] since; ago

syn·ec·do·che (si nek′də kē) *n.* [< ML. < L. < Gr., ult. < *syn-*, together + *ekdechesthai*, to receive] a figure of speech in which a part is used for a whole, a whole for a part, an individual for a class, a class for an individual, or a material for a thing

made of that material (Examples: *bread* for *food*, *the army* for *a soldier*, or *denims* for *trousers*)

syn·er·gism (sin′ər jiz′m) *n.* [< ModL. < Gr. < *syn-*, together + *ergon*, work] the simultaneous action of separate agencies which, together, have a greater total effect than the sum of their individual effects: said esp. of drugs: also **syn′er·gy** (-jē) — **syn′er·gis′tic** *adj.* —**syn′er·gis′ti·cal·ly** *adv.*

Synge (siŋ), (Edmund) **John Mil·ling·ton** (mil′iŋ tən) 1871-1909; Ir. dramatist

syn·od (sin′əd) *n.* [OE. *sinoth*, ult. < Gr. *synodos*, a meeting < *syn-*, together + *hodos*, way] **1.** a council of churches or church officials; specif., a high governing body in any of certain Christian churches **2.** any assembly or council —**syn′od·al** *adj.*

syn·od·i·cal (si näd′i k′l) *adj.* **1.** of a synod **2.** *Astron.* of or having to do with conjunction, esp. with the period of time between two successive conjunctions of the same heavenly bodies Also **syn·od′ic** —**syn·od′i·cal·ly** *adv.*

syn·o·nym (sin′ə nim) *n.* [< L. < Gr. < *syn-*, together + *onyma*, a name] **1.** a word having the same or nearly the same meaning as another in the same language [*"little"* is a *synonym* of *"small"*] **2.** the name of something used for the name of something else closely associated with it [*"the press"* is a *synonym* for *"journalists"*] —**syn′o·nym′ic, syn′o·nym′i·cal** *adj.*

syn·on·y·mize (si nän′ə mīz′) *vt.* **-mized′, -miz′ing** to give a synonym or synonyms for (a word)

syn·on·y·mous (si nän′ə məs) *adj.* [see prec.] of the same or nearly the same meaning —**syn·on′y·mous·ly** *adv.*

syn·on·y·my (-mē) *n., pl.* **-mies** **1.** the study of synonyms **2.** a list or listing of synonyms, esp. one in which slight differences in meaning between the synonyms are pointed out **3.** the quality of being synonymous; sameness or near sameness of meaning

syn·op·sis (si näp′sis) *n., pl.* **-ses** (-sēz) [LL. < Gr. < *syn-*, together + *opsis*, a seeing] a short outline or review of the main points, as of a story; summary —see SYN. at ABRIDGMENT

☆**syn·op·size** (-sīz) *vt.* **-sized, -siz·ing** to make a synopsis of; summarize

syn·op·tic (-tik) *adj.* **1.** of or giving a synopsis, summary, or general view **2.** giving an account from the same point of view: said esp. [*often* S-] of the first three Gospels Also **syn·op′ti·cal** —**syn·op′ti·cal·ly** *adv.*

syn·o·vi·a (si nō′vē ə) *n.* [ModL. < ?] the clear, albuminous lubricating fluid secreted by the membranes of joint cavities, tendon sheaths, etc. —**syn·o′vi·al** *adj.*

syn·tac·tic (sin tak′tik) *adj.* of or in accordance with the rules of syntax: also **syn·tac′ti·cal** —**syn·tac′ti·cal·ly** *adv.*

syn·tax (sin′taks) *n.* [< Fr. < LL. < Gr., ult. < *syn-*, together + *tassein*, to arrange] *Gram.* **1.** the way words are put together and related to one another in sentences; sentence structure **2.** the branch of grammar dealing with this

syn·the·sis (sin′thə sis) *n., pl.* **-ses′** (-sēz′) [Gr. < *syn-*, together + *tithenai*, to place] **1.** the putting together of parts or elements so as to form a whole **2.** a whole formed in this way **3.** *Chem.* the formation of a complex compound by the combining of two or more simpler compounds, elements, or radicals —**syn′the·sist** *n.*

syn·the·size (-sīz′) *vt.* **-sized′, -siz′ing** **1.** to bring together into a whole by synthesis [a composition which *synthesizes* ragtime and the blues] **2.** to form by bringing together separate parts; specif., *Chem.* to produce by synthesis rather than by extraction, refinement, etc.

syn·the·siz·er (-sī′zər) *n.* a person or thing that synthesizes; ☆specif., an electronic music device that produces sounds not made by ordinary musical instruments

syn·thet·ic (sin thet′ik) *adj.* **1.** of, involving, or using synthesis **2.** produced by synthesis; specif., produced by synthesizing chemicals rather than by using natural products [*synthetic* rubber] **3.** not real or genuine; artificial [*synthetic* enthusiasm] **4.** using inflection rather than word order and function words to express relationships of syntax [Latin is a *synthetic* language] Also **syn·thet′i·cal** —*n.* something synthetic —**syn·thet′i·cal·ly** *adv.*

synthetic resin any of a large class of complex organic compounds formed from simpler molecules by polymerization, used esp. in making plastics

syph·i·lis (sif′ə lis) *n.* [ModL. < *Syphilus*, hero of a Latin poem (1530)] a disease caused by a spirochete and usually passed on during sexual intercourse or gotten in the womb before birth —**syph′i·lit′ic** *adj., n.*

sy·phon (sī′fən) *n., vi., vt. var. sp. of* SIPHON

Syr. **1.** Syria **2.** Syriac **3.** Syrian

Syr·a·cuse (sir′ə kyoos′, -kyooz′) **1.** [after the Gr. city-state] city in central N.Y.: pop. 197,000 (met. area 636,000) **2.** seaport on the SE coast of Sicily (in ancient times, a Gr. city-state): pop. 105,000

Syr Dar·ya (sir där′yä) river in central U.S.S.R., flowing from Uzbek S.S.R. into the Aral Sea: c. 1,700 mi.

Syr·i·a (sir′ē ə) **1.** region of ancient times at the E end of the Mediterranean **2.** country in the NW part of this region: 71,227 sq. mi.; pop. 6,451,000; cap. Damascus

Syr·i·ac (sir′ē ak′) *n.* the ancient Aramaic language of Syria, used from the 3d cent. A.D. to the 13th

Syr·i·an (sir′ē ən) *adj.* of Syria, its people, their language, etc. —*n.* **1.** a member of the Semitic people of Syria **2.** their modern Arabic dialect

sy·rin·ga (sə rin′gə) *n.* [ModL., genus name < Gr. *syrinx* (see SYRINGE): from former use in making pipes] **1.** *same as* LILAC (senses 1 & 2) **2.** *earlier name for* MOCK ORANGE

sy·ringe (sə rinj′, sir′inj) *n.* [< ML. < Gr. *syringos*, genitive of *syrinx*, a reed, pipe] **1.** a device consisting of a narrow tube with a rubber bulb or piston at one end by means of which a liquid can be drawn in and then pushed out in a stream: used to inject fluids into, or extract fluids from, body cavities, to wash out wounds, etc. **2.** *short for* HYPODERMIC SYRINGE —*vt.* **-ringed′, -ring′ing** to wash, inject, etc. with a syringe

SYRINGE

syr·inx (sir′inks) *n., pl.* **sy·rin·ges** (sə rin′jēz), **syr·inx·es** [ModL. < Gr., a pipe] **1.** the vocal organ of songbirds, at or near the base of the trachea **2.** *same as* PANPIPE

syr·up (sir′əp, sur′-) *n.* [< OFr. < ML. < Ar. *sharāb*, a drink] any sweet, thick liquid; specif., *a)* a solution made by boiling sugar with water and, often, flavored *b)* *short for* MAPLE SYRUP, CORN SYRUP, etc. —**syr′up·y** *adj.*

sys·tem (sis′təm) *n.* [< LL. < Gr. *systēma*, ult. < *syn-*, together + *histanai*, to set] **1.** a group of things or parts working together or connected in some way so as to form a whole [a solar *system*, school *system*, *system* of highways] **2.** a set of principles, rules, etc. linked in an orderly way to show a logical plan [an economic *system*] **3.** a method or plan of classifying or arranging [a seating *system*] **4.** *a)* an established way of doing something; method; procedure [her *system* for training dogs] *b)* orderliness or careful planning in one's way of doing things [she studies without much *system*] **5.** *a)* the body as a whole [the poison spread throughout his *system*] *b)* a number of organs acting together to perform one of the main bodily functions [the nervous *system*] **6.** a related series of natural objects or elements, as rivers **7.** *Geol.* a major division of stratified rocks comprising the rocks laid down during a period —see SYN. at METHOD

sys·tem·at·ic (sis′tə mat′ik) *adj.* **1.** based on or forming a system [a *systematic* philosophy] **2.** according to a system, method, or plan; regular; orderly [a *systematic* search] **3.** orderly in planning or doing things; methodical [a *systematic* person] **4.** of or having to do with classification Also **sys′tem·at′i·cal** —see SYN. at ORDERLY —**sys′tem·at′i·cal·ly** *adv.*

sys·tem·a·tize (sis′təm ə tīz′) *vt.* **-tized′, -tiz′ing** to form into a system; arrange according to a system; make systematic —**sys′tem·a·ti·za′tion** *n.* —**sys′tem·a·tiz′er** *n.*

sys·tem·ic (sis tem′ik) *adj.* of a system; specif., *Physiol.* of or affecting the entire organism or bodily system —☆*n.* any of a group of pesticides that are absorbed into the tissues of plants, making the plants poisonous to insects, etc. that feed on them —**sys·tem′i·cal·ly** *adv.*

sys·tem·ize (sis′tə mīz′) *vt.* **-ized′, -iz′ing** *same as* SYSTEMATIZE —**sys′tem·i·za′tion** *n.*

☆**systems analysis** an engineering technique that breaks down complex technical, social, etc. problems into basic elements whose relationships are studied and programmed into a complete and unified system —**systems analyst**

☆**systems engineering** a branch of engineering using computer science, facts from systems-analysis studies, etc. to design systems for operating certain kinds of organizations —**systems engineer**

sys·to·le (sis′tə lē′) *n.* [ModL. < Gr. *systolē*, ult. < *syn-*, together + *stellein*, to send] the usual rhythmic contraction of the heart, esp. of the ventricles, during which the blood is pushed out from the heart into the arteries —**sys·tol·ic** (sis täl′ik) *adj.*

Szcze·cin (shche tsēn′) river port in NW Poland, on the Oder: pop. 335,000

T

T, t (tē) *n.*, *pl.* **T's, t's** **1.** the twentieth letter of the English alphabet **2.** the sound of *T* or *t*

T (tē) *n.* an object shaped like T —*adj.* shaped like T —**to a T** to perfection; exactly

't it: a contraction, as in *'twas, do't*

-t *var. of* -ED (in some past participles and adjectives derived from them) *[slept]*

T. **1.** tablespoon(s) **2.** Territory **3.** Testament **4.** Tuesday

t. **1.** teaspoon(s) **2.** temperature **3.** tense **4.** time **5.** ton(s) **6.** town(ship) **7.** transitive **8.** troy

Ta *Chem.* tantalum

tab[1] (tab) *n.* [< ?] **1.** a small, flat loop or strap fastened to something *[he hung his jacket by the tab]* **2.** a projecting part fastened to a card or paper, used in filing **3.** *Aeron.* an auxiliary airfoil set into the back edge of a larger control surface, as an aileron —*vt.* **tabbed, tab'bing** **1.** to provide with tabs **2.** to select or name *[she was tabbed the best prospect for future stardom]*

tab[2] (tab) ☆*n.* [prob. < TABULATE] [Colloq.] **1.** a bill or check, as for expenses **2.** total cost or expenses —☆**keep tabs** (or **a tab**) **on** [Colloq.] to follow or watch every move of; check on —☆**pick up the tab** [Colloq.] to pay the bill or total cost

tab[3] (tab) *n. shortened form of:* **1.** TABLET **2.** TABULATOR —*vt.* **tabbed, tab'bing** *shortened form of* TABULATE

tab·ard (tab'ərd) *n.* [OFr. *tabart*] **1.** a loose, heavy jacket worn outdoors as by peasants in the Middle Ages **2.** a cloak having short sleeves and decorated with his coat of arms, worn by a knight over his armor **3.** a herald's official coat, decorated with his lord's coat of arms

Ta·bas·co (tə bas'kō) [< *Tabasco*, a Mexican state] ☆*a trademark for* a hot sauce made from a kind of red pepper

tab·by (tab'ē) *n.*, *pl.* **-bies** [< Fr. < ML. < Ar. *'attābi*, quarter of Baghdad where it was made] **1.** a silk taffeta with wavy markings **2.** a gray or brown cat with dark stripes **3.** any pet cat, esp. a female —*adj.* having dark stripes over gray or brown

tab·er·na·cle (tab'ər nak''l) *n.* [< LL. < L. *tabernaculum*, a tent, dim. of *taberna*, a hut] **1.** formerly, a temporary shelter, as a tent **2.** [T-] *a)* the holy sanctuary carried by the Jews in their wanderings from Egypt to Palestine: Ex. 25–27 *b)* later, the Jewish Temple **3.** a shrine, niche, etc. covered by a canopy **4.** a place of worship, esp. one seating many people **5.** a container for consecrated Hosts, usually in the center of the altar at the back —**tab'er·nac'u·lar** (-yə lər) *adj.*

ta·bes dor·sa·lis (tā'bēz dôr sā'lis, -sal'is) [ModL. < L. *tabes*, a wasting away + *dorsualis*, of the back] a chronic disease of the nervous system, usually caused by syphilis and characterized by loss of reflexes, lack of muscular coordination, etc.

ta·ble (tā'b'l) *n.* [OFr. < L. *tabula*, a board, tablet] **1.** orig., a thin slab of metal, stone, or wood, used for inscriptions; tablet **2.** *a)* a piece of furniture consisting of a flat top set on legs *b)* such a table set with food for a meal *[invited to eat at the captain's table]* *c)* food served at a meal *[sharing his table with friends]* *d)* the people seated at a table *[our table played bridge]* **3.** a large, flat-topped piece of furniture or equipment used for games, as a working surface, etc. *[pool table, examining table]* **4.** *a)* a compact, orderly list *[a table of contents]* *b)* a

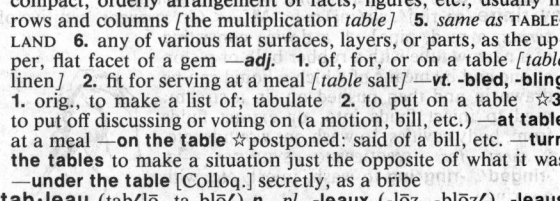
TABARD

compact, orderly arrangement of facts, figures, etc., usually in rows and columns *[the multiplication table]* **5.** *same as* TABLELAND **6.** any of various flat surfaces, layers, or parts, as the upper, flat facet of a gem —*adj.* **1.** of, for, or on a table *[table linen]* **2.** fit for serving at a meal *[table salt]* —*vt.* **-bled, -bling** **1.** orig., to make a list of; tabulate **2.** to put on a table *[table linen]* **3.** to put off discussing or voting on (a motion, bill, etc.) —**at table** at a meal —**on the table** ☆postponed: said of a bill, etc. —**turn the tables** to make a situation just the opposite of what it was —**under the table** [Colloq.] secretly, as a bribe

tab·leau (tab'lō, ta blō') *n.*, *pl.* **-leaux** (-lōz, -blōz'), **-leaus** [Fr. < OFr. *tablel*, dim. of *table*: see prec.] **1.** a striking, dramatic scene or picture **2.** a representation of a scene, picture, etc. by a person or group in costume, posing silently without moving

ta·ble·cloth (tā'b'l klôth', -kläth') *n.* a cloth for covering a table, esp. at meals

ta·ble d'hôte (tä'b'l dōt', tab''l) *pl.* **ta'bles d'hôte'** (-b'lz, -'lz) [Fr., lit., table of the host] a complete meal with courses as specified, served at a restaurant or hotel for a set price: distinguished from A LA CARTE

ta·ble·land (tā'b'l land') *n.* a high, broad, level region; plateau

table linen tablecloths, napkins, etc.

ta·ble·spoon (-spōōn') *n.* **1.** *a)* a large spoon used for serving food *b)* *same as* SOUPSPOON **2.** a spoon used as a measuring unit in cooking, equal to 3 teaspoonfuls or 1/2 fluid ounce **3.** *same as* TABLESPOONFUL

ta·ble·spoon·ful (-fool) *n.*, *pl.* **-fuls** as much as a tablespoon will hold

tab·let (tab'lit) *n.* [< MFr. dim. of *table*: see TABLE] **1.** a flat, thin piece of stone, metal, etc., esp. one with words written on it or carved into it **2.** a smooth, flat leaf of wood, metal, etc., used to write on **3.** a writing pad containing sheets of paper fastened at one edge **4.** a small, flat piece of some hard substance, as medicine, soap, etc.

table tennis a game somewhat like tennis in miniature, played on a table with a small celluloid or plastic ball and wooden paddles

ta·ble·ware (tā'b'l wer') *n.* dishes, glassware, silverware, etc. for use at meals

table wine a wine to be served with meals, with from 8 to 13 percent alcohol

Tab·loid (tab'loid) [TABL(ET) + -OID] *a trademark for* a small tablet of medicine —*n.* [t-] a newspaper with pages about half the usual size, many pictures, and short, often sensational, news stories —*adj.* [t-] condensed; short

TABLE TENNIS

ta·boo (ta bōō', tə-) *n.* [Tongan *tabu*] **1.** *a)* among some Polynesian peoples, a sacred rule which does not allow certain people or things to be touched, talked about, etc. *b)* the system of such rules **2.** any custom or tradition in a society, which makes something forbidden *[a taboo against using certain words in polite speech]* —*adj.* **1.** sacred and forbidden by taboo **2.** forbidden by custom, tradition, etc. —*vt.* **1.** to put under taboo **2.** to prohibit or forbid

ta·bor (tā′bər) *n.* [OFr. *tabur* < Per. *tabīrah*] a small drum, formerly used by a fife player to beat out a rhythm to accompany himself Also sp. **ta′bour**

tab·o·ret (tab′ər it, tab′ə ret′) *n.* [OFr., a stool, dim. of *tabur:* see prec.] **1.** a small tabor **2.** a stool Also sp. **tab′ou·ret**

Ta·briz (tä brēz′) city in NW Iran: pop. 468,000

ta·bu (ta bōō′, tə-) *n., adj., vt. var. sp. of* TABOO

tab·u·lar (tab′yə lər) *adj.* [< L. < *tabula:* see TABLE] **1.** flat like a table [*tabular* rock] **2.** *a)* of or arranged in tables or columns [*tabular* data] *b)* calculated by using tables —**tab′u·lar·ly** *adv.*

ta·bu·la ra·sa (tab′yə lə rä′sə) [< L. *tabula*, tablet + *rasa*, fem. pp. of *radere*, to erase] a blank tablet; clean slate [the mind of a newborn infant may be thought of as a *tabula rasa*]

tab·u·late (tab′yə lāt′; *for adj.* -lit) *vt.* **-lat·ed**, **-lat·ing** [< L. *tabula* (see TABLE) + -ATE¹] to put (facts, statistics, etc.) in a table or columns; arrange systematically —*adj.* having a flat surface —**tab′u·la′tion** *n.*

tab·u·la·tor (-lāt′ər) *n.* a person or thing that tabulates; specif., a device or key for setting stops on a typewriter carriage, as for typing columns

tac·a·ma·hac (tak′ə mə hak′) *n.* [< Sp. < Nahuatl *tecomahca*] **1.** a strong-smelling gum resin used in ointments and incenses **2.** any of several trees producing this resin

ta·chom·e·ter (ta käm′ə tər, tə-) *n.* [< Gr. *tachos*, speed + -METER] a device that indicates or measures the revolutions per minute of a revolving shaft —**ta·chom′e·try** *n.*

tac·it (tas′it) *adj.* [< Fr. < L. pp. of *tacere*, to be silent] not expressed openly, but implied or understood; silent [his smile gave *tacit* approval] —**tac′it·ly** *adv.* —**tac′it·ness** *n.*

tac·i·turn (tas′ə turn′) *adj.* [< Fr. < L. < *tacere:* see prec.] almost always silent; not liking to talk —see SYN. at SILENT —**tac′i·tur′ni·ty** *n.* —**tac′i·turn′ly** *adv.*

Tac·i·tus (tas′ə təs), (Publius Cornelius) 55?–117? A.D.; Rom. historian

tack (tak) *n.* [MDu. *tacke*, a twig, point] **1.** a short nail or pin with a sharp point and a somewhat large, flat head **2.** a long, loose stitch used in sewing, as to baste a hem **3.** a zigzag course, or movement in such a course **4.** a course of action [taking a new *tack*] **5.** *Naut. a)* a rope for holding securely the forward lower corner of some sails *b)* the corner thus held *c)* the direction in which a ship is moving in relation to the position of the sails *d)* a change of direction made by changing the position of the sails *e)* a course against the wind *f)* any of a series of zigzag movements in such a course **6.** a horse's equipment, as saddles, bridles, etc. —*vt.* **1.** to fasten with tacks [to *tack* down a carpet] **2.** to fasten loosely, as with long stitches **3.** to add or attach as something extra [to *tack* an amendment onto a bill] **4.** *Naut. a)* to change the course of (a ship) by turning its bow into the wind *b)* to maneuver (a ship) against the wind by a series of tacks —*vi.* **1.** *a)* to tack a ship *b)* to change its course by being tacked: said of a ship **2.** to go in a zigzag course **3.** to change suddenly one's course of action —**tack′er** *n.*

WIND

TACKING

tack·le (tak′l; *in nautical usage, often* tā′k'l) *n.* [MDu. *takel*, pulley, rope] **1.** apparatus; equipment; gear [fishing *tackle*] **2.** a system of ropes and pulleys, used to lower, raise, or move weights **3.** the act or an instance of tackling, as in football **4.** Football the player next to either end on the offensive or defensive line **5.** *Naut.* the ropes and pulleys used to raise and lower a ship's sails —*vt.* **tack′led**, **tack′ling** **1.** to fasten with tackle **2.** to harness (a horse) **3.** to take hold of; seize **4.** to undertake to do, solve, or deal with [to *tackle* a problem] **5.** *Football* to stop or throw down (an opponent carrying the ball) —*vi.* *Football* to tackle an opponent —**tack′ler** *n.*

tack room a room near a stable in which tack (sense 6) is kept

tack·y¹ (tak′ē) *adj.* **tack′i·er**, **tack′i·est** [< *tack*, stickiness & -Y²] sticky, as varnish, glue, etc. before completely dry —**tack′i·ness** *n.*

☆**tack·y²** (tak′ē) *adj.* **tack′i·er**, **tack′i·est** [< *tacky*, a hillbilly < ?] [Colloq.] unfashionable or shabby, as in appearance —**tack′i·ness** *n.*

☆**ta·co** (tä′kō) *n., pl.* **-cos** [AmSp.] a Mexican dish consisting of a fried, folded tortilla filled with chopped meat, shredded lettuce, etc.

Ta·co·ma (tə kō′mə) [AmInd., lit., snowy peak] seaport in W Wash., on Puget Sound: pop. 155,000

☆**tac·o·nite** (tak′ə nīt′) *n.* [< *Taconic* Range in Vt. and Mass.] a low-grade iron ore

tact (takt) *n.* [Fr. < L. pp. of *tangere*, to touch] a sense of the right thing to say or do without offending; skill in dealing with people

tact·ful (takt′fəl) *adj.* having or showing tact —**tact′ful·ly** *adv.* —**tact′ful·ness** *n.*

tac·tic (tak′tik) *n.* [< ModL. < Gr.: see TACTICS] **1.** *same as* TACTICS **2.** a detail of tactics; skillful move

tac·ti·cal (tak′ti k'l) *adj.* **1.** of or having to do with tactics, esp. in military or naval maneuvers **2.** characterized by or showing skill in tactics —**tac′ti·cal·ly** *adv.*

tac·ti·cian (tak tish′ən) *n.* an expert in tactics

tac·tics (tak′tiks) *n.pl.* [Gr. (*ta*) *taktika*, lit., (the) matters of arrangement < *tassein*, to arrange] **1.** *a)* [*with sing. v.*] the science of maneuvering military and naval forces in battle in trying to gain an advantage *b)* actions based on this science **2.** any methods used to bring about some result, esp. skillful methods

tac·tile (tak′t'l; *chiefly Brit.* -tīl) *adj.* [Fr. < L. *tactilis* < *tangere*, to touch] **1.** that can be perceived by the touch; tangible **2.** of, having, or related to the sense of touch —**tac·til′i·ty** (-til′ə tē) *n.*

tact·less (takt′lis) *adj.* not having or showing tact —**tact′less·ly** *adv.* —**tact′less·ness** *n.*

tad·pole (tad′pōl′) *n.* [ME. *tadde*, toad + *poll*, head] the larva of frogs and toads, having gills and a tail and living in water

Ta·dzhik Soviet Socialist Republic (tä′jik) republic of the U.S.S.R., in C Asia: 55,250 sq. mi.; pop. 2,900,000; cap. Dushanbe: also **Ta·dzhik·i·stan** (tä jēk′i stän′)

tael (tāl) *n.* [Port. < Malay *tahil*, a weight] **1.** any of various units of weight of E Asia **2.** formerly, a Chinese unit of money

ta·'en (tān) [Archaic] taken

taf·fe·ta (taf′i tə) *n.* [< OFr., ult. < Per. < *tāftan*, to weave] a fine, rather stiff fabric of silk, nylon, acetate, etc., with a sheen —*adj.* like or made of taffeta

TADPOLE
(in three stages)

taff·rail (taf′rāl′) *n.* [< Du. *tafereel*, a panel, ult. < L. *tabula:* see TABLE] the rail around a ship's stern

taf·fy (taf′ē) *n.* [< ?] a chewy candy made of sugar or molasses boiled down and pulled: see TOFFEE

Taft (taft), **William Howard** 1857–1930; 27th president of the U.S. (1900–13); chief justice of the U.S. (1921–30)

tag (tag) *n.* [prob. < Scand.] **1.** orig., a hanging end, as on a torn skirt **2.** any hanging part or loosely attached end **3.** a hard-tipped end, as of metal, on a cord or lace ☆**4.** a card, paper, ticket, etc. attached to something as a label or for identification, etc. [a price *tag*] **5.** a word or phrase that describes a person or thing; epithet **6.** the sentence or sentences ending a speech, story, play, etc. **7.** a children's game in which one player, called "it," chases the others until he touches, or tags, one of them, making him "it" in turn ☆**8.** *Baseball* the act of tagging —*vt.* **tagged, tag′ging** **1.** to provide with a tag; put a tag on **2.** to identify or label; call by an epithet [she was soon *tagged* as a rebel] **3.** to choose or select [he was *tagged* for the job] ☆**4.** to overtake and touch as in the game of tag ☆**5.** *Baseball* to touch (a base runner) with the ball, thus putting him out **6.** [Colloq.] to hit hard **7.** [Colloq.] to follow close behind —*vi.* [Colloq.] to follow close behind a person or thing (usually with *along, after*, etc.) [when he left for school, the dog *tagged* along] —**tag′ger** *n.*

Ta·ga·log (tä gä′läg, -lôg) *n.* **1.** *pl.* **-logs, -log** a member of a Malayan people of the Philippine Islands **2.** their Indonesian language

tag end 1. any loosely attached or hanging end **2.** the last part of something; remnant

fat, āpe, cär; ten, ēven; is, bīte; gō, hôrn, tōōl, lōōk; oil, out; up, fur; get; joy; yet; chin; she; thin, then; zh, leisure; ŋ, ring; ə for *a* in *ago*, *e* in *agent*, *i* in *sanity*, *o* in *comply*, *u* in *focus*; ' as in *able* (ā′b'l); Fr. bâl; ë, Fr. coeur; ö, Fr. feu; ô, Fr. coq; ü, Fr. duc; r, Fr. cri; H, G. ich; kh, G. doch; ‡foreign; ☆ Americanism; < derived from. See inside front cover.

Ta·gore (tä′gôr, tə gôr′), Sir **Ra·bin·dra·nath** (rə bēn′drə nät′) 1861–1941; Hindu poet

Ta·gus (tä′gəs) river flowing west across C Spain & Portugal into the Atlantic

Ta·hi·ti (tə hēt′ē, tä-) chief island of the Society Islands, in the South Pacific —**Ta·hi·ti·an** (tə hēsh′ən, tä-; -hēt′ē ən) *adj., n.*

Ta·hoe (tä′hō), Lake [< AmInd. *tah-oo*, lake] lake on the border between Calif. & Nev.

Tai (tī) *n., adj.* same as THAI

tai·ga (tī′gə) *n.* [Russ.] the forests of cone-bearing trees in the far northern regions of Eurasia and North America

tail[1] (tāl) *n.* [OE. *tægel*] **1.** the rear end of an animal's body, esp. when forming a distinct, movable part that extends beyond the backbone **2.** anything like an animal's tail in form or position [the *tail* of a shirt] **3.** the part that trails behind a comet and gives off light **4.** the hind, last, bottom, or inferior part of anything **5.** [*often pl.*] the reverse side of a coin **6.** *a)* the rear section of an aircraft, rocket, or missile *b)* a set of stabilizing planes at the rear of an airplane ☆**7.** [*pl.*] [Colloq.] *a)* a swallow-tailed coat *b)* full-dress attire for men **8.** [Colloq.] a person who follows another, esp. in order to keep watch on him —*adj.* **1.** at the rear **2.** from the rear [a *tail* wind] —*vt.* **1.** to provide with a tail **2.** to fasten at or by the tail **3.** to fasten one end of (a brick, board, etc.) into a wall, etc. ☆**4.** [Slang] to follow closely, esp. in order to keep watch on —*vi.* **1.** to move along in a rambling line [five embarrassed boys *tailed* out of the room] **2.** to become gradually smaller or fainter (with *off* or *away*) [her voice *tailed* off into silence] ☆**3.** [Colloq.] to follow close behind —☆**on one's tail** following one closely —**turn tail** to run from danger, difficulty, etc. —**tail′less** *adj.* —**tail′like** *adj.*

tail[2] (tāl) *n.* [< OFr. < *taillier*: see TAILOR] same as ENTAIL (*n.* 2 & 3) —*adj.* limited in a specific way as to inheritance

☆**tail·back** (tāl′bak′) *n.* *Football* the offensive back farthest from the line of scrimmage

tailed (tāld) *adj.* having a (specified kind of) tail: usually in combination [*bobtailed*]

tail end **1.** the rear or bottom end of anything **2.** the concluding part of anything

☆**tail·gate** (tāl′gāt′) *n.* a board or gate at the back of a wagon, truck, station wagon, etc.: it can be removed or swung down for loading, etc.: also **tail′board′** —*vi., vt.* **-gat′ed, -gat′ing** to drive too closely behind (another vehicle) —**tail′gat′er** *n.*

tail·ing (tāl′iŋ) *n.* **1.** [*pl.*] waste or refuse left in milling, mining, etc. **2.** the part of a projecting brick, stone, etc. fastened into a wall

tail·light (tāl′līt′) *n.* a light, usually red, at the rear of a vehicle to warn vehicles coming from behind

TAILGATE

tai·lor (tā′lər) *n.* [< OFr. < *taillier*, to cut < LL. *taliare*, to split < L. *talea*, a twig] a person who makes, repairs, or alters suits, coats, etc. —*vi.* to work as a tailor —*vt.* **1.** to make (clothes) by tailor's work **2.** to make clothes for **3.** to make, change, etc. so as to meet certain conditions [a movie *tailored* for young people] **4.** to fashion (women's garments) with trim, simple lines —**tai′lor·ing** *n.*

tai·lor·bird (-bʉrd′) *n.* any of several small Asiatic and African birds that stitch leaves together to camouflage and hold their nests

tai·lored (tā′lərd) *adj.* having trim, simple lines, as some women's garments, or specially fitted, as slipcovers

tai·lor-made (tā′lər mād′) *adj.* made by or as by a tailor; specif., *a)* having trim, simple lines; tailored *b)* made-to-order or made to meet a particular need

tail·piece (tāl′pēs′) *n.* **1.** a part forming the end of something **2.** the piece of wood at the lower end of a violin, cello, etc., to which the strings are attached: see illustration at VIOLIN **3.** a short beam with one end tailed in a wall and the other supported by a header **4.** *Printing* an ornamental design, as at the end of a chapter

☆**tail·pipe** (-pīp′) *n.* **1.** an exhaust pipe at the rear of an automotive vehicle **2.** the exhaust duct of a jet engine

tail·race (-rās′) *n.* the lower part of a millrace, through which water flows after turning a water wheel

tail·spin (-spin′) *n.* **1.** same as SPIN (*n.* 4) **2.** a state of rapidly increasing depression or confusion

tail·stock (-stäk′) *n.* the adjustable part of a lathe, which holds the work to be turned

tail wind a wind blowing in the same direction as the course of a ship or aircraft

taint (tānt) *vt.* [prob. a merging of ME. *taynten*, to touch + Anglo-Fr. *teinter*, to color, ult. < L. *tingere*, to wet] **1.** to affect with something harmful, unpleasant, etc.; spoil, infect, etc. [water *tainted* by chemicals] **2.** to make morally corrupt [her character was not *tainted* by the evil she saw] —*n.* a trace of something that harms, spoils, corrupts, etc. —**taint′less** *adj.*

Tai·pei, Tai·peh (tī′pe′) capital of Taiwan: pop. 1,700,000

Tai·wan (tī′wän′) island province of China, off the SE coast: seat of the Kuomintang government: 13,885 sq. mi.; pop. 14,964,000; cap. Taipei —**Tai′wan′i·an** *adj., n.*

Tai·yü·an (tī′yü än′) city in N China: pop. 1,500,000

Taj Ma·hal (täzh′ mə häl′, täj′) large tomb at Agra, India, built (1630?–48?) by a Mogul emperor for his favorite wife

ta·ka (tä′kä) *n., pl.* **-ka** [< Sans. *tŏnkŏ*, silver coins] see MONETARY UNITS, table (Bangladesh)

take (tāk) *vt.* **took, tak′en, tak′ing** [OE. *tacan* < ON. *taka*] **1.** to get possession of by force or skill; capture, seize, etc. [the soldiers *took* the city] **2.** *a)* to win (a game, a trick at cards, etc.) *b)* to capture (an opponent's piece in chess or checkers) **3.** to get hold of; grasp [he *took* her in his arms] **4.** to affect; attack [*taken* with a fit] **5.** to capture the fancy of; charm [we were *taken* by her wit] **6.** to get into one's hand or hold [he *took* the pen and began to write] **7.** to eat, drink, etc. for nourishment or as medicine **8.** to enter into a special relationship with [to *take* a wife] **9.** to buy [he *took* the first suit he tried on] **10.** to rent, lease, etc. [to *take* a cottage] **11.** to get regularly by paying for [to *take* a newspaper] **12.** to assume as a responsibility, task, etc. [to *take* a job, *take* a vow] **13.** to assume (a symbol of duty or office, etc.) [the president *took* the chair] **14.** to join or support (one side in a contest, disagreement, etc.) **15.** to assume as if granted or due one [to *take* the blame, to *take* deductions] **16.** to choose; select [*take* five cards from the deck] **17.** to use [*take* a mop to the floor] **18.** *a)* to travel by [to *take* a bus] *b)* to set out on; follow [*take* that path] **19.** to go to for shelter, safety, etc. [to *take* cover] **20.** to consider [to *take* a matter seriously] **21.** *a)* to occupy [take a chair] *b)* to use up [it *took* all day] **22.** to require; need [it *takes* money] **23.** to derive (a name, quality, etc.) from something or someone **24.** to get or draw from a source, as for quotation [he *took* a verse from the Bible] **25.** to obtain by observation, experiment, etc. [*take* her temperature] **26.** to be enrolled as a student in (a course, etc.) **27.** to write down [to *take* notes] **28.** to make (a photograph, picture, etc.) **29.** to make an impression of [*take* his fingerprints] **30.** to win (a prize, etc.) **31.** to undergo or endure [to *take* punishment] **32.** to occupy oneself or engage in [to *take* a nap] **33.** to accept (something offered) [to *take* advice] **34.** to have a specified reaction to [to *take* a joke in earnest] **35.** to manage to get over, through, etc. [the horse *took* the jump] **36.** to be affected by [he *took* cold] **37.** to absorb (a dye, polish, etc.) **38.** to understand [he *took* her remarks as praise] **39.** to suppose [he *took* her to be a clerk] **40.** to have or feel (an emotion, etc.) [*take* pity] **41.** to do; perform [to *take* a walk] **42.** to conduct; lead [this path *takes* you home] **43.** to escort [*take* a friend to lunch] **44.** to carry [to *take* a book with one] **45.** to remove as by stealing **46.** to bring to an end [cancer *takes* many lives] **47.** to subtract [*take* two from four] **48.** to direct (oneself) **49.** [Colloq.] to aim [he *took* a jab at me] **50.** [Slang] to cheat; trick **51.** *Gram.* to be used with [a transitive verb *takes* an object] —*vi.* **1.** to get possession **2.** to take root; begin growing: said of a plant **3.** to catch [the fire *took* rapidly] **4.** to gain public favor; be popular **5.** to be effective in action, etc. [the vaccination *took*] **6.** to detract (*from*) [nothing *took* from the scene's beauty] **7.** to go [to *take* to the hills] **8.** [Colloq. or Dial.] to become (sick) —*n.* **1.** the act or process of taking **2.** something taken **3.** *a)* the amount taken [the day's *take* of fish] *b)* [Slang] money received; receipts **4.** a movie scene photographed with an uninterrupted run of the camera **5.** any of a series of recordings or tapes of a performance, from which one will be selected for release to the public —see SYN. at BRING —☆**on the take** [Slang] willing to take bribes, etc. —**take after** **1.** to be, act, or look like **2.** to run after: also **take out** (or **off**) **after** —**take amiss** to become offended at (an act) —**take back** to withdraw (something said, etc.) —**take down** **1.** to separate into its parts; take apart. **2.** to humble (a person) **3.** to put in writing; record —☆**take five** (or **ten**, etc.) take a five (or ten, etc.) minute break, as from working —**take for** **1.** to consider to be **2.** to mistake for —**take in** **1.** to admit; receive **2.** to make smaller **3.** to include

4. to understand **5.** to cheat; trick ☆**6.** to visit or view [to *take in* the sights] —**take it** [Slang] ☆to withstand hardship, criticism, etc. —☆**take it out on** [Colloq.] to make (another) suffer for one's own anger, irritation, etc. —**take off 1.** to go away **2.** to deduct **3.** to leave the ground or water in flight: said of an aircraft **4.** [Colloq.] to start **5.** [Colloq.] to imitate; mimic —**take on 1.** to acquire; assume **2.** to employ **3.** to undertake (a task, etc.) **4.** to play against; oppose **5.** [Colloq.] to show strong feeling, esp. anger or sorrow —**take one's time** to be unhurried —**take out 1.** to remove **2.** to apply for and get **3.** [Colloq.] to escort —**take over** to begin controlling, managing, etc. —**take to 1.** to apply oneself to (work, etc.) **2.** to become fond of —**take up 1.** to make tighter or shorter **2.** to pay off (a mortgage, note, etc.) **3.** to absorb (a liquid) **4.** to accept (a challenge, bet, etc.) **5.** to resume (something interrupted) **6.** to become interested in (an occupation, belief, etc.) **7.** to occupy (space or time) —**take upon (or on) oneself 1.** to take the responsibility for **2.** to begin (to do something) —**take up with** [Colloq.] to become a friend or companion of —**tak′a·ble, take′a·ble** *adj.* —**tak′er** *n.*

☆**take-home pay** (tāk′hōm′) wages or salary after deductions for income tax, social security, etc. have been made

tak·en (tāk′'n) *pp.* of TAKE

take·off (tāk′ôf) *n.* **1.** the act of leaving the ground, as in an airplane by jumping **2.** the place from which one leaves the ground ☆**3.** the starting point or early stages of something **4.** [Colloq.] an amusing imitation as done in making fun of someone; burlesque Also **take′-off′**

take·out (-out′) *n.* a taking out —*adj.* ☆describing or of prepared food sold by a restaurant to be taken away and eaten elsewhere Also **take′-out′**

take·o·ver (-ō′vər) *n.* the act of seizing power or getting control in a nation, organization, etc.: also **take′-o′ver**

tak·ing (tāk′iŋ) *adj.* attractive; charming [a *taking* smile] —*n.* **1.** the act of one that takes **2.** something taken; catch **3.** [*pl.*] earnings; profits —**tak′ing·ly** *adv.*

talc (talk) *n.* [Fr. < Ar. *ṭalq*] **1.** a soft mineral, magnesium silicate, used to make talcum powder, lubricants, etc. **2.** *shortened form of* TALCUM POWDER —*vt.* **talcked** or **talced, talck′ing** or **talc′ing** to use talc on

tal·cum (**powder**) (tal′kəm) a powder for the body and face made of powdered, purified talc, usually perfumed

tale (tāl) *n.* [OE. *talu*] **1.** something told or related **2.** a story of events that are true or made-up; narrative **3.** a piece of harmful gossip **4.** a falsehood; lie **5.** [Archaic] a tally; count —see SYN. at STORY¹

tale·bear·er (tāl′ber′ər) *n.* a person who spreads gossip, tells secrets, etc.: also **tale′tell′er** (-tel′ər) —**tale′bear′ing** *adj., n.*

tal·ent (tal′ənt) *n.* [OE. *talente* < L. < Gr. *talanton*, a unit of money, weight] **1.** any of various large units of weight or of money in ancient times in Greece, Rome, the Middle East, etc. **2.** any natural ability or power [to develop one's *talents*] **3.** a special, superior ability in an art, science, craft, etc. [a *talent* for acting] **4.** people who have talent [encouraging local *talent*] —**tal′ent·ed** *adj.*

SYN.—**talent** implies a natural ability to do a certain thing and suggests that the ability has been or can be developed through training, practice, etc. [a *talent* for drawing]; **gift** suggests a special ability that is thought of as having been given, as by nature, rather than gotten through effort [a *gift* for making friends]; **aptitude** implies a special ability which makes it likely that one can do a certain kind of work easily and well [aptitude tests]; **faculty** implies a special ability or skill that is either natural or acquired [she has developed the *faculty* of getting along with others]; **knack** implies an ability, gained through practice or experience, to do something easily and cleverly [the *knack* of writing limericks]; **genius** may imply any great natural ability [he has a *genius* for always saying the right thing], but more often suggests an extraordinary natural power to do creative, original work in the arts or sciences [the *genius* of Leonardo da Vinci]

☆**talent scout** a person whose work is seeking out talented persons who can be trained or used as movie actors, professional athletes, etc.

ta·ler (tä′lər) *n., pl.* **ta′ler** [G.: see DOLLAR] a former German silver coin

ta·les·man (tālz′mən, tā′lēz-) *n., pl.* **-men** *Law* a person summoned to fill a vacancy in a jury when the regular jury panel lacks the proper number

ta·li (tā′lī) *n. alt. pl.* of TALUS¹

tal·i·pes (tal′ə pēz′) *n.* [ModL. < L. *talus*, an ankle + *pes*, a foot] *same as* CLUBFOOT

tal·i·pot (tal′ə pät′) *n.* [Beng. *tālipāt*, palm leaf < Sans.] a palm tree of the East Indies, with very large leaves used for fans, umbrellas, etc.: also **talipot palm**

TALIPOT

tal·is·man (tal′is mən, -iz-) *n., pl.* **-mans** [Fr. < Ar. < MGr. *telesma*, a consecrated object] **1.** a ring, stone, etc. carved with figures supposed to bring good luck, keep away evil, etc. **2.** anything supposed to have magic power; a charm —**tal′is·man′ic** (-man′ik), **tal′is·man′i·cal** *adj.*

talk (tôk) *vi.* [ME. *talken*, prob. based on OE. *talian*, to reckon] **1.** to put ideas into spoken words, or exchange ideas by spoken words; speak **2.** to express ideas by some means other than speech [to *talk* in sign language] **3.** to speak of unimportant matters; chatter **4.** to gossip **5.** to confer; consult [she *talked* with her lawyer before signing the paper] **6.** to make noises suggestive of speech [teaching the parrot to *talk*] **7.** to reveal secret information **8.** to make a somewhat informal speech —*vt.* **1.** to put into spoken words; utter [to *talk* nonsense] **2.** to use in speaking [to *talk* Spanish] **3.** to discuss [to *talk* sports] **4.** to put into a specified condition by talking [to *talk* oneself hoarse] —*n.* **1.** *a)* the act of talking *b)* conversation **2.** an informal speech [he gave a *talk* on gardening] **3.** a conference [*talks* between the company and the union] **4.** gossip [there is *talk* going around about him] **5.** the subject of conversation, gossip, etc. [the *talk* of the town] **6.** empty, frivolous discussion **7.** a particular kind of speech; dialect, etc. **8.** sounds, as by an animal, suggestive of speech —see SYN. at SPEAK and SPEECH —**big talk** [Slang] bragging talk —☆**talk back** to answer disrespectfully or rudely —**talk big** [Slang] to boast —**talk down** to silence by talking louder, longer, or more effectively than —**talk down to** to talk to (a person) in a simple way, as if one does not consider him to be very intelligent or important —**talk out** to discuss (a problem, etc.) at length in an effort to reach an understanding —**talk over 1.** to discuss **2.** to persuade (a person) by talking —**talk up** ☆**1.** to promote or praise in discussion **2.** to speak loudly and clearly ☆**3.** to speak boldly, frankly, etc. —**talk′er** *n.*

☆**talk·a·thon** (tôk′ə thän′) *n.* [TALK + (MAR)ATHON] any period of talking carried on for a very long time

talk·a·tive (-tiv) *adj.* talking, or fond of talking, a great deal; loquacious —**talk′a·tive·ness** *n.*

SYN.—**talkative**, which implies a fondness for talking often and at length, is, unlike the other terms here, usually used in favorable descriptions with no suggestion of contempt [a witty, *talkative* girl]; **loquacious** usually implies a tendency to talk without stopping or to keep up a seemingly endless flow of chatter [a *loquacious* teacher who went on lecturing after the bell rang]; **garrulous** implies a tendency to talk at great length and in a boring, rambling way about unimportant matters [a *garrulous* old man]; **voluble** suggests a continuous flow of smooth, glib talk [a *voluble* orator] —ANT. taciturn, reserved

☆**talking book** a recording of a reading of a book, etc. for use esp. by the blind

talking picture *earlier name for* a motion picture that has a sound track on the film: also [Colloq.] ☆**talk′ie** (-ē) *n.*

☆**talking point** a point that is stressed because it seems to be one that will help in winning an argument

talk·ing-to (tôk′iŋ too′) *n.* [Colloq.] a rebuke; scolding

talk·y (tôk′ē) *adj.* **1.** talkative **2.** containing too much talk, or dialogue [a *talky* novel] —**talk′i·ness** *n.*

tall (tôl) *adj.* [< OE. (ge)tæl, swift] **1.** of more than normal height or stature **2.** having a specified height [five feet *tall*] ☆**3.** [Colloq.] hard to believe; exaggerated [a *tall* tale] ☆**4.** [Colloq.] large [a *tall* drink] —see SYN. at HIGH —**tall′ish** *adj.* —**tall′ness** *n.*

Tal·la·has·see (tal′ə has′ē) [< Creek Indian name] capital of Fla., in the N part: pop. 72,000

Tal·ley·rand (tal′ē rand′; Fr. tà lā rän′) (born *Charles Maurice de Talleyrand-Périgord*) 1754–1838; Fr. statesman & diplomat

Tal·linn (tàl′lin) capital of the Estonian S.S.R., on the Gulf of Finland: pop. 363,000: also sp. **Tallin**

tal·lit, tal·lith (tä lēt′, täl′is) *n.* [< LHeb. < *ṭālal*, to cover] *Judaism* a fringed shawl worn by men during morning prayer: see Deut. 22:12

tal·low (tal′ō) *n.* [prob. < MLowG. *talg*] the pale-yellow solid fat extracted from the natural fat of cattle, sheep, etc., used in making candles, soaps, lubricants, etc. —*vt.* to cover or smear with tallow —**tal′low·y** *adj.*

TALLIT

tal·ly (tal′ē) *n., pl.* **-lies** [Anglo-L. *talia* < L. *talea*, a stick] **1.** *a)* orig., a stick that has notches representing the amount of a debt *b)* anything used in keeping a record of an account or score **2.** an account, reckoning, or score [keep a *tally* of what you spend] **3.** an identifying tag or label —*vt.* **-lied, -ly·ing** **1.** to put on or as on a tally; record [we *tallied* two runs in the ninth inning] **2.** to count (usually with *up*) [*tally* up the score] —*vi.* **1.** to tally something **2.** to score a point or points in a game **3.** to agree; correspond [his story of what happened doesn't *tally* with hers]

tal·ly·ho (tal′ē hō′; *for n. & v.,* tal′ē hō′) *interj.* [altered < Fr. *taïaut*] the cry of a hunter when he sees the fox —*n., pl.* **-hos′** **1.** a cry of "tallyho" **2.** a coach drawn by four horses —*vi.* to cry "tallyho"

Tal·mud (täl′mood, tal′-; -məd) *n.* [LHeb. *talmūdh*, lit., learning < Heb. *lāmadh*, to learn] the writings which form the Jewish civil and religious law —**Tal·mud′ic, Tal·mud′i·cal** *adj.* —**Tal′mud·ism** *n.* —**Tal′mud·ist** *n.*

tal·on (tal′ən) *n.* [< OFr., ult. < L. *talus*, an ankle] **1.** the claw of a bird of prey, or, sometimes, of an animal **2.** a human finger or hand that looks like a claw or is used like a claw —**tal′oned** *adj.*

ta·lus¹ (tā′ləs) *n., pl.* **-lus·es, -li** (-lī) [ModL. < L., an ankle] **1.** the anklebone **2.** the entire ankle

ta·lus² (tā′ləs) *n.* [Fr. < OFr. *talu* < L. *talutium*, surface indication of gold under the earth] **1.** a slope **2.** a pile of rock debris at the foot of a cliff or below a rock face

tam (tam) *n. short for* TAM-O′-SHANTER

☆**ta·ma·le** (tə mä′lē) *n.* [< MexSp. < Nahuatl *tamalli*] a native Mexican food of minced meat and red peppers rolled in cornmeal, wrapped in corn husks, and cooked by baking, steaming, etc.

☆**tam·a·rack** (tam′ə rak′) *n.* [< Algonquian] **1.** an American larch tree, usually found in swamps **2.** its wood

tam·a·rind (tam′ə rind) *n.* [< Sp. < Ar. *tamr hindī*, date of India] **1.** a tropical tree with yellow flowers and brown pods with an acid pulp **2.** its pods, used in foods, medicine, etc.

tam·a·risk (tam′ə risk) *n.* [< LL. < L. *tamarix*] any of a group of trees or shrubs with slender branches and feathery flower clusters, often grown for a windbreak

tam·ba·la (täm bä′lä) *n., pl.* **ma′tam·ba′la** (mä′-) [native term, lit., rooster] *see* MONETARY UNITS, table (Malawi)

tam·bour (tam′boor) *n.* [< MFr. < OFr. < Ar. *tanbūr*, stringed instrument < Per.] **1.** a drum **2.** a frame consisting of two hoops, one fitting closely inside the other, used to stretch and hold cloth for embroidery ☆**3.** a door, panel, etc. as in a cabinet, made of narrow, wooden slats that slide in grooves, as around curves —*vt., vi.* to embroider on a tambour

tam·bour·a, tam·bur·a (täm boor′ə) *n.* [Per. *tambūra*] a lutelike instrument of India, usually with four strings

tam·bou·rine (tam′bə rēn′) *n.* [Fr., dim. of *tambour:* see TAMBOUR] a shallow, single-headed hand drum having jingling metal disks in the rim: played by shaking, hitting with the hand, etc. —**tam′bou·rin′ist** *n.*

TAMBOURINE

tame (tām) *adj.* **tam′er, tam′est** [OE. *tam*] **1.** taken from a wild state and trained for use by man or as a pet: said of animals **2.** gentle and easy to manage; docile **3.** not lively or interesting; dull [the old sailor found life in the village rather *tame*] —*vt.* **tamed, tam′ing** **1.** to make (wild animals) tame **2.** to make gentle, easy to manage, or spiritless; subdue **3.** to make less intense; soften —*vi.* to become tame —**tam′a·ble, tame′a·ble** *adj.* —**tame′ly** *adv.* —**tame′ness** *n.* —**tam′er** *n.*

tame·less (tām′lis) *adj.* **1.** not tamed **2.** not tamable

Tam·er·lane (tam′ər lān′) [< *Timur lenk*, Timur the lame] 1336?-1405; Mongol warrior whose conquests extended from the Black Sea to the upper Ganges

Tam·il (tam′′l, täm′-, tum′-) *n.* **1.** *pl.* **-ils, -il** any of a Tamil-speaking people of southern India and northern Ceylon **2.** the Dravidian language of the Tamils, ancient or modern

☆**Tam·ma·ny** (tam′ə nē) *n.* [altered < *Tamanend*, a 17th-c. Am. Indian chief] a powerful Democratic political organization of New York City, incorporated in 1789: also **Tammany Society, Tammany Hall** —*adj.* of Tammany's practices, members, etc.

Tam·muz (tä′mooz) *n.* [Heb.] *see* JEWISH CALENDAR

tam-o′-shan·ter (tam′ə shan′tər) *n.* [< main character of R. Burns's poem "Tam o'Shanter"] a Scottish cap with a round, flat top

tamp (tamp) *vt.* [< ? TAMPION] **1.** in blasting, to pack clay, sand, etc. around the charge in (the drill hole) **2.** to pack or pound (*down*) by a series of blows or taps [to *tamp* down tobacco in a pipe]

Tam·pa (tam′pə) [< AmInd. village name] seaport in WC Fla., on an arm (**Tampa Bay**) of the Gulf of Mexico: pop. 278,000 (met. area, incl. St. Petersburg, 1,013,000)

TAM-O′-SHANTER

tamp·er¹ (tam′pər) *n.* a person or thing that tamps; specif., any of various instruments or tools for tamping

tam·per² (tam′pər) *vi.* [var. of TEMPER] [Archaic] to plot; scheme —**tamper with** **1.** to make secret, illegal arrangements with, as by bribing [to *tamper with* a witness] **2.** to handle or interfere with in a way that is wrong or so as to damage, etc. [someone had *tampered* with the lock] —**tam′per·er** *n.*

Tam·pe·re (täm′pe re) city in SW Finland: pop. 156,000

Tam·pi·co (tam pē′kō; *Sp.* täm pē′kð) seaport in E Mexico, on the Gulf of Mexico: pop. 196,000

tam·pi·on (tam′pē ən) *n.* [< Fr. *tampon* < *tapon*, a bung < Frank.] a plug or stopper put in the muzzle of a gun that is not in use

tam·pon (tam′pän) *n.* [Fr.: see prec.] a plug of cotton or other absorbent material put into a body cavity, wound, etc. to stop bleeding or absorb secretions —*vt.* to put a tampon into

tan (tan) *n.* [MFr. < ML. *tannum*] **1.** *same as* TANBARK **2.** tannin or a solution made from it **3.** *a)* a yellowish-brown color *b)* such a color given to fair skin as by exposure to the sun —*adj.* **tan′ner, tan′nest** yellowish-brown —*vt.* **tanned, tan′ning** **1.** to change (hide) into leather by soaking in tannin **2.** to produce a tan color in, as by exposure to the sun **3.** [Colloq.] to whip severely; flog —*vi.* to become tanned

tan tangent

tan·a·ger (tan′ə jər) *n.* [ModL. *tanagra* < Port. < Tupi *tangara*] any of various small, new-world songbirds: the males usually are brilliantly colored

tan·bark (tan′bärk′) *n.* any bark containing tannin, used to tan hides and, after the tannin has been taken out, to cover race tracks, circus rings, etc.

tan·dem (tan′dəm) *adv.* [orig. punning use of L. *tandem*, at length (of time)] one behind another; in single file [five dogs hitched *tandem* to a sled] —*n.* **1.** a two-wheeled carriage drawn by horses harnessed tandem **2.** a team, as of horses, harnessed tandem **3.** a bicycle with two seats and sets of pedals placed tandem **4.** a relationship between two persons or things in which they cooperate and help each other [to work in *tandem*] —*adj.* having two parts or things placed tandem

Ta·ney (tô′nē), **Roger B(rooke)** 1777-1864; U.S. jurist; chief justice of the U.S. (1836-64)

tang (tang) *n.* [ON. *tangi*, a sting] **1.** a point or prong on a knife, file, etc. that fits into the handle **2.** a strong, sharp taste or odor [a spicy *tang*] **3.** a touch or trace (*of*) **4.** a special or characteristic flavor, quality, etc. [pronunciations with a strong Scottish *tang*] —*vt.* to provide (a knife, etc.) with a tang

Tan·gan·yi·ka (tan′gan yē′kə) **1.** mainland region of Tanzania: formerly a Brit. trust territory **2.** Lake, lake in EC Africa, between Tanganyika and Zaire

☆**tan·ge·lo** (tan′jə lō′) *n., pl.* **-los′** [TANG(ERINE) + (*pom*)*elo*, grapefruit] a fruit produced by crossing a tangerine with a grapefruit

tan·gent (tan′jənt) *adj.* [< L. prp. of *tangere*, to touch] **1.** touching **2.** *Geom.* touching and not intersecting a curved line or surface at one point only: said of a line or plane —*n.* **1.** *Geom.* a tangent line, curve, or surface **2.** *Trigonometry* the ratio of the side opposite a given acute angle (in a right triangle) to the adjacent side —see **SYN.** at ADJACENT —**go** (or **fly**) **off at** (or **on**) **a tangent** to change suddenly from one subject or line of action to another —**tan′gen·cy** *n.*

tan·gen·tial (tan jen′shəl) *adj.* **1.** of or like a tangent **2.** drawn as a tangent **3.** going off at a tangent **4.** merely touching on a subject [*wasting time on tangential matters*] **—tan·gen′tial·ly** *adv.*

tan·ge·rine (tan′jə rēn′, tan′jə rēn′) *n.* [< Fr. *Tanger*, Tangier] **1.** a variety of mandarin orange with a deep, reddish-yellow color and segments that are easily separated **2.** a deep, reddish-yellow color

tan·gi·ble (tan′jə b'l) *adj.* [< LL. *tangibilis* < L. *tangere*, to touch] **1.** that can be touched or felt by touch; having actual form and substance **2.** that can be appraised for value [*tangible assets*] **3.** that can be understood; definite; objective [there is no *tangible* basis for his fears] **—n.** [*pl.*] property that can be appraised for value; material things —see SYN. at PERCEPTIBLE **— tan′gi·bil′i·ty, tan′gi·ble·ness** *n.* **—tan′gi·bly** *adv.*

Tan·gier (tan jir′) seaport in N Morocco, on the Strait of Gibraltar: pop. 170,000

tan·gle (taŋ′g'l) *vt.* **-gled, -gling** [prob. var. of ME. *taglen*, to entangle] **1.** to hinder, obstruct, or confuse as by circling, entwining, etc. [a series of sounds that *tangled* his tongue] **2.** to catch as in a net or snare; trap [her feet became *tangled* in the garden hose] **3.** to make a knot or snarl of [the cat *tangled* the yarn] **—vi.** **1.** to become tangled **2.** [Colloq.] to quarrel or fight **—n.** **1.** a twisted, confused mass, as of string, branches, etc.; snarl **2.** a jumbled, confused condition [a *tangle* of words] **3.** a perplexed state **—tan′gler** *n.*

tan·go (taŋ′gō) *n.,* *pl.* **-gos** [AmSp.] **1.** a S. American dance with long gliding steps and dips **2.** music for this **—vi.** **-goed, -go·ing** to dance the tango

tan·gram (taŋ′grəm) *n.* [prob. coinage modeled on ANAGRAM] a Chinese puzzle made by cutting a square into five triangles, a square, and a rhomboid, and using these pieces to form various figures and designs

Tang·shan (täŋ′shän′) city in NE China, near Tientsin: pop. 812,000

tang·y (taŋ′ē) *adj.* **tang′i·er, tang′i·est** having a tang, or sharp flavor, esp. a pleasantly sharp one **—tang′i·ness** *n.*

TANGRAM

tank (taŋk) *n.* [< Sp. & Port. *tanque* < *estancar*, to stop the flow of] **1.** any large container for liquid or gas [an oil *tank*, a swimming *tank*] **2.** [name chosen to conceal secret manufacture] an armored, self-propelled combat vehicle armed with guns and moving on tractor treads ☆**3.** [Slang] a jail cell, esp. one for new prisoners **—vt.** to put or store in a tank **—tank up** [Colloq.] **1.** to supply with or get a full tank of gasoline ☆**2.** to drink much liquor **—tank′ful′** *n., pl.* **-fuls′**

tank·age (taŋ′kij) *n.* **1.** the amount that a tank or tanks can hold **2.** *a)* the storage of fluids, gases, etc. in tanks *b)* the charge for such storage **3.** waste from slaughtered animals, dried for use as fertilizer or feed

tank·ard (taŋ′kərd) *n.* [ME.] a large drinking cup with a handle and, often, a hinged lid

☆**tank car** a railroad car that is a large tank on wheels, for carrying liquids and gases

☆**tanked** (taŋkt) *adj.* [Colloq.] drunk: also **tanked up**

tank·er (taŋ′kər) *n.* **1.** a ship with large tanks in the hull for carrying a cargo of oil or other liquids ☆**2.** a plane with a cargo of gasoline for refueling another plane in flight

tank farming *same as* HYDROPONICS

☆**tank top** [orig. used in swimming tanks] a knitted shirt, like an undershirt but with wider shoulder straps

☆**tank town** **1.** a railroad stop where locomotives stop to get water **2.** any small or unimportant town

☆**tank truck** a motor truck built with a tank for transporting gasoline, oil, or other liquids

tan·ner (tan′ər) *n.* a person whose work is tanning hides

tan·ner·y (-ē) *n., pl.* **-ner·ies** a place where hides are tanned

tan·nic (tan′ik) *adj.* of, like, or obtained from tanbark or tannin

tannic acid a yellowish substance, $C_{14}H_{10}O_9$, gotten from oak bark, gallnuts, etc. and used in tanning, medicine, etc.

tan·nin (tan′in) *n. same as* TANNIC ACID

tan·sy (tan′zē) *n., pl.* **-sies** [OFr. *tanesie*, ult. < LL. *tanacetum* < ?] any of various strong-smelling plants with clusters of small, yellow flowers

tan·ta·lize (tan′tə līz′) *vt.* **-lized′, -liz′ing** [< TANTALUS + -IZE] to tease or disappoint by promising or showing something wanted and then withholding it **—tan′ta·li·za′tion** *n.* **—tan′ta·liz′er** *n.* **—tan′ta·liz′ing·ly** *adv.*

tan·ta·lum (tan′tə ləm) *n.* [ModL. < TANTALUS: from the difficulty in extracting it from its ore] a rare chemical element that is a steel-blue metal, used to make surgical instruments, parts of radio tubes and aircraft, etc.: symbol, Ta; at. wt., 180.948; at. no., 73

Tan·ta·lus (tan′tə ləs) *Gr. Myth.* a king whose punishment in the lower world was to stand in water that always receded when he tried to drink it and under branches of fruit he could never reach

tan·ta·mount (tan′tə mount′) *adj.* [< Anglo-Fr. < OFr. *tant* (< L. *tantus*, so much) + *amonter* (see AMOUNT)] almost the same as; equal in value, effect, etc. (*to*) [the king's wishes were *tantamount* to orders]

tan·trum (tan′trəm) *n.* [< ?] a strong outburst of rage, frustration, etc.; childish fit of bad temper

Tan·za·ni·a (tan′zə nē′ə, tän′-) country in E Africa, consisting of a mainland section (*Tanganyika*) and Zanzibar: a member of the Commonwealth: 362,820 sq. mi.; pop. 13,634,000; cap. Dar es Salaam **—Tan′za·ni′an** *adj., n.*

Tao·ism (dou′iz'm, tou′-) *n.* [Chin. *tao*, the way + -ISM] a Chinese religion and philosophy based on the teachings of Lao-tse and stressing simplicity, selflessness, etc. **—Tao′ist** *n., adj.* **— Tao·is′tic** *adj.*

tap¹ (tap) *vt.* **tapped, tap′ping** [OFr. *taper*, prob. echoic] **1.** to strike lightly [he *tapped* my shoulder] **2.** to strike something lightly with [he *tapped* the chalk against the blackboard] **3.** to make or do by tapping [to *tap* out a rhythm on a drum] ☆**4.** to choose, as for membership in a club **5.** to repair (a shoe) by adding a thickness of leather, etc. to the heel or sole **—vi.** **1.** to strike a light, rapid blow or a series of such blows **2.** to do a tap dance **3.** to move with a tapping sound **—n.** **1.** a light, rapid blow, or the sound made by it **2.** the leather, etc. added in tapping a shoe **3.** a small metal plate attached to the heel or toe of a shoe, as for tap dancing **—tap′per** *n.*

tap² (tap) *n.* [OE. *tæppa*] **1.** a device for controlling the flow of liquid in a pipe, barrel, etc.; faucet **2.** a plug, cork, etc. for stopping a hole in a container holding a liquid **3.** a draining of liquid from a body cavity **4.** a tool used to cut threads in a female screw ☆**5.** the act of wiretapping ☆**6.** a place in an electrical circuit where a connection can be made **—vt.** **tapped, tap′ping** **1.** to put a tap or spigot on **2.** to make a hole in for drawing off liquid [to *tap* a sugar maple] **3.** to pull out the plug from **4.** to draw (liquid) from a container, cavity, etc. **5.** to make use of [to *tap* new resources] **6.** to make a connection with (an electric circuit, water main, etc.); specif., ☆to wiretap (a telephone line) **7.** to cut threads on the inner surface of (a nut, pipe, etc.) **8.** [Slang] to borrow or get money from **—on tap** **1.** ready to be drawn, as liquid from a cask that has been tapped **2.** [Colloq.] ready for consideration or action **—tap′-per** *n.*

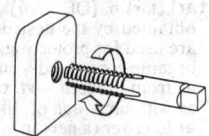

TAP (sense 4)

ta·pa (tä′pä) *n.* [< native Polynesian name] an unwoven cloth made in the Pacific islands from the treated inner bark of a mulberry tree

tap dance a dance performed with sharp, loud taps of the foot, toe, or heel at each step **—tap′-dance′** *vi.* **-danced′, -danc′ing —tap′-danc′er** *n.*

tape (tāp) *n.* [OE. *tæppe*, a fillet] **1.** a strong, narrow, woven strip of cotton, linen, etc. used for binding, tying, etc. **2.** a narrow strip or band of steel, paper, etc. **3.** a strip of cloth stretched above the finishing line of a race **4.** *short for:* *a)* TAPE MEASURE *b)* ADHESIVE TAPE, MASKING TAPE, etc. **—vt.** **taped, tap′ing** **1.** to put tape on or around, as for binding, tying, etc. **2.** to measure by using a tape measure **3.** to record (sound, video material, computer data, etc.) on magnetic tape **—tap′er** *n.*

☆**tape deck** a simplified magnetic-tape assembly, without its own amplifier or speaker but having tape reels, drive, and recording and playback heads

---

fat, āpe, cär; ten, ēven; is, bīte; gō, hôrn, to͞ol, lo͝ok; oil, out; up, fur; get; joy; yet; chin; she; thin, then; zh, leisure; ŋ, ring; ə for a in ago, e in agent, i in sanity, o in comply, u in focus; ′ as in able (ā′b'l); Fr. bal; ë, Fr. coeur; ö, Fr. feu; Fr. mon; ô, Fr. coq; ü, Fr. duc; r, Fr. cri; H, G. ich; kh, G. doch; ‡foreign; ☆ Americanism; < derived from. See inside front cover.

tape measure a tape with marks in inches, feet, etc. for measuring: also **tape/line/** (-līn′) *n.*

ta·per (tā′pər) *n.* [OE. *tapur*] **1.** a slender candle **2.** a long wick coated with wax, used for lighting candles, lamps, etc. **3.** any feeble light **4.** a gradual decrease in width or thickness [the *taper* of a pyramid] —*vt., vi.* **1.** to decrease gradually in width or thickness [a sword *tapers* to a point] **2.** to lessen; diminish [her voice *tapered* off to a whisper] Often with *off*

tape-re·cord (tāp′ri kôrd′) *vt.* to record on magnetic tape

tape recorder a device for recording sound on magnetic tape and for playing it back after it is recorded: see MAGNETIC RECORDING

tap·es·try (tap′is trē) *n., pl.* **-tries** [< MFr. < OFr. *tapis*, a carpet, ult. < Gr. dim. of *tapēs*, a carpet] a heavy cloth woven with decorative designs and pictures, used as a wall hanging, furniture covering, etc. —*vt.* **-tried, -try·ing** to decorate as with a tapestry: usually used in the past participle, *tapestried*

tape·worm (tāp′wurm′) *n.* any of various flatworms that live as parasites in the intestines of man and other vertebrates

tap·i·o·ca (tap′ē ō′kə) *n.* [Port. & Sp. < Tupi < *ty*, juice + *pya*, heart + *oc*, to squeeze out] a starchy substance prepared from the root of the cassava plant, used in puddings, etc.

ta·pir (tā′pər) *n., pl.* **ta′pirs, ta′pir:** see PLURAL, II, D, 1 [Sp. < Tupi *tapyra*] any of several large, hoglike mammals found mostly in tropical America: tapirs have flexible snouts and feed on plants

tap·pet (tap′it) *n.* [TAP[1] + -ET] in an engine or machine, a part that sticks out so as to move or be moved by another part each time it comes into contact with it

TAPIR
(2½–3½ ft. high at shoulder)

tap·room (tap′rōōm′) *n. same as* BARROOM

tap·root (-rōōt′, -rōōt′) *n.* [TAP[2] + ROOT[1]] a main root, growing almost straight down, from which branch roots spread out: see illustration at ROOT

taps (taps) *n.* [< TAP[1], because orig. a drum signal] ☆a bugle call to put out the lights for the night, as in an army camp: also sounded at a military funeral

tar[1] (tär) *n.* [OE. *teru*] **1.** a thick, sticky, brown to black liquid obtained by the destructive distillation of wood, coal, etc.: tars are used for protecting and preserving surfaces, in making many organic compounds, etc. **2.** loosely, any of the solids in smoke, as from tobacco —*vt.* **tarred, tar′ring** to cover or smear with or as with tar —*adj.* of, like, or covered with tar —☆**tar and feather** to cover (a person) with tar and feathers, as in punishment by mob action

tar[2] (tär) *n.* [< TAR(PAULIN)] [Colloq.] a sailor

tar·an·tel·la (tar′ən tel′ə) *n.* [It., dim. of TARANTO] **1.** a fast, whirling southern Italian dance for couples **2.** music for this

Ta·ran·to (tə ran′tō; It. tä′rän tô′) seaport in SE Italy, on an inlet (**Gulf of Taranto**) of the Ionian Sea: pop. 219,000

ta·ran·tu·la (tə ran′chōō lə) *n., pl.* **-las, -lae** (-lē) [ML. < It. < TARANTO because such spiders found nearby] ☆**1.** a large, hairy, somewhat poisonous spider of the southwestern U.S. and tropical America **2.** a similar spider of S Europe

tar·boosh (tär bōōsh′) *n.* [Ar. *ṭarbūsh*] a brimless cap of cloth or felt shaped like a cone with the top cut off, worn by Moslem men

TARANTULA
(body to 3½ in.; legs to 5 in.)

tar·dy (tär′dē) *adj.* **-di·er, -di·est** [< OFr. < L. *tardus*, slow] **1.** slow in moving, acting, etc. **2.** late, delayed, or habitually slow or late —**tar′di·ly** *adv.* —**tar′di·ness** *n.*

tare[1] (ter) *n.* [< or akin to MDu. *tarwe*, wheat] **1.** any of several vetches **2.** the seed of any of these plants **3.** *Bible* a weed, perhaps the darnel

tare[2] (ter) *n.* [< MFr. < It. < Ar. *taraḥa*, to reject] the deduction of the weight of a container, wrapper, etc. from the total weight to determine the weight of the contents —*vt.* **tared, tar′ing** to find out, allow for, or mark the tare of

tar·get (tär′git) *n.* [< MFr. dim. of *targe*, a shield < Frank.] **1.** orig., a small, round shield **2.** *a)* a thing aimed at in archery, rifle practice, etc., as a flat board marked with circles, one inside the other *b)* any object that is shot at, bombarded, etc. **3.** an objective; goal [the *target* of the charity drive is $50,000] **4.** an object of criticism or ridicule [she was the *target* of their

sneers] **5.** a metallic insert in the anode of an X-ray tube, at which the cathode rays are aimed and from which X-rays issue —*vt.* to set a target, or goal, for

☆**target date** a date aimed at, as for starting or completing something

tar·iff (tar′if) *n.* [< It. < Ar. *ta′rif*, information] **1.** a list or system of taxes upon exports or, esp., imports **2.** a tax of this kind, or its rate **3.** any list of prices, charges, etc. ☆**4.** [Colloq.] any bill, charge, etc. —*vt.* **1.** to set a tariff on **2.** to fix the price of according to a tariff

Ta·rim River (tä′rēm′, dä′-) river in NW China, flowing from the Tien Shan into E Sinkiang region: c. 1,300 mi.

tar·la·tan, tar·le·tan (tär′lə tən) *n.* [Fr. *tarlatane*] a thin, stiff, open-weave muslin

Tar·mac (tär′mak) [< TAR[1] + MAC(ADAM)] *a trademark for* a coal-tar material used in paving —*n.* [t-] [Chiefly Brit.] a road, airport runway, etc. paved with crushed stone and tar

tarn (tärn) *n.* [< or akin to ON. *tjörn*] a small mountain lake

tar·na·tion (tär nā′shən) *interj., n.* [prob. < ′tar(nal), dial. form of ETERNAL + (DAM)NATION] *dial. var. of* DAMNATION: used to add emphasis [what in *tarnation* is that?]

tar·nish (tär′nish) *vt.* [< MFr. *ternir*, to make dim, prob. < OHG. *tarnjan*, to conceal] **1.** to dull the luster of or discolor the surface of (a metal) as by exposure to the air **2.** to soil or damage; bring dishonor to [to *tarnish* one's reputation] —*vi.* **1.** to lose luster; discolor, as from oxidation **2.** to become soiled, dishonored, etc. —*n.* **1.** a being tarnished; dullness **2.** the dull, discolored film on a tarnished surface **3.** a stain; blemish —**tar′nish·a·ble** *adj.*

ta·ro (tä′rō) *n., pl.* **-ros** [Tahitian] **1.** a large, tropical Asiatic plant cultivated for its edible tubers which are the source of poi **2.** the tuber of this plant

tar·ot (tar′ō, -ət; ta rō′) *n.* [Fr., ult. < Ar. *taraḥa*, to remove] [often T-] any of a set of playing cards with pictures of symbolic figures, used in fortunetelling

☆**tarp** (tärp) *n.* [Colloq.] *shortened form of* TARPAULIN

☆**tar paper** a heavy paper soaked with tar, used as a base for roofing, etc.

tar·pau·lin (tär pô′lin, tär′pə lin) *n.* [TAR[1] + -paulin, prob. < *palling* < PALL[2], a covering] **1.** canvas coated with a waterproofing compound **2.** a sheet of this for spreading over something to keep it dry

tar·pon (tär′pən, -pän) *n., pl.* **-pons, -pon:** see PLURAL, II, D, 1 [< ?] a large, silvery game fish of the herring group, found in the warmer parts of the western Atlantic

Tar·quin (tär′kwin) (*Lucius Tarquinius Superbus*) real or legendary Etruscan king of Rome (534?–510? B.C.)

tar·ra·gon (tar′ə gän′) *n.* [Sp. < Ar. < Gr. *drakōn*, dragon] **1.** an old-world wormwood whose fragrant leaves are used for seasoning **2.** these leaves

tar·ry[1] (tar′ē) *vi.* **-ried, -ry·ing** [prob. < OE. *tergan*, to vex, merged with OFr. *targer*, to delay < L. *tardus*, slow] **1.** to delay, be slow, etc. [don't *tarry* along the way] **2.** to stay for a time, esp. longer than intended [we *tarried* in the park until sundown] —see SYN. at STAY[3] —**tar′ri·er** *n.*

tar·ry[2] (tär′ē) *adj.* **-ri·er, -ri·est** **1.** of or like tar **2.** covered or smeared with tar —**tar′ri·ness** *n.*

tar·sal (tär′s′l) *adj.* of the tarsus —*n.* a tarsal bone or plate. See illustration at SKELETON

tar·si·er (tär′sē ər) *n.* [Fr. < *tarse*, TARSUS, from the foot structure] any of several small primates of the East Indies and the Philippines, with very large eyes and a long tail: they live in trees and are active at night

Tar·sus (tär′səs) city in S Turkey, near the Mediterranean: birthplace of the Apostle Paul: pop. 57,000

tar·sus (tär′səs) *n., pl.* **-si** (-sī) [ModL. < Gr. *tarsos*, flat of the foot] **1.** the human ankle, consisting of seven bones **2.** *Zool. a)* a group of bones in the ankle region of the hind limbs of vertebrates having four limbs *b)* the fifth segment from the base of an insect leg

TARSIER
(head & body 3–7 in. long; tail 5–10 in. long)

tart[1] (tärt) *adj.* [OE. *teart*] **1.** sharp in taste; sour; acid **2.** sharp in meaning; cutting [a *tart* answer] —see SYN. at SOUR —**tart′ly** *adv.* —**tart′ness** *n.*

tart[2] (tärt) *n.* [MFr. *tarte*] **1.** a small shell of pastry filled with jam, jelly, etc. **2.** in England, a small pie filled with fruit or jam and often having a top crust

tart[3] (tärt) *n.* [< prec., orig., slang term of affection] a prostitute or any woman of loose morals

tar·tan (tär′t'n) *n.* [prob. < MFr. *tiretaine*, a cloth of mixed fibers, ult. < L. *Tyrus*, TYRE] **1.** woolen cloth with a woven plaid pattern, esp. as worn in the Scottish Highlands, where each clan has its own pattern **2.** any plaid cloth or pattern **3.** a garment made of tartan —*adj.* of or made of tartan

Tar·tar (tär′tər) *n.* [< ML. *Tartarus* < Per. *Tātār*] **1.** same as TATAR **2.** [*usually* t-] a bad-tempered person who is hard to deal with —*adj.* of Tatary or the Tatars —**catch a tartar** to attack or oppose someone too strong for one

tar·tar (tär′tər) *n.* [< ML. < MGr. *tartaron* < ? Ar.] **1.** a potassium salt of tartaric acid forming a reddish, crustlike deposit in wine casks: in purified form called CREAM OF TARTAR **2.** a hard deposit on the teeth, consisting of saliva proteins, food deposits, calcium phosphate, etc.

tartar emetic a poisonous salt of tartaric acid used in medicine to cause vomiting, in dyeing as a mordant, etc.

tar·tar·ic (tär tar′ik, -tär′-) *adj.* of, containing, or derived from tartar or tartaric acid

tartaric acid a colorless, crystalline acid, $C_4H_6O_6$, found in fruit juices, etc. and obtained commercially from tartar: it is used in dyeing, photography, medicine, etc.

tar·tar sauce (tär′tər) [< Fr.] a sauce, as for seafood, consisting of mayonnaise with chopped pickles, olives, capers, etc.: also sp. **tartare sauce**

Tar·ta·rus (tär′tər əs) *Gr. Myth.* **1.** an abyss below Hades **2.** same as HADES (sense 1 *a*)

Tar·ta·ry (tär′tər ē) same as TATARY

tar·trate (tär′trāt) *n.* a salt or ester of tartaric acid

☆**Tar·zan** (tär′zan, -zən) *n.* [after *Tarzan*, jungle-raised hero of stories by E. R. Burroughs (1875–1950), U.S. writer] [*also* t-] a very strong, forceful, and agile man: often used humorously

Tash·kent (täsh kent′) capital of the Uzbek S.S.R., in the E part: pop. 1,385,000

task (task) *n.* [< ONormFr. < ML. *tasca*, for *taxa*, a tax < L. *taxare*, to rate, TAX] **1.** a piece of work that one must do **2.** any piece of work **3.** any difficult undertaking [invalids sometimes find eating a *task*] —*vt.* **1.** to assign a task to **2.** to put a strain on; tax [to *task* one's memory] —**take to task** to find fault with; scold

☆**task force 1.** a specially trained military unit that is given a specific mission or task **2.** any group that has a specific project to carry out

task·mas·ter (task′mas′tər) *n.* a person who gives tasks or hard work to others to do, esp. a strict or demanding person

Tas·man (täs′män; *E.* taz′mən), **A·bel Jans·zoon** (ä′bəl yän′sōn) 1603?–59; Du. navigator, esp. in the Pacific

Tas·ma·ni·a (taz mā′nē ə, -mān′yə) **1.** island south of Victoria, Australia **2.** state of Australia made up of this island & smaller nearby islands —**Tas·ma′ni·an** *adj., n.*

Tasmanian devil a flesh-eating mammal of Tasmania: the female has a pouch in which she carries her young

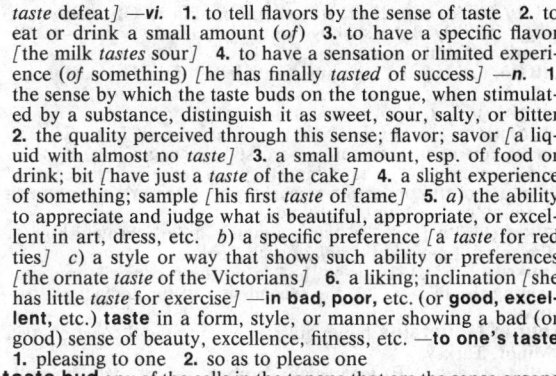

TASMANIAN DEVIL
(to 4 ft. long,
including tail)

Tass (täs) [< the initial letters of the full name] a Soviet agency for gathering and distributing news

tasse (tas) *n.* [MFr., pouch] any of a series of jointed metal plates forming a skirtlike protection of armor for the lower body: see illustration at ARMOR

tas·sel (tas′'l) *n.* [OFr., a knob] **1.** an ornamental tuft of threads, cords, etc. of equal length, hanging loosely from a knob or knot **2.** something like this; specif., the tassellike tuft of corn silk on an ear of corn —*vt.* **-seled** or **-selled, -sel·ing** or **-sel·ling** to put tassels on —☆*vi.* to grow tassels, as corn

Tas·so (täs′sō; *E.* tas′ō), **Tor·qua·to** (tôr kwä′tō) 1544–95; It. epic poet

taste (tāst) *vt.* **tast′ed, tast′ing** [OFr. *taster*, to touch, taste] **1.** to test the flavor of by putting a little in one's mouth [*taste* this to see if it needs salt] **2.** to detect the flavor of by the sense of taste [I *taste* garlic in the salad] **3.** to eat or drink, esp. a small amount of [he just *tasted* his food] **4.** to experience [to

taste defeat] —*vi.* **1.** to tell flavors by the sense of taste **2.** to eat or drink a small amount (*of*) **3.** to have a specific flavor [the milk *tastes* sour] **4.** to have a sensation or limited experience (*of* something) [he has finally *tasted* of success] —*n.* **1.** the sense by which the taste buds on the tongue, when stimulated by a substance, distinguish it as sweet, sour, salty, or bitter **2.** the quality perceived through this sense; flavor; savor [a liquid with almost no *taste*] **3.** a small amount, esp. of food or drink; bit [have just a *taste* of the cake] **4.** a slight experience of something; sample [his first *taste* of fame] **5.** *a)* the ability to appreciate and judge what is beautiful, appropriate, or excellent in art, dress, etc. *b)* a specific preference [a *taste* for red ties] *c)* a style or way that shows such ability or preferences [the ornate *taste* of the Victorians] **6.** a liking; inclination [she has little *taste* for exercise] —**in bad, poor,** etc. (or **good, excellent,** etc.) **taste** in a form, style, or manner showing a bad (or good) sense of beauty, excellence, fitness, etc. —**to one's taste 1.** pleasing to one **2.** so as to please one

taste bud any of the cells in the tongue that are the sense organs of taste

taste·ful (tāst′fəl) *adj.* having or showing good taste [*tasteful* décor] —**taste′ful·ly** *adv.* —**taste′ful·ness** *n.*

taste·less (-lis) *adj.* **1.** *a)* without taste or flavor; flat; insipid *b)* dull; uninteresting **2.** lacking good taste; in poor taste —**taste′less·ly** *adv.* —**taste′less·ness** *n.*

tast·er (tās′tər) *n.* a person who tastes; specif., one employed to test the quality of wines, teas, etc. by tasting

tast·y (tās′tē) *adj.* **tast′i·er, tast′i·est 1.** that tastes good; flavorful **2.** [Now Rare] same as TASTEFUL —**tast′i·ly** *adv.* —**tast′i·ness** *n.*

tat[1] (tat) *vt.* **tat′ted, tat′ting** [< TATTING] to make by tatting —*vi.* to do tatting

tat[2] (tat) *n.* [< ? TAP[1]] *see* TIT FOR TAT

ta·ta·mi (tə tä′mē) *n., pl.* **-mi, -mis** [Jpn.] a floor mat woven of rice straw, used traditionally in Japanese homes for sitting on, as when eating

Ta·tar (tät′ər) *n.* [Per.] **1.** a member of any of the Mongolian and Turkic tribes that invaded W Asia and E Europe in the Middle Ages **2.** any of a Turkic people living in a region of east-central European Russia and in parts of Asia **3.** any of their Turkic languages —*adj.* of the Tatars or their languages

Ta·ta·ry (tät′ə rē) vast region in Europe & Asia under the control of Tatar tribes in the late Middle Ages

'ta·ter, ta·ter (tāt′ər) *n. dial. form of* POTATO

tat·ter (tat′ər) *n.* [prob. < ON. *töturr*, rags] **1.** a torn and hanging shred or piece, as of a garment **2.** a separate shred or scrap; rag **3.** [*pl.*] torn, ragged clothes —*vt., vi.* to reduce to tatters; make or become ragged

tat·ter·de·mal·ion (tat′ər di māl′yən, -mal′-) *n.* [< prec. + ?] a person in torn, ragged clothes; ragamuffin

tat·tered (tat′ərd) *adj.* **1.** torn and ragged [*tattered* clothes] **2.** wearing torn and ragged clothes [a *tattered* child]

tat·ting (tat′iŋ) *n.* [prob. < Brit. dial. *tat*, to tangle] **1.** a fine lace made by looping and knotting thread that is wound on a hand shuttle **2.** the act of making this

tat·tle (tat′'l) *vi.* **-tled, -tling** [prob. < MDu. *tatelen*, of echoic origin] **1.** to talk in a foolish way; chatter **2.** to tell others' secrets [he *tattled* to the teacher] —*n.* foolish talk; chatter —**tat′tler** *n.*

☆**tat·tle·tale** (-tāl′) *n.* a person who tells the secrets of others; informer; talebearer: now chiefly a word used by children

tat·too[1] (ta tōo′) *vt.* **-tooed′, -too′ing** [< Tahitian *tatau*] **1.** to puncture (the skin) with a needle and put in colors so as to leave permanent marks or designs **2.** to make (marks or designs) on the skin in this way —*n., pl.* **-toos′** a tattooed mark or design —**tat·too′er, tat·too′ist** *n.*

tat·too[2] (ta tōo′) *n., pl.* **-toos′** [< Du. < *tap toe*, shut the tap: a signal for closing barrooms] **1.** *a)* a signal on a drum, bugle, etc. summoning soldiers, etc. to their quarters at night *b)* in England, a military spectacle featuring music, marching, etc. **2.** a loud drumming, rapping, etc. [his fingers beat a *tattoo* on the table] —*vt., vi.* **-tooed′, -too′ing** to beat or tap

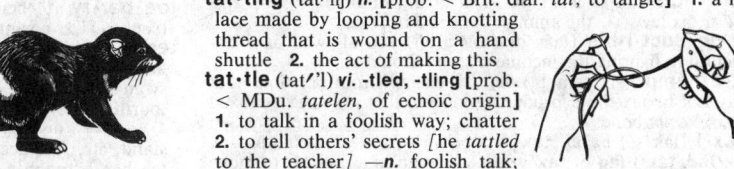

TATTING

tat·ty (tat′ē) *adj.* **-ti·er, -ti·est** [prob. akin to OE. *taetteca*, a rag] [Chiefly Brit.] shabby, worn out, tawdry, etc. —**tat′ti·ly** *adv.* —**tat′ti·ness** *n.*

tau (tô, tou) *n.* [Gr.] the nineteenth letter of the Greek alphabet (T, τ)

taught (tôt) *pt. & pp. of* TEACH

taunt (tônt, tänt) *vt.* [< ? Fr. *tant pour tant*, tit for tat] **1.** to make fun of in scornful or sarcastic language; jeer at **2.** to drive or provoke by taunting [they *taunted* him into leaving] —*n.* a scornful or jeering remark; gibe —see SYN. at RIDICULE —**taunt′er** *n.* —**taunt′ing·ly** *adv.*

taupe (tōp) *n.* [Fr. < L. *talpa*, a mole] a dark, brownish gray, the color of moleskin —*adj.* of such a color

Tau·rus (tôr′əs) [L., a bull] **1.** a northern constellation containing the Pleiades **2.** the second sign of the zodiac: see ZODIAC

Taurus Mountains mountain range along the S coast of Asia Minor, Turkey

taut (tôt) *adj.* [ME. *toght*, tight, prob. < pp. of *togen*, to pull] **1.** tightly stretched, as a rope **2.** strained; tense [a *taut* smile] **3.** trim, tidy, well-disciplined, etc. [a *taut* ship] —**taut′ly** *adv.* —**taut′ness** *n.*

taut·en (tôt′ən) *vt., vi.* to make or become taut

tau·to- [< Gr. < *to auto*, the same] *a combining form meaning* the same [tautology]

☆**tau·tog** (tô täg′) *n.* [< Algonquian pl. of *tautau*, a blackfish] a black or greenish food fish found off the Atlantic coast of the U.S.

tau·tol·o·gy (tô täl′ə jē) *n., pl.* **-gies** [< LL. < Gr.: see TAUTO- & -LOGY] **1.** needless repetition of an idea in a different word, phrase, etc.; redundancy, as "necessary essentials" **2.** an instance of this —**tau·to·log·i·cal** (tôt′ə läj′i k'l) *adj.* —**tau′to·log′i·cal·ly** *adv.*

tav·ern (tav′ərn) *n.* [< OFr. < L. *taberna*] **1.** a place where liquors, beer, etc. are sold and drunk; saloon; bar **2.** an inn

taw (tô) *n.* [< ?] **1.** a fancy marble used to shoot with in playing marbles **2.** the line from which the players shoot

taw·dry (tô′drē) *adj.* **-dri·er, -dri·est** [< *St. Audrey*, esp. in *St. Audrey laces*, sold at St. Audrey's fair, Norwich, England] cheap and showy; gaudy; sleazy —see SYN. at GAUDY —**taw′dri·ly** *adv.* —**taw′dri·ness** *n.*

taw·ny (tô′nē) *adj.* **-ni·er, -ni·est** [< OFr. pp. of *tanner*, to tan] brownish-yellow; tan —*n.* a tawny color —**taw′ni·ness** *n.*

tax (taks) *vt.* [< MFr. < L. *taxare*, to appraise < base of *tangere*, to touch] **1.** orig., to determine the value of; assess **2.** to require (a person) to pay a percentage of his income, property value, etc. for the support of a government **3.** to put a tax on (income, property, purchases, etc.) **4.** to put a burden or strain on [his pranks *tax* my patience] **5.** to accuse; charge [to be *taxed* with negligence] —*n.* **1.** a payment that one must make to help support a government, usually a percentage of income, property value, sales price, etc. **2.** a heavy demand; burden; strain —**tax′a·bil′i·ty** *n.* —**tax′a·ble** *adj.* —**tax′er** *n.*

tax·a·tion (tak sā′shən) *n.* **1.** a taxing or being taxed **2.** a tax or tax levy **3.** the amount collected in taxes

tax-de·duct·i·ble (taks′di duk′tə b'l) *adj.* allowed as a deduction in figuring the income tax one should pay

tax-ex·empt (-ig zempt′) *adj.* **1.** exempt from taxation; that may not be taxed **2.** producing income that may not be taxed [tax-exempt bonds]

☆**tax·i** (tak′sē) *n., pl.* **tax′is** *shortened form of* TAXICAB —*vi.* **tax′ied, tax′i·ing** or **tax′y·ing 1.** to go in a taxi **2.** to move slowly along the ground or on water as an airplane does before taking off or after landing —*vt.* **1.** to carry in a taxi **2.** to cause (an airplane) to taxi

☆**tax·i·cab** (-kab′) *n.* [< *taxi(meter) cab*] an automobile in which passengers are carried for a fare shown on a meter

tax·i·der·my (tak′si dur′mē) *n.* [< Gr. *taxis*, arrangement + *derma*, a skin] the art of preparing, stuffing, and mounting the skins of animals so as to make them look lifelike —**tax′i·der′mal, tax′i·der′mic** *adj.* —**tax′i·der′mist** *n.*

tax·i·me·ter (tak′sē mēt′ər) *n.* [Fr. *taximètre* < G. < ML. *taxa*, a tax + -*meter*, -METER] an automatic device in taxicabs that shows the amount of fare owed

tax·is (tak′sis) *n.* [ModL. < Gr. *taxis*, arrangement] *Biol.* the movement of a cell or organism toward or away from some outside influence

☆**taxi stand** a place where taxicabs are stationed for hire

tax·on (tak′sän) *n., pl.* **tax′a** (-sə) [< TAXONOMY] any of the natural groups, as a species, genus, etc., into which plants and animals are classified

tax·on·o·my (tak sän′ə mē) *n.* [< Fr.< Gr. *taxis*, arrangement + *nomos*, a law] the science of classifying things, esp. plants and animals into natural, related groups such as species and genera —**tax′o·nom′ic** (-sə näm′ik), **tax′o·nom′i·cal** *adj.* —**tax′o·nom′i·cal·ly** *adv.* —**tax·on′o·mist** *n.*

tax·pay·er (taks′pā′ər) *n.* a person who pays taxes

☆**tax shelter** a financial investment made mainly to get expenses and other deductions which can be used to reduce one's income tax

tax stamp a stamp that shows a tax has been paid

tax·us (tak′səs) *n., pl.* **tax′us** [ModL. < L.] *same as* YEW (*n.* 1)

Tay·lor (tā′lər) [after Zachary TAYLOR] city in SE Mich.: suburb of Detroit: pop. 70,000

Tay·lor (tā′lər) **1.** Jer·e·my (jer′ə mē), 1613–67; Eng. bishop & religious writer **2.** Zach·a·ry (zak′ər ē), 1784–1850; U.S. general in the Mexican War; 12th president of the U.S. (1849–50)

Tb *Chem.* terbium

TB, T.B., tb, t.b. tuberculosis

T-bar (tē′bär′) *n.* ☆a T-shaped bar that hangs from an endless cable and is used to pull two skiers at a time uphill as they stand on their skis

Tbi·li·si (t'bi li sē′) capital of the Georgian S.S.R.: pop. 889,000

☆**T-bone steak** (tē′bōn′) a steak from the loin, with a T-shaped bone, containing some tenderloin

tbs., tbsp. tablespoon; tablespoons

Tc *Chem.* technetium

Tchai·kov·sky (chī kôf′skē), **Peter Il·ich** (il′yich) 1840–93; Russ. composer: also **Pētr Il·yich Tschai·kow·sky** (pyô′tr′ il·yēch′ chī kôf′skē)

Tchekov *var. sp. of* CHEKHOV: also **Tchekhov**

TD touchdown: also **td**

Te *Chem.* tellurium

tea (tē) *n.* see PLURAL, II, D, 3 [Chin. dial. *t'e*, for Mandarin *ch'a*, tea] **1.** a white-flowered, evergreen shrub grown in warm parts of Asia for its young leaves, which are prepared by drying, etc. for use in making a common drink **2.** the dried, prepared leaves **3.** the drink made by steeping these in hot water, etc. **4.** a drink like tea made from some other plant or from a meat extract [sassafras *tea*, beef *tea*] **5.** [Chiefly Brit.] a light meal, usually with tea, in the late afternoon **6.** a social gathering in the afternoon at which tea, coffee, etc. are served ☆**7.** [Slang] marijuana

TEA (leaves, flowers & plant)

☆**tea bag** a small, porous bag with tea leaves in it, for putting into hot water to make a cup of tea

☆**tea ball** a hollow metal ball with many holes in it, used to hold tea leaves in making tea

tea·ber·ry (tē′ber′ē) *n., pl.* **-ries 1.** *same as* WINTERGREEN (sense 1) **2.** a wintergreen berry

teach (tēch) *vt.* **taught, teach′ing** [OE. *tæcan*] **1.** to show or help to learn how to do something; instruct [she *taught* him to swim] **2.** to give lessons to; guide the study of [he *teaches* fourth grade] **3.** to give lessons in (a subject) [to *teach* art] **4.** to give knowledge, insight, etc. to; cause to know, understand, etc. [the accident *taught* her to be careful] —*vi.* to be a teacher —**teach′a·bil′i·ty, teach′a·ble·ness** *n.* —**teach′a·ble** *adj.*

SYN.—**teach** is the most common word for the giving of knowledge or for showing how to do something, usually by spending time with each student [he *taught* her how to skate]; **instruct** implies teaching according to some system, usually in a particular subject [she *instructs* in chemistry]; **educate** stresses the development of the abilities and skills of a student in various ways and in various subjects, esp. in institutions of higher learning [he was *educated* in European universities]; **train** implies the development of a particular ability or skill, or instruction directed toward a particular job, career, etc. [he was *trained* as a mechanic]; **school** sometimes suggests training that helps one to do something difficult [he *schooled* himself to ignore insults]

teach·er (tē′chər) *n.* a person who teaches, esp. in a school or college —**teach′er·ship′** *n.*

☆**teach-in** (tēch′in′) *n.* a long, special meeting, as at a college or university, with lectures and debate on a current issue, esp. one held to protest against some policy

teach·ing (tē′chiŋ) *n.* **1.** the action of one who teaches; profession of a teacher **2.** something taught; precept, doctrine, etc.: *usually in pl.*

tea·cup (tē′kup′) *n.* **1.** a cup for drinking tea, etc. **2.** a teacupful

tea·cup·ful (-fool′) *n., pl.* **-fuls′** as much as a teacup will hold, about four fluid ounces

tea·house (tē′hous′) *n.* in the Orient, a place where tea and other refreshments are served

teak (tēk) *n.* [< Port. < native word *tēkka*] **1.** a large East Indian tree with hard, yellowish-brown wood used for shipbuilding, furniture, etc. **2.** its wood: also **teak′wood′**

tea·ket·tle (tē′ket′'l) *n.* a covered kettle with a spout and handle, used to boil water for tea, etc.

teal (tēl) *n.* [ME. *tele*] **1.** *pl.* **teals, teal:** see PLURAL, II, D, 1 any of several small, short-necked freshwater wild ducks **2.** a dark greenish blue: also **teal blue**

team (tēm) *n.* [OE., offspring] **1.** two or more horses, oxen, etc. harnessed to the same vehicle or plow **2.** a draft animal or animals and the vehicle drawn **3.** a group of people working together on a project or playing together against opponents in games —*vt., vi.* to join together in a team (often with *up*) —*adj.* of or done by a team

team·mate (tē′māt′) *n.* a fellow team member

☆**team·ster** (-stər) *n.* one whose occupation is driving teams or trucks for hauling loads

☆**team teaching** teaching by several teachers working together with a group of students to explore relationships among various subject areas

team·work (-wurk′) *n.* the action or effort of people working together as a group

tea party a social gathering at which tea is served

tea·pot (tē′pät′) *n.* a pot with a spout, handle, and lid, for brewing and pouring tea

tear¹ (ter) *vt.* **tore, torn, tear′ing** [OE. *teran*, to rend] **1.** to pull apart by force; rip; rend [to *tear* cloth] **2.** to make (a hole, etc.) by tearing **3.** to wound by tearing; lacerate [skin *torn* and bruised] **4.** to split into opposed groups; disrupt [a country *torn* by civil war] **5.** to divide by doubt, etc. [*torn* between duty and desire] **6.** to remove as by tearing, pulling, etc. (with *up, out, off,* etc.) [to *tear* a plant up by its roots] —*vi.* **1.** to be torn [this paper *tears* easily] **2.** to move with force or speed; rush [*tearing* around the race track] —*n.* **1.** the act of tearing **2.** a torn place; rip ☆**3.** [Slang] a spree —**tear at** to pull at violently in an effort to tear or remove [*tearing at* the bandage] — **tear down** to take apart; wreck, demolish, etc. [to *tear down* a building] —**tear into** [Colloq.] to attack or criticize violently [*tearing into* their rivals] —**tear′er** *n.*

SYN.—**tear** implies a pulling apart by force, so as to leave ragged edges [to *tear* paper wrapping]; **rip** suggests sudden or great force in tearing, especially along a seam or in a straight line [to *rip* a hem]; **rend**, a somewhat literary term, emphasizes a violent tearing or splitting [the tree was *rent* by a bolt of lightning]

tear² (tir) *n.* [OE.] **1.** a drop of the salty fluid that keeps the eyeball moist and flows from the eye in weeping **2.** any tearlike drop **3.** [*pl.*] sorrow; grief [a life filled with *tears*] —*vi.* to flow with tears [onions make my eyes *tear*] —**in tears** weeping — **tear′less** *adj.*

tear·drop (tir′dräp′) *n.* a tear —*adj.* tear-shaped

tear·ful (-fəl) *adj.* **1.** in tears; weeping **2.** causing tears; sad —**tear′ful·ly** *adv.* —**tear′ful·ness** *n.*

tear gas (tir) a gas that makes the eyes sore and blinds them with tears —**tear′-gas′** *vt.* **-gassed′, -gas′sing**

tear·ing (ter′iŋ) *adj.* violent; furious; rushing

☆**tear-jerk·er** (tir′jur′kər) *n.* [Slang] a play, movie, etc. that is sad in a too sentimental way —**tear′-jerk′ing** *adj.*

tea·room (tē′rōōm′) *n.* a restaurant that serves tea, coffee, light lunches, etc. and caters chiefly to women

tea rose a kind of rose having a sweet odor

tear·y (tir′ē) *adj.* **tear′i·er, tear′i·est** **1.** tearful; crying **2.** of or like tears —**tear′i·ly** *adv.* —**tear′i·ness** *n.*

tease (tēz) *vt.* **teased, teas′ing** [OE. *tæsan*] **1.** *a)* to card or comb (flax, wool, etc.) *b)* to raise a nap on (cloth) with teasels *c)* to fluff (the hair) by brushing or combing the hair ends toward the scalp **2.** to bother or annoy by mocking, poking fun, etc. **3.** to pester with repeated requests [*teasing* her mother for candy] **4.** to tantalize [dreams of success kept *teasing* them] —*vi.* to tease someone —*n.* **1.** a teasing or being teased **2.** a person who teases —**teas′er** *n.* —**teas′ing·ly** *adv.*

tea·sel (tē′z'l) *n.* [< OE. < base of *tæsan*, to tease] **1.** a bristly plant (esp. the **fuller's teasel**) with prickly, cylindrical flower heads **2.** a dried flower head of the fuller's teasel, used to raise a nap on cloth **3.** any device for raising a nap on cloth —*vt.* **-seled** or **-selled, -sel·ing** or **-sel·ling** to nap (cloth) with teasels —**tea′sel·er, tea′sel·ler** *n.*

tea·spoon (tē′spōōn′) *n.* **1.** a spoon for stirring tea, coffee, etc. and eating some soft foods **2.** *same as* TEASPOONFUL

tea·spoon·ful (-fool′) *n., pl.* **-fuls′** as much as a teaspoon holds; 1/3 tablespoonful (1 ⅓ fluid drams)

teat (tēt, tit) *n.* [< OFr. *tete* < Gmc.] the nipple of a breast or udder

tea·zel, tea·zle (tē′z'l) *n., vt. same as* TEASEL

Te·bet, Te·beth (tā vāt′, tā′vəs) *n.* [Heb.] *see* JEWISH CALENDAR

TEASEL

tech. **1.** technical **2.** technology

tech·ne·ti·um (tek nē′shē əm) *n.* [ModL. < Gr. < *technē*, an art] a metallic chemical element obtained in the fission of uranium: symbol, Tc; at. wt., 97(?); at. no., 43

tech·nic (tek′nik; *for n. 1 also* tek nēk′) *adj.* [< Gr. < *technē*, an art] *same as* TECHNICAL —*n.* **1.** *same as* TECHNIQUE **2.** [*pl.*, *with sing. or pl. v.*] the study or principles of an art

tech·ni·cal (tek′ni k'l) *adj.* [prec. + -AL] **1.** dealing with the practical, industrial, or mechanical arts or the applied sciences [a *technical* school] **2.** of or used in a specific science, art, craft, etc. [*technical* terms] **3.** of or showing technique [*technical* skill] **4.** according to principles or rules [a *technical* difference] **5.** involving or using technicalities [a *technical* discussion] —**tech′ni·cal·ly** *adv.*

tech·ni·cal·i·ty (tek′nə kal′ə tē) *n., pl.* **-ties** **1.** the state or quality of being technical **2.** a technical point, term, method, etc. [the *technicalities* of radio repair] **3.** a minute, formal point or detail brought to bear upon a main issue [found guilty on a legal *technicality*]

technical knockout *Boxing* a victory won when the opponent, though not knocked out, is so badly hurt that the referee stops the match

☆**technical sergeant** *U.S. Air Force* the second grade of enlisted man, just below master sergeant

tech·ni·cian (tek nish′ən) *n.* a person skilled in the technicalities of some subject or in the technique of some art or science

☆**Tech·ni·col·or** (tek′ni kul′ər) *a trademark for* a certain process of making color motion pictures —*n.* [t-] **1.** this process **2.** bright colors —**tech′ni·col′ored** *adj.*

tech·nique (tek nēk′) *n.* [Fr. < Gr.: see TECHNIC] **1.** the method of procedure (as to practical or formal details) in creating an artistic work or carrying out a scientific or mechanical operation **2.** the degree of expertness shown in this **3.** any method of doing a thing

tech·no- [< Gr. *technē*, an art] *a combining form meaning:* **1.** art, science, skill **2.** technical, technological [*technocracy*]

☆**tech·noc·ra·cy** (tek näk′rə sē) *n.* [prec. + -CRACY] government by scientists and engineers —**tech′no·crat′** (-nə krat′) *n.* —**tech′no·crat′ic** *adj.*

tech·no·log·i·cal (tek′nə läj′i k'l) *adj.* **1.** of technology **2.** resulting from technical progress in the use of machinery and automation Also **tech′no·log′ic** —**tech′no·log′i·cal·ly** *adv.*

tech·nol·o·gy (tek näl′ə jē) *n.* [Gr. *technologia*, systematic treatment] **1.** the science or study of the practical or industrial arts, applied sciences, etc. **2.** the terms used in a science, art, etc. **3.** science as it is put to use in actual practice or to work out practical problems; applied science **4.** a method, process, etc. for handling a specific technical problem —**tech·nol′o·gist** *n.*

tec·ton·ic (tek tän′ik) *adj.* [< LL. < Gr. < *tektōn*, a builder] designating, of, or pertaining to the processes that produce changes in the earth's crust

Te·cum·seh (ti kum′sə) 1768?–1813; chief of the Shawnee Indians

ted (ted) *vt.* **ted′ded, ted′ding** [prob. < ON. *tethja*, to manure] to spread or scatter (newly cut grass) for drying as hay —**ted′der** *n.*

---

fat, āpe, cär; ten, ēven; is, bīte; gō, hôrn, tōōl, look; oil, out; up, fur; get; joy; yet; chin; she; thin, then; zh, leisure; ŋ, ring; ə for *a* in *ago*, *e* in *agent*, *i* in *sanity*, *o* in *comply*, *u* in *focus*; ′ as in *able* (ā′b'l); Fr. bál; ë, Fr. coeur; ö, Fr. feu; Fr. mon; ô, Fr. coq; ü, Fr. duc; r, Fr. cri; H, G. ich; kh, G. doch; ‡foreign; ☆ Americanism; < derived from. See inside front cover.

☆**ted·dy bear** (ted′ē) [< *Teddy* (*Theodore*) Roosevelt] a child's stuffed toy made to look like a bear cub

Te De·um (tē dē′əm, tā dā′ōom) [LL.] **1.** a Christian hymn beginning *Te Deum laudamus* (We praise thee, O God) **2.** music for this hymn

te·di·ous (tē′dē əs, tē′jəs) *adj.* full of tedium; tiresome; boring —**te′di·ous·ly** *adv.* —**te′di·ous·ness** *n.*

te·di·um (-dē əm) *n.* [L. *taedium* < *taedet*, it offends] the condition or quality of being tiresome, boring, or monotonous

tee[1] (tē) *n., pl.* **tees 1.** the letter T, t **2.** anything shaped like T —*adj.* shaped like T —**to a tee** exactly

tee[2] (tē) *n.* [< prec.: the mark was orig. T-shaped] a mark aimed at in quoits, curling, etc.

tee[3] (tē) *n.* [prob. < Scot. dial. *teaz*] **1.** a small, pointed holder of wood, plastic, etc. on which a golf ball is put to be driven **2.** the place at each hole from which a golfer makes his first stroke —*vt., vi.* **teed, tee′ing** to put (a ball) on a tee —**tee off 1.** to play a golf ball from a tee **2.** to begin ☆**3.** [Slang] to make angry or disgusted

tee-hee (tē′hē′) *interj., n.* [ME.: echoic] the sound of a titter or snicker —*vi.* **-heed′, -hee′ing** to titter or snicker

teem[1] (tēm) *vi.* [OE. *tieman*, to bear < base of *team*, progeny] to be full; abound; swarm [a river *teeming* with fish]

teem[2] (tēm) *vi.* [ON. *taema*, to empty] to rain heavily

teen (tēn) *n.* [< OE. *tien*, ten] **1.** [*pl.*] the years from thirteen through nineteen (of a century or a person's age) **2.** *same as* TEEN-AGER —*adj. same as* TEEN-AGE

teen-age (tēn′āj′) *adj.* **1.** in one's teens **2.** of, like, or for persons in their teens Also **teen′age′**

☆**teen-ag·er** (-āj′ər) *n.* a person in the teens

tee·ny (tē′nē) *adj.* **-ni·er, -ni·est** *colloq. var. of* TINY: also **teen·sy** (tēn′sē)

☆**teen·y-bop·per** (tē′nē bäp′ər) *n.* [< TEEN + -Y[1] + BOP + -ER] [Slang] a young teen-ager, esp. a girl, of the 1960's, following the latest fads

tee·ny-wee·ny (-wē′nē) *adj.* [Colloq.] very small; tiny: also **teen·sy-ween·sy** (tēn′sē wēn′sē)

☆**tee·pee** (tē′pē) *n. alt. sp. of* TEPEE

☆**tee shirt** *same as* T-SHIRT

tee·ter (tēt′ər) *vi.* [dial. *titter* < ON. *titra*, to tremble] to totter, wobble, etc. —*vt.* to cause to teeter —*n. shortened form of* TEETER-TOTTER

☆**tee·ter·board** (-bôrd′) *n. same as* SEESAW

tee·ter-tot·ter (-tät′ər, -tŏt′-) *n., vi. same as* SEESAW

teeth (tēth) *n. pl. of* TOOTH

teethe (tēth) *vi.* **teethed, teeth′ing** to grow teeth; cut one's teeth

☆**teeth·ing ring** (tē′thiŋ) a ring of ivory, plastic, etc. for teething babies to bite on

teeth·ridge (tēth′rij′) *n.* the ridge of gum along the inside of the upper front teeth

tee·to·tal (tē tōt′'l, tē′tōt′'l) *adj.* [formed by repeating the first letter of TOTAL] **1.** [Colloq.] entire; complete **2.** of or in favor of teetotalism —**tee·to′tal·er, tee·to′tal·ler** *n.* —**tee·to′tal·ly** *adv.*

tee·to·tal·ism (-iz'm) *n.* the principle or practice of never drinking any alcoholic liquor —**tee·to′tal·ist** *n.*

☆**Tef·lon** (tef′län) *a trademark for* a tough, insoluble polymer used in making nonsticking coatings, as for cooking utensils, and in gaskets, bearings, etc.

Te·gu·ci·gal·pa (te gōo′sē gäl′pä) capital of Honduras, in the SC part: pop. 219,000

teg·u·ment (teg′yoo mənt) *n.* [< L. *tegere*, to cover] *same as* INTEGUMENT

te·hee (tē′hē′) *interj., n., vi.* **-heed′, -hee′ing** *var. of* TEE-HEE

Teh·rán, Te·he·ran (te hrän′; *E.* te ə rän′, -ran′) capital of Iran, in the NC part: pop. 3,150,000

Te·huan·te·pec (te wän′tə pek′, -wän′tə pek′) **1. Gulf of,** arm of the Pacific, off the S coast of Mexico **2. Isthmus of,** narrowest part of Mexico, between this gulf & the Gulf of Mexico

Teil·hard de Char·din (te yàr′ də shàr dan′), **Pierre** 1881–1955; Fr. paleontologist, geologist, & philosopher

☆**tek·tite** (tek′tīt) *n.* [< Gr. *tēktos*, molten < *tēkein*, to melt + -ITE] any of certain small, dark-green to black glassy objects, assumed to have come to earth from outer space

tel- *same as:* **1.** TELE- **2.** TELO-

tel. 1. telegram **2.** telegraph **3.** telephone

Tel A·viv-Jaf·fa (tel′ä vēv′yäf′ə, tel′ə vēv′jaf′ə) seaport in W Israel, made up of the former cities of Tel Aviv & Jaffa: pop. 383,000: usually called **Tel Aviv**

tel·e- *a combining form meaning:* **1.** [< Gr. < *tēle*, far off] at, over, from, or to a distance [*telegraph*] **2.** [< TELE(VISION)] of or by television [*telecast*]

tel·e·cast (tel′ə kast′) *vt., vi.* **-cast′** or **-cast′ed, -cast′ing** [TELE- + (BROAD)CAST] to broadcast by television —*n.* a television broadcast —**tel′e·cast′er** *n.*

tel·e·com·mu·ni·ca·tion (tel′ə kə myōō′nə kā′shən) *n.* [*also pl.*, *with sing. or pl. v.*] communication by radio, telephone, telegraph, television, etc.

tel·e·gen·ic (tel′ə jen′ik) *adj.* [TELE- + -GENIC] that looks attractive on television: said esp. of persons

☆**tel·e·gram** (tel′ə gram′) *n.* [TELE- + -GRAM] a message sent by telegraph

tel·e·graph (-graf′) *n.* [< Fr.: see TELE- & -GRAPH] an apparatus or system for sending messages, orig. in Morse code, by electric impulses through a wire or by means of radio waves —*vt.* **1.** to send (a message) by telegraph to (someone) **2.** [Colloq.] to let another know without meaning to (something one plans to do), as by a look —*vi.* to send a telegram —**te·leg·ra·pher** (tə leg′rə fər), **te·leg′ra·phist** *n.* —**tel′e·graph′ic** *adj.* —**tel′e·graph′i·cal·ly** *adv.*

te·leg·ra·phy (tə leg′rə fē) *n.* **1.** the operation of telegraph apparatus **2.** the sending of messages by telegraph

tel·e·ki·ne·sis (tel′ə ki nē′sis) *n.* [ModL. < TELE- + Gr. *kinēsis*, motion] the causing of an object to move supposedly by means of psychic forces and not by means of any physical force —**tel′e·ki·net′ic** (-net′ik) *adj.*

Te·lem·a·chus (tə lem′ə kəs) *Gr. Legend* the son of Odysseus and Penelope, who helped his father slay his mother's suitors

Te·le·mann (tā′lə män′), **Ge·org Phi·lipp** (gā ôrk′ fē′lip) 1681–1767; Ger. composer

tel·e·mark (tel′ə märk′) *n.* [after *Telemark*, region in S Norway] *Skiing* a turning movement during which the outer ski is pushed forward and turned in at a widening angle

tel·e·me·ter (tel′ə mēt′ər, tə lem′ə tər) *n.* [TELE- + -METER] a device for measuring temperature, radiation, etc. at a remote point, as in outer space, and transmitting the information, esp. by radio, to a distant receiver on earth —*vt., vi.* to transmit by telemeter —**tel′e·met′ric** (-met′rik) *adj.*, **tel′e·met′ri·cal·ly** *adv.* —**te·lem·e·try** (tə lem′ə trē) *n.*

te·le·ol·o·gy (tē′lē äl′ə jē, tel′ē-) *n.* [ModL. < Gr. *telos*, an end + *-logia* (see -LOGY)] **1.** the fact or quality of being directed toward a definite end or goal **2.** a belief that what happens or occurs in nature is determined by an overall design or purpose, not just by mechanical causes —**te′le·o·log′i·cal** (-ə läj′i k'l) *adj.* —**te′le·ol′o·gist** *n.*

te·lep·a·thy (tə lep′ə thē) *n.* [TELE- + -PATHY] the supposed sending of messages from one mind to another by some means other than by speaking, seeing, etc. —**tel·e·path·ic** (tel′ə path′ik) *adj.* —**tel′e·path′i·cal·ly** *adv.* —**tel·e·path′ist** *n.*

tel·e·phone (tel′ə fōn′) *n.* [TELE- + -PHONE] ☆an instrument or system for sending sounds over distances by changing them into electric impulses that are sent through a wire and then changed back into sounds —*vi.* **-phoned′, -phon′ing** to talk over a telephone —*vt.* **1.** to convey (a message) by telephone **2.** to speak to or reach (a person) by telephone —**tel′e·phon′er** *n.* —**tel′e·phon′ic** (-fän′ik) *adj.* —**tel′e·phon′i·cal·ly** *adv.*

te·leph·o·ny (tə lef′ə nē) *n.* the science of sending sounds over distances by telephone

tel·e·pho·to (tel′ə fōt′ō) *adj.* **1.** telephotographic **2.** describing or of a camera lens producing a large image of a distant object —[T-] *a trademark for* a telephotograph (sense 2) or a system of telephotography

tel·e·pho·to·graph (tel′ə fōt′ə graf′) *n.* **1.** a photograph taken with a telephoto lens **2.** a photograph sent by telephotography —*vt., vi.* **1.** to take (photographs) with a telephoto lens **2.** to send (photographs) by telephotography

tel·e·pho·tog·ra·phy (-fə täg′rə fē) *n.* **1.** photography done with a telephoto lens **2.** the science or process of sending photographs over distances by changing light rays into electric signals which are sent over wire or radio channels —**tel′e·pho′to·graph′ic** (-fōt′ə graf′ik) *adj.*

tel·e·por·ta·tion (-pôr tā′shən) *n.* [TELE- + (TRANS)PORTATION] in theory, the transportation of matter through space by changing it into energy and then changing it back to the original matter when it reaches its destination

tel·e·print·er (tel′ə prin′tər) *n. chiefly Brit. term for* TELETYPEWRITER

☆**Tel·e·Promp·Ter** (tel′ə prämp′tər) *a trademark for* an electronic device that unrolls a speech, etc. line by line so that the speaker can read it aloud on television without letting the audience see it —*n.* (written **teleprompter**) this device

☆**tel·e·ran** (tel′ə ran′) *n.* [*tele*(*vision*) *r*(*adar*) *a*(*ir*) *n*(*avigation*)] the sending to aircraft by television of data received by radar, as an aid to navigation

tel·e·scope (tel′ə skōp′) *n.* [< It. < ModL. < Gr.: see TELE- & -SCOPE] an instrument for making distant objects, as stars, seem nearer and larger: it consists of a tube or tubes containing lenses in a *refracting telescope*, the image is focused directly on a lens; in a *reflecting telescope*, the image is focused on a concave mirror —*adj.* having parts that slide one inside another —*vi.* **-scoped′, -scop′ing** to slide or be forced one inside another like the tubes of a collapsible telescope —*vt.* **1.** to cause to telescope; force together by telescoping **2.** to condense; shorten

tel·e·scop·ic (tel′ə skäp′ik) *adj.* **1.** of a telescope **2.** seen or gotten by using a telescope **3.** that can be seen only through a telescope **4.** able to see far away; farseeing **5.** having sections that slide one inside another [a *telescopic* drinking cup] Also **tel′e·scop′i·cal** —**tel′e·scop′i·cal·ly** *adv.*

☆**tel·e·thon** (tel′ə thän′) *n.* [TELE(VISION) + (MARA)THON] a campaign, as on a lengthy telecast, asking for support for a cause, as by pledged donations made by telephone

☆**Tel·e·type** (tel′ə tīp′) *a trademark for* a form of teletypewriter —*n.* [*often* **t-**] communication by means of Teletype —*vt., vi.* **-typed′, -typ′ing** [*often* **t-**] to send (messages) by Teletype —**tel′e·typ′er, tel′e·typ′ist** *n.*

☆**tel·e·type·writ·er** (tel′ə tīp′rīt′ər) *n.* a form of telegraph in which the message is typed on a keyboard that sends electric signals to a machine that prints the words

tel·e·vise (tel′ə vīz′) *vt., vi.* **-vised′, -vis′ing** to send pictures of by television —**tel′e·vi′sor** *n.*

tel·e·vi·sion (-vizh′ən) *n.* [TELE- + VISION] **1.** the process of sending pictures of scenes or views by radio waves or, sometimes, by wire, in which light rays are changed by a camera tube into electric signals that are picked up by a receiver that changes the signals into electron beams that are projected against the screen of a picture tube, reproducing the original image **2.** television broadcasting as an industry, art, etc.; also, its facilities and related activities **3.** a television receiving set —*adj.* of, in, or by television

tel·ex (tel′eks) *n.* [TEL(ETYPEWRITER) + EX(CHANGE)] **1.** a teletypewriter with a telephone dial for making connections **2.** a message sent by this —*vt.* to send (a message) by telex

tell (tel) *vt.* **told, tell′ing** [OE. *tellan*, lit., to calculate] **1.** orig., to count one by one [there were ten present all *told*] **2.** to give an account of (a story, etc.) in speech or writing; narrate; relate **3.** to express in words; utter [to *tell* the truth] **4.** to report; announce [*telling* the news far and wide] **5.** to make known; disclose [don't *tell* the secret] **6.** to recognize; distinguish [I can *tell* the difference] **7.** to decide; know [he can't *tell* when to go] **8.** to let know; inform [*tell* me about the game] **9.** to request; order [*tell* him to leave] **10.** to say definitely [it's there, I *tell* you] —*vi.* **1.** to give an account or description (of something) [the book *tells* of his early life] **2.** to be evidence or an indication (of something) [his worn looks *tell* of his suffering] **3.** to reveal something, esp. secrets [I'll never *tell*] **4.** to produce a result or have a marked effect [the strain is beginning to *tell*] —**tell off 1.** to count and separate from the total [to *tell off* volunteers for the job] **2.** [Colloq.] to scold severely [he really *told* her *off*] —**tell on 1.** to make weary, worn-out, etc. [the work is *telling on* her] **2.** [Colloq.] to tell secrets about [he *told on* his brother] —**tell′a·ble** *adj.*

SYN.—**tell** is the basic term meaning to give the facts or details of some circumstance or occurrence [*tell* me what happened]; **relate** suggests the orderly telling of something that one has personally experienced, seen, or heard [*relate* your dream to us]; **recount** suggests the telling of things one after another, just as they occurred, and in great detail [to *recount* one's adventures]; **narrate** suggests the telling of something as in a story or novel, by developing a plot, building up to a climax, etc. [to *narrate* the story of the flood], and **report** suggests the giving to others of information about something that one has seen, observed, studied, etc. [to *report* the results of the experiment] —see also SYN. at REVEAL

Tell (tel), **William** in Swiss legend, a hero in the fight for independence from Austria, who was forced by a tyrant to shoot an apple off his son's head with bow and arrow

tell·er (tel′ər) *n.* **1.** a person who tells (a story, etc.) **2.** a person who counts; specif., *a*) one who counts votes *b*) a bank clerk who pays out or receives money

tell·ing (tel′iŋ) *adj.* **1.** effective; forceful [a *telling* blow] **2.** that tells or reveals much [a *telling* gesture] —**tell′ing·ly** *adv.*

tell·tale (-tāl′) *n.* **1.** a person who tells secrets; talebearer; informer **2.** something that reveals a secret **3.** a device that indicates or records information —*adj.* revealing a secret [the *telltale* jam on his face showed he had stolen the tarts]

tel·lu·ri·um (te loor′ē əm) *n.* [ModL. < L. *tellus*, the earth] a rare chemical element that is white and brittle and used in alloys: symbol, Te; at. wt., 127.60; at. no., 52

tel·ly (tel′ē) *n.* [Brit. Colloq.] television

tel·o- [< Gr. *telos*, an end] *a combining form meaning* end

tel·pher, tel·fer (tel′fər) *n.* [< TEL(E)- + Gr. *pherein*, to BEAR¹] a car powered by electric current, that hangs from overhead cables and runs on them —**tel′pher·age** *n.*

Tel·u·gu (tel′ə gōō′) *n.* **1.** a Dravidian language of S India **2.** *pl.* **-gus′, -gu′** a member of a Dravidian people speaking this language —*adj.* of Telugu or the Telugus Also **Tel′e·gu′**

☆**tem·blor** (tem′blôr, -blər; *Sp.* tem blôr′) *n., pl.* **-blors;** *Sp.* **-blo′res** (-blô′res) [Sp. < *temblar*, to tremble] *same as* EARTHQUAKE

te·mer·i·ty (tə mer′ə tē) *n.* [< L. < *temere*, rashly] foolish or rash boldness; recklessness

SYN.—**temerity** refers to a rashness or a foolish boldness that comes from not taking into account possible dangers or risks [he had the *temerity* to run across the freeway]; **audacity** suggests either taking too much for granted or going directly against the customs, morals, etc. accepted by most people [the town was shocked by the *audacity* of the movie]; **effrontery**, always indicating strong disapproval by the one using the term, implies a being rude or without shame in doing or saying something not considered proper, courteous, etc. [his *effrontery* in pushing ahead of everyone else]; **nerve, cheek, brass,** and **gall** are colloquial terms used instead of effrontery or audacity but **gall** is stronger than the others in suggesting shocking action or speech

temp. **1.** temperature **2.** temporary

Tem·pe (tem′pē) [after Vale of *Tempe*, river valley in E Greece] city in SC Ariz.: suburb of Phoenix: pop. 63,000

tem·per (tem′pər) *vt.* [< OE. & OFr., both < L. *temperare*, to regulate < *tempus*, a period] **1.** to make suitable or less strong by mingling with another thing; moderate [*temper* blame with praise] **2.** *a*) to bring to the desired texture, hardness, etc. by treating in some way [to *temper* steel by heating and sudden cooling] *b*) to toughen, as by hardship **3.** *Music* to adjust the pitch of (a note, instrument, etc.) to some temperament —*vi.* to become tempered —*n.* **1.** a being tempered; specif., the degree of hardness and toughness of a metal **2.** frame of mind; disposition [in a bad *temper*] **3.** mental calm; composure: now only in **lose** (or **keep**) **one's temper 4.** a tendency to get angry [to have a *temper*] **5.** anger; rage [to fly into a *temper*] **6.** something used to temper a mixture, etc. —see SYN. at DISPOSITION and MOOD¹

tem·per·a (tem′pər ə) *n.* [It. < *temperare* < L.: see TEMPER] **1.** *a*) a way of painting that uses pigments mixed with size, casein, or egg to produce a dull finish *b*) the paint so used **2.** a water-base paint used as for posters

tem·per·a·ment (tem′prə mənt, -pər ə mənt, -pər mənt) *n.* [L. *temperamentum*, proper mixing < *temperare*: see TEMPER] **1.** one's usual frame of mind or natural disposition **2.** a nature that makes one excitable, moody, etc. **3.** *Music* a system of adjustment of the intervals between the tones of an instrument —see SYN. at DISPOSITION

tem·per·a·men·tal (tem′prə men′t'l, -pər ə men′t'l, -pər men′t'l) *adj.* **1.** of or caused by temperament **2.** having a nature that is easily upset or excited **3.** behaving in strange or unexpected ways —**tem′per·a·men′tal·ly** *adv.*

tem·per·ance (tem′pər əns, -prəns) *n.* [< MFr. < L. < prp. of *temperare*: see TEMPER] **1.** a being temperate or moderate; self-restraint **2.** the drinking of little or no alcoholic liquor

tem·per·ate (tem′pər it, -prit) *adj.* [< L. pp. of *temperare*, to TEMPER] **1.** moderate in indulging the appetites; specif., drinking little or no alcoholic liquor **2.** moderate in one's actions, speech, etc. **3.** showing restraint [a *temperate* reply] **4.** nei-

TELE-
SCOPIC
CUP

---

ther very hot nor very cold: said of a climate, etc. —see **SYN.** at MODERATE —**tem′per·ate·ly** adv. —**tem′per·ate·ness** n.

Temperate Zone either of two zones of the earth (**North Temperate Zone** and **South Temperate Zone**) between the tropics and the polar circles: see illustration at ZONE

tem·per·a·ture (tem′prə chər, tem′pər ə-) n. [< L. < temperatus, temperate] the degree of hotness or coldness of anything, usually as measured on a thermometer; specif., a) the degree of heat of a living body; also, an excess of this over the normal (about 98.6°F or 37°C in man) b) the degree of heat of the atmosphere

tem·pered (tem′pərd) adj. 1. having been given the desired texture, hardness, etc. [tempered steel] 2. modified by other qualities, etc. [justice tempered with mercy] 3. having a (specified) temper [bad-tempered] 4. Music adjusted to a temperament

tem·pest (tem′pist) n. [< OFr., ult. < L. tempestas, portion of time, weather < tempus, time] 1. a violent storm with high winds, esp. one that also brings rain, hail, or snow 2. a violent outburst; tumult

tem·pes·tu·ous (tem pes′chōō wəs) adj. 1. of or like a tempest; stormy 2. violent; turbulent [tempestuous emotions] —**tem·pes′tu·ous·ly** adv. —**tem·pes′tu·ous·ness** n.

Tem·plar (tem′plər) n. [from occupying quarters near the site of Solomon's Temple in Jerusalem] same as KNIGHT TEMPLAR

tem·plate, tem·plet (tem′plit) n. [< Fr., dim. of temple < L. templum, small timber] 1. a pattern, usually a thin plate, for forming an accurate copy of an object or shape 2. Archit. a) a short stone or timber placed under a beam to help spread the pressure evenly b) a beam for supporting joists over a doorway, etc.

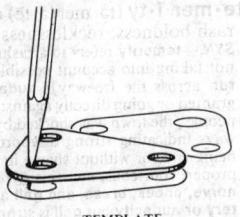

TEMPLATE

tem·ple[1] (tem′p'l) n. [< OE. & OFr., both < L. templum, orig., space marked out] 1. a building for the worship of a god or gods 2. [T-] any of three buildings for worshiping Jehovah, built at different times by the Jews in ancient Jerusalem 3. the synagogue of a Reform, or sometimes Conservative, congregation 4. a Christian church 5. a building, usually a fairly large one, serving some purpose [a Masonic temple] —**tem′pled** adj.

tem·ple[2] (tem′p'l) n. [< OFr. < VL. < L. tempora, the temples, pl. of tempus, temple of the head] 1. the flat area at either side of the forehead, above and behind the eye ☆2. either of the sidepieces of a pair of eyeglasses

tem·po (tem′pō) n., pl. -pos, -pi (-pē) [It. < L. tempus, time] 1. the speed at which a piece of music is performed 2. rate of activity; pace [the tempo of modern living]

tem·po·ral[1] (tem′pər əl, -prəl) adj. [L. temporalis < tempus, time] 1. lasting only for a time; transitory; not eternal [temporal happiness] 2. of this world; not spiritual [temporal matters] 3. having to do with the laws of a state rather than of a church; civil or secular 4. of or limited by time [temporal measurements] —n. a temporal thing, power, etc. —**tem′po·ral·ly** adv.

tem·po·ral[2] (tem′pər əl, -prəl) adj. [LL. temporalis < L. tempora: see TEMPLE[2]] of or near the temple or temples (of the head)

temporal bone either of a pair of compound bones forming the sides of the skull

tem·po·ral·i·ty (tem′pə ral′ə tē) n., pl. -ties 1. the quality or state of being temporal 2. [usually pl.] the revenues or properties belonging to a church

tem·po·rar·y (tem′pə rer′ē) adj. [< L. < tempus, time] lasting only for a time; not permanent —**tem·po·rar·i·ly** (tem′pə·rer′ə lē, tem′pə rer′ə lē) adv. —**tem′po·rar′i·ness** n.

tem·po·rize (tem′pə rīz′) vi. -rized′, -riz′ing [MFr. temporiser < ML. < L. tempus, time] 1. to act or speak in a way one thinks is popular or will give one an advantage rather than in a right way 2. a) to put off making a decision, or to agree for a while, so as to gain time b) to bargain or deal (with a person) so as to gain time —**tem′po·ri·za′tion** n. —**tem′po·riz′er** n.

tempt (tempt) vt. [< OFr. < LL. temptare < L., to try the strength of] 1. orig., to test; try 2. to entice (a person) to do or want something that is wrong, forbidden, etc. 3. to be inviting or enticing to; attract 4. to provoke or risk provoking [he tempted fate by driving with a bad tire] —see **SYN.** at LURE — **tempt′a·ble** adj. —**tempt′er** n. —**tempt′ress** n.fem.

temp·ta·tion (temp tā′shən) n. 1. a tempting or being tempted 2. something that tempts

tempt·ing (temp′tiŋ) adj. that tempts; enticing; attractive — **tempt′ing·ly** adv.

tem·pu·ra (tem′pōō rä′, tem pōōr′ə) n. [Jpn., lit., fried food] a Japanese dish of seafood or vegetables dipped in an egg batter and deep-fried [shrimp tempura]

‡**tem·pus fu·git** (tem′pəs fyōō′jit) [L.] time flies

ten (ten) adj. [OE.] totaling one more than nine —n. 1. the cardinal number between 9 and 11; 10; X 2. anything having ten units or members, or numbered ten 3. [Colloq.] a ten-dollar bill

ten. 1. tenor 2. Music tenuto

ten·a·ble (ten′ə b'l) adj. [Fr. < OFr. < tenir: see TENANT] that can be held, defended, or believed [tenable theories] —**ten′a·bil·i·ty, ten′a·ble·ness** n. —**ten′a·bly** adv.

te·na·cious (tə nā′shəs) adj. [< L. tenacis, genitive of tenax, holding fast < tenere, to hold] 1. holding firmly [a tenacious grip] 2. that keeps or retains something for a long time [a tenacious memory] 3. holding together strongly; tough [a tenacious wood] 4. clinging; sticky [tenacious burs] 5. persistent; stubborn [tenacious courage] —**te·na′cious·ly** adv. —**te·na′cious·ness** n.

te·nac·i·ty (tə nas′ə tē) n. the quality or state of being tenacious —see **SYN.** at PERSEVERANCE

ten·an·cy (ten′ən sē) n., pl. -cies 1. the condition of being a tenant 2. the length of time that one is a tenant 3. any holding of property, an office, etc.

ten·ant (ten′ənt) n. [OFr., orig. prp. of tenir, to hold < L. tenere] 1. a person who pays rent to occupy or use land, a building, etc. 2. one that lives or dwells in a specified place —vt. to live in as a tenant —**ten′ant·a·ble** adj. —**ten′ant·less** adj.

tenant farmer a person who farms land owned by another and pays rent in cash or in a share of the crops

ten·ant·ry (ten′ən trē) n., pl. -ries 1. all the tenants of a place 2. occupancy by a tenant

☆**ten-cent store** (ten′sent′) same as FIVE-AND-TEN-CENT STORE

tench (tench) n., pl. tench′es, tench: see PLURAL, II, D, 1 [< OFr. < LL. tinca] a common European freshwater fish related to the carp

Ten Commandments Bible the ten laws forming the fundamental moral code of Israel, given to Moses by God on Mount Sinai: Ex. 20:2–17; Deut. 5:6–22

tend[1] (tend) vt. [see ATTEND] 1. to take care of; watch over; attend to [to tend the sick] 2. to be in charge of; manage [to tend a store] —vi. to pay attention; attend [tending to business]

tend[2] (tend) vi. [< OFr. < L. tendere, to stretch < IE. base ten-, to stretch] 1. to move or go in a certain direction; extend [to tend east] 2. to be likely or apt; incline [tending to boast] 3. to lead (to or toward) a specified result) [this tends to reassure us]

tend·ance (ten′dəns) n. the act of tending or taking care of

tend·en·cy (ten′dən sē) n., pl. -cies [< ML. < L. prp. of tendere, to stretch] 1. an inclination to move or act in a particular direction or way; leaning; bias [a tendency to criticize] 2. a course toward some purpose, object, or result; drift [understood the tendency of these remarks]

SYN.—tendency refers to an inclination or disposition to move in a particular direction or act in a certain way, esp. as a result of some inborn or natural quality [he has a tendency to exaggerate]; **trend** suggests the movement of most of the individuals or elements of a group, culture, activity, etc. toward a certain goal or in a certain direction [a trend in literature toward realism; an upward business trend]; **current** suggests a stronger and more definite movement than trend and one less likely to change direction [the currents of modern thought]; **drift** suggests a being carried or driven toward some goal or a moving in a direction not clearly set or seen in advance [the drift of the nation toward dictatorship; I finally caught the drift of his remarks]; **tenor** is used of any activity or procedure that keeps to a steady, clear course [the even tenor of her daily life] or of the intended meaning or basic idea of something spoken or written [the tenor of the Bill of Rights]

ten·den·tious (ten den′shəs) adj. [< G., ult. < ML. tendentia, TENDENCY] showing a deliberate tendency or aim; esp., advancing a particular point of view: also sp. **ten·den′cious** —**tenden′tious·ly** adv. —**ten·den′tious·ness** n.

ten·der[1] (ten′dər) adj. [< OFr. < L. tener, soft] 1. soft or delicate and easily chewed, broken, cut, etc. [a tender steak] 2. physically weak; frail 3. immature; young [the tender age of five] 4. of soft quality or delicate tone [the tender night air] 5. needing careful handling; ticklish [a tender subject] 6. gentle or light, as a touch 7. a) affectionate, loving, etc. [a tender smile] b) thoughtful; careful; considerate [in the tender care of a loving father] **8.** *a)* that is hurt or feels pain easily; sensitive [a *tender* skin] *b)* sensitive to impressions, emotions, etc. [a *tender* conscience] *c)* sensitive to others' feelings; compassionate [a *tender* heart] —**ten′der·ly** *adv.* —**ten′der·ness** *n.*

ten·der² (ten′dər) *vt.* [< Fr. < L. *tendere*, to stretch] **1.** to offer as payment for something owed **2.** to present for acceptance; offer (an invitation, apology, etc.) —*n.* **1.** an offer of money, services, etc. as to pay for something owed **2.** a formal offer, as of marriage, a contract, etc. ☆**3.** money, etc. offered in payment —see **SYN.** at OFFER —**ten′der·er** *n.*

tend·er³ (ten′dər) *n.* **1.** a person who tends, or has charge of, something **2.** *a)* a ship to supply or service another ship, a submarine, etc. *b)* a boat for carrying passengers, etc. to or from a ship close to shore **3.** the railroad car behind a steam locomotive for carrying its coal and water

☆**ten·der·foot** (-foŏt′) *n., pl.* **-foots′, -feet′ 1.** a newcomer, specif. to the hardships of ranching and outdoor life in the West **2.** a beginner in the Boy Scouts

ten·der·heart·ed (-här′tid) *adj.* having a tender heart; quick to feel pity —**ten′der·heart′ed·ly** *adv.* —**ten′der·heart′ed·ness** *n.*

ten·der·ize (ten′də rīz′) *vt.* **-ized′, -iz′ing** to make (meat) tender, as by adding a substance that softens tissues —**ten′der·i·za′tion** *n.* —**ten′der·iz·er** *n.*

☆**ten·der·loin** (ten′dər loin′) *n.* **1.** a cut of beef or pork from the tenderest muscle of the loin **2.** [usually T-] a city district full of vice and crime that can be a source of graft for the police

ten·di·ni·tis (ten′də nīt′əs) *n.* [< ModL.: see TENDON & -ITIS] inflammation of a tendon

ten·don (ten′dən) *n.* [ML. *tendo* < Gr. < *teinein*, to stretch] any of the cords of tough, fibrous tissue connecting muscles to bones or other parts; sinew —**ten′di·nous** (-də nəs) *adj.*

ten·dril (ten′drəl) *n.* [prob. < OFr. *tendrum*, ult. < L. *tener*, soft] a threadlike part of a climbing plant, serving to support it by clinging to or coiling around an object

ten·e·brous (ten′ə brəs) *adj.* [< L. < *tenebrae*, darkness] dark; gloomy: also **te·neb·ri·ous** (tə neb′rē əs)

ten·e·ment (ten′ə mənt) *n.* [< OFr. < ML. < L. *tenere*, to hold] **1.** *Law* land, buildings, etc. that someone else has given one the right to hold **2.** a house where people live **3.** a suite of rooms, or an apartment, that is rented **4.** *same as* TENEMENT HOUSE

☆**tenement house** an apartment building, now specif. one in the slums that is run-down and overcrowded

Ten·er·ife (ten′ə rēf′; *Sp.* te ne rē′fe) largest island of the Canary Islands: 795 sq. mi.

ten·et (ten′it) *n.* [L., he holds] a principle, doctrine, or belief held as a truth, as by some group —see **SYN.** at DOCTRINE

ten·fold (ten′fōld′) *adj.* [see -FOLD] **1.** having ten parts **2.** having ten times as much or as many —*adv.* ten times as much or as many

☆**ten-gal·lon hat** (ten′gal′ən) a wide-brimmed felt hat with a high, round crown, orig. worn by cowboys

Ten·nes·see (ten′ə sē′) [< *Tanasi*, Cherokee village name] **1.** EC State of the U.S.: 42,244 sq. mi.; pop. 3,924,000; cap. Nashville: abbrev. **Tenn., TN 2.** river flowing from NE Tenn. through N Ala. & W Tenn. into the Ohio River —**Ten′nes·se′an** *adj., n.*

☆**Tennessee Valley Authority** a Federal corporation organized in 1933 to provide cheap electric power, flood control, irrigation, etc. by developing the entire valley of the Tennessee River, esp. by building dams and reservoirs

☆**Tennessee walking horse** any of a breed of saddle horse with an easy, ambling gait

ten·nis (ten′is) *n.* [prob. < Anglo-Fr. *tenetz*, hold (imperative) < OFr. *tenir*: see TENANT] **1.** a game (officially **lawn tennis**), usually played outdoors, in which two or four players using rackets hit a ball back and forth over a net dividing a marked rectangular area (**tennis court**): see illustration at RACKET **2.** a similar but more complex old indoor game (**court tennis**), the ball being in addition bounced against walls

tennis shoe *same as* SNEAKER (sense 2)

Ten·ny·son (ten′ə s'n), **Alfred,** 1st Baron Tennyson, 1809–92; Eng. poet: called *Alfred, Lord Tennyson* —**Ten′ny·so′ni·an** (-sō′nē ən) *adj.*

ten·on (ten′ən) *n.* [< MFr. < *tenir:* see TENANT] a part of a piece of wood, etc. cut to stick out so that it will fit into a hole (*mortise*) in another piece to make a joint: see illustration at MORTISE —*vt., vi.* **1.** to make a tenon (on) **2.** to joint by mortise and tenon

ten·or (ten′ər) *n.* [< OFr. < L. < *tenere*, to hold] **1.** general course or tendency [the even *tenor* of his life] **2.** general meaning; drift [the *tenor* of the discussion] **3.** [because the tenor voice "held" the melody] *a)* the usual range of the highest singing voice of men: see also COUNTERTENOR *b)* a voice or singer with such a range *c)* a musical instrument with a similar range *d)* a part for such a voice or instrument —*adj.* of, in, for, or having this range —see **SYN.** at TENDENCY

tenor clef *see* C CLEF

ten·pen·ny (ten′pen′ē, -pə nē) *adj.* **1.** worth ten (esp. Brit.) pennies **2.** designating a size of nails, three inches long

ten·pins (-pinz′) *n.pl.* **1.** [*with sing. v.*] the game of bowling in which ten pins are used **2.** the pins

tense¹ (tens) *adj.* **tens′er, tens′est** [< L. pp. of *tendere*, to stretch] **1.** stretched tight; strained; taut **2.** feeling, showing, or causing mental strain; anxious **3.** *Phonet.* pronounced with the jaw and tongue relatively rigid: said of certain vowels as *e* in *he*: opposed to LAX —*vt., vi.* **tensed, tens′ing** to make or become tense —**tense′ly** *adv.* —**tense′ness** *n.*

tense² (tens) *n.* [< OFr. < L. *tempus*, time] any form or set of forms of a verb that show the time of the action or condition

ten·sile (ten′s'l) *adj.* **1.** of or under tension [*tensile* stress] **2.** capable of being stretched [*tensile* materials]: also **ten′si·ble** (-sə b'l) —**ten·sil′i·ty** (-sil′ə tē) *n.*

tensile strength resistance to lengthwise stress, measured (in weight per unit area) by the greatest load pulling in the direction of length that a given substance can bear without tearing apart

ten·sion (ten′shən) *n.* **1.** a tensing or being tensed **2.** mental or nervous strain; tense feeling **3.** a state of strained relations [international *tension*] **4.** a device to regulate tautness of thread, etc. **5.** *same as* VOLTAGE **6.** *a)* stress on a material by forces tending to cause extension *b)* a force exerting such stress —*vt.* to subject to tension —**ten′sion·al** *adj.*

ten·sor (ten′sər, -sôr) *n.* [ModL. < L. pp. of *tendere*, to stretch] any muscle that stretches a body part

tent (tent) *n.* [< OFr. < L. pp. of *tendere*, to stretch] **1.** a portable shelter consisting of canvas, etc. stretched over poles and attached to stakes **2.** anything like a tent; specif., *short for* OXYGEN TENT —*adj.* of or like a tent [a *tent* theater] —*vi.* to live in a tent [*tenting* in the desert] —*vt.* **1.** to lodge in tents **2.** to cover as with a tent

ten·ta·cle (ten′tə k'l) *n.* [ModL. *tentaculum* < L. *tentare*, to touch] **1.** any of various long, slender, flexible growths, as at the head or mouth of some invertebrates, used for grasping, feeling, etc. **2.** *Bot.* any of various sensitive hairs on some leaves, as of certain insect-eating plants —**ten·tac′u·lar** (-tak′yə lər) *adj.*

ten·ta·tive (ten′tə tiv) *adj.* [LL. *tentativus* < pp. of L. *tentare*, to try] made or done as a test or for the time being; not definite or final —**ten′ta·tive·ly** *adv.* —**ten′ta·tive·ness** *n.*

☆**tent caterpillar** any of the caterpillars that live in colonies in large, tentlike webs spun among tree branches

ten·ter (ten′tər) *n.* [see TENT] a frame to stretch cloth on for even drying —*vt.* to stretch on a tenter

ten·ter·hook (-hoŏk′) *n.* any of the hooked nails that hold cloth stretched on a tenter —**on tenterhooks** in suspense

tenth (tenth) *adj.* [OE. *teogotha*] **1.** coming after nine others in a series; 10th **2.** designating any of the ten equal parts of something —*n.* **1.** the one following the ninth **2.** any of the ten equal parts of something; 1/10 —**tenth′ly** *adv.*

tent stitch [< ? TENT] an embroidery stitch forming a series of parallel slanting lines

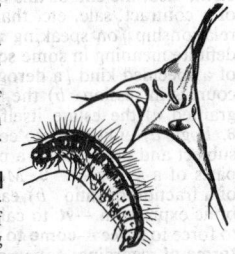

TENT CATERPILLAR & WEB

ten·u·ous (ten′yoo wəs) *adj.* [< L. *tenuis*, thin + -OUS] **1.** slender or fine, as a fiber **2.** not dense; rare, as air high up **3.** slight; flimsy [*tenuous* evidence] —see SYN. at THIN —**te·nu·i·ty** (tə noo′ə tē, -nyoo′-), **ten′u·ous·ness** *n.* —**ten′u·ous·ly** *adv.*

ten·ure (ten′yər, -yoor) *n.* [< MFr. < *tenir*: see TENANT] **1.** the act or right of holding property, an office, etc. **2.** the period or conditions of this **3.** the holding of a position in teaching, civil service, etc. on a permanent basis after meeting specified requirements

te·nu·to (tə noot′ō) *adj.* [It., pp. of *tenere*, to hold] *Music* held for the full value, as a note

☆**te·pee** (tē′pē) *n.* [< Siouan < *ti*, to dwell + *pi*, used for] a cone-shaped tent of animal skins, used by the Indians of the Great Plains

tep·id (tep′id) *adj.* [< L. < *tepere*, to be slightly warm] slightly warm; lukewarm —**te·pid·i·ty** (tə pid′ə tē), **tep′id·ness** *n.* —**tep′id·ly** *adv.*

☆**te·qui·la** (tə kē′lə) *n.* [AmSp. < Nahuatl *Tequila*, a Mexican district] **1.** a strong alcoholic liquor of Mexico, distilled from pulque or mescal **2.** a Mexican agave that is a source of tequila and mescal

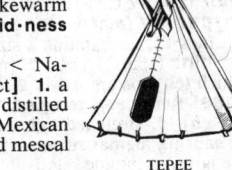
TEPEE

ter. **1.** terrace **2.** territory

ter·a- (ter′ə) [< Gr. *teras*, monster] *a combining form meaning* one trillion [*terahertz*]

ter·bi·um (tur′bē əm) *n.* [ModL. < *Ytterby*, town in Sweden] a metallic chemical element of the rare-earth group: symbol, Tb; at. wt., 158.924; at. no., 65

Ter Borch (tur bôrkh′), **Ge·rard** (gā′rärt) 1617–81; Du. painter: also written **Ter′borch**

terce (turs) *n.* [< OFr. < L. *tertia*, fem. of *tertius*, third] [*often* T-] *Eccles.* the third of the seven canonical hours

ter·cen·te·nar·y (tur′sen ten′ər ē, tər sen′tə ner′ē) *adj., n., pl.* **-nar·ies** [< L. *ter*, three times + CENTENARY] *same as* TRICENTENNIAL: also **ter′cen·ten′ni·al** (-ten′ē əl)

ter·cet (tur′sit, tər set′) *n.* [Fr. < It. dim. of *terzo*, a third < L. *tertius*] a group of three lines that rhyme

ter·e·binth (ter′ə binth′) *n.* [< MFr., ult. < Gr. *terebinthos*] a small European tree whose cut bark yields a turpentine

Ter·ence (ter′əns) [L. *Terentius*, name of a Roman gens] **1.** a masculine name: dim. **Terry** **2.** (L. name *Publius Terentius Afer*) 190?–159? B.C.; Rom. writer of comedies

Te·re·sa (tə rē′sə, *Sp.* te re′sä) **1.** [var. of THERESA] a feminine name **2.** Saint, 1515–82; Sp. Carmelite nun: called **Teresa of A·vi·la** (ä′vē lä′)

ter·gi·ver·sate (tur′ji vər sāt′) *vi.* **-sat·ed, -sat·ing** [< L. pp. of *tergiversari* < *tergum*, the back + *versari*, to turn] **1.** to desert a cause, party, etc. **2.** to be clever or tricky in avoiding responsibility —**ter′gi·ver·sa′tion** *n.* —**ter′gi·ver·sa′tor** *n.*

ter·i·ya·ki (ter′ē yä′kē) *n.* [Jpn.] meat or fish marinated or dipped in soy sauce and broiled, grilled, or barbecued: a Japanese dish

term (turm) *n.* [< OFr. < L. *terminus*, a limit < IE. base *ter-*, to cross over] **1.** a set date, as for paying something owed for or ending something **2.** a set period of time; specif., *a)* a division of a school year, as a semester ☆*b)* the period set for holding an office *c)* the normal period between conception and birth; also, the end of this period; childbirth **3.** [*pl.*] conditions of a contract, sale, etc. that limit or define it **4.** [*pl.*] personal relationship [on speaking *terms*] **5.** a word or phrase having definite meaning in some science, art, etc. **6.** a word or phrase of a specified kind [a derogatory *term*] **7.** *Law a)* the time a court is in session *b)* the length of time for which an estate is granted *c)* the estate itself *d)* time allowed a debtor to pay **8.** *Logic a)* either of two concepts with a stated relation, as the subject and predicate of a proposition *b)* any one of the three parts of a syllogism **9.** *Math. a)* either of the two quantities of a fraction or ratio *b)* each quantity in a series or in an algebraic expression —*vt.* to call by a term; name —**bring to terms** to force to agree —**come to terms** to arrive at an agreement —**in terms of** regarding; concerning

ter·ma·gant (tur′mə gənt) *n.* [< OFr. *Tervagant*, a supposed Moslem deity] a quarrelsome, scolding woman; shrew

term·er (tur′mər) *n.* a person serving a specified term, esp. in prison [a third-*termer*]

ter·mi·na·ble (tur′mi nə b'l) *adj.* **1.** that can be terminated or ended **2.** that comes to an end after a specified time, as a contract —**ter′mi·na·bil′i·ty, ter′mi·na·ble·ness** *n.* —**ter′mi·na·bly** *adv.*

ter·mi·nal (tur′mə n'l) *adj.* [L. *terminalis*] **1.** of, at, or forming the end or extremity of something [a *terminal* bud] **2.** occurring at the end of a series; concluding; final [a *terminal* payment] **3.** of or in the final stages of a fatal disease [*terminal* cancer] **4.** in or of a term or set period of time [*terminal* examinations] **5.** of, at, or forming the end of a transportation line [a *terminal* city] —*n.* **1.** a terminating part; end; extremity **2.** a connective device or point on an electric circuit or conductor ☆**3.** *a)* either end of a transportation line *b)* a station or city there or at any important point of the line —see SYN. at LAST[1] —**ter′mi·nal·ly** *adv.*

☆**terminal leave** the final leave given to a member of the armed forces just before his discharge, made up of days of leave he has coming that he has not used

ter·mi·nate (tur′mə nāt′) *vt.* **-nat·ed, -nat·ing** [< L. pp. of *terminare*, to end < *terminus*, a limit] **1.** to form the end or limit of; finish or bound [this show *terminated* his acting career] **2.** to put an end to; stop [to terminate a discussion] —*vi.* **1.** to come to an end [the road *terminates* at the river] —see SYN. at CLOSE[2] —**ter′mi·na′tive** *adj.* —**ter′mi·na′tor** *n.*

ter·mi·na·tion (tur′mə nā′shən) *n.* **1.** a terminating or being terminated **2.** the end or limit **3.** *Linguis.* the end of a word; specif., an ending that shows inflection —**ter′mi·na′tion·al** *adj.*

ter·mi·nol·o·gy (tur′mə näl′ə jē) *n., pl.* **-gies** the terms or special words used in some science, art, work, etc. —**ter′mi·no·log′i·cal** (-nə läj′i k'l) *adj.* —**ter′mi·no·log′i·cal·ly** *adv.* —**ter′mi·nol′o·gist** *n.*

term insurance life insurance for only a specified period of time

ter·mi·nus (tur′mə nəs) *n., pl.* **-ni′** (-nī′), **-nus·es** [L., a limit] **1.** a boundary or limit **2.** a boundary stone or marker **3.** an end; final point or goal **4.** either end of a transportation line

ter·mite (tur′mīt) *n.* [L. *termitis*, genitive of *termes*, wood-boring worm] a pale-colored, antlike insect with a soft body, that lives in colonies and is very destructive to wooden structures

term·less (turm′lis) *adj.* **1.** having no limit or end **2.** not limited; unconditional

☆**term paper** a long paper or report that a student is required to write for a course during a school term

tern (turn) *n.* [< ON. *therna*] any of several sea birds related to the gulls, but smaller, with a more slender body and beak and a deeply forked tail

ter·na·ry (tur′nər ē) *adj.* [< L. < *terni*, three each] **1.** made up of three parts; threefold; triple **2.** third in rank or order **3.** *Chem.* composed of three different atoms, elements, etc.

ter·nate (tur′nāt) *adj.* [ModL., ult. < L. *terni*, three each] **1.** consisting of three **2.** arranged in threes, as some leaves —**ter′nate·ly** *adv.*

ter·pene (tur′pēn) *n.* [G. *terpen*] any of a series of isomeric hydrocarbons of the general formula $C_{10}H_{16}$, found in resins, etc.

Terp·sich·o·re (tərp sik′ə rē′) *Gr. Myth.* the Muse of dancing

terp·si·cho·re·an (turp′si kə rē′ən) *adj.* **1.** [T-] of Terpsichore **2.** having to do with dancing

terr. **1.** terrace **2.** territory

ter·race (ter′əs) *n.* [OFr., walled platform < It. *terrazzo* < L. *terra*, earth] **1.** *a)* a raised, flat mound of earth with sloping sides *b)* any of a series of flat platforms of earth with sloping sides, rising one above another, as on a hillside **2.** an unroofed, paved area next to a house and overlooking a lawn or garden **3.** a balcony or deck outside an apartment **4.** a flat roof, esp. of a house of Spanish or Oriental architecture **5.** *a)* a row of houses, esp. of houses joined together, on ground raised from the street *b)* a street in front of such houses: often used in street names ☆**6.** a parklike strip in the middle of a boulevard —*vt.* **-raced, -rac·ing** to form into or surround with a terrace [slopes *terraced* to stop erosion]

TERRACE (sense 2)

ter·ra cot·ta (ter′ə kät′ə) [It., lit., baked earth < L.] **1.** a hard, brown-red earthenware, usually not glazed, used for pottery, sculpture, etc. **2.** its brown-red color —**ter′ra-cot′ta** *adj.*

terra fir·ma (fur′mə) [L.] firm earth; solid ground

ter·rain (tə rān′, ter′ān) *n.* [Fr. < L. < *terra*, earth] ground or an area of land, esp. with regard to its special features or its fitness for some use [hilly *terrain*]

☆**Ter·ra·my·cin** (ter'ə mī's'n) [< L. *terra*, earth + MYC(O)- + -IN[1]] *a trademark for* an antibiotic derived from cultures of a soil fungus

ter·rane (tə rān', ter'ān) *n.* [see TERRAIN] *Geol.* a rock formation or series of related formations

☆**ter·ra·pin** (ter'ə pin) *n.* [< Algonquian] **1.** any of several American freshwater or tidewater turtles; specif., *same as* DIAMONDBACK **2.** its edible flesh

ter·rar·i·um (tə rer'ē əm) *n., pl.* **-i·ums, -i·a** (-ə) [ModL. < L. *terra*, earth + *-arium* as in *aquarium*] **1.** an enclosure for keeping small land animals **2.** a glass container for a garden of small plants

TERRARIUM

ter·raz·zo (tə raz'ō, tə rät'sō) *n.* [It., lit., TERRACE] flooring made of small chips of marble set in cement and polished

Ter·re Haute (ter'ə hōt', hut') [Fr., lit., high land] city in W Ind., on the Wabash: pop. 70,000

ter·res·tri·al (tə res'trē əl) *adj.* [< L. *terrestris* < *terra*, earth] **1.** of this world; worldly; mundane [*terrestrial* pleasures] **2.** of or representing the earth [a *terrestrial* globe] **3.** made up of land, not water [the *terrestrial* parts of the world] **4.** living on land rather than in water, in trees, etc. **5.** growing in the ground —*n.* an inhabitant of the earth —see SYN. at EARTHLY —**ter·res'tri·al·ly** *adv.*

ter·ret (ter'it) *n.* [< OFr. *toret*, dim. of *tour*, a turn] any of the rings on a harness, through which the reins pass

ter·ri·ble (ter'ə b'l) *adj.* [OFr. < L. *terribilis* < *terrere*, to frighten] **1.** causing terror; fearful; dreadful [a *terrible* earthquake] **2.** extreme; intense; severe [*terrible* suffering] **3.** [Colloq.] very bad, unpleasant, disagreeable, etc. [a *terrible* movie] —**ter'ri·ble·ness** *n.* —**ter'ri·bly** *adv.*

ter·ri·er (ter'ē ər) *n.* [MFr. (*chien*) *terrier*, hunting (dog) < *terrier*, burrow, ult. < L. *terra*, earth] any of various breeds of active, typically small dog, orig. bred to burrow after small game

ter·rif·ic (tə rif'ik) *adj.* [< L. < base of *terrere*, to frighten + -FIC] **1.** causing great fear; terrifying; dreadful [a *terrific* storm] **2.** [Colloq.] *a)* unusually great, intense, etc. [a *terrific* burst of energy] *b)* unusually fine, admirable, enjoyable, etc. [a *terrific* actor] —**ter·rif'i·cal·ly** *adv.*

ter·ri·fy (ter'ə fī') *vt.* **-fied'**, **-fy'ing** [L. *terrificare* < *terrificus*, TERRIFIC] to fill with terror; frighten greatly; alarm —see SYN. at AFRAID —**ter'ri·fy'ing·ly** *adv.*

ter·ri·to·ri·al (ter'ə tôr'ē əl) *adj.* **1.** of territory or land [*territorial* expansion] **2.** of or limited to a specific territory or district [*territorial* waters] ☆**3.** [T-] of a Territory or Territories **4.** [often T-] organized regionally for home defense [the British *Territorial* Army] **5.** displaying territoriality —*n.* [T-] [Chiefly Brit.] a member of a Territorial defense force —**ter'ri·to'ri·al·ly** *adv.*

ter·ri·to·ri·al·i·ty (ter'ə tôr'ē al'ə tē) *n.* **1.** the condition of being territorial **2.** the pattern of behavior shown by an animal in defending its territory

ter·ri·to·ry (ter'ə tôr'ē) *n., pl.* **-ries** [L. *territorium* < *terra*, earth] **1.** the land and waters under the control of a nation, state, ruler, etc. **2.** a part of a country or empire that does not have all the rights of a major division; specif., ☆*a)* [T-] formerly, a part of the U.S. not a State and having an appointed governor *b)* [T-] a similar region in Canada or Australia **3.** any large area of land; region ☆**4.** an assigned area [a traveling salesman's *territory*] **5.** the place or range of action, existence, thought, etc. [he tried to cover too much *territory* in his speech] **6.** the area which an animal or pair of animals lives in and defends against intruders

ter·ror (ter'ər) *n.* [< MFr. < L. < *terrere*, to frighten] **1.** intense fear **2.** *a)* a person or thing causing intense fear [bandits who were the *terror* of the West] *b)* the quality of causing dread; terribleness [his threats held no *terror* for me] **3.** a program of terrorism **4.** [Colloq.] a very annoying or unmanageable person, esp. a child

ter·ror·ism (ter'ər iz'm) *n.* **1.** the use of force or threats to frighten people and cause them to obey, esp. by a government or

political group **2.** the frightened condition produced in this way —**ter'ror·ist** *n., adj.* —**ter'ror·is'tic** *adj.*

ter·ror·ize (-īz') *vt.* **-ized'**, **-iz'ing** **1.** to fill with terror **2.** to force to do something, make obey, etc. by filling with terror —**ter'ror·i·za'tion** *n.* —**ter'ror·iz'er** *n.*

ter·ry (ter'ē) *n., pl.* **-ries** [prob. < Fr. pp. of *tirer*, to draw] cloth having a pile in which the loops are left uncut: also **terry cloth**

terse (turs) *adj.* **ters'er**, **ters'est** [< L. pp. of *tergere*, to wipe] using no more words than are needed to be clear; very concise —see SYN. at CONCISE —**terse'ly** *adv.* —**terse'ness** *n.*

ter·tial (tur'shəl) *adj.* [< L. *tertius*, third] designating or of the third row of flight feathers on a bird's wing —*n.* a tertial feather

ter·tian (tur'shən) *adj.* [< L. *tertius*, third] occurring every other day —*n.* a tertian fever or disease

ter·ti·ar·y (tur'shē er'ē, -shə rē) *adj.* [< L. < *tertius*, third] **1.** of the third rank, order, formation, etc.; third **2.** [T-] *Geol.* designating or of the first period in the Cenozoic Era —*n., pl.* **-ar'ies** a tertial feather —**the Tertiary** the Tertiary Period or its rocks: see GEOLOGIC TIME CHART

Tes·la (tes'lə), **Ni·ko·la** (nik'ə lə) 1856–1943; U.S. inventor, born in Croatia

tes·sel·late (tes'ə lāt'; *for adj.* -lit) *vt.* **-lat'ed**, **-lat'ing** [< L. < *tessella*, little square stone] to lay out or pave in a mosaic pattern of small, square blocks —*adj.* arranged in such a pattern; tessellated —**tes'sel·la'tion** *n.*

tes·ser·a (tes'ər ə) *n., pl.* **-ser·ae** (-ē) [L., square piece] any of the small pieces used in mosaic work

test[1] (test) *n.* [OFr., cup used in assaying < L. *testum*, earthen vessel < *testa*, a shell] **1.** *a)* an examination or trial, as to prove the value or find out the nature of something [a *test* of one's courage] *b)* a method or process, or a standard or criterion, used in making such an examination or trial [the real *test* of a material is how well it wears] **2.** an event, situation, etc. that tries a person's qualities [the delay was a *test* of his patience] **3.** a set of questions, problems, etc. for finding out a person's knowledge, abilities, etc.; examination [an algebra *test*; a driver's *test*] **4.** *Chem. a)* a trial or reaction for identifying a substance *b)* the reagent used in the procedure —*vt.* to subject to a test; try —*vi.* **1.** to give or take a test for diagnosis, function, etc. [to *test* for blood sugar] **2.** to be rated as the result of a test [to *test* high in mathematics] —see SYN. at TRIAL —**test'a·ble** *adj.*

test[2] (test) *n.* [L. *testa*, a shell] the hard outer covering of certain animals, as the shell of clams

Test. Testament

tes·ta (tes'tə) *n., pl.* **-tae** (-tē) [ModL. < L., a shell] *Bot.* the hard outer covering of a seed

tes·ta·ceous (tes tā'shəs) *adj.* [L. *testaceus*, consisting of brick or shell < *testa*, a shell] **1.** of or like shells **2.** having a hard shell **3.** *Biol.* light reddish-brown

tes·ta·ment (tes'tə mənt) *n.* [< OFr. < LL. < L., ult. < *testis*, a witness] **1.** orig., a covenant, esp. one between God and man **2.** [T-] *a)* either of the two parts of the Christian Bible, the *Old Testament* and the *New Testament* *b)* [Colloq.] a copy of the New Testament **3.** *a)* a statement, act, etc. showing that something is a fact, is true, etc. [a *testament* to his good sense] *b)* a statement of beliefs, etc. **4.** *Law* a will: now rare except in **last will and testament** —**tes'ta·men'ta·ry** (-men'tə rē), **tes'ta·men'tal** *adj.*

tes·tate (tes'tāt) *adj.* [< L. pp. of *testari*, to testify, make a will] having made and left a legally valid will —*n.* a person who has died testate —**tes'ta·cy** (-tə sē) *n.*

tes·ta·tor (tes'tāt ər, tes tāt'-) *n.* a person who has made a will, esp. one who has died leaving a valid will —**tes·ta'trix** (-tā'triks) *n.fem., pl.* **tes'tri·ces'** (-tri sēz')

test ban an agreement between or among nuclear powers to stop testing nuclear weapons, esp. in the atmosphere

test case *Law* **1.** a case that is likely to be used as a precedent ☆**2.** a case entered into for the purpose of testing whether a particular law is constitutional

test·er[1] (tes'tər) *n.* a person or thing that tests

tes·ter[2] (tes'tər) *n.* [< OFr. *testiere*, headpiece < L. *testa*, a shell] a canopy, as over a bed

tes·tes (tes'tēz) *n. pl. of* TESTIS

tes·ti·cle (tes'ti k'l) *n.* [< L. dim. of *testis*, testicle] either of

---

fat, āpe, cär; ten, ēven; is, bīte; gō, hôrn, tōol, look; oil, out; up, fur; get; joy; yet; chin; she; thin, *th*en; zh, leisure; ŋ, ring; ə for *a* in *ago*, *e* in *agent*, *i* in *sanity*, *o* in *comply*, *u* in *focus*; ' as in *able* (ā'b'l); Fr. bâl; ë, Fr. coeur; ö, Fr. feu; Fr. mon; ô, Fr. coq; ü, Fr. duc; ℸ, Fr. cri; H, G. ich; kh, G. doch; ‡foreign; ☆ Americanism; < derived from. See inside front cover.

tes·ti·fy (tes′tə fī′) *vi.* **-fied′, -fy′ing** [< L. *testificari* < *testis*, a witness + *facere*, to make] **1.** to state that something has happened or is a fact; give evidence, esp. under oath in court **2.** to be evidence or an indication [his look *testifies* to his rage] —*vt.* **1.** to give as evidence; declare, esp. under oath in court **2.** to be evidence of; indicate —**tes′ti·fi·ca′tion** *n.* —**tes′ti·fi′er** *n.*

tes·ti·mo·ni·al (tes′tə mō′nē əl) *n.* **1.** a statement telling about a person's qualifications, good character, etc. or praising a product, service, etc. **2.** something given or done to show thanks or to honor someone

tes·ti·mo·ny (tes′tə mō′nē) *n., pl.* **-nies** [< L. < *testis*, a witness] **1.** a statement that something has happened or is a fact, esp. one made under oath in court **2.** any form of evidence; indication [his smile was *testimony* of his joy] **3.** a public statement, as of religious belief

tes·tis (tes′tis) *n., pl.* **-tes** (-tēz) [L.] *same as* TESTICLE

tes·tos·ter·one (tes täs′tə rōn′) *n.* [TEST(IS) + -o- + STER(OL) + -ONE] a male sex hormone produced by the testicles or a synthetic compound used in place of this

test pilot a pilot who tests new or newly designed airplanes in flight, to find out about their fitness for use

test-tube (tes′tōōb′, -tyōōb′) *adj.* **1.** made in or as in a test tube; experimental **2.** produced by artificial insemination [a *test-tube* baby]

test tube a tube of thin, clear glass closed at one end, used in chemical experiments, etc.

tes·tu·do (tes tōō′dō, -tyōō′-) *n., pl.* **-di·nes** (-də nēz′) [L., tortoise (shell)] in ancient Rome, **1.** a movable shelter with a roof, used for protection by soldiers **2.** a protection formed by a group of soldiers by overlapping their shields above their heads

tes·ty (tes′tē) *adj.* **-ti·er, -ti·est** [< Anglo-Fr. < OFr. *teste*, the head < L. *testa*, a shell] easily angered or annoyed; irritable; touchy —**tes′ti·ly** *adv.* —**tes′ti·ness** *n.*

tet·a·nus (tet′'n əs) *n.* [L. < Gr. *tetanos*, spasm, lit., stretched] an acute infectious disease, often fatal, caused by the toxin of a bacillus which usually enters the body through wounds: it causes spasms and stiffness of the muscles, esp. in the jaw and neck; lockjaw

tet·a·ny (tet′'n ē) *n.* [ModL. *tetania*: see TETANUS] an abnormal condition characterized by spasms of the muscles

tetched (techt) *adj.* [Dial. or Humorous] touched; slightly insane

tetch·y (tech′ē) *adj.* **tetch′i·er, tetch′i·est** [prob. < OFr. *teche*, a spot + -Y²] touchy; irritable; peevish —**tetch′i·ly** *adv.* —**tetch′i·ness** *n.*

tête-à-tête (tāt′ə tāt′) *n.* [Fr., lit., head-to-head] **1.** a private talk between two people ☆**2.** an S-shaped seat on which two people can sit facing each other —*adj.* for or of two people in private —*adv.* together privately [to speak *tête-à-tête*]

teth·er (teth′ər) *n.* [prob. < ON. *tjōthr*] a rope or chain fastened to an animal so as to keep it within certain limits —*vt.* to fasten with a tether —**at the end of one's tether** at the end of one's endurance, resources, etc.

☆**teth·er·ball** (-bôl′) *n.* **1.** a game for two people who hit at a ball hanging by a cord from a pole in an attempt to make the cord coil around the pole **2.** the ball used

tet·ra (tet′rə) *n.* [< ModL. < old genus name] a colorful tropical American fish, often kept in aquariums: the **neon tetra** is a popular variety

tet·ra- [Gr. < base of *tettares*, four] *a combining form meaning* four: also, before a vowel, **tetr-**

tet·ra·chlo·ride (tet′rə klôr′īd) *n.* any chemical compound with four chlorine atoms in each molecule

tet·ra·chord (tet′rə kôrd′) *n.* [< TETRA- & CHORD²] *Music* a series of four tones within the interval of a fourth

tet·ra·cy·cline (tet′rə sī′klin, -klīn) *n.* [< TETRA- + CYCL(IC) + -INE⁴] a yellow, crystalline powder prepared synthetically or obtained from certain microorganisms: used as an antibiotic

tet·rad (tet′rad) *n.* [< Gr. *tetras*, four] a group or set of four

☆**tet·ra·eth·yl lead** (tet′rə eth′'l) a heavy, colorless, poisonous compound of lead, added to gasoline to increase power and prevent engine knock

tet·ra·gon (tet′rə gän′) *n.* [< LL. < Gr.: see TETRA- & -GON] a plane figure with four angles and four sides; quadrangle

te·trag·o·nal (te trag′ə n'l) *adj.* **1.** of, or having the form of, a tetragon; quadrangular **2.** designating a crystal form in which the three axes intersect at right angles and the two horizontal axes are equal

tet·ra·he·dron (tet′rə hē′drən) *n., pl.* **-drons, -dra** (-drə) [ModL. < LGr.: see TETRA- & -HEDRON] a solid figure with four triangular faces —**tet′ra·he′dral** *adj.*

TETRAHEDRON

te·tral·o·gy (te tral′ə jē) *n., pl.* **-gies** [< Gr.: see TETRA- & -LOGY] any series of four related plays, operas, novels, etc.

te·tram·er·ous (te tram′ər əs) *adj.* [TETRA- + -MEROUS] *Biol.* made up of four parts or divisions

te·tram·e·ter (te tram′ə tər) *n.* [< LL. < Gr.: see TETRA- & -METER] **1.** a line of verse containing four metrical feet **2.** verse made up of such lines —*adj.* having four metrical feet

tet·ra·pod (tet′rə päd′) *n.* [TETRA- + -POD] a vertebrate that has four legs or leglike appendages: mammals, birds, reptiles, and amphibians are tetrapods

te·trarch (tē′trärk, tē′-) *n.* [< LL. < L. < Gr.: see TETRA- & -ARCH] in the ancient Roman Empire, the ruler of part (orig. a fourth part) of a province —**te·trarch′ic** *adj.*

te·trarch·y (-trär kē) *n., pl.* **-trarch·ies** **1.** the rule or territory of a tetrarch **2.** government by four persons

tet·ra·va·lent (tet′rə vā′lənt) *adj.* **1.** having a valence of four **2.** *same as* QUADRIVALENT (sense 1)

tet·rode (tet′rōd) *n.* [TETR(A)- + -ODE] an electron tube having four electrodes

te·trox·ide (te träk′sīd) *n.* any oxide with four atoms of oxygen in each molecule

tet·ter (tet′ər) *n.* [OE. *teter*] any of various skin diseases, as eczema, characterized by itching

Teut. **1.** Teuton **2.** Teutonic

Teu·ton (tōōt′'n, tyōōt′-) *n.* **1.** a member of the Teutones **2.** a member of any Teutonic people; esp., a German

Teu·to·nes (tōōt′'n ēz′, tyōōt′-) *n.pl.* [L.] an ancient tribe, either Teutonic or Celtic, that lived in Jutland

Teu·ton·ic (tōō tän′ik, tyōō-) *adj.* **1.** of the ancient Teutons **2.** German **3.** designating or of a group of north European peoples including the German, Scandinavian, Dutch, English, etc. **4.** *Linguis.* earlier var. of GERMANIC —**Teu·ton′i·cal·ly** *adv.*

Tex·as (tek′səs) [Sp. < AmInd. *techas*, allies (against the Apaches)] SW State of the U.S., on the Gulf of Mexico & the Mexican border: 267,339 sq. mi.; pop. 11,197,000; cap. Austin: abbrev. **Tex., TX** —**Tex′an** *adj., n.*

☆**Texas fever** an infectious disease of cattle caused by a parasite that enters the red blood cells

☆**Texas leaguer** *Baseball* a safely hit fly ball that falls between the infield and outfield

☆**Texas tower** [from its resemblance to oil rigs off the *Texas* coast] an offshore platform on foundations planted in the sea bottom, for beacons, radar installations, etc.

text (tekst) *n.* [< OFr. < L. *textus*, fabric < pp. of *texere*, to weave] **1.** the exact or original words of an author or speaker **2.** any of the forms or editions in which a written work exists **3.** the main part of the matter on a printed page, not including notes, pictures, etc. **4.** *a)* a passage from the Bible used as the topic of a sermon *b)* any topic or subject dealt with **5.** *shortened form of* TEXTBOOK

text·book (tekst′book′) *n.* a book containing the basic information on a subject and used in teaching or studying

tex·tile (teks′tīl, -t'l, -til) *adj.* [< L. *textilis* < *textus*: see TEXT] **1.** having to do with weaving or woven fabrics [the *textile* industry] **2.** that has been or can be woven [a *textile* fabric] —*n.* **1.** a fabric made by weaving, knitting, etc.; cloth **2.** raw material suitable for this, as cotton, wool, nylon, etc.

tex·tu·al (teks′chōo wəl) *adj.* of, contained in, or based on a text [*textual* criticism] —**tex′tu·al·ly** *adv.*

tex·ture (teks′chər) *n.* [< L. < *texere*: see TEXT] **1.** the look and feel of a fabric as caused by the arrangement, size, etc. of its threads **2.** the structure or composition of anything, esp. in the way it looks or feels on the surface [stucco has a rough *texture*] —*vt.* **-tured, -tur·ing** to cause to have a particular texture —**tex′tur·al** *adj.* —**tex′tur·al·ly** *adv.*

☆**TGIF, T.G.I.F.** Thank God It's Friday: used with emphasis to show relief at the end of the workweek

☆**T-group** (tē′grōōp′) *n.* [t(*raining*) group] a group taking part in sensitivity training

-th¹ [< OE.] *a suffix meaning:* **1.** the act of [*stealth*] **2.** the state or quality of being or having [*wealth*]

-th² [< OE.] a suffix used in forming ordinal numerals [*fourth, fifteenth*]: also, after a vowel, **-eth**

-th³ [< OE.: see -ETH²] *contracted form of* -ETH² *[hath, doth]*

Th *Chem.* thorium

Th. Thursday

Thack·er·ay (thak'ər ē), **William Make·peace** (māk'pēs') 1811-63; Eng. novelist

Thai (tī) *n.* **1.** a group of Asian languages considered to belong to the Sino-Tibetan language family **2.** the official language of Thailand **3.** *pl.* **Thais, Thai** *a)* a member of a group of Thai-speaking peoples of SE Asia *b)* a native or inhabitant of Thailand —*adj.* of Thailand, its people, culture, etc.

Thai·land (tī'land, -lənd) **1.** country in SE Asia, on the Indochinese & Malay peninsulas: 198,456 sq. mi.; pop. 35,814,000; cap. Bangkok **2. Gulf of,** arm of the South China Sea between the Malay & Indochinese peninsulas

thal·a·mus (thal'ə məs) *n., pl.* **-mi'** (-mī') [ModL. < L. < Gr. *thalamos,* inner room] **1.** *Anat.* a mass of gray matter at the base of the brain, that passes sensory impulses along to the cerebrum **2.** *Bot.* the receptacle of a flower —**tha·lam·ic** (thə lam'ik) *adj.*

tha·las·sic (thə las'ik) *adj.* [< Fr. < Gr. *thalassa,* sea] of the sea or ocean; marine

Tha·les (thā'lēz) 636?-546 B.C.; Gr. philosopher

Tha·li·a (thə lī'ə, thāl'yə) *Gr. Myth.* **1.** the Muse of comedy and pastoral poetry **2.** one of the three Graces

thal·li·um (thal'ē əm) *n.* [ModL. < Gr. *thallos,* green shoot: from its green spectrum line] a soft, poisonous, metallic chemical element: symbol, Tl; at. wt., 204.37; at. no., 81

thal·lo·phyte (thal'ə fīt') *n.* [see THALLUS & -PHYTE] any of a primary division of plants including the bacteria, algae, fungi, and lichens —**thal'lo·phyt'ic** (-fit'ik) *adj.*

thal·lus (thal'əs) *n., pl.* **-li** (-ī), **-lus·es** [ModL. < Gr. *thallos,* young shoot] the plant body of a thallophyte, showing no clear distinction of roots, stem, or leaves —**thal'loid** (-oid) *adj.*

Thames (temz) river in S England, flowing east through London into the North Sea

than (than, then; *unstressed* thən, th'n) *conj.* [< OE. *thenne,* orig., then] a word used: *a)* to introduce the second part of a comparison *[A is taller than B] b)* to indicate an exception *[none other than Sue]* —*prep.* compared to: in *than whom* and *than which [a writer than whom* there is none finer]

than·a·tol·o·gy (than'ə täl'ə jē) *n.* [< Gr. *thanatos,* death + -LOGY] the study of death, esp. of the medical and psychological problems connected with dying —**than'a·tol'o·gist** *n.*

thane (thān) *n.* [OE. *thegen*] **1.** in early England, one of a class of freemen who got land from the king or a lord in return for military services **2.** in early Scotland, a person of rank who got land from the king

thank (thaŋk) *vt.* [OE. *thancian*] **1.** to express appreciation to, as by saying "thank you" **2.** to hold responsible; blame: an ironic use *[she can be thanked* for our failure] —**thank you** shortened form of I thank you

thank·ful (thaŋk'fəl) *adj.* feeling or showing thanks; grateful — **thank'ful·ly** *adv.* —**thank'ful·ness** *n.*

thank·less (-lis) *adj.* **1.** not feeling or showing thanks; ungrateful **2.** unappreciated *[a thankless task]* —**thank'less·ly** *adv.* —**thank'less·ness** *n.*

thanks (thaŋks) *n.pl.* the act or fact of thanking someone for something; an expression of gratitude *[I owe you thanks]* — *interj.* I thank you —**thanks to 1.** thanks be given to **2.** on account of *[thanks* to the tail wind, the plane arrived early]

thanks·giv·ing (thaŋks'giv'iŋ) *n.* **1.** the act of giving thanks, esp. in a formal and public way or in a prayer of thanks to God ☆**2.** [T-] *a)* a U.S. holiday observed on the fourth Thursday of November as a day of giving thanks and feasting: it commemorates the Pilgrims' celebration of the good harvest of 1621 *b)* a similar Canadian holiday on the second Monday of October In full, **Thanksgiving Day**

Thant (thänt, thônt), **U** (ōō) 1909-74; Burmese diplomat; secretary-general of the United Nations (1962-71)

that (that; *unstressed* thət) *pron., pl.* **those** [OE. *thæt*] *as a demonstrative pronoun:* **1.** the person or thing there *[that* is the book I want] **2.** the person or thing mentioned before or understood *[that* is what he told me] **3.** the thing farther away than or in some way different from another *[this* suit is a better fit than *that]* **4.** [*pl.*] certain people *[those* who know] *as a relative pronoun, now often left out, esp. in sense* 1: **1.** who,

whom, or which *[the road (that)* we took] **2.** where; at which *[the place that* I saw her] **3.** when; in which *[the year that* he died] —*adj., pl.* **those 1.** designating the one mentioned before or understood *[that* girl is Joan] **2.** designating the thing farther away or different in some way *[this* house is larger than *that* one] **3.** designating a person or thing not described but well known *[that* certain feeling] —*conj. used:* **1.** to introduce a noun clause expressing a supposed or actual fact *[that* he's gone is obvious] **2.** to introduce an adverbial clause expressing purpose *[they* died *that* we might live] **3.** to introduce an adverbial clause expressing result *[she* ran so fast *that* I lost her] **4.** to introduce an adverbial clause expressing cause *[I'm* sorry *that* you're ill] **5.** to introduce an incomplete sentence expressing surprise, desire, etc. *[oh, that* she were here!] —*adv.* **1.** to that extent; so *[I* can't see *that* far] : also used colloquially before an adjective modified by a clause showing result *[I'm that* tired I could drop] ☆**2.** [Colloq.] very; so very: used in negative sentences, phrases, etc. *[I* didn't like the book *that* much] —**all that** [Colloq.] so very *[he* isn't *all that* rich] —☆**at that** [Colloq.] **1.** at that point: also **with that 2.** all things considered; even so —**that is 1.** to be specific **2.** in other words — **that's that!** that is settled!

thatch (thach) *n.* [OE. *thæc*] **1.** *a)* a roof or roofing of straw, rushes, palm leaves, etc. *b)* material for such a roof: also **thatch'ing 2.** any of various palms whose leaves are used for thatch: also **thatch palm 3.** the hair growing on the head —*vt.* [OE. *theccan*] to cover with or as with thatch

thau·ma·tur·gy (thô'mə tur'jē) *n.* [< Gr. < *thaumatos,* genitive of *thauma,* a wonder + *ergon,* work] the supposed working of miracles; magic —**thau'ma·tur'gic, thau'ma·tur'gi·cal** *adj.*

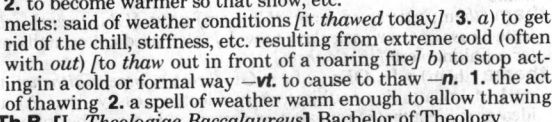

THATCHED
ROOF

thaw (thô) *vi.* [OE. *thawian*] **1.** *a)* to melt: said of ice, snow, etc. *b)* to become unfrozen: said of frozen foods **2.** to become warmer so that snow, etc. melts: said of weather conditions *[it thawed* today] **3.** *a)* to get rid of the chill, stiffness, etc. resulting from extreme cold (often with *out) [to thaw* out in front of a roaring fire] *b)* to stop acting in a cold or formal way —*vt.* to cause to thaw —*n.* **1.** the act of thawing **2.** a spell of weather warm enough to allow thawing

Th.B. [L. *Theologiae Baccalaureus*] Bachelor of Theology

Th.D. [L. *Theologiae Doctor*] Doctor of Theology

the (thə; *before vowels* thi, thē) *adj., definite article* [OE. *se* (nominative masculine article) with *th-* < other case & gender forms] **1.** *the* (as opposed to *a, an*) refers to a particular person or thing, as: *a)* that (one) being spoken of *[the* story ended] *b)* that (one) which is present, close, etc. *[the* day is hot] *c)* that (one) designated, as by a title *[the* Ohio (River)] *d)* that (one) considered best, outstanding, etc. *[that's the* hotel in town] : usually italicized in print *e)* that (one) belonging to a person previously mentioned *[take* me by *the* hand] *f)* that (one) considered as a unit of purchase, etc. *[ten* cents *the* dozen] *g)* one specified period of time *[the* fifties] *h)* [Colloq.] that (one) in a specified relationship to one *[the* wife] **2.** *the* is used to refer to that one of a number of persons or things which is identified by a modifier, as by an attributive adjective or a relative clause *[the* back door; *the* man who called] **3.** *the* is used: *a)* before a noun that names a whole group or class *[the* cow is a domestic animal] *b)* before an adjective used as a noun *[the* good, *the* true] —*adv.* **1.** that much; to that extent *[the* better to see you with] **2.** by how much . . . by that much; to what extent . . . to that extent: used in a correlative construction expressing comparison *[the* sooner, *the* better]

the·a·ter, the·a·tre (thē'ə tər) *n.* [< OFr. < L. < Gr. *theatron* < base of *theasthai,* to view] **1.** a place or building where plays, motion pictures, etc. are presented **2.** any place like a theater, esp. a lecture hall, surgical clinic, etc., having rows of seats on a sloping floor **3.** any scene of events *[the* Asian *theater* of war] **4.** *a)* the art of writing or putting on plays *b)* all the people engaged in putting on plays, esp. live plays

☆**the·a·ter-in-the-round** (-in thə round') *n.* same as ARENA THEATER

the·at·ri·cal (thē at′ri k'l) *adj.* **1.** having to do with the theater, a play, actors, etc. [a *theatrical* company] **2.** characteristic of the theater; dramatic; esp., artificial or emotional in a showy way [stalking off in *theatrical* manner] Also **the·at′ric** —**the·at′ri·cal·ism**, **the·at′ri·cal′i·ty** (-kal′ə tē) *n.* —**the·at′ri·cal·ly** *adv.*

the·at·ri·cal·ize (-īz′) *vt.* **-ized′**, **-iz′ing 1.** to make theatrical; give a dramatic, sometimes overly dramatic, quality to **2.** to put into a theatrical setting —**the·at′ri·cal·i·za′tion** (-ə zā′shən) *n.*

the·at·ri·cals (-k'lz) *n.pl.* performances of stage plays, esp. by amateurs

the·at·rics (thē at′riks) *n.pl.* **1.** [with *sing. v.*] the art of the theater **2.** things done or said in a showy, theatrical way; histrionics

Thebes (thēbz) **1.** ancient city in S Egypt, on the Nile **2.** chief city of ancient Boeotia, EC Greece —**The·ban** (thē′bən) *adj., n.*

the·ca (thē′kə) *n., pl.* **-cae** (-sē) [ModL. < L. < Gr. *thēkē*, a case] **1.** *Bot.* a spore case, sac, or capsule **2.** *Zool., Anat.* any sac enclosing an organ or a whole organism, as the covering of an insect pupa —**the′cal** *adj.* —**the′cate** (-kit) *adj.*

thee (thē) *pron.* [OE. *the*] *objective case of* THOU: also formerly used in place of *thou* by Friends (Quakers) [*thee* is kind]

theft (theft) *n.* [OE. *thiefth*] the act or an instance of stealing; larceny

thegn (thān) *n.* [OE.] *var. of* THANE

their (ther; *unstressed* thər) *adj.* [ON. *theirra*] of, belonging to, made by, or done by them [*their* books; *their* arrival]: often used colloquially after a singular subject [everyone has had *their* lunch]

theirs (therz) *pron.* that or those belonging to them: used without a following noun [that book is *theirs*, *theirs* are better]: also used after *of* to indicate possession [a friend of *theirs*]

the·ism (thē′iz'm) *n.* [THE(O)- + -ISM] **1.** belief in a god or gods **2.** belief in one God who is creator and ruler of the universe —**the′ist** *n., adj.* —**the·is′tic**, **the·is′ti·cal** *adj.* —**the·is′ti·cal·ly** *adv.*

Thel·ma (thel′mə) [< ?, but often a var. of SELMA] a feminine name

them (them; *unstressed* thəm, th'm, əm) *pron.* [ON. *theim*] objective case of THEY [ask *them* to wait]: also used colloquially after a linking verb [that's *them*]

theme (thēm) *n.* [< OFr. < L. < Gr. *thema* < base of *tithenai*, to put] **1.** *a)* a topic or subject, as of a lecture, essay, etc. *b)* an idea or subject that is repeated or presented in a number of ways in a work of art, literature, etc. to unify it **2.** a short essay, esp. one written as a school assignment **3.** *a)* a short melody used as the subject of a musical composition *b)* a musical phrase upon which variations are developed ☆**4.** the main song of a movie, musical, etc., or the music used to identify a radio or television program: also **theme song** —**the·mat·ic** (thē mat′ik) *adj.* —**the·mat′i·cal·ly** *adv.*

The·mis·to·cles (thə mis′tə klēz′) 525?–460? B.C.; Athenian statesman & naval commander

them·selves (them selvz′, thəm-) *pron.* a form of the third person plural pronoun, used: *a)* for added emphasis [they built it *themselves*] *b)* as a reflexive [they hurt *themselves*] *c)* as a kind of noun meaning "their real or true selves" [they are not *themselves* today]

then (then) *adv.* [see THAN] **1.** at that time [he was young *then*] **2.** soon afterward; next in time [he took his hat and *then* left] **3.** next in order [first comes one and *then* two] **4.** in that case; accordingly [if he read it, *then* he knows] **5.** besides; moreover [I like to walk, and *then* it's cheaper] **6.** at another time [now it's warm, *then* cold] —*adj.* being such at that time [the *then* mayor] —*n.* that time [by *then*, they were gone] —**but then** but on the other hand —**then and there** at that time and in that place; at once —**what then?** what would happen in that case?

thence (thens, thens) *adv.* [OE. *thanan*] **1.** from that place [to Boston and *thence* to Maine] **2.** from that time; thenceforth [a year *thence*] **3.** on that account; therefore [he was sick and *thence* quite weak]

thence·forth (thens′fôrth′, thens′-) *adv.* from that time onward; thereafter: also **thence′for′ward**, **thence′for′wards**

the·o- [< Gr. *theos*, god] *a combining form meaning* a god or God: also, before a vowel, *the-*

the·oc·ra·cy (thē äk′rə sē) *n., pl.* **-cies** [< Gr.: see THEO- & -CRACY] **1.** lit., the rule of a state by God or a god **2.** government by priests or clergy claiming to rule with divine authority **3.** a country so governed —**the·o·crat** (thē′ə krat′) *n.* —**the′o·crat′ic**, **the′o·crat′i·cal** *adj.* —**the′o·crat′i·cal·ly** *adv.*

the·od·o·lite (thē äd′'l īt′) *n.* [ModL. *theodelitus*] a surveying instrument used to measure vertical and horizontal angles —**the·od′o·lit′ic** (-ə lit′ik) *adj.*

The·o·dore (thē′ə dôr′) [< L. < Gr. < *theos*, god + *dōron*, gift] a masculine name: dim. *Ted*, *Teddy*

The·od·o·ric (thē äd′ər ik) 454?–526 A.D.; king of the Ostrogoths (474–526)

The·o·do·si·us I (thē′ə dō′shē əs, -shəs) (*Flavius Theodosius*) 346?–395 A.D.; Rom. general; emperor of Rome (379–395): called *the Great*

theol. **1.** theologian **2.** theology

the·o·lo·gi·an (thē′ə lō′jən, -jē ən) *n.* a student of or a specialist in theology or a theology

the·o·log·i·cal (thē′ə läj′i k'l) *adj.* of, based on, or offering instruction in, theology or a theology: also **the′o·log′ic** —**the′o·log′i·cal·ly** *adv.*

theological virtues in *Christianity*, the three virtues (faith, hope, and charity) added to the cardinal virtues

the·ol·o·gize (thē äl′ə jīz′) *vt.* **-gized′**, **-giz′ing** to put into theological terms —*vi.* to speculate theologically —**the·ol′o·giz′er** *n.*

the·ol·o·gy (thē äl′ə jē) *n., pl.* **-gies** [< LL. < Gr.: see THEO- & -LOGY] **1.** the study of God and of religious beliefs **2.** a system of religious beliefs, as that of a particular religion

the·o·rem (thē′ə rəm, thir′əm) *n.* [< Fr. < L. < Gr. *theōrēma* < *theōrein*, to view] **1.** a statement that is not self-evident but that can be proved from accepted premises and so is taken to be a law or principle **2.** a statement of relations in an equation or formula **3.** *Math.* a statement of something to be proved

the·o·ret·i·cal (thē′ə ret′i k'l) *adj.* **1.** of or having to do with theory [a *theoretical* science] **2.** limited to or based on theory; not practical; hypothetical [only a *theoretical* knowledge of the subject] **3.** tending to theorize; speculative [a *theoretical* person] Also **the′o·ret′ic** —**the′o·ret′i·cal·ly** *adv.*

the·o·re·ti·cian (thē′ə rə tish′ən) *n.* a person who theorizes, esp. one who specializes in the theory of some art, science, etc.: also **the′o·rist** (-rist)

the·o·rize (thē′ə rīz′) *vi.* **-rized′**, **-riz′ing** to form a theory or theories; speculate —**the′o·ri·za′tion** *n.* —**the′o·riz′er** *n.*

the·o·ry (thē′ə rē, thir′ē) *n., pl.* **-ries** [< Fr. < LL. < Gr. < *theōrein*, to view] **1.** an idea or plan as to how something might be done [a practical *theory* for controlling pollution] **2.** a careful, orderly statement of the principles of something [Aristotle's *theory* of right and wrong] **3.** an explanation of how or why something happens, esp. one that is based on scientific study and observation and that has been proved true in part **4.** that branch of an art or science dealing with knowledge of its principles and methods rather than with its practice [studying music *theory*] **5.** popularly, an opinion, guess, etc. [my *theory* is that he's lying]

SYN.—**theory**, as compared here, implies a general principle for which there is much evidence explaining how something works or comes to be [the *theory* of evolution]; **hypothesis** implies an explanation which, although there is little evidence for it, is assumed to be true, esp. as a basis for further experimenting [the nebular *hypothesis*]; **law** implies an exact principle that has been worked out by observing how certain events in nature occur over and over again under the same conditions [the *law* of the conservation of energy]

theory of games *same as* GAME THEORY

the·os·o·phy (thē äs′ə fē) *n.* [< ML. < LGr., ult. < Gr. *theos*, god + *sophos*, wise] **1.** *pl.* **-phies** any of various philosophies or religions that seek mystical knowledge of the nature of God and the cosmos through meditation, revelation, etc. **2.** [often **T-**] the doctrines of a modern sect (Theosophical Society) that has in its beliefs elements of Buddhism and Brahmanism —**the′o·soph′ic** (-ə säf′ik), **the′o·soph′i·cal** *adj.* —**the′o·soph′i·cal·ly** *adv.* —**the·os′o·phist** *n.*

ther·a·peu·tic (ther′ə pyōōt′ik) *adj.* [ModL. < Gr., ult. < *therapeuein*, to nurse] **1.** *a)* used to cure or heal; curative *b)* done to preserve health [*therapeutic* abortion] **2.** of therapeutics Also **ther′a·peu′ti·cal** —**ther′a·peu′ti·cal·ly** *adv.*

ther·a·peu·tics (-iks) *n.pl.* [with *sing. v.*] the branch of medicine that deals with the treatment and cure of diseases; therapy

ther·a·py (ther′ə pē) *n., pl.* **-pies** [ModL. < Gr. < *therapeuein*, to nurse] the treatment of disease or of any physical or mental disorder by medical or physical means: often used in compounds [hydrotherapy] —☆**ther′a·pist** *n.*

there (ther) *adv.* [OE. *ther*] **1.** at or in that place: often used for

DIAGRAM OF THEODOLITE (A, vertical angles; B, horizontal angles)

added emphasis [John *there* is a good boy] **2.** toward, to, or into that place [go *there*] **3.** at that point in action, speech, etc. [*there* he paused] **4.** in that matter, respect, etc. [*there* you are wrong] **5.** right now [*there* goes the whistle] *There* is also used: *a*) in exclamations showing approval, etc. [*there's* a fine fellow!] *b*) in introducing sentences in which the real subject follows the verb [*there* are three men here] *c*) in place of the name, as in greeting a person [hi *there*!] —*n.* that place or point [we left *there* at six] —*interj.* an exclamation expressing defiance, dismay, satisfaction, sympathy, etc. [*there, there!* don't worry] —(**not**) **all there** [Colloq.] (not) sound of mind

there·a·bouts (ther′ə bouts′) *adv.* **1.** near that place **2.** near that time **3.** near that number, amount, degree, etc. Also **there′a·bout′**

there·af·ter (ther af′tər) *adv.* **1.** after that; from then on **2.** [Archaic] accordingly

there·at (-at′) *adv.* **1.** at that place; there **2.** at that time **3.** for that reason

there·by (-bī′) *adv.* **1.** by that means **2.** connected with that [*thereby* hangs a tale]

there·for (-fôr′) *adv.* for this; for that; for it [he paid the rent and requested a receipt *therefor*]

there·fore (ther′fôr′) *adv.* for this or that reason; consequently; hence: often used like a conjunction [he missed the bus and *therefore* was late]

there·from (ther frum′, -främ′) *adv.* from this; from that; from it

there·in (-in′) *adv.* **1.** in there; in or into that place or thing [the box and all the contents *therein*] **2.** in that matter, detail, etc. [*therein* you are wrong]

there·in·af·ter (ther′in af′tər) *adv.* in the following part of that document, speech, etc.

there·in·to (ther in′tōō) *adv.* **1.** into that place or thing **2.** into that matter, condition, etc.

there·of (-uv′) *adv.* **1.** of that **2.** concerning that **3.** from that as a cause, reason, etc.

there·on (-än′) *adv.* **1.** on that **2.** same as THEREUPON

there's (therz) **1.** there is **2.** there has

The·re·sa (tə rē′sə) **1.** [< Fr. or Port. < L. *Therasia* < ? Gr. *therizein*, to reap] a feminine name **2.** Saint, *same as* Saint TERESA

there·to (ther tōō′) *adv.* **1.** to that place, thing, etc.: also **there·un·to** (ther un′tōō, ther′un tōō′) **2.** [Archaic] besides

there·to·fore (ther′tə fôr′, ther′tə fôr′) *adv.* up to then; until that time; before that

there·un·der (ther un′dər) *adv.* **1.** under that; under it **2.** under the terms stated there

there·up·on (ther′ə pän′, ther′ə pän′) *adv.* **1.** just after that **2.** as a result of that **3.** on that subject, etc.

there·with (ther with′, -*with*′) *adv.* **1.** along with that **2.** in addition to that **3.** by that method or means **4.** just after that

there·with·al (ther′with ôl′) *adv.* **1.** in addition; besides **2.** [Obs.] along with that

ther·mal (thur′m'l) *adj.* [Fr. < Gr. *thermē*, heat] **1.** having to do with heat, hot springs, etc. **2.** warm or hot ☆**3.** designating or of a loosely knitted material with air spaces to help hold in body heat [*thermal* underwear] —*n.* a rising column of warm air, caused by the uneven heating of the earth or sea by the sun —**ther′mal·ly** *adv.*

thermal barrier the speed limit beyond which the high temperatures caused by atmospheric friction would damage or destroy a given spacecraft, rocket, etc.

☆**thermal pollution** the discharge of heated liquid or air into lakes, rivers, etc., as by an industry or nuclear power plant, causing such a rise in the water temperature as to affect the life cycles of organisms within the water and disturb the ecological balance

thermal spring a spring whose water has a temperature higher than that of the air in the place where it is located

ther·mic (thur′mik) *adj.* of or caused by heat

therm·i·on (thurm′ī′ən, thur′mē-) *n.* [THERM(O)- + ION] a negative or positive ion sent out by a substance heated to a glowing state

therm·i·on·ic (thurm′ī än′ik, thur′mē-) *adj.* of or working by means of thermions [*thermionic* current]

therm·i·on·ics (thurm′ī än′iks, thur′mē-) *n.pl.* [*with sing. v.*] the study and science of thermionic activity

thermionic tube an electron tube having a cathode electrically heated in order to cause electrons or ions to be sent out

☆**therm·is·tor** (thər mis′tər, thur′mis′-) *n.* [THERM(O)- + (RES)ISTOR] a resistor made of semiconductor material, whose electrical resistance decreases as temperature rises: used to measure temperature, microwave power, etc.

Ther·mit (thur′mit) [G. < Gr. *thermē*, heat + G. *it*, -ITE¹] *a trademark for* a mixture of aluminum powder and iron oxide, which produces great heat when it burns and is used in welding, incendiary bombs, etc. —*n.* [t-] such a mixture

ther·mo- [< Gr. *thermē*, heat] *a combining form meaning:* **1.** heat [*thermodynamics*] **2.** thermoelectric [*thermocouple*] Also, before a vowel, **therm-**

ther·mo·chem·is·try (thur′mō kem′is trē) *n.* the branch of chemistry that deals with the relationship of heat to chemical change —**ther′mo·chem′i·cal** *adj.*

ther·mo·cou·ple (thur′mə kup′'l) *n.* a pair of conductors, each of a different metal, joined together: when the junction is heated, the voltage across it is in proportion to the rise in temperature: also called **thermoelectric couple**

ther·mo·dy·nam·ic (thur′mō dī nam′ik) *adj.* **1.** of or having to do with thermodynamics **2.** caused or operated by heat converted into power —**ther′mo·dy·nam′i·cal·ly** *adv.*

ther·mo·dy·nam·ics (-dī nam′iks) *n.pl.* [*with sing. v.*] the branch of physics dealing with the relationship between heat and other forms of energy, esp. mechanical energy, and with the change of energy from one form to another

ther·mo·e·lec·tric (-i lek′trik) *adj.* of or having to do with the direct relations between heat and electricity: also **ther′mo·e·lec′tri·cal** —**ther′mo·e·lec′tri·cal·ly** *adv.*

ther·mo·e·lec·tric·i·ty (-i lek′tris′ə tē) *n.* electricity produced by heating the junction between two different metal conductors

ther·mo·gram (thur′mə gram′) *n.* [THERMO- + -GRAM] a record made by a thermograph

ther·mo·graph (-graf′) *n.* [THERMO- + -GRAPH] a thermometer for recording changes in temperature automatically

ther·mo·junc·tion (thur′mō junk′shən) *n.* the point of contact between the two conductors of a thermocouple

ther·mo·la·bile (-lā′b'l, -lā′bil) *adj.* [THERMO- + LABILE] describing or of substances, as some toxins, enzymes, etc., that are destroyed or lose their properties when heated to 55°C or above —**ther′mo·la·bil′i·ty** (-lā bil′ə tē) *n.*

ther·mom·e·ter (thər mäm′ə tər) *n.* [< Fr.: see THERMO- & -METER] an instrument for measuring temperatures, as a sealed glass tube, marked off in degrees, in which mercury, colored alcohol, etc. rises or falls as it expands or contracts from changes in temperature: see FAHRENHEIT, CELSIUS —**ther·mo·met·ric** (thur′mə met′rik) *adj.* —**ther′mo·met′ri·cal·ly** *adv.*

ther·mo·nu·cle·ar (thur′mō nōō′klē ər, -nyōō′-) *adj.* *Physics* **1.** designating or of a reaction in which light atomic nuclei fuse at temperatures of millions of degrees into heavier nuclei **2.** designating, of, or using the heat energy released in nuclear fusion [a *thermonuclear* reactor]

ther·mo·phile (thur′mə fīl′) *n.* [THERMO- + -PHILE] an organism adapted to living at high temperatures, as some bacteria and algae —**ther′mo·phil′ic** (-fil′ik) *adj.*

ther·mo·pile (thur′mə pīl′) *n.* [THERMO- + PILE¹] a device consisting of a series of thermocouples, used for measuring very small changes in temperature or for producing thermoelectric current

ther·mo·plas·tic (thur′mə plas′tik) *adj.* becoming soft and moldable on being heated: said of certain plastics —*n.* a thermoplastic substance

Ther·mop·y·lae (thər mäp′ə lē) in ancient Greece, a mountain pass on the E coast: scene of a battle (480 B.C.) in which the Persians destroyed a Spartan army

CLINICAL THERMOMETERS (top, oral; bottom, rectal)

---

fat, āpe, cär; ten, ēven; is, bīte; gō, hôrn, tōōl, lōōk; oil, out; up, fur; get; joy; yet; chin; she; thin, *th*en; zh, leisure; ŋ, ring; ə for *a* in *ago*, *e* in *agent*, *i* in *sanity*, *o* in *comply*, *u* in *focus*; ′ as in *able* (ā′b'l); Fr. bâl; ë, Fr. coeur; ö, Fr. feu; Fr. mon; ô, Fr. coq; ü, Fr. duc; r, Fr. cri; H, G. ich; kh, G. doch; ‡foreign; ☆ Americanism; < derived from. See inside front cover.

ther·mos (thur′məs) *n.* [Gr. *thermos,* hot] a bottle, flask, or jug with two walls enclosing a vacuum, used for keeping liquids at almost their original temperature for several hours: in full, **thermos bottle** (or **flask** or **jug**)

ther·mo·set·ting (thur′mō set′iŋ) *adj.* becoming permanently hard and unmoldable when once subjected to heat: said of certain plastics

ther·mo·sta·ble (thur′mō stā′b'l) *adj.* [THERMO- + STABLE[1]] describing or of substances, as some toxins, enzymes, etc., that can be heated to temperatures above 55°C without losing their properties —**ther′mo·sta·bil′i·ty** (-stə bil′ə tē) *n.*

ther·mo·stat (thur′mə stat′) *n.* [THERMO- + -STAT] 1. a device for regulating temperature, esp. one that automatically controls a heating unit 2. a device that sets off a sprinkler, etc. at a certain heat —**ther′mo·stat′ic** *adj.* —**ther′mo·stat′i·cal·ly** *adv.*

ther·mo·tax·is (thur′mə tak′sis) *n.* [ModL.: see THERMO- & TAXIS] 1. *Biol.* movement of an organism toward or from a source of heat 2. *Physiol.* the normal regulation of body temperature —**ther′mo·tax′ic,** **ther′mo·tac′tic** (-tik) *adj.*

ther·mot·ro·pism (thər mät′rə piz'm) *n.* [THERMO- + -TROPISM] *Biol.* growth or movement toward or away from a source of heat —**ther′mo·trop′ic** (-thur′mə träp′ik) *adj.*

the·sau·rus (thi sôr′əs) *n., pl.* **-ri** (-ī), **-rus·es** [L. < Gr. *thēsauros,* a treasure] 1. a treasury or storehouse 2. a book containing a store of words; specif., a book of synonyms and antonyms

these (thēz) *pron., adj. pl. of* THIS

The·seus (thē′sōōs, -syōōs, -sē əs) *Gr. Legend* the chief hero of Attica, king of Athens, famous esp. for his killing of the Minotaur —**The·se·an** (thi sē′an) *adj.*

the·sis (thē′sis) *n., pl.* **the·ses** (-sēz) [L. < Gr. *thesis,* a placing < base of *tithenai,* to put] 1. a statement or idea defended in argument 2. a formal and lengthy research paper, esp. one presented as part of the requirements for a master's degree 3. *Logic* an unproved statement assumed as a premise

Thes·pi·an (thes′pē ən) *adj.* [after *Thespis,* Greek poet of 6th c. B.C., supposed originator of Greek tragedy] [*often* **t-**] having to do with the drama; dramatic —*n.* [*often* **t-**] an actor or actress: used in a humorous or affected way

Thes·sa·lo·ni·ans (thes′ə lō′nē ənz) either of two books of the New Testament which were epistles from the Apostle Paul to the Christians of Thessalonica: abbrev. **Thess.**

Thes·sa·lon·i·ca (thes′ə län′i kə, -ə lə nī′kə) *ancient name of* SALONIKA

Thes·sa·ly (thes′ə lē) division of E Greece, on the Aegean Sea: an ancient region (see map at GREECE) —**Thes·sa·li·an** (the sā′lē ən) *adj., n.*

the·ta (thāt′ə, thēt′ə) *n.* the eighth letter of the Greek alphabet (Θ, θ, ϑ)

thews (thyōōz) *n.pl., sing.* **thew** [OE. *theaw,* custom, habit] 1. muscular power; bodily strength 2. muscles or sinews —**thew′y** *adj.* **thew′i·er, thew′i·est**

they (thā) *pron. for sing. see* HE, SHE, IT [< ON. *their*] 1. the persons, animals, or things being talked about [the boys knew *they* had won] 2. people in general [*they* say it's so] The case forms of the third personal plural pronoun are: *they,* nominative; *them,* objective; *their* and *theirs,* possessive; *themselves,* intensive and reflexive

they'd (thād) 1. they had 2. they would

they'll (thāl, thel) 1. they will 2. they shall

they're (ther, thā′ər) they are

they've (thāv) they have

thi- *same as* THIO-

thi·a·mine (thī′ə mēn′, -min) *n.* [altered < THI(O)- + (VIT)AMIN] vitamin B₁, a white, crystalline compound, $C_{12}H_{17}ON_4SCl$, found in cereal grains, egg yolk, liver, etc., or prepared synthetically: a lack of this vitamin results in beriberi and certain nervous disorders: also **thi′a·min** (-min)

Thi·bet (ti bet′) *var. of* TIBET —**Thi·bet′an** *adj., n.*

thick (thik) *adj.* [OE. *thicce*] 1. of relatively great depth or width from side to side [a *thick* board] 2. having large diameter in relation to length [a *thick* pipe] 3. measured between opposite surfaces [a wall six inches *thick*] 4. dense; compact; specif., *a)* marked by abundant, close growth; luxuriant [*thick* woods] *b)* great in number and close together [a *thick* crowd] *c)* flowing or pouring slowly; not thin [*thick* soup] *d)* dense and heavy [*thick* smoke] *e)* covered to some depth [a road

THERMOS
BOTTLE
(in cross
section)

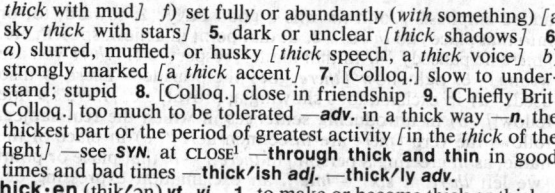

thick with mud] *f)* set fully or abundantly (*with* something) [a sky *thick* with stars] 5. dark or unclear [*thick* shadows] 6. *a)* slurred, muffled, or husky [*thick* speech, a *thick* voice] *b)* strongly marked [a *thick* accent] 7. [Colloq.] slow to understand; stupid 8. [Colloq.] close in friendship 9. [Chiefly Brit. Colloq.] too much to be tolerated —*adv.* in a thick way —*n.* the thickest part or the period of greatest activity [in the *thick* of the fight] —see SYN. at CLOSE[1] —**through thick and thin** in good times and bad times —**thick′ish** *adj.* —**thick′ly** *adv.*

thick·en (thik′ən) *vt., vi.* 1. to make or become thick or thicker 2. to make or become more complicated [the plot *thickened*] —**thick′en·er** *n.*

thick·en·ing (-iŋ) *n.* 1. the action of one that thickens 2. a substance used to thicken 3. the thickened part

thick·et (thik′it) *n.* [OE. *thiccet* < *thicce,* thick] a thick growth of shrubs, underbrush, or small trees

thick·head·ed (thik′hed′id) *adj.* stupid —**thick′head′ed·ness** *n.*

thick·ness (-nis) *n.* 1. the quality of being thick 2. the measure of how thick a thing is 3. a layer [three *thicknesses* of cloth]

thick·set (-set′) *adj.* 1. planted thickly or closely [*thickset* trees] 2. thick in body; stocky —*n.* [Archaic] a thicket

thick-skinned (-skind′) *adj.* 1. having a thick skin 2. not easily hurt by criticism, insults, etc.

thief (thēf) *n., pl.* **thieves** (thēvz) [OE. *theof*] a person who steals, esp. secretly

thief knot a kind of knot: see illustration at KNOT

thieve (thēv) *vt., vi.* **thieved, thiev′ing** [OE. *theofian* < *theof,* a thief] to steal

thiev·er·y (thēv′ər ē) *n., pl.* **-er·ies** the act or practice of stealing or an instance of this; theft

thiev·ish (-ish) *adj.* 1. in the habit of stealing 2. of or like a thief; stealthy; sneaky —**thiev′ish·ly** *adv.* —**thiev′ish·ness** *n.*

thigh (thī) *n.* [OE. *theoh*] the part of the leg between the knee and the hip

thigh·bone (thī′bōn′) *n.* the largest and longest bone in the body, from the hip to the knee; femur: also **thigh bone**

thill (thil) *n.* [OE. *thille,* a stake, pole] either of the two shafts between which a horse is hitched to a wagon

thim·ble (thim′b'l) *n.* [OE. *thymel* < *thuma,* a thumb] 1. a small cap of metal, plastic, etc. worn as a protection on the finger that pushes the needle in sewing 2. anything like this; esp., a grooved metal ring inserted in a loop of rope, etc. to prevent wear

thim·ble·ful (-fool′) *n., pl.* **-fuls′** 1. as much as a thimble will hold 2. a very small quantity

thim·ble·rig (-rig′) *n. same as* SHELL GAME —*vt., vi.* **-rigged′, -rig′ging** to cheat or swindle, as in this game —**thim′ble·rig′ger** *n.*

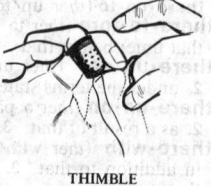

THIMBLE

thin (thin) *adj.* **thin′ner, thin′nest** [OE. *thynne*] 1. of relatively little depth or width from side to side [a *thin* board] 2. having small diameter in relation to length [*thin* thread] 3. having little fat or flesh; slender 4. not dense or compact; specif., *a)* scanty in growth; sparse [*thin* hair] *b)* small in size or number [*thin* receipts] *c)* flowing or pouring quickly; watery [*thin* soup] *d)* not dense or heavy [*thin* smoke] *e)* rarefied, as air at high altitudes 5. not deep and strong; weak, faint, dim, etc. [*thin* colors, a *thin* voice] 6. light or sheer, as fabric 7. easily seen through; flimsy [a *thin* excuse] 8. lacking vigor, interest, etc.; slight, weak, vapid, etc. [a *thin* plot, a *thin* argument] —*adv.* in a thin way —*vt., vi.* **thinned, thin′ning** to make or become thin or thinner: often with *out, down,* etc. —**thin′ly** *adv.* —**thin′ness** *n.* —**thin′nish** *adj.*

SYN.—**thin** implies relatively little width from one surface or side of a thing to the opposite and may suggest lack of fleshiness or fullness; **slender** and **slim** imply a thinness that is more or less pleasing in proportion but may suggest a being short of the amount needed or wanted [a *slender* income; a *slim* possibility]; **lean,** implying an absence of fat, suggests a lack of richness or productiveness [*lean* years]; **slight** implies smallness and lightness or delicateness in form or structure and may suggest smallness in amount, extent, importance, etc. [a *slight* figure, difference, etc.]; **tenuous** implies extreme physical thinness or fineness and may suggest weakness in content, substance, etc. [a *tenuous* film, plot, etc.] —**ANT.** thick, substantial

thine (thīn) *pron.* [OE. *thin*] [Archaic or Poet.] that or those belonging to thee (you): absolute form of THY [a friend of *thine,* this is *thine*] —*adj.* [Archaic or Poet.] thy: used before a word beginning with a vowel or silent *h*

thing[1] (thiŋ) *n.* [OE., a council, hence, "matter discussed, thing"] **1.** any matter, affair, or concern [how are *things?*] **2.** a happening, act, deed, incident, etc. [to do great *things*] **3.** an end to be achieved, a step in a process, etc. [the next *thing* is to mix thoroughly] **4.** that which exists in a distinct or individual way [all *things* in the universe]; specif., *a*) a real object or substance, not a quality, idea, etc. [paintings and other beautiful *things*] *b*) an organism [living *things*] *c*) an item, detail, etc. [look at each *thing* on the list] *d*) the object or idea referred to by a word, symbol, or sign *e*) an object of thought; idea [think the right *things*] **5.** *a*) [*pl.*] personal belongings; also, clothes or clothing [pick up your *things*] *b*) a dress, garment, etc. [not a *thing* to wear] **6.** a person or animal thought of with pity, affection, or contempt [poor *thing!*] **7.** something mentioned but unnamed [where did you buy that *thing?*] **8.** [Colloq.] a point of dispute; issue [he made a *thing* of it] ☆**9.** [Colloq.] a strong, often neurotic liking, fear, dislike, etc. [to have a *thing* about flying] —☆**do one's (own) thing** [Colloq.] to express one's unique personality in one's own way of life, activities, etc. —**see things** [Colloq.] to have hallucinations —**the thing 1.** that which is wise, basic, etc. **2.** that which is the height of fashion

‡**thing**[2] (tiŋ; *E.* thiŋ) *n.* [ON., assembly] a Scandinavian legislative body

thing·a·ma·bob, thing·um·a·bob (thiŋ′ə mə bäb′) *n.* [Colloq.] same as THINGAMAJIG: also **thing′um·bob′**

thing·a·ma·jig, thing·um·a·jig (-jig′) *n.* [extension of older *thingum,* THING[1]] [Colloq.] any device or gadget: joking substitute for a name not known or temporarily forgotten

think[1] (thiŋk) *vt.* **thought, think′ing** [OE. *thencan*] **1.** to form or have in the mind [think good thoughts] **2.** to judge; consider [I *think* her charming] **3.** to believe, expect, or imagine [I *think* I can go] **4.** to work out or solve by reasoning [to *think* a problem through] **5.** [Now Rare] to intend [thinking to do right] **6.** *a*) to have in mind; form an idea of [think what may be] *b*) to recall; recollect [think what joy was ours] **7.** to have constantly in mind [think success] —*vi.* **1.** to use the mind; reflect or reason [think before you act] **2.** to have an opinion, belief, judgment, etc. [I just *think* so; we *think* highly of him] **3.** to remember (with *of* or *about*) [think of the past] **4.** to give thought or be thoughtful [he *thinks* about the future; she *thinks* of the problems of others] **5.** to discover or invent [they *think* of new formulas all the time] —*n.* [Colloq.] the act of thinking [give it a good *think*] —*adj.* [Colloq.] having to do with thinking —**think (all) the world of** to admire or love greatly —**think better of 1.** to form a more favorable opinion of **2.** to make a wiser decision about, after further thought —**think fit** to regard as proper —**think little (or nothing) of 1.** to attach little (or no) importance to **2.** to have little (or no) doubt about —**think on (or upon)** [Archaic] to give thought to —**think out 1.** to think about to a conclusion: also **think through 2.** to work out by thinking —**think out loud** to speak one's thoughts as they come to one: also **think aloud** —**think over** to give thought to; ponder well —**think twice** to think over carefully —**think up** to invent, plan, etc. by thinking —**think′a·ble** *adj.* —**think′er** *n.*

SYN.—**think** is the general word meaning to use the mind so as to form ideas, reach conclusions, etc. [learn to *think* clearly]; **reason** implies a logical order of thought, starting with what is known or thought to be true and going on to a definite conclusion [he *reasoned* that she would accept]; **cogitate** is used, sometimes humorously, of a person who is, or appears to be, thinking hard [the baby frowned and seemed to be *cogitating*]; **reflect** implies a turning of one's thoughts on or back on a subject and suggests deep or quiet continued thought [he *reflected* on the day's events]; **speculate** implies a reasoning on the basis of information that is not complete or certain and therefore emphasizes that the opinions formed are guesses [to *speculate* on the possibility of life on Mars]; **deliberate** implies careful and thorough thinking on a matter in order to arrive at a conclusion [the jury *deliberated* on the case]

think[2] (thiŋk) *v.impersonal pt.* **thought** [OE. *thyncan*] to seem: obs., except in archaic METHINKS, METHOUGHT

think·ing (thiŋk′iŋ) *adj.* **1.** that thinks or can think; rational **2.** given to thought; reflective —*n.* thought —**put on one's thinking cap** to begin careful thinking about a problem

☆**think tank (or factory)** [Slang] a group of experts organized to do intensive research and problem solving, using computers, etc.

thin·ner (thin′ər) *n.* a person or thing that thins; esp., a substance added, as turpentine to paint, for thinning

thin-skinned (-skind′) *adj.* **1.** having a thin skin **2.** easily hurt by criticism, insults, etc.

thi·o- [< Gr. *theion,* brimstone] *a combining form meaning* sulfur, used to show the replacement of oxygen by sulfur

☆**Thi·o·kol** (thī′ə kôl′, -kōl′) [arbitrary coinage] *a trademark for* any of various synthetic rubbery compounds used as sealants and sealing adhesives

thi·o·pen·tal (sodium) (thī′ə pen′tal, -tôl, -t'l) [THIO- + PENT(A)- + -AL] a yellowish-white powder, $C_{11}H_{17}N_2O_2SNa$, injected into the veins in solution as a general anesthetic and hypnotic

thi·o·sul·fate (thī′ō sul′fāt) *n.* a salt of thiosulfuric acid; esp., sodium thiosulfate

thi·o·sul·fu·ric acid (thī′ō sul fyoor′ik) [THIO- + SULFURIC] an unstable acid, $H_2S_2O_3$, whose salts are used in photography, bleaching, etc.

third (thurd) *adj.* [OE. *thridda*] **1.** coming after two others in a series; 3d or 3rd **2.** next below the second in rank, value, merit, etc. **3.** designating any of the three equal parts of something —*adv.* in the third place, rank, group, etc. —*n.* **1.** the one following the second **2.** any person, thing, class, etc. that is third **3.** any of the three equal parts of something; 1/3 **4.** the third forward gear ratio of a motor vehicle transmission **5.** *Music a*) the third tone of an ascending diatonic scale, or a tone two degrees above or below any given tone in such a scale *b*) the interval between two such tones, or a combination of them —**third′ly** *adv.*

☆**third base** *Baseball* the base between second base and home plate, located on the pitcher's right

third-class (thurd′klas′) *adj.* **1.** of the class, rank, excellence, etc. next below the second **2.** designating or of accommodations next below the second ☆**3.** designating or of a lower-cost class of mail limited to merchandise weighing less than 16 oz. or bulk mailing of identical circulars, advertisements, etc. —*adv.* **1.** with third-class travel accommodations ☆**2.** as or by third-class mail

third degree ☆[Colloq.] harsh or brutal treatment and questioning of a prisoner in order to force a confession or information —**third′-de·gree′** *adj.*

third dimension 1. *a*) the dimension of depth in something *b*) the quality of having, or of seeming to have, depth, or solidity **2.** the quality of being true to life or seeming real —**third′-di·men′sion·al** *adj.*

third estate formerly, the common people as distinguished from the nobility and clergy: see ESTATE (sense 2)

third·ly (thurd′lē) *adv.* in the third place; third

third party ☆**1.** a political party competing against the two major parties in a two-party system **2.** a person other than the principals in a case or matter

third person that form of a pronoun (as *he* or *they*) or verb (as *is* or *are*) which refers to the one or ones spoken of

☆**third rail** an extra rail used in some electric railroads for supplying power

third-rate (-rāt′) *adj.* **1.** third in quality, rank, etc.; third-class **2.** inferior; very poor —**third′-rat′er** *n.*

third world [*often* T- W-] the underdeveloped or new nations of the world, esp. of Africa and Asia, thought of as forming a group independent of the great powers

thirst (thurst) *n.* [OE. *thurst*] **1.** the feeling of discomfort or dryness caused by a desire or need for water **2.** [Colloq.] a craving for a specific liquid, esp. for alcoholic liquor **3.** any strong desire; craving [a *thirst* for knowledge] —*vi.* **1.** to be thirsty **2.** to have a strong desire or craving

thirst·y (thurs′tē) *adj.* **thirst′i·er, thirst′i·est** **1.** wanting to drink; feeling thirst **2.** *a*) lacking water or moisture; dry [*thirsty* fields] *b*) very absorbent [a *thirsty* blotter] **3.** having a strong desire; craving [*thirsty* for power] —**thirst′i·ly** *adv.* —**thirst′i·ness** *n.*

thir·teen (thur′tēn′) *adj.* [OE. *threotyne*] three more than ten —*n.* the cardinal number between twelve and fourteen; 13; XIII

thir·teenth (-tēnth′) *adj.* **1.** coming after twelve others in a series; 13th **2.** designating any of the thirteen equal parts of something —*n.* **1.** the one following the twelfth **2.** any of the thirteen equal parts of something; 1/13

---

fat, āpe, cär; ten, ēven; is, bīte; gō, hôrn, too͞l, look; oil, out; up, fur; get; joy; yet; chin; she; thin, *th*en; zh, leisure; ŋ, ring; ə for *a* in ago, e in agent, i in sanity, o in comply, u in focus; ′ as in able (ā′b'l); Fr. bal; ë, Fr. coeur; ö, Fr. feu; Fr. mon; ô, Fr. coq; ü, Fr. duc; r, Fr. cri; H, G. ich; kh, G. doch; ‡ foreign; ☆ Americanism; < derived from. See inside front cover.

thir·ti·eth (thur′tē ith) *adj.* **1.** coming after twenty-nine others in a series; 30th **2.** designating any of the thirty equal parts of something —*n.* **1.** the one following the twenty-ninth **2.** any of the thirty equal parts of something; 1/30

thir·ty (thur′tē) *adj.* [OE. *thritig* < *thri*, three + *-tig*, -TY²] three times ten —*n., pl.* **-ties** **1.** the cardinal number between twenty-nine and thirty-one; 30; XXX ☆**2.** this number used to signify the end of a dispatch, story, etc., as for a newspaper —**the thirties** the numbers or years, as of a century, from thirty through thirty-nine

thir·ty-sec·ond note (thurt′ē sek′ənd) *Music* a note having 1/32 the duration of a whole note: see illustration at NOTE

this (this) *pron., pl.* **these** [OE. *thes*, masc., *this*, neut.] **1.** the person or thing here [*this* is your pen] **2.** the thing that is nearer than or in some way different from another [*this* is larger than that; *this* is more likely to happen than that] **3.** the thing that is being, or is about to be, mentioned or presented [now hear *this*] —*adj., pl.* **these 1.** designating the person or thing here [*this* man, *this* pencil] **2.** designating the thing that is nearer than or in some way different from another [*this* desk is smaller than that one; *this* possibility is more likely than that] **3.** designating something that is being, or is about to be, mentioned or presented [hear *this* song] **4.** [Colloq.] designating a particular but unspecified person or thing [there's *this* lady in Iowa] —*adv.* to this extent; so [it was *this* big]

this·tle (this′'l) *n.* [OE. *thistel*] any of various plants of the composite family, with prickly leaves and heads of white, purple, etc. flowers; esp., the **Scotch thistle** with white down and lavender flowers —**this·tly** (this′lē) *adj.*

this·tle·down (-doun′) *n.* the down attached to the flower head of a thistle

thith·er (thith′ər, thith′-) *adv.* [OE. *thider*] to or toward that place; there —*adj.* on or toward that side; farther

thith·er·to (-tōō′; thith′ər tōō′, thith′-) *adv.* until that time; till then

thith·er·ward (-wərd) *adv.* [Rare] toward that place; thither: also **thith′er·wards**

tho, tho' (thō) *conj., adv.* shortened sp. of THOUGH

thole (thōl) *n.* [OE. *thol*] a pin or either of a pair of pins set upright into the side of a boat for an oar to turn against in rowing: also **thole′pin′** (-pin′)

Thom·as (täm′əs) [LL. < Gr. < Ar. *te̊'oma*, lit., a twin] **1.** a masculine name: dim. *Tom, Tommy* **2.** *Bible* one of the twelve apostles, who doubted at first the resurrection of Jesus: John 20:24–29 **3. Dyl·an (Marlais)** (dil′ən), 1914–53; Welsh poet **4. George Henry**, 1816–70; Union general in the Civil War

Tho·mism (tō′miz'm) *n.* the teachings in theology and philosophy of Thomas Aquinas and his followers —**Tho′mist** (-mist) *adj., n.* —**Tho·mis′tic** *adj.*

Thomp·son (tämp′s'n, täm′-) **1. Benjamin**, Count Rumford, 1753–1814; Brit. scientist & statesman, born in America **2. Francis**, 1859–1907; Eng. poet

☆**Thompson submachine gun** [< the co-inventor, J. T. *Thompson* (1860–1940), U.S. army officer] *a trademark for* a type of submachine gun: see SUBMACHINE GUN

thong (thôŋ) *n.* [OE. *thwang*] **1.** a narrow strip of leather, etc. used as a lace, strap, etc. **2.** a whiplash, as of braided strips of hide

Thor (thôr) *Norse Myth.* the god of thunder, war, and strength, and the son of Odin

tho·rac·ic (thô ras′ik, thə-) *adj.* of, in, or near the thorax

tho·ra·co- (thôr′ə kō) *a combining form meaning* the thorax (and): also, before a vowel, **thorac-**

tho·rax (thôr′aks) *n., pl.* **-rax·es, -ra·ces′** (-ə sēz′) [L. < Gr. *thorax*] **1.** in man and other higher vertebrates, the part of the body between the neck and the abdomen, containing the heart and lungs; chest **2.** the middle one of the three main segments of an insect's body

☆**Tho·ra·zine** (thôr′ə zēn′) [*thor-* (< ?) + (CHLORPROM)-AZINE] *a trademark for* CHLORPROMAZINE

Thor·eau (thôr′ō, thə rō′), **Henry David** (born *David Henry Thoreau*) 1817–62; U.S. naturalist & writer

tho·ri·um (thôr′ē əm) *n.* [ModL. < THOR] a rare, grayish, radioactive chemical element, used in making electronic equip-

THISTLE

THORAX

ment and as a nuclear fuel: symbol, Th; at. wt., 232.038; at. no., 90 —**tho′ric** *adj.*

thorn (thôrn) *n.* [OE.] **1.** *a*) a short, hard, sharp-pointed growth on a branch or stem *b*) any small tree or shrub bearing thorns; esp., *same as* HAWTHORN **2.** anything that keeps troubling or annoying one: usually in the phrase **thorn in one's side** (or **flesh**) **3.** in Old English, the runic character (þ), standing for the sound of English *th* in both *thick* and *they*

thorn apple ☆**1.** *same as* HAWTHORN *b*) its applelike fruit; haw ☆**2.** a jimson weed or similar plant

thorn·y (thôr′nē) *adj.* **thorn′i·er, thorn′i·est 1.** full of thorns; prickly **2.** difficult or full of obstacles, trouble, pain, etc. —**thorn′i·ness** *n.*

thor·o (thur′ō, -ə) *adj.* shortened sp. of THOROUGH

tho·ron (thôr′än) *n.* [ModL. < THORIUM] a radioactive isotope of radon, resulting from the disintegration of thorium

thor·ough (thur′ō, -ə) *prep., adv.* [ME. *thoruh*, a var. of *through*, THROUGH] *obs. form of* THROUGH —*adj.* **1.** complete in every way; with nothing left out, undone, etc. [a *thorough* checkup; a *thorough* knowledge of the subject] **2.** that is completely (the thing specified); absolute [a *thorough* rascal] **3.** very exact, accurate, and painstaking, esp. with regard to details [a *thorough* worker] —**thor′ough·ly** *adv.* —**thor′ough·ness** *n.*

thor·ough·bred (thur′ə bred′) *adj.* of pure or unmixed breed, as a horse or dog; pedigreed —*n.* **1.** a thoroughbred animal; specif. [T-], any of the breed of horses developed for racing at a gallop **2.** a cultured, well-bred person

thor·ough·fare (-fer′) *n.* a public street open at both ends, esp. one through which there is much traffic; main road

thor·ough·go·ing (-gō′iŋ) *adj.* very thorough; specif., *a*) precise and painstaking [a *thoroughgoing* investigation] *b*) absolute; out-and-out [a *thoroughgoing* scoundrel]

those (thōz) *adj., pron.* [OE. *thas*] *pl. of* THAT

thou (thou) *pron.* [OE. *thu*] the nominative second person singular of the personal pronoun: formerly used in familiar address but now replaced by *you* except in poetic, religious, and some dialectal use: *thee* is the objective case form, *thy* or *thine* the possessive, and *thyself* the intensive and reflexive

though (thō) *conj.* [< OE. *theah* & cognate ON. *tho*] **1.** in spite of the fact that; notwithstanding that [*though* it rained, he went] **2.** and yet; nevertheless; however [they will probably win, *though* no one thinks so] **3.** even if; supposing that [*though* he may fail, he will have tried] —*adv.* however; nevertheless [she sings well, *though*]

thought¹ (thôt) *n.* [OE. *thoht*] **1.** the act or process of thinking [she was deep in *thought*] **2.** the power of reasoning; intellect; imagination [animals lack *thought*] **3.** what one thinks; idea, opinion, plan, etc. [let me have your *thoughts* on the matter] **4.** the ideas, opinions, etc. prevailing at a given time or place or among a given group [modern *thought* in education] **5.** attention; consideration [give it a moment's *thought*] **6.** intention or expectation [no *thought* of leaving] **7.** a little; trifle [be a *thought* more careful] —see SYN. at IDEA

thought² (thôt) *pt. & pp. of* THINK¹

thought·ful (thôt′fəl) *adj.* **1.** full of thought; meditative **2.** showing thought; serious [a *thoughtful* essay] **3.** heedful, careful, etc.; esp., considerate of others —**thought′ful·ly** *adv.* —**thought′ful·ness** *n.*

SYN.—**thoughtful**, as compared here, implies a thinking of the comfort or well-being of others, as by figuring out in advance what they might need or want [it was *thoughtful* of you to call]; **considerate** implies a thoughtful or sympathetic regard for others shown by putting them at ease and keeping them from being uncomfortable, embarrassed, worried, etc. [a *considerate* host]; **attentive** implies a constant thoughtfulness as shown by repeated acts of consideration, courtesy, or devotion [an *attentive* escort]

thought·less (-lis) *adj.* **1.** not stopping to think; careless **2.** not given proper thought; hasty or rash [a *thoughtless* remark] **3.** not considerate of others —**thought′less·ly** *adv.* —**thought′less·ness** *n.*

thou·sand (thou′z'nd) *n.* [OE. *thusend*] **1.** ten hundred; 1,000; M **2.** an indefinite but very large number [I've told you *thousands* of times] —*adj.* amounting to one thousand in number

thou·sand·fold (-fōld′) *adj.* [see -FOLD] having a thousand times as much or as many —*adv.* a thousand times as much or as many: with *a*

☆**Thousand Island dressing** a salad dressing made of mayonnaise with ketchup, minced pickles, etc.

Thousand Islands group of c.1,000 islands in the St. Lawrence River at the outlet of Lake Ontario, some part of N.Y. State & some of Ontario, Canada

thou·sandth (thou′z′ndth) *adj.* **1.** coming last in a series of a thousand **2.** designating any of the thousand equal parts of something —*n.* **1.** the thousandth one of a series **2.** any of the thousand equal parts of something; 1/1000

Thrace (thrās) **1.** ancient region in the E Balkan Peninsula: see map at MACEDONIA **2.** modern region in the SE Balkan Peninsula divided between Greece & Turkey —**Thra·cian** (thrā′shən) *adj., n.*

thrall (thrôl) *n.* [OE. *thræl* < ON.] **1.** orig., a slave or bondman **2.** a person completely under the influence of someone or something **3.** slavery [held in *thrall*]

thrall·dom, thral·dom (thrôl′dəm) *n.* the condition of being a thrall; servitude; slavery

thrash (thrash) *vt.* [OE. *therscan*, to beat] **1.** *same as* THRESH **2.** to make move violently or wildly [a bird *thrashing* its wings] **3.** to give a severe beating to; flog **4.** to defeat soundly —*vi.* **1.** *same as* THRESH **2.** to move or toss about violently [*thrashing* in agony] **3.** to make one's way by thrashing [*thrashing* through the water] —*n.* the act of thrashing —see SYN. at BEAT —**thrash out** to settle by much discussion —**thrash over** to go over (a problem, etc.) in great detail

thrash·er[1] (thrash′ər) *n.* a person or thing that thrashes

thrash·er[2] (thrash′ər) *n.* [E. dial. *thresher*] ☆any of a group of gray to brownish American songbirds having a long, stiff tail and a long bill like the thrush

thread (thred) *n.* [OE. *thræd*] **1.** *a)* a light, fine, stringlike length of two or more fibers or strands of spun cotton, silk, etc. twisted together and used in sewing *b)* a similar fine length of material such as nylon, plastic, glass, or metal *c)* the fine, stringy filament that a spider, silkworm, etc. produces from within its body *d)* a fine, stringy length of syrup, etc. **2.** any thin line, stratum, vein, ray, etc. **3.** something like a thread in being long, continuous, connected, etc. [the *thread* of a story] **4.** the spiral ridge of a screw, bolt, nut, etc. ☆**5.** [*pl.*] [Slang] a suit, or clothes generally —*vt.* **1.** *a)* to put a thread through the eye of (a needle, etc.) *b)* to arrange thread for use on (a sewing machine) **2.** to string (beads, etc.) on or as if on a thread **3.** to cut or mold a thread (sense 4) on or in (a screw, pipe, etc.) **4.** to interweave with or as if with threads **5.** *a)* to pass through by twisting, turning, or weaving in and out [to *thread* the streets] *b)* to make (one's way) in this way —*vi.* **1.** to go along in a winding way ☆**2.** to form a thread when dropped from a spoon: said of boiling syrup beginning to thicken — **thread′er** *n.* —**thread′like′** *adj.*

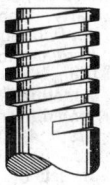

THREAD
OF A
BOLT

thread·bare (thred′ber′) *adj.* **1.** worn down so that the threads show; having the nap worn off [*threadbare* rugs] **2.** wearing worn-out clothes; shabby [a *threadbare* beggar] **3.** that has lost freshness or novelty; stale [a *threadbare* argument]

thread·worm (-wurm′) *n.* any of various threadlike worms that live as parasites in the intestines

thread·y (-ē) *adj.* **thread′i·er, thread′i·est 1.** of or like a thread; stringy; fibrous **2.** forming threads; thick; viscid: said of liquids **3.** thin, weak, feeble, etc. [a *thready* voice] — **thread′i·ness** *n.*

threat (thret) *n.* [OE. *threat*, a throng] **1.** a warning that one plans to harm another, esp. if a certain thing is done or not done [a bully's *threats*] **2.** *a)* a sign of something dangerous or harmful about to happen [the *threat* of war] *b)* a source of possible danger or harm [a *threat* to free speech]

threat·en (thret′'n) *vt.* [OE. *threatnian*] **1.** *a)* to make threats against [*threatening* them with arrest] *b)* to warn of (punishment, injury, etc.) in a threat [*threatened* death to all who disobeyed] **2.** *a)* to be a sign of (possible danger, harm, etc.) [clouds *threatening* snow] *b)* to be a source of possible danger, harm, etc. to [an epidemic *threatens* the city] —*vi.* **1.** to make threats **2.** to be a sign or source of possible danger, etc. — **threat′en·er** *n.* —**threat′en·ing·ly** *adv.*

SYN.—**threaten** implies a warning by words, actions, conditions, etc. of something harmful or evil that will be done or will happen unless there is some kind of change [they *threatened* to put him in jail; pollution *threatens* civilization]; **menace** stresses the frightening or hostile nature of that which threatens [the *menacing* movement of his hand toward his revolver]

three (thrē) *adj.* [OE. *threo, thrie*] totaling one more than two

—*n.* **1.** the cardinal number between two and four; 3; III **2.** anything having three units or members, or numbered three

☆**three-base hit** (thrē′bās′) *Baseball* a hit by which a batter reaches third base safely: also [Slang] **three′-bag′ger** (-bag′ər) *n.*

☆**3-D** (thrē′dē′) *adj.* producing or meant to produce an effect of three dimensions [a *3-D* movie] —*n.* a system or effect that gives a three-dimensional look to visual images, as in movies

three-deck·er (-dek′ər) *n.* **1.** a ship with three decks **2.** any structure with three levels **3.** [Colloq.] a sandwich made with three slices of bread

three-di·men·sion·al (-də men′shən 'l) *adj.* **1.** *a)* of or having three dimensions *b)* appearing to have depth or thickness in addition to height and width **2.** having a lifelike quality [a *three-dimensional* novel]

three·fold (-fōld′) *adj.* [see -FOLD] **1.** having three parts **2.** having three times as much or as many —*adv.* three times as much or as many

three-mile limit (-mīl′) the outer limit of a zone of water extending three miles offshore, sometimes regarded as the limit to a country's right to control, use, etc.

three·pence (thrip′ns, thrup′-, threp′-) *n.* **1.** the sum of three British pennies **2.** a British coin of this value, not minted for general circulation since 1971

three·pen·ny (thrē′pen′ē, thrip′ə nē) *adj.* **1.** worth or costing threepence **2.** of small worth; cheap

three·ply (-plī′) *adj.* having three thicknesses, interwoven layers, strands, etc.

three-quar·ter (-kwôr′tər) *adj.* of or involving three fourths

three R's, the *see* R

three·score (thrē′skôr′) *adj.* sixty

three·some (-səm) *n.* a group of three persons

thren·o·dy (thren′ə dē) *n., pl.* **-dies** [< Gr. < *threnos*, lamentation + *ōidē*, song] a song of lamentation; dirge —**thre·nod·ic** (thri näd′ik) *adj.* —**thren′o·dist** *n.*

thresh (thresh) *vt.* [earlier form of THRASH] **1.** to beat out (grain) from its husk, as with a flail **2.** to beat grain out of (husks) **3.** to beat or strike as with a flail —*vi.* **1.** to thresh grain **2.** to toss about; thrash —**thresh out** to settle by much discussion; thrash out

thresh·er (thresh′ər) *n.* **1.** a person who threshes **2.** a machine for threshing grain: also **threshing machine 3.** a large shark with a long tail

thresh·old (thresh′ōld, -hōld) *n.* [OE. *therscold*] **1.** *same as* DOORSILL **2.** the entrance or beginning point of something [at the *threshold* of a new career] **3.** *Physiol., Psychol.* the point at which a stimulus is just strong enough for one to become aware of it or for it to cause a response [the *threshold* of pain]

threw (thrōō) *pt.* of THROW

thrice (thrīs) *adv.* [ME. *thries*] **1.** three times **2.** threefold **3.** very much; fully [*thrice* blessed]

thrift (thrift) *n.* [ON. < *thrifast*, to THRIVE] **1.** orig., a thriving **2.** careful management of one's money or resources; economy; frugality **3.** a small plant with narrow leaves and small white, pink, red, or purplish flowers —**thrift′less** *adj.* —**thrift′less·ly** *adv.* —**thrift′less·ness** *n.*

thrift·y (thrift′ē) *adj.* **thrift′i·er, thrift′i·est 1.** practicing or showing thrift; economical **2.** thriving; prospering [*thrifty* plants] —**thrift′i·ly** *adv.* —**thrift′i·ness** *n.*

SYN.—**thrifty** implies a clever managing of one's money or resources, usually so as to save some part of it [a *thrifty* housewife]; **frugal** suggests a spending only for what is really necessary, as the simplest of food and clothing, and the avoiding of all luxuries [*frugal* country folk]; **sparing** implies a holding back in spending, even to the point of doing without what most people would consider necessary [*sparing* to the point of being miserly]; **economical** implies careful management of one's money or resources so as to avoid all wastefulness [it is often *economical* to buy in large quantities]; **provident** stresses careful management with an eye to future needs [*provident* parents] —**ANT. lavish, prodigal, wasteful**

thrill (thril) *vi., vt.* [OE. *thyr(e)lian*, to pierce < *thyrel*, hole < *thurh*, through] **1.** to feel or cause to feel keen emotional excitement; tingle or make tingle with excitement [a *thrilling* movie] **2.** to quiver or cause to quiver; shake [to *thrill* with fear] —*n.* **1.** a thrilling or being thrilled; tremor, as of excitement [a *thrill* of joy] **2.** the quality of thrilling, or the ability to thrill [the *thrill* of water-skiing] **3.** something that causes emotional excitement [her first plane ride was a *thrill*]

---

fat, āpe, cär; ten, ēven; is, bīte; gō, hôrn, tōōl, look; oil, out; up, fur; get; joy; yet; chin; she; thin, *th*en; zh, leisure; ŋ, ring; ə for *a* in *ago, e* in *agent, i* in *sanity, o* in *comply, u* in *focus*; ′ as in *able* (ā′b'l); Fr. bal; ë, Fr. coeur; ö, Fr. feu; ô, Fr. mo*n*; ô, Fr. coq; ü, Fr. duc; r, Fr. cri; H, G. ich; kh, G. doch; ‡ foreign; ☆ Americanism; < derived from. See inside front cover.

thrill·er (thril′ər) *n.* a novel, movie, etc. full of suspense, esp. [Chiefly Brit.] one dealing with crime and detection

thrips (thrips) *n., pl.* **thrips** [L. < Gr. *thrips*, woodworm] any of a group of very small insects that harm plants by sucking their juices

thrive (thrīv) *vi.* **thrived** or **throve, thrived** or **thriv·en** (thriv′'n), **thriv′ing** [< ON. *thrifast*, to prosper < *thrifa*, to grasp] **1.** to prosper or flourish; be successful; grow rich and strong **2.** to grow vigorously or luxuriantly [plants *thrive* under her care]

thro', thro (thrōō) *prep., adv., adj.* archaic shortened form of THROUGH

throat (thrōt) *n.* [OE. *throte*] **1.** the front part of the neck **2.** the upper part of the passage from the mouth and nose to the stomach and lungs, including the pharynx and the upper part of the larynx, trachea, and esophagus **3.** any narrow, throatlike passage or part [the *throat* of a bottle] —**jump down someone's throat** [Colloq.] to attack or criticize someone suddenly and violently —**stick in one's throat** to be hard for one to say, as from reluctance

-throat·ed (thrōt′id) *a combining form meaning* having a (specified kind of) throat [ruby-*throated*]

throat·y (-ē) *adj.* **throat′i·er, throat′i·est 1.** produced in the throat, as some sounds or tones **2.** characterized by such sounds; husky [a *throaty* voice] —**throat′i·ly** *adv.* —**throat′i·ness** *n.*

throb (thräb) *vi.* **throbbed, throb′bing** [ME. *throbben*] **1.** to beat, pulsate, vibrate, etc. **2.** to beat strongly or fast; palpitate, as the heart under exertion **3.** to tingle or quiver with excitement —*n.* **1.** the act of throbbing **2.** a beat or pulsation, esp. a strong one of the heart —**throb′ber** *n.* —**throb′bing·ly** *adv.*

throe (thrō) *n.* [prob. < OE. *thrawu*, pain] a spasm or pang of pain: *usually used in pl.* [the *throes* of childbirth, death *throes*] —**in the throes of** in the act of struggling with (a problem, task, etc.)

throm·bin (thräm′bin) *n.* [< Gr. *thrombos*, a clot] the enzyme of the blood that causes clotting by forming fibrin

throm·bo·sis (thräm bō′sis) *n.* [ModL. < Gr. < *thrombos*, a clot] coagulation of the blood in the heart or a blood vessel, forming a clot —**throm·bot′ic** (-bät′ik) *adj.*

throne (thrōn) *n.* [< OFr. < L. < Gr. *thronos*, a seat] **1.** the chair on which a king, cardinal, etc. sits on formal or ceremonial occasions **2.** the power or rank of a king, etc.; sovereignty [the king lost his *throne* in the revolution] **3.** a sovereign ruler, etc. [orders from the *throne*] —*vt., vi.* **throned, thron′ing** to enthrone or be enthroned

throng (thrôŋ) *n.* [OE. (ge)thrang < thringan, to crowd] **1.** a great number of people gathered together; crowd **2.** any great number of things massed or considered together; multitude —*vi.* to gather together, move, or press in a throng; crowd [thronging into the hall] —*vt.* to crowd into or around [to *throng* a theater] —see SYN. at CROWD

throt·tle (thrät′'l) *n.* [prob. dim. of THROAT] **1.** [Rare] the throat or windpipe **2.** the valve that regulates the amount of fuel vapor entering an internal-combustion engine or controls the flow of steam in a steam line: also **throttle valve 3.** the lever or pedal that controls this valve —*vt.* **-tled, -tling 1.** to choke; strangle **2.** to stop the freedom of speech or action of; suppress [to *throttle* the press] **3.** *a)* to reduce the flow of (fuel vapor, etc.) by means of a throttle *b)* to lessen the speed of (an engine, vehicle, etc.) by this or similar means —*vi.* to choke or suffocate —**throt′tler** *n.*

THROTTLE
OF INTERNAL-
COMBUSTION
ENGINE

through (thrōō) *prep.* [OE. *thurh*] **1.** *a)* in one side and out the other side of; from end to end of [to drive *through* a tunnel] *b)* from one part of to another [birds fly *through* the air] **2.** in the midst of; among **3.** by way of [she left *through* the back door] **4.** over the entire extent of [searching all *through* the house] **5.** to various places in; around [touring *through* France] **6.** *a)* from the beginning to the end of [*through* the summer] ☆*b)* up to and including [*through* Friday] **7.** without making a stop for [to go *through* a red light] **8.** past the difficulties of [to come *through* hard times] **9.** by means of [*through* her help] **10.** as a result of; because of [*through* error] —*adv.* **1.** in one side and out the other; from end to end [fell all the way *through*] **2.** from the beginning to the end [to read a book *through*] **3.** completely to the end [see it *through*] **4.** thoroughly; completely: also **through and through** [soaked *through*] —*adj.* **1.** extending from one place

to another [a *through* street] ☆**2.** traveling to the destination without stops [a *through* train] **3.** arrived at the end; finished [*through* with an assignment] **4.** at the end of one's usefulness, resources, etc. [*through* in politics] **5.** having no further dealings, etc. (*with* someone or something)

through·out (thrōō out′) *prep.* all the way through; in or during every part of [*throughout* the week] —*adv.* **1.** in or through every part; everywhere [flimsy *throughout*] **2.** from start to finish; during the whole time [staying hopeful *throughout*]

☆**through·way** (thrōō′wā′) *n.* same as EXPRESSWAY

throve (thrōv) *alt. pt. of* THRIVE

throw (thrō) *vt.* **threw, thrown, throw′ing** [OE. *thrawan*, to twist] **1.** to twist strands of (silk, etc.) into thread or yarn **2.** to send through the air by a fast motion of the arm; fling, hurl, toss, etc. [to *throw* a ball] **3.** to discharge through the air from a catapult, gun, etc. [cannon *throwing* shells on the fort] **4.** to cause to fall; upset [*thrown* by a horse] **5.** to move or send rapidly [they *threw* troops into the battle] **6.** to put suddenly and forcibly into a specified place, condition, or situation [*thrown* into confusion] **7.** *a)* to cast (dice) *b)* to make (a specified cast) at dice [to *throw* a five] **8.** to cast off; shed [snakes *throw* their skins] **9.** to move (the lever of a switch, clutch, etc.) or connect, disconnect, etc. by so doing **10.** *a)* to direct, cast, turn, etc. (with *at, on, upon*, etc.) [to *throw* a glance, a light, a shadow, etc.] *b)* to deliver (a punch) **11.** to cause (one's voice) to seem to come from some other source, as a ventriloquist does **12.** to put (blame *on*, obstacles *before*, etc.) ☆**13.** [Colloq.] to lose (a game, race, etc.) on purpose ☆**14.** [Colloq.] to give (a party, dance, etc.) ☆**15.** [Colloq.] to have (a fit, tantrum, etc.) **16.** [Colloq.] to confuse or upset [the question *threw* him] **17.** *Ceramics* to shape on a potter's wheel —*vi.* to cast or hurl something —*n.* **1.** the act of one who throws; a cast **2.** the distance something is or can be thrown [a stone's *throw*] ☆**3.** *a)* a spread for draping over a sofa, etc. *b)* a woman's light scarf or wrap **4.** *a)* the motion of a moving part, as a cam, eccentric, etc. *b)* the extent of such a motion —**throw away 1.** to rid oneself of; discard **2.** to waste **3.** to fail to make use of [to *throw away* a chance] **4.** to deliver (a line or lines) in an offhand way: said of an actor or comedian —**throw cold water on** to discourage by showing no interest or by criticizing —**throw in 1.** to engage (a clutch) or cause (gears) to mesh **2.** to add extra or free **3.** to add to others [he *threw in* his own comment] **4.** [Colloq.] to join (*with*) in cooperative action —**throw off 1.** *a)* to rid oneself of *b)* to recover from **2.** to mislead **3.** to expel, emit, etc. [to *throw off* sparks] —**throw on** to put on (a garment) hastily —**throw oneself at** to try very hard to win the affection or love of —**throw oneself into** to take part in with great vigor —**throw oneself on** (or **upon**) to ask for (someone's mercy, etc.) for oneself —**throw open 1.** to open completely and suddenly [to *throw* the door *open*] **2.** to remove all restrictions from [*throwing open* membership in the club] —**throw out 1.** to discard **2.** to reject or remove, often with force **3.** to emit **4.** to give (a hint or suggestion) **5.** to disengage (a clutch) ☆**6.** *Baseball* to throw the ball to a teammate who in turn retires (a runner) —**throw over 1.** to give up; abandon **2.** to jilt —**throw together 1.** to make or assemble hurriedly **2.** to cause to become acquainted [*thrown together* in army life] —**throw up 1.** to give up or abandon **2.** to vomit **3.** to construct rapidly ☆**4.** to mention repeatedly (*to* someone), as in reproach —**throw′er** *n.*

SYN.—**throw** is the general word meaning to cause to move through the air by a rapid movement of the arm, etc.; **cast**, the preferred word in special uses [to *cast* a fishing line], generally has a more archaic or formal quality [they *cast* stones at him]; to **toss** is to throw lightly or carelessly and, usually, with an upward or sidewise motion [to *toss* a coin]; **hurl** and **fling** both imply a throwing with force or violence, but **hurl** suggests that the object thrown moves swiftly for some distance [to *hurl* a spear], while **fling** suggests that the object is thrust sharply so that it strikes a surface with considerable force [she *flung* the plate to the floor]; **pitch** implies a throwing with a definite aim or in a definite direction [to *pitch* a baseball]

throw·a·way (thrō′ə wā′) *n.* a leaflet, handbill, etc. given out as in the streets or from house to house —*adj.* ☆**1.** meant to be discarded after use [a *throwaway* bottle] **2.** purposely casual or offhand, as a remark

throw·back (-bak′) *n.* **1.** a throwing back; check or stop **2.** a return to an earlier or more primitive type or condition **3.** an instance of this

☆**throw rug** same as SCATTER RUG

thru (thrōō) *prep., adv., adj.* shortened sp. of THROUGH

thrum[1] (thrum) *n.* [OE., a ligament] **1.** *a)* the row of warp thread ends left on a loom when the web is cut off *b)* any of these ends **2.** any short end thread or fringe

thrum[2] (thrum) *vt., vi.* **thrummed, thrum′ming** [echoic] **1.** to strum (a guitar, banjo, etc.) **2.** to drum (on) with the fingers —*n.* the act or sound of thrumming

thrush[1] (thrush) *n.* [OE. *thrysce*] any of a large group of songbirds, some plain-colored, others having a spotted or bright breast, including the robin, wood thrush, blackbird, etc.

thrush[2] (thrush) *n.* [prob. akin to Dan. *trøske*] a disease, esp. of infants, caused by a fungus that forms milky white lesions on the mouth, lips, and throat

thrust (thrust) *vt.* **thrust, thrust′ing** [ON. *thrysta* < IE. *treud-*, to squeeze] **1.** to push with sudden force; shove [he *thrust* the books into her hand] **2.** to pierce; stab [the boar was *thrust* through] **3.** to force or impose (oneself or another) upon someone else or into some position or situation [he *thrust* himself into leadership] —*vi.* **1.** to push or shove against something [to *thrust* against a door] **2.** to make a stab or lunge, as with a sword [to parry and *thrust*] **3.** to force one's way (*into, through,* etc.) [they *thrust* into the forest] **4.** to extend, as in growth [trees that *thrust* high] —*n.* **1.** a thrusting; specif., *a)* a sudden, forceful push *b)* a stab, as with a sword *c)* any sudden attack [a *thrust* over the border] **2.** continuous pressure of one part against another, as of a rafter against a wall **3.** *a)* the driving force of a propeller in the line of its shaft *b)* the forward force produced by the gases rushing out rearward from a jet or rocket engine **4.** *a)* forward movement; impetus [the *thrust* of science] *b)* energy; drive [creative *thrust*] ☆**5.** the basic meaning or purpose [the *thrust* of a speech] —see SYN. at PUSH

thrust·er (thrus′tər) *n.* **1.** a person or thing that thrusts ☆**2.** a rocket used to maneuver a spacecraft

☆**thru·way** (thrōō′wā′) *n.* same as EXPRESSWAY

Thu·cyd·i·des (thōō sid′ə dēz′) 460?–400? B.C.; Athenian historian

thud (thud) *vi.* **thud′ded, thud′ding** [prob. ult. < OE. *thyddan*, to strike] to hit or fall with a dull sound —*n.* **1.** a heavy blow **2.** a dull sound, as of a heavy object dropping on a soft, solid surface

thug (thug) *n.* [Hindi *thag* < Sans. *sthaga*, a rogue] **1.** [*also* **T**-] a member of a former religious organization in India that murdered and robbed **2.** a rough, brutal hoodlum, gangster, robber, etc. —**thug′ger·y** *n.* —**thug′gish** *adj.*

thu·li·um (thōō′lē əm) *n.* [ModL. < (ULTIMA) THULE] a metallic chemical element of the rare-earth group: symbol, Tm; at. wt., 168.934; at. no., 69

thumb (thum) *n.* [OE. *thuma*] **1.** the short, thick finger of the human hand that is nearest the wrist **2.** a corresponding part in some other animals **3.** that part of a glove, etc. which covers the thumb —*vt.* **1.** to handle, turn, soil, etc. as with the thumb **2.** [Colloq.] to ask for or get (a ride) or make (one's way) in hitchhiking by gesturing with the thumb extended —**all thumbs** clumsy; fumbling —☆**thumb one's nose** to raise one's thumb to the nose in a coarse gesture of defiance or contempt —**thumbs down** a signal of disapproval —**thumbs up** a signal of approval —**thumb through** to quickly turn and glance through the pages of —**under one's thumb** under one's influence

thumb index an index to the sections of a reference book, consisting of a series of rounded notches cut in the front edge of a book with a tab bearing a label at the base of each notch —**thumb′-in′dex** *vt.*

thumb·nail (thum′nāl′) *n.* **1.** the nail of the thumb **2.** something as small as a thumbnail —*adj.* very small or brief [a *thumbnail* sketch]

thumb·screw (-skrōō′) *n.* **1.** a screw with a head shaped in such a way that it can be turned with the thumb and forefinger **2.** a former instrument of torture for squeezing the thumbs

☆**thumb·tack** (-tak′) *n.* a tack with a wide, flat head, that can be pressed into a board, etc. with the thumb

thump (thump) *n.* [echoic] **1.** a blow with something heavy and blunt **2.** the dull sound made by such a blow —*vt.* **1.** to strike with a thump or thumps **2.** to thrash; beat severely —*vi.* **1.** to hit or fall with a thump **2.** to make a dull, heavy sound; pound; throb [his heart was *thumping*] —**thump′er** *n.*

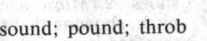

THUMBSCREW

thump·ing (thum′piŋ) *adj.* **1.** that thumps **2.** [Colloq.] very large; whopping —**thump′ing·ly** *adv.*

thun·der (thun′dər) *n.* [OE. *thunor*] **1.** the sound that is heard after a flash of lightning, caused by the sudden heating and expanding of air by electrical discharge **2.** any loud, rumbling sound like this [the *thunder* of cannon] **3.** an outburst of threatening or angry words [the *thunder* of an accusation] Also used in mild oaths [yes, by *thunder!*]: also **thun·der·a′tion** —*vi.* **1.** to produce thunder [it is *thundering*] **2.** to make, or move with, a sound like thunder [a *thundering* herd of bison] **3.** to make strong denunciations, etc. [to *thunder* against modern ways] —*vt.* to say, strike, etc. with the sound or violence of thunder —**steal someone's thunder** to lessen the force of someone's statement or action by saying or doing it first —**thun′der·er** *n.*

thun·der·bolt (-bōlt′) *n.* **1.** a flash of lightning with the thunder heard after it **2.** something that stuns or acts with sudden force or violence

thun·der·clap (-klap′) *n.* **1.** a clap, or loud crash, of thunder **2.** anything like this in being sudden, startling, violent, etc.

thun·der·cloud (-kloud′) *n.* a storm cloud charged with electricity and producing lightning and thunder

thun·der·head (-hed′) *n.* a round mass of cumulus clouds coming before a thunderstorm

thun·der·ous (-əs) *adj.* **1.** full of or making thunder **2.** making a noise like thunder [*thunderous* applause] —**thun′der·ous·ly** *adv.*

thun·der·show·er (-shou′ər), **thun·der·squall** (-skwôl′), **thun·der·storm** (-stôrm′) *n.* a shower (or squall or storm) with thunder and lightning

thun·der·struck (-struk′) *adj.* amazed or shocked as if struck by a thunderbolt: also **thun·der·strick·en** (-strik′'n)

Thur·ber (thur′bər), James (Grover) 1894–1961; U.S. writer, humorist, & cartoonist

thu·ri·ble (thoor′ə b'l, thur′-) *n.* [< L. < *thuris*, genitive of *thus*, incense < Gr. *thyos*, sacrifice] same as CENSER

Thu·rin·gi·a (thoo rin′jē ə) region of SW East Germany —**Thu·rin′gi·an** *adj., n.*

Thurs., Thur. Thursday

Thurs·day (thurz′dē, -dā) *n.* [< OE. < ON. *Thorsdagr*, Thor's day] the fifth day of the week

Thurs·days (-dēz, -dāz) *adv.* on or during every Thursday [*Thursdays* he bowls]

thus (thus) *adv.* [OE.] **1.** in this or that manner; in the way just stated or in the following manner [do it *thus*] **2.** to this or that degree or extent; so [*thus* far] **3.** consequently; therefore; hence [he is ill and *thus* absent] **4.** for example

[Map of East Germany / West Germany / Czechoslovakia showing THURINGIA, Erfurt, Bavaria] THURINGIA

thwack (thwak) *vt.* [prob. echoic] to strike with something flat; whack —*n.* a blow with something flat

thwart (thwôrt) *adj.* [ON. *thvert*, transverse] lying across something else —*adv., prep.* archaic var. of ATHWART —*n.* **1.** a rower's seat extending across a boat **2.** a brace extending across a canoe —*vt.* to keep from doing or being done; block or hinder (a person, plans, etc.) [the teacher *thwarted* their efforts to cheat]

thy (thī) *adj.* [ME. *thi* < *thin*, thy] of, belonging to, or done by thee: archaic or poet. var. of *your*: see also THINE, THOU

thyme (tīm) *n.* [< MFr. < L. < Gr. *thymon* < *thyein*, to offer sacrifice] any of various shrubby plants or herbs of the mint family, with white, pink, or red flowers and fragrant leaves used to flavor food —**thym′ic** *adj.*

thy·mine (thī′mēn, -min) *n.* [G. *thymin* < Gr. *thymos*, spirit + G. *-in*, -INE[4]] a white, crystalline base, $C_5H_6N_2O_2$, one of the substances forming the genetic code in DNA molecules

thy·mol (thī′môl, -mōl) *n.* [THYM(E) + -OL[1]] a colorless compound, $C_{10}H_{14}O$, extracted from thyme or made synthetically: used as an antiseptic, as in mouthwashes

thy·mus (thī′məs) *n.* [ModL. < Gr. *thymos*] a ductless, glandlike body near the throat: its function is not clearly known and it disappears in the adult: also **thymus gland** —**thy′mic** *adj.*

---

fat, āpe, cär; ten, ēven; is, bīte; gō, hôrn, tōōl, lŏŏk; oil, out; up, fur; get; joy; yet; chin; she; thin, then; zh, leisure; ŋ, ring; ə for a in ago, e in agent, i in sanity, o in comply, u in focus; ' as in able (ā′b'l); Fr. bäl; ë, Fr. coeur; ö, Fr. feu; Fr. mon; ô, Fr. coq; ü, Fr. duc; r, Fr. cri; H, G. ich; kh, G. doch; ‡foreign; ☆ Americanism; < derived from. See inside front cover.

thy·roid (thī′roid) *adj.* [ModL. < Gr. < *thyreos*, door-shaped shield < *thyra*, door + *-eidēs*, -OID] **1.** designating or of a large ductless gland near the trachea, secreting the hormone thyroxine, which regulates body growth and metabolism **2.** designating or of the principal cartilage of the larynx, forming the Adam's apple —*n.* **1.** the thyroid gland **2.** the thyroid cartilage **3.** a preparation of the thyroid gland of certain animals, used in treating goiter, etc.: also **thyroid extract**

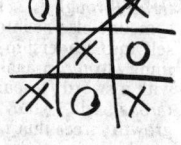

THYROID

thy·rox·ine (thī räk′sēn, -sin) *n.* [THYR(OID) + OX(Y)-¹ + -INE⁴] a colorless, crystalline compound, $C_{15}H_{11}I_4NO_4$, the active hormone of the thyroid gland, often made synthetically and used in treating goiter, etc.: also **thy·rox′in** (-sin)

thyr·sus (thur′səs) *n.,* pl. **-si** (-sī) [L. < Gr. *thyrsos*] *Gr. Myth.* a staff tipped with a pine cone and sometimes entwined with ivy, carried by Dionysus, the satyrs, etc.

thy·self (thī self′) *pron. reflexive or intensive form of* THOU: an archaic or poet. var. of *yourself*

ti (tē) *n.* [altered < *si*: see GAMUT, SOL-FA] *Music* a syllable representing the seventh tone of the diatonic scale

Ti *Chem.* titanium

ti·ar·a (tē er′ə, -ar′ə, -är′ə; tī-) *n.* [L. < Gr. *tiara*] **1.** an ancient Persian headdress **2.** the Pope's triple crown **3.** a woman's coronetlike headdress, often jeweled

Ti·ber (tī′bər) river in C Italy, flowing from the Apennines south through Rome into the Tyrrhenian Sea

Ti·ber·i·as (tī bir′ē əs), **Sea of** *same as* the Sea of GALILEE

Ti·ber·i·us (tī bir′ē əs) (*Tiberius Claudius Nero Caesar*) 42 B.C.–37 A.D.; Rom. emperor (14 A.D.–37 A.D.)

Ti·bet (ti bet′) autonomous region of SW China, north of the Himalayas: 471,660 sq. mi.; cap. Lhasa

Ti·bet·an (ti bet′'n) *adj.* of Tibet, its people, their language, etc. —*n.* **1.** a member of the Mongolic people of Tibet **2.** the Sino-Tibetan language of Tibet

tib·i·a (tib′ē ə) *n.,* pl. **-i·ae** (-i ē′), **-i·as** [L.] **1.** the inner and thicker of the two bones of the leg below the knee; shinbone **2.** a corresponding bone in the leg of other vertebrates —**tib′i·al** *adj.*

tic (tik) *n.* [Fr. < ?] a twitching of a muscle, esp. of the face, that is not consciously controlled

tick¹ (tik) *n.* [prob. < Gmc. echoic base] **1.** a light clicking or tapping sound, as that made by a clock **2.** a mark made to check off items; check mark (✔, ✓, etc.) **3.** [Brit. Colloq.] a moment; instant —*vi.* **1.** to make a tick or ticks, as a clock **2.** [Colloq.] to function; work *[what makes him tick?]* —*vt.* **1.** to mark or count by a tick or ticks *[his watch ticked away the seconds]* **2.** [Chiefly Brit.] to check off (an item in a list, etc.) with a tick (usually with *off*)

tick² (tik) *n.* [OE. *ticia*] any of a large group of bloodsucking arachnids that are parasitic on man, cattle, sheep, etc., including many species that transmit diseases

tick³ (tik) *n.* [ult. < L. < Gr. *thēkē*, a case] **1.** the cloth case that is filled with cotton, feathers, etc. to form a mattress or pillow **2.** [Colloq.] *same as* TICKING

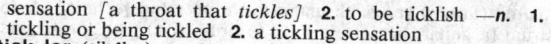

TICK
(¼ in. long)

tick⁴ (tik) *n.* [< TICKET] [Chiefly Brit. Colloq.] credit; trust *[to buy something on tick]*

tick·er (tik′ər) *n.* a person or thing that ticks; specif., ☆*a*) a telegraphic device that records stock market quotations, etc. on paper tape (**ticker tape**) *b*) [Old Slang] a watch *c*) [Slang] the heart

tick·et (tik′it) *n.* [< obs. Fr. *etiquet* (now *étiquette*), a ticket] **1.** a printed card or piece of paper that gives one a specified right, as to attend a theater, ride a bus, etc. **2.** a label or tag, as on a piece of merchandise, giving the size, price, etc. ☆**3.** the list of candidates nominated by a political party in an election; slate ☆**4.** [Colloq.] a summons to court for a traffic violation —*vt.* **1.** to label or tag with a ticket ☆**2.** to issue a ticket to

tick·ing (tik′iŋ) *n.* [see TICK³] a strong, heavy cloth, often striped, used for casings of mattresses, pillows, etc.

tick·le (tik′'l) *vt.* **-led, -ling** [ME. *tikelen*] **1.** to please, gratify, etc.: often used in slang phrases, as **tickled pink** (or **silly, to death,** etc.) **2.** to amuse *[the joke really tickled her]* **3.** to touch or stroke lightly so as to cause twitching, laughter, etc. *[to tickle someone's ear]* —*vi.* **1.** to have a scratching or tingling

sensation *[a throat that tickles]* **2.** to be ticklish —*n.* **1.** a tickling or being tickled **2.** a tickling sensation

tick·ler (tik′lər) *n.* **1.** a person or thing that tickles ☆**2.** a memorandum pad, file, etc. for reminding one of things that need to be taken care of at certain future dates

tick·lish (tik′lish) *adj.* **1.** sensitive to tickling *[ticklish under the arms]* **2.** very sensitive or easily upset; touchy *[ticklish about politics]* **3.** needing careful handling; delicate *[a ticklish situation]* —**tick′lish·ly** *adv.* —**tick′lish·ness** *n.*

tick-tack-toe, tic-tac-toe (tik′tak tō′) *n.* a game in which two players take turns marking either X's or O's in an open block of nine squares, the object being to complete a line of three of one's mark first

tick-tock (tik′täk′) *n.* the sound made by a clock —*vi.* to make this sound

Ti·con·der·o·ga (tī′kän də rō′gə), **Fort** [< Iroquoian, lit., between two lakes] former fort in northeastern N.Y., taken from the British by Am. Revolutionary soldiers in 1775

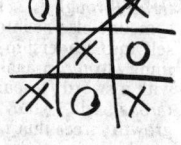

TICK-TACK-TOE

tid·al (tīd′'l) *adj.* of, having, caused by, determined by, or dependent on a tide or tides —**tid′al·ly** *adv.*

tidal wave 1. in popular usage, an unusually great, destructive wave sent inshore by an earthquake or a very strong wind ☆**2.** any great, widespread movement, expression of feeling, etc.

tid·bit (tid′bit′) *n.* [dial. *tid*, small object + BIT²] a choice bit of food, gossip, etc.

tid·dly·winks (tid′lē wiŋks′, tid′'l ē-) *n.* a game in which the players try to snap little colored disks into a cup by pressing their edges with a larger disk: also **tid′dle·dy·winks′** (-'l dē wiŋks′)

tide (tīd) *n.* [OE. *tid*, time] **1.** a period of time: now only in combination *[Eastertide]* **2.** *a*) the alternate rise and fall of the surface of oceans, seas, etc., caused by the attraction of the moon and sun: it occurs twice in each period of 24 hours and 50 minutes *b*) *same as* FLOOD TIDE **3.** something that rises and falls like the tide **4.** a stream, current, trend, etc. *[the tide of public opinion]* **5.** [Archaic] an opportune time —*adj. same as* TIDAL —*vi.* **tid′ed, tid′ing** to surge like a tide —*vt.* to carry as with the tide —**tide over** to help along for a time, esp. through a time of difficulty —**turn the tide** to reverse a condition

☆**tide·land** (tīd′land′, -lənd) *n.* **1.** land covered by water at high tide and uncovered at low tide **2.** [*pl.*] loosely, land under water just beyond this and within territorial limits

tide·mark (-märk′) *n.* the high-water mark or, sometimes, the low-water mark of the tide

tide·wa·ter (-wôt′ər, -wät′-) *n.* **1.** water, as in some streams along a coastline, that is affected by the tide ☆**2.** an area in which water is affected by the tide —*adj.* of or along a tidewater

ti·dings (tī′diŋz) *n.pl.* [OE. *tidung*] news; information

ti·dy (tī′dē) *adj.* **-di·er, -di·est** [ult. < OE. *tid*, time] **1.** neat in personal appearance, ways, etc.; orderly *[a tidy housekeeper]* **2.** neat; in order; trim *[a tidy apartment]* **3.** [Colloq.] *a*) fairly good; satisfactory *[a tidy arrangement]* *b*) rather large; considerable *[a tidy sum]* —*vt., vi.* **-died, -dy·ing** to make (things) tidy (often with *up*) —*n., pl.* **-dies** *same as* ANTIMACASSAR —see SYN. at NEAT¹ —**ti′di·ly** *adv.* —**ti′di·ness** *n.*

tie (tī) *vt.* **tied, ty′ing** [OE. *tigan* < base of *teag*, a rope] **1.** to fasten or bind together or to something else, as with string or rope made secure by knotting, etc. *[to tie someone's hands; to tie a boat to a pier]* **2.** to tighten and knot the laces, strings, etc. of *[to tie one's shoes]* **3.** *a*) to make (a knot or bow) *b*) to make a knot or bow in *[to tie a necktie]* **4.** to join or bind in any way *[tied by common interests]* **5.** to confine; restrict *[tied to the house while convalescing]* **6.** to equal (the score, record, etc.) of (opponents, a rival, etc.) **7.** *Music* to connect with a tie —*vi.* to make a tie *[to tie easily]* —*n.* **1.** a string, cord, etc. used to tie things **2.** something that joins, binds, etc.; bond *[a business tie; ties of friendship]* **3.** something that confines or restricts *[legal ties]* **4.** short for NECKTIE **5.** a beam, rod, etc. that holds together and strengthens parts of a building ☆**6.** any of the parallel crossbeams to which the rails of a railroad are fastened **7.** *a*) an equality of scores, votes, etc. in a contest *b*) a contest in which scores, etc. are equal **8.** [*pl.*] low, laced shoes **9.** *Music* a curved line joining two notes of the same pitch, showing that the tone is to be held without a break —*adj.* that has been tied, or made equal *[a tie score]* —**tie down** to confine; restrain; restrict *[tied down by household duties]* —☆**tie in** **1.** to bring into or have a connection **2.** to make or be consistent, harmonious, etc. *[his report ties in with hers]* —**tie off** to close off passage through by tying with something *[to tie* *off* an artery] —**tie up** **1.** to tie securely **2.** to wrap up and tie with string, etc. **3.** to moor (a ship or boat) to a dock ☆**4.** to block or hinder [communications were *tied up*] **5.** to cause to be already in use, committed, etc. [the gym is *tied up* for today] **SYN.**—**tie** suggests the connection of one thing with another by means of a rope, string, etc. which can be knotted [to *tie* a horse to a hitching post]; **bind** suggests the use of an encircling band which holds two or more things firmly together [to *bind* someone's arms]; **fasten** implies a joining of one thing to another in various ways, as by tying, binding, gluing, nailing, pinning, etc. [to *fasten* a mirror to the wall]; **attach** emphasizes the joining of two or more things in order to keep them together as a unit [to *attach* tags to a package] —**ANT.** separate, part

tie·back (tī′bak′) *n.* ☆**1.** a sash, ribbon, tape, etc. used to tie curtains or draperies to one side ☆**2.** a curtain with a tieback

tie beam a horizontal beam serving as a tie (*n.* 5)

tie clasp a decorative clasp for fastening a necktie to the shirt front: also **tie clip, tie bar**

tie-dye (tī′dī′) *n.* **1.** a method of dyeing designs on cloth by tightly tying bunches of it with thread, etc. so that the dye affects only exposed parts **2.** cloth so decorated or a design so made —*vt.* **-dyed′, -dye′ing** to dye in this way

☆**tie-in** (tī′in′) *adj.* designating or of a sale in which an item in demand can be bought only along with some other item —*n.* **1.** a tie-in sale or advertisement **2.** a connection or relationship

tie line ☆**1.** a direct telephone line between extensions in one or more PBX systems ☆**2.** a line used to connect one electric power or transportation system with another

Tien Shan (tyen shän) mountain system in C Asia, extending across the Kirghiz S.S.R. & Sinkiang, China

Tien·tsin (tin′tsin′; *Chin.* tyen′jin′) seaport in NE China, on an arm of the Yellow Sea: pop. c. 4,000,000

tie·pin (tī′pin′) *n.* same as **STICKPIN**

Tie·po·lo (tye′pō lō), **Gio·van·ni Bat·tis·ta** (jō vän′nē bät-tēs′tä) 1696–1770; Venetian painter

tier[1] (tir) *n.* [< MFr. *tire*, order] any of a series of layers or rows, as of seats, arranged one above or behind another —*vt., vi.* to arrange or be arranged in tiers —**tiered** *adj.*

ti·er[2] (tī′ər) *n.* a person or thing that ties

tierce (turs) *n.* [often **T-**] same as **TERCE**

tie rod **1.** a horizontal rod serving as a tie (*n.* 5) **2.** a rod connecting a front wheel of an automotive vehicle to the steering mechanism

Tier·ra del Fue·go (tyer′rä del fwe′gō; *E.* tē er′ə del′ foo-ā′gō) **1.** a group of islands at the tip of S. America, divided between Argentina & Chile **2.** chief island of this group See map at Strait of MAGELLAN

☆**tie tack** an ornamental pin with a short point that fits into a snap, used to fasten a necktie to the shirt front

tie-up (tī′up′) *n.* ☆**1.** a temporary stoppage or interruption of work, traffic, etc. **2.** connection, relation, or involvement

tiff (tif) *n.* [? related to **SNIFF**] **1.** a slight fit of anger or bad humor **2.** a slight quarrel; spat —*vi.* to be in or have a tiff

tif·fin (tif′in) *n., vi.* Anglo-Ind. term for **LUNCH**

ti·ger (tī′gər) *n., pl.* **-gers, -ger:** see PLURAL, II, D, 1 [< OE. & OFr., both < L. < Gr. *tigris*] **1.** a large, flesh-eating animal of the cat family, native to Asia, having a tawny coat striped with black **2.** a person who moves or acts with force, violence, etc. —☆**have a tiger by the tail** to find oneself in a situation more difficult to handle than one expected —**ti′ger·ish** *adj.*

tiger beetle any of various brightly colored beetles, often striped, whose larvae burrow in soil and feed on other insects

tiger lily a lily having orange flowers with purplish-black spots

tiger moth any of a group of moths with brightly striped or spotted wings

tiger's eye a semiprecious, yellow-brown stone: also **ti′ger·eye′** *n.*

tight (tīt) *adj.* [< OE. *-thight*, strong] **1.** made so that water, air, etc. cannot pass through [a *tight* boat] **2.** drawn, packed, spaced, etc. closely together [a *tight* weave; a *tight* schedule of events] **3.** [Dial.] snug; trim; neat **4.** fixed securely; firm [a *tight* joint] **5.** fully stretched; taut; not slack or loose [a *tight* wire] **6.** fitting so closely as to be uncomfortable [*tight* shoes] **7.** strict [*tight* control] **8.**

TIGER LILY

difficult to manage: esp. in the phrase **a tight corner** (or **squeeze**, etc.), a difficult situation **9.** showing strain [a *tight* smile] **10.** almost even or tied [a *tight* race] **11.** sharp: said of a spiral, turn, etc. **12.** *a)* difficult to get; scarce [money is *tight* when interest rates on loans are high] *b)* characterized by such scarcity [a *tight* market for steel] **13.** concise: said of language, style, etc. **14.** [Colloq.] stingy **15.** [Slang] drunk —*adv.* in a tight manner; esp., *a)* securely or firmly [hold *tight*] *b)* [Colloq.] soundly [sleep *tight*] —**sit tight** to keep one's opinion or position and wait —**tight′ly** *adv.* —**tight′ness** *n.*

-tight (tīt) [< prec.] *a combining form meaning* not letting (something specified) in or out [watertight, airtight]

tight·en (tīt′'n) *vt., vi.* to make or become tight or tighter —**tight′en·er** *n.*

tight·fist·ed (tīt′fis′tid) *adj.* stingy

tight-fit·ting (-fit′iŋ) *adj.* fitting very tight

tight-knit (-nit′) *adj.* **1.** tightly knit **2.** well organized

tight-lipped (-lipt′) *adj.* **1.** having the lips closed tightly **2.** not saying much; keeping secrets

tight·rope (-rōp′) *n.* a rope stretched tight on which acrobats do balancing acts

tights (tīts) *n.pl.* a garment that fits tightly over the legs and the lower part of the body, worn by acrobats, dancers, etc.

☆**tight·wad** (tīt′wäd′, -wôd′) *n.* [TIGHT + WAD] [Slang] a stingy person; miser

ti·glon (tī′glän′, -glən) *n.* (TIG(ER) + L(I)ON) the offspring of a male tiger and a female lion: also **ti′gon** (-gän′, -gən)

ti·gress (tī′gris) *n.* a female tiger

Ti·gris (tī′gris) river flowing from EC Turkey through Iraq, joining the Euphrates to form the Shatt-al-Arab

Ti·jua·na (tē wä′nə, tē′ə wä′-; *Sp.* tē hwä′nä) city in Baja California, on the U.S. border: pop. 335,000

tike (tīk) *n.* same as **TYKE**

til·bu·ry (til′bər ē) *n., pl.* **-ries** [< *Tilbury*, a London coach builder] a light, two-wheeled carriage for two persons

til·de (til′də) *n.* [Sp. < L. *titulus*, title, sign] a diacritical mark (~) used in various ways, as over an *n* in Spanish to indicate a palatal nasal sound (ny), as in *señor*

Til·den (til′d'n), **Samuel Jones** 1814–86; U.S. politician

tile (tīl) *n.* [OE. *tigele*, ult. < L. *tegula*] **1.** *a)* a thin piece of glazed or unglazed, fired clay, stone, etc. used for roofing, flooring, decorative borders, bathroom walls, etc. *b)* a similar piece of plastic, asphalt, etc., used to cover floors, walls, etc. **2.** tiles collectively **3.** a drain of semicircular tiles or earthenware pipe **4.** burnt-clay, hollow blocks, used variously in construction **5.** any of the pieces in mah-jongg or some other games —*vt.* **tiled, til′ing** to cover with tiles —**til′er** *n.*

til·ing (tīl′iŋ) *n.* **1.** the action of a person who tiles **2.** tiles collectively **3.** a covering of tiles

till[1] (til) *prep., conj.* [OE. *til*] same as **UNTIL**

till[2] (til) *vt., vi.* [OE. *tilian*, lit., to strive for] to work (land) in raising crops, as by plowing, fertilizing, etc.; cultivate —**till′a·ble** *adj.*

till[3] (til) *n.* [< ? ME. *tillen*, to draw] **1.** a drawer or tray, as in a store counter, for keeping money **2.** ready cash

till·age (til′ij) *n.* **1.** the tilling of land **2.** land that is tilled

till·er[1] (til′ər) *n.* [< OFr. < ML. *telarium*, roller in a loom < L. *tela*, a web] a bar or handle for turning a boat's rudder

till·er[2] (til′ər) *n.* a person who tills the soil

tilt (tilt) *vt.* [prob. < OE. *tealt*, shaky] **1.** to cause to slope or slant; tip [to *tilt* a table] **2.** *a)* to poise or thrust (a lance) in or as in a tilt *b)* to charge at (one's opponent) in a tilt —*vi.* **1.** to slope; incline [the shack *tilts* to the left] **2.** to poise or thrust one's lance (*at* one's opponent) in a tilt **3.** to take part in a tilt or joust **4.** to dispute, argue, contend, etc. [to *tilt* with a lecturer] —*n.* **1.** a contest in which two knights on horseback thrust with lances in an attempt to unseat each other **2.** any spirited contest, dispute, etc. between persons **3.** *a)* the act of tilting, or sloping *b)* a slope or slant —(**at) full tilt** at full speed; with the greatest force —**tilt′er** *n.*

TILLER

tilth (tilth) *n.* [OE. < *tilian*: see TILL²] **1.** a tilling of land **2.** tilled land

Tim. Timothy

tim·bal (tim′b'l) *n.* [< Fr. < Sp. < Ar. < *al*, the + *tabl*, drum] *same as* KETTLEDRUM

tim·bale (tim′b'l) *n.* [Fr.: see prec.] **1.** a custardlike dish made with chicken, lobster, fish, etc. and baked in a small drum-shaped mold **2.** a type of fried or baked pastry shell, filled with a cooked food

tim·ber (tim′bər) *n.* [OE.] **1.** wood for building houses, ships, etc. **2.** a large, heavy piece of wood prepared for use in building; beam **3.** trees or forests; timberland **4.** personal quality or character [a man of his *timber*] **5.** a wooden rib of a ship —*vt.* to provide, build, or prop up with timbers —*adj.* of or for timber —*interj.* a warning shout by a lumberman that a cut tree is about to fall —**tim′bered** *adj.* —**tim′ber·ing** *n.*

timber hitch *Naut.* a knot used for tying a rope to a spar

☆**tim·ber·land** (tim′bər land′) *n.* land with trees suitable for timber; wooded land

☆**tim·ber·line** (-līn′) *n.* the line above or beyond which trees do not grow, as on mountains or in polar regions

timber wolf *same as* GRAY WOLF

tim·bre (tam′bər, tim′-) *n.* [Fr., earlier, sound of a bell < MFr. < OFr., ult. < Gr. *tympanon*, a drum] the quality of sound, apart from pitch or loudness, that makes one voice or musical instrument different from another

tim·brel (tim′brəl) *n.* [< OFr.: see prec.] an ancient type of tambourine

Tim·buk·tu (tim′buk tōō′, tim buk′tōō) town in C Mali, near the Niger River: pop. 9,000

time (tīm) *n.* [OE. *tima*] **1.** the past, present, and future; every minute there has been or ever will be **2.** a system of measuring the passing of hours [solar *time*, standard *time*] **3.** the period between two events or during which something exists, happens, or acts [an hour's *time*] **4.** [*usually pl.*] a period of history [medieval *times*, Lincoln's *time*] **5.** *a*) a period characterized by a certain state of affairs or a specific experience [a *time* of peace, have a good *time*] *b*) [*usually pl.*] conditions as they are [*times* are bad] **6.** a set period or term, as a lifetime or a term of imprisonment, apprenticeship, military service, etc. [to serve *time*] **7.** a period necessary, sufficient, measured, etc. for something [*time* for play, a baking *time* of ten minutes] **8.** *a*) the period worked or to be worked by an employee *b*) the hourly rate of pay for the regular working hours [to get double *time* for holiday work] **9.** rate of speed in marching, driving, etc. [quick *time*] **10.** a precise instant, minute, hour, day, year, etc., determined by clock or calendar [the *time* is 5:17 P.M.] **11.** the point at which something happens; occasion [game *time* is 2:00 P.M.] **12.** the usual or set moment for something to happen, begin, or end [*time* to get up]; specif., ☆one's turn [a *time* at bat] **13.** the suitable or proper moment [now is the *time* to act] **14.** any one of a series of moments at which the same thing happens, is done, etc. [for the fifth *time*, *time* and *time* again] **15.** *Music a*) the grouping of rhythmic beats into measures of equal length *b*) the characteristic rhythm of a piece of music in terms of this grouping [waltz *time*] *c*) the rate of speed at which a composition is played; tempo *d*) the length of a note or rest ☆**16.** *Sports same as* TIMEOUT —*interj. Sports* a signal that a period of play or activity is ended or that play is being stopped for a short time —*vt.* **timed, tim′ing 1.** to arrange the time of so as to be acceptable or suitable, favorable, etc. [he *timed* his visit to find her at home] **2.** to adjust, set, etc. so as to be alike in time [*time* your watch with mine] **3.** to set the length of (a syllable or musical note) as a unit of rhythm **4.** to measure or record the pace, speed, etc. of [to *time* a runner] —*adj.* **1.** having to do with time **2.** set to explode, open, etc. at a given time [a *time* bomb] **3.** payable later [a *time* loan] ☆**4.** designating or of any of a series of payments made over a period of time —**abreast of the times** up to date **2.** informed about current matters —**against time** trying to finish in a given time —☆**ahead of time** sooner than due; early —**at one time 1.**

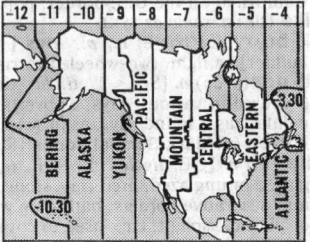

TIME ZONES

together **2.** earlier; formerly —**at the same time 1.** together **2.** nonetheless; however —**at times** occasionally; sometimes —**behind the times** out-of-date; old-fashioned —**behind time** late —**do time** [Colloq.] to serve a prison term —**for the time being** for the present; temporarily —**from time to time** at intervals; now and then —**in good time 1.** at the proper time **2.** in a short time; quickly —**in no time** very quickly —**in time 1.** eventually **2.** before it is too late **3.** keeping the set tempo, pace, etc. —**make time** to travel, work, etc. at a fast rate of speed [we made (good) *time* between Boston and Albany] —**many a time** often; frequently —**on time** ☆**1.** at the set time; punctual(ly) ☆**2.** to be paid for in installments over a period of time [buying a car on *time*] —**pass the time of day** to exchange a few words of greeting, etc. —**time after time** again and again; continually: also **time and again** —☆**time of one's life** [Colloq.] an experience of great pleasure for one —**time on one's hands** a period of time with nothing to do —**time was** there was a time [*time was* when I enjoyed music like that]

time and a half a rate of payment one and a half times the usual rate, as for working overtime

☆**time capsule** a container holding articles of the present time, buried or preserved for a future age

☆**time clock** a clock with a device for marking on a card (**timecard**) the time at which an employee begins and ends a work period

time exposure 1. a relatively long exposure of photographic film, generally for more than half a second **2.** a photograph taken in this way

time-hon·ored (tīm′än′ərd) *adj.* honored because it is very old or has been in use for a long time

time·keep·er (-kē′pər) *n.* **1.** *same as* TIMEPIECE **2.** a person who keeps track of time, as in some sports, or one who keeps a record of the hours worked by employees

time-lapse (-laps′) *adj.* of a technique of photographing a slow process, as the growth of a plant, on motion-picture film by exposing single frames at widely spaced intervals: the film is projected at regular speed to show the process speeded up

time·less (-lis) *adj.* **1.** unending **2.** eternal **3.** not limited to a specific time; always valid or true [*timeless* art] —**time′less·ly** *adv.* —**time′less·ness** *n.*

time limit a fixed period of time during which something must be done or ended

☆**time lock** a lock with a mechanism that keeps it from being opened before the time set

time·ly (-lē) *adj.* **-li·er, -li·est** happening, done, said, etc. at a suitable time; well-timed; opportune —**time′li·ness** *n.*

SYN.—*timely* applies to that which happens or is done at a proper or suitable time, esp. at such a time as to be of help or use [a *timely* interruption]; *opportune* refers to that which comes at just the right time, often as if by accident, so that it meets the needs of the occasion exactly [the *opportune* arrival of a supply train]; *seasonable* applies to that which is well suited to the season of the year or to the moment or occasion [*seasonable* weather; a *seasonable* hint]

time·out (-out′) *n.* ☆*Sports*, etc. a short period of time during which play in a game is stopped

time·piece (-pēs′) *n.* any device for measuring and recording time; esp., a clock or watch

tim·er (tī′mər) *n.* **1.** *same as*: *a*) TIMEKEEPER *b*) STOPWATCH ☆**2.** in internal-combustion engines, a mechanism for causing the spark to be produced in the cylinder at the right time **3.** a device for timing, or automatically starting and stopping, some mechanism

times (tīmz) *prep.* multiplied by: symbol, × [two *times* three is six]

time·sav·ing (tīm′sā′viŋ) *adj.* that saves time because of greater efficiency, etc. —**time′sav′er** *n.*

time·serv·er (-sur′vər) *n.* a person who tries to get a more important position, more money, etc. by changing his opinions to suit the mood of the times or to please those in power; toady —**time′serv′ing** *n., adj.*

☆**time sharing** a system allowing a computer to be used for a number of tasks fed in from different locations at the same time

time signature *Music* a sign, usually like a numerical fraction, coming after the key signature and showing the time, or tempo

time study a study of the time it takes a worker to do a certain task and of the movements he makes in doing it: such studies are usually made in order to find ways of increasing efficiency: in full, **time and motion study**

time·ta·ble (-tā′b'l) *n.* a schedule of the times when certain things are to happen, esp. of the times of arrival and departure of planes, trains, buses, etc.

time-test·ed (-tes′tid) *adj.* having value proved by long use or experience

time warp the condition or process of being moved from one point in time to another, as in science fiction

time·worn (-wôrn′) *adj.* **1.** showing signs of wear or damage because of age or long use **2.** overused; trite [a *time-worn* plot for a novel]

☆**time zone** *see* STANDARD TIME and illustration at TIME

tim·id (tim′id) *adj.* [< L. < *timere,* to fear] **1.** easily frightened or shy **2.** showing lack of self-confidence [a *timid* reply] —**ti-mid·i·ty** (tə mid′ə tē), **tim′id·ness** *n.* —**tim′id·ly** *adv.*

tim·ing (tī′miŋ) *n.* **1.** the arranging or setting of the speed or time of doing something so as to get the best results [the *timing* of an engine, of a golfer's swing, of an announcement, etc.] **2.** measurement of time, as with a stopwatch

Ti·mor (tē′môr, ti môr′) island of Indonesia, in the SE Malay Archipelago: c. 13,000 sq. mi.

tim·or·ous (tim′ər əs) *adj.* [< MFr. < ML. < L. *timor,* fear] **1.** full of fear or easily frightened; timid **2.** showing or caused by timidity —**tim′or·ous·ly** *adv.* —**tim′or·ous·ness** *n.*

Tim·o·thy (tim′ə thē) [< Fr. < L. < Gr. < *timē,* honor + *theos,* god] **1.** a masculine name **2.** *Bible a)* a disciple of the Apostle Paul *b)* either of the epistles from the Apostle Paul to Timothy, books of the New Testament

tim·o·thy (tim′ə thē) *n.* [after *Timothy* Hanson, who took the seed to the Carolinas, c. 1720] ☆a perennial grass with long spikes, widely grown for hay

tim·pa·ni (tim′pə nē) *n.pl., sing.* **-pa·no′** (-nō′) [It.: see TYMPANUM] kettledrums; esp., a set of kettledrums of different pitches played by one person in an orchestra —**tim′pa·nist** *n.*

Ti·mur (tē mo͞or′) *see* TAMERLANE

tin (tin) *n.* [OE.] **1.** a soft, silver-white, metallic chemical element, easily shaped at ordinary temperatures: symbol, Sn; at. wt., 118.69; at. no., 50 **2.** *same as* TIN PLATE **3.** *a)* a pan, box, etc. made of tin plate *b)* [Chiefly Brit.] a can used for preserving food; also, its contents —*vt.* **tinned, tin′ning** **1.** to cover or plate with tin **2.** [Chiefly Brit.] to put in cans for preservation; can

tin·a·mou (tin′ə mo͞o′) *n.* [Fr. < Carib name, *tinamu*] a bird of South and Central America that looks like the partridge and quail, but is related to the ostrich

☆**tin can** **1.** a can used for preserving food **2.** [Slang] *same as* DESTROYER (sense 2)

tinc·ture (tiŋk′chər) *n.* [< L. *tinctura* < pp. of *tingere,* to dye] **1.** orig., a dye **2.** a light color; tint; tinge **3.** a slight trace, smattering, etc. [there is some *tincture* of truth in what she says] **4.** a medicinal substance in a solution of alcohol or alcohol and water [tincture of quinine] —*vt.* **-tured, -tur·ing** **1.** to color lightly; tint; tinge **2.** to give a slight trace to [a message *tinctured* with hope]

TINAMOU
(to 18 in. long)

tin·der (tin′dər) *n.* [OE. *tynder*] any dry material that catches fire easily, esp. as formerly used for starting a fire from a spark made by flint and steel struck together

tin·der·box (-bäks′) *n.* **1.** formerly, a metal box for holding tinder, flint, and steel for starting a fire **2.** any object, building, etc. that can catch fire easily **3.** any place or situation in which trouble, war, etc. is likely to flare up

tine (tīn) *n.* [OE. *tind*] a slender, pointed part that sticks out; prong [the *tines* of a fork] —**tined** *adj.*

tin·e·a (tin′ē ə) *n.* [< L., a gnawing worm, moth] any of various skin diseases caused by a fungus; esp., ringworm

tin ear [Colloq.] ☆a seeming inability to hear music or a certain kind of music with understanding or appreciation

tin·foil (tin′foil′) *n.* a very thin sheet or sheets of tin or an alloy of tin and lead, etc., used as a wrapping for food products, in insulation, etc.

ting[1] (tiŋ) *n.* [echoic] a single, light, ringing sound, as of a small bell being struck —*vt., vi.* to make or cause to make a ting

‡**ting**[2] (tiŋ) *n. same as* THING[2]

ting-a-ling (tiŋ′ə liŋ′) *n.* the sound of a small bell ringing again and again

tinge (tinj) *vt.* **tinged, tinge′ing** or **ting′ing** [L. *tingere,* to dye] **1.** to color slightly; give a tint to [northern lights *tinged* the sky] **2.** to give a trace, slight flavor or odor, shade, etc. to [joy *tinged* with sorrow] —*n.* **1.** a slight coloring; tint **2.** a slight trace, flavor, odor, etc.

tin·gle (tiŋ′g'l) *vi.* **-gled, -gling** [< ME. var. of *tinklen,* to tinkle] **1.** to have a prickling or stinging feeling, as from cold, excitement, etc. **2.** to cause this feeling —*n.* this feeling —**tin′-gler** *n.* —**tin′gling·ly** *adv.* —**tin′gly** *adj.* **-gli·er, -gli·est**

☆**tin god** a person who is not worthy of the honor or respect he demands or receives

☆**tin·horn** (tin′hôrn′) *adj.* [Slang] cheap, showy, and phony —*n.* [Slang] a tinhorn person, esp. a gambler

tin·ker (tiŋ′kər) *n.* [< ?] **1.** a person who mends pots, pans, etc., usually one who travels about doing this **2.** a person who can make all kinds of minor repairs **3.** a clumsy or unskillful worker; bungler —*vi.* **1.** to work as a tinker **2.** to make clumsy attempts to mend something **3.** to fuss with something in a useless or careless way; putter —**tin′ker·er** *n.*

tinker's damn (or **dam**) [< prec. + DAMN: with reference to the low social standing and profane speech of tinkers] something of no value: esp. in **not worth a tinker's damn**

☆**Tin·ker·toy** (tiŋ′kər toi′) *a trademark for* a toy set of wooden dowels, joints, wheels, etc., used by children to form structures —*n.* [**t-**] anything looking like or suggesting such a structure

tin·kle (tiŋ′k'l) *vi.* **-kled, -kling** [echoic] to make a series of light, clinking sounds like those of a very small bell —*vt.* **1.** to cause to tinkle **2.** to show, signal, etc. by tinkling —*n.* the act or sound of tinkling —**tin′kler** *n.* —**tin′kly** *adj.* **-kli·er, -kli·est**

☆**tin liz·zie** (liz′ē) [orig. nickname of an early model of Ford automobile] any cheap or old automobile

tin·ner (tin′ər) *n.* **1.** a tin miner **2.** *same as* TINSMITH

tin·ny (tin′ē) *adj.* **-ni·er, -ni·est** **1.** of or producing tin **2.** like tin; bright but cheap; not well-made [tinny jewelry] **3.** of or like the sound made in striking a tin object [tinny music] —**tin′-ni·ly** *adv.* —**tin′ni·ness** *n.*

☆**Tin Pan Alley** **1.** the center of popular music publishing in New York City **2.** the publishers, writers, and promoters of popular music

tin plate thin sheets of iron or steel plated with tin —**tin′-plate′** *vt.* **-plat′ed, -plat′ing**

tin·sel (tin′s'l, -z′l) *n.* [< MFr. *estincelle* < OFr.: see STENCIL] **1.** formerly, a cloth partly woven with glittering threads of gold, silver, etc. **2.** thin sheets, strips, or threads of tin, metal foil, etc., used for decoration, as on Christmas trees **3.** something that looks showy and fine but is really cheap and of little value —*adj.* **1.** made of or decorated with tinsel **2.** showy but of little value —*vt.* **-seled** or **-selled, -sel·ing** or **-sel·ling** **1.** to make glitter as with tinsel **2.** to give a showy, gaudy look to —**tin′sel·ly** *adj.*

tin·smith (tin′smith′) *n.* a person who works with tin or tin plate; maker of tinware: also **tin′man,** *pl.* **-men**

tint (tint) *n.* [< L. pp. of *tingere,* to dye] **1.** a delicate color or hue; tinge **2.** a color or shading of a color, esp. with reference to its mixture with white [several *tints* of green] **3.** a dye for the hair —*vt.* to give a tint to —**tint′er** *n.*

☆**tin·tin·nab·u·la·tion** (tin′ti nab′yo͞o lā′shən) *n.* [< L. *tintinnabulum,* little bell] the ringing sound of bells

Tin·to·ret·to (tēn′tô ret′tô; *E.* tin′tə ret′ō), **Il** (ēl) (born *Jacopo Robusti*) 1518–94; Venetian painter

☆**tin·type** (tin′tīp′) *n.* an old kind of photograph taken directly on a sensitized plate of enameled tin or iron

tin·ware (-wer′) *n.* pots, pans, etc. of tin plate

ti·ny (tī′nē) *adj.* **-ni·er, -ni·est** [< ME. *tine,* a little (something)] very small; minute —**see** SYN **at** SMALL —**ti′ni·ly** *adv.* —**ti′niness** *n.*

-tion (shən) [< Fr. < OFr. < L. *-tionis,* genitive of *-tio*] a suffix meaning: **1.** the act of [correction] **2.** the state of being [elation] **3.** the thing that is [creation]

-tious (shəs) [< Fr. < L. *-tiosus*] a suffix used to form adjectives from nouns ending in -TION [cautious]

tip[1] (tip) *n.* [ME. *tippe*] **1.** the pointed or rounded end or top of something [the *tip* of the nose] **2.** something attached to the end [a rubber *tip* on a cane] **3.** a top or apex, as of a mountain —*vt.* **tipped, tip′ping** **1.** to make a tip on **2.** to cover the tip or tips of [darts *tipped* with poison] **3.** to be the tip of

tip² (tip) *vt.* **tipped, tip′ping** [akin ? to prec.] **1.** to strike lightly and sharply; tap **2.** to give a small present of money to (a waitress, porter, etc.) for some service **3.** [Colloq.] to give secret information to (often with *off*) [to *tip off* the police about a robbery] ☆**4.** *Baseball* *a)* to hit (the ball) so that it glances off the bat *b)* to glance off (the bat, glove, etc.): said of the ball —*vi.* to give a tip or tips [a customer who *tips* generously] —*n.* **1.** a light, sharp blow; tap **2.** a piece of secret information [a *tip* on the race] **3.** a suggestion, hint, warning, etc. **4.** a small present of money given to a waitress, porter, etc. for services; gratuity —**tip one's hand** (or **mitt**) [Slang] to reveal one's plans, etc., often without meaning to —**tip′per** *n.*

tip³ (tip) *vt.* **tipped, tip′ping** [< ?] **1.** to overturn or upset [he *tipped* over his glass] **2.** to cause to tilt or slant [she *tipped* the bowl toward herself] **3.** to raise (one's hat) slightly in greeting someone —*vi.* **1.** to tilt or slant **2.** to overturn or topple [the cart *tipped* over] —*n.* a tipping or being tipped; tilt; slant —**tip the scales at** to weigh (a specified amount)

☆**tip-off** (tip′ôf′) *n.* a giving of secret information, a hint, warning, etc.

Tip·pe·ca·noe (tip′ē kə nōo′) **1.** [< Algonquian, lit., place of the sucker (fish)] river in N Ind., flowing southwest into the Wabash **2.** *nickname of* William Henry Harrison

tip·pet (tip′it) *n.* [prob. dim. of ME. *tippe*, tip¹] **1.** formerly, a long, hanging part of a hood, cape, or sleeve **2.** a scarflike garment of fur, wool, etc. for the neck and shoulders, hanging down in front **3.** a long, black scarf worn by Anglican clergymen

tip·ple¹ (tip′'l) *vi., vt.* **-pled, -pling** [prob. < ME. *tipelar*, tavern-keeper < ?] to drink (alcoholic liquor) regularly and often —*n.* alcoholic liquor —**tip′pler** *n.*

☆**tip·ple²** (tip′'l) *n.* [< TIP³ + -LE²] an apparatus for emptying coal, etc. from a mine car

TIPPET

tip·py (tip′ē) *adj.* **-pi·er, -pi·est** [Colloq.] that tips easily; not steady; shaky

tip·py-toe, tip·py·toe (-tō′) *n., adj., adv., vi.* **-toed′, -toe′ing** *colloq. var. of* TIPTOE

tip·ster (tip′stər) *n.* [Colloq.] a person who sells tips, as to people betting on horse races, buying and selling stocks, etc.

tip·sy (tip′sē) *adj.* **-si·er, -si·est** **1.** that tips easily; not steady **2.** somewhat drunk —**tip′si·ly** *adv.* —**tip′si·ness** *n.*

tip·toe (tip′tō′) *n.* the tip of a toe or the tips of the toes —*vi.* **-toed′, -toe′ing** to walk quietly or carefully on one's tiptoes —*adj.* **1.** standing on one's tiptoes **2.** quiet or careful —*adv.* on tiptoe —**on tiptoe** **1.** on one's tiptoes **2.** eager or eagerly **3.** quietly or carefully

tip·top (-täp′) *n.* [TIP¹ + TOP¹] **1.** the highest point; very top **2.** [Colloq.] the highest in quality or excellence; best —*adj., adv.* **1.** at the highest point, or top **2.** [Colloq.] at the highest point of excellence, health, etc. [I'm feeling *tiptop* today]

ti·rade (tī′rād, tī rād′) *n.* [Fr. < It. *tirata*, a volley < pp. of *tirare*, to fire] a long, angry or scolding speech; harangue

Ti·ra·na (ti rä′nə) capital of Albania, in the central part: pop. 169,000: also, Albanian **Ti·ra·në** (tē rä′nə)

tire¹ (tīr) *vt., vi.* **tired, tir′ing** [OE. *tiorian*] **1.** to make or become unable to go on because of a need for rest; exhaust [the hike *tired* me] **2.** to make or become bored or impatient, as by dull talk

tire² (tīr) *n.* [prob. var. of ME. *atir*, equipment] a hoop of iron or rubber, or a rubber tube filled with air, fixed around the wheel of a vehicle to form a tread —*vt.* **tired, tir′ing** to furnish with tires

tired (tīrd) *adj.* **1.** exhausted; weary **2.** stale; trite [a *tired* joke] —**tired′ly** *adv.* —**tired′ness** *n.*

SYN.—**tired** is used of one who has been drained of much strength and energy through hard work, boredom, impatience, etc. [*tired* from mowing the lawn]; **weary** (or **wearied**) suggests such a great loss of energy or interest that one feels unable or unwilling to continue [*weary* of study]; **exhausted** implies a total draining of strength and energy, as after a long, hard climb; **fatigued** refers to one who has lost so much energy through long exercise or effort that rest and sleep are essential [*fatigued* at the end of the political campaign]

tire·less (tīr′lis) *adj.* that does not become tired —**tire′less·ly** *adv.* —**tire′less·ness** *n.*

tire·some (-səm) *adj.* **1.** tiring; boring **2.** annoying; irksome

[her *tiresome* habit of never arriving on time] —**tire′some·ly** *adv.* —**tire′some·ness** *n.*

Ti·rich Mir (tē′rich mir′) mountain in N Pakistan: highest peak of the Hindu Kush: 25,230 ft.

ti·ro (tī′rō) *n., pl.* **-ros** *var. sp. of* TYRO

Tir·ol (tir′äl, tī′rōl, ti rōl′) E Alpine region in W Austria & N Italy —**Ti·ro·le·an** (ti rō′lē ən), *n.* —**Ti·ro·lese** (tir′ə lēz′) *adj., n., pl.* -lese

'tis (tiz) it is

Tish·ah b'Ab (tē shä′ bə äv′, tish′ə bôv′) a Jewish fast day commemorating the destruction of the Temple, observed on the 9th day of Ab

Tish·ri (tish rē′, tish′rē) *n.* *see* JEWISH CALENDAR

tis·sue (tish′ōo; *chiefly Brit.* tis′yōo) *n.* [< OFr. *tissu* < pp. of *tistre* < L. *texere*, to weave] **1.** cloth; esp., light, thin cloth, as gauze **2.** a tangled mass or series; mesh; network; web [a *tissue* of lies] **3.** a piece of soft, absorbent paper, used as a throwaway handkerchief, as toilet paper, etc. **4.** *a) same as* TISSUE PAPER *b)* a sheet of tissue paper **5.** *Biol. a)* the substance of an organic body or organ, made up of cells and the material between them *b)* any substance of this kind having a particular purpose [epithelial *tissue*]

tissue culture **1.** the process of growing tissue artificially in a special, sterile culture medium **2.** the tissue thus grown

tissue paper very thin, unglazed, nearly transparent paper, as for wrapping things, making tracings, etc.

Ti·sza (tē′sə) river in E Europe, flowing from the Ukraine through Hungary & Yugoslavia into the Danube: c. 800 mi.

tit¹ (tit) *n.* [TIT(MOUSE)] a titmouse or other small bird

tit² (tit) *n.* [OE.] *same as* TEAT

Tit. Titus

Ti·tan (tīt′'n) *poetic name for* HELIOS —*n.* **1.** *Gr. Myth.* any of a race of giant gods who were overthrown by the gods of Olympus **2.** [t-] any person or thing of great size or power —*adj.* [also t-] *same as* TITANIC —**Ti′tan·ess** *n.fem.*

Ti·ta·ni·a (ti tä′nē ə, tī-) in early folklore, the queen of fairyland and wife of Oberon

Ti·tan·ic (tī tan′ik) *adj.* **1.** of or like the Titans **2.** [t-] of great size, strength, or power —**ti·tan′i·cal·ly** *adv.*

ti·ta·ni·um (tī tä′nē əm, ti-) *n.* [ModL. < Gr. pl. of *Titan*, a Titan] a silvery or dark-gray, shiny, metallic chemical element found in various minerals and used to remove oxygen from molten steel: symbol, Ti; at. wt., 47.90; at. no., 22

titanium dioxide a compound, TiO_2, used esp. as a white pigment

tit·bit (tit′bit) *n. chiefly Brit. var of* TIDBIT

tit for tat [var. of earlier *tip for tap*: see TIP²] this in return for that, as blow for blow

tithe (tīth) *n.* [OE. *teothe*, a tenth] **1.** one tenth of the annual produce of one's land or of one's annual income, paid as a contribution to support a church or its clergy **2.** *a)* a tenth part *b)* any small part **3.** any tax or levy —*vt., vi.* **tithed, tith′ing** to pay a tithe of (one's income, etc.) —**tith′a·ble** *adj.* —**tith′er** *n.*

Ti·tian (tish′ən) (It. name *Tiziano Vecellio*) 1490?-1576; Venetian painter

ti·tian (tish′ən) *n.* [from the hair color in many of *Titian's* portraits] reddish yellow

Ti·ti·ca·ca (tit′ē kä′kə; *Sp.* tē′tē kä′kä), Lake largest lake in S. America, on the border of SE Peru & W Bolivia

tit·il·late (tit′'l āt′) *vt.* **-lat·ed, -lat·ing** [< L. pp. of *titillare*, to tickle] **1.** *same as* TICKLE **2.** to excite or stimulate in a pleasant way —**tit′il·lat′er** *n.* —**tit′il·la′tion** *n.* —**tit′il·la′tive** *adj.*

tit·i·vate (tit′ə vāt′) *vt., vi.* **-vat·ed, -vat·ing** [prob. < TIDY, with imitation Latin suffix] to dress up; spruce up —**tit′i·va′tion** *n.*

tit·lark (tit′lärk) *n.* [TIT¹ + LARK¹] *same as* PIPIT

ti·tle (tīt′'l) *n.* [OFr. < L. *titulus*] **1.** the name of a book, chapter, poem, picture, piece of music, play, etc. **2.** *a) short for* TITLE PAGE *b)* a literary work having a particular title [50 new *titles* in the publisher's fall catalog] **3.** a word or phrase that describes; epithet [Freud has the *title* "father of psychoanalysis"] **4.** a word used to show the rank, office, occupation, etc. of a person ["Duke," "Mayor," and "Dr." are *titles*] **5.** a claim or right [he has no *title* to treat me that way] **6.** *Law a)* a

---

WEST GERMANY / BAVARIA / SWITZ. / TIROL / AUSTRIA / ITALY

TIROL

right to ownership, esp. of real estate *b*) evidence of such a right *c*) a document stating such a right; deed *d*) a division of a law book, statute, etc., usually larger than a section or article **7.** a championship *[the heavyweight title]* **8.** *Motion Pictures, TV* words shown on the screen that give credits, translations, etc. —*vt.* **-tled, -tling** to give a title to; name; entitle

ti·tled (-'ld) *adj.* having a title, esp. of nobility

title deed a document that proves who has title to property

ti·tle·hold·er (-hōl'dər) *n.* the holder of a title; specif., the winner of a championship, as in some sport

title page the page in the front of a book that gives the title, author, publisher, etc.

title role (or **part** or **character**) the character in a play, movie, etc. whose name is used as or in its title

☆**ti·tlist** (tīt'list) *n.* a titleholder in some sport

tit·mouse (tit'mous') *n., pl.* **-mice'** (-mīs') [ME. *titemose,* prob. < *tit-,* little + OE. *mase,* titmouse] a small bird found throughout the world except in S. America and Australia; ☆esp., the **tufted titmouse**, with a crest on the head, common in the eastern U.S.

Ti·to (tē'tō), Marshal (born *Josip Broz*) 1892–1980; Communist party leader of Yugoslavia; president (1953–80)

ti·trate (tī'trāt) *vt.* **-trat·ed, -trat·ing** [< Fr. *titrer* < *titre,* a standard < OFr. *title,* TITLE + -ATE[1]] to test by titration

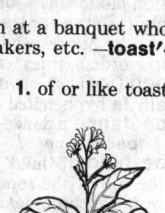

TUFTED TITMOUSE
(to 6 in. long)

ti·tra·tion (tī trā'shən) *n. Chem.* the process of finding out how much of a substance is in a known volume of a solution by measuring how much of a solution of known concentration must be added to produce a given reaction

tit-tat-toe (tit'tat tō') *n.* same as TICK-TACK-TOE

tit·ter (tit'ər) *vi.* [echoic] to laugh in a silly or nervous way, as if trying to hold back the sound; giggle —*n.* a silly or nervous laugh; giggle —**see** SYN. at LAUGH —**tit'ter·er** *n.*

tit·tle (tit''l) *n.* [ME. *title,* orig. same word as TITLE] **1.** formerly, a dot or other small mark used as a diacritical mark **2.** a very small particle; iota; jot

tit·tle-tat·tle (tit''l tat''l) *n., vi.* **-tled, -tling** [< repetition of sounds of TATTLE] gossip; chatter

tit·u·lar (tich'ə lər; *chiefly Brit.* tit'yə-) *adj.* [< L. *titulus,* a title] **1.** of, or having the nature of, a title **2.** having a title **3.** existing only in title; in name only *[a titular leader]* —**tit'u·lar·ly** *adv.*

Ti·tus (tīt'əs) *Bible* a book of the New Testament, which was an epistle of the Apostle Paul to his disciple Titus

tiz·zy (tiz'ē) *n., pl.* **-zies** [< ?] [Colloq.] a state of wild excitement, esp. over some unimportant matter

TKO, T.K.O. *Boxing abbrev. of* TECHNICAL KNOCKOUT

Tl *Chem.* thallium

TLC, T.L.C., t.l.c. tender, loving care

Tm *Chem.* thulium

TM trademark

☆**T-man** (tē'man') *n., pl.* **T'-men** (-men') [< T(reasury)-man] [Colloq.] a law-enforcement agent of the U.S. Department of the Treasury

TN Tennessee

tn. 1. ton(s) **2.** training

TNT, T.N.T. trinitrotoluene

to (tōō; *unstressed* tōo, tə) *prep.* [OE.] **1.** *a*) in the direction of; toward *[turn to the left]* *b*) in the direction of and reaching *[he went to Boston]* **2.** as far as *[wet to the skin]* **3.** into a condition of *[a rise to fame]* **4.** on, onto, against, at, next, etc. *[tie it to the post]* **5.** *a*) until *[from noon to night]* *b*) before *[the time is ten to six]* **6.** for the purpose of *[come to my aid]* **7.** *a*) as concerns; with regard to *[open to attack]* *b*) in the opinion of *[it seems to me]* **8.** producing or resulting in *[torn to pieces]* **9.** with; along with *[add this to the rest]* **10.** belonging with *[the key to this house]* **11.** as compared with; as against *[a score of 7 to 0]* **12.** *a*) in agreement with *[not to my taste]* *b*) in response to *[the dog comes to my whistle]* **13.** making up; in or for each *[four quarts to a gallon]* **14.** to the limit of *[moderate*

to high in price] **15.** with (a specified person or thing) as the receiver, or indirect object, of the action *[give the book to her]* **16.** in honor of *[a toast to you]* *To* is also used as a sign of the infinitive *[it was easy to read]* —*adv.* **1.** forward *[his hat is on wrong side to]* **2.** in the normal position; esp., shut or closed *[the door was blown to]* **3.** to the matter at hand *[they turned to and devoured the cake]* —**to and fro** back and forth

toad (tōd) *n.* [OE. *tade*] **1.** any of a group of tailless, leaping amphibians with a rough, warty skin, that live on moist land rather than in water, except during breeding **2.** a person thought of as disgusting, worthless, etc.

toad·fish (tōd'fish') *n., pl.* **-fish', -fish'es:** see FISH any of various scaleless fishes with froglike heads, found in shallow places off the Atlantic coast of N. America

TOAD
(½–9 in. long)

toad·stool (-stōōl') *n.* a mushroom; esp., in popular usage, any poisonous mushroom

toad·y (tōd'ē) *n., pl.* **toad·ies** [short for *toadeater,* quack doctor's assistant who pretended to eat poisonous toads and then drank the quack's cure-all] a person who flatters others in order to get things from them: also **toad'eat·er** —*vt., vi.* **toad'-ied, toad'y·ing** to be a toady (to); flatter —**toad'y·ism** *n.*

to-and-fro (tōō'ən frō') *adj.* moving forward and backward

toast[1] (tōst) *vt.* [< OFr., ult. < L. pp. of *torrere,* to parch] **1.** to brown the surface of (bread, etc.) by heating **2.** to warm thoroughly *[toast yourself by the fire]* —*vi.* to become toasted —*n.* sliced bread browned by heat —**toast'er** *n.*

toast[2] (tōst) *n.* [< the toasted spiced bread formerly put in the wine] **1.** a person, thing, idea, etc. in honor of which people raise their glasses and drink **2.** *a*) the act of so drinking in honor of some person, etc. *b*) a brief statement of praise, good wishes, etc. made just before so drinking **3.** any person greatly admired *[she is the toast of New York]* —*vt., vi.* to propose or drink a toast (to) —**toast'er** *n.*

toast·mas·ter (tōst'mas'tər) *n.* the person at a banquet who offers toasts, introduces after-dinner speakers, etc. —**toast'-mis'tress** (-mis'trəs) *n.fem.*

toast·y (tōs'tē) *adj.* **toast'i·er, toast'i·est 1.** of or like toast **2.** warm and comfortable or cozy

Tob. Tobit

to·bac·co (tə bak'ō) *n., pl.* **-cos** [Sp. *tobaco* < WInd., pipe in which the Indians smoked the plant] **1.** any of various plants of the nightshade family, with large leaves and white, yellow, greenish, or purple flowers, esp. a species widely grown for its leaves **2.** these leaves, prepared for smoking, chewing, or for use as snuff **3.** cigars, cigarettes, snuff, etc. **4.** the use of tobacco for smoking, etc.

to·bac·co·nist (tə bak'ə nist) *n.* [Chiefly Brit.] a dealer in tobacco and other smoking supplies

To·ba·go (tō bā'gō, tə-) island in the West Indies, northeast of Trinidad: 116 sq. mi. See TRINIDAD AND TOBAGO

To·bit (tō'bit) a book of the Apocrypha

to·bog·gan (tə bäg'ən) *n.* [CanadFr. *tabagan* < Algonquian] a long, narrow, flat sled without runners, curved back at the front end: now used for coasting downhill —*vi.* **1.** to coast, travel, etc. on a toboggan **2.** to go down rapidly *[prices tobogganned]* —**to·bog'gan·er, to·bog'gan·ist** *n.*

To·bol (tō bōl'y') river in W Siberia, flowing from the S Urals northeastward into the Irtysh: 1,042 mi.

To·by (tō'bē) *n., pl.* **-bies** [< *Toby,* dim. of *Tobias,* ult. < Heb. *tōbhīyāh,* lit., the lord is good] a jug or mug for ale or beer shaped like a fat man with a three-cornered hat: also **Toby jug**

TOBACCO
PLANT

TOBOGGAN

To·can·tins (tō/kän tēns/) river flowing from central Brazil northward into the Pará River: c. 1,700 mi.

toc·ca·ta (tə kät/ə) *n.* [It. < pp. of *toccare*, to touch < L.] a composition in free style for the organ, piano, etc., often used as a prelude of a fugue

to·coph·er·ol (tō käf/ə rôl', -rōl') *n.* [< Gr. *tokos*, childbirth + *pherein*, to BEAR[1] + -OL[1]] any of the four related oils that make up vitamin E and are present chiefly in wheat-germ oil, cottonseed oil, lettuce, etc.

Tocque·ville (tōk vēl'; *E.* tōk/vil), **A·lex·is** (Charles Henri Maurice Clérel) de (à lek sē/ də) 1805–59; Fr. writer & statesman

toc·sin (täk/sin) *n.* [Fr. < MFr. < Pr. < *toc*, a stroke + *senh*, a bell < L. *signum*, a sign] **1.** *a)* an alarm bell *b)* its sound **2.** any alarm

to·day (tə dā/) *adv.* [OE. *to dæg*] **1.** on or during the present day [do it *today*] **2.** in the present time or age; nowadays [few people read Whittier's poetry] —*n.* **1.** the present day [*today's* game] **2.** the present time or period [*today's* fashions] Also, esp. formerly, **to-day**

tod·dle (täd/'l) *vi.* **-dled, -dling** [? < TOTTER + -LE[2]] to walk with short, uncertain steps, as a child does —*n.* the act of toddling —**tod/dler** *n.*

tod·dy (täd/ē) *n., pl.* **-dies** [Anglo-Ind. < Hindi *tārī*, fermented sap < *tār*, palm tree] **1.** the sweet or fermented sap of various East Indian palms, used as a beverage **2.** a drink of brandy, whiskey, etc. mixed with hot water, sugar, and, usually, spices: also **hot toddy**

to-do (tə dōō/) *n.* [Colloq.] a commotion; fuss

toe (tō) *n.* [OE. *ta*] **1.** *a)* any of the parts at the end of the foot *b)* the front part of the foot *c)* that part of a shoe, sock, etc. which covers the toes **2.** anything like a toe in location, shape, or purpose —*vt.* **toed, toe/ing 1.** to touch, kick, etc. with the toes [the runners *toed* the starting line] **2.** *a)* to drive (a nail) slantingly *b)* to fasten with nails so driven; toenail —*vi.* ☆ to stand, walk, or be formed so that the toes are in a specified position [to *toe* in] —**on one's toes** [Colloq.] mentally or physically alert —**step (or tread) on someone's toes** to offend someone, esp. by not respecting his rights —**toe the line (or mark)** to follow orders, rules, etc. exactly —**toe/like/** *adj.*

toed (tōd) *adj.* having (a specified kind or number of) toes: usually in hyphenated compounds [three-*toed*]

toe dance a dance performed on the tips of the toes, as in ballet —**toe/-dance/** *vi.* **-danced/, -danc/ing** —**toe/-danc/er** *n.*

toe·hold (tō/hōld') *n.* **1.** a small space or ledge for supporting the toe of the foot in climbing, etc. **2.** any means of getting over difficulties, gaining entry, etc. [I need some kind of *toehold* in the business world if I am to succeed] **3.** *Wrestling* a hold in which one wrestler twists the other's foot

toe·less (-lis) *adj.* **1.** having no toe or toes **2.** having the toe open [*toeless* shoes]

toe·nail (-nāl') *n.* **1.** the nail of a toe **2.** *Carpentry* a nail driven in on a slant —*vt. Carpentry* to fasten with a toenail

toff (täf, tôf) *n.* [< *toft*, var. of TUFT] [Brit. Slang] **1.** a wealthy upper-class person **2.** a well-dressed man

tof·fee, tof·fy (tôf/ē, täf/-) *n.* [later Brit. form of TAFFY] a hard, chewy candy made with brown sugar or molasses and, often, nuts; kind of taffy

tog (täg, tôg) *n.* [prob. ult. < L. *toga*, TOGA] [*pl.*] [Colloq.] clothes [tennis *togs*] —*vt.* **togged, tog/-ging** [Colloq.] to put clothes on; dress (usually with *up* or *out*) [*togged* out in a fancy gown]

to·ga (tō/gə) *n., pl.* **-gas, -gae** (-jē) [L. < *tegere*, to cover] **1.** in ancient Rome, a loose, one-piece outer garment worn in public by citizens **2.** a robe of office —**to/gaed** (-gəd) *adj.*

to·geth·er (tə geth/ər) *adv.* [< OE. < *to* (see TO) + *gædre*, together < base of *gaderian*, to gather] **1.** in or into one gathering, group, or place [the family ate *together*] **2.** in or into contact, collision, union, etc. [the cars skidded *together*] **3.** thought of as a group [he won more than all of us *together*] **4.** *a)* with one another; in association [to live *together*] *b)* by working together [*together* they lifted the sofa] **5.** at the same time [shots fired *together*] **6.** one after another; continuously [he worked for two days *together*] **7.** in or into agreement, cooperation, etc. [let's get *together*] **8.** in or into a unified whole [to put all the pieces *together*] —☆*adj.* [Slang] having fully developed one's abilities, ambitions, etc.

to·geth·er·ness (-nis) *n.* the spending of much time together, as by a family in leisure-time activities, esp. in an effort to bring about a more stable, friendly relationship

tog·ger·y (täg/ər ē, tôg/-) *n.* [Colloq.] clothes; togs

tog·gle (täg/'l) *n.* [prob. < dial. *tuggle* < TUG + -LE[2]] **1.** a rod, pin, or bolt for putting through a loop of a rope, a link of a chain, etc. to make an attachment, prevent slipping, etc. **2.** a toggle joint or a device having one —*vt.* **-gled, -gling** to provide or fasten with a toggle

toggle joint a knee-shaped joint made up of two bars pivoted together at one end: pressure put on the joint to straighten it sends opposite, outward pressure to the open ends

toggle switch a switch consisting of a lever moved back and forth through a small arc to open or close an electric circuit

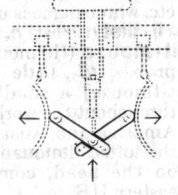

TOGGLE JOINT
(arrows indicate direction of pressure)

To·go (tō/gō) country in W Africa, on the Atlantic, east of Ghana: 21,853 sq. mi.; pop. 1,914,000; cap. Lomé —**To/go·lese/** (-lēz/) *adj., n., pl.* **-lese**

toil[1] (toil) *vi.* [Anglo-Fr. *toiler*, to strive < OFr. < L. *tudiculare*, to stir about, ult. < *tudes*, mallet] **1.** to work hard and continuously **2.** to go or move slowly with pain or effort [to *toil* up a hill] —*n.* hard, exhausting work or effort —see SYN. at WORK —**toil/er** *n.*

toil[2] (toil) *n.* [OFr. *toile* < L. *tela*, a web] **1.** [Archaic] a net for trapping **2.** [*pl.*] any snare like a net

toi·let (toi/lit) *n.* [MFr. *toilette* < *toile*, cloth: see prec.] **1.** formerly, a dressing table **2.** the act of dressing or grooming oneself **3.** dress; attire ☆**4.** *a)* a room, shelter, etc. for ridding the body of waste; specif., a small room with a bowl-shaped fixture for this purpose that flushes with water *b)* such a fixture —*adj.* **1.** of or for grooming oneself [*toilet* articles] ☆**2.** for a toilet (*n.* 4 *b*) [a *toilet* brush] —**make one's toilet** [Now Rare] to bathe, dress, arrange one's hair, etc.

toilet paper (or **tissue**) soft, absorbent paper, for cleaning oneself after ridding the body of waste

toi·let·ry (toi/lə trē) *n., pl.* **-ries** soap, lotion, cologne, etc. used in cleaning and grooming oneself

toi·lette (twä let/, toi-) *n.* [Fr.: see TOILET] **1.** the process of grooming oneself, including bathing, hairdressing, dressing, etc.: said of women **2.** dress or manner of dress; attire

toilet training the training of a young child to use a toilet when he needs to rid his body of waste

toilet water a perfumed, slightly alcoholic liquid applied to the skin after bathing, shaving, etc.

toil·some (toil/səm) *adj.* requiring toil, or hard work; laborious —**toil/some·ly** *adv.* —**toil/some·ness** *n.*

toil·worn (-wôrn') *adj.* worn out by toil or showing the effects of toil [a *toilworn* face]

To·kay (tō kā/) *n.* **1.** a sweet, rich wine made in Tokay, Hungary **2.** any wine like this **3.** a large, sweet grape used for the wine

toke (tōk) *n.* [? < TOKEN] ☆[Slang] a puff on a cigarette, esp. one of marijuana or hashish

to·ken (tō/k'n) *n.* [OE. *tacn*] **1.** a sign or symbol [this gift is a *token* of my affection] **2.** something used as a sign of authority, identity, etc. **3.** a keepsake **4.** a piece of stamped metal for use in place of money, as for fare on a bus, etc. —*vt.* to be a token of —*adj.* **1.** by way of a token, symbol, etc. [a *token* gesture] **2.** merely pretended; having only the appearance of; slight [*token* resistance] —see SYN. at PLEDGE —**by the same token** following from this —**in token of** as evidence of

to·ken·ism (-iz'm) *n.* the process of acting on a principle, meeting a demand, etc., but in a very small, merely formal way; specif., ☆token integration of Negroes, as in schools, jobs, etc.

To·ky·o (tō/kē ō'; *Jap.* tō/kyō') capital of Japan, on the S coast of Honshu: pop. 8,907,000 (met. area 19,500,000) —**To/ky·o·ite** (-īt') *n.*

☆**tol·bu·ta·mide** (täl byōōt/ə mīd') *n.* [TOL(U) + BUT(YRIC) + AMIDE] a drug that releases insulin from the pancreas, used in the treatment of diabetes

told (tōld) *pt. & pp. of* TELL —**all told** all (being) counted; in all [there were ten *all told*]

tole (tōl) *n.* [Fr. *tôle*, sheet iron < *table*, TABLE] a type of metalware coated with lacquer or enamel, used for trays, lamps, etc.

To·le·do (tə lē/dō; *also for 2, Sp.* tō lā/thō) **1.** [after the city

TOENAIL

in Spain] port in NW Ohio, on Lake Erie: pop. 384,000 (met. area 693,000) **2.** city in C Spain: pop. 40,000 —*n.*, *pl.* **-dos** a fine-tempered sword or sword blade made in Toledo, Spain

tol·er·a·ble (täl′ər ə b'l) *adj.* **1.** that can be tolerated or put up with; endurable [a *tolerable* burden] **2.** fairly good; passable [a *tolerable* dinner] **3.** [Colloq.] in fairly good health [feeling *tolerable*] —**tol′er·a·bil′i·ty** *n.* —**tol′er·a·bly** *adv.*

tol·er·ance (-əns) *n.* **1.** a tolerating or being tolerant, esp. of the beliefs, customs, etc. of others, even though these are not like one's own **2.** the amount of variation allowed from a standard; specif., the difference between the allowable maximum and minimum sizes of some mechanical part **3.** *Med.* the ability to resist the effects of a drug, etc. taken over a period of time or in larger and larger doses

tol·er·ant (-ənt) *adj.* **1.** having or showing tolerance of others' beliefs, customs, etc. **2.** *Med.* of or having tolerance —**tol′er·ant·ly** *adv.*

tol·er·ate (täl′ə rāt′) *vt.* **-at′ed, -at′ing** [< L. pp. of *tolerare*, to bear] **1.** to allow; permit [I won't *tolerate* such talk] **2.** to recognize and respect (others' beliefs, customs, etc.) without sharing them **3.** to put up with; bear [she can't *tolerate* cats] **4.** *Med.* to have tolerance for (a specific drug, etc.) —see **SYN.** at BEAR[1] —**tol′er·a·tive** *adj.* —**tol′er·a′tor** *n.*

tol·er·a·tion (täl′ə rā′shən) *n.* tolerance; esp., freedom to hold religious views that differ from the established ones

Tol·ki·en (tōl′kē ən), **J(ohn) R(onald) R(euel)** 1892–1973; Eng. novelist & scholar

toll[1] (tōl) *n.* [OE., prob. ult. < Gr. *telos*, tax] **1.** a tax or charge for a privilege, esp. for permission to use a bridge, highway, etc. **2.** the right to demand toll **3.** a charge for some service, as for a long-distance telephone call **4.** the number lost, taken, etc. [the storm took a heavy *toll* of lives]

toll[2] (tōl) *vt.* [< ? OE. *-tillan*, to touch] **1.** to ring (a church bell, etc.) slowly and with regular strokes, as when someone dies **2.** to sound (the hour, a knell, etc.) by such ringing **3.** to announce, summon, etc. by such ringing —*vi.* to sound or ring slowly: said of a bell —*n.* **1.** the act or sound of tolling a bell **2.** a single stroke of the bell —**toll′er** *n.*

toll bar a bar, gate, etc. for stopping traffic at a point where toll is taken

toll·booth (tōl′bo͞oth′) *n.* ☆a booth at which toll is collected, as before vehicles enter a toll road

toll bridge a bridge at which toll is paid for passage

toll call a long-distance telephone call, for which there is a charge beyond the local rate

toll·gate (-gāt′) *n.* a gate for stopping traffic at a point where toll is taken

toll·keep·er (-kēp′ər) *n.* a person who collects tolls at a tollgate

toll road a road on which toll must be paid

Tol·stoy (tōl stoi′, E. täl′stoi, tōl′-), **Count Lev** (E. **Leo**) **Ni·ko·la·ye·vich** (lyev nē′kô lä′ye vich) 1828–1910; Russ. novelist & social theorist: also sp. **Tolstoi**

Tol·tec (täl′tek, tōl′-) *n.* any of a group of Nahuatl Indians who lived in Mexico before the rise of the Aztecs —*adj.* of the Toltecs or their culture: also **Tol′tec·an**

to·lu (balsam) (tō lo͞o′) [< Sp. < *Tolú*, seaport in Colombia] a sweet-smelling resin obtained from a S. American tree: it is used in cough syrups, etc.

tol·u·ene (täl′yo͞o wēn′) *n.* [TOLU + (BENZ)ENE] a liquid hydrocarbon, C_7H_8, first obtained from tolu balsam but now from coal tar, petroleum, etc.: it is used in making dyes, explosives, etc.: also **tol′u·ol** (-wôl′, -wōl′)

tom (täm) *n.* [< *Tom*, dim. of THOMAS] the male of some animals, esp. of the cat —*adj.* male [a *tom* turkey]

☆**tom·a·hawk** (täm′ə hôk′) *n.* [< Algonquian] a light ax with a head of stone, used by North American Indians as a tool and a weapon —*vt.* to hit, cut, or kill with a tomahawk

Tom and Jerry (jer′ē) ☆a hot drink made of rum, etc., beaten eggs, sugar, water or milk, and nutmeg

to·ma·to (tə māt′ō, -mät′ō) *n., pl.* **-toes** [< Sp. < Nahuatl *tomatl*] **1.** a red or yellowish

TOMAHAWK

fruit with a juicy pulp, used as a vegetable **2.** the plant that it grows on

tomb (to͞om) *n.* [< Anglo-Fr. < LL. < Gr. *tymbos*] **1.** a vault, chamber, or grave for the dead **2.** a burial monument —**the tomb** death —**tomb′less** *adj.* —**tomb′like′** *adj.*

tom·boy (täm′boi′) *n.* a girl who behaves or plays like an active boy —**tom′boy′ish** *adj.* —**tom′boy′ish·ly** *adv.* —**tom′boy′ish·ness** *n.*

tomb·stone (to͞om′stōn′) *n.* a stone put on a tomb or grave usually telling who is buried there

tom·cat (täm′kat′) *n.* a male cat

☆**tom·cod** (täm′käd′) *n.* **1.** a small, codlike saltwater food fish of the northern Atlantic coast **2.** a similar fish of the Pacific coast

Tom Collins *see* COLLINS

Tom, Dick, and Harry everyone; anyone: usually used to show contempt [don't take the advice of every *Tom, Dick, and Harry*]

tome (tōm) *n.* [Fr. < L. < Gr. *tomos*, piece cut off] **1.** orig., any volume of a work of several volumes **2.** a book, esp. a large or serious one

tom·fool (täm′fo͞ol′) *n.* a foolish, stupid, or silly person —*adj.* foolish, stupid, or silly

tom·fool·er·y (-ər ē) *n., pl.* **-er·ies** foolish or silly behavior; nonsense

Tom·my (täm′ē) *n., pl.* **-mies** [< *Tommy Atkins* (for *Thomas Atkins*, fictitious name used in Brit. army sample forms)] [*also* t-] name used for any private in the British army

☆**Tommy gun** *alternate trademark for* THOMPSON SUBMACHINE GUN —*n.* a submachine gun

tom·my·rot (täm′ē rät′) *n.* [Slang] nonsense; foolishness

to·mor·row (tə mär′ō, -môr′ō) *adv.* [OE. *to morgen*] **1.** on the day after today **2.** at some time in the future —*n.* **1.** the day after today **2.** some time in the future Also, esp. formerly, **to-morrow**

Tom Thumb **1.** a tiny hero of English folk tales **2.** any midget or small person

tom·tit (täm′tit′) *n.* [Chiefly Brit.] a titmouse or any of various other small birds

tom-tom (täm′täm′) *n.* [Hindi *tam-tam*] a simple kind of drum with a small head, usually beaten with the hands

-to·my (tə mē) [< Gr. < *temnein*, to cut] a combining form meaning: **1.** a dividing [dichotomy] **2.** a surgical operation [lithotomy]

ton (tun) *n.* [var. of TUN] **1.** a unit of weight equal to 2,000 pounds avoirdupois, commonly used in the U.S., Canada, South Africa, etc.: in full, **short ton 2.** a unit of weight equal to 2,240 pounds avoirdupois, commonly used in Great Britain: in full, **long ton 3.** *same as* METRIC TON **4.** a unit of internal capacity of ships, equal to 100 cubic feet: in full, **register ton 5.** a unit of carrying capacity of ships, usually equal to 40 cubic feet: in full, **measurement ton, freight ton 6.** a unit for measuring displacement of ships, equal to 35 cubic feet: it is nearly equal to the volume of a long ton of sea water: in full, **displacement ton** ☆**7.** a unit of cooling capacity of an air conditioner, equal to 12,000 B.t.u. per hour **8.** [often *pl.*][Colloq.] a very large amount or number [*tons* of fun] Abbrev. **T., t., tn.** (*sing.* & *pl.*)

ton·al (tō′n'l) *adj.* of a tone or tonality —**ton′al·ly** *adv.*

to·nal·i·ty (tō nal′ə tē) *n., pl.* **-ties 1.** quality of tone **2.** *Art* the color scheme in a painting **3.** *Music a) same as* KEY[1] *b)* tonal character as determined by the relationship of the tones to the keynote

tone (tōn) *n.* [< OFr. < L. < Gr. *tonos* < *teinein*, to stretch] **1.** *a)* a vocal or musical sound *b)* its quality [the clear *tone* of an oboe] **2.** an intonation, pitch, modulation, etc. of the voice that expresses a particular feeling [a *tone* of contempt] **3.** a way of wording or expressing things that shows a certain attitude [the friendly *tone* of her letter] **4.** normal elasticity [rubber that has lost its *tone*] **5.** *a)* the style, character, spirit, etc. of a place or period [the calm, rational *tone* of the 18th century] *b)*

TOM-TOM

distinctive style; elegance [paintings that gave the room *tone*]
6. a quality of color; tint or shade [three *tones* of green] **7.**
Linguis. the relative height of pitch with which a syllable, word,
etc. is pronounced **8.** *Music* a) a sound of distinct pitch (as
distinguished from a noise) that may be put into harmonic relation with other such sounds b) the simple tone of a musical
sound as distinguished from its overtones c) any one of the full
intervals of a diatonic scale; whole step **9.** *Painting* the effect
produced by the combination of light, shade, and color **10.**
Physiol. the normal, healthy condition of an organ, muscle, etc.
[exercise improves muscle *tone*]: see also TONUS —*vt.* **toned,**
ton′ing 1. [Rare] *same as* INTONE **2.** to give a tone to, as of
color or sound **3.** to change the tone of —*vi.* to take on a tone
—**tone down 1.** to make or become less bright, sharp, etc.;
soften **2.** to make (something written or said) less harsh —
tone in with to blend or harmonize with —**tone up** to make or
become brighter, sharper, or stronger —**tone′less** *adj.* —**tone′-**
less·ly *adv.* —**tone′less·ness** *n.* —**ton′er** *n.*
tone arm the pivoted arm containing the pickup on a record
player
tone color *same as* TIMBRE
tone-deaf (tōn′def′) *adj.* not able to tell the difference between
different musical tones —**tone′-deaf′ness** *n.*
tone poem *same as* SYMPHONIC POEM
tone row (or **series**) *see* TWELVE-TONE
☆**tong**¹ (tôŋ, täŋ) *vt.* to seize, collect, handle, or hold with tongs
—*vi.* to use tongs
☆**tong**² (tôŋ, täŋ) *n.* [Chin. *t'ang,* a meeting place] a Chinese
association, society, etc.
Ton·ga (täŋ′gə) country on a group of islands (**Tonga Islands**)
in the South Pacific, east of Fiji: a member of the Commonwealth: 270 sq. mi.; pop. 86,000: see map at FIJI
Ton·gan (-gən) *n.* **1.** a native of Tonga **2.** the Polynesian
language of the Tongans
tongs (tôŋz, täŋz) *n.pl.* [*sometimes with sing. v.*] [OE. *tange*] a
device for seizing or lifting objects,
with two arms pivoted or hinged
together: also called **pair of tongs**
tongue (tuŋ) *n.* [OE. *tunge*] **1.** the
movable muscular part attached to the
floor of the mouth: it is used in eating,
tasting, and (in man) speaking **2.** an
animal's tongue used as food **3.** a)
the act or power of speaking [have
you lost your *tongue?*] b) a manner
or style of speaking [a glib *tongue*] **4.**

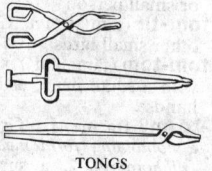

TONGS

a language or dialect [the French *tongue*] **5.** something like a
tongue in shape, position, motion, or use; specif., a) the flap
under the laces of a shoe b) the clapper of a bell c) the pole
of a wagon, etc. d) the projecting tenon of a tongue-and-
groove joint e) a narrow strip of land stretching into a sea, river, etc. f) a long, narrow flame —*vt.* **tongued, tongu′ing**
1. [Archaic] to speak **2.** to touch, lick, etc. with the tongue
3. *Music* to play by tonguing: see TONGUING —*vi.* **1.** to stick
out like a tongue **2.** *Music* to use tonguing: see TONGUING —
find one's tongue to get back the ability to talk, as after shock
—**hold one's tongue** to keep oneself from speaking —**on every-**
one's tongue spoken as common gossip —**on the tip of one's**
(or the) tongue almost said or remembered —**speak in tongues**
to utter sounds that cannot be understood, as while in a religious
trance; engage in glossolalia —**tongue′less** *adj.* —**tongue′like′**
adj.
tongue-and-groove joint (tuŋ′n grōōv′) a kind of joint in
which a tongue or tenon on one board fits exactly into a groove
in another
tongued (tuŋd) *adj.* having a (specified kind of) tongue: usually
in compounds [sharp-*tongued*]
tongue-lash (tuŋ′lash′) *vt.* [Colloq.] to scold or criticize harshly
—**tongue′-lash′ing** *n.*
tongue-tie (-tī′) *n.* limited motion of the tongue, caused by a
short frenum and making it impossible to speak properly —*vt.*
-tied′, -ty′ing to make tongue-tied
tongue-tied (-tīd′) *adj.* **1.** having a condition of tongue-tie
2. not able to speak because one is embarrassed, amazed, etc.
tongue twister a phrase or sentence hard to speak fast (Example: six sheiks' sick sheep)
tongu·ing (tuŋ′iŋ) *n.* the use of the tongue in playing a musical
wind instrument, esp. for more accurate playing of rapid notes
ton·ic (tän′ik) *adj.* [< Gr. < *tonos:* see TONE] **1.** a) of or producing good muscle tone, or tension b) characterized by continuous muscular contraction [a *tonic* spasm] **2.** giving

strength or energy; stimulating [swimming has a *tonic* effect]
3. *Music* designating or based on a keynote [a *tonic* chord] —
n. **1.** anything that stimulates or gives energy; specif., a) a drug,
medicine, etc. for increasing body tone b) a hair or scalp dressing **2.** a carbonated beverage flavored with a little quinine and
served in a mixed drink with gin, vodka, etc.; quinine water **3.**
Music the basic tone of a diatonic scale; keynote —**ton′i·cal-**
ly *adv.*
tonic accent *Phonet.* emphasis given to a syllable by changing,
esp. by raising, the pitch rather than by stress
to·nic·i·ty (tō nis′ə tē) *n.* the quality or condition of being
tonic; esp., normal muscle tension; tonus
to·night (tə nīt′) *adv.* [OE. *to niht*] on or during the present or
coming night —*n.* this night or the night about to come Also,
esp. formerly, **to-night**
Ton·kin (tän′kin, täŋ′-) region & former Fr. state in NE Indochina: now part of North Vietnam
Ton·le Sap (tän′lä säp′) lake in central Cambodia: 1,000 sq.
mi. (about three times larger in flood season)
ton·nage (tun′ij) *n.* **1.** a duty or tax on ships, based on tons
carried **2.** the total shipping, in tons, of a country or port **3.**
the amount in tons a ship can carry **4.** weight in tons
ton·neau (tu nō′) *n., pl.* **-neaus′, -neaux′** (-nōz′) [Fr., lit., a
cask] an enclosed rear compartment for passengers in an early
type of automobile
ton·sil (tän′s'l) *n.* [L. *tonsillae, pl.*] either of a pair of oval
masses of lymphoid tissue, one on each side of the throat at the
back of the mouth —**ton′sil·lar** *adj.*
ton·sil·lec·to·my (tän′sə lek′tə mē) *n., pl.* **-mies** the surgical
removal of the tonsils
ton·sil·li·tis (-līt′əs) *n.* inflammation of the tonsils —**ton′sil-**
lit′ic (-lit′ik) *adj.*
ton·so·ri·al (tän sôr′ē əl) *adj.* [< L. < *tonsor,* clipper < pp. of
tondere, to clip] of a barber or barbering: often used in a humorous way [a *tonsorial* artist]
ton·sure (tän′shər) *n.* [< MFr. < L. *tonsura* < pp. of *tondere,* to
clip] **1.** the act of shaving a man's head,
esp. on top, when he becomes a priest or
monk **2.** the part of the head left bare by
doing this —*vt.* **-sured, -sur·ing** to shave
the head of, esp. in this way
ton·tine (tän′tēn, tän tēn′) *n.* [Fr. < It.,
after L. *Tonti,* 17th-c. banker of Naples]
a fund to which a group of persons give
money, which finally goes to that person
or persons still living after a specified time
to·nus (tō′nəs) *n.* [ModL. < L. < Gr.
tonos: see TONE] the slight continuous
tightening of a normal muscle at rest

TONSURE

☆**ton·y** (tō′nē) *adj.* **ton′i·er, ton′i·est**
[Old Slang] high-toned; luxurious; stylish
too (tōō) *adv.* [< TO] **1.** in addition; also [you come *too*]
2. more than enough [the hat is *too* big] **3.** very; extremely
[it's *too* good!] Often used only to emphasize [I will *too* go] or
as an adjective with *much, many* [*too* much to see]
took (tōōk) *pt. of* TAKE
tool (tōōl) *n.* [OE. *tol*] **1.** any implement, instrument, etc. held
in the hand and used for some work, as a knife, saw, or shovel
2. a) the working part of a power-driven machine, as a drill,
jigsaw blade, etc. b) the whole machine; machine tool **3.**
anything used to get something done [books are *tools* of educa-
tion] **4.** a person used by another to accomplish his purposes,
esp. when these are illegal or dishonest —*vt.* **1.** to shape or
work with a tool **2.** to provide tools or machinery for (a factory, etc.): often with *up* **3.** to put designs, etc. on (leather, etc.)
with tools —*vi.* **1.** to use a tool or tools **2.** to get or install the
tools, equipment, etc. needed [the automobile plant is *tooling* up
for next year's models] **3.** to go in a vehicle [he *tooled* along
the highway in his new car] —**tool′er** *n.* —**tool′ing** *n.*
tool·box (tōōl′bäks′) *n.* a box or chest in which tools are kept:
also **tool chest**
tool·mak·er (-mā′kər) *n.* a machinist who makes, maintains,
and repairs machine tools —**tool′mak′ing** *n.*
tool·room (-rōōm′) *n.* a room, as in a machine shop, where
tools are stored when not being used, or kept while being repaired, etc.
toot (tōōt) *vi.* [prob. via LowG. *tuten* < echoic base] **1.** to blow
a horn, whistle, etc. in short blasts **2.** to sound in short blasts:
said of a horn, etc. —*vt.* **1.** to cause to sound in short blasts
2. to sound (tones, etc.) as on a horn —*n.* **1.** a short blast of a
horn, etc. ☆**2.** [Slang] a drinking spree

tooth (to͞oth; *for v. also* to͞oth) *n., pl.* **teeth** (tēth) [OE. *toth*] **1.** *a)* any of a set of hard, bonelike parts in the jaws of most vertebrates, used for biting, tearing, and chewing *b)* any similar part in invertebrates *c)* [*pl.*] *same as* DENTURE **2.** a toothlike part, as on a saw, comb, gearwheel, etc. **3.** an appetite or taste for something [*a sweet tooth*] **4.** something biting, piercing, etc. like a tooth [*the teeth of the storm*] **5.** an effective means of giving force to something [*to put teeth into a law*] —*vt.* **1.** to provide with teeth **2.** to make jagged; indent —*vi.* to mesh or interlock, as gears — **armed** (or **dressed**) **to the teeth** as armed (or dressed up) as one can be —**get** (or **sink**) **one's teeth into** to become fully occupied with —**in the teeth of 1.** directly against **2.** in opposition to; defying —**show one's teeth** to show hostility; threaten angrily —**tooth and nail** with all one's strength or resources —**tooth′less** *adj.*

tooth·ache (-āk′) *n.* pain in or near a tooth

tooth·brush (-brush′) *n.* a brush for cleaning the teeth

toothed (to͞otht, to͞othd) *adj.* **1.** having teeth: often used in hyphenated compounds [*big-toothed*] **2.** having notches [*a toothed leaf*]

toothed whale any of a main division of whales, as the sperm whale, that have cone-shaped teeth

tooth·paste (to͞oth′pāst′) *n.* a paste used in cleaning the teeth with a toothbrush

tooth·pick (-pik′) *n.* a very small, pointed stick for getting bits of food free from between the teeth

tooth powder a powder used like toothpaste

tooth shell *same as* SCAPHOPOD

tooth·some (-səm) *adj.* pleasing to the taste; tasty —**tooth′some·ly** *adv.* —**tooth′some·ness** *n.*

tooth·y (-ē) *adj.* **tooth′i·er, tooth′i·est** having or showing teeth that stick out or are noticeable [*a toothy smile*] —**tooth′i·ly** *adv.* —**tooth′i·ness** *n.*

too·tle (to͞ot′'l) *vi.* **-tled, -tling** [TOOT + -LE²] to keep tooting softly —*n.* the act or sound of tootling

top¹ (täp) *n.* [OE.] **1.** the head or the crown of the head [*from top to toe*] **2.** the highest part, point, or surface of anything [*the top of a hill, page, etc.*] **3.** the part of a plant growing above the ground [*beet tops*] **4.** an uppermost part or covering; specif., *a)* a lid, cap, cover, etc. *b)* a folding roof of an automobile *c)* the upper part of a two-piece garment *d)* a platform around the head of each lower mast on a sailing ship **5.** one first in order, excellence, importance, etc.; specif., *a)* the highest degree, pitch, rank, position, etc. [*he shouted at the top of his voice; she is at the top of her class*] *b)* a person of highest rank, etc. *c)* the choicest part; pick [*the top of the crop*] *d)* the beginning, as of something being rehearsed [*take it from the top*] ☆*e)* *Baseball* the first half (*of* an inning) **6.** *Sports a)* a stroke hitting the ball near its top *b)* the forward spin given the ball by such a stroke —*adj.* of or at the top; highest, greatest, foremost, etc. [*a top student*] —*vt.* **topped, top′ping 1.** to take off the top of (a plant, etc.) **2.** to put a top on [*to top a cake with icing*] **3.** to be a top for [*snow topped the mountain*] **4.** to reach or go over the top of **5.** to be more than in amount, height, etc. [*the fish topped 75 pounds*] **6.** to be better, more effective, etc. than; outdo [*he tops them all at golf*] **7.** to be at the top of; head; lead [*our team topped the league*] **8.** *Sports* to hit (a ball) near its top, giving it a forward spin —*vi.* to top someone or something —**off the top** [Slang] from gross income —☆**off the top of one's head** speaking offhand, without careful thought —**on top** at the top; successful —**on top of 1.** on or at the top of **2.** resting upon **3.** in addition to; besides **4.** following right after **5.** controlling successfully —**over the top 1.** over the front of a trench, as in attacking **2.** going beyond the quota or goal —**(the) tops** [Slang] the very best —**top off** to complete by adding a finishing touch —☆**top out** to level off

top² (täp) *n.* [OE.] a child's cone-shaped toy, spun on its pointed end —**sleep like a top** to sleep soundly

to·paz (tō′paz) *n.* [< OFr. < L. < Gr. *topazos*] **1.** a crystalline mineral that is a silicate of aluminum and fluorine; esp., a clear, yellow variety used as a gem **2.** a yellow variety of quartz

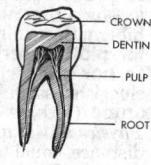

TOOTH

☆**top banana** [prob. from the banana-shaped soft club carried by burlesque comedians] [Slang] **1.** a top performer in show business; specif., the star comedian in a burlesque show **2.** the most important person in any group

top boot a boot reaching to just below the knee, esp. such a boot topped with a band of a different color

☆**top·coat** (täp′kōt′) *n.* a lightweight overcoat

top dog [Slang] the person, company, etc. in a controlling or leading position, esp. over others that are competing

top-drawer (-drôr′) *adj.* of first importance, rank, etc.

top-dress·ing (-dres′iŋ) *n.* material applied to a surface, as fertilizer —**top′-dress** *vt.*

tope (tōp) *vt., vi.* **toped, top′ing** [Fr. *toper*, to accept a bet] [Archaic] to drink much (alcoholic liquor)

to·pee (tō pē′, tō′pē) *n.* [Hindi *topi*] in India, a pith helmet worn as a sunshade

To·pe·ka (tə pē′kə) [? Siouan, lit., good place to dig potatoes] capital of Kans., on the Kansas River: pop. 125,000

top·er (tō′pər) *n.* a person who topes; drunkard

top-flight (täp′flīt′) *adj.* [Colloq.] best; first-rate

top·gal·lant (täp′gal′ənt, tə gal′-) *adj.* next above the topmast —*n.* a topgallant mast, sail, etc.

top hat a tall, black hat, usually of silk, worn by men in formal dress

top-heav·y (täp′hev′ē) *adj.* too heavy at the top and therefore likely to fall over —**top′-heav′i·ness** *n.*

to·pi (tō pē′, tō′pē) *n.* *same as* TOPEE

to·pi·ar·y (tō′pē er′ē) *adj.* describing or of the art of trimming and training shrubs or trees into unusual or ornamental shapes —*n., pl.* **-ar′ies** topiary art or work

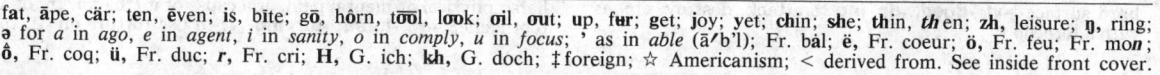

TOP HAT

top·ic (täp′ik) *n.* [< L. < Gr. *ta topika*, title of a book on rhetoric by Aristotle, ult. < *topos*, a place] **1.** the subject of a writing, speech, discussion, etc. **2.** a heading or item in an outline

top·i·cal (-i k'l) *adj.* **1.** of, using, or arranged by topics [*a topical outline*] **2.** having to do with topics of the day; of current or local interest [*a topical joke*] **3.** *Med.* of or for a particular part of the body [*a topical lotion*] —**top′i·cal·i·ty** (-kal′ə tē) *n.* —**top′i·cal·ly** *adv.*

top kick [Mil. Slang] *same as* FIRST SERGEANT

top·knot (täp′nät′) *n.* **1.** a knot of feathers, ribbons, etc. worn as a headdress **2.** a tuft of hair or feathers on the crown of the head

top·less (-lis) *adj.* without a top; specif., ☆of or wearing a costume that exposes the breasts

top-lev·el (-lev′'l) *adj.* **1.** of or by persons of the highest office or rank **2.** in or of the highest office or rank

top·loft·y (-lôf′tē) *adj.* [Colloq.] lofty in manner; haughty —**top′loft′i·ly** *adv.* —**top′loft′i·ness** *n.*

top·mast (täp′məst, -mast′) *n.* the second mast above the deck of a sailing ship, supported by the lower mast

☆**top·min·now** (täp′min′ō) *n.* a small fish that feeds at the surface and produces its young fully formed

top·most (täp′mōst′) *adj.* at the very top

☆**top-notch** (-näch′) *adj.* [Colloq.] first-rate; excellent

to·pog·ra·phy (tə päg′rə fē) *n., pl.* **-phies** [< LL. < Gr.: see TOPIC & -GRAPHY] **1.** *a)* the science of showing on maps, charts, etc. the surface features of a region, such as hills, rivers, and roads *b)* such features **2.** surveying done to discover and measure such features **3.** a study of some part or system of the body showing the relationship, size, shape, etc. of its parts **4.** a similar study of something, as the mind or the atom, regarded as a whole made up of parts —**to·pog′ra·pher** *n.* —**top·o·graph·ic** (täp′ə graf′ik), **top′o·graph′i·cal** *adj.* —**top′o·graph′i·cal·ly** *adv.*

to·pol·o·gy (tə päl′ə jē) *n., pl.* **-gies** [< Gr. *topos*, a place + -LOGY] **1.** *same as* TOPOGRAPHY (senses 3 & 4) **2.** *Math.* the study of those properties of geometric figures that remain unchanged even when under distortion —**top·o·log·i·cal** (täp′ə läj′i k'l) *adj.* —**to·pol′o·gist** *n.*

top·per (täp′ər) *n.* **1.** a person or thing that tops **2.** [Colloq.] *a)* *same as* TOP HAT *b)* a woman's short topcoat

top·ping (-iŋ) *n.* something that forms the top of, or is put on top of, something else, as a sauce on food —*adj.* [Brit. Colloq.] excellent; first-rate

top·ple (täp″'l) *vi.* **-pled, -pling** [< TOP¹, *v.* + -LE²] **1.** to fall (over) from top-heaviness, etc. **2.** to lean as if about to fall over; totter —*vt.* **1.** to cause to topple **2.** to overthrow

top·sail (täp's'l, -sāl') *n.* **1.** in a square-rigged sailing ship, the square sail, or either of a pair of square sails, next above the lowest sail on a mast **2.** in a fore-and-aft-rigged sailing ship, the small sail set above the gaff

top-se·cret (-sē'krit) *adj.* designating or of the most highly restricted military or government information

☆**top sergeant** *colloq. var. of* FIRST SERGEANT

top·side (-sīd') *n.* [*usually pl.*] the part of a ship's side above the waterline —*adv.* on or to an upper deck or the main deck of a ship

☆**top·soil** (-soil') *n.* the upper layer of soil, usually darker and richer than the subsoil

top·sy·tur·vy (täp'sē tur'vē) *adv., adj.* [prob. < *top*, highest part + ME. *terven*, to roll] **1.** upside down; reversed **2.** in confusion or disorder —*n.* a topsy-turvy condition

toque (tōk) *n.* [Fr.] a woman's small, round hat that fits close to the head

to·rah, to·ra (tō'rə, tō rä') *n.* [Heb.] *Judaism* **1.** *a)* learning, law, instruction, etc. *b)* [*also* T-] the whole of Jewish religious literature, including the Scripture, the Talmud, etc. **2.** [*usually* T-] *a)* the Pentateuch *b) pl.* **-roth, -rot** (-ras, -rōt') a parchment scroll containing the Pentateuch

torch (tôrch) *n.* [OFr. *torche*, ult. < L. *torquere*, to twist] **1.** a flaming light that can be carried in the hand, as a long piece of burning wood, etc. with resin in it **2.** anything viewed as enlightening, inspiring, etc. [*the torch of science*] **3.** a device that can be carried about, for producing a very hot flame, used in welding, etc., as a blowtorch **4.** [Brit.] a flashlight —*vt.* ☆[Slang] to set fire to, as in arson —☆**carry a** (or **the**) **torch for** [Slang] to love (someone), esp. without having one's love returned

torch·bear·er (tôrch'ber'ər) *n.* **1.** a person who carries a torch **2.** a person or leader who enlightens or inspires others

torch·light (tôrch'līt') *n.* the light of a torch or torches —☆ *adj.* done or carried on by torchlight

tore (tôr) *pt. of* TEAR¹

tor·e·a·dor (tôr'ē ə dôr') *n.* [Sp. < *torear*, to fight bulls, ult. < L. *taurus*, a bull] a bullfighter: term no longer used

to·re·ro (tə rer'ō; *Sp.* tô re'rô) *n., pl.* **-ros** (-rōz; *Sp.* -rôs) [Sp. < LL. < L. *taurus*, a bull] a bullfighter, esp. a matador

to·ri·i (tôr'i ē') *n., pl.* **-ri·i'** [Jpn.] a gateway at the entrance to a Shinto temple, consisting of two uprights supporting a curved horizontal beam, with a straight crosspiece just below

TOQUE

TORII

To·ri·no (tô rē'nô) *It. name of* TURIN

tor·ment (tôr'ment; *for v., usually* tôr ment') *n.* [< OFr. < L. *tormentum*, a rack, torture < *torquere*, to twist] **1.** great pain, physical or mental; agony **2.** something that causes pain, anxiety, or annoyance —*vt.* **1.** to make suffer greatly, in body or mind **2.** to annoy, harass, or tease —**see** **SYN.** at BAIT —**tor·ment'ing·ly** *adv.* —**tor·men'tor, tor·ment'er** *n.*

torn (tôrn) *pp. of* TEAR¹

tor·na·do (tôr nā'dō) *n., pl.* **-does, -dos** [< Sp. *tronada*, thunder < L. *tonare*, to thunder] ☆**1.** a rapidly whirling column of air, usually seen as a slender, funnel-shaped cloud that usually destroys everything in its narrow path **2.** any whirlwind or hurricane —☆**tor·nad'ic** (-nad'ik) *adj.*

To·ron·to (tə rän'tō) capital of Ontario, Canada, on Lake Ontario: pop. 633,000 (met. area 2,803,000)

tor·pe·do (tôr pē'dō) *n., pl.* **-does** [L., numbness < *torpere*, to be stiff] **1.** *same as* ELECTRIC RAY ☆**2.** a large, cigar-shaped missile: it is launched under water, where it moves under its own power until it hits something in its path, as an enemy ship **3.** any of various other explosive devices, as an underwater mine **4.** a small firework that explodes when thrown against a hard surface —*vt.* **-doed, -do·ing** to attack, destroy, etc. as with a torpedo

☆**torpedo boat** a small, fast warship for attacking with torpedoes

tor·pid (tôr'pid) *adj.* [< L. < *torpere*, to be numb] **1.** having lost for a time all or part of the power of feeling or motion, as a hibernating animal; dormant **2.** sluggish or slow and dull —**tor·pid'i·ty, tor'pid·ness** *n.* —**tor'pid·ly** *adv.*

tor·por (tôr'pər) *n.* **1.** a state of being dormant or inactive **2.** sluggishness; dullness; apathy —**see SYN.** at LETHARGY

torque (tôrk) *n.* [< L. *torques*, a twisted metal necklace] **1.** *Physics* a twisting effect made on a body by a force acting at a distance, equal to the force times its distance from the center of rotation **2.** popularly, any force that causes rotation

torque converter a device that uses fluid to pass torque along and increase its force

Tor·que·ma·da (tôr'ke mä'thä; *E.* tôr'ki mä'də), **To·más de** (tô mäs' *the*) 1420–98; Sp. Dominican monk; first Grand Inquisitor of the Spanish Inquisition

torque wrench a wrench that shows, as on a dial, the amount of torque used in tightening a bolt, nut, etc.

Tor·rance (tôr'əns) [after J. *Torrance*, local landowner] city in SW Calif.: suburb of Los Angeles: pop. 135,000

tor·rent (tôr'ənt, tär'-) *n.* [Fr. < L. *torrens*, burning, rushing, prp. of *torrere*, to parch] **1.** a swift, rushing stream, esp. of water **2.** a flood or rush [*a torrent* of words, mail, etc.] **3.** a very heavy fall of rain —**tor·ren·tial** (tô ren'shəl, tə-) *adj.* —**tor·ren'tial·ly** *adv.*

Tor·re·ón (tô'rä ôn') city in NC Mexico: pop. 257,000

Tor·ri·cel·li (tôr'rē chel'lē; *E.* tôr'i chel'ē), **E·van·ge·lis·ta** (e'vän je lēs'tä) 1608–47; It. physicist: discovered principle of the barometer

tor·rid (tôr'id, tär'-) *adj.* [< L. < *torrere*, to parch] **1.** dried by intense heat or caused to undergo intense heat, esp. of the sun; scorched; parched; arid [*a torrid desert*] **2.** so hot as to parch or scorch [*the torrid sun*] **3.** highly passionate, emotional, etc. —**tor·rid·i·ty** (tô rid'ə tē), **tor'rid·ness** *n.* —**tor'rid·ly** *adv.*

Torrid Zone the area of the earth's surface between the Tropic of Cancer & the Tropic of Capricorn and divided by the equator: see illustration at ZONE

tor·sion (tôr'shən) *n.* [< MFr. < LL. < pp. of L. *torquere*, to twist] **1.** a twisting or being twisted **2.** *Mech. a)* the stress produced in a rod, wire, etc. from having one end twisted while the other is held firm or twisted in the opposite direction *b)* the tendency of a rod, etc. so twisted to untwist again —**tor'sion·al** *adj.* —**tor'sion·al·ly** *adv.*

torsion bar a metal bar that can bend under torsion, part of the wheel suspension on some automotive vehicles

tor·so (tôr'sō) *n., pl.* **-sos, -si** (-sē) [It. < L. < Gr. *thyrsos*, a stem] **1.** the trunk of the human body **2.** a statue showing this, esp. one with the head and limbs missing

tort (tôrt) *n.* [< OFr. < ML. < L. pp. of *torquere*, to twist] *Law* a wrongful act, injury, or damage (not involving a breach of contract), for which a civil action can be brought

torte (tôrt) *n.* [G. < It. < LL. *torta*, twisted bread] a rich cake, variously made, as of eggs, chopped nuts, and crumbs

tor·ti·col·lis (tôr'ti käl'is) *n.* [ModL. < L. *tortus*, twisted + *collum*, the neck] *Med.* a condition of continuing and uncontrollable tightening of the neck muscles, causing the head to be twisted to an abnormal position

☆**tor·til·la** (tôr tē'ə) *n.* [Sp., dim. of *torta*, a cake: see TORTE] a griddlecake of unleavened cornmeal, now sometimes of flour: a staple food throughout Mexico

tor·toise (tôr'təs) *n., pl.* **-tois·es, -toise:** see PLURAL, II, D, 1 [< ML. *tortuca*, ult. < ? LGr. *tartarouchos*, demon] a turtle, esp. one that lives on land: see TURTLE

tortoise shell 1. the hard, mottled, yellow-and-brown shell of some turtles used, esp. formerly, in making combs, etc. **2.** a synthetic substance like this **3.** any of several black and yellow-brown butterflies —**tor'toise-shell'** *adj.*

tor·to·ni (tôr tō'nē) *n.* [prob. altered < It. *tortone*, lit., big tart] an ice cream made with heavy cream, maraschino cherries, almonds, etc.

tor·tu·ous (tôr'choo wəs) *adj.* [Anglo-Fr. < L. *tortuosus* < pp. of *torquere*, to twist] **1.** full of twists and turns; winding; crooked [*a tortuous river*] **2.** not straightforward; tricky or dishonest [*tortuous* thinking] —**tor'tu·os'i·ty** (-wäs'ə tē) *n., pl.* **-ties** —**tor'tu·ous·ly** *adv.* —**tor'tu·ous·ness** *n.*

tor·ture (tôr'chər) *n.* [Fr. < LL. *tortura* < pp. of L. *torquere*, to twist] **1.** the causing of great pain, as in order to punish someone or make him confess **2.** a method of doing this **3.** any harsh physical or mental pain, or a cause of it [the *torture* of a toothache] —*vt.* **-tured, -tur·ing 1.** to use torture on **2.** to cause extreme physical or mental pain to *[he was tortured by doubts]* **3.** to twist (meaning, etc.) —**tor′tur·er** *n.* —**tor′tur·ous** *adj.* —**tor′tur·ous·ly** *adv.*

to·rus (tôr′əs) *n., pl.* **-ri** (-ī) [L., a bulge] **1.** a large, convex molding used at the base of columns, etc. **2.** *Bot.* the receptacle of a flower stalk **3.** *Geom.* a figure shaped like a doughnut that is formed by the revolution of a circle about any line in its plane and external to it

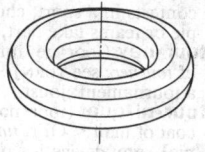

TORUS (sense 3)

To·ry (tôr′ē) *n., pl.* **-ries** [< Ir. *tōruidhe*, robber < *tōir*, to pursue] **1.** formerly, a member of one of the two major political parties of England: orig. opposed to Whig: changed officially c. 1830 to *Conservative* **2.** in the American Revolution, a person who showed or favored continued loyalty to Great Britain **3.** *[often* t-*]* any very conservative person —*adj.* *[also* t-*]* of or being a Tory — **To′ry·ism** *n.*

Tos·ca·ni·ni (täs′kə nē′nē, tôs′-), **Ar·tu·ro** (är toor′ō) 1867-1957; It. orchestral conductor, esp. in the U.S.

toss (tôs, täs) *vt.* [prob. < Scand.] **1.** to throw or pitch about; buffet *[a boat tossed by a storm]* ☆**2.** to mix (esp. a salad) lightly **3.** to throw; specif., to throw upward lightly from the hand *[to toss a ball]* **4.** to throw in or pass about (ideas, remarks, etc.) **5.** to lift quickly; jerk upward *[tossed her head in disdain]* **6.** to toss up with (someone *for* something): see phrase below —*vi.* **1.** to be tossed or thrown about *[the kite tossed in the wind]* **2.** to fling oneself about in sleep, etc. *[to toss and turn at night]* **3.** to toss up: see phrase below —*n.* **1.** a tossing or being tossed **2.** a tossing up: see phrase below **3.** the distance that something is or can be tossed —see SYN. at THROW —**toss off 1.** to make, do, write, etc. quickly and casually **2.** to drink quickly, all at once —**toss up** to toss a coin to decide something according to which side lands uppermost — **toss′er** *n.*

toss·up (tôs′up′, täs′-) *n.* **1.** the act of tossing a coin to decide something according to which side lands uppermost **2.** an even chance

tost (tôst, täst) *archaic pt. & pp. of* TOSS

tot[1] (tät) *n.* [prob. < Scand.] **1.** a young child **2.** [Chiefly Brit.] a small drink of alcoholic liquor

tot[2] (tät) *vt., vi.* **tot′ted, tot′ting** [contr. < TOTAL] [Chiefly Brit. Colloq.] to add; total (usually with *up*)

tot. total

to·tal (tōt′'l) *adj.* [< MFr. < ML. < L. *totus*, all] **1.** making up the (or a) whole; entire *[the total amount is ten dollars]* **2.** complete; utter *[a total loss]* —*n.* the whole amount or number —*vt.* **-taled** or **-talled, -tal·ing** or **-tal·ling 1.** to find the total of; add *[to total a column of figures]* **2.** to equal a total of; add up to *[his golf score totals 89]* ☆**3.** [Slang] to wreck completely *[the crash totaled his car]* —*vi.* to amount (*to*) as a whole —**to′tal·ly** *adv.*

to·tal·i·tar·i·an (tō tal′ə ter′ē ən, tō′tal ə-) *adj.* [TOTAL + (AUTHOR)ITARIAN] designating, of, or like a government or state in which one political group maintains complete control under a dictatorship and bans all others Also **to·tal·is·tic** (tōt′'l is′tik), **to′tal·ist** —*n.* a person favoring such a government or state —**to·tal′i·tar′i·an·ism** *n.*

to·tal·i·ty (tō tal′ə tē) *n., pl.* **-ties 1.** the fact or condition of being total **2.** the total amount or sum

to·tal·i·za·tor (tōt′'l i zāt′ər) *n.* a machine used in parimutuel betting to register bets and, usually, compute odds and payoffs while bets are being placed: also **to′tal·i·sa′tor, to′tal·iz′er**

☆**tote**[1] (tōt) *vt.* **tot′ed, tot′ing** [prob. of Afr. origin] [Colloq.] **1.** to carry or haul **2.** to be armed with (a gun, etc.) —*n.* **1.** [Colloq.] *a)* a toting *b)* something toted; load **2.** *short for* TOTE BAG —**tot′er** *n.*

tote[2] (tōt) *vt.* **tot′ed, tot′ing** *shortened form of* TOTAL (usually with *up*)

tote[3] (tōt) *n. shortened form of* TOTALIZATOR

tote bag ☆a large handbag of cloth, etc. in which one can carry shoes, small packages, etc.

tote board [Colloq.] a large board facing the grandstand at a race track, on which the bets, odds, and payoffs recorded by a totalizator are flashed

to·tem (tōt′əm) *n.* [< Algonquian] **1.** among primitive peoples, an animal or natural object thought to be related by blood to a given family or clan and taken as its symbol **2.** an image of this —**to·tem·ic** (tō tem′ik) *adj.* —**to′tem·ism** *n.* —**to′tem·ist** *n.*

totem pole a pole or post carved and painted with totems, often put up in front of their dwellings by Indian tribes of northwestern N. America

toth·er, t'oth·er, 'toth·er (tuth′ər) *adj., pron.* [Chiefly Dial.] that (or the) other

tot·ter (tät′ər) *vi.* [prob. < Scand.] **1.** to rock or shake as if about to fall **2.** to be on the point of collapse **3.** to be unsteady on one's feet; stagger —*n.* a tottering —see SYN. at STAGGER —**tot′ter·ing** *adj.* —**tot′ter·ing·ly** *adv.* —**tot′ter·y** *adj.*

tou·can (tōō′kan) *n.* [Fr. < Port. < Tupi *tucana*] a brightly colored, fruit-eating bird of tropical America, with a very large beak

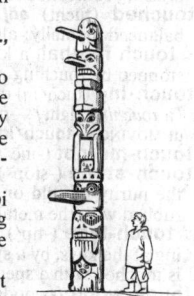

TOTEM POLE

touch (tuch) *vt.* [OFr. *tochier*] **1.** to put the hand, finger, etc. on, so as to feel **2.** to bring into contact with something else *[touch* a match to kindling*]* **3.** to be or come into contact with *[the desk touches the wall]* **4.** to border on; adjoin *[where the land touches the sea]* **5.** to strike lightly *[touching his pencil on the desk]* **6.** to affect by contact *[water won't touch these grease spots]* **7.** to injure slightly *[frost touched these plants]* **8.** to give a light tint, appearance, etc. to *[clouds touched with pink]* **9.** to stop at (a port, etc.) in passing: said of a ship **10.** to lay hands on; handle; use *[don't touch the papers on my desk]* **11.** to handle or affect so as to hurt or damage *[their house wasn't touched by the tornado]* **12.** to taste or take any of *[didn't touch his supper]* **13.** to come up to; reach *[the thermometer touched 90° today]* **14.** to compare with; equal *[cooking that can't touch hers]* **15.** to take or use wrongfully **16.** to deal with or refer to, esp. in passing **17.** to have to do with; concern *[a subject that touches our welfare]* **18.** to make feel pity, sympathy, gratefulness, etc. *[your kindness touches me]* **19.** to hurt the feelings of; pain *[touched him to the quick]* **20.** [Slang] to ask for and get a loan or gift of money from **21.** *Geom.* to be tangent to —*vi.* **1.** to touch a person or thing **2.** to be or come in contact *[the car bumpers touched]* **3.** to come near to something; verge (*on* or *upon*) *[strange behavior touching on madness]* **4.** to have a bearing (*on, upon*) *[studies that touch on this problem]* **5.** to treat a topic, esp. slightly or in passing (with *on, upon*) *[the speaker touched on many subjects]* **6.** to stop briefly (at a port, etc.) during a voyage **7.** *Geom.* to be tangent —*n.* **1.** a touching or being touched; specif., a light tap, stroke, etc. **2.** the sense by which physical objects are felt **3.** a feeling so caused; feel *[the cloth has a velvety touch]* **4.** a special quality, skill, or manner *[he lost his touch]* **5.** an effect of being touched; specif., *a)* a mark, impression, etc. left by touching *b)* a small, skillful change or addition in a painting, story, etc. *[the artist put in a few touches to darken the portrait]* **6.** a very small amount, degree, etc.; specif., *a)* a trace, tinge, etc. *[a touch of humor]* *b)* a slight attack *[a touch of the flu]* **7.** formerly, a touchstone **8.** contact or communication *[keep in touch]* **9.** [Slang] *a)* the act of asking for a loan or gift of money, or a getting of it thus *[to make a touch]* *b)* money so gotten *c)* a person with reference to how easily money can be so gotten from him *[an easy touch]* **10.** *Music* *a)* the way that a performer strikes the keys of a piano, etc. *[a delicate touch]* *b)* the way that the keys of a piano, etc. respond to the fingers *[a piano with a heavy touch]* —**touch down** to land: said of an aircraft or spacecraft —**touch off 1.** to represent accurately or aptly **2.** to make explode; fire **3.** to produce (esp. a violent reaction, etc.) by minor changes or additions —**touch up** to improve or finish (a painting, story, etc.) by minor changes or additions —**touch′a·bil′i·ty** *n.* — **touch′a·ble** *adj.* —**touch′er** *n.*

touch and go an uncertain, risky, or dangerous situation — **touch-and-go** (tuch′ən gō′) *adj.*

☆**touch·back** (tuch′bak′) *n. Football* a play in which a player grounds the ball behind his own goal line when the ball was caused to pass the goal line by an opponent

☆**touch·down** (-doun′) *n.* **1.** a touching down, or landing **2.** *Football* *a)* a scoring play in which a player grounds the ball on or past the opponent's goal line *b)* a score of six points so made

tou·ché (tōō shā′) *interj.* [Fr.] *Fencing* touched: said when one's opponent scores a point by a touch of his foil: also used in praising someone for his witty reply, etc.

touched (tucht) *adj.* **1.** emotionally moved **2.** slightly unbalanced mentally: also **touched in the head**

☆**touch football** a kind of football in which the ball carrier is stopped by touching rather than tackling him

touch·ing (tuch′iŋ) *adj.* that makes one feel pity, sympathy, etc. [a *touching* sight] —*prep.* with regard to; concerning —see SYN. at MOVING —**touch′ing·ly** *adv.*

touch-me-not (-mē nät′) *n. same as* JEWELWEED

touch·stone (-stōn′) *n.* **1.** a black stone formerly used to test the purity of gold or silver by the streak left on it when it was rubbed with the metal **2.** any test of genuineness

☆**touch-type** (-tīp′) *vi.* **-typed′, -typ′ing** to type without looking at the keys, by a system (**touch system**) in which a given key is touched with a specific finger —**touch′-typ′ist** *n.*

touch·wood (-wood′) *n.* dried, decayed wood or dried fungus used as tinder; punk

touch·y (tuch′ē) *adj.* **touch′i·er, touch′i·est** [TOUCH + -Y²] **1.** easily offended or irritated; oversensitive **2.** very risky [a *touchy* situation] —**touch′i·ly** *adv.* —**touch′i·ness** *n.*

tough (tuf) *adj.* [OE. *toh*] **1.** that will bend, twist, etc. without tearing or breaking [*tough* rubber] **2.** not easily cut or chewed [*tough* steak] **3.** sticky; thick [*tough* putty] **4.** *a)* physically strong; hardy [a *tough* pioneer] *b)* mentally or morally firm **5.** hard to influence; stubborn [a *tough* customer] **6.** practical and realistic [a *tough* bargainer] ☆**7.** overly aggressive; rough or brutal [don't get *tough* with me] **8.** *a)* very difficult [a *tough* situation] *b)* violent [a *tough* fight] **9.** [Colloq.] unfavorable; bad [a *tough* break] ☆**10.** [Slang] fine; excellent —☆*n.* a rough or brutal person; thug —see SYN. at STRONG —**tough′ly** *adv.* — **tough′ness** *n.*

tough·en (tuf′'n) *vt., vi.* to make or become tough or tougher

tough·ie, tough·y (-ē) *n., pl.* **-ies** [Colloq.] **1.** a tough person; ruffian **2.** a difficult problem or situation

tough-mind·ed (-mīn′did) *adj.* shrewd and unsentimental; practical; realistic —**tough′-mind′ed·ness** *n.*

Tou·lon (tōō län′; *Fr.* tōō lōn′) seaport in SE France, on the Mediterranean: pop. 175,000

Tou·louse (tōō lōōz′) city in S France, on the Garonne River: pop. 371,000

Tou·louse-Lau·trec (tōō lōōz′lō trek′), **Hen·ri (Marie Raymond) de** (än rē′ də) 1864–1901; Fr. painter

tou·pee (tōō pā′) *n.* [Fr. *toupet*, dim. of OFr. *toup*, tuft of hair] a man's wig, esp. one for a bald spot

tour (toor) *n.* [< MFr. < OFr. < *tourner*, to TURN] **1.** a turn or shift of work; esp., a period of duty or military service at a single place: in full, **tour of duty 2.** a long trip, as for sightseeing **3.** any trip, as for inspection; round; circuit; specif., a trip, as by a theatrical company, to give performances, etc. in various cities —*vi.* to go on a tour —*vt.* **1.** to take a tour through **2.** to take (a play, etc.) on tour —**on tour** touring, as to give performances, lectures, etc.

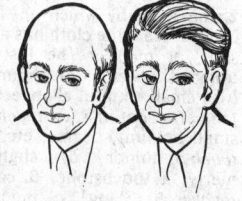
MAN WITH AND
WITHOUT TOUPEE

tour de force (toor′ də fôrs′) *pl.* **tours′ de force′** (toor′) [Fr.] a very unusual or skillful production, performance, etc., sometimes a merely clever one

☆**touring car** an early type of open automobile, often with a folding top, seating five or more passengers

tour·ism (toor′iz'm) *n.* tourist travel, esp. when thought of as a source of income for a country or business —**tour·is′tic** *adj.*

tour·ist (-ist) *n.* **1.** a person who makes a tour, esp. for pleasure **2.** tourist class —*adj.* **1.** of or for tourists **2.** designating or of the lowest-priced accommodations, as on a ship [*tourist* class] —*adv.* in or by means of tourist class [to travel *tourist*]

☆**tourist court** *same as* MOTEL

☆**tourist home** a private home in which bedrooms are rented to tourists or travelers

tour·ma·line (toor′mə lin, -lēn′) *n.* [Fr., ult. < Sinh. *tōramalli*, a carnelian] a crystalline mineral that is a complex silicate, commonly black but also colored or transparent, used as a gemstone and in optical equipment

tour·na·ment (toor′nə mənt, tur′-) *n.* [< OFr. < *tornier:* see TOURNEY] **1.** in the Middle Ages, a contest in which knights on horseback tried to unseat one another with lances **2.** a series of contests in a sport, chess, or bridge, in which a number of people or teams take part, trying to win the championship

tour·ney (toor′nē, tur′-) *n., pl.* **-neys** [< OFr. *torneier* < base of *tourner:* see TURN] *same as* TOURNAMENT —*vi.* to take part in a tournament; joust

tour·ni·quet (toor′nə kit, tur′-; -kā′) *n.* [Fr. < MFr. *turniquet*, coat of mail < OFr. *tunicle* < L. dim. of *tunica*, tunic] any device for pressing on a blood vessel to stop bleeding in an emergency, as a bandage twisted about a leg or arm and released from time to time

Tours (toor; *Fr.* tōōr) city in WC France, on the Loire: pop. 128,000

tou·sle (tou′z'l) *vt.* **-sled, -sling** [< ME. *tusen*, to pull] to make untidy, or muss up; rumple [*tousled* hair] —*n.* a tousled condition, mass of hair, etc.

Tous·saint L'Ou·ver·ture (tōō san′ lōō ver-tür′) (born *Pierre François Dominique Toussaint*) 1743?–1803; Haitian Negro liberator & general

tout (tout) *vi., vt.* [OE. *totian*, to peep] [Colloq.] **1.** to try to get (customers, votes, etc.) **2.** to praise or recommend (a person or thing) highly **3.** *a)* esp. in England, to spy on (racehorses) to get betting tips ☆*b)* to sell such tips on (racehorses) —*n.* [Colloq.] a person who touts —**tout′er** *n.*

‡**tout de suite** (tōōt swēt′) [Fr.] immediately

tou·zle (tou′z'l) *n., vt.* **-zled, -zling** *var. of* TOUSLE

tow¹ (tō) *vt.* [OE. *togian*] to pull as by a rope or chain —*n.* **1.** a towing or being towed **2.** something towed **3.** a towline —**in tow 1.** being towed **2.** as one's companion or follower **3.** under one's control

tow² (tō) *n.* [OE. *tow-*, for spinning] the coarse and broken fibers of hemp, flax, etc. before spinning

tow·age (tō′ij) *n.* **1.** a towing or being towed **2.** the charge for this

to·ward (tôrd; *also for prep.* tə wôrd′; *also, and for adj. usually,* tō′ərd) *prep.* [OE. *toweard:* see TO & -WARD] **1.** in the direction of [the house faces *toward* the park] **2.** so as to face [he turned it *toward* the window] **3.** in a way aimed at or tending to [steps *toward* peace] **4.** having to do with; about [my attitude *toward* it] **5.** close to [*toward* noon] **6.** in order to get; for [saving *toward* a car] **7.** so as to help pay for [to contribute *toward* a new library] —*adj.* [Archaic or Rare] **1.** favorable **2.** easy to manage **3.** at hand **4.** in progress

to·wards (tôrdz, tə wôrdz′) *prep. same as* TOWARD

tow·boat (tō′bōt′) *n. same as* TUGBOAT

tow·el (tou′'l, toul) *n.* [< OFr. *toaille* < Frank.] a piece of absorbent cloth or paper for wiping or drying things —*vt.* **-eled** or **-elled, -el·ing** or **-el·ling** to wipe or dry with a towel —**throw** (or **toss,** etc.) **in the towel** [Colloq.] to admit defeat; give up — **towel off** to dry oneself, as after bathing

tow·el·ing, tow·el·ling (-iŋ) *n.* material for making towels

tow·er¹ (tou′ər) *n.* [OE. *torr* & OFr. *tur*, both < L. *turris*] **1.** a building that is much higher than it is long or wide, either standing alone or as part of another building **2.** such a building used as a fortress or prison **3.** a person or thing like a tower in height, strength, etc. —*vi.* to rise high or stand high like a tower [the giraffe *towers* over other animals] —**tow′ered** *adj.*

tow·er² (tō′ər) *n.* a person or thing that tows

tow·er·ing (tou′ər iŋ) *adj.* **1.** that towers; very high or tall [a *towering* steeple] **2.** very great, intense, etc. [a *towering* rage] —see SYN. at HIGH

Tower of London a fortress on the Thames in London: in historic times it served as a palace and, later, as a prison

☆**tow·head** (tō′hed′) *n.* **1.** a head of pale-yellow hair **2.** a person having such hair —**tow′head′ed** *adj.*

☆**tow·hee** (tou′hē, tō′-) *n.* [echoic] any of various small, N. American sparrows that feed on the ground

tow·line (tō′līn′) *n.* a rope, chain, etc. for towing

town (toun) *n.* [OE. *tun*] **1.** a group of houses and buildings, larger than a village but smaller than a city **2.** a city or other thickly populated urban place ☆**3.** *a)* in parts of the U.S., *same as* TOWNSHIP *b)* in New England and some other States, a unit of local government whose affairs are conducted by a town meeting **4.** the business center of a city [to go into *town*] **5.** the people of a town [a friendly *town*] —*adj.* of or for a town

—go to town [Slang] **1.** to go on a spree **2.** to act fast and efficiently ☆**3.** to be very successful **—**☆**on the town** [Colloq.] out for a good time at the theater, nightclubs, etc.

town clerk an official in charge of the records, legal business, etc. of a town

town crier a person who formerly cried public announcements through the streets of a village or town

town hall a building in a town, housing the offices of public officials, the council chamber, etc.

town house 1. a city residence, esp. of a person who also owns a country residence ☆**2.** a dwelling, usually two-story, that is one of a number of dwellings built and joined together as a unit

☆**town meeting 1.** a meeting of the people of a town **2.** esp. in New England, a meeting of the qualified voters of a town to act upon town business

town·ship (-ship′) *n.* **1.** orig., in England, a parish or division of a parish **2.** in parts of the U.S., a division of a county making up a unit of local government **3.** in New England, *same as* TOWN (sense 3 *b*) **4.** a unit of territory in the U.S. land survey, generally six miles square **5.** in Canada, a subdivision of a province

towns·man (tounz′mən) *n., pl.* **-men 1.** a person who lives in, or has been raised in, a town **2.** any of the persons who live in the same town where one lives

towns·peo·ple (-pē′p'l) *n.pl.* **1.** the people of a town **2.** people raised in a town or city Also **towns′folk′** (-fōk′)

☆**tow·path** (tō′path′) *n.* a path alongside a canal, for men or animals towing canalboats

tow·rope (-rōp′) *n.* a rope used in towing

☆**tow truck** a truck equipped for towing away vehicles that are not able to operate, are not legally parked, etc.

tox·e·mi·a (täk sē′mē ə) *n.* [ModL.: see TOXIC & -EMIA] a condition in which poisonous substances, esp. toxins from bacteria, etc., are in the bloodstream: also sp. **tox·ae′mi·a —tox·e′mic** (-mik) *adj.*

tox·ic (täk′sik) *adj.* [< ML. < L. *toxicum,* a poison < Gr. *toxikon,* orig., poison for arrows < *toxon,* a bow] **1.** of, affected by, or caused by a toxin **2.** acting as a poison **—tox·ic′i·ty** (-sis′ə tē) *n.*

tox·i·co- [< Gr. *toxikon:* see prec.] *a combining form meaning* poison: also, before a vowel, **tox′ic-**

tox·i·col·o·gy (täk′si käl′ə jē) *n.* [< Fr.: see TOXIC & -LOGY] the science dealing with poisons and their effects and with antidotes for poisons **—tox′i·co·log′ic** (-kə läj′ik), **tox′i·co·log′i·cal** *adj.* **—tox′i·co·log′i·cal·ly** *adv.* **—tox′i·col′o·gist** *n.*

tox·in (täk′sin) *n.* [TOX(IC) + -IN¹] **1.** any of various poisonous compounds produced by some microorganisms and causing certain diseases **2.** any of various similar poisons produced by certain plants or animals Toxins injected into animals or man usually cause antitoxins to form

tox·oid (täk′soid) *n.* [TOX(IN) + -OID] a toxin that has been treated, as with chemicals, so that its poisonous qualities are removed but it can still be used as an antigen

toy (toi) *n.* [< ? MDu. *toi,* finery] **1.** a thing of little value or importance; trifle **2.** a bauble; trinket **3.** a plaything, esp. one for children **4.** anything small; specif., a dog of a kind that is bred to be small **—adj. 1.** being or like a toy [a *toy* spaniel] **2.** of or for toys [a *toy* chest] **3.** made as a toy or as a small model [a *toy* stove] **—vi.** to play or trifle (*with* a thing, idea, etc.) **—see SYN.** at TRIFLE

☆**to·yon** (tō′yən) *n.* [AmSp.] a large evergreen shrub or tree of the rose family, with clusters of white flowers and bright-red berries, native to California

toy·shop (toi′shäp′) *n.* a shop where toys are sold

tp. township

T-R transmit-receive

tr. 1. trace **2.** transitive **3.** translated **4.** translation **5.** translator **6.** transpose **7.** treasurer **8.** trustee

trace¹ (trās) *n.* [< OFr. < *tracier,* ult. < L. pp. of *trahere,* to draw] **1.** a mark, footprint, etc. left by a person, animal, or thing that has passed by [no human *trace* on the island] ☆**2.** a beaten path or trail **3.** a mark left by a past person, thing, or event; sign [*traces* of war] **4.** a very small amount [a *trace* of anger] **5.** something traced, drawn, recorded, etc., as a mark, sketch, etc. **6.** the visible line or spot moving across the face of a cathode-ray tube **7.** *Chem.* a very small amount, usually one so small that it cannot be measured **—vt. traced, trac′ing 1.** [Now Rare] to move along (a path, route, etc.) **2.** to follow the trail of; track [to *trace* a lion to his den] **3.** *a)* to follow the development or course of [to *trace* the history of Rome back to Caesar] *b)* to find (a source, date, etc.) in this way **4.** to discover by investigating traces of (a prehistoric thing, etc.) **5.** to draw, outline, etc. **6.** to ornament with tracery **7.** to copy (a drawing, etc.) by following its lines on a transparent sheet placed over it **8.** to record by a curved, broken, or wavy line, as in a seismograph **—vi. 1.** to follow a path, route, etc. **2.** to go back or date back in time [this statue *traces* to the early Greeks] **—trace′a·bil′i·ty, trace′a·ble·ness** *n.* **—trace′a·ble** *adj.* **—trace′a·bly** *adv.*

trace² (trās) *n.* [< OFr. pl. of *trait:* see TRAIT] either of two straps, chains, etc. by which a horse, ox, etc. is connected to the vehicle drawn **—kick over the traces** to shake off control

trace element 1. a chemical element, as copper, zinc, etc., essential in a proper diet, but only in very small quantities **2.** any element present in very small quantities in an organism, soil, water, etc.

trac·er (trā′sər) *n.* **1.** one that traces; specif., *a)* a person who traces designs, etc. on transparent paper *b)* a person who traces lost or missing articles, persons, etc. *c)* an instrument for tracing designs on cloth, etc. ☆**2.** a request sent out to try to find a letter, package, etc. missing in transport **3.** *same as* TRACER BULLET (OR SHELL) **4.** an element or other substance put into an animal body and used to follow biochemical reactions, to locate diseased cells, etc.

tracer bullet (or **shell**) a bullet or shell that leaves a trail of smoke or fire to mark its course and help in adjusting aim

trac·er·y (-ē) *n., pl.* **-er·ies** [< TRACE¹ + -ERY] any graceful design of lines that come together or cross in various ways, as in a stained-glass window

tra·che·a (trā′kē ə; *chiefly Brit.* trə kē′ə) *n., pl.* **-che·ae′** (-ē′), **-che·as** [ML. < LL. < Gr. *tracheia* (*arteria*), rough (windpipe)] **1.** the tube through which most land vertebrates breathe, coming from the larynx and dividing into the bronchi: see illustration at EPIGLOTTIS **2.** any of the minute tubes branching through the bodies of insects, etc. and bringing in air **—tra′che·al** *adj.*

TRACERY

tra·che·o- *a combining form meaning:* **1.** of the trachea **2.** the trachea and Also, before a vowel, **trache-**

tra·che·ole (trā′kē ōl′) *n.* [< TRACHE(O)- + -ole, dim. suffix < Fr. < L.] any of the very small, thin-walled respiratory tubes coming from the ends of the smallest insect tracheae

tra·che·ot·o·my (trā′kē ät′ə mē) *n., pl.* **-mies** [see -TOMY] the surgical operation of making an incision or cut in the trachea

tra·cho·ma (trə kō′mə) *n.* [< Gr. < *trachys,* rough] a contagious infection of the conjunctiva and cornea, caused by a virus **—tra·cho′ma·tous** (-käm′ə təs, -kō′məs-) *adj.*

trac·ing (trā′siŋ) *n.* **1.** the action of one that traces **2.** something made by tracing, as a copy of a drawing, or a line traced by a recording instrument

track (trak) *n.* [MFr. *trac,* a track] **1.** a mark or marks left by a person, animal, or thing in passing, as a footprint or rut **2.** a trace or vestige **3.** a beaten path or trail **4.** a course or line of motion or action; route [on the right *track* to solving the problem] **5.** a series of ideas, events, etc. **6.** a path or circuit laid out for running, horse racing, etc. **7.** a pair of parallel metal rails on which the wheels of trains, etc. run ☆**8.** the distance in inches between parallel wheels, as of an automobile **9.** either of the two endless belts on tanks, some tractors, etc. on which they move ☆**10.** *a)* athletic sports performed on a track, as running, hurdling, etc. *b)* track and field sports together **11.** *a) same as* SOUND TRACK *b)* any of the bands on a phonograph record *c)* any of the parallel recording surfaces along a magnetic tape **12.** *Motion Pictures* a shot taken by a camera on a moving vehicle: also **tracking shot —vt. 1.** *a)* to follow the track or footprints of [we *tracked* the fox to its den] *b)* to follow (a path, etc.) **2.** to trace by means of marks, signs, evidence, etc. [they *tracked* the criminal through three States]

3. to plot the path of and record data from (an aircraft, spacecraft, etc.) using a telescope, radar, etc. **4.** to tread or travel **5.** *a)* to leave footprints, etc. on *[the boys tracked* up the clean floor*]* ☆*b)* to leave in the form of tracks *[to track* dirt over the floor*]* —*vi.* **1.** to be in alignment, as wheels, or a phonograph pickup in a record groove **2.** *Motion Pictures* to move the camera on a vehicle in taking a shot —☆**in one's tracks** where one is at the moment —**keep track of** to go on knowing about or being informed about —**lose track of** to fail to stay informed about —☆**make tracks** [Colloq.] to go or leave hurriedly —**on** (or **off) the track** keeping to (or straying from) the subject or goal —**track down 1.** to go after until caught **2.** to investigate or search for until found —**track′er** *n.* —**track′less** *adj.*

☆**track·age** (trak′ij) *n.* **1.** all the tracks of a railroad **2.** *a)* permission for a railroad to use the tracks of another railroad *b)* a charge for this

track and field a sport, as in schools, in which a series of contests is held in running, jumping, shot-putting, discus-throwing, etc.

☆**tracking station** a station equipped to track the path of a spacecraft, satellite, etc. and record data from it

☆**track·man** (-mən) *n., pl.* **-men** one whose work is laying and repairing railroad tracks: also **track′lay′er**

☆**track man** an athlete who competes in track or field events, as a runner, hurdler, discus thrower, etc.

tract[1] (trakt) *n.* [< L. < pp. of *trahere,* to draw] **1.** formerly, *a)* length of time *b)* a period of time **2.** a large stretch of land, etc. **3.** *Anat., Zool.* a system of parts or organs having some special function *[the digestive tract]*

tract[2] (trakt) *n.* [< LL. < L. pp. of *tractare:* see TRACTABLE] a pamphlet, esp. one on a religious or political subject

trac·ta·ble (trak′tə b'l) *adj.* [< L. < *tractare,* to drag < *trahere,* to draw] **1.** easily managed, taught, etc.; docile *[a tractable horse]* **2.** easily worked or shaped; malleable *[a tractable metal]* —see SYN. at OBEDIENT —**trac′ta·bil′i·ty, trac′ta·ble·ness** *n.* —**trac′ta·bly** *adv.*

trac·tion (trak′shən) *n.* [< ML. < L. *tractus,* pp. of *trahere,* to draw] **1.** a pulling or drawing, as of a load, or a being pulled or drawn **2.** the condition of having a leg, arm, the head, etc. pulled, usually by means of some apparatus, in order to bring a fractured or dislocated bone into place or to relieve pressure **3.** the power used by a locomotive, etc. *[electric traction]* **4.** the power, as of tires on pavement, to grip or hold to a surface while moving, without slipping —**trac′tive** *adj.*

☆**trac·tor** (trak′tər) *n.* [ModL. < L.: see TRACTION] **1.** a powerful, motor-driven vehicle with large rear wheels or endless belt treads, for pulling farm machinery, hauling loads, etc. **2.** a truck with a driver's cab and no body, for hauling one or more trailers

☆**trac·tor-trail·er** (-trā′lər) *n.* a combination of a tractor and a trailer or semitrailer, used in trucking

TRACTOR

trade (trād) *n.* [MLowG., a track < OS. *trada,* a trail] **1.** *a)* a means of earning one's living; occupation *b)* skilled work; craft *[the plumber's trade]* *c)* all the persons or companies in a particular line of business *[the book trade]* **2.** buying and selling, or bartering; commerce *[trade* between nations*]* **3.** business of a specified kind *[the tourist trade]* **4.** customers; clientele *[this sale will bring in the trade]* **5.** a purchase or sale; deal *[a poor trade* in stock on the market*]* **6.** an exchange; swap *[an even trade* of his marbles for my jackknife*]* **7.** *[pl.]* the trade winds —*adj.* **1.** of trade or commerce **2.** of, by, or for the trade (n. 1 c) *[a trade* journal*]* **3.** of the members in the trades, or crafts, etc. *[trade* unions*]*: also **trades** —*vi.* **trad′ed, trad′ing 1.** to carry on a business *[this company trades* in tea*]* **2.** to have business dealings *[our country trades* with other countries*]* **3.** to make an exchange (*with* someone) **4.** [Colloq.] to be a customer (*at* a specified store, etc.) —*vt.* **1.** to exchange; barter *[I traded* my stamp collection for his camera*]* **2.** to buy and sell (stocks, etc.) —☆**trade in** to give (one's used car, etc.) as part of the purchase price of a new one —**trade on** (or **upon)** to take advantage of; exploit *[he traded* on his war record to get votes*]* —**trad′a·ble, trade′a·ble** *adj.*

☆**trade-in** (trād′in′) *n.* **1.** a used car, etc. given or taken as part payment toward a new one **2.** a deal involving such a car, etc. **3.** the amount allowed as part payment

trade·mark (-märk′) *n.* a symbol, design, word, etc. used by a manufacturer or dealer to identify his products as different from those of competitors: usually registered and protected by law —*vt.* **1.** to put a trademark on (a product) **2.** to register (a symbol, word, etc.) as a trademark

trade name 1. the name by which a product is commonly known in trade **2.** a name, often a trademark or service mark, used by a company to describe a product, service, etc. **3.** the name under which a company carries on business

☆**trade-off** (-ôf′) *n.* an exchange; esp., the giving up of one benefit, advantage, etc. in order to gain another considered more desirable: also **trade′off′**

trad·er (trā′dər) *n.* **1.** a person who trades; merchant **2.** a ship used in trade

trade route a regular route used by trading ships, caravans, etc.

trade school a school where a trade or trades are taught

trades·man (trādz′mən) *n., pl.* **-men** [Chiefly Brit.] a person in business; esp., a storekeeper —**trades′wom′an** *n.fem., pl.* **-wom′en**

trades·peo·ple (-pē′p'l) *n.pl.* people in business; esp., storekeepers: also **trades′folk**

trade union *same as* LABOR UNION: also [Chiefly Brit.] **trades union** —**trade′-un′ion** *adj.* —**trade unionism** —**trade unionist**

trade wind [earlier *trade,* adv., steadily, in phr. *to blow trade*] a wind that blows steadily toward the equator from the northeast in the tropics north of the equator and from the southeast in the tropics south of the equator

☆**trading post** a store or station in an outpost, settlement, etc., where trading is done, as with natives

trading stamp any of the stamps given along with purchases by some merchants to customers, who can then exchange them for merchandise

tra·di·tion (trə dish′ən) *n.* [< MFr. < L. < pp. of *tradere,* to deliver] **1.** *a)* the handing down by word of mouth of beliefs, customs, stories, etc. from generation to generation *b)* a belief, custom, etc. so handed down **2.** any long-established custom or practice **3.** any unwritten religious teachings thought of as coming from the founder or earliest prophet of a religion —**tra·di′tion·less** *adj.*

tra·di·tion·al (-'l) *adj.* of, handed down by, or conforming to tradition; conventional: also **tra·di′tion·ar′y** (-er′ē) —**tra·di′tion·al·ly** *adv.*

tra·di·tion·al·ism (-'l iz'm) *n.* the following of tradition or a clinging to traditions —**tra·di′tion·al·ist, tra·di′tion·ist** *n.* —**tra·di′tion·al·is′tic** *adj.*

tra·duce (trə d$\overline{oo}$s′, -dy$\overline{oo}$s′) *vt.* **-duced′, -duc′ing** [L. *traducere,* to disgrace < *tra(ns),* across + *ducere,* to lead] **1.** to say untrue or mean things about; slander **2.** to turn against; betray —**tra·duce′ment** *n.* —**tra·duc′er** *n.*

Tra·fal·gar (trə fal′gər; *Sp.* trä′fäl gär′), **Cape** cape on the SW coast of Spain, at the entrance of the Strait of Gibraltar: site of a naval battle (1805) in which Nelson's Brit. fleet defeated Napoleon's fleet

traf·fic (traf′ik) *n.* [< Fr. < It. < *trafficare,* to trade < L. *trans,* across + It. *ficcare,* to bring] **1.** buying and selling; trade, sometimes of a wrong or illegal kind *[traffic* in drugs*]* **2.** dealings or business *[I'll have no traffic* with his kind*]* **3.** *a)* the movement or number of cars along a street, pedestrians along a sidewalk, etc. *[to direct traffic* on city streets*]* *b)* the cars, pedestrians, etc. **4.** the amount of business done in a given period, as measured by the number of passengers or customers, the amount of freight handled, etc. —*adj.* of traffic or its regulation *[a traffic* light*]* —*vi.* **-ficked, -fick·ing 1.** to carry on traffic, esp. illegal business *[I'll traffic* in drugs*]* **2.** to have dealings (*with* someone) —**traf′fick·er** *n.*

☆**traffic circle** a street in the form of a circle which has several streets coming into it, with vehicles traveling in one direction only

☆**traffic court** a local court having authority over those charged with violating laws that control the movement of traffic on streets and highways

traffic island a platform or area marked in a roadway to separate lanes for traffic traveling in opposite directions or to provide a protected place for persons crossing the roadway on foot

☆**traffic light** (or **signal**) a set of signal lights for traffic, as where streets meet, that tell cars or walkers to go (green light), prepare to stop (yellow light), or stop (red light)

trag·a·canth (trag′ə kanth′) *n.* [< Fr. < L. < Gr. < *tragos,* goat + *akantha,* thorn] **1.** a white or reddish gum that has no taste and is used as a thickener and emulsifier in foodstuffs, drugs, etc. **2.** any of certain Asiatic plants that produce this gum

tra·ge·di·an (trə jē′dē ən) *n.* an actor of tragedy

tra·ge·di·enne (trə jē′dē en′) *n.* an actress of tragedy

trag·e·dy (traj′ə dē) *n., pl.* **-dies** [< MFr. < L. < Gr. *tragōidia* < *tragos*, goat + *ōidē*, song: prob. from the goatskin costume of the performers acting as satyrs] **1.** a serious play having a sad or unfortunate ending brought about by fate, a moral weakness in a character, social conditions, etc. **2.** the branch of drama made up of such plays **3.** the writing or acting of such plays **4.** a novel or any narrative like such a play in theme, tone, etc. **5.** the tragic element or quality as it appears in literature or life **6.** a very sad or tragic event

trag·ic (traj′ik) *adj.* **1.** of, like, or having to do with tragedy [a *tragic* actor; a *tragic* tale] **2.** bringing great harm, suffering, etc.; very sad, unfortunate, etc. [a *tragic* accident; a *tragic* misunderstanding] **3.** suitable to tragedy [a *tragic* voice] Also **trag′i·cal** —*n.* the tragic element or quality in art or life —**trag′i·cal·ly** *adv.* —**trag′i·cal·ness** *n.*

trag·i·com·e·dy (traj′ə käm′ə dē) *n., pl.* **-dies** **1.** a play, novel, etc. combining tragic and comic elements **2.** a situation or incident in life like this —**trag′i·com′ic, trag′i·com′i·cal** *adj.* —**trag′i·com′i·cal·ly** *adv.*

tra·gus (trā′gəs) *n., pl.* **-gi** (-jī) [LL. < Gr. *tragos*, hairy part of the ear, lit., goat] the fleshy part at the front of the external ear, partly going over the opening of the ear

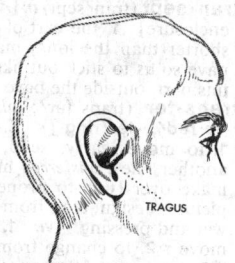

TRAGUS

trail (trāl) *vt.* [< MFr., ult. < L. *tragula*, sledge < *trahere*, to drag] **1.** *a)* to drag or let drag behind one *b)* to bring along behind [*trailing* exhaust fumes] *c)* to pull or tow **2.** *a)* to make (a path, etc.), as by treading down *b)* to make a path in (grass, etc.) **3.** to follow the tracks of [they *trailed* the wounded animal for three hours] **4.** to hunt by tracking **5.** to follow or lag behind (another or others) in movement, a contest, etc. **6.** *Mil.* to carry (a rifle, etc.) in one hand, with the muzzle tilted forward and the butt near the ground —*vi.* **1.** to be drawn along behind one [the bride's veil *trailed* on the floor] **2.** to grow along the ground, etc., as some plants **3.** to extend in an irregular line; straggle **4.** to flow behind in a long, thin stream, wisp, etc. [black smoke *trailed* from the exhaust pipe] **5.** *a)* to follow or lag behind [the children *trailed* along after us] *b)* to be losing, as in a sports contest [to *trail* by 13 points] **6.** to track game: said of hounds **7.** to grow gradually weaker, dimmer, etc. (with *off* or *away*) [her voice *trailed* off into a whisper] —*n.* **1.** something that trails behind [a *trail* of dust] **2.** a mark, scent, etc. left by a person, animal, or thing that has passed ☆**3.** a rough path made across country, as by repeated passage **4.** a train of events, etc. following something [a *trail* of debts followed his illness] **5.** a part of a gun carriage, which may be lowered to the ground to form a rear brace

☆**trail·blaz·er** (trāl′blā′zər) *n.* **1.** a person who blazes a trail or path **2.** a pioneer in any field —**trail′blaz′ing** *n.*

trail·er (trā′lər) *n.* **1.** one that trails another ☆**2.** a cart or van designed to be pulled by an automobile or truck (esp. a tractor, *n.* 2), for hauling freight, animals, a boat, etc. ☆**3.** a closed vehicle designed to be pulled by a motor vehicle and equipped as a place to live or work in: see also MOBILE HOME ☆**4.** a selection of scenes from a coming motion picture, used to advertise it

☆**trailer park** an area, usually with piped water, electricity, etc., designed to provide rental space for trailers, esp. mobile homes to be parked for a long or a short time: also **trailer camp, trailer court**

☆**trailing arbutus** (trā′liŋ) *same as* ARBUTUS (sense 2)

trailing edge *Aeron.* the rear edge of an airfoil, propeller blade, etc.

train (trān) *n.* [< OFr. < *trahiner*, to draw on, ult. < L. *trahere*, to pull] **1.** something that drags along behind, as a part of a gown that trails **2.** a group of followers or attendants in a procession; retinue, as of a king **3.** a group of persons, animals, vehicles, etc. moving in a line; procession; caravan [a wagon *train*] **4.** the persons, vehicles, etc. carrying supplies, ammunition, food, etc. for combat troops [a supply *train*] **5.** a series of

events that follow some happening [war brought famine in its *train*] **6.** any connected series [a *train* of thought] **7.** a line of gunpowder used to set off an explosive charge **8.** a series of connected parts for passing on motion [a gear *train*] **9.** a line of connected railroad cars pulled or pushed by a locomotive —*vt.* **1.** to guide the growth of (a plant) by tying, pruning, etc. **2.** to cause to undergo certain action, exercises, etc. so as to bring to a desired condition [a surgeon's hand *trained* to be steady] **3.** to guide the mental, moral, etc. development of; bring up; rear [they *trained* their children to be kind] **4.** to teach so as to make fully skilled [to *train* airplane pilots] **5.** to teach (animals) to do tricks or obey commands **6.** to make fit for some sport, as by exercise, practice, etc. **7.** to aim (a gun, binoculars, etc.) at something [she *trained* her opera glasses on the stage] **8.** [Colloq.] to teach (a child, puppy, etc.) to move the bowels and urinate in the place intended for this —*vi.* to give or get training —see SYN. at TEACH —**train′a·ble** *adj.* —**train′er** *n.*

train·ee (trā nē′) *n.* a person who is being given vocational training, military training, etc. —**train·ee′ship′** *n.*

train·ing (trān′iŋ) *n.* **1.** the lessons, practice, drills, etc. given by one who trains or received by one who is being trained **2.** the process of being trained for some sport, as by exercise, practice, etc.

☆**train·man** (-mən) *n., pl.* **-men** a person who works on a railroad train or in a railroad yard; esp., a brakeman

traipse (trāps) *vi., vt.* **traipsed, traips′ing** [< ?] [Dial. or Colloq.] to walk or wander in an aimless or lazy way —*n.* [Dial. or Colloq.] the act of traipsing

trait (trāt) *n.* [Fr., a line < L. pp. of *trahere*, to draw] a special quality or feature, as of personality [a sense of humor is his finest *trait*] —see SYN. at QUALITY

trai·tor (trāt′ər) *n.* [OFr. < L. < pp. of *tradere*, to betray] a person who betrays his country, cause, friends, etc.; one guilty of treason or treachery —**trai′tress** *n.fem.*

trai·tor·ous (-əs) *adj.* **1.** of or like a traitor; treacherous **2.** of or involving treason; treasonable —see SYN. at FAITHLESS —**trai′tor·ous·ly** *adv.* —**trai′tor·ous·ness** *n.*

Tra·jan (trā′jən) (L. name *Marcus Ulpius Trajanus*) 53?–117 A.D.; Rom. emperor (98–117), born in Spain

tra·jec·to·ry (trə jek′tə rē) *n., pl.* **-ries** [< ML. < L. pp. of *trajicere* < *tra(ns)*, across + *jacere*, to throw] the curved path of something thrown or shot through space, esp. that of a projectile

tram (tram) *n.* [prob. < LowG. *traam*, a beam] **1.** an open railway car used in mines: also **tram′car′** **2.** [Brit.] *a)* a streetcar; trolley car: also **tram′car′** *b)* a streetcar line: also **tram′line′, tram′way′** —*vt., vi.* **trammed, tram′ming** to carry or ride in a tram

tram·mel (tram′'l) *n.* [< MFr. < ML. *tremaculum*, kind of fishing net < L. *tres*, three + *macula*, a mesh] **1.** *a)* a fishing net with three layers of mesh *b)* a fowling net Also **trammel net** **2.** a shackle for a horse, esp. one to teach ambling **3.** [usually pl.] something that hinders freedom of action **4.** a device with links, etc. for hanging a pothook in a fireplace **5.** an instrument for drawing ellipses —*vt.* **-meled** or **-melled, -mel·ing** or **-mel·ling** **1.** to entangle as in a trammel **2.** to hinder, restrain, or shackle [*trammeled* by harsh laws] —**tram′mel·er, tram′mel·ler** *n.*

tramp (tramp) *vi.* [< or akin to LowG. *trampen*, to trample] **1.** *a)* to walk with heavy steps *b)* to step heavily; stamp [the horse *tramped* on my foot] **2.** *a)* to travel about on foot; hike [we *tramped* through the woods] *b)* to travel as or like a vagabond, hobo, etc. —*vt.* **1.** to step on heavily; trample **2.** to walk or ramble through —*n.* **1.** a person who travels about on foot doing odd jobs or begging; hobo; vagrant **2.** the sound of heavy steps **3.** a journey on foot; hike [a *tramp* through the forest] **4.** a freight ship that has no regular schedule, arranging for cargo, etc. as it goes along —see SYN. at VAGRANT —**tramp′er** *n.*

tram·ple (tram′p'l) *vi.* **-pled, -pling** [< ME. *trampen* (see TRAMP) + -LE²] to step heavily (*on* something) —*vt.* to crush, destroy, etc. as by stepping heavily on [a herd of cattle *trampled* the crops] —*n.* the sound of trampling —**trample under foot** to crush or hurt by or as by trampling: also **trample on** (or **upon**) —**tram′pler** *n.*

tram·po·line (tram′pə lēn′, -lin; tram′pə lēn′) *n.* [< It. *trampolino*, a springboard] ☆a sheet of strong canvas stretched tightly on a frame, used as a kind of springboard in acrobatic tumbling —**tram′po·lin′er, tram′po·lin′ist** *n.*

trance (trans) *n.* [< OFr. < L. *transire*, to die: see TRANSIT] **1.** a state brought on by hysteria, hypnosis, etc., in which a person seems to be conscious but is unable to move or act of his own will **2.** a stunned condition; daze, stupor, etc. **3.** the condition of being completely lost in thought or meditation **4.** the state a spiritualist medium is in while supposedly communicating with the dead

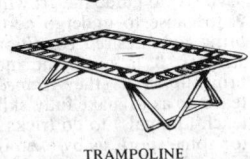

TRAMPOLINE

tran·quil (traŋ′kwəl, tran′-) *adj.* -quil·er or -quil·ler, -quil·est or -quil·lest [L. *tranquillus*] calm, quiet, peaceful, etc. [*tranquil* waters, a *tranquil* mood] —see SYN. at CALM — **tran′quil·ly** *adv.*

tran·quil·ize, tran·quil·lize (traŋ′kwə līz′, tran′-) *vt., vi.* -ized′ or -lized′, -iz′ing or -liz′ing to make or become tranquil; specif., to calm by the use of a tranquilizer —**tran′quil·i·za′tion, tran′quil·li·za′tion** *n.*

tran·quil·iz·er, tran·quil·liz·er (-lī′zər) *n.* any of certain drugs used in calming persons suffering from nervous tension, anxiety, etc.

tran·quil·li·ty, tran·quil·i·ty (traŋ kwil′ə tē, tran-) *n.* the quality or state of being tranquil; calmness, etc.

trans- [L. < *trans*, across] *a prefix meaning:* **1.** on or to the other side of, over, across, through [*transatlantic*] **2.** so as to change completely [*transliterate*] **3.** above and beyond, transcending [*transsonic*]

trans. 1. transaction(s) **2.** transitive **3.** translated **4.** translation **5.** transportation

trans·act (tran sakt′, -zakt′) *vt.* [< L. pp. of *transigere* < *trans-*, across + *agere*, to drive] to carry on, conduct, or complete (business, etc.) —**trans·ac′tor** *n.*

trans·ac·tion (-sak′shən, -zak′-) *n.* **1.** a transacting or being transacted **2.** something transacted; specif., *a)* a business deal *b)* [*pl.*] a record of the matters dealt with at a formal meeting —**trans·ac′tion·al** *adj.*

trans·al·pine (trans al′pīn, tranz-; -pin) *adj.* on the other (the northern) side of the Alps, from Rome

trans·at·lan·tic (trans′ət lan′tik, tranz′-) *adj.* **1.** crossing the Atlantic [a *transatlantic* flight] **2.** on the other side of the Atlantic

Trans·cau·ca·sia (trans′kô kā′zhə, -shə) that part of the Caucasus south of the Caucasus Mountains, containing the republics of Armenia, Azerbaijan, & Georgia —**Trans′cau·ca′sian** *adj., n.*

☆**trans·ceiv·er** (tran sē′vər) *n.* [TRANS(MITTER) + (RE)CEIVER] **1.** a device in a single housing, working sometimes as a radio transmitter and at other times as a radio receiver **2.** an electronic device that transmits and receives exact reproductions of printed material, pictures, etc. over a telephone line

tran·scend (tran send′) *vt.* [L. *transcendere* < *trans-*, over + *scandere*, to climb] **1.** to go beyond the limits of; exceed [his story *transcends* belief] **2.** to be superior to; surpass; excel [her beauty *transcends* that of others] —*vi.* to be transcendent

tran·scend·ent (-sen′dənt) *adj.* **1.** far beyond the usual or ordinary; superior [her *transcendent* wisdom] **2.** *Theol.* existing apart from the material universe —**tran·scend′ence, tran·scend′en·cy** *n.* —**tran·scend′ent·ly** *adv.*

tran·scen·den·tal (tran′sen den′t'l) *adj.* **1.** *same as:* *a)* TRANSCENDENT (sense 1) *b)* SUPERNATURAL **2.** abstract; metaphysical **3.** of transcendentalism **4.** *Math.* that cannot be a root of any algebraic equation with rational coefficients — **tran′scen·den′tal·ly** *adv.*

tran·scen·den·tal·ism (-iz'm) *n.* **1.** any of various philosophies seeking to discover the nature of reality by investigating the process of thought rather than the things that are thought about ☆**2.** the philosophical ideas of Emerson and some other 19th-cent. New Englanders, based on a search for reality through spiritual intuition **3.** popularly, any unclear, impractical, or idealistic thought —**tran′scen·den′tal·ist** *n., adj.*

☆**trans·con·ti·nen·tal** (trans′kän tə nen′t'l) *adj.* **1.** that crosses a (or the) continent [a *transcontinental* flight] **2.** on the other side of a (or the) continent —**trans′con·ti·nen′tal·ly** *adv.*

tran·scribe (tran skrīb′) *vt.* -scribed′, -scrib′ing [< L. < *trans-*, over + *scribere*, to write] **1.** to write or type out in full (shorthand notes, a speech, etc.) **2.** to translate or transliterate **3.** to arrange (a piece of music) for an instrument, etc. other than that for which it was originally written **4.** *Radio & TV* to record (a program, commercial, etc.) for broadcast later —**tran·scrib′er** *n.*

tran·script (tran′skript′) *n.* **1.** something made by transcribing; written, typewritten, or printed copy **2.** any copy or reproduction, ☆esp. one that is official, as a copy of a student's record in school or college

tran·scrip·tion (tran skrip′shən) *n.* **1.** the act or process of transcribing **2.** a transcript; copy **3.** an arrangement of a piece of music for an instrument, voice, etc. other than that for which it was originally written **4.** a recording made for radio or television broadcasting; also, the act of using such recordings —**tran·scrip′tion·al** *adj.*

trans·duc·er (trans doos′ər, tranz-; -dyoos′-) *n.* [< L. < *trans-*, over + *ducere*, to lead + -ER] any of various devices that transmit energy from one system to another, sometimes one that changes the form of the energy

tran·sect (tran sekt′) *vt.* [< TRANS- + pp. of L. *secare*, to cut] to cut across —**tran·sec′tion** *n.*

tran·sept (tran′sept) *n.* [< ModL. < L. *trans-*, across + *septum*, enclosure] **1.** the part of a cross-shaped church that is usually shorter than the long, main section, or nave and crosses the nave so as to stick out like arms at each side **2.** either arm of this part, outside the nave

trans·fer (trans fur′; *also, & for n. always,* trans′fər) *vt.* -ferred′, -fer′ring [< L. < *trans-*, across + *ferre*, to BEAR[1]] **1.** to move, carry, send, etc. from one person or place to another [he *transferred* his notes to another notebook] **2.** to make over (title to property, etc.) to another **3.** to move (a picture, design, etc.) from one surface to another, as by making wet and pressing —*vi.* **1.** to transfer oneself or be transferred; move ☆**2.** to change from one school, college, etc. to another ☆**3.** to change from one bus, train, etc. to another —*n.* **1.** a transferring or being transferred **2.** one that is transferred; specif., a picture or design transferred or to be transferred from one surface to another ☆**3.** a ticket allowing the bearer to change from one bus, train, etc. to another ☆**4.** a document permitting a transfer ☆**5.** a person who transfers or is transferred [he is a *transfer* from another school] —**trans·fer′a·ble, trans·fer′ra·ble** *adj.* —**trans·fer′al, trans·fer′ral** *n.* — **trans·fer′rer,** *Law* **trans·fer′or** *n.*

trans·fer·ee (trans′fər ē′) *n.* a person who is transferred or to whom something is transferred

trans·fer·ence (trans fur′əns, trans′fər-) *n.* **1.** a transferring or being transferred **2.** a transferring of the feelings that one had toward a certain person in the past, esp. in childhood, and that one has repressed, to another person in the present, esp. to one's psychoanalyst

trans·fig·u·ra·tion (trans fig′yoo rā′shən, trans′fig-) *n.* a change in form or looks —[T-] **1.** *Bible* the change in the appearance of Jesus on the mountain: Matt. 17 **2.** a church festival (Aug. 6) commemorating this

trans·fig·ure (trans fig′yər) *vt.* -ured, -ur·ing [L. *transfigurare*: see TRANS- & FIGURE] **1.** to change the figure, form, or appearance of; transform [a new dress and hairdo *transfigured* her] **2.** to make seem splendid or glorious [he was *transfigured* by his deep love] —see SYN. at TRANSFORM —**trans·fig′ur·er** *n.*

trans·fix (trans fiks′) *vt.* [< L. pp. of *transfigere* < *trans-*, through + *figere*, to fix] **1.** to pierce through as with an arrow **2.** to fasten in this way; impale **3.** to make unable to move, as if pierced through [*transfixed* with horror] —**trans·fix′ion** *n.*

trans·form (trans fôrm′) *vt.* [L. *transformare*, ult. < *trans-*, over + *forma*, a shape] **1.** to change the form or appearance of [a vase of roses *transformed* the drab room] **2.** to change the condition, character, or function of [the barn has been *transformed* into a house] **3.** *Elec.* to change (voltage, current, etc.) by use of a transformer **4.** *Math.* to change (an algebraic expression or equation) to a different form having the same value **5.** *Physics* to change (one form of energy) into another —*vi.* [Rare] to be or become transformed —**trans·form′a·ble** *adj.* — **trans·form′a·tive** *adj.*

SYN.—**transform** implies a change either in outer form or inner nature, in use, etc. [she was *transformed* into a happy girl]; **transmute** suggests a change in basic nature that seems almost like a miracle [*transmuted* from a shy youth into a man about town]; **convert** implies a change in details so as to be suitable for a new use [to *convert* an attic into an apartment]; **metamorphose** suggests a surprising change produced as if by magic [a tadpole is *metamorphosed* into a frog]; **transfigure** implies a change in outward appearance which seems to make splendid or glorious [her plain features *transfigured* with tenderness] —see also **SYN.** at CHANGE

trans·for·ma·tion (trans′fər mā′shən) *n.* **1.** a transforming or being transformed ☆**2.** *Linguis.* the process or result of getting, by applying certain rules, all the sentences of a given language from a basic group of simple, declarative sentences —**trans′for·ma′tion·al** *adj.*

trans·form·er (trans fôr′mər) *n.* **1.** a person or thing that transforms **2.** *Elec.* a device for transferring electric energy from one alternating-current circuit to another, usually with a change in voltage, current, etc.

trans·fuse (trans fyoōz′) *vt.* -fused′, -fus′ing [< L. pp. of *transfundere* < *trans-*, across + *fundere*, to pour] **1.** to pour in or spread through; instill [the victory *transfused* new courage into the team] **2.** *Med.* *a)* to transfer or introduce (blood, saline solution, etc.) into a blood vessel, usually a vein *b)* to give a transfusion to —**trans·fus′er** *n.* —**trans·fus′i·ble** *adj.* —**trans·fu′sive** *adj.*

trans·fu·sion (-fyoō′zhən) *n.* a transfusing, esp. of blood

trans·gress (trans gres′, tranz-) *vt.* [< Fr. < L. pp. of *transgredi* < *trans-*, over + *gradi*, to step] **1.** to overstep or break (a law, commandment, etc.) **2.** to go beyond (a limit, boundary, etc.) —*vi.* to break a law, commandment, etc.; sin —**trans·gres′sive** *adj.* —**trans·gres′sor** *n.*

trans·gres·sion (-gresh′ən) *n.* a transgressing or breaking of a law, duty, etc.; sin

tran·ship (tran ship′) *vt.* var. sp. of TRANSSHIP

tran·sient (tran′shənt) *adj.* [< L. prp. of *transire*: see TRANSIT] **1.** *a)* passing away with time; temporary [*transient* glories] *b)* passing quickly [*transient* pleasures] ☆**2.** staying for only a short time [a *transient* lodger] —*n.* ☆a transient person or thing [*transients* at a hotel] —**tran′sience, tran′sien·cy** *n.* —**tran′sient·ly** *adv.*

SYN.—**transient** applies to that which lasts or stays but a short time [a *transient* guest, feeling, etc.]; **transitory** refers to that which by its very nature must sooner or later pass or end [an animal's life is *transitory*]; **ephemeral** applies to that which is very short-lived [the *ephemeral* popularity of a best seller]; **momentary** implies lasting for a moment or a very short time [a *momentary* delay]; **evanescent** applies to that which appears for a moment and then fades quickly away [*evanescent* mental images]; **fleeting** implies of a thing that it passes swiftly and cannot be held [a *fleeting* thought] —**ANT.** lasting, permanent

☆**tran·sis·tor** (tran zis′tər, -sis′-) *n.* [TRAN(SFER) + (RE)SISTOR] a small, solid-state electronic device used instead of an electron tube, esp. in hearing aids and very small radios

☆**tran·sis·tor·ize** (-tə rīz′) *vt.* -ized′, -iz′ing to equip with transistors

trans·it (tran′sit, -zit) *n.* [< L. pp. of *transire* < *trans-*, over + *ire*, to go] **1.** *a)* passage through or across *b)* a transition; change **2.** *a)* the act of carrying or being carried from one place to another [goods in *transit*] *b)* a system of public transportation in a city: see also RAPID TRANSIT **3.** an instrument used by surveyors for measuring horizontal angles: in full, **transit theodolite 4.** *Astron. a)* the passage that a heavenly body seems to make across a given meridian or through the field of a telescope *b)* the similar passage of a smaller heavenly body across the disk of a larger one —*vt., vi.* to make a transit (through or across)

TRANSIT

tran·si·tion (tran zish′ən, -sish′-; Brit. -sizh′-) *n.* **1.** *a)* a passing from one condition, activity, place, etc. to another [the *transition* from war to peace] *b)* the period of this **2.** a word, phrase, sentence, etc. that relates one element or topic to another that follows **3.** *Music a)* a shifting from one key to another; modulation *b)* same as BRIDGE[1] —**tran·si′tion·al** *adj.* —**tran·si′tion·al·ly** *adv.*

tran·si·tive (tran′sə tiv, -zə-) *adj.* taking a direct object to complete the meaning: said of certain verbs —*n.* a transitive verb —**tran′si·tive·ly** *adv.*

tran·si·to·ry (tran′sə tôr′ē, -zə-) *adj.* of a passing nature; not lasting; temporary [*transitory* fame] —see **SYN.** at TRANSIENT —**tran′si·to′ri·ly** *adv.* —**tran′si·to′ri·ness** *n.*

transl. 1. translated **2.** translation

trans·late (trans lāt′, tranz-; trans′lāt, tranz′-) *vt.* -lat′ed, -lat′ing [< L. *translatus*, used as pp. of *transferre*, to TRANSFER] **1.** to change from one place or condition to another; specif., *Theol.* to carry up to heaven without death **2.** to put into the words of a different language [to *translate* a French poem into English] **3.** to change into another medium or form [*translate* ideas into action] **4.** to put into different words; rephrase —*vi.* **1.** to make a translation into another language **2.** to be capable of being translated [his plays *translate* easily] —**trans·lat′a·ble** *adj.* —**trans·la′tor** *n.*

trans·la·tion (-lā′shən) *n.* **1.** a translating or being translated **2.** writing or speech translated into another language —**trans·la′tion·al** *adj.*

trans·lit·er·ate (trans lit′ə rāt′, tranz-) *vt.* -at′ed, -at′ing [< TRANS- + L. *litera*, letter + -ATE[1]] to write or spell (words, letters, etc. in one alphabet) in corresponding characters of another alphabet —**trans·lit′er·a′tion** *n.*

trans·lu·cent (trans loō′s'nt, tranz-) *adj.* [< L. prp. of *translucere* < *trans-*, through + *lucere*, to shine] **1.** orig., shining through **2.** letting light pass but spreading it so that objects on the other side cannot be clearly seen [frosted glass is *translucent*]: also **trans·lu′cid** (-sid) —**trans·lu′cence, trans·lu′cen·cy** *n.* —**trans·lu′cent·ly** *adv.*

trans·mi·grate (trans mī′grāt, tranz-) *vi.* -grat·ed, -grat·ing [< L. pp. of *transmigrare*: see TRANS- & MIGRATE] **1.** to move from one region, country, etc. to another **2.** in some religions, to pass into another body at death: said of the soul —**trans·mi′gra·tor** *n.* —**trans·mi′gra·to′ry** (-grə tôr′ē) *adj.*

trans·mi·gra·tion (trans′mī grā′shən, tranz′-) *n.* the act or process of transmigrating; specif., the supposed passing of the soul at death into some other body

trans·mis·si·ble (trans mis′ə b'l, tranz-) *adj.* capable of being transmitted —**trans·mis′si·bil′i·ty** *n.*

trans·mis·sion (-mish′ən) *n.* **1.** *a)* a transmitting or being transmitted *b)* something transmitted **2.** the part of an automobile, etc. that sends the power from the engine to the wheels, as by gears **3.** the passage of radio waves through space between the transmitting station and the receiving station —**trans·mis′sive** *adj.*

trans·mit (-mit′) *vt.* -mit′ted, -mit′ting [< L. < *trans-*, over + *mittere*, to send] **1.** to send or cause to go from one person or place to another; transfer; convey [to *transmit* a letter] **2.** to pass along (a disease, etc.) **3.** to hand down to others by heredity, inheritance, etc. [color blindness may be *transmitted*] **4.** to communicate (news, etc.) **5.** *a)* to cause (light, heat, etc.) to pass through some medium [the sun *transmits* heat and light] *b)* to allow the passage of; conduct [water *transmits* sound] **6.** to carry (force, movement, etc.) from one mechanical part to another **7.** to send out (radio or television broadcasts, etc.) by electromagnetic waves —*vi.* to send out radio or television signals —**trans·mit′tal, trans·mit′tance, trans·mit′tan·cy** *n.* —**trans·mit′ti·ble, trans·mit′ta·ble** *adj.*

trans·mit·ter (trans mit′ər; for 2, often trans′mit ər, tranz′-) *n.* **1.** a person who transmits **2.** a thing that transmits; specif., *a)* the part of a telegraphic instrument by which messages are sent *b)* the part of a telephone, behind the mouthpiece, that changes sound into electric impulses for transmission *c)* the device that produces and sends out radio waves

trans·mu·ta·tion (trans′myoō tā′shən, tranz′-) *n.* **1.** a transmuting or being transmuted **2.** the changing of base metals into gold and silver as sought by alchemists in the Middle Ages **3.** *Chem.* the changing of atoms of one element into atoms of a different isotope, or element, as by nuclear bombardment —**trans′mu·ta′tion·al** *adj.* —**trans·mut′a·tive** (-myoōt′ə tiv) *adj.*

trans·mute (trans myoōt′, tranz-) *vt., vi.* -mut′ed, -mut′ing [< L. < *trans-*, over + *mutare*, to change] to change from one form, nature, substance, etc. into another; transform —see **SYN.** at TRANSFORM —**trans·mut′a·bil′i·ty** *n.* —**trans·mut′a·ble** *adj.* —**trans·mut′a·bly** *adv.*

trans·na·tion·al (-nash′ə n'l) *adj.* beyond the limits, interests, etc. of a single nation

trans·o·ce·an·ic (trans′ō shē an′ik, tranz′-) *adj.* **1.** crossing or spanning the ocean **2.** from or on the other side of the ocean

tran·som (tran′səm) *n.* [prob. < L. *transtrum,* crossbeam] **1.** a horizontal crossbar across the top or middle of a window or the top of a door ☆**2.** a small window directly over a door or window, usually hinged to the transom **3.** any crosspiece, as the horizontal beam of a gallows

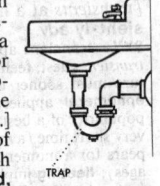

TRANSOM

tran·son·ic (tran sän′ik) *adj.* designating, of, or moving at a speed within the range of change from subsonic to supersonic speed

trans·pa·cif·ic (trans′pə sif′ik) *adj.* **1.** crossing or spanning the Pacific **2.** on the other side of the Pacific

trans·par·en·cy (trans per′ən sē, -par′-) *n.* **1.** a transparent state or quality: also **trans·par′ence 2.** *pl.* **-cies** something transparent; specif., a positive film or slide having a picture, etc. that can be seen through when light shines through it or that can be projected on a screen

trans·par·ent (-ənt) *adj.* [< ML. prp. of *transparere* < L. *trans-,* through + *parere,* to appear] **1.** transmitting light rays so that objects on the other side may be clearly seen [*transparent glass*] **2.** so fine in texture or open in mesh as to be seen through; sheer; gauzy [a *transparent veil*] **3.** easily understood, recognized, or detected; obvious [a *transparent lie*] —**trans·par′ent·ly** *adv.* —**trans·par′ent·ness** *n.*

tran·spire (tran spīr′) *vt.* **-spired′, -spir′ing** [< Fr. < ML. < L. *trans-,* through + *spirare,* to breathe] to cause (vapor, moisture, etc.) to pass through tissue or certain other substances, esp. through the pores of the skin or the surface of leaves, etc. —*vi.* **1.** to give off vapor, moisture, etc. as through pores **2.** to be given off, exhaled, etc. **3.** to leak out; become known ☆**4.** to come to pass; happen [what *transpired* while I was gone?]: thought of by some people to be a loose or incorrect meaning —see SYN. at HAPPEN —**tran′spi·ra′tion** (-spə rā′shən) *n.*

trans·plant (trans plant′; *for n.* trans′plant′) *vt.* [< LL.: see TRANS- & PLANT] **1.** to dig up (a growing plant) from one place and plant or put in another **2.** to remove (people) from one place and resettle in another **3.** to transfer (tissue or an organ) by surgery from one individual or part of the body to another; graft —*vi.* to be capable of being transplanted [that sort of shrub does not *transplant* well] —*n.* **1.** a transplanting **2.** something transplanted, as a body organ or seedling —**trans·plant′a·ble** *adj.* —**trans·plan·ta′tion** *n.* —**trans·plant′er** *n.*

tran·spon·der (tran spän′dər) *n.* [TRAN(SMITTER) + (RE)SPOND + -ER] a radio or radar transceiver that automatically transmits electrical signals when put into action by a specific signal

trans·port (trans pôrt′; *for n.* trans′pôrt) *vt.* [< MFr. < L. *trans-,* over + *portare,* to carry] **1.** to carry from one place to another, esp. over long distances [to *transport* goods by train or truck] **2.** to carry away with emotion; enrapture [*transported* with delight] **3.** to send to a place far away as a punishment —*n.* **1.** a transporting; transportation **2.** strong emotion, esp. of delight or joy **3.** a ship, airplane, train, etc. used for transporting soldiers, freight, etc. **4.** a transported convict —see SYN. at ECSTASY —**trans·port′a·bil′i·ty** *n.* —**trans·port′a·ble** *adj.* —**trans·port′er** *n.*

trans·por·ta·tion (trans′pər tā′shən) *n.* **1.** a transporting or being transported **2.** *a)* a means or system of carrying things *b)* the work or business of transporting passengers or goods ☆**3.** fare or a ticket for being transported

trans·pose (trans pōz′) *vt.* **-posed′, -pos′ing** [MFr. *transposer:* see TRANS- & POSE] **1.** to change the usual or relative order or position of; interchange [he mistakenly *transposed* the *e* and the *i* in "weird"] **2.** to transfer (an algebraic term) from one side of an equation to the other, reversing the plus or minus value **3.** to rewrite or play (a musical composition) in a different key —*vi.* to play music in a different key —**trans·pos′a·bil′i·ty, trans·pos′a·ble·ness** *n.* —**trans·pos′a·ble** *adj.* —**trans·pos′er** *n.* —**trans·po·si′tion** (-pə zish′ən) *n.*

☆**trans·sex·u·al** (tran sek′shōō wəl, trans-) *n.* a person who would like to be of the opposite sex, or one whose sex has been changed by means of surgery and hormone injections —**trans·sex′u·al·ism** *n.*

trans·ship (tran ship′, trans-) *vt.* **-shipped′, -ship′ping** to transfer from one ship, train, truck, etc. to another for reshipment —**trans·ship′ment** *n.*

trans·son·ic (-sän′ik) *adj.* same as TRANSONIC

☆**tran·stage** (tran′stāj′) *n.* [TRAN(S)- + STAGE] an unmanned, third-stage rocket that can be restarted in space and that can change orbit, perform maneuvers, etc.

tran·sub·stan·ti·a·tion (tran′səb stan′shē ā′shən) *n.* [< ML. < pp. of *transubstantiare* < L. *trans-,* over + *substantia,* substance] **1.** a changing of one substance into another **2.** *R.C. & Orthodox Eastern Ch.* the doctrine that, in the Eucharist, the whole substances of the bread and wine are changed into the body and blood of Christ, while only the appearance, taste, etc. of bread and wine remain

trans·u·ran·ic (trans′yōō ran′ik, tranz′-) *adj.* designating or of the elements, as plutonium, having atomic numbers higher than that of uranium: also **trans′u·ra′ni·um** (-rā′nē əm)

Trans·vaal (trans väl′, tranz-) province of South Africa, in the NE part

trans·ver·sal (trans vur′səl) *adj.* same as TRANSVERSE —*n.* a line that intersects two or more other lines —**trans·ver′sal·ly** *adv.*

trans·verse (trans vurs′, tranz-; *also, and for n. usually,* trans′vurs, tranz′-) *adj.* [< L. pp. of *transvertere:* see TRAVERSE] lying, situated, placed, etc. across; crosswise —*n.* a transverse part, beam, etc. —**trans·verse′ly** *adv.*

transverse colon the central portion of the large intestine, crossing the abdomen: see illustration at INTESTINE

trans·ves·tite (trans ves′tīt, tranz-) *n.* [< TRANS- + L. *vestire,* to clothe + -ITE] a person who gets sexual pleasure from dressing in the clothes of the opposite sex —**trans·ves′tism, trans·ves′ti·tism** (-tiz′m) *n.*

Tran·syl·va·ni·a (tran′sil vā′nē ə, -vān′yə) plateau region in C Romania —**Tran′syl·va′ni·an** *adj., n.*

Transylvanian Alps range of the Carpathian Mountains, in central and SW Romania

trap¹ (trap) *n.* [OE. *træppe*] **1.** any device for catching animals; gin, snare, etc. **2.** any scheme or ambush designed to catch or trick unsuspecting persons [a question that was a *trap* to get the truth from him] **3.** any of various devices for preventing the escape of gas, bad odors, etc., as a U-shaped part in a drainpipe **4.** a device for throwing disks into the air to be shot at in trapshooting **5.** a light, two-wheeled carriage with springs **6.** same as TRAPDOOR ☆**7.** [*pl.*] the cymbals, blocks, etc. attached to a set of drums, as in a jazz band **8.** [Slang] the mouth **9.** *Golf* same as SAND TRAP —*vt.* **trapped, trap′ping 1.** to catch as in a trap; entrap **2.** to hold back or seal off by a trap **3.** to furnish with a trap or traps ☆**4.** *Sports* to grab (a ball) just as it bounces from the ground —*vi.* to set traps to catch animals, ☆esp. for their furs

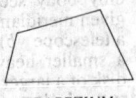

TRAP

trap² (trap) *n.* [< Sw. < *trappa,* stair] **1.** any of several dark-colored, igneous rocks; esp., such a rock, as basalt, used in roadmaking **2.** a geologic structure with oil or gas inside Also **trap′rock′**

trap³ (trap) *vt.* **trapped, trap′ping** [< OFr. *drap,* cloth] to cover with trappings; caparison —*n.* [*pl.*] [Colloq.] personal belongings, clothes, etc.

trap·door (trap′dôr′) *n.* a hinged or sliding door in a roof, ceiling, or floor

tra·peze (tra pēz′, trə-) *n.* [Fr. < ModL.: see TRAPEZIUM] a short horizontal bar, hung at a height by two ropes, on which gymnasts, acrobats, etc. swing and do stunts

tra·pe·zi·um (tra pē′zē əm) *n., pl.* **-zi·ums, -zi·a** (-ə) [ModL. < Gr. dim. of *trapeza,* table < *tra-,* for *tetra,* four + *peza,* a foot] **1.** a plane figure with four sides no two of which are parallel **2.** [Brit.] same as TRAPEZOID (sense 1) **3.** a small bone of the wrist near the base of the thumb

TRAPEZIUM

trap·e·zoid (trap′ə zoid′) *n.* [ModL. < Gr.: see prec. & -OID] **1.** a plane figure with four sides only two of which are parallel **2.** [Brit.] same as TRAPEZIUM (sense 1) **3.** a small bone of the wrist near the base of the index finger —*adj.* shaped like a trapezoid: also **trap′e·zoi′dal**

TRAPEZOID

trap·per (trap′ər) *n.* a person who traps; esp., one who traps fur-bearing animals for their skins

trap·pings (-iŋz) *n.pl.* [see TRAP³] **1.** a highly decorated covering for a horse; caparison **2.** highly decorated clothing **3.** the things that go along with something and are an outward sign of it [the *trappings* of success]

Trap·pist (trap′ist) *n.* [< Fr. < (*La*) *Trappe,* abbey in Normandy] a monk of a branch of the Cistercian order, living under a vow of silence —*adj.* of the Trappists

trap·shoot·ing (trap′shōōt′iŋ) *n.* the sport of shooting at clay pigeons, or disks, sprung into the air from traps —**trap′shoot′-er** n.

trash (trash) n. [prob. < Scand.] **1.** parts that have been broken off, stripped off, etc., esp. leaves, twigs, etc. **2.** anything thrown away as worthless; rubbish **3.** worthless, unnecessary, disgusting, or foolish matter [literary trash] **4.** a person or people thought of as having a bad reputation —vt. [Slang] to destroy (property) as by vandalism, arson, etc.

trash·y (trash′ē) adj. **trash′i·er, trash′i·est** containing, consisting of, or like trash; worthless —**trash′i·ness** n.

‡**trat·tor·i·a** (trät′tô rē′ä) n., pl. **-i·e** (-e) [It. < trattore, innkeeper] a small, inexpensive restaurant in Italy

trau·ma (trou′mə, trô′-) n., pl. **-mas, -ma·ta** (-mə tə) [ModL. < Gr.] **1.** Med. a bodily injury, wound, or shock **2.** Psychiatry an emotional shock which has a lasting effect on the mind —**trau·mat′ic** (-mat′ik) adj. —**trau·mat′i·cal·ly** adv.

trau·ma·tize (-tīz′) vt. **-tized, -tiz′ing 1.** Med. to injure or wound (tissues) **2.** Psychiatry to cause to undergo a trauma

trav·ail (trav′āl, trə vāl′) n. [OFr. < VL. tripalium, a torture device < tria, three + palus, a stake] **1.** very hard work **2.** the pains of childbirth **3.** intense pain; agony —vi. **1.** to toil or work hard **2.** to suffer the pains of childbirth —see SYN. at WORK

trav·el (trav′l) vi. **-eled** or **-elled, -el·ing** or **-el·ling** [var. of TRAVAIL] **1.** to go from one place to another; make a journey [they traveled across the State] **2.** to go from place to place as a traveling salesman **3.** to move, pass, or be transmitted [light travels faster than sound] **4.** to move in a given course: said of mechanical parts, etc. ☆**5.** Basketball to move (usually more than two steps) while holding the ball **6.** [Colloq.] to associate or spend time (with) **7.** [Colloq.] to move with speed [this car can really travel] —vt. **1.** to make a journey over or through [to travel a road] **2.** [Colloq.] to cause to pass along [the cattle were traveled to market] —n. **1.** the act or process of traveling **2.** [pl.] a) trips, journeys, tours, etc. b) an account of these **3.** movement of any kind **4.** a) mechanical motion, esp. back-and-forth motion b) the distance of a mechanical stroke, etc. —**trav′el·er, trav′el·ler** n.

travel agency an agency that makes travel plans for tourists and other travelers, as by making reservations for them at hotels or for airplane flights, boat trips, etc. —**travel agent**

trav·eled, trav·elled (trav′ld) adj. **1.** that has traveled much **2.** much used by travelers [a traveled road]

☆**traveler's check** a check, usually one of a set, issued by a bank, etc. and sold to a traveler who signs it when it is issued and again in the presence of the one cashing it

☆**traveling salesman** a salesman who travels for a business firm, trying to get orders for his goods

☆**trav·e·logue, trav·e·log** (trav′ə lôg′, -läg′) n. **1.** a lecture describing travels, usually given along with the showing of pictures **2.** a motion picture of travels

trav·erse (tra vʉrs′, trə-; also, & for n. & adj. always, trav′ərs) vt. **-ersed′, -ers′ing** [< OFr. < L. pp. of transvertere < trans-, over + vertere, to turn] **1.** a) to pass over, across, or through [pioneers traversed the plains in covered wagons] b) to go back and forth over or along **2.** to go counter to; oppose **3.** to examine carefully **4.** to turn (a gun, etc.) sideways —vi. **1.** to cross over **2.** to move back and forth over a place, etc. **3.** to swivel or pivot **4.** to move across a mountain slope, as in skiing, in a slanting direction —n. **1.** something that traverses or crosses; specif., a) a crossbar, crossbeam, etc. b) a gallery, loft, etc. crossing a building **2.** a traversing or passing across or through **3.** a device that causes a traversing movement **4.** a way across **5.** a zigzag course taken by a vessel —adj. **1.** lying across **2.** describing or of drapes and the rods for them hung in pairs so that they can be drawn together or apart by pulling cords at the side —**trav′ers·a·ble** adj. —**trav′ers′al** n. —**trav′ers·er** n.

trav·er·tine (trav′ər tēn′, -tin) n. [< It., ult. < L. (lapis) Tiburtinus, (stone) by Tibur, ancient It. city] a light-colored limestone that forms in deposits around springs, lakes, etc. full of lime

trav·es·ty (trav′is tē) n., pl. **-ties** [< Fr. pp. of travestir, to disguise < It. < L. trans-, over + vestire, to dress] **1.** an exaggerated imitation of something done in such a way as to make it seem ridiculous; burlesque **2.** a crude or ridiculous example (of

something) [a trial that was a travesty of justice] —vt. **-tied, -ty·ing** to make a travesty of —see SYN. at CARICATURE

tra·vois (trə voi′) n., pl. **-vois′** (-voiz′), **-vois′es** (-voi′zəz) [CanadFr. < travail, a load < Fr.: see TRAVAIL] a crude sledge of the N. American Plains Indians with two poles or shafts for dragging a net or platform along with a horse, dog, etc.: also **tra·voise′** (-voiz′)

trawl (trôl) n. [< ? MDu. traghel, a dragnet] **1.** a large, baglike net dragged by a boat along the bottom of a fishing bank: also **trawl′net′** ☆**2.** a long line supported by buoys, from which many short fishing lines are hung: also **trawl line** —vt., vi. to fish or catch with a trawl

trawl·er (trô′lər) n. a boat used in trawling

tray (trā) n. [OE. treg, wooden board] **1.** a flat piece of wood, metal, etc. with a low rim, for holding or carrying food or other things **2.** a tray with its contents [a tray of food] **3.** a shallow, removable box like a tray that fits inside a trunk, cabinet, etc.

TRAWL

treach·er·ous (trech′ər əs) adj. **1.** not loyal or faithful; betraying or likely to betray **2.** seeming safe, reliable, etc. but not really so [treacherous rocks] —see SYN. at FAITHLESS —**treach′er·ous·ly** adv. —**treach′er·ous·ness** n.

treach·er·y (-ē) n., pl. **-er·ies** [< OFr. < trichier, to trick, cheat] **1.** a betraying of trust or faith; disloyalty or treason **2.** an act of disloyalty or treason

trea·cle (trē′k'l) n. [< OFr. < L. < Gr. thēriakē, remedy for venomous bites < thērion, dim. of thēr, wild beast] [Brit.] molasses —**trea′cly** (-klē) adj.

tread (tred) vt. **trod, trod′den** or **trod, tread′ing** [OE. tredan < IE. base dra-, to run, step, from which also comes TRAP] **1.** to walk on, in, along, over, etc. [we trod the dusty road for hours] **2.** to do or follow by walking, dancing, etc. [to tread the measures gaily] **3.** to press or beat with the feet; trample [to tread grapes in making wine] **4.** to keep down or overcome, as if by stepping on **5.** to have sexual intercourse with: said of male birds —vi. **1.** to move on foot; walk **2.** to set one's foot (on, across, etc.) **3.** to press or beat with the feet; trample (on or upon) **4.** to have sexual intercourse: said of birds —n. **1.** the act, manner, or sound of treading [we heard his heavy tread on the stairs] **2.** something on which a person or thing treads or moves, as the part of a shoe sole, wheel, etc. that touches the ground, the endless belt over cogged wheels of a tractor, etc., the horizontal surface of a stair step, etc. **3.** a) the thick outer layer of an automotive tire b) the depth or pattern of grooves in this layer —**tread the boards** to act in plays —**tread water** pt. & pp. now usually **tread′ed** to keep the body upright and the head above water in swimming by moving the legs up and down —**tread′er** n.

trea·dle (tred′'l) n. [< OE. < tredan: see prec.] a lever or pedal moved by the foot to turn a wheel —vi. **-dled, -dling** to work a treadle

tread·mill (tred′mil′) n. **1.** a mill wheel turned by persons treading steps built around its outer edge, or by an animal treading an endless belt **2.** any monotonous routine of duties, work, etc. that never seems to end

treas. **1.** treasurer **2.** treasury

trea·son (trē′z'n) n. [< OFr. < L. < pp. of tradere, to deliver up < trans-, over + dare, to give] **1.** [Now Rare] a betraying of trust or faith **2.** a betraying of one's country, esp. by helping the enemy in time of war

trea·son·a·ble (-ə b'l) adj. of or involving treason; traitorous: also **trea′son·ous** —**trea′son·a·ble·ness** n. —**trea′son·a·bly** adv.

treas·ure (trezh′ər) n. [< OFr. < L. < Gr. thēsauros] **1.** money, gold, jewels, etc. collected and stored up **2.** any person or thing that is loved or greatly valued —vt. **-ured, -ur·ing 1.** to save up (money, etc.) for future use **2.** to value greatly; cherish [I treasure their friendship] —see SYN. at APPRECIATE

treas·ur·er (trezh′ər ər) n. a person in charge of a treasure or treasury; specif., an officer in charge of the funds of a government, corporation, society, etc. —**treas′ur·er·ship′** n.

treas·ure-trove (-trōv′) n. [< Anglo-Fr. < OFr. tresor, treasure + *trové*, pp. of *trover*, to find] **1.** treasure found hidden, the original owner of which is not known **2.** any valuable discovery

treas·ur·y (-ē) *n., pl.* **-ur·ies 1.** a place where treasure is kept **2.** a place where public or private funds are kept, recorded, etc. **3.** the funds or revenues of a state, corporation, club, etc. **4.** [T-] the department of government in charge of issuing money, collecting taxes, etc. **5.** a collection of valuable works of art, literature, etc.

treasury note ☆any of the interest-bearing notes issued by the U.S. Treasury and maturing within one to five years

treat (trēt) *vi.* [< OFr. *traiter* < L. *tractare*, drag with force < *trahere*, to draw] **1.** to discuss terms (*with* a person or *for* a settlement) **2.** to deal with a subject; speak or write (*of*) **3.** to pay the cost of another's entertainment [it's my turn to *treat*] —*vt.* **1.** to deal with (a subject) in writing, speech, music, etc. in a specified style **2.** to act toward (a person, animal, etc.) in a specified manner [we were *treated* well] **3.** to act toward in a specified way [he *treated* it as a joke] **4.** *a)* to pay for the food, drink, etc. of (another) *b)* to provide with something that pleases **5.** to expose to some process or substance, esp. one that has a chemical effect [the water is *treated* with chlorine] **6.** to give medical or surgical care to (someone) or for (some illness) —*n.* **1.** a meal, drink, etc. paid for by someone else **2.** anything that gives great pleasure [it was a *treat* to hear the children sing] **3.** *a)* the act of treating or entertaining *b)* one's turn to treat —**treat′a·bil′i·ty** *n.* —**treat′a·ble** *adj.* —**treat′er** *n.*

trea·tise (trēt′is) *n.* [< Anglo-Fr., ult. < OFr. *traiter:* see TREAT] a formal article or book dealing with some subject in a detailed way

treat·ment (trēt′mənt) *n.* **1.** act, manner, method, etc. of treating [kind *treatment*] **2.** the use of medicine, surgery, etc. to try to cure or heal

trea·ty (trēt′ē) *n., pl.* **-ties** [< OFr. *traité*, ult. < pp. of L. *tractare*, to manage] a formal agreement between two or more nations, relating to peace, alliance, trade, etc.

Treb·i·zond (treb′ə zänd′) empire (1204–1461) on the SE coast of the Black Sea

tre·ble (treb′'l) *adj.* [< OFr. < L. *triplus*, triple] **1.** triple **2.** of, for, or performing the treble **3.** high-pitched or shrill —*n.* **1.** the highest part in musical harmony; soprano **2.** a singer or instrument that takes this part **3.** a high-pitched voice or sound —*vt., vi.* **-bled, -bling** to make or become three times as much or as many —**tre′bly** *adv.*

treble clef *Music* a sign on a staff, showing the position of G above middle C on the second line: see illustration at CLEF

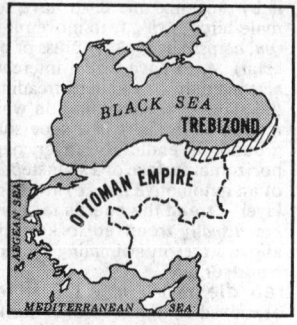

TREBIZOND (c. 1450)

tree (trē) *n.* [OE. *treow*] **1.** a large, woody perennial plant with one main trunk which develops many branches **2.** a treelike bush or shrub [a rose *tree*] **3.** a wooden beam, bar, post, etc. [a clothes *tree*] **4.** anything that looks like a tree; specif., *short for* FAMILY TREE —*vt.* **treed, tree′ing** ☆**1.** to chase up a tree [the dogs *treed* a possum] **2.** to stretch (a shoe, etc.) on a shoe tree —**up a tree** [Colloq.] in a situation without escape; cornered —**tree′less** *adj.* —**tree′like′** *adj.*

tree fern a tropical fern with a woody trunk

tree frog any of various frogs that live in trees: many are called *tree toads*

☆**tree lawn** in some cities, the strip of ground between a street and its parallel sidewalk, often planted with a lawn and trees: also **tree′lawn′**

tree·nail (trē′nāl′; tren′'l, trun′-) *n.* [< ME. < *tre*, wood + *nayle*, nail] a dry wooden peg used to join timbers, esp. in shipbuilding: it swells when wet so as to fit tight

tree of heaven a fast-growing ailanthus

tree squirrel any of various squirrels that live in trees, as the gray squirrel, the red squirrel, etc.

☆**tree surgery** treatment of damaged trees as by filling holes, cutting branches, etc. —**tree surgeon**

☆**tree toad** see TREE FROG

tree·top (trē′täp′) *n.* the topmost part of a tree

tre·foil (trē′foil) *n.* [< Anglo-Fr. < L. < *tri-*, three + *folium*, a leaf] **1.** a plant with leaves divided into three leaflets, as the clover **2.** a design or decoration shaped like such a leaf

TREFOILS

trek (trek) *vi.* **trekked, trek′king** [Afrik. < Du. *trekken*, to draw] **1.** in South Africa, to travel by ox wagon **2.** to travel slowly or with difficulty **3.** [Colloq.] to go, esp. on foot —*n.* **1.** in South Africa, a journey made by ox wagon **2.** a journey or leg of a journey **3.** a migration **4.** [Colloq.] a short trip, esp. on foot —**trek′ker** *n.*

trel·lis (trel′is) *n.* [< OFr., ult. < L. *trilix*, triple-twilled] an openwork structure of thin, crossed strips, esp. of wood, on which vines are trained to grow; lattice —*vt.* **1.** to furnish with, or train on, a trellis **2.** to cross or interweave like a trellis

trem·a·tode (trem′ə tōd′, trē′mə-) *n.* [< ModL. < Gr. < *trēmatos*, genitive of *trēma*, a hole + *eidos*, form] any of various parasitic flatworms; fluke —*adj.* of a trematode

trem·ble (trem′b'l) *vi.* **-bled, -bling** [< OFr. < VL., ult. < L. *tremere*] **1.** to shake uncontrollably from cold, fear, excitement, etc.; shiver [her hand *trembled*] **2.** to feel great fear or worry [the warning made them *tremble*] **3.** to quake, totter, vibrate, etc. [the earth *trembled* from the shock wave] **4.** to quaver [a *trembling* voice] —*n.* **1.** a trembling **2.** [*sometimes pl.*] a fit of trembling —see SYN. at SHAKE —**trem′bler** *n.* —**trem′bling·ly** *adv.* —**trem′bly** *adj.*

tre·men·dous (tri men′dəs) *adj.* [< L. *tremendus* < *tremere*, to TREMBLE] **1.** such as to make one tremble; terrifying **2.** *a)* very large; great [a *tremendous* building] *b)* [Colloq.] wonderful, amazing, etc. [a *tremendous* opportunity] —see SYN. at ENORMOUS —**tre·men′dous·ly** *adv.* —**tre·men′dous·ness** *n.*

trem·o·lo (trem′ə lō′) *n., pl.* **-los′** [It. < L.: see TREMULOUS] **1.** a trembling effect produced by rapidly repeating the same musical tone **2.** a device, as in an organ, for producing such a tone

trem·or (trem′ər; *occas.* trē′mər) *n.* [< OFr. < L. < *tremere*, to TREMBLE] **1.** a trembling, shaking, etc. **2.** a vibrating motion **3.** a nervous thrill; trembling sensation **4.** a trembling sound —**trem′or·ous** *adj.*

trem·u·lous (trem′yoo ləs) *adj.* [L. *tremulus* < *tremere*, to TREMBLE] **1.** trembling; quivering **2.** fearful; timid **3.** marked by or showing trembling or quivering [*tremulous* excitement, *tremulous* handwriting] Also **trem′u·lant** —**trem′u·lous·ly** *adv.* —**trem′u·lous·ness** *n.*

tre·nail (trē′nāl′; tren′'l, trun′-) *n.* same as TREENAIL

trench (trench) *vt.* [< OFr. < ? L. *truncare*, to cut off] **1.** to cut, slice, gash, etc. **2.** to dig a ditch or ditches in **3.** to surround or fortify with trenches —*vi.* **1.** to dig a ditch or ditches **2.** to trespass (*on* or *upon* another's land, rights, etc.) **3.** to border (*on*); come close —*n.* **1.** a deep furrow **2.** a long, narrow ditch with earth banked in front, used to protect soldiers in battle

trench·ant (tren′chənt) *adj.* [< OFr.: see prec.] **1.** orig., cutting; sharp **2.** to the point; keen; incisive [*trenchant* words] **3.** forceful; strong [a *trenchant* argument] **4.** sharp and clear; distinct [a *trenchant* pattern] —see SYN. at INCISIVE —**trench′an·cy** *n.* —**trench′ant·ly** *adv.*

trench coat a belted raincoat in a military style

trench·er (tren′chər) *n.* [Archaic] **1.** a wooden platter for carving and serving meat **2.** *a)* food served on a trencher *b)* a supply of food

trench·er·man (-mən) *n., pl.* **-men** an eater; esp., one who eats much and heartily

trench fever an infectious disease transmitted by body lice, in which there is returning fever, muscular pains, etc.

trench foot a diseased condition of the feet resulting from long exposure to wet and cold, as of soldiers in trenches

trench mortar (or **gun**) any of various portable mortars for shooting projectiles in a high curved path and at a short distance

trench mouth an infectious disease of the mouth and throat in which the mucous membranes have open sores

trend (trend) *vi.* [OE. *trendan*] **1.** to stretch, turn, bend, etc. in a specific direction [the river *trends* northward] **2.** to have a general tendency or course:

TRENCH
COAT

said of events, opinions, etc. —*n.* **1.** the general direction of a river, road, etc. **2.** the general tendency or course, as of events, a discussion, etc. **3.** a current or popular style, as in fashions —see SYN. at TENDENCY

trend·y (trend′ē) *adj.* **trend′i·er, trend′i·est** [Colloq.] of or in the latest style, or trend; faddish —**trend′i·ly** *adv.* —**trend′i·ness** *n.*

Trent (trent) **1.** city in N Italy: pop. 87,000: It. name **Tren·to** (tren′tô) **2.** river in C England, flowing northeast into the North Sea **3.** Council of, the council of the Roman Catholic Church held from time to time at Trent, 1545–63, to act against the effects of the Reformation

Tren·ton (tren′tən) [after Wm. *Trent* (1655–1724), colonist] capital of N.J., on the Delaware River: pop. 105,000

tre·pan (tri pan′) *n.* [< ML. < Gr. < *trypan*, to bore] **1.** an early form of the trephine **2.** a heavy boring tool —*vt.* **-panned′, -pan′ning** *same as* TREPHINE —**trep·a·na·tion** (trep′ə nā′shən) *n.*

tre·pang (tri paŋ′) *n.* [Malay *tĕripang*] a boiled, smoked, and dried sea cucumber, used in the Orient for making soup

tre·phine (tri fīn′, -fēn′) *n.* [formed (after TREPAN) < L. *tres*, three + *fines*, ends] a type of small circular saw used in surgery to remove disks of bone from the skull —*vt.* **-phined′, -phin′ing** to operate on with a trephine —**treph·i·na·tion** (tref′ə nā′shən) *n.*

trep·i·da·tion (trep′ə dā′shən) *n.* [< L. < pp. of *trepidare*, to tremble < *trepidus*, disturbed] **1.** tremulous or trembling movement **2.** fearful uncertainty or worry

tres·pass (tres′pəs; *also, esp. for v.*, -pas′) *vi.* [< OFr., ult. < L. *trans-*, across + VL. word no longer known] **1.** to go beyond the limits of what is considered right or moral; transgress **2.** to go on another's property without permission or right **3.** to break in on; intrude [to *trespass* on one's privacy] **4.** *Law* to commit a trespass —*n.* a trespassing; specif., *a*) a moral wrong *b*) a breaking in on; intrusion *c*) *Law* an illegal act done with force against another's person, rights, or property —**tres′pass·er** *n.*

tress (tres) *n.* [< OFr. < ? Frank.] **1.** orig., a braid of hair **2.** a lock of human hair **3.** [*pl.*] a woman's or girl's hair, esp. when long and falling loosely

-tress (tris) *a suffix meaning* female [*actress*]: see also -ESS

tres·tle (tres′'l) *n.* [< OFr., ult. < L. *transtrum*, a beam] **1.** a frame consisting of a horizontal beam fastened to two pairs of spreading legs, used to support planks to form a table, etc. **2.** a framework of uprights and cross-pieces, supporting a bridge, etc.; also, such a bridge

☆**tres·tle·work** (-wurk′) *n.* a system of trestles for supporting a bridge, etc.

Tre·vel·yan (tri vil′yən, -vel′-), **George Macaulay** 1876–1962; Eng. historian

TRESTLE

trey (trā) *n.* [< OFr. < L. *tres*, three] **1.** a playing card with three spots **2.** the side of a die bearing three spots, or a throw of the dice totaling three

tri- [< Fr., L., or Gr.] *a combining form meaning:* **1.** having or involving three [*triangular*] **2.** triply, in three ways [*trilingual*] **3.** three times, into three [*trisect*] **4.** every third [*triannual*] **5.** *Chem.* having three atoms, groups, or equivalents of (the thing specified) [*tribasic*]

tri·a·ble (trī′ə b'l) *adj.* that can be tried or tested, esp. in a law court —**tri′a·ble·ness** *n.*

tri·ac·e·tate (trī as′ə tāt′) *n.* a compound containing three acetate radicals in the molecule

tri·ad (trī′ad) *n.* [< LL. < Gr. < *treis*, three] **1.** a group of three persons, things, etc. **2.** a musical chord of three tones, esp. one consisting of a root tone and its third and fifth: a triad with a major third and perfect fifth is called a *major triad;* a triad with a minor third and perfect fifth is called a *minor triad* —**tri·ad′ic** *adj.*

tri·age (trē äzh′) *n.* [Fr. < *trier*, to sift] a system of deciding in what order battlefield injuries will receive medical treatment, according to immediate need, chance of survival, etc.

tri·al (trī′əl, trīl) *n.* [Anglo-Fr. < *trier*, to try] **1.** *a*) a trying, testing, etc.; test [a *trial* of his courage] *b*) a testing of qualifications, progress, etc. [to give a new product a *trial*] *c*) an

experiment **2.** *a*) a being tried by suffering, temptation, etc. [friends are needed in a time of *trial*] *b*) suffering, hardship, trouble, etc., or the cause of this [the *trials* of pioneer life; a child who has been a great *trial* to her parents] **3.** a formal examination of the facts of a case by a court of law to decide whether a charge or claim is true **4.** an attempt; effort [to give up after three unsuccessful *trials*] —*adj.* **1.** of or having to do with a trial or trials [a *trial* lawyer] **2.** of or for trying, testing, etc. [a *trial* run of a play] —**on trial** in the process of being tried SYN.—**trial** implies the trying of a person or thing in order to find out his or its worth, usefulness, etc. in actual performance [all new employees are on *trial* for six months]; **experiment** is applied to any action or process that is used to discover something not yet known, to test one's theories or conclusions, or to show how something works [laboratory *experiments*]; **test** suggests a thorough examination or trial of a thing under controlled conditions and with fixed standards in mind [a *test* of a new spacecraft]

trial and error the process of trying or testing over and over again, improving the methods used in the light of errors made, until the right result is found —**tri′al-and-er′ror** *adj.*

trial balance a statement of the debit and credit balances of all open accounts in a double-entry bookkeeping ledger made as a check to see if the balances are equal

☆**trial balloon** **1.** *same as* PILOT BALLOON **2.** an action, statement, etc. made to test public opinion on an issue

trial jury *same as* PETIT JURY

tri·an·gle (trī′aŋ′g'l) *n.* [< MFr. < L.: see TRI- & ANGLE[1]] **1.** a plane figure having three angles and three sides **2.** any three-sided or three-cornered figure, area, etc. **3.** a situation involving three persons **4.** a musical instrument consisting of a steel rod bent into a triangle: it makes a high-pitched, tinkling sound when struck

TRIANGLES

tri·an·gu·lar (trī aŋ′gyə lər) *adj.* **1.** of or shaped like a triangle; having three corners **2.** of or involving three persons, parts, etc. **3.** having bases that are triangles, as a prism —**tri·an·gu·lar′i·ty** (-ler′ə tē) *n.* —**tri·an′gu·lar·ly** *adv.*

tri·an·gu·late (trī aŋ′gyə lāt′; *for adj. usually* -lit) *vt.* **-lat′ed, -lat′ing** **1.** to divide into triangles **2.** to survey (a region) by triangulation **3.** to make triangular —*adj.* of, like, or marked with triangles

tri·an·gu·la·tion (trī aŋ′gyə lā′shən) *n. Surveying* the finding out of the distance between points on the earth's surface by means of calculations based on the division of an area into connected triangles and the measurement of their angles

Tri·as·sic (trī as′ik) *adj.* [< ModL. < LL. *trias*, TRIAD (because divisible into three groups) + -IC] designating or of the first period of the Mesozoic Era —**the Triassic** the Triassic Period or its rocks: see GEOLOGIC TIME CHART

trib·al (trī′b'l) *adj.* of a tribe or tribes —**tri′bal·ly** *adv.*

trib·al·ism (trī′b'l iz'm) *n.* tribal organization, culture, loyalty, etc. —**trib′al·ist** *n., adj.*

tribe (trīb) *n.* [L. *tribus*, any of the divisions (orig. three) of the ancient Romans] **1.** a group of persons, families, or clans believed to have a common ancestor and living together under a leader or chief **2.** any group of people with the same occupation, ideas, etc. **3.** a subdivision of a subfamily of plants or animals **4.** loosely, any group of plants or animals classified together **5.** [Colloq.] a family

tribes·man (trībz′mən) *n., pl.* **-men** a member of a tribe

trib·u·la·tion (trib′yə lā′shən) *n.* [< OFr. < LL. < *tribulare*, to afflict < L., to press < *tribulum*, threshing tool] **1.** great misery or distress; deep sorrow **2.** the cause of this; an affliction; trial

tri·bu·nal (trī byōō′n'l, tri-) *n.* [L.: see TRIBUNE[1]] **1.** the judge's seat or bench in a courtroom **2.** a court of justice

trib·une[1] (trib′yōōn; *in a newspaper name often* tri byōōn′) *n.* [< L. *tribunus* < *tribus*, TRIBE] **1.** in ancient Rome, *a*) any of several officials whose duty it was to protect the rights and interests of the lower classes *b*) any of six officers taking turns commanding a legion **2.** a defender of the rights of the people —**trib′une·ship′** *n.*

trib·une[2] (trib′yōōn) *n.* [Fr. < It. < L.: see TRIBUNAL, sense 1] a raised platform or dais for speakers

trib·u·tar·y (trib′yōō ter′ē) *adj.* **1.** paying tribute [a *tributary* region] **2.** under another's control; subject [a *tributary* nation] **3.** owed or paid as tribute [*tributary* money] **4.** *a)* making additions; contributory [*tributary* resources] *b)* flowing into a larger one [a *tributary* stream] —*n.*, *pl.* **-ar·ies 1.** a tributary nation or ruler **2.** a tributary stream or river

trib·ute (trib′yo͞ot) *n.* [< MFr. < L. pp. of *tribuere*, to allot, pay < *tribus*, TRIBE] **1.** money that one nation is forced to pay to another, more powerful nation **2.** any forced payment **3.** something given, done, or said which shows gratitude, honor, or praise

SYN.—**tribute**, the most general of these words, is used of spoken or written praise or of praise that is shown or implied in some other way [the poem was a *tribute* to her beauty; his success was a *tribute* to his teachers]; **encomium** suggests high praise expressed in a formal and sometimes excessive way [heaping *encomiums* on a political candidate]; **eulogy** refers to formal praise of a lofty kind, especially praise of a person who has just died [the chaplain delivered the *eulogy*]; **panegyric** suggests the very highest praise, full of detail and expressed in poetic or highly formal language [the Roman orator's *panegyric* on the emperor]

trice (trīs) *vt.* **triced, tric′ing** [MDu. *trisen*, to pull < *trise*, windlass] to haul up and tie with a small line [to *trice* up a sail] —*n.* [< *at a trice*, with one pull] a very short time; instant: now only in **in a trice**

tri·cen·ten·ni·al (trī′sen ten′ē əl) *adj.* happening once in a period of 300 years —☆*n.* a 300th anniversary

tri·ceps (trī′seps) *n.*, *pl.* **-ceps** or **-ceps·es** [ModL. < L. < *tri-*, three + *caput*, a head] a muscle having three points of origin, esp. the muscle at the back of the upper arm that extends the forearm

tri·cer·a·tops (trī ser′ə täps′) *n.* [ModL. < *tri-*, three + *cerat-*, horn + Gr. *ōps*, eye] a huge, plant-eating dinosaur with a large crest over the neck and a long horn above each eye

tri·chi·na (tri kī′nə) *n.*, *pl.* **-nae** (-nē) [ModL. < Gr. *trichinos*, hairy < *thrix*, hair] a very small worm whose larvae infest the intestines and muscles of man, pigs, etc., causing trichinosis —**tri·chi′nal** *adj.*

TRICERATOPS
(to 30 ft. long, including tail)

trich·i·no·sis (trik′ə nō′sis) *n.* a disease caused by trichinae: it is characterized by fever, diarrhea, muscular pains, etc. and is usually acquired by eating undercooked pork from an infected hog

trick (trik) *n.* [ONormFr. *trique* < OFr. *trichier*, to cheat] **1.** something that is done to fool, cheat, outwit, etc.; ruse; stratagem **2.** *a)* a piece of playful mischief; prank *b)* a deception or illusion [the light played a *trick* on his eyes] **3.** a foolish or mean act **4.** a clever or skillful act intended to amuse; specif., *a)* an act of jugglery, sleight of hand, etc. *b)* a feat performed by a trained animal **5.** the art or knack of doing a thing easily, skillfully, quickly, etc. [the *trick* of making good gravy] **6.** a personal mannerism [his *trick* of tugging at his ear] **7.** a turn at work; shift [during my *trick* at the ship's wheel] **8.** *Card Games* the cards played and won in a single round —*vt.* to deceive, cheat, outwit, fool, etc. —*adj.* **1.** of, for, or using tricks [*trick* photography] **2.** that tricks [a *trick* question] **3.** not always working right [a *trick* knee] —**do** (or **turn**) **the trick** to bring about the desired result —**trick out** (or **up**) to dress up; adorn

SYN.—**trick** is the common word for an action or device in which cleverness and craftiness are used to outwit others either in order to cheat or deceive them or simply in fun [a gambler's *trick*; a magic *trick*]; **ruse** suggests something meant to cover up one's real intentions or the truth [her apparent illness was merely a *ruse*]; **stratagem** is a fairly complicated ruse by means of which one tries to outwit an enemy or opponent [military *stratagems*]; **maneuver** suggests the clever manipulation of persons or situations to suit one's purposes [a political *maneuver*]; **artifice** suggests some especially clever or imaginative means of bringing about a result, and does not necessarily imply any intention to trick or deceive [the *artifices* of a skilled debater]; **wile** implies a tricky way of acting that is both sly and appealing [womanly *wiles*] —see also SYN. at CHEAT

trick·er·y (trik′ər ē) *n.*, *pl.* **-er·ies** the use of tricks to cheat, outwit, etc.; deception; fraud

trick·le (trik′'l) *vi.* **-led, -ling** [prob. < ME. *striken*, to strike] **1.** to flow slowly in a thin stream or fall in drops **2.** to move little by little [the crowd *trickled* away] —*vt.* to cause to trickle —*n.* a thin flow or drip

☆**trick or treat!** give me a treat or I will play a trick on you!: traditional greeting used by children on Halloween as they go from door to door in costume asking for treats

trick·ster (trik′stər) *n.* a person who tricks; cheat

trick·sy (-sē) *adj.* **-si·er, -si·est 1.** full of tricks; playful; mischievous **2.** *same as* TRICKY —**trick′si·ness** *n.*

trick·y (trik′ē) *adj.* **trick′i·er, trick′i·est 1.** using deceptive tricks; full of trickery [a *tricky* opponent] **2.** difficult; complicated [a *tricky* problem] —see SYN. at SLY —**trick′i·ly** *adv.* —**trick′i·ness** *n.*

tri·clin·ic (trī klin′ik) *adj.* [< TRI- + Gr. *klinein*, to incline + -IC] designating a crystal form with three unequal axes, three unequal angles, and no right angles: see illustration at CRYSTAL

tri·col·or (trī′kul′ər) *n.* a flag having three stripes, each of a different color, esp. the flag of France —*adj.* having three colors

tri·corn, tri·corne (-kôrn) *adj.* [< Fr. < L. < *tri-*, three + *cornu*, horn] having three horns or corners —*n.* a tricorn hat

tri·cot (trē′kō) *n.* [Fr. < *tricoter*, to knit, ult. < MDu.] **1.** a thin fabric that is either knitted or woven to look knitted **2.** a type of ribbed cloth for dresses

tri·cus·pid (trī kus′pid) *adj.* [< L.: see TRI- & CUSP] **1.** having three cusps, or points [a *tricuspid* tooth]: also **tri·cus′pi·date** (-pə·dāt′) **2.** designating or of a valve with three flaps, between the right auricle and right ventricle of the heart —*n.* a tricuspid tooth or valve

tri·cy·cle (trī′si k'l) *n.* [Fr.] a light, three-wheeled vehicle worked by pedals, esp. one for children

TRICORN

tri·dent (trīd′'nt) *n.* [< L. < *tri-*, three + *dentis*, genitive of *dens*, a tooth] a three-pronged spear

tri·den·tate (trī den′tāt) *adj.* having three teeth, prongs, or points

tried (trīd) *pt.* & *pp. of* TRY —*adj.* **1.** tested; proved [a *tried* recipe] **2.** trustworthy; faithful [a friend, *tried* and true]

tri·en·ni·al (trī en′ē əl) *adj.* [< L. < *tri-*, three + *annus*, a year] **1.** happening every three years **2.** lasting three years —*n.* a triennial event —**tri·en′ni·al·ly** *adv.*

tri·er (trī′ər) *n.* a person or thing that tries

Tri·este (trē est′; *It.* trē es′te) seaport in NE Italy, on an inlet (**Gulf of Trieste**) of the Adriatic: pop. 278,000

tri·fa·cial (trī fā′shəl) *adj.*, *n. same as* TRIGEMINAL

tri·fid (trī′fid) *adj.* [< L. < *tri-*, three + base of *findere*, to divide] divided into three parts by deep clefts, as some leaves

tri·fle (trī′f'l) *n.* [< OFr. dim. of *truffe*, deception] **1.** something of little value or importance **2.** a small amount; bit **3.** a small sum of money **4.** an English dessert made of spongecake spread with jam and covered with custard, whipped cream, etc. —*vi.* **-fled, -fling 1.** to talk or act in a joking way; deal lightly [not a person to *trifle* with] **2.** to play or toy (*with* something) —*vt.* to spend idly; waste [*trifling* time away] —**tri′fler** *n.*

SYN.—**trifle** is the general term meaning to deal with in a way which shows little real interest or seriousness [to *trifle* with a person, an idea, etc.]; **flirt** implies a light, shallow interest that moves quickly from one person or thing to another [she's always *flirting* with men]; **dally** implies a playing with a subject or thing that one has little or no intention of taking seriously [to *dally* with painting]; **toy** suggests a trifling or dallying with no purpose beyond that of killing time in an amusing way [to *toy* with an idea]

tri·fling (-fliŋ) *adj.* **1.** not at all serious; frivolous; fickle **2.** not important; trivial —see SYN. at PETTY

☆**tri·fo·cal** (trī fō′k'l, trī′fō′-) *adj.* adjusted to three different focal lengths —*n.* **1.** a lens with one part ground for close focus, one for intermediate focus (about 30 inches), and one for distant focus **2.** [*pl.*] a pair of glasses with such lenses

tri·fo·li·ate (trī fō′lē it, -āt′) *adj.* having three leaves

trig[1] (trig) *adj.* [< ON. *tryggr*, true] [Chiefly Brit.] **1.** trim; neat **2.** in good condition

TRIFOCALS

trig[2] (trig) *n. shortened form of* TRIGONOMETRY

trig., trigon. 1. trigonometric(al) **2.** trigonometry

tri·gem·i·nal (trī jem′ə n'l) *adj.* [< ModL. < L. < *tri-*, three + *geminus*, twin] designating or of either of a pair of cranial nerves, each of which divides into three branches supplying the head and face —*n.* a trigeminal nerve

trig·ger (trig′ər) *n.* [< Du. < *trekken*, to pull] a lever, etc.

which when pulled or pressed releases a catch, spring, etc.; esp., the small lever pressed back by the finger in firing a gun —*vt.* **1.** to fire or set into action with a trigger **2.** to set off (an action) *[the fight triggered a riot]* —☆**quick on the trigger** [Colloq.] **1.** quick to fire a gun **2.** quick to act, reply, etc.; alert

☆**trig·ger-hap·py** (-hap′ē) *adj.* [Colloq.] quick to use force, make war, etc.

tri·glyc·er·ide (trī glis′ər īd′) *n.* [TRI- + GLYCERIDE] any of a group of esters of fatty acids and glycerol, found in the blood and thought to be a factor in atherosclerosis

trig·o·nal (trig′ə n'l) *adj.* [L. *trigonalis*] **1.** of a triangle; triangular **2.** designating a crystal form with three equal axes, three equal angles, and no right angles

trig·o·nom·e·try (trig′ə näm′ə trē) *n.* [< ModL. < Gr. *trigōnon*, triangle + *-metria*, measurement] the branch of mathematics dealing with the ratios between the sides of a right triangle with reference to either acute angle (*trigonometric functions*), the relations between these ratios, and use of these facts in finding the unknown sides or angles of any triangle —**trig·o·no·met·ric** (-nə met′rik), **trig′o·no·met′ri·cal** *adj.* —**trig′o·no·met′ri·cal·ly** *adv.*

tri·graph (trī′graf′) *n.* three letters representing one sound (Example: *eau* in *bureau*)

tri·he·dral (trī hē′drəl) *adj.* [TRI- + -HEDRAL] having three sides or faces *[a trihedral angle]* —*n.* a figure formed by three lines, each in a different plane, that intersect at a point

trike (trīk) *n.* [Colloq.] *same as* TRICYCLE

tri·lat·er·al (trī lat′ər əl) *adj.* three-sided

tri·lin·gual (trī liŋ′gwəl) *adj.* in or using three languages

trill (tril) *n.* [< It. < *trillare*, of echoic origin] **1.** a moving rapidly back and forth between one tone and another just above it, in singing or playing **2.** a bird's warble **3.** *a)* a rapid vibration of the tongue or uvula, as in pronouncing *r* in some languages *b)* an *r*, etc. so pronounced —*vt., vi.* to speak, sing, or play with a trill —**trill′er** *n.*

tril·lion (tril′yən) *n.* [Fr. < *tri-*, TRI- + (*mi*)*llion*] ☆**1.** in the U.S. and France, the number represented by 1 followed by 12 zeros **2.** in Great Britain and Germany, the number represented by 1 followed by 18 zeros —*adj.* amounting to one trillion —**tril′lionth** *adj., n.*

tril·li·um (tril′ē əm) *n.* [ModL., genus name < L. *tri-*, three] a plant of the lily family, with three leaves and a flower with three petals

tri·lo·bate (trī lō′bāt) *adj.* having three lobes, as some leaves: also **tri·lo′bat·ed, tri′lobed′** (-lōbd′)

tri·lo·bite (trī′lə bīt′) *n.* [< ModL.: see TRI-, LOBE, & -ITE] an extinct sea arthropod with the body divided by two furrows into three parts: a common fossil in Paleozoic rocks —**tri′lo·bit′ic** (-bit′ik) *adj.*

tril·o·gy (tril′ə jē) *n., pl.* **-gies** [Gr. *trilogia*: see TRI- & -LOGY] a set of three plays, novels, etc. which form a related group, although each is a complete work

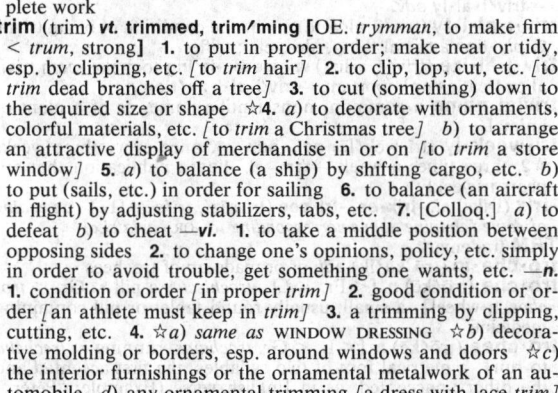

TRILLIUM

trim (trim) *vt.* **trimmed, trim′ming** [OE. *trymman*, to make firm < *trum*, strong] **1.** to put in proper order; make neat or tidy, esp. by clipping *[to trim hair]* **2.** to clip, lop, cut, etc. *[to trim dead branches off a tree]* **3.** to cut (something) down to the required size or shape ☆**4.** *a)* to decorate with ornaments, colorful materials, etc. *[to trim a Christmas tree]* *b)* to arrange an attractive display of merchandise in or on *[to trim a store window]* **5.** *a)* to balance (a ship) by shifting cargo, etc. *b)* to put (sails, etc.) in order for sailing **6.** to balance (an aircraft in flight) by adjusting stabilizers, tabs, etc. **7.** [Colloq.] *a)* to defeat *b)* to cheat —*vi.* **1.** to take a middle position between opposing sides **2.** to change one's opinions, policy, etc. simply in order to avoid trouble, get something one wants, etc. —*n.* **1.** condition or order *[in proper trim]* **2.** good condition or order *[an athlete must keep in trim]* **3.** a trimming by clipping, cutting, etc. **4.** ☆*a)* *same as* WINDOW DRESSING ☆*b)* decorative molding or borders, esp. around windows and doors ☆*c)* the interior furnishings or the ornamental metalwork of an automobile *d)* any ornamental trimming *[a dress with lace trim]*

5. *a)* the condition of being ready to sail: said of a vessel *b)* the position of a vessel in the water in relation to the horizontal *c)* correct position in the water: a ship is **in trim** if it is stable and floating evenly, **out of trim** if not *d)* the adjustment of sails, etc. in a vessel **6.** something trimmed off —*adj.* **trim′mer, trim′mest 1.** orderly; neat **2.** well-proportioned; smartly designed **3.** in good condition —*adv.* in a trim way —see SYN. at NEAT[1] —**trim one's sails** to adjust one's opinions, actions, etc. to meet changing conditions —**trim′ly** *adv.* —**trim′mer** *n.* —**trim′ness** *n.*

trim·er·ous (trim′ər əs) *adj.* [TRI- + -MEROUS] having the parts in sets of three *[a trimerous flower]*

tri·mes·ter (trī mes′tər, trī′mes-) *n.* [< Fr. < L. < *tri-*, three + *mensis*, month] **1.** a three-month period **2.** in some colleges and universities, any of three periods into which the school year is divided

trim·e·ter (trim′ə tər) *n.* [< L. < Gr.: see TRI- & METER[1]] **1.** a line of verse containing three metrical feet **2.** verse consisting of trimeters —*adj.* having three metrical feet

trim·ming (trim′iŋ) *n.* **1.** the action of one that trims **2.** that which trims; specif., *a)* decoration *b)* [*pl.*] side dishes of a meal *[steak with all the trimmings]* **3.** [*pl.*] parts trimmed off

tri·month·ly (trī munth′lē) *adj.* happening or appearing every three months

tri·nal (trī′n'l) *adj.* [< LL. < L. *trinus*, triple < *tres*, three] threefold; triple: also **tri′na·ry** (-nər ē), **trine** (trīn)

Trin·i·dad (trin′ə dad′; Sp. trē nē thäth′) island in the West Indies, off the NE coast of Venezuela: see next entry: 1,864 sq. mi. —**Trin′i·dad′i·an** *adj., n.*

Trinidad and Tobago country in the West Indies, made up of the islands of Trinidad & Tobago: a member of the Commonwealth: 1,980 sq. mi.; pop. 1,030,000; cap. Port-of-Spain

Trin·i·tar·i·an (trin′ə ter′ē ən) *adj.* **1.** of, about, or believing in the Trinity **2.** [t-] of a trinity —*n.* one who believes in the Trinity —**Trin′i·tar′i·an·ism** *n.*

tri·ni·tro·tol·u·ene (trī nī′trō täl′yoo wēn′) *n.* [TRI- + NITRO- + TOLUENE] a high explosive, $CH_3C_6H_2(NO_2)_3$, derived from toluene and used for blasting, in artillery shells, etc.: also **tri·ni′tro·tol′u·ol′** (-wôl′, -wōl′): abbrev. TNT

trin·i·ty (trin′ə tē) *n., pl.* **-ties** [< OFr. < L. < *trinus*, triple] **1.** a unit formed of three persons or things **2.** [T-] *Christian Theol.* the union of the three divine persons (Father, Son, and Holy Spirit, or Holy Ghost) in one Godhead

Trinity Sunday the Sunday after Pentecost, dedicated to the Trinity

trin·ket (triŋ′kit) *n.* [ONormFr. *trenquet*] **1.** a small piece of inexpensive jewelry, etc. **2.** a trifle or toy

tri·no·mi·al (trī nō′mē əl) *adj.* [TRI- + (BI)NOMIAL] composed of three terms —*n.* **1.** a mathematical expression consisting of three terms connected by plus or minus signs **2.** a three-word scientific name of a plant or animal, noting the genus, species, and subspecies

tri·o (trē′ō) *n., pl.* **tri′os** [Fr. < It. < *tri-*, TRI- (after *duo*, DUO)] **1.** a group of three **2.** *Music a)* a composition for three voices or instruments *b)* the three performers of such a composition *c)* the middle section of a minuet, scherzo, etc., orig. written in three parts

tri·ode (trī′ōd) *n.* [TRI- + (ELECTR)ODE] an electron tube containing three electrodes (an anode, cathode, and control grid)

tri·o·let (trī′ə lit, trē′ō let′) *n.* [Fr., perhaps a special use of *triolet*, clover] a poem or stanza having eight lines and two rhymes, the first line being repeated as the fourth and seventh, and the second as the eighth: the rhyme scheme is *abaaaabab*

tri·ox·ide (trī äk′sīd) *n.* an oxide having three oxygen atoms to the molecule

trip (trip) *vi.* **tripped, trip′ping** [OFr. *treper* < Gmc.] **1.** to walk, run, or dance with light, rapid steps; skip; caper *[she tripped gaily about the room]* **2.** to stumble, esp. by catching the foot **3.** to make a mistake *[I tripped on the spelling of "rhythm"]* **4.** to be started or put in operation by means of a catch, pawl, etc. ☆**5.** [Slang] to experience a trip (*n.* 6) —*vt.* **1.** to make stumble **2.** to cause to make a mistake **3.** to catch in a lie, error, etc. (often with *up*) **4.** *a)* to release (a spring, wheel, etc.), as by moving a catch *b)* to start or operate by such action —*n.* **1.** a light, quick step **2.** a going to or from a place, or to a place and returning; journey, esp. a short one

3. *a)* a stumble *b)* a maneuver to cause this **4.** a mistake **5.** *a)* a device, as a pawl, for tripping a part *b)* its action ☆**6.** [Slang] *a)* the hallucinations, sensations, etc. produced by a psychedelic drug, esp. LSD *b)* a certain way of living, behaving, thinking, etc. —**trip the light fantastic** to dance

SYN.—**trip** strictly implies a fairly short course of travel, although it is also commonly used to mean the same thing as **journey** [a vacation *trip*]; **journey**, a more formal word, implies travel of some length, usually over land, and does not necessarily suggest the idea of return [the *journey* was filled with hardships]; **voyage** is used of a long journey by water [a *voyage* across the Atlantic]; **jaunt** is applied to a short, casual trip taken for pleasure or recreation [a *jaunt* to the city]; **expedition** is applied to a journey taken by an organized group for some definite purpose [an archaeological *expedition*]

tri·par·tite (trī pär′tīt) *adj.* [< L. < *tri-*, three + *partitus*, PARTITE] **1.** divided into three parts **2.** having three corresponding parts or copies **3.** made or existing between three parties, as an agreement —**tri·par′tite·ly** *adv.*

tripe (trīp) *n.* [< MFr., prob. ult. < Ar. *tharb*, entrails, lit., fold of fat] **1.** part of the stomach of an ox or similar animal, used as food **2.** [Slang] anything worthless, disgusting, etc.; nonsense

☆**trip·ham·mer** (trip′ham′ər) *n.* a heavy, power-driven hammer, raised and then let fall over and over again by means of a tripping device: also **trip hammer**

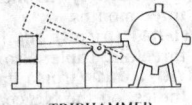

TRIPHAMMER

tri·ple (trip′'l) *adj.* [Fr. < L. *triplus*: see the *v.*] **1.** consisting of three; threefold **2.** done, said, etc. three times **3.** three times as much, as many, etc. **4.** *Music* having three beats to the measure [*triple* time] —*n.* **1.** a triple amount, number, etc. ☆**2.** *Baseball* same as THREE-BASE HIT —*vt.* **tri′pled**, **tri′pling** [< ML. < L. *triplus*, threefold < *tri-*, TRI- + *-plus*, as in *duplus*, double] **1.** to make three times as much or as many ☆**2.** *Baseball* to advance (a runner) by hitting a triple —*vi.* **1.** to be tripled ☆**2.** *Baseball* to hit a triple

☆**triple play** *Baseball* a play in which three players are put out

tri·ple-space (-spās′) *vt., vi.* **-spaced′**, **-spac′ing** to type (copy) so as to leave two full spaces between lines

trip·let (trip′lit) *n.* [TRIPL(E) + -ET] **1.** a group of three, usually of one kind; specif., *a)* a group of three lines of poetry, usually rhyming *b)* a group of three musical notes to be performed in the time of two of the same value **2.** any of three offspring born at a single birth

tri·plex (trip′leks, trī′pleks) *adj.* [L. < *tri-*, TRI-, + *-plex*, -fold] triple; threefold < *tri-*, TRI- + *-plus* —*n.* a thing that is triplex

trip·li·cate (trip′lə kit; *for v.* -kāt′) *adj.* [< L. pp. of *triplicare*, to treble < *triplex*, threefold] **1.** threefold **2.** designating the third of three identical copies —*n.* any of three identical copies —*vt.* **-cat′ed**, **-cat′ing** to make three identical copies of —**in triplicate** in three identical copies —**trip′li·ca′tion** *n.*

tri·ply (trip′lē) *adv.* in a triple amount or degree

tri·pod (trī′päd) *n.* [< L. < Gr. < *tri-*, three + *pous*, a foot] **1.** a three-legged caldron, stool, etc. **2.** a three-legged support for a camera, etc.

Trip·o·li (trip′ə lē) **1.** one of the two capitals of Libya, on the NW coast: pop. 245,000 **2.** seaport on the NW coast of Lebanon: pop. 150,000

trip·per (trip′ər) *n.* **1.** one that trips; specif., a device for tripping or releasing a catch, pawl, etc. **2.** [Brit. Colloq.] a person who takes a trip; tourist

trip·ping (-iŋ) *adj.* moving lightly and quickly; nimble —**trip′ping·ly** *adv.*

trip·tych (trip′tik) *n.* [< Gr. *triptychos*, threefold < *tri-*, three + *ptychē*, a fold] **1.** an ancient writing tablet of three leaves hinged together **2.** a set of three panels with pictures, carvings, etc., often hinged together and hung above an altar

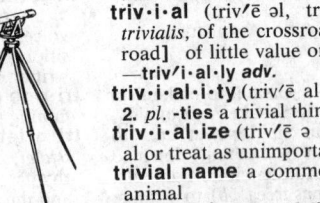

TRIPOD FOR A TELESCOPE

tri·reme (trī′rēm) *n.* [< L. < *tri-*, three + *remus*, an oar] an ancient Greek or Roman galley, usually a warship, with three banks of oars on each side

tri·sect (trī sekt′, trī′sekt) *vt.* [< TRI- + L. pp. of *secare*, to cut] **1.** to cut into three parts **2.** *Geom.* to divide into three equal parts —**tri·sec′tion** *n.* —**tri·sec′tor** *n.*

tri·shaw (trī′shô′) *n.* [< TRI- + (JINRIKI)SHA] same as PEDICAB

Tris·tram (tris′trəm) *Medieval Legend* a knight who is involved in a tragic romance with a princess, Isolde: also **Tris′tam** (-təm), **Tris′tan** (-tən)

tri·syl·la·ble (trī sil′ə b'l, trī′sil′-) *n.* a word of three syllables —**tri·syl·lab·ic** (trī′si lab′ik) *adj.*

trite (trīt) *adj.* **trit′er**, **trit′est** [L. *tritus*, pp. of *terere*, to wear out < IE. base *ter-*, to rub, bore] worn out by constant use; no longer fresh, original, etc.; stale —**trite′ly** *adv.* —**trite′ness** *n.*

SYN.—**trite** is applied to an expression or idea which has been used so often that it has lost its original freshness and force (e.g., "like a bolt from the blue"); **hackneyed** refers to expressions which through constant use have become just about meaningless (e.g., "last but not least"); **stereotyped** applies to those fixed expressions which seem almost sure to be used in certain situations (e.g., "I point with pride" in a political speech); **commonplace** is used of any obvious remark or idea that is familiar to just about everybody and is used merely as a matter of course and without any real thought (e.g., "it isn't the heat, it's the humidity") —**ANT.** original, fresh

trit·i·um (trit′ē əm, trish′-) *n.* [ModL. < Gr. *tritos*, third] a radioactive isotope of hydrogen with an atomic weight of 3: it decays by beta-particle emission and is used in thermonuclear bombs, as a radioactive tracer, etc.

Tri·ton (trīt′'n) **1.** *Gr. Myth.* a sea god with the head and upper body of a man and the tail of a fish **2.** the larger of Neptune's two moons —**[t-]** **1.** *a)* a sea snail with a long, spiral shell *b)* the shell **2.** an old-world salamander

trit·u·rate (trich′ə rāt′) *vt.* **-rat′ed**, **-rat′ing** [< LL. pp. of *triturare*, to grind < L. < *tritus*: see TRITE] to rub, crush, or grind into very fine particles; pulverize —*n.* something triturated —**trit′u·ra·ble** *adj.* —**trit′u·ra′tion** *n.* —**trit′u·ra′tor** *n.*

tri·umph (trī′əmf) *n.* [< OFr. < L. *triumphus*, akin to Gr. *thriambos*, hymn to Bacchus] **1.** in ancient Rome, a procession celebrating a victorious general's return **2.** a victory; success **3.** great joy over a victory, success, etc. [he smiled in *triumph* when he won the race] —*vi.* **1.** to be victorious, successful, etc. **2.** to rejoice or exult over victory, success, etc.

tri·um·phal (trī um′f'l) *adj.* **1.** of, like, or having to do with a triumph **2.** celebrating a triumph [a *triumphal* procession]

tri·um·phant (trī um′fənt) *adj.* **1.** victorious; successful [the *triumphant* team] **2.** showing great joy in victory, etc. [a *triumphant* shout] —**tri·um′phant·ly** *adv.*

tri·um·vir (trī um′vər) *n., pl.* **-virs**, **-vi·ri′** (-vi rī′) [L. < *trium virum*, of three men] in ancient Rome, any of three officials who had equal power and ruled together —**tri·um′vi·ral** *adj.*

tri·um·vi·rate (-it) *n.* **1.** the office or term of a triumvir **2.** government by three men **3.** any group of three who hold control together **4.** any group of three

tri·une (trī′yōon) *adj.* [< TRI- + L. *unus*, one] being three in one [a *triune* God] —**tri·u′ni·ty** *n.*

tri·va·lent (trī vā′lənt) *adj.* **1.** having a valence of three **2.** having three valences —**tri·va′lence**, **tri·va′len·cy** *n.*

triv·et (triv′it) *n.* [OE. *trefet* < L. *tripes*, tripod] **1.** a three-legged stand for holding pots, kettles, etc. over or near a fire **2.** a small stand with short legs, for hot dishes to rest on

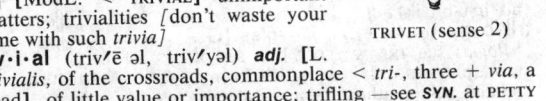

TRIVET (sense 2)

triv·i·a (triv′ē ə) *n.pl.* [*often with sing. v.*] [ModL. < TRIVIAL] unimportant matters; trivialities [don't waste your time with such *trivia*]

triv·i·al (triv′ē əl, triv′yəl) *adj.* [L. *trivialis*, of the crossroads, commonplace < *tri-*, three + *via*, a road] of little value or importance; trifling —see SYN. at PETTY —**triv′i·al·ly** *adv.*

triv·i·al·i·ty (triv′ē al′ə tē) *n.* **1.** the condition of being trivial **2.** *pl.* **-ties** a trivial thing, idea, etc.; trifle

triv·i·al·ize (triv′ē ə līz′) *vt.* **-ized′**, **-iz′ing** to make seem trivial or treat as unimportant —**triv′i·al·i·za′tion** *n.*

trivial name a common, nonscientific name, as of a plant or animal

tri·week·ly (trī wēk′lē) *adj., adv.* **1.** once every three weeks ☆**2.** three times a week —☆*n., pl.* **-lies** a publication that appears triweekly

-trix (triks) *pl.* **-trix·es**, **-tri·ces** (tri sēz′, trī′sēz) [L.] *an ending of some feminine nouns corresponding to* -OR [*aviatrix*]

TRM trademark

tro·cha·ic (trō kā′ik) *adj.* of or made up of trochees

tro·che (trō′kē) *n.* [< Fr. < LL. *trochiscus*, a pill < Gr. < *trochos*, a wheel] a small, usually round tablet or pill containing medicine

tro·chee (trō′kē) *n.* [< L. < Gr. *trochaios*, running < *trechein*, to run] a metrical foot of two syllables, the first accented and the other unaccented, as in English verse (Example: "Péter, | Péter, | púmpkin | éater")

trod (träd) *pt. & alt. pp.* of TREAD

trod·den (träd′'n) *alt. pp.* of TREAD

trode (trōd) *archaic pt.* of TREAD

trog·lo·dyte (träg′lə dīt′) *n.* [< L. < Gr. < *trōglē*, a cave + *dyein*, to enter] **1.** any of the prehistoric people who lived in caves; cave man **2.** a person who lives alone, as a hermit **3.** anyone who lives in a crude, primitive way —**trog′lo·dyt′ic** (-dit′ik) *adj.*

troi·ka (troi′kə) *n.* [Russ. < *troe*, three] **1.** *a)* a Russian vehicle drawn by three horses abreast *b)* the horses **2.** any group of three; esp., three persons who hold control together

Troi·lus (troi′ləs, trō′i ləs) *Gr. Legend* a son of King Priam: in Chaucer and Shakespeare, Troilus was the lover of the unfaithful Cressida

Trois-Ri·vières (trwä rē vyer′) city in S Quebec, Canada, on the St. Lawrence: pop. 58,000: Eng. name *Three Rivers*

Tro·jan (trō′jən) *adj.* of ancient Troy, its people, etc. —*n.* **1.** a native or inhabitant of ancient Troy **2.** a strong, hardworking, determined person

Trojan horse *Gr. Legend* a huge, hollow wooden horse filled with Greek soldiers and left at the gates of Troy: when the Trojans brought it into the city, the soldiers crept out and opened the gates to the Greek army

Trojan War *Gr. Legend* the ten-year war waged against Troy by the Greeks to get back Helen: see HELEN OF TROY

troll[1] (trōl) *vt., vi.* [ME. *trollen*, to roll, wander] **1.** to roll; revolve **2.** *a)* to sing the parts of (a round, etc.) in succession *b)* to sing in a strong or full voice **3.** to fish (*for* or *in*) with a moving line, esp. one with a revolving lure pulled through the water behind a moving boat —*n.* a lure, or a lure and line, used in trolling —**troll′er** *n.*

troll[2] (trōl) *n.* [ON.] in Scandinavian folklore, a giant or dwarf that lives underground or in a cave

trol·ley (träl′ē) *n., pl.* **-leys** [< TROLL[1]] **1.** a carriage, basket, etc. hanging from wheels which run on an overhead track ☆**2.** a device, as a grooved wheel at the end of a pole, to carry electric current from an overhead wire to the motor of a streetcar, etc. ☆**3.** a trolley car; streetcar **4.** [Brit.] a low cart —*vt., vi.* **-leyed, -ley·ing** ☆to carry or go on a trolley —☆**off one's trolley** [Slang] crazy; insane

☆**trolley bus** an electric bus that gets its power from overhead wires by means of trolleys but does not run on tracks

☆**trolley car** an electric streetcar that gets its power from an overhead wire by means of a trolley

trol·lop (träl′əp) *n.* [prob. < G. *trolle*, a wench] a woman whose sexual behavior is loose and immoral; specif., a prostitute

Trol·lope (träl′əp), **Anthony** 1815–82; Eng. novelist

trol·ly (träl′ē) *n., pl.* **-lies**, *vt., vi.* **-lied**, **-ly·ing** *var. of* TROLLEY

trom·bone (träm bōn′, träm′bōn) *n.* [It. < *tromba*, a trumpet < OHG. *trumba*] a large brass-wind instrument with a flared bell at one end of a long tube bent parallel to itself twice and having either a section that slides in or out (**slide trombone**) or valves (**valve trombone**) —**trom·bon′ist** *n.*

tromp (trämp) *vi., vt. var. of* TRAMP

‡**trompe l'oeil** (trōnp lĕ′y′) [Fr., lit., trick of the eye] **1.** a painting, etc. so realistic that it gives the illusion of being the actual thing rather than a painting **2.** any such illusion

-tron (trän) [Gr.] *a combining form meaning* instrument

Trond·heim (trôn′hām) seaport on a fjord in central Norway: pop. 126,000

troop (troop) *n.* [< Fr. < OFr. < ML. *troppus*, a flock] **1.** a group of persons or animals; band, herd, etc. **2.** loosely, a great number; lot [a whole *troop* of errors] **3.** [*pl.*] soldiers **4.** a subdivision of a cavalry regiment, corresponding to an infantry company **5.** a unit of Boy Scouts or Girl Scouts under an adult leader —*vi.* to gather or move in a group or crowd [the students *trooped* into the hall]

SYN.—**troop** is applied to a group of people organized as a unit [a cavalry *troop*] or working or acting together [a *troop* of happy children]; **troupe** is now the usual term for a group of performers in a theater, circus, etc. [the dance *troupe* will perform in London and Paris]; **company** is the general word for any group of people associated in any of various ways [he spoke to the assembled *company*]; **band** suggests a fairly small group of people joined together for some common purpose [a brass *band*; a *band* of thieves]

TROMBONE

troop·er (troo′pər) *n.* [TROOP + -ER] **1.** an enlisted soldier in the cavalry **2.** a cavalry horse **3.** a mounted policeman ☆**4.** [Colloq.] a member of the police force of a State

troop·ship (troop′ship′) *n.* a ship for carrying troops

trope (trōp) *n.* [< L. < Gr. *tropos*, a turning < *trepein*, to turn] *same as* FIGURE OF SPEECH

tro·phy (trō′fē) *n., pl.* **-phies** [< MFr. < L. < Gr. *tropaion*, token of an enemy's defeat, ult. < *trepein*, to turn] **1.** something taken from a defeated enemy and kept as a memorial of victory **2.** an animal skin, head, etc. displayed to show one's hunting skill **3.** a prize, usually a silver cup, awarded in a sports contest, etc. **4.** any memento

-tro·phy (trə fē) [Gr. *-trophia* < *trephein*, to nourish] *a combining form meaning* nutrition, growth [hypertrophy]

trop·ic (träp′ik) *n.* [< LL. < Gr. *tropikos*, of a turn (of the sun at the solstices) < *tropē*, a turn] **1.** *Astron.* either of two circles of the celestial sphere (the **Tropic of Cancer**, c. 23½° north, and the **Tropic of Capricorn**, c. 23½° south) parallel to the celestial equator: they are the limits of the apparent north-and-south journey of the sun: see illustration at ZONE **2.** *Geog. a)* either of two parallels of latitude corresponding to these, on either side of the earth's equator *b)* [*also* **T-**] [*pl.*] the region of the earth between these latitudes, noted for its hot climate —*adj.* of the tropics; tropical

-trop·ic (träp′ik, trō′pik) [< Gr. < *trepein*, to turn + -IC] *a combining form meaning* turning, changing, or otherwise responding to a (specified kind of) stimulus [phototropic]: also **-troph·ic** (träf′ik)

trop·i·cal (träp′i k'l) *adj.* of, in, characteristic of, or suitable for the tropics [a *tropical* storm] —**trop′i·cal·ly** *adv.*

tropical fish any of various usually brightly colored fish, orig. from the tropics, kept in an aquarium (**tropical aquarium**) maintained at a constant, warm temperature

Tropical Zone *same as* TORRID ZONE

tropic bird any of various tropical sea birds having white feathers with black markings and a pair of long tail feathers

tro·pism (trō′piz'm) *n.* [< next entry] the tendency of a plant or animal to grow or turn toward or away from an external stimulus such as light —**tro·pis′tic** *adj.*

-tro·pism (trə piz'm) [< TROPE + -ISM] *a combining form meaning* tropism [heliotropism]: also **-tro·py** (trə pē)

trop·o·sphere (träp′ə sfir′, trō′pə-) *n.* [< Fr. < Gr. *tropos* (see TROPE) + Fr. *sphère* (see SPHERE)] the atmosphere from the earth's surface to the stratosphere, reaching from 6 to 12 miles, in which clouds form and the temperature usually decreases with altitude —**trop′o·spher′ic** (-sfer′ik, -sfir′-) *adj.*

‡**trop·po** (trôp′pô) *adv.* [It.] too; too much so: a direction in music, as in *allegro non troppo*, not too fast

trot (trät) *vi.* **trot′ted**, **trot′ting** [< OFr. < OHG. *trottōn*, to tread] **1.** to move, ride, go, etc. at a trot **2.** to hurry; run —*vt.* to make trot —*n.* **1.** a gait of a horse, etc. in which a front leg and the opposite hind leg are moved at the same time **2.** a person's gait between a walk and a run **3.** a horse race for trotters ☆**4.** [Slang] *same as* PONY (*n.* 3) —**trot out** [Colloq.] to bring out for others to see or admire

troth (trôth, trōth, träth) *n.* [ult. < OE. *treowth*, truth] [Archaic] **1.** faithfulness; loyalty **2.** truth: chiefly in **in troth**, truly; indeed **3.** one's pledged word; promise: see also PLIGHT ONE'S TROTH (at PLIGHT[2]) —*vt.* [Archaic] to pledge to marry

trot·line (trät′līn′) *n.* a strong fishing line suspended over the water and holding many short lines bearing baited hooks

Trot·sky (trät′skē; *Russ.* trôt′-), **Le·on** (lē′än) (born *Lev Davidovich Bronstein*) 1879–1940; Russ. revolutionist & writer: exiled (1929) —**Trot′sky·ism** *n.* —**Trot′sky·ite**, **Trot′sky·ite′** (-īt′) *adj., n.*

trot·ter (trät′ər) *n.* **1.** an animal that trots; esp., a horse bred and trained for trotting races **2.** the foot of a sheep or pig used as food

trou·ba·dour (troo′bə dôr′) *n.* [Fr. < Pr. < *trobar*, to compose in verse] any of a class of lyric poets and poet-musicians who lived in southern France and northern Italy in the 11th, 12th, and 13th cent. and wrote poems of love and chivalry

trou·ble (trub′'l) *vt.* **-bled**, **-bling** [OFr. *trubler*, ult. < LL. *turbidare*, to trouble < L. *turbidus*, turbid] **1.** to disturb or stir up [*troubled* waters] **2.** to worry; harass; perturb [her son's absence *troubled* her] **3.** to cause pain or discomfort to [troubled by headaches] **4.** to put to an extra effort; cause inconvenience to [don't *trouble* yourself to rise] **5.** to annoy, bother, etc. [don't *trouble* her with such trivial matters] —*vi.* to take pains; bother [don't *trouble* to return it] —*n.* **1.** a state of mental distress; worry [a mind free of *trouble*] **2.** *a*) a misfortune or mishap *b*) a difficult situation [that might get you into *trouble*] *c*) a condition of needing to be repaired, fixed, etc. [tire *trouble*] **3.** a cause of annoyance, distress, etc. [the puppy was a constant *trouble*] **4.** public or civil disorder **5.** bother; pains [take the *trouble* to listen] **6.** an illness; ailment [heart *trouble*]

trou·ble·mak·er (-mā′kər) *n.* a person who is always making trouble for others; esp., one who stirs up others to quarrel, complain, rebel, etc. —**trou′ble·mak′ing** *n.*

☆**trou·ble-shoot·er** (-shōōt′ər) *n.* a person whose work is to find and repair or eliminate mechanical breakdowns or other sources of trouble —**trou′ble-shoot′ing** *n.*

trou·ble·some (-səm) *adj.* full of or causing trouble, difficulty, inconvenience, etc. [a troublesome cough] —**trou′ble·some·ly** *adv.* —**trou′ble·some·ness** *n.*

trou·blous (trub′ləs) *adj.* [Chiefly Literary] **1.** troubled; disturbed **2.** *same as* TROUBLESOME

trough (trôf) *n.* [OE. *trog*] **1.** a long, narrow, open container for holding water or food for animals **2.** a vessel of similar shape, as for kneading something **3.** a gutter, esp. under the edges of a roof, for carrying off rainwater **4.** a long, narrow hollow, as between waves **5.** a low point in business activity, etc. **6.** a long, narrow area of low barometric pressure

trounce (trouns) *vt.* **trounced, trounc′ing** [< ?] **1.** to beat; thrash **2.** [Colloq.] to defeat, esp. soundly —**trounc′er** *n.*

☆**troupe** (trōōp) *n.* [Fr.] a group, esp. of actors, singers, etc.; company —*vi.* **trouped, troup′ing** to travel as a member of a troupe —**see SYN.** at TROOP —**troup′er** *n.*

trou·sers (trou′zərz) *n.pl.* [< obs. *trouse* < ScotGael. *triubhas*] an outer garment, esp. for men and boys, reaching from the waist usually to the ankles and divided into separate coverings for the legs; pants —**trou′ser** *adj.*

trous·seau (trōō′sō, trōō sō′) *n., pl.* **-seaux** (-sōz), **-seaus** [Fr. < OFr., dim. of *trousse*, a bundle] a bride's outfit of clothes, linen, etc.

trout (trout) *n., pl.* **trout, trouts**: see PLURAL, II, D, 2 [OE. *truht* < LL. < Gr. *trōktēs*, kind of fish < *trōgein*, to gnaw] any of various food and game fishes related to but smaller than the salmon and found chiefly in fresh water

trow (trō, trou) *vi., vt.* [OE. *treowian* < *treow*, faith] [Archaic] to believe, think, suppose, etc.

trow·el (trou′əl) *n.* [< MFr. < LL. < L. *trulla* < *trua*, ladle] **1.** a tool with a thin, flat, rectangular blade for smoothing plaster **2.** a tool with a thin, flat, pointed blade for applying and shaping mortar, as in bricklaying **3.** a tool with a pointed scoop for digging in a garden —*vt.* **-eled** or **-elled, -el·ing** or **-el·ling** to spread, smooth, shape, dig, etc. with a trowel

Troy (troi) **1.** ancient city in NW Asia Minor **2.** [after prec.] city in eastern N.Y., on the Hudson: pop. 63,000

troy (troi) *adj.* by or in troy weight

troy weight [< *Troyes*, a city in France] a system of weights for gold, silver, precious stones, etc.: see TABLES OF WEIGHTS AND MEASURES in Supplements

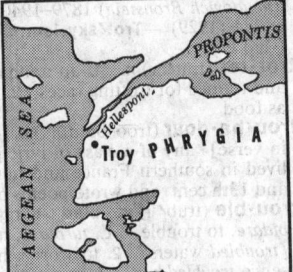

TROWELS
(A, brick; B, garden)

tru·ant (trōō′ənt) *n.* [OFr., a beggar < Celt.] **1.** a pupil who stays away from school without permission **2.** a person who neglects his work or duties —*adj.* **1.** that is a truant **2.** idle; lazy —**tru′an·cy** (-ən sē) *n., pl.* **-cies** —**tru′ant·ly** *adv.*

☆**truant officer** a school official dealing with truants: now usually called *attendance officer*

truce (trōōs) *n.* [OE. *treow*, compact, faith] **1.** a period during a war when fighting stops for a time by agreement of both sides **2.** any pause in quarreling, conflict, trouble, etc.

TROY (c. 1200 B.C.)

truck[1] (truk) *n.* [prob. < L. < Gr. *trochos*, a wheel < *trechein*, to run] **1.** a small, solid wheel, esp. for a gun carriage **2.** a small, wooden disk with holes for ropes, esp. at the top of a flagpole or mast **3.** a frame with wheels at one end and handles at the other, used to carry trunks, crates, etc.: also **hand truck 4.** a low frame or platform on wheels, for carrying heavy loads, as in a warehouse ☆**5.** an automotive vehicle for hauling loads along highways, streets, etc. **6.** a swiveling frame with two or more pairs of wheels, under each end of a railroad car, etc. —*vt.* to carry on a truck —*vi.* **1.** to do trucking **2.** to drive a truck as one's work

truck[2] (truk) *vt., vi.* [MFr. *troquer* < ?] to exchange; barter —*n.* **1.** *same as* BARTER **2.** payment of wages in goods instead of money **3.** small commercial articles **4.** small articles of little value ☆**5.** vegetables raised for sale in markets **6.** [Colloq.] dealings [have no further *truck* with them] **7.** [Colloq.] trash; rubbish

truck·age (truk′ij) *n.* **1.** transportation of goods by truck **2.** the charge for this

truck·er[1] (-ər) *n.* **1.** a truck driver **2.** a person or company doing trucking Also **truck′man** (-mən), *pl.* **-men**

truck·er[2] (-ər) *n.* ☆ a truck farmer

☆**truck farm** a farm where vegetables are grown for sale in markets —**truck farmer** —**truck farming**

truck·ing (-iŋ) *n.* the business of carrying goods by truck

truck·le (truk′'l) *n.* [< L. *trochlea*, a pulley < Gr. < *trochos*, a wheel] **1.** *orig.*, a small wheel **2.** *short for* TRUCKLE BED —*vi.* **-led, -ling** to be overly humble and willing to obey; give in too easily (*to*) [it's disgusting the way he *truckles* to his boss]

truckle bed *same as* TRUNDLE BED

truc·u·lent (truk′yoo lənt) *adj.* [< L. < *trucis*, genitive of *trux*] **1.** fierce; savage **2.** harsh; scathing [his *truculent* remarks] **3.** ready to fight —**truc′u·lence, truc′u·len·cy** *n.* —**truc′u·lent·ly** *adv.*

Tru·deau (trōō′dō; Fr. trü dō′), **Pierre El·li·ott** (el′ē ət) 1921– ; prime minister of Canada (1968–79; 1980–)

trudge (truj) *vi.* **trudged, trudg′ing** [< ?] to walk, esp. in a tired way or with effort —*n.* a walk, esp. a long or tiring one

trudg·en stroke (truj′ən) [after J. *Trudgen*, 19th-cent. Eng. swimmer] a swimming stroke in which a double overarm motion and a scissors kick are used: also **trudg′en** *n.*

true (trōō) *adj.* **tru′er, tru′est** [OE. *treowe*] **1.** faithful; loyal [remaining *true* to his wife] **2.** reliable; certain [a *true* indication] **3.** that agrees with fact; not false [a *true* story] **4.** *a*) conforming to an original, standard, etc. [*true* weight] *b*) exact; accurate; correct [a *true* copy] **5.** rightful; lawful [the *true* heirs] **6.** accurately fitted, placed, or shaped [the board is *true*] **7.** *a*) genuine; authentic [a *true* diamond] *b*) rightly so called [a *true* scholar] **8.** [Archaic] honest, virtuous, or truthful —*adv.* **1.** truly, truthfully, accurately, etc. [he shot *true* to the mark] **2.** *Biol.* without variation [a plant that breeds *true*] —*vt.* **trued, tru′ing** or **true′ing** to fit, place, or shape accurately (often with *up*) —*n.* that which is true; truth or reality (with *the*) —**come true** to happen as predicted, hoped, or expected —**in** (or **out of**) **true** that is (or is not) properly set, adjusted, etc. —**true to form** behaving as might be expected —**true′ness** *n.*

SYN.—**true, actual,** and **real** are often used, with almost no difference in meaning, to indicate that something exists in fact or is what it is said to be; but in precise use **true** implies agreement with some standard or model [a *true* poet] or agreement with the facts or with what actually exists [the *true* story of her life], **actual** is used of something that exists or occurred in fact, not something imaginary, theoretical, etc. [an *actual* historical event], and **real** implies exact agreement between what something is and what it seems or pretends to be [*real* rubber, *real* courage]

true bill a bill of indictment, stating the charges against someone accused of a crime, which a grand jury finds to be based on enough evidence to require a trial

true-blue (trōō′blōō′) *adj.* very loyal; staunch

☆**true-false test** (trōō′fôls′) a test, as of knowledge, made up of a series of statements which are to be identified as either "true" or "false"

true·heart·ed (-här′tid) *adj.* **1.** loyal; faithful **2.** honest or sincere —**true′heart′ed·ness** *n.*

true-life (-līf′) *adj.* like what happens in real life; true to reality [a *true-life* story]

true·love (-luv′) *n.* (one's) sweetheart; a loved one

truelove knot a kind of bowknot that is hard to untie, a symbol of lasting love: also **true′-lov′er's knot**

true ribs ribs that are attached by cartilage directly to the breastbone; in man, the upper seven pairs of ribs

truf·fle (truf′′l, trŏŏ′f′l) *n.* [< Fr. < OIt. *truffa*, ult. < L. *tuber*, a knob] any of a group of fungi that grow underground and are used as food, esp. a European kind regarded as a delicacy

tru·ism (trŏŏ′iz′m) *n.* a statement which is so obviously true or widely known to be true that it hardly seems necessary to say it —**tru·is′tic** *adj.*

tru·ly (trŏŏ′lē) *adv.* **1.** in a true manner; accurately, faithfully, etc. [to report the facts *truly*] **2.** in fact; really [it is *truly* a beautiful day]

Tru·man (trŏŏ′mən), **Harry S.** 1884–1972; 33d president of the U.S. (1945–53)

trump[1] (trump) *n.* [altered < TRIUMPH] **1.** any playing card of a suit that ranks higher than any other suit during the playing of a hand **2.** [*occas. pl. with sing. v.*] a suit of trumps **3.** [Colloq.] a fine person —*vt.* **1.** to take (a trick, card, etc.) with a trump **2.** to outdo; surpass —*vi.* to play a trump —**trump up** to make up (a charge against someone, an excuse, etc.) in order to deceive

trump[2] (trump) *n., vi., vt.* [OFr. *trompe*] *archaic var. of* TRUMPET

trump·er·y (trum′pər ē) *n., pl.* **-er·ies** [< MFr. < *tromper*, to deceive] **1.** something showy but worthless **2.** nonsense —*adj.* showy but worthless

trum·pet (trum′pit) *n.* [< MFr. dim. of *trompe*, trumpet] **1.** a brass-wind instrument with a blaring tone, made of a long, looped tube flared at the end opposite the mouthpiece **2.** something shaped like a trumpet; esp., *same as* EAR TRUMPET **3.** a sound like that of a trumpet —*vi.* **1.** to blow a trumpet **2.** to make a sound like a trumpet [the elephant *trumpeted* in anger] —*vt.* **1.** to sound on or as on a trumpet **2.** to announce loudly [he *trumpeted* his innocence to all who were present]

☆**trumpet creeper** a climbing vine of the southern U.S., with red, trumpet-shaped flowers: also **trumpet vine**

TRUMPET

trum·pet·er (-ər) *n.* **1.** a trumpet player **2.** a long-legged, long-necked S. American bird having a loud cry ☆**3.** *same as* TRUMPETER SWAN **4.** a domestic pigeon with feathered feet and a rounded crest

☆**trumpeter swan** a N. American wild swan with a loud cry

☆**trumpet honeysuckle** an American honeysuckle with reddish, trumpet-shaped flowers

trun·cate (trun′kāt) *vt.* **-cat·ed, -cat·ing** [< L. pp. of *truncare*, to cut off < *truncus*, a stem] to shorten by cutting; lop —*adj. same as* TRUNCATED —**trun·ca′tion** *n.*

trun·cat·ed (-id) *adj.* **1.** cut short or appearing as if cut short **2.** having the vertex cut off by a plane [a *truncated* cone]

trun·cheon (trun′chən) *n.* [< OFr., ult. < L. *truncus*, a stem] **1.** a staff carried as a symbol of authority **2.** [Chiefly Brit.] a policeman's stick

trun·dle (trun′d'l) *n.* [OE. *trendel*, a circle < *trendan*, to roll] **1.** a small wheel **2.** *short for* TRUNDLE BED —*vt., vi.* **-dled, -dling** **1.** to roll along **2.** to move on or as if on wheels

trundle bed a low bed on small wheels, that can be rolled under a higher bed when not in use

trunk (truŋk) *n.* [< OFr. < L. *truncus*, trunk, orig., mutilated] **1.** the main stem of a tree **2.** a human body or animal body, not including the head and limbs **3.** the thorax of an insect **4.** the main part of a nerve, blood vessel, etc. **5.** a long, flexible snout, as of an elephant **6.** a large, reinforced box for carrying a traveler's clothes, etc. **7.** a large, long, boxlike pipe, etc. that conveys air, water, etc. **8.** [*pl.*] *same as* TRUNK HOSE ☆**9.** [*pl.*] men's shorts worn for boxing, swimming, etc. ☆**10.** *short for* TRUNK LINE ☆**11.** a compartment in an automobile, usually in the rear, for a spare tire, luggage, etc.

trunk·fish (truŋk′fish′) *n., pl.* **-fish′, -fish′es:** see FISH a tropical fish whose body is covered with bony plates

trunk hose full, baggy short trousers reaching about halfway down the thigh, worn in the 16th and 17th cent.

☆**trunk line** a main line of a railroad, telephone system, etc.

trun·nion (trun′yən) *n.* [Fr. *trognon*, a stump] either of two projecting pins on each side of a cannon, on which it pivots

truss (trus) *vt.* [OFr. *trousser*] **1.** orig., to tie into a bundle **2.** to tie or bind (often with *up*) [they *trussed* up the prisoner's arms and legs] **3.** to skewer or bind the wings, etc. of (a fowl)

before cooking **4.** to support or strengthen with a truss —*n.* **1.** a bundle or pack **2.** an iron band around a mast, for holding a yard in place **3.** a rigid framework of beams, struts, etc. for supporting a roof, bridge, etc. **4.** a device, usually a pad on a belt, worn to support a hernia

trust (trust) *n.* [ON. *traust*] **1.** *a)* firm belief in the honesty, reliability, etc. of some person or thing; faith [I put little *trust* in such methods] *b)* the one trusted [the Lord is our *trust*] **2.** confident expectation, hope, etc. [have *trust* in the future] **3.** *a)* the fact of having confidence placed in one *b)* the responsibility resulting from this [she lived up to her *trust*] **4.** care; custody [the valuables were placed in my *trust*] **5.** something entrusted to one; charge [the children's welfare is her *trust*] **6.** confidence in a purchaser's intention or future ability to pay for goods, etc.; credit [to sell on *trust*] **7.** *a)* a group of business corporations under the control of a single board of trustees, who are able to eliminate competition, fix prices, etc. *b) same as* CARTEL (sense 3) **8.** *Law a)* confidence placed in a person by allowing him to hold and manage property for another's benefit *b)* property managed by a trustee or trustees —*vi.* to have trust or faith; be confident [I can help only if you *trust* in me] —*vt.* **1.** to have trust in; rely on, etc. [I don't *trust* that shaky ladder] **2.** to commit (something) *to* a person's care [he *trusted* the book to them] **3.** to put something confidently in the charge of [to *trust* a lawyer with one's case] **4.** to allow to do something without fear of the outcome [I can't *trust* her to drive in bad weather] **5.** to believe or suppose [I *trust* you know we'll all be there] **6.** to hope [I *trust* that they will be happy] **7.** to grant business credit to [the grocer will *trust* us for another week] —*adj.* **1.** relating to a trust or trusts [*trust* management] **2.** held in trust [a *trust* fund] **3.** acting as a trustee [a *trust* company] —see SYN. at BELIEF and MONOPOLY —**in trust** in the condition of being entrusted to another's care —**trust to** to rely on [don't *trust to* luck] —**trust′a·ble** *adj.* —**trust′er** *n.*

☆**trust company** **1.** a company formed to act as a trustee **2.** a bank organized to handle trusts and to carry on all banking operations except issuing bank notes

trus·tee (trus tē′) *n.* **1.** a person or company that is put in charge of another's property or affairs **2.** a nation under whose control a trust territory is placed **3.** any of a group of persons appointed to manage the affairs of a college, hospital, etc. —*vt.* **-teed′, -tee′ing** to place under the control of a trustee or trustees

trus·tee·ship (-ship′) *n.* **1.** the position or work of a trustee **2.** *a)* the authority given by the United Nations to a country to manage a trust territory *b)* the state or fact of being a trust territory

trust·ful (trust′fəl) *adj.* full of trust or confidence in another or others; trusting —**trust′ful·ly** *adv.* —**trust′ful·ness** *n.*

trust fund money, stock, etc. held in trust

trust·ing (trus′tiŋ) *adj.* that trusts; trustful —**trust′ing·ly** *adv.*

trust territory a territory placed by the United Nations under the control of a country that manages the affairs of the territory

trust·wor·thy (trust′wur′thē) *adj.* **-thi·er -thi·est** worthy of trust; dependable; reliable —see SYN. at RELIABLE —**trust′wor′-thi·ly** *adv.* —**trust′wor′thi·ness** *n.*

trust·y (trus′tē) *adj.* **trust′i·er, trust′i·est** that can be relied upon; dependable [my *trusty* old car] —*n., pl.* **trust′ies** a trusted person; ☆*specif.*, a convict who is given special privileges because he has behaved well —see SYN. at RELIABLE —**trust′i·ly** *adv.* —**trust′i·ness** *n.*

truth (trŏŏth) *n., pl.* **truths** (trŏŏthz, trŏŏths) [OE. *treowth*] **1.** the quality or state of being true; specif., *a)* orig., loyalty *b)* sincerity; honesty *c)* the quality of being in agreement with reality or facts *d)* reality; actual existence *e)* agreement with a standard, rule, etc.; correctness **2.** that which is true [did the newspaper print the *truth* about him?] **3.** an established or proven fact, etc. **4.** a particular belief or teaching thought of by the speaker as the true one (often with *the*) —**in truth** truly; in fact —**of a truth** certainly

truth drug an anesthetic or hypnotic, as thiopental sodium, believed to make a person who takes it willing to answer questions: also ☆**truth serum**

truth·ful (trŏŏth′fəl) *adj.* **1.** telling the truth; honest [a *truthful* person] **2.** agreeing with fact or reality [a *truthful* account] —**truth′ful·ly** *adv.* —**truth′ful·ness** *n.*

---

try (trī) *vt.* **tried, try'ing** [OFr. *trier,* ult. < ? L. pp. of *terere,* to thresh grain] **1.** to melt down (fat, etc.) to get (the oil): usually with *out* **2.** *a)* to examine and decide (a case) in a law court *b)* to determine legally the guilt or innocence of (a person) **3.** to put to the proof; test [*try* your luck] **4.** to test the faith, patience, etc. of; afflict [he was sorely *tried*] **5.** to put to a severe test or strain [the long climb *tried* her strength] **6.** to test the effect of; experiment with [*try* this recipe] **7.** to attempt; endeavor [*try* to forget] **8.** to attempt to open (a door or window) in testing to see whether it is locked —*vi.* **1.** to make an effort, attempt, etc. **2.** to experiment —*n., pl.* **tries** an attempt; effort; trial —**try on** to test the fit or appearance of (a garment) by putting it on —**try one's hand at** to attempt (to do something), esp. for the first time —**try out** ☆**1.** to test the quality, value, etc. of, as by using ☆**2.** to test one's fitness, as for a place on a team, a part in a play, etc.
SYN.—**try** is the simple, direct word for making some effort to do something [*try* to come], but specifically it implies experimenting to test or prove something [I'll *try* your recipe]; **attempt,** somewhat more formal, suggests a setting out to accomplish something but often implies failure [she had *attempted* to wallpaper the bedroom]; **endeavor** suggests hard work and determined effort in the face of difficulties [we shall *endeavor* to recover your lost suitcase]; **essay** suggests an experimenting to test whether something difficult can be done [he will not *essay* the high jump]; **strive** suggests a determined, serious effort to accomplish something [*strive* to win]; **struggle** suggests an effort involving much toil and strain to overcome difficulties or free oneself from something that is holding one back [she *struggled* to reach the top]

try·ing (trī'iŋ) *adj.* that tries one's patience; hard to bear; annoying [I've had a *trying* day] —**try'ing·ly** *adv.*
☆**try·out** (trī'out') *n.* [Colloq.] a chance to prove, or a test to determine, one's fitness for a place on a team, a part in a play, etc.
tryp·a·no·some (trip'ə nə sōm') *n.* [< ModL. < Gr. *trypanon,* borer + ModL. *-soma, -SOME*[3]] any of a group of flagellate protozoans that live as parasites in the blood of man and other vertebrates, are usually transmitted by an insect bite, and often cause serious diseases, as sleeping sickness
tryp·sin (trip'sin) *n.* [G., prob. < Gr. *tryein,* to wear away + G. (*pe*)*psin:* see PEPSIN] a digestive enzyme in the pancreatic juice: it changes proteins into peptides —**tryp'tic** *adj.*
try·sail (trī's'l, -sāl') *n.* [< naut. phr. *a try,* position of lying to in a storm] a small fore-and-aft sail used to keep a vessel's bow pointing into the wind in a storm
try square an instrument for testing the accuracy of square work and for marking off right angles
tryst (trist, trīst) *n.* [OFr. *triste,* hunting station] **1.** an appointment to meet at a certain time and place, esp. one made secretly by lovers **2.** *a)* a meeting held by appointment *b)* the place of such a meeting: also **trysting place** —**tryst'er** *n.*

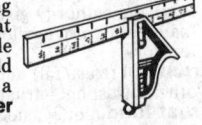
TRY SQUARE

tsar (tsär, zär) *n. var. sp. of* CZAR —**tsar'dom** *n.* —**tsar'ism** *n.* —**tsar'ist** *adj., n.*
Tschaikowsky *see* TCHAIKOVSKY
tset·se fly (tset'sē, tsēt'-, set'-, sēt'-) [Afrik. < the Bantu name] any of several small flies of central and southern Africa, including the one that carries sleeping sickness
☆**T-shirt** (tē'shurt') *n.* [so named because T-shaped] a knitted sport shirt or undershirt with short sleeves and no collar, pulled on over the head
Tsi·nan (jē'nän') city in NE China: pop. 882,000
Tsing·tao (chiŋ'dou') seaport in NE China, on the Yellow Sea: pop. 1,144,000
tsk *interj., n.* a clicking or sucking sound made with the tongue to express disapproval, sympathy, etc. —*vi.* to utter "tsks"
tsp. **1.** teaspoon(s) **2.** teaspoonful(s)
T square a T-shaped ruler for drawing parallel lines
tsu·na·mi (tsoo nä'mē) *n.* [Jpn. < *tsu,* a harbor + *nami,* wave] a huge sea wave caused by a disturbance under water, as an earthquake: popularly, but inaccurately, called *tidal wave* —**tsu·na'mic** (-mik) *adj.*
tsu·tsu·ga·mu·shi disease (tsoo'tsoo gə moo'shē) [< Jpn., lit., dangerous insect] an Asian disease transmitted to man by the bite of the larva of a mite: it causes fever and a rash
Tu. Tuesday
tu·a·ta·ra (too'ə tä'rə) *n.* [< Maori < *tua,* back + *tara,* spine] a primitive reptile that resembles a lizard and is found on islands near

T SQUARE

New Zealand: it has a row of spines in the middle of the back and a well-developed third eye
tub (tub) *n.* [MDu. *tubbe*] **1.** *a)* a round, open, wooden container, usually formed of staves and hoops fastened around a flat bottom *b)* any large, open container of metal, etc., as for washing clothes *c)* as much as a tub will hold **2.** *a) short for* BATHTUB *b)* [Brit. Colloq.] a bath in a tub **3.** [Colloq.] a slow-moving, clumsy ship or boat —*vt.* **tubbed, tub'bing** **1.** [Colloq.] to wash in a tub **2.** [Brit. Colloq.] to bathe (oneself) —**tub'ba·ble** *adj.* —**tub'ber** *n.*
tu·ba (too'bə, tyoo'-) *n., pl.* **tu'bas, tu'bae** (-bē) [L., a trumpet] a large, brass-wind musical instrument with a full, deep tone
tub·by (tub'ē) *adj.* **-bi·er, -bi·est** **1.** shaped like a tub **2.** short and fat — **tub'bi·ness** *n.*
tube (toob, tyoob) *n.* [Fr. < L. *tubus,* a pipe] **1.** *a)* a slender, hollow cylinder or pipe of metal, glass, rubber, etc., in which gases and liquids can flow or be kept *b)* an instrument, part, organ, etc. that looks like a tube [a bronchial *tube*] **2.** a rubber casing filled with air and used, esp. formerly, with an outer casing to form an automotive tire **3.** a long, slender container made of soft metal, plastic, etc., with a screw cap at one end, from which toothpaste, glue, etc. can be squeezed out ☆**4.** *short for:* ELECTRON TUBE *b)* VACUUM TUBE **5.** *a)* an underground tunnel for a railroad, subway, etc. *b)* [Brit. Colloq.] a subway —*vt.* **tubed, tub'ing** **1.** to provide with, place in, or pass through a tube or tubes **2.** to make tubular —☆**down the tube (or tubes)** [Colloq.] in or into a condition of failure, defeat, etc. —☆**the tube** [Colloq.] television —**tub'al** *adj.* —**tu'bate** *adj.* —**tube'like'** *adj.*

TUBA

tube foot any of the many water-filled tubes that stand out from the body in most echinoderms, used in moving about, handling food, etc.
☆**tube·less tire** (toob'lis, tyoob'-) a tire for an automotive vehicle, consisting of a single air-filled unit without an inner tube
tu·ber (too'bər, tyoo'-) *n.* [L., lit., a swelling] **1.** a short, thickened, fleshy part of an underground stem, as a potato **2.** a tubercle or swelling
tu·ber·cle (too'bər k'l, tyoo'-) *n.* [L. *tuberculum,* dim. of *tuber:* see prec.] **1.** a small, rounded part growing out from a bone or from the root of a plant **2.** any abnormal hard nodule or swelling; specif., the typical lumpy swelling of tuberculosis
tubercle bacillus the bacterium causing tuberculosis
tu·ber·cu·lar (too bur'kyə lər, tyoo-) *adj.* **1.** of, like, or having tubercles **2.** of or having tuberculosis **3.** caused by the tubercle bacillus Also **tu·ber'cu·lous** (-ləs) —*n.* a person having tuberculosis
tu·ber·cu·lin (-lin) *n.* a sterile solution prepared from a culture of the tubercle bacillus and injected into the skin as a test for tuberculosis
tu·ber·cu·lo·sis (too bur'kyə lō'sis, tyoo-) *n.* [ModL.: see TUBERCLE & -OSIS] an infectious disease caused by the tubercle bacillus and causing tubercles to form in body tissues; specif., tuberculosis of the lungs; consumption
tube·rose (toob'rōz', tyoob'-) *n.* [ModL. < L. *tuberosus,* TUBEROUS] a perennial Mexican plant with a tuberous root and white, sweet-smelling flowers
tu·ber·os·i·ty (too'bə räs'ə tē, tyoo'-) *n., pl.* **-ties** **1.** a being tuberous **2.** a rounded swelling, as on a bone for the attachment of a muscle or tendon
tu·ber·ous (too'bər əs, tyoo'-) *adj.* [< Fr. < L. *tuberosus:* see TUBER & -OUS] **1.** covered with rounded, wartlike swellings; knobby **2.** of, like, or having a tuber or tubers Also **tu'ber·ose'** (-ōs')
tuberous root a tuberlike root without buds or scale leaves, as of the dahlia —**tu'ber·ous-root'ed** *adj.*
tu·bi·fex (too'bə feks', tyoo'-) *n., pl.* **-fex·es, -fex'** [ModL. < L. *tubus,* a pipe + *-fex* < *facere,* to make] a small freshwater worm, found esp. in polluted waters and often used as food for aquarium fish
tub·ing (toob'iŋ, tyoob'-) *n.* **1.** a series or system of tubes **2.** material in the form of a tube **3.** a piece or length of tube
tu·bu·lar (too'byə lər, tyoo'-) *adj.* [< L. dim. of *tubus,* a pipe] **1.** of or shaped like a tube **2.** made with tubes Also **tu'bu·late** (-lit) —**tu'bu·lar'i·ty** (-lar'ə tē) *n.* —**tu'bu·lar·ly** *adv.*

tu·bule (tōōb′yool, tyōōb′-) *n.* a small tube, esp. one that is a part of an animal or plant

tuck[1] (tuk) *vt.* [< MDu. *tucken*, to tuck & related OE. word *tucian*, to tug] **1.** to pull up or gather up in a fold or folds, so as to make shorter [*to tuck up* one's skirt for wading] **2.** to sew a fold or folds in (a garment) **3.** *a)* to push the edges of (a sheet, shirt, etc.) under or in, in order to keep firmly in place (usually with *up, in,* etc.) *b)* to cover or wrap snugly [*tuck* the baby in bed] **4.** to put or press snugly into a small space; fit [to *tuck* shoes in a suitcase] **5.** to put into a hidden, empty, or isolated spot [a cabin *tucked* in the hills] —*vi.* **1.** to draw together; pucker **2.** to make tucks —*n.* a sewed fold in a garment —**tuck away** to put aside, as for future use —**tuck in** to pull or draw in (one's chin, stomach, etc.)

☆**tuck**[2] (tuk) *n.* shortened form of TUXEDO

tuck·er (tuk′ər) *n.* **1.** a person or device that makes tucks **2.** a neck and shoulder covering formerly worn with a low-cut dress or blouse by women **3.** [Austral. Slang] food

☆**tuck·er**[2] (tuk′ər) *vt.* [prob. < *tuck,* in obs. sense "to punish, rebuke"] [Colloq.] to tire (*out*); weary

Tuc·son (tōō′sän, tōō sän′) [Sp. < Pima *tu-uk-so-on,* black base, after a dark stratum in a nearby mountain] city in S Ariz.: pop. 263,000

Tu·cu·mán (tōō kōō män′) city in N Argentina: pop. 366,000

Tu·dor (tōō′dər, tyōō′-) ruling family of England (1485–1603) —*adj.* designating or of a style of architecture popular under the Tudors, having shallow moldings, much paneling, slightly rounded arches, etc.

Tues·day (tōōz′dē, tyōōz′-; -dā) *n.* [OE. *Tiwes dæg,* lit., day of the god of war *Tiw*] the third day of the week: abbrev. **Tues.**

Tues·days (-dēz, -dāz) *adv.* on or during every Tuesday

tu·fa (tōō′fə, tyōō′-) *n.* [It. *tufo* < L. *tofus*] a porous rock formed of calcium carbonate, etc. deposited near the mouth of a mineral spring, geyser, etc. —**tu·fa′ceous** (-fā′shəs) *adj.*

tuff (tuf) *n.* [< Fr. < It. *tufo,* TUFA] a porous rock formed from volcanic ash, dust, etc. —**tuff·a′ceous** (-ā′shəs) *adj.*

tuf·fet (tuf′ət) *n.* [< TUFT] **1.** a tuft of grass **2.** [by misunderstanding of a nursery rhyme] a low stool

tuft (tuft) *n.* [OFr. *tufe,* prob. < L. *tufa,* helmet crest] **1.** a bunch of hairs, feathers, grass, etc. growing or tied closely together **2.** *a)* the fluffy ball forming the end of any of the clusters of threads drawn tightly through a quilt, etc. to hold the padding in place *b)* a decorative button to which such a tuft is fastened —*vt.* **1.** to provide or decorate with a tuft or tufts **2.** to keep the padding of (a quilt, mattress, etc.) in place by regularly spaced tufts —*vi.* to grow in or form into tufts —**tuft′er** *n.* —**tuft′y** *adj.*

tuft·ed (tuf′tid) *adj.* **1.** having or decorated with tufts **2.** formed into or growing in a tuft or tufts

tug (tug) *vi.* **tugged, tug′ging** [prob. < ON. *toga,* to draw] **1.** to pull hard [she *tugged* at the bell rope] **2.** to labor; toil; struggle —*vt.* **1.** to pull at with force; strain at [the baby *tugged* the cat's tail] **2.** to drag; haul [he *tugged* the trunk out of the locker] **3.** to tow with a tugboat —*n.* **1.** a hard pull [a *tug* on the shoelace broke it] **2.** a great effort or a struggle, strain, etc. **3.** a rope, chain, strap, etc. used for pulling; esp., a trace of a harness **4.** shortened form of TUGBOAT —see **SYN.** at PULL —**tug′ger** *n.*

tug·boat (tug′bōt′) *n.* a small, powerful boat used for towing or pushing ships, barges, etc.

tug of war **1.** a contest in which two teams pull at opposite ends of a rope, each trying to drag the other across a central line **2.** any hard struggle

tu·grik (tōō′grik) *n.* [Mongol. *dughurik,* lit., wheel] see MONETARY UNITS, table (Mongolia)

Tui·ler·ies (twē′lər ēz; *Fr.* twēl rē′) former royal palace in Paris, burned in 1871: the site is now a public garden

TUGBOAT

tu·i·tion (tōō wish′ən, tyōō-) *n.* [< OFr. < L. *tuitio,* protection < pp. of *tueri,* to protect] **1.** the fee paid for being taught, esp. at a college or private school **2.** [Now Rare] teaching; instruction —**tu·i′tion·al** *adj.*

Tu·la (tōō′lä) city in central European R.S.F.S.R.: pop. 462,000

☆**tu·la·re·mi·a** (tōō′lə rē′mē ə) *n.* [ModL. < *Tulare* County, California + -EMIA] an infectious disease of rodents, esp. rabbits, that is transmitted to man by the handling of flesh from an infected animal or by the bite of certain insects: also sp. **tu·la·rae′mi·a** —**tu′la·re′mic** *adj.*

☆**tu·le** (tōō′lē) *n.* [Sp. < Nahuatl *tullin,* bulrush] either of two large bulrushes found in lakes and marshes of the southwestern U.S.

tu·lip (tōō′lip, tyōō′-) *n.* [< Fr. < Turk. *tülbend,* TURBAN: the flower resembles a turban] **1.** any of various plants that grow from a bulb and have long, pointed leaves and a large, cup-shaped flower **2.** the flower or bulb

☆**tulip tree** a N. American tree of the magnolia family, with tulip-shaped, greenish-yellow flowers, and long, conelike fruit: also called **tulip poplar**

☆**tu·lip·wood** (-wood′) *n.* **1.** the light, soft wood of the tulip tree, used for furniture, etc. **2.** any of several woods having streaks of color

tulle (tōōl; *Fr.* tül) *n.* [< *Tulle,* city in France] a thin, fine netting of silk, rayon, nylon, etc., used for veils, scarfs, etc.

Tul·ly (tul′ē) Englished name of (Marcus) Tullius (CICERO)

Tul·sa (tul′sə) [< Creek Indian name] city in NE Okla., on the Arkansas River: pop. 332,000

tum·ble (tum′b'l) *vi.* **-bled, -bling** [OE. *tumbian,* to jump, dance] **1.** to do somersaults, handsprings, or similar acrobatic feats **2.** *a)* to fall suddenly or helplessly [she slipped and *tumbled* down the steps] *b)* to undergo a sudden drop or downfall [prices *tumbled,* the government *tumbled*] **3.** to stumble or trip **4.** to toss or roll about [puppies *tumbling* about in the pile of leaves] **5.** to move in a quick, disorderly manner [the boys *tumbled* out of the house] **6.** [Colloq.] to understand suddenly (with *to*) —*vt.* **1.** to cause to tumble **2.** to put into disorder as by tossing here and there —*n.* **1.** a tumbling; specif., *a)* a somersault, handspring, etc. *b)* a fall [to take a *tumble*] **2.** a messy or confused condition —**give** (or **get**) **a tumble** [Colloq.] to give (or get) some favorable or affectionate notice, attention, etc.

☆**tum·ble·bug** (-bug′) *n.* any of various beetles that roll and bury balls of dung, in which they deposit their eggs and in which the larvae develop

tum·ble·down (-doun′) *adj.* that looks ready to fall down; dilapidated

tum·bler (tum′blər) *n.* **1.** an acrobat or gymnast who does somersaults, handsprings, etc. **2.** a kind of pigeon that does somersaults in flight **3.** *a)* an ordinary drinking glass with no foot or stem *b)* its contents **4.** a part of a lock whose position must be changed by a key in order to release the bolt **5.** a device for tumbling things about

☆**tum·ble·weed** (tum′b'l wēd′) *n.* any of various plants which break off near the ground in autumn and are blown about by the wind

tum·brel, tum·bril (tum′brəl) *n.* [< MFr. < *tomber,* to fall] **1.** a farmer's cart that can be tilted for emptying **2.** any of the carts used to carry prisoners to the guillotine during the French Revolution

tu·me·fac·tion (tōō′mə fak′shən, tyōō′-) *n.* **1.** a swelling up or becoming swollen **2.** a swollen part

tu·me·fy (tōō′mə fī′, tyōō′-) *vt., vi.* **-fied′, -fy′ing** [< L. < *tumere,* to swell + *facere,* to make] to swell or cause to swell

tu·mes·cence (tōō mes′'ns, tyōō-) *n.* [< L. prp. of *tumescere,* to swell up] **1.** the act of swelling **2.** a swollen part —**tu·mes′cent** *adj.*

tu·mid (tōō′mid, tyōō′-) *adj.* [< L. < *tumere,* to swell] **1.** swollen; bulging **2.** sounding important but not really so; pompous [a *tumid* style of writing] —**tu·mid′i·ty** *n.* —**tu′mid·ly** *adv.*

tum·my (tum′ē) *n., pl.* **-mies** stomach: a child's word

tu·mor (tōō′mər, tyōō′-) *n.* [L. < *tumere,* to swell] a swelling on some part of the body; esp., an abnormal growth of tissue in some part of the body, that is either harmless or harmful: Brit. sp. **tu′mour** —**tu′mor·ous** *adj.*

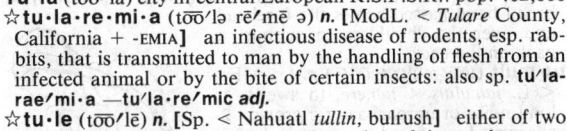

TUMBLEWEED

☆**tump·line** (tump′līn) *n.* [*tump*, a tumpline < AmInd.] a broad band passed across the forehead and over the shoulders to support a pack on the back

tu·mult (tōō′mult, tyōō′-) *n.* [< MFr. < L. *tumultus* < *tumere*, to swell] **1.** loud noise or uproar, as of a crowd **2.** an excited, confused, or disturbed condition [the news left us in a *tumult*]

tu·mul·tu·ous (tōō mul′chōō wəs) *adj.* **1.** full of or characterized by tumult; wild and noisy; uproarious [a *tumultuous* greeting for the hero] **2.** making a tumult [a *tumultuous* crowd] **3.** greatly disturbed [*tumultuous* emotions] —**tu·mul′tu·ous·ly** *adv.* —**tu·mul′tu·ous·ness** *n.*

tu·mu·lus (tōō′myə ləs, tyōō′-) *n.*, *pl.* **-li′** (-lī′), **-lus·es** [L., a mound] an artificial mound, esp. an ancient burial mound

tun (tun) *n.* [OE. *tunne*, large cask & OFr. *tonne*, both < ML. *tunna* < Celt.] **1.** a large cask, esp. one for wine, beer, or ale **2.** a measure of capacity for liquids, usually 252 gallons —*vt.* **tunned, tun′ning** to store in a tun or tuns

☆**tu·na¹** (tōō′nə, tyōō′-) *n.*, *pl.* **tu′na, tu′nas:** see PLURAL, II, D, 2 [AmSp. < Sp. < Ar. < L. *thunnus*] **1.** a large ocean fish of the mackerel group: also called **bluefin tuna 2.** any of various related fishes, as the albacore **3.** the oily flesh of the tuna, often canned for food: also called **tuna fish**

tu·na² (tōō′nə, tyōō′-) *n.* [Sp., of WInd. origin] any of various prickly pears

tun·a·ble (tōōn′ə b′l, tyōō′-) *adj.* that can be tuned: also sp. **tune′a·ble** —**tun′a·ble·ness** *n.*

tun·dra (tun′drə, tōōn′-) *n.* [Russ.] any large, flat, treeless plain in the arctic regions

tune (tōōn, tyōōn) *n.* [ME., var. of *tone*, TONE] **1.** a series of musical tones with a regular rhythm; melody; air **2.** the condition of having correct musical pitch, or of being in key; also, harmony; concord: now chiefly in phrases **in tune, out of tune** [a violin that is *in tune;* a person *out of tune* with the times] —*vt.* **tuned, tun′ing 1.** to adjust (a musical instrument) to some standard of pitch [to *tune* a piano] **2.** to adapt (music, the voice, etc.) to some pitch, tone, etc. **3.** to adjust (an electronics circuit, a motor, etc.) to the proper or desired performance —*vi.* to be in tune; harmonize —see SYN. at MELODY —**call the tune** to be in control —**change one's tune** to change one's attitude or manner: also **sing a different tune** —**to the tune of** [Colloq.] to the amount of —**tune in 1.** to adjust a radio or television receiver to a given frequency or channel so as to receive (a specified station, program, etc.) ☆**2.** [Slang] to become or make aware, knowing, etc. —**tune out 1.** to adjust a radio or television receiver so as to get rid of (interference, etc.) **2.** [Slang] to stop paying attention to, showing interest in, etc. —**tune up 1.** to adjust (musical instruments) to the same pitch **2.** to put (an engine) into good working condition

tune·ful (tōōn′fəl, tyōō′-) *adj.* full of tunes or melody; musical; melodious —**tune′ful·ly** *adv.* —**tune′ful·ness** *n.*

tune·less (-lis) *adj.* not musical or melodious —**tune′less·ly** *adv.* —**tune′less·ness** *n.*

tun·er (tōō′nər, tyōō′-) *n.* a person or thing that tunes; specif., *a)* a person who tunes musical instruments [a piano *tuner*] *b)* the part of a radio receiver that detects signals

tune·up, tune-up (tōōn′up′, tyōōn′-) *n.* an adjusting, as of an engine, to the proper condition

tung oil (tuŋ) [< Chin. *yu-t'ung* < *yu*, oil + *t'ung*, name of the tree] a fast-drying oil from the seeds of a subtropical tree (**tung tree**), used in paints, varnishes, etc.

tung·sten (tuŋ′stən) *n.* [Sw. < *tung*, heavy + *sten*, stone] a hard, heavy, gray-white, metallic chemical element, used in steel, electric lamp filaments, etc.: symbol, W; at. wt., 183.85; at. no., 74

tu·nic (tōō′nik, tyōō′-) *n.* [L. *tunica*] **1.** a garment like a loose gown worn by men and women in ancient Greece and Rome **2.** a blouse reaching to the hips or lower, often worn with a belt **3.** [Chiefly Brit.] a short coat forming part of the uniform of soldiers, policemen, etc. **4.** *Biol.* a covering membrane or tissue

tu·ni·ca (tōō′ni kə, tyōō′-) *n.*, *pl.* **-cae′** (-sē′) [ModL.: see TU-NIC] *Anat.*, *Zool.* an enclosing or covering layer of tissue or membrane, as of the ovaries

tu·ni·cate (tōō′ni kit, tyōō′-; -kāt′) *adj.* [< L. pp. of *tunicare,* to put on a tunic] *Bot.*, *Zool.* covered with or having a tunic or tunics: also **tu′ni·cat′ed** (-kāt′id) —*n.* any of several sea animals having a saclike body enclosed by a thick cellulose tunic

tuning fork a small steel instrument with two prongs, which when struck sounds a certain fixed tone: it is used as a guide in tuning instruments, in testing hearing, etc.

Tu·nis (tōō′nis, tyōō′-) capital of Tunisia, on an inlet (**Gulf of Tunis**) of the Mediterranean: pop. 642,000

Tu·ni·sia (tōō nē′zhə, tyōō-; -nish′ə, -nish′ē ə) country in N Africa, on the Mediterranean: 48,332 sq. mi.; pop. 5,137,000; cap. Tunis —**Tu·ni′sian** *adj., n.*

tun·nel (tun′l) *n.* [MFr. *tonnelle,* vault < OFr. dim. of *tonne,* a tun] **1.** an underground or underwater passageway for automobiles, trains, etc. **2.** an animal's burrow **3.** any tunnellike passage, as one in a mine —*vt.* **-neled** or **-nelled, -nel·ing** or **-nel·ling 1.** to make a tunnel through or under **2.** to make (one's way) by digging a tunnel —*vi.* to make a tunnel —**tun′nel·er, tun′nel·ler** *n.*

tun·ny (tun′ē) *n.*, *pl.* **-nies, -ny:** see PLURAL, II, D, 1 [< MFr. < L. < Gr. *thynnos*] *same as* TUNA¹ (senses 1 & 2)

☆**tu·pe·lo** (tōō′pə lō′) *n.*, *pl.* **-los′** [< Creek Indian *ito,* tree + *opilwa,* a swamp] **1.** any of several gum trees of the southern U.S. **2.** the fine-textured wood of any of these trees, used for mallets, furniture, etc.

Tu·pi (tōō pē′, tōō′pē) *n.* [Tupi, comrade] **1.** *pl.* **Tu·pis′, Tu·pi′** any member of a group of S. American Indian tribes living chiefly along the lower Amazon **2.** their language

tup·pence (tup′ns) *n. same as* TWOPENCE

tuque (tōōk, tyōōk) *n.* [CanadFr. < Fr. *toque,* a cap] a kind of knitted winter cap

tur·ban (tur′bən) *n.* [< MFr. < It. or Port. < Turk. *tülbend,* dial. form of *dülbend* < Per.] **1.** a covering for the head worn by Moslems, etc., consisting of a cloth wound in folds about the head, often over a cap **2.** any head covering or hat like this — **tur′baned** *adj.*

tur·bel·lar·i·an (tur′bə ler′ē ən) *n.* [< ModL. < L. dim. of *turba,* a crowd + -AN] any of a group of flatworms found chiefly in water and having a leaf-shaped body covered with cilia

tur·bid (tur′bid) *adj.* [< L. < *turba,* a crowd] **1.** not clear; full of dirt or mud; cloudy [a *turbid* pond] **2.** thick or dark, as clouds or smoke **3.** confused or muddled, as in thought —**tur·bid′i·ty, tur′bid·ness** *n.* —**tur′bid·ly** *adv.*

tur·bi·nate (tur′bə nit, -nāt′) *adj.* [< L. < *turbinis,* genitive of *turbo,* a whirl] **1.** shaped like a cone resting on its apex [a *turbinate* shell] **2.** shaped like a spiral; specif., *Anat., Zool.* designating or of certain spongy bones in the passages of the nose Also **tur′bi·nat′ed** (-nāt′id) —*n.* a turbinate shell or bone

tur·bine (tur′bin, -bīn) *n.* [Fr. < L. *turbo,* a whirl] an engine driven by the pressure of steam, water, air, etc. against the curved vanes of a wheel on a shaft

tur·bo- [< TURBINE] *a combining form meaning* consisting of or driven by a turbine

tur·bo·fan (tur′bō fan′) *n.* a turbojet engine in which additional thrust is obtained from the part of the air that bypasses the engine and is speeded up by a fan: in full, **turbofan engine**

tur·bo·jet (-jet′) *n.* **1.** a jet engine with a turbine-driven air compressor that compresses the air used in burning the fuel: the resulting hot gases are used to rotate the turbine before they form the jet that propels the aircraft: in full, **turbojet engine 2.** an aircraft propelled by such an engine

tur·bo·prop (-präp′) *n.* [TURBO- + PROP(ELLER)] **1.** a turbojet engine whose turbine shaft drives a propeller that develops most of the thrust, some being added by a jet of the turbine exhaust gases: in full, **turboprop engine 2.** an aircraft propelled by such an engine

tur·bo·su·per·charg·er (-sōō′pər chär′jər) *n.* a device using a turbine driven by exhaust gases to compress air before delivering it to the intake of a reciprocating engine: used to maintain air-intake pressure at high altitudes

tur·bot (tur′bət; *now sometimes* -bō) *n.*, *pl.* **-bot, -bots:** see PLURAL, II, D, 2 [< OFr. *tourbout*] **1.** a large European flatfish, highly thought of as food **2.** any of several American flounders

tur·bu·lent (tur′byə lənt) *adj.* [Fr. < L. < *turba,* a crowd] full of uproar or wild disorder; specif., *a)* marked by or causing

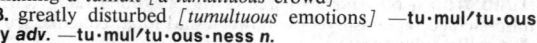

TUMPLINE

TUNING FORK

TURBAN

turmoil; disorderly [a *turbulent* crowd] *b)* violently stirred up or excited [*turbulent* feelings] *c)* full of violent motion [*turbulent* air currents] —**tur·bu·lence, tur·bu·len·cy** *n.* —**tur·bu·lent·ly** *adv.*

tu·reen (too rēn′) *n.* [MFr. *terrine,* earthen vessel, ult. < L. *terra,* earth] a large, deep dish with a lid, for serving soup, etc.

turf (turf) *n., pl.* **turfs,** esp. Brit. **turves** (turvz) [OE.] **1.** *a)* a surface layer of earth containing grass and its roots; sod *b)* a piece of this layer **2.** peat, or a piece of it for use as fuel ☆**3.** [Slang] one's own neighborhood, etc. thought of as an area which no stranger, intruder, etc. should be allowed to enter —*vt.* to cover with turf —**the turf 1.** a track for horse racing **2.** the sport of horse racing

turf·man (turf′mən) *n., pl.* **-men** an owner, trainer, etc. of racehorses

Tur·ge·nev (toor gā′nyif), **I·van** (**Sergeevich**) (ē vän′) 1818–83; Russ. novelist: also sp. **Turgenieff, Turgeniev**

tur·ges·cent (tur jes′'nt) *adj.* [< L. prp. of *turgescere,* to swell up] becoming turgid or swollen —**tur·ges′cence** *n.*

tur·gid (tur′jid) *adj.* [< L. *turgidus* < *turgere,* to swell] **1.** swollen or puffed up **2.** so full of long words and hard language that the meaning is unclear —see SYN. at BOMBASTIC —**tur·gid′i·ty, tur′gid·ness** *n.* —**tur′gid·ly** *adv.*

tur·gor (tur′gər) *n.* [LL. < L. *turgere,* to swell] the normal swollen condition of living animal and plant cells due to pressure of the cell contents against the cell membrane

Tu·rin (toor′in, tyoor′-; too rin′, tyoo-) city in NW Italy, on the Po River: pop. 1,177,000

Turk (turk) *n.* **1.** a native or inhabitant of Turkey; esp., a member of the Moslem people of Turkey or, formerly, of the Ottoman Empire **2.** a member of any of the peoples speaking Turkic languages See also YOUNG TURK

Turk. 1. Turkey **2.** Turkish

Tur·ke·stan (tur′ki stan′, -stän′) region in central Asia, stretching from the Caspian Sea to the Gobi Desert, inhabited by Turkic-speaking peoples

Tur·key (tur′kē) country occupying Asia Minor & a SE part of the Balkan Peninsula: 301,381 sq. mi.; pop. 36,162,000; cap. Ankara

tur·key (tur′kē) *n., pl.* **-keys, -key:** see PLURAL, II, D, 1 [orig. applied to the guinea fowl, sometimes imported through Turkey and for a time identified with the Am. fowl] ☆**1.** *a)* a large N. American bird with a small head and spreading tail, widely domesticated and bred as poultry *b)* its flesh, used as food ☆**2.** [Slang] a failure [his only Broadway play was a *turkey*] ☆**3.** *Bowling* three strikes in a row —☆**talk turkey** [Colloq.] to talk plainly and directly

☆**turkey buzzard** a dark-colored vulture of temperate and tropical America, having a naked, reddish head: also called **turkey vulture**

Tur·ki (toor′kē, tur′-) *n.* **1.** the Turkic languages as a group or any Turkic language **2.** a member of any Turkic people —*adj.* designating or of the Turkic languages or the peoples who speak them

Tur·kic (tur′kik) *adj.* **1.** designating or of a subfamily of Altaic languages, including Turkish **2.** designating or of the peoples who speak any of these languages —*n.* the Turkic languages

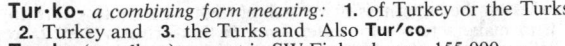

TURKEY BUZZARD
(wingspread
to 6 ft.)

Turk·ish (tur′kish) *adj.* of Turkey, the Turks, their language, etc. —*n.* **1.** the Turkic language of Turkey: in full, **Ottoman-Turkish 2.** loosely, *same as* TURKIC

Turkish bath a public bath in which the bather, after a period of heavy sweating in a room of hot air or steam, is washed and massaged

Turkish Empire *same as* OTTOMAN EMPIRE

Turkish towel [*also* t-] a thick cotton towel of terry cloth

Tur·ki·stan (tur′ki stan′, -stän′) *same as* TURKESTAN

Turk·men Soviet Socialist Republic (turk′men) republic of the U.S.S.R., in C Asia, on the Caspian Sea: 188,400 sq. mi.; pop. 2,200,000: also **Turk′men·i·stan′** (-i stan′, -i stän′) — **Turk·me·ni·an** (turk mē′nē ən) *adj.*

Tur·ko- *a combining form meaning:* **1.** of Turkey or the Turks **2.** Turkey and **3.** the Turks and Also **Tur′co-**

Tur·ku (toor′koo) seaport in SW Finland: pop. 155,000

tur·mer·ic (tur′mər ik) *n.* [< MFr. < ML. *terra merita,* lit., deserving earth < ?] **1.** an East Indian plant whose root in powdered form is used as a yellow dye, seasoning, etc. **2.** this root or the powder made from it

tur·moil (tur′moil) *n.* [*tur-* (< ? TURBULENT) + MOIL] a very excited or confused condition; tumult; commotion; uproar

turn (turn) *vt.* [< OE. *turnian* & OFr. *tourner,* both < L. *tornare,* to turn in a lathe, etc. < Gr. *tornos,* a lathe] **1.** to make (a wheel, etc.) move about a center or axis; rotate; revolve **2.** to move around or partly around [to *turn* a key, handle, etc.] **3.** to do (a somersault, cart wheel, etc.) **4.** to give a rounded shape to, as on a lathe **5.** to give a graceful form to [to *turn* a pretty phrase] **6.** to change the position or direction of [*turn* your chair around] **7.** to think about; ponder [he *turned* my situation over in his mind] **8.** *a)* to bend, fold, etc. [*turn* the sheet back] *b)* to twist (one's ankle) **9.** to move so that the underside is on top, and vice versa; reverse; invert [to *turn* pages, a collar, the soil, etc.] **10.** to make upside down, topsy-turvy, etc. **11.** to upset (the stomach) **12.** to change the course of; deflect; divert [to *turn* a blow] **13.** *a)* to cause to change intentions, actions, etc. [to *turn* someone from his purpose] *b)* to change in feelings, attitudes, etc. [to *turn* people against someone] **14.** to go around (a corner, etc.) **15.** to reach or pass [she has just *turned* 21] **16.** to reverse the course of; repel [to *turn* an attack] **17.** to drive, set, let go, etc. in some way [the dog was *turned* loose] **18.** to direct, point, aim, etc. [eyes *turned* ahead, thoughts *turned* to the past] **19.** to put to a specified use; apply [he *turned* his hand to writing] **20.** to change from one form, condition, etc. to another [to *turn* cream into butter] **21.** to exchange for [to *turn* produce into hard cash] **22.** to translate or paraphrase **23.** to disturb mentally [sorrow has *turned* her brain] **24.** to make sour [hot weather will *turn* milk] **25.** to affect in some way [*turned* sick by the sight] **26.** to change the color of [the first frost starts to *turn* the leaves] —*vi.* **1.** to rotate, revolve, pivot, etc. [he *turned* on his heel and walked out] **2.** to move around or partly around [the key won't *turn*] **3.** to reel; whirl [my head is *turning*] **4.** to become curved or bent **5.** to reverse position so that bottom becomes top **6.** to become upset, as the stomach **7.** to change or reverse one's or its course or direction [the tide *turned*] **8.** to consult; refer (*to*) **9.** to go or apply (*to*) for help **10.** to direct or shift one's attention, abilities, etc. [he *turned* to music for relaxation] **11.** to make a sudden attack (*on* or *upon*) [the dog *turned* on him] **12.** to reverse one's feelings, loyalty, etc. [he *turned* against his sister] **13.** to depend (*on* or *upon*) [the outcome *turns* on whether he will agree] **14.** to become [to *turn* bitter with age] **15.** to change into another form [the rain *turned* to sleet] **16.** to become rancid, sour, etc. **17.** to change color, as leaves in the fall —*n.* **1.** the act of turning around; rotation, as of a wheel, handle, etc. **2.** a single twist, coil, winding, etc. [make one more *turn* with the rope] **3.** a musical ornament of four tones, with the tones above and below the main tone alternating with it **4.** a change or reversal of position, course, or direction [a *turn* to the right; the *turn* of the tide] **5.** a short walk or ride, as for exercise [to take a *turn* around the block] **6.** the place where a change in direction occurs; bend; curve [a *turn* in the road] **7.** *a)* a change in condition, events, health, etc. [a *turn* for the better] *b)* same as TURNING POINT **8.** the time of change [at the *turn* of the century] **9.** a sudden, brief shock [his shout gave me quite a *turn*] **10.** an action or deed [to do someone a good *turn*] **11.** a period of activity [a *turn* at gardening] **12.** an attack of illness, dizziness, etc. **13.** the right, duty, or chance to do something, esp. in regular order [his *turn* at bat] **14.** an act in a variety show **15.** a form, manner, detail, etc. [a quaint *turn* to her speech] **16.** natural tendency [a curious *turn* of mind] —**at every turn** in every instance; constantly —**by turns** one after another in regular order —☆**call the turn** to predict successfully —**in turn** in proper order —**out of turn 1.** not in proper order **2.** at the wrong time; esp., unwisely [to talk *out of turn*] —**take turns** to speak, do, etc. one after another in regular order —**to a turn** perfectly —**turn and turn about** one after another in regular order; alternately —**turn down** ☆**1.** to reject (the request, advice, etc. of someone) **2.**

to lessen the brightness or volume of (light or sound) —**turn in** 1. to make a turn into; enter [*turn in* that driveway] ☆2. to deliver; hand in [*turn in* your homework] ☆3. to inform on or hand over, as to the police 4. to give back 5. [Colloq.] to go to bed —**turn off** 1. *a*) to leave (a road, etc.); *b*) to branch off: said of a road, etc. 2. to shut off [*turn off* the water] 3. to stop showing suddenly [to *turn off* a smile] ☆4. [Slang] to cause (someone) to become bored, uninterested, annoyed, etc. —**turn on** 1. to start; make go on, flow, etc. [*turn on* the radio] 2. to show suddenly [to *turn on* the charm] ☆3. [Slang] *a*) to stimulate with or as with a psychedelic drug; make or become happy, excited, etc. *b*) to be attracted to —**turn out** 1. to put out (a light) 2. to put outside 3. to drive out; dismiss 4. to come or gather [to *turn out* for a picnic] 5. to make; produce [she *turns out* good pies] 6. to result [how did it all *turn out?*] 7. to prove to be [he *turned out* to be a good worker] 8. to become 9. to equip, dress, etc. 10. [Colloq.] to get out of bed —**turn over** 1. to change or reverse the position of, as by rolling 2. to shift one's position, as from one side to the other 3. to begin, or make begin, to operate, as an engine 4. to think about; ponder 5. to hand over; give 6. to put to a different use; convert 7. to sell and replace (a stock of goods) 8. to do business to the amount of —**turn to** to get to work —**turn up** 1. to fold back or over upon itself 2. to lift up or turn face up 3. to increase the speed, force, loudness, etc. of, as by turning a control 4. to make a turn onto or into (a street, etc.) 5. to have an upward direction 6. to happen 7. to arrive 8. to find or be found

SYN.—**turn**, the most general word here, implies motion around, or partly around, a center or axis [a wheel *turns*]; **rotate** implies movement of a body around its own center or axis [the earth *rotates* on its axis]; **revolve** is sometimes substituted for **rotate**, but in exact use it suggests movement, usually circular or elliptical, around a center outside itself [the earth *revolves* around the sun]; **gyrate** implies movement in a spiral course, as by a tornado; **spin** and **whirl** suggest very fast and continuous rotation or revolution [a top *spins*; the leaves *whirled* about the yard]

turn·a·bout (turn′ə bout′) *n.* 1. a turning about, as to face the other way 2. a shift or reversal of loyalty, opinion, etc.; about-face

turn·buck·le (-buk′'l) *n.* a metal loop with opposite internal threads in each end for the threaded ends of two rods or ringbolts, used as a connecting device that can be turned to tighten or loosen either the rods or wires attached to the ring-bolts

TURNBUCKLE

turn·coat (-kōt′) *n.* a person who goes over to the opposite side or party; renegade; traitor

turn·down (-doun′) *adj.* having the upper part folded down [a *turndown* collar] —*n.* a rejection [his *turndown* of the offer]

turn·er (tur′nər) *n.* 1. a thing that turns or is used for turning [a pancake *turner*] 2. a person who turns; specif., one who operates a lathe

Tur·ner (tur′nər) 1. J(oseph) M(allord) W(illiam), 1775–1851; Eng. painter 2. Nat (nat), 1800–31; U.S. Negro slave, who led an unsuccessful revolt (1831)

turn·ing (tur′niŋ) *n.* 1. the action of a person or thing that turns 2. a place where a road, etc. turns or turns off 3. the art or process of shaping things on a lathe

turning point 1. a point at which something turns or changes direction 2. a point in time at which a very important change occurs; crisis

tur·nip (tur′nip) *n.* [prob. < TURN or < Fr. *tour*, in sense of "round" + ME. *nepe* < OE. < L. *napus*, a turnip] 1. *a*) a plant of the mustard family, with edible, hairy leaves and a roundish, light-colored root used as a vegetable *b*) *same as* RUTABAGA 2. the root of either of these plants

turn·key (turn′kē′) *n., pl.* **-keys′** a person in charge of the keys of a prison; warder; jailer

turn·off (-ôf′) *n.* 1. the act of turning off ☆2. a place where one turns off; esp., a road or ramp leading off a highway

turn·out (-out′) *n.* 1. the act of turning out 2. a gathering of people, as for a meeting 3. an amount produced 4. *a*) a wider part of a narrow road, as for passing *b*) a railroad siding 5. a carriage with its horse or horses

turn·o·ver (-ō′vər) *n.* 1. a turning over; specif., *a*) an upset *b*) a change from one side, opinion, etc. to another 2. a small pie made by folding one half of the crust back over the other 3. *a*) the number of times a stock of goods is sold and replaced during a given period *b*) the amount of business done during a given period in terms of the money used in buying and

selling 4. *a*) the number of workers hired as replacements during a given period *b*) the ratio of this to the average number of workers employed —*adj.* that is turned over [a *turnover* collar]

turn·pike (-pīk′) *n.* [ME. *turnpyke*, a spiked barrier across a road: see TURN & PIKE[4]] 1. *same as* TOLLGATE 2. a toll road, esp. one that is an expressway

turn·stile (-stīl′) *n.* a post with revolving horizontal bars, often coin-operated, used at an entrance to admit persons one at a time

turn·stone (-stōn′) *n.* a small shore bird resembling a plover, that turns over pebbles in search of food

turn·ta·ble (-tā′b'l) *n.* a round platform that turns; specif., *a*) such a platform for holding a phonograph record while it is being played *b*) such a platform with tracks, used to turn a locomotive around

turn·up (turn′up′) *adj.* that turns up or is turned up

TURNSTILE

‡**Turn·ver·ein** (toorn′fer īn′; *E.* turn′fə rīn′) *n.* [G. < *turnen*, to exercise + *verein*, a club] a club of gymnasts

tur·pen·tine (tur′pən tīn′) *n.* [< OFr. < L., ult. < Gr. *terebinthos*, a tree yielding turpentine] 1. any of the various oleoresins obtained from pines and other coniferous trees: in full, **gum turpentine** 2. a colorless, volatile oil distilled from such oleoresins and used in paints, in medicine, etc.: in full, **spirits** (or **oil**) **of turpentine** —*vt.* **-tined′, -tin′ing** to apply turpentine to —**tur′pen·tin′ic** (-tin′ik), **tur′pen·tin′ous** (-tī′nəs) *adj.*

tur·pi·tude (tur′pə tōōd′, -tyōōd′) *n.* [MFr. < L. < *turpis*, vile] the condition of being wicked, evil, or corrupt

turps (turps) *n.pl.* [*with sing. v.*] *same as* TURPENTINE (*n.* 2)

tur·quoise (tur′koiz, -kwoiz) *n.* [< MFr. fem. of OFr. *turqueis*, Turkish: orig. brought to western Europe through Turkey] 1. a greenish-blue, semiprecious stone, a hydrous phosphate of aluminum containing a small amount of copper 2. a greenish blue —*adj.* greenish-blue Also sp. **tur′quois**

tur·ret (tur′it) *n.* [< OFr. dim. of *tour*: see TOWER[1]] 1. a small tower on a building, usually at a corner 2. *a*) a low, armored, usually revolving structure for guns, as on a warship, tank, etc. *b*) a transparent dome for a gun and gunner, as on a bomber 3. an attachment for a lathe, drill, etc., consisting of a block holding several cutting tools, which may be turned to place any of the tools in a position to be used —**tur′ret·ed** *adj.*

tur·tle (tur′t'l) *n., pl.* **-tles, -tle** [altered (after TURTLEDOVE) < Fr. *tortue*, tortoise] 1. any of various land and water reptiles having a toothless beak and a soft body covered by a hard shell into which most kinds can pull the head, tail, and four legs: land species are usually called *tortoise* 2. the flesh of some turtles, used as food 3. *archaic var. of* TURTLEDOVE —*vi.* **-tled, -tling** to hunt for turtles —**turn turtle** to turn upside down

tur·tle·back (-bak′) *n.* an arched structure built over the deck of a ship as a protection against heavy seas

tur·tle·dove (-duv′) *n.* [OE. *turtle* < L. *turtur*, of echoic origin] 1. any of several wild doves known for their sad cooing and the love that the mates seem to show toward each other 2. *same as* MOURNING DOVE

tur·tle·neck (-nek′) *n.* ☆1. a high, closefitting, turndown collar on a pullover sweater, shirt, etc. ☆2. a sweater, shirt, etc. with such a neck

Tus·ca·loo·sa (tus′kə lōō′sə) [< Choctaw < *taska*, warrior + *lusa*, black] city in WC Ala., near Birmingham: pop. 66,000

Tus·ca·ny (tus′kə nē) region of central Italy, on the Ligurian & Tyrrhenian seas: chief city, Florence: see map at LIGURIA — **Tus′can** *adj., n.*

Tus·ca·ro·ra (tus′kə rôr′ə) *n.* [< the native name, lit., hemp gatherers] 1. *pl.* **-ras, -ra** a member of a tribe of Iroquoian Indians at one time living in Virginia and North Carolina, but later in New York and Ontario 2. their Iroquoian language

tush[1] (tush) *interj., n.* an exclamation expressing blame, impatience, contempt, etc.

tush[2] (tush) *n.* [< OE. *tucs*: see TUSK] *same as* TUSK

TURTLENECK SWEATER

tusk (tusk) *n.* [OE. *tucs*] 1. in elephants,

wild boars, etc., a very long, pointed tooth, usually one of a pair, that sticks out of the mouth **2.** any tusklike tooth or part —*vt.* to dig, gore, etc. with a tusk —**tusked** *adj.* —**tusk'like'** *adj.*

tusk·er (tus'kər) *n.* an animal with tusks, as an elephant

tus·sah (tus'ə) *n.* [< Hindi < Sans. *tasara*, lit., a shuttle] **1.** an Asiatic silkworm that produces a coarse, tough silk **2.** this silk: also **tussah silk** Also sp. **tus'sore, tus'sor** (tus'ôr)

tus·sle (tus''l) *n., vi.* **-sled, -sling** [LME. *tusen*, to pull + -LE²] struggle; wrestle; scuffle

tus·sock (tus'ək) *n.* [prob. < ME. (*to*)*tusen*, to rumple + -*ok*, little] a thick tuft or clump of grass, sedge, twigs, etc. —**tus'sock·y** (-ē) *adj.*

tussock moth any of a large group of moths whose caterpillars are covered with long tufts of hair: many harm certain trees

tut (tut) *interj., n.* a sound made to show that one is impatient, annoyed, angry, etc. —*vi.* **tut'ted, tut'ting** to utter "tuts"

Tut·ankh·a·men (to͞ot'äŋk ä'mən) fl. c. 1355 B.C.; Egyptian king of the 18th dynasty: also sp. **Tutankhamun**

☆**tu·tee** (to͞o tē', tyo͞o-) *n.* [TUT(OR) + -EE] a person who is being tutored

tu·te·lage (to͞ot''l ij, tyo͞ot'-) *n.* [< L. *tutela*, protection] **1.** guardianship; care, protection, etc. **2.** teaching; instruction **3.** the condition of being under a guardian or tutor

tu·te·lar·y (-er'ē) *adj.* [< L. < *tutela*: see prec.] **1.** watching over or protecting [each Roman family had its *tutelary* gods] **2.** of or serving as a guardian [granted *tutelary* responsibility by the court] Also **tu'te·lar** (-ər) —*n., pl.* **-lar'ies** a tutelary god, spirit, etc.

tu·tor (to͞ot'ər, tyo͞ot'-) *n.* [< MFr. < L. < pp. of *tueri*, to guard] **1.** a teacher who teaches one student at a time; private teacher **2.** a legal guardian of a minor **3.** in English universities, an official in charge of the studies of an undergraduate ☆**4.** in some U.S. colleges, a teacher ranking below an instructor —*vt.* to act as a tutor to; esp., to teach (students) one at a time —*vi.* **1.** to act as a tutor **2.** [Colloq.] to be taught by a tutor —**tu'tor·age, tu'tor·ship'** *n.*

tu·to·ri·al (to͞o tôr'ē əl, tyo͞o-) *adj.* of a tutor or tutors —*n.* a class in a tutorial system

tutorial system a system of instruction in which a tutor directs the studies of each of a small group of students

tut·ti (to͞ot'ē) *adj.* [It., ult. < L. *totus*, all] *Music* for all instruments or voices —*n., pl.* **-tis** **1.** a passage played or sung by all performers **2.** the sound of such a passage

☆**tut·ti-frut·ti** (to͞ot'ē fro͞ot'ē) *n.* [It., all fruits] **1.** ice cream or other sweet food containing bits of candied fruits **2.** a flavoring combining a number of fruit flavors

tu·tu (to͞o'to͞o) *n.* [Fr.] a very short, full skirt worn by women ballet dancers

Tu·tu·i·la (to͞o'to͞o ē'lä) chief island of American Samoa, in the South Pacific: chief town, Pago Pago

Tu·va·lu (to͞o'və lo͞o') country consisting of a group of nine islands in the WC Pacific: 10 sq. mi.; pop. 6,000

☆**tux** (tuks) *n. same as* TUXEDO

☆**tux·e·do** (tək sē'dō) *n., pl.* **-dos** [< the name of a country club near *Tuxedo* Lake, N.Y.] **1.** a man's tailless jacket for semiformal evening wear, orig. black and with satin lapels **2.** a suit with such a jacket, worn with a dark bow tie

tu·yère (twē yer', to͞o-; twir) *n.* [< Fr. < *tuyau*, a pipe] the nozzle through which air is forced into a blast furnace or forge

TUTU

TV (tē'vē') *n., pl.* **TVs, TV's** television or a television receiving set

TVA, T.V.A. Tennessee Valley Authority

☆**TV dinner** [because it can conveniently be eaten while viewing television] a frozen, precooked dinner packaged in a tray for heating and serving

twa (twä) *adj., n.* [OE.] Scot. var. of TWO

twad·dle (twäd''l) *n.* [prob. akin to TATTLE] foolish, empty talk or writing; nonsense —*vt., vi.* **-dled, -dling** to talk or write in a foolish or meaningless manner; prattle —**twad'dler** *n.*

twain (twān) *n., adj.* [OE. *twegen*, two] archaic var. of TWO

Twain (twān), **Mark** see Samuel Langhorne CLEMENS

twang (twaŋ) *n.* [echoic] **1.** a quick, sharp, vibrating sound, as of a plucked string **2.** *a*) a sharp, nasal way of speaking *b*) a dialect characterized by such a way of speaking —*vi., vt.* **1.** to make or cause to make a twang, as a bowstring, banjo, etc. **2.** to speak or say with a twang **3.** to shoot or be released with a twang, as an arrow —**twang'y** *adj.*

'twas (twuz, twäz; *unstressed* twəz) it was

twat·tle (twät''l) *n., vi., vt.* **-tled, -tling** var. of TWADDLE

tweak (twēk) *vt.* [OE. *twiccan*, to twitch] to give a sudden, twisting pinch to [to *tweak* someone's nose] —*n.* such a pinch

tweed (twēd) *n.* [< misreading of *tweel*, Scot. form of TWILL; later assoc. with the *Tweed*, river in Scotland] **1.** a wool fabric with a rough surface, in a twill weave of two or more colors **2.** a suit, etc. of this **3.** [*pl.*] clothes of tweed

twee·dle·dum and twee·dle·dee (twēd''l dum''n twēd''l dē') [echoic of musical sounds] two persons or things so much alike that it is hard to tell them apart

tweed·y (twēd'ē) *adj.* **tweed'i·er, tweed'i·est** **1.** of or like tweed **2.** *a*) often wearing tweeds *b*) well-dressed in an informal way, fond of outdoor activities, etc. —**tweed'i·ness** *n.*

'tween (twēn) *prep.* [Poet.] between

tweet (twēt) *n., interj.* [echoic] the high, chirping sound of a small bird —*vi.* to make this sound

tweet·er (twēt'ər) *n.* in a set of two or more loudspeakers, a small, high-fidelity speaker for reproducing high-frequency sounds: see also WOOFER

tweeze (twēz) *vt.* **tweezed, tweez'ing** [back-formation < TWEEZERS] [Colloq.] to pluck with or as with tweezers

tweez·ers (twē'zərz) *n.pl.* [*with sing. or pl. v.*] [< obs. *tweeze*, surgical set < Fr. pl. of *étui*, a case] small pincers for plucking out hairs, handling little objects, etc.: also **tweezer** or **pair of tweezers**

twelfth (twelfth) *adj.* [OE. *twelfta*] **1.** coming after eleven others in a series; 12th **2.** designating any of the twelve equal parts of something —*n.* **1.** the one following the eleventh **2.** any of the twelve equal parts of something; 1/12

Twelfth Day the twelfth day (Jan. 6) after Christmas; Epiphany: the evening before, or sometimes the evening of, this day is called **Twelfth Night**

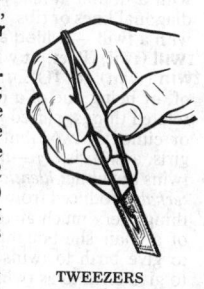

TWEEZERS

twelve (twelv) *adj.* [OE. *twelf*] two more than ten —*n.* **1.** the cardinal number between eleven and thirteen; 12; XII **2.** any group of twelve persons or things; dozen —**the Twelve** the Twelve Apostles

Twelve Apostles the twelve disciples chosen by Jesus to go forth to teach the gospel

twelve·fold (twelv'fōld') *adj.* **1.** having twelve parts **2.** having twelve times as much or as many —*adv.* twelve times as much or as many

twelve·mo (-mō) *adj., n., pl.* **-mos** same as DUODECIMO

twelve·month (-munth') *n.* a year

twelve-tone (-tōn') *adj.* designating or of a modern system of writing music in which the composer arranges the twelve tones of the chromatic scale into some fixed order (*tone row*) and then uses this arrangement in developing his theme

twen·ti·eth (twen'tē ith) *adj.* **1.** coming after nineteen others in a series; 20th **2.** designating any of the twenty equal parts of something —*n.* **1.** the one following the nineteenth **2.** any of twenty equal parts of something; 1/20

twen·ty (twen'tē) *adj.* [OE. *twegentig*] two times ten —*n., pl.* **-ties** **1.** the cardinal number between nineteen and twenty-one; 20; XX ☆**2.** [Colloq.] a twenty-dollar bill —**the twenties** the numbers or years, as of a century, from twenty through twenty-nine

twen·ty·fold (-fōld') *adj.* **1.** having twenty parts **2.** having twenty times as much or as many —*adv.* twenty times as much or as many

twen·ty-one (-wun') *n.* ☆a gambling game at cards in which each player's aim is to get from the dealer cards totaling twenty-one points or as close as possible to that total without going over it; blackjack

twen·ty-twen·ty (or **20/20**) **vision** (twen′tē twen′tē) normal keenness of vision, which is the ability to see clearly at twenty feet what the normal eye can see

'twere (twɐr) [Poet.] it were

twerp (twɐrp) *n.* [< ? or akin to Dan. *tver*, perverse] [Slang] a person thought of as unimportant, contemptible, etc.

twice (twīs) *adv.* [OE. *twiges* < *twiga*] **1.** two times *[he asked twice]* **2.** two times as much or as many; twofold; doubly *[he is twice the athlete you are]*

twice-told (twīs′tōld′) *adj.* **1.** told twice **2.** stale; trite

twid·dle (twid′'l) *vt.* **-dled, -dling** [prob. < TW(IST) + (D)IDDLE¹] to twirl or play with lightly —*vi.* **1.** to toy with some object **2.** to be busy about unimportant things —*n.* a light, twirling motion, as with the thumbs —**twiddle one's thumbs 1.** to twirl one's thumbs idly around one another **2.** to be idle —**twid′dler** *n.* —**twid′dly** *adj.*

twig (twig) *n.* [OE. *twigge*] a small branch or shoot of a tree or shrub

twig·gy (twig′ē) *adj.* **-gi·er, -gi·est 1.** thin, delicate, etc. like a twig **2.** full of or covered with twigs

twi·light (twī′līt′) *n.* [ME. < *twi-*, two + LIGHT¹] **1.** *a)* the soft, dim light just after sunset or, sometimes, just before sunrise *b)* the period from sunset to dark **2.** any growing darkness **3.** a condition of gradual decline *[in the twilight of the actor's career]* —*adj.* of or like twilight

twilight sleep a state of partial loss of consciousness brought on by the injection of morphine and scopolamine, formerly used to lessen the pains of childbirth

twi·lit (twī′lit) *adj.* illuminated by or as if by the soft, dim light of twilight

twill (twil) *n.* [OE. *twilic*, woven of double thread, ult. < L. *bilix*, with a double thread] **1.** a cloth woven so as to have parallel diagonal lines or ribs **2.** the pattern of this weave —*vt.* to weave with a twill —**twilled** *adj.*

'twill (twil) [Poet.] it will

twin (twin) *adj.* [OE. *twinn* & ON. *tvinnr*, double] **1.** consisting of, or being one of a pair of, two separate but similar or closely related things; paired *[twin gables on the house]* **2.** being two, or either of two, that have been born at the same birth *[twin girls, a twin sister]* —*n.* **1.** either of two born at the same birth: twins are either *identical* (produced from the same ovum) or *fraternal* (produced from separate ova) **2.** either of two persons or things very much alike in appearance, shape, etc. *[it is the twin of a chair she bought yesterday]* —*vi.* **twinned, twin′ning 1.** to give birth to twins **2.** to be paired (with another) —*vt.* **1.** to give birth to as twins **2.** to pair or couple

☆**twin bill** [Colloq.] *same as:* **1.** DOUBLE FEATURE **2.** DOUBLE-HEADER

twine (twīn) *n.* [OE. *twin*, double thread] **1.** a strong thread, string, or cord of two or more strands twisted together **2.** something formed by twining or twisting things together —*vt.* **twined, twin′ing 1.** *a)* to twist together; intertwine *b)* to form in this way **2.** to wreathe or wind (one thing) around or with another *[she twined a rope around the branch]* **3.** to encircle, enfold, etc. *[a wreath twining his brow]* —*vi.* **1.** to twist, interlace, etc. *[the ivy twined around the post]* **2.** to twist and turn *[a path twines up the mountain]* —**twin′ing·ly** *adv.*

twin-en·gined (twin′en′jənd) *adj.* powered by two engines: said of an airplane: also **twin′-en′gine**

twinge (twinj) *vt., vi.* **twinged, twing′ing** [OE. *twengan*, to squeeze] to have or cause to have a sudden, brief pain or pang —*n.* **1.** a sudden, brief pain or pang **2.** a sudden, brief feeling of guilt, shame, etc.; qualm *[a twinge of conscience]*

☆**twi-night, twi·night** (twī′nīt′) *adj.* [TWI(LIGHT) + NIGHT] *Baseball* designating a double-header that starts in the late afternoon and continues into the evening

twin·kle (twiŋ′k'l) *vi.* **-kled, -kling** [OE. *twinclian*] **1.** to shine with quick flashes of light, as some stars; sparkle **2.** to light up, as with amusement: said of the eyes **3.** to move about quickly and lightly, as a dancer's feet; flicker —*vt.* to make twinkle —*n.* **1.** a wink of the eye **2.** a quick flash of amusement, etc. in the eye **3.** a quick flash of light; sparkle **4.** the instant that it takes to wink —**twin′kler** *n.*

twin·kling (-kliŋ) *n.* **1.** the action of a thing that twinkles **2.** *a)* the winking of an eye *b)* the very brief time it takes to wink; instant

twin·screw (twin′skrōō′) *adj.* having two screw propellers, usually rotating in opposite directions, as some ships

twirl (twɐrl) *vt., vi.* [prob. < Scand.] **1.** to rotate rapidly; spin **2.** to whirl in a circle **3.** to twist or coil *[to twirl one's mustache]* ☆**4.** *Baseball* to pitch —*n.* **1.** a twirling or being

twirled **2.** something twirled; specif., a twist, coil, curl, etc. —**twirl′er** *n.*

twirp (twɐrp) *n.* [Slang] *var. of* TWERP

twist (twist) *vt.* [< OE. *-twist*, a rope (in *mæst-twist*, rope to stay a mast)] **1.** to wind (strands of cotton, silk, etc.) around one another, as in spinning or in making thread, cord, etc. **2.** to wreathe; twine **3.** to wind (thread, rope, etc.) around something **4.** to make (one's or its way) by turning one way and then another **5.** to give spiral shape to by turning the ends in opposite directions **6.** *a)* to cause to undergo torsion *b)* to put out of shape in this way; wrench; sprain *[to twist one's ankle]* **7.** *a)* to change the normal or usual shape of (the face, etc.) *b)* to cause to be malformed *[fingers twisted with arthritis]* **8.** to confuse or disturb mentally or emotionally *[a twisted personality]* **9.** to change or distort the meaning of *[twisting his enemy's words without regard for truth]* **10.** to cause to turn around or rotate *[twist the lid to take it off]* **11.** to break off by turning the end (often with *off*) *[to twist the stem from an apple]* —*vi.* **1.** to undergo twisting and thus take on a spiral or coiled form *[the wire twists easily]* **2.** to spiral, coil, twine, etc. (*around* or *about* something) **3.** to revolve or rotate **4.** to turn to one side **5.** to wind or meander, as a path **6.** to squirm; writhe *[a bored child twisting and turning in his seat]* **7.** to move in a curved path, as a ball —*n.* **1.** a strong, closely twisted silk thread ☆**2.** a twisted roll of tobacco leaves **3.** a loaf of bread or roll made of twisted pieces of dough **4.** a knot, etc. made by twisting **5.** a sliver of peel from a lemon, lime, etc. twisted and added to a drink for flavor **6.** a twisting or being twisted *[a twist to the left]* **7.** a spin given to a ball in throwing or striking it **8.** stress due to torsion, or the degree of this **9.** a changing of the normal or usual shape, as of the face **10.** a wrench or sprain **11.** a turning aside; turn; bend **12.** a place at which something twists *[a twist in the road]* **13.** a personal liking or leaning, esp. an eccentric one; quirk **14.** a misleading change, as of meaning **15.** a different or unexpected meaning, method, slant, etc. *[a new twist to an old story]*

twist·er (twis′tər) *n.* **1.** a person or thing that twists; specif., a thrown or batted ball that has been given a twist *[he hit a twister to the shortstop]* ☆**2.** a tornado or cyclone

twit¹ (twit) *vt.* **twit′ted, twit′ting** [< OE. *ætwitan* < *æt*, at + *witan*, to accuse] to blame, tease, taunt, etc., esp. by reminding of a fault or mistake —*n.* a reproach or taunt

twit² (twit) *n.* [< TWITTER¹] ☆a state of nervous excitement

twitch (twich) *vt., vi.* [< OE. *twiccian*, to pluck] **1.** to pull (at) with a quick, slight jerk; pluck **2.** to move with a quick, slight jerk, often due to muscle spasm *[a rabbit's nose twitches]* **3.** to ache with a sudden, sharp pain —*n.* **1.** a quick, slight jerk **2.** a sudden, quick motion, esp. one caused by muscle spasm; tic *[a twitch of the mouth]* **3.** a sudden, sharp pain; twinge

twit·ter¹ (twit′ər) *vi.* [ME. *twiteren*: orig. echoic] **1.** to make a series of light, sharp vocal sounds; chirp, as birds do **2.** *a)* to talk in a rapid or excited manner; chatter *b)* to giggle **3.** to tremble with excitement, etc. —*vt.* to say in a twittering manner —*n.* **1.** the act or sound of twittering **2.** a condition of trembling excitement; flutter *[in a twitter while waiting for the curtain to rise]* —**twit′ter·er** *n.* —**twit′ter·y** *adj.*

twit·ter² (twit′ər) *n.* a person who twits

'twixt (twikst) *prep.* [Poet.] betwixt

two (tōō) *adj.* [OE. *twa*] totaling one more than one —*n.* **1.** the cardinal number between one and three; 2; II **2.** anything having two units or members, or numbered two —**in two** in two parts —**put two and two together** to reach an obvious conclusion by considering several facts together

☆**two-base hit** (tōō′bās′) a double in baseball

☆**two-bit** (-bit′) *adj.* **1.** [Colloq.] worth twenty-five cents **2.** [Slang] *a)* cheap and showy *b)* unimportant, inferior, etc.

☆**two bits** [Colloq.] twenty-five cents

☆**two-by-four** (tōō′bə fôr′, -bī-) *adj.* **1.** that measures two inches (or feet, etc.) by four inches (or feet, etc.) **2.** [Colloq.] small, narrow, cramped, etc. —*n.* any length of untrimmed lumber two inches thick and four inches wide: in the building trades, a trimmed piece approximately 1 ½ by 3 ½ inches

two-edged (-ejd′) *adj.* **1.** that has two cutting edges **2.** that can have two different meanings *[a two-edged remark]*

two-faced (-fāst′) *adj.* **1.** having two faces **2.** not sincere or honest; false; hypocritical —**two′-fac′ed·ly** (-fās′id lē) *adv.*

two-fist·ed (-fis′tid) *adj.* [Colloq.] **1.** able to use both fists ☆**2.** strong and forceful

two·fold (-fōld′) *adj.* **1.** having two parts; double **2.** having twice as much or as many —*adv.* twice as much or as many

two-hand·ed (-han′did) *adj.* **1.** that needs to be used or held with both hands [a *two-handed* sword] **2.** worked by two people [a *two-handed* saw] **3.** for two people, as a card game **4.** having two hands **5.** using both hands equally well

two-leg·ged (-leg′id, -legd′) *adj.* having two legs

two·pence (tup′′ns) *n.* **1.** two pence, or two British pennies **2.** a former British coin of this value

two·pen·ny (tup′ə nē; *also, esp. of nails,* tōō′pen′ē) *adj.* **1.** worth or costing twopence **2.** cheap; worthless **3.** designating a size of nails one inch long

two-piece (tōō′pēs′) *adj.* consisting of two separate parts [a *two-piece* bathing suit]

two-ply (-plī′) *adj.* **1.** having two thicknesses, layers, strands, etc. **2.** woven double

two-sid·ed (-sīd′id) *adj.* **1.** having two sides **2.** that can be understood, interpreted, etc. in two ways [a *two-sided* question]

two·some (-səm) *n.* **1.** two people; a couple **2.** two people playing a round of golf together

two-step (-step′) *n.* **1.** a ballroom dance in 2/4 time **2.** a piece of music for this dance

☆**two-time** (tōō′tīm′) *vt.* **-timed′, -tim′ing** [Slang] to trick or mislead; esp., to be unfaithful to (one's wife or husband, or one's lover) —**two′-tim′er** *n.*

'twould (twood) [Poet.] it would

two-way (tōō′wā′) *adj.* **1.** having separate lanes for vehicles going in opposite directions [a *two-way* street] **2.** involving the same obligations, privileges, etc. toward each other by two parties, nations, etc. [a *two-way* cultural exchange] **3.** involving two persons, groups, etc. [a *two-way* political race] **4.** a) used for both transmitting and receiving [a *two-way* radio] b) moving or allowing movement in two directions [a *two-way* faucet] **5.** that can be used in two ways [a *two-way* raincoat]

twp. township

TX Texas

-ty¹ (tē, ti) [< OFr. *-té* < L. *-tas*] *a suffix meaning* quality of, condition of [*novelty*]

-ty² (tē, ti) [OE. *-tig*] *a suffix meaning* tens, times ten [*sixty*]

Ty·burn (tī′bərn) a place where criminals were executed in London, England, in what is now Hyde Park

☆**ty·coon** (tī kōōn′) *n.* [< Jap. < Chin. *ta*, great + *kiun*, prince] **1.** a title applied by foreigners to the former shogun of Japan **2.** a wealthy, powerful businessman, industrialist, etc.

ty·ing (tī′iŋ) *prp. of* TIE

tyke (tīk) *n.* [ON. *tik*, a bitch] **1.** [Colloq.] a small child **2.** [Chiefly Brit. Dial.] a dog, esp. a mongrel or cur

Ty·ler (tī′lər) [after John TYLER] city in E Tex.: pop. 58,000

Ty·ler (tī′lər), **John** 1790–1862; 10th president of the U.S. (1841–45)

tym·pa·ni (tim′pə nē) *n.pl., sing.* **-no′** (-nō′) *var. of* TIMPANI — **tym′pa·nist** *n.*

tym·pan·ic membrane (tim pan′ik) a thin membrane that separates the middle ear from the external ear and vibrates when struck by sound waves; eardrum

tym·pa·num (tim′pə nəm) *n., pl.* **-nums, -na** (-nə) [L., a drum < Gr. *tympanon*] **1.** *Anat.* same as: a) MIDDLE EAR b) TYMPANIC MEMBRANE **2.** a drum or drumhead **3.** *Archit.* a) the recessed space, usually triangular, enclosed by the slanting cornices of a pediment b) the space enclosed by an arch and the top of the door or window below it —**tym·pan′ic** (-pan′ik) *adj.*

Tyn·dale (tin′d'l), **William** 1494?–1536; Eng. religious reformer & translator of the Bible: executed for heresy

typ·al (tīp′'l) *adj.* of, relating to, or used as a type

type (tīp) *n.* [< LL. < L. < Gr. *typos*, a figure, model < *typtein*, to strike] **1.** a person, thing, or event that represents another, esp. another that it is thought will appear later; symbol; token; sign **2.** the general form, plan, style, etc. of a particular class or group [that's not the *type* of shoe I wanted] **3.** a class, group, etc. having characteristics in common [a new *type* of airplane]: usually followed by *of*, but in colloquial use *of* is often omitted **4.** a person, animal, or thing that is representative or characteristic of a class or group [he is a Harvard Law School *type*] **5.** a perfect example; model;

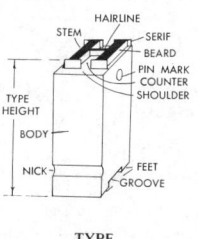

TYPE

pattern [the Greek temple has been the *type* for many public buildings] **6.** *Biol.* a single specimen on which the description and name of a taxon has been based **7.** *Printing* a) a rectangular piece of metal or, sometimes, wood, with a raised letter, figure, etc. in reverse on its upper end b) a set of such pieces c) the letters, etc. printed or mechanically reproduced from such pieces [small *type* is hard to read] —*vt.* **typed, typ′ing 1.** to classify according to type [to *type* a blood sample; to be *typed* as a villain in the theater] **2.** to write with a typewriter; typewrite —*vi.* to use a typewriter —**typ′a·ble, type′a·ble** *adj.*

SYN.—**type** is used of a group or category made up of persons or things that share certain special characteristics clearly setting them apart from the members of related groups or categories [a new *type* of shock absorber]; **kind** basically refers to a group or division found in nature [the rodent *kind*], but it is sometimes used, like *sort*, to refer to a less clearly defined group [all *sorts*, or *kinds*, of games]; **nature**, in exact use, refers to a grouping whose special characteristics are natural and basic [earthquakes and other phenomena of that *nature*]

-type (tīp) [< Gr. *typos*: see TYPE] *a combining form meaning*: **1.** type, example [*prototype*] **2.** stamp, print, printing type [*monotype*]

type·cast (tīp′kast′) *vt.* **-cast′, -cast′ing** to cast (an actor) repeatedly in the same type of part

type-cast (tīp′kast′) *vt., vi.* **-cast′, -cast′ing** to cast (type)

type·face (-fās′) *n.* same as FACE (*n.* 10)

type metal an alloy of tin, lead, and antimony, and sometimes copper, used for making type, etc.

☆**type·script** (-skript′) *n.* typewritten matter

type·set (-set′) *vt.* **-set′, -set′ting** to set in type

type·set·ter (-set′ər) *n.* **1.** a person who sets type; compositor **2.** a machine for setting type —**type′set′ting** *n., adj.*

☆**type·write** (-rīt′) *vt., vi.* **-wrote′, -writ′ten, -writ′ing** to write with a typewriter: now usually shortened to *type*

☆**type·writ·er** (-rīt′ər) *n.* **1.** a writing machine with a keyboard, for making letters, figures, etc. that look like printed ones **2.** *earlier term for* TYPIST

type·writ·ing (-rīt′iŋ) *n.* **1.** the act, skill, or process of using a typewriter **2.** writing done on a typewriter

ty·phoid (tī′foid) *n.* [TYPH(US) + -OID] **1.** orig., any typhuslike disorder **2.** a serious disease caused by a bacillus and spread as by infected food or drinking water: it causes fever, intestinal disorders, etc.: in full, **typhoid fever** —**ty·phoi′dal** *adj.*

ty·phoon (tī fōōn′) *n.* [< Chin. dial. *tai-fung*, lit., great wind] any violent tropical cyclone originating in the western Pacific, esp. in the South China Sea —**ty·phon′ic** (-fän′ik) *adj.*

ty·phus (tī′fəs) *n.* [ModL. < Gr. *typhos*, a fever] a serious infectious disease caused by a rickettsia transmitted to man by fleas, lice, etc., and causing fever, red spots on the skin, etc.: in full, **typhus fever** —**ty′phous** (-fəs) *adj.*

typ·i·cal (tip′i k'l) *adj.* **1.** serving as a type; symbolic **2.** having the particular characteristics, qualities, etc. of a class, group, etc.; representative [a church *typical* of Gothic style] **3.** belonging to a type; characteristic [a snail moving with *typical* slowness] —**typ′i·cal·ly** *adv.* —**typ′i·cal·ness, typ′i·cal·i·ty** (-kal′ə tē) *n.*

typ·i·fy (tip′ə fī′) *vt.* **-fied′, -fy′ing** [see TYPE & -FY] **1.** to be a type of; symbolize **2.** to have or show the particular characteristics of; be typical of [Tom Sawyer *typified* the American boy] —**typ′i·fi·ca′tion** *n.*

typ·ist (tīp′ist) *n.* a person who operates a typewriter, esp. one whose work is typing

☆**ty·po** (tī′pō) *n., pl.* **-pos** [Colloq.] a typographical error; mechanical mistake made in setting type or in typing

ty·po- [< Gr. *typos*: see TYPE] *a combining form meaning* type

ty·pog·ra·pher (tī päg′rə fər) *n.* a person skilled in typography; printer, compositor, etc.

ty·po·graph·i·cal (tī′pə graf′i k'l) *adj.* of typography; having to do with the setting of type, printing, etc.: also **ty′po·graph′ic** —**ty′po·graph′i·cal·ly** *adv.*

ty·pog·ra·phy (tī päg′rə fē) *n.* [< Fr. < ML.: see TYPO- & -GRAPHY] **1.** the art or process of printing from type **2.** the art or process of setting and arranging type for printing **3.** the arrangement, style, or appearance of matter printed from type

Tyr (tir) *Norse Myth.* the god of war and son of Odin

ty·ran·ni·cal (ti ran′i k'l, tī-) *adj.* **1.** of or suited to a tyrant; arbitrary; despotic **2.** harsh, cruel, unjust, etc. Also **ty·ran′nic** —**ty·ran′ni·cal·ly** *adv.*

ty·ran·ni·cide (-ə sīd′) *n.* **1.** the act of killing a tyrant **2.** a person who kills a tyrant

tyr·an·nize (tir′ə nīz′) *vi.* **-nized′, -niz′ing 1.** to govern as a tyrant **2.** to use power in a harsh or cruel way —*vt.* to treat tyrannically; oppress *[a captain who tyrannized his crew]* — **tyr′an·niz′er** *n.*

☆**ty·ran·no·saur** (ti ran′ə sôr′, tī-) *n.* [< ModL. < Gr. *tyran-nos,* tyrant + -SAURUS] any of various huge, two-footed, flesh-eating dinosaurs of the Cretaceous Period in N. America: also **ty·ran′no·saur′us** (-əs)

tyr·an·nous (tir′ə nəs) *adj.* tyrannical; cruel, harsh, unjust, etc. —**tyr′an·nous·ly** *adv.*

tyr·an·ny (tir′ə nē) *n., pl.* **-nies 1.** the office, authority, government, etc. of a tyrant, or absolute ruler **2.** harsh and unjust government; despotism **3.** very cruel and unjust use of power or authority **4.** harshness; strictness **5.** a tyrannical act

ty·rant (tī′rənt) *n.* [< OFr. < L. < Gr. *tyrannos*] **1.** a ruler with absolute authority; specif., in ancient

TYRANNOSAUR
(to 47 ft. long)

Greece, such a ruler who seized power illegally **2.** a cruel, unjust ruler; despot **3.** any person who uses his authority in a cruel or unjust manner *[her father is a tyrant]*

tyrant flycatcher any of a group of American flycatchers

Tyre (tīr) seaport in SW Lebanon, on the Mediterranean: center of ancient Phoenician culture: pop. 12,000 —**Tyr·i·an** (tir′ē ən) *adj., n.*

tyre (tīr) *n. Brit. sp. of* TIRE²

Tyrian purple (or **dye**) **1.** a purple or crimson dye used by the ancient Romans and Greeks: it was made from certain mollusks, originally at Tyre **2.** bluish red

ty·ro (tī′rō) *n., pl.* **-ros** [ML. < L. *tiro,* recruit] a beginner in learning something; novice

Tyr·ol (tir′əl, tī′rōl, ti rōl′) *same as* TIROL —**Ty·ro·le·an** (ti rō′lē ən) *adj., n.* —**Tyr·o·lese** (tir′ə lēz′) *adj., n., pl.* **-lese′**

Tyr·rhe·ni·an Sea (ti rē′nē ən) part of the Mediterranean, between the W coast of Italy & the islands of Corsica & Sardinia

tzar (tsär, zär) *n. var. of* CZAR —**tzar′dom** *n.* —**tzar′ism** *n.* —**tzar′ist** *adj., n.*

tzar·e·vitch (tsär′ə vich, zär′-) *n. var. of* CZAREVITCH

tza·ri·na (tsä rē′nə, zä-) *n. var. of* CZARINA: also **tza·rit′za** (-rēt′sə)

tzet·ze fly (tset′sē, tsē′tsē) *var. of* TSETSE FLY

Tzu·po (dzoo′pō′) city in Shantung province, NE China: pop. 875,000

U

U, u (yo͞o) *n., pl.* **U's, u's** **1.** the twenty-first letter of the English alphabet **2.** a sound of *U* or *u*

U (yo͞o) *n.* **1.** something shaped like U **2.** *Chem.* uranium — *adj.* shaped like U

U., U **1.** Union **2.** United **3.** University

U., U, u., u unit; units

U.A.R. United Arab Republic

U.A.W., UAW United Automobile, Aerospace, and Agricultural Implement Workers of America

U·ban·gi (o͞o bäŋ′gē, yo͞o baŋ′-) river in C Africa, flowing from N Zaire west & south into the Congo River

u·biq·ui·tous (yo͞o bik′wə təs) *adj.* [see UBIQUITY & -OUS] present, or seeming to be present, everywhere at the same time; omnipresent —see *SYN.* at OMNIPRESENT —**u·biq′ui·tous·ly** *adv.* —**u·biq′ui·tous·ness** *n.*

u·biq·ui·ty (-tē) *n.* [< Fr. < L. *ubique*, everywhere] the state, fact, or capacity of being, or seeming to be, everywhere at the same time; omnipresence

U-boat (yo͞o′bōt′) *n.* [< G. *U-boot*, abbrev. of *Unterseeboot*, undersea boat] a German submarine

U bolt a U-shaped bolt with threads and a nut at each end

u.c. *Printing* upper case

U·ca·ya·li (o͞o′kä yä′lē) river in E Peru, flowing north to join the Marañón & form the Amazon: c. 1,200 mi.

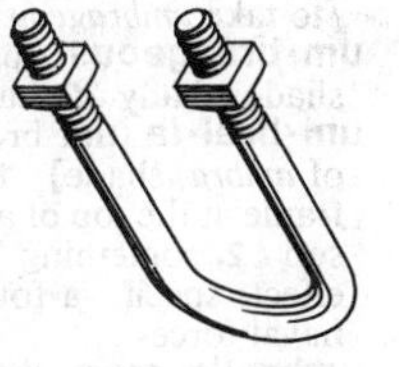

ud·der (ud′ər) *n.* [OE. *udr*] a large, baglike, milk-producing gland with two or more teats, as in cows

U·fa (o͞o fä′) city in eastern European R.S.F.S.R., in the western foothills of the Urals: pop. 773,000

☆**UFO** (yo͞o′fō, yo͞o′ef ō′) *n., pl.* **UFOs, UFO's** [*u*(*nidentified*) *f*(*lying*) *o*(*bject*)] any of a number of unidentified objects reported, esp. since 1947, to have been seen flying at varying heights and speeds and variously thought to be hallucinations, secret military missiles, spacecraft from another planet, etc.

U·gan·da (yo͞o gan′də, o͞o gän′dä) country in EC Africa: a member of the Commonwealth: 93,981 sq. mi.; pop. 10,127,000; cap. Kampala —**U·gan′dan** (-dən) *adj., n.*

ugh (oͦokh, uH, oͦo, ug, *etc.*) *interj.* [echoic] an exclamation of disgust, horror, etc.

ug·li (ug′lē) *n.* [altered < UGLY: from its misshapen appearance] a Jamaican citrus fruit that is a three-way cross between a grapefruit, orange, and tangerine: also called **ugli fruit**

ug·li·fy (ug′lə fī′) *vt.* **-fied′, -fy′ing** to make ugly; disfigure

ug·ly (ug′lē) *adj.* **-li·er, -li·est** [< ON. *uggligr*, fearful < *uggr*, fear] **1.** unpleasing to look at; unsightly [an *ugly* shack] **2.** bad, unpleasant, disgusting, etc. [an *ugly* lie] **3.** dangerous; threatening [*ugly* storm clouds] **4.** [Colloq.] ill-tempered; cross [an *ugly* mood] —**ug′li·ly** *adv.* —**ug′li·ness** *n.*

ugly duckling [from a story by H. C. Andersen] a very plain child or unpromising thing that in time becomes or could become beautiful, important, etc.

U·gri·an (o͞o′grē ən, yo͞o′-) *adj.* **1.** designating or of a group of Finno-Ugric peoples of W Siberia and Hungary **2.** *same as*

U BOLT

Ugric (*adj.* 1) —*n.* **1.** a member of any of the Ugrian peoples **2.** *same as* UGRIC

U·gric (-grik) *adj.* **1.** designating or of a branch of the Finno-Ugric subfamily of languages including Hungarian (Magyar) **2.** *same as* UGRIAN (*adj.* 1) —*n.* the Ugric languages

uh (u, un) *interj.* **1.** *same as* HUH **2.** a sound made in speaking, as while searching for a word

UHF, U.H.F., uhf, u.h.f. ultrahigh frequency

uh-huh (ə hu′; *for 2* un′un′) *interj.* **1.** an exclamation indicating: *a*) a "yes" reply *b*) that one is listening closely **2.** *var. of* UH-UH

uh-uh (un′un′, -un′) *interj.* an exclamation indicating a "no" reply

U.K. United Kingdom

u·kase (yo͞o′kās, -kāz; yo͞o kās′, -kāz′) *n.* [Russ. *ukaz*, edict] **1.** in Czarist Russia, an order of the Czar **2.** any official order or decree

U·krain·i·an (yo͞o krā′nē ən, -krī′-) *adj.* of the Ukraine, its people, their language, etc. —*n.* **1.** a native or inhabitant of the Ukraine **2.** the East Slavic language of the Ukrainians, very closely related to Russian

Ukrainian Soviet Socialist Republic republic of the U.S.S.R., in the SW European part: 231,990 sq. mi.; pop. 47,100,000; cap. Kiev: also called **the U·kraine** (yo͞o krān′)

☆**u·ku·le·le** (yo͞o′kə lā′lē; *Haw.* oͦo′koo lā′lä) *n.* [Haw., lit., flea] a musical instrument having four strings, like a small guitar: also [Colloq.] **uke** (yo͞ok)

UL, U.L. Underwriters' Laboratories

U·lan Ba·tor (o͞o′län bä′tôr) capital of the Mongolian People's Republic, in the NC part: pop. 254,000

ul·cer (ul′sər) *n.* [< L. *ulceris*, genitive of *ulcus*, ulcer] **1.** an open sore with pus, as on the skin or stomach lining **2.** any condition or influence that is rotten or corrupting [slums are the *ulcers* of our cities]

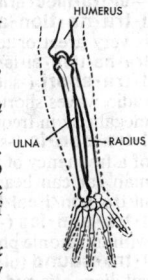

UKULELE

ul·cer·ate (ul′sə rāt′) *vt., vi.* **-at′ed, -at′ing** [< L. pp. of *ulcerare*] to have or cause to have an ulcer or ulcers [an *ulcerated* stomach] —**ul′cer·a′tion** *n.* —**ul′cer·a′tive** *adj.*

ul·cer·ous (-sər əs) *adj.* **1.** having an ulcer or ulcers **2.** of or like an ulcer or ulcers

-ule (yo͞ol, yool) [< Fr. < L. *-ulus, -ula, -ulum*] *a suffix meaning* little [sporule]

-u·lent (yo͞o lənt) [< Fr. < L. *-ulentus*] *a suffix meaning* full of [fraudulent]

ul·na (ul′nə) *n., pl.* **-nae** (-nē) **, -nas** [ModL. < L., the elbow] **1.** the larger of the two bones of the forearm, on the side opposite the thumb **2.** a similar bone in the forelimb of other vertebrates —**ul′nar** (-nər) *adj.*

-u·lose (yo͞o lōs′) [< L. *-ulosus*] *a suffix meaning* characterized by, marked by [granulose]

HUMERUS

ULNA — RADIUS

---

fat, āpe, cär; ten, ēven; is, bīte; gō, hôrn, to͞ol, loͦok; oil, out; up, fur; get; joy; yet; chin; she; thin, *th*en; zh, leisure; ŋ, ring; ə for *a* in *ago*, *e* in *agent*, *i* in *sanity*, *o* in *comply*, *u* in *focus*; ′ as in *able* (ā′b'l); Fr. bal; ë, Fr. coeur; ö, Fr. feu; Fr. mo*n*; o�, Fr. coq; ü, Fr. duc; r, Fr. cri; H, G. ich; kh, G. doch; ‡foreign; ☆ Americanism; < derived from. See inside front cover.

-u·lous (yoo ləs) [< L. *-ulosus*] *a suffix meaning* tending to, characterized by [*populous*]

Ul·ster (ul′stər) **1.** former province of Ireland, divided to form Northern Ireland and a province (*Ulster*) of Ireland **2.** [Colloq.] Northern Ireland —**Ul′ster·man** (-mən) *n., pl.* -**men**

ul·ster (ul′stər) *n.* [< ULSTER, where fabric for such coats was orig. made] a long, loose, heavy overcoat

ult. 1. ultimate **2.** ultimately **3.** ultimo

ul·te·ri·or (ul tir′ē ər) *adj.* [L.] **1.** lying beyond or on the farther side **2.** later, following, or future **3.** beyond what is openly said or made known [an *ulterior* motive] —**ul·te′ri·or·ly** *adv.*

ul·ti·ma (ul′ti mə) *n.* [L., fem. of *ultimus*, last] the last syllable of a word

ul·ti·mate (ul′tə mit) *adj.* [< LL. pp. of *ultimare*, to come to an end < L. *ultimus*, last] **1.** beyond which it is impossible to go; farthest [the *ultimate* limits of space] **2.** final; last [an *ultimate* decision] **3.** most basic; fundamental; primary [the *ultimate* goodness of man] **4.** greatest or highest possible; maximum [the flood water reached its *ultimate* level] —*n.* something ultimate [the *ultimate* in pleasure] —see SYN. at LAST¹ —**ul′ti·ma·cy** (-mə sē), **ul′ti·mate·ness** *n.* —**ul′ti·mate·ly** *adv.*

ul·ti·ma Thu·le (ul′ti mə thoo′lē) [L.] **1.** among the ancients, the northernmost region of the world **2.** any far-off, unknown region

ul·ti·ma·tum (ul′tə māt′əm) *n., pl.* -**tums**, -**ta** (-ə) [ModL. < LL., neut. pp. of *ultimare:* see ULTIMATE] a final offer or demand presented to another in a dispute, esp. with a threat to break off relations, use force, etc. if it is refused

ul·ti·mo (ul′tə mō′) *adv.* [L. *ultimo* (*mense*), (in the) last (month)] in the preceding month: an old-fashioned usage [yours of the 13th (day) *ultimo* received]

ul·tra (ul′trə) *adj.* [L., beyond] going beyond the usual limit; extreme [she is an *ultra* optimist] —*n.* a person whose beliefs, as in politics, are extreme, unreasonable, etc.

ul·tra- [L.] *a prefix meaning:* **1.** beyond [*ultraviolet*] **2.** beyond what is usual, reasonable, etc. [*ultramodern*] **3.** beyond the range of [*ultramicroscopic*]

ul·tra·cen·tri·fuge (ul′trə sen′trə fyooj′) *n.* a high-speed centrifuge for separating colloidal and other very small particles from larger particles in a mixture —*vt.* -**fuged′**, -**fug′ing** to cause to undergo the action of an ultracentrifuge

ul·tra·con·serv·a·tive (ul′trə kən sur′və tiv) *adj.* extremely conservative —*n.* an ultraconservative person

ul·tra·high frequency (ul′trə hī′) any radio frequency between 300 and 3,000 megahertz

ul·tra·ma·rine (ul′trə mə rēn′) *adj.* [< ML.: see ULTRA- & MARINE] **1.** beyond the sea **2.** deep-blue —*n.* **1.** a blue coloring matter orig. made from powdered lapis lazuli **2.** any similar coloring matter made from other substances **3.** a deep blue

ul·tra·mi·cro·scope (-mī′krə skōp′) *n.* an instrument using scattered light to allow observation of objects, as colloidal particles, too small to be seen with an ordinary microscope —**ul′tra·mi·cros′co·py** (-mī kräs′kə pē) *n.*

ul·tra·mi·cro·scop·ic (-mī′krə skäp′ik) *adj.* **1.** too small to be seen with an ordinary microscope **2.** of an ultramicroscope —**ul′tra·mi·cro·scop′i·cal·ly** *adv.*

ul·tra·mod·ern (-mäd′ərn) *adj.* modern to an extreme degree —**ul′tra·mod′ern·ism** *n.* —**ul′tra·mod′ern·ist** *n.*

ul·tra·na·tion·al·ism (-nash′ən ′l iz'm) *n.* nationalism that is very great or too great —**ul′tra·na′tion·al·ist** *adj., n.* —**ul′tra·na′tion·al·is′tic** *adj.*

ul·tra·short (-shôrt′) *adj.* very short; specif., designating or of radio waves shorter than 10 meters in wavelength and above 30 megahertz in frequency

ul·tra·son·ic (-sän′ik) *adj.* [ULTRA- + SONIC] designating or of a frequency of mechanical vibrations above the range the human ear can hear, i.e., above 20,000 vibrations per second —**ul′tra·son′i·cal·ly** *adv.*

ul·tra·son·ics (-sän′iks) *n.pl.* [*with sing. v.*] the science dealing with ultrasonic phenomena

ul·tra·sound (ul′trə sound′) *n.* ultrasonic waves used in medical diagnosis and therapy, in surgery, etc.

ul·tra·vi·o·let (ul′trə vī′ə lit) *adj.* **1.** lying just beyond the violet end of the visible spectrum and having wavelengths shorter than 4,000 angstroms **2.** of or producing light rays of such wavelengths —*n.* ultraviolet radiation

ul·u·late (yool′yoo lāt′, ul′-) *vi.* -**lat′ed**, -**lat′ing** [< L. pp. of *ululare*, to howl: echoic] **1.** to howl or hoot **2.** to wail or weep loudly —**ul′u·lant** (-lənt) *adj.* —**ul′u·la′tion** *n.*

U·lys·ses (yoo lis′ēz) [L.] *same as* ODYSSEUS

um·bel (um′b'l) *n.* [L. *umbella:* see UMBRELLA] a cluster of flowers with stalks that are nearly equal in length and that grow from the same point —**um′bel·late** (-it, -āt′), **um′bel·lat′ed** *adj.* —**um′bel·late′ly** *adv.*

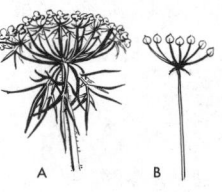

UMBEL
(A, compound; B, simple)

um·bel·lif·er·ous (um′bə lif′ər-əs) *adj.* having an umbel or umbels, as plants of the parsley family

um·ber (um′bər) *n.* [< Fr. < It. (*terra d′*)*ombra*, lit., (earth of) shade, prob. < L. *umbra*, a shade] **1.** a kind of earth containing oxides of manganese and iron, used as a coloring matter: raw umber is yellowish-brown; umber that has been heated to a very high temperature (*burnt umber*) is reddish-brown **2.** a yellowish-brown or reddish-brown color —*adj.* of the color of raw umber or burnt umber —*vt.* to color with or as with umber

um·bil·i·cal (um bil′i k'l) *adj.* **1.** of or like an umbilicus or an umbilical cord **2.** located at or near the navel **3.** joined together by or as if by an umbilical cord —☆*n.* **1.** a cable for supplying oxygen, power, etc. to an astronaut or aquanaut when he goes outside his craft **2.** a cable for testing parts of a spacecraft, removed just before liftoff

umbilical cord a cordlike structure that connects a fetus with the placenta: it is cut at birth, the navel being formed at the point where it was attached to the fetus

um·bil·i·cus (um bil′i kəs, um′bi lī′kəs) *n., pl.* -**ci**′ (-sī′, -sī) [L.] **1.** *same as* NAVEL **2.** a hollow place that resembles a navel, as the hilum of a seed

um·bra (um′brə) *n., pl.* -**brae** (-brē), -**bras** [L., a shade] **1.** a shade or shadow **2.** the dark cone of shadow projecting from a planet or satellite on the side opposite the sun: see illustration at ECLIPSE

um·brage (um′brij) *n.* [OFr. < L. < *umbra*, a shade] **1.** [Obs.] shade; shadow **2.** foliage that gives shade **3.** a feeling of hurt and anger over what one takes to be an insult or slight; offense [to take *umbrage* at a remark] —see SYN. at OFFENSE

um·bra·geous (um brā′jəs) *adj.* [see UMBRAGE] **1.** giving shade; shady **2.** easily offended —**um·bra′geous·ly** *adv.*

um·brel·la (um brel′ə) *n.* [< It. < L. < *umbella*, parasol, dim. of *umbra*, shade] **1.** cloth, plastic, etc. stretched over a folding frame at the top of a stick, used for protection against the rain or sun **2.** something like this in appearance or in its protective effect; specif., a force of aircraft sent up to protect ground or naval forces

umbrella tree ☆**1.** an American magnolia with clusters of long leaves at the ends of the branches, bad-smelling white flowers, and reddish fruit **2.** any of various trees with leaves shaped like an umbrella or growing in umbrellalike clusters

Um·bri·a (um′brē ə; *It.* oom′brē ä′) region in central Italy: in ancient times a district extending from the Tiber to the Adriatic —**Um′bri·an** *adj., n.*

u·mi·ak, u·mi·ack (oo′mē ak′) *n.* [Esk.] a large, open boat made of skins stretched on a wooden frame, used by Eskimos

UMIAK

um·laut (oom′lout) *n.* [G. < *um*, about + *laut*, a sound] *Linguis.* **1.** *a)* a change in the sound of a vowel, caused by the influence of another vowel that at one time came immediately after it in a word *b)* a vowel resulting from such a change **2.** the diacritical mark (¨) placed over such a vowel, esp. in German, to show umlaut —*vt.* to sound or write with an umlaut

ump (ump) *n., vt., vi. shortened form of* UMPIRE

um·pire (um′pīr) *n.* [ME. *oumpere* (by faulty separation of *a noumpere*) < MFr. *nomper*, uneven, hence third person < *non*, not + *per*, even] **1.** a person chosen to give a decision in a dispute; arbiter **2.** an official who rules on the plays of a game, as in baseball —*vt., vi.* -**pired**, -**pir·ing** to act as umpire (in or of)

ump·teen (ump′tēn′) *adj.* [Slang] a great number of; very many —**ump′teenth′** *adj.*

UMW, U.M.W. United Mine Workers of America

un- (un; *unstressed, also* ən) *either of two prefixes meaning:* **1.** [OE. *un-*] not, lack of, the opposite of [*unhappy, untruth*] **2.** [OE. *un-, on-, and-*] the reverse or removal of: added to verbs to show a reversal of the action of the verb [*unfasten*] and to nouns to form verbs showing a removal or release from the thing, state, etc. shown by the noun [*unhand*]; sometimes *un-* is used simply to add emphasis [*unloosen*] The list at the bottom of this page and the following pages includes many of the more common compounds formed with *un-* (either prefix) that do not have special meanings

UN, U.N. United Nations

un·a·ble (un ā′b'l) *adj.* not able; lacking the ability, means, or power to do something

un·a·bridged (un′ə brijd′) *adj.* not abridged, or shortened: often applied to a large dictionary that is not a shortened version of a larger work

un·ac·com·pa·nied (un′ə kum′pə nēd) *adj.* **1.** not accompanied **2.** *Music* without an accompaniment

un·ac·count·a·ble (un′ə koun′tə b'l) *adj.* **1.** that cannot be explained or accounted for; strange [*an unaccountable accident*] **2.** not responsible [*he is unaccountable to you*] —**un′ac·count′a·bil′i·ty** *n.* —**un′ac·count′a·bly** *adv.*

un·ac·count·ed-for (-koun′tid fôr′) *adj.* not explained

un·ac·cus·tomed (-ə kus′təmd) *adj.* **1.** not accustomed or used [*unaccustomed to wealth*] **2.** not usual; strange [*an unaccustomed action*]

un·ad·vised (-əd vīzd′) *adj.* **1.** without counsel or advice **2.** thoughtlessly hasty; indiscreet —**un′ad·vis′ed·ly** (-vīz′id lē) *adv.* —**un′ad·vis′ed·ness** *n.*

un·af·fect·ed (-ə fek′tid) *adj.* **1.** not affected, or influenced **2.** without affectation; sincere and natural —see **SYN.** at SINCERE —**un′af·fect′ed·ly** *adv.* —**un′af·fect′ed·ness** *n.*

un-A·mer·i·can (-ə mer′ə kən) *adj.* not American; esp., thought of as not conforming to the principles, policies, etc. of the U.S. —**un′-A·mer′i·can·ism** *n.*

U·na·mu·no (ōō′nä mōō′nō), **Mi·guel de** (mē gel′ *the*) 1864-1936; Sp. philosopher & writer

u·nan·i·mous (yōō nan′ə məs) *adj.* [< L. < *unus*, one + *animus*, the mind] **1.** agreeing completely; united in opinion **2.** showing, or based on, complete agreement [*a unanimous vote*] —**u·na·nim·i·ty** (yōō′nə nim′ə tē) *n.* —**u·nan′i·mous·ly** *adv.*

un·ap·proach·a·ble (un′ə prōch′ə b'l) *adj.* **1.** not approachable; hard to be friendly with; aloof **2.** having no rival or equal; unmatched [*unapproachable* skill] —**un′ap·proach′a·bil′i·ty** *n.* —**un′ap·proach′a·bly** *adv.*

un·arm (un ärm′) *vt.* same as DISARM

un·armed (-ärmd′) *adj.* having no weapons, esp. firearms, or armor; defenseless

un·as·sail·a·ble (un′ə sāl′ə b'l) *adj.* not assailable; specif., *a*) that cannot be successfully attacked *b*) that cannot be successfully denied [*unassailable* arguments] —**un′as·sail′a·ble·ness, un′as·sail′a·bil′i·ty** *n.* —**un′as·sail′a·bly** *adv.*

un·as·sum·ing (-ə sōō′miŋ, -syōō′-) *adj.* not bold, showy, or forward; modest —**un′as·sum′ing·ly** *adv.* —**un′as·sum′ing·ness** *n.*

un·at·tached (-ə tacht′) *adj.* **1.** not attached or fastened **2.** not connected with any organization; independent **3.** not engaged or married **4.** *Law* not taken as security for a judgment

un·a·vail·ing (-ə vā′liŋ) *adj.* not bringing success; useless; futile [*her unavailing* efforts] —**un′a·vail′ing·ly** *adv.*

un·a·void·a·ble (-ə void′ə b'l) *adj.* that cannot be avoided; inevitable —**un′a·void′a·ble·ness** *n.* —**un′a·void′a·bly** *adv.*

un·a·ware (-ə wer′) *adj.* not aware or conscious [*unaware* of danger] —*adv.* same as UNAWARES —**un′a·ware′ness** *n.*

un·a·wares (-ə werz′) *adv.* **1.** without knowing or being aware **2.** unexpectedly; by surprise [*to sneak up on someone unawares*]

un·backed (un bakt′) *adj.* **1.** without a back or backing **2.** having no backers, supporters, etc.

un·bal·ance (-bal′əns) *vt.* **-anced, -anc·ing 1.** to throw out of balance **2.** to disturb the working of (the mind) —*n.* the condition of being unbalanced

un·bal·anced (-bal′ənst) *adj.* **1.** not balanced or equal [*an unbalanced* budget] **2.** not sane or normal in mind

un·bar (-bär′) *vt.* **-barred′, -bar′ring** to unbolt or unlock

un·bear·a·ble (-ber′ə b'l) *adj.* that cannot be put up with or tolerated —**un·bear′a·ble·ness** *n.* —**un·bear′a·bly** *adv.*

un·beat·a·ble (-bēt′ə b'l) *adj.* **1.** that cannot be defeated **2.** that cannot be improved on [*an unbeatable* suggestion]

un·beat·en (-bēt′'n) *adj.* **1.** not struck, pounded, etc. **2.** not walked on or traveled over **3.** not defeated or improved upon

un·be·com·ing (un′bi kum′iŋ) *adj.* not appropriate or suited to one's appearance, status, character, etc. [*an unbecoming* dress, *unbecoming* behavior] —see **SYN.** at IMPROPER —**un′be·com′ing·ly** *adv.* —**un′be·com′ing·ness** *n.*

un·be·known (-bi nōn′) *adj.* unknown or unnoticed; without one's knowledge (usually with *to*): also **un′be·knownst′** (-nōnst′) [*unbeknown* to me she began writing poetry]

un·be·lief (-bə lēf′) *n.* a withholding or lack of belief, esp. in religion

un·be·liev·a·ble (-bə lēv′ə b'l) *adj.* beyond belief; astounding; incredible —**un′be·liev′a·bly** *adv.*

un·be·liev·er (-bə lē′vər) *n.* **1.** a person who does not believe; doubter **2.** a person who does not accept any, or any particular, religious belief

un·be·liev·ing (-bə lē′viŋ) *adj.* not believing; doubting; skeptical —**un′be·liev′ing·ly** *adv.*

un·bend (un bend′) *vt., vi.* **-bent′** or **-bend′ed, -bend′ing 1.** to make or become relaxed or more natural [*after the interview, he unbent* and told some jokes] **2.** to make or become straight again

un·bend·ing (-ben′diŋ) *adj.* not bending; specif., *a*) rigid; stiff *b*) not giving in; firm *c*) cool; reserved; stern —*n.* a relaxation of control, harshness, etc. —**un·bend′ing·ly** *adv.* —**un·bend′ing·ness** *n.*

un·bi·ased, un·bi·assed (-bī′əst) *adj.* without bias or prejudice; impartial; fair —see **SYN.** at FAIR[1]

un·bid·den (-bid′'n) *adj.* **1.** not commanded **2.** without being asked, wanted, etc.; uninvited [*she walked in unbidden*] Also **un·bid′**

---

un′a·bashed′	un′ad·ver·tised′	un′ap·par′ent	un′as·sort′ed
un′a·bat′ed	un′ad·vis′a·ble	un′ap·peal′a·ble	un′as·sured′
un′ab·bre′vi·at′ed	un′af·fil′i·at′ed	un′ap·peal′ing	un′at·tain′a·ble
un′a·bet′ted	un′a·fraid′	un′ap·peas′a·ble	un′at·tempt′ed
un′ab·solved′	un′ag·gres′sive	un′ap·pe·tiz′ing	un′at·tend′ed
un′ab·sorbed′	un·aid′ed	un′ap·pre′ci·at′ed	un′at·test′ed
un′ac·a·dem′ic	un·aimed′	un′ap·pre′ci·a·tive	un′at·tired′
un·ac′cent·ed	un·a·like′	un′ap·proached′	un′at·trac′tive
un′ac·cept′a·ble	un′al·lied′	un′ap·pro′pri·at′ed	un′au·then′tic
un′ac·cli′mat·ed	un′al·low′a·ble	un·apt′	un′au·then′ti·cat′ed
un′ac·com′mo·dat′ed	un′al·loyed′	un·ar′mored	un′au·thor′ized′
un′ac·com′mo·dat′ing	un·al′ter·a·ble	un·ar′tis·tic	un′a·vail′a·ble
un′ac·com′plished	un·al′tered	un′as·cer·tained′	un′a·venged′
un′ac·cred′it·ed	un′am·big′u·ous	un′a·shamed′	un′a·vowed′
un′ac·knowl′edged	un′am·bi′tious	un·asked′	un′a·wak′ened
un′ac·quaint′ed	un′am·pli·fied′	un′as·pi′rat·ed	un·awed′
un′a·dapt′a·ble	un′a·mus′ing	un′as·pir′ing	un·baked′
un′ad·just′a·ble	un′an·nounced′	un′as·signed′	un·bap′tized′
un′a·dorned′	un′an′swer·a·ble	un′as·sim′i·lat′ed	un·bathed′
un′a·dul′ter·at′ed	un′an·tic′i·pat′ed	un′as·sist′ed	un′be·fit′ting
un′ad·ven′tur·ous	un′a·pol′o·get′ic	un′as·so′ci·at′ed	un·belt′ed

---

un·bind (-bīnd′) *vt.* **-bound′, -bind′ing** **1.** to untie; unfasten **2.** to release from bonds, controls, etc.

un·blessed, un·blest (-blest′) *adj.* **1.** not blessed **2.** unhappy; wretched

un·blush·ing (-blush′iŋ) *adj.* **1.** not blushing **2.** without feeling any shame —**un·blush′ing·ly** *adv.*

un·bolt (-bōlt′) *vt., vi.* to draw back the bolt or bolts of (a door, etc.); unbar; open

un·bolt·ed[1] (-bōlt′id) *adj.* not fastened with a bolt

un·bolt·ed[2] (-bōlt′id) *adj.* not bolted or sifted, as flour

un·born (-bôrn′) *adj.* **1.** not born **2.** still within the mother's uterus **3.** yet to come or be; future [*unborn* generations]

un·bos·om (-booz′əm, -boo͞o′zəm) *vt., vi.* to tell or reveal (one's feelings, secrets, etc.) —**unbosom oneself** to express (oneself) openly about one's feelings, etc.

un·bound·ed (-boun′did) *adj.* **1.** without bounds or limits **2.** not held back; uncontrolled [with *unbounded* enthusiasm]

un·bowed (-boud′) *adj.* **1.** not bowed or bent **2.** not giving in; unsubdued

un·bri·dled (-brī′d'ld) *adj.* **1.** having no bridle on, as a horse **2.** not controlled; unrestrained [an *unbridled* temper]

un·bro·ken (-brō′k'n) *adj.* not broken; specif., *a)* whole; intact *b)* not tamed [an *unbroken* horse] *c)* continuous; uninterrupted [an *unbroken* silence] *d)* not bettered or surpassed [an *unbroken* record]

un·buck·le (-buk′'l) *vt.* **-led, -ling** to unfasten the buckle or buckles of

un·bur·den (-burd′'n) *vt.* **1.** to free from a burden **2.** to free or ease (oneself or one's mind) by making known (something hard to bear)

un·but·ton (-but′'n) *vt., vi.* to unfasten the buttons of (a garment, etc.)

un·but·toned (-but′'nd) *adj.* **1.** with buttons unfastened **2.** free and easy; casual; informal

un·called-for (un kôld′fôr′) *adj.* **1.** not needed **2.** unnecessary and out of place; impertinent [an *uncalled-for* remark]

un·can·ny (-kan′ē) *adj.* **1.** strange or mysterious, esp. in a way that is frightening or unsettling; weird [the empty house had an *uncanny* look] **2.** so remarkable, keen, etc. as to seem unnatural [an *uncanny* sense of hearing] —see SYN. at WEIRD —**un·can′ni·ly** *adv.* —**un·can′ni·ness** *n.*

un·cap (-kap′) *vt.* **-capped′, -cap′ping** to remove the cap from (a bottle, etc.)

un·cared-for (-kerd′fôr′) *adj.* not cared for or looked after; neglected

un·cer·e·mo·ni·ous (un′ser ə mō′nē əs) *adj.* **1.** less ceremonious than is expected; informal **2.** so brief or abrupt as to be rude [his *unceremonious* departure] —**un′cer·e·mo′ni·ous·ly** *adv.* —**un′cer·e·mo′ni·ous·ness** *n.*

un·cer·tain (un surt′'n) *adj.* **1.** *a)* not surely or certainly known; questionable [the plane's departure time is *uncertain*] *b)* not sure or certain in knowledge; doubtful [he looked *uncertain* of what to do] **2.** not definite; vague [an *uncertain* number] **3.** likely to change; not steady; varying [*uncertain* weather] —**un·cer′tain·ly** *adv.* —**un·cer′tain·ness** *n.*

un·cer·tain·ty (-tē) *n.* **1.** lack of certainty; doubt **2.** *pl.* **-ties** something uncertain

SYN.—**uncertainty** may imply only a lack of complete sureness [*uncertainty* about a date of birth] or it may suggest such vagueness as to make anything more than guesswork impossible [the *uncertainty* of the future]; **doubt** implies such a lack of sureness, as because of a shortage of evidence, that no decision or certain opinion can be reached [there is *doubt* about his guilt]; **dubiety** suggests uncertainty that is marked by a wavering between conclusions; **skepticism** implies the habit of mind of a person who refuses to believe without clear and convincing proof —ANT. conviction, assurance, certitude

uncertainty principle in quantum mechanics, the axiom that it is impossible to measure exactly and at the same time two related quantities, as both the position and momentum of an electron

un·char·i·ta·ble (-char′i tə b'l) *adj.* harsh or severe, as in judging or dealing with others; unkind, selfish, unhelpful, tending to find fault, etc. —**un·char′i·ta·ble·ness** *n.* —**un·char′i·ta·bly** *adv.*

un·chart·ed (-chär′tid) *adj.* not marked on a chart or map; unexplored or unknown

un·chris·tian (-kris′chən) *adj.* **1.** not having or practicing a Christian religion **2.** not in agreement with the principles of Christianity; not worthy of a Christian [a cruel, *unchristian* act]

un·church (-church′) *vt.* **1.** to deprive (a person) of membership in a given church **2.** to deprive (a congregation) of its rights as a church

un·ci·al (un′shē əl, -shəl) *adj.* [< L. < *uncia*, an inch] designating or of a form of large, rounded, handwritten letter used in Greek and Latin manuscripts between 300 and 900 A.D. —*n.* **1.** an uncial letter **2.** an uncial manuscript **3.** uncial handwriting

un·ci·form (un′si fôrm′) *adj.* [ModL. < L. *uncus*, a hook + -*formis*, -FORM] shaped like a hook

un·ci·nate (un′si nit, -nāt′) *adj.* [L. *uncinatus*, ult. < *uncus*, a hook] bent like a hook; hooked

un·cir·cum·cised (un sur′kəm sīzd′) *adj.* **1.** not circumcised; specif., not Jewish; gentile **2.** [Archaic] heathen

un·civ·il (un siv′'l) *adj.* not civil or courteous; ill-mannered —see SYN. at RUDE —**un·civ′il·ly** *adv.*

un·civ·i·lized (-siv′ə līzd′) *adj.* **1.** not civilized; barbarous **2.** far from civilization

un·clad (-klad′) *adj.* wearing no clothes; naked

un·clasp (-klasp′) *vt.* **1.** to unfasten the clasp of **2.** to release from a clasp or grasp

un·cle (uŋ′k'l) *n.* [OFr. < L. *avunculus*, one's mother's brother] **1.** the brother of one's father or mother **2.** the husband of one's aunt **3.** [Colloq.] any elderly man: a term of address — ☆**say** (or **cry**) **uncle** to surrender or admit defeat

un·clean (un klēn′) *adj.* **1.** dirty; filthy; foul **2.** not pure according to religious laws **3.** morally impure; unchaste, obscene, etc. —**un·clean′ness** *n.*

un·clean·ly[1] (-klen′lē) *adj.* not cleanly; unclean; dirty [an *uncleanly*, unhealthful room] —**un·clean′li·ness** *n.*

un·clean·ly[2] (-klēn′lē) *adv.* in an unclean manner

un·clench (-klench′) *vt., vi.* to open: said of something clenched, or clinched: also **un·clinch′** (-klinch′)

☆**Uncle Sam** [< abbrev. U.S.] [Colloq.] the U.S. (government or people), pictured as a tall man with chin whiskers, dressed in a red, white, and blue suit

☆**Uncle Tom** [after an elderly Negro slave in H. B. STOWE's antislavery novel, *Uncle Tom's Cabin* (1852)] a Negro whose behavior toward whites is thought of as being too humble or flattering: a term showing contempt —**Uncle Tom′ism**

un·cloak (un klōk′) *vt., vi.* **1.** to remove a cloak or other covering (from) **2.** to reveal; expose

un·close (-klōz′) *vt., vi.* **-closed′, -clos′ing** to open

un·clothe (-klōth′) *vt.* **-clothed′** or **-clad′, -cloth′ing** to strip of or as of clothes; uncover; divest

un·coil (-koil′) *vt., vi.* to take out of a coiled condition; unwind

un·blam′a·ble	un·bur′ied	un·change′a·ble	un·clas′si·fied
un·bleached′	un·burned′	un·changed′	un·cleaned′
un·blem′ished	un·burnt′	un·chap′er·oned′	un·clear′
un·blink′ing	un·busi′ness·like′	un′char·ac·ter·is′tic	un·cleared′
un·bought′	un·caged′	un·charged′	un·clipped′
un·bound′	un·can′celed	un·char′tered	un·clog′
un·braced′	un′ca·non′i·cal	un·chaste′	un·cloud′ed
un·braid′	un·car′ing	un·chas′tened	un·clut′tered
un·branched′	un·car′pet·ed	un·checked′	un·coat′ed
un·brand′ed	un·cat′a·loged′	un·cher′ished	un·cocked′
un·break′a·ble	un·caught′	un·chewed′	un′col·lect′a·ble
un·breath′a·ble	un·ceas′ing	un·chilled′	un′col·lect′ed
un·bridge′a·ble	un·cel′e·brat′ed	un·chiv′al·rous	un′col·lect′i·ble
un·broth′er·ly	un·cen′sored	un·cho′sen	un·col′o·nized′
un·bruised′	un·cen′sured	un·chris′tened	un·col′ored
un·brushed′	un·cer′ti·fied′	un·claimed′	un·combed′
un·budg′et·ed	un·chain′	un·clar′i·fied	un′com·bin′a·ble
un·built′	un·chal′lenged	un·clas′si·fi′a·ble	un′com·bined′

un·com·fort·a·ble (-kumf'tər b'l, -kum'fər tə b'l) *adj.*
1. not comfortable; feeling discomfort 2. not pleasant or agreeable; causing discomfort [*uncomfortable* new shoes; an *uncomfortable* pause in the conversation] 3. ill at ease [she is *uncomfortable* with strangers] —**un·com'fort·a·bly** *adv.*

un·com·mit·ted (un'kə mit'id) *adj.* 1. not committed or carried out, as a crime 2. not bound or pledged, as to certain principles 3. not having taken a position; neutral 4. not imprisoned 5. not committed to a mental hospital

un·com·mon (un käm'ən) *adj.* 1. not common; rare; not usual 2. strange; remarkable; extraordinary —see SYN. at RARE¹ —**un·com'mon·ly** *adv.* —**un·com'mon·ness** *n.*

un·com·mu·ni·ca·tive (un'kə myōō'nə kāt'iv, -ni kə tiv) *adj.* not communicative; tending to keep one's opinions, feelings, etc. to oneself; reserved; taciturn —**un'com·mu'ni·ca'tive·ly** *adv.* —**un'com·mu'ni·ca'tive·ness** *n.*

un·com·pro·mis·ing (un käm'prə mī'ziŋ) *adj.* not giving in at all; firm; inflexible

un·con·cern (un'kən surn') *n.* 1. lack of interest; indifference 2. lack of concern, or worry

un·con·cerned (-kən surnd') *adj.* not concerned; specif., *a)* not interested *b)* not worried or anxious —see SYN. at INDIFFERENT —**un'con·cern'ed·ly** (-sur'nid lē) *adv.*

un·con·di·tion·al (-kən dish'ən 'l) *adj.* not depending on any conditions; absolute [an *unconditional* guarantee] —**un'con·di'tion·al·ly** *adv.*

un·con·di·tioned (-kən dish'ənd) *adj.* 1. *same as* UNCONDITIONAL 2. *Psychol.* not a result of conditioning; natural; inborn [an *unconditioned* reflex]

un·con·scion·a·ble (un kän'shən ə b'l) *adj.* 1. not guided or held back by conscience; unscrupulous 2. unreasonable, excessive, etc. [he kept me waiting for an *unconscionable* length of time] —**un·con'scion·a·bly** *adv.*

un·con·scious (-kän'shəs) *adj.* 1. not conscious; unable to feel and think [*unconscious* from a blow on the head] 2. not aware [*unconscious* of his mistake] 3. not doing or done on purpose [an *unconscious* habit] —**the unconscious** *Psychoanalysis* the sum of all memories, thoughts, feelings, etc. of which the individual is not conscious but which influence his emotions and behavior —**un·con'scious·ly** *adv.* —**un·con'scious·ness** *n.*

un·con·sid·ered (un'kən sid'ərd) *adj.* 1. not considered; not kept in mind 2. not a result of careful thinking [a hasty, *unconsidered* remark]

un·con·sti·tu·tion·al (un'kän stə tōō'shən 'l, -tyōō'-) *adj.* not in agreement with or permitted by a constitution, specif. the U.S. Constitution —☆**un'con·sti·tu'tion·al'i·ty** (-shə nal'ə tē) *n.* —**un'con·sti·tu'tion·al·ly** *adv.*

un·con·ven·tion·al (un'kän ven'shən 'l) *adj.* not conforming to customary, formal, or accepted practices, standards, etc. [an *unconventional* tennis serve] —**un'con·ven·tion·al'i·ty** (-shə nal'ə tē) *n.* —**un'con·ven'tion·al·ly** *adv.*

un·cork (un kôrk') *vt.* 1. to pull the cork out of 2. [Colloq.] to let out, let loose, etc. [she *uncorked* a wild scream]

un·count·ed (-koun'tid) *adj.* 1. not counted 2. too many to be counted; innumerable

un·cou·ple (-kup'l) *vt.* **-pled, -pling** to unfasten (things joined together); disconnect —*vi.* to become unfastened

un·couth (-kōōth') *adj.* [OE. *uncuth*, unknown < *un-*, not + *cuth*, pp. of *cunnan*, to know] 1. awkward; clumsy; ungainly 2. uncultured; crude; boorish [*uncouth* manners] —**un·couth'ly** *adv.* —**un·couth'ness** *n.*

un·cov·er (-kuv'ər) *vt.* 1. to make known; disclose 2. to lay bare by removing a covering 3. to remove the cover or protection from 4. to remove the hat, cap, etc. from (the head), as in showing respect —*vi.* to take off one's hat, etc., as in showing respect

un·cross (-krôs') *vt.* to change back from a crossed position [to *uncross* one's legs]

unc·tion (uŋk'shən) *n.* [L. *unctio* < *ungere*, to anoint] 1. *a)* the act of anointing, as in medical treatment or a religious ceremony *b)* the oil, ointment, etc. used for this 2. anything that soothes or comforts 3. *a)* a very emotional or deeply serious manner of speaking or behaving, esp. about religious matters *b)* such a manner when it is pretended or seems put on

unc·tu·ous (uŋk'choo wəs) *adj.* [< ML. < L. *unctum*, ointment < *ungere*, to anoint] 1. of, like, or characteristic of an ointment; oily or greasy 2. making a false show of deep or sincere feeling, as in trying to persuade; too smooth in speech, manners, etc. —**unc'tu·os'i·ty** (-wäs'ə tē), **unc'tu·ous·ness** *n.* —**unc'tu·ous·ly** *adv.*

un·cut (un kut') *adj.* not cut; specif., *a)* having untrimmed margins: said of the pages of a book *b)* not ground to shape: said of a gem *c)* not abridged or shortened

un·daunt·ed (-dôn'tid, -dän'-) *adj.* not daunted; not afraid or discouraged; undismayed [*undaunted* by defeat] —**un·daunt'ed·ly** *adv.*

un·de·ceive (un'di sēv') *vt.* **-ceived', -ceiv'ing** to cause to be no longer deceived, mistaken, or misled

un·de·cid·ed (-di sīd'id) *adj.* 1. that is not decided or settled [an *undecided* issue] 2. not having come to a decision [we remain *undecided*] —**un'de·cid'ed·ly** *adv.* —**un'de·cid'ed·ness** *n.*

un·de·ni·a·ble (-di nī'ə b'l) *adj.* 1. that cannot be denied [what you say is *undeniable*] 2. unquestionably good or excellent [a book of *undeniable* worth] —**un'de·ni'a·bly** *adv.*

un·der (un'dər) *prep.* [OE.] 1. in, at, or to a position down from; below [*under* the chair] 2. beneath the surface of [*under* water] 3. below and to the other side of [to drive *under* a bridge] 4. covered or concealed by [a vest *under* a coat] 5. *a)* lower in authority, position, etc. than [a rank just *under* that of captain] *b)* lower in value, amount, etc. than [to buy *under* cost] *c)* lower than the required degree of [*under* age] 6. *a)* subject to the control, government, direction, influence, etc. of [he served *under* two presidents] *b)* bound by [*under* oath] *c)* receiving the effect of; undergoing [*under* repair] 7. with the character, disguise, etc. of [*under* an alias] 8. in (the desig-

un·come'ly	un'con·gealed'	un·cooked'	un·dat'ed
un·com'fort·ed	un'con·gen'ial	un'co·op'er·a·tive	un'de·bat'a·ble
un·com'mis'sioned	un'con·nect'ed	un'co·or'di·nat'ed	un'de·cayed'
un·com'pen·sat'ed	un'con·quer·a·ble	un'cor·rect'ed	un'de·ci'pher·a·ble
un·com·plain'ing	un'con·quered	un'cor·rob'o·rat'ed	un'de·clared'
un·com'plet'ed	un'con·sci·en'tious	un'cor·rupt'ed	un'de·clin'a·ble
un·com'pli·cat'ed	un'con·se'crat'ed	un·count'a·ble	un'dec'o·rat'ed
un·com·pli·men'ta·ry	un'con·soled'	un·crate'	un'de·feat'a·ble
un·com·ply'ing	un'con·sol'i·dat'ed	un·cred'it·ed	un'de·feat'ed
un·com'pound'ed	un'con·strained'	un·crit'i·cal	un'de·fend'ed
un·com·pre·hend'ing	un'con·strict'ed	un·crowd'ed	un'de·filed'
un·com·pressed'	un'con·sumed'	un·crowned'	un'de·fin'a·ble
un·con·cealed'	un'con·tam'i·nat'ed	un·crys'tal·lized'	un'de·fined'
un·con·cil'i·at'ed	un'con·tem·plat'ed	un·cul'ti·va·ble	un'de·liv'er·a·ble
un·con·clud'ed	un'con·test'ed	un·cul'ti·vat'ed	un'de·mand'ing
un·con·demned'	un'con·tra·dict'a·ble	un·cul'tured	un'dem·o·crat'ic
un·con·densed'	un'con·trived'	un·curbed'	un'de·mon'stra·ble
un·con·du'cive	un'con·trol'la·ble	un·cured'	un'de·mon'stra·tive
un·con·fessed'	un'con·trolled'	un·curl'	un'de·nied'
un·con·fined'	un'con·vert'ed	un·cur'tailed'	un'de·nom'i·na'tion·al
un·con·firmed'	un'con·vinced'	un·cush'ioned	un'de·pend'a·ble
un·con·fused'	un'con·vinc'ing	un·dam'aged	un'de·pre'ci·at'ed

nated category) [spiders are classified *under* arachnids] **9.** during the rule of [France *under* Louis XV] **10.** being the subject of [the question *under* discussion] **11.** because of [*under* the circumstances] **12.** by the authority of [*under* her signature] —*adv.* **1.** in or to a lower position; beneath [to pass *under*] **2.** beneath the surface, as of water [to sink *under*] **3.** in or to a subordinate condition [their ruler kept them *under*] **4.** so as to be covered or concealed [the car was snowed *under*] **5.** less in amount, value, etc. [it cost two dollars or *under*] —*adj.* lower in position, authority, rank, amount, degree, etc. [the *under* portion]

un·der- [OE.] *a prefix meaning:* **1.** in, on, to, or from a lower place or side; beneath or below [*undershirt*] **2.** in an inferior or subordinate position or rank [*undergraduate*] **3.** too little, not enough, below normal [*underdeveloped*]: the list below includes some common compounds formed with *under* that can be understood if *too little* or *not enough* is added to the meaning of the base word

underactive	undermanned
underbake	underpopulated
underconsumption	underprice
undercook	undersubscribe
underemphasize	undersupply
underexercise	undertrained

☆**un·der·a·chieve** (un'dər ə chēv') *vi.* **-chieved'**, **-chiev'ing** to fail to do as well in school studies as might be expected from scores made on intelligence tests —**un'der·a·chieve'ment** *n.* —**un'der·a·chiev'er** *n.*

un·der·act (-akt') *vt., vi.* to act (a theatrical role) with too little emphasis or too great restraint

un·der·age (-āj') *adj.* **1.** not of full or mature age **2.** below the age required by law

un·der·arm (un'dər ärm') *adj.* **1.** under the arm; in the armpit **2.** *same as* UNDERHAND (sense 1) —*adv. same as* UNDERHAND (sense 1)

un·der·bel·ly (-bel'ē) *n.* **1.** the lower, rear part of an animal's belly **2.** any vulnerable or unprotected area or part that can be easily attacked

un·der·bid (un'dər bid'; *for n.* un'dər bid') *vt., vi.* **-bid'**, **-bid'ding** **1.** to bid lower than (another person) **2.** to bid less than the worth of —*n.* a lower or inadequate bid

un·der·bod·y (un'dər bäd'ē) *n.* **1.** the underpart of an animal's body **2.** the undersurface of a vehicle

un·der·bred (un'dər bred') *adj.* **1.** lacking good manners; ill-bred; impolite **2.** not of pure breed

☆**un·der·brush** (un'dər brush') *n.* small trees, shrubs, etc. that grow beneath large trees in woods or forests

un·der·buy (un'dər bī') *vt., vi.* **-bought'**, **-buy'ing** **1.** to buy at less than the real value **2.** to buy more cheaply than (another or others)

un·der·cap·i·tal·ize (-kap'ə tə līz') *vt., vi.* **-ized'**, **-iz'ing** to provide (a business) with too little capital for it to be successful —**un'der·cap'i·tal·i·za'tion** *n.*

un·der·car·riage (un'dər kar'ij) *n.* a supporting frame or structure, as of an automobile

un·der·charge (un'dər chärj'; *for n.* un'dər chärj') *vt., vi.* **-charged'**, **-charg'ing** **1.** to charge too low a price (to) **2.** to provide with too little or low a charge —*n.* a charge that is too little or low

☆**un·der·class** (un'dər klas') *n.* the class of people at the lowest social and economic level, with less income than is needed to maintain themselves

☆**un·der·class·man** (un'dər klas'mən) *n., pl.* **-men** a freshman or sophomore

un·der·clothes (un'dər klōz', -klōthz') *n.pl. same as* UNDERWEAR: also **un'der·cloth'ing** (-klōth'iŋ)

un·der·coat (-kōt') *n.* **1.** a coating of tarlike material applied to the undersurface of a car, etc. to retard rust, etc. **2.** a coat of paint, varnish, etc. applied as a first coat or before the final coat Also **un'der·coat'ing** —*vt.* to apply an undercoat to

un·der·cool (un'dər kool') *vt., vi. same as* SUPERCOOL

☆**un·der·cov·er** (-kuv'ər) *adj.* acting or done in secret

un·der·cur·rent (un'dər kur'ənt) *n.* **1.** a current flowing below another or beneath the surface **2.** an underlying tendency, opinion, etc., usually one that is kept hidden and not expressed openly

un·der·cut (un'dər kut'; *for v.* un'dər kut') *n.* **1.** a cut made below another so as to leave an overhang **2.** *Sports* an undercutting; a thing undercut —*adj.* that is undercut —*vt.* **-cut'**, **-cut'ting** **1.** to make an undercut (sense 1) in **2.** to cut out the underpart of **3.** to undersell or work for lower wages than [he *undercut* his business

rival] **4.** to weaken the position of; undermine [she *undercut* his reputation] **5.** *Sports* to strike (a ball) with a slanting downward motion, as in golf, or to chop with an underhand stroke, as in tennis, esp. so as to give backspin to the ball —*vi.* to undercut someone or something

un·der·de·vel·op (un'dər di vel'əp) *vt.* **1.** to develop to a point below what is needed **2.** to develop (a photographic film, etc.) for too short a time or with a weak developer

un·der·de·vel·oped (-əpt) *adj.* not developed to a desirable degree; specif., poorly developed economically and having few or no industries [*underdeveloped* nations]

un·der·do (-doo') *vt.* **-did'**, **-done'**, **-do'ing** to do less than is usual, needed, or desired

☆**un·der·dog** (un'dər dôg') *n.* **1.** the one that is losing, as in a contest **2.** a person who is handicapped or has been treated unjustly, unfairly, etc.

un·der·done (un'dər dun') *adj.* not cooked enough, as meat

un·der·em·ployed (-im ploid') *adj.* **1.** employed at less than full time **2.** working at low-skilled, poorly paid jobs when one can do more skilled work —**the underemployed** underemployed people —**un'der·em·ploy'ment** *n.*

un·der·es·ti·mate (-es'tə māt'; *for n.* -mit) *vt., vi.* **-mat'ed**, **-mat'ing** to set too low an estimate on or for —*n.* an estimate that is too low —**un'der·es'ti·ma'tion** *n.*

un·der·ex·pose (-ik spōz') *vt.* **-posed'**, **-pos'ing** to expose (a photographic film, etc.) to inadequate light or for too short a time —**un'der·ex·po'sure** (-spō'zhər) *n.*

un·der·feed (-fēd') *vt.* **-fed'**, **-feed'ing** to feed less than is needed

un·der·foot (un'dər foot') *adv., adj.* **1.** under the foot or feet ☆**2.** in the way, as of one walking

un·der·fur (un'dər fur') *n.* the softer, finer fur under the outer coat of some animals, as beavers or seals

un·der·gar·ment (-gär'mənt) *n.* a piece of underwear

un·der·gird (un'dər gurd') *vt.* **-gird'ed** or **-girt'**, **-gird'ing** **1.** to gird or strengthen from the bottom side [to *undergird* a bridge] **2.** to supply support for [to *undergird* a theory]

un·der·go (-gō') *vt.* **-went'**, **-gone'**, **-go'ing** to have happen to one; experience; endure; go through

un·der·grad·u·ate (-graj'oo wit) *n.* a student at a university or college who has not yet received a bachelor's degree

un·der·ground (un'dər ground'; *for n.* -ground') *adj.* **1.** occurring, working, etc. beneath the surface of the earth **2.** done or working in secret; undercover **3.** describing or of newspapers, movies, etc. that are unconventional, experimental, radical, etc. and not usually intended to make money —*adv.* **1.** beneath the surface of the earth **2.** in or into secrecy or hiding —*n.* **1.** the entire region beneath the surface of the earth **2.** a group of people working secretly against the government in power or against enemy forces occupying their country **3.** [Brit.] a subway

underground railroad **1.** a subway: also **underground railway** ☆**2.** [*often* U- R-] in the U.S. before the Civil War, a system set up by abolitionists to help fugitive slaves to escape to Free States and Canada

un·der·growth (-grōth') *n. same as* UNDERBRUSH

un·der·hand (un'dər hand') *adj.* **1.** performed with the arm below the level of the shoulder [an *underhand* throw] **2.** *same as* UNDERHANDED (sense 1) —*adv.* **1.** with an underhand motion **2.** underhandedly; secretly; slyly

un·der·hand·ed (un'dər han'did) *adj.* **1.** secret, sly, deceitful, etc. [*underhanded* dealings] **2.** lacking workers, players, etc.; shorthanded —see SYN. at SECRET —**un'der·hand'ed·ly** *adv.* —**un'der·hand'ed·ness** *n.*

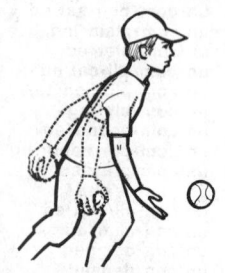

UNDERHAND PITCH

un·der·lay (un'dər lā'; *for n.* un'dər lā') *vt.* **-laid'**, **-lay'ing** **1.** to cover the bottom of [the leather is *underlaid* with felt] **2.** to raise or support with something laid underneath [trusses *underlay* the roof] —*n.* something laid underneath; specif., patches of paper laid under type to raise it

un·der·lie (-lī') *vt.* **-lay'**, **-lain'**, **-ly'ing** **1.** to lie under or beneath [rock *underlies* the field] **2.** to form the basis or foundation of [what evidence *underlies* this theory?]

un·der·line (un'dər līn'; *also, for v.*, un'dər līn') *vt.* **-lined'**, **-lin'ing** **1.** to draw a line beneath; underscore [to *underline* a word] **2.** to stress or emphasize [he *underlined* his warning by shouting] —*n. same as* UNDERSCORE

un·der·ling (un′dər liŋ) *n.* [OE.: see UNDER- & -LING[1]] a person who must carry out the orders of others above him; inferior: a term used to show contempt

un·der·lin·ing (-līn′iŋ) *n.* a garment lining formed of pieces cut to the shape of and attached to the sections of a garment, which are then sewed together

un·der·lip (-lip′) *n.* the lower lip

un·der·ly·ing (un′dər lī′iŋ) *adj.* **1.** lying under; placed beneath [an *underlying* layer of clay] **2.** fundamental; basic [the *underlying* cause] **3.** really there but not easily seen or usually noticed [an *underlying* trend]

un·der·mine (un′dər mīn′, un′dər mīn′) *vt.* **-mined′, -min′ing** **1.** to dig beneath, so as to form a tunnel or mine [to *undermine* a fort] **2.** to wear away and weaken the supports of [erosion is *undermining* the wall] **3.** to injure, weaken, or impair, esp. in a slow or stealthy way [his health has been *undermined* by his smoking]

un·der·most (un′dər mōst′) *adj., adv.* lowest in place, position, rank, etc.

un·der·neath (un′dər nēth′) *adv.* [OE. *underneothan*] **1.** under; below; beneath **2.** at a lower level —*prep.* **1.** under; below; beneath **2.** under the form, appearance, or authority of [*underneath* his cold manner he's warmhearted] —*adj.* under or lower —*n.* the underpart

un·der·nour·ish (-nur′ish) *vt.* to provide with less food than is needed for health and growth —**un′der·nour′ish·ment** *n.*

☆**un·der·pants** (un′dər pants′) *n.pl.* an undergarment, long or short, for the lower part of the body, with a separate opening for each leg

un·der·part (-pärt′) *n.* the lower part or side, as of an animal's body or an airplane's fuselage

☆**un·der·pass** (-pas′) *n.* a passageway under something; esp., a road that runs under a railway or highway

un·der·pay (un′dər pā′) *vt., vi.* **-paid′, -pay′ing** to pay too little, or less than is right —**un′der·pay′ment** *n.*

un·der·pin (-pin′) *vt.* **-pinned′, -pin′ning** to support or strengthen from beneath, as with props

un·der·pin·ning (un′dər pin′iŋ) *n.* **1.** a supporting structure, esp. one placed beneath a wall **2.** a support or prop ☆**3.** [*pl.*] [Colloq.] the legs

un·der·play (un′dər plā′) *vt., vi.* **1.** to act (a role or scene) in a manner intended to be subtle and restrained **2.** *same as* UNDERACT

un·der·priv·i·leged (-priv′′l ijd, -priv′lijd) *adj.* deprived of basic social rights and security because of being poor, discriminated against, etc. —**the underprivileged** underprivileged people

un·der·pro·duce (-prə dōōs′, -dyōōs′) *vt., vi.* **-duced′, -duc′ing** to produce in a quantity that fails to meet the need or demand —**un′der·pro·duc′tion** *n.*

un·der·rate (-rāt′) *vt.* **-rat′ed, -rat′ing** to rate, assess, or estimate too low

un·der·score (un′dər skôr′; *for n.* un′dər skôr′) *vt.* **-scored′, -scor′ing** *same as* UNDERLINE —*n.* a line drawn under a word, passage, etc., as for emphasis

un·der·sea (-sē′) *adj., adv.* beneath the surface of the sea: also **un′der·seas′** (-sēz′) *adv.*

un·der·sec·re·tar·y (-sek′rə ter′ē) *n., pl.* **-tar′ies** an assistant secretary: in U.S. government, **under secretary**

un·der·sell (-sel′) *vt.* **-sold′, -sell′ing** **1.** to sell at a lower price than (another seller) ☆**2.** to publicize or promote in a restrained or inadequate manner

☆**un·der·sexed** (-sekst′) *adj.* having a weaker than normal sexual drive or interest

un·der·sher·iff (un′dər sher′if) *n.* a deputy sheriff

☆**un·der·shirt** (un′dər shurt′) *n.* a collarless, usually sleeveless undergarment worn under an outer shirt, esp. by men and boys

un·der·shoot (un′dər shōōt′) *vt.* **-shot′, -shoot′ing** **1.** to shoot or fall short of (a target, mark, etc.) **2.** to bring an aircraft down short of (the runway, etc.) in landing it —*vi.* to shoot or go short of the mark

☆**un·der·shorts** (un′dər shôrts′) *n.pl.* short underpants worn by men and boys

un·der·shot (-shät′) *adj.* **1.** with the lower part jutting out past the upper [an *undershot* jaw] **2.** driven by water flowing along the lower part [an *undershot* water wheel]

un·der·side (-sīd′) *n.* the side or surface underneath

un·der·sign (un′dər sīn′) *vt.* to sign one's name at the end of (a letter, document, etc.) —**the undersigned** the person or persons undersigning

un·der·sized (-sīzd′) *adj.* smaller in size than is usual, average, or proper: also **un′der·size′**

UNDERSHOT WHEEL

un·der·slung (-sluŋ′) *adj.* **1.** attached to the underside of the axles: said of an automobile frame **2.** projecting: said of the lower jaw

un·der·staffed (un′dər staft′) *adj.* having too small a staff; having fewer personnel than needed

un·der·stand (un′dər stand′) *vt.* **-stood′, -stand′ing** [OE. *understandan*, lit., to stand under] **1.** to get or know the meaning of [do you *understand* the question?] **2.** to get as an idea or notion from what is heard, known, etc.; infer [I *understand* you're new here] **3.** to take as meant or meaning; interpret [he *understood* my silence as disapproval] **4.** to take for granted or as a fact [it is *understood* no one is to leave] **5.** to supply mentally (an idea, word, etc.) in order to make the grammar clear [in the sentence "She is taller than I," the word "am" is *understood* at the end] **6.** to get as information; learn [we *understand* he's the coach] **7.** to know clearly or fully the nature, character, etc. of [he *understands* his job] **8.** to know the feelings of and have sympathy toward [no one *understands* me] —*vi.* **1.** to have understanding, comprehension, etc., either in general or with reference to something specific [she *understands* quickly] **2.** to be informed; believe [he has left, I *understand*] —**un′der·stand′a·ble** *adj.* —**un′der·stand′a·bly** *adv.*

SYN.—*understand* and *comprehend* are both used to imply clear perception of the meaning of something, but *understand* stresses the full awareness or knowledge arrived at, while *comprehend* stresses the process of grasping something mentally [a foreigner may *comprehend* the words of some phrase of American slang without actually *understanding* what the whole phrase means]; *appreciate* implies a clear, sensitive and careful perception of the exact worth or value of something [to *appreciate* the skills needed for such a task]

un·der·stand·ing (-iŋ) *n.* **1.** the act, state, or feeling of a person who understands; comprehension, knowledge, sympathetic awareness, etc. [his talk gave us a better *understanding* of the problem] **2.** the power to think, learn, judge, etc.; intelligence; sense [a man of keen *understanding*] **3.** an explanation or interpretation [tell us your *understanding* of the poem] **4.** *a)* agreement, as of ideas, intentions, etc. among persons *b)* an agreement, esp. one that settles a dispute or is informal [the feuding families have reached an *understanding*] —*adj.* that understands; having or showing comprehension, sympathy, etc. [an *understanding* friend] —**un′der·stand′ing·ly** *adv.*

un·der·state (un′dər stāt′) *vt.* **-stat′ed, -stat′ing** **1.** to make a weaker statement of than is allowed by truth, accuracy, or importance [don't *understate* your case] **2.** to express in a restrained style [*understated* grief] —**un′der·state′ment** *n.*

un·der·stood (-stood′) *pt. & pp. of* UNDERSTAND —*adj.* **1.** agreed upon **2.** taken for granted; assumed

un·der·stud·y (un′dər stud′ē) *n., pl.* **-ies** an actor or actress who learns the part of another and stands ready to play the part when necessary —*vt., vi.* **-stud′ied, -stud′y·ing** **1.** to act as an understudy (to) **2.** to learn (a part) as an understudy

un·der·sur·face (-sur′fis) *n. same as* UNDERSIDE

un·der·take (un′dər tāk′) *vt.* **-took′, -tak′en, -tak′ing** **1.** to enter into or upon (a task, journey, etc.); take upon oneself; agree to do **2.** to give a promise or pledge that; contract [he *undertook* to be their guide] **3.** to promise; guarantee [he *undertook* his nephew's education]

un·der·tak·er (un′dər tā′kər; *for 2* un′dər tā′kər) *n.* **1.** a person who undertakes something **2.** *earlier term for* FUNERAL DIRECTOR

un·der·tak·ing (un′dər tā′kiŋ; *also, & for 3 always,* un′dər tā′kiŋ) *n.* **1.** something undertaken; task; enterprise **2.** a promise; guarantee **3.** the business of an undertaker (sense 2) **4.** the act of one who undertakes a task, etc.

fat, āpe, cär; ten, ēven; is, bīte; gō, hôrn, tōōl, look; oil, out; up, fur; get; joy; yet; chin; she; thin, then; zh, leisure; ŋ, ring; ə for a in ago, e in agent, i in sanity, o in comply, u in focus; ′ as in able (ā′b'l); Fr. bal; ë, Fr. coeur; ö, Fr. feu; Fr. mon; ô, Fr. coq; ü, Fr. duc; r, Fr. cri; H, G. ich; kh, G. doch; ‡foreign; ☆ Americanism; < derived from. See inside front cover.

un·der-the-count·er (un′dər *th*ə koun′tər) *adj.* [Colloq.] done, sold, given, etc. secretly in an unlawful or unethical way: also **un′der-the-ta′ble**

un·der·things (-thiŋz′) *n.pl.* women's or girls' underwear

un·der·tone (-tōn′) *n.* **1.** a low tone of sound or voice **2.** a subdued or background color **3.** any underlying quality, factor, element, etc. [an *undertone* of horror]

un·der·tow (-tō′) *n.* [UNDER- + TOW¹] a current of water moving beneath the surface water and in a different direction, as seaward under the surf

un·der·val·ue (un′dər val′yōō) *vt.* **-ued, -u·ing 1.** to value too low, or below the real worth **2.** to regard or esteem too lightly —**un′der·val′u·a′tion** *n.*

☆**un·der·waist** (un′dər wāst′) *n.* an undergarment worn under a waist

un·der·wa·ter (un′dər wôt′ər, -wät′ər) *adj.* **1.** being, done, etc. beneath the surface of the water **2.** used or for use under water —*adv.* beneath the surface of the water

un·der·way (un′dər wā′) *adj.* not at anchor or moored or aground: said of a ship

un·der·wear (un′dər wer′) *n.* clothing worn under one's outer clothes, usually next to the skin, as undershirts, undershorts, slips, bras, etc.

un·der·weight (un′dər wāt′; *also for adj.* un′dər wāt′) *adj.* below what is normal, desirable, or allowed in weight —*n.* less weight than is needed, desired, or allowed

un·der·went (un′dər went′) *pt. of* UNDERGO

un·der·world (un′dər wurld′) *n.* **1.** the mythical world of the dead; Hades **2.** the criminal members of society, or those people who live a life of vice or crime, regarded as a group or class

un·der·write (un′dər rīt′) *vt.* **-wrote′, -writ′ten, -writ′ing 1.** to write under something written; subscribe to, as by one's signature **2.** to agree to buy (an issue of stocks, bonds, etc.) on a given date and at a fixed price, or to guarantee the purchase of (stocks or bonds to be made available to the public) **3.** to agree to pay for the cost of (an undertaking, etc.) **4.** *a)* to sign one's name to (an insurance policy), thus accepting liability *b)* to write an insurance policy for; insure *c)* to take on liability to the amount of (a specified sum) —**un′der·writ′er** *n.*

un·de·sir·a·ble (un′di zīr′ə b'l) *adj.* not desirable; not pleasing or wanted; objectionable —*n.* an undesirable person —**un′de·sir′a·bil′i·ty** *n.* —**un′de·sir′a·bly** *adv.*

un·dies (un′dēz) *n.pl.* [Colloq.] women's or girls' underwear

un·do (un dōō′) *vt.* **-did′, -done′, -do′ing 1.** *a)* to release or untie (a fastening) *b)* to open (a parcel, door, etc.) by this means **2.** to reverse or do away with (something done or its effect) [to *undo* a verdict] **3.** to ruin or destroy [the enemy is completely *undone*] **4.** to upset or perturb [she was *undone* by his criticism] —**un·do′er** *n.*

un·do·ing (-iŋ) *n.* **1.** the act of reversing something that has been done or its effect **2.** ruin or the cause of ruin

un·done¹ (un dun′) *pp. of* UNDO —*adj.* **1.** ruined, disgraced, etc. **2.** emotionally upset; greatly perturbed

un·done² (un dun′) *adj.* not done; not performed, accomplished, completed, etc.

un·doubt·ed (-dout′id) *adj.* not doubted or called in question; certain —**un·doubt′ed·ly** *adv.*

un·draw (-drô′) *vt., vi.* **-drew′, -drawn′, -draw′ing** to draw (a curtain, drapes, etc.) open, back, or aside

un·dreamed (-drēmd′) *adj.* not even dreamed (*of*) or imagined [glory *undreamed* of]: also **un·dreamt′** (-dremt′)

un·dress (un dres′; *for n. usually* un′dres′) *vt.* **1.** to take off the clothing of; strip **2.** to remove the dressing from (a wound) —*vi.* to take off one's clothes; strip —*n.* **1.** the state of being naked, partly clothed, in a robe, etc. **2.** ordinary clothing or informal dress, as opposed to uniform, full dress, etc.

Und·set (ōōn′set), **Si·grid** (si′gri; *E.* si′grid) 1882–1949; Norw. novelist

un·due (un dōō′, -dyōō′) *adj.* **1.** not yet due or payable [*undue* bills] **2.** not suitable; improper [*undue* flippancy] **3.** too much; excessive [*undue* haste]

un·du·lant (un′joo lənt, -dyoo-; -doo-) *adj.* moving in or as in waves; undulating

undulant fever a form of brucellosis, transmitted to man from domestic animals or their products, and marked by a fever that keeps coming back, sweating, and pains in the joints

un·du·late (-lāt′; *for adj. usually* -lit) *vt.* **-lat′ed, -lat′ing** [< L. *undulatus*, undulated, ult. < *unda*, a wave] **1.** to cause to move in waves **2.** to give a wavy form, surface, etc. to —*vi.* **1.** to move in waves [an *undulating* worm] **2.** to have a wavy form, surface, etc. [*undulating* plains] —*adj.* having a wavy form, margin, or surface: also **un′du·lat′ed** —**un′du·la·to′ry** *adj.*

un·du·la·tion (un′joo lā′shən, -dyoo-, -doo-) *n.* **1.** an undulating or undulating motion **2.** a wavy, curving form or outline, esp. one of a series **3.** *Physics* wave motion, as of light or sound, or a wave or vibration

un·du·ly (un dōō′lē, -dyōō′-) *adv.* beyond what is proper or right; too much [*unduly* alarmed]

un·dy·ing (-dī′iŋ) *adj.* not dying; immortal or eternal

un·earned (-urnd′) *adj.* **1.** not earned by work or service; specif., obtained as a return on an investment [*unearned* income] **2.** not deserved; unmerited

un·earth (-urth′) *vt.* **1.** to dig up from out of the earth **2.** to bring to light; discover or disclose

un·earth·ly (-urth′lē) *adj.* **1.** not, or as if not, of this earth [an *unearthly* light] **2.** supernatural; ghostly [an *unearthly* apparition] **3.** weird; mysterious [*unearthly* noises] **4.** [Colloq.] fantastic, outlandish, etc. [an *unearthly* costume] —see SYN. at WEIRD —**un·earth′li·ness** *n.*

un·eas·y (-ē′zē) *adj.* **-eas′i·er, -eas′i·est 1.** having, showing, or allowing no ease of body or mind; uncomfortable **2.** awkward; constrained [an *uneasy* smile] **3.** worried; anxious —**un·ease′, un·eas′i·ness** *n.* —**un·eas′i·ly** *adv.*

un·ed·it·ed (-ed′it id) *adj.* **1.** not edited for publication **2.** not put together for presentation [an *unedited* film]

un·em·ploy·a·ble (un′im ploi′ə b'l) *adj.* not employable; specif., that cannot be employed because of age, physical disability, mental retardation, etc. —*n.* an unemployable person

un·em·ployed (-im ploid′) *adj.* **1.** not employed; having no job or work **2.** not being used; idle [*unemployed* resources] —**the unemployed** people who are out of work

un·em·ploy·ment (-im ploi′mənt) *n.* **1.** the state of being unemployed **2.** the number or percentage of persons in the normal labor force who are out of work

un·de·served′	un′dip·lo·mat′ic	un′dis·tract′ed	un′e·co·nom′i·cal
un·de·serv′ing	un′di·rect′ed	un′dis·tressed′	un·ed′i·fy·ing
un·des′ig·nat·ed	un·dis·cern′i·ble	un′dis·trib′ut·ed	un·ed′u·cat·ed
un·de·sign′ing	un′dis·cern′ing	un′dis·turbed′	un·ef·faced′
un·de·sired′	un·dis·charged′	un′di·ver′si·fied′	un′e·man′ci·pat·ed
un·de·sir′ous	un′dis·ci·plined′	un′di·vert′ed	un′em·bar′rassed
un·de·stroyed′	un′dis·closed′	un′di·vest′ed	un·em·bel′lished
un′de·tach′a·ble	un′dis·cour′aged	un′di·vid′ed	un′e·mo′tion·al
un′de·tect′ed	un′dis·cov′er·a·ble	un′di·vulged′	un·em·phat′ic
un′de·ter′mi·na·ble	un′dis·cov′ered	un·doc′u·ment′ed	un·emp′tied
un′de·terred′	un′dis·crim′i·nat′ing	un·dog·mat′ic	un′en·closed′
un′de·vel′oped	un′dis·cussed′	un′do·mes′tic	un′en·cum′bered
un′de·vi′at·ing	un′dis·guised′	un′do·mes′ti·cat·ed	un·end′ing
un′de·voured′	un′dis·mayed′	un·drained′	un′en·dorsed′
un′de·vout′	un′dis·pelled′	un′dra·mat′ic	un′en·dowed′
un′dif·fer·en′ti·at′ed	un′dis·posed′	un·draped′	un·en·dur′a·ble
un′dif·fused′	un′dis·put′ed	un·dried′	un·en·force′a·ble
un′di·gest′ed	un′dis·sect′ed	un·drink′a·ble	un′en·gaged′
un′di·gest′i·ble	un′dis·solved′	un·du′ti·ful	un′en·joy′a·ble
un·dig′ni·fied′	un′dis·tilled′	un·dyed′	un′en·light′ened
un′di·lut′ed	un′dis·tin′guish·a·ble	un·eat′a·ble	un′en·riched′
un′di·min′ished	un′dis·tin′guished	un·eat′en	un′en·rolled′
un·dimmed′	un′dis·tort′ed	un′e·clipsed′	un′en·slaved′

un·e·qual (un ē′kwəl) *adj.* **1.** not equal, as in size, strength, ability, value, rank, amount, etc. [they received *unequal* shares] **2.** *a*) not balanced or symmetrical [*unequal* margins] *b*) that matches contestants, etc. unequal in size, strength, etc. [an *unequal* battle] **3.** not even, regular, etc.; variable [an *unequal* flow] **4.** not having the necessary ability, power, courage, etc. (to) [he is *unequal* to the task] —*n.* one that is not equal to another —**un·e′qual·ly** *adv.*

un·e·qualed, un·e·qualled (-ē′kwəld) *adj.* not equaled; unmatched; unrivaled; supreme

un·e·quiv·o·cal (un′i kwiv′ə k′l) *adj.* not equivocal; not ambiguous; very clear in meaning; plain [an *unequivocal* answer of "No!"] —**un′e·quiv′o·cal·ly** *adv.*

un·err·ing (un ur′iŋ, -er′-) *adj.* **1.** free from error [*unerring* judgment] **2.** not missing or failing; sure; exact [with *unerring* regularity] —**un·err′ing·ly** *adv.*

UNESCO (yōō nes′kō) United Nations Educational, Scientific, and Cultural Organization

un·e·ven (un ē′vən) *adj.* not even; specif., *a*) not level, smooth, or flat; rough; irregular [*uneven* ground] *b*) not equal in size, amount, etc. [pencils of *uneven* length] *c*) not uniform; varying [an *uneven* rhythm] *d*) not equally balanced or matched [*uneven* forces] *e*) that leaves a remainder when divided by two; odd [nine is an *uneven* number] —**un·e′ven·ly** *adv.* —**un·e′ven·ness** *n.*

un·ex·am·pled (un′ig zam′p′ld) *adj.* with nothing like it before; without precedent [*unexampled* bravery]

un·ex·cep·tion·a·ble (-ik sep′shə nə b′l) *adj.* not exceptionable; without flaw or fault; not calling for even the slightest criticism [*unexceptionable* behavior] —**un′ex·cep′tion·a·bly** *adv.*

un·ex·cep·tion·al (-ik sep′shən ′l) *adj.* **1.** not uncommon or unusual; ordinary [another *unexceptional* day] **2.** that does not allow for any exception [an *unexceptional* rule] **3.** *same as* UNEXCEPTIONABLE: regarded by some as a loose usage —**un′ex·cep′tion·al·ly** *adv.*

un·ex·pect·ed (-ik spek′tid) *adj.* not expected; unforeseen —**un′ex·pect′ed·ly** *adv.* —**un′ex·pect′ed·ness** *n.*

un·fail·ing (un fāl′iŋ) *adj.* **1.** not failing; constant [his *unfailing* courtesy] **2.** never ceasing or falling short; inexhaustible [an *unfailing* supply] **3.** always reliable; certain [an *unfailing* sign of success] —**un·fail′ing·ly** *adv.*

un·fair (-fer′) *adj.* **1.** not just or impartial; biased; inequitable [an *unfair* decision] **2.** dishonest or unethical in business dealings [*unfair* competitors] —**un·fair′ly** *adv.* —**un·fair′ness** *n.*

un·faith·ful (-fāth′fəl) *adj.* **1.** failing to stay loyal or to keep a vow, promise, etc.; faithless [an *unfaithful* lover] **2.** not true, accurate, or reliable; untrustworthy [an *unfaithful* translation] **3.** guilty of adultery —**un·faith′ful·ly** *adv.* —**un·faith′ful·ness** *n.*

un·fa·mil·iar (un′fə mil′yər) *adj.* **1.** not familiar or well-known; strange [a part of town *unfamiliar* to him] **2.** not knowing about; not acquainted (*with* something) [she is un-

familiar with his plays] —**un′fa·mil′i·ar′i·ty** (-yar′ə tē, -ē ar′-) *n.* —**un′fa·mil′iar·ly** *adv.*

un·fas·ten (un fas′′n) *vt.* to open or make loose; untie, unlock, undo, etc. —*vi.* to become unfastened

un·fa·vor·a·ble (-fā′vər ə b′l, -fāv′rə b′l) *adj.* not favorable; opposed, harmful, disadvantageous, inauspicious, etc. [an *unfavorable* review of a book] —**un·fa′vor·a·bly** *adv.*

un·feel·ing (-fēl′iŋ) *adj.* **1.** without feeling; that cannot feel **2.** hardhearted; cruel [his *unfeeling* refusal to help] —**un·feel′ing·ly** *adv.*

un·feigned (-fānd′) *adj.* genuine; real; sincere [with *unfeigned* joy] —**un·feign′ed·ly** (-fān′id lē) *adv.*

un·fin·ished (-fin′isht) *adj.* **1.** not finished or completed **2.** having no finish, or final coat, as of paint

un·fit (-fit′) *adj.* **1.** not meeting requirements; not fit or suitable [a movie *unfit* for children] **2.** not physically or mentally fit [*unfit* for military service] **3.** not fitted for a given purpose [food *unfit* to eat] —*vt.* **-fit′ted, -fit′ting** to make unfit [the accident *unfitted* him for work] —**un·fit′ly** *adv.* —**un·fit′ness** *n.*

un·fix (-fiks′) *vt.* to unfasten; loosen

un·flap·pa·ble (-flap′ə b′l) *adj.* [see FLAP, *n.* 4] [Colloq.] not easily excited or upset; calm

un·fledged (-flejd′) *adj.* **1.** not fully fledged; unfeathered, as a young bird **2.** immature; undeveloped

un·flinch·ing (-flin′chiŋ) *adj.* steadfast; resolute; unyielding —**un·flinch′ing·ly** *adv.*

un·fold (-fōld′) *vt.* **1.** to open and spread out (something folded) [to *unfold* a newspaper] **2.** to lay open to view; reveal, disclose, display, or explain [to *unfold* plans] **3.** to open up; unwrap [*unfold* the bandage] —*vi.* **1.** to become unfolded, as the blossom of a flower **2.** to develop fully [as the plot of the play *unfolded*]

un·for·tu·nate (-fôr′chə nit) *adj.* **1.** *a*) having bad luck; unlucky *b*) bringing, or coming by, bad luck; unfavorable [an *unfortunate* event] **2.** not suitable or successful [an *unfortunate* choice] —*n.* an unfortunate person —**un·for′tu·nate·ly** *adv.*

un·found·ed (-foun′did) *adj.* not founded on fact or truth; baseless [an *unfounded* rumor]

un·freeze (-frēz′) *vt.* **-froze′, -froz′en, -freez′ing 1.** to cause to thaw [to *unfreeze* meat] ☆**2.** to remove financial controls from (prices, wages, etc.)

un·fre·quent·ed (un′frē kwent′id, un frē′kwənt-) *adj.* seldom visited or frequented [an older, *unfrequented* resort]

un·friend·ed (un fren′did) *adj.* having no friends; friendless

un·friend·ly (-frend′lē) *adj.* **1.** not friendly or kind; hostile **2.** not favorable or propitious —**un·friend′li·ness** *n.*

un·frock (-fräk′) *vt.* **1.** to remove a frock from **2.** to take away from (a priest or minister) the right to continue to be a member of the clergy

un·furl (-furl′) *vt., vi.* to open or unfold (a flag, sail, etc.) that has been furled

un·gain·ly (-gān′lē) *adj.* **1.** awkward; clumsy **2.** coarse and unattractive —**un·gain′li·ness** *n.*

un′en·tan′gled	un′ex·cused′	un·feared′	un′fore·seen′
un′en·ter·pris′ing	un′ex·e·cut′ed	un·fea′si·ble	un′for·est·ed
un′en·ter·tain′ing	un′ex·er·cised′	un·feath′ered	un′for·feit·ed
un′en·thu′si·as′tic	un′ex·pend′a·ble	un·fed′	un′forged′
un′en·ti′tled	un′ex·pe′ri·enced	un·fed′er·at′ed	un′for·get′ta·ble
un′en′vi·a·ble	un′ex·pired′	un·felt′	un′for·giv′a·ble
un·en′vied	un′ex·plain′a·ble	un·fem′i·nine	un′for·giv′en
un·en′vi·ous	un′ex·plained′	un·fenced′	un′for·giv′ing
un′e·quipped′	un′ex·plod′ed	un′fer·ment′ed	un′for·got′ten
un′es·cort′ed	un′ex·ploit′ed	un·fer′til·ized′	un·formed′
un′es·sen′tial	un′ex·plored′	un·fet′tered	un′for·mu·lat′ed
un′es·tab′lished	un′ex·posed′	un·fil′i·al	un′for·sak′en
un′es·ti·mat′ed	un′ex·pressed′	un·filled′	un′for·ti·fied′
un·eth′i·cal	un′ex·pur′gat·ed	un·fil′tered	un·fought′
un′e·vent′ful	un′ex·tend′ed	un·fired′	un·framed′
un′ex·act′ing	un′ex·tin′guished	un·fit′ting	un·free′
un′ex·ag′ger·at·ed	un·fad′ed	un·flag′ging	un·fruit′ful
un′ex·am′ined	un·fad′ing	un·flat′ter·ing	un·ful′fulled′
un′ex·celled′	un·fal′ter·ing	un·fla′vored	un·fund′ed
un′ex·change′a·ble	un·fash′ion·a·ble	un·for·bid′den	un·fun′ny
un′ex·cit′a·ble	un·fath′om·a·ble	un·forced′	un·fur′nished
un′ex·cit′ing	un·fath′omed	un′fore·see′a·ble	un·gar′nished

Un·ga·va (uŋ gā′və, -gä′-) region in N Quebec, Canada, between Labrador & Hudson Bay

un·glued (-glōōd′) *adj.* broken open; separated: said of things glued together —☆**come unglued** [Slang] to become emotionally upset and very disturbed

un·god·ly (-gäd′lē) *adj.* **1.** not godly or religious; impious [*ungodly* practices] **2.** sinful; wicked [an *ungodly* life] **3.** [Colloq.] outrageous; dreadful [an *ungodly* noise] —*adv.* [Colloq.] outrageously; dreadfully [it's *ungodly* early] —**un·god′li·ness** *n.*

un·gov·ern·a·ble (-guv′ər nə b'l) *adj.* that cannot be governed or controlled; unruly —**un·gov′ern·a·bly** *adv.*

un·gra·cious (-grā′shəs) *adj.* **1.** rude; discourteous; impolite **2.** unpleasant; unattractive —**un·gra′cious·ly** *adv.* —**un·gra′cious·ness** *n.*

un·guard·ed (-gärd′id) *adj.* **1.** unprotected **2.** without guile or cunning; open [a clear, *unguarded* gaze] **3.** careless; thoughtless; imprudent [in an *unguarded* moment] —**un·guard′ed·ly** *adv.*

un·guent (uŋ′gwənt) *n.* [L. *unguentum* < *unguere*, to anoint] a salve or ointment —**un·guen·tar·y** (-gwən ter′ē) *adj.*

un·guis (uŋ′gwis) *n., pl.* **un·gues** (-gwēz) [L., a nail] a nail, claw, or hoof: also **un′gu·la** (-gyōō lə), *pl.* **-lae** (-lē′)

un·gu·late (-gyōō lit, -lāt′) *adj.* [< L. *ungula*, a hoof] having hoofs; of or belonging to a former group of all mammals having hoofs —*n.* a mammal having hoofs

un·hal·lowed (un hal′ōd) *adj.* **1.** not hallowed or consecrated; unholy **2.** wicked; profane

un·hand (-hand′) *vt.* to loose or release from the hand or hands or one's grasp; let go of

un·hand·y (-han′dē) *adj.* **-hand′i·er**, **-hand′i·est 1.** not handy, convenient, or easy to reach **2.** not clever with the hands; awkward —**un·hand′i·ly** *adv.* —**un·hand′i·ness** *n.*

un·hap·py (-hap′ē) *adj.* **-pi·er**, **-pi·est 1.** unlucky; unfortunate **2.** sad; wretched; sorrowful **3.** not suitable [an *unhappy* choice] —**un·hap′pi·ly** *adv.* —**un·hap′pi·ness** *n.*

un·health·y (-hel′thē) *adj.* **-health′i·er**, **-health′i·est 1.** having or showing poor health; sickly; not well **2.** harmful to health; unwholesome [an *unhealthy* climate] **3.** harmful to morals [an *unhealthy* movie] **4.** dangerous or risky [an *unhealthy* situation] —**un·health′i·ly** *adv.* —**un·health′i·ness** *n.*

un·heard (-hurd′) *adj.* **1.** not perceived by the ear **2.** not given a hearing or listened to [his warning went *unheard*]

un·heard-of (-hurd′uv′) *adj.* **1.** not heard of before; unprecedented **2.** unacceptable or outrageous [*unheard-of* behavior]

un·hinge (-hinj′) *vt.* **-hinged′**, **-hing′ing 1.** *a)* to remove from the hinges *b)* to remove the hinges from **2.** to dislodge or detach **3.** to throw (the mind, etc.) into confusion; unbalance or upset

un·his·tor·ic (un′his tôr′ik, -tär′-) *adj.* not historic or historical; specif., *Linguis.* not having a historical basis; accidental, as the *b* in *thumb:* also **un′his·tor′i·cal**

un·hitch (un hich′) *vt.* **1.** to free from a hitch [to *unhitch* a horse] **2.** to unfasten; release; detach

un·ho·ly (-hō′lē) *adj.* **-li·er**, **-li·est 1.** not sacred, hallowed, or consecrated [*unholy* ground] **2.** wicked; profane; impious [*unholy* deeds] **3.** [Colloq.] outrageous; dreadful [*unholy* glee] —**un·ho′li·ness** *n.*

un·hook (-hook′) *vt.* **1.** to remove or loosen from a hook [to *unhook* a fish] **2.** to undo or unfasten the hook or hooks of [to *unhook* a dress] —*vi.* to become unhooked

un·hoped-for (-hōpt′fôr′) *adj.* not to be hoped for; not expected [*unhoped-for* good luck]

un·horse (-hôrs′) *vt.* **-horsed′**, **-hors′ing 1.** to make (a rider) fall from a horse **2.** to overthrow (an opponent)

un·hu·man (-hyōō′mən, -yōō′-) *adj.* **1.** *rare var. of: a)* INHUMAN *b)* SUPERHUMAN **2.** not human in kind, quality, etc. [*unhuman* creatures] —**un·hu′man·ly** *adv.*

u·ni- [< L. *unus*, one] *a combining form meaning* having or consisting of one only [*unicellular*]

U·ni·ate, U·ni·at (yōō′nē at, -at′) *n.* [< Russ. *uniyat*, ult. < L. *unus*, one: from union with the Roman Church] a member of the Eastern Church (sense 1 *b*)

u·ni·cam·er·al (yōō′nə kam′ər əl) *adj.* [< UNI- + LL. *camera*, a chamber] having only one group in the lawmaking body

UNICEF (yōō′nə sef′) United Nations International Children's Emergency Fund

u·ni·cel·lu·lar (yōō′nə sel′yōō lər) *adj.* having or consisting of a single cell

u·ni·corn (yōō′nə kôrn′) *n.* [< OFr. < L. < *unus*, one + *cornu*, a horn] a mythical horselike animal with a single horn growing from the center of its forehead

☆**u·ni·cy·cle** (yōō′nə sī′k'l) *n.* a riding device with only one wheel, which is straddled by the rider

unidentified flying object *same as* UFO

u·ni·fi·ca·tion (yōō′nə fi kā′shən) *n.* the act of unifying or the state of being unified

u·ni·form (yōō′nə fôrm′) *adj.* [< MFr. < L. < *unus*, one + *-formis*, -form] **1.** always the same; not varying in form, rate, degree, manner, etc. [a *uniform* speed] **2.** having the same form, appearance, etc. as others of the same class [a row of *uniform* houses] **3.** consistent in action, effect, etc. [a *uniform* policy] —*n.* the official or special clothes worn by the members of a particular group, as policemen or soldiers —*vt.* ☆to clothe or supply with a uniform —see SYN. at STEADY —**uniform with** having the same form, appearance, etc. as —**u′ni·form′ly** *adv.*

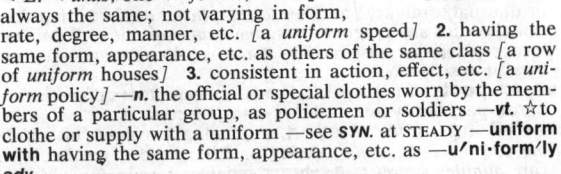

UNICORN

u·ni·formed (-fôrmd′) *adj.* wearing a uniform

u·ni·form·i·ty (yōō′nə fôr′mə tē) *n., pl.* **-ties** state, quality, or instance of being uniform

u·ni·fy (yōō′nə fī′) *vt., vi.* **-fied′**, **-fy′ing** [< MFr. < LL. *unificare:* see UNI- & -FY] to combine into one; become or make united; consolidate —**u′ni·fi′a·ble** *adj.* —**u′ni·fi′er** *n.*

u·ni·lat·er·al (yōō′nə lat′ər əl) *adj.* **1.** of, occurring on, or affecting one side only [*unilateral* paralysis] **2.** involving one only of several parties; done by one only [a *unilateral* decision] **3.** taking into account one side only of a matter; one-sided [a *unilateral* view] **4.** turned to, or having its parts on, one side —**u′ni·lat′er·al·ism** *n.* —**u′ni·lat′er·al·ly** *adv.*

u·ni·lin·e·ar (-lin′ē ər) *adj.* of or following a single, consistent path of development or progression

un·im·peach·a·ble (un′im pēch′ə b'l) *adj.* that cannot be doubted, questioned, or discredited; irreproachable —**un′im·peach′a·bly** *adv.*

un·im·proved (un′im prōōvd′) *adj.* **1.** not bettered, improved, or developed [*unimproved* land, with no buildings on it] **2.** not used to good advantage **3.** not improved in health

---

un·gath′ered	un·guid′ed	un·her′ald·ed	un·im′i·tat′ed
un·gen′er·ous	un·ham′pered	un·he·ro′ic	un·im·paired′
un·gen′tle·man·ly	un·han′dled	un·hes′i·tat′ing	un·im·pas′sioned
un·gen′u·ine	un·hand′some	un·hin′dered	un·im·ped′ed
un·gift′ed	un·hanged′	un·hired′	un·im·ple·ment′ed
un·gird′	un·hard′ened	un·hon′ored	un·im·por′tance
un·glazed′	un·harmed′	un·housed′	un·im·por′tant
un·glo′ri·fied′	un·harm′ful	un·hung′	un·im·pos′ing
un·gloved′	un′har·mo′ni·ous	un·hur′ried	un·im·preg′nat·ed
un·grace′ful	un·har′ness	un·hurt′	un·im·pressed′
un·grad′ed	un·har′rowed	un·hy′gi·en′ic	un·im·pres′sion·a·ble
un·grad′u·at·ed	un·har′vest·ed	un·hy′phen·at′ed	un·im·pres′sive
un′gram·mat′i·cal	un·hatched′	un·i·den′ti·fied	un·in·cor′po·rat′ed
un·grate′ful	un·healed′	un·id·i·o·mat′ic	un·in·dulged′
un·grat′i·fied′	un·health′ful	un·il·lu·mi·nat′ed	un·in·dus′tri·al·ized′
un·greased′	un·heat′ed	un·il·lus·trat′ed	un·in·dus′tri·ous
un·ground′ed	un·heed′ed	un′im·ag′i·na·ble	un·in·fect′ed
un·grudg′ing	un·heed′ing	un′im·ag′i·na·bly	un·in·fest′ed
un·guess′a·ble	un·help′ful	un′im·ag′i·na′tive	un′in·flect′ed

un·in·hib·it·ed (-in hib′it id) *adj.* without inhibition; esp., free from the usual social or psychological restraints

un·in·ter·est·ed (un in′trist id, -in′tər ist-) *adj.* not interested; indifferent —**un·in′ter·est·ed·ly** *adv.*

un·ion (yoōn′yən) *n.* [< MFr. < LL. < L. < *unus,* one] **1.** a uniting or being united; combination; junction; specif., *a*) a grouping together of nations, political groups, etc. for some specific purpose *b*) marriage **2.** something united; a whole made up of united parts; specif., *a*) an organization or confederation uniting various individuals, political units, etc. *b*) *short for* LABOR UNION **3.** a device symbolizing political union, used in a flag or ensign, as the white stars on a blue field in the U.S. flag **4.** a building used for social recreation on a college campus: in full, **student union 5.** a device for joining together parts; esp., a coupling for linking the ends of pipes **6.** *Math.* a set containing all the elements of two or more given sets, with no element listed more than once —see *SYN.* at ALLIANCE and UNITY —☆**the Union** the United States of America

☆**union card** a card which identifies one as a member in good standing of a particular labor union

☆**union catalog** a library catalog combining the catalogs of different libraries or different divisions

Union City [formed by the union of two older towns] city in northeastern N.J.: suburb of Jersey City: pop. 59,000

un·ion·ism (yoōn′yən iz′m) *n.* **1.** *a*) the principle of union *b*) support of this principle or of a specified union **2.** the system or principles of labor unions ☆**3.** [U-] loyalty to the Federal union of the U.S., esp. during the Civil War —**un′ion·ist** *n.*

un·ion·ize (-īz′) *vt.* -ized′, -iz′ing **1.** to organize (a group of workers) into a labor union **2.** to bring under the rules, standards, etc. of a labor union [to *unionize* an industry] —*vi.* to join or organize a labor union —**un′ion·i·za′tion** *n.*

union jack 1. a jack or flag consisting only of a union, esp. of the union of a national flag **2.** [U- J-] the national flag of the United Kingdom

Union of South Africa *former name of* SOUTH AFRICA

Union of Soviet Socialist Republics country in E Europe & N Asia, extending from the Baltic Sea to the Pacific: it is a union of fifteen federated republics: 8,603,000 sq. mi.; pop. 258,000,000; cap. Moscow

☆**union shop** a factory, business, etc. operating under a contract with a labor union, which requires that all new workers must join the union after being hired

☆**union suit** a suit of men's or boys' underwear combining shirt and drawers in a single garment

u·nique (yoō nēk′) *adj.* [Fr. < L. *unicus,* single < *unus,* one] **1.** that is the only one; sole [a *unique* specimen] **2.** having no like or equal; unparalleled [a *unique* accomplishment] **3.** highly unusual, extraordinary, etc.: a common usage still objected to by some —**u·nique′ly** *adv.* —**u·nique′ness** *n.*

☆**u·ni·sex** (yoō′nə seks′) *adj.* [Colloq.] designating or of a fashion, as in clothing, that is the same for men and women

u·ni·sex·u·al (yoō′nə sek′shoō wəl) *adj.* having one sex (male or female) only; not hermaphroditic —**u′ni·sex′u·al′i·ty** (-shoō wal′ə tē) *n.* —**u′ni·sex′u·al·ly** *adv.*

u·ni·son (yoō′nə sən, -zən) *n.* [MFr. < ML. < L. *unus,* one + *sonus,* a sound] **1.** sameness of musical pitch, as of two or more voices or tones **2.** agreement; harmony —**in unison 1.** singing or playing the same note at the same time **2.** with all the voices or instruments performing the same part **3.** uttering the same words, or producing the same sound, at the same time

u·nit (yoō′nit) *n.* [< UNITY] **1.** *a*) the smallest whole number; one *b*) the number in the position just to the left of the decimal point **2.** any fixed quantity, amount, measure, etc. used as a standard [the ounce is a *unit* of weight]; specif., the amount of a drug, vaccine, etc. needed to produce a given result **3.** *a*) a single person or group, esp. as a part of a whole [an army *unit*] *b*) a single, distinct part, esp. one used for a special purpose [the lens *unit* of a camera]

U·ni·tar·i·an (yoō′nə ter′ē ən) *n.* **1.** a person who does not accept the doctrine of the Trinity, believing rather that God exists as only one person or being **2.** a member of a Christian denomination based on this belief and showing tolerance of differing religious views —*adj.* **1.** of Unitarians or their beliefs **2.** [u-] *same as* UNITARY —**U′ni·tar′i·an·ism** *n.*

u·ni·tar·y (yoō′nə ter′ē) *adj.* **1.** of a unit or units **2.** of, based on, or characterized by unity **3.** having the nature of or used as a unit

unit character *Genetics* a character or trait determined by a single gene or gene pair

u·nite (yoō nīt′) *vt., vi.* -nit′ed, -nit′ing [< L. pp. of *unire,* to unite < *unus,* one] **1.** to put or join together so as to make one; combine into a whole [the two sects *united* to form a new church] **2.** *a*) to bring or come together in a common activity, shared interest, etc.; join through fellowship, agreement, etc. [they *united* in singing the anthem] *b*) to join in marriage —see *SYN.* at JOIN

u·nit·ed (yoō nīt′id) *adj.* **1.** combined; joined [the *united* armies of the allies] **2.** of or resulting from joint action or association [a *united* charity drive] **3.** in agreement [we are *united* on that point] —**u·nit′ed·ly** *adv.* —**u·nit′ed·ness** *n.*

United Arab Emirates country consisting of seven Arab sheikdoms in E Arabia, on the Persian Gulf: 32,300 sq. mi.; pop. 179,000

United Arab Republic *former name* (1961-71) *of* EGYPT

United Church of Christ a Protestant denomination formed by a merger of denominations in 1957

United Kingdom country in W Europe, consisting of England, Scotland, Wales, Northern Ireland, the Channel Islands, & the Isle of Man: 94,217 sq. mi.; pop. 55,730,000; cap. London: in full, **United Kingdom of Great Britain and Northern Ireland**

☆**United Nations** an international organization of nations pledged to promote world peace and security under a charter signed in 1945 by 50 nations: 100 additional members had been admitted by 1980: headquarters, New York City

United States of America country made up of the N. American area extending from the Atlantic Ocean to the Pacific Ocean between Canada and Mexico, together with Alaska & Hawaii: 3,615,211 sq. mi.; pop. 219,530,000 (1979 est.); cap. Washington: also called **United States**

u·ni·tive (yoō′nə tiv) *adj.* tending to produce unity

u·nit·ize (yoō′nə tīz′) *vt.* -ized′, -iz′ing to make into a single unit —**u′nit·i·za′tion** *n.*

unit magnetic pole a magnetic pole that, when placed in a vacuum at a distance of one centimeter from an equal and like pole, will repel it with a force of one dyne

unit pricing a system of pricing goods, esp. food items, by also showing the price for a standard unit, as for an ounce or pint, to make it easier to compare prices

u·ni·ty (yoō′nə tē) *n., pl.* -ties [< OFr. < L. *unitas* < *unus,* one] **1.** the state of being one, or united; oneness **2.** a single, separate thing **3.** harmony; agreement; concord [different opinions brought into *unity*] **4.** *a*) unification *b*) a unified group or body **5.** a whole that is a union of related parts **6.** *a*) an arrangement of parts in a work of art or literature, that will produce a single effect *b*) an effect so produced **7.** steadiness of purpose, action, etc. **8.** *Math.* any quantity, magnitude, etc. identified as a unit, or 1

SYN. —**unity** implies the oneness, as in spirit, aims, interests, feelings, etc., of that which is made up of various parts or individuals [national *unity*]; **union** implies the state of being united into a single organization for a common purpose [a labor *union*]; **solidarity** implies such firm and complete unity in an organization, group, class, etc. as to make for the greatest possible strength in influence, action, etc. [political *solidarity*]

Univ. 1. Universalist **2.** University

u·ni·va·lent (yoō′nə vā′lənt, yoō niv′ə lənt) *adj. Chem.* **1.** having one valence **2.** having a valence of one —**u′ni·va′lence, u′ni·va′len·cy** *n.*

un·in′flu·enced	un′in·spired′	un′in·tel′li·gi·ble	un′in·ven′tive
un·in·formed′	un′in·struct′ed	un′in·tend′ed	un′in·vest′ed
un′in·hab′it·a·ble	un′in·sur′a·ble	un′in·ten′tion·al	un′in·vit′ed
un·in·hab′it·ed	un′in·sured′	un′in·ter·est·ing	un′in·vit′ing
un·in·i′ti·at·ed	un·in′te·grat·ed	un′in·ter·rupt′ed	un′in·volved′
un·in·jured	un·in·tel′li·gent	un′in·tim′i·dat·ed	un′is′sued

u·ni·valve (yo͞o'nə valv') *n.* **1.** a mollusk having a one-piece shell, as a snail **2.** such a one-piece shell —*adj.* **1.** having a one-piece shell **2.** having one valve only: also **u'ni·valved'**

u·ni·ver·sal (yo͞o'nə vur's'l) *adj.* [< OFr. < L.: see UNIVERSE] **1.** present or occurring everywhere [a nearly *universal* pollutant in the air we breathe] **2.** of, for, or including all or the whole; not limited [a *universal* human need] **3.** broad in knowledge, interests, etc. [a *universal* mind] **4.** that can be used for all or most kinds, forms, sizes, etc. [a *universal* voltage regulator] **5.** used, intended to be used, or understood by all [a *universal* sign of grief] **6.** *Logic* saying something about every member of a specified class ["all men are mortal" is a *universal* proposition] —*n.* **1.** short for UNIVERSAL JOINT **2.** *Logic* a universal proposition —**u'ni·ver'sal·ness** *n.*
SYN. —**universal** is used of that which applies to every case or individual, without exception, in the class, category, etc. concerned [a *universal* practice among primitive peoples]; **general** refers to that which applies to all or nearly all of the members of a group or class [a *general* favorite among college students]; **generic** is used of that which applies to every member of a class or, specif. in biology, of a genus [a *generic* name]

u·ni·ver·sal·ism (-iz'm) *n.* **1.** *same as* UNIVERSALITY **2.** [U-] the theological doctrine that all souls will eventually be saved

U·ni·ver·sal·ist (-ist) *n.* a believer in Universalism, ☆specif. a member of a U.S. Protestant denomination now merged with the Unitarians —*adj.* ☆of Universalism or Universalists

u·ni·ver·sal·i·ty (yo͞o'nə vər sal'ə tē) *n., pl.* **-ties 1.** quality, state, or instance of being universal **2.** unlimited range, application, occurrence, etc.; comprehensiveness

u·ni·ver·sal·ize (yo͞o'nə vər sal'īz') *vt.* **-ized', -iz'ing** to make universal —**u'ni·ver'sal·i·za'tion** *n.*

universal joint (or **coupling**) a joint or coupling that allows the parts joined to swing in any direction, esp. one used to transmit rotary motion from one shaft to another not in line with it, as in the drive shaft of an automobile

u·ni·ver·sal·ly (yo͞o'nə vur's'l ē) *adv.* **1.** in every case [*universally* true] **2.** in every part or place [a custom practiced *universally*]

universal suffrage suffrage for all adult citizens

u·ni·verse (yo͞o'nə vurs') *n.* [L. *universum* < *unus*, one + pp. of *vertere*, to turn] **1.** the whole system of all the things that exist; the cosmos **2.** the world as the scene of human activity

UNIVERSAL JOINT

u·ni·ver·si·ty (yo͞o'nə vur'sə tē) *n., pl.* **-ties** [< MFr. < ML. < L. *universitas*, the whole, a society < *universus*: see prec.] **1.** an educational institution of the highest level, made up of one or more undergraduate colleges and, usually, graduate and professional schools **2.** the buildings, students, faculty, or administrators of a university

un·joint (un joint') *vt.* **1.** to separate (a joint) **2.** to separate the joints of

un·just (-just') *adj.* not just or right; unfair —**un·just'ly** *adv.* —**un·just'ness** *n.*

un·kempt (-kempt') *adj.* [UN- + *kempt*, pp. of dial. *kemben*, to comb] **1.** not combed **2.** not tidy or neat; messy —**see SYN** at SLOVENLY —**un·kempt'ness** *n.*

un·kind (-kīnd') *adj.* not kind or considerate; hurting the feelings of others; harsh, cruel, etc. —**un·kind'ness** *n.*

un·kind·ly (-kīnd'lē) *adj. same as* UNKIND —*adv.* in an unkind manner —**un·kind'li·ness** *n.*

un·known (-nōn') *adj.* **1.** not in one's knowledge, acquaintance, etc.; unfamiliar (*to*) [a fact *unknown* to most citizens] **2.** not discovered, identified, etc. [containing an *unknown* amount of water] —*n.* an unknown person, thing, or quantity

un·lace (-lās') *vt.* **-laced', -lac'ing** to undo or unfasten the laces of

un·lash (-lash') *vt.* to untie or loosen (something lashed, or tied with a rope, etc.)

un·latch (-lach') *vt., vi.* to open by releasing a latch

un·law·ful (-lô'fəl) *adj.* **1.** against the law; illegal **2.** against moral or ethical standards; immoral —**un·law'ful·ly** *adv.* —**un·law'ful·ness** *n.*

un·lead·ed (-led'id) *adj.* not mixed with tetraethyl lead: said of gasoline

un·learn (-lurn') *vt., vi.* to forget (something learned) by a conscious effort, as in retraining

un·learn·ed (-lur'nid; *for 2* -lurnd') *adj.* **1.** *a*) not learned or educated; ignorant *b*) showing a lack of learning or education **2.** *a*) not learned [*unlearned* lessons] *b*) known without conscious effort or study [*unlearned* tact] —**un·learn'ed·ly** *adv.*

un·leash (-lēsh') *vt.* to release from or as from a leash

un·less (ən les') *conj.* [earlier *on lesse that*, at less than] in any case other than; except if [he won't go *unless* she does]

un·let·tered (un let'ərd) *adj.* **1.** *a*) not educated; ignorant *b*) not knowing how to read or write; illiterate **2.** not marked with letters —**see SYN**·at IGNORANT

un·like (-līk') *adj.* not alike; different; dissimilar —*prep.* **1.** not like; different from [a case *unlike* any one before] **2.** not characteristic of [it's *unlike* her to cry] —**un·like'ness** *n.*

un·like·ly (-līk'lē) *adj.* **1.** not likely; improbable [an *unlikely* story] **2.** not likely to succeed [an *unlikely* candidate] —*adv.* in an unlikely manner; improbably [he may, not *unlikely*, join us] —**un·like'li·hood', un·like'li·ness** *n.*

un·lim·ber[1] (-lim'bər) *adj.* not limber; stiff [*unlimber* fingers] —*vi., vt.* to make or become limber, or supple [tossing a ball to *unlimber* his arm]

un·lim·ber[2] (-lim'bər) *vt., vi.* **1.** to prepare (a field gun) for use by taking off the limber **2.** to get ready for action

un·lim·it·ed (-lim'it id) *adj.* **1.** without limits or restrictions [*unlimited* power] **2.** without boundaries [*unlimited* space]

un·list·ed (-lis'tid) *adj.* not listed; specif., *a*) not publicly listed [an *unlisted* telephone number] *b*) not admitted for trading on the stock exchange: said of securities

un·load (-lōd') *vt.* **1.** *a*) to remove (a load, cargo, etc.) *b*) to take a load or cargo from [to *unload* a truck] **2.** *a*) to express or tell (one's troubles, etc.) freely *b*) to relieve of something that troubles, burdens, etc. **3.** to remove the charge from (a gun) **4.** to get rid of [a company trying to *unload* surplus stock] —*vi.* to unload something

un·lock (-läk') *vt.* **1.** *a*) to open (a lock) *b*) to open the lock of (a door, etc.) **2.** to let loose as if by opening a lock; release [to *unlock* a flood of tears] **3.** to cause to separate [to *unlock* clenched jaws] **4.** to make known; reveal [to *unlock* a secret] —*vi.* to get unlocked

un·looked-for (-lo͞okt'fôr') *adj.* not expected or foreseen

un·loose (-lo͞os') *vt.* **-loosed', -loos'ing** to make or let loose; set free, unfasten, etc.: also **un·loos'en**

un·luck·y (-luk'ē) *adj.* **-luck'i·er, -luck'i·est** not lucky; having or bringing bad luck; unfortunate —**un·luck'i·ly** *adv.*

un·make (-māk') *vt.* **-made', -mak'ing 1.** to cause to be as before; make go back to the original condition **2.** to ruin; destroy **3.** to remove from a position or rank

un·man (-man') *vt.* **-manned', -man'ning** to make lose courage, confidence, or other qualities generally thought of as those that a man should have [the ghastly sight *unmanned* him]

un·man·ly (-man'lē) *adj.* **-li·er, -li·est** not manly; specif., cowardly, weak, effeminate, etc. —**un·man'li·ness** *n.*

un·manned (-mand') *adj.* not manned; ☆specif., without a crew aboard and operating by automatic or remote control

un·man·ner·ly (-man'ər lē) *adj.* having or showing poor manners; rude —*adv.* rudely —**un·man'ner·li·ness** *n.*

un·mask (-mask') *vt.* **1.** to remove a mask or disguise from **2.** to reveal the true nature, purpose, etc. of [to *unmask* a spy] —*vi.* to take off a mask or disguise

un·jad'ed	un·la'dy·like'	un·link'	un·man'i·fest'ed
un·joined'	un·la·ment'ed	un·lit'	un'man·u·fac'tur·a·ble
un'ju·di'cial	un·laun'dered	un·live'ly	un'man·u·fac'tured
un·jus'ti·fi'a·ble	un·leased'	un·lo'cat·ed	un·marked'
un·kept'	un·leav'ened	un·lov'a·ble	un·mar'ket·a·ble
un·kissed'	un·lev'ied	un·loved'	un·marred'
un·knit'	un·li'censed	un·love'ly	un·mar'ried
un·knot'	un·life'like'	un·lov'ing	un·mas'tered
un·know'a·ble	un·light'ed	un·lu'bri·cat'ed	un·match'a·ble
un·know'ing	un·lik'a·ble	un·mag'ni·fied'	un·matched'
un·la'beled	un·like'a·ble	un·mal'le·a·ble	un·mat'ed
un·la'bored	un·lined'	un·man'age·a·ble	un·mat'ted

un·mean·ing (-mēn′iŋ) *adj.* **1.** lacking in meaning or sense; meaningless **2.** showing no sense or intelligence; expressionless

un·meet (-mēt′) *adj.* [Now Rare] not meet, or fit; unsuitable

un·men·tion·a·ble (un men′shən ə b'l) *adj.* not fit to be mentioned; not nice to talk about —*n.* [*pl.*] unmentionable things; specif., underwear: a humorous usage

un·mer·ci·ful (-mur′si fəl) *adj.* having or showing no mercy; cruel; pitiless —**un·mer′ci·ful·ly** *adv.*

un·mind·ful (-mīnd′fəl) *adj.* not mindful; heedless; careless [*unmindful* of the needs of others]

un·mis·tak·a·ble (un′mis tāk′ə b'l) *adj.* that cannot be mistaken or misunderstood; clear; plain —**un′mis·tak′a·bly** *adv.*

un·mit·i·gat·ed (un mit′ə gāt′id) *adj.* **1.** not lessened or eased [*unmitigated* suffering] **2.** out-and-out; complete; absolute [an *unmitigated* fool] —**un·mit′i·gat·ed·ly** *adv.*

un·mor·al (-môr′'l) *adj. var. of* AMORAL

un·moved (-mōōvd′) *adj.* **1.** not moved from its place **2.** firm or unchanged in purpose **3.** not having one's feelings stirred; not affected [*unmoved* by their suffering]

un·muz·zle (-muz′'l) *vt.* **-zled, -zling 1.** to remove a muzzle from (a dog, etc.) **2.** to stop censoring

un·nat·u·ral (-nach′ər əl) *adj.* not natural; specif., *a*) abnormal; strange *b*) artificial, affected, or strained [an *unnatural* smile] *c*) abnormally evil or cruel —see SYN. at IRREGULAR —**un·nat′u·ral·ly** *adv.* —**un·nat′u·ral·ness** *n.*

un·nec·es·sar·y (-nes′ə ser′ē) *adj.* not necessary or required; needless —**un′nec′es·sar′i·ly** *adv.*

un·nerve (-nurv′) *vt.* **-nerved′, -nerv′ing 1.** to cause to lose one's courage, self-control, etc. **2.** to make nervous

un·num·bered (-num′bərd) *adj.* **1.** not counted **2.** *same as* INNUMERABLE **3.** having no identifying number

un·oc·cu·pied (-äk′yə pīd′) *adj.* **1.** having no occupant; vacant; empty **2.** at leisure; idle

un·or·gan·ized (-ôr′gə nīzd′) *adj.* **1.** having no organic structure **2.** not having or following any regular order, system,

or organization **3.** not having or belonging to a labor union

un·pack (-pak′) *vt.* **1.** to open and remove the packed contents of [to *unpack* a suitcase] **2.** to take from a crate, trunk, etc. [to *unpack* books] —*vi.* to empty a packed trunk, suitcase, etc.

un·par·al·leled (-par′ə leld′) *adj.* that has no parallel, equal, or counterpart; unmatched

un·par·lia·men·ta·ry (-pär′lə men′tər ē, -trē) *adj.* contrary to parliamentary law or usage

un·peg (-peg′) *vt.* **-pegged′, -peg′ging 1.** to remove a peg or pegs from **2.** to unfasten or detach in this way

un·peo·ple (-pē′p'l) *vt.* **-pled, -pling** to reduce the population of; depopulate

un·pin (-pin′) *vt.* **-pinned′, -pin′ning 1.** to remove a pin or pins from **2.** to unfasten or detach in this way

un·pleas·ant (-plez′'nt) *adj.* not pleasant; offensive; disagreeable —**un·pleas′ant·ly** *adv.* —**un·pleas′ant·ness** *n.*

un·plumbed (-plumd′) *adj.* **1.** not sounded or measured with or as with a plumb [*unplumbed* depths] **2.** not fully plumbed or understood [an *unplumbed* mystery]

un·polled (-pōld′) *adj.* **1.** *a*) not questioned in a poll *b*) not having voted *c*) not cast or registered: said of votes **2.** not having the horns, branches, etc. cut off

un·pop·u·lar (-päp′yə lər) *adj.* not popular; not liked by the public or by most people —**un′pop·u·lar′i·ty** (-yə lar′ə tē) *n.*

un·prac·ticed (-prak′tist) *adj.* **1.** not practiced; not done or used regularly or often **2.** not skilled or experienced [an *unpracticed* speaker]

un·prec·e·dent·ed (-pres′ə den′tid) *adj.* having no precedent; not done or known before; unheard-of; novel

un·prej·u·diced (-prej′ə dist) *adj.* without prejudice or bias; impartial; fair

un·prin·ci·pled (-prin′sə p'ld) *adj.* without good moral principles; unscrupulous

un·print·a·ble (-print′ə b'l) *adj.* not printable; not fit to be printed, as because of obscenity

---

un·meant′
un·meas′ur·a·ble
un·meas′ured
un′me·chan′i·cal
un·med′i·cat′ed
un·med′i·tat′ed
un′me·lo′di·ous
un·melt′ed
un·mend′ed
un·men′tioned
un·mer′ce·nar′y
un·mer′it·ed
un′me·thod′i·cal
un·mil′i·tar′y
un·milled′
un·min′gled
un′mis·tak′en
un·mixed′
un·mod′i·fied
un·mod′u·lat′ed
un·mois′tened
un·mold′
un·mo·lest′ed
un·mol′li·fied′
un·moor′
un·mort′gaged
un·mo′ti·vat′ed
un·mount′ed
un·mourned′
un·mov′a·ble
un·mov′ing
un·mown′
un·muf′fle
un·mur′mur·ing
un·mu′si·cal
un·mys′ti·fied′
un·nail′
un·nam′a·ble
un·name′a·ble

un·named′
un·nat′u·ral·ized′
un·nav′i·ga·ble
un·nav′i·gat′ed
un·need′ed
un·need′ful
un·neigh′bor·ly
un·not′ed
un·no′tice·a·ble
un·no′ticed
un·nur′tured
un′ob·jec′tion·a·ble
un′o·bliged′
un′o·blig′ing
un′ob·scured′
un′ob·serv′ant
un′ob·served′
un′ob·serv′ing
un′ob·struct′ed
un′ob·tain′a·ble
un′ob·tru′sive
un′of·fend′ing
un′of·fen′sive
un·of′fered
un·of·fi′cial
un·of·fi′cious
un·oiled′
un·o′pen
un·o′pened
un′op·posed′
un′op·pressed′
un′or·dained′
un·o·rig′i·nal
un′or·na·men′tal
un′or·na·ment′ed
un′or·tho·dox′
un′os·ten·ta′tious
un·owned′
un·ox′i·dized′

un·pac′i·fied′
un·paid′
un·paid′-for′
un·pain′ful
un·paint′ed
un·paired′
un·pal′at·a·ble
un·par′don·a·ble
un·par′doned
un·part′ed
un·pas′teur·ized′
un·patched′
un·pat′ent·ed
un·pa·tri·ot′ic
un·paved′
un·peace′ful
un·pen′e·trat′ed
un·pen′sioned
un′per·ceived′
un′per·ceiv′ing
un′per·cep′tive
un′per·fect′ed
un′per·formed′
un′per·plexed′
un′per·suad′a·ble
un′per·suad′ed
un′per·sua′sive
un′per·turbed′
un′phil·o·soph′ic
un′phil·o·soph′i·cal
un·picked′
un·pierced′
un·pile′
un·pit′ied
un·pit′y·ing
un·placed′
un·planned′
un·plant′ed
un·play′a·ble

un·played′
un·pleas′ing
un·pledged′
un·pli′a·ble
un·ploughed′
un·plowed′
un·plucked′
un·plug′
un′po·et′ic
un′po·et′i·cal
un·point′ed
un·poised′
un·po′lar·ized′
un·pol′ished
un′po·lit′i·cal
un·pol·lut′ed
un·pop′u·lat′ed
un·posed′
un·post′ed
un′pre·dict′a·ble
un′pre·med′i·tat′ed
un′pre·pared′
un′pre·pos·sess′ing
un′pre·scribed′
un′pre·sent′a·ble
un′pre·served′
un·pressed′
un′pre·tend′ing
un′pre·ten′tious
un′pre·vent′a·ble
un·priced′
un·print′ed
un·priv′i·leged
un·probed′
un·proc′essed′
un′pro·cur′a·ble
un′pro·duc′tive
un·pro′faned′
un′pro·fessed′

---

un·pro·fes·sion·al (un′prə fesh′ən ′l) *adj.* **1.** breaking the rules of a given profession **2.** not of, typical of, or belonging to a profession —**un′pro·fes′sion·al·ly** *adv.*

un·qual·i·fied (un kwäl′ə fīd′) *adj.* **1.** lacking the necessary qualifications; not fit **2.** not limited; complete [an *unqualified* success] —**un·qual′i·fied′ly** *adv.*

un·ques·tion·a·ble (-kwes′chən ə b′l) *adj.* not to be questioned, doubted, or disputed; certain —**un·ques′tion·a·bly** *adv.*

un·ques·tioned (-kwes′chənd) *adj.* not questioned; specif., *a*) not asked questions; not interrogated *b*) not disputed; undoubted; accepted [his *unquestioned* skill as a writer]

un·qui·et (-kwī′ət) *adj.* not quiet; restless, disturbed, uneasy, anxious, etc. —*n.* an unquiet state —**un·qui′et·ly** *adv.* —**un·qui′et·ness** *n.*

un·quote (un′kwōt′) *interj.* ☆I end the quotation: used in speech after a quotation

un·rav·el (un rav′′l) *vt.* **-eled** or **-elled, -el·ing** or **-el·ling** **1.** to undo (something woven, tangled, etc.); separate the threads of **2.** to make clear; solve [to *unravel* a mystery] —*vi.* to become unraveled —**un·rav′el·ment** *n.*

un·read (-red′) *adj.* **1.** not read, as a book **2.** having read little or nothing [an *unread* person]

un·read·a·ble (-rēd′ə b′l) *adj.* not readable; specif., *a*) not legible; badly written or printed *b*) too dull, difficult, etc. to read [an *unreadable* novel]

un·read·y (-red′ē) *adj.* **1.** not ready; unprepared, as for action **2.** not prompt or alert; slow —**un·read′i·ness** *n.*

un·re·al (-rē′əl, -rēl′) *adj.* not real; imaginary, false, etc. —**un′re·al′i·ty** (-rē′ al′ə tē) *n., pl.* **-ties**

un·re·al·is·tic (un′rē ə lis′tik) *adj.* dealing with ideas or matters in a way that is not realistic; impractical; visionary —**un′re·al·is′ti·cal·ly** *adv.*

un·rea·son (un rē′z′n) *n.* lack of reason; irrationality

un·rea·son·a·ble (-ə b′l) *adj.* not reasonable; specif., *a*) having or showing little sense or judgment [in an *unreasonable* mood] *b*) beyond the limits of what is reasonable; excessive [an *unreasonable* price] —see SYN. at IRRATIONAL —**un·rea′son·a·ble·ness** *n.* —**un·rea′son·a·bly** *adv.*

un·rea·son·ing (-iŋ) *adj.* lacking reason or judgment; irrational —**un·rea′son·ing·ly** *adv.*

☆**un·re·con·struct·ed** (un′rē kən struk′tid) *adj.* **1.** not reconstructed **2.** holding to an earlier way of life or point of view that most people no longer accept or believe in

un·reel (un rēl′) *vt., vi.* to unwind as from a reel

un·re·gen·er·ate (un′ri jen′ər it) *adj.* **1.** not spiritually reborn **2.** refusing to change one's way of living, thinking, etc.; stubborn [an *unregenerate* conservative] Also **un′re·gen′er·at′ed**

un·re·lent·ing (-ri len′tiŋ) *adj.* **1.** refusing to give in or relent **2.** without mercy or compassion **3.** not relaxing or slowing up, as in effort —**un′re·lent′ing·ly** *adv.*

un·re·li·gious (-ri lij′əs) *adj.* **1.** same as IRRELIGIOUS **2.** not involving religion; nonreligious

un·re·mit·ting (-ri mit′iŋ) *adj.* not stopping, relaxing, or slowing down; persistent —**un′re·mit′ting·ly** *adv.*

un·re·served (-ri zurvd′) *adj.* not reserved; specif., *a*) frank or open in speech or behavior *b*) not limited; complete; total [such *unreserved* enthusiasm is rare] *c*) not set aside for advance sale [*unreserved* seats] —**un′re·serv′ed·ly** (-zur′vid lē) *adv.*

un·rest (un rest′) *n.* a troubled or disturbed state; restlessness; specif., angry, rebellious dissatisfaction

un·rid·dle (-rid′′l) *vt.* **-dled, -dling** to solve or explain (a riddle, mystery, etc.)

un·right·eous (-rī′chəs) *adj.* **1.** not righteous; wicked; sinful **2.** not right; unjust; unfair —**un·right′eous·ly** *adv.* —**un·right′eous·ness** *n.*

un·rip (-rip′) *vt.* **-ripped′, -rip′ping** to rip open; take apart or detach by ripping

un·ripe (-rīp′) *adj.* **1.** not ripe or mature; green **2.** not yet fully developed [*unripe* plans] —**un·ripe′ness** *n.*

un·ri·valed, un·ri·valled (-rī′v′ld) *adj.* having no rival, equal, or competitor; matchless; peerless

un·roll (-rōl′) *vt.* **1.** to open or spread out (something rolled up) **2.** to show; display —*vi.* to become unrolled

un·ruf·fled (-ruf′′ld) *adj.* not ruffled or disturbed; calm; smooth; serene —see SYN. at COOL

un·rul·y (-rōō′lē) *adj.* **-rul′i·er, -rul′i·est** [< ME. < un-, not + reuly, orderly] hard to control, restrain, or keep in order; disobedient, disorderly, etc. —**un·rul′i·ness** *n.*

un·sad·dle (-sad′′l) *vt.* **-dled, -dling** **1.** to take the saddle off (a horse, etc.) **2.** to throw from the saddle; unhorse —*vi.* to take the saddle off a horse, etc.

un·said (-sed′) *pt. & pp. of* UNSAY —*adj.* not expressed

un·sat·u·rat·ed (-sach′ə rāt′id) *adj.* **1.** not saturated **2.** *Chem. a*) capable of dissolving more of the solute than has been dissolved *b*) designating an organic compound with a

un·prof′it·a·ble	un′re·cip′ro·cat′ed	un′re·nowned′	un′re·turned′
un′pro·gres′sive	un′re·claim′a·ble	un′rent′a·ble	un′re·vealed′
un·prom′is·ing	un′re·claimed′	un′rent′ed	un′re·venged′
un·prompt′ed	un′rec·og·niz′a·ble	un′re·paid′	un′re·versed′
un·pro·nounce′a·ble	un′rec′og·nized′	un′re·pair′a·ble	un′re·viewed′
un·pro·nounced′	un′rec·om·mend′ed	un′re·paired′	un′re·vised′
un·pro·pi′tious	un′rec·om·pensed′	un′re·pealed′	un′re·voked′
un·pro·por′tion·ate	un′rec·on·cil′a·ble	un′re·pent′ant	un′re·ward′ed
un·pro·posed′	un′rec·on·ciled′	un′re·pent′ing	un′re·ward′ing
un·pros′per·ous	un′re·cord′ed	un′re·place′a·ble	un·rhe·tor′i·cal
un·pro·tect′ed	un′re·cov′er·a·ble	un′re·placed′	un·rhymed′
un·proved′	un′rec′ti·fied′	un′re·plen′ished	un·rhyth′mic
un·prov′en	un′re·deemed′	un′re·port′ed	un·rhyth′mi·cal
un·pro·vid′ed	un′re·fined′	un′rep·re·sent′a·tive	un·right′ful
un·pro·voked′	un′re·flect′ed	un′rep·re·sent′ed	un·rip′ened
un·pruned′	un′re·flect′ing	un′re·pressed′	un·ro·man′tic
un·pub′lished	un′re·formed′	un′re·prieved′	un·roof′
un·punc′tu·al	un′re·freshed′	un′rep′ri·mand′ed	un·round′ed
un·pun′ished	un′re·gard′ed	un′re·quest′ed	un·ruled′
un·purged′	un′reg·is·tered	un′re·quit′ed	un·safe′
un·pur′i·fied′	un′reg′u·lat′ed	un′re·sent′ful	un·saint′ly
un·quench′a·ble	un′re·hearsed′	un′re·signed′	un·sal′a·ble
un·quenched′	un′re·lat′ed	un′re·sist′ant	un·sal′a·ried
un·ques′tion·ing	un′re·laxed′	un′re·sist′ing	un·sale′a·ble
un·quot′a·ble	un′re·li·a·bil′i·ty	un′re·solved′	un·salt′ed
un·quot′ed	un′re·li′a·ble	un′re·spon′sive	un·sam′pled
un·ran′somed	un′re·lieved′	un·rest′ed	un·sanc′ti·fied′
un·rat′ed	un′re·mem′e·died	un·rest′ful	un·sanc′tioned
un·rat′i·fied′	un′re·mem′bered	un′re·strain′a·ble	un·san′i·tar′y
un·reach′a·ble	un′re·morse′ful	un′re·strained′	un·sat′ed
un·re′al·iz′a·ble	un′re·mov′a·ble	un′re·straint′	un·sa′tia·ble
un·re′al·ized′	un′re·moved′	un′re·strict′ed	un·sa′ti·at′ed
un·rea′soned	un′re·mu′ner·at′ed	un′re·tard′ed	un·sat·is·fac′to·ri·ly
un′re·buked′	un′re·mu′ner·a′tive	un′re·ten′tive	un·sat·is·fac′to·ry
un′re·ceived′	un′re·newed′	un′re·tract′ed	un·sat′is·fied′
un′re·cep′tive		un′re·trieved′	un·sat′is·fy′ing

double or triple bond between carbon atoms, capable of combining with other elements or compounds by adding on at the bond

un·sa·vor·y (-sā′vər ē) *adj.* **1.** orig., tasteless **2.** unpleasant to taste or smell [*unsavory* odors] **3.** unpleasant or disgusting, esp. so as to seem immoral [an *unsavory* scandal] —**un·sa′vor·i·ly** *adv.* —**un·sa′vor·i·ness** *n.*

un·say (-sā′) *vt.* **-said′, -say′ing** to take back or retract (what has been said)

un·scathed (-skā*th*d′) *adj.* not hurt; unharmed

un·schooled (-skōōld′) *adj.* **1.** not educated or trained **2.** not gotten or changed by schooling; natural

☆**un·scram·ble** (-skram′b'l) *vt.* **-bled, -bling** to cause to be no longer scrambled, disordered, or mixed up; specif., *Electronics* to make (incoming scrambled signals) clear and understandable at the receiver —**un·scram′bler** *n.*

un·screw (-skrōō′) *vt.* **1.** to remove a screw or screws from **2.** *a)* to remove or loosen by removing a screw or screws, or by turning [to *unscrew* the hinges on a door; to *unscrew* a jar lid] *b)* to remove a threaded top, cover, etc. from (a jar, etc.) —*vi.* to become unscrewed

un·scru·pu·lous (-skrōō′pyə ləs) *adj.* not scrupulous; paying no attention to what is right or proper; not honest [*unscrupulous* business practices] —**un·scru′pu·lous·ly** *adv.* —**un·scru′pu·lous·ness** *n.*

un·seal (-sēl′) *vt.* **1.** to break or remove the seal of **2.** to open by or as by breaking a seal

un·search·a·ble (-surch′ə b'l) *adj.* that cannot be searched into or understood; mysterious —**un·search′a·bly** *adv.*

un·sea·son·a·ble (-sē′z'n ə b'l) *adj.* **1.** not usual for the season [*unseasonable* heat] **2.** coming at the wrong time; untimely [an *unseasonable* remark] —**un·sea′son·a·ble·ness** *n.* —**un·sea′son·a·bly** *adv.*

un·seat (-sēt′) *vt.* **1.** to make fall from a seat, saddle, etc. **2.** to force out of office, an important position, etc.

un·seem·ly (-sēm′lē) *adj.* not seemly; not proper or decent; unbecoming —*adv.* in an unseemly way —see **SYN.** at IMPROPER —**un·seem′li·ness** *n.*

un·self·ish (-sel′fish) *adj.* not selfish; putting the good of others above one's own interests; generous —**un·self′ish·ly** *adv.* —**un·self′ish·ness** *n.*

un·set·tle (-set′'l) *vt.* **-tled, -tling** to make unsettled, shaky, troubled, etc.; disturb, displace, disorder, or disarrange [the news *unsettled* her] —*vi.* to become unsettled —**un·set′tle·ment** *n.*

un·set·tled (-set′'ld) *adj.* **1.** not settled; not in order, not stable, not decided or determined, etc. [*unsettled* weather; an *unsettled* argument] **2.** not paid or disposed of, as a debt or estate ☆**3.** having no settlers [*unsettled* lands] **4.** not established in a

place to live [new in town and still *unsettled*] —**un·set′tled·ness** *n.*

un·sex (-seks′) *vt.* to deprive of the qualities thought of as characteristic of one's sex

un·shack·le (-shak′'l) *vt.* **-led, -ling** **1.** to loosen or remove the shackles from **2.** to free

un·sheathe (-shē*th*′) *vt.* **-sheathed′, -sheath′ing** to remove (a sword, knife, etc.) from a sheath

un·ship (-ship′) *vt.* **-shipped′, -ship′ping** **1.** to unload from a ship **2.** to remove from its proper place on a ship or boat [to *unship* an oar]

un·sight·ly (-sīt′lē) *adj.* not pleasant to look at; ugly —**un·sight′li·ness** *n.*

un·skilled (-skild′) *adj.* not skilled; specif., having, showing, or needing no special skill or training [digging ditches is *unskilled* labor]

un·skill·ful (-skil′fəl) *adj.* not skillful; awkward; clumsy —**un·skill′ful·ly** *adv.* —**un·skill′ful·ness** *n.*

un·snap (-snap′) *vt.* **-snapped′, -snap′ping** to undo the snap or snaps of, so as to loosen or detach

un·snarl (-snärl′) *vt.* to remove the snarls from; untangle

un·so·cia·ble (-sō′shə b'l) *adj.* **1.** avoiding others; not sociable or friendly **2.** not helping to bring about sociability —**un·so′cia·bil′i·ty, un·so′cia·ble·ness** *n.* —**un·so′cia·bly** *adv.*

un·so·cial (-sō′shəl) *adj.* having or showing a dislike for the company of others —**un·so′cial·ly** *adv.*

SYN.—**unsocial** implies a dislike for the society or company of others [an *unsocial* neighbor]; **asocial** implies complete lack of concern for the interests, welfare, etc. of others and often suggests great selfishness [the frequent *asocial* behavior of very young children]; **antisocial** applies to that which is believed to be harmful to society or to social institutions [the anarchist's *antisocial* teachings] —**ANT.** social

un·sol·der (-säd′ər) *vt.* **1.** to take apart (things soldered together) **2.** to disunite; separate

un·so·phis·ti·cat·ed (un′sə fis′tə kāt′id) *adj.* not sophisticated; innocent, simple, unworldly, etc. —see **SYN.** at NAIVE —**un′so·phis′ti·cat·ed·ly** *adv.* —**un′so·phis′ti·ca′tion** *n.*

un·sound (un sound′) *adj.* not sound or free from fault or weakness; specif., *a)* not normal or healthy [an *unsound* mind] *b)* not safe, firm, or solid [an *unsound* ship] *c)* not safe financially [an *unsound* bank] *d)* not accurate, sensible, etc. [an *unsound* plan] *e)* light: said of sleep —**un·sound′ly** *adv.* —**un·sound′ness** *n.*

un·spar·ing (-sper′iŋ) *adj.* **1.** not sparing or stinting; generous in giving; lavish [*unsparing* charity] **2.** not merciful; harsh [*unsparing* criticism] —**un·spar′ing·ly** *adv.*

un·speak·a·ble (-spēk′ə b'l) *adj.* **1.** that cannot be spoken **2.** hard to describe or speak about because so great, bad, etc. [*unspeakable* joy, *unspeakable* tortures] —**un·speak′a·bly** *adv.*

---

un·saved′	un′se·lect′ed	un·shod′	un·sof′tened
un·scal′a·ble	un′se·lec′tive	un·shorn′	un·soiled′
un·scaled′	un·sent′	un·short′ened	un·sold′
un·scanned′	un′sen·ti·men′tal	un·shrink′a·ble	un·sol′dier·ly
un·scarred′	un·sep′a·rat′ed	un·shrink′ing	un′so·lic′it·ed
un·scent′ed	un·served′	un·shriv′en	un′so·lid′i·fied′
un·sched′uled	un·serv′ice·a·ble	un·shrunk′	un·solv′a·ble
un·schol′ar·ly	un·set′	un·shuf′fled	un·solved′
un′sci·en·tif′ic	un·sev′ered	un·shut′	un·sort′ed
un′sci·en·tif′i·cal·ly	un·sewn′	un·shut′tered	un·sought′
un·scorched′	un·shad′ed	un·sift′ed	un·sound′ed
un·scraped′	un·shad′owed	un·sight′ed	un·soured′
un·scratched′	un·shak′a·ble	un·signed′	un·sowed′
un·screened′	un·shake′a·ble	un·si′lenced	un·sown′
un·scrip′tur·al	un·shak′en	un·sim′pli·fied′	un·spe′cial·ized′
un·sculp′tured	un·shamed′	un·sing′a·ble	un′spe·cif′ic
un·sealed′	un·shaped′	un·sink′a·ble	un′spec·i·fied′
un·sea′soned	un·shape′ly	un·sis′ter·ly	un′spec·tac′u·lar
un·sea′wor·thy	un·shared′	un·sized′	un·spent′
un·sec′ond·ed	un·sharp′ened	un·skep′ti·cal	un·spilled′
un′se·cured′	un·shaved′	un·slack′ened	un·spir′it·u·al
un·seed′ed	un·shav′en	un·slaked′	un·spoiled′
un·see′ing	un·shed′	un·sleep′ing	un·spo′ken
un·seen′	un·shelled′	un·sliced′	un·sport′ing
un·seg′ment·ed	un·shel′tered	un·smil′ing	un·sports′man·like′
un·seg′re·gat′ed	un·shield′ed	un·smoked′	un·spot′ted

---

fat, āpe, cär; ten, ēven; is, bīte; gō, hôrn, tōōl, lŏŏk; oil, out; up, fur; get; joy; yet; chin; she; thin, *th*en; zh, leisure; ŋ, ring; ə for *a* in *ago, e* in *agent, i* in *sanity, o* in *comply, u* in *focus*; ′ as in *able* (ā′b'l); Fr. bâl; ë, Fr. coeur; ö, Fr. feu; Fr. mon; ô, Fr. coq; ü, Fr. duc; *r*, Fr. cri; H, G. ich; kh, G. doch; ‡foreign; ☆ Americanism; < derived from. See inside front cover.

un·sta·ble (-stā'b'l) *adj.* not stable; specif., *a)* not fixed, firm, or steady [an *unstable* foundation] *b)* changeable [the *unstable* weather of spring] *c)* easily upset or disturbed emotionally *d)* Chem., Physics tending to change form or break down —**un·sta·ble·ness** *n.* —**un·sta·bly** *adv.*

un·stead·y (-sted'ē) *adj.* not steady; specif., *a)* not firm or stable; shaky *b)* changeable; wavering *c)* not regular in habits, purpose, or behavior; erratic —*vt.* **-stead'ied, -stead'y·ing** to make unsteady —**un·stead'i·ly** *adv.* —**un·stead'i·ness** *n.*

un·step (-step') *vt.* **-stepped', -step'ping** *Naut.* to remove (a mast) from its step or socket

un·stick (-stik') *vt.* **-stuck', -stick'ing** to loosen or free (something stuck)

un·stop (-stäp') *vt.* **-stopped', -stop'ping** 1. to remove the stopper from 2. to clear (a blocked pipe, etc.)

un·strap (-strap') *vt.* **-strapped', -strap'ping** to loosen or remove the strap or straps of

un·string (-striŋ') *vt.* **-strung', -string'ing** 1. to loosen or remove the string or strings of 2. to remove from a string 3. to make nervous, weak, upset, etc.

un·struc·tured (-struk'chərd) *adj.* not organized in a precise, formal way; loose, free, open, etc.

un·strung (-struŋ') *adj.* 1. nervous, upset, etc. 2. having the string(s) loosened or removed, as a bow

un·stud·ied (-stud'ēd) *adj.* 1. not learned or achieved by study or conscious effort [his *unstudied* skill as a speaker] 2. spontaneous; natural; unaffected [her *unstudied* enthusiasm]

un·sub·stan·tial (un'səb stan'shəl) *adj.* not substantial; specif., *a)* having no material substance *b)* flimsy; light [made of an *unsubstantial* material] *c)* not based on fact or truth; unreal [her *unsubstantial* hopes] —**un'sub·stan'ti·al·i·ty** (-stan'shē al'ə tē) *n.* —**un'sub·stan'tial·ly** *adv.*

un·suit·a·ble (un sōōt'ə b'l, -syōōt'-) *adj.* not suitable; unbecoming; inappropriate —**un·suit'a·bly** *adv.*

un·sung (-suŋ') *adj.* 1. not sung 2. not honored or praised, as in song or poetry [an *unsung* hero]

un·sus·pect·ed (un'sə spek'tid) *adj.* 1. not believed guilty, bad, harmful, etc. 2. not imagined to exist, be probable, etc. [an *unsuspected* danger] —**un'sus·pect'ed·ly** *adv.*

un·tan·gle (un taŋ'g'l) *vt.* **-gled, -gling** 1. to free from a snarl or tangle; disentangle [to *untangle* a rope] 2. to free from confusion; clear up; put in order [to *untangle* a mystery]

un·taught (-tôt') *adj.* 1. not taught or educated 2. got without being taught; natural [an *untaught* skill]

un·ten·a·ble (-ten'ə b'l) *adj.* 1. not tenable; that cannot be defended [an *untenable* position] —**un'ten·a·bil'i·ty, un·ten'a·ble·ness** *n.*

un·thank·ful (-thaŋk'fəl) *adj.* 1. not thankful; ungrateful 2. thankless; unappreciated —**un·thank'ful·ly** *adv.* —**un·thank'ful·ness** *n.*

un·think·a·ble (-thiŋk'ə b'l) *adj.* 1. that cannot be thought about or imagined; inconceivable [*unthinkable* cruelty] 2. not to be considered; impossible [it is *unthinkable* that he would do such a thing] —**un·think'a·bly** *adv.*

un·think·ing (-thiŋk'iŋ) *adj.* 1. showing lack of thought or of consideration for others; thoughtless [an *unthinking* reaction; an *unthinking* remark] 2. lacking the ability to think; not rational —**un·think'ing·ly** *adv.*

un·thread (-thred') *vt.* 1. to draw the thread from 2. to disentangle; unravel 3. to find one's way through (a maze, etc.)

un·ti·dy (-tī'dē) *adj.* **-di·er, -di·est** not tidy or neat; slovenly, messy, etc. —see SYN. at SLOVENLY —**un·ti'di·ness** *n.*

un·tie (-tī') *vt.* **-tied', -ty'ing** 1. to loosen or undo (something tied or knotted) 2. to free, as from difficulty, control, etc. 3. to untangle —*vi.* to become untied

un·til (un til', ən-) *prep.* [ME. *untill* < *un-* (see UNTO) + *till*, till] 1. up to the time of; till [*until* payday] 2. before (a specified time) [not *until* tomorrow] —*conj.* 1. up to the time when or that [*until* I go] 2. to the point, degree, etc. that [heat water *until* it boils] 3. before [don't leave *until* he does]

un·time·ly (un tīm'lē) *adj.* 1. before the usual or expected time; premature [his *untimely* death] 2. at the wrong time; inopportune [an *untimely* remark] —*adv.* too soon or at the wrong time —**un·time'li·ness** *n.*

un·to (un'tōō, -too) *prep.* [ME. *un-*, until + *to*, to] *archaic or poet. var. of:* 1. TO 2. UNTIL

un·told (un tōld') *adj.* 1. not told or made known [a story left *untold*] 2. too great, numerous, etc. to be counted, measured, or described [*untold* wealth]

un·touch·a·ble (-tuch'ə b'l) *adj.* that cannot or should not be touched —*n.* 1. an untouchable person or thing 2. in India, formerly, one who was not supposed to touch or be touched by higher-caste Hindus —**un'touch·a·bil'i·ty** *n.*

un·to·ward (un tō'ərd, -tôrd') *adj.* 1. inappropriate, improper, unseemly, etc. [an *untoward* remark] 2. not favorable or fortunate [*untoward* circumstances]

un·trav·eled, un·trav·elled (un trav'l'd) *adj.* 1. not used by travelers [an *untraveled* road] 2. not having done much traveling, esp. to distant places

un·tried (-trīd') *adj.* 1. not tested or proved [an *untried* recipe] 2. not tried in court

un·true (un trōō') *adj.* 1. not correct; false 2. not agreeing with a standard or rule 3. not faithful or loyal —**un·tru'ly** *adv.*

un·truth (-trōōth') *n.* 1. the quality or state of being untrue; falsity 2. an untrue statement; falsehood; lie

un·truth·ful (-trōōth'fəl) *adj.* 1. that is not the truth; untrue [an *untruthful* report] 2. telling a lie or lies, esp. often —**un·truth'ful·ly** *adv.* —**un·truth'ful·ness** *n.*

un·tu·tored (-tōōt'ərd, -tyōōt'-) *adj.* 1. not tutored or taught; uneducated 2. simple; naive; unsophisticated —see SYN. at IGNORANT

un·sprung'	un'sup·port'a·ble	un·taint'ed	un·tired'
un·squan'dered	un'sup·port'ed	un·tal'ent·ed	un·tir'ing
un·stained'	un'sup·pressed'	un·talked'-of'	un·ti'tled
un·stamped'	un·sure'	un·tam'a·ble	un·torn'
un·stand'ard·ized'	un'sur·mount'a·ble	un·tamed'	un·touched'
un·starched'	un'sur·pass'a·ble	un·tanned'	un·trace'a·ble
un·starred'	un'sur·passed'	un·tapped'	un·traced'
un·stat'ed	un'sur·prised'	un·tar'nished	un·tracked'
un·states'man·like'	un'sus·cep'ti·ble	un·tast'ed	un·trained'
un·stemmed'	un'sus·pect'ing	un·taxed'	un·tram'meled
un·ster'i·lized'	un'sus·pi'cious	un·teach'a·ble	un'trans·fer'a·ble
un·stint'ed	un'sus·tained'	un·tech'ni·cal	un'trans·ferred'
un·stint'ing	un·swayed'	un·tem'pered	un'trans·lat'a·ble
un·stitched'	un·sweet'ened	un·ten'ant·ed	un'trans·lat'ed
un·stop'pa·ble	un·swept'	un·tend'ed	un'trans·mit'ted
un·strained'	un·swerv'ing	un·ter'ri·fied'	un·trapped'
un·strat'i·fied'	un·swol'len	un·test'ed	un'tra·versed'
un·stressed'	un·sworn'	un·teth'ered	un·treat'ed
un·stri'at·ed	un'sym·met'ri·cal	un·thanked'	un·trimmed'
un·stuffed'	un'sym·pa·thet'ic	un·thatched'	un·trod'
un'sub·dued'	un'sym·pa·thet'i·cal·ly	un·thawed'	un·trod'den
un'sub·mis'sive	un'sym·pa·thiz'ing	un·the·at'ri·cal	un·trou'bled
un'sub·si·dized'	un'sys·tem·at'ic	un·thought'ful	un·trust'wor'thy
un'sub·stan'ti·at·ed	un'sys·tem·at'i·cal·ly	un·thought'-of'	un·tuft'ed
un'suc·cess'ful	un'sys'tem·a·tized'	un·thrift'y	un·tun'a·ble
un·suit'ed	un·tab'u·lat'ed	un·tick'et·ed	un·tuned'
un·sul'lied	un·tack'	un·till'a·ble	un·tune'ful
un·sunk'	un·tact'ful	un·tilled'	un·turned'
un'su·per·vised'	un·tagged'	un·tinged'	un·twilled'

un·twine (-twīn′) *vt.* **-twined′, -twin′ing** to undo (something twined or twisted); disentangle or unwind —*vi.* to become untwined

un·twist (-twist′) *vt., vi.* to turn in the opposite direction so as to loosen or separate; untwine

un·used (-yoozd′) *adj.* **1.** not in use [*unused* space] **2.** that has never been used [*unused* clothing] **3.** not accustomed [*unused* to traveling]

un·u·su·al (-yoo′zhoo wəl) *adj.* not usual or common; rare; remarkable —see SYN. at RARE¹ —**un·u′su·al·ly** *adv.* —**un·u′su·al·ness** *n.*

un·ut·ter·a·ble (-ut′ər ə b′l) *adj.* that cannot be talked about or described —**un·ut′ter·a·bly** *adv.*

un·var·nished (-vär′nisht) *adj.* **1.** not varnished **2.** plain; simple; unadorned [the *unvarnished* truth]

un·veil (un vāl′) *vt.* to reveal as by removing a veil or covering from —*vi.* to take off a veil; reveal oneself

un·veil·ing (-iŋ) *n.* a formal removal of a covering from a new statue, tombstone, etc., as during a ceremony

un·voiced (un voist′) *adj.* **1.** not spoken or expressed **2.** *Phonet.* same as VOICELESS

un·war·y (-wer′ē) *adj.* not watchful or on one's guard; not alert to possible danger, trickery, etc. —**un·war′i·ly** *adv.* —**un·war′i·ness** *n.*

un·wea·ried (-wir′ēd) *adj.* **1.** not weary or tired **2.** never wearying; tireless; indefatigable

un·well (-wel′) *adj.* not well; ailing; ill; sick

un·wept (-wept′) *adj.* **1.** not shed [*unwept* tears] **2.** not wept for; unmourned

un·whole·some (-hōl′səm) *adj.* not wholesome; specif., *a)* harmful to body or mind *b)* unhealthy or unhealthy-looking *c)* morally bad —**un·whole′some·ly** *adv.* —**un·whole′some·ness** *n.*

un·wield·y (-wēl′dē) *adj.* hard to handle, use, control, etc. because of large size or weight or awkward shape [an *unwieldy* crate] —**un·wield′i·ness** *n.*

un·will·ing (-wil′iŋ) *adj.* **1.** not willing or inclined; reluctant [*unwilling* to take the blame] **2.** done, given, etc. against one's will [*unwilling* permission] —**un·will′ing·ly** *adv.*

un·wind (-wīnd′) *vt.* **-wound′, -wind′ing 1.** to wind off or undo (something wound) **2.** to uncoil **3.** to untangle **4.** to relax —*vi.* to become unwound, relaxed, etc.

un·wise (-wīz′) *adj.* not wise; not showing good judgment; foolish —**un·wise′ly** *adv.*

un·wit·ting (-wit′iŋ) *adj.* **1.** not knowing; unaware [*unwitting* of the danger around her] **2.** not done on purpose; not intended [an *unwitting* insult] —**un·wit′ting·ly** *adv.*

un·wont·ed (-wun′tid, -wôn′-) *adj.* not common, usual, or habitual; rare [her *unwonted* harshness shocked us] —**un·wont′ed·ly** *adv.*

un·world·ly (-wurld′lē) *adj.* **1.** not of this world; unearthly **2.** not concerned with the affairs, pleasures, etc. of this world; otherworldly **3.** not worldly-wise; unsophisticated

un·wor·thy (-wur′thē) *adj.* **-thi·er, -thi·est 1.** lacking merit or value; worthless **2.** not deserving [*unworthy* of such honors]

3. not fit or suitable [that remark is *unworthy* of a gentleman] —**un·wor′thi·ly** *adv.* —**un·wor′thi·ness** *n.*

un·wrap (-rap′) *vt.* **-wrapped′, -wrap′ping** to take off the wrapping of; open or undo (something wrapped) —*vi.* to become unwrapped

un·writ·ten (-rit′'n) *adj.* **1.** not in writing; not written or printed [an *unwritten* agreement] **2.** operating only through custom or tradition [an *unwritten* rule] **3.** not written on; blank

unwritten law law based on custom, usage, court decisions, etc. rather than on the action of a lawmaking body

un·yoke (-yōk′) *vt.* **-yoked′, -yok′ing 1.** to remove a yoke from [to *unyoke* oxen] **2.** to separate or disconnect

☆**un·zip** (-zip′) *vt., vi.* **-zipped′, -zip′ping 1.** to open (a zipper) **2.** to open the zipper of (a garment, etc.)

up¹ (up) *adv.* [OE.] **1.** to a higher place [to climb *up*] **2.** in or on a higher position or level [to stay *up* in the air] **3.** in a direction or place thought of as higher or above [moving *up* to Iowa from Texas] **4.** above the horizon [the sun comes *up* at dawn] **5.** to a later period [from childhood *up*] **6.** to a higher condition or rank [he has come *up* in the world] **7.** to a higher amount, degree, etc. [to go *up* in price] **8.** *a)* in or into a standing or upright position [to stand *up*] *b)* out of bed [he gets *up* before me in the morning] **9.** into action, view, discussion, etc. [to bring a matter *up*] **10.** aside; away; by [lay *up* grain] **11.** so as to be even with in space, time, degree, etc. [keep *up* with the times] **12.** so as to be tightly closed, bound, packed, etc. [tie the package *up*] **13.** completely [eat it *up*] **14.** so as to stop [to rein *up* a horse] ☆**15.** *Baseball* to one's turn at batting; at bat **16.** *Naut.* windward **17.** *Sports & Games* ahead (by a specified number of points, goals, etc.) ☆**18.** [Colloq.] served in a cocktail glass without ice cubes The adverb *up* is also used with verbs: *a)* to form combinations having special meanings (Example: when did she show *up*?) *b)* to add emphasis (Example: dress *up*) *c)* as an addition with little or no meaning (Example: light *up* a cigarette) —*prep.* **1.** to, toward, or at a higher place, condition, rank, etc. on or in [climb *up* the ladder] **2.** at, along, or toward a more distant part of [*up* the road] **3.** toward the source or against the flow, etc. of [*up* the river] **4.** in or toward the interior or more northerly part of (a country, territory, etc.) —*adj.* **1.** being in or directed toward a higher position, condition, etc. [his hand is *up*] **2.** *a)* above the ground [the new grass is *up*] *b)* above the horizon [the sun is *up*] **3.** higher in amount, degree, etc. [rents are *up*] **4.** *a)* standing or upright [the fence post is *up*] *b)* out of bed [he's not *up* yet] **5.** active, excited, etc. [her anger was *up*] **6.** even with in space, time, etc. **7.** in the inner or higher part of a country, etc. **8.** at an end; over [time is *up*] **9.** [Colloq.] happening [what's *up*?] ☆**10.** *Baseball* at bat —*n.* **1.** an upward slope, movement, course, etc. **2.** a period or state of prosperity, good luck, etc. —*vi.* **upped, up′ping** [Colloq.] to get up; rise: also used, sometimes without inflection, to give added force to a second verb [he *up* and left] —*vt.* [Colloq.] **1.** to put up, lift up, or take up **2.** to cause to rise [to *up* prices] —☆**on the up and up** [Slang] honest —☆**up against** [Colloq.] faced with —☆**up against it** in difficulty, esp. financial difficulty —**up and around** (or **about**) out of bed and active again, as after an illness —**up and doing** busy; active —**up for** **1.** presented or considered for (an elective office, election, sale, auction, etc.) **2.** before a court for (trial) or on (a charge) —**up on** (or **in**) [Colloq.] well-informed about —**up front** [Colloq.] ☆**1.** very honest; candid ☆**2.** ahead of time; in advance —**ups and downs** good periods and bad periods —**up to** [Colloq.] **1.** doing or getting ready to do; scheming [up to mischief] **2.** equal to (a task, etc.); capable of (doing, undertaking, etc.) **3.** as many as [up to four may play] **4.** as far as [up to here] ☆**5.** dependent upon ☆**6.** resting upon as a duty [the decision is entirely up to her] —**up with!** give or restore power, favor, etc. to!

up[2] (up) *adv.* [phonetic respelling of AP(IECE)] apiece; each [the score is seven up]

up- *a combining form meaning* up [uphill]

☆**up·and·com·ing** (up/'n kum'iŋ) *adj.* **1.** full of energy and ideas, alert, and promising **2.** gaining in importance or reputation

up-and-down (-doun') *adj.* **1.** going alternately up and down, to and fro, etc. **2.** variable; changing; fluctuating

u·pas (yōō'pəs) *n.* [short for Malay *pohon upas*, tree of poison] **1.** a tall Javanese tree of the mulberry family, whose whitish bark produces a poisonous juice [the juice

up·beat (up'bēt') *n.* **1.** an upward trend; upswing **2.** *Music* an upward stroke made by a conductor to show an unaccented beat —*adj.* lively; cheerful; optimistic [a movie with an *upbeat* ending]

up·braid (up brād') *vt.* [< OE. < *up-*, up + *bregdan*, to pull, shake] to find fault with harshly or bitterly; criticize sharply —see SYN. at SCOLD

up·bring·ing (up'briŋ'iŋ) *n.* the training and education one gets while growing up; rearing; nurture

☆**up·chuck** (-chuk') *vi., vt., n.* [Slang] *same as* VOMIT

up·com·ing (-kum'iŋ) *adj.* coming soon; forthcoming

up·coun·try (-kun'trē) *adj.* of or located in the interior of a country —*n.* the interior of a country —*adv.* ☆in or toward the interior of a country

up·date (up dāt') *vt.* **-dat'ed, -dat'ing** to bring up to date; make agree with the most recent facts, methods, ideas, etc.

up·draft (up'draft') *n.* an upward air current

up·end (up end') *vt., vi.* **1.** to turn or stand on end **2.** to upset or topple

☆**up·grade** (up'grād'; *for v. usually* up grād') *n.* an upward slope, esp. in a road —*adj., adv.* uphill; upward — *vt.* **-grad'ed, -grad'ing** **1.** to promote to a more skilled job at higher pay **2.** to raise in importance, value, etc. —**on the upgrade** becoming more important, stronger, healthier, etc.

up·growth (up'grōth') *n.* **1.** upward growth; rise or development **2.** anything produced by this

up·heav·al (up hē'v'l) *n.* **1.** an upheaving, as of part of the earth's crust by an earthquake **2.** a sudden, violent change, as a revolution

up·heave (-hēv') *vt.* **-heaved'** or **-hove', -heav'ing** to heave or lift up —*vi.* to rise as if forced up

up·hill (up'hil') *adv.* **1.** toward the top of a hill **2.** with difficulty —*adj.* **1.** going or sloping up **2.** requiring great effort [an *uphill* battle against disease]

up·hold (up hōld') *vt.* **-held', -hold'ing** **1.** to hold up; raise **2.** to keep from falling; support **3.** to give moral support to **4.** to decide in favor of; support against opposition [to *uphold* the right of every citizen to vote] —see SYN. at SUPPORT —**up·hold'er** *n.*

☆**up·hol·ster** (up hōl'stər, ə pōl'-) *vt.* [altered < ME. *upholder*, dealer in secondhand goods < *upholden*, to repair] to fit out (furniture, etc.) with covering, padding, springs, etc. —**up·hol'ster·er** *n.*

up·hol·ster·y (-stər ē, -strē) *n., pl.* **-ster·ies** **1.** the materials used in upholstering **2.** the business or work of upholstering

up·keep (up'kēp') *n.* **1.** the act of keeping buildings, equipment, etc. in good working condition; maintenance **2.** the cost of this **3.** state of repair

up·land (-lənd, -land') *n.* land higher than the land around it —*adj.* of or located in upland

up·lift (up lift'; *for n.* up'lift') *vt.* **1.** to lift up; elevate [trees with *uplifted* branches] **2.** to raise to a higher moral, social, or cultural level —☆*n.* **1.** *a)* the act or process of uplifting *b)* any influence, movement, etc. aimed at uplifting society **2.** *Geol.* a raising of land above the surrounding area —**up·lift'er** *n.*

up·most (up'mōst') *adj. same as* UPPERMOST

up·on (ə pän') *prep.* on, or up and on: *upon* can usually be used in place of *on*, the choice depending on idiom, sentence rhythm, etc.

up·per (up'ər) *adj.* **1.** higher in place or physical position [an *upper* floor] **2.** farther north or farther inland [the *upper* Mississippi] **3.** higher in rank, authority, etc. [the *upper* levels of the administration] **4.** [U-] *Geol.* later: used of a division of a period —*n.* **1.** the part of a shoe or boot above the sole ☆**2.** [Colloq.] an upper berth **3.** [Slang] any drug containing a stimulant; esp., an amphetamine —☆**on one's uppers** [Colloq.] **1.** wearing shoes with soles worn through **2.** in need; poor

upper case [see CASE[2], *n.* 6] capital-letter type used in printing, as distinguished from the small letters (*lower case*) —**up'per-case'** *adj.* —**up'per-case'** *vt.* **-cased', -cas'ing**

upper class the social class above the middle class; rich, socially well-known, or aristocratic class

☆**up·per·class·man** (up'ər klas'mən) *n., pl.* **-men** a junior or senior in a high school or college

upper crust ☆[Colloq.] *same as* UPPER CLASS

up·per·cut (up'ər kut') *n. Boxing* a short, swinging blow directed upward, as to the chin —*vt., vi.* **-cut', -cut'ting** to hit with an uppercut

upper hand the position of advantage or control [his opponent has the *upper hand*]

Upper House [*often* u- h-] in a legislature having two branches, the branch that is smaller and over which the voters have less control, as the U.S. Senate

up·per·most (up'ər mōst') *adj.* highest in place, power, authority, etc.; topmost; foremost [the thought was *uppermost* in his mind] —*adv.* in the highest place, rank, etc.

Upper Vol·ta (väl'tə) country in W Africa, north of Ghana: 108,880 sq. mi.; pop. 5,384,000; cap. Ouagadougou

☆**up·pi·ty** (up'ə tē) *adj.* [Colloq.] snobbish, overly proud, haughty, etc. —**up'pi·ty·ness** *n.*

Upp·sa·la (oop'sä'lä; *E.* up'sə lə) city in EC Sweden: pop. 102,000: also sp. **Up'sa·la**

up·raise (up rāz') *vt.* **-raised', -rais'ing** to raise up

up·rear (-rir') *vt.* **1.** to lift up **2.** to erect; build —*vi.* to rise up

up·right (up'rīt'; *also for adv.* up rīt') *adj.* **1.** standing or directed straight up; erect [*upright* pickets in a fence] **2.** honest and just; honorable —*adv.* in an upright position [to stand *upright*] —*n.* **1.** the state of being upright or vertical **2.** something having an upright position, as a vertical post [a lake house built on *uprights*] **3.** *short for* UPRIGHT PIANO —**up'right'ly** *adv.* —**up'right'ness** *n.*

SYN.—**upright** suggests unbending inner strength and straightness of moral character; **honest** implies complete fairness and openness in one's dealings with others and emphasizes freedom from lying or cheating; **just**, when it refers to things, emphasizes fairness and, when used of people, stresses high moral behavior and judgment; **honorable** implies behavior in strict keeping with what is considered to be morally right, esp. in one's social class, profession, etc. —**ANT. dishonest, unjust**

upright piano a piano with a vertical, rectangular body

up·rise (up rīz') *vi.* **-rose', -ris'en, -ris'ing** **1.** to rise; get up; move up, rise into view, swell, etc. **2.** to rise in revolt —*n.* **1.** the act of rising up **2.** an upward slope

up·ris·ing (up'rīz'iŋ) *n.* the action of rising up; specif., a revolt —see SYN. at REBELLION

up·roar (-rôr') *n.* [Du. *oproer*, a stirring up] **1.** a noisy, confused condition; loud commotion; tumult [his remark threw the meeting into an *uproar*] **2.** loud, confused noise; din —see SYN. at NOISE

UPRIGHT PIANO

up·roar·i·ous (up rôr'ē əs) *adj.* **1.** making or marked by, an uproar; tumultuous **2.** *a)* loud and excited, as laughter *b)* causing such laughter [an *uproarious* joke] —**up·roar'i·ous·ly** *adv.* —**up·roar'i·ous·ness** *n.*

up·root (up rōōt', -root') *vt.* **1.** to tear up by the roots **2.** to destroy or remove completely [to *uproot* poverty]

up·set (up set'; *for n. and occas. adj.* up'set') *vt.* **-set', -set'ting** **1.** *a)* to tip over; overturn [to *upset* a vase] *b)* to defeat unexpectedly [our team *upset* the champions] **2.** *a)* to disturb the order or working of [to *upset* a busy schedule] *b)* to disturb mentally, emotionally, or physically [the bad news *upset* him] **3.** *Mech.* to shorten and thicken (a red-hot piece of iron) by beating on the end; swage —*vi.* to become overturned —*n.* **1.** an upsetting or being upset; specif., *a)* an overturning *b)* an unexpected defeat *c)* a disturbance or disorder, esp. an emotional or physical one **2.** *Mech. a)* a swage used for up-setting *b)* an upset piece or part —*adj.* **1.** tipped over; overturned **2.** disturbed or disordered [*upset* plans]

upset price the price fixed as the minimum at which something will be sold at an auction

up·shot (up′shät′) *n.* [orig., the final shot in an archery match] the conclusion; result; outcome

up·side (-sīd′) *n.* the upper side or part

upside down 1. with the top side or part underneath **2.** in disorder; topsy-turvy [we turned the room *upside down* looking for the book] —*up′side-down′ adj.*

☆**upside-down cake** a cake baked with a bottom layer of fruit and turned upside down before serving

up·si·lon (yōōp′sə län′, up′-; -lən) *n.* [Gr.] the twentieth letter of the Greek alphabet (Υ, υ)

up·stage (up′stāj′; *for v.* up stāj′) *adv.* toward or at the rear of a stage —*adj.* **1.** of or having to do with the rear of a stage **2.** haughty and aloof —*vt.* **-staged′, -stag′ing** to draw attention, as of an audience, to oneself by taking it away from (another), as by moving upstage

up·stairs (up′sterz′) *adv.* **1.** up the stairs **2.** on or to an upper floor or higher level —*adj.* located on an upper floor [*an upstairs* room] —*n.* an upper floor or floors —**kick upstairs** [Colloq.] to promote from a position of power to one that seems higher but is really less powerful

up·stand·ing (up stan′diŋ) *adj.* **1.** standing straight; erect **2.** upright in character and behavior; honorable

up·start[1] (up′stärt′) *n.* a person who has recently come into wealth, power, etc., esp. one who is bold and pushing in a way that annoys others; parvenu —*adj.* of or like an upstart

up·start[2] (up stärt′) *vi.* to start, or spring, up

☆**up·state** (up′stāt′) *n.* that part of a State farther to the north or away from a large city; esp., the northern part of New York —*adj., adv.* in, to, or from upstate —*up′stat′er n.*

up·stream (-strēm′) *adv., adj.* in the direction against the current of a stream

up·surge (up surj′; *for n.* up′surj′) *vi.* **-surged′, -surg′ing** to surge up —*n.* a surge upward

up·sweep (up′swēp′; *for v.* up swēp′) *n.* **1.** a sweep or curve upward **2.** an upswept hairdo —*vt., vi.* **-swept′, -sweep′ing** to sweep or curve upward

up·swept (up′swept′) *adj.* **1.** curved upward **2.** designating or of a style of hairdo in which the hair is combed up in the back and piled on the top of the head

up·swing (up′swiŋ′; *for v.* up swiŋ′) *n.* a swing or trend upward; specif., an upward trend in business —*vi.* **-swung′, -swing′ing 1.** to swing upward **2.** to advance or improve

up·sy-dai·sy (up′sə dā′zē, up′sē-) *interj.* [baby-talk based on UP[1]] up you go: said playfully as when lifting a baby

up·take (up′tāk′) *n.* the act of taking up; a drawing up, absorbing, etc. —☆**quick (or slow) on the uptake** [Colloq.] quick (or slow) to understand or react

up·thrust (-thrust′) *n.* **1.** an upward push or thrust **2.** an upheaval of a part of the earth's crust

☆**up-tight, up·tight** (up′tīt′) *adj.* [Slang] **1.** very tense, nervous, anxious, etc. **2.** too conventional or strict in attitudes **3.** in a bad way or state Also **up tight**

up-to-date (up′tə dāt′) *adj.* **1.** going up to the present time; having the latest facts, ideas, etc. [an *up-to-date* report] **2.** keeping up with what is most recent, modern, etc. [*up-to-date* styles] —*up′-to-date′ness n.*

up·town (up′toun′) *adj., adv.* of, in, like, to, or toward the upper part of a city or town, usually the part away from the main business district —☆*n.* the uptown section

up·turn (up turn′; *for n.* up′turn′) *vt., vi.* to turn up, upward, or over —*n.* an upward turn, curve, or trend [business took a sharp *upturn*] —*up′turned′ adj.*

up·ward (up′wərd) *adv., adj.* **1.** toward a higher place, position, degree, etc. **2.** from an earlier to a later time [*moving upward* through history] **3.** beyond (a specified price, amount, etc.) [tickets cost one dollar and *upward*] Also **up′wards** *adv.* —**upwards (or upward) of** more than —*up′ward·ly adv.*

up·wind (up′wind′) *adv., adj.* in the direction from which the wind is blowing or usually blows

Ur (ʉr) ancient Sumerian city on the Euphrates River, in what is now S Iraq

u·ra·cil (yoor′ə sil) *n.* [UR(O)- + AC(ETIC) + -IL(E)] a crystalline base, $C_4H_4O_2N_2$, found in ribonucleic acid

U·ral (yoor′əl) **1.** [*pl.*] mountain system in the western R.S.F.S.R., traditionally thought of as the boundary between Europe & Asia: also **Ural Mountains 2.** a river flowing from the S section of these mountains into the Caspian Sea

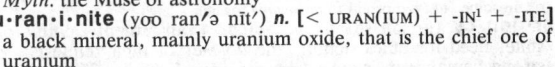

URALS

U·ral-Al·ta·ic (-al tā′ik) *n.* the group of languages which includes, among others, the Uralic and Altaic families —*adj.* **1.** designating or of this group of languages **2.** of the peoples speaking these languages

U·ral·ic (yoo ral′ik, -rā′lik) *adj.* designating or of the family of languages including Finno-Ugric and Samoyed —*n.* this family of languages Also **U·ra′li·an** (-rā′lē ən)

U·ra·ni·a (yoo rā′nē ə) *Gr. Myth.* the Muse of astronomy

u·ran·i·nite (yoo ran′ə nīt′) *n.* [< URAN(IUM) + -IN[1] + -ITE] a black mineral, mainly uranium oxide, that is the chief ore of uranium

u·ra·ni·um (yoo rā′nē əm) *n.* [ModL. < URANUS, the planet] a very hard, heavy, radioactive metallic chemical element: it is found only in combination, and its isotopes are important in work on atomic energy, esp. the isotope **U 235**, which can undergo continuous fission, and the more plentiful isotope **U 238**, from which plutonium is made: symbol, U; at. wt., 238.03; at. no., 92

U·ra·nus (yoor′ə nəs, yoo rā′nəs) **1.** a Greek god who was the symbol of the heavens and was the father of the Titans, Furies, and Cyclopes: he was overthrown by his son Cronus (Saturn) **2.** a planet of the solar system, seventh in distance from the sun: diameter, c. 29,500 mi.

u·rate (yoor′āt) *n.* a salt of uric acid

ur·ban (ʉr′bən) *adj.* [< L. < *urbs*, a city] **1.** of, in, or making up a city or town **2.** characteristic of the city as distinguished from the country

Ur·ban II (ʉr′bən) 1042?-99; Pope (1088–99)

ur·bane (ʉr bān′) *adj.* [< L.: see URBAN] polite and courteous in a smooth, polished way; refined —see SYN. at SUAVE —**ur·bane′ly** *adv.* —**ur·bane′ness n.**

ur·ban·ism (ʉr′bən iz'm) *n.* **1.** *a)* urban life, organization, problems, etc.; life in the cities *b)* the study of this **2.** a condition in which most of the people in a country live in the cities —*ur′ban·ist n., adj.*

ur·ban·ite (-īt′) *n.* a person living in a city

ur·ban·i·ty (ʉr ban′ə tē) *n., pl.* **-ties 1.** the quality of being urbane; refined politeness **2.** [*pl.*] refined courtesies; amenities

ur·ban·ize (ʉr′bə nīz′) *vt.* **-ized′, -iz′ing** to change from rural to urban; cause to be like a city —*ur′ban·i·za′tion n.*

☆**ur·ban·ol·o·gist** (ʉr′bə näl′ə jist) *n.* [URBAN + -o- + -LOG(Y) + -IST] an expert in urban problems

☆**urban renewal** the improving of older urban areas that have fallen into poor condition, as by clearing slums and building new housing projects, etc.

ur·chin (ʉr′chin) *n.* [< OFr. < L. *ericius*, a hedgehog < *er*, hedgehog] **1.** *same as* SEA URCHIN **2.** a small boy, or any youngster, esp. one who is mischievous

Ur·du (oor′dōō) *n.* an Indic language, a form of Hindi written with Arabic characters: an official language of Pakistan

-ure (ər) [Fr. < L. *-ura*] *a suffix meaning:* **1.** act or result of being [*exposure*] **2.** a thing or group that [*legislature*] **3.** state of being [*composure*]

u·re·a (yoo rē′ə, yoor′ē ə) *n.* [ModL. < Fr. < Gr. *ouron*, urine] a soluble, crystalline solid, $CO(NH_2)_2$, found in the urine of mammals or produced synthetically: used in making plastics, adhesives, etc. —*u·re′al, u·re′ic adj.*

u·re·mi·a (yoo rē′mē ə, -rēm′yə) *n.* [ModL. < Gr. *ouron*, urine + *haima*, blood] an illness caused by the presence in the blood of waste products normally gotten rid of in the urine — **u·re′mic** adj.

u·re·ter (yoo rēt′ər, yoor′ə tər) n. [ModL. < Gr. < *ourein,* to urinate] a duct or tube that carries urine from a kidney to the bladder or cloaca —**u·re′ter·al, u·re·ter·ic** (yoor′ə ter′ik) adj.

u·re·thra (yoo rē′thrə) n., pl. **-thrae** (-thrē) **-thras** [LL. < Gr. < *ouron,* urine] the canal through which urine is discharged from the bladder in most mammals: in the male, semen is also discharged through the urethra —**u·re′thral** adj.

U·rey (yoor′ē), **Harold Clay·ton** (klā′t'n) 1893– ; U.S. chemist

urge (ʉrj) vt. **urged, urg′ing** [L. *urgere,* to press hard] **1.** to press upon the attention; speak strongly in favor of [to *urge* caution] **2.** to plead with; ask or try to persuade earnestly; exhort [they *urged* him to finish college] **3.** to drive or force onward; impel [he *urged* his mule up the hill] —vi. **1.** to put forth arguments, claims, etc. in a earnest, forceful way [to *urge* against hasty action] **2.** to exert a force that drives or impels, as to action —n. **1.** the act of urging **2.** an impulse or inner drive to do a certain thing [an *urge* to sneeze; the *urge* to become a writer] —**urg′er** n.

SYN.—**urge** implies a strong effort to persuade someone to do something, as by pleading, argument, or forceful recommendation [he *urged* us to accept the offer]; **exhort** implies an earnest urging to action or conduct considered proper or right [the minister *exhorted* his flock to work for peace]; **press** suggests a continuous and forceful urging that is hard to resist [we *pressed* him to stay]; **importune** implies continued efforts to break down resistance against a demand or request, often to the point of being annoying or tiresome [not too proud to *importune* for help]

ur·gen·cy (ʉr′jən sē) n., pl. **-cies 1.** an urgent quality or state; need for quick action [the *urgency* of their request] **2.** strong demand; insistence [the *urgency* of public opinion] **3.** something urgent

ur·gent (ʉr′jənt) adj. [MFr. < L. prp. of *urgere,* to urge] **1.** calling for haste, immediate action, etc.; pressing [an *urgent* situation] **2.** demanding in a strong and serious way; insistent [an *urgent* call for help] —**ur′gent·ly** adv.

-ur·gy (ʉr′jē) [< Gr. < *-ourgos,* worker < *ergon,* work] a combining form meaning a working with or by means of (something specified) [zymurgy]

u·ric (yoor′ik) adj. of, contained in, or derived from urine

uric acid a white, odorless, crystalline substance, $C_5H_4N_4O_3$, found in urine

u·ri·nal (yoor′ə n'l) n. **1.** a portable container used, as in a sickbed, by men for urinating **2.** a fixture with a drain, for use by men in urinating

☆**u·ri·nal·y·sis** (yoor′ə nal′ə sis) n., pl. **-ses′** (-sēz′) chemical or microscopic analysis of the urine

u·ri·nar·y (yoor′ə ner′ē) adj. **1.** of urine **2.** of the organs involved in secreting and discharging urine

u·ri·nate (yoor′ə nāt′) vi. **-nat′ed, -nat′ing** to discharge urine from the body —vt. to discharge as or with the urine —**u′ri·na′tion** n. —**u′ri·na′tive** adj.

u·rine (yoor′in) n. [OFr. < L. *urina*] in mammals, the yellowish fluid containing urea and other waste products, secreted from the blood by the kidneys, passed to the bladder, and discharged from time to time through the urethra

u·ri·no- [< L. *urina,* urine] a combining form meaning urine, urinary tract: also, before a vowel, **urin-**

u·ri·no·gen·i·tal (yoor′ə nō jen′ə t'l) adj. same as UROGENITAL

urn (ʉrn) n. [L. *urna*] **1.** a) a vase, esp. one with a foot or pedestal b) a container for the ashes of a cremated body **2.** a metal container with a faucet, used for making or serving coffee, tea, etc.

u·ro- [< Gr. *ouron,* urine] a combining form meaning urine, urination, urinary tract: also, before a vowel, **ur-**

u·ro·gen·i·tal (yoor′ō jen′ə t'l) adj. designating or of the urinary and genital organs; genitourinary

u·rol·o·gy (yoo räl′ə jē) n. the branch of medicine dealing with the urogenital or urinary system and its diseases —**u·ro·log·ic** (yoor′ə läj′ik), **u′ro·log′i·cal** adj. —**u·rol′o·gist** n.

u·ros·co·py (yoo räs′kə pē) n., pl. **-pies** examination of the urine, as for the diagnosis of disease —**u·ro·scop·ic** (yoor′ə skäp′ik) adj.

Ur·sa Major (ʉr′sə) [L., lit., Great Bear] the most easily seen constellation in the northern sky: it contains the seven stars which form the Big Dipper

Ursa Minor [L., lit., Little Bear] the northernmost constella-

URN

tion: it contains the Little Dipper, with the North Star at the end of its handle

ur·sine (ʉr′sīn, -sin) adj. [< L. < *ursus,* a bear] of or like a bear or the bear family; bearlike

Ur·su·la (ʉr′sə lə) [ML., dim. of L. *ursa,* she-bear] **1.** a feminine name **2.** Saint, a legendary Christian Brit. princess said to have lived in the 4th cent.

Ur·su·line (-lin, -līn) n. [< ModL.: after Saint URSULA] R.C.Ch. any member of a teaching order of nuns founded c.1537 —adj. of this order

ur·ti·car·i·a (ʉr′tə ker′ē ə) n. [ModL. < L. *urtica,* a nettle] same as HIVES —**ur′ti·car′i·al** adj.

U·ru·guay (yoor′ə gwā′, -gwī′; Sp. ōō′rōō gwī′) **1.** country in southeastern S. America, on the Atlantic: 72,171 sq. mi.; pop. 2,886,000; cap. Montevideo **2.** river in southeastern S. America, flowing into the Río de la Plata —**U′ru·guay′an** adj., n.

u·rus (yoor′əs) n. [L. < Gmc.] same as AUROCHS (sense 1)

us (us) pron. [OE.] objective case of WE (Ex.: tell *us* the story): also used colloquially after a linking verb (Ex.: that's *us*)

U.S., US United States

USA, U.S.A. 1. United States of America **2.** United States Army

us·a·ble, use·a·ble (yōō′zə b'l) adj. that can be used; fit, convenient, or ready for use —**us′a·bil′i·ty, us′a·ble·ness** n. —**us′a·bly** adv.

USAF, U.S.A.F. United States Air Force

us·age (yōō′sij, -zij) n. **1.** the act, way, or extent of using; treatment [shoes scuffed from hard *usage*] **2.** a long-continued or long-established practice; custom; habit **3.** the way in which a word, phrase, etc. is used in speaking or writing, or an instance of this ["a turkey" meaning "a failure" is a slang *usage*]

USCG, U.S.C.G. United States Coast Guard

USDA United States Department of Agriculture

use (yōōz; for n. yōōs) vt. **used** (yōōzd; for vt. 6 & vi., with the following "to," yōōs′tə or yōōs′too), **us′ing** [< OFr., ult. < L. *usus,* pp. of *uti,* to use] **1.** to put or bring into action or service [she *used* the vacuum cleaner] **2.** to practice; exercise [use your judgment] **3.** to behave toward; treat [to *use* a friend badly] **4.** to do away with by using; consume, expend, etc. [to *use* up one's energy] **5.** a) to smoke or chew (tobacco) b) to take or consume habitually [to *use* drugs] **6.** to make familiar or accustom so that one can put up with (used in the passive voice) [she's *used* to hard work] **7.** to exploit or treat (a person) as a means to some selfish end —vi. to be accustomed; be in the habit (now used only in the past tense, with an infinitive, generally meaning "did in an earlier time") [she *used* to read a lot; he *used* to live in Iowa] —n. **1.** a using or being used [the *use* of atomic energy for power] **2.** the ability to use [he lost the *use* of his leg] **3.** the right or permission to use [to grant a friend the *use* of one's car] **4.** the need or opportunity to use [no further *use* for his services] **5.** a way of using [to be taught the *use* of the typewriter] **6.** the quality that makes a thing useful; usefulness [what's the *use* of your worrying?] **7.** the object or purpose for which something is used; function, service, or benefit [the many *uses* of electric power] **8.** custom; habit; practice **9.** Law a) the enjoyment of property, as from occupying or employing it b) profit or benefit, esp. that of property held in trust by another —**have no use for 1.** to have no need of ☆**2.** to dislike strongly —**in use** being used —**make use of** to use; have occasion to use —**put to use** to use

SYN.—**use** implies the putting of a thing into action or service for a given purpose, esp. its intended purpose, or, in the case of a person treated as a thing, for one's own selfish purposes [to *use* a pencil, a suggestion, etc.; he *used* his brother to advance himself]; **employ**, a more formal term, implies the putting to useful work of something not in use at that moment [to *employ* a vacant lot as a playground] and, with reference to persons, suggests a providing of work and pay [he *employs* five mechanics]; **utilize** implies the putting of something to a practical or profitable use [to *utilize* byproducts]

used (yōōzd) pt. & pp. of USE —adj. **1.** that has been used **2.** same as SECONDHAND

use·ful (yōōs′fəl) adj. that can be used; serviceable; helpful —**use′ful·ly** adv. —**use′ful·ness** n.

use·less (-lis) adj. **1.** having no use; not serviceable; worthless [a *useless* gadget] **2.** to no purpose [it is *useless* for you to complain]—see SYN. at FUTILE —**use′less·ly** adv. —**use′less·ness** n.

us·er (yōō′zər) n. a person or thing that uses; specif., ☆a person who uses drugs; addict

U-shaped (yōō′shāpt′) adj. having the shape of a U

ush·er (ush′ər) n. [OFr. *uissier* < L. *ostiarius* < *ostium,* door] **1.** an official doorkeeper **2.** a person whose duty it is to show people to their seats in a theater, church, etc. **3.** any of the groom's attendants at a wedding —**vt. 1.** to show the way to or conduct (others) to seats, etc. **2.** to herald or bring [the atom bomb *ushered* in a new age] —**vi.** to act as an usher

☆**ush·er·ette** (ush′ə ret′) **n.** a woman or girl usher, as in a theater

USIA, U.S.I.A. United States Information Agency

USIS, U.S.I.S. United States Information Service

U.S.M., USM 1. United States Mail **2.** United States Mint

USMC, U.S.M.C. United States Marine Corps

USN, U.S.N. United States Navy

USNG, U.S.N.G. United States National Guard

USO, U.S.O. United Service Organizations

U.S.P., U.S.Pharm. United States Pharmacopoeia

U.S.S., USS United States Ship, Steamer, or Steamship

U.S.S.R., USSR Union of Soviet Socialist Republics

u·su·al (yōō′zhoo wəl, -zhwəl, -zhəl) **adj.** [< MFr. < LL. *usualis* < L. *usus:* see USE] such as is most often seen, heard, used, etc.; common; ordinary; customary —**as usual** in the usual way —**u′su·al·ly** *adv.* —**u′su·al·ness** *n.*

SYN.—**usual** applies to that which past experience has shown to be the normal, common, thus expected thing [the *usual* results, greeting, answer, etc.]; **customary** refers to that which fits with the usual practices of some individual or with the existing customs of some group [his *customary* mid-morning coffee; it was *customary* to dress formally for dinner]; **habitual** implies a fixed practice that results from repeated acts [her *habitual* tardiness]; **wonted** is a somewhat literary substitute for **customary** or **habitual** [behaving in their *wonted* manner]; **accustomed** may be substituted for **customary** but suggests less strongly a fixed custom [he sat in his *accustomed* place]. —**ANT.** extraordinary, unusual

u·su·fruct (yōō′zyoo frukt′, -zoo-, -soo-) **n.** [< LL. < L. *usus,* a use + *fructus,* a fruit] *Law* the right to use and enjoy the advantages and profits of the property of another without changing or damaging the property —**u′su·fruc′tu·ar′y** (-fruk′choo wer′ē) *adj., n., pl.* -**ar′ies**

u·su·rer (yōō′zhoor rər) *n.* a person who practices usury

u·su·ri·ous (yōō zhoor′ē əs) *adj.* **1.** practicing usury **2.** of or involving usury —**u·su′ri·ous·ly** *adv.* —**u·su′ri·ous·ness** *n.*

u·surp (yōō surp′, -zurp′) *vt., vi.* [< MFr. < L. *usurpare* < *usus,* a use + *rapere,* to seize] to take and hold (power, position, rights, etc.) by force or without right —**u·surp′er** *n.*

u·sur·pa·tion (yōō′sər pā′shən, -zər-) *n.* unlawful or violent taking of a throne, power, etc.

u·su·ry (yōō′zhoo rē) *n., pl.* -**ries** [< ML. < L. *usura* < *usus:* see USE] **1.** the lending of money at interest, now specif. at a rate of interest that is too high or against the law **2.** interest at such a high rate

usw, u.s.w. [G. *und so weiter*] and so forth

U·tah (yōō′tô, -tä) [< Sp. < tribal name, lit. ? hill dwellers] Western State of the U.S.: 84,916 sq. mi.; pop. 1,059,000; cap. Salt Lake City: abbrev. Ut., UT —**U′tah·an** *adj., n.*

Ute (yōōt, yōōt′ē) *n.* [see UTAH] **1.** *pl.* **Utes, Ute** any member of a tribe of Shoshonean Indians living mainly in Colorado and Utah **2.** their Shoshonean language

u·ten·sil (yōō ten′s'l) *n.* [< MFr. < L. < *utensilis,* fit for use < *uti,* to use] a tool or container used for a particular purpose, now esp. one used in a kitchen [cooking *utensils*]

u·ter·ine (yōōt′ər in, yōō′tə rīn′) *adj.* **1.** of the uterus **2.** having the same mother but a different father [*uterine* sisters]

u·ter·us (yōōt′ər əs) *n., pl.* **u′ter·i′** (-ī′) [L.] a hollow, muscular organ of female mammals in which the ovum is deposited and the embryo and fetus are developed; womb

U Thant *see* THANT

U·ti·ca (yōō′ti kə) [after an ancient city in N Africa] city in central N.Y., on the Mohawk River: pop. 92,000

u·til·i·tar·i·an (yoo til′ə ter′ē ən) *adj.* **1.** of or having utility; useful **2.** stressing usefulness over beauty, etc. **3.** of or believing in utilitarianism —**n.** a person who believes in utilitarianism

u·til·i·tar·i·an·ism (-iz′m) *n.* **1.** the doctrine that the value of anything is determined solely by its usefulness **2.** the doctrine that the purpose of all action should be to bring about the greatest happiness of the greatest number **3.** utilitarian character or quality

u·til·i·ty (yoo til′ə tē) *n., pl.* -**ties** [< OFr. < L. < *utilis,* useful < *uti,* to use] **1.** usefulness **2.** something useful **3.** *a)* something useful to the public, esp. the service of electricity, gas, wa-

ter, etc. *b)* a company providing such a service: see also PUBLIC UTILITY **4.** *Econ.* the power to satisfy the needs or wants of humanity —**adj. 1.** for practical use with little attention to beauty **2.** useful or used in a number of ways ☆**3.** *Baseball* able to substitute in several positions [*utility* infielder]

☆**utility room** a room containing various household appliances and equipment, as for heating, laundry, cleaning, etc.

u·ti·lize (yōōt′'l īz′) *vt.* -**lized′, -liz′ing** to put to use; make practical or profitable use of [to *utilize* atomic power for peaceful purposes] Brit. sp. **u′ti·lise** —see SYN. at USE —**u′ti·liz′a·ble** *adj.* —**u′ti·li·za′tion** *n.* —**u′ti·liz′er** *n.*

ut·most (ut′mōst′) *adj.* [OE. *utemest,* double superl. of *ut,* out] **1.** most distant; farthest [the *utmost* regions of the earth] **2.** of or to the greatest or highest degree, amount, etc.; greatest [a meeting of the *utmost* importance] —**n.** the most that is possible [straining his muscles to the *utmost*]

U·to-Az·tec·an (yōōt′ō az′tek ən) *adj.* designating or of a large American Indian linguistic family of the western U.S., Mexico, and Central America —**n.** the Uto-Aztecan family of languages, including Shoshone, Nahuatl, Pima, etc.

U·to·pi·a (yoo tō′pē ə) [ModL. < Gr. *ou,* not + *topos,* a place] an imaginary island described in a book of the same name by Sir Thomas More (1516) as having a perfect political and social system —**n.** [*often* **u-**] **1.** any imaginary place, state, or situation of perfection **2.** any idealistic scheme for a perfect society

U·to·pi·an (-ən) *adj.* **1.** of or like Utopia **2.** [*often* **u-**] having or based on ideas imagining perfection in social and political organization; idealistic; visionary —**n. 1.** an inhabitant of Utopia **2.** [*often* **u-**] a person who believes in a utopia, esp. of a social or political nature; visionary —**u·to′pi·an·ism** *n.*

U·trecht (yōō′trekt; *Du.* ü′treHt) city in the C Netherlands: pop. 279,000

u·tri·cle (yōō′tri k'l) *n.* [< Fr. < L. dim. of *uter,* leather bag] a small sac, vesicle, or baglike part: also **u·tric·u·lus** (yoo-trik′yə ləs), *pl.* -**li′** (-lī′) —**u·tric′u·lar** *adj.*

U·tril·lo (ōō tril′ō; *Fr.* ōō trē lō′), **Maurice** 1883-1955; Fr. painter

ut·ter[1] (ut′ər) *adj.* [OE. *uttera,* compar. of *ut,* out] complete; total; absolute [*utter* joy; an *utter* fool] —**ut′ter·ly** *adv.* —**ut′ter·ness** *n.*

ut·ter[2] (ut′ər) *vt.* [< ME. < *utter,* outward < *ut,* out] **1.** orig., to give out; put forth; now esp., to pass (counterfeit money, forged checks, etc.) **2.** to make or express with the voice [to *utter* a cry, to *utter* a thought] **3.** to express in any way —**ut′ter·a·ble** *adj.* —**ut′ter·er** *n.*

ut·ter·ance (ut′ər əns, ut′rəns) *n.* **1.** the act, power, or way of uttering [to give *utterance* to an idea] **2.** something uttered or said

ut·ter·most (ut′ər mōst′) *adj., n.* same as UTMOST

U-turn (yōō′turn′) *n.* a turning completely around, esp. of a vehicle within the width of a street or road, so as to head in the opposite direction

UV, uv ultraviolet

u·ve·a (yōō′vē ə) *n.* [< L. *uva,* a grape] the iris, ciliary body, and choroid, together forming the colored layer of the eye —**u′ve·al** *adj.*

u·vu·la (yōō′vyə lə) *n., pl.* -**las, -lae′** (-lē′) [ML., dim. of L. *uva,* a grape] the small, fleshy part of the soft palate hanging down above the back of the tongue

u·vu·lar (-lər) *adj.* **1.** of or having to do with the uvula **2.** *Phonet.* pronounced with a vibration of the uvula, or with the back of the tongue near or touching the uvula —**n.** a uvular sound —**u′vu·lar·ly** *adv.*

UVULA

ux·o·ri·al (ək sôr′ē əl, əg zôr′-) *adj.* [see UXORIOUS] of or like a wife —**ux·or′i·al·ly** *adv.*

ux·o·ri·ous (-əs) *adj.* [< L. < *uxor,* wife] fond of or devoted to one's wife in a way that seems extreme —**ux·o′ri·ous·ly** *adv.* —**ux·o′ri·ous·ness** *n.*

Uz·bek (ooz′bek, uz′-) *n.* **1.** a member of a Turkic people living in the region of the Uzbek S.S.R. **2.** the Turkic language of the Uzbeks **Also Uz′beg** (-beg)

Uzbek Soviet Socialist Republic republic of the U.S.S.R., in C Asia: 173,546 sq. mi.; pop. 12,000,000; cap. Tashkent: also **Uz·bek·i·stan** (ooz′bek i stan′, uz′-; -stän′)

---

fat, āpe, cär; ten, ēven; is, bīte; gō, hôrn, tōōl, look; oil, out; up, fur; get; joy; yet; chin; she; thin, then; zh, leisure; ŋ, ring; ə for a in ago, e in agent, i in sanity, o in comply, u in focus; ' as in able (ā′b'l); Fr. bal; ë, Fr. coeur; ö, Fr. feu; Fr. mon; ô, Fr. coq; ü, Fr. duc; r, Fr. cri; H, G. ich; kh, G. doch; ‡foreign; ☆ Americanism; < derived from. See inside front cover.

V, v (vē) *n., pl.* **V's, v's** **1.** the twenty-second letter of the English alphabet **2.** the sound of *V* or *v*

V (vē) *n.* **1.** something shaped like V **2.** a Roman numeral for 5 ☆**3.** [Colloq.] a five-dollar bill **4.** *Chem.* vanadium —*adj.* shaped like V

V, v **1.** *Math.* vector **2.** velocity **3.** victory **4.** volt(s)

v. **1.** [L. *vice*] in the place of **2.** [G. *von*] of **3.** [L. *vide*] see **4.** verb **5.** *pl.* **vv.** verse **6.** version **7.** versus **8.** vice- **9.** village **10.** *pl.* **vv.** violin **11.** voice **12.** volt **13.** voltage **14.** volume

VA, V.A. Veterans Administration

Va., VA Virginia

va·can·cy (vā′kən sē) *n., pl.* **-cies** **1.** the state of being vacant; emptiness **2.** *a)* empty space *b)* a vacant space; gap, blank, opening, etc. **3.** lack of intelligence, interest, or thought **4.** an unoccupied position or office **5.** a room, apartment, etc. available for rent

va·cant (vā′kənt) *adj.* [< OFr. < L. prp. of *vacare*, to be empty] **1.** having nothing in it, as a space; empty [a *vacant* lot] **2.** not held, filled, or occupied, as a position, a seat, a house, etc. **3.** free from work or activity [*vacant* time] **4.** without thought, interest, etc. [a *vacant* mind, stare, etc.] —see SYN. at EMPTY — **va′cant·ly** *adv.* —**va′cant·ness** *n.*

va·cate (vā′kāt) *vt.* **-cat·ed, -cat·ing** [< L. pp. of *vacare*, to be empty] **1.** to make vacant; specif., to leave (an office, position, etc.) or move out of (a house, room, etc.) **2.** *Law* to make no longer binding; void; annul —*vi.* to make an office, position, house, etc. vacant

va·ca·tion (vā kā′shən, və-) *n.* [< MFr. < L. *vacatio*] **1.** a rest or relief from something ☆**2.** a period of time when one stops working, going to school, etc. in order to rest and have recreation **3.** [Rare] a vacating **4.** *Law* a formal recess between terms of court —*vi.* to take one's vacation —☆**va·ca′tion·er, va·ca′tion·ist** *n.*

va·ca·tion·land (-land′) *n.* an area that attracts vacationers because it has recreational facilities, historic sights, etc.

vac·ci·nate (vak′sə nāt′) *vt.* **-nat·ed, -nat·ing** to inject with a specific vaccine in order to prevent disease, as in immunizing against smallpox —*vi.* to practice vaccination —**vac′ci·na′tor** *n.*

vac·ci·na·tion (vak′sə nā′shən) *n.* **1.** the act or practice of vaccinating **2.** the scar on the skin where the vaccine has been applied

vac·cine (vak sēn′; vak′sēn, -sin) *n.* [L. *vaccinus*, from cows < *vacca*, a cow: from use of cowpox virus in smallpox vaccine] any preparation of killed microorganisms, living weakened organisms, etc. introduced into the body to produce immunity to a specific disease by causing antibodies to be formed —**vac′ci·nal** *adj.*

vac·il·late (vas′ə lāt′) *vi.* **-lat·ed, -lat·ing** [< L. pp. of *vacillare*] **1.** to sway to and fro; waver **2.** to move back and forth or up and down; fluctuate or oscillate [the pointer on the scales *vacillated*] **3.** to waver in mind; be unable to decide [to *vacillate* between going and staying] —see SYN. at HESITATE —**vac′il·lat′ing** *adj.* —**vac′il·lat′ing·ly** *adv.* —**vac′il·la′tion** *n.* —**vac′il·la′tor** *n.*

va·cu·i·ty (va kyōō′ə tē) *n., pl.* **-ties** [< L. < *vacuus*, empty] **1.** the condition of being empty; emptiness **2.** an empty space; void or vacuum **3.** lack of intelligence, interest, or thought **4.** something senseless or silly

vac·u·ole (vak′yoo wōl′) *n.* [Fr. < L. *vacuus*, empty] *Biol.* a fluid-filled cavity within the plasma membrane of a cell, believed

to get rid of excess water or wastes —**vac′u·o·lar** (-wə- lər, vak′yoo wō′lər) *adj.*

vac·u·ous (vak′yoo wəs) *adj.* [L. *vacuus*] **1.** empty **2.** showing lack of intelligence or thought; stupid; senseless; inane [a *vacuous* smile] **3.** lacking purpose; idle [a bored, *vacuous* life] —**vac′u·ous·ly** *adv.* —**vac′u·ous·ness** *n.*

vac·u·um (vak′yoo wəm; *also,* & *for adj.* & *v. usually,* vak′yoom) *n., pl.* **-u·ums, -u·a** (-yoo wə) [L., neut. sing. of *vacuus*, empty] **1.** a space with nothing at all in it **2.** an enclosed space, as that inside a vacuum tube, out of which most of the air or gas has been taken, as by pumping **3.** a space or condition of emptiness caused as by the removal of something important; void [the *vacuum* created in the party by the death of their leader] ☆**4.** *short for* VACUUM CLEANER —*adj.* **1.** of a vacuum **2.** used to make a vacuum **3.** having a vacuum **4.** working by suction or the creation of a partial vacuum —*vt., vi.* to clean with a vacuum cleaner: in full, **vac′u·um-clean′**

vacuum bottle (or **flask** or **jug**) *same as* THERMOS

vacuum cleaner a machine for cleaning carpets, floors, upholstery, etc. by suction: also **vacuum sweeper**

vacuum gauge an instrument for measuring the pressure of the air or gas in a partial vacuum

☆**vacuum-packed** (-pakt′) *adj.* packed in an airtight container from which most of the air was taken out before sealing, so as to keep the contents fresh

vacuum pump a pump used to draw air or gas out of a sealed space

vacuum tube an electron tube from which as much air has been taken out as possible

va·de me·cum (vā′dē mē′kəm, vä′-) [L., lit., go with me] something carried about by a person for constant use, reference, etc., as a handbook

Va·duz (vä′doots) capital of Liechtenstein: pop. 4,000

vag·a·bond (vag′ə bänd′) *adj.* [< MFr. < L. *vagabundus*, strolling about < *vagari*, to wander] **1.** moving from place to place; wandering [a *vagabond* tribe] **2.** of, having to do with, or living an unsettled, drifting, irresponsible life; vagrant; shiftless [*vagabond* habits] **3.** aimlessly following an irregular course; drifting —*n.* **1.** a person who wanders from place to place, having no fixed abode **2.** a tramp **3.** an idle, disreputable, or shiftless person —*vi.* to wander —see SYN. at VAGRANT —**vag′a·bond′age, vag′a·bond′ism** *n.* —**vag′a·bond′ish** *adj.*

va·gar·y (və ger′ē, -gar′-; vā′gər ē) *n., pl.* **-gar′ies** [< L. *vagari*, to wander] **1.** an odd, eccentric, or unexpected action **2.** an odd, whimsical, or freakish idea or notion —**va·gar′i·ous** *adj.* —**va·gar′i·ous·ly** *adv.*

va·gi·na (və jī′nə) *n., pl.* **-nas, -nae** (-nē) [L., a sheath] a sheath or sheathlike part; specif., in female mammals, the canal leading from the vulva to the uterus —**vag·i·nal** (vaj′ə n'l, və- jī′n'l) *adj.*

vag·i·nate (vaj′ə nit, -nāt′) *adj.* **1.** having a vagina or sheath; sheathed **2.** like a sheath

va·gran·cy (vā′grən sē) *n., pl.* **-cies** [< VAGRANT] **1.** a wandering in thought or talk; digression **2.** a wandering from place to place **3.** shiftless or lazy wandering without money or work, as of tramps, beggars, etc.: often a statutory offense chargeable as a misdemeanor

va·grant (vā′grənt) *n.* [prob. < Anglo-Fr. < OFr. *walcrer*, to wander: influenced prob. by L. *vagari*, to wander] a person who wanders from place to place; esp., one without a regular job, supporting himself by begging, etc.; vagabond, tramp,

---

etc. —*adj.* **1.** wandering from place to place; roaming; nomadic **2.** of, characteristic of, or living the life of a vagrant **3.** following no fixed direction or course; random, wayward, etc. —**va′grant·ly** *adv.*

SYN.—**vagrant** refers to a person without a fixed home who wanders about from place to place, supporting himself by begging, etc., and in legal usage refers to any such person whose way of living makes him a public nuisance and who may therefore be arrested; **vagabond**, orig. implying laziness, roguishness, etc., now often suggests no more than a carefree, roaming existence; **bum**, **tramp**, and **hobo** are informal substitutes for **vagrant** and **vagabond**, in some senses, but **bum** specifically brings to mind a homeless drunkard who never works, **tramp**, a vagrant who lives by begging or by doing odd jobs, and **hobo**, a migratory laborer who follows seasonal work

vague (vāg) *adj.* **va′guer, va′guest** [Fr. < L. *vagus*, wandering] **1.** not clearly or exactly expressed or stated [a *vague* answer] **2.** not definite in shape or form [*vague* figures in the fog] **3.** not sharp, certain, or exact in thought or feeling [*vague* about his plans; a *vague* longing] **4.** not known or determined; uncertain —see **SYN.** at OBSCURE —**vague′ly** *adv.* —**vague′ness** *n.*

va·gus (vā′gəs) *n., pl.* **va′gi** (-jī) [ModL. < L., wandering] either of a pair of cranial nerves acting upon the larynx, lungs, heart, esophagus, and most of the abdominal organs: also **vagus nerve** —**va′gal** (-g'l) *adj.*

va·hi·ne (vä hē′nä) *n.* [Tahitian] a Polynesian woman, esp. of Tahiti

vain (vān) *adj.* [< OFr. < L. *vanus*, empty] **1.** having no real value or meaning; worthless, empty, etc. [*vain* promises] **2.** with little or no result; not successful; futile, fruitless, etc. [a *vain* attempt] **3.** having or showing too high an opinion of oneself, one's looks, one's ability, etc.; conceited —**in vain 1.** without success; uselessly [pleading *in vain* for help] **2.** without the proper respect; profanely —**vain′ly** *adv.* —**vain′ness** *n.*

SYN.—**vain** applies to that which has little or no real value, worth, or meaning [*vain* sacrifices]; **idle** refers to that which has no practical use or purpose because it can never be brought into being or have a real effect [*idle* hopes, *idle* talk]; **empty** and **hollow** are used of that which has only an outward show of being real, genuine, etc. [*empty* threats, *hollow* pleasures] —see also **SYN.** at FUTILE

vain·glo·ri·ous (vān′glôr′ē əs) *adj.* [< ML.: see VAINGLORY] **1.** boastfully vain and proud of oneself **2.** characterized by boastful vanity —**vain′glo′ri·ous·ly** *adv.* —**vain′glo′ri·ous·ness** *n.*

vain·glo·ry (vān′glôr′ē, vān glôr′ē) *n.* [< OFr. < L. *vana gloria*, empty boasting: see VAIN & GLORY] **1.** extreme self-pride and boastfulness **2.** vain show or empty pomp

val·ance (val′əns, vāl′-) *n.* [< ? *Valence*, city in France] **1.** a short drapery or curtain hanging from the edge of a bed, shelf, etc., often to the floor **2.** a short drapery or covering of wood or metal across the top of a window —**val′anced** *adj.*

vale[1] (vāl) *n.* [< OFr. < L. *vallis*] [Poet.] *same as* VALLEY

‡va·le[2] (vā′lē, wä′lā) *interj., n.* [L.] farewell

val·e·dic·tion (val′ə dik′shən) *n.* [< L. pp. of *valedicere* < *vale*, farewell (imper. of *valere*, to be well) + *dicere*, to say] **1.** a saying farewell **2.** a farewell speech or statement

☆**val·e·dic·to·ri·an** (val′ə dik tôr′ē ən) *n.* in schools and colleges, the student, usually the one ranking highest in the class in scholarship, who delivers the valedictory

val·e·dic·to·ry (val′ə dik′tər ē) *adj.* said or done at parting, by way of farewell; spoken as a valediction —*n., pl.* **-ries** a farewell speech, esp. one delivered at graduation

va·lence (vā′ləns) *n.* [< ML., ult. < L. prp. of *valere*, to be strong] *Chem.* **1.** the combining power of an element or radical, as measured by the number of hydrogen or chlorine atoms which one radical or one atom of the element will combine with or replace (for example, oxygen has a *valence* of two, so that one atom of oxygen combines with two hydrogen atoms to form the water molecule, H_2O) **2.** any of the units of valence which a particular element may have Also **va′len·cy,** *pl.* **-cies**

valence electrons the electrons in the outermost shell of an atom, which largely determine its properties

Va·len·ci·a (və len′shē ə, -shə, -sē ə; *Sp.* vä len′thyä) **1.** region & former kingdom in E Spain, on the Mediterranean **2.** seaport in this region: pop. 624,000

Va·len·ci·ennes (və len′sē enz′) *n.* [after *Valenciennes*, city in N France] a fine lace having a simple floral pattern and a net background: also **Valenciennes lace**

-va·lent (vā′lənt) [< L. *valens:* see VALENCE] *Chem. a suffix meaning:* **1.** having a specified valence **2.** having a specified number of valences

VALENCIA

Val·en·tine (val′ən tīn′), Saint 3d cent. A.D.; Christian martyr of Rome

val·en·tine (val′ən tīn′) *n.* **1.** a sweetheart to whom one sends a message of affection on Saint Valentine's Day **2.** a greeting card or gift sent on this day

Va·le·ri·an (və lir′ē ən) (L. name *Publius Licinius Valerianus*) 190?–after 260 A.D.; Roman emperor (253–260)

va·le·ri·an (və lir′ē ən) *n.* [< MFr. < ML. *valeriana*] **1.** any of various plants with clusters or spikes of white, pink, red, or purplish flowers **2.** a drug made from the roots of some of these plants, formerly used as a sedative

val·et (val′it, val′ā; *Fr.* vȧ lā′) *n.* [Fr., a groom < OFr. *vaslet*, young man, page] **1.** a man's personal manservant who takes care of the man's clothes, helps him in dressing, etc. **2.** an employee, as of a hotel, who cleans or presses clothes, etc. ☆**3.** a rack for hanging a change of clothing for a man —*vt., vi.* to serve (a person) as a valet

val·e·tu·di·nar·i·an (val′ə tōō′də ner′ē ən) *n.* [< L. < *valetudo*, state of health, sickness < *valere*, to be strong] **1.** a person in poor health; invalid **2.** a person who worries constantly about his health —*adj.* **1.** in poor health; sickly **2.** anxiously concerned about one's health Also **val′e·tu′di·nar′y,** *pl.* **-nar′ies**

Val·hal·la (val hal′ə) *Norse Myth.* the great hall where Odin receives and feasts the souls of heroes fallen bravely in battle: also **Val·hall′**

val·iant (val′yənt) *adj.* [< OFr. prp. of *valoir* < L. *valere*, to be strong] courageous; brave [a *valiant* struggle for freedom] —see **SYN.** at BRAVE —**val′iance, val′ian·cy** *n.* —**val′iant·ly** *adv.*

val·id (val′id) *adj.* [< Fr. < L. *validus*, strong < *valere*, to be strong] **1.** having legal force; binding under law [a *valid* deed or will] **2.** well-grounded on principles or evidence, as an argument; sound **3.** producing or able to produce the desired results; effective [a *valid* method] **4.** *Logic* correctly derived or inferred according to the rules of logic —**val′id·ly** *adv.* —**val′idness** *n.*

val·i·date (val′ə dāt′) *vt.* **-dat′ed, -dat′ing** [< ML. pp. of *validare*] **1.** to give legal force to; declare (a will, etc.) legally valid **2.** to prove to be valid [a witness who *validated* my story] —see **SYN.** at CONFIRM —**val′i·da′tion** *n.*

va·lid·i·ty (və lid′ə tē) *n., pl.* **-ties** the state, quality, or fact of being valid in law or in argument, proof, etc.

va·lise (və lēs′) *n.* [Fr. < It. *valigia* < ?] a piece of hand luggage: an old-fashioned term

Val·kyr·ie (val kir′ē, val′ki rē) *n. Norse Myth.* any of the maidens of Odin who lead the souls of heroes slain in battle to Valhalla —**Val·kyr′i·an** *adj.*

Val·la·do·lid (val′ə dō′lid; *Sp.* vä′lyä thō lēth′) city in NC Spain: pop. 212,000

Val·le·jo (və lā′hō, -ō) [after M. *Vallejo* (1807–90), owner of the site] seaport in W Calif., north of Oakland: pop. 67,000

Val·let·ta (vä let′ä) seaport & capital of Malta, on the island of Malta: pop. 16,000

val·ley (val′ē) *n., pl.* **-leys** [< OFr. < L. *vallis*] **1.** a stretch of low land lying between hills or mountains **2.** the land drained or watered by a great river system [the Nile *valley*] **3.** any long dip or hollow

---

fat, āpe, cär; ten, ēven; is, bīte; gō, hôrn, tōōl, lᴏᴏk; ᴏil, ᴏut; up, fur; get; joy; yet; chin; she; thin, then; zh, leisure; ŋ, ring; ə for a in ago, e in agent, i in sanity, o in comply, u in focus; ' as in able (ā′b'l); Fr. bȧl; ë, Fr. coeur; ö, Fr. feu; Fr. mon; ô, Fr. coq; ü, Fr. duc; r, Fr. cri; H, G. ich; kh, G. doch; ‡foreign; ☆ Americanism; < derived from. See inside front cover.

Valley Forge [after an iron *forge* on *Valley* Creek] village in SE Pa.: the place where Washington and his troops camped in the winter of 1777–78

Val·ois (val wä′) **1.** former duchy in NC France **2.** ruling family of France (1328–1589)

val·or (val′ər) *n.* [< OFr. < LL. < L. *valere*, to be strong] great courage or bravery: also, Brit. sp., **val′our** —**val′or·ous** *adj.* —**val′or·ous·ly** *adv.* —**val′or·ous·ness** *n.*

☆**val·or·i·za·tion** (val′ər i zā′shən) *n.* [Port. *valorização*, ult. < LL. *valor*, VALOR] a fixing of prices, usually by government action, as by buying up a product at the fixed price —**val′or·ize′** (-ə rīz′) *vt.*, *vi.* **-ized′**, **-iz′ing**

Val·pa·rai·so (val′pə rā′zō, -rī′sō) seaport in C Chile: pop. 296,000: also **Val·pa·ra·i·so** (*Sp.* väl′pä rä ē′sō)

‡**valse** (väls) *n.* [Fr.] a waltz

val·u·a·ble (val′yoo b'l, -yoo wə b'l) *adj.* **1.** having value; esp., having great value in terms of money [a *valuable* diamond] **2.** thought of as precious, useful, worthy, etc. [*valuable* knowledge] —*n.* an article of value, esp. one of small size, as a piece of jewelry: *usually used in pl.* **val′u·a·ble·ness** *n.* —**val′u·a·bly** *adv.*

val·u·ate (val′yoo wāt′) *vt.* **-at′ed**, **-at′ing** to set a value on; appraise —**val′u·a′tor** *n.*

val·u·a·tion (val′yoo wā′shən) *n.* **1.** the act of determining the value of anything; evaluation [we took the pearls to a jeweler for a *valuation*] **2.** determined or estimated value [the car was sold for less than its *valuation*] **3.** estimation of the worth, merit, etc. of anything —**val′u·a′tion·al** *adj.*

val·ue (val′yoo) *n.* [< OFr. pp. of *valoir*, to be strong, to be worth < L. *valere*] **1.** a fair or proper exchange [to pay for *value* received] **2.** the worth of a thing in money or goods at a certain time [the *value* of a house] **3.** estimated or appraised worth [the dealer placed a low *value* on her old car] **4.** purchasing power [the changing *value* of the dollar] **5.** that quality of a thing that makes it more or less desirable, useful, etc. [the *value* of true friendship] **6.** [*pl.*] the social principles, goals, or standards held by an individual, class, society, etc. **7.** numerical order assigned to a playing card, etc. **8.** *Art a)* relative lightness or darkness of a color *b)* the effect produced by the use of light and shade **9.** *Math.* the quantity for which a symbol stands [to find the *value* of x] **10.** *Music* the relative length of time a note, tone, or rest is held **11.** *Phonet.* the quality of a speech sound [the several *values* of a vowel in English] —*vt.* **-ued**, **-u·ing** **1.** to estimate the value of; appraise [the property was *valued* at $2,000] **2.** to place a certain estimate of worth on in a scale of values [to *value* health above wealth] **3.** to think highly of; prize [I *value* your friendship] —**see SYN.** at APPRECIATE **and** WORTH —**val′ue·less** *adj.* —**val′u·er** *n.*

val·ue-add·ed tax (val′yoo ad′əd) a tax placed on the cost of a product at each stage of its production and finally included in the cost to the consumer as a kind of indirect sales tax

val·ued (-yood) *adj.* **1.** estimated; appraised [a painting *valued* at $1,000] **2.** highly thought of; esteemed [a *valued* friend]

value judgment an estimate made of the worth, goodness, etc. of a person, action, event, etc., esp. when such a judgment is not called for or desired

val·vate (val′vāt) *adj.* [L. *valvatus*, having folding doors < *valva*: see VALVE] **1.** having a valve or valves **2.** *Bot. a)* meeting without overlapping, as petals, etc. *b)* opening by valves, as a pea pod

valve (valv) *n.* [L. *valva*, leaf of a folding door] **1.** a sluice gate **2.** *Anat.* a fold of tissue which allows body fluids to flow in one direction only, or opens and closes a tube, etc. **3.** *Bot.* any of the parts into which a seed capsule separates **4.** *Mech. a)* any device in a pipe, etc. that allows a flow in one direction only, or controls or stops the flow by means of a flap, lid, plug, etc. *b)* this flap, lid, plug, etc. **5.** *Music* a device, as in the trumpet, that opens a branch to the main tube, lengthening the air column and lowering the pitch **6.** *Zool.* one of the parts making up the shell of a mollusk, clam, etc. —*vt.*, *vi.* **valved**, **valv′ing** **1.** to fit with a valve or valves **2.** to control the flow of (a fluid) by means of a valve —**valve′less** *adj.* —**valve′like′** *adj.*

val·vu·lar (val′vyə lər) *adj.* **1.** having the form or action of a valve **2.** having a valve or valves **3.** of a valve or valves; esp., of the valves of the heart Also **val′var** (-vər)

☆**va·moose** (va moos′) *vi.*, *vt.* **-moosed′**, **-moos′ing** [Sp.

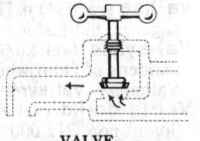

VALVE
(in a faucet)

vamos, let us go] [Old Slang] to leave quickly; go away (from) hurriedly: also **va·mose′** (-mōs′) **-mosed′**, **-mos′ing**

vamp[1] (vamp) *n.* [< OFr. *avampié* < *avant*, before + *pié*, a foot] **1.** the part of a boot or shoe covering the instep and, in some styles, also the toes **2.** something patched up to seem new **3.** *Music* a simple phrase, esp. a series of chords, used as an introduction, between numbers, etc. —*vt.* **1.** to put a vamp on (a shoe, etc.) **2.** to patch (*up*); repair **3.** to invent; fabricate —*vi. Music.* to play a vamp

vamp[2] (vamp) *n. shortened form of* VAMPIRE (sense 3) —*vt.* to seduce or trick (a man) by the use of feminine charms —*vi.* to act the part of a vamp

vam·pire (vam′pīr) *n.* [Fr. < G. *vampir*; of Slav. orig.] **1.** *Folklore* a corpse that comes alive at night and sucks the blood of sleeping persons **2.** a person who without pity takes from others all that he can **3.** a beautiful but wicked woman who seduces men and leads them to their ruin **4.** *shortened form of* VAMPIRE BAT —**vam′pir·ism** *n.*

vampire bat 1. a tropical American bat that lives on the blood of animals **2.** any of various other bats mistakenly believed to be bloodsuckers

van[1] (van) *n.* [abbrev. < VANGUARD] **1.** the front of an army or fleet when advancing **2.** the foremost position in a line, movement, etc., or those in this position

van[2] (van) *n.* [< CARAVAN] **1.** a closed truck or wagon for carrying furniture, etc. **2.** [Brit.] *a)* a closed railway car for baggage, etc. *b)* a delivery wagon or truck

va·na·di·um (və nā′dē əm) *n.* [ModL. < ON. *Vanadis*, a name of Freya, goddess of love] a silver-white metal that is a chemical element: symbol, V; at. wt., 50.942; at. no., 23

vanadium steel a steel alloy containing 0.15 to 0.25 percent vanadium to harden and toughen it

☆**Van Al·len (radiation) belt** (van al′ən) [after J. A. *Van Allen* (1914–), U.S. physicist] a doughnut-shaped belt of high-intensity radiation encircling the earth at varying levels, starting at an altitude of c. 600 mi.

Van Bu·ren (van byoor′ən), **Martin** 1782–1862; 8th president of the U.S. (1837–41)

Van·cou·ver (van koo′vər) **1.** island of British Columbia, Canada, off the SW coast **2.** seaport in SW British Columbia, opposite this island: pop. 410,000 (met. area 1,166,000)

Van·dal (van′d'l) *n.* **1.** a member of an East Germanic tribe that overran Gaul, Spain, etc., destroying and plundering, and sacked Rome in 455 A.D. **2.** [v-] a person who destroys or spoils things on purpose, esp. works of art, public property, etc. —*adj.* **1.** of the Vandals: also **Van·dal·ic** (van dal′ik) **2.** [v-] like a vandal; brutally destructive

van·dal·ism (-iz'm) *n.* brutal destruction of public or private property, esp. of that which is beautiful —**van′dal·is′tic** *adj.*

van·dal·ize (-īz′) *vt.* **-ized′**, **-iz′ing** to destroy or damage (public or private property) on purpose

☆**Van de Graaff generator** (van′di gräf′) [after R. J. *Van de Graaff* (1901–), U.S. physicist] an electrostatic generator using an insulating belt to produce potentials of millions of volts

Van·der·bilt (van′dər bilt), **Cor·nel·ius** (kôr nēl′yəs) 1794–1877; U.S. capitalist & industrialist

Van Dyck (van dīk′), Sir **Anthony** 1599–1641; Fl. painter, in England after 1632: also sp. **Van·dyke′**

Van·dyke (beard) (van dīk′) a closely trimmed, pointed beard, as seen in portraits by Van Dyck

vane (vān) *n.* [OE. *fana*, a flag] **1.** *same as* WEATHER VANE **2.** any of several flat or curved pieces set around an axle and turned about it by moving air, water, etc. [the *vanes* of a windmill] or mechanically turned to move the air, water, etc. [the *vanes* of a turbine] **3.** a plate or strip of metal fixed to a rocket, missile, etc. to give balance or guidance **4.** the web or flat part of a feather —**vaned** *adj.* —**vane′less** *adj.*

van Eyck (vän īk′), **Jan** (yän) 1385?–1441; Fl. painter

van Gogh (van gō′, gôkh′; *Du.* vän khôkh′), **Vincent** 1853–90; Du. painter

van·guard (van′gärd′) *n.* [< OFr. < *avant*, before + *garde*, guard] **1.** the front part of an army in an advance; the van **2.** the leading position or persons in a movement

VANDYKE
BEARD

va·nil·la (və nil′ə) *n.* [ModL., genus name < Sp. dim. of *vaina*, a pod < L. *vagina*, a sheath] **1.** any of various climbing tropical American orchids with sweet-smelling flowers **2.** the podlike capsule (**vanilla bean**) of some of these plants **3.** a flavoring made from these capsules —**va·nil′lic** *adj.*

va·nil·lin (və nil′in, van′ə lin) *n.* a sweet-smelling, white, crystalline substance, $C_8H_8O_3$, produced from the vanilla bean or made synthetically and used for flavoring

van·ish (van′ish) *vi.* [< OFr., ult. < L. *evanescere*: see EVANESCE] **1.** to go or pass suddenly from sight [the sun *vanished* beneath the horizon] **2.** to stop existing; come to an end [the passenger pigeon has *vanished*] —**van′ish·er** *n.*

vanishing point 1. the point where parallel lines going away from the observer seem to come together **2.** a time, place, or stage at which something disappears

van·i·ty (van′ə tē) *n., pl.* -**ties** [< OFr. < L. < *vanus*, vain] **1.** any thing or act that is vain, useless, or worthless **2.** a being vain, or worthless; futility **3.** a being vain, or overly proud of oneself, one's possessions, etc. ☆**4.** *short for* VANITY CASE ☆**5.** *same as* DRESSING TABLE **6.** a cabinet in a bathroom with a washbowl set in the top

vanity case a woman's small traveling case fitted for carrying cosmetics, toilet articles, etc.

☆**vanity press** (or **publisher**) a press or publishing house that publishes books only at the author's own expense

van·quish (vaŋ′kwish, van′-) *vt.* [< OFr. < L. *vincere*, to conquer] **1.** to conquer or defeat in battle **2.** *a)* to defeat in any conflict, as in argument *b)* to overcome (a feeling, condition, etc.); suppress —see SYN. at CONQUER —**van′quish·er** *n.*

van·tage (van′tij) *n.* [see ADVANTAGE] **1.** a position more favorable than that of an opponent **2.** a position that allows a clear and broad view: also **vantage point**

van·ward (van′wərd) *adj.* in the van, or front, as of an army —*adv.* toward the van

Van·zet·ti (van zet′ē), **Bar·to·lo·me·o** (bär′tō lō mā′ō) 1888-1927; It. anarchist in the U.S.: see SACCO

vap·id (vap′id) *adj.* [L. *vapidus*] **1.** having no taste or flavor [a *vapid* drink] **2.** lifeless; dull; boring [*vapid* talk] —see SYN. at INSIPID —**vap·id·i·ty** (va pid′ə tē), *pl.* -**ties**, **vap′id·ness** *n.* —**vap′id·ly** *adv.*

va·por (vā′pər) *n.* [< Anglo-Fr. < MFr. < L. *vapor*] **1.** *a)* visible particles of moisture floating in the air, as fog, mist, or steam *b)* anything, as smoke, fumes, etc., given off in a cloud **2.** the gaseous form of any substance that is usually a liquid or solid **3.** [*pl.*] [Archaic] gloomy or low spirits (often with *the*) —*vi.* **1.** to rise or pass off as vapor; evaporate **2.** to give off vapor **3.** to brag or bluster —*vt. same as* VAPORIZE —**va′por·er** *n.* —**va′por·ish** *adj.* —**va′por·like′** *adj.*

va·por·ize (vā′pə rīz′) *vt., vi.* -**ized′**, -**iz′ing** to change into vapor, as by heating or spraying —**va′por·iz′a·ble** *adj.* —**va′por·i·za′tion** *n.*

va·por·iz·er (-rī′zər) *n.* a device for vaporizing liquids, esp. one for making steam or vaporizing medicated liquid to ease breathing

☆**vapor lock** a blocking of the flow of fuel in an internal-combustion engine as the result of vaporized fuel in the fuel line, caused by too much heat

va·por·ous (vā′pər əs) *adj.* **1.** giving off or forming vapor **2.** full of vapor; foggy; misty **3.** like vapor **4.** *a)* fleeting, fanciful, etc.: said of things, ideas, etc. *b)* given to such ideas or talk Also **va′por·y** —**va′por·ous·ly** *adv.* —**va′por·ous·ness, va′por·os′i·ty** (-pə räs′ə tē) *n.*

vapor pressure the pressure at any given temperature of a vapor in equilibrium with its liquid or solid form: also called **vapor tension**

vapor trail a white trail of condensed water vapor in the wake of an aircraft: also called **contrail**

va·pour (-pər) *n., vi., vt.* Brit. sp. of VAPOR

☆**va·que·ro** (vä ker′ō) *n., pl.* -**ros** [Sp. < *vaca*, a cow < L. *vacca*] in the Southwest, a man who herds cattle; cowboy

var. 1. variant(s) **2.** variation **3.** variety **4.** various

Va·ra·na·si (və rän′ə sē′) city in NE India, on the Ganges: pop. 490,000

var·i·a·ble (ver′ē ə b'l, var′-) *adj.* **1.** likely to change or vary; changeable, fickle, etc. [in a *variable* mood] **2.** that can be changed or varied [a *variable* price] **3.** *Biol.* tending to differ in some way from the type **4.** *Math.* having no fixed value —*n.* **1.** anything changeable; thing that varies **2.** *Math. a)* a quantity that may have a number of different values *b)* a symbol for such a quantity **3.** *Naut.* a shifting wind —**var′i·a·bil′i·ty, var′i·a·ble·ness** *n.* —**var′i·a·bly** *adv.*

variable star a star whose brightness varies from time to time, usually in regular periods

var·i·ance (ver′ē əns, var′-) *n.* **1.** a varying or being variant **2.** degree or amount of change or difference **3.** official permission to bypass regulations, esp. zoning laws of a city **4.** a quarrel; dispute **5.** *Accounting* the difference between actual costs of production and the expected costs —**at variance** not in agreement; conflicting

var·i·ant (-ənt) *adj.* varying; different; esp., different in some way from others of the same kind —*n.* anything that is variant, as a different spelling of the same word

var·i·a·tion (ver′ē ā′shən, var′-) *n.* **1.** *a)* the act, fact, or process of varying; change in form, condition, extent, etc. [a *variation* in style] *b)* the degree or amount of such change [a *variation* of ten feet] **2.** *same as* DECLINATION (sense 3) **3.** a thing that is somewhat different from another of the same kind **4.** *Biol.* a differing from the usual or parental type in structure or form **5.** *Music* the repetition of a melody or theme with changes in harmony, rhythm, key, etc. —**var′i·a′tion·al** *adj.*

var·i·cel·la (var′ə sel′ə) *n.* [ModL., dim. of *variola*: see VARIOLA] *same as* CHICKEN POX —**var′i·cel′loid** (-oid) *adj.*

var·i·col·ored (ver′i kul′ərd, var′-) *adj.* of several or many colors

var·i·cose (var′ə kōs′) *adj.* [L. *varicosus* < *varicis*, genitive of *varix*, enlarged vein] **1.** abnormally and irregularly swollen [*varicose* veins] **2.** resulting from varicose veins [*varicose* ulcer] —**var′i·cos′i·ty** (-käs′ə tē) *n.*

var·ied (ver′ēd, var′-) *adj.* **1.** of different kinds; various [a program of *varied* entertainment] **2.** showing different colors; variegated **3.** changed; altered —**var′ied·ly** *adv.*

var·i·e·gate (ver′ē ə gāt′, ver′ə gāt′; var′-) *vt.* -**gat′ed, -gat′ing** [< L. pp. of *variegare* < *varius*, various] **1.** to make varied in appearance, as by marking with different colors in streaks, spots, etc. **2.** to give variety to; diversify —**var′i·e·gat′ed** *adj.* —**var′i·e·ga′tion** *n.*

va·ri·e·tal (və rī′ə t'l) *adj.* of or being a variety [*varietal* forms of a plant species]

va·ri·e·ty (və rī′ə tē) *n., pl.* -**ties** [< Fr. < L. *varietas*] **1.** the condition of being varied or not always the same; change [*variety* is the spice of life] **2.** any of the various forms of something; sort; kind [*varieties* of cloth] **3.** a number of different kinds [a *variety* of fruits, a *variety* of merchandise] **4.** a subdivision of a species, as of a plant [*varieties* of corn] —*adj.* of or in a variety show [a *variety* act]

variety meat meat other than flesh; specif., any of the edible organs, as the liver, kidneys, heart, etc.

variety show a show made up of different kinds of acts, as comic skits, songs, dances, etc.

☆**variety store** a retail store that sells a wide variety of items, mostly of a small and inexpensive kind

var·i·form (ver′ə fôrm′, var′-) *adj.* having various forms

va·ri·o·la (və rī′ə lə) *n.* [ModL. < ML. < L. *varius*, various, mottled] *same as* SMALLPOX

var·i·om·e·ter (ver′ē äm′ə tər, var′-) *n.* [VARIO(US) + -METER] **1.** a device for determining variations of magnetic force esp. at different places on the earth **2.** *Radio* a unit consisting of a coil that can be rotated within a fixed coil to vary inductance

var·i·o·rum (ver′ē ôr′əm, var′-) *n.* [L., of various (scholars)] **1.** an edition or text, as of a literary work, with notes by various editors, scholars, etc. **2.** an edition containing different versions of a text —*adj.* of or being a variorum

var·i·ous (ver′ē əs, var′-) *adj.* [L. *varius*, diverse] **1.** differing one from another; of several kinds [cars of *various* makes] **2.** *a)* several or many [found in *various* parts of the country] *b)* individual; distinct [bequests to the *various* heirs] **3.** many-sided; versatile *[the* various *bounty of nature]* **4.** characterized by variety; varied in nature or appearance —**var′i·ous·ly** *adv.*

va·ris·tor (və ris′tər) *n.* [VAR(IOUS) + (RES)ISTOR] a semiconductor device whose resistance drops as the voltage is increased

var·let (vär′lit) *n.* [OFr., var. of *vaslet:* see VALET] [Archaic] **1.** an attendant **2.** a scoundrel; knave

var·mint, var·ment (vär′mənt) *n.* [dial. var. of VERMIN] [Dial. or Colloq.] a person or animal regarded as troublesome or objectionable

var·nish (vär′nish) *n.* [< OFr. < ML. *veronix,* a resin < Gr. *Berenikē,* an ancient city] **1.** *a)* a preparation made of resins dissolved in oil (**oil varnish**) or in alcohol, turpentine, etc. (**spirit varnish**), used to give a hard, glossy surface to wood, etc. *b)* any of various natural or prepared products similarly used **2.** the hard, glossy surface produced **3.** an outward show or look of smoothness or polish; gloss *[a varnish of politeness]* —*vt.* **1.** to cover with varnish **2.** to smooth over in a false way *[to varnish a lie with an innocent look]* —**var′nish·er** *n.*

va·room (və rōōm′) *n., vi. var. of* VROOM

var·si·ty (vär′sə tē) *n., pl.* -**ties** [contr. & altered < UNIVERSITY] the main team representing a university, college, or school in games or contests against others —*adj.* designating or of such a team

var·y (ver′ē, var′-) *vt.* **var′ied, var′y·ing** [< OFr. < L. *variare* < *varius,* various] **1.** to change in form, nature, etc.; alter *[to vary an approach to a problem]* **2.** to make different from one another *[to vary the assignments]* **3.** to give variety to *[to vary one's reading]* —*vi.* **1.** to be or become different; differ or change *[the objects vary in shape]* **2.** to deviate or depart *(from)* *[versions that vary from the original]* —see **SYN.** at CHANGE —**var′i·er** *n.*

vas (vas) *n., pl.* **va·sa** (vā′sə) [L., a vessel] *Anat., Biol.* a vessel or duct —**va·sal** (vā′s'l) *adj.*

Va·sa·ri (vä zä′rē), **Gior·gio** (jôr′jō) 1511–74; It. architect, painter, & biographer of artists

vas·cu·lar (vas′kyə lər) *adj.* [< ModL. < L. *vasculum,* dim. of *vas,* a vessel] **1.** *Anat., Zool.* of or consisting of vessels carrying blood or lymph **2.** *Bot.* of, consisting of, or having special cells, xylem, and phloem that carry water and food, as ferns and seed plants

vascular bundle a unit of the conducting system of higher plants, consisting chiefly of xylem and phloem

vas de·fe·rens (vas def′ə renz′) *pl.* **va·sa de·fe·ren·ti·a** (vā′sə def′ə ren′shē ə) [ModL. < L. *vas,* a vessel + *deferens,* carrying down] the duct that carries sperm from the testicle to the ejaculatory duct of the penis

vase (vās, vāz; *chiefly Brit.* väz) *n.* [< Fr. < L. *vas,* a vessel, dish] an open container of metal, glass, pottery, etc. used for decoration, holding flowers, etc.

vas·ec·to·my (va sek′tə mē, -zek′-) *n., pl.* -**mies** [VAS(O)- + -ECTOMY] the cutting and tying off of part of the vas deferens to prevent the passing of sperm: used as a form of birth control

☆**Vas·e·line** (vas′ə lēn′) [coinage < G. *was(ser),* water + Gr. *el(aion),* oil + -INE⁴] *a trademark for* PETROLATUM —*n.* [v-] petrolatum, or petroleum jelly

vas·o- [< L. *vas,* a vessel] *a combining form meaning:* **1.** blood vessels *[vasomotor]* **2.** vas deferens *[vasectomy]* **3.** vasomotor *[vasoinhibitor]* Also, before a vowel, **vas-**

vas·o·con·stric·tor (vas′ō kən strik′tər) *adj.* [prec. + CON-STRICTOR] narrowing the blood vessels —*n.* a nerve or drug doing this —**vas′o·con·stric′tion** *n.*

vas·o·di·la·tor (-dī′lāt′ər) *adj.* [VASO- + DILATOR] widening the blood vessels —*n.* a nerve or drug doing this —**vas′o·dil′a·ta′tion** (-dil′ə tā′shən), **vas′o·di·la′tion** *n.*

vas·o·in·hib·i·tor (-in hib′ə tər) *n.* [VASO- + INHIBITOR] a drug or other agent slowing down or checking the action of the vasomotor nerves —**vas′o·in·hib′i·to·ry** (-tôr′ē) *adj.*

vas·o·mo·tor (-mōt′ər) *adj.* [VASO- + MOTOR] controlling the narrowing and widening of blood vessels, as certain nerves

vas·o·pres·sin (-pres′'n) *n.* [VASO- + PRESS(URE) + -IN¹] a hormone of the pituitary gland that increases blood pressure

vas·o·pres·sor (-pres′ər) *n.* [VASO- + PRESS(URE) + -OR] a substance causing a rise in blood pressure

vas·sal (vas′'l) *n.* [OFr. < ML. *vassalus* < *vassus,* servant < Celt.] **1.** a person in the feudal system who held land in return for loyalty, military help, etc. to an overlord **2.** an underling, servant, slave, etc. —*adj.* of, like, or being a vassal —**vas′sal·age** (-ij) *n.*

vast (vast) *adj.* [L. *vastus*] very great in size, extent, amount, degree, etc. —**vast′ly** *adv.* —**vast′ness** *n.*

Väs·te·ras (ves′tə rôs′) city in SC Sweden: pop. 113,000

vast·y (vas′tē) *adj.* **vast′i·er, vast′i·est** [Archaic] vast; immense; huge

vat (vat) *n.* [< OE. *fæt,* a cask] a large tank, tub, or cask for holding liquids as for use in a manufacturing process —*vt.* **vat′-ted, vat′ting** to put or store in a vat

Vat·i·can (vat′i k'n) **1.** the palace of the Pope, a group of buildings in Vatican City **2.** the government or authority of the Pope —*adj.* **1.** of the Vatican **2.** naming either of two Roman Catholic Councils held in Vatican City in 1869–70 (**Vatican I**) and 1962–65 (**Vatican II**)

Vatican City independent state inside the city of Rome, with the Pope as its head: 108 acres; pop. c. 1,000

va·tic·i·nal (və tis′ə n'l) *adj.* having to do with prophecy or the foretelling of things to come; prophetic

vaude·ville (vōd′vil, vôd′-; vō′də-, vô′də-) *n.* [Fr. < *Vau-de-Vire,* a valley in Normandy, famous for light, merry songs] ☆a stage show made up of a variety of acts, including songs, dances, comic skits, acrobatics, etc.; also, such entertainment generally —☆**vaude·vil′lian** (-vil′yən) *n., adj.*

Vaughan (vôn) **1.** [< a family name] a masculine name: also sp. **Vaughn 2.** Henry, 1622–95; Eng. poet

Vaughan Williams, Ralph 1872–1958; Eng. composer

vault¹ (vôlt) *n.* [< OFr., ult. < L. *volvere,* to roll] **1.** an arched roof, ceiling, etc. of stone, brick, etc. **2.** an arched chamber or space, esp. when underground **3.** a cellar room used for storage **4.** *a)* a burial chamber *b)* a concrete or metal container into which the casket is placed at burial ☆**5.** a secure room for the safekeeping of valuables or money, as in a bank **6.** the sky as a vault-like canopy —*vt.* **1.** to cover with a vault *[to vault a passageway]* **2.** to build as a vault *[to vault a roof]* —*vi.* to curve like a vault *[the bridge vaults above the river]* —**vault′ed** *adj.*

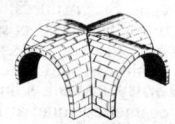

GROINED VAULT

vault² (vôlt) *vi.* [< MFr. < OIt. *voltare,* ult. < L. *volvere,* to roll] to leap as over a barrier, esp. putting the hands on the barrier or using a long pole —*vt.* to vault over *[to vault a fence]* —*n.* a vaulting —**vault′er** *n.*

vault·ing¹ (vôl′tiŋ) *n.* **1.** the arched work forming a vault **2.** a vault or vaults

vault·ing² (vôl′tiŋ) *adj.* **1.** that vaults or leaps **2.** reaching too far or beyond one's abilities *[vaulting ambition]*

vaunt (vônt, vänt) *vi., vt.* [< OFr. < LL. *vanitare* < L. *vanus,* vain] to boast or brag (of) —*n.* a boast or brag —**vaunt′ed** *adj.* —**vaunt′er** *n.*

v.aux. auxiliary verb

vb. 1. verb **2.** verbal

VC, V.C. Viet Cong

V.C. 1. Vice-Consul **2.** Victoria Cross

VD, V.D. venereal disease

☆**V-Day** (vē′dā′) *n.* Victory Day

've *contraction of* HAVE *[we've seen it]*

Ve·a·dar (vā′ä där′, vē′ä där′) *n.* [Heb.] a recurring extra month of the Jewish year: see JEWISH CALENDAR

veal (vēl) *n.* [OFr. *veel* < L. dim. of *vitulus,* a calf] **1.** the flesh of a young calf, used as food **2.** a vealer

☆**veal·er** (vēl′ər) *n.* a calf, esp. as intended for food

Veb·len (veb′lən), **Thor·stein (Bunde)** (thôr′stīn) 1857–1929; U.S. political economist & social scientist

vec·tor (vek′tər) *n.* [ModL. < L., a carrier < pp. of *vehere,* to carry] **1.** *Biol.* an animal, as an insect, that passes a disease-producing organism on from one host to another **2.** *Math. a)* a quantity that is measurable and also has direction, such as a force or velocity *b)* a line of a particular direction and length, representing such a quantity —**vec′to·ri·al** (-tôr′ē əl) *adj.*

Ve·da (vā′də, vē′-) *n.* [Sans. *veda,* knowledge] any or all of the four ancient sacred books of Hinduism, consisting of psalms, chants, sacred formulas, etc. —**Ve·da·ic** (vi dā′ik), **Ve′dic** *adj.*

Ve·dan·ta (vi dän′tə, -dan′-) *n.* [Sans. < *veda,* knowledge + *anta,* an end] a system of Hindu philosophy based on the Vedas —**Ve·dan′tic** *adj.* —**Ve·dan′tism** *n.*

☆**V-E Day** (vē′ē′) May 8, 1945, the official date of Germany's surrender ending the European phase of World War II

vee (vē) *n.* the letter V, v, or anything shaped like it —*adj.* shaped like V

☆**Veep** (vēp) *n.* [< *veepee* (for V.P.)] [sometimes **v**-] [Colloq.] a vice-president; specif., the U.S. Vice President

veer (vir) *vi.* [altered < Fr. *virer,* to turn around] **1.** to change direction; shift; turn *[the car veered suddenly to the left]* **2.** to change about; shift from one opinion, purpose, etc. to another

3. to shift clockwise: said of the wind —*vt.* to turn or swing; change the course of [he *veered* the truck to the center lane] —*n.* a change of direction —see SYN. at DEVIATE —**veer′ing·ly** *adv.*

☆**veer·y** (vir′ē) *n., pl.* **veer′ies** [prob. echoic] a brown and cream-colored thrush of the eastern U.S.

Ve·ga (vē′gə, vā′-) [ML. < Ar.] a very bright star in the constellation Lyra

Ve·ga (ve′gä), **Lo·pe de** (lô′pe *the*) 1562–1635; Sp. dramatist & poet

veg·e·ta·ble (vej′tə b′l, vej′ə tə-) *adj.* [< ML. *vegetabilis*, vegetative < LL., animating < L. *vegetare:* see VEGETATE] **1.** of plants in general [the *vegetable* kingdom] **2.** of, like, or from vegetables [*vegetable* oil] —*n.* **1.** any plant, as distinguished from something animal or mineral **2.** *a)* any plant that is eaten whole or in part, raw or cooked *b)* the part of such a plant used as food, as the root (for example, a carrot), tuber (a potato), seed (a pea), fruit (a tomato), stem (celery), leaf (lettuce), etc. **3.** a person thought of as like a vegetable, esp. one who leads a dull, inactive life or one who is unconscious

vegetable butter any of various vegetable fats that are solid at ordinary temperatures

vegetable ivory the fully ripe, ivorylike seed of a S. American palm, used to make buttons, ornaments, etc.

vegetable marrow [Chiefly Brit.] any of various long, smooth-skinned types of summer squash

vegetable oil any of various liquid fats that come from the fruits or seeds of plants, used in food products, etc

veg·e·tal (vej′ə t′l) *adj.* of, like, or from plants or vegetables

veg·e·tar·i·an (vej′ə ter′ē ən) *n.* [VEGET(ABLE) + -ARIAN] a person who chooses to eat no meat for reasons of health or because of feelings against the killing of animals: some vegetarians eat only vegetables, fruits, grains, and nuts, others also eat milk, cheese, eggs, and the like —*adj.* **1.** of vegetarians, their beliefs, etc. **2.** consisting only of vegetables, fruits, etc. —**veg′e·tar′i·an·ism** *n.*

veg·e·tate (vej′ə tāt′) *vi.* **-tat′ed, -tat′ing** [< L. pp. of *vegetare* < *vegetus*, lively < *vegere*, to quicken] **1.** to grow as plants **2.** to exist with little mental and physical activity; lead a dull, inactive life

veg·e·ta·tion (vej′ə tā′shən) *n.* **1.** the act or process of vegetating **2.** plant life in general **3.** dull, inactive, unthinking existence —**veg′e·ta′tion·al** *adj.*

veg·e·ta·tive (vej′ə tāt′iv) *adj.* **1.** of plants or plant growth **2.** growing as plants **3.** designating or of the functions or parts of plants not related to reproduction [leaves and other *vegetative* parts] **4.** helping plant growth [*vegetative* loams] **5.** dull and inactive [a *vegetative* life] **6.** of or relating to asexual reproduction, as by bulbs in plants or by budding in some lower animals Also **veg′e·tive** (-tiv) —**veg′e·ta′tive·ly** *adv.* —**veg′e·ta′tive·ness** *n.*

ve·he·ment (vē′ə mənt) *adj.* [< MFr. < L. *vehemens*, eager < *vehere*, to carry] **1.** acting or moving with great force; violent [a *vehement* storm] **2.** full of or showing very strong feeling; intense, fervent, impassioned, etc. [a *vehement* argument] —**ve′he·mence, ve′he·men·cy** *n.* —**ve′he·ment·ly** *adv.*

ve·hi·cle (vē′ə k′l, vē′hi-) *n.* [< Fr. < L. *vehiculum*, carriage < *vehere*, to carry] **1.** a means of carrying persons or things, esp. over land or in space, as an automobile, bicycle, sled, spacecraft, etc. **2.** a means by which something is expressed, passed along, etc. [television as a *vehicle* for advertising] **3.** a play as a means of presenting a specified actor or company **4.** *Painting* a liquid, as water or oil, with which pigments are mixed for use **5.** *Pharmacy* a substance, as a syrup, in which medicines are given

ve·hic·u·lar (vē hik′yoo lər) *adj.* of or for vehicles [a *vehicular* tunnel]

veil (vāl) *n.* [< ONormFr. < L. *vela*, pl. of *velum*, cloth] **1.** a piece of light fabric, as net or gauze, worn, esp. by women, over the face or head to hide the features or as a decoration **2.** anything cloth, curtain, etc. used to hide or separate things **3.** anything that covers or hides [a *veil* of mist, a *veil* of silence] **4.** *a)* a part of a nun's headdress, draped along the face and over the shoulders *b)* the state or life of a nun: chiefly in **take the veil,** to become a nun —*vt.* to cover, hide, etc. with or as with a veil —**veiled** *adj.* —**veil′like′** *adj.*

veil·ing (vāl′iŋ) *n.* **1.** a veil **2.** fabric for veils

vein (vān) *n.* [< OFr. < L. *vena*] **1.** any of the system of tubes bringing blood back to the heart from all parts of the body **2.** any riblike support in an insect wing **3.** any of the fine lines, or ribs, in a leaf **4.** a layer of mineral, rock, etc. in a fissure or zone of different rock; lode **5.** a streak or marking of a color or substance different from the surrounding material, as in marble **6.** *a)* a distinctive quality or strain running through something [a *vein* of humor] *b)* course or tenor of thought, feeling, action, etc. **7.** a temporary state of mind; mood [in a serious *vein*] —*vt.* **1.** to mark as with veins [a cheese heavily *veined* with mold] **2.** to branch out through like veins [a network of rivers *vein* the land] —**veined** *adj.*

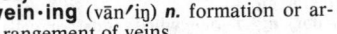

VEINS
(left: in arm;
top right: in leaf;
bottom right: in
insect wings)

vein·ing (vān′iŋ) *n.* formation or arrangement of veins

vein·let (-lit) *n.* same as VENULE: also **vein′ule** (-yoōl)

vein·y (-ē) *adj.* **vein′i·er, vein′i·est** full of veins or veinlike markings

ve·lar (vē′lər) *adj.* **1.** of a velum; esp., of the soft palate **2.** *Phonet.* pronounced with the back of the tongue touching or near the soft palate, as the sound of *k* followed by a back vowel like (oō) —*n.* a velar sound

Ve·láz·quez (ve läth′keth; *E.* və las′kes, -kwez), **Die·go (Rodríguez de Silva y)** (dye′gô) 1599–1660; Sp. painter: also **Ve·lás·quez** (ve läs′keth)

☆**Vel·cro** (vel′krō) [arbitrary formation < VEL(VET)] *a trademark for* a nylon material made with both a surface of tiny hooks and one of pile: matching strips are used in garments, etc. as fasteners, easily pressed together or pulled apart —*n.* this material

veld, veldt (velt) *n.* [Afrik. < MDu. *veld*, a field] in South Africa, open grassy country

vel·le·i·ty (və lē′ə tē) *n., pl.* **-ties** [< ML. < L. *velle*, to wish] a mere wish; inclination

vel·lum (vel′əm) *n.* [MFr. *velin*, vellum < OFr. *veel:* see VEAL] **1.** a fine parchment used for writing on or for binding books **2.** a manuscript on vellum **3.** a strong paper resembling vellum —*adj.* of or like vellum

ve·loc·i·pede (və läs′ə pēd′) *n.* [< Fr. < L. *velocis*, genitive of *velox*, swift + *pedis*, genitive of *pes*, a foot] **1.** any of various early bicycles or tricycles **2.** [Now Rare] a child's tricycle

ve·loc·i·ty (və läs′ə tē) *n., pl.* **-ties** [< Fr. < L. *velox:* see prec.] **1.** quickness of motion or action; speed [to move with great *velocity*] **2.** rate of change of position, or rate of motion in a particular direction, in relation to time [a wind *velocity* of 15 miles per hour]

ve·lo·drome (vē′lə drōm′, vel′ə-) *n.* [< Fr. < *velo*, VELOCIPEDE + -*drome*, -DROME] an indoor arena with a track banked for bicycle races

ve·lour, ve·lours (və loor′) *n., pl.* **ve·lours′** [Fr.: see VELURE] a fabric with a soft nap like velvet, used for upholstery, draperies, hats, clothing, etc.

ve·lum (vē′ləm) *n., pl.* **-la** (-lə) [L., a veil] *Biol.* any of various veillike membranous partitions or coverings; specif., *same as* SOFT PALATE

ve·lure (və loor′) *n.* [Fr. *velours* < OFr. < LL. *villosus*, shaggy < *villus*, shaggy hair] velour or velvetlike fabric

vel·vet (vel′vit) *n.* [< OFr. < VL. *villutus* < L. *villus*, shaggy hair] **1.** a rich fabric of silk, rayon, nylon, etc. with a soft, thick pile **2.** anything with a surface like that of velvet ☆**3.** [Old Slang] extra or clear profit or gain —*adj.* **1.** made of or covered with velvet **2.** smooth or soft like velvet —**vel′vet·y** *adj.*

☆**velvet ant** any of various wasps that resemble ants, often covered with brightly colored hairs: the females are wingless

vel·vet·een (vel′və tēn′) *n.* a cotton cloth with a short, thick pile, resembling velvet

ve·na ca·va (vē′nə kā′və) *pl.* **ve′nae ca′vae** (vē′nē kā′vē) [ModL. < L. *vena*, vein + *cava*, fem. of *cavus*, hollow] *Anat.*

either of two large veins carrying blood to the right atrium of the heart: see illustration at HEART

ve·nal (vē'n'l) *adj.* [L. *venalis*, salable < *venum*, sale] **1.** that can readily be bribed or corrupted [a *venal* judge] **2.** characterized by bribery or corruption [*venal* politics] —**ve·nal·i·ty** (-nal'ə tē) *n., pl.* **-ties** —**ve'nal·ly** *adv.*

ve·na·tion (vē nā'shən) *n.* [< L. *vena*, a vein] **1.** an arrangement or system of veins, as in an insect's wing or a leaf **2.** such veins as a group

vend (vend) *vt., vi.* [< Fr. < L. *vendere*, contr. < *venum dare*, to offer for sale] to sell, esp. by peddling

vend·ee (ven'dē') *n.* the person to whom a thing is sold

ven·det·ta (ven det'ə) *n.* [It. < L. *vindicta*, vengeance] **1.** a feud in which relatives of a murdered or wronged person seek vengeance on the guilty person or his family **2.** any bitter quarrel or feud —**ven·det'tist** *n.*

vend·i·ble, vend·a·ble (ven'də b'l) *adj.* [see VEND] capable of being sold —*n.* something vendible —**vend'i·bil'i·ty** *n.* —**vend'i·bly** *adv.*

vending machine a coin-operated machine for selling certain kinds of articles, refreshments, etc.

ven·dor, vend·er (ven'dər) *n.* **1.** one who vends, or sells; seller **2.** *same as* VENDING MACHINE

ve·neer (və nir') *vt.* [G. *furnieren* < Fr. *fournir*, to furnish] **1.** to cover with a thin layer of finer material; esp., to cover (wood) with wood of a finer quality **2.** to make outwardly attractive [to *veneer* a flaw] **3.** to glue (thin wood layers) together to form plywood —*n.* **1.** a thin layer used to veneer something; also, any of the layers used in making plywood **2.** a surface appearance that hides what is below [a *veneer* of culture]

ve·neer·ing (-iŋ) *n.* material used for veneer

ven·er·a·ble (ven'ər ə b'l, ven'rə b'l) *adj.* [see VENERATE] **1.** worthy of respect or reverence by reason of age, dignity, character, etc. [a *venerable* old man] **2.** impressively ancient, historic, or hallowed [a *venerable* building] —**ven'er·a·bil'i·ty** *n.* —**ven'er·a·bly** *adv.*

ven·er·ate (ven'ə rāt) *vt.* **-at·ed, -at·ing** [< L. pp. of *venerari*, to worship] to feel or show deep respect for; revere —see SYN. at REVERE¹ —**ven'er·a'tor** *n.*

ven·er·a·tion (ven'ə rā'shən) *n.* **1.** a venerating or being venerated **2.** a feeling of deep respect or reverence **3.** an act showing this —see SYN. at AWE

ve·ne·re·al (və nir'ē əl) *adj.* [< L. *venereus* < *veneris*, genitive of *venus*, love] **1.** of or relating to sexual love or intercourse **2.** *a)* that is usually passed on by sexual intercourse with a person having the disease, as syphilis and gonorrhea *b)* infected with a venereal disease *c)* of or dealing with venereal disease [a *venereal* clinic]

ven·er·y¹ (ven'ər ē) *n.* [< L. *Veneris*, genitive of *Venus*, Venus, love] [Archaic] the satisfying of sexual need; sexual intercourse

ven·er·y² (ven'ər ē) *n.* [< MFr. < *vener*, to hunt < L. *venari*] [Archaic] the hunting of game; the chase

Ve·ne·ti·a (və nē'shē ə, -shə) **1.** ancient district at the head of the Adriatic, north of the Po River: with Istria it formed a Roman province **2.** *same as* VENETO

Ve·ne·tian (və nē'shən) *adj.* of Venice, its people, culture, etc. —*n.* a native or inhabitant of Venice

Venetian blind [*also* v- b-] a window blind made of a number of thin, horizontal slats that can be set at any angle to regulate the light and air passing through or drawn up by cords to the window top

Ve·ne·to (ve'ne tô') region of N Italy, on the Adriatic: chief city, Venice

Ve·ne·zi·a (ve ne'tsyä) *It. name of* VENICE

Ven·e·zue·la (ven'i zwā'lə, -zwē'-; *Sp.* ve'ne swe'lä) country in northern S. America, on the Caribbean Sea: 352,143 sq. mi.; pop. 10,399,000; cap. Caracas —**Ven'e·zue'lan** *adj., n.*

venge·ance (ven'jəns) *n.* [OFr. < *venger*, to avenge < L. *vindicare*: see VINDICATE] **1.** the return of an injury for an injury, in punishment; an avenging; revenge **2.** the desire to make such a return —**with a vengeance 1.** with great force or fury **2.** to an extreme or unusual degree

venge·ful (venj'fəl) *adj.* **1.** wanting or seeking vengeance; vindictive [a *vengeful* opponent] **2.** arising from a desire for vengeance: said of actions or feelings [*vengeful* spite] **3.** inflicting vengeance [a *vengeful* weapon] —see SYN. at VINDICTIVE —**venge'ful·ly** *adv.* —**venge'ful·ness** *n.*

VENETIAN BLIND

ve·ni·al (vē'nē əl, vēn'yəl) *adj.* [OFr. < LL. *venialis* < L. *venia*, grace] **1.** that can be forgiven, pardoned, or excused, as an error or fault **2.** *R.C.Ch.* not causing spiritual death: said of sins not regarded as serious —**ve'ni·al·ly** *adv.*

Ven·ice (ven'is) seaport in N Italy built on more than 100 small islands in an inlet (**Gulf of Venice**) at the N end of the Adriatic: pop. 368,000

ven·in (ven'in) *n.* [VEN(OM) + -IN¹] any of the specific poisonous substances of animal venoms

ve·ni·re (və nī'rē) *n.* [L., to come] **1.** *short for* VENIRE FACIAS **2.** a list or group of people from among whom a jury or juries will be selected

venire fa·ci·as (fā'shē as') [ML., cause to come] *Law* a writ issued by a judge to a sheriff or coroner, instructing him to summon persons to serve as jurors

☆**ve·ni·re·man** (və nī'rē mən) *n., pl.* **-men** a member of a venire (sense 2)

ven·i·son (ven'i s'n, -z'n; *Brit.* ven'zən) *n.* [< OFr. < L. < pp. of *venari*, to hunt] the flesh of deer, used as food

ven·om (ven'əm) *n.* [< OFr. < L. *venenum*, a poison] **1.** the poison secreted by some snakes, spiders, insects, etc., injected into the victim by bite or sting **2.** bitter feeling; spite; malice [a look full of *venom*]

ven·om·ous (-əs) *adj.* **1.** full of venom; poisonous [a *venomous* sting] **2.** full of spite or ill will; malicious [a *venomous* remark] **3.** able to inject venom by bite or sting [a *venomous* snake] —**ven'om·ous·ly** *adv.* —**ven'om·ous·ness** *n.*

ve·nous (vē'nəs) *adj.* [L. *venosus*] **1.** *a)* of a vein or veins *b)* having veins or full of veins; veiny **2.** designating blood being carried in the veins back to the heart and lungs: venous blood has given up oxygen and taken up carbon dioxide —**ve'nous·ly** *adv.*

vent¹ (vent) *n.* [OFr. *venter*, to blow, ult. < L. *ventus*, a wind] **1.** an opening or hole for a gas, liquid, etc. to pass through or escape; outlet; passage **2.** a way of letting out or expressing something; expression or release [giving *vent* to anger] ☆**3.** a small triangular window, as in a car door, for letting air in without a direct draft **4.** the opening in a volcano through which it erupts **5.** the anal opening in animals; esp., the outlet of the cloaca in birds, reptiles, etc. —*vt.* **1.** to make a vent in **2.** to let (steam, gas, etc.) out through an opening **3.** to give release or expression to [to *vent* one's grief]

vent² (vent) *n.* [< OFr., ult. < L. pp. of *findere*, to split] a vertical slit in a garment, esp. one put in the back or sides of a coat —*vt.* to make a vent or vents in

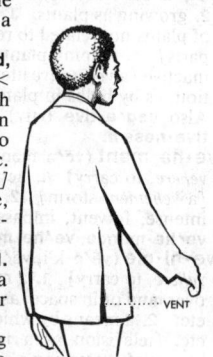

ven·ti·late (ven't'l āt') *vt.* **-lat·ed, -lat·ing** [< L. pp. of *ventilare*, to fan < *ventus*, a wind] **1.** *a)* to circulate fresh air in (a room, etc.) *b)* to circulate in (a room, etc.): said of fresh air **2.** to put a vent in so as to let air, gas, etc. escape [to *ventilate* a shipping box] **3.** to examine and discuss (a grievance, etc.) openly **4.** to aerate (blood); oxygenate

ven·ti·la·tion (ven't'l ā'shən) *n.* **1.** the act or process of ventilating **2.** a system or means of circulating fresh air indoors

ven·ti·la·tor (ven't'l āt' ər) *n.* a thing that ventilates; esp., any device used to bring in fresh air and drive out foul air

ven·tral (ven'trəl) *adj.* [Fr. < L. *ventralis* < *venter*, belly] of, on, or near the belly —**ven'tral·ly** *adv.*

ven·tri·cle (ven'tri k'l) *n.* [< L. dim. of *venter*, belly] *Anat., Zool.* a cavity; specif., *a)* either of the two lower chambers of the heart which receive blood from the atria and pump it into the arteries: see illustration at HEART *b)* any of the four small continuous cavities within the brain —**ven·tric'u·lar** (-trik'yə lər) *adj.*

ven·tril·o·quism (ven tril'ə kwiz'm) *n.* [< L. < *venter*, belly + *loqui*, to speak + -ISM] the art or practice of speaking so that the voice seems to come from some source other than the speaker, as from a small dummy held by the speaker: also **ven·tril'o·quy** (-kwē) —**ven·tril'o·quist** *n.* —**ven·tril'o·quis'tic** *adj.* —**ven·tril'o·quize** (-kwīz') *vi., vt.* **-quized', -quiz'ing**

Ven·tu·ra (ven toor'ə) *n.* [< (*San Buena*)*ventura* (the official name) < Sp., lit., saint of good fortune] city in SW Calif., northwest of Los Angeles: pop. 56,000

ven·ture (ven'chər) *n.* [< ME. *aventure*: see ADVENTURE]

1. a risky undertaking; esp., a business enterprise in which there is danger of loss as well as chance for profit **2.** an action, investment, etc. involving a risk [her *venture* into a stage career] **3.** chance; fortune: now only in **at a venture,** by mere chance —*vt.* **-tured, -tur·ing 1.** to risk; hazard [to *venture* one's fortune] **2.** to take the risk of; brave [to *venture* the weather] **3.** to express (an opinion, etc.) at the risk of being criticized, etc. —*vi.* to do or go at some risk [unwilling to *venture* further] — **ven′tur·er** *n.*

ven·ture·some (-səm) *adj.* **1.** willing to take chances; bold; daring **2.** full of risks or danger; risky; hazardous —**ven′ture·some·ly** *adv.* —**ven′ture·some·ness** *n.*

ven·tu·ri (tube) (ven toor′ē) [after G. B. *Venturi* (1746–1822), It. physicist] a short tube with a narrow throat that increases the velocity and lowers the pressure of a fluid flowing through it: used to measure fluid flow, to regulate the mixture in a carburetor, etc.

ven·tur·ous (ven′chər əs) *adj. same as* VENTURESOME —**ven′-tur·ous·ly** *adv.* —**ven′tur·ous·ness** *n.*

ven·ue (ven′yōō, -ōō) *n.* [OFr., arrival < *venir,* to come < L. *venire*] *Law* **1.** the county or locality in which a cause of action or a crime occurs **2.** the county or locality in which a jury is selected and a case tried —**change of venue** *Law* the substitution of another place of trial, as when the jury or court is likely to be prejudiced

ven·ule (ven′yōōl) *n.* [< L. dim. of *vena,* vein] **1.** *Anat.* a small vein **2.** *Biol.* any small branch of a vein in a leaf or in an insect wing —**ven′u·lar** (-yoo lər) *adj.*

Ve·nus (vē′nəs) [L., lit., love] **1.** *Rom. Myth.* the goddess of love and beauty: identified with the Greek goddess Aphrodite **2.** a planet in the solar system, second in distance from the sun: diameter, c.7,600 mi. —*n.* **1.** a statue or image of Venus **2.** a very beautiful woman

☆**Ve·nus′ fly·trap** (vē′nəs flī′trap′) a white-flowered swamp plant native to the Carolinas, having leaves with two hinged blades that snap shut and so trap insects

Ve·nu·sian (vi nōō′shən) *adj.* of the planet Venus —*n.* an imagined inhabitant of the planet Venus

Ver·a (vir′ə) [Russ. *Vjera,* faith; also L. fem. of *verus,* true] a feminine name

ve·ra·cious (və rā′shəs) *adj.* [< L. < *verus,* true] **1.** habitually truthful; honest [a *veracious* witness] **2.** true; accurate [a *veracious* report] —**ve·ra′-cious·ly** *adv.* —**ve·ra′cious·ness** *n.*

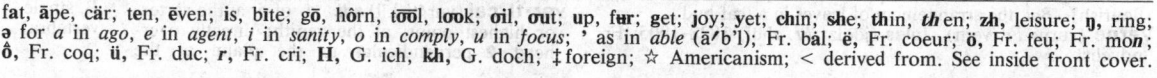

VENUS' FLYTRAP

ve·rac·i·ty (və ras′ə tē) *n., pl.* **-ties** [< ML. < L. *verus,* true] **1.** the quality of being veracious, or truthful, accurate, etc. **2.** that which is true; truth —see SYN. at HONESTY

Ver·a·cruz (ver′ə krōōz′; *Sp.* ve′rä krōōs′) seaport in E Mexico, on the Gulf of Mexico: pop. 242,000

ve·ran·da, ve·ran·dah (və ran′də) *n.* [Anglo-Ind. < Port. *varanda,* a balcony < *vara,* a pole < L., forked stick] an open porch, usually roofed, along the outside of a building

verb (vurb) *n.* [< OFr. < L. *verbum,* a word] **1.** any of a class of words expressing action, a state of being, or a happening and forming the main part of a predicate: see also AUXILIARY VERB, LINKING VERB **2.** any group of words used as a verb —*adj.* of, or functioning as, a verb

ver·bal (vur′b'l) *adj.* **1.** of, in, or by means of words [a *verbal* image] **2.** concerned merely with words rather than with facts, ideas, or actions [empty, *verbal* praise] **3.** oral rather than written [a *verbal* contract] **4.** *Gram.* of, like, or derived from a verb [a *verbal* noun] —*n. Gram.* a verbal noun or other word derived from a verb: in English, gerunds, infinitives, and participles are verbals —see SYN. at ORAL —**ver′bal·ly** *adv.*

ver·bal·ism (-iz'm) *n.* **1.** an expression in one or more words; word or word phrase [a slang *verbalism*] **2.** words only, without any real meaning [their protest is mere *verbalism*]

ver·bal·ist (-ist) *n.* **1.** a person skilled in verbal expression **2.** a person who gives more importance to words than to the facts or ideas they convey

ver·bal·ize (vur′bə līz′) *vi.* **-ized′, -iz′ing 1.** to be wordy, or verbose **2.** to communicate in words [she *verbalizes* skillfully]

—*vt.* **1.** to express in words [it is hard to *verbalize* that idea] **2.** to change (a noun, etc.) into a verb —**ver′bal·i·za′tion** *n.* —**ver′bal·iz′er** *n.*

verbal noun *Gram.* a noun derived from a verb and acting in some respects like a verb: in English it is either a noun ending in -*ing* (a gerund) or an infinitive (Examples: *walking* is healthful, *to err* is human)

ver·ba·tim (vər bāt′əm) *adv.* [ML. < L. *verbum,* a word] word for word; in exactly the same words [to repeat a conversation *verbatim*] —*adj.* following the original, word for word [a *verbatim* account]

ver·be·na (vər bē′nə) *n.* [ModL., genus name < L., foliage] any of a group of ornamental plants with spikes or clusters of red, white, or purplish flowers

ver·bi·age (vur′bē ij) *n.* [Fr. < OFr. < L. *verbum,* a word] the use of more words than are needed to be clear; wordiness

ver·bose (vər bōs′) *adj.* [L. *verbosus,* full of words < *verbum,* a word] using or containing too many words; wordy; long-winded —see SYN. at WORDY —**ver·bose′ly** *adv.* —**ver·bos′i·ty** (-bäs′ə tē), **ver·bose′ness** *n.*

‡**ver·bo·ten** (fer bō′tən) *adj.* [G.] forbidden; prohibited

VERBENA

ver·dant (vur′d'nt) *adj.* [prob. < VERD(URE) + -ANT] **1.** green [*verdant* grass] **2.** covered with green vegetation [*verdant* land] **3.** inexperienced; immature [in one's *verdant* youth] —**ver′dan·cy** (-d'n sē) *n.*

Verde (vurd), **Cape** peninsula on the Atlantic coast of Senegal: westernmost point of Africa

Ver·di (ver′dē), **Giu·sep·pe (Fortunino Francisco)** (jōō-zep′pe) 1813–1901; It. operatic composer

ver·dict (vur′dikt) *n.* [< Anglo-Fr. < ML. < L. *vere,* truly + *dictum,* a thing said < *dicere,* to say] **1.** *Law* the decision reached by a jury at the end of a trial **2.** any decision or judgment

ver·di·gris (vur′di grēs′, -gris) *n.* [< MFr. < OFr. < *verd,* green + *de,* of + *Grece,* Greece] a green or greenish-blue coating that forms on brass, bronze, or copper

Ver·dun (ver dun′, vur-; *Fr.* ver dėn′) **1.** city in NE France, on the Meuse River: scene of a battle of World War I **2.** city in SW Quebec, Canada: suburb of Montreal: pop. 77,000

ver·dure (vur′jər) *n.* [OFr. < *verd,* green] **1.** the fresh green color of growing things **2.** green vegetation —**ver′dured** *adj.* —**ver′dur·ous** *adj.*

verge¹ (vurj) *n.* [< OFr. < L. *virga,* rod] **1.** *a)* the edge, brink, or margin [the *verge* of a forest, on the *verge* of hysteria] *b)* [Brit.] a grassy border, as along a road **2.** an enclosing or surrounding line or border **3.** a rod or staff symbolic of an office —*vi.* **verged, verg′ing** to be on the verge, brink, or border (usually with *on* or *upon*) [streets *verging* on a slum area; talk *verging* on the ridiculous]

verge² (vurj) *vi.* **verged, verg′ing** [L. *vergere*] **1.** to tend or incline (*to* or *toward*) [new tariff laws *verging* toward free trade] **2.** to be in the process of change into something else; pass gradually (*into*) [dawn *verging* into daylight]

verg·er (vur′jər) *n.* [see VERGE¹ & -ER] **1.** a person who carries a staff of office before a bishop, etc. **2.** a church caretaker or usher

Ver·gil (vur′jəl) *var. of* VIRGIL —**Ver·gil′i·an** (-jil′ē ən) *adj.*

ver·i·est (ver′ē ist) *adj.* [superl. of VERY, *adj.*] being such to the highest degree; utter [the *veriest* nonsense]

ver·i·fi·ca·tion (ver′ə fi kā′shən) *n.* a verifying or being verified; establishment or confirmation of the truth or accuracy of a fact, theory, etc.

ver·i·fy (ver′ə fī′) *vt.* **-fied′, -fy′ing** [< MFr. < ML. < L. *verus,* true + *-ficare,* -FY] **1.** to prove to be true by demonstration, evidence, etc.; confirm or substantiate [to *verify* a theory by experiments] **2.** to test the accuracy of, as by comparison with a standard [to *verify* a measurement] **3.** *Law* to affirm on oath —see SYN. at CONFIRM —**ver′i·fi′a·ble** *adj.* —**ver′i·fi′a·bly** *adv.* —**ver′i·fi′er** *n.*

ver·i·ly (ver′ə lē) *adv.* [Archaic] in very truth; truly

ver·i·sim·i·lar (ver′ə sim′ə lər) *adj.* [< L. < *verus,* true + *similis,* like] seeming to be true or real; likely

fat, āpe, cär; ten, ēven; is, bīte; gō, hôrn, tōōl, look; oil, out; up, fur; get; joy; yet; chin; she; thin, then; zh, leisure; ŋ, ring; ə for *a* in *ago, e* in *agent, i* in *sanity, o* in *comply, u* in *focus;* ′ as in *able* (ā′b'l); Fr. bâl; ë, Fr. coeur; ö, Fr. feu; ô, Fr. mon; ô̱, Fr. coq; ü, Fr. duc; ʀ, Fr. cri; ʜ, G. ich; kh, G. doch; ‡foreign; ☆ Americanism; < derived from. See inside front cover.

ver·i·si·mil·i·tude (ver′ə si mil′ə tōōd′, -tyōōd′) *n.* [< L.: see prec.] **1.** the appearance of being true or real [the *verisimilitude* of the characters in a novel] **2.** something having the mere appearance of being true or real [an argument full of deceptive *verisimilitudes*]

ver·i·ta·ble (ver′i tə b′l) *adj.* [< OFr. < L. *veritas*, truth] being such in truth or fact; actual [a *veritable* feast] —**ver′i·ta·bly** *adv.*

ver·i·ty (ver′ə tē) *n., pl.* **-ties** [< OFr. < L. *veritas*, truth < *verus*, true] **1.** the condition of being true or real [to doubt the *verity* of a rumor] **2.** a truth or reality, esp. one that is regarded as basic [the eternal *verities*]

ver·juice (vur′jōōs′) *n.* [< MFr. < *vert*, green + *jus*, juice] **1.** the sour, acid juice of green, or unripe, fruit **2.** sourness of temper, looks, etc.

Ver·laine (ver len′), **Paul** (pōl) 1844–96; Fr. poet

Ver·meer (vər mer′; *E.* vər mir′), **Jan** (yän) 1632–75; Du. painter: also called *Jan van der Meer van Delft*

ver·meil (vur′mil) *n.* [OFr. < LL. *vermiculus*, kermes < L. dim. of *vermis*, a worm] **1.** [Poet.] the color vermilion **2.** gilded silver, bronze, or copper

ver·mi- [< L. *vermis*, a worm] *a combining form meaning* worm [*vermicide*]

ver·mi·cel·li (vur′mə sel′ē, -chel′ē) *n.* [It., little worms < L. dim. of *vermis*, a worm] pasta like spaghetti, but in thinner strings

ver·mi·cide (vur′mə sīd′) *n.* [VERMI- + -CIDE] a drug or other agent used to kill worms, esp. intestinal worms

ver·mic·u·lar (vər mik′yə lər) *adj.* [< ModL. < L. dim. of *vermis*, a worm] **1.** *a)* wormlike in shape or movement *b)* having twisting lines, ridges, etc. that look like worm tracks [a *vermicular* surface] **2.** of, made by, or caused by worms Also **ver·mic′u·late** (-lit), **ver·mic′u·lat′ed** (-lāt′id)

☆**ver·mic·u·lite** (vər mik′yə līt′) *n.* [< L.: see prec. & -ITE] mica in the form of tiny scales that expand when heated: used for insulation, water adsorption, etc.

ver·mi·form (vur′mə fôrm′) *adj.* [VERMI- + -FORM] shaped like a worm

vermiform appendix *see* APPENDIX (sense 2)

ver·mi·fuge (vur′mə fyōōj′) *n.* [VERMI- + -FUGE] a medicine that expels worms from the intestines

ver·mil·ion (vər mil′yən) *n.* [< OFr. < *vermeil*, bright-red: see VERMEIL] **1.** *a)* bright-red mercuric sulfide, used as a pigment *b)* any of several other red pigments resembling this **2.** a bright red or scarlet —*adj.* of the color vermilion

ver·min (vur′min) *n., pl.* **-min** [< OFr. < L. *vermis*, a worm] **1.** *a)* any of various insects, bugs, or small animals regarded as pests because destructive, disease-carrying, etc., as flies, lice, or rats *b)* such pests as a group **2.** [Chiefly Brit.] birds or animals that kill game on preserves **3.** a vile, disgusting person or persons —**ver′min·ous** *adj.*

Ver·mont (vər mänt′) [< Fr. *Verd Mont*, green mountain] New England State of the U.S.: 9,609 sq. mi.; pop. 444,000; cap. Montpelier: abbrev. **Vt., VT** —**Ver·mont′er** *n.*

ver·mouth (vər mōōth′) *n.* [Fr. < G. *wermut*, wormwood] a sweet or dry, fortified white wine flavored with herbs, used in cocktails and as an aperitif

ver·nac·u·lar (vər nak′yə lər) *adj.* [L. *vernaculus*, native < *verna*, a native-born slave] **1.** using the native language of a place [a *vernacular* writer] **2.** commonly spoken by the people of a particular country or place [a *vernacular*, as distinguished from the literary, dialect] **3.** of or in the native language **4.** native to a place [*vernacular* arts] **5.** designating or of the common name, rather than the scientific Latin name, of an animal or plant —*n.* **1.** the native language or dialect of a country or place **2.** the common, everyday language of ordinary people in a particular locality **3.** the special language of people in a particular work, group, etc. [the *vernacular* of the underworld] **4.** a vernacular word or term —see SYN. at DIALECT —**ver·nac′u·lar·ism** *n.* —**ver·nac′u·lar·ly** *adv.*

ver·nal (vur′n′l) *adj.* [L. *vernalis* < *vernus* < *ver*, spring] **1.** of or happening in the spring [the *vernal* equinox] **2.** springlike; fresh, warm, and mild [a *vernal* breeze] **3.** fresh and young; youthful [*vernal* beauty] —**ver′nal·ly** *adv.*

ver·nal·ize (-īz′) *vt.* **-ized′, -iz′ing** to stimulate the growth and flowering of (a plant) by artificially shortening the dormant period —**ver′nal·i·za′tion** *n.*

ver·na·tion (vər nā′shən) *n.* [< ModL. < pp. of L. *vernare*, to flourish] *Bot.* the arrangement of leaves in a leaf bud

Verne (vurn; *Fr.* vern), **Jules** (jōōlz; *Fr.* zhül) 1828–1905; Fr. novelist

ver·ni·er (vur′nē ər, -nir) *n.* [after P. *Vernier*, 17th-c. Fr. mathematician] a short, graduated scale that slides along a longer graduated instrument and is used to indicate fractional parts of divisions, as in a micrometer: also **vernier scale**

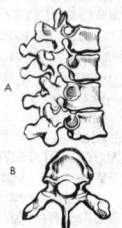

a = 527

VERNIER

Ve·ro·na (və rō′nə; *It.* ve rô′nä) city in N Italy: pop. 259,000 —**Ver·o·nese** (ver′ə nēz′) *adj., n.*

Ve·ro·ne·se (ve′rô ne′se; *E.* ver′ə-nēz′), **Pa·o·lo** (pä′ô lô′) (born *Paolo Cagliari*) 1528–88; Venetian painter, born in Verona

Ve·ron·i·ca (və rän′i kə) [ML.] a feminine name —*n.* [v-] **1.** [ModL.] *same as* SPEEDWELL **2.** *Bullfighting* a slow, pivoting movement made by a matador, with his cape held out, as the bull charges past him

Ver·sailles (ver sī′, -sālz′; *Fr.* ver sä′y′) city in NC France, near Paris: the Allies & Germany signed a peace treaty here (1919) ending World War I: pop. 95,000

ver·sa·tile (vur′sə t′l; *chiefly Brit.* -tīl′) *adj.* [Fr. < L. < pp. of *versare*, whirl about < *vertere*, to turn] **1.** *a)* competent in many things; able to turn easily from one subject or occupation to another [a *versatile* artist who did painting, sculpture, and ceramics] *b)* adaptable to many uses or functions [a *versatile* piece of furniture] **2.** *Biol.* turning or moving freely, as the anther of a flower or the antenna of an insect —**ver′sa·tile·ly** *adv.* —**ver′sa·til′i·ty** (-til′ə tē) *n.*

verse (vurs) *n.* [< OE. & OFr. < L. *versus*, a turning, row, pp. of *vertere*, to turn < IE. base *wer-*, to turn] **1.** a single line of poetry having meter **2.** *a)* poetry in general; sometimes, specif., poems of a light or amusing nature *b)* poetry having a certain meter, rhyme, etc. [blank *verse*, trochaic *verse*] **3.** *a)* a single poem *b)* the poetry of a particular writer, period, etc. **4.** a stanza or other short subdivision of a poem **5.** any of the single, usually numbered, short divisions of a chapter of the Bible —*vt., vi.* **versed, vers′ing** [Now Rare] *same as* VERSIFY

versed (vurst) *adj.* [< L. pp. of *versari*, to be busy] acquainted by experience and study; skilled or learned (*in* a subject)

ver·si·cle (vur′si k′l) *n.* [< L. *versiculus*, dim. of *versus*, a verse] a short verse or sentence, esp. one said or sung in a religious service and followed by a response

ver·si·fi·ca·tion (vur′sə fi kā′shən) *n.* **1.** the act of versifying **2.** the art, practice, or theory of poetic composition **3.** the form or metrical structure of a poem

ver·si·fy (vur′sə fī′) *vi.* **-fied′, -fy′ing** [< MFr. < L. < *versus*: see VERSE & -FY] to compose verses —*vt.* **1.** to tell about or describe in verse **2.** to put into verse form —**ver′si·fi′er** *n.*

ver·sion (vur′zhən, -shən) *n.* [Fr. < ML. < L. *versus*: see VERSE] **1.** *a)* a translation *b)* [often V-] a translation of the Bible **2.** an account giving one point of view [two *versions* of the accident] **3.** a particular form or variation, sometimes as adapted to another art form [a revised *version* of a play; the movie *version* of the novel] —**ver′sion·al** *adj.*

†**vers li·bre** (ver lē′br′) *French term for* FREE VERSE

ver·so (vur′sō) *n., pl.* **-sos** [ModL. (*folio*) *verso*, on (the page) turned] *Printing* any left-hand page of a book; back of a leaf: opposed to RECTO

verst (vurst, verst; *Russ.* vyôrst) *n.* [< Russ. *versta*] a former Russian unit of linear measure, equal to c.3,500 feet

ver·sus (vur′səs) *prep.* [ML. < L., toward < *vertere*, to turn] **1.** in contest against [our team *versus* theirs] **2.** in contrast with; as an alternative to [peace *versus* war]

ver·te·bra (vur′tə brə) *n., pl.* **-brae** (-brē′), **-bras** [L., a joint < *vertere*, to turn] any of the bones that make up the spinal column, or backbone —**ver′te·bral** *adj.*

ver·te·brate (-brit, -brāt′) *adj.* [< L.: see prec.] **1.** having a backbone, or spinal column **2.** of or belonging to the vertebrates —*n.* any of a large group of animals, including all mammals, fishes, birds, reptiles, and amphibians, that have a backbone and a brain and cranium

ver·tex (vur′teks) *n., pl.* **-tex·es, -ti·ces′** (-tə-sēz′) [L., the top, the turning point < *vertere*, to turn] **1.** *a)* the highest point; top; apex *b)* *same as* ZENITH **2.** *Geom. a)* the point where the two sides of an angle intersect *b)* any corner point of a triangle, square, cube, etc.

ver·ti·cal (vur′ti k′l) *adj.* **1.** of or at the vertex, or highest point; at the zenith; directly overhead **2.** perpendicular to the plane of the

VERTEBRAE
(A, section of spinal column; B, single vertebra)

horizon or to a level surface; upright; straight up or down [a *vertical* fall]; a *vertical* fall] **3.** of or including the different levels, as in the manufacture and distribution of some product —*n.* **1.** a vertical line, plane, etc. **2.** upright position [push the beam back to the *vertical*] —**ver′ti·cal′i·ty** (-kal′ə tē) *n.* —**ver′ti·cal·ly** *adv.*

vertical union *same as* INDUSTRIAL UNION

ver·ti·ces (vur′tə sēz′) *n. alt. pl. of* VERTEX

ver·ti·cil (vur′tə sil) *n.* [L. *verticillus,* dim. of *vertex,* a whirl] *Bot.* a circle of leaves, flowers, etc. on a stem; whorl —**ver·tic·il·late** (vər tis′'l it, -āt′) *adj.*

ver·tig·i·nous (vər tij′ə nəs) *adj.* **1.** of, having, or causing vertigo; dizzy or dizzying [to feel *vertiginous,* a *vertiginous* height] **2.** whirling; spinning **3.** unstable; inconstant —**ver·tig′i·nous·ly** *adv.*

ver·ti·go (vur′ti gō′) *n., pl.* **-goes, ver·tig·i·nes** (vər tij′ə nēz′) [L. < *vertere,* to turn] *Med.* a condition in which one has the feeling of whirling or of having the surroundings whirling about one, so that one tends to lose one's balance; dizziness

ver·tu (vər tōō′, vur′tōō) *n. same as* VIRTU

ver·vain (vur′vān) *n.* [< OFr. < L. *verbena,* foliage] any of a number of verbenas

verve (vurv) *n.* [Fr. < OFr., caprice < L. *verba,* words] **1.** vigor and energy; liveliness; spirit; dash

ver·y (ver′ē) *adj.* **ver′i·er, ver′i·est** [< OFr., ult. < L. *verus,* true] **1.** in the fullest sense; complete; utter [the *very* opposite of the truth] **2.** same; identical [the *very* hat she lost] **3.** exactly right, suitable, etc.; precise [the *very* one I want] **4.** even (the): used to add emphasis [the *very* rafters shook] **5.** actual [caught in the *very* act] —*adv.* **1.** in a high degree; exceedingly [*very* hot] **2.** truly; really: used to add emphasis [the *very* same person] —*see* SYN *at* SAME

very high frequency any radio frequency between 30 and 300 megahertz

very low frequency any radio frequency between 10 and 30 kilohertz

Ver·y signal (or **light**) (ver′ē, vir′ē) [after E. W. *Very,* 19th-c. U.S. ordnance expert] a colored flare fired from a special pistol (**Very pistol**) for signaling at night

ves·i·cant (ves′i kənt) *adj.* [< L. *vesica,* a blister] causing blisters —*n.* a vesicant agent, as mustard gas Also **ves′i·ca·to′ry** (-kə tôr′ē) *adj., n., pl.* **-to′ries**

ves·i·cate (ves′i kāt′) *vt., vi.* **-cat′ed, -cat′ing** [< L. *vesica,* a bladder, blister] to blister —**ves′i·ca′tion** *n.*

ves·i·cle (ves′i k'l) *n.* [< Fr. < L. dim. of *vesica,* bladder] **1.** a small, membranous cavity, sac, or cyst; specif., a blister **2.** *Geol.* a small, spherical cavity in volcanic rock —**ve·sic·u·lar** (və sik′yə lər), **ve·sic′u·late** (-lit) *adj.*

Ves·pa·si·an (ves pā′zhē ən, -zhən) (L. name *Titus Flavius Sabinus Vespasianus*) 9–79 A.D.; Roman emperor (69–79)

ves·per (ves′pər) *n.* [L.] **1.** *a*) orig., evening *b*) [Poet.] [V-] *same as* EVENING STAR **2.** an evening prayer or service; specif., [*pl.*] [*often* V-] *a*) *R.C.Ch.* the sixth of the seven canonical hours, recited or sung in the late afternoon *b*) *Anglican Ch. same as* EVENSONG —*adj.* **1.** of evening **2.** of vespers

ves·per·tine (ves′pər t'n, -tīn′) *adj.* [< L. < *vesper,* evening] **1.** of or happening in the evening **2.** blooming, active, etc. in the evening, as some plants or animals

ves·pine (ves′pīn, -pin) *adj.* [< L. *vespa,* a wasp] of or like wasps

Ves·puc·ci, A·me·ri·go (ves pōōt′chē), (ä′me rē′gō) (L. name *Americus Vespucius*) 1451?–1512; It. navigator

ves·sel (ves′'l) *n.* [< OFr. < LL. dim. of L. *vas,* a vessel] **1.** a utensil for holding something, as a bowl, pot, tub, etc. **2.** a ship or large boat **3.** *a*) *Anat., Zool.* a tube or duct containing or circulating a body fluid *b*) *Bot.* a water-conducting tube in the xylem

vest (vest) *n.* [< Fr. < It. < L. *vestis,* a garment] **1.** *a*) a short, tightfitting, sleeveless garment worn, esp. under a suit coat, by men; waistcoat *b*) a similar, jacketlike garment worn by women *c*) a piece set into a bodice,

VEST

resembling the front of a man's vest **2.** a girl's undershirt **3.** [Brit.] any undershirt —*vt.* **1.** to dress, as in church vestments; clothe **2.** to place (some right, power, or property) in the control of a person or group (with *in*) [ownership was *vested* in the tenants] **3.** to provide or invest (a person or group) (*with* some right, power, or property) [he was *vested* with full authority] —*vi.* **1.** to put on garments or vestments **2.** to become vested (*in* a person), as property

Ves·ta (ves′tə) [L.] *Rom. Myth.* the goddess of the hearth

ves·tal (ves′t'l) *adj.* **1.** of or sacred to Vesta **2.** of the vestal virgins **3.** chaste; pure —*n.* **1.** *short for* VESTAL VIRGIN **2.** a chaste woman; specif., a virgin

vestal virgin in ancient Rome, any of the virgin priestesses of Vesta, who tended the sacred fire in her temple

vest·ed (ves′tid) *adj.* **1.** not depending upon anything; fixed; absolute [a *vested* right] **2.** including a vest [a *vested* suit]

vested interest 1. an established right that cannot be done away with, as to some future benefit **2.** [*pl.*] the powerful persons and groups that own and control industry, business, etc.

☆**vest·ee** (ves tē′) *n. dim. of* VEST (*n.* 1 *c*)

ves·ti·bule (ves′tə byōōl′) *n.* [L. *vestibulum,* entrance hall] **1.** a small entrance hall, either to a building or a room ☆**2.** the enclosed passage between passenger cars of a train **3.** *Anat., Zool.* any cavity or space serving as an entrance to another cavity or space [the *vestibule* of the inner ear leading into the cochlea] —**ves·tib·u·lar** (ves tib′yə lər) *adj.*

ves·tige (ves′tij) *n.* [Fr. < L. *vestigium,* a footprint] **1.** a trace or remaining bit of something once present or whole [*vestiges* of an ancient wall, not a *vestige* of hope] **2.** *Biol.* an organ or part not so fully developed or functional as it once was in the embryo or species: also **ves·tig·i·um** (ves tij′ē əm), *pl.* **-i·a** (-ə) —**ves·tig′i·al** (-tij′ē əl, -tij′əl) *adj.* —**ves·tig′i·al·ly** *adv.*

vest·ing (ves′tiŋ) *n.* the keeping by an employee of all or part of his pension rights regardless of whether or not he changes employers, retires early, etc.

vest·ment (vest′mənt) *n.* [< OFr. < L. *vestimentum* < *vestire,* to clothe] **1.** a garment; esp., an official robe or gown **2.** *Eccles.* any of the garments worn by clergymen, etc. during religious services

vest-pock·et (vest′päk′it) *adj.* **1.** small enough to fit into a vest pocket [a *vest-pocket* dictionary] **2.** very small

ves·try (ves′trē) *n., pl.* **-tries** [< OFr. < L. *vestiarium,* a wardrobe < *vestis,* a garment] **1.** a room in a church, where vestments and sacred vessels are kept **2.** a room in a church, used for prayer meetings, Sunday school, etc. **3.** *Anglican & Episcopal Ch.* a group of church members who manage the business affairs of the church

ves·try·man (-mən) *n., pl.* **-men** a member of a vestry

ves·ture (ves′chər) *n.* [< OFr. < VL. < L. *vestire,* to clothe] [Now Rare] **1.** clothing **2.** a covering —*vt.* **-tured, -tur·ing** [Rare or Archaic] to clothe or cover

Ve·su·vi·us (və sōō′vi əs) active volcano in S Italy, on the Bay of Naples (see POMPEII) —**Ve·su′vi·an** *adj.*

vet¹ (vet) *n. shortened form of* VETERINARIAN —*vt.* **vet′ted, vet′ting** [Colloq.] **1.** to examine or treat as a veterinarian does **2.** to examine or evaluate thoroughly

☆**vet²** (vet) *n. shortened form of* VETERAN

vet. 1. veteran **2.** veterinarian **3.** veterinary

vetch (vech) *n.* [< ONormFr. < L. *vicia,* vetch] any of a number of leafy, climbing or trailing plants of the legume family, used chiefly as fodder or fertilizer

vet·er·an (vet′ər ən, vet′rən) *adj.* [L. *veteranus* < *veteris,* genitive of *vetus,* old] **1.** having had long experience in some kind of work or in military service **2.** of a veteran or veterans —*n.* **1.** a person with much experience in some kind of work **2.** a person who has served in the armed forces of a country, esp. in war

☆**Veterans Administration** a consolidated Federal agency administering all laws on benefits for military veterans

VETCH

☆**Veterans Day** a legal holiday in the U.S. honoring all veter-

---

ans of the armed forces: observed (except for a period from 1971 to 1977) on ARMISTICE DAY

vet·er·i·nar·i·an (vet′ər ə ner′ē ən, vet′rə ner′-) *n.* a person who practices veterinary medicine or surgery

vet·er·i·nar·y (vet′ər ə ner′ē, vet′rə-) *adj.* [< L. < *veterina,* beasts of burden] designating or of the branch of medicine dealing with the treatment of diseases and injuries in animals, esp. domestic animals —*n., pl.* **-nar′ies** *same as* VETERINARIAN

ve·to (vē′tō) *n., pl.* **-toes** [L., I forbid < *vetare,* to forbid] **1.** *a)* an order forbidding some proposed act; prohibition *b)* the power to prevent action thus **2.** the constitutional right or power of a ruler or legislature to reject bills passed by another branch of the government; specif., ☆in the U.S., *a)* the power of the President to refuse to sign a bill passed by Congress *b)* a similar power held by the governors of States *c)* the exercise of this power ☆**3.** a document or message giving the reasons of the executive for rejecting a bill: also **veto message 4.** the power of any of the five permanent members of the Security Council of the United Nations to prevent an action by casting a negative vote —*vt.* **-toed, -to·ing 1.** to prevent (a bill) from becoming law by veto **2.** to forbid; prohibit; refuse consent to

vex (veks) *vt.* [< MFr. < L. *vexare,* to agitate] **1.** to disturb, annoy, irritate, etc., esp. by some small, repeated action /their constant chatter *vexes* me/ **2.** to cause to feel pain; distress /*vexed* with a headache/ **3.** to keep discussing (a matter, question, etc. that is difficult to solve or settle) —see SYN. at ANNOY —**vexed** *adj.* —**vex·ed·ly** (vek′sid lē) *adv.* —**vex′er** *n.*

vex·a·tion (vek sā′shən) *n.* **1.** a vexing or being vexed **2.** something that vexes; cause of annoyance or distress /he was a great *vexation* to his sisters/

vex·a·tious (-shəs) *adj.* characterized by or causing vexation; annoying, troublesome, etc. /his *vexatious* habit of interrupting/ —**vex·a′tious·ly** *adv.* —**vex·a′tious·ness** *n.*

vex·ing (vek′sin) *adj.* that vexes —**vex′ing·ly** *adv.*

VFR Visual Flight Rules

V.F.W., VFW Veterans of Foreign Wars

VHF, V.H.F., vhf, v.h.f. very high frequency

VI, V.I. Virgin Islands (of the United States)

vi., v.i. intransitive verb

v.i. [L. *vide infra*] see below

vi·a (vī′ə, vē′ə) *prep.* [L. < *via,* a way] **1.** by way of; passing through /from Rome to London *via* Paris/ **2.** by means of /via airmail/

vi·a·ble (vī′ə b′l) *adj.* [Fr., ult. < L. *vita,* life] **1.** *a)* able to live; specif., developed enough to be able to live outside the uterus /a premature but *viable* infant/ *b)* capable of growing /*viable* seeds/ **2.** workable; likely to survive or be effective /a *viable* economy, *viable* ideas/ —**vi′a·bil′i·ty** *n.* —**vi′a·bly** *adv.*

vi·a·duct (vī′ə dukt′) *n.* [L. *via* (see VIA) + (AQUE)DUCT] a bridge consisting of a series of short spans supported on piers or towers, usually for carrying a road or railroad over a valley, gorge, etc.

vi·al (vī′əl) *n.* [< OFr. < OPr., ult. < Gr. *phialē,* shallow cup] a small bottle, usually of glass, for holding medicine or other liquids; phial

‡**vi·a me·di·a** (vī′ə mē′dē ə, vē′ə mā′-) [L.] a middle way; course between two extremes

vi·and (vī′ənd) *n.* [< OFr., ult. < L. *vivere,* to live] **1.** an article of food **2.** *[pl.]* food, esp. fine, costly food

vi·at·i·cum (vī at′i kəm) *n., pl.* **-ca** (-kə), **-cums** [L. < *viaticus,* of a way or road < *via,* way] **1.** money or supplies for a journey **2.** *[often* V-] the Eucharist as given to a person dying or in danger of death

☆**vibes** (vībz) *n.pl.* **1.** [Colloq.] *same as* VIBRAPHONE **2.** [< VIBRATION(s)] [Slang] qualities in a person or thing that are thought of as being like vibrations which produce an emotional reaction in others

☆**vi·bra·harp** (vī′brə härp′) *n. same as* VIBRAPHONE

vi·brant (vī′brənt) *adj.* [< L. prp. of *vibrare,* to vibrate] **1.** quivering; vibrating /vibrant harp strings/ **2.** full and rich; resonant /vibrant tones/ **3.** full of life and activity; lively /vibrant streets/ **4.** energetic, sparkling, vivacious, etc. /a *vibrant* woman/ —**vi′bran·cy** *n.* —**vi′brant·ly** *adv.*

vi·bra·phone (vī′brə fōn′) *n.* [VIBRA(TE) + -PHONE] a musical instrument like the marimba but having electrically operated valves in the resonators, that produce a gentle vibrato —**vi′bra·phon′ist** *n.*

vi·brate (vī′brāt) *vt.* **-brat·ed, -brat·ing** [< L. pp. of *vibrare,* to vibrate] **1.** to set in to-and-fro motion; oscillate **2.** to cause to quiver —*vi.* **1.** to swing back and forth; oscillate, as a pendulum **2.** to move rapidly back and forth; quiver, as a plucked string **3.** to resound; echo /the hall *vibrated* with cheers/ **4.** to feel very excited; thrill

vi·bra·tile (vī′brə til, -tīl′) *adj.* **1.** of or characterized by vibration **2.** capable of vibrating or being vibrated **3.** having a vibrating motion —**vi′bra·til′i·ty** *n.*

vi·bra·tion (vī brā′shən) *n.* **1.** the action of vibrating; esp., rapid movement back and forth; quivering **2.** *Physics a)* rapid, periodic, to-and-fro motion or oscillation of an elastic body or the particles of a fluid, as in transmitting sound *b)* a single, complete oscillation —**vi·bra′tion·al** *adj.*

vi·bra·to (vi brät′ō, vē-) *n., pl.* **-tos** [It.] *Music* a mild throbbing quality in the sound of a voice or instrument, produced by a slight but rapid variation in pitch by means of a slight movement of the finger on a violin string, a slight wavering of the tone in singing, etc.

vi·bra·tor (vī′brāt′ər) *n.* something that vibrates, as an electrical device used in massage, etc.

vi·bra·to·ry (vī′brə tôr′ē) *adj.* **1.** of, like, or causing vibration **2.** vibrating or capable of vibration

vi·bur·num (vī bur′nəm) *n.* [ModL., genus name < L., the wayfaring tree] any of various shrubs or small trees related to the honeysuckle and bearing white flowers

vic·ar (vik′ər) *n.* [< OFr. < L. *vicarius* < *vicis,* a change] **1.** a person who acts in place of another; deputy **2.** *Anglican Ch.* a parish priest who is not a rector and who is paid a salary from the tithes **3.** *Protestant Episcopal Ch.* a minister in charge of one chapel in a parish **4.** *R.C.Ch. a)* a church officer acting as deputy of a bishop *b)* [V-] the Pope: in full, **Vicar of Christ**

vic·ar·age (-ij) *n.* **1.** the residence of a vicar **2.** the salary of a vicar **3.** the position or duties of a vicar

vicar apostolic *pl.* **vicars apostolic** *R.C.Ch.* a bishop chosen for a region where no regular see has yet been organized

vic·ar·gen·er·al (vik′ər jen′ər əl) *n., pl.* **vic′ars-gen′er·al 1.** *Anglican Ch.* a layman serving as administrative deputy to an archbishop or bishop **2.** *R.C.Ch.* a priest, etc. acting as administrative deputy to a bishop or to the general superior of a religious order

vi·car·i·al (vī ker′ē əl, vi-) *adj.* **1.** of or acting as a vicar **2.** delegated /*vicarial* powers/

vi·car·i·ous (vī ker′ē əs, vi-) *adj.* [L. *vicarius,* substituted < *vicis,* a change] **1.** *a)* taking the place of another /a *vicarious* ruler/ *b)* handled by one person as the deputy of another; delegated /*vicarious* powers/ **2.** *a)* done or undergone by one person in place of another /*vicarious* punishment/ *b)* felt as if one were actually taking part in another's experience /a *vicarious* thrill/ —**vi·car′i·ous·ly** *adv.* —**vi·car′i·ous·ness** *n.*

vice¹ (vīs) *n.* [< OFr. < L. *vitium*] **1.** *a)* an evil or wicked action, habit, or characteristic /greed is her worst *vice*/ *b)* evil or wicked behavior; depravity or corruption /leading a life of *vice*/ *c)* prostitution **2.** any minor fault, failing, defect, etc. —**see** SYN. at FAULT —**vice′less** *adj.*

vi·ce² (vī′sē, -sə) *prep.* [L.: see VICE-] in the place of

vice³ (vīs) *n., vt. chiefly Brit. sp. of* VISE

vice- [< L. *vice,* in the place of another, abl. of *vicis:* see VICAR] *a prefix meaning* one who acts in the place of; subordinate; deputy /vice-president/

vice admiral a naval officer next in rank above a rear admiral and below an admiral —**vice admiralty**

vice-con·sul (vīs′kän′s'l) *n.* an officer who is subordinate to or a substitute for a consul —**vice′-con′su·lar** *adj.* —**vice′con′su·late** (-it) *n.* —**vice′-con′sul·ship′** *n.*

vice-ge·rent (vīs′jir′ənt) *n.* [< ML. < L. < *vice* (see VICE-) + *gerere,* to direct] a person appointed by another to exercise the latter's power and authority; deputy —*adj.* of a vicegerent: also **vice′ge′ral** —**vice′ge′ren·cy** *n.*

vice-pres·i·dent (vīs′prez′i dənt) *n.* **1.** *a)* an officer next in rank below a president, acting in his place during his absence or incapacity ☆*b)* [V- P-] the elected officer of this rank in the U.S. government: he succeeds to the Presidency if the President dies or otherwise leaves office: usually written **Vice President 2.** any of several officers of a company, etc., each in charge of a department —☆**vice′-pres′i·den·cy** *n.* —☆**vice′-pres′i·den′tial** *adj.*

vice·re·gal (vīs′rē′g'l) *adj.* of a viceroy

vice·re·gent (-rē′jənt) *n.* a deputy of a regent

vice·roy (vīs′roi) *n.* [MFr. < *vice-* (see VICE-) + *roy,* a king < L. *rex*] **1.** a person ruling a country, colony, etc. as the deputy of a sovereign ☆**2.** a red-and-black American butterfly much like the monarch butterfly but smaller

vice·roy·al·ty (vīs′roi′əl tē) *n., pl.* **-ties** the office or term of office of, or the area ruled by, a viceroy: also **vice′roy·ship′**

vice squad a police squad with responsibility for eliminating or controlling prostitution, gambling, etc.

vi·ce ver·sa (vī′sē vur′sə, vī′sə; vīs′) [L.] the order being reversed; the other way around; conversely [we like her and *vice versa*—that is, she likes us]

Vi·chy (vish′ē, vē′shē; *Fr.* vē shē′) city in C France: capital of unoccupied France (1940–44): pop. 31,000

vi·chy·ssoise (vē′shē swäz′, vish′ē-) *n.* [Fr.] a thick cream soup of potatoes, onions, etc., usually served cold

Vichy (water) **1.** a sparkling mineral water found at Vichy **2.** a natural or manufactured water like this

vic·i·nage (vis′ə nij) *n.* [< MFr., ult. < L. *vicinus:* see VICINITY] *same as* VICINITY

vi·cin·i·ty (və sin′ə tē) *n., pl.* **-ties** [< L. < *vicinus*, near < *vicus*, village] **1.** a being near or close by; nearness [two theaters in close *vicinity*] **2.** nearby or surrounding region; neighborhood [in the *vicinity* of the stadium]

vi·cious (vish′əs) *adj.* [< OFr. < L. < *vitium*, a vice] **1.** *a)* wicked or evil; depraved [a *vicious* criminal] *b)* tending to make evil or corrupt [a *vicious* effect] **2.** full of faults or errors [a *vicious* argument] **3.** likely to attack or bite one; bad-tempered [a *vicious* dog] **4.** meant to harm; spiteful; mean and cruel [a *vicious* rumor] **5.** very intense, sharp, etc. [a *vicious* blow] — **vi′cious·ly** *adv.* —**vi′cious·ness** *n.*

SYN.—**vicious** suggests extremely wicked or cruel behavior or habits [a *vicious* tyrant]; **villainous** suggests the evil or immorality of a villain or scoundrel [a *villainous* attack]; **iniquitous** implies the absence of all goodness or justice and a lack of concern with moral principles [his *iniquitous* trampling on human rights]; **nefarious** implies shocking wickedness and a total disregard of law or morality [a *nefarious* scheme for robbing the poor]; **infamous** suggests wickedness so great that it is, or should be, known of and condemned by most people [an *infamous* crime] —**ANT.** virtuous, righteous

vicious circle **1.** a situation in which the solution of one problem creates another problem, the solution of which simply brings back the first problem, often in a more troublesome form **2.** an illogical argument in which the conclusion depends on a premise which itself depends on the conclusion

vi·cis·si·tude (vi sis′ə tood′, -tyood′) *n.* [Fr. < L. *vicissitudo* < *vicis*, a turn] **1.** a condition of constant or regular change **2.** [*pl.*] unpredictable changes or variations that keep occurring in life, fortune, etc.; shifting circumstances; ups and downs —**see** SYN. at DIFFICULTY —**vi·cis′si·tu′di·nous** *adj.*

Vicks·burg (viks′burg) [after Rev. N. Vick (?-1819), early settler] city in W Miss., on the Mississippi River: captured by Grant in the Civil War (1863): pop. 25,000

vic·tim (vik′təm) *n.* [L. *victima*] **1.** a person or animal killed as a sacrifice to a god **2.** someone or something killed, destroyed, etc. [*victims* of war] **3.** a person who is cheated, tricked, bullied, etc. [a *victim* of swindlers]

vic·tim·ize (vik′tə mīz′) *vt.* **-ized′, -iz′ing** to make a victim of [*victimized* by a blackmailer] —**vic′tim·i·za′tion** *n.* —**vic′tim·iz′er** *n.*

Vic·tor (vik′tər) [L.: see VICTOR] a masculine name

vic·tor (vik′tər) *n.* [L. < pp. of *vincere*, to conquer] the winner in a battle, struggle, etc.

Victor Emmanuel II 1820–78; king of Sardinia (1849–61) & the first king of Italy (1861–78)

Victor Emmanuel III 1869–1947; king of Italy (1900–46): abdicated & the monarchy dissolved (1946)

Vic·to·ri·a¹ (vik tôr′ē ə, -tôr′yə) **1.** [L., VICTORY] a feminine name: dim. *Vicky* **2.** (**Alexandrina**), 1819–1901; queen of Great Britain & Ireland (1837–1901) —*n.* [after Queen *Victoria*] [v-] **1.** a four-wheeled carriage for two passengers, with a folding top and a high seat for the coachman **2.** a S. American waterlily with large leaves up to seven feet wide and large, night-blooming flowers

VICTORIA

Vic·to·ri·a² (vik tôr′ē ə, -tôr′yə) **1.** state of Australia, in the SE part **2.** capital of Hong Kong: pop., of met. area, 2,800,000 **3.** capital of British Columbia, Canada, on Vancouver Island: pop. 63,000 **4. Lake,** lake in E Africa, bounded by Kenya, Uganda, & Tanzania

Victoria Cross the highest British military decoration, given for exceptional bravery

Victoria Day a legal holiday in Canada, celebrated on the Monday immediately preceding May 25

Victoria Falls waterfall of the Zambezi River, between Rhodesia & Zambia: c. 350 ft. high; c. 1 mi. wide

Victoria Land land region of Antarctica, along the Ross Sea

Vic·to·ri·an (-ən, -yən) *adj.* **1.** of or characteristic of the time when Victoria was queen of England **2.** like the ideas, customs, etc. of this time, thought of as prudish, fussy, stuffy, etc. —*n.* a person of the time of Queen Victoria —**Vic·to′ri·an·ism** *n.*

vic·to·ri·ous (vik tôr′ē əs, -tôr′yəs) *adj.* **1.** having won a victory; triumphant **2.** of, typical of, or bringing about victory — **vic·to′ri·ous·ly** *adv.*

vic·to·ry (vik′tər ē, -trē) *n., pl.* **-ries** [< OFr. < L. *victoria* < *victor*, VICTOR] **1.** the decisive winning of a battle or war **2.** success in any struggle [a football *victory*; *victory* over disease]

vict·ual (vit′'l) *n.* [< MFr. < LL. < L. *victualis*, of food < *victus*, food < pp. of *vivere*, to live] **1.** [Archaic or Dial.] food or other provisions **2.** [*pl.*] [Dial. or Colloq.] articles of food —*vt.* **-ualed** or **-ualled, -ual·ing** or **-ual·ling** to supply with victuals —*vi.* to lay in a supply of food

vict·ual·er, vict·ual·ler (-ər) *n.* **1.** formerly, a person who supplied victuals, as to an army **2.** [Brit.] an innkeeper

vi·cu·ña (vī koon′yə, -koon′ə; vi-) *n., pl.* **-ñas, -ña:** see PLURAL, II, D, 1 [Sp., of Quechuan origin] **1.** an animal related to the llama and alpaca, found wild in the S. American Andes: it has soft, shaggy wool **2.** this wool **3.** a fabric made from it or in imitation of it

‡**vi·de** (vī′dē, vē′dā) [L.] see: used to direct attention to a particular page, book, etc.

‡**vide an·te** (an′tē) [L.] see before (in the book, etc.)

‡**vide in·fra** (in′frə) [L.] see below; see further on (in the book, etc.)

‡**vi·de·li·cet** (vi del′ə sit) *adv.* [L. < *videre licet*, it is permitted to see] that is; namely

VICUÑA
(to 40 in. high at shoulder)

vid·e·o (vid′ē ō′) *adj.* [L., I see] **1.** of or used in television **2.** designating or of the picture portion of a telecast: see AUDIO —*n. same as* TELEVISION

vid·e·o·cas·sette (-ka set′, -kə-) *n.* a cassette containing videotape, for use in a videotape recorder

video game an electronic device attached to a television set, that produces images on the screen, which are controlled by players competing in any of various games

vid·e·o·phone (vid′ē ō fōn′) *n.* a telephone combined with a television receiver and transmitter so that users can see one another while talking

vid·e·o·tape (vid′ē ō tāp′) *n.* a magnetic tape on which the video and audio portions of a telecast can be recorded as for later broadcasting

‡**vide su·pra** (soo′prə) [L.] see above; see earlier (in the book, etc.)

☆**vid·i·con** (vid′ə kän) *n.* [VID(EO) + ICON(OSCOPE)] a TV camera pickup tube in which optical images are scanned by an electron beam for transmission

vie (vī) *vi.* **vied, vy′ing** [< OFr. < L. *invitare*, to invite] to be a rival or rivals; compete as in a contest [they *vied* with us for first place] —**vi′er** *n.*

Vi·en·na (vē en′ə) capital of Austria, on the Danube: pop. 1,642,000 —**Vi·en·nese** (vē′ə nēz′) *adj., n., pl.* **-nese′**

Vien·tiane (vyen tyän′) capital of Laos, on the Mekong River: pop. c.150,000

Vi·et Cong (vē′et käŋ′, vyet) Communist guerrilla forces in South Vietnam (1954–1976): also **Vi′et·cong′** *n.*

Vi·et·nam (vē′ət näm′, vyet′-; -nam′) country on the E coast of the Indochinese Peninsula: divided, 1954–76, into two republics (**North Vietnam** and **South Vietnam**): 129,607 sq. mi.; pop. 47,872,000; cap. Hanoi See map at INDOCHINA Also sp. **Viet-Nam, Viet Nam** —**Vi′et·nam·ese′, Vi′et-Nam·ese′** (-nə mēz′, -mēs′) *adj., n., pl.* **-ese′**

view (vyōō) *n.* [< OFr. < *veoir,* to see < L. *videre*] **1.** the act of seeing or looking; examination *[taking a closer view]* **2.** sight or vision; esp., range of vision *[within view]* **3.** mental examination or survey *[a correct view of the situation]* **4.** *a)* that which is seen; scene or prospect *[admiring the view from the bridge]* *b)* a picture or photograph of such a scene **5.** a way of thinking about something; opinion *[her views on politics]* **6.** an object; aim; goal *[with a view to helping]* **7.** a general survey *[a view of world literature]* —*vt.* **1.** to look at with great care; inspect *[the landlord viewed the damage]* **2.** to see *[a large crowd viewed the fireworks]* **3.** to think about; consider *[after you have viewed the problem from all sides]* **4.** to think of in a particular way *[I view the plan with scorn]* —**in view 1.** in sight **2.** being thought about, or considered **3.** as a goal aimed at **4.** in expectation; as a hope —**in view of** because of —**on view** displayed publicly —**with a view to 1.** with the purpose of **2.** with a hope of; looking forward to

SYN· —**view** is the general word for that which can be seen *[the view is cut off by the next building]*; **prospect** suggests a view from a position that allows one to look out over a wide area and to a great distance *[a grand prospect of snowy mountains and deep valleys]*; **scene** suggests an attractive or dramatic view of objects, persons, etc. placed or arranged as they might be in a painting or a play *[a peaceful country scene]*; **vista** suggests a distant view seen through a long, narrow passage *[at the end of the valley lay a vista of rolling hills and winding rivers]* —**see also SYN·** at OPINION and SEE

view·er (vyōō′ər) *n.* **1.** a person who views a scene, television show, etc.; spectator **2.** an optical device for allowing an individual to look at slides, filmstrips, etc.

view·find·er (-fīn′dər) *n. same as* FINDER (sense 2)

view·less (-lis) *adj.* **1.** without a view, or prospect **2.** [Rare] invisible **3.** having or expressing no opinions

view·point (-point′) *n.* a way of thinking about and judging matters; point of view

vi·ges·i·mal (vī jes′ə m'l) *adj.* [< L., ult. < *viginti,* twenty] **1.** of or based on the number twenty **2.** twentieth

vig·il (vij′əl) *n.* [< OFr. < L. < *vigil,* awake < *vigere,* to be lively] **1.** the act or a time of staying awake during the usual hours of sleep as in order to keep watch over or guard something; watch *[the nurse's vigil by the patient's bedside]* **2.** *Eccles.* the evening or day before a festival, or the church services held then

vig·i·lance (vij′ə ləns) *n.* the quality or state of being vigilant; watchfulness

☆**vigilance committee** a group that sets itself up, without legal authority, to punish crime and keep order

vig·i·lant (vij′ə lənt) *adj.* [Fr. < L. prp. of *vigilare,* to watch < *vigil,* awake] staying watchful and alert to danger or trouble — **see SYN·** at WATCHFUL —**vig′i·lant·ly adv.**

☆**vig·i·lan·te** (vij′ə lan′tē) *n.* [Sp., vigilant] a member of a vigilance committee

vi·gnette (vin yet′) *n.* [Fr., dim. < *vigne,* a vine] **1.** an ornamental design or illustration used in a book, magazine, etc., as at the beginning or end of a chapter or section **2.** a picture or photograph shading off gradually at the edges and thus having no clear border **3.** a short literary sketch or description —*vt.* **-gnet′ted, -gnet′ting** to make a vignette of —**vi·gnet′-tist n.**

vig·or (vig′ər) *n.* [< OFr. < L. < *vigere,* to be strong] **1.** strength and energy of body or mind; vitality **2.** active or healthy growth *[the vigor of a plant]* **3.** intensity or force *[the vigor of her refusal]* Also, Brit. sp., **vig′-our**

vig·or·ous (vig′ər əs) *adj.* **1.** strong; robust *[a vigorous old man]* **2.** of, characterized by, or requiring vigor *[vigorous growth]* **3.** forceful; powerful *[a vigorous writing style]* —**vig′or·ous·ly adv.** —**vig′or·ous·ness n.**

vik·ing (vī′kiŋ) *n.* [ON. *vikingr]* [*also* V-] any of the Scandinavian pirates who raided the coasts of Europe from the 8th to the 10th centuries

vil. village

vile (vīl) *adj.* [< OFr. < L. *vilis,* cheap, base] **1.** morally base or evil; wicked *[vile crimes]* **2.** repulsive; disgusting *[vile language]* **3.** degrading; low *[vile prison conditions]* **4.** ex-

VIGNETTE
(and
original
picture)

tremely disagreeable or inferior; very bad *[vile weather]* —**see SYN·** at BASE² —**vile′ly adv.** —**vile′ness n.**

vil·i·fy (vil′ə fī′) *vt.* **-fied′, -fy′ing** [LL. *vilificare:* see VILE & -FY] to use foul or insulting language about; slander; defame — **vil′i·fi·ca′tion n.** —**vil′i·fi′er n.**

vil·la (vil′ə) *n.* [It. < L.] **1.** a house or estate in the country or on the outskirts of a city, esp. when large or luxurious **2.** [Brit.] a small suburban house

Vi·lla (vē′yä), **Fran·cis·co** (frän sēs′kō) (born *Doroteo Arango)* 1877?-1923; Mex. revolutionary leader: called *Pancho Villa*

vil·lage (vil′ij) *n.* [< OFr. < L. < *villa,* a country house] **1.** a group of houses in the country, larger than a hamlet and smaller than a town **2.** such a community incorporated as a municipality **3.** all the people of a village —*adj.* of a village — **vil′lag·er n.**

vil·lain (vil′ən) *n.* [< OFr. < VL. *villanus,* a farm servant < L. *villa,* a farm] **1.** a person guilty of or likely to commit great crimes; evil or wicked person; scoundrel **2.** a wicked character in a novel, play, etc. who opposes the hero **3.** *same as* VILLEIN —**vil′lain·ess n.fem.**

vil·lain·ous (vil′ə nəs) *adj.* **1.** of or like a villain; evil; wicked **2.** very bad or disagreeable *[villainous weather]* —**see SYN·** at VICIOUS —**vil′lain·ous·ly adv.**

vil·lain·y (-ē) *n., pl.* **-lain·ies 1.** the fact or state of being villainous **2.** villainous conduct **3.** a villainous act; wicked, detestable, or criminal deed

Vil·la-Lo·bos (vē′lä lō′bŏŏs; *E.* vē′lə lō′bəs), **Hei·tor** (ā tôr′) 1887?-1959; Brazilian composer

vil·la·nelle (vil′ə nel′) *n.* [Fr. < It. *villanella,* a rural song, ult. < L. *villa,* a farm] a poem having usually five three-line stanzas and a final four-line stanza, and with only two rhymes throughout

-ville (vil) [< Fr. *ville,* town, city] *a combining form meaning:* **1.** town, city *[Evansville]* ☆**2.** place or condition characterized by: used in making up slang words *["dullsville"]*

vil·lein (vil′ən) *n.* [see VILLAIN] in feudal England, any of a class of serfs who by the 13th cent. had become freemen in their legal relations to all except their lord —**vil′lein·age n.**

Vil·lon (vē yōn′), **Fran·çois** (frän swä′) (born *François de Montcorbier* or *des Loges)* 1431-?; Fr. poet

vil·lus (vil′əs) *n., pl.* **vil′li** (-ī) [L., shaggy hair] **1.** *Anat.* any of numerous hairlike growths on certain mucous membranes of the body, as of the small intestine, serving to secrete mucus and absorb fats, etc. **2.** *Bot.* any of the long, soft hairs on certain plants —**vil·los·i·ty** (vi läs′ə tē) *n., pl.* **-ties** —**vil′lous** (-əs) *adj.*

Vil·ni·us (vil′nē ŏŏs′) capital of the Lithuanian S.S.R.: pop. 372,000: Russ. name **Vil·na** (vēl′nä; *E.* vil′nə)

☆**vim** (vim) *n.* [prob. echoic, but thought to be < L. *vim,* acc. of *vis,* strength] energy; vigor

‡**vin** (van; *Anglicized* vin) *n.* [Fr.] wine

vi·na·ceous (vī nā′shəs) *adj.* [< L. < *vinum,* wine] **1.** of or like wine or grapes **2.** wine-colored; red

vin·ai·grette (vin′i gret′) *n.* [Fr. < *vinaigre,* vinegar] a small ornamental box or bottle with holes in the lid, used for holding vinegar, smelling salts, etc.

vinaigrette sauce a sauce made of vinegar, oil, herbs, etc. and used esp. on cold meats

Vin·cent (vin′s'nt) [< LL. < prp. of *vincere,* to conquer] a masculine name

Vin·cent's angina (vin′s'nts) [after J. H. *Vincent* (1862-1950), Fr. physician] *same as* TRENCH MOUTH: also called **Vincent's infection**

Vinci, Leonardo da *see* DA VINCI

vin·ci·ble (vin′sə b'l) *adj.* [< L. < *vincere,* to overcome] that can be overcome or defeated —**vin′ci·bil′i·ty n.**

vin·cu·lum (viŋ′kyŏŏ ləm) *n., pl.* **-la** (-lə) [L. < *vincere,* to bind] **1.** that which binds; bond **2.** *Math.* a line drawn over two or more terms to show that they are to be treated together (Example: a – x + y)

vin·di·cate (vin′də kāt′) *vt.* **-cat′ed, -cat′ing** [< L. pp. of *vindicare,* to claim; < *vim,* acc. of *vis,* force + *dicere,* to say] **1.** to clear from criticism, blame, suspicion, etc. *[Smith's confession vindicated Brown]* **2.** to defend (a cause, etc.) against opposition *[to vindicate a claim]* **3.** to show to be true or right; justify *[she vindicated their belief in her]* —**see SYN·** at ABSOLVE — **vin′di·ca′tive** (-kāt′iv, vin dik′ə tiv), **vin′di·ca·to·ry** (-di tôr′ē) *adj.* —**vin′di·ca′tor n.**

vin·di·ca·tion (vin′də kā′shən) *n.* **1.** a vindicating or being vindicated **2.** a fact or circumstance that shows something to be true or right [his repayment of the money was a *vindication* of their trust]

vin·dic·tive (vin dik′tiv) *adj.* [< L. *vindicta*, revenge (see VIN-DICATE) + -IVE] **1.** wanting to get revenge **2.** said or done in revenge [*vindictive* punishment] —**vin·dic′tive·ly** *adv.* —**vin·dic′tive·ness** *n.*

SYN.—**vindictive** stresses the unforgiving nature of one who has a deep-seated desire to get even with another for a wrong, injury, etc. [*vindictive* feelings]; **vengeful** and **revengeful** suggest not a mere desire to get even but the actual, active seeking of revenge [a *vengeful*, or *revengeful*, enemy]; **spiteful** implies a mean, nasty desire to cause another harm or unhappiness in order to get even [*spiteful* gossip]

vine (vīn) *n.* [< OFr. < L. < *vinum*, wine] **1.** *a)* any plant with a long, thin stem that grows along the ground or climbs a wall or other support by means of tendrils, etc. *b)* the stem of such a plant **2.** *same as* GRAPEVINE (sense 1) —**vine′like** *adj.*

vin·e·gar (vin′i gər) *n.* [< MFr. < *vin*, wine + *aigre*, sour < L. *acris*, acrid] a sour liquid containing acetic acid, made by fermenting cider, wine, malt, etc.: it is used to flavor or preserve foods

vin·e·gar·y (vin′i gər ē) *adj.* **1.** of or like vinegar **2.** sour in speech, mood, nature, etc.; ill-tempered Also **vin′e·gar·ish**

vine·yard (vin′yərd) *n.* a piece of land where grapevines are grown

vin·i- [< L. *vinum*, wine] *a combining form meaning* wine grapes or wine [*viniculture*]

vin·i·cul·ture (vin′i kul′chər) *n.* [VINI- + CULTURE] the cultivation of wine grapes —**vin′i·cul′tur·al** *adj.* —**vin′i·cul′tur·ist** *n.*

Vin·land (vin′lənd) region, now believed to be part of N. America, discovered by Norsemen c.1000 A.D.

‡**vi·no** (vē′nô) *n.* [It. & Sp.] wine

vi·nous (vī′nəs) *adj.* [< L. < *vinum*, wine] **1.** of, having the nature of, or characteristic of wine **2.** *a)* fond of drinking wine *b)* resulting from drinking wine —**vi·nos′i·ty** (-näs′ə tē) *n.*

Vin·son (vin′sən), **Fred(erick) M(oore)** 1890-1953; U.S. jurist; chief justice of the U.S. (1946-53)

vin·tage (vin′tij) *n.* [< OFr. < L. *vindemia* < *vinum*, wine + *demere*, to remove] **1.** *a)* the crop of grapes from a certain vineyard or grape-growing region in a single season *b)* the wine, esp. a prized wine, of a particular region in a specified year **2.** the act or season of gathering grapes or of making wine **3.** the type or model of a particular year or period [a car of prewar *vintage*] —*adj.* **1.** *a)* of a good vintage; choice [*vintage* wine] *b)* representative of the best [*vintage* short stories] **2.** dating from a period long past [*vintage* clothes]

vint·ner (vint′nər) *n.* [< OFr. < ML. *vinetum*, a vineyard] a merchant who sells wine

vin·y (vī′nē) *adj.* **vin′i·er**, **vin′i·est** **1.** of or like vines **2.** filled or covered with vines

vi·nyl (vī′n'l) *n.* [< L. *vinum*, wine + -YL] the univalent radical, $CH_2:CH-$, derived from ethylene: various vinyl compounds are polymerized to form resins and plastics

vi·ol (vī′əl) *n.* [MFr. *viole* < OPr. *viula* < ?] any of an early family of stringed instruments, usually with six strings, frets, and a flat back: used in sizes from the treble viol to the bass viol

vi·o·la¹ (vē ō′lə, vī-) *n.* [It. < OPr. *viula*, viol] a stringed instrument of the violin family, slightly larger than a violin and tuned a fifth lower

vi·o·la² (vī′ə lə, vī ō′lə) *n.* [< L., a violet] any of various violets developed from a pansy

vi·o·la·ble (vī′ə lə b'l) *adj.* that can be, or is likely to be, violated —**vi′o·la·bil′i·ty**, **vi′o·la·ble·ness** *n.* —**vi′o·la·bly** *adv.*

vi·o·la da gam·ba (vē ō′lə də gam′bə, gäm′-) [It., lit., viol for the leg] an early instrument of the viol family, held between the knees and having about the same range as the cello

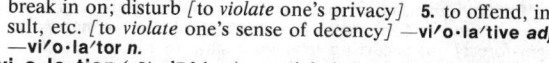

VIOL

vi·o·late (vī′ə lāt′) *vt.* **-lat′ed**, **-lat′ing** [< L. pp. of *violare*, to use force] **1.** to break (a law, rule, promise, etc.); fail to keep or observe **2.** to assault sexually; esp., to rape (a woman) **3.** to treat (something sacred) with disrespect; desecrate **4.** to

break in on; disturb [to *violate* one's privacy] **5.** to offend, insult, etc. [to *violate* one's sense of decency] —**vi′o·la′tive** *adj.* —**vi′o·la′tor** *n.*

vi·o·la·tion (vī′ə lā′shən) *n.* a violating or being violated; specif., *a)* failure to keep or observe a law, rule, etc. *b)* rape *c)* treatment of something sacred with disrespect *d)* disturbance [*violation* of the peace]

vi·o·lence (vī′ə ləns) *n.* [< MFr. < L. < *violentus*, violent] **1.** physical force used to cause injury or damage **2.** intense, powerful force [the *violence* of the hurricane] **3.** *a)* unjust or unfeeling use of force or power, as in violating another's rights, privacy, etc. *b)* the harm done by this [his insults did *violence* to our sense of decency] **4.** strong feeling; fury [to attack a speech with *violence*] **5.** a twisting of a sense, phrase, etc. so as to change the meaning [a *violent* deed or act

vi·o·lent (-lənt) *adj.* **1.** *a)* acting with or showing great physical force that causes damage or injury [*violent* blows with the fists] *b)* acting with or marked by unlawful force [*violent* overthrow of the government] **2.** caused by violence [a *violent* death] **3.** *a)* showing strong feeling; furious; passionate [*violent* language] *b)* emotionally disturbed and uncontrollable [panic made them *violent*] **4.** very strong; severe; intense [a *violent* storm] —**vi′o·lent·ly** *adv.*

vi·o·let (vī′ə lit) *n.* [< OFr. < L. *viola*, a violet] **1.** *a)* any of a number of related short plants with white, blue, purple, or yellow flowers *b)* the flower of any of these plants **2.** any of various similar but unrelated plants, as the African violet **3.** a bluish-purple color —*adj.* bluish-purple

violet ray 1. the shortest ray of the visible spectrum **2.** loosely, an ultraviolet ray

vi·o·lin (vī′ə lin′) *n.* [< It. dim. of *viola*, a viol] any instrument of the modern family of stringed instruments played with a bow and having four strings and no frets; specif., the smallest and highest-pitched instrument of this family, held horizontally under the chin

vi·o·lin·ist (-ist) *n.* a violin player

vi·ol·ist (vī′əl ist; *for 2* vē ō′list) *n.* **1.** a viol player **2.** a viola player

vi·o·lon·cel·lo (vē′ə län chel′ō, vī′ə lən-) *n., pl.* **-los** [It., dim. of *violone*, bass viol < *viola*, viol] *same as* CELLO —**vi′o·lon·cel′list** *n.*

VIP, V.I.P. [Colloq.] very important person

vi·per (vī′pər) *n.* [OFr. < L. *vipera* < ? *vivus*, living + *parere*, to bear] **1.** *a)* any of a family of poisonous snakes found in Europe, Africa, and Asia, including the puff adder (sense 1), etc. *b)* *same as* PIT VIPER *c)* *same as* ADDER (sense 1) **2.** a mean or untrustworthy person —**vi′per·ine** (-in, -īn′) *adj.*

vi·per·ous (-əs) *adj.* of, having the nature of, or like a viper; esp., spiteful or untrustworthy: also **vi′per·ish** —**vi′per·ous·ly** *adv.* —**vi′per·ous·ness** *n.*

vi·ra·go (vi rā′gō, vī-; -rä′-) *n., pl.* **-goes, -gos** [OE. < L., a manlike maiden < *vir*, a man] a loud, quarrelsome, bad-tempered woman; shrew

vi·ral (vī′rəl) *adj.* of, involving, or caused by a virus

☆**vir·e·o** (vir′ē ō′) *n., pl.* **-e·os** [L., a type of finch] any of a number of small American songbirds that have olive-green or gray feathers and feed on insects

vi·res·cent (vī res′'nt, vi-) *adj.* [< L. prp. of *virescere* < *virere*, to be green] **1.** turning or becoming green **2.** greenish —**vi·res′cence** *n.*

Vir·gil (vur′jəl) [< L. *Vergilius*, name of the Roman gens to which the poet belonged] **1.** a masculine name **2.** (L. name *Publius Vergilius Maro*) 70-19 B.C.; Roman poet: author of the *Aeneid* —**Vir·gil·i·an** (-jil′ē ən) *adj.*

vir·gin (vur′jin) *n.* [< OFr. < L. *virginis*, genitive of *virgo*, a maiden] a person, esp. a woman, who has not had sexual intercourse —[V-] *Astron. same as* VIRGO —*adj.* **1.** being a virgin

VIOLIN & BOW
(A, scroll; B, pegs; C, neck; D, fingerboard; E, waist; F, tailpiece; G, chinboard)

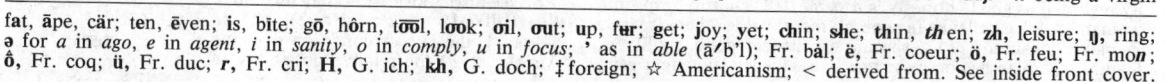

fat, āpe, cär; ten, ēven; is, bīte; gō, hôrn, tōōl, lㄛㄛk; oil, out; up, fur; get; joy; yet; chin; she; thin, *th*en; zh, leisure; ŋ, ring; ə for *a* in *ago*, *e* in *agent*, *i* in *sanity*, *o* in *comply*, *u* in *focus*; ' as in *able* (ā′b'l); Fr. bâl; ë, Fr. coeur; ö, Fr. feu; Fr. mon; ô, Fr. coq; ü, Fr. duc; r, Fr. cri; H, G. ich; kh, G. doch; ‡foreign; ☆ Americanism; < derived from. See inside front cover.

2. like a virgin; chaste; modest **3.** untouched, pure, clean, etc. [*virgin* snow] **4.** *a)* not yet used, explored, etc. by man [*a virgin* forest] *b)* occurring in a pure state in nature [*virgin* silver]; also, obtained directly from an ore **5.** being the first [a *virgin* effort] —**the Virgin** Mary, the mother of Jesus

vir·gin·al[1] (vur′ji n′l) *adj.* **1.** of or like a virgin; maidenly **2.** pure; fresh; unsullied —**vir′gin·al·ly** *adv.*

vir·gin·al[2] (vur′ji n′l) *n.* [prob. akin to prec.: reason for name is uncertain] a harpsichord; esp., a small, rectangular harpsichord of the 16th cent., placed on a table or in the lap to be played

VIRGINAL

Virgin Birth *Christian Theol.* the doctrine that Mary gave birth to Jesus although she was still a virgin and that she was his only human parent

Vir·gin·ia (vur jin′yə, -ē ə) **1.** [L., fem. of *Virginius*, name of a Roman gens] a feminine name **2.** [after ELIZABETH I, the *Virgin* Queen] Southern State of the U.S., on the Atlantic: 40,815 sq. mi.; pop. 4,648,000; cap. Richmond: abbrev. **Va., VA** —**Vir·gin′·ian** *adj., n.*

Virginia Beach city in SE Va., on the Atlantic, near Norfolk: pop. 172,000

☆**Virginia cowslip** (or **bluebell**) a woodland plant with clusters of blue or purple, bell-shaped flowers

☆**Virginia creeper** *same as* WOODBINE (sense 2)

☆**Virginia deer** *same as* WHITE-TAILED DEER

☆**Virginia reel** **1.** a folk dance, the American variety of the reel, performed by a number of couples facing each other in two parallel lines **2.** music for this dance

Virgin Islands group of islands in the West Indies, east of Puerto Rico: *a)* **British Virgin Islands** easternmost islands of this group, constituting a Brit. territory: 59 sq. mi.; pop. 10,000 *b)* **Virgin Islands of the United States** the islands of this group closest to Puerto Rico, constituting a territory of the U.S.: 132 sq. mi.; pop. 63,000; cap. Charlotte Amalie: abbrev. **VI, V.I.**

Virgin Islands National Park national park on the third largest island (*St. John*) of the Virgin Islands of the U.S.

vir·gin·i·ty (vər jin′ə tē) *n.* the state or fact of being a virgin; maidenhood, chastity, etc.

Virgin Mary Mary, the mother of Jesus

Virgin Queen *a name given to* ELIZABETH I

vir·gin's-bow·er (vur′jinz bou′ər) *n.* a climbing variety of clematis, with small, white flowers

virgin wool wool that has never before been processed

Vir·go (vur′gō) [L., lit., virgin] **1.** a large constellation between Leo and Libra **2.** the sixth sign of the zodiac: see ZODIAC

vir·gule (vur′gyool) *n.* [Fr. < L. dim. of *virga*, a twig] a short, diagonal line (/) used between two words to show that either can be used (and/or), in dates or fractions (3/8), to express "per" (feet/second), etc.

vir·i·des·cent (vir′ə des′′nt) *adj.* [< LL., ult. < *viridis*, green] greenish —**vir′i·des′cence** *n.*

vir·ile (vir′əl; *chiefly Brit.* -īl) *adj.* [< L. < *vir*, a man] **1.** of or characteristic of an adult man; masculine; male **2.** manly; strong, forceful, vigorous, etc. [a *virile* writing style] **3.** able to engage in sexual intercourse; potent —see SYN. at MALE — **vir′ile·ly** *adv.* —**vi·ril·i·ty** (vi ril′ə tē) *n.*

vi·rol·o·gy (vī räl′ə jē) *n.* [< VIR(US) + -*o*- + -LOGY] the study of viruses and virus diseases —**vi·ro·log·ic** (vī′rə läj′ik), **vi′ro·log′i·cal** *adj.* —**vi·rol′o·gist** *n.*

vir·tu (vər too′, vur′too) *n.* [It. < L. *virtus*, virtue] **1.** a love of, or taste for, artistic objects **2.** such objects as a group **3.** the quality of being so artistic, rare, etc. as to interest a collector

vir·tu·al (vur′choo wəl) *adj.* being such practically or in effect, although not in actual fact or name [although we have met, he is a *virtual* stranger to me] —**vir′tu·al′i·ty** (-wal′ə tē) *n.*

vir·tu·al·ly (-choo wəl ē, -choo lē) *adv.* in effect although not in fact; for all practical purposes [*virtually* identical]

vir·tue (vur′choo) *n.* [< OFr. < L. *virtus*, manliness, worth] **1.** general moral excellence; right action and thinking; goodness or morality [*virtue* is its own reward] **2.** a specific moral quality regarded as good [honesty is a *virtue*] **3.** chastity, esp. in a woman **4.** *a)* excellence in general; merit; value [there is *virtue* in planning ahead] *b)* a specific excellence; good quality or feature [the plan has many *virtues*] **5.** efficacy; potency; esp.,

healing power, as of a medicine —**by** (or **in**) **virtue of** because of; on the grounds of —**make a virtue of necessity** to do what has to be done as if one really wanted to do it

vir·tu·os·i·ty (vur′choo wäs′ə tē) *n., pl.* **-ties** [< VIRTUOSO + -ITY] great skill in the practice of one of the fine arts, esp. in the playing of music

vir·tu·o·so (vur′choo wō′sō) *n., pl.* **-sos, -si** (-sē) [It., skilled] **1.** orig., *a)* a person with a broad interest in the arts or sciences *b)* a person with highly cultivated artistic tastes **2.** a person having great skill in the practice of some fine art, esp. in the playing of music —*adj.* of or like that of a virtuoso: also **vir′tu·os′ic** (-wäs′ik, -wō′sik)

vir·tu·ous (vur′choo wəs) *adj.* **1.** having, or characterized by, moral virtue; good, moral, etc. **2.** chaste: said of a woman —see SYN. at MORAL —**vir′tu·ous·ly** *adv.* —**vir′tu·ous·ness** *n.*

vir·u·lent (vir′yoo lənt, -oo-) *adj.* [< L. *virulentus* < *virus*, a poison] **1.** *a)* extremely poisonous or harmful; deadly [a *virulent* mixture] *b)* bitterly spiteful; full of hate [a *virulent* speech] **2.** *Med. a)* serious and spreading rapidly: said of a disease *b)* highly infectious: said of a microorganism —**vir·u·lence, vir′u·len·cy** *n.* —**vir′u·lent·ly** *adv.*

vi·rus (vī′rəs) *n.* [L., a poison < IE. base *weis-*, to flow] **1.** orig., venom, as of a snake **2.** *a)* a form of matter smaller than any of the bacteria, that can multiply in living cells and cause disease in animals or plants [smallpox, measles, the flu, etc. are caused by *viruses*]: see also FILTERABLE VIRUS *b)* a disease caused by a virus **3.** an evil or harmful influence [the *virus* of hate]

vi·sa (vē′zə) *n.* [Fr. < L. pp. of *videre*, to see] an endorsement on a passport, showing that it has been examined by the proper officials of a country and the passport holder has permission to enter that country —*vt.* **-saed, -sa·ing** **1.** to put a visa on (a passport) **2.** to give a visa to (someone)

vis·age (viz′ij) *n.* [< OFr. < L. *visus*, a look < pp. of *videre*, to see] the face; countenance [his stern *visage*] —see SYN. at FACE —**vis′aged** *adj.*

vis-à-vis (vē′zə vē′) *adj., adv.* [Fr.] face to face; opposite — *prep.* **1.** face to face with **2.** in relation to [analyzing Japan's industrial growth *vis-à-vis* that of China]

Visc. 1. Viscount **2.** Viscountess Also **Vis., Visct.**

vis·cer·a (vis′ər ə) *n.pl., sing.* **vis′cus** (-kəs) [L.] the internal organs of the body, as the heart, lungs, liver, intestines, etc.; specif., in popular usage, the intestines

vis·cer·al (-əl) *adj.* **1.** of, like, or affecting the viscera **2.** emotional, instinctive, etc. rather than intellectual [a *visceral* reaction] —**vis′cer·al·ly** *adv.*

vis·cid (vis′id) *adj.* [< LL. < L. *viscum*, birdlime] thick and sticky, like glue or syrup; viscous —**vis·cid·i·ty** (vi sid′ə tē) *n.* —**vis′cid·ly** *adv.*

vis·cose (vis′kōs) *adj.* **1.** *same as* VISCOUS **2.** of or made of viscose —*n.* a thick, sticky solution made by treating cellulose with sodium hydroxide and carbon disulfide: used in making cellophane and rayon thread and fabrics (**viscose rayon**)

vis·cos·i·ty (vis käs′ə tē) *n., pl.* **-ties** **1.** a viscous quality or state **2.** *Physics* the internal friction of a fluid, caused by molecular attraction, which makes it resist a tendency to flow [fluids of low *viscosity* flow freely]

vis·count (vī′kount) *n.* [< OFr. < ML. *vice comes*: see VICE- & COUNT[2]] a nobleman ranking below an earl or count and above a baron —**vis′count·cy, vis′count·y, vis′count·ship′** *n.*

vis·count·ess (vī′koun tis) *n.* **1.** the wife of a viscount **2.** a noblewoman having the same rank as a viscount

vis·cous (vis′kəs) *adj.* [< LL. < L. *viscum*, birdlime] **1.** thick and sticky, like glue or syrup; viscid **2.** *Physics* having viscosity —**vis′cous·ly** *adv.* —**vis′cous·ness** *n.*

vise (vīs) *n.* [< OFr. < L. *vitis*, a vine, lit., that which winds] a device having two jaws opened and closed by a screw, lever, etc., used for holding an object firmly while it is being worked on —*vt.* **vised, vis′ing** to hold or squeeze with or as with a vise — **vise′like′** *adj.*

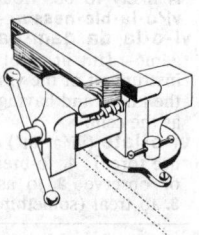

VISE

vi·sé (vē′zā, vē zā′) *n., vt.* **-séed, -sé·ing** [Fr.] *same as* VISA

Vish·nu (vish′noo) *Hinduism* the second member of the trinity (Brahma, Vishnu, and Siva), called "the Preserver": see also KRISHNA —**Vish′nu·ism** *n.*

vis·i·bil·i·ty (viz′ə bil′ə tē) *n., pl.* **-ties** **1.** the fact or condition of being visible **2.** *a)* the relative possibility of being seen under the conditions of distance, light, and atmosphere that exist at a certain time [the poor *visibility* of dark clothing at night] b) the maximum distance at which things can be seen [fog reduced *visibility* to 500 feet]

vis·i·ble (viz′ə b'l) *adj.* [< OFr. < L. *visibilis* < pp. of *videre*, to see] **1.** that can be seen [a barely *visible* scar] **2.** that can be perceived; evident; manifest [*visible* poverty] —**vis′i·ble·ness** *n.* —**vis′i·bly** *adv.*

Vis·i·goth (viz′ə gäth′, -gôth′) *n.* any of the West Goths who invaded the Roman Empire late in the 4th cent. A.D. and set up a kingdom in France and Spain —**Vis′i·goth′ic** *adj.*

vi·sion (vizh′ən) *n.* [< OFr. < L. *visio* < pp. of *videre*, to see < IE. base *w(e)di-*, to see] **1.** the act or power of seeing; sight [he wears glasses to improve his *vision*] **2.** a) something supposedly seen by other than normal sight, as in a dream, trance, etc. b) the experience of having seen something in this way **3.** a mental image [*visions* of power] **4.** a) the ability to perceive something not actually visible, as through keen foresight [a project made possible by one man's *vision*] b) power of imagination [a statesman of great *vision*] **5.** something or someone of great beauty [she was a *vision* in her new gown] —*vt.* to see as in a vision —**vi′sion·al** *adj.*

vi·sion·ar·y (-er′ē) *adj.* **1.** of, like, or seen in a vision **2.** a) imaginary b) not realistic; impractical [a *visionary* scheme] **3.** seeing or likely to see visions **4.** having or tending to have impractical ideas —*n.*, *pl.* **-ar′ies 1.** a person who sees visions **2.** a person who has impractical ideas; dreamer —**see SYN** at IMAGINARY

vis·it (viz′it) *vt.* [< OFr. < L. *visitare* < *visere*, to go to see < pp. of *videre*, to see] **1.** to go or come to see (someone) out of friendship or for business or professional reasons [to *visit* cousins, a doctor, etc.] **2.** to stay with as a guest [they *visited* us for two days] **3.** to go or come to (a place) as in order to inspect or look at [to *visit* Paris] **4.** to occur or come to [*visited* by an odd idea] **5.** to come upon or afflict [a drought *visited* the land] **6.** to inflict (punishment, suffering, etc.) upon (someone) [to *visit* devastation upon the inhabitants] —*vi.* to visit someone or something; specif., ☆a) to make a social call (often with *with*) b) to stay with someone as a guest ☆c) [Colloq.] to chat, as during a visit —*n.* the act of visiting; specif., a) a social call b) a stay as a guest c) an official call, as of a doctor ☆d) [Colloq.] a friendly conversation or chat —**vis′it·a·ble** *adj.*

vis·it·ant (viz′it ənt) *n.* **1.** a visitor **2.** a migratory bird in any of its temporary stopping places

vis·it·a·tion (viz′ə tā′shən) *n.* **1.** a visiting; esp., an official visit as to inspect **2.** any trouble looked on as punishment sent by God —**the Visitation** *R.C.Ch.* **1.** the visit of the Virgin Mary to Elizabeth: Luke 1:39–56 **2.** a church feast (July 2) commemorating this —**vis′it·a′tion·al** *adj.* —**vis·it·a·to·ri·al** (viz′i tə tôr′ē əl), **vis′i·to′ri·al** *adj.*

vis·it·ing card (viz′i tin) *same as* CALLING CARD

☆**visiting fireman** [Colloq.] **1.** an important visitor who is given special treatment, esp. any of a group of important visitors **2.** a tourist, about town, etc. who spends money freely

vis·i·tor (viz′it ər) *n.* a person making a visit

vi·sor (vī′zər) *n.* [< Anglo-Fr. < OFr. < *vis*, a face] **1.** a) in armor, the movable part of a helmet that could be lowered to cover the upper part of the face b) a movable section of safety glass, that is part of a protective head covering, as for welders ☆**2.** the brim of a cap, sticking out in front to shade the eyes **3.** an adjustable shade over the windshield in a car, for shading the eyes —**vi′-sored** *adj.*

☆**VISTA** (vis′tə) [*V*(olunteers) *i*(n) *S*(ervice) *t*(o) *A*(merica)] a U.S. government program using volunteers who work at improving living conditions in poverty-stricken areas of the U.S.

vis·ta (vis′tə) *n.* [< It., ult. < L. *videre*, to see] **1.** a view, esp. one seen through a long passage, as between rows of houses or trees **2.** a mental view of a series of events [a book that provides a sweeping *vista* of ancient history] —**see SYN** at VIEW —**vis′taed** *adj.*

Vis·tu·la (vis′choo lə) river in Poland, flowing from the Carpathian Mountains into the Baltic Sea

VISORS

vis·u·al (vizh′oo wəl) *adj.* [< LL. < L. *visus*, a sight < pp. of *videre*, to see] **1.** of, connected with, based on, or used in seeing [*visual* aids] **2.** that is or can be seen; visible [*visual* evidence] —**vis′u·al·ly** *adv.*

visual aids motion pictures, slides, charts, etc. (but not books) used in teaching, illustrating lectures, etc.

vis·u·al·ize (vizh′oo wə līz′, -oo līz′) *vt.* **-ized′, -iz′ing** to form a mental image of (something not visible) [trying to *visualize* the room as it will look after the changes are made] —*vi.* to form a mental image —**vis′u·al·i·za′tion** *n.*

vi·tal (vīt′'l) *adj.* [< MFr. < L. < *vita*, life] **1.** of or having to do with life [*vital* organs] **2.** a) necessary to life [*vital* organs] b) destroying life; fatal [*vital* wounds] **3.** very important; essential [her help is *vital* to the success of our plan] **4.** full of life and vigor; energetic [a *vital* personality] —*n.* [*pl.*] **1.** the vital organs, as the heart, brain, etc. **2.** the essential parts of anything —**see SYN** at LIVING —**vi′tal·ly** *adv.* —**vi′tal·ness** *n.*

vi·tal·ism (-iz′m) *n.* the doctrine that the life in living organisms is caused and carried on by a basic force (**vital force or principle**) that is different from all physical and chemical forces —**vi′tal·ist** *n., adj.* —**vi′tal·is′tic** *adj.*

vi·tal·i·ty (vī tal′ə tē) *n., pl.* **-ties 1.** power to live or go on living **2.** power to endure or survive [the Constitution has shown great *vitality*] **3.** mental or physical energy; vigor

vi·tal·ize (vīt′'l īz′) *vt.* **-ized′, -iz′ing 1.** to make vital; give life to **2.** to make lively or energetic —**vi′tal·i·za′tion** *n.*

Vi·tal·li·um (vī tal′ē əm) *a trademark for* an alloy of cobalt, chromium, and molybdenum, used in bone surgery, etc.

vital statistics data on births, deaths, marriages, etc.

vi·ta·min (vīt′ə min; *Brit.* vit′-) *n.* [< L. *vita*, life + AMINE: from the earlier, incorrect idea that these substances all contain amino acids] any of a number of complex organic substances found in foods and essential for the normal functioning of the body —**vi′ta·min′ic** *adj.*

vitamin A a fat-soluble alcohol found in fish-liver oil, egg yolk, butter, etc. or derived from carotene in carrots and other vegetables: a deficiency of this vitamin results in night blindness: it occurs in two forms, **vitamin A₁** and **vitamin A₂**

vitamin B (**complex**) a group of unrelated water-soluble substances, including: a) **vitamin B₁** (see THIAMINE) b) **vitamin B₂** (see RIBOFLAVIN) c) **vitamin B₆** (see PYRIDOXINE) d) NIACIN e) PANTOTHENIC ACID f) BIOTIN: also called **vitamin H** g) INOSITOL h) PARA-AMINOBENZOIC ACID i) CHOLINE j) FOLIC ACID k) **vitamin B₁₂** a complex vitamin, essential for normal growth and used esp. in treating pernicious anemia

vitamin C *same as* ASCORBIC ACID

vitamin D any of several fat-soluble vitamins found in fish-liver oils, milk, egg yolk, etc.: a deficiency of this vitamin tends to produce rickets: this group includes **vitamin D₂**, **vitamin D₃**, **vitamin D₄**, and **vitamin D₅**

vitamin E the tocopherols as a group, necessary for fertility in some animals

vitamin H *same as* BIOTIN

vitamin K a fat-soluble vitamin that promotes blood clotting: **vitamin K₁** is found chiefly in alfalfa leaves and **vitamin K₂** chiefly in fish meal: **vitamin K₃** and **vitamin K₄** are prepared synthetically

vi·ti·ate (vish′ē āt′) *vt.* **-at′ed, -at′ing** [< L. pp. of *vitiare* < *vitium*, a VICE¹] **1.** to make imperfect or faulty; spoil [the use of faulty statistics *vitiated* her argument] **2.** to weaken morally; debase [his character was *vitiated* by laziness] **3.** to make legally ineffective [the lack of a signature *vitiated* the contract] —**vi′ti·a′tion** *n.* —**vi′ti·a′tor** *n.*

vit·i·cul·ture (vit′ə kul′chər, vīt′-) *n.* [< L. *vitis*, a vine + CULTURE] the cultivation of grapes —**vit′i·cul′tur·al** *adj.* —**vit′i·cul′tur·ist** *n.*

vit·re·ous (vit′rē əs) *adj.* [< L. < *vitrum*, glass] **1.** a) of or like glass; glassy b) derived from or made of glass **2.** of the vitreous body —**vit′re·ous·ness** *n.*

vitreous body (or **humor**) the transparent, colorless, jellylike substance that fills the eyeball between the retina and lens: see illustration at EYE

vit·ri·fy (vit′rə fī′) *vt., vi.* **-fied′, -fy′ing** [< Fr. < L. *vitrum*, glass + Fr. *-fier*, -FY] to change into glass or a substance like glass by fusion due to heat —**vit′ri·fi′a·ble** *adj.* —**vit′ri·fi·ca′-tion**, (-fi kā′shən), **vit′ri·fac′tion** (-fak′shən) *n.*

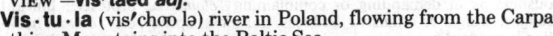

vit·rine (vi trēn′) *n.* [Fr., ult. < L. *vitrum*, glass] a glass display case for art objects, curios, etc.

vit·ri·ol (vit′rē əl, -ōl′) *n.* [< MFr. < ML. *vitriolum* < LL. < L. *vitreus*, glassy] **1.** *a)* any of several sulfates of metals, as of copper (*blue vitriol*), of iron (*green vitriol*), of zinc (*white vitriol*), etc. *b)* *same as* SULFURIC ACID: in full, **oil of vitriol 2.** sharpness or bitterness, as in speech or writing —*vt.* **-oled** or **-olled**, **-ol·ing** or **-ol·ling** to treat as with vitriol

vit·ri·ol·ic (vit′rē äl′ik) *adj.* **1.** of, like, or derived from a vitriol **2.** very sharp or bitter [*vitriolic* talk]

vit·tle (vit′'l) *n., v. obs.* or *dial. var. of* VICTUAL

vi·tu·per·ate (vī tōō′pə rāt′, vi-; -tyōō′-) *vt.* **-at′ed, -at′ing** [< L. pp. of *vituperare* < *vitium*, a fault + *parare*, to make ready] to scold or talk about in an extremely harsh way; berate —see SYN. at SCOLD —**vi·tu′per·a·tion** *n.* —**vi·tu′per·a′tive** *adj.* —**vi·tu′per·a′tive·ly** *adv.* —**vi·tu′per·a′tive·ness** *n.*

‡**vi·va** (vē′vä) *interj.* [It., Sp.] (long) live (someone or something specified)!: an exclamation of praise

vi·va·ce (vi vä′chā) *adj., adv.* [It.] *Music* in a lively, spirited manner: a direction to the performer

vi·va·cious (vi vā′shəs, vī-) *adj.* [< L. *vivacis*, genitive of *vivax* < *vivere*, to live] full of life and energy; spirited; lively —**vi·va′cious·ly** *adv.* —**vi·va′cious·ness** *n.*

Vi·val·di (vē väl′dē; *E.* vi-), **An·to·nio** (än tô′nyô) 1675?–1741; It. composer

vi·var·i·um (vī ver′ē əm) *n., pl.* **-i·ums, -i·a** (-ə) [L., ult. < *vivere*, to live] an enclosed place for keeping and studying animals, with conditions very much like those of their natural environment

VIVARIUM

vi·va vo·ce (vī′və vō′sē) [ML., with living voice] by word of mouth; orally [an order given *viva voce*] —**vi′va-vo′ce** *adj.*

‡**vive** (vēv) *interj.* [Fr.] (long) live (someone or something specified)!: an exclamation of praise

Viv·i·an (viv′ē ən, viv′yən) [L. *Vivianus* < *vivus*, alive] a masculine or feminine name

viv·id (viv′id) *adj.* [< L. < *vivere*, to live] **1.** full of life; lively; striking [a *vivid* personality] **2.** bright and strong: said of colors, light, etc. **3.** forming or giving a clear picture in the mind [a *vivid* imagination, a *vivid* description] **4.** clearly brought to mind, as a memory —**viv′id·ly** *adv.* —**viv′id·ness** *n.*

viv·i·fy (viv′ə fī′) *vt.* **-fied′, -fy′ing** [< Fr. < LL. < L. *vivus*, alive + *facere*, to make] **1.** to give life to; animate **2.** to make more lively, active, striking, etc. —**viv′i·fi·ca′tion** *n.*

vi·vip·a·rous (vī vip′ər əs) *adj.* [< L. < *vivus*, alive + *parere*, to produce] bearing living young (as most mammals and some other animals do) instead of laying eggs: opposed to OVIPAROUS —**vi·vip′a·rous·ly** *adv.*

viv·i·sect (viv′ə sekt′) *vt., vi.* to practice vivisection (on) —**viv′i·sec′tor** *n.*

viv·i·sec·tion (viv′ə sek′shən) *n.* [< L. *vivus*, alive + SECTION] surgical operations or other experiments done on living animals for scientific purposes, as in studying diseases and trying to find cures for them —**viv′i·sec′tion·al** *adj.*

viv·i·sec·tion·ist (-ist) *n.* a person who practices or favors the practice of vivisection for the good of science

vix·en (vik′s'n) *n.* [ME. (southern dial.) *fixen* < OE. *fyxe*, she-fox] **1.** a female fox **2.** a bad-tempered, shrewish woman —**vix′en·ish** *adj.* —**vix′en·ish·ly** *adv.*

viz., viz (viz; *often read* "namely") [ML., altered < contr. for L. *videlicet*] videlicet; that is; namely

viz·ard (viz′ərd) *n.* [altered < *visar*, var. of VISOR] a mask, as for disguise

vi·zier (vi zir′, viz′yər) *n.* [< Turk. < Ar. *wazir*, lit., bearer of burdens < *wazara*, to bear a burden] in Moslem countries, a high officer in the government; esp., a minister of state: also sp. **vi·zir′** —**vi·zier′ate** (-it, -āt), **vi·zier′ship** *n.* —**vi·zier′i·al** *adj.*

viz·or (vī′zər) *n. alt. sp. of* VISOR

V-J Day (vē′jā′) the day on which the fighting with Japan officially ended in World War II (Aug. 15, 1945) or the day of formal surrender (Sept. 2, 1945)

VL. Vulgar Latin

Vla·di·vos·tok (vlad′i väs′täk; *Russ.* vlä′di vôs tôk′) seaport in southeastern R.S.F.S.R., on the Pacific: pop. 442,000

Vla·minck (vlä mank′), **Mau·rice de** (mô rēs′ də) 1876–1958; Fr. painter

VLF, V.L.F., vlf, v.l.f. very low frequency

Vl·ta·va (v′l′tä vä) river in W Czechoslovakia, flowing northward into the Elbe

V-neck (vē′nek′) *n.* a neckline V-shaped in front

voc. vocative

vocab. vocabulary

vo·ca·ble (vō′kə b'l) *n.* [Fr. < L. *vocabulum* < *vocare*, to call] a word; esp., a word thought of as a unit of sounds or letters rather than as a unit of meaning

vo·cab·u·lar·y (vō kab′yə ler′ē, və-) *n., pl.* **-lar·ies** [< ML. < L. *vocabulum*, a word: see prec.] **1.** a list of words, usually in alphabetical order with their meanings, as in a dictionary or glossary **2.** all the words of a language, or all those used by a particular person, class, profession, etc.

vo·cal (vō′k'l) *adj.* [< L. *vocalis* < *vocis*, genitive of *vox*, VOICE] **1.** *a)* made by the voice; esp., spoken; oral [*vocal* sounds] *b)* sung or to be sung [*vocal* music] **2.** having a voice; able to speak or make oral sounds **3.** of, used in, connected with, or belonging to the voice [*vocal* organs] **4.** full of voices [a *vocal* crowd] **5.** speaking freely or strongly [she was *vocal* in the fight for women's rights] **6.** *Phonet. same as:* VOCALIC *b)* VOICED —*n.* **1.** a vocal sound **2.** the part of a popular song that is sung, not the parts played by the instruments —**vo′cal·ly** *adv.*

vocal cords either of two pairs of membranous cords or folds in the larynx, consisting of a thicker upper pair (**false vocal cords**) and a lower pair (**true vocal cords**): voice is produced when air from the lungs causes the lower (true) cords to vibrate

vo·cal·ic (vō kal′ik) *adj.* **1.** *a)* of, or having the nature of, a vowel *b)* made up mainly or entirely of vowels **2.** producing or involving vowel change —**vo·cal′i·cal·ly** *adv.*

vo·cal·ist (vō′k'l ist) *n.* a singer

vo·cal·ize (vō′k'l īz′) *vt.* **-ized′, -iz′ing 1.** to express with the voice; say or sing **2.** *Phonet. a)* to change into or use as a vowel *b)* to voice —*vi.* to make vocal sounds; speak or sing; specif., to do a singing exercise, using various vowel sounds —**vo′cal·i·za′tion** *n.* —**vo′cal·iz′er** *n.*

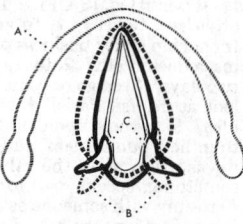
VOCAL CORDS
(A, thyroid cartilage; B, vocal cords at rest; C, vocal cords in use)

vo·ca·tion (vō kā′shən) *n.* [< LL. < L. < *vocare*, to call] **1.** *a)* a call or will to carry on some work or enter a certain career, esp. a religious one *b)* the work or career toward which one believes himself to be called **2.** any trade, profession, or occupation

vo·ca·tion·al (-'l) *adj.* **1.** of a vocation, trade, occupation, etc. **2.** designating or of education, training, etc. intended to prepare one for an occupation, sometimes specif. in a trade [to study mechanics or stenography at a *vocational* school] —**vo·ca′tion·al·ism** *n.* —**vo·ca′tion·al·ly** *adv.*

☆**vocational guidance** the work of testing and interviewing persons in order to guide them toward the choice of a suitable vocation

voc·a·tive (väk′ə tiv) *adj.* [< OFr. < L. < pp. of *vocare*, to call < *vox*, the VOICE] *Gram.* in certain inflected languages, designating or of the case showing the person or thing addressed —*n.* **1.** the vocative case **2.** a word in this case —**voc′a·tive·ly** *adv.*

vo·cif·er·ate (vō sif′ə rāt′) *vt., vi.* **-at′ed, -at′ing** [< L. pp. of *vociferari* < *vox*, voice + *ferre*, to bear] to cry out or shout loudly or with strong feeling; clamor —**vo·cif′er·ant** (-ər ənt) *adj.* —**vo·cif′er·a′tion** *n.* —**vo·cif′er·a′tor** *n.*

vo·cif·er·ous (vō sif′ər əs) *adj.* loud and noisy in making one's feelings known; clamorous —**vo·cif′er·ous·ly** *adv.* —**vo·cif′er·ous·ness** *n.*

SYN.—**vociferous** suggests loud and uncontrolled shouting or crying out [a *vociferous* mob, *vociferous* cheers]; **clamorous** suggests an urgent vociferousness in demanding or complaining [*clamorous* protests]; **blatant** suggests vulgar or offensive loudness, noisiness, uproar, etc. [*blatant* heckling]; **strident** suggests a harsh, grating loudness [a *strident* voice]; **boisterous** suggests uncontrolled high spirits in noisemaking [*boisterous* singing at the party]; **obstreperous** implies unruly behavior that is noisy or rough in resisting control [an *obstreperous* child]

vod·ka (väd′kə) *n.* [Russ., dim. of *voda*, water] a colorless alcoholic liquor distilled from wheat, rye, etc.

vogue (vōg) *n.* [Fr., a fashion, lit., a rowing < *voguer*, to row < MLowG.] **1.** the accepted fashion at any particular time; mode: often with *the* **2.** general acceptance; popularity [coming into *vogue*] —see SYN. at FASHION —*adj.* in vogue: also **voguish** (vō′gish)

voice (vois) *n.* [< OFr. < L. *vocis*, genitive of *vox*, a voice < IE. base *wekw-*, to speak] **1.** sound made through the mouth, esp. by human beings in talking, singing, etc. **2.** the ability to make such sounds [to lose one's *voice*] **3.** any sound, influence, etc. thought of as like speech or the human voice [the *voice* of the sea, the *voice* of one's conscience] **4.** a specified or distinctive quality of vocal sound [an angry *voice*] **5.** *a*) an expressed wish, choice, opinion, etc. [the *voice* of the people] *b*) the right to express one's choice, opinion, etc.; vote [to have a *voice* in one's government] **6.** the act of putting into words what one thinks or feels [giving *voice* to his doubts] **7.** the means by which something is expressed [a newspaper known to be the *voice* of the administration] **8.** *Gram.* a form of a verb showing the connection between the subject and the verb, either as performing (**active voice**) or receiving (**passive voice**) the action **9.** *Music a*) the quality of a person's singing [a good *voice*] *b*) a singer *c*) any of the individual parts sung or played together in a musical composition **10.** *Phonet.* sound made by vibrating the vocal cords with air forced from the lungs, as in pronouncing all vowels and such consonants as (b), (d), (g), (m), etc. —*vt.* **voiced, voic′ing** **1.** to say or express in words **2.** *Music* to regulate the tone of (organ pipes, etc.) **3.** *Phonet.* to pronounce by letting the voice sound through the vocal cords —**in voice** with the voice in good condition, as for singing —**with one voice** unanimously —**voic′er** *n.*

voice box *same as* LARYNX

voiced (voist) *adj.* **1.** having a voice **2.** having (a specified kind of) voice [deep-*voiced*] **3.** expressed by the voice **4.** *Phonet.* made by vibrating the vocal cords with air forced from the lungs [*m*, *v*, *z*, etc. are voiced consonants]

voice·less (vois′lis) *adj.* **1.** having no voice; mute **2.** not speaking or spoken **3.** *Phonet.* not voiced [*p*, *t*, *k*, etc. are *voiceless* consonants] —**voice′less·ly** *adv.* —**voice′-less·ness** *n.*

SYN.—**voiceless** is applied to one who has no voice, either from birth or through loss [the throat operation left him *voiceless*]; **speechless** usually implies temporary or momentary loss of the ability to speak [*speechless* with horror]; **dumb** implies a lack of the power of speech and is now more often applied to animals and objects than to persons [a *dumb* beast]; **mute** is applied to persons unable to speak, specif. as because of deafness from birth and not through lack of or injury to the speech organs —**ANT.** articulate

voice-o·ver (-ō′vər) *n.* the voice commenting or narrating off camera, as for a television commercial

☆**voice·print** (-print′) *n.* a pattern of wavy lines, etc. made from a person's voice by an electronic device

void (void) *adj.* [< OFr., ult. < L. *vacivus* < *vacare*, to be empty] **1.** not occupied; vacant: said of a position or office **2.** *a*) having nothing in it; empty *b*) lacking; devoid (of) [*void* of sense] **3.** useless; ineffective **4.** *Law* of no legal force; not binding; invalid [a *void* contract] —*n.* **1.** an empty space or vacuum **2.** *a*) total absence of something normally present *b*) a feeling of emptiness or loss [the *void* left by his death] —*vt.* **1.** *a*) to empty (the contents of something) *b*) to discharge (urine or feces) **2.** to make void; annul [to *void* an agreement] —*vi.* to move the bowels or, esp., to urinate —see SYN. at EMPTY and NULLIFY —**void′a·ble** *adj.* —**void′er** *n.*

‡**voi·là** (wvä lä′) [Fr., see there] behold; there it is: often used as an interjection

voile (voil) *n.* [Fr., a veil] a thin, sheer fabric, as of cotton

vol. 1. volcano **2.** *pl.* **vols.** volume **3.** volunteer

vo·lant (vō′lənt) *adj.* [Fr. < L. prp. of *volare*, to fly] **1.** flying or capable of flying **2.** nimble; quick **3.** *Heraldry* represented as flying

vol·a·tile (väl′ə t'l; *chiefly Brit.* -tīl′) *adj.* [MFr. < L. < *volare*, to fly] **1.** vaporizing or evaporating quickly, as alcohol **2.** *a*) unstable or explosive [a *volatile* social condition] *b*) moving suddenly and often from one idea, interest, feeling, etc. to another; changeable *c*) not lasting long; fleeting —**vol′a·til′i·ty** (-til′ə tē), **vol′a·tile·ness** *n.*

vol·a·til·ize (väl′ə t'l īz′) *vt.*, *vi.* -ized′, -iz′ing to make or become volatile; evaporate —**vol′a·til·i·za′tion** *n.*

vol·can·ic (väl kan′ik) *adj.* **1.** of, from, or produced by a volcano [*volcanic* rock] **2.** having volcanoes [a *volcanic* island] **3.** like a volcano; likely to explode; violent [a *volcanic* temper] —**vol·can′i·cal·ly** *adv.*

volcanic glass natural glass, as obsidian, formed by the very rapid cooling of molten lava

vol·can·ism (väl′kə niz'm) *n.* volcanic activity or phenomena

vol·ca·no (väl kā′nō) *n.*, *pl.* **-noes, -nos** [It. < L. *Volcanus*, VULCAN] **1.** an opening in the earth's crust through which molten rock (*lava*), rock fragments, gases, ashes, etc. are thrown up from the earth's interior **2.** a cone-shaped hill or mountain, chiefly of volcanic materials, built up around the opening, usually so as to form a crater

vole (vōl) *n.* [earlier *vole mouse* < Scand., as in Norw. *voll*, field + MOUSE] any of a number of small rodents with a fat body and short tail

Vol·ga (väl′gə, vōl′-; *Russ.* vôl′gä) river in western R.S.F.S.R., flowing southeastward into the Caspian Sea

Vol·go·grad (väl′gə grad′; *Russ.* vôl′gô grät′) city in SC European R.S.F.S.R., on the Volga: pop. 818,000

vo·li·tion (vō lish′ən, və-) *n.* [Fr. < ML. *volitio*, ult. < L. *velle*, to will] the act or power of using the will in deciding or making a choice [of his own *volition* he apologized] —see SYN. at WILL[1] —**vo·li′tion·al** *adj.*

vol·i·tive (väl′ə tiv) *adj.* **1.** of the will **2.** *Gram.* expressing a wish, as a verb, mood, etc.

vol·ley (väl′ē) *n.*, *pl.* **-leys** [MFr. *volee*, ult. < L. pp. of *volare*, to fly] **1.** *a*) the shooting of a number of guns or other weapons at the same time *b*) the missiles shot in this way **2.** a burst of words or acts suggestive of this [a *volley* of curses] **3.** *Sports a*) the flight of a ball, etc. before it touches the ground *b*) a return of a ball, etc. before it touches the ground *c*) loosely, any series of shots back and forth, as in tennis, esp. in warming up —*vt.*, *vi.* **-leyed, -ley·ing** **1.** to shoot or be shot in a volley **2.** *Sports* to return (the ball, etc.) as a volley; take part in a volley —**vol′ley·er** *n.*

☆**vol·ley·ball** (-bôl′) *n.* **1.** a game played on a court by two teams who hit a large, light, inflated ball back and forth over a high net with the hands, each team trying to return the ball before it touches the ground **2.** this ball

vol·plane (väl′plān) *vi.* **-planed′, -plan′ing** [Fr. *vol plané* < *voler*, to fly + *plané*, pp. of *planer*, to glide] to glide down as or in an airplane with the engine cut off —*n.* such a glide

vols. volumes

volt[1] (vōlt) *n.* [< Fr. < It. < L. pp. of *volvere*, to turn about] **1.** a turning movement of a horse, sideways around a center **2.** *Fencing* a leap to avoid a thrust

volt[2] (vōlt) *n.* [after A. *Volta* (1745–1827), It. physicist] the mks unit of electromotive force or difference in potential between two points in an electric circuit that will send a current of one ampere through a resistance of one ohm

Vol·ta (väl′tə) river in Ghana, flowing south into the Gulf of Guinea: c. 300 mi.

volt·age (vōl′tij) *n.* electromotive force, or difference in electrical potential, expressed in volts

vol·ta·ic (väl tā′ik, vōl-) *adj.* **1.** designating or of electricity produced by chemical action; galvanic **2.** used in so producing electricity

voltaic battery 1. a battery made up of voltaic cells **2.** *same as* VOLTAIC CELL

voltaic cell a device for producing an electric current by the action of two plates of different metals in an electrolyte

voltaic pile *same as* PILE[1] (*n.* 5)

VOLCANO
(A, crater; B, conduit through which molten rock & gases rise to surface; C, parasitic cone; D, ashes & lava; E, sedimentary & metamorphic rock; F, igneous rock; G, reservoir of hot magma)

fat, āpe, cär; ten, ēven; is, bīte; gō, hôrn, tōōl, lŏŏk; ôil, out; up, fur; get; joy; yet; chin; she; thin, then; zh, leisure; ŋ, ring; ə for *a* in *ago*, *e* in *agent*, *i* in *sanity*, *o* in *comply*, *u* in *focus*; ′ as in *able* (ā′b'l); Fr. bal; ë, Fr. coeur; ö, Fr. feu; Fr. mon; ô, Fr. coq; ü, Fr. duc; r, Fr. cri; H, G. ich; kh, G. doch; ‡foreign; ☆ Americanism; < derived from. See inside front cover.

Vol·taire (vōl ter′, väl-; *Fr.* vôl ter′) (born *François Marie Arouet*) 1694–1778; Fr. writer & philosopher

vol·tam·e·ter (väl tam′ə tər, vōl-) *n.* an electrolytic cell for measuring an electric current by the amount of gas freed or metal deposited from an electrolyte

volt·am·me·ter (vōlt′am′mēt′ər) *n.* an instrument for measuring either voltage or amperage

volt·am·pere (-am′pir) *n.* a unit of electric power equal to the product of one volt and one ampere

volt·me·ter (-mēt′ər) *n.* an instrument for measuring voltage

vol·u·ble (väl′yoo b'l) *adj.* [Fr. < L. *volubilis* < pp. of *volvere*, to roll] **1.** talking very much and easily; talkative, glib, etc. **2.** *Bot.* twining or twisting, as a vine —see SYN. at TALKATIVE — **vol′u·bil′i·ty** *n.* —**vol′u·bly** *adv.*

vol·ume (väl′yoom, -yəm) *n.* [MFr. < L. *volumen*, a scroll < pp. of *volvere*, to roll] **1.** *a)* a collection of written or printed sheets bound together; book [the many *volumes* in his library] *b)* any of the books of a set [*Volume* III of the encyclopedia] **2.** a set of the issues of a periodical over a fixed period of time, usually a year **3.** the amount of space occupied in three dimensions; cubic contents [the *volume* of this box is 27 cubic feet, or .765 cubic meter] **4.** *a)* a quantity, bulk, mass, or amount [a large *volume* of sales] *b)* a large quantity [*volumes* of oil gushed from the well] **5.** the strength or loudness of sound [lower the *volume* of the radio] **6.** *Music* fullness of tone —see SYN. at BULK — **speak volumes** to be very meaningful

vol·u·met·ric (väl′yoo met′rik) *adj.* of or based on the measurement of volume: also **vol′u·met′ri·cal** —**vol′u·met′ri·cal·ly** *adv.*

vo·lu·mi·nous (və loo′mə nəs) *adj.* **1.** writing, producing, or made up of enough to fill volumes [the *voluminous* works of Dickens] **2.** of great volume; large; bulky; full [a *voluminous* skirt] —**vo·lu′mi·nos′i·ty** (-näs′ə tē) *n.* —**vo·lu′mi·nous·ly** *adv.*

vol·un·tar·y (väl′ən ter′ē) *adj.* [< L. < *voluntas*, free will, ult. < *velle*, to will] **1.** brought about by one's own free choice; given or done of one's own free will [*voluntary* gifts] **2.** acting as such willingly or without being asked [a *voluntary* guide] **3.** done purposely; intentional [*voluntary* manslaughter] **4.** controlled by the will [*voluntary* muscles] **5.** having free will or the power of free choice [man is a *voluntary* agent] **6.** made up of volunteers [a *voluntary* army] —*n., pl.* **-tar′ies** an organ solo played for a church service —**vol′un·tar′i·ly** *adv.*

SYN.—**voluntary** implies the use of one's own free choice or will in an action, whether or not outside influences are at work [*voluntary* services]; **intentional** applies to that which is done on purpose for a definite reason and is in no way accidental [an *intentional* snub]; **deliberate** implies a full awareness of the significance of what one intends to do and of its effects [a *deliberate* attempt to cheat us]; **willful** implies stubborn determination to have one's own way despite influences, arguments, advice, etc. in opposition [a *willful* refusal]

vol·un·teer (väl′ən tir′) *n.* [< obs. Fr. *volontaire*, a voluntary] **1.** a person who offers to do something of his own free will **2.** a person who enlists in the armed forces of his own free will —*adj.* **1.** of or made up of volunteers [a *volunteer* regiment] **2.** serving as a volunteer [a *volunteer* nurse] **3.** same as VOLUNTARY —*vt.* to offer or give of one's own free will [to *volunteer* information] —*vi.* to enter or offer to enter into any service of one's own free will; enlist [to *volunteer* for military service]

vo·lup·tu·ar·y (və lup′choo wer′ē) *n., pl.* **-ar′ies** [see VOLUPTUOUS] a person mainly interested in luxurious living and sensual pleasures —*adj.* of or characterized by luxury and sensual pleasures

vo·lup·tu·ous (-choo wəs) *adj.* [< L. < *voluptas*, pleasure] **1.** full of, producing, or characterized by sensual pleasures [a *voluptuous* feast] **2.** fond of luxury, the pleasures of the senses, etc. **3.** suggesting, or arising from, sensual pleasure **4.** sexually attractive because of a full, shapely figure [a *voluptuous* woman] —**vo·lup′tu·ous·ly** *adv.* —**vo·lup′tu·ous·ness** *n.*

vo·lute (və loot′) *n.* [< L. < pp. of *volvere*, to roll] **1.** a spiral or twisting form; whorl **2.** *Archit.* a spiral scroll, as of an Ionic capital **3.** *Zool.* any of the turns or whorls of a spiral shell —*adj.* spiraled: also **vo·lut′ed** —**vo·lu′tion** *n.*

vo·mer (vō′mər) *n.* [ModL. < L., plowshare] a thin, flat bone forming part of the septum separating the nasal passages

vom·it (väm′it) *n.* [< L. < pp. of *vomere*] matter thrown up from the stomach —*vi., vt.* **1.** to throw up (the contents of the stomach) through the mouth **2.** to throw out or be thrown out with force; belch forth [the cannons *vomited* smoke and fire] —**vom′it·er** *n.*

‡von (fôn; *E.* vän) *prep.* [G.] of; from: a prefix in many names of German and Austrian families, esp. of the nobility

☆**voo·doo** (voo′doo) *n., pl.* **-doos** [Creole Fr. < a WAfr. word] **1.** a primitive religion based on a belief in magic, witchcraft, and charms, that began in Africa and is still practiced, chiefly by natives of the West Indies **2.** a person who practices voodoo **3.** a voodoo charm, object, etc. —*adj.* of voodoos or their practices, beliefs, etc. —*vt.* to affect by voodoo magic —**voo′doo·ism** *n.* —**voo′doo·ist** *n.* —**voo′doo·is′tic** *adj.*

vo·ra·cious (vô rā′shəs, və-) *adj.* [L. *voracis*, genitive of *vorax* < *vorare*, to devour] **1.** greedy in eating; ravenous; gluttonous **2.** very greedy or eager in some desire or pursuit [a *voracious* reader] —**vo·ra′cious·ly** *adv.* —**vo·rac′i·ty** (-ras′ə tē), **vo·ra′cious·ness** *n.*

Vo·ro·nezh (vô rô′nesh) city in SC European R.S.F.S.R., near the Don; pop. 660,000

-vo·rous (və rəs) [< L. < *vorare*, to devour] *a combining form meaning* feeding on, eating [*omnivorous*]

vor·tex (vôr′teks) *n., pl.* **vor·tex·es, vor′ti·ces′** (-tə sēz′) [L. < *vertere*, to turn] **1.** a whirling mass of water forming a vacuum at its center, into which anything caught in the motion is drawn; whirlpool **2.** a whirl of air; whirlwind **3.** any activity, situation, etc. that is like a whirl in its rush, power to cause disaster, etc. —**vor′ti·cal** *adj.* —**vor′ti·cal·ly** *adv.*

vor·ti·cel·la (vôr′tə sel′ə) *n., pl.* **-cel′lae** (-ē) [ModL., dim. < L. *vortex*: see VORTEX] any of a group of one-celled animals living in water, with a bell-shaped body on a thin stem used to hold onto another object

Vosges (Mountains) (vōzh) mountain range in NE France, west of the Rhine

vot·a·ble (vōt′ə b'l) *adj.* that can be submitted to a vote

vo·ta·ry (vōt′ə rē) *n., pl.* **-ries** [< L. pp. of *vovere*, to vow + -ARY] **1.** *a)* a person bound by religious vows, as a monk *b)* a devout worshiper **2.** a devoted supporter; one who is devoted to some cause or interest [a *votary* of music] Also **vo′ta·rist** —**vo′ta·ress** (-ris) *n.fem.*

vote (vōt) *n.* [L. *votum*, a vow < pp. of *vovere*, to vow] **1.** a decision on a proposal, etc., or a choice between candidates for office **2.** *a)* the expression of such a decision or choice *b)* the ballot, voice, etc. by which it is expressed **3.** the right to make such a decision, etc.; suffrage **4.** *a)* all the votes together [to get out the *vote*] *b)* a specified group of voters, or their votes [the farm *vote*] **5.** [Archaic] a vow —*vi.* **vot′ed, vot′ing** to give or cast a vote [for whom did you *vote*?] —*vt.* **1.** *a)* to decide, choose, pass, or authorize by vote [Congress *voted* new taxes] *b)* to give or grant by vote *c)* to support (a specified party) in voting **2.** to declare by general opinion [we *voted* the picnic a success] **3.** [Colloq.] to suggest [I *vote* we leave now] —**vote down** to defeat by voting —**vote in** to elect —**vote out** to defeat (the person presently in office) in an election —**vote′less** *adj.*

vot·er (vōt′ər) *n.* a person who has a right to vote; elector, esp. one who actually votes

☆**voting machine** a machine on which the votes in an election are cast, registered, and counted

vo·tive (vōt′iv) *adj.* [L. *votivus* < *votum*: see VOTE] given, done, etc. in fulfillment of a vow [*votive* offerings]

vouch (vouch) *vt.* [< OFr. < L. *vocare*, to call < *vox*, a VOICE] to uphold by demonstration or evidence; testify —*vi.* **1.** to give one's word, a guarantee, etc. [his friends *vouch* for his honesty] **2.** to act as or be evidence or a guarantee [references *vouching* for his ability]

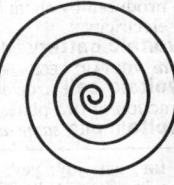

VOTING MACHINE

vouch·er (vou′chər) *n.* **1.** a person who vouches, as for the truth of a statement **2.** a paper giving evidence of or attesting to the payment or receipt of money, the accuracy of an account, etc.

vouch·safe (vouch sāf′) *vt.* **-safed′, -saf′ing** [< ME. *vouchen safe*, to vouch as safe] to be kind or gracious enough to give or grant [to *vouchsafe* a reply] —**vouch·safe′ment** *n.*

vous·soir (voo swär′) *n.* [Fr. < OFr., ult. < L. pp. of *volvere*, to roll] *Archit.* any of the wedge-shaped stones of which an arch or vault is built

VOLUTE

vow (vou) *n.* [< OFr. < L. *votum:* see VOTE] **1.** a solemn promise or pledge, as one made to God or with God as one's witness, binding oneself to an act, way of life, etc. [marriage *vows*] **2.** a solemn declaration —*vt.* **1.** to promise solemnly [he *vowed* to love her always] **2.** to swear solemnly to do, get, etc. [he *vowed* revenge] **3.** to declare in a forceful or earnest way [she *vowed* that she had never heard such noise] —*vi.* to make a vow —**take vows** to enter a religious order —**vow′er** *n.*

vow·el (vou′əl, voul) *n.* [< MFr. < L. *vocalis* (*littera*), vocal (letter) < *vox,* a VOICE] **1.** any speech sound made by letting the voiced breath pass through without stopping it with the tongue, teeth, or lips: see also CONSONANT **2.** a letter, as *a, e, i, o, u,* and sometimes *y,* representing such a sound —*adj.* of a vowel or vowels

‡**vox** (väks) *n., pl.* **vo·ces** (vō′sēz) [L.] voice

‡**vox po·pu·li** (päp′yoo lī′) [L.] the voice of the people; public opinion or sentiment: abbrev. **vox pop.**

voy·age (voi′ij) *n.* [< OFr. < L. *viaticum,* provision for a journey < *via,* way] **1.** a journey by water [an ocean *voyage*] **2.** a journey by aircraft or spacecraft —*vi.* **-aged, -ag·ing** to make a voyage; travel —*vt.* to sail or travel over or on —see SYN. at TRIP —**voy′ag·er** *n.*

‡**vo·ya·geur** (vwä yá zhër′) *n., pl.* **-geurs′** (-zhër′) [Fr.] in Canada, **1.** formerly, a person who transported goods and men for the fur companies **2.** any woodsman or boatman of the wilds

Voy·ag·eurs National Park (voi′ij ərz) national park in a lake region of northernmost Minn., on the border of Ontario, Canada

vo·yeur (vwä yur′, voi ur′) *n.* [Fr. < *voir,* to see] a person who has an exaggerated interest in viewing sexual objects or activities to get sexual satisfaction; peeping Tom —**vo·yeur′ism** *n.* —**vo′yeur·is′tic** *adj.*

V.P., VP Vice-President

V.Rev. Very Reverend

vroom (vroom) *n.* [echoic] the sound made by a motor vehicle in accelerating —*vi.* [Colloq.] to make, or move off with, such a sound

vs. versus

v.s. [L. *vide supra*] see above

V-shaped (vē′shāpt′) *adj.* shaped like the letter V

Vt., VT Vermont

vt., v.t. transitive verb

☆**VTOL** [*v*(*ertical*) *t*(*ake*)*o*(*ff and*) *l*(*anding*)] an aircraft, usually other than a helicopter, that can take off and land vertically

VTR video tape recorder

V-type engine (vē′tīp′) a gasoline engine in which the cylinders are set at an angle in two banks forming a V

Vul·can (vul′k'n) *Rom. Myth.* the god of fire and of metalworking —**Vul·ca′ni·an** (-kā′nē ən) *adj.*

vul·can·ite (vul′kə nīt′) *n.* [< prec. + -ITE] a hard rubber made by treating crude rubber with a large amount of sulfur and intense heat; ebonite: used in combs, electrical insulation, etc.

vul·can·ize (-nīz′) *vt., vi.* **-ized′, -iz′ing** [< VULCAN + -IZE] to treat (crude rubber) with sulfur and heat in order to make it

stronger and more elastic —**vul′can·i·za′tion** *n.* —**vul′can·iz′er** *n.*

Vulg. Vulgate

vul·gar (vul′gər) *adj.* [< L. *vulgaris* < *vulgus,* the common people] **1.** of the great mass of people in general; common; popular [a *vulgar* superstition] **2.** of or in the language commonly spoken by the people **3.** *a*) characterized by a lack of culture, refinement, taste, etc.; crude; boorish [a *vulgar* joke] *b*) indecent or obscene [*vulgar* language] —see SYN. at COARSE —**vul′gar·ly** *adv.* —**vul′gar·ness** *n.*

vul·gar·i·an (vul ger′ē ən, -gar′-) *n.* a vulgar person; esp., a rich person with coarse, showy manners or tastes

vul·gar·ism (vul′gər iz'm) *n.* **1.** a word, phrase, etc. that is used widely but is thought of as nonstandard, coarse, or obscene **2.** vulgar behavior, quality, etc.; vulgarity

vul·gar·i·ty (vul gar′ə tē) *n.* **1.** the state or quality of being vulgar, crude, etc. **2.** *pl.* **-ties** a vulgar act, habit, usage in speech, etc.

vul·gar·ize (vul′gə rīz′) *vt.* **-ized′, -iz′ing** to make vulgar; specif., *a*) to make coarse, crude, etc. *b*) to popularize —**vul′gar·i·za′tion** *n.* —**vul′gar·iz′er** *n.*

Vulgar Latin the everyday speech of the Roman people, from which the Romance languages developed

Vul·gate (vul′gāt, -git) *n.* [ML. *vulgata* (*editio*), popular (edition)] **1.** a Latin version of the Bible prepared in the 4th cent., that is authorized by the Roman Catholic Church **2.** [v-] the vernacular, or common speech —*adj.* **1.** of or in the Vulgate **2.** [v-] of or in the vernacular, or common speech

vul·ner·a·ble (vul′nər ə b'l) *adj.* [< LL. < L. *vulnerare,* to wound < *vulneris,* genitive of *vulnus,* a wound] **1.** that can be wounded or physically injured [a *vulnerable* spot on the body] **2.** *a*) open to, or easily hurt by, criticism or attack [a *vulnerable* reputation] *b*) affected by a specified influence, temptation, etc. [an officeholder *vulnerable* to political pressure] **3.** open to attack by armed forces [a *vulnerable* position] **4.** *Bridge* open to increased penalties or increased bonuses: said of a team which has won one game —**vul′ner·a·bil′i·ty** *n.* —**vul′ner·a·bly** *adv.*

vul·pine (vul′pīn, -pin) *adj.* [< L. < *vulpes,* a fox] **1.** of or like a fox or foxes **2.** clever, sly, etc.

vul·ture (vul′chər) *n.* [L. *vultur*] **1.** a large bird related to the eagles and hawks, with a naked head: vultures feed on the remains of dead animals ☆**2.** *same as* TURKEY BUZZARD **3.** a greedy, ruthless person who preys on others —**vul′tur·ous** *adj.*

vul·va (vul′və) *n., pl.* **-vae** (-vē), **-vas** [ModL. < L., womb] the outer genital organs of the female —**vul′val, vul′var** *adj.* —**vul′vate** (-vāt, -vit) *adj.*

vv. **1.** verses **2.** violins

v.v. vice versa

vy·ing (vī′iŋ) *adj.* that vies; that competes

VULTURE
(to 32 in. long; wingspread to 6 ft.)

W, w (dub′′l yoo, -yə) *n., pl.* **W's, w's** **1.** the twenty-third letter of the English alphabet **2.** the sound of *W* or *w*

W *Chem.* tungsten

W, w watt; watts

W, W., w, w. **1.** west **2.** western

W. **1.** Wales **2.** Washington **3.** Wednesday **4.** Welsh

W., w. **1.** watt(s) **2.** weight **3.** width **4.** won

w. **1.** week(s) **2.** wide **3.** wife **4.** with

WA Washington (State)

Wa·bash (wô′bash) [< Algonquian stream and tribal name] river flowing from W Ohio across Ind. into the Ohio River

wab·ble (wäb′′l) *n., vt., vi.* **-bled, -bling** *var. of* WOBBLE

☆**Wac** (wak) *n.* a member of the Women's Army Corps

WAC Women's Army Corps

wack·y (wak′ē) *adj.* **wack′i·er, wack′i·est** [< ? WHACK + -Y²] [Slang] ☆odd, silly, or crazy —**wack′i·ly** *adv.* —**wack′i·ness** *n.*

Wa·co (wā′kō) [< AmInd. tribal name] city in EC Tex.: pop. 95,000

wad (wäd, wôd) *n.* [ML. *wadda*, wadding < ?] **1.** a small, soft mass or ball, as a handful of cotton, crumpled paper, etc. **2.** a lump or small, firm mass [a *wad* of chewing gum] **3.** a mass of soft material used for padding, packing, etc. **4.** a plug stuffed against a charge to keep it firmly in place, as in a muzzleloading gun ☆**5.** [Colloq.] a roll of paper money ☆**6.** [Slang] a large amount, esp. of money —*vt.* **wad′ded, wad′ding 1.** to press together, or roll up (paper, etc.) into a wad **2.** to plug or stuff with a wad [to *wad* putty into a crack] **3.** to line or pad with wadding **4.** to hold (a charge) in place by a wad —**wad′der** *n.*

Wad·den·zee, Wad·den Zee (väd′ən zā′) section of the North Sea stretching into the Netherlands: formerly, the N part of the Zuider Zee

wad·ding (wäd′iŋ, wôd′-) *n.* any soft material for use in padding, packing, stuffing, etc.; esp., cotton made up into loose, fluffy sheets

wad·dle (wäd′′l, wôd′-) *vi.* **-dled, -dling** [< WADE + -LE²] to walk with short steps, swaying from side to side, as a duck —*n.* **1.** the act of waddling **2.** a waddling way of walking —**wad′dler** *n.*

wade (wād) *vi.* **wad′ed, wad′ing** [OE. *wadan*, to go] **1.** to walk through water, mud, snow, or anything that slows one down **2.** to walk and splash about in shallow water in play **3.** to get through with difficulty [to *wade* through a book] ☆**4.** [Colloq.] to start or attack with vigor (with *in* or *into*) [to *wade* into the work; to *wade* into a person for lying] —*vt.* to go across or through by wading [to *wade* a stream] —*n.* an act of wading

wad·er (wād′ər) *n.* **1.** a person or thing that wades **2.** *same as* WADING BIRD **3.** *a)* [*pl.*] high waterproof boots ☆*b)* [*usually pl.*] waterproof trousers with bootlike parts for the feet, worn by fishermen, etc. for wading in deep water

wa·di (wä′dē) *n., pl.* **-dis, -dies** [Ar. *wādī*] in Arabia, N Africa, etc., **1.** a valley, ravine, etc. that is dry except during the rainy season **2.** the rush of water that flows through it Also sp. **wa′dy,** *pl.* **-dies**

wading bird any of various long-legged shore birds that wade the shallows and marshes for food, as the crane, heron, rail, coot, sandpiper, and snipe

☆**wading pool** a shallow pool of water, esp. a small, movable unit in which little children can wade and play

☆**Waf** (waf) *n.* a member of the WAF

WAF Women in the Air Force

wa·fer (wā′fər) *n.* [< ONormFr. *waufre* < MDu. *wafel*] **1.** *a)* a thin, flat, crisp cracker or cookie *b)* anything that looks like this, as a thin, flat disk of candy **2.** a thin cake of unleavened bread used in the Eucharist **3.** a small disk of sticky paper, used as a seal on letters, documents, etc.

☆**waf·fle¹** (wäf′′l, wôf′-) *n.* [Du. *wafel*] a crisp batter cake with small, square hollows, baked in a waffle iron —*adj.* having a surface like a waffle: also **waf′fled**

waf·fle² (wäf′′l, wôf′-) *vi.* **-fled, -fling** [orig., to yelp < echoic *waff*, to yelp] [Chiefly Brit. Colloq.] to speak or write in a wordy, vague, or unsure manner —*n.* [Chiefly Brit. Colloq.] talk or writing of this kind

☆**waffle iron** a utensil or appliance for cooking waffles, having two flat, studded plates pressed together so that the waffle bakes between them

waft (waft, wäft) *vt.* [< obs. *wafter*, a convoy < Du. *wachter*, lit., a watcher] to carry or move (objects, sounds, smells, etc.) lightly through the air or over water —*vi.* **1.** to float, as in the air [cooking odors *wafted* through the hall-way] **2.** to blow gently: said of breezes —*n.* **1.** an odor, sound, etc. carried through the air **2.** a puff or gust of wind **3.** a wafting movement —**waft′-er** *n.*

WAFFLE IRON

wag¹ (wag) *vt.* **wagged, wag′ging** [prob. < ON. *vaga*, to rock] **1.** *a)* to cause to move rapidly back and forth, up and down, etc. [the dog *wagged* his tail] *b)* to shake (a finger) or nod (the head), as in scolding or agreeing **2.** to move (the tongue) in talking, esp. in idle gossip —*vi.* **1.** to move rapidly back and forth, up and down, etc. **2.** to keep moving in talk, esp. in gossip: said of the tongue —*n.* the act or an instance of wagging —**wag′ger** *n.*

wag² (wag) *n.* [prob. < obs. *waghalter*, a gallows bird, rogue] a comical or humorous person; joker

wage (wāj) *vt.* **waged, wag′ing** [< ONormFr. *wagier* < *wage* (OFr. *gage*), a pledge < Frank.] to take part in or carry on (a war, campaign, etc.) —*n.* **1.** [*often pl.*] money paid to an employee for work done, usually on an hourly, daily, or piecework basis **2.** [*usually pl., formerly with sing. v.*] what is given in return; recompense; requital [“The *wages* of sin is death”]

SYN.—**wage** (or **wages**) applies to money paid an employee at regular periods of time, as at hourly or piecework rates, esp. for skilled or manual labor; **salary** applies to fixed amounts usually paid monthly or twice a month, esp. to clerical or professional workers; **stipend** is a somewhat overly formal substitute for **salary**, or it is applied to a fixed payment, as an amount of money granted to a student; **fee** applies to the payment requested or given for professional services, as of a doctor, lawyer, etc.: **pay** is the general term that may be substituted for any of these words

wage earner a person who works for wages

wa·ger (wā′jər) *n.* [< ONormFr.: see WAGE] the act of betting or something bet —*vt., vi.* to bet —**wa′ger·er** *n.*

wage scale a schedule of the rates of wages paid for work or jobs of specified kinds in a given industry, plant, locality, etc.

☆**wage·work·er** (wāj′wur′kər) *n.* a person who works for wages

wag·ger·y (wag′ər ē) *n., pl.* **-ger·ies** **1.** mischievous humor of a playful or joking kind **2.** a joke; esp., a practical joke

wag·gish (wag′ish) *adj.* **1.** of or like a wag or joker; comical [a *waggish* fellow] **2.** playful; joking [a *waggish* remark] —**wag′gish·ly** *adv.*

wag·gle (wag′'l) *vt.* **-gled, -gling** [< WAG[1] + -LE[2]] to wag, esp. with short, quick movements —*vi.* to wobble —*n.* the act of waggling —**wag′gly** *adj.*

wag·gon (wag′ən) *n., vt., vi. Brit. var. of* WAGON

Wag·ner (väg′nər), **(Wilhelm) Rich·ard** (riH′ärt) 1813-83; Ger. composer

Wag·ne·ri·an (väg nir′ē ən) *adj.* **1.** of or like Richard Wagner or his music, theories, etc. **2.** designating or of a soprano, tenor, etc. specializing in Wagner's operas —*n.* an admirer of Wagner's music, theories, etc.

wag·on (wag′ən) *n.* [Du. *wagen*] **1.** *a)* a four-wheeled vehicle for carrying heavy loads *b)* a small cart used by children at play ☆**2.** *short for: a)* PATROL WAGON *b)* STATION WAGON **3.** [Brit.] a railroad freight car —*vt., vi.* to carry or move (goods) in a wagon —☆**fix someone's wagon** [Slang] to hurt someone in some way so as to get even with him —**hitch one's wagon to a star** to set oneself an ambitious goal —☆**on (or off) the wagon** [Slang] no longer (or once again) drinking alcoholic liquors

wag·on·er (-ər) *n.* a person who drives a wagon

wag·on·ette (wag′ə net′) *n.* [dim. of WAGON] a four-wheeled carriage with two seats set lengthwise facing each other behind the driver's seat

‡**wag·on-lit** (vȧ gōn lē′) *n., pl.* **wag·ons-lits** (-gōn lē′) [Fr.] in Europe, a railroad sleeping car

wag·on·load (wag′ən lōd′) *n.* the amount a wagon holds

wagon train a line of wagons traveling together, as one carrying military supplies, or one in which pioneers crossed the Western plains

wag·tail (wag′tāl′) *n.* **1.** a small bird related to the pipits, having a long tail that wags up and down ☆**2.** any of various similar birds, as an American water thrush

☆**wa·hi·ne** (wä hē′nä) *n.* [Maori & Haw.] a Polynesian woman, esp. of Hawaii

☆**wa·hoo**[1] (wä′hōō, wä hōō′) *n.* [< Dakota *wanhu*] any of several N. American shrubs having brilliant red fruits or leaves

☆**wa·hoo**[2] (wä′hōō, wä hōō′) *n., pl.* **-hoo, -hoos:** see PLURAL, II, D, 2 [< ?] a large game and food fish, related to the mackerels and found in warm seas

☆**wa·hoo**[3] (wä hōō′, wä′hōō) *interj.* [Western] a shout expressing great enthusiasm, joy, etc.

waif (wāf) *n.* [ONormFr., prob. < ON.] **1.** anything found that is without an owner, as a stray animal **2.** a person without home or friends; esp., a homeless child

Wai·ki·ki (wī′kē kē′, wī′kē kē′) [Haw., spurting water] famous bathing beach in Honolulu, Hawaii

wail (wāl) *vi.* [< ON. *væla* < *væ*, woe] **1.** to show grief or pain by long, loud cries **2.** to make a sad, crying sound [the wind wails] **3.** *Jazz* [Slang] to play in an inspired way —*vt.* [Archaic] **1.** to express deep sorrow for; lament; mourn **2.** to cry out in mourning —*n.* **1.** a long cry of grief or pain **2.** a sound like this **3.** the act of wailing —**wail′er** *n.* —**wail′ful** *adj.* —**wail′ful·ly** *adv.*

Wailing Wall same as WESTERN WALL

wain (wān) *n.* [OE. *wægn*] [Archaic or Dial.] a wagon or cart

wain·scot (wān′skət, -skät′) *n.* [< MDu. *wagenschot*] **1.** a lining or paneling of wood, etc. on the walls of a room, often on the lower part only **2.** the lower part of the walls of a room when finished differently from the upper part —*vt.* **-scot·ed** or **-scot·ted, -scot·ing** or **-scot·ting** to line (a wall, etc.) with wainscoting

wain·scot·ing, wain·scot·ting (-iŋ) *n.* **1.** same as WAINSCOT **2.** material used to wainscot

wain·wright (wān′rīt′) *n.* [WAIN + WRIGHT] a person who builds or repairs wagons

waist (wāst) *n.* [< base of OE. *weaxan*, to grow] **1.** the part of the body between the ribs and the hips **2.** *a)* the part of a garment that covers the waist *b)* same as WAISTLINE (sense 2) *c)* the part of a garment covering the body from the shoulders to the waistline *d)* a blouse **3.** the middle part or middle, narrow part of something

waist·band (wāst′band′) *n.* a band that fits around the waist, esp. one at the top of a skirt, trousers, etc.

waist·cloth (-klôth′) *n.* same as LOINCLOTH

waist·coat (wes′kət, wāst′kōt′) *n.* **1.** [Brit.] a man's vest **2.** a similar garment worn by women —**waist′coat·ed** *adj.*

waist-high (wāst′hī′) *adj.* reaching up to the waist

waist·line (wāst′lin′) *n.* **1.** the line of the waist, between the ribs and the hips **2.** *a)* the narrow part of a woman's dress, etc., worn at the waist or above or below it as styles change *b)* the line where the waist and skirt of a dress join **3.** the distance around the waist

WAISTLINES

wait (wāt) *vi.* [ONormFr. *waitier* < Frank.: for IE. base see WAKE[1]] **1.** to stay in place or remain in readiness or in anticipation (*until* something expected happens or *for* someone to arrive or catch up) **2.** to be ready [dinner is *waiting* for us] **3.** to remain undone for a time [that job will have to *wait*] **4.** to serve food [to *wait* at table; to *wait* on a person] —*vt.* **1.** to be, remain, or delay in expectation of [to *wait* orders; *wait* one's turn] **2.** [Colloq.] to delay serving (a meal) as in waiting for someone [we'll *wait* dinner for you] —*n.* the act or a period of waiting [an hour's *wait*] —see SYN. at STAY[3] —**lie in wait (for)** to wait so as to catch after planning an ambush or trap (for) —**wait on (or upon) 1.** to act as a servant to **2.** to call on or visit (a person) in order to pay one's respects, ask a favor, etc. **3.** to be a result of; depend on **4.** to serve (a customer, etc.) as a clerk, waiter, etc. **5.** [Dial. or Colloq.] to wait for; await —**wait out** to remain inactive during the time of —**wait table** to serve food as a waiter or servant to people at a table —**wait up 1.** to put off going to bed until someone expected arrives or something expected happens **2.** [Colloq.] to stop and wait for someone to catch up

Waite (wāt), **Mor·ri·son Rem·ick** (môr′i s'n rem′ik) 1816-88; U.S. jurist; chief justice of the U.S. (1874-88)

wait·er (wāt′ər) *n.* **1.** a person who waits or awaits **2.** a man who waits on table, as in a restaurant **3.** a tray for carrying dishes; salver

wait·ing (-iŋ) *adj.* **1.** that waits **2.** of or for a wait —*n.* **1.** the act of one that waits **2.** a period of waiting —**in waiting** in attendance, as on a king or other royal person

waiting game a delaying or postponing action until one has the advantage

waiting list a list of those applying, as for a vacancy or an item in short supply, in the order that they have applied

waiting room a room in which people wait, as in a railroad station, a dentist's office, etc.

wait·ress (wā′tris) *n.* a woman or girl who waits on table, as in a restaurant

waive (wāv) *vt.* **waived, waiv′ing** [< Anglo-Fr. *waiver*, to renounce < ON. *veifa*, to fluctuate] **1.** to give up or do without (a right, claim, etc.) **2.** to keep from insisting on or taking advantage of [to *waive* formalities] **3.** to put off; postpone [to *waive* a question] —see SYN. at RELINQUISH

waiv·er (wā′vər) *n. Law* **1.** a waiving, or giving up voluntarily, of a right, claim, etc. **2.** a formal written statement of this

wake[1] (wāk) *vi.* **woke** or **waked, waked** (or, occas. Brit., **wok′en** or **woke**), **wak′ing** [< OE. *wacian*, to be awake & *wacan*, to arise, both < IE. base *weg-*, to be active] **1.** to come out of sleep or a state like sleep; awake (often with *up*) **2.** to be or stay awake **3.** to become active again (often with *up*) **4.** to become alert [to *wake* to a danger] **5.** [Chiefly Dial.] *pt. & pp.* **waked** to hold a wake —*vt.* **1.** to cause to wake from or as from sleep (often with *up*) **2.** to stir up or excite (feelings, etc.) **3.** [Chiefly Dial.] *pt. & pp.* **waked** to hold a wake over (a corpse) —*n.* an all-night watch over a corpse before burial

wake[2] (wāk) *n.* [ON. *vök*, a hole in the ice] **1.** the track left in the water by a moving boat or ship **2.** any track left behind [the storm left wreckage in its *wake*] —**in the wake of** following close behind

wake·ful (wāk′fəl) *adj.* **1.** keeping awake **2.** alert; watchful [*wakeful* guards] **3.** *a)* unable to sleep *b)* sleepless [a *wakeful* night] —**wake′ful·ly** *adv.* —**wake′ful·ness** *n.*

Wake Island (wāk) coral atoll in the N Pacific between Midway & Guam: a U.S. territory

wake·less (wāk′lis) *adj.* unbroken; deep: said of sleep

wak·en (wāk′'n) *vi., vt.* [OE. *wacnian*] to become awake or cause to wake; become active or stir into action; wake up —see SYN. at STIR[1] —**wak′en·er** *n.*

wake·rob·in (wāk′räb′in) *n.* ☆1. *same as* TRILLIUM 2. [Brit.] any of several plants of the arum family

Wa·la·chi·a (wä lā′kē ə) region in S Romania —**Wa·la′·chi·an** *adj., n.*

Wald·helm (vält′hīm), **Kurt** (koort) 1918– ; Austrian diplomat; secretary-general of the United Nations (1972–)

☆**Wal·dorf salad** (wôl′-dôrf) [after the old hotel *Waldorf-Astoria* in New York City] a salad made of diced apples, celery, and walnuts, with mayonnaise

wale (wāl) *n.* [OE. *walu,* a weal] 1. a raised line made on the skin by a slash of a whip, etc.; welt 2. *a)* a ridge on the surface of cloth, as corduroy *b)* texture of cloth 3. [*pl.*] heavy planks fastened to the outside of the hull of a wooden ship —*vt.* **waled, wal′ing** 1. to mark (the skin) with wales 2. to make (cloth, etc.) with wales

WALACHIA

Wales (wālz) division of the United Kingdom, occupying a peninsula of WC Great Britain, on St. George's Channel: 8,016 sq. mi.; pop. 2,662,000; chief city, Cardiff

walk (wôk) *vi.* [OE. *wealcan,* to roll < IE. base *wel-,* to turn, roll, from which also comes L. *volvere*] 1. to move along on foot at a normal pace by placing one foot (or, with four-footed animals, two feet) on the ground before lifting the other (or others) 2. to appear after death [ghosts are said to *walk* in this old house] 3. to follow a certain course, way of life, etc. [let us *walk* in peace] ☆4. Baseball to get a walk ☆5. Basketball same as TRAVEL — *vt.* 1. to go through, along, over, etc. by walking [to *walk* the deck] 2. to cause (a horse, dog, etc.) to walk, as for exercise 3. to push (a bicycle, etc.) while walking alongside 4. to go along with (a person) on a walk [I'll *walk* you home] 5. to bring to a specified state by walking [to *walk* oneself to exhaustion] ☆6. *Baseball a)* to give a walk to (a batter) *b)* to force (a run) *in* by doing this when the bases are loaded —*n.* 1. the act of walking 2. a stroll or hike [an afternoon *walk*] 3. a route taken in walking 4. a distance to walk [an hour's *walk* from here] 5. the pace of one who walks 6. a way of walking [I knew her by her *walk*] 7. a particular position in life, area of activity, etc. [people from all *walks* of life] 8. a path set apart for walking [the park has gravel *walks*] 9. an enclosure for grazing or exercising animals ☆10. *Baseball* an advancing to first base on four balls (see BALL, *n.* 7) —**walk (all) over** [Colloq.] 1. to defeat completely 2. to rule over in a harsh or bullying way —**walk away from** to get ahead of easily —**walk away with** 1. to steal 2. to win easily —**walk off** 1. to go away, esp. without warning 2. to get rid of (fat, etc.) by walking —**walk off with** 1. to steal 2. to win (something), esp. easily —**walk out** ☆to go on strike —☆**walk out on** [Colloq.] to leave; desert; abandon — **walk′ing** *adj., n.*

walk·a·way (wôk′ə wā′) *n.* an easily won victory

walk·er (-ər) *n.* 1. a person or animal that walks ☆2. a frame on wheels for use by babies who are learning to walk ☆3. a somewhat similar frame without wheels, used as a support in walking by convalescents, etc.

☆**walk·ie-talk·ie** (wôk′ē tôk′ē) *n.* a small radio transmitter and receiver that can be carried by one person: also **walk′y-talk′y,** *pl.* **-talk′ies**

☆**walk-in** (-in′) *adj.* large enough for one to walk inside [a *walk-in* closet] —*n.* a walk-in closet, etc.

☆**walking papers** [Colloq.] dismissal from a job

walking stick 1. a stick carried when walking; cane 2. an insect resembling a twig: also **walk′ing·stick′** *n.*

walk-on (wôk′än′) *n.* a minor role in which an actor has no speaking lines or just a very few

☆**walk·out** (-out′) *n.* 1. a strike of workers 2. a sudden departure of people, as from a meeting, in a show of protest

walk·o·ver (-ō′vər) *n.* an easily won victory

WALKER

walk-through (-throo′) *n.* an early rehearsal of a play in which the actors begin to carry out actions on stage

☆**walk-up** (-up′) *n.* 1. an upstairs apartment in a building without an elevator 2. the building itself

☆**walk·way** (-wā′) *n.* a path, passage, etc. for pedestrians, esp. one that is sheltered

wall (wôl) *n.* [OE. *weall* < L. *vallum,* a rampart < *vallus,* a stake] 1. an upright structure of wood, stone, etc., built to enclose, divide, support, or protect [the *walls* of a room, building, garden, etc.] 2. [*usually pl.*] a surrounding fortification 3. anything like a wall in appearance or use [a *wall* of secrecy; the *walls* of the chest] —*adj.* of, on, in, or along a wall —*vt.* 1. to furnish, enclose, divide, etc. with or as with a wall [to *wall* a room with books; to *wall* off the old wing; a mind *walled* in by fears] 2. to close up (an opening) with a wall (usually with *up*) —**drive** (or **push**) **to the wall** to place in a desperate position — **drive** (or **send,** etc.) **up the wall** [Colloq.] to make wild with anger, pain, worry, etc. —**go to the wall** 1. to be defeated 2. to fail in business —**off the wall** [Slang] 1. unsound of mind; crazy 2. very odd or unusual; eccentric —**walled** *adj.* —**wall′·less** *adj.* —**wall′-like′** *adj.*

wal·la·by (wäl′ə bē) *n., pl.* **-bies, -by:** see PLURAL, II, D, 1 [< Australian native name] any of various small or medium-sized marsupials related to the kangaroos

Wal·lace (wôl′is, wäl′-) 1. [ult. < Anglo-Fr. *Waleis* or ME. *Walisc,* foreign, WELSH] a masculine name: dim. **Wally** 2. **Al·fred Rus.sel** (rus″l), 1823–1913; Eng. naturalist 3. **Henry A**(gard), 1888–1965; U.S. politician 4. **Sir William,** 1272?–1305?; Scot. leader in the struggle against the English

wal·la·roo (wäl′ə rōo′) *n.* [< Australian native name] a large kangaroo with a stocky body and broad, thickly padded feet

wall·board (wôl′bôrd′) *n.* material, as of gypsum, made up into sheets for covering walls, ceilings, etc. in place of plaster, etc.

Wal·len·stein (väl′ən shtīn′; *E.* wôl′ən stīn′), **Al·brecht von** (äl′breHt fôn) 1583–1634; Austrian general

wal·let (wäl′it, wôl′-) *n.* [ME. *walet* < ?] 1. formerly, a knapsack ☆2. a flat pocket case, as of leather, with sections for paper money, cards, etc.; billfold

wall·eye (wôl′ī′) *n.* [< ff.] 1. an eye, as of a horse, with a whitish iris or white, cloudy cornea 2. an eye that turns outward, showing more white than is normal 3. any of several fishes with large eyes that seem to be staring

wall·eyed (-īd′) *adj.* [< ON., ult. < *vagl,* a beam + *eygr,* having eyes] 1. having a walleye or walleyes 2. having large, staring eyes, as some fishes

☆**walleyed pike** a N. American freshwater food and game fish of the perch family

wall·flow·er (-flou′ər) *n.* 1. any of a number of garden plants having racemes of yellow, orange, etc. flowers 2. [Colloq.] a person, esp. a girl, who merely looks on at a dance from shyness or lack of a partner

Wal·loon (wä loon′) *n.* [Fr. *Wallon*] 1. a member of a people living mostly in southern and southeastern Belgium and nearby parts of France 2. the French dialect of the Walloons

wal·lop (wäl′əp, wôl′-) *vt.* [< ONormFr. *waloper* (OFr. *galoper*), to gallop < Frank.] [Colloq.] 1. to beat soundly 2. to strike hard 3. to defeat completely —*n.* [Colloq.] 1. a hard blow 2. the power to strike a hard blow ☆3. a thrill

wal·lop·ing (-iŋ) *adj.* [Colloq.] very large; enormous —*n.* [Colloq.] 1. a beating 2. a complete defeat

wal·low (wäl′ō, wôl′-) *vi.* [OE. *wealwian,* to roll around] 1. to roll about, as in mud, dust, etc. 2. to roll and pitch, as a ship 3. to indulge oneself in or revel in some feeling, way of life, etc. [to *wallow* in self-pity, to *wallow* in riches] —*n.* 1. a wallowing ☆2. a place where animals wallow —**wal′low·er** *n.*

wall·pa·per (wôl′pā′pər) *n.* paper for covering the walls or ceiling of a room —*vt.* to put wallpaper on

Wall Street 1. a street in lower Manhattan, New York City: main U.S. financial center 2. U.S. financiers and their power, policies, etc., or the U.S. money market

wall-to-wall (wôl′tə wôl′) *adj.* 1. that completely covers a floor [*wall-to-wall* carpeting] 2. [Colloq.] *a)* in very large numbers or amounts [a *wall-to-wall* crowd] *b)* taking care of everything [*wall-to-wall* health care]

wal·nut (wôl′nut′, -nət) *n.* [< OE. < *wealh,* foreign + *hnutu,* a nut] 1. any of a number of related trees, valued for their nuts and wood 2. their edible nut, having a hard, crinkled shell and a two-lobed seed 3. their wood, used for furniture, paneling, etc. 4. the brown color of black walnut wood ☆5. *local name for* SHAGBARK

Wal·pole (wôl′pōl, wäl′-) **1. Horace,** 4th Earl of Orford, (born *Horatio Walpole*) 1717–97; Eng. writer **2. Sir Robert,** 1st Earl of Orford, 1676–1745; Eng. statesman; prime minister (1721–42): father of *Horace*

Wal·pur·gis Night (väl poor′gis) the eve of May Day (April 30), when witches supposedly gathered for an orgy: also [G.] **Wal·pur·gis·nacht** (väl poor′gis nächt′)

wal·rus (wôl′rəs, wäl′-) *n., pl.* **-rus·es, -rus:** see PLURAL, II, D, 1 [Du. < Dan. *hvalros,* prob. < ON. *hross-hvalr,* lit., horse whale] a large sea mammal of the seal family, having two tusks sticking out from the upper jaw, a thick mustache, a thick hide, and a heavy layer of blubber —*adj.* like that of a walrus [a *walrus* mustache]

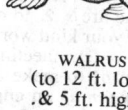

WALRUS
(to 12 ft. long & 5 ft. high)

Wal·ter (wôl′tər) [< ONormFr. < Frank. < *waldan,* to rule + *heri,* army; also < G. *Walther* < OHG.] a masculine name: dim. *Walt*

Wal·tham (wôl′tham, -thəm) [? after *Waltham* Abbey, England, home of the 1st settlers] city in E Mass.: suburb of Boston: pop. 62,000

Wal·ton (wôl′t'n), **I·zaak** (ī′zək) 1593–1683; Eng. writer

waltz (wôlts, wôls) *n.* [< G. < *walzen,* to roll, dance about] **1.** a ballroom dance for couples, in 3/4 time **2.** music for this dance or in its rhythm —*adj.* of, for, or typical of a waltz —*vi.* **1.** to dance a waltz **2.** to move lightly and quickly **3.** [Colloq.] to move effortlessly and successfully [to *waltz* through life] —*vt.* to dance with in a waltz —**waltz′er** *n.*

Wal·vis Bay (wôl′vis) **1.** seaport on the coast of South West Africa **2.** small territory of South Africa surrounding this seaport

☆**wam·pum** (wäm′pəm) *n.* [< Algonquian] **1.** small beads made of shells and used by N. American Indians as money, for ornament, etc. **2.** [Slang] money

wan (wän, wôn) *adj.* **wan′ner, wan′nest** [OE. *wann,* dark] **1.** sickly pale; pallid [a *wan* complexion] **2.** weak, as when one is sick, sad, or tired [a *wan* smile] —see SYN. at PALE[1] —**wan′ly** *adv.* —**wan′ness** *n.*

wand (wänd, wônd) *n.* [ON. *vondr*] **1.** a thin, easily bent switch, as of a young tree **2.** a rod carried as a symbol of authority; scepter **3.** any rod of supposed magic power

wan·der (wän′dər, wôn′-) *vi.* [OE. *wandrian*] **1.** to move or go about aimlessly; ramble; roam [to *wander* about a city] **2.** to go to a place in a casual or indirect way; stroll [to *wander* into a room] **3.** *a)* to stray (*from* a path, course, etc.) *b)* to stray from home, friends, etc. (often with *off*) **4.** to go astray in mind or purpose; specif., *a)* to drift away from a subject, as in discussion *b)* to be disordered, rambling, etc. [his thoughts *wandered*] **5.** to take a winding course, as a river **6.** to move idly from one object to another: said of the eyes, etc. —*vt.* to roam through, in, or over [to *wander* the world] —**wan′der·er** *n.* —**wan′der·ing** *adj., n.* —**wan′der·ing·ly** *adv.*

wan·der·lust (-lust′) *n.* [G.] a strong feeling of wanting to wander or travel

wane (wān) *vi.* **waned, wan′ing** [OE. *wanian*] **1.** to seem to grow gradually smaller: said of the moon in the phases after it has become full **2.** to become less intense, bright, strong, etc.; weaken [his interest in sports *waned*] **3.** to lessen in power, importance, etc. **4.** to approach the end [the day *wanes*] —*n.* **1.** the act of waning **2.** a period of waning —**on the wane** getting smaller, weaker, etc.; waning

SYN.—**wane** implies a fading or weakening of that which has reached a high point of force, greatness, etc. [the actor's fame *waned* as he grew older]; **abate** suggests a continued lessening in degree, force, etc. [the fever is *abating*]; **ebb,** applied specifically to a changing force, refers to one of the periods of going back or down [their *ebbing* fortunes]; **subside** suggests a quieting or lessening of violent activity or feeling [her anger had *subsided*] —ANT. **wax, increase, revive**

wan·gle (waŋ′g'l) *vt.* **-gled, -gling** [altered < ? WAGGLE] [Colloq.] **1.** to get or bring about by sly or tricky means, clever dealing, etc. [he *wangled* some passes to the theater] **2.** to falsify or manipulate for a selfish or dishonest purpose —*vi.* [Colloq.] to make use of tricky and indirect methods to achieve one's aims —**wan′gler** *n.*

Wan·kel engine (väŋ′k'l, waŋ′-) [after F. *Wankel* (1902–), G. engineer] a rotary internal-combustion engine having a spinning piston and relatively few parts

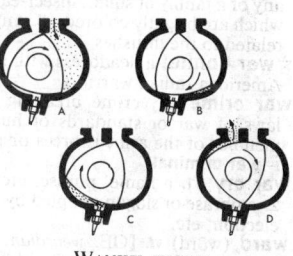

WANKEL ENGINE
(A, intake; B, compression; C, ignition; D, exhaust)

want (wänt, wônt) *vt.* [ON. *vanta*] **1.** to have too little of; lack [he *wants* kindness] **2.** to be short by (a specified amount) [it *wants* two minutes of noon] **3.** to feel that one would like to have, do, get, etc.; wish or long for; desire [do you *want* soup? I *want* to visit Paris] **4.** *a)* to wish to see or speak with (someone) [*wanted* on the phone] *b)* to wish to capture, as for arrest [*wanted* by the police] **5.** [Chiefly Brit.] to require; need [this matter *wants* attention] *Want* is also used colloquially with the meaning *ought* or *should* [you *want* to be careful] —*vi.* **1.** to have a need or lack [to *want* for money] **2.** to be needy or very poor ["waste not, *want* not"] —*n.* **1.** a scarcity; shortage; lack [to starve for *want* of food] **2.** a being needy or very poor [a family in *want*] **3.** a wish for something; craving **4.** something needed; need —see SYN. at DESIRE and LACK and POVERTY —**want′er** *n.*

☆**want ad** [Colloq.] a classified advertisement, as in a newspaper, stating that one wants a job, an apartment, an employee, etc.

want·ing (wän′tiŋ, wôn′-) *adj.* **1.** absent; lacking [a coat with buttons *wanting*] **2.** not up to some standard [weighed and found *wanting*] —*prep.* **1.** lacking (something); without [a watch *wanting* a minute hand] **2.** minus; less [a year, *wanting* one week] —**wanting in** having not enough of (some quality, etc.)

wan·ton (wän′t'n, wôn′-) *adj.* [< OE. < *wan,* lacking + *togen,* pp. of *teon,* to bring up] **1.** orig., not disciplined [*wanton* boys] **2.** sexually loose or unrestrained [a *wanton* woman] **3.** [Poet.] frisky, playful, lively, capricious, etc. [*wanton* winds] **4.** without reason, sense, or mercy [*wanton* cruelty] **5.** recklessly ignoring justice, decency, morality, etc. [*wanton* disregard of human rights] **6.** [Now Rare] luxuriant or extravagant —*n.* a wanton person or thing; esp., a sexually promiscuous woman —*vi.* to be wanton —**wan′ton·ly** *adv.* —**wan′ton·ness** *n.*

☆**wap·i·ti** (wäp′ə tē) *n., pl.* **-tis, -ti:** see PLURAL, II, D, 1 [< Algonquian] the American elk, the largest N. American deer, with large, branching antlers and a short tail

war (wôr) *n.* [ONormFr. *werre,* strife < Frank.] **1.** open armed conflict between countries or between groups within the same country **2.** any fight or struggle [the *war* against disease] **3.** military operations as a science —*adj.* of, used in, or resulting from war —*vi.* **warred, war′ring 1.** to carry on war **2.** to struggle; strive —**at war** in a state of active armed conflict —**declare war (on) 1.** to make a formal declaration of being at war (with) **2.** to announce one's hostility (to) —**go to war 1.** to enter into a war **2.** to join the armed forces during a war

WAPITI
(54–60 in. high at shoulder)

War between the States the U.S. Civil War (1861–65): term used generally in the South

war·ble[1] (wôr′b'l) *vt.* **-bled, -bling** [ONormFr. *werbler* < Frank.] **1.** to sing (notes, etc.) with trills, quavers, runs, etc., as a bird **2.** to express in song —*vi.* **1.** to sing in a melodious way, with trills, etc. **2.** to make a musical sound; babble, as a stream ☆**3.** same as YODEL —*n.* **1.** an act of warbling **2.** a warbling sound; trill

war·ble[2] (wôr′b'l) *n.* [prob. < Scand.] a swelling under the hide of an animal, caused by the larva of the warble fly or botfly

warble fly any of a group of two-winged flies whose larvae burrow beneath the hides of cattle, horses, etc., producing warbles

fat, āpe, cär; ten, ēven; is, bīte; gō, hôrn, tōōl, lôôk; oil, out; up, fur; get; joy; yet; chin; she; thin, then; zh, leisure; ŋ, ring; ə for *a* in *ago, e* in *agent, i* in *sanity, o* in *comply, u* in *focus;* ′ as in *able* (ā′b'l); Fr. bal; ë, Fr. coeur; ö, Fr. feu; ô, Fr. coq; ü, Fr. duc; r, Fr. cri; H, G. ich; kh, G. doch; ‡ foreign; ☆ Americanism; < derived from. See inside front cover.

war·bler (wôr′blər) *n.* **1.** a bird or person that warbles ☆**2.** any of a family of small, insect-eating, new-world birds, many of which are brightly colored **3.** any of a family of small songbirds related to the thrushes

☆**war bonnet** a headdress with long feathers, worn by some N. American Indian warriors

war crime any crime breaking international law or accepted laws of war or standards of humane behavior, done as by a member of the armed forces or government of a nation at war —**war criminal**

war cry 1. a name, phrase, etc. shouted in a charge or battle **2.** a phrase or slogan adopted by a party in any struggle, contest, election, etc.

ward (wôrd) *vt.* [OE. *weardian*, to protect, guard] **1.** to turn aside; fend off [to *ward* off a blow, a disaster, etc.] **2.** [Rare] to guard —*n.* **1.** a guarding: now only in *watch and ward* **2.** a being under guard **3.** *a*) a child or person not able to manage his own affairs who is placed under the care of a guardian or court *b*) any person under another's care **4.** each of the divisions of a jail or prison **5.** a division of a hospital [a maternity *ward*] **6.** a division of a city or town, for purposes of administration, voting, etc. **7.** a means of defense **8.** a defensive position, as in fencing **9.** *a*) a ridge in a lock that allows only the right key to enter *b*) the notch in a key that fits this ridge

-ward (wərd) [< OE. -*weard* < base of *weorthan*, to become] *a suffix meaning* in a (specified) direction or course [*backward*]

Ward (wôrd), **Ar·te·mus** (är′ti məs) (pseud. of *Charles Farrar Browne*) 1834–67; U.S. humorist

☆**war dance** a ceremonial dance performed as by some American Indian tribes before battle or after victory

war·den (wôr′d'n) *n.* [< ONormFr. < OFr. *gardein*] **1.** a person who guards, or has charge of, something; keeper [a game *warden*] **2.** the chief official of a prison **3.** in England, a governing officer in certain hospitals, colleges, etc. **4.** in Connecticut, the chief executive of a borough **5.** *same as* CHURCHWARDEN —**war′den·ship′** *n.*

ward·er (wôr′dər) *n.* **1.** a watchman **2.** a person who guards an entrance **3.** [Chiefly Brit.] a warden in a jail

☆**ward heeler** a person who works in a ward for a political party or boss, as in getting votes: a term showing contempt

ward·robe (wôrd′rōb′) *n.* **1.** a closet or tall cabinet with hangers for holding clothes **2.** a room where clothes are kept, as a room in a theater for costumes **3.** one's supply of clothes [a spring *wardrobe*]

ward·room (wôrd′rōōm′) *n.* in a warship, a compartment used for eating and relaxing by commissioned officers, except, usually, the captain

-wards (wərdz) *same as* -WARD

ward·ship (wôrd′ship′) *n.* **1.** guardianship; custody, as of a minor **2.** the condition of being a ward

ware (wer) *n.* [OE. *waru*] **1.** anything that a merchant, peddler, etc. has to sell: *usually used in pl.* [the *wares* of a store] **2.** a specified kind of merchandise or manufactured thing: used in compounds [*hardware*, *glassware*] **3.** pottery or a specified kind of pottery

ware·house (wer′hous′; *for v.*, *usually* -houz′) *n.* a building where wares, or goods, are stored —*vt.* **-housed′**, **-hous′ing** to store in a warehouse —**ware′house′man** (-mən) *n., pl.* **-men**

war·fare (wôr′fer′) *n.* **1.** the action of waging war; armed struggle **2.** fighting or conflict of any kind

☆**war·far·in** (wôr′fə rin) *n.* [W(isconsin) A(lumni) R(esearch) F(oundation) + (coum)arin, a chemical] a crystalline powder used as a rat poison and, in medicine, to prevent the clotting of blood

war game 1. training in military tactics in which maps and small figures are used to represent ground, troops, etc. **2.** [*pl.*] practice maneuvers for military forces

☆**war hawk** *same as* HAWK[1] (*n.* 2)

war·head (wôr′hed′) *n.* the forward section of a self-propelled missile, etc. containing the explosive charge

war horse 1. a horse used in battle **2.** [Colloq.] a person who has taken part in many struggles **3.** [Colloq.] a symphony, play, opera, etc. performed so often as to seem stale and trite For 2 & 3 now usually **war′horse′** *n.*

war·i·ly (wer′ə lē) *adv.* in a wary manner; cautiously

war·i·ness (-ē nis) *n.* the quality or state of being wary

war·like (wôr′līk′) *adj.* **1.** fit for, fond of, or ready for war; bellicose [*warlike* generals] **2.** of or suitable to war [a *warlike* expedition] **3.** threatening war [a *warlike* editorial]

war·lock (wôr′läk′) *n.* [OE. *wǣrloga*, a traitor, liar] a sorcerer or wizard; a male witch

war·lord (wôr′lôrd′) *n.* **1.** a high military officer in a warlike nation **2.** a local ruler or leader with a military following, as formerly in China

warm (wôrm) *adj.* [OE. *wearm* < IE. *gwher-*, hot] **1.** *a*) having or giving off a little heat [a *warm* iron] *b*) giving off pleasurable heat [a *warm* fire] *c*) hot [a *warm* night] **2.** *a*) overheated, as with exercise *b*) such as to make one heated [*warm* work] **3.** effective in keeping body heat in [*warm* clothing] **4.** marked by lively disagreement, as an argument **5.** hearty; ardent; enthusiastic [*warm* encouragement] **6.** *a*) friendly or sincere [a *warm* welcome, *warm* thanks] *b*) sympathetic or loving [a *warm* heart] **7.** suggesting warmth [yellow, orange, and red are *warm* colors] **8.** newly made; fresh, as a scent or trail **9.** [Colloq.] close to discovering something **10.** [Colloq.] disagreeable; uncomfortable [we'll make it *warm* for him] —*adv.* so as to be warm —*vt., vi.* **1.** to make or become warm [*warm* yourself by the fire] **2.** to make or become interested, pleased, friendly, etc. [your kind words *warmed* my heart; she *warmed* to him after only a few meetings] —**warm up 1.** *a*) to make or become warm *b*) to make or become warm enough to work efficiently [to *warm up* an engine] **2.** to reheat (cooked food, etc.): also **warm over 3.** to practice or exercise before a game, contest, performance, etc. —**warm′er** *n.* —**warm′ish** *adj.* —**warm′ly** *adv.* —**warm′ness** *n.*

warm·blood·ed (wôrm′blud′id) *adj.* **1.** having a body heat that stays the same, independent of and usually warmer than that of the surroundings, as mammals and birds **2.** having warmth of feeling; ardent —**warm′blood′ed·ness** *n.*

☆**warmed-o·ver** (wôrmd′ō′vər) *adj.* **1.** reheated [*warmed-over* hash] **2.** presented again, without significant change [*warmed-over* ideas]

warm front *Meteorol.* the forward edge of an advancing mass of warm air replacing colder air

warm·heart·ed (wôrm′här′tid) *adj.* kind, sympathetic, friendly, etc. —**warm′heart′ed·ly** *adv.* —**warm′heart′ed·ness** *n.*

warming pan a long-handled, covered pan for holding live coals: formerly used to warm beds

war·mon·ger (wôr′muŋ′gər, -mäŋ′-) *n.* a person or agency that is in favor of war or tries to bring about a war —**war′mon′ger·ing** *adj., n.*

warmth (wôrmth) *n.* **1.** *a*) the state or quality of being warm *b*) mild heat **2.** *a*) excitement or strong feeling; enthusiasm or ardor *b*) friendly or affectionate feelings or nature *c*) slight anger **3.** a warm effect gotten by using red, yellow, or orange

WARMING PAN

☆**warm-up** (wôrm′up′) *n.* the act or an instance of practicing or exercising before a game, contest, performance, etc.

warn (wôrn) *vt.* [OE. *wearnian*] **1.** to tell (a person) of a danger, coming evil, etc. **2.** to advise to be careful about certain acts [*warned* against littering the park] **3.** to let know in advance [signaling to *warn* us that he would turn] **4.** to give notice to (a person) to stay or keep (*off*, *away*, etc.) —*vi.* to give warning —**warn′er** *n.*

warn·ing (wôr′niŋ) *n.* **1.** the act of one that warns, or the state of being warned **2.** something that warns [pain in the body is a *warning* of trouble] —*adj.* that warns —**warn′ing·ly** *adv.*

War of American Independence *Brit. name for* AMERICAN REVOLUTION

War of 1812 a war (1812–15) between the U.S. and Great Britain

warp (wôrp) *n.* [OE. *wearp*, the base of *weorpan*, to throw] **1.** *a*) a twist or bend in wood *b*) any similar distortion **2.** a mental twist, quirk, bias, etc. **3.** a rope run from a ship to a dock, etc., used to pull the vessel into position **4.** *a*) *Weaving* the threads running lengthwise in the loom and crossed by the weft or woof *b*) foundation; base —*vt.* **1.** to bend or twist out of shape [rain and heat had *warped* the boards] **2.** to turn from what is right, natural, etc.; distort [a *warped* mind] **3.** to move (a ship) by pulling on a line fastened to a dock, etc. —*vi.* **1.** to become bent or twisted out of shape **2.** to turn aside from the natural or right course —**warp′er** *n.*

☆**war paint 1.** coloring matter applied to the face and body, as by some American Indian tribes, in preparation for war **2.** [Slang] *a*) ceremonial dress *b*) women's cosmetics

☆**war·path** (wôr′path′) *n.* the path taken by American Indians on a warlike expedition —**on the warpath 1.** at war, ready for war, etc. **2.** angry; ready to fight

war·plane (wôr′plān′) *n.* any airplane for use in war

war·rant (wôr′ənt, wär′-) *n.* [< ONormFr. (OFr. *garant*), a warrant < Frank.] **1.** *a)* authorization, as by the law *b)* a good reason for some act, belief, etc.; justification **2.** something that guarantees some event or result **3.** a written paper that gives the right to do something; specif., *a)* authorization for the payment or receipt of money *b) Law* a writ authorizing an officer to make an arrest, seizure, search, etc. *c) Mil.* the certificate of appointment to the grade of warrant officer —*vt.* **1.** *a)* to give (someone) authorization to do something *b)* to authorize the doing of something **2.** to be a good reason for (an act, belief, etc.); justify [his mistake does not *warrant* strong criticism] **3.** *a)* to guarantee the quality, quantity, etc. of (goods) to a purchaser *b)* to guarantee to (the purchaser) that goods sold are as described **4.** [Colloq.] to state with confidence [I *warrant* he'll be late] —**war′rant·a·ble** *adj.*

war·ran·tee (wôr′ən tē′, wär′-) *n. Law* a person to whom a warranty is given

warrant officer an officer of the U.S. armed forces ranking above an enlisted man but below a commissioned officer and holding his office on a warrant instead of a commission

war·ran·tor (wôr′ən tôr′, wär′-; -tər) *n. Law* a person who warrants, or gives warranty: also **war′rant·er** (-tər)

war·ran·ty (-tē) *n., pl.* **-ties** [see WARRANT] **1.** official authorization **2.** a good reason, as for an opinion or action **3.** *Law* a guarantee; specif., *a)* a guarantee of something in a contract, as to a purchaser that goods sold him are as described or will be repaired or replaced if found faulty within a specified time *b)* an agreement by which the seller of real estate guarantees the security of the title

War·ren[1] (wôr′ən, wär′-) **1.** [< ONormFr. < ? OHG. *Warin,* name of a people mentioned by Tacitus] a masculine name **2. Earl,** 1891–1974; U.S. jurist; chief justice of the U.S. (1953–69)

War·ren[2] (wôr′ən, wär′-) **1.** [after Dr. J. *Warren* (1741–75)] city in SE Mich.: suburb of Detroit: pop. 179,000 **2.** [after M. *Warren,* 19th-cent. U.S. surveyor] city in NE Ohio: pop. 63,000: see YOUNGSTOWN

war·ren (wôr′ən, wär′-) *n.* [< ONormFr. < OFr. *warir,* to preserve < Frank.] **1.** a space or limited area in which rabbits breed or are numerous **2.** any building or buildings crowded like a rabbit warren

war·ri·or (wôr′ē ər, wôr′yər; wär′-) *n.* [< ONormFr. < *werrier,* to make war < *werre,* WAR] a man experienced in fighting or war; soldier

War·saw (wôr′sô) capital of Poland, on the Vistula River: pop. 1,284,000

war·ship (wôr′ship′) *n.* any ship for use in war, as a battleship, destroyer, etc.

wart (wôrt) *n.* [OE. *wearte*] **1.** a small, usually hard growth on the skin, caused by a virus **2.** a small growth on a plant — **wart′y** *adj.* **wart′i·er, wart′i·est**

War·ta (vär′tä) river in Poland, flowing from the S part northwest into the Oder: 502 mi.

wart hog a wild African hog with large, curved tusks, and a number of warts below the eyes

war·time (wôr′tīm′) *n.* a time of war —*adj.* of or in such a time

☆**war whoop** a loud shout or yell uttered, as by N. American Indians, on going into battle, etc.

War·wick (wôr′wik) [after an Earl of *Warwick* (England), friend of the founder] city on the SE coast of R.I.: suburb of Providence: pop. 84,000

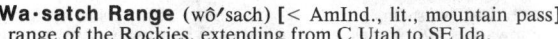

WART HOG
(2–2½ ft. high at shoulder)

War·wick (wôr′ik, wär′-), **Earl** of, (*Richard Neville*) 1428–71; Eng. statesman & military leader

war·y (wer′ē) *adj.* **war′i·er, war′i·est** [< archaic adj. *ware,* watchful + -Y²] **1.** cautious; on one's guard [a *wary* patrol] **2.** showing caution [a *wary* look] —**wary of** careful of

was (wuz, wäz; *unstressed* wəz) [OE. *wæs*] *the first and third person singular in the past tense of* BE

Wa·satch Range (wô′sach) [< AmInd., lit., mountain pass] range of the Rockies, extending from C Utah to SE Ida.

wash (wôsh, wäsh) *vt.* [OE. *wæscan*] **1.** to clean by means of water or other liquid, often with soap, etc. [to *wash* one's hands, a car, etc.] **2.** to make clean in a religious or moral sense; purify [*washed* of all guilt] **3.** to wet, moisten, or drench [rain *washed* the streets] **4.** to cleanse by licking, as a cat does **5.** to flow over, past, or against: said of a sea, waves, etc. **6.** to soak (*out*), flush (*off*), or carry (*away*) by the action of water [to *wash* out dirt; a bridge *washed* away by the flood] **7.** *a)* to make by flowing over and wearing away substance [rain *washed* gullies in the bank] *b)* to cut into or erode [the flood *washed* out the road] **8.** to be a cleansing agent for [soap that will *wash* silks] **9.** to cover with a thin coating of paint or metal [silverware *washed* with gold] **10.** *Chem.* to pass (a gas) over or through a liquid in order to remove soluble matter **11.** *Mining* to pass water through or over (earth, etc.) in order to separate (ore, precious stones, etc.) —*vi.* **1.** to wash oneself or one's hands, face, etc. (often with *up*) **2.** to wash clothes **3.** to undergo washing, esp. without fading, etc. [good muslin *washes* well] **4.** to be removed by washing [the stain *washed* out] **5.** to be worn or carried away by the action of water [the bridge *washed* out] **6.** to sweep, beat, or flow (*over, against, along, up,* etc.) as in waves [a feeling of tenderness *washed* over him] **7.** [Brit. Colloq.] to withstand a test [his story won't *wash*] —*n.* **1.** *a)* the act or an instance of washing ☆*b)* a place where something is washed [an auto *wash*] **2.** a quantity of clothes, etc. washed, or to be washed [to hang out the *wash*] **3.** watery garbage, as for feeding hogs; swill; hogwash **4.** *a)* the rush or flow of water or waves *b)* the sound of this *c)* the eddy of water caused by a propeller, oars, etc. *d)* a disturbed eddy of air left behind a moving airplane, propeller, etc.; slipstream **5.** wear or erosion caused by the action of water **6.** silt, mud, etc. carried and dropped by running water **7.** earth from which metals, ores, etc. may be washed **8.** *a)* low ground which is flooded part of the time and partly dry the rest *b)* a bog; marsh ☆**9.** in the western U.S., the bed of a stream when it runs dry **10.** a thin coating of paint or metal **11.** any of various liquids for cosmetic or medicinal use [mouthwash] **12.** weak liquor or liquid food ☆**13.** [Colloq.] water, beer, etc. drunk after strong liquor; chaser —*adj.* that can be washed without damage [a *wash* dress] — **come out in the wash** [Slang] to be revealed or explained sooner or later —**wash down 1.** to clean by washing **2.** to follow (food, a drink of whiskey, etc.) with a drink, as of water —**wash out** ☆[Slang] to drop or be dropped from a course, esp. in military aviation, because of failure

Wash. Washington (State)

wash·a·ble (wôsh′ə b'l, wäsh′-) *adj.* that can be washed without damage —☆*n.* a washable fabric or garment

☆**wash-and-wear** (-'n wer′) *adj.* designating or of fabrics or garments that need little or no ironing after washing

wash·board (-bôrd′) *n.* ☆a board or frame with a ridged surface of metal, glass, etc. used for scrubbing dirt out of clothes

wash·bowl (-bōl′) *n.* ☆a bowl or basin for use in washing one's hands and face, etc., esp. a bathroom fixture fitted with water faucets and a drain: also **wash′ba·sin** (-bā′s'n)

☆**wash·cloth** (-klôth′) *n.* a small cloth, usually of terry, used in washing the face or body

wash·day (-dā′) *n.* a day when the clothes and linens of a household are washed

washed-out (wôsht′out′, wäsht′-) *adj.* **1.** faded in color, specif. from washing **2.** [Colloq.] tired; spiritless **3.** [Colloq.] tired-looking; pale and wan

washed-up (-up′) *adj.* **1.** cleaned up **2.** [Colloq.] tired; exhausted ☆**3.** [Slang] finished; done for; having failed

wash·er (wôsh′ər, wäsh′-) *n.* **1.** a person who washes **2.** a flat disk or ring of metal, rubber, etc., used to make a seat for the head of a bolt or for a nut or faucet valve, to lock a nut in place, to provide packing, etc. **3.** a machine for washing something

WASHER

wash·er·wom·an (-woom′ən) *n., pl.* **-wom′en** a woman whose work is washing clothes, etc. —**wash′er·man** (-mən) *n.masc., pl.* **-men**

wash goods washable fabrics or garments

wash·ing (wôsh′iŋ, wäsh′-) *n.* **1.** the act of a person or thing that washes **2.** clothes, etc. washed or to be washed, esp. at one time **3.** matter obtained or removed by washing **4.** a thin coating, as of metal, put on in liquid form

washing machine a machine for washing clothes, linens, etc., now usually one working automatically; washer

washing soda sodium carbonate in the form of crystals, used in washing clothes, etc.

Wash·ing·ton (wôsh′iŋ tən, wäsh′-) [after G. WASHINGTON] **1.** NW coastal State of the U.S.: 68,192 sq. mi.; pop. 3,409,000; cap. Olympia: abbrev. **Wash., WA 2.** capital of the U.S., occupying the same area as the District of Columbia: pop. 757,000 (met. area, including parts of Md. & Va., 2,861,000) —**Wash·ing·to′ni·an** (-tō′nē ən) *adj., n.*

Wash·ing·ton (wôsh′iŋ tən, wäsh′-) **1. Book·er T**(aliaferro) (book′ər), 1856-1915; U.S. Negro educator & author **2. George,** 1732-99; 1st president of the U.S. (1789-97); commander in chief of the Continental army

Washington (National) Monument white marble obelisk in Washington, D.C., on a mall west of the Capitol, in memory of George Washington: 555 ft. high

Washington's Birthday February 22, George Washington's birthday: it is celebrated as a legal holiday in most States on the third Monday in February

wash·out (wôsh′out′, wäsh′-) *n.* ☆**1.** the washing away of soil, rocks, etc. by a sudden, strong flow of water ☆**2.** a hole made by such washing away, as in a road **3.** [Slang] a complete failure

☆**wash·rag** (-rag′) *n. same as* WASHCLOTH

☆**wash·room** (-rōōm′) *n.* **1.** a room for washing **2.** *same as* RESTROOM

wash·stand (-stand′) *n.* **1.** a table holding a bowl and pitcher, etc. for washing the face and hands **2.** a washbowl that is a bathroom fixture

wash·tub (-tub′) *n.* a tub for washing clothes, etc.; often, a metal tub fixed in place with water faucets and a drain

wash·wom·an (-woom′ən) *n., pl.* **-wom′en** *same as* WASHERWOMAN

wash·y (-ē) *adj.* **wash′i·er, wash′i·est 1.** watery; weak **2.** weak in color; pale **3.** without force or substance; insipid

was·n't (wuz′′nt, wäz′-) was not

☆**WASP, Wasp** (wäsp, wôsp) *n.* a white Anglo-Saxon Protestant

wasp (wäsp, wôsp) *n.* [OE. *wæsp*] any of a large, worldwide group of winged insects with a narrow body, biting mouthparts, and, in the females and workers, a sharp sting — **wasp′like′** *adj.* —**wasp′y** *adj.* **wasp′i·er, wasp′i·est**

wasp·ish (wäs′pish, wôs′-) *adj.* **1.** of or like a wasp **2.** having a narrow waist **3.** bad-tempered; snappish — **wasp′ish·ly** *adv.* —**wasp′ish·ness** *n.*

wasp waist a very narrow or tightly corseted waist

was·sail (wäs′′l, was′-; -āl) *n.* [< ON. *ves heill,* lit., be hearty] **1.** a toast formerly given in drinking to a person's health **2.** the spiced ale or other liquor drunk when making this toast **3.** a party with much drinking, esp. at Christmas time —*vi., vt.* to drink a wassail (to) —**was′sail·er** *n.*

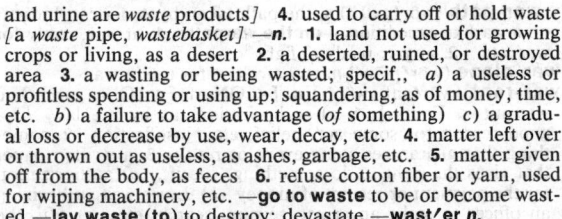

WASP
(1/2–3 in. long)

Was·ser·mann test (wäs′ər mən) [after A. von *Wassermann* (1866-1925), G. bacteriologist] a blood test for syphilis

wast (wäst; *unstressed* wəst) *archaic second person singular in the past tense of* BE: *used with* thou

wast·age (wās′tij) *n.* **1.** loss by use, spoiling, etc. **2.** the process of wasting **3.** anything wasted, or the amount of this

waste (wäst) *vt.* **wast′ed, wast′ing** [ONormFr. *waster* < L. *vastare,* to lay waste] **1.** to destroy or ruin [locusts *wasted* the fields] **2.** to wear away; use up [soil *wasted* by erosion] **3.** to make weak or feeble [a man *wasted* by age and disease] **4.** to use up or spend without need, gain, or purpose; squander [he *wastes* money and time] **5.** to fail to take advantage of [to *waste* an opportunity] ☆**6.** [Mil. Slang] to kill —*vi.* **1.** to lose strength, health, flesh, etc., as by disease [in her old age, she *wasted* away] **2.** to be used up or worn down gradually —*adj.* **1.** not used or usable for growing crops or living, as a desert; wild; barren; desolate **2.** left over; no longer of use [*waste* paper] **3.** given off from the bowels, kidneys, etc. [feces

and urine are *waste* products] **4.** used to carry off or hold waste [a *waste* pipe, *wastebasket*] —*n.* **1.** land not used for growing crops or living, as a desert **2.** a deserted, ruined, or destroyed area **3.** a wasting or being wasted; specif., *a)* a useless or profitless spending or using up; squandering, as of money, time, etc. *b)* a failure to take advantage (*of* something) *c)* a gradual loss or decrease by use, wear, decay, etc. **4.** matter left over or thrown out as useless, as ashes, garbage, etc. **5.** matter given off from the body, as feces **6.** refuse cotton fiber or yarn, used for wiping machinery, etc. —**go to waste** to be or become wasted —**lay waste (to)** to destroy; devastate —**wast′er** *n.*

SYN.—**waste** is the general word for any stretch of land which cannot be used to grow crops or to live on; a **desert** is an empty, dry, usually sandy area of land; **wilderness** refers to an uninhabited area in which a lack of paths or trails makes it difficult to find one's way, specif. an area thickly covered with trees and underbrush

waste·bas·ket (wāst′bas′kit) *n.* a basket or other open container for wastepaper, bits of trash, etc.: also **wastepaper basket**

waste·ful (-fəl) *adj.* using more than is necessary; squandering; extravagant [a *wasteful* person, *wasteful* practices] —**waste′ful·ly** *adv.* —**waste′ful·ness** *n.*

waste·land (-land′) *n.* land that is barren, empty, ruined, etc.

waste·pa·per (-pā′pər) *n.* paper thrown away after use or as useless: also **waste paper**

wast·ing (wās′tiŋ) *adj.* **1.** that can ruin or destroy [a *wasting* war] **2.** that can injure health, as a disease —**wast′ing·ly** *adv.*

wast·rel (wās′trəl) *n.* **1.** a person who wastes; esp., a spendthrift **2.** a good-for-nothing

watch (wäch, wôch) *n.* [OE. *wæcce* < base of *wacian,* to be awake] **1.** the act or fact of keeping awake, esp. in order to protect or guard **2.** *a)* close observation for a time, as to find out something *b)* alert, careful guarding [the dog keeps *watch* over the house] **3.** a person or group on duty to protect or guard **4.** [*pl.*] hours (of the night): only in the phrase **watches of the night 5.** the period of duty of a guard **6.** a small timepiece carried in the pocket, worn on the wrist, etc. **7.** *a)* any of the periods of duty (usually four hours) into which the day is divided on shipboard *b)* the part of the ship's crew on duty during any such period —*vi.* **1.** to stay awake at night; keep vigil, as in tending a sick person **2.** to be on the alert; keep guard **3.** to look; observe **4.** to be looking or waiting attentively (with *for*) [*watch* for your chance] —*vt.* **1.** to guard **2.** to observe carefully; keep one's eyes on [to *watch* the setting sun] **3.** to keep informed about [I've *watched* his career with interest] **4.** to wait for and look for [to *watch* one's chance] **5.** to keep watch over; tend (a flock, baby, etc.) —**on the watch** watching; on the lookout —☆**watch oneself** to be careful or cautious —☆**watch out** to be alert and on one's guard —**watch over** to protect from harm —**watch′er** *n.*

☆**watch·band** (wäch′band′, wôch′-) *n.* a band of leather, metal, cloth, etc. for holding a watch on the wrist

watch·case (-kās′) *n.* the metal case, or outer covering, of a watch

watch·dog (-dôg′, -däg′) *n.* **1.** a dog kept to guard property **2.** a person or group that keeps watch to prevent waste, dishonest practices, etc.

watch fire a fire kept burning at night as a signal or for the use of those staying awake to guard

watch·ful (-fəl) *adj.* watching closely; alert [a *watchful* guard] —**watch′ful·ly** *adv.* —**watch′ful·ness** *n.*

SYN.—**watchful** is the general word implying a paying careful attention and being ready to protect against danger or seize an opportunity [under the *watchful* eye of the Secret Service]; **vigilant** implies an active, sharp watchfulness that must go on without a letup [a *vigilant* sentry]; **alert** implies a quickness of mind and a readiness to take fast action [*alert* to the danger before them]; **wide-awake** implies an alertness to opportunities rather than to dangers and suggests an awareness of all the surrounding circumstances [a *wide-awake* young salesman]

watch·mak·er (-mā′kər) *n.* a person who makes or repairs watches —**watch′mak′ing** *n.*

watch·man (-mən) *n., pl.* **-men** a person hired to watch or guard, esp. at night

watch night a religious service held on New Year's Eve: also **watch meeting** or **watch-night service**

watch pocket a small pocket, usually in a vest or trousers, for carrying a watch

watch·tow·er (-tou′ər) *n.* a high tower from which a sentinel watches for enemies, forest fires, etc.; lookout

watch·word (-wurd′) *n.* **1.** a secret word that must be spoken to a guard in order to pass; password **2.** a slogan; esp., the slogan or cry of a group or party

wa·ter (wôt′ər, wät′-) *n.* [OE. *wæter* < IE. base *wed-*, water, wet] **1.** the colorless, transparent liquid that forms springs, rivers, lakes, oceans, etc., and falls as rain: a compound of hydrogen and oxygen, H_2O, it freezes at 32°F (0°C) and boils at 212°F (100°C) **2.** [*often pl.*] a large body of water, as a river, lake, sea, etc. **3.** water with reference to its depth, its surface, its level, etc. [*ten feet of water*, under *water*, high *water*] **4.** [*pl.*] the water of mineral springs **5.** any body fluid or secretion, as urine, saliva, tears, etc. **6.** a solution of any substance, often a gas, in water [*ammonia water*] **7.** *a)* the degree of clearness and brightness of a precious stone [a diamond of the first *water*] *b)* degree of quality or trueness to type [an artist of the first *water*] **8.** a wavy, shiny finish given to linen, silk, etc., or to a metal surface **9.** *Finance* an illegal issue of watered stock —*vt.* **1.** to supply with water; specif., *a)* to give (animals) water to drink *b)* to give water to (soil, crops, etc.), as by sprinkling, irrigating, etc. *c)* to soak or moisten with water (often with *down*) *d)* to make weaker by adding water [to *water* the milk] **2.** to give a wavy, shiny look to the finish of (silk, etc.) **3.** *Finance* to add illegally to the total face value of (stock) without increasing assets to justify this —*vi.* **1.** to fill with tears: said of the eyes **2.** to secrete or fill with saliva [his mouth *watered*] **3.** to take on a supply of water **4.** to drink water: said of animals —*adj.* **1.** of or for water [*water* pipes] **2.** in or on water [*water* sports] **3.** growing in or living on or near water [*water* plants, *water* birds] **4.** *a)* worked by water [a *water* wheel] *b)* created by running water [*water* power] —**by water** by ship or boat —**hold water** to remain or prove sound, logical, etc. [the argument won't *hold water*] —**like water** too freely: said of money spent, etc. —**make one's mouth water** to create a desire or appetite in one —**make** (or **pass**) **water** to urinate —**water down** to weaken the power or effectiveness of —**wa′ter·er** *n.* —**wa′ter·less** *adj.*

Water Bearer *same as* AQUARIUS

☆**water bed** a bed consisting of a plastic bag filled with water and held in a frame, often with an attached heating element: also **wa′ter·bed′** *n.*

water beetle any of various beetles that live in freshwater ponds and streams

water bird a swimming or wading bird

water boatman any of various water bugs that swim about by movement of their fringed, oarlike hind legs

wa·ter·borne (-bôrn′) *adj.* floating on or carried by water

wa·ter·buck (-buk′) *n.,* *pl.* **-buck′**, **-bucks′**: see PLURAL, II, D, 2 an African antelope having curved horns, found near rivers and streams

water buffalo a slow, powerful, oxlike animal of S Asia, Malaya, and the Philippine Islands, used for pulling loads

water bug 1. any of various insects that live on or near water ☆**2.** loosely, *same as* COCKROACH

Wa·ter·bur·y (wôt′ər ber′ē, wät′-) [from the many streams there] city in WC Conn.: pop. 108,000

water chestnut ☆**1.** a Chinese sedge, growing in clumps in water ☆**2.** its button-shaped tuber, used in cooking

WATERBUCK
(2½–4 ft. high at shoulder)

water clock a mechanism for measuring time by the fall or flow of water; clepsydra

water closet *same as* TOILET (*n.* 4)

wa·ter·col·or (-kul′ər) *n.* **1.** coloring matter mixed with water for use as a paint **2.** a painting done with such paints **3.** the art of painting with watercolors —*adj.* painted with watercolors —**wa′ter·col′or·ist** *n.*

wa·ter·cooled (-kōōld′) *adj.* kept from overheating by having water passed around or through it, as in pipes or a water jacket [a *water-cooled* engine] —**wa′ter·cool′** *vt.*

☆**water cooler** a device for cooling water, esp. by refrigeration, for drinking

wa·ter·course (-kôrs′) *n.* **1.** a stream of water; river, brook, etc. **2.** a channel for water, as a canal or stream bed

wa·ter·craft (-kraft′) *n.* **1.** skill in water sports, boating, etc. **2.** *pl.* **-craft′** a boat, ship, or other water vehicle

wa·ter·cress (-kres′) *n.* a plant of the mustard family, growing generally in running water: its leaves are used in salads, etc.

water cure *same as* HYDROTHERAPY

wa·ter·fall (-fôl′) *n.* a steep fall of water, as of a stream, from a height; cascade

wa·ter·fowl (-foul′) *n.,* *pl.* **-fowls′**, **-fowl′**: see PLURAL, II, D, 1 a bird that lives on or near the water, esp. one that swims

☆**wa·ter·front** (-frunt′) *n.* **1.** land at the edge of a stream, harbor, etc. **2.** the part of a city or town on such land

☆**water gap** a break in a mountain ridge, with a stream flowing through it

water gas a fuel gas that is a poisonous mixture of hydrogen, carbon dioxide, carbon monoxide, and nitrogen, made by forcing steam through hot coke

☆**Wa·ter·gate** (-gāt′) *n.* [after *Watergate*, building in Washington, D.C., where Dem. Party hdqrs. were burglarized (1972) under direction of govt. officials] a scandal that involves officials who violate public trust by engaging in various crimes and corrupt practices in order to stay in power

water gate a gate controlling the flow of water; floodgate

water gauge 1. a gauge for measuring the level or flow of water in a stream or channel **2.** a device, as a glass tube, that shows the water level in a tank, boiler, etc.

water glass 1. a drinking glass; tumbler; goblet **2.** *same as* WATER GAUGE (sense 2) **3.** sodium silicate or, sometimes, potassium silicate, usually dissolved in water to form a syrupy liquid used as an adhesive, as a preservative for eggs, etc. Also **wa′ter·glass′** *n.*

water hole 1. a dip or hole in the surface of the ground, in which water collects; pool; pond **2.** a hole in the ice on a body of water

☆**water hyacinth** a floating plant with showy lavender flowers, native to S. America: now often a hindrance to water traffic in the southern U.S., esp. Florida

water ice [Brit.] water and sugar flavored and frozen

wa·ter·i·ness (-ē nis) *n.* the state or quality of being watery

wa·ter·ing place (-iŋ) **1.** a place at a stream, lake, etc. where animals go to drink **2.** [Chiefly Brit.] a resort or spa with mineral springs for drinking or bathing or with a beach for swimming, water sports, etc.

watering pot (or **can**) a can with a spout, often having a nozzle with holes, for watering plants, etc.

water jacket a casing for holding water that circulates, placed around something to be cooled or kept at a constant temperature, esp. around the cylinders of an internal-combustion engine

water jump a strip, ditch, or channel of water that a horse must jump, as in a steeplechase

water level 1. *a)* the surface of still water *b)* the height of this **2.** *same as: a)* WATER TABLE *b)* WATERLINE (senses 1 & 2)

wa·ter·lil·y (-lil′ē) *n.,* *pl.* **-lil′ies 1.** any of various water plants having large, flat, floating leaves and showy flowers in many colors **2.** the flower of such a plant

wa·ter·line (-līn′) *n.* **1.** the line to which the surface of the water comes on the side of a ship or boat **2.** any of several lines parallel to this, marked on the hull of a ship, indicating how far the ship has sunk in the water when it is fully or partly loaded, or unloaded ☆**3.** a pipe, tube, etc. connected to a source of water

WATERLILY

wa·ter·logged (-lôgd′, -lägd′) *adj.* **1.** soaked or filled with water so as to be heavy and slow in movement: said of boats or floating objects **2.** soaked with water; swampy

Wa·ter·loo (wôt′ər lōō′, wät′-; wôt′ər lōō′, wät′-) **1.** [after the Belgian town] city in NE Iowa: pop. 76,000 **2.** town in C Belgium: scene of Napoleon's final defeat (1815) —*n.* any complete defeat

water main a main pipe in a system of water pipes

wa·ter·man (wôt′ər mən, wät′-) *n.,* *pl.* **-men** a person who works on or with boats; esp., an oarsman —**wa′ter·man·ship′** *n.*

wa·ter·mark (-märk′) *n.* **1.** a mark showing the limit to which water has risen **2.** *Papermaking a)* a faint mark in paper, produced by pressure of a raised design, as in the mold *b)* the design —*vt.* **1.** to mark (paper) with a watermark **2.** to mark or stamp (a design) as a watermark

wa·ter·mel·on (-mel′ən) *n.* **1.** a large, edible fruit with a hard, green rind and juicy, pink or red pulp having many seeds **2.** the vine on which it grows

water mill a mill whose machinery is driven by water

☆**water moccasin** a large, poisonous, olive-brown pit viper found along or in rivers and swamps in the southeastern U.S.: often confused with various harmless water snakes

water nymph *Gr. & Rom. Myth.* a goddess having the form of a lovely young girl, supposed to live in a stream, pool, lake, etc.

water of crystallization water that occurs in crystalline substances and can be removed by heat: the loss of water usually results in the loss of crystalline structure

water of hydration water which is chemically combined with a substance to form a hydrate and which can be removed, as by heating

water ouzel any of several birds of Europe, Asia, and America; esp., the **American dipper** of western N. America that dives and swims in mountain streams

water pipe 1. a pipe for carrying water **2.** a smoking pipe in which the smoke is drawn through water; hookah

water pistol a toy gun that shoots water in a stream

water plant any plant living under water or with only the roots in or under water

water polo a water game played with a round, partly inflated ball by two teams of seven swimmers

water power 1. the power of running or falling water, used to drive machinery, etc. **2.** a fall of water that can be so used Also **wa′ter·pow′er** *n.*

wa·ter·proof (-proof′) *adj.* that keeps out water completely; esp., treated with rubber, plastic, etc. so that water will not come through —*n.* **1.** waterproof material **2.** [Chiefly Brit.] a raincoat, etc. of waterproof material —*vt.* to make waterproof — **wa′ter·proof′er** *n.*

water rat 1. any of various rodents that live on the banks of streams and ponds ☆**2.** *same as* MUSKRAT

wa·ter·re·pel·lent (-ri pel′ənt) *adj.* that repels water but is not thoroughly waterproof

water scorpion a sticklike, four-winged insect having a long breathing tube at the rear end of the abdomen

wa·ter·shed (-shed′) *n.* **1.** a stretch of high land dividing the areas drained by different river systems ☆**2.** the area drained by a river system **3.** a very important turning point

wa·ter·side (-sīd′) *n.* land at the edge of a body of water —*adj.* of, at, or on the waterside

☆**wa·ter·ski** (-skē′) *vi.* **-skied′**, **-ski′ing** to be towed, as a sport, on skilike boards (**water skis**) by a line attached to a speedboat —**wa′ter·ski′er** *n.*

water snake any of numerous saltwater or freshwater snakes; esp., a thick-bodied, nonpoisonous freshwater snake

wa·ter·soak (-sōk′) *vt.* to soak with or in water

water softener 1. a chemical compound added to hard water to make it soft, or free from mineral salts **2.** a tank, etc. in which water is filtered through chemicals to make it soft

wa·ter·sol·u·ble (-säl′yoo b′l) *adj.* that can be dissolved in water

WATER-SKIER

water spaniel either of two breeds of spaniel having a curly coat and used in hunting to bring back waterfowl that have been shot down

wa·ter·spout (-spout′) *n.* **1.** a hole, pipe, or spout from which water runs **2.** a tornado occurring over water, appearing as a whirling column of spray

water sprite in folklore, a spirit, nymph, etc. living in or haunting the water

water strider a narrow-bodied insect having long legs with which it moves swiftly on the surface of ponds, etc.

water table the level below which the ground is saturated with water

water thrush ☆any of several N. American warblers, usually found near streams

wa·ter·tight (-tīt′) *adj.* **1.** so tightly put together that no water can get in or through **2.** well thought out, with no weak points: said of an argument, plan, etc. —**wa′ter·tight′ness** *n.*

Wa·ter·ton Lakes National Park (wôt′ər tən, wät′-) na-

tional park in S Alberta, Canada: with Glacier National Park of Montana, it forms **Waterton-Glacier International Peace Park**

water tower 1. a tank raised above the ground, used for water storage and for keeping equal pressure on a water system ☆**2.** a firefighting apparatus that can be used to lift high-pressure hoses, etc. to great height

water vapor water in the form of mist or tiny scattered particles, esp. when below the boiling point, as in the air: distinguished from STEAM

wa·ter·way (-wā′) *n.* **1.** a channel through or along which water runs **2.** any body of water wide enough and deep enough for boats, ships, etc.

water wheel 1. a wheel with paddles turned by running water, used to give power **2.** a wheel with buckets on its rim, used for lifting water

water wings a device, filled with air, used to keep one afloat while learning to swim

wa·ter·works (-wurks′) *n.pl.* [*often with sing. v.*] **1.** a system of reservoirs, pumps, etc. used to bring a water supply to a city, etc. **2.** a pumping station in such a system

wa·ter·worn (-wôrn′) *adj.* worn, smoothed, or polished by the action of running water

wa·ter·y (-ē) *adj.* **1.** of or like water [the fish in his *watery* home] **2.** containing or full of water [*watery* soil] **3.** thin, diluted, weak, etc. [*watery* soup] **4.** tearful [*watery* eyes] **5.** in or consisting of water [a *watery* grave] **6.** soft or soggy [a *watery* cake]

Wat·ling Island (wät′liŋ) *same as* SAN SALVADOR (island): also **Wat′lings Island**

☆**WATS** (wäts) *n.* [*w(ide) a(rea) t(elecommunications) s(ervice)*] a telephone service which ties a customer into the long-distance network through special lines so that he can make calls to all telephones in a particular area or areas at a special rate

Wat·son (wät′s'n, wôt′-), **James Dewey** 1928– ; U.S. biochemist: helped determine the structure of DNA

watt (wät, wôt) *n.* [after J. WATT] the unit of power, equal to one joule per second or to the power developed by a current of one ampere under one volt of pressure

Watt (wät, wôt), **James** 1736–1819; Scot. engineer & inventor: noted for his development of the steam engine

watt·age (wät′ij, wôt′-) *n.* **1.** amount of electrical power, expressed in watts **2.** the amount of watts required to operate a given appliance or device

Wat·teau (vä tō′; *E.* wä tō′), (Jean) An·toine (än twän′) 1684–1721; Fr. painter

watt-hour (wät′our′, wôt′-) *n.* a unit of electrical energy or work, equal to one watt acting for one hour

wat·tle (wät′'l, wôt′-) *n.* [OE. *watul*] **1.** sticks woven together with twigs or branches, used for walls, roofs, etc. **2.** [*pl.*] rods or poles used as the support of a thatched roof **3.** in Australia, any of various acacias **4.** a fleshy, often brightly colored piece of skin that hangs from the throat of a cock, turkey, etc., or of some lizards —*adj.* made of or roofed with wattle or wattles —*vt.* **-tled**, **-tling 1.** to weave (sticks, twigs, etc.) together so as to form a structure **2.** to build of wattle

WATTLES

watt·me·ter (wät′mēt′ər, wôt′-) *n.* an instrument for measuring in watts the power in an electric circuit

Wa·tu·si (wä too′sē) *n., pl.* **-sis**, **-si** any member of a tall, cattle-owning people of Burundi and Rwanda, in east central Africa: also **Wa·tut′si** (-too t′sē)

Wau·ke·gan (wô kē′gən) [< Algonquian, lit., trading place] city in NE Ill., on Lake Michigan: pop. 65,000

waul (wôl) *vi., n.* wail, squall, or howl

Wau·wa·to·sa (wô′wə tō′sə) [< AmInd. *wawatosi*, ? firefly] city in SE Wis.: suburb of Milwaukee: pop. 59,000

Wave (wāv) *n.* a member of the WAVES

wave (wāv) *vi.* **waved**, **wav′ing** [OE. *wafian*] **1.** to move up and down or back and forth in a curving motion; sway to and fro [the flag *waves*] **2.** to greet or signal by moving a hand, arm, etc. to and fro [the crowd *waved* as he passed] **3.** to have the form of a series of curves [hair that *waves* naturally] —*vt.* **1.** to cause to wave or sway to and fro **2.** to shake or swing (a weapon) in a threatening way; brandish **3.** *a)* to move or swing (something) as a signal *b)* to signal (something) by doing this [to *wave* farewell] *c)* to signal to (someone) by doing this [he *waved* us on] **4.** to arrange (hair, etc.) in a series of curves —*n.* **1.** *a)* a ridge or swell moving along the surface of a body of water, etc. *b)* something that suggests this as when wind blows over a field of grain **2.** a curve or series of curves, as in the hair, etc. **3.** a motion to and fro or up and down, as that made by the hand in signaling **4.** something like a wave in action or form; specif., a sudden increase or rise that builds up and then goes down *[a crime wave; a wave of anger; a wave of new settlers]* **5.** *[pl.]* [Poet.] water; esp., the sea **6.** *Physics* a vibration or state of motion that is passed along from one particle in a medium to the next in a given direction, as in the transmission of light, sound, etc. —**make waves** to cause trouble over a situation that seems to be calmly accepted by others — **wave′less** *adj.* —**wave′like′** *adj.* —**wav′er** *n.*

wave band *Radio & TV* a specific range of radio-wave frequencies

wave·length (wāv′leŋkth, -leŋth) *n. Physics* the distance, measured in the direction of a wave, from any given point to the next point in the same phase: also **wave length**

wave·let (-lit) *n.* a little wave; ripple

wave mechanics the mathematical treatment of the behavior of submicroscopic particles of matter that exhibit both particle and wave phenomena

wa·ver (wā′vər) *vi.* [< ME. < *waven,* to WAVE] **1.** to sway to and fro; flutter **2.** to show doubt or be uncertain *[he never wavered in his decision to study law]* **3.** to become unsteady; falter *[the battle line wavered and broke]* **4.** to tremble: said of the voice, etc. **5.** to flicker: said of light —*n.* a wavering —see SYN. at HESITATE —**wa′ver·er** *n.* —**wa′ver·ing·ly** *adv.* —**wa′ver·y** *adj.*

WAVES (wāvz) [orig. *W(omen) A(ppointed for) V(oluntary) E(mergency) S(ervice)]* the women's branch of the U.S. Navy

wav·y (wā′vē) *adj.* **wav′i·er, wav′i·est** **1.** having waves; full of waves *[wavy hair]* **2.** moving in a wavelike motion *[fields of wavy grain]* —**wav′i·ness** *n.*

wax[1] (waks) *n.* [OE. *weax]* **1.** an easily molded, dull-yellow substance secreted by bees for building cells; beeswax: it is used for candles, modeling, etc. **2.** any substance like this; specif., *a)* paraffin *b)* earwax *c)* sealing wax —*vt.* to rub, polish, cover, or treat with wax —**wax′like′** *adj.*

wax[2] (waks) *vi.* **waxed, waxed** or archaic **wax′en, wax′ing** [OE. *weaxan,* to grow] **1.** to get larger, stronger, fuller, etc. *[the moon waxes and wanes]* **2.** to become *[to wax angry]*

☆**wax bean** **1.** a variety of kidney bean with long, narrow, yellow pods **2.** the immature pod cooked as a vegetable

wax·ber·ry (waks′ber′ē) *n., pl.* **-ries** same as: **1.** SNOWBERRY (senses 1 & 3) ☆**2.** BAYBERRY (sense 1)

wax·en (wak′s'n) *adj.* **1.** made of, or covered with, wax *[a waxen candle]* **2.** like wax, as in being pale, soft, easily molded, etc. *[his waxen face]*

wax insect an insect that secretes a waxy substance sometimes used commercially; specif., a Chinese scale insect

☆**wax myrtle** an evergreen shrub native to eastern N. America and having grayish-white berries coated with a wax used for candles; bayberry

wax palm **1.** same as CARNAUBA **2.** a palm of the Andes that produces a wax used to make candles, polishes, etc.

wax paper a kind of paper made moistureproof by a wax, or paraffin, coating: also **waxed paper**

wax·wing (waks′wiŋ′) *n.* any of a group of birds with silky-brown feathers, a showy crest, and red, waxy tips on its wings

wax·work (-wurk′) *n.* **1.** work, as objects, figures, etc., made of wax **2.** a human figure made of wax

wax·works (-wurks′) *n.pl.* [with sing. v.] an exhibition of wax figures made to look like famous or notorious persons: also **wax museum**

wax·y (wak′sē) *adj.* **wax′i·er, wax′i·est** **1.** full of, covered with, or made of wax **2.** like wax in nature or appearance —**wax′i·ness** *n.*

way (wā) *n.* [OE. *weg* < IE. base *wegh-,* to go] **1.** a road, highway, street, path, etc. *[the Appian Way of ancient Rome was a paved road]* **2.** room for pass-

CEDAR WAXWING
(to 7 in. long)

ing; an opening, as in a crowd *[clear a way for the ambulance]* **3.** a route or course from one place to another: often used in compounds *[highway, railway, one-way street]* **4.** a specified route or direction *[on the way to town]* **5.** course or habits of life *[to fall into evil ways]* **6.** a method of doing something *[do it this way]* **7.** a usual or typical manner of living, acting, etc. *[to change one's ways]* **8.** manner or style *[smiling in a friendly way]* **9.** distance *[a long way off]*: also [Colloq.] **ways** **10.** direction of movement or action *[look this way]* **11.** a point or detail; particular *[to be right in some ways]* **12.** what one desires; wish; will *[to get one's own way]* **13.** range, as of experience *[that never came my way]* **14.** relationship as to those taking part *[a four-way agreement]* **15.** [Colloq.] a (specified) state or condition *[he is in a bad way]* **16.** [Colloq.] a district; locality *[out our way]* **17.** *[pl.]* a timber framework on which a ship is built and along which it slides in launching **18.** *Naut.* a ship's movement through water —*adv.* [Colloq.] away; far *[way behind]* —see SYN. at METHOD —**by the way** **1.** as a new but related point; incidentally **2.** on or beside the way —**by way of** **1.** passing through; via *[to Rome by way of Paris]* **2.** as a way, method, or means of *[it was done by way of showing thanks]* — **come one's way** **1.** to come to one **2.** to turn out successfully for one: also **go one's way** —**give way** **1.** to withdraw; yield **2.** to break down —**give way to** **1.** to step aside for; yield to **2.** to give expression to *[to give way to tears]* —**go out of the (or one's) way** to make a special effort —**in the way** in such a position as to keep from passing, going on, etc. —**lead the way** to be a guide or example —**make one's way** **1.** to advance or proceed **2.** to succeed by one's own efforts —**make way** **1.** to clear a passage **2.** to make progress —**on the way out** **1.** becoming unfashionable or unpopular **2.** dying —**out of the way** **1.** in a position so as not to hinder, etc. **2.** taken care of; settled **3.** out of existence; (put) to death **4.** not on the right, direct, or usual route **5.** *a)* improper; wrong *b)* unusual —**see one's way (clear)** **1.** to be willing to (do something) **2.** to find it possible —**the way** how; as *[with things the way they are]* — **under way** **1.** moving; advancing **2.** *Naut. see* UNDERWAY

way·bill (wā′bil′) *n.* ☆a paper giving a list of goods and shipping instructions, sent with the goods being shipped

way·far·er (-fer′ər) *n.* a person who travels, esp. from place to place on foot —**way′far′ing** *adj., n.*

way·lay (wā′lā′, wā′lā′) *vt.* **-laid′, -lay′ing** **1.** to lie in wait for and attack; ambush *[waylaid by robbers]* **2.** to wait for and stop so as to speak with *[waylay the boss and ask him now]* — **way′lay′er** *n.*

Wayne (wān) **1.** [< surname *Wayne]* a masculine name **2. Anthony,** 1745-96; Am. general in the Revolutionary War: called *Mad Anthony Wayne*

Way of the Cross same as STATIONS OF THE CROSS

☆**way-out** (wā′out′) *adj.* [Colloq.] characterized by ideas, ways of behaving, etc. that are not yet accepted by most people; very unconventional, experimental, nonconformist, etc.

-ways (wāz) [< *way* (see WAY) + *-s]* a suffix meaning in a (specified) direction, position, or manner *[endways]:* same as -WISE (sense 1)

ways and means **1.** methods and resources that can be used by a person, company, etc. **2.** methods of raising money, as for government

way·side (wā′sīd′) *n.* the area close to the side of a road —*adj.* on, near, or along the side of a road —**go by the wayside** to be put aside or discarded

☆**way station** a small railroad station between more important ones, where through trains stop only if signalled

way·ward (-wərd) *adj.* [see AWAY & -WARD] **1.** insisting on having one's own way; headstrong, willful, disobedient, etc. **2.** not regular or steady; changeable; erratic *[wayward breezes]* —**way′ward·ly** *adv.* —**way′ward·ness** *n.*

way·worn (-wôrn′) *adj.* tired from traveling

W.B., W/B waybill

w.c. **1.** water closet **2.** without charge

W.C.T.U. Women's Christian Temperance Union

we (wē) *pron. for sing. see* I [OE.] **1.** the persons speaking or writing: sometimes used by a person in referring to two or more persons including himself and often the person or persons being spoken or written to, or by a monarch, author, editor, etc. in referring to himself **2.** you: used in speaking to a child, invalid, etc. *[shall we take a nap now?]* The case forms of the first personal plural pronoun are: **we,** nominative; **us,** objective; **our,** possessive; **ourselves,** intensive and reflexive

weak (wēk) *adj.* [ON. *veikr*] **1.** *a)* lacking in strength of body or muscle; not physically strong *b)* lacking energy; feeble; infirm *[weak from illness]* **2.** lacking in skill or strength for combat or competition *[a weak team]* **3.** lacking in moral strength or will power *[a person of weak character]* **4.** lacking in mental power *[a weak mind]* **5.** *a)* lacking ruling power, or authority *[a weak government]* *b)* having few resources, little wealth, etc. *[a weak nation]* **6.** lacking in force or effectiveness *[weak discipline]* **7.** *a)* not strong in material or construction; easily broken, bent, etc. *[a weak railing]* *b)* not secure; unable to hold up against an attack, etc. *[a weak fort]* **8.** *a)* not functioning normally or well: said of a body organ or part *[weak eyes]* *b)* easily upset; queasy *[a weak stomach]* **9.** suggesting moral or physical weakness *[a weak chin]* **10.** lacking in volume, intensity, etc.; faint *[a weak voice]* **11.** lacking the usual or proper strength *[weak tea]* **12.** poor or lacking in something specified *[weak in grammar]* **13.** unconvincing; faulty *[a weak argument]* **14.** *Chem.* having a low ion concentration, as certain acids and bases **15.** *Gram.* inflected by adding a suffix such as *-ed, -d* rather than by an internal vowel change: said of regular verbs **16.** *Phonet.* unstressed or lightly stressed *[a weak syllable]* —**weak′ish** *adj.*
SYN.—weak, the most general of these words, implies having very little, or less than normal, physical, mental, or moral strength *[a weak muscle, mind, character, etc.]*; **feeble** is used of that which is so weak or ineffective as to be pitiable *[a feeble old man, a feeble joke]*; **frail** refers to that which is extremely delicate or weak, or easily broken or shattered *[a frail body, frail support]*; **infirm** suggests a loss of strength or soundness, as through illness or old age *[his infirm old grandfather]*; **decrepit** implies a being broken down or worn out, as by old age or long use *[a decrepit old horse, a decrepit sofa]* —**ANT. strong, sturdy, robust**

weak·en (wēk′'n) *vt., vi.* to make or become weak or weaker
SYN.—weaken, the most general of these words, implies a lessening of strength, power, soundness, etc. *[weakened by disease, to weaken an argument]*; **debilitate** suggests a partial or temporary weakening, as by disease or lack of self-control and harmful habits *[debilitated by fever; debilitated by constantly staying up too late]*; **enervate** implies a lessening of force, vigor, energy, liveliness, etc., as through soft, easy living *[enervated by idleness and too much sleep]* —**ANT. strengthen, energize**

☆**weak·fish** (-fish′) *n., pl.* **-fish′, -fish′es:** see FISH [< obs. Du. < *week,* soft + *visch,* a fish] any of several ocean fishes used for food, esp. a species found along the eastern coast of the U.S.

weak-kneed (wēk′nēd′) *adj.* **1.** having weak knees **2.** lacking courage, firmness of purpose, etc.

weak·ling (-liŋ) *n.* **1.** a person or animal that is physically weak **2.** a person of weak character —*adj.* weak; feeble

weak·ly (-lē) *adj.* **-li·er, -li·est** sickly; feeble; weak —*adv.* in a weak way —**weak′li·ness** *n.*

weak-mind·ed (-mīn′did) *adj.* **1.** having or showing a lack of firm purpose; indecisive **2.** mentally retarded —**weak′-mind′ed·ness** *n.*

weak·ness (-nis) *n.* **1.** the state of being weak **2.** a weak point; fault, as in one's character **3.** a special liking that is hard to control *[weakness for pickles]* **4.** something of which one is unreasonably fond *[candy is my weakness]* —see SYN. at FAULT

weak sister ☆[Slang] one who is cowardly, unreliable, etc.

weal¹ (wēl) *n.* [var. of WALE] a mark, line, or ridge raised on the skin, as by a blow; welt

weal² (wēl) *n.* [OE. *wela*] a prosperous state; well-being; welfare *[the public weal]*

wealth (welth) *n.* [see WEAL² & -TH¹] **1.** *a)* much money or property; riches *b)* the state of being rich; affluence *[a man of wealth]* **2.** a large amount; abundance *[a wealth of ideas]* **3.** valuable products or contents *[the wealth of the oceans]* **4.** *Econ. a)* everything having value that can be measured in terms of price *b)* any useful material thing capable of being bought and sold

wealth·y (wel′thē) *adj.* **wealth′i·er, wealth′i·est 1.** having wealth; rich **2.** characterized by or suggestive of wealth *[a wealthy suburb]* **3.** abounding (*in* something) *[wealthy in natural resources]* —see SYN. at RICH —**wealth′i·ly** *adv.* —**wealth′i·ness** *n.*

wean (wēn) *vt.* [OE. *wenian*] **1.** to get (a child or young animal) used to food other than its mother's milk; now, often, to cause to give up drinking milk from a bottle with a nipple **2.** to cause (a person) to lose interest in something, break a habit, etc. *[using good books to wean her away from TV]* —**wean′er** *n.*

weap·on (wep′ən) *n.* [OE. *wæpen*] **1.** any instrument or device used for fighting, as a club, gun, bomb, etc. **2.** any means of

attack or defense *[a cat's claws are its weapons; his best weapon is silence]*

weap·on·ry (-rē) *n.* **1.** the design and production of weapons **2.** all of the weapons a nation has for use in war

wear¹ (wer) *vt.* **wore, worn, wear′ing** [OE. *werian*] **1.** to have or carry (clothing, jewelry, a weapon, etc.) on the body **2.** to have or show in one's expression or appearance *[to wear a smile]* **3.** to damage, use up, etc. by constant use, friction, etc. (often with *away*) *[rubbing has worn away the finish]* **4.** to bring to a specified state by use *[to wear a coat to rags]* **5.** to make by the friction of rubbing, flowing, etc. *[to wear a hole in the rug]* **6.** to tire or exhaust (a person) —*vi.* **1.** to become damaged, used up, etc. by constant use, friction, etc. *[shoes starting to wear]* **2.** to hold up in spite of use; last *[a fabric that wears well]* **3.** to become in time; grow gradually *[his courage is wearing thin]* **4.** to pass away gradually: said of time *[the day wore on]* **5.** to have an irritating or tiring effect (*on*) *[noise wearing on his nerves]* —*n.* **1.** a wearing or being worn *[a dress for holiday wear]* **2.** things, esp. clothes, worn, or for wearing, on the body *[men's wear]*: often in combination *[sportswear]* **3.** damage, loss, etc. from use, friction, etc. *[the soles show considerable wear]* **4.** the ability to last in spite of use *[a lot of wear left in the tire]* —**wear down 1.** to lose or cause to lose thickness or height by use, friction, etc. **2.** to tire out; exhaust **3.** to overcome by constant effort *[to wear down an enemy]* —**wear off** to pass away gradually *[the effects wore off]* —**wear out 1.** to make or become useless from continued wear or use **2.** to tire out; exhaust —**wear′er** *n.*

wear² (wer) *vt.* **wore, worn, wear′ing** [altered < *veer* (to let out)] to turn (a ship) about by swinging its bow away from the wind —*vi.* to turn about by having the bow swung away from the wind

wear·a·ble (wer′ə b'l) *adj.* that can be worn; suitable for wear —*n.* [*pl.*] garments; clothing —**wear′a·bil′i·ty** *n.*

wear and tear loss and damage resulting from use

wear·ing (-iŋ) *adj.* **1.** of or for wear *[wearing apparel]* **2.** causing wear *[the wearing action of dripping water]* **3.** tiring or exhausting *[a wearing task]* —**wear′ing·ly** *adv.*

wea·ri·some (wir′ē səm) *adj.* causing weariness; tiring or tiresome —**wea′ri·some·ly** *adv.* —**wea′ri·some·ness** *n.*

wear·proof (wer′prōof′) *adj.* that resists wearing out

wea·ry (wir′ē) *adj.* **-ri·er, -ri·est** [OE. *werig*] **1.** tired; worn out **2.** having little or no patience, interest, etc. left; bored (with *of*) *[weary of reading novels]* **3.** tiring *[weary work]* **4.** tiresome; annoying *[weary excuses]* —*vt., vi.* **-ried, -ry·ing** to make or become weary —see SYN. at TIRED —**wea′ri·ly** *adv.* —**wea′ri·ness** *n.*

wea·sand (wē′z'nd) *n.* [OE. *wæsend*] the gullet; esophagus

wea·sel (wē′z'l) *n., pl.* **-sels, -sel:** see PLURAL, II, D, 1 [OE. *wesle*] **1.** an agile, flesh-eating mammal related to the marten, with a long, slender body, short legs, and a long, bushy tail: they feed on rats, birds, eggs, etc. **2.** a sly or sneaky person —*vi.* **1.** to use weasel words **2.** [Colloq.] to avoid doing something one is supposed to do (with *out*) —**wea′sel·ly** *adj.*

WEASEL
(6–14 in. long, including tail)

☆**weasel words** words or remarks that are deliberately misleading or unclear

weath·er (weth′ər) *n.* [OE. *weder*] **1.** the general condition (as to temperature, moisture, cloudiness, etc.) of the atmosphere at a particular time and place **2.** disagreeable atmospheric conditions; storm, rain, etc. *[protected against the weather]* —*vt.* **1.** to expose to the weather or atmosphere, as for airing, drying, seasoning, etc. **2.** to wear away, discolor, etc. by exposure to the atmosphere **3.** to get through safely *[to weather a storm]* **4.** *Naut.* to pass to the windward of (a cape, reef, etc.) —*vi.* **1.** to become worn, discolored, etc. by exposure to the weather **2.** to undergo such exposure in a specified way *[it weathers well]* —*adj.* **1.** designating or of the side of a ship, etc. toward the wind; windward **2.** exposed to the elements *[a weather deck]* —☆**under the weather** [Colloq.] **1.** not feeling well; ill **2.** somewhat drunk

weath·er-beat·en (-bēt′'n) *adj.* showing the effect of weather, as, *a)* stained, damaged, or worn *b)* sunburned, roughened, etc. *[the sailor's weather-beaten face]*

weath·er·board (-bôrd′) *n.* a clapboard; piece of siding

weath·er·bound (-bound′) *adj.* delayed or halted by bad weather, as a ship, airplane, etc.

☆**Weather Bureau** *former name of the* NATIONAL WEATHER SERVICE

weath·er·cock (-käk′) *n.* **1.** a weather vane in the form of a rooster **2.** a fickle or changeable person or thing

weather eye **1.** an eye alert to signs of changing weather **2.** a close watch for any change

weath·er·glass (-glas′) *n.* same as BAROME-TER (sense 1)

weath·er·ing (-iŋ) *n. Geol.* the effects of the forces of weather on rock surfaces, as in forming soil, sand, etc.

weath·er·man (-man′) *n., pl.* **-men′** (-men′) ☆ a person who forecasts the weather, or, esp., one who reports weather conditions and weather forecasts, as on television

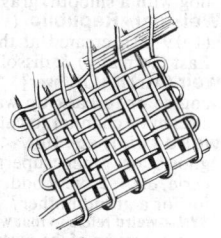
WEATHERCOCK

☆**weather map** a map or chart that shows weather conditions in a certain area at a given time by indicating barometric pressures, temperatures, wind direction, etc.

weath·er·proof (-pro͞of′) *adj.* that can be exposed to wind, rain, snow, etc. without being damaged —*vt.* to make weatherproof

weather station a post or office where weather conditions are recorded and studied and forecasts are made

☆**weath·er·strip** (-strip′) *n.* a thin strip of metal, felt, wood, etc., put along the edges of a door or window to keep out drafts, rain, etc.: also **weather strip** —*vt.* **-stripped′, -strip′ping** to provide with weatherstrips: also **weath′er-strip′**

☆**weath·er·strip·ping** (-strip′iŋ) *n.* **1.** same as WEATHER-STRIP **2.** a collection or group of weatherstrips

weather vane a shaped piece of metal, etc., set up high to swing in the wind and show which way the wind is blowing

weath·er·wise (-wīz′) *adj.* **1.** skilled in predicting the weather **2.** skilled in predicting shifts of opinion, feeling, etc.

weath·er·worn (-wôrn′) *adj.* same as WEATHER-BEATEN

weave (wēv) *vt.* **wove** or, chiefly for *vt.* 6 & *vi.* 3, **weaved, wo′-ven** or **wove** or, chiefly for *vt.* 6 & *vi.* 3, **weaved, weav′ing** [OE. *wefan*] **1.** *a)* to make (a fabric), esp. on a loom, by interlacing threads or yarns *b)* to form (threads) into a fabric **2.** *a)* to construct in the mind [to *weave* a plot] *b)* to form (incidents, etc.) into a story, poem, etc. **3.** *a)* to make by interlacing twigs, straw, etc. [to *weave* baskets] *b)* to interlace (twigs, straw, etc.) so as to make something **4.** to twist (something) into, through, or among [to *weave* flowers into one's hair] **5.** to spin (a web): said of spiders, etc. **6.** *a)* to cause (a vehicle, etc.) to move from side to side or in and out *b)* to make (one's way) by moving thus —*vi.* **1.** to do weaving **2.** to become interlaced **3.** to move from side to side or in and out [*weaving* through traffic] —*n.* a method or pattern of weaving [burlap has a loose *weave*]

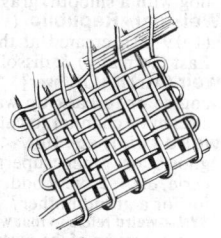
WEAVING

weav·er (wē′vər) *n.* **1.** a person who weaves; esp., one whose work is weaving **2.** same as WEAVERBIRD

weav·er·bird (-burd′) *n.* any of a group of old-world birds resembling finches, that weave domed nests of sticks, grass, and other vegetation

web (web) *n.* [OE. *webb*] **1.** any woven fabric; esp., a length of cloth being woven on a loom or just taken off **2.** the network spun by a spider or by the larvae of certain insects **3.** a carefully woven trap **4.** anything put together in a careful or complicated way [a *web* of lies] **5.** *Anat.* a tissue or membrane **6.** *Mech.* the plate joining the flanges of a girder, rail, etc. **7.** *Printing* a large roll of paper for use in a type of rotary press (**web press**) **8.** *Zool. a)* the vane of a feather *b)* a membrane joining the toes of various water birds, water animals, etc. —*vt.* **webbed, web′bing** **1.** to join by a web **2.** to cover as with a web **3.** to catch as in a web —**web′like′** *adj.*

webbed (webd) *adj.* **1.** formed like a web or made of webbing **2.** joined by a web [*webbed* toes] **3.** having the toes joined by a web [a *webbed* foot]

web·bing (web′iŋ) *n.* **1.** a strong, tough fabric woven in strips and used for belts, in upholstery, etc. **2.** a membrane joining

the toes, as of a duck or frog **3.** a part like this, as between the thumb and forefinger of a baseball glove **4.** a netlike structure of interwoven cords, etc., as that forming the hitting surface of a tennis racket

We·ber (vā′bər) **1. Carl Ma·ri·a (Friedrich Ernst) von** (mä rē′ä fôn), 1786–1826; Ger. composer **2. Max,** 1864–1920; Ger. sociologist

We·bern (vā′bərn), **An·ton (von)** (än′tôn) 1883–1945; Austrian composer

web·foot (web′fŏŏt′) *n., pl.* **-feet** **1.** a foot with the toes webbed **2.** an animal with webbed feet —**web′-foot′ed** *adj.*

Web·ster (web′stər) **1. Daniel,** 1782–1852; U.S. statesman & orator **2. John,** 1580?–1625?; Eng. dramatist **3. Noah,** 1758–1843; U.S. lexicographer —**Web·ster′i·an** (-stir′ē ən) *adj.*

web-toed (web′tōd′) *adj.* having webfeet

☆**web·worm** (-wurm′) *n.* any of various caterpillars that spin large, irregular webs

wed (wed) *vt.* **wed′ded, wed′ded** or **wed, wed′ding** [OE. *weddian*] **1.** to marry; specif., *a)* to take for one's husband or wife *b)* to conduct the marriage ceremony for **2.** to join closely [a project that *weds* science and art] —*vi.* to get married

we'd (wēd) **1.** we had **2.** we should **3.** we would

Wed. Wednesday

wed·ded (wed′id) *adj.* **1.** married **2.** devoted [*wedded* to one's work] **3.** joined [*wedded* by common interests]

Wed·dell Sea (wed′əl, wə del′) section of the Atlantic, along the coast of Antarctica, southeast of S. America

wed·ding (wed′iŋ) *n.* [OE. *wedding*] **1.** the act or ceremony of getting married, or the festivities that go with it **2.** a marriage anniversary [a golden *wedding*] **3.** a joining together —see SYN. at MARRIAGE

wedding ring a ring put on the bride's finger by the groom during the marriage ceremony; also, a ring sometimes given to the groom by the bride during the ceremony

wedge (wej) *n.* [OE. *wecg*] **1.** a piece of wood, metal, etc. tapering to a thin edge that can be driven into a narrow opening: used to split wood, lift heavy weights, etc. **2.** anything shaped like this [a *wedge* of pie]; specif., *a) Golf* an iron with much loft, used as for shots out of sand traps ☆*b)* same as WEDGIE **3.** any action or procedure used to open the way for a change —*vt.* **wedged, wedg′ing** **1.** to split as with a wedge **2.** to fix in place by driving a wedge under, beside, etc. [to *wedge* a door open] **3.** to pack (*in*) or crowd together [we were *wedged* in like sardines] —*vi.* to push or be forced like a wedge [he *wedged* through the door] —**wedge′like′** *adj.* —**wedg′y** *adj.*

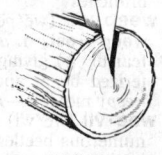
WEDGE

☆**wedg·ie** (wej′ē) *n.* a woman's shoe having a wedgelike piece under the heel so as to form a solid sole, flat from heel to toe

Wedg·wood (ware) (wej′wŏŏd′) [after J. *Wedgwood*, 18th-c. Eng. potter] *a trademark for* a fine English pottery, usually with raised figures in white on a tinted background

wed·lock (wed′läk′) *n.* [< OE. < *wed*, a pledge + *-lac*, an offering] the state of being married —see SYN. at MARRIAGE

Wednes·day (wenz′dē, -dā) *n.* [OE. *Wodnes dæg*, Woden's day] the fourth day of the week

Wednes·days (-dēz, -dāz) *adv.* on or during every Wednesday

wee (wē) *adj.* **we′er, we′est** [OE. *wege*] **1.** very small; tiny **2.** very early [in the *wee* hours of the morning]

weed (wēd) *n.* [OE. *weod*] **1.** any unwanted, uncultivated plant, esp. one growing rapidly and in large numbers and crowding out a desired crop, spoiling a lawn, etc. **2.** [Colloq.] *a)* tobacco: with *the b)* a cigar or cigarette **3.** something useless —*vt.* **1.** to remove weeds from (a garden, etc.) **2.** to remove as useless, harmful, etc.: often with *out* [to *weed* out faded pictures from an album] —*vi.* to remove weeds, etc. — **weed′er** *n.* —**weed′like′** *adj.*

weed-kill·er (wēd′kil′ər) *n.* same as HERBICIDE

weeds (wēdz) *n.pl.* [< OE. *wæde*, a garment] black mourning clothes, esp. those worn by a widow

weed·y (wēd′ē) *adj.* **weed′i·er, weed′i·est** **1.** full of weeds **2.** of or like a weed, as in rapid growth **3.** lean, lanky, awkward, etc. —**weed′i·ness** *n.*

week (wēk) *n.* [OE. *wicu*] **1.** a period of seven days, esp. one beginning with Sunday and ending with Saturday **2.** the hours or days of work in a seven-day period [a 40-hour *week*] —**week after week** every week —**week by week** each week —**week in, week out** every week

week·day (wēk′dā′) *n.* **1.** any day of the week except Sunday (or, as in Judaism, Saturday) **2.** any day not in the weekend —*adj.* of, for, or on a weekday

week·days (-dāz′) *adv.* on or during every weekday or most weekdays

week·end, week-end (-end′) *n.* the period from Friday night or Saturday to Monday morning: also **week end** —*adj.* of, for, or on a weekend —*vi.* to spend the weekend (*at* or *in* a specified place)

week·ends (-endz′) *adv.* on or during every weekend or most weekends

week·ly (-lē) *adj.* **1.** done, happening, appearing, etc. once a week or every week [a *weekly* visit] **2.** of a week, or of each week [a *weekly* wage] —*adv.* once a week; every week —*n., pl.* **-lies** a periodical published once a week

ween (wēn) *vi., vt.* [OE. *wenan*] [Archaic] to think; suppose; imagine

☆**wee·nie, wee·ny**[1] (wē′nē) *n., pl.* **-nies** [Colloq.] *same as* WIENER

wee·ny[2] (wē′nē) *adj.* **-ni·er, -ni·est** [WEE + (TI)NY] [Colloq.] small; tiny

weep (wēp) *vi.* **wept, weep′ing** [OE. *wepan*] **1.** to show strong emotion, usually grief or sorrow, by shedding tears **2.** to lament or mourn (with *for*) **3.** to form drops of moisture condensed from the air [cold pipes *weep* in hot weather] **4.** to give off liquid, as a wound, the stem of a plant, etc. —*vt.* **1.** to weep for; lament **2.** to shed (tears, etc.) —*n.* [*often pl.*] a fit of weeping —**weep′er** *n.*

weep·ing (wē′piŋ) *n.* the act of one who or that which weeps —*adj.* **1.** that weeps tears or other liquid **2.** having graceful, drooping branches —**weep′ing·ly** *adv.*

weeping willow a Chinese willow with delicate, drooping branches

weep·y (wē′pē) *adj.* **weep′i·er, weep′i·est** **1.** *a)* tending to weep; tearful *b)* giving off liquid **2.** characterized by or apt to cause weeping [a *weepy* movie] —**weep′i·ness** *n.*

wee·vil (wē′v'l) *n.* [OE. *wifel*] any of numerous beetles, esp. those with projecting beaks, including many species that feed, esp. as larvae, on cotton, fruits, grain, etc. —**wee′vil·y, wee′vil·ly** *adj.*

weft (weft) *n.* [OE. *weft* < base of *wefan*, to weave] **1.** in weaving, the woof **2.** something woven

WEEPING WILLOW
(tree & leaf)

weigh[1] (wā) *vt.* [OE. *wegan*, to carry] **1.** to find out the weight of by means of a scale or balance [to *weigh* potatoes] **2.** to have a (specified) weight [it *weighs* ten pounds]: regarded as a *vi.* when used with an adverb **3.** *same as* WEIGHT (*vt.* 1) **4.** to lift or balance (an object) in the hand(s) in order to estimate its heaviness **5.** to measure out as by weight [to *weigh* out two pounds of candy] **6.** *a)* to consider and choose carefully [to *weigh* one's words] *b)* to consider carefully in order to make a choice [to *weigh* one plan against another] **7.** to hoist, or lift (an anchor): a sailor's term —*vi.* **1.** to have importance or influence [his word *weighed* heavily with the jury] **2.** to be a burden (with *on* or *upon*) [his crime *weighed* on his mind] **3.** to hoist anchor: a sailor's term —see SYN. at CONSIDER —**weigh down** **1.** to make bend down as with added weight **2.** to bear down on so as to worry or depress —**weigh in** **1.** to weigh (a boxer, jockey, etc.) before or after a contest to find out if his weight is what it is supposed to be **2.** to be so weighed —**weigh′a·ble** *adj.* —**weigh′er** *n.*

weigh[2] (wā) *n. var. of* WAY: used only in the phrase **under weigh**, making progress, advancing: see UNDERWAY

weight (wāt) *n.* [OE. *wiht* < *wegan*, to carry] **1.** a quantity weighing a specified amount **2.** heaviness; the quality a thing has because of the pull of gravity on it **3.** how much a thing weighs or should weigh **4.** *a)* any unit of heaviness, as an ounce, pound, etc. *b)* any system of such units [troy *weight*]: see TABLES OF WEIGHTS AND MEASURES in Supplements *c)* a piece of metal, etc. of a specific standard heaviness, used in weighing [put the two-ounce *weight* on the balance] **5.** any block or

mass used for its heaviness; specif., *a)* one used to hold light things down [a *paperweight*] *b)* one used to drive a mechanism [clock *weights*] *c)* one lifted for exercise **6.** *a)* any heavy thing or load *b)* a burden of responsibility, sorrow, etc. **7.** importance or consequence [a matter of great *weight*] **8.** influence, power, or authority [to throw one's *weight* to the losing side] **9.** the relative thickness or heaviness of a fabric or article of clothing [a suit of summer *weight*] **10.** *Sports a)* any of the classifications for boxers and wrestlers based on what they weigh *b)* the number of pounds a horse must carry for a race, including the weight of the jockey, saddle, and, often, added lead weights —*vt.* **1.** to add weight to [to *weight* a ship with ballast] **2.** to burden [*weighted* down with sorrow] **3.** to control or manipulate so as to favor a particular side [*weighted* evidence] —see SYN. at IMPORTANCE —**by weight** as determined by weighing —**carry weight** to be important, have influence, etc. —**pull one's weight** to do one's share —**throw one's weight around** to use one's authority or rank to gain an advantage

weight·less (wāt′lis) *adj.* having little or no apparent weight; specif., free of or offsetting the pull of gravity —**weight′less·ly** *adv.* —**weight′less·ness** *n.*

weight lifting the athletic exercise or competitive sport of lifting barbells —**weight lifter**

weight·y (-ē) *adj.* **weight′i·er, weight′i·est** **1.** very heavy **2.** hard to bear; burdensome [*weighty* responsibilities] **3.** very important; serious [*weighty* matters of state] **4.** influential, powerful, etc. [influenced by several *weighty* motives] —see SYN. at HEAVY —**weight′i·ly** *adv.* —**weight′i·ness** *n.*

Wei·ma·ra·ner (vī′mə rän′ər, wī′-) *n.* [< *Weimar* (see next entry), where the breed was developed] any of a breed of lean, medium-sized hunting dog with a smooth, gray coat

WEIGHT LIFTER

Wei·mar Republic (vī′mär; *E.* wī′mär) German Republic (1919–33), created at the city of Weimar (in what is now SW East Germany) & dissolved after Hitler became chancellor

weir (wir) *n.* [OE. *wer*] **1.** a low dam built in a river to change its course or to back up water, as for a mill **2.** a fence built in a stream or channel to catch fish

weird (wird) *adj.* [ult. < OE. *wyrd*, fate] **1.** of or suggestive of ghosts or other supernatural things; unearthly, mysterious, eerie, etc. **2.** very odd, strange, queer, etc. [rather *weird* behavior for a grandmother] —**weird′ly** *adv.* —**weird′ness** *n.*
SYN.—**weird** refers to that which is extremely mysterious or strange, esp. in ways suggestive of the supernatural [a *weird* experience]; **eerie** is used of that which causes a vague, superstitious feeling of uneasiness or fear [*eerie* noises in the night]; **uncanny** applies to that which is so unusual that no normal or natural explanation of it seems possible [her *uncanny* ability to guess correctly]; **unearthly** is used of that which is so strange or extraordinary as to seem to belong to another world [an *unearthly* light]

weird·o (wir′dō) *n., pl.* **-os** [Slang] a person or thing that is weird, eccentric, bizarre, etc.: also **weird′ie** (-dē)

Weird Sisters the three Fates

Weiz·mann (vīts′män; *E.* wīts′mən), **Cha·im** (khī′im) 1874–1952; Israeli chemist & Zionist leader, born in Russia; first president of Israel (1948–52)

Welch (welch, welsh) *adj., n. var. of* WELSH

welch (welch, welsh) *vi.* [Slang] *var. of* WELSH

wel·come (wel′kəm) *adj.* [< OE. *wilcuma*, a welcome guest < *willa*, pleasure + *cuma*, a guest] **1.** gladly received [a *welcome* guest] **2.** agreeable; pleasing [*welcome* news] **3.** gladly allowed or invited [you are *welcome* to use the library] **4.** under no obligation ["you're *welcome*" is the usual reply to "thank you"] —*n.* words or action used in greeting [a hearty *welcome*] —*interj.* you are welcome: used as a word used in greeting —*vt.* **-comed, -com·ing** **1.** to greet with pleasure and hospitality [to *welcome* guests] **2.** to receive with pleasure or satisfaction [to *welcome* criticism] **3.** to meet, receive, or acknowledge in a specified way [the outlaw was *welcomed* with a burst of gunfire] —**bid welcome** to receive with cordial greetings —☆**wear out one's welcome** to come too often or stay too long —**wel′com·er** *n.*

☆**welcome mat** a doormat: chiefly in **put out the welcome mat,** to welcome enthusiastically

weld (weld) *vt.* [altered < obs. *well*, to weld] **1.** to join (pieces of metal, etc.) by heating until they melt together or can be hammered or pressed together **2.** to join together; unite [to *weld* the unrelated events into an interesting story] —*vi.* to be welded or capable of being welded [this metal *welds* easily] —*n.* **1.** a welding or being welded **2.** the joint formed by welding — **weld′a·bil′i·ty** *n.* —**weld′a·ble** *adj.* —**weld′er** *n.*

wel·fare (wel′fer′) *n.* [see WELL² & FARE] **1.** condition of health, happiness, and comfort; well-being **2.** aid by government agencies for the poor, unemployed, etc. **3.** *same as* WELFARE WORK —**on welfare** receiving government aid because of poverty, unemployment, etc.

welfare state a nation in which the government takes responsibility for the welfare of the citizens, with regard to employment, medical care, social security, etc.

welfare work the organized effort of a community or group to improve the living conditions of its needy members —**welfare worker**

wel·kin (wel′kin) *n.* [OE. *wolcen*] [Archaic or Poet.] the sky thought of as forming a curved roof above the earth

well¹ (wel) *n.* [OE. *wella*, akin to *weallan*, to boil up] **1.** a natural spring and pool **2.** a hole sunk into the earth to get water, gas, oil, etc. **3.** a well-supplied source [this book is a *well* of information] **4.** any shaft like a well; esp., *a)* an open shaft in a building for a staircase *b)* a shaft in a building or between buildings to let in light and air *c)* an elevator shaft *d) Naut.* an enclosed place for the pumps in the hold of a ship **5.** any of various containers for liquid, as an inkwell **6.** a depression in a platter, broiler, etc. for catching meat juices —*vi., vt.* to pour forth as from a well; gush (*up, forth, down, out,* etc.) [pity *welled* up in her heart]

well² (wel) *adv.* **bet′ter, best** [OE. *wel*] **1.** in a pleasing or desirable way; satisfactorily [the work is going *well*] **2.** in a proper or friendly way [to treat a person *well*] **3.** skillfully [to sing *well*] **4.** fittingly [they were *well* rewarded] **5.** *a)* in comfort and plenty [to live *well*] *b)* to one's advantage [to marry *well*] **6.** with good reason; in justice [you may *well* ask] **7.** to a considerable degree, extent, etc. [they are *well* tanned] **8.** thoroughly [stir it *well*] **9.** with certainty; definitely [you know *well* why] **10.** intimately; closely [to know a person *well*] **11.** in good spirit; with good grace [he took the news *well*] *Well* is also used in hyphenated compounds, to mean *properly, satisfactorily, thoroughly,* etc. [*well*-defined] —*adj.* **1.** proper, right, etc. [it is *well* that he came] **2.** in good health [to be *well* again] **3.** in good condition [all is *well*] —*interj.* an exclamation used to express surprise, agreement, resignation, etc., or to introduce a remark —see SYN. at HEALTHY —**as well 1.** besides; in addition **2.** with equal reason or effect [you could *as well* stay home] —**as well as 1.** just as much or as good as **2.** in addition to [for pleasure *as well as* profit] —**wish someone well** to wish someone success or good luck

we'll (wēl, wil) **1.** we shall **2.** we will

well-ad·vised (wel′əd vīzd′) *adj.* showing or resulting from careful thought or sound advice; wise; prudent [a *well-advised* decision]

Wel·land (Ship) Canal (wel′ənd) canal of the St. Lawrence Seaway, in Ontario, Canada, between Lake Ontario & Lake Erie: see map at ST. LAWRENCE SEAWAY

well-ap·point·ed (wel′ə poin′tid) *adj.* excellently furnished or equipped [a *well-appointed* office]

well-a·way (wel′ə wā′) *interj.* [ME. *wei la wei*, lit., woe! lo! woe!] [Archaic] alas!: also **well′a·day′** (-dā′)

well-bal·anced (wel′bal′ənst) *adj.* **1.** carefully balanced, adjusted, etc. [a *well-balanced* meal] **2.** sane, sensible, and reliable [a *well-balanced* individual]

well-be·haved (-bi hāvd′) *adj.* behaving well; polite

well-be·ing (-bē′iŋ) *n.* the state of being well, happy, or prosperous; welfare

well-be·loved (-bi luvd′, -luv′id) *adj.* **1.** deeply loved **2.** highly respected: used in formal speaking or writing

well-born (-bôrn′) *adj.* born into a family of high social position

well-bred (-bred′) *adj.* **1.** showing good breeding; courteous and considerate **2.** of good stock: said of animals

well-chos·en (-chō′z'n) *adj.* chosen with care; appropriate

well-con·tent (-kən tent′) *adj.* thoroughly pleased or satisfied: also **well′-con·tent′ed**

well-dis·posed (-dis pōzd′) *adj.* **1.** suitably or properly placed or arranged **2.** inclined to be friendly, kindly, or favorable (*toward* a person) or receptive (*to* an idea, etc.)

well-done (-dun′) *adj.* **1.** done with skill and efficiency **2.** thoroughly cooked: said esp. of meat

well-fa·vored (wel′fā′vərd) *adj.* handsome; pretty

well-fed (-fed′) *adj.* showing the effect of eating much good food; specif., plump or fat

well-fixed (-fikst′) *adj.* [Colloq.] ☆wealthy; well-to-do

well-found·ed (-foun′did) *adj.* based on facts, good evidence, or sound judgment [a *well-founded* suspicion]

well-groomed (-grōōmd′) *adj.* **1.** carefully cared for [a *well-groomed* horse, a *well-groomed* lawn] **2.** clean and neat; carefully washed, combed, dressed, etc.

well-ground·ed (-groun′did) *adj.* **1.** having a thorough basic knowledge of a subject [*well-grounded* in mathematics] **2.** based on good reasons; well-founded

well-head (wel′hed′) *n.* **1.** the source of a spring of water; spring **2.** any source; fountainhead

☆**well-heeled** (wel′hēld′) *adj.* [Slang] rich; prosperous

well-in·formed (-in fôrmd′) *adj.* **1.** having thorough knowledge of a subject **2.** knowing a great deal about many subjects, esp. those of current interest

Wel·ling·ton (wel′iŋ tən) capital of New Zealand; seaport on S North Island: pop. (of urban area) 179,000

Wel·ling·ton (wel′iŋ tən), 1st Duke of, (Arthur *Wellesley*) 1769–1852; Brit. general & statesman, born in Ireland

Wellington (boot) [after prec.] [*also* w- b-] a knee-high, waterproof boot

well-in·ten·tioned (wel′in ten′shənd) *adj.* having or showing good or kindly intentions, but often with bad results

well-knit (-nit′) *adj.* having a strong, compact, or sturdy structure

well-known (-nōn′) *adj.* **1.** widely or generally known; famous **2.** thoroughly known

well-made (-mād′) *adj.* **1.** skillfully and carefully put together [a *well-made* table] **2.** having a clever, skillfully arranged plot [a *well-made* play]

well-man·nered (-man′ərd) *adj.* polite; courteous

well-mean·ing (-mē′niŋ) *adj.* **1.** having good or kindly intentions [a *well-meaning* but annoying individual] **2.** said or done with good intentions, but often unwisely or with bad results: also **well′-meant′** (-ment′)

well-nigh (-nī′) *adv.* very nearly; almost

well-off (-ôf′) *adj.* **1.** in a favorable or fortunate condition or situation **2.** wealthy; well-to-do

well-or·dered (-ôr′dərd) *adj.* properly or carefully organized

well-pre·served (-pri zurvd′) *adj.* in good condition or looking good in spite of age

well-read (-red′) *adj.* **1.** having read much (*in* a subject) [*well-read* in history] **2.** having a wide knowledge of books as a result of having read much

well-round·ed (-roun′did) *adj.* **1.** well planned for proper balance [a *well-rounded* program] **2.** showing interest, ability, etc. in many fields **3.** shapely

Wells (welz), **H(erbert) G(eorge)** 1866–1946; Eng. novelist & historian

well-spo·ken (wel′spō′k'n) *adj.* **1.** speaking in a skillful, courteous, well-educated manner **2.** suitable and well-chosen or well-expressed: said of words, remarks, etc.

well-spring (wel′spriŋ) *n.* **1.** a spring or fountainhead **2.** a supply that is always full [a *wellspring* of facts]

well-thought-of (wel′thôt′uv′) *adj.* having a good reputation; of good repute

well-timed (-tīmd′) *adj.* timely; opportune

well-to-do (-tə dōō′) *adj.* prosperous; well-off; wealthy —see SYN. at RICH

well-turned (-turnd′) *adj.* **1.** gracefully shaped [a *well-turned* ankle] **2.** expressed or worded well [a *well-turned* phrase]

well-wish·er (-wish′ər) *n.* a person who wishes well to another or to a cause, movement, etc. —**well′-wish′ing** *adj., n.*

well-worn (-wôrn′) *adj.* **1.** much worn; much used **2.** overused; trite [a *well-worn* joke]

Welsh (welsh, welch) *adj.* of Wales, its people, their language, etc. —*n.* the Brythonic language spoken in Wales —**the Welsh** the people of Wales

welsh (welsh, welch) *vi.* [< ?] [Slang] to cheat by failing to pay a debt [to *welsh* on a bet] —**welsh′er** *n.*

Welsh cor·gi (kôr′gē) [WELSH + W. *corgi* < *corr*, dwarf + *ci*, dog] either of two breeds of short-legged dog with a foxlike head, orig. from Wales

Welsh·man (welsh′mən, welch′-) *n., pl.* **-men** a native or inhabitant of Wales

Welsh rabbit [orig. a humorous usage] a dish of melted cheese, often mixed with ale or beer, served on crackers or toast: also **Welsh rarebit**

Welsh terrier a wire-haired terrier closely resembling the Airedale but smaller, orig. from Wales

welt (welt) *n.* [ME. *welte*] **1.** a strip of leather sewn into the seam between the sole and upper of a shoe to strengthen the seam **2.** a strip of material placed at an edge or seam of a garment, etc. for ornamentation or added strength **3.** *a)* a ridge raised on the skin by the blow of a whip, etc. *b)* such a blow — *vt.* **1.** to furnish with a welt **2.** to raise welts on (the body) **3.** [Colloq.] to beat severely; thrash

wel·ter (wel′tər) *vi.* [MDu. *welteren*] **1.** to roll about or wallow, as a pig in mud **2.** to be deeply involved [to *welter* in sin] **3.** to be soaked, stained, etc. [to *welter* in blood] —*n.* **1.** a tossing and tumbling, as of waves **2.** a confusion; turmoil [fighting through a *welter* of bargain hunters]

wel·ter·weight (wel′tər wāt′) *n.* [prob. < WELT (*vt.* 3) + -ER + WEIGHT] a boxer or wrestler between a lightweight and a middleweight (in boxing, 136–147 pounds)

Wel·ty (wel′tē), **Eu·dor·a** (yōō dôr′ə) 1909–; U.S. short-story writer & novelist

wen (wen) *n.* [OE. *wenn*] a cyst filled with oily matter that has been retained, esp. one on the scalp

wench (wench) *n.* [OE. *wencel*, a child] **1.** a girl or young woman: now used to show contempt or said in a joking way **2.** [Archaic] *a)* a country girl *b)* a female servant *c)* a woman whose sexual behavior is loose and immoral —*vi.* to spend much time with women whose sexual behavior is loose and immoral

wend (wend) *vt.* **wend′ed** or archaic **went, wend′ing** [OE. *wendan*, to turn] to proceed on (one's way) [we *wended* our way home]

went (went) [old pt. of WEND, used to replace missing form of GO] *pt. of* GO

wept (wept) *pt. & pp. of* WEEP

were (wur; *unstressed* wər) [OE. *wæron*] *the second person singular and first, second, and third person plural in the past tense of* BE: *also the past subjunctive in all persons*

we're (wir) we are

weren't (wurnt) were not

were·wolf (wir′woolf′, wur′-, wer′-) *n., pl.* **-wolves** (-woolvz′) [< OE. < *wer*, a man + *wulf*, a wolf] *Folklore* a person changed into a wolf or able to take the form of a wolf at will: also sp. **wer′wolf′**, *pl.* **wer′wolves′**

wert (wurt; *unstressed* wərt) *the archaic second person singular in the past tense and past subjunctive of* BE: *used with* thou

wes·kit (wes′kit) *n.* [< WAISTCOAT] a vest or waistcoat

Wes·ley (wes′lē, wez′-) **1.** [< the surname *Wesley*] a masculine name **2. Charles,** 1707–88; Eng. clergyman: brother of *John* **3. John,** 1703–91; Eng. clergyman & founder of the Methodist Church

Wes·ley·an (wes′lē ən, wez′-) *adj.* of John Wesley or the Methodist Church —*n.* a follower of John Wesley; Methodist — **Wes′ley·an·ism** *n.*

Wes·sex (wes′iks) former Anglo-Saxon kingdom in S England

west (west) *n.* [OE.] **1.** the direction to the left of a person facing north; direction in which sunset occurs (270° on the compass, opposite east) **2.** a region or district in or toward this direction **3.** [W-] the Western Hemisphere, or the Western Hemisphere and Europe; the Occident **4.** [W-] the Western Roman Empire —*adj.* **1.** in, of, to, or toward the west **2.** from the west [a *west* wind] **3.** [W-] designating the western part of a country, etc. [*West* Africa] —*adv.* in or toward the west —**the West** ☆**1.** the western part of the U.S., esp. the region west of the Mississippi **2.** the U.S. and its non-Communist allies in Europe and the Western Hemisphere

West (west), **Benjamin** 1738–1820; Am. painter, in England after 1763

West Al·lis (al′is) [after the *Allis*-Chalmers Co. there] city in SE Wis.: suburb of Milwaukee: pop. 72,000

West Berlin W section of Berlin, forming a separate city associated with West Germany: pop. 2,141,000: see BERLIN

☆**west·bound** (west′bound′) *adj.* going westward

West Co·vi·na (kō vē′nə) [*Covina* said locally to mean "place of vines"] city in SW Calif.: suburb of Los Angeles: pop. 68,000

West End W section of London, England

west·er·ly (wes′tər lē) *adj., adv.* **1.** toward the west **2.** from the west —*n., pl.* **-lies** a wind from the west

west·ern (wes′tərn) *adj.* **1.** in, of, or toward the west [the

western sky] **2.** from the west [a *western* wind] **3.** [W-] of or characteristic of the West —*n.* ☆a story, motion picture, etc. about cowboys or frontiersmen in the western U.S.

Western Australia state of Australia, occupying the W third of the continent

Western Church that part of the Catholic Church which recognizes the Pope and follows the Latin Rite; the Roman Catholic Church

west·ern·er (wes′tər nər) *n.* a native or inhabitant of the west, ☆specif. [W-] of the western part of the U.S.

Western Hemisphere that half of the earth that includes North & South America

west·ern·ize (wes′tərn īz′) *vt.* **-ized′, -iz′ing** to make western in character, habits, ideas, etc. —**west′ern·i·za′tion** *n.*

west·ern·most (-mōst′) *adj.* farthest west

☆**Western (omelet)** an omelet prepared with diced green pepper, onion, and ham

Western Reserve section of the Northwest Territory, on Lake Erie: reserved for settlers by Conn. when its other western lands were ceded to the Federal government in 1786

Western Roman Empire the W part of the Roman Empire, from 395 A.D., when its parts were formed by the division of the Roman Empire, until 476 A.D. when it was overthrown

Western Samoa country in the South Pacific, consisting of two large islands & several small ones: a member of the Commonwealth: 1,130 sq. mi.; pop. 146,000

Western Wall a high wall in Jerusalem believed to be part of the western section of the wall surrounding Herod's Temple: Jews have traditionally gathered at this site for prayer

West Germany a country in NC Europe: 95,735 sq. mi.; pop. 59,974,000; cap. Bonn: see GERMANY

West Haven city in SW Conn., on Long Island Sound: suburb of New Haven: pop. 53,000

West Indies large group of islands between N. America & S. America: it includes the Greater Antilles, Lesser Antilles, & Bahamas —**West Indian**

West·ing·house (wes′tiŋ hous′), **George** 1846–1914; U.S. inventor & manufacturer

West Ir·i·an (ir′ē ən) province of Indonesia, occupying the W half of the island of New Guinea: c.160,000 sq. mi.

West·land (west′lənd, -land′) [from its location in the county] city in SE Mich.: suburb of Detroit: pop. 87,000

West·min·ster (west′min′stər) metropolitan borough of London, on the Thames: site of the Houses of Parliament

Westminster Abbey Gothic church in Westminster where English monarchs are crowned: burial place for English monarchs and other famous persons

west-north·west (west′nôrth′west′, -nôr-) *n.* the direction halfway between due west and northwest; 22°30′ north of due west —*adj., adv.* **1.** in or toward this direction **2.** from this direction

West Palm Beach city in SE Fla., on a lagoon opposite Palm Beach: pop. 57,000

West·pha·li·a (west fā′lē ə, -fāl′yə) region in West Germany, on the Rhine: formerly a duchy, a kingdom, & a province of Prussia

West Point military reservation in southeastern N.Y., on the west bank of the Hudson: site of the U.S. Military Academy

west-south·west (west′-south′west′, -sou-) *n.* the direction halfway between due west and southwest; 22°30′ south of due west —*adj., adv.* **1.** in or toward this direction **2.** from this direction

West Virginia E State of the U.S., northwest of Va.: 24,181 sq. mi.; pop. 1,744,000; cap. Charleston: abbrev. **W.Va., WV** —**West Virginian**

west·ward (-wərd) *adv., adj.* toward the west: also **west′wards** *adv.* —*n.* a westward direction, point, or region

west·ward·ly (-lē) *adv., adj.* **1.** toward the west **2.** from the west [a *westwardly* wind]

wet (wet) *adj.* **wet′ter, wet′test** [OE. *wæt*] **1.** covered or soaked with water or other liquid [*wet* streets, *wet* socks] **2.** rainy; misty [a *wet* day] **3.** not yet dry [*wet* paint] **4.** pre-

WESTPHALIA (1812)

served or bottled in a liquid **5.** using, or done with or in, water or other liquid [*wet* sanding] ☆**6.** permitting or favoring the sale of alcoholic liquors [a *wet* town] —*n.* water, rain, moisture, etc. [out there working in the *wet*] —*vt., vi.* **wet** or **wet′- ted, wet′ting 1.** to make or become wet (often with *through* or *down*) [he *wet* his lips] **2.** to make (a bed, oneself, etc.) wet by urination —☆**all wet** [Slang] wrong; in error —**wet behind the ears** [Colloq.] young and inexperienced —**wet′ly** *adv.* —**wet′- ness** *n.* —**wet′ta·ble** *adj.* —**wet′ter** *n.* —**wet′tish** *adj.*
SYN.—**wet** is applied to something covered or soaked with water or other liquid [*wet* hands, laundry, etc.] or to something not yet dry [*wet* plaster]; **damp** implies slight, usually undesirable or unpleasant wetness [a *damp* room]; **dank** suggests a disagreeable, chilling, unhealthful dampness [a *dank* fog]; **moist** implies slight wetness but, unlike **damp**, often suggests that the absence of dryness is desirable [*moist* air]; **humid** suggests air so filled with moisture as to cause discomfort [a hot, *humid* day] —**ANT.** dry

☆**wet·back** (wet′bak′) *n.* [from the fact that many enter by swimming or wading the Rio Grande] [Colloq.] a Mexican agricultural laborer who illegally enters the U.S. to work

wet blanket a person or thing that causes people to feel less enthusiastic, happy, etc.

wet cell a voltaic cell in which the electrolyte is a liquid

weth·er (weth′ər) *n.* [OE.] a castrated male sheep

wet·land (wet′land′) *n.* [*usually pl.*] swamps or marshes, ☆esp. as an area preserved for wildlife

wet nurse a woman hired to breast-feed another woman's child —**wet-nurse** (wet′nurs′) *vt.* **-nursed′, -nurs′ing**

wet suit a closefitting, usually one-piece suit of rubber, worn by skin divers for warmth

we've (wēv) we have

wf, w.f. *Printing* wrong font

WGmc. West Germanic

whack (hwak, wak) *vt., vi.* [echoic] [Colloq.] to hit or slap with a sharp sound —*n.* [Colloq.] a blow that makes a sharp sound; also, this sound —**at a** (or **one**) **whack** [Colloq.] at one time and quickly or without pausing —☆**have** (or **take**) **a whack at** [Colloq.] **1.** to aim a blow at **2.** to make an attempt at —☆**out of whack** [Colloq.] not in proper working condition —**whack off** [Colloq.] to separate or remove as by a chopping blow —**whack′er** *n.*

whack·ing (hwak′iŋ, wak′-) *adj.* [Chiefly Brit. Colloq.] big; huge

whack·y (-ē) *adj.* **-i·er, -i·est** [Slang] *same as* WACKY

whale[1] (hwāl, wāl) *n., pl.* **whales, whale**: see PLURAL, II, D, 1 [OE. *hwæl*] any of various large mammals that live in the sea and have a fishlike form, with a flat, horizontal tail and with front limbs modified into flippers; esp., any of the larger mammals of this kind (up to 100 ft. in length), as distinguished from the porpoises and dolphins: see TOOTHED WHALE, WHALEBONE WHALE —*vi.* **whaled, whal′ing** to hunt whales —☆**a whale of a** [Colloq.] an exceptionally large, fine, etc. example of (a class of persons or things)

whale[2] (hwāl, wāl) *vt.* **whaled, whal′ing** [prob. var. of WALE] [Colloq.] to beat; whip; thrash

☆**whale·boat** (hwāl′bōt′, wāl′-) *n.* **1.** a long rowboat, pointed at both ends: used formerly by whalers **2.** a similar boat, often one with a motor (**motor whaleboat**) used as a ship's lifeboat

whale·bone (-bōn′) *n.* **1.** the tough, elastic material hanging in fringed sheets from the upper jaw or palate of whalebone whales: it strains out the tiny sea animals on which they feed **2.** something made of whalebone

whalebone whale any of a main division of whales, as the blue whale, having whalebone in the mouth and no teeth

whal·er (hwā′lər, wā′-) *n.* **1.** a ship used in whaling **2.** a man whose work is whaling: also ☆**whale′man,** *pl.* **-men**

whal·ing (-liŋ) *n.* the work or trade of hunting and killing whales for their blubber, whalebone, etc.

wham (hwam, wam) *interj.* a sound imitating a heavy blow or explosion —*n.* a heavy blow or impact —*vt., vi.* **whammed, wham′ming** to strike, explode, etc. loudly

☆**wham·my** (hwam′ē, wam′-) *n., pl.* **-mies** [Slang] a jinx or the evil eye: usually in **put a** (or **the**) **whammy on**

WET SUIT

whang (hwaŋ, waŋ) *vt.* [echoic] to strike with a heavy blow —*vi.* to make a loud noise by hitting —*n.* **1.** a loud, echoing noise **2.** a whack or blow

whap (hwäp, wäp) *vt., vi., n.* **whapped, whap′ping** [Colloq.] *same as* WHOP

wharf (hwôrf, wôrf) *n., pl.* **wharves** (hwôrvz, wôrvz), **wharfs** [OE. *hwerf,* a dam < base of *hweorfan,* to turn] a platform built along or out from the shore, where ships can dock and load or unload; pier; dock —*vt.* **1.** to bring to a wharf; moor at a wharf **2.** to unload or store on a wharf

wharf·age (-ij) *n.* **1.** the use of a wharf, as for loading or unloading a ship **2.** a fee charged for this **3.** wharves as a group

Whar·ton (hwôr′t'n, wôr′-), **Edith** (born *Edith Newbold Jones*) 1862–1937; U.S. novelist

what (hwut, hwät, wut, wät; *unstressed* hwət, wət) *pron.* [OE. *hwæt,* neut. of *hwa,* who] **1.** which thing, event, etc.: used in asking questions or in asking someone to repeat, explain, specify, etc. [*what* is that object? you told him *what?*] **2.** that which or those which: used as a relative pronoun [to know *what* one wants, not *what* it once was] —*n.* the nature (*of* an event) [the *what* and why of his exile] —*adj.* **1.** which or which kind of [*what* man told you that? I know *what* books you like] **2.** as much as or as many as [*what* time (or men) you need] **3.** how great, surprising, etc.: in exclamations [*what* joy!] —*adv.* **1.** in what respect? to what degree? how? [*what* does it matter?] **2.** in some manner or degree; in part; partly (usually with *with*) [*what* with singing and joking, the time passed quickly] **3.** how greatly, surprisingly, etc. [*what* sad news!] —*conj.* that: in **but what,** but that [never doubt *but what* he loves you] —*interj.* an exclamation of surprise, anger, etc. [*what!* no dinner?] —**and what not** and other things of all sorts —**what about** what do you think, know, etc. concerning? —**what for 1.** why? **2.** [Slang] punishment [you'll get *what for*] —☆**what have you** [Colloq.] anything similar [games, toys, or *what have you*] —**what if 1.** what would happen if **2.** what difference would it make if —**what's what** [Colloq.] the real facts of the matter —**what the (heck, devil,** etc.) **1.** an exclamation of surprise **2.** what: used for added force —**what though** no matter if

what·ev·er (hwut ev′ər, wət-) *pron.* what: used for emphasis; specif., *a*) which thing, event, etc.: used in questions [*whatever* can it be?] *b*) anything that [tell her *whatever* you like] *c*) no matter what [*whatever* you do, don't rush] *d*) [Colloq.] anything at all [she reads novels, biographies, or *whatever*] —*adj.* **1.** of no matter what type, degree, etc. [make *whatever* repairs are needed] **2.** being who it may be [*whatever* man told you that, it isn't true] **3.** of any kind [no plans *whatever*] Also [Poet.] **what·e'er** (-er′)

what·not (hwut′nät′, hwät′-, wut′-, wät′-) *n.* a set of open shelves for displaying small art objects, knickknacks, etc.

what's (hwuts, hwäts, wuts, wäts) what is

what·so·ev·er (hwut′sō ev′ər, hwät′-, wut′-, wät′-) *pron., adj.* whatever: also [Poet.] **what′so·e'er** (-er′)

wheal[1] (hwēl, wēl) *n.* [akin to OE. *hwelian,* to suppurate] **1.** formerly, a pustule; pimple **2.** a small, raised patch of skin, as from an insect bite or hives

wheal[2] (hwēl, wēl) *n. same as* WEAL[1]

wheat (hwēt, wēt) *n.* see PLURAL, II, D, 3 [OE. *hwæte*] **1.** any of a group of cereal grasses with dense spikes that grow upright and bear grains that are threshed to remove the chaff **2.** such grain, used for flour, cereals, pasta, etc.

☆**wheat cake** a pancake made with whole-wheat flour

wheat·en (hwēt′'n, wēt′-) *adj.* **1.** made of wheat or wheat flour **2.** of the pale-yellow color of wheat

☆**wheat germ 1.** the embryo of the wheat kernel, milled out as an oily flake **2.** the milled flakes, used as a vitamin supplement

whee (hwē, wē) *interj.* an exclamation expressing joy, excitement, etc.

whee·dle (hwē′d'l, wē′-) *vt., vi.* **-dled, -dling** [< ? G. *wedeln,* to wag the tail, hence to flatter] **1.** to influence or persuade (a person) by flattery, soothing words, coaxing, etc. **2.** to get (something) by coaxing or flattery —**whee′dler** *n.*

WHEAT

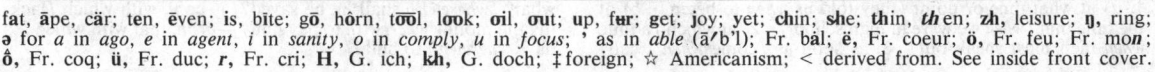

wheel (hwēl, wēl) *n.* [OE. *hweol*] **1.** a solid disk, or a circular frame connected by spokes to a central hub, capable of turning on a central axis **2.** anything like a wheel in shape, movement, etc. **3.** a device having as its main part a wheel or wheels; specif., *a)* a medieval torture instrument that was a circular frame on which a victim was painfully stretched *b)* a wheel with projecting handles, to control a ship's rudder *c) short for* POTTER'S WHEEL, SPINNING WHEEL, etc. ☆*d)* [Colloq.] a bicycle ☆*e)* [*pl.*] [Slang] an automobile **4.** [*usually pl.*] the moving or controlling forces or agencies [the *wheels* of progress] **5.** a turning movement, specif. one made by a line of ships, troops, etc. ☆**6.** [Slang] an important or influential person: also **big wheel** —*vt., vi.* **1.** to move or roll on wheels or in a wheeled vehicle [to *wheel* a grocery cart] **2.** to turn or cause to turn as on an axis; rotate, revolve, pivot, etc. **3.** to move or cause to move in a circle [birds *wheeling* about overhead] **4.** to turn so as to reverse direction, attitude, etc. (often with *about*) [the deer *wheeled* and faced the dogs] —**at the wheel 1.** steering a ship, car, etc. **2.** in charge; directing activities —☆**wheel and deal** [Slang] to behave in a daring, aggressive way, as in a business deal —**wheel of fortune** the changes, good and bad, that occur in life —**wheels within wheels** a complicated series of related events, motives, etc.

wheel and axle a grooved wheel fixed to a shaft or drum, used for lifting weights: the turning of the wheel by a rope in the groove winds a rope on the shaft or drum

wheel·bar·row (-bar′ō, -ber′ō) *n.* a small kind of cart in which small loads can be carried, having a single wheel in front, two legs in back, and two shafts with handles for raising the vehicle off its legs and pushing or pulling it —*vt.* to carry in a wheelbarrow

wheel·base (-bās′) *n.* in a motor vehicle, the distance in inches from the center of the hub of a front wheel to the center of the hub of the back wheel on the same side of the vehicle

wheel·chair (-cher′) *n.* ☆a chair mounted on large wheels, used in moving about by persons unable to walk

wheeled (hwēld, wēld) *adj.* **1.** having a wheel or wheels [a *wheeled* vehicle] **2.** having wheels of a specified number or kind [four-*wheeled*]

wheel·er (hwēl′ər, wēl′-) *n.* **1.** a person or thing that wheels **2.** *same as* WHEEL HORSE (sense 1) **3.** something with a specified kind or number of wheels [two-*wheeler*]

☆**wheel·er-deal·er** (hwēl′ər dēl′ər, wēl′-) *n.* [Slang] a person who wheels and deals: see phrase at entry WHEEL

wheel horse 1. the horse, or one of the horses, harnessed nearest the front wheels of a vehicle ☆**2.** a person who works especially hard and effectively in any job or project

☆**wheel·house** (-hous′) *n. same as* PILOTHOUSE

wheel·wright (-rīt′) *n.* a person who makes and repairs wagon and carriage wheels

wheeze (hwēz, wēz) *vi.* **wheezed, wheez′ing** [ON. *hvæsa*, to hiss] **1.** to breathe hard with a whistling, breathy sound, as in asthma **2.** to make a sound like this [the old organ *wheezed*] —*vt.* to utter with a sound of wheezing —*n.* **1.** an act or sound of wheezing **2.** [Slang] a trite remark or joke —**wheez′er** *n.* —**wheez′ing·ly** *adv.*

wheez·y (hwē′zē, wē′-) *adj.* **wheez′i·er, wheez′i·est** wheezing or characterized by wheezing —**wheez′i·ly** *adv.*

whelk[1] (hwelk, welk) *n.* [OE. *wioluc*] any of various large sea snails with spiral shells, esp. those species used in Europe for food

whelk[2] (hwelk, welk) *n.* [OE. *hwylca*] **1.** a pimple or pustule **2.** *same as* WEAL[1]

whelm (hwelm, welm) *vt.* [? merging of OE. *-hwelfan*, to overwhelm, with *helmian*, to cover] **1.** to put under water; submerge **2.** to overpower or crush

WHELK
(3 in. long)

whelp (hwelp, welp) *n.* [OE. *hwelp*] **1.** a young dog; puppy **2.** a young lion, tiger, wolf, etc.; cub **3.** a youth or child: a term showing contempt —*vt., vi.* to give birth to (whelps)

when (hwen, wen; *unstressed* hwən, wən) *adv.* [OE. *hwænne*] **1.** *a)* at what time? [*when* did they leave?] *b)* on what occasion or under what circumstances? [*when* do you double the final consonant?] *c)* at what point? [*when* shall I stop pouring?] **2.** earlier and in other circumstances [I knew him *when*] —*conj.* **1.** *a)* at what time or point [they told us *when* to begin] *b)* at the time that [*when* we were in high school] **2.** at which [a time *when* men must speak out] **3.** as soon as [come *when* I call]

4. at whatever time that [he rested *when* he could] **5.** although [to object *when* there's no reason to do so] **6.** if [how can he help *when* they won't let him?] —*pron.* what time or which time [until *when* will you stay?] —*n.* the time or moment (*of* an event) [the *when* and where of his arrest]

when·as (hwen az′, wen-) *conj.* [Archaic] **1.** when **2.** inasmuch as **3.** whereas

whence (hwens, wens) *adv.* [OE. *hwanan*] from what place, source, cause, etc.; from where [*whence* do you come? *whence* did he get his facts?] —*conj.* **1.** to the place from which [return *whence* you came] **2.** because of which fact [one shoe was badly worn, *whence* I deduced that he limped]

whence·so·ev·er (hwens′sō ev′ər, wens′-) *adv., conj.* from whatever place, source, or cause

when·ev·er (hwen ev′ər, wen-, hwən-, wən-) *adv.* [Colloq.] when: used for emphasis [*whenever* will he learn?] —*conj.* at whatever time; on whatever occasion [visit us *whenever* you can] Also [Poet.] **when′e′er′** (-er′)

when·so·ev·er (hwen′sō ev′ər, wen′-) *adv., conj.* whenever: used for emphasis: also [Poet.] **when′so·e′er′** (-er′)

where (hwer, wer; *unstressed* hwər, wər) *adv.* [OE. *hwær*] **1.** in or at what place? [*where* is the car?] **2.** to or toward what place? [*where* did he go?] **3.** in what situation? [*where* will we be if we lose?] **4.** in what way? [*where* is she to blame?] **5.** from what place or source? [*where* did you find out?] —*conj.* **1.** in or at what place [he knows *where* it is] **2.** in or at which place [we came home, *where* we ate dinner] **3.** in or at the place or situation in which [he is *where* he should be] **4.** in whatever place, situation, or respect in which [there is never peace *where* men are greedy] **5.** *a)* to or toward the place to which [he'll go *where* we go] *b)* to a place in which [send help *where* it's needed] **6.** to or toward whatever place [go where you please] **7.** [Colloq.] *same as* WHEREAS NOTE The use of *where* in place of *that* to introduce a noun clause is objected to by some [I see *where* taxes are going up] —*pron.* **1.** the place or situation in, at, or to which [it is a mile from *where* he lives] **2.** what or which place [*where* are you from?] —*n.* the place (*of* an event) [the when and *where* of his arrest]

where·a·bouts (hwer′ə bouts′, wer′-) *adv.* near or at what place? where? [*whereabouts* are we?] —*n.* the place where a person or thing is [do you know his *whereabouts*?]

where·as (hwer az′, wer-, hwər-, wər-) *conj.* **1.** in view of the fact that: used at the beginning of a formal document [*whereas* the following incidents have occurred] **2.** but on the other hand; while [she is slender, *whereas* he is stout] —*n., pl.* **-as·es** a statement beginning with "whereas"

where·at (-at′) *adv.* [Archaic] at what? [*whereat* was he angry?] —*conj.* [Archaic] at which point [he left, *whereat* she began to weep]

where·by (-bī′) *adv.* [Archaic] by what? how? [*whereby* did you expect to profit?] —*conj.* by which; by means of which [a plan *whereby* to make money]

where·fore (hwer′fôr′, wer′-) *adv.* [Archaic] for what reason or purpose? why? [*wherefore* are you angry?] —*conj.* **1.** for which [the reason *wherefore* we have met] **2.** because of which; therefore [we are victorious, *wherefore* let us rejoice] —*n.* the reason; cause [explaining the whys and *wherefores* of the plan]

where·from (hwer frum′, wer-) *adv., conj.* from which

where·in (-in′) *adv.* [Archaic] in what way? how? [*wherein* is it wrong?] —*conj.* in which [the room *wherein* he lay]

where·of (-uv′) *adv., conj.* of what, which, or whom [the things *whereof* he spoke]

where·on (-än′) *adv.* [Archaic] on what? [*whereon* do you rely?] —*conj.* on which [the hill *whereon* we stand]

where·so·ev·er (hwer′sō ev′ər, wer′-) *adv., conj.* wherever: used for emphasis: also [Poet.] **where′so·e′er′** (-er′)

where·to (hwer tōō′, wer-) *adv.* to what? toward what place, direction, or end? —*conj.* to which [the place *whereto* they hasten]

where·up·on (hwer′ə pän′, wer′-; hwer′ə pän, wer′-) *adv.* [Archaic] upon what? whereon? —*conj.* **1.** upon which [the ground *whereupon* he had fallen] **2.** at which; as a result of which [she told a joke, *whereupon* he laughed]

wher·ev·er (hwer ev′ər, wer-, hwər-, wər-) *adv.* [Colloq.] where: used for emphasis [*wherever* did you hear that?] —*conj.* in, at, or to whatever place or situation [he thinks of us, *wherever* he is] Also [Poet.] **wher·e′er′** (-er′)

where·with (hwer with′, wer-; -with′) *adv.* [Archaic] with what? [*wherewith* shall he be saved?] —*conj.* with which [lacking the money *wherewith* to pay him] —*pron.* that with which [to have *wherewith* to build]

where·with·al (hwer′with ôl′, wer′-; -with-) *n.* what is needed to get something done; necessary means, esp. money (usually with *the*) [the *wherewithal* to continue one's education] —*adv., conj.* archaic var. of WHEREWITH

wher·ry (hwer′ē, wer′-) *n., pl.* **-ries** [< ? ME. *whirren*, to whir, with idea of fast movement] **1.** a light rowboat used on rivers **2.** a racing scull for one person **3.** [Brit.] a large, broad, but light barge —*vt.* **-ried, -ry·ing** to transport in a wherry

whet (hwet, wet) *vt.* **whet′ted, whet′ting** [OE. *hwettan* < *hwæt*, sharp] **1.** to sharpen by rubbing or grinding (the edge of a knife or tool); hone **2.** to make stronger; stimulate [to *whet* the appetite] —*n.* **1.** an act of whetting **2.** something that whets

wheth·er (hweth′ər, weth′ər) *conj.* [OE. *hwæther*] **1.** if it is true or likely that [ask *whether* she will help] **2.** in either case that [*whether* it rains or snows] **3.** either [*whether* by accident or design] —*whether or no* in any case

whet·stone (hwet′stōn′, wet′-) *n.* a stone with a rough surface, for sharpening knives or other edged tools

whew (hyo͞o, hwo͞o) *interj.* [echoic] an exclamation of relief, surprise, disgust, etc.

whey (hwā, wā) *n.* [OE. *hwæg*] the thin, watery part of milk, which separates from the thicker part (curds) after coagulation, as in cheesemaking —**whey′ey** (-ē) *adj.*

whey·face (hwā′fās′, wā′-) *n.* **1.** a pale face **2.** a person having such a face —**whey′faced′** *adj.*

which (hwich, wich) *pron.* [OE. *hwylc*] **1.** what one (or ones) of the persons, things, or events mentioned or implied? [*which* do you want?] **2.** the one (or ones) that [he knows *which* he wants] **3.** that: used to refer to the thing or event just mentioned [her hat, *which* is blue; the boat *which* sank] **4.** any that; whichever [take *which* you like] **5.** a thing or fact that [you are late —*which* reminds me, where is Joe?] —*adj.* **1.** what one or ones (of the number mentioned or implied) [*which* man (or men) came?] **2.** whatever [try *which* plan you like] **3.** being the one just mentioned [he is old, *which* fact is important]

which·ev·er (hwich ev′ər, wich-) *pron., adj.* **1.** any one (of two or more) [he may choose *whichever* (desk) he likes] **2.** no matter which [*whichever* (desk) he chooses, they won't be pleased]

which·so·ev·er (hwich′sō ev′ər, wich′-) *pron., adj.* whichever: used for emphasis

whick·er (hwik′ər, wik′-) *vi.* [echoic] to neigh or whinny

whiff (hwif, wif) *n.* [echoic] **1.** a light puff or gust of air or wind; breath **2.** a slight gust of odor; faint smell [a *whiff* of garlic] **3.** an inhaling or exhaling of tobacco smoke ☆**4.** [Colloq.] an unsuccessful attempt to hit the ball in golf, baseball, etc. —*vt.* **1.** to blow with a puff or gust; waft ☆**2.** [Colloq.] to cause (a batter) to strike out in baseball —*vi.* **1.** to blow or move in puffs ☆**2.** [Colloq.] to miss the ball, as in golf, or strike out, as in baseball —**whiff′er** *n.*

whif·fle (hwif′'l, wif′-) *vi.* **-fled, -fling** [WHIFF + -LE²] **1.** to blow in gusts: said of the wind **2.** to shift or veer about; vacillate —*vt.* to blow or scatter as with a puff of wind —**whiff′fler** *n.*

whiffle ball a small, hollow plastic ball with holes in it that reduce the distance it can travel when struck, as with a bat

☆**whif·fle·tree** (-trē′) *n.* var. of WHIPPLE-TREE

WHIFFLE BALL

Whig (hwig, wig) *n.* [< *whiggamore* (applied to Scot. Presbyterians who marched on Edinburgh in 1648) < WScot. < *whig*, a cry to urge on horses + *mare*, a horse] **1.** a member of a political party in England (fl. 18th to mid-19th cent.) which favored increased popular rights: it later became the Liberal Party ☆**2.** in the American Revolution, a person who opposed Great Britain and supported the Revolution ☆**3.** a member of an American political party (c.1836–1856) opposing the Democratic Party —*adj.* of or being a Whig —**Whig′gish** *adj.* — **Whig′gism, Whig′ger·y** *n.*

while (hwīl, wīl) *n.* [OE. *hwil*] a period of time [a short *while*] —*conj.* **1.** during or throughout the time that [we talked *while* we ate] **2.** at the same time that [*while* you're up, close the door] **3.** *a)* although [*while* she isn't pretty, she is charming] *b)* whereas; and on the other hand [the walls are green, *while* the ceiling is white] —*vt.* **whiled, whil′ing** to spend (time) in a

pleasant way [to *while* away the hours] —**between whiles** now and then; at intervals —**the while** during this very time —**worth (one's) while** worth the time it takes one

whiles (hwīlz, wīlz) *adv.* [Chiefly Scot.] same as SOMETIMES — *conj.* [Archaic or Dial.] same as WHILE

whi·lom (hwī′ləm, wī′-) *adv.* [OE. *hwilum*, dative pl. of *hwil*, while] [Archaic] at one time; formerly —*adj.* formerly such; former [their *whilom* friends]

whilst (hwīlst, wīlst) *conj.* [Chiefly Brit., or U.S. Dial.] same as WHILE

whim (hwim, wim) *n.* [short for WHIM-WHAM] a sudden thought or wish to do something, without any particular reason; idle and passing notion [on a *whim*, he climbed aboard the bus]

whim·brel (hwim′brəl, wim′-) *n.* [prob. echoic of its cry] a small European curlew

whim·per (hwim′pər, wim′-) *vi.* [? akin to WHINE] to make low, broken, crying sounds —*vt.* to say with a whimper —*n.* a whimpering sound or cry —**whim′per·er** *n.* —**whim′per·ing·ly** *adv.*

whim·si·cal (hwim′zi k'l, wim′-) *adj.* **1.** full of whims or whimsy; having odd notions [a *whimsical* inventor] **2.** different in an odd way; fanciful [a *whimsical* costume] **3.** unpredictable —**whim′si·cal·ly** *adv.*

whim·si·cal·i·ty (hwim′zi kal′ə tē, wim′-) *n.* **1.** the quality of being whimsical: also **whim′si·cal·ness 2.** *pl.* **-ties** a whimsical speech, idea, or action

whim·sy (hwim′zē, wim′-) *n., pl.* **-sies** [prob. < WHIM-WHAM] **1.** an odd notion that comes to one suddenly; whim **2.** quaint or fanciful humor [poems full of *whimsy*] Also sp. **whim′sey,** *pl.* **-seys**

whim-wham (hwim′hwam′, wim′wam′) *n.* [< ?] an odd notion; whim —☆**the whim-whams** [Colloq.] a nervous feeling; the jitters

whin (hwin, win) *n.* [prob. < Scand.] same as FURZE

whin·chat (hwin′chat′, win′-) *n.* [WHIN + *chat*, a warbler] a brown and buff migrating European songbird

whine (hwīn, wīn) *vi.* **whined, whin′ing** [OE. *hwinan*] **1.** *a)* to utter an irritated, high-pitched sound, as in complaint, distress, etc. [a *whining* child] *b)* to make a drawn-out, high-pitched sound [a *whining* machine] **2.** to complain or beg in a childish, undignified way [she kept *whining* about her troubles] —*vt.* to say with a whine —*n.* **1.** the act or sound of whining **2.** a complaint spoken in a whining tone —**whin′er** *n.* —**whin′i·ness** *n.* —**whin′ing·ly** *adv.* —**whin′y, whin′ey** *adj.*

☆**whing·ding** (hwiŋ′diŋ′, wiŋ′-) *n.* [Slang] same as WINGDING

whin·ny (hwin′ē, win′ē) *vi.* **-nied, -ny·ing** [prob. < or akin to WHINE] to neigh in a low, gentle way: said of a horse —*vt.* to express with a whinny —*n., pl.* **-nies** the sound of whinnying

whip (hwip, wip) *vt.* **whipped, whip′ping** [MDu. *wippen*, to swing] **1.** to move, pull, throw, etc. suddenly (usually with *out, off, up,* etc.) [to *whip* out a knife] **2.** to strike, as with a strap, rod, etc.; lash; beat **3.** to drive, urge, etc. by or as by whipping **4.** to strike as a whip does [the rain *whipped* her face] **5.** to wind (cord or thread) around (a rope, etc.), so as to prevent fraying **6.** to beat (eggs, cream, etc.) into a froth with a fork, whisk, mixer, etc. **7.** to sew (a seam, etc.) with a loose, overcasting or overhand stitch **8.** [Colloq.] to defeat, as in a contest —*vi.* **1.** to move, go, etc. quickly and suddenly [he *whipped* through the door] **2.** to flap about in a whiplike manner [flags *whipping* in the wind] —*n.* **1.** an instrument for striking or beating a person or animal, usually a rod with a lash attached to one end **2.** a blow, cut, etc. made with or as with a whip **3.** a person who uses a whip, as a coachman **4.** an officer of a political party in Congress, Parliament, etc. who enforces party discipline, attendance, etc.: also **party whip 5.** a whipping motion **6.** a dessert made of sugar and whipped cream, beaten egg whites, etc., and often fruit —**whip into shape** [Colloq.] to bring by strong action into a desired condition —**whip up 1.** to stir up; excite [to *whip up* enthusiasm] **2.** [Colloq.] to prepare quickly and efficiently [to *whip up* a lunch] —**whip′per** *n.*

whip·cord (hwip′kôrd′, wip′-) *n.* **1.** a hard, twisted or braided cord used for whiplashes, etc. **2.** a strong worsted cloth with small, diagonal ribs

whip hand 1. the hand in which a driver holds his whip **2.** the position of advantage or control

whip·lash (-lash′) *n.* **1.** the lash of a whip ☆**2.** a sudden, sharp jolting of the neck backward and then forward, as caused by the impact of a rear-end automobile collision

whipped cream rich sweet cream stiffened as by whipping and used as a topping on desserts, etc.: also **whip cream**

whip·per·snap·per (hwip′ər snap′ər, wip′-) *n.* [< *whip-snapper*, one who snaps whips] a young or unimportant person who does not seem to show proper respect for those older or more important than himself

whip·pet (hwip′it, wip′-) *n.* [dim. < WHIP] a swift dog like a small greyhound, used in racing

whip·ping (-iŋ) *n.* **1.** a flogging or beating, as in punishment **2.** cord, twine, etc. used to whip, or bind

whipping boy *same as* SCAPEGOAT (sense 2)

whipping cream sweet cream with a high percentage of butterfat, that can be whipped until stiff

whipping post a post to which those who break the law are tied to be whipped as a punishment

whip·ple·tree (hwip′′l trē′, wip′-) *n.* [< WHIP + TREE] *same as* SINGLE-TREE

☆**whip·poor·will** (hwip′ər wil′, wip′-) *n.,* *pl.* **-wills′, -will′:** see PLURAL, II, D, 1 [echoic] a grayish bird of eastern N. America, one of the goatsuckers

whip·saw (hwip′sô′, wip′-) *n.* a long-bladed saw; esp., a cross-cut saw with a handle at each end, for use by two persons

whip·stitch (-stich′) *vt., vi. Sewing* to overcast or whip —*n.* a stitch made in this way

whip·stock (-stäk′) *n.* the handle of a whip

whir, whirr (hwur, wur) *vi., vt.* **whirred, whir′ring** [prob. < Scand.] to fly, revolve, vibrate, etc. with a whizzing or buzzing sound —*n.* a sound like this, as of a propeller

whirl (hwurl, wurl) *vi.* [ON. *hvirfla*] **1.** to move rapidly in a circular manner or as in an orbit [the dancers *whirled* around the room] **2.** to rotate or spin fast; gyrate **3.** to move, go, etc. swiftly [the car *whirled* up the hill] **4.** to seem to spin; reel [my head is *whirling*] —*vt.* **1.** to cause to rotate, revolve, etc. rapidly **2.** to move, carry, etc. with a rotating motion [the wind *whirled* the leaves] —*n.* **1.** the act of whirling **2.** a whirling motion **3.** something whirling or being whirled [a *whirl* of dust] **4.** a series of parties, etc. [the social *whirl*] **5.** a noisy commotion; uproar; stir **6.** a confused or dizzy condition [my head is in a *whirl*] —see SYN. at TURN —☆**give it a whirl** [Colloq.] to try something; make an attempt —**whirl′er** *n.*

whirl·i·gig (hwur′li gig′, wur′-) *n.* [see WHIRL & GIG[1]] **1.** a child's toy that whirls or spins **2.** a merry-go-round **3.** a whirling motion

whirligig beetle a small, bluish-black beetle that darts about in circles on the surface of ponds, streams, etc.

whirl·pool (hwurl′pool′, wurl′-) *n.* **1.** water whirling rapidly in a circle into which floating objects are drawn; eddy of water **2.** anything like a whirlpool [a *whirlpool* of emotion]

☆**whirlpool bath** a bath, as used in hydrotherapy, in which a device causes a current of warm water to swirl around

whirl·wind (-wind′) *n.* **1.** a current of air whirling violently upward in a spiral that has a forward motion **2.** anything like a whirlwind, as in violent or destructive force —*adj.* carried on as fast as possible [a *whirlwind* courtship]

whirl·y·bird (hwur′lē burd′, wur′-) *n. colloq. term for* HELICOPTER

whish (hwish, wish) *vi.* [echoic] to move with a soft, rushing sound; whiz; swish —*n.* a sound so made

whisk (hwisk, wisk) *n.* [ON. *visk*, a brush] **1.** *a)* the act of brushing with a quick, light, sweeping motion *b)* such a motion **2.** a small bunch of straw, hair, etc. used for brushing **3.** a kitchen utensil consisting of wire loops fixed in a handle, for whipping eggs, etc. —*vt.* **1.** to move, remove, brush (*away, off, out,* etc.) with a quick, sweeping motion [to *whisk* out a handkerchief; to *whisk* off crumbs] **2.** [Chiefly Brit.] to whip (eggs, cream, etc.) —*vi.* to move quickly, nimbly, or briskly [the cat *whisked* under the sofa]

whisk broom a small, short-handled broom for brushing clothes, etc.

whisk·er (hwis′kər, wis′-) *n.* [see WHISK &

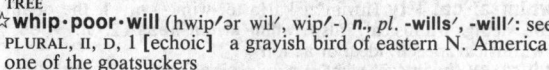

WHIPPET
(18–22 in. high at shoulder)

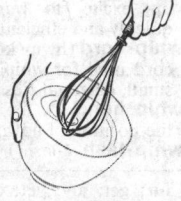

WHISK

-ER] **1.** [*pl.*] the hair growing on a man's face; esp., the beard on the cheeks **2.** *a)* a hair of a man's beard *b)* any of the long, bristly hairs growing on the upper lip of a cat, rat, etc. —**whisk′ered, whisk′er·y** *adj.*

whis·key (hwis′kē, wis′kē) *n., pl.* **-keys, -kies** [short for *usquebaugh* < IrGael. *uisce*, water + *beathadh*, life] **1.** a strong alcoholic liquor distilled from the fermented mash of grain, esp. of rye, wheat, corn, or barley **2.** a drink of whiskey —*adj.* of, for, or made with whiskey Also sp. **whis′ky,** *pl.* **-kies** NOTE In the U.S. and Ireland, the usual spelling is **whiskey;** in Great Britain and Canada, it is **whisky**

whis·per (hwis′pər, wis′-) *vi.* [OE. *hwisprian*] **1.** to speak very softly, esp. without vibration of the vocal cords **2.** to talk in a quiet or sneaky way, as in gossiping or plotting **3.** to make a soft, rustling sound [the breeze *whispered* in the tall grass] —*vt.* **1.** to say very softly, esp. by whispering **2.** to tell (something) to (someone) privately or as a secret —*n.* **1.** a whispering; soft, low speech produced with breath but, usually, without vibrating the vocal cords [to speak in a *whisper*] **2.** something whispered; a secret, hint, rumor, etc. **3.** a soft, rustling sound — **whis′per·er** *n.* —**whis′per·ing** *adj., n.* —**whis′per·ing·ly** *adv.* —**whis′per·y** *adj.*

☆**whispering campaign** the spreading, by word of mouth, of rumors intended to harm the reputation of a political candidate, cause, etc.

whist[1] (hwist, wist) *interj.* [echoic] [Archaic or Dial.] hush!

whist[2] (hwist, wist) *n.* [< earlier *whisk*] a card game usually played by two pairs of players, similar to bridge

whis·tle (hwis′′l, wis′-) *vi.* **-tled, -tling** [OE. *hwistlian*] **1.** *a)* to make a clear, shrill sound by forcing breath between the teeth or through puckered lips *b)* to make a similar sound by sending steam through a small opening **2.** to make a clear, shrill cry: said of some birds and animals **3.** to move, pass, go, etc. with a high, shrill sound, as the wind **4.** *a)* to blow a whistle *b)* to have its whistle blown, as a train —*vt.* **1.** to produce (a tune, etc.) by whistling **2.** to call, signal, etc. by whistling —*n.* **1.** a device for making whistling sounds **2.** the act or sound of whistling —**wet one's whistle** to take a drink —**whistle for** to seek or expect but fail to get —☆**whistle in the dark** to pretend to be sure of oneself —**whis′tler** *n.* —**whis′tling** *adj., n.*

Whis·tler (hwis′lər, wis′-), **James Ab·bott Mc·Neill** (ab′ət mək nēl′) 1834–1903; U.S. painter & etcher in England

☆**whistle stop** **1.** a small town, orig. one at which a train stopped only upon signal **2.** a brief stop in a small town as part of a tour, esp. in a political campaign —**whis′tle-stop′** *vi.* **-stopped′, -stop′ping**

whit (hwit, wit) *n.* [Early ModE. respelling of OE. *wiht*, a wight] the least bit; jot [not a *whit* the wiser]

white (hwit, wit) *adj.* **whit′er, whit′est** [OE. *hwit*] **1.** having the color of pure snow or milk; of the color of reflected light containing all of the visible rays of the spectrum: opposite to black: see COLOR **2.** of a light or pale color; specif., *a)* gray; silvery *b)* very blond *c)* pale; wan [a face *white* with terror] *d)* light-yellow or amber [*white* wines] *e)* blank, as a space unmarked by printing *f)* snowy [a *white* Christmas] **3.** colorless [*white* creme de menthe] **4.** clothed in white [the *White* Friars] **5.** pure; innocent **6.** free from evil intent; harmless [*white* magic] **7.** *a)* having a light-colored skin; Caucasoid *b)* of or controlled by Caucasoids ☆**8.** [Slang] honest; fair —*n.* **1.** white color **2.** the state of being white; specif., *a)* fairness of complexion *b)* purity; innocence **3.** a white or light-colored part or thing, as the albumen of an egg, the white part of the eyeball, the light-colored part of meat, wood, etc., a white garment, white wine, white pigment, etc. **4.** [*also* W-] a person with a light-colored skin; Caucasoid —*vt.* **whit′ed, whit′ing** to make white; whiten —**bleed white** to drain (a person) completely of money, resources, etc. —**white′ly** *adv.* —**white′ness** *n.*

white ant *popular name for* TERMITE

white·bait (-bāt′) *n., pl.* **-bait** **1.** any of various small, silvery European fishes, as young herring, used as food ☆**2.** a smelt of the Pacific coast of N. America

☆**white bass** (bas) a silvery food and game fish found in fresh water in eastern N. America

white birch ☆**1.** *same as* PAPER BIRCH **2.** a European birch with silvery-white bark, widely grown in the U.S.

white blood cell *same as* LEUKOCYTE: also called **white blood corpuscle**

white bread bread of a light color, made from finely sifted wheat flour

☆**white bush** (scallop) a variety of summer squash having a saucer-shaped, white fruit, scalloped around the edges

white·cap (-kap′) *n.* a wave with its crest broken into white foam

☆**white cedar 1.** *a)* an evergreen tree growing in swampy land in the eastern U.S. *b)* its soft, light-colored wood, used for shingles, etc. **2.** *a)* the American arborvitae, growing in the northeastern U.S. *b)* its soft, brittle wood

white clover a creeping species of clover with white flower clusters, grown in lawns and as a forage plant

white-col·lar (-käl′ər) *adj.* [from the formerly typical white shirt worn by such workers] ☆designating or of people who hold jobs as clerks, salesmen, professional workers, etc.

☆**white-collar crime** a crime, as fraud, embezzlement, etc., committed by a person in business, government, or a profession in connection with his work

whited sepulcher a hypocrite: Matt. 23:27

white elephant 1. an albino elephant, thought of as sacred by the Thais, Burmese, etc. **2.** something of little profit or use that costs a lot to keep up ☆**3.** any object that its owner no longer wants to keep but that others may want to own or buy

white feather [from belief that a white feather in a gamecock's tail shows bad breeding, hence cowardice] a symbol of cowardice: chiefly in **show the white feather,** to behave in a cowardly way

White·field (hwit′fēld′, wit′-), **George** 1714–70; Eng. Methodist evangelist

white·fish (hwit′fish′, wit′-) *n., pl.* **-fish′, -fish′es:** see FISH **1.** any of various white or silvery food fishes of the salmon family, found in the lakes of the northern U.S. and Canada **2.** any of various other whitish fishes, as the **ocean whitefish** of southern California waters **3.** *same as* BELUGA (sense 2)

white flag a white banner or cloth held up as a sign that one wants a truce or is willing to surrender

☆**white·fly** (-flī′) *n., pl.* **-flies′** any of various tiny whitish insects, often harmful to plants

White Friar a Carmelite friar: so called from the white mantle worn by these friars

white gold gold alloyed with nickel, zinc, etc., to give it a white, platinumlike appearance: used in jewelry

white-haired (-herd′) *adj.* **1.** having white or very light hair **2.** [Colloq.] *same as* FAIR-HAIRED (sense 2)

White·hall (hwit′hôl′, wit′-) a street in London where several government offices are located —*n.* the British government

white·head (-hed′) *n.* a small, whitish lump of fatty matter clogging a skin pore

white heat 1. the degree of intense heat (beyond red heat) at which metal, etc. glows white **2.** a state of very great emotion, excitement, etc.

White·horse (hwīt′hôrs′, wīt′-) capital of the Yukon Territory, Canada, in the S part: pop. 13,000

white-hot (hwīt′hät′, wīt′-) *adj.* **1.** glowing white with heat **2.** extremely angry, excited, enthusiastic, etc.

White House, the ☆**1.** official residence of the President of the U.S.: a white mansion in Washington, D.C. ☆**2.** the executive branch of the U.S. government

white lead 1. a poisonous, heavy, white powder, basic lead carbonate, $2PbCO_3 \cdot Pb(OH)_2$, used as a paint pigment, for pottery glazes, etc. **2.** any of several white pigments containing lead, as lead sulfate

white lie a lie about something unimportant, often one told to spare someone's feelings

white light *Physics* light, as sunlight, made up of rays of all the wavelengths ranging from red to violet

☆**white lightning** [Slang] homemade corn whiskey

white-liv·ered (-liv′ərd) *adj.* cowardly; craven

white matter whitish nerve tissue of the brain and spinal cord, consisting chiefly of nerve fibers

white meat any light-colored meat, as veal, pork, the breast of poultry, etc.

White Mountains [from the appearance of the higher peaks] range of the Appalachian system, in northern N.H.

whit·en (hwīt′'n, wīt′-) *vt., vi.* to make or become white or whiter —**whit′en·er** *n.* —**whit′en·ing** *n.*

white oak 1. any of a number of oaks having whitish or grayish bark and hard wood **2.** the wood of any such tree, used in barrels, furniture, etc.

white·out (-out′) *n.* a weather condition occurring in polar regions, in which the snowy ground and white sky blend so that one's sense of direction and distance disappears

white paper an official government report

white pepper pepper ground from the husked, dried seeds of the nearly ripe pepper berry

☆**white perch** a small, silvery food fish found in coastal waters and streams of the eastern U.S.

☆**white pine 1.** *a)* a pine of eastern N. America, with needles in groups of five and soft, light wood *b)* this wood **2.** any of various pines with needles in groups of five

White Plains [? after the AmInd. *quaropas,* white marshes] city in southeastern N.Y., near New York City: pop. 50,000

white poplar 1. a large, old-world poplar having lobed leaves with white or gray down on the undersides, now widespread in the U.S. ☆**2.** *same as: a)* TULIP TREE *b)* TULIPWOOD (sense 1)

☆**white potato** *same as* POTATO (sense 2 *a*)

white race loosely, the Caucasoid group of mankind

☆**white room** a room which is completely free of dirt, germs, etc. and in which temperature, humidity, and pressure are controlled: used in making and repairing delicate instruments, preventing infection, etc.

White Russia *same as* BYELORUSSIAN SOVIET SOCIALIST REPUBLIC

White Russian 1. a native or inhabitant of White Russia; Byelorussian **2.** any of the Russians who fought against the Bolsheviks (Reds) in the Russian civil war

white sale a sale of sheets, towels, linens, etc. held in a store

white sauce a sauce for vegetables, meat, fish, etc., made of fat or butter, flour, milk or stock, and seasoning

White Sea arm of the Arctic Ocean, extending into northwestern U.S.S.R.

white slave a woman lured or forced into or held in prostitution for the profit of others —**white′-slave′** *adj.* —**white slaver** —**white slavery**

☆**white-tailed deer** (-tāld′) a common American deer having a tail that is white on the undersurface, a white-spotted red coat in summer, and a brownish-gray coat in winter: also **white′tail′** *n.*

white tie 1. a white bow tie, properly worn with a swallow-tailed coat **2.** a swallow-tailed coat and its accessories

☆**white·wall** (-wôl′) *adj.* designating or of a pneumatic tire with a circular white band on the outer sidewall: also **white′-wall′** —*n.* a whitewall tire

white·wash (-wôsh′, -wäsh′) *n.* **1.** a mixture of lime, whiting, size, water, etc., for whitening walls, etc. **2.** *a)* a covering up of faults or mistakes as in an effort to avoid blame *b)* something said or done for this purpose ☆**3.** [Colloq.] *Sports* a defeat in which the loser scores no points —*vt.* **1.** to cover with whitewash **2.** to cover up the faults, defects, or mistakes of ☆**3.** [Colloq.] *Sports* to defeat (an opponent) without allowing him to score —**white′wash′er** *n.* —**white′wash′ing** *n.*

WHITE-TAILED DEER
(to 3¹/₂ ft. high
at shoulder)

white water foaming, whitish water, as in rapids, whitecaps, etc.

white whale *same as* BELUGA (sense 2)

whith·er (hwith′ər, with′-) *adv.* [OE. *hwider*] to what place, condition, etc.? where? —*conj.* **1.** to which place, condition, etc. **2.** wherever *Where* is now almost always used in place of *whither*

whith·er·so·ev·er (hwith′ər sō ev′ər, with′-) *adv., conj.* [Archaic] to whatever place; wheresoever

whit·ing[1] (hwīt′iŋ, wīt′-) *n., pl.* **-ings, -ing:** see PLURAL, II, D, 1 [MDu. *wijting < wit,* white] any of numerous unrelated ocean food fishes of N. America, Europe, and Australia, including several hakes and kingfishes

whit·ing[2] (hwīt′iŋ, wīt′-) *n.* [see WHITE, *v.* + -ING] powdered chalk used in making paints, inks, etc.

whit·ish (hwīt′ish, wīt′-) *adj.* somewhat white —**whit′ish·ness** *n.*

---

whit·low (hwit′lō, wit′-) *n.* [ME. *whitflawe:* of disputed origin] *same as* FELON[2]

Whit·man (hwit′mən, wit′-), **Walt**(er) 1819–92; U.S. poet

Whit·ney (hwit′nē, wit′-), Eli 1765–1825; U.S. inventor, esp. of the cotton gin

Whit·ney (hwit′nē), **Mount** [after J. *Whitney* (1819–96), U.S. geologist] mountain of the Sierra Nevada Range, EC Calif.: highest in the U.S. outside of Alas., 14,495 ft.

Whit·sun (hwit′s'n, wit′-) *adj.* of or celebrated on Whitsunday or at Whitsuntide

Whit·sun·day (hwit′sun′dē, wit′-; -dā; -s'n dā) *n.* [OE. *Hwita Sunnandæg*, white Sunday] *same as* PENTECOST (sense 2)

Whit·sun·tide (-s'n tīd′) *n.* the week beginning with Whitsunday, esp. the first three days of that week

Whit·ti·er (hwit′ē ər, wit′-) [after J. G. WHITTIER] city in SW Calif.: suburb of Los Angeles: pop. 73,000

Whit·ti·er (hwit′ē ər, wit′-), **John Green·leaf** (grēn′lēf′) 1807–92; U.S. poet

whit·tle (hwit′'l, wit′-) *vt.* **-tled, -tling** [OE. *thwitan*, to cut] **1.** *a)* to cut thin shavings from (wood) with a knife *b)* to carve (an object) in this way **2.** to reduce, destroy, etc. gradually, as if by whittling: usually with *down, away*, etc. [to *whittle* down costs] —*vi.* to whittle wood —**whit′tler** *n.*

whit·y (hwīt′ē, wīt′-) *adj.* **whit′i·er, whit′i·est** *same as* WHITISH

whiz, whizz (hwiz, wiz) *vi.* **whizzed, whiz′zing** [echoic] **1.** to make the buzzing or hissing sound of something moving swiftly through the air **2.** to speed by with or as with this sound [the bus *whizzed* by him] —*vt.* to cause to whiz —*n.* **1.** a whizzing sound or movement ☆**2.** [Slang] a person who is very quick, clever, or skilled at something [a *whiz* at math] —**whiz′zing·ly** *adv.*

who (hōō) *pron.*, obj. **whom**, poss. **whose** [OE. *hwa*] **1.** what or which person or persons: used to introduce a question [*who* is he? I don't know *who* he is] **2.** *a)* (the, or a, person or persons) that: used to introduce a relative clause [the man *who* came to dinner] *b)* any person or persons that ["*who* steals my purse steals trash"] NOTE The use of *who* rather than *whom* as the object of a verb or preposition [*who* did you see? *who* was it written by?] is widespread, but is objected to by some —**who's who** who the important people are

WHO World Health Organization

whoa (hwō, wō, hō) *interj.* [for HO] stop!: used esp. in directing a horse to stand still

☆**who·dun·it** (hōō dun′it) *n.* [Colloq.] a mystery novel, play, etc.: see MYSTERY[1] (sense 2 *b*)

who·ev·er (-ev′ər) *pron.* **1.** any person that; whatever person [*whoever* wins gets a prize] **2.** no matter what person [*whoever* said it, it's not so] **3.** what person? who?: used for emphasis [*whoever* told you that?]

whole (hōl) *adj.* [OE. *hal*] **1.** healthy; not diseased or injured **2.** not broken, damaged, defective, etc.; intact [a *whole* yolk] **3.** containing all the elements or parts; complete [a *whole* set, *whole* blood] **4.** not divided up; in a single unit [a *whole* cheese] **5.** being the entire amount, extent, etc. [the *whole* week] **6.** having both parents in common [a *whole* brother] **7.** *Arith.* not mixed or fractional [25 is a *whole* number] —*n.* **1.** the entire amount, extent, etc.; totality [the *whole* of his fortune was left to charity] **2.** a complete organization of parts; unity or system [our 50 separate States form a *whole*] —**as a whole** as a complete unit; altogether —☆**made out of whole cloth** completely imaginary or false —**on the whole** all things considered; in general —**whole′ness** *n.*

whole blood blood for transfusion from which none of the elements has been removed

☆**whole·heart·ed** (hōl′här′tid) *adj.* doing or done with all one's energy, enthusiasm, etc.; sincere [*wholehearted* support] —**whole′heart′ed·ly** *adv.* —**whole′heart′ed·ness** *n.*

whole-hog (hōl′hôg′, -häg′) *adj., adv.* [Slang] ☆holding back nothing; thorough(ly); complete(ly)

whole milk milk from which none of the butterfat or other elements have been removed

whole note *Music* a note held four times as long as a quarter note: see illustration at NOTE

whole number zero or any positive or negative multiple of 1; integer [28 is a *whole number*]

whole·sale (hōl′sāl′) *n.* the selling of goods in relatively large quantities, esp. to retailers who then sell them at higher prices to consumers —*adj.* **1.** of, connected with, or taking part in such selling [a *wholesale* dealer, a *wholesale* price] **2.** widespread or general [*wholesale* criticism] —*adv.* **1.** in wholesale amounts or at wholesale prices [buying *wholesale*] **2.** in a widespread or

general way [to reject proposals *wholesale*] —*vt., vi.* **-saled′, -sal′ing** to sell wholesale —**whole′sal′er** *n.*

whole·some (hōl′səm) *adj.* [see WHOLE & -SOME[1]] **1.** good for one's health or well-being; healthful [*wholesome* food] **2.** tending to improve the mind or character [a *wholesome* book for children] **3.** full of health and vigor [a *wholesome* girl] **4.** suggesting health [a *wholesome* smile] —**whole′some·ly** *adv.* —**whole′some·ness** *n.*

whole tone *Music* an interval consisting of two adjacent semitones: also **whole step**

☆**whole-wheat** (-hwēt′) *adj.* **1.** made of the entire cleaned kernels of wheat [*whole-wheat* flour] **2.** made of whole-wheat flour [*whole-wheat* bread]

who'll (hōōl) **1.** who shall **2.** who will

whol·ly (hō′lē, hōl′lē) *adv.* to the whole amount or degree; totally; entirely [*wholly* dependent on his family]

whom (hōōm) *pron.* objective case of WHO: see note at WHO on the use of *who* and *whom*

whom·ev·er (hōōm ev′ər) *pron.* objective case of WHOEVER

whomp (hwämp) *vt.* [echoic] **1.** to beat, strike, thump, etc. **2.** to defeat soundly —*n.* the act or sound of whomping

whom·so·ev·er (hōōm′sō ev′ər) *pron.* objective case of WHOSOEVER

whoop (hōōp, hwōōp, wōōp, wŏŏp) *n.* [OFr. *houper*, to cry out] **1.** a loud shout, cry, etc., as of excitement, joy, etc. **2.** a hoot, as of an owl **3.** the gasping sound made when a breath of air is taken in following a fit of coughing in whooping cough —*vi., vt.* to utter, or utter with, a whoop or whoops —*interj.* an exclamation of excitement, joy, etc. —☆**not worth a whoop** [Colloq.] worth nothing at all —☆**whoop it** (or **things**) **up** [Slang] **1.** to create a noisy disturbance, as in celebrating **2.** to create enthusiasm (*for*) —**whoop′er** *n.*

☆**whoop-de-do, whoop-de-doo** (hōōp′dē dōō′, hwōōp′-) *n.* [< WHOOP] [Colloq.] noisy or excited activity, commotion, or fuss; hoopla, ballyhoo, to-do, etc.

whoop·ee (wōō′pē, hwōō′-, wŏŏ′-, hwŏŏ′-) *interj.* [< WHOOP] an exclamation of great joy, delight, etc. —*n.* **1.** a shout of "whoopee!" ☆**2.** noisy fun —☆**make whoopee** [Slang] to have fun in a noisy way

whoop·ing cough (hōō′piŋ, hoŏ′-) an infectious disease, usually affecting children, in which there are repeated attacks of coughing that end in a whoop

☆**whooping crane** a large, white N. American crane noted for its whooping call: now nearly extinct

whoops (hwoops, woops, hwŏŏps, wŏŏps) *interj.* an exclamation uttered as upon losing one's balance or making an embarrassing slip of the tongue

whoosh (hwoosh, woosh) *vi., vt.* [echoic] to make or cause to make a hissing or rushing sound while moving swiftly through the air —*n.* this sound —*interj.* an exclamation imitating this or expressing surprise, fatigue, etc.

whop (hwäp, wäp) *vt., vi.* **whopped, whop′ping** [prob. echoic] [Colloq.] **1.** to beat, strike, etc. **2.** to defeat soundly —*n.* [Colloq.] a sharp, loud blow, thump, etc.

whop·per (hwäp′ər, wäp′-) *n.* [< prec.] [Colloq.] **1.** anything that is very large **2.** a great lie

whop·ping (-iŋ) *adj.* [< WHOP + -ING] [Colloq.] very large or great; colossal

WHOOPING CRANE
(to 4 ft. high)

whore (hôr) *n.* [OE. *hore* < or akin to ON. *hora*] a woman who has sexual intercourse with many men; esp., a prostitute —*vi.* **whored, whor′ing** **1.** to be a whore **2.** to have sexual intercourse with whores —**whor′ish** *adj.*

who're (hōō′ər, hoŏr) who are

whorl (hwôrl, wôrl, hwʉrl, wʉrl) *n.* [< dial. var. of WHIRL] anything arranged in a circle or circles, or having a coiled or spiral appearance; specif., *a)* a type of fingerprint pattern formed by circular ridges *b) Bot.* a circular growth of leaves, petals, etc. about the same point on a stem *c) Zool.* any of the turns in a spiral shell —**whorled** *adj.*

whor·tle·ber·ry (hwʉr′t'l ber′ē, wʉr′-) *n., pl.* **-ries** [< Brit. dial. form of earlier *hurtleberry* < OE. *horte*] **1.** *a)* a European plant having pink flowers and blue or blackish, edible berries *b)* any of these berries ☆**2.** *same as* HUCKLEBERRY

who's (hōōz) **1.** who is **2.** who has

whose (hōōz) *pron.* [OE. *hwæs*] that or those belonging to whom [*whose* is this?] —*adj.* of, belonging to, made, or done by whom or which [the woman *whose* car was stolen]

whose·so·ev·er (hōōz'sō ev'ər) *pron.* of whomsoever

☆**who·sis** (hōō'zis) *n.* [shortened from *who is this*] [Slang] a person or thing whose name is not known or is forgotten

who·so (hōō'sō) *pron.* [OE. *hwa swa*] [Archaic] whoever; whosoever

who·so·ev·er (hōō'sō ev'ər) *pron.* whoever: used for emphasis

whr. watt-hour

why (hwī, wī) *adv.* [OE. *hwi,* instrumental case of *hwæt,* what] for what reason, cause, or purpose? [*why* did he go? he told her *why* he went] —*conj.* **1.** because of which [there is no reason *why* you should go] **2.** the reason for which [that is *why* she went] —*n., pl.* **whys** the reason, cause, etc. [never mind the *why*] —*interj.* an exclamation used to show surprise, impatience, etc. or to introduce a remark

whyd·ah (**bird**) (hwid'ə, wid'-) [altered < *widow bird*] any of several chiefly brown-and-black West African weaverbirds

WI Wisconsin

Wich·i·ta (wich'ə tô') [< AmInd.] city in S Kans., on the Arkansas River: pop. 277,000

Wichita Falls [see prec.] city in NC Tex.: pop. 98,000

wick (wik) *n.* [OE. *weoca*] a piece of cord or tape, or a thin bundle of threads, in a candle, oil lamp, cigarette lighter, etc., that absorbs the fuel and, when lighted, burns with a steady flame

wick·ed (wik'id) *adj.* [ME. < *wikke,* evil, akin to OE. *wicce,* witch] **1.** morally bad or wrong; acting or done with an evil purpose [a *wicked* scheme] **2.** painful, unpleasant, etc. [a *wicked* blow on the head] **3.** naughty; mischievous ☆**4.** [Slang] skillful [he plays a *wicked* game of golf] —**wick'ed·ly** *adv.* —**wick'ed·ness** *n.*

wick·er (wik'ər) *n.* [< Scand.] **1.** a thin, easily bent twig; withe **2.** *a)* twigs or long, woody strips woven together, as in making baskets or furniture *b) same as* WICKERWORK (sense 1) —*adj.* made of or covered with wicker

wick·er·work (-wurk') *n.* **1.** things made of wicker **2.** *same as* WICKER (sense 2 *a)*

wick·et (wik'it) *n.* [ONormFr. *wiket* < Gmc.] **1.** a small door or gate, esp. one set in or near a larger one **2.** a small window or opening, as in a ticket office **3.** a small gate for regulating the flow of water, as to a water wheel **4.** *Cricket a)* either of two sets of three vertical sticks (*stumps*) each, with two small pieces (*bails*) resting on top of them *b)* the playing space between the two wickets ☆**5.** *Croquet* any of the small wire arches through which the balls must be hit; hoop

wick·et·keep·er (-kē'pər) *n. Cricket* the fielder whose position is just behind the batsman's wicket

☆**wick·i·up** (wik'ē up') *n.* [< Algonquian name] a kind of hut made by covering an oval-shaped frame with grass, brush, etc., used by the nomadic Indians of the southwestern U.S.

Wick·liffe, Wic·lif (wik'lif) *variants of* WYCLIFFE

wide (wīd) *adj.* **wid'er, wid'est** [OE. *wid*] **1.** reaching over a large area; esp., measuring more from side to side than is usual [a *wide* bed] **2.** of a specified distance from side to side [two miles *wide*] **3.** large or not limited in size, amount, or degree [a *wide* variety of items] **4.** roomy; ample; full [*wide* pants] **5.** opened as far as possible [eyes *wide* with fear] **6.** far from the point, issue, etc. aimed at [*wide* of the mark] —*adv.* **1.** over a relatively large area; widely [to travel far and *wide*] **2.** to a large or full extent; fully [*wide* open] **3.** so as to miss the point, issue, etc. aimed at; astray [her shot went *wide*] —see SYN· at BROAD —**wide'ly** *adv.* —**wide'ness** *n.*

-wide (wīd) *a combining form meaning* existing or reaching throughout [nationwide]

wide-an·gle (wīd'aŋ'g'l) *adj.* **1.** designating or of a kind of camera lens covering a wide angle of view **2.** designating or of any of several systems using one or more movie cameras (and projectors) and a very wide, curved screen

wide-a·wake (-ə wāk') *adj.* **1.** fully awake **2.** watchful and

WICKIUP

ready, as for an opportunity; alert —see SYN· at WATCHFUL

wide-eyed (-īd') *adj.* with the eyes wide open, as in surprise

wid·en (wīd''n) *vt., vi.* to make or become wide or wider

wide-o·pen (wīd'ō'p'n) *adj.* **1.** opened wide ☆**2.** not having or enforcing laws against prostitution, gambling, liquor sales, etc. [a *wide-open* city]

☆**wide receiver** *Football* a player eligible to receive a pass who usually takes a position to one side at some distance from the other members of the offensive team

wide·spread (-spred') *adj.* **1.** spread out widely [with *widespread* arms] **2.** happening, found, etc. over a wide area [*widespread* damage from the storm]

widg·eon (wij'ən) *n., pl.* **-eons, -eon:** see PLURAL, II, D, 1 [prob. < MFr. *vigeon*] any of various wild ducks found near rivers and lakes, having a head that is white on top

☆**wid·get** (wij'it) *n.* [altered < GADGET] a small gadget

wid·ow (wid'ō) *n.* [OE. *widewe*] **1.** a woman whose husband has died and who has not remarried ☆**2.** *Cards* a group of cards dealt into a separate pile, typically for the use of the highest bidder ☆**3.** [Colloq.] a woman whose husband is often away taking part in a certain sport, hobby, etc. [a golf *widow*] —*vt.* to cause to become a widow [*widowed* by the war] —**wid'ow·hood'** *n.*

wid·ow·er (wid'ə wər) *n.* a man whose wife has died and who has not remarried

widow's mite a small gift or contribution freely given by one who can scarcely afford it: Mark 12:41–44

widow's peak a point formed by hair growing down in the middle of a forehead

width (width, witth) *n.* [< WIDE, by analogy with LENGTH] **1.** a being wide; wideness **2.** the distance from side to side [a river 500 yards in *width*] **3.** a piece of something of a certain width [two *widths* of cloth]

wield (wēld) *vt.* [OE. *wealdan* & *wieldan*] **1.** to handle and use (a tool or weapon), esp. with skill and control **2.** to have and use (power, influence, etc.); exercise —**wield'er** *n.*

wield·y (wēl'dē) *adj.* **wield'i·er, wield'i·est** that can be wielded easily; manageable

Wien (vēn) *Ger. name of* VIENNA

☆**wie·ner** (wē'nər) *n.* [short for G. *Wiener wurst,* Vienna sausage] a smoked link sausage of beef or beef and pork, etc.; frankfurter: also **wie'ner·wurst'** (-wurst')

Wie·ner (wē'nər), **Nor·bert** (nôr'bərt) 1894–1964; U.S. mathematician & pioneer in cybernetics

Wies·ba·den (vēs'bäd''n) city in W West Germany, on the Rhine: pop. 261,000

wife (wīf) *n., pl.* **wives** (wīvz) [OE. *wif*] **1.** orig., a woman: still so used in *midwife, housewife,* etc. **2.** a married woman —**take to wife** to marry (a specified woman) —**wife'hood'** *n.* —**wife'less** *adj.* —**wife'ly** *adj.* **-li·er, -li·est**

wig (wig) *n.* [shortened < PERIWIG] **1.** a false covering of real or synthetic hair for the head, worn as part of a costume, to hide baldness, etc. **2.** *same as* TOUPEE —*vt.* **wigged, wig'ging** to furnish with a wig or wigs —**wig'less** *adj.*

wi·geon (wij'ən) *n. var. of* WIDGEON

wig·gle (wig''l) *vt., vi.* **-gled, -gling** [prob. < MLowG. *wiggen,* to move to and fro] to move with short, twisting motions from side to side —*n.* the act or an instance of wiggling

wig·gler (wig'lər) *n.* **1.** a person or thing that wiggles **2.** the larva of a mosquito; wriggler

wig·gly (-lē) *adj.* **-gli·er, -gli·est 1.** that wiggles; wiggling [a *wiggly* worm] **2.** wavy [a *wiggly* line]

wight (wīt) *n.* [OE. *wiht*] [Archaic] a human being; person

Wight (wīt), **Isle of** island in the English Channel, off the S coast of England, that is an English county

☆**wig·let** (wig'lit) *n.* a small wig; specif., a woman's hairpiece for use along with her own hair

wig·wag (wig'wag') *vt., vi.* **-wagged', -wag'ging** [< obs. *wig,* to move + WAG¹] **1.** to move back and forth; wag **2.** to send (a message) by waving flags, lights, etc. back and forth according to a code —*n.* the sending of messages in this way

WIDOW'S PEAK

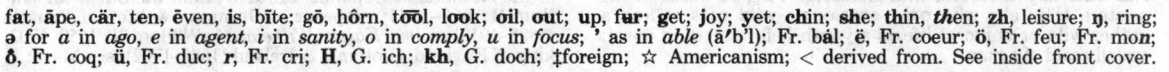

fat, āpe, cär, ten, ēven, is, bīte; gō, hôrn, tōol, look; oil, out; up, fur; get; joy; yet; chin; she; thin, *th*en; zh, leisure; ŋ, ring; ə for *a* in *ago, e* in *agent, i* in *sanity, o* in *comply, u* in *focus;* ' as in *able* (ā'b'l); Fr. bál; ë, Fr. coeur; ö, Fr. feu; Fr. mon; ∂, Fr. coq; ü, Fr. duc; r, Fr. cri; H, G. ich; kh, G. doch; ‡foreign; ☆ Americanism; < derived from. See inside front cover.

☆**wig·wam** (wig′wäm, -wôm) *n.* [< Algonquian] a shelter made by the Indians of eastern and central N. America, consisting of a framework of arched poles covered with bark, leaves, branches, etc.

Wil·ber·force (wil′bər fôrs′), **William** 1759–1833; Eng. statesman & opponent of slavery

Wil·bur (wil′bər) [OE. *Wilburh:* prob. < a place name meaning "willow town"] a masculine name

☆**wil·co** (wil′kō) *interj.* [*wil*(*l*) *co*(*mply*)] I will comply with your request: used as a reply in voice radio communications

WIGWAM

wild (wīld) *adj.* [OE. *wilde*] **1.** living or growing in its original, natural state; not tamed or cultivated by man [*wild* flowers, *wild* animals] **2.** not lived in or used for farming; overgrown, waste, etc. [*wild* land] **3.** not civilized; savage [a *wild* tribe] **4.** not controlled; unruly, rough, lawless, etc. [*wild* children] **5.** lacking social or moral control; characterized by immoral or rowdy pleasure seeking [a *wild* rake, a *wild* party] **6.** violent or stormy [*wild* seas] **7.** *a)* very excited or enthusiastic [*wild* with delight, *wild* about French food] *b)* angered, frantic, crazed, etc. [*wild* with desperation] **8.** in a state of disorder, confusion, etc. [*wild* hair] **9.** reckless, fantastic, crazy, etc. [a *wild* scheme] **10.** missing the target [a *wild* shot] **11.** *Cards* having any value specified by the holder: said of a card —*adv.* in a wild way [to shoot *wild*] —*n.* [*usually pl.*] a wilderness or wasteland —**run wild** to grow, exist, or behave in an uncontrolled way — **wild′ly** *adv.* —**wild′ness** *n.*

wild boar a type of hog living wild in Europe, Asia, and Africa: the ancestor of domestic hogs

wild card **1.** *Cards* a card that has been declared wild ☆**2.** *Sports* any of the teams that, in addition to those that finish in first and sometimes second place, qualify for the championship play-offs

wild carrot a common weed with finely divided leaves and clusters of white flowers: the ancestor of the garden carrot

wild·cat (wīld′kat′) *n., pl.* **-cats′, -cat′:** see PLURAL, II, D, 1 **1.** *a)* any of various fierce, medium-sized animals of the cat family, as the lynx or bobcat *b)* a house cat that has escaped from its home and is no longer tame: in this sense, usually **wild cat** **2.** a person who has a fierce temper ☆**3.** a risky business scheme ☆**4.** an oil well drilled in an area not known before to have oil **5.** *Naut.* a drum on a windlass, that meshes with the links of a chain cable —*adj.* ☆**1.** unsound or financially risky [a *wildcat* scheme] ☆**2.** *a)* operating in an illegal or unethical way *b)* not officially authorized [a *wildcat* strike] —☆*vi.* **-cat′· ted, -cat′ting 1.** to drill for oil in an area not known to have oil **2.** to take part in wildcat enterprises —☆**wild′cat′ter** *n.*

Wilde (wīld), **Oscar** (**Fingal O′Flahertie Wills**) 1854–1900; Brit. playwright, poet, & novelist, born in Ireland

wil·de·beest (wil′də bēst′, vil′-) *n., pl.* **-beests′, -beest′:** see PLURAL, II, D, 1 [Afrik. < Du. *wild,* wild + *beeste,* beast] *same as* GNU

Wil·der (wīl′dər) **Thorn·ton** (**Niven**) (thôrn′t′n) 1897–1975; U.S. novelist & playwright

wil·der·ness (wil′dər nis) *n.* [< ME. *wilderne,* wild place (< OE. < *wilde,* wild + *deor,* animal) + -*nesse,* -NESS] **1.** wasteland or overgrown land with no settlers **2.** a large, confused tangle [a *wilderness* of streets and alleys] —**see SYN** at WASTE

wild-eyed (wīld′īd′) *adj.* **1.** staring in a wild, confused, or insane way **2.** very impractical or foolish [*wild-eyed* ideas]

wild·fire (-fīr′) *n.* a fire that spreads fast and is hard to put out [the rumors spread like *wildfire*]

wild·flow·er (-flou′ər) *n.* any flowering plant growing wild in fields, woods, etc. Also **wild flower**

wild·fowl (-foul′) *n., pl.* **-fowls′, -fowl′:** see PLURAL, II, D, 1 a wild bird, esp. a game bird, as a wild duck, pheasant, etc.: also **wild fowl**

wild-goose chase (-gōōs′) any search or undertaking as hopeless as trying to catch a wild goose by chasing it

wild hog *same as:* **1.** WILD BOAR **2.** PECCARY

wild·ing (wīl′diŋ) *n.* **1.** a wild plant; esp., a wild apple tree **2.** the fruit of such a plant

wild·life (wīld′līf′) *n.* wild animals and birds as a group

wild oats any of several wild grasses growing as weeds in the western U.S.: also **wild oat** —**sow one′s wild oats** to lead a rather wild or immoral life as a youth before settling down: usually said of a man

wild pansy an uncultivated pansy, esp. a European type with petals in combinations of white, yellow, and purple

☆**wild pitch** *Baseball* a pitch so badly thrown that the catcher is unable to control it, letting a runner move up to another base

wild rice **1.** a tall grass of the U.S. and Canada, found in swampy borders of lakes and streams **2.** its edible grain

wild rose any of various roses growing wild, as eglantine

wild type the typical form that a kind of plant has under natural conditions

☆**Wild West** [*also* w- W-] the western U.S. in its frontier days of lawlessness

wild·wood (wīld′wood′) *n.* a natural woodland or forest

wile (wīl) *n.* [Late OE. *wil* < OE. *wigle,* magic] a sly or clever trick used to fool or lure someone [using flattery and other *wiles* to gain her confidence] —*vt.* **wiled, wil′ing** to use wiles on in order to lure —**see SYN** at TRICK —**wile away** to while away (time): by confusion with *while*

Wil·fred, Wil·frid (wil′frid) [< OE. < *willa,* a wish, WILL¹ + *frith,* peace] a masculine name

wil·ful (wil′fəl) *adj. var. of* WILLFUL

Wil·hel·mi·na (wil′hel mē′nə) [< G. fem. of *Wilhelm:* see WILLIAM] a feminine name

Wilkes-Bar·re (wilks′bar′ē, -ber′ē; -ə) [after J. *Wilkes,* 18th-c. Eng. political reformer & Col. I. *Barré,* Brit. officer] city in NE Pa.: pop. 59,000

Wil·kins (wil′kinz), **Maurice H**(**ugh**) **F**(**rederick**) 1916– ; Eng. biophysicist: helped determine the structure of DNA

will¹ (wil) *n.* [OE. *willa*] **1.** the power of making a reasoned choice or decision or of controlling one′s own actions [a strong or weak *will;* free *will*] **2.** *a)* strong and fixed purpose; determination [where there′s a *will* there′s a way] *b)* energy and enthusiasm [to work with a *will*] **3.** attitude toward others [a person of good *will*] **4.** the desire, purpose, choice, etc. of a certain person or group [what is your *will*?] **5.** a legal document in which a person tells what he wants done with his money and property after he dies —*vt.* **1.** to have as the object of one′s will; desire; want [to *will* another′s happiness] **2.** to control or influence by the power of the will [he *willed* her to do as he wished] **3.** to leave (property, etc.) to someone by a will —*vi.* **1.** to use one′s will [to succeed by *willing*] **2.** to choose or prefer [to do as one *wills*] —**at will** when one wishes —**will′a·ble** *adj.* —**will′·less** *adj.*

SYN.—**will** refers to the power of making choices and controlling one′s own actions or to an intention resulting from the use of this power [freedom of the *will,* her *will* to succeed]; **volition** emphasizes the use of the will in making a choice or decision [he came of his own *volition*]

will² (wil; *unstressed* wəl) *v., pt.* **would** [OE. *willan*] **1.** a helping verb used to express the future: it has been the rule to use *will* in the second and third persons and *shall* in the first person to show simple future, and to reverse these in order to show determination; however, *will* is now ordinarily used in all persons except in the most formal writing **2.** a helping verb used to express: *a)* willingness [*will* you do me a favor?] *b)* ability or capacity [it will hold another quart] *c)* habit, custom, liking, or certainty [boys *will* be boys] *d)* expectation, guessing, etc. [that *will* be his wife with him, I suppose] See also SHALL —*vt., vi.* to wish; desire [do what (or as) you *will*]

Wil·lard (wil′ərd) **1.** [< the surname *Willard*] a masculine name **2. Frances** (**Elizabeth Caroline**), 1839–98; U.S. temperance leader

will call the department, as of a large store, at which articles are held to be picked up, as when paid for

willed (wild) *adj.* having a will, esp. a specified kind of will: used in hyphenated compounds [strong-*willed*]

Wil·lem·stad (wil′əm stät′, vil′-) capital of the Netherlands Antilles, on the island of Curaçao: pop. 44,000

☆**wil·let** (wil′it) *n., pl.* **-lets, -let:** see PLURAL, II, D, 1 [echoic of its cry] a large, gray-and-white, long-legged wading bird of N. and S. America, living along shallow shores

will·ful (wil′fəl) *adj.* **1.** done or said on purpose [*willful* lies] **2.** always wanting one′s own way; doing as one pleases; self-willed [his *willful* daughter] —**see SYN** at VOLUNTARY —**will′ful·ly** *adv.* —**will′ful·ness** *n.*

Wil·liam (wil′yəm) [< ONormFr. < OHG. < *willeo,* WILL¹ + *helm,* protection] **1.** a masculine name **2. William I** *a)* 1027?–87; duke of Normandy who conquered England (see Battle of HASTINGS); king of England (1066–87): called *William the Conqueror b)* 1533–84; prince of Orange (1544–84); founder of the Netherlands republic: called *William the Silent* **3. William II** 1859–1941; emperor of Germany & king of Prussia (1888–1918): called *Kaiser Wilhelm* **4. William III** 1650–1702; king of England, Scotland, & Ireland (1689–1702): see MARY II

Wil·liams (wil′yəmz) **1. Roger,** 1603?–83; Eng. colonist in America: founder of Rhode Island **2. Tennessee,** (born *Thomas Lanier Williams*) 1914– ; U.S. playwright

Wil·liams·burg (wil′yəmz burg′) [after WILLIAM III] city in SE Va.; colonial capital of Va., now restored to its 18th-cent. appearance

☆**wil·lies** (wil′ēz) *n.pl.* [< ?] [Slang] a state of nervousness; jitters: with *the*

will·ing (wil′iŋ) *adj.* **1.** ready or agreeing (*to* do something) [*willing* to try] **2.** doing, giving, etc. or done, given, etc. readily or gladly; voluntary [a *willing* helper, *willing* service] —**will′ing·ly** *adv.* —**will′ing·ness** *n.*

wil·li·waw, wil·ly·waw (wil′i wô′) *n.* [< an Austral. term for WHIRLWIND] a sudden, violent, cold wind blowing down from mountain passes toward the coast in far northern or southern regions

will-o′-the-wisp (wil′ə *th*ə wisp′) *n.* [earlier *Will* (personal name) *with the wisp*] **1.** a light seen moving over marshes at night: see also IGNIS FATUUS **2.** any hope or goal that leads one on but is impossible to reach

wil·low (wil′ō) *n.* [OE. *welig*] **1.** *a)* any of a group of trees and shrubs bearing catkins and usually narrow leaves: the twigs of certain species can be bent easily for weaving baskets, chair seats, etc. *b)* the wood of any of these trees **2.** [orig. made of willow] [Colloq.] a baseball bat or cricket bat

wil·low·y (wil′ə wē) *adj.* **1.** covered or shaded with willows [a *willowy* river bank] **2.** like a willow; specif., *a)* gracefully slender [she has a *willowy* figure] *b)* easily bent or able to bend easily; pliant, supple, lithe, etc.

will·pow·er (wil′pou′ər) *n.* strength of will, mind, or purpose; self-control [use *willpower* to break a bad habit]

wil·ly-nil·ly (wil′ē nil′ē) *adv.* [contr. < *will I, nill I: nill* < OE. *nyllan* < *ne,* not + *willan,* to WILL[1]] whether one wishes it or not; willingly or unwillingly —*adj.* that is or happens whether one wishes it or not

Wil·ming·ton (wil′miŋ tən) [after S. Compton (1673?–1743), Earl of *Wilmington*] seaport in N Del., on the Delaware River: pop. 80,000

Wil·son (wil′s′n) **1. Edmund,** 1895–1972; U.S. writer & critic **2. (Thomas) Wood·row** (wood′rō), 1856–1924; 28th president of the U.S. (1913–21)

Wil·son, Mount [after B. D. *Wilson,* early settler] mountain of the Coast Ranges, SW Calif., near Pasadena: site of an astronomical observatory

Wilson (cloud) chamber [after C. T. R. *Wilson* (1869–1959), Scot. physicist] *same as* CLOUD CHAMBER

wilt[1] (wilt) *vi.* [var. of obs. *welk,* to wither] **1.** to become limp, as from heat or lack of water; wither; droop: said of plants **2.** to become weak or faint; languish [*wilting* under the hard work] **3.** to lose courage [to *wilt* under fire or attack] —*vt.* to cause to wilt —*n.* the act of wilting or condition of being wilted

wilt[2] (wilt) *archaic second person singular in the present tense of* WILL[2]*: used with* thou

Wil·ton (wilt′′n) *n.* [< *Wilton,* England, where first made] a kind of carpet with a velvety pile of cut loops: also **Wilton carpet, Wilton rug**

wil·y (wī′lē) *adj.* **wil′i·er, wil′i·est** full of wiles; crafty; sly —see SYN. at SLY —**wil′i·ness** *n.*

wim·ble (wim′b′l) *n.* [< Anglo-Fr. < MDu. *wimmel,* an auger] any of various tools for boring, as a gimlet, auger, etc. —*vt.* **-bled, -bling** to bore with a wimble

Wim·ble·don (wim′b′l dən) city in SE England: suburb of London: scene of international lawn tennis matches

wim·ple (wim′p′l) *n.* [OE. *wimpel*] a woman's head covering of medieval times consisting of a cloth arranged about the head, cheeks, chin, and neck: now worn only by certain nuns —*vt.* **-pled, -pling 1.** to clothe as with a wimple **2.** to lay in folds **3.** to cause to ripple —*vi.* **1.** to lie in folds **2.** to ripple

win (win) *vi.* **won, win′ning** [OE. *winnan,* to fight] **1.** *a)* to gain a victory; be victorious; triumph (sometimes with *out*) *b)* to finish in first place in a race, contest, etc. **2.** to succeed in reaching or achieving a specified state or place (with various prepositions, adverbs,

WIMPLE

etc.) [to *win* back to health] —*vt.* **1.** to get by effort, struggle, etc.; specif., *a)* to gain through accomplishment [to *win* distinctions] *b)* to achieve (one's point, demands, etc.) *c)* to gain (a prize or award) in competition *d)* to earn (a livelihood, etc.) **2.** to be victorious in (a contest, dispute, etc.) **3.** to get to with effort [they *won* the hilltop by noon] **4.** to influence or persuade: often with *over* [to *win* someone over to one's side] **5.** *a)* to gain the sympathy, favor, etc. of [to *win* a supporter] *b)* to gain (someone's sympathy, etc.) **6.** to persuade to marry one —*n.* **1.** [Colloq.] an act of winning; victory, as in a contest **2.** *Racing* first position at the finish

wince (wins) *vi.* **winced, winc′ing** [< Anglo-Fr. var. of OFr. *guenchir* < Frank.] to draw back slightly, usually twisting the face, as in pain —*n.* the act of wincing —**winc′er** *n.*

winch (winch) *n.* [OE. *wince*] **1.** a crank with a handle for turning something, as a grindstone **2.** a machine for lifting or pulling, having a drum turned by a crank or motor: a rope or cable tied to the load is wound on this drum —*vt.* to lift or pull with a winch

☆**Win·ches·ter (rifle)** (win′ches′tər, -chis-) [after O. F. *Winchester* (1810–80), U.S. arms manufacturer] *a trademark for* a type of repeating rifle

wind[1] (wīnd) *vt.* **wound** or rarely **wind′ed, wind′ing** [OE. *windan*] **1.** *a)* to turn, or make revolve [to *wind* a crank] *b)* to move as by cranking **2.** *a)* to coil (string, ribbon, etc.) around itself or around something else [*winding* a bandage around his toe] *b)* to cover by encircling with something [to *wind* a spool with thread] **3.** *a)* to make (one's way) in a winding or twisting course *b)* to make move in such a course **4.** to introduce indirectly [*winding* his prejudices through all his writings] **5.** to lift or pull as with a winch (often with *up*) **6.** to tighten the spring of (a clock, etc.) as by turning a stem —*vi.* **1.** to move or go in a twisting or curving course [the river *winds* through the valley] **2.** to appear in a way that is indirect, roundabout, etc. **3.** to coil or spiral (*about* or *around* something) [the grapevine *wound* around the tree] **4.** to undergo winding [this clock *winds* easily] —*n.* **1.** the act of winding **2.** a single turn of something wound **3.** a turn; twist; bend; curve [a *wind* in the road] —**wind up 1.** to wind into a ball, etc. **2.** to entangle or involve [problems that are *wound up* in the matter] **3.** to bring or come to an end; finish [to *wind up* the day's work] **4.** to make very tense, nervous, excited, etc. ☆**5.** *Baseball* to swing the arm in getting ready to pitch the ball —**wind′er** *n.*

wind[2] (wind; *for n., also poet.* wīnd) *n.* [OE.] **1.** air that is moving **2.** a strong, fast-moving air current; gale **3.** an air current bearing a scent, as in hunting [to lose (the) *wind* of the fox] **4.** figuratively, air thought of as bearing information, showing trends, etc. [rumors in the *wind*] **5.** breath or the power of breathing [to get the *wind* knocked out of one] **6.** *a)* foolish or empty talk *b)* bragging; pomposity **7.** gas in the stomach or intestines **8.** [*pl.*] the wind instruments of an orchestra, or the players of these —*vt.* **1.** to expose to the wind, as for drying; air **2.** to get or follow the scent of **3.** to put out of breath [to be *winded* by a long run] **4.** to rest (a horse, etc.) so as to allow recovery of breath —**break wind** to let out gas from the bowels —**get** (or **have**) **wind of** to get (or have) information or a hint about —**how the wind blows** (or **lies**) what the trend of affairs, public opinion, etc. is —**in the teeth of the wind** straight against the wind: also **in the wind's eye** —**in the wind** happening or about to happen —**into the wind** in the direction from which the wind is blowing —**take the wind out of one's sails** to suddenly take away one's advantage, confidence, enthusiasm, etc. —**wind′less** *adj.* —**wind′less·ness** *n.*

wind[3] (wīnd) *vt., vi.* **wound** or rarely **wind′ed, wind′ing** [< prec.] [Poet.] **1.** to blow (a horn, etc.) **2.** to sound (a signal, etc.) as on a horn

wind·age (win′dij) *n.* **1.** the disturbance of air around a moving projectile **2.** the moving of a projectile from its course by the wind, or the degree of this

wind·bag (wind′bag′) *n.* [Colloq.] a person who talks much but says little of importance

wind·blown (-blōn′) *adj.* **1.** blown by the wind **2.** twisted in growth by the prevailing wind: said of a tree

wind·borne (-bôrn′) *adj.* carried by the wind, as pollen

☆**wind·break** (-brāk′) *n.* a hedge, fence, or row of trees that serves as a protection from wind

☆**Wind·break·er** (-brā′kər) *a trademark for* a warm sports jacket of leather, wool, etc., having a closefitting elastic waistband and cuffs —*n.* [w-] such a jacket

wind-bro·ken (-brō′k'n) *adj.* having the heaves: see HEAVES

wind·burn (-bʉrn′) *n.* a roughened, reddened, sore condition of the skin, caused by overexposure to the wind

Wind Cave National Park national park in SW S.Dak.: it contains a limestone cavern (**Wind Cave**)

wind chimes a cluster of small chimes or ornaments of glass, ceramic, etc., hung so that they strike one another and tinkle when blown by the wind: also **wind bells**

wind cone *same as* WINDSOCK

wind·fall (-fôl′) *n.* **1.** something blown down by the wind, as fruit from a tree **2.** any money or gain that one gets without expecting it

wind·flow·er (-flou′ər) *n. same as* ANEMONE (sense 1)

☆**wind gap** a narrow pass in a mountain ridge, formerly the bed of a small stream

wind gauge **1.** *same as* ANEMOMETER **2.** an attachment on a gun sight for measuring the degree the gun must be turned to the side in order to act against the force of the wind

Wind·hoek (vint′hook) capital of South West Africa (Namibia), in the central part: pop. 65,000

wind·i·ly (win′də lē) *adv.* in a windy manner

wind·i·ness (-dē nis) *n.* a windy quality or condition

wind·ing (wīn′diŋ) *n.* **1.** the action or effect of a person or thing that winds; a coiling, twining, turn, bend, etc. **2.** something that winds or is wound around an object, as the wire in the armature of a motor; also, a single turn of this —*adj.* that winds, turns, coils, spirals, etc.

winding sheet a cloth in which the body of a dead person is wrapped for burial; shroud

wind instrument (wind) a musical instrument sounded by blowing air, esp. breath, through it, as a flute, trumpet, etc.

☆**wind·jam·mer** (wind′jam′ər) *n. Naut.* a sailing ship, esp. a large one, or one of its crew

wind·lass (wind′ləs) *n.* [ON. *vindass* < *vinda*, to WIND[1] + *ass*, a beam] a winch, esp. a simple one worked by a crank —*vt., vi.* to lift, pull, etc. with a windlass

wind·mill (wind′mil′) *n.* a machine made to go by the wind blowing on a wheel of vanes at the top of a tower: it gives power for grinding grain, pumping water, etc. —**fight (or tilt at) windmills** to fight imaginary opponents: from Don Quixote's mistaking windmills for giants —*vt., vi.* to rotate like a windmill

WINDLASS

win·dow (win′dō) *n.* [< ON. < *vindr*, WIND[2] + *auga*, an eye] **1.** *a)* an opening in a building, vehicle, etc., to let in light or air or to look through, usually having a pane or panes of glass, etc. set in a frame that is usually movable *b)* any such pane or frame **2.** any similar opening **3.** the transparent panel of a window envelope **4.** *same as* LAUNCH WINDOW **5.** any part of the frequency spectrum of the earth's atmosphere through which light, heat, or radio waves can get to the earth's surface —*vt.* to provide with a window or windows —**win′dow·less** *adj.*

window box a long, narrow box on or outside a window ledge, for growing plants

window dressing **1.** the display of goods and trimmings in a store window to attract customers **2.** any display or attempt to make something seem better than it really is —**window dresser**

window envelope an envelope with a transparent panel, through which the address on the letter, bill, etc. inside can be seen

win·dow·pane (-pān′) *n.* a pane of glass in a window

window seat a seat built in beneath a window or windows and usually containing storage space

☆**window shade** a shade for a window, esp. one of stiffened, opaque material on a roller

win·dow·shop (-shäp′) *vi.* **-shopped′, -shop′ping** to look at displays of goods in store windows without entering the stores to buy —**win′dow-shop′per** *n.*

win·dow·sill (-sil′) *n.* the sill of a window

wind·pipe (wind′pīp′) *n. same as* TRACHEA (sense 1)

wind·proof (-proof′) *adj.* that the wind cannot blow through, blow out, etc. [*a windproof* coat, a *windproof* lighter]

wind·row (-rō′) *n.* **1.** a row of hay or of grain, etc. raked together to dry **2.** a row of dry leaves, dust, etc. swept together by the wind —*vt.* to rake or sweep into windrows

☆**wind·shield** (-shēld′) *n.* in automobiles, etc., a transparent screen in front, as of glass, to protect the riders from wind, etc.: also, chiefly Brit., **wind′screen′**

wind·sock (-säk′) *n.* a long, cone-shaped cloth bag, open at both ends and attached to the top of a mast, as at an airfield, to show wind direction: also called **wind sleeve**

Wind·sor[1] (win′zər) ruling family of Great Britain since 1917

Wind·sor[2] (win′zər) **1.** city in SE England, on the Thames: site of Windsor Castle **2.** port in SE Ontario, Canada, opposite Detroit: pop. 193,000

Windsor Castle a royal residence since the time of William the Conqueror, located in Windsor, England

Windsor chair a style of wooden chair, esp. popular in 18th-cent. England and America, with spreading legs, a spindle back, and usually a saddlelike seat

Windsor knot a form of double slipknot in a four-in-hand necktie, resulting in a wider, thicker knot

wind·storm (wind′stôrm′) *n.* a storm with a strong wind but little or no rain, hail, etc.

wind-swept (-swept′) *adj.* swept by or exposed to winds

☆**wind tee** a large T-shaped weather vane placed on a landing field to show wind direction to aircraft

WINDSOR
CHAIR

☆**wind tunnel** a tunnellike chamber through which air is forced and in which scale models of airplanes, etc. are tested to determine the effects of wind pressure

wind·up (wīnd′up′) *n.* **1.** a winding up, or conclusion; close; end ☆**2.** *Baseball* the swinging of the arm when getting ready to pitch the ball

wind·ward (wind′wərd, win′dərd) *n.* the direction from which the wind blows —*adv.* toward the wind —*adj.* **1.** moving windward **2.** on the side from which the wind blows Opposed to LEEWARD

Wind·ward Islands (wind′wərd) S group of islands in the Lesser Antilles of the West Indies, extending from the Leeward Islands southward to Trinidad

wind·y (win′dē) *adj.* **wind′i·er, wind′i·est** **1.** with much wind [a *windy* day] **2.** swept by strong winds [a *windy* city] **3.** violent like wind [*windy* anger] **4.** *a)* without substance; empty, flimsy, etc. *b)* long-winded, pompous, boastful, etc. **5.** *same as* FLATULENT

wine (wīn) *n.* [OE. *win*, ult. < L. *vinum*] **1.** the fermented juice of grapes, used as an alcoholic beverage and in cooking, etc. **2.** the fermented juice of other fruits or plants, used as a beverage [dandelion *wine*] **3.** a dark, purplish red like that of red wine —*vt., vi.* **wined, win′ing** to provide with or drink wine: usually in **wine and dine,** to entertain with much food, drink, etc.

wine·bib·ber (wīn′bib′ər) *n.* a person given to drinking much or too much wine —**wine′bib′bing** *adj., n.*

wine cellar **1.** a cellar where wine is stored **2.** a stock of wine

wine-col·ored (-kul′ərd) *adj.* having the color of red wine; dark purplish-red

wine gallon the old English gallon of 231 cu. in., now the standard gallon in the U.S.

wine·glass (-glas′) *n.* a small glass, usually stemmed, for serving wine —**wine′glass·ful′** *n., pl.* **-fuls′**

wine·grow·ing (-grō′iŋ) *n.* the art or process of growing grapes and making wine from them —**wine′grow′er** *n.*

wine press a vat in which grapes are trampled, or a machine for pressing them, to remove the juice for making wine

☆**win·er·y** (wīn′ər ē) *n., pl.* **-er·ies** an establishment where wine is made

☆**Wine·sap** (wīn′sap′) *n.* a dark-red winter apple

wine·skin (wīn′skin′) *n.* a large bag for holding wine, made of the skin of an animal

wing (wiŋ) *n.* [< ON. pl. of *vaengr*] **1.** *a)* either of the pair of feathered parts that a bird spreads out from its side in flying *b)* any of the paired parts used like this for flying, in other creatures [bats' *wings* have a webbing of skin connecting bones that are like those in other mammals' forelimbs; most insects have two pairs of membranous *wings*] *c)* any of various winglike parts used by certain animals for gliding, as the pectoral fin of a flying fish **2.** either of a pair of winglike parts that angels, dragons, etc. are thought of as having **3.** something used as or like a wing; esp., *a* (or the) main supporting surface of an airplane **4.** something like a wing in its position or relation to the main part; esp., *a)* a distinct part of a building, often at one side or added later or having a special use *[the east* wing; *the surgical* wing *of a hospital]* b) either side of a theater stage out of sight of the audience c) any winglike part, as on some seeds **5.** a group having a winglike relation to another group; specif., a) the right or left section of an army, fleet, etc. b) a section or group, as of a political party, holding specified views, as of a leftist or rightist kind **6.** in hockey, a position forward and right (or left) of center, or a player lining up at this position **7.** a) any of various air force units; specif., ☆*U.S. Air Force,* a unit larger than a group and smaller than a division b) *[pl.]* the insignia worn by pilots and crew of military aircraft **8.** a flying or soaring, or a means of doing this: now chiefly in **give wing to, take wing** (see phrases below) **9.** *[Slang]* a person's arm; specif., ☆*Baseball* a pitcher's throwing arm —*vt.* **1.** to provide with wings **2.** a) to cause to fly or speed as on wings *[to* wing *an arrow at a target]* b) to make (one's way) by flying c) to go through or over by flying **3.** to carry or move as by flight **4.** to wound, as with a bullet, in the wing, arm, etc. —*vi.* to go swiftly as on wings; fly —**give wing** (or **wings**) **to** to make able to fly or soar on or as if on wings —**on the wing 1.** flying, or while in flight **2.** in motion or while moving or traveling —**on wings of** filled with joy or rapture by *[on wings of* song*]* —**take wing 1.** to take flight; fly away **2.** to become joyous, inspired, etc. —**under one's wing** under one's protection, patronage, etc. —**wing′less** *adj.*

wing chair an upholstered armchair with a high back and high sides, or wings

☆**wing·ding** (wiŋ′diŋ′) *n.* **[<** ?] *[Slang]* **1.** an event, party, etc. that is very joyous, lively, etc. **2.** something very striking, exciting, etc. of its kind

winged (wiŋd; *often poet.* wiŋ′id) *adj.* **1.** having wings or winglike parts **2.** moving, esp. swiftly, on or as if on wings **3.** grand; noble *[winged* words*]*

☆**wing nut** a nut with sides sticking out so that it can be turned with the thumb and forefinger: see illustration at NUT

wing·span (wiŋ′span′) *n.* the distance between the tips of an airplane's wings

wing·spread (-spred′) *n.* **1.** the distance between the tips of a pair of fully spread wings **2.** *same as* WINGSPAN

WING CHAIR

wing tip ☆**1.** a man's shoe with a decorative piece of leather over the vamp: the piece is peaked toward the tongue and has holes on it and along the upper edge of its wing-shaped sides ☆**2.** this piece of leather Also **wing′-tip′, wing′tip′** *n.*

wink (wiŋk) *vi.* [OE. *wincian*] **1.** to close the eyelids and open them again quickly **2.** a) to close and open an eyelid quickly so as to signal, etc. b) to be closed and opened thus: said of the eye **3.** to shine or twinkle in flashes of light *[the* winking *stars]* —*vt.* **1.** to make (the eyes or an eye) wink **2.** to move, remove, etc. by winking *[to* wink *back tears]* **3.** to signal, etc. by winking —*n.* **1.** the act of winking **2.** a very short time; instant *[she was there in a* wink; *he didn't sleep a* wink*]* **3.** a signal, etc. given by winking **4.** a twinkle —**wink at** to pretend not to notice (some wrongdoing)

SYN.—**wink** usually implies that the quick closing and opening of one or both eyelids one or more times is done on purpose *[he* winked *at her knowingly]*; **blink** implies a rapid series of such movements, usually done as a reflex without thinking and with the eyes half-shut *[to* blink *in the harsh sunlight]*

wink·er (wiŋk′ər) *n.* **1.** a person or thing that winks **2.** a blinder (for a horse) **3.** *[Colloq.]* an eyelash or an eye

win·kle[1] (wiŋ′k'l) *n.* **1.** *short for* PERIWINKLE[2] **2.** a large snail very harmful to oysters and clams

win·kle[2] (wiŋ′k'l) *vt.* **-kled, -kling** **[<** ?] *[Colloq.]* to pry or force from cover, secrecy, etc. (with *out, out of,* etc.)

win·ner (win′ər) *n.* one that wins; esp., *[Colloq.]* one that seems destined to win or be successful

win·ning (-iŋ) *adj.* **1.** that wins; victorious **2.** attractive; charming *[a* winning *smile]* —*n.* **1.** victory **2.** *[pl.]* something won, esp. money —**win′ning·ly** *adv.*

Win·ni·peg (win′ə peg′) **1.** capital of Manitoba, Canada, on the Red River: pop. 257,000 (met. area 509,000) **2. Lake,** large lake in SC Manitoba

win·now (win′ō) *vt.* [OE. *windwian* < *wind,* WIND[2]] **1.** a) to blow the chaff from (grain) b) to blow off (chaff) **2.** to blow away; scatter **3.** to analyze or examine carefully so as to separate the various elements; sift **4.** a) to separate out (poor or useless parts) b) to sort out or extract (good or useful parts) —*vi.* to winnow grain —*n.* **1.** a winnowing **2.** an apparatus for winnowing —**win′now·er** *n.*

☆**win·o** (wī′nō) *n., pl.* **-os** *[Slang]* a person, esp. an alcoholic, who habitually gets drunk on wine, esp. cheap wine

win·some (win′səm) *adj.* [OE. *wynsum,* pleasant] attractive in a sweet, pleasant way; charming —**win′some·ly** *adv.* —**win′some·ness** *n.*

Win·ston-Sa·lem (win′stən sā′ləm) [ult. after Maj. J. *Winston* (1746–1815) & SALEM] city in north central N.C., near Greensboro: pop. 133,000

win·ter (win′tər) *n.* [OE.] **1.** the coldest season of the year, following autumn **2.** a year as marked by this season *[a man of eighty* winters*]* **3.** any period thought of, like winter, as a time of decline, trouble, etc. *[the* winter *of his career]* —*adj.* **1.** of, typical of, or suitable for winter *[winter* sports*]* **2.** that will keep during the winter *[winter* apples*]* **3.** planted in the fall to be harvested in the spring *[winter* wheat*]* —*vi.* **1.** to pass the winter *[we* winter *in Florida]* **2.** to be supplied with food and shelter in the winter —*vt.* to keep or maintain during the winter *[they* winter *the circus in the South]* —**win′ter·er** *n.*

win·ter·ber·ry (-ber′ē) *n., pl.* **-ries** ☆any of several tall hollies of eastern N. America with thin leaves and bright red, black, purple, or yellow berries that last over winter

win·ter·green (-grēn′) *n.* ☆**1.** an evergreen plant with small, rounded leaves, white flowers, and red berries ☆**2.** a substance (oil of wintergreen) made from these leaves or from birch bark or synthetically, used in medicine and as a flavoring ☆**3.** its sharp flavor

☆**win·ter·ize** (-īz′) *vt.* **-ized, -iz′ing** to put into condition for winter *[to* winterize *a car with antifreeze]*

☆**win·ter·kill** (-kil′) *vt., vi.* to kill or die by exposure to winter cold: said of plants

winter solstice the time in the Northern Hemisphere when the sun is farthest south of the celestial equator; December 21 or 22

☆**winter squash** any of several squashes, as the acorn squash, with a hard rind and good keeping qualities

win·ter·time (-tīm′) *n.* the season of winter

Win·throp (win′thrəp), **John** 1588–1649; Eng. colonist in America; 1st governor of the colony (*Massachusetts Bay Colony*) founded at Salem, Mass.; also, his son, 1606–76; governor of Connecticut colony (1657, 1659–76)

win·try (win′trē) *adj.* **-tri·er, -tri·est** of or like winter; cold, gloomy, etc. *[a* wintry *day, a* wintry *stare]*: also **win′ter·y** (-tər ē, -trē) —**win′tri·ly** (-trə lē) *adv.* —**win′tri·ness** (-trē nis) *n.*

win·y (wī′nē) *adj.* **win′i·er, win′i·est** like wine in taste, smell, color, etc.

wipe (wīp) *vt.* **wiped, wip′ing** [OE. *wipian*] **1.** a) to rub with a cloth, etc., as for cleaning or drying b) to clean or dry in this manner *[wipe* the dishes*]* **2.** to rub or pass (a cloth, etc.) over something **3.** to apply by wiping *[wipe* oil over the surface*]* **4.** to remove as by wiping (with *away, off,* etc.) *[to* wipe *dust off a table]* —*n.* a wiping —**wipe out 1.** to remove; erase **2.** to kill off **3.** to destroy —**wip′er** *n.*

wipe·out (wīp′out′) *n. [Slang]* any fall, failure, etc.

wire (wīr) *n.* [OE. *wir*] **1.** metal that has been drawn into a long thread **2.** a length of this, used for conducting electric current, tying bales, etc. **3.** wire netting or other wirework **4.** anything made of wire or wirework, as a telephone cable, a snare, etc. **5.** a) telegraph *[reply by* wire*]* b) a telegram ☆**6.** *Horse Racing* a wire above the finish line of a race —*adj.* made of wire or wirework —*vt.* **wired, wir′ing** **1.** to furnish, connect, bind, etc. with wire *[to* wire *a vine to a stake]* **2.** to supply with a system of wires for electric current *[to* wire *a house]* **3.** to telegraph —*vi.* to telegraph —☆**down to the wire** to the very last moments —☆**get (in) under the wire** to enter or achieve barely on time —☆**pull wires** to get what one wants through one's friends' influence —**wire′like′** *adj.*

wire·draw (wīr′drô′) *vt.* **-drew′, -drawn′, -draw′ing** **1.** to draw (metal) into wire **2.** to draw out, with too much detail, hairsplitting, etc. *[wiredrawn* arguments*]*

wire gauge a device for measuring the diameter of wire, thickness of sheet metal, etc.: it usually consists of a disk with notches of different sizes along its edge

WIRE GAUGE

wire·hair (-her′) *n.* a fox terrier with a wiry coat: also **wire-haired terrier**

wire-haired (-herd′) *adj.* having stiff and coarse, or wiry, hair

wire·less (-lis) *adj.* **1.** without wire or wires; specif., sending or sent by radio waves instead of by electric current in wires **2.** [Chiefly Brit.] *same as* RADIO —*n.* **1.** *same as:* a) WIRELESS TELEGRAPHY b) [Chiefly Brit.] RADIO **2.** a message sent by wireless —*vt., vi.* to communicate (with) by wireless

wireless telegraphy (or **telegraph**) telegraphy by radio-transmitted signals

wireless telephone a telephone operating by radio-transmitted signals —**wireless telephony**

wire netting netting of woven wire, used in various sizes for fences and the like

Wire·pho·to (-fōt′ō) *a trademark for:* **1.** a system of reproducing photographs at a distance by means of electric signals transmitted by wire **2.** a photograph so produced

☆**wire·pull·er** (-pool′ər) *n.* a person who gets what he wants through his friends' influence —**wire′pull′ing** *n.*

wire service a business organization that sends news stories, features, etc. by direct telegraph to subscribing or member newspapers and radio and television stations

☆**wire·tap** (-tap′) *vi., vt.* **-tapped′, -tap′ping** to make a secret connection with (a telephone line) in order to overhear or record private conversations —*n.* **1.** the act or an instance of wiretapping **2.** a device used in wiretapping —*adj.* of or relating to wiretapping —**wire′tap′per** *n.*

wire·work (-wurk′) *n.* netting, mesh, etc. made of wire

wire·worm (-wurm′) *n.* any of the thin, hard-bodied, wormlike larvae of click beetles that often live underground and attack the roots of crops

wir·ing (wīr′iŋ) *n.* **1.** the action of a person or thing that wires **2.** a system of wires, as to provide a house with electricity —*adj.* **1.** that wires **2.** used in wiring

wir·y (wīr′ē) *adj.* **wir′i·er, wir′i·est 1.** of wire **2.** like wire in shape and substance; stiff [*wiry* hair] **3.** lean, sinewy, and strong: said of persons and animals **4.** produced by or as if by a vibrating wire [a *wiry* sound] —**wir′i·ness** *n.*

wis (wis) *vt.* [< ME. *iwis*, certainly: erroneously understood as "I know"] [Archaic] to suppose; imagine; deem

Wis·con·sin (wis kän′s'n) [< Fr. < Algonquian] Middle Western State of the U.S.: 56,154 sq. mi.; pop. 4,418,000; cap. Madison: abbrev. **Wis., WI** —**Wis·con′sin·ite′** (-īt′) *n.*

wis·dom (wiz′dəm) *n.* [OE. < *wis*, WISE¹ + *-dom*, -DOM] **1.** the quality of being wise; good judgment, based on knowledge, experience, etc.; sagacity [the *wisdom* to save money for old age] **2.** learning; knowledge; erudition [the *wisdom* of the ages] **3.** wise teaching **4.** a wise plan or course of action —see SYN. at INFORMATION

Wisdom of Solomon one of the books of the Apocrypha: called **Wisdom** in the Douay Bible

wisdom tooth the back tooth on each side of each jaw in human beings, appearing usually between the ages of 17 and 25

wise¹ (wīz) *adj.* **wis′er, wis′est** [OE. *wis* < IE. base *weid-*, to see, from which also comes L. *videre*] **1.** having or showing good judgment; sagacious [a *wise* judge] **2.** prompted by wisdom; judicious; sound [a *wise* saying] **3.** having information; informed [no *wiser* after reading the book] **4.** learned or scholarly [a *wise* professor] **5.** shrewd; cunning ☆**6.** [Slang] *a)* annoyingly self-assured, knowing, etc. *b)* disrespectful; fresh —☆**be (or get) wise to** [Slang] to be (or become) aware of —☆**get wise** [Slang] **1.** to become aware of the true facts **2.** to become disrespectful —☆**put wise (to)** [Slang] to give (someone) information, etc. (about) —☆**wise up** [Slang] to make or become informed —**wise′ly** *adv.* —**wise′ness** *n.*

SYN.—**wise** implies the ability to judge and deal with persons, situations, etc. rightly, based on a broad range of knowledge, experience, and understanding [a *wise* parent]; **sage** suggests the great wisdom of age, experience, and philosophical thought [*sage* advice]; **judicious** implies the ability to make wise decisions based on sound judgment [a *judicious* approach to a problem]; **prudent** suggests the wisdom of one who is able to recognize the most suitable or careful course of action in practical matters [a *prudent* policy] —ANT. foolish, stupid

wise² (wīz) *n.* [OE.] way; manner: used chiefly in phrases, as **in no wise, in this wise,** etc.

-wise (wīz) [< prec.] *a suffix meaning:* **1.** in a (specified) direction, position, or manner [*sidewise*]: same as -WAYS **2.** in the same way or direction as [*clockwise*] **3.** with regard to; in connection with [*weatherwise, budgetwise*]

wise·a·cre (wīz′ā′kər) *n.* [< MDu. < OHG. *wizzago*, a prophet] a person who acts as though he were much wiser than he really is

☆**wise·crack** (-krak′) *n.* [Slang] a joke or clever remark, often one that shows a lack of respect or of seriousness —*vi.* [Slang] to make wisecracks —*vt.* [Slang] to say as a wisecrack —**wise′-crack′er** *n.*

☆**wise guy** [Slang] a person who is boldly and annoyingly conceited, knowing, etc.; smart aleck

wi·sent (vē′zənt) *n.* [G. < OHG. *wisunt*, BISON] *same as* AUROCHS (sense 2)

wish (wish) *vt.* [OE. *wyscan*] **1.** to have a longing for; want; desire [you may have whatever you *wish*] **2.** to have or express a desire about [to *wish* the day were over, to *wish* her good luck] **3.** to bid [to *wish* a person good morning] **4.** to request [he *wishes* her to leave] **5.** to pass off; impose (with *on*) [he *wished* the job on me] —*vi.* **1.** to have a desire; long or yearn (*for* something) **2.** to make a wish —*n.* **1.** a wishing; desire for something [I have no wish to hear it] **2.** something wished for [he got his *wish*] **3.** a polite request with some of the force of an order [we obeyed his *wishes*] **4.** [*pl.*] expressed desire for a person's well-being, good fortune, etc. [to offer one's best *wishes*] —see SYN. at DESIRE —**wish′er** *n.*

wish·bone (wish′bōn′) *n.* [from its use as a sign of whose wish will come true when it is pulled apart by two persons] the forked bone in front of the breastbone of most birds

wish·ful (-fəl) *adj.* having or showing a wish; desirous; longing —**wish′ful·ly** *adv.* —**wish′ful·ness** *n.*

wishful thinking thinking in which one explains facts in terms of what he would like to believe

wish·y-wash·y (wish′ē wôsh′ē, -wäsh′ē) *adj.* [redupl. of WASHY] [Colloq.] **1.** watery; insipid; thin **2.** not strong or definite in character; weak [*wishy-washy* ideas]

wisp (wisp) *n.* [prob. < Scand.] **1.** a small bunch or tuft [a *wisp* of straw, hair, etc.] **2.** a thin, filmy bit or puff [a *wisp* of smoke] **3.** something delicate, frail, etc. [a *wisp* of a girl] **4.** *same as* WILL-O'-THE-WISP —*vt.* to roll into a wisp —**wisp′y** *adj.* **wisp′i·er, wisp′i·est**

wist (wist) *pt. & pp.* of WIT²

☆**wis·ter·i·a** (wis tir′ē ə) *n.* [ModL., after C. *Wistar* (1761–1818), U.S. anatomist] a twining shrub of the legume family, with showy clusters of bluish, white, pink, or purple flowers: also **wis·tar′i·a** (-ter′-)

wist·ful (wist′fəl) *adj.* [altered (after WISHFUL) < earlier *wistly*, attentive] showing longing or a vague yearning or sadness [the memory brought a *wistful* smile to his face] —**wist′ful·ly** *adv.* —**wist′ful·ness** *n.*

WISTERIA
(flowers & leaves)

wit¹ (wit) *n.* [OE.] **1.** [*pl.*] powers of thinking and reasoning, esp. in a normal, effective way [frightened out of his *wits*] **2.** alert, practical intelligence; good sense **3.** *a)* the ability to make lively, clever remarks expressed in a surprising, concise, or ironic way *b)* a person having this ability, or speech or writing in which it is expressed —**at one's wits' end** at a loss as to what to do —**keep (or have) one's wits about one** to stay alert, as in an emergency, and be able to deal with things —**live by one's wits** to live by trickery or craftiness

SYN.—**wit** refers to the ability to see contradictions, weaknesses, etc. in people and things and to make quick, sharp, often sarcastic remarks about them that delight or entertain; **humor** is applied to the ability to see and express that which is comical, or ridiculous, but suggests a kindly or sympathetic quality in the use of this ability to amuse others; **irony** refers to the humor that is implied in the difference between what is actually said and the meaning that is intended or in the difference between appearance and reality in life

wit² (wit) *vt., vi.* **wist, wit′ting** [OE. *witan*] [Archaic] to know or learn *Wit* is conjugated in the present tense: (I) *wot*, (thou) *wost* or *wot(t)est*, (he, she, it) *wot* or *wot(t)eth*, (we, ye, they) *wite* or *witen* —**to wit** that is to say; namely

witch (wich) **n.** [OE. *wicce*, fem. of *wicca*, sorcerer] **1.** a person, now specif. a woman, who is imagined to have magic power, esp. with the help of the devil; sorceress: see also WARLOCK **2.** an ugly and ill-tempered old woman —**vt. 1.** to put a magic spell on **2.** to charm; fascinate

witch·craft (wich′kraft′) **n. 1.** *a*) the power or practices of witches; black magic; sorcery *b*) an instance of this **2.** fascinating attraction or charm

witch doctor among certain tribes, esp. in Africa, a person who practices a type of primitive medicine involving the use of magic, witchcraft, etc.

witch·er·y (wich′ər ē) **n.,** *pl.* **-er·ies 1.** witchcraft; sorcery **2.** great charm; fascination

witch·es'-broom (wich′iz broōm′) **n.** an abnormal growth of closely bunched, thin twigs at the ends of branches of various woody plants, caused by fungi, viruses, etc.

☆**witch grass** [altered < QUITCH (GRASS)] a weedy N. American grass with hairy leaves and slim, spreading panicles

witch hazel [OE. *wice*] **1.** a shrub with yellow flowers and woody fruit **2.** a lotion made with an extract from the leaves and bark of this shrub

witch hunt [after the cruel treatment of persons once imagined to be witches] an investigation usually carried on with much publicity, supposedly to uncover activities aimed at overthrowing the government but really to harass and weaken political opposition —**witch hunter**

witch·ing (wich′iŋ) **n.** witchcraft —**adj.** that witches; fascinating; bewitching —**witch′ing·ly adv.**

with (with, with) **prep.** [OE., orig., against] **1.** against [to argue *with* a friend] **2.** *a*) alongside of; near to [the wrench is *with* the pliers on the top shelf] *b*) in the company of [I saw Mary *with* her father] *c*) into; among [mix blue *with* red] **3.** as an associate, or companion, of [he played golf *with* me] **4.** *a*) as a member of [to sing *with* a quartet] *b*) working for [*with* the firm 20 years] **5.** in regard to; concerning [pleased *with* her gift] **6.** in the same terms as; compared to [having equal standing *with* the others] **7.** as well as [he can run *with* the best] **8.** of the same opinions as [I'm *with* you] **9.** on the side of [he voted *with* the Tories] **10.** in the opinion of [it's all right *with* me] **11.** as a result of [faint *with* hunger] **12.** *a*) by means of; using [stir *with* a spoon] *b*) by [filled *with* air] **13.** having received [*with* your permission, he'll go] **14.** having or showing [a boy *with* red hair, to enter *with* confidence, to play *with* skill] **15.** in the keeping, care, etc. of [leave the baby *with* me] **16.** *a*) added to [those, *with* the ones we have, will be enough] *b*) including [*with* the newcomers, the class is large] **17.** in spite of [*with* all her faults, I love her still] **18.** *a*) at the same time as [to rise *with* the chickens] *b*) in the same direction as [to travel *with* the sun] *c*) in the same degree as; in proportion to [wages varying *with* skills] *d*) in the course of [grief lessens *with* time] **19.** to; onto [join one end *with* the other] **20.** from [to part *with* money] **21.** after [*with* that remark, he left] —**with that** after that

with- [OE. < prec.] *a combining form meaning:* **1.** away, back [*withdraw*] **2.** against, from [*withhold*]

with·al (with ôl′, with-) **adv. 1.** besides; as well [a strong lad and brave *withal*] **2.** despite that; notwithstanding [poor but proud *withal*] **3.** [Archaic] with that; therewith —**prep.** [Archaic] with: used following its object

with·draw (with drô′, with-) **vt.** **-drew′, -drawn′, -draw′ing 1.** to take back or draw back; remove [to *withdraw* one's hand] **2.** to take back (something said, offered, etc.) —**vi. 1.** to move back; go away; retreat [she *withdrew* behind the curtain] **2.** to remove oneself [*from* an organization, activity, association with other people, etc.] —see SYN. at GO —**with·draw′er n.**

with·draw·al (-drô′əl) **n. 1.** the act of withdrawing **2.** a giving up the use of a narcotic drug to which one has become addicted, typically accompanied by unpleasant effects on the body and mind (**withdrawal symptoms**)

with·drawn (-drôn′) *pp. of* WITHDRAW —**adj.** withdrawing within oneself; shy, reserved, unsociable, etc.

withe (with, with, wīth) **n.** [OE. *withthe*] a tough twig of willow, etc. that is easily bent and used for binding things —**vt. withed, with′ing** to bind with withes

with·er (with′ər) **vi.** [< ME. var. of *wederen*, lit., to weather] **1.** to dry up; shrivel [plants *withering* in the heat, a face wither-

ing with age] **2.** to lose strength; weaken [our hopes soon *withered*] —**vt. 1.** to cause to wither **2.** to make lose courage or be ashamed [her *withering* scorn]

SYN.—**wither** implies a drying up, decaying, wilting, fading, etc., as from a loss of natural juices [apples *withering* on the bough]; **shrivel** implies a shrinking, wrinkling, or curling, as from being exposed to very great heat [blossoms *shriveling* in the hot sun]; **wizen** implies a shrinking and wrinkling, as from great age, lack of proper nourishment, etc. [the *wizened* face of the old beggar]

with·ers (with′ərz) **n.pl.** [OE. *withre*, resistance < *wither*, against] the highest part of the back of a horse, etc., between the shoulder blades

with·hold (with hōld′, with-) **vt. -held′, -hold′ing 1.** *a*) to hold back; keep back; check [to *withheld* his anger] ☆*b*) to take out or deduct (taxes, etc.) from wages or salary **2.** to keep from giving; refuse [to *withhold* approval] —**vi.** to hold back; refrain; forbear

☆**withholding tax** the amount of income tax withheld from employees' wages or salaries

with·in (with in′, with-) **adv.** [OE. *withinnan*] **1.** on or to the inside **2.** indoors [cold outdoors, but warm *within*] **3.** inside the body, mind, spirit, etc. —**prep. 1.** in the inner part of; inside [stay *within* the house] **2.** not beyond in space, time, extent, etc.; in the scope or range of [*within* a mile of home; *within* one's experience] **3.** inside the limits of [*within* the law] —**n.** the inside or the interior

with·out (-out′) **adv.** [OE. *withutan*] **1.** on the outside [a shed freshly painted within and *without*] **2.** outdoors —**prep. 1.** at, on, or to the outside of [they stood *without* the gates] **2.** beyond [*without* his reach] **3.** not with; lacking [shoes *without* laces] **4.** free from [a man *without* fear] **5.** in a way that avoids [to pass by *without* speaking] —**n.** the outside or the exterior —**conj.** [Dial.] unless —**go** (or **do**) **without** to manage or get along although lacking something mentioned before

with·stand (with stand′, with-) **vt., vi. -stood′, -stand′ing** to oppose, resist, or survive, esp. in a successful way [these trees can *withstand* cold winters] —see SYN. at OPPOSE

with·y (with′ē, with′ē) **n.,** *pl.* **with′ies** [OE. *withig*] *same as* WITHE

wit·less (wit′lis) **adj.** lacking wit or intelligence; foolish —**wit′less·ly adv.** —**wit′less·ness n.**

wit·ling (wit′liŋ) **n.** one who believes himself to be a wit

wit·ness (wit′nis) **n.** [OE. *gewitnes*, knowledge, testimony] **1.** evidence; testimony [to bear false *witness*] **2.** a person who saw, or can give a firsthand account of, something **3.** a person who gives evidence in court **4.** a person who watches a contract, will, etc. being signed and then, as proof that he did, signs it himself **5.** something serving as evidence —**vt. 1.** to be or give proof of [her tears *witnessed* her sadness] **2.** to act as witness of (a contract, will, etc.) **3.** to be present at; see personally [to *witness* a sports event] **4.** to be the scene of [this field *witnessed* a battle] —**vi. 1.** to give, or serve as, evidence **2.** to testify to religious beliefs or faith —**bear witness** to be or give evidence

☆**witness stand** the place from which a witness gives his testimony in a law court: also, Brit., **wit′ness-box′ n.**

wit·ted (wit′id) **adj.** having (a specified kind of) wit: used in hyphenated compounds [slow-*witted*]

Wit·ten·berg (wit′'n burg′; *G.* vit′ən berk′) city in central East Germany, on the Elbe: the Reformation originated here in 1517: pop. 47,000

wit·ti·cism (wit′ə siz'm) **n.** [< WITTY + -*cism*, as in CRITICISM] a witty remark

wit·ting (wit′iŋ) **adj.** [ME. *wytting*] done knowingly; intentional —**wit′ting·ly adv.**

wit·ty (wit′ē) **adj. -ti·er, -ti·est** [OE. *wittig*] having or showing wit; cleverly amusing [a *witty* person, a *witty* remark] —**wit′ti·ly adv.** —**wit′ti·ness n.**

SYN.—**witty** implies a sharp, amusing cleverness and quickness in seeing and commenting, sometimes in a sarcastic way, on the contradictions, weakness, etc. in people and things; **humorous** connotes more friendliness, gentleness, etc. in saying or doing something that is intentionally comical or amusing; **facetious** suggests an attempt to be witty or humorous that is unsuccessful because it is not proper or is in bad taste; **jocular** implies a happy or playful nature characterized by the desire to amuse others; **jocose** suggests a mildly mischievous quality in joking or jesting —**ANT. serious, solemn, sober**

Wit·wa·ters·rand (wit wôt′ərz rand′, -wät′-; -ränt′) region in NE South Africa, containing rich gold fields

wive (wīv) *vi., vt.* **wived, wiv′ing** [OE. *wifian*] [Archaic] to marry (a woman)

wi·vern (wī′vərn) *n. same as* WYVERN

wives (wīvz) *n. pl. of* WIFE

☆**wiz** (wiz) *n. shortened form of* WIZARD (*n.* 2)

wiz·ard (wiz′ərd) *n.* [ME. *wisard*, prob. < *wis*, WISE[1] + *-ard*, -ARD] **1.** a magician; sorcerer **2.** [Colloq.] a person very gifted or clever at a specified activity [a *wizard* at designing electronic equipment] —*adj.* **1.** of wizards or wizardry **2.** magic —**wiz′ard·ly** *adv.*

wiz·ard·ry (-rē) *n.* witchcraft; magic; sorcery

wiz·en (wiz′'n, wēz′-) *vt., vi.* [OE. *wisnian*] to dry up; wither; shrivel —*adj. same as* WIZENED —see SYN. at WITHER

wiz·ened (-'nd) *adj.* dried up; withered; shriveled [the old man's *wizened* face]

wk. *pl.* **wks. 1.** week **2.** work

WL, w.l. 1. waterline **2.** wavelength

Wm. William

WNW, W.N.W., w.n.w. west-northwest

WO, W.O. Warrant Officer

woad (wōd) *n.* [OE. *wad*] any of a group of plants of the mustard family, esp. a plant (**dyer's woad**) with yellow flowers and leaves that yield a blue dye

wob·ble (wäb′'l) *vi.* **-bled, -bling** [prob. < LowG. *wabbeln*] **1.** to move from side to side in an unsteady way **2.** to shake as jelly does **3.** to be uncertain; waver in mind —*vt.* to cause to wobble —*n.* a wobbling motion —**wob′bler** *n.* —**wob′bli·ness** *n.* —**wob′bly** *adj.* **-bli·er, -bli·est**

Wo·den, Wo·dan (wōd′'n) the chief Germanic god, identified with the Norse god Odin

woe (wō) *n.* [OE. *wa*] **1.** great sorrow; grief [a tale of *woe*] **2.** a cause of sorrow; trouble [the *woes* of King Lear] —*interj.* alas! Also [Archaic] **wo**—see SYN. at SORROW

woe·be·gone (wō′bi gôn′, -gän′) *adj.* **1.** [Archaic] woeful **2.** showing woe; looking sad or mournful

woe·ful (-fəl) *adj.* **1.** full of woe; sad; mournful **2.** of, causing, or involving woe [*woeful* neglect] **3.** pitiful; wretched; miserable [*woeful* poverty] —**woe′ful·ly** *adv.* —**woe′ful·ness** *n.*

wok (wäk, wôk) *n.* [Chin.] a metal cooking pan with a bowl-shaped bottom, often used with a ring-like stand

woke (wōk) *alt. pt. & occas. Brit. pp. of* WAKE[1]

wok·en (wō′k'n) *occas. Brit. pp. of* WAKE[1]

wold (wōld) *n.* [OE. *wald*] a high, hilly land without trees

wolf (woolf) *n., pl.* **wolves** [OE. *wulf*] **1.** *a)* any of a group of wild, flesh-eating, doglike mammals, esp. the gray wolf, found throughout the Northern Hemisphere *b)* the fur of a wolf **2.** *a)* a fierce, cruel, or greedy person ☆*b)* [Slang] a man who is bold in seeking sexual relations with many women —*vt.* to eat greedily (often with *down*) —**cry wolf** to give a false alarm —**keep the wolf from the door** to manage to have enough to live on —**wolf in sheep's clothing** a person who hides evil intentions behind a good-natured manner —**wolf′ish** *adj.* —**wolf′ish·ly** *adv.* —**wolf′ish·ness** *n.*

☆**wolf·ber·ry** (woolf′ber′ē) *n., pl.* **-ries** a strong plant with pink flowers and white, spongy berries

Wolfe (woolf) **1. James,** 1727–59; Eng. general: defeated the Fr. forces under Montcalm at Quebec (1759) **2. Thomas (Clayton),** 1900–38; U.S. novelist

wolf·hound (woolf′hound′) *n.* a large dog of any of several breeds formerly used for hunting wolves: see IRISH WOLFHOUND, BORZOI (*Russian wolfhound*)

wolf·ram (wool′frəm) *n.* [G. < *wolf*, wolf + MHG. *ram*, dirt] *same as* TUNGSTEN

wolf·ram·ite (-frə mīt′) *n.* [< G.: see prec.] a brownish or blackish mineral, a compound of tungsten (wolfram), iron, and manganese: the main ore of tungsten

wolfs·bane (woolfs′bān′) *n. same as* ACONITE (sense 1)

wolf spider any of a group of active hunting spiders that are wanderers, living in the ground and not building webs

Wol·sey (wool′zē), **Thomas** 1475?–1530; Eng. statesman & cardinal; chief Chancellor (1515–29) under Henry VIII

Wol·ver·hamp·ton (wool′vər hamp′tən) city in WC England, near Birmingham: pop. 264,000

wol·ver·ine (wool′və rēn′, wool′və rēn′) *n., pl.* **-ines′, -ine′:** see PLURAL, II, D, 1 [< WOLF, prob. because of its fierceness] **1.** a stocky, fierce, flesh-eating mammal with thick fur, found in the northern U.S., northern Eurasia, and Canada: the European variety is the GLUTTON (sense 3) **2.** its fur Also, Brit. sp., **wol′ver·ene′**

WOLVERINE
(2½–3½ ft. long,
including tail;
12–16 in. high
at shoulder)

wolves (woolvz) *n. pl. of* WOLF

wom·an (woom′ən) *n., pl.* **wom′en** (wim′in) [OE. *wifman* < *wif*, a female + *mann*, a human being] **1.** an adult, female human being **2.** women as a group ["*Woman's* work is never done"] **3.** a female servant **4.** *a)* [Dial.] a wife *b)* a sweetheart or a mistress **5.** womanly qualities or characteristics [it's the *woman* in her] —*adj.* female [a *woman* dentist]

SYN.—**woman** is the standard general term for the adult human being of the sex that bears children; **female**, referring specif. to sex, is applied to plants and animals, but is regarded as a disrespectful substitute for **woman** [that strong-minded *female* is here again], except when used in statistical tables and scientific writings; **lady**, used specif. of a woman of the upper classes and once common as the polite form for any woman, is now avoided as a general substitute for **woman**, except in such formulas as "*ladies and gentlemen*"

wom·an·hood (-hood′) *n.* **1.** the condition of being a woman **2.** womanly qualities **3.** women; womankind

wom·an·ish (-ish) *adj.* like, characteristic of, or suitable to a woman; feminine or effeminate —see SYN. at FEMALE —**wom′an·ish·ly** *adv.* —**wom′an·ish·ness** *n.*

wom·an·ize (-īz′) *vt.* **-ized′, -iz′ing** to make effeminate —*vi.* [Colloq.] to have sexual intercourse with many women —**wom′an·iz′er** *n.*

wom·an·kind (-kīnd′) *n.* women in general

wom·an·like (-līk′) *adj.* womanly

wom·an·ly (-lē) *adj.* **1.** like a woman; womanish **2.** characteristic of or fit for a woman [a *womanly* figure] —see SYN. at FEMALE —**wom′an·li·ness** *n.*

woman suffrage the right of women to vote in governmental elections —**wom′an-suf′fra·gist** *n.*

womb (woom) *n.* [OE. *wamb*] **1.** *same as* UTERUS **2.** any place in which something is contained, developed, etc. [the *womb* of time]

wom·bat (wäm′bat) *n.* [altered < Australian native name] a burrowing animal that looks like a small bear, found in Australia, Tasmania, and several Pacific islands: the female carries her young in a pouch

wom·en (wim′in) *n. pl. of* WOMAN

wom·en·folk (-fōk′) *n.pl.* [Dial. or Colloq.] women; womankind: also **wom′en·folks′**

women's rights the rights claimed by and for women of equal privileges and opportunities with men: also **woman's rights**

won[1] (wun) *pt. & pp. of* WIN

won[2] (wän) *n., pl.* **won** [Korean < Chin. *yüan*, round] the monetary unit of North Korea and South Korea: see MONETARY UNITS, table

won·der (wun′dər) *n.* [OE. *wundor*] **1.** a person, thing, or event so unusual as to cause surprise, amazement, etc.; marvel **2.** the feeling of surprise, amazement, etc. caused by something strange, remarkable, etc. [gazing in *wonder* at the comet] **3.** a miracle —*vi.* **1.** to feel wonder; marvel [to *wonder* at the miracles of modern science] **2.** to have curiosity, sometimes mixed with doubt [I *wonder* about his sudden change of mind] —*vt.* to have curiosity or doubt about; want to know [I *wonder* what he meant] —**do wonders for** to make a remarkable improvement in —**no wonder!** now I know why! —**won′der·er** *n.*

won·der·ful (-fəl) *adj.* **1.** that causes wonder; marvelous; amazing **2.** [Colloq.] very good; excellent —**won′der·ful·ly** *adv.* —**won′der·ful·ness** *n.*

won·der·land (-land′) *n.* an imaginary land or place full of wonders, or a real place like this

won·der·ment (-mənt) *n.* wonder or amazement

won·der·struck (-struk′) *adj.* struck with wonder, surprise, admiration, etc.: also **won′der-strick′en** (-strik′'n)

won·der·work·er (-wurk′ər) *n.* a person who performs miracles

won·drous (wun′drəs) *adj.* wonderful —*adv.* wonderfully; remarkably [a maiden *wondrous* fair] —**won′drous·ly** *adv.*

wont (wōnt, wônt, wunt, wänt) *adj.* [ult. < OE. *wunian*, to be used to] accustomed [he was *wont* to rise early] —*n.* usual practice; habit [it is his *wont* to dine late] —see SYN. at HABIT

won't (wōnt) [contr. < ME. *wol not*] will not

wont·ed (wōn'tid, wôn'-, wun'-, wän'-) *adj.* customary; accustomed [in his *wonted* manner] —see SYN. at USUAL

won ton (wän' tän') a Chinese dish consisting of folded pieces of noodle dough filled with ground meat and boiled: served in a broth (**won-ton soup**) or fried

woo (woo) *vt.* [OE. *wogian*] **1.** to try to get the love of; seek as a mate; court **2.** to try to get; seek [to *woo* fame] **3.** to try to persuade; coax; urge [a comedian *wooing* his audience for applause] —*vi.* to court a person —**woo'er** *n.*

wood (wood) *n.* [OE. *wudu*] **1.** [*usually pl.*] a thick growth of trees; forest or grove **2.** the hard substance under the bark of trees and shrubs **3.** trees cut and prepared for use in making things; lumber or timber **4.** wood used as fuel; firewood **5.** something made of wood; specif., *a*) a wooden cask [whiskey aged in *wood*] *b*) [*pl.*] woodwind instruments *c*) *Golf* any of a set of numbered clubs with wooden heads having various lofts: see illustration at GOLF CLUB —*adj.* **1.** made of wood; wooden **2.** for cutting, shaping, or holding wood **3.** growing or living in woods —*vt.* **1.** to plant trees thickly over **2.** to furnish with wood, esp. for fuel —*vi.* to get a supply of wood —☆**out of the woods** [Colloq.] out of difficulty, danger, etc.

Wood (wood), **Grant** (grant) 1892-1942; U.S. painter

wood alcohol *same as* METHANOL

wood anemone any of several anemones that grow as wildflowers in woodlands

wood·bine (wood'bīn') *n.* [OE. *wudubinde*: see WOOD & BIND] **1.** a European climbing honeysuckle ☆**2.** a climbing vine growing in eastern N. America, with green flower clusters and dark-blue berries; Virginia creeper

wood block a block of wood, esp. one used in making a woodcut —**wood'block'** *adj.*

wood·carv·ing (-kär'viŋ) *n.* **1.** the art or craft of carving wood by hand to make art objects, decorative moldings, etc. **2.** an object so made —**wood'carv'er** *n.*

☆**wood·chuck** (-chuk') *n.* [altered < Algonquian name] a common N. American marmot, an animal that burrows in the ground and spends the winter in a kind of sleep; groundhog

wood·cock (-käk') *n., pl.* **-cocks'**, **-cock'**: see PLURAL, II, D, 1 **1.** a European game bird with short legs and a long bill ☆**2.** a smaller, related game bird of eastern N. America

wood·craft (-kraft') *n.* **1.** skill or training in matters relating to the woods, as camping, hunting, etc. **2.** *same as: a*) WOODWORKING *b*) WOODCARVING

wood·cut (-kut') *n.* **1.** a wooden block engraved with a design, etc. **2.** a print made from this

☆**wood·cut·ter** (-kut'ər) *n.* a person who chops down trees, cuts wood, etc. —**wood'cut'ting** *n.*

☆**wood duck** a brightly colored N. American duck that nests in hollow trees near woodland lakes

wood·ed (-id) *adj.* covered with trees or woods

wood·en (wood''n) *adj.* **1.** made of wood **2.** stiff, clumsy, or lifeless [a *wooden* expression on his face] **3.** dull; insensitive —**wood'en·ly** *adv.* —**wood'en·ness** *n.*

wood engraving 1. the art or process of engraving on wood **2.** *same as* WOODCUT —**wood engraver**

wood·en·head·ed (wood''n hed'id) *adj.* [Colloq.] dull; stupid —**wood'en·head'ed·ness** *n.*

wooden horse *same as* TROJAN HORSE

wood·en·ware (-wer') *n.* bowls, dishes, etc. made of wood

☆**wood ibis** a large, white, heronlike stork found in the wooded swamps of the southern U.S.

wood·land (wood'land'; *also, and for adj. always,* -lənd) *n.* land covered with woods or trees —*adj.* of, living in, or relating to the woods —**wood'land·er** *n.*

wood louse *same as* SOW BUG

wood·man (-mən) *n., pl.* **-men** *same as* WOODSMAN

wood·note (-nōt') *n.* a sound of a forest bird or animal

wood nymph a nymph that lives in the woods; dryad

wood·peck·er (-pek'ər) *n.* any of various tree-climbing birds that have a strong, pointed bill used to drill holes in bark to get insects

wood·pile (-pīl') *n.* a pile of wood, esp. of firewood

wood pulp pulp made from wood fiber, used in paper manufacture

wood·ruff (-ruf') *n.* [OE. *wudurofe*] a plant with small white, pink, or blue, lily-shaped flowers

wood screw a metal screw with a sharp point and a coarse thread, for use in wood

wood·shed (-shed') *n.* a shed for storing firewood

woods·man (woodz'mən) *n., pl.* **-men 1.** a person who lives or works in the woods, as a hunter, woodcutter, etc. **2.** a person at home in the woods or skilled in woodcraft

wood sorrel any of a group of creeping plants with white, pink, red, or yellow, five-petaled flowers

☆**woods·y** (wood'zē) *adj.* **woods'i·er**, **woods'i·est** of, characteristic of, or like the woods —**woods'i·ness** *n.*

wood tar a dark, sticky, syruplike substance obtained by the destructive distillation of wood

wood thrush ☆ a large, brown thrush of eastern N. America, having a sweet, clear song: also called ☆**wood robin**

wood turning the art or process of turning, or shaping, wood on a lathe —**wood'-turn'er** *n.* —**wood'-turn'ing** *n.*

wood·wind (wood'wind') *n.* **1.** [*pl.*] the wind instruments of an orchestra that were originally made of wood, including clarinets, oboes, bassoons, flutes, and English horns: some are now made of metal **2.** any of these instruments —*adj.* of or for such instruments

wood·work (-wurk') *n.* **1.** work done in wood **2.** things made of wood, esp. the interior moldings, doors, etc. of a house

wood·work·ing (-wur'kiŋ) *n.* the art or work of making things out of wood —*adj.* of woodworking —**wood'work'er** *n.*

wood·worm (-wurm') *n.* any of a number of insect larvae that live on and burrow in wood

wood·y (wood'ē) *adj.* **wood'i·er**, **wood'i·est 1.** covered with trees; wooded **2.** consisting of or forming wood [a *woody* plant] **3.** like wood —**wood'i·ness** *n.*

woof¹ (woof, woof) *n.* [OE. *owef* < *o-* (< *on*) + *-wef* < base of *wefan*, to weave] **1.** the horizontal threads crossing the warp in a woven fabric; weft **2.** a woven fabric

woof² (woof) *n.* a gruff barking sound of or like that of a dog —*vi.* to make such a sound

woof·er (woof'ər) *n.* [prec. + -ER] in a set of two or more loudspeakers, a large, high-fidelity speaker for reproducing low-frequency sounds: see also TWEETER

wool (wool) *n.* see PLURAL, II, D, 3 [OE. *wull* < IE. base *wel-*, hair, wool] **1.** *a*) the soft, curly hair of sheep *b*) the hair of some other animals, as the goat, llama, or alpaca **2.** *a*) yarn spun from the fibers of such hair *b*) cloth, clothing, etc. made of this yarn **3.** anything that looks or feels like wool —*adj.* of wool or woolen material —☆**all wool and a yard wide** genuine —☆**pull the wool over someone's eyes** to deceive or trick someone —**wool'like'** *adj.*

wool·en (wool'ən) *adj.* **1.** made of wool **2.** of or relating to wool or woolen cloth —*n.* [*pl.*] woolen goods or clothing Also, chiefly Brit. sp., **wool'len**

wool·gath·er·ing (-gath'ər iŋ) *n.* absent-mindedness or daydreaming —**wool'gath'er·er** *n.*

wool·grow·er (-grō'ər) *n.* a person who raises sheep for wool —**wool'grow'ing** *n.*

wool·ly (wool'ē) *adj.* **-li·er**, **-li·est 1.** of or like wool **2.** bearing wool **3.** covered with wool or something like wool in texture ☆**4.** rough and uncivilized: chiefly in **wild and woolly 5.** confused; fuzzy [*woolly* ideas] —*n., pl.* **-lies 1.** [Western] a sheep **2.** a woolen garment; specif., [*pl.*] long underwear —**wool'li·ness** *n.*

wool·ly-head·ed (-hed'id) *adj.* confused, unclear, impractical, etc. in thought: also **wool'ly-mind'ed** (-mīn'did)

wool·pack (wool'pak') *n.* **1.** a large cloth bag in which to pack wool or fleece for sale **2.** a bale of wool **3.** a fleecy cumulus cloud

REDHEADED WOODPECKER (to 10 in. long)

WOODCHUCK (head & body to 15 in. long; tail to 6 in. long)

wool·y (wool′ē) *adj.* **wool′i·er, wool′i·est, *n., pl.* wool′ies** *same as* WOOLLY —**wool′i·ness** *n.*

☆**wooz·y** (wōō′zē, wooz′ē) *adj.* **wooz′i·er, wooz′i·est** [prob. < *wooze,* var. of OOZE[1]] [Colloq.] **1.** dizzy, faint, and sickish **2.** befuddled, as from drink —**wooz′i·ly** *adv.* —**wooz′i·ness** *n.*

Worces·ter (woos′tər) [after *Worcester,* city in E England] city in C Mass.: pop. 177,000

Worces·ter·shire sauce (woos′tər shir′) [orig. made in *Worcester,* England] a spicy sauce for meats, poultry, etc., containing soy, vinegar, etc.

word (wurd) *n.* [OE. < IE. base *wer-,* to speak] **1.** *a)* a spoken sound or group of sounds having meaning and used as a single unit of speech: a word consists of at least one base morpheme with or without prefixes or suffixes *b)* a letter or group of letters, written or printed, representing such a unit of language **2.** a brief statement; remark [a *word* of advice] **3.** a promise [he gave his *word*] **4.** news; information [no *word* from home] **5.** *a)* a password or signal *b)* a command; order [he gave the *word* to begin] **6.** [*usually pl.*] *a)* talk; speech [the President's *words* on this occasion] *b)* lyrics or text of music that is sung **7.** [*pl.*] a quarrel; dispute; argument **8.** an ordered combination of characters with meaning, regarded as a unit and stored in a computer —*vt.* to put into words; phrase [a beautifully *worded* description] —**a good word** a favorable comment; bit of praise —**be as good as one's word** to live up to one's promises —**by word of mouth** by speech; orally —**have a word with** to have a short talk with —**have no words for** to be unable to describe —**in a word** in short; briefly —**in so many words** exactly and plainly —**man** (or **woman**) **of his** (or **her**) **word** one who keeps his promises —**of many** (or **few**) **words** talkative (or untalkative) —**take one at one's word** to believe that a person means what he says and act accordingly —**take the words out of one's mouth** to say what one was about to say oneself —**the Word 1.** the Bible: also **Word of God 2.** the spirit of God as revealed in Jesus: John 1:1 **3.** *same as* GOSPEL (sense 1) —**(upon) my word!** indeed! —**word for word** in exactly the same words

word·age (wurd′ij) *n.* words or the number of words

word·book (-book′) *n.* a dictionary; lexicon

word-for-word (-fər wurd′) *adj.* in exactly the same words

word·ing (-iŋ) *n.* choice and arrangement of words; diction

word·less (-lis) *adj.* **1.** without words; speechless **2.** not expressed or not capable of being expressed in words —**word′less·ly** *adv.* —**word′less·ness** *n.*

word of honor pledged word; solemn promise

word order the arrangement of words in a phrase, clause, or sentence

word processing a computerized system in which letters, forms, etc. are prepared, edited, stored, and reproduced, as by using an electronic typewriter

Words·worth (wurdz′wurth), **William** 1770–1850; Eng. poet

word·y (wur′dē) *adj.* **word′i·er, word′i·est** using many or too many words; verbose —**word′i·ly** *adv.* —**word′i·ness** *n.*

SYN. —**wordy** is the general term implying the use of more words in speaking or writing than are needed to say what is meant [a *wordy* document]; **verbose** suggests a wordiness that becomes confusing, tiresome, pompous, etc. [a *verbose* political speech]; **prolix** suggests the drawing out of what is said with all kinds of unnecessary little details that are very dull or boring [his *prolix* sermons]; **diffuse** suggests a wordiness that results from wandering from one point to another instead of sticking to the subject [a rambling, *diffuse* harangue]; **redundant** implies the use of unnecessary or repetitious words [*redundant* writing] —**ANT·** concise, terse, pithy

wore (wôr) *pt. of* WEAR[1]

work (wurk) *n.* [OE. *weorc* < IE. base *werg-,* to do] **1.** the use of physical or mental energy or skill in doing or making something; labor **2.** employment at a job [out of *work*] **3.** occupation, profession, business, trade, craft, etc. **4.** *a)* something one is making, doing, or acting upon; task [to take *work* home] *b)* the amount of this [a day's *work*] **5.** something that has been or is to be made or done; specif., *a)* an act; deed: *usually used in pl.* [good *works*] *b)* [*pl.*] collected writings [the *works* of Poe] *c)* [*pl.*] engineering structures, as bridges, dams, etc. [public *works*] *d)* a fortification [an *earthwork*] *e)* needlework; embroidery [*fancywork*] *f)* *same as* WORK OF ART **6.** [*pl., with sing. v.*] a place where work is done, as a factory [*ironworks*] **7.** workmanship [superior *work*] **8.** the action of, or effect produced by, natural forces [the dunes are the *work* of the wind] **9.** *Mech.* transference of force from one body or system to another, measured by the product of the force and the amount of displacement in the line of force [the *work* done by a pulley] —*adj.* of, for, or used in work [*work* tools] —*vi.* **worked** or

wrought, work′ing 1. to use effort or energy to do or make something; do work; labor; toil **2.** to be employed [where do you *work?*] **3.** *a)* to do its work; operate; act [this drill *works* by electric power] *b)* to operate effectively [the radio won't *work* without new batteries] **4.** to be fermenting [the wine is *working*] **5.** to produce results or exert an influence [let it *work* in her mind] **6.** to be handled, kneaded, etc. [putty that *works* easily] **7.** to move, proceed, etc. slowly and with or as with difficulty [to *work* toward an objective] **8.** to move, twitch, etc. as from agitation [his face *worked* with emotion] **9.** to change into a specified condition, as by repeated movement [the handle *worked* loose] —*vt.* **1.** to cause; bring about [her idea *worked* wonders] **2.** to mold; shape [to *work* silver] **3.** to sew, embroider, etc. [to *work* a sampler] **4.** to solve (a mathematical problem or a puzzle) **5.** to handle; knead [to *work* dough] **6.** to bring into a specified condition, as by moving back and forth [to *work* a nail loose] **7.** to cultivate (soil) [the farmer *works* his land] **8.** to cause to function; operate; use [to *work* a pump] **9.** to cause fermentation in **10.** to cause to work [to *work* a crew hard] **11.** to influence; persuade [*work* her around to your ideas] **12.** to make (one's way, etc.) by work or effort [to *work* one's way to the top] **13.** to provoke; rouse [to *work* oneself into a rage] **14.** to carry on activity in, along, etc.; cover [a salesman *working* his territory] **15.** [Colloq.] to make use of, esp. by clever dealing [*work* your connections] —**at work** working —☆**get** (or **give someone**) **the works** [Slang] to be (or cause someone to be) the victim of an ordeal —**in the works** [Colloq.] in the process of being planned or done —**make short** (or **quick**) **work of** to deal with or dispose of quickly —**out of work** unemployed —☆**shoot the works** [Slang] **1.** to risk everything on one chance **2.** to make a supreme effort —**the works 1.** the working parts (of a watch, clock, etc.) ☆**2.** [Colloq.] all possible extras; everything that can be included: also **the whole works** —**work in** to insert or be inserted [to *work in* some new ideas] —**work off 1.** to get rid of, as by exertion [to *work off* excess energy] ☆**2.** to pay (a debt or obligation) by work instead of money —**work on** (or **upon**) **1.** to influence [the suggestion *worked* strongly *on* them] **2.** to try to persuade [*work on* her and get her to agree] —**work out 1.** to make its way out, as from being embedded [the sliver is *working out*] **2.** to exhaust (a mine, etc.) **3.** *same as* WORK OFF (sense 2) **4.** to accomplish **5.** to solve [to *work out* a crossword puzzle] **6.** to result in some way [it will *work out* for the best] **7.** to develop; elaborate [to *work out* a plan] **8.** to engage in a workout —**work over** ☆[Colloq.] to subject to harsh or cruel treatment —**work up 1.** to advance; rise [the story *works up* to a climax] **2.** to develop; elaborate [to *work up* sharp contrasts] **3.** to arouse; excite [don't get all *worked up*]

SYN. —**work** is the general word for effort put forth in doing or making something, whether physical or mental, easy or difficult, pleasant or unpleasant, etc.; **labor** more often implies strenuous physical work [sentenced to three years at hard *labor*]; **travail**, now a somewhat literary word, suggests painful exertion or oppressive labor [wearied by long *travail*]; **toil** implies long, exhausting work, whether physical or mental [years of *toil* in research] —**ANT·** rest, play

work·a·ble (wur′kə b'l) *adj.* **1.** that can be worked **2.** practicable; feasible —**work′a·bil′i·ty, work′a·ble·ness** *n.*

work·a·day (wur′kə dā′) *adj.* **1.** of or suitable for working days; everyday [*workaday* clothes] **2.** commonplace; ordinary

☆**work·a·hol·ic** (wur′kə hôl′ik, -häl′-) *n.* [< WORK + ALCOHOLIC] a person who feels a need to work all the time

work basket a basket for holding sewing equipment

work·bench (wurk′bench′) *n.* a table at which work is done, as by a mechanic, carpenter, etc.

work·book (-book′) *n.* ☆**1.** a book of questions and exercises for use by students **2.** a book of operating instructions **3.** a book containing a record of work planned or done

work·box (-bäks′) *n.* a box for work tools and materials

work·day (-dā′) *n.* **1.** a day on which work is done; working day ☆**2.** the part of a day during which work is done [a 7-hour *workday*] —*adj. same as* WORKADAY

work·er (wur′kər) *n.* **1.** a person, animal, or thing that works; specif., a person who works for a living **2.** a person who works for a cause, etc. [a party *worker*] **3.** any of various sterile female ants, bees, etc. that do work for the colony

work farm a farm on which the workers are short-term prisoners convicted of less serious crimes

work force the total number of people that are working or are available for work in a nation, region, plant, etc.

work·horse (wurk′hôrs′) *n.* **1.** a horse used for working, as for pulling a plow **2.** a steady, responsible worker with a heavy workload **3.** a durable machine, vehicle, etc.

work·house (-hous´) *n.* **1.** in England, formerly, a poorhouse ☆**2.** a kind of jail where the prisoners are put to work while serving short sentences for minor crimes

work·ing (wʉr´kiŋ) *adj.* **1.** that works; doing work **2.** of, for, or used in work *[a working* day, *working* clothes*]* **3.** sufficient to get work done *[a working* majority*]* **4.** on which further work may be based *[a working* hypothesis*]* —*n.* **1.** the act or process of a person or thing that works **2.** *[usually pl.]* a part of a mine, quarry, etc. where work is or has been done

working capital the part of a company's capital that can be converted readily into cash

working class workers as a class, esp. industrial workers; wage earners —**work´ing-class´** *adj.*

working day 1. a day on which work is done, esp. as distinguished from a Sunday, holiday, etc. **2.** the part of a day during which work is done; specif., the number of hours each day that an employee is required to work

work·ing·man (-man´) *n., pl.* **-men´** (-men´) a worker; esp., an industrial or manual worker; wage earner; laborer

working papers any official papers that legalize the employment of a minor or of an alien

work·ing·wom·an (-woom´ən) *n., pl.* **-wom´en** a woman worker; esp., a woman industrial or manual worker

work·load (wʉrk´lōd´) *n.* the amount of work assigned to be completed within a given period of time

work·man (wʉrk´mən) *n., pl.* **-men 1.** *same as* WORKINGMAN **2.** a craftsman

work·man·like (-līk´) *adj.* characteristic of a good workman; skillful: also **work´man·ly**

work·man·ship (-ship´) *n.* **1.** skill of a workman; craftsmanship **2.** something produced by this skill

workmen's compensation money paid to an employee for injury or disease suffered in connection with his work, under an insurance system supervised by the government and contributed to by employers

work of art 1. something produced in one of the fine arts, as a painting, sculpture, etc. **2.** anything made, performed, etc. with great skill and beauty

☆**work·out** (wʉrk´out´) *n.* **1.** a period of doing exercises for physical fitness or in athletic training **2.** any exercise, work, etc. requiring great effort

work·room (-rōōm´) *n.* a room in which work is done

work sheet 1. a sheet of paper showing a record of work, working time, etc., or used for working notes **2.** a sheet of paper with exercises, problems, etc. to be worked on directly by students

work·shop (-shäp´) *n.* **1.** a room or building where work is done **2.** a seminar or series of meetings for intensive study, work, etc. in some field *[a writers' workshop]*

work song a folk song sung by laborers, as in the fields, with a marked rhythm matching the rhythm of their work

work·ta·ble (-tā´b'l) *n.* a table at which work is done, esp. one with drawers for tools, materials, etc.

☆**work·week** (-wēk´) *n.* the total number of hours or days worked in a week for the regular wage or salary

work·wom·an (-woom´ən) *n., pl.* **-wom´en** *same as* WORKINGWOMAN

world (wʉrld) *n.* [OE. *werold*] **1.** *a)* the planet earth *b)* the whole universe *c)* any heavenly body imagined as being inhabited *[worlds* in space*]* **2.** the earth and its inhabitants **3.** *a)* mankind *b)* people generally *[the* news startled the *world]* **4.** *a)* *[also* W-*]* some part of the earth *[the* Old *World]* *b)* some period of history, its society, etc. *[the* ancient *world]* *c)* any sphere or domain *[the* animal *world]* *d)* any sphere of human activity *[the world* of music*]* **5.** individual experience, outlook, etc. *[his world* is narrow*]* **6.** *a)* the usual social or everyday life of people, as apart from a life devoted to religious or spiritual matters *[to* give up the *world]* *b)* people leading the usual social life **7.** *[often pl.]* a large amount; great deal *[to* do a *world* (or *worlds)* of good*]* —**bring into the world** to give birth to — **come into the world** to be born —**for all the world 1.** for any reason or consideration at all **2.** in every respect; exactly *[she* looks *for all the world* like her mother*]* —**in the world 1.** on earth or in the universe; anywhere *[where in the world* could you find this?*]* **2.** at all; ever *[how in the world* did you know?*]* —☆**on top of the world** [Colloq.] filled with joy, pride, etc.;

jubilant —☆**out of this world** [Slang] exceptionally fine; extraordinary; remarkable —**world without end** forever

☆**world-beat·er** (wʉrld´bēt´ər) *n.* [Colloq.] a person or thing that is a great success or has the qualities needed to become one

world·ling (-liŋ) *n.* a worldly person

world·ly (wʉrld´lē) *adj.* **-li·er, -li·est 1.** of or limited to this world; temporal or secular **2.** devoted to or concerned with the affairs, pleasures, etc. of this world: also **world´ly-mind´ed 3.** worldly-wise —see SYN. at EARTHLY —**world´li·ness** *n.*

world·ly-wise (-wīz´) *adj.* wise in the ways or affairs of the world; sophisticated

world power a nation or organization large or powerful enough to have a worldwide influence

☆**World Series** [*also* w- s-] an annual series of games between the winning teams of the two major U.S. baseball leagues to decide the championship

world-shak·ing (wʉrld´shā´kiŋ) *adj.* of great importance, effect, or influence; momentous

☆**World War I** the war (1914–18) between the Allies (Great Britain, France, Russia, the U.S., Italy, Japan, etc.) and the Central Powers (Germany, Austria-Hungary, etc.)

☆**World War II** the war (1939–45) between the United Nations (Great Britain, France, the Soviet Union, the U.S., etc.) and the Axis (Germany, Italy, Japan, etc.)

world-wea·ry (wʉrld´wir´ē) *adj.* weary of the world; bored with living

world·wide (-wīd´) *adj.* extending throughout the world

worm (wʉrm) *n.* [OE. *wyrm*, serpent] **1.** any of many long, slender, soft-bodied, creeping animals, as the annelids, roundworms, etc. **2.** popularly, *a)* an insect larva, as a grub *b)* any of several mollusks, as the shipworms *c)* any of various wormlike animals, as the rotifer **3.** a person looked down on as being too meek, wretched, etc. **4.** something thought of as being wormlike because of its spiral shape; specif., a short, rotating screw that meshes with the teeth of a worm wheel or a rack **5.** *[pl.] Med.* any disease or disorder caused by parasitic worms in the intestines, etc. —*vi.* to move, proceed, etc. like a worm, in a winding, creeping, or roundabout manner *[don't* try to *worm* out of this*]* —*vt.* **1.** to bring about, get, make, etc. in a winding, creeping, or roundabout manner *[to worm* one's way through underbrush; to *worm* out information*]* **2.** to rid of worms; esp., to purge of intestinal worms —**worm´er** *n.* —**worm´like´** *adj.*

worm-eat·en (wʉrm´ēt´'n) *adj.* **1.** eaten into by worms, termites, etc. **2.** worn-out, out-of-date, etc.

worm gear 1. *same as* WORM WHEEL **2.** a gear consisting of a worm and worm wheel

worm·hole (-hōl´) *n.* a hole made, as in wood, by a worm, termite, etc.

Worms (vôrmz; *E.* wʉrmz) city in West Germany, on the Rhine: scene of an assembly (*Diet of Worms*), 1521, at which Martin Luther was condemned for heresy

worm wheel a toothed wheel designed to gear with the thread of a worm

worm·wood (wʉrm´wood´) *n.* [altered by folk etym. < OE. *wermod*] **1.** any of various strong-smelling plants; esp., a Eurasian perennial that yields a bitter-tasting, dark-green oil (**wormwood oil**) used in making absinthe **2.** a bitter, unpleasant experience

worm·y (wʉr´mē) *adj.* **worm´i·er, worm´i·est 1.** containing a worm or worms; worm-infested **2.** *same as* WORM-EATEN **3.** like a worm **4.** debased; groveling —**worm´i·ness** *n.*

worn (wôrn) *pp. of* WEAR[1] —*adj.* **1.** showing the effects of use, wear, etc. *[worn* soles*]* **2.** damaged by use or wear *[a worn* thread on a screw*]* **3.** showing the effects of worry or anxiety *[a worn* face*]* **4.** exhausted; spent *[barren, worn* land*]*

worn-out (wôrn´out´) *adj.* **1.** used or worn until no longer effective, usable, or serviceable **2.** exhausted; tired out

wor·ri·ment (wʉr´ē mənt) *n.* **1.** a worrying or being worried; mental disturbance; anxiety **2.** a cause of worry

wor·ri·some (-səm) *adj.* **1.** causing worry or anxiety **2.** having a tendency to worry —**wor´ri·some·ly** *adv.*

wor·ry (wʉr´ē) *vt.* **-ried, -ry·ing** [OE. *wyrgan*, to strangle] **1.** *a)* to treat roughly, as with continual biting *[a dog worrying* a bone*]* *b)* to pluck at, touch, etc. repeatedly in a nervous way

WORM GEAR

[to *worry* a loose tooth with the tongue] **2.** to annoy; bother [stop *worrying* me with trifles] **3.** to cause to feel troubled or uneasy [his absence *worried* her] —*vi.* **1.** to bite or tear (*at* an object) with the teeth **2.** to be anxious, troubled, etc. [why *worry?*] **3.** to manage to get (*along* or *through*) in the face of difficulties —*n., pl.* **-ries 1.** the act of worrying **2.** a troubled state of mind; anxiety **3.** something that causes anxiety [money is the least of his *worries*] —see SYN. at CARE —**wor'ri·er** *n.*

☆**wor·ry·wart** (-wôrt) *n.* [WORRY + WART] [Colloq.] a person who tends to worry, esp. over trivial details

worse (wʉrs) *adj. compar.* of BAD[1] & ILL [OE. *wiersa*] **1.** *a)* bad, evil, harmful, unpleasant, etc. to a degree greater than another or others; less good [an even *worse* mistake; a *worse* winter than last year's] *b)* of poorer quality or condition [cheaper but *worse* equipment] **2.** in poorer health; more ill [the patient is *worse* today] **3.** in a less satisfactory situation —*adv. compar.* of BADLY & ILL in a worse manner; to a worse extent [he behaved *worse* than ever] —*n.* that which is worse [I have *worse* to report] —**for the worse** to a worse condition —**worse off** in a worse condition

wors·en (wʉr's'n) *vt., vi.* [orig., a dial. word < prec. + -EN] to make or become worse

wor·ship (wʉr'ship) *n.* [< OE.: see WORTH & -SHIP] **1.** *a)* deep respect and great honor paid to a deity; veneration *b)* a church service or other rite showing this [to attend *worship*] **2.** very great love, regard, or admiration [*worship* of a hero] **3.** [Chiefly Brit.] a title of honor (preceded by *your* or *his*) used in addressing certain officials —*vt.* **-shiped** or **-shipped, -ship·ing** or **-ship·ping 1.** to show religious reverence for **2.** to have very great love or admiration for —*vi.* to take part in a religious service [freedom to *worship* as they pleased] —see SYN. at REVERE[1] —**wor'ship·er, wor'ship·per** *n.*

wor·ship·ful (-fəl) *adj.* **1.** [Chiefly Brit.] honorable; respected: used as a title of respect **2.** feeling or offering great devotion or respect [*worshipful* followers] —**wor'ship·ful·ly** *adv.* —**wor'ship·ful·ness** *n.*

worst (wʉrst) *adj. superl.* of BAD[1] & ILL [OE. *wyrsta*] **1.** *a)* bad, evil, harmful, unpleasant, etc. in the greatest degree [the *worst* consequences] *b)* of the lowest quality or condition [the *worst* movie I ever saw] **2.** in the least satisfactory situation —*adv. superl.* of BADLY & ILL in the worst manner; to the worst extent [this hurt me *worst*] —*n.* that which is worst [the *worst* that could happen] —*vt.* to get the better of; defeat [to *worst* an opponent] —**at worst** under the worst circumstances —**if (the) worst comes to (the) worst** if the worst possible thing happens —☆**(in) the worst way** [Slang] very much; greatly —**make the worst of** to be pessimistic about

wor·sted (woos'tid, wʉr'stid) *n.* [after *Worsted*, now *Worstead*, England, where first made] **1.** a smooth, hard-twisted thread or yarn made from long-staple wool **2.** fabric made from this —*adj.* made of worsted

wort[1] (wʉrt) *n.* [< OE. *wyrt-* (in compounds)] a liquid prepared with malt which, after fermenting, becomes beer, ale, etc.

wort[2] (wʉrt) *n.* [OE. *wyrt*, a root] a plant or herb: now usually in compounds [liverwort]

worth (wʉrth) *n.* [OE. *weorth* < IE. base *wer-*, to turn] **1.** the value of a thing in terms of money [the net *worth* of a business] **2.** the quality that makes a person or thing have value for others or deserve their esteem; merit [I know his *worth* as a friend; those ideas have great *worth*] **3.** the quantity of something that may be had for a given sum [a dime's *worth* of nuts] **4.** wealth; possessions [to calculate one's *worth*] —*adj.* [with prepositional force] **1.** deserving or worthy of; meriting [it is *worth* the effort] **2.** equal in value to (something specified) [a book *worth* $10] **3.** having wealth amounting to [a man *worth* half a million dollars] —☆**for all one is worth** to the utmost —☆**put in one's two cents' worth** to give one's opinion

SYN.—**worth** and **value** both refer to the amount of money or goods a thing can be exchanged for [the *worth* or *value* of the jewels]; when the terms are distinguished, **worth** refers to the basic excellence of a thing as judged by its moral or cultural qualities and the like, while **value** refers to excellence as measured by how useful, important, profitable, etc. a thing is [the true *worth* of Shakespeare's plays cannot be measured by their *value* to the commercial theater]

worth·less (wʉrth'lis) *adj.* without worth or merit; useless, valueless, etc. —**worth'less·ly** *adv.* —**worth'less·ness** *n.*

worth·while (-hwīl', -wīl') *adj.* important or valuable enough to repay time or effort spent; of true value

wor·thy (wʉr'thē) *adj.* **-thi·er, -thi·est 1.** having worth, value, or merit [a *worthy* idea] **2.** deserving; meriting (often with *of* or an infinitive) [*worthy* of promotion; *worthy* to be elected]

—*n., pl.* **-thies** a person of outstanding worth or importance: often used in a joking way [the village *worthies*] —**wor'thi·ly** *adv.* —**wor'thi·ness** *n.*

wot (wät) *the first and third person singular in the present tense of* WIT[2]

would (wood; *unstressed* wəd) *v.* [OE. *wolde*, pt. of *willan*, to will] **1.** *pt. of* WILL[2] **2.** a helping verb used: *a)* to express condition [he *would* go if you *would*] *b)* in an indirect quotation to express futurity [he said that he *would* stop] *c)* to express habitual action in the past [Sundays he *would* sleep late] *d)* to soften a request [*would* you please leave?] **3.** I wish [*would* that she were here] See also SHOULD

would-be (wood'bē') *adj.* **1.** wishing or pretending to be [a *would-be* expert] **2.** intended to be [a *would-be* help]

would·n't (wood''nt) would not

wouldst (woodst) *archaic second person singular in the past tense of* WILL[2]: *used with* thou: also **would·est** (wood'ist)

wound[1] (woond) *n.* [OE. *wund*] **1.** an injury in which the skin or other tissue is broken, cut, torn, etc. **2.** any hurt to the feelings, honor, etc. —*vt., vi.* to inflict a wound on or upon (someone); injure —**the wounded** persons wounded, esp. in warfare

wound[2] (wound) **1.** *pt. & pp.* of WIND[1] **2.** *pt. & pp.* of WIND[3]

wove (wōv) *pt. & alt. pp.* of WEAVE

wo·ven (wōv'n) *alt. pp.* of WEAVE

wow[1] (wou) *interj.* an exclamation of surprise, pleasure, pain, etc. —*n.* ☆[Slang] a remarkable, successful, exciting, etc. person or thing —☆*vt.* [Slang] to be a great success with

☆**wow**[2] (wou) *n.* [echoic] a distortion in reproduced sound, caused by variations in speed of the turntable, tape, etc. either in recording or playing

WPA, W.P.A. Works Progress (later, Work Projects) Administration

wpm words per minute

wrack[1] (rak) *n.* [< OE. *wræc*, misery & MDu. *wrak*, a wreck] **1.** ruin; destruction: now chiefly in **wrack and ruin 2.** seaweed, etc. cast up on shore

wrack[2] (rak) *vt.* [< RACK[1]] *same as* RACK[1]; esp., to subject to very great mental or physical suffering; torture

wraith (rāth) *n.* [Scot., ult. < ON. *vorthr*, guardian < *vartha*, to guard] **1.** a ghost **2.** a ghostlike figure of a person supposedly seen just before his death

wran·gle[1] (raŋ'g'l) *vi.* **-gled, -gling** [< ME. *wringen*, to WRING + -LE[2]] **1.** to quarrel angrily and noisily **2.** to argue; dispute —*vt.* to argue (a person) *into* or *out of* something —*n.* an angry, noisy dispute or quarrel —see SYN. at QUARREL[2]

wran·gle[2] (raŋ'g'l) *vt.* **-gled, -gling** [< WRANGLER[2]] ☆to herd (livestock, esp. saddle horses)

wran·gler[1] (raŋ'glər) *n.* [WRANGLE[1] + -ER] a person who wrangles, or argues, esp. in a noisy or angry way

wran·gler[2] (raŋ'glər) *n.* [< (*horse*) *wrangler*, partial transl. of AmSp. *caballerango*, a groom] ☆a cowboy who herds livestock, esp. saddle horses

wrap (rap) *vt.* **wrapped** or **wrapt, wrap'ping** [ME. *wrappen*] **1.** *a)* to wind or fold (a covering) around something [*wrap* the bandage around your arm] *b)* to cover by this means [he was *wrapped* in a blanket] **2.** to envelop; hide; conceal [a town *wrapped* in fog] **3.** to enclose and fasten in a wrapper of paper, etc. [a box *wrapped* for mailing] **4.** to wind or fold [to *wrap* one's arms around someone] —*vi.* to twine, extend, coil, etc. (usually with *over, around,* etc.) [the loose wire has *wrapped* around the cylinder] —*n.* **1.** an outer covering or outer garment [the guests put their *wraps* in the closet] **2.** [*pl.*] secrecy; censorship [plans kept under *wraps*] —**wrapped up in 1.** devoted to; absorbed in (work, etc.) **2.** involved in [*wrapped up in* too many activities] —**wrap up 1.** to enfold in a covering **2.** to put on warm clothing ☆**3.** [Colloq.] *a)* to bring to an end [to *wrap up* a meeting] *b)* to give a concluding report, etc. on (a news story)

wrap·a·round (rap'ə round') *adj.* **1.** that has a full-length opening and is wrapped around the body [a *wraparound* skirt] **2.** molded, etc. so as to curve [a *wraparound* windshield] —*n.* a wraparound garment, esp. a skirt

wrap·per (-ər) *n.* **1.** a person or thing that wraps **2.** that in which something is wrapped; covering; cover **3.** a woman's dressing gown **4.** a baby's robe

wrap·ping (-iŋ) *n.* [often *pl.*] the material, as paper, in which something is wrapped

wrap-up (-up') *n.* ☆**1.** [Colloq.] *a)* the concluding event, action, etc. in a sequence *b)* a concluding, summarizing report, etc. ☆**2.** [Slang] a quick, easy sale or the customer to whom the sale is made

wrasse (ras) *n., pl.* **wrass'es, wrasse:** see PLURAL, II, D, 1 [Corn. *wrach*] any of various fishes with spiny fins and bright coloring, found esp. in tropical seas

wras·tle (ras'l) *n., vi., vt.* **-tled, -tling** *dial. or colloq. var. of* WRESTLE: also **wras'sle -sled, -sling**

wrath (rath; *chiefly Brit.* rôth) *n.* [OE. *wrǣththo < wrath*, wroth] **1.** intense anger; rage **2.** any action carried out in great anger, esp. for punishment or vengeance —see SYN. at ANGER

wrath·ful (rath'fəl) *adj.* **1.** full of wrath; extremely angry **2.** resulting from or expressing wrath —**wrath'ful·ly** *adv.* —**wrath'ful·ness** *n.*

wreak (rēk) *vt.* [OE. *wrecan,* to revenge] **1.** to let out (one's anger, malice, etc.) freely, in words or actions **2.** to inflict (vengeance), cause (havoc), etc. —**wreak'er** *n.*

wreath (rēth) *n., pl.* **wreaths** (rēthz) [OE. *writha,* a ring < *writhan,* to twist] **1.** a twisted band or ring of leaves, flowers, etc. **2.** something suggesting this in shape [*wreaths* of smoke] —**wreath'like'** *adj.*

wreathe (rēth) *vt.* **wreathed, wreath'ing** **1.** to coil, twist, or entwine, esp. so as to form a wreath [to *wreathe* flowers] **2.** to coil, twist, or entwine around; encircle [clouds *wreathe* the hills] **3.** to decorate with wreaths [the *wreathed* victors] **4.** to cover or envelop [a face *wreathed* in smiles] —*vi.* **1.** to have a twisting or coiling movement [smoke *wreathing* upward] **2.** to form a wreath [ivy *wreathing* around a pillar]

WREATH

wreck (rek) *n.* [Anglo-Fr. *wrec* < ON. *vrek,* driftwood, wreckage] **1.** goods or wreckage cast ashore after a shipwreck **2.** *a)* the disabling or destruction of a ship by a storm or other disaster; shipwreck *b)* a ship thus disabled or destroyed **3.** the remains of anything that has been destroyed or badly damaged **4.** a person in very poor health **5.** a wrecking or being wrecked; ruin —*vt.* **1.** to destroy or damage badly [to *wreck* a car in a collision] **2.** to tear down (a building, etc.) **3.** to overthrow; thwart; ruin [the rain *wrecked* our plans] **4.** to destroy the health of [drugs *wrecked* them] —*vi.* **1.** to be wrecked **2.** to work as a wrecker

wreck·age (rek'ij) *n.* **1.** a wrecking or being wrecked **2.** the remains of something that has been wrecked

wreck·er (-ər) *n.* **1.** a person or thing that wrecks **2.** a person who causes ruin, obstruction, etc. **3.** a person, car, train, etc. that salvages or clears away wrecks; specif., a truck equipped to tow away wrecked or disabled automobiles **4.** a person whose work is tearing down old buildings, motor vehicles, etc., salvaging usable materials and parts

wreck·ing (-iŋ) *n.* the act or work of a wrecker —*adj.* engaged in or used in dismantling wrecks

☆**wrecking bar** a crowbar with a chisellike point at one end and a curved claw at the other

wren (ren) *n.* [OE. *wrenna*] any of various small, insect-eating songbirds having a long bill, rounded wings, and a stubby, erect tail

Wren (ren), Sir **Christopher** 1632–1723; Eng. architect

wrench (rench) *n.* [OE. *wrenc,* a trick] **1.** a sudden, sharp twist or pull **2.** an injury caused by a twist or jerk, as to the back **3.** a sudden feeling of anguish, grief, etc., as at parting with someone **4.** any of a number of tools used for holding and turning nuts, bolts, pipes, etc. —*vt.* **1.** to twist, pull, or jerk violently **2.** to injure (a part of the body) with a twist or wrench **3.** to twist or distort (a meaning, statement, etc.) —*vi.* to pull or tug (*at* something) with a wrenching movement

wrest (rest) *vt.* [OE. *wrǣstan*] **1.** to pull or force away violently with a twisting motion [to *wrest* a weapon from an enemy] **2.** to take by force; usurp [to *wrest* power from the people] **3.** to distort or change the true meaning, purpose, etc. of —*n.* a wresting; a twist; wrench

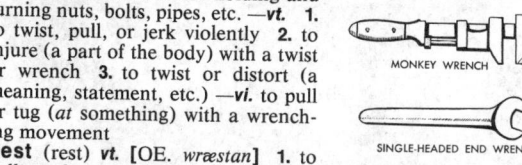

STILLSON WRENCH

MONKEY WRENCH

SINGLE-HEADED END WRENCH

TYPES OF WRENCH

wres·tle (res'l) *vi., vt.* **-tled, -tling** [< OE. *wrǣstan,* to twist + -LE[2]] **1.** to struggle hand to hand with (an opponent) in an attempt to throw or force him to the ground without striking blows **2.** to struggle hard (*with* a problem, etc.) or struggle to move or lift (something) —*n.* **1.** a wrestling; wrestling bout **2.** a struggle or contest —**wres'tler** *n.*

wres·tling (-liŋ) *n.* a form of sport in which the opponents wrestle, or struggle hand to hand

wretch (rech) *n.* [OE. *wrecca,* an outcast] **1.** a miserable or unhappy person **2.** a person who is despised or scorned

wretch·ed (rech'id) *adj.* [OE. *wrǣcc*] **1.** very unhappy; miserable; unfortunate [to feel *wretched*] **2.** causing misery [*wretched* slums] **3.** bad in quality; very poor or unsatisfactory [a *wretched* meal] **4.** deserving to be despised; hateful; vile [a *wretched* traitor] —**wretch'ed·ly** *adv.* —**wretch'ed·ness** *n.*

wrig·gle (rig'l) *vi.* **-gled, -gling** [MLowG. *wriggeln*] **1.** to twist and turn to and fro; squirm [to *wriggle* impatiently in one's seat] **2.** to move along with a twisting, writhing motion [to *wriggle* through a hole in the fence] **3.** to make one's way by tricky or shifty means; dodge [to *wriggle* out of a difficulty] —*vt.* **1.** to cause to wriggle [to *wriggle* one's fingers] **2.** to bring into a specified condition by wriggling [she *wriggled* her foot out of the shoe] —*n.* a wriggling movement —**wrig'gly** *adj.* **-gli·er, -gli·est**

wrig·gler (-lər) *n.* **1.** a person or thing that wriggles **2.** the larva of a mosquito; wiggler

wright (rīt) *n.* [OE. *wyrhta < wyrcan,* to work] a person who makes or builds something: used chiefly in compounds [*shipwright, playwright*]

Wright (rīt) **1.** Frank Lloyd, 1869–1959; U.S. architect **2.** Orville (ôr'vil), 1871–1948 & his brother Wilbur, 1867–1912; U.S. inventors of the first airplane to be flown successfully **3.** Richard, 1908–60; U.S. writer, esp. of novels

wring (riŋ) *vt.* **wrung** or rare **winged, wring'ing** [OE. *wringan*] **1.** *a)* to squeeze, press, or twist, esp. so as to force out water or other liquid [to *wring* out a washcloth] *b)* to force out (water, etc.) by this means **2.** to clasp and twist (the hands) together in distress, pain, etc. **3.** to wrench or twist with force or violence [to kill a chicken by *wringing* its neck] **4.** to get by force, threats, persistence, etc. [to *wring* a confession from a suspect] **5.** to cause to feel anguish, pity, etc. [the story *wrung* her heart] —*n.* the act of wringing; a twist

wring·er (riŋ'ər) *n.* **1.** a person or thing that wrings **2.** a device with two rollers close together between which wet clothes are run to squeeze out the water

wrin·kle[1] (riŋ'k'l) *n.* [prob. < OE. *(ge)wrinclod,* pp. of *(ge)wrinclian,* to wind about] **1.** a small ridge or furrow in a normally smooth surface, caused by contraction, folding, etc. [*wrinkles* in a shirt collar] **2.** a crease or pucker in the skin [a face full of *wrinkles*] —*vt., vi.* **-kled, -kling** to contract or pucker into small ridges or creases [to *wrinkle* one's forehead] —**wrin'kly** *adj.* **-kli·er, -kli·est**

wrin·kle[2] (riŋ'k'l) *n.* [prob. ult. < OE. *wrenc,* a trick] [Colloq.] a clever or novel trick, idea, or device

wrist (rist) *n.* [OE.] **1.** the joint or part of the arm between the hand and the forearm; carpus **2.** the corresponding part in an animal **3.** the part of a sleeve, glove, etc. covering the wrist —☆**a slap** (or **tap**) **on the wrist** a token punishment, less severe than seems called for

wrist·band (rist'band') *n.* a band that goes around the wrist, as on the cuff of a sleeve

wrist·let (-lit) *n.* **1.** a closefitting band or strip of material worn around the wrist, as for warmth **2.** a bracelet

wrist·lock (-läk') *n.* a wrestling hold in which one wrestler gets a grip on his opponent's wrist and twists his arm

wrist pin the stud or pin by which the connecting rod is attached to a wheel, crank, etc.

wrist·watch (-wäch', -wôch') *n.* a watch worn on a strap or band that fits around the wrist

writ (rit) *n.* [OE. < *writan,* to write] **1.** [Rare or Archaic] something written **2.** a formal legal document ordering or prohibiting some action

write (rīt) *vt.* **wrote, writ'ten, writ'ing;** archaic *pt. & pp.* **writ** [OE. *writan,* to scratch, write] **1.** *a)* to form (words, letters, etc.) on a surface, esp. with a pen or pencil *b)* to form the words, letters, etc. of [*write* your name] **2.** to spell (a word, etc.) [words *written* the same are often pronounced differently]

3. to know (a language, its alphabet, etc.) well enough to communicate in writing **4.** to be the author or composer of (literary or musical material) [Dickens *wrote* novels; Mozart *wrote* symphonies] **5.** to fill in (a check, printed form, etc.) with the writing required [*write* a money order for $10] **6.** to cover with writing [he *wrote* 10 pages] **7.** to say in a letter or written message [he *wrote* that he was ill] **8.** to send a letter or note to [*write* me every day] **9.** to record (information) in a computer's memory or on a tape, etc. for use by a computer **10.** to leave signs or evidence of [greed was *written* on his face] —*vi.* **1.** to form words, letters, etc. on a surface, esp. with a pen or pencil [children learning to *write*] **2.** to write books or other literary matter [he *writes* for a living] **3.** to write a letter [I *wrote* last month and am still waiting for an answer] **4.** to produce writing of a specified kind [to *write* legibly] —**write down** **1.** to put into written form [*write* his words *down* exactly] **2.** to discredit in writing [to *write down* an opponent] **3.** to write in a very simple, patronizing way [to *write down* to children] — **write in** ☆to vote for (someone not officially on a ballot) by inserting his name on the ballot —**write off** **1.** to cancel or remove from accounts (bad debts, etc.) **2.** to drop from consideration —**write out** **1.** to put into writing **2.** to write in full —**write up** to write an account of [to *write up* a news story]

writ·er (rīt′ər) *n.* a person who writes, esp. one whose work or occupation is writing, as an author, journalist, etc.

writer's cramp a cramp of the muscles of the hand and fingers, from writing for too long a time

☆**write-up** (rīt′up′) *n.* [Colloq.] a written report or description, often a favorable account, as for publicity

writhe (rīth) *vt.* **writhed, writh′ing** [OE. *writhan*, to twist] to cause to twist or turn; contort [his face was *writhed* with rage] —*vi.* **1.** to make twisting or turning movements; squirm [to *writhe* with pain] **2.** to suffer the distress of one who feels very embarrassed, frustrated, etc. —*n.* a writhing movement

writ·ing (rīt′iŋ) *n.* **1.** the act of a person who writes **2.** something written, as a letter, document, etc. **3.** written form [to put a request in *writing*] **4.** *short for* HANDWRITING **5.** a literary work **6.** the profession or occupation of a writer **7.** the art, style, etc. of literary composition —*adj.* **1.** that writes **2.** used in writing

writ·ten (rit′'n) *pp.* of WRITE —*adj.* put down in a form to be read; not spoken or oral [a *written* message]

Wroc·ław (vrôts′läf) city in SW Poland, on the Oder River: pop. 514,000

wrong (rôŋ) *adj.* [OE. *wrang* < ON. *rangr*, twisted] **1.** not just, moral, etc.; unlawful, immoral, or improper [it is *wrong* to steal] **2.** not in accordance with an established standard, intended or required action, etc. [the *wrong* method] **3.** not suitable or appropriate [the *wrong* time to object] **4.** *a)* not the one that is true, correct, wanted, etc.; incorrect [a *wrong* answer] *b)* acting, believing, etc. incorrectly; in error; mistaken [we were *wrong* to take his word for it] **5.** in an unsatisfactory or bad condition [everything is *wrong* today] **6.** not working properly [what's *wrong* with the light?] **7.** designating the unfinished, inner, or under side [the *wrong* side of a fabric] —*adv.* in a wrong manner, direction, etc.; incorrectly —*n.* **1.** that which is wrong, esp. an unjust or immoral act [he knows right from *wrong*; you do him a *wrong* to accuse him] **2.** *Law* a violation of a legal right —*vt.* **1.** to treat badly or unjustly; injure [he *wronged* his wife and children by leaving] **2.** to think badly of without real justification —see SYN. at INJUSTICE —**get (someone**

or **something) wrong** [Colloq.] to fail to understand (someone or something) properly —**go wrong** **1.** to turn out badly **2.** to change from good behavior to bad —**in the wrong** not on the side supported by truth, justice, etc. —**wrong′er** *n.* —**wrong′ly** *adv.* —**wrong′ness** *n.*

wrong·do·ing (rôŋ′dōō′iŋ) *n.* any act or behavior that is wrong, wicked, unlawful, etc. —**wrong′do′er** *n.*

wrong·ful (-fəl) *adj.* **1.** full of wrong; unjust, unfair, or injurious **2.** without legal right; unlawful —**wrong′ful·ly** *adv.* —**wrong′ful·ness** *n.*

wrong·head·ed (-hed′id) *adj.* stubborn in sticking to wrong opinions, ideas, etc.; perverse —**wrong′head′ed·ly** *adv.* —**wrong′head′ed·ness** *n.*

wrote (rōt) *pt.* of WRITE

wroth (rôth; *chiefly Brit.* rōth) *adj.* [OE. *wrath*] angry; wrathful; incensed

wrought (rôt) *alt. pt. & pp.* of WORK —*adj.* **1.** formed; fashioned [a beautifully *wrought* bracelet] **2.** shaped by hammering or beating: said of metals [*wrought* silver] **3.** worked out with care [a well-*wrought* argument] **4.** decorated; ornamented [*wrought* ivory]

wrought iron a kind of iron that contains some slag and very little carbon: it is tough but easy to work or shape and is used in fences, grillwork, etc. —**wrought′-i′ron** *adj.*

wrought-up (rôt′up′) *adj.* very disturbed or excited

wrung (ruŋ) *pt. & pp.* of WRING

wry (rī) *adj.* **wri′er, wri′est** [OE. *wrigian*, to turn] **1.** turned or bent to one side; twisted; distorted [a *wry* mouth] **2.** made by twisting or distorting the features [a *wry* face] **3.** ironic or bitter [*wry* humor] —**wry′ly** *adv.* —**wry′ness** *n.*

wry·neck (rī′nek′) *n.* **1.** a condition in which the neck is twisted by a muscle spasm **2.** a bird related to the woodpecker, noted for its habit of twisting its neck

WSW, W.S.W., w.s.w. west-southwest

wt. weight

Wu·han (wōō′hän′) city in EC China, on the Yangtze: pop. 2,500,000

‡**Wun·der·kind** (voon′dər kint′) *n., pl.* **-kin′der** (-kin′dər) [G. < *wunder*, wonder + *kind*, child] a child prodigy

Wup·per·tal (voop′ər täl′) city in the Ruhr Basin of West Germany: pop. 414,000

wurst (wurst, woorst; *G.* voorsht) *n.* [G.] sausage: often used in combination [*bratwurst, knackwurst*]

W.Va., WV West Virginia

Wy·an·dotte (wī′ən dät′) *n.* [< Iroquoian name for the Huron Indians] any of a breed of American chickens

Wy·att (wī′ət), Sir **Thomas** 1503?–42; Eng. poet

wych-elm (wich′elm′) *n.* [< OE. *wice*, applied to trees with pliant branches + ELM] **1.** a small variety of elm native to Europe and N Asia **2.** its wood

Wych·er·ley (wich′ər lē), **William** 1640?–1716; Eng. dramatist

Wyc·liffe (or **Wyc·lif**) (wik′lif), **John** 1324?–84; Eng. religious reformer: made the first complete translation of the Bible into English

Wy·o·ming (wī ō′miŋ) [< Algonquian, lit., large plains] **1.** Western State of the U.S.: 97,914 sq. mi.; pop. 332,000; cap. Cheyenne; abbrev. **Wyo., WY** **2.** city in SW Mich.: suburb of Grand Rapids: pop. 57,000 —**Wy·o′ming·ite′** (-īt′) *n.*

wy·vern (wī′vərn) *n.* [< ONormFr. *wivre* < OFr. < L. *vipera*, viper, serpent] *Heraldry* a two-legged dragon with wings and a barbed tail

X

X, x (eks) *n., pl.* **X's, x's** **1.** the twenty-fourth letter of the English alphabet **2.** a sound of *X* or *x*

X (eks) *n.* **1.** a mark shaped like X, used to represent the signature of a person who cannot write, to mark a particular point on a map or diagram, etc. **2.** the Roman numeral for 10: it subtracts ten units when placed before a larger numeral (for example, XL = 40) **3.** a person or thing unknown or unrevealed —*adj.* shaped like X

☆**X** a motion-picture rating meaning that no one under the age of seventeen is to be admitted

x *a symbol for:* **1.** *Math. a)* an unknown quantity *b)* times (in multiplication) *[3 × 3 = 9] c)* an abscissa **2.** *a)* by *[3 ft. × 4 ft.] b)* power of magnification (in optical instruments) *c)* one's choice or answer (on a ballot, test, etc.)

x (eks) *vt.* **x-ed** or **x'd, x-ing** or **x'ing** **1.** to show (one's choice, etc.) by marking with an X **2.** to cross out (words or letters) with an X or X's

xan·the·in (zan′thē in) *n.* [Fr. *xanthéine*] the water-soluble part of the yellow pigment in some plants

xan·thic (zan′thik) *adj.* [< Fr.: see XANTHO- & -IC] **1.** yellow **2.** of or having to do with xanthine

xan·thine (zan′thēn, -thin) *n.* [Fr.: see XANTHO- & -IN¹] a white, crystalline nitrogenous compound present in blood, urine, and certain plants

Xan·thip·pe (zan tip′ē) 5th cent. B.C.; wife of Socrates: her name has become proverbial for the nagging wife

xan·tho- (zan′thō, -thə) [< Gr. *xanthos*, yellow] *a combining form meaning* yellow: also, before a vowel, **xanth-**

xan·thous (zan′thəs) *adj.* [Gr. *xanthos*] yellow

Xa·vi·er (zā′vē ər, zav′ē-; zāv′yər), Saint **Francis** 1506–52; Sp. Jesuit missionary

x-ax·is (eks′ak′sis) *n., pl.* **x′-ax′es** (-sēz) *Math.* the horizontal axis along which the abscissa is measured

X chromosome *Genetics* one of the sex chromosomes: see SEX CHROMOSOME

Xe *Chem.* xenon

xe·bec (zē′bek) *n.* [< Fr. *chébec*, ult. < Ar. *shabbāk*] a small, three-masted ship with overhanging bow and stern: once common in the Mediterranean

xen·o- [< Gr. *xenos*] *a combining form meaning:* **1.** stranger, foreigner *[xenophobia]* **2.** strange, foreign Also, before a vowel, **xen-**

xe·non (zē′nän, zen′än) *n.* [Gr., neut. of *xenos*, strange] a chemical element that is a heavy, colorless gas: it is found in the air in very small quantities and is used in electron tubes, lasers, etc.: symbol, Xe; at. wt., 131.30; at. no., 54

xen·o·pho·bi·a (zen′ə fō′bē ə, zē′nə-) *n.* [ModL.: see XENO- & -PHOBIA] fear or hatred of strangers or foreigners —**xen′o·phobe′** (-fōb′) *n.* —**xen′o·pho′bic** (-fō′bik) *adj.*

Xen·o·phon (zen′ə fən) 430?–355? B.C.; Gr. historian, essayist, & military leader

☆**xe·rog·ra·phy** (zi räg′rə fē) *n.* [< Gr. *xēros*, dry + -GRA-PHY] a process for copying printed or written material, etc., in which an image of the material is electrically charged on a surface and attracts oppositely charged dry ink particles, which are then fused in place —**xe·ro·graph·ic** (zir′ə graf′ik) *adj.*

xe·roph·i·lous (zi räf′ə ləs) *adj.* [< Gr. *xēros*, dry + -PHILOUS] thriving in a hot, dry climate —**xe·roph′i·ly** *n.*

xe·ro·phyte (zir′ə fīt′) *n.* [< Gr. *xēros*, dry + -PHYTE] a plant adapted to grow under very dry or desert conditions —**xe′ro·phyt′ic** (-fit′ik) *adj.*

☆**Xe·rox** (zir′äks) *a trademark for* a device for copying printed or written material, etc. by xerography —*n.* a copy made by such a device —*vt., vi.* to reproduce by such a device

Xer·xes I (zurk′sēz) 519?–465? B.C.; king of Persia (486?–465?): son of DARIUS I: called *the Great*

Xho·sa (kō′sä, -zä; *the k is actually a click*) *n.* **1.** *pl.* **Xho′sas, Xho′sa** any member of a people living in Cape Province, South Africa **2.** their Bantu language, characterized by clicks Also sp. **Xo′sa**

xi (zī, sī; *Gr.* ksē) *n.* [Gr.] the fourteenth letter of the Greek alphabet (Ξ, ξ)

Xin·gu (shiŋ gōō′) river in NC Brazil, flowing north into the Amazon: c. 1,200 mi.

Xmas (kris′məs; *popularly* eks′məs) *n.* [X (chi), 1st letter in Gr. *Christos*, Christ + -MAS] *same as* CHRISTMAS

X-ray (eks′rā′) *n.* **1.** an electromagnetic ray or radiation of very short wavelength produced by the bombardment of a metal by a stream of electrons, as in a vacuum tube: X-rays can pass through solid substances and are widely used in medicine to study the bones, organs, etc. inside the body and to diagnose and treat certain disorders **2.** a photograph made by means of X-rays —*adj.* of, by, or having to do with X-rays —*vt.* to examine, treat, or photograph with X-rays Also **X ray, x-ray, x ray**

xy·lem (zī′ləm, -lem) *n.* [G. < Gr. *xylon*] the woody tissue of a plant, which gives support to the softer tissues and contains vessels or cells that conduct water, minerals, etc.

xy·lo- [< Gr. *xylon*] *a combining form meaning* wood *[xylophone]*: also, before a vowel, **xyl-**

xy·lo·phone (zī′lə fōn′) *n.* [XYLO- + -PHONE] a musical instrument consisting of a series of wooden bars graduated in length so as to sound the notes of the scale when struck with small wooden hammers —**xy′lo·phon′ist** (-fō′nist, zī läf′ə nist) *n.*

xy·lose (zī′lōs) *n.* [XYL(O)- + -OSE¹] a colorless sugar derived from wood, straw, corncobs, etc. and used in dyeing, diabetic foods, etc.

XYLOPHONE

---

fat, āpe, cär; ten, ēven; is, bīte; gō, hôrn, tōol, look; oil, out; up, fur; get; joy; yet; chin; she; thin, *th*en; zh, leisure; ŋ, ring; ə for *a* in *ago, e* in *agent, i* in *sanity, o* in *comply, u* in *focus*; ' as in *able* (ā′b'l); Fr. bâl; ë, Fr. coeur; ö, Fr. feu; Fr. mo*n*; ô, Fr. coq; ü, Fr. duc; r, Fr. cri; H, G. ich; kh, G. doch; ‡foreign; ☆ Americanism; < derived from. See inside front cover.

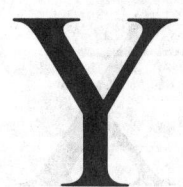

Y

Y, y (wī) *n., pl.* **Y's, y's** **1.** the twenty-fifth letter of the English alphabet **2.** a sound of *Y* or *y*

Y (wī) *n.* **1.** something shaped like Y **2.** *Chem.* yttrium —*adj.* shaped like Y

y *Math. a symbol for:* **1.** the second of a set of unknown quantities, *x* usually being the first **2.** an ordinate

-y[1] (ē, i) [ME. *-y, -i, -ie,* prob. < OFr.] *a suffix meaning* little, dear: used in forming diminutives, nicknames, and terms of endearment [*kitty, Billy*]

-y[2] (ē, i) [OE. *-ig*] *a suffix meaning:* **1.** having, full of, or characterized by [*dirty*] **2.** somewhat; rather [*chilly*] **3.** tending to [*sticky*] **4.** suggestive of, somewhat like [*wavy*] In some words, *-y* simply adds force without changing the meaning [*vasty*]

-y[3] (ē, i) [< OFr. *-ie* < L. *-ia* < or akin to Gr. *-ia*] *a suffix meaning:* **1.** quality or condition of (being) [*jealousy*] **2.** a shop or goods of a specified kind [*bakery*] **3.** a group of a specified kind [*soldiery*]

-y[4] (ē, i) [< Anglo-Fr. *-ie* < L. *-ium*] *a suffix meaning* action of [*inquiry, entreaty*]

Y, Y. *short for* YMCA, YMHA, YWCA, YWHA

y. **1.** yard(s) **2.** year(s)

yacht (yät) *n.* [Du. *jacht,* short for *jaghtschip,* pursuit ship] a large boat or small ship for pleasure cruises, races, etc. —*vi.* to sail in a yacht —**yacht′ing** *n.*

yachts·man (yäts′mən) *n., pl.* **-men** a person who owns or sails a yacht —**yachts′man·ship′** *n.*

yack (yak) *vi., n. var. of* YAK[2]

yah (yä, ya) *interj.* a shout of scorn, defiance, etc.

Ya·hoo (yä′hōō) *n.* **1.** in Swift's *Gulliver's Travels,* any of a race of coarse, brutish creatures having the form and vices of man **2.** [y-] a vicious, coarse person

Yah·weh, Yah·we (yä′we) [Heb.: see JEHOVAH] God: a form of the Hebrew name in the Scriptures: also **Yah·ve, Yah·veh** (yä′ve)

yak[1] (yak) *n., pl.* **yaks, yak:** see PLURAL, II, D, 1 [Tibet. *gyak*] a stocky, long-haired wild ox of Tibet and C Asia, often used as a beast of burden

☆**yak**[2] (yak; *also, for n.* 2, yäk) *vi.* **yakked, yak′king** [echoic] [Slang] to talk much or idly; chatter —*n.* [Slang] **1.** idle talk or chatter **2.** *a)* a loud laugh, esp. as audience response to comedy *b)* a joke or comic routine that gets such a laugh Also, for *vi. & n.* (sense 1), **yak′-yak′, yak·e·ty-yak** (yak′ə tē yak′) —**yak′ker** *n.*

YAK
(to 5 ft. high at shoulder)

Ya·lu (yä′lōō′) river flowing along the Manchuria–North Korea border into the Yellow Sea

yam (yam) *n.* [Port. *inhame,* prob. < WAfr. name] **1.** *a)* the edible, starchy root of a climbing plant grown in tropical regions *b)* this plant ☆**2.** [South] the sweet potato

ya·mal·ka, ya·mul·ka (yäm′əl kə) *n. var. of* YARMULKE

yam·mer (yam′ər) *vi., vt.* [OE. *geomerian,* to lament] [Colloq. or Dial.] **1.** to whine or complain (about) **2.** to shout, yell, etc. —*n.* [Colloq. or Dial.] the act or sound of yammering —**yam′mer·er** *n.*

yang (yäŋ, yaŋ) *n.* [< Chin. dial.] in Chinese philosophy, the active, positive, masculine force or principle in the universe: see YIN

Yang·tze (yaŋ′sē; *Chin.* yän′tse′) river in C China, flowing from Tibet into the East China Sea: c. 3,400 mi.

☆**Yank** (yaŋk) *n.* [Slang] a Yankee; esp., a U.S. soldier in World Wars I and II —*adj.* [Slang] of or like a Yank or Yanks

yank (yaŋk) *n.* [< ?] ☆[Colloq.] a sudden, strong pull; jerk —*vt., vi.* [Colloq.] to jerk

Yan·kee (yaŋ′kē) *n.* [< ? Du. *Jan Kees* (taken as pl.) < *Jan,* John + *Kees* < *kaas,* cheese: a disparaging nickname applied by Dutch colonists in America to English settlers] ☆**1.** a native or inhabitant of New England ☆**2.** *a)* a native or inhabitant of a Northern State; Northerner *b)* a Union soldier in the Civil War ☆**3.** a native or inhabitant of the U.S. —☆*adj.* of or like Yankees —☆**Yan′kee·dom** *n.*

☆**Yankee Doo·dle** (dōō′d'l) an old American song, popular during the Revolutionary War

‡**Yan·qui** (yäŋ′kē) *n., pl.* **-quis** (-kēs) *American Spanish respelling of* YANKEE (sense 3)

Ya·oun·dé (yä′ōōn dā′) capital of Cameroun, in the SW part: pop. 130,000

yap (yap) *vi.* **yapped, yap′ping** [echoic] **1.** to make a sharp, high-pitched bark or yelp **2.** [Slang] to talk noisily and stupidly —*n.* **1.** a sharp, high-pitched bark or yelp **2.** [Slang] *a)* noisy, stupid talk *b)* a crude, noisy person *c)* the mouth —**yap′per** *n.* —**yap′ping·ly** *adv.*

yard[1] (yärd) *n.* [OE. *gierd,* a rod] **1.** *a)* a measure of length, equal to 3 feet, or 36 inches *b)* a cubic yard [a *yard* of topsoil] **2.** *Naut.* a slender rod or spar fastened across a mast to support a sail or to hold signal flags, lights, etc. **3.** [Slang] one hundred dollars or, sometimes, one thousand dollars

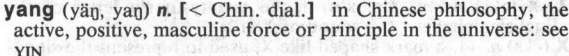

YARDS

yard[2] (yärd) *n.* [OE. *geard,* enclosure] **1.** the ground around or next to a house or other building [*churchyard, farmyard*] **2.** a pen, etc. for livestock or poultry **3.** a place in the open used for a particular purpose, work, etc. [a navy *yard,* a lumber*yard*] **4.** a place where deer, moose, etc. gather and feed in winter **5.** a railroad center where trains are made up, serviced, switched, etc. —*vt.* to put, keep, or enclose in a yard

yard·age (yär′dij) *n.* **1.** measurement in yards **2.** the length of something so measured ☆**3.** distance covered in carrying a football forward

yard·arm (yärd′ärm′) *n. Naut.* either end of a yard supporting a square sail, signal lights, etc.

yard goods cloth fabrics made in standard width, usually sold by the yard

yard·man (-mən) *n., pl.* **-men** a man who works in a yard

☆**yard·mas·ter** (-mas′tər) *n.* a man in charge of a railroad yard

☆**yard·stick** (-stik′) *n.* **1.** a measuring stick one yard long **2.** any standard used in judging, comparing, etc.

yar·mul·ke (yär′məl kə) *n.* [Yid. < Pol. *yarmułka*] a skullcap often worn by Jewish men and boys at prayer or study, at meals, etc.: also **yar′mel·ke, yar′mel·ke**

yarn (yärn) *n.* [OE. *gearn*] **1.** a strand or thread of spun wool, silk, cotton, nylon, glass, etc., for weaving, knitting, rope-making, etc. **2.** [Colloq.] a tale or story, esp. one that seems exaggerated —*vi.* [Old Colloq.] to tell yarns —**spin a yarn** [Colloq.] to tell a yarn

Ya·ro·slavl, Ya·ro·slavl' (yä′rô släv′l′) city in W European R.S.F.S.R., on the Volga: pop. 517,000

yar·row (yar′ō) *n.* [OE. *gæruwe*] a plant of the composite family, having a strong smell, finely divided leaves, and clusters of small, pink or white flowers

yat·a·ghan, yat·a·gan (yat′ə gan′, -gən) *n.* [Turk. *yātāghan*] a type of Turkish short saber with a double-curved blade and a handle without a guard

yat·ter (yat′ər) *vi.* [prob. < YA(K)² + (CHA)TTER] [Slang] to talk on and on about unimportant things

☆**yau·pon** (yô′pən) *n.* [< AmInd. *yop*, a shrub] an evergreen holly of the southeastern U.S.: its leaves are sometimes used as a substitute for tea

yaw (yô) *vi.* [ON. *jaga*, to sway] **1.** to swing back and forth across its course, as a ship pushed by high waves **2.** to turn or swing about the vertical axis, as an aircraft, spacecraft, etc. —*vt.* to cause to yaw —*n.* an act of yawing

yawl (yôl) *n.* [< MLowG. *jolle* or Du. *jol*] **1.** a ship's boat **2.** a sailboat like a ketch, but with the short mizzenmast behind the rudderpost

yawn (yôn) *vi.* [prob. merging of OE. *ginian* & *ganian*, both meaning "to gape"] **1.** to open the mouth wide and breathe in deeply, as one often does automatically when sleepy or bored **2.** to open wide; gape [a *yawning* hole] —*vt.* to express with a yawn —*n.* the act of yawning —**yawn′er** *n.*

YAWL

yawp (yôp) *vi.* [ME. *yolpen*] **1.** to utter a loud, harsh call or cry **2.** [Slang] to talk noisily and stupidly —*n.* the act or sound of yawping —**yawp′er** *n.*

yaws (yôz) *n.pl.* [*with sing. v.*] [of Carib origin] an infectious disease of tropical regions, caused by a spirochete and characterized by a rash and sores on the skin

y-ax·is (wī′ak′sis) *n., pl.* **y′-ax′es** (-sēz) *Math.* the vertical axis along which the ordinate is measured

Yb *Chem.* ytterbium

Y chromosome *Genetics* one of the sex chromosomes: see SEX CHROMOSOME

y·clept, y·cleped (i klept′) *pp.* [OE. *geclypod*, pp. of *clipian*, to call] [Archaic] called; named [a knight *yclept* Sir Bors]

yd. *pl.* **yd., yds.** yard

ye¹ (*thə, thi, thē; now often* yē) *adj. archaic form of* THE: *y* was substituted by early printers for the thorn þ, the Old and Middle English character representing the sound (*th*) or (*th*)

ye² (yē; *unstressed* yi) *pron.* [OE. *ge*] [Archaic] you

yea (yā) *adv.* [OE. *gea*] **1.** yes: used to show agreement **2.** indeed; truly —*n.* an answer or vote of "yes" —*Interj.* ☆a cry used in cheering on an athletic team

☆**yeah** (ya, ye, ye′ə, *etc.*) *adv.* [Colloq.] yes

yean (yēn) *vt., vi.* [< an OE. word thought to be *ge-eanian*] to bring forth (young): said of a sheep or goat

yean·ling (yēn′liŋ) *n.* a lamb or kid —*adj.* newborn

year (yir) *n.* [OE. *gear*] **1.** a period of 365 days (in leap year, 366 days) divided into 12 months (from Jan. 1 through Dec. 31) **2.** the period (365 days, 5 hours, 48 minutes, and 46 seconds) spent by the sun in its apparent passage from vernal equinox to vernal equinox: the year of the seasons: also **tropical** or **solar year 3.** the period (365 days, 6 hours, 9 minutes, and 9.54 seconds) spent by the sun in its apparent passage from a fixed star and back to the same position again: also **sidereal year 4.** a period of 12 lunar months, as in the Jewish calendar: also **lunar year 5.** the period of time in which any planet makes its revolution around the sun **6.** a period of 12 calendar months starting from any date [six *years* ago] **7.** a calendar year of a specified number in an era [the *year* 500 B.C.] **8.** a particular annual period of less than 365 days [a school *year*] **9.** [*pl.*] *a*) age [old for her *years*] *b*) time; esp., a long time [*years* ago] —**year after year** every year —**year by year** each year —**year in, year out** every year

year·book (yir′book′) *n.* a book published each year, as one with statistics and data of the past year, one with pictures and reports of a school's graduating class, etc.

year·ling (yir′liŋ, yur′-) *n.* an animal one year old or in its second year —*adj.* being a year old

year·long (yir′lôŋ′) *adj.* continuing for a full year [a *yearlong* celebration]

year·ly (-lē) *adj.* **1.** lasting a year [the earth's *yearly* revolution around the sun] **2.** done, happening, etc. once a year, or every year [a *yearly* event] **3.** of a year, or each year [her *yearly* income] —*adv.* annually; every year [we visit them *yearly*]

yearn (yurn) *vi.* [OE. *gyrnan* < *georn*, eager] **1.** to be filled with longing or desire [to *yearn* for fame] **2.** to feel tenderness or sympathy —**yearn′er** *n.*

yearn·ing (yur′niŋ) *n.* deep longing, desire, etc.

year-round (yir′round′) *adj.* open, in use, operating, etc. throughout the year

yea·say·er (yā′sā′ər) *n.* [YEA + SAY + -ER] a person who is optimistic, confident, etc. in his attitude toward life

yeast (yēst) *n.* [OE. *gist*] **1.** any of various single-celled fungi that live on sugary solutions, ferment sugars to form alcohol and carbon dioxide, and are used in making beer, whiskey, etc. and as a leavening in baking: also **yeast plant 2.** *a*) the yellowish, moist mass of yeast plants occurring as a froth on fermenting solutions *b*) this substance dried in flakes or granules or pressed into cakes **3.** foam; froth **4.** something that causes excitement, activity, disturbance, etc. —**yeast′like′** *adj.*

yeast·y (yēs′tē) *adj.* **yeast′i·er, yeast′i·est 1.** of, like, or containing yeast **2.** frothy; foamy **3.** light; frivolous **4.** very active, excited, stirred up, etc. —**yeast′i·ness** *n.*

Yeats (yāts), **William Butler** 1865–1939; Ir. poet, playwright, & essayist

yech (yek, yuk) *interj.* a gagging sound made in the throat to show disgust, contempt, etc.: also sp. **yecch**

☆**yegg** (yeg) *n.* [< ?] [Old Slang] a criminal; esp., a safecracker or burglar

yell (yel) *vi.* [OE. *giellan*] to cry out loudly; shout; scream —*vt.* to utter by yelling —*n.* **1.** a loud outcry or shout; scream ☆**2.** a rhythmic cheer given in unison, as by students at a football game —**yell′er** *n.*

yel·low (yel′ō) *adj.* [OE. *geolu*] **1.** of the color of gold, butter, or ripe lemons **2.** having a yellowish skin ☆**3.** [Colloq.] cowardly ☆**4.** featuring news stories that are sensational and in poor taste [*yellow* journalism] —*n.* **1.** a yellow color; color between orange and green in the spectrum **2.** a yellow pigment or dye **3.** the yolk of an egg —*vt., vi.* to make or become yellow —**yel′low·ish** *adj.* —**yel′low·ness** *n.*

☆**yel·low-bel·ly** (-bel′ē) *n., pl.* **-lies** [Slang] a contemptible coward —**yel′low-bel′lied** *adj.*

yel·low·bird (-burd′) *n.* a bird yellow in color, as the yellow warbler, the American goldfinch, etc.

☆**yel·low-dog contract** (-dôg′) a contract, now illegal, by which a new employee agrees not to join a labor union

☆**yellow fever** a tropical disease caused by a virus carried to man by the bite of the **yellow-fever mosquito**, and marked by fever, yellowing of the skin, vomiting, etc.

yel·low-green algae (-grēn′) a group of algae that contain a yellowish or brownish pigment that hides the chlorophyll

yel·low·ham·mer (-ham′ər) *n.* [ult. < OE. *geolu*, yellow + *amore*, kind of finch] **1.** a small European finch having a yellow head, neck, and breast ☆**2.** a flicker with a red mark on the head and with wings colored golden on the underside

☆**yellow jack 1.** *same as* YELLOW FEVER **2.** a yellow flag used as a signal of quarantine

☆**yellow jacket** any of several social wasps or hornets having bright-yellow markings

Yel·low·knife (yel′ō nif′) town on Great Slave Lake in NW Canada; capital of Northwest Territories: pop. 8,000

yel·low·legs (-legz′) *n., pl.* **-legs′** ☆either of two black-and-white American sandpipers having long, yellow legs

☆**Yellow Pages** [*also* y- p-] the section or volume of a telephone directory, printed on yellow paper, containing classified listings of subscribers according to business, profession, etc.

☆**yellow pine 1.** any of several N. American pines having yellowish wood **2.** this wood

Yellow River *same as* HWANG HO

Yellow Sea arm of the East China Sea, between China & Korea
☆**yel·low-shaft·ed flicker** (or **woodpecker**) (-shaf′tid) *same as* YELLOWHAMMER (sense 2)
Yel·low·stone (yel′ō stōn′) [transl. of Fr. name, ? transl. of native name] river flowing from NW Wyo. through Mont. into the Missouri River
Yellowstone National Park national park mostly in NW Wyo., containing geysers, boiling springs, etc.
☆**yellow streak** a tendency to be cowardly
yel·low·tail (-tāl′) *n., pl.* **-tails′, -tail′:** see PLURAL, II, D, 1 ☆any of several fishes having a yellowish tail, as a rockfish of the Pacific coast of the U.S.
yel·low·throat (-thrōt′) *n.* ☆any of various American warblers with a yellow breast and throat
☆**yellow warbler** a small, bright-yellow N. American warbler
yel·low·wood (-wood′) *n.* **1.** any of several trees with yellow wood, esp. ☆one of the southeastern U.S. **2.** its wood
yel·low·y (yel′ə wē) *adj.* somewhat yellow
yelp (yelp) *vi.* [OE. *gielpan,* to boast] **1.** to utter a short, sharp cry or bark, as a dog **2.** to cry out sharply, as in pain —*vt.* to express by yelping —*n.* a short, sharp cry or bark —**yelp′er** *n.*
Yem·en (yem′ən) **1.** country in S Arabia, on the Red Sea: c. 75,000 sq. mi.; pop. 5,000,000; cap. San′a: in full, **Yemen Arab Republic 2.** country in S Arabia, on the Arabian Sea, east of Yemen (sense 1): c. 110,000 sq. mi.; pop. 1,475,000; cap. Aden: in full, **People's Democratic Republic of Yemen** —**Yem′en·ite′** (-ə nīt′), **Yem′e·ni** (-ə nē) *adj., n.*
yen[1] (yen) *n., pl.* **yen** [Jpn. < Chin. *yüan,* round] the monetary unit of Japan: see MONETARY UNITS, table
yen[2] (yen) *n.* [Chin. *yăn,* opium] ☆[Colloq.] a strong longing or desire —*vi.* **yenned, yen′ning** [Colloq.] to have a yen (*for*); long; yearn
Ye·ni·sei, Ye·ni·sey (ye′ni sā′) river in C Siberian R.S.F.S.R., flowing north into the Arctic Ocean: c. 2,600 mi.
yen·ta, yen·te (yen′tə) *n.* [Yid.] a woman gossip or busybody
yeo·man (yō′mən) *n., pl.* **-men** [ME. *yeman,* prob. contr. < *yung man,* young man] **1.** orig., *a)* a manservant in a royal or noble household *b)* a freeholder of a class below the gentry **2.** [Brit.] *a)* a small landowner *b) same as* YEOMAN OF THE GUARD *c)* a member of the yeomanry (sense 2) **3.** *U.S. Navy* a petty officer who performs clerical and secretarial duties —*adj.* of or like yeomen: see also YEOMAN'S SERVICE
yeo·man·ly (-lē) *adj.* **1.** of, like, or fit for a yeoman **2.** brave; sturdy —*adv.* in a yeomanly manner
yeoman of the (royal) guard any of the 100 men forming a ceremonial guard for the English royal family
yeo·man·ry (-rē) *n.* **1.** yeomen as a group **2.** a British volunteer cavalry force that is part of the Territorial Army
yeoman's service very good, useful, or loyal service or assistance: also **yeoman service**
☆**yep** (yep) *adv.* [Slang] yes
-yer (yər) *same as* -IER: usually after *w,* as in *lawyer*
Ye·re·van (ye re vän′) capital of the Armenian S.S.R., at the foot of Mt. Ararat: pop. 767,000
yes (yes) *adv.* [OE. *gese,* prob. < *gea,* yea + *si,* be it so] **1.** aye; yea; it is so: the opposite of NO, used to express agreement, consent, etc. **2.** not only that, but more; moreover [ready, *yes,* eager to help] *Yes* is sometimes used alone in questioning to mean "What is it?" or as a polite way of showing interest —*n., pl.* **yes′es 1.** the act of saying *yes* **2.** a positive vote, or a person who casts such a vote —*vt., vi.* **yessed, yes′sing** to say *yes* (to)
ye·shi·va (yə shē′və; *Heb.* ye shē vä′) *n., pl.* **-vas;** *Heb.* **-vot′** (-vōt′) [< Heb. *yeshīväh,* lit., a sitting] **1.** a school or college for Talmudic studies; esp., a seminary for the training of Orthodox rabbis **2.** a Jewish school combining religious and secular studies
☆**yes man** [Slang] a person who expresses approval of every suggestion or opinion offered by his superior
yes·ter (yes′tər) *adj.* [< YESTERDAY] **1.** of yesterday **2.** previous to this Usually in combination [yestereve, yesteryear]
yes·ter·day (yes′tər dē, -dā′) *n.* [< OE. < *geostran,* yesterday + *dæg,* day] **1.** the day before today **2.** a recent day or time **3.** [usually pl.] time gone by —*adv.* **1.** on the day before today **2.** recently —*adj.* of yesterday [yesterday morning]
yes·ter·year (-yir′) *n., adv.* [Poet.] **1.** last year **2.** (in) recent years
yet (yet) *adv.* [OE. *giet*] **1.** up to now or to the time specified; thus far [he hasn't gone *yet*] **2.** at the present time; now [we can't leave *yet*] **3.** still; even now [there is *yet* a chance for peace] **4.** at some future time; sooner or later [she will thank you *yet*] **5.** now or at a particular time, as continuing from an earlier time [we could hear her *yet*] **6.** in addition; still [he was *yet* more kind] **7.** as much as; even [he did not come, nor *yet* write] **8.** now, after all the time that has gone by [hasn't he finished *yet?*] **9.** nevertheless [he was rich, *yet* lonely —*conj.* nevertheless; however [she seems happy, *yet* she is troubled] —**as yet** up to now
ye·ti (yet′ē) *n.* [Tibet.] [*often* Y-] *same as* ABOMINABLE SNOWMAN
yew (yōō) *n.* [OE. *iw*] **1.** an evergreen shrub or tree with red, waxy cones and a fine-grained, elastic wood **2.** the wood, used esp. for making archers' bows
Yg·dra·sil, Ygg·dra·sill (ig′drə sil′) [ON.] *Norse Myth.* the huge ash tree whose roots and branches hold together the universe
Yid·dish (yid′ish) *n.* [Yid. *yidish* < G. *jüdisch,* Jewish, ult. < L. *Judaeus,* a Jew] a language developed from medieval High German, spoken by East European Jews and their descendants in other countries: it is written in the Hebrew alphabet and contains elements of Hebrew, Russian, Polish, English, etc.: abbrev. **Yid.** —*adj.* of or in this language

YEW
(leaves & shrub)

yield (yēld) *vt.* [OE. *gieldan,* to pay] **1.** to produce; specif., *a)* to give or furnish as a natural process [the orchard *yields* a good crop] *b)* to give in return; produce as a result, profit, etc. [an investment that *yielded* high profits] **2.** to give up under pressure; surrender [to *yield* the city to the invaders] **3.** to give; concede; grant [to *yield* the right of way; to *yield* a point] —*vi.* **1.** to produce or bear [a mine that has *yielded* poorly] **2.** to give up; surrender [to *yield* to a demand] **3.** to give way to physical force [the gate *yielded* to our pushing] **4.** to give place (often with *to*); specif., *a)* to let another (motorist) have the right of way *b)* to give up willingly a right, position, etc. [I *yield* to the Senator from Utah] —*n.* **1.** the amount yielded or produced [a *yield* of 26 bushels per acre] **2.** the earnings received from investment in stocks, bonds, etc. **3.** the force in kilotons or megatons of a nuclear or thermonuclear explosion —**yield′er** *n.*
SYN.—**yield** implies a giving way under the pressure of force, persuasion, etc. [to *yield* to his pleas]; **capitulate** implies surrender to a force that one has neither the strength nor will to resist any longer [to *capitulate* to the will of the majority]; **succumb** emphasizes the weakness of the one who gives way or the overwhelming power of that which makes one yield [he *succumbed* to her charms]; **defer** implies a yielding to another because of respect for his authority, knowledge, etc. [to *defer* to the nurse's judgment] —see also SYN. at SURRENDER —ANT. resist
yield·ing (yēl′diŋ) *adj.* **1.** bending easily; flexible **2.** giving in easily; submissive; obedient
yin (yin) *n.* [< Chin. dial.] in Chinese philosophy, the passive, negative, feminine force or principle in the universe: see YANG
☆**yip** (yip) *n.* [echoic] [Colloq.] a yelp, or bark —*vi.* **yipped, yip′ping** [Colloq.] to yelp, or bark
yipe (yīp) *interj.* an exclamation of pain, fear, alarm, etc.
yip·pee (yip′ē) *interj.* an exclamation of joy, delight, etc.
-yl (il; *now rarely* ēl) [< Gr. *hylē,* wood] *Chem.* a combining form meaning: **1.** a monovalent hydrocarbon radical [ethyl] **2.** a radical containing oxygen [hydroxyl]
YMCA, Y.M.C.A. Young Men's Christian Association
YMHA, Y.M.H.A. Young Men's Hebrew Association
☆**yock** (yäk) *n.* [var. of YAK[2]] [Slang] a loud laugh or something causing loud laughter; yak: also sp. **yok**
yo·del (yō′d'l) *vt., vi.* **-deled** or **-delled, -del·ing** or **-del·ling** [G. *jodeln*] to sing with sudden changes back and forth between one's normal voice and a falsetto —*n.* **1.** the act or sound of yodeling **2.** a song sung in this way —**yo′del·er, yo′del·ler** *n.*
yo·ga (yō′gə) *n.* [Sans., union] **1.** *Hinduism* a discipline by which one seeks to reach a state of oneness with the universal soul by thinking deeply, placing the body in certain unusual positions, breathing in a controlled way, etc. **2.** a system of exercising involving such positions, breathing, etc. —**yo′gic** (-gik) *adj.*
yo·gi (yō′gē) *n., pl.* **-gis** a person who practices yoga: also **yo′gin** (-gin)
yo·gurt (yō′gərt) *n.* [Turk. *yōghurt*] a thick, semisolid food made from milk fermented by a bacterium: often prepared with various flavors: also sp. **yo′ghurt, yo′ghourt**

yoke (yōk) *n.*, *pl.* **yokes**: for 2, usually **yoke** [OE. *geoc* < IE. base *yeu-*, to join] **1.** a wooden frame with loops at either end, fitted around the necks of a pair of oxen, etc. to harness them **2.** a pair of animals harnessed together [a *yoke* of oxen] **3.** the condition of being under another's power or control; bondage [the peasants threw off their *yoke*] **4.** something that binds, unites, etc. [a *yoke* of friendship] **5.** something like a yoke, as a frame that fits over the shoulders for carrying pails, etc. **6.** a part of a garment fitted closely around the shoulders or hips to support the gathered parts below [the *yoke* of a shirt] —*vt.* **yoked, yok′ing 1.** to put a yoke on **2.** to harness (an animal) to (a plow, etc.) **3.** to join together —*vi.* to be joined together

YOKE
(on pair of oxen)

yo·kel (yō′k'l) *n.* [prob. < dial. *yokel*, green woodpecker] a person living in a rural area; rustic: a term showing contempt

Yo·ko·ha·ma (yō′kə hä′mə; *Jpn.* yô′kô hä′mä) seaport on the S coast of Honshu, Japan: pop. 1,789,000

yolk (yōk) *n.* [OE. *geolca*] **1.** the yellow part of an egg **2.** *Biol.* the protein and fat in an ovum, which provide food for the growing embryo —**yolked, yolk′y** *adj.*

yolk sac a sac containing yolk that is attached to and supplies food for the embryos of birds, fishes, and reptiles

Yom Kip·pur (yäm kip′ər, yôm; *Heb.* yōm′ kē pōōr′) a Jewish holiday, the Day of Atonement, a fast day observed on the 10th day of Tishri

yon (yän) *adj., adv.* [OE. *geon*] [Archaic or Dial.] yonder

yond (yänd) *adj., adv.* [OE. *geond*] [Archaic or Dial.] yonder

yon·der (yän′dər) *adj.* [ME.] **1.** farther; more distant [the *yonder* side of the building] **2.** being at a distance, but within sight; that or those over there [go to *yonder* village] —*adv.* at or in that place; over there

Yon·kers (yäŋ′kərz) [< Du. *De Jonkers* (*Land*), the young nobleman's (land)] city in southeastern N.Y., on the Hudson: suburb of New York City: pop. 204,000

☆**yoo-hoo** (yōō′hōō′) *interj., n.* a shout or call used to attract someone's attention

yore (yôr) *adv.* [OE. *geara*] [Obs.] long ago —*n.* time long past: now only in **of yore**, of long ago

York[1] (yôrk) ruling family of England (1461–85) —**York′ist** *adj., n.*

York[2] (yôrk) **1.** city in N England: pop. 104,000 **2.** [after YORKSHIRE] city in SE Pa.: pop. 50,000

York·shire (yôrk′shir) former large county of N England: in 1975 it was divided into three counties

Yorkshire pudding a batter of flour, eggs, and milk baked in the drippings of roasting meat

Yorkshire terrier a small terrier, with long, silky hair, first bred in Yorkshire, England

York·town (yôrk′toun′) [after the Duke of *York*, later CHARLES I] town in SE Va.: scene of the surrender of Cornwallis to Washington (1781)

Yo·sem·i·te National Park (yō sem′ə tē) [< AmInd., lit., grizzly bears, killers] national park in EC Calif., in the Sierra Nevadas: notable for its steep-walled valley (**Yosemite Valley**) & its high waterfalls (**Yosemite Falls**)

you (yōō; *unstressed* yŏŏ, yə) *pron.* [OE. *eow*, dat. & acc. pl. of *ge*, YE[2]] **1.** the person or persons to whom one is speaking or writing: the case forms of the second personal pronoun are: *you*, nominative and objective (sing. & pl.); *your* and *yours*, possessive (sing. & pl.); and *yourselves* (pl.), intensive and reflexive **2.** a person or people generally [*you* never can tell!]

you-all (yōō ôl′, yôl) *pron.* ☆*Southern colloq.* for YOU: chiefly used as a plural form

you'd (yōōd; *unstressed* yŏŏd, yəd) **1.** you had **2.** you would

you'll (yōōl; *unstressed* yŏŏl, yəl) **1.** you will **2.** you shall

young (yuŋ) *adj.* [OE. *geong* < IE. base *yuwen-*, young] **1.** being in an early period of life or growth [a *young* actor; a *young*

YORKSHIRE
TERRIER
(8 in. high
at shoulder)

tree] **2.** characteristic of youth in quality, appearance, etc.; fresh; vigorous [*young* for his age] **3.** of youth or early life [her *young* days] **4.** lately begun; in an early stage [a *young* industry] **5.** lacking experience or practice; immature; green **6.** younger than another of the same name or family [*young* Jones or his father] —*n.* **1.** young people [humor that appeals to *young* and old] **2.** offspring, esp. young offspring, as a group [a bear and her *young*] —**with young** pregnant —**young′ish** *adj.* —**young′ness** *n.*

SYN.—**young** is the general word for one in an early period of life and suggests the energy, strength, freshness, immaturity, etc. characteristic of this period [a *young* child, man, etc.; *young* ideas]; **youthful** applies to one who is, or appears to be, in the period between childhood and maturity or to that which is suitable for such a person [a *youthful* executive, *youthful* clothes]; **juvenile** applies to that which has to do with, is suited to, or is intended for young persons [*juvenile* delinquency, behavior, books, etc.]; **puerile** is used of adults and adult behavior showing a childish lack of maturity [*puerile* impatience]; **adolescent** applies to one in the period between puberty and maturity and especially suggests the awkwardness, emotionalism, etc. of this period [*adolescent* yearnings] —**ANT. old, mature**

Young (yuŋ), **Brig·ham** (brig′əm) 1801–77; U.S. Mormon leader

☆**young·ber·ry** (yuŋ′ber′ē) *n.*, *pl.* **-ries** [after B. *Young*, 19th-c. U.S. horticulturist] **1.** a large, sweet, dark-purple berry, a cross between a blackberry and a dewberry **2.** the trailing bramble bearing this fruit

young blood 1. young people; youth **2.** youthful energy, vigor, strength, ideas, etc.

young·ling (yuŋ′liŋ) *n.* **1.** a young person; youth **2.** a young animal or plant —*adj.* young

young·ster (-stər) *n.* **1.** a child **2.** a youth

Youngs·town (yuŋz′toun′) [after J. *Young*, an early (c. 1800) settler] city in NE Ohio: pop. 140,000 (met. area, with Warren, 536,000)

Young Turk [orig., member of early 20th-c. revolutionary party in Turkey] [also **y- T-**] any of a group of younger people seeking to take control of an organization, political party, etc. from the older, usually conservative, people in power

your (yŏŏr, yôr; *unstressed* yər) *possessive pronominal adj.* [OE. *eower*] of, belonging to, made by, or done by you [*your* book; *your* work]: also used before some titles [*your* Honor]

you're (yŏŏr, yōŏr; *unstressed* yər) you are

yours (yŏŏrz, yôrz) *pron.* that or those belonging to you: used without a following noun [that book is *yours*, *yours* are better]: also used after *of* to indicate possession [a friend of *yours*]

your·self (yər self′, yŏŏr-) *pron.*, *pl.* **-selves′** (-selvz′) **1.** a form of the 2d person singular pronoun, used: *a*) as an intensive [you *yourself* went] *b*) as a reflexive [you hurt *yourself*] *c*) as a kind of noun meaning "your real or true self" [you are not *yourself* today] **2.** *same as* ONESELF [it is best to do it *yourself*]

yours truly 1. a phrase used before the signature in ending a letter **2.** [Colloq.] I or me

youth (yōōth) *n.*, *pl.* **youths** (yōōths, yōōthz) [OE. *geoguthe*] **1.** the state or quality of being young, fresh, lively, etc. [to recapture one's *youth*] **2.** the period of life coming between childhood and maturity; adolescence **3.** an early stage of growth or existence, as of a country **4.** young people as a group [a club for the *youth* of our town] **5.** a young person; esp., a young man

youth·ful (yōōth′fəl) *adj.* **1.** young; not yet old or mature [a *youthful* widow] **2.** of, like, or fit for a young person [*youthful* styles] **3.** fresh; vigorous; active [still *youthful* at eighty] **4.** new; early; in an early stage —see SYN. at YOUNG —**youth′fully** *adv.* —**youth′ful·ness** *n.*

youth hostel any of a system of supervised shelters providing cheap lodging for young people on bicycle tours, hikes, etc.

you've (yōōv; *unstressed* yŏŏv, yəv) you have

yow (you) *interj.* an exclamation of pain, surprise, etc.

yowl (youl) *vi.* [< ON. *gaula*] to utter a long, mournful cry; howl —*n.* such a cry

☆**yo-yo** (yō′yō′) *n.* [< Tagalog name: the toy came to the U.S. from the Philippines] **1.** a spoollike toy attached to one end of a string upon which it may be made to spin up and down **2.** [Slang] a person who is dull or stupid

Y·pres (ē′pr′) town in NW Belgium, near the Fr. border: center of heavy fighting in World War I

---

fat, āpe, cär; ten, ēven; is, bīte; gō, hôrn, tōōl, lŏŏk; oil, out; up, fur; get; joy; yet; chin; she; thin, then; zh, leisure; ŋ, ring; ə for a in ago, e in agent, i in sanity, o in comply, u in focus; ' as in able (ā′b'l); Fr. bâl; ë, Fr. coeur; ö, Fr. feu; Fr. mon; ô, Fr. coq; ü, Fr. duc; r, Fr. cri; H, G. ich; kh, G. doch; ‡foreign; ☆ Americanism; < derived from. See inside front cover.

yr. **1.** year; years **2.** younger **3.** your

yrs. **1.** years **2.** yours

yt·ter·bi·um (i tur′bē əm) *n.* [ModL. < *Ytterby*, Sweden] a scarce, silvery, metallic chemical element of the rare-earth group: symbol, Yb; at. wt., 173.04; at. no., 70

yt·tri·um (it′rē əm) *n.* [ModL. < *Ytterby*, Sweden] a rare, silvery, metallic chemical element: symbol, Y; at. wt., 88.905; at. no., 39

yu·an (yōō än′) *n.* [Chin. *yüan*, round] the basic monetary unit of China: see MONETARY UNITS, table

Yu·ca·tán, Yu·ca·tan (yōō′kä tän′; *E.* yōō′kə tan′) peninsula containing SE Mexico, British Honduras, & part of W Guatemala: it stretches north into the Gulf of Mexico

yuc·ca (yuk′ə) *n.* [ModL., genus name < Sp. *yuca*] **1.** a plant of the U.S. and Latin America, having stiff, sword-shaped leaves and white flowers in an erect raceme **2.** its flower

☆**yuck** (yuk) *n.* [Slang] something unpleasant, disgusting, etc. —*interj.* an exclamation expressing distaste, disgust, etc.: also sp. **yuch, yucch**

☆**yuck·y** (yuk′ē) *adj.* **-i·er, -i·est** [Slang] unpleasant, disgusting, etc.

Yu·go·slav (yōō′gō släv′, -gə-) *adj.* of Yugoslavia or its people: also **Yu′go·slav′ic** —*n.* a member of a Slavic people, including

YUCCA

Serbs, Croats, and Slovenes, who live in Yugoslavia Also **Yu′go·sla′vi·an** (-slä′vē ən, -släv′yən)

Yu·go·sla·vi·a (yōō′gō slä′vē ə, -gə släv′yə) country in the NW Balkan Peninsula, on the Adriatic: 98,766 sq. mi.; pop. 20,672,000; cap. Belgrade

☆**yuk** (yuk) *n.* [echoic] [Slang] a loud laugh of amusement, or something causing such a laugh —*vi.* **yukked, yuk′king** [Slang] to laugh loudly Also sp. **yuck**

Yu·kon (yōō′kän) **1.** territory of NW Canada, east of Alas.: 207,076 sq. mi.; pop. 22,000; cap. Whitehorse: in full, **Yukon Territory** : abbrev. **Y.T.** **2.** river flowing through this territory & Alas. into the Bering Sea

Yukon Standard Time *see* STANDARD TIME

yule (yōōl) *n.* [OE. *geol*] Christmas or the Christmas season

yule log a large log formerly used as a foundation for the ceremonial Christmas Eve fire

yule·tide (yōōl′tīd′) *n.* Christmas time

yum (yum) *interj.* [echoic: see YUMMY] excellent; delicious

yum·my (yum′ē) *adj.* **-mi·er, -mi·est** [echoic of a sound made in showing pleasure at a taste] [Colloq.] very tasty; delectable; delicious *[a yummy cake]*

☆**yup** (yup) *adv.* [Slang] yes

yurt (yoort) *n.* [< Russ. *yurta*, lit., dwelling] a circular tent of felt or skins on a framework of poles, used by the nomads of Mongolia

YWCA, Y.W.C.A. Young Women's Christian Association

YWHA, Y.W.H.A. Young Women's Hebrew Association

Z

Z, z (zē; *Brit. & Canad.* zed) *n.*, *pl.* **Z's, z's** 1. the twenty-sixth and last letter of the English alphabet 2. the sound of Z or z 3. *a symbol for* the last in a sequence or group

Z (zē; *Brit. & Canad.* zed) *n.* an object shaped like Z —*adj.* shaped like Z

z *Math. a symbol for:* 1. the third in a set of unknown quantities, *x* and *y* usually being the first two 2. a variable

Z., z. 1. zero 2. zone

Za·greb (zä′greb) city in NW Yugoslavia; capital of Croatia: pop. 457,000

Za·ire, Za·ïre (zä ir′) 1. country in C Africa, on the equator: a former Belgian colony: 905,563 sq. mi.; pop. 22,477,000; cap. Kinshasa 2. *same as* CONGO (River)

za·ire (zä ir′) *n.*, *pl.* **za·ire′** [< Port., prob. < Kongo *nzadi*, big river] the monetary unit of Zaire: see MONETARY UNITS, table

Zam·be·zi (zam bē′zē) river in S Africa, flowing through Zambia & Mozambique into the Indian Ocean: c. 1,600 mi.

Zam·bi·a (zam′bē ə) country in S Africa: a member of the Commonwealth: 290,323 sq. mi.; pop. 4,336,000; cap. Lusaka

za·ny (zā′nē) *n.*, *pl.* **-nies** [< Fr. < It. *zanni*, orig., a shortened pronunciation of *Giovanni*, John] 1. a clown or buffoon 2. a silly or foolish person; simpleton —*adj.* **-ni·er, -ni·est** of or like a zany; specif., *a*) comical in a crazy way *b*) foolish or crazy —**za′ni·ly** *adv.* —**za′ni·ness** *n.*

Zan·zi·bar (zan′zə bär′) 1. group of islands off the E coast of Africa, forming a part of Tanzania 2. largest island of this group: 640 sq. mi.

☆**zap** (zap) *vt., vi.* **zapped, zap′ping** [echoic] [Slang] to move, strike, stun, kill, etc. with sudden speed and force —*n.* [Slang] energy, verve, pep, etc. —*interj.* an exclamation used to express sudden, swift action

Za·po·rozh·e, Za·po·rozh·ye (zä′pô rôzh′ye) city in the SE Ukrainian S.S.R., on the Dnepr: pop. 658,000

Za·ra·go·za (thä′rä gô′thä) city in NE Spain: pop. 657,000

Zar·a·thus·tra (zar′ə thŏŏs′trə) *Persian name of* ZOROASTER

zeal (zēl) *n.* [< LL. *zelus* < Gr. *zēlos*] very great enthusiasm, as in working for a cause; strong interest or devotion; fervor —see **SYN.** at PASSION

Zea·land (zē′lənd) largest island of Denmark, between Jutland & Sweden: 2,912 sq. mi.; chief city, Copenhagen

zeal·ot (zel′ət) *n.* [< LL. < Gr. *zēlōtēs* < *zēlos*, zeal] a person who shows zeal for something, esp. too much zeal; fanatic —**zeal′ot·ry** *n.*

SYN.—zealot implies great, often too great, devotion to a cause and intense activity in its support *[zealots of reform]*; **fanatic** suggests the unreasonable attitude of one who goes to such length to preserve or carry out his beliefs *[an antismoking fanatic]*; an **enthusiast** is one who shows a strong, eager, lively interest in an activity, cause, etc. *[a sports enthusiast]*

zeal·ous (zel′əs) *adj.* full of or showing zeal; very eager; enthusiastic *[a zealous patriot]* —**zeal′ous·ly** *adv.* —**zeal′ous·ness** *n.*

ze·bec, ze·beck (zē′bek) *n. same as* XEBEC

ze·bra (zē′brə; *Brit. & Canad., also* zeb′rə) *n.*, *pl.* **-bras, -bra:** see PLURAL, II, D, 1 [Port., prob. ult. < L. *equiferus*, a wild horse] any of several swift African mammals related to the horse, with dark stripes on a white or tan body

zebra fish any of a number of unrelated fishes with barred, zebralike markings, often kept in aquariums

ze·bu (zē′byōō) *n.*, *pl.* **-bus, -bu:** see PLURAL, II, D, 1 [Fr. *zébu* < ?] an oxlike farm animal of Asia and Africa: it has a large hump and short, curving horns: see BRAHMAN (sense 2)

ZEBU
(5–5½ ft. high at shoulder)

Zech·a·ri·ah (zek′ə rī′ə) *Bible* 1. a Hebrew prophet of the 6th cent. B.C. 2. the book containing his prophecies: abbrev. **Zech.**

zed (zed) *n.* [< MFr. < LL. < Gr. *zēta*] *Brit. & usual Canad. name for* the letter Z, z

zee (zē) *n.*, *pl.* **zees** the letter Z, z

‡**Zeit·geist** (tsīt′gīst′) *n.* [G., time spirit] the general state or trend of thought and feeling in a period of history

Zen (zen) *n.* [Jpn. < Chin., ult. < Sans. *dhyāna*, meditation] 1. a Japanese Buddhist sect that seeks understanding of reality not in traditional scripture but through deep thought that makes no use of reasoning or study 2. the beliefs and practices of this sect

Zend (zend) *n.* [Per., interpretation] the Middle Persian translation of and commentary on the Zoroastrian Avesta

Zend-A·ves·ta (zend′ə ves′tə) *n.* the sacred writings of the Zoroastrians

Zeng·er (zeŋ′ər, -gər), **John Peter** 1697–1746; Am. journalist & publisher, born in Germany

ze·nith (zē′nith; *Brit.* zen′ith) *n.* [< MFr. < ML. *cenit* < Ar. *semt*, road < L. *semita*, path] 1. the point in the sky directly overhead: that point of the celestial sphere directly opposite to the nadir 2. the highest point; peak *[at the zenith of his career]* —see **SYN.** at SUMMIT

Ze·no (zē′nō) 334?–261? B.C.; Gr. philosopher: founder of Stoicism

Ze·no·bi·a (zə nō′bē ə) 3d cent. A.D.; queen of Palmyra

Zeph·a·ni·ah (zef′ə nī′ə) *Bible* 1. a Hebrew prophet of the 7th cent. B.C. 2. the book containing his prophecies: abbrev. **Zeph.**

zeph·yr (zef′ər) *n.* [< L. < Gr. *zephyros*] 1. the west wind 2. a soft, gentle breeze 3. a soft, lightweight yarn or cloth

zep·pe·lin (zep′ə lin, zep′lin) *n.* [after F. von Zeppelin (1838–1917), G. inventor] *[often Z-]* a type of airship designed around 1900

ze·ro (zir′ō, zē′rō) *n.*, *pl.* **-ros, -roes** [Fr. *zéro* < It. < Ar. *ṣifr*, CIPHER] 1. the symbol or numeral 0; cipher; naught 2. the point, marked 0, from which positive or negative quantities are measured on a scale, as on thermometers 3. a temperature that causes a thermometer to register zero 4. nothing *[four minus four equals zero]* 5. the lowest point *[his chances sank to zero]* —*adj.* 1. of or at zero 2. without measurable value 3. designating or of visibility limited to very short distances, as in flying —*vt.* **-roed, -ro·ing** to adjust (an instrument, etc.) to a zero point from which all positive or negative readings are to be made — **zero in** to aim (a gun or guns) directly at a target —**zero in on**

fat, āpe, cär; ten, ēven; is, bīte; gō, hôrn, tōōl, lŏŏk; ŏil, ŏut; up, fur; get; joy; yet; chin; she; thin, then; zh, leisure; ŋ, ring; ə for *a* in *ago*, *e* in *agent*, *i* in *sanity*, *o* in *comply*, *u* in *focus*; ′ as in *able* (ā′b'l); Fr. bál; ë, Fr. coeur; ö, Fr. feu; Fr. mon; ô, Fr. coq; ü, Fr. duc; r, Fr. cri; H, G. ich; kh, G. doch; ‡ foreign; ☆ Americanism; < derived from. See inside front cover.

1. to adjust gunfire so as to be aiming directly at (a target) **2.** to concentrate attention on; focus on

☆**ze·ro-base** (zir′ō bās′) *adj.* [from the idea of starting at zero] describing a way of preparing a budget, in which each proposed item is judged anew without taking into account any earlier budget: also **ze′ro-based′**

zero gravity a condition in which gravitational attraction is zero; weightlessness

zero hour 1. the time set for beginning an attack or other military action **2.** any very important moment; critical point

☆**zero (population) growth** a condition in a given population in which the birthrate equals the death rate so that the number of people remains the same

zest (zest) *n.* [Fr. *zeste*, orange peel used to give flavor] **1.** stimulating or exciting quality; flavor; relish [danger adds *zest* to an acrobat's work] **2.** keen enjoyment; gusto (often with *for*) [a *zest* for life; to work with *zest*] —**zest′ful** *adj.* —**zest′ful·ly** *adv.* —**zest′ful·ness** *n.* —**zest′y** *adj.*

ze·ta (zāt′ə, zēt′ə) *n.* [Gr.] the sixth letter of the Greek alphabet (Z, ζ)

Zeus (zōōs) the supreme god of the ancient Greeks, son of Cronus and Rhea: identified with the Roman god Jupiter

zig·gu·rat (zig′oo rat) *n.* [Assyr. *ziqquratu*, height] an ancient Assyrian or Babylonian temple built in the form of a pyramid with each story smaller than the one below it

zig·zag (zig′zag′) *n.* [Fr.] **1.** a series of short, sharp angles or turns in alternate directions, as in a line or course **2.** a design, path, etc. in the form of a zigzag [lightning made a *zigzag* in the sky] —*adj.* having the form of a zigzag [*zigzag* stitching] —*adv.* in a zigzag course —*vt.*, *vi.* -**zagged′**, -**zag′ging** to move or form in a zigzag [the rabbit *zigzagged* across the field]

☆**zilch** (zilch) *n.* [nonsense syllable] [Slang] nothing; zero

☆**zil·lion** (zil′yən) *n.* [arbitrary coinage, after MILLION] [Colloq.] a very large, indefinite number

Zim·ba·bwe (zim bä′bwe) country in S Africa, north of South Africa: formerly called RHODESIA: 150,333 sq. mi.; pop. 6,930,000; cap. Salisbury

zinc (ziŋk) *n.* [G. *zink*] a bluish-white, metallic chemical element, used as a protective coating for iron, in electric batteries and in alloys, and, in the form of salts, in medicines: symbol, Zn; at. wt., 65.37; at. no., 30 —*vt.* **zincked** or **zinced**, **zinck′ing** or **zinc′ing** to coat or treat with zinc; galvanize —**zinc′ic** (-ik), **zinc′ous** (-əs), **zinck′y**, **zink′y**, **zinc′y** *adj.*

zinc ointment an ointment containing zinc oxide

zinc oxide a white powder, ZnO, used as a pigment and in making glass, cosmetics, ointments, etc.

zinc sulfide a yellowish-white, crystalline powder, ZnS, having the property of luminescence, used in making television screens and luminous watch faces, as a pigment, etc.

zinc white zinc oxide used as a white pigment

zing (ziŋ) *n.* [echoic] [Slang] **1.** a shrill, high-pitched sound, as of something moving at high speed **2.** energy, zest, etc. —*vi.* [Slang] to make a zing —**zing′y** *adj.* **zing′i·er**, **zing′i·est**

Zin·jan·thro·pus (zin jan′thrə pəs) *n.* [ModL. < Ar. *Zīnj*, East Africa + Gr. *anthrōpos*, man] a type of primitive man who lived about 1,500,000 years ago

zin·ni·a (zin′ē ə, zin′yə) *n.* [ModL., after J. G. *Zinn*, 18th-c. G. botanist] a plant of the composite family, with brightly colored flowers, native to N. and S. America

Zi·on (zī′ən) **1.** the hill in Jerusalem on which the Temple was built: a symbol of the center of Jewish national life **2.** *a)* Jerusalem *b)* the land of Israel **3.** the Jewish people **4.** heaven

Zi·on·ism (-iz'm) *n.* a movement formerly for reestablishing, now for supporting, the Jewish national state of Israel —**Zi′on·ist** *n.*, *adj.* —**Zi′on·is′tic** *adj.*

Zion National Park national park in SW Utah, noted for its spectacular rock formations

zip (zip) *n.* [echoic] **1.** a short, sharp hissing sound, as of a passing bullet **2.** [Colloq.] energy; force; vim **3.** [Slang] a score of zero —☆*vi.* **zipped**, **zip′ping 1.** to make, or move with, a zip **2.** [Colloq.] to act or move with speed or energy [we *zipped* through our work] **3.** to become fastened or unfastened by means of a zipper —☆*vt.* to fasten or unfasten with a zipper

☆**ZIP code** (zip) [z(oning) i(mprovement) p(lan)] a system for

ZINNIA

speeding up mail deliveries, under which the post office assigns a code number to individual areas and places

☆**zip·per** (zip′ər) *n.* **1.** a person or thing that zips **2.** a device used to fasten and unfasten two edges of material: it consists of two rows of interlocking teeth worked by a sliding part

zip·py (zip′ē) *adj.* -**pi·er**, -**pi·est** [< ZIP + -Y²] [Colloq.] full of energy; lively; brisk

zir·con (zur′kän) *n.* [G. *zirkon*, ult. < Per. *zargūn*, gold-colored < *zar*, gold] a crystalline silicate of zirconium, ZrSiO₄, colored yellow, brown, red, etc.: transparent varieties are used as gems

zir·co·ni·um (zər kō′nē əm) *n.* [ModL.: see prec.] a soft, gray or black, metallic chemical element used in alloys, ceramics, etc.: symbol, Zr; at. wt., 91.22; at. no., 40

zirconium oxide zirconium dioxide, ZrO₂, a heavy, white powder used in making furnace linings, pigments, etc.

zit (zit) *n.* [< ?] [Slang] a pimple, esp. one on the face

zith·er (zith′ər, zith′-) *n.* [G. < L. < Gr. *kithara*, a lute] a musical instrument having from thirty to forty strings stretched across a soundboard and played with a plectrum and the fingers

zło·ty (zlô′tē) *n.*, *pl.* -**tys** [Pol., lit., golden] the monetary unit of Poland: see MONETARY UNITS, table

Zn *Chem.* zinc

zo- *same as* ZOO-: used before a vowel

-zo·a (zō′ə) [ModL. < Gr. *zōia*, pl. of *zōion*, an animal] *a combining form used in zoology to form names of groups* [Protozoa]

zo·di·ac (zō′dē ak′) *n.* [< MFr. < L. < Gr. *zōdiakos* (*kyklos*),

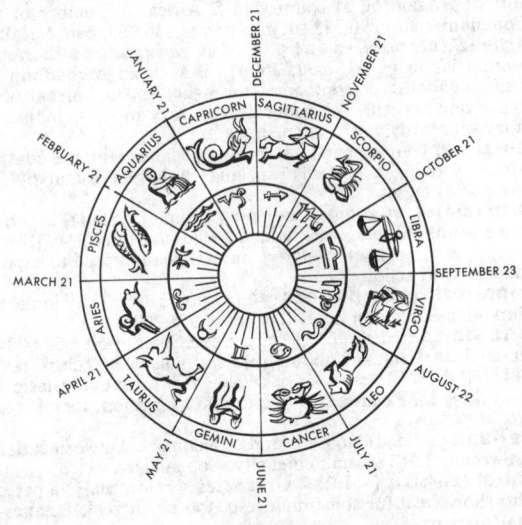

ZITHER

ZODIAC

lit., (circle) of animals < *zōidion*, dim. of *zōion*, animal] **1.** an imaginary belt in the heavens extending on either side of the apparent path of the sun and including the paths of the moon and the principal planets: it is divided into twelve equal parts, or signs, named for constellations **2.** a diagram representing this: used in astrology —**zo·di·a·cal** (-dī′ə k'l) *adj.*

-zo·ic (zō′ik) *a suffix meaning:* **1.** [< Gr. < *zōon*, animal + -*ikos*, -IC] having a (specified) animal way of life [saprozoic] **2.** [< Gr. `zōē, life + -IC] of, relating to, or being a geologic era having a (specified) type of life [Cenozoic]

Zo·la (zō lä′; *E.* zō′lə), **É·mile** (**Édouard Charles Antoine**) (ā mēl′) 1840–1902; Fr. novelist

☆**zom·bie** (zäm′bē) *n.* [of Afr. origin] **1.** in West Indian superstition, a dead person supposedly brought back by magic power to a form of life in which he can be made to move or act as he is ordered **2.** [Slang] *a)* a person like a zombie as in seeming to lack vitality, emotion, etc. *b)* a weird, eccentric, or unattractive person For sense 1, also sp. **zom′bi**

zon·al (zōn′'l) *adj.* **1.** of or having to do with a zone or zones **2.** formed or divided in zones; zoned

zone (zōn) *n.* [Fr. < L. < Gr. *zōnē* < *zōnnynai*, to gird] **1.** *a)* an encircling band, stripe, etc. different in color, structure, etc. from what surrounds it *b)* formerly, a belt or girdle **2.** any of the five great divisions into which the earth's surface is marked off by imaginary lines: see TORRID ZONE, TEMPERATE ZONE, and FRIGID ZONE **3.** any region or area thought of as different from others because of its particular use, crops, geological features, etc. [a canal *zone,* cotton *zone*] ☆**4.** *a)* any area of a city set apart by law for a particular use, as for homes, businesses, etc. *b)* any space along a street or road limited in use by traffic regulations [no parking *zone*] ☆**5.** *a)* any of the numbered sections into which a metropolitan area is divided to make mail delivery easier *b)* any of a series of areas marked off around a given point, each having a different postage rate for goods shipped from that point **6.** *short for* TIME ZONE **7.** *Sports* any of the areas into which a football field, basketball court, etc. is divided, as for defense —*vt.* **zoned, zon′ing 1.** to mark off into zones; ☆*specif.,* *a)* to divide (a city, etc.) into zones for particular uses, as for homes, parks, etc. *b)* to limit to a certain use by dividing a city, etc. into such zones [an area *zoned* for industry] **2.** to encircle; surround

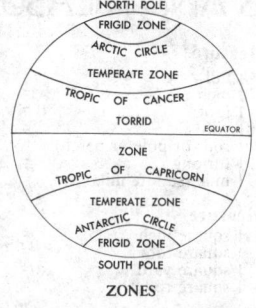

NORTH POLE
FRIGID ZONE
ARCTIC CIRCLE
TEMPERATE ZONE
TROPIC OF CANCER
TORRID
EQUATOR
ZONE
TROPIC OF CAPRICORN
TEMPERATE ZONE
ANTARCTIC CIRCLE
FRIGID ZONE
SOUTH POLE
ZONES

☆**zonked** (zäŋkt) *adj.* [pp. of *zonk,* to strike, beat] [Slang] highly intoxicated or under the influence of a drug

zoo (zōō) *n.* [< ZOO(LOGICAL GARDEN)] **1.** a place where wild animals are kept for the public to see **2.** a collection of wild animals

zoo- [< Gr. *zōion,* an animal] *a combining form meaning:* **1.** animal, animals [*zoology*] **2.** zoology and [*zoogeography*] Words beginning with *zoo-* are sometimes written **zoö-**

zo·o·ge·og·ra·phy (zō′ə jē äg′rə fē) *n.* the science dealing with the geographical distribution of animals —**zo′o·ge·og′ra·pher** *n.* —**zo′o·ge′o·graph′ic** (-jē′ə graf′ik), **zo′o·ge′o·graph′i·cal** *adj.* —**zo′o·ge′o·graph′i·cal·ly** *adv.*

zo·og·ra·phy (zō äg′rə fē) *n.* [ZOO- + -GRAPHY] the branch of zoology dealing with the description of animals, their habits, etc. —**zo·og′ra·pher** *n.* —**zo·o·graph·ic** (zō′ə graf′ik), **zo′o·graph′i·cal** *adj.*

zo·oid (zō′oid) *n.* [ZO- + -OID] **1.** an animal organism produced by fission, budding, etc. rather than by sexual means **2.** any of the individual members of a compound organism, as the coral —**zo·oi·dal** (zō oi′d'l) *adj.*

zool. **1.** zoological **2.** zoology

zoological garden *same as* ZOO (sense 1)

zo·ol·o·gy (zō äl′ə jē) *n.* [< ModL.: see ZOO- & -LOGY] **1.** the branch of biology that deals with animals, their life, growth, classification, etc. **2.** the animal life of an area; fauna **3.** the characteristics of an animal or an animal group —**zo′o·log′i·cal** (-ə läj′i k'l), **zo′o·log′ic** *adj.* —**zo′o·log′i·cal·ly** *adv.* —**zo·ol′o·gist** *n.*

zoom (zōōm) *vi.* [echoic] **1.** to make a loud, low-pitched, buzzing or humming sound **2.** to move with a zooming sound [cars *zooming* past] **3.** to climb suddenly and sharply: said of an airplane **4.** to rise rapidly [prices *zoomed*] **5.** to focus a camera by using a zoom lens —*vt.* to cause to zoom —*n.* **1.** the act or sound of zooming **2.** *same as* ZOOM LENS —*adj.* equipped with a zoom lens

zoom lens a system of lenses, as in a movie or TV camera, that can be rapidly adjusted for close-up shots or distance views while keeping the image in focus

-zo·on (zō′än) [ModL. < Gr. *zōion,* an animal] *a combining form meaning animal or living being* [*spermatozoon*]

zo·o·phyte (zō′ə fīt′) *n.* [< ModL. < Gr.: see ZOO- & -PHYTE] any animal, as a coral, sponge, etc., that looks and grows somewhat like a plant —**zo′o·phyt′ic** (-fit′ik), **zo′o·phyt′i·cal** *adj.*

zo·o·spore (zō′ə spôr′) *n. Bot.* an asexual spore, esp. of certain fungi or algae, that is able to move about usually by means of cilia or flagella —**zo′o·spor′ic, zo·os′po·rous** (-äs′pə rəs) *adj.*

zo·ri (zôr′ē) *n., pl.* **zo′ris, zo′ri** [Jpn.] a flat sandal of a Japanese style, with a thong passing between the big toe and the toe next to it

Zo·ro·as·ter (zō′rō as′tər, zôr′ō as′-) ? 6th or 7th cent. B.C.; Per. religious leader: founder of Zoroastrianism —**Zo′ro·as′tri·an** (-trē ən) *adj., n.*

Zo·ro·as·tri·an·ism (-trē ən iz'm) *n.* the religious system of the ancient Persians, teaching that the spirit of good will eventually triumph over the spirit of evil

Zou·ave (zōō äv′, zwäv) *n.* [Fr. < Ar. *Zwāwa,* an Algerian tribe] **1.** a member of a former infantry unit in the French army that wore a colorful Oriental uniform **2.** a member of any military group having a similar uniform

zounds (zoundz) *interj.* [altered < the oath (*by*) *God's wounds*] [Archaic] a mild oath expressing surprise or anger

☆**zow·ie** (zou′ē) *interj.* an exclamation expressing excitement, enthusiasm, admiration, etc.

zoy·si·a (zoi′sē ə) *n.* [ModL., after Karl von *Zois,* 18th-c. G. botanist] ☆a creeping, wiry grass used for lawns in warm, dry regions

Zr *Chem.* zirconium

zuc·chet·to (zōō ket′ō, -ə; *It.* tsōō ket′tô) *n., pl.* **-tos** [It. **-ti** (-tē) [< It. < *zucca,* a gourd] *R.C.Ch.* a skullcap worn by clergymen: a priest's is black, a bishop's purple, a cardinal's red, and the Pope's white

☆**zuc·chi·ni** (zōō kē′nē) *n., pl.* **-ni, -nis** [It., pl. of *zucchino,* dim. of *zucca,* a gourd] a type of summer squash that has a green skin and is shaped somewhat like a cucumber

Zui·der Zee, Zuy·der Zee (zī′dər zē′; *Du.* zöi′dər zā′) former arm of the North Sea, which extended into the Netherlands: the S section (now called IJSSELMEER) was shut off from the North Sea by dikes: see also WADDENZEE

Zu·lu (zōō′lōō) *n.* **1.** *pl.* **-lus, -lu** any member of a cattle-owning people living in Natal province, South Africa **2.** their Bantu language —*adj.* of the Zulus, their language, etc.

Zu·lu·land (zōō′lōō land′) region, formerly a Zulu kingdom, in Natal province, South Africa, on the Indian Ocean

Zu·ñi (zōōn′yē) *n.* [AmSp. < AmInd.] **1.** *pl.* **-ñis, -ñi** any member of a tribe of American Indians living in a pueblo in western New Mexico **2.** their language —**Zu′ñi·an** *adj., n.*

Zur·ba·rán (thōōr′bä rän′), **Fran·cis·co de** (frän thēs′kô the) 1598–1664; Sp. painter

Zur·ich (zoor′ik) city in N Switzerland: pop. 428,000: also written **Zür·ich** (*G.* tsü′riH)

☆**zwie·back** (swē′bak, swī′-, tswē′-, zwī′-; -bäk; *G.* tsvē′-bäk′) *n.* [G. < *zwie-,* twice + *backen,* to bake] a kind of bread or biscuit that is sliced and toasted after being baked

Zwing·li (tsviŋ′lē; *E.* zwiŋ′glē, swiŋ′-), **Ul·rich** (ool′riH) or **Hul·dreich** (hool′drīH) 1484–1531; Swiss Protestant reformer —**Zwing′li·an** *adj., n.*

zy·go·mat·ic (zī′gə mat′ik) *adj.* [< ModL. < Gr. < *zygoun,* to yoke] of, relating to, or located in the bony arch on either side of the face just below the eye in many vertebrates: the arch includes several bony growths and the cheekbone

zy·go·spore (zī′gə spôr′) *n.* a thick-walled, resting spore formed by the union of two similar gametes, as in certain fungi and algae

zy·gote (zī′gōt, zig′ōt) *n.* [< Gr. *zygōtos,* yoked < *zygon,* a yoke] a cell formed by the union of male and female gametes; fertilized egg cell before it divides —**zy·got′ic** (-gät′ik) *adj.*

zy·mase (zī′mās) *n.* [Fr.: see ZYME & -ASE] an enzyme, present in yeast, that promotes fermentation by breaking down glucose and some other carbohydrates into alcohol and carbon dioxide

zyme (zīm) *n.* [Gr. *zymē,* a leaven] [Obs.] a ferment or enzyme

zy·mo- [< Gr. *zymē,* a leaven] *a combining form meaning* fermentation [*zymology*]: also, before a vowel, **zym-**

zy·mo·gen (zī′mə jən) *n. Biochem.* an inactive form of an enzyme that can be made active

zy·mol·o·gy (zī mäl′ə jē) *n.* [ZYMO- + -LOGY] the science dealing with fermentation —**zy′mo·log′ic** (-mə läj′ik), **zy′mo·log′i·cal** *adj.* —**zy·mol′o·gist** *n.*

zy·mur·gy (zī′mər jē) *n.* [ZYM(O)- + -URGY] the branch of chemistry dealing with fermentation, as applied in wine making, brewing, etc.

TABLES OF WEIGHTS AND MEASURES

Linear Measure

	1 mil	=	0.0254 millimeter
1,000 mils	= 1 inch	=	2.54 centimeters
12 inches	= 1 foot	=	0.3048 meter
3 feet	= 1 yard	=	0.9144 meter
5 1/2 yards or 16 1/2 feet	= 1 rod (or pole or perch)	=	5.029 meters
40 rods	= 1 furlong	=	201.168 meters
8 furlongs or 1,760 yards or 5,280 feet	= 1 mile (statute mile)	=	1.6093 kilometers

Square Measure

	1 square inch	=	6.452 square centimeters
144 square inches	= 1 square foot	=	929.03 square centimeters
9 square feet	= 1 square yard	=	0.8361 square meter
30 1/4 square yards	= 1 square rod	=	25.292 square meters
160 square rods or 4,840 square yards or 43,560 square feet	= 1 acre	=	0.4047 hectare
640 acres	= 1 square mile	=	259.00 hectares or 2.590 square kilometers

Cubic Measure

	1 cubic inch	= 16.387	cubic centimeters
1,728 cubic inches	= 1 cubic foot	= 0.0283	cubic meter
27 cubic feet	= 1 cubic yard	= 0.7646	cubic meter
16 cubic feet	= 1 cord foot (used in measuring cordwood)	= 0.453	cubic meter
8 cord feet or 128 cubic feet	= 1 cord	= 3.625	cubic meters

Nautical Measure

6 feet	= 1 fathom	= 1.829 meters
100 fathoms	= 1 cable's length (ordinary) (In the U.S. Navy 120 fathoms or 720 feet, or 219.456 meters, = 1 cable's length.)	
10 cables' length	= 1 international nautical mile (6,076.11549 feet, by international agreement)	= 1.852 kilometers (exactly)
1 international nautical mile	= 1.150779 statute miles (the length of a minute of longitude at the equator)	
60 international nautical miles	= 1 degree of a great circle of the earth = 69.047 statute miles	

Dry Measure

	1 pint	=	33.60 cubic inches =	0.5506 liter
2 pints	= 1 quart	=	67.20 cubic inches =	1.1012 liters
8 quarts	= 1 peck	=	537.61 cubic inches =	8.8098 liters
4 pecks	= 1 bushel	=	2,150.42 cubic inches =	35.2390 liters

Liquid Measure

1 gill	= 4 fluid ounces (see next table)	=	7.219 cubic inches =	0.1183 liter
4 gills	= 1 pint	=	28.875 cubic inches =	0.4732 liter
2 pints	= 1 quart	=	57.75 cubic inches =	0.9464 liter
4 quarts	= 1 gallon	=	231 cubic inches =	3.7854 liters

The British imperial gallon (4 imperial quarts) = 277.42 cubic inches = 4.546 liters.
The barrel in Great Britain equals 36 imperial gallons, in the United States, usually 31 1/2 gallons.

Apothecaries' Fluid Measure

	1 minim	=	0.0038 cubic inch	= 0.0616 milliliter
60 minims	= 1 fluid dram	=	0.2256 cubic inch	= 3.6966 milliliters
8 fluid drams	= 1 fluid ounce	=	1.8047 cubic inches	= 0.0296 liter
16 fluid ounces	= 1 pint	=	28.875 cubic inches	= 0.4732 liter

See table immediately preceding for quart and gallon equivalents.

Circular (or Angular) Measure

60 seconds (")	= 1 minute (')
60 minutes	= 1 degree (°)
90 degrees	= 1 quadrant or 1 right angle
180 degrees	= 2 quadrants or 1 straight angle
4 quadrants or 360 degrees	= 1 circle

Avoirdupois Weight

	1 grain	=	0.0648 gram
27.34 grains	= 1 dram	=	1.772 grams
16 drams or 437.5 grains	= 1 ounce	=	28.3495 grams
16 ounces or 7,000 grains	= 1 pound	=	453.59 grams
100 pounds	= 1 hundredweight	=	45.36 kilograms
2,000 pounds	= 1 ton (short ton)	=	907.18 kilograms

In Great Britain, 14 pounds (6.35 kilograms) = 1 stone, 112 pounds (50.80 kilograms) = 1 hundredweight, and 2,240 pounds (1,016.05 kilograms) = 1 long ton.

Troy Weight
(Used in weighing gold, silver, and precious stones)

		1 grain	=	0.00648	gram
	3.086 grains	= 1 carat	=	200.00	milligrams
	24 grains	= 1 pennyweight	=	1.5552	grams
20 pennyweights or 480	grains	= 1 ounce	=	31.1035	grams
12 ounces or 5,760	grains	= 1 pound	=	373.24	grams

Apothecaries' Weight
(Used in pharmacy)

		1 grain	=	0.0648	gram
	20 grains	= 1 scruple	=	1.296	grams
	3 scruples	= 1 dram	=	3.888	grams
8 drams or 480	grains	= 1 ounce	=	31.1035	grams
12 ounces or 5,760	grains	= 1 pound	=	373.24	grams

THE METRIC SYSTEM
Linear Measure

	1 millimeter	=	0.03937	inch
10 millimeters	= 1 centimeter	=	0.3937	inch
10 centimeters	= 1 decimeter	=	3.937	inches
10 decimeters	= 1 meter	=	39.37	inches or 3.2808 feet
10 meters	= 1 decameter	=	393.7	inches
10 decameters	= 1 hectometer	=	328.08	feet
10 hectometers	= 1 kilometer	=	0.621	mile or 3,280.8 feet

Square Measure

	1 square millimeter	=	0.00155	square inch
100 square millimeters	= 1 square centimeter	=	0.15499	square inch
100 square centimeters	= 1 square decimeter	=	15.499	square inches
100 square decimeters	= 1 square meter	=	1,549.9	square inches or 1.196 square yards
100 square meters	= 1 square decameter	=	119.6	square yards
100 square decameters	= 1 square hectometer	=	2.471	acres
100 square hectometers	= 1 square kilometer	=	0.386	square mile or 247.1 acres

Land Measure

1 square meter	= 1 centiare	=	1,549.9	square inches
100 centiares	= 1 are	=	119.6	square yards
100 ares	= 1 hectare	=	2.471	acres
100 hectares	= 1 square kilometer	=	0.386	square mile or 247.1 acres

Volume Measure

1,000 cubic millimeters	= 1 cubic centimeter	=	0.06102	cubic inch
1,000 cubic centimeters	= 1 cubic decimeter	=	61.023	cubic inches or 0.0353 cubic foot
1,000 cubic decimeters	= 1 cubic meter (called a *stere* in measuring cordwood)	=	35.314	cubic feet or 1.308 cubic yards

Capacity Measure

10 milliliters	= 1 centiliter	=	0.338	fluid ounce
10 centiliters	= 1 deciliter	=	3.38	fluid ounces or 0.1057 liquid quart
10 deciliters	= 1 liter	=	1.0567	liquid quarts or 0.9081 dry quart
10 liters	= 1 decaliter	=	2.64	gallons or 0.284 bushel
10 decaliters	= 1 hectoliter	=	26.418	gallons or 2.838 bushels
10 hectoliters	= 1 kiloliter	=	264.18	gallons or 35.315 cubic feet

Weights

10 milligrams	= 1 centigram	=	0.1543	grain or 0.000353 ounce (avdp.)
10 centigrams	= 1 decigram	=	1.5432	grains
10 decigrams	= 1 gram	=	15.432	grains or 0.035274 ounce (avdp.)
10 grams	= 1 decagram	=	0.3527	ounce
10 decagrams	= 1 hectogram	=	3.5274	ounces
10 hectograms	= 1 kilogram	=	2.2046	pounds
10 kilograms	= 1 myriagram	=	22.046	pounds
10 myriagrams	= 1 quintal	=	220.46	pounds
10 quintals	= 1 metric ton	=	2,204.6	pounds

METRIC CONVERSION TABLES

Conversion _to_ Metric Units	Conversion _from_ Metric Units

LINEAR MEASURE

To convert	Multiply by	To convert	Multiply by
inches to millimeters	25.4	millimeters to inches	0.039
inches to centimeters	2.54	centimeters to inches	0.394
feet to meters	0.305	meters to feet	3.281
yards to meters	0.914	meters to yards	1.094
miles to kilometers	1.609	kilometers to miles	0.621

SQUARE MEASURE

To convert	Multiply by	To convert	Multiply by
sq. inches to sq. centimeters	6.452	sq. centimeters to sq. inches	0.155
sq. feet to sq. meters	0.093	sq. meters to sq. feet	10.764
sq. yards to sq. meters	0.836	sq. meters to sq. yards	1.196
acres to hectares	0.405	hectares to acres	2.471

CUBIC MEASURE

To convert	Multiply by	To convert	Multiply by
cu. inches to cu. centimeters	16.387	cu. centimeters to cu. inches	0.061
cu. feet to cu. meters	0.028	cu. meters to cu. feet	35.315
cu. yards to cu. meters	0.765	cu. meters to cu. yards	1.308

LIQUID MEASURE

To convert	Multiply by	To convert	Multiply by
fluid ounces to liters	0.03	liters to fluid ounces	33.814
quarts to liters	0.946	liters to quarts	1.057
gallons to liters	3.785	liters to gallons	0.264
imperial gallons to liters	4.546	liters to imperial gallons	0.220

WEIGHTS

To convert	Multiply by	To convert	Multiply by
ounces avoirdupois to grams	28.35	grams to ounces avoirdupois	0.035
pounds avoirdupois to kilograms	0.454	kilograms to pounds avoirdupois	2.205
tons to metric tons	0.907	metric tons to tons	1.102

TEMPERATURE

Fahrenheit thermometer		Celsius (or Centigrade) thermometer
32°F	freezing point of water	0°C
212°F	boiling point of water	100°C
98.6°F	body temperature	37°C

To find degrees Celsius, subtract 32 from degrees Fahrenheit and divide by 1.8.
To find degrees Fahrenheit, multiply degrees Celsius by 1.8 and add 32.